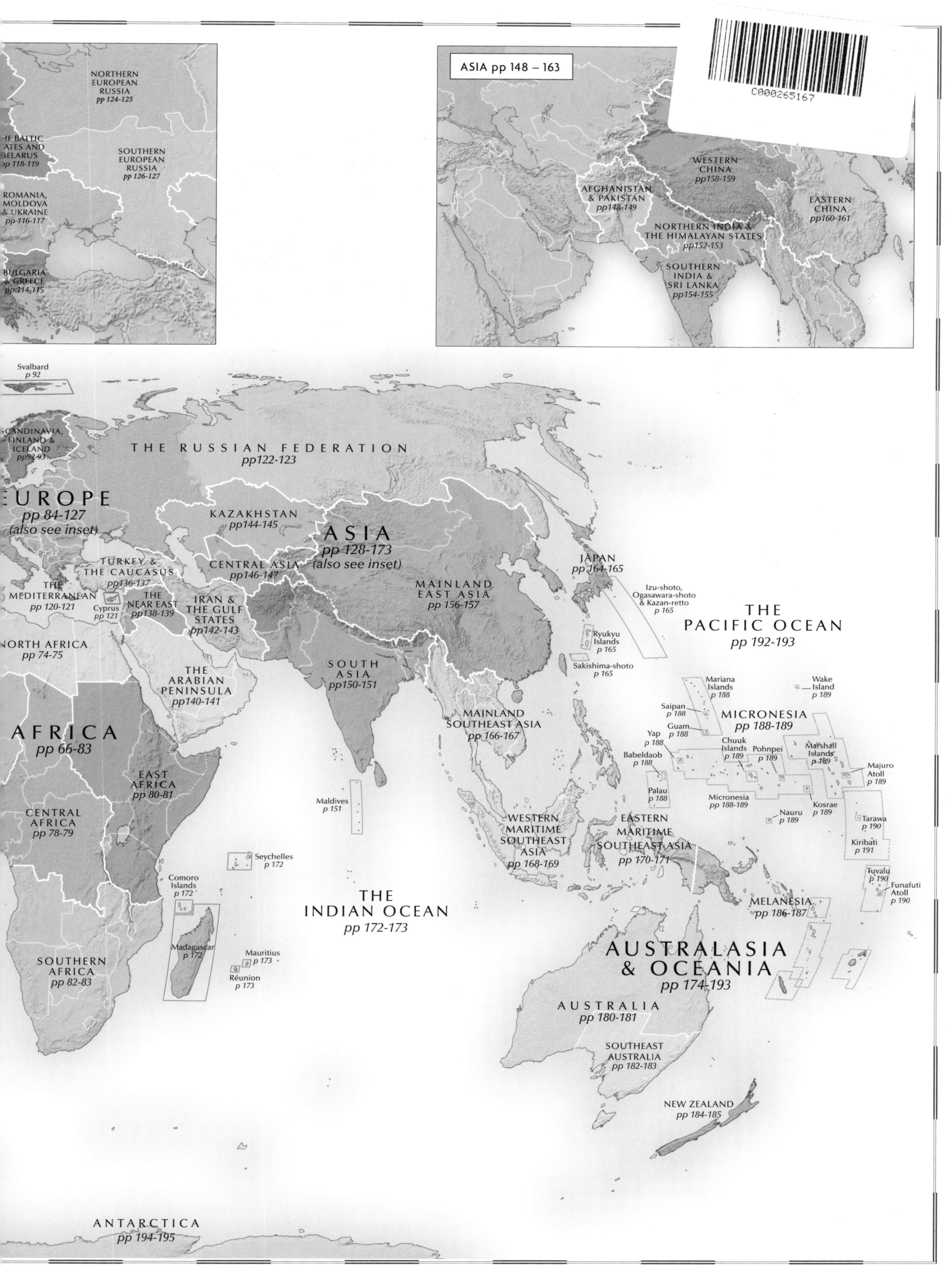

WORLD ATLAS

CONCISE

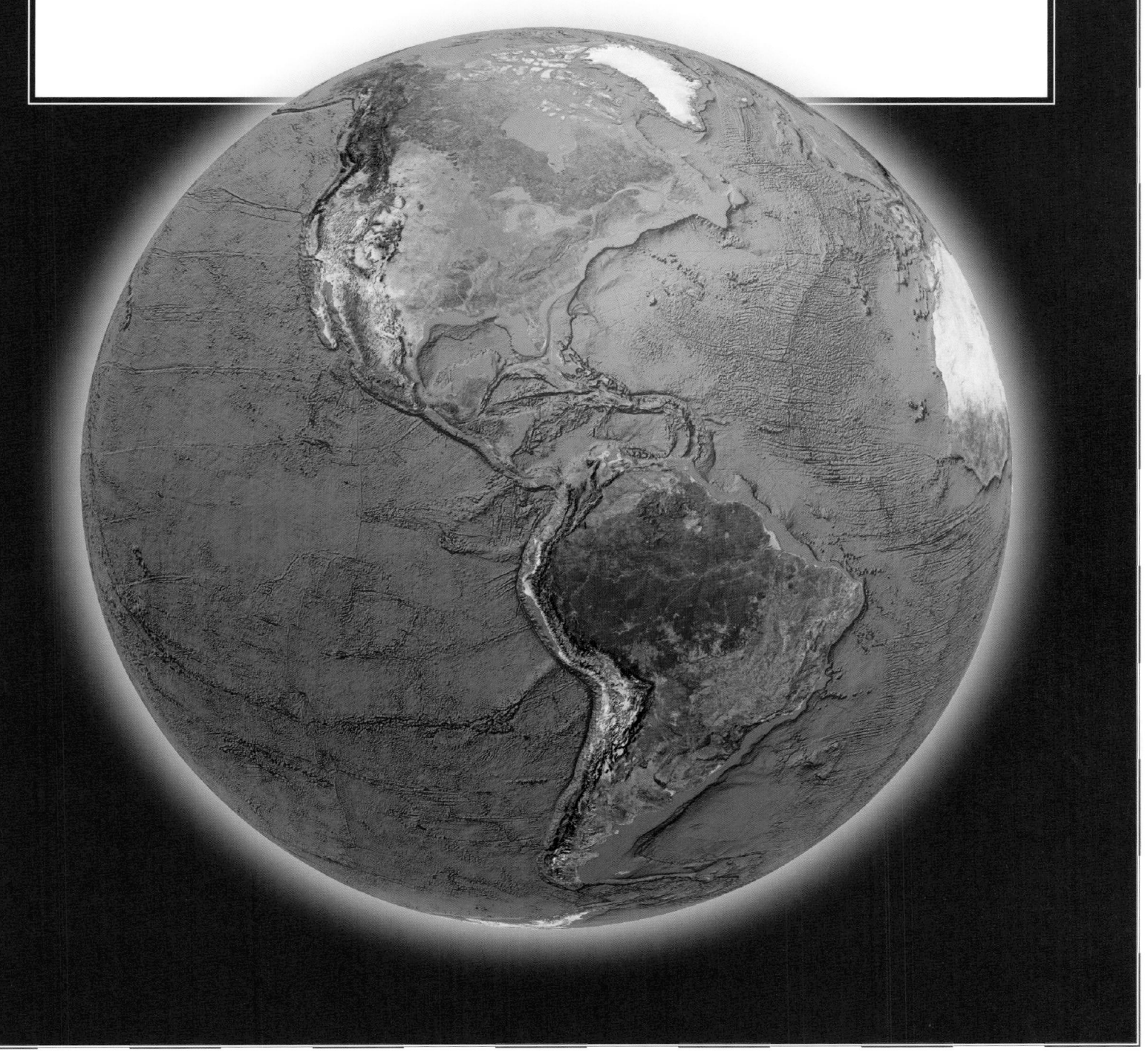

London • New York • Melbourne • Munich • Delhi

WORLD ATLAS

CONCISE

LONDON, NEW YORK, MELBOURNE, MUNICH, DELHI

FOR THE FIFTH EDITION

Publisher Jonathan Metcalf **Art Director** Philip Ormerod **Associate Publisher** Liz Wheeler
Managing Cartographer David Roberts **Senior Cartographic Editor** Simon Mumford **Designers** Encompass Graphics Ltd, Brighton, UK • Philip Rowles
Cartographers Paul Eames • Iorwerth Watkins **Jacket Designer** Philip Ormerod **Production Controller** Linda Dare **Production Editor** Joanna Byrne

General Geographical Consultants

Physical Geography Denys Brunsden, Emeritus Professor, Department of Geography, King's College, London
Human Geography Professor J Malcolm Wagstaff, Department of Geography, University of Southampton
Place Names Caroline Burgess, Permanent Committee on Geographical Names, London
Boundaries International Boundaries Research Unit, Mountjoy Research Centre, University of Durham

Digital Mapping Consultants

DK Cartopia developed by George Galfalvi and XMap Ltd, London
Professor Jan-Peter Muller, Department of Photogrammetry and Surveying, University College, London
Cover globes, planets and information on the Solar System provided by Philip Eales and Kevin Tildsley, Planetary Visions Ltd, London

Regional Consultants

North America Dr David Green, Department of Geography, King's College, London • Jim Walsh, Head of Reference, Wessell Library, Tufts University, Medford, Massachussetts
South America Dr David Preston, School of Geography, University of Leeds **Europe** Dr Edward M Yates, formerly of the Department of Geography, King's College, London
Africa Dr Philip Amis, Development Administration Group, University of Birmingham • Dr Ieuan Ll Griffiths, Department of Geography, University of Sussex
Dr Tony Binns, Department of Geography, University of Sussex
Central Asia Dr David Turnock, Department of Geography, University of Leicester **South and East Asia** Dr Jonathan Rigg, Department of Geography, University of Durham
Australasia and Oceania Dr Robert Allison, Department of Geography, University of Durham

Acknowledgments

Digital terrain data created by Eros Data Center, Sioux Falls, South Dakota, USA. Processed by GVS Images Inc, California, USA and Planetary Visions Ltd, London, UK
Cambridge International Reference on Current Affairs (CIRCA), Cambridge, UK • Digitization by Robertson Research International, Swanley, UK • Peter Clark
British Isles maps generated from a dataset supplied by Map Marketing Ltd/European Map Graphics Ltd in combination with DK Cartopia copyright data

DORLING KINDERSLEY CARTOGRAPHY

Editor-in-Chief Andrew Heritage **Managing Cartographer** David Roberts **Senior Cartographic Editor** Roger Bullen
Editorial Direction Louise Cavanagh **Database Manager** Simon Lewis **Art Direction** Chez Picthall

Cartographers

Pamela Alford • James Anderson • Caroline Bowie • Dale Buckton • Tony Chambers • Jan Clark • Bob Croser • Martin Darlison • Damien Demaj • Claire Ellam • Sally Gable
Jeremy Hepworth • Geraldine Horner • Chris Jackson • Christine Johnston • Julia Lunn • Michael Martin • Ed Merritt • James Mills-Hicks • Simon Mumford • John Plumer
John Scott • Ann Stephenson • Gail Townsley • Julie Turner • Sarah Vaughan • Jane Voss • Scott Wallace • Iorwerth Watkins • Bryony Webb • Alan Whitaker • Peter Winfield

Digital Maps Created in DK Cartopia by
Tom Coulson • Thomas Robertshaw
Philip Rowles • Rob Stokes
Managing Editor
Lisa Thomas
Editors
Thomas Heath • Wim Jenkins • Jane Oliver
Siobhan Ryan • Elizabeth Wyse
Editorial Research
Helen Dangerfield • Andrew Rebeiro-Hargrave
Additional Editorial Assistance
Debra Clapson • Robert Damon • Ailsa Heritage
Constance Novis • Jayne Parsons • Chris Whitwell

Placenames Database Team
Natalie Clarkson • Ruth Duxbury • Caroline Falce • John Featherstone • Dan Gardiner
Ciárán Hynes • Margaret Hynes • Helen Rudkin • Margaret Stevenson • Annie Wilson
Senior Managing Art Editor
Philip Lord
Designers
Scott David • Carol Ann Davis • David Douglas • Rhonda Fisher
Karen Gregory • Nicola Liddiard • Paul Williams
Illustrations
Ciárán Hughes • Advanced Illustration, Congleton, UK
Picture Research
Melissa Albany • James Clarke • Anna Lord
Christine Rista • Sarah Moule • Louise Thomas

First published in Great Britain in 2001 by Dorling Kindersley Limited, 80 Strand, London WC2R 0RL.

A Penguin Company

Second Edition 2003. Reprinted with revisions 2004. Third Edition 2005. Fourth Edition 2008. Fifth Edition 2011.

A CIP catalogue record for this book is available from the British Library.

ISBN: 978-1-4053-6313-6

Printed and bound by Star Standard, Singapore.

Discover more at **www.dk.com**

Introduction

EVERYTHING YOU NEED TO KNOW ABOUT OUR PLANET TODAY

For many, the outstanding legacy of the twentieth century was the way in which the Earth shrank. In the third millennium, it is increasingly important for us to have a clear vision of the world in which we live. The human population has increased fourfold since 1900. The last scraps of *terra incognita* – the polar regions and ocean depths – have been penetrated and mapped. New regions have been colonized and previously hostile realms claimed for habitation. The growth of air transport and mass tourism allows many of us to travel further, faster, and more frequently than ever before. In doing so we are given a bird's-eye view of the Earth's surface denied to our forebears.

At the same time, the amount of information about our world has grown enormously. Our multimedia environment hurls uninterrupted streams of data at us, on the printed page, through the airwaves and across our television, computer, and phone screens; events from all corners of the globe reach us instantaneously, and are witnessed as they unfold. Our sense of stability and certainty has been eroded; instead, we are aware that the world is in a constant state of flux and change. Natural disasters, man-made cataclysms, and conflicts between nations remind us daily of the enormity and fragility of our domain. The ongoing threat of international terrorism throws into very stark relief the difficulties that arise when trying to 'know' or 'understand' our planet and its many cultures.

The current crisis in our 'global' culture has made the need greater than ever before for everyone to possess an atlas. The **CONCISE** WORLD **ATLAS** has been conceived to meet this need. At its core, like all atlases, it seeks to define where places are, to describe their main characteristics, and to locate them in relation to other places. Every attempt has been made to make the information on the maps as clear, accurate, and accessible as possible using the latest digital cartographic techniques. In addition, each page of the atlas provides a wealth of further information, bringing the maps to life. Using photographs, diagrams, 'at-a-glance' maps, introductory texts, and captions, the atlas builds up a detailed portrait of those features – cultural, political, economic, and geomorphological – that make each region unique and which are also the main agents of change.

This fifth edition of the **CONCISE** WORLD **ATLAS** incorporates hundreds of revisions and updates affecting every map and every page, distilling the burgeoning mass of information available through modern technology into an extraordinarily detailed and reliable view of our world.

CONTENTS

THE WORLD

ATLAS OF THE WORLD

North America

South America

Africa

Europe

Asia

Australasia & Oceania

INDEX–GAZETTEER

Key to maps

Regional

Physical features

elevation

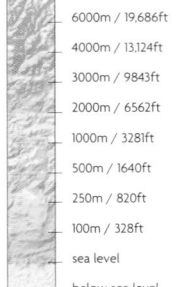

6000m / 19,686ft
4000m / 13,124ft
3000m / 9843ft
2000m / 6562ft
1000m / 3281ft
500m / 1640ft
250m / 820ft
100m / 328ft
sea level
below sea level

▲ elevation above sea level (mountain height)
▲ volcano
✕ pass
▼ elevation below sea level (depression depth)

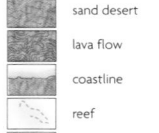

sand desert
lava flow
coastline
reef
atoll

sea depth

sea level
-250m / -820ft
-500m / -1640ft
-1000m / -3281ft
-2000m / -6562ft
-3000m / -9843ft

▲ seamount / guyot symbol
▼ undersea spot depth

Drainage features

main river
secondary river
tertiary river
minor river
main seasonal river
secondary seasonal river
canal
waterfall
rapids
dam
perennial lake
seasonal lake
perennial salt lake
seasonal salt lake
reservoir
salt flat / salt pan
marsh / salt marsh
mangrove
wadi
○ spring / well / waterhole / oasis

Ice features

ice cap / sheet
ice shelf
glacier / snowfield

summer pack ice limit

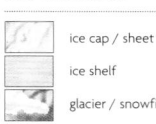
winter pack ice limit

Communications

━━━━ motorway / highway
----- motorway / highway (under construction)
━━━━ major road
──── minor road
→···→ tunnel (road)
──── main line
──── minor line
→···→ tunnel (rail)
✈ international airport

Borders

▬▬▬ full international border
■ ■ ■ ■ undefined international border
▬ ▬ ▬ disputed de facto border
▬·▬·▬ disputed territorial claim border
━ ━ ━ indication of country extent (Pacific only)
━·━·━ indication of dependent territory extent (Pacific only)
●●●●●●● demarcation/ cease fire line
▬▬▬ autonomous / federal region border
──── 2nd order internal administrative border
──── 3rd order internal administrative border

Settlements

▢ built up area

settlement population symbols

■ more than 5 million
◉ 1 million to 5 million
◎ 500,000 to 1 million
◎ 100,000 to 500,000
⊕ 50,000 to 100,000
○ 10,000 to 50,000
○ fewer than 10,000

■●● country/dependent territory capital city
■●● autonomous / federal region / 2nd order internal administrative centre
■●● 3rd order internal administrative centre

Miscellaneous features

====== ancient wall
◇ site of interest
⊙ scientific station

Graticule features

──── lines of latitude and longitude / Equator
---- Tropics / Polar circles
45° degrees of longitude / latitude

Typographic key

Physical features

landscape features ... *Namib Desert*
Massif Central
ANDES
headland .... *Nordkapp*
elevation / volcano / pass .... Mount Meru 4556 m
drainage features .... *Lake Geneva*
rivers / canals spring / well / waterhole / oasis / waterfall / rapids / dam .... *Mekong*
ice features .... *Vatnajökull*
sea features .... *Golfe de Lion*
Andaman Sea
INDIAN OCEAN
undersea features .... *Barracuda Fracture Zone*

Regions

country .... **ARMENIA**
dependent territory with parent state ..... **NIUE (to NZ)**
region outside feature area .... ANGOLA
autonomous / federal region .... MINAS GERAIS
2nd order internal administrative region .... **MINSKAYA VOBLASTS'**
3rd order internal administrative region .... Vaucluse
cultural region .... New England

Settlements

capital city .... **BEIJING**
dependent territory capital city .... FORT-DE-FRANCE
other settlements ... **Chicago**
Adana
Tizi Ozou
Yonezawa
Farnham

Miscellaneous

sites of interest / miscellaneous .... *Valley of the Kings*
Tropics / Polar circles .... *Antarctic Circle*

How to use this Atlas

The atlas is organized by continent, moving eastwards from the International Date Line. The opening section describes the world's structure, systems and its main features. The Atlas of the World which follows, is a continent-by-continent guide to today's world, starting with a comprehensive insight into the physical, political and economic structure of each continent, followed by integrated mapping and descriptions of each region or country.

The world

The introductory section of the Atlas deals with every aspect of the planet, from physical structure to human geography, providing an overall picture of the world we live in. Complex topics such as the landscape of the Earth, climate, oceans, population and economic patterns are clearly explained with the aid of maps, diagrams drawn from the latest information.

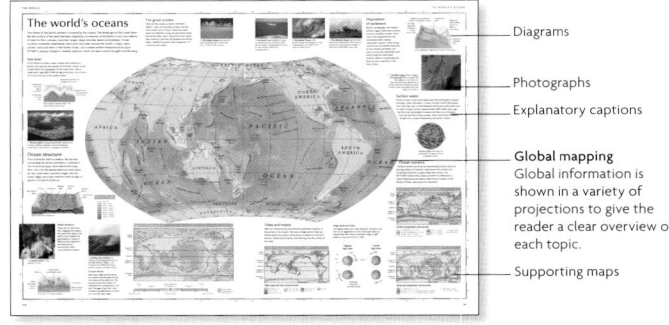

Diagrams
Photographs
Explanatory captions
Global mapping Global information is shown in a variety of projections to give the reader a clear overview of each topic.
Supporting maps

The political continent

The political portrait of the continent is a vital reference point for every continental section, showing the position of countries relative to one another, and the relationship between human settlement and geographic location. The complex mosaic of languages spoken in each continent is mapped, as is the effect of communications networks on the pattern of settlement.

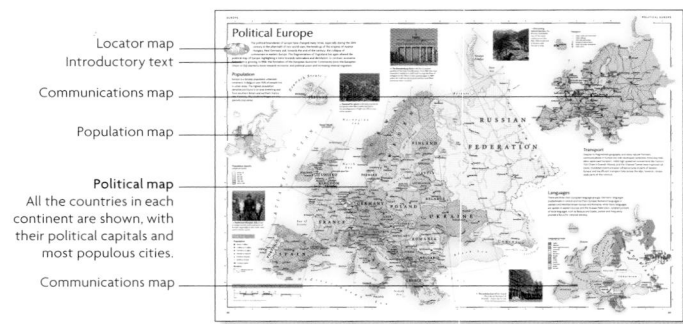

Locator map
Introductory text
Communications map
Population map
Political map All the countries in each continent are shown, with their political capitals and most populous cities.
Communications map

Continental resources

The Earth's rich natural resources, including oil, gas, minerals and fertile land, have played a key role in the development of society. These pages show the location of minerals and agricultural resources on each continent, and how they have been instrumental in dictating industrial growth and the varieties of economic activity across the continent.

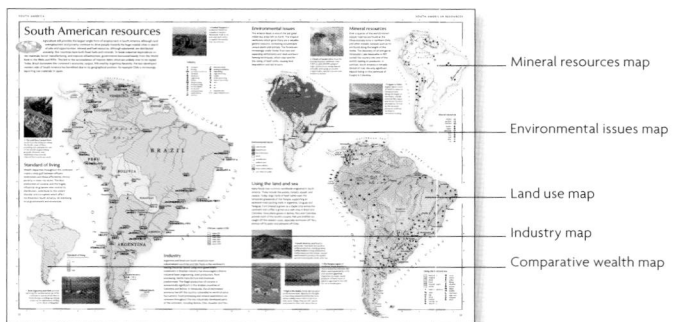

Mineral resources map
Environmental issues map
Land use map
Industry map
Comparative wealth map

The physical continent

The astonishing variety of landforms, and the dramatic forces that created and continue to shape the landscape, are explained in the continental physical spread. Cross-sections, illustrations and terrain maps highlight the different parts of the continent, showing how nature's forces have produced the landscapes we see today.

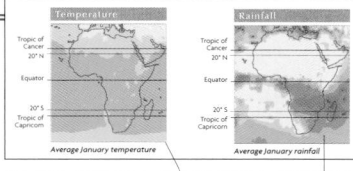

Climate charts
Rainfall and temperature charts clearly show the continental patterns of rainfall and temperature.

Climate map
Climatic regions vary across each continent. The map displays the differing climatic regions, as well as daily hours of sunshine at selected weather stations.

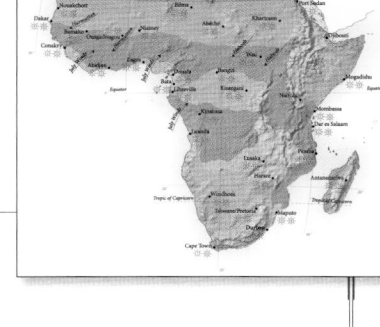

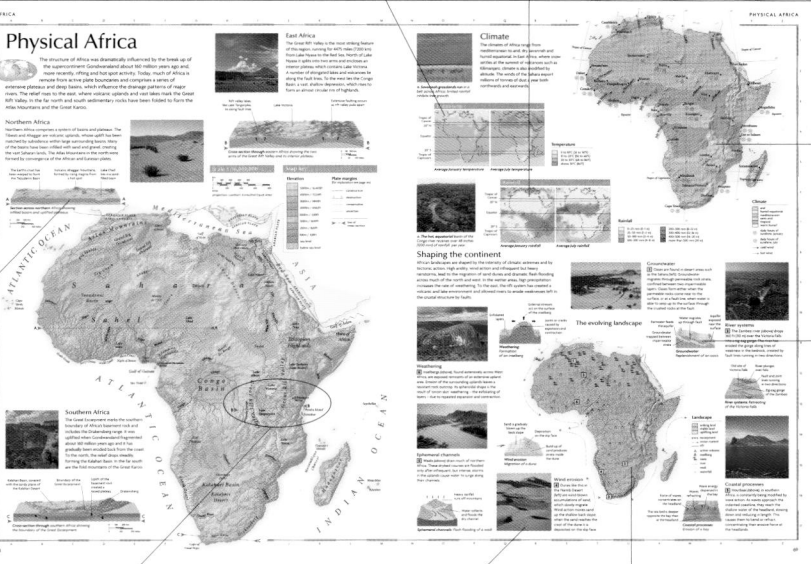

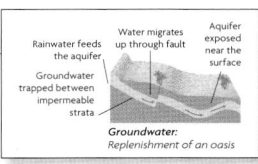

Groundwater:
Replenishment of an oasis

Landform diagrams
The complex formation of many typical landforms is summarized in these easy-to-understand illustrations.

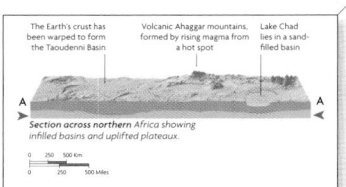

Cross-sections
Detailed cross-sections through selected parts of the continent show the underlying geomorphic structure.

Main physical map
Detailed satellite data has been used to create an accurate and visually striking picture of the surface of the continent.

Photographs
A wide range of beautiful photographs bring the world's regions to life.

Landscape evolution map
The physical shape of each continent is affected by a variety of forces which continually sculpt and modify the landscape. This map shows the major processes which affect different parts of the continent.

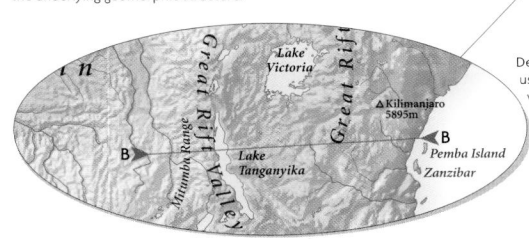

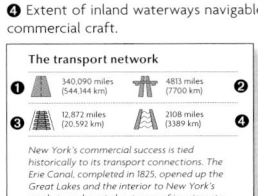

Regional mapping

The main body of the Atlas is a unique regional map set, with detailed information on the terrain, the human geography of the region and its infrastructure. Around the edge of the map, additional 'at-a-glance' maps, give an instant picture of regional industry, land use and agriculture. The detailed terrain map (shown in perspective), focuses on the main physical features of the region, and is enhanced by annotated illustrations, and photographs of the physical structure.

Key to transport symbols
❶ Extent of national paved road network.
❷ Extent of motorways, freeways or major national highways.
❸ Extent of commercial rail network.
❹ Extent of inland waterways navigable by commercial craft.

The transport network

❶	340,090 miles (544,344 km)	4813 miles (7700 km)	❷
❸	12,872 miles (20,592 km)	2108 miles (3389 km)	❹

New York's commercial success is tied historically to its transport connections. The Erie Canal, completed in 1825, opened up the Great Lakes and the interior to New York's markets and carried a stream of immigrants into the Midwest.

Transport network
The differing extent of the transport network for each region is shown here, along with key facts about the transport system.

Regional Locator
This small map shows the location of each country in relation to its continent.

Key to main map
A key to the population symbols and land heights accompanies the main map.

World locator
This locates the continent in which the region is found on a small world map.

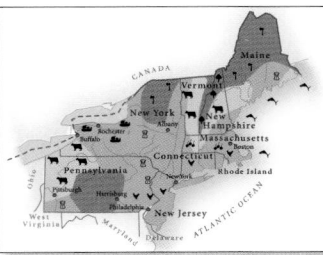

Land use map
This shows the different types of land use which characterize the region, as well as indicating the principal agricultural activities.

Map keys
Each supporting map has its own key.

Grid reference
The framing grid provides a location reference for each place listed in the Index.

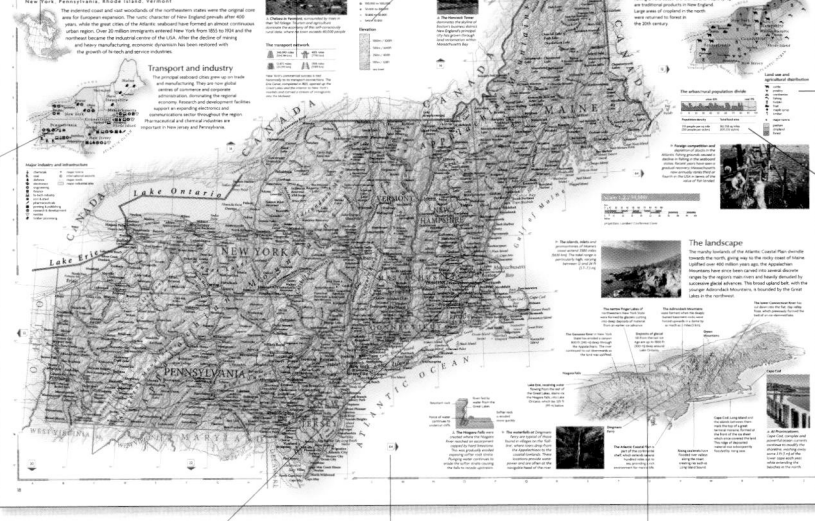

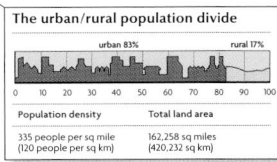

The urban/rural population divide

urban 83%   rural 17%

0 10 20 30 40 50 60 70 80 90 100

Population density	Total land area
335 people per sq mile (120 people per sq km)	162,258 sq miles (420,232 sq km)

Urban/rural population divide
The proportion of people in the region who live in urban and rural areas, as well as the overall population density and land area are clearly shown in these simple graphics.

Transport and industry map
The main industrial areas are mapped, and the most important industrial and economic activities of the region are shown.

Continuation symbols
These symbols indicate where adjacent maps can be found.

Landscape map
The computer-generated terrain model accurately portrays an oblique view of the landscape. Annotations highlight the most important geographic features of the region.

Main regional map
A wealth of information is displayed on the main map, building up a rich portrait of the interaction between the physical landscape and the human and political geography of each region. The key to the regional maps can be found on page viii.

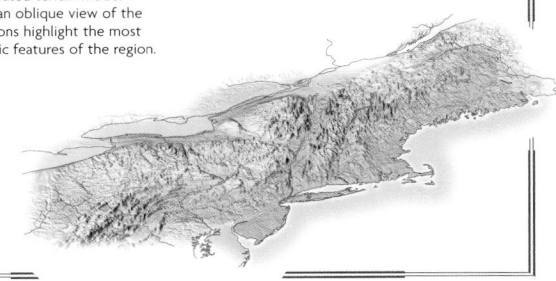

The Solar System

Nine major planets, their satellites and countless minor planets (asteroids) orbit the Sun to form the Solar System. The Sun, our nearest star, creates energy from nuclear reactions deep within its interior, providing all the light and heat which make life on Earth possible. The Earth is unique in the Solar System in that it supports life: its size, gravitational pull and distance from the Sun have all created the optimum conditions for the evolution of life. The planetary images seen here are composites derived from actual spacecraft images (not shown to scale).

Orbits

All the Solar System's planets and dwarf planets orbit the Sun in the same direction and (apart from Pluto) roughly in the same plane. All the orbits have the shapes of ellipses (stretched circles). However in most cases, these ellipses are close to being circular: only Pluto and Eris have very elliptical orbits. Orbital period (the time it takes an object to orbit the Sun) increases with distance from the Sun. The more remote objects not only have further to travel with each orbit, they also move more slowly.

Ceres
(dwarf planet)

Mercury   Venus   Earth   Mars

Jupiter

The Sun

- ⊖ *Diameter: 864,948 miles (1,392,000 km)*
- ● *Mass: 1990 million million million million tons*

The Sun was formed when a swirling cloud of dust and gas contracted, pulling matter into its centre. When the temperature at the centre rose to 1,000,000°C, nuclear fusion – the fusing of hydrogen into helium, creating energy – occurred, releasing a constant stream of heat and light.

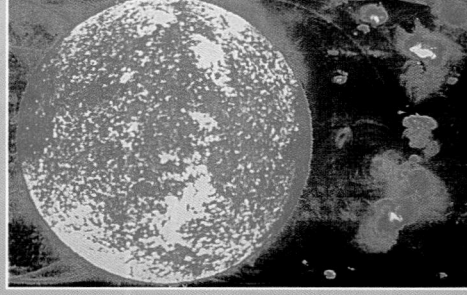

▲ *Solar flares are sudden bursts of energy from the Sun's surface. They can be 125,000 miles (200,000 km) long.*

The formation of the Solar System

The cloud of dust and gas thrown out by the Sun during its formation cooled to form the Solar System. The smaller planets nearest the Sun are formed of minerals and metals. The outer planets were formed at lower temperatures, and consist of swirling clouds of gases.

Solar eclipse

A solar eclipse occurs when the Moon passes between Earth and the Sun, casting its shadow on Earth's surface. During a total eclipse *(below)*, viewers along a strip of Earth's surface, called the area of totality, see the Sun totally blotted out for a short time, as the umbra (Moon's full shadow) sweeps over them. Outside this area is a larger one, where the Sun appears only partly obscured, as the penumbra (partial shadow) passes over.

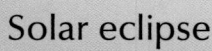
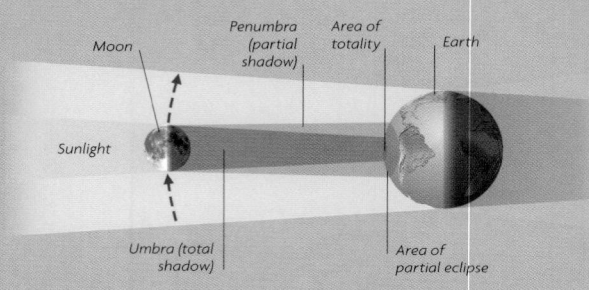

Moon

Penumbra *(partial shadow)*   Area of totality   Earth

Sunlight

Umbra *(total shadow)*   Area of partial eclipse

PLANETS

	MERCURY	VENUS	EARTH	MARS	JUPITER	SATURN	URANUS	NEPTUNE
DIAMETER	3029 miles (4875 km)	7521 miles (12,104 km)	7928 miles (12,756 km)	4213 miles (6780 km)	88,846 miles (142,984 km)	74,898 miles (120,536 km)	31,763 miles (51,118 km)	30,775 miles (49,528 km)
AVERAGE DISTANCE FROM THE SUN	36 mill. miles (57.9 mill. km)	67.2 mill. miles (108.2 mill. km)	93 mill. miles (149.6 mill. km)	141.6 mill. miles (227.9 mill. km)	483.6 mill. miles (778.3 mill. km)	889.8 mill. miles (1431 mill. km)	1788 mill. miles (2877 mill. km)	2795 mill. miles (4498 mill. km)
ROTATION PERIOD	58.6 days	243 days	23.93 hours	24.62 hours	9.93 hours	10.65 hours	17.24 hours	16.11 hours
ORBITAL PERIOD	88 days	224.7 days	365.26 days	687 days	11.86 years	29.37 years	84.1 years	164.9 years
SURFACE TEMPERATURE	-180°C to 430°C (-292°F to 806°F)	480°C (896°F)	-70°C to 55°C (-94°F to 131°F)	-120°C to 25°C (-184°F to 77 °F)	-110°C (-160°F)	-140°C (-220°F)	-200°C (-320°F)	-200°C (-320°F)

DWARF PLANETS

	CERES	PLUTO	ERIS
DIAMETER	590 miles (950 km)	1432 miles (2304 km)	1429-1553 miles (2300-2500 km)
AVERAGE DISTANCE FROM THE SUN	257 mill. miles (414 mill. km)	3675 mill. miles (5915 mill. km)	6344 mill. miles (10,210 mill. km)
ROTATION PERIOD	9.1 hours	6.38 days	not known
ORBITAL PERIOD	4.6 years	248.6 years	557 years
SURFACE TEMPERATURE	-107°C (-161°F)	-230°C (-380°F)	-243°C (-405°F)

AVERAGE DISTANCE FROM THE SUN

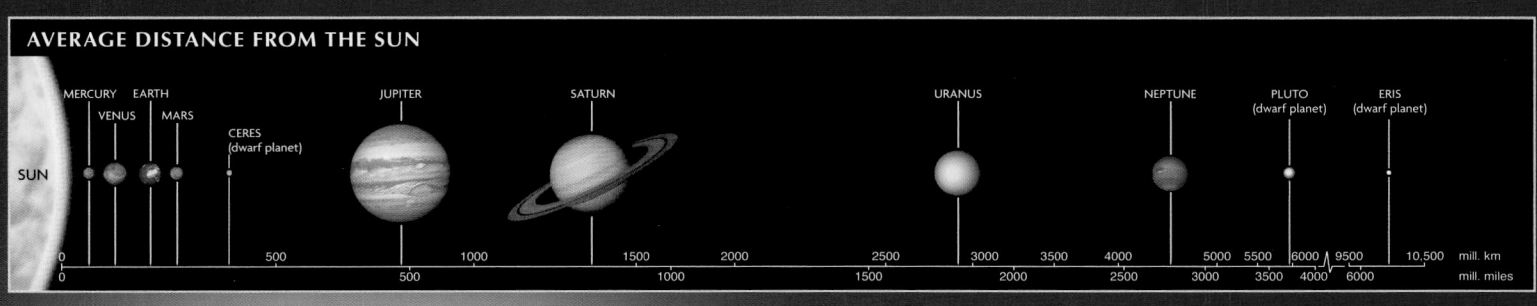

SUN · MERCURY · VENUS · EARTH · MARS · CERES (dwarf planet) · JUPITER · SATURN · URANUS · NEPTUNE · PLUTO (dwarf planet) · ERIS (dwarf planet)

0 · 500 · 1000 · 1500 · 2000 · 2500 · 3000 · 3500 · 4000 · 5000 5500 · 6000 9500 · 10,500 mill. km
0 · 500 · 1000 · 1500 · 2000 · 2500 · 3000 · 3500 · 4000 6000 mill. miles

Saturn

Uranus

Neptune

Eris (dwarf planet)

Pluto (dwarf planet)

Space debris

Millions of objects, remnants of planetary formation, circle the Sun in a zone lying between Mars and Jupiter: the asteroid belt. Fragments of asteroids break off to form meteoroids, which can reach the Earth's surface. Comets, composed of ice and dust, originated outside our Solar System. Their elliptical orbit brings them close to the Sun and into the inner Solar System.

▲ *Meteor Crater in* Arizona is *4200 ft (1300 m) wide and 660 ft (200 m) deep. It was formed over 10,000 years ago.*

Possible and actual meteorite craters

Map key
◦ Possible impact craters
◦ Meteorite impact craters

The Earth's atmosphere

During the early stages of the Earth's formation, ash, lava, carbon dioxide and water vapour were discharged onto the surface of the planet by constant volcanic eruptions. The water formed the oceans, while carbon dioxide entered the atmosphere or was dissolved in the oceans. Clouds, formed of water droplets, reflected some of the Sun's radiation back into space. The Earth's temperature stabilized and early life forms began to emerge, converting carbon dioxide into life-giving oxygen.

▲ *It is thought that the gases that make up the Earth's atmosphere originated deep within the interior, and were released many millions of years ago during intense volcanic actvity, similar to this eruption at Mount St. Helens.*

▲ *The orbit of* Halley's Comet *brings it close to the Earth every 76 years. It last visited in 1986.*

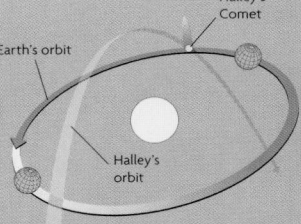

Halley's Comet

Earth's orbit

Halley's orbit

Orbit of Halley's Comet around the Sun

The physical world

The Earth's surface is constantly being transformed: it is uplifted, folded and faulted by tectonic forces; weathered and eroded by wind, water and ice. Sometimes change is dramatic, the spectacular results of earthquakes or floods. More often it is a slow process lasting millions of years. A physical map of the world represents a snapshot of the ever-evolving architecture of the Earth. This terrain map shows the whole surface of the Earth, both above and below the sea.

Map key

Geographical regions

- ice
- tundra
- needleleaf forest
- broadleaf forest
- cultivated land
- hot desert
- cold desert
- tropical grassland
- tropical rainforest
- mountain
- submarine regions

Scale 1:73,000,000

Km
0 250 500 1000 1500 2000

Miles
0 250 500 1000 1500 2000

projection: Wagner VII

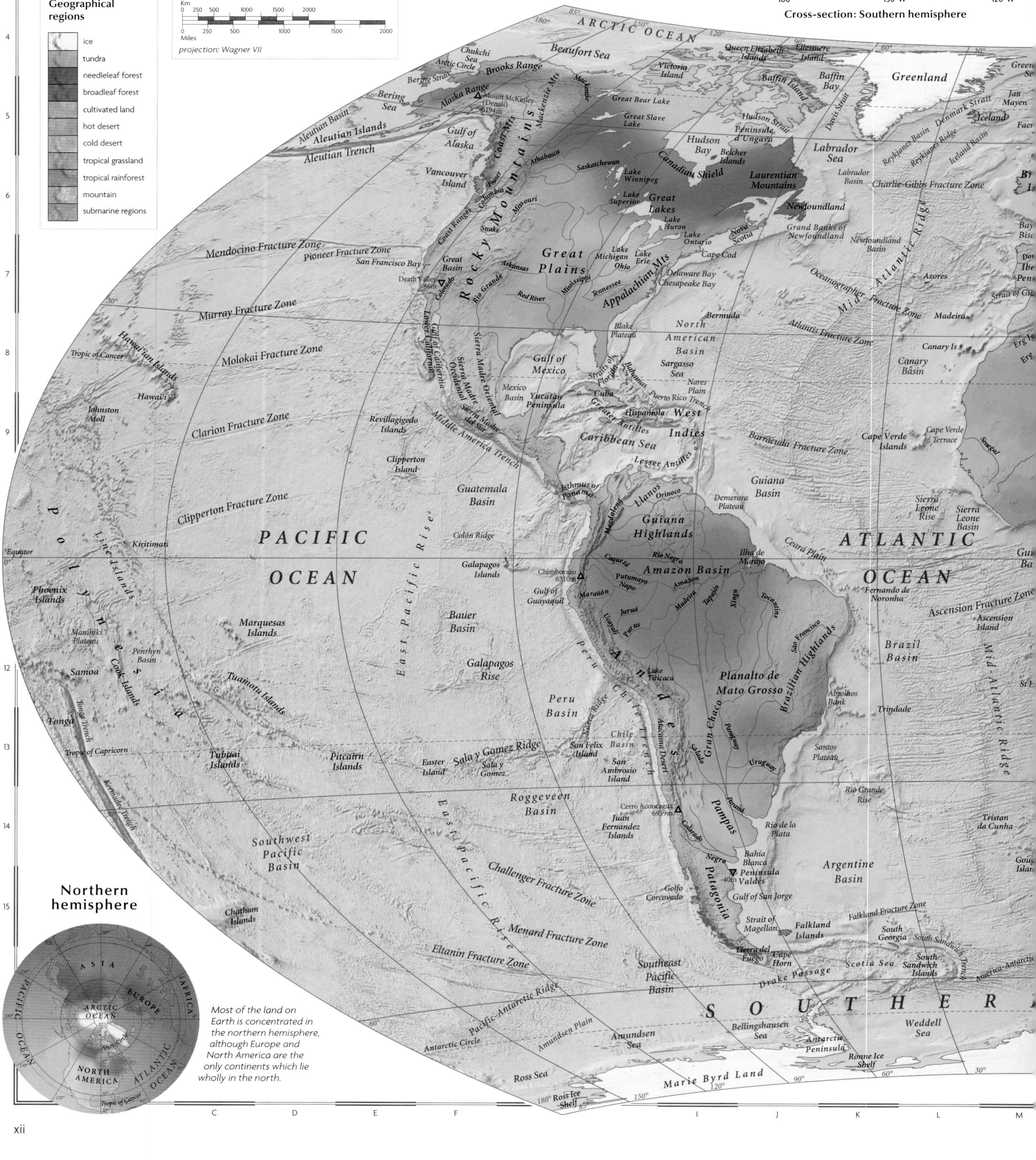

The world in section

These cross-sections around the Earth, one in the northern hemisphere; one straddling the Equator, reveal the limited areas of land above sea level in comparison with the extent of the sea floor. The greater erosive effects of weathering by wind and water limit the upward elevation of land above sea level, while the deep oceans retain their dramatic mountain and trench profiles.

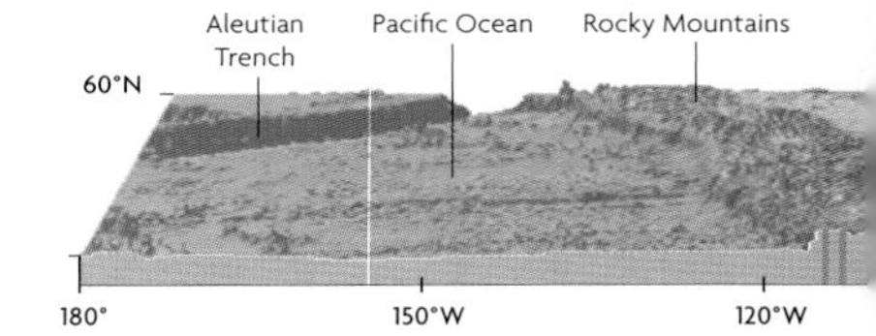

Aleutian Trench Pacific Ocean Rocky Mountains
60°N
180° 150°W 120°W
Cross-section: Northern hemisphere

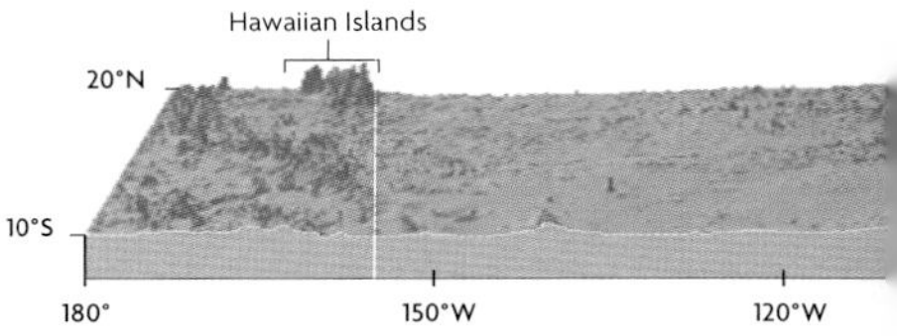

Hawaiian Islands
20°N
10°S
180° 150°W 120°W
Cross-section: Southern hemisphere

Northern hemisphere

Most of the land on Earth is concentrated in the northern hemisphere, although Europe and North America are the only continents which lie wholly in the north.

xii

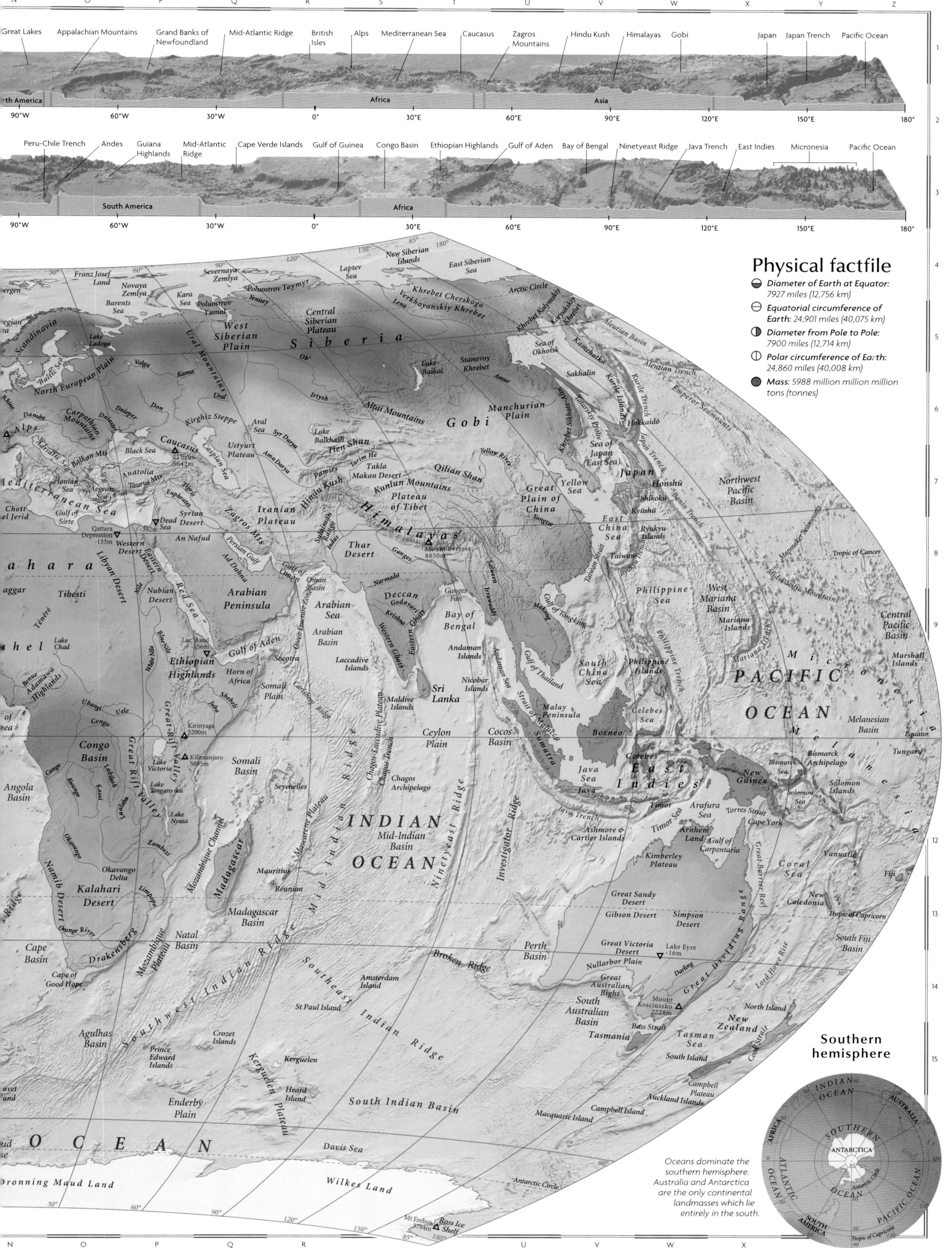

Physical factfile

- **Diameter of Earth at Equator:** 7927 miles (12,756 km)
- **Equatorial circumference of Earth:** 24,901 miles (40,075 km)
- **Diameter from Pole to Pole:** 7900 miles (12,714 km)
- **Polar circumference of Earth:** 24,860 miles (40,008 km)
- **Mass:** 5988 million million million tons (tonnes)

Southern hemisphere

Oceans dominate the southern hemisphere. Australia and Antarctica are the only continental landmasses which lie entirely in the south.

Structure of the Earth

The Earth as it is today is just the latest phase in a constant process of evolution which has occurred over the past 4.5 billion years. The Earth's continents are neither fixed nor stable; over the course of the Earth's history, propelled by currents rising from the intense heat at its centre, the great plates on which they lie have moved, collided, joined together, and separated. These processes continue to mould and transform the surface of the Earth, causing earthquakes and volcanic eruptions and creating oceans, mountain ranges, deep ocean trenches and island chains.

Inside the Earth

The Earth's hot inner core is made up of solid iron, while the outer core is composed of liquid iron and nickel. The mantle nearest the core is viscous, whereas the rocky upper mantle is fairly rigid. The crust is the rocky outer shell of the Earth. Together, the upper mantle and the crust form the lithosphere.

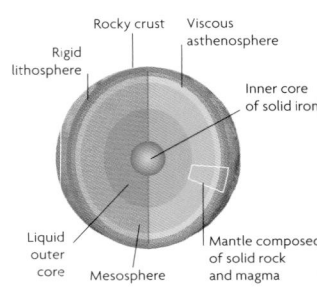

Rigid lithosphere / Rocky crust / Viscous asthenosphere / Inner core of solid iron / Mantle composed of solid rock and magma / Mesosphere / Liquid outer core

The dynamic Earth

The Earth's crust is made up of eight major (and several minor) rigid continental and oceanic tectonic plates, which fit closely together. The positions of the plates are not static. They are constantly moving relative to one another. The type of movement between plates affects the way in which they alter the structure of the Earth. The oldest parts of the plates, known as shields, are the most stable parts of the Earth and little tectonic activity occurs here.

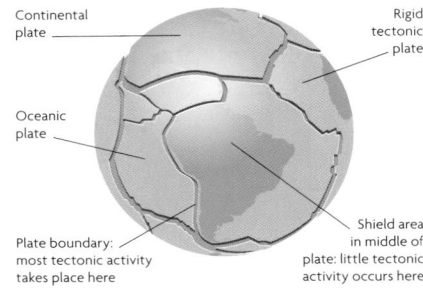

Continental plate / Rigid tectonic plate / Oceanic plate / Plate boundary: most tectonic activity takes place here / Shield area in middle of plate: little tectonic activity occurs here

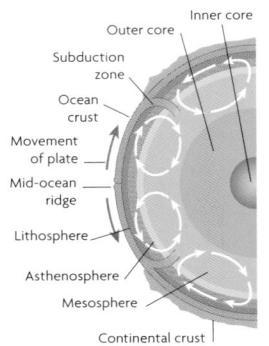

Inner core / Outer core / Subduction zone / Ocean crust / Movement of plate / Mid-ocean ridge / Lithosphere / Asthenosphere / Mesosphere / Continental crust

Convection currents

Deep within the Earth, at its inner core, temperatures may exceed 8100°F (4500°C). This heat warms rocks in the mesosphere which rise through the partially molten mantle, displacing cooler rocks just below the solid crust, which sink, and are warmed again by the heat of the mantle. This process is continually repeated, creating convection currents which form the moving force beneath the Earth's crust.

Plate boundaries

The boundaries between the plates are the areas where most tectonic activity takes place. Three types of movement occur at plate boundaries: the plates can either move towards each other, move apart, or slide past each other. The effect this has on the Earth's structure depends on whether the margin is between two continental plates, two oceanic plates or an oceanic and continental plate.

◀ **The Mid-Atlantic Ridge** rises above sea level in Iceland, producing geysers and volcanoes.

Mid-ocean ridges

Mid-ocean ridges are formed when two adjacent oceanic plates pull apart, allowing magma to force its way up to the surface, which then cools to form solid rock. Vast amounts of volcanic material are discharged at these mid-ocean ridges which can reach heights of 10,000 ft (3000 m).

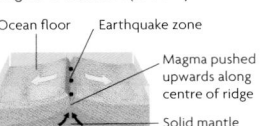

Ocean floor / Earthquake zone / Magma pushed upwards along centre of ridge / Solid mantle

Formation of a mid-ocean ridge

▲ **Mount Pinatubo is** an active volcano, lying on the Pacific 'Ring of Fire'.

Ocean plates meeting

△△ Oceanic crust is denser and thinner than continental crust; on average it is 3 miles (5 km) thick, while continental crust averages 18–24 miles (30–40 km). When oceanic plates of similar density meet, the crust is contorted as one plate overrides the other, forming deep sea trenches and volcanic island arcs above sea level.

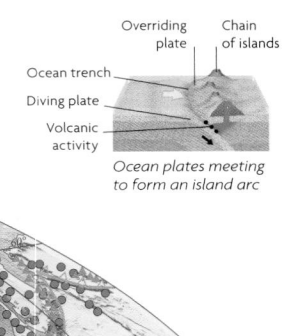

Overriding plate / Chain of islands / Ocean trench / Diving plate / Volcanic activity

Ocean plates meeting to form an island arc

Tectonic activity

- - - - - uncertain plate boundary
▲ volcanic zone
● earthquake zone
● hot spot
ⵛⵛⵛⵛ rift valley

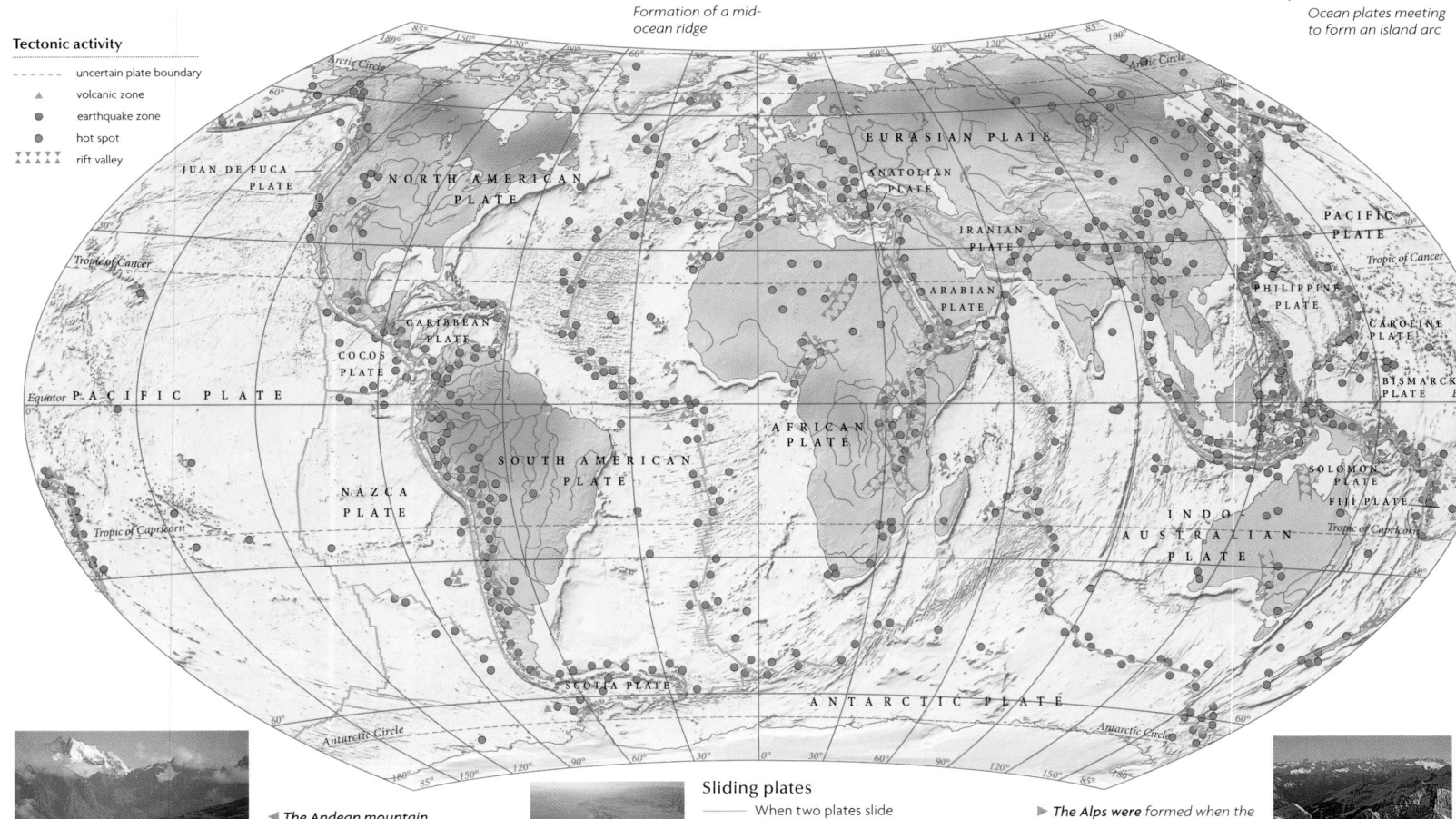

JUAN DE FUCA PLATE / NORTH AMERICAN PLATE / EURASIAN PLATE / ANATOLIAN PLATE / IRANIAN PLATE / PACIFIC PLATE / CARIBBEAN PLATE / ARABIAN PLATE / PHILIPPINE PLATE / CAROLINE PLATE / COCOS PLATE / PACIFIC PLATE / BISMARCK PLATE / AFRICAN PLATE / SOUTH AMERICAN PLATE / SOLOMON PLATE / FIJI PLATE / NAZCA PLATE / INDO AUSTRALIAN PLATE / SCOTIA PLATE / ANTARCTIC PLATE

Arctic Circle / Tropic of Cancer / Equator / Tropic of Capricorn / Antarctic Circle

Diving plates

△△ When an oceanic and a continental plate meet, the denser oceanic plate is driven underneath the continental plate, which is crumpled by the collision to form mountain ranges. As the ocean plate plunges downward, it heats up, and molten rock (magma) is forced up to the surface.

◀ **The Andean mountain** chain is the typical result of the impact of a diving plate.

Oceanic plate dives under continental plate / Mountains thrust up by collision / Earthquake zone / Continental plate

Diving plate

▲ **The deep fracture** caused by the sliding plates of the San Andreas Fault can be clearly seen in parts of California.

Sliding plates

When two plates slide past each other, friction is caused along the fault line which divides them. The plates do not move smoothly, and the uneven movement causes earthquakes.

Plate / Plate / Fault line / Earthquake zone

Sliding plates

▶ **The Alps were** formed when the African Plate collided with the Eurasian Plate, about 65 million years ago.

Plate buckles as it collides / Mountains thrust upwards / Earthquake zone / Crust thickens in response to the impact

Continental plates colliding to form a mountain range

Colliding plates

△△△ When two continental plates collide, great mountain chains are thrust upwards as the crust buckles and folds under the force of the impact.

Continental drift

Although the plates which make up the Earth's crust move only a few centimetres in a year, over the millions of years of the Earth's history, its continents have moved many thousands of kilometres, to create new continents, oceans and mountain chains.

1: Cambrian period

570–510 million years ago. Most continents are in tropical latitudes. The supercontinent of Gondwanaland reaches the South Pole.

2: Devonian period

408–362 million years ago. The continents of Gondwanaland and Laurentia are drifting northwards.

3: Carboniferous period

362–290 million years ago. The Earth is dominated by three continents; Laurentia, Angaraland and Gondwanaland.

4: Triassic period

245–208 million years ago. All three major continents have joined to form the super-continent of Pangea.

5: Jurassic period

208–145 million years ago. The super-continent of Pangea begins to break up, causing an overall rise in sea levels.

6: Cretaceous period

145–65 million years ago. Warm shallow seas cover much of the land; sea levels are about 80 ft (25 m) above present levels.

7: Tertiary period

65–2 million years ago. Although the world's geography is becoming more recognizable, major events such as the creation of the Himalayan mountain chain, are still to occur during this period.

Continental shields

The centres of the Earth's continents, known as shields, were established between 2500 and 500 million years ago; some contain rocks over three billion years old. They were formed by a series of turbulent events: plate movements, earthquakes and volcanic eruptions. Since the Pre-Cambrian period, over 570 million years ago, they have experienced little tectonic activity, and today, these flat, low-lying slabs of solidified molten rock form the stable centres of the continents. They are bounded or covered by successive belts of younger sedimentary rock.

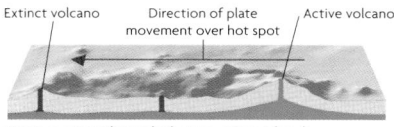

The Hawai'ian island chain

A hot spot lying deep beneath the Pacific Ocean pushes a plume of magma from the Earth's mantle up through the Pacific Plate to form volcanic islands. While the hot spot remains stationary, the plate on which the islands sit is moving slowly. A long chain of islands has been created as the plate passes over the hot spot.

Extinct volcano | Direction of plate movement over hot spot | Active volcano

Cross-section through the Hawai'ian Islands

Evolution of the Hawai'ian Islands

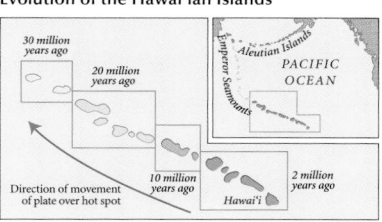

Creation of the Himalayas

Between 10 and 20 million years ago, the Indian subcontinent, part of the ancient continent of Gondwanaland, collided with the continent of Asia. The Indo-Australian Plate continued to move northwards, displacing continental crust and uplifting the Himalayas, the world's highest mountain chain.

Movements of India

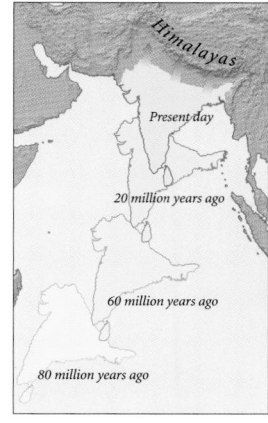

Force of collision pushes up mountains

Cross-section through the Himalayas

▲ **The Himalayas were** uplifted when the Indian subcontinent collided with Asia.

The Earth's geology

The Earth's rocks are created in a continual cycle. Exposed rocks are weathered and eroded by wind, water and chemicals and deposited as sediments. If they pass into the Earth's crust they will be transformed by high temperatures and pressures into metamorphic rocks or they will melt and solidify as igneous rocks.

Sandstone

[8] Sandstones are sedimentary rocks formed mainly in deserts, beaches and deltas. Desert sandstones are formed of grains of quartz which have been well rounded by wind erosion.

▲ **Rock stacks** of desert sandstone, at Bryce Canyon National Park, Utah, USA.

◀ **Extrusive igneous rocks** are formed during volcanic eruptions, as here in Hawai'i.

Andesite

[7] Andesite is an extrusive igneous rock formed from magma which has solidified on the Earth's crust after a volcanic eruption.

Gneiss

[1] Gneiss is a metamorphic rock made at great depth during the formation of mountain chains, when intense heat and pressure transform sedimentary or igneous rocks.

▲ **Gneiss formations in** Norway's Jotunheimen Mountains.

◀ **Basalt columns at** Giant's Causeway, Northern Ireland, UK.

Basalt

[2] Basalt is an igneous rock, formed when small quantities of magma lying close to the Earth's surface cool rapidly.

Limestone

[3] Limestone is a sedimentary rock, which is formed mainly from the calcite skeletons of marine animals which have been compressed into rock.

▲ **Limestone hills, Guilin,** China.

Coral

[4] Coral reefs are formed from the skeletons of millions of individual corals.

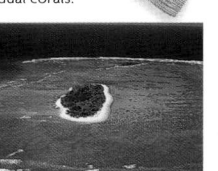

▲ **Great Barrier Reef,** Australia.

Geological regions

- continental shield
- sedimentary cover
- coral formation
- igneous rock types

Mountain ranges

- Alpine (new)
- Hercynian (old)
- Caledonian (ancient)

Schist

[6] Gchist is a metamorphic rock formed during mountain building, when temperature and pressure are comparatively high. Both mudstones and shales reform into schist under these conditions.

▶ **Schist formations in** the Atlas Mountains, northwestern Africa.

Granite

[5] Granite is an intrusive igneous rock formed from magma which has solidified deep within the Earth's crust. The magma cools slowly, producing a coarse-grained rock.

▶ **Namibia's Namaqualand Plateau** is formed of granite.

Shaping the landscape

The basic material of the Earth's surface is solid rock: valleys, deserts, soil, and sand are all evidence of the powerful agents of weathering, erosion, and deposition which constantly shape and transform the Earth's landscapes. Water, either flowing continually in rivers or seas, or frozen and compacted into solid sheets of ice, has the most clearly visible impact on the Earth's surface. But wind can transport fragments of rock over huge distances and strip away protective layers of vegetation, exposing rock surfaces to the impact of extreme heat and cold.

Coastal water

The world's coastlines are constantly changing; every day, tides deposit, sift and sort sand, and gravel on the shoreline. Over longer periods, powerful wave action erodes cliffs and headlands and carves out bays.

► *A low, wide* sandy beach on South Africa's Cape Peninsula is continually re-shaped by the action of the Atlantic waves.

▲ *The sheer chalk* cliffs at Seven Sisters in southern England are constantly under attack from waves.

Water

Less than 2% of the world's water is on the land, but it is the most powerful agent of landscape change. Water, as rainfall, groundwater and rivers, can transform landscapes through both erosion and deposition. Eroded material carried by rivers forms the world's most fertile soils.

▲ *Waterfalls such as* the Iguaçu Falls on the border between Argentina and southern Brazil, erode the underlying rock, causing the falls to retreat.

Groundwater

In regions where there are porous rocks such as chalk, water is stored underground in large quantities; these reservoirs of water are known as aquifers. Rain percolates through topsoil into the underlying bedrock, creating an underground store of water. The limit of the saturated zone is called the water table.

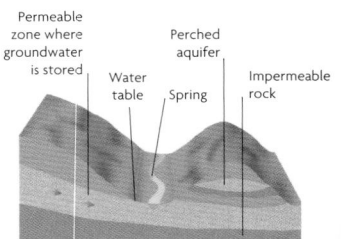
Storage of groundwater in an aquifer

World river systems

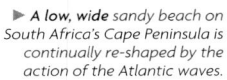
drainage basin

World river systems:
Sediment deposited annually per drainage basin

Rivers

Rivers erode the land by grinding and dissolving rocks and stones. Most erosion occurs in the river's upper course as it flows through highland areas. Rock fragments are moved along the river bed by fast-flowing water and deposited in areas where the river slows down, such as flat plains, or where the river enters seas or lakes.

River valleys

Over long periods of time rivers erode uplands to form characteristic V-shaped valleys with smooth sides.

River valley erosion

Deltas

When a river deposits its load of silt and sediment (alluvium) on entering the sea, it may form a delta. As this material accumulates, it chokes the mouth of the river, forcing it to create new channels to reach the sea.

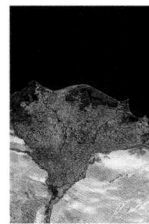
► *The Nile forms* a broad delta as it flows into the Mediterranean.

Drainage basins

The drainage basin is the area of land drained by a major trunk river and its smaller branch rivers or tributaries. Drainage basins are separated from one another by natural boundaries known as watersheds.

The drainage basin of the Po river, northern Italy.

Meanders

In their lower courses, rivers flow slowly. As they flow across the lowlands, they form looping bends called meanders.

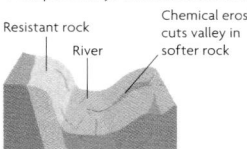
◄ *Mud is deposited* by China's Yellow River in its lower course.

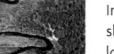

▲ *The Mississippi River* forms meanders as it flows across the southern US.

▲ *The meanders of* Utah's San Juan River have become deeply incised.

Deposition

When rivers have deposited large quantities of fertile alluvium, they are forced to find new channels through the alluvium deposits, creating braided river systems.

Landslides

Heavy rain and associated flooding on slopes can loosen underlying rocks, which crumble, causing the top layers of rock and soil to slip.

► *A huge landslide* in the Swiss Alps has left massive piles of rocks and pebbles called scree.

Gullies

In areas where soil is thin, rainwater is not effectively absorbed, and may flow overland. The water courses downhill in channels, or gullies, and may lead to rapid erosion of soil.

▲ *A deep gully* in the French Alps caused by the scouring of upper layers of turf.

Ice

During its long history, the Earth has experienced a number of glacial episodes when temperatures were considerably lower than today. During the last Ice Age, 18,000 years ago, ice covered an area three times larger than it does today. Over these periods, the ice has left a remarkable legacy of transformed landscapes.

Glaciers

Glaciers are formed by the compaction of snow into 'rivers' of ice. As they move over the landscape, glaciers pick up and carry a load of rocks and boulders which erode the landscape they pass over, and are eventually deposited at the end of the glacier.

▲ *A massive glacier* advancing down a valley in southern Argentina.

Post-glacial features

When a glacial episode ends, the retreating ice leaves many features. These include depositional ridges called moraines, which may be eroded into low hills known as drumlins; sinuous ridges called eskers; kames, which are rounded hummocks; depressions known as kettle holes; and windblown loess deposits.

Glacial valleys

Glaciers can erode much more powerfully than rivers. They form steep-sided, flat-bottomed valleys with a typical U-shaped profile. Valleys created by tributary glaciers, whose floors have not been eroded to the same depth as the main glacial valley floor, are called hanging valleys

▲ *The U-shaped profile* and piles of morainic debris are characteristic of a valley once filled by a glacier.

▲ *A series of* hanging valleys high up in the Chilean Andes.

▲ *The profile of* the Matterhorn has been formed by three cirques lying 'back-to-back'.

Cirques

Cirques are basin-shaped hollows which mark the head of a glaciated valley. Where neighboring cirques meet, they are divided by sharp rock ridges called arêtes. It is these arêtes which give the Matterhorn its characteristic profile.

Fjords

Fjords are ancient glacial valleys flooded by the sea following the end of a period of glaciation. Beneath the water, the valley floor can be 4000 ft (1300 m) deep.

▲ *A fjord fills* a former glacial valley in southern New Zealand.

Periglaciation

Periglacial areas occur near to the edge of ice sheets. A layer of frozen ground lying just beneath the surface of the land is known as permafrost. When the surface melts in the summer, the water is unable to drain into the frozen ground, and so 'creeps' downhill, a process known as solifluction.

Past and present world ice-cover and glacial features

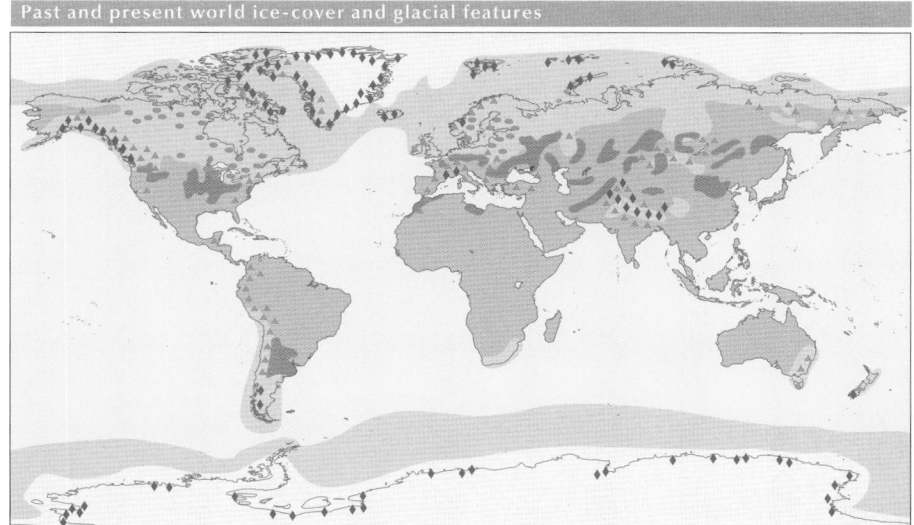

Post-glacial landscape features

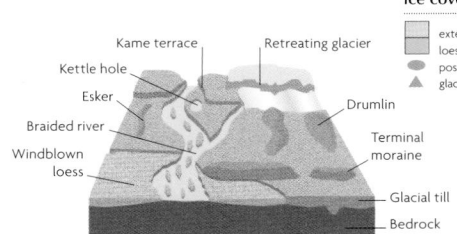

Kame terrace — Retreating glacier
Kettle hole
Esker
Braided river — Drumlin
Windblown loess — Terminal moraine
— Glacial till
— Bedrock

Post-glacial landscape features

Past and present world ice cover and glacial features

- extent of last Ice Age
- loess deposits
- post-glacial feature
- glacial feature
- present day ice cover
- glacial field

Ice shattering

Water drips into fissures in rocks and freezes, expanding as it does so. The pressure weakens the rock, causing it to crack, and eventually to shatter into polygonal patterns.

▲ *Irregular polygons show* through the sedge-grass tundra in the Yukon, Canada.

Wind

Strong winds can transport rock fragments great distances, especially where there is little vegetation to protect the rock. In desert areas, wind picks up loose, unprotected sand particles, carrying them over great distances. This powerfully abrasive debris is blasted at the surface by the wind, eroding the landscape into dramatic shapes.

Deposition

The rocky, stony floors of the world's deserts are swept and scoured by strong winds. The smaller, finer particles of sand are shaped into surface ripples, dunes, or sand mountains, which rise to a height of 650 ft (200 m). Dunes usually form single lines, running perpendicular to the direction of the prevailing wind. These long, straight ridges can extend for over 100 miles (160 km).

Dunes

Dunes are shaped by wind direction and sand supply. Where sand supply is limited, crescent-shaped barchan dunes are formed.

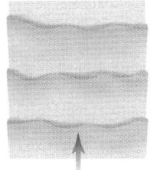

Wind direction

Prevailing winds and dust trajectories

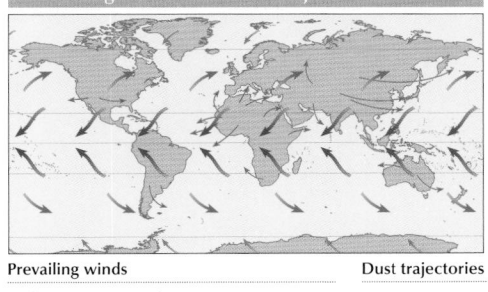

Prevailing winds
- northeast trade
- southeast trade
- westerly
- westerly
- polar easterly
- polar easterly

Dust trajectories
- trajectory of aeolian dust

Hot and cold deserts

Main desert types
- hot arid
- semi-arid
- cold polar

▲ *Barchan dunes in the* Arabian Desert.

▲ *Complex dune system in* the Sahara.

Heat

Fierce sun can heat the surface of rock, causing it to expand more rapidly than the cooler, underlying layers. This creates tensions which force the rock to crack or break up. In arid regions, the evaporation of water from rock surfaces dissolves certain minerals within the water, causing salt crystals to form in small openings in the rock. The hard crystals force the openings to widen into cracks and fissures.

▲ *The cracked and* parched floor of Death Valley, California. This is one of the hottest deserts on Earth.

Types of dune

Transverse dune *Barchan dune* *Linear dune* *Star dune*

Temperature

Most of the world's deserts are in the tropics. The cold deserts which occur elsewhere are arid because they are a long way from the rain-giving sea. Rock in deserts is exposed because of lack of vegetation and is susceptible to changes in temperature; extremes of heat and cold can cause both cracks and fissures to appear in the rock.

Desert abrasion

Abrasion creates a wide range of desert landforms from faceted pebbles and wind ripples in the sand, to large-scale features such as yardangs (low, streamlined ridges), and scoured desert pavements.

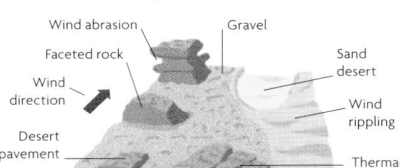

Wind abrasion — Gravel
Faceted rock
Wind direction — Sand desert
Desert pavement — Wind rippling
— Thermal fracturing

Features of a desert surface

◄ *This dry valley* at Ellesmere Island in the Canadian Arctic is an example of a cold desert. The cracked floor and scoured slopes are features also found in hot deserts.

The world's oceans

Two-thirds of the Earth's surface is covered by the oceans. The landscape of the ocean floor, like the surface of the land, has been shaped by movements of the Earth's crust over millions of years to form volcanic mountain ranges, deep trenches, basins and plateaux. Ocean currents constantly redistribute warm and cold water around the world. A major warm current, such as El Niño in the Pacific Ocean, can increase surface temperature by up to 10°F (8°C), causing changes in weather patterns which can lead to both droughts and flooding.

The great oceans

There are five oceans on Earth: the Pacific, Atlantic, Indian and Southern oceans, and the much smaller Arctic Ocean. These five ocean basins are relatively young, having evolved within the last 80 million years. One of the most recent plate collisions, between the Eurasian and African plates, created the present-day arrangement of continents and oceans.

▲ *The Indian Ocean* accounts for approximately 20% of the total area of the world's oceans.

Sea level

If the influence of tides, winds, currents and variations in gravity were ignored, the surface of the Earth's oceans would closely follow the topography of the ocean floor, with an underwater ridge 3000 ft (915 m) high producing a rise of up to 3 ft (1 m) in the level of the surface water.

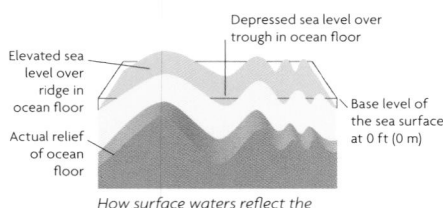

Elevated sea level over ridge in ocean floor

Depressed sea level over trough in ocean floor

Actual relief of ocean floor

Base level of the sea surface at 0 ft (0 m)

How surface waters reflect the relief of the ocean floor

▲ *The low relief* of many small Pacific islands such as these atolls at Huahine in French Polynesia makes them vulnerable to changes in sea level.

Ocean structure

The continental shelf is a shallow, flat sea-bed surrounding the Earth's continents. It extends to the continental slope, which falls to the ocean floor. Here, the flat abyssal plains are interrupted by vast, underwater mountain ranges, the mid-ocean ridges, and ocean trenches which plunge to depths of 35,828 ft (10,920 m).

Flat-topped guyot

Trench   Seamount   Abyssal plain   Oceanic ridge

Volcanic island

Continental shelf

Typical sea-floor features

Ocean depth

	Sea level
	200m / 656ft
	1000m / 3281ft
	2000m / 6562ft
	3000m / 9843ft
	4000m / 13,124ft
	5000m / 16,400ft
	6000m / 19,686ft

Black smokers

These vents in the ocean floor disgorge hot, sulphur-rich water from deep in the Earth's crust. Despite the great depths, a variety of lifeforms have adapted to the chemical-rich environment which surrounds black smokers.

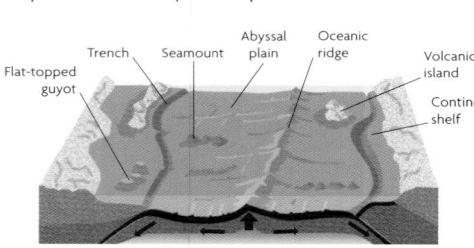

▲ *A black smoker* in the Atlantic Ocean.

▲ *Surtsey, near Iceland,* is a volcanic island lying directly over the Mid-Atlantic Ridge. It was formed in the 1960s following intense volcanic activity nearby.

Ocean floors

Mid-ocean ridges are formed by lava which erupts beneath the sea and cools to form solid rock. This process mirrors the creation of volcanoes from cooled lava on the land. The ages of sea floor rocks increase in parallel bands outwards from central ocean ridges.

Chimney   Plume of hot mineral laden water

Water percolates into the sea floor

Ocean floor

Water heated by hot basalt

Formation of black smokers

Ages of the ocean floor

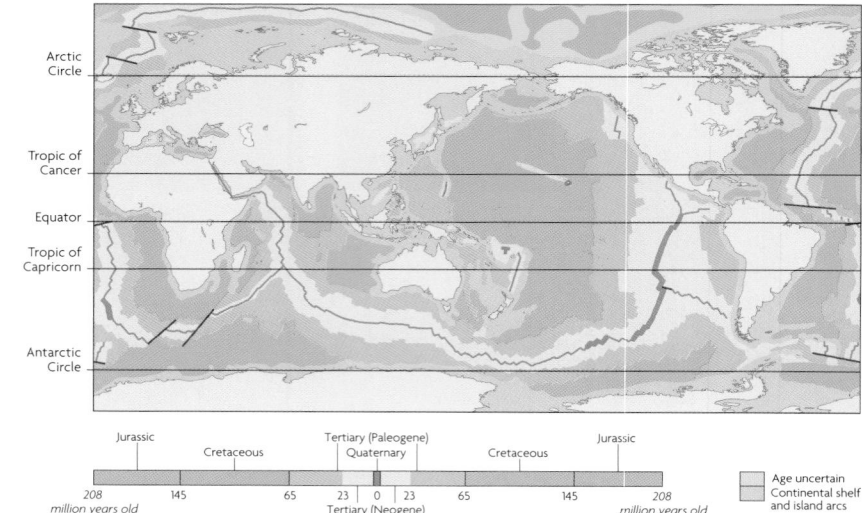

Arctic Circle
Tropic of Cancer
Equator
Tropic of Capricorn
Antarctic Circle

Jurassic	Cretaceous	Tertiary (Paleogene) Quaternary	Cretaceous	Jurassic

208 million years old — 145 — 65 — 23 0 23 — 65 — 145 — 208 million years old
Tertiary (Neogene)

Age uncertain
Continental shelf and island arcs

Map labels

Arctic Circle · Barents Sea · Kara Sea · Laptev Sea · ARCTIC · East Siberian Sea · North Sea · Baltic Sea · EUROPE · ASIA · Sea of Okhotsk · Adriatic Sea · Black Sea · Caspian Sea · Mediterranean Sea · Sea of Japan (East Sea) · Kurile Trench · Emperor Seamounts · Japan Trench · Northwest Pacific Basin · Persian Gulf · Yellow Sea · East China Sea · Taiwan Strait · Mid-Pacific Mountains · Tropic of Cancer · Red Sea · Arabian Sea · Bay of Bengal · Philippine Sea · Mariana Trench · AFRICA · Carlsberg Ridge · Chagos-Laccadive Plateau · Gulf of Thailand · South China Sea · Celebes Sea · Sunda Shelf · Strait of Malacca · Melanesian Basin · Gulf of Guinea · Equator · INDIAN · Bismarck Sea · Somali Basin · Mid-Indian Basin · Arafura Sea · Solomon Sea · Mozambique Channel · Mid-Indian Ridge · Ninetyeast Ridge · Timor Sea · Coral Sea · Angola Basin · Mascarene Plateau · Great Barrier Reef · Madagascar Basin · AUSTRALIA · Tropic of Capricorn · Mozambique Plateau · Perth Basin · Cape Basin · Tasman Sea · Agulhas Basin · OCEAN · South Australian Basin · Bass Strait · Southwest Indian Ridge · Kerguelen Plateau · Southeast Indian Ridge · Walvis Ridge · South Indian Basin · Enderby Plain · SOUTHERN · Antarctic Circle · ANTARCTICA

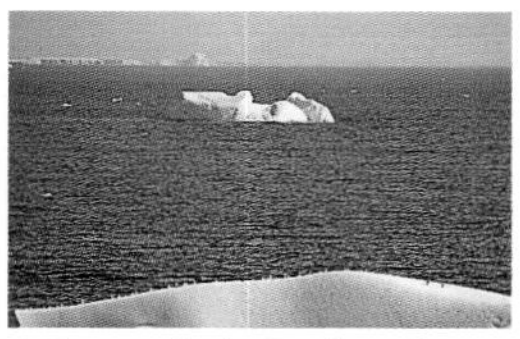

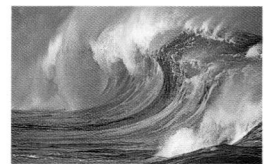

▲ **Currents in the** *Southern Ocean are driven by some of the world's fiercest winds, including the Roaring Forties, Furious Fifties and Shrieking Sixties.*

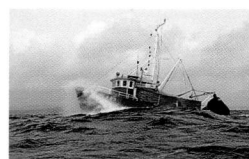

▲ ***The Pacific Ocean*** *is the world's largest and deepest ocean, covering over one-third of the surface of the Earth.*

▲ ***The Atlantic Ocean*** *was formed when the landmasses of the eastern and western hemispheres began to drift apart 180 million years ago.*

Deposition of sediment

Storms, earthquakes, and volcanic activity trigger underwater currents known as turbidity currents which scour sand and gravel from the continental shelf, creating underwater canyons. These strong currents pick up material deposited at river mouths and deltas, and carry it across the continental shelf and through the underwater canyons, where it is eventually laid down on the ocean floor in the form of fans.

Sediment accumulates at head of underwater canyon
Continental shelf
Rocks and Other debris, flow from shelf to ocean floor
Recently-deposited sediments overlay older rocks
Deep sea turbidity flow

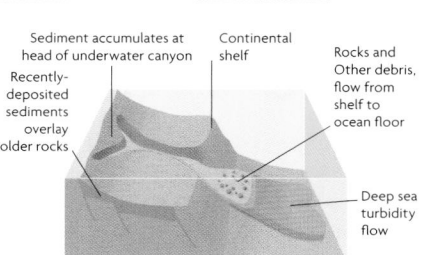

How sediment is deposited on the ocean floor

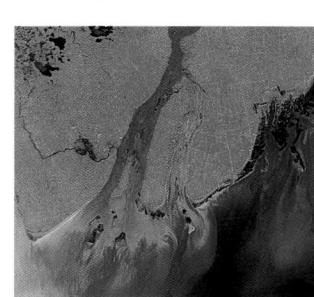

► ***Satellite image of*** *the Yangtze (Chang Jiang) Delta, in which the land appears red. The river deposits immense quantities of silt into the East China Sea, much of which will eventually reach the deep ocean floor.*

CEAN
Beaufort Sea
Baffin Bay
Greenland Sea
Arctic Circle
Davis Strait
Hudson Strait
Hudson Bay
Labrador Sea
Gulf of Alaska
Newfoundland Basin
Mid-Atlantic Ridge
NORTH AMERICA
Mendocino Fracture Zone
Murray Fracture Zone
North American Basin
Gulf of Mexico
ATLANTIC
Sargasso Sea
Canary Basin
Tropic of Cancer
Molokai Fracture Zone
Hawaiian Ridge
Yucatan Basin
Middle America Trench
Clarion Fracture Zone
Caribbean Sea
Barracuda Fracture Zone
PACIFIC
Guatemala Basin
Clipperton Fracture Zone
Central Pacific Basin
Equator
East Pacific Rise
SOUTH AMERICA
Peru Basin
Peru Chile Trench
Brazil Basin
Nazca Ridge
Chile Basin
OCEAN
Tropic of Capricorn
Sala y Gomez Ridge
Rio Grande Rise
OCEAN
Southwest Pacific Basin
Argentine Basin
Mid-Atlantic Ridge
Pacific-Antarctic Ridge
OCEAN
Southeast Pacific Basin
Scotia Sea
South Sandwich Trench
Amundsen Sea
Bellingshausen Sea
Antarctic Circle
Weddell Sea

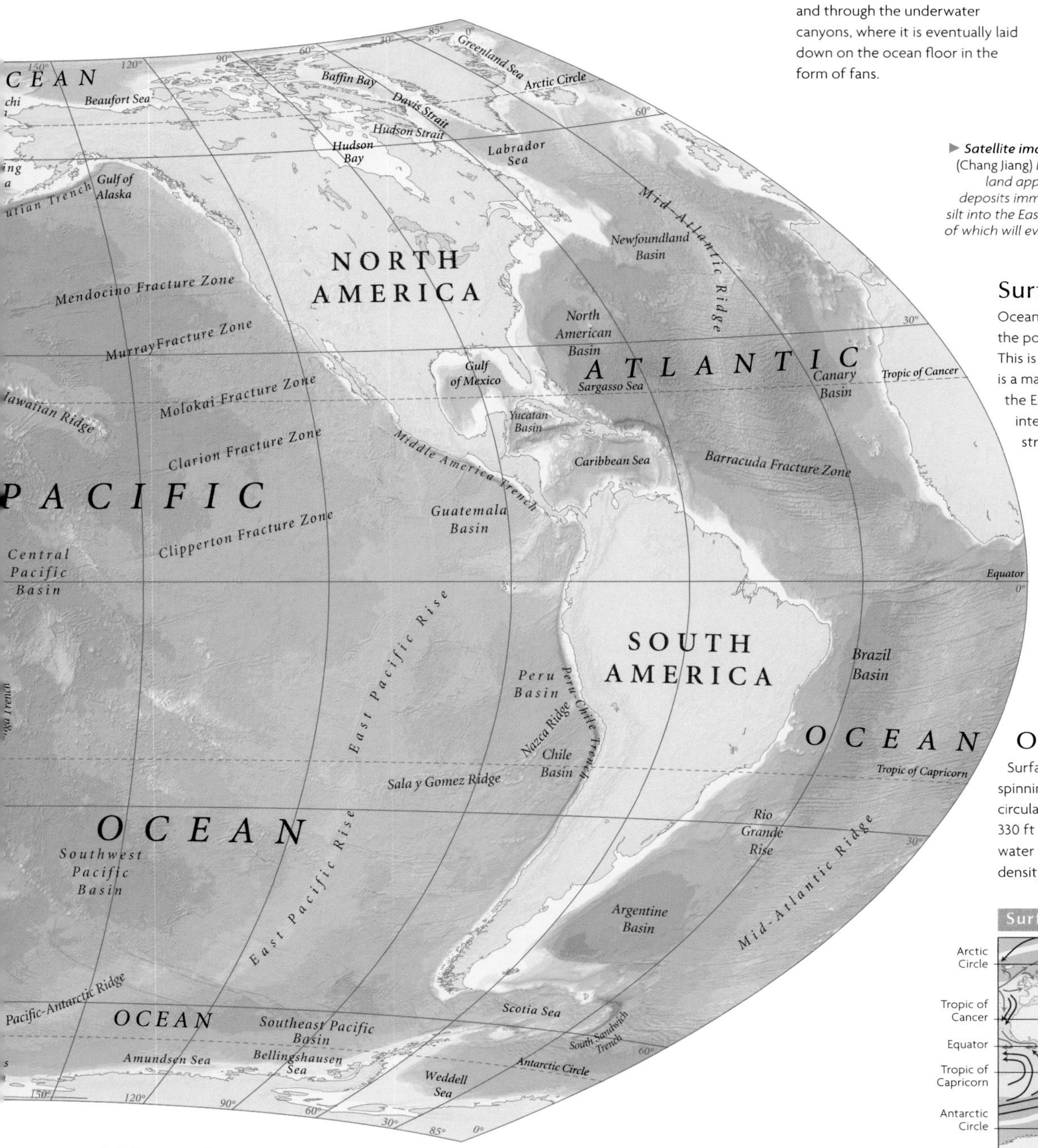

Surface water

Ocean currents move warm water away from the Equator towards the poles, while cold water is, in turn, moved towards the Equator. This is the main way in which the Earth distributes surface heat and is a major climatic control. Approximately 4000 million years ago, the Earth was dominated by oceans and there was no land to interrupt the flow of the currents, which would have flowed as straight lines, simply influenced by the Earth's rotation.

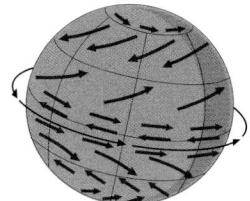

Idealized globe showing the movement of water around a landless Earth.

Ocean currents

Surface currents are driven by the prevailing winds and by the spinning motion of the Earth, which drives the currents into circulating whirlpools, or gyres. Deep sea currents, over 330 ft (100 m) below the surface, are driven by differences in water temperature and salinity, which have an impact on the density of deep water and on its movement.

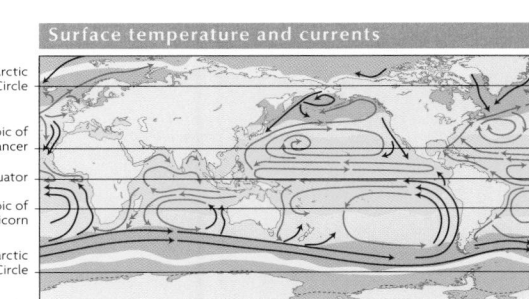

Surface temperature and currents
Arctic Circle
Tropic of Cancer
Equator
Tropic of Capricorn
Antarctic Circle

Surface temperature and currents

- Ice-shelf (below 0°C / 32°F)
- Sea-ice* (average) below -2°C / 28°F
- Sea-water -2–0°C / 28–32°F
- 0–10°C / 32–50°F
- 10–20°C / 50–68°F
- 20–30°C / 68–86°F
- warm current
- cold current

* Sea-water freezes at -1.9°C / 28.4°F

Tides and waves

Tides are created by the pull of the Sun and Moon's gravity on the surface of the oceans. The levels of high and low tides are influenced by the position of the Moon in relation to the Earth and Sun. Waves are formed by wind blowing over the surface of the water.

Tidal range and wave environments
Arctic Circle
Tropic of Cancer
Equator
Tropic of Capricorn
Antarctic Circle

Tidal range and wave environments

- less than 2m / 7ft
- 2–4m / 7–13ft
- greater than 4m / 13ft
- east coast swell
- west coast swell
- tropical cyclone
- storm wave
- ice-shelf

High and low tides

The highest tides occur when the Earth, the Moon and the Sun are aligned *(below left)*. The lowest tides are experienced when the Sun and Moon align at right angles to one another *(below right)*.

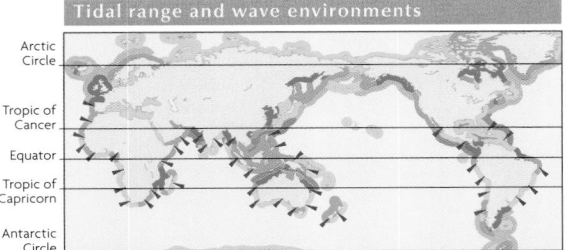

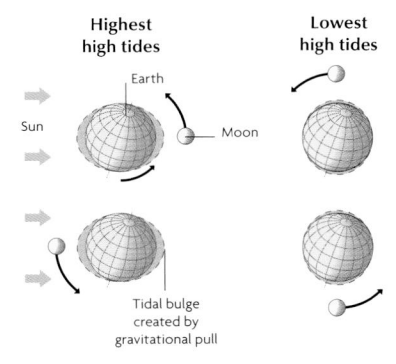

Highest high tides
Lowest high tides
Earth
Sun
Moon
Tidal bulge created by gravitational pull

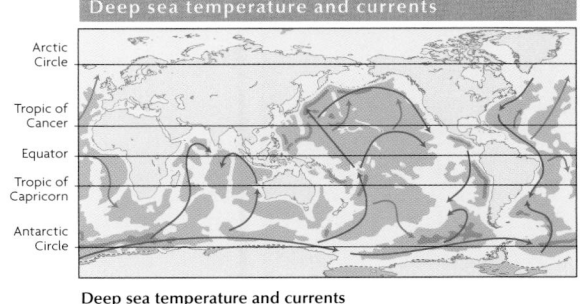

Deep sea temperature and currents
Arctic Circle
Tropic of Cancer
Equator
Tropic of Capricorn
Antarctic Circle

Deep sea temperature and currents

- Ice-shelf (below 0°C / 32°F)
- Sea-water -2–0°C / 28–32°F (below 5000m / 16,400ft)
- Sea-water 0–5°C / 32–41°F (below 4000m / 13,120ft)
- Primary currents
- Secondary currents

The global climate

The Earth's climatic types consist of stable patterns of weather conditions averaged out over a long period of time. Different climates are categorized according to particular combinations of temperature and humidity. By contrast, weather consists of short-term fluctuations in wind, temperature and humidity conditions. Different climates are determined by latitude, altitude, the prevailing wind and circulation of ocean currents. Longer-term changes in climate, such as global warming or the onset of ice ages, are punctuated by shorter-term events which comprise the day-to-day weather of a region, such as frontal depressions, hurricanes and blizzards.

The atmosphere, wind and weather

The Earth's atmosphere has been compared to a giant ocean of air which surrounds the planet. Its circulation patterns are similar to the currents in the oceans and are influenced by three factors; the Earth's orbit around the Sun and rotation about its axis, and variations in the amount of heat radiation received from the Sun. If both heat and moisture were not redistributed between the Equator and the poles, large areas of the Earth would be uninhabitable.

◄ *Heavy fogs,* as here in southern England, form as moisture-laden air passes over cold ground.

Temperature

The world can be divided into three major climatic zones, stretching like large belts across the latitudes: the tropics which are warm; the cold polar regions and the temperate zones which lie between them. Temperatures across the Earth range from above 30°C (86°F) in the deserts to as low as -55°C (-70°F) at the poles. Temperature is also controlled by altitude; because air becomes cooler and less dense the higher it gets, mountainous regions are typically colder than those areas which are at, or close to, sea level.

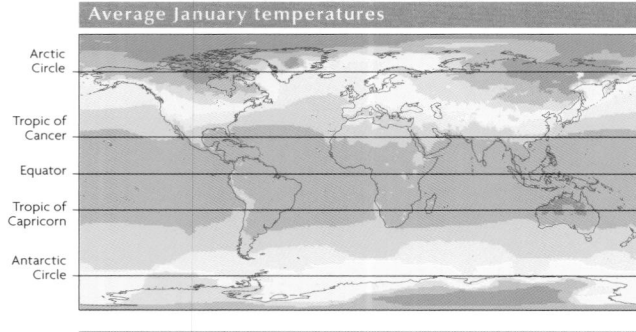
Average January temperatures

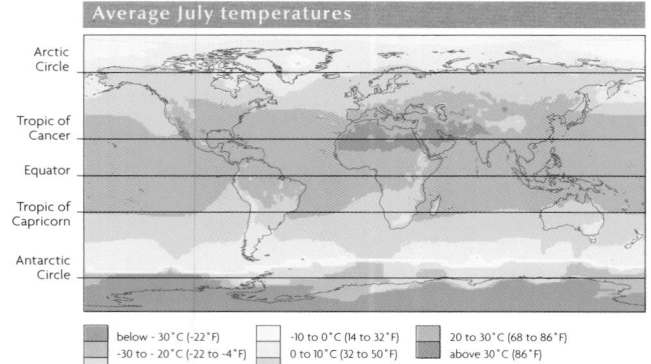
Average July temperatures

below - 30°C (-22°F)
-30 to - 20°C (-22 to -4°F)
-20 to - 10°C (-4 to 14°F)
-10 to 0°C (14 to 32°F)
0 to 10°C (32 to 50°F)
10 to 20°C (50 to 68°F)
20 to 30°C (68 to 86°F)
above 30°C (86°F)

Global air circulation

Air does not simply flow from the Equator to the poles, it circulates in giant cells known as Hadley and Ferrel cells. As air warms it expands, becoming less dense and rising; this creates areas of low pressure. As the air rises it cools and condenses, causing heavy rainfall over the tropics and slight snowfall over the poles. This cool air then sinks, forming high pressure belts. At surface level in the tropics these sinking currents are deflected polewards as the westerlies and towards the equator as the trade winds. At the poles they become the polar easterlies.

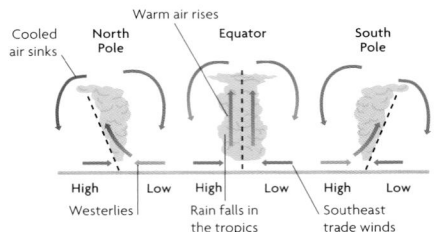
Warm air rises
Cooled air sinks
North Pole
Equator
South Pole
High | Low | High | Low | High | Low
Westerlies | Rain falls in the tropics | Southeast trade winds

▲ *The Antarctic pack ice* expands its area by almost seven times during the winter as temperatures drop and surrounding seas freeze.

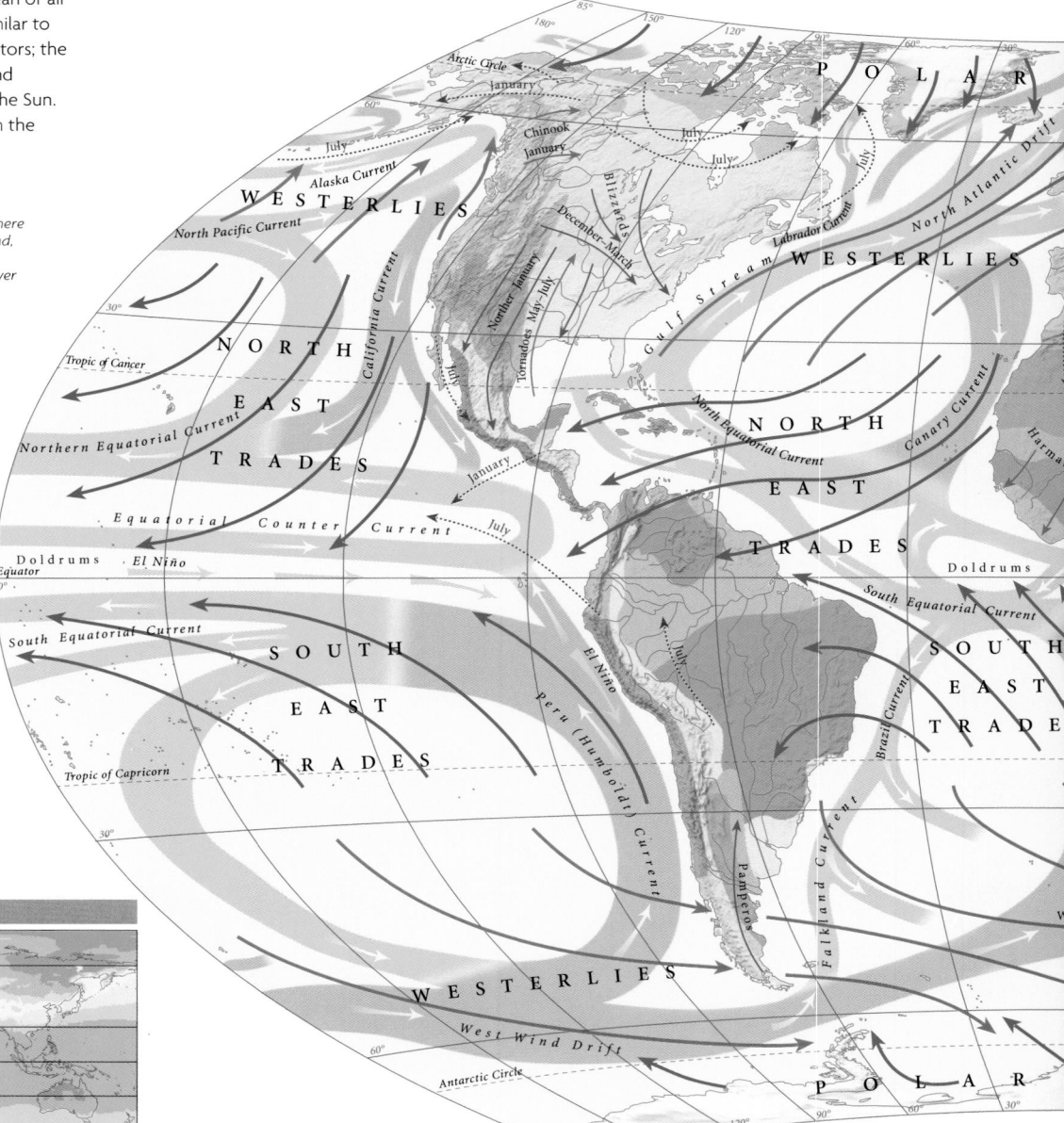

Climatic change

The Earth is currently in a warm phase between ice ages. Warmer temperatures result in higher sea levels as more of the polar ice caps melt. Most of the world's population lives near coasts, so any changes which might cause sea levels to rise, could have a potentially disastrous impact.

▲ *This ice fair,* painted by Pieter Brueghel the Younger in the 17th century, shows the Little Ice Age which peaked around 300 years ago.

The greenhouse effect

Gases such as carbon dioxide are known as 'greenhouse gases' because they allow shortwave solar radiation to enter the Earth's atmosphere, but help to stop longwave radiation from escaping. This traps heat, raising the Earth's temperature. An excess of these gases, such as that which results from the burning of fossil fuels, helps trap more heat and can lead to global warming.

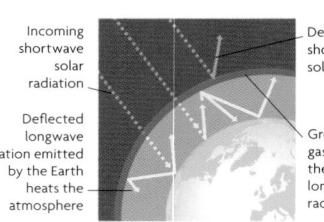
Incoming shortwave solar radiation
Deflected shortwave solar radiation
Deflected longwave radiation emitted by the Earth heats the atmosphere
Greenhouse gases prevent the escape of longwave radiation

◄ *The islands of the Caribbean, Mexico's Gulf coast and the southeastern USA are often hit by hurricanes formed far out in the Atlantic.*

Oceanic water circulation

In general, ocean currents parallel the movement of winds across the Earth's surface. Incoming solar energy is greatest at the Equator and least at the poles. So, water in the oceans heats up most at the Equator and flows polewards, cooling as it moves north or south towards the Arctic or Antarctic. The flow is eventually reversed and cold water currents move back towards the Equator. These ocean currents act as a vast system for moving heat from the Equator towards the poles and are a major influence on the distribution of the Earth's climates.

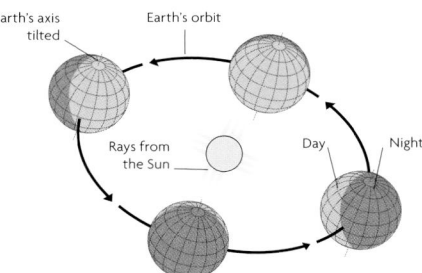

▲ *In marginal climatic zones years of drought can completely dry out the land and transform grassland to desert.*

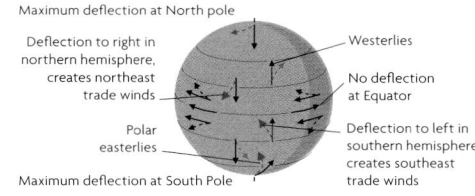

▲ *The wide range of environments found in the Andes is strongly related to their altitude, which modifies climatic influences. While the peaks are snow-capped, many protected interior valleys are semi-tropical.*

Tilt and rotation

The tilt and rotation of the Earth during its annual orbit largely control the distribution of heat and moisture across its surface, which correspondingly controls its large-scale weather patterns. As the Earth annually rotates around the Sun, half its surface is receiving maximum radiation, creating summer and winter seasons. The angle of the Earth means that on average the tropics receive two and a half times as much heat from the Sun each day as the poles.

Earth's axis tilted
Earth's orbit
Rays from the Sun
Day
Night

The Coriolis effect

The rotation of the Earth influences atmospheric circulation by deflecting winds and ocean currents. Winds blowing in the northern hemisphere are deflected to the right and those in the southern hemisphere are deflected to the left, creating large-scale patterns of wind circulation, such as the northeast and southeast trade winds and the westerlies. This effect is greatest at the poles and least at the Equator.

Maximum deflection at North pole

Deflection to right in northern hemisphere, creates northeast trade winds
Westerlies
No deflection at Equator
Polar easterlies
Deflection to left in southern hemisphere, creates southeast trade winds

Maximum deflection at South Pole

Precipitation

When warm air expands, it rises and cools, and the water vapour it carries condenses to form clouds. Heavy, regular rainfall is characteristic of the equatorial region, while the poles are cold and receive only slight snowfall. Tropical regions have marked dry and rainy seasons, while in the temperate regions rainfall is relatively unpredictable.

▲ *Monsoon rains, which affect southern Asia from May to September, are caused by sea winds blowing across the warm land.*

▲ *Heavy tropical rainstorms occur frequently in Papua New Guinea, often causing soil erosion and landslides in cultivated areas.*

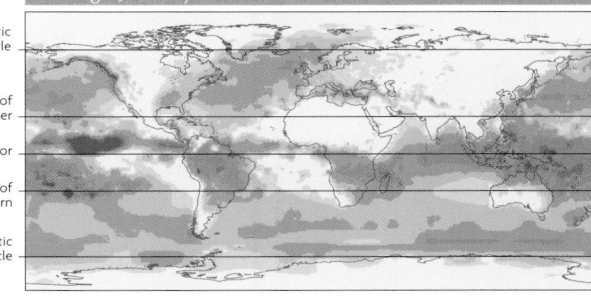

Average January rainfall

Arctic Circle
Tropic of Cancer
Equator
Tropic of Capricorn
Antarctic Circle

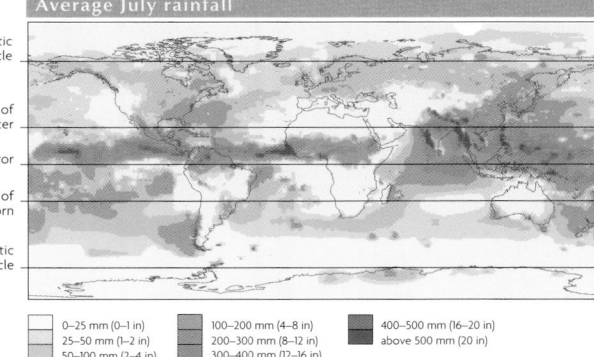

Average July rainfall

Arctic Circle
Tropic of Cancer
Equator
Tropic of Capricorn
Antarctic Circle

0–25 mm (0–1 in)
25–50 mm (1–2 in)
50–100 mm (2–4 in)
100–200 mm (4–8 in)
200–300 mm (8–12 in)
300–400 mm (12–16 in)
400–500 mm (16–20 in)
above 500 mm (20 in)

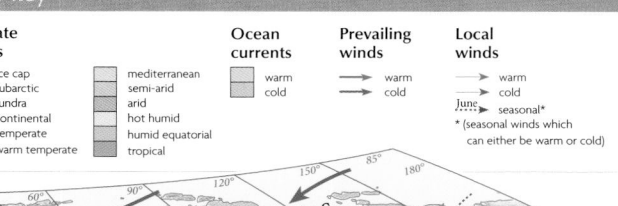

▲ *The intensity of some blizzards in Canada and the northern USA can give rise to snowdrifts as high as 10 ft (3 m).*

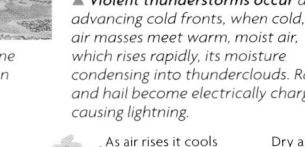

▲ *The Atacama Desert in Chile is one of the driest places on Earth, with an average rainfall of less than 2 inches (50 mm) per year.*

▲ *Violent thunderstorms occur along advancing cold fronts, when cold, dry air masses meet warm, moist air, which rises rapidly, its moisture condensing into thunderclouds. Rain and hail become electrically charged, causing lightning.*

The rainshadow effect

When moist air is forced to rise by mountains, it cools and the water vapour falls as precipitation, either as rain or snow. Only the dry, cold air continues over the mountains, leaving inland areas with little or no rain. This is called the rainshadow effect and is one reason for the existence of the Mojave Desert in California, which lies east of the Coast Ranges.

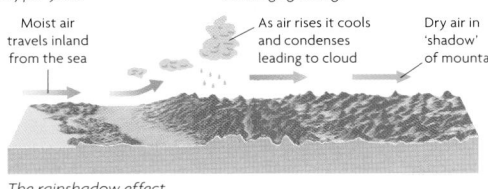

Moist air travels inland from the sea
As air rises it cools and condenses leading to cloud
Dry air in 'shadow' of mountain

The rainshadow effect

Life on Earth

A unique combination of an oxygen-rich atmosphere and plentiful water is the key to life on Earth. Apart from the polar ice caps, there are few areas which have not been colonized by animals or plants over the course of the Earth's history. Plants process sunlight to provide them with their energy, and ultimately all the Earth's animals rely on plants for survival. Because of this reliance, plants are known as primary producers, and the availability of nutrients and temperature of an area is defined as its primary productivity, which affects the quantity and type of animals which are able to live there. This index is affected by climatic factors – cold and aridity restrict the quantity of life, whereas warmth and regular rainfall allow a greater diversity of species.

Biogeographical regions

The Earth can be divided into a series of biogeographical regions, or biomes, ecological communities where certain species of plant and animal co-exist within particular climatic conditions. Within these broad classifications, other factors including soil richness, altitude and human activities such as urbanization, intensive agriculture and deforestation, affect the local distribution of living species within each biome.

Polar regions
A layer of permanent ice at the Earth's poles covers both seas and land. Very little plant and animal life can exist in these harsh regions.

Tundra
A desolate region, with long, dark freezing winters and short, cold summers. With virtually no soil and large areas of permanently frozen ground known as permafrost, the tundra is largely treeless, though it is briefly clothed by small flowering plants in the summer months.

Needleleaf forests
With milder summers than the tundra and less wind, these areas are able to support large forests of coniferous trees.

Broadleaf forests
Much of the northern hemisphere was once covered by deciduous forests, which occurred in areas with marked seasonal variations. Most deciduous forests have been cleared for human settlement.

Temperate rainforests
In warmer wetter areas, such as southern China, temperate deciduous forests are replaced by evergreen forest.

Deserts
Deserts are areas with negligible rainfall. Most hot deserts lie within the tropics; cold deserts are dry because of their distance from the moisture-providing sea.

Mediterranean
Hot, dry summers and short winters typify these areas, which were once covered by evergreen shrubs and woodland, but have now been cleared by humans for agriculture.

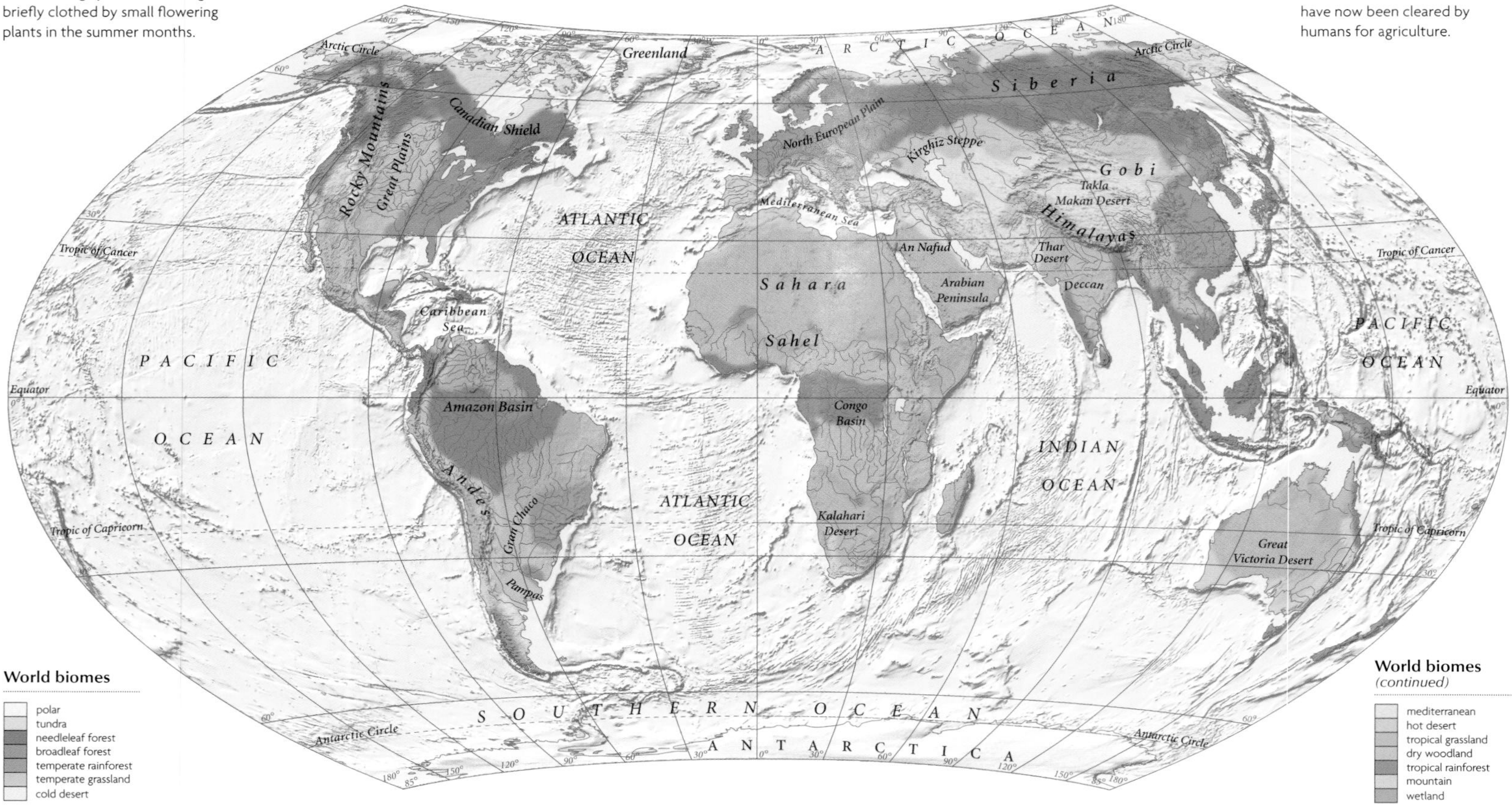

World biomes
- polar
- tundra
- needleleaf forest
- broadleaf forest
- temperate rainforest
- temperate grassland
- cold desert

World biomes
(continued)
- mediterranean
- hot desert
- tropical grassland
- dry woodland
- tropical rainforest
- mountain
- wetland

Tropical and temperate grasslands
The major grassland areas are found in the centres of the larger continental landmasses. In Africa's tropical savannah regions, seasonal rainfall alternates with drought. Temperate grasslands, also known as steppes and prairies are found in the northern hemisphere, and in South America, where they are known as the pampas.

Dry woodlands
Trees and shrubs, adapted to dry conditions, grow widely spaced from one another, interspersed by savannah grasslands.

Tropical rainforests
Characterized by year-round warmth and high rainfall, tropical rainforests contain the highest diversity of plant and animal species on Earth.

Mountains
Though the lower slopes of mountains may be thickly forested, only ground-hugging shrubs and other vegetation will grow above the tree line which varies according to both altitude and latitude.

Wetlands
Rarely lying above sea level, wetlands are marshes, swamps and tidal flats. Some, with their moist, fertile soils, are rich feeding grounds for fish and breeding grounds for birds. Others have little soil structure and are too acidic to support much plant and animal life.

Biodiversity

The number of plant and animal species, and the range of genetic diversity within the populations of each species, make up the Earth's biodiversity. The plants and animals which are endemic to a region – that is, those which are found nowhere else in the world – are also important in determining levels of biodiversity. Human settlement and intervention have encroached on many areas of the world once rich in endemic plant and animal species. Increasing international efforts are being made to monitor and conserve the biodiversity of the Earth's remaining wild places.

Animal adaptation

The degree of an animal's adaptability to different climates and conditions is extremely important in ensuring its success as a species. Many animals, particularly the largest mammals, are becoming restricted to ever-smaller regions as human development and modern agricultural practices reduce their natural habitats. In contrast, humans have been responsible – both deliberately and accidentally – for the spread of some of the world's most successful species. Many of these introduced species are now more numerous than the indigenous animal populations.

Polar animals

The frozen wastes of the polar regions are able to support only a small range of species which derive their nutritional requirements from the sea. Animals such as the walrus *(left)* have developed insulating fat, stocky limbs and double-layered coats to enable them to survive in the freezing conditions.

Desert animals

Many animals which live in the extreme heat and aridity of the deserts are able to survive for days and even months with very little food or water. Their bodies are adapted to lose heat quickly and to store fat and water. The Gila monster *(above)* stores fat in its tail.

Amazon rainforest

The vast Amazon Basin is home to the world's greatest variety of animal species. Animals are adapted to live at many different levels from the treetops to the tangled undergrowth which lies beneath the canopy. The sloth *(below)* hangs upside down in the branches. Its fur grows from its stomach to its back to enable water to run off quickly.

Diversity of animal species

Number of
animal species per country

- more than 2000
- 1000–1999
- 700–999
- 400–699
- 200–399
- 100–199
- 0–99
- data not available

Marine biodiversity

The oceans support a huge variety of different species, from the world's largest mammals like whales and dolphins down to the tiniest plankton. The greatest diversities occur in the warmer seas of continental shelves, where plants are easily able to photosynthesize, and around coral reefs, where complex ecosystems are found. On the ocean floor, nematodes can exist at a depth of more than 10,000 ft (3000 m) below sea level.

High altitudes

Few animals exist in the rarefied atmosphere of the highest mountains. However, birds of prey such as eagles and vultures *(above)*, with their superb eyesight can soar as high as 23,000 ft (7000 m) to scan for prey below.

Urban animals

The growth of cities has reduced the amount of habitat available to many species. A number of animals are now moving closer into urban areas to scavenge from the detritus of the modern city *(left)*. Rodents, particularly rats and mice, have existed in cities for thousands of years, and many insects, especially moths, quickly develop new colouring to provide them with camouflage.

Endemic species

Isolated areas such as Australia and the island of Madagascar, have the greatest range of endemic species. In Australia, these include marsupials such as the kangaroo *(below)*, which carry their young in pouches on their bodies. Destruction of habitat, pollution, hunting, and predators introduced by humans, are threatening this unique biodiversity.

Plant adaptation

Environmental conditions, particularly climate, soil type and the extent of competition with other organisms, influence the development of plants into a number of distinctive forms. Similar conditions in quite different parts of the world create similar adaptations in the plants, which may then be modified by other, local, factors specific to the region.

Cold conditions

In areas where temperatures rarely rise above freezing, plants such as lichens *(left)* and mosses grow densely, close to the ground.

Rainforests

Most of the world's largest and oldest plants are found in rainforests; warmth and heavy rainfall provide ideal conditions for vast plants like the world's largest flower, the rafflesia *(left)*.

Hot, dry conditions

Arid conditions lead to the development of plants whose surface area has been reduced to a minimum to reduce water loss. In cacti *(above)*, which can survive without water for months, leaves are minimal or not present at all.

Ancient plants

Some of the world's most primitive plants still exist today, including algae, cycads and many ferns *(above)*, reflecting the success with which they have adapted to changing conditions.

Resisting predators

A great variety of plants have developed devices including spines *(above)*, poisons, stinging hairs and an unpleasant taste or smell to deter animal predators.

Diversity of plant species

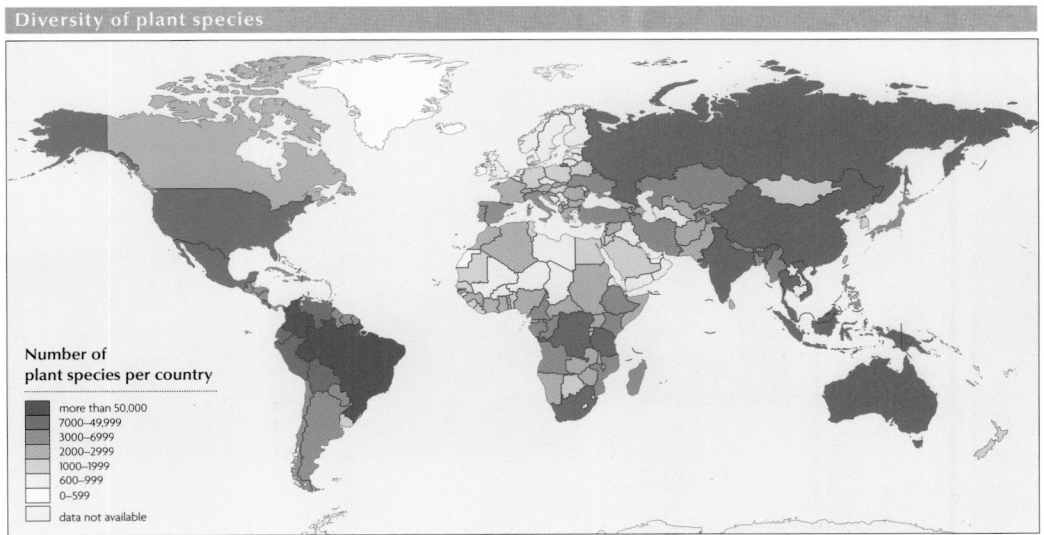

Number of
plant species per country

- more than 50,000
- 7000–49,999
- 3000–6999
- 2000–2999
- 1000–1999
- 600–999
- 0–599
- data not available

Weeds

Weeds such as bindweed *(above)* are fast-growing, easily dispersed, and tolerant of a number of different environments, enabling them to quickly colonize suitable habitats. They are among the most adaptable of all plants.

Population and settlement

The Earth's population is projected to rise from its current level of about 6.5 billion to reach some 10 billion by 2025. The global distribution of this rapidly growing population is very uneven, and is dictated by climate, terrain, natural and economic resources. The great majority of the Earth's people live in coastal zones, and along river valleys. Deserts cover over 20% of the Earth's surface, but support less than 5% of the world's population. It is estimated that over half of the world's population live in cities – most of them in Asia – as a result of mass migration from rural areas in search of jobs. Many of these people live in the so-called 'megacities', some with populations as great as 40 million.

Patterns of settlement

The past 200 years have seen the most radical shift in world population patterns in recorded history.

Nomadic life

All the world's peoples were hunter-gatherers 10,000 years ago. Today nomads, who live by following available food resources, account for less than 0.0001% of the world's population. They are mainly pastoral herders, moving their livestock from place to place in search of grazing land.

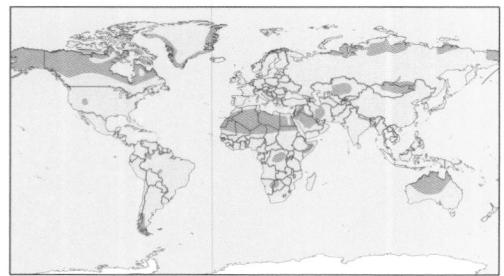

Nomadic population

▮ Nomadic population area

The growth of cities

In 1900 there were only 14 cities in the world with populations of more than a million, mostly in the northern hemisphere. Today, as more and more people in the developing world migrate to towns and cities, there are 29 cities whose population exceeds 5 million, and around 440 million-cities.

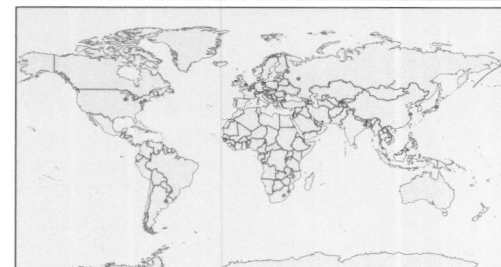

Million-cities in 1900

• Cities over 1 million population

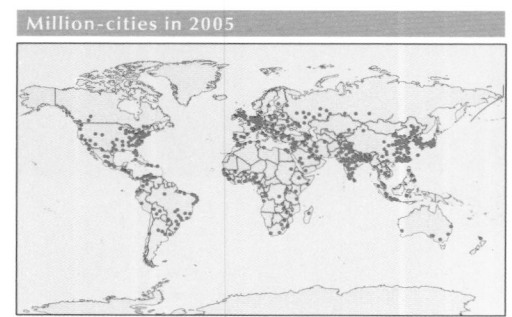

Million-cities in 2005

• Cities over 1 million population

North America

The eastern and western seaboards of the USA, with huge expanses of interconnected cities, towns and suburbs, are vast, densely-populated megalopolises. Central America and the Caribbean also have high population densities. Yet, away from the coasts and in the wildernesses of northern Canada the land is very sparsely settled.

▲ **Vancouver on Canada's** west coast, grew up as a port city. In recent years it has attracted many Asian immigrants, particularly from the Pacific Rim.

▲ **North America's central** plains, the continent's agricultural heartland, are thinly populated and highly productive.

Europe

With its temperate climate, and rich mineral and natural resources, Europe is generally very densely settled. The continent acts as a magnet for economic migrants from the developing world, and immigration is now widely restricted. Birth rates in Europe are generally low, and in some countries, such as Germany, the populations have stabilized at zero growth, with a fast-growing elderly population.

▲ **Many European cities,** like Siena, once reflected the 'ideal' size for human settlements. Modern technological advances have enabled them to grow far beyond the original walls.

▲ **Within the densely-populated** Netherlands the reclamation of coastal wetlands is vital to provide much-needed land for agriculture and settlement.

Population density
(inhabitants per sq km)

- 200–1000
- 100–200
- 50–100
- 20–50
- 10–20
- 5–10
- 1–5
- Less than 1

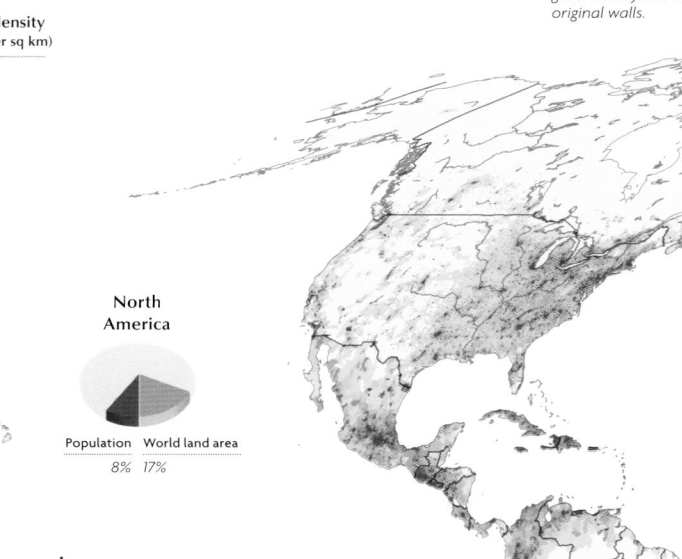

North America
Population 8% | World land area 17%

Europe
Population 11% | World land area 7.1%

Africa
Population 14% | World land area 20.2%

South America
Population 6% | World land area 11.8%

South America

Most settlement in South America is clustered in a narrow belt in coastal zones and in the northern Andes. During the 20th century, cities such as São Paulo and Buenos Aires grew enormously, acting as powerful economic magnets to the rural population. Shanty towns have grown up on the outskirts of many major cities to house these immigrants, often lacking basic amenities.

▲ **Many people in** western South America live at high altitudes in the Andes, both in cities and in villages such as this one in Bolivia.

▲ **Venezuela is one** of the most highly urbanized countries in South America, with nearly 90% of the population living in cities such as Caracas.

Africa

▲ **Cities such as** Nairobi (above), Cairo and Johannesburg have grown rapidly in recent years, although only Cairo has a significant population on a global scale.

The arid climate of much of Africa means that settlement of the continent is sparse, focusing in coastal areas and fertile regions such as the Nile Valley. Africa still has a high proportion of nomadic agriculturalists, although many are now becoming settled, and the population is predominantly rural.

▲ **Traditional lifestyles and** homes persist across much of Africa, which has a higher proportion of rural or village-based population than any other continent.

Asia

Most Asian settlement originally centred around the great river valleys such as the Indus, the Ganges and the Yangtze. Today, almost 60% of the world's population lives in Asia, many in burgeoning cities – particularly in the economically-buoyant Pacific Rim countries. Even rural population densities are high in many countries; practices such as terracing in Southeast Asia making the most of the available land.

▲ **Many of China's** cities are now vast urban areas with populations of more than 5 million people.

▲ **This stilt village** in Bangladesh is built to resist the regular flooding. Pressure on land, even in rural areas, forces many people to live in marginal areas.

Population structures

Population pyramids are an effective means of showing the age structures of different countries, and highlighting changing trends in population growth and decline. The typical pyramid for a country with a growing, youthful population, is broad-based *(left)*, reflecting a high birth rate and a far larger number of young rather than elderly people. In contrast, countries with populations whose numbers are stabilizing have a more balanced distribution of people in each age band, and may even have lower numbers of people in the youngest age ranges, indicating both a high life expectancy, and that the population is now barely replacing itself *(right)*. The Russian Federation *(centre)* shows a marked decline in population due to a combination of a high death rate and low birth rate. The government has taken steps to reverse this trend by providing improved child support and health care. Immigration is also seen as vital to help sustain the population.

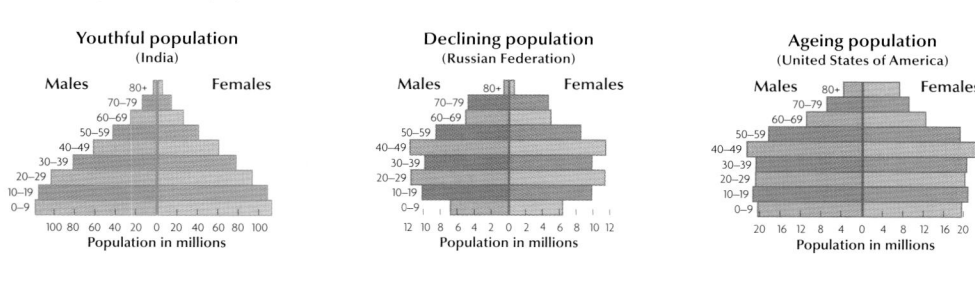

Youthful population
(India)

Declining population
(Russian Federation)

Ageing population
(United States of America)

Population growth

Improvements in food supply and advances in medicine have both played a major role in the remarkable growth in global population, which has increased five-fold over the last 150 years. Food supplies have risen with the mechanization of agriculture and improvements in crop yields. Better nutrition, together with higher standards of public health and sanitation, have led to increased longevity and higher birth rates.

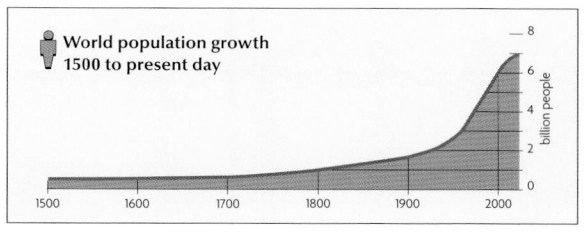

World population growth 1500 to present day

World nutrition

Two-thirds of the world's food supply is consumed by the industrialized nations, many of which have a daily calorific intake far higher than is necessary for their populations to maintain a healthy body weight. In contrast, in the developing world, about 800 million people do not have enough food to meet their basic nutritional needs.

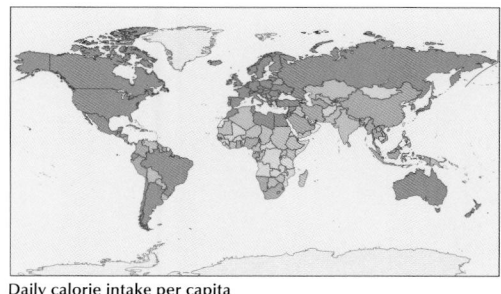

Daily calorie intake per capita

- above 3000
- 2500–2999
- 2000–2499
- below 2000
- data not available

World life expectancy

Improved public health and living standards have greatly increased life expectancy in the developed world, where people can now expect to live twice as long as they did 100 years ago. In many of the world's poorest nations, inadequate nutrition and disease, means that the average life expectancy still does not exceed 45 years.

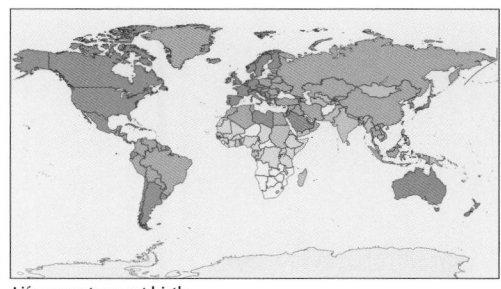

Life expectancy at birth

- above 75 years
- 65–74 years
- 55–64 years
- 45–54 years
- below 44 years
- data not available

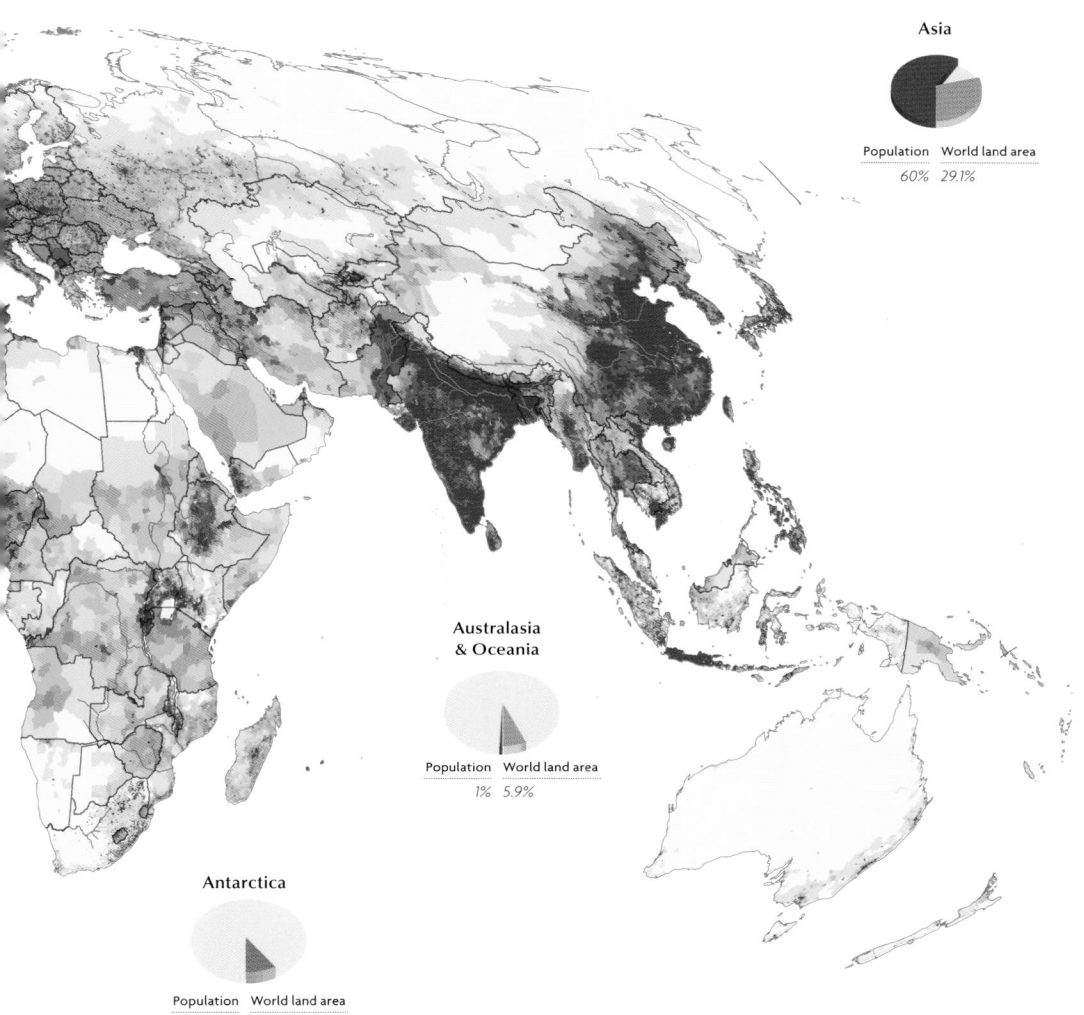

Asia

Population 60%   World land area 29.1%

Australasia & Oceania

Population 1%   World land area 5.9%

Antarctica

Population 0%   World land area 8.9%

Australasia and Oceania

This is the world's most sparsely settled region. The peoples of Australia and New Zealand live mainly in the coastal cities, with only scattered settlements in the arid interior. The Pacific islands can only support limited populations because of their remoteness and lack of resources.

► *Brisbane, on Australia's Gold Coast is the most rapidly expanding city in the country. The great majority of Australia's population lives in cities near the coasts.*

◄ *The remote highlands of Papua New Guinea are home to a wide variety of peoples, many of whom still subsist by traditional hunting and gathering.*

Average world birth rates

Birth rates are much higher in Africa, Asia and South America than in Europe and North America. Increased affluence and easy access to contraception are both factors which can lead to a significant decline in a country's birth rate.

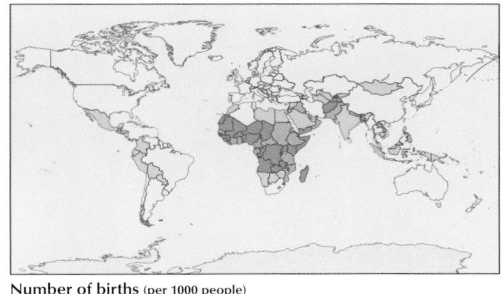

Number of births (per 1000 people)

- above 40
- 30–39
- 20–29
- below 20
- data not available

World infant mortality

In parts of the developing world infant mortality rates are still high; access to medical services such as immunization, adequate nutrition and the promotion of breast-feeding have been important in combating infant mortality.

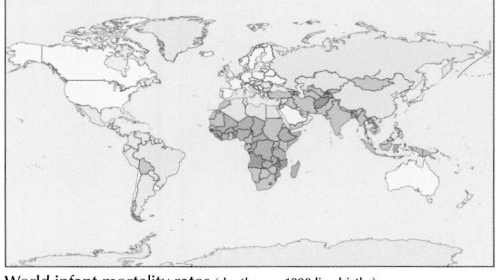

World infant mortality rates (deaths per 1000 live births)

- above 125
- 75–124
- 35–74
- 15–34
- below 15
- data not available

The economic system

The wealthy countries of the developed world, with their aggressive, market-led economies and their access to productive new technologies and international markets, dominate the world economic system. At the other extreme, many of the countries of the developing world are locked in a cycle of national debt, rising populations and unemployment. The state-managed economies of the former communist bloc began to be dismantled during the 1990s, and China is emerging as a major economic power following decades of isolation.

Trade blocs

International trade blocs are formed when groups of countries, often already enjoying close military and political ties, join together to offer mutually preferential terms of trade for both imports and exports. Increasingly, global trade is dominated by three main blocs: the EU, NAFTA, and ASEAN. They are supplanting older trade blocs such as the Commonwealth, a legacy of colonialism.

Trade blocs

EU	NAFTA	ASEAN	LAIA
CACM	SADC	ECOWAS	CEEAC

International trade flows

World trade acts as a stimulus to national economies, encouraging growth. Over the last three decades, as heavy industries have declined, services – banking, insurance, tourism, airlines and shipping – have taken an increasingly large share of world trade. Manufactured articles now account for nearly two-thirds of world trade; raw materials and food make up less than a quarter of the total.

Shipping

Ships carry 80% of international cargo, and extensive container ports, where cargo is stored, are vital links in the international transport network.

Multinationals

Multinational companies are increasingly penetrating inaccessible markets. The reach of many American commodities is now global.

Primary products

Many countries, particularly in the Caribbean and Africa, are still reliant on primary products such as rubber and coffee, which makes them vulnerable to fluctuating prices.

Service industries

Service industries such as banking, tourism and insurance were the fastest-growing industrial sector in the last half of the 20th century. Lloyds of London is the centre of the world insurance market.

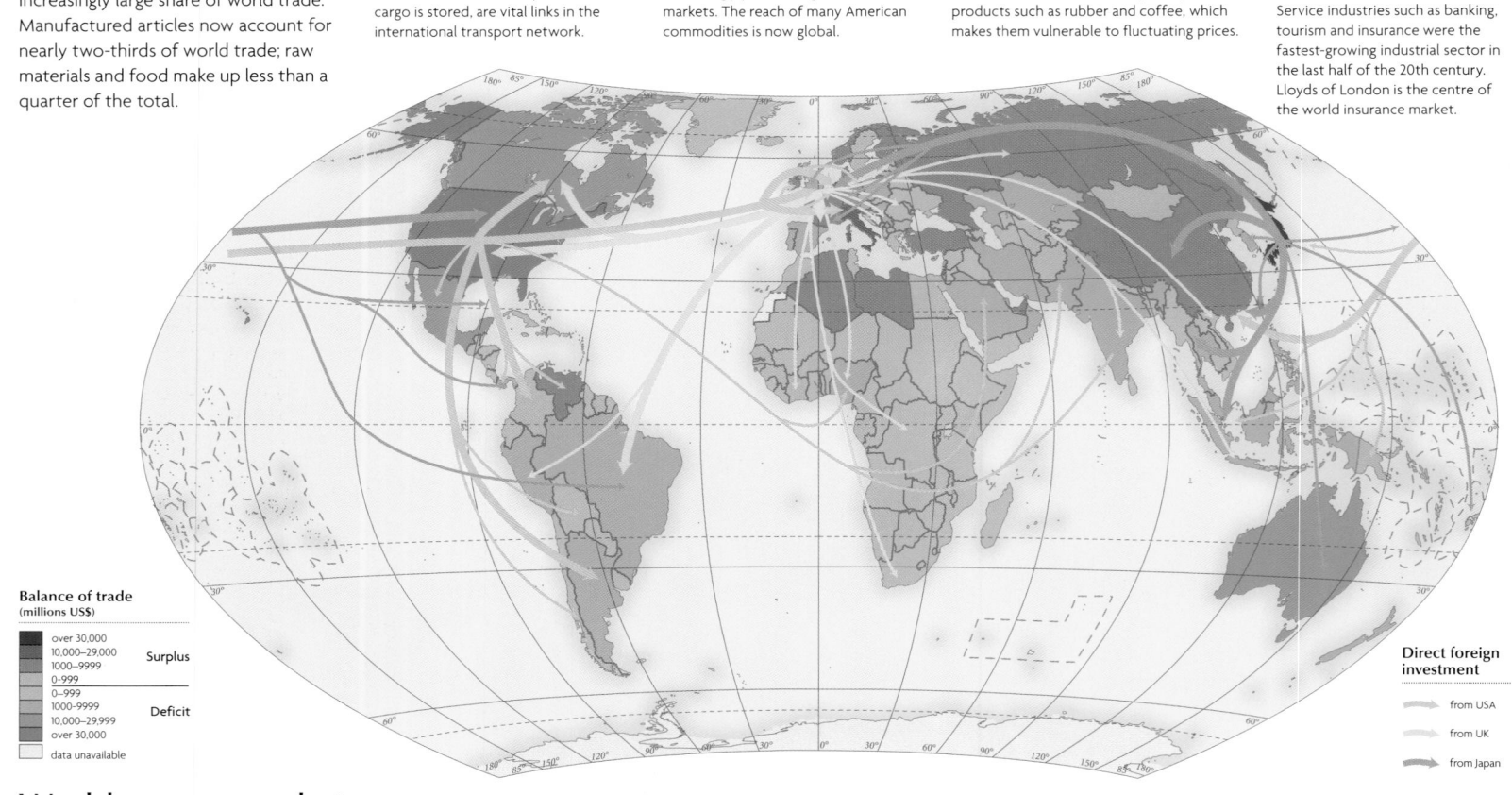

Balance of trade
(millions US$)

over 30,000	
10,000–29,000	
1000–9999	Surplus
0–999	
0–999	
1000–9999	
10,000–29,999	Deficit
over 30,000	
data unavailable	

Direct foreign investment

from USA

from UK

from Japan

World money markets

The financial world has traditionally been dominated by three major centres – Tokyo, New York and London, which house the headquarters of stock exchanges, multinational corporations and international banks. Their geographic location means that, at any one time in a 24-hour day, one major market is open for trading in shares, currencies and commodities. Since the late 1980s, technological advances have enabled transactions between financial centres to occur at ever-greater speed, and new markets have sprung up throughout the world.

New stock markets

New stock markets are now opening in many parts of the world, where economies have recently emerged from state controls. In Moscow and Beijing, and several countries in eastern Europe, newly-opened stock exchanges reflect the transition to market-driven economies.

The developing world

International trade in capital and currency is dominated by the rich nations of the northern hemisphere. In parts of Africa and Asia, where exports of any sort are extremely limited, home-produced commodities are simply sold in local markets.

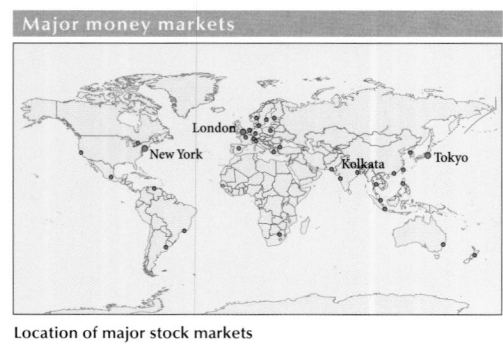

Major money markets

Location of major stock markets

● Major stock markets

▲ *The Tokyo Stock Market* crashed in 1990, leading to slow-down in the growth of the world's most powerful economy, and a refocusing on economic policy away from export-led growth and towards the domestic market.

▲ *Dealers at the* Kolkata Stock Market. The Indian economy has been opened up to foreign investment and many multinationals now have bases there.

▲ *Markets have thrived* in communist Vietnam since the introduction of a liberal economic policy.

World wealth disparity

A global assessment of Gross Domestic Product (GDP) by nation reveals great disparities. The developed world, with only a quarter of the world's population, has 80% of the world's manufacturing income. Civil war, conflict and political instability further undermine the economic self-sufficiency of many of the world's poorest nations.

Urban sprawl

Cities are expanding all over the developing world, attracting economic migrants in search of work and opportunities. In cities such as Rio de Janeiro, housing has not kept pace with the population explosion, and squalid shanty towns (favelas) rub shoulders with middle-class housing.

▲ *The favelas of* Rio de Janeiro sprawl over the hills surrounding the city.

Agricultural economies

In parts of the developing world, people survive by subsistence farming – only growing enough food for themselves and their families. With no surplus product, they are unable to exchange goods for currency, the only means of escaping the poverty trap. In other countries, farmers have been encouraged to concentrate on growing a single crop for the export market. This reliance on cash crops leaves farmers vulnerable to crop failure and to changes in the market price of the crop.

Urban decay

Although the USA still dominates the global economy, it faces deficits in both the federal budget and the balance of trade. Vast discrepancies in personal wealth, high levels of unemployment, and the dismantling of welfare provisions throughout the 1980s have led to severe deprivation in several of the inner cities of North America's industrial heartland.

▲ *Cities such as* Detroit have been badly hit by the decline in heavy industry.

Booming cities

Since the 1980s the Chinese government has set up special industrial zones, such as Shanghai, where foreign investment is encouraged through tax incentives. Migrants from rural China pour into these regions in search of work, creating 'boomtown' economies.

◀ *Foreign investment has* encouraged new infrastructure development in cities like Shanghai.

Economic 'tigers'

The economic 'tigers' of the Pacific Rim – China, Singapore, and South Korea – have grown faster than Europe and the USA over the last decade. Their export- and service-led economies have benefited from stable government, low labour costs, and foreign investment.

▲ *Hong Kong, with* its fine natural harbour, is one of the most important ports in Asia.

Comparative world wealth

[world map]

World economies - average GDP per capita (US$)
- above 20,000
- 5000–20,000
- 2000–5000
- below 2000
- data unavailable

▲ *The Ugandan uplands* are fertile, but poor infrastructure hampers the export of cash crops.

▲ *A shopping arcade* in Paris displays a great profusion of luxury goods.

The affluent West

The capital cities of many countries in the developed world are showcases for consumer goods, reflecting the increasing importance of the service sector, and particularly the retail sector, in the world economy. The idea of shopping as a leisure activity is unique to the western world. Luxury goods and services attract visitors, who in turn generate tourist revenue.

Tourism

In 2004, there were over 700 million tourists worldwide. Tourism is now the world's biggest single industry, employing 130 million people, though frequently in low-paid unskilled jobs. While tourists are increasingly exploring inaccessible and less-developed regions of the world, the benefits of the industry are not always felt at a local level. There are also worries about the environmental impact of tourism, as the world's last wildernesses increasingly become tourist attractions.

◀ *In rural Southeast Asia,* babies are given medical checks by UNICEF as part of a global aid programme sponsored by the UN.

▲ *Botswana's Okavango Delta* is an area rich in wildlife. Tourists make safaris to the region, but the impact of tourism is controlled.

Money flows

Foreign investment in the developing world during the 1970s led to a global financial crisis in the 1980s, when many countries were unable to meet their debt repayments. The International Monetary Fund (IMF) was forced to reschedule the debts and, in some cases, write them off completely. Within the developing world, austerity programmes have been initiated to cope with the debt, leading in turn to high unemployment and galloping inflation. In many parts of Africa, stricken economies are now dependent on international aid.

Tourist arrivals

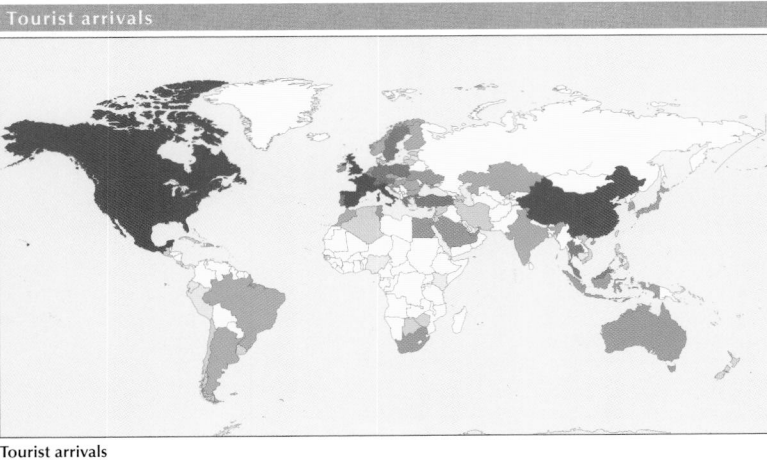

Tourist arrivals
- over 20 million
- 10–20 million
- 5–10 million
- 2.5–5 million
- 1–2.5 million
- 700,000–999,000
- under 700,000
- data unavailable

International debt

[world map]

International debt (as percentage of GNI)
- over 100%
- 70–99%
- 50–69%
- 30–49%
- 10–29%
- below 10%
- data unavailable

The political world

There are 195 independent countries in the world today. With the exception of Antarctica, where territorial claims have been deferred by international treaty, every land area of the Earth's surface either belongs to, or is claimed by, one country or another. The largest country in the world is the Russian Federation, the smallest is Vatican City. Some 60 overseas dependent territories remain, administered variously by France, Australia, Denmark, New Zealand, Norway, Portugal, the UK, the US and the Netherlands.

International borders

The map shows three main types of boundary between states. Full borders represent internationally agreed and recognized territorial boundaries. Undefined borders exist where no fixed boundary between states has been demarcated; the boundaries indicated in this way show approximate areas of sovereignty. A disputed border is indicated where a *de facto* territorial boundary exists, which is not agreed or is subject to arbitration.

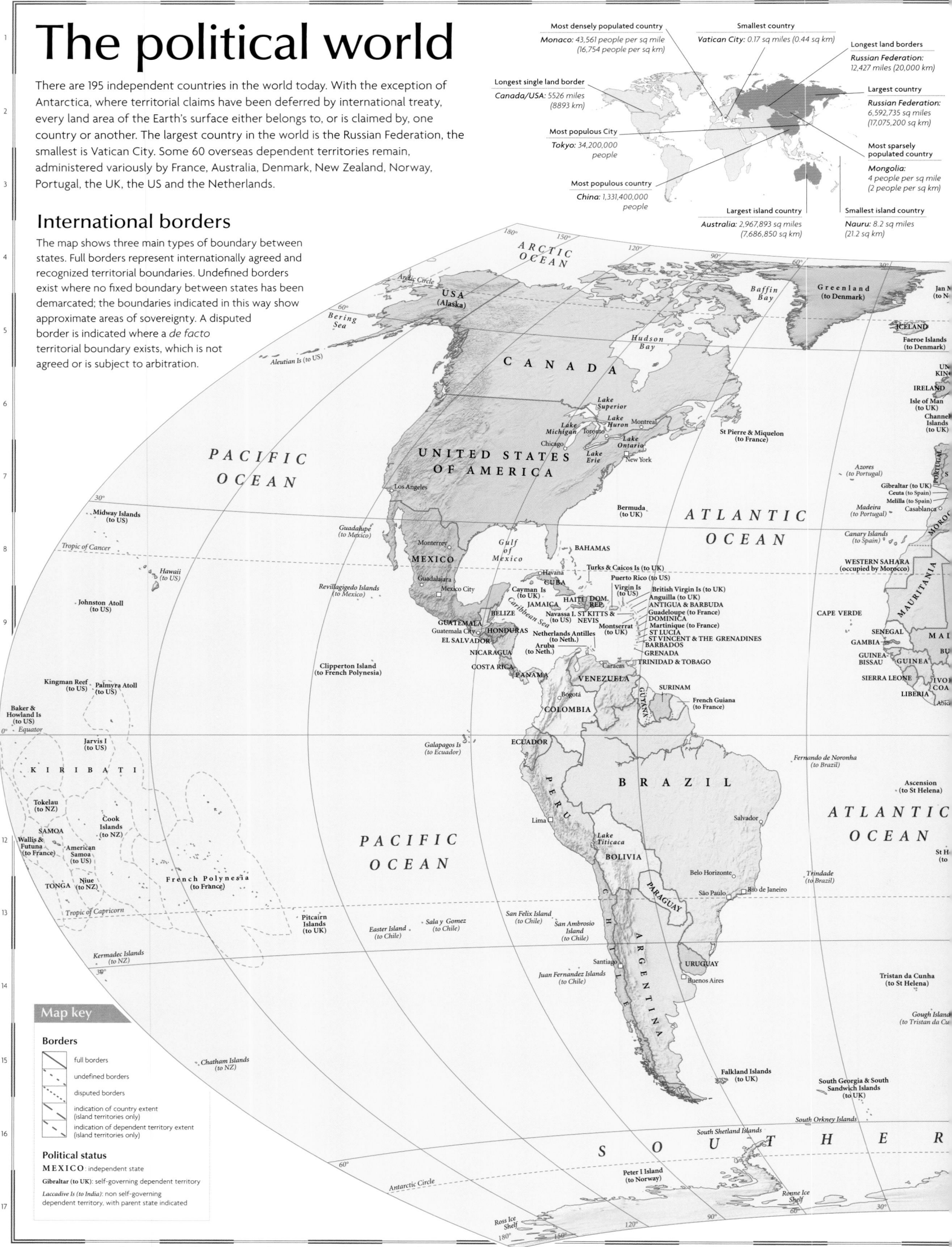

Most densely populated country
Monaco: 43,561 people per sq mile (16,754 people per sq km)

Smallest country
Vatican City: 0.17 sq miles (0.44 sq km)

Longest land borders
Russian Federation: 12,427 miles (20,000 km)

Longest single land border
Canada/USA: 5526 miles (8893 km)

Largest country
Russian Federation: 6,592,735 sq miles (17,075,200 sq km)

Most populous City
Tokyo: 34,200,000 people

Most sparsely populated country
Mongolia: 4 people per sq mile (2 people per sq km)

Most populous country
China: 1,331,400,000 people

Largest island country
Australia: 2,967,893 sq miles (7,686,850 sq km)

Smallest island country
Nauru: 8.2 sq miles (21.2 sq km)

Map key

Borders

- full borders
- undefined borders
- disputed borders
- indication of country extent (island territories only)
- indication of dependent territory extent (island territories only)

Political status

MEXICO: independent state

Gibraltar (to UK): self-governing dependent territory

Laccadive Is (to India): non self-governing dependent territory, with parent state indicated

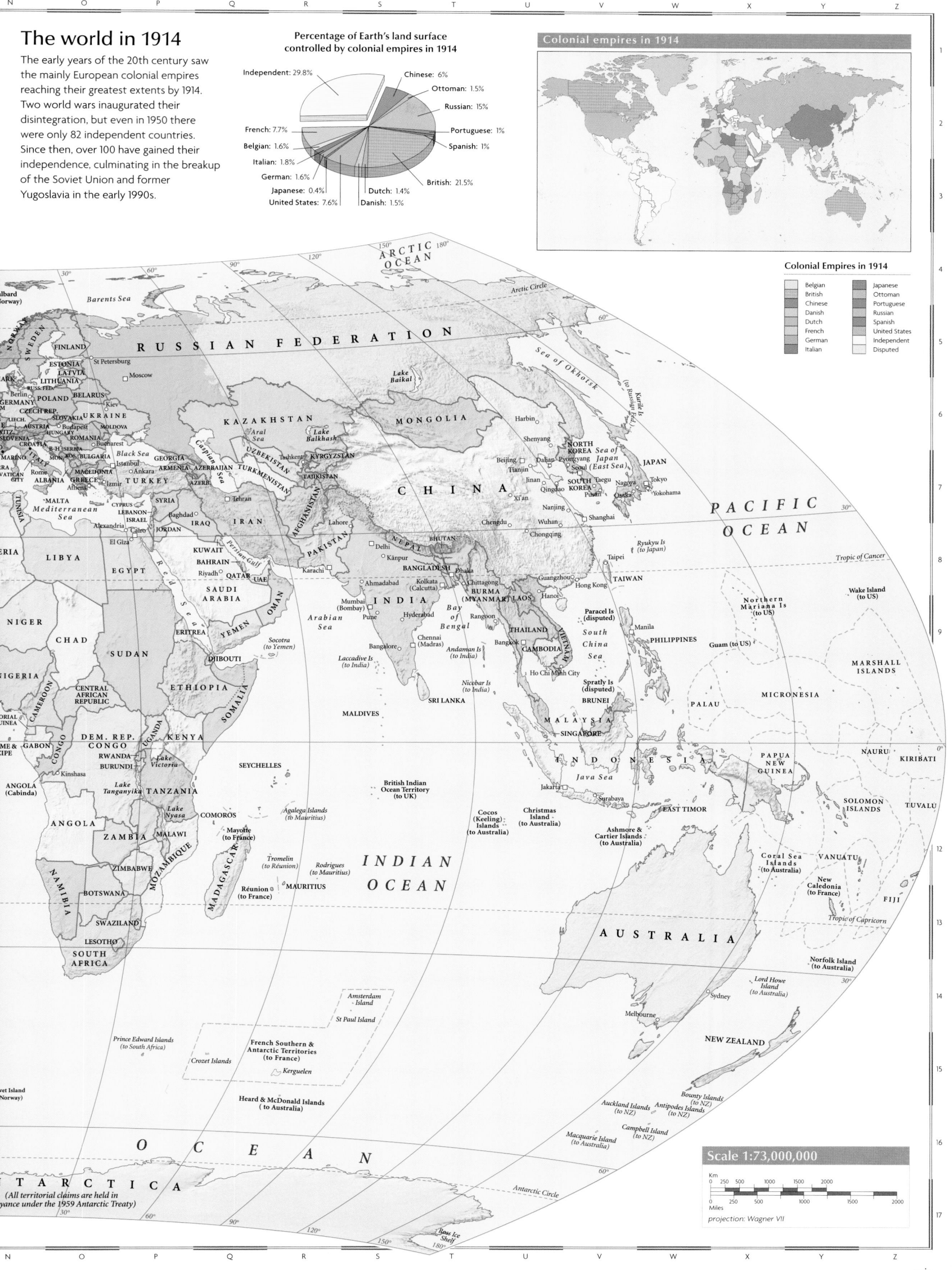

The world in 1914

The early years of the 20th century saw the mainly European colonial empires reaching their greatest extents by 1914. Two world wars inaugurated their disintegration, but even in 1950 there were only 82 independent countries. Since then, over 100 have gained their independence, culminating in the breakup of the Soviet Union and former Yugoslavia in the early 1990s.

Percentage of Earth's land surface controlled by colonial empires in 1914

- Independent: 29.8%
- Chinese: 6%
- Ottoman: 1.5%
- Russian: 15%
- French: 7.7%
- Portuguese: 1%
- Belgian: 1.6%
- Spanish: 1%
- Italian: 1.8%
- German: 1.6%
- British: 21.5%
- Japanese: 0.4%
- Dutch: 1.4%
- United States: 7.6%
- Danish: 1.5%

Colonial empires in 1914

Colonial Empires in 1914

- Belgian
- British
- Chinese
- Danish
- Dutch
- French
- German
- Italian
- Japanese
- Ottoman
- Portuguese
- Russian
- Spanish
- United States
- Independent
- Disputed

Scale 1:73,000,000

projection: Wagner VII

States and boundaries

There are over 190 sovereign states in the world today; in 1950 there were only 82. Over the last half-century national self-determination has been a driving force for many states with a history of colonialism and oppression. As more borders have been added to the world map, the number of international border disputes has increased.

In many cases, where the impetus towards independence has been religious or ethnic, disputes with minority groups have also caused violent internal conflict. While many newly-formed states have moved peacefully towards independence, successfully establishing government by multiparty democracy, dictatorship by military regime or individual despot is often the result of the internal power-struggles which characterize the early stages in the lives of new nations.

The nature of politics

Democracy is a broad term: it can range from the ideal of multiparty elections and fair representation to, in countries such as Singapore, a thin disguise for single-party rule. In despotic regimes, on the other hand, a single, often personal authority has total power; institutions such as parliament and the military are mere instruments of the dictator.

◀ *The stars and* stripes of the US flag are a potent symbol of the country's status as a federal democracy.

Types of government

Multiparty democracy for more than 10 yrs
Multiparty democracy within last 10 yrs
Single-party government
Military regime
Theocracy
Monarchy
Non-party system
Transitional regime

� Current civil unrest

The changing world map

Decolonization

In 1950, large areas of the world remained under the control of a handful of European countries *(page xxviii)*. The process of decolonization had begun in Asia, where, following the Second World War, much of south and southeast Asia sought and achieved self-determination. In the 1960s, a host of African states achieved independence, so that by 1965, most of the larger tracts of the European overseas empires had been substantially eroded. The final major stage in decolonization came with the break-up of the Soviet Union and the Eastern bloc after 1990. The process continues today as the last toeholds of European colonialism, often tiny island nations, press increasingly for independence.

▲ *Icons of communism,* including statues of former leaders such as Lenin and Stalin, were destroyed when the Soviet bloc was dismantled in 1989, creating several new nations.

▲ *Iran has been* one of the modern world's few true theocracies; Islam has an impact on every aspect of political life.

▲ *North Korea is* an independent communist republic. Power is concentrated in the hands of Kim Jong Il.

◀ *Saddam Hussein, former* autocratic leader of Iraq, promoted an extreme personality cult for over 20 years. He was ousted by a US-led coalition in 2003.

◀ *South Africa became* a democracy in 1994, when elections ended over a century of white minority rule.

New nations 1945–1965

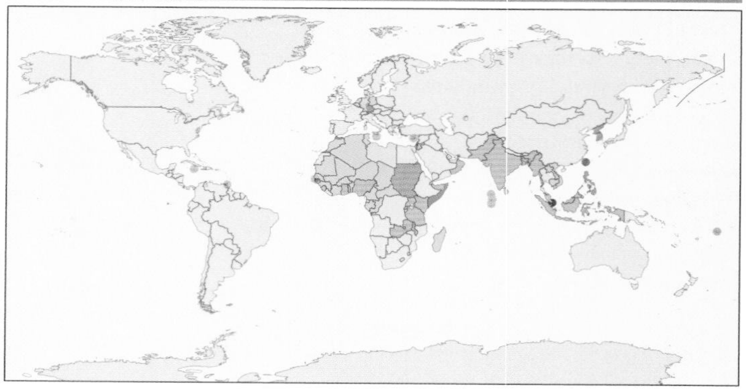

New nations 1965–present

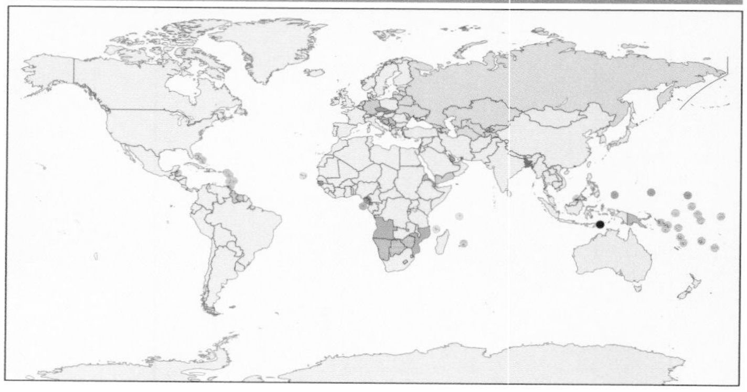

Administration at the time of independence

Australia
Aust/NZ/UK
Belgium
China
Czechoslovakia
Egypt/UK
Ethiopia
France
France/UK
Indonesia
Italy
Japan

Malaysia
Netherlands
New Zealand
Pakistan
Portugal
South Africa
Spain
UK
Unified country
USA
USSR
Yugoslavia

▲ *In Brunei the* Sultan has ruled by decree since 1962; power is closely tied to the royal family. The Sultan's brothers are responsible for finance and foreign affairs.

USA (Alaska)
Bering Sea
CANADA
Hudson Bay
Great Lakes
PACIFIC OCEAN
UNITED STATES OF AMERICA
Tropic of Cancer
Gulf of Mexico
MEXICO
BAHAMAS
CUBA
JAMAICA HAITI DOM. REP.
BELIZE
GUATEMALA EL SALVADOR HONDURAS
NICARAGUA
COSTA RICA PANAMA
ST KITTS & NEVIS
ANTIGUA & BARBUDA
DOMINICA
GRENADA
BARBADOS
ST LUCIA
ST VINCENT & THE GRENADINES
TRINIDAD & TOBAGO
CAPE VERDE
VENEZUELA GUYANA SURINAM
French Guiana (to France)
COLOMBIA
ECUADOR
PERU
BRAZIL
BOLIVIA
CHILE
PARAGUAY
ARGENTINA
URUGUAY
PACIFIC OCEAN
ATLANTIC OCEAN
Equator
KIRIBATI
Tokelau (to NZ)
Cook Islands (to NZ)
SAMOA
American Samoa (to US)
TONGA
Niue (to NZ)
French Polynesia (to France)
Pitcairn Islands (to UK)
Tropic of Capricorn
Arctic Circle
Baffin Bay
Greenland (to Denmark)
ARCTIC OCEAN
Barents Sea
ICELAND
IRELAND
UNITED KINGDOM
ATLANTIC OCEAN
PORTUGAL
SPAIN
MOROCCO
WESTERN SAHARA (occupied by Morocco)
MAURITANIA
SENEGAL
GAMBIA
GUINEA-BISSAU
GUINEA
SIERRA LEONE
LIBERIA
MALI
BURKINA
IVORY COAST
GHANA
TOGO
BENIN
NIGER
NIGERIA
CHAD
CAMEROON
EQ. GUINEA
SAO TOME & PRINCIPE
GABON
CONGO
DEM. REP. CONGO
ANGOLA (Cabinda)
ANGOLA
NAMIBIA
BOTSWANA
ZAMBIA
ZIMBABWE
MOZAMBIQUE
SWAZILAND
LESOTHO
SOUTH AFRICA
NORWAY
FINLAND
SWEDEN
DENMARK
GERM.
NETH.
BEL.
LUX.
FRANCE
SWITZ.
ITALY
ESTONIA
LATVIA
LITHUANIA
RUSS. FED. (Kaliningrad)
POLAND
BELARUS
UKRAINE
MOLD.
ROM.
AUSTRIA
HUNG.
SLOVENIA
CROATIA
BOS. & HERZ.
SERB.
MACED.
ALB.
GREECE
BULGARIA
RUSSIAN FEDERATION
KAZAKHSTAN
MONGOLIA
CHINA
Lake Baikal
Aral Sea
Ozero Balkhash
UZBEKISTAN
TURKMENISTAN
KYRG.
TAJ.
AFGHAN.
PAKISTAN
NEPAL
BHUTAN
INDIA
Caspian Sea
Black Sea
GEORGIA
ARM. AZERB.
TURKEY
SYRIA
IRAQ
IRAN
KUWAIT
SAUDI ARABIA
BAHRAIN
QATAR
U.A.E.
OMAN
YEMEN
Persian Gulf
JORDAN
ISRAEL
LEB.
CYPRUS
Mediterranean Sea
TUNISIA
ALGERIA
LIBYA
EGYPT
SUDAN
ERITREA
DJIBOUTI
ETHIOPIA
SOMALIA
CENTRAL AFRICAN REP.
UGANDA
KENYA
RWANDA
BURUNDI
TANZANIA
Lake Victoria
Lake Tanganyika
Lake Nyasa
MALAWI
COMOROS
MADAGASCAR
MAURITIUS
SEYCHELLES
MALDIVES
SRI LANKA
Bay of Bengal
BANGLADESH
BURMA
THAILAND
LAOS
VIETNAM
CAMBODIA
MALAYSIA
SINGAPORE
BRUNEI
INDONESIA
PHILIPPINES
TAIWAN
NORTH KOREA
SOUTH KOREA
JAPAN
Sea of Okhotsk
Sea of Japan
NORTH Sea
South China Sea
Java Sea
EAST TIMOR
PAPUA NEW GUINEA
AUSTRALIA
NEW ZEALAND
PACIFIC OCEAN
Northern Mariana Is (to US)
Guam (to US)
MARSHALL ISLANDS
PALAU
MICRONESIA
NAURU
KIRIBATI
TUVALU
SOLOMON ISLANDS
VANUATU
New Caledonia (to France)
FIJI
Tropic of Cancer
Tropic of Capricorn
Equator
INDIAN OCEAN
Arabian Sea
Arctic Circle
MONACO
VAT. CITY
ANDORRA
SAN MARINO
MALTA
SLOVAKIA
CZECH REP.
KOSOVO
MONT.
French Southern & Antarctic Territories (to France)
Antarctic Circle
ANTARCTICA
(All territorial claims are held in abeyance under the 1959 Antarctic Treaty)

Lines on the map

The determination of international boundaries can use a variety of criteria. Many of the borders between older states follow physical boundaries; some mirror religious and ethnic differences; others are the legacy of complex histories of conflict and colonialism, while others have been imposed by international agreements or arbitration.

Post-colonial borders

When the European colonial empires in Africa were dismantled during the second half of the 20th century, the outlines of the new African states mirrored colonial boundaries. These boundaries had been drawn up by colonial administrators, often based on inadequate geographical knowledge. Such arbitrary boundaries were imposed on people of different languages, racial groups, religions and customs. This confused legacy often led to civil and international war.

▲ **The conflict that** has plagued many African countries since independence has caused millions of people to become refugees.

Physical borders

Many of the world's countries are divided by physical borders: lakes, rivers, mountains. The demarcation of such boundaries can, however, lead to disputes. Control of waterways, water supplies and fisheries are frequent causes of international friction.

Enclaves

The shifting political map over the course of history has frequently led to anomalous situations. Parts of national territories may become isolated by territorial agreement, forming an enclave. The West German part of the city of Berlin, which until 1989 lay a hundred miles (160 km) within East German territory, was a famous example.

Antarctica

When Antarctic exploration began a century ago, seven nations, Australia, Argentina, Britain, Chile, France, New Zealand and Norway, laid claim to the new territory. In 1961 the Antarctic Treaty, now signed by 45 nations, agreed to hold all territorial claims in abeyance.

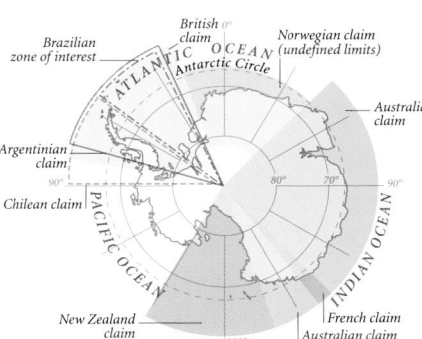

World boundaries

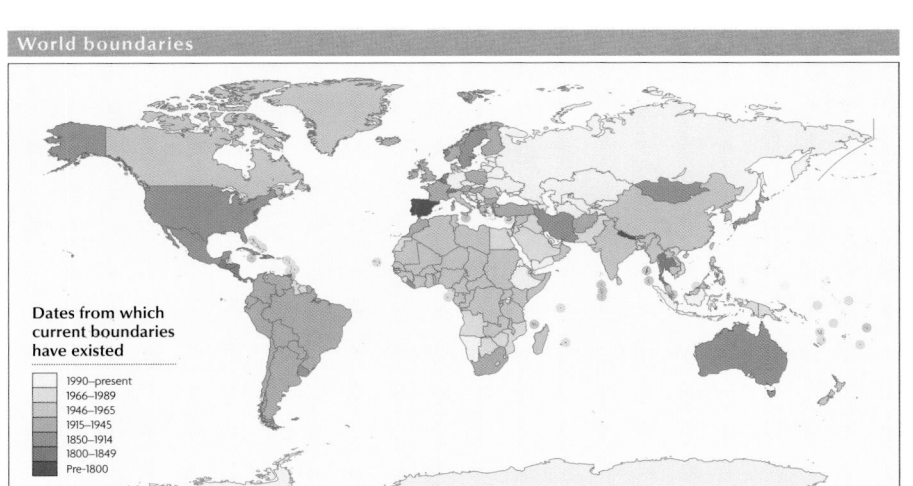

Dates from which current boundaries have existed

- 1990–present
- 1966–1989
- 1946–1965
- 1915–1945
- 1850–1914
- 1800–1849
- Pre-1800

▲ **Since the independence** of Lithuania and Belarus, the peoples of the Russian enclave of Kaliningrad have become physically isolated.

Geometric borders

Straight lines and lines of longitude and latitude have occasionally been used to determine international boundaries; and indeed the world's second longest continuous international boundary, between Canada and the USA, follows the 49th Parallel for over one-third of its course. Many Canadian, American and Australian internal administrative boundaries are similarly determined using a geometric solution.

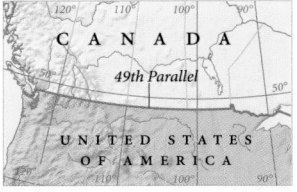

▲ **Different farming techniques** in Canada and the USA clearly mark the course of the international boundary in this satellite map.

Lake borders

Countries which lie next to lakes usually fix their borders in the middle of the lake. Unusually the Lake Nyasa border between Malawi and Tanzania runs along Tanzania's shore.

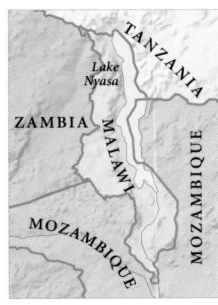

▲ **Complicated agreements between** colonial powers led to the awkward division of Lake Nyasa.

River borders

Rivers alone account for one-sixth of the world's borders. Many great rivers form boundaries between a number of countries. Changes in a river's course and interruptions of its natural flow can lead to disputes, particularly in areas where water is scarce. The centre of the river's course is the nominal boundary line.

▲ **The Danube forms** all or part of the border between nine European nations.

Mountain borders

Mountain ranges form natural barriers and are the basis for many major borders, particularly in Europe and Asia. The watershed is the conventional boundary demarcation line, but its accurate determination is often problematic.

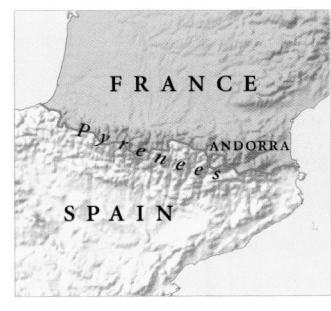

▲ **The Pyrenees form** a natural mountain border between France and Spain.

Shifting boundaries – Poland

Borders between countries can change dramatically over time. The nations of eastern Europe have been particularly affected by changing boundaries. Poland is an example of a country whose boundaries have changed so significantly that it has literally moved around Europe. At the start of the 16th century, Poland was the largest nation in Europe. Between 1772 and 1795, it was absorbed into Prussia, Austria and Russia, and it effectively ceased to exist. After the First World War, Poland became an independent country once more, but its borders changed again after the Second World War following invasions by both Soviet Russia and Nazi Germany.

▲ **In 1634, Poland** was the largest nation in Europe, its eastern boundary reaching towards Moscow.

▲ **From 1772–1795, Poland** was gradually partitioned between Austria, Russia and Prussia. Its eastern boundary receded by over 100 miles (160 km).

▲ **Following the First** World War, Poland was reinstated as an independent state, but it was less than half the size it had been in 1634.

▲ **After the Second** World War the Baltic Sea border was extended westwards, but much of the eastern territory was annexed by Russia.

International disputes

There are more than 60 disputed borders or territories in the world today. Although many of these disputes can be settled by peaceful negotiation, some areas have become a focus for international conflict. Ethnic tensions have been a major source of territorial disagreement throughout history, as has the ownership of, and access to, valuable natural resources. The turmoil of the post-colonial era in many parts of Africa is partly a result of the 19th century 'carve-up' of the continent, which created potential for conflict by drawing often arbitrary lines through linguistic and cultural areas.

Jammu and Kashmir

Disputes over Jammu and Kashmir have caused three serious wars between India and Pakistan since 1947. Pakistan wishes to annex the largely Muslim territory, while India refuses to cede any territory or to hold a referendum, and also lays claim to the entire territory. Most international maps show the 'line of control' agreed in 1972 as the *de facto* border. In addition India has territorial disputes with neighbouring China. The situation is further complicated by a Kashmiri independence movement, active since the late 1980s.

▲ **Indian army troops** maintain their positions in the mountainous terrain of northern Kashmir.

North and South Korea

Since 1953, the *de facto* border between North and South Korea has been a ceasefire line which straddles the 38th Parallel and is designated as a demilitarized zone. Both countries have heavy fortifications and troop concentrations behind this zone.

▲ **Heavy fortifications** on the border between North and South Korea.

▲ The so-called 'green line' divides Cyprus into Greek and Turkish sectors.

Cyprus

Cyprus was partitioned in 1974, following an invasion by Turkish troops. The south is now the Greek Cypriot Republic of Cyprus, while the self-proclaimed Turkish Republic of Northern Cyprus is recognized only by Turkey.

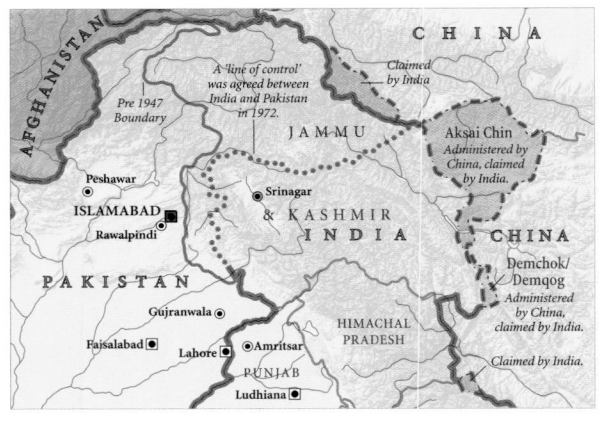

Conflicts and international disputes

- Countries contributing troops to coalition force in Iraq (as of 2008)
- Major active territorial or border disputes
- Countries involved in internal conflict
- Active territorial or border disputes and internal conflict

The Falkland Islands

The British dependent territory of the Falkland Islands was invaded by Argentina in 1982, sparking a full-scale war with the UK. In 1995, the UK and Argentina reached an agreement on the exploitation of oil reserves around the islands.

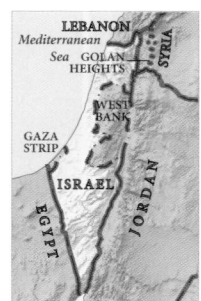
◄ **British warships** in Falkland Sound during the 1982 war with Argentina.

Israel

Israel was created in 1948 following the 1947 UN Resolution (147) on Palestine. Until 1979 Israel had no borders, only ceasefire lines from a series of wars in 1948, 1967 and 1973. Treaties with Egypt in 1979 and Jordan in 1994 led to these borders being defined and agreed. Negotiations over Israeli settlements and Palestinian self-government have seen little effective progress since 2000.

Former Yugoslavia

Following the disintegration in 1991 of the communist state of Yugoslavia, the breakaway states of Croatia and Bosnia and Herzegovina came into conflict with the 'parent' state (consisting of Serbia and Montenegro). Warfare focused on ethnic and territorial ambitions in Bosnia. The tenuous Dayton Accord of 1995 sought to recognize the post-1990 borders, whilst providing for ethnic partition and required international peace-keeping troops to maintain the terms of the peace.

▲ **Most claimant states** have small military garrisons on the Spratly Islands.

The Spratly Islands

The site of potential oil and natural gas reserves, the Spratly Islands in the South China Sea have been claimed by China, Vietnam, Taiwan, Malaysia and the Philippines since the Japanese gave up a wartime claim in 1951.

Palestinian control
Mixed control
Israeli settlement block
● Israeli settlement
○ Palestinian settlement
— West Bank fence

▲ **Barbed-wire fences** surround a settlement in the Golan Heights.

■ Republika Srpska
□ Federacija Bosna i Hercegovina

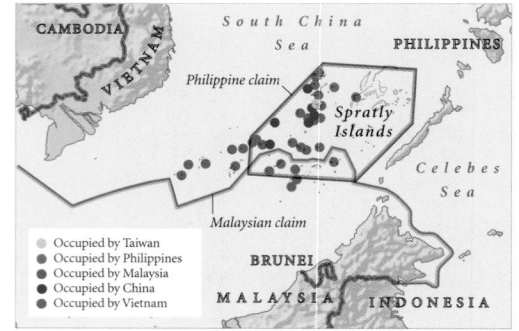
● Occupied by Taiwan
● Occupied by Philippines
● Occupied by Malaysia
● Occupied by China
● Occupied by Vietnam

ATLAS
OF THE WORLD

THE MAPS IN THIS ATLAS ARE ARRANGED CONTINENT BY CONTINENT, STARTING

FROM THE INTERNATIONAL DATE LINE, AND MOVING EASTWARDS. THE MAPS PROVIDE

A UNIQUE VIEW OF TODAY'S WORLD, COMBINING TRADITIONAL CARTOGRAPHIC

TECHNIQUES WITH THE LATEST REMOTE-SENSED AND DIGITAL TECHNOLOGY.

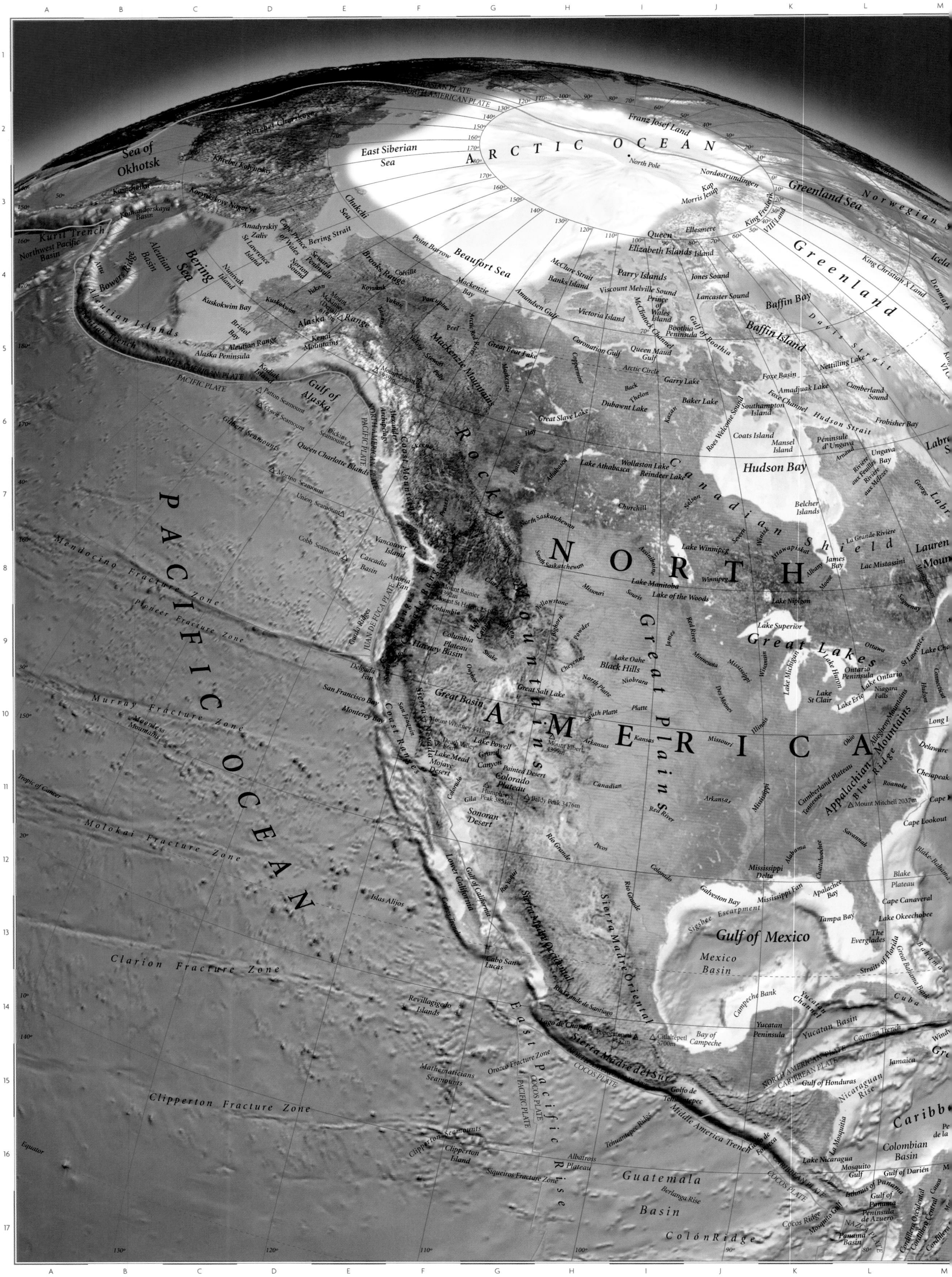

A B C D E F G H I J K L M

1
2
3
4
5
6
7
8
9
10
11
12
13
14
15
16
17

EURASIAN PLATE
NORTH AMERICAN PLATE

Northern Chukotka
Sea of Okhotsk
East Siberian Sea
ARCTIC OCEAN
North Pole
Franz Josef Land
Nordøstrundingen
Greenland Sea
Norwegian Sea
Khrebet Kolymskiy
Kamchatka
Chukchi Sea
Morris Jesup
Kap
King Frederik VIII Land
Greenland
Kurit Trench
Northwest Pacific Basin
Komandorskaya Basin
Anadyrskiy Zaliv
Cape Prince of Wales
Bering Strait
Seward Peninsula
Point Barrow
Beaufort Sea
McClure Strait
Banks Island
Parry Islands
Queen Elizabeth Islands
Ellesmere Island
King Christian X Land
King Frederik VIII Land
Icela(nd)
Denmark Strait

Bering Sea
Aleutian Islands
St Lawrence Island
Nunivak Island
Norton Sound
Brooks Range
Colville
Mackenzie Bay
Amundsen Gulf
Victoria Island
Viscount Melville Sound
Prince of Wales Island
McClintock Channel
Boothia Peninsula
Gulf of Boothia
Baffin Bay
Baffin Island
Davis Strait

Bowers Ridge
Amu
Aleutian Trench
Kuskokwim Bay
Bristol Bay
Aleutian Range
Alaska Peninsula
Kodiak Island
Kenai Peninsula
Gulf of Alaska
Yukon
Kuskokwim
Mount McKinley (Denali)
Alaska Range
Peel
Arctic Red River
Yukon
Mackenzie
Mackenzie Mountains
Great Bear Lake
Coronation Gulf
Queen Maud Gulf
Arctic Circle
Garry Lake
Back
Foxe Basin
Amadjuak Lake
Nettilling Lake
Cumberland Sound
Frobisher Bay

NORTH AMERICAN PLATE
PACIFIC PLATE
Patton Seamount
Giacomini Seamount
Wickills Seamount
PACIFIC PLATE
Alexander Archipelago
Skeena
Kuskokwim Mountains
Rocky
Liard
Hay
Great Slave Lake
Thelon
Dubawnt Lake
Baker Lake
Kazan
Roes Welcome Sound
Southampton Island
Foxe Channel
Hudson Strait
Coats Island
Mansel Island
Péninsule d'Ungava
Rivière aux Feuilles
Rivière aux Mélèzes
Ungava Bay
Arnaud
Labr

Morton Seamount
Union Seamount
Queen Charlotte Islands
Coast Mountains
Lake Athabasca
Wollaston Lake
Reindeer Lake
Hudson Bay
Belcher Islands
La Grande Rivière
Attawapiskat
George
Labr

Cobb Seamount
Vancouver Island
Cascadia Basin
Astoria Fan
Mountains
Churchill
North Saskatchewan
Nelson
NORTH
Canadian Shield
Lauren
Moun

Mendocino Fracture Zone
Mount Rainier
Mount St Helens
Columbia
Columbia Plateau
Yellowstone
Missouri
South Saskatchewan
Lake Manitoba
Lake Winnipeg
Winnipeg
Lake of the Woods
Souris
Red River
Lake Nipigon
Lake Superior
Great Lakes
Moose
Albany
James Bay
Lac Mistassini
Severn

Pioneer Fracture Zone
Gorda Ridges
JUAN DE FUCA PLATE
Delgada Fan
Harney Basin
Snake
Columbia
Bighorn
Powder
Cheyenne
Lake Oahe
Black Hills
Niobrara
Minnesota
Mississippi
Wisconsin
Lake Michigan
Lake Huron
Ontario Peninsula
Ottawa
Lake Ontario
Lake St Clair
Lake Erie
Niagara Falls
St Lawrence

Murray Fracture Zone
Meinesz Seamounts
San Francisco Bay
Monterey Bay
San Joaquin
Coast Ranges
Great Basin
Great Salt Lake
North Platte
South Platte
Platte
Des Moines
Illinois
AMERICA
Great Plains
Allegheny Mountains
Delaware
Long I(sland)
Chesapeak(e)
Cape

Mount Whitney 4418m
Sierra Nevada
Death Valley
Mojave Desert
Lake Mead
Lake Powell
Grant
Grand Canyon
Painted Desert
Colorado Plateau
Humphreys Peak
Baldy Peak 3476m
Mount Elbert 4399m
Arkansas
Kansas
Canadian
Missouri
Cumberland Plateau
Tennessee
Blue Ridge
Appalachian Mountains
Mount Mitchell 2037m
Roanoke
Cape

Tropic of Cancer
Molokai Fracture Zone
Sonoran Desert
Gila
Colorado
Rio Grande
Pecos
Arkansas
Red River
Alabama
Chattahoochee
Savannah
Cape Lookout

Clarion Fracture Zone
Islas Alijos
Lower California
Gulf of California
Rio Grande
Colorado
Mississippi Delta
Galveston Bay
Mississippi Fan
Apalachee Bay
Tampa Bay
Blake Plateau
Cape Canaveral
Lake Okeechobee
Sigsbee Escarpment
Gulf of Mexico
Mexico Basin
The Everglades
Straits of Florida
Great Bahama

Revillagigedo Islands
Cabo San Lucas
Sierra Madre Occidental
Rio Grande de Santiago
Campeche Bank
Yucatan Channel
Yucatan Basin
Cuba
Cayman Trench

PACIFIC OCEAN
Mathematicians Seamounts
East Pacific Rise
Lago de Chapala
Popocatepetl
Citlaltepetl 5700m
Sierra Madre Oriental
Bay of Campeche
Yucatan Peninsula
Jamaica
Gr

Clipperton Fracture Zone
Orozco Fracture Zone
COCOS PLATE
PACIFIC PLATE
Sierra Madre del Sur
Golfo de Tehuantepec
NORTH AMERICAN PLATE
CARIBBEAN PLATE
Gulf of Honduras
Nicaraguan Rise
Caribb(ean)
Colombian Basin

Clipperton Seamounts
Clipperton Island
Albatross Plateau
Siqueiros Fracture Zone
Guatemala Basin
Berlanga Rise
Tehuantepec Ridge
Middle America Trench
Lake Managua
Lake Nicaragua
Mosquito Gulf
Gulf of Darién
Cocos Ridge
COCOS PLATE
Mosquito Coast
Isthmus of Panama
Gulf of Panama
Peninsula de Azuero
Cordillera Occidental
Cordillera

Equator
Colón Ridge
Cocos Basin
Panama Basin
NAZCA PLATE

50°
60°
70°
150°
160°
170°
180°
170°
160°
40°
30°
20°
10°
130°
120°
110°
100°
90°
80°
70°
60°
50°
40°
30°
20°
10°
0°
140°
150°
160°
170°
130°
120°
110°

North America

North America is the world's third largest continent with a total area of 9,358,340 sq miles (24,238,000 sq km) including Greenland and the Caribbean islands.

It lies wholly within the Northern Hemisphere.

- ⬤ **Greatest extent, North–South:** 4600 miles / 7400 km
- ▢ **Greatest extent, East–West:** 3500 miles / 5700 km

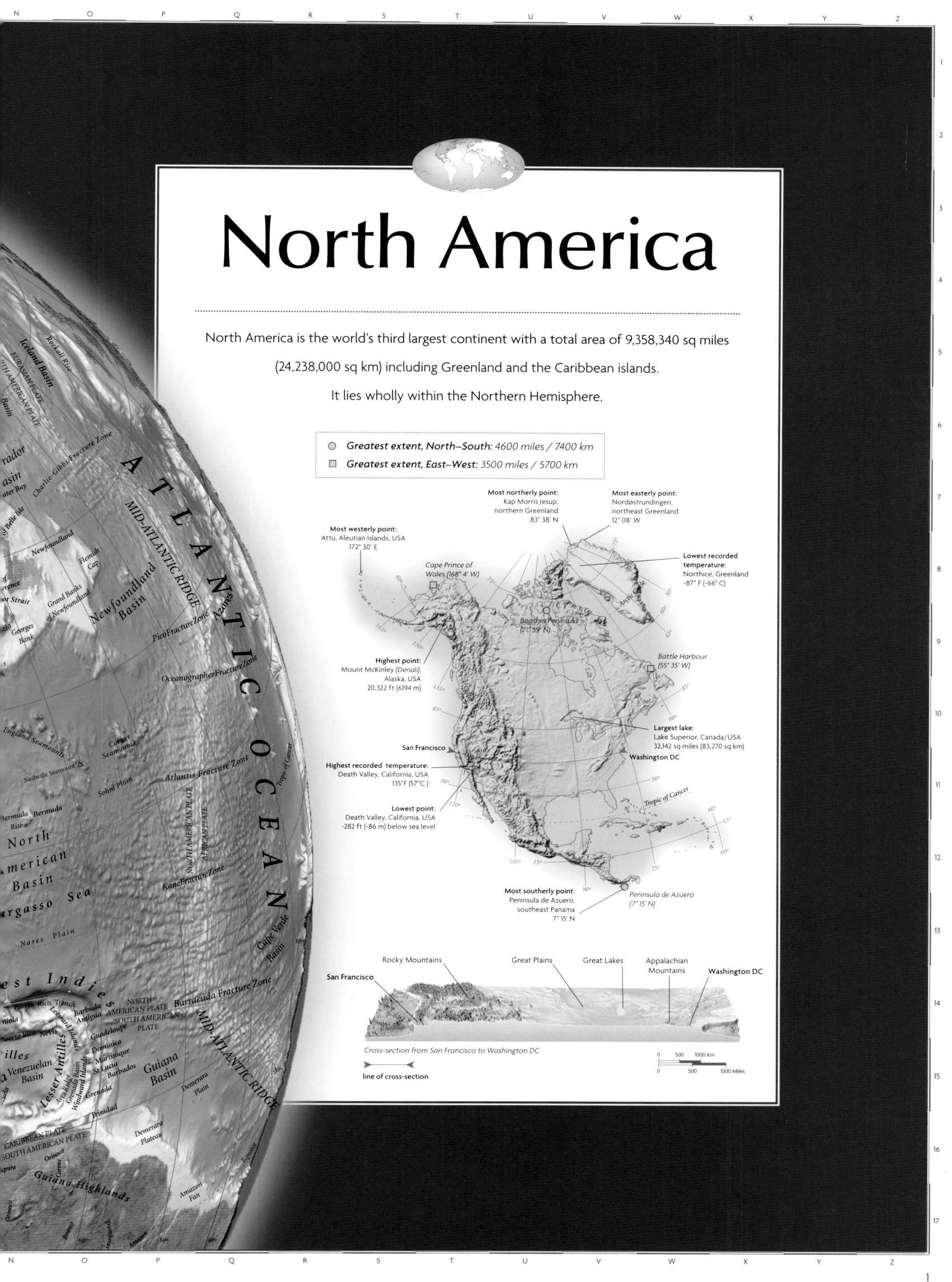

Most northerly point:
Kap Morris Jesup,
northern Greenland
83° 38' N

Most easterly point:
Nordøstrundingen,
northeast Greenland
12° 08' W

Most westerly point:
Attu, Aleutian Islands, USA
172° 30' E

Lowest recorded temperature:
Northice, Greenland
-87° F (-66° C)

Cape Prince of
Wales (168° 4' W)

Boothia Peninsula
(71° 59' N)

Highest point:
Mount McKinley (Denali),
Alaska, USA
20,322 ft (6194 m)

Battle Harbour
(55° 35' W)

Largest lake:
Lake Superior, Canada/USA
32,142 sq miles (83,270 sq km)

San Francisco

Washington DC

Highest recorded temperature:
Death Valley, California, USA
135°F (57°C)

Lowest point:
Death Valley, California, USA
-282 ft (-86 m) below sea level

Tropic of Cancer

Most southerly point:
Península de Azuero,
southeast Panama
7° 15' N

Península de Azuero
(7° 15' N)

Rocky Mountains | Great Plains | Great Lakes | Appalachian Mountains | Washington DC

San Francisco

Cross-section from San Francisco to Washington DC

line of cross-section

0   500   1000 Km
0   500   1000 Miles

Iceland Basin
EURASIAN PLATE
NORTH AMERICAN PLATE

Rockall Rise

Charlie-Gibbs Fracture Zone

rador
asin
ater Bay

ATLANTIC
MID-ATLANTIC RIDGE

Newfoundland

Flemish Cap

Azores

Grand Banks of Newfoundland

Newfoundland Basin

PicoFractureZone

Georges Bank

or Strait
rence

OceanographerFractureZone

OCEAN

England Seamounts

Corner Seamounts

Nashville Seamount

Sohm Plain

Atlantis Fracture Zone

NORTH AMERICAN PLATE
AFRICAN PLATE

Bermuda *Bermuda Rise*

North
American
Basin

KaneFractureZone

argasso Sea

Nares Plain

Cape Verde Basin

West Indies

NORTH AMERICAN PLATE
Barracuda Fracture Zone

Puerto Rico Trench
Barbuda
Antigua
Guadeloupe
SOUTH AMERICAN PLATE

MID-ATLANTIC RIDGE

miola
uerto Rico *Nevis*
illes
Venezuelan Basin
Lesser Antilles
St Lucia
Martinique
Dominica
Barbados
Windward *Grenada*
Grenada Basin
Trinidad

Guiana Basin

Demerara Plain

CARIBBEAN PLATE
SOUTH AMERICAN PLATE

Orinoco
Guiana Highlands

Amazon Fan

Equator

Physical North America

The North American continent can be divided into a number of major structural areas: the Western Cordillera, the Canadian Shield, the Great Plains and Central Lowlands, and the Appalachians. Other smaller regions include the Gulf Atlantic Coastal Plain which borders the southern coast of North America from the southern Appalachians to the Great Plains. This area includes the expanding Mississippi Delta. A chain of volcanic islands, running in an arc around the margin of the Caribbean Plate, lie to the east of the Gulf of Mexico.

The Western Cordillera

About 80 million years ago the Pacific and North American plates collided, uplifting the Western Cordillera. This consists of the Aleutian, Coast, Cascade and Sierra Nevada mountains, and the inland Rocky Mountains. These run parallel from the Arctic to Mexico.

The weight of the ice sheet, 1.8 miles (3 km) thick, has depressed the land to 0.6 miles (1 km) below sea level

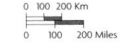

▲ This computer-generated view shows the ice-covered island of Greenland without its ice cap.

Strata have been thrust eastward along fault lines

Volcanic rock

The Rocky Mountain Trench is the longest linear fault on the continent

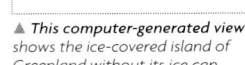

B　　　　　　　　　　　　　　　　　　　　　　　B

Cross-section through the Western Cordillera showing direction of mountain building.

The Canadian Shield

Spanning northern Canada and Greenland, this geologically stable plain forms the heart of the continent, containing rocks over two billion years old. A long history of weathering and repeated glaciation has scoured the region, leaving flat plains, gentle hummocks, numerous small basins and lakes, and the bays and islands of the Arctic.

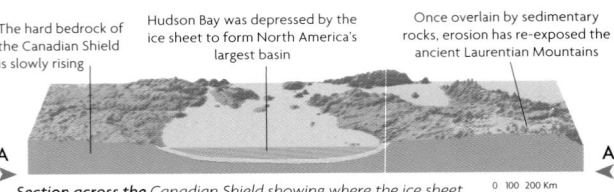

The hard bedrock of the Canadian Shield is slowly rising

Hudson Bay was depressed by the ice sheet to form North America's largest basin

Once overlain by sedimentary rocks, erosion has re-exposed the ancient Laurentian Mountains

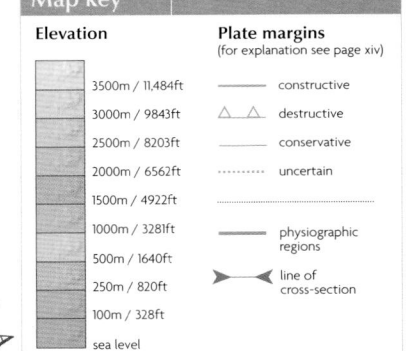

A　　　　　　　　　　　　　　　　　　　　　　A

Section across the Canadian Shield showing where the ice sheet has depressed the underlying rock and formed bays and islands.

Map key

Elevation

- 3500m / 11,484ft
- 3000m / 9843ft
- 2500m / 8203ft
- 2000m / 6562ft
- 1500m / 4922ft
- 1000m / 3281ft
- 500m / 1640ft
- 250m / 820ft
- 100m / 328ft
- sea level

Plate margins (for explanation see page xiv)

- —— constructive
- △ △ destructive
- —— conservative
- ⋯⋯ uncertain
- —— physiographic regions
- ◄——► line of cross-section

Scale 1:42,000,000

projection: Lambert Azimuthal Equal Area

The Great Plains and Central Lowlands

Deposits left by retreating glaciers and rivers have made this vast flat area very fertile. In the north this is the result of glaciation, with deposits up to one mile (1.7 km) thick, covering the basement rock. To the south and west, the massive Missouri/Mississippi river system has for centuries deposited silt across the plains, creating broad, flat flood plains and deltas.

Sedimentary layers overlay domed basement rock

Upland rivers drain south towards the Mississippi Basin

Confluence of the Missouri and Mississippi rivers

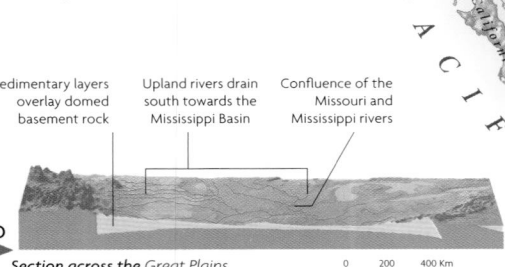

D　　　　　　　　　　　　　　　　　　　D

Section across the Great Plains and Central Lowlands showing river systems and structure.

The Appalachians

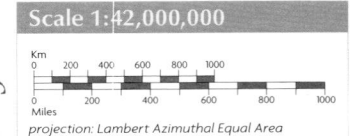

The Appalachian Mountains, uplifted about 400 million years ago, are some of the oldest in the world. They have been lowered and rounded by erosion and now slope gently towards the Atlantic across a broad coastal plain.

Horizontal strata

Sedimentary strata folded and faulted into ridges and valleys

Softer strata has been crumpled against the harder basement rock

Hard basement rock

C　　　　　　　　　　　　　　C

Cross-section through the Appalachians showing the numerous folds, which have subsequently been weathered to create a rounded relief.

Map labels

ASIA
Bering Strait
Beaufort Sea
Bering Sea
Aleutian Islands
Aleutian Range
Brooks Range
Alaska Range
Mount McKinley 6194m
Mackenzie Delta
Gulf of Alaska
NORTH AMERICAN PLATE
PACIFIC PLATE
Coast Mountains
Mackenzie Mountains
Mackenzie
Great Bear Lake
Great Slave Lake
Lake Athabasca
Reindeer Lake
Rocky Mountains
WESTERN CORDILLERA
Cascade Range
Mount Rainier 4392m
Mount St Helens 2549m
Great Basin
Sierra Nevada
San Joaquin
San Andreas Fault
Death Valley -86m
Great Salt Lake
Mojave Desert
Grand Canyon
Colorado Plateau
Colorado
Sonoran Desert
Lower California
Sierra Nevada
Gulf of California
Sierra Madre Occidental
Sierra Madre Oriental
Sierra Madre del Sur
Rio Grande
Volcán Pico de Orizaba 5700m
Yucatán Peninsula
Isthmus of Panama
COCOS PLATE
CARIBBEAN PLATE
Lake Nicaragua
CARIBBEAN PLATE
SOUTH AMERICAN PLATE
SOUTH AMERICA
Caribbean Sea
Lesser Antilles
Greater Antilles
West Indies
Nova Scotia
Cape Cod
Newfoundland
Laurentian Mountains
Labrador
Labrador Sea
Hudson Bay
Hudson Strait
Foxe Basin
Baffin Island
Baffin Bay
Davis Strait
Greenland
ATLANTIC OCEAN
CANADIAN SHIELD
CENTRAL LOWLANDS
GREAT PLAINS
Lake Winnipeg
Lake Manitoba
Lake Superior
Lake Huron
Lake Michigan
Lake Ontario
Lake Erie
Great Lakes
St Lawrence
APPALACHIAN MOUNTAINS
Ohio
Arkansas
Missouri
Mississippi
GULF ATLANTIC COASTAL PLAIN
Mississippi Delta
Gulf of Mexico
PACIFIC OCEAN

Climate

North America's climate includes extremes ranging from freezing Arctic conditions in Alaska and Greenland, to desert in the southwest, and tropical conditions in southeastern Florida, the Caribbean and Central America. Central and southern regions are prone to severe storms including tornadoes and hurricanes.

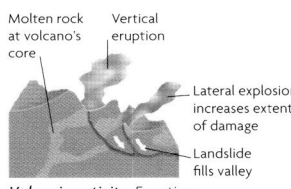

▲ *'Tornado alley' in the Mississippi Valley suffers frequent tornadoes.*

▲ *Much of the southwest is semi-desert; receiving less than 12 inches (300 mm) of rainfall a year.*

Climate

	ice cap
	tundra
	subarctic
	cool continental
	warm humid
	semi-arid
	arid
	humid equatorial
	tropical
☀	daily hours of sunshine, January
☀	daily hours of sunshine, July
→	direction of hurricanes
⊛	tornado zones

Temperature

Average January temperature

Average July temperature

Temperature

	below -30°C (-22°F)		0 to 10°C (32 to 50°F)
	-30 to -20°C (-22 to -4°F)		10 to 20°C (50 to 68°F)
	-20 to -10°C (-4 to 14°F)		20 to 30°C (68 to 86°F)
	-10 to 0°C (14 to 32°F)		above 30°C (86°F)

Rainfall

Average January rainfall

Average July rainfall

Rainfall

	0–25 mm (0–1 in)
	25–50 mm (1–2 in)
	50–100 mm (2–4 in)
	100–200 mm (4–8 in)
	200–300 mm (8–12 in)
	300–400 mm (12–16 in)
	400–500 mm (16–20 in)
	more than 500 mm (20 in)

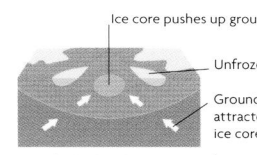

◄ *The lush, green mountains of the Lesser Antilles receive annual rainfalls of up to 360 inches (9000 mm).*

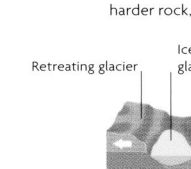

(map of North America with cities: Nome, Fairbanks, Aklavik, Kugluktuk, Resolute, Eismitte, Iqaluit, Haines Junction, Juneau, Fort Vermillon, Fort St John, Churchill, Happy Valley – Goose Bay, Torbay, Vancouver, Medicine Hat, Winnipeg, Montréal, Boise, Sioux City, Toronto, Salt Lake City, San Francisco, Denver, New York, Las Vegas, Phoenix, Atlanta, Cape Hatteras, Los Angeles, Little Rock, Guaymas, Houston, Miami, Nassau, Chihuahua, New Orleans, Santo Domingo, Fort-de-France, Mérida, Kingston, Acapulco, San Salvador, San José)

Shaping the continent

Glacial processes affect much of northern Canada, Greenland and the Western Cordillera. Along the western coast of North America, Central America and the Caribbean, underlying plates moving together lead to earthquakes and volcanic eruptions. The vast river systems, fed by mountain streams, constantly erode and deposit material along their paths.

Volcanic activity

1 Mount St Helens volcano *(right)* in the Cascade Range erupted violently in May 1980, killing 57 people and levelling large areas of forest. The lateral blast filled a valley for 15 miles (25 km) with debris.

Molten rock at volcano's core — Vertical eruption — Lateral explosion increases extent of damage — Landslide fills valley

Volcanic activity: *Eruption of Mount St Helens*

Seismic activity

5 The San Andreas Fault *(above)* places much of the North America's west coast under constant threat from earthquakes. It is caused by the Pacific Plate grinding past the North American Plate at a faster rate, though in the same direction.

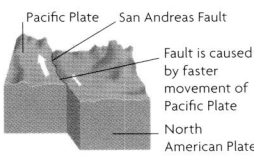

Pacific Plate — San Andreas Fault — Fault is caused by faster movement of Pacific Plate — North American Plate

Seismic activity: *Action of the San Andreas Fault*

River erosion

6 The Grand Canyon *(above)* in the Colorado Plateau was created by the downward erosion of the Colorado River, combined with the gradual uplift of the plateau, over the past 30 million years. The contours of the canyon formed as the softer rock layers eroded into gentle slopes, and the hard rock layers into cliffs. The depth varies from 3855–6560 ft (1175–2000 m).

Soft rock is easily eroded into gentle slopes — Hard rock resists erosion — Colorado River cuts down through rock

River Erosion: *Formation of the Grand Canyon*

Periglaciation

2 The ground in the far north is nearly always frozen: the surface thaws only in summer. This freeze-thaw process produces features such as pingos *(left)*; formed by the freezing of groundwater. With each successive winter ice accumulates producing a mound with a core of ice.

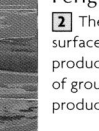

Ice core pushes up ground to form pingo — Unfrozen lake — Groundwater attracted to ice core

Periglaciation: *Formation of a pingo in the Mackenzie Delta*

The evolving landscape

Post-glacial lakes

3 A chain of lakes from Great Bear Lake to the Great Lakes *(above)* was created as the ice retreated northwards. Glaciers scoured hollows in the softer lowland rock. Glacial deposits at the lip of the hollows, and ridges of harder rock, trapped water to form lakes.

Retreating glacier — Ice-scoured hollow filled with glacial meltwater to form a lake — Harder rock creates a barrier between lakes — Softer lowland rock

Post-glacial lakes: *Formation of the Great Lakes*

Landscape

	limestone region
	sinking land
	stable land
	uplifting land
▲	active volcano
⋯	area of tectonic activity
- - -	limit of permafrost
—	maximum limit of glaciation
→	ocean current

Weathering

4 The Yucatan Peninsula is a vast, flat limestone plateau in southern Mexico. Weathering action from both rainwater and underground streams has enlarged fractures in the rock to form caves and hollows, called sinkholes *(above)*.

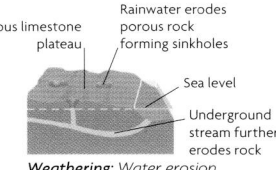

Porous limestone plateau — Rainwater erodes porous rock forming sinkholes — Sea level — Underground stream further erodes rock

Weathering: *Water erosion on the Yucatan Peninsula*

Political North America

Democracy is well established in some parts of the continent but is a recent phenomenon in others. The economically dominant nations of Canada and the USA have a long democratic tradition but elsewhere, notably in the countries of Central America, political turmoil has been more common. In Nicaragua and Haiti, harsh dictatorships have only recently been superseded by democratically-elected governments. North America's largest countries, Canada, Mexico and the USA have federal state systems, sharing political power between national and state governments. The USA has intervened militarily on several occasions in Central America and the Caribbean to protect its strategic interests.

Transport

In the 19th century, railways were used to open up the North American continent. Air transport is now more common for long distance passenger travel, although railways are still extensively used for bulk freight transport. Waterways, like the Mississippi River, are important for the transport of bulk materials, and the Panama Canal is a vital link between the Pacific Ocean and the Caribbean. In the 20th century, road transport increased massively in North America, with the introduction of cheap, mass-produced motor cars and extensive highway construction.

◄ *This busy suburban* interchange in Los Angeles is part of the USA's Interstate freeway system. Construction of the 55,000 mile (88,500 km) freeway network began in the 1950s, and it now connects most major cities, and carries one-fifth of the USA's road traffic.

Transport

— major roads and motorways
— major railways
— major canals
--- international borders
● transport intersections
✛ international airports
✛ major ports

▲ *The 40 mile* (65 km) long Panama Canal cuts through the Isthmus of Panama, a narrow strip of land connecting North and South America. Opened in 1914, the canal reduced the journey between the Atlantic and Pacific oceans by almost 8000 nautical miles (14,800 km).

◄ *Low-density housing* developments such as this one on the outskirts of Phoenix, Arizona, reflect the USA's abundance of land and a dispersed population, dependent on the motor car for personal mobility.

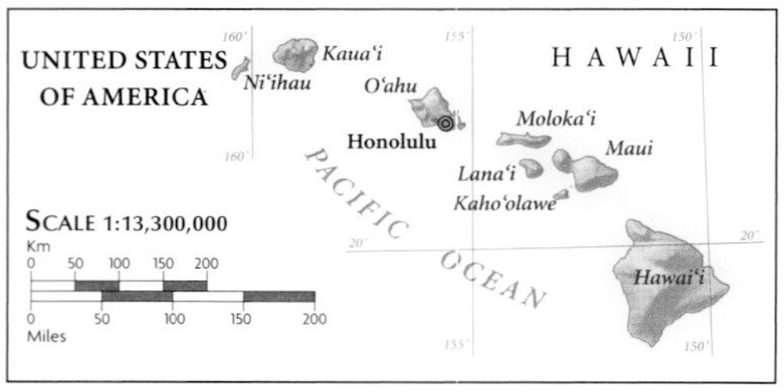

UNITED STATES OF AMERICA

SCALE 1:13,300,000

HAWAI'I

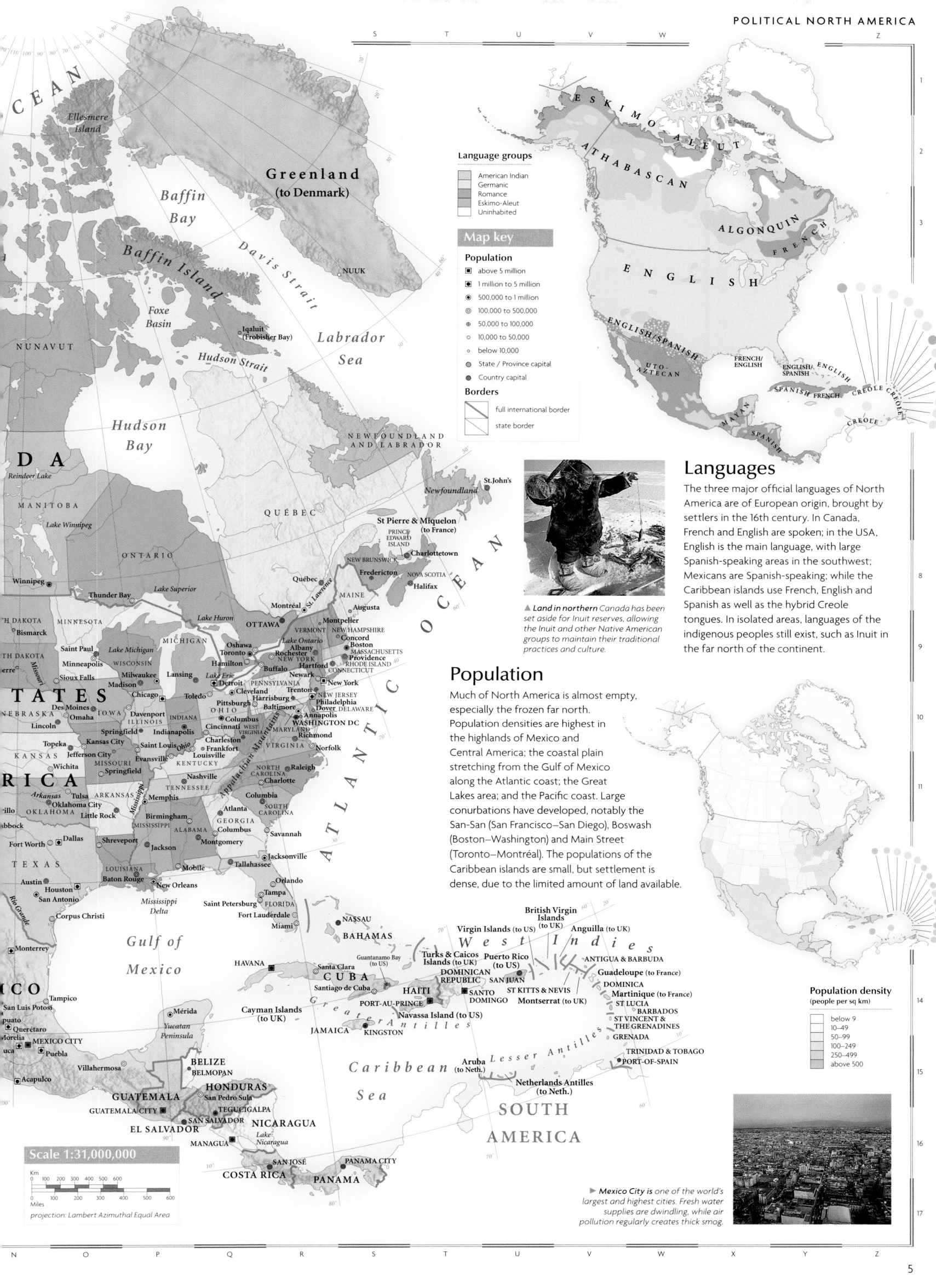

Language groups
- American Indian
- Germanic
- Romance
- Eskimo-Aleut
- Uninhabited

Map key

Population
- ▣ above 5 million
- ◉ 1 million to 5 million
- ◉ 500,000 to 1 million
- ◎ 100,000 to 500,000
- ⊕ 50,000 to 100,000
- ○ 10,000 to 50,000
- ∘ below 10,000
- State / Province capital
- Country capital

Borders
- full international border
- state border

Languages

The three major official languages of North America are of European origin, brought by settlers in the 16th century. In Canada, French and English are spoken; in the USA, English is the main language, with large Spanish-speaking areas in the southwest; Mexicans are Spanish-speaking; while the Caribbean islands use French, English and Spanish as well as the hybrid Creole tongues. In isolated areas, languages of the indigenous peoples still exist, such as Inuit in the far north of the continent.

▲ *Land in northern Canada has been set aside for Inuit reserves, allowing the Inuit and other Native American groups to maintain their traditional practices and culture.*

Population

Much of North America is almost empty, especially the frozen far north. Population densities are highest in the highlands of Mexico and Central America; the coastal plain stretching from the Gulf of Mexico along the Atlantic coast; the Great Lakes area; and the Pacific coast. Large conurbations have developed, notably the San-San (San Francisco–San Diego), Boswash (Boston–Washington) and Main Street (Toronto–Montréal). The populations of the Caribbean islands are small, but settlement is dense, due to the limited amount of land available.

Population density
(people per sq km)
- below 9
- 10–49
- 50–99
- 100–249
- 250–499
- above 500

▶ *Mexico City is one of the world's largest and highest cities. Fresh water supplies are dwindling, while air pollution regularly creates thick smog.*

Scale 1:31,000,000

Km
0 100 200 300 400 500 600
Miles
0 100 200 300 400 500 600

projection: Lambert Azimuthal Equal Area

5

North American resources

The two northern countries of Canada and the USA are richly endowed with natural resources which have helped to fuel economic development. The USA is the world's largest economy, although today it is facing stiff competition from the Far East. Mexico has relied on oil revenues but there are hopes that the North American Free Trade Agreement (NAFTA), will encourage trade growth with Canada and the USA. The poorer countries of Central America and the Caribbean depend largely on cash crops and tourism.

Industry

The modern, industrialized economies of the USA and Canada contrast sharply with those of Mexico, Central America and the Caribbean. Manufacturing is especially important in the USA; vehicle production is concentrated around the Great Lakes, while electronic and hi-tech industries are increasingly found in the western and southern states. Mexico depends on oil exports and assembly work, taking advantage of cheap labour. Many Central American and Caribbean countries rely heavily on agricultural exports.

◄ *After its purchase* from Russia in 1867, Alaska's frozen lands were largely ignored by the USA. Oil reserves similar in magnitude to those in eastern Texas were discovered in Prudhoe Bay, Alaska in 1968. Freezing temperatures and a fragile environment hamper oil extraction.

Standard of living

The USA and Canada have one of the highest overall standards of living in the world. However, many people still live in poverty, especially in inner city ghettos and some rural areas. Central America and the Caribbean are markedly poorer than their wealthier northern neighbours. Haiti is the poorest country in the western hemisphere.

Standard of living
(UN human development index)

high

low

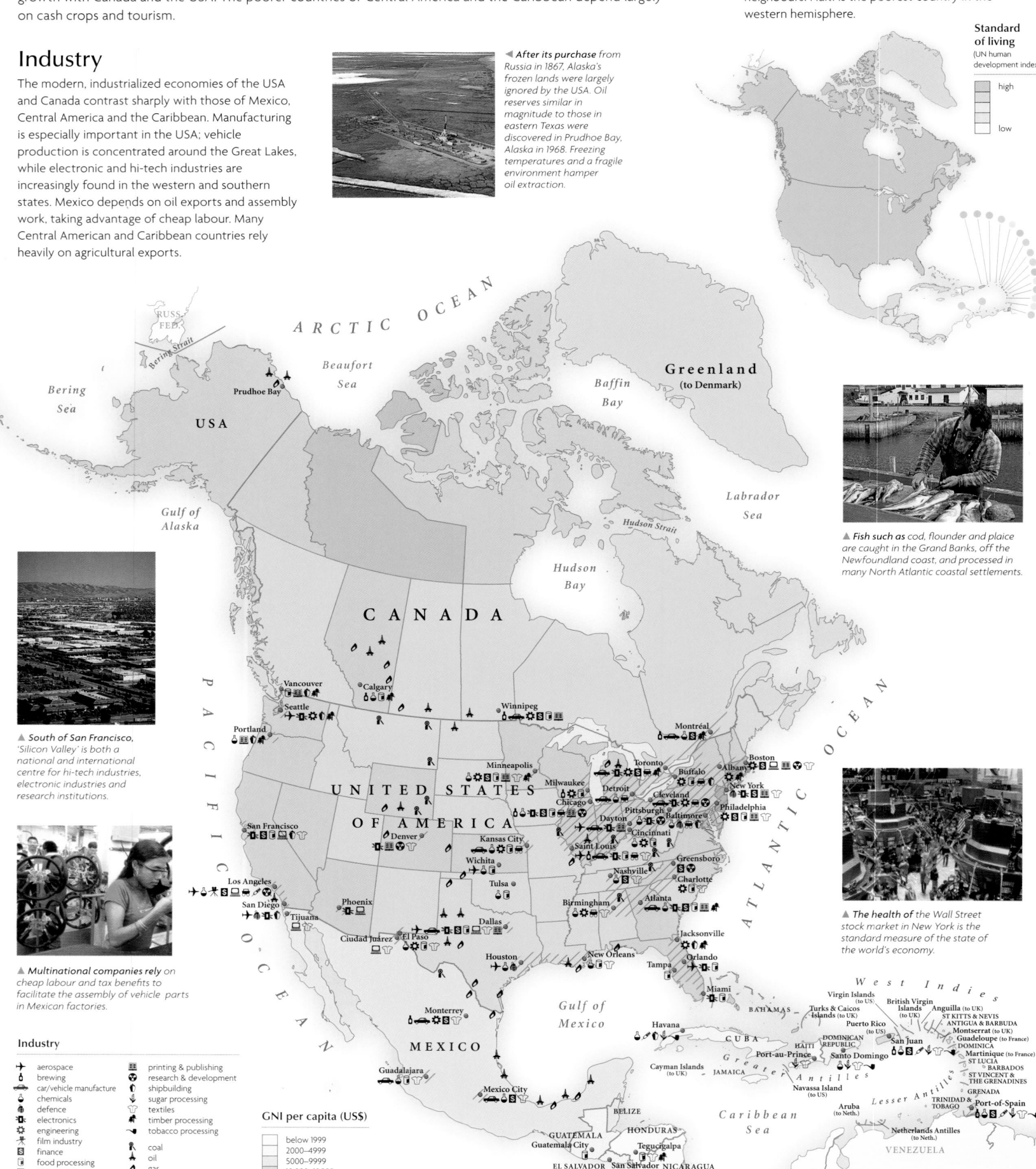

▲ *South of San Francisco*, 'Silicon Valley' is both a national and international centre for hi-tech industries, electronic industries and research institutions.

▲ *Multinational companies rely* on cheap labour and tax benefits to facilitate the assembly of vehicle parts in Mexican factories.

▲ *Fish such as* cod, flounder and plaice are caught in the Grand Banks, off the Newfoundland coast, and processed in many North Atlantic coastal settlements.

▲ *The health of* the Wall Street stock market in New York is the standard measure of the state of the world's economy.

Industry

- ✈ aerospace
- brewing
- 🚗 car/vehicle manufacture
- chemicals
- defence
- electronics
- ✿ engineering
- film industry
- 💲 finance
- food processing
- 💻 hi-tech industry
- iron & steel
- pharmaceuticals
- printing & publishing
- research & development
- shipbuilding
- sugar processing
- textiles
- timber processing
- tobacco processing
- coal
- oil
- gas
- ● industrial cities
- ⬚ major industrial areas

GNI per capita (US$)

- below 1999
- 2000–4999
- 5000–9999
- 10,000–19,999
- 20,000–24,999
- above 25,000

N O P Q R S T U V W X Y Z

Environmental issues

Many fragile environments are under threat throughout the region. In Haiti, all the primary rainforest has been destroyed, while air pollution from factories and cars in Mexico City is amongst the worst in the world. Elsewhere, industry and mining pose threats, particularly in the delicate arctic environment of Alaska where oil spills have polluted coastlines and decimated fish stocks.

Environmental issues

- national parks
- acid rain
- tropical forest
- forest destroyed
- desert
- desertification
- polluted rivers
- radioactive contamination
- marine pollution
- heavy marine pollution
- poor urban air quality

▲ **Wild bison** graze in Yellowstone National Park, the world's first national park. Designated in 1872, geothermal springs and boiling mud are among its natural spectacles, making it a major tourist attraction.

Mineral resources

Fossil fuels are exploited in considerable quantities throughout the continent. Coal mining in the Appalachians is declining but vast open pits exist further west in Wyoming. Oil and natural gas are found in Alaska, Texas, the Gulf of Mexico, and the Canadian West. Canada has large quantities of nickel, while Jamaica has considerable deposits of bauxite, and Mexico has large reserves of silver.

Mineral resources

- oil field
- gas field
- coal field
- bauxite
- copper
- gold
- iron
- lead
- nickel
- phosphates
- silver
- uranium

▲ **In addition to** fossil fuels, North America is also rich in exploitable metallic ores. This vast, mile-deep (1.6 km) pit is a copper mine in New Mexico.

▲ **In agriculturally marginal** areas where the soil is either too poor, or the climate too dry for crops, cattle ranching proliferates – especially in Mexico and the western reaches of the Great Plains.

Using the land and sea

Abundant land and fertile soils stretch from the Canadian prairies to Texas creating North America's agricultural heartland. Cereals and cattle ranching form the basis of the farming economy, with corn and soya beans also important. Fruit and vegetables are grown in California using irrigation, while Florida is a leading producer of citrus fruits. Caribbean and Central American countries depend on cash crops such as bananas, coffee and sugar cane, often grown on large plantations. This reliance on a single crop can leave these countries vulnerable to fluctuating world crop prices.

◄ **Sugar cane is** Cuba's main agricultural crop, and is grown and processed throughout the Caribbean. Fermented sugar is used to make rum.

◄ **The Great Plains** support large-scale arable farming throughout central North America. Corn is grown in a belt south and west of the Great Lakes, while further west where the climate is drier, wheat is grown.

Using the land and sea

- cropland
- forest
- ice cap
- mountain region
- pasture
- tundra
- wetland
- desert
- major conurbations
- cattle
- goats
- pigs
- poultry
- reindeer
- sheep
- bananas
- citrus fruits
- coffee
- corn (maize)
- cotton
- fishing
- fruit
- maple syrup
- peanuts
- rice
- shellfish
- soya beans
- sugar cane
- timber
- tobacco
- vineyards
- wheat

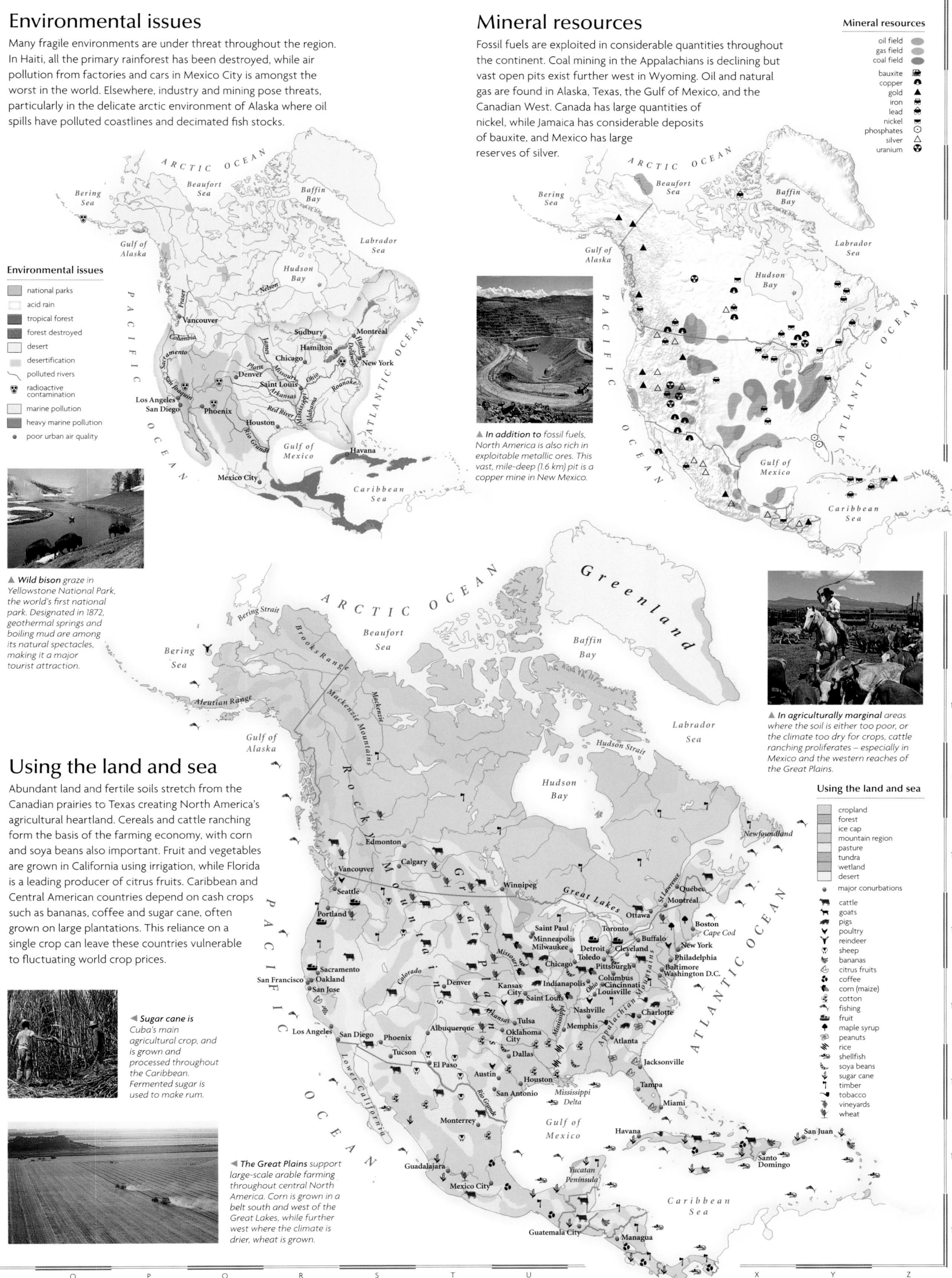

7

Canada

Canada is the second largest country in the world, and with only about one-tenth of its land area inhabited, it is one of the most sparsely populated. Canada became a confederation in 1867, though Newfoundland did not join until 1949. As a founding member of the UN and of the Commonwealth, Canada has played an important role in international affairs. A constitutional crisis, focusing on the French-speaking Québécois, and Inuit and Native American land rights, dominated politics in the 1990s. In 1999, part of the Northwest Territories, Nunavut, became a self-governing homeland for the Inuit.

◄ *The Selwyn Mountains* in northwestern Canada form part of the Rocky Mountains. The highest point, Keele Peak, rises to 9750 ft (2972 m).

Transport and industry

Abundant energy in the form of coal, oil, natural gas and hydro-electric power underpins Canadian industry. Over 75% of manufacturing is concentrated in the Great Lakes–St. Lawrence region, including prospering aerospace, transport and hi-tech industries. Across Canada as a whole, manufacturing has developed around a diversified, high-quality resource base and a wide range of metallic and non-metallic minerals.

◄ *Canada has one* of the world's highest rates of energy consumption per person. It is endowed with vast hydro-electric potential from which more than 60% of its electricity requirements are generated.

Major industry and infrastructure

- ✈ aerospace
- 🚗 car manufacture
- ⚗ chemicals
- ⚙ engineering
- food processing
- 🖥 hi-tech industry
- ♨ hydro-electric power
- ◊ oil & gas
- ⛏ mining
- timber processing
- ■ capital cities
- ● major towns
- ⊕ international airports
- — major roads
- ▨ major industrial areas

The transport network

🛣	309,019 miles (497,375 km)	⛴	10,500 miles (16,900 km)
🚂	8049 miles (12,995 km)	⚓	1864 miles (3000 km)

In recent years the road network has been expanded, especially links to remote areas. Meanwhile, for long-distance travel, air transport now supersedes the declining rail network, which focuses mainly on east–west routes.

Using the land and sea

The majority of Canada's agricultural land is found in the prairies, which cover 140 million acres (57 million ha) and support wheat and grain-fed cattle. More specialized crops, such as fruit and vegetables, are grown in pockets of agricultural land in the east and west. Of Canada's many islands, only Prince Edward Island has notable farmland. Further north, boreal forests, exploited for timber, run in an almost unbroken arc, giving way to uncultivable tundra and ice sheets in the far north.

The urban/rural population divide

urban 77%   rural 23%

0 10 20 30 40 50 60 70 80 90 100

Population density	Total land area
9 people per sq mile (3 people per sq km)	3,559,294 sq miles (9,220,970 sq km)

Land use and agricultural distribution

- 🐄 cattle
- 🌾 cereals
- 🎣 fishing
- 🍎 fruit
- 🌲 timber
- ■ capital cities
- ● major towns
- pasture
- cropland
- forest
- wetland
- mountain region
- barren
- tundra

◄ *The climate and* topography of the prairies makes them ideally suited to farming. Long summer days, moderate temperatures, limited rainfall and flat plains provide excellent conditions for wheat farming.

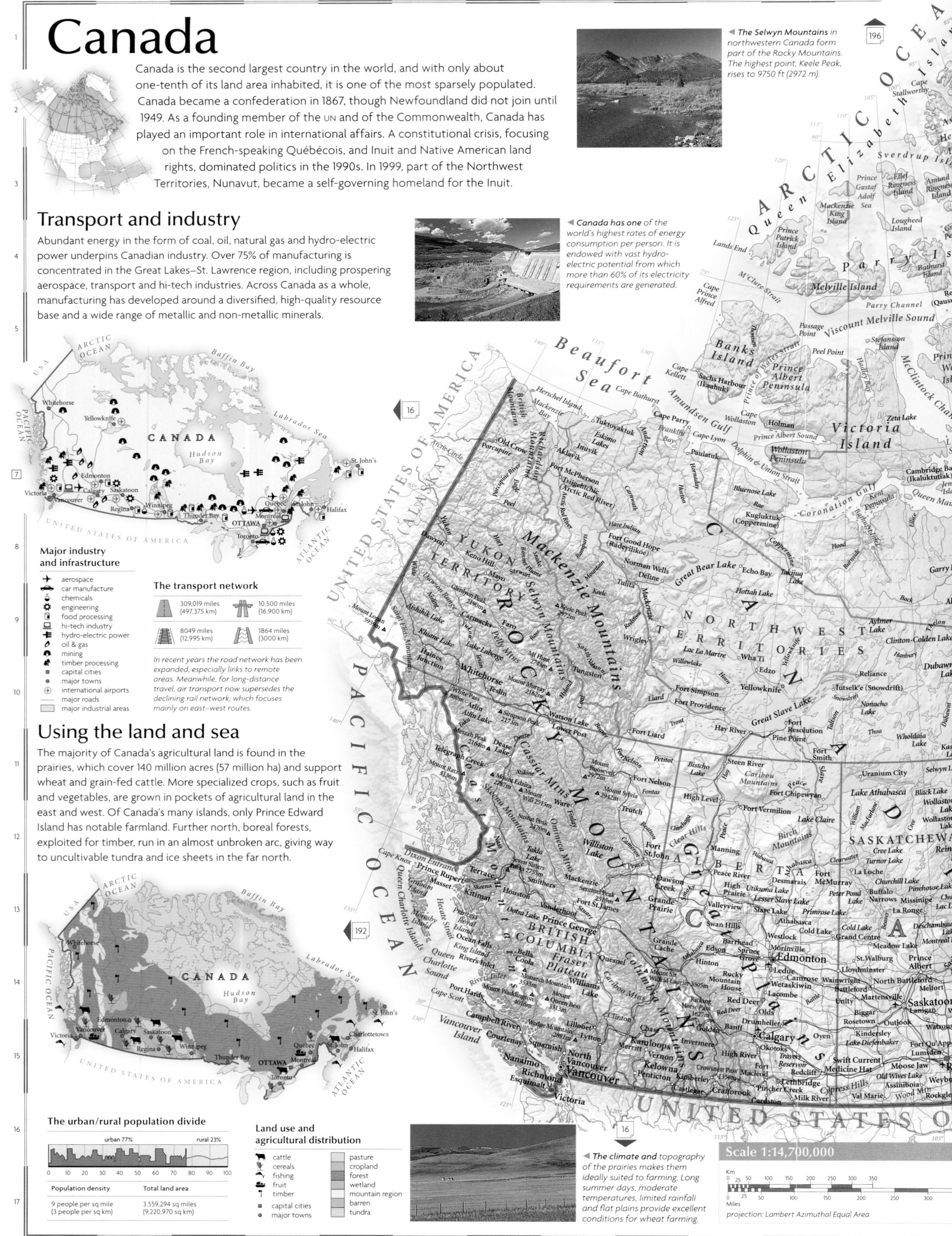

Scale 1:14,700,000

Km 25 50   100   150   200   250   300   350

Miles 0 25   50   100   150   200   250   300

projection: Lambert Azimuthal Equal Area

The landscape

Glaciers on islands in the Arctic Ocean are the last remnants of the ice sheet that once covered and shaped Canada. Hudson Bay is the centre of the Canadian Shield, a huge, eroded plateau marked at its southern extremity by a string of lakes running southeastwards from Great Bear Lake to the Great Lakes. In contrast to the rolling relief of the Shield and the central lowland region, the Rocky Mountains rise to peaks of over 13,000 ft (4000 m), stretching 500 miles (800 km) along the west coast.

▶ **Permanently frozen ground** known as permafrost is common in Canada's northern tundra. It thickens further north, becoming hundreds of metres deep in parts of the Arctic.

Permanently frozen ground

Top layer thaws in the summer

Marginal areas of permafrost thaw in summer

Unfrozen ground where temperature is more moderate

The Mackenzie river, flowing north over the permafrost, forms a wide river channel with many tributaries. Together with the Peel river it has created a long, narrow delta at its mouth. The entire river freezes during the winter.

Fertile prairies stretch from the southern rim of the Canadian Shield, south into the USA.

Exposure to three phases of mountain-building and subsequent erosion over millions of years has moulded the ancient Canadian Shield into a series of basins and ridges.

▲ **Along the northeastern** coast of Baffin Island the mountains rise to 8000 ft (2440 m). Glaciers move down through the valleys to the sea, eroding wide U-shaped valleys.

The Rocky Mountains were formed some 80 million years ago, when the Pacific plate was driven under the North American plate, forcing up the land.

The Great Lakes lie on the Canada–USA border. The basins they now occupy were fashioned by repeated ice advance. At one time, Lakes Superior, Huron and Michigan formed a single large lake, Lake Nipissing.

The St. Lawrence River is 2350 miles (3782 km) long. It flows from the western shore of Lake Superior through the Great Lakes and on to the Atlantic Ocean. From December to April, the St. Lawrence Seaway freezes between Lake Ontario and Montréal.

▶ **The Great Lakes** are drained by the St. Lawrence River which flows down through a wide tectonic depression. It forms a broad estuary for much of its course, the width varying from 1.2 miles (1.9 km) in the upper reaches to 90 miles (145 km) at its mouth.

Isolated pillars, known as hoodoos near Red Deer river in the badlands of Alberta are a product of wind and water erosion, especially flash floods. The badlands lie in the rain shadow of the Rocky Mountains, which creates a semi-arid climate.

Map key

Population
- ▣ 1 million to 5 million
- ◉ 500,000 to 1 million
- ◎ 100,000 to 500,000
- ⊕ 50,000 to 100,000
- ⊙ 10,000 to 50,000
- ○ below 10,000

Elevation
- 6000m / 19,686ft
- 4000m / 13,124ft
- 3000m / 9843ft
- 2000m / 6562ft
- 1000m / 3281ft
- 500m / 1640ft
- 250m / 820ft
- 100m / 328ft
- sea level

Canada:
WESTERN PROVINCES

Alberta, British Columbia, Manitoba,
Saskatchewan, Yukon Territory

The mountains of the west coast, incorporating British Columbia and
the Yukon Territory, descend into the vast, flat prairies of Alberta,
Saskatchewan and Manitoba. The empty lands and fertile soils of
the prairie provinces attracted migrants, and the descendants of
early European immigrants still make up a large proportion of
the population. The mechanization of agriculture has
reduced the need for labour, and rural population
densities remain low. The majority of the people live
within 100 miles (160 km) of the southern Canada–USA
border, and in British Columbia, one of the leading Canadian provinces in
terms of economic wealth. The Yukon Territory, in the far north, remains a
relatively unspoilt wilderness, containing large, untapped mineral reserves.
This province has a significant population of Native Americans,
many of whom maintain a traditional lifestyle.

Using the land and sea

Wheat farming is the economic mainstay of Alberta, Manitoba and
Saskatchewan, which contain 82% of farmland in Canada. Cattle
are also raised on the prairies. Forestry and fishing are the most
prominent resource-based industries in British Columbia. Despite
the mountainous terrain, fruit and specialized grains can be grown
in the Okanagan and Fraser valleys.

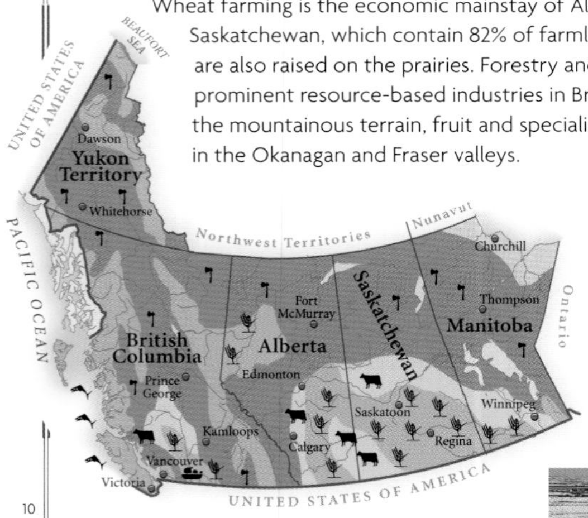

Land use and agricultural distribution

- cattle
- cereals
- fishing
- fruit
- timber
- major towns

- pasture
- cropland
- forest
- wetland
- barren
- tundra

The urban/rural population divide

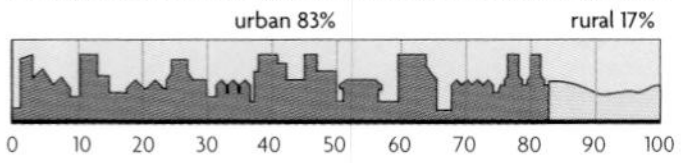

urban 83%   rural 17%

0 10 20 30 40 50 60 70 80 90 100

Population density	Total land area
8 people per sq mile (3 people per sq km)	1,230,547 sq miles (3,187,120 sq km)

▲ Large, highly-mechanized and
often very specialized farms,
requiring huge investment but little
labour, characterize modern
farming in the prairies.

Transport and industry

The western provinces contain a wealth of mineral resources.
Alberta holds the bulk of Canada's fossil fuels; the other
provinces contain reserves of metallic ores, such as zinc, lead
and silver. Isolation from markets has slowed the development
of manufacturing, restricting it to the large cities like Vancouver,
Winnipeg and Calgary. Hydro-electric power is widely
exploited, although there is increasing concern about potential
ecological damage.

The transport network

🛣	82,438 miles (135,145 km)
	6459 miles (10,401 km)
🚆	24,041 miles (38,694 km)
⚓	None

The transport network of the
western provinces is dominated
by east–west routes that weave
through mountain passes and
spread across the plains. Access
to some northern areas is
restricted to air travel.

Major industry and infrastructure

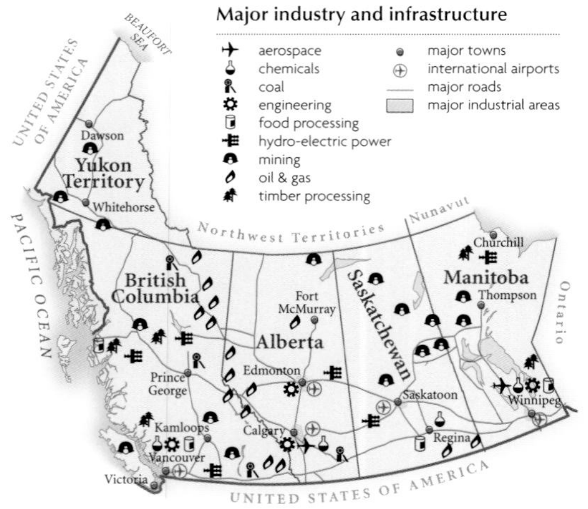

- ✈ aerospace
- chemicals
- coal
- ⚙ engineering
- food processing
- hydro-electric power
- mining
- oil & gas
- timber processing

- major towns
- ⊕ international airports
- major roads
- major industrial areas

▲ The Fraser River valley is a major
area of settlement in British
Columbia. Railways cross the
Rocky Mountains via this valley.

▲ Established in 1907,
Jasper National Park lies
in the heart of the Rocky
Mountains. It is noted for
its spectacular alpine
scenery and contains
part of the large
Columbia Icefield.

◄ Much of the Yukon Territory
is uninhabited tundra. Industry
is based on the extraction of
mineral resources, and to a
lesser extent, on the scattered
forests of the south.

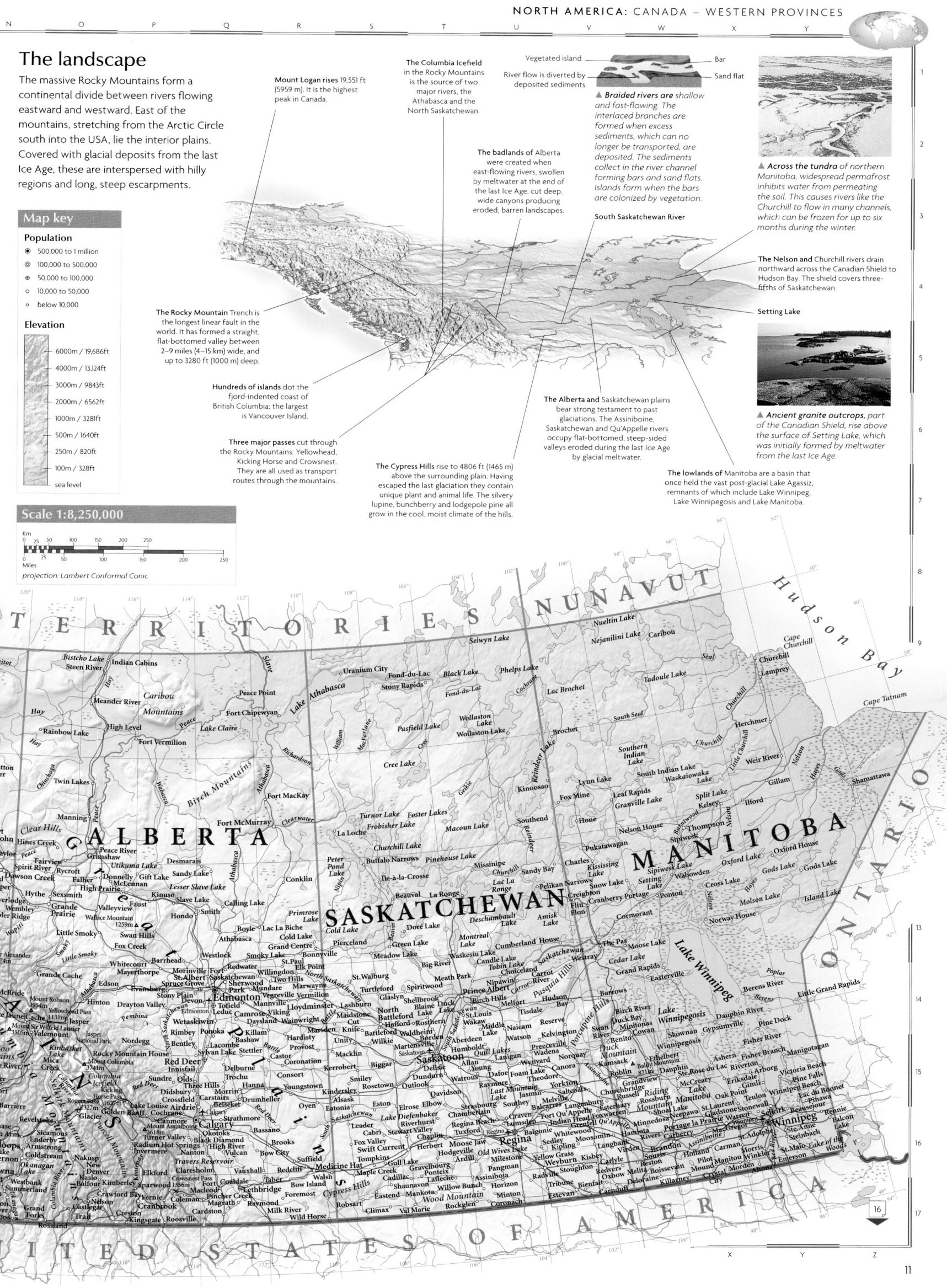

The landscape

The massive Rocky Mountains form a continental divide between rivers flowing eastward and westward. East of the mountains, stretching from the Arctic Circle south into the USA, lie the interior plains. Covered with glacial deposits from the last Ice Age, these are interspersed with hilly regions and long, steep escarpments.

Map key

Population

- ◉ 500,000 to 1 million
- ◎ 100,000 to 500,000
- ⊕ 50,000 to 100,000
- ○ 10,000 to 50,000
- ○ below 10,000

Elevation

- 6000m / 19,686ft
- 4000m / 13,124ft
- 3000m / 9843ft
- 2000m / 6562ft
- 1000m / 3281ft
- 500m / 1640ft
- 250m / 820ft
- 100m / 328ft
- sea level

Scale 1:8,250,000

Km
0 25 50   100   150   200   250

Miles
0   25 50   100   150   200   250

projection: Lambert Conformal Conic

Mount Logan rises 19,551 ft (5959 m). It is the highest peak in Canada.

The Columbia Icefield in the Rocky Mountains is the source of two major rivers, the Athabasca and the North Saskatchewan.

The badlands of Alberta were created when east-flowing rivers, swollen by meltwater at the end of the last Ice Age, cut deep, wide canyons producing eroded, barren landscapes.

Vegetated island — *Bar*
River flow is diverted by deposited sediments — *Sand flat*

▲ **Braided rivers are** shallow and fast-flowing. The interlaced branches are formed when excess sediments, which can no longer be transported, are deposited. The sediments collect in the river channel forming bars and sand flats. Islands form when the bars are colonized by vegetation.

South Saskatchewan River

▲ **Across the tundra** of northern Manitoba, widespread permafrost inhibits water from permeating the soil. This causes rivers like the Churchill to flow in many channels, which can be frozen for up to six months during the winter.

The Nelson and Churchill rivers drain northward across the Canadian Shield to Hudson Bay. The shield covers three-fifths of Saskatchewan.

Setting Lake

The Rocky Mountain Trench is the longest linear fault in the world. It has formed a straight, flat-bottomed valley between 2–9 miles (4–15 km) wide, and up to 3280 ft (1000 m) deep.

Hundreds of islands dot the fjord-indented coast of British Columbia; the largest is Vancouver Island.

Three major passes cut through the Rocky Mountains: Yellowhead, Kicking Horse and Crowsnest. They are all used as transport routes through the mountains.

The Cypress Hills rise to 4806 ft (1465 m) above the surrounding plain. Having escaped the last glaciation they contain unique plant and animal life. The silvery lupine, bunchberry and lodgepole pine all grow in the cool, moist climate of the hills.

The Alberta and Saskatchewan plains bear strong testament to past glaciations. The Assiniboine, Saskatchewan and Qu'Appelle rivers occupy flat-bottomed, steep-sided valleys eroded during the last Ice Age by glacial meltwater.

▲ **Ancient granite outcrops**, part of the Canadian Shield, rise above the surface of Setting Lake, which was initially formed by meltwater from the last Ice Age.

The lowlands of Manitoba are a basin that once held the vast post-glacial Lake Agassiz, remnants of which include Lake Winnipeg, Lake Winnipegosis and Lake Manitoba.

Canada: EASTERN PROVINCES

New Brunswick, Newfoundland & Labrador, Nova Scotia, Ontario, Prince Edward Island, Québec, *St Pierre & Miquelon (to France)*

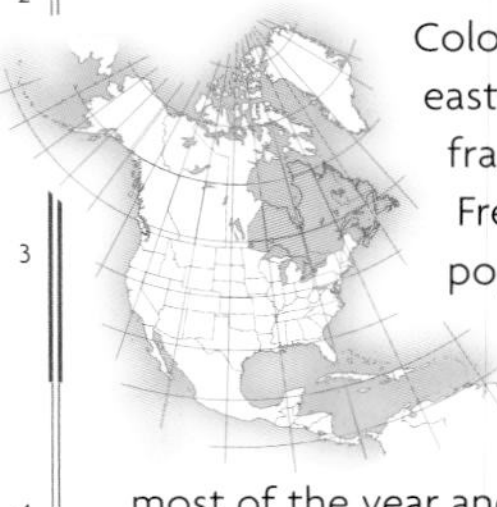

Colonized by both the English and the French during the 16th century, Canada's eastern provinces are still marked by their dual influences. They contain the last fragment of once-sizeable French territories, the islands of St Pierre and Miquelon. French remains Canada's second official language and Québec's first language. The population of the eastern provinces is highly concentrated in the south, especially along the border with the USA. A recent decline in fishing in the Atlantic provinces has encouraged a steady flow of westerly migration to more prosperous regions. The north, around Hudson Bay, remains snow-covered for most of the year and the indigenous Inuit people make up the bulk of its sparse population.

◄ *Rocher Percé, is 290 ft (88 m) high. Lying off the southeastern coast of Québec, it is a sanctuary for sea birds.*

Scale 1:7,750,000

Km
0 25 50 100 150 200

Miles
0 25 50 100 150 200

projection: Lambert Conformal Conic

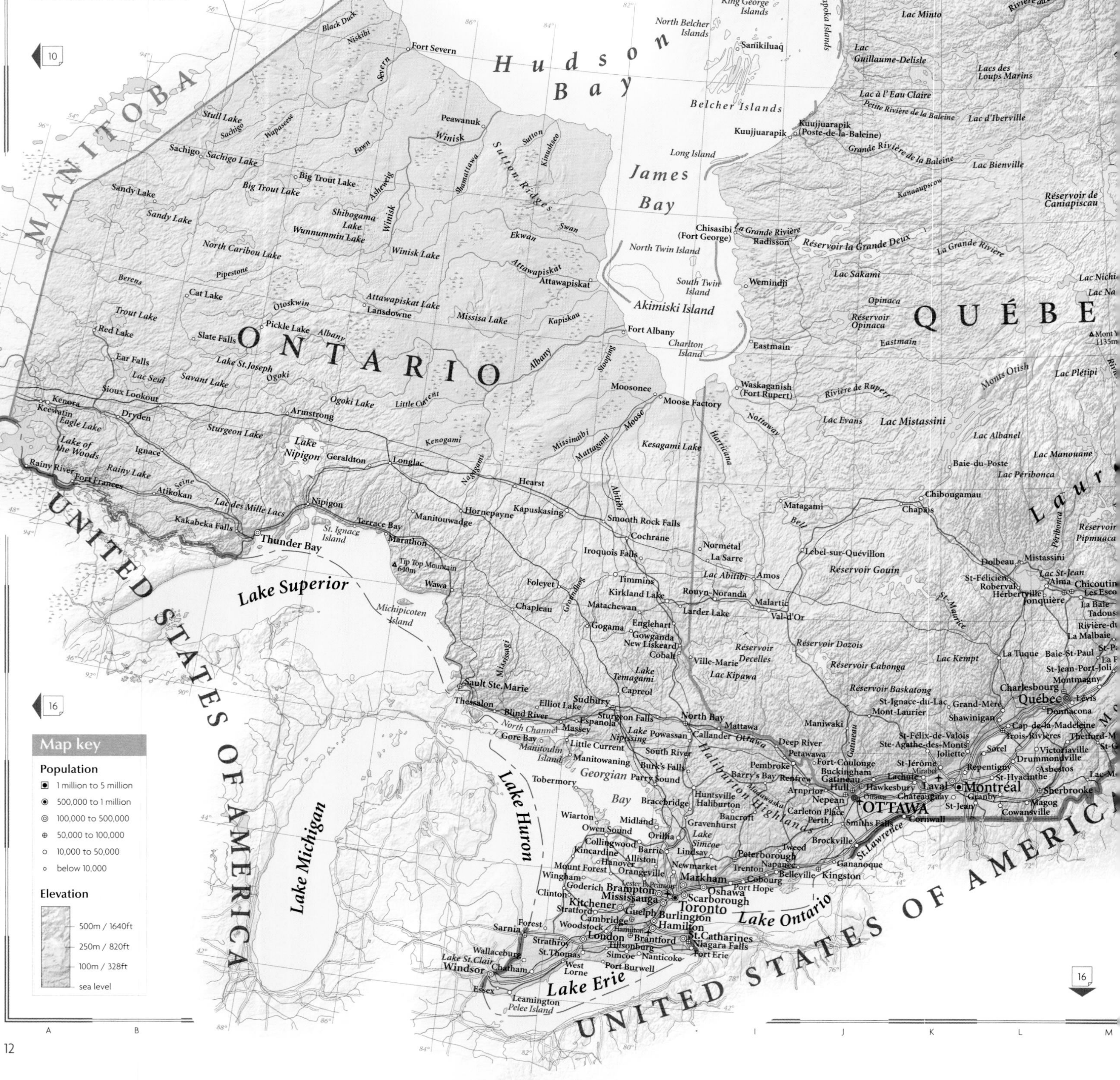

Map key

Population

- ◉ 1 million to 5 million
- ◉ 500,000 to 1 million
- ▣ 100,000 to 500,000
- ▪ 50,000 to 100,000
- ○ 10,000 to 50,000
- ∘ below 10,000

Elevation

- 500m / 1640ft
- 250m / 820ft
- 100m / 328ft
- sea level

MANITOBA

ONTARIO

UNITED STATES OF AMERICA

NUNAVUT

Péninsule d' Ungava

QUÉBEC

Hudson Bay

James Bay

Hudson S

Lake Superior, Lake Michigan, Lake Huron, Lake Erie, Lake Ontario, Georgian Bay

Toronto, Ottawa, Montréal, Québec, Sudbury, Thunder Bay, Windsor, London, Hamilton

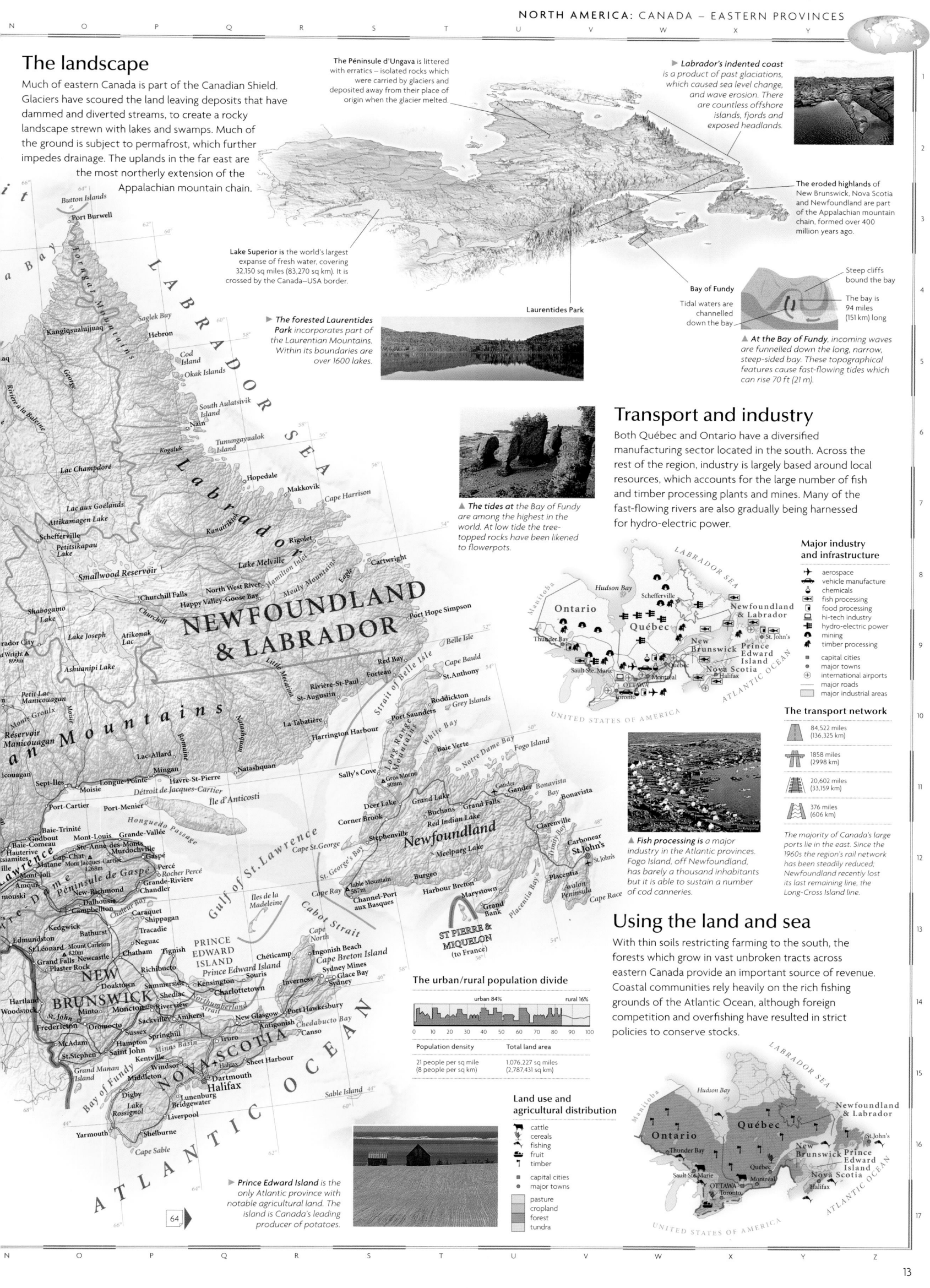

The landscape

Much of eastern Canada is part of the Canadian Shield. Glaciers have scoured the land leaving deposits that have dammed and diverted streams, to create a rocky landscape strewn with lakes and swamps. Much of the ground is subject to permafrost, which further impedes drainage. The uplands in the far east are the most northerly extension of the Appalachian mountain chain.

The Péninsule d'Ungava is littered with erratics – isolated rocks which were carried by glaciers and deposited away from their place of origin when the glacier melted.

► Labrador's indented coast is a product of past glaciations, which caused sea level change, and wave erosion. There are countless offshore islands, fjords and exposed headlands.

The eroded highlands of New Brunswick, Nova Scotia and Newfoundland are part of the Appalachian mountain chain, formed over 400 million years ago.

Lake Superior is the world's largest expanse of fresh water, covering 32,150 sq miles (83,270 sq km). It is crossed by the Canada–USA border.

Laurentides Park

Steep cliffs bound the bay

Bay of Fundy
Tidal waters are channelled down the bay

The bay is 94 miles (151 km) long

▲ At the Bay of Fundy, incoming waves are funnelled down the long, narrow, steep-sided bay. These topographical features cause fast-flowing tides which can rise 70 ft (21 m).

► The forested Laurentides Park incorporates part of the Laurentian Mountains. Within its boundaries are over 1600 lakes.

▲ The tides at the Bay of Fundy are among the highest in the world. At low tide the tree-topped rocks have been likened to flowerpots.

Transport and industry

Both Québec and Ontario have a diversified manufacturing sector located in the south. Across the rest of the region, industry is largely based around local resources, which accounts for the large number of fish and timber processing plants and mines. Many of the fast-flowing rivers are also gradually being harnessed for hydro-electric power.

Major industry and infrastructure

✈ aerospace
🚗 vehicle manufacture
chemicals
🐟 fish processing
food processing
🖥 hi-tech industry
hydro-electric power
⛏ mining
🌲 timber processing

■ capital cities
• major towns
international airports
— major roads
major industrial areas

The transport network

84,522 miles (136,325 km)

1858 miles (2998 km)

20,602 miles (33,159 km)

376 miles (606 km)

The majority of Canada's large ports lie in the east. Since the 1960s the region's rail network has been steadily reduced; Newfoundland recently lost its last remaining line, the Long-Cross Island line.

▲ Fish processing is a major industry in the Atlantic provinces. Fogo Island, off Newfoundland, has barely a thousand inhabitants but it is able to sustain a number of cod canneries.

Using the land and sea

With thin soils restricting farming to the south, the forests which grow in vast unbroken tracts across eastern Canada provide an important source of revenue. Coastal communities rely heavily on the rich fishing grounds of the Atlantic Ocean, although foreign competition and overfishing have resulted in strict policies to conserve stocks.

The urban/rural population divide

urban 84%   rural 16%

0 10 20 30 40 50 60 70 80 90 100

Population density	Total land area
21 people per sq mile (8 people per sq km)	1,076,227 sq miles (2,787,431 sq km)

Land use and agricultural distribution

🐄 cattle
🌾 cereals
🐟 fishing
🍎 fruit
🌲 timber

■ capital cities
• major towns

pasture
cropland
forest
tundra

► Prince Edward Island is the only Atlantic province with notable agricultural land. The island is Canada's leading producer of potatoes.

64

13

Southeastern Canada

Southern Ontario, Southern Québec

The southern parts of Québec and Ontario form the economic heart of Canada. The two provinces are divided by their language and culture; in Québec, French is the main language, whereas English is spoken in Ontario. Separatist sentiment in Québec has led to a provincial referendum on the question of a sovereignty association with Canada. The region contains Canada's capital, Ottawa and its two largest cities: Toronto, the centre of commerce and Montréal, the cultural and administrative heart of French Canada.

▶ *Niagara Falls lies* on the border between Canada and the USA. It comprises a system of two falls: American Falls, in New York, is separated from Horseshoe Falls, in Ontario, by Goat Island. Horseshoe Falls, seen here, plunges 184 ft (56 m) and is 2500 ft (762 m) wide.

▲ *The port at* Montréal is situated on the St. Lawrence Seaway. A network of 16 locks allows sea-going vessels access to routes once plied by fur-trappers and early settlers.

Transport and industry

The cities of southern Québec and Ontario, and their hinterlands, form the heart of Canadian manufacturing industry. Toronto is Canada's leading financial centre, and Ontario's motor and aerospace industries have developed around the city. A major centre for nickel mining lies to the north of Toronto. Most of Québec's industry is located in Montréal, the oldest port in North America. Chemicals, paper manufacture and the construction of transport equipment are leading industrial activities.

Major industry and infrastructure

car manufacture	textiles
chemicals	paper industry
engineering	timber processing
finance	capital cities
food processing	major towns
hi-tech industry	international airports
mining	major roads
iron & steel	major industrial areas

The transport network

The opening of the St. Lawrence Seaway in 1959 finally allowed ocean-going ships (up to 24,000 tons (tonnes)) access to the interior of Canada, creating a vital trading route.

Map key

Population

- 1 million to 5 million
- 500,000 to 1 million
- 100,000 to 500,000
- 50,000 to 100,000
- 10,000 to 50,000
- below 10,000

Elevation

- 500m / 1640ft
- 250m / 820ft
- 100m / 328ft
- sea level

▶ *Montréal, on the* banks of the St. Lawrence River, is Québec's leading metropolitan centre and one of Canada's two largest cities – Toronto is the other. Montréal clearly reflects French culture and traditions.

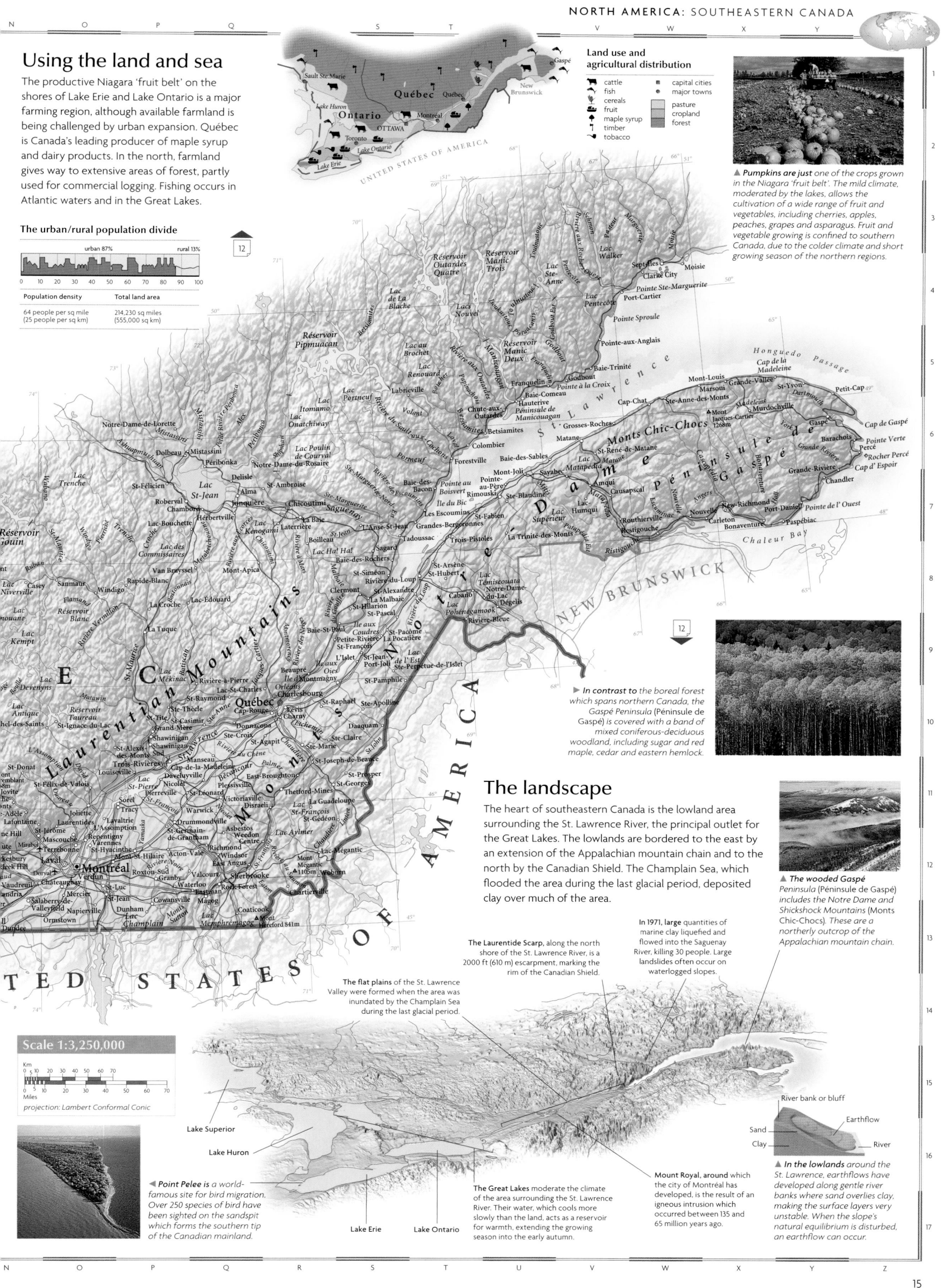

Using the land and sea

The productive Niagara 'fruit belt' on the shores of Lake Erie and Lake Ontario is a major farming region, although available farmland is being challenged by urban expansion. Québec is Canada's leading producer of maple syrup and dairy products. In the north, farmland gives way to extensive areas of forest, partly used for commercial logging. Fishing occurs in Atlantic waters and in the Great Lakes.

Land use and agricultural distribution

- cattle
- fish
- cereals
- fruit
- maple syrup
- timber
- tobacco
- capital cities
- major towns
- pasture
- cropland
- forest

▲ *Pumpkins are just* one of the crops grown in the Niagara 'fruit belt'. The mild climate, moderated by the lakes, allows the cultivation of a wide range of fruit and vegetables, including cherries, apples, peaches, grapes and asparagus. Fruit and vegetable growing is confined to southern Canada, due to the colder climate and short growing season of the northern regions.

The urban/rural population divide

urban 87%   rural 13%

Population density	Total land area
64 people per sq mile (25 people per sq km)	214,230 sq miles (555,000 sq km)

▶ *In contrast to* the boreal forest which spans northern Canada, the Gaspé Peninsula (Péninsule de Gaspé) is covered with a band of mixed coniferous-deciduous woodland, including sugar and red maple, cedar and eastern hemlock.

The landscape

The heart of southeastern Canada is the lowland area surrounding the St. Lawrence River, the principal outlet for the Great Lakes. The lowlands are bordered to the east by an extension of the Appalachian mountain chain and to the north by the Canadian Shield. The Champlain Sea, which flooded the area during the last glacial period, deposited clay over much of the area.

▲ *The wooded Gaspé* Peninsula (Péninsule de Gaspé) includes the Notre Dame and Shickshock Mountains (Monts Chic-Chocs). These are a northerly outcrop of the Appalachian mountain chain.

The Laurentide Scarp, along the north shore of the St. Lawrence River, is a 2000 ft (610 m) escarpment, marking the rim of the Canadian Shield.

In 1971, large quantities of marine clay liquefied and flowed into the Saguenay River, killing 30 people. Large landslides often occur on waterlogged slopes.

The flat plains of the St. Lawrence Valley were formed when the area was inundated by the Champlain Sea during the last glacial period.

Scale 1:3,250,000

Km
0 10 20 30 40 50 60 70
Miles
0 10 20 30 40 50 60 70

projection: Lambert Conformal Conic

Lake Superior
Lake Huron

◀ *Point Pelee is a* world-famous site for bird migration. Over 250 species of bird have been sighted on the sandspit which forms the southern tip of the Canadian mainland.

Lake Erie
Lake Ontario

The Great Lakes moderate the climate of the area surrounding the St. Lawrence River. Their water, which cools more slowly than the land, acts as a reservoir for warmth, extending the growing season into the early autumn.

Mount Royal, around which the city of Montréal has developed, is the result of an igneous intrusion which occurred between 135 and 65 million years ago.

River bank or bluff
Earthflow
Sand
Clay
River

▲ *In the lowlands* around the St. Lawrence, earthflows have developed along gentle river banks where sand overlies clay, making the surface layers very unstable. When the slope's natural equilibrium is disturbed, an earthflow can occur.

15

The United States of America

COTERMINOUS USA (FOR ALASKA AND HAWAII SEE PAGES 38-39)

The USA's progression from frontier territory to economic and political superpower has taken less than 200 years. The 48 coterminous states, along with the outlying states of Alaska and Hawaii, are part of a federal union, held together by the guiding principles of the US Constitution, which enshrines the ideals of democracy and liberty for all. Abundant fertile land and a rich resource-base fuelled and sustained the USA's economic development. With the spread of agriculture and the growth of trade and industry came the need for a larger workforce, which was supplied by millions of immigrants, many seeking an escape from poverty and political or religious persecution. Immigration continues today, particularly from Central America and Asia.

▲ *Washington DC was* established as the site for the nation's capital in 1790. It is home to the seat of national government, on Capitol Hill, as well as the President's official residence, the White House.

▶ *The clear waters* of Niagara Falls cascade 190 ft (58 m) into the gorge below. It is one of America's most famous spectacles and a leading tourist attraction. The falls are slowly receding and the gorge may one day stretch from Lake Ontario to Lake Erie.

▲ *Mount Rainier is a* dormant volcano in the Cascade Range, Washington. This 14,090 ft (4392 m) peak is flanked by the most extensive glacier outside Alaska.

Scale 1:12,700,000

Km
0 25 50 100 150 200 250 300 350 400

Miles
0 25 50 100 150 200 250 300 350 400

projection: Lambert Azimuthal Equal Area

Transport and industry

The USA has been the industrial powerhouse of the world since the Second World War, pioneering mass-production and the consumer lifestyle. Initially, heavy engineering and manufacturing in the northeast led the economy. Today, heavy industry has declined and the USA's economy is driven by service and financial industries, with the most important being defence, hi-tech and electronics.

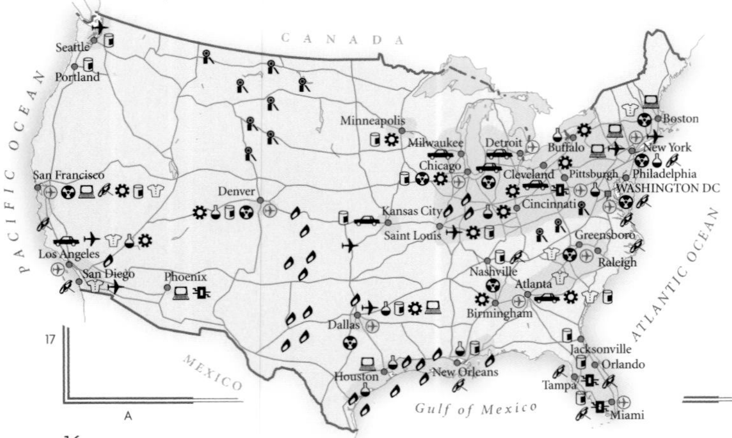

The transport network

3,875,040 miles (6,240,000 km)	52,388 miles (84,361 km)
148,308 miles (235,238 km)	25,467 miles (41,009 km)

Transport in the USA is dominated by the car which, with the extensive Interstate Highway system, allows great personal mobility. Today, internal air flights between major cities provide the most rapid cross-country travel.

Major industry and infrastructure

- aerospace
- car manufacture
- chemicals
- coal
- electronics
- engineering
- food processing
- hi-tech industry
- oil & gas
- research & development
- textiles
- tourism
- capital cities
- major towns
- international airports
- major roads
- major industrial areas

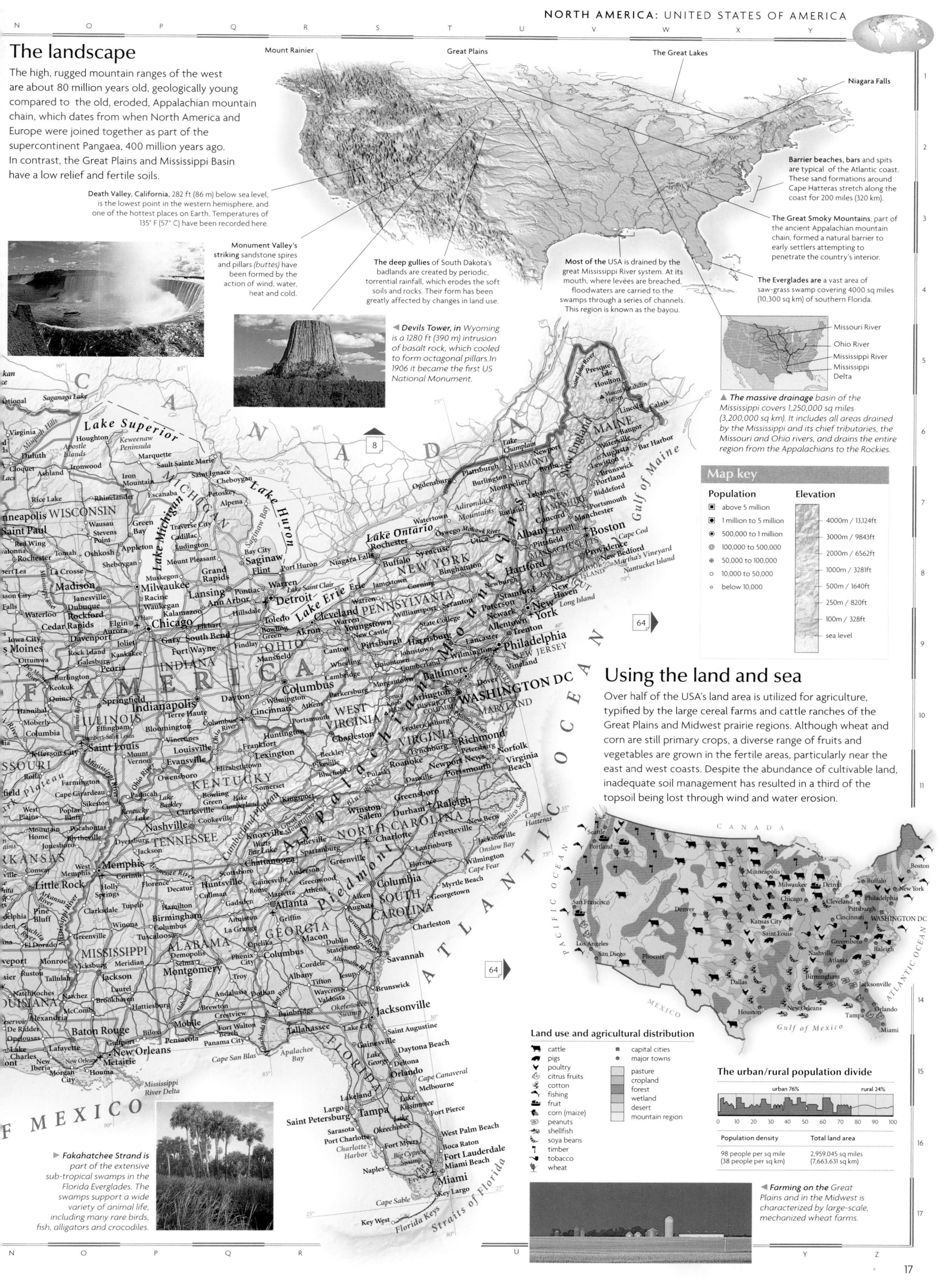

The landscape

The high, rugged mountain ranges of the west are about 80 million years old, geologically young compared to the old, eroded, Appalachian mountain chain, which dates from when North America and Europe were joined together as part of the supercontinent Pangaea, 400 million years ago. In contrast, the Great Plains and Mississippi Basin have a low relief and fertile soils.

Death Valley, California, 282 ft (86 m) below sea level, is the lowest point in the western hemisphere, and one of the hottest places on Earth. Temperatures of 135° F (57° C) have been recorded here.

Monument Valley's striking sandstone spires and pillars *(buttes)* have been formed by the action of wind, water, heat and cold.

The deep gullies of South Dakota's badlands are created by periodic, torrential rainfall, which erodes the soft soils and rocks. Their form has been greatly affected by changes in land use.

◀ *Devils Tower, in Wyoming is a 1280 ft (390 m) intrusion of basalt rock, which cooled to form octagonal pillars. In 1906 it became the first US National Monument.*

Most of the USA is drained by the great Mississippi River system. At its mouth, where levées are breached, floodwaters are carried to the swamps through a series of channels. This region is known as the bayou.

Barrier beaches, bars and spits are typical of the Atlantic coast. These sand formations around Cape Hatteras stretch along the coast for 200 miles (320 km).

The Great Smoky Mountains, part of the ancient Appalachian mountain chain, formed a natural barrier to early settlers attempting to penetrate the country's interior.

The Everglades are a vast area of saw-grass swamp covering 4000 sq miles (10,300 sq km) of southern Florida.

▲ *The massive drainage* basin of the Mississippi covers 1,250,000 sq miles (3,200,000 sq km). It includes all areas drained by the Mississippi and its chief tributaries, the Missouri and Ohio rivers, and drains the entire region from the Appalachians to the Rockies.

Map key

Population

- ▣ above 5 million
- ▣ 1 million to 5 million
- ◉ 500,000 to 1 million
- ◎ 100,000 to 500,000
- ⊕ 50,000 to 100,000
- ⊙ 10,000 to 50,000
- ○ below 10,000

Elevation

- 4000m / 13,124ft
- 3000m / 9843ft
- 2000m / 6562ft
- 1000m / 3281ft
- 500m / 1640ft
- 250m / 820ft
- 100m / 328ft
- sea level

Using the land and sea

Over half of the USA's land area is utilized for agriculture, typified by the large cereal farms and cattle ranches of the Great Plains and Midwest prairie regions. Although wheat and corn are still primary crops, a diverse range of fruits and vegetables are grown in the fertile areas, particularly near the east and west coasts. Despite the abundance of cultivable land, inadequate soil management has resulted in a third of the topsoil being lost through wind and water erosion.

▶ *Fakahatchee Strand is* part of the extensive sub-tropical swamps in the Florida Everglades. The swamps support a wide variety of animal life, including many rare birds, fish, alligators and crocodiles.

Land use and agricultural distribution

- 🐄 cattle
- 🐖 pigs
- 🦃 poultry
- citrus fruits
- cotton
- fishing
- fruit
- corn (maize)
- peanuts
- shellfish
- soya beans
- timber
- tobacco
- wheat
- ■ capital cities
- • major towns
- pasture
- cropland
- forest
- wetland
- desert
- mountain region

The urban/rural population divide

urban 76% rural 24%

0 10 20 30 40 50 60 70 80 90 100

Population density	Total land area
98 people per sq mile (38 people per sq km)	2,959,045 sq miles (7,663,631 sq km)

◀ *Farming on the* Great Plains and in the Midwest is characterized by large-scale, mechanized wheat farms.

USA: NORTHEASTERN STATES

Connecticut, Maine, Massachusetts, New Hampshire, New Jersey, New York, Pennsylvania, Rhode Island, Vermont

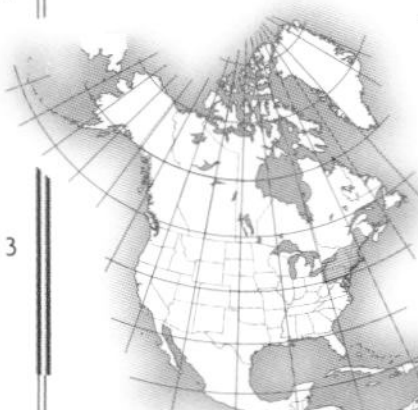

The indented coast and vast woodlands of the northeastern states were the original core area for European expansion. The rustic character of New England prevails after 400 years, while the great cities of the Atlantic seaboard have formed an almost continuous urban region. Over 20 million immigrants entered New York from 1855 to 1924 and the northeast became the industrial centre of the USA. After the decline of mining and heavy manufacturing, economic dynamism has been restored with the growth of hi-tech and service industries.

▲ *Chelsea in Vermont,* surrounded by trees in their fall foliage. Tourism and agriculture dominate the economy of this self-consciously rural state, where no town exceeds 40,000 people.

Transport and industry

The principal seaboard cities grew up on trade and manufacturing. They are now global centres of commerce and corporate administration, dominating the regional economy. Research and development facilities support an expanding electronics and communications sector throughout the region. Pharmaceutical and chemical industries are important in New Jersey and Pennsylvania.

The transport network

340,090 miles (544,144 km)	4813 miles (7700 km)
12,872 miles (20,592 km)	2108 miles (3389 km)

New York's commercial success is tied historically to its transport connections. The Erie Canal, completed in 1825, opened up the Great Lakes and the interior to New York's markets and carried a stream of immigrants into the Midwest.

Map key

Population
- above 5 million
- 1 million to 5 million
- 500,000 to 1 million
- 100,000 to 500,000
- 50,000 to 100,000
- 10,000 to 50,000
- below 10,000

Elevation
- 1000m / 3281ft
- 500m / 1640ft
- 250m / 820ft
- 100m / 328ft
- sea level

Major industry and infrastructure
- chemicals
- coal
- defence
- electronics
- engineering
- finance
- hi-tech industry
- iron & steel
- pharmaceuticals
- printing & publishing
- research & development
- textiles
- timber processing
- major towns
- international airports
- major roads
- major industrial area

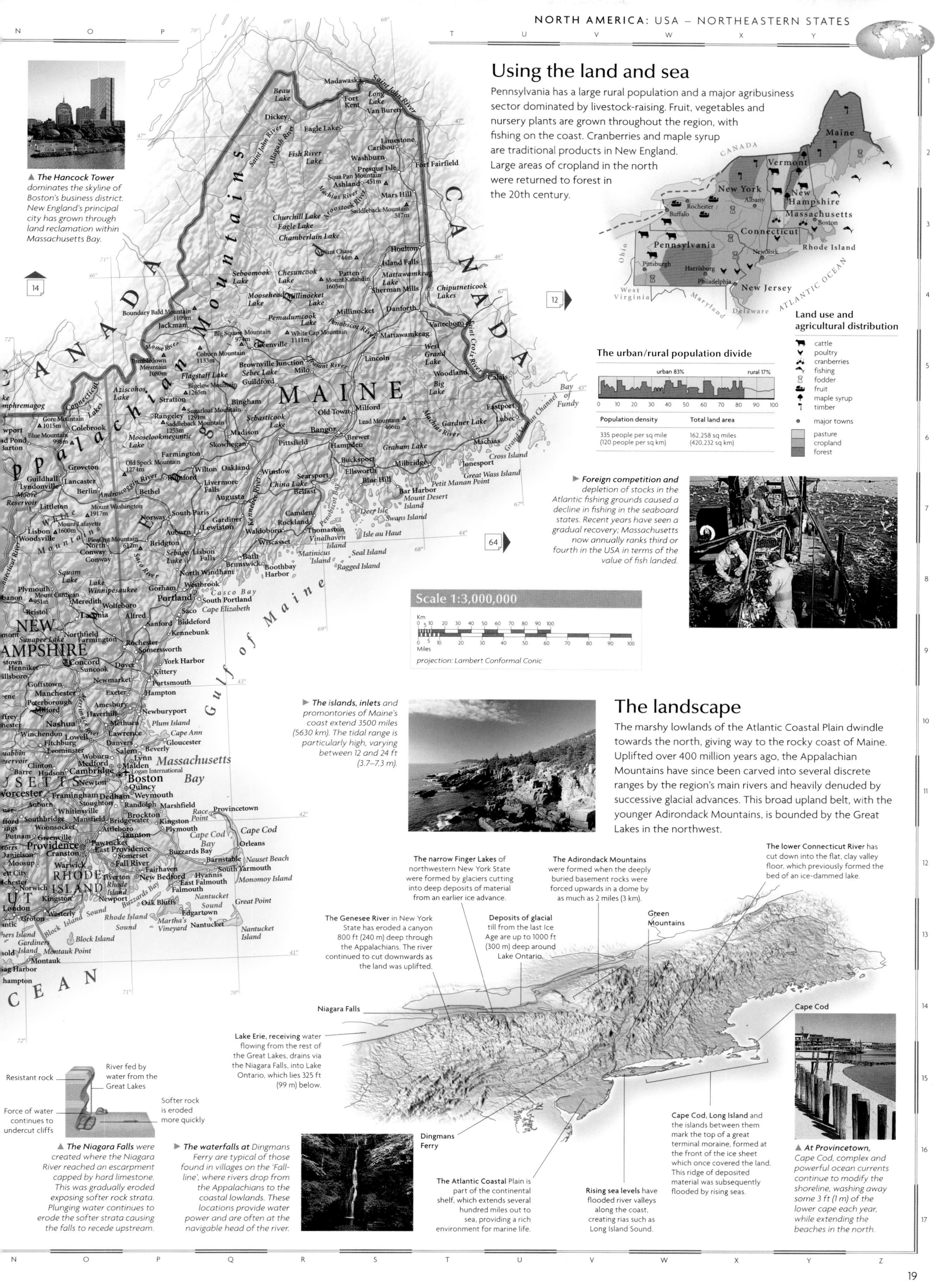

▲ **The Hancock Tower** dominates the skyline of Boston's business district. New England's principal city has grown through land reclamation within Massachusetts Bay.

Using the land and sea

Pennsylvania has a large rural population and a major agribusiness sector dominated by livestock-raising. Fruit, vegetables and nursery plants are grown throughout the region, with fishing on the coast. Cranberries and maple syrup are traditional products in New England. Large areas of cropland in the north were returned to forest in the 20th century.

The urban/rural population divide

urban 83%   rural 17%

0 10 20 30 40 50 60 70 80 90 100

Population density	Total land area
335 people per sq mile (120 people per sq km)	162,258 sq miles (420,232 sq km)

Land use and agricultural distribution

- cattle
- poultry
- cranberries
- fishing
- fodder
- fruit
- maple syrup
- timber
- major towns
- pasture
- cropland
- forest

▶ **Foreign competition and depletion of stocks** in the Atlantic fishing grounds caused a decline in fishing in the seaboard states. Recent years have seen a gradual recovery; Massachusetts now annually ranks third or fourth in the USA in terms of the value of fish landed.

Scale 1:3,000,000

Km
0 5 10 20 30 40 50 60 70 80 90 100

Miles
0 5 10 20 30 40 50 60 70 80 90 100

projection: Lambert Conformal Conic

▶ **The islands, inlets** and promontories of Maine's coast extend 3500 miles (5630 km). The tidal range is particularly high, varying between 12 and 24 ft (3.7–7.3 m).

The landscape

The marshy lowlands of the Atlantic Coastal Plain dwindle towards the north, giving way to the rocky coast of Maine. Uplifted over 400 million years ago, the Appalachian Mountains have since been carved into several discrete ranges by the region's main rivers and heavily denuded by successive glacial advances. This broad upland belt, with the younger Adirondack Mountains, is bounded by the Great Lakes in the northwest.

The narrow Finger Lakes of northwestern New York State were formed by glaciers cutting into deep deposits of material from an earlier ice advance.

The Adirondack Mountains were formed when the deeply buried basement rocks were forced upwards in a dome by as much as 2 miles (3 km).

The lower Connecticut River has cut down into the flat, clay valley floor, which previously formed the bed of an ice-dammed lake.

The Genesee River in New York State has eroded a canyon 800 ft (240 m) deep through the Appalachians. The river continued to cut downwards as the land was uplifted.

Deposits of glacial till from the last Ice Age are up to 1000 ft (300 m) deep around Lake Ontario.

Green Mountains

Niagara Falls

Cape Cod

Lake Erie, receiving water flowing from the rest of the Great Lakes, drains via the Niagara Falls, into Lake Ontario, which lies 325 ft (99 m) below.

Dingmans Ferry

Cape Cod, Long Island and the islands between them mark the top of a great terminal moraine, formed at the front of the ice sheet which once covered the land. This ridge of deposited material was subsequently flooded by rising seas.

▲ **The Niagara Falls** were created where the Niagara River reached an escarpment capped by hard limestone. This was gradually eroded exposing softer rock strata. Plunging water continues to erode the softer strata causing the falls to recede upstream.

Resistant rock

River fed by water from the Great Lakes

Force of water continues to undercut cliffs

Softer rock is eroded more quickly

▶ **The waterfalls at** Dingmans Ferry are typical of those found in villages on the 'Fall-line', where rivers drop from the Appalachians to the coastal lowlands. These locations provide water power and are often at the navigable head of the river.

The Atlantic Coastal Plain is part of the continental shelf, which extends several hundred miles out to sea, providing a rich environment for marine life.

Rising sea levels have flooded river valleys along the coast, creating rias such as Long Island Sound.

▲ **At Provincetown,** Cape Cod, complex and powerful ocean currents continue to modify the shoreline, washing away some 3 ft (1 m) of the lower cape each year, while extending the beaches in the north.

USA: MID-EASTERN STATES

Delaware, District of Columbia, Kentucky,
Maryland, North Carolina, South Carolina,
Tennessee, Virginia, West Virginia

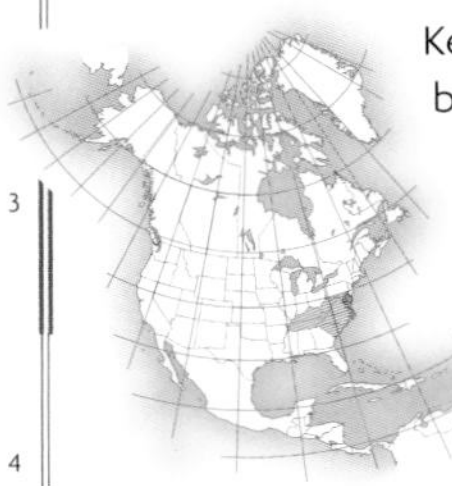

Key events in the history of the USA took place in this diverse region, which became the front line in the Civil War of 1861–65 between North and South. Strong regional contrasts exist between the fertile coastal plains, the isolated upcountry of the Appalachian Mountains and the cotton-growing areas of the Mississippi lowlands to the west. Whilst coal mining, a traditional industry in the Appalachians, has declined in recent years leaving much rural poverty, service industries elsewhere have increased, especially in the US federal capital, Washington DC.

Transport and industry

In the urbanized northeast, manufacturing remains important, alongside a burgeoning service sector. North Carolina is a major centre for industrial research and development. Traditional industries include Tennessee whiskey, and textiles in South Carolina. The decline of open-cast coal mining in the Appalachians has been hastened by environmental controls, although adventure-tourism is a flourishing new industry.

Major industry and infrastructure

- adventure-tourism
- car manufacture
- coal
- electronics
- engineering
- finance
- food processing
- hi-tech industry
- mining
- research & development
- textiles
- capital cities
- major towns
- international airports
- major roads
- major industrial areas

The transport network

452,218 miles (723,548 km)	5737 miles (8267 km)
18,336 miles (29,503 km)	4404 miles (7081 km)

Tennessee's rivers are part of an important inland bulk-transport network. Memphis is connected with New Orleans in the south, and with cities as distant as Minneapolis, Sioux City, Chicago and Pittsburgh, via the Mississippi and its tributaries.

The landscape

The eastern tributaries of the Mississippi drain the interior lowlands. The Cumberland Plateau and the parallel ranges of the Appalachians have been successively uplifted and eroded over time, with the eastern side reduced to a series of foothills known as the Piedmont. The broad coastal plain gradually falls away into salt marshes, lagoons and offshore bars, broken by flooded estuaries along the shores of the Atlantic.

Map key

Population
- ◉ 500,000 to 1 million
- ◎ 100,000 to 500,000
- ⊕ 50,000 to 100,000
- ⊙ 10,000 to 50,000
- ○ below 10,000

Elevation
- 6000m / 19,686ft
- 4000m / 13,124ft
- 3000m / 9843ft
- 2000m / 6562ft
- 1000m / 3281ft
- 500m / 1640ft
- 250m / 820ft
- 100m / 328ft
- sea level

Scale 1:3,250,000

Km 0 5 10 20 30 40 50 60 70 80

Miles 0 5 10 20 30 40 50 60 70 80

projection: Lambert Conformal Conic

▲ The Bluegrass region of Kentucky centres on the town of Lexington. This exceptionally fertile rolling plain is well known for its thoroughbred horse-breeding ranches.

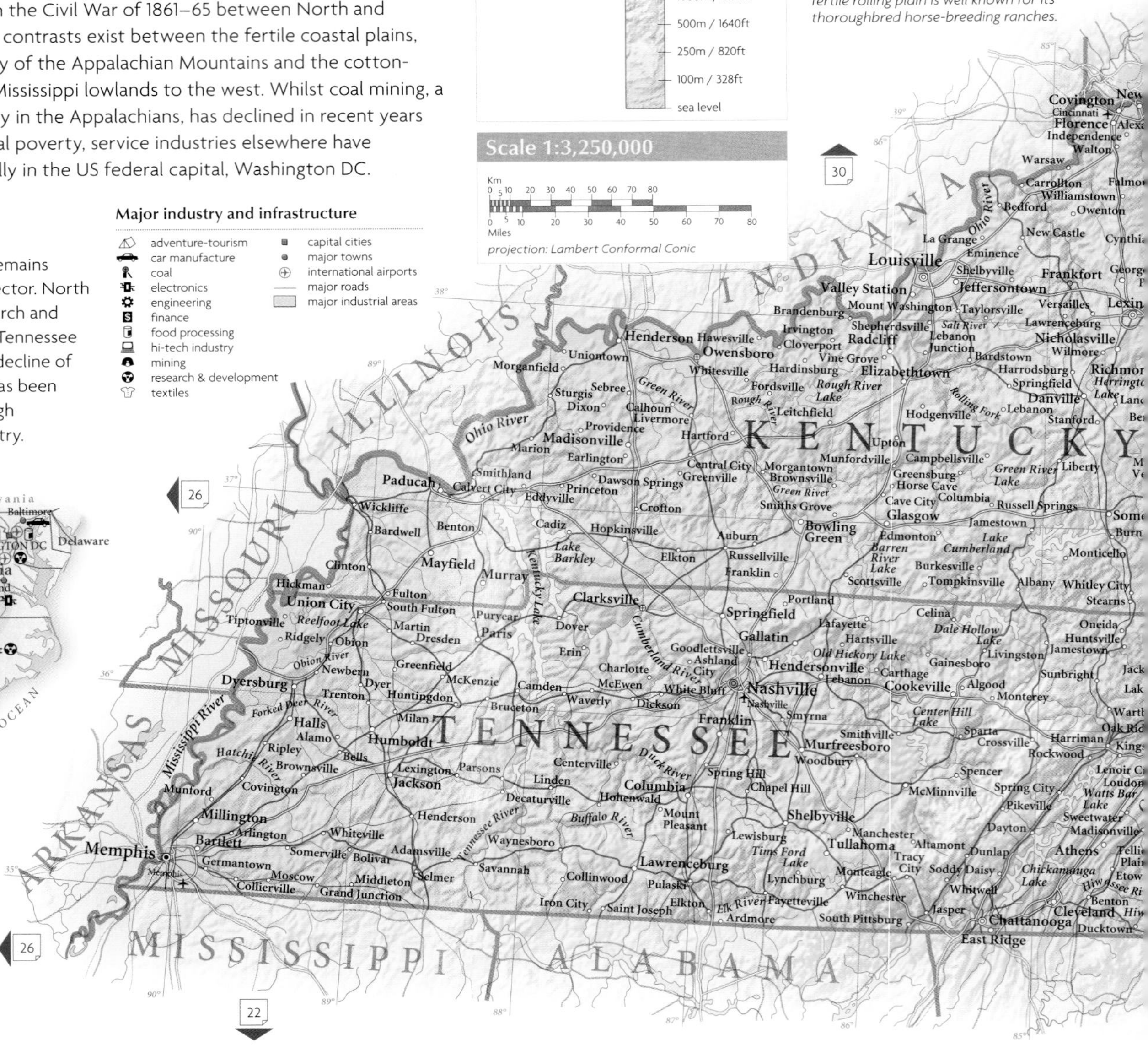

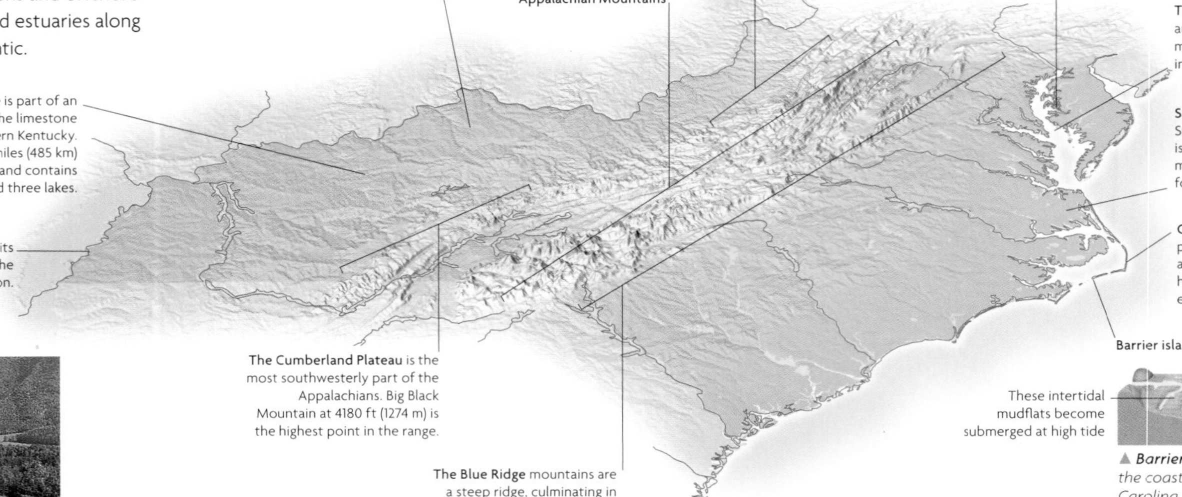

Natural Bridge in eastern Kentucky is an arch 78 ft (26 m) long and 65 ft (20 m) high. It has been shaped from resistant sandstone by gradual weathering processes, which removed the softer rock lying underneath.

The Allegheny Mountains form the northwestern edge of the Appalachian mountain chain. Continuous folding has formed rich seams of bituminous coal.

◄ Farmland on the eastern shores of Chesapeake Bay is sustained by artificial drainage. The area also provides refuge for a variety of waterfowl.

Appalachian Mountains

The many inlets of Chesapeake Bay are the flooded tributaries of the main river valley, which have been inundated by rising sea levels.

The Mammoth Cave is part of an extensive cave system in the limestone region of southwestern Kentucky. It stretches for over 300 miles (485 km) on five different levels and contains three rivers and three lakes.

Salt marshes such as Great Dismal Swamp, develop where the coast is sheltered. Vast areas of such marshland have been reclaimed for farmland and settlement.

The Mississippi River and its tributary the Ohio River form the western border of the region.

Cape Hatteras is the easternmost point of an offshore barrier island; a wave-deposited sand-bar which has become permanent, establishing its own vegetation.

Barrier islands

These intertidal mudflats become submerged at high tide

Tidal inlet

Barrier island

The Cumberland Plateau is the most southwesterly part of the Appalachians. Big Black Mountain at 4180 ft (1274 m) is the highest point in the range.

The Blue Ridge mountains are a steep ridge, culminating in Mount Mitchell, the highest point in the Appalachians, at 6684 ft (2037 m).

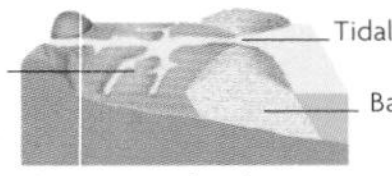

▲ Barrier islands are common along the coasts of North and South Carolina. As sea levels rise, wave action builds up ridges of sand and pebbles parallel to the coast, separated by lagoons or intertidal mudflats, which are flooded at high tide.

◄ The Great Smoky Mountains form the western escarpment of the Appalachians. The region is heavily forested, with over 130 species of tree.

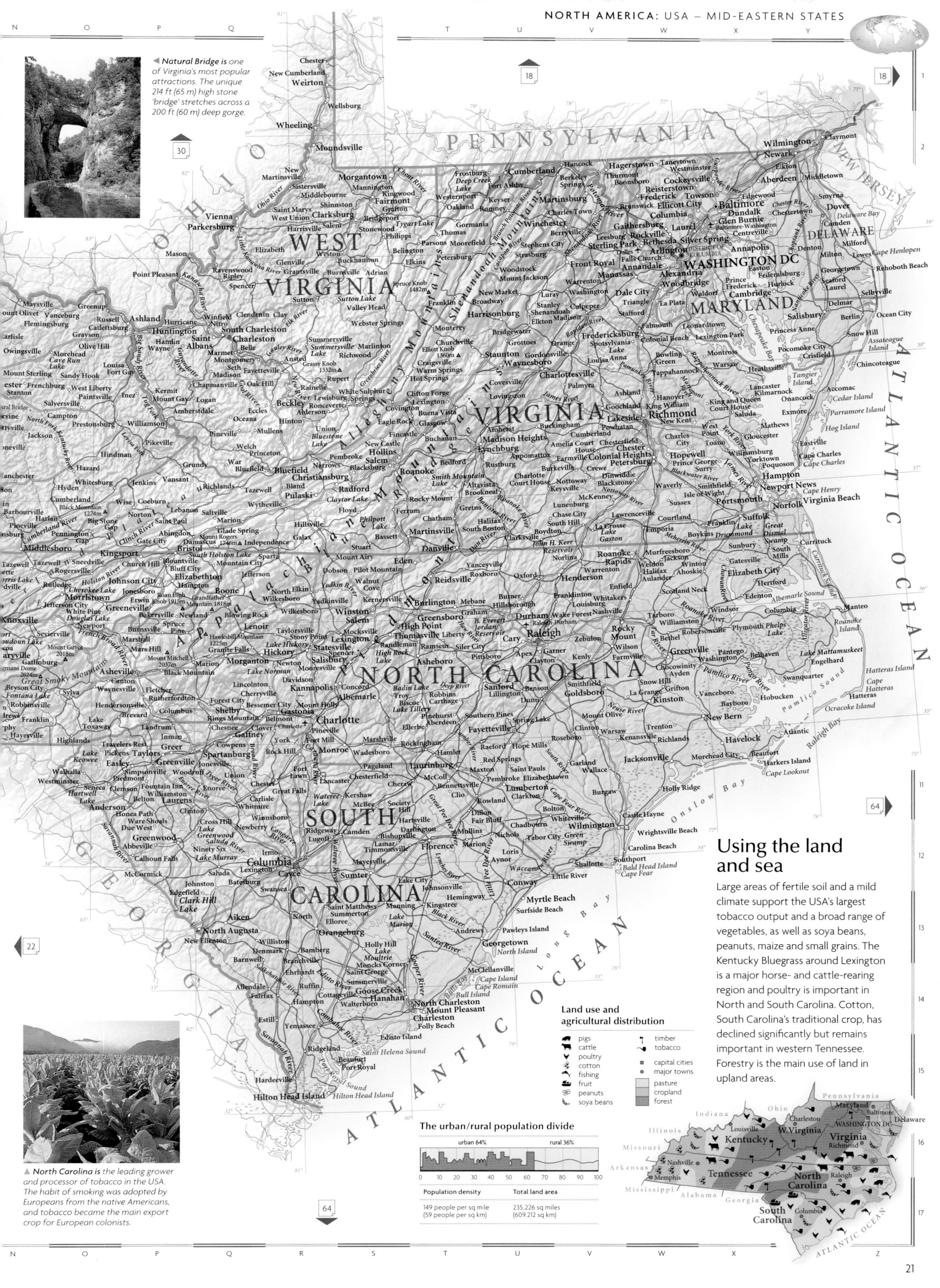

◀ *Natural Bridge is one of Virginia's most popular attractions. The unique 214 ft (65 m) high stone 'bridge' stretches across a 200 ft (60 m) deep gorge.*

▲ *North Carolina is the leading grower and processor of tobacco in the USA. The habit of smoking was adopted by Europeans from the native Americans, and tobacco became the main export crop for European colonists.*

Using the land and sea

Large areas of fertile soil and a mild climate support the USA's largest tobacco output and a broad range of vegetables, as well as soya beans, peanuts, maize and small grains. The Kentucky Bluegrass around Lexington is a major horse- and cattle-rearing region and poultry is important in North and South Carolina. Cotton, South Carolina's traditional crop, has declined significantly but remains important in western Tennessee. Forestry is the main use of land in upland areas.

Land use and agricultural distribution

- pigs
- cattle
- poultry
- cotton
- fishing
- fruit
- peanuts
- soya beans
- timber
- tobacco
- ■ capital cities
- ● major towns
- pasture
- cropland
- forest

The urban/rural population divide

urban 64%   rural 36%

0 10 20 30 40 50 60 70 80 90 100

Population density

149 people per sq mile
(59 people per sq km)

Total land area

235,226 sq miles
(609,212 sq km)

USA: SOUTHERN STATES

Alabama, Florida, Georgia, Louisiana, Mississippi

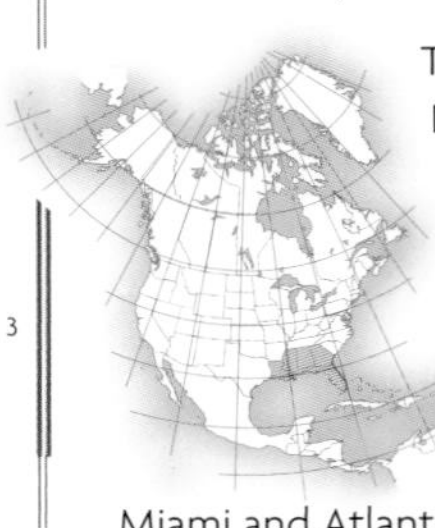

The South has maintained a separate identity and outlook throughout the history of the USA. Defeat in the American Civil War (1861–65) brought chronic poverty to the Confederate states, while the subsequent liberation of four million black slaves began a struggle not resolved until the 1960s, when the Civil Rights movement achieved an end to legal racial segregation. Since then many parts of the region have experienced rapid change: tourism and retirement communities, together with agriculture, have fuelled growth in Florida whilst defence-related industries have boosted the growth of cities such as Miami and Atlanta. Despite these changes, many people retain a strong attachment to their history: in Louisiana, French is still spoken in Cajun communities near the coast.

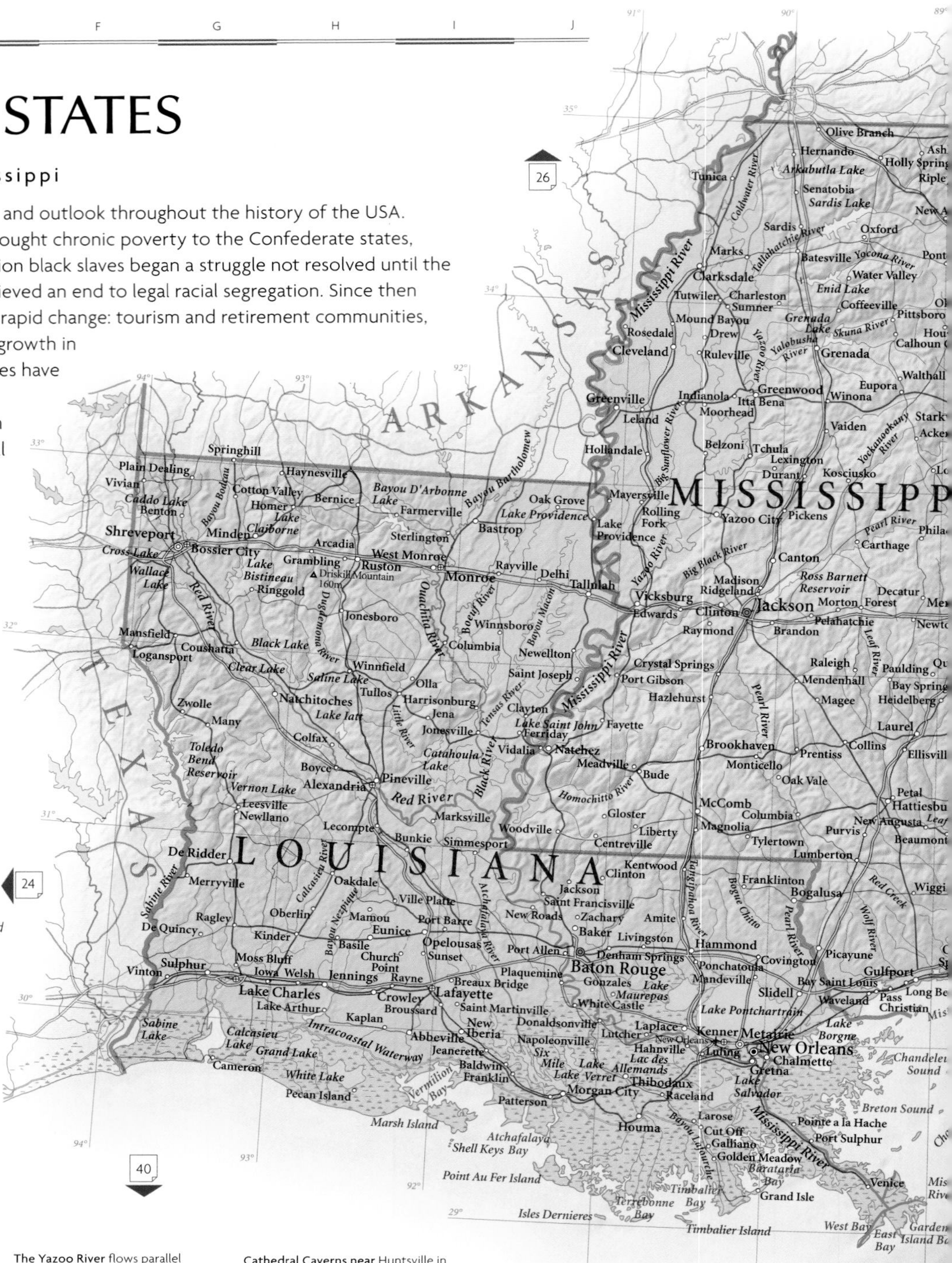

Transport and industry

Florida's tourist trade is only part of a flourishing service sector, which has swelled the principal cities of the south. Petroleum and mineral extraction has made the Gulf coast a major industrial region. Traditional textile production remains important in Georgia, while advanced new industries have grown from the NASA Space Program.

The transport network

441,625 miles (706,600 km)	
5116 miles (8186 km)	
16,597 miles (26,555 km)	
6179 miles (9942 km)	

Atlanta's Hartsfield International airport is one of the busiest in the world. A dramatic rise in the use of regional air transport has helped to integrate the major cities of the southern states.

◀ *The French Quarter is the traditional cultural centre of New Orleans. The city, extensively damaged by Hurricane Katrina in 2005, once thrived on the cotton trade but now relies mainly on tourism and on oil from the Gulf of Mexico.*

Major industry and infrastructure

✈	aerospace	♦	oil
🚗	car manufacture	▽	textiles
chemicals		⊙	tourism
coal		•	major towns
defence		⊕	international airports
electronics			major roads
engineering			major industrial areas
food processing			

▲ *The cypress swamps of the Mississippi Delta form in the backswamps behind the levées of the river and in the multitude of subsiding delta basins.*

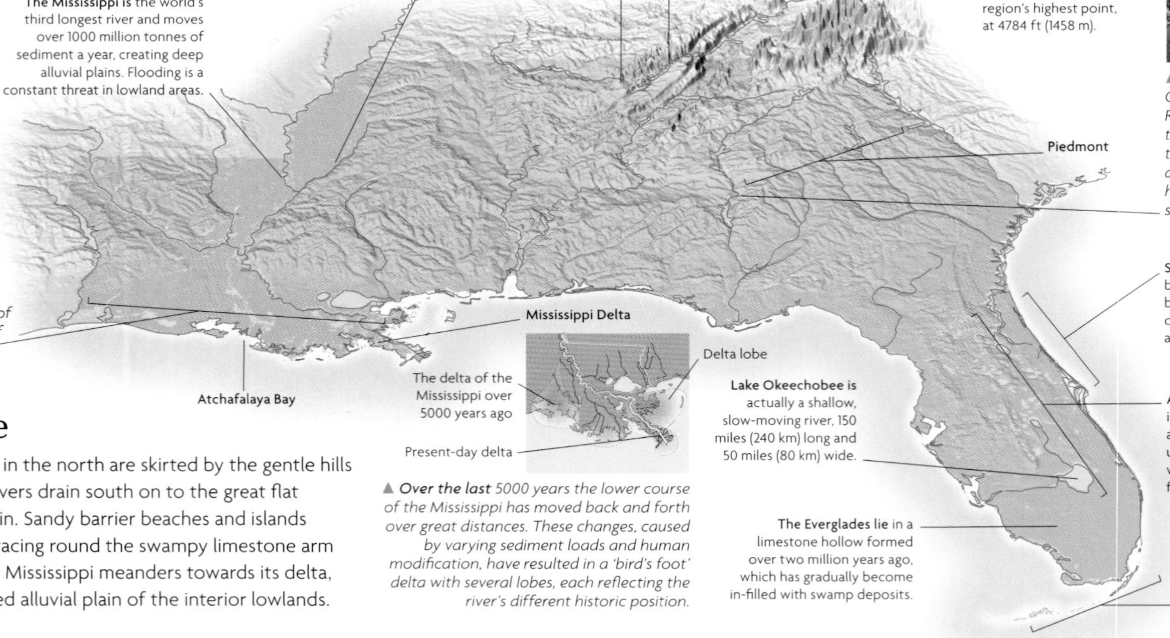

The landscape

The Blue Ridge mountains in the north are skirted by the gentle hills of the Piedmont, whose rivers drain south on to the great flat expanse of the coastal plain. Sandy barrier beaches and islands dominate the sea shore, tracing round the swampy limestone arm of Florida. In the west, the Mississippi meanders towards its delta, crossing the thickly mantled alluvial plain of the interior lowlands.

The Yazoo River flows parallel to the Mississippi through a common flood plain. The confluence of the rivers is deferred downstream because flood deposition has built the Mississippi channel up above the level of the Yazoo.

The Mississippi is the world's third longest river and moves over 1000 million tonnes of sediment a year, creating deep alluvial plains. Flooding is a constant threat in lowland areas.

Cathedral Caverns near Huntsville in Alabama is a system of vast limestone caves, with a main opening 1000 ft (300 m) high and 150 ft (50 m) wide.

At De Soto Falls, Alabama, the Little River descends into the deepest canyon east of the Mississippi, with sheer cliff walls up to 700 ft (230 m) high.

Brasstown Bald in the Blue Ridge mountains of Georgia is the region's highest point, at 4784 ft (1458 m).

▲ *In Providence Canyon, Georgia, the Chattahoochee River has cut straight down through the sandy bedrock, to leave sheer rock faces and pinnacles, which have been smoothed by subsequent weathering.*

Piedmont

Sand bars, deposited by waves breaking offshore, form barrier beaches along much of the coastline, creating sheltered lagoons and salt marshes behind them.

Mississippi Delta

Delta lobe

Lake Okeechobee is actually a shallow, slow-moving river, 150 miles (240 km) long and 50 miles (80 km) wide.

Atchafalaya Bay

The delta of the Mississippi over 5000 years ago

Present-day delta

▲ *Over the last 5000 years the lower course of the Mississippi has moved back and forth over great distances. These changes, caused by varying sediment loads and human modification, have resulted in a 'bird's foot' delta with several lobes, each reflecting the river's different historic position.*

Across Florida the coastal plain is mostly less than 75 ft (25 m) above sea level. The land is underlain by limestone, pitted with hollows which have been filled by over 10,000 lakes.

The Everglades lie in a limestone hollow formed over two million years ago, which has gradually become in-filled with swamp deposits.

Florida Keys

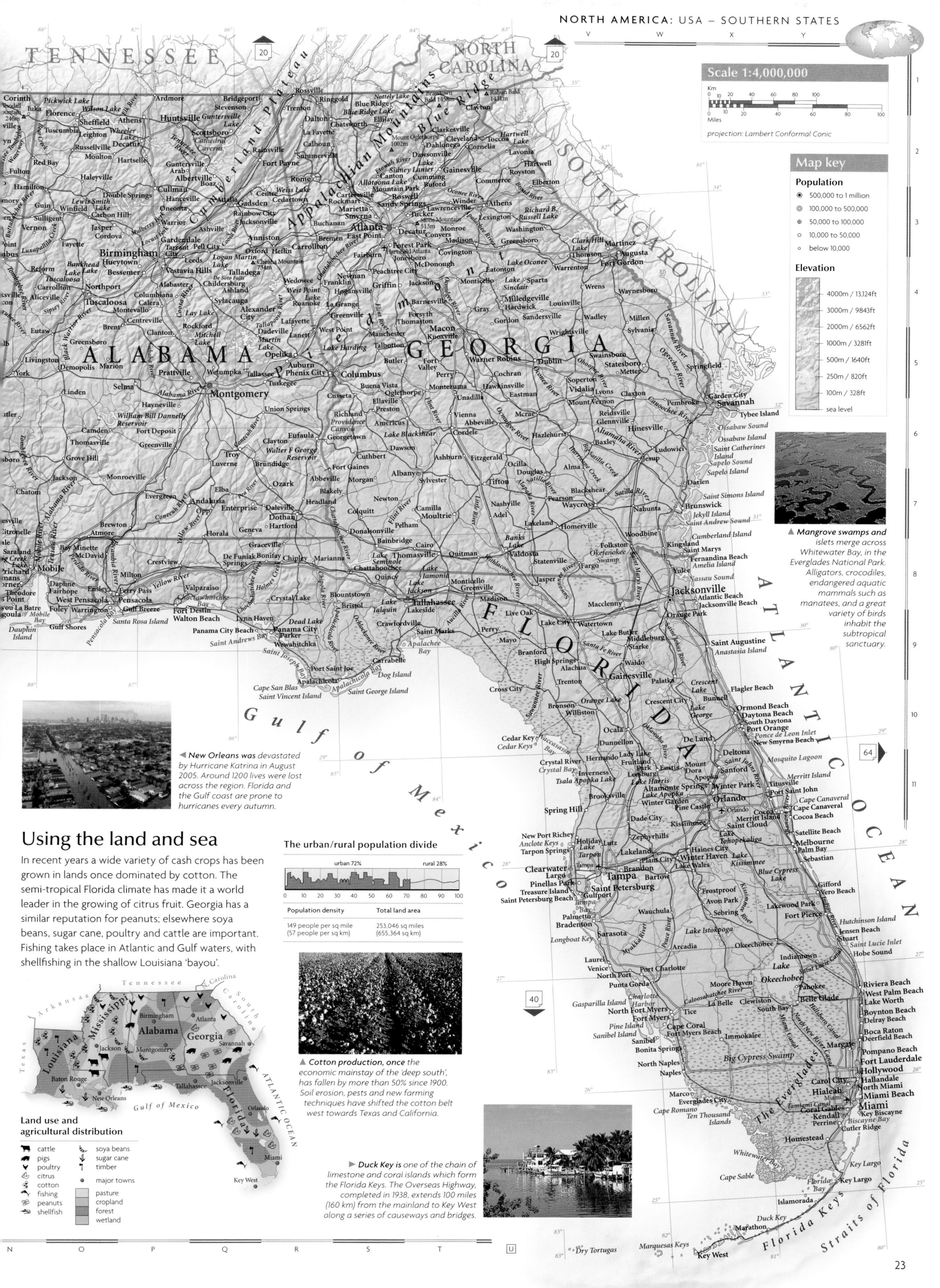

Scale 1:4,000,000

projection: Lambert Conformal Conic

Map key

Population
- 500,000 to 1 million
- 100,000 to 500,000
- 50,000 to 100,000
- 10,000 to 50,000
- below 10,000

Elevation
- 4000m / 13,124ft
- 3000m / 9843ft
- 2000m / 6562ft
- 1000m / 3281ft
- 500m / 1640ft
- 250m / 820ft
- 100m / 328ft
- sea level

▲ *Mangrove swamps and islets merge across Whitewater Bay, in the Everglades National Park. Alligators, crocodiles, endangered aquatic mammals such as manatees, and a great variety of birds inhabit the subtropical sanctuary.*

◄ *New Orleans was devastated by Hurricane Katrina in August 2005. Around 1200 lives were lost across the region. Florida and the Gulf coast are prone to hurricanes every autumn.*

Using the land and sea

In recent years a wide variety of cash crops has been grown in lands once dominated by cotton. The semi-tropical Florida climate has made it a world leader in the growing of citrus fruit. Georgia has a similar reputation for peanuts; elsewhere soya beans, sugar cane, poultry and cattle are important. Fishing takes place in Atlantic and Gulf waters, with shellfishing in the shallow Louisiana 'bayou'.

The urban/rural population divide

urban 72%   rural 28%

0 10 20 30 40 50 60 70 80 90 100

Population density	Total land area
149 people per sq mile (57 people per sq km)	253,046 sq miles (655,364 sq km)

▲ *Cotton production, once the economic mainstay of the 'deep south', has fallen by more than 50% since 1900. Soil erosion, pests and new farming techniques have shifted the cotton belt west towards Texas and California.*

▶ *Duck Key is one of the chain of limestone and coral islands which form the Florida Keys. The Overseas Highway, completed in 1938, extends 100 miles (160 km) from the mainland to Key West along a series of causeways and bridges.*

Land use and agricultural distribution
- cattle
- pigs
- poultry
- citrus
- cotton
- fishing
- peanuts
- shellfish
- soya beans
- sugar cane
- timber
- major towns
- pasture
- cropland
- forest
- wetland

23

USA: Texas

First explored by Spaniards moving north from Mexico in search of gold, Texas was controlled by Spain and then Mexico, before becoming an independent republic in 1836, and joining the Union of States in 1845. During the 19th century, many of the migrants who came to Texas raised cattle on the abundant land; in the 20th century, they were joined by prospectors attracted by the promise of oil riches. Today, although natural resources, especially oil, still form the basis of its wealth, the diversified Texan economy includes thriving hi-tech and finance industries. The major urban centres, home to 80% of the population, lie in the south and east, and include Houston, the 'oil-city', and Dallas–Fort Worth. Hispanic influences remain strong, especially in the south and west.

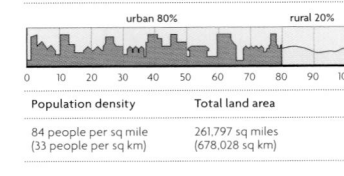

▲ **Dallas was founded** in 1841 as a prairie trading post and its development was stimulated by the arrival of railroads. Cotton and then oil funded the town's early growth. Today, the modern, high-rise skyline of Dallas reflects the city's position as a leading centre of banking, insurance and the petroleum industry in the southwest.

Using the land

Cotton production and livestock-raising, particularly cattle, dominate farming, although crop failures and the demands of local markets have led to some diversification. Following the introduction of modern farming techniques, cotton production spread out from the east to the plains of western Texas. Cattle ranches are widespread, while sheep and goats are raised on the dry Edwards Plateau.

▲ **The huge cattle** ranches of Texas developed during the 19th century when land was plentiful and could be acquired cheaply. Today, more cattle and sheep are raised in Texas than in any other state.

Land use and agricultural distribution

- cattle
- goats
- sheep
- cereals
- cotton
- • major towns
- pasture
- cropland
- forest
- barren

The urban/rural population divide

urban 80%   rural 20%

Population density	Total land area
84 people per sq mile (33 people per sq km)	261,797 sq miles (678,028 sq km)

The landscape

Texas is made up of a series of massive steps descending from the mountains and high plains of the west and northwest to the coastal lowlands in the southeast. Many of the state's borders are delineated by water. The Rio Grande flows from the Rocky Mountains to the Gulf of Mexico, marking the border with Mexico.

▲ **Cap Rock Escarpment** juts out from the plains, running 200 miles (320 km) from north to south. Its height varies from 300 ft (90 m) rising to sheer cliffs up to 1000 ft (300 m).

The Llano Estacado or Staked Plain in northern Texas is known for its harsh environment. In the north, freezing winds carrying ice and snow sweep down from the Rocky Mountains, and to the south, sandstorms frequently blow up, scouring anything in their paths. Flash floods, in the wide, flat river beds that remain dry for most of the year, are another hazard.

The Guadalupe Mountains lie in the southern Rocky Mountains. They incorporate Guadalupe Peak, the highest in Texas, rising 8749 ft (2667 m).

The Red River flows for 1300 miles (2090 km), marking most of the northern border of Texas. A dam and reservoir along its course provide vital irrigation and hydro-electric power to the surrounding area.

The Rio Grande flows from the Rocky Mountains through semi-arid land, supporting sparse vegetation. The river actually shrinks along its course, losing more water through evaporation and seepage than it gains from its tributaries and rainfall.

Big Bend National Park

Edwards Plateau is a limestone outcrop. It is part of the Great Plains, bounded to the southeast by the Balcones Escarpment, which marks the southerly limit of the plains.

◄ **Flowing through** 1500 ft (450 m) high gorges, the shallow, muddy Rio Grande makes a 90° bend, which marks the southern border of Big Bend National Park, giving it its name. The area is a mixture of forested mountains, deserts and canyons.

Sabine River

Extensive forests of pine and cypress grow in the eastern corner of the coastal lowlands where the average rainfall is 45 inches (1145 mm) a year. This is higher than the rest of the state and over twice the average in the west.

In the coastal lowlands of southeastern Texas the Earth's crust is warping, causing the land to subside and allowing the sea to invade. Around Galveston, the rate of downward tilting is 6 inches (15 cm) per year. Erosion of the coast is also exacerbated by hurricanes.

Laguna Madre in southern Texas has been almost completely cut off from the sea by Padre Island. This sand bank was created by wave action, carrying and depositing material along the coast. The process is known as longshore drift.

Padre Island

Oil deposits

Oil trapped by fault

Oil deposits migrate through reservoir rocks such as shale

Oil accumulates beneath impermeable cap rock

Impermeable rock strata

Salt dome

▲ **Oil deposits are** found beneath much of Texas. They collect as oil migrates upwards through porous layers of rock until it is trapped, either by a cap of rock above a salt dome, or by a fault line which exposes impermeable rock through which the oil cannot rise.

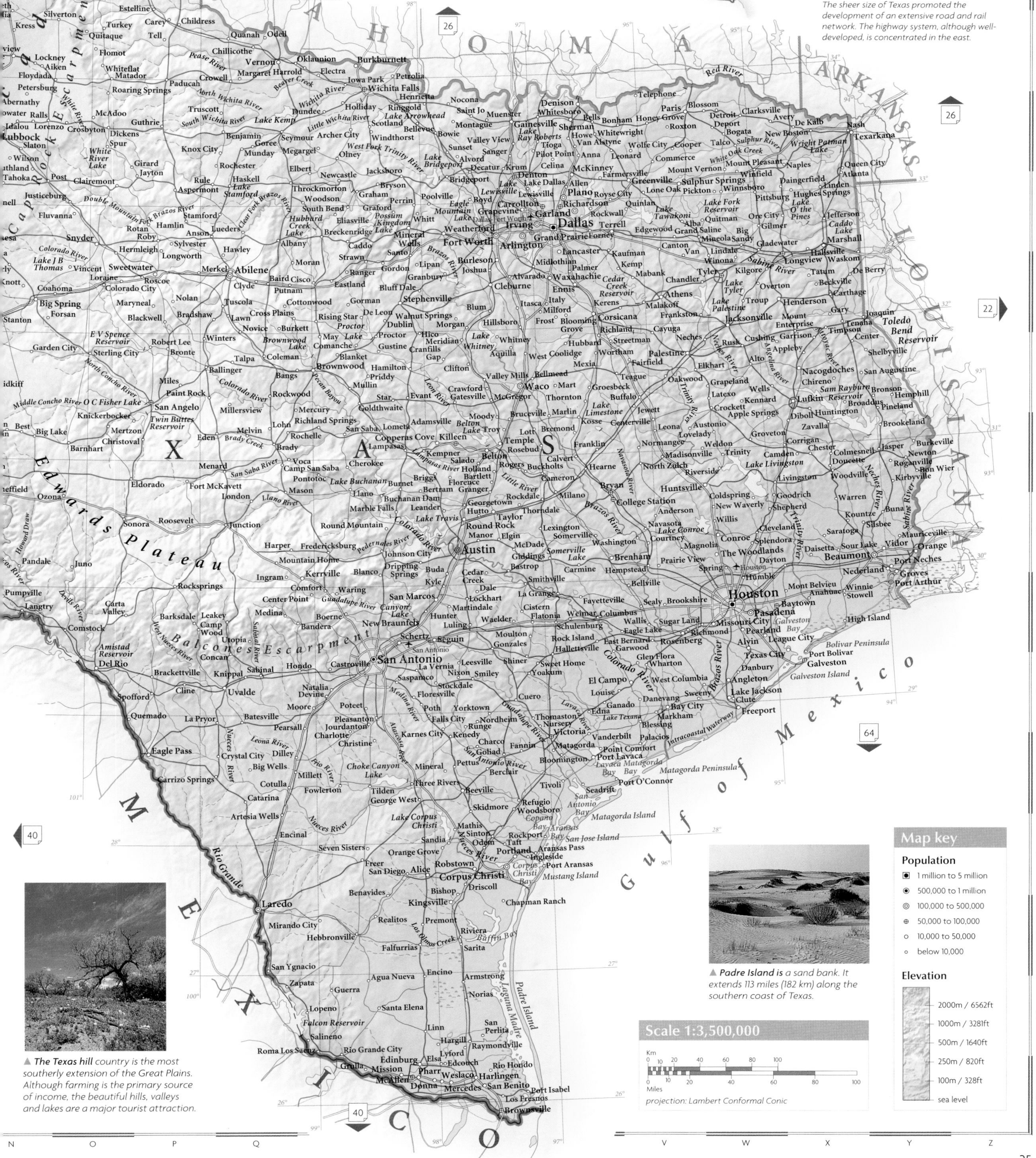

Transport and industry

Industry in the 20th century was largely concentrated on the processing of local raw materials, especially oil – deposits were discovered under 65% of the state's area. The technological demands of the oil industry and defence-related institutions, particularly NASA, have stimulated the development of numerous electronics and hi-tech firms which, alongside many national corporate headquarters, are based in Dallas–Fort Worth and Houston.

Major industry and infrastructure

- chemicals
- defence
- engineering
- finance
- food processing
- gas
- hi-tech industry
- mining
- oil
- textiles
- major towns
- international airports
- major roads
- major industrial areas

The transport network

293,509 miles (496,614 km)		3229 miles (5166 km)	
10,681 miles (17,089 km)		845 miles (1359 km)	

The sheer size of Texas promoted the development of an extensive road and rail network. The highway system, although well-developed, is concentrated in the east.

Map key

Population

- 1 million to 5 million
- 500,000 to 1 million
- 100,000 to 500,000
- 50,000 to 100,000
- 10,000 to 50,000
- below 10,000

Elevation

- 2000m / 6562ft
- 1000m / 3281ft
- 500m / 1640ft
- 250m / 820ft
- 100m / 328ft
- sea level

▲ *Padre Island is a sand bank. It extends 113 miles (182 km) along the southern coast of Texas.*

▲ *The Texas hill country is the most southerly extension of the Great Plains. Although farming is the primary source of income, the beautiful hills, valleys and lakes are a major tourist attraction.*

Scale 1:3,500,000

Km 0 10 20 40 60 80 100

Miles 0 10 20 40 60 80 100

projection: Lambert Conformal Conic

25

USA: SOUTH MIDWESTERN STATES

Arkansas, Kansas, Missouri, Oklahoma

The expansion of the USA focused on this region in the mid-19th century. Settlers spread from the confluence of the Missouri and Mississippi rivers up onto the Great Plains. This treeless expanse, which early explorers had called the 'Great American Desert', was turned into one of the world's richest agricultural regions; but periodic droughts, coupled with over-intensive farming, led to the 'Dustbowl' soil erosion crisis of the 1930s, the abandonment of many farms, and a mass exodus to the west coast. The land has since recovered, although the mechanization of agriculture has led to a decline in the rural population. In recent years, suburban residential development has spread rapidly across the wooded Ozark Plateau in the east of the region.

Transport and industry

The processing of agricultural products, such as brewing and meat packing, has been traditionally important in these states. In Kansas and Oklahoma, diversified manufacturing now supplements income from fossil fuels; Wichita has become a world centre for aeronautical engineering, an industry which also employs many people in neighbouring Missouri.

Major industry and infrastructure

- ✈ aerospace
- ✿ engineering
- Ⓢ finance
- ⬛ food processing
- ◊ gas
- ⬣ mining
- ⚓ oil
- ⬛ vehicle manufacture
- ● major towns
- ⊕ international airports
- — major roads
- ⬛ major industrial areas

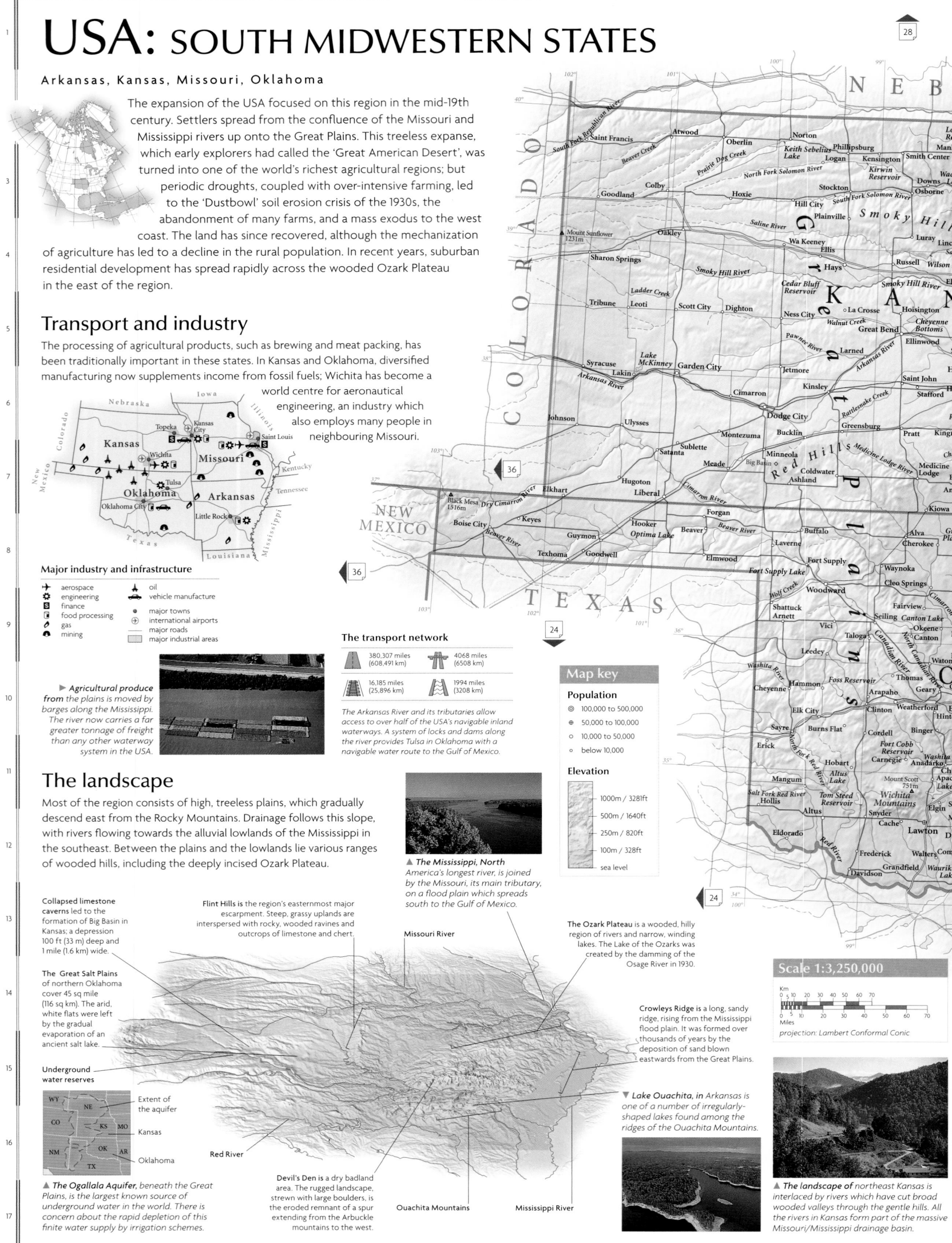

▶ *Agricultural produce from the plains is moved by barges along the Mississippi. The river now carries a far greater tonnage of freight than any other waterway system in the USA.*

The transport network

380,307 miles (608,491 km)	4068 miles (6508 km)
16,185 miles (25,896 km)	1994 miles (3208 km)

The Arkansas River and its tributaries allow access to over half of the USA's navigable inland waterways. A system of locks and dams along the river provides Tulsa in Oklahoma with a navigable water route to the Gulf of Mexico.

The landscape

Most of the region consists of high, treeless plains, which gradually descend east from the Rocky Mountains. Drainage follows this slope, with rivers flowing towards the alluvial lowlands of the Mississippi in the southeast. Between the plains and the lowlands lie various ranges of wooded hills, including the deeply incised Ozark Plateau.

▲ *The Mississippi, North America's longest river, is joined by the Missouri, its main tributary, on a flood plain which spreads south to the Gulf of Mexico.*

Map key

Population
- ◎ 100,000 to 500,000
- ⊕ 50,000 to 100,000
- ○ 10,000 to 50,000
- ○ below 10,000

Elevation
- 1000m / 3281ft
- 500m / 1640ft
- 250m / 820ft
- 100m / 328ft
- sea level

Collapsed limestone caverns led to the formation of Big Basin in Kansas; a depression 100 ft (33 m) deep and 1 mile (1.6 km) wide.

The Great Salt Plains of northern Oklahoma cover 45 sq mile (116 sq km). The arid, white flats were left by the gradual evaporation of an ancient salt lake.

Underground water reserves

Flint Hills is the region's easternmost major escarpment. Steep, grassy uplands are interspersed with rocky, wooded ravines and outcrops of limestone and chert.

Missouri River

The Ozark Plateau is a wooded, hilly region of rivers and narrow, winding lakes. The Lake of the Ozarks was created by the damming of the Osage River in 1930.

Crowleys Ridge is a long, sandy ridge, rising from the Mississippi flood plain. It was formed over thousands of years by the deposition of sand blown eastwards from the Great Plains.

Scale 1:3,250,000

Km
0 10 20 30 40 50 60 70

Miles
0 5 10 20 30 40 50 60 70

projection: Lambert Conformal Conic

▼ *Lake Ouachita, in Arkansas is one of a number of irregularly-shaped lakes found among the ridges of the Ouachita Mountains.*

▲ *The Ogallala Aquifer, beneath the Great Plains, is the largest known source of underground water in the world. There is concern about the rapid depletion of this finite water supply by irrigation schemes.*

Devil's Den is a dry badland area. The rugged landscape, strewn with large boulders, is the eroded remnant of a spur extending from the Arbuckle mountains to the west.

Ouachita Mountains

Red River

Mississippi River

▲ *The landscape of northeast Kansas is interlaced by rivers which have cut broad wooded valleys through the gentle hills. All the rivers in Kansas form part of the massive Missouri/Mississippi drainage basin.*

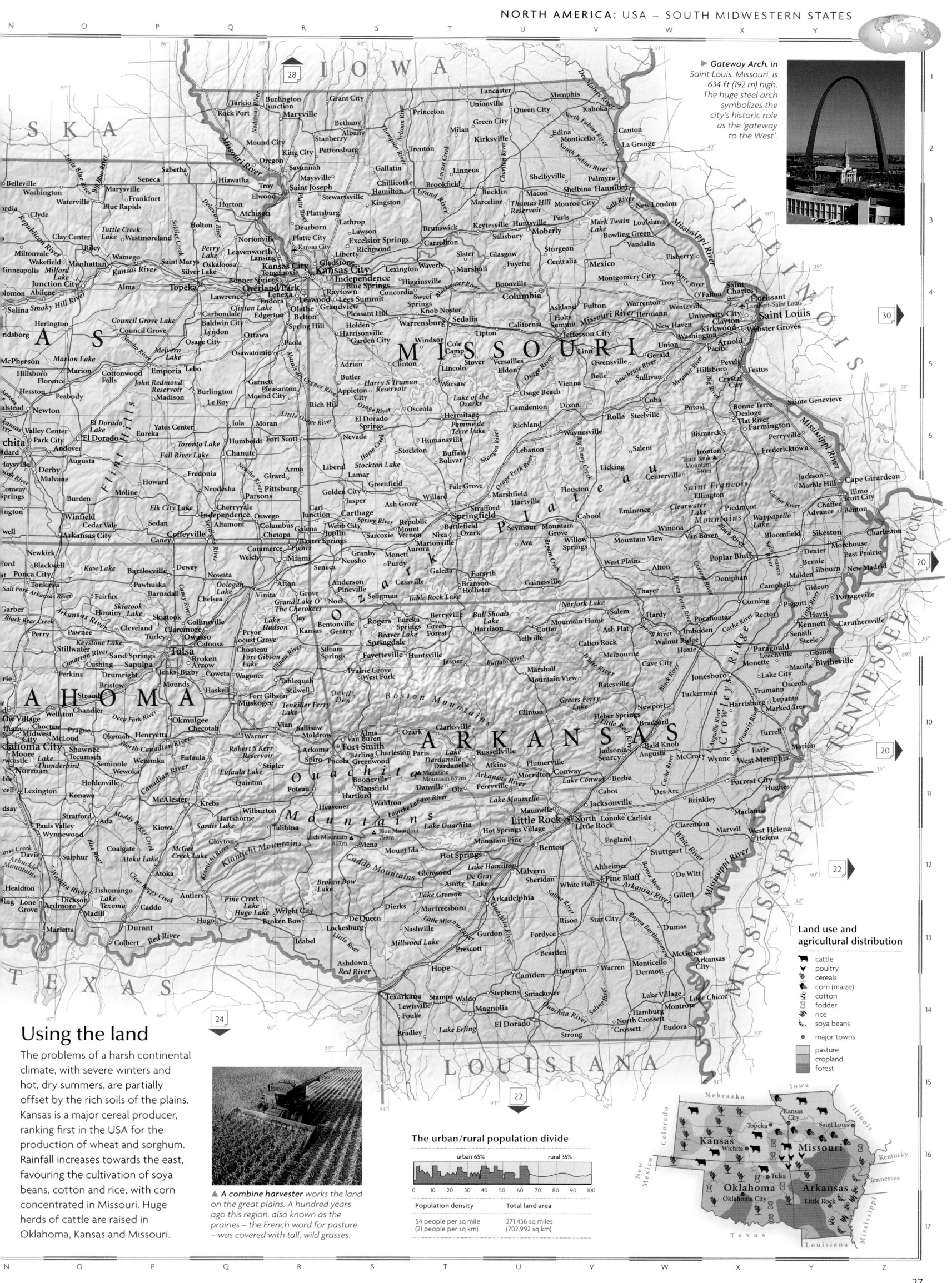

▶ *Gateway Arch*, in Saint Louis, Missouri, is 634 ft (192 m) high. The huge steel arch symbolizes the city's historic role as the 'gateway to the West'.

Using the land

The problems of a harsh continental climate, with severe winters and hot, dry summers, are partially offset by the rich soils of the plains. Kansas is a major cereal producer, ranking first in the USA for the production of wheat and sorghum. Rainfall increases towards the east, favouring the cultivation of soya beans, cotton and rice, with corn concentrated in Missouri. Huge herds of cattle are raised in Oklahoma, Kansas and Missouri.

▲ *A combine harvester* works the land on the great plains. A hundred years ago this region, also known as the prairies – the French word for pasture – was covered with tall, wild grasses.

The urban/rural population divide

urban 65%   rural 35%

0 10 20 30 40 50 60 70 80 90 100

Population density	Total land area
54 people per sq mile (21 people per sq km)	271,436 sq miles (702,992 sq km)

Land use and agricultural distribution

- cattle
- poultry
- cereals
- corn (maize)
- cotton
- fodder
- rice
- soya beans
- major towns
- pasture
- cropland
- forest

USA: UPPER PLAINS STATES

Iowa, Minnesota, Nebraska, North Dakota, South Dakota

Lying at the very heart of the North American continent, much of this region was acquired from France as part of the Louisiana Purchase in 1803. The area was largely by-passed by the early waves of westward migrants. When Europeans did settle, during the 19th century, they displaced the Native Americans who lived on the plains. The settlers planted arable crops and raised cattle on the immensely fertile prairie land, founding an agrarian tradition which flourishes today. Most of this region remains rural; of the five states, only in Minnesota has there been significant diversification away from agriculture and resource-based industries into the hi-tech and service sectors.

Using the land

The popular image of these states as agricultural is entirely justified; prairies stretch uninterrupted across most of the area. Croplands fall into two regions: the wheat belt of the plains, and the corn belt of the central USA. Cash crops, such as soya beans, are grown to supplement incomes. Livestock, particularly pigs and cattle, are raised throughout this region.

▶ *Dark, fertile prairie* soils in the southeast provide Minnesota's most productive farmland. Hot, humid summers create a long growing season for corn cultivation.

Land use and agricultural distribution

- cattle
- pigs
- corn (maize)
- soya beans
- wheat
- • major towns
- pasture
- cropland
- forest
- wetland

The urban/rural population divide

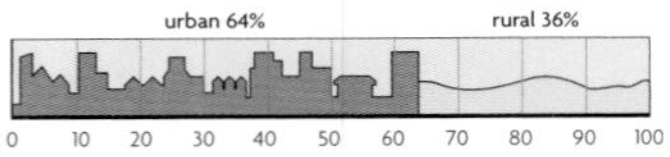

urban 64%   rural 36%

0 10 20 30 40 50 60 70 80 90 100

Population density	Total land area
31 people per sq mile (12 people per sq km)	357,212 sq miles (925,143 sq km)

Transport and industry

Food processing and the production of farm machinery are supported by the large agricultural sector. Mineral exploitation is also an important activity: gold is mined in the ore-rich Black Hills of South Dakota, and both North Dakota and Nebraska are emerging as major petroleum producers.

▶ *Water erosion along* the Little Missouri River has carried away sedimentary deposits, creating rugged landscapes known as badlands.

The transport network

504,522 miles (807,235 km)		3422 miles (5475 km)	
16,940 miles (27,104 km)		683 miles (1098 km)	

Nebraska's central location has made it an important transport artery for east–west traffic. Minnesota's road network radiates out from the hub of the twin cities, Minneapolis–Saint Paul.

Major industry and infrastructure

- coal
- engineering
- electronics
- finance
- food processing
- oil & gas
- mining
- • major towns
- ⊕ international airports
- — major roads
- major industrial areas

The landscape

These states straddle the Great Plains and the lowlands of the central USA, with Minnesota lying in a transition zone between the eastern forests and the prairies. The region was shaped by repeated ice advances and retreats, leaving a flat relief, broken only by the numerous lakes and broad river networks which drain the prairies.

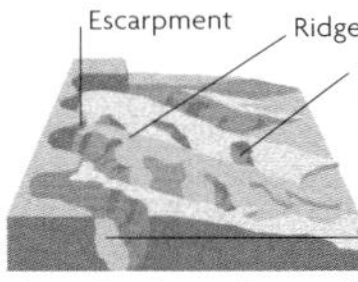

Escarpment   Ridge

In permeable strata hollows are formed by small mudslides

Water flowing into gullies erodes back the escarpment

▲ *Badlands are formed* by stormwater run-off which flows down the impermeable strata of the escarpment and saturates the permeable strata leading to mudslides and the formation of gullies.

North Dakota Badlands

The Minnesota landscape contains many post-glacial features, including its numerous lakes, boulder-strewn hills and mineral-rich deposits.

▲ *In the badlands* of North and South Dakota, horizontal layers of sandstone have been eroded by rivers, leaving a landscape of narrow gullies, sharp crests and pinnacles.

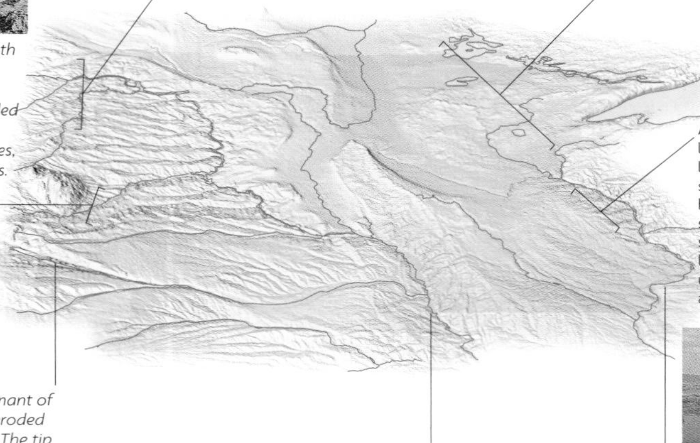

South Dakota Badlands

Although it escaped the last glaciation, the limestone bedrock of southeastern Minnesota has been eroded by surface and subterranean streams, leaving a network of underground caverns and steepsided valleys.

▲ *Chimney Rock is a remnant of* an ancient land surface, eroded by the North Platte River. The tip of its spire stands 500 ft (150 m) above the plain.

Missouri River

Mississippi River

◀ *In northeastern Iowa,* the Mississippi and its tributaries have deeply incised the underlying bedrock creating a hilly terrain, with bluffs standing 300 ft (90 m) above the valley.

▶ **Along the shores** of Lake Superior in Minnesota, the average number of frost-free days can be as few as 90, and frosts may occur in any month of the year.

CANADA

NORTH DAKOTA

SOUTH DAKOTA

MINNESOTA

NEBRASKA

IOWA

MISSOURI

KANSAS

WISCONSIN

ILLINOIS

Lake Superior

Map key

Population

⊚ 100,000 to 500,000
⊕ 50,000 to 100,000
○ 10,000 to 50,000
∘ below 10,000

Elevation

2000m / 6562ft
1000m / 3281ft
500m / 1640ft
250m / 820ft
100m / 328ft
sea level

Scale 1:3,500,000

Km
0 10 20 40 60 80 100 120

Miles
0 10 20 40 60 80 100 120

projection: Lambert Conformal Conic

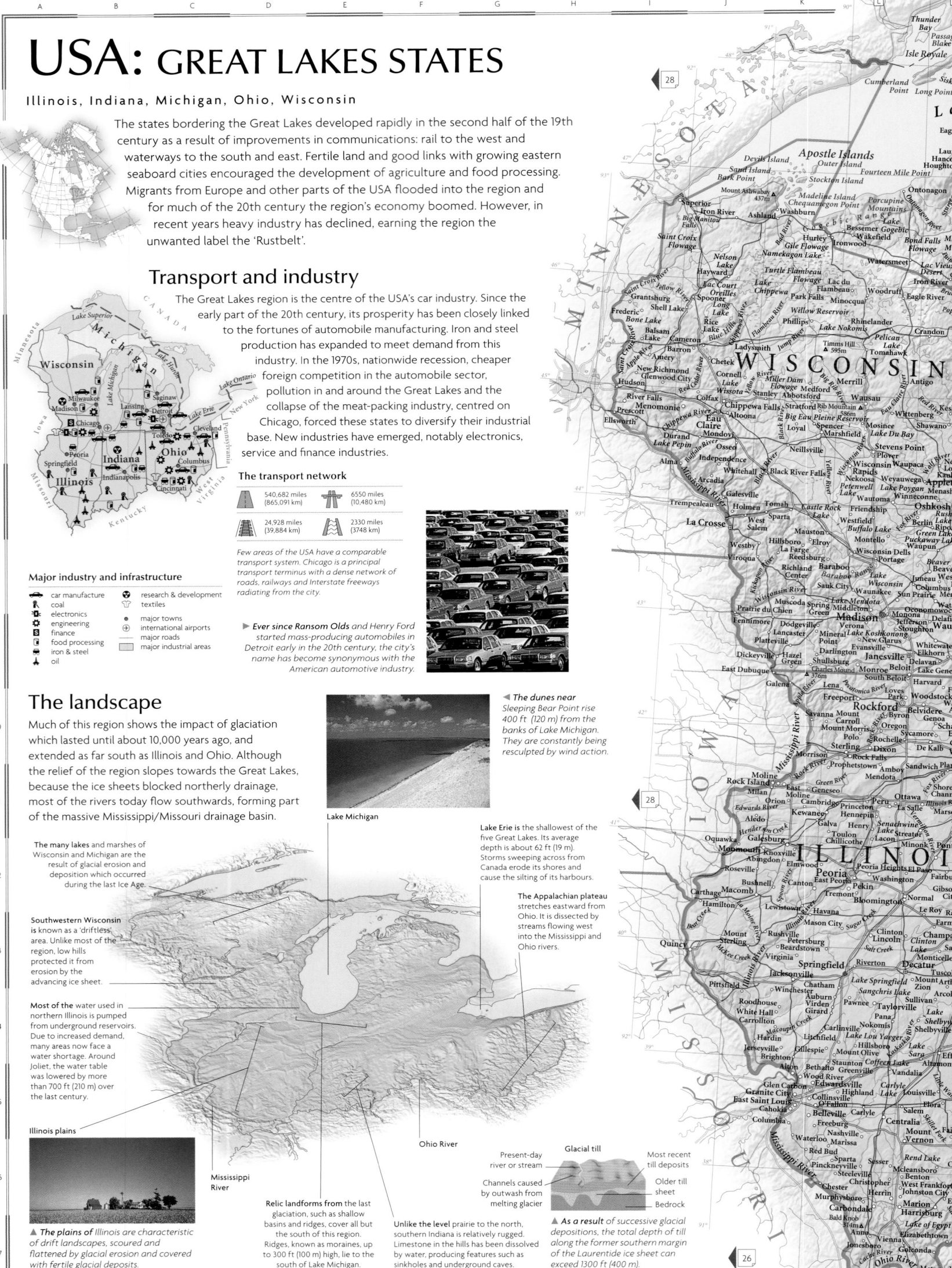

USA: GREAT LAKES STATES

Illinois, Indiana, Michigan, Ohio, Wisconsin

The states bordering the Great Lakes developed rapidly in the second half of the 19th century as a result of improvements in communications: rail to the west and waterways to the south and east. Fertile land and good links with growing eastern seaboard cities encouraged the development of agriculture and food processing. Migrants from Europe and other parts of the USA flooded into the region and for much of the 20th century the region's economy boomed. However, in recent years heavy industry has declined, earning the region the unwanted label the 'Rustbelt'.

Transport and industry

The Great Lakes region is the centre of the USA's car industry. Since the early part of the 20th century, its prosperity has been closely linked to the fortunes of automobile manufacturing. Iron and steel production has expanded to meet demand from this industry. In the 1970s, nationwide recession, cheaper foreign competition in the automobile sector, pollution in and around the Great Lakes and the collapse of the meat-packing industry, centred on Chicago, forced these states to diversify their industrial base. New industries have emerged, notably electronics, service and finance industries.

The transport network

540,682 miles (865,091 km)	6550 miles (10,480 km)
24,928 miles (39,884 km)	2330 miles (3748 km)

Few areas of the USA have a comparable transport system. Chicago is a principal transport terminus with a dense network of roads, railways and Interstate freeways radiating from the city.

▶ Ever since Ransom Olds and Henry Ford started mass-producing automobiles in Detroit early in the 20th century, the city's name has become synonymous with the American automotive industry.

Major industry and infrastructure

- car manufacture
- coal
- electronics
- engineering
- finance
- food processing
- iron & steel
- oil
- research & development
- textiles
- major towns
- international airports
- major roads
- major industrial areas

The landscape

Much of this region shows the impact of glaciation which lasted until about 10,000 years ago, and extended as far south as Illinois and Ohio. Although the relief of the region slopes towards the Great Lakes, because the ice sheets blocked northerly drainage, most of the rivers today flow southwards, forming part of the massive Mississippi/Missouri drainage basin.

◀ The dunes near Sleeping Bear Point rise 400 ft (120 m) from the banks of Lake Michigan. They are constantly being resculpted by wind action.

Lake Michigan

Lake Erie is the shallowest of the five Great Lakes. Its average depth is about 62 ft (19 m). Storms sweeping across from Canada erode its shores and cause the silting of its harbours.

The Appalachian plateau stretches eastward from Ohio. It is dissected by streams flowing west into the Mississippi and Ohio rivers.

The many lakes and marshes of Wisconsin and Michigan are the result of glacial erosion and deposition which occurred during the last Ice Age.

Southwestern Wisconsin is known as a 'driftless' area. Unlike most of the region, low hills protected it from erosion by the advancing ice sheet.

Most of the water used in northern Illinois is pumped from underground reservoirs. Due to increased demand, many areas now face a water shortage. Around Joliet, the water table was lowered by more than 700 ft (210 m) over the last century.

Illinois plains

Mississippi River

Ohio River

Glacial till

Present-day river or stream

Channels caused by outwash from melting glacier

Most recent till deposits

Older till sheet

Bedrock

▲ The plains of Illinois are characteristic of drift landscapes, scoured and flattened by glacial erosion and covered with fertile glacial deposits.

Relic landforms from the last glaciation, such as shallow basins and ridges, cover all but the south of this region. Ridges, known as moraines, up to 300 ft (100 m) high, lie to the south of Lake Michigan.

Unlike the level prairie to the north, southern Indiana is relatively rugged. Limestone in the hills has been dissolved by water, producing features such as sinkholes and underground caves.

▲ As a result of successive glacial depositions, the total depth of till along the former southern margin of the Laurentide ice sheet can exceed 1300 ft (400 m).

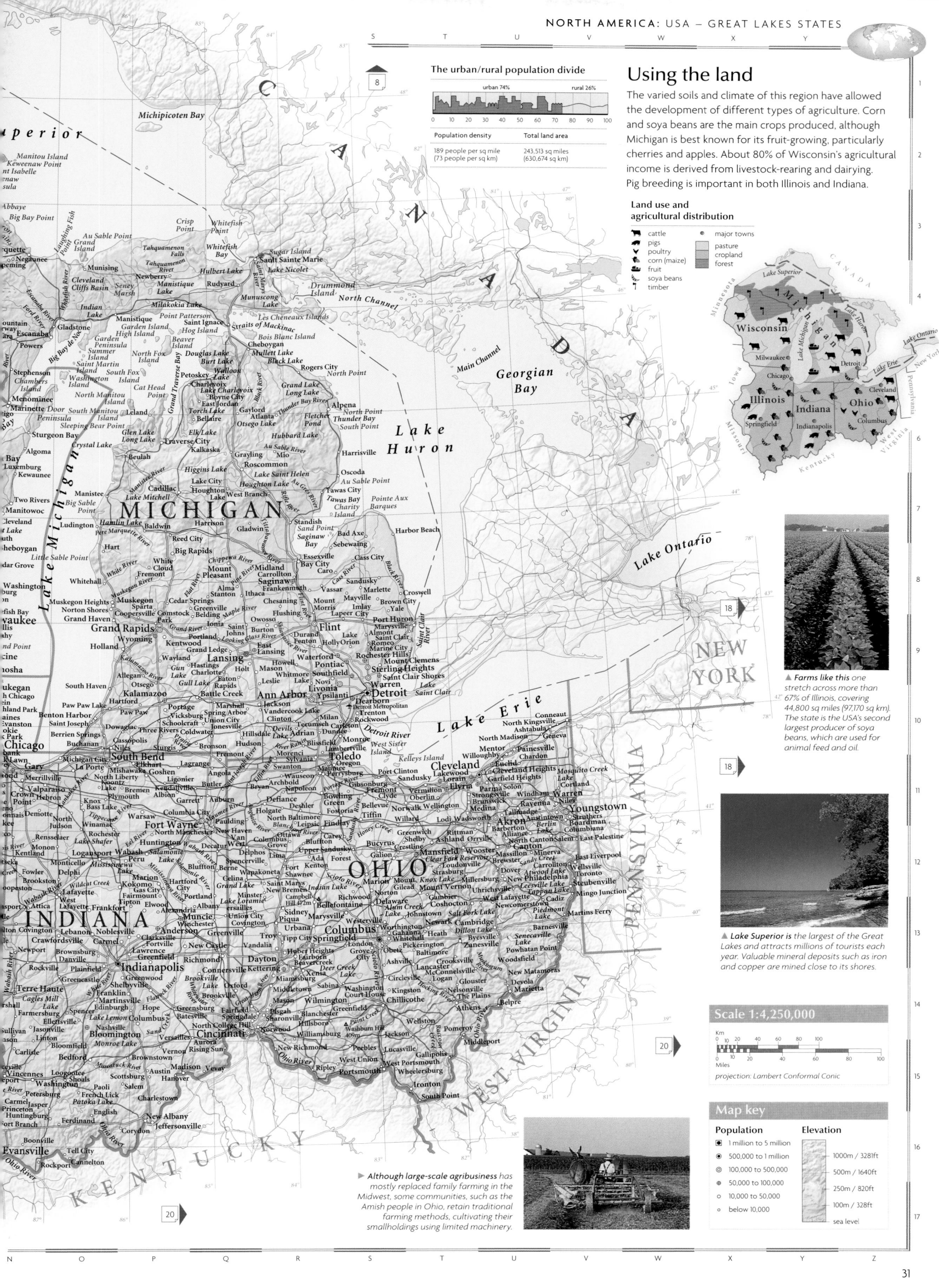

The urban/rural population divide

urban 74%   rural 26%

Population density	Total land area
189 people per sq mile (73 people per sq km)	243,513 sq miles (630,674 sq km)

Using the land

The varied soils and climate of this region have allowed the development of different types of agriculture. Corn and soya beans are the main crops produced, although Michigan is best known for its fruit-growing, particularly cherries and apples. About 80% of Wisconsin's agricultural income is derived from livestock-rearing and dairying. Pig breeding is important in both Illinois and Indiana.

Land use and agricultural distribution

- cattle
- pigs
- poultry
- corn (maize)
- fruit
- soya beans
- timber
- major towns
- pasture
- cropland
- forest

▲ *Farms like this one stretch across more than 67% of Illinois, covering 44,800 sq miles (97,170 sq km). The state is the USA's second largest producer of soya beans, which are used for animal feed and oil.*

▲ *Lake Superior is the largest of the Great Lakes and attracts millions of tourists each year. Valuable mineral deposits such as iron and copper are mined close to its shores.*

Scale 1:4,250,000

projection: Lambert Conformal Conic

Map key

Population
- ▣ 1 million to 5 million
- ◉ 500,000 to 1 million
- ◎ 100,000 to 500,000
- ⊕ 50,000 to 100,000
- ⊙ 10,000 to 50,000
- ⊙ below 10,000

Elevation
- 1000m / 3281ft
- 500m / 1640ft
- 250m / 820ft
- 100m / 328ft
- sea level

▶ *Although large-scale agribusiness has mostly replaced family farming in the Midwest, some communities, such as the Amish people in Ohio, retain traditional farming methods, cultivating their smallholdings using limited machinery.*

USA: NORTH MOUNTAIN STATES

Idaho, Montana, Oregon, Washington, Wyoming

The remoteness of the northwestern states, coupled with the rugged landscape, ensured that this was one of the last areas settled by Europeans in the 19th century. Fur-trappers and gold-prospectors followed the Snake River westwards as it wound its way through the Rocky Mountains. The states of the northwest have pioneered many conservationist policies, with the USA's first national park opened at Yellowstone in 1872. More recently, the Cascades and Rocky Mountains have become havens for adventure tourism. The mountains still serve to isolate the western seaboard from the rest of the continent. This isolation has encouraged west coast cities to expand their trade links with countries of the Pacific Rim.

▲ *The Snake River* has cut down into the basalt of the Columbia Basin to form Hells Canyon, the deepest in the USA, with cliffs up to 7900 ft (2408 m) high.

Using the land

Wheat farming in the east gives way to cattle ranching as rainfall decreases. Irrigated farming in the Snake River valley produces large yields of potatoes and other vegetables. Dairying and fruit-growing take place in the wet western lowlands between the mountain ranges.

▶ *Fine-textured, volcanic soils* in the hilly Palouse region of eastern Washington are susceptible to erosion.

The urban/rural population divide

urban 74%   rural 26%

0 10 20 30 40 50 60 70 80 90 100

Population density	Total land area
26 people per sq mile (10 people per sq km)	487,970 sq miles (1,263,716 sq km)

Scale 1:4,250,000

Km
0 10 20   40   60   80   100
Miles
0 10   20   40   60   80   100

projection: Lambert Conformal Conic

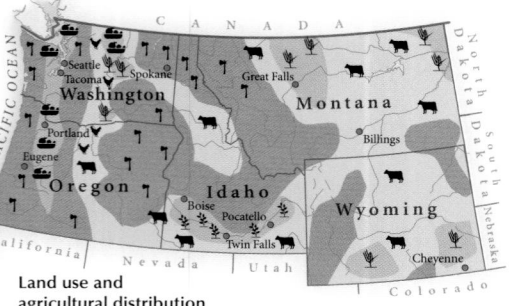

Land use and agricultural distribution

- cattle
- poultry
- cereals
- fruit
- potatoes
- timber
- major towns
- pasture
- cropland
- forest

Transport and industry

Minerals and timber are extremely important in this region. Uranium, precious metals, copper and coal are all mined, the latter in vast open-cast pits in Wyoming; oil and natural gas are extracted further north. Manufacturing, notably related to the aerospace and electronics industries, is important in western cities.

The transport network

347,857 miles (556,571 km)	
4200 miles (6720 km)	
12,354 miles (19,766 km)	
1108 miles (1782 km)	

Major industry and infrastructure

- adventure tourism
- aerospace
- coal
- chemicals
- electronics
- food processing
- mining
- oil & gas
- timber processing
- major towns
- international airports
- major roads
- major industrial areas

The Union Pacific Railroad has been in service across Wyoming since 1867. The route through the Rocky Mountains is now shared with the Interstate 80, a major east–west highway.

◀ *Seattle lies in* one of Puget Sound's many inlets. The city receives oil and other resources from Alaska, and benefits from expanding trade across the Pacific.

◀ *Crater Lake, Oregon,* is 6 miles (10 km) wide and 1800 ft (600 m) deep. It marks the site of a volcanic cone, which collapsed after an eruption within the last 7000 years.

The landscape

The Rocky Mountains are flanked by lower parallel ranges, which spread onto the Great Plains in the east and surmount the broad lava plateau which extends westwards. The Cascade Range divides the Columbia Basin from the coastlands, where the low areas skirting Puget Sound are broken by the steep, volcanic Olympic Mountains and the wooded hills of the Coast Ranges.

Molten rock cools, forming parallel columns

Surrounding strata eroded away

Molten rock wells up from the Earth's core

▲ *Devil's Tower in* Wyoming is an igneous intrusion, formed below the Earth's surface. Molten rock intruded through cracks in the overlying strata and cooled. Over time, the softer rock layers have been eroded away, leaving only the tower standing.

Glacial valleys on the seaward side of the Olympic Mountains receive about 142 inches (3600 mm) of rain per year, supporting the only true rainforest of the northern hemisphere.

Puget Sound

Mount St Helens erupted in 1980, killing 57 people and devastating a huge area.

Columbia Basin

Grand Coulee and the lesser *coulées* (ravines) were cut by cataclysmic floods, from the release of an ice-dammed lake, at the end of the last Ice Age.

The Continental Divide, or watershed, crosses the Lewis Range. From here, rivers flow east to Hudson Bay, south to the Gulf of Mexico and west to the Pacific Ocean.

► *Piney Buttes are the* remnants of an older, higher land surface gradually weathered and eroded into isolated outcrops with flat tops and steep sides.

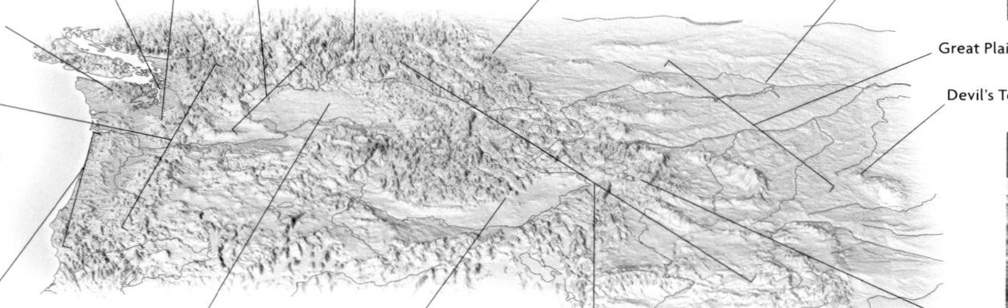

Great Plains

Devil's Tower

The Cascades are glacially scoured volcanic mountains, the highest of which is Mount Rainier, a dormant volcano at 14,409 ft (4392 m).

Coast Ranges

The plateaux of the Columbia and Snake rivers represent one of the world's largest accumulations of lava. Over 5 million years ago, successive flows of molten basalt buried the existing land surface by up to 450 ft (150 m).

The contorted rock shapes at 'Craters of the Moon' National Monument in Idaho were left 2000 years ago by the sporadic upwelling of viscous lava from fissures in the basalt plateau.

Rocky Mountains

▲ *Water from the* hot springs in Yellowstone National Park deposits minerals as it cools in rock pools. Long periods of deposition have created these rock terraces.

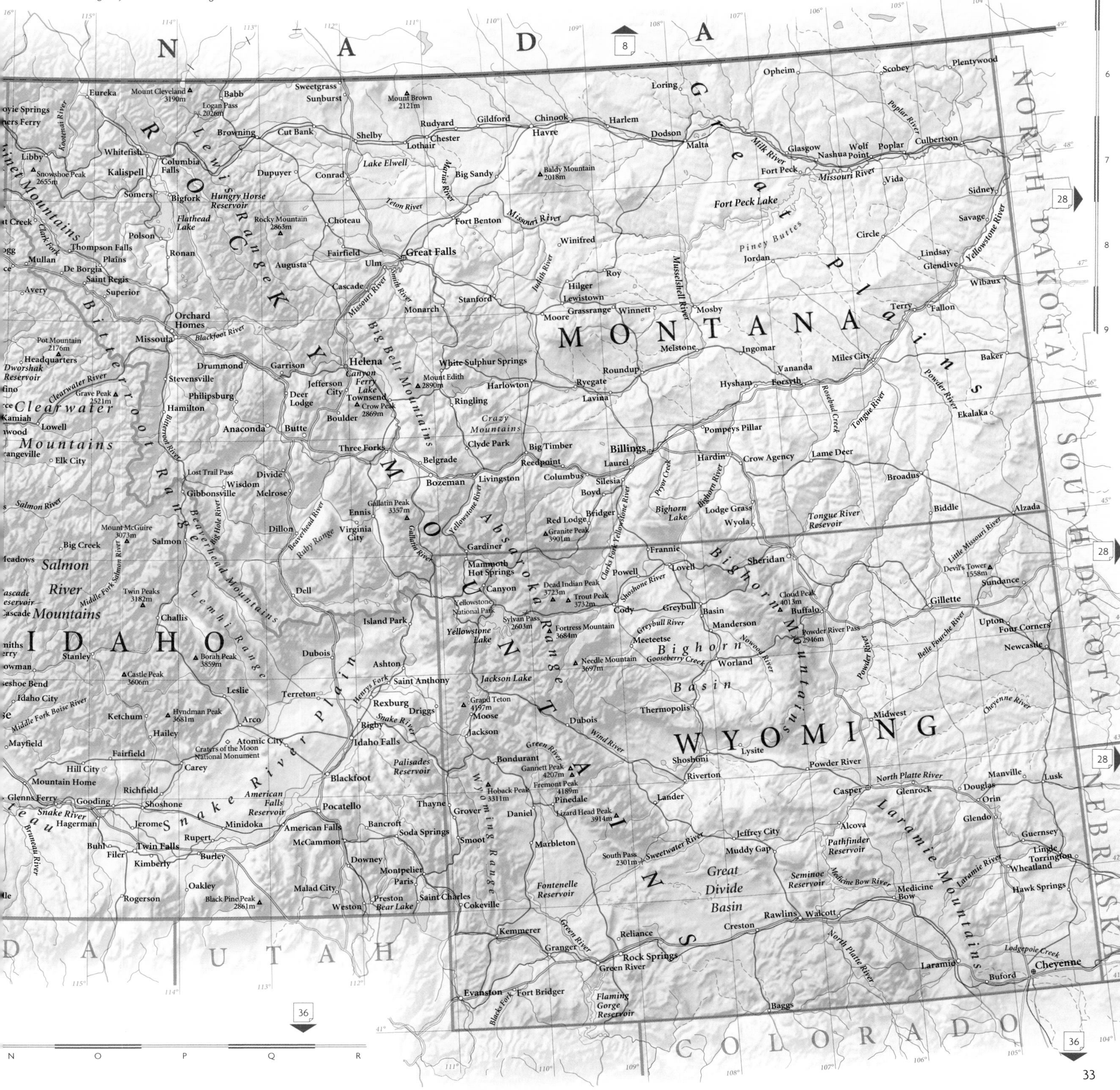

[Map of North Mountain States showing Montana, Wyoming, Idaho, with neighbouring Canada, North Dakota, South Dakota, Nebraska, Colorado, Utah]

Selected map labels:

CANADA

NORTH DAKOTA · SOUTH DAKOTA · NEBRASKA

MONTANA · WYOMING · IDAHO · UTAH · COLORADO

ROCKY MOUNTAINS · Great Plains · Bitterroot Range · Beaverhead Mountains · Lemhi Range · Absaroka Range · Bighorn Mountains · Laramie Mountains · Cascade Mountains · Salmon River Mountains · Clearwater Mountains · Crazy Mountains · Bighorn Basin · Great Divide Basin

Eureka, Mount Cleveland 3190m, Logan Pass 2026m, Babb, Browning, Cut Bank, Sweetgrass, Sunburst, Mount Brown 2121m, Rudyard, Gildford, Chinook, Harlem, Loring, Opheim, Scobey, Plentywood, Shelby, Lothair, Chester, Havre, Dodson, Malta, Glasgow, Nashua, Wolf Point, Poplar, Culbertson

Libby, Whitefish, Kalispell, Columbia Falls, Dupuyer, Conrad, Big Sandy, Baldy Mountain 2018m, Fort Peck, Fort Peck Lake, Sidney, Savage, Wibaux

Somers, Bigfork, Hungry Horse Reservoir, Flathead Lake, Choteau, Fort Benton, Winifred, Jordan, Circle, Lindsay, Glendive

Polson, Ronan, Augusta, Fairfield, Ulm, Great Falls, Hilger, Roy, Piney Buttes, Terry, Fallon

Missoula, Orchard Homes, Cascade, Monarch, Stanford, Lewistown, Moore, Grassrange, Winnett, Mosby, Ingomar, Vananda, Forsyth, Miles City, Baker

Helena, Garrison, White Sulphur Springs, Mount Edith 2890m, Harlowton, Ryegate, Lavina, Roundup, Melstone, Hysham, Ekalaka

Deer Lodge, Boulder, Townsend, Crow Peak 2869m, Ringling, MONTANA, Pompeys Pillar, Broadus, Biddle, Alzada

Anaconda, Butte, Three Forks, Belgrade, Clyde Park, Big Timber, Columbus, Laurel, Billings, Hardin, Crow Agency, Lame Deer

Bozeman, Livingston, Reedpoint, Boyd, Silesia, Bridger, Lodge Grass, Wyola

Ennis, Gallatin Peak 3357m, Red Lodge, Granite Peak 3901m, Bighorn Lake, Tongue River Reservoir

Dillon, Virginia City, Gardiner, Frannie, Sheridan, Devil's Tower 1558m, Sundance, Gillette, Upton, Four Corners, Newcastle

Mammoth Hot Springs, Canyon, Dead Indian Peak 3723m, Powell, Lovell, Cloud Peak 4013m, Buffalo

Island Park, Yellowstone National Park, Sylvan Pass 2603m, Trout Peak 3732m, Cody, Greybull, Basin, Manderson, Powder River Pass 2946m

Ashton, Saint Anthony, Jackson Lake, Fortress Mountain 3684m, Yellowstone Lake, Meeteetse, Worland

Terreton, Rexburg, Driggs, Grand Teton 4197m, Moose, Needle Mountain 3697m, Thermopolis, BIGHORN BASIN

Rigby, Idaho Falls, Jackson, Dubois, WYOMING

Bondurant, Green River, Shoshoni, Lysite, Midwest

Shoshone, Blackfoot, Pocatello, Thayne, Daniel, Pinedale, Fremont Peak 4189m, Riverton, Lander, Powder River, Casper, Glenrock, Orin, Douglas, Manville, Lusk

Craters of the Moon National Monument, Carey, American Falls Reservoir, Palisades Reservoir, Hoback Peak 3311m, Gannett Peak 4207m, Lizard Head Peak 3914m, Jeffrey City, Alcova, Glendo, Guernsey

Pocatello, American Falls, Soda Springs, Grover, Marbleton, South Pass 2301m, Muddy Gap, Pathfinder Reservoir, Medicine Bow

Twin Falls, Burley, McCammon, Downey, Montpelier, Paris, Smoot, Fontenelle Reservoir, Great Divide Basin, Seminoe Reservoir, Rawlins, Walcott, Medicine Bow, Hawk Springs

Malad City, Weston, Saint Charles, Cokeville, Kemmerer, Granger, Reliance, Creston, Laramie Mountains, Ledgepole Creek

Evanston, Fort Bridger, Rock Springs, Green River, Flaming Gorge Reservoir, Baggs, Laramie, Buford, Cheyenne

UTAH · COLORADO

USA: CALIFORNIA & NEVADA

The 'Gold Rush' of 1849 attracted the first major wave of European settlers to the USA's west coast. The pleasant climate, beautiful scenery and dynamic economy continue to attract immigrants – despite the ever-present danger of earthquakes – and California has become the USA's most populous state. The population is concentrated in the vast conurbations of Los Angeles, San Francisco and San Diego; new immigrants include people from South Korea, the Philippines, Vietnam and Mexico. Nevada's arid lands were initially exploited for minerals; in recent years, revenue from mining has been superseded by income from the tourist and gambling centres of Las Vegas and Reno.

Map key

Population

- ◪ 1 million to 5 million
- ◎ 500,000 to 1 million
- ◍ 100,000 to 500,000
- ◌ 50,000 to 100,000
- ○ 10,000 to 50,000
- · below 10,000

Elevation

- 4000m / 13,124ft
- 3000m / 9843ft
- 2000m / 6562ft
- 1000m / 3281ft
- 500m / 1640ft
- 250m / 820ft
- 100m / 328ft
- sea level

Scale 1:3,250,000

Km 0 5 10 20 30 40 50 60 70 80
Miles 0 5 10 20 30 40 50 60 70 80

projection: Lambert Conformal Conic

Transport and industry

Nevada's rich mineral reserves ushered in a period of mining wealth which has now been replaced by revenue generated from gambling. California supports a broad set of activities including defence-related industries and research and development facilities. 'Silicon Valley', near San Francisco, is a world leading centre for micro-electronics, while tourism and the Los Angeles film industry also generate large incomes.

◀ Gambling was legalized in Nevada in 1931. Las Vegas has since become the centre of this multi-million dollar industry.

Major industry and infrastructure

- ✈ aerospace
- 🚗 car manufacture
- ✗ defence
- 🎬 film industry
- $ finance
- 🍴 food processing
- ♣ gambling
- 🖥 hi-tech industry
- ⛏ mining
- ⚕ pharmaceuticals
- ☢ research & development
- ✄ textiles
- ⚑ tourism
- • major towns
- ✈ international airports
- — major roads
- ▭ major industrial areas

The transport network

| 211,459 miles (338,334 km) | 2944 miles (4710 km) |
| 7822 miles (12,595 km) | 190 miles (360 km) |

In California, the motor vehicle is a vital part of daily life, and an extensive freeway system runs throughout the state, cementing its position as the most important mode of transport.

The landscape

The broad Central Valley divides California's coastal mountains from the Sierra Nevada. The San Andreas Fault, running beneath much of the state, is the site of frequent earth tremors and sometimes more serious earthquakes. East of the Sierra Nevada, the landscape is characterized by the basin and range topography with stony deserts and many salt lakes.

Extensive cracking (faulting) uplifted a series of ridges

Rising molten rock causes stretching of the Earth's crust

As ridges are eroded they fill intervening valleys with sediments

▲ Molten rock (magma) welling up to form a dome in the Earth's interior, causes the brittle surface rocks to stretch and crack. Some areas were uplifted to form mountains (ranges), while others sunk to form flat valleys (basins).

◀ The General Sherman sequoia tree in Sequoia National Park is 2500 years old and at 275 ft (84 m) is one of the largest living things on earth.

Most of California's agriculture is confined to the fertile and extensively irrigated Central Valley, running between the Coast Ranges and the Sierra Nevada. It incorporates the San Joaquin and Sacramento valleys.

The dramatic granitic rock formations of Half Dome and El Capitan, and the verdant coniferous forests, attract millions of visitors annually to Yosemite National Park in the Sierra Nevada.

Sierra Nevada

The Great Basin dominates most of Nevada's topography containing large open basins, punctuated by eroded features such as buttes and mesas. River flow tends to be seasonal, dependent upon spring showers and winter snow melt.

Wheeler Peak is home to some of the world's oldest trees, bristlecone pines, which live for up to 5000 years.

When the Hoover Dam across the Colorado River was completed in 1936, it created Lake Mead, one of the largest artificial lakes in the world, extending for 115 miles (285 km) upstream.

The San Andreas Fault is a transverse fault which extends for 650 miles (1050 km) through California. Major earthquakes occur when the land either side of the fault moves at different rates. San Francisco was devastated by an earthquake in 1906.

Death Valley

Amargosa Desert

▲ The Sierra Nevada create a 'rainshadow', preventing rain from reaching much of Nevada. Pacific air masses, passing over the mountains, are stripped of their moisture.

▶ Named by migrating settlers in 1849, Death Valley is the driest, hottest place in North America, as well as being the lowest point on land in the western hemisphere, at 282 ft (86 m) below sea level.

The sparsely populated Mojave Desert receives less than 8 inches (200 mm) of rainfall a year. It is used extensively for weapons-testing and military purposes.

The Salton Sea was created accidentally between 1905 and 1907 when an irrigation channel from the Colorado River broke out of its banks and formed this salty 300 sq mile (777 sq km), land-locked lake.

Using the land

California is the USA's leading agricultural producer, although low rainfall makes irrigation essential. The long growing season and abundant sunshine allow many crops to be grown in the fertile Central Valley including grapes, citrus fruits, vegetables and cotton. Almost 17 million acres (6.8 million hectares) of California's forests are used commercially. Nevada's arid climate and poor soil are largely unsuitable for agriculture; 85% of its land is state owned and large areas are used for underground testing of nuclear weapons.

Land use and agricultural distribution

- 🐄 cattle
- 🍊 citrus fruits
- 🍎 fruit
- irrigation
- 🌲 timber
- vineyards
- • major towns
- pasture
- cropland
- forest
- desert

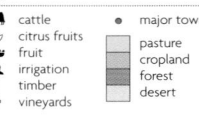

▲ Without considerable irrigation, this fertile valley at Palm Springs would still be part of the Sonoran Desert. California's farmers account for about 80% of the state's total water usage.

The urban/rural population divide

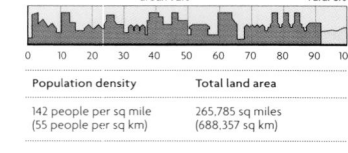

urban 92%   rural 8%

0 10 20 30 40 50 60 70 80 90 100

Population density	Total land area
142 people per sq mile (55 people per sq km)	265,785 sq miles (688,357 sq km)

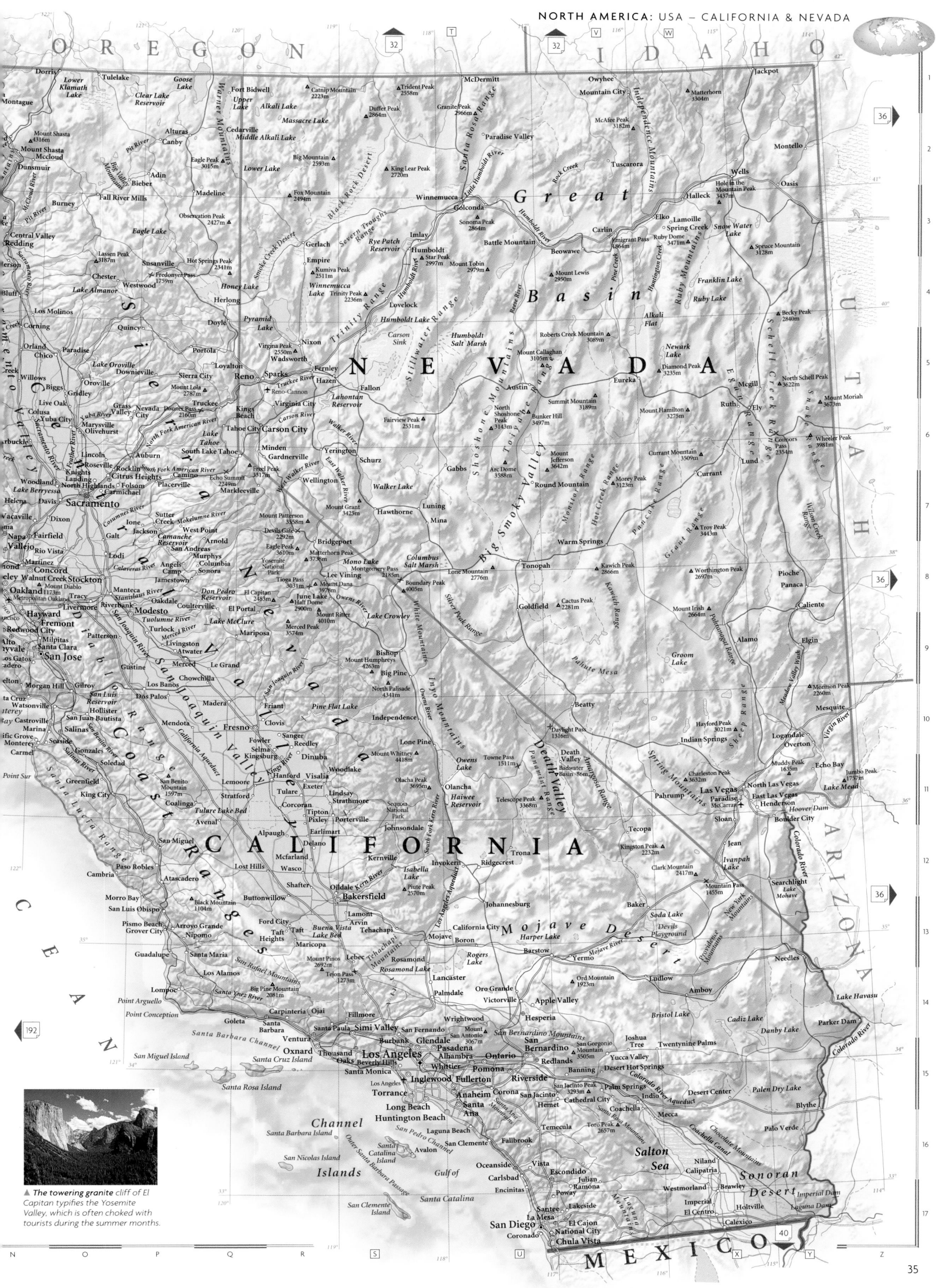

▲ The towering granite cliff of El Capitan typifies the Yosemite Valley, which is often choked with tourists during the summer months.

USA: SOUTH MOUNTAIN STATES

Arizona, Colorado, New Mexico, Utah

This arid region, characterized by expansive plateaux and spectacular canyons is home to several distinct peoples. The ruins of cliff dwellings built a thousand years ago by the Anasazi people still exist today, and native Americans own one-third of the land in Arizona. Spanish and Mexican conquest and settlement left a hispanic presence which is strongest in New Mexico. The Mormons, who came to the Great Salt Lake seeking religious freedom in 1847, were among the earliest Anglo-American settlers and now make up over 70% of Utah's population. The region's mineral wealth drove rapid development in the 20th century, yet the constraints of a fragile environment, including widespread water shortages, may limit prospects for growth.

The landscape

The arid, rocky expanse of the Colorado Plateau is dissected by immense canyons of the Colorado River. Desert lies to the north and south and branches of the Rocky Mountains run to the east and west. The Great Salt Lake and Desert lie within the Great Basin, a barren region of parallel mountain ranges which extends into Arizona.

When water evaporates it leaves a salt pan

Water level of lake varies according to quantity of run-off received from snow melt

Mudflats

Lake is fed by seasonal snow melt

▲ *The Great Salt* Lake is an ephemeral lake; it can remain dry for extended periods, leaving a pan of evaporated mineral salts in its centre.

Over 13 million years of weathering has created thousands of spires and pinnacles from the alternating rock strata of Bryce Canyon.

Lake Powell

The Rio Grande has its source in several meltwater streams, which have cut deep valleys into the platform of the San Juan Mountains.

Sand dunes, 600 ft (180 m) high, have been deposited in San Luis Valley, by winds funnelled through the San Juan and Sangre de Cristo mountains in the Rockies.

The parallel basins and ridges, which run north-south along the Great Basin, reflect a major series of block-faults in the underlying bedrock.

Parts of the Grand Canyon, which cuts through the Colorado Plateau, are 16 miles (25 km) wide. The Colorado River has cut down 6262 ft (2000 m), exposing rock strata more than 2 billion years old.

Rainbow Bridge is the world's largest natural arch. The 309 ft (94 m) span probably began to grow when the sandstone spur of a meandering creek was breached during a flash flood.

The striking colour effects seen in the Painted Desert come from minerals such as gypsum and haematite, combined with ambient heat and dust.

Petrified Forest

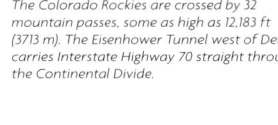

▶ *In the arid* landscape of Petrified Forest National Park in Arizona, the grain of prehistoric trees has been preserved as a fossil imprint in the rocks. The bog-preserved trees were gradually turned to stone by seeping mineral-rich water.

Shifting gypsum sands produce a constantly changing land surface, overwhelming plants and any other obstacles in Tularosa Valley.

Carlsbad Caverns

▶ *The intricate stalactites* of Carlsbad Caverns have grown with the seepage of calcium-rich water, over the last 100,000 years. The huge caves are home to around 100,000 Mexican freetail bats.

Transport and industry

New industries have helped reduce the region's dependence on the extraction of minerals and fossil fuels. Precision manufacture has grown rapidly, particularly in Arizona and Colorado. Salt Lake City and Denver are well-established financial centres and New Mexico, the USA's main producer of uranium, is a prominent region for nuclear research. Colorado is the USA's most important centre for winter sports.

The transport network

232,434 miles (373,986 km)	4059 miles (6515 km)
8627 miles (13,881 km)	none

The Colorado Rockies are crossed by 32 mountain passes, some as high as 12,183 ft (3713 m). The Eisenhower Tunnel west of Denver carries Interstate Highway 70 straight through the Continental Divide.

Major industry and infrastructure

- chemicals
- coal
- defence
- finance
- food processing
- hi-tech industry
- oil & gas
- mining
- research & development
- winter sports
- • major towns
- ✈ international airports
- — major roads
- ▢ major industrial areas

▲ *Glen Canyon Dam* on the Colorado river was completed in 1964. It provides hydro-electric power and irrigation water as part of a long-term federal project to harness the river.

◀ *The flat tablelands* (mesas), and the isolated pinnacles (buttes) which rise from the floor of Monument Valley are the resistant remnants of an earlier land surface, gradually cut back by erosion under arid conditions.

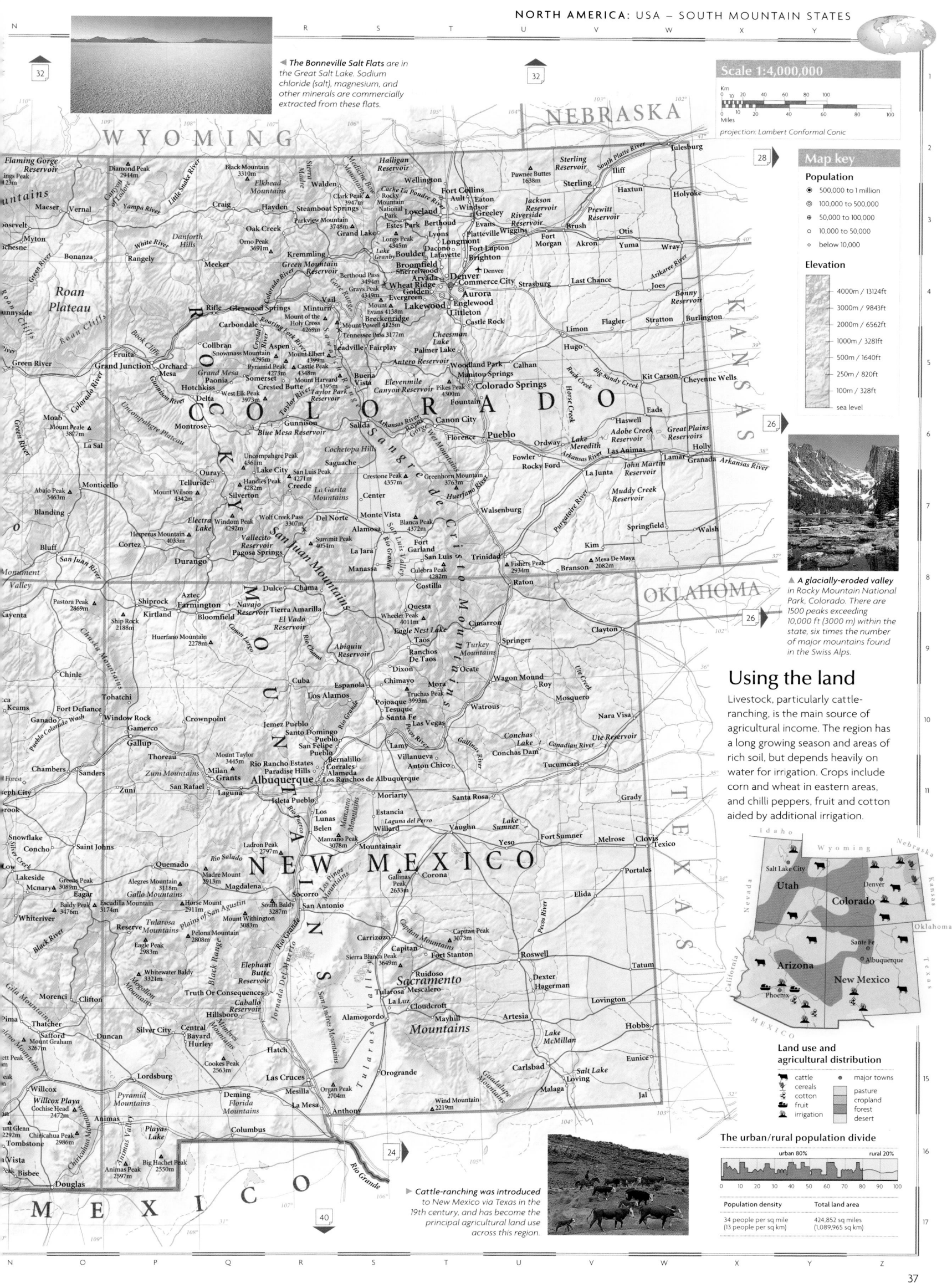

◄ *The Bonneville Salt Flats are in the Great Salt Lake. Sodium chloride (salt), magnesium, and other minerals are commercially extracted from these flats.*

Scale 1:4,000,000

Km
Miles

projection: Lambert Conformal Conic

Map key

Population

- ⊙ 500,000 to 1 million
- ◎ 100,000 to 500,000
- ⊕ 50,000 to 100,000
- ⊙ 10,000 to 50,000
- ○ below 10,000

Elevation

- 4000m / 13124ft
- 3000m / 9843ft
- 2000m / 6562ft
- 1000m / 3281ft
- 500m / 1640ft
- 250m / 820ft
- 100m / 328ft
- sea level

▲ *A glacially-eroded valley in Rocky Mountain National Park, Colorado. There are 1500 peaks exceeding 10,000 ft (3000 m) within the state, six times the number of major mountains found in the Swiss Alps.*

Using the land

Livestock, particularly cattle-ranching, is the main source of agricultural income. The region has a long growing season and areas of rich soil, but depends heavily on water for irrigation. Crops include corn and wheat in eastern areas, and chilli peppers, fruit and cotton aided by additional irrigation.

Land use and agricultural distribution

- cattle
- cereals
- cotton
- fruit
- irrigation
- • major towns
- pasture
- cropland
- forest
- desert

The urban/rural population divide

urban 80%   rural 20%

Population density	Total land area
34 people per sq mile (13 people per sq km)	424,852 sq miles (1,089,965 sq km)

▶ *Cattle-ranching was introduced to New Mexico via Texas in the 19th century, and has become the principal agricultural land use across this region.*

37

USA: HAWAII

The 122 islands of the Hawai'ian archipelago – which are part of Polynesia – are the peaks of the world's largest volcanoes. They rise approximately 6 miles (9.7 km) from the floor of the Pacific Ocean. The largest, the island of Hawai'i, remains highly active. Hawaii became the USA's 50th state in 1959. A tradition of receiving immigrant workers is reflected in the islands' ethnic diversity, with peoples drawn from around the rim of the Pacific. Only 9% of the current population are native Polynesians.

▲ The island of Moloka'i is formed from volcanic rock. Mature sand dunes cover the rocks in coastal areas.

Using the land and sea

The ice-free coastline of Alaska provides access to salmon fisheries and more than 129 million acres (52.2 million ha) of forest. Most of Alaska is uncultivable, and around 90% of food is imported. Barley, hay and hothouse products are grown around Anchorage, where dairy farming is also concentrated.

The urban/rural population divide

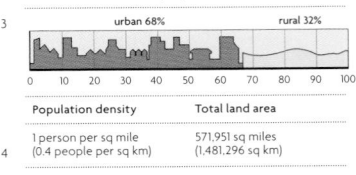

urban 68%	rural 32%

Population density	Total land area
1 person per sq mile (0.4 people per sq km)	571,951 sq miles (1,481,296 sq km)

◄ A raft of timber from the Tongass forest is hauled by a tug, bound for the pulp mills of the Alaskan coast between Juneau and Ketchikan.

Transport and industry

Tourism dominates the economy, with over 90% of the population employed in services. The naval base at Pearl Harbor is also a major source of employment. Industry is concentrated on the island of O'ahu and relies mostly on imported materials, while agricultural produce is processed locally.

The transport network

4102 miles (6600 km)		43 miles (69 km)	
none		none	

Hawaii relies on ocean-surface transportation. Honolulu is the main focus of this network, bringing foreign trade and the markets of mainland USA to Hawaii's outer islands.

Major industry and infrastructure

🏭 food processing	● major towns	
⚓ military base	⊕ international airports	
textiles	—— major roads	
tourism	major industrial areas	

◄ *Haleakala's extinct volcanic crater is the world's largest. The giant caldera, containing many secondary cones, is 2000 ft (600 m) deep and 20 miles (32 km) in circumference.*

Scale 1:4,000,000

Km
0 20 40 60 80 100

Miles
0 20 40 60 80 100

projection: Lambert Conformal Conic

Map key

Population
- ◉ 100,000 to 500,000
- ⊕ 50,000 to 100,000
- ○ 10,000 to 50,000
- ○ below 10,000

Elevation
- 4000m / 13,124ft
- 3000m / 9843ft
- 2000m / 6562ft
- 1000m / 3281ft
- 500m / 1640ft
- 250m / 820ft
- 100m / 328ft
- sea level

Using the land and sea

The volcanic soils are extremely fertile and the climate hot and humid on the lower slopes, supporting large commercial plantations growing sugar cane, bananas, pineapples and other tropical fruit, as well as nursery plants and flowers. Some land is given to pasture, particularly for beef and dairy cattle.

Land use and agricultural distribution
- 🐂 cattle
- 🐟 fishing
- 🍍 fruit
- sugar cane
- ● major towns
- pasture
- cropland
- forest
- mountain region

▶ *The island of Kaua'i is one of the wettest places in the world, receiving some 450 inches (11,500 mm) of rain a year.*

The urban/rural population divide

urban 89%	rural 11%

Population density	Total land area
189 people per sq mile (73 people per sq km)	6,423 sq miles (16,636 sq km)

Map key

Population
- ◉ 100,000 to 500,000
- ⊕ 50,000 to 100,000
- ○ 10,000 to 50,000
- ○ below 10,000

Elevation
- 4000m / 13,124ft
- 3000m / 9843ft
- 2000m / 6562ft
- 1000m / 3281ft
- 500m / 1640ft
- 250m / 820ft
- 100m / 328ft
- sea level

Scale 1:9,000,000

Km
0 25 50 100 150 200 250

Miles
0 25 50 100 150 200 250

projection: Lambert Conformal Conic

USA: ALASKA

Almost 650,000 people live in Alaska, a wilderness of ice, forest, mountains and plains, purchased from Russia in 1867 and twice the size of Texas. The discovery of large oil reserves has brought prosperity to the USA's 'last frontier', while advancing the need to preserve natural habitats and the traditional livelihoods of indigenous peoples such as the Aleuts and Inupiaq.

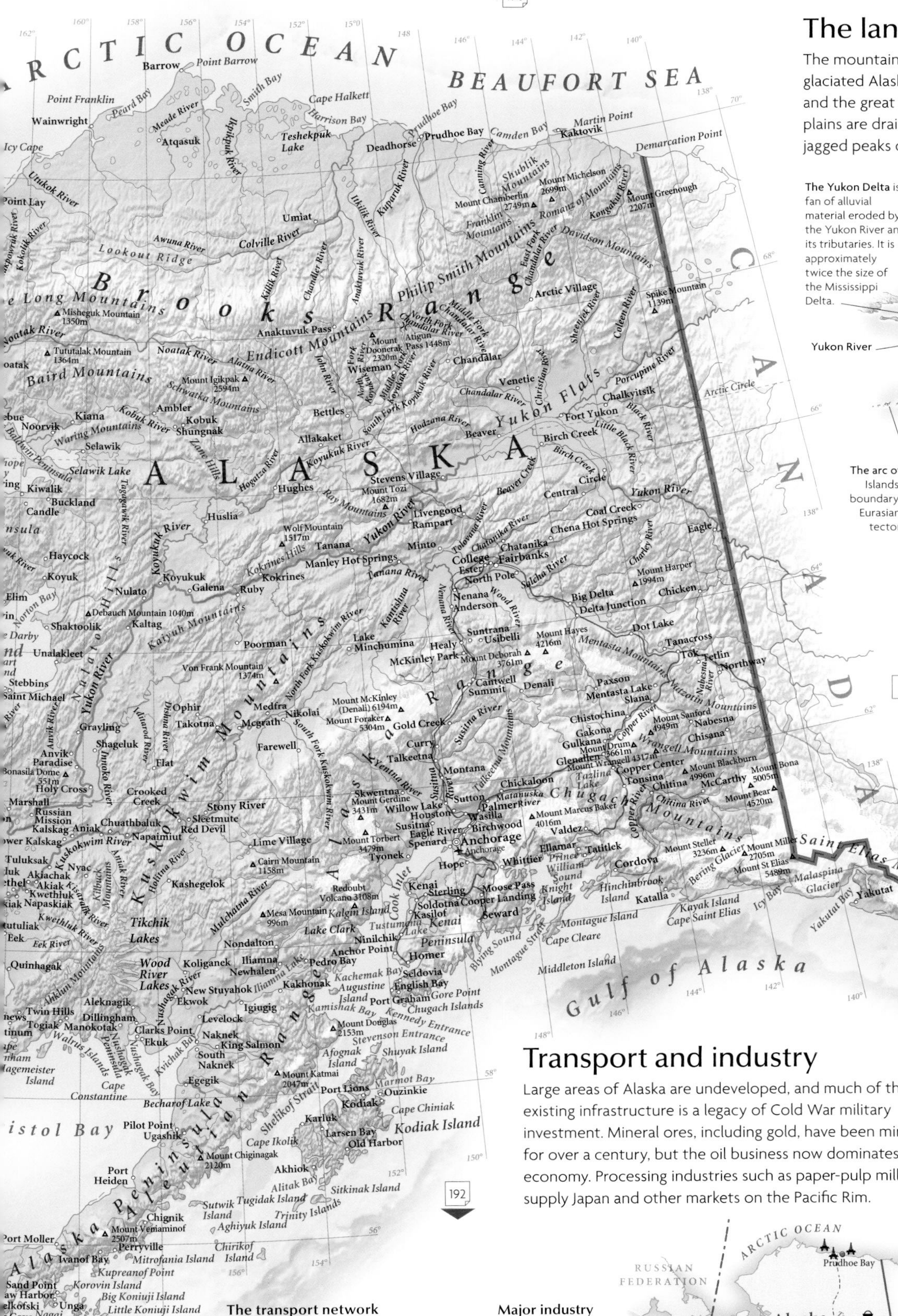

The landscape

The mountains of the Pacific coast culminate in the heavily glaciated Alaska Range and extend west, to the Alaska Peninsula and the great volcanic arc of the Aleutian Islands. The interior plains are drained by the Yukon River and bounded by the bare, jagged peaks of the Brooks Range to the north.

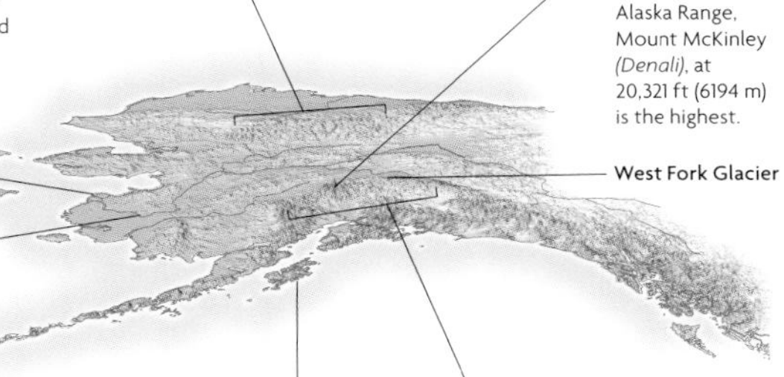

The Yukon Delta is a fan of alluvial material eroded by the Yukon River and its tributaries. It is approximately twice the size of the Mississippi Delta.

Brooks Range

The ten highest mountains in the USA are all in the Alaska Range, Mount McKinley (Denali), at 20,321 ft (6194 m) is the highest.

West Fork Glacier

Yukon River

The arc of the Aleutian Islands marks the boundary between the Eurasian and Pacific tectonic plates.

Fjords are found along the coast where valleys, deeply excavated by large glaciers, were inundated by rising seas.

Alaska Range

▲ *By August, the Alaska Range is covered with autumnal tundra vegetation.*

West Fork Glacier

The surging ice mass shears along the glacier margin

Deep crevasses divide the front of the surging glacier into large ice blocks

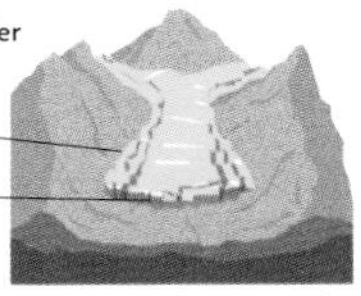

▲ *Surging glaciers make rapid and dramatic advances, normally after periods of snow accumulation. West Fork Glacier in the Susitna River Basin travelled 2.5 miles (4 km) in 1987.*

Transport and industry

Large areas of Alaska are undeveloped, and much of the existing infrastructure is a legacy of Cold War military investment. Mineral ores, including gold, have been mined for over a century, but the oil business now dominates the economy. Processing industries such as paper-pulp mills supply Japan and other markets on the Pacific Rim.

Land use and agricultural distribution

- fishing
- reindeer
- fruit
- • major towns
- forest
- barren
- tundra

The transport network

13,524 miles (21,760 km)		49 miles (78 km)	
482 miles (772 km)		none	

Over 40 million gallons (182 million litres) of oil are pumped through the Trans-Alaska Pipeline every day. The oil takes six days to travel the 789 miles (1262 km) from Prudhoe Bay to Valdez.

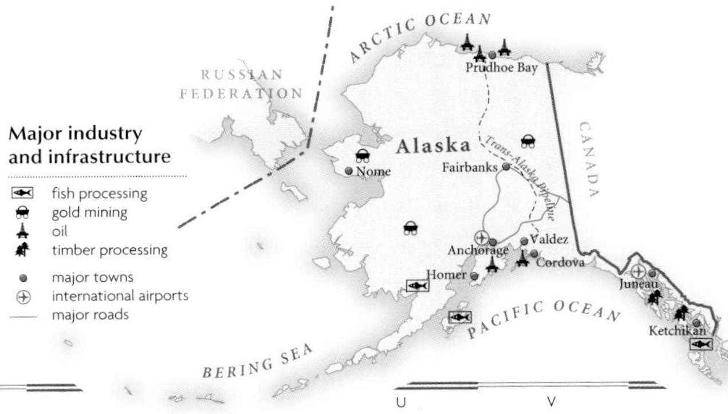

Major industry and infrastructure

- fish processing
- gold mining
- oil
- timber processing
- major towns
- international airports
- major roads

▲ *The Trans-Alaska Pipeline has carried crude oil from Prudhoe Bay since 1977. The oilfield is the USA's largest and is estimated to be equal in size to the biggest oilfields of the Persian Gulf.*

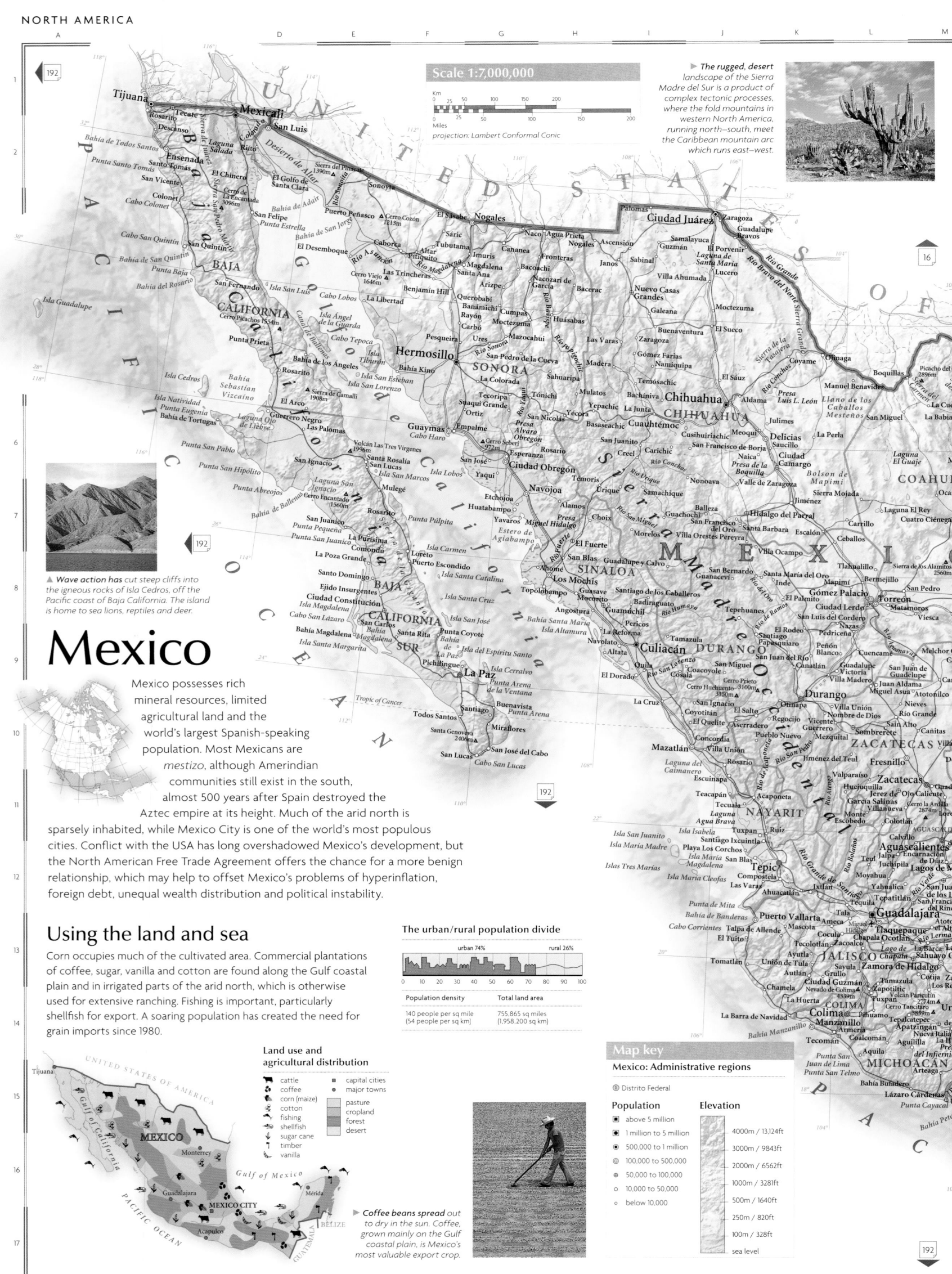

Mexico

Mexico possesses rich mineral resources, limited agricultural land and the world's largest Spanish-speaking population. Most Mexicans are *mestizo*, although Amerindian communities still exist in the south, almost 500 years after Spain destroyed the Aztec empire at its height. Much of the arid north is sparsely inhabited, while Mexico City is one of the world's most populous cities. Conflict with the USA has long overshadowed Mexico's development, but the North American Free Trade Agreement offers the chance for a more benign relationship, which may help to offset Mexico's problems of hyperinflation, foreign debt, unequal wealth distribution and political instability.

Using the land and sea

Corn occupies much of the cultivated area. Commercial plantations of coffee, sugar, vanilla and cotton are found along the Gulf coastal plain and in irrigated parts of the arid north, which is otherwise used for extensive ranching. Fishing is important, particularly shellfish for export. A soaring population has created the need for grain imports since 1980.

▲ *Wave action has* cut steep cliffs into the igneous rocks of Isla Cedros, off the Pacific coast of Baja California. The island is home to sea lions, reptiles and deer.

▶ *The rugged, desert* landscape of the Sierra Madre del Sur is a product of complex tectonic processes, where the fold mountains running north–south, meet the Caribbean mountain arc which runs east–west.

▶ *Coffee beans spread* out to dry in the sun. Coffee, grown mainly on the Gulf coastal plain, is Mexico's most valuable export crop.

Scale 1:7,000,000
projection: Lambert Conformal Conic

The urban/rural population divide

urban 74% — rural 26%

Population density	Total land area
140 people per sq mile (54 people per sq km)	755,865 sq miles (1,958,200 sq km)

Land use and agricultural distribution

- cattle
- coffee
- corn (maize)
- cotton
- fishing
- shellfish
- sugar cane
- timber
- vanilla
- capital cities
- major towns
- pasture
- cropland
- forest
- desert

Map key

Mexico: Administrative regions

① Distrito Federal

Population
- above 5 million
- 1 million to 5 million
- 500,000 to 1 million
- 100,000 to 500,000
- 50,000 to 100,000
- 10,000 to 50,000
- below 10,000

Elevation
- 4000m / 13,124ft
- 3000m / 9843ft
- 2000m / 6562ft
- 1000m / 3281ft
- 500m / 1640ft
- 250m / 820ft
- 100m / 328ft
- sea level

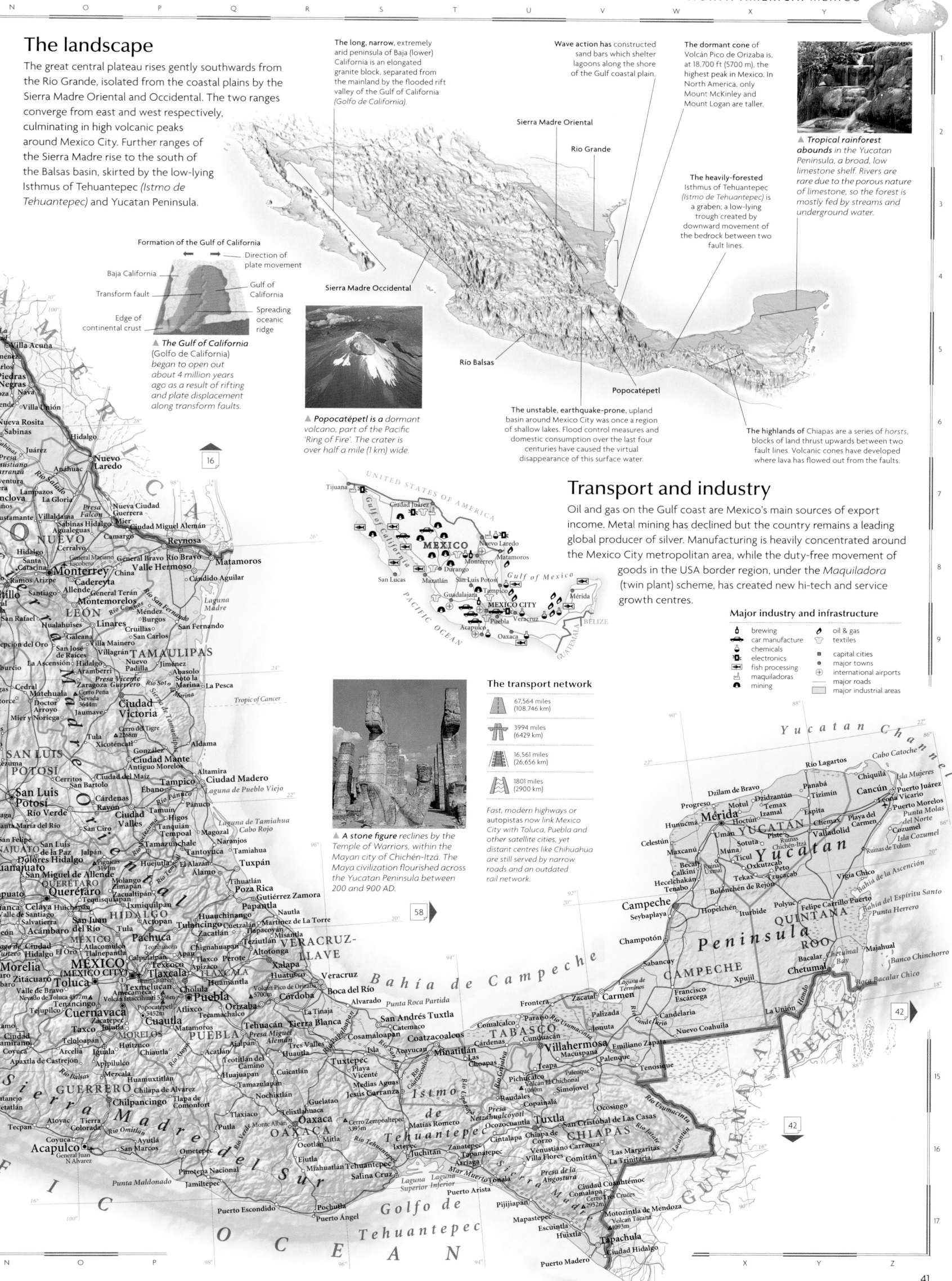

The landscape

The great central plateau rises gently southwards from the Rio Grande, isolated from the coastal plains by the Sierra Madre Oriental and Occidental. The two ranges converge from east and west respectively, culminating in high volcanic peaks around Mexico City. Further ranges of the Sierra Madre rise to the south of the Balsas basin, skirted by the low-lying Isthmus of Tehuantepec (Istmo de Tehuantepec) and Yucatan Peninsula.

The long, narrow, extremely arid peninsula of Baja (lower) California is an elongated granite block, separated from the mainland by the flooded rift valley of the Gulf of California (Golfo de California).

Wave action has constructed sand bars which shelter lagoons along the shore of the Gulf coastal plain.

The dormant cone of Volcán Pico de Orizaba is, at 18,700 ft (5700 m), the highest peak in Mexico. In North America, only Mount McKinley and Mount Logan are taller.

▲ Tropical rainforest abounds in the Yucatan Peninsula, a broad, low limestone shelf. Rivers are rare due to the porous nature of limestone, so the forest is mostly fed by streams and underground water.

The heavily-forested Isthmus of Tehuantepec (Istmo de Tehuantepec) is a graben; a low-lying trough created by downward movement of the bedrock between two fault lines.

Formation of the Gulf of California

Direction of plate movement
Baja California
Transform fault
Gulf of California
Edge of continental crust
Spreading oceanic ridge

▲ The Gulf of California (Golfo de California) began to open out about 4 million years ago as a result of rifting and plate displacement along transform faults.

▲ Popocatépetl is a dormant volcano, part of the Pacific 'Ring of Fire'. The crater is over half a mile (1 km) wide.

The unstable, earthquake-prone, upland basin around Mexico City was once a region of shallow lakes. Flood control measures and domestic consumption over the last four centuries have caused the virtual disappearance of this surface water.

The highlands of Chiapas are a series of horsts, blocks of land thrust upwards between two fault lines. Volcanic cones have developed where lava has flowed out from the faults.

Transport and industry

Oil and gas on the Gulf coast are Mexico's main sources of export income. Metal mining has declined but the country remains a leading global producer of silver. Manufacturing is heavily concentrated around the Mexico City metropolitan area, while the duty-free movement of goods in the USA border region, under the Maquiladora (twin plant) scheme, has created new hi-tech and service growth centres.

Major industry and infrastructure

- brewing
- car manufacture
- chemicals
- electronics
- fish processing
- maquiladoras
- mining
- oil & gas
- textiles
- ■ capital cities
- ● major towns
- ✈ international airports
- — major roads
- major industrial areas

The transport network

67,564 miles (108,746 km)

3994 miles (6429 km)

16,561 miles (26,656 km)

1801 miles (2900 km)

Fast, modern highways or autopistas now link Mexico City with Toluca, Puebla and other satellite cities, yet distant centres like Chihuahua are still served by narrow roads and an outdated rail network.

▲ A stone figure reclines by the Temple of Warriors, within the Mayan city of Chichén-Itzá. The Maya civilization flourished across the Yucatan Peninsula between 200 and 900 AD.

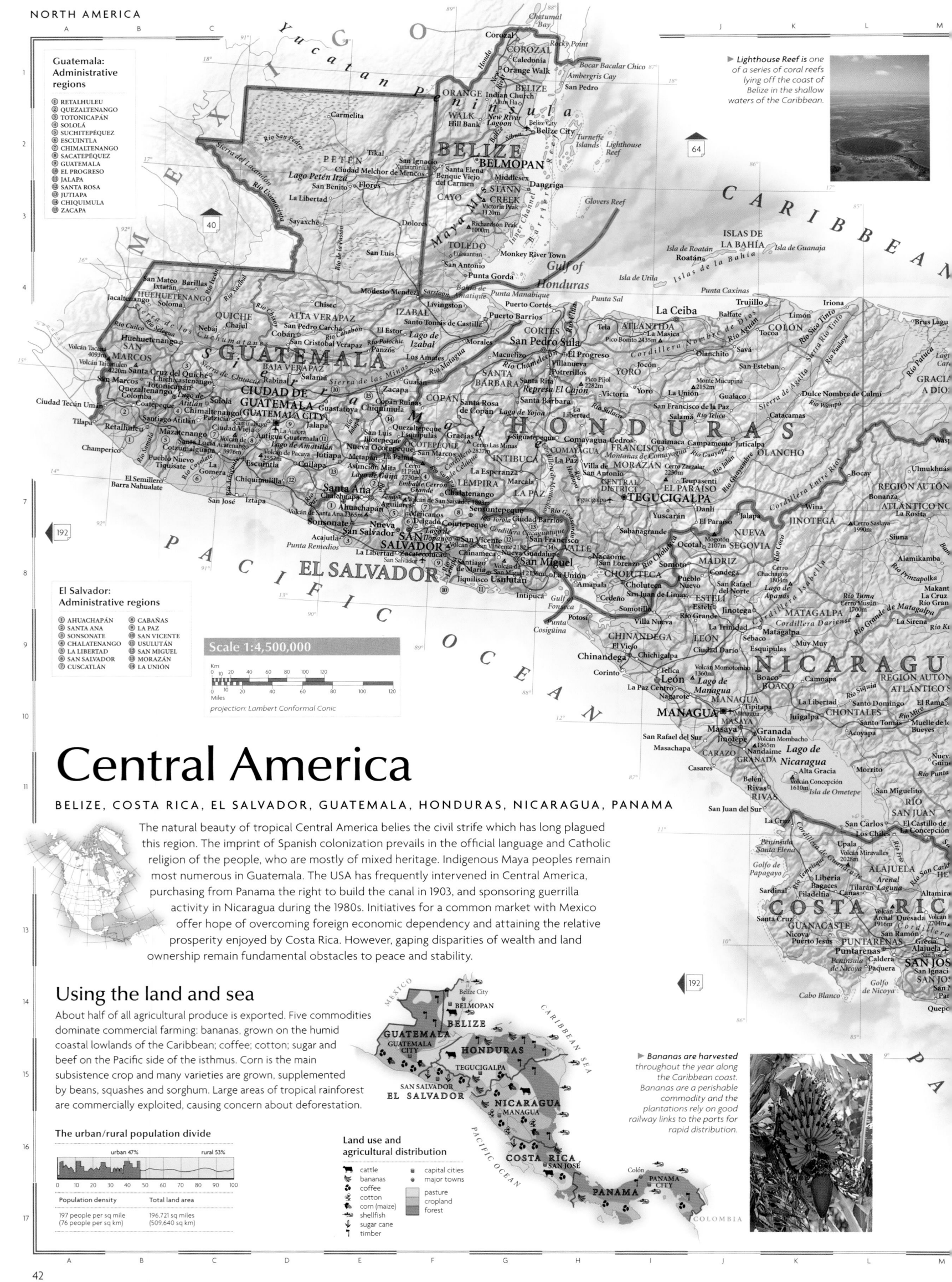

Guatemala: Administrative regions

① RETALHULEU
② QUEZALTENANGO
③ TOTONICAPÁN
④ SOLOLÁ
⑤ SUCHITEPÉQUEZ
⑥ ESCUINTLA
⑦ CHIMALTENANGO
⑧ SACATEPÉQUEZ
⑨ GUATEMALA
⑩ EL PROGRESO
⑪ JALAPA
⑫ SANTA ROSA
⑬ JUTIAPA
⑭ CHIQUIMULA
⑮ ZACAPA

► *Lighthouse Reef is one of a series of coral reefs lying off the coast of Belize in the shallow waters of the Caribbean.*

El Salvador: Administrative regions

① AHUACHAPÁN
② SANTA ANA
③ SONSONATE
④ CHALATENANGO
⑤ LA LIBERTAD
⑥ SAN SALVADOR
⑦ CUSCATLÁN
⑧ CABAÑAS
⑨ LA PAZ
⑩ SAN VICENTE
⑪ USULUTÁN
⑫ SAN MIGUEL
⑬ MORAZÁN
⑭ LA UNIÓN

Scale 1:4,500,000

Km 0 20 40 60 80 100 120
Miles 0 20 40 60 80 100 120

projection: Lambert Conformal Conic

Central America

BELIZE, COSTA RICA, EL SALVADOR, GUATEMALA, HONDURAS, NICARAGUA, PANAMA

The natural beauty of tropical Central America belies the civil strife which has long plagued this region. The imprint of Spanish colonization prevails in the official language and Catholic religion of the people, who are mostly of mixed heritage. Indigenous Maya peoples remain most numerous in Guatemala. The USA has frequently intervened in Central America, purchasing from Panama the right to build the canal in 1903, and sponsoring guerrilla activity in Nicaragua during the 1980s. Initiatives for a common market with Mexico offer hope of overcoming foreign economic dependency and attaining the relative prosperity enjoyed by Costa Rica. However, gaping disparities of wealth and land ownership remain fundamental obstacles to peace and stability.

Using the land and sea

About half of all agricultural produce is exported. Five commodities dominate commercial farming: bananas, grown on the humid coastal lowlands of the Caribbean; coffee; cotton; sugar and beef on the Pacific side of the isthmus. Corn is the main subsistence crop and many varieties are grown, supplemented by beans, squashes and sorghum. Large areas of tropical rainforest are commercially exploited, causing concern about deforestation.

► *Bananas are harvested throughout the year along the Caribbean coast. Bananas are a perishable commodity and the plantations rely on good railway links to the ports for rapid distribution.*

The urban/rural population divide

urban 47%   rural 53%
0 10 20 30 40 50 60 70 80 90 100

Population density
197 people per sq mile
(76 people per sq km)

Total land area
196,721 sq miles
(509,640 sq km)

Land use and agricultural distribution

- cattle
- bananas
- coffee
- cotton
- corn (maize)
- shellfish
- sugar cane
- timber
- ▪ capital cities
- • major towns
- pasture
- cropland
- forest

42

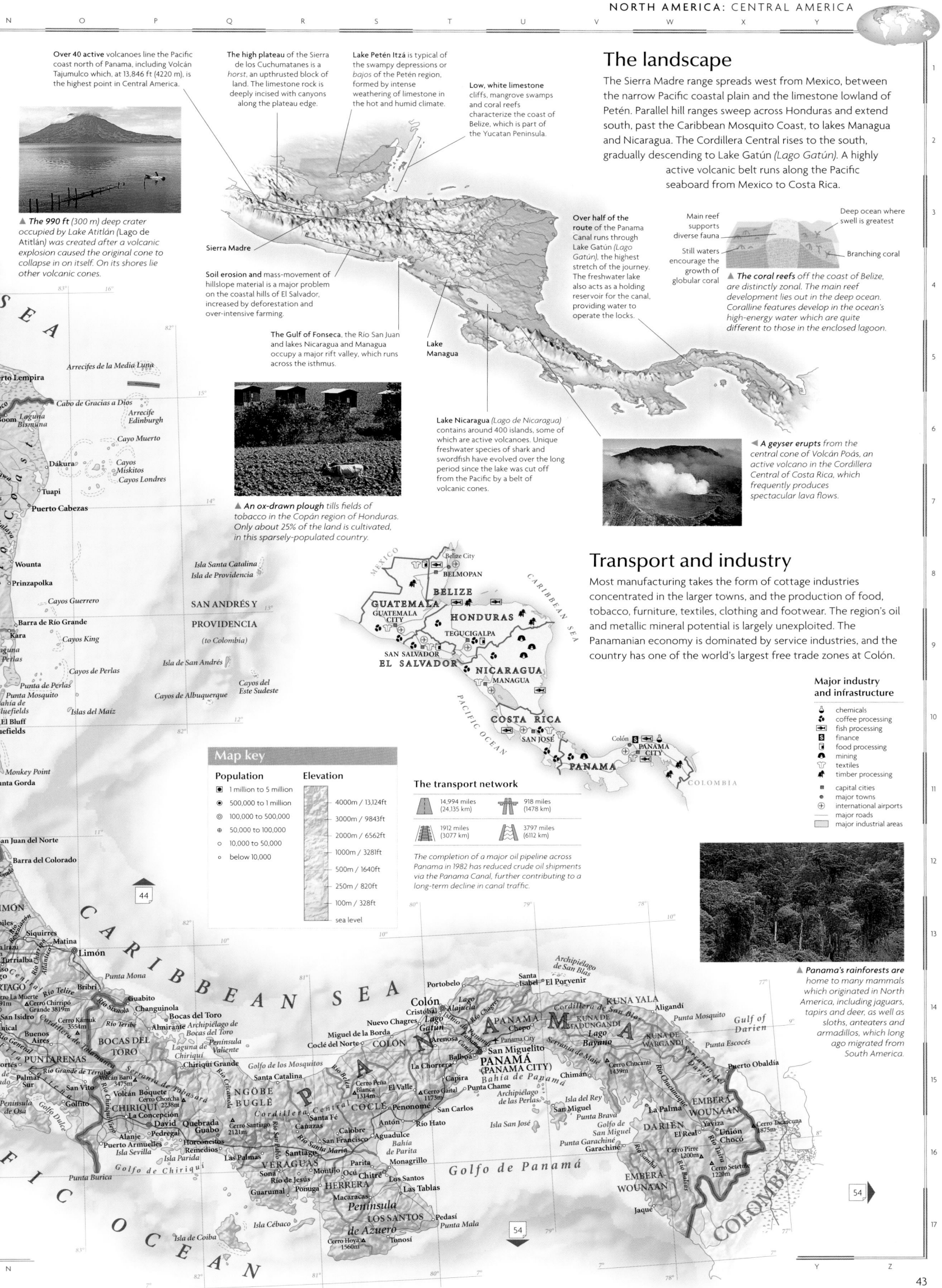

Over 40 active volcanoes line the Pacific coast north of Panama, including Volcán Tajumulco which, at 13,846 ft (4220 m), is the highest point in Central America.

▲ *The 990 ft (300 m) deep crater occupied by Lake Atitlán (Lago de Atitlán) was created after a volcanic explosion caused the original cone to collapse in on itself. On its shores lie other volcanic cones.*

The high plateau of the Sierra de los Cuchumatanes is a *horst*, an upthrusted block of land. The limestone rock is deeply incised with canyons along the plateau edge.

Lake Petén Itzá is typical of the swampy depressions or *bajos* of the Petén region, formed by intense weathering of limestone in the hot and humid climate.

Low, white limestone cliffs, mangrove swamps and coral reefs characterize the coast of Belize, which is part of the Yucatan Peninsula.

Sierra Madre

Soil erosion and mass-movement of hillslope material is a major problem on the coastal hills of El Salvador, increased by deforestation and over-intensive farming.

The Gulf of Fonseca, the Rio San Juan and lakes Nicaragua and Managua occupy a major rift valley, which runs across the isthmus.

Lake Managua

Over half of the route of the Panama Canal runs through Lake Gatún (*Lago Gatún*), the highest stretch of the journey. The freshwater lake also acts as a holding reservoir for the canal, providing water to operate the locks.

The landscape

The Sierra Madre range spreads west from Mexico, between the narrow Pacific coastal plain and the limestone lowland of Petén. Parallel hill ranges sweep across Honduras and extend south, past the Caribbean Mosquito Coast, to lakes Managua and Nicaragua. The Cordillera Central rises to the south, gradually descending to Lake Gatún (*Lago Gatún*). A highly active volcanic belt runs along the Pacific seaboard from Mexico to Costa Rica.

Main reef supports diverse fauna
Still waters encourage the growth of globular coral
Deep ocean where swell is greatest
Branching coral

▲ *The coral reefs off the coast of Belize, are distinctly zonal. The main reef development lies out in the deep ocean. Coralline features develop in the ocean's high-energy water which are quite different to those in the enclosed lagoon.*

Lake Nicaragua (*Lago de Nicaragua*) contains around 400 islands, some of which are active volcanoes. Unique freshwater species of shark and swordfish have evolved over the long period since the lake was cut off from the Pacific by a belt of volcanic cones.

▲ *An ox-drawn plough tills fields of tobacco in the Copán region of Honduras. Only about 25% of the land is cultivated, in this sparsely-populated country.*

◀ *A geyser erupts from the central cone of Volcán Poás, an active volcano in the Cordillera Central of Costa Rica, which frequently produces spectacular lava flows.*

Transport and industry

Most manufacturing takes the form of cottage industries concentrated in the larger towns, and the production of food, tobacco, furniture, textiles, clothing and footwear. The region's oil and metallic mineral potential is largely unexploited. The Panamanian economy is dominated by service industries, and the country has one of the world's largest free trade zones at Colón.

Major industry and infrastructure

- chemicals
- coffee processing
- fish processing
- finance
- food processing
- mining
- textiles
- timber processing

- ■ capital cities
- ● major towns
- ✈ international airports
- — major roads
- ▢ major industrial areas

Map key

Population
- 1 million to 5 million
- 500,000 to 1 million
- 100,000 to 500,000
- 50,000 to 100,000
- 10,000 to 50,000
- below 10,000

Elevation
- 4000m / 13,124ft
- 3000m / 9843ft
- 2000m / 6562ft
- 1000m / 3281ft
- 500m / 1640ft
- 250m / 820ft
- 100m / 328ft
- sea level

The transport network

14,994 miles (24,135 km)
918 miles (1478 km)
1912 miles (3077 km)
3797 miles (6112 km)

The completion of a major oil pipeline across Panama in 1982 has reduced crude oil shipments via the Panama Canal, further contributing to a long-term decline in canal traffic.

▲ *Panama's rainforests are home to many mammals which originated in North America, including jaguars, tapirs and deer, as well as sloths, anteaters and armadillos, which long ago migrated from South America.*

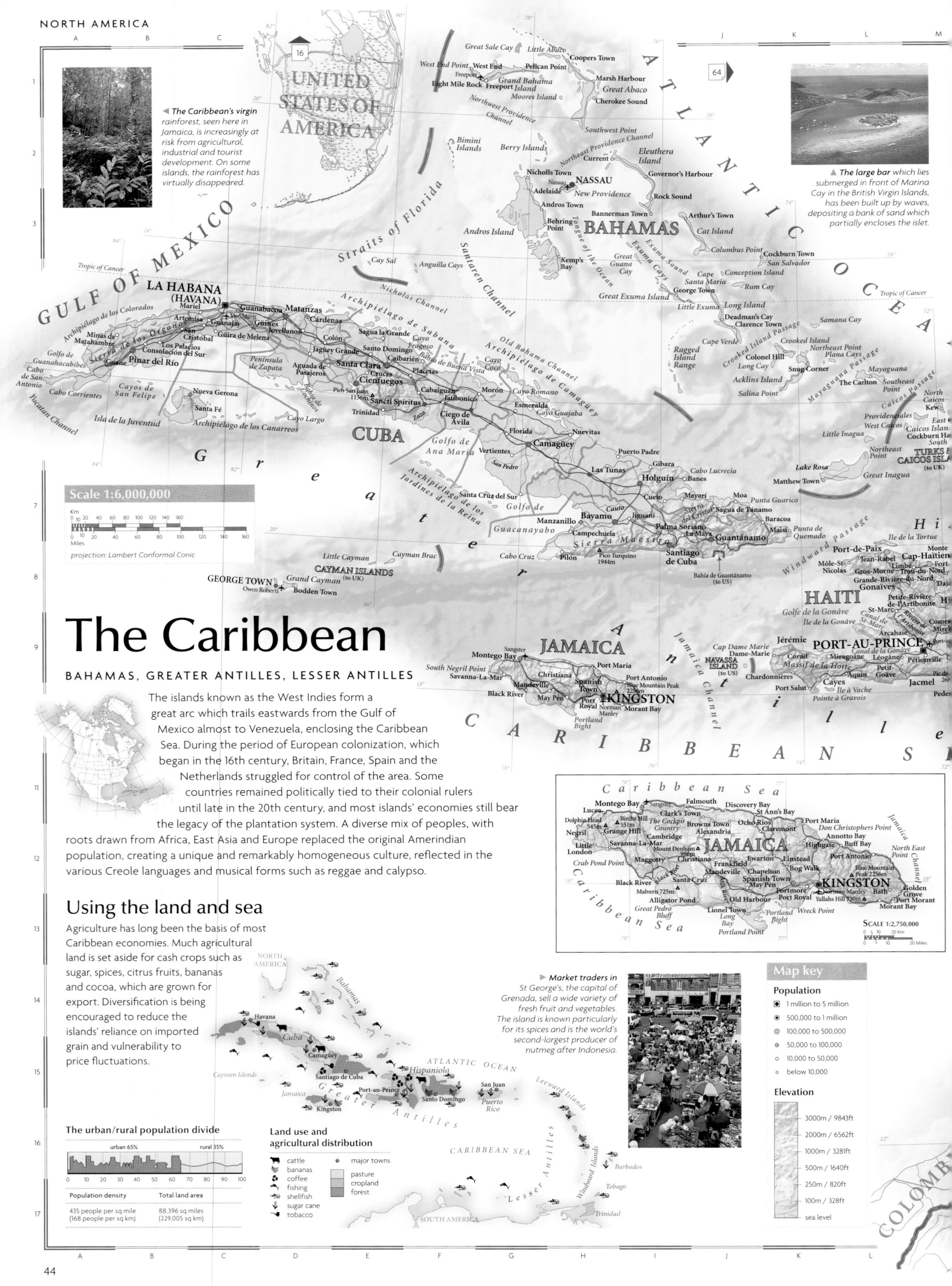

The Caribbean's virgin rainforest, seen here in Jamaica, is increasingly at risk from agricultural, industrial and tourist development. On some islands, the rainforest has virtually disappeared.

The large bar which lies submerged in front of Marina Cay in the British Virgin Islands, has been built up by waves, depositing a bank of sand which partially encloses the islet.

The Caribbean

BAHAMAS, GREATER ANTILLES, LESSER ANTILLES

The islands known as the West Indies form a great arc which trails eastwards from the Gulf of Mexico almost to Venezuela, enclosing the Caribbean Sea. During the period of European colonization, which began in the 16th century, Britain, France, Spain and the Netherlands struggled for control of the area. Some countries remained politically tied to their colonial rulers until late in the 20th century, and most islands' economies still bear the legacy of the plantation system. A diverse mix of peoples, with roots drawn from Africa, East Asia and Europe replaced the original Amerindian population, creating a unique and remarkably homogeneous culture, reflected in the various Creole languages and musical forms such as reggae and calypso.

Using the land and sea

Agriculture has long been the basis of most Caribbean economies. Much agricultural land is set aside for cash crops such as sugar, spices, citrus fruits, bananas and cocoa, which are grown for export. Diversification is being encouraged to reduce the islands' reliance on imported grain and vulnerability to price fluctuations.

Scale 1:6,000,000
projection: Lambert Conformal Conic

SCALE 1:2,750,000

Market traders in St George's, the capital of Grenada, sell a wide variety of fresh fruit and vegetables. The island is known particularly for its spices and is the world's second-largest producer of nutmeg after Indonesia.

Map key

Population
- 1 million to 5 million
- 500,000 to 1 million
- 100,000 to 500,000
- 50,000 to 100,000
- 10,000 to 50,000
- below 10,000

Elevation
- 3000m / 9843ft
- 2000m / 6562ft
- 1000m / 3281ft
- 500m / 1640ft
- 250m / 820ft
- 100m / 328ft
- sea level

The urban/rural population divide
urban 65% / rural 35%

Population density: 435 people per sq mile (168 people per sq km)
Total land area: 88,396 sq miles (229,005 sq km)

Land use and agricultural distribution
- cattle
- bananas
- coffee
- fishing
- shellfish
- sugar cane
- tobacco
- major towns
- pasture
- cropland
- forest

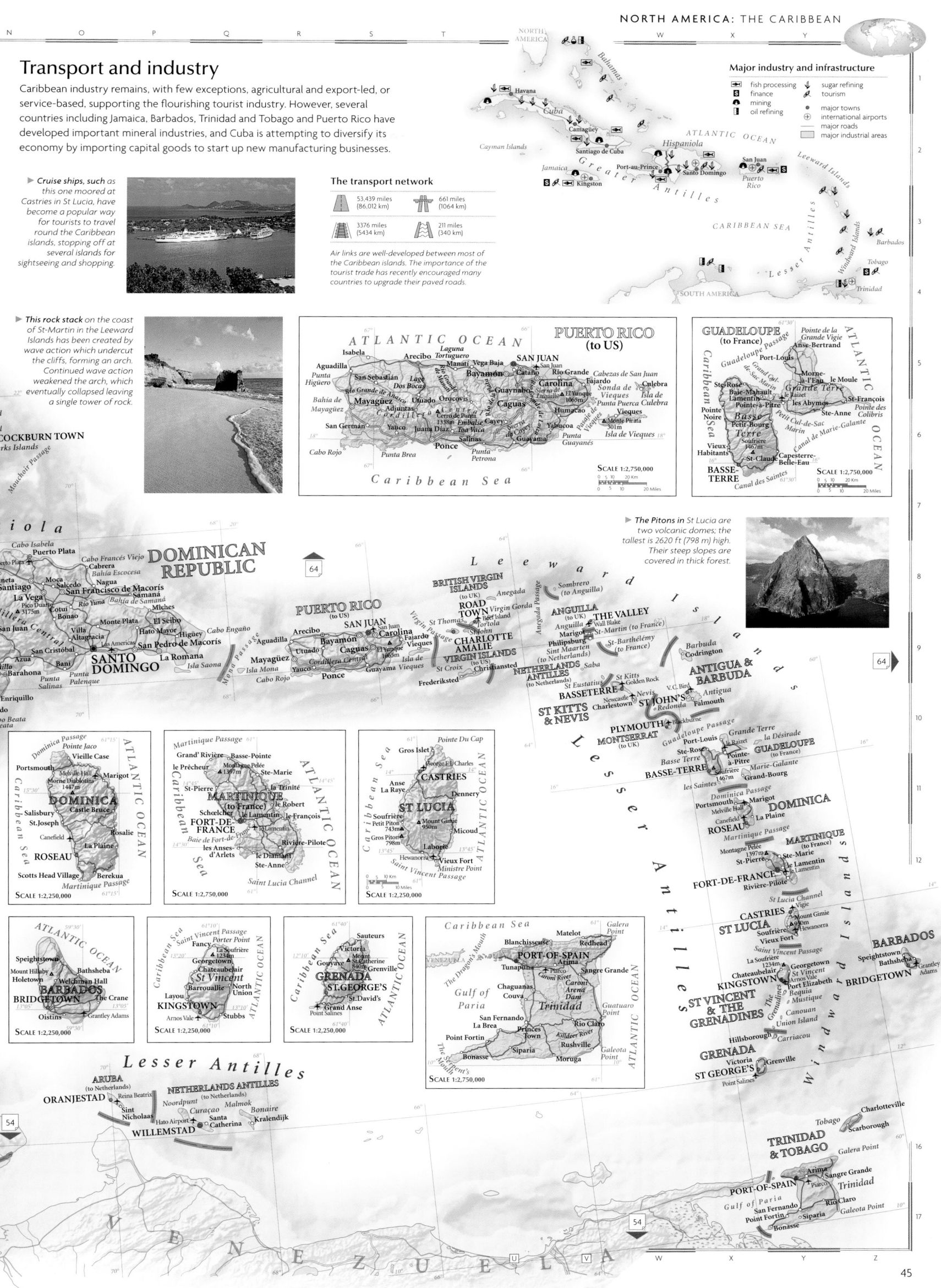

Transport and industry

Caribbean industry remains, with few exceptions, agricultural and export-led, or service-based, supporting the flourishing tourist industry. However, several countries including Jamaica, Barbados, Trinidad and Tobago and Puerto Rico have developed important mineral industries, and Cuba is attempting to diversify its economy by importing capital goods to start up new manufacturing businesses.

▶ *Cruise ships, such as* this one moored at Castries in St Lucia, have become a popular way for tourists to travel round the Caribbean islands, stopping off at several islands for sightseeing and shopping.

Major industry and infrastructure

- fish processing
- finance
- mining
- oil refining
- sugar refining
- tourism
- major towns
- international airports
- major roads
- major industrial areas

The transport network

53,439 miles (86,012 km)	661 miles (1064 km)
3376 miles (5434 km)	211 miles (340 km)

Air links are well-developed between most of the Caribbean islands. The importance of the tourist trade has recently encouraged many countries to upgrade their paved roads.

▶ *This rock stack* on the coast of St-Martin in the Leeward Islands has been created by wave action which undercut the cliffs, forming an arch. Continued wave action weakened the arch, which eventually collapsed leaving a single tower of rock.

▶ *The Pitons in* St Lucia are two volcanic domes; the tallest is 2620 ft (798 m) high. Their steep slopes are covered in thick forest.

PUERTO RICO (to US)
SCALE 1:2,750,000

GUADELOUPE (to France)
SCALE 1:2,750,000

DOMINICA
SCALE 1:2,250,000

MARTINIQUE (to France)
SCALE 1:2,750,000

ST LUCIA
SCALE 1:2,250,000

BARBADOS
SCALE 1:2,250,000

ST VINCENT
SCALE 1:2,250,000

GRENADA
SCALE 1:2,250,000

TRINIDAD & TOBAGO
SCALE 1:2,750,000

South America

Reaching from the humid tropics down into the cold south Atlantic, South America has an area of 6,886,000 sq miles (17,835,000 sq km). There are 12 separate countries, with the largest, Brazil, covering almost half the continent.

○ *Greatest extent, North–South: 4750 miles / 7640 km*
□ *Greatest extent, East–West: 3100 miles / 4990 km*

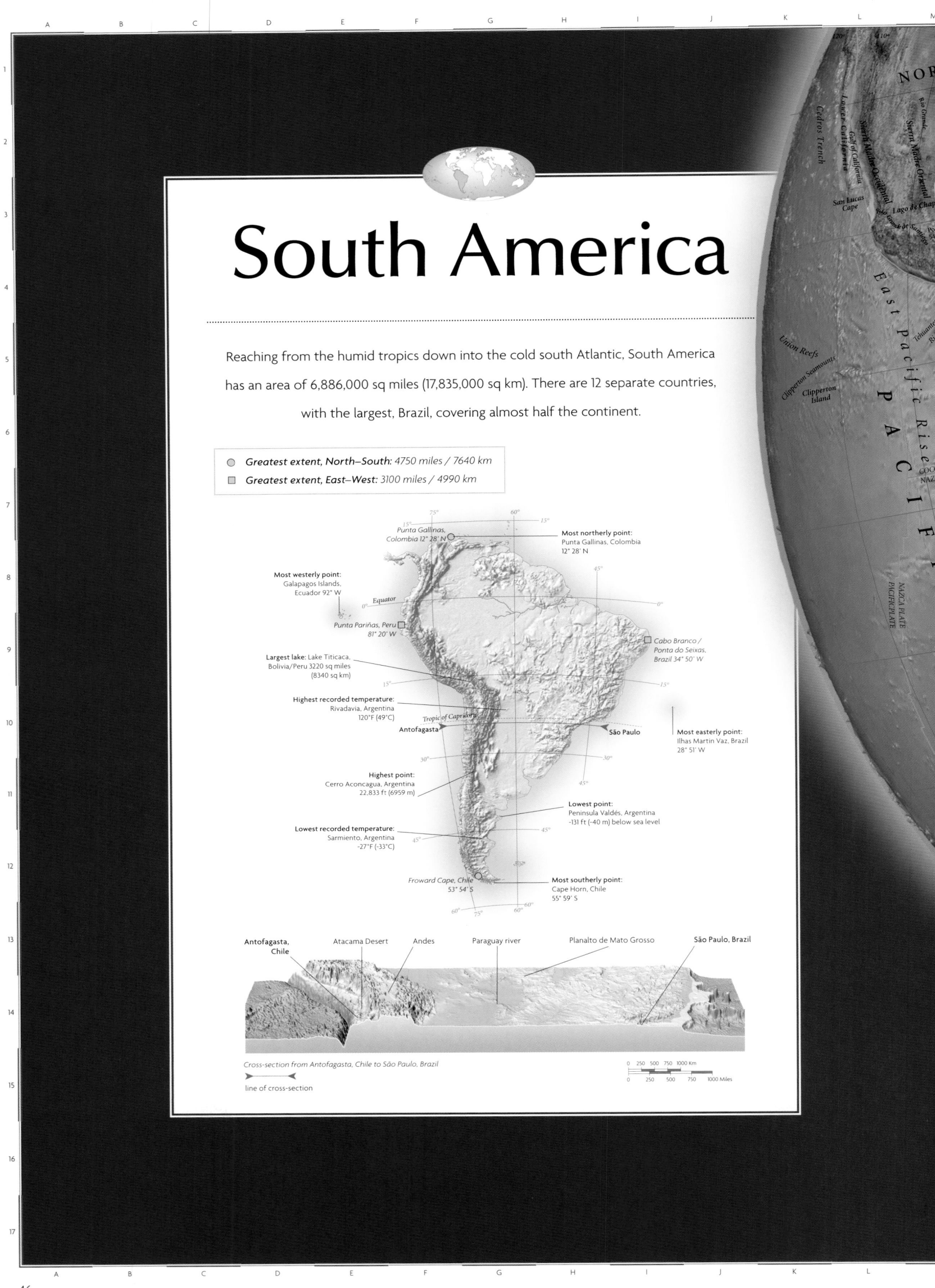

Punta Gallinas, Colombia 12° 28' N

Most northerly point:
Punta Gallinas, Colombia
12° 28' N

Most westerly point:
Galapagos Islands,
Ecuador 92° W

Equator

Punta Pariñas, Peru
81° 20' W

Cabo Branco /
Ponta do Seixas,
Brazil 34° 50' W

Largest lake: Lake Titicaca,
Bolivia/Peru 3220 sq miles
(8340 sq km)

Highest recorded temperature:
Rivadavia, Argentina
120°F (49°C)

Tropic of Capricorn

Antofagasta

São Paulo

Most easterly point:
Ilhas Martin Vaz, Brazil
28° 51' W

Highest point:
Cerro Aconcagua, Argentina
22,833 ft (6959 m)

Lowest point:
Peninsula Valdés, Argentina
-131 ft (-40 m) below sea level

Lowest recorded temperature:
Sarmiento, Argentina
-27°F (-33°C)

Froward Cape, Chile
53° 54' S

Most southerly point:
Cape Horn, Chile
55° 59' S

Antofagasta, Chile | Atacama Desert | Andes | Paraguay river | Planalto de Mato Grosso | São Paulo, Brazil

Cross-section from Antofagasta, Chile to São Paulo, Brazil

line of cross-section

0 250 500 750 1000 Km
0 250 500 750 1000 Miles

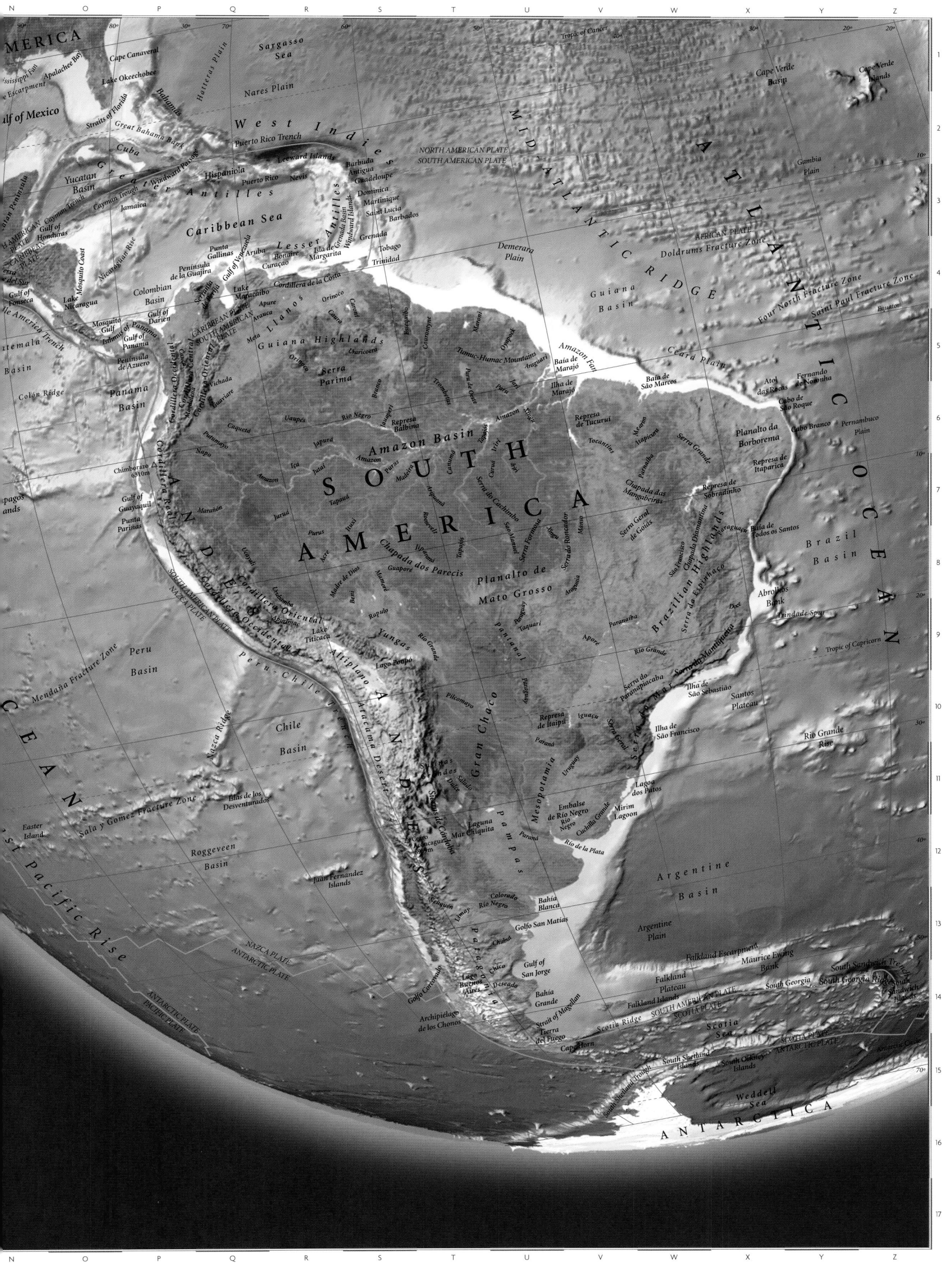

N O P Q R S T U V W X Y Z

AMERICA

Mississippi Fan
Apalachee Bay
Cape Canaveral
Cape Canaveral
Sargasso Sea
Cape Verde
Cape Verde Islands

Escarpment
Lake Okeechobee
Hatteras Plain
Nares Plain
Cape Verde Basin

Gulf of Mexico
Straits of Florida
Great Bahama Bank
Bahamas
West Indies
Cape Verde Basin

Yucatan Peninsula
Cuba
Puerto Rico Trench
Barbuda
Gumbia Plain

Yucatan Basin
Jamaica
Hispaniola
Puerto Rico
Leeward Islands
Barbuda
Antigua
Guadeloupe
NORTH AMERICAN PLATE
SOUTH AMERICAN PLATE

Cayman Trough
Windward Passage
Dominica
AFRICAN PLATE

Gulf of Honduras
Caribbean Sea
Lesser Antilles
Martinique
Saint Lucia
Barbados
Doldrums Fracture Zone

Gulf of Fonseca
Mosquito Coast
Punta Gallinas
Aruba
Grenada
Tobago
Demerara Plain

Nicaraguan Rise
Peninsula de la Guajira
Curaçao
Isla de Margarita
Trinidad
Guiana Basin

Colombian Basin
Lake Maracaibo
Cordillera de la Costa
Four North Fracture Zone

Mosquito Gulf
Gulf of Darien
Apure
Orinoco
Saint Paul Fracture Zone

Isthmus of Panama
Llanos
Guayana Highlands
Casiquiare
Ceará Plain
Equator

Peninsula de Azuero
Cordillera Occidental
Serra Parima
Uaricoera
Tumuc-Humac Mountains
Amazon Fan
Atol das Rocas
Fernando de Noronha

Colón Ridge
Cordillera Oriental
Orinoco
Branco
Pará de Oeste
Araguari
Baía de Marajó
Cabo de São Roque

Panama Basin
Chimborazo 6310m
Napo
Putumayo
Uaupés
Rio Negro
Trombetas
Ilha de Marajó
Baía de São Marcos
Planalto da Borborema
Cabo Branco
Pernambuco Plain

Gulf of Guayaquil
Caquetá
Içá
Japurá
Represa Balbina
SOUTH
Amazon
Xingu
Represa de Tucuruí
Mearim
Atapicuru
Serra Grande
Represa de Itaparica

Galápagos Islands
Punta Parinas
Marañón
Jutaí
Juruá
Purus
Amazon
Madeira
Tapajós
Purus
Tocantins
Parnaíba
Chapada das Mangabeiras

Peru Basin
Cordillera Real
Uçayali
AMERICA
Araguaia
São Francisco
Chapada Diamantina
Represa de Sobradinho

Mendaña Fracture Zone
Chapada dos Parecis
Guaporé
Planalto de Mato Grosso
Serra Roncador
Serra Gerais de Goiás
Brazilian Highlands
Serra do Espinhaço
Baía de Todos os Santos

Nazca Ridge
Madre de Dios
Beni
Paraná
Serra Formosa
Xingu
Manso
Doce
Brazil Basin

Cordillera Occidental
Rapulo
Yungas
Rio Grande
Tocantins
Paranaíba
Abrolhos Bank

Chile Basin
Altiplano
Lake Titicaca
Lago Poopó
A N D E S
Pantanal
Apore
Rio Grande
Serra da Mantiqueira
Trindade Spur

Islas de los Desventurados
Pilcomayo
Gran Chaco
Paraguay
Uruguay
Serra do Paranapiacaba
Ilha de São Sebastião
Santos Plateau
Tropic of Capricorn

Sala y Gomez Fracture Zone
Atacama Desert
Represa de Itaipú
Iguaçu
Serra Geral
Ilha de São Francisco

Easter Island
Roggeveen Basin
Laguna Mar Chiquita
Mesopotamia
Paraná
Embalse de Río Negro
Lagoa dos Patos
Rio Grande Rise

Juan Fernandez Islands
Aconcagua 6959m
Córdoba
P a m p a s
Río Negro
Mirim Lagoon
Cuchilla Grande

East Pacific Rise
Colorado
Río Negro
Rio de la Plata

NAZCA PLATE
Bahía Blanca
Argentine Basin

ANTARCTIC PLATE
Limay
Chubut
Golfo San Matías
Argentine Plain

ANTARCTIC PLATE
PACIFIC PLATE
Lago Buenos Aires
Chico
Gulf of San Jorge
Falkland Escarpment
Maurice Ewing Bank
South Sandwich Trench

Golfo Corcovado
Deseado
Bahía Grande
Falkland Plateau
South Georgia
South Georgia Ridge
South Sandwich Islands

Archipiélago de los Chonos
Strait of Magellan
Falkland Islands
SOUTH AMERICAN PLATE
Scotia Sea

Tierra del Fuego
Scotia Ridge
SCOTIA PLATE

Cape Horn
South Shetland Islands
South Orkney Islands
SCOTIA PLATE
ANTARCTIC PLATE
Antarctic Circle

South Shetland Trough
Weddell Sea

ANTARCTICA

Physical South America

Three major physiographic regions characterize South America. The oldest, the ancient Brazilian Shield and the smaller Guiana and Patagonian shields, form the stable core of the continent. Stretching along the entire west coast are the younger Andean fold mountains with many summits rising to 20,000 ft (6100 m). These two diverse regions are separated by a number of sedimentary basins carrying South America's large river systems to the sea. These include the massive Amazon Basin and the basin of the Gran Chaco.

The Amazon Basin and Guiana Shield

The Amazon river occupies a large depression in the Earth's crust, formed by the uplift of the Andes. It is covered by thick volcanic deposits and layers of alluvium – these have been laid down by the Amazon's many tributaries. To the north is the smaller Guiana Shield.

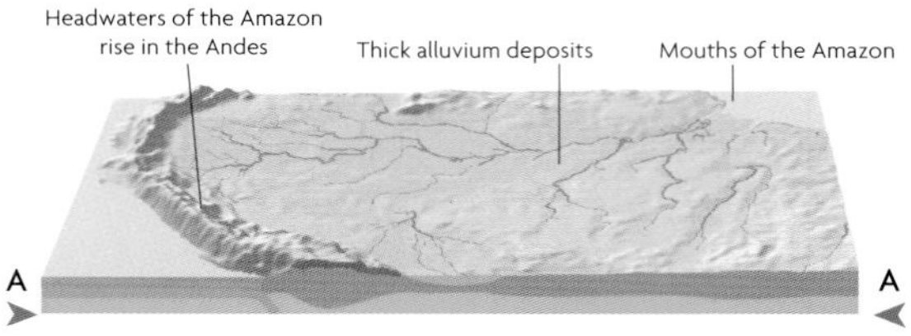

Headwaters of the Amazon rise in the Andes · Thick alluvium deposits · Mouths of the Amazon

A — A

Section across northern South America showing Amazon Basin and its drainage pattern.

0 500 1000 Km
0 500 1000 Miles

Scale 1:30,500,000

Km 0 200 400 600 800
Miles 0 200 400 600 800

projection: Lambert Azimuthal Equal Area

The Andean Uplands

The Andean Uplands run along the west coast of South America. They are being uplifted as the Nazca Plate is subducted beneath the South American Plate. They contain some of the world's largest volcanoes, such as Cotopaxi, and Lake Titicaca which occupies a dormant site. The far south has many large ice-sheets and a fragmented coastline.

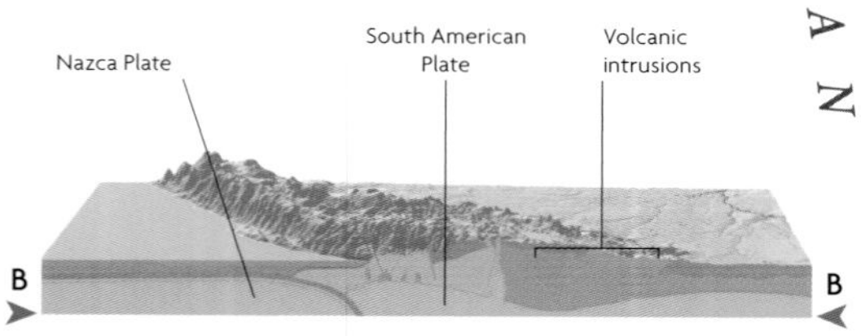

Nazca Plate · South American Plate · Volcanic intrusions

B — B

Cross-section through the Andes showing the subduction of the Nazca Plate beneath the South American Plate.

0 200 400 Km
0 200 400 Miles

The Brazilian Shield and Gran Chaco

The immense Brazilian Shield underlies more than one-third of South America. It is pitted with numerous volcanic intrusions, and a large basaltic plateau exists between the Paraná river and the Atlantic Ocean. The flat Gran Chaco lies to the west of the shield, covered by sedimentary deposits eroded from the Andes, and transported by South America's mighty rivers.

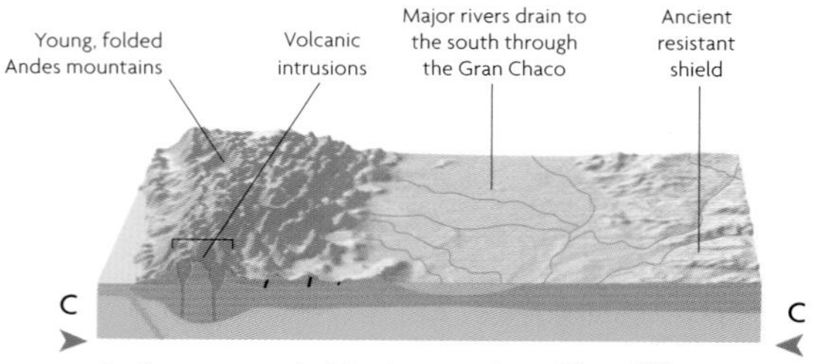

Young, folded Andes mountains · Volcanic intrusions · Major rivers drain to the south through the Gran Chaco · Ancient resistant shield

C — C

Section across central South America showing the flat basin of the Gran Chaco and the ancient Brazilian Shield.

0 200 400 Km
0 200 400 Miles

Map key

Elevation

6000m / 19,686ft
4000m / 13,124ft
3000m / 9843ft
2000m / 6562ft
1000m / 3281ft
500m / 1640ft
250m / 820ft
100m / 328ft
sea level

Plate margins
(for explanation see page xiv)

constructive
destructive
conservative
uncertain

physiographic regions

line of cross-section

Map labels

Punta Gallinas
Gulf of Venezuela
Lake Maracaibo
Gulf of Darien
Gulf of Panama
Cauca
Magdalena
Orinoco
Llanos
Pakaraima Mountains
GUIANA SHIELD
Guiana Highlands
Tumuc-Humac Mountains
Cordillera Occidental
Cordillera Central
Cordillera Oriental
Rio Negro
Branco
Japurá
Represa Balbina
Amazon
Ilha de Marajó
Cabo de São Roque
Cordillera Real
Cotopaxi 5897m
Chimborazo 6310m
Putumayo
Amazon
Amazon Basin
Purus
Madeira
Tapajós
Xingu
Serra dos Carajás
Planalto da Borborema
Gulf of Guayaquil
Marañón
Juruá
Serra de Cachimbo
Serra Formosa
Araguaia
Tocantins
Represa de Sobradinho
Punta Negra
Nevado Huascarán 6768m
Ucayali
Madre de Dios
Chapada dos Parecis
Guaporé
Planalto de Mato Grosso
Serra do Roncador
Serra Dourada
São Francisco
BRAZILIAN SHIELD
Brazilian Highlands
Lake Titicaca
Altiplano
Lago Poopó
Pantanal
Serra do Espinhaço
PACIFIC OCEAN
ATLANTIC OCEAN
COCOS PLATE
NAZCA PLATE
Pilcomayo
Serra de Maracaju
Serra do Caiapó
Paraná
Serra da Mantiqueira
SOUTH AMERICAN PLATE
NAZCA PLATE
ANDEAN SYSTEM
Atacama Desert
Gran Chaco
Paraguay
Uruguay
Serra Geral
Serra do Mar
Cerro Ojos del Salado 6880m
Mesopotamia
Lagoa dos Patos
Cerro Aconcagua 6959m
Pampas
Paraná
Mirim Lagoon
Salado
Río de la Plata
Colorado
Río Negro
PATAGONIAN SHIELD
Patagonia
Isla de Chiloé
Península Valdés
Lago Colhué Huapí
Lago Chico
Gulf of San Jorge
Deseado
Golfo de Peñas
Bahía Grande
ANTARCTIC PLATE
Strait of Magellan
Tierra del Fuego
Falkland Islands
SOUTH AMERICAN PLATE
SCOTIA PLATE
Cape Horn

Climate

The climate of South America is influenced by three principal factors: the seasonal shift of high pressure air masses over the tropics, cold ocean currents along the western coast, affecting temperature and precipitation, and the mountain barrier produced by the Andes, which creates a rain shadow over much of the south.

▲ *Mild winters and cool summers typify the extensive Pampas grasslands of Argentina.*

▲ *Chile's hyper-arid Atacama Desert is renowned as one of the driest places on Earth.*

Climate
- tundra
- cool continental
- warm humid
- semi-arid
- arid
- humid equatorial
- tropical
- ☼ daily hours of sunshine, January
- ☼ daily hours of sunshine, July
- → cold wind

Temperature

Average January temperature

Average July temperature

Temperature
- below -30°C (-22°F)
- -30 to -20°C (-22 to -4°F)
- -20 to -10°C (-4 to 14°F)
- -10 to 0°C (14 to 32°F)
- 0 to 10°C (32 to 50°F)
- 10 to 20°C (50°F)
- 20 to 30°C (68 to 86°F)
- above 30°C (86°F)

Rainfall

Average January rainfall

Average July rainfall

Rainfall
- 0–25 mm (0–1 in)
- 25–50 mm (1–2 in)
- 50–100 mm (2–4 in)
- 100–200 mm (4–8 in)
- 200–300 mm (8–12 in)
- 300–400 mm (12–16 in)
- 400–500 mm (16–20 in)
- more than 500 mm (20 in)

▲ *Tropical conditions are found across over half of South America. When both rainfall and temperatures are high, hot humid rainforests prevail.*

Shaping the continent

South America's active tectonic belt has been extensively folded over millions of years; landslides are still frequent in the mountains. The large river systems that erode the mountains flow across resistant shield areas, depositing sediment. Present-day glaciation affects the distinctive landscape of the far south.

Mass movement

6 Debris slides are common in the highlands of South America *(left)*. They occur where soil on a slope is saturated by rainwater and therefore less stable. The actual slides are often triggered by earthquakes.

- Scarp face left after soil has moved to the base of the slope
- Failure plane
- Toe of debris slide

Mass movement: A section of a debris slide

Chemical weathering

1 Table mountains *(left)* are the eroded remnants of an ancient upland. As water percolates along cracks in these high, flat-topped mountains it forms intricate cave systems. Chemical weathering also isolates large blocks which then collapse, accumulating as rockfalls at the foot of scarp slopes.

- Smooth summit dissected by deep gorges
- Rainfall
- Run-off surges down caverns as waterfalls

Chemical weathering: Erosion of the Guyana Shield

The evolving landscape

River systems

2 Along the Amazon *(above)* there is a great variation in rates of erosion. As the headwaters of the Amazon flow down from the Andes, they erode and transport vast quantities of sediment, and are known as whitewaters. Across the shield areas erosion rates are very low. These rivers, carrying rotting vegetation, are called blackwaters.

- Whitewater river
- Blackwater river
- Little erosion in shield areas
- Confluence of whitewater with blackwater

River systems: Suspended sediments in the Amazon

Folding

5 Folding occurs beneath the surface under high temperatures and pressures. Rocks become sufficiently malleable to flow and not fracture as tectonic plates collide. In the Valley of the Moon in Chile *(above)*, anticlines (or upfolds) and synclines (or troughs) have been exploited by erosion.

- Fold axis
- Anticline
- Syncline
- Fold axis

Folding: Synclines and anticlines

Deposition

4 Large alluvial fans are found extensively across South America *(above)*. Confined mountain rivers, carrying large quantities of eroded material, emerge from a mountain gorge onto the plains, where they deposit their load in huge fans.

- Confined stream in the mountains
- Subsequent fan
- Mountain front
- Fan forms as stream emerges onto the plain

Deposition: Formation of an alluvial fan

Landscape

- uplifting land
- stable land
- sinking land
- glacier
- → ocean current
- ▽ aluvial fan
- ▲ inselberg
- river

- Unstable front in deep water, where ice is fracturing
- Original extent of glacier
- Icebergs
- Stable front
- Glacier was grounded against a shoal

Glaciation: Retreating glacier in Patagonia

Glaciation

3 As fjord glaciers in Patagonia *(above)* retreat, they become grounded on shoals. In deeper water the base of the glacier becomes unstable, and icebergs break off (calve) until the glacier snout grounds once more.

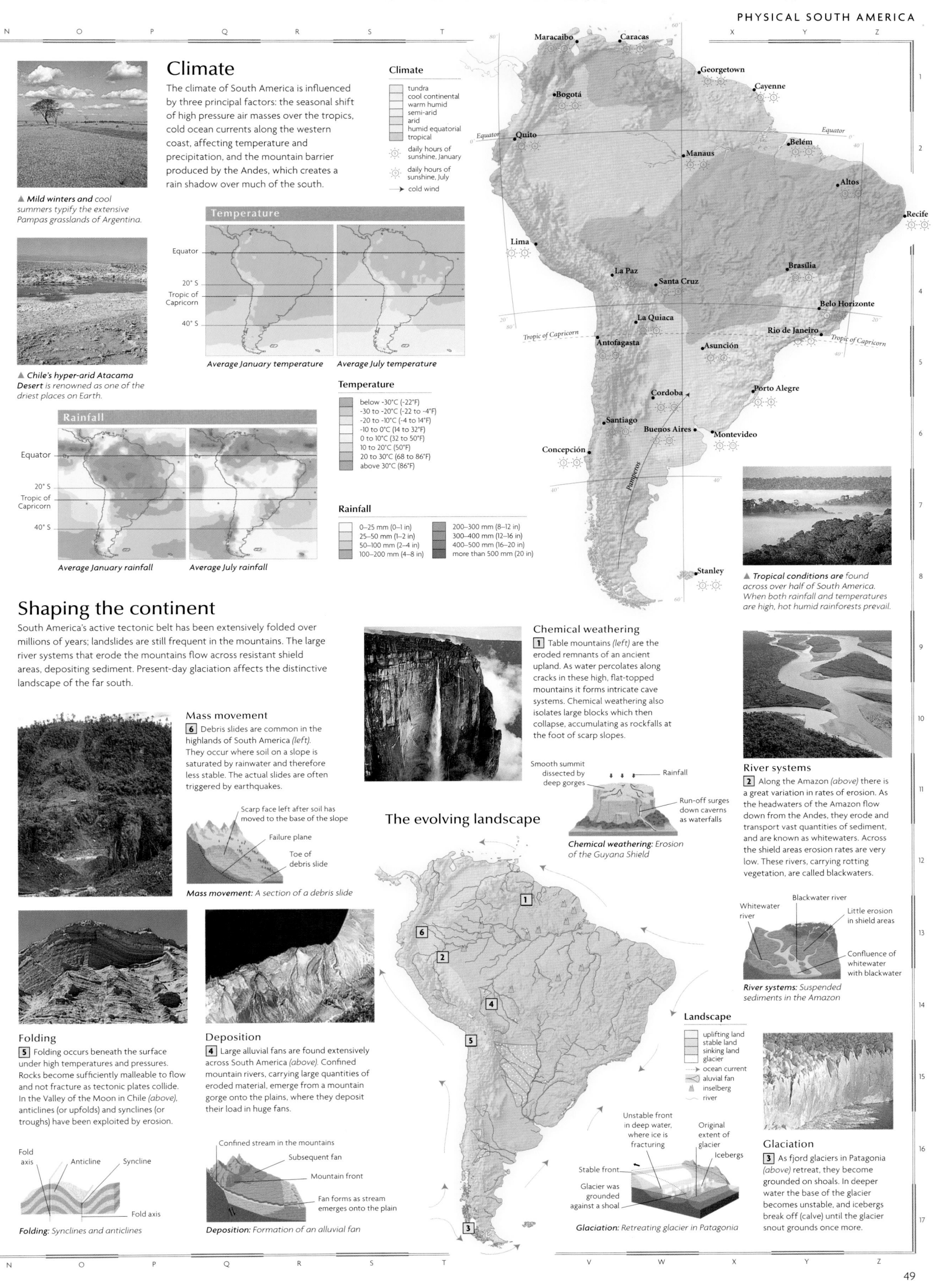

Maracaibo, Caracas, Georgetown, Cayenne, Bogotá, Quito, Belém, Manaus, Altos, Recife, Lima, La Paz, Santa Cruz, Brasília, Belo Horizonte, La Quiaca, Rio de Janeiro, Antofagasta, Asunción, Cordoba, Porto Alegre, Santiago, Buenos Aires, Montevideo, Concepción, Stanley

Equator, Tropic of Capricorn, Pamperos

Political South America

Modern South America's political boundaries have their origins in the territorial endeavours of explorers during the 16th century, who claimed almost the entire continent for Portugal and Spain. The Portuguese land in the east later evolved into the federal states of Brazil, while the Spanish vice-royalties eventually emerged as separate independent nation-states in the early 19th century. South America's growing population has become increasingly urbanized, with the expansion of coastal cities into large conurbations like Rio de Janeiro and Buenos Aires. In Brazil, Argentina, Chile and Uruguay, a succession of military dictatorships has given way to fragile, but strengthening, democracies.

◀ *Europe retains a* small foothold in South America. Kourou in French Guiana was the site chosen by the European Space Agency to launch the Ariane rocket. As a result of its status as a French overseas department, French Guiana is actually part of the European Union.

Scale 1:24,000,000

Km
0 100 200 300 400 500 600 700 800

Miles
0 100 200 300 400 500 600 700 800

projection: Lambert Azimuthal Equal Area

Transport

Most major road and rail routes are confined to the coastal regions by the forbidding natural barriers of the Andes mountains and the Amazon Basin. Few major cross-continental routes exist, although Buenos Aires serves as a transport centre for the main rail links to La Paz and Valparaíso, while the construction of the Trans-Amazon and Pan-American Highways have made direct road travel possible from Recife to Lima and from Puerto Montt up the coast into central America. A new waterway project is proposed to transform the Paraguay river into a major shipping route, although it involves considerable wetland destruction.

▶ *South America's most* extensive rail network is centred on the Argentinian capital, Buenos Aires. The construction of new rail lines from this important port, allowed the colonization of the Pampas lands for agriculture.

Languages

Prior to European exploration in the 16th century, a diverse range of indigenous languages were spoken across the continent. With the arrival of Iberian settlers, Spanish became the dominant language, with Portuguese spoken in Brazil, and Native American languages such as Quechua and Guaraní, becoming concentrated in the continental interior. Today this pattern persists, although successive European colonization has led to Dutch being spoken in Surinam, English in Guyana, and French in French Guiana, while in large urban areas, Japanese and Chinese are increasingly common.

Transport

— major roads and motorways
— major railways
- - - international borders
• transport intersections
⊕ international airports
⊕ major ports

Map labels:
Barranquilla, Cartagena, Ciénaga, Maracaibo, La Guaira, Caracas, La Cruz, Cúcuta, San Cristóbal, Bucaramanga, Georgetown, Buenaventura, Cali, Bogotá, Paramaribo, Cayenne, Quito, Guayaquil, Manaus, Santarém, Belém, São Luís, Fortaleza, Trans-Amazon Highway, Teresina, Porto Franco, Picos, Salgueiro, Recife, Humaitá, Juazeiro, Maceió, Porto Velho, Barreiras, Feira de Santana, Aracaju, Callao, Lima, Cuiabá, Brasília, Salvador, La Paz, Santa Cruz, Goiânia, Arequipa, Arica, São José do Rio Preto, Belo Horizonte, Campo Grande, Vitória, Ourinhos, Antofagasta, Salta, Asunción, Apucarana, São Paulo, Santos, Curitiba, Paranaguá, San Miguel de Tucumán, Resistencia, Coquimbo, Córdoba, Sante Fe, Santa Maria, Porto Alegre, Mendoza, San Luis, Rio Cuarto, Rosario, Rio Grande, Valparaíso, Santiago, Mercedes, Buenos Aires, San Rafael, Montevideo, Talcahuano, Concepción, Neuquén, Mar del Plata, Zapala, Bahía Blanca, Puerto Montt, Comodoro Rivadavia, Punta Arenas

Language groups
□ American Indian
□ Germanic
■ Romance

Language map labels: SPANISH, CARIBAN, ARAWAKAN, ENGLISH, DUTCH, FRENCH, QUECHUA, AYMARA, PORTUGUESE, GUARANI, SPANISH, GERMAN, GERMAN, GERMAN

▶ *Chile's main port,* Valparaíso, is a vital national shipping centre, in addition to playing a key role in the growing trade with Pacific nations. The country's awkward, elongated shape means that sea transport is frequently used for internal travel and communications in Chile.

▲ *Indigenous South American* lifestyles have not been totally submerged by European cultures and languages. The continental interior, and particularly the Amazon Basin, is still home to many different ethnic peoples.

▶ *Lima's magnificent* cathedral reflects South America's colonial past with its unmistakably Spanish style. In July 1821, Peru became the last Spanish colony on the mainland to declare independence.

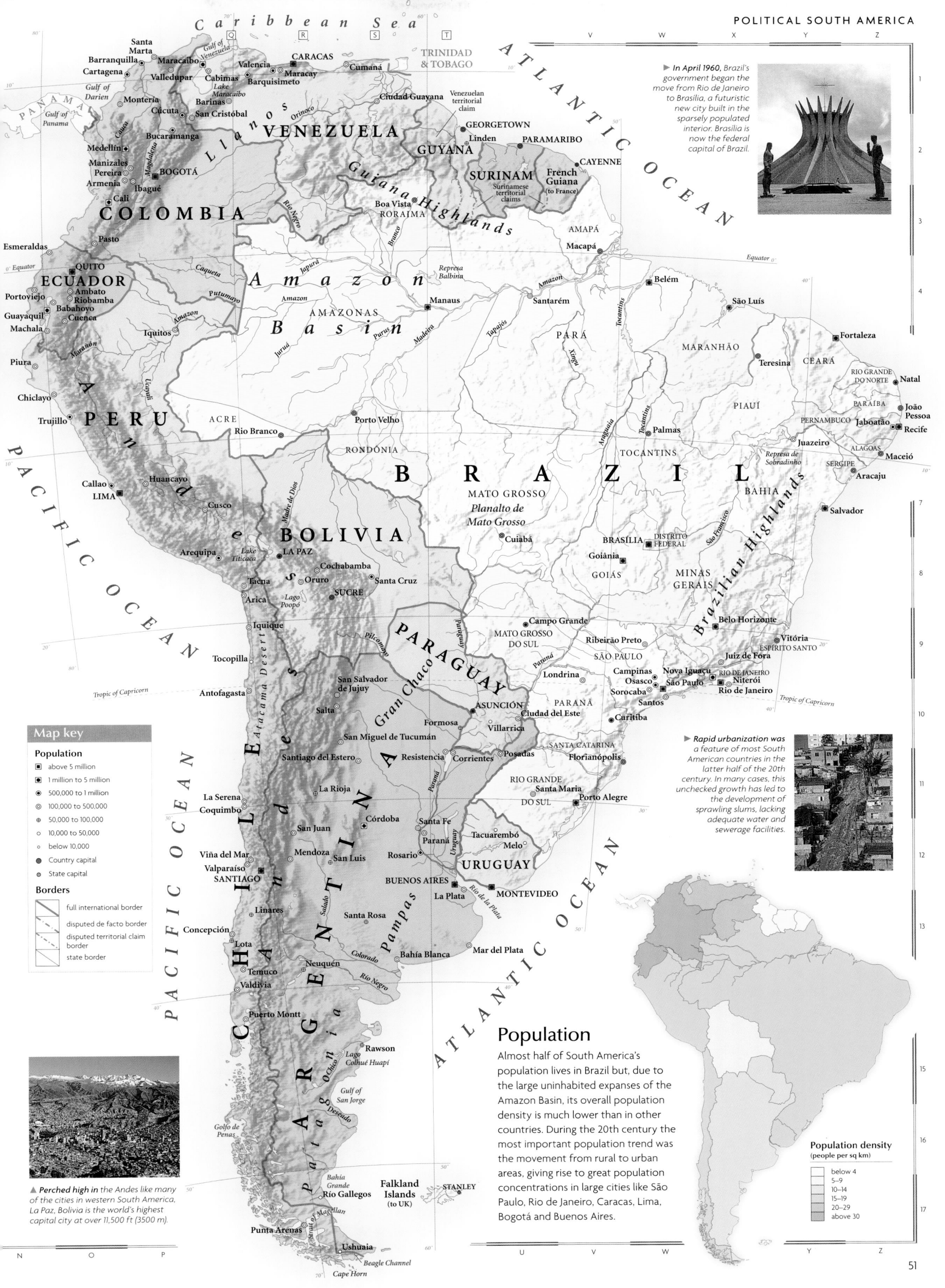

Caribbean Sea

TRINIDAD & TOBAGO

ATLANTIC OCEAN

VENEZUELA

Santa Marta
Barranquilla
Cartagena
Maracaibo
Valledupar
Valencia
CARACAS
Maracay
Cumaná
Cabimas
Barquisimeto
Monteria
Cúcuta
Barinas
San Cristóbal
Ciudad Guayana
Venezuelan territorial claim

Medellín
Manizales
Pereira
Armenia
Ibagué
BOGOTÁ
Cali

COLOMBIA

GEORGETOWN
Linden
PARAMARIBO
GUYANA
SURINAM
CAYENNE
French Guiana (to France)
Surinamese territorial claims

Boa Vista
RORAIMA

AMAPÁ

Esmeraldas
QUITO
Pasto

ECUADOR
Portoviejo
Ambato
Riobamba
Guayaquil
Babahoyo
Cuenca
Machala

Macapá

Belém

Santarém

São Luís

Fortaleza

Piura
Chiclayo

PERU

Iquitos

Amazon
AMAZONAS
Basin

Manaus

PARÁ

MARANHÃO

Teresina

CEARÁ

RIO GRANDE DO NORTE
Natal
PARAÍBA
João Pessoa
Jaboatão
Recife

Trujillo

Rio Branco
ACRE
Porto Velho
RONDÔNIA

B R A Z I L

PIAUÍ
PERNAMBUCO
Juazeiro
ALAGOAS
Maceió
SERGIPE
Aracaju

Callao
LIMA
Huancayo
Cusco

BOLIVIA
Arequipa
Lake Titicaca
LA PAZ
Cochabamba
Oruro
Santa Cruz
SUCRE
Arica
Lago Poopó

MATO GROSSO
Planalto de Mato Grosso
Cuiabá

BRASÍLIA
DISTRITO FEDERAL
Goiânia
GOIÁS

TOCANTINS
Palmas

BAHIA
Brazilian Highlands
Represa de Sobradinho

Salvador

MINAS GERAIS
Belo Horizonte

Iquique
Tocopilla

Atacama Desert

Campo Grande
MATO GROSSO DO SUL
Ribeirão Preto

Vitória
ESPÍRITO SANTO

Antofagasta

PARAGUAY

San Salvador de Jujuy
Salta
Formosa
Gran Chaco
ASUNCIÓN
Ciudad del Este
Villarrica

SÃO PAULO
Londrina
Campinas
Osasco
Sorocaba
Nova Iguaçu
São Paulo
Santos
RIO DE JANEIRO
Niterói
Rio de Janeiro
Juiz de Fora
PARANÁ
Curitiba

San Miguel de Tucumán
Santiago del Estero
Resistencia
Corrientes
Posadas
SANTA CATARINA
Florianópolis

La Serena
Coquimbo
La Rioja

A R G E N T I N A

San Juan

Córdoba
Santa Fe
Paraná

RIO GRANDE DO SUL
Santa Maria
Porto Alegre

Viña del Mar
Valparaíso
SANTIAGO
Mendoza
San Luis
Rosario

Tacuarembó
Melo
URUGUAY

Linares

BUENOS AIRES
La Plata
MONTEVIDEO

Santa Rosa

Pampas

Concepción
Lota
Neuquén
Rio Negro

Bahía Blanca
Mar del Plata

Temuco
Valdivia

Patagonia

Puerto Montt

Lago Colhué Huapí
Rawson
Gulf of San Jorge

Falkland Islands (to UK)
STANLEY

Bahía Grande
Rio Gallegos

Punta Arenas

Ushuaia

Beagle Channel
Cape Horn

PACIFIC OCEAN

ATLANTIC OCEAN

Map key

Population
- ▪ above 5 million
- ◪ 1 million to 5 million
- ◩ 500,000 to 1 million
- ⊡ 100,000 to 500,000
- ⊕ 50,000 to 100,000
- ○ 10,000 to 50,000
- ○ below 10,000
- ● Country capital
- ● State capital

Borders
- full international border
- disputed de facto border
- disputed territorial claim border
- state border

► *In April 1960, Brazil's government began the move from Rio de Janeiro to Brasília, a futuristic new city built in the sparsely populated interior. Brasília is now the federal capital of Brazil.*

► *Rapid urbanization was a feature of most South American countries in the latter half of the 20th century. In many cases, this unchecked growth has led to the development of sprawling slums, lacking adequate water and sewerage facilities.*

▲ *Perched high in the Andes like many of the cities in western South America, La Paz, Bolivia is the world's highest capital city at over 11,500 ft (3500 m).*

Population

Almost half of South America's population lives in Brazil but, due to the large uninhabited expanses of the Amazon Basin, its overall population density is much lower than in other countries. During the 20th century the most important population trend was the movement from rural to urban areas, giving rise to great population concentrations in large cities like São Paulo, Rio de Janeiro, Caracas, Lima, Bogotá and Buenos Aires.

Population density
(people per sq km)
- below 4
- 5–9
- 10–14
- 15–19
- 20–29
- above 30

South American resources

Agriculture still provides the largest single form of employment in South America, although rural unemployment and poverty continue to drive people towards the huge coastal cities in search of jobs and opportunities. Mineral and fuel resources, although substantial, are distributed unevenly; few countries have both fossil fuels and minerals. To break industrial dependence on raw materials, boost manufacturing, and improve infrastructure, governments borrowed heavily from the World Bank in the 1960s and 1970s. This led to the accumulation of massive debts which are unlikely ever to be repaid. Today, Brazil dominates the continent's economic output, followed by Argentina. Recently, the less-developed western side of South America has benefited due to its geographical position; for example Chile is increasingly exporting raw materials to Japan.

◀ *Ciudad Guayana is a planned industrial complex in eastern Venezuela, built as an iron and steel centre to exploit the nearby iron ore reserves.*

Industry

✈	aerospace	✐	pharmaceuticals
♭	brewing	⊞	printing & publishing
⊟	car/vehicle manufacture	⚓	shipbuilding
⚗	chemicals	↓	sugar processing
✿	electronics	⟂	textiles
✿	engineering	♣	timber processing
Ⅰ	finance	✿	tobacco processing
▭	fish processing	✿	wine
▭	food processing	♦	oil
▭	hi-tech industry	⚬	gas
▬	iron & steel	•	industrial cities
▼	meat processing	▱	major industrial areas
△	metal refining		
✿	narcotics		

▲ *The cold Peru Current flows north from the Antarctic along the Pacific coast of Peru, providing rich nutrients for one of the world's largest fishing grounds. However, over-exploitation has severely reduced Peru's anchovy catch.*

Standard of living

Wealth disparities throughout the continent create a wide gulf between affluent landowners and those afflicted by chronic poverty in inner-city slums. The illicit production of cocaine, and the hugely influential drug barons who control its distribution, contribute to the violent disorder and corruption which affect northwestern South America, de-stabilizing local governments and economies.

Standard of living
(UN human development index)

low

high

▶ *Both Argentina and Chile are now exploring the southernmost tip of the continent in search of oil. Here in Punta Arenas, a drilling rig is being prepared for exploratory drilling in the Strait of Magellan.*

GNI per capita (US$)

below 999
1000–1999
2000–2999
3000–3999
4000–4999
above 5000

Industry

Argentina and Brazil are South America's most industrialized countries and São Paulo is the continent's leading industrial centre. Long-term government investment in Brazilian industry has encouraged a diverse industrial base; engineering, steel production, food processing, textile manufacture and chemicals predominate. The illegal production of cocaine is economically significant in the Andean countries of Colombia and Bolivia. In Venezuela, the oil-dominated economy has left the country vulnerable to world oil price fluctuations. Food processing and mineral exploitation are common throughout the less industrially developed parts of the continent, including Bolivia, Chile, Ecuador and Peru.

Caribbean Sea
PANAMA
Gulf of Panama
VENEZUELA
Barranquilla
Cartagena
Maracaibo
Barquisimeto
Caracas
Valencia
Ciudad Guayana
Georgetown
Paramaribo
GUYANA
SURINAM
French Guiana (to France)
Medellín
Bogotá
Cali
COLOMBIA
ATLANTIC OCEAN
Quito
ECUADOR
Guayaquil
Iquitos
Amazon Basin
Manaus
Belém
BRAZIL
Fortaleza
Natal
Chiclayo
Chimbote
PERU
Lima
Cusco
Recife
Maceió
Salvador
BOLIVIA
La Paz
Santa Cruz
Sucre
Brasília
Arequipa
Arica
Iquique
Chuquicamata
Belo Horizonte
Antofagasta
PARAGUAY
São Paulo
Rio de Janeiro
Asunción
Ciudad del Este
Curitiba
San Miguel de Tucumán
Corrientes
Porto Alegre
Córdoba
Santa Fe
Rosario
URUGUAY
Rio Grande
Valparaíso
Mendoza
Montevideo
Santiago
Buenos Aires
Talca
ARGENTINA
Concepción
CHILE
Valdivia
Neuquén
Bahía Blanca
PACIFIC OCEAN
Comodoro Rivadavia
Gulf of San Jorge
Falkland Islands (to UK)
Bahía Grande
Punta Arenas
Strait of Magellan
Cape Horn
ATLANTIC OCEAN

Environmental issues

The Amazon Basin is one of the last great wilderness areas left on Earth. The tropical rainforests which grow there are a valuable genetic resource, containing innumerable unique plants and animals. The forests are increasingly under threat from new and expanding settlements and 'slash and burn' farming techniques, which clear land for the raising of beef cattle, causing land degradation and soil erosion.

▲ *Clouds of smoke* billow from the burning Amazon rainforest. Over 11,500 sq miles (30,000 sq km) of virgin rainforest are being cleared annually, destroying an ancient, irreplaceable, natural resource and biodiverse habitat.

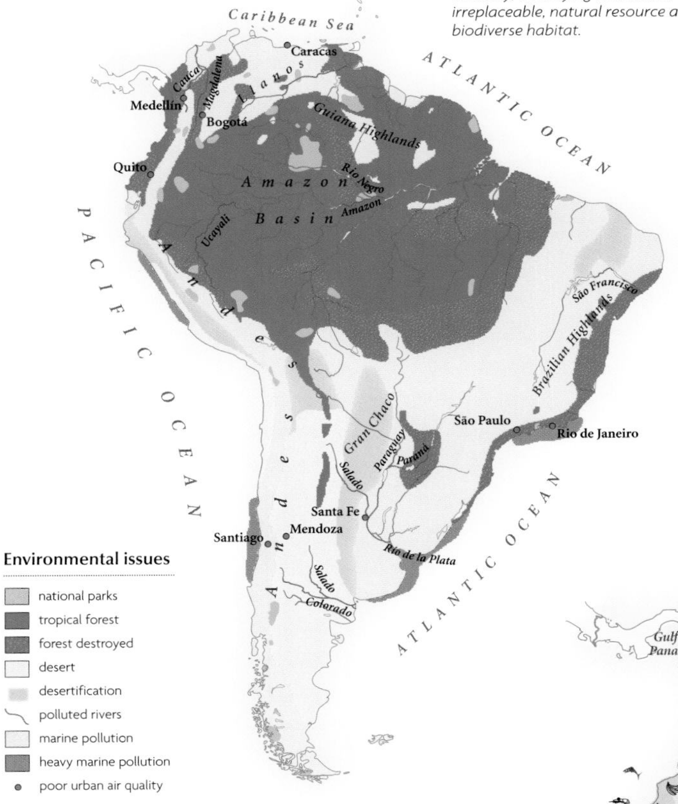

Mineral resources

Over a quarter of the world's known copper reserves are found at the Chuquicamata mine in northern Chile, and other metallic minerals such as tin are found along the length of the Andes. The discovery of oil and gas at Venezuela's Lake Maracaibo in 1917 turned the country into one of the world's leading oil producers. In contrast, South America is virtually devoid of coal, the only significant deposit being on the peninsula of Guajira in Colombia.

◀ *Copper is Chile's* largest export, most of which is mined at Chuquicamata. Along the length of the Andes, metallic minerals like copper and tin are found in abundance, formed by the excessive pressures and heat involved in mountain-building.

Mineral resources

oil field	
gas field	
coal field	
bauxite	copper
diamonds	gold
iron	lead
silver	tin

Environmental issues

- national parks
- tropical forest
- forest destroyed
- desert
- desertification
- polluted rivers
- marine pollution
- heavy marine pollution
- poor urban air quality

Using the land and sea

Many foods now common worldwide originated in South America. These include the potato, tomato, squash, and cassava. Today, large herds of beef cattle roam the temperate grasslands of the Pampas, supporting an extensive meat-packing trade in Argentina, Uruguay and Paraguay. Corn (maize) is grown as a staple crop across the continent and coffee is grown as a cash crop in Brazil and Colombia. Coca plants grown in Bolivia, Peru and Colombia provide most of the world's cocaine. Fish and shellfish are caught off the western coast, especially anchovies off Peru, shrimps off Ecuador and pilchards off Chile.

◀ *South America, and* Brazil in particular, now leads the world in coffee production, mainly growing Coffea Arabica in large plantations. Coffee beans are harvested, roasted and brewed to produce the world's second most popular drink, after tea.

◀ *The Pampas region* of southeast South America is characterized by extensive, flat plains, and populated by cattle and ranchers (gauchos). Argentina is a major world producer of beef, much of which is exported to the USA for use in hamburgers.

◀ *High in the Andes,* hardy alpacas graze on the barren land. Alpacas are thought to have been domesticated by the Incas, whose nobility wore robes made from their wool. Today, they are still reared and prized for their soft, warm fleeces.

Using the land and sea

- barren land
- cropland
- desert
- forest
- mountain region
- pasture
- major conurbations
- cattle
- pigs
- sheep
- bananas
- corn (maize)
- citrus fruits
- cocoa
- cotton
- coffee
- fishing
- oil palms
- peanuts
- rubber
- shellfish
- soya beans
- sugar cane
- vineyards
- wheat

Northern South America

COLOMBIA, GUYANA, SURINAM, VENEZUELA, French Guiana (to France)

Fringed by the Pacific and Atlantic oceans and the Caribbean Sea, South America's northern region has a rich range of natural resources, some exploited for centuries by colonial powers including the Spanish, French, Dutch and British, others still to be fully explored. The prospects for further economic development in Colombia, Guyana and Surinam are blighted by drug-related violence and political instability. Venezuela, despite huge incomes from its oil reserves, remains less developed in other industrial sectors. French Guiana is an overseas *département* of France, now seeking greater autonomy. Most of the major population centres, such as Bogotá, have grown up in the temperate conditions of the high Andes or, like Caracas, at strategic points along the Caribbean coast.

▶ *Flowers grown in Colombia are exported all over the world, and include fine carnations and roses. Here, workers are cutting roses which have been grown in plastic greenhouses.*

Map key

Population
- ▣ 1 million to 5 million
- ◉ 500,000 to 1 million
- ◎ 100,000 to 500,000
- ⊕ 50,000 to 100,000
- ○ 10,000 to 50,000
- ∘ below 10,000

Elevation
- 4000m / 13,124ft
- 3000m / 9843ft
- 2000m / 6562ft
- 1000m / 3281ft
- 500m / 1640ft
- 250m / 820ft
- 100m / 328ft
- sea level

◀ *Scattered farms and villages have grown up on the gentle slopes of this Colombian river valley, utilizing the fertile soils for farming.*

Scale 1:7,250,000

Km 0 25 50 100 150 200
Miles 0 25 50 100 150 200

projection: Lambert Azimuthal Equal Area

▲ *Large open squares like the Plaza de Bolívar in Bogotá are characteristic of many cities founded by the Spanish.*

▲ *The Orinoco river flows from its source in the southern Guiana Highlands to form a broad delta on Venezuela's Atlantic coast. One of its distributary channels opens into a wide bay called the Serpent's Mouth.*

Transport and industry

Many mineral resources are mined in Colombia, including fuels, gold and precious and semi-precious stones. Revenues from coffee and exports of illegal narcotics are crucial to the economy. Venezuela's major economic activity is the oil industry around Lake Maracaibo (Lago de Maracaibo). Sugar and bauxite are exported from Guyana and Surinam.

The transport network

🛣	31,720 miles (51,054 km)
🛤	3411 miles (5490 km)
🚂	2448 miles (3940 km)
⚓	22,429 miles (36,100 km)

Rivers are an important means of transport in Colombia; many are extensively navigable. The Pan-American Highway runs through Colombia. In Venezuela, much infrastructure investment is linked to the oil industry.

Major industry and infrastructure

- chemicals
- finance
- food processing
- iron & steel
- narcotics
- mining
- oil
- oil refining
- pharmaceuticals
- textiles
- timber processing
- ▪ capital cities
- major towns
- ⊕ international airports
- — major roads
- major industrial areas

▲ Vast oil reserves around Lake Maracaibo (Lago de Maracaibo) form the focus of Venezuelan industry. Incomes from oil are used to invest in other industries and in the development of infrastructure.

Using the land

The Andean basins support cereals and potatoes. Livestock graze at higher altitudes and on the drier tropical grasslands known as the llanos; hardy goats are reared in scrubland areas. Grown at higher elevations, coffee is an important cash crop, as is cotton, sugar cane, bananas, citrus fruits, cocoa and rice, farmed on the Caribbean lowlands. Coca is the most widely-grown narcotic plant, with heroin poppies grown in Colombia and marijuana in lowland areas throughout the region.

The urban/rural population divide

urban 80%   rural 20%

0 10 20 30 40 50 60 70 80 90 100

Population density	Total land area
78 people per sq mile (30 people per sq km)	1,111,317 sq miles (2,879,060 sq km)

Land use and agricultural distribution

- cattle
- goats
- bananas
- cereals
- coffee
- cotton
- sugar cane
- ▪ capital cities
- major towns
- pasture
- cropland
- forest
- wetlands
- mountain region

The landscape

At its northernmost reaches, in western Colombia and Venezuela, the great Andean mountain chain splits into three distinct ranges: the Cordillera Oriental, Cordillera Central and Cordillera Occidental, intercut by a complex series of lesser ranges and basins. The relief becomes lower toward the coast and the interior plains of the northern Amazon Basin, rising again into the tropical hills of the Guiana Highlands.

▲ The Sierra Nevada de Santa Marta is a granite massif which rises sharply from the Caribbean lowlands to snow-covered peaks, the tallest of which is 18,947 ft (5775 m) high.

Lake Maracaibo (Lago de Maracaibo) is not a true lake but a shallow inlet of the Caribbean Sea. It is the main source of Venezuela's oil.

The drainage basin of the Magdalena River and the Cauca, its main tributary, covers over 20% of Colombia's total surface area.

In the Guiana Highlands, Venezuela's most remote region, the ancient crystalline rocks contain deposits of iron ore, gold and diamonds.

Angel Falls (Salto Ángel), at 3212 ft (979 m), is the world's highest waterfall.

Igneous intrusions into the crystalline plateau which forms most of central Guyana have led to the formation of the many rapids which characterize Guyana's rivers.

Guiana Shield

- Alluvial plains
- Inselbergs
- Table mountains

▲ The Guiana Shield is one of the oldest land surfaces in the world – probably formed more than 4 billion years ago. Chemical weathering over millions of years has created flat-topped table mountains and large numbers of inselbergs.

Over 80% of Surinam is covered by tropical rainforest.

Cordillera Occidental

Cordillera Central

Cordillera Oriental

Colombia's eastern lowlands are known locally as llanos, meaning grasslands.

▶ The Potaru river descends 741 ft (226 m) over a sandstone ledge at the Kaieteur Falls in Guyana.

Most of the land in French Guiana is low-lying; here, the rocks of the Guiana Highlands have been eroded by rivers flowing towards the sea.

55

Western South America

BOLIVIA, ECUADOR, PERU

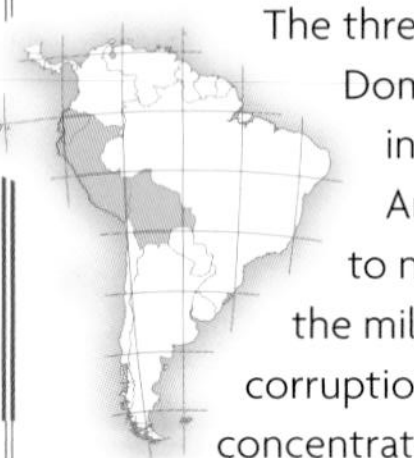

The three states of Western South America share a similar geography and recent history. Dominated by the Inca empire until Spanish conquest in the 16th century, they achieved independence from Spain in the early 19th century. The precipitous terrain of the Andes presents severe difficulties for overland transport and continues to be a barrier to national unity and stability. Although Ecuador is now a relatively stable democracy, the military is highly influential in Peru and Bolivia, while the drug trade and associated corruption discourages external aid and economic progress. Wealth and power are still largely concentrated in the hands of a small elite of families, who attained their position during the Spanish colonial period. Energy resources and political recognition for the indigenous peoples are becoming increasingly important issues, particularly in Bolivia.

▶ *Ecuador's capital city, Quito, lies high in the Andes, nestling between snow-capped peaks. At 9350 ft (2850 m), Quito is the second highest capital in the world – La Paz in Bolivia is the highest.*

The landscape

Bolivia, Peru and Ecuador each possess a high Andean mountain region and an eastern region consisting of tropical lowlands and the Andean slope leading down to them. Towards the south of the region, the mountains widen to form the high plateau of the Altiplano. Peru and Ecuador also have fertile, lowland coastal plains. A wide variety of environments include *selva* (tropical rainforest), *montaña* (mountain forest) and grassland.

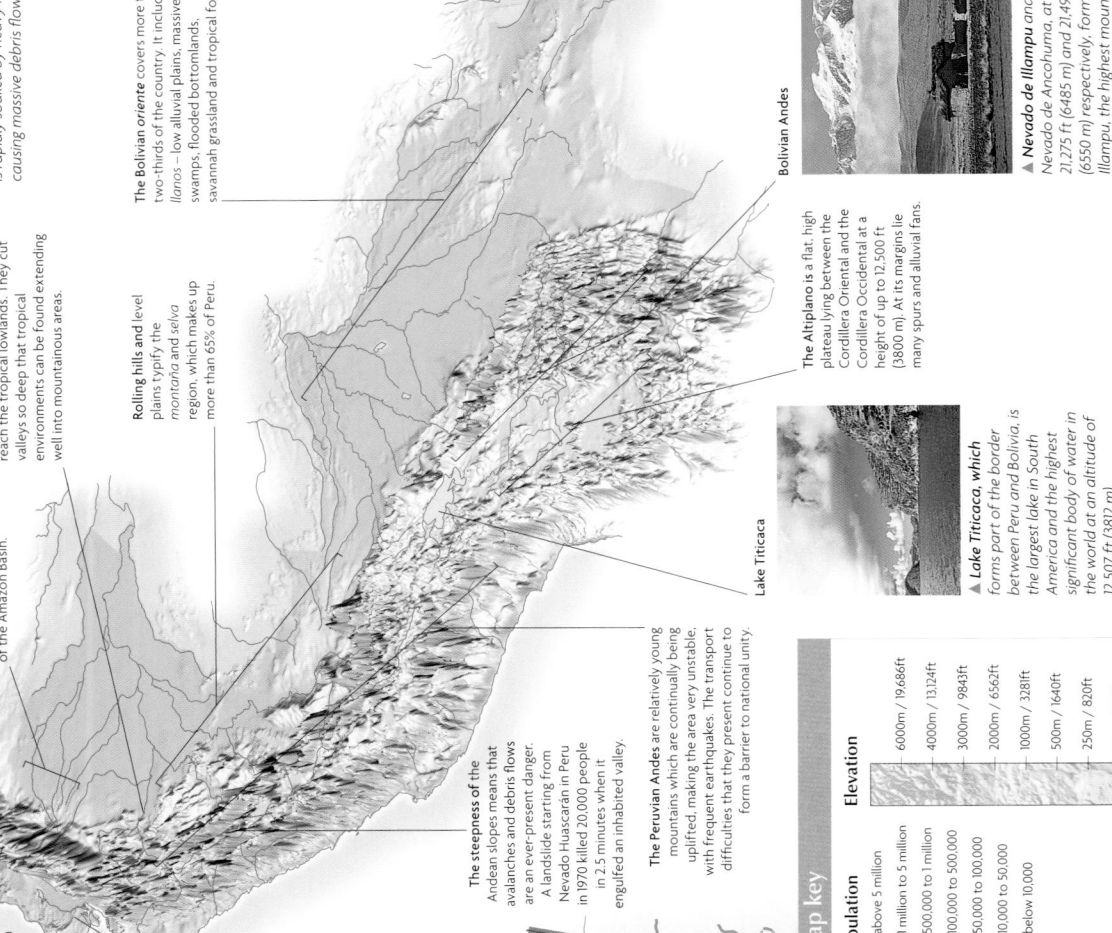

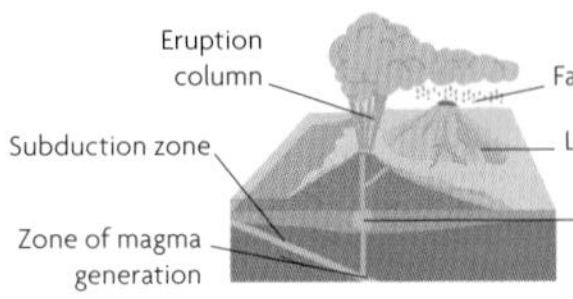

▲ *There are many large and active volcanoes in the Andes. Magma generated in the heart of the volcano erupts in a huge cloud of ash. Ash-fall deposits are common throughout the Andes and the rock produced is known as andesite. This is rapidly soaked by heavy rain, causing massive debris flows.*

Eruption column
Subduction zone
Zone of magma generation
Falling ash
Lava flows
Magma chamber

The Bolivian *oriente* covers more than two-thirds of the country. It includes *llanos* – low alluvial plains, massive swamps, flooded bottomlands, savannah grassland and tropical forests.

Fast-flowing tributaries of the Amazon, which rise in the Andes, run eastwards through the front ranges to reach the tropical lowlands. They cut valleys so deep that tropical environments can be found extending well into mountainous areas.

Much of eastern Ecuador is covered by the tropical rainforest of the Amazon Basin.

Rolling hills and level plains typify the *montaña* and *selva* region, which makes up more than 65% of Peru.

Cotopaxi is the world's highest active volcano, with a peak 19,347 ft (5897 m) high. A massive eruption in 1877 caused a mudflow which destroyed everything in its path for 150 miles (240 km).

The coastal flood plains are the source of Ecuador's richest soils, enabling the cultivation of a wide range of crops.

The steepness of the Andean slopes means that avalanches and debris flows are an ever-present danger. A landslide starting from Nevado Huascarán in Peru in 1970 killed 20,000 people in 25 minutes when it engulfed an inhabited valley.

The Peruvian Andes are relatively young mountains which are continually being uplifted, making the area very unstable, with frequent earthquakes. The transport difficulties that they present continue to form a barrier to national unity.

Bolivian Andes

▲ *Nevado de Illampu and Nevado de Ancohuma, at 21,275 ft (6485 m) and 21,490 ft (6550 m) respectively, form Illampu, the highest mountain in the Bolivian Andes.*

The Altiplano is a flat, high plateau lying between the Cordillera Oriental and the Cordillera Occidental at a height of up to 12,500 ft (3800 m). At its margins lie many alluvial spurs and alluvial fans.

Lake Titicaca

▲ *Lake Titicaca, which forms part of the border between Peru and Bolivia, is the largest lake in South America and the highest significant body of water in the world at an altitude of 12,507 ft (3812 m).*

Scale 1:8,500,000

Map key

Population

■ above 5 million
■ 1 million to 5 million
◉ 500,000 to 1 million
⊕ 100,000 to 500,000
○ 50,000 to 100,000
○ 10,000 to 50,000
○ below 10,000

Elevation

6000m / 19,686ft
4000m / 13,124ft
3000m / 9843ft
2000m / 6562ft
1000m / 3281ft
500m / 1640ft
250m / 820ft
100m / 328ft
sea level

Ecuador: Administrative regions
1 CARCHI
2 TUNGURAHUA
3 BOLÍVAR
4 CHIMBORAZO
5 ZAMORA CHINCHIPE

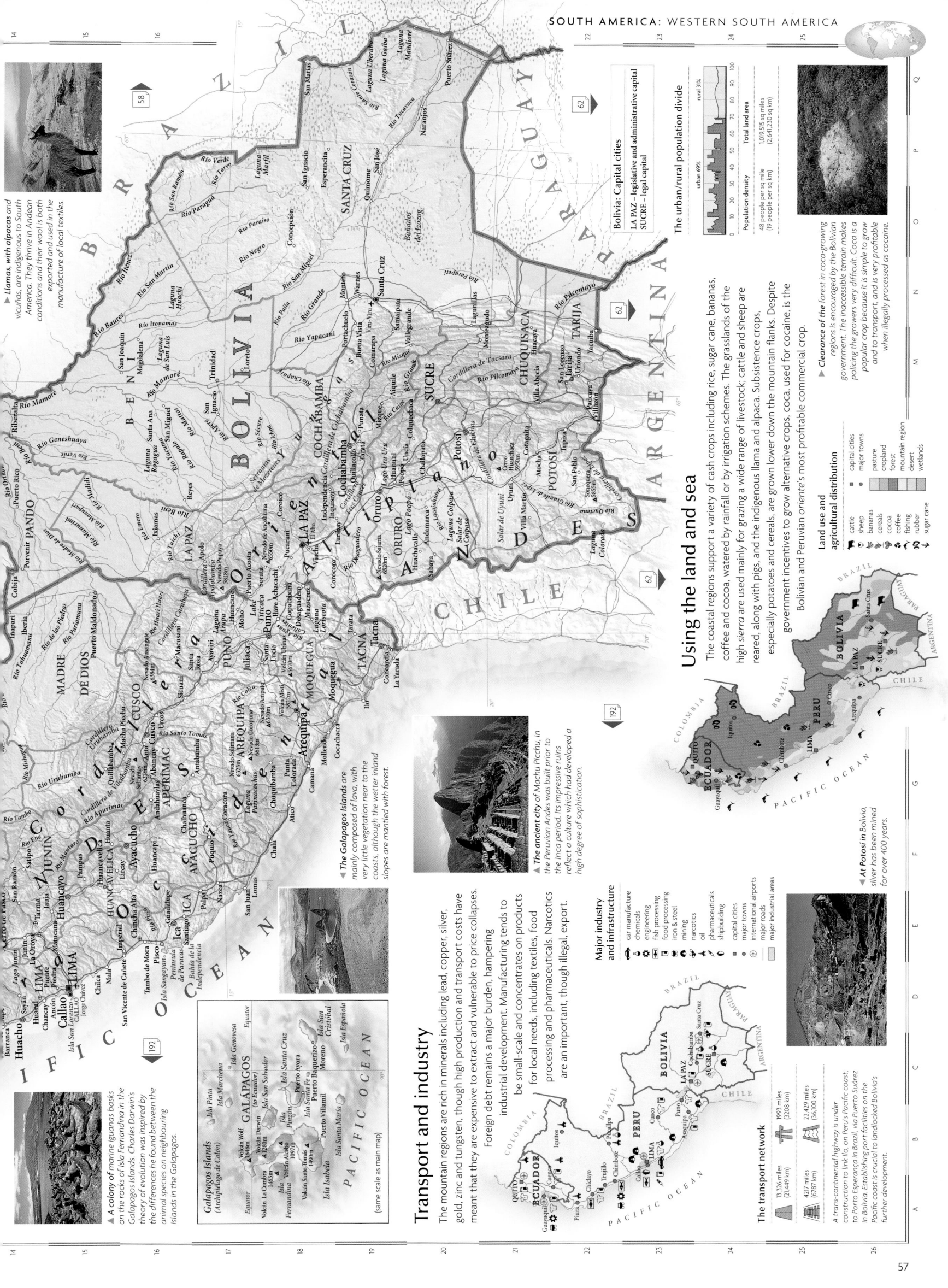

▲ *Llamas, with alpacas and vicuñas, are indigenous to South America. They thrive in Andean conditions and their wool is both exported and used in the manufacture of local textiles.*

Bolivia: Capital cities
LA PAZ – legislative and administrative capital
SUCRE – legal capital

The urban/rural population divide

rural 31%
urban 69%

Population density
48 people per sq mile
(19 people per sq km)

Total land area
1,019,515 sq miles
(2,641,230 sq km)

▲ *Clearance of the forest in coca-growing regions is encouraged by the Bolivian policing the growers very difficult. Coca is a popular crop because it is simple to grow and to transport, and is very profitable when illegally processed as cocaine.*

Using the land and sea

The coastal regions support a variety of cash crops including rice, sugar cane, bananas, coffee and cocoa, watered by rainfall or by irrigation schemes. The grasslands of the high *sierra* are used mainly for grazing a wide range of livestock; cattle and sheep are reared, along with pigs, and the indigenous llama and alpaca. Subsistence crops, especially potatoes and cereals, are grown lower down the mountain flanks. Despite government incentives to grow alternative crops, coca, used for cocaine, is the Bolivian and Peruvian oriente's most profitable commercial crop.

Land use and agricultural distribution

cattle, sheep, bananas, cereals, cocoa, coffee, fishing, rubber, sugar cane

capital cities, major towns
pasture, cropland, forest, mountain region, desert, wetlands

▲ *The Galapagos Islands are mainly composed of lava, with very little vegetation near to the coasts, although the wetter inland slopes are mantled with forest.*

▲ *The ancient city of Machu Picchu, in the Peruvian Andes was built prior to the Inca period. Its impressive ruins reflect a culture which had developed a high degree of sophistication.*

▲ *A colony of marine iguanas basks on the rocks of Isla Fernandina in the Galapagos Islands. Charles Darwin's theory of evolution was inspired by the differences he found between the animal species on neighbouring islands in the Galapagos.*

Galapagos Islands
(Archipiélago de Colón)
(to Ecuador)

(same scale as main map)

Transport and industry

The mountain regions are rich in minerals including lead, copper, silver, gold, zinc and tungsten, though high production and transport costs have meant that they are expensive to extract and vulnerable to price collapses. Foreign debt remains a major burden, hampering industrial development. Manufacturing tends to be small-scale and concentrates on products for local needs, including textiles, food processing and pharmaceuticals. Narcotics are an important, though illegal, export.

▲ *At Potosí in Bolivia, silver has been mined for over 400 years.*

Major industry and infrastructure

car manufacture, chemicals, engineering, fish processing, food processing, iron & steel, mining, narcotics, oil, pharmaceuticals, shipbuilding

capital cities, major towns, international airports, major roads, major industrial areas

The transport network

13,326 miles (21,449 km)
1993 miles (3208 km)
4217 miles (6787 km)
22,429 miles (36,100 km)

A trans-continental highway is under construction to link Ilo, on Peru's Pacific coast, to Porto Esperança in Brazil, via Puerto Suárez in Bolivia. Establishing port facilities on the Pacific coast is crucial to landlocked Bolivia's further development.

Brazil

Brazil is the largest country in South America, with a population of 191 million – almost half the combined total of the continent. The 26 states which make up the federal republic of Brazil are administered from the purpose-built capital, Brasília. Tropical rainforest, covering more than one-third of the country, contains rich natural resources, but great tracts are sacrificed to agriculture, industry and urban expansion on a daily basis. Most of Brazil's multi-ethnic population now live in cities, some of which are vast areas of urban sprawl; São Paulo is one of the world's biggest conurbations, with more than 20 million inhabitants. Although prosperity is a reality for some, many people still live in great poverty, and mounting foreign debts continue to damage Brazil's prospects of economic advancement.

Using the land

Brazil has immense natural resources, including minerals and hardwoods, many of which are found in the fragile rainforest. Brazil is the world's leading coffee grower and a major producer of livestock, sugar and orange juice concentrate. Soya beans for animal feed, particularly for poultry feed, have become the country's most significant crop.

Land use and agricultural distribution

- cattle
- pigs
- sheep
- citrus fruits
- coffee
- cotton
- soya beans
- sugar cane
- timber

- ● capital cities
- ○ major towns

- pasture
- cropland
- forest

The landscape

The Amazon Basin, containing the largest area of tropical rainforest on Earth, covers nearly half of Brazil. It is bordered by two shield areas: in the south by the Brazilian Highlands, and in the north by the Guiana Highlands. The east coast is dominated by a great escarpment which runs for 1600 miles (2565 km).

The ancient Brazilian Highlands have a varied topography. Their plateaux, hills and deep valleys are bordered by highly-eroded mountains containing important mineral deposits. They are drained by three great river systems, the Amazon, the Paraguay–Paraná and the São Francisco.

The São Francisco Basin has a climate unique in Brazil. Known as the 'drought polygon', it has almost no rain during the dry season, leading to regular disastrous droughts.

The northeastern scrublands are known as the *caatinga*, a virtually impenetrable thorny woodland, sometimes intermixed with cacti where water is scarce.

The famous Sugar Loaf Mountain (*Pão de Açúcar*) which overlooks Rio de Janeiro is a fine example of a volcanic plug a domed core of solidified lava left after the slopes of the original volcano have eroded away.

Deep natural harbours such as Baía de Guanabara were created where the steep slopes of the Serra da Mantiqueira plunge directly into the ocean.

The Amazon Basin is the largest river basin in the world. The Amazon river and over a thousand tributaries drain an area of 2,375,000 sq miles (6,150,000 sq km) and carry one-fifth of the world's fresh water out to sea.

Guiana Highlands

Brazil's highest mountain is the Pico da Neblina which was only discovered in 1962. It is 9888 ft (3014 m) high.

The flood plains which border the Amazon river are made up of a variety of different features including shallow lakes and swamps, mangrove forests in the tidal delta area and fertile levées on river banks and point bars.

Pantanal wetlands

▼ *Large-scale gullies are* common in Brazil, particularly on hillslopes from which vegetation has been removed. Gullies grow headwards (up the slope) aided by a combination of erosion through water seepage and rainwater runoff.

Direction of growth
Overland water flow
Gully
Hillslope gullying
Rainfall
Water seeps through hillslope

▲ *The Pantanal region in the south of Brazil is an extension of the Gran Chaco plain. The swamps and marshes of this area are renowned for their beauty, and abundant and unique wildlife, including wildfowl and these caimans, a type of crocodile.*

▼ *The Iguaçu river surges over the spectacular Iguaçu Falls (Saltos do Iguaçu) towards the Paraná river. Falls like these are increasingly under pressure from large-scale hydro-electric projects such as that at Itaipú.*

▲ *The fecundity of parts of Brazil's rainforest results from exceptionally high levels of rainfall and the quantities of silt deposited by the Amazon river system.*

The urban/rural population divide

urban 78%
rural 22%

Population density	Total land area
55 people per sq mile (21 people per sq km)	3,286,472 sq miles (8,511,970 sq km)

Map key

Population
- ■ above 5 million
- ◉ 1 million to 5 million
- ◎ 500,000 to 1 million
- ⊙ 100,000 to 500,000
- ⊙ 50,000 to 100,000
- ○ 10,000 to 50,000
- ○ below 10,000

Elevation
- 3000m / 9843ft
- 2000m / 6562ft
- 1000m / 3281ft
- 500m / 1640ft
- 250m / 820ft
- 100m / 328ft
- sea level

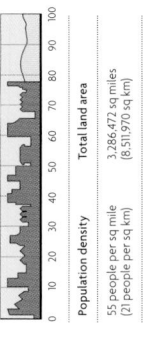

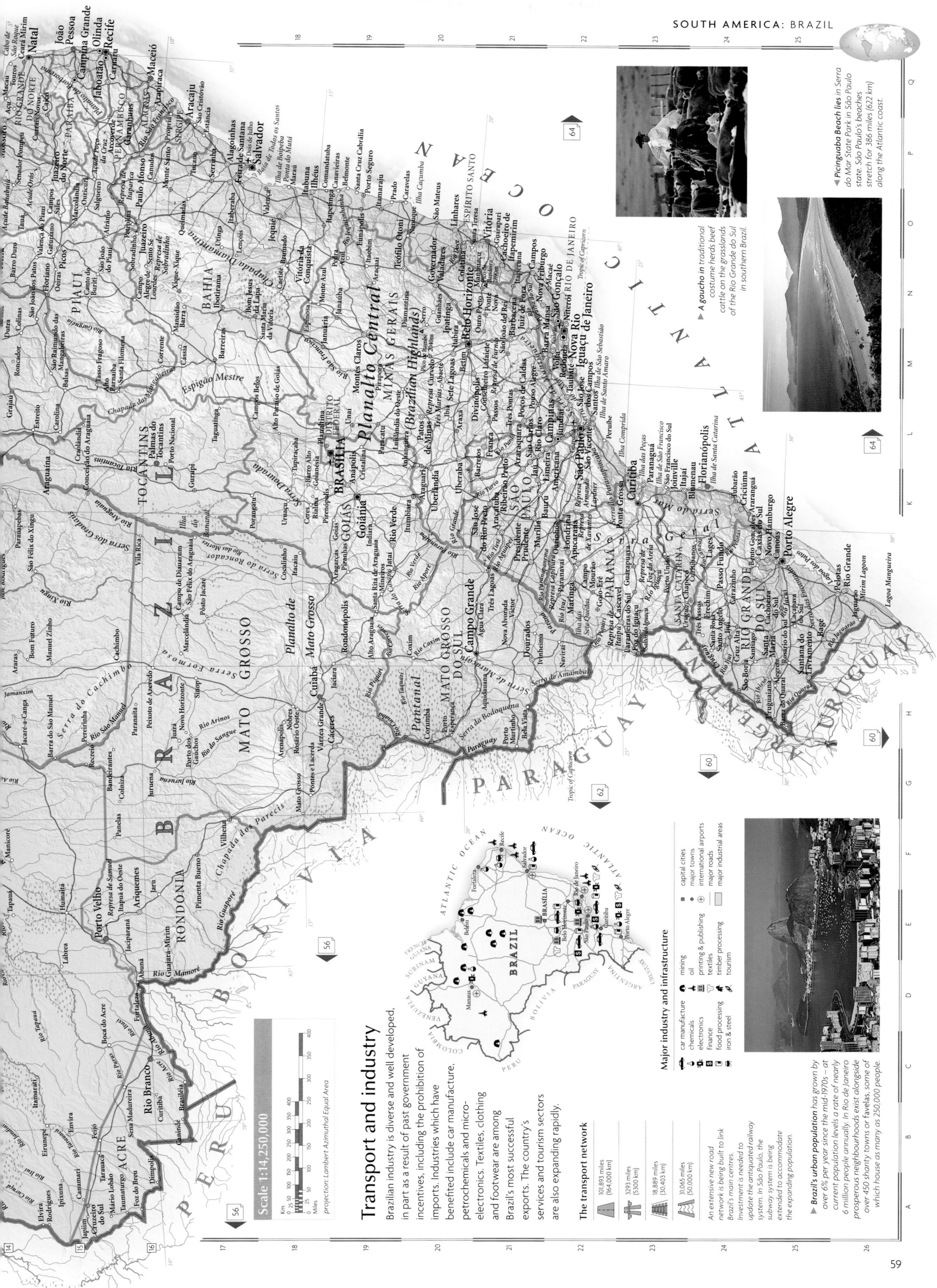

A gaucho in traditional costume herds beef cattle on the grasslands of the Rio Grande do Sul in southern Brazil.

▼ Picinguaba Beach lies in Serra do Mar State Park in São Paulo state. São Paulo's beaches stretch for 386 miles (622 km) along the Atlantic coast.

Transport and industry

Brazilian industry is diverse and well developed, in part as a result of past government incentives, including the prohibition of imports. Industries which have benefited include car manufacture, petrochemicals and microelectronics. Textiles, clothing and footwear are among Brazil's most successful exports. The country's services and tourism sectors are also expanding rapidly.

The transport network

101,893 miles (164,000 km)

3293 miles (5300 km)

18,889 miles (30,403 km)

31,065 miles (50,000 km)

An extensive new road network is being built to link Brazil's main centres. Investment is needed to update the antiquated railway system. In São Paulo, the subway system is being extended to accommodate the expanding population.

Scale 1:14,250,000

Km
0   50 100 150 200 250 300 350 400
0 25 50 100 150 200 250 300 350 400
Miles

projection: Lambert Azimuthal Equal Area

Major industry and infrastructure

- car manufacture
- chemicals
- electronics
- finance
- food processing
- iron & steel
- mining
- oil
- printing & publishing
- textiles
- timber processing
- tourism

- capital cities
- major towns
- international airports
- major roads
- major industrial areas

▲ Brazil's urban population has grown by over 6% per year since the mid-1970s – at current population levels a rate of nearly 6 million people annually. In Rio de Janeiro prosperous neighbourhoods exist alongside over 450 shanty towns or favelas, some of which house as many as 250,000 people.

Eastern South America

URUGUAY, NORTHEAST ARGENTINA, SOUTHEAST BRAZIL

The vast conurbations of Rio de Janeiro, São Paulo and Buenos Aires form the core of South America's highly-urbanized eastern region. São Paulo state, with over 40 million inhabitants, is among the world's 20 most powerful economies, and São Paulo is the fastest growing city on the continent. Rio de Janeiro and Buenos Aires, transformed in the last hundred years from port cities to great metropolitan areas each with more than 10 million inhabitants, typify the unstructured growth and wealth disparities of South America's great cities. In Uruguay, two fifths of the population lives in the capital, Montevideo, which faces Buenos Aires across the River Plate (Rio de la Plata). Immigration from the countryside has created severe pressure on the urban infrastructure, particularly on available housing, leading to a profusion of crowded shanty settlements (favelas or barrios).

Using the land

Most of Uruguay and the Pampas of northern Argentina are devoted to the rearing of livestock, especially cattle and sheep, which are central to both countries' economies. Soya beans, first produced in Brazil's Rio Grande do Sul, are now more widely grown for large-scale export, as are cereals, sugar cane and grapes. Subsistence crops, including potatoes, corn and sugar beet, are grown on the remaining arable land.

Transport and industry

Southeast Brazil is home to much of the important motor and capital goods industry, largely based around São Paulo; iron and steel production is also concentrated in this region. Uruguay's economy continues to be based mainly on the export of livestock products including meat and leather goods. Buenos Aires is Argentina's chief port, and the region has a varied and sophisticated economic base including service-based industries such as finance and publishing, as well as primary processing.

Major industry and infrastructure

- car manufacture
- chemicals
- engineering
- finance
- food processing
- iron & steel
- meat processing
- printing & publishing
- shipbuilding
- textiles
- timber processing
- capital cities
- major towns
- international airports
- major roads
- major industrial areas

The transport network

Throughout the region, road networks need to be expanded to cope with urban development. Plans are underway to build a bridge over the River Plate (Rio de la Plata) to link Colonia and Buenos Aires.

▲ *The Itaipú dam on the Paraná river is one of the largest hydro-electric projects in the world, jointly financed by Brazil and Paraguay.*

Map key

Population
- ■ above 5 million
- ■ 1 million to 5 million
- ◉ 500,000 to 1 million
- ◎ 100,000 to 500,000
- ⊕ 50,000 to 100,000
- ○ 10,000 to 50,000
- ∘ below 10,000

Elevation
- 2000m / 6562ft
- 1000m / 3281ft
- 500m / 1640ft
- 250m / 820ft
- 100m / 328ft
- sea level

Scale 1:7,000,000

projection: Lambert Azimuthal Equal Area

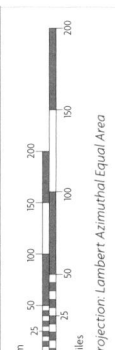

▲ *Soya beans are harvested, pressed, and processed into soya cake, which is used as animal feed. The cake is fed mainly to chickens on large-scale factory farms, and the growth in soya production has been an important factor in the expansion of the Brazilian poultry trade.*

Land use and agricultural distribution

- cattle
- sheep
- cereals
- coffee
- fruit
- soya beans
- sugar cane
- major cities
- major towns
- pasture
- cropland
- forest
- wetlands
- barren land

▼ *The rolling grasslands of Uruguay are ideally suited to the rearing of cattle, which are concentrated in great herds throughout the region.*

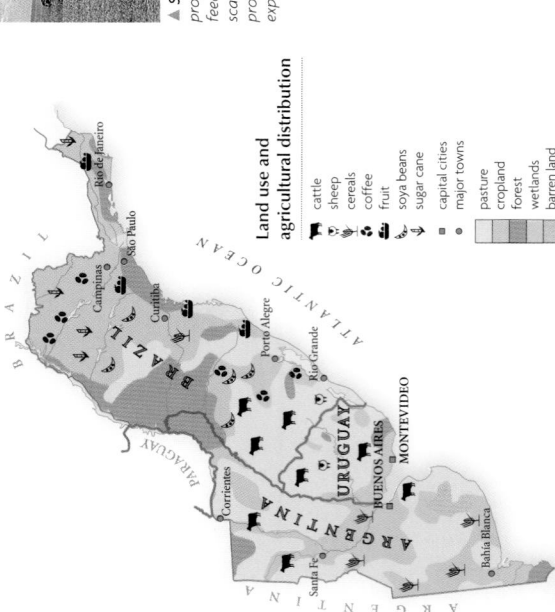

▲ *Rio de Janeiro's annual carnival, Mardi Gras, which ushers in the start of Lent, is an extravagant five-day parade through the city, characterized by fantastically decorated floats,*

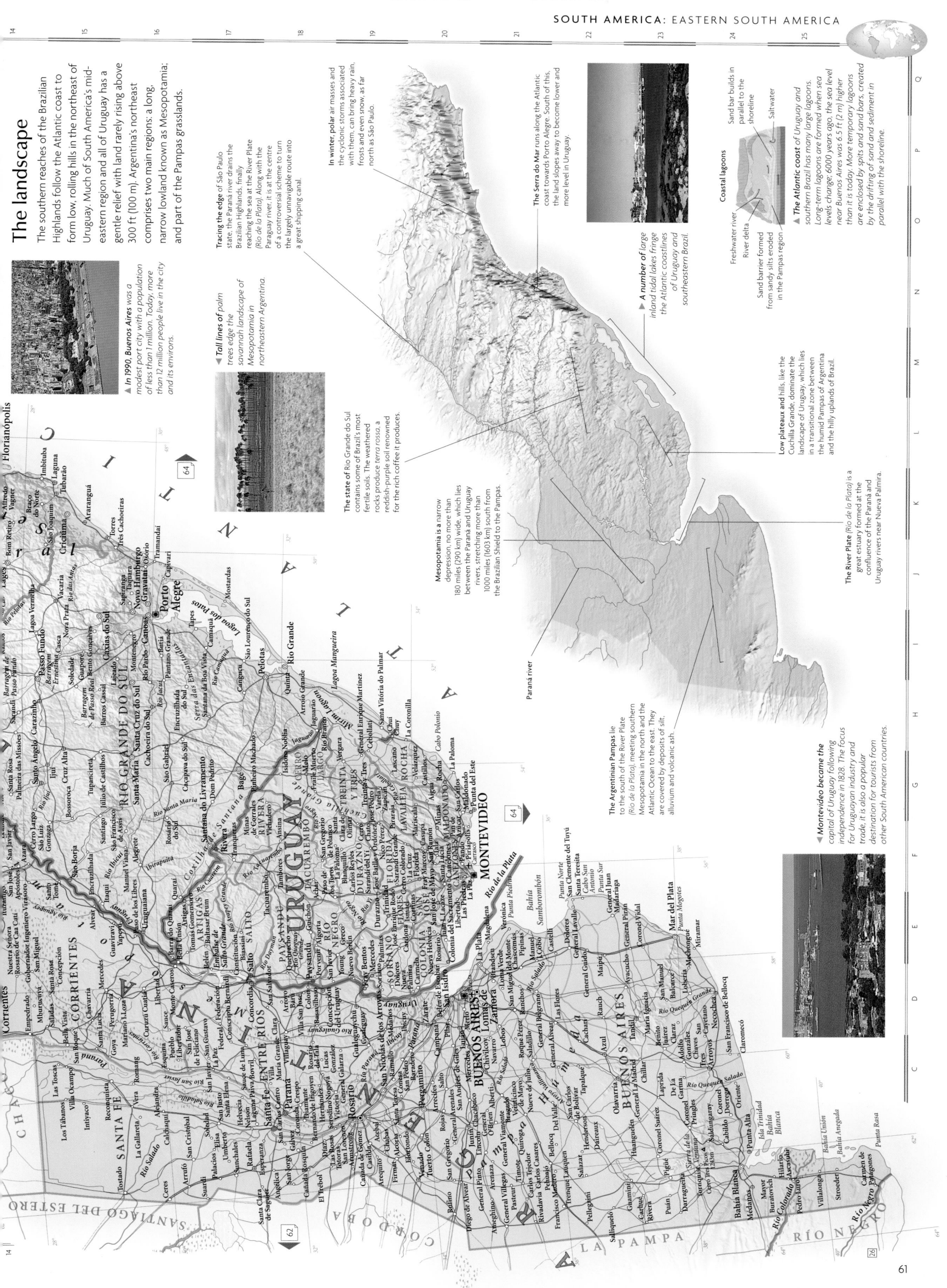

The landscape

The southern reaches of the Brazilian Highlands follow the Atlantic coast to form low, rolling hills in the northeast of Uruguay. Much of South America's mid-eastern region and all of Uruguay has a gentle relief with land rarely rising above 300 ft (100 m). Argentina's northeast comprises two main regions: a long, narrow lowland known as Mesopotamia; and part of the Pampas grasslands.

▲ *In 1990, Buenos Aires was a modest port city with a population of less than 1 million. Today, more than 12 million people live in the city and its environs.*

Tracing the edge of São Paulo state, the Paraná river drains the Brazilian Highlands, finally reaching the sea at the River Plate (Río de la Plata). Along with the Paraguay river, it is at the centre of a controversial scheme to turn the largely unnavigable route into a great shipping canal.

▼ *Tall lines of palm trees edge the savannah landscape of Mesopotamia in northeastern Argentina.*

The state of Rio Grande do Sul contains some of Brazil's most fertile soils. The weathered rocks produce terra rossa a reddish-purple soil renowned for the rich coffee it produces.

In winter, polar air masses and the cyclonic storms associated with them, can bring heavy rain, frosts and even snow, as far north as São Paulo.

The Serra do Mar runs along the Atlantic coast towards Porto Alegre. South of this, the land slopes away to become lower and more level in Uruguay.

▲ *A number of large inland tidal lakes fringe the Atlantic coastlines of Uruguay and southeastern Brazil.*

Low plateaus and hills, like the Cuchilla Grande, dominate the landscape of Uruguay, which lies in a transitional zone between the humid Pampas of Argentina and the hilly uplands of Brazil.

Coastal lagoons

Sand bar builds in parallel to the shoreline
Saltwater
Freshwater river
River delta
Sand barrier formed from sandy silts eroded in the Pampas region

▲ *The Atlantic coast of Uruguay and southern Brazil has many large lagoons. Long-term lagoons are formed when sea levels change: 6000 years ago, the sea level near Buenos Aires was 6.5 ft (2 m) higher than it is today. More temporary lagoons are enclosed by spits and sand bars, created by the drifting of sand and sediment in parallel with the shoreline.*

Mesopotamia is a narrow depression, no more than 180 miles (290 km) wide, which lies between the Paraná and Uruguay rivers, stretching more than 1000 miles (1603 km) south from the Brazilian Shield to the Pampas.

Paraná river

The River Plate (Río de la Plata) is a great estuary formed at the confluence of the Paraná and Uruguay rivers near Nueva Palmira.

The Argentinian Pampas lie to the south of the River Plate (Río de la Plata), meeting southern Mesopotamia in the north and the Atlantic Ocean to the east. They are covered by deposits of silt, alluvium and volcanic ash.

▼ *Montevideo became the capital of Uruguay following independence in 1828. The focus for Uruguayan industry and trade, it is also a popular destination for tourists from other South American countries.*

Southern South America

ARGENTINA, CHILE, PARAGUAY

South America's cone-shaped southern region is shared by Argentina and Chile, two overwhelmingly urbanized nations whose populations live mainly in or around the capital cities, Buenos Aires and Santiago. The people are largely *mestizo* or of European origin; in the early 20th century Argentina absorbed waves of new European immigrants, many from Italy and Germany. Paraguay is far less urbanized than its neighbours, with a homogeneous population of mixed Spanish and Guaraní origin, who retain their Indian roots through the Guaraní language. Though most Paraguayans live in the southeast, near Asunción, the indigenous Indians live in the sparsely populated Gran Chaco. The Gran Chaco is also home to some of Argentina's minority indigenous peoples, who otherwise live mainly in Andean regions. Chile's estimated 800,000 Mapuche Indians live almost exclusively in the south.

Transport and industry

Food processing and agricultural exports remain a fundamental part of Argentina's economy. The growth of manufacturing is regularly hampered by hyper-inflation and massive foreign debts. The world's most important copper-producer and one of the top twenty gold producers, Chile also has a thriving wine and grape industry. Most Paraguayan exports involve primary processing, although domestic goods are produced for home markets.

Argentina's state transport system is undergoing privatization, though the outmoded rail network requires updating. Paraguay requires foreign investment to upgrade its roads and railways. Essential internal air routes, especially across the Andes, are well developed in all three countries.

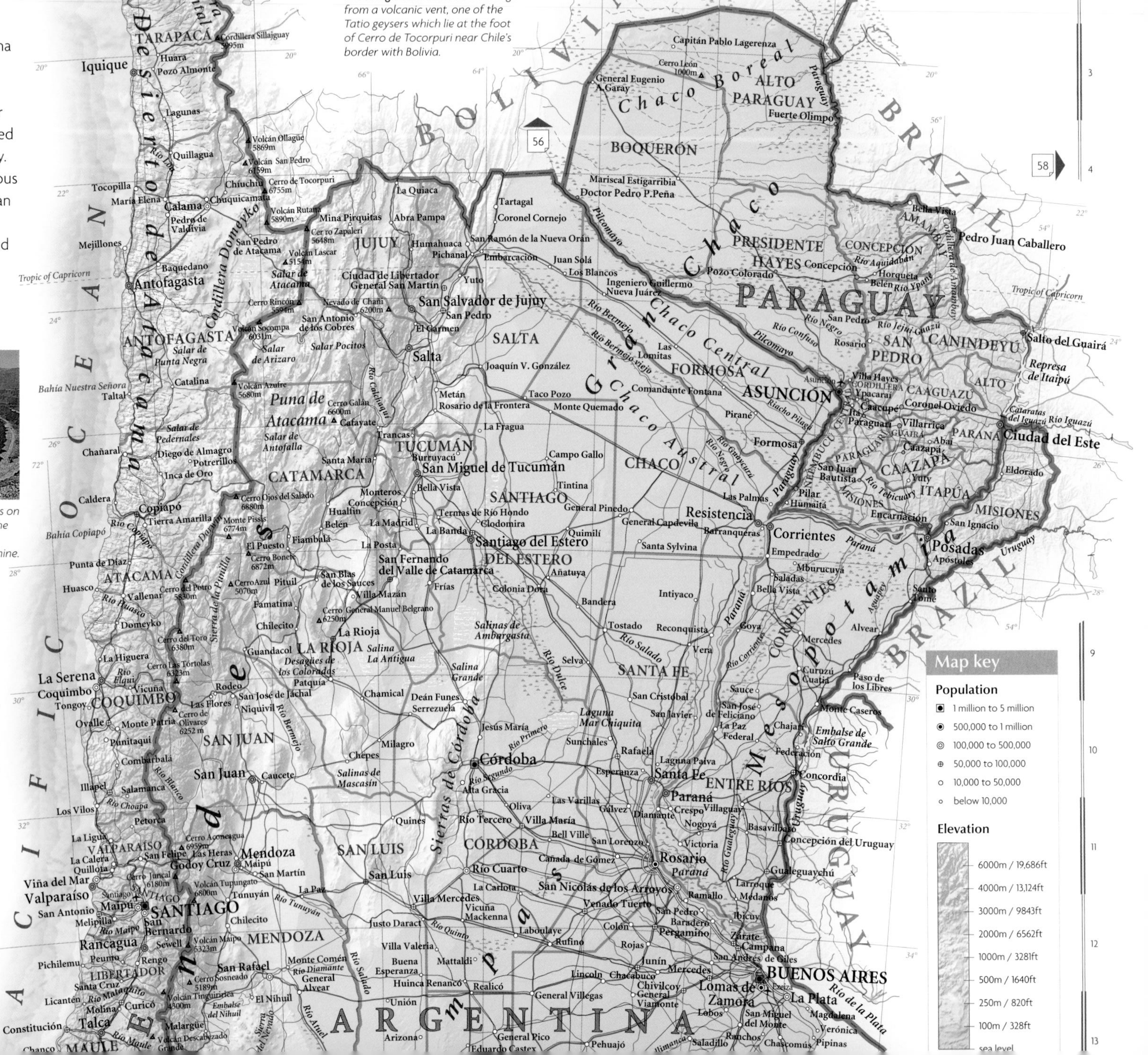

Major industry and infrastructure

- chemicals
- engineering
- food processing
- meat processing
- mining
- oil
- textiles
- timber processing
- capital cities
- major towns
- international airports
- major roads
- major industrial areas

The transport network

55,062 miles (93,453 km)	3038 miles (4889 km)
26,881 miles (43,153 km)	9180 miles (14,775 km)

▲ *Floodwaters cover the land in the Gran Chaco, partly submerging its vegetation of fan palms and hyacinths.*

▲ *Boiling water and steam emerge from a volcanic vent, one of the Tatio geysers which lie at the foot of Cerro de Tocorpuri near Chile's border with Bolivia.*

▲ *Chuquicamata copper mine, lies on a desert plateau near Calama in the Andes of northern Chile. It is the world's largest open-cast copper mine.*

Map key

Population
- 1 million to 5 million
- 500,000 to 1 million
- 100,000 to 500,000
- 50,000 to 100,000
- 10,000 to 50,000
- below 10,000

Elevation
- 6000m / 19,686ft
- 4000m / 13,124ft
- 3000m / 9843ft
- 2000m / 6562ft
- 1000m / 328ft
- 500m / 1640ft
- 250m / 820ft
- 100m / 328ft
- sea level

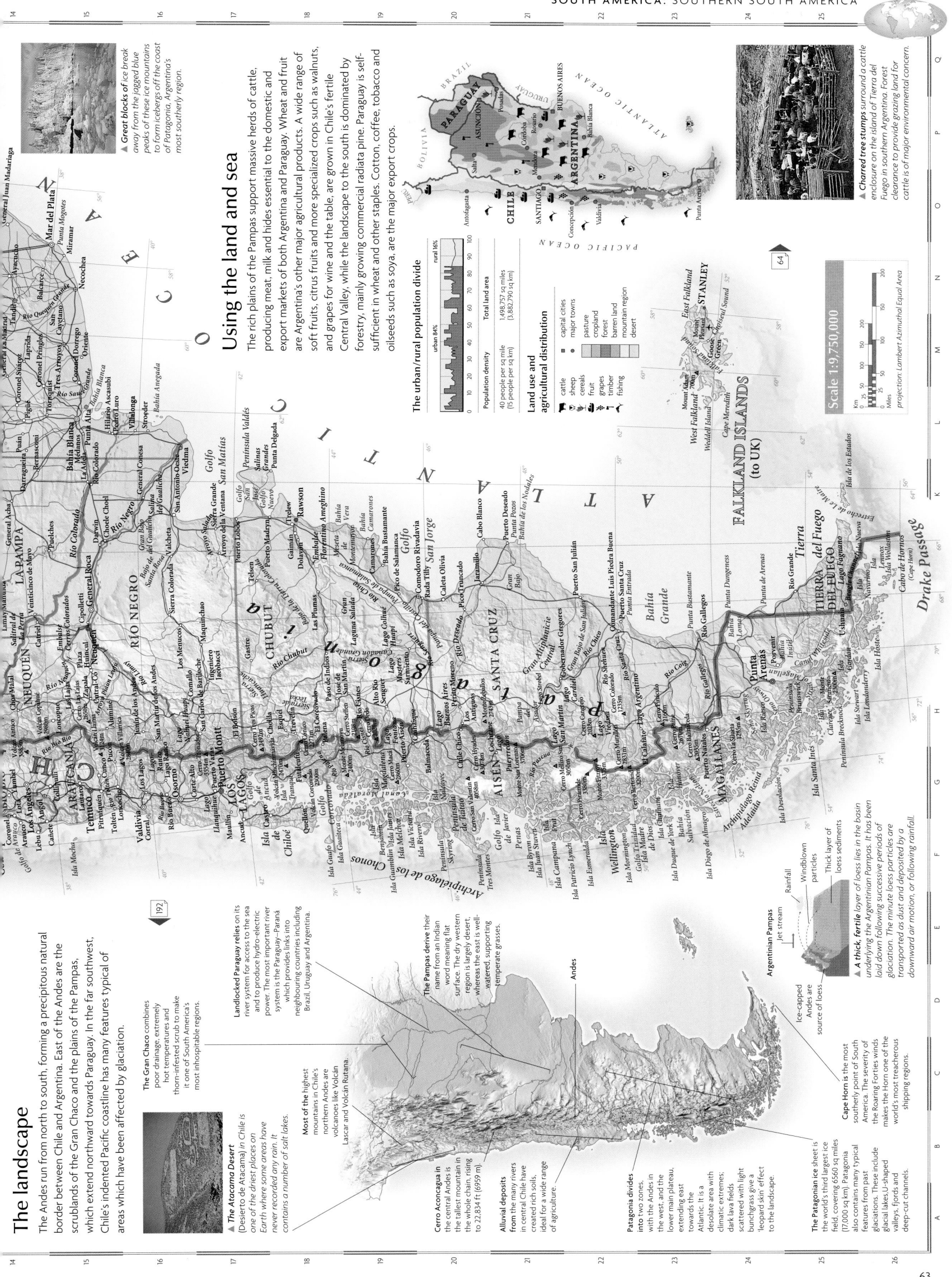

The landscape

The Andes run from north to south, forming a precipitous natural border between Chile and Argentina. East of the Andes are the scrublands of the Gran Chaco and the plains of the Pampas, which extend northward towards Paraguay. In the far southwest, Chile's indented Pacific coastline has many features typical of areas which have been affected by glaciation.

▲ Great blocks of ice break away from the jagged blue peaks of these ice mountains to form icebergs off the coast of Patagonia, Argentina's most southerly region.

▲ The Atacama Desert (Desierto de Atacama) in Chile is one of the driest places on Earth where some areas have never recorded any rain. It contains a number of salt lakes.

The Gran Chaco combines poor drainage, extremely hot temperatures and thorn-infested scrub to make it one of South America's most inhospitable regions.

Landlocked Paraguay relies on its river system for access to the sea and to produce hydro-electric power. The most important river system is the Paraguay–Paraná which provides links into neighbouring countries including Brazil, Uruguay and Argentina.

Most of the highest mountains in Chile's northern Andes are volcanoes like Volcán Lascar and Volcán Rutana.

Cerro Aconcagua in the central Andes is the tallest mountain in the whole chain, rising to 22,834 ft (6959 m).

Alluvial deposits from the many rivers in central Chile have created rich soils, ideal for a wide range of agriculture.

Patagonia divides into two zones, with the Andes in the west, and the lower main plateau, extending east towards the Atlantic. It is a desolate area with climatic extremes; dark lava fields scattered with light bunchgrass give a 'leopard skin' effect to the landscape.

The Patagonian ice sheet is the world's third largest ice field, covering 6560 sq miles (17,000 sq km). Patagonia also contains many typical features from past glaciations. These include glacial lakes, U-shaped valleys, fjords and deep-cut channels.

The Pampas derive their name from an Indian word meaning flat surface. The dry western region is largely desert, whereas the east is well-watered, supporting temperate grasses.

Cape Horn is the most southerly point of South America. The severity of the Roaring Forties winds makes the Horn one of the world's most treacherous shipping regions.

Ice-capped Andes are source of loess

Andes

Argentinian Pampas

Rainfall
Jet stream
Windblown particles
Thick layer of loess sediments

▲ A thick, fertile layer of loess lies in the basin underlying the Argentinian Pampas. It has been laid down following successive periods of glaciation. The minute loess particles are transported as dust and deposited by a downward air motion, or following rainfall.

Using the land and sea

The rich plains of the Pampas support massive herds of cattle, producing meat, milk and hides essential to the domestic and export markets of both Argentina and Paraguay. Wheat and fruit are Argentina's other major agricultural products. A wide range of soft fruits, citrus fruits and more specialized crops such as walnuts, and grapes for wine and the table, are grown in Chile's fertile Central Valley, while the landscape to the south is dominated by forestry, mainly growing commercial radiata pine. Paraguay is self-sufficient in wheat and other staples. Cotton, coffee, tobacco and oilseeds such as soya, are the major export crops.

The urban/rural population divide

Population density
40 people per sq mile
(15 people per sq km)

Land use and agricultural distribution

capital cities
major towns
pasture
cropland
forest
barren land
mountain region
desert

cattle
sheep
cereals
fruit
grapes
fishing
timber

▲ Charred tree stumps surround a cattle enclosure on the island of Tierra del Fuego in southern Argentina. Forest clearance to provide grazing land for cattle is of major environmental concern.

Scale 1:9,750,000

projection: Lambert Azimuthal Equal Area

The Atlantic Ocean

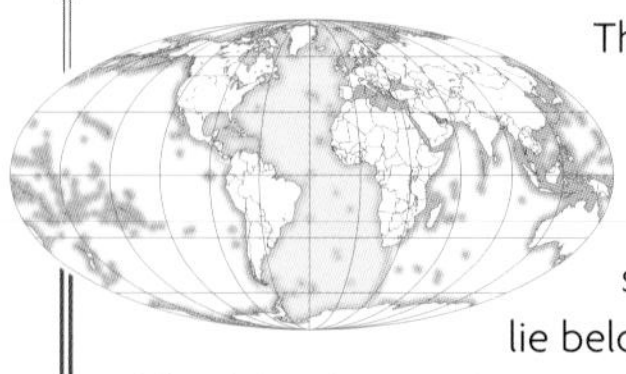

The Atlantic is the youngest of the world's oceans, formed about 180 million years ago when the landmasses of the eastern and western hemispheres separated. Its underwater topography is dominated by the Mid-Atlantic Ridge, a huge mountain system running north to south along the centre of the ocean. Although most of the ridge's peaks lie below the sea, some emerge as volcanic islands, like Iceland and the Azores.

The Atlantic contains a wealth of resources, including substantial oil and gas reserves and rich fishing grounds. Until the 1950s, the north Atlantic was the world's busiest shipping route; cheaper air transport and alternative routes have shifted patterns of world trade.

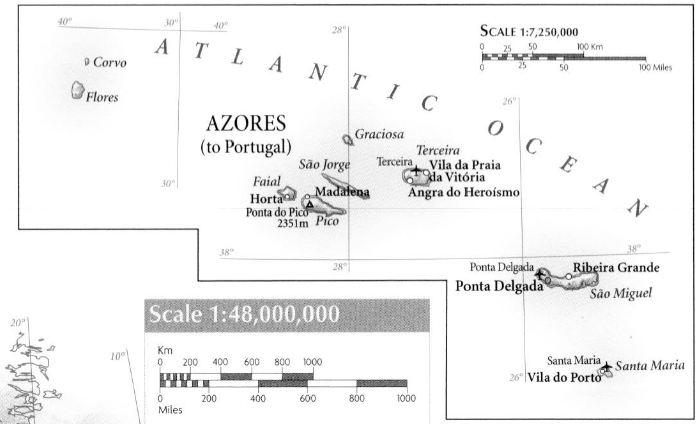

Resources

Development of the oil and gas reserves in the Atlantic began in the 1940s around the Gulf of Mexico. Since then other areas have been exploited, including the North Sea, the west coast of Africa and the area east of Newfoundland and Nova Scotia. There is also extensive mining of sand, gravel and shell deposits by the USA and UK. For centuries, the north Atlantic's fishing grounds have been utilized more heavily than other oceans, leading to a serious decline in many fish stocks.

Resources
(including wildlife)
- fish
- whales
- aggregates
- oil & gas
- major towns
- major ports

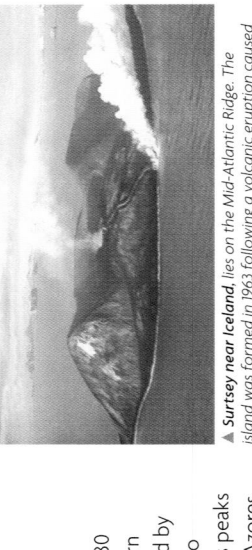

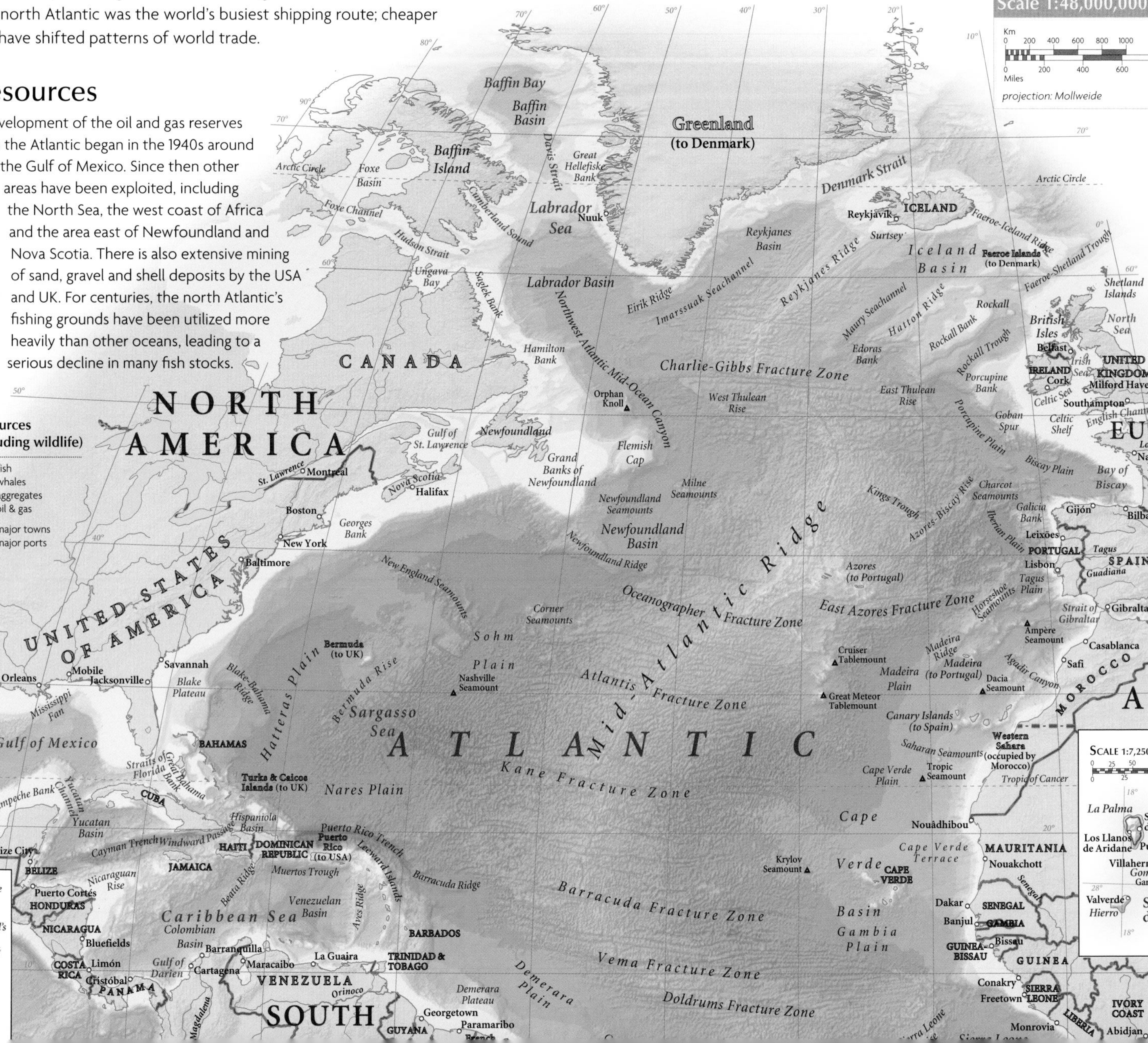

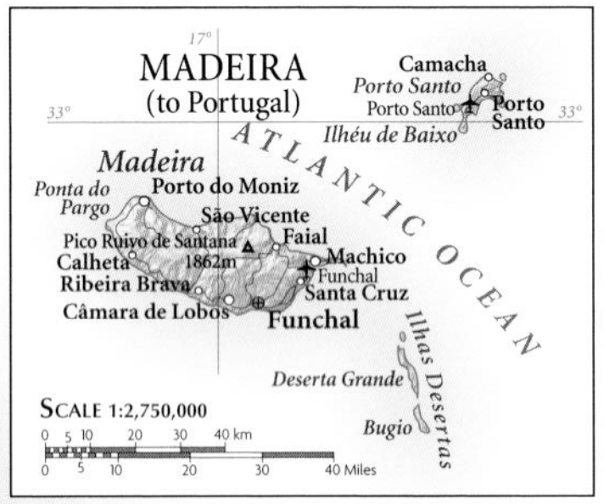

▲ *Surtsey near Iceland*, lies on the Mid-Atlantic Ridge. The island was formed in 1963 following a volcanic eruption caused by sea-floor spreading.

▲ *Fishing in the seas* around northwestern Europe dates back over 1500 years. The high nutrient content of the seas makes them ideal breeding grounds for many species of fish.

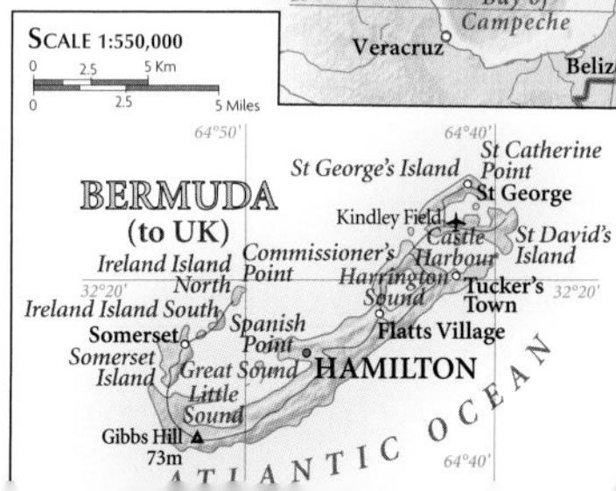

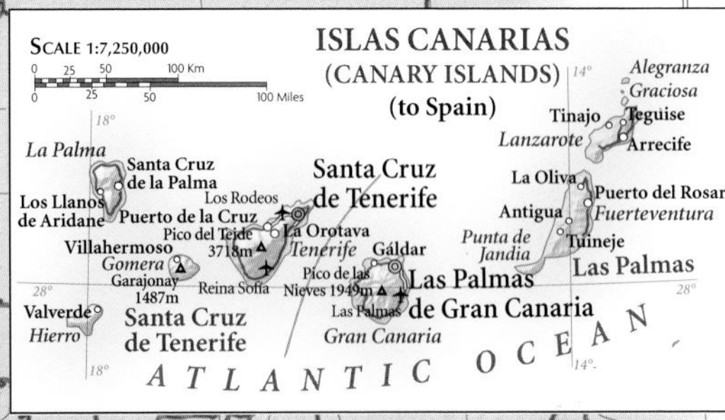

▲ *On 5 January 1993*, the oil tanker Braer ran aground in the Shetland Islands, spilling 83,660 tons (85,000 tonnes) of light crude oil into the ocean, devastating the local marine ecosystem.

SCALE 1:48,000,000

projection: Mollweide

AZORES (to Portugal)

SCALE 1:7,250,000

Corvo, Flores, Graciosa, São Jorge, Terceira, Faial, Horta, Ponta do Pico 2351m, Pico, Madalena, Pico, Angra do Heroísmo, Vila da Praia, Vila Vitória, Santa Cruz, Santa Maria, Vila do Porto, Ribeira Grande, São Miguel, Ponta Delgada, Ponta Delgada

MADEIRA (to Portugal)

SCALE 1:2,750,000

Madeira, Porto Santo, Camacha, Porto Santo, Ilhéu de Baixo, Ponta do Pargo, Porto do Moniz, Pico Ruivo de Santana, São Vicente, Faial, Calheta, Ribeira Brava, Câmara de Lobos, Machico, Santa Cruz, Funchal, Ilhas Desertas, Deserta Grande, Bugio

ISLAS CANARIAS (CANARY ISLANDS) (to Spain)

SCALE 1:7,250,000

Alegranza, Graciosa, La Oliva, Lanzarote, Teguise, Puerto del Rosario, Arrecife, Tinajo, Antigua, Fuerteventura, Punta de Jandía, La Palma, Santa Cruz de Tenerife, Los Rodeos, Los Llanos de Aridane, Villahermoso, Gomera, Garajonay 1487m, Valverde, Hierro, Puerto de la Cruz, Orotava, Pico del Teide 3718m, Nieves 1949m, Santa Cruz de Tenerife, Reina Sofía, Gáldar, Las Palmas de Gran Canaria, Gran Canaria, Las Palmas, Santa Cruz de Tenerife

BERMUDA (to UK)

SCALE 1:550,000

St George's Island, Ireland Island North, Ireland Island South, Somerset Island, St Catherine Point, St George, St David's Island, Kindley Field, Harrington Sound, Tucker's Town, Spanish Point, HAMILTON, Platts Village, Commissioner's Point, Great Sound, Spittal Pond, Gibbs Hill, Elbow Beach

Map labels (ocean/land features):

NORTH AMERICA, SOUTH AMERICA, EUROPE, AFRICA, CANADA, UNITED STATES OF AMERICA, GREENLAND (to Denmark), ICELAND, IRELAND, UNITED KINGDOM, FRANCE, SPAIN, PORTUGAL, MOROCCO, ALGERIA, WESTERN SAHARA (occupied by Morocco), MAURITANIA, SENEGAL, GAMBIA, GUINEA-BISSAU, GUINEA, SIERRA LEONE, LIBERIA, IVORY COAST, GHANA, TOGO, BENIN, NIGERIA, CAPE VERDE, MEXICO, BELIZE, GUATEMALA, HONDURAS, NICARAGUA, COSTA RICA, PANAMA, CUBA, JAMAICA, HAITI, DOMINICAN REPUBLIC, BAHAMAS, Turks & Caicos Islands (to UK), Puerto Rico (to USA), VENEZUELA, GUYANA, COLOMBIA, TRINIDAD & TOBAGO, BARBADOS, Bermuda (to UK)

ATLANTIC OCEAN, Mid-Atlantic Ridge, Reykjanes Ridge, Charlie-Gibbs Fracture Zone, Azores-Biscay Rise, Azores Fracture Zone, East Azores Fracture Zone, Atlantis Fracture Zone, Kane Fracture Zone, Barracuda Fracture Zone, Vema Fracture Zone, Doldrums Fracture Zone, Oceanographer Fracture Zone, Sargasso Sea, Hatteras Plain, Nares Plain, Sohm Plain, Newfoundland Basin, Labrador Sea, Labrador Basin, Baffin Bay, Baffin Basin, Davis Strait, Denmark Strait, Iceland Basin, Rockall Trough, Rockall Bank, Porcupine Bank, Porcupine Plain, Biscay Plain, Iberian Plain, Madeira Plain, Canary Basin, Cape Verde Basin, Cape Verde Plain, Gambia Plain, Gambia Basin, Sierra Leone Basin, Demerara Plain, Demerara Plateau, Caribbean Sea, Gulf of Mexico, Grand Banks of Newfoundland

Reykjavík, Nuuk, St John's, Halifax, Boston, New York, Baltimore, Savannah, Jacksonville, Mobile, New Orleans, Tampico, Veracruz, Belize City, Puerto Cortés, Bluefields, Cristóbal, Barranquilla, Cartagena, Maracaibo, La Guaira, Georgetown, Paramaribo, Cork, Belfast, Southampton, Milford Haven, Nantes, Bordeaux, Bilbao, Gijón, Leixões, Lisbon, Casablanca, Safi, Nouâdhibou, Nouakchott, Dakar, Banjul, Bissau, Conakry, Freetown, Monrovia, Abidjan, Accra, Lomé, Cotonou, Lagos, Porto-Novo, Las Palmas, Santa Cruz de Tenerife, Funchal, Ponta Delgada

Globe inset labels: Reykjavík, Rotterdam, Gibraltar, New York, New Orleans, Sargasso Sea, Caribbean Sea, La Guaira, Cristóbal, Rio de Janeiro, Buenos Aires, Cape Town, Lagos, NORTH AMERICA, SOUTH AMERICA, EUROPE, AFRICA, ANTARCTICA, ATLANTIC OCEAN, Weddell Sea, Scotia Sea

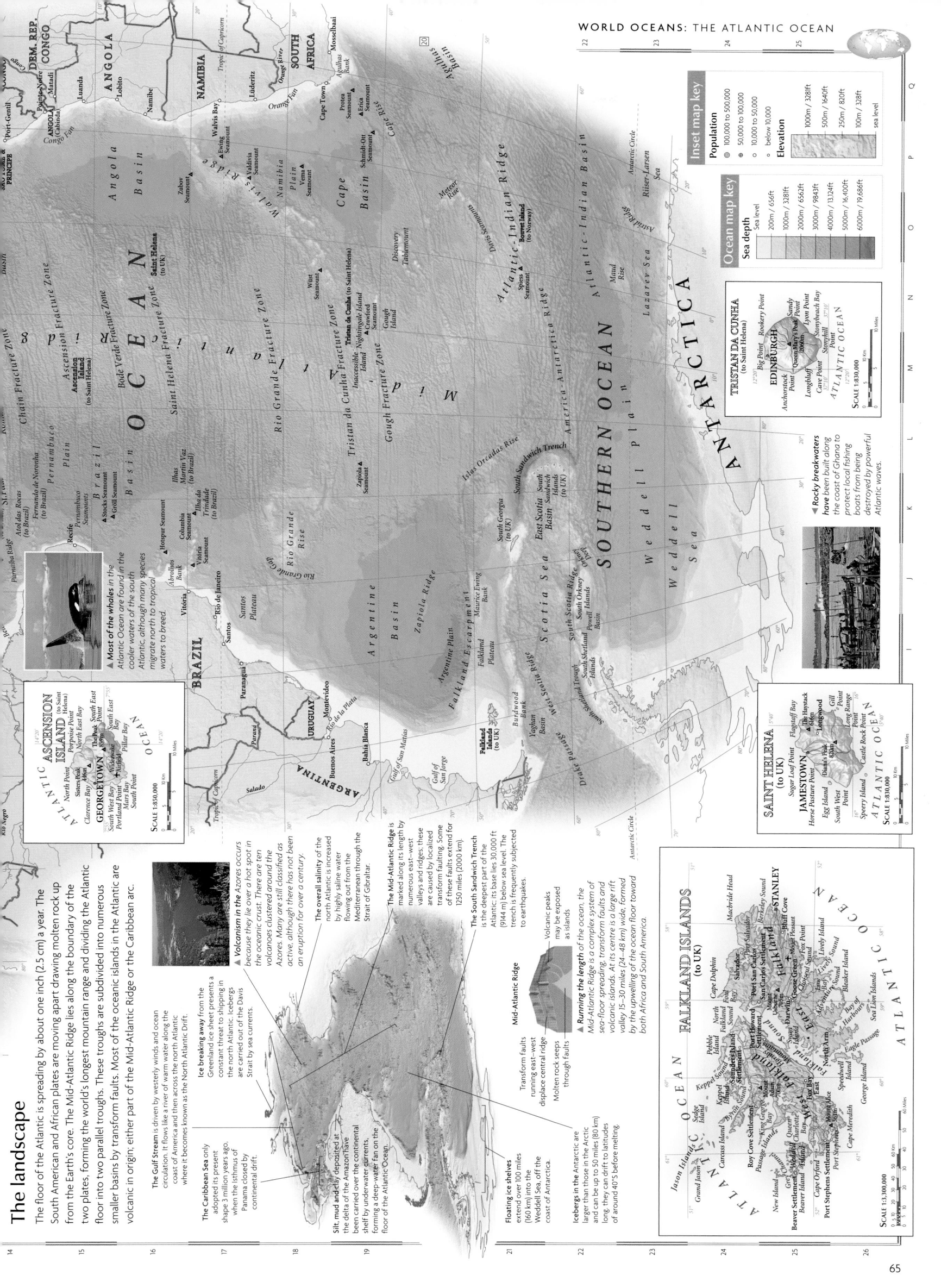

The landscape

The floor of the Atlantic is spreading by about one inch (2.5 cm) a year. The South American and African plates are moving apart drawing molten rock up from the Earth's core. The Mid-Atlantic Ridge lies along the boundary of the two plates, forming the world's longest mountain range and dividing the Atlantic floor into two parallel troughs. These troughs are subdivided into numerous smaller basins by transform faults. Most of the oceanic islands in the Atlantic are volcanic in origin; either part of the Mid-Atlantic Ridge or the Caribbean arc.

The Gulf Stream is driven by westerly winds and ocean circulation. It flows like a river of warm water along the coast of America and then across the north Atlantic where it becomes known as the North Atlantic Drift.

The Caribbean Sea only adopted its present shape 3 million years ago, when the isthmus of Panama closed by continental drift.

Silt, mud and clay deposited at the delta of the Amazon have been carried over the continental shelf by underwater currents, forming a deep-water fan on the floor of the Atlantic Ocean.

Icebergs in the Antarctic are larger than those in the Arctic and can be up to 50 miles (80 km) long; they can drift to latitudes of around 40°S before melting.

Floating ice shelves extend over 100 miles (160 km) into the Weddell Sea, off the coast of Antarctica.

Ice breaking away from the Greenland ice sheet presents a constant threat to shipping in the north Atlantic. Icebergs are carried out of the Davis Strait by sea currents.

▲ **Volcanism in the Azores** occurs because they lie over a hot spot in the oceanic crust. There are ten volcanoes clustered around the Azores. Many are still classified as active, although there has not been an eruption for over a century.

The overall salinity of the north Atlantic is increased by highly saline water flowing out from the Mediterranean through the Strait of Gibraltar.

The Mid-Atlantic Ridge is marked along its length by numerous east–west valleys and ridges; these are caused by localized transform faulting. Some of these faults extend for 1250 miles (2000 km).

The South Sandwich Trench is the deepest part of the Atlantic; its base lies 30,000 ft (9144 m) below sea level. The trench is frequently subjected to earthquakes.

▲ **Most of the whales** in the Atlantic Ocean are found in the cooler waters of the south Atlantic, although many species migrate north to tropical waters to breed.

Transform faults running east–west displace central ridge

Molten rock seeps through faults

Volcanic peaks may be exposed as islands

Mid-Atlantic Ridge

▲ **Running the length** of the ocean, the Mid-Atlantic Ridge is a complex system of sea-floor spreading, transform faults and volcanic islands. At its centre is a large rift valley 15–30 miles (24–48 km) wide, formed by the upwelling of the ocean floor toward both Africa and South America.

◀ **Rocky breakwaters have been built** along the coast of Ghana to protect local fishing boats from being destroyed by powerful Atlantic waves.

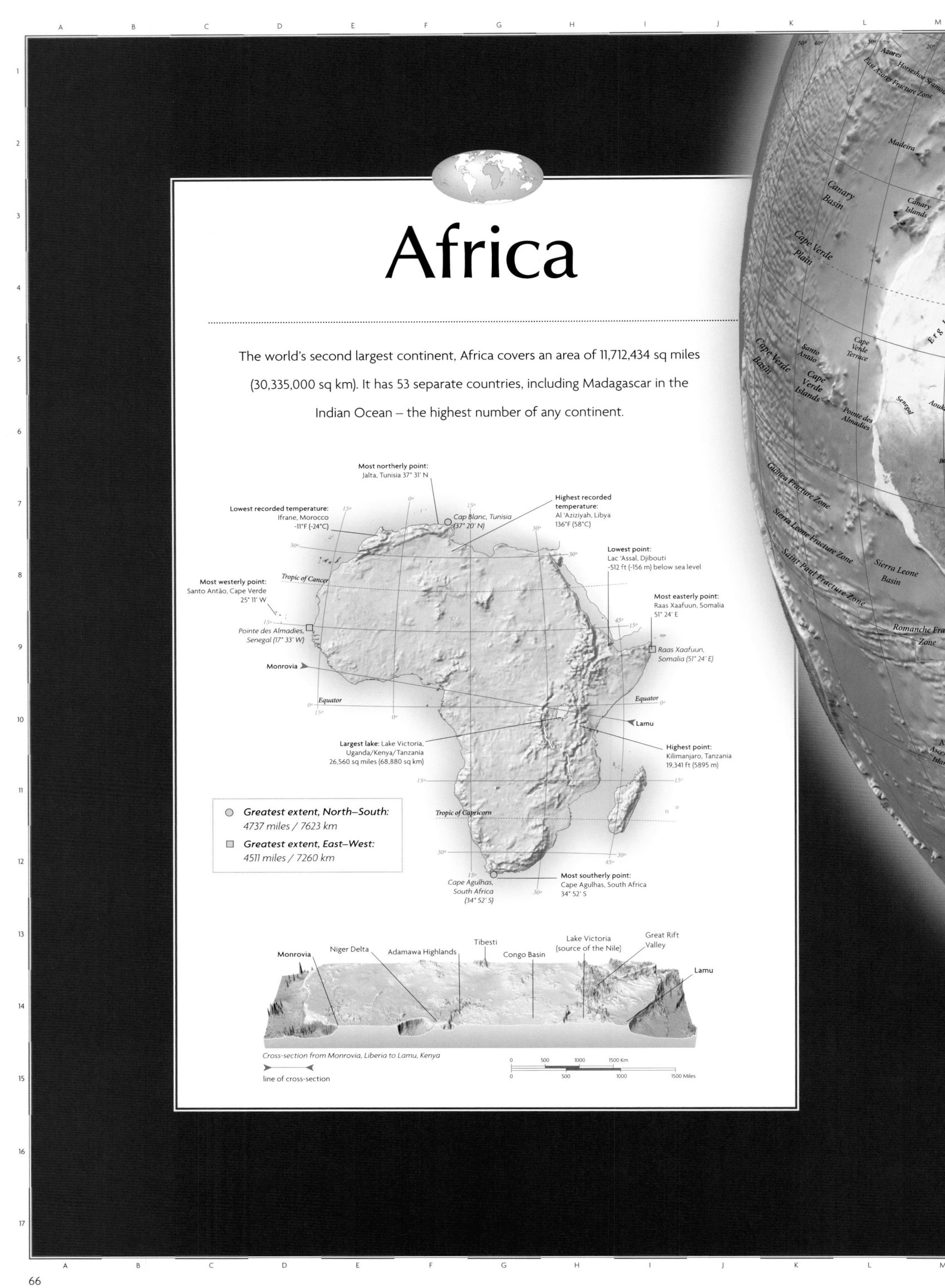

Africa

The world's second largest continent, Africa covers an area of 11,712,434 sq miles (30,335,000 sq km). It has 53 separate countries, including Madagascar in the Indian Ocean – the highest number of any continent.

Most northerly point:
Jalta, Tunisia 37° 31' N

Lowest recorded temperature:
Ifrane, Morocco
-11°F (-24°C)

Cap Blanc, Tunisia
(37° 20' N)

Highest recorded temperature:
Al 'Aziziyah, Libya
136°F (58°C)

Lowest point:
Lac 'Assal, Djibouti
-512 ft (-156 m) below sea level

Most westerly point:
Santo Antão, Cape Verde
25° 11' W

Tropic of Cancer

Most easterly point:
Raas Xaafuun, Somalia
51° 24' E

*Pointe des Almadies,
Senegal (17° 33' W)*

*Raas Xaafuun,
Somalia (51° 24' E)*

Monrovia

Equator

Equator

Lamu

Largest lake: Lake Victoria,
Uganda/Kenya/Tanzania
26,560 sq miles (68,880 sq km)

Highest point:
Kilimanjaro, Tanzania
19,341 ft (5895 m)

○ **Greatest extent, North–South:**
4737 miles / 7623 km

□ **Greatest extent, East–West:**
4511 miles / 7260 km

Tropic of Capricorn

Most southerly point:
Cape Agulhas, South Africa
34° 52' S

*Cape Agulhas,
South Africa
(34° 52' S)*

Monrovia | Niger Delta | Adamawa Highlands | Tibesti | Congo Basin | Lake Victoria (source of the Nile) | Great Rift Valley | Lamu

Cross-section from Monrovia, Liberia to Lamu, Kenya

line of cross-section

0   500   1000   1500 Km

0   500   1000   1500 Miles

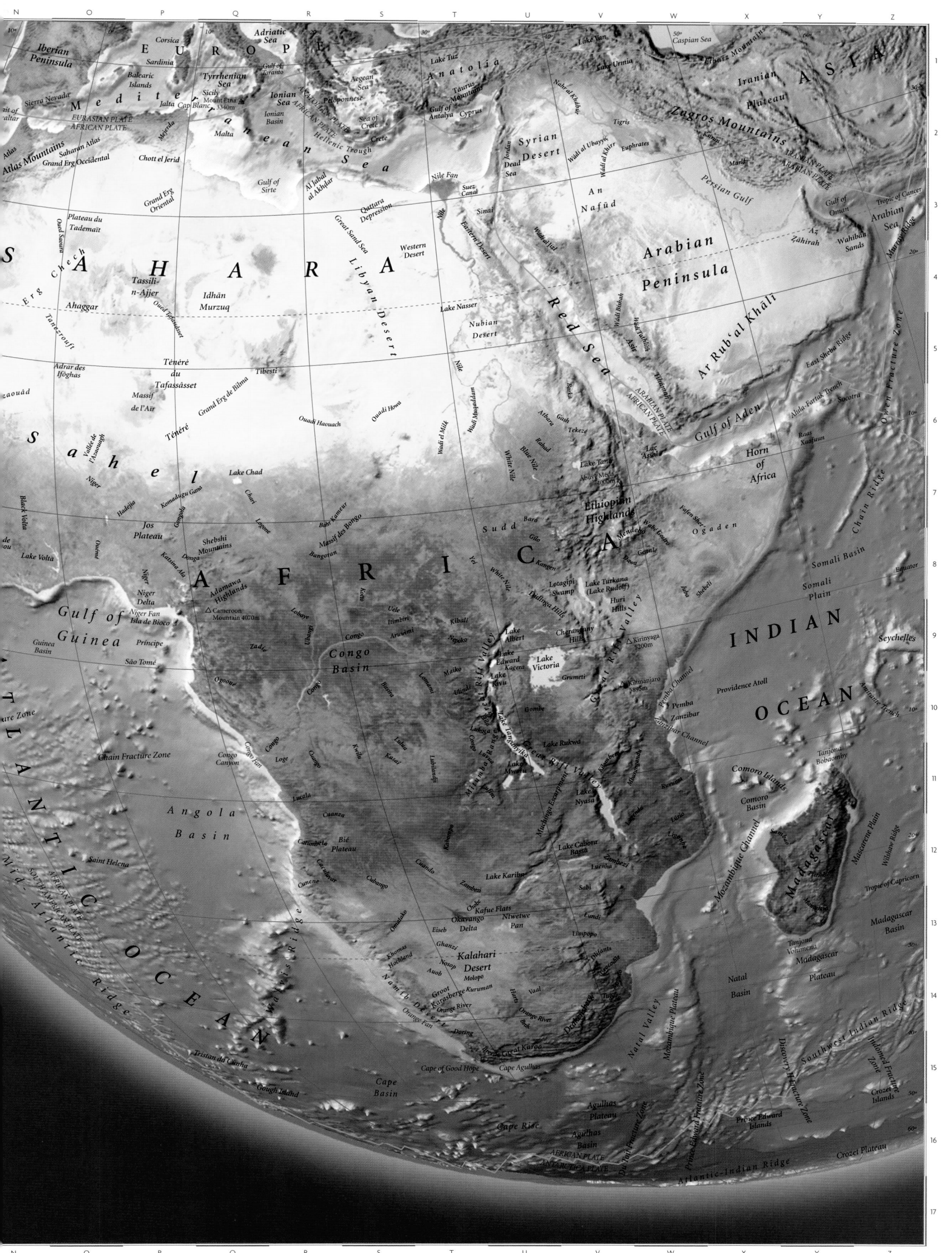

Physical Africa

The structure of Africa was dramatically influenced by the break up of the supercontinent Gondwanaland about 160 million years ago and, more recently, rifting and hot spot activity. Today, much of Africa is remote from active plate boundaries and comprises a series of extensive plateaux and deep basins, which influence the drainage patterns of major rivers. The relief rises to the east, where volcanic uplands and vast lakes mark the Great Rift Valley. In the far north and south sedimentary rocks have been folded to form the Atlas Mountains and the Great Karoo.

Northern Africa

Northern Africa comprises a system of basins and plateaux. The Tibesti and Ahaggar are volcanic uplands, whose uplift has been matched by subsidence within large surrounding basins. Many of the basins have been infilled with sand and gravel, creating the vast Saharan lands. The Atlas Mountains in the north were formed by convergence of the African and Eurasian plates.

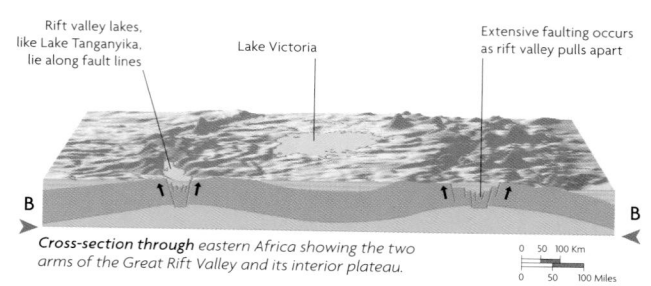

The Earth's crust has been warped to form the Taoudenni Basin

Volcanic Ahaggar mountains, formed by rising magma from a hot spot

Lake Chad lies in a sand-filled basin

Section across northern Africa showing infilled basins and uplifted plateaux.

East Africa

The Great Rift Valley is the most striking feature of this region, running for 4475 miles (7200 km) from Lake Nyasa to the Red Sea. North of Lake Nyasa it splits into two arms and encloses an interior plateau which contains Lake Victoria. A number of elongated lakes and volcanoes lie along the fault lines. To the west lies the Congo Basin, a vast, shallow depression, which rises to form an almost circular rim of highlands.

Rift valley lakes, like Lake Tanganyika, lie along fault lines

Lake Victoria

Extensive faulting occurs as rift valley pulls apart

Cross-section through eastern Africa showing the two arms of the Great Rift Valley and its interior plateau.

Scale 1:40,000,000

projection: Lambert Azimuthal Equal Area

Map key

Elevation

5000m / 16,405ft
4000m / 13,124ft
3000m / 9843ft
2000m / 6562ft
1000m / 3281ft
500m / 1640ft
250m / 820ft
100m / 328ft
sea level
below sea level

Plate margins (for explanation see page xiv)

— constructive
△ destructive
— conservative
···· uncertain
line of cross-section

Southern Africa

The Great Escarpment marks the southern boundary of Africa's basement rock and includes the Drakensberg range. It was uplifted when Gondwanaland fragmented about 160 million years ago and it has gradually been eroded back from the coast. To the north, the relief drops steadily, forming the Kalahari Basin. In the far south are the fold mountains of the Great Karoo.

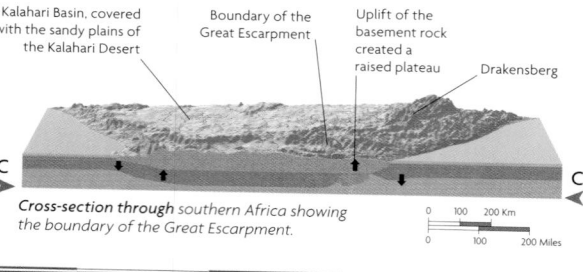

Kalahari Basin, covered with the sandy plains of the Kalahari Desert

Boundary of the Great Escarpment

Uplift of the basement rock created a raised plateau

Drakensberg

Cross-section through southern Africa showing the boundary of the Great Escarpment.

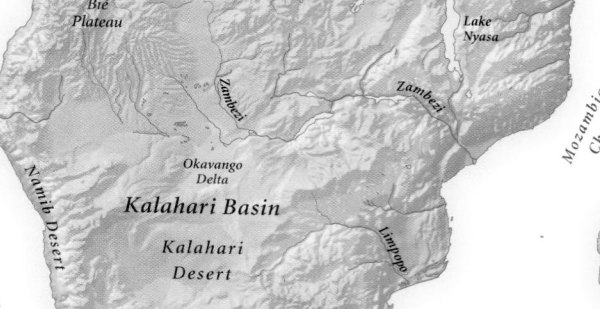

Climate

The climates of Africa range from mediterranean to arid, dry savannah and humid equatorial. In East Africa, where snow settles at the summit of volcanoes such as Kilimanjaro, climate is also modified by altitude. The winds of the Sahara export millions of tonnes of dust a year both northwards and eastwards.

▲ Savannah grasslands run in a belt across Africa; limited rainfall inhibits tree growth.

Temperature

Average January temperature

Average July temperature

Temperature
- 0 to 10°C (32 to 50°F)
- 10 to 20°C (50 to 68°F)
- 20 to 30°C (68 to 86°F)
- above 30°C (86°F)

Rainfall

Average January rainfall

Average July rainfall

Rainfall
- 0–25 mm (0–1 in)
- 25–50 mm (1–2 in)
- 50–100 mm (2–4 in)
- 100–200 mm (4–8 in)
- 200–300 mm (8–12 in)
- 300–400 mm (12–16 in)
- 400–500 mm (16–20 in)
- more than 500 mm (20 in)

▲ The hot, equatorial basin of the Congo river receives over 48 inches (1200 mm) of rainfall per year.

Climate
- arid
- humid equatorial
- mediterranean
- semi-arid
- tropical
- warm humid
- ☼ daily hours of sunshine, January
- ☼ daily hours of sunshine, July
- → cold wind
- → hot wind

Shaping the continent

African landscapes are shaped by the intensity of climatic extremes and by tectonic action. High aridity, wind action and infrequent but heavy rainstorms, lead to the migration of sand dunes and dramatic flash flooding across much of the north and west. In the wetter areas, high precipitation increases the rate of weathering. To the east, the rift system has created a volcanic and lake environment and allowed rivers to erode weaknesses left in the crustal structure by faults.

Groundwater

1 Oases are found in desert areas such as the Sahara *(left)*. Groundwater migrates through permeable rock strata, confined between two impermeable layers. Oases form either when the permeable rocks come near to the surface, or at a fault line, when water is able to seep up to the surface through the crushed rocks at the fault.

External stresses act on the surface of the inselberg

Exfoliated layers

Joints or cracks caused by expansion and contraction

Weathering: Formation of an inselberg

The evolving landscape

Rainwater feeds the aquifer

Water migrates up through fault

Aquifer exposed near the surface

Groundwater trapped between impermeable strata

Groundwater: Replenishment of an oasis

River systems

2 The Zambezi river *(above)* drops 360 ft (110 m) over the Victoria Falls into a zig-zag gorge. The river has eroded the gorge along lines of weakness in the bedrock, created by fault lines running in two directions.

Old site of Victoria Falls

River plunges over falls

Fault and joint lines running in two directions

Zig-zag gorge of the Zambezi

River systems: Retreating of the Victoria Falls

Weathering

6 Inselbergs *(above)*, found extensively across West Africa, are exposed remnants of an extensive upland area. Erosion of the surrounding uplands leaves a resistant rock outcrop. Its spheroidal shape is the result of 'onion-skin' weathering – the exfoliating of layers – due to repeated expansion and contraction.

Ephemeral channels

5 Wadis *(above)* drain much of northern Africa. These drybed courses are flooded only after infrequent, but intense, storms in the uplands cause water to surge along their channels.

Heavy rainfall runs off mountains

Water collects and floods the dry channel

Ephemeral channels: Flash flooding of a wadi

Sand is gradually blown up the back slope

Deposition on the slip face

Build up of sand produces strata inside the dune

Wind erosion: Migration of a dune

Wind erosion

4 Dunes like this in the Namib Desert *(left)* are wind-blown accumulations of sand, which slowly migrate. Wind action moves sand up the shallow back slope; when the sand reaches the crest of the dune it is deposited on the slip face.

Landscape
- sinking land
- stable land
- uplifting land
- ∨∨∨ escarpment
- → ocean current
- — rift
- ▲ active volcano
- ⛰ inselberg
- ⚓ oasis
- — river
- ⋯ wadi
- ⚡ waterfall

Wave energy dispersed in the bay

Waves refracting

Force of waves concentrates on the headland

The sea bed is deeper opposite the bay than at the headland

Coastal processes: Erosion of a bay

Coastal processes

3 Houtbaai *(above)*, in southern Africa, is constantly being modified by wave action. As waves approach the indented coastline, they reach the shallow water of the headland, slowing down and reducing in length. This causes them to bend or refract, concentrating their erosive force at the headlands.

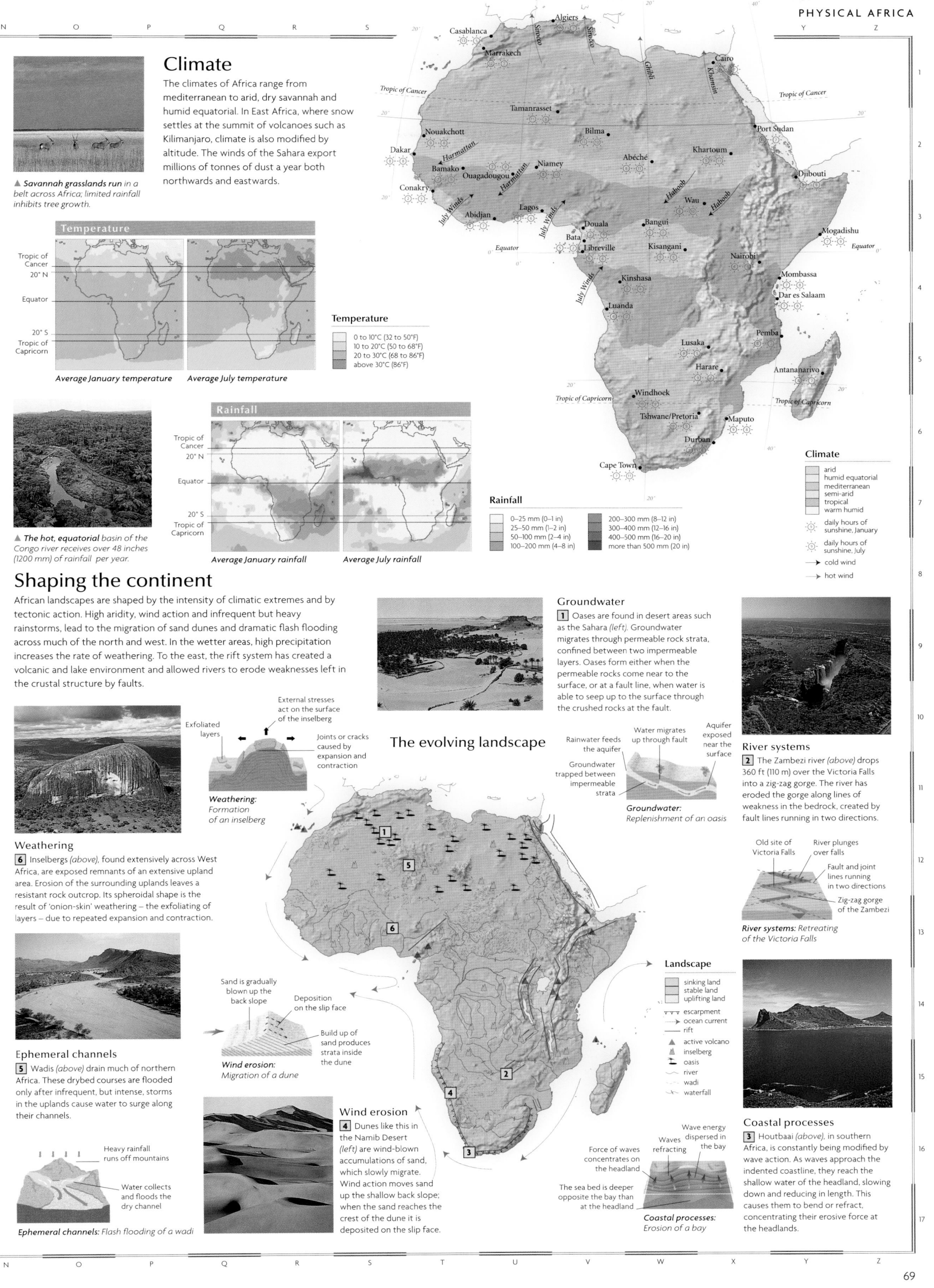

Map labels: Algiers, Casablanca, Marrakech, Sirocco, Sirocco, Ghibli, Cairo, Khamsin, Tamanrasset, Nouakchott, Bilma, Khartoum, Port Sudan, Dakar, Abéché, Harmattan, Niamey, Bamako, Ouagadougou, Conakry, Wau, Haboob, Haboob, Djibouti, Abidjan, Lagos, Juby Winds, Douala, Bangui, Mogadishu, Bata, Libreville, Kisangani, Equator, July Winds, Kinshasa, Nairobi, Mombassa, Dar es Salaam, Luanda, Pemba, Lusaka, Harare, Antananarivo, Windhoek, Tropic of Capricorn, Tshwane/Pretoria, Maputo, Durban, Cape Town

Political Africa

The political map of modern Africa only emerged following the end of the Second World War. Over the next half-century, all of the countries formerly controlled by European powers gained independence from their colonial rulers – only Liberia and Ethiopia were never colonized. The post-colonial era has not been an easy period for many countries, but there have been moves towards multi-party democracy across much of the continent. In South Africa, democratic elections replaced the internationally-condemned apartheid system only in 1994. Other countries have still to find political stability; corruption in government and ethnic tensions are serious problems. National infrastructures, based on the colonial transport systems built to exploit Africa's resources, are often inappropriate for independent economic development.

Languages

Three major world languages act as *lingua francas* across the African continent: Arabic in North Africa; English in southern and eastern Africa and Nigeria; and French in Central and West Africa, and in Madagascar. A huge number of African languages are spoken as well – over 2000 have been recorded, with more than 400 in Nigeria alone – reflecting the continuing importance of traditional cultures and values. In the north of the continent, the extensive use of Arabic reflects Middle Eastern influences while Bantu is widely-spoken across much of southern Africa.

Language groups

- Afro-Asiatic (Hamito-Semitic)
- Niger-Congo
- Nilo-Saharan
- Khoisan
- Indo-European
- Austronesian

Official African languages

- French
- English
- Arabic
- Portuguese
- Swahili
- Amharic
- Spanish
- French/English
- French/Arabic
- French/Malagasy
- English/Swahili
- Arabic/Somali

▲ *Islamic influences are* evident throughout North Africa. The Great Mosque at Kairouan, Tunisia, is Africa's holiest Islamic place.

▲ *In northeastern Nigeria,* people speak Kanuri – a dialect of the Nilo-Saharan language group.

Transport

African railways were built to aid the exploitation of natural resources, and most offer passage only from the interior to the coastal cities, leaving large parts of the continent untouched – five land-locked countries have no railways at all. The Congo, Nile and Niger river networks offer limited access to land within the continental interior, but have a number of waterfalls and cataracts which prevent navigation from the sea. Many roads were developed in the 1960s and 1970s, but economic difficulties are making the maintenance and expansion of the networks difficult.

▶ *South Africa has the* largest concentration of railways in Africa. Over 20,000 miles (32,000 km) of routes have been built since 1870.

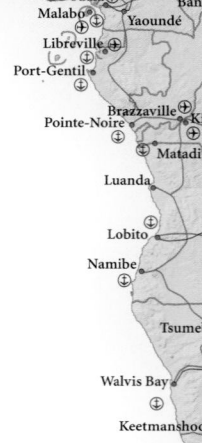

▲ *Traditional means of* transport, such as the camel, are still widely used across the less accessible parts of Africa.

◀ *The Congo river,* though not suitable for river transport along its entire length, forms a vital link for people and goods in its navigable inland reaches.

Transport

- major roads and motorways
- major railways
- major canal
- international borders
- ● transport intersections
- ⊕ international airports
- ◉ major ports

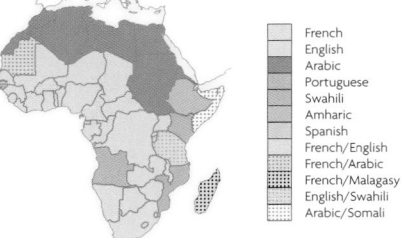

MOROCC
Casabla
Saf
Marrak
Agadir
Canary Islands (to Spain)
LAÂYOUNE
Western Sahara (Occupied by Morocco)
Tropic of Cancer
Madeira (to Portugal)

CAPE VERDE
PRAIA
NOUAKCHOTT
Senegal
DAKAR
Kaolack
BANJUL
GAMBIA
GUINEA-BISSAU
BISSAU
BAMAKO
GUINEA
CONAKRY
Koidu
FREETOWN
SIERRA LEONE
MONROVIA
YAMOUSSOUK
IV
CO
LIBERIA
S
MAURITANI

Ceuta (to Spain)
Tanger
Rabat
Casablanca
Agadir
Algiers
Oran
Skikda
Tunis
Tripoli
Alexandria
Port Said
Suez Canal
Cairo
Suez
Nouâdhibou
Tamanrasset
Aswân
Wadi Halfa
Port Sudan
Nouakchott
Dakar
Banjul
Bissau
Bamako
Agadez
Niamey
Ouagadougon
Kano
Maiduguri
Ndjamena
Nyala
Khartoum
Massawa
Assab
Djibouti
Conakry
Freetown
Monrovia
Cotonou
Accra
Lome
Lagos
Abidjan
Warri
Douala
Malabo
Yaoundé
Bangui
Addis Ababa
Libreville
Port-Gentil
Kisangani
Kampala
Mogadishu
Nairobi
Brazzaville
Kinshasa
Bukavu
Mombasa
Pointe-Noire
Matadi
Kananga
Kalemie
Dodoma
Dar es Salaam
Luanda
Mbeya
Lobito
Lubumbashi
Nampula
Namibe
Lusaka
Livingstone
Harare
Beira
Tsumeb
Bulawayo
Walvis Bay
Windhoek
Antananarivo
Toamasina
Tshwane/Pretoria
Maputo
Keetmanshoop
Johannesburg
Durban
Cape Town
Port Elizabeth

ARABIC
BERBER
TUAREG
TEDA
FULANI
MANDINGO
MOSI
HAUSA
KANURI
AKAN
YORUBA
EVE
IBO
DINKA
AZANDE
TIGRAI
AMHARA
GALLA
BEJA
SOMALI
MASAI
SWAHILI
BANTU
SAN
KHOI
MALAGASY
AFRIKAANS

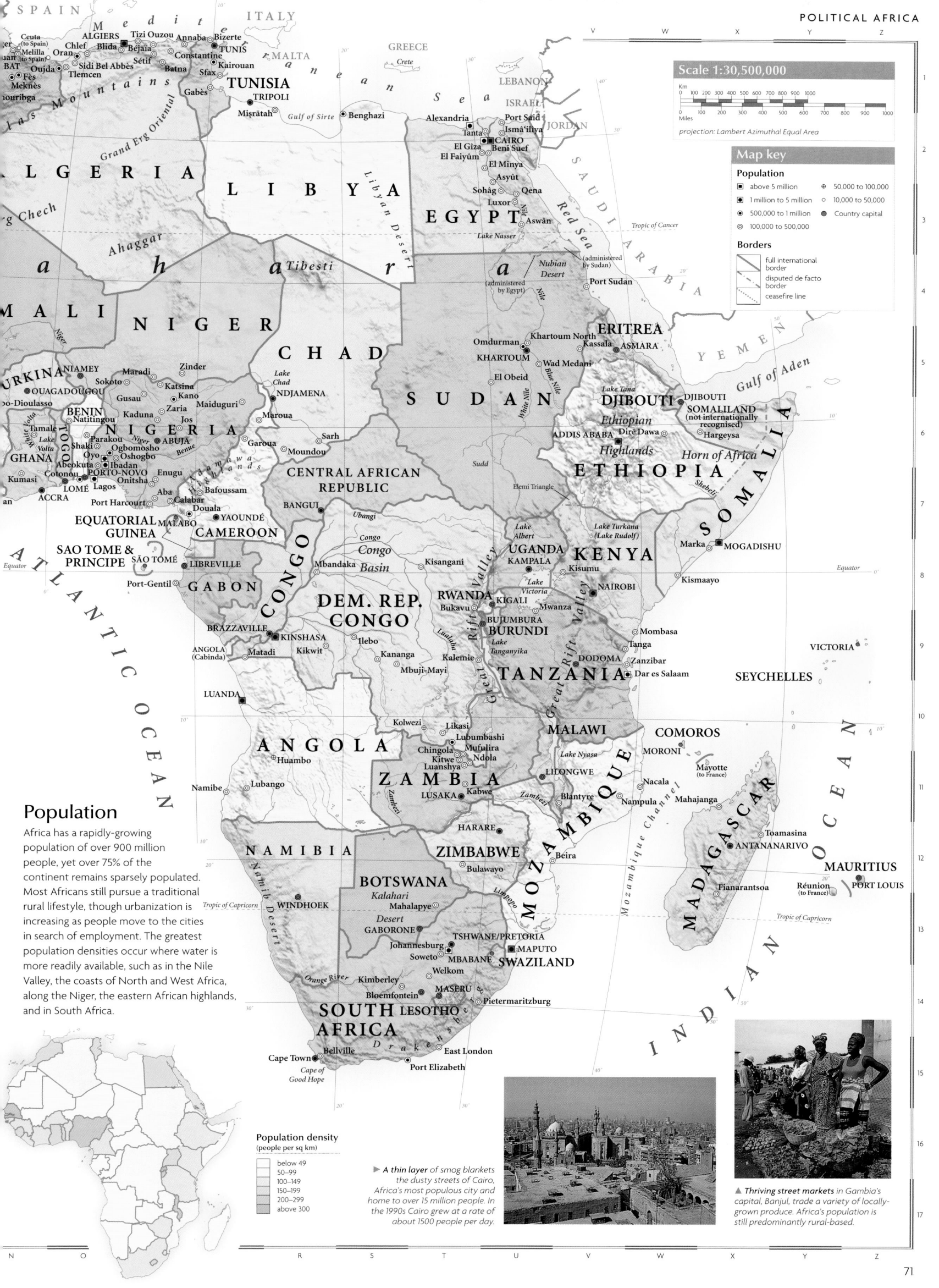

Scale 1:30,500,000

projection: Lambert Azimuthal Equal Area

Map key

Population
- ■ above 5 million
- ■ 1 million to 5 million
- ◉ 500,000 to 1 million
- ◉ 100,000 to 500,000
- ⊕ 50,000 to 100,000
- ○ 10,000 to 50,000
- ● Country capital

Borders
- full international border
- disputed de facto border
- ceasefire line

Population

Africa has a rapidly-growing population of over 900 million people, yet over 75% of the continent remains sparsely populated. Most Africans still pursue a traditional rural lifestyle, though urbanization is increasing as people move to the cities in search of employment. The greatest population densities occur where water is more readily available, such as in the Nile Valley, the coasts of North and West Africa, along the Niger, the eastern African highlands, and in South Africa.

Population density
(people per sq km)
- below 49
- 50–99
- 100–149
- 150–199
- 200–299
- above 300

▶ **A thin layer** of smog blankets the dusty streets of Cairo, Africa's most populous city and home to over 15 million people. In the 1990s Cairo grew at a rate of about 1500 people per day.

▲ **Thriving street markets** in Gambia's capital, Banjul, trade a variety of locally-grown produce. Africa's population is still predominantly rural-based.

71

African resources

The economies of most African countries are dominated by subsistence and cash crop agriculture, with limited industrialization. Manufacturing industry is largely confined to South Africa. Many countries depend on a single resource, such as copper or gold, or a cash crop, such as coffee, for export income, which can leave them vulnerable to fluctuations in world commodity prices. In order to diversify their economies and develop a wider industrial base, investment from overseas is being actively sought by many African governments.

Industry

Many African industries concentrate on the extraction and processing of raw materials. These include the oil industry, food processing, mining and textile production. South Africa accounts for over half of the continent's industrial output with much of the remainder coming from the countries along the northern coast. Over 60% of Africa's workforce is employed in agriculture.

◄ *The unspoilt natural* splendour of wildlife reserves, like the Serengeti National Park in Tanzania, attract tourists to Africa from around the globe. The tourist industry in Kenya and Tanzania is particularly well developed, where it accounts for almost 10% of GNI.

Standard of living

Since the 1960s most countries in Africa have seen significant improvements in life expectancy, healthcare and education. However, 28 of the 30 most deprived countries in the world are African, and the continent as a whole lies well behind the rest of the world in terms of meeting many basic human needs.

Standard of living
(UN human development index)

high

low

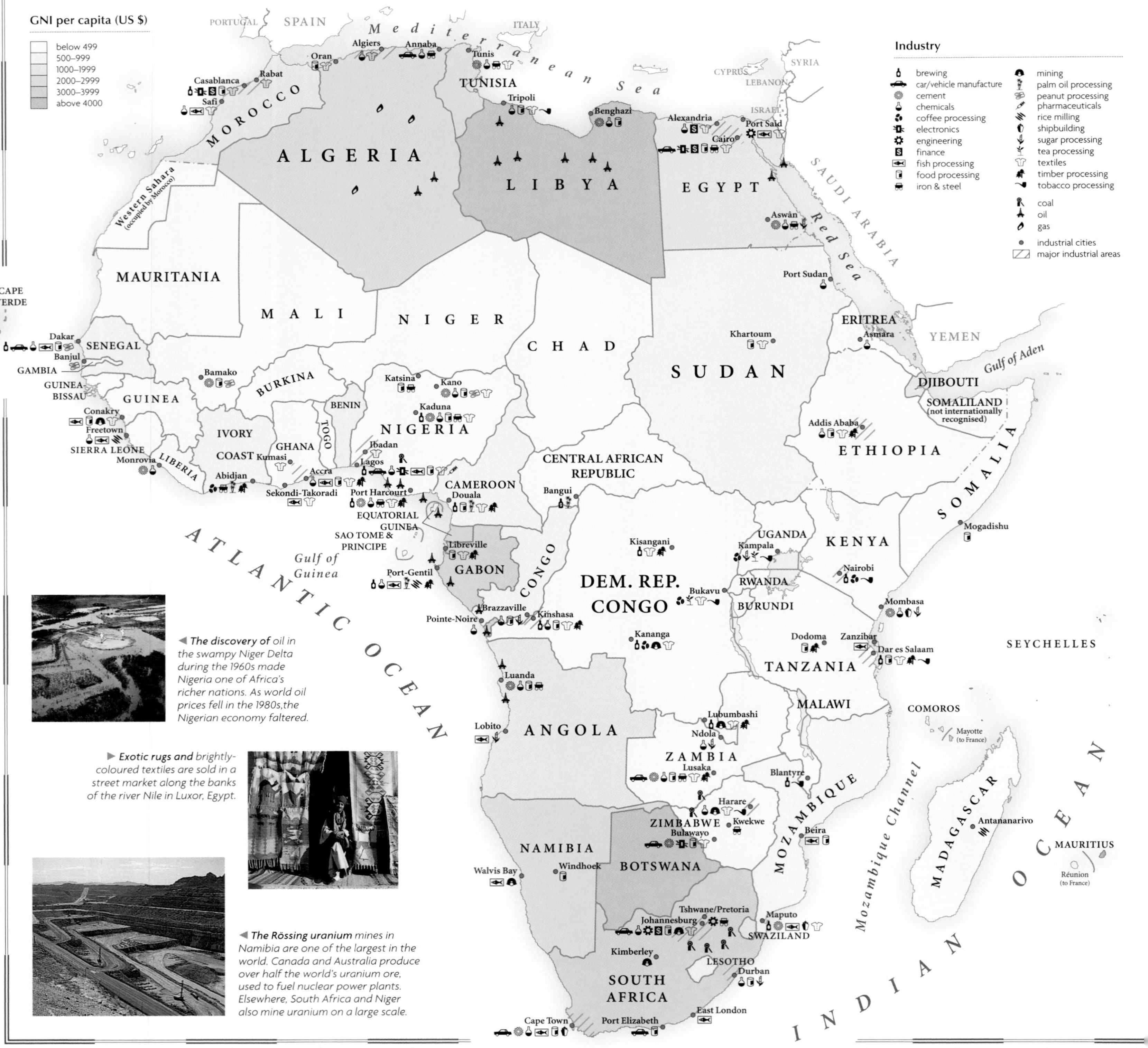

GNI per capita (US $)

below 499
500–999
1000–1999
2000–2999
3000–3999
above 4000

Industry

brewing	mining
car/vehicle manufacture	palm oil processing
cement	peanut processing
chemicals	pharmaceuticals
coffee processing	rice milling
electronics	shipbuilding
engineering	sugar processing
finance	tea processing
fish processing	textiles
food processing	timber processing
iron & steel	tobacco processing

coal
oil
gas

● industrial cities
major industrial areas

◄ *The discovery of* oil in the swampy Niger Delta during the 1960s made Nigeria one of Africa's richer nations. As world oil prices fell in the 1980s, the Nigerian economy faltered.

► *Exotic rugs and* brightly-coloured textiles are sold in a street market along the banks of the river Nile in Luxor, Egypt.

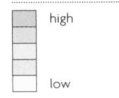

◄ *The Rössing uranium* mines in Namibia are one of the largest in the world. Canada and Australia produce over half the world's uranium ore, used to fuel nuclear power plants. Elsewhere, South Africa and Niger also mine uranium on a large scale.

PORTUGAL SPAIN *Mediterranean Sea* ITALY CYPRUS SYRIA LEBANON ISRAEL

Algiers Annaba Tunis
Oran
Casablanca Rabat
Safi
MOROCCO
TUNISIA
Tripoli
Benghazi Alexandria Port Said SAUDI ARABIA
Cairo
ALGERIA
LIBYA
EGYPT
Aswân
Red Sea

Western Sahara (occupied by Morocco)

MAURITANIA
CAPE VERDE
MALI NIGER CHAD SUDAN Khartoum ERITREA Asmara YEMEN
Port Sudan

Dakar SENEGAL Bamako BURKINA Katsina Kano DJIBOUTI *Gulf of Aden*
Banjul
GAMBIA
GUINEA-BISSAU GUINEA Kaduna SOMALILAND (not internationally recognised)
Conakry Ibadan NIGERIA Addis Ababa ETHIOPIA
Freetown IVORY GHANA BENIN TOGO Lagos CENTRAL AFRICAN REPUBLIC
SIERRA LEONE COAST Kumasi SOMALIA
Monrovia LIBERIA Abidjan Accra CAMEROON Bangui
Sekondi-Takoradi Port Harcourt Douala Mogadishu
EQUATORIAL GUINEA UGANDA KENYA
SAO TOME & PRINCIPE Libreville Kisangani Kampala
GABON DEM. REP. RWANDA Nairobi
Gulf of Guinea Port-Gentil CONGO CONGO Bukavu Mombasa
Brazzaville BURUNDI
Pointe-Noire Kinshasa Kanaga Dodoma Zanzibar SEYCHELLES
Luanda TANZANIA Dar es Salaam
ATLANTIC OCEAN
Lobito ANGOLA Lubumbashi MALAWI COMOROS
Ndola Mayotte (to France)
ZAMBIA Lusaka Blantyre MADAGASCAR
Harare Beira Antananarivo
ZIMBABWE Kwekwe MAURITIUS
Walvis Bay Windhoek Bulawayo MOZAMBIQUE Réunion (to France)
NAMIBIA BOTSWANA *Mozambique Channel*
Tshwane/Pretoria Maputo
Johannesburg SWAZILAND
Kimberley LESOTHO Durban
SOUTH AFRICA *INDIAN OCEAN*
Cape Town Port Elizabeth East London

Environmental issues

One of Africa's most serious environmental problems occurs in marginal areas such as the Sahel where scrub and forest clearance, often for cooking fuel, combined with overgrazing, are causing desertification. Game reserves in southern and eastern Africa have helped to preserve many endangered animals, although the needs of growing populations have led to conflict over land use, and poaching is a serious problem.

Environmental issues

- national parks
- tropical forest
- forest destroyed
- desert
- desertification
- polluted rivers
- radioactive contamination
- marine pollution
- heavy marine pollution
- poor urban air quality

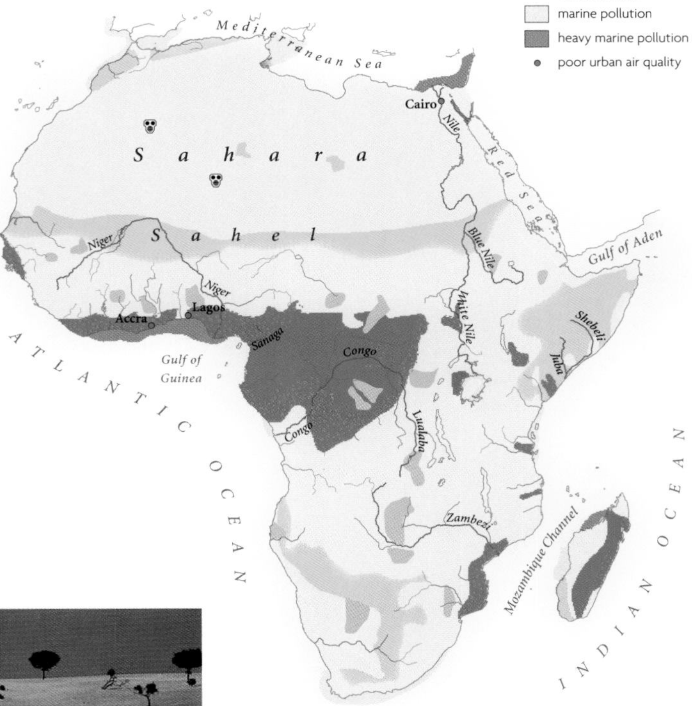

▲ **The Sahel's delicate** natural equilibrium is easily destroyed by the clearing of vegetation, drought and overgrazing. This causes the Sahara to advance south, engulfing the savannah grasslands.

Mineral resources

Africa's ancient plateaux contain some of the world's most substantial reserves of precious stones and metals. About 15% of the world's gold is mined in South Africa; Zambia has great copper deposits; and diamonds are mined in Botswana, Dem. Rep. Congo and South Africa. Oil has brought great economic benefits to Algeria, Libya and Nigeria.

Mineral resources

- oil field
- gas field
- coal field
- bauxite
- copper
- diamonds
- gold
- iron
- phosphates
- tin
- uranium

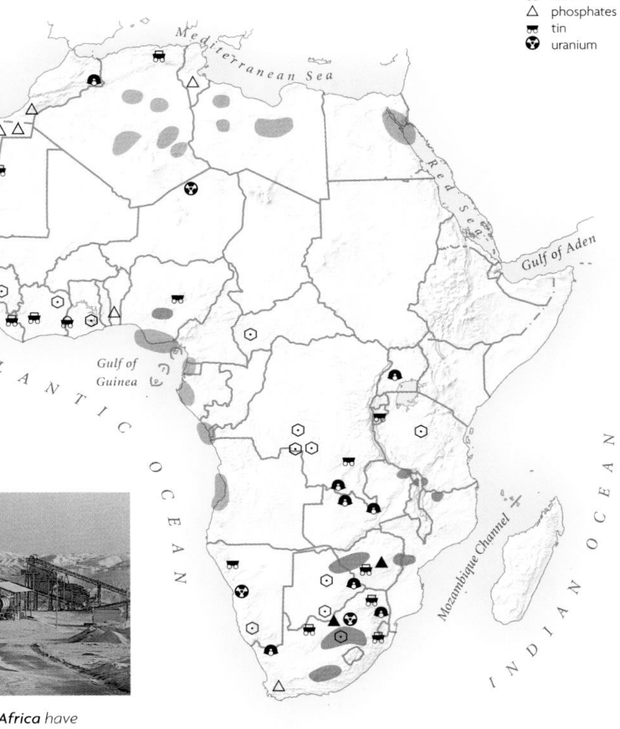

▲ **North and West Africa** have large deposits of white phosphate minerals, which are used in making fertilizers. Morocco, Senegal, and Tunisia are among the continent's leading producers.

▲ **Workers on a tea plantation** gather one of Africa's most important cash crops, providing a valuable source of income. Coffee, rubber, bananas, cotton and cocoa are also widely grown as cash crops.

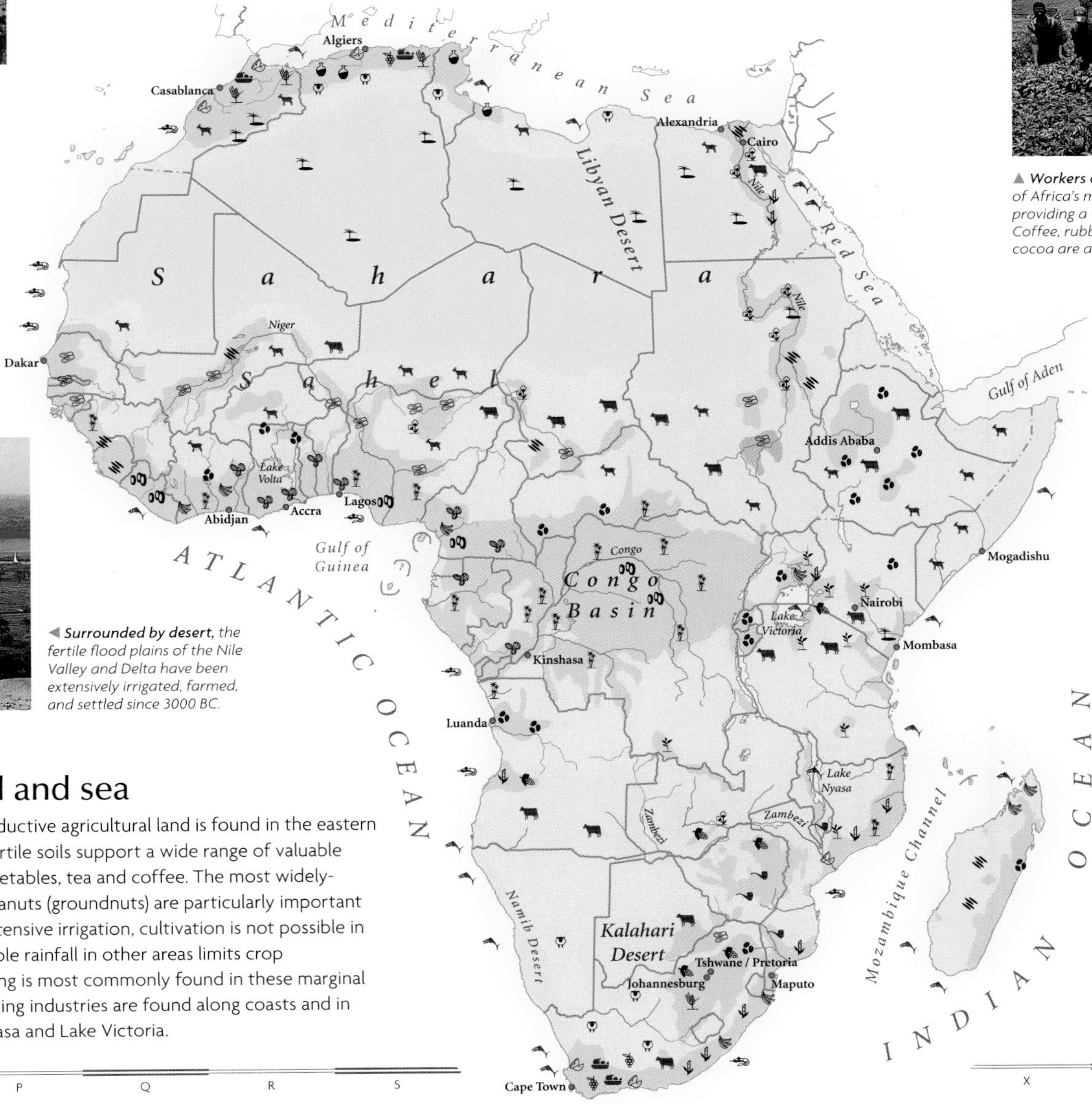

Using the land and sea

Some of Africa's most productive agricultural land is found in the eastern volcanic uplands, where fertile soils support a wide range of valuable export crops including vegetables, tea and coffee. The most widely-grown grain is corn and peanuts (groundnuts) are particularly important in West Africa. Without intensive irrigation, cultivation is not possible in desert regions and unreliable rainfall in other areas limits crop production. Pastoral herding is most commonly found in these marginal lands. Substantial local fishing industries are found along coasts and in vast lakes such as Lake Nyasa and Lake Victoria.

◄ **Surrounded by desert**, the fertile flood plains of the Nile Valley and Delta have been extensively irrigated, farmed, and settled since 3000 BC.

Using the land and sea

- cropland
- desert
- forest
- pasture
- wetland
- major conurbations
- cattle
- goats
- cereals
- sheep
- bananas
- corn (maize)
- citrus fruits
- cocoa
- cotton
- coffee
- dates
- fishing
- fruit
- oil palms
- olives
- peanuts
- rice
- rubber
- shellfish
- sugar cane
- tea
- tobacco
- vineyards
- wheat

North Africa

ALGERIA, EGYPT, LIBYA, MOROCCO, TUNISIA, WESTERN SAHARA

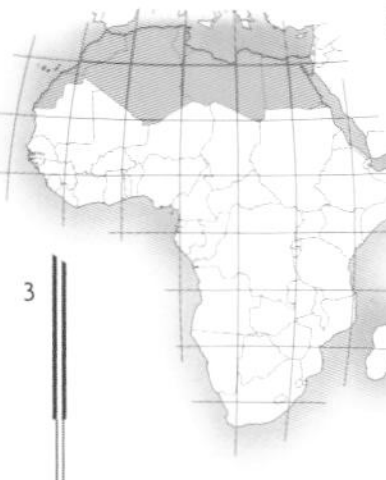

Fringed by the Mediterranean along the northern coast and by the arid Sahara in the south, North Africa reflects the influence of many invaders, both European and, most importantly, Arab, giving the region an almost universal Islamic flavour and a common Arabic language. The countries lying to the west of Egypt are often referred to as the Maghreb, an Arabic term for 'west'. Today, Morocco and Tunisia exploit their culture and landscape for tourism, while rich oil and gas deposits aid development in Libya and Algeria, despite political turmoil. Egypt, with its fertile, Nile-watered agricultural land and varied industrial base, is the most populous nation.

▲ *These rock piles* in Algeria's Ahaggar mountains are the result of weathering caused by extremes of temperature. Great cracks or joints appear in the rocks, which are then worn and smoothed by the wind.

The landscape

The Atlas Mountains, which extend across much of Morocco, northern Algeria and Tunisia, are part of the fold mountain system which also runs through much of southern Europe. They recede to the south and east, becoming a steppe landscape before meeting the Sahara desert which covers more than 90% of the region. The sediments of the Sahara overlie an ancient plateau of crystalline rock, some of which is more than four billion years old.

Map key

Population
- ■ above 5 million
- ◨ 1 million to 5 million
- ◉ 500,000 to 1 million
- ◎ 100,000 to 500,000
- ⊕ 50,000 to 100,000
- ○ 10,000 to 50,000
- ○ below 10,000

Elevation
- 4000m / 13,124ft
- 3000m / 9843ft
- 2000m / 6562ft
- 1000m / 3281ft
- 500m / 1640ft
- 250m / 820ft
- 100m / 328ft
- sea level

Scale 1:12,250,000

projection: Lambert Azimuthal Equal Area

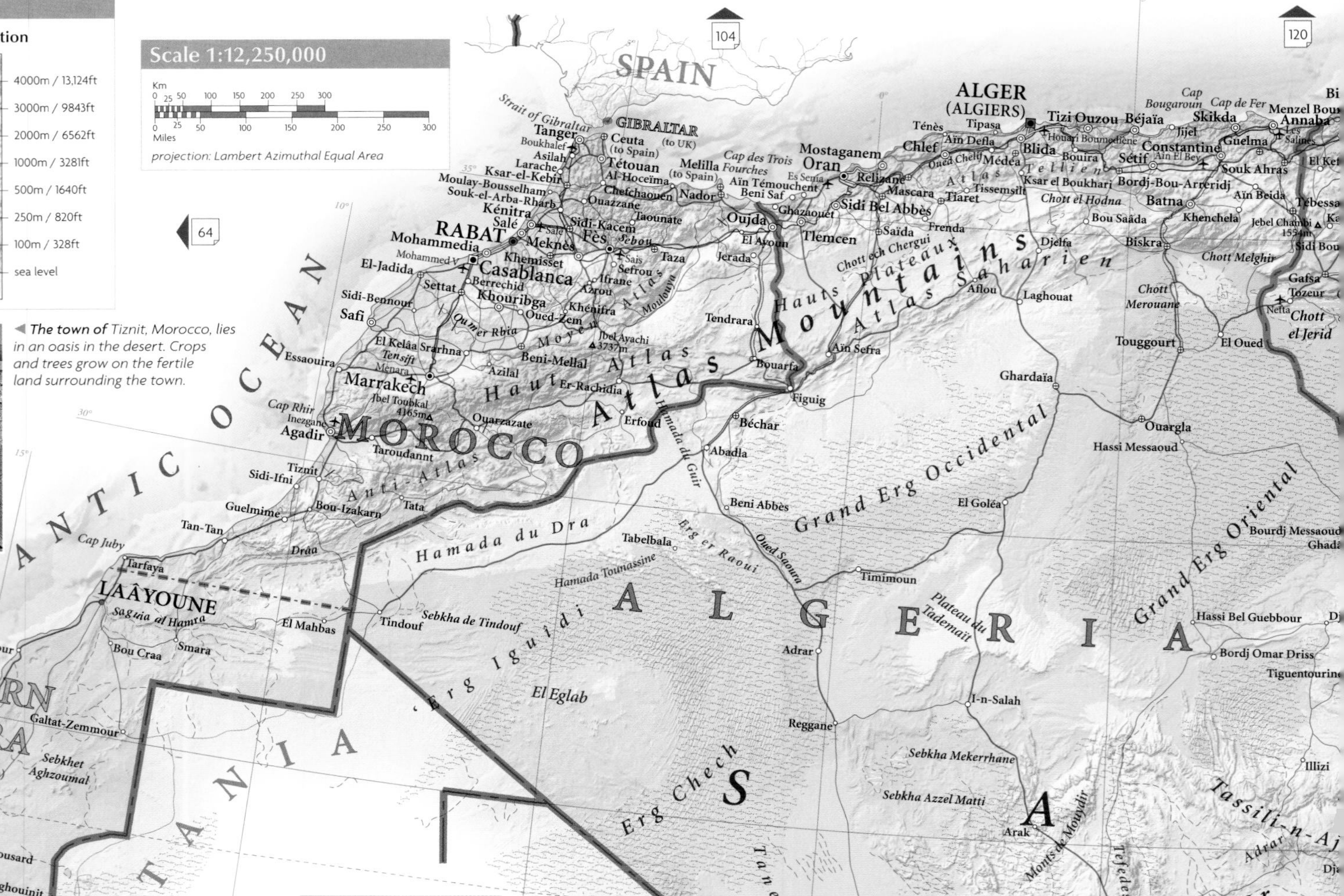

◀ *The town of* Tiznit, Morocco, lies in an oasis in the desert. Crops and trees grow on the fertile land surrounding the town.

▶ *The Grand Erg Occidental* is one of Algeria's great Saharan sand seas. Wind force and direction determines the nature of landforms such as the linear or seif dunes in the foreground.

Using the land and sea

Sheltered valleys in the Atlas Mountains, the Nile Valley and Delta, and the Mediterranean coast are the main sources of good farming land. A wide variety of valuable crops including cereals, rice and cotton, and woods such as cedar and cork, are grown. Typical Mediterranean crops such as olives, figs, dates and citrus fruits also thrive in these areas. The Nile Valley is particularly fertile, and most of Egypt's population lives close to the river. Elsewhere, irrigation is essential to improve crop yields on the desert margins.

The urban/rural population divide

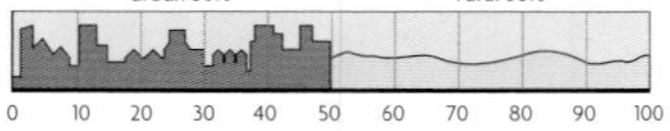

urban 50%	rural 50%

0 10 20 30 40 50 60 70 80 90 100

Population density
65 people per sq mile
(25 people per sq km)

Total land area
2,215,020 sq miles
(5,738,394 sq km)

Land use and agricultural distribution
- goats
- sheep
- cereals
- citrus fruits
- cork
- cotton
- dates
- fishing
- olives
- vineyards
- ■ capital cities
- ● major towns
- pasture
- cropland
- forest
- desert

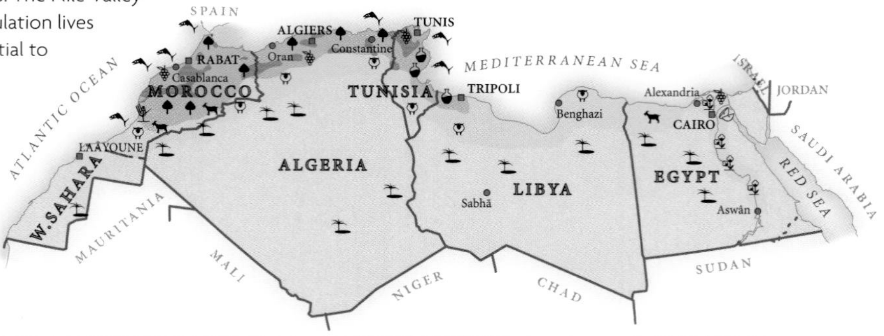

▲ *Many North African* nomads, such as the Bedouin, maintain a traditional pastoral lifestyle on the desert fringes, moving their herds of sheep, goats and camels from place to place – crossing country borders in order to find sufficient grazing land.

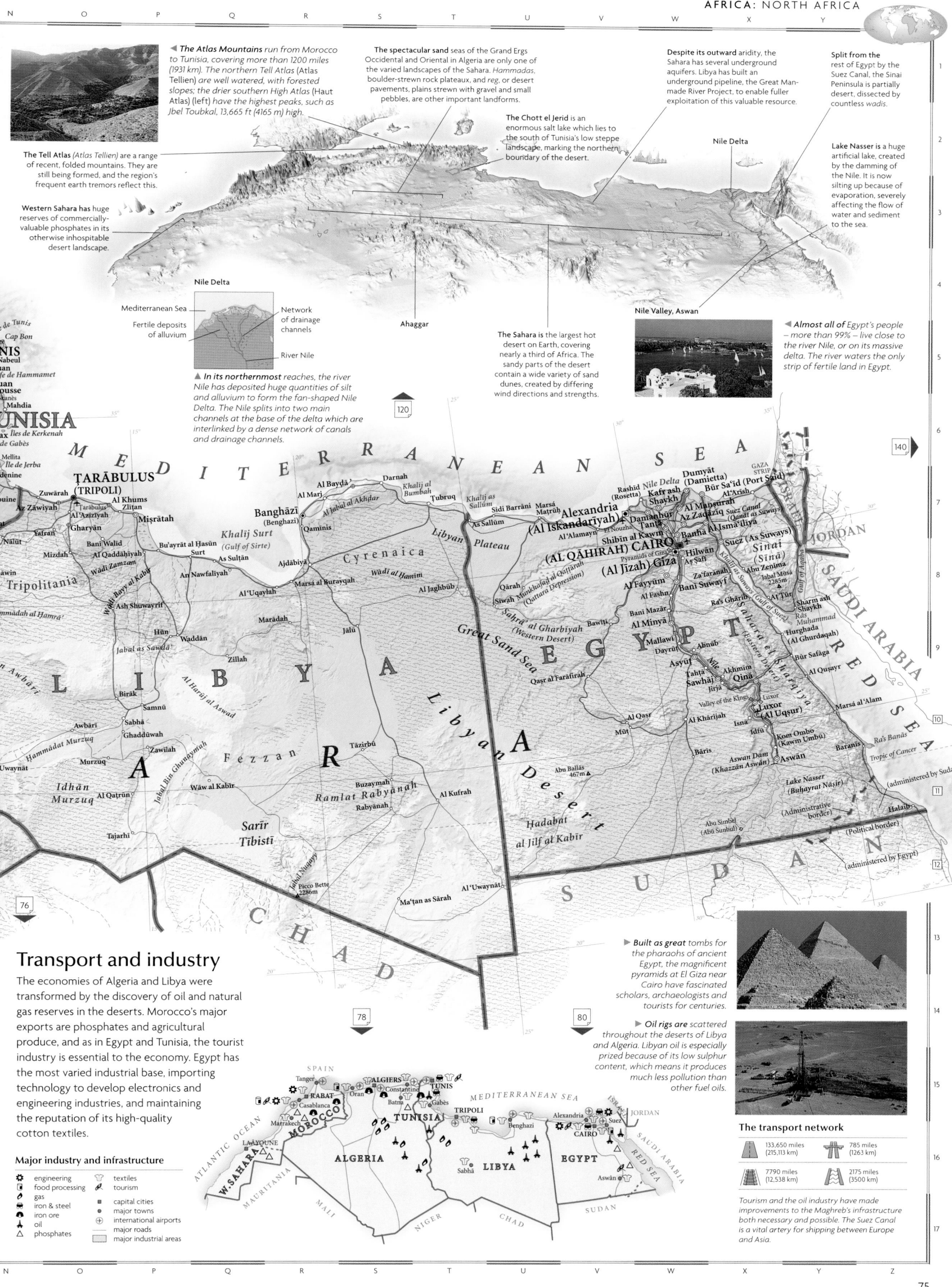

◀ **The Atlas Mountains** run from Morocco to Tunisia, covering more than 1200 miles (1931 km). The northern Tell Atlas (Atlas Tellien) are well watered, with forested slopes; the drier southern High Atlas (Haut Atlas) (left) have the highest peaks, such as Jbel Toubkal, 13,665 ft (4165 m) high.

The spectacular sand seas of the Grand Ergs Occidental and Oriental in Algeria are only one of the varied landscapes of the Sahara. *Hammadas*, boulder-strewn rock plateaux, and *reg*, or desert pavements, plains strewn with gravel and small pebbles, are other important landforms.

Despite its outward aridity, the Sahara has several underground aquifers. Libya has built an underground pipeline, the Great Man-made River Project, to enable fuller exploitation of this valuable resource.

Split from the rest of Egypt by the Suez Canal, the Sinai Peninsula is partially desert, dissected by countless *wadis*.

The Chott el Jerid is an enormous salt lake which lies to the south of Tunisia's low steppe landscape, marking the northern boundary of the desert.

The Tell Atlas (Atlas Tellien) are a range of recent, folded mountains. They are still being formed, and the region's frequent earth tremors reflect this.

Nile Delta

Lake Nasser is a huge artificial lake, created by the damming of the Nile. It is now silting up because of evaporation, severely affecting the flow of water and sediment to the sea.

Western Sahara has huge reserves of commercially-valuable phosphates in its otherwise inhospitable desert landscape.

Nile Delta

Mediterranean Sea

Network of drainage channels

Fertile deposits of alluvium

River Nile

Ahaggar

The Sahara is the largest hot desert on Earth, covering nearly a third of Africa. The sandy parts of the desert contain a wide variety of sand dunes, created by differing wind directions and strengths.

Nile Valley, Aswan

◀ **Almost all of** Egypt's people – more than 99% – live close to the river Nile, or on its massive delta. The river waters the only strip of fertile land in Egypt.

▲ **In its northernmost** reaches, the river Nile has deposited huge quantities of silt and alluvium to form the fan-shaped Nile Delta. The Nile splits into two main channels at the base of the delta which are interlinked by a dense network of canals and drainage channels.

Transport and industry

The economies of Algeria and Libya were transformed by the discovery of oil and natural gas reserves in the deserts. Morocco's major exports are phosphates and agricultural produce, and as in Egypt and Tunisia, the tourist industry is essential to the economy. Egypt has the most varied industrial base, importing technology to develop electronics and engineering industries, and maintaining the reputation of its high-quality cotton textiles.

▶ **Built as great** tombs for the pharaohs of ancient Egypt, the magnificent pyramids at El Giza near Cairo have fascinated scholars, archaeologists and tourists for centuries.

▶ **Oil rigs are** scattered throughout the deserts of Libya and Algeria. Libyan oil is especially prized because of its low sulphur content, which means it produces much less pollution than other fuel oils.

Major industry and infrastructure

- ⚙ engineering
- 🏭 food processing
- ⛽ gas
- 🏭 iron & steel
- ▲ iron ore
- ⛏ oil
- △ phosphates

- 🧵 textiles
- ⚓ tourism

- ■ capital cities
- ● major towns
- △ international airports
- — major roads
- major industrial areas

The transport network

🛣 133,650 miles (215,113 km)		🌉 785 miles (1263 km)	
🚂 7790 miles (12,538 km)		⚓ 2175 miles (3500 km)	

Tourism and the oil industry have made improvements to the Maghreb's infrastructure both necessary and possible. The Suez Canal is a vital artery for shipping between Europe and Asia.

75

West Africa

BENIN, BURKINA, CAPE VERDE, GAMBIA, GHANA, GUINEA, GUINEA-BISSAU, IVORY COAST, LIBERIA, MALI, MAURITANIA, NIGER, NIGERIA, SENEGAL, SIERRA LEONE, TOGO

West Africa is an immensely diverse region, encompassing the desert landscapes and mainly Muslim populations of the southern Saharan countries, and the tropical rainforests of the more humid south, with a great variety of local languages and cultures. The rich natural resources and accessibility of the area were quickly exploited by Europeans; most of the Africans taken by slave traders came from this region, causing serious depopulation. The very different influences of West Africa's leading colonial powers, Britain and France, remain today, reflected in the languages and institutions of the countries they once governed.

▶ The dry scrub of the Sahel is only suitable for grazing herd animals like these cattle in Mali.

Transport and industry

Abundant natural resources including oil and metallic minerals are found in much of West Africa, although investment is required for their further exploitation. Nigeria experienced an oil boom during the 1970s but subsequent growth has been sporadic. Most industry in other countries has a primary basis, including mining, logging and food processing.

The transport network

🛣 62,154 miles (100,038 km)		🚉 1037 miles (1669 km)	
🛤 6752 miles (10,867 km)		✈ 10,192 miles (16,405 km)	

The road and rail systems are most developed near the coasts. Some of the land-locked countries remain disadvantaged by the difficulty of access to ports, and their poor road networks.

Major industry and infrastructure

- chemicals
- cotton spinning
- food processing
- mining
- oil
- palm oil processing
- peanut processing
- textiles
- vehicle manufacture
- ● capital cities
- ● major towns
- ✈ international airports
- — major roads
- major industrial areas

Scale 1:10,000,000

Km 0 25 50 100 150 200 250

Miles 0 25 50 100 150 200 250

projection: Lambert Azimuthal Equal Area

Map key

Population
- ▣ 1 million to 5 million
- ◉ 500,000 to 1 million
- ◎ 100,000 to 500,000
- ⊕ 50,000 to 100,000
- ○ 10,000 to 50,000
- ◦ below 10,000

Elevation
- 2000m / 6562ft
- 1000m / 3281ft
- 500m / 1640ft
- 250m / 820ft
- 100m / 328ft
- sea level

CAPE VERDE

Santo Antão, Pombas, Ilhas de Barlavento, Pedra Lume, Mindelo, Ribeira Brava, Amilcar Cabral, Sal, São Vicente, São Nicolau, Boa Vista, João Barrosa

ATLANTIC OCEAN

Tarrafal, Maio, Fogo, São Filipe, Santiago, Maio, PRAIA

Ilhas de Sotavento

(same scale as main map)

◀ The southern regions of West Africa still contain great swathes of tropical rainforest, including some of the world's most prized hardwood trees, such as mahogany and iroko.

Using the land and sea

The humid southern regions are most suitable for cultivation; in these areas, cash crops such as coffee, cotton, cocoa and rubber are grown in large quantities. Peanuts (groundnuts) are grown throughout West Africa. In the north, advancing desertification has made the Sahel increasingly unviable for cultivation, and pastoral farming is more common. Great herds of sheep, cattle and goats are grazed on the savannah grasses, and fishing is important in coastal and delta areas.

▲ The Gambia, mainland Africa's smallest country, produces great quantities of peanuts (groundnuts). Winnowing is used to separate the nuts from their stalks.

Land use and agricultural distribution

- goats
- sheep
- cocoa
- coffee
- cotton
- oil palms
- peanuts
- rubber
- shellfish
- ■ capital cities
- ● major towns
- pasture
- cropland
- forest
- desert

The urban/rural population divide

urban 36%   rural 64%

0 10 20 30 40 50 60 70 80 90 100

Population density	Total land area
104 people per sq mile (40 people per sq km)	2,337,137 sq miles (6,054,760 sq km)

▲ **Inselbergs, found across** the Sahel, are isolated hills, or outcrops, formed where the surrounding plain has eroded away, leaving only the more resistant remnants of the original plateau.

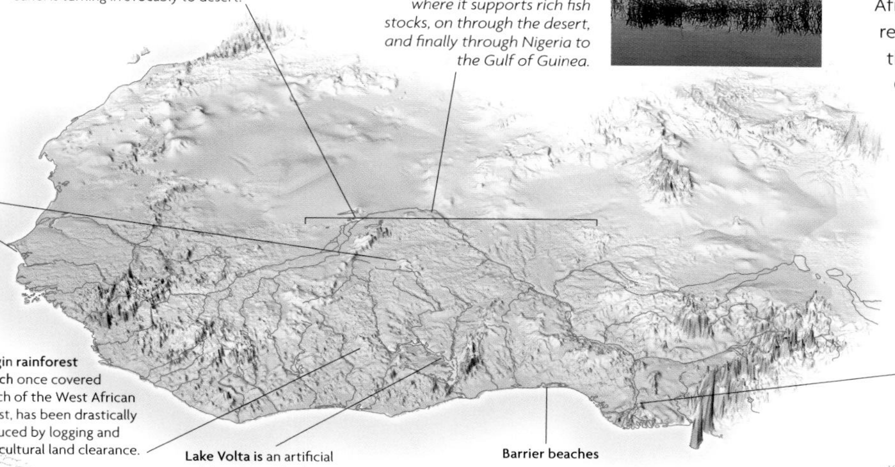

The dry grasslands of the Sahel border the southern reaches of the Sahara. Over-grazing, drought and the cutting down of trees for firewood, means that much of the Sahel is turning irrevocably to desert.

▶ **The Niger river** flows for 2600 miles (4181 km) from Fouta Djallon, on the plateau of Guinea, via southern Mali, where it supports rich fish stocks, on through the desert, and finally through Nigeria to the Gulf of Guinea.

The landscape

There are two major topographical areas in West Africa: the northern deserts are part of the Saharan region which stretches across the whole continent; the grasslands of the Sahel and the southern Guinea coast are part of Africa's central plateau. The landscape is generally low, rarely rising above 1500 ft (457 m) and consists mainly of plains, broken by an occasional high plateau or mountain range.

Two types of coastline characterize West Africa. Swampy, muddy coasts colonized by mangroves occur on river deltas and where ocean currents are weak, like the coast of Senegal. Sandy beaches, with barrier ridges and lagoons, form where currents are stronger.

Virgin rainforest which once covered much of the West African coast, has been drastically reduced by logging and agricultural land clearance.

Lake Volta is an artificial lake, created by the damming of the Volta river. It links the drier northern areas with the coast and is intended to provide fresh water for drinking, fisheries and irrigation.

As it nears the Gulf of Guinea, the Niger forks into many strands. When the river floods, alluvium is deposited over a wide area. This creates fertile soils, able to support both crops and livestock.

Barrier beaches
Fluvial deposits
River dammed by barrier beach
Lagoon
Barrier beach
Estuarine deposits

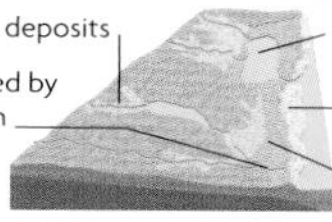

▲ **Along much of** the West African coast, barrier beaches have built up and dammed river mouths, forming fluvial and estuarine plains.

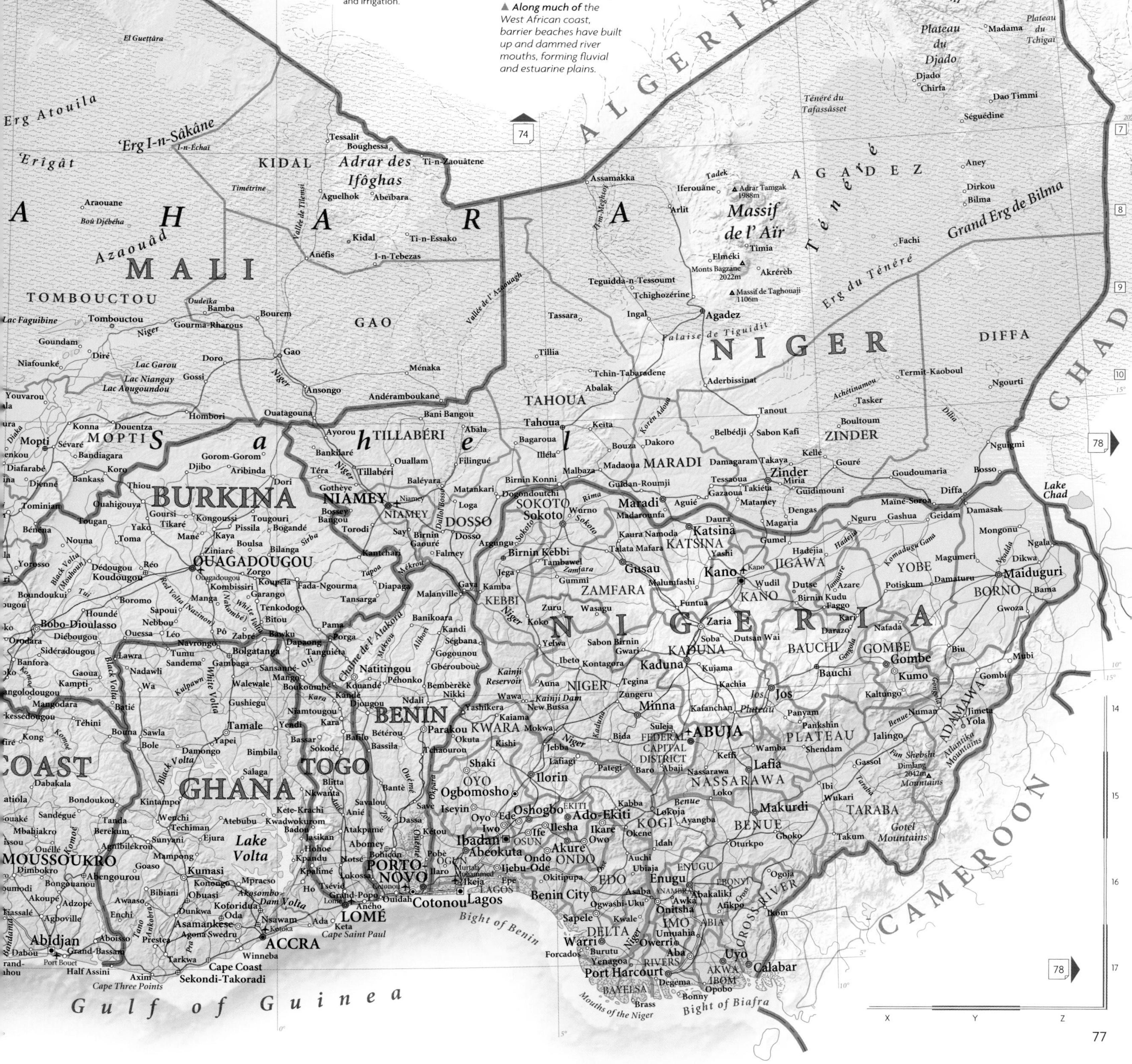

(Map of West Africa showing countries including Algeria, Libya, Mali, Niger, Chad, Burkina, Nigeria, Benin, Togo, Ghana, Cameroon, and the Gulf of Guinea with numerous cities, rivers, and geographic features)

Central Africa

CAMEROON, CENTRAL AFRICAN REPUBLIC, CHAD, CONGO, DEM. REP. CONGO, EQUATORIAL GUINEA, GABON, SAO TOME & PRINCIPE

The great rainforest basin of the Congo river embraces most of remote Central Africa. The interior was largely unknown to Europeans until late in the 19th century, when its tribal kingdoms were split – principally between France and Belgium – with Sao Tome and Principe the lone Portuguese territory, and Equatorial Guinea controlled by Spain. Open democracy and regional economic integration are important goals for these nations – several of which have only recently emerged from restrictive regimes – and investment is needed to improve transport infrastructures. Many of the small, but fast-growing and increasingly urban population, speak French, the regional *lingua franca*, along with several hundred Pygmy, Bantu and Sudanic dialects.

Transport and industry

Large reserves of valuable minerals are found in Central Africa: copper, cobalt and diamonds are mined in Dem. Rep. Congo and manganese in Gabon. Congo, Cameroon, Gabon and Equatorial Guinea have oil deposits and oil has also been recently discovered in Chad. Goods such as palm oil and rubber are processed for export.

▲ *The ancient rocks of Dem. Rep. Congo hold immense and varied mineral reserves. This open pit copper mine is at Kolwezi in the far south.*

Major industry and infrastructure

- 🍺 brewing
- ⚗ chemicals
- ◆ cobalt
- ⛏ copper
- ◆ diamonds
- 🍴 food processing
- manganese
- 🛢 oil
- palm oil processing
- 👕 textiles
- tin
- ■ capital cities
- ▪ major towns
- ✈ international airports
- major roads
- ⊕ major industrial areas

The transport network

🛣	102,747 miles (165,774 km)
🚂	3985 miles (6414 km)
✈	37 miles (60 km)
⛴	14,110 miles (22,710 km)

The Trans-Gabon railway, which began operating in 1987, has opened up new sources of timber and manganese. Elsewhere, much investment is needed to update and improve road, rail and water transport.

The landscape

Lake Chad lies in a desert basin bounded by the volcanic Tibesti mountains in the north, plateaux in the east and, in the south, the broad watershed of the Congo basin. The vast circular depression of the Congo is isolated from the coastal plain by the granite Massif du Chaillu. To the northwest, the volcanoes and fold mountains of the Cameroon Ridge (*Dorsale Camerounaise*) extend as islands into the Gulf of Guinea. The high fold mountains fringing the east of the Congo Basin fall steeply to the lakes of the Great Rift Valley.

The Tibesti mountains are the highest in the Sahara. They were pushed up by the movement of the African Plate over a hot spot, which first formed the northern Ahaggar mountains and is now thought to lie under the Great Rift Valley.

The Congo river is second only to the Amazon in the volume of water it carries, and in the size of its drainage basin.

Lake Tanganyika, the world's second deepest lake, is the largest of a series of linear 'ribbon' lakes occupying a trench within the Great Rift Valley.

Rich mineral deposits in the 'Copper Belt' of Dem. Rep. Congo were formed under intense heat and pressure when the ancient African Shield was uplifted to form the region's mountains.

▲ *Virgin tropical rainforest covers the Ruwenzori range on the borders of Dem. Rep. Congo and Uganda.*

▲ *A plug of resistant lava, at the southwestern end of the Cameroon Ridge (Dorsale Camerounaise), is all that remains of an eroded volcano.*

The volcanic massif of Cameroon Mountain occupies an area which remains volcanically active.

The lake-like expansion of the Congo river at Stanley Pool is the lowest point of the interior basin, although the river still descends more than 1000 ft (300 m) to reach the sea.

Lake Chad is the remnant of an inland sea, which once occupied much of the surrounding basin. A series of droughts since the 1970s has reduced the area of this shallow freshwater lake to about 1000 sq miles (2599 sq km).

Massif du Chaillu

Gulf of Guinea

▲ *The Congo river flows sluggishly through the rainforest of the interior basin. Towards the coast, the river drops steeply in a series of waterfalls and cataracts. At this point, the erosional power of the river becomes so great that it has formed a deep submarine canyon offshore.*

Broad, shallow basin

Waterfalls and cataracts

Submarine canyon

▲ *The vast sand flats surrounding Lake Chad were once covered by water. Changing climatic patterns caused the lake to shrink, and desert now covers much of its previous area.*

Map key

Population
- ⬤ 1 million to 5 million
- ◉ 500,000 to 1 million
- ◉ 100,000 to 500,000
- ◎ 50,000 to 100,000
- ◦ 10,000 to 50,000
- ◦ below 10,000

Elevation
- 4000m / 13,124ft
- 3000m / 9843ft
- 2000m / 6562ft
- 1000m / 3281ft
- 500m / 1640ft
- 250m / 820ft
- 100m / 328ft
- sea level

Scale 1:10,500,000

projection: Lambert Azimuthal Equal Area

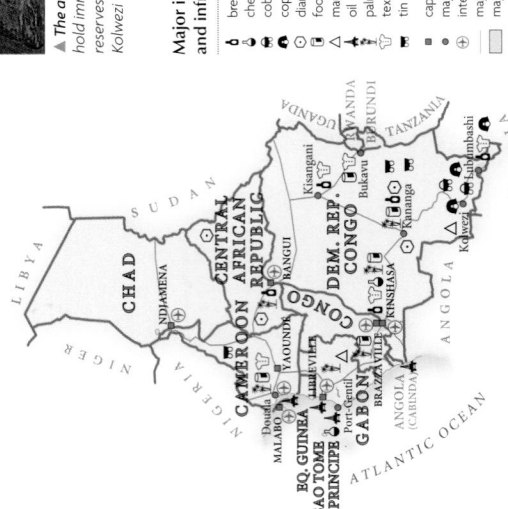

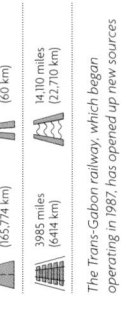

74

76

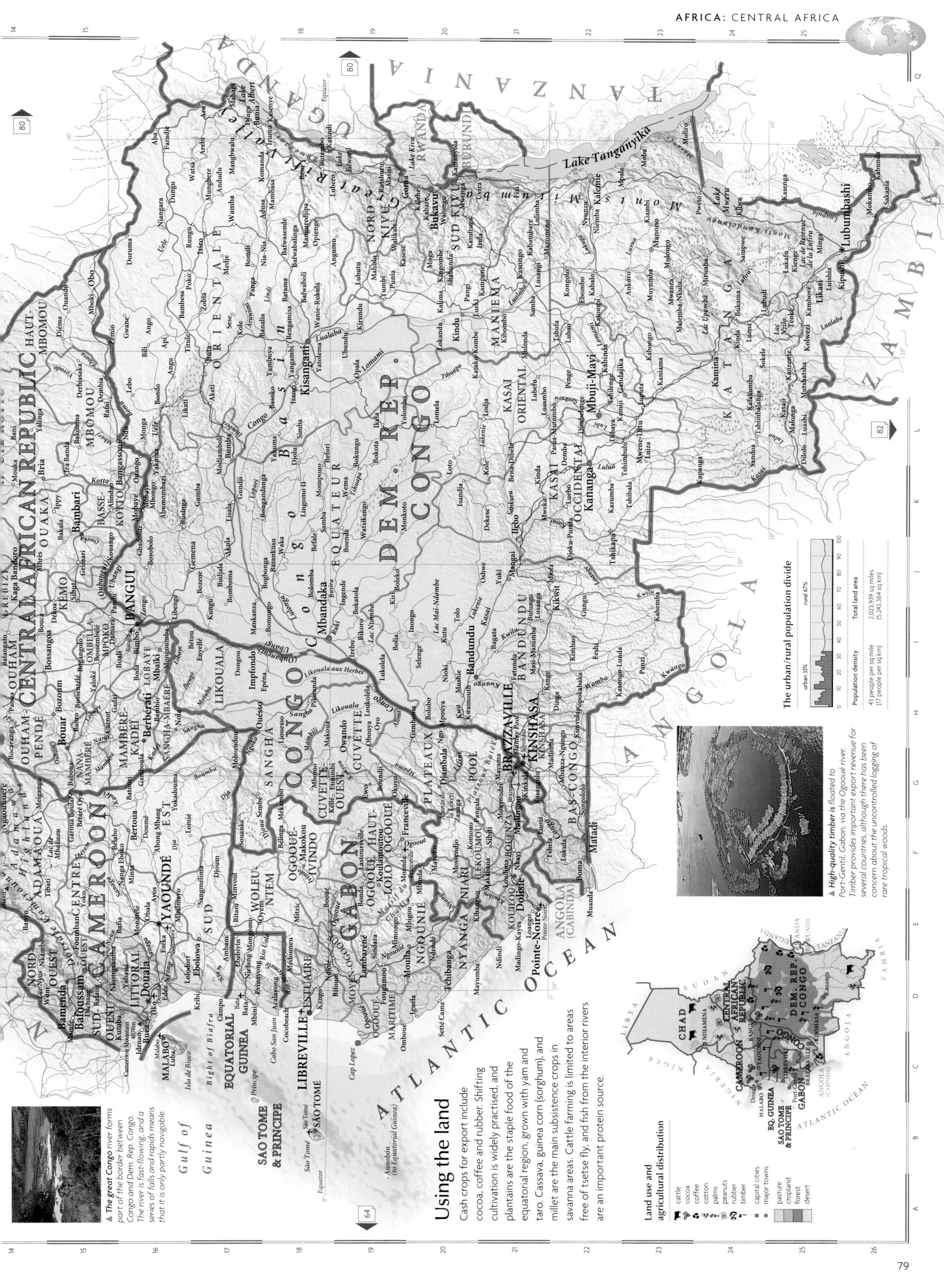

RWANDA
BURUNDI
Lake Tanganyika
TANZANIA
UGANDA
ZAMBIA

CENTRAL AFRICAN REPUBLIC

HAUT-MBOMOU
OUAKA
MBOMOU
BASSE-KOTTO
KEMO
OMBELLA-MPOKO
NANA-MAMBÉRÉ
MAMBÉRÉ-KADÉÏ
SANGHA-MBAÉRÉ
LOBAYE

ORIENTALE

BANGUI

NORD-KIVU
SUD-KIVU
MANIEMA

B a s s i n

C o n g o

DEM. REP. CONGO

ÉQUATEUR

Kisangani

KASAI ORIENTAL
KASAI OCCIDENTAL

Mbuji-Mayi
Kananga

KATANGA

Lubumbashi

Mbandaka

BANDUNDU

BAS-CONGO
KINSHASA
BRAZZAVILLE

ANGOLA

CAMEROON

YAOUNDÉ

LITTORAL
Douala
OUEST
NORD
SUD
CENTRE
EST
ADAMAOUA

EQUATORIAL GUINEA
MALABO

LIBREVILLE

GABON

ESTUAIRE
OGOOUÉ-MARITIME
MOYEN-OGOOUÉ
NGOUNIÉ
NYANGA
WOLEU-NTEM
OGOOUÉ-IVINDO
OGOOUÉ-LOLO
HAUT-OGOOUÉ

CONGO

CUVETTE
CUVETTE-OUEST
SANGHA
LIKOUALA
PLATEAUX
POOL
LÉKOUMOU
NIARI
KOUILOU
BOUENZA

SAO TOMÉ
& PRINCIPE
SÃO TOMÉ

Pointe-Noire

Gulf of Guinea

ATLANTIC OCEAN

Bight of Biafra

ANGOLA (CABINDA)

Equator

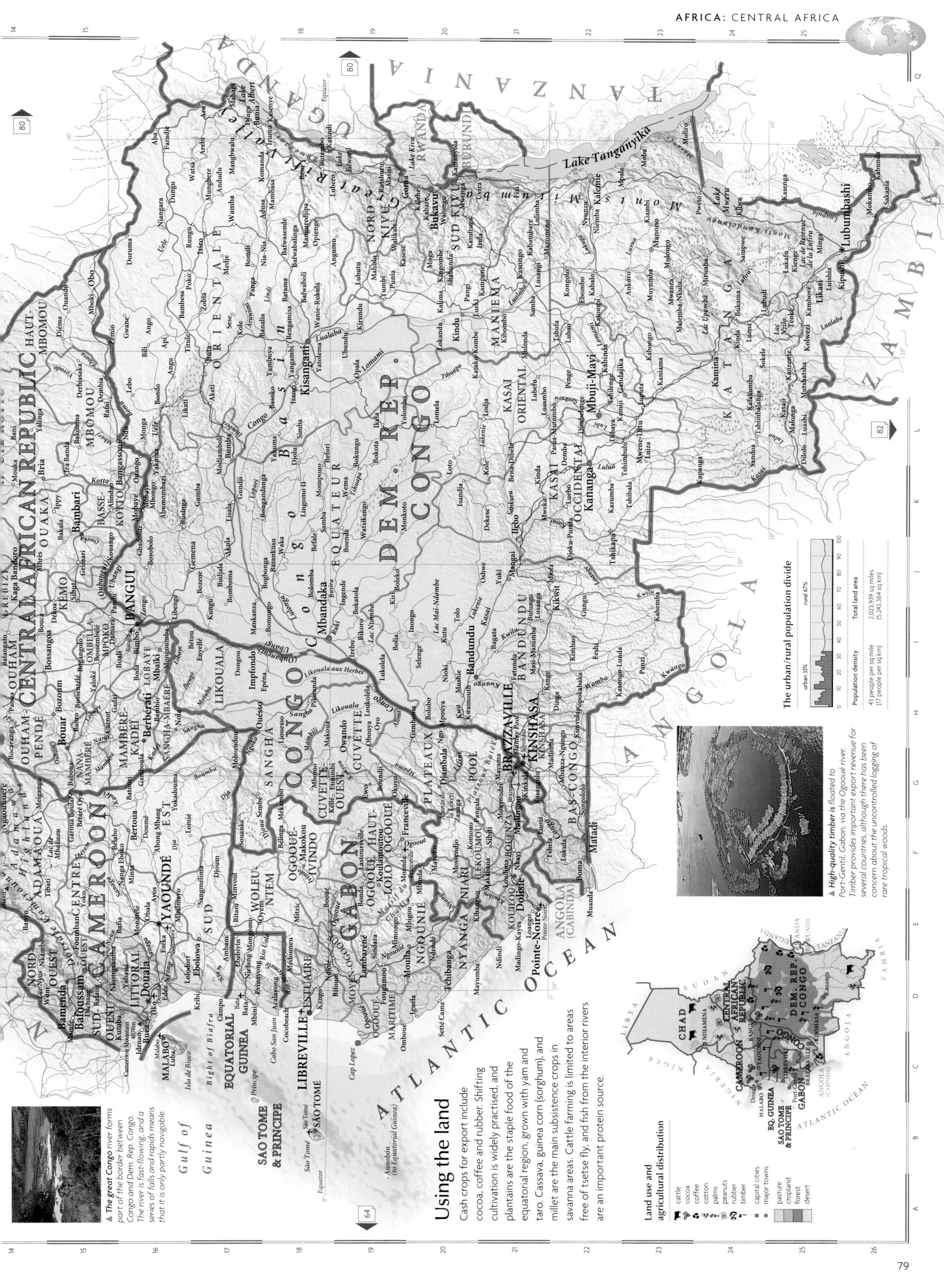

▲ *The great Congo river forms part of the border between Congo and Dem. Rep. Congo. The river is fast-flowing, and a series of falls and rapids means that it is only partly navigable.*

Using the land

Cash crops for export include cocoa, coffee and rubber. Shifting cultivation is widely practised, and plantains are the staple food of the equatorial region, grown with yam and taro. Cassava, guinea corn (sorghum), and millet are the main subsistence crops in savanna areas. Cattle farming is limited to areas free of tsetse fly, and fish from the interior rivers are an important protein source.

Land use and agricultural distribution

- cattle
- cocoa
- coffee
- cotton
- palms
- peanuts
- rubber
- timber
- capital cities
- major towns
- pasture
- cropland
- forest
- desert

▲ *High-quality timber is floated to Port-Gentil, Gabon, via the Ogooué river. Timber provides important export revenue for several countries, although there has been concern about the uncontrolled logging of rare tropical woods.*

The urban/rural population divide

urban 33%   rural 67%

Population density	Total land area
43 people per sq mile (17 people per sq km)	2,023,939 sq miles (5,243,364 sq km)

LIBYA
NIGER
CHAD
SUDAN
NIGERIA
CENTRAL AFRICAN REPUBLIC
CAMEROON
EQ. GUINEA
SAO TOMÉ & PRINCIPE
GABON
CONGO
DEM. REP. CONGO
UGANDA
RWANDA
BURUNDI
TANZANIA
ANGOLA
ZAMBIA
ANGOLA (CABINDA)
ATLANTIC OCEAN

N'DJAMENA
BANGUI
MALABO
YAOUNDÉ
Port-Gentil
LIBREVILLE
SÃO TOMÉ
BRAZZAVILLE
KINSHASA

East Africa

BURUNDI, DJIBOUTI, ERITREA, ETHIOPIA, KENYA, RWANDA, SOMALIA, SUDAN, TANZANIA, UGANDA

The countries of East Africa divide into two distinct cultural regions. Sudan and the 'Horn' nations have been influenced by the Middle East; Ethiopia was the home of one of the earliest Christian civilizations, and Sudan reflects both Muslim and Christian influences, while the southern countries share a closer cultural affinity with other sub-Saharan nations. Some of Africa's most densely populated countries lie in this region, and the needs of a growing number of people have put pressure on marginal lands and fragile environments. Although most East African economies remain strongly agricultural, Kenya has developed a varied industrial base.

The landscape

East Africa's most significant landscape feature is the Great Rift Valley, which formed during the most recent phase of continental movement when the rigid basement rocks cracked and buckled. Great blocks of land were raised and lowered, creating huge flat-bottomed valleys and steep escarpments, sometimes covered by volcanic extrusions in highland areas.

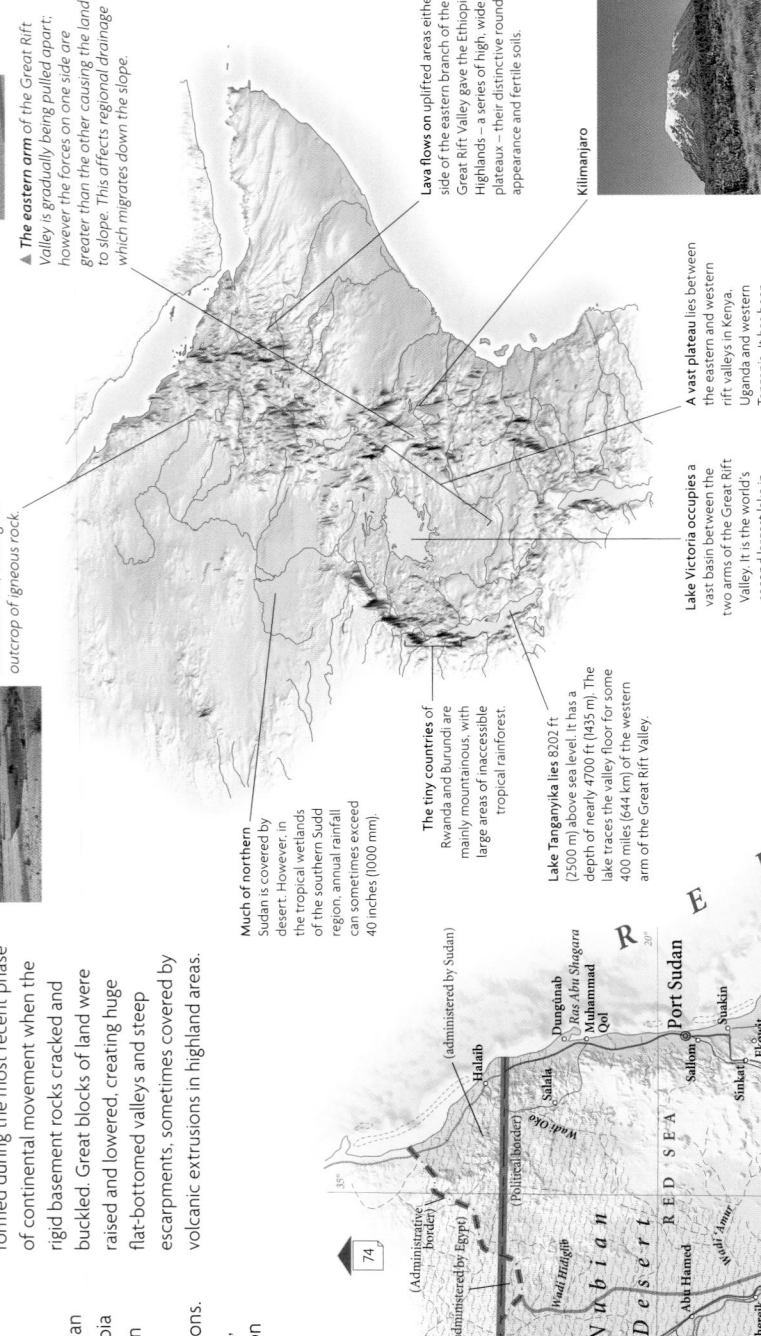

Central block slopes towards main fault

Ephemeral lake forms at far edge of slope

Boundary fault

▲ *The eastern arm* of the Great Rift Valley is gradually being pulled apart; however the forces on one side are greater than the other causing the land to slope. This affects regional drainage which migrates down the slope.

▼ *This dome at* Gonder, in Ethiopia, is a volcanic intrusion, formed when molten rock pushed up the surface of the Earth and then solidified, leaving an outcrop of igneous rock.

Lava flows on uplifted areas either side of the eastern branch of the Great Rift Valley gave the Ethiopian Highlands – a series of high, wide plateaux – their distinctive rounded appearance and fertile soils.

Kilimanjaro

▲ *An extinct volcano,* Kilimanjaro is Africa's highest mountain, rising 19,340 ft (5895 m). Once famed for its snow-capped peak, this has almost completely melted due to changing climatic conditions.

A vast plateau lies between the eastern and western rift valleys in Kenya, Uganda and western Tanzania. It has been levelled by long periods of erosion to form a peneplain, but is dotted with inselbergs – outcrops of more resistant rocks.

Lake Victoria occupies a vast basin between the two arms of the Great Rift Valley. It is the world's second largest lake in terms of surface area, extending 26,560 sq miles (68,880 sq km). The lake contains numerous islands and coral reefs.

Lake Tanganyika lies 8202 ft (2500 m) above sea level. It has a depth of nearly 4700 ft (1435 m). The lake traces the valley floor for some 400 miles (644 km) of the western arm of the Great Rift Valley.

The tiny countries of Rwanda and Burundi are mainly mountainous, with large areas of inaccessible tropical rainforest.

Much of northern Sudan is covered by desert. However, in the tropical wetlands of the southern Sudd region, annual rainfall can sometimes exceed 40 inches (1000 mm).

▼ *The Kassala region* in eastern Sudan is watered by the Atbara river, an important tributary of the Nile. Most of the population is engaged in agriculture, growing cotton and cereals.

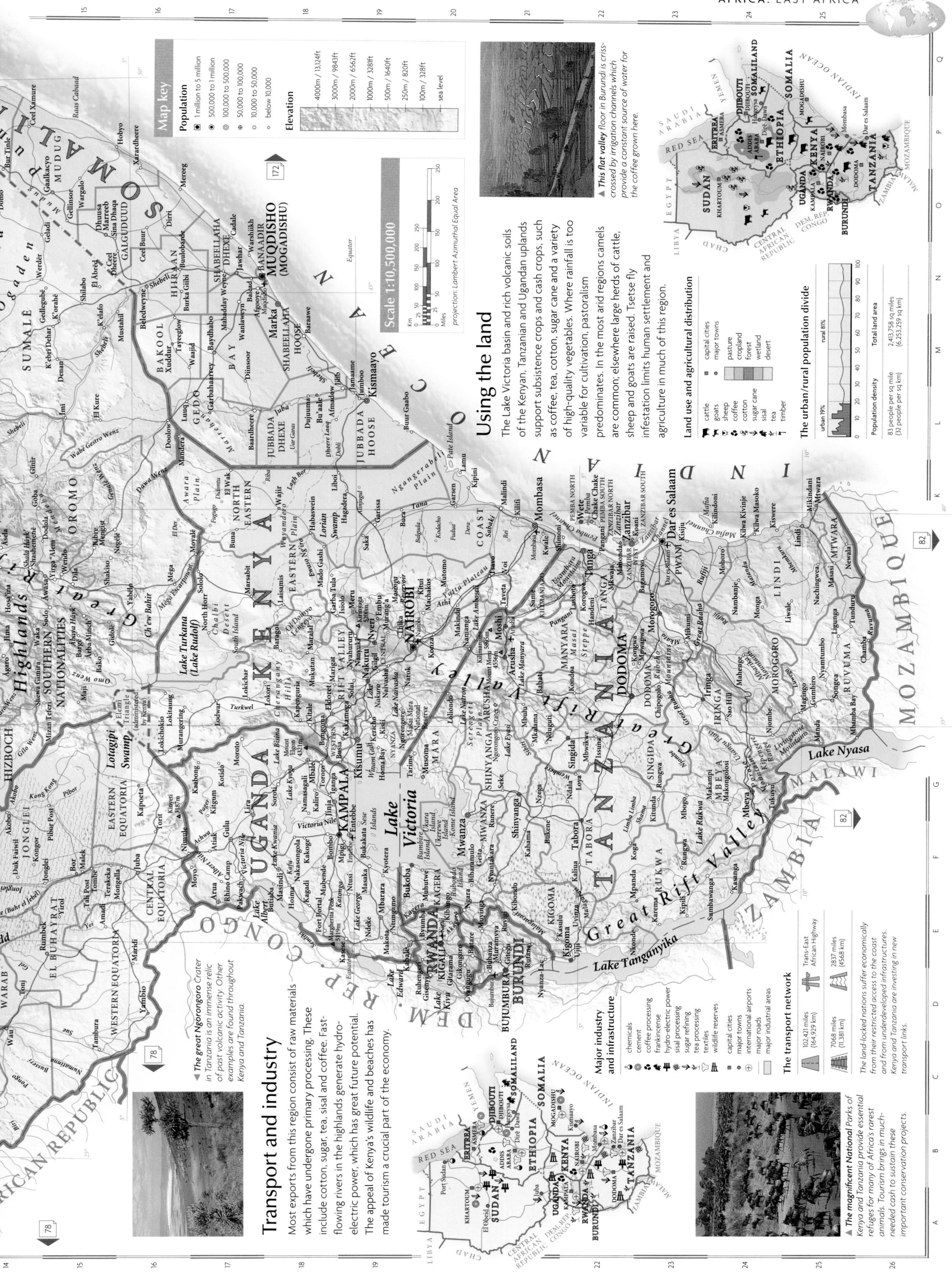

Map key

Population
- ● 1 million to 5 million
- ◉ 500,000 to 1 million
- ◎ 100,000 to 500,000
- ⊕ 50,000 to 100,000
- ○ 10,000 to 50,000
- ○ below 10,000

Elevation
- 4000m / 13124ft
- 3000m / 9843ft
- 2000m / 6562ft
- 1000m / 3281ft
- 500m / 1640ft
- 250m / 820ft
- 100m / 328ft
- sea level

Scale 1:10,500,000

projection: Lambert Azimuthal Equal Area

▲ *This flat valley floor in Burundi is criss-crossed by irrigation channels which provide a constant source of water for the coffee grown here.*

Using the land

The Lake Victoria basin and rich volcanic soils of the Kenyan, Tanzanian and Ugandan uplands support subsistence crops and cash crops, such as coffee, tea, cotton, sugar cane and a variety of high-quality vegetables. Where rainfall is too variable for cultivation, pastoralism predominates. In the most arid regions camels are common; elsewhere large herds of cattle, sheep and goats are raised. Tsetse fly infestation limits human settlement and agriculture in much of this region.

Land use and agricultural distribution

- cattle
- goats
- sheep
- coffee
- cotton
- sugar cane
- sisal
- tea
- timber

- ■ capital cities
- ◻ major towns
- pasture
- cropland
- forest
- wetland
- desert

The urban/rural population divide

urban 19% / rural 81%

Population density	Total land area
83 people per sq mile (32 people per sq km)	2,413,758 sq miles (6,253,259 sq km)

Transport and industry

Most exports from this region consist of raw materials which have undergone primary processing. These include cotton, sugar, tea, sisal and coffee. Fast-flowing rivers in the highlands generate hydro-electric power, which has great future potential. The appeal of Kenya's wildlife and beaches has made tourism a crucial part of the economy.

▲ *The great Ngorongoro Crater in Tanzania is an immense relic of past volcanic activity. Other examples are found throughout Kenya and Tanzania.*

Major industry and infrastructure

- chemicals
- cement
- coffee processing
- frankincense
- hydro-electric power
- sugar refining
- sisal processing
- tea processing
- textiles
- wildlife reserves
- ■ capital cities
- ◻ major towns
- international airports
- major roads
- major industrial areas

The transport network

		Trans-East African Highway
102,421 miles (164,929 km)		
7068 miles (11,381 km)	2837 miles (4568 km)	

The land-locked nations suffer economically from their restricted access to the coast and from underdeveloped infrastructures. Kenya and Tanzania are investing in new transport links.

▲ *The magnificent National Parks of Kenya and Tanzania provide essential refuges for many of Africa's rarest animals. Tourism brings in much-needed cash to sustain these important conservation projects.*

Southern Africa

ANGOLA, BOTSWANA, LESOTHO, MALAWI, MOZAMBIQUE, NAMIBIA, SOUTH AFRICA, SWAZILAND, ZAMBIA, ZIMBABWE

Africa's vast southern plateau has been a contested homeland for disparate peoples for many centuries. The European incursion began with the slave trade and quickened in the 19th century, when the discovery of enormous mineral wealth secured South Africa's regional economic dominance. The struggle against white minority rule led to strife in Namibia, Zimbabwe, and the former Portuguese territories of Angola and Mozambique. South Africa's notorious apartheid laws, which denied basic human rights to more than 75% of the people, led to the state being internationally ostracized until 1994, when the first fully democratic elections inaugurated a new era of racial justice.

Transport and industry

South Africa, the world's largest exporter of gold, has a varied economy which generates about 75% of the region's income and draws migrant labour from neighbouring states. Angola exports petroleum; Botswana and Namibia rely on diamond mining; and Zambia is seeking to diversify its economy to compensate for declining copper reserves.

▲ Almost all new mining ventures in Zimbabwe are now subject to government control. This mine at Bindura in northeastern Zimbabwe produces nickel, one of the country's top three minerals in terms of economic value.

Major industry and infrastructure

- 🚗 car manufacture
- coal
- copper
- ◇ diamonds
- ⊙ food processing
- gold
- oil
- textiles
- uranium
- wildlife reserves

- ■ capital cities
- major towns
- ✈ international airports
- major roads
- major industrial areas

The landscape

Most of southern Africa rests on a concave plateau comprising the Kalahari basin and a mountainous fringe, skirted by a coastal plain which widens out in Mozambique. The plateau extends north, towards the Planalto de Bié in Angola, the Congo Basin and the lake-filled troughs of the Great Rift Valley. The eastern region is drained by the Zambezi and Limpopo rivers, and the Orange is the major western river.

At Victoria Falls, the Zambezi river has cut a spectacular gorge taking advantage of large joints in the basalt, which were first formed as the lava cooled and contracted.

▶ The fast-flowing Zambezi river cuts a deep, wide channel as it flows along the Zimbabwe/Zambia border.

The Okavango/Cubango river flows from the Planalto de Bié to the swamplands of the Okavango Delta, one of the world's largest inland deltas, where it divides into countless distributary channels, feeding out into the desert.

Lake Nyasa occupies one of the deep troughs of the Great Rift Valley, where the land has been displaced downwards by as much as 3000 ft (920 m).

Great Rift Valley

Limpopo river

Bushveld intrusion

Volcanic lava, over 250 million years old, caps the peaks of the Drakensberg range, which lie on the mountainous rim of southern Africa's interior plateau.

Broad, flat-topped mountains characterize the Great Karoo, which have been cut from level rock strata under extremely arid conditions.

The mountains of the Little Karoo are composed of sedimentary rocks which have been substantially folded and faulted.

The Orange River, one of the longest in Africa, rises in Lesotho and is the only major river in the south which flows westward, rather than to the east coast.

Planalto de Bié

Namib Desert

The Kalahari Desert is the largest continuous sand surface in the world. Iron oxide gives a distinctive red colour to the windblown sand, which, in eastern areas covers the bedrock by over 200 ft (60 m).

Thousands of years of evaporating water have produced the Etosha Pan, one of the largest salt flats in the world. Lake and river sediments in the area indicate that the region was once less arid.

Khorixas, Namibia

▲ Finger Rock, near Khorixas, Namibia is a remnant of a former land surface, which has been denuded by erosion over the last 5 million years. These occasional stacks of partially weathered rocks interrupt the plains of the dry southern interior.

The transport network

84,213 miles (135,609 km)	746 miles (1202 km)
23,208 miles (37,372 km)	3815 miles (6144 km)

Southern Africa's Cape-gauge rail network is by far the largest in the continent. About two-thirds of the 20,000 mile (32,000 km) system lies within South Africa. Lines such as the Harare–Bulawayo route have become corridors for industrial growth.

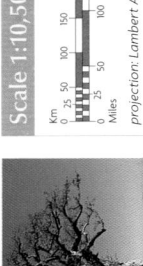

▲ Following a series of droughts, this baobab tree in Zimbabwe now stands alone in a field once filled by sugar cane. The thick trunk and small leaves of the baobab help it to conserve water, enabling it to survive even in drought conditions.

Map key

Population
- ■ 1 million to 5 million
- ◉ 500,000 to 1 million
- ◎ 100,000 to 500,000
- ⊕ 50,000 to 100,000
- ⊙ 10,000 to 50,000
- ○ below 10,000

Elevation
- 3000m / 9843ft
- 2000m / 6562ft
- 1000m / 3281ft
- 500m / 1640ft
- 250m / 820ft
- 100m / 328ft
- sea level

South Africa: Capital cities
TSHWANE / PRETORIA – administrative capital
CAPE TOWN – legislative capital
BLOEMFONTEIN – judicial capital

▲ The Bushveld intrusion lies on South Africa's high 'veld'. Molten magma intruded into the Earth's crust creating a saucer-shaped feature, more than 180 miles (300 km) across, containing regular layers of precious minerals, overlain by a dome of granite.

Granite
Chromite
Bushveld intrusion
Gabbro and peridotite
Magnetite
Platinum minerals

Scale 1:10,500,000

projection: Lambert Azimuthal Equal Area

Km 0 25 50 100 150 200 250 300
Miles 0 25 50 100 150 200 250 300

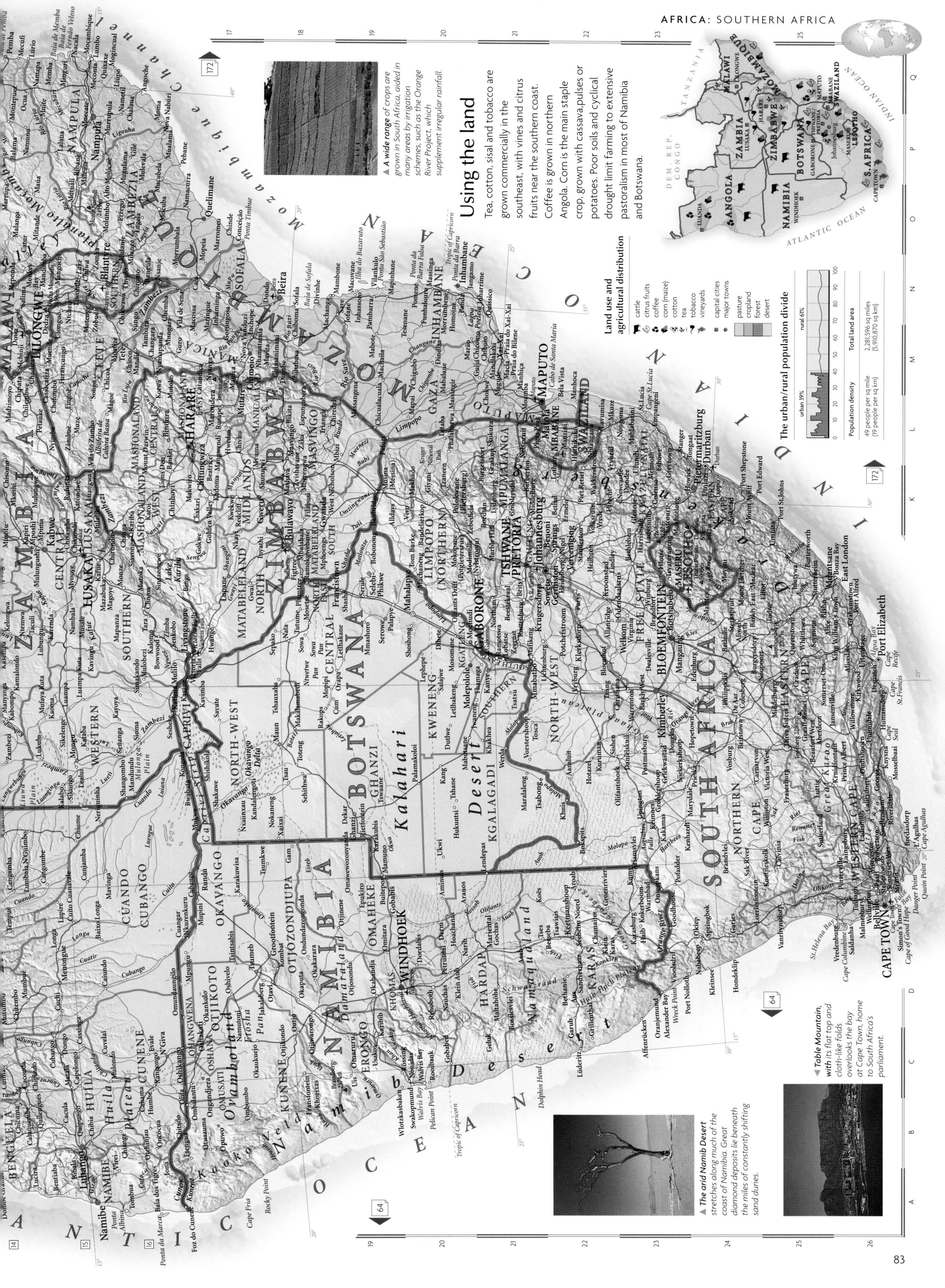

▲ A wide range of crops are grown in South Africa, aided in many areas by irrigation schemes, such as the Orange River Project, which supplement irregular rainfall.

Using the land

Tea, cotton, sisal and tobacco are grown commercially in the southeast, with vines and citrus fruits near the southern coast. Coffee is grown in northern Angola. Corn is the main staple crop, grown with cassava,pulses or potatoes. Poor soils and cyclical drought limit farming to extensive pastoralism in most of Namibia and Botswana.

Land use and agricultural distribution

cattle
citrus fruits
coffee
corn (maize)
cotton
tea
tobacco
vineyards
capital cities
major towns

pasture
cropland
forest
desert

The urban/rural population divide

urban 39%   rural 61%

Population density   49 people per sq mile
(19 people per sq km)

Total land area   2,281,596 sq miles
(5,910,870 sq km)

▲ The arid Namib Desert stretches along much of the coast of Namibia. Great diamond deposits lie beneath the miles of constantly shifting sand dunes.

▼ Table Mountain, with its flat top and cloth-like folds overlooks the bay at Cape Town, home to South Africa's parliament.

83

ARCTIC OCEAN
North Pole

Ellesmere Island

Greenland

King Frederik
VIII Land

King Christian X Land

Greenland
Sea

Spitsbergen

NORTH AMERICAN PLATE
EURASIAN PLATE

Laptev Sea

Ostrov
Rudol'fa
Franz Josef Land

Severnaya
Zemlya

Poluostrov Taymyr

Kara Sea

Mys
Flissingsky

Barents
Sea

Bjørnøya

Barents
Trough

Nordkinn
North Cape

Novaya Zemlya

Poluostrov Yamal

Kara Strait

Gulf of Ob

Yenisey

Baydaratskaya Guba

Jan Mayen Fracture Zone
Jan Mayen

Kolbeinsey Ridge

Iceland
Plateau

Tromsøflaket
Fugløya Bank

Murmansk Rise

Ostrov
Kolguyev
Poluostrov
Kanin

Pechora

West Siberian
Plain

Ob'

Arctic Circle

Denmark Strait

Bjargtangar

Iceland
Basin

Reykjanes Ridge

Iceland
Vatnajökull

Faeroe-Iceland Ridge

Norwegian Sea

Vesterålen

Voring Plateau

Kebnekaise
2117m

Lofoten

Inarijärvi

Torneälven

Kola Peninsula
Ozero
Imandra

White Sea

Onega Bay

Ozero
Vygozero

Northern Dvina

Timanskiy Kryazh

Gora Narodnaya
1895m

Pechora

U r a l   M o u n t a i n s

Mezen'

Vychegda

Norwegian
Basin

Scandinavia

Kemijoki

Oulujoki

Lake
Ladoga

Ozero
Beloye

Vaga

Sukhona

Kama

Chusovaya

Talbot

Faeroe Islands

Bill Baileys
Bank
Faeroe-Shetland Trough
Shetland
Islands

Viking Bank

Traena
Bank

Gáldhøpiggen
2469m

Ljungan

Ljusnan

Gilnia

Umeälven

Gulf of Bothnia

Åland

Gulf of Finland

Lake
Onega

Onega

Svir

Rybinsk
Reservoir

Gor'ky
Reservoir

Vetluga

Yoshkar

Kuybyshev
Reservoir

Belaya

Hatton Ridge

Rockall
Rise

Feni Ridge

Rockall Trough

Outer Hebrides

Orkney Islands

North
Sea

Jutland
Bank

Skagerrak

Great
Fisher
Bank

Kattegat

Vänern

Vättern

Gotland

Gulf of
Riga

Baltic Sea

Lake Ilmen

Lake Pskov

Msta

Lake
Peipus

Moskva

Oka

Klyazma

Sura

Rybinsk
Reservoir

Kuybyshev
Reservoir

Ben Nevis
1343m

Grampian
Mountains

North Channel
Pennines

Porcupine
Plain

British
Isles

Ireland
Shannon

Irish Sea

Snowdon
1085m

Britain

Trent

Severn

Thames

Dogger
Bank

Frisian Islands

Elbe

Oder

Warta

Vistula

Bug

Western Dvina

Neman

North European Plain

Dnieper

Byelozero

Pripet
Marshes

Desna

Central Russian Upland

Seym

Don

Donets

Khoper

Tsimlyansk
Reservoir

Kirghiz S

Celtic Sea
Celtic
Shelf

St. George's
Channel

Bristol Channel

Land's End

English Channel

Channel Islands

E U R O P E

Ardennes

Rhine

Seine

Marne

Meuse

Moselle

Harz

Danube

Lake Constance

Kiev
Reservoir

Kremenchuk
Reservoir

Dniester Podil's'ka Vysochina

Pivdennyy Buh

Dnieper Lowlands

Dnieper

Dniester

Don

Manych

Yergeni

Volga

Azores-Biscay Rise

Charcot Seamounts

Theta Gap
Galicia
Bank

Biscay
Plain

Bay of
Biscay

Loire

Cher

Vienne

Vosges
Black
Forest

Jura

Lake Geneva

Saône

Massif
Central

Mont
Blanc
4807m

A L P S

Lake Garda

Bakony

Drava

Lake Balaton

Great
Hungarian
Plain

Tisza

Carpathian Mountains

Siret

Prut

Black Sea Lowland

Sea of
Azov

Crimea

Kuban'

Volga Upland

Iberian
Plain

Condillera Cantábrica

I b e r i a n

Miño

Aragón

Duero

Ebro

Douro

Dordogne

Lot

Garonne

Cévennes

Po

Ligurian
Sea

Arno

Adriatic Sea

Dinaric Alps

Apennines

Balkan Mountains

Danube

Transylvanian Alps

Black Sea

Gorringe
Ridge

Iberian
Plain

Sistema Central

Sistema Ibérica

P e n i n s u l a

Guadiana

Tagus

Guadalquivir

Júcar

Sierra Morena

Segura

Sistemas Béticos
Sierra Nevada

Gulf of
Valencia

Balearic Islands

Corsica

Strait of Bonifacio

Gulf of Lion

Sardinia

Algerian Basin

Tiber

Corno Grande
2912m

Tyrrhenian

Adriatic
Basin

Lake
Ohrid

Lake Scutari

Lake
Presba

Rhodope Mountains

Maritsa

Sea of
Marmara

Bosporus

EURASIAN
ANATOLIAN PLATE

Aegean
Sea

Anatolia

Lake Tuz

Cabo
da Roca

Tagus Plain

Cape
Saint Vincent

Horseshoe Seamounts

Ampère Seamount

Seine Plain
Seine Seamount

Punta de
Tarifa

Strait of
Gibraltar

Alboran Sea

Rif

Oued Chelif
Sebou

Tell Atlas

Tyrrhenian
Sea

Tyrrhenian
Basin

M e d i t e r r a n e a n

EURASIAN PLATE
AFRICAN PLATE

Mount Etna
3340m

Malta

Sicily

Strait of Messina

Ionian Sea

Ionian Basin

Strait of Taranto

Peloponnese

Mirtoan
Sea

Sea of Crete

Gávdos

Mediterranean Ridge

Kárpathos
Basin

Crete

Kásos Strait

Taurus Mountains

Rhodes

Gulf of
Antalya

Cyprus

Cyprus
Basin

AFRICAN PLATE

Madeira

Dacia Seamount

Açgadir Canyon

Oumer Rbia

Moulouya

Middle Atlas

High Atlas

A t l a s   M o u n t a i n s

Saharan Atlas

Chott el Jerid

Levantine Basin

Nile Fan

Canary Islands

Grand Erg Occidental

Grand Erg Oriental

Gulf of
Sirte

Qattara Depression
-133m

Western Desert

Libyan Desert

Suez Canal

Gulf of Si

Nile

Erg Iguidi

Erg Chech

S A H A R A

A F R I C A

84

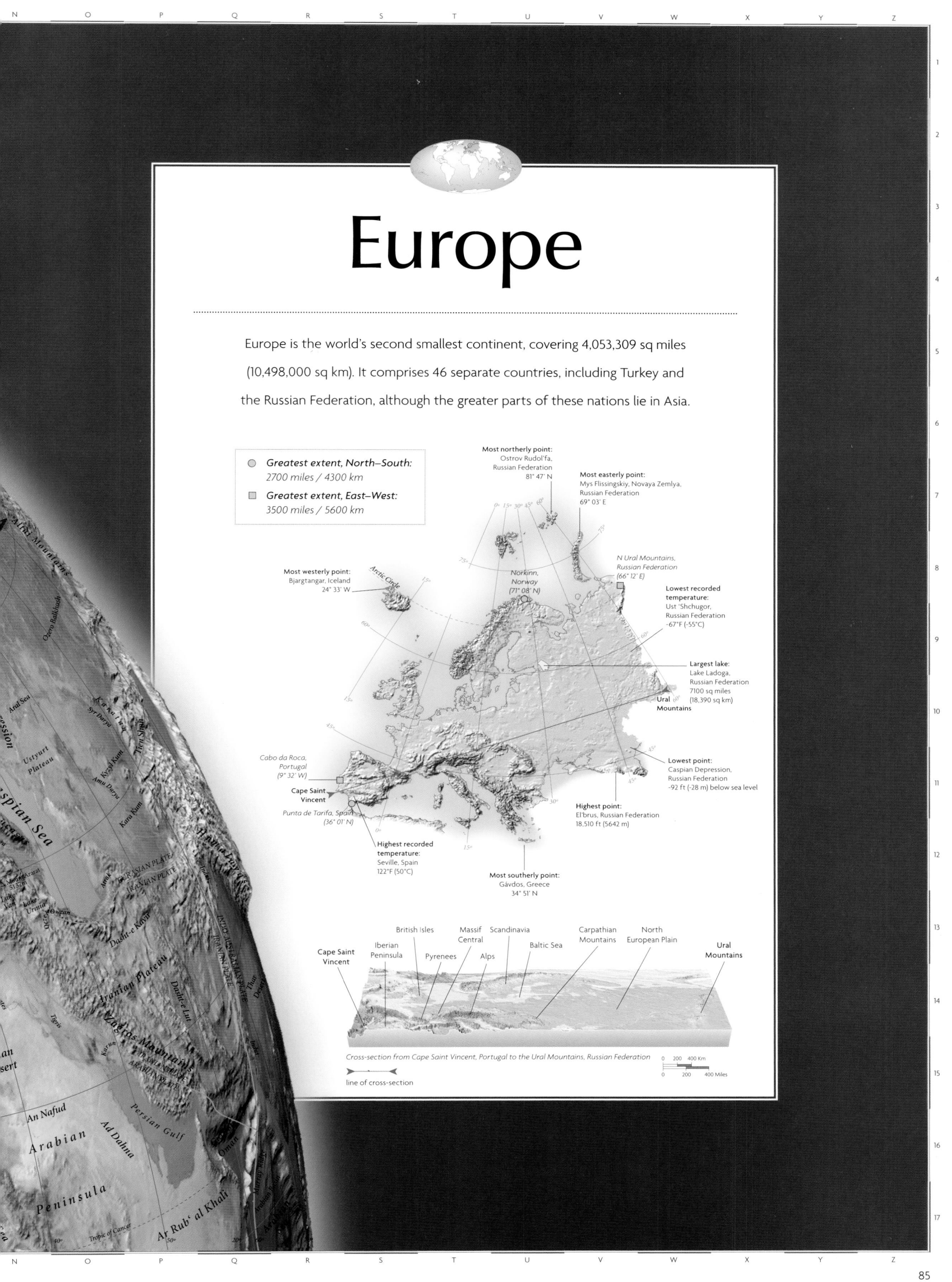

Europe

Europe is the world's second smallest continent, covering 4,053,309 sq miles (10,498,000 sq km). It comprises 46 separate countries, including Turkey and the Russian Federation, although the greater parts of these nations lie in Asia.

- **Greatest extent, North–South:** 2700 miles / 4300 km
- **Greatest extent, East–West:** 3500 miles / 5600 km

Most northerly point: Ostrov Rudol'fa, Russian Federation 81° 47' N

Most easterly point: Mys Flissingskiy, Novaya Zemlya, Russian Federation 69° 03' E

N Ural Mountains, Russian Federation (66° 12' E)

Most westerly point: Bjargtangar, Iceland 24° 33' W

Norkinn, Norway (71° 08' N)

Lowest recorded temperature: Ust 'Shchugor, Russian Federation -67°F (-55°C)

Largest lake: Lake Ladoga, Russian Federation 7100 sq miles (18,390 sq km)

Ural Mountains

Cabo da Roca, Portugal (9° 32' W)

Cape Saint Vincent

Punta de Tarifa, Spain (36° 01' N)

Lowest point: Caspian Depression, Russian Federation -92 ft (-28 m) below sea level

Highest point: El'brus, Russian Federation 18,510 ft (5642 m)

Highest recorded temperature: Seville, Spain 122°F (50°C)

Most southerly point: Gávdos, Greece 34° 51' N

Cross-section from Cape Saint Vincent, Portugal to the Ural Mountains, Russian Federation

line of cross-section

Cape Saint Vincent — Iberian Peninsula — British Isles — Pyrenees — Massif Central — Alps — Scandinavia — Baltic Sea — Carpathian Mountains — North European Plain — Ural Mountains

0   200   400 Km
0   200   400 Miles

Physical Europe

The physical diversity of Europe belies its relatively small size. To the northwest and south it is enclosed by mountains. The older, rounded Atlantic Highlands of Scandinavia and the British Isles lie to the north and the younger, rugged peaks of the Alpine Uplands to the south. In between lies the North European Plain, stretching 2485 miles (4000 km) from The Fens in England to the Ural Mountains in Russia. South of the plain lies a series of gently folded sedimentary rocks separated by ancient plateaux, known as massifs.

The North European Plain

Rising less than 1000 ft (300 m) above sea level, the North European Plain strongly reflects past glaciation. Ridges of both coarse moraine and finer, windblown deposits have accumulated over much of the region. The ice sheet also diverted a number of river channels from their original courses.

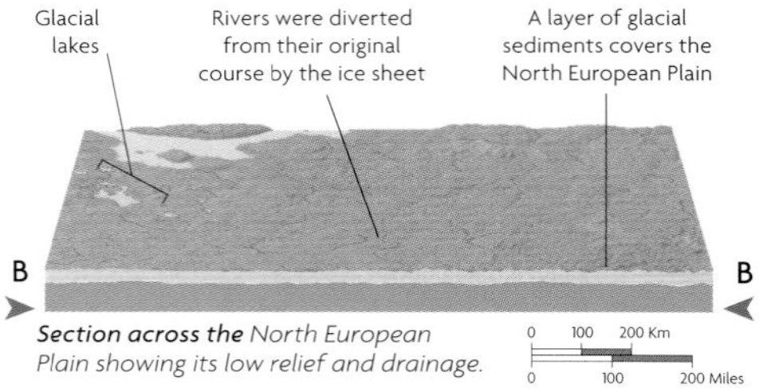

Glacial lakes · Rivers were diverted from their original course by the ice sheet · A layer of glacial sediments covers the North European Plain

Section across the North European Plain showing its low relief and drainage.

0 100 200 Km
0 100 200 Miles

The Atlantic Highlands

The Atlantic Highlands were formed by compression against the Scandinavian Shield during the Caledonian mountain-building period over 500 million years ago. The highlands were once part of a continuous mountain chain, now divided by the North Sea and a submerged rift valley.

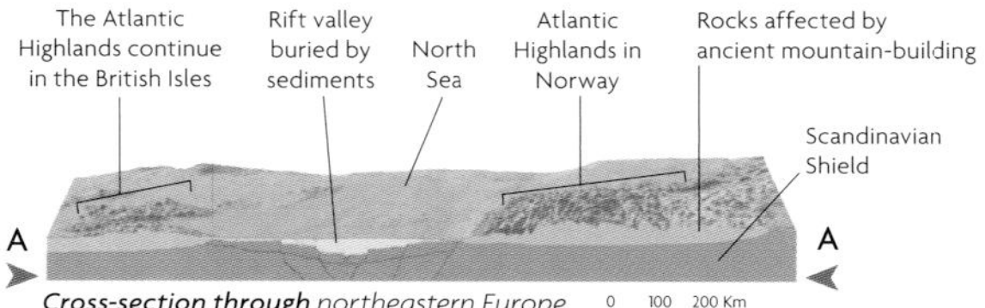

The Atlantic Highlands continue in the British Isles · Rift valley buried by sediments · North Sea · Atlantic Highlands in Norway · Rocks affected by ancient mountain-building · Scandinavian Shield

Cross-section through northeastern Europe showing the continuous mountain chain and rift valley system.

0 100 200 Km
0 100 200 Miles

Scale 1:25,500,000

Km
0 100 200 300 400 500 600
Miles
0 100 200 300 400 500 600

projection: Lambert Azimuthal Equal Area

Map key

Elevation

4000m / 13,124ft
3000m / 9843ft
2000m / 6562ft
1000m / 3281ft
500m / 1640ft
250m / 820ft
100m / 328ft
sea level

Plate margins
(for explanation see page xiv)

constructive
destructive
conservative
uncertain
physiographic regions
line of cross-section

Map labels

NORTH AMERICAN PLATE · EURASIAN PLATE · Iceland · ATLANTIC OCEAN · Norwegian Sea · Faeroe Islands · Shetland Islands · Outer Hebrides · British Isles · Ireland · Shannon · Britain · The Fens · Thames · English Channel · Seine · Loire · Bay of Biscay · PLATEAUX AND LOWLANDS · Pyrenees · Massif Central · Mt Blanc 4807m · ALPS · Iberian Peninsula · Ebro · Douro · Guadalquivir · Tagus · EURASIAN PLATE · AFRICAN PLATE · Corsica · Balearic Islands · Sardinia · Apennines · Po · Tyrrhenian Sea · Sicily · Etna 3263m · Mediterranean Sea · Ionian Sea · Adriatic Sea · Dinaric Alps · Vesuvius 1171m · Balkan Mountains · Peloponnese · Crete · Aegean Sea · ANATOLIAN PLATE · AFRICAN PLATE · ALPINE UPLANDS · Rhine · Elbe · Weser · Harz · Ardennes · Oder · Vistula · Danube · Carpathian Mountains · Great Hungarian Plain · Dniester · Dnieper · Don · Volga · Volga Uplands · Caspian Sea · Sea of Azov · Crimea · Black Sea · Caucasus · El'brus 5642m · ASIA · ATLANTIC HIGHLANDS · Kölen · Kola Peninsula · White Sea · SCANDINAVIAN SHIELD · Gulf of Bothnia · Vänern · Vättern · Jylland · North Sea · Baltic Sea · Gulf of Riga · Western Dvina · Lake Ladoga · Lake Onega · Northern Dvina · Central Russian Upland · Novaya Zemlya · Ostrov Kolguyev · Barents Sea · Kara Sea · Ural Mountains · NORTH EUROPEAN PLAIN

The Alpine Uplands

The collision of the African and European continents, which began about 65 million years ago, folded and then uplifted a series of mountain ranges running across southern Europe and into Asia. Two major lines of folding can be traced: one includes the Pyrenees, the Alps and the Carpathian Mountains; the other incorporates the Apennines and the Dinaric Alps.

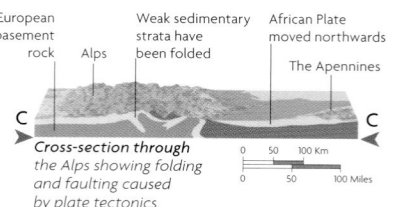

European basement rock · Alps · Weak sedimentary strata have been folded · African Plate moved northwards · The Apennines

Cross-section through the Alps showing folding and faulting caused by plate tectonics.

0 50 100 Km
0 50 100 Miles

The plateaux and lowlands

The uplifted plateaux or massifs of southern central Europe are the result of long-term erosion, later followed by uplift. They are the source areas of many of the rivers which drain Europe's lowlands. In some of the higher reaches, fractures have enabled igneous rocks from deep in the Earth to reach the surface.

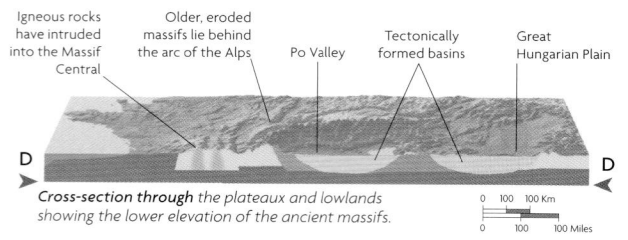

Igneous rocks have intruded into the Massif Central · Older, eroded massifs lie behind the arc of the Alps · Po Valley · Tectonically formed basins · Great Hungarian Plain

Cross-section through the plateaux and lowlands showing the lower elevation of the ancient massifs.

0 100 Km
0 100 Miles

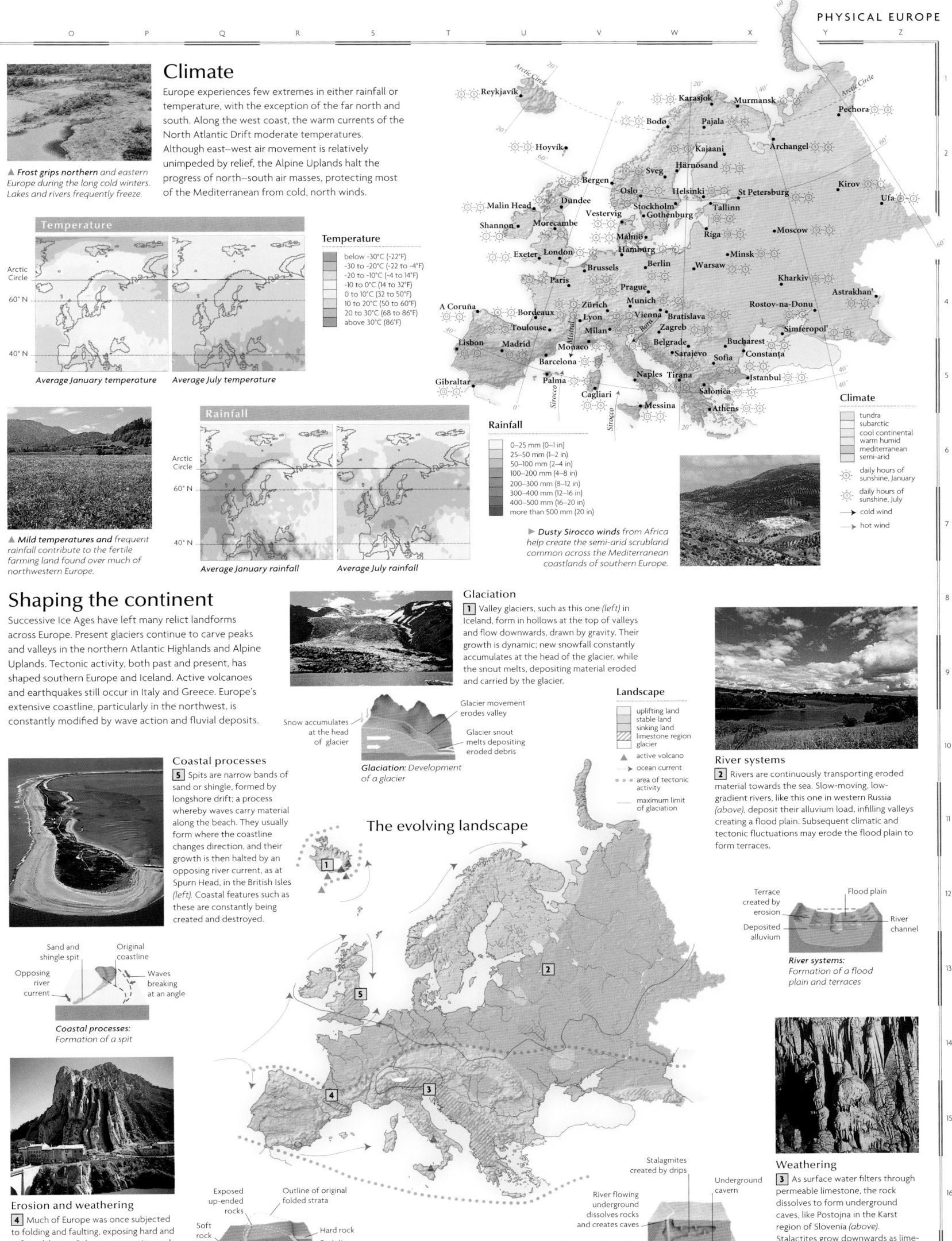

Climate

Europe experiences few extremes in either rainfall or temperature, with the exception of the far north and south. Along the west coast, the warm currents of the North Atlantic Drift moderate temperatures. Although east–west air movement is relatively unimpeded by relief, the Alpine Uplands halt the progress of north–south air masses, protecting most of the Mediterranean from cold, north winds.

▲ *Frost grips northern and eastern Europe during the long cold winters. Lakes and rivers frequently freeze.*

Temperature

Temperature
- below -30°C (-22°F)
- -30 to -20°C (-22 to -4°F)
- -20 to -10°C (-4 to 14°F)
- -10 to 0°C (14 to 32°F)
- 0 to 10°C (32 to 50°F)
- 10 to 20°C (50 to 60°F)
- 20 to 30°C (68 to 86°F)
- above 30°C (86°F)

Arctic Circle
60° N
40° N

Average January temperature   *Average July temperature*

Rainfall

Rainfall
- 0–25 mm (0–1 in)
- 25–50 mm (1–2 in)
- 50–100 mm (2–4 in)
- 100–200 mm (4–8 in)
- 200–300 mm (8–12 in)
- 300–400 mm (12–16 in)
- 400–500 mm (16–20 in)
- more than 500 mm (20 in)

Arctic Circle
60° N
40° N

Average January rainfall   *Average July rainfall*

▲ *Mild temperatures and frequent rainfall contribute to the fertile farming land found over much of northwestern Europe.*

▶ *Dusty Sirocco winds from Africa help create the semi-arid scrubland common across the Mediterranean coastlands of southern Europe.*

Climate
- tundra
- subarctic
- cool continental
- warm humid
- mediterranean
- semi-arid

☼ daily hours of sunshine, January
☼ daily hours of sunshine, July
→ cold wind
→ hot wind

Shaping the continent

Successive Ice Ages have left many relict landforms across Europe. Present glaciers continue to carve peaks and valleys in the northern Atlantic Highlands and Alpine Uplands. Tectonic activity, both past and present, has shaped southern Europe and Iceland. Active volcanoes and earthquakes still occur in Italy and Greece. Europe's extensive coastline, particularly in the northwest, is constantly modified by wave action and fluvial deposits.

Glaciation

1 Valley glaciers, such as this one *(left)* in Iceland, form in hollows at the top of valleys and flow downwards, drawn by gravity. Their growth is dynamic; new snowfall constantly accumulates at the head of the glacier, while the snout melts, depositing material eroded and carried by the glacier.

Snow accumulates at the head of glacier
Glacier movement erodes valley
Glacier snout melts depositing eroded debris

Glaciation: Development of a glacier

Landscape
- uplifting land
- stable land
- sinking land
- limestone region
- glacier
- ▲ active volcano
- → ocean current
- ⋯ area of tectonic activity
- — maximum limit of glaciation

Coastal processes

5 Spits are narrow bands of sand or shingle, formed by longshore drift; a process whereby waves carry material along the beach. They usually form where the coastline changes direction, and their growth is then halted by an opposing river current, as at Spurn Head, in the British Isles *(left)*. Coastal features such as these are constantly being created and destroyed.

Sand and shingle spit
Original coastline
Opposing river current
Waves breaking at an angle

Coastal processes: Formation of a spit

The evolving landscape

River systems

2 Rivers are continuously transporting eroded material towards the sea. Slow-moving, low-gradient rivers, like this one in western Russia *(above)*, deposit their alluvium load, infilling valleys creating a flood plain. Subsequent climatic and tectonic fluctuations may erode the flood plain to form terraces.

Terrace created by erosion
Flood plain
Deposited alluvium
River channel

River systems: Formation of a flood plain and terraces

Erosion and weathering

4 Much of Europe was once subjected to folding and faulting, exposing hard and soft rock layers. Subsequent erosion and weathering has worn away the softer strata, leaving up-ended layers of hard rock as in the French Pyrenees *(above)*.

Exposed up-ended rocks
Outline of original folded strata
Soft rock
Hard rock
Fault line
Folded rock strata

Erosion and weathering: Modification of a fold

Weathering

3 As surface water filters through permeable limestone, the rock dissolves to form underground caves, like Postojna in the Karst region of Slovenia *(above)*. Stalactites grow downwards as lime-enriched water seeps from roof fractures; stalagmites grow upwards where drips splash down.

Stalagmites created by drips
Underground cavern
River flowing underground dissolves rocks and creates caves
Stalactites formed by seeping water

Weathering: Formation of a cave

Political Europe

The political boundaries of Europe have changed many times, especially during the 20th century in the aftermath of two world wars, the break-up of the empires of Austria-Hungary, Nazi Germany and, towards the end of the century, the collapse of communism in eastern Europe. The fragmentation of Yugoslavia has again altered the political map of Europe, highlighting a trend towards nationalism and devolution. In contrast, economic federalism is growing. In 1958, the formation of the European Economic Community (now the European Union or EU) started a move towards economic and political union and increasing internal migration.

▲ *The Brandenburg Gate* in Berlin is a potent symbol of German reunification. From 1961, the road beneath it ended in a wall, built to stop the flow of refugees to the West. It was opened again in 1989 when the wall was destroyed and East and West Germany were reunited.

Population

Europe is a densely populated, urbanized continent; in Belgium over 90% of people live in urban areas. The highest population densities are found in an area stretching east from southern Britain and northern France, into Germany. The northern fringes are only sparsely populated.

▲ *Demand for space* in densely populated European cities like London has led to the development of high-rise offices and urban sprawl.

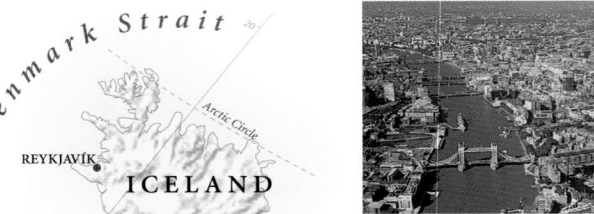

Population density
(people per sq km)

	below 49
	50–99
	100–149
	150–199
	200–299
	above 300

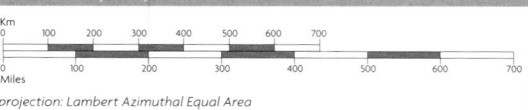

▲ *Traditional lifestyles still* persist in many remote and rural parts of Europe, especially in the south, east, and in the far north.

Map key

Population

- ▣ above 5 million
- ▣ 1 million to 5 million
- ◉ 500,000 to 1 million
- ◎ 100,000 to 500,000
- ⊕ 50,000 to 100,000
- ○ 10,000 to 50,000
- ● Country capital

Borders

⬚	full international border

Scale 1:17,250,000

Km
0   100   200   300   400   500   600   700

Miles
0   100   200   300   400   500   600   700

projection: Lambert Azimuthal Equal Area

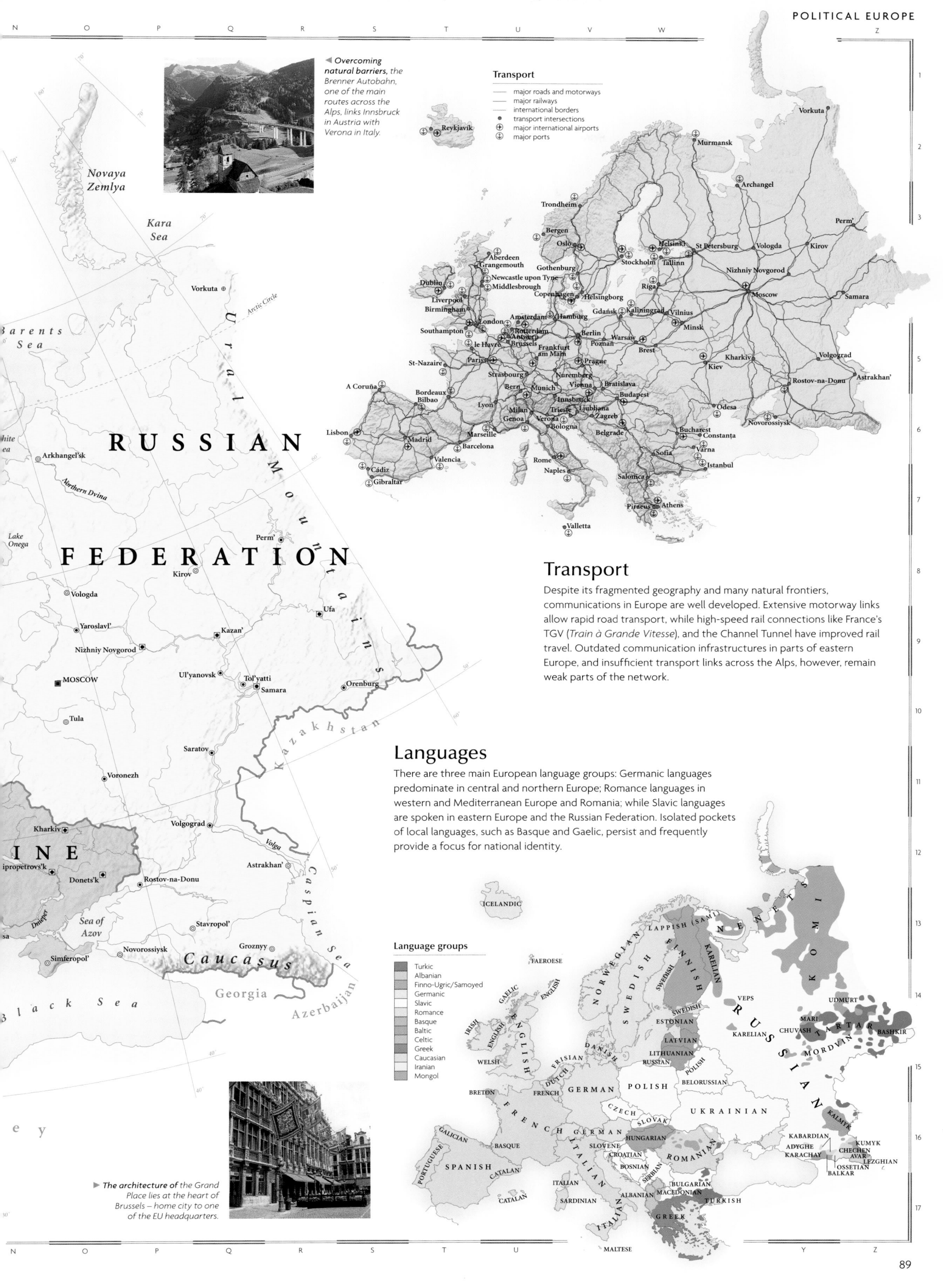

◀ *Overcoming natural barriers*, the Brenner Autobahn, one of the main routes across the Alps, links Innsbruck in Austria with Verona in Italy.

Transport

Despite its fragmented geography and many natural frontiers, communications in Europe are well developed. Extensive motorway links allow rapid road transport, while high-speed rail connections like France's TGV (*Train à Grande Vitesse*), and the Channel Tunnel have improved rail travel. Outdated communication infrastructures in parts of eastern Europe, and insufficient transport links across the Alps, however, remain weak parts of the network.

Languages

There are three main European language groups: Germanic languages predominate in central and northern Europe; Romance languages in western and Mediterranean Europe and Romania; while Slavic languages are spoken in eastern Europe and the Russian Federation. Isolated pockets of local languages, such as Basque and Gaelic, persist and frequently provide a focus for national identity.

▶ *The architecture of* the Grand Place lies at the heart of Brussels – home city to one of the EU headquarters.

Transport
— major roads and motorways
— major railways
— international borders
• transport intersections
⊕ major international airports
⊕ major ports

Language groups
- Turkic
- Albanian
- Finno-Ugric/Samoyed
- Germanic
- Slavic
- Romance
- Basque
- Baltic
- Celtic
- Greek
- Caucasian
- Iranian
- Mongol

European resources

Europe's large tracts of fertile, accessible land, combined with its generally temperate climate, have allowed a greater percentage of land to be used for agricultural purposes than in any other continent. Extensive coal and iron ore deposits were used to create steel and manufacturing industries during the 19th and 20th centuries. Today, although natural resources have been widely exploited, and heavy industry is of declining importance, the growth of hi-tech and service industries has enabled Europe to maintain its wealth.

Industry

Europe's wealth was generated by the rise of industry and colonial exploitation during the 19th century. The mining of abundant natural resources made Europe the industrial centre of the world. Adaptation has been essential in the changing world economy, and a move to service-based industries has been widespread except in eastern Europe, where heavy industry still dominates.

▲ Countries like Hungary are still struggling to modernize inefficient factories left over from extensive, centrally-planned industrialization during the communist era.

◄ Frankfurt am Main is an example of a modern service-based city. The skyline is dominated by headquarters from the worlds of banking and commerce.

▲ Other power sources are becoming more attractive as fossil fuels run out; 16% of Europe's electricity is now provided by hydro-electric power.

Standard of living

Living standards in western Europe are among the highest in the world, although there is a growing sector of homeless, jobless people. Eastern Europeans have lower overall standards of living – a legacy of stagnated economies.

Standard of living
(UN human development index)

- low
- high
- data not available

▶ Skiing brings millions of tourists to the slopes each year, which means that even unproductive, marginal land is used to create wealth in the French, Swiss, Italian and Austrian Alps.

GNI per capita (US $)

- below 1999
- 2000–4999
- 5000–9999
- 10,000–19,999
- 20,000–24,999
- above 25,000

Industry

Symbol	Industry	Symbol	Industry	Symbol	Industry
✈	aerospace	⬚	food processing	🍇	wine
⚓	brewing	⬛	hi-tech industry	⚒	coal
🚗	car/vehicle manufacture	⚙	iron & steel	●	oil
⚗	chemicals	⬛	pharmaceuticals	◗	gas
⚔	defence	⬛	printing & publishing		
⚡	electronics	⚓	shipbuilding	●	industrial cities
⚙	engineering	▽	textiles	▨	major industrial areas
$	finance	🌲	timber processing		

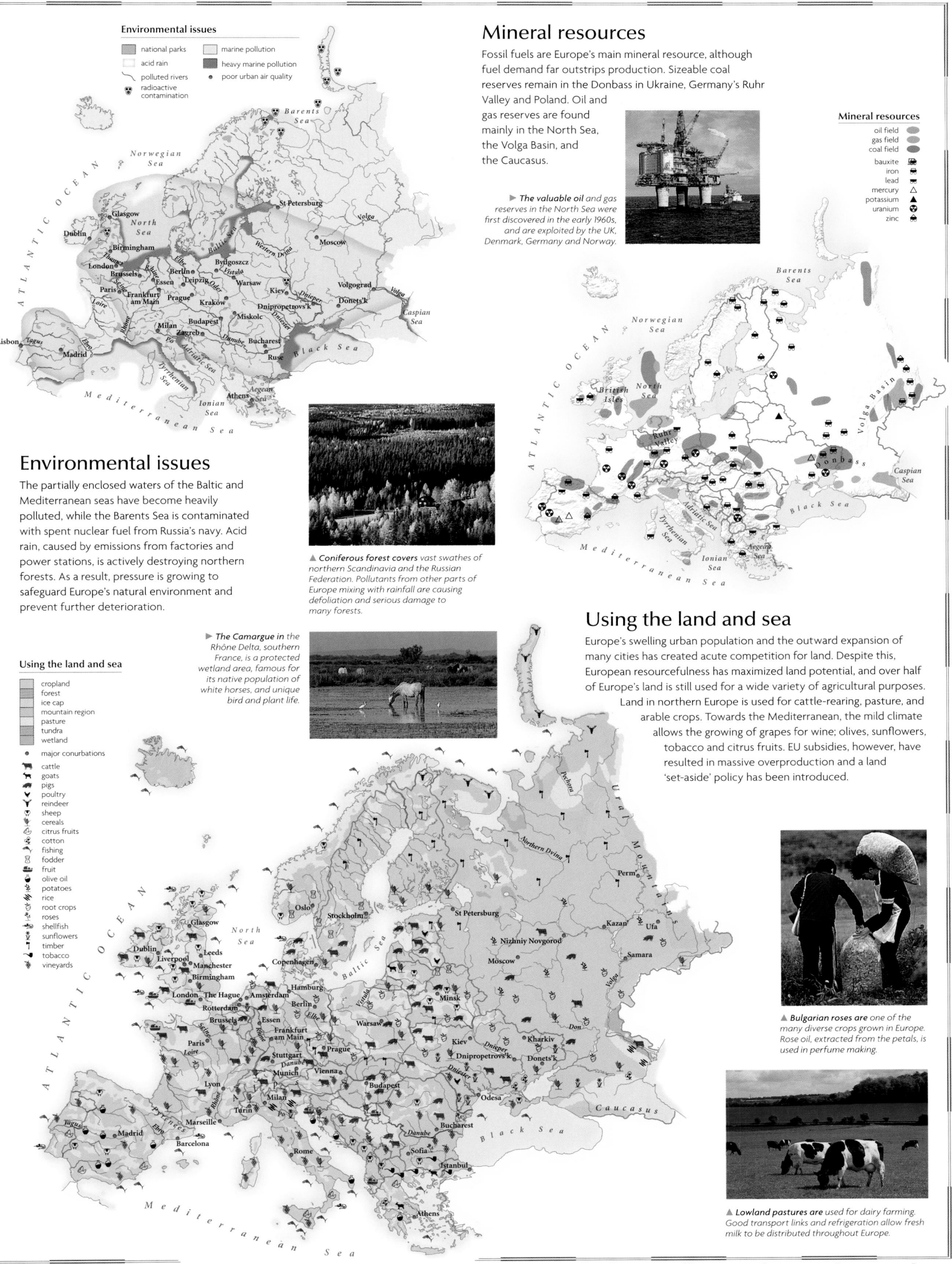

Mineral resources

Fossil fuels are Europe's main mineral resource, although fuel demand far outstrips production. Sizeable coal reserves remain in the Donbass in Ukraine, Germany's Ruhr Valley and Poland. Oil and gas reserves are found mainly in the North Sea, the Volga Basin, and the Caucasus.

▶ *The valuable oil* and gas reserves in the North Sea were first discovered in the early 1960s, and are exploited by the UK, Denmark, Germany and Norway.

Environmental issues

- national parks
- acid rain
- polluted rivers
- radioactive contamination
- marine pollution
- heavy marine pollution
- poor urban air quality

Mineral resources

- oil field
- gas field
- coal field
- bauxite
- iron
- lead
- mercury
- potassium
- uranium
- zinc

Environmental issues

The partially enclosed waters of the Baltic and Mediterranean seas have become heavily polluted, while the Barents Sea is contaminated with spent nuclear fuel from Russia's navy. Acid rain, caused by emissions from factories and power stations, is actively destroying northern forests. As a result, pressure is growing to safeguard Europe's natural environment and prevent further deterioration.

▲ *Coniferous forest covers* vast swathes of northern Scandinavia and the Russian Federation. Pollutants from other parts of Europe mixing with rainfall are causing defoliation and serious damage to many forests.

▶ *The Camargue in* the Rhône Delta, southern France, is a protected wetland area, famous for its native population of white horses, and unique bird and plant life.

Using the land and sea

Europe's swelling urban population and the outward expansion of many cities has created acute competition for land. Despite this, European resourcefulness has maximized land potential, and over half of Europe's land is still used for a wide variety of agricultural purposes. Land in northern Europe is used for cattle-rearing, pasture, and arable crops. Towards the Mediterranean, the mild climate allows the growing of grapes for wine; olives, sunflowers, tobacco and citrus fruits. EU subsidies, however, have resulted in massive overproduction and a land 'set-aside' policy has been introduced.

Using the land and sea

- cropland
- forest
- ice cap
- mountain region
- pasture
- tundra
- wetland
- major conurbations
- cattle
- goats
- pigs
- poultry
- reindeer
- sheep
- cereals
- citrus fruits
- cotton
- fishing
- fodder
- fruit
- olive oil
- potatoes
- rice
- root crops
- roses
- shellfish
- sunflowers
- timber
- tobacco
- vineyards

▲ *Bulgarian roses are* one of the many diverse crops grown in Europe. Rose oil, extracted from the petals, is used in perfume making.

▲ *Lowland pastures are* used for dairy farming. Good transport links and refrigeration allow fresh milk to be distributed throughout Europe.

Scandinavia, Finland & Iceland

DENMARK, NORWAY, SWEDEN, FINLAND, ICELAND

Jutting into the Arctic Circle, this northern swathe of Europe has some of the continent's harshest environments, but benefits from great reserves of oil, gas and natural evergreen forests. While most early settlers came from the south, migrants to Finland came from the east, giving it a distinct language and culture. Since the late 19th century, the Scandinavian states have developed strong egalitarian traditions. Today, their welfare benefits systems are among the most extensive in the world, and standards of living are high. The Lapps, or Sami, maintain their traditional lifestyle in the northern regions of Norway, Sweden and Finland.

The landscape

Glaciers up to 10,000 ft (3000 m) deep covered most of Scandinavia and Finland during the last Ice Age. The effects of glaciation mark the entire landscape, from the mountains to the lowlands, across the tundra landscape of Lapland, and the lake districts of Sweden and Finland.

Geysers are a by-product of Iceland's volcanic activity. Geysir, Iceland's largest spring, gives them their name.

Lapland, north of the Arctic Circle, is an area of undulating fells and plains known as tundra. The subsoil is permanently frozen and therefore impermeable. There are many peat bogs. Pools reappear in the summer when the surface thaws.

▼ **Finland's landscape was** fashioned by ice action. Glaciers gouged out its distinctive shallow lake basins, such as Oulujärvi, and left debris called moraines in their wake.

Oulujärvi

Area of maximum yearly uplift 0.3 in/yr (9 mm/yr)

▲ **Scandinavia is still** recovering from the last Ice Age, when ice depressed the land by 2000 ft (600 m). This gradual uplift is known as isostatic rebound.

Slower rates of uplift 0.1 in/yr (3 mm/yr)

Sjælland coast

▲ **On the coast of** Sjælland, these cliffs have been eroded by the sea, exposing layers of chalk and limestone.

Fjords

▲ **The fjords on the western** coast of Norway were once gentle river valleys. Their deep floors and steep sides were carved out by glaciers during the last Ice Age, and they were later flooded by the sea.

Halti mountain is Finland's highest point, at 4356 ft (1328 m).

The Lofoten Islands were one of the first areas exposed as the ice sheet melted.

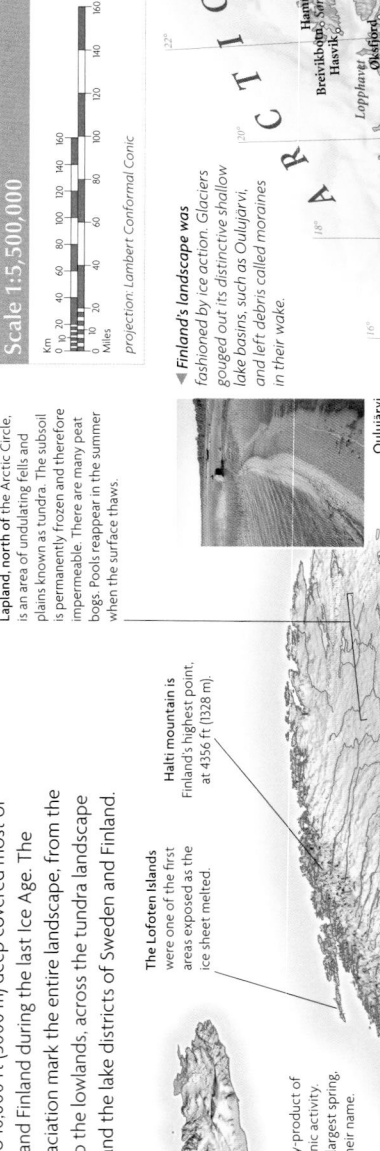

Using the land and sea

The cold climate, short growing season, poorly developed soil, steep slopes, and exposure to high winds across northern regions means that most agriculture is concentrated, with the population, in the south. Most of Finland and much of Norway and Sweden are covered by dense forests of pine, spruce and birch, which supply the timber industries.

Land use and agricultural distribution

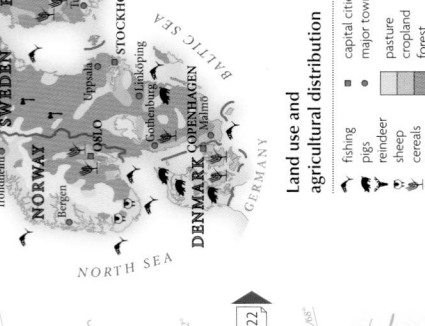

capital cities
major towns

fishing
pigs
reindeer
sheep
cereals
timber

pasture
cropland
forest
mountain region
tundra

The urban/rural population divide

urban 77%
rural 23%

Population density
51 people per sq mile

Total land area
473,970 sq miles
(1,227,610 sq km)

SCALE 1:9,000,000
projection: Lambert Conformal Conic

Scale 1:5,500,000
projection: Lambert Conformal Conic

(same scale as main map)

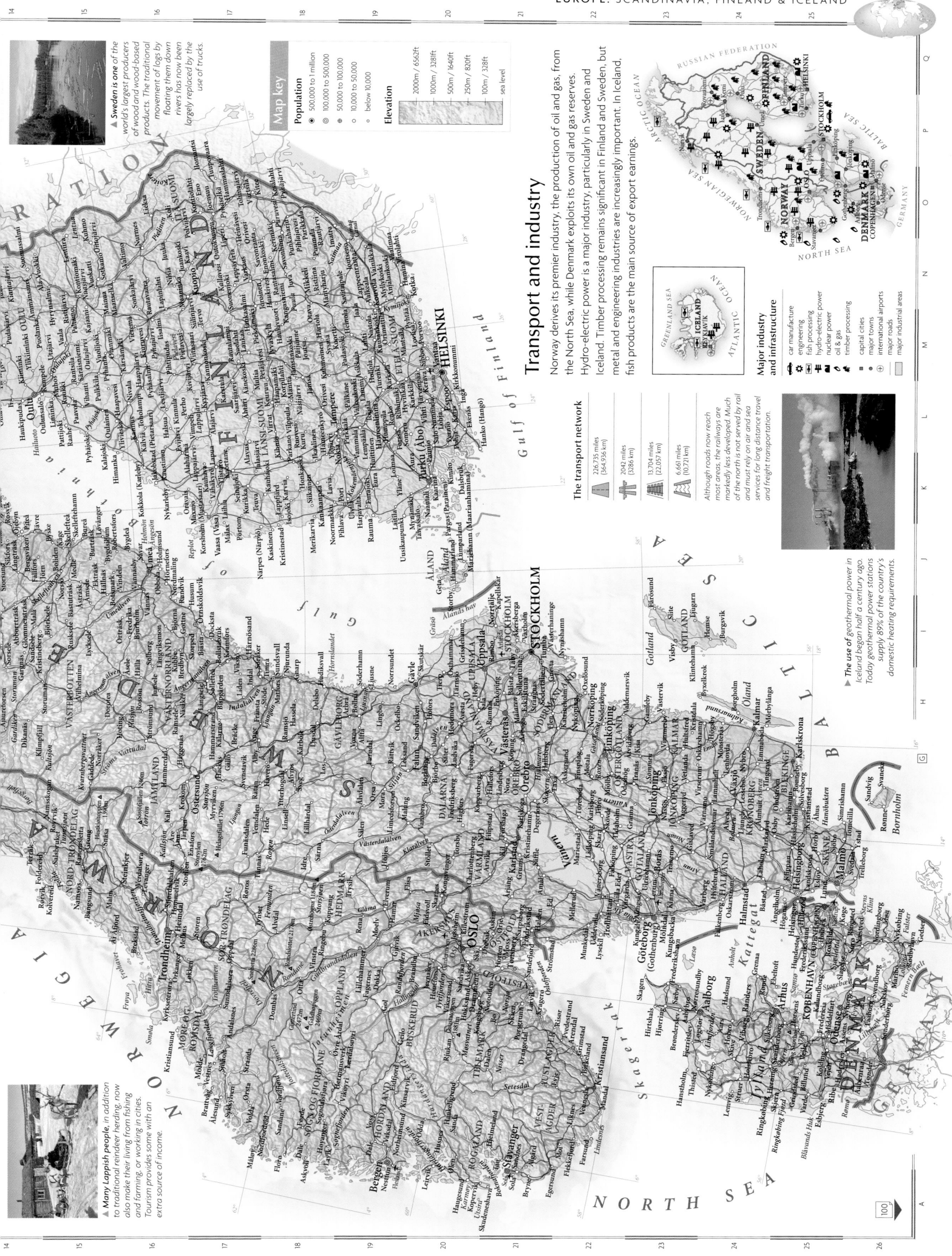

Transport and industry

Norway derives its premier industry, the production of oil and gas, from the North Sea, while Denmark exploits its own oil and gas reserves. Hydro-electric power is a major industry, particularly in Sweden and Iceland. Timber processing remains significant in Finland and Sweden, but metal and engineering industries are increasingly important. In Iceland, fish products are the main source of export earnings.

Major industry and infrastructure

- car manufacture
- engineering
- fish processing
- hydro-electric power
- nuclear power
- oil & gas
- timber processing
- capital cities
- major cities
- major towns
- international airports
- major roads
- major industrial areas

The transport network

226,735 miles (364,936 km)	2042 miles (3286 km)
13,704 miles (22,057 km)	6,661 miles (10,721 km)

Although roads now reach most areas, the railways are markedly less developed. Much of the north is not served by rail and must rely on air and sea services for long distance travel and freight transportation.

▲ The use of geothermal power in Iceland began half a century ago. Today geothermal power stations supply 89% of the country's domestic heating requirements.

▲ Sweden is one of the world's largest producers of wood and wood-based products. The traditional movement of logs by floating them down rivers has now been largely replaced by the use of trucks.

▲ Many Lappish people, in addition to traditional reindeer herding, now also make their living from fishing and farming, or working in cities. Tourism provides some with an extra source of income.

Map key

Population
- ⊙ 500,000 to 1 million
- ◉ 100,000 to 500,000
- ⊕ 50,000 to 100,000
- ○ 10,000 to 50,000
- ○ below 10,000

Elevation
- 2000m / 6562ft
- 1000m / 3281ft
- 500m / 1640ft
- 250m / 820ft
- 100m / 328ft
- sea level

Southern Scandinavia

SOUTHERN NORWAY, SOUTHERN SWEDEN, DENMARK

Scandinavia's economic and political hub is the more habitable and accessible southern region. Many of the area's major cities are on the southern coasts, including Oslo and Stockholm, the capitals of Norway and Sweden. In Denmark, most of the population and the capital, Copenhagen, are located on its many islands. A cultural unity links the three Scandinavian countries. Their main languages, Danish, Swedish and Norwegian, are mutually intelligible, and they all retain their monarchies, although the parliaments have legislative control.

Using the land

Agriculture in southern Scandinavia is highly mechanized although farms are small. Denmark is the most intensively farmed country and its western pastureland is used mainly for pig farming. Cereal crops including wheat, barley and oats, predominate in eastern Denmark and in the far south of Sweden. Southern Norway and Sweden have large tracts of forest which are exploited for logging.

The urban/rural population divide

urban 87%   rural 13%

Total land area
173,487 sq miles
(456,564 sq km)

Population density
112 people per sq mile
(43 people per sq km)

Land use and agricultural distribution

● capital cities
○ major towns

pasture
cropland
forest
mountain region

cattle
pigs
sheep
cereals
fodder
root crops
timber

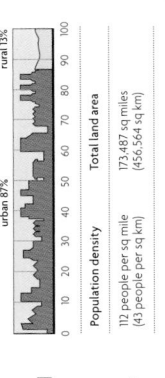

▲ In Norway winters are longer and colder inland than in coastal areas, where the warm current of the North Atlantic Drift moderates the climate.

The landscape

Southern Scandinavia, with the exception of Norway, has a flatter terrain than the rest of the region. Denmark and southern Sweden are both extensions of the North European Plain. In this area, because of glacial deposition rather than erosion, the soils are deeper and more fertile.

Acid rain, caused by industrial pollution carried north from elsewhere in Europe, harms plant and animal life in Scandinavian forests and lakes. The region's surface rocks lack lime to neutralize the acid, so making the problem more serious.

▲ In the past, glaciers such as this one in Olden, Norway, were much larger. Today, many are retreating to yield the spectacular glacial scenery.

Distinctive low ridges, called eskers, are found across southern Sweden. They are formed from sand and gravel deposits left by retreating glaciers.

▲ Limestone pillars eroded by the sea dot the coast of Gotland and surrounding islands.

The lakes of southern Sweden remain from a period when the land was completely flooded. As the ice which covered the area melted, the land rose, leaving lakes in shallow, ice-scoured depressions. Sweden has over 90,000 lakes.

The peak of Glittertind in the Jotunheimen mountains is 8110 ft (2472 m) high.

Vänern in Sweden is the largest lake in Scandinavia. It covers an area of 2080 sq miles (5390 sq km).

Denmark's flat and fertile soils are formed on glacial deposits between 100–160 ft (30–50 m) deep.

When the ice retreated the valley was flooded by the sea

Old valley floor

Sognefjorden

Erosion by glaciers deepened existing river valleys

Sea level

▲ Sognefjorden is the deepest of Norway's many fjords. It drops to 4291 ft (1308 m) below sea level.

Map key

Scale 1:3,250,000

projection: Lambert Conformal Conic

Population
◉ 500,000 to 1 million
◎ 100,000 to 500,000
⊕ 50,000 to 100,000
○ 10,000 to 50,000
○ below 10,000

Elevation
2000m / 6562ft
1000m / 3281ft
500m / 1640ft
250m / 820ft
100m / 328ft
sea level

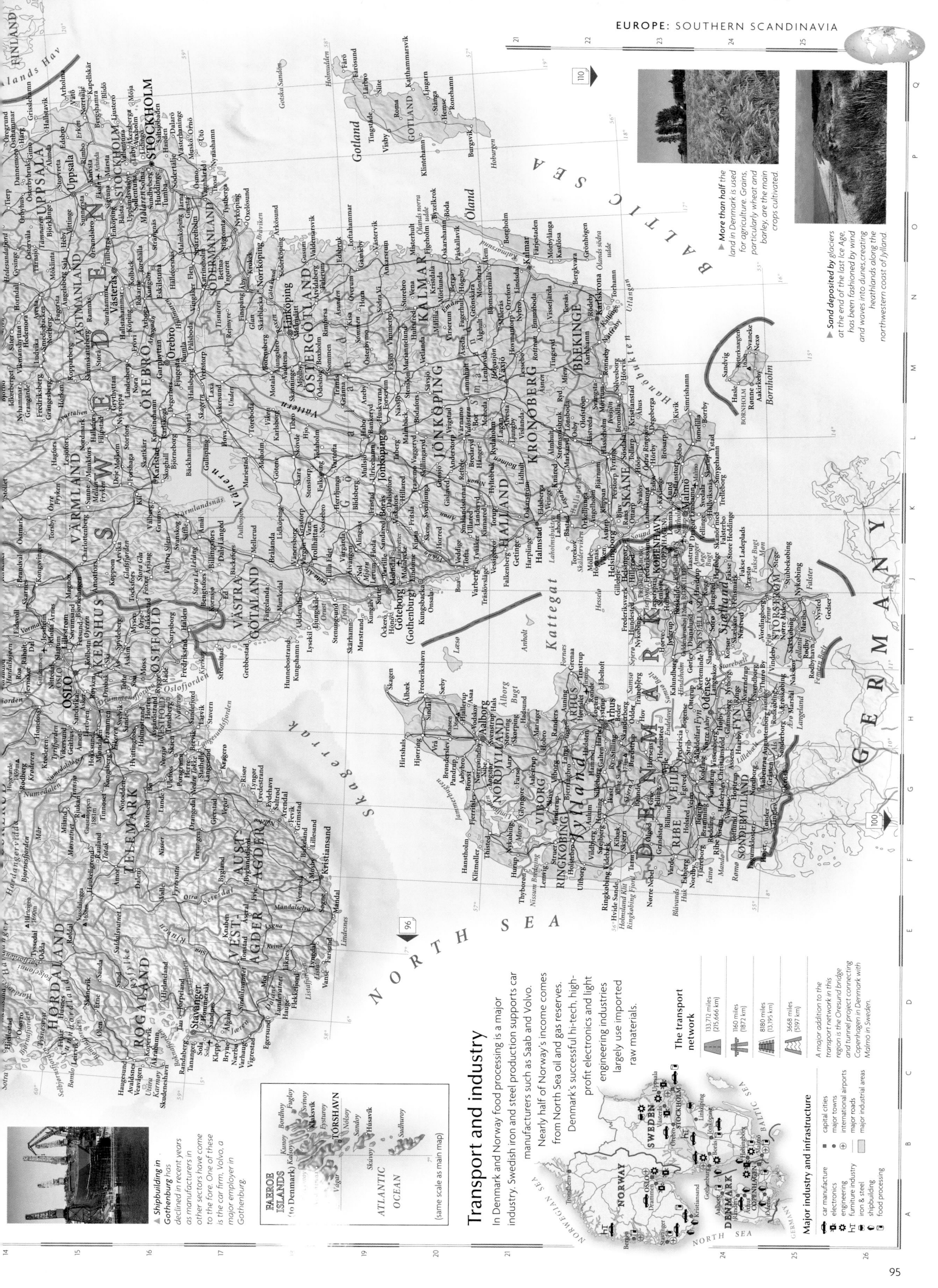

▲ More than half the land in Denmark is used for agriculture. Grains, particularly wheat and barley, are the main crops cultivated.

▲ Sand deposited by glaciers at the end of the last Ice Age, has been fashioned by wind and waves into dunes, creating heathlands along the northwestern coast of Jylland.

▲ Shipbuilding in Gothenburg has declined in recent years as manufacturers in other sectors have come to the fore. One of these is the car firm, Volvo, a major employer in Gothenburg.

Transport and industry

In Denmark and Norway food processing is a major industry. Swedish iron and steel production supports car manufacturers such as Saab and Volvo. Nearly half of Norway's income comes from North Sea oil and gas reserves. Denmark's successful hi-tech, high-profit electronics and light engineering industries largely use imported raw materials.

The transport network

133,712 miles (215,166 km)
1160 miles (1872 km)
8180 miles (13,195 km)
3668 miles (5197 km)

A major addition to the transport network in this region is the Øresund bridge and tunnel project connecting Copenhagen in Denmark with Malmo in Sweden.

Major industry and infrastructure

- ● capital cities
- ● major towns
- ⊕ international airports
- major roads
- major industrial areas

Major industry:
- car manufacture
- electronics
- engineering
- furniture industry
- iron & steel
- shipbuilding
- food processing

FAEROE ISLANDS (to Denmark)
TÓRSHAVN
ATLANTIC OCEAN
(same scale as main map)

The British Isles

UNITED KINGDOM, IRELAND

The British Isles have for centuries played a central role in European and world history. England, Wales, Scotland and Northern Ireland together form the United Kingdom (UK), while the southern portion of Ireland is an independent country, self-governing since 1921. Although England has tended to be the politically and economically dominant partner in the UK, the Scots, Welsh and Irish maintain independent cultures, distinct national identities and languages. Southeastern England is the most densely populated part of this crowded region, with over eight million people living in and around the London area.

▲ The valley of Glen Coe in the Scottish Highlands is a U-shaped valley, typical of the north and west of the British Isles, where glaciers shaped much of the landscape.

Transport and industry

The British Isles' industrial base was founded primarily on coal, iron and textiles, based largely in the north. Today, the most productive sectors include hi-tech industries clustered mainly in southeastern England, chemicals, finance and the service sector, particularly tourism.

Major industry and infrastructure

- car manufacture
- chemicals
- engineering
- hi-tech industry
- iron & steel
- tourism
- capital cities
- major towns
- international airports
- major roads
- major industrial areas

The transport network

285,947 miles (460,240 km)	2023 miles (3578 km)
11,825 miles (19,032km)	3976 miles (6400 km)

The UK's congested roads have become a major focus of environmental concern in recent years. No longer an island, the UK was finally linked to continental Europe by the Channel Tunnel in 1994.

▼ Clew Bay in western Ireland, is characteristic of the heavily indented west coast, where deep wide-mouthed bays separate the mountains of Mayo, Donegal and Kerry as they thrust out into the Atlantic Ocean.

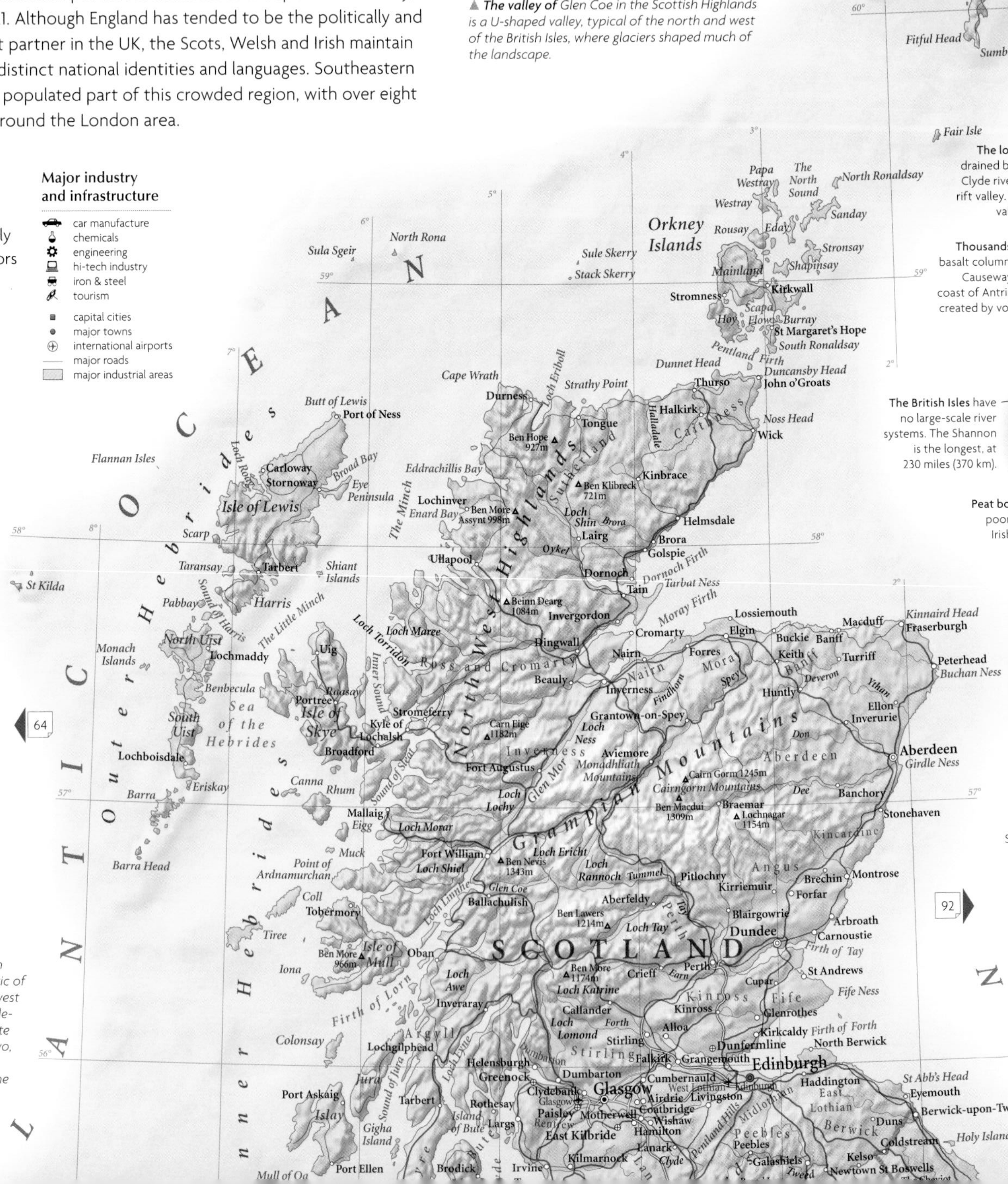

The landscape

Rugged uplands dominate the landscape of Scotland, Wales and northern England. All the peaks in the British Isles over 4000 ft (1219 m) lie in highland Scotland. Lowland England rises into several ranges of rolling hills, including the older Mendips, and the Cotswolds and the Chilterns, which were formed at the same time as the Alps in southern Europe.

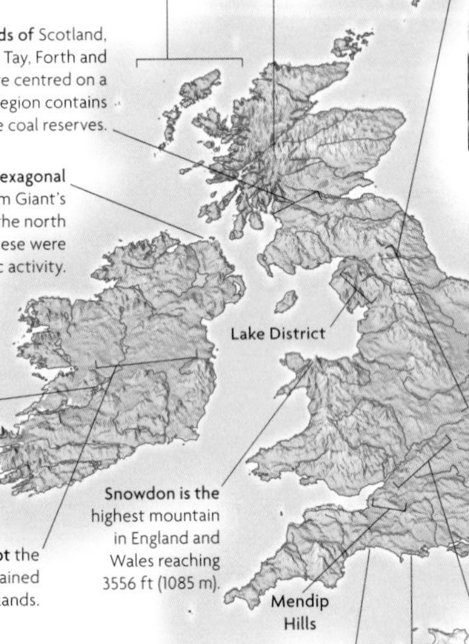

▲ Ullswater in the Lake District fills a deep valley formed by glacial erosion.

The Fens are a low-lying area reclaimed from the sea.

The Pennines, sometimes called 'the backbone of England' are formed of limestones and grits.

The Chiltern Hills

The Cotswold Hills are characterized by a series of limestone ridges overlooking clay vales.

Ben Nevis at 4409 ft (343 m) is the highest peak in the UK.

Over 600 islands, mostly uninhabited, lie west and north of the Scottish mainland

Lake District

Mendip Hills

Snowdon is the highest mountain in England and Wales reaching 3556 ft (1085 m)

The lowlands of Scotland, drained by the Tay, Forth and Clyde rivers, are centred on a rift valley. The region contains valuable coal reserves.

Thousands of hexagonal basalt columns form Giant's Causeway on the north coast of Antrim. These were created by volcanic activity.

The British Isles have no large-scale river systems. The Shannon is the longest, at 230 miles (370 km).

Peat bogs dot the poorly-drained Irish lowlands.

▼ Dartmoor, studded with tors, is an exposed part of a vast granite dome, formed when molten rock intruded into the Earth's crust.

▲ Coastal erosion around the British Isles forms striking features such as this limestone arch, Durdle Door in Dorset.

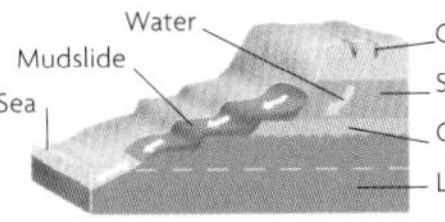

Durdle Door

Black Ven, Lyme Regis

- Cracks
- Sandstone
- Clay
- Limestone
- Water
- Mudslide
- Sea

▲ Much of the south coast is subject to landslides. Following rain, porous sandstones feed water into the underlying, less permeable clays which then crumble and slide into the sea.

Map key

Population

- ■ above 5 million
- ⊡ 1 million to 5 million
- ⊙ 500,000 to 1 million
- ⊕ 100,000 to 500,000
- ⊕ 50,000 to 100,000
- ⊕ 10,000 to 50,000
- ∘ below 10,000

Elevation

- 1000m / 328ft
- 500m / 1640ft
- 250m / 820ft
- 100m / 328ft
- sea level

SCOTLAND

West Highlands

Northwest Highlands

Grampian Mountains

ORKNEY ISLANDS

SHETLAND ISLANDS

Hebrides

Inner Hebrides

Outer Hebrides

The Minch

NORTH SEA

ATLANTIC OCEAN

IRELAND

UNITED KINGDOM

LONDON

DUBLIN

English Channel

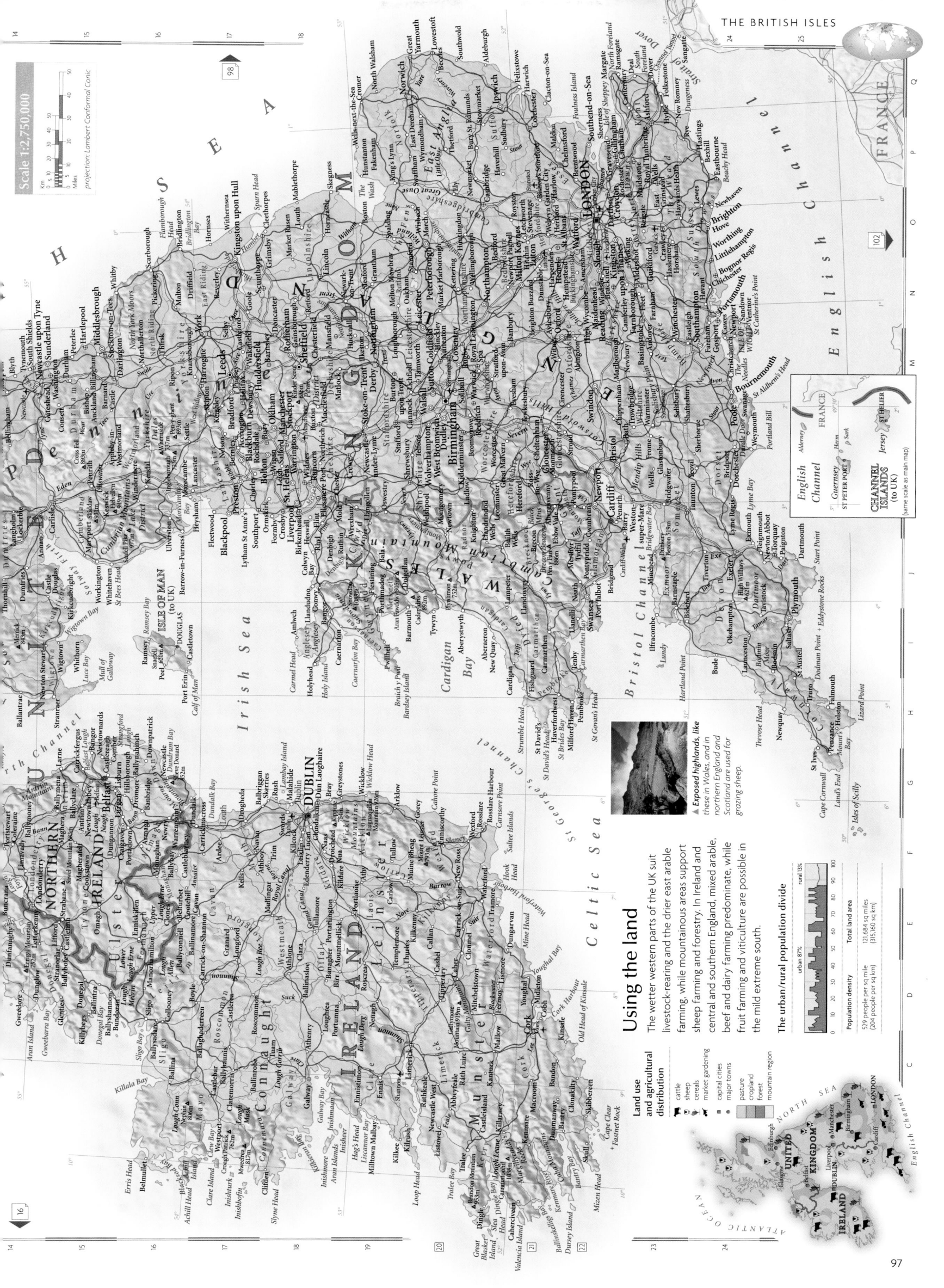

Scale 1:2,750,000
projection: Lambert Conformal Conic

Exposed highlands, like these in Wales, and in northern England and Scotland are used for grazing sheep.

Using the land

The wetter western parts of the UK suit livestock-rearing and the drier east arable farming, while mountainous areas support sheep farming and forestry. In Ireland and central and southern England, mixed arable, beef and dairy farming predominate, while fruit farming and viticulture are possible in the mild extreme south.

Land use and agricultural distribution

- cattle
- sheep
- cereals
- market gardening
- capital cities
- major towns
- pasture
- cropland
- forest
- mountain region

The urban/rural population divide

urban 87% rural 13%

Population density	Total land area
529 people per sq mile (204 people per sq km)	121,684 sq miles (315,160 sq km)

CHANNEL ISLANDS (to UK) (same scale as main map)
English Channel
FRANCE
Alderney
Guernsey
ST PETER PORT
Herm
Sark
Jersey ST HELIER

The Low Countries

BELGIUM, LUXEMBOURG, NETHERLANDS

One of northwestern Europe's strategic crossroads, the Low Countries are united by a common history in which they have often been a battleground in European wars. For over a thousand years they were ruled by foreign powers. Even after they achieved independence, the three countries maintained close links, later forming the world's first totally free labour and goods market, the Benelux Economic Union, which became the core of the European Community (now the European Union or EU). These states have remained at the forefront of wider European co-operation; Brussels, The Hague and Luxembourg are hosts to major institutions of the EU.

The landscape

The main geographical regions of the Netherlands are the northern glacial heathlands, the low-lying lands of the Rhine and Maas/Meuse, the reclaimed polders, and the dune coast and islands. Belgium includes part of the Ardennes, together with the coalfields on its northern flanks, and the fertile Flanders plain.

Since the Middle Ages the people of the Netherlands have used ditches and drainage dykes to reclaim land from the sea. These reclaimed areas are known as polders.

Sea — Polder — Drainage ditch

Dune system

Sand dunes

▲ Extensive sand dune systems along the coast have prevented flooding of the land. Behind the dunes, marshy land is drained to form polders, usable land suitable for agriculture.

Schoorl

▼ Heathlands, like these at Schoorl, are found along the coast of the Netherlands. Much of the coast was breached by the sea in the 5th century, creating its distinctive inlets and islands.

▲ One-third of the Netherlands lies below sea level and flooding is a constant threat. Barrages have been built across the mouths of many rivers to contain floodwaters.

The parallel valleys of the Maas/Meuse and Rhine rivers were created when the Rhine was deflected from its previous course by the ice sheet which formed during the last Ice Age.

Silts and sands eroded by the Rhine throughout its course are deposited in a delta on the west coast of the Netherlands.

The loess soils of the Flanders Plain in western Belgium provide excellent conditions for arable farming.

Hautes Fagnes is the highest part of Belgium. The bogs and streams in this upland region result from high rainfall and low temperatures.

Ardennes

▼ Uplifted and folded 220 million years ago, the Ardennes have since been reduced to relatively level plateaux, then sharply incised by rivers such as the Maas/Meuse.

Transport and industry

In the western Netherlands, a massive, sprawling industrialized zone encompasses many new hi-tech and service industries. Belgium's central region has emerged as the country's light manufacturing and services centre. Luxembourg city is home to more than 160 banks and the European headquarters of many international companies.

The transport network

✈ 140,588 miles (226,281 km)		⚓ 2565 miles (4129 km)	
	4099 miles (6598 km)		4134 miles (6653 km)

The Low Countries hold a key position on the North Sea, containing Europe's two largest ports, Rotterdam and Antwerp, which are connected to a comprehensive system of inland waterways.

Major industry and infrastructure

- ✈ aerospace
- finance
- ⚙ engineering
- 💻 hi-tech industry
- pharmaceuticals
- textiles
- ■ capital cities
- • major towns
- ⊕ international airports
- major roads
- major industrial areas

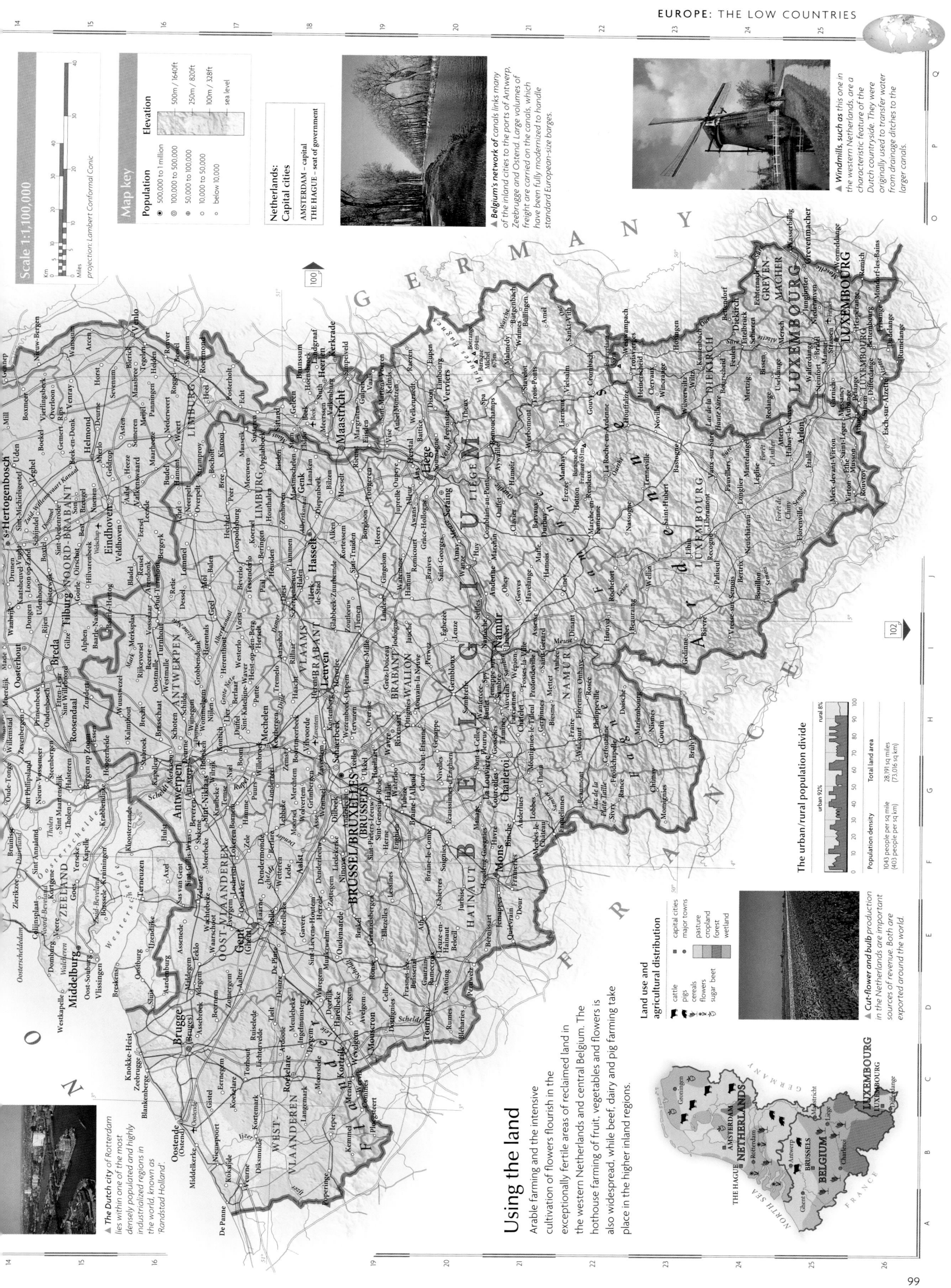

Scale 1:1,100,000

projection: Lambert Conformal Conic

Map key

Population
- ◉ 500,000 to 1 million
- ◎ 100,000 to 500,000
- ⊕ 50,000 to 100,000
- ⊙ 10,000 to 50,000
- ∘ below 10,000

Elevation
- 500m / 1640ft
- 250m / 820ft
- 100m / 328ft
- sea level

Netherlands:
Capital cities
AMSTERDAM – capital
THE HAGUE – seat of government

▲ *Belgium's network* of canals links many of the inland cities to the ports of Antwerp, Zeebrugge and Ostend. Large volumes of freight are carried on the canals, which have been fully modernized to handle standard European-size barges.

▲ *Windmills, such as* this one in the western Netherlands, are a characteristic feature of the Dutch countryside. They were originally used to transfer water from drainage ditches to the larger canals.

Using the land

Arable farming and the intensive cultivation of flowers flourish in the exceptionally fertile areas of reclaimed land in the western Netherlands and central Belgium. The hothouse farming of fruit, vegetables and flowers is also widespread, while beef, dairy and pig farming take place in the higher inland regions.

Land use and agricultural distribution
- capital cities
- major towns
- pasture
- cropland
- forest
- wetland
- cattle
- pigs
- cereals
- flowers
- sugar beet

▲ *Cut-flower and bulb* production in the Netherlands are important sources of revenue. Both are exported around the world.

The urban/rural population divide

urban 92% rural 8%

Population density	Total land area
1043 people per sq mile (403 people per sq km)	28,191 sq miles (73,016 sq km)

▲ *The Dutch city of* Rotterdam lies within one of the most densely populated and highly industrialized regions in the world, known as 'Randstad Holland'.

99

Germany

Despite the devastation of its industry and infrastructure during the Second World War and its separation from eastern Germany during the Cold War, West Germany made a rapid recovery in the following generation to become Europe's most formidable economic power. When the Berlin Wall was dismantled in 1989, the two halves of Germany were politically united for the first time in 40 years. Complete social and economic unity remain a longer term goal, as East German industry and society adapt to a free market. Germany has been a key player in the creation of the European Union (EU) and in moves toward a single European currency.

Using the land

Germany has a large, efficient agricultural sector, and produces more than three-quarters of its own food. The major crops grown are cereals and sugar beet on the more fertile soils, and root crops, rye, oats and fodder on the poorer soils of the northern plains and central uplands. Southern Germany is also a principal producer of high quality wines. Vineyards cover the slopes surrounding the Rhine and its tributaries.

Land use and agricultural distribution
- cattle
- pigs
- cereals
- sugar beet
- vineyards
- capital cities
- major towns
- pasture
- cropland
- forest

The urban/rural population divide

urban 87%   rural 13%

Population density
612 people per sq mile
(236 people per sq km)

Total land area
137,804 sq miles
(356,910 sq km)

▲ *The Moselle river flows through the Rhine State Uplands (Rheinisches Schiefergebirge). During a period of uplift, pre-existing river meanders were deeply incised, to form its present dramatic contours.*

The landscape

The plains of northern Germany, the volcanic plateaux and mountains of the central uplands, and the Bavarian Alps are the three principal geographic regions in Germany. North to south the land rises steadily from barely 300 ft (90 m) in the plains to 6500 ft (2000 m) in the Bavarian Alps, which are a small but distinct region in the far south.

▲ *The heathlands of northern Germany are covered by glacial deposits of sandy outwash soil which makes them largely infertile. They support only sheep and solitary trees.*

Much of the landscape of northern Germany has been shaped by glaciation. During the last Ice Age, the ice sheet advanced as far the northern slopes of the central uplands.

▲ *Part of the floor of the Rhine Rift Valley was let down between two parallel faults in the Earth's crust.*

Fault lines
Rhine
Downfaulted block

Lüneburg Heath (Lüneburger Heide)

Müritz lake covers 45 sq miles (117 sq km), but is only 108 ft (33 m) deep. It lies in a shallow valley formed by meltwater flowing out from a retreating ice sheet. These valleys are known as Urstromtäler.

The Harz Mountains were formed 300 million years ago. They are block-faulted mountains, formed when a section of the Earth's crust was thrust up between two faults.

Zugspitze, the highest peak in Germany at 9719 ft (2962 m), was formed during the Alpine mountain-building period, 30 million years ago.

The Danube rises in the Black Forest (Schwarzwald) and flows east, across a wide valley, on its course to the Black Sea.

Rhine Rift Valley

The Rhine is Germany's principal waterway and one of Europe's longest rivers, flowing 820 miles (1320 km).

▼ *The Elbe flows in wide meanders across the north German plain to the North Sea. At its mouth it is 10 miles (16 km) wide.*

Elbe river

Scale 1:2,500,000
projection: Lambert Conformal Conic

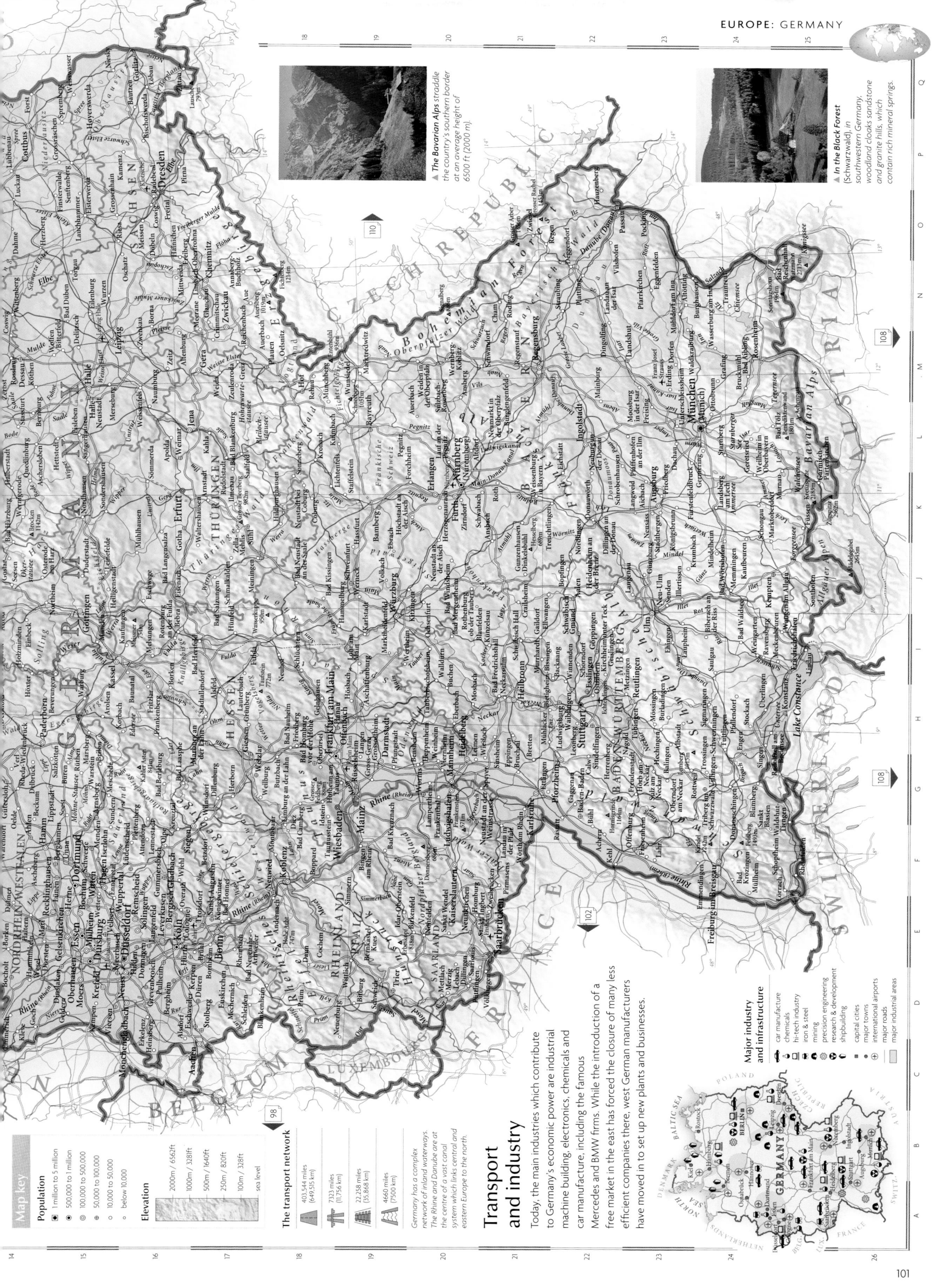

▲ *The Bavarian Alps straddle the country's southern border at an average height of 6500 ft (2000 m).*

▲ *In the Black Forest (Schwarzwald), in southwestern Germany, woodland cloaks sandstone and granite hills, which contain rich mineral springs.*

Map Key

Population

- ■ 1 million to 5 million
- ◉ 500,000 to 1 million
- ● 100,000 to 500,000
- ⊕ 50,000 to 100,000
- ∘ 10,000 to 50,000
- · below 10,000

Elevation

- 2000m / 6562ft
- 1000m / 3281ft
- 500m / 1640ft
- 250m / 820ft
- 100m / 328ft
- sea level

The transport network

- 403,544 miles (649,515 km)
- 7323 miles (11,756 km)
- 22,258 miles (35,868 km)
- 4660 miles (7500 m)

Germany has a complex network of inland waterways. The Rhine and Danube are at the centre of a vast canal system which links central and eastern Europe to the north.

Transport and industry

Today, the main industries which contribute to Germany's economic power are industrial machine building, electronics, chemicals and car manufacture, including the famous Mercedes and BMW firms. While the introduction of a free market in the east has forced the closure of many less efficient companies there, west German manufacturers have moved in to set up new plants and businesses.

Major industry and infrastructure

- car manufacture
- chemicals
- hi-tech industry
- iron & steel
- mining
- precision engineering
- research & development
- shipbuilding
- ⊞ capital cities
- ■ major cities
- ∘ major towns
- ✈ international airports
- major roads
- major industrial areas

101

France

FRANCE, MONACO

A major centre of culture and fashion, and a leading producer of both industrial and agricultural goods, France is a key player in the push towards European unity. The founder of modern Republican government in the 18th century, France has been closely involved in European events for many centuries. The Paris Basin is the most highly populated area; Île de France is home to over 11 million people. Large parts of rural France remain thinly populated, particularly the mountainous Massif Central, Pyrenees and southern Alps.

◀ The chalk cliffs of Normandy (Normandie) and southeastern England form part of a single geological region, now divided in two by the English Channel.

The landscape

France's landscape was fashioned by two phases of mountain-building. The northwestern peninsula, the Massif Central and the Vosges date from 220 million years ago. The complex folds of the Alps and Pyrenees, the gently-folded Jura, and the low-lying sedimentary areas of the Paris, Garonne and Rhône basins started to form 65 million years ago.

The coast of Brittany (Bretagne) is highly indented where deep valleys in the northwestern peninsula were drowned by the sea.

The Normandy (Normandie) coastline is characterized by high chalk cliffs.

The coastline of France is 2141 miles (3427 km) long.

▲ The Paris Basin consists of a layered sequence of sedimentary rocks. Fertile soils over much of the area make good agricultural land.

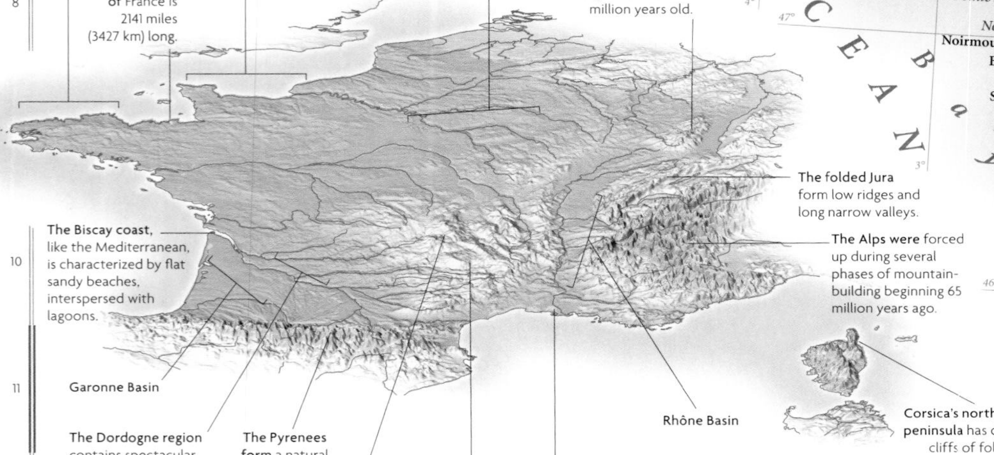

The gently rounded summits of the Vosges are over 200 million years old.

The folded Jura form low ridges and long narrow valleys.

The Alps were forced up during several phases of mountain-building beginning 65 million years ago.

The Biscay coast, like the Mediterranean, is characterized by flat sandy beaches, interspersed with lagoons.

Garonne Basin

The Dordogne region contains spectacular examples of limestone scenery including caves and gorges.

The Pyrenees form a natural border between France and Spain.

The ancient Massif Central, disturbed by the formation of the Alps, was subject to volcanism that only ceased during the last 10,000 years.

Rhône Delta

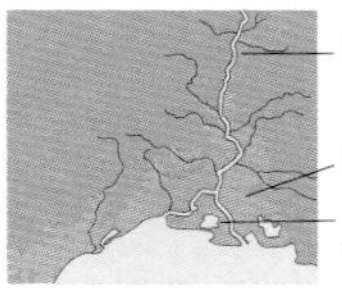

Rhône
Delta plain
The marshes of the Camargue

Rhône Basin

Corsica's northeastern peninsula has dramatic cliffs of folded limestone.

◀ The volcanic landscape of the Auvergne where the cones of its extinct volcanoes have worn away to leave 'plugs' of lava.

▲ Deposition in the Rhône Delta is wave-dominated. Sea currents carry river sediments extending the delta plain westwards.

Transport and industry

Today the main French growth industries are hi-tech, including micro-electronics, telecommunications and aerospace. Other important sectors are the nuclear industry, only rivalled in scale by that of the USA, car manufacture, dominated by the giants Renault and Peugeot and a highly diversified tourist industry.

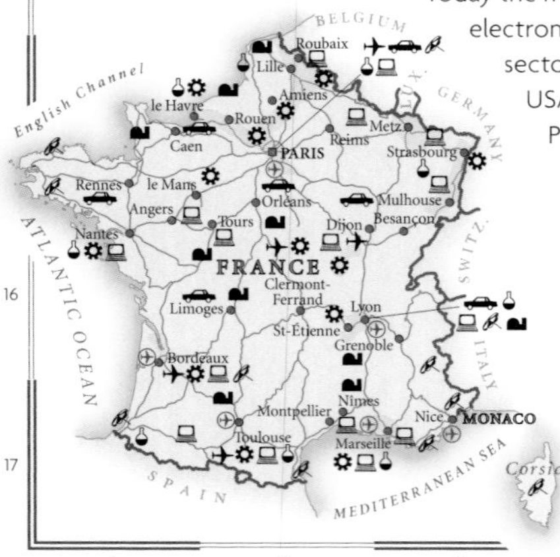

Major industry and infrastructure

✈ aerospace industry
⚙ car manufacture
⚗ chemicals
✿ engineering
▯ hi-tech industry
☢ nuclear power
✎ tourism

■ capital cities
● major towns
✈ international airports
— major roads
▭ major industrial areas

The transport network

555,473 miles (894,050 km)
7305 miles (11,758 km)
10,399 miles (16,737 km)
1159 miles (1863 km)

The French TGV (Train à Grande Vitesse) leads the world in high-speed train technology, and provides a service which can be faster, door-to-door, than air travel.

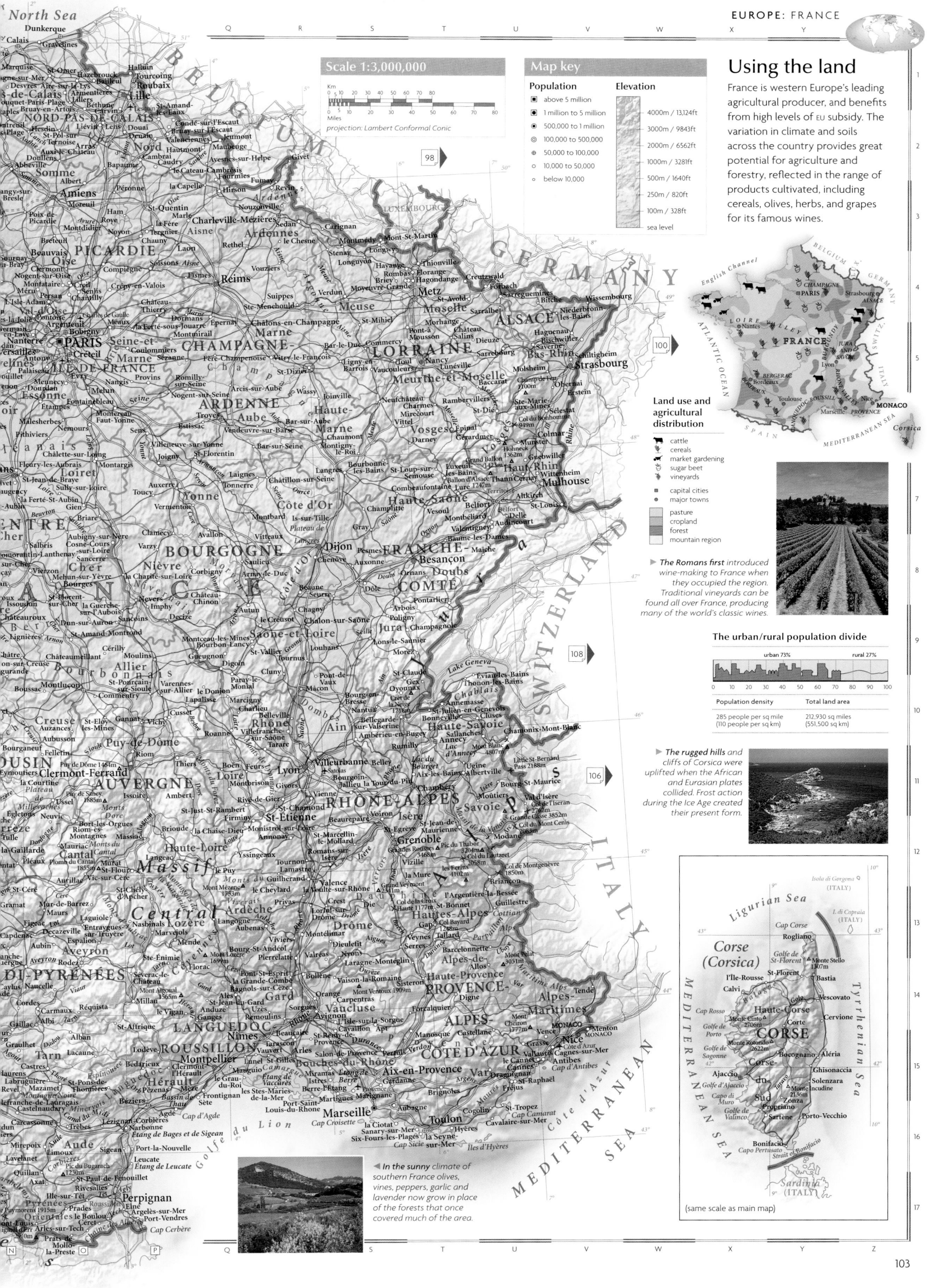

Using the land

France is western Europe's leading agricultural producer, and benefits from high levels of EU subsidy. The variation in climate and soils across the country provides great potential for agriculture and forestry, reflected in the range of products cultivated, including cereals, olives, herbs, and grapes for its famous wines.

Scale 1:3,000,000

projection: Lambert Conformal Conic

Map key

Population
- above 5 million
- 1 million to 5 million
- 500,000 to 1 million
- 100,000 to 500,000
- 50,000 to 100,000
- 10,000 to 50,000
- below 10,000

Elevation
- 4000m / 13,124ft
- 3000m / 9843ft
- 2000m / 6562ft
- 1000m / 3281ft
- 500m / 1640ft
- 250m / 820ft
- 100m / 328ft
- sea level

Land use and agricultural distribution
- cattle
- cereals
- market gardening
- sugar beet
- vineyards
- capital cities
- major towns
- pasture
- cropland
- forest
- mountain region

▶ The Romans first introduced wine-making to France when they occupied the region. Traditional vineyards can be found all over France, producing many of the world's classic wines.

The urban/rural population divide

urban 73%   rural 27%

Population density	Total land area
285 people per sq mile (110 people per sq km)	212,930 sq miles (551,500 sq km)

▶ The rugged hills and cliffs of Corsica were uplifted when the African and Eurasian plates collided. Frost action during the Ice Age created their present form.

◀ In the sunny climate of southern France olives, vines, peppers, garlic and lavender now grow in place of the forests that once covered much of the area.

Corse (Corsica)

(same scale as main map)

103

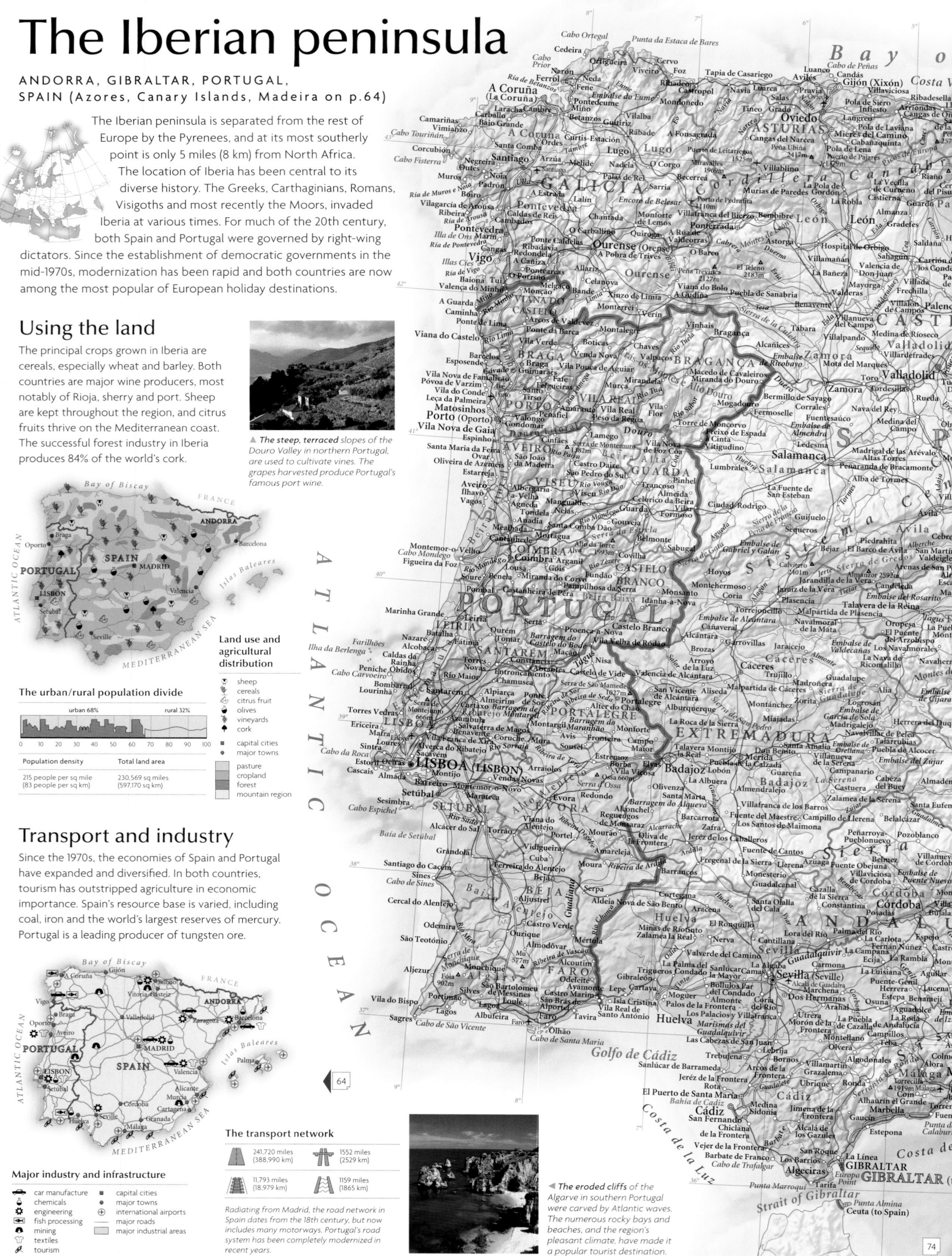

The Iberian peninsula

ANDORRA, GIBRALTAR, PORTUGAL,
SPAIN (Azores, Canary Islands, Madeira on p.64)

The Iberian peninsula is separated from the rest of Europe by the Pyrenees, and at its most southerly point is only 5 miles (8 km) from North Africa. The location of Iberia has been central to its diverse history. The Greeks, Carthaginians, Romans, Visigoths and most recently the Moors, invaded Iberia at various times. For much of the 20th century, both Spain and Portugal were governed by right-wing dictators. Since the establishment of democratic governments in the mid-1970s, modernization has been rapid and both countries are now among the most popular of European holiday destinations.

Using the land

The principal crops grown in Iberia are cereals, especially wheat and barley. Both countries are major wine producers, most notably of Rioja, sherry and port. Sheep are kept throughout the region, and citrus fruits thrive on the Mediterranean coast. The successful forest industry in Iberia produces 84% of the world's cork.

▲ The steep, terraced slopes of the Douro Valley in northern Portugal, are used to cultivate vines. The grapes harvested produce Portugal's famous port wine.

Land use and agricultural distribution

- sheep
- cereals
- citrus fruit
- olives
- vineyards
- cork
- capital cities
- major towns
- pasture
- cropland
- forest
- mountain region

The urban/rural population divide

urban 68%   rural 32%

0 10 20 30 40 50 60 70 80 90 100

Population density	Total land area
215 people per sq mile (83 people per sq km)	230,569 sq miles (597,170 sq km)

Transport and industry

Since the 1970s, the economies of Spain and Portugal have expanded and diversified. In both countries, tourism has outstripped agriculture in economic importance. Spain's resource base is varied, including coal, iron and the world's largest reserves of mercury. Portugal is a leading producer of tungsten ore.

Major industry and infrastructure

- car manufacture
- chemicals
- engineering
- fish processing
- mining
- textiles
- tourism
- capital cities
- major towns
- international airports
- major roads
- major industrial areas

The transport network

241,720 miles (388,990 km)	1552 miles (2529 km)
11,793 miles (18,979 km)	1159 miles (1865 km)

Radiating from Madrid, the road network in Spain dates from the 18th century, but now includes many motorways. Portugal's road system has been completely modernized in recent years.

◄ The eroded cliffs of the Algarve in southern Portugal were carved by Atlantic waves. The numerous rocky bays and beaches, and the region's pleasant climate, have made it a popular tourist destination.

The climate in northwestern Spain is milder in both summer and winter than in the rest of the country, creating a verdant environment, more commonly associated with northwestern Europe.

Map key

Population
- ◉ 1 million to 5 million
- ◉ 500,000 to 1 million
- ◉ 100,000 to 500,000
- ⊕ 50,000 to 100,000
- ○ 10,000 to 50,000
- ○ below 10,000

Elevation
- 3000m / 9843ft
- 2000m / 6562ft
- 1000m / 3281ft
- 500m / 1640ft
- 250m / 820ft
- 100m / 328ft
- sea level

Scale 1:3,000,000

Km 0 5 10 20 30 40 50 60 70 80
Miles 0 10 20 30 40 50 60 70 80

projection: Lambert Conformal Conic

Bay of Biscay · *Pyrenees* · *Golfo de Valencia* · *MEDITERRANEAN SEA* · *Islas Baleares (Balearic Islands)* · *Costa Brava* · *Costa del Azahar* · *Costa Blanca* · *Costa del Sol* · *Alboran Sea* · *Golfo de Mazarrón* · *Golfo de Almería*

Major cities and regions: PAIS VASCO, Bilbao, Donostia-San Sebastián, Pamplona (Iruña), Vitoria-Gasteiz, Logroño, NAVARRA, LA RIOJA, ARAGÓN, Zaragoza, Huesca, Teruel, CATALUÑA, Barcelona, Girona, Lleida (Lérida), Tarragona, ANDORRA, ANDORRA LA VELLA, MADRID, Guadalajara, Cuenca, CASTILLA-LA MANCHA, Albacete, Ciudad Real, PAÍS VALENCIANO, Valencia, Castellón de la Plana, Alicante (Alacant), Elche (Elx), MURCIA, Murcia, Cartagena, Granada, Almería, Jaén, ILLES BALEARS, Palma, Mallorca (Majorca), Menorca (Minorca), Ibiza (Eivissa)

The landscape

A vast plateau, the Meseta dominates the centre of the peninsula, enclosed by the Cordillera Cantábrica to the north and the Sierra Morena to the south. It is drained by three major rivers, the Douro/Duero, the Tagus, and the Guadalquivir. The peninsula experiences great variations in climate and rainfall, both regionally and locally.

▲ *The Pyrenees form Iberia's northeastern boundary, running for 270 miles (440 km), dividing the peninsula from the rest of Europe.*

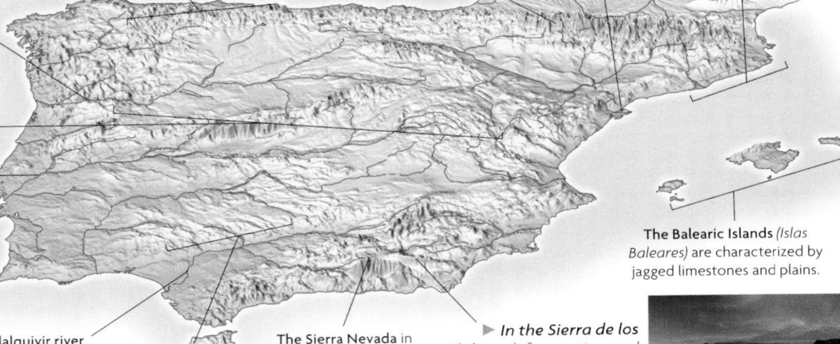

The Ebro river has formed the peninsula's largest delta. Recently, sediment flows have been seriously disturbed by nearby reservoirs.

On the northeastern coast sea level changes are evident from wave-cut beaches which rise up to 200 ft (60 m) above the present sea level.

- Cordillera Cantábrica
- Douro/Duero river
- The Meseta plateau averages 1970 ft (600 m) in height and is now largely dry and treeless.
- Tagus River

The Guadalquivir river brings vital irrigation water to the plains, and like many of Iberia's rivers, is prone to flooding.

Sierra Morena

The Sierra Nevada in southern Spain contain Iberia's highest peak, Mulhacén, which rises 11,418 ft (3481 m).

The Balearic Islands *(Islas Baleares)* are characterized by jagged limestones and plains.

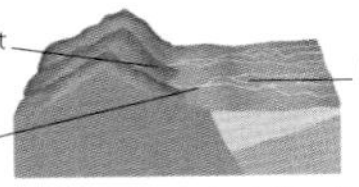

▶ *In the Sierra de los Filabres deforestation and overgrazing, which cause soil erosion, have created semi-desert badlands.*

▲ *Pediments are characteristic of semi-arid lands across Iberia. A pediment is a flat, low-lying, eroded platform, cut into the bedrock. Weathered material is transported by streams and deposited in broad fan shapes on the pediment.*

Mountain front · Weathered material · Pediment

Peñón de Alhucemas (to Spain) · Melilla (to Spain) · Islas Chafarinas (to Spain) · Isla de Alborán

The Italian peninsula

ITALY, SAN MARINO, VATICAN CITY

The Italian peninsula is a land of great contrasts. Until unification in 1861, Italy was a collection of independent states, whose competitiveness during the Renaissance resulted in the architectural and artistic magnificence of cities such as Rome, Florence and Venice. The majority of Italy's population and economic activity is concentrated in the north, centred on the sophisticated industrial city of Milan. Southern Italy, the *Mezzogiorno*, has a harsh and difficult terrain, and remains far less developed than the north. Attempts to attract industry and investment in the south are frequently deterred by the entrenched network of organized crime and corruption.

The landscape

The mainly mountainous and hilly Italian peninsula took its present form following a collision between the African and Eurasian tectonic plates. The Alps in the northwest rise to a high point of 15,772 ft (4807 m) at Mont Blanc (*Monte Bianco*) on the French border, while the Apennines (*Appennino*) form a rugged backbone, running along the entire length of the country.

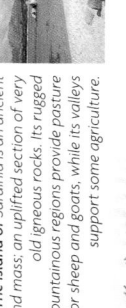
Costa Smeralda

▲ *The island of Sardinia is an ancient land mass, an uplifted section of very old igneous rocks. Its rugged mountainous regions provide pasture for sheep and goats, while its valleys support some agriculture.*

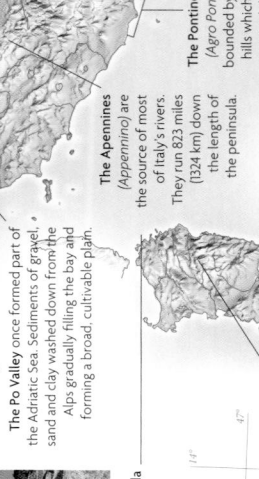
Mont Blanc (*Monte Bianco*)

▲ *The Dolomites* (Alpi Dolomitiche) *are formed of thick limestones, overlying weaker marine strata. They have distinctive serrated peaks and many massive landslides occur.*

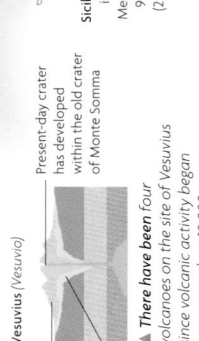

The distinctive square shape of the Gulf of Taranto (*Golfo di Taranto*) was defined by numerous block faults. Earthquakes are common in this region.

The Apennines (*Appennino*) are the source of most of Italy's rivers. They run 823 miles (1324 km) down the length of the peninsula.

The Pontine Marshes (*Agro Pontino*) are bounded by low sand hills which prevent natural drainage.

The Po Valley once formed part of the Adriatic Sea. Sediments of gravel, sand and clay washed down from the Alps gradually filling the bay and forming a broad, cultivable plain.

Sardinia is the second largest island in the Mediterranean Sea. The highest point is Punta La Marmora at 6017 ft (1834 m).

The Strait of Messina (*Stretto di Messina*) is between 2 and 12 miles (3–19 km) wide, and is a rich fishing ground.

Sicily is the largest island in the Mediterranean at 9926 sq miles (25,708 sq km).

The southwestern tip of Sicily lies 95 miles (152 km) from the north African mainland and is part of the same geological region.

Vesuvius (*Vesuvio*)

Present-day crater has developed within the old crater of Monte Somma

▲ *There have been four volcanoes on the site of Vesuvius since volcanic activity began here more than 10,000 years ago.*

Vesuvius (*Vesuvio*)
Monte Somma
Old crater

Using the land

Italy produces 95% of its own food. The best farming land is in the Po Valley in northern Italy, where soft wheat and rice are grown. Irrigation is essential to agriculture in much of the south. Italy is a major producer and exporter of citrus fruits, olives, tomatoes and wine.

The urban/rural population divide

urban 67%
rural 33%

Population density	Total land area
506 people per sq mile (195 people per sq km)	116,320 sq miles (301,270 sq km)

Land use and agricultural distribution

- capital cities
- major towns
- pasture
- cropland
- forest
- cattle
- cereals
- citrus fruits
- olive oil
- rice
- vineyards

Scale 1:2,750,000

Km
0 5 10 20 30 40 50 60 70

Miles
0 5 10 20 30 40 50 60 70

projection: Lambert Conformal Conic

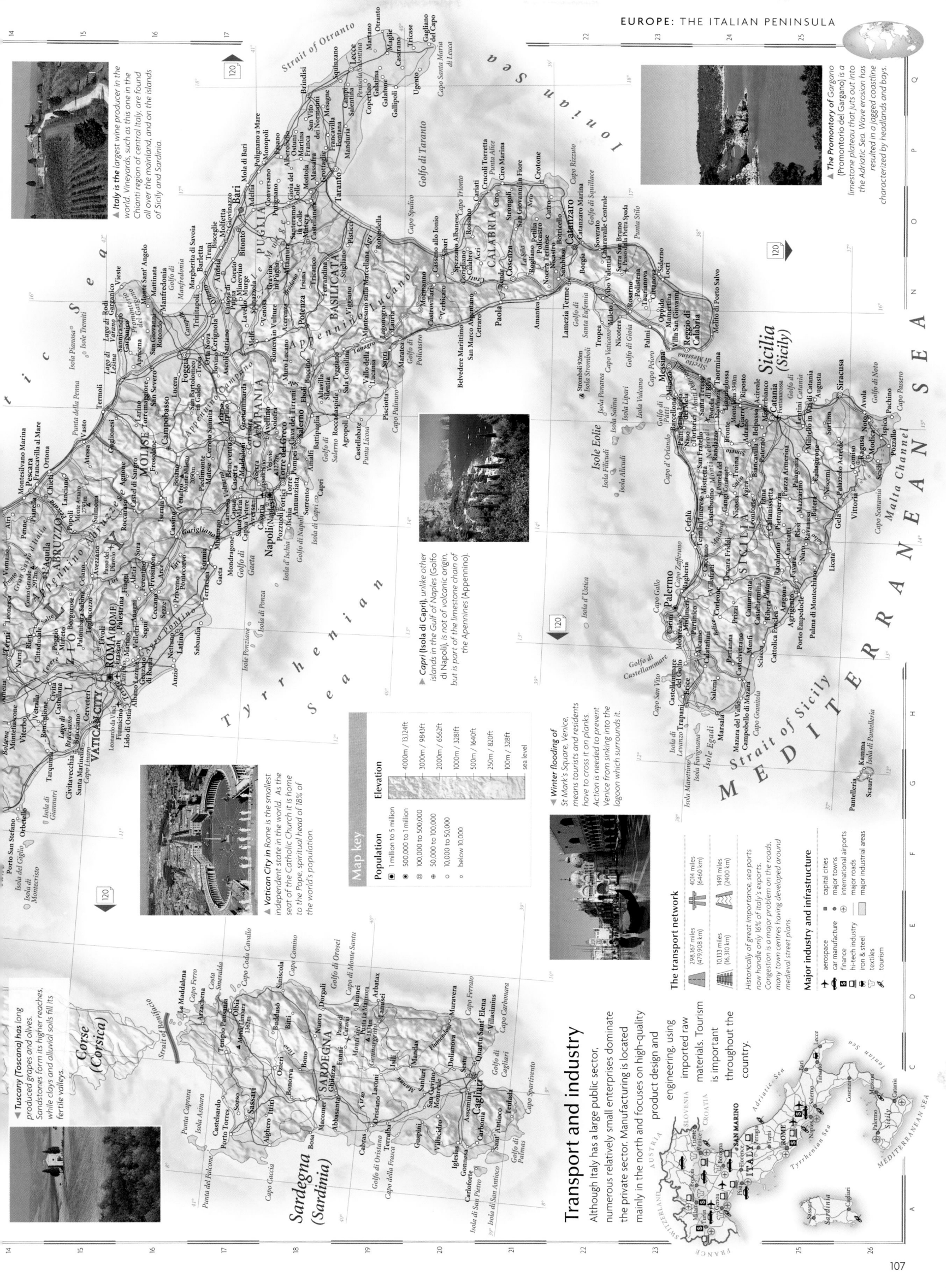

▲ *Italy is the largest wine producer in the world. Vineyards, such as this one in the Chianti region of central Italy, are found all over the mainland, and on the islands of Sicily and Sardinia.*

▲ *The Promontory of Gargano (Promontorio del Gargano) is a limestone plateau that juts out into the Adriatic Sea. Wave erosion has resulted in a jagged coastline characterized by headlands and bays.*

▲ *Capri (Isola di Capri), unlike other islands in the Gulf of Naples (Golfo di Napoli), is not of volcanic origin, but is part of the limestone chain of the Apennines (Appennino).*

▲ *Vatican City in Rome is the smallest independent state in the world. As the seat of the Catholic Church it is home to the Pope, spiritual head of 18% of the world's population.*

▼ *Winter flooding of St Mark's Square, Venice, means tourists and residents have to cross it on planks. Action is needed to prevent Venice from sinking into the lagoon which surrounds it.*

▲ *Tuscany (Toscana) has long produced grapes and olives. Sandstones form its higher reaches, while clays and alluvial soils fill its fertile valleys.*

Map key

Population

- ◉ 1 million to 5 million
- ⊙ 500,000 to 1 million
- ⊛ 100,000 to 500,000
- ⊕ 50,000 to 100,000
- ○ 10,000 to 50,000
- ∘ below 10,000

Elevation

	4000m / 13,124ft
	3000m / 9843ft
	2000m / 6562ft
	1000m / 3281ft
	500m / 1640ft
	250m / 820ft
	100m / 328ft
	sea level

The transport network

✈	298,167 miles (479,908 km)	404 miles (6460 km)
	10,133 miles (16,310 km)	1491 miles (2400 km)

Historically of great importance, sea ports now handle only 16% of Italy's exports. Congestion is a major problem on the roads, many town centres having developed around medieval street plans.

Major industry and infrastructure

- ✈ aerospace
- Ⓢ car manufacture
- finance
- hi-tech industry
- iron & steel
- textiles
- tourism

- ● capital cities
- ■ major towns
- ⊕ international airports
- major roads
- ☐ major industrial areas

Transport and industry

Although Italy has a large public sector, numerous relatively small enterprises dominate the private sector. Manufacturing is located mainly in the north and focuses on high-quality product design and engineering, using imported raw materials. Tourism is important throughout the country.

The Alpine states

AUSTRIA, LIECHTENSTEIN, SLOVENIA, SWITZERLAND

The Alpine countries of Austria, Switzerland, Liechtenstein and Slovenia form a narrow strip across western Europe's geographical core, lying on the main north–south trading routes across the Alps. Switzerland, politically neutral since 1815, is an important international meeting place and houses one of the headquarters of the United Nations, although it only became a member in 2002. Austria, once at the heart of the great Habsburg Empire has been a fully independent nation since 1955, and maintains a deserved reputation as an international centre of culture. Slovenia declared independence from the former Yugoslavia in 1991 and despite initial economic hardship, is now starting to achieve the prosperity enjoyed by its Alpine neighbours.

◄ **The Matterhorn, on** the Swiss-Italian border, is one of the highest mountains in the Alps, at 14,692 ft (4478 m). The term 'horn' refers to its distinctive peak, formed by three glaciers eroding hollows, known as cirques, in each of its sides.

Using the land

The Alpine region's mountainous terrain discourages cultivation over much of the land area. The primary agricultural activity is the raising of dairy and beef cattle on the pasture land of the lower mountain slopes. Austria is self-supporting in grains, and crops such as wheat, barley and grapes are grown on the east Austrian lowlands. Woodlands are more prevalent in the eastern Alps; both Austria and Slovenia have large tracts of forest.

Land use and agricultural distribution

- cattle
- pigs
- cereals
- vineyards
- capital cities
- major towns
- pasture
- cropland
- forest
- mountain region

The landscape

The Alps occupy three-fifths of Switzerland, most of southern Austria and the northwest of Slovenia. They were formed by the collision of the African and Eurasian tectonic plates, which began 65 million years ago. Their complex geology is reflected in the differing heights and rock types of the various ranges. The Rhine flows along Liechtenstein's border with Switzerland, creating a broad flood plain in the north and west of Liechtenstein. In the far northeast and east are a number of lowland regions, including the Vienna Basin, Burgenland and the plain of the Danube. Slovenia's major rivers flow across the lower eastern regions; in the west, the rivers flow largely underground through the limestone Karst region.

Original height after uplift and folding
Folded strata are overturned creating a *nappe*
Eurasian Plate
Present-day height of Alps
African Plate

▲ **The convergence of** the African and Eurasian plates compressed and folded huge masses of rock strata. As the plates continued to move together, the folded strata were overturned, creating complex nappes. Much of the rock strata has since been eroded, resulting in the current topography of the Alps.

▲ **Constricted as it** cuts through ridges in the Alps, the Danube meanders across the lowlands, where uplift combined with river erosion has deepened meanders.

The Vienna Basin lies mainly below 390 ft (120 m). It gradually subsided and filled with sediment as the Alps were uplifted.

Neusiedler See straddles the border of Austria and Hungary; the area around it provides some of the best wine-growing land in Austria.

The Austrian Alps comprise three distinct mountain ranges, separated by deep trenches. The northern and southern ranges are rugged limestones, while the Tauern range is formed of crystalline rocks.

The mountains of the Jura form a natural border between Switzerland and France. Their marine limestones date from over 200 million years ago. When the Alps were formed the Jura were folded into a series of parallel ridges and troughs.

Tectonic activity has resulted in dramatic changes in land height over very short distances. Lake Geneva, lying at 1221 ft (372 m) is only 43 miles (70 km) away from the 15,772 ft (4807 m) peak of Mont Blanc, on the France–Italy border.

The Bernese Alps (Berner Alpen) contain the Aletsch, which at 15 miles (24 km) is the longest Alpine glacier.

The Rhine, like other major Alpine rivers, follows a broad, flat trough between the mountains. Along part of its course, the Rhine forms the boundary between Switzerland and Liechtenstein.

The first road through the Brenner Pass was built in 1772, although it has been used as a mountain route since Roman times. It is the lowest of the main Alpine passes at 4298 ft (1374 m).

Karst region

► **The deep, blue** lakes of the Karst region are part of a drainage network which runs largely underground through this limestone area.

The limestone cave system at Postojna extends for more than 10 miles (16 km) and includes caverns reaching 125 ft (40 m) in height and width.

The Tauern range in the central Austrian Alps contains the highest mountain in Austria, the towering Grossglockner, rising 12,461 ft (3798 m).

The urban/rural population divide

urban 66%   rural 34%

Population density: 314 people per sq mile (121 people per sq km)

Total land area: 56,135 sq miles (145,390 sq km)

◄ *In this mountainous region, the flatter, more accessible areas are often used for both cattle grazing and recreation.*

◄ *These converging glaciers are marked by dark lines of moraine. This eroded material is carried by glaciers, and deposited as the ice melts.*

Scale 1:2,000,000

projection: Lambert Conformal Conic

Map key

Population
- ◉ 1 million to 5 million
- ◉ 500,000 to 1 million
- ◎ 100,000 to 500,000
- ⊕ 50,000 to 100,000
- ○ 10,000 to 50,000
- ○ below 10,000

Elevation
- 4000m / 13,124ft
- 3000m / 9843ft
- 2000m / 6562ft
- 1000m / 3281ft
- 500m / 1640ft
- 250m / 820ft
- 100m / 328ft
- sea level

► *The Austrian Tirol contains some of the most spectacular Alpine scenery. Snow cover is a permanent feature in the highest reaches.*

Transport and industry

All four nations concentrate on high-quality manufacturing and services. Austrian iron and steel production is complemented by construction industries; and Slovenia, traditionally the industrial powerhouse of the western Balkans has increasingly diversified industries. Liechtenstein and Switzerland, lacking raw materials, produce pharmaceuticals and precision instruments, such as watches, and act as international banking centres. The spectacular scenery of the region encourages tourism all year round.

The transport network

- 181,107 miles (291,497 km)
- 2116 miles (3405 km)
- 6368 miles (10,249 km)
- 993 miles (1598 km)

Tunnels and passes through the Alps are an important feature of this region. The NEAT project, providing two new high-speed rail links between Basel and Milan, was given approval in 1992.

Major industry and infrastructure
- car manufacture
- chemicals
- engineering
- finance
- food processing
- iron & steel
- pharmaceuticals
- textiles
- tourism
- watch making
- winter sports
- ■ capital cities
- major towns
- international airports
- major roads
- major industrial areas

▲ *The Schönbrunn Palace in Vienna was the summer residence of the Habsburg monarchy. Today, it is a major tourist attraction.*

Central Europe

CZECH REPUBLIC, HUNGARY, POLAND, SLOVAKIA

When Slovakia and the Czech Republic became separate countries in 1993, they joined Hungary and Poland in a new role as independent nation states, following centuries of shifting boundaries and imperial strife. This turbulent history bequeathed the region a rich cultural heritage, shared through the works of its many great writers and composers, and celebrated in the vibrant historic capitals of Prague, Budapest and Warsaw. Having shaken off years of Soviet domination in 1989, these states are confronting the challenge of winning commercial investment to modernize outmoded industries as they integrate their economies with those of the European Union.

Transport and industry

Heavy industry has dominated post-war life in Central Europe. Poland has large coal reserves, having inherited the Silesian coalfield from Germany after the Second World War, allowing the export of large quantities of coal, along with other minerals. Hungary specializes in consumer goods and services, while Slovakia's industrial base is still relatively small. The Czech Republic's traditional glassworks and breweries bring some stability to its precarious Soviet-built manufacturing sector.

Major industry and infrastructure

- car manufacture
- chemicals
- engineering
- food processing
- mining
- shipbuilding
- tourism

- ■ capital cities
- ● major towns
- ✈ international airports
- — major roads
- ▭ major industrial areas

The transport network

213,997 miles (344,600 km)	817 miles (1315 km)
27,479 miles (44,249 km)	3784 miles (6094 km)

The huge growth of tourism and business has prompted major investment in the transport infrastructure, with new road-building schemes within and between the main cities of the region.

▲ Budapest, the capital of Hungary, straddles the Danube. It comprises the historic towns of Buda, on the west bank, and Pest, which contains the Parliament Building, seen here on the far bank.

The landscape

The forested Carpathian Mountains, uplifted with the Alps, lie southeast of the older Bohemian Massif, which contains the Sudeten and Krusné Hory (Erzgebirge) ranges. They divide the fertile plains of the Danube to the south and the Vistula (Wisła), which flows north across vast expanses of glacial deposits into the Baltic Sea.

Hot mineral springs occur where geothermally heated water wells up through faults and fractures in the rocks of the Sudeten Mountains.

Pomerania is a sandy coastal region of glacially-formed lakes stretching west from the Vistula (Wisła).

Longshore currents moving east along the Baltic coast have built a 40 mile (65 km) spit composed of material from the Vistula (Wisła) river.

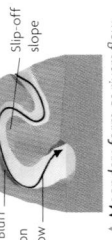

▲ The Biebrza river has left meanders and oxbow lakes as it flows across low-lying ground.

Gerlachovský štít, in the Tatra Mountains, is Slovakia's highest mountain, at 8711ft (2655 m).

Carpathian Mountains

Danube river

Slip-off slope

Bluff

Direction of flow

▲ Meanders form as rivers flow across plains at a low gradient. A steep cliff or bluff, forms on the outside curve, and a gentler slip-off slope on the inside bend.

The Great Hungarian Plain formed by the flood plain of the Danube is a mixture of steppe and cultivated land, covering nearly half of Hungary's total area.

The Slovak Ore Mountains (Slovenské Rudohorie) are noted for their mineral resources, including high-grade iron ore.

Bohemian Massif

Krusné Hory (Erzgebirge)

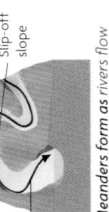

▼ The Berounka river cuts through the precipitous wooded landscape of the Bohemian Massif, banked by a broad flood plain.

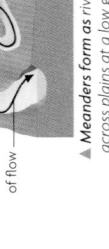

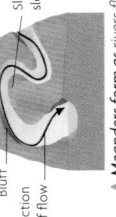

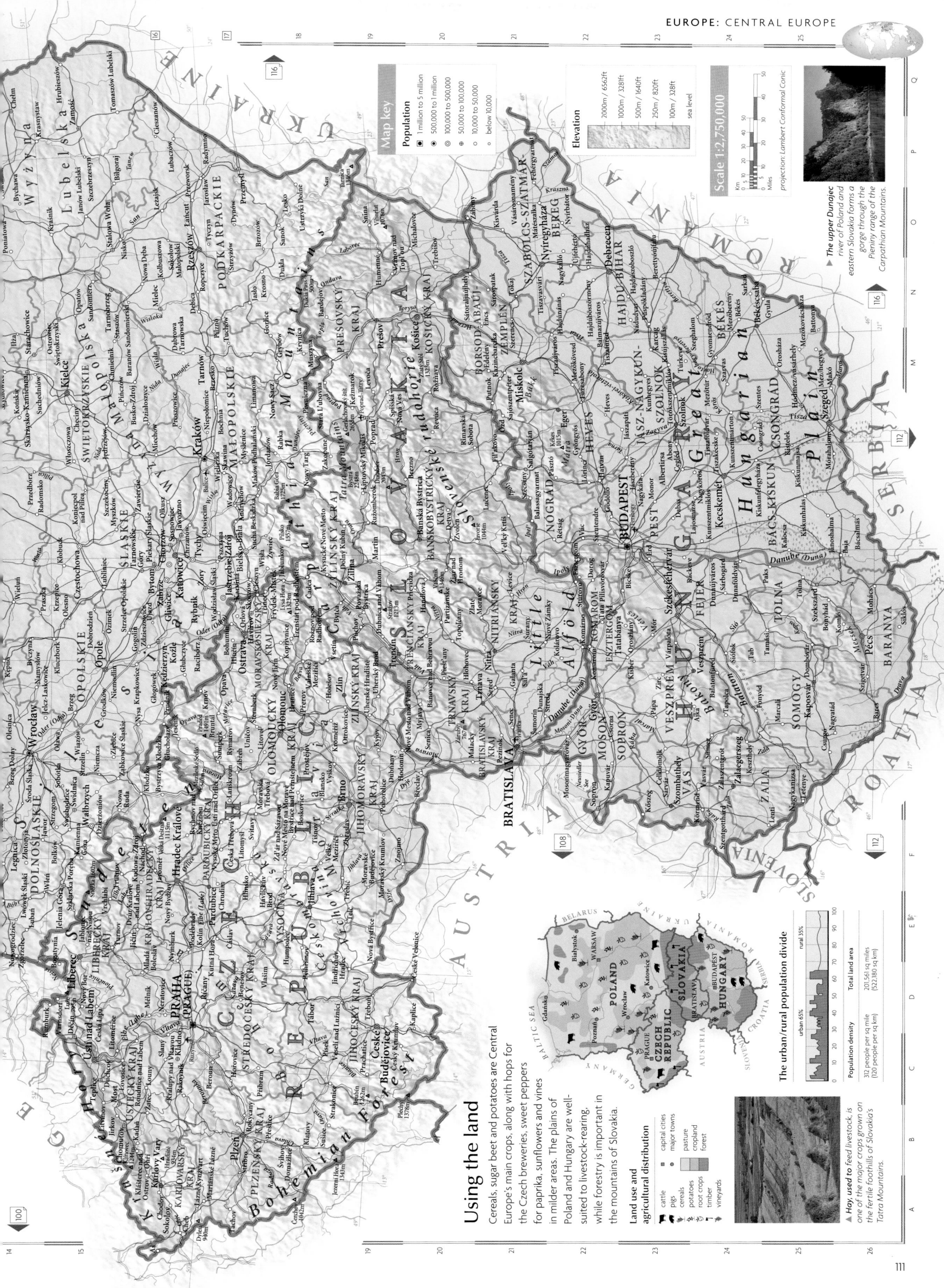

Map key

Population
- ◉ 1 million to 5 million
- ◉ 500,000 to 1 million
- ◎ 100,000 to 500,000
- ○ 50,000 to 100,000
- ○ 10,000 to 50,000
- ○ below 10,000

Elevation
- 2000m / 6562ft
- 1000m / 3281ft
- 500m / 1640ft
- 250m / 820ft
- 100m / 328ft
- sea level

Scale 1:2,750,000

projection: Lambert Conformal Conic

▶ The upper Dunajec river of Poland and eastern Slovakia forms a gorge through the Pieniny range of the Carpathian Mountains.

Using the land

Cereals, sugar beet and potatoes are Central Europe's main crops, along with hops for the Czech breweries, sweet peppers for paprika, sunflowers and vines in milder areas. The plains of Poland and Hungary are well-suited to livestock-rearing, while forestry is important in the mountains of Slovakia.

Land use and agricultural distribution

- cattle
- pigs
- cereals
- potatoes
- root crops
- timber
- vineyards
- ● capital cities
- ● major towns
- pasture
- cropland
- forest

The urban/rural population divide

| | urban 65% | rural 35% |

Population density
312 people per sq mile
(120 people per sq km)

Total land area
201,561 sq miles
(522,180 sq km)

▲ Hay, used to feed livestock, is one of the major crops grown on the fertile foothills of Slovakia's Tatra Mountains.

Southeast Europe

ALBANIA, BOSNIA & HERZEGOVINA, CROATIA, KOSOVO, MACEDONIA, MONTENEGRO, SERBIA

For 46 years the federation of Yugoslavia held together the most diverse ethnic region in Europe, along the picturesque mountain hinterland of the Dalmatian coast. Economic collapse resulted in internal tensions. In the early 1990s, civil war broke out in both Croatia and Bosnia as the ethnic populations struggled to establish their own exclusive territories. Peace was only restored by the UN after NATO launched air strikes in 1995. Montenegro voted to split from Serbia in 2006. More recently, Kosovo controversially declared independence from Serbia in 2008, although this may take some time to be fully recognized. Neighbouring Albania is slowly improving its fragile economy but remains one of Europe's poorest nations.

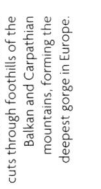

▲ *Hot, dry summers* and mild winters offer excellent conditions for viticulture in Montenegro. The precipitous Dinaric Alps have kept this region relatively isolated for centuries.

The landscape

The Tisza, Sava and Drava rivers drain the broad northern lowland, meeting the Danube after it crosses the Hungarian border. In the west, the Dinaric Alps divide the Adriatic Sea from the interior. Mainland valleys and elongated islands run parallel to the steep Dalmatian (*Dalmacija*) coastline, following alternating bands of resistant limestone.

Polijes in the Kosovo region

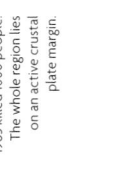

Sheer limestone walls enclose all sides

Flat *polje* floor

Underground drainage along joints in the rock

Spring at foot of cliff

▲ *Rain and underground* water dissolve limestone along massive vertical joints (cracks). This creates poljes: depressions several miles across with steep walls and broad, flat floors.

At Iron Gate (*Derdap*), on the border with Romania, the Danube narrows and cuts through foothills of the Balkan and Carpathian mountains, forming the deepest gorge in Europe.

A major earthquake at Skopje, Macedonia, in 1963 killed 1000 people. The whole region lies on an active crustal plate margin.

Lake Ohrid

▲ *Lake Ohrid borders* Albania and Macedonia. Ohrid is the deepest lake in the western Balkans, reaching depths of 938 ft (286 m).

The river flood plains of the Pannonian Basin are flanked by terraces of gravel and wind-blown glacial deposits known as loess.

At least 70% of the fresh water in the western Balkans drains eastwards into the Black Sea, mostly via the Danube (*Dunav*).

Tisza river

Drava river

Sava river

A series of river valleys breaking through the Dinaric Alps from the lowlands of western Albania give access to the interior.

The elongated islands, promontories and straits of the Dalmatian (*Dalmacija*) coast were formed as the Adriatic Sea rose to flood valleys running parallel to the shore.

Dalmatian (*Dalmacija*) coast

▲ *Limestone cliffs along the* Dalmatian (*Dalmacija*) shoreline are heavily eroded, as salt water dissolves the rock along existing horizontal cracks, or joints. This tends to form a platform of rock at the foot of the cliff.

Map key

Population

- ⬛ 1 million to 5 million
- ◉ 500,000 to 1 million
- ◎ 100,000 to 500,000
- ⊕ 50,000 to 100,000
- ○ 10,000 to 50,000
- ○ below 10,000

Elevation

- 2000m / 6562ft
- 1000m / 3281ft
- 500m / 1640ft
- 250m / 820ft
- 100m / 328ft
- sea level

▲ *The Tara river is one of Montenegro's major rivers. It flows into the Danube via the Drina and Sava rivers. Along its course the Tara has eroded spectacular gorges up to 3280 ft (1000 m) deep.*

Land use and agricultural distribution

- 🐖 pigs
- 🐑 sheep
- 🌾 cereals
- 🍎 fruit
- 🫒 olives
- 🌲 timber
- tobacco
- vineyards
- ■ capital cities
- ● major towns
- pasture
- cropland
- forest
- mountain region

The urban/rural population divide

urban 51% | rural 49%

Population density: 240 people per sq mile (93 people per sq km)

Total land area: 95,038 sq miles (246,278 sq km)

Transport and industry

Processing industries based on the region's wealth of mineral reserves predominate in Albania and Macedonia. In other regions, industrial plants have been commandeered, if not destroyed in the war and mineral extraction has severely declined. The fast-flowing rivers found throughout the Dinaric Alps are exploited to generate hydro-electric power.

▲ *The historic centre of Mostar in southern Bosnia, with its famous 16th-century Turkish bridge, was destroyed by shelling during 1993. The town was formerly the capital of Herzegovina.*

In February 2008, Kosovo (a UN Protectorate within Serbia since 1999) declared independence. Although recognized by several countries, this decision has proved controversial with other states wary of setting a precedent for separatist groups within their own borders. It is therefore likely to be some time before Kosovo becomes universally recognized.

Major industry and infrastructure

- △ aluminum refining
- car manufacture
- chemicals
- engineering
- food processing
- hydro-electric power
- mining
- shipbuilding
- textiles
- timber processing
- ■ capital cities
- ● major towns
- ⊕ international airports
- major roads

The transport network

46,996 miles (75,642 km)

685 miles (1103 km)

5413 miles (8713 km)

879 miles (1415 km)

The war resulted in the destruction or disintegration of infrastructure for transport, communications and power supply, though this is now in the process of recovery.

▲ *Industrial processing plants were established throughout Albania by the Hoxha regime, which collapsed in 1992. They remain incongruous among the villages of one of Europe's most conservative rural societies.*

▲ *The ancient Croatian port of Dubrovnik was one of the former Yugoslavia's most popular tourist resorts and an important point of access to the sea along the Dalmatian (Dalmacija) coast. Shelling of the old city by Serb forces in 1991 provoked international condemnation.*

Using the land

Crops of wheat, maize, sugar beet, vegetables and fruit are widely grown. The hilly terrain is suited to forestry and livestock farming. The mild, mediterranean climate of the coastal regions provides ideal conditions for growing vines and olives. Albania's largely agricultural economy has been adversely affected by the recent dismantling of state farms.

▼ *Sweet red peppers are dried in the sun, ready to make paprika. Macedonia's economy is mainly agricultural and its fertile soils support a broad range of crops.*

Bulgaria & Greece

Including EUROPEAN TURKEY

Greece is renowned as the original hearth of western civilization. The rugged terrain and numerous islands have profoundly affected its development, creating a strong agricultural and maritime tradition.

In the past 50 years, this formerly rural society has rapidly urbanized, with one third of the population now living in the capital, Athens, and in the northern city of Salonica. Bulgaria, dominated for centuries by the Ottoman Turks, became part of the eastern bloc after the Second World War, only slowly emerging from Soviet influence in 1989. Moves towards democracy led to some instability in Bulgaria and Greece, now outweighed by the challenge of integration with the European Union.

The landscape

Bulgaria's Balkan mountains divide the Danubian Plain (*Dunavska Ravnina*) and Maritsa Basin, meeting the Black Sea in the east along sandy beaches. The steep Rhodope Mountains form a natural barrier with Greece, while the younger Pindus form a rugged central spine which descends into the Aegean Sea to give a vast archipelago of over 2000 islands, the largest of which is Crete.

Mount Olympus is the mythical home of the Greek Gods and, at 9570 ft (2917 m), is the highest mountain in Greece.

Ancient metamorphic rock, formed miles below the surface

Limestone rocks exposed by erosion of metamorphic rocks

Younger limestones created in shallow seas

▲ **Mount Olympus** is a composite of rocks formed by two major tectonic events. First the older metamorphic rocks were thrust over the limestones, then two million years ago regional warping and subsequent erosion, re-exposed the limestone.

The Peloponnese consist of several mountainous peninsulas, linked to the mainland by the Isthmus of Corinth. The Corinth Canal (*Dioryga Korinthou*), built in 1893, cuts through the isthmus, linking the Aegean and Ionian seas.

The Danube, Europe's second longest river, forms most of Bulgaria's northern border. The Danubian plain (*Dunavska Ravnina*), extending from the southern bank, is extremely fertile.

▲ **The Arda river** cuts through the Rhodope Mountains in rugged, rocky gorges.

The islands of Crete, Kythira, Karpathos and Rhodes are part of an arc which bends southeastwards from the Peloponnese, forming the southern boundary of the Aegean.

▲ **Layers of black** volcanic ash still cover the island of Santorini. This volcano last erupted 3500 years ago, but still shows signs of volcanic activity.

Balkan Mountains
Maritsa Basin
Pindus Mountains
Rhodope Mountains
Rhodes
Karpathos
Crete
Kythira
Mount Olympus
Corinth Canal (*Dioryga Korinthou*)

Transport and industry

Soviet investment introduced heavy industry into Bulgaria, and the processing of agricultural produce, such as tobacco, is important throughout the country. Both countries have substantial shipyards and Greece has one of the world's largest merchant fleets. Many small craft workshops, producing textiles and processed foods, are clustered around Greek cities. The service and construction sectors have profited from the successful tourist industry.

Major industry and infrastructure

- ⚙ chemicals
- ✷ engineering
- 🏭 food processing
- ⚓ shipbuilding
- ✦ textiles
- ✈ tourism
- ■ capital cities
- • major towns
- ✈ international airports
- major roads
- major industrial areas

The transport network

🚆	103,930 miles (167,630 km)
✈	345 miles (557 km)
🚂	4346 miles (6995 km)
🛣	294 miles (474 km)

Bulgaria's railways require investment to revive its outdated infrastructure. In Greece, despite a developing road network, ferry-boats remain the most effective form of transport in many areas.

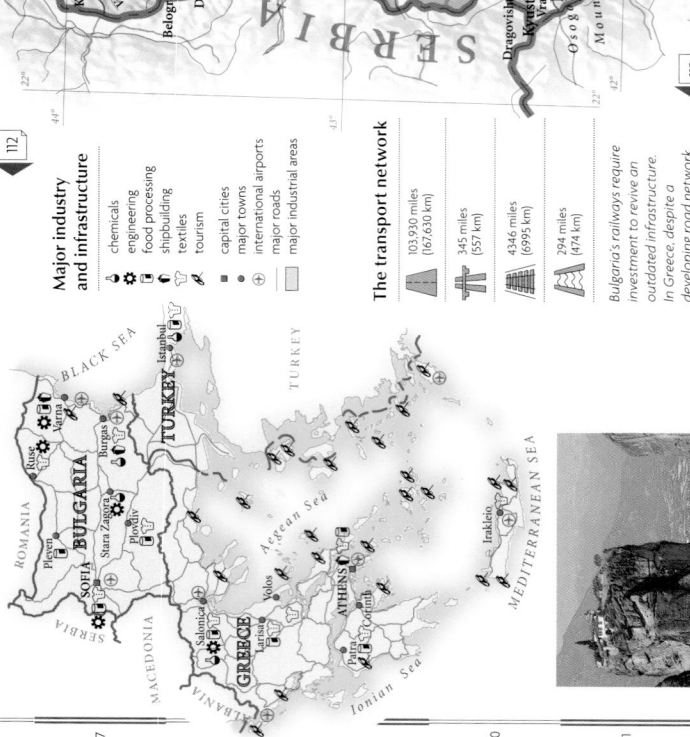

▲ A **towering pinnacle** at Metéora in central Greece is home to the monastery of Roussanou. The 24 rock towers which dominate the plain of Thessaly (*Thessalia*) are remnants of an old plateau. Long-term weathering along fissures in the rock has worn away the rest of the plateau.

Scale 1:2,750,000

projection: Lambert Conformal Conic

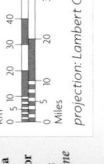
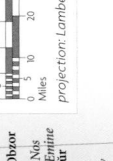
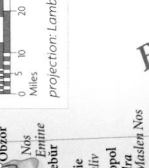
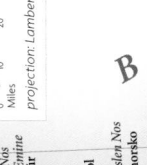
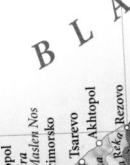
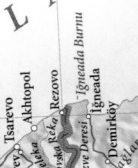

BLACK SEA

ROMANIA
SERBIA
MACEDONIA
BULGARIA
TURKEY
GREECE
ALBANIA

Aegean Sea
Ionian Sea
MEDITERRANEAN SEA

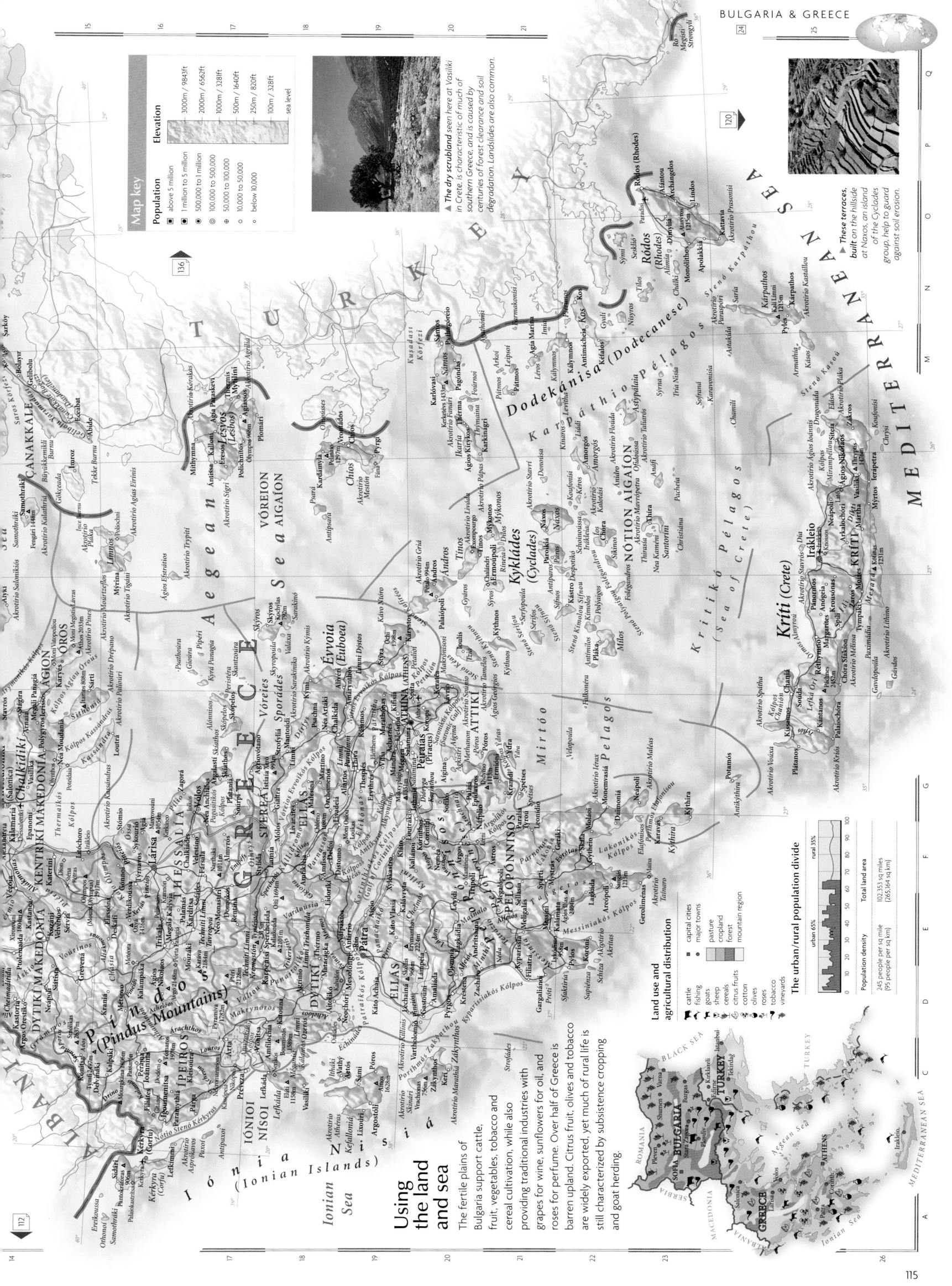

Map key

Population

- ■ above 5 million
- ◉ 1 million to 5 million
- ◎ 500,000 to 1 million
- ⊕ 100,000 to 500,000
- ⊖ 50,000 to 100,000
- ○ 10,000 to 50,000
- ○ below 10,000

Elevation

- 3000m / 9843ft
- 2000m / 6562ft
- 1000m / 328ft
- 500m / 1640ft
- 250m / 820ft
- 100m / 328ft
- sea level

▲ *The dry scrubland seen here at Vasiliki in Crete, is characteristic of much of southern Greece, and is caused by centuries of forest clearance and soil degradation. Landslides are also common.*

▲ *These terraces, built on the hillside at Naxos, an island of the Cyclades group, help to guard against soil erosion.*

Using the land and sea

The fertile plains of Bulgaria support cattle, fruit, vegetables, tobacco and cereal cultivation, while also providing traditional industries with grapes for wine, sunflowers for oil, and roses for perfume. Over half of Greece is barren upland. Citrus fruit, olives and tobacco are widely exported, yet much of rural life is still characterized by subsistence cropping and goat herding.

Land use and agricultural distribution

- ■ capital cities
- • major towns

- cattle
- fishing
- goats
- sheep
- cereals
- cotton
- olives
- roses
- tobacco
- vineyards
- citrus fruits

- pasture
- cropland
- forest
- mountain region

The urban/rural population divide

urban 65%   rural 35%

Population density	Total land area
245 people per sq mile (95 people per sq km)	102,353 sq miles (265,164 sq km)

Romania, Moldova & Ukraine

The industrial, social and cultural make-up of Romania and the former Soviet states of Moldova and Ukraine still bear the imprint of their communist past. As part of the USSR, Ukraine was a leading agricultural, industrial and energy producer. These industries, like those in Moldova and Romania, are now being reoriented more firmly towards western markets. As a result of shifting borders, and Soviet policy actively encouraging Russian immigration into other Soviet states like Ukraine and Moldova, all three countries now contain large numbers of foreign nationals. Moldovans and Romanians are still close in terms of language and culture, although Moldova is striving to remain an independent nation.

Using the land

The fertile black soils of Ukraine, often called 'the breadbasket of Europe', have enabled the cultivation of a variety of cereals and vegetables, which are widely exported. Romania and Moldova also grow cereals, sunflowers and vegetables, and are noted for the quality of their wines.

◀ The fertile lands and tolerant climate of Moldova are ideally suited to growing grapes for wine.

Land use and agricultural distribution

- cattle
- pigs
- poultry
- sheep
- cereals
- cotton
- sugar beet
- sunflowers
- vineyards

- ■ capital cities
- ● major towns

- pasture
- cropland
- forest
- wetland

The urban/rural population divide

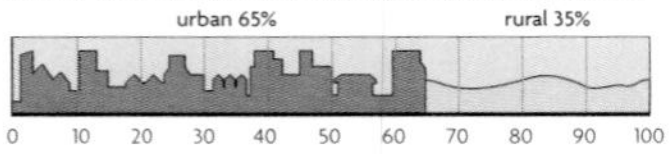

urban 65% | rural 35%

0 10 20 30 40 50 60 70 80 90 100

Population density	Total land area
222 people per sq mile (86 people per sq km)	334,947 sq miles (867,740 sq km)

◀ Glacial lakes are found throughout the Transylvanian Alps (Carpatii Meridionali), although the mountains no longer have any permanent snow cover.

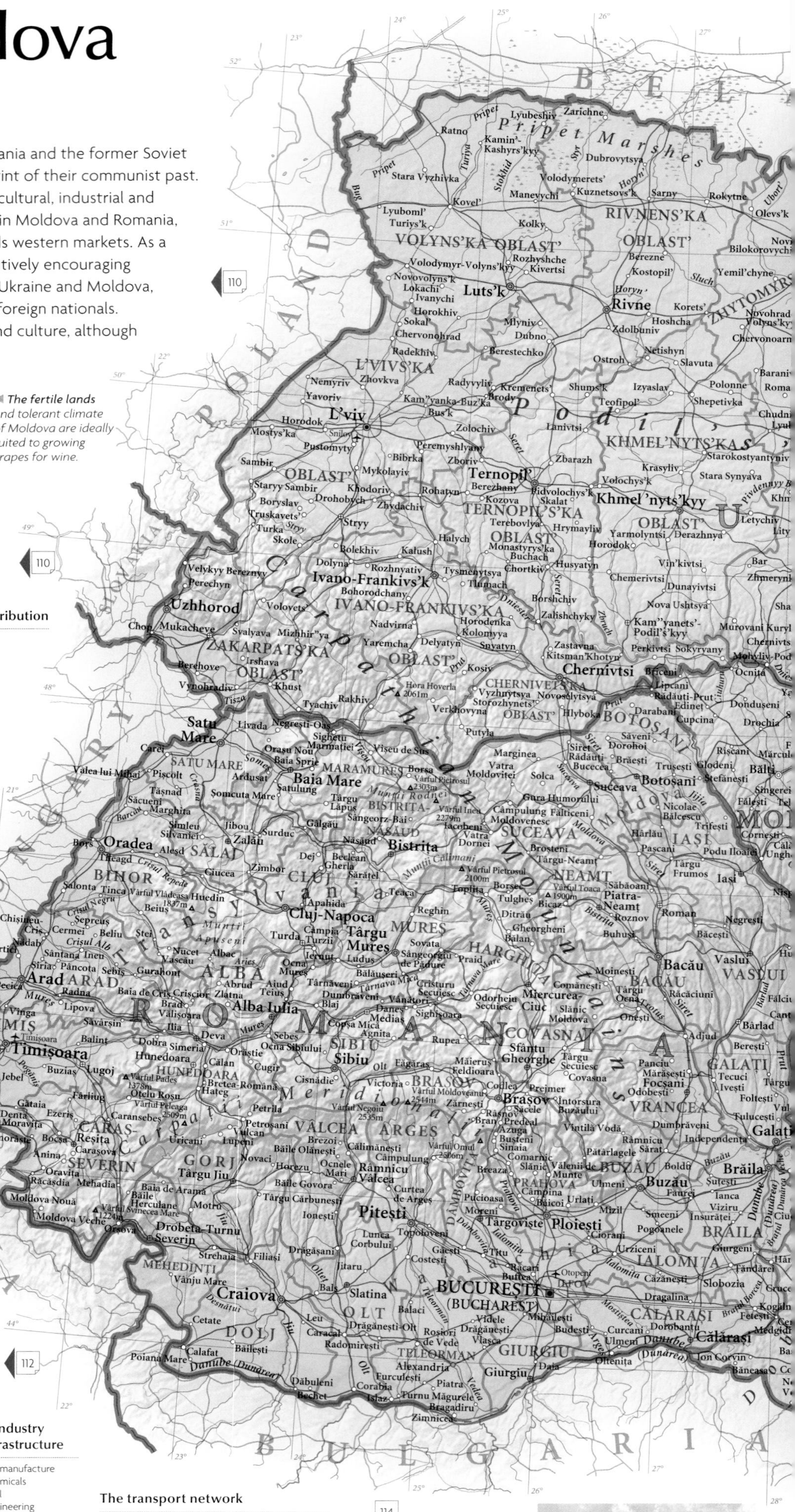

Transport and industry

Heavy industry using local raw materials characterizes much of this region. The industrial heartland of Ukraine, specializing in metal and machine-building industries, is based around its vast mineral reserves in the Donbass region. In Moldova, food processing draws on produce from its agricultural sector. Romanian industry relies both on local raw materials and imported iron, steel and oil.

Major industry and infrastructure

- car manufacture
- chemicals
- coal
- engineering
- food processing
- mining
- oil & gas
- textiles
- tourism

- ■ capital cities
- ● major towns
- ⊕ international airports
- — major roads
- major industrial areas

The transport network

170,707 miles (274,757 km)		1170 miles (1883 km)	
21,474 miles (34,563 km)		4130 miles (6647 km)	

Increased industrialization has necessitated the upgrading of road and rail networks in all three countries. Modernization has tended to focus only on major cities and industrial areas.

▶ During the 1960s and 1970s, many industries, like this carbon factory, developed using the mineral resources on the flanks of the Transylvanian Alps (Carpatii Meridionali).

Scale 1:3,500,000

Km
0 5 10 20 30 40 50 60 70 80 90 100
Miles
0 10 20 30 40 50 60 70 80 90 100

projection: Lambert Conformal Conic

Map key

Population
- ◉ 1 million to 5 million
- ⊙ 500,000 to 1 million
- ◎ 100,000 to 500,000
- ⊕ 50,000 to 100,000
- ○ 10,000 to 50,000
- ∘ below 10,000

Elevation
- 2000m / 6562ft
- 1000m / 3281ft
- 500m / 1640ft
- 250m / 820ft
- 100m / 328ft
- sea level

▲ The Swallow's Nest castle at Yalta is one of many tourist resorts on the Crimean (Krym) coast, dubbed the 'Russian Riviera'.

The landscape

Vast flat lowlands and gently rolling hills cover most of southeastern Europe. In the southwest, the Carpathian Mountains form a gentle arc. To the south of the Carpathian Mountains lies the Danube Plain, across which the Danube river flows to the Black Sea. To the north and east, the hills of Moldova level out into low plains, running east to the steppes of Ukraine.

▶ Divided into crystalline massifs, the southern arm of the Carpathian Mountains, the Transylvanian Alps (Carpatii Meridionali), extend 170 miles (274 km) across southwestern Romania.

Uplifted and folded at the same time as the Alps, some 250 miles (400 km) of the eastern Carpathian Mountains contain ancient volcanic cones and craters.

The Apuseni Mountains (Muntii Apuseni) are rich in mineral deposits, including gold and iron ore.

Transylvanian Alps (Carpatii Meridionali)

The Danube forms a natural border between Romania and Bulgaria.

The Codrii Hills dominate the landscape of central Moldova; they are intersected by deep, flat valleys and ravines.

Steppe landscape covers two-thirds of Ukraine. These flat, treeless grasslands extend from central Europe to central Asia.

Most of the major rivers in southeastern Europe, like the Danube, the Dniester and Dnieper flow south and east to the Black Sea.

The three branches of the Danube Delta (Delta Dunării) form a triangle of wetlands covering some 1950 sq miles (5050 sq km).

Old glaciated valley

Water has eroded a new post-glacial valley

▲ Balkas are common throughout Ukraine. They are large U-shaped valleys, formed during the last Ice Age, which contain narrower, deep valleys. These were incised by a sudden flow of water, following an ice melt.

Anti-clockwise currents have created the sandspits which fringe the Sea of Azov.

At Kryms'ki Hory, three flat-topped, parallel limestone ridges run 80 miles (128 km) along the southern coast of the Crimean (Krym) Peninsula.

The Baltic states & Belarus

BELARUS, ESTONIA, LATVIA, LITHUANIA, Kaliningrad

Occupying Europe's main corridor to Russia, the four distinct cultures of Estonia, Latvia, Lithuania and Belarus share a history of struggle for nationhood against the interests of more powerful neighbours. As the first republics to declare their independence from the Soviet Union in 1990–91, the Baltic states of Estonia, Latvia and Lithuania sought an economic role in the EU, while reaffirming their European cultural roots through the church and a strong musical tradition. Meanwhile, Belarus has shown economic and political allegiance to Russia by joining the Commonwealth of Independent States.

▲ *The seaport of Riga* is Latvia's capital and the centre of economic and cultural life. With a 32% Russian minority in Latvia, language and the right to national citizenship are key issues.

Using the land

Across the four nations cattle and pig farming are widespread, together with diverse arable crops, including flax for making linen, potatoes used to produce vodka, cereals and other vegetables. Almost a third of the land is forested; demand for timber has increased the importance of forest management.

Land use and agricultural distribution

cattle · pigs · cereals · flax · potatoes · timber · capital cities · major towns · pasture · cropland · forest · wetland

The urban/rural population divide

urban 69% rural 31%

Population density: 122 people per sq mile (47 people per sq km)
Total land area: 145,006 sq miles (375,656 sq km)

▲ *A pine forest* in northern Belarus. Conifers in the north give way to hardwood forest further south. Timber mills are supplied with logs floated along the country's many navigable waterways.

▲ *The Western Dvina* river provides hydro-electric power and, during the summer months, access to the Baltic Sea. The lower course of the river freezes from December to April.

Map key

Population: 1 million to 5 million; 500,000 to 1 million; 100,000 to 500,000; 50,000 to 100,000; 10,000 to 50,000; below 10,000

Elevation: 250m / 820ft; 100m / 328ft; sea level

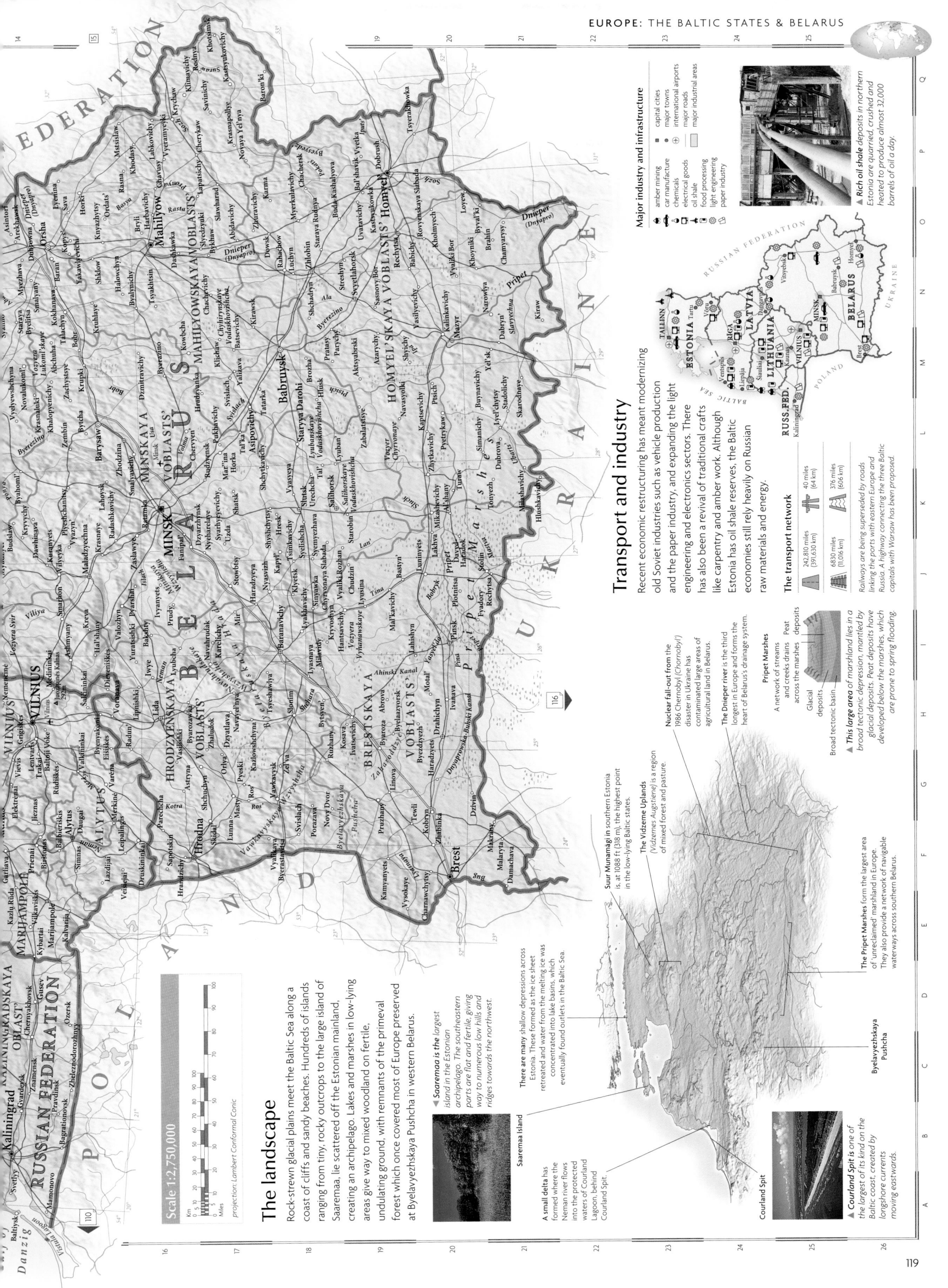

The landscape

Rock-strewn glacial plains meet the Baltic Sea along a coast of cliffs and sandy beaches. Hundreds of islands ranging from tiny, rocky outcrops to the large island of Saaremaa, lie scattered off the Estonian mainland, creating an archipelago. Lakes and marshes in low-lying areas give way to mixed woodland on fertile, undulating ground, with remnants of the primeval forest which once covered most of Europe preserved at Byelavyezhskaya Pushcha in western Belarus.

▼ *Saaremaa is the largest island in the Estonian archipelago. The southeastern parts are flat and fertile, giving way to numerous low hills and ridges towards the northwest.*

There are many shallow depressions across Estonia. These formed as the ice sheet retreated and water from the melting ice was concentrated into lake basins, which eventually found outlets in the Baltic Sea.

A small delta has formed where the Neman river flows into the protected waters of Courland Lagoon, behind Courland Spit.

Saaremaa Island

Courland Spit

▲ *Courland Spit is one of the largest of its kind on the Baltic coast, created by longshore currents moving eastwards.*

Scale 1:2,750,000

projection: Lambert Conformal Conic

Suur Munamägi in southern Estonia is, at 1088 ft (318 m), the highest point in the low-lying Baltic states.

The Videzemes Uplands (*Vidzemes Augstiene*) is a region of mixed forest and pasture.

Nuclear fall-out from the 1986 Chernobyl (*Chornobyl*) disaster in Ukraine has contaminated large areas of agricultural land in Belarus.

The Dnieper river is the third longest in Europe and forms the heart of Belarus's drainage system.

Pripet Marshes
A network of streams and creeks drains across the marshes

Peat deposits
Glacial deposits
Broad tectonic basin

▲ *This large area of marshland lies in a broad tectonic depression, mantled by glacial deposits. Peat deposits have developed below the marshes, which are prone to spring flooding.*

The Pripet Marshes form the largest area of 'unreclaimed' marshland in Europe. They also provide a network of navigable waterways across southern Belarus.

Byelavyezhskaya Pushcha

Transport and industry

Recent economic restructuring has meant modernizing old Soviet industries such as vehicle production and the paper industry, and expanding the light engineering and electronics sectors. There has also been a revival of traditional crafts like carpentry and amber work. Although Estonia has oil shale reserves, the Baltic economies still rely heavily on Russian raw materials and energy.

The transport network

242,810 miles (391,630 km)	40 miles (64 km)
6830 miles (11,016 km)	376 miles (606 km)

Railways are being superseded by roads linking the ports with eastern Europe and Russia. A highway connecting the three Baltic capitals with Warsaw has been proposed.

Major industry and infrastructure

amber mining
car manufacture
chemicals
electrical goods
oil shale
food processing
light engineering
paper industry

capital cities
major towns
international airports
major roads
major industrial areas

▲ *Rich oil shale deposits in northern Estonia are quarried, crushed and heated to produce almost 32,000 barrels of oil a day.*

119

The Mediterranean

The Mediterranean Sea stretches over 2500 miles (4000 km) east to west, separating Europe from Africa. At its most westerly point it is connected to the Atlantic Ocean through the Strait of Gibraltar. In the east, the Suez canal, opened in 1869, gives passage to the Indian Ocean. In the northeast, linked by the Sea of Marmara, lies the Black Sea. The Mediterranean is bordered by almost 30 states and territories, and more than 100 million people live on its shores and islands. Throughout history, the Mediterranean has been a focal area for many great empires and civilizations, reflected in the variety of cultures found on its shores. Since the 1960s, development along the southern coast of Europe has expanded rapidly to accommodate increasing numbers of tourists and to enable the exploitation of oil and gas reserves. This has resulted in rising levels of pollution, threatening the future of the sea.

▲ **Monaco is just** one of the luxurious resorts scattered along the Riviera, which stretches along the coast from Cannes in France to La Spezia in Italy. The region's mild winters and hot summers have attracted wealthy tourists since the early 19th century.

The landscape

The Mediterranean Sea is almost totally landlocked, joined to the Atlantic Ocean through the Strait of Gibraltar, which is only 8 miles (13 km) wide. Lying on an active plate margin, sea floor movements have formed a variety of basins, troughs and ridges. A submarine ridge running from Tunisia to the island of Sicily divides the Mediterranean into two distinct basins. The western basin is characterized by broad, smooth abyssal (or ocean) plains. In contrast, the eastern basin is dominated by a large ridge system, running east to west.

The narrow Strait of Gibraltar inhibits water exchange between the Mediterranean Sea and the Atlantic Ocean, producing a high degree of salinity and a low tidal range within the Mediterranean. The lack of tides has encouraged the build-up of pollutants in many semi-enclosed bays.

Main surface current

Dense currents sink below surface

Denser, more saline currents flow back to Atlantic

▲ **Because the Mediterranean** is almost enclosed by land, its circulation is quite different to the oceans. There is one major current which flows in from the Atlantic and moves east. Currents flowing back to the Atlantic are denser and flow below the main current.

Industrial pollution flowing from the Dnieper and Danube rivers has destroyed a large proportion of the fish population that used to inhabit the upper layers of the Black Sea.

The Ionian Basin is the deepest in the Mediterranean, reaching depths of 16,800 ft (5121 m).

The edge of the Eurasian Plate is edged by a continental shelf. In the Mediterranean Sea this is widest at the Ebro Fan where it extends 60 miles (96 km).

Oxygen in the Black Sea is dissolved only in its upper layers; at depths below 230–300 ft (70–100 m) the sea is 'dead' and can support no lifeforms other than specially-adapted bacteria.

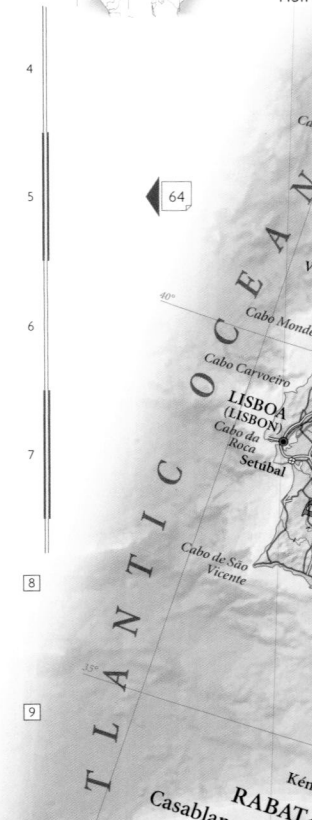

◀ **The Atlas Mountains** are a range of fold mountains which lie in Morocco and Algeria. They run parallel to the Mediterranean, forming a topographical and climatic divide between the Mediterranean coast and the western Sahara.

An arc of active submarine, island and mainland volcanoes, including Etna and Vesuvius, lie in and around southern Italy. The area is also susceptible to earthquakes and landslides.

Nutrient flows into the eastern Mediterranean, and sediment flows to the Nile Delta have been severely lowered by the building of the Aswan Dam across the Nile in Egypt. This is causing the delta to shrink.

The Suez Canal, opened in 186_ extends 100 miles (160 km) fro_ Port Said to the Gulf of Suez.

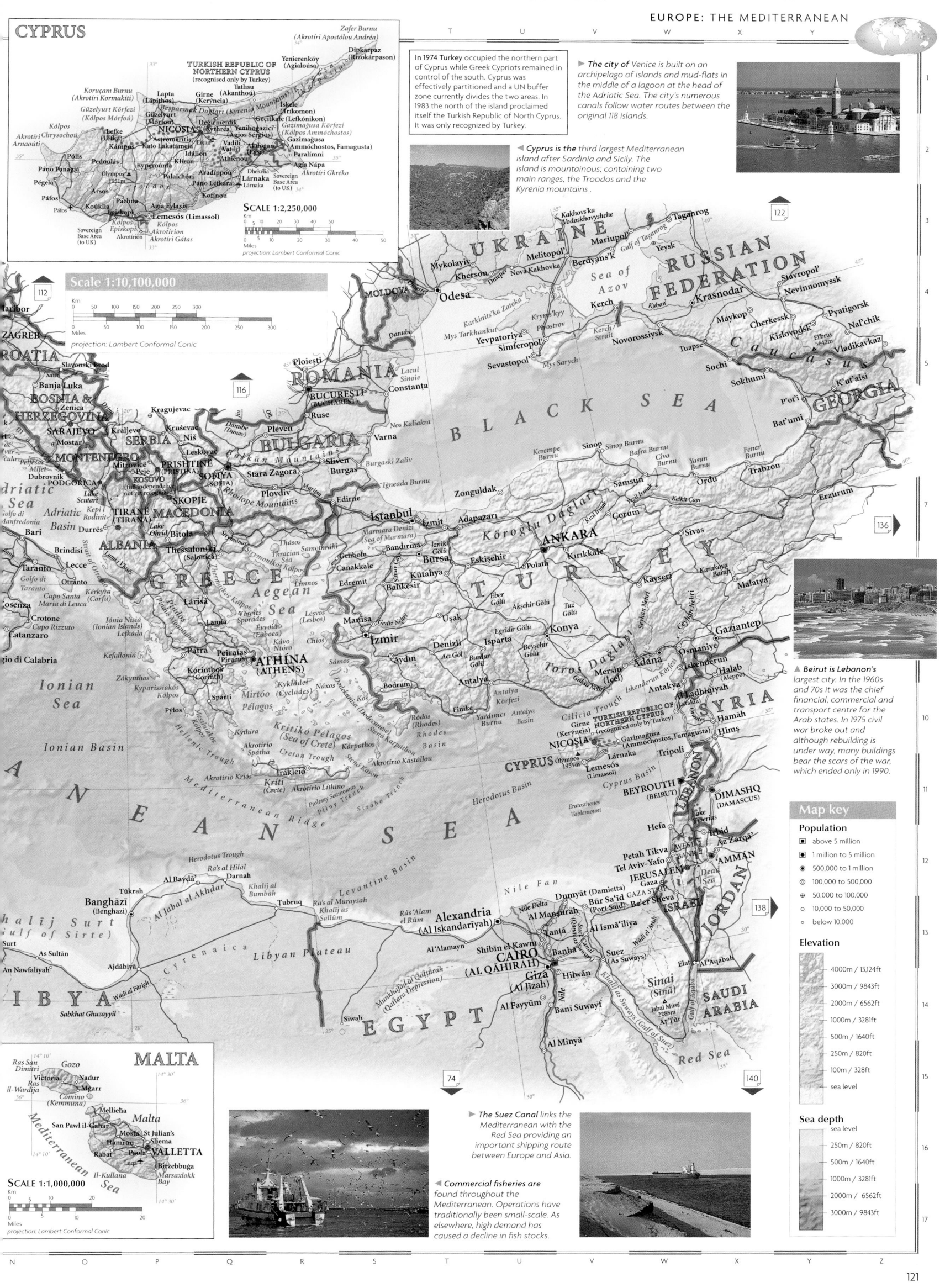

CYPRUS

SCALE 1:2,250,000

projection: Lambert Conformal Conic

Scale 1:10,100,000

projection: Lambert Conformal Conic

In 1974 Turkey occupied the northern part of Cyprus while Greek Cypriots remained in control of the south. Cyprus was effectively partitioned and a UN buffer zone currently divides the two areas. In 1983 the north of the island proclaimed itself the Turkish Republic of North Cyprus. It was only recognized by Turkey.

▶ *The city of* Venice is built on an archipelago of islands and mud-flats in the middle of a lagoon at the head of the Adriatic Sea. The city's numerous canals follow water routes between the original 118 islands.

◀ *Cyprus is the* third largest Mediterranean island after Sardinia and Sicily. The island is mountainous; containing two main ranges, the Troodos and the Kyrenia mountains.

▲ *Beirut is Lebanon's* largest city. In the 1960s and 70s it was the chief financial, commercial and transport centre for the Arab states. In 1975 civil war broke out and although rebuilding is under way, many buildings bear the scars of the war, which ended only in 1990.

Map key

Population
- above 5 million
- 1 million to 5 million
- 500,000 to 1 million
- 100,000 to 500,000
- 50,000 to 100,000
- 10,000 to 50,000
- below 10,000

Elevation
- 4000m / 13,124ft
- 3000m / 9843ft
- 2000m / 6562ft
- 1000m / 3281ft
- 500m / 1640ft
- 250m / 820ft
- 100m / 328ft
- sea level

Sea depth
- sea level
- 250m / 820ft
- 500m / 1640ft
- 1000m / 3281ft
- 2000m / 6562ft
- 3000m / 9843ft

MALTA

SCALE 1:1,000,000

projection: Lambert Conformal Conic

▶ *The Suez Canal* links the Mediterranean with the Red Sea providing an important shipping route between Europe and Asia.

◀ *Commercial fisheries are* found throughout the Mediterranean. Operations have traditionally been small-scale. As elsewhere, high demand has caused a decline in fish stocks.

The Russian Federation

The Cold War era of global relations was concluded in 1991 with the formal dissolution of the Soviet Union. The Russian Federation declared its separate sovereignty from the foundering communist empire following independence declarations from a number of former Soviet republics. As the leading member of the Commonwealth of Independent States, the Russian Federation has a central role in the development of post-Soviet Eurasia. Crossing 11 time zones, the Russian Federation is almost twice the size of the USA, and with more than 150 ethnic minorities and 21 autonomous republics, regionalist dissent within its own territory remains a danger.

THE RUSSIAN FEDERATION: ADMINISTRATIVE REGIONS

124-125

126-127

The administrative area names in European Russia have been omitted west of the Ural Mountains. Please refer to pages 124–125 and 126–127 where these areas are shown at a larger scale.

▶ *Summer beds of* moss and lichen scatter a 90% surface cover of ice across the islands of Franz Josef Land (Zemlya Frantsa-Iosifa), the northernmost land in the eastern hemisphere.

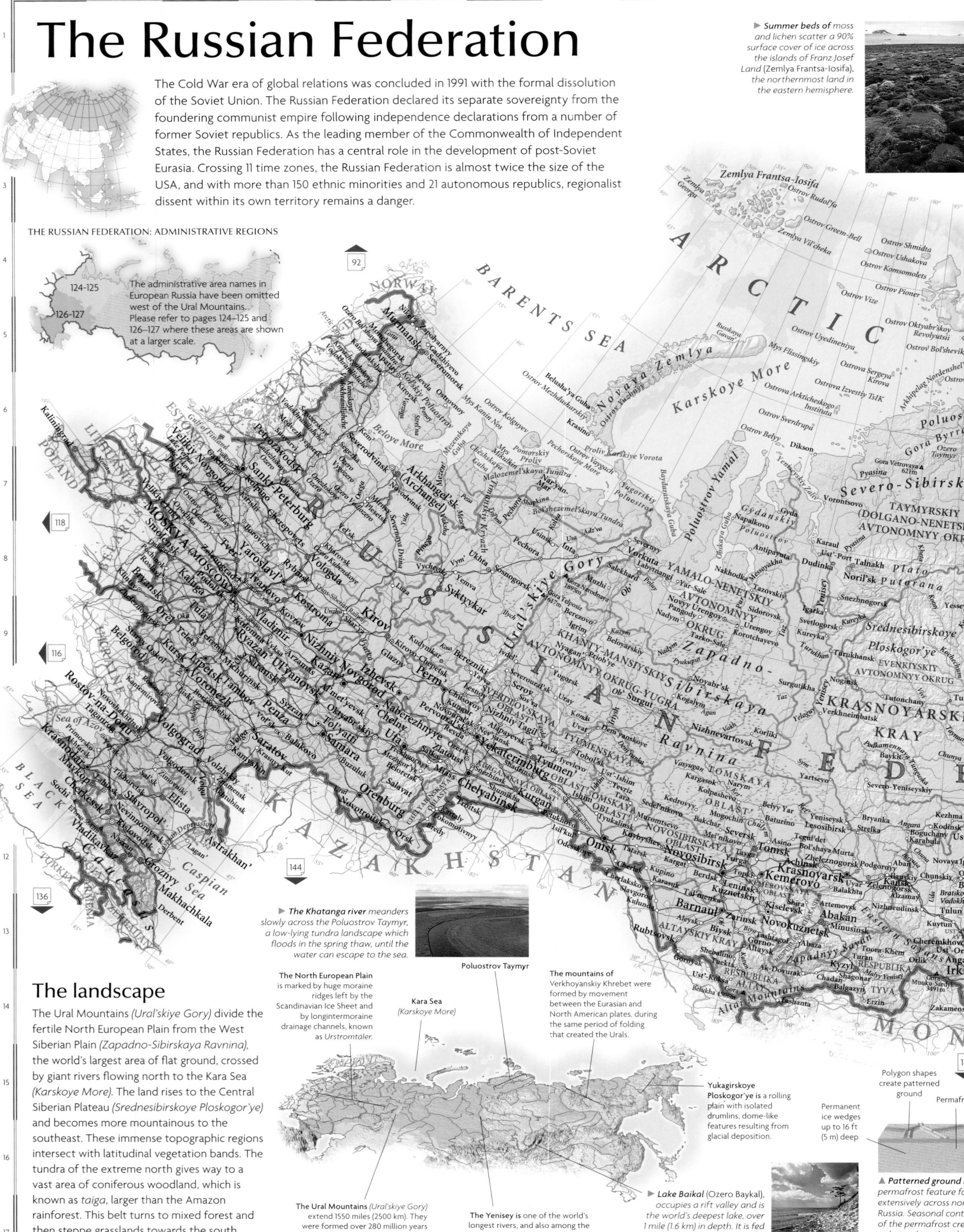

The landscape

The Ural Mountains (*Ural'skiye Gory*) divide the fertile North European Plain from the West Siberian Plain (*Zapadno-Sibirskaya Ravnina*), the world's largest area of flat ground, crossed by giant rivers flowing north to the Kara Sea (*Karskoye More*). The land rises to the Central Siberian Plateau (*Srednesibirskoye Ploskogor'ye*) and becomes more mountainous to the southeast. These immense topographic regions intersect with latitudinal vegetation bands. The tundra of the extreme north gives way to a vast area of coniferous woodland, which is known as *taiga*, larger than the Amazon rainforest. This belt turns to mixed forest and then steppe grasslands towards the south.

▶ *The Khatanga river* meanders slowly across the Poluostrov Taymyr, a low-lying tundra landscape which floods in the spring thaw, until the water can escape to the sea.

Poluostrov Taymyr

The North European Plain is marked by huge moraine ridges left by the Scandinavian Ice Sheet and by longintermoraine drainage channels, known as *Urstromtäler*.

Kara Sea (*Karskoye More*)

The mountains of Verkhoyanskiy Khrebet were formed by movement between the Eurasian and North American plates, during the same period of folding that created the Urals.

Yukagirskoye Ploskogor'ye is a rolling plain with isolated drumlins, dome-like features resulting from glacial deposition.

Permanent ice wedges up to 16 ft (5 m) deep

Polygon shapes create patterned ground

Permafrost

▲ *Patterned ground is* permafrost feature found extensively across north Russia. Seasonal contraction of the permafrost form polygonal cracks, which filled by ice wedges.

The Ural Mountains (*Ural'skiye Gory*) extend 1550 miles (2500 km). They were formed over 280 million years ago, folded as the East European and Siberian plates moved closer together.

The Yenisey is one of the world's longest rivers, and also among the most languid, dropping only 500 ft (152 m) over 1200 miles (2000 km).

▶ *Lake Baikal* (Ozero Baykal), occupies a rift valley and is the world's deepest lake, over 1 mile (1.6 km) in depth. It is fed by over 300 rivers and drained by just one, the Angara.

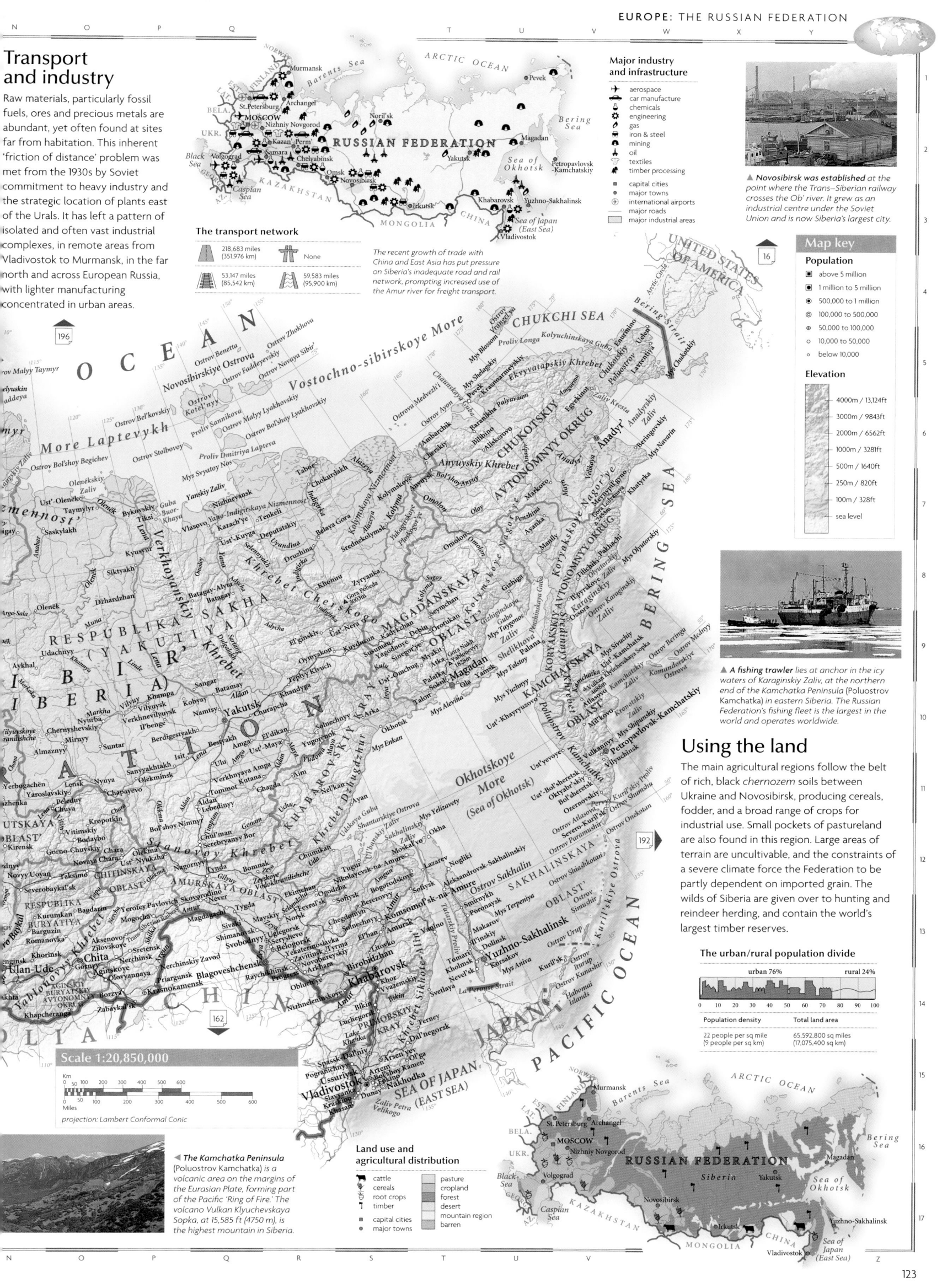

Transport and industry

Raw materials, particularly fossil fuels, ores and precious metals are abundant, yet often found at sites far from habitation. This inherent 'friction of distance' problem was met from the 1930s by Soviet commitment to heavy industry and the strategic location of plants east of the Urals. It has left a pattern of isolated and often vast industrial complexes, in remote areas from Vladivostok to Murmansk, in the far north and across European Russia, with lighter manufacturing concentrated in urban areas.

The transport network

218,683 miles (351,976 km)	None		
53,147 miles (85,542 km)		59,583 miles (95,900 km)	

The recent growth of trade with China and East Asia has put pressure on Siberia's inadequate road and rail network, prompting increased use of the Amur river for freight transport.

Major industry and infrastructure

- ✈ aerospace
- 🚗 car manufacture
- ⚗ chemicals
- ⚙ engineering
- ▲ gas
- ⚒ iron & steel
- ⛏ mining
- ♦ oil
- ⊽ textiles
- ■ timber processing
- ■ capital cities
- ● major towns
- ✈ international airports
- — major roads
- major industrial areas

▲ *Novosibirsk was established at the point where the Trans–Siberian railway crosses the Ob' river. It grew as an industrial centre under the Soviet Union and is now Siberia's largest city.*

Map key

Population
- ■ above 5 million
- ◉ 1 million to 5 million
- ◉ 500,000 to 1 million
- ◎ 100,000 to 500,000
- ⊕ 50,000 to 100,000
- ○ 10,000 to 50,000
- ○ below 10,000

Elevation
- 4000m / 13,124ft
- 3000m / 9843ft
- 2000m / 6562ft
- 1000m / 3281ft
- 500m / 1640ft
- 250m / 820ft
- 100m / 328ft
- sea level

▲ *A fishing trawler lies at anchor in the icy waters of Karaginskiy Zaliv, at the northern end of the Kamchatka Peninsula (Poluostrov Kamchatka) in eastern Siberia. The Russian Federation's fishing fleet is the largest in the world and operates worldwide.*

Using the land

The main agricultural regions follow the belt of rich, black *chernozem* soils between Ukraine and Novosibirsk, producing cereals, fodder, and a broad range of crops for industrial use. Small pockets of pastureland are also found in this region. Large areas of terrain are uncultivable, and the constraints of a severe climate force the Federation to be partly dependent on imported grain. The wilds of Siberia are given over to hunting and reindeer herding, and contain the world's largest timber reserves.

The urban/rural population divide

urban 76%   rural 24%

0 10 20 30 40 50 60 70 80 90 100

Population density	Total land area
22 people per sq mile (9 people per sq km)	65,592,800 sq miles (17,075,400 sq km)

Scale 1:20,850,000

Km
0 50 100 200 300 400 500 600

Miles
0 50 100 200 300 400 500 600

projection: Lambert Conformal Conic

◀ *The Kamchatka Peninsula (Poluostrov Kamchatka) is a volcanic area on the margins of the Eurasian Plate, forming part of the Pacific 'Ring of Fire.' The volcano Vulkan Klyuchevskaya Sopka, at 15,585 ft (4750 m), is the highest mountain in Siberia.*

Land use and agricultural distribution

- 🐄 cattle
- cereals
- root crops
- timber
- ■ capital cities
- ● major towns
- pasture
- cropland
- forest
- desert
- mountain region
- barren

Northern European Russia

Reaching into the Arctic Circle, this region of lakeland, forest and tundra is historically bound to Europe by St Petersburg, the old imperial capital of Tsarist Russia and home to a third of the region's population. Communist rule from Moscow left the north politically marginalized, contributing to the present problems of outmoded industry, poor infrastructure and serious environmental neglect. However, with borders embracing Finland, Norway, the Baltic and the northern sea route to the Atlantic, the region's success in foreign trade is now of prime importance to the Russian economy.

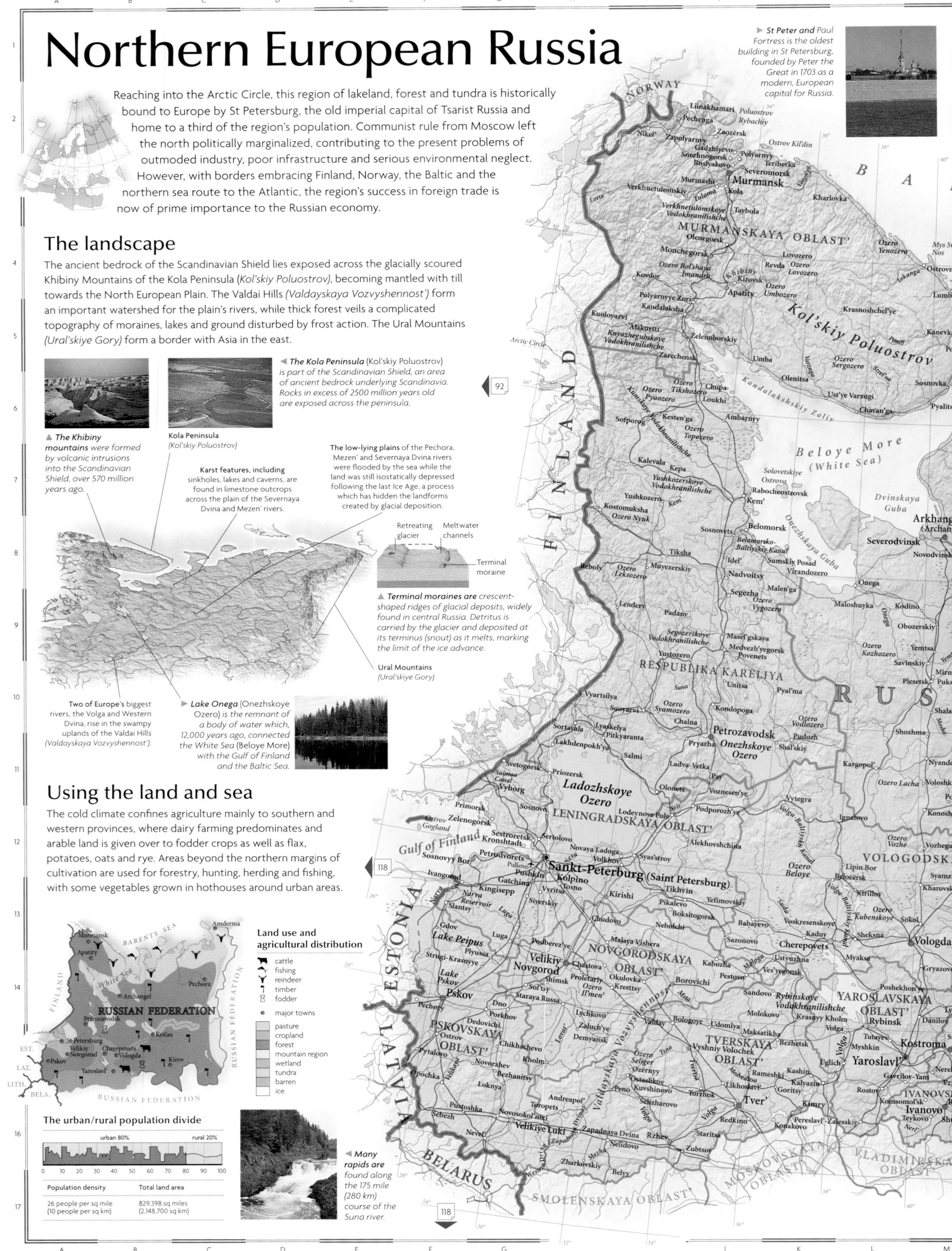

▶ St Peter and Paul Fortress is the oldest building in St Petersburg, founded by Peter the Great in 1703 as a modern, European capital for Russia.

The landscape

The ancient bedrock of the Scandinavian Shield lies exposed across the glacially scoured Khibiny Mountains of the Kola Peninsula (Kol'skiy Poluostrov), becoming mantled with till towards the North European Plain. The Valdai Hills (Valdayskaya Vozvyshennost') form an important watershed for the plain's rivers, while thick forest veils a complicated topography of moraines, lakes and ground disturbed by frost action. The Ural Mountains (Ural'skiye Gory) form a border with Asia in the east.

◀ The Kola Peninsula (Kol'skiy Poluostrov) is part of the Scandinavian Shield, an area of ancient bedrock underlying Scandinavia. Rocks in excess of 2500 million years old are exposed across the peninsula.

▲ The Khibiny mountains were formed by volcanic intrusions into the Scandinavian Shield, over 570 million years ago.

Kola Peninsula (Kol'skiy Poluostrov)

Karst features, including sinkholes, lakes and caverns, are found in limestone outcrops across the plain of the Severnaya Dvina and Mezen' rivers.

The low-lying plains of the Pechora, Mezen' and Severnaya Dvina rivers were flooded by the sea while the land was still isostatically depressed following the last Ice Age, a process which has hidden the landforms created by glacial deposition.

Retreating glacier   Meltwater channels

Terminal moraine

▲ Terminal moraines are crescent-shaped ridges of glacial deposits, widely found in central Russia. Detritus is carried by the glacier and deposited at its terminus (snout) as it melts, marking the limit of the ice advance.

Ural Mountains (Ural'skiye Gory)

Two of Europe's biggest rivers, the Volga and Western Dvina, rise in the swampy uplands of the Valdai Hills (Valdayskaya Vozvyshennost').

▶ Lake Onega (Onezhskoye Ozero) is the remnant of a body of water which, 12,000 years ago, connected the White Sea (Beloye More) with the Gulf of Finland and the Baltic Sea.

Using the land and sea

The cold climate confines agriculture mainly to southern and western provinces, where dairy farming predominates and arable land is given over to fodder crops as well as flax, potatoes, oats and rye. Areas beyond the northern margins of cultivation are used for forestry, hunting, herding and fishing, with some vegetables grown in hothouses around urban areas.

Land use and agricultural distribution

- cattle
- fishing
- reindeer
- timber
- fodder
- major towns

pasture
cropland
forest
mountain region
wetland
tundra
barren
ice

RUSSIAN FEDERATION

The urban/rural population divide

urban 80%   rural 20%

0 10 20 30 40 50 60 70 80 90 100

Population density	Total land area
26 people per sq mile (10 people per sq km)	829,398 sq miles (2,148,700 sq km)

◀ Many rapids are found along the 175 mile (280 km) course of the Suna river.

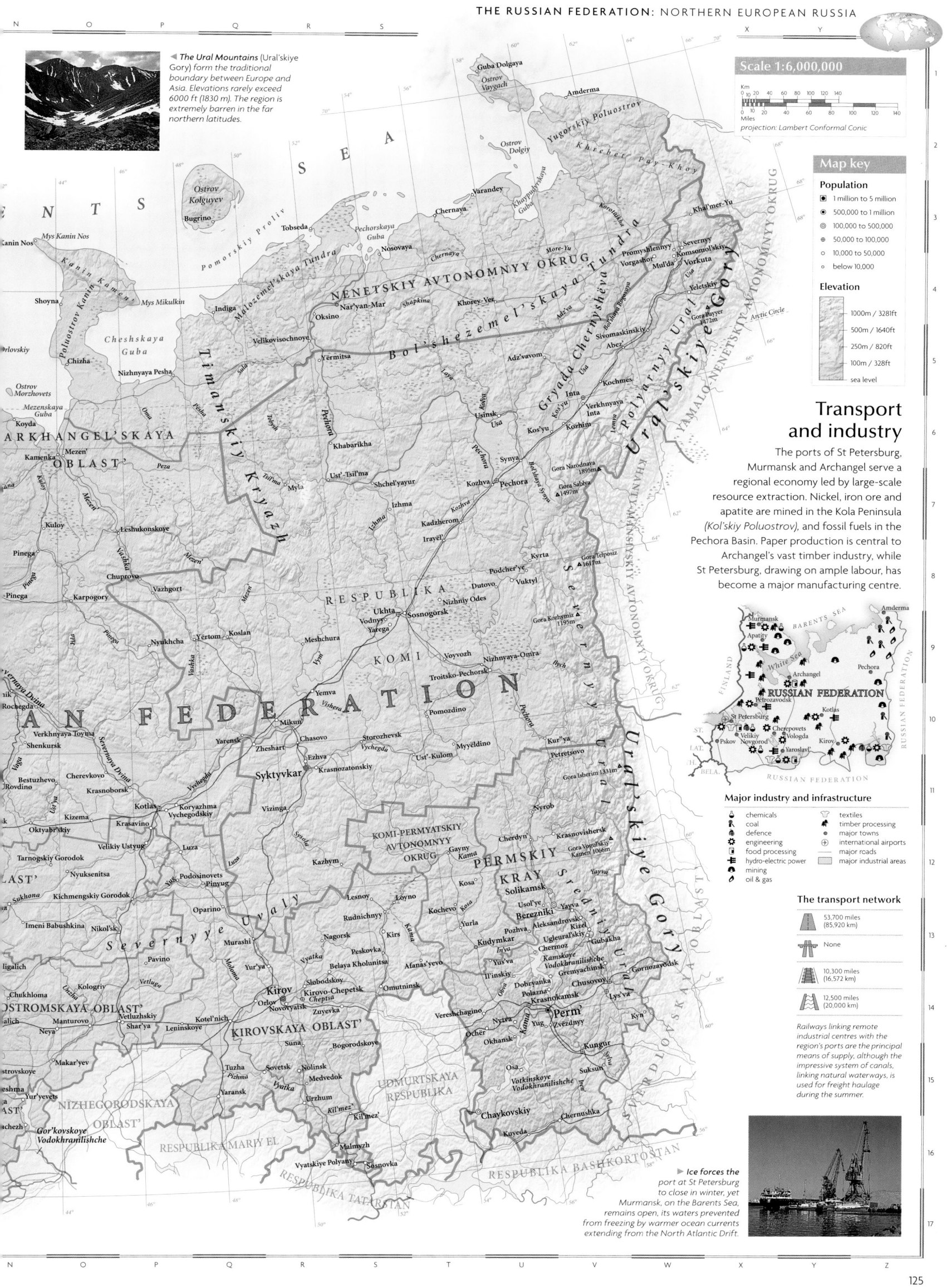

◀ *The Ural Mountains* (Ural'skiye Gory) *form the traditional boundary between Europe and Asia. Elevations rarely exceed 6000 ft (1830 m). The region is extremely barren in the far northern latitudes.*

Scale 1:6,000,000

projection: Lambert Conformal Conic

Map key

Population

- ▣ 1 million to 5 million
- ◉ 500,000 to 1 million
- ◎ 100,000 to 500,000
- ⊕ 50,000 to 100,000
- ○ 10,000 to 50,000
- ∘ below 10,000

Elevation

- 1000m / 3281ft
- 500m / 1640ft
- 250m / 820ft
- 100m / 328ft
- sea level

Transport and industry

The ports of St Petersburg, Murmansk and Archangel serve a regional economy led by large-scale resource extraction. Nickel, iron ore and apatite are mined in the Kola Peninsula (*Kol'skiy Poluostrov*), and fossil fuels in the Pechora Basin. Paper production is central to Archangel's vast timber industry, while St Petersburg, drawing on ample labour, has become a major manufacturing centre.

Major industry and infrastructure

- ⚗ chemicals
- ⛏ coal
- defence
- ⚙ engineering
- 🍴 food processing
- hydro-electric power
- ⚒ mining
- ◗ oil & gas
- ⊤ textiles
- timber processing
- • major towns
- ✈ international airports
- — major roads
- ▢ major industrial areas

The transport network

- 53,700 miles (85,920 km)
- None
- 10,300 miles (16,572 km)
- 12,500 miles (20,000 km)

Railways linking remote industrial centres with the region's ports are the principal means of supply, although the impressive system of canals, linking natural waterways, is used for freight haulage during the summer.

▶ *Ice forces the port at St Petersburg to close in winter, yet Murmansk, on the Barents Sea, remains open, its waters prevented from freezing by warmer ocean currents extending from the North Atlantic Drift.*

125

► Kaliningrad has been a Russian enclave since 1945. The port is an important centre for the Russian Federation's Baltic fishing fleet.

◄ St Basil's Cathedral, completed in 1561, stands in Moscow's Red Square next to the Kremlin; the original fortified stronghold of the city.

Southern European Russia

This region, divided from Asia by desert, seas and mountains, has exerted a powerful influence both east and west since the 13th century. Over 70 years of Communist rule produced a highly urbanized, industrial society dominated by Moscow, which was the capital of the Soviet Union until 1991. Almost two-thirds of the Russian Federation's population live in this core area, with a relatively high *per capita* share of its wealth. However, the rapid growth of a market economy has caused great social upheaval, with rising crime and political instability.

The landscape

Ancient folds in the deep sedimentary strata of the North European Plain have created a sequence of high and low regions. The Central Russian Upland (Srednerusskaya Vozvyshennost') in the west is deeply incised by rivers draining into the lowland of the Oka and Don rivers. In the east the Volga, Europe's longest river, flows south to the Caspian Sea, dividing the Volga Uplands (Privolzhskaya Vozvyshennost') from the foothills of the Ural Mountains (Ural'skiye Gory). The Caucasus mountains and the Black Sea form a natural border to the southwest.

▲ A plantation of Scots pine helps consolidate the loose sandy soils of the Meshchera Lowland (Meshcherskaya Nizina), which lies on the bed of an old glacial lake.

The Smolensk-Moscow Upland (Smolensko-Moskovskaya Vozvyshennost') is a series of terminal moraine ridges marking the southern extent of the last glaciation.

Glacial till covers the bedrock to the north of the North European Plain, giving a gentle surface relief.

The lowland of the Oka and Don rivers lies over a broad trough, between the upfolds of the Volga Uplands (Privolzhskaya Vozvyshennost') to the east, and the Central Russian Upland (Srednerusskaya Vozvyshennost') to the west.

The southern Ural Mountains (Ural'skiye Gory) consist of several parallel ranges of ancient fold mountains running from north to south.

Central Russian Upland (Srednerusskaya Vozvyshennost').

The flood plain of the Volga forms a long oasis of verdant vegetation, contrasting with the aridity of the surrounding Caspian hinterland.

The marshlands of the Volga Delta are visited by over 260 species of bird each year, migrating between South Africa and Arctic Siberia.

The Caspian Depression is a large downfold (or syncline) which became flooded, forming the Caspian Sea. The shoreline is 98 ft (30 m) below sea level.

Salt dome

Salt dome is forced up and through the rock strata

Sedimentary strata

Salts are forced upwards by denser overlying strata

◄ The Caucasus mountains run from the Black Sea to the Caspian Sea. They include El' brus which, at 18,511 ft (5642 m), is the highest point in Europe. It is still uplifting at a rate of 0.4 inches (10 mm) per year.

Drifting sand occupies large areas of the south, forming dunes up to 50 ft (15 m) high.

▲ Salt domes, rounded hills up to 500 ft (150 m) high, are produced as less dense rock salts are displaced under the extreme pressure of denser, overlying strata and forced up towards the surface creating domes. They are widespread in the Caspian Depression.

Map key

Population
- above 5 million
- 1 million to 5 million
- 500,000 to 1 million
- 100,000 to 500,000
- 50,000 to 100,000
- 10,000 to 50,000
- below 10,000

Elevation
- 4000m / 13,124ft
- 3000m / 9843ft
- 2000m / 6562ft
- 1000m / 3281ft
- 500m / 1640ft
- 250m / 820ft
- 100m / 328ft
- sea level

Scale 1:6,000,000
projection: Lambert Conformal Conic

Using the land

In the cold, humid north and in the southern Urals (Ural'skiye Gory), small grains, potatoes and flax are commonly rotated with legumes which support livestock farming. The rich chernozem (or black earth) areas support diverse crops such as sugar beet, hemp, sunflowers, millet and vegetables. Further south, aridity restricts husbandry to extensive grazing, with intensive fruit and rice cultivation along the oasis of the Volga.

The urban/rural population divide

urban 71% rural 29%

Population density
119 people per sq mile
(46 people per sq km)

Total land area
705,916 sq miles
(1,828,800 sq km)

Land use and agricultural distribution
- sheep
- flax
- potatoes
- rice
- sunflowers
- sugar beet
- timber
- capital cities
- major towns
- pasture
- cropland
- forest
- wetland
- mountain region
- tundra

Transport and industry

Manufacturing is largely based around Moscow and the Volga region, which became a major industrial area during the Second World War. Both Moscow and Nizhniy Novgorod are centres of skilled labour for light manufacturing and engineering. Most of Russia's main chemical plants are located along the Volga, and one of the world's largest car factories was recently opened in Tol'yatti. Processing and machine construction plants use oil, gas and hydro-electric power from the Volga Basin and metallic minerals from the Urals (Ural'skiye Gory) and Kursk.

Industrial plants are massed along the Volga. Environmental stress from decades of unbridled industrial development has prompted widespread concern about pollution levels.

The transport network
- 250,000 miles (402,000 km)
- None
- 28,000 miles (44,800 km)
- 16,300 miles (26,080 km)

Seventy private and national flag airlines have been created from the reorganization of the state airline Aeroflot, which maintained the world's largest fleet of aircraft during the Soviet era.

Major industry and infrastructure
- aerospace
- car manufacture
- chemicals
- defence
- electronics
- engineering
- gas
- mining
- oil
- textiles
- capital cities
- major towns
- international airports
- major roads
- major industrial areas

Asia

Asia, the world's largest continent, covers 16,838,365 sq miles (43,608,000 sq km).
It comprises 49 separate countries, including 97% of Turkey and 72% of the
Russian Federation. Almost 60% of the world's population lives in Asia.

- ● **Greatest extent, North–South:**
  4000 miles / 6440 km
- ■ **Greatest extent, East–West:**
  6000 miles / 9650 km

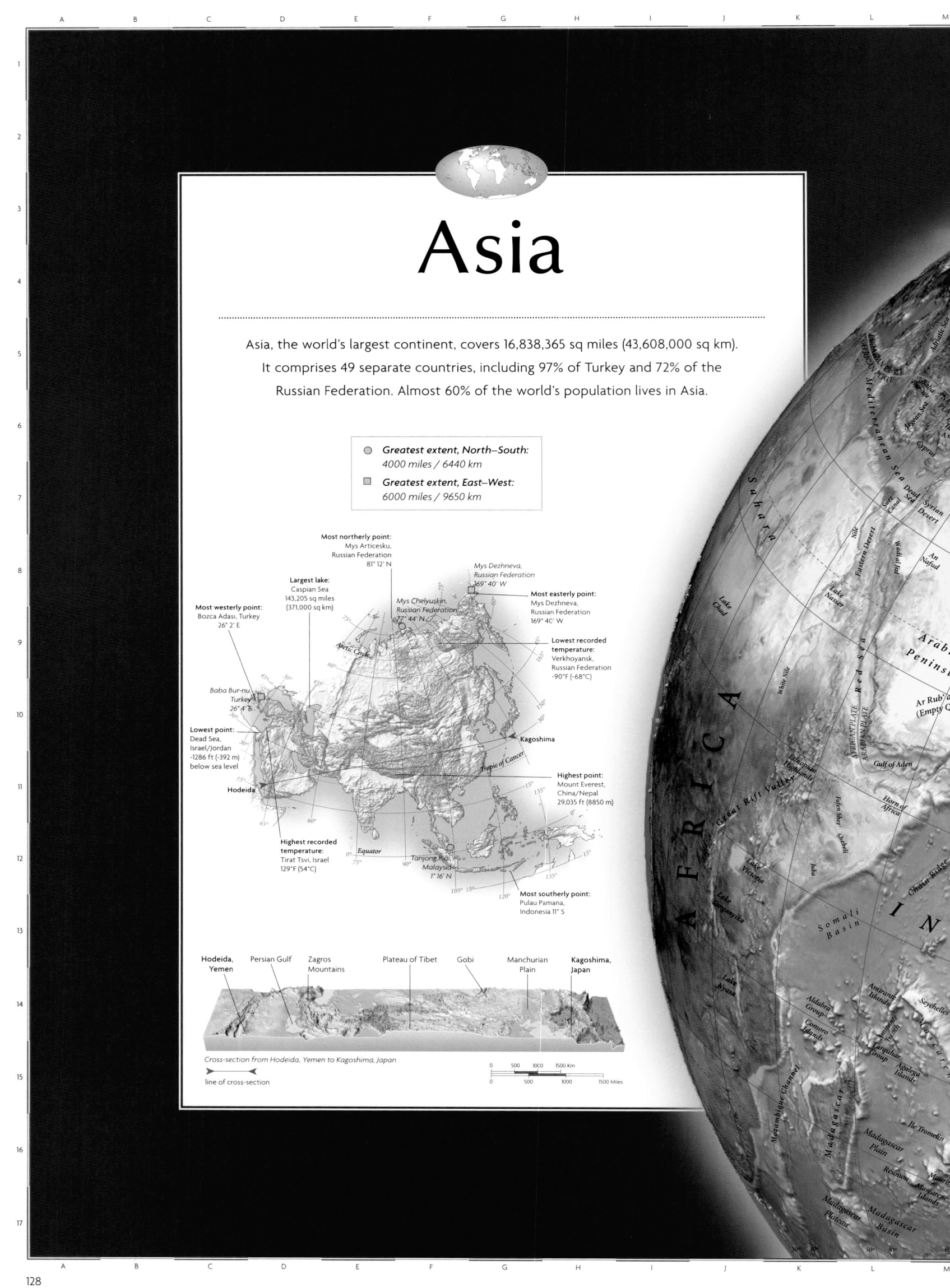

Most northerly point:
Mys Articesku,
Russian Federation
81° 12' N

Largest lake:
Caspian Sea
143,205 sq miles
(371,000 sq km)

Mys Chelyuskin,
Russian Federation
77° 44' N

Mys Dezhneva,
Russian Federation
169° 40' W

Most easterly point:
Mys Dezhneva,
Russian Federation
169° 40' W

Most westerly point:
Bozca Adası, Turkey
26° 2' E

**Lowest recorded
temperature:**
Verkhoyansk,
Russian Federation
-90°F (-68°C)

Baba Bur-nu,
Turkey
26° 4' E

Arctic Circle

Lowest point:
Dead Sea,
Israel/Jordan
-1286 ft (-392 m)
below sea level

● **Kagoshima**

Highest point:
Mount Everest,
China/Nepal
29,035 ft (8850 m)

▲ **Hodeida**

Tropic of Cancer

**Highest recorded
temperature:**
Tirat Tsvi, Israel
129°F (54°C)

Equator

Tanjong Piai,
Malaysia
1° 16' N

Most southerly point:
Pulau Pamana,
Indonesia 11° S

Hodeida,   Persian Gulf   Zagros   Plateau of Tibet   Gobi   Manchurian   **Kagoshima,**
Yemen   Mountains   Plain   **Japan**

Cross-section from Hodeida, Yemen to Kagoshima, Japan

⟵▶ line of cross-section

0	500	1000	1500 Km
0	500	1000	1500 Miles

ARCTIC OCEAN
North Pole
NORTH AMERICAN PLATE
EURASIAN PLATE

Norwegian Sea
Scandinavia
North Sea
Gulf of Bothnia
Baltic Sea
Gulf of Finland
EUROPE
North European Plain
Russian Upland
Central
Caspian Depression
Caucasus
Caspian Sea
Usyurt Plateau
Turan Lowland
Kara Kum
Syr Darya
Kirghiz Steppe
Sarysu
Lake Balkhash
Chu
Ili
ASIA
Turan Lowland
Iranian Plateau
Zagros Mountains
EURASIAN PLATE
IRANIAN PLATE
Great Salt Desert
Rigestan
Hindu Kush
Pamirs
Tien Shan
Dzungaria
Altai Mountains
Tarim Basin
Takla Makan Desert
Kunlun Mountains
Plateau of Tibet
Himalayas
Plateau of Mongolia
Gobi
Nan Shan
Qilian Shan
Ordos Desert
Wutai Shan
Qinghai Hu
Bayan Har Shan

West Siberian Plain
Ural Mountains
Central Siberian Plateau
Lake Baikal
Stanovoy Khrebet
Manchurian Plain
Sea of Okhotsk
Kamchatka
Kuril Trench

Siberia
North Siberian Lowland
Lena
Sea of Japan (East Sea)
Bo Hai
Korea Bay
Yellow Sea
Cheju-do
East China Sea
PACIFIC OCEAN
Japan Trench
Ryukyu Islands
Taiwan
Taiwan Strait

Great Plain of China
Yellow River
Han Shui
Yangtze
Hong Hu
Dongting Hu
Tai Hu

Arabian Sea
Arabian Basin
Strait of Hormuz
Gulf of Oman
INDO-AUSTRALIAN PLATE
Thar Desert
Punjab Plains
Deccan
Western Ghats
Eastern Ghats
Coromandel Coast
Malabar Coast
Laccadive Islands
Cape Comorin
Gulf of Mannar
Sri Lanka
Maldives

INDIAN OCEAN
Ceylon Plain
Chagos-Laccadive Plateau
Ninetyeast Ridge
Mid-Indian Basin
Chagos Bank
Chagos Trench
Nikitin Seamount
Cocos Basin

Bay of Bengal
Mouths of the Ganges
Ganges
Brahmaputra
Khasi Hills
Arakan Yoma
Gulf of Martaban
Andaman Islands
Andaman Sea
Gulf of Thailand
Isthmus of Kra
Nicobar Islands
Mouths of the Mekong
South China Sea
Philippine Sea
Philippine Basin
Mindoro
Panay
Palawan
Sulu Sea
Mindanao
Celebes Sea

Malay Peninsula
Strait of Malacca
Danau Toba
Sumatra
Tanjong Piai
Gunung Kerinci
Pulau Bangka
Greater Sunda Islands
Borneo
Natuna Islands
Sunda Shelf
Java Sea
East Indies
Java
Java Trench
Sunda Trough
Bali
Lesser Sunda Islands
Molucca Sea
Halmahera
New Guinea Trench
Banda Sea
Arafura Sea
Timor Trough

Cocos Islands
Christmas Island
Investigator Ridge

AUSTRALIA

Physical Asia

The structure of Asia can be divided into two distinct regions. The landscape of northern Asia consists of old mountain chains, shields, plateaux and basins, like the Ural Mountains in the west and the Central Siberian Plateau to the east. To the south of this region, are a series of plateaux and basins, including the vast Plateau of Tibet and the Tarim Basin. In contrast, the landscapes of southern Asia are much younger, formed by tectonic activity beginning about 65 million years ago, leading to an almost continuous mountain chain running from Europe, across much of Asia, and culminating in the mighty Himalayan mountain belt, formed when the Indo-Australian Plate collided with the Eurasian Plate. They are still being uplifted today. North of the mountains lies a belt of deserts, including the Gobi and the Takla Makan. In the far south, tectonic activity has formed narrow island arcs, extending over 4000 miles (7000 km). To the west lies the Arabian Shield, once part of the African Plate. As it was rifted apart from Africa, the Arabian Plate collided with the Eurasian Plate, uplifting the Zagros Mountains.

Coastal Lowlands and Island Arcs

The coastal plains that fringe Southeast Asia contain many large delta systems, caused by high levels of rainfall and erosion of the Himalayas, the Plateau of Tibet and relict loess deposits. To the south is an extensive island archipelago, lying on the drowned Sunda Shelf. Most of these islands are volcanic in origin, caused by the subduction of the Indo-Australian Plate beneath the Eurasian Plate.

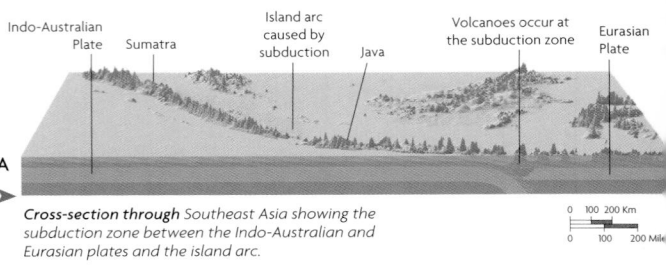

Cross-section through Southeast Asia showing the subduction zone between the Indo-Australian and Eurasian plates and the island arc.

The Indian Shield and Himalayan System

The large shield area beneath the Indian subcontinent is between 2.5 and 3.5 billion years old. As the floor of the southern Indian Ocean spread, it pushed the Indian Shield north. This was eventually driven beneath the Plateau of Tibet. This process closed up the ancient Tethys Sea and uplifted the world's highest mountain chain, the Himalayas. Much of the uplifted rock strata was from the seabed of the Tethys Sea, partly accounting for the weakness of the rocks and the high levels of erosion found in the Himalayas.

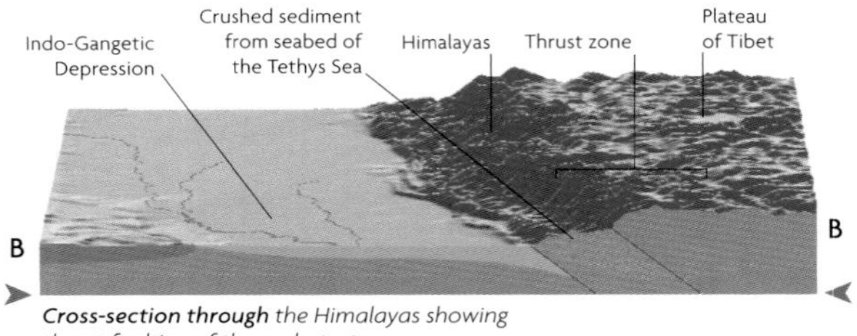

Cross-section through the Himalayas showing thrust faulting of the rock strata.

East Asian Plains and Uplands

Several, small, isolated shield areas, such as the Shandong Peninsula, are found in east Asia. Between these stable shield areas, large river systems like the Yangtze and the Yellow River have deposited thick layers of sediment, forming extensive alluvial plains. The largest of these is the Great Plain of China, the relief of which does not rise above 300 ft (100 m).

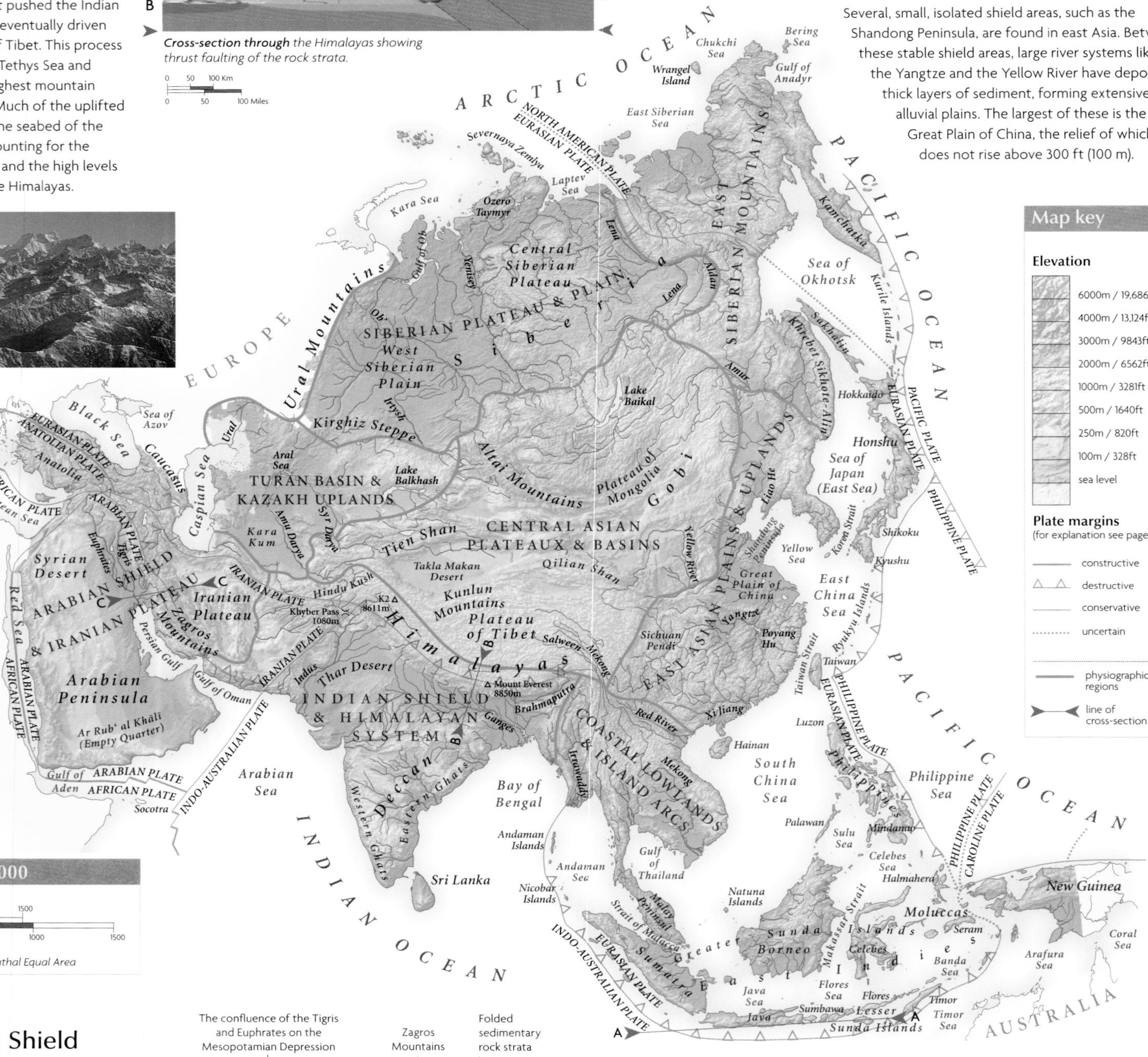

Scale 1:63,000,000

projection: Lambert Azimuthal Equal Area

Map key

Elevation

- 6000m / 19,686ft
- 4000m / 13,124ft
- 3000m / 9843ft
- 2000m / 6562ft
- 1000m / 3281ft
- 500m / 1640ft
- 250m / 820ft
- 100m / 328ft
- sea level

Plate margins
(for explanation see page xiv)

- constructive
- destructive
- conservative
- uncertain
- physiographic regions
- line of cross-section

The Arabian Shield and Iranian Plateau

Approximately five million years ago, rifting of the continental crust split the Arabian Plate from the African Plate and flooded the Red Sea. As this rift spread, the Arabian Plate collided with the Eurasian Plate, transforming part of the Tethys seabed into the Zagros Mountains which run northwest-southeast across western Iran.

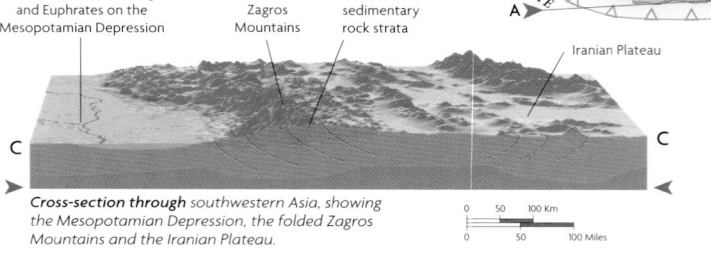

Cross-section through southwestern Asia, showing the Mesopotamian Depression, the folded Zagros Mountains and the Iranian Plateau.

Climate

he climate of Asia exhibits marked differences from region to region, with reezing polar conditions in the north, hot and cold deserts in central regions nd subtropical conditions throughout the south. Much of this variation can e attributed to enormous mountain barriers and internal depressions found cross the continent. Monsoon winds, which reverse semi-annually, cause lternate wet and dry seasons across southern Asia. These air asses moving north from the ocean are stripped of their oisture over the Himalayas causing arid onditions across the Plateau of ibet. Both the south and east re susceptible to tropical yclones or typhoons.

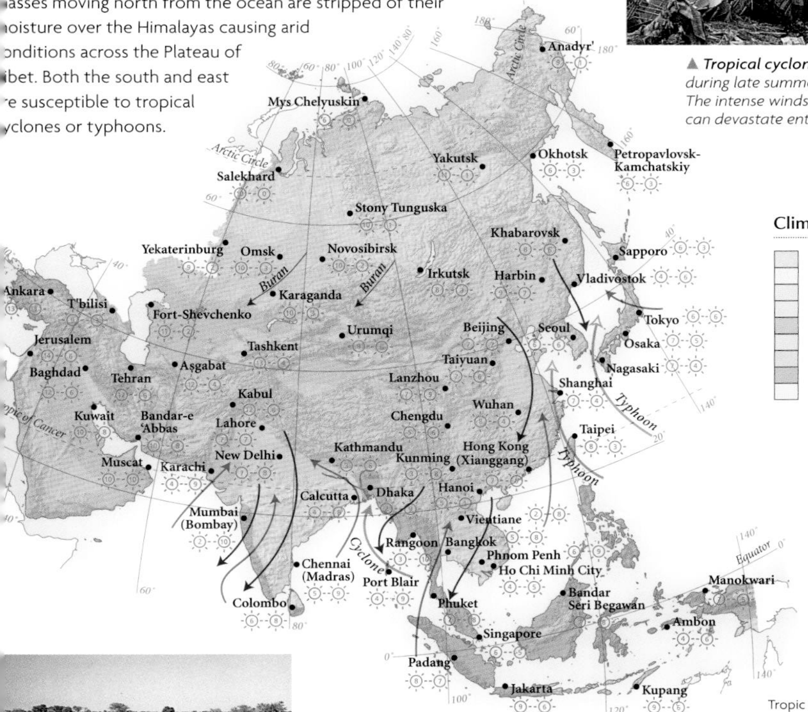

▲ *Tropical cyclones occur* principally *during late summer and early autumn. The intense winds and heavy rainfall can devastate entire villages.*

Temperature

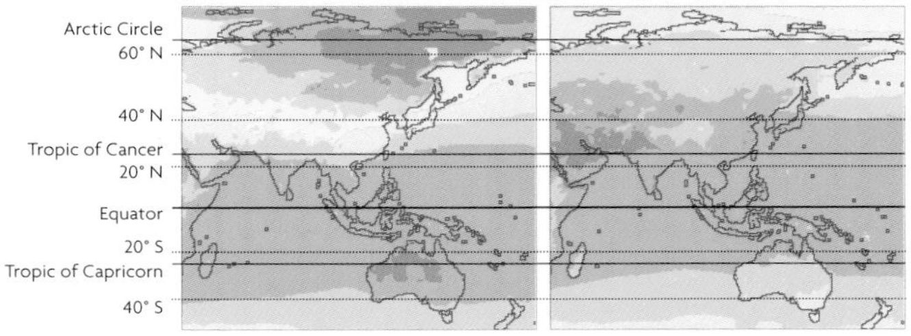

Average January temperature *Average July temperature*

Temperature

below -30°C (-22°F)	0 to 10°C (32 to 50°F)
-30 to -20°C (-22 to -4°F)	10 to 20°C (50°F)
-20 to -10°C (-4 to 14°F)	20 to 30°C (68 to 86°F)
-10 to 0°C (14 to 32°F)	above 30°C (86°F)

Climate

tundra	☀ daily hours of sunshine, January
subarctic	
cool continental	☀ daily hours of sunshine, July
warm humid	
mediterranean	→ cyclone
semi-arid	→ typhoon
arid	→ cold/dry monsoon
humid equatorial	→ warm/wet monsoon
tropical	→ cold wind

▶ *The Gobi Desert experiences major extremes in climate, with winter temperatures sometimes falling below -40°C (-40°F) and summer temperatures exceeding 45°C (113°F).*

Rainfall

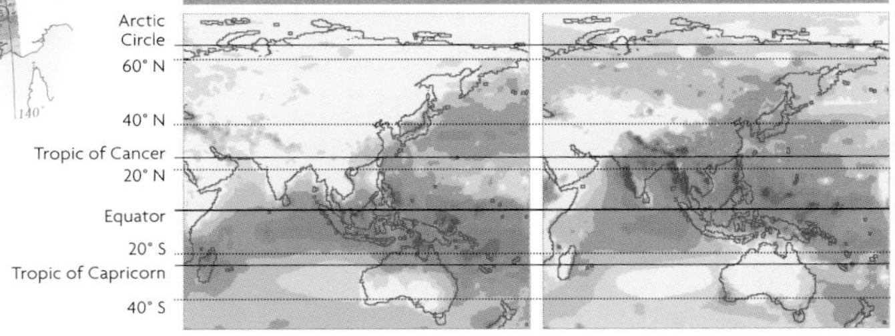

Average January rainfall *Average July rainfall*

Rainfall

0 –25 mm (0–1 in)
25–50 mm (1–2 in)
50–100 mm (2–4 in)
100–200 mm (4–8 in)
200–300 mm (8–12 in)
300–400 mm (12–16 in)
400–500 mm (16–20 in)
more than 500 mm (20 in)

◀ *Through India, the* southwest monsoon, which brings heavy rainfall from May to September, accounts for 80% of annual precipitation.

Shaping the landscape

n the north, melting of extensive permafrost leads to typical eriglacial features such as thermokarst. In the arid areas wind action ransports sand creating extensive dune systems. An active tectonic argin in the south causes continued uplift, and volcanic and seismic ctivity, but also high rates of weathering and erosion. Across the ontinent, huge rivers erode and transport vast quantities of ediment depositing it on the plains or forming large deltas.

River systems

1 Vast river systems flow across Asia, many originating in the Himalayas and the Plateau of Tibet. Seasonal melting of snow and monsoon rains swell the river flow leading to flooding and erosion. The Yellow River *(right)* gets its colour from the high level of eroded material from the loess plateau.

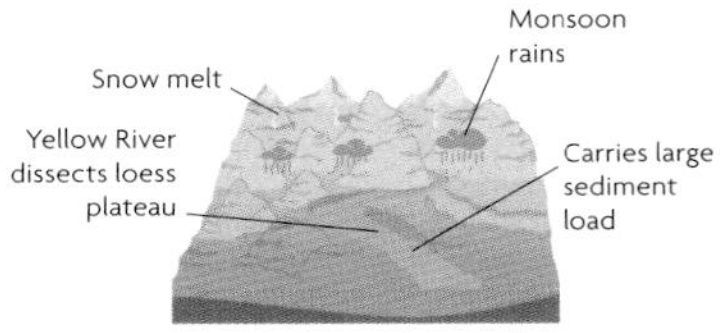

Monsoon rains
Snow melt
Yellow River dissects loess plateau
Carries large sediment load

River systems: erosion of the loess plateau by the yellow river

Chemical weathering

2 Tower karsts are widespread across south China *(left)* and Vietnam. It is thought the karstic towers were formed under a soil cover, where small depressions in the limestone bedrock began to be weathered by soil water acids, eventually creating larger hollows. This process continued over millions of years, deepening the hollows and leaving steep-sided limestone hills.

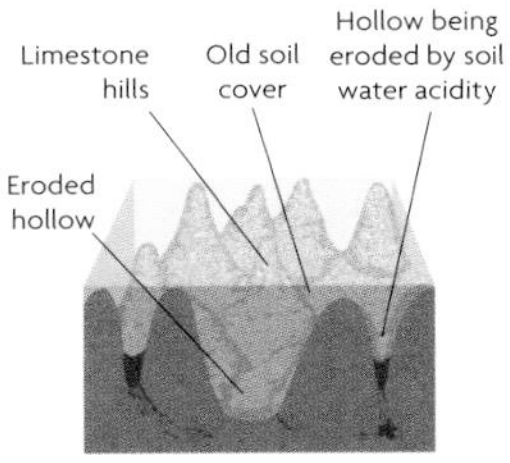

Limestone hills
Old soil cover
Hollow being eroded by soil water acidity
Eroded hollow

Chemical weathering: formation of tower karst

Sedimentation

4 The Ganges/Brahmaputra is a tide-dominated delta *(below)*. The two rivers transport huge quantities of mountain sediment, which is deposited on the delta plain. This debris is then redistributed by tidal currents, to form extensions to the bars, beach ridges and deltaic deposits.

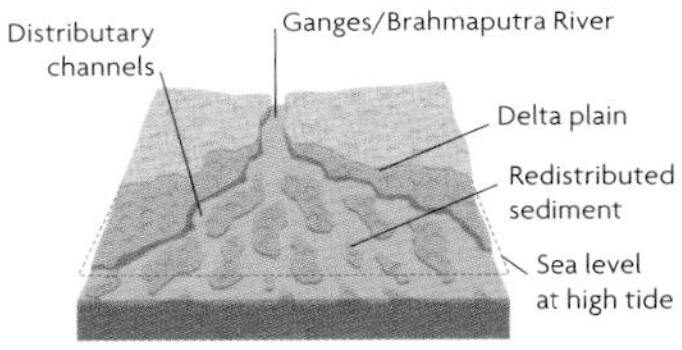

Distributary channels
Ganges/Brahmaputra River
Delta plain
Redistributed sediment
Sea level at high tide

Sedimentation: the destruction of a delta

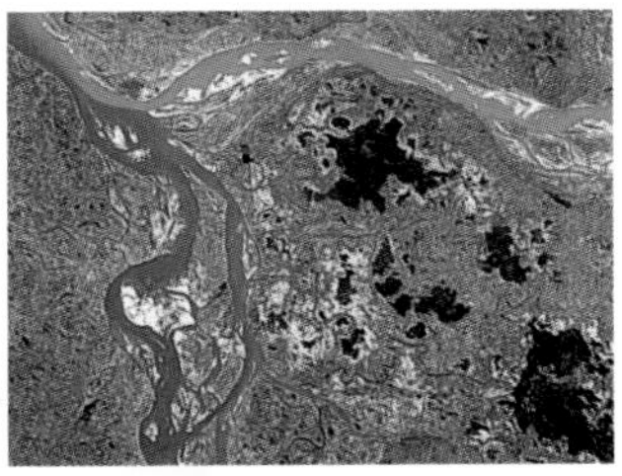

olcanic activity

Volcanic eruptions ccur frequently across outheast Asia's island arcs *elow)*. Low-level ruptions occur when roundwater, superheated y underlying magma, ecomes pressurized, rcing hot fluid and rocks o through cracks in the olcanic cone. This is known a phreatic eruption.

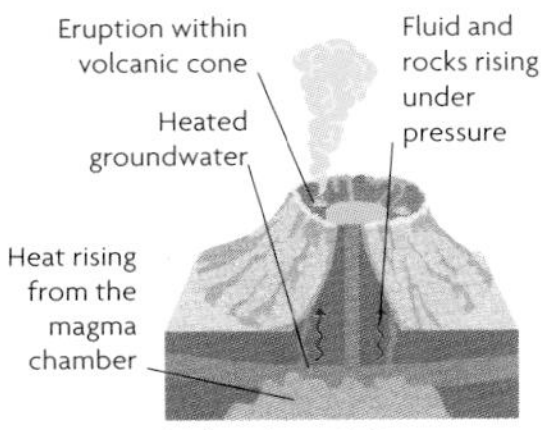

Eruption within volcanic cone
Fluid and rocks rising under pressure
Heated groundwater
Heat rising from the magma chamber

Volcanic activity: a phreatic eruption

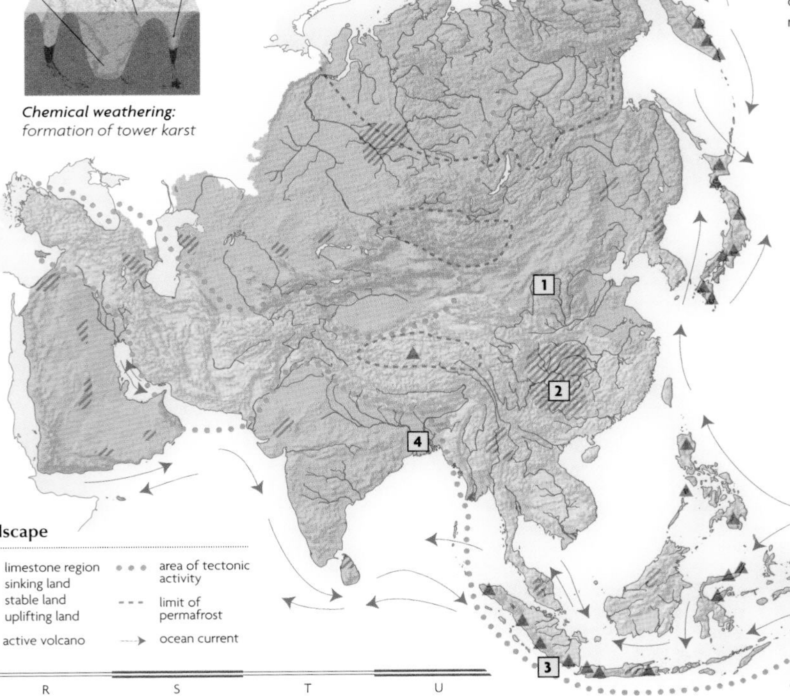

Landscape

limestone region	••• area of tectonic activity
sinking land	
stable land	– – limit of permafrost
uplifting land	
▲ active volcano	→ ocean current

Political Asia

Asia is the world's largest continent, encompassing many different and discrete realms, from the desert Arab lands of the southwest to the subtropical archipelago of Indonesia; from the vast barren wastes of Siberia to the fertile river valleys of China and South Asia, seats of some of the world's most ancient civilizations. The collapse of the Soviet Union has fragmented the north of the continent into the Siberian portion of the Russian Federation, and the new republics of Central Asia. Strong religious traditions heavily influence the politics of South and Southwest Asia. Hindu and Muslim rivalries threaten to upset the political equilibrium in South Asia where India – in terms of population – remains the world's largest democracy. Communist China, another population giant, is reasserting its position as a world political and economic power, while on its doorstep, the dynamic Pacific Rim countries, led by Japan, continue to assert their worldwide economic force.

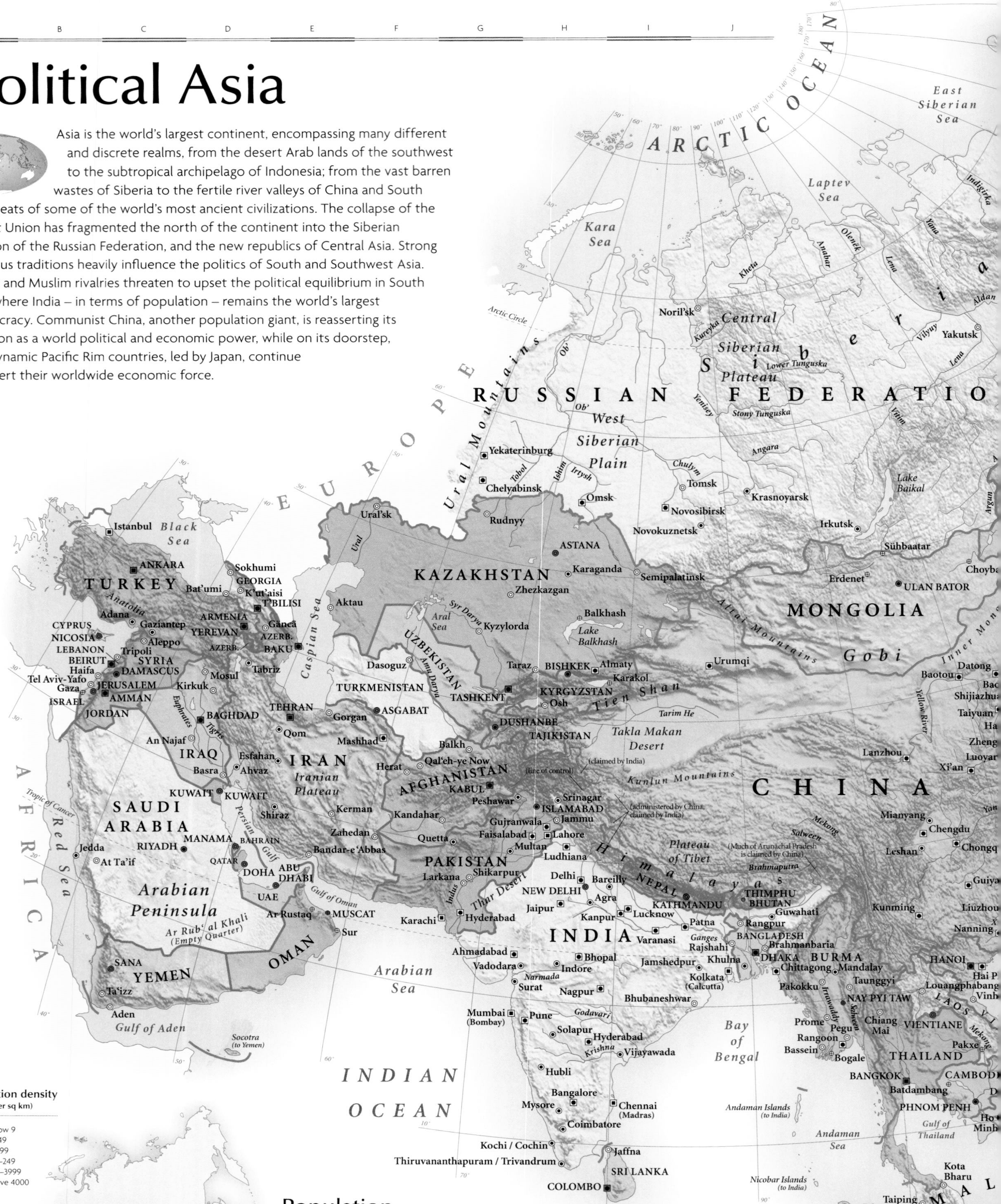

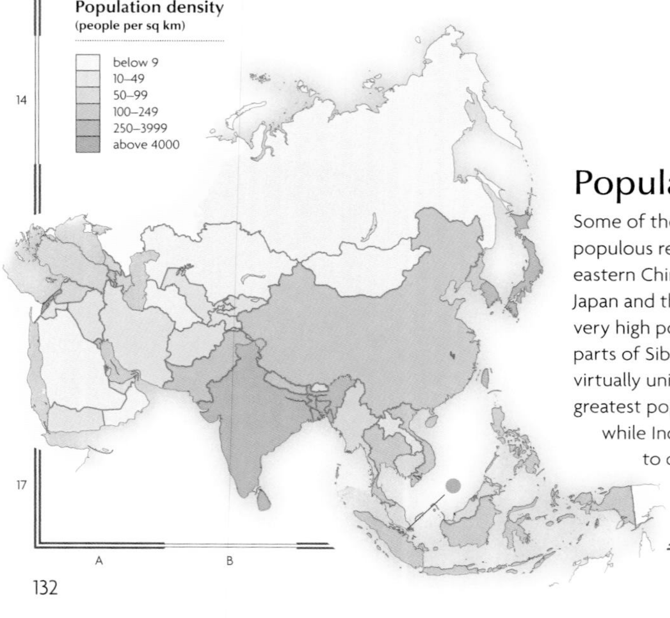

Population density
(people per sq km)

- below 9
- 10–49
- 50–99
- 100–249
- 250–3999
- above 4000

Population

Some of the world's most populous and least populous regions are in Asia. The plains of eastern China, the Ganges river plains in India, Japan and the Indonesian island of Java, all have very high population densities; by contrast parts of Siberia and the Plateau of Tibet are virtually uninhabited. China has the world's greatest population – 20% of the globe's total – while India, with the second largest, is likely to overtake China within 30 years.

◀ *Kolkata's 13 million inhabitants bustle through a maze of crowded, narrow streets. Population densities in India's largest city reach almost 85,000 per sq mile (33,000 per sq km).*

Map labels

ARCTIC OCEAN
East Siberian Sea
Kara Sea
Laptev Sea
Kheta
Olenek
Lena
Indigirka
Yana
Anabar
Vilyuy
Yakutsk
Aldan
Arctic Circle
Noril'sk
Kureyka
Lower Tunguska
Central Siberian Plateau
S i b e r i a
Ob'
RUSSIAN FEDERATION
Stony Tunguska
Yenisey
Angara
Chulym
Lake Baikal
Bac
E U R O P E
Ural Mountains
West Siberian Plain
Ural
Tobol
Ishim
Irtysh
Yekaterinburg
Chelyabinsk
Omsk
Tomsk
Novosibirsk
Novokuznetsk
Krasnoyarsk
Irkutsk
Sühbaatar
Choybal
ULAN BATOR
Erdenet
Ural'sk
Rudnyy
ASTANA
KAZAKHSTAN
Karaganda
Semipalatinsk
MONGOLIA
Altai Mountains
Gobi
Inner Mon
Istanbul
Black Sea
ANKARA
Sokhumi
GEORGIA
Bat'umi
K'ut'aisi
T'BILISI
TURKEY
Anatolia
Adana
Gaziantep
ARMENIA
YEREVAN
Ganca
AZERB.
BAKU
CYPRUS
NICOSIA
Aleppo
AZERB.
Aktau
Syr Darya
Kyzylorda
Balkhash
Lake Balkhash
Taraz
Urumqi
Tien Shan
BISHKEK
Almaty
Datong
Baotou
Shijiazhu
LEBANON
Tripoli
SYRIA
BEIRUT
Haifa
DAMASCUS
Mosul
Tabriz
Caspian Sea
Dasoguz
UZBEKISTAN
Amu Darya
TASHKENT
Karakol
KYRGYZSTAN
Osh
Tarim He
Lanzhou
Taiyuan
Tel Aviv-Yafo
Gaza
JERUSALEM
AMMAN
Kirkuk
TURKMENISTAN
ASGABAT
DUSHANBE
TAJIKISTAN
Takla Makan Desert
Ha
Zheng
ISRAEL
JORDAN
BAGHDAD
TEHRAN
Gorgan
Qom
Balkh
(claimed by India)
CHINA
Luoyar
Xi'an
An Najaf
Esfahan
IRAN
Mashhad
Qal'eh-ye Now
Herat
(line of control)
Kunlun Mountains
IRAQ
Basra
Ahvaz
Iranian Plateau
AFGHANISTAN
KABUL
(administered by China, claimed by India)
Mianyang
Chengdu
KUWAIT
KUWAIT
Kerman
Kandahar
Peshawar
Srinagar
ISLAMABAD
Jammu
Plateau of Tibet
(Much of Arunachal Pradesh is claimed by China)
Leshan
Chongq
SAUDI ARABIA
Shiraz
Zahedan
Quetta
Gujranwala
Faisalabad
Lahore
Salween
Mekong
MANAMA
BAHRAIN
Bandar-e 'Abbas
Multan
Ludhiana
Brahmaputra
Kunming
Liuzhou
Jedda
RIYADH
QATAR
Larkana
PAKISTAN
Shikarpur
Delhi
Bareilly
H i m a l a y a s
THIMPHU
Guwahati
Nanning
At Ta'if
DOHA
ABU DHABI
UAE
Gulf of Oman
Ar Rustaq
MUSCAT
Karachi
Hyderabad
NEW DELHI
Agra
NEPAL
KATHMANDU
BHUTAN
Rangpur
Guiya
Arabian Peninsula
Ar Rub' al Khali (Empty Quarter)
Sur
Jaipur
Kanpur
Lucknow
Patna
BANGLADESH
Brahmanbaria
SANA
YEMEN
OMAN
Arabian Sea
Ahmadabad
Vadodara
Bhopal
Indore
Jamshedpur
Khulna
DHAKA
Chittagong
BURMA
Mandalay
HANOI
Ta'izz
Narmada
Surat
Nagpur
INDIA
Kolkata (Calcutta)
Pakokku
Taunggyi
Aden
Gulf of Aden
Socotra (to Yemen)
Mumbai (Bombay)
Pune
Godavari
Krishna
Hyderabad
Vijayawada
Bhubaneshwar
Irrawaddy
Prom
Pegu
Chiang Mai
LAOS
VIENTIANE
Vinh
Pakxe
INDIAN OCEAN
Solapur
Bay of Bengal
Rangoon
Bassein
Bogale
THAILAND
Hubli
Bangalore
Mysore
Chennai (Madras)
Coimbatore
Andaman Islands (to India)
BANGKOK
Batdambang
CAMBO
Kochi / Cochin
Jaffna
Andaman Sea
PHNOM PENH
Ho Chi Minh
Thiruvananthapuram / Trivandrum
SRI LANKA
COLOMBO
Nicobar Islands (to India)
Gulf of Thailand
Kota Bharu
Taiping
MAL
KUALA LUM
Medan
PUTRAJAYA
SINGAPO
SINGAPO
Equator
Jam
Sumatra
Padang
Palembang
JAKA
AFRICA
Tropic of Cancer
Red Sea
Euphrates
Tigris
Persian Gulf
Thar Desert
Indus
Ganges
Rajshahi
Varanasi

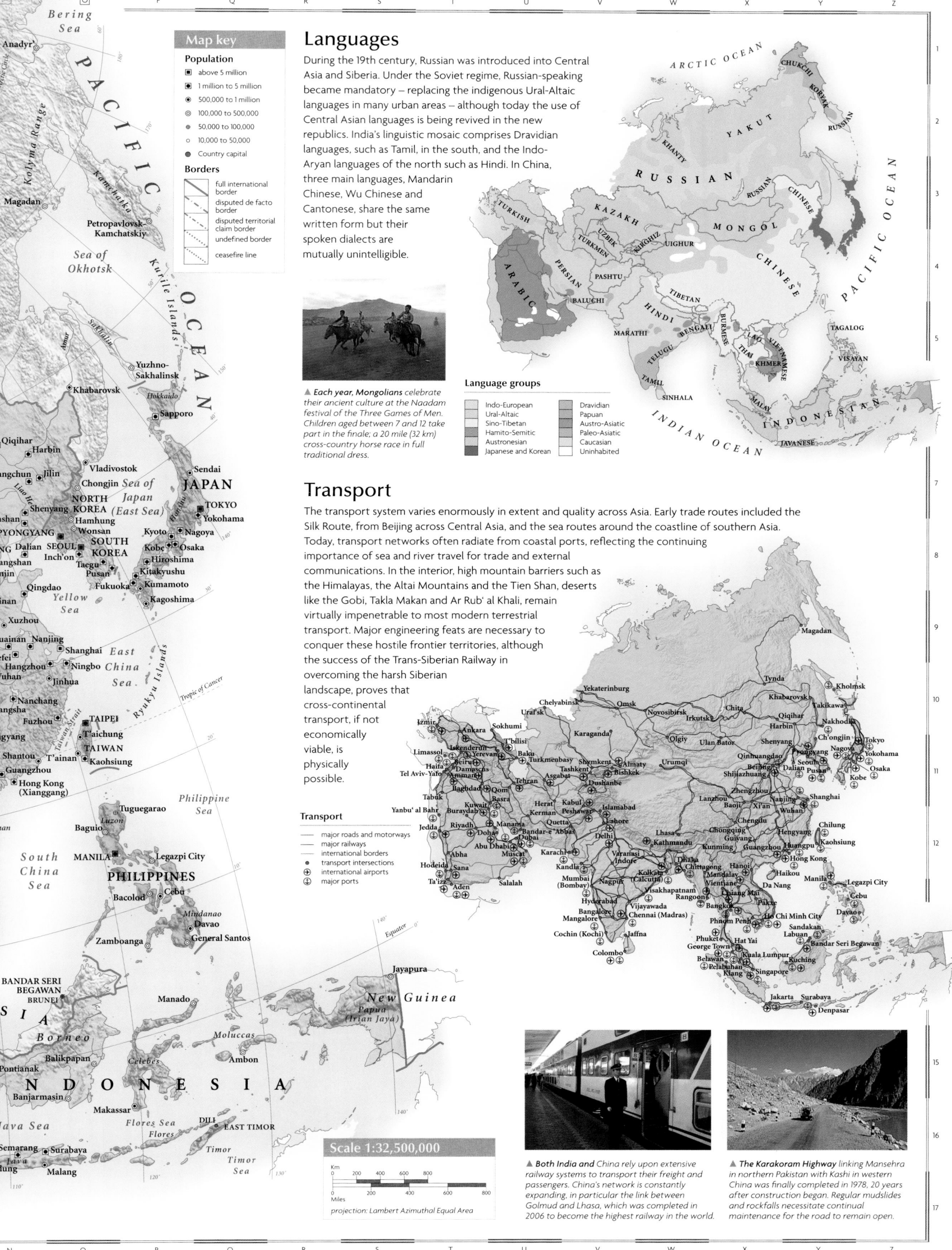

Map key

Population
- ▪ above 5 million
- ▪ 1 million to 5 million
- ◉ 500,000 to 1 million
- ◎ 100,000 to 500,000
- ⊕ 50,000 to 100,000
- ○ 10,000 to 50,000
- ● Country capital

Borders
- full international border
- disputed de facto border
- disputed territorial claim border
- undefined border
- ceasefire line

Languages

During the 19th century, Russian was introduced into Central Asia and Siberia. Under the Soviet regime, Russian-speaking became mandatory – replacing the indigenous Ural-Altaic languages in many urban areas – although today the use of Central Asian languages is being revived in the new republics. India's linguistic mosaic comprises Dravidian languages, such as Tamil, in the south, and the Indo-Aryan languages of the north such as Hindi. In China, three main languages, Mandarin Chinese, Wu Chinese and Cantonese, share the same written form but their spoken dialects are mutually unintelligible.

▲ *Each year, Mongolians celebrate their ancient culture at the Naadam festival of the Three Games of Men. Children aged between 7 and 12 take part in the finale; a 20 mile (32 km) cross-country horse race in full traditional dress.*

Language groups
- Indo-European
- Ural-Altaic
- Sino-Tibetan
- Hamito-Semitic
- Austronesian
- Japanese and Korean
- Dravidian
- Papuan
- Austro-Asiatic
- Paleo-Asiatic
- Caucasian
- Uninhabited

Transport

The transport system varies enormously in extent and quality across Asia. Early trade routes included the Silk Route, from Beijing across Central Asia, and the sea routes around the coastline of southern Asia. Today, transport networks often radiate from coastal ports, reflecting the continuing importance of sea and river travel for trade and external communications. In the interior, high mountain barriers such as the Himalayas, the Altai Mountains and the Tien Shan, deserts like the Gobi, Takla Makan and Ar Rub' al Khali, remain virtually impenetrable to most modern terrestrial transport. Major engineering feats are necessary to conquer these hostile frontier territories, although the success of the Trans-Siberian Railway in overcoming the harsh Siberian landscape, proves that cross-continental transport, if not economically viable, is physically possible.

Transport
- major roads and motorways
- major railways
- international borders
- ● transport intersections
- ⊕ international airports
- ⊕ major ports

Scale 1:32,500,000

Km
0   200   400   600   800
Miles
0   200   400   600   800

projection: Lambert Azimuthal Equal Area

▲ *Both India and China rely upon extensive railway systems to transport their freight and passengers. China's network is constantly expanding, in particular the link between Golmud and Lhasa, which was completed in 2006 to become the highest railway in the world.*

▲ *The Karakoram Highway linking Mansehra in northern Pakistan with Kashi in western China was finally completed in 1978, 20 years after construction began. Regular mudslides and rockfalls necessitate continual maintenance for the road to remain open.*

Asian resources

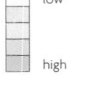

Although agriculture remains the economic mainstay of most Asian countries, the number of people employed in agriculture has steadily declined, as new industries have been developed during the past 30 years. China, Indonesia, Malaysia, Thailand and Turkey have all experienced far-reaching structural change in their economies, while the breakup of the Soviet Union has created a new economic challenge in the Central Asian republics. The countries of the Persian Gulf illustrate the rapid transformation from rural nomadism to modern, urban society which oil wealth has brought to parts of the continent. Asia's most economically dynamic countries, Japan, Singapore, South Korea, and Taiwan, fringe the Pacific Ocean and are known as the Pacific Rim. In contrast, other Southeast Asian countries like Laos and Cambodia remain both economically and industrially underdeveloped.

Industry

East Asian industry leads the continent in both productivity and efficiency; electronics, hi-tech industries, car manufacture and shipbuilding are important. The so-called economic 'tigers' of the Pacific Rim are Japan, South Korea and Taiwan and in recent years China has rediscovered its potential as an economic superpower. Heavy industries such as engineering, chemicals, and steel typify the industrial complexes along the corridor created by the Trans-Siberian Railway, the Fergana Valley in Central Asia, and also much of the huge industrial plain of east China. The discovery of oil in the Persian Gulf has brought immense wealth to countries that previously relied on subsistence agriculture on marginal desert land.

Industry

✈ aerospace	🏭 printing & publishing
🍺 brewing	⚓ shipbuilding
🚗 car/vehicle manufacture	↓ sugar processing
🏛 cement	⚲ tea processing
⚗ chemicals	✦ textiles
⚡ electronics	☘ timber processing
⚙ engineering	⚶ tobacco processing
$ finance	⛏ coal
🐟 fish processing	♦ oil
🍴 food processing	▲ gas
🖥 hi-tech industry	• industrial cities
⬛ iron & steel	▱ major industrial areas
⚕ pharmaceuticals	

Standard of living

Despite Japan's high standards of living, and Southwest Asia's oil-derived wealth, immense disparities exist across the continent. Afghanistan remains one of the world's most underdeveloped nations, as do the mountain states of Nepal and Bhutan. Further rapid population growth is exacerbating poverty and overcrowding in many parts of India and Bangladesh.

Standard of living
(UN human development index)

⬜	low
⬛	high

▲ On a small island at the southern tip of the Malay Peninsula lies Singapore, one of the Pacific Rim's most vibrant economic centres. Multinational banking and finance form the core of the city's wealth.

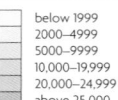

GNI per capita (US$)

⬜	below 1999
	2000–4999
	5000–9999
	10,000–19,999
	20,000–24,999
⬛	above 25,000

▲ Iron and steel, engineering and shipbuilding typify the heavy industry found in eastern China's industrial cities, especially the nation's leading manufacturing centre, Shanghai.

◀ Traditional industries are still crucial to many rural economies across Asia. Here, on the Vietnamese coast, salt has been extracted from seawater by evaporation and is being loaded into a van to take to market.

ARCTIC OCEAN

PACIFIC OCEAN

RUSSIAN FEDERATION

Sea of Okhotsk

Yakutsk

Trans-Siberian Railway

Yekaterinburg
Chelyabinsk
Magnitogorsk
Omsk
Novosibirsk
Kemerovo
Krasnoyarsk
Bratsk
Khabarovsk
Novokuznetsk
Irkutsk
Karaganda

KAZAKHSTAN

Vladivostok
JAPAN
Harbin
NORTH KOREA
Tokyo
Nagoya
Kobe

Aral Sea

Caspian Sea

Istanbul
Izmir
Ankara
TURKEY
GEORGIA
Tbilisi
ARMENIA
Yerevan
AZERB.
Baku

CYPRUS
LEBANON
Beirut
SYRIA
Damascus
Tel Aviv-Yafo
ISRAEL
JORDAN
Amman
Kirkuk
Baghdad
IRAQ
Basra
Isfahan
Tehran
IRAN

UZBEKISTAN
Tashkent
TURKMENISTAN
Asgabat
Dushanbe
TAJIKISTAN
Farghona
KYRGYZSTAN
Almaty

Urumqi

MONGOLIA
Ulan Bator

Shenyang
Beijing
Tianjin
Pyongyang
Dalian
SOUTH KOREA
Seoul
Pusan
Qingdao

CHINA

Taiyuan
Jinan
Lanzhou
Zhengzhou
Xi'an
Nanjing
Shanghai
Wuhan

Kuwait
KUWAIT
SAUDI ARABIA
Ad Damman
BAHRAIN
Riyadh
QATAR
Abu Dhabi
UAE
Dubai
Jedda

AFGHANISTAN
Rawalpindi
Lahore
PAKISTAN
Karachi
Ahmadabad

Persian Gulf
Gulf of Oman

Red Sea

OMAN

YEMEN

Gulf of Aden

Arabian Sea

Delhi
Kanpur
NEPAL
BHUTAN
INDIA
Indore
Jamshedpur
BANGLADESH
Dhaka
Chittagong
Kolkata (Calcutta)
Mumbai (Bombay)
Nagpur

Chengdu
Chongqing
Kunming

Guangzhou
Hong Kong

Taipei
TAIWAN

BURMA
Mandalay

Hanoi
LAOS
VIETNAM
Da Nang
South China Sea

Manila
PHILIPPINES

Rangoon
THAILAND
Bangkok
CAMBODIA

Bangalore
Chennai (Madras)

SRI LANKA

INDIAN OCEAN

Ho Chi Minh City

MALAYSIA
BRUNEI
Kuala Lumpur
Singapore
SINGAPORE

INDONESIA

Jakarta
Surabaya
EAST TIMOR

Environmental issues

The transformation of Uzbekistan by the former Soviet Union into the world's fifth largest producer of cotton led to the diversion of several major rivers for irrigation. Starved of this water, the Aral Sea diminished in volume by over 75% since 1960, irreversibly altering the ecology of the area. Heavy industries in eastern China have polluted coastal waters, rivers and urban air, while in Burma, Malaysia and Indonesia, ancient hardwood rainforests are felled faster than they can regenerate.

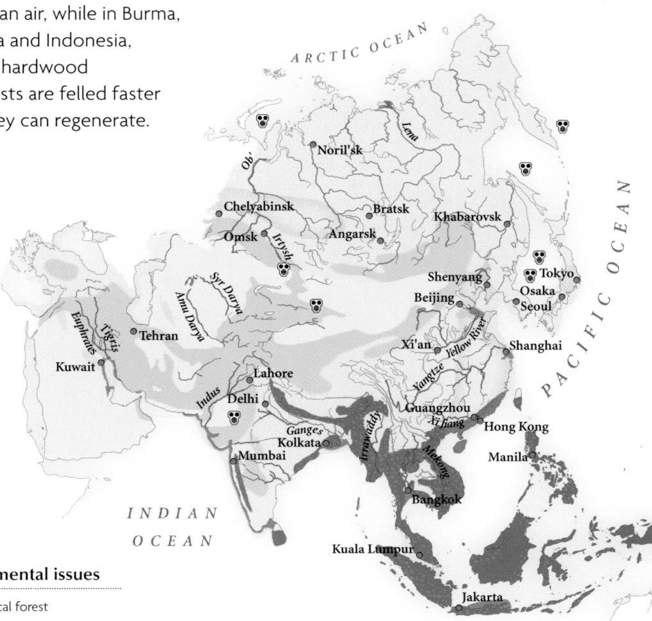

▲ *Although Siberia remains* a quintessentially frozen, inhospitable wasteland, vast untapped mineral reserves – especially the oil and gas of the West Siberian Plain – have lured industrial development to the area since the 1950s and 1960s.

Environmental issues

- ■ tropical forest
- ■ forest destroyed
- □ desert
- ▨ desertification
- □ acid rain
- ⌁ polluted rivers
- ▨ marine pollution
- ▨ heavy marine pollution
- ☢ radioactive contamination
- • poor urban air quality

◄ *The long-term environmental* impact of the Gulf War (1991) is still uncertain. As Iraqi troops left Kuwait, equipment was abandoned to rust and thousands of oil wells were set alight, pouring crude oil into the Persian Gulf.

Mineral resources

At least 60% of the world's known oil and gas deposits are found in Asia; notably the vast oil fields of the Persian Gulf, and the less-exploited oil and gas fields of the Ob' basin in west Siberia. Immense coal reserves in Siberia and China have been utilized to support large steel industries. Southeast Asia has some of the world's largest deposits of tin, found in a belt running down the Malay Peninsula to Indonesia.

Mineral resources

- ▨ oil field
- ▨ gas field
- ▨ coal field
- ◖ chromite
- ⬤ copper
- ▲ gold
- ■ iron
- ◭ lead
- △ nickel
- ⊙ platinum
- ⬚ tin
- ◉ wolfram

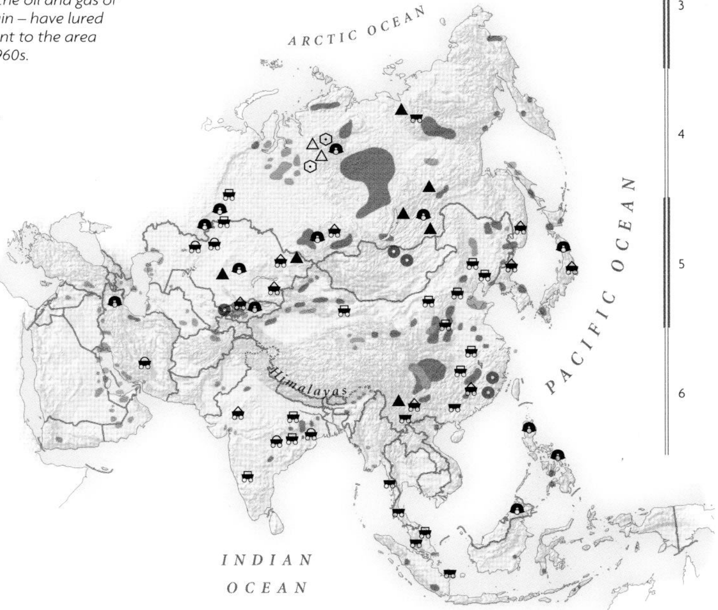

Using the land and sea

Vast areas of Asia remain uncultivated as a result of unsuitable climatic and soil conditions. In favourable areas such as river deltas, farming is intensive. Rice is the staple crop of most Asian countries, grown in paddy fields on waterlogged alluvial plains and terraced hillsides, and often irrigated for higher yields. Across the black earth region of the Eurasian steppe in southern Siberia and Kazakhstan, wheat farming is the dominant activity. Cash crops, like tea in Sri Lanka and dates in the Arabian Peninsula, are grown for export, and provide valuable income. The sovereignty of the rich fishing grounds in the South China Sea is disputed by China, Malaysia, Taiwan, the Philippines and Vietnam, because of potential oil reserves.

▲ *Date palms have* been cultivated in oases throughout the Arabian Peninsula since antiquity. In addition to the fruit, palms are used for timber, fuel, rope, and for making vinegar, syrup and a liquor known as arrack.

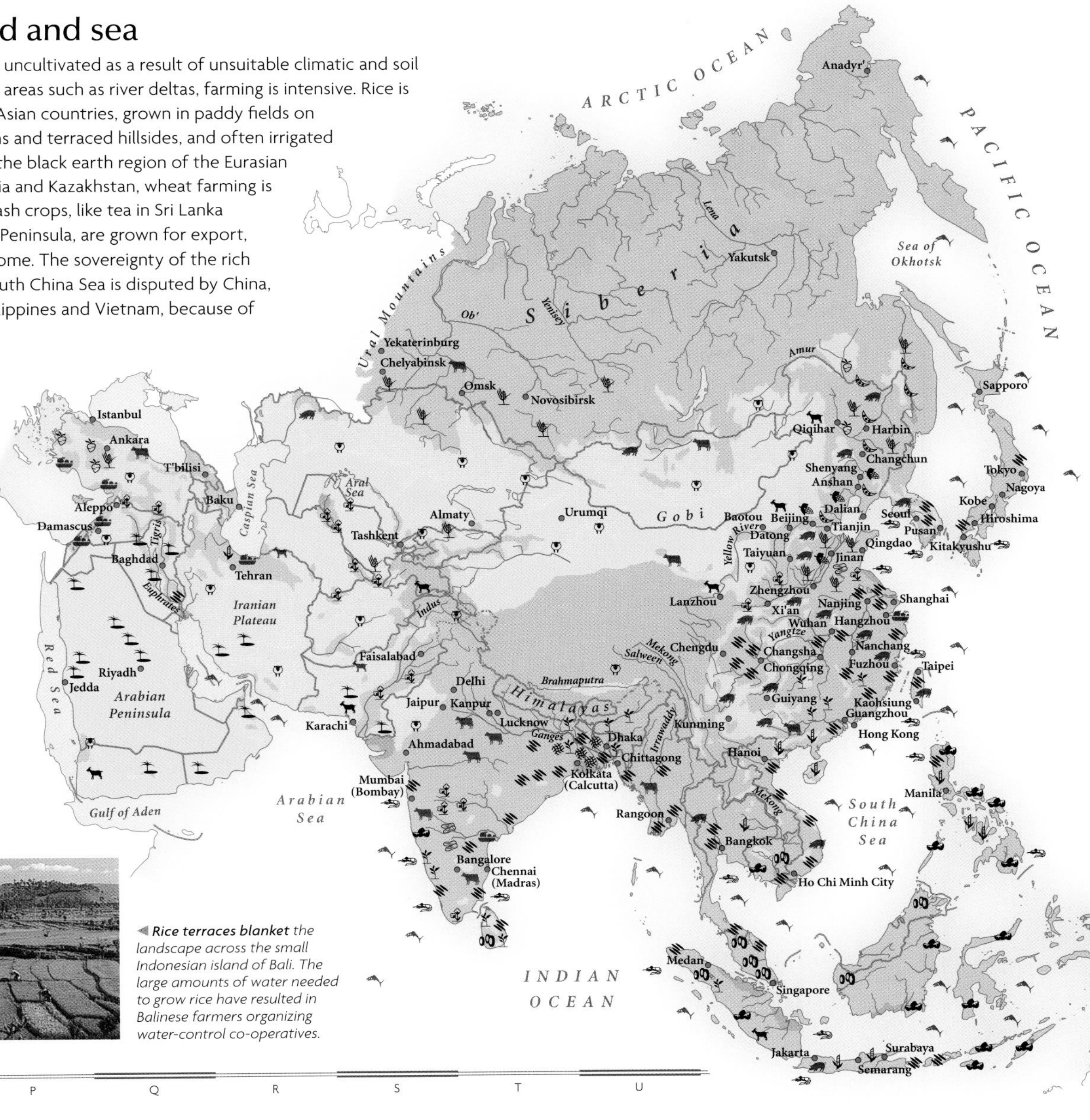

Using the land and sea

- ▨ cropland
- ▨ desert
- ▨ forest
- ▨ mountain region
- ▨ pasture
- ▨ tundra
- ▨ wetland
- • major conurbations
- cattle
- pigs
- goats
- sheep
- coconuts
- corn (maize)
- cotton
- dates
- fishing
- fruit
- jute
- peanuts
- rice
- rubber
- shellfish
- soya beans
- sugar beet
- sugar cane
- tea
- timber
- wheat

◄ *Rice terraces blanket* the landscape across the small Indonesian island of Bali. The large amounts of water needed to grow rice have resulted in Balinese farmers organizing water-control co-operatives.

Turkey & the Caucasus

ARMENIA, AZERBAIJAN, GEORGIA, TURKEY

This region occupies the fragmented junction between Europe, Asia and the Russian Federation. Sunni Islam provides a common identity for the secular state of Turkey, which the revered leader Kemal Atatürk established from the remnants of the Ottoman Empire after the First World War. Turkey has a broad resource base and expanding trade links with Europe, but the east is relatively undeveloped and strife between the state and a large Kurdish minority has yet to be resolved. Georgia is similarly challenged by ethnic separatism, while the Christian state of Armenia and the mainly Muslim and oil-rich Azerbaijan are locked in conflict over the territory of Nagorno-Karabakh.

Transport and industry

Turkey leads the region's well-diversified economy. Petrochemicals, textiles, engineering and food processing are the main industries. Azerbaijan is able to export oil, while the other states rely heavily on hydro-electric power and imported fuel. Georgia produces precision machinery. War and earthquake damage have devastated Armenia's infrastructure.

▲ **Azerbaijan has substantial** oil reserves, located in and around the Caspian Sea. They were some of the earliest oilfields in the world to be exploited.

Major industry and infrastructure

- carpet weaving
- cement
- chemicals
- coal
- engineering
- food processing
- oil
- textiles
- tourism
- vehicle manufacture
- ■ capital cities
- ■ major towns
- ⊕ international airports
- —— major roads
- major industrial areas

Using the land and sea

Turkey is largely self-sufficient in food. The irrigated Black Sea coastlands have the world's highest yields of hazelnuts. Tobacco, cotton, sultanas, tea and figs are the region's main cash crops and a great range of fruit and vegetables are grown. Wine grapes are among the labour-intensive crops which allow full use of limited agricultural land in the Caucasus. Sturgeon fishing is particularly important in Azerbaijan.

Land use and agricultural distribution

- cattle
- goats
- cotton
- fishing
- fruit
- hazelnuts
- olives
- sugar beet
- tobacco
- vineyards
- ● capital cities
- major towns
- pasture
- cropland
- forest

The urban/rural population divide

urban 72%   rural 28%

0 10 20 30 40 50 60 70 80 90 100

Population density	Total land area
238 people per sq mile (92 people per sq km)	368,912 sq miles (955,730 sq km)

The transport network

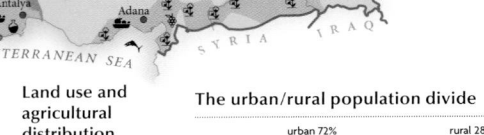

114,867 miles (184,882 km)

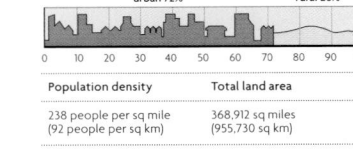

5778 miles (9300 km)

8120 miles (13,069 km)

745 miles (1200 km)

Physical and political barriers have severely limited communications between Armenia, Georgia and Azerbaijan. Turkey has a relatively well-developed transport network.

▲ **For many centuries,** Istanbul has held tremendous strategic importance as a crucial gateway between Europe and Asia. Founded by the Greeks as Byzantium, the city became the centre of the East Roman Empire and was known as Constantinople to the Romans. From the 15th century onwards the city became the centre of the great Ottoman Empire.

The landscape

The deeply-eroded hills and salty basins of the Anatolian Plateau are bordered by several mountain ranges along the Black Sea coast, and the limestone Taurus Mountains *(Toros Daglari)* in the south. A lowland trough divides the Caucasus and the Lesser Caucasus, which form a formidable barrier of peaks in the north.

Limestone weathering in the Anatolian Plateau

Eroded gully
High plateau
Layers of tephra
Remnant landforms

▲ **In central Turkey**, rainwater has chemically weathered away numerous layers of limestone, leaving isolated outcrops and pinnacles and deep eroded gullies.

▶ **The Caucasus are** fold mountains, which formed around the same time as the Taurus Mountains (Toros Daglari) around 65 million years ago and have since been modified by volcanic erruptions.

Lava has flowed over large areas of the Lesser Caucasus within the last five million years, producing extensive basalt plateaux.

The straits of the Bosporus and the Dardanelles, respectively linking the Black and Mediterranean seas with the Sea of Marmara, formed after the last Ice Age, when a rising sea level caused these former river valleys to be flooded.

Many of the rivers crossing the Anatolian Plateau never reach the sea, but drain into salt marshes and shallow salt lakes such as Lake Tuz *(Tuz Gölü)*, where much of the water is lost to evaporation.

Anatolian Plateau

▲ **The white rock terraces** at Pamukkale in western Turkey were formed when underground water, heated by volcanic activity, dissolved minerals in the rocks. When the water reached the surface and evaporated the minerals were left behind in these extraordinary formations.

The earthquake that struck Armenia in 1988 killed over 55,000 people and devastated the country's infrastructure.

The volcanic cone of Mount Ararat is the highest peak in Turkey, with an altitude of 16,853 ft (5137 m).

Long, parallel mountain ranges run from east to west into the Aegean Sea, which has risen since the last Ice Age to form a drowned coastline of numerous islands and extended inlets.

Pamukkale

The folded peaks of the Taurus Mountains *(Toros Daglari)* were formed 60–65 million years ago, at the same time as the Alps. The rock is mainly limestone, with deep caves, gorges and underground rivers.

The Cilician Gates *(Gülek Bogazi)*, a major pass through the Taurus Mountains *(Toros Daglari)*, is the point where streams flow from the interior plateau onto the lowland of Adana.

Thick, temperate forest veils the seaward slopes of the Kaçkar Daglari. The southern slopes, which lie in a rainshadow, are dry and barren.

The granite massif near Surami divides the lowlands of Georgia from the oil-rich basin of Azerbaijan's Kura river, which has built a large delta into the Caspian Sea.

The shallow, saline Lake Van *(Van Gölü)* is the largest lake in Turkey. Dry terraces mark a previous shoreline 181 ft (55 m) above the present water level.

Map key

Population

- ▣ above 5 million
- ◙ 1 million to 5 million
- ◉ 500,000 to 1 million
- ◎ 100,000 to 500,000
- ⊕ 50,000 to 100,000
- ○ 10,000 to 50,000
- ○ below 10,000

Elevation

- 4000m / 13,124ft
- 3000m / 9843ft
- 2000m / 6562ft
- 1000m / 3281ft
- 500m / 1640ft
- 250m / 820ft
- 100m / 328ft
- sea level

▶ **Since the 6th century BC**, the pinnacles and caves of east-central Anatolia have been utilized as dwellings. Many are still inhabited today.

Scale 1:4,500,000

Km
0 10 20   40   60   80   100 120

Miles
0 10 20   40   60   80   100 120

projection: Lambert Conformal Conic

▲ **The fisheries of** Azerbaijan are noted for their hauls of sturgeon, and the Caspian Sea accounts for 80% of the world's total catch. However, stocks are now under serious threat due to overfishing.

▲ **Traditional steam baths** are found throughout the region, and are used for socializing as well as for bathing.

The Near East

IRAQ, ISRAEL, JORDAN, LEBANON, SYRIA

Some of the world's oldest civilizations developed in this region – the Fertile Crescent – which is venerated by Jews, Muslims and Christians, but torn by competing religious, ethnic and national claims to the land. Turkish Ottoman rule ended with the First World War and the region was divided into areas administered by Britain and France. The UN endorsed calls for a Jewish homeland in what was then Palestine and in 1948 the state of Israel was declared. Hostility towards the Jewish state led to a series of wars with its Arab neighbours. After 2000, attempts to broker peaceful resolutions with both the Palestinian population and with adjacent Arab states were hampered by a revival of Islamic militarism and conflicting international interests in the oil-rich region. This led to an Israeli retrenchment and culminated in a US-led invasion of Iraq in 2003, which toppled the Ba'athist regime of Saddam Hussein in the name of a 'war on terror'.

Using the land and sea

Water scarcity limits cropland to the north and to areas watered principally by the Tigris, Euphrates and Jordan rivers. In Israel, new irrigation techniques are allowing cultivation in the arid Negev. Wheat is the chief grain and large areas of scrub support livestock herding. Commercial produce includes dates, tobacco, citrus fruits, olives, grapes and cotton, which is Syria's main export crop. Fishing is still important in the Mediterranean.

The urban/rural population divide

urban 70%   rural 30%

0 10 20 30 40 50 60 70 80 90 100

Population density	Total land area
217 people per sq mile (84 people per sq km)	325,460 sq miles (843,160 sq km)

Land use and agricultural distribution

- sheep
- cereals
- citrus fruits
- cotton
- dates
- fishing
- rice
- tobacco

- ▪ capital cities
- • major towns

- pasture
- cropland
- wetland
- desert

Transport and industry

The petrochemical industry is well established, and central to the economies of Syria and Iraq, which was the world's second largest oil exporter before the war with Iran which began in 1980. Lebanon has traditionally been a centre for commerce, while Israel has a well-diversified economy with an expanding tourist industry, despite few natural resources.

The transport network

- 49,859 miles (80,249 km)
- 1365 miles (2197 km)
- 3826 miles (6158 km)
- 1171 miles (1885 km)

Jordan's sea port of Al 'Aqabah is connected to Damascus in Syria by road and rail. This route to the Red Sea provides for large exports of phosphate and trade with states in the Persian Gulf.

Major industry and infrastructure

- car manufacture
- cement
- chemicals
- electronics
- finance
- food processing
- iron & steel
- oil
- oil refining
- textiles

- ▪ capital cities
- • major towns
- ⊕ international airports
- major roads
- major industrial areas

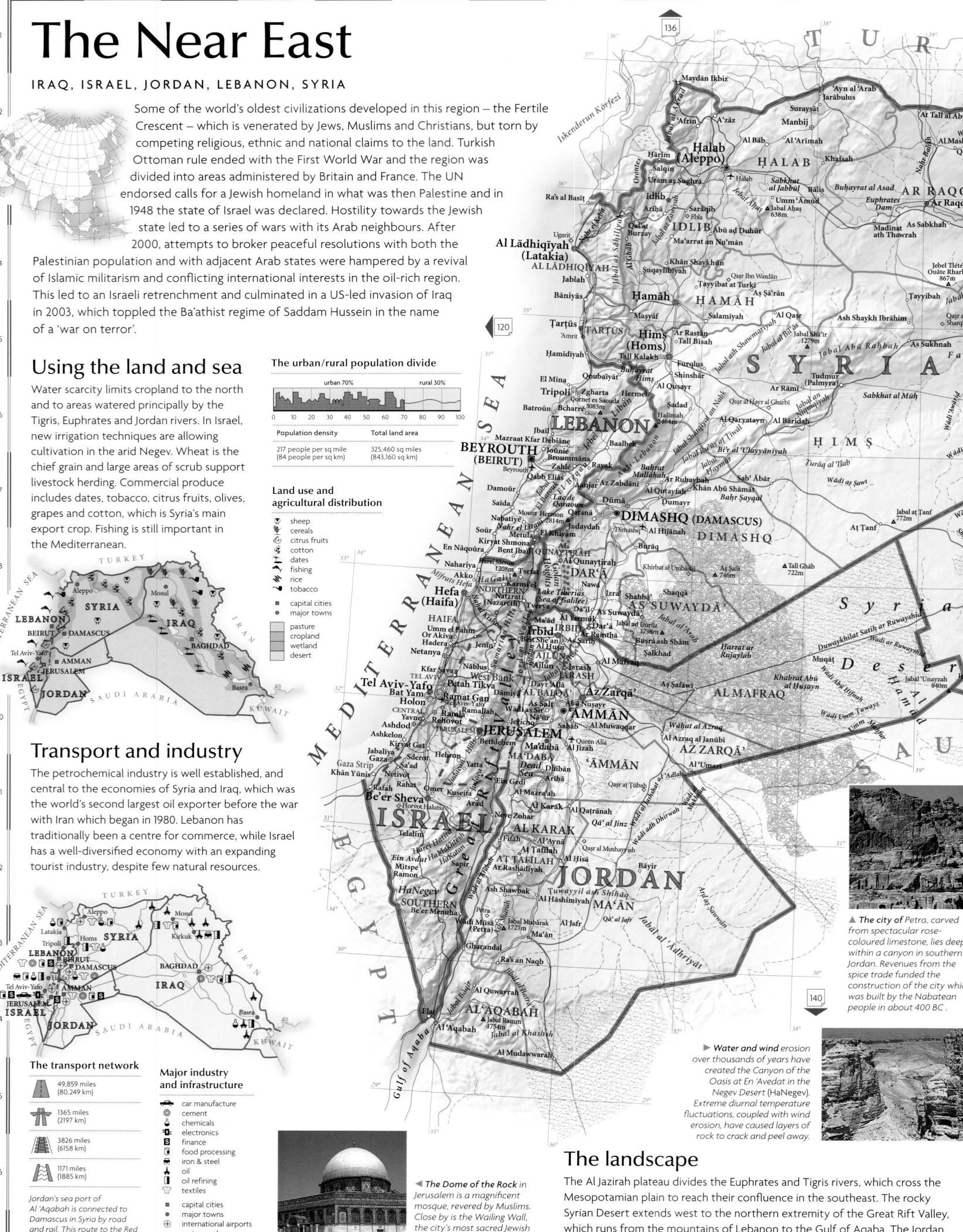

◄ The Dome of the Rock in Jerusalem is a magnificent mosque, revered by Muslims. Close by is the Wailing Wall, the city's most sacred Jewish landmark and the Church of the Holy Sepulchre, a famous Christian place of worship.

▲ The city of Petra, carved from spectacular rose-coloured limestone, lies deep within a canyon in southern Jordan. Revenues from the spice trade funded the construction of the city which was built by the Nabatean people in about 400 BC.

▶ Water and wind erosion over thousands of years have created the Canyon of the Oasis at En 'Avedat in the Negev Desert (HaNegev). Extreme diurnal temperature fluctuations, coupled with wind erosion, have caused layers of rock to crack and peel away.

The landscape

The Al Jazirah plateau divides the Euphrates and Tigris rivers, which cross the Mesopotamian plain to reach their confluence in the southeast. The rocky Syrian Desert extends west to the northern extremity of the Great Rift Valley, which runs from the mountains of Lebanon to the Gulf of Aqaba. The Jordan river flows south along this trough into the Dead Sea, divided from the Mediterranean coastal plain by a steep-sided plateau.

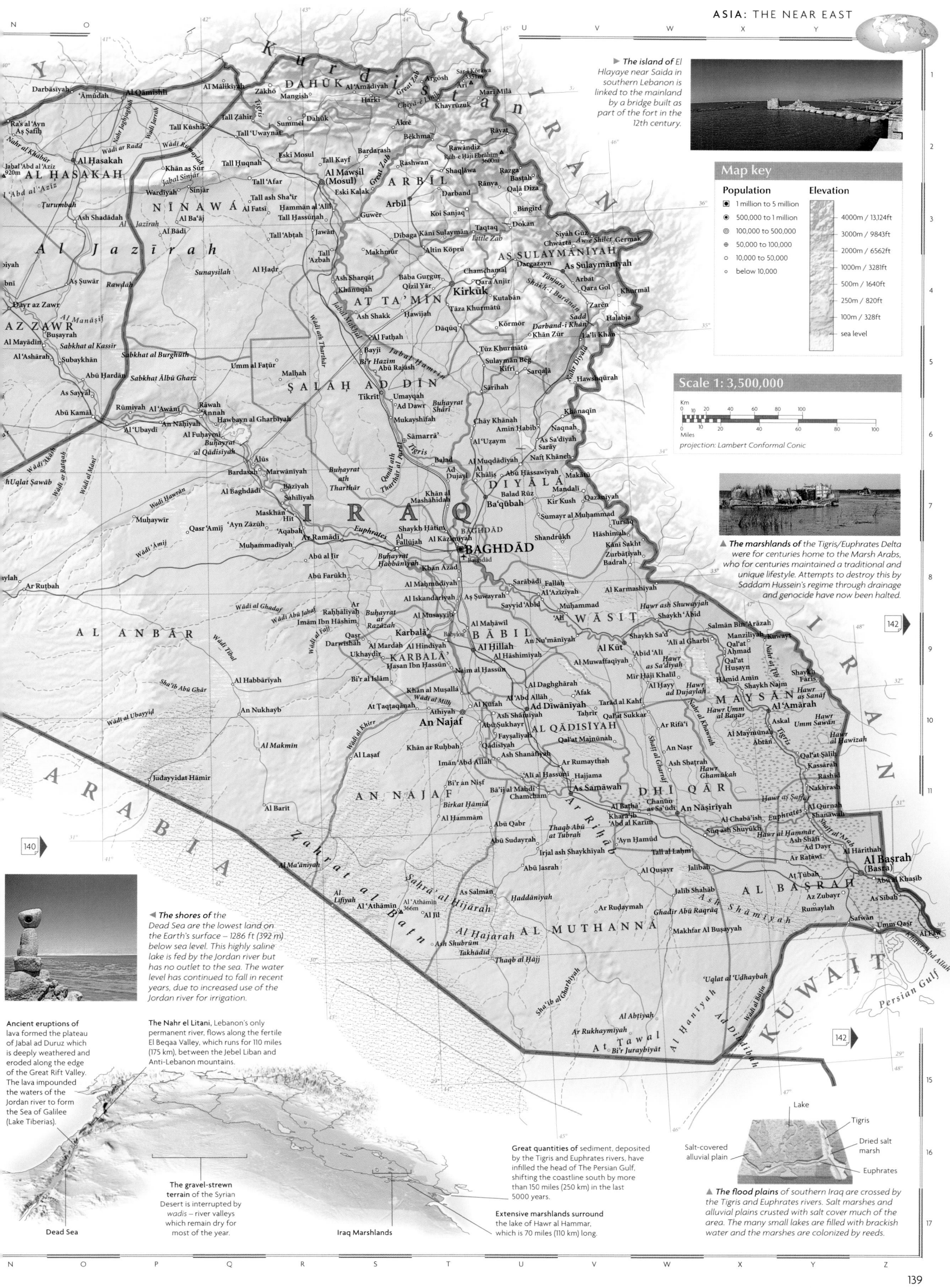

▶ The island of El Hlayaye near Saida in southern Lebanon is linked to the mainland by a bridge built as part of the fort in the 12th century.

Map key

Population
- ◉ 1 million to 5 million
- ◉ 500,000 to 1 million
- ⊙ 100,000 to 500,000
- ⊕ 50,000 to 100,000
- ○ 10,000 to 50,000
- ∘ below 10,000

Elevation
- 4000m / 13,124ft
- 3000m / 9843ft
- 2000m / 6562ft
- 1000m / 3281ft
- 500m / 1640ft
- 250m / 820ft
- 100m / 328ft
- sea level

Scale 1: 3,500,000

Km
0 10 20 40 60 80 100
Miles
0 10 20 40 60 80 100

projection: Lambert Conformal Conic

▲ The marshlands of the Tigris/Euphrates Delta were for centuries home to the Marsh Arabs, who for centuries maintained a traditional and unique lifestyle. Attempts to destroy this by Saddam Hussein's regime through drainage and genocide have now been halted.

◀ The shores of the Dead Sea are the lowest land on the Earth's surface – 1286 ft (392 m) below sea level. This highly saline lake is fed by the Jordan river but has no outlet to the sea. The water level has continued to fall in recent years, due to increased use of the Jordan river for irrigation.

Ancient eruptions of lava formed the plateau of Jabal ad Duruz which is deeply weathered and eroded along the edge of the Great Rift Valley. The lava impounded the waters of the Jordan river to form the Sea of Galilee (Lake Tiberias).

Dead Sea

The Nahr el Litani, Lebanon's only permanent river, flows along the fertile El Beqaa Valley, which runs for 110 miles (175 km), between the Jebel Liban and Anti-Lebanon mountains.

The gravel-strewn terrain of the Syrian Desert is interrupted by wadis – river valleys which remain dry for most of the year.

Iraq Marshlands

Great quantities of sediment, deposited by the Tigris and Euphrates rivers, have infilled the head of The Persian Gulf, shifting the coastline south by more than 150 miles (250 km) in the last 5000 years.

Extensive marshlands surround the lake of Hawr al Hammar, which is 70 miles (110 km) long.

Lake
Tigris
Dried salt marsh
Salt-covered alluvial plain
Euphrates

▲ The flood plains of southern Iraq are crossed by the Tigris and Euphrates rivers. Salt marshes and alluvial plains crusted with salt cover much of the area. The many small lakes are filled with brackish water and the marshes are colonized by reeds.

The Arabian Peninsula

BAHRAIN, KUWAIT, OMAN, QATAR, SAUDI ARABIA, UNITED ARAB EMIRATES (UAE), YEMEN

Huge expanses of desert cover much of the Arabian Peninsula, limiting settlement to oases, the mountains along the Red Sea and coastal belts. The most populous area is the fertile highlands of Yemen. The Islamic faith and Arabic language give the region a cultural and religious unity, and the Saudi city of Mecca *(Makkah)* is Islam's most holy place, visited by over two million pilgrims each year. More than half the world's oil reserves are contained in this region, and the exploitation of oil and gas has brought great wealth, particularly to Saudi Arabia. Yemen and Oman are the least developed of the Arabian states, with large rural populations. Within Saudi Arabia over 86% of the people live in urban areas.

Using the land

Most of the Arabian Peninsula is unsuited to settled agriculture, making irrigation and land reclamation projects essential. The narrow coastal plain and isolated oases, commonly amounting to less than 1% of the land area, are used to cultivate grains, coffee and exotic fruits. Goats, sheep and camels are widespread throughout the region.

The urban/rural population divide

urban 64%	rural 36%

0 10 20 30 40 50 60 70 80 90 100

Population density	Total land area
50 people per sq mile (19 people per sq km)	1,147,856 sq miles (2,973,720 sq km)

Land use and agricultural distribution

- goats
- sheep
- cereals
- coffee
- dates
- fruit
- capital cities
- major towns
- pasture
- cropland
- desert

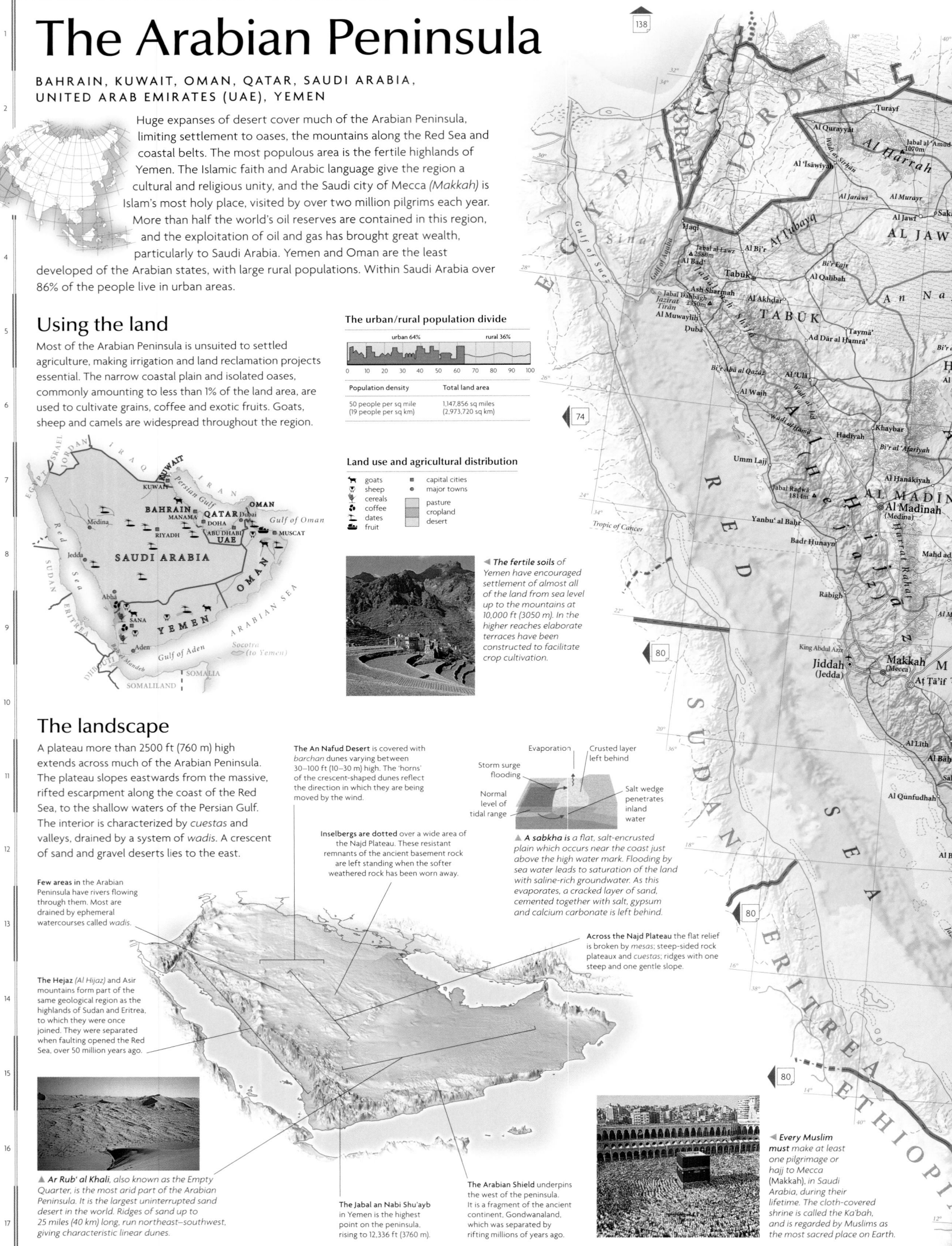

◄ **The fertile soils** of Yemen have encouraged settlement of almost all of the land from sea level up to the mountains at 10,000 ft (3050 m). In the higher reaches elaborate terraces have been constructed to facilitate crop cultivation.

The landscape

A plateau more than 2500 ft (760 m) high extends across much of the Arabian Peninsula. The plateau slopes eastwards from the massive, rifted escarpment along the coast of the Red Sea, to the shallow waters of the Persian Gulf. The interior is characterized by *cuestas* and valleys, drained by a system of *wadis*. A crescent of sand and gravel deserts lies to the east.

Few areas in the Arabian Peninsula have rivers flowing through them. Most are drained by ephemeral watercourses called *wadis*.

The An Nafud Desert is covered with *barchan* dunes varying between 30–100 ft (10–30 m) high. The 'horns' of the crescent-shaped dunes reflect the direction in which they are being moved by the wind.

Inselbergs are dotted over a wide area of the Najd Plateau. These resistant remnants of the ancient basement rock are left standing when the softer weathered rock has been worn away.

▲ **A sabkha is** a flat, salt-encrusted plain which occurs near the coast just above the high water mark. Flooding by sea water leads to saturation of the land with saline-rich groundwater. As this evaporates, a cracked layer of sand, cemented together with salt, gypsum and calcium carbonate is left behind.

Across the Najd Plateau the flat relief is broken by *mesas*; steep-sided rock plateaux and *cuestas*; ridges with one steep and one gentle slope.

The Hejaz *(Al Hijaz)* and Asir mountains form part of the same geological region as the highlands of Sudan and Eritrea, to which they were once joined. They were separated when faulting opened the Red Sea, over 50 million years ago.

▲ **Ar Rub' al Khali**, also known as the Empty Quarter, is the most arid part of the Arabian Peninsula. It is the largest uninterrupted sand desert in the world. Ridges of sand up to 25 miles (40 km) long, run northeast–southwest, giving characteristic linear dunes.

The Jabal an Nabi Shu'ayb in Yemen is the highest point on the peninsula, rising to 12,336 ft (3760 m).

The Arabian Shield underpins the west of the peninsula. It is a fragment of the ancient continent, Gondwanaland, which was separated by rifting millions of years ago.

◄ **Every Muslim must** make at least one pilgrimage or *hajj* to Mecca (Makkah), in Saudi Arabia, during their lifetime. The cloth-covered shrine is called the Ka'bah, and is regarded by Muslims as the most sacred place on Earth.

138

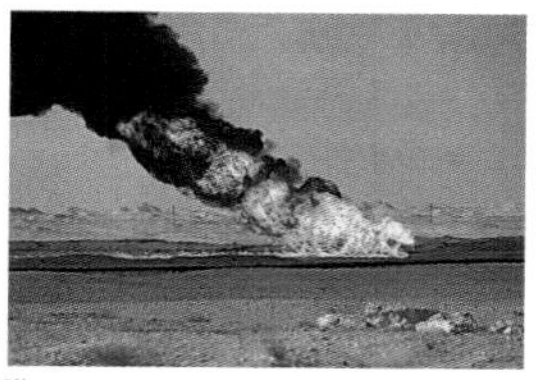

◄ *Saudi Arabia contains the world's largest oil reserves, lying mainly along the Persian Gulf coast. Each day the region produces around 10 million barrels of oil. Here, in the desert, excess oil is being burnt off.*

Transport and industry

The extraction and refining of oil and gas are the major industrial activities in the Arabian Peninsula. The region also has an active construction sector, with many Arab cities reflecting the wealth generated by the oil industry. The service sector is dominated by financial and technical institutions, which, like the construction sector, mainly serve the oil industry. Traditional handicrafts such as carpet-weaving are found in rural areas.

The transport network

- 44,832 miles (72,159 km)
- 673 miles (1083 km)
- 670 miles (1078 km)
- none

Internal surface transport is poorly developed across the peninsula. Along the coast, commercial routes have developed, but connections between bordering states rely on major airports.

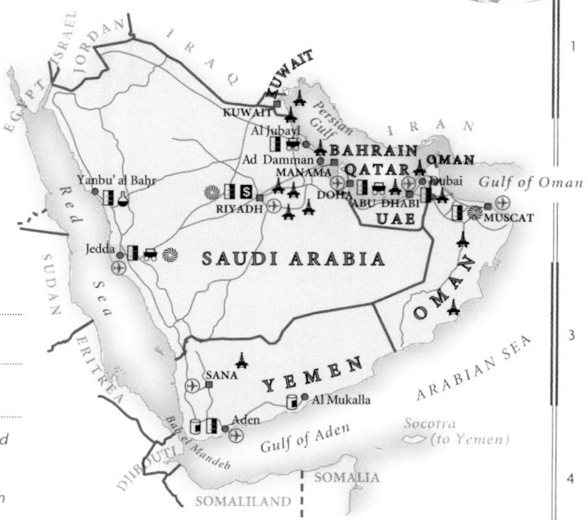

Major industry and infrastructure

- cement
- chemicals
- iron & steel
- oil
- oil refining
- food processing
- capital cities
- major towns
- international airports
- major roads
- major industrial areas

► *Seasonal watercourses or wadis drain much of the interior of the Arabian Peninsula. Although they remain dry for much of the year, they are prone to flash floods after heavy rains.*

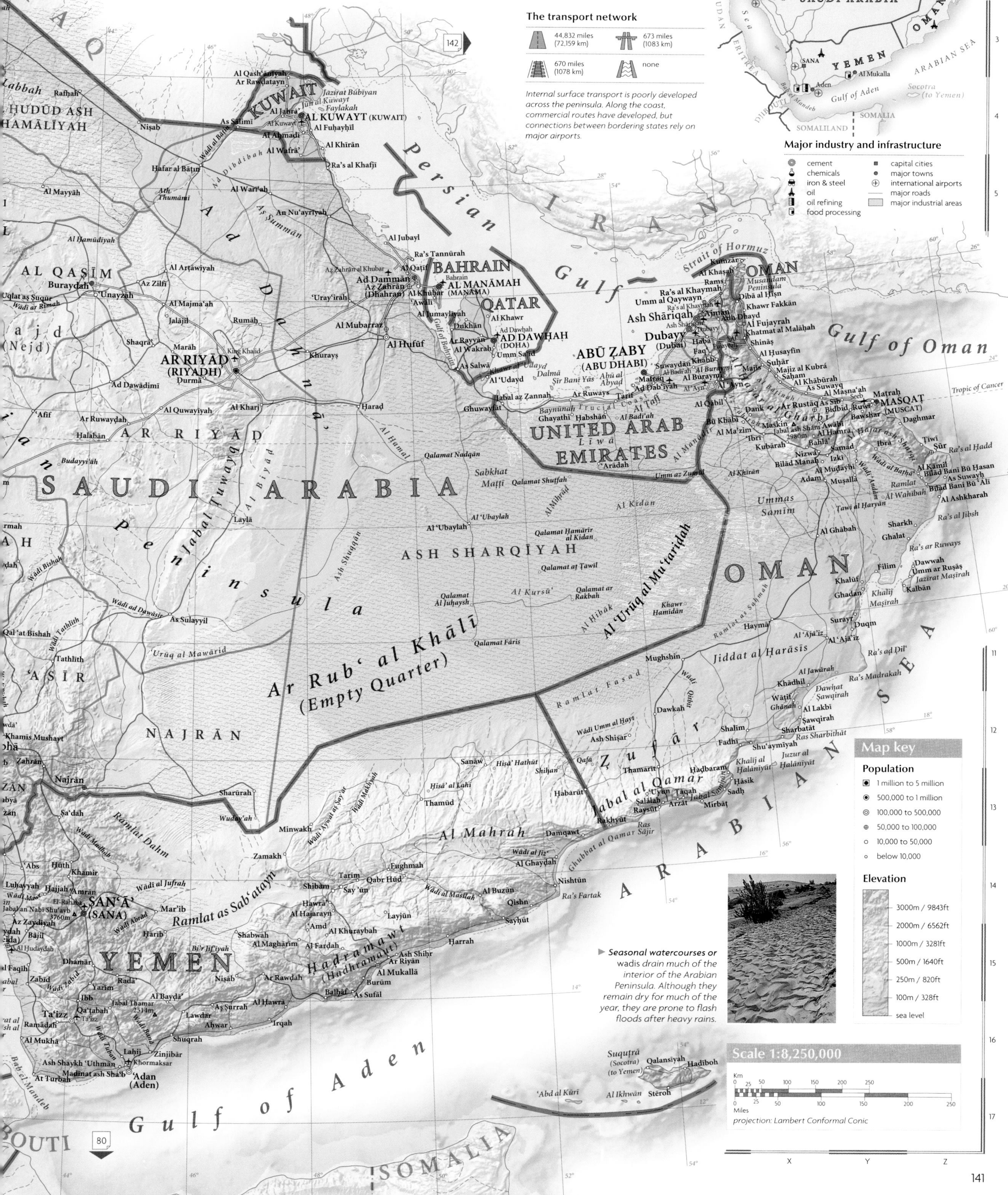

Map key

Population

- 1 million to 5 million
- 500,000 to 1 million
- 100,000 to 500,000
- 50,000 to 100,000
- 10,000 to 50,000
- below 10,000

Elevation

- 3000m / 9843ft
- 2000m / 6562ft
- 1000m / 3281ft
- 500m / 1640ft
- 250m / 820ft
- 100m / 328ft
- sea level

Scale 1:8,250,000

Km 0 25 50 100 150 200 250

Miles 0 25 50 100 150 200 250

projection: Lambert Conformal Conic

142

80

Iran & the Gulf states

BAHRAIN, IRAN, KUWAIT, QATAR, UNITED ARAB EMIRATES (UAE)

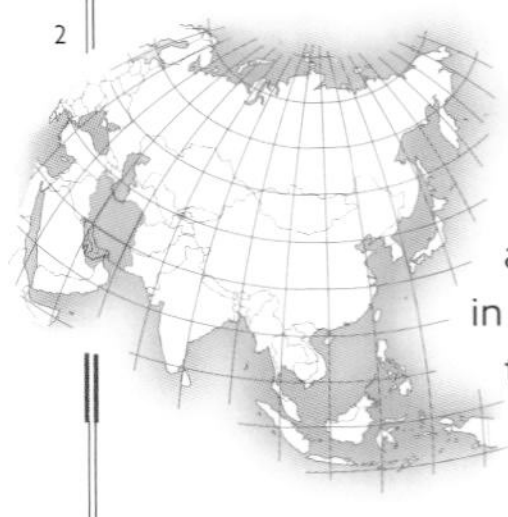

The discovery of oil in the Persian Gulf in the 1930s brought great wealth to the surrounding states. The revenue was largely used to modernize industry and infrastructure, initiating great social change in these formerly agrarian countries. Today, over 90% of the people in the Gulf states live in urban areas, and foreign nationals make up a sizeable proportion of the population in Kuwait, Qatar and the United Arab Emirates. The importance of control of the oil reserves has led to a number of territorial disputes, including most recently the Iran–Iraq War (1980-88) and the First Gulf War (1991). Islam is practised almost exclusively throughout the region and two distinct strands are found; Sunni Muslims in Qatar, Kuwait and UAE, and Shi'a Muslims in Iran and Bahrain. In 1979 Iran became the world's largest theocracy.

The landscape

The land rises steeply from the fragmented coastal lowlands bordering the Persian Gulf, to reach Iran's interior plateau, bounded by heavily-eroded mountain chains. An unstable plate boundary runs northwest to southeast across Iran causing frequent earthquakes. On the sandy west coast of the Persian Gulf, the relief is generally flat, with patches of salt marsh. Bahrain consists of two groups of islands, which are mostly small and rocky.

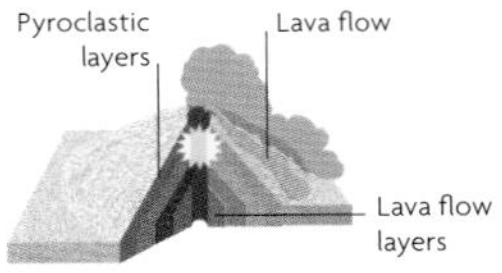

Pyroclastic layers
Lava flow
Lava flow layers

▲ **Qolleh-ye Damavand** in the Elburz Mountains is a composite volcano. It comprises layers of lava and pyroclasts – fragmentary rocks which accumulate on the slopes of the volcano after being ejected into the air.

▲ **Marine sediments from** deep beneath the ancient Tethys Sea have been uplifted to form the Elburz Mountains, which stretch along the shores of the Caspian Sea, northern Iran.

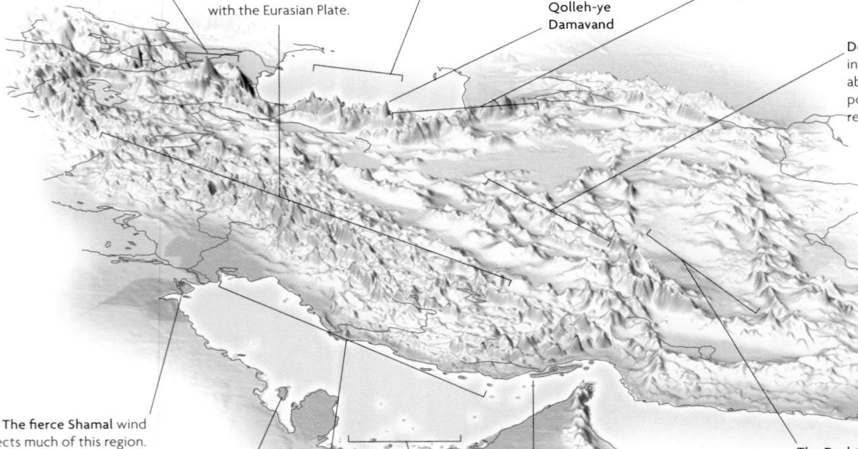

Lava and ash from previous volcanic activity cover a 200 mile (320 km) stretch from the border with Azerbaijan to the Caspian Sea.

Iran's two mountain chains, the Zagros and Elburz, were uplifted at the same time as the Alps in Europe, when the African Plate collided with the Eurasian Plate.

Caspian Sea

Qolleh-ye Damavand

Dominated by a vast, semi-arid interior plateau, most of Iran lies above 1640 ft (500 m). The region is poorly drained with many of its basins remaining dry for months at a time.

The fierce Shamal wind affects much of this region. Every summer it blows dust south from the flood plains of the Tigris and Euphrates, reducing visibility to such **an extent that** Kuwait International Airport is frequently forced to close.

Autumn winds blowing across the Persian Gulf can reach speeds of up to 95 mph (150 kmph) causing severe storms, squalls and waterspouts.

The Dasht-e Lut

Prolific springs tapping artesian water make cultivation possible across the north of Bahrain's main island. This provides a sharp contrast to the sandy plains in the south and west.

The oilfields of the Persian Gulf are formed from marine shale deposits lying in sedimentary basins at the margins of the Zagros Mountains.

Numerous islands lie along the southern coast of the Persian Gulf. Some of these are salt domes, created when less dense salts were displaced and forced up to the surface by denser, overlying strata.

◀ **The Dasht-e Lut** covers a large portion of eastern Iran with its dry, wind-eroded plain of scattered sandstone pillars and salty depressions. During the summer, temperatures soar, making it one of the world's hottest, driest places.

◀ **All of the** Gulf states have commercial fishing fleets. Before the discovery of oil, fishing was the region's leading industry.

Using the land and sea

Along the coast of the Caspian Sea, desalinated water allows fruits and vegetables to be produced, although water shortages and desert soils still limit farming. Sheep are the most important livestock raised in Iran and commercial forests cover the northwest of the country. Shrimp stocks were decimated by pollution during the Gulf War, but fishing remains important for domestic and export markets.

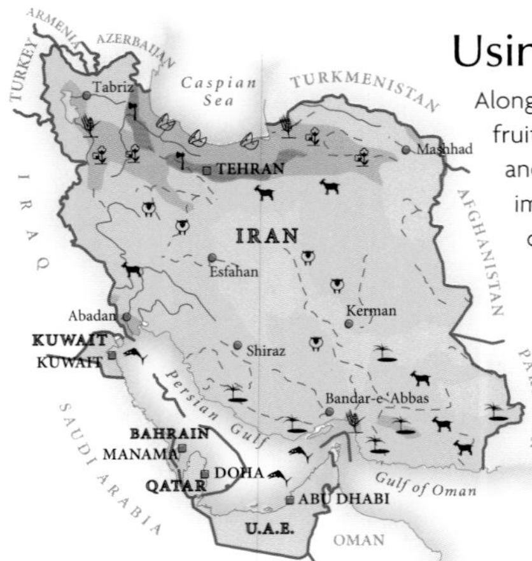

◀ **The Kuwait Towers** in the centre of Kuwait are symbols of the vast wealth oil has brought to the country. Before 1960, the city had only one main street and was surrounded by a mud wall.

Land use and agricultural distribution

- goats
- sheep
- cereals
- citrus fruits
- cotton
- dates
- fishing
- timber
- capital cities
- major towns
- pasture
- cropland
- forest
- desert
- wetland

The urban/rural population divide

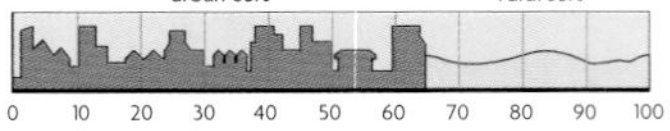

urban 65%   rural 35%

0 10 20 30 40 50 60 70 80 90 100

Population density	Total land area
112 people per sq mile (43 people per sq km)	642,883 sq miles (1,665,500 sq km)

◄ *Many volcanoes lie in Iran's 1200 mile (1930 km) volcanic belt, including the country's highest peak, the now-extinct Qolleh-ye Damavand at 18,600 ft (5671 m).*

146

► *Extensive oil and gas exploitation in the Gulf region has allowed the economic transformation of the Gulf states. Consequently, many of these states have a hugely improved per capita income compared to the 1960's.*

Transport and industry

Both onshore and offshore oil reserves are exploited throughout the region. Kuwait not only extracts but also refines 80% of its oil. Bahrain has diversified its economy to become the main commercial and financial centre in the Persian Gulf. Iran produces a wide range of products: textile mills are widespread and carpet-weaving is an important export industry.

Major industry and infrastructure

- carpet manufacture
- chemicals
- finance
- food processing
- oil
- oil refining
- textiles
- capital city
- major towns
- international airports
- major roads
- major industrial areas

The transport network

63,543 miles (102,274 km)	884 miles (1423 km)
3822 miles (6151 km)	562 miles (904 km)

Major towns and neighbouring countries are linked by adequate road networks, although rural areas are less well served. Bahrain is linked to the mainland by a 15 mile (25 km) long causeway.

Map key

Population

- above 5 million
- 1 million to 5 million
- 500,000 to 1 million
- 100,000 to 500,000
- 50,000 to 100,000
- 10,000 to 50,000
- below 10,000

Elevation

- 4000m / 13,124ft
- 3000m / 9843ft
- 2000m / 6562ft
- 1000m / 3281ft
- 500m / 1640ft
- 250m / 820ft
- 100m / 328ft
- sea level

Scale 1:6,000,000

Km
0 20 40 60 80 100 120 140 160 180 200

Miles
0 20 40 60 80 100 120 140 160 180 200

projection: Lambert Conformal Conic

Map labels

TURKMENISTAN
AFGHANISTAN
PAKISTAN
OMAN
UNITED ARAB EMIRATES
QATAR
BAHRAIN
IRAN

Caspian Sea
Persian Gulf
Gulf of Oman
Strait of Hormuz
Makran Coast
Tropic of Cancer

Koppeh Dagh
Alborz (Elburz Mountains)
Kūhhā-ye Kūhhā
Dasht-e Kavir
Iranian Plateau
Dasht-e Lūt
Zagros Mountains
Makran

GOLESTĀN, MĀZANDARĀN, SEMNĀN, KHORĀSĀN-E SHEMĀLĪ, KHORĀSĀN-E RAZAVĪ, KHORĀSĀN-E JANŪBĪ, QOM, ESFAHĀN, YAZD, KERMĀN, FĀRS, HORMOZGĀN, SĪSTĀN VA BALŪCHESTĀN, CHAHĀR MAHALL VA BAKHTĪĀRĪ

TEHRĀN, Mashhad, Gorgan, Bojnūrd, Sārī, Qom, Esfahān, Yazd, Kermān, Shīrāz, Zāhedān, Bandar-e 'Abbās, Bandar-e Būshehr, AD DAWHAH (DOHA), ABŪ ZABY (ABU DHABI), Dubayy (Dubai)

143

Kazakhstan

Abundant natural resources lie in the immense steppe grasslands, deserts and central plateau of the former Soviet republic of Kazakhstan. An intensive programme of industrial and agricultural development to exploit these resources during the Soviet era resulted in catastrophic industrial pollution, including fallout from nuclear testing and the shrinkage of the Aral Sea. Since independence, the government has encouraged foreign investment and liberalized the economy to promote growth. The adoption of Kazakh as the national language is intended to encourage a new sense of national identity in a state where living conditions for the majority remain harsh, both in cramped urban centres and impoverished rural areas.

Transport and industry

The single most important industry in Kazakhstan is mining, based around extensive oil deposits near the Caspian Sea, the world's largest chromium mine, and vast reserves of iron ore. Recent foreign investment has helped to develop industries including food processing and steel manufacture, and to expand the exploitation of mineral resources. The Russian space programme is still based at Baykonyr, near Kyzylorda in central Kazakhstan.

Major industry and infrastructure

- ⬡ chemicals
- ⚙ engineering
- 🐟 fish processing
- ▣ food processing
- ■ iron & steel
- △ metallurgy
- ⛏ mining
- ⚓ oil
- ■ capital cities
- ● major towns
- ⊕ international airports
- — major roads
- ▢ major industrial areas

The transport network

🛣 48,263 miles (77,680 km)

🛤 none

🚃 8483 miles (13,660 km)

🚃 3900 miles (2423 km)

Industrial areas in the north and east are well-connected to Russia. Air and rail links with Germany and China have been established through foreign investment. Better access to Baltic ports is being sought.

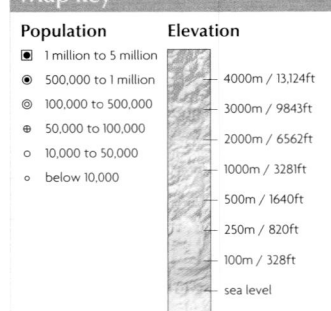

◀ *An open-cast coal mine in Kazakhstan. Foreign investment is being actively sought by the Kazakh government in order to fully exploit the potential of the country's rich mineral reserves.*

Map key

Population

- ▣ 1 million to 5 million
- ◉ 500,000 to 1 million
- ◎ 100,000 to 500,000
- ⊕ 50,000 to 100,000
- ● 10,000 to 50,000
- ○ below 10,000

Elevation

- 4000m / 13,124ft
- 3000m / 9843ft
- 2000m / 6562ft
- 1000m / 3281ft
- 500m / 1640ft
- 250m / 820ft
- 100m / 328ft
- sea level

Using the land and sea

The rearing of large herds of sheep and goats on the steppe grasslands forms the core of Kazakh agriculture. Arable cultivation and cotton-growing in pasture and desert areas was encouraged during the Soviet era, but relative yields are low. The heavy use of fertilizers and the diversion of natural water sources for irrigation has degraded much of the land.

Land use and agricultural distribution

- 🐄 cattle
- 🐐 goats
- 🐑 sheep
- 🌿 cotton
- 🐟 fishing
- 🌾 wheat
- ■ capital cities
- ● major towns
- ▢ pasture
- ▢ cropland
- ▢ forest
- ▢ mountain region
- ▢ desert

The urban/rural population divide

urban 56%	rural 44%

0　10　20　30　40　50　60　70　80　90　100

Population density	Total land area
16 people per sq mile (6 people per sq km)	1,048,878 sq miles (2,717,300 sq km)

◀ *The nomadic peoples who moved their herds around the steppe grasslands are now largely settled, although echoes of their traditional lifestyle, in particular their superb riding skills, remain.*

Scale 1:7,000,000

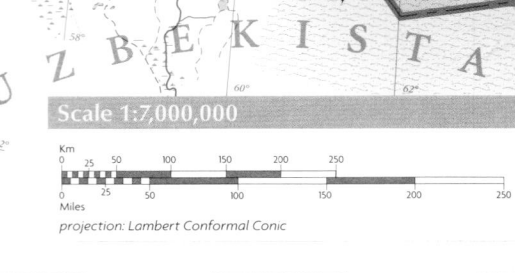

projection: Lambert Conformal Conic

The landscape

Stretching more than 1250 miles (2000 km) from the Caspian Sea in the west to China in the east, more than 40% of Kazakhstan is covered by steppe grasslands which give way to barren desert in the south. The land rises eastwards towards the mineral-rich central plateau, to form the Altai Mountains.

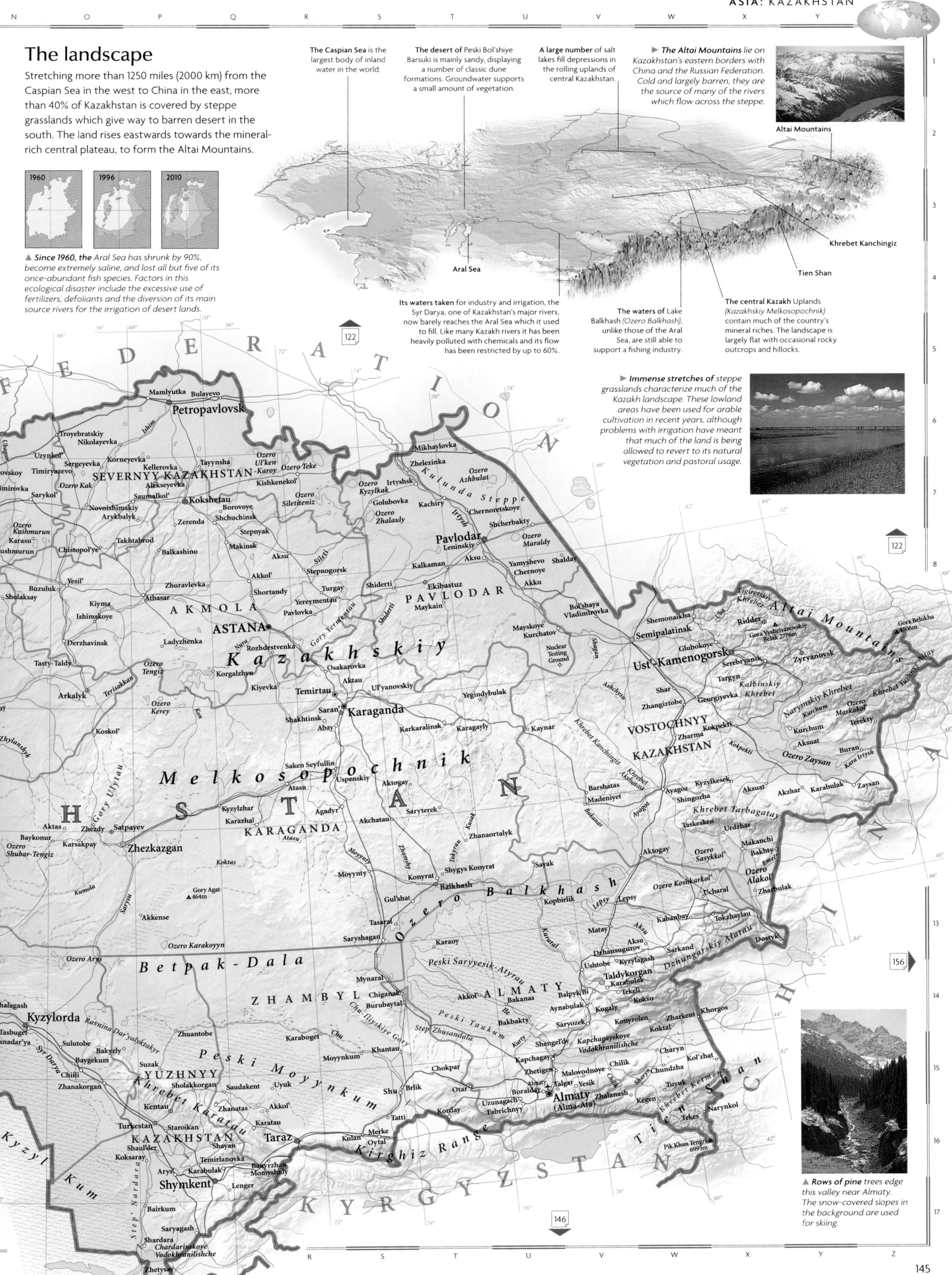

1960 **1996** **2010**

▲ *Since 1960, the* Aral Sea has shrunk by 90%, become extremely saline, and lost all but five of its once-abundant fish species. Factors in this ecological disaster include the excessive use of fertilizers, defoliants and the diversion of its main source rivers for the irrigation of desert lands.

The Caspian Sea is the largest body of inland water in the world.

The desert of Peski Bol'shiye Barsuki is mainly sandy, displaying a number of classic dune formations. Groundwater supports a small amount of vegetation.

A large number of salt lakes fill depressions in the rolling uplands of central Kazakhstan.

▶ *The Altai Mountains* lie on Kazakhstan's eastern borders with China and the Russian Federation. Cold and largely barren, they are the source of many of the rivers which flow across the steppe.

Altai Mountains

Khrebet Kanchingiz

Tien Shan

Aral Sea

Its waters taken for industry and irrigation, the Syr Darya, one of Kazakhstan's major rivers, now barely reaches the Aral Sea which it used to fill. Like many Kazakh rivers it has been heavily polluted with chemicals and its flow has been restricted by up to 60%.

The waters of Lake Balkhash (Ozero Balkhash), unlike those of the Aral Sea, are still able to support a fishing industry.

The central Kazakh Uplands (Kazakhskiy Melkosopochnik) contain much of the country's mineral riches. The landscape is largely flat with occasional rocky outcrops and hillocks.

▶ *Immense stretches of* steppe grasslands characterize much of the Kazakh landscape. These lowland areas have been used for arable cultivation in recent years, although problems with irrigation have meant that much of the land is being allowed to revert to its natural vegetation and pastoral usage.

▲ *Rows of pine* trees edge this valley near Almaty. The snow-covered slopes in the background are used for skiing.

Central Asia

KYRGYZSTAN, TAJIKISTAN, TURKMENISTAN, UZBEKISTAN

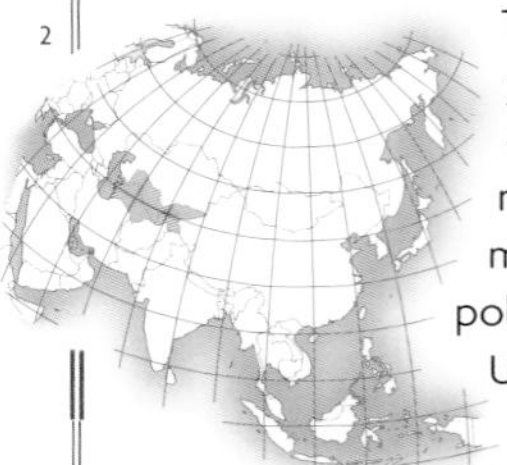

The four republics that declared independence in 1991 were created in the early years of the Soviet Union, promoting ethnic divisions in a region whose common focus, since the 8th century, has been Islam. Traditional rural and nomadic ways of life have survived the Soviet era, while the benefits of modern industry and grand irrigation schemes have resulted in severe pollution in the delicate, arid environment of the steppe, particularly in Uzbekistan. Many ethnic minority groups are scattered among the four republics, with isolated communities in the mountains of Kyrgyzstan.

The current Islamic revival has brought hope of greater regional unity, in spite of religious factionalism which, in 1992, plunged Tajikistan into civil war.

▲ **The southern shoreline** of the Aral Sea has retreated over 30 miles (48 km) since 1960. A major cause is the diversion of water from the Amu Darya river for irrigation via the Kara Kum Canal (Garagum Kanaly).

◄ **The desert of** the Kara Kum (Garagum) occupies over 70% of Turkmenistan; its wind-scoured surface of dune ridges and depressions severely limits human settlement.

Map key

Population
- ◉ 1 million to 5 million
- ◎ 500,000 to 1 million
- ⊚ 100,000 to 500,000
- ⊕ 50,000 to 100,000
- ⊙ 10,000 to 50,000
- ○ below 10,000

Elevation
- 6000m / 19,686ft
- 4000m / 13,124ft
- 3000m / 9843ft
- 2000m / 6562ft
- 1000m / 3281ft
- 500m / 1640ft
- 250m / 820ft
- 100m / 328ft
- sea level

Transport and industry

Fossil fuels are extracted and processed in all four states, with scope for further exploitation. Agriculture provides raw materials for many industries, including food and textiles processing, and the manufacture of leather goods, clothing and carpets. Farm machinery is also produced.

The transport network

73,658 miles (118,555 km)	87 miles (140 km)
4773 miles (7683 km)	1180 miles (1900 km)

The Kara Kum Canal (Garagumskiy Kanal) runs for 870 miles (1400 km) from the Amu Darya river to the Caspian Sea. The canal is principally used for irrigation but is navigable for 280 miles (450 km).

Major industry and infrastructure

- carpet weaving
- chemicals
- engineering
- food processing
- oil & gas
- textiles
- ■ capital cities
- major towns
- ⊕ international airports
- major roads
- major industrial areas

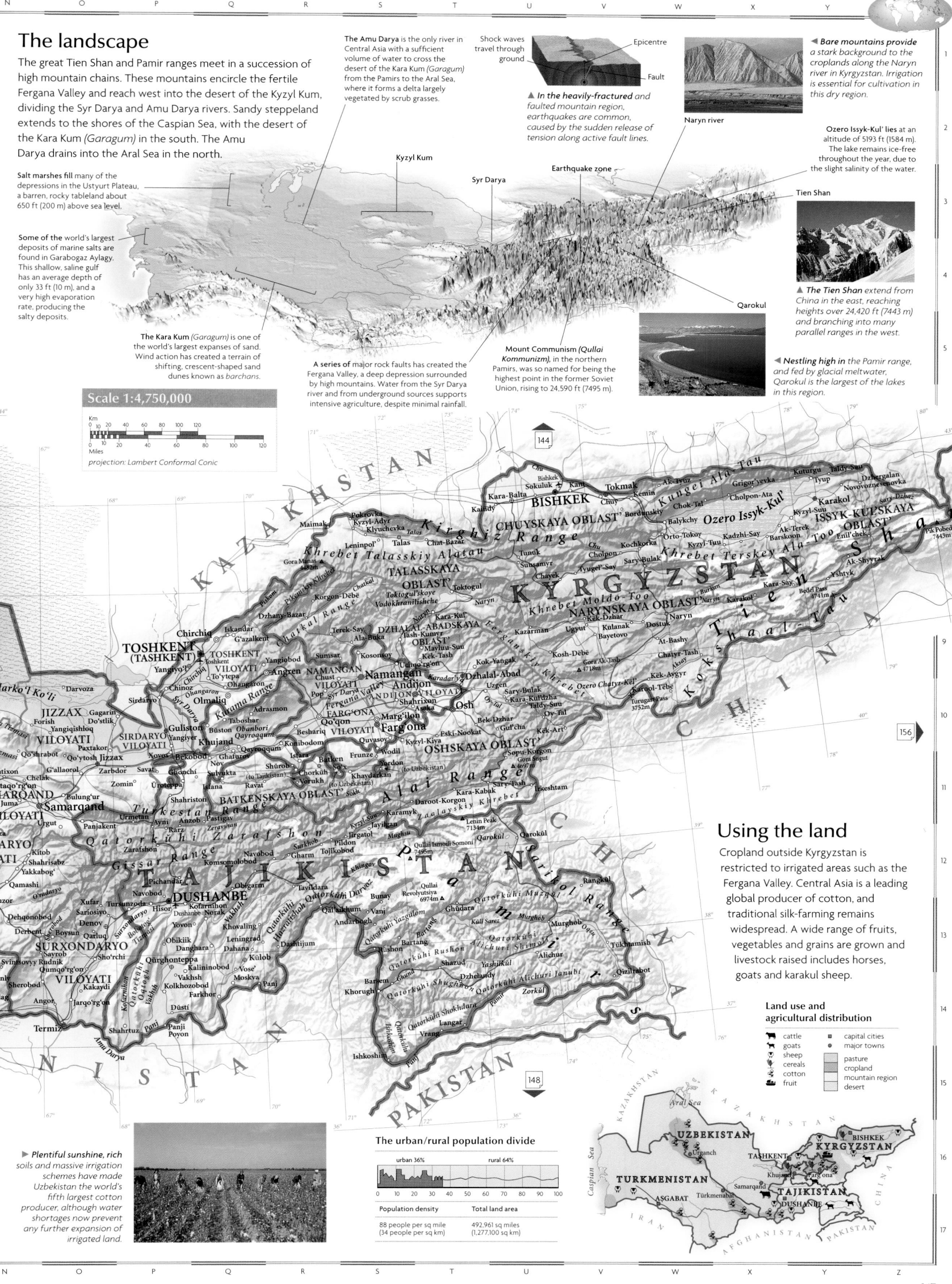

The landscape

The great Tien Shan and Pamir ranges meet in a succession of high mountain chains. These mountains encircle the fertile Fergana Valley and reach west into the desert of the Kyzyl Kum, dividing the Syr Darya and Amu Darya rivers. Sandy steppeland extends to the shores of the Caspian Sea, with the desert of the Kara Kum (Garagum) in the south. The Amu Darya drains into the Aral Sea in the north.

Salt marshes fill many of the depressions in the Ustyurt Plateau, a barren, rocky tableland about 650 ft (200 m) above sea level.

Some of the world's largest deposits of marine salts are found in Garabogaz Aylagy. This shallow, saline gulf has an average depth of only 33 ft (10 m), and a very high evaporation rate, producing the salty deposits.

The Kara Kum (Garagum) is one of the world's largest expanses of sand. Wind action has created a terrain of shifting, crescent-shaped sand dunes known as barchans.

A series of major rock faults has created the Fergana Valley, a deep depression surrounded by high mountains. Water from the Syr Darya river and from underground sources supports intensive agriculture, despite minimal rainfall.

The Amu Darya is the only river in Central Asia with a sufficient volume of water to cross the desert of the Kara Kum (Garagum) from the Pamirs to the Aral Sea, where it forms a delta largely vegetated by scrub grasses.

Shock waves travel through ground

Epicentre

Fault

▲ **In the heavily-fractured** and faulted mountain region, earthquakes are common, caused by the sudden release of tension along active fault lines.

Kyzyl Kum

Syr Darya

Earthquake zone

Naryn river

◄ **Bare mountains provide** a stark background to the croplands along the Naryn river in Kyrgyzstan. Irrigation is essential for cultivation in this dry region.

Ozero Issyk-Kul' lies at an altitude of 5193 ft (1584 m). The lake remains ice-free throughout the year, due to the slight salinity of the water.

Tien Shan

▲ **The Tien Shan** extend from China in the east, reaching heights over 24,420 ft (7443 m) and branching into many parallel ranges in the west.

Mount Communism (Qullai Kommunizm), in the northern Pamirs, was so named for being the highest point in the former Soviet Union, rising to 24,590 ft (7495 m).

Qarokul

◄ **Nestling high in** the Pamir range, and fed by glacial meltwater, Qarokul is the largest of the lakes in this region.

Scale 1:4,750,000

Km
0 10 20 40 60 80 100 120
Miles
0 10 20 40 60 80 100 120

projection: Lambert Conformal Conic

Using the land

Cropland outside Kyrgyzstan is restricted to irrigated areas such as the Fergana Valley. Central Asia is a leading global producer of cotton, and traditional silk-farming remains widespread. A wide range of fruits, vegetables and grains are grown and livestock raised includes horses, goats and karakul sheep.

Land use and agricultural distribution

- cattle
- goats
- sheep
- cereals
- cotton
- fruit
- ■ capital cities
- • major towns
- pasture
- cropland
- mountain region
- desert

▶ **Plentiful sunshine, rich** soils and massive irrigation schemes have made Uzbekistan the world's fifth largest cotton producer, although water shortages now prevent any further expansion of irrigated land.

The urban/rural population divide

urban 36%   rural 64%

0 10 20 30 40 50 60 70 80 90 100

Population density	Total land area
88 people per sq mile (34 people per sq km)	492,961 sq miles (1,277,100 sq km)

Afghanistan & Pakistan

Pakistan was created by the partition of British India in 1947, becoming the western arm of a new Islamic state for Indian Muslims; the eastern sector, in Bengal, seceded to become the separate country of Bangladesh in 1971. Over half of Pakistan's 158 million people live in the Punjab, at the fertile head of the great Indus Basin. The river sustains a national economy based on irrigated agriculture, including cotton for the vital textiles industry. Afghanistan, a mountainous, landlocked country, with an ancient and independent culture, has been wracked by war since 1979. Factional strife escalated into an international conflict in late 2001, as US-led troops ousted the militant and fundamentally Islamist *taliban* regime as part of their 'war on terror'.

◄ *The town of* Bamian lies high in the Hindu Kush west of Kabul. Between the 2nd and 5th centuries two huge statues of Buddha were carved into the nearby rock, the largest of which stood 125 ft (38 m) high. The statues were destroyed by the taliban *regime in March 2001.*

Transport and industry

Pakistan is highly dependent on the cotton textiles industry, although diversified manufacture is expanding around cities such as Karachi and Lahore. Afghanistan's limited industry is based mainly on the processing of agricultural raw materials and includes traditional crafts such as carpet-making.

Major industry and infrastructure

- carpet weaving
- chemicals
- engineering
- finance
- food processing
- iron & steel
- oil & gas
- textiles
- capital cities
- major towns
- international airports
- major roads
- major industrial areas

The transport network

96,154 miles (154,763 km)

211 miles (340 km)

4852 miles (7814 km)

745 miles (1200 km)

The Karakoram Highway was completed after 20 years of construction in 1978. It breaches the Himalayan mountain barrier providing a commercial motor route linking lowland Pakistan and China.

► *The Karakoram Highway* is one of the highest major roads in the world. It took over 24,000 workers almost 20 years to complete.

The landscape

Afghanistan's topography is dominated by the mountains of the Hindu Kush, which spread south and west into numerous mountain spurs. The dry plateau of southwestern Afghanistan extends into Pakistan and the hills which overlook the great Indus Basin. In northern Pakistan the Hindu Kush, Himalayan and Karakoram ranges meet to form one of the world's highest mountain regions.

◄ *The Hunza river* rises in the northern Karakoram Range, running for 120 miles (193 km) before joining the Gilgit river.

Hunza river

► *The arid Hindu Kush* makes much of Afghanistan uninhabitable, with over 50% of the land lying above 6500 ft (2000 m).

The plains and foothills which extend from the northern slopes of the Hindu Kush are part of the great grassy steppe lands of Central Asia.

Hindu Kush

K2 (Mount Godwin Austen), in the Karakoram Range, is the second highest mountain in the world, at an altitude of 28,251 ft (8611 m).

Some of the largest glaciers outside the polar regions are found in the Karakoram Range, including Siachen Glacier (Siachen Muztagh), which is 40 miles (72 km) long.

Frequent earthquakes mean that mountain-building processes are continuing in this region, as the Indo-Australian Plate drifts northwards, colliding with the Eurasian Plate.

Himalayas

Mountain chains running southwest from the Hindu Kush into Pakistan form a barrier to the humid winds which blow from the Indian Ocean, creating arid conditions across southern Afghanistan.

The soils of the Punjab plain are nourished by enormous quantities of sediment, carried from the Himalayas by the five tributaries of the Indus river.

The Indus Basin is part of the Indus-Ganges lowland, a vast depression which has been filled with layers of sediment over the last 50 million years. These deposits are estimated to be over 16,400 ft (5000 m) deep.

The Indus Delta is prone to heavy flooding and high levels of salinity. It remains a largely uncultivated wilderness area.

Glacis covered by coarse-grained sediment

Sediments washed down from mountains accumulate on glacis slopes

Fine sediments deposited on salt flats are removed by wind erosion.

Bedrock

▲ *Glacis are gentle,* debris-covered slopes which lead into salt flats or deserts. They typically occur at the base of mountains in arid regions such as Afghanistan.

Map labels

TURKMENISTAN · UZBEKISTAN · TAJIKISTAN · CHINA
Mazar-e Sharif · Herat · KABUL · Peshawar · ISLAMABAD · Rawalpindi · Lahore · AFGHANISTAN · Kandahar · Quetta · Faisalabad · Multan · Bahawalpur · PAKISTAN · Sukkur · IRAN · INDIA · Karachi · Hyderabad · ARABIAN SEA

146 · 142 · 142

TURKMENISTAN
Kāriz-e Elyās · Towraghoudi · Bālā Morghāb · Selseleh-ye
Qarah Bāgh · Kushk · BĀDGHIS
Eslām Qal'eh · Qal'eh-ye Now · Qādes
Kūhestān · Dasht-e Hamdam Āb
Zendeh Jān · Herāt · GHOW
Ghūriān · HERĀT
Namakzar · AFGH
Shindand · Farāh Rūd · Kūh-e Chehel Abdāl
Dak · Dasht-e Bābūs · FARĀH
Anār Darreh · Farāh · Delārām
Now Zād
Hāmūn-e Sāberi · Dasht-e Khāsh · Gereshk
Hāmūn-e Pūzak · NĪMRŪZ · Lashkar Gāh
Chakhānsūr · Shelleh-ye Padeh Tal
Zaranj · Dasht-e Mārgow · Darvīshān · Kūchnay Darweysh
HELMAND
Dasht-e Gowd-e Zereh · Daryā-ye Helmand · Deh Shū
Chāgai Hills · Hāmūn-i Lora
Nok Kundi · Yakmach · Dālbandin
Dasht-i Tāhlāb · Tāhlāb
Hāmūn-i Māshkel
BAL
Kamarod
Sīāhān Ran · Tagas
Panjgūr
Central Makr
Ispikān · As
Nihing · Malar
Mand · Nasrābād · Kech · Hoshāb
Turbat
Dasht
Suntsar · Khor Kalamat
Jīwani · Gwādar · Pasni · Astola Island · Ormāra
Gwādar West Bay · Gwādar East Bay

Scale 1:5,000,000

Km
0 10 20 40 60 80 100 120 140 160

Miles
0 10 20 40 60 80 100 120 140 160

projection: Lambert Conformal Conic

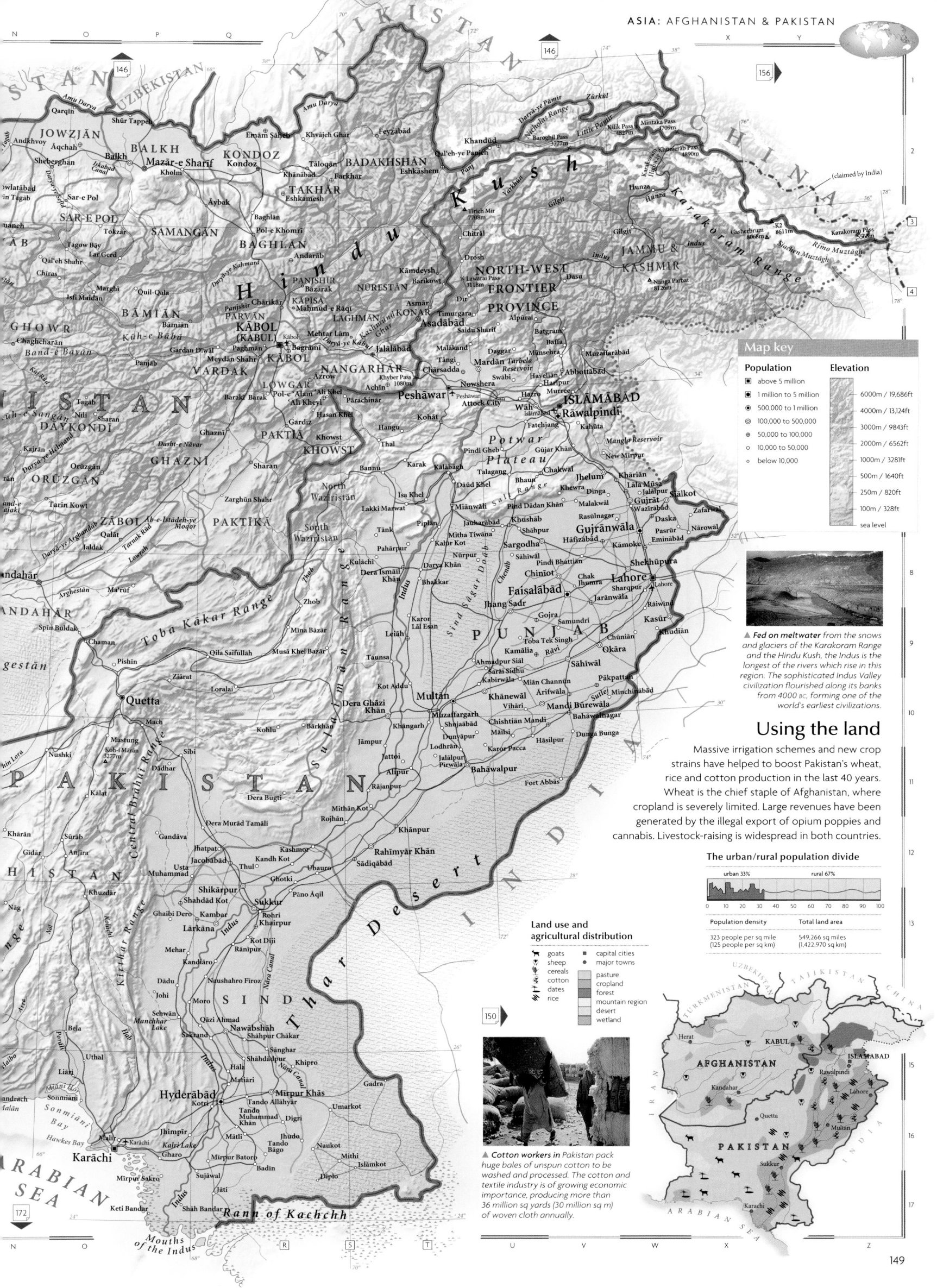

Map key

Population

- ■ above 5 million
- ■ 1 million to 5 million
- ◉ 500,000 to 1 million
- ◎ 100,000 to 500,000
- ⊙ 50,000 to 100,000
- ○ 10,000 to 50,000
- ∘ below 10,000

Elevation

- 6000m / 19,686ft
- 4000m / 13,124ft
- 3000m / 9843ft
- 2000m / 6562ft
- 1000m / 3281ft
- 500m / 1640ft
- 250m / 820ft
- 100m / 328ft
- sea level

▲ *Fed on meltwater from the snows and glaciers of the Karakoram Range and the Hindu Kush, the Indus is the longest of the rivers which rise in this region. The sophisticated Indus Valley civilization flourished along its banks from 4000 BC, forming one of the world's earliest civilizations.*

Using the land

Massive irrigation schemes and new crop strains have helped to boost Pakistan's wheat, rice and cotton production in the last 40 years. Wheat is the chief staple of Afghanistan, where cropland is severely limited. Large revenues have been generated by the illegal export of opium poppies and cannabis. Livestock-raising is widespread in both countries.

The urban/rural population divide

urban 33%   rural 67%

Population density	Total land area
323 people per sq mile (125 people per sq km)	549,266 sq miles (1,422,970 sq km)

Land use and agricultural distribution

- goats
- sheep
- cereals
- cotton
- dates
- rice
- ■ capital cities
- • major towns
- pasture
- cropland
- forest
- mountain region
- desert
- wetland

▲ *Cotton workers in Pakistan pack huge bales of unspun cotton to be washed and processed. The cotton and textile industry is of growing economic importance, producing more than 36 million sq yards (30 million sq m) of woven cloth annually.*

South Asia

BANGLADESH, BHUTAN, INDIA, MALDIVES, NEPAL, PAKISTAN, SRI LANKA

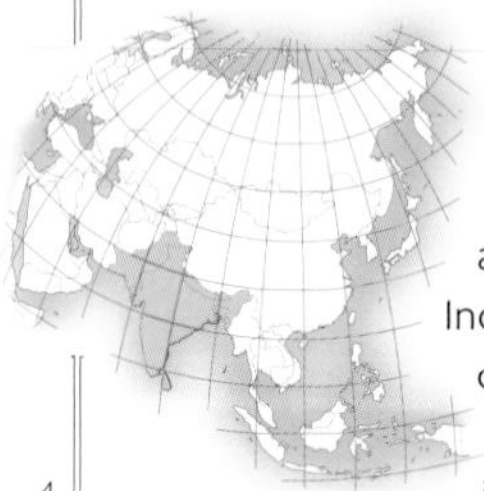

More than one-fifth of the world's population lives in the south Asian subcontinent. Great cultural diversity has come from a long succession of foreign invaders, including Hindu Aryans, Islamic Moguls and the British, whose empire incorporated the princely states of the Maharajas and extended to the borders of Nepal and Bhutan in the Himalayas.

Independent since 1947, India is the world's largest democracy, and at the current rate of growth, may overtake China as the world's most populous country during the 21st century. There are points of tension in the region over claims for independence by the Sikhs in the Indian Punjab and the Tamil separatists in Sri Lanka, and the long-standing dispute with Pakistan over Jammu and Kashmir in the north.

The landscape

South Asia is effectively isolated from the rest of Asia by desert along the western flank of Pakistan, and a continuous wall of mountains, dominated by the Himalayas, to the north and east. The great basins of the Indus and Ganges separate this mountain fringe from the rolling plateau of the Indian peninsula, which is bordered by a line of coastal hills, the Eastern and Western Ghats.

▼ *The towering Karakoram and Hindu Kush ranges, formed at the same time as the Himalayas, dominate Pakistan's northern borders. K2 on the border of northern Pakistan is the second highest mountain on Earth, at 28,251 ft (8611 m).*

▲ *The Indus valley near Skardu in northern Pakistan has been partially infilled by great quantities of eroded sediment. Most of this is carried from the region's bare slopes by swollen rivers during the spring thaw and mass movement activity.*

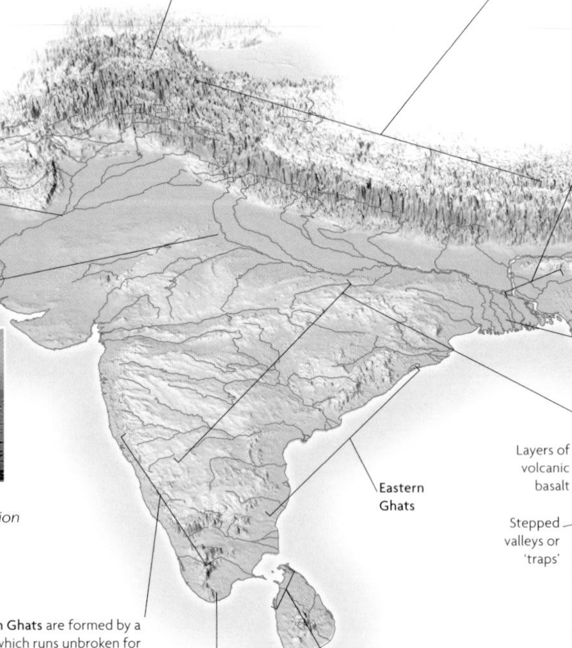

The Himalayas are the highest and most extensive mountain system in the world. They were formed when the Indo-Australian Plate collided with the Eurasian Plate about 40 million years ago, thrusting up huge masses of land and creating a 'ripple effect', which formed lesser mountain ranges in Tibet and Southeast Asia. Mount Everest is the world's tallest mountain at 29,035 ft (8850 m).

Almost all of Bangladesh lies in the immense delta formed by the Ganges and the Brahmaputra which merge and flow out into the Bay of Bengal.

Ganges delta

Deccan plateau

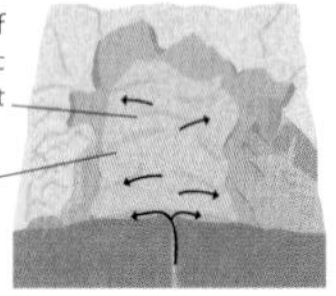

▲ *The Deccan plateau covers an area of more than 123,553 sq miles (320,000 sq km). It is formed of deep layers of volcanic basalt, reaching thicknesses of more than 9800 ft (3000 m) towards the coast. Distinctive stepped valleys cut in the basalt plateau by rivers are known as 'traps'.*

Layers of volcanic basalt

Stepped valleys or 'traps'

Eastern Ghats

Coastal deposition has formed many typical features along the western coast of Sri Lanka. These include spits and bars, sometimes enclosing lagoons.

Trivandrum in southern India normally receives the first of the monsoon rains, which are essential to south Asian agriculture and moderate the extreme summer heat. The monsoon then moves northwards over a period of about two months.

The Western Ghats are formed by a fault scarp which runs unbroken for more than 930 miles (1500 km). They reach their highest point at the southern Cardamom Hills.

▲ *Rivers flowing from the Himalayas into a broad depression in northern India have formed marshes around Bharatpur. They are now a sanctuary for numerous bird species.*

Bharatpur

The Indus river flows more than 1970 miles (3180 km) from southwestern Tibet to its mouth on the Arabian Sea. It has an estimated catchment area of 450,000 sq miles (1,165,500 sq km).

The coast of western Pakistan is a staircase of folded rock strata caused by successive periods of rapid uplift.

150

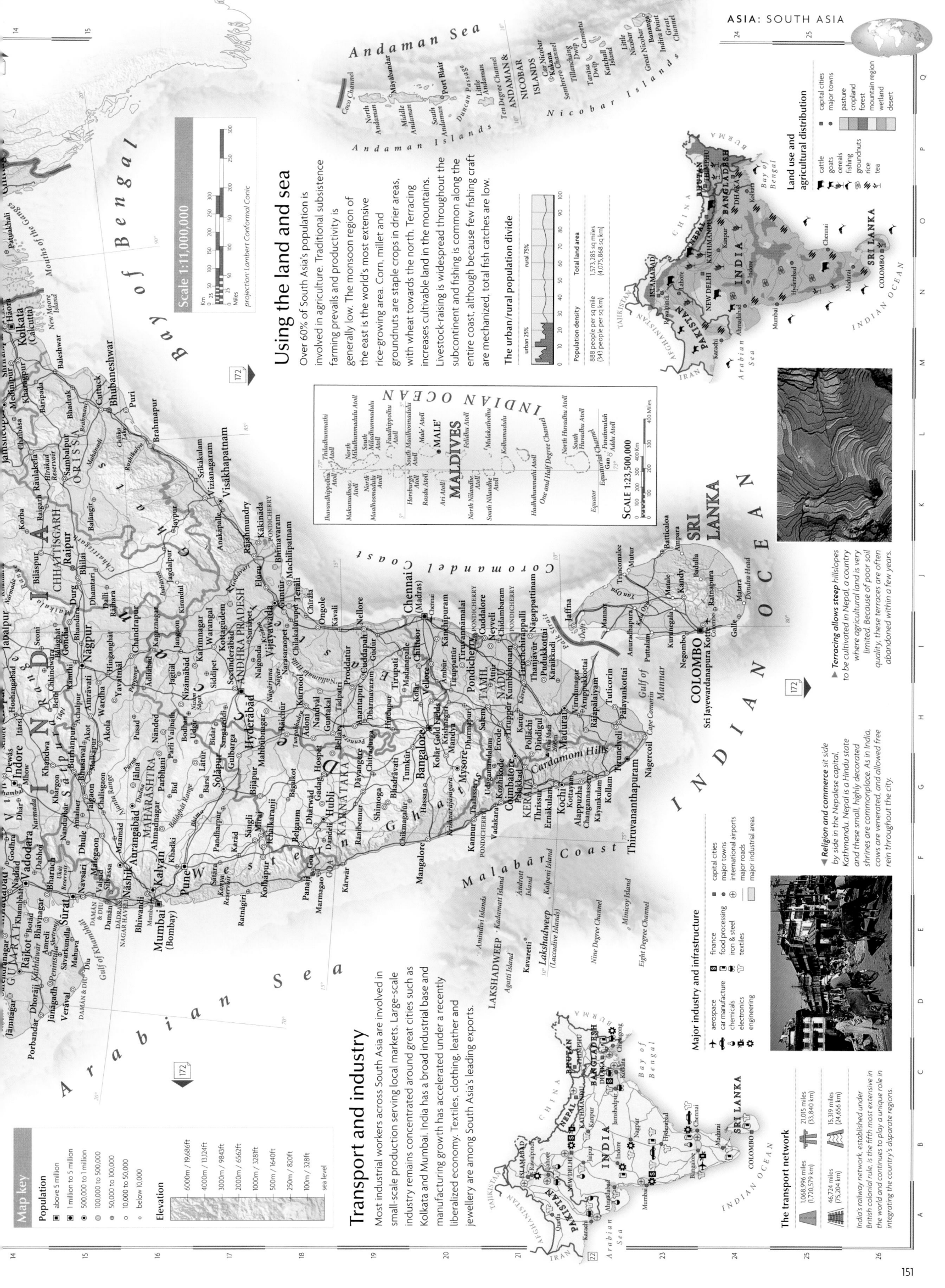

Map key

Population

- ▪ above 5 million
- ● 1 million to 5 million
- ⊙ 500,000 to 1 million
- ⊕ 100,000 to 500,000
- ○ 50,000 to 100,000
- ○ 10,000 to 50,000
- ○ below 10,000

Elevation

- 6000m / 19,686ft
- 4000m / 13,124ft
- 3000m / 9843ft
- 2000m / 6562ft
- 1000m / 3281ft
- 500m / 1640ft
- 250m / 820ft
- 100m / 328ft
- sea level

Scale 1:11,000,000

projection: Lambert Conformal Conic

Using the land and sea

Over 60% of South Asia's population is involved in agriculture. Traditional subsistence farming prevails and productivity is generally low. The monsoon region of the east is the world's most extensive rice-growing area. Corn, millet and groundnuts are staple crops in drier areas, with wheat towards the north. Terracing increases cultivable land in the mountains. Livestock-raising is widespread throughout the subcontinent and fishing is common along the entire coast, although because few fishing craft are mechanized, total fish catches are low.

The urban/rural population divide

rural 75%

urban 25%

Population density	Total land area
888 people per sq mile (343 people per sq km)	1,573,285 sq miles (4,075,868 sq km)

Land use and agricultural distribution

- 🐄 cattle
- 🐐 goats
- 🐟 fishing
- 🌾 cereals
- 🥜 groundnuts
- 🍃 tea
- 🌾 rice

- capital cities
- major towns
- pasture
- cropland
- forest
- mountain region
- rice
- wetland
- desert

▲ **Terracing allows steep hillsides** to be cultivated in Nepal, a country where agricultural land is very limited. Because of poor soil quality, these terraces are often abandoned within a few years.

Transport and industry

Most industrial workers across South Asia are involved in small-scale production serving local markets. Large-scale industry remains concentrated around great cities such as Kolkata and Mumbai. India has a broad industrial base and manufacturing growth has accelerated under a recently liberalized economy. Textiles, clothing, leather and jewellery are among South Asia's leading exports.

Major industry and infrastructure

- ✈ aerospace
- 🚗 car manufacture
- chemicals
- electronics
- ⚙ engineering
- $ finance
- food processing
- iron & steel
- ✂ textiles
- major industrial areas

- ▪ capital cities
- ● major towns
- ✈ international airports
- major roads

▼ **Religion and commerce sit side by side** in the Nepalese capital, Kathmandu. Nepal is a Hindu state and these small, highly decorated shrines are commonplace. As in India, cows are venerated, and allowed free rein throughout the city.

The transport network

🚗 1,068,996 miles (1,720,579 km)	🛤 21,015 miles (33,840 km)
✈ 46,724 miles (75,204 km)	⚓ 15,319 miles (24,656 km)

India's railway network, established under British colonial rule, is the fifth most extensive in the world and continues to play a unique role in integrating the country's disparate regions.

MALDIVES

MALE'

SCALE 1:23,500,000

Northern India & the Himalayan states

BANGLADESH, BHUTAN, NEPAL, Arunachal Pradesh, Assam, Bihar, Chandigarh, Delhi, Haryana, Himachal Pradesh, Jammu & Kashmir, Jharkhand, Manipur, Meghalaya, Mizoram, Nagaland, Punjab, Rajasthan, Sikkim, Tripura, Uttarakhand, Uttar Pradesh, West Bengal

The Ganges and Brahmaputra river basins and the massive mountain barrier of the Himalayas define this region's landscape and have served to reinforce potent cultural and religious differences among its people. Hinduism pervades most aspects of national life and is a growing political force within India, a secular country which also encompasses the centre of Sikhism at Amritsar and the world's largest Muslim minority. Nepal is a crowded mountain state, which faces severe ecological problems from deforestation, while the tiny Himalayan Buddhist kingdom of Bhutan is emerging from long-term isolation, to welcome selected visitors. The Muslim state of Bangladesh, formerly East Pakistan, is one of the world's most densely populated countries and one of the poorest, with more than 145 million people living largely on the massive Ganges/Brahmaputra delta. Many Bangladeshis live under threat of repeated, catastrophic floods.

◄ *The Golden Temple* in Amritsar, the most sacred shrine of the Sikh religion, was the scene of violent clashes between Sikh separatists and government forces in 1984.

Scale 1:6,500,000

projection: Lambert Conformal Conic

Map key

Population
- ◉ 1 million to 5 million
- ◎ 500,000 to 1 million
- ⊚ 100,000 to 500,000
- ⊕ 50,000 to 100,000
- ○ 10,000 to 50,000
- ∘ below 10,000

Elevation
- 6000m / 19,686ft
- 4000m / 13,124ft
- 3000m / 9843ft
- 2000m / 6562ft
- 1000m / 3281ft
- 500m / 1640ft
- 250m / 820ft
- 100m / 328ft
- sea level

Transport and industry

Textiles, engineering, chemicals and electronics are leading industries in north India. The plateau of Chota Nagpur provides ore for iron and steel production in the major industrial region northeast of Kolkata. Bangladesh processes jute and Nepal has a small manufacturing sector based on agricultural produce, while Bhutan's limited industry is concentrated in the southern lowland area.

Major industry and infrastructure
- adventure tourism
- car manufacture
- chemicals
- coal
- electronics
- engineering
- finance
- food processing
- iron & steel
- jute processing
- oil
- tea processing
- textiles
- capital cities
- major towns
- international airports
- major roads
- major industrial areas

The transport network

Over 60% of Bangladesh's internal trade is carried by boat. The country has a very disjointed land transport network, with no bridges over the Brahmaputra and few road crossings on the Ganges river.

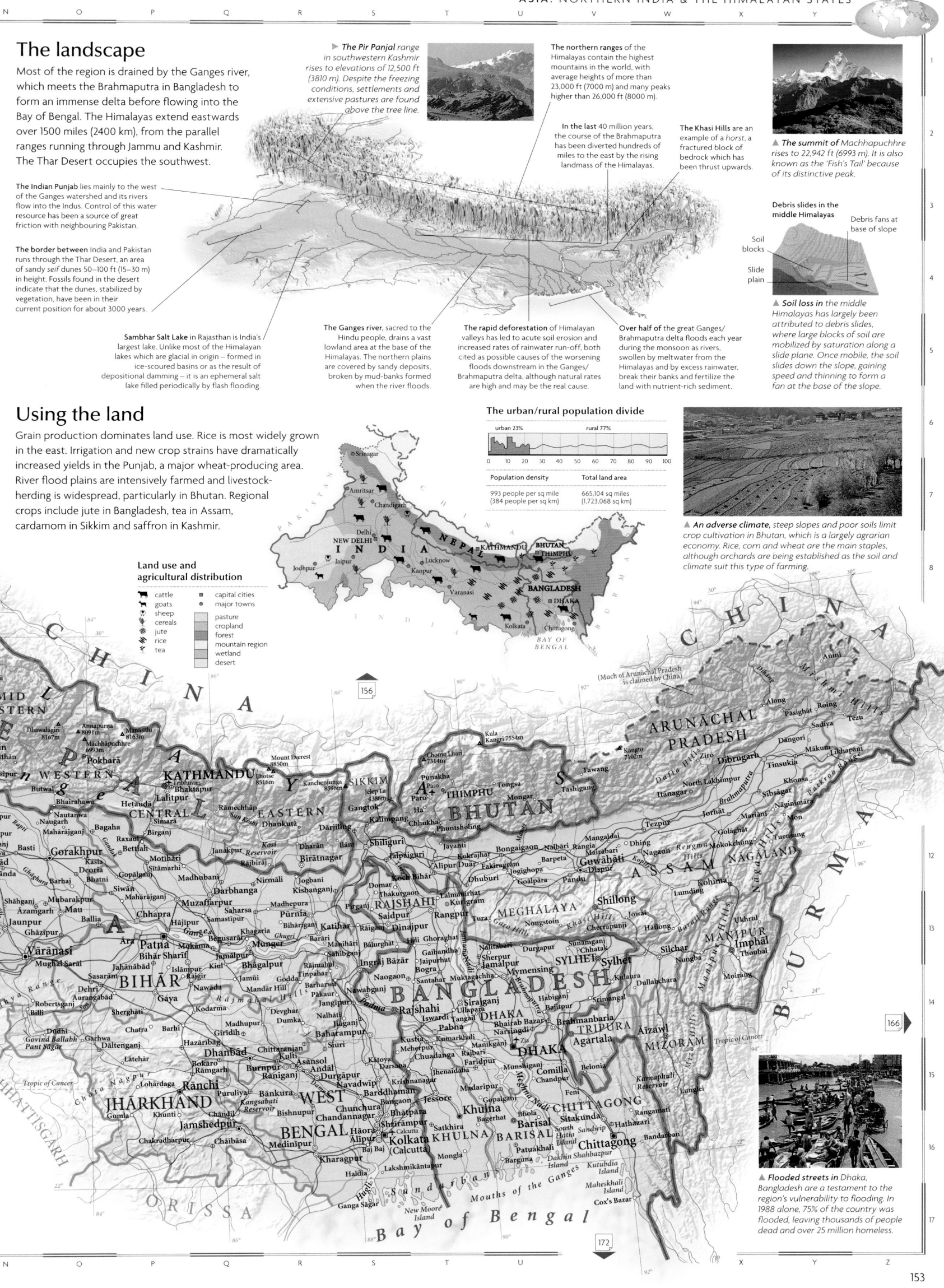

The landscape

Most of the region is drained by the Ganges river, which meets the Brahmaputra in Bangladesh to form an immense delta before flowing into the Bay of Bengal. The Himalayas extend eastwards over 1500 miles (2400 km), from the parallel ranges running through Jammu and Kashmir. The Thar Desert occupies the southwest.

The Indian Punjab lies mainly to the west of the Ganges watershed and its rivers flow into the Indus. Control of this water resource has been a source of great friction with neighbouring Pakistan.

The border between India and Pakistan runs through the Thar Desert, an area of sandy *seif* dunes 50–100 ft (15–30 m) in height. Fossils found in the desert indicate that the dunes, stabilized by vegetation, have been in their current position for about 3000 years.

Sambhar Salt Lake in Rajasthan is India's largest lake. Unlike most of the Himalayan lakes which are glacial in origin – formed in ice-scoured basins or as the result of depositional damming – it is an ephemeral salt lake filled periodically by flash flooding.

The Ganges river, sacred to the Hindu people, drains a vast lowland area at the base of the Himalayas. The northern plains are covered by sandy deposits, broken by mud-banks formed when the river floods.

The rapid deforestation of Himalayan valleys has led to acute soil erosion and increased rates of rainwater run-off, both cited as possible causes of the worsening floods downstream in the Ganges/Brahmaputra delta, although natural rates are high and may be the real cause.

Over half of the great Ganges/Brahmaputra delta floods each year during the monsoon as rivers, swollen by meltwater from the Himalayas and by excess rainwater, break their banks and fertilize the land with nutrient-rich sediment.

The Pir Panjal range in southwestern Kashmir rises to elevations of 12,500 ft (3810 m). Despite the freezing conditions, settlements and extensive pastures are found above the tree line.

The northern ranges of the Himalayas contain the highest mountains in the world, with average heights of more than 23,000 ft (7000 m) and many peaks higher than 26,000 ft (8000 m).

In the last 40 million years, the course of the Brahmaputra has been diverted hundreds of miles to the east by the rising landmass of the Himalayas.

The Khasi Hills are an example of a *horst*, a fractured block of bedrock which has been thrust upwards.

▲ *The summit of* Machhapuchhre rises to 22,942 ft (6993 m). It is also known as the 'Fish's Tail' because of its distinctive peak.

Debris slides in the middle Himalayas

Debris fans at base of slope
Soil blocks
Slide plain

▲ *Soil loss in* the middle Himalayas has largely been attributed to debris slides, where large blocks of soil are mobilized by saturation along a slide plane. Once mobile, the soil slides down the slope, gaining speed and thinning to form a fan at the base of the slope.

Using the land

Grain production dominates land use. Rice is most widely grown in the east. Irrigation and new crop strains have dramatically increased yields in the Punjab, a major wheat-producing area. River flood plains are intensively farmed and livestock-herding is widespread, particularly in Bhutan. Regional crops include jute in Bangladesh, tea in Assam, cardamom in Sikkim and saffron in Kashmir.

The urban/rural population divide

urban 23%   rural 77%

0 10 20 30 40 50 60 70 80 90 100

Population density	Total land area
993 people per sq mile (384 people per sq km)	665,104 sq miles (1,723,068 sq km)

▲ *An adverse climate,* steep slopes and poor soils limit crop cultivation in Bhutan, which is a largely agrarian economy. Rice, corn and wheat are the main staples, although orchards are being established as the soil and climate suit this type of farming.

Land use and agricultural distribution

- cattle
- goats
- sheep
- cereals
- jute
- rice
- tea
- capital cities
- major towns
- pasture
- cropland
- forest
- mountain region
- wetland
- desert

▲ *Flooded streets in* Dhaka, Bangladesh are a testament to the region's vulnerability to flooding. In 1988 alone, 75% of the country was flooded, leaving thousands of people dead and over 25 million homeless.

(Much of Arunāchal Pradesh is claimed by China)

Southern India & Sri Lanka

SRI LANKA, Andhra Pradesh, Chhattisgarh, Dadra & Nagar Haveli, Daman & Diu, Goa, Gujarat, Karnataka, Kerala, Lakshadweep, Madhya Pradesh, Maharashtra, Orissa, Pondicherry, Tamil Nadu

The unique and highly independent southern states reflect the diverse and decentralized nature of India, which has fourteen official languages. The southern half of the peninsula lay beyond the reach of early invaders from the north and retained the distinct and ancient culture of Dravidian peoples such as the Tamils, whose language is spoken in preference to Hindi throughout southern India. The interior plateau of southern India is less densely populated than the coastal lowlands, where the European colonial imprint is strongest. Urban and industrial growth is accelerating, but southern India's vast population remains predominantly rural. The island of Sri Lanka has two distinct cultural groups; the mainly Buddhist Sinhalese majority, and the Tamil minority whose struggle for a homeland in the northeast has led to prolonged civil war.

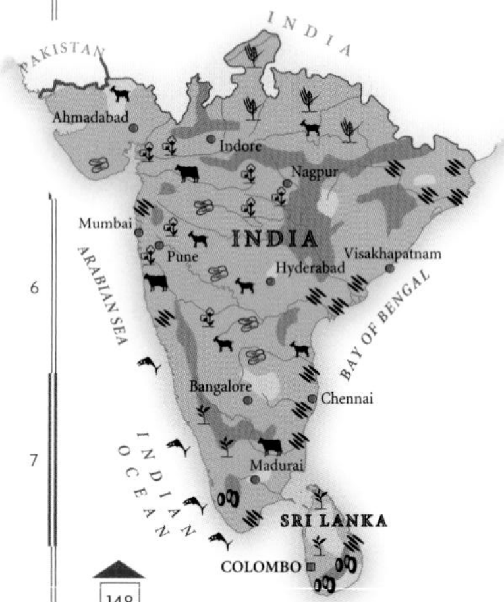

Using the land and sea

Rice is the main staple in the east, in Sri Lanka and along the humid Malabar Coast. Groundnuts are grown on the Deccan plateau, with wheat, corn and chickpeas, towards the north. Sri Lanka is a leading exporter of tea, coconuts and rubber. Cotton plantations supply local mills around Nagpur and Mumbai. Fishing supports many communities in Kerala and the Laccadive Islands.

Land use and agricultural distribution

- cattle
- goats
- cereals
- cotton
- fishing
- groundnuts
- rice
- rubber
- tea
- capital cities
- major towns

pasture
cropland
forest
wetland

The urban/rural population divide

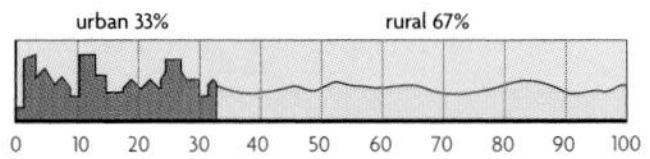

urban 33%   rural 67%

Population density	Total land area
730 people per sq mile (282 people per sq km)	698,295 sq miles (1,809,054 sq km)

The landscape

The undulating Deccan plateau underlies most of southern India; it slopes gently down towards the east and is largely enclosed by the Ghats coastal hill ranges. The Western Ghats run continuously along the Arabian Sea coast, while the Eastern Ghats are interrupted by rivers which follow the slope of the plateau and flow across broad lowlands into the Bay of Bengal. The plateaux and basins of Sri Lanka's central highlands are surrounded by a broad plain.

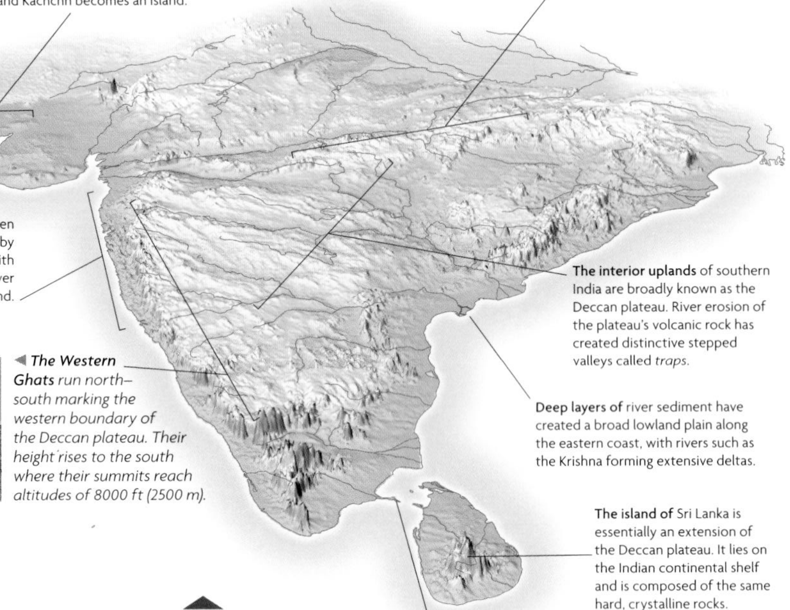

Along the northern boundary of the Deccan plateau, old basement rocks are interspersed with younger sedimentary strata. This creates spectacular scarplands, cut by numerous waterfalls along the softer sedimentary strata.

The interior uplands of southern India are broadly known as the Deccan plateau. River erosion of the plateau's volcanic rock has created distinctive stepped valleys called traps.

Deep layers of river sediment have created a broad lowland plain along the eastern coast, with rivers such as the Krishna forming extensive deltas.

The island of Sri Lanka is essentially an extension of the Deccan plateau. It lies on the Indian continental shelf and is composed of the same hard, crystalline rocks.

The Rann of Kachchh tidal marshes encircle the low-lying Kachchh peninsula. For several months during the rainy season the water level of the marshes rises and Kachchh becomes an island.

The Konkan coast, which runs between Daman and Goa, is characterized by rocky headlands, and bays with crescent-shaped beaches. Flooded river valleys known as rias extend inland.

▼ The Western Ghats run north–south marking the western boundary of the Deccan plateau. Their height rises to the south where their summits reach altitudes of 8000 ft (2500 m).

Ocean currents cause sediment build up

Sri Lanka

Relict of ancient tombolo

Adam's Bridge

Adam's Bridge

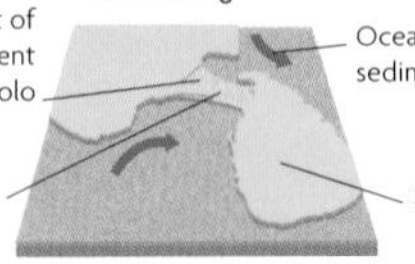

▲ Adam's Bridge (Rama's Bridge) is a chain of sandy shoals lying about 4 ft (1.2 m) under the sea between India and Sri Lanka. They once formed the world's longest tombolo, or land bridge, before the sea level began to rise several thousand years ago.

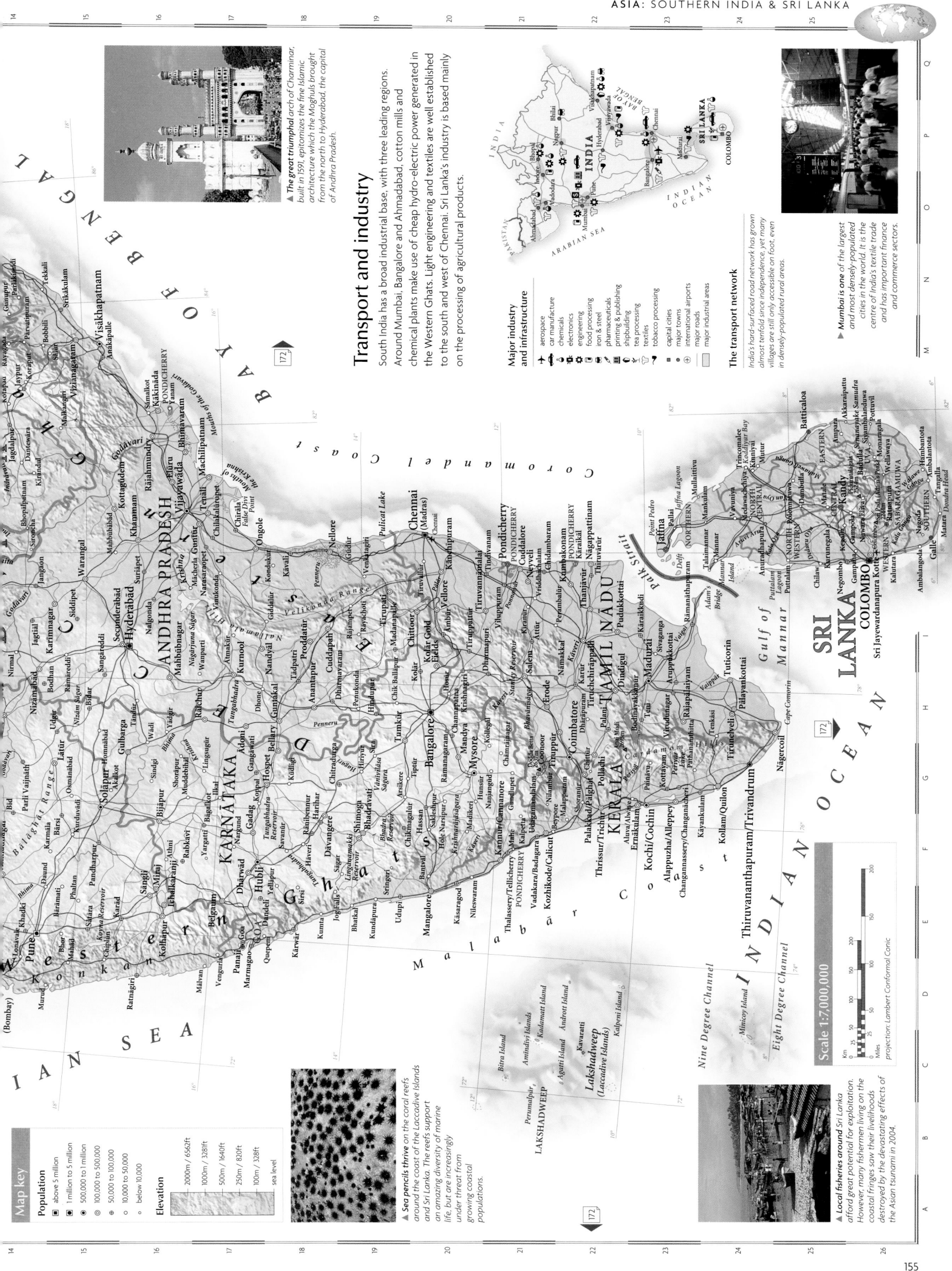

▲ **The great triumphal** arch of Charminar, built in 1591, epitomizes the fine Islamic architecture which the Moghuls brought from the north to Hyderabad, the capital of Andhra Pradesh.

Transport and industry

South India has a broad industrial base, with three leading regions. Around Mumbai, Bangalore and Ahmadabad, cotton mills and chemical plants make use of cheap hydro-electric power generated in the Western Ghats. Light engineering and textiles are well established to the south and west of Chennai. Sri Lanka's industry is based mainly on the processing of agricultural products.

Major industry and infrastructure

- aerospace
- car manufacture
- chemicals
- electronics
- engineering
- food processing
- iron & steel
- pharmaceuticals
- printing & publishing
- shipbuilding
- tea processing
- textiles
- tobacco processing
- capital cities
- major towns
- international airports
- major roads
- major industrial areas

The transport network

India's hard-surfaced road network has grown almost tenfold since independence, yet many villages are still only accessible on foot, even in densely-populated rural areas.

▲ **Mumbai is one** of the largest and most densely-populated cities in the world. It is the centre of India's textile trade and has important finance and commerce sectors.

Map key

Population
- ■ above 5 million
- ■ 1 million to 5 million
- ◉ 500,000 to 1 million
- ◎ 100,000 to 500,000
- ⊕ 50,000 to 100,000
- ○ 10,000 to 50,000
- ○ below 10,000

Elevation
- 2000m / 6562ft
- 1000m / 3281ft
- 500m / 1640ft
- 250m / 820ft
- 100m / 328ft
- sea level

▲ **Sea pencils thrive** on the coral reefs around the coast of the Laccadive Islands and Sri Lanka. The reefs support an amazing diversity of marine life, but are increasingly under threat from growing coastal populations.

▲ **Local fisheries around** Sri Lanka afford great potential for exploitation. However, many fishermen living on the coastal fringes saw their livelihoods destroyed by the devastating effects of the Asian tsunami in 2004.

Scale 1:7,000,000

projection: Lambert Conformal Conic

Mainland East Asia

CHINA, MONGOLIA, NORTH KOREA, SOUTH KOREA, TAIWAN

China, the world's most populous nation, has an unbroken cultural history, longer than that of any other country, and is rapidly emerging as a leading world power. When Mao Zedong established Communist rule in 1949, China had become a backward feudal empire, stricken by civil war and over a century of European and Japanese incursions. The closed regime withstood the traumas of rapid industrialization, communalized farming and the brutal purges of the Cultural Revolution but, since the 1980s has introduced economic reforms, led by expanded foreign trade. China's population is heavily concentrated in the east and, despite accelerating urban growth, remains predominantly rural. One cultural group, the Han, make up over 90% of the people, while five 'Autonomous Regions' have been established in the south and west for the main ethnic minorities.

Transport and industry

Large-scale industrial growth has always been a priority of the Communist government. Metals and machine production, chemicals and engineering are among the leading industries, concentrated in the major cities of the east coast. Textiles and clothing manufacture, the main consumer goods sector, is relatively well dispersed, with a few significant centres such as Shanghai, Beijing and Hong Kong.

Major industry and infrastructure

- car manufacture
- chemicals
- electronics
- engineering
- finance
- food processing
- iron & steel
- shipbuilding
- textiles

- capital cities
- major towns
- international airports
- major roads
- major industrial areas

The transport network

829,790 miles (1,335,571 km)	12,740 miles (20,506 km)
43,976 miles (70,780 km)	70,991 miles (114,262 km)

Ever-increasing demand for rail transportation has led to major improvement and expansion of the network, notably the 690 mile (1100 km) link between Golmud and Lhasa opened in 2006.

◄ Coal is China's most abundant mineral resource. This mine at Fuxin in Liaoning province is used to provide coal for a nearby power station.

The landscape

The East Asian landmass is arranged in three distinct levels, the highest of which is the Plateau of Tibet in the southwest. The arid uplands of northwestern China form a barren middle step. The main rivers flow eastward from these two platforms to the East China and South China sea coasts, across a broad region of alluvial lowlands and low hills.

▲ The Plateau of Tibet occupies about a quarter of China's total area. The Yangtze, Mekong, Indus and Brahmaputra rivers all originate in the south and east of the plateau.

The Himalayas extend along the southwestern edge of the Plateau of Tibet, forming a continuous mountain barrier over 1500 miles (2500 km) long.

Warm, humid conditions have caused intensive erosion of south China's karst areas, producing spectacular jagged peaks and vast caves in the limestone.

The Gobi Desert extends across the Nei Mongol Gaoyuan; a vast saucer-shaped upland surrounded by a rim of higher mountains.

Tarim Basin *(Tarim Pendi)*

Plateau of Tibet

The loess plateau of northern China is the world's greatest expanse of loess, a loose soil made up of wind-blown material. The plateau has been heavily eroded by tributaries of the Yellow River.

Shifting sand dunes are found in the arid west of the northeast China Plain, while the eastern part of this great expanse is wet and swampy.

River-eroded fine soils

Thick blanket of loess

▲ Because of its very small grain-size, loess has been easily transported and deposited by winds which scour the plains, and in northern China, deposits of loess can be up to 3000 ft (1000 m) thick. Loess-based soils are very fertile, but clearing land for agriculture quickly destabilizes the soil and allows it to be eroded.

Paektu-san

North China Plain

The Yangtze is China's longest river and the principal navigable waterway.

Sichuan Pendi

▲ Gansu province, through which the ancient Silk Route passes on its way to the west, is characterized by extensive loess deposits which are terraced and used for crop cultivation.

◄ Paektu-san, at 9023 ft (2750 m), is North Korea's highest peak; an extinct volcanic cone now filled by a crater lake.

◄ Although it is over 30 years since his death, the legacy of Chairman Mao Zedong, architect of the Great Proletariat Cultural Revolution, is still very much in evidence across China's landscape. In 1959 Mao launched a 20-year period of industrialization and socio-economic realignment, rejecting western ideals and social codes.

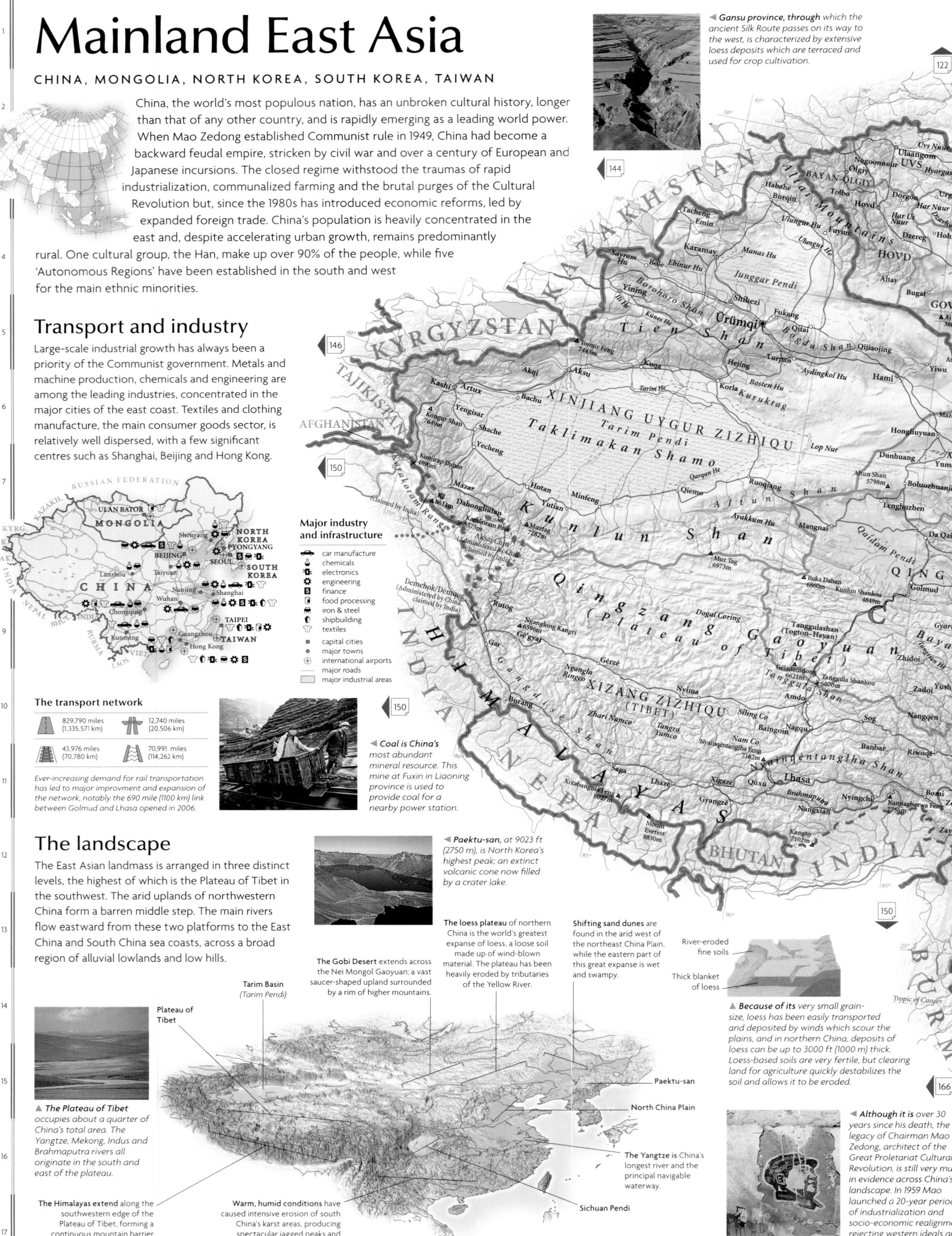

Scale 1:14,000,000

Km
0 25 50 100 150 200 250 300 350 400
Miles
0 25 50 100 150 200 250 300 350 400

projection: Lambert Conformal Conic

Map key

Population
- □ above 5 million
- ▣ 1 million to 5 million
- ◉ 500,000 to 1 million
- ◎ 100,000 to 500,000
- ◍ 50,000 to 100,000
- ○ 10,000 to 50,000
- ○ below 10,000

Elevation
- 6000m / 19,686ft
- 4000m / 13,124ft
- 3000m / 9843ft
- 2000m / 6562ft
- 1000m / 3281ft
- 500m / 1640ft
- 250m / 820ft
- 100m / 328ft
- sea level

Using the land and sea

Around 90% of China is unsuitable for cultivation, being either climatically or topographically adverse, or lacking sufficiently fertile soils. Most of the west is used for nomadic herding, while farmland is concentrated in the eastern monsoon region, with rice grown in the tropical and subtropical south. Cereals and soya beans predominate as rainfall and temperatures decline further north.

Land use and agricultural distribution

- pigs
- sheep
- corn (maize)
- cotton
- fishing
- fruit
- rice
- sugar cane
- soya beans

- ■ capital cities
- ● major towns
- pasture
- cropland
- forest
- mountain region

◄ **The Great Wall** of China remains one of the world's largest-ever construction projects, and is so vast that it is visible from space. Sections were added as late as 1640 and it runs for over 4000 miles (6400 km) from the Yellow Sea to Central Asia.

The urban/rural population divide

urban 32%   rural 68%

0 10 20 30 40 50 60 70 80 90 100

Population density	Total land area
325 people per sq mile (125 people per sq km)	4,288,672 sq miles (11,110,550 sq km)

RUSSIAN FEDERATION

Western China

Gansu, Ningxia, Qinghai, Tibet, Xinjiang

The plateaux and basins of China's dry, desolate western domain are sparsely populated and largely undeveloped, although they have rich mineral reserves; they also form a critical buffer zone for China, in a geographically important and culturally sensitive part of the Asian continent. Across most of the west, the Han Chinese are outnumbered by a range of cultural groups, including the Uygur, the largest group of the various semi-nomadic Muslim peoples from Central Asia. The remote, inhospitable Plateau of Tibet is the world's coldest and highest plateau. It has been occupied by the Chinese since 1950. Tibet is one of western China's five 'Autonomous Regions', but its reclusive Buddhist culture has been systematically undermined by the Chinese government.

Map key

Population
- ◉ 1 million to 5 million
- ◉ 500,000 to 1 million
- ⊕ 100,000 to 500,000
- ⊕ 50,000 to 100,000
- ○ 10,000 to 50,000
- ○ below 10,000

Elevation
- 6000m / 19,686ft
- 4000m / 13,124ft
- 3000m / 9843ft
- 2000m / 6562ft
- 1000m / 3281ft
- 500m / 1640ft
- 250m / 820ft
- 100m / 328ft
- sea level

Scale 1:7,750,000

projection: Lambert Conformal Conic

▲ *The Lhasa He* is one of the many rivers which drain the vast Plateau of Tibet. From its source in the Nyainqêntanglha Shan range and fed by the spring meltwater, it eventually joins the upper Brahmaputra 40 miles (65 km) southwest of Lhasa.

Using the land

Agriculture is constrained by the cold, dry climate and lack of fertile soils in the region, although irrigation and glasshouse farming are increasing agricultural potential. Large quantities of fruit, like melons and grapes, are grown at the oases of Hami and Turpan in Xinjiang, and new irrigation schemes have greatly increased cotton and wheat production in the Tarim Basin (*Tarim Pendi*). Most of the great area of Tibet and Qinghai is devoted to pastoralism. Sheep are the principal livestock.

Land use and agricultural distribution
- goats
- sheep
- cereals
- cotton
- grapes
- melons
- oases
- major towns
- pasture
- cropland
- forest
- mountain region
- desert

▲ *The Potala Palace*, in Tibet's capital, Lhasa, was the former residence of the Dalai Lama, Tibetan Buddhism's spiritual leader. Tibet remains only sparsely populated; forming over 20% of China's landmass, it supports fewer than 1% of its population.

The landscape

The Himalayas mark the southwestern edge of the Plateau of Tibet, an extreme mountain wilderness which occupies nearly a quarter of China's total area. A large structural depression, the Qaidam Pendi, lies at its northeastern edge. The Kunlun mountain chain isolates the plateau from the desert to the north, where the Tien Shan range forms a spur between the Tarim Basin (Tarim Pendi) and Dzungarian Basin (Junggar Pendi).

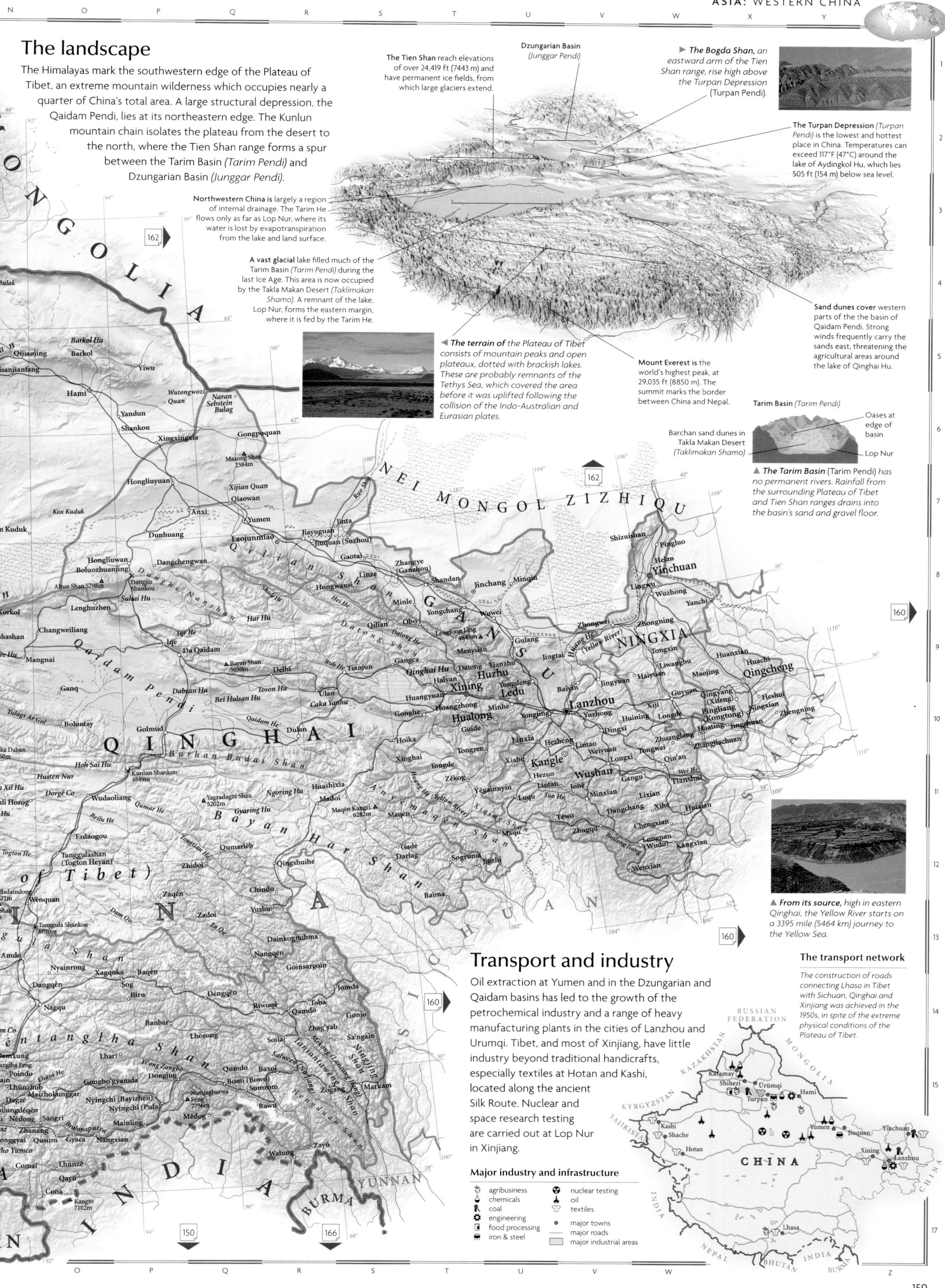

The Tien Shan reach elevations of over 24,419 ft (7443 m) and have permanent ice fields, from which large glaciers extend.

Dzungarian Basin (Junggar Pendi)

► **The Bogda Shan**, an eastward arm of the Tien Shan range, rise high above the Turpan Depression (Turpan Pendi).

The Turpan Depression (Turpan Pendi) is the lowest and hottest place in China. Temperatures can exceed 117°F (47°C) around the lake of Aydingkol Hu, which lies 505 ft (154 m) below sea level.

Northwestern China is largely a region of internal drainage. The Tarim He flows only as far as Lop Nur, where its water is lost by evapotranspiration from the lake and land surface.

A vast glacial lake filled much of the Tarim Basin (Tarim Pendi) during the last Ice Age. This area is now occupied by the Takla Makan Desert (Taklimakan Shamo). A remnant of the lake, Lop Nur, forms the eastern margin, where it is fed by the Tarim He.

◄ **The terrain of** the Plateau of Tibet consists of mountain peaks and open plateaus, dotted with brackish lakes. These are probably remnants of the Tethys Sea, which covered the area before it was uplifted following the collision of the Indo-Australian and Eurasian plates.

Mount Everest is the world's highest peak, at 29,035 ft (8850 m). The summit marks the border between China and Nepal.

Sand dunes cover western parts of the the basin of Qaidam Pendi. Strong winds frequently carry the sands east, threatening the agricultural areas around the lake of Qinghai Hu.

Tarim Basin (Tarim Pendi)

Barchan sand dunes in Takla Makan Desert (Taklimakan Shamo)

Oases at edge of basin

Lop Nur

▲ **The Tarim Basin** (Tarim Pendi) has no permanent rivers. Rainfall from the surrounding Plateau of Tibet and Tien Shan ranges drains into the basin's sand and gravel floor.

▲ **From its source**, high in eastern Qinghai, the Yellow River starts on a 3395 mile (5464 km) journey to the Yellow Sea.

Transport and industry

Oil extraction at Yumen and in the Dzungarian and Qaidam basins has led to the growth of the petrochemical industry and a range of heavy manufacturing plants in the cities of Lanzhou and Urumqi. Tibet, and most of Xinjiang, have little industry beyond traditional handicrafts, especially textiles at Hotan and Kashi, located along the ancient Silk Route. Nuclear and space research testing are carried out at Lop Nur in Xinjiang.

The transport network

The construction of roads connecting Lhasa in Tibet with Sichuan, Qinghai and Xinjiang was achieved in the 1950s, in spite of the extreme physical conditions of the Plateau of Tibet.

Major industry and infrastructure

- agribusiness
- chemicals
- coal
- engineering
- food processing
- iron & steel
- nuclear testing
- oil
- textiles
- major towns
- major roads
- major industrial areas

159

Eastern China

TAIWAN, Anhui, Beijing, Chongqing, Fujian, Guangdong, Guangxi, Guizhou, Hainan, Hebei, Henan, Hubei, Hunan, Jiangsu, Jiangxi, Shaanxi, Shandong, Shanghai, Shanxi, Sichuan, Tianjin, Yunnan, Zhejiang

The east is China's heartland. Massive industrial development since 1949 has transformed much of the densely populated rural landscape, in a region still prone to flooding and drought. Over 30 cities have populations of over a million, including the giant metropolis of Shanghai and the capital Beijing, which has been China's cultural and political centre since the 13th century. The ethnically diverse southwest and the oil-rich interior provinces of Sichuan and Shaanxi have largely missed out on the remarkable economic growth occurring in designated free-trade areas along the coasts of the South and East China seas. The republic of Taiwan was established in 1949 by Chinese nationalists ousted from the mainland by the victorious Communist forces. Taiwan now has one of the strongest economies in the world but its sovereignty is not recognized by China. Hong Kong provides a major international trade link for China; a 99-year 'lease' period of British control was concluded in 1997.

▲ **North of the** Qin Ling range in Shaanxi province, is an agriculturally fertile region covered with fine, wind-blown deposits and known as the loess plateau. The loose sediments are vulnerable to water erosion.

Using the land and sea

This is a region of intensive cultivation. Wheat, millet, sorghum and cotton are the main crops of the Yellow River basin. South from Sichuan, rice becomes the principal crop, grown with wheat, corn and cotton along the Yangtze river. Tea is produced in the hills and sugar cane along the coast of the southeast, where flat land is limited. Pigs and poultry are raised in great numbers.

Land use and agricultural distribution

- cattle
- pigs
- cereals
- corn (maize)
- cotton
- fishing
- peanuts
- rice
- sugar cane
- tea
- capital cities
- major towns
- pasture
- cropland
- forest
- mountain region

▲ **On the hills** above the North China Plain, slopes are terraced to utilize the rich loess soils of the Taihang Shan range.

Map key

Population
- above 5 million
- 1 million to 5 million
- 500,000 to 1 million
- 100,000 to 500,000
- 50,000 to 100,000
- 10,000 to 50,000
- below 10,000

Elevation
- 6000m / 19,686ft
- 4000m / 13,124ft
- 3000m / 9843ft
- 2000m / 6562ft
- 1000m / 3281ft
- 500m / 1640ft
- 250m / 820ft
- 100m / 328ft
- sea level

Scale 1:8,500,000

projection: Lambert Conformal Conic

◄ **The former Portuguese** territory of Macao, with its colonial architecture, bars and casinos, reverted to Chinese rule in 1999.

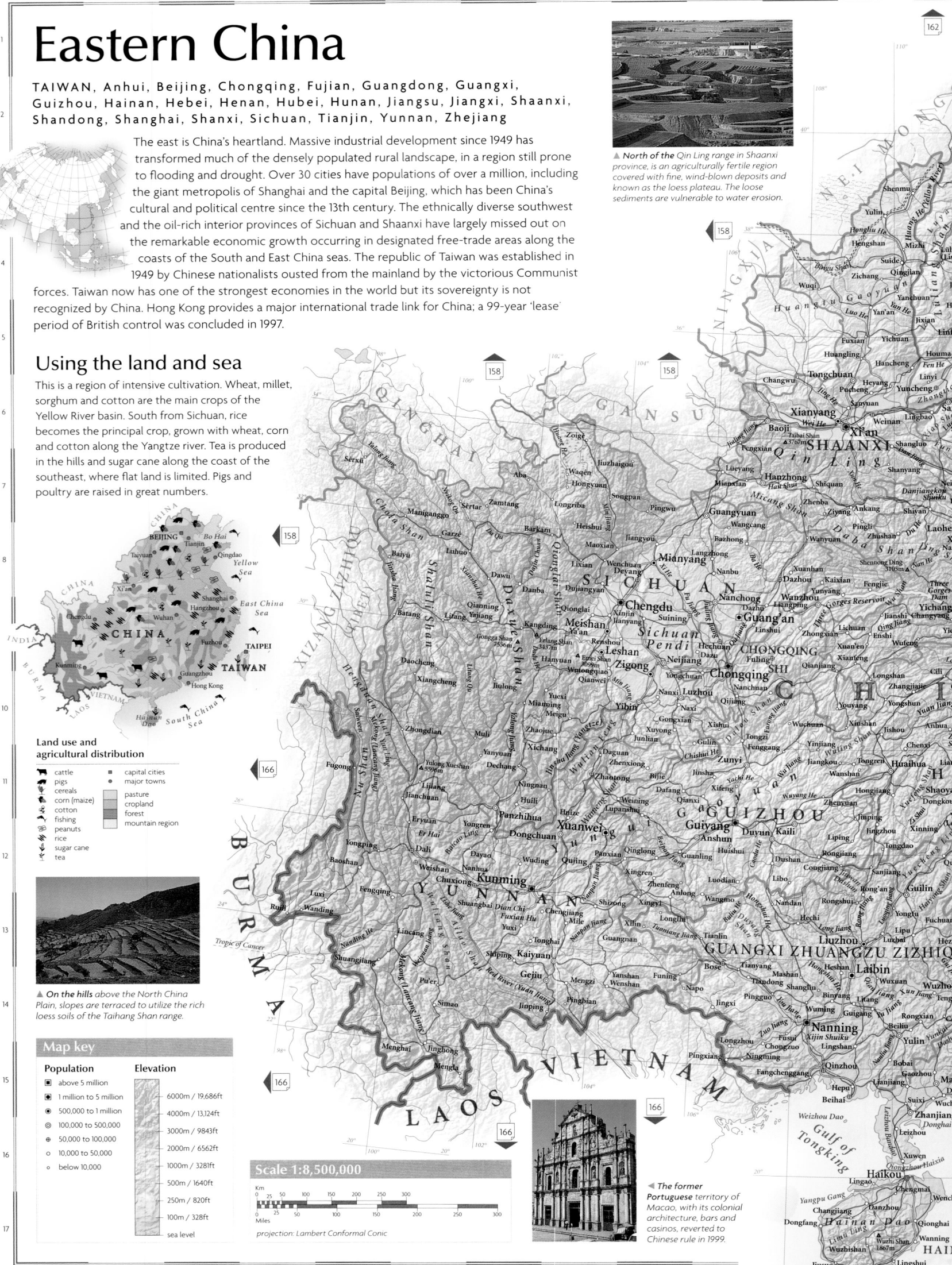

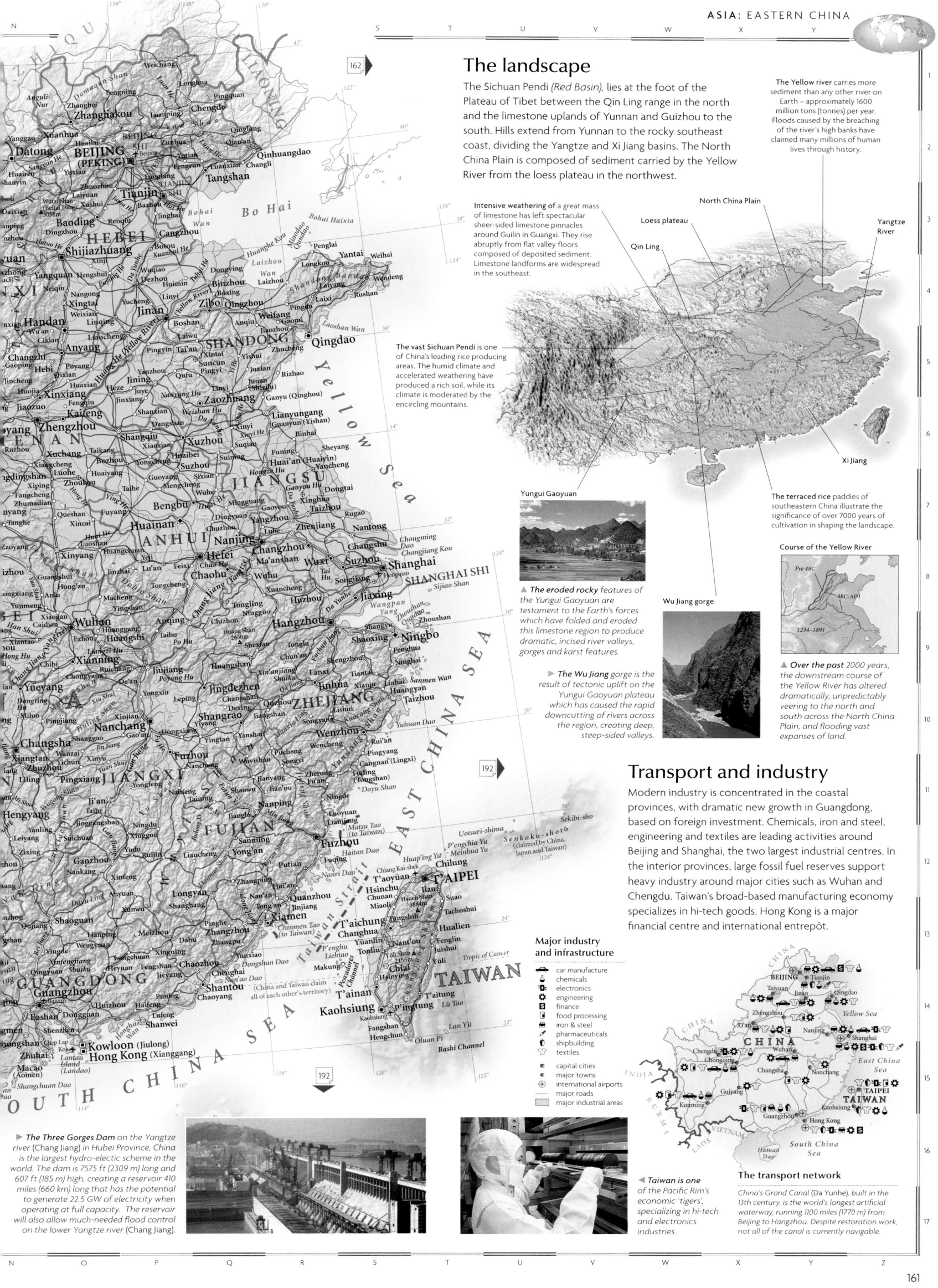

The landscape

The Sichuan Pendi (Red Basin), lies at the foot of the Plateau of Tibet between the Qin Ling range in the north and the limestone uplands of Yunnan and Guizhou to the south. Hills extend from Yunnan to the rocky southeast coast, dividing the Yangtze and Xi Jiang basins. The North China Plain is composed of sediment carried by the Yellow River from the loess plateau in the northwest.

The Yellow river carries more sediment than any other river on Earth – approximately 1600 million tons (tonnes) per year. Floods caused by the breaching of the river's high banks have claimed many millions of human lives through history.

Intensive weathering of a great mass of limestone has left spectacular sheer-sided limestone pinnacles around Guilin in Guangxi. They rise abruptly from flat valley floors composed of deposited sediment. Limestone landforms are widespread in the southeast.

The vast Sichuan Pendi is one of China's leading rice producing areas. The humid climate and accelerated weathering have produced a rich soil, while its climate is moderated by the encircling mountains.

Yungui Gaoyuan

▲ The eroded rocky features of the Yungui Gaoyuan are testament to the Earth's forces which have folded and eroded this limestone region to produce dramatic, incised river valleys, gorges and karst features.

▶ The Wu Jiang gorge is the result of tectonic uplift on the Yungui Gaoyuan plateau which has caused the rapid downcutting of rivers across the region, creating deep, steep-sided valleys.

Wu Jiang gorge

The terraced rice paddies of southeastern China illustrate the significance of over 7000 years of cultivation in shaping the landscape.

Course of the Yellow River

Pre 4BC

4BC–AD1

1234–1891

▲ Over the past 2000 years, the downstream course of the Yellow River has altered dramatically, unpredictably veering to the north and south across the North China Plain, and flooding vast expanses of land.

Transport and industry

Modern industry is concentrated in the coastal provinces, with dramatic new growth in Guangdong, based on foreign investment. Chemicals, iron and steel, engineering and textiles are leading activities around Beijing and Shanghai, the two largest industrial centres. In the interior provinces, large fossil fuel reserves support heavy industry around major cities such as Wuhan and Chengdu. Taiwan's broad-based manufacturing economy specializes in hi-tech goods. Hong Kong is a major financial centre and international entrepôt.

Major industry and infrastructure

- car manufacture
- chemicals
- electronics
- engineering
- finance
- food processing
- iron & steel
- pharmaceuticals
- shipbuilding
- textiles

- capital cities
- major towns
- international airports
- major roads
- major industrial areas

The transport network

China's Grand Canal (Da Yunhe), built in the 13th century, is the world's longest artificial waterway, running 1100 miles (1770 m) from Beijing to Hangzhou. Despite restoration work, not all of the canal is currently navigable.

▶ The Three Gorges Dam on the Yangtze river (Chang Jiang) in Hubei Province, China is the largest hydro-electic scheme in the world. The dam is 7575 ft (2309 m) long and 607 ft (185 m) high, creating a reservoir 410 miles (660 km) long that has the potential to generate 22.5 GW of electricity when operating at full capacity. The reservoir will also allow much-needed flood control on the lower Yangtze river (Chang Jiang).

◀ Taiwan is one of the Pacific Rim's economic 'tigers', specializing in hi-tech and electronics industries.

Northeastern China, Mongolia & Korea

MONGOLIA, NORTH KOREA, SOUTH KOREA, Heilongjiang, Inner Mongolia, Jilin, Liaoning

This northerly region has for centuries been a domain of shifting borders and competing colonial powers. Mongolia was the heartland of Chinghiz Khan's vast Mongol empire in the 13th century, while northeastern China was home to the Manchus, China's last ruling dynasty (1644–1911). The mineral and forest wealth of the northeast helped make this China's principal region of heavy industry, although the outdated state factories now face decline. South Korea's state-led market economy has grown dramatically and Seoul is now one of the world's largest cities. The austere communist regime of North Korea has isolated itself from the expanding markets of the Pacific Rim and faces continuing economic stagnation.

▲ *The Eurasian steppe* stretches from the mouth of the Danube in Europe, to Mongolia. In Mongolia, nomadic people have lived in felt huts called yurts or gers, for thousands of years.

Map key

Population

- ■ above 5 million
- ▣ 1 million to 5 million
- ◉ 500,000 to 1 million
- ◎ 100,000 to 500,000
- ⊕ 50,000 to 100,000
- ⊙ 10,000 to 50,000
- ○ below 10,000

Elevation

- 4000m / 13,124ft
- 3000m / 9843ft
- 2000m / 6562ft
- 1000m / 3281ft
- 500m / 1640ft
- 250m / 820ft
- 100m / 328ft
- sea level

Scale 1:7,750,000

Km
0 25 50   100   150   200

Miles
0 25   50   100   150   200

projection: Lambert Conformal Conic

The landscape

The great North China Plain is largely enclosed by mountain ranges including the Great and Lesser Khingan Ranges (*Da Hinggan Ling* and *Xiao Hinggan Ling*) in the north, and the Changbai Shan, which extend south into the rugged peninsula of Korea. The broad steppeland plateau of Nei Mongol Gaoyuan borders the southeastern edge of the great cold desert of the Gobi which extends west across the southern reaches of Mongolia. In northwest Mongolia the Altai Mountains and various lesser ranges are interspersed with lakeland basins.

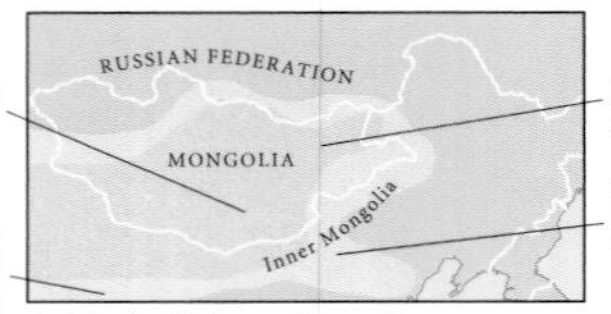

▲ *Much of Mongolia* and Inner Mongolia is a vast desert area. To the south and east, a semi-arid region extends into China proper.

▲ *The Gobi desert* stretches from Central Asia, through Mongolia and into China. Bare rock surfaces, rather than sand dunes, typify the cold desert landscape of the Gobi.

Tributaries of the Amur river follow U-shaped valleys through the Great Khingan Range (*Da Hinggan Ling*). These were cut by ice-age glaciers between 3 and 10 million years ago.

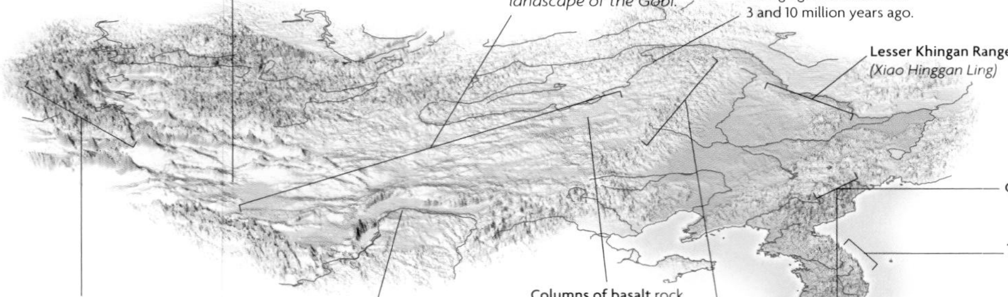

The Altai Mountains are the highest and longest of the mountain ranges which extend into Mongolia from the northwest. These mountains provide one of the last refuges for the endangered snow leopard.

The Yellow River sweeps north around the Ordos Desert (*Mu Us Shadi*), bringing water to an otherwise barren region.

Columns of basalt rock protrude in occasional clusters from the flat surface of the eastern Gobi. Their regular, six-sided form was produced when the rock cooled and contracted from its molten state.

Great Khingan Range (*Da Hinggan Ling*)

A crater lake occupies the 9023 ft (2750 m) snowy summit of the extinct volcano Paektu-san, the highest peak in the mountains of the Changbai Shan.

◀ *The wooded mountain* range of T'aebaek-sanmaek forms the backbone of the Korean peninsula, running north–south along the eastern coastline.

Gobi
Semi-arid zone
Desert zone
Ordos Desert (Mu Us Shadi)

RUSSIAN FEDERATION
MONGOLIA
Inner Mongolia

Lesser Khingan Range (Xiao Hinggan Ling)
Changbai Shan
T'aebaek-sanmaek

Transport and industry

North Korea's centrally-planned economy is strongly oriented towards heavy industry, while South Korea has a broad manufacturing base which includes textiles, steel, electronics, and one of the world's largest shipbuilding industries. Mongolia and Inner Mongolia's great mineral resource potential is largely undeveloped. The heavy industrial region around Shenyang produces iron, steel, chemicals and cement on a massive scale.

Major industry and infrastructure

- car manufacture
- chemicals
- coal
- electronics
- engineering
- finance
- food processing
- iron & steel
- pharmaceuticals
- shipbuilding
- textiles
- capital cities
- major towns
- international airports
- major roads
- major industrial areas

▲ Ulan Bator, the Mongolian capital bears many of the hallmarks of Soviet-style central planning, the result of economic and industrial assistance from the Soviet Union following Mongolian independence in 1921.

The transport network

Liaoning has China's most comprehensive railway network, the legacy of the Japanese occupation of Manchuria in the 20th century. The railways are used primarily for freight transport.

▶ While North Korea has remained politically and economically isolated from the rest of the world, South Korea has enjoyed immense economic growth. It has benefited considerably from US economic aid in the aftermath of the Korean war of 1950–1953.

Using the land and sea

Mongolia and Inner Mongolia rely heavily on livestock farming, with only about 1% of the land area cultivated. Northeastern China produces wheat, corn, soya beans and sugar beet. The cool climate limits the range of crops and large upland areas of the northeast remain forested. Rice is the staple food of North and South Korea. The latter has become a leading ocean-fishing nation.

Land use and agricultural distribution

- goats
- pigs
- sheep
- corn (maize)
- fishing
- rice
- soya beans
- sugar beet
- wheat
- capital cities
- major towns
- pasture
- cropland
- forest
- mountain region
- desert

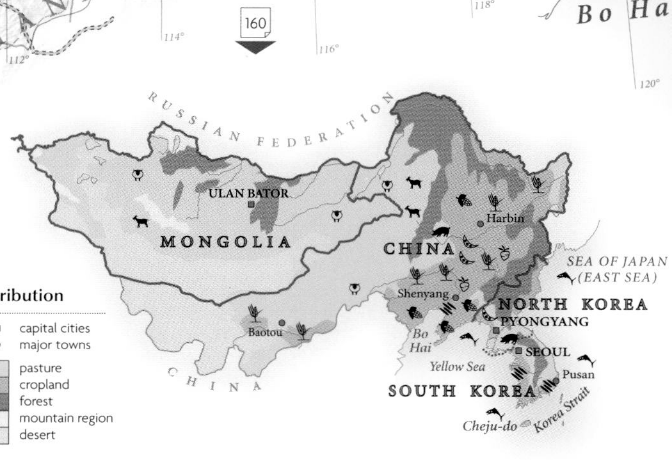

Japan

In the years since the end of the Second World War, Japan has become the world's most dynamic industrial nation. The country comprises a string of over 4000 islands which lie in a great northeast to southwest arc in the northwest Pacific. Four major islands: Hokkaido, Honshu, Shikoku and Kyushu are home to the great majority of Japan's population of 128 million people, although the mountainous terrain of the central region means that most cities are situated on the coast. A densely populated industrial belt stretches along much of Honshu's southern coast, including Japan's crowded capital, Tokyo. Alongside its spectacular economic growth and the increasing westernization of its cities, Japan still maintains a most singular culture, reflected in its traditional food, formal behavioural codes, unique Shinto religion and a deep reverence for the emperor.

Using the land and sea

Although only about 11% of Japan is suitable for cultivation, substantial government support, a favourable climate and intensive farming methods enable the country to be virtually self-sufficient in rice production. Northern Hokkaido, the largest and most productive farming region, has an open terrain and climate similar to that of the US Midwest, and produces over half of Japan's cereal requirements. Farmers are being encouraged to diversify by growing fruit, vegetables and wheat, as well as raising livestock.

Land use and agricultural distribution

- cattle
- pigs
- fishing
- cereals
- citrus fruits
- fruit
- herbs
- rice
- root crops
- tobacco
- ■ capital cities
- ● major towns

- pasture
- cropland
- forest

The urban/rural population divide

urban 78% rural 22%

0 10 20 30 40 50 60 70 80 90 100

Population density	Total land area
885 people per sq mile (342 people per sq km)	145,869 sq miles (377,800 sq km)

The landscape

The islands of Japan lie on the Pacific 'Ring of Fire', and form a series of clearly defined arcs. The largely mountainous landscape was formed very recently in geological terms. Volcanic eruptions and earthquakes continue to reshape the terrain and to shake the country's complex infrastructure. There is no one continuous mountain range; the mountains divide into many small land blocks separated by lowlands and dissected by numerous river valleys.

Sea of Japan (East Sea)
Active volcanic island
Japan Trench (subduction zone)

▲ **Japan is part** of an arc of volcanic islands, formed by the Pacific Plate diving under the Eurasian Plate. This process generates intense stress which is periodically released as earthquakes.

◀ **Mount Fuji is** Japan's highest mountain, rising 12,388 ft (3776 m) above the Kanto Plain in the central region of Honshu. The flat land below is suitable for growing crops such as tea. Like many Japanese mountains, it is revered as a sacred site.

Mount Fuji

A number of rivers which emerge from the volcanic parts of northwestern Honshu are so highly acidic that their water is unsuitable for irrigation and consumption.

▶ **Trees cling to** the sheer slopes of the waterfalls on the northern island of Hokkaido. The island's climate is similar to that in northern Europe, with long, cold winters and short, warm summers.

▶ **Cutting terraces maximizes** the limited agricultural land, enabling Japan to produce large quantities of rice.

In much of Kyushu the coast is subsiding, giving a highly indented coastline. In some places, former hilltops are barely visible above the current sea level.

The Inland Sea (Seto-naikai) has resulted from the depression of faulted blocks which has allowed sea water to invade the region between northern Shikoku and western Honshu.

Strong southeasterly winds blowing onshore during the winter create sand dunes which extend for miles along the eastern coasts.

Biwa-ko is the largest lake in Japan, covering 260 sq miles (673 sq km) in central Honshu. The depression in which it lies was created by recent faulting of the underlying rocks.

There are over 60 active volcanoes – like Asahi-dake, Hokkaido's highest peak – throughout Japan. This accounts for more than 10% of the world's total.

Rising land on the Pacific coast of Honshu leads to typical features such as raised beaches, some lying over 1000 ft (300 m) above sea level.

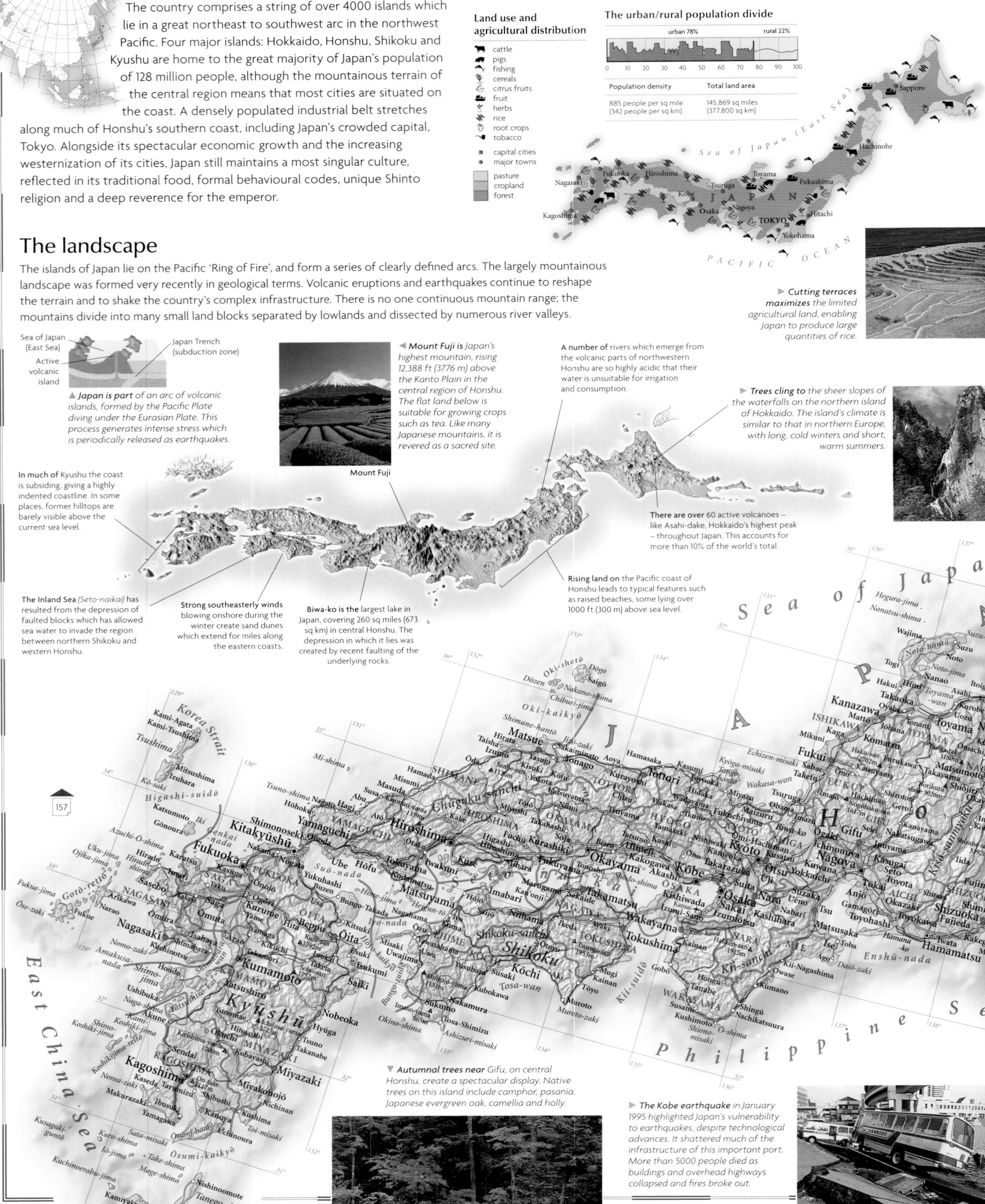

▼ **Autumnal trees near** Gifu, on central Honshu, create a spectacular display. Native trees on this island include camphor, pasania, Japanese evergreen oak, camellia and holly.

▶ **The Kobe earthquake** in January 1995 highlighted Japan's vulnerability to earthquakes, despite technological advances. It shattered much of the infrastructure of this important port. More than 5000 people died as buildings and overhead highways collapsed and fires broke out.

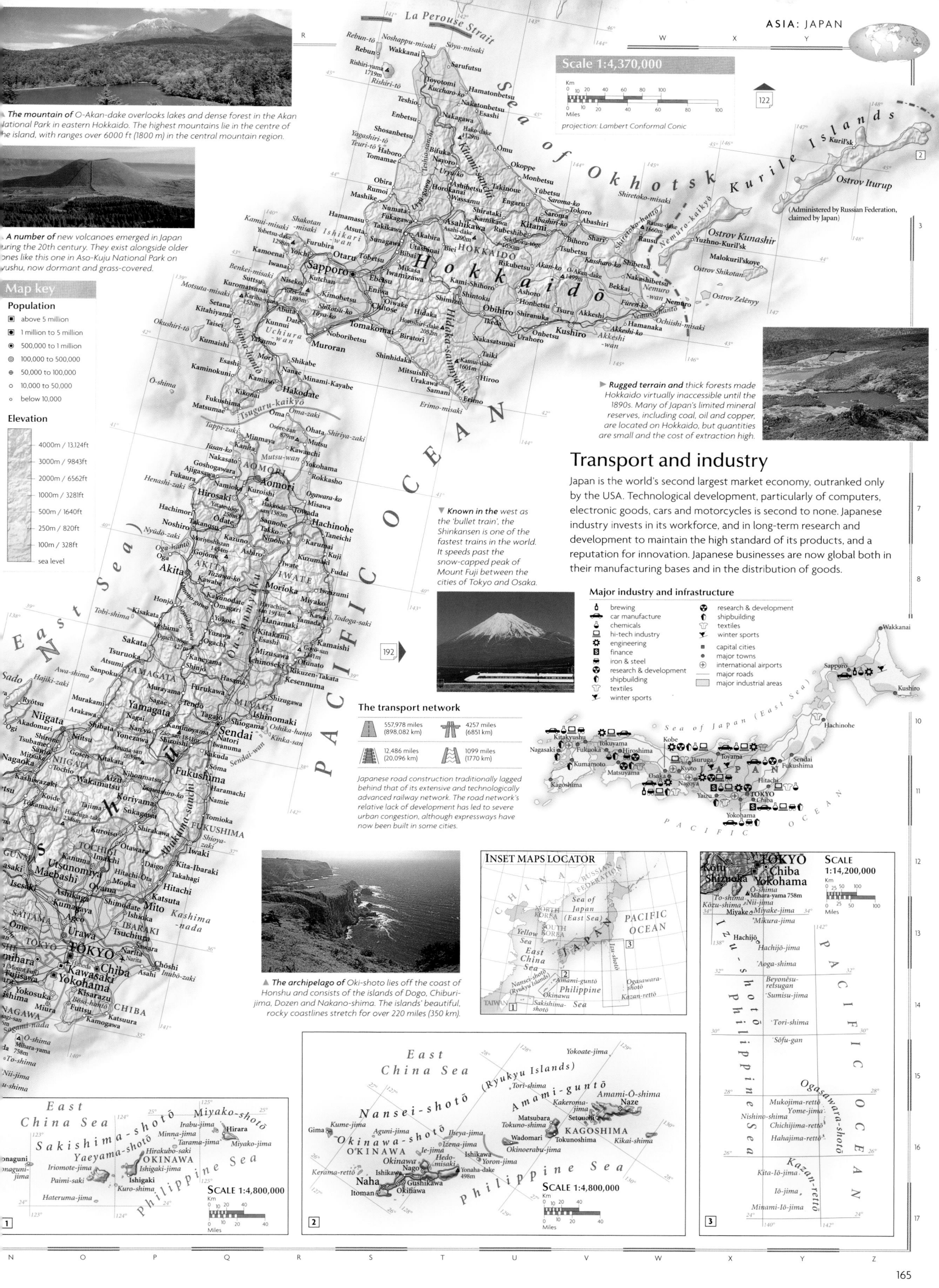

The mountain of O-Akan-dake overlooks lakes and dense forest in the Akan National Park in eastern Hokkaido. The highest mountains lie in the centre of the island, with ranges over 6000 ft (1800 m) in the central mountain region.

A number of new volcanoes emerged in Japan during the 20th century. They exist alongside older ones like this one in Aso-Kuju National Park on Kyushu, now dormant and grass-covered.

Map key

Population
- above 5 million
- 1 million to 5 million
- 500,000 to 1 million
- 100,000 to 500,000
- 50,000 to 100,000
- 10,000 to 50,000
- below 10,000

Elevation
- 4000m / 13,124ft
- 3000m / 9843ft
- 2000m / 6562ft
- 1000m / 3281ft
- 500m / 1640ft
- 250m / 820ft
- 100m / 328ft
- sea level

Scale 1:4,370,000

projection: Lambert Conformal Conic

▶ *Rugged terrain and thick forests made Hokkaido virtually inaccessible until the 1890s. Many of Japan's limited mineral reserves, including coal, oil and copper, are located on Hokkaido, but quantities are small and the cost of extraction high.*

Transport and industry

Japan is the world's second largest market economy, outranked only by the USA. Technological development, particularly of computers, electronic goods, cars and motorcycles is second to none. Japanese industry invests in its workforce, and in long-term research and development to maintain the high standard of its products, and a reputation for innovation. Japanese businesses are now global both in their manufacturing bases and in the distribution of goods.

▼ *Known in the west as the 'bullet train', the Shinkansen is one of the fastest trains in the world. It speeds past the snow-capped peak of Mount Fuji between the cities of Tokyo and Osaka.*

Major industry and infrastructure
- brewing
- car manufacture
- chemicals
- hi-tech industry
- engineering
- finance
- iron & steel
- research & development
- shipbuilding
- textiles
- winter sports
- research & development
- shipbuilding
- textiles
- winter sports
- capital cities
- major towns
- international airports
- major roads
- major industrial areas

The transport network

557,978 miles (898,082 km)	4257 miles (6851 km)
12,486 miles (20,096 km)	1099 miles (1770 km)

Japanese road construction traditionally lagged behind that of its extensive and technologically advanced railway network. The road network's relative lack of development has led to severe urban congestion, although expressways have now been built in some cities.

INSET MAPS LOCATOR

SCALE 1:14,200,000

▲ *The archipelago of Oki-shoto lies off the coast of Honshu and consists of the islands of Dogo, Chiburi-jima, Dozen and Nakano-shima. The islands' beautiful, rocky coastlines stretch for over 220 miles (350 km).*

SCALE 1:4,800,000 (inset 1)

SCALE 1:4,800,000 (inset 2)

Mainland Southeast Asia

BURMA, CAMBODIA, LAOS, THAILAND, VIETNAM

Thickly forested mountains, intercut by the broad valleys of five great rivers characterize the landscape of Southeast Asia's mainland countries. Agriculture remains the main activity for much of the population, which is concentrated in the river flood plains and deltas. Linked ethnic and cultural roots give the region a distinct identity. Most people on the mainland are Theravada Buddhists, and the Philippines is the only predominantly Christian country in Southeast Asia. Foreign intervention began in the 16th century with the opening of the spice trade; Cambodia, Laos and Vietnam were French colonies until the end of the Second World War, Burma was under British control. Only Thailand was never colonized. Today, Thailand is poised to play a leading role in the economic development of the Pacific Rim, and Laos and Vietnam have begun to mend the devastation of the Vietnam War, and to develop their economies. With continuing political instability and a shattered infrastructure, Cambodia faces an uncertain future, while Burma is seeking investment and the ending of its long isolation from the world community.

▲ *The Irrawaddy river is Burma's vital central artery, watering the ricefields and providing a rich source of fish, as well as an important transport link, particularly for local traffic.*

The landscape

A series of mountain ranges runs north–south through the mainland, formed as the result of the collision between the Eurasian Plate and the Indian subcontinent, which created the Himalayas. They are interspersed by the valleys of a number of great rivers. On their passage to the sea these rivers have deposited sediment, forming huge, fertile flood plains and deltas.

The coastline of the Isthmus of Kra

Longshore drift
Eroded coastline
Spit
Lagoon
Wave attack

◄ *The east and west coasts of the Isthmus of Kra differ greatly. The tectonically uplifting west coast is exposed to the harsh south-westerly monsoon and is heavily eroded. On the east coast, longshore currents produce depositional features such as spits and lagoons.*

Hkakabo Razi is the highest point in mainland Southeast Asia. It rises 19,300 ft (5885 m) at the border between China and Burma.

Mountains dominate the Laotian landscape with more than 90% of the land lying more than 600 ft (180 m) above sea level. The mountains of the Chaine Annamitique form the country's eastern border.

The Red River delta in northern Vietnam is fringed to the north by steep-sided, round-topped limestone hills, typical of karst scenery.

The Irrawaddy river runs virtually north–south, draining the plains of northern Burma. The Irrawaddy delta is the country's main rice-growing area.

Salween River

Isthmus of Kra

◄ *The fast-flowing waters of the Mekong river cascade over this waterfall in Champasak province in Laos. The force of the water erodes rocks at the base of the fall.*

▲ *The coast of the Isthmus of Kra, in southeast Thailand has many small, precipitous islands like these, formed by chemical erosion on limestone, which is weathered along vertical cracks. The humidity of the climate in Southeast Asia increases the rate of weathering.*

Malay Peninsula

Tonle Sap, a freshwater lake, drains into the Mekong delta via the Mekong river. It is the largest lake in Southeast Asia.

The Mekong river flows through southern China and Burma, then for much of its length forms the border between Laos and Thailand, flowing through Cambodia before terminating in a vast delta on the southern Vietnamese coast.

Using the land and sea

The fertile flood plains of rivers such as the Mekong and Salween, and the humid climate, enable the production of rice throughout the region. Cambodia, Burma and Laos still have substantial forests, producing hardwoods such as teak and rosewood. Cash crops include tropical fruits such as coconuts, bananas and pineapples, rubber, oil palm, sugar cane and the jute substitute, kenaf. Pigs and cattle are the main livestock raised. Large quantities of marine and freshwater fish are caught throughout the region.

▲ *Commercial logging – still widespread in Burma – has now been stopped in Thailand because of over-exploitation of the tropical rainforest.*

The urban/rural population divide

urban 30%   rural 70%

0 10 20 30 40 50 60 70 80 90 100

Population density	Total land area
345 people per sq mile (133 people per sq km)	733,828 sq miles (1,901,110 sq km)

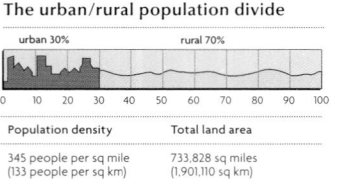

Land use and agricultural distribution

- cattle
- pigs
- bananas
- coconuts
- fishing
- oil palms
- rice
- rubber
- sugar cane
- timber

- ■ capital cities
- ● major towns

- pasture
- cropland
- forest
- wetland

Transport and industry

Industrial manufacturing has become increasingly important in Thailand and Vietnam in recent years. The assembling of component-based electrical and electronic goods is becoming more common throughout this region, with foreign companies benefiting from low labour costs and the upgrading of technology. The economies of Burma and Cambodia are still based on agricultural produce and the processing of raw materials. Tin is the region's most important metal, and nickel, copper and chromite are also mined, although the quantities produced are not significant on a global scale. Thailand's successful tourist industry is the country's highest earner of foreign exchange.

The transport network

82,958 miles (133,524 km)	267 miles (430 km)
7500 miles (12,071 km)	28,585 miles (46,008 km)

Transport development has concentrated on the building of road networks. Water and sea transport remain important, although air links have impr oved, particularly in Thailand and the Philippines.

Major industry and infrastructure

⚗	chemicals	🔥	oil & gas	■	capital cities
⚙	electronics	⛏	mining	●	major towns
⚙	engineering	🚢	shipbuilding	⊕	international airports
$	finance	👕	textiles	—	major roads
🍴	food processing	🌲	timber processing	▨	major industrial areas
🏭	iron & steel				

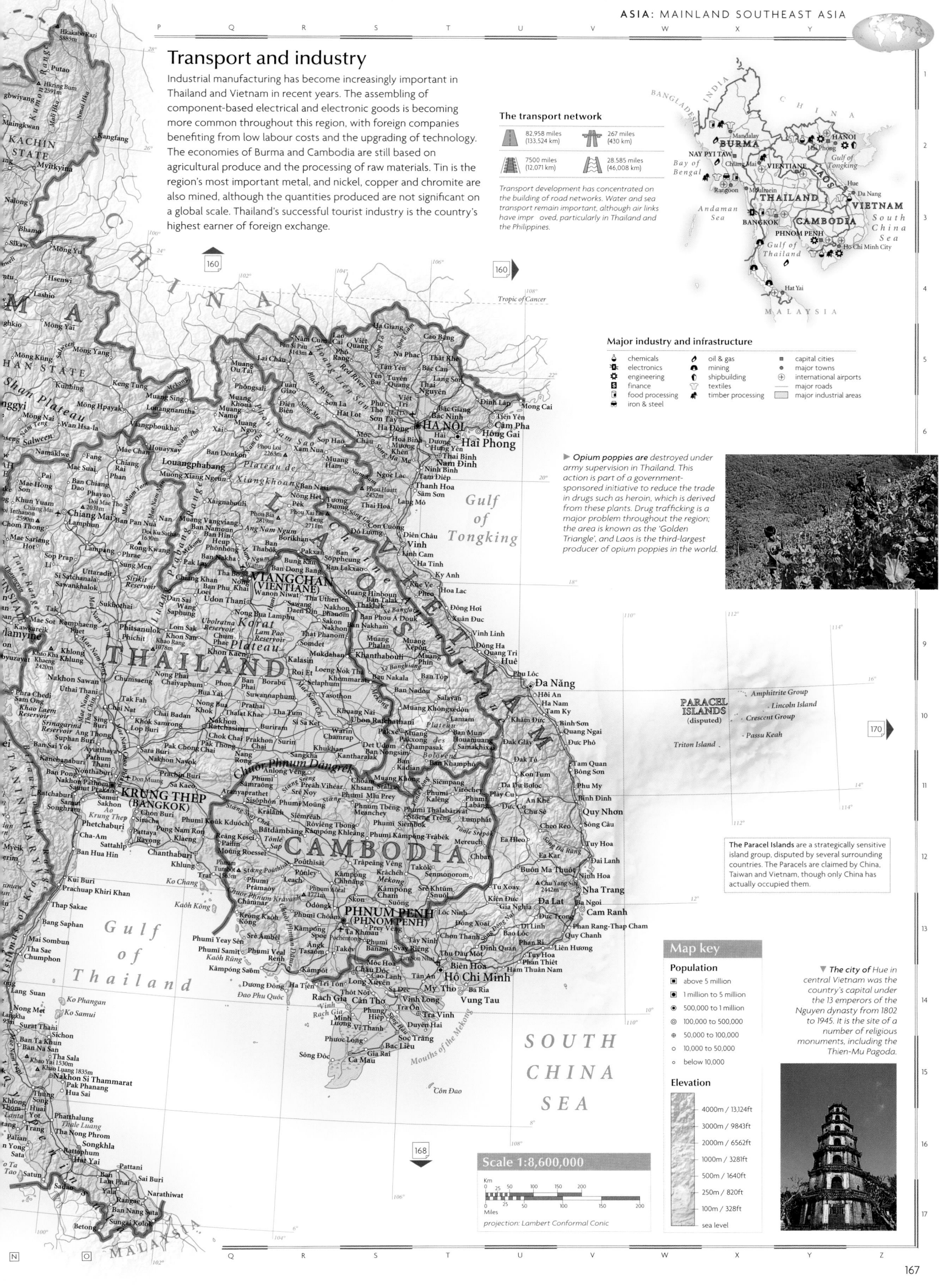

▶ **Opium poppies are** destroyed under army supervision in Thailand. This action is part of a government-sponsored initiative to reduce the trade in drugs such as heroin, which is derived from these plants. Drug trafficking is a major problem throughout the region; the area is known as the 'Golden Triangle', and Laos is the third-largest producer of opium poppies in the world.

The Paracel Islands are a strategically sensitive island group, disputed by several surrounding countries. The Paracels are claimed by China, Taiwan and Vietnam, though only China has actually occupied them.

▼ **The city of** Hue in central Vietnam was the country's capital under the 13 emperors of the Nguyen dynasty from 1802 to 1945. It is the site of a number of religious monuments, including the Thien-Mu Pagoda.

Map key

Population

■	above 5 million
◼	1 million to 5 million
◉	500,000 to 1 million
◎	100,000 to 500,000
⊕	50,000 to 100,000
○	10,000 to 50,000
○	below 10,000

Elevation

	4000m / 13,124ft
	3000m / 9843ft
	2000m / 6562ft
	1000m / 3281ft
	500m / 1640ft
	250m / 820ft
	100m / 328ft
	sea level

Scale 1:8,600,000

projection: Lambert Conformal Conic

Western Maritime Southeast Asia

BRUNEI, INDONESIA, MALAYSIA, SINGAPORE

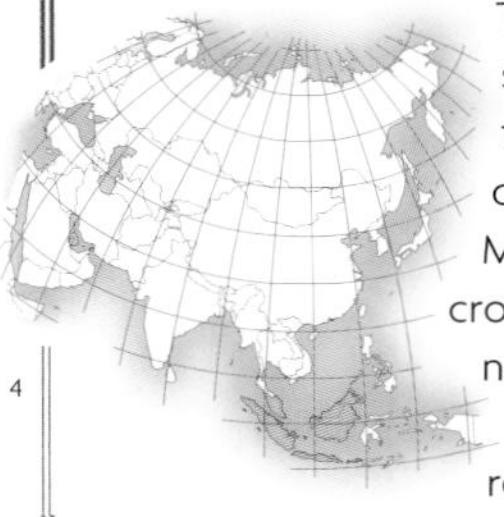

The world's largest archipelago, Indonesia's myriad islands stretch 3100 miles (5000 km) eastwards across the Pacific, from the Malay Peninsula to western New Guinea. Only about 1500 of the 13,677 islands are inhabited and the huge, predominently Muslim population is unevenly distributed, with some two-thirds crowded onto the western islands of Java, Madura and Bali. The national government is trying to resettle large numbers of people from these islands to other parts of the country to reduce population pressure there. Malaysia, split between the mainland and the east Malaysian states of Sabah and Sarawak on Borneo, has a diverse population, as well as a fast-growing economy, although the pace of its development is still far outstripped by that of Singapore. This small island nation is the financial and commercial capital of Southeast Asia. The Sultanate of Brunei in northern Borneo, one of the world's last princely states, has an extremely high standard of living, based on its oil revenues.

The landscape

Indonesia's western islands are characterized by rugged volcanic mountains cloaked with dense tropical forest, which slope down to coastal plains covered by thick alluvial swamps. The Sunda Shelf, an extension of the Eurasian Plate, lies between Java, Bali, Sumatra and Borneo. These islands' mountains rise from a base below the sea, and they were once joined together by dry land, which has since been submerged by rising sea levels.

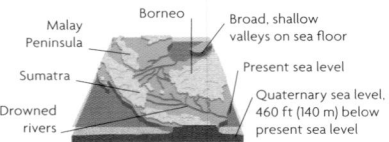

The Sunda Shelf underlies this whole region. It is one of the largest submarine shelves in the world, covering an area of 714,285 sq miles (1,850,000 sq km). During the early Quaternary period, when sea levels were lower, the shelf was exposed.

◀ *Danau (lake) Toba* in Sumatra fills an enormous caldera 18 miles (30 km) wide and 62 miles (100 km) long – the largest in the world. It was formed through a combination of volcanic action and tectonic activity.

Malay Peninsula has a rugged east coast, but the west coast, fronting the Strait of Malacca, has many sheltered beaches and bays. The two coasts are divided by the Banjaran Titiwangsa, which run the length of the peninsula.

◀ *The river of* Sungai Mahakam cuts through the central highlands of Borneo, the third largest island in the world, with a total area of 290,000 sq miles (757,050 sq km). Although mountainous, Borneo is one of the most stable of the Indonesian islands, with little volcanic activity.

The island of Krakatau *(Pulau Rakata)*, lying between Sumatra and Java, was all but destroyed in 1883, when the volcano erupted. The release of gas and dust into the atmosphere disrupted cloud cover and global weather patterns for several years.

Gunung Kinabalu is the highest peak in Malaysia, rising 13,455 ft (4101 m).

Indonesia has more than 220 volcanoes, most of which are still active. They are strung out along the island arc from Sumatra through the Lesser Sunda Islands, into the Moluccas and Celebes.

Transport and industry

Singapore has a thriving economy based on international trade and finance. Annual trade through the port is among the highest of any in the world. Indonesia's western islands still depend on natural resources, particularly petroleum, gas and wood, although the economy is rapidly diversifying with manufactured exports including garments, consumer electronics and footwear. A high-profile aircraft industry has developed in Bandung on Java. Malaysia has a fast-growing and varied manufacturing sector, although oil, gas and timber remain important resource-based industries.

▶ *Ranks of gleaming* skyscrapers, new motorways and infrastructure construction reflect the investment which is pouring into Southeast Asian cities like the Malaysian capital, Kuala Lumpur. Traditional housing and markets still exist amidst the new developments. Many of the city's inhabitants subsist at a level far removed from the prosperity implied by its outward modernity.

Malaysia: Capital cities

KUALA LUMPUR – capital
PUTRAJAYA – administrative capital

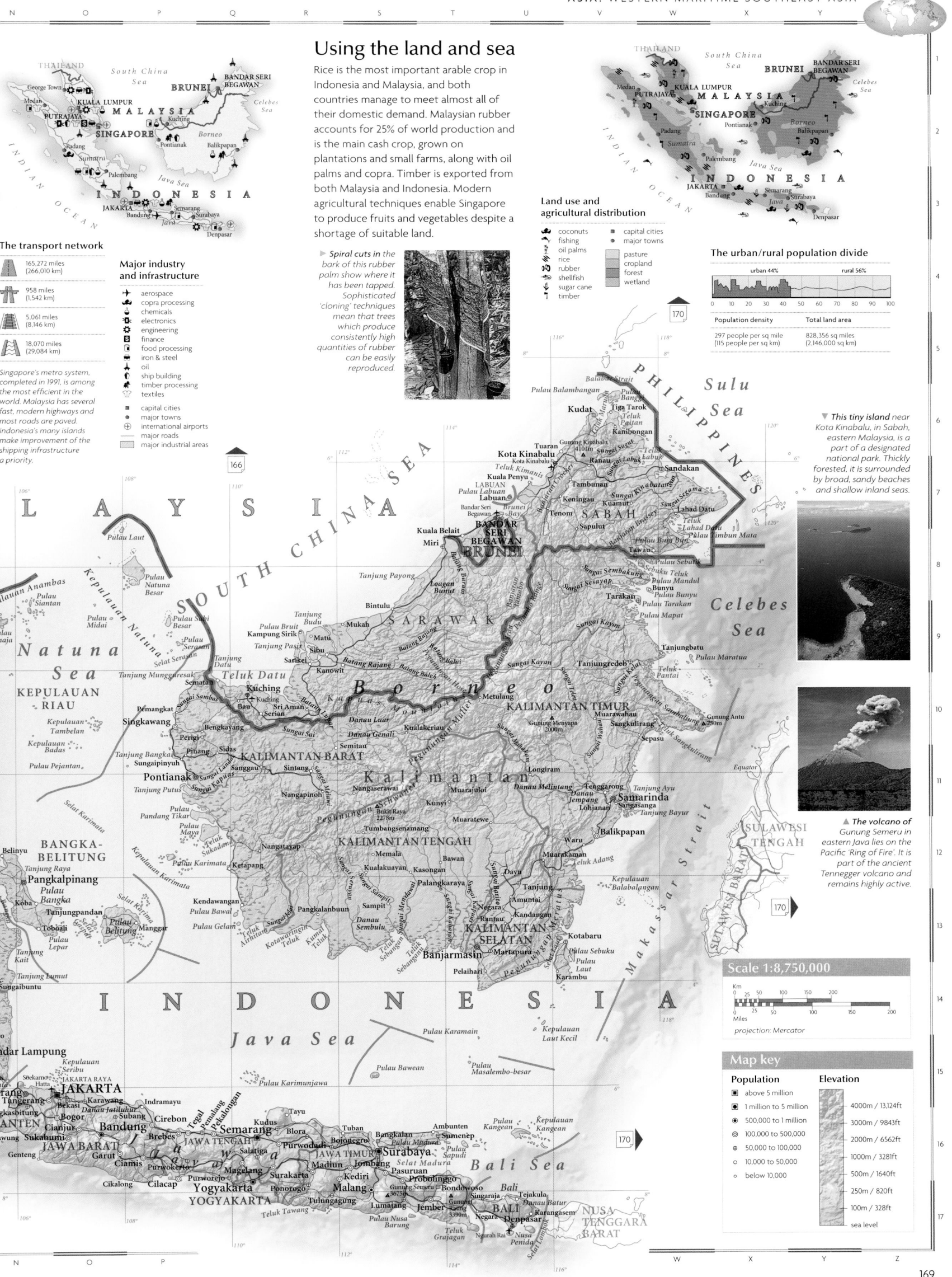

Using the land and sea

Rice is the most important arable crop in Indonesia and Malaysia, and both countries manage to meet almost all of their domestic demand. Malaysian rubber accounts for 25% of world production and is the main cash crop, grown on plantations and small farms, along with oil palms and copra. Timber is exported from both Malaysia and Indonesia. Modern agricultural techniques enable Singapore to produce fruits and vegetables despite a shortage of suitable land.

▶ *Spiral cuts in the bark of this rubber palm show where it has been tapped. Sophisticated 'cloning' techniques mean that trees which produce consistently high quantities of rubber can be easily reproduced.*

The transport network

🛣	165,272 miles (266,010 km)
🛤	958 miles (1,542 km)
🚂	5,061 miles (8,146 km)
✈	18,070 miles (29,084 km)

Singapore's metro system, completed in 1991, is among the most efficient in the world. Malaysia has several fast, modern highways and most roads are paved. Indonesia's many islands make improvement of the shipping infrastructure a priority.

Major industry and infrastructure

- ✈ aerospace
- 🥥 copra processing
- 🧪 chemicals
- 💡 electronics
- ⚙ engineering
- 💲 finance
- 🍴 food processing
- ⛏ iron & steel
- 🛢 oil
- ⚓ ship building
- 🪵 timber processing
- 👕 textiles
- ■ capital cities
- ● major towns
- ⊕ international airports
- — major roads
- ▭ major industrial areas

Land use and agricultural distribution

- 🥥 coconuts
- 🎣 fishing
- 🌴 oil palms
- 🌾 rice
- rubber
- 🐚 shellfish
- 🌿 sugar cane
- 🌲 timber
- ■ capital cities
- ● major towns
- pasture
- cropland
- forest
- wetland

The urban/rural population divide

urban 44%   rural 56%

0 10 20 30 40 50 60 70 80 90 100

Population density	Total land area
297 people per sq mile (115 people per sq km)	828,356 sq miles (2,146,000 sq km)

▼ *This tiny island near Kota Kinabalu, in Sabah, eastern Malaysia, is a part of a designated national park. Thickly forested, it is surrounded by broad, sandy beaches and shallow inland seas.*

▲ *The volcano of Gunung Semeru in eastern Java lies on the Pacific 'Ring of Fire'. It is part of the ancient Tennegger volcano and remains highly active.*

Scale 1:8,750,000

Km 0 25 50 100 150 200

Miles 0 25 50 100 150 200

projection: Mercator

Map key

Population
- ▣ above 5 million
- ▪ 1 million to 5 million
- ◉ 500,000 to 1 million
- ◎ 100,000 to 500,000
- ⊕ 50,000 to 100,000
- ○ 10,000 to 50,000
- ○ below 10,000

Elevation
- 4000m / 13,124ft
- 3000m / 9843ft
- 2000m / 6562ft
- 1000m / 3281ft
- 500m / 1640ft
- 250m / 820ft
- 100m / 328ft
- sea level

Eastern Maritime Southeast Asia

EAST TIMOR, INDONESIA, PHILIPPINES

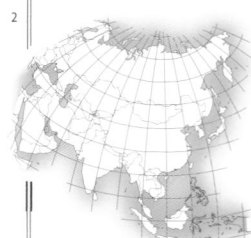

The Philippines takes its name from Philip II of Spain who was king when the islands were colonized during the 16th century. Almost 400 years of Spanish, and later US, rule have left their mark on the country's culture; English is widely spoken and over 90% of the population is Christian. The Philippines' economy is agriculturally based – inadequate infrastructure and electrical power shortages have so far hampered faster industrial growth. Indonesia's eastern islands are less economically developed than the rest of the country. Papua (Irian Jaya), which constitutes the western portion of New Guinea, is one of the world's last great wildernesses. East Timor is the newest independent state in the world, gaining full autonomy in 2002.

▲ *The traditional boat-shaped* houses of the Toraja people in Sulawesi. Although now Christian, the Toraja still practice the animist traditions and rituals of their ancestors. They are famous for their elaborate funeral ceremonies and burial sites in cliffside caves.

The landscape

Located on the Pacific 'Ring of Fire' the Philippines' 7100 islands are subject to frequent earthquakes and volcanic activity. Their terrain is largely mountainous, with narrow coastal plains and interior valleys and plains. Luzon and Mindanao are by far the largest islands and comprise roughly 66% of the country's area. Indonesia's eastern islands are mountainous and dotted with volcanoes, both active and dormant.

▶ *Lake Taal on* the Philippines island of Luzon lies within the crater of an immense volcano that erupted twice in the 20th century, first in 1911 and again in 1965, causing the deaths of more than 3200 people.

The Spratly Islands are a strategically sensitive island group, disputed by several surrounding countries. The Spratlys are claimed by China, Taiwan, Vietnam, Malaysia and the Philippines and are particularly important as they lie on oil and gas deposits.

Mindanao has five mountain ranges many of which have large numbers of active volcanoes. Lying just west of the Philippines Trench, which forms the boundary between the colliding Philippine and Eurasian plates, the entire island chain is subject to earthquakes and volcanic activity.

The 1000 islands of the Moluccas are the fabled Spice Islands of history, whose produce attracted traders from around the globe. Most of the northern and central Moluccas have dense vegetation and rugged mountainous interiors where elevations often exceed 3000 feet (9144 m).

▲ *Bohol in the* southern Philippines is famous for its so-called 'chocolate hills'. There are more than 1000 of these regular mounds on the island. The hills are limestone in origin, the smoothed remains of an earlier cycle of erosion. Their brown appearance in the dry season gives them their name.

The four-pronged island of Celebes is the product of complex tectonic activity which ruptured and then reattached small fragments of the Earth's crust to form the island's many peninsulas.

Coral islands such as Timor in eastern Indonesia show evidence of very recent and dramatic movements of the Earth's plates. Reefs in Timor have risen by as much as 4000 ft (1300 m) in the last million years.

The Pegunungan Jayawijaya range in central Papua (Irian Jaya) contains the world's highest range of limestone mountains, some with peaks more than 16,400 ft (5000 m) high. Heavy rainfall and high temperatures, which promote rapid weathering, have led to the creation of large underground caves and river systems such as the river of Sungai Baliem.

Using the land and sea

Indonesia's eastern islands are less intensively cultivated than those in the west. Coconuts, coffee and spices such as cloves and nutmeg are the major commercial crops while rice, corn and soya beans are grown for local consumption. The Philippines' rich, fertile soils support year-round production of a wide range of crops. The country is one of the world's largest producers of coconuts and a major exporter of coconut products, including one-third of the world's copra. Although much of the arable land is given over to rice and corn, the main staple food crops, tropical fruits such as bananas, pineapples and mangos, and sugar cane are also grown for export.

Land use and agricultural distribution

- coconuts
- fishing
- rice
- rubber
- shellfish
- sugar cane
- ■ capital cities
- ● major towns
- pasture
- cropland
- forest
- wetland

The urban/rural population divide

urban 45%	rural 55%

0 10 20 30 40 50 60 70 80 90 100

Population density	Total land area
258 people per sq mile (160 people per sq km)	654,771 sq miles (1,053,755 sq km)

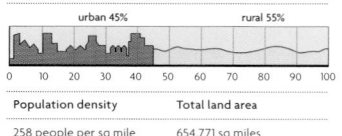

◀ *The terracing of* land to restrict soil erosion and create flat surfaces for agriculture is a common practice throughout Southeast Asia, particularly where land is scarce. These terraces are on Luzon in the Philippines.

▲ *More than two-thirds* of Papua's (Irian Jaya) land area is heavily forested and the population of around 1.5 million live mainly in isolated tribal groups using more than 80 distinct languages.

Map labels

SOUTH CHINA SEA

SPRATLY ISLANDS (disputed)

MALAYSI

KALIMANTAN TIMUR

KALIMANTAN SELATAN

Palawan
Quezo
Brooke's Point
Balabac Island
Balabac Strait
Caga
Tawi

Luzon Strait
Luzon
Baguio
Philippine Sea
MANILA
South China Sea
PHILIPPINES
Sulu Sea
Zamboanga
Mindanao
Butuan
Davao
Cebu
MALAYSIA
Celebes Sea
Manado
PACIFIC OCEAN
Halmahera
Maluku (Moluccas)
Celebes
Ceram
Ambon
Banda Sea
Makassar
Jayapura
New Guinea
PAPUA NEW GUINEA
INDONESIA
Arafura Sea
Lombok
Sumbawa
Sumba
Flores
DILI
EAST TIMOR
Timor
Kupang
Timor Sea
INDIAN OCEAN
Java Sea
Equator
Kepulu
Te
NUSA TENGGA
Mataram
Bayan
Gunung Tambora
Sumbawabesar
Pulau
Lombok
Kaliwang
Kuta
Gunung Lekan
Ampla

168

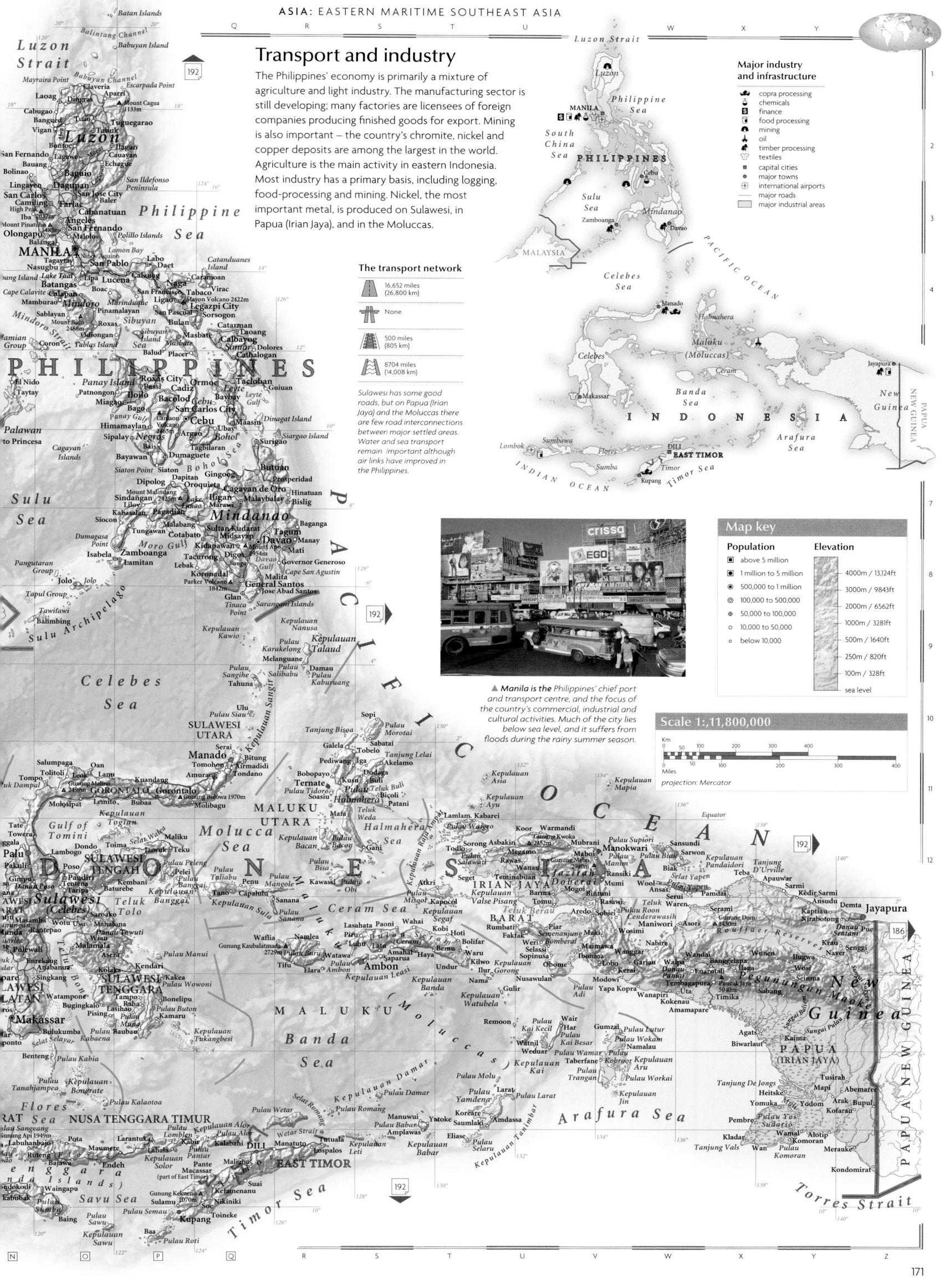

Transport and industry

The Philippines' economy is primarily a mixture of agriculture and light industry. The manufacturing sector is still developing; many factories are licensees of foreign companies producing finished goods for export. Mining is also important – the country's chromite, nickel and copper deposits are among the largest in the world. Agriculture is the main activity in eastern Indonesia. Most industry has a primary basis, including logging, food-processing and mining. Nickel, the most important metal, is produced on Sulawesi, in Papua (Irian Jaya), and in the Moluccas.

Major industry and infrastructure

- copra processing
- chemicals
- finance
- food processing
- mining
- oil
- timber processing
- textiles
- capital cities
- major towns
- international airports
- major roads
- major industrial areas

The transport network

- 16,652 miles (26,800 km)
- None
- 500 miles (805 km)
- 8704 miles (14,008 km)

Sulawesi has some good roads, but on Papua (Irian Jaya) and the Moluccas there are few road interconnections between major settled areas. Water and sea transport remain important although air links have improved in the Philippines.

▲ **Manila is the** Philippines' chief port and transport centre, and the focus of the country's commercial, industrial and cultural activities. Much of the city lies below sea level, and it suffers from floods during the rainy summer season.

Map key

Population
- above 5 million
- 1 million to 5 million
- 500,000 to 1 million
- 100,000 to 500,000
- 50,000 to 100,000
- 10,000 to 50,000
- below 10,000

Elevation
- 4000m / 13,124ft
- 3000m / 9843ft
- 2000m / 6562ft
- 1000m / 3281ft
- 500m / 1640ft
- 250m / 820ft
- 100m / 328ft
- sea level

Scale 1:,11,800,000

projection: Mercator

The Indian Ocean

Despite being the smallest of the three major oceans, the evolution of the Indian Ocean was the most complex. The ocean basin was formed during the break up of the supercontinent Gondwanaland, when the Indian subcontinent moved northeast, Africa moved west and Australia separated from Antarctica. Like the Pacific Ocean, the warm waters of the Indian Ocean are punctuated by coral atolls and islands. About one-fifth of the world's population – over 1000 million people – live on its shores. Those people living along the northern coasts are constantly threatened by flooding and typhoons caused by the monsoon winds.

The landscape

The Indian Ocean began forming about 150 million years ago, but in its present form it is relatively young, only about 36 million years old. Along the three subterranean mountain chains of its mid-ocean ridge the seafloor is still spreading. The Indian Ocean has fewer trenches than other oceans and only a narrow continental shelf around most of its surrounding land.

Sediments come from Ganges/Brahmaputra river system

Submarine canyons transport sediment to fan – some of these are more than 1500 miles (2500 km) long

Sri Lanka

▲ *The Ganges Fan* is one of the world's largest submarine accumulations of sediment, extending far beyond Sri Lanka. It is fed by the Ganges/Brahmaputra river system, whose sediment is carried through a network of underwater canyons at the edge of the continental shelf.

The mid-oceanic ridge runs from the Arabian Sea. It diverges east of Madagascar, one arm runs southwest to join the Mid-Atlantic Ridge, the other branches southeast, joining the Pacific-Antarctic Ridge, southeast of Tasmania.

The Ninetyeast Ridge takes its name from the line of longitude it follows. It is the world's longest and straightest under-sea ridge.

Two of the world's largest rivers flow into the Indian Ocean; the Indus and the Ganges/Brahmaputra. Both have deposited enormous fans of sediment.

Indus River

▶ A large proportion of the coast of Thailand, on the Isthmus of Kra, is stabilized by mangrove thickets. They act as an important breeding ground for wildlife.

The relief of Madagascar rises from a low-lying coastal strip in the east, to the central plateau. The plateau is also a major watershed separating Madagascar's three main river basins.

▶ *The central group* of the Seychelles are mountainous, granite islands. They have a narrow coastal belt and lush, tropical vegetation cloaks the highlands.

The Kerguelen Islands in the Southern Ocean were created by a hot spot in the Earth's crust. The islands were formed in succession as the Antarctic Plate moved slowly over the hot spot.

The Java Trench is the world's longest, it runs 1600 miles (2570 km) from the southwest of Java, but is only 50 miles (80 km) wide.

The circulation in the northern Indian Ocean is controlled by the monsoon winds. Biannually these winds reverse their pattern, causing a reversal in the surface currents and alternative high and low pressure conditions over Asia and Australia.

Resources

Many of the small islands in the Indian Ocean rely exclusively on tuna-fishing and tourism to maintain their economies. Most fisheries are artisanal, although large-scale tuna-fishing does take place in the Seychelles, Mauritius and the western Indian Ocean. Other resources include oil in The Gulf, pearls in the Red Sea and tin from deposits off the shores of Burma, Thailand and Indonesia.

▶ *The recent use* of large drag nets for tuna-fishing has not only threatened the livelihoods of many small-scale fisheries, but also caused widespread environmental concern about the potential impact on other marine species.

Resources (including wildlife)

fish	△	tin deposits
penguins	●	tourism
shellfish		
whales	●	major towns
oil & gas	⊕	major ports

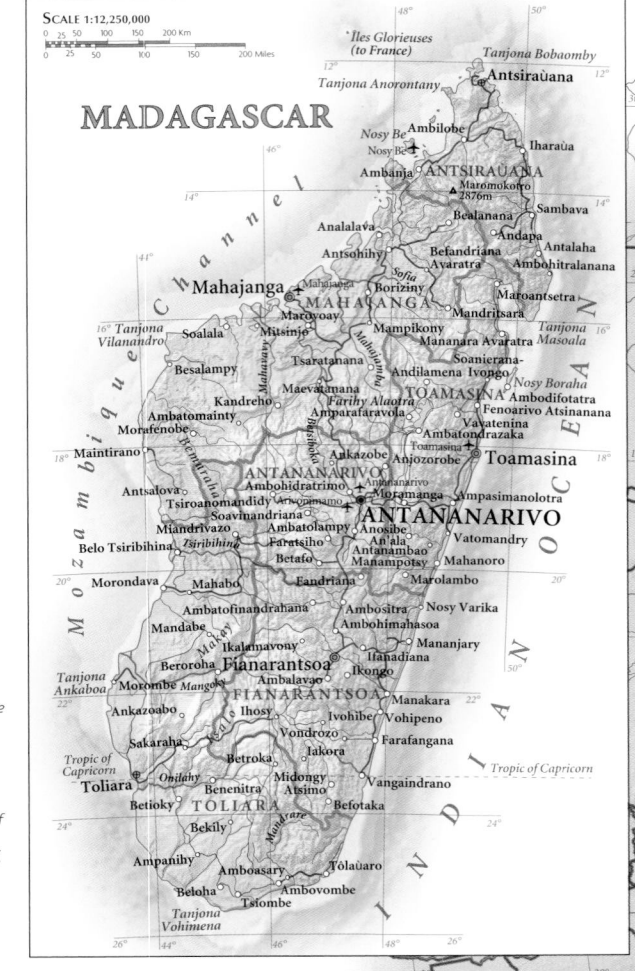

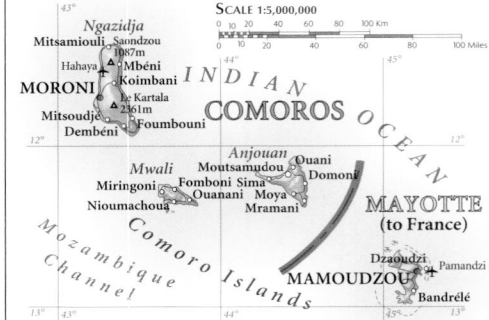

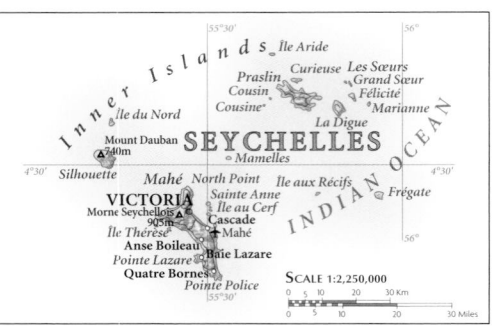

▲ *Coral reefs support* an enormous diversity of animal and plant life. Many species of tropical fish, like these squirrel fish, live and feed around the profusion of reefs and atolls in the Indian Ocean.

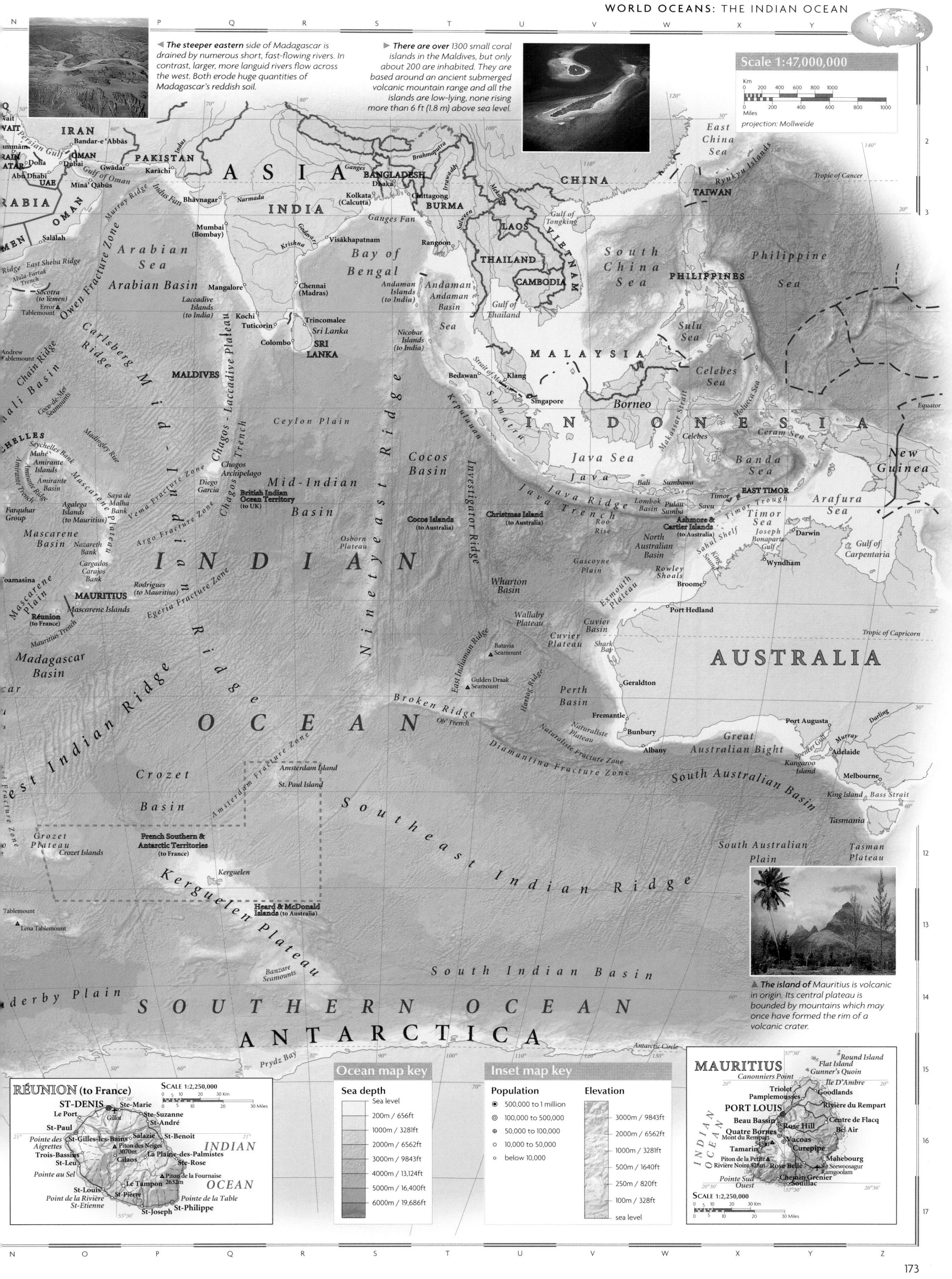

◄ *The steeper eastern* side of Madagascar is drained by numerous short, fast-flowing rivers. In contrast, larger, more languid rivers flow across the west. Both erode huge quantities of Madagascar's reddish soil.

► *There are over* 1300 small coral islands in the Maldives, but only about 200 are inhabited. They are based around an ancient submerged volcanic mountain range and all the islands are low-lying, none rising more than 6 ft (1.8 m) above sea level.

Scale 1:47,000,000

Km
0 200 400 600 800 1000

Miles
0 200 400 600 800 1000

projection: Mollweide

▲ *The island of* Mauritius is volcanic in origin. Its central plateau is bounded by mountains which may once have formed the rim of a volcanic crater.

Ocean map key

Sea depth

Sea level
200m / 656ft
1000m / 3281ft
2000m / 6562ft
3000m / 9843ft
4000m / 13,124ft
5000m / 16,400ft
6000m / 19,686ft

Inset map key

Population
- 500,000 to 1 million
- 100,000 to 500,000
- 50,000 to 100,000
- 10,000 to 50,000
- below 10,000

Elevation
3000m / 9843ft
2000m / 6562ft
1000m / 3281ft
500m / 1640ft
250m / 820ft
100m / 328ft
sea level

RÉUNION (to France)

SCALE 1:2,250,000

ST-DENIS   Ste-Marie
Le Port   Ste-Suzanne
Gillot   Ste-André
St-Paul
Pointe des   St-Gilles-les-Bains   Salazie   St-Benoit
Aigrettes   Piton des Neiges
Trois-Bassins   3070m   La Plaine-des-Palmistes
St-Leu   Cilaos   Ste-Rose
Pointe au Sel
Piton de la Fournaise
St-Louis   Le Tampon   2632m
Point de la Rivière   St-Pierre   Pointe de la Table
St-Etienne   St-Joseph   St-Philippe
INDIAN OCEAN

MAURITIUS

Round Island
Flat Island
Gunner's Quoin
Cannonniers Point
Triolet   Goodlands
Pamplemousses
PORT LOUIS   Rivière du Rempart
Beau Bassin   Rose Hill   Centre de Flacq
Quatre Bornes   Mont du Rempart   Bel Air
Tamarin   Vacoas
Piton de la Petite   Rose Belle   Mahebourg
Rivière Noire 828m   Curepipe
Pointe Sud   Chemin Grenier   Sir Seewoosagur
Ouest   Souillac   Ramgoolam

SCALE 1:2,250,000
INDIAN OCEAN

Australasia & Oceania

Australasia and Oceania, covering a land area of 3,285,048 sq miles (8,508,238 sq km), takes in 14 countries including the continent of Australia, New Zealand, Papua New Guinea and many island groups scattered across the Pacific Ocean.

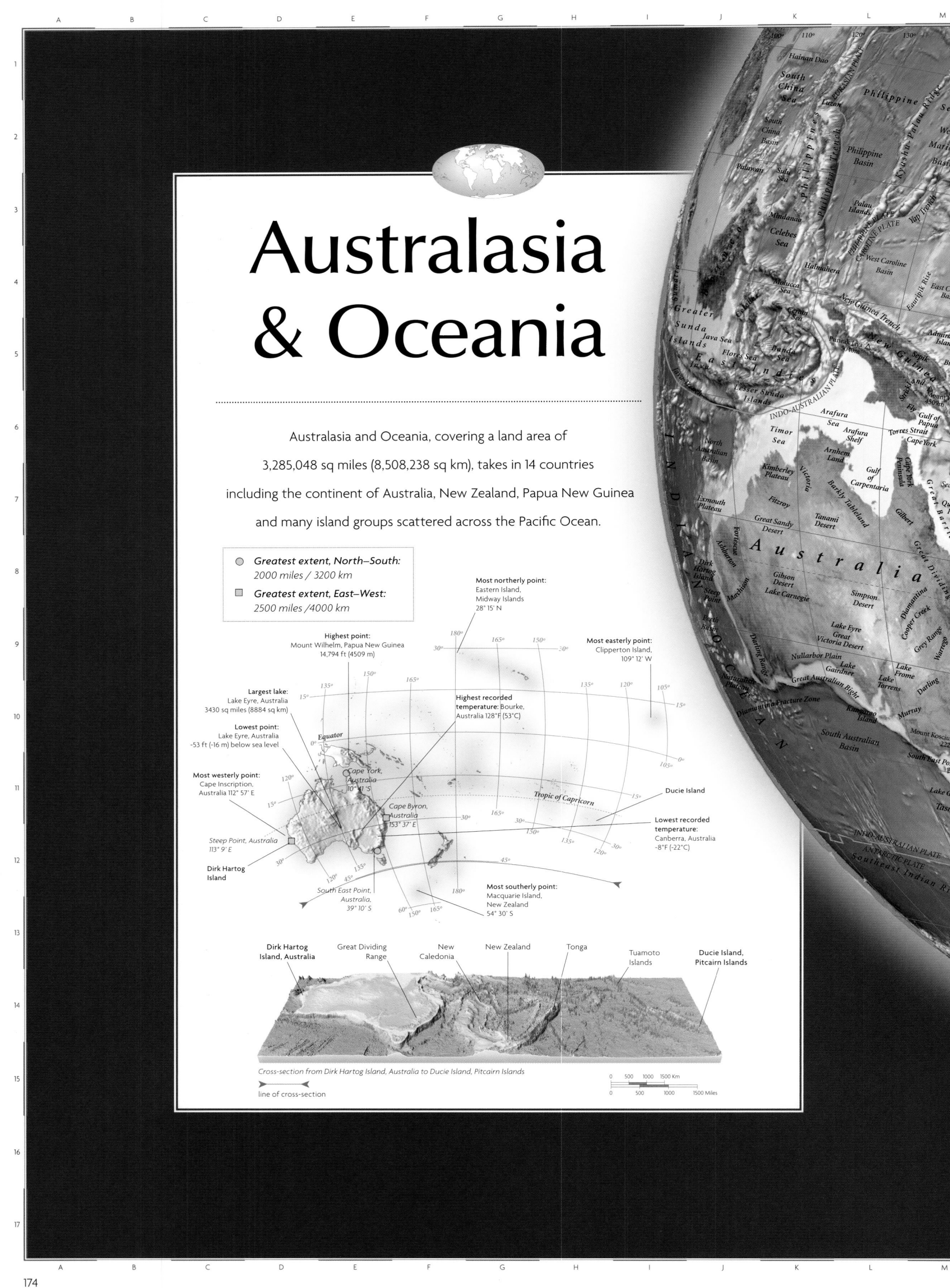

- **Greatest extent, North–South:**
  2000 miles / 3200 km
- **Greatest extent, East–West:**
  2500 miles /4000 km

Most northerly point:
Eastern Island,
Midway Islands
28° 15' N

Highest point:
Mount Wilhelm, Papua New Guinea
14,794 ft (4509 m)

Most easterly point:
Clipperton Island,
109° 12' W

Largest lake:
Lake Eyre, Australia
3430 sq miles (8884 sq km)

Highest recorded temperature: Bourke,
Australia 128°F (53°C)

Lowest point:
Lake Eyre, Australia
-53 ft (-16 m) below sea level

Most westerly point:
Cape Inscription,
Australia 112° 57' E

Cape York,
Australia
10° 41' S

Ducie Island

Cape Byron,
Australia
153° 37' E

Lowest recorded temperature:
Canberra, Australia
-8°F (-22°C)

Steep Point, Australia
113° 9' E

Dirk Hartog Island

*South East Point,
Australia,
39° 10' S*

Most southerly point:
Macquarie Island,
New Zealand
54° 30' S

Dirk Hartog Island, Australia | Great Dividing Range | New Caledonia | New Zealand | Tonga | Tuamoto Islands | Ducie Island, Pitcairn Islands

Cross-section from Dirk Hartog Island, Australia to Ducie Island, Pitcairn Islands

line of cross-section

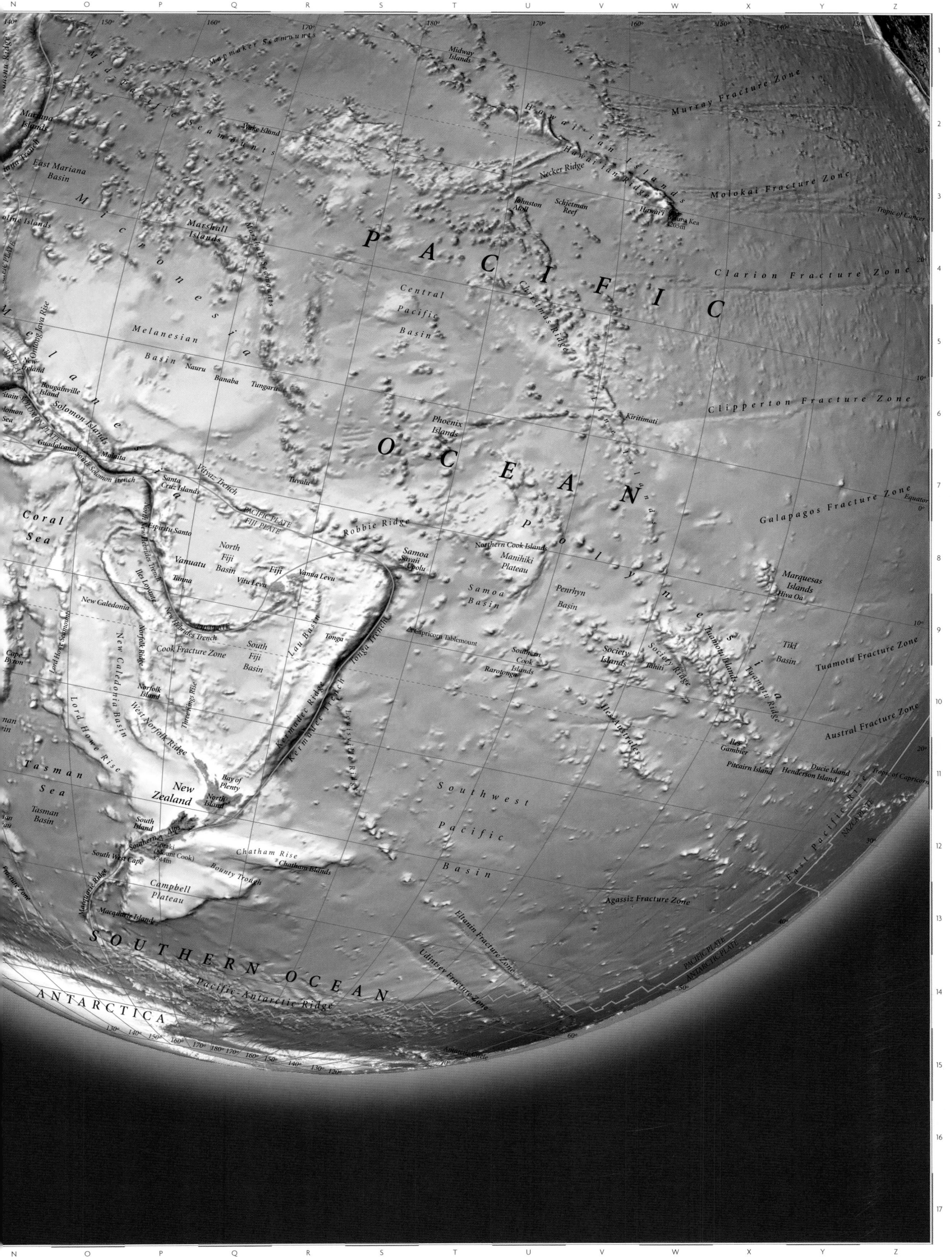

N O P Q R S T U V W X Y Z

1
2
3
4
5
6
7
8
9
10
11
12
13
14
15
16
17

N O P Q R S T U V W X Y Z

150° 160° 170° 180° 170° 160° 150° 140° 130°

30°
Tropic of Cancer
20°
10°
0° Equator
10°
20°
Tropic of Capricorn
30°
40°

Mid Pacific Seamounts

Marcus-Necker Seamounts

Midway Islands

Murray Fracture Zone

Hawaiian Islands

Necker Ridge

Molokai Fracture Zone

Schjetman Reef

Johnston Atoll

Hawai'i Mauna Kea 4205m

Clarion Fracture Zone

Wake Island

East Mariana Basin

Mariana Islands

Micronesia

Caroline Islands

Marshall Islands

Marshall Islands

Marshall Seamounts

P A C I F I C

Central Pacific Basin

Christmas Ridge

Clipperton Fracture Zone

ONTONG JAVA PLATEAU

Ontong Java Rise

Melanesia

Melanesian Basin

Nauru

Banaba

Tungaru

Phoenix Islands

O C E A N

Kiritimati

Galapagos Fracture Zone

Bougainville Island

Solomon Islands

Guadalcanal

South Solomon Trench

Malaita

Santa Cruz Islands

Vityaz Trench

Tuvalu

Robbie Ridge

Polynesia

Line Islands

Equator

Coral Sea

PACIFIC PLATE
FIJI PLATE

North Fiji Basin

Samoa Savaii Upolu

Northern Cook Islands

Manihiki Plateau

Marquesas Islands
Hiva Oa

North West Espiritu Santo

Vanuatu

Fiji

Vanua Levu

Penrhyn Basin

Vitu Levu

Tanna

New Hebrides Trench

Ile Loyaute

Samoa Basin

Society Islands

Society Ridge

Tuamotu Islands

Tiki Basin

New Caledonia

South Fiji Basin

Capricorn Tablemount

Southern Cook Islands

Tahiti

Tuamotu Ridge

Tuamotu Fracture Zone

Norfolk Ridge

Cook Fracture Zone

Lau Basin

Tonga

Rarotonga

Norfolk Island

New Caledonia Basin

West Norfolk Ridge

Three Kings Rise

Tonga Trench

Kermadec Ridge

Louisville Ridge

Manihiki

Austral Fracture Zone

Cape Byron

Lord Howe Seamounts

Lord Howe Rise

Bay of Plenty

North Island

Gambier

Ile Gambier

Pitcairn Island

Ducie Island

Henderson Island

Southwest

Tasman Sea

New Zealand

Kermadec Trench

Pacific

East Pacific Rise

Tropic of Capricorn

Tasman Basin

South Island

Southern Alps Aoraki (Mount Cook) 3744m

Chatham Rise

Chatham Islands

Basin

NAZCA PLATE

South West Cape

Bounty Trough

Campbell Plateau

Agassiz Fracture Zone

Fracture Zone

Macquarie Ridge

Macquarie Island

Eltanin Fracture Zone

PACIFIC PLATE
ANTARCTIC PLATE

S O U T H E R N   O C E A N

Udintsev Fracture Zone

Pacific-Antarctic Ridge

A N T A R C T I C A

130° 140° 150° 160° 170° 180° 170° 160° 150° 140° 130°

60°

70°

Antarctic Circle

Political Australasia & Oceania

Vast expanses of ocean separate this geographically fragmented realm, characterized more by each country's isolation than by any political unity. Australia's and New Zealand's traditional ties with the United Kingdom, as members of the Commonwealth, are now being called into question as Australasian and Oceanian nations are increasingly looking to forge new relationships with neighbouring Asian countries like Japan. External influences have featured strongly in the politics of the Pacific Islands; the various territories of Micronesia were largely under US control until the late 1980s, and France, New Zealand, the USA and the UK still have territories under colonial rule in Polynesia. Nuclear weapons-testing by Western superpowers was widespread during the Cold War period, but has now been discontinued.

◄ *Western Australia's mineral* wealth has transformed its state capital, Perth, into one of Australia's major cities. Perth is one of the world's most isolated cities – over 2500 miles (4000 km) from the population centres of the eastern seaboard.

Scale 1:35,500,000

Km
0 200 400 600 800

Miles
0 200 400 600 800

projection: Lambert Azimuthal Equal Area

Population

Density of settlement in the region is generally low. Australia is one of the least densely populated countries on Earth with over 80% of its population living within 25 miles (40 km) of the coast – mostly in the southeast of the country. New Zealand, and the island groups of Melanesia, Micronesia and Polynesia, are much more densely populated, although many of the smaller islands remain uninhabited.

Population density
(people per sq km)

below 4
5-24
25-49
50-99
100-199
200-299
above 300

▲ *The myriad of* small coral islands which are scattered across the Pacific Ocean are often uninhabited, as they offer little shelter from the weather, often no fresh water, and only limited food supplies.

◄ *The planes of* the Australian Royal Flying Doctor Service are able to cover large expanses of barren land quickly, bringing medical treatment to the most inaccessible and far-flung places.

Northern Mariana Islands (to US)

Philippine Sea

Saipan

Guam (to US)
HAGÅTNA

Bikini Atoll

Yap

Caroline Chuuk Pohnpei ●PALIKIR
Ralik

MELEKEOK
Babeldaob ●

Caroline Islands

Kosrae

PALAU

MICRONESIA

Melanesia

NAURU

PAPUA NEW GUINEA

Bismarck Sea New Ireland
Wewak New Rabaul
Madang Britain *Solomon Islands*
Ubai Bougainville
Mount Arawa Island SOLOMON
Hagen Lae *Solomon* New HONIARA ISLAND
Tapini *Sea* Georgia Guadalcanal
Islands Santa Cruz
PORT MORESBY Islands

VANU...
Espiritu Santo
Malekula
PORT-V...

Arafura Sea Torres Strait
Coral New Caledonia
Sea Coral Sea Islands (to France)
(to Australia) NOUMÉA

Darwin ● Cape P
Arnhem York
Land Peninsula
Timor Katherine Gulf of
Sea Joseph Carpentaria Cairns
Bonaparte
Gulf Normanton
Wyndham Townsville Mackay
Kimberley NORTHERN Hughenden
Plateau Mount Isa
Derby Tennant Creek Rockhampton
Tanami QUEENSLAND
Broome Desert Barcaldine
TERRITORY
Port Hedland Alice Springs Charleville Miles Brisbane
Great Sandy Simpson Toowoomba
Desert Desert Cunnamulla Grafton
AUSTRALIA Norfolk
Hamersley Range Lake Eyre Bourke (to Aus
North Barwon
Gibson SOUTH AUSTRALIA Wilcannia NEW Lord Howe Island
Desert Lake Torrens SOUTH WALES (to Australia)
Carnarvon WESTERN AUSTRALIA Dubbo
Great Victoria Lake Everard Port Augusta Newcastle
Desert Lake Gairdner Campbelltown Sydney
Mount Magnet Ceduna Whyalla Murray Wagga Wagga Wollongong
CANBERRA
Kalgoorlie Adelaide Bendigo AUSTRALIAN
Geraldton Great Australian Kangaroo Horsham CAPITAL TERRITORY *Tasman*
Bight Island Ballarat VICTORIA *Sea*
Perth Mount Gambier Melbourne
Esperance Geelong
Albany Bass Strait Launceston
TASMANIA
Tasmania Hobart

INDIAN OCEAN
Tropic of Capricorn
Nullarbor Plain
Great Dividing Range
Flinders Ranges
Grey Range
Darling

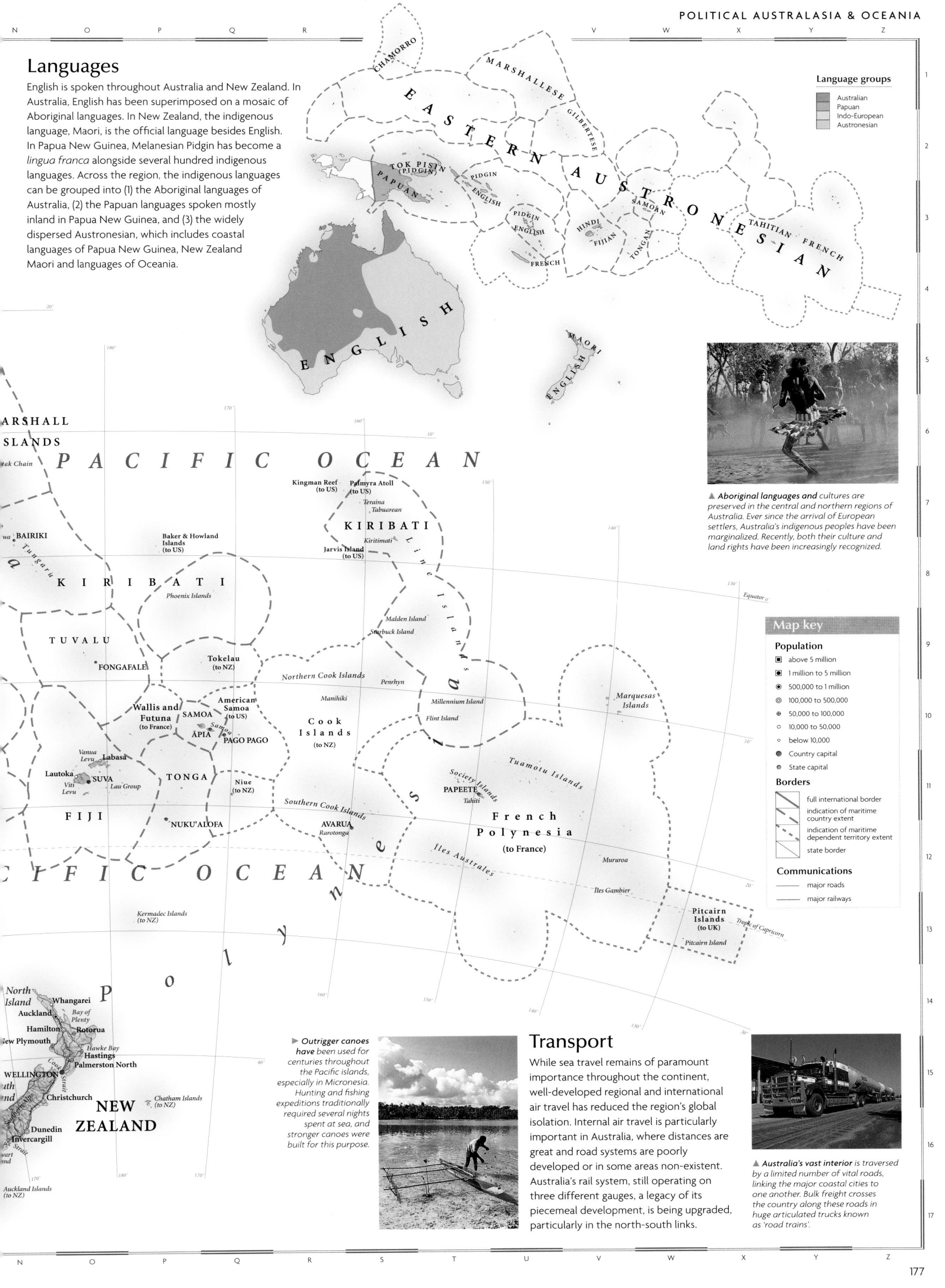

Languages

English is spoken throughout Australia and New Zealand. In Australia, English has been superimposed on a mosaic of Aboriginal languages. In New Zealand, the indigenous language, Maori, is the official language besides English. In Papua New Guinea, Melanesian Pidgin has become a *lingua franca* alongside several hundred indigenous languages. Across the region, the indigenous languages can be grouped into (1) the Aboriginal languages of Australia, (2) the Papuan languages spoken mostly inland in Papua New Guinea, and (3) the widely dispersed Austronesian, which includes coastal languages of Papua New Guinea, New Zealand Maori and languages of Oceania.

Language groups

- Australian
- Papuan
- Indo-European
- Austronesian

▲ *Aboriginal languages and* cultures are preserved in the central and northern regions of Australia. Ever since the arrival of European settlers, Australia's indigenous peoples have been marginalized. Recently, both their culture and land rights have been increasingly recognized.

Map key

Population

- ▣ above 5 million
- ◉ 1 million to 5 million
- ◉ 500,000 to 1 million
- ◉ 100,000 to 500,000
- ⊕ 50,000 to 100,000
- ○ 10,000 to 50,000
- ○ below 10,000
- ● Country capital
- ⊙ State capital

Borders

- full international border
- indication of maritime country extent
- indication of maritime dependent territory extent
- state border

Communications

- —— major roads
- —— major railways

► *Outrigger canoes have* been used for centuries throughout the Pacific islands, especially in Micronesia. Hunting and fishing expeditions traditionally required several nights spent at sea, and stronger canoes were built for this purpose.

Transport

While sea travel remains of paramount importance throughout the continent, well-developed regional and international air travel has reduced the region's global isolation. Internal air travel is particularly important in Australia, where distances are great and road systems are poorly developed or in some areas non-existent. Australia's rail system, still operating on three different gauges, a legacy of its piecemeal development, is being upgraded, particularly in the north-south links.

▲ *Australia's vast interior is* traversed by a limited number of vital roads, linking the major coastal cities to one another. Bulk freight crosses the country along these roads in huge articulated trucks known as 'road trains'.

177

Australasian & Oceanian resources

Natural resources are of major economic importance throughout Australasia and Oceania. Australia in particular is a major world exporter of raw materials such as coal, iron ore and bauxite, while New Zealand's agricultural economy is dominated by sheep-raising. Trade with western Europe has declined significantly in the last 20 years, and the Pacific Rim countries of Southeast Asia are now the main trading partners, as well as a source of new settlers to the region. Australasia and Oceania's greatest resources are its climate and environment; tourism increasingly provides a vital source of income for the whole continent.

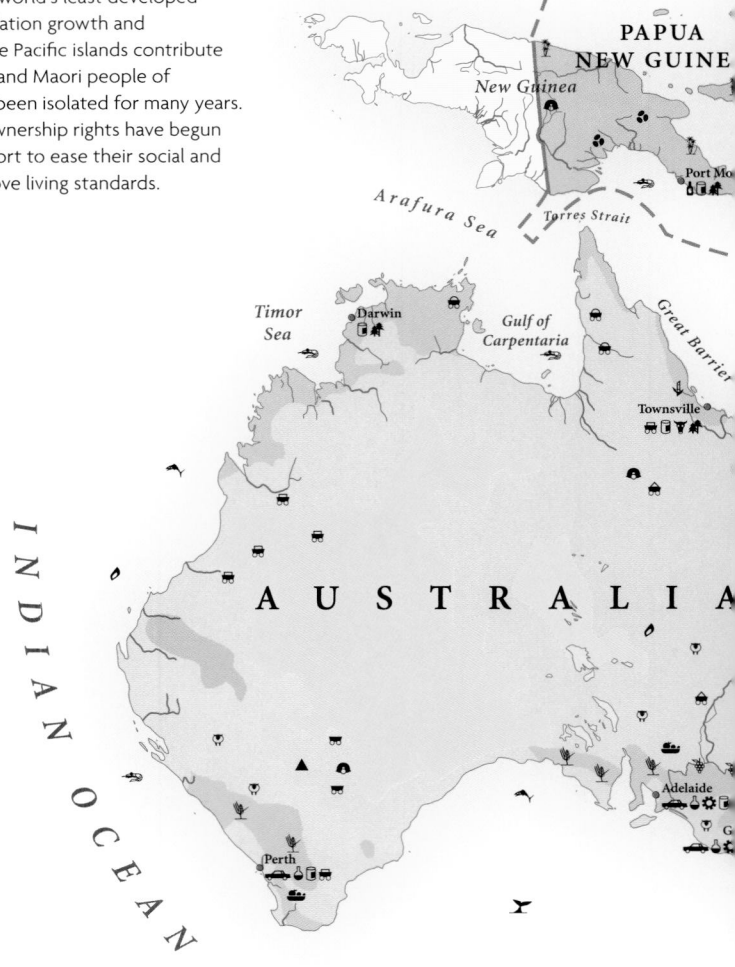

▲ *The largely unpolluted* waters of the Pacific Ocean support rich and varied marine life, much of which is farmed commercially. Here, oysters are gathered for market off the coast of New Zealand's South Island.

▶ *Huge flocks of* sheep are a common sight in New Zealand, where they outnumber people by 12 to 1. New Zealand is one of the world's largest exporters of wool and frozen lamb.

Standard of living

In marked contrast to its neighbour, Australia, with one of the world's highest life expectancies and standards of living, Papua New Guinea is one of the world's least developed countries. In addition, high population growth and urbanization rates throughout the Pacific islands contribute to overcrowding. The Aboriginal and Maori people of Australia and New Zealand have been isolated for many years. Recently, their traditional land ownership rights have begun to be legally recognized in an effort to ease their social and economic isolation, and to improve living standards.

Standard of living
(UN human development index)

- low
- high
- figures unavailable

Environmental issues

The prospect of rising sea levels poses a threat to many low-lying islands in the Pacific. Nuclear weapons-testing, once common throughout the region, was finally discontinued in 1996. Australia's ecological balance has been irreversibly altered by the introduction of alien species. Although it has the world's largest underground water reserve, the Great Artesian Basin, the availability of fresh water in Australia remains critical. Periodic droughts combined with over-grazing lead to desertification and increase the risk of devastating bush fires, and occasional flash floods.

Environmental issues

- national parks
- tropical forest
- forest destroyed
- desert
- desertification
- polluted rivers
- radioactive contamination
- marine pollution
- heavy marine pollution
- poor urban air quality

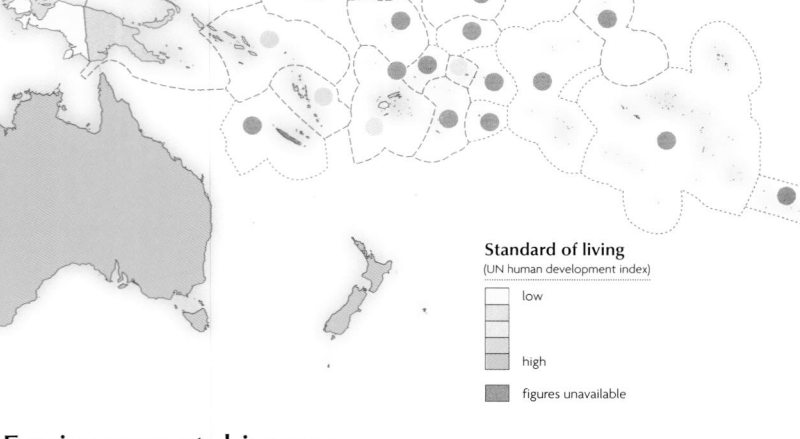

▲ *In 1946 Bikini Atoll,* in the Marshall Islands, was chosen as the site for Operation Crossroads – investigating the effects of atomic bombs upon naval vessels. Further nuclear tests continued until the early 1990s. The long-term environmental effects are unknown.

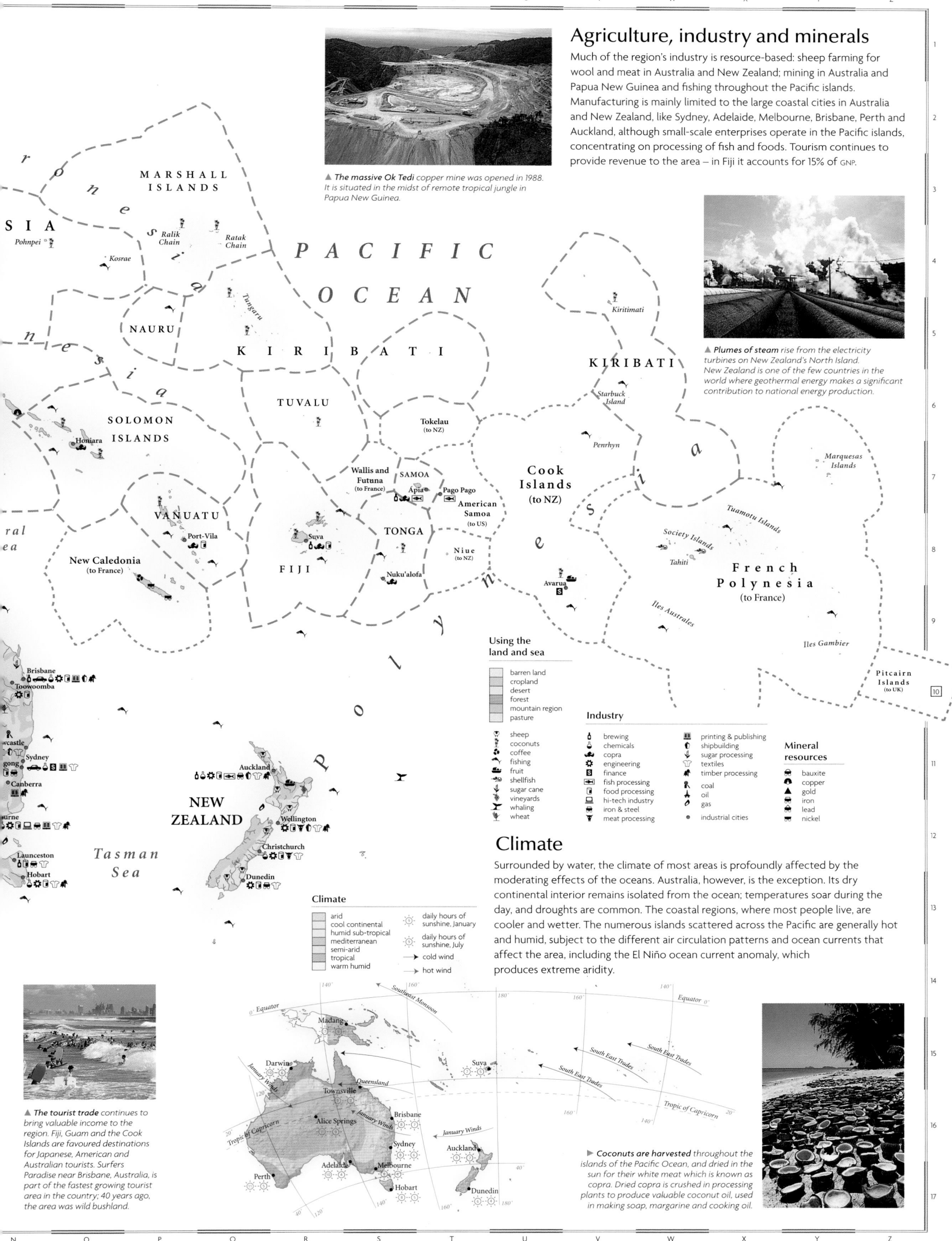

Agriculture, industry and minerals

Much of the region's industry is resource-based: sheep farming for wool and meat in Australia and New Zealand; mining in Australia and Papua New Guinea and fishing throughout the Pacific islands. Manufacturing is mainly limited to the large coastal cities in Australia and New Zealand, like Sydney, Adelaide, Melbourne, Brisbane, Perth and Auckland, although small-scale enterprises operate in the Pacific islands, concentrating on processing of fish and foods. Tourism continues to provide revenue to the area – in Fiji it accounts for 15% of GNP.

▲ **The massive Ok Tedi** copper mine was opened in 1988. It is situated in the midst of remote tropical jungle in Papua New Guinea.

▲ **Plumes of steam** rise from the electricity turbines on New Zealand's North Island. New Zealand is one of the few countries in the world where geothermal energy makes a significant contribution to national energy production.

Using the land and sea

- barren land
- cropland
- desert
- forest
- mountain region
- pasture

Industry

- sheep
- coconuts
- coffee
- fishing
- fruit
- shellfish
- sugar cane
- vineyards
- whaling
- wheat

- brewing
- chemicals
- copra
- engineering
- finance
- fish processing
- food processing
- hi-tech industry
- iron & steel
- meat processing

- printing & publishing
- shipbuilding
- sugar processing
- textiles
- timber processing
- coal
- oil
- gas
- industrial cities

Mineral resources

- bauxite
- copper
- gold
- iron
- lead
- nickel

Climate

Surrounded by water, the climate of most areas is profoundly affected by the moderating effects of the oceans. Australia, however, is the exception. Its dry continental interior remains isolated from the ocean; temperatures soar during the day, and droughts are common. The coastal regions, where most people live, are cooler and wetter. The numerous islands scattered across the Pacific are generally hot and humid, subject to the different air circulation patterns and ocean currents that affect the area, including the El Niño ocean current anomaly, which produces extreme aridity.

Climate

- arid
- cool continental
- humid sub-tropical
- mediterranean
- semi-arid
- tropical
- warm humid

- ☼ daily hours of sunshine, January
- ☼ daily hours of sunshine, July
- → cold wind
- → hot wind

▲ **The tourist trade** continues to bring valuable income to the region. Fiji, Guam and the Cook Islands are favoured destinations for Japanese, American and Australian tourists. Surfers Paradise near Brisbane, Australia, is part of the fastest growing tourist area in the country; 40 years ago, the area was wild bushland.

▶ **Coconuts are harvested** throughout the islands of the Pacific Ocean, and dried in the sun for their white meat which is known as copra. Dried copra is crushed in processing plants to produce valuable coconut oil, used in making soap, margarine and cooking oil.

179

Australia

Australia is the world's smallest continent, a stable landmass lying between the Indian and Pacific oceans. Previously home to its aboriginal peoples only, since the end of the 18th century immigration has transformed the face of the country. Initially settlers came mainly from western Europe, particularly the UK, and for years Australia remained wedded to its British colonial past. More recent immigrants have come from eastern Europe, and from Asian countries such as Japan, South Korea and Indonesia. Australia is now forging strong trading links with these 'Pacific Rim' countries and its economic future seems to lie with Asia and the Americas, rather than Europe, its traditional partner.

Using the land

Over 104 million sheep are dispersed in vast herds around the country, contributing to a major export industry. Cattle-ranching is important, particularly in the west. Wheat, and grapes for Australia's wine industry, are grown mainly in the south. Much of the country is desert, unsuitable for agriculture unless irrigation is used.

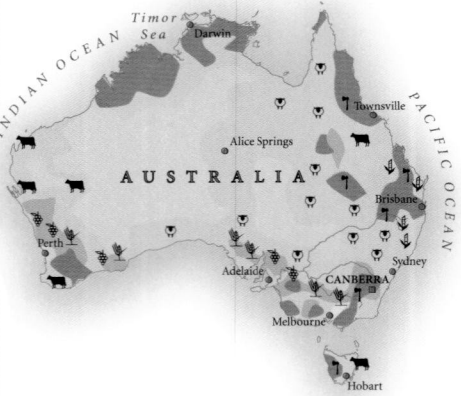

The urban/rural population divide

urban 85%   rural 15%

0 10 20 30 40 50 60 70 80 90 100

Population density	Total land area
6 people per sq mile (2 people per sq km)	2,967,893 sq miles (7,686,850 sq km)

Land use and agricultural distribution

- cattle
- sheep
- cereals
- sugar cane
- timber
- vineyards
- capital cities
- major towns
- pasture
- cropland
- forest
- desert
- mountain region

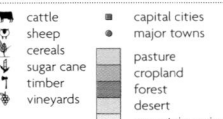

▲ *Lines of ripening* vines stretch for miles in Barossa Valley, a major wine-growing region near Adelaide.

▲ *The Great Barrier Reef* is the world's largest area of coral islands and reefs. It runs for about 1240 miles (2000 km) along the Queensland coast.

The landscape

Australia consists of many eroded plateaux, lying firmly in the middle of the Indo-Australian Plate. It is the world's flattest continent, and the driest, after Antarctica. The coasts tend to be more hilly and fertile, especially in the east. The mountains of the Great Dividing Range form a natural barrier between the eastern coastal areas and the flat, dry plains and desert regions of the Australian 'outback.'

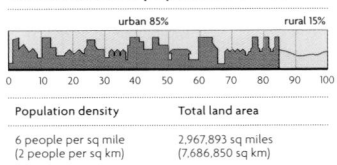

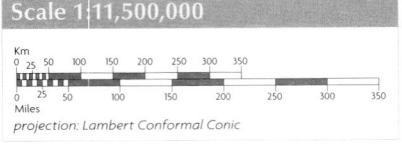

◀ *Uluru (Ayers Rock),* the world's largest free-standing rock, is a massive outcrop of red sandstone in Australia's desert centre. Wind and sandstorms have ground the rock into the smooth curves seen here. Uluru is revered as a sacred site by many aboriginal peoples.

Scale 1:11,500,000

Km
0 25 50   100   150   200   250   300   350

Miles
0 25 50   100   150   200   250   300   350

projection: Lambert Conformal Conic

Map key

Population
- 1 million to 5 million
- 500,000 to 1 million
- 100,000 to 500,000
- 50,000 to 100,000
- 10,000 to 50,000
- below 10,000

Elevation
- 2000m / 6562ft
- 1000m / 3281ft
- 500m / 1640ft
- 250m / 820ft
- 100m / 328ft
- sea level

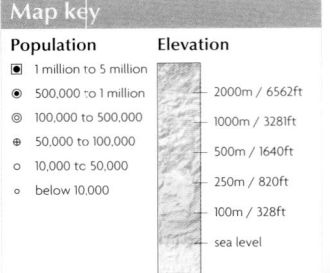

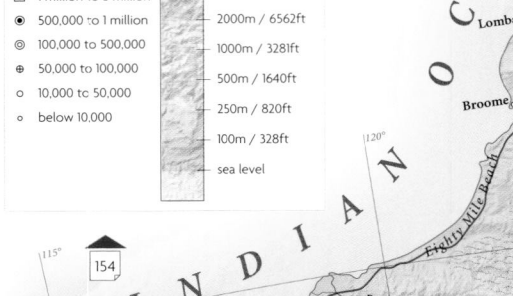

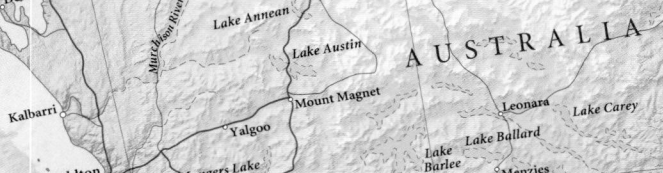

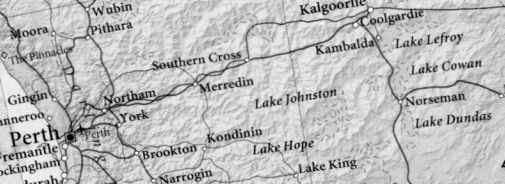

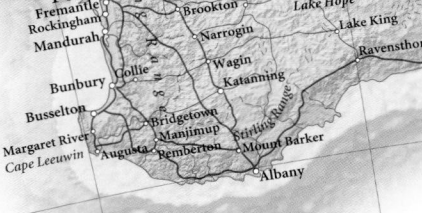

The ancient Kimberley Plateau is the source of some of Australia's richest mineral deposits, including diamonds.

Uluru (Ayers Rock)

Arnhem Land

The tropical rain forest of the Cape York Peninsula contains more than 600 different varieties of tree.

Great Artesian Basin

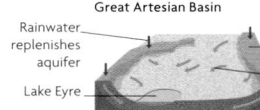

▲ *The Pinnacles are a* series of rugged sandstone pillars. Their strange shapes have been formed by water and wind erosion.

More than half of Australia rests on a uniform shield over 600 million years old. It is one of the Earth's original geological plates.

The Nullarbor Plain is a low-lying limestone plateau which is so flat that the Trans-Australian Railway runs through it in a straight line for more than 300 miles (483 km).

The Simpson Desert has a number of large salt pans, created by the evaporation of past rivers and now sourced by seasonal rains. Some are crusted with gypsum, but most are covered by common salt crystals.

The Lake Eyre basin, lying 51 ft (16 m) below sea level, is one of the largest inland drainage systems in the world, covering an area of more than 500,000 sq miles (1,300,000 sq km).

The Great Dividing Range forms a watershed between east- and west-flowing rivers. Erosion has created deep valleys, gorges and waterfalls where rivers tumble over escarpments on their way to the sea.

Australian Alps

Tasmania has the same geological structure as the Australian Alps. During the last period of glaciation, 18,000 years ago, sea levels were some 300 ft (100 m) lower and it was joined to the mainland.

Great Artesian Basin

Rainwater replenishes aquifer

Lake Eyre

Aquifers from which artesian water is obtained

Underground water movements

▲ *The Great Artesian Basin underlies* nearly 20% of the total area of Australia, providing a valuable store of underground water, essential to Australian agriculture. The ephemeral rivers which drain the northern part of the basin have highly braided courses and, in consequence, the area is known as 'channel country.'

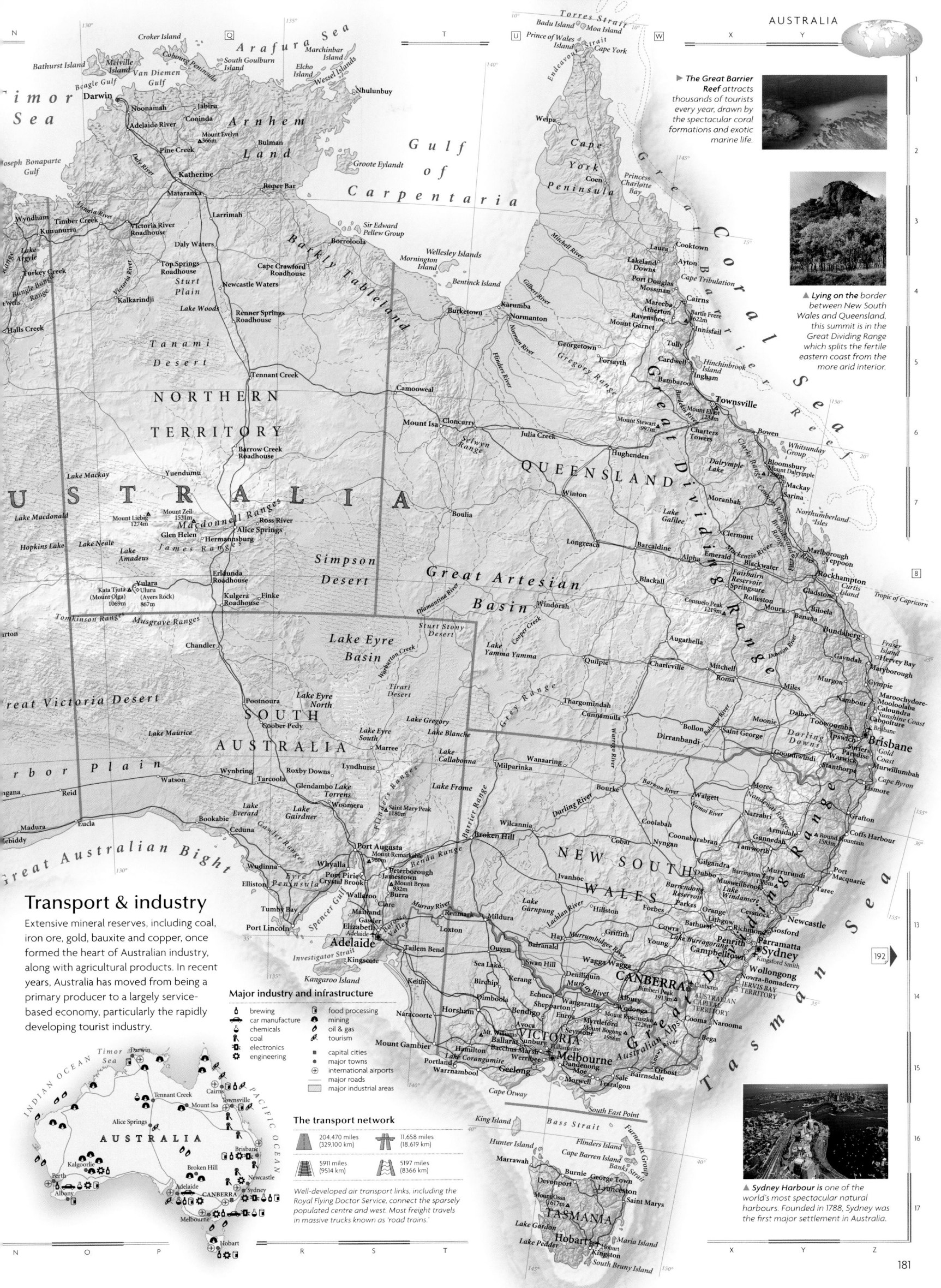

▶ *The Great Barrier Reef* attracts thousands of tourists every year, drawn by the spectacular coral formations and exotic marine life.

▲ *Lying on the* border between New South Wales and Queensland, this summit is in the Great Dividing Range which splits the fertile eastern coast from the more arid interior.

Transport & industry

Extensive mineral reserves, including coal, iron ore, gold, bauxite and copper, once formed the heart of Australian industry, along with agricultural products. In recent years, Australia has moved from being a primary producer to a largely service-based economy, particularly the rapidly developing tourist industry.

Major industry and infrastructure

- brewing
- car manufacture
- chemicals
- coal
- electronics
- engineering
- food processing
- mining
- oil & gas
- tourism
- capital cities
- major towns
- international airports
- major roads
- major industrial areas

The transport network

204,470 miles (329,100 km)	11,658 miles (18,619 km)
5911 miles (9514 km)	5197 miles (8366 km)

Well-developed air transport links, including the Royal Flying Doctor Service, connect the sparsely populated centre and west. Most freight travels in massive trucks known as 'road trains.'

▲ *Sydney Harbour is* one of the world's most spectacular natural harbours. Founded in 1788, Sydney was the first major settlement in Australia.

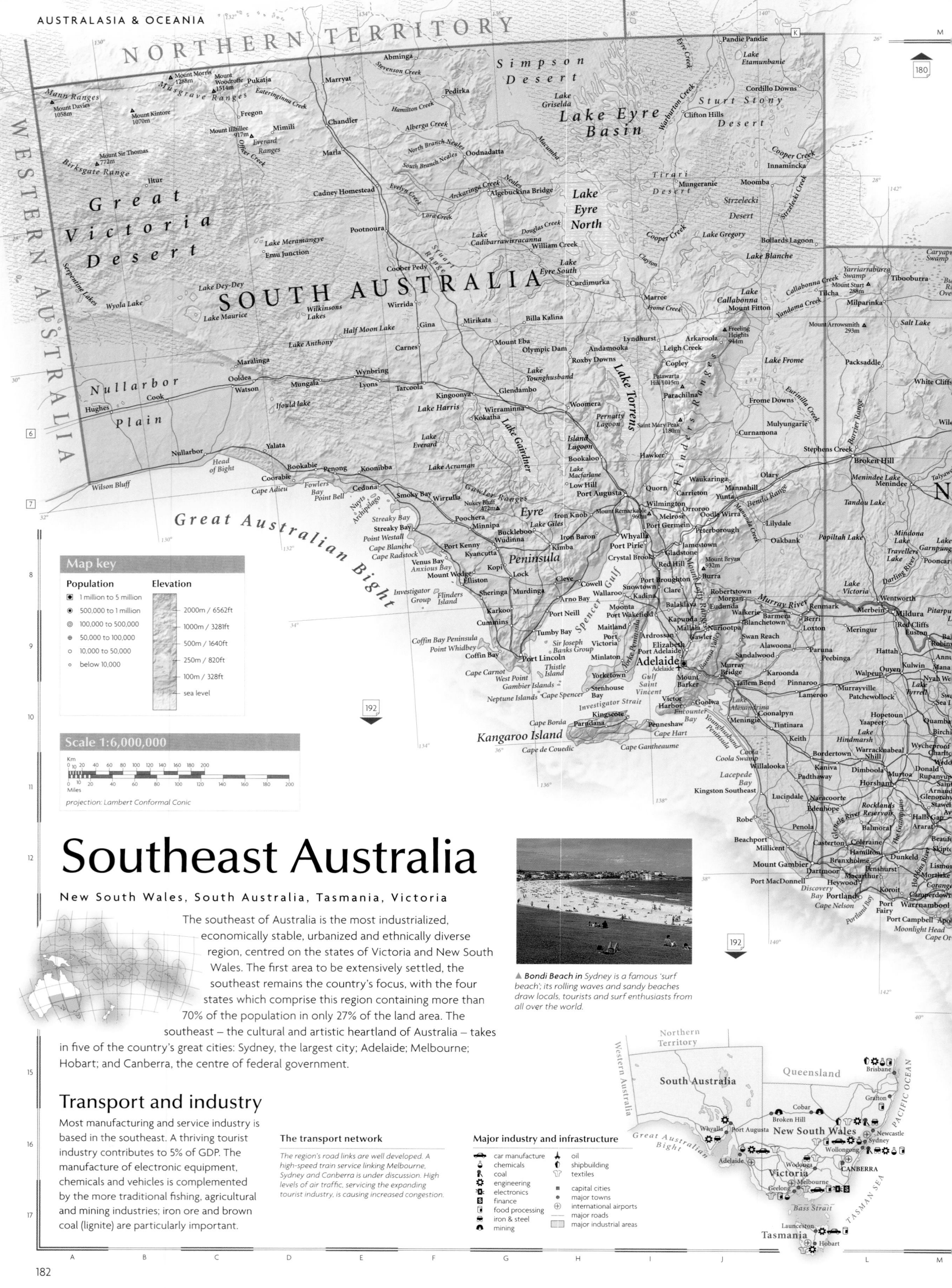

NORTHERN TERRITORY

Simpson Desert

Lake Eyre Basin

Sturt Stony Desert

Great Victoria Desert

SOUTH AUSTRALIA

WESTERN AUSTRALIA

Nullarbor Plain

Great Australian Bight

Map key

Population
- ▣ 1 million to 5 million
- ◉ 500,000 to 1 million
- ◎ 100,000 to 500,000
- ⊕ 50,000 to 100,000
- ○ 10,000 to 50,000
- ○ below 10,000

Elevation
- 2000m / 6562ft
- 1000m / 3281ft
- 500m / 1640ft
- 250m / 820ft
- 100m / 328ft
- sea level

Scale 1:6,000,000

Km
0 10 20 40 60 80 100 120 140 160 180 200

Miles
0 10 20 40 60 80 100 120 140 160 180 200

projection: Lambert Conformal Conic

Eyre Peninsula

Kangaroo Island

Southeast Australia

New South Wales, South Australia, Tasmania, Victoria

The southeast of Australia is the most industrialized, economically stable, urbanized and ethnically diverse region, centred on the states of Victoria and New South Wales. The first area to be extensively settled, the southeast remains the country's focus, with the four states which comprise this region containing more than 70% of the population in only 27% of the land area. The southeast – the cultural and artistic heartland of Australia – takes in five of the country's great cities: Sydney, the largest city; Adelaide; Melbourne; Hobart; and Canberra, the centre of federal government.

▲ *Bondi Beach in Sydney is a famous 'surf beach'; its rolling waves and sandy beaches draw locals, tourists and surf enthusiasts from all over the world.*

Transport and industry

Most manufacturing and service industry is based in the southeast. A thriving tourist industry contributes to 5% of GDP. The manufacture of electronic equipment, chemicals and vehicles is complemented by the more traditional fishing, agricultural and mining industries; iron ore and brown coal (lignite) are particularly important.

The transport network

The region's road links are well developed. A high-speed train service linking Melbourne, Sydney and Canberra is under discussion. High levels of air traffic, servicing the expanding tourist industry, is causing increased congestion.

Major industry and infrastructure

- 🚗 car manufacture
- ⚗ chemicals
- ⚙ coal
- ⚙ engineering
- 💡 electronics
- 💰 finance
- 🍴 food processing
- ⚒ iron & steel
- ⛏ mining
- ⚓ oil
- 🚢 shipbuilding
- 👕 textiles
- ● capital cities
- ○ major towns
- ✈ international airports
- major roads
- ▦ major industrial areas

Using the land and sea

The western flanks of the Great Dividing Range and the northern deserts of South Australia support massive herds of sheep and cattle, while more intensive stock-rearing occurs near the cities. Sugar cane is the most important industrial crop, and cereals including wheat, maize, barley and sorghum are also grown. Grapes, citrus and orchard fruits are among the wide range of fruit and vegetables cultivated in this region. Tasmania's forestry and fishing contributes to over one-third of the state's exports.

▲ The fertile Darling Downs, known as the 'breadbasket of Australia', support a wide range of crops including cereals, sugar cane and fruit.

▶ The Murray River has its source in the eastern uplands of the Great Dividing Range. Fed by melting snow, it runs for 1609 miles (2589 km), and has sufficient volume to reach the ocean southeast of Adelaide despite a minimal gradient for most of its lower reaches.

The urban/rural population divide

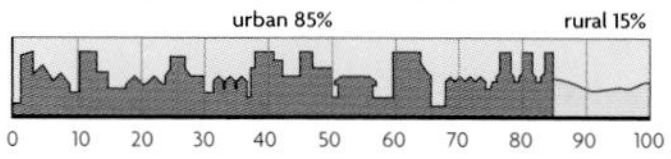

urban 85%   rural 15%

Population density	Total land area
18 people per sq mile (7 people per sq km)	778,022 sq miles (2,015,600 sq km)

Land use and agricultural distribution

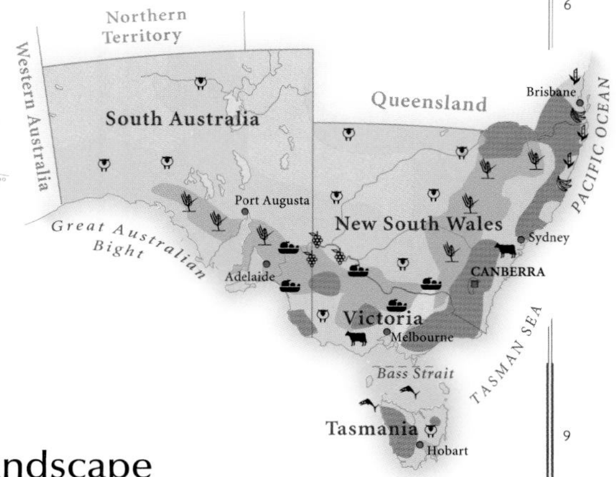

- cattle
- sheep
- bananas
- fishing
- fruit
- sugar cane
- vineyards
- wheat
- ■ capital cities
- ● major towns
- pasture
- cropland
- forest
- desert
- mountain region

The landscape

The southern half of the Great Dividing Range runs parallel to the eastern coast of Victoria and New South Wales as far as Tasmania, which, though divided from the mainland is part of the same mountain chain. South Australia comprises the Australian shield and half of the dry, flat Nullarbor Plain. The Murray/Darling river basin is the only major river system.

◀ The heavily folded Flinders Ranges is part of an arc of sedimentary rocks reaching northward from Kangaroo Island.

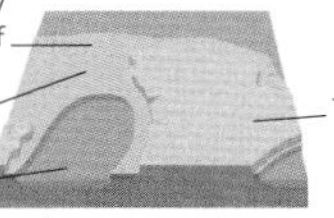

Shallow continental shelf
Past land link
Bass Strait
Tasmania

▲ Tasmania is part of Australia's eastern highlands, separated from the mainland by 155 miles (250 km) of the Bass Strait. In the recent geological past, dry land links between Tasmania and Victoria would have been possible during periods of world-wide glaciation, when the sea level was more than 180 ft (55 m) below that of present sea levels.

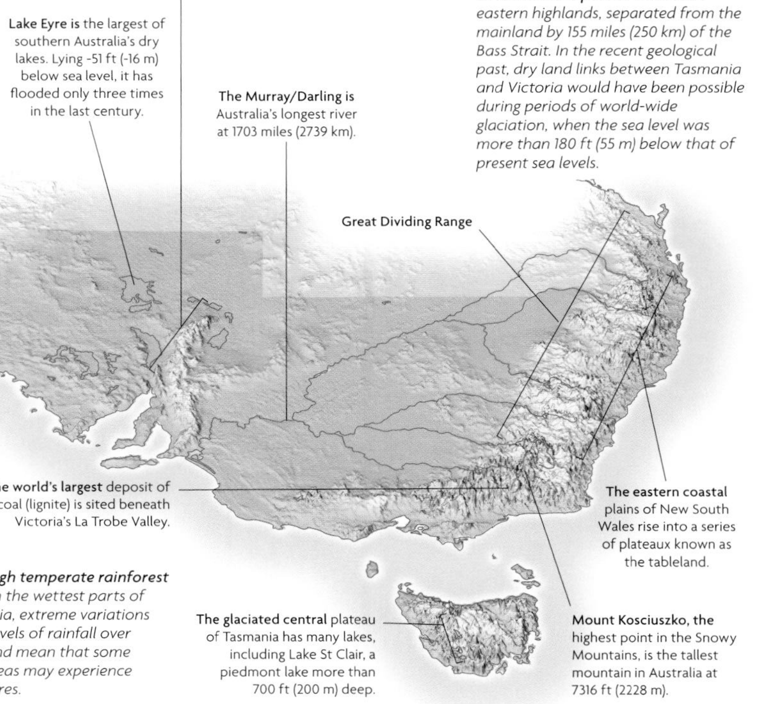

Lake Eyre is the largest of southern Australia's dry lakes. Lying -51 ft (-16 m) below sea level, it has flooded only three times in the last century.

The Musgrave and Everard ranges form bare, rounded hills made up of ancient granite and gneiss.

The Murray/Darling is Australia's longest river at 1703 miles (2739 km).

Great Dividing Range

The eastern part of the Nullarbor Plain has many sinkholes, eroded by rainwater, which run underground to form a system of long caves in the limestone rocks.

The world's largest deposit of brown coal (lignite) is sited beneath Victoria's La Trobe Valley.

The eastern coastal plains of New South Wales rise into a series of plateaux known as the tableland.

◀ Though temperate rainforest grows in the wettest parts of Tasmania, extreme variations in the levels of rainfall over the island mean that some drier areas may experience forest fires.

The glaciated central plateau of Tasmania has many lakes, including Lake St Clair, a piedmont lake more than 700 ft (200 m) deep.

Mount Kosciuszko, the highest point in the Snowy Mountains, is the tallest mountain in Australia at 7316 ft (2228 m).

Tasmania

192

New Zealand

Lying 1500 miles east-southeast of Australia, New Zealand was originally settled by the Maori, a people with Polynesian roots. It was one of the last major landmasses to be visited by Europeans. The islands' rugged topography means that most settlement has concentrated in coastal areas. People of European origin make up about 70% of the population of 4 million, following immigration from the 1920s onwards. Many recent settlers have come from Asia, including India and China, and a number of the Pacific islands. Although the Maori now make up a minority of less than half a million, their ancient claims to at least half of national territory are gaining increasing legal credence.

The landscape

New Zealand comprises two large islands and many scattered smaller islands. On South Island the Alpine Fault marks the boundary between the Pacific and Indo-Australian plates. Tectonic activity has strongly influenced the formation of the Southern Alps, snow-capped mountains with several peaks over 9800 ft (3000 m). North Island has a lower and less extensive mountain region, containing forested hills, a central volcanic plateau and downlands.

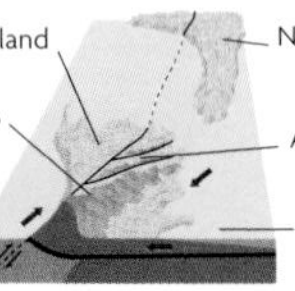

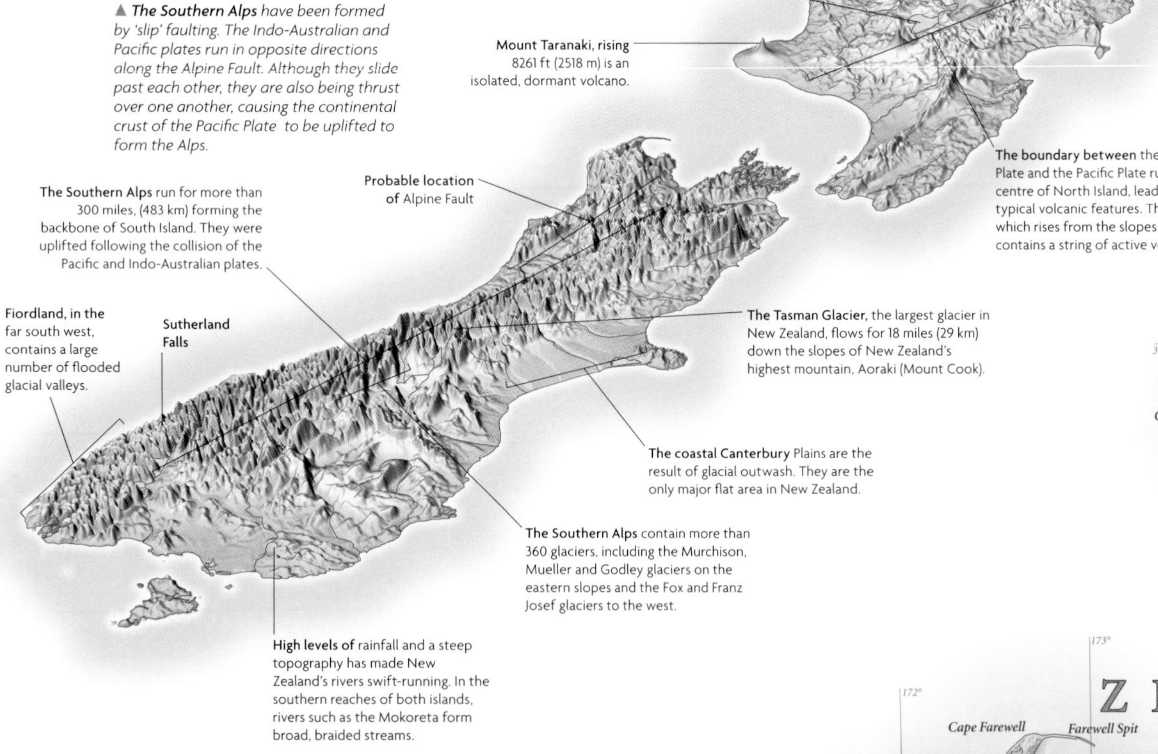

▲ Clouds of steam rise from White Island, an active, offshore volcano lying in the Bay of Plenty, off the northern coast of North Island.

Scale 1:3,000,000
projection: Lambert Conformal Conic

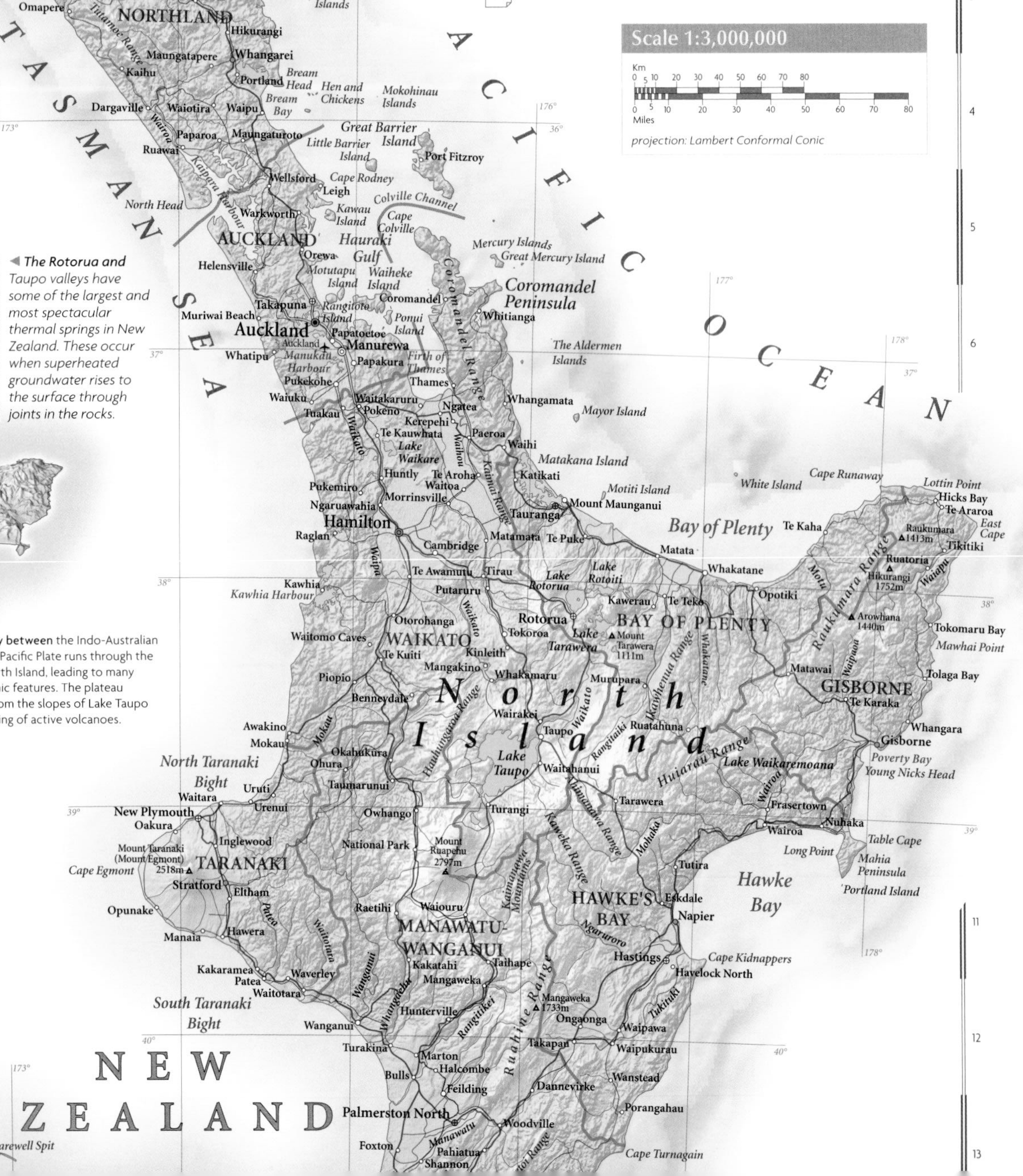

192

▼ The Northland region is characterized by many coastal inlets. These are lined by mangrove swamps, signalling the change to a subtropical climate in the far north of the island.

Northland

▼ The Rotorua and Taupo valleys have some of the largest and most spectacular thermal springs in New Zealand. These occur when superheated groundwater rises to the surface through joints in the rocks.

Rotorua

The boundary between the Indo-Australian Plate and the Pacific Plate runs through the centre of North Island, leading to many typical volcanic features. The plateau which rises from the slopes of Lake Taupo contains a string of active volcanoes.

Mountain-building in the Southern Alps

North Island
Alpine Fault
Pacific Plate
South Island
Southern Alps
Indo-Australian Plate

▲ The Southern Alps have been formed by 'slip' faulting. The Indo-Australian and Pacific plates run in opposite directions along the Alpine Fault. Although they slide past one another, they are also being thrust over one another, causing the continental crust of the Pacific Plate to be uplifted to form the Alps.

The Southern Alps run for more than 300 miles (483 km) forming the backbone of South Island. They were uplifted following the collision of the Pacific and Indo-Australian plates.

Fiordland, in the far south west, contains a large number of flooded glacial valleys.

Sutherland Falls

Probable location of Alpine Fault

Lake Taupo is New Zealand's largest inland lake. It occupies the crater of an extinct volcano.

Mount Taranaki, rising 8261 ft (2518 m) is an isolated, dormant volcano.

The Tasman Glacier, the largest glacier in New Zealand, flows for 18 miles (29 km) down the slopes of New Zealand's highest mountain, Aoraki (Mount Cook).

The coastal Canterbury Plains are the result of glacial outwash. They are the only major flat area in New Zealand.

The Southern Alps contain more than 360 glaciers, including the Murchison, Mueller and Godley glaciers on the eastern slopes and the Fox and Franz Josef glaciers to the west.

High levels of rainfall and a steep topography has made New Zealand's rivers swift-running. In the southern reaches of both islands, rivers such as the Mokoreta form broad, braided streams.

PACIFIC OCEAN

TASMAN SEA

NEW ZEALAND

North Island

South Island

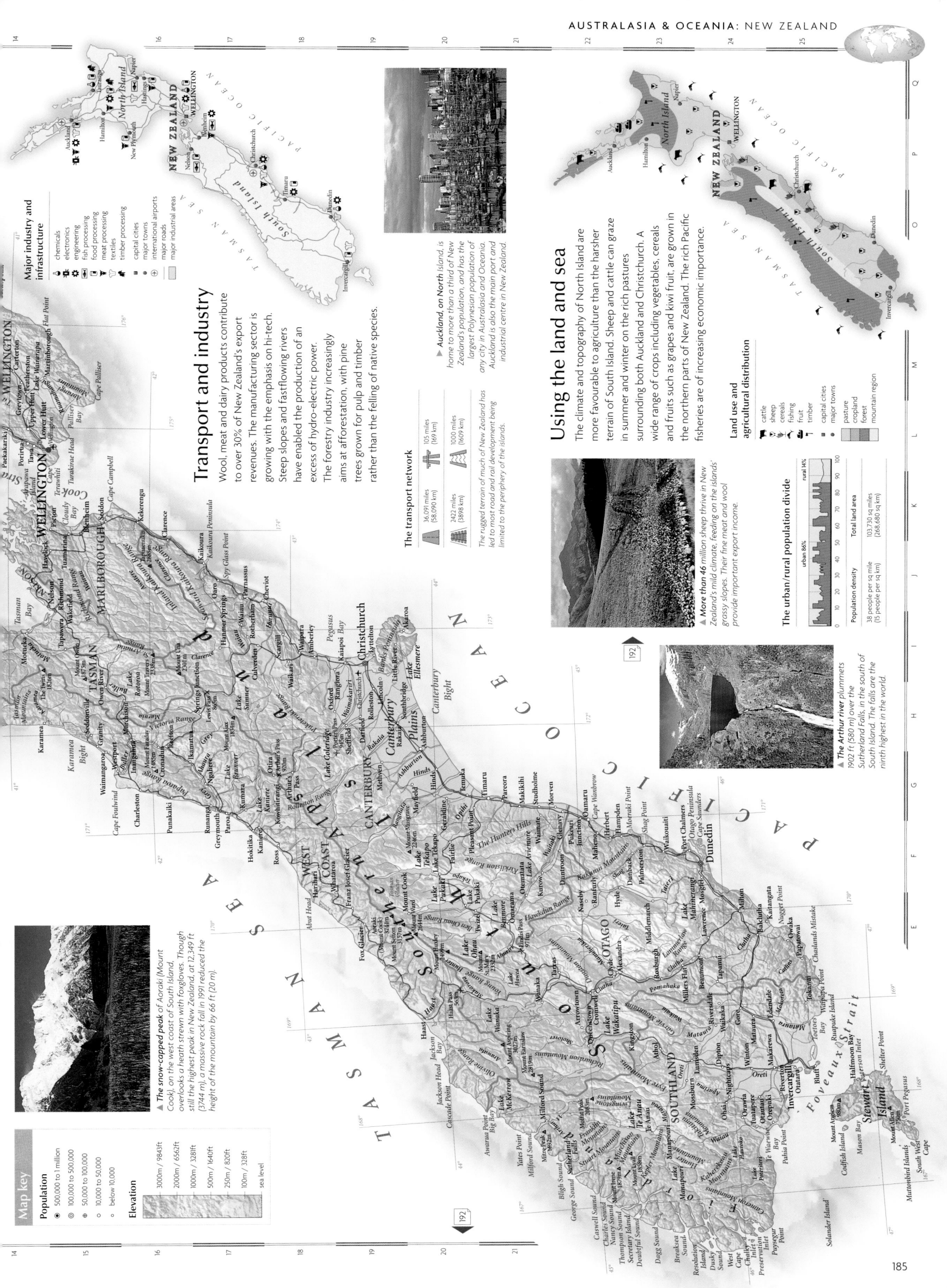

Transport and industry

Wool, meat and dairy products contribute to over 30% of New Zealand's export revenues. The manufacturing sector is growing with the emphasis on hi-tech. Steep slopes and fastflowing rivers have enabled the production of an excess of hydro-electric power. The forestry industry increasingly aims at afforestation, with pine trees grown for pulp and timber rather than the felling of native species.

Major industry and infrastructure

- chemicals
- electronics
- engineering
- fish processing
- food processing
- meat processing
- textiles
- timber processing
- capital cities
- major towns
- international airports
- major roads
- major industrial areas

▲ *Auckland, on North Island, is home to more than a third of New Zealand's population, and has the largest Polynesian population of any city in Australasia and Oceania. Auckland is also the main port and industrial centre in New Zealand.*

The transport network

36,091 miles (58,090 km)	105 miles (169 km)
2422 miles (3898 km)	1000 miles (1609 km)

The rugged terrain of much of New Zealand has led to most road and rail development being limited to the periphery of the islands.

Using the land and sea

The climate and topography of North Island are more favourable to agriculture than the harsher terrain of South Island. Sheep and cattle can graze in summer and winter on the rich pastures surrounding both Auckland and Christchurch. A wide range of crops including vegetables, cereals and fruits such as grapes and kiwi fruit, are grown in the northern parts of New Zealand. The rich Pacific fisheries are of increasing economic importance.

▲ *More than 46 million sheep thrive in New Zealand's mild climate, feeding on the islands' grassy slopes. Their fine meat and wool provide important export income.*

▲ *The Arthur river plummets 1902 ft (580 m) over the Sutherland Falls, in the south of South Island. The falls are the ninth highest in the world.*

Land use and agricultural distribution

- cattle
- sheep
- cereals
- fishing
- fruit
- timber
- capital cities
- major towns
- pasture
- cropland
- forest
- mountain region

The urban/rural population divide

urban 86%   rural 14%

Population density	Total land area
38 people per sq mile (15 people per sq km)	103,730 sq miles (268,680 sq km)

Map key

Population
- 500,000 to 1 million
- 100,000 to 500,000
- 50,000 to 100,000
- 10,000 to 50,000
- below 10,000

Elevation
- 3000m / 9843ft
- 2000m / 6562ft
- 1000m / 3281ft
- 500m / 1640ft
- 250m / 820ft
- 100m / 328ft
- sea level

▲ *The snow-capped peak of Aoraki (Mount Cook), on the west coast of South Island, overlooks a heath strewn with foxgloves. Though still the highest peak in New Zealand, at 12,349 ft (3744 m), a massive rock fall in 1991 reduced the height of the mountain by 66 ft (20 m).*

Melanesia

FIJI, New Caledonia *(to France)*, PAPUA NEW GUINEA, SOLOMON ISLANDS, VANUATU

Lying in the southwest Pacific Ocean, northeast of Australia and south of the Equator, the islands of Melanesia form one of the three geographic divisions (along with Polynesia and Micronesia) of Oceania. Melanesia's name derives from the Greek melas, 'black', and nesoi, 'islands'. Most of the larger islands are volcanic in origin. The smaller islands tend to be coral atolls and are mainly uninhabited. Rugged mountains, covered by dense rainforest, take up most of the land area. Melanesian's cultivate yams, taro, and sweet potatoes for local consumption and live in small, usually dispersed, homesteads.

▲ *Huli tribesmen from Southern Highlands Province in Papua New Guinea parade in ceremonial dress, their powdered wigs decorated with exotic plumage and their faces and bodies painted with coloured pigments.*

Map key

Population
- ◉ 100,000 to 500,000
- ⊕ 50,000 to 100,000
- ○ 10,000 to 50,000
- ○ below 10,000

Elevation

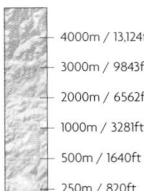

- 4000m / 13,124ft
- 3000m / 9843ft
- 2000m / 6562ft
- 1000m / 3281ft
- 500m / 1640ft
- 250m / 820ft
- 100m / 328ft
- sea level

Transport and Industry

The processing of natural resources generates significant export revenue for the countries of Melanesia. The region relies mainly on copra, tuna and timber exports, with some production of cocoa and palm oil. The islands have substantial mineral resources including the world's largest copper reserves on Bougainville Island; gold, and potential oil and natural gas. Tourism has become the fastest growing sector in most of the countries' economies.

◀ *On New Caledonia's main island, relatively high interior plateaux descend to coastal plains. Nickel is the most important mineral resource, but the hills also harbour metallic deposits including chrome, cobalt, iron, gold, silver and copper.*

◀ *Lying close to the banks of the Sepik river in northern Papua New Guinea, this building is known as the Spirit House. It is constructed from leaves and twigs, ornately woven and trimmed into geometric patterns. The house is decorated with a mask and topped by a carved statue.*

▲ *On one of Vanuatu's many islands, beach houses stand at the water's edge, surrounded by coconut palms and other tropical vegetation. The unspoilt beaches and tranquillity of its islands are drawing ever-larger numbers of tourists to Vanuatu.*

The transport network

🛣	1236 miles (1990 km)	⛆ None	
🚆	370 miles (595 km)	✈	6924 miles (11,143 km)

As most of the islands of Melanesia lie off the major sea and air routes, services to and from the rest of the world are infrequent. Transport by road on rugged terrain is difficult and expensive.

Major industry and infrastructure

- ♨ beverages
- ☕ coffee processing
- copra processing
- 🍴 food processing
- ⛏ mining
- ☷ textiles
- ⚒ timber processing
- tourism
- ■ capital cities
- ● major towns
- ✈ international airports
- major roads

The Landscape

Melanesia comprises high, volcanic islands, low coral islands and continental islands. New Guinea is part of the Australian continental platform, and is separated from it only by the shallow flooding of the Torres Strait. The plate margin of the Pacific and Indo-Australian plates cuts through mainland Papua New Guinea. Volcanic activity, resulting from the collision of these plates, has sculpted much of Melanesia's landscape.

The Star Mountains include some of the most remote terrain on Earth. The area is rich in gold and copper.

The lowland plains in the south and north of Papua New Guinea's main island are swampy, and contain some fertile alluvial soils. This contrasts with the mountainous islands in the rest of the country where soils are generally thin and nutrients are retained in the existing vegetation.

Southern Papua New Guinea is part of the Indo-Australian Plate. New Guinea only became separated physically from Australia about 8000-years ago following the flooding of the Torres Strait.

▶ Papua New Guinea's rivers, though fairly short, carry extremely high sediment loads, largely due to soil erosion. This is caused by a combination of very steep slopes and heavy rainfall, and is made worse by forest clearance, particularly 'slash and burn' techniques and road or mine operations.

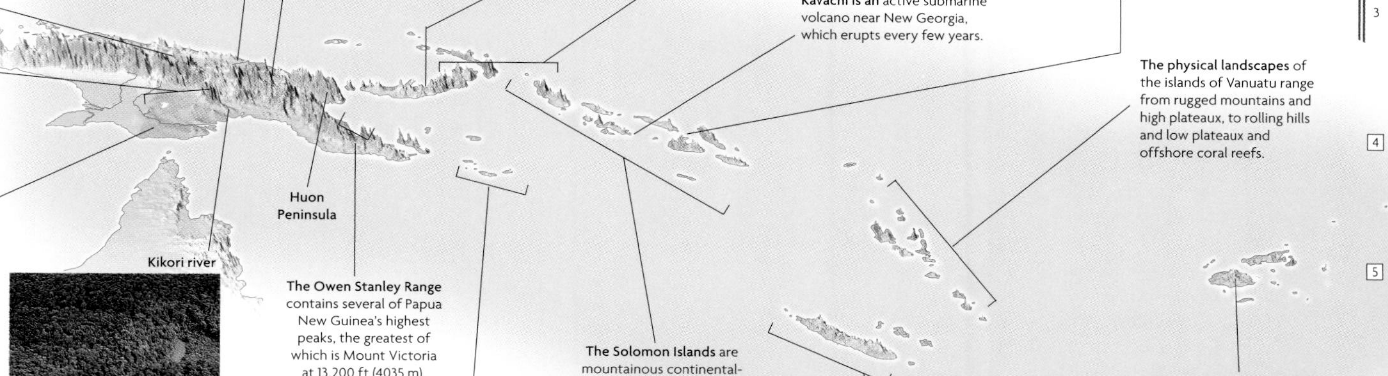

The Sepik river drains the lowlands north of the Central Range, flowing eastward into the Bismarck Sea.

The Bismarck Range is precipitous, rugged and covered in dense vegetation, rising to 14,793 ft (4509-m) at Mount Wilhelm in central Papua New Guinea.

Huon Peninsula

Kikori river

The Owen Stanley Range contains several of Papua New Guinea's highest peaks, the greatest of which is Mount Victoria at 13,200 ft (4035 m).

The Louisiade Archipelago contains 10 volcanic islands and numerous coral islets. Tagula Island is the largest of the islands, containing the archipelago's highest peak at 2645 ft (806 m).

Most of Papua New Guinea's outlying islands, including New Britain, Bougainville Island and New Ireland, are precipitous and of volcanic origin.

Kavachi is an active submarine volcano near New Georgia, which erupts every few years.

The Solomon Islands are mountainous continental-type islands with largely andesitic volcanoes.

New Caledonia's main island is surrounded by coral reef that extends from the Huon island group in the north, to Île des Pins in the south.

◀ The slopes of this extinct volcano near Talasea on the island of New Britain have been almost entirely colonized by rainforest vegetation.

▲ A series of coral reefs can be seen in the clear waters off Cape Esperance on the island of Guadalcanal in the Solomons.

The physical landscapes of the islands of Vanuatu range from rugged mountains and high plateaux, to rolling hills and low plateaux and offshore coral reefs.

Viti Levu, the largest of Fiji's islands, contains the country's highest mountain, Mount Victoria at 4339 ft (1323 m).

Huon Peninsula

Caves and undercut cliffs mark former shoreline
Former level of beach
Current beach
Stream cuts down through recently exposed land

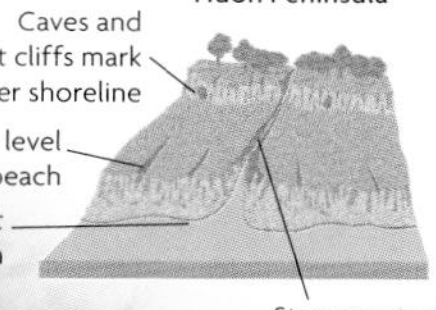

Uplift of the land in tectonically active regions can lead to former coastlines being lifted beyond the reach of the sea. New cliffs and caves are formed at a lower level, and rivers cut down through the lower land to reach sea level once more.

Using the land and sea

Almost 60% of the population of Melanesia is engaged in agriculture and animal husbandry at a subsistence level. Coconuts and cocoa are grown for export revenue. Over 80% of the land area is cloaked by tropical forest and woodlands, which have proved to be a rich timber source. In coastal areas, fishing, mainly for tuna, is a staple industry.

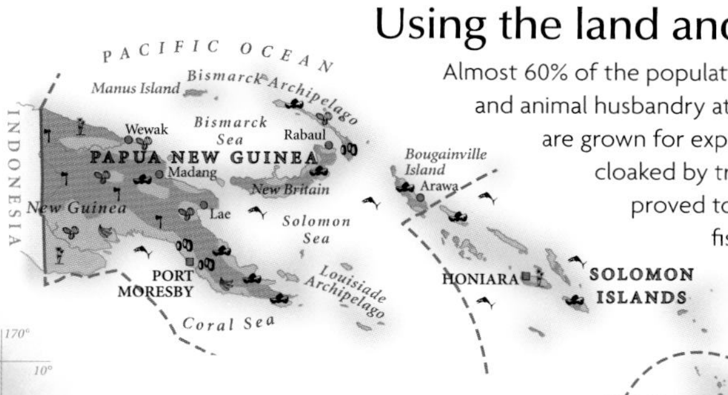

PACIFIC OCEAN
INDONESIA
Manus Island
Bismarck Archipelago
Wewak
Bismarck Sea
PAPUA NEW GUINEA
Madang
Rabaul
New Britain
New Guinea
Lae
Bougainville Island
Arawa
Solomon Sea
PORT MORESBY
Louisiade Archipelago
HONIARA
SOLOMON ISLANDS
Coral Sea

PACIFIC OCEAN
Coral Sea
VANUATU
FIJI
NEW CALEDONIA (to France)
PORT-VILA
SUVA
NOUMÉA

The urban/rural population divide

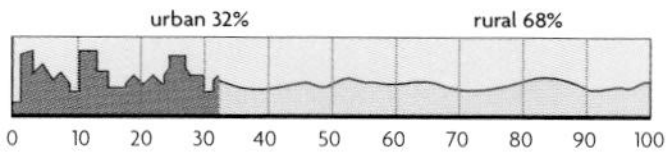

urban 32%   rural 68%

0 10 20 30 40 50 60 70 80 90 100

Population density	Total land area
32 people per sq mile (12 people per sq km)	205,354 sq miles (332,008 sq km)

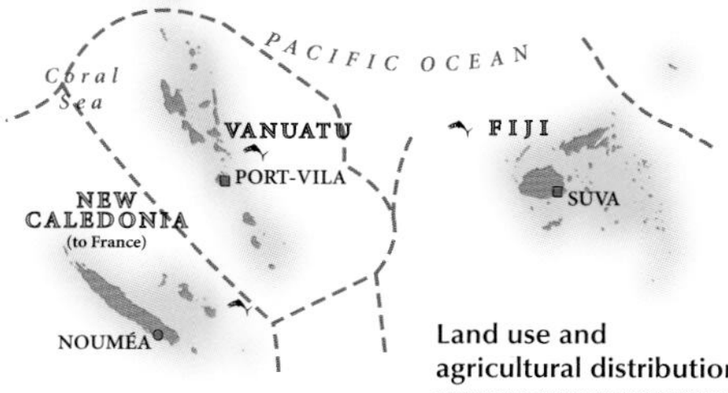

◀ Abaca Eco-tourist Park near Lautoka on the island of Viti Levu in western Fiji is one of a number of projects aimed at combining tourism with awareness about the environment. The government and people of Fiji are keen to protect the unique ecology of the islands and prevent further damage to the coral reefs. Until the recent ending of nuclear testing in the Pacific by Western nations, Fiji lay downwind of some of the main testing sites.

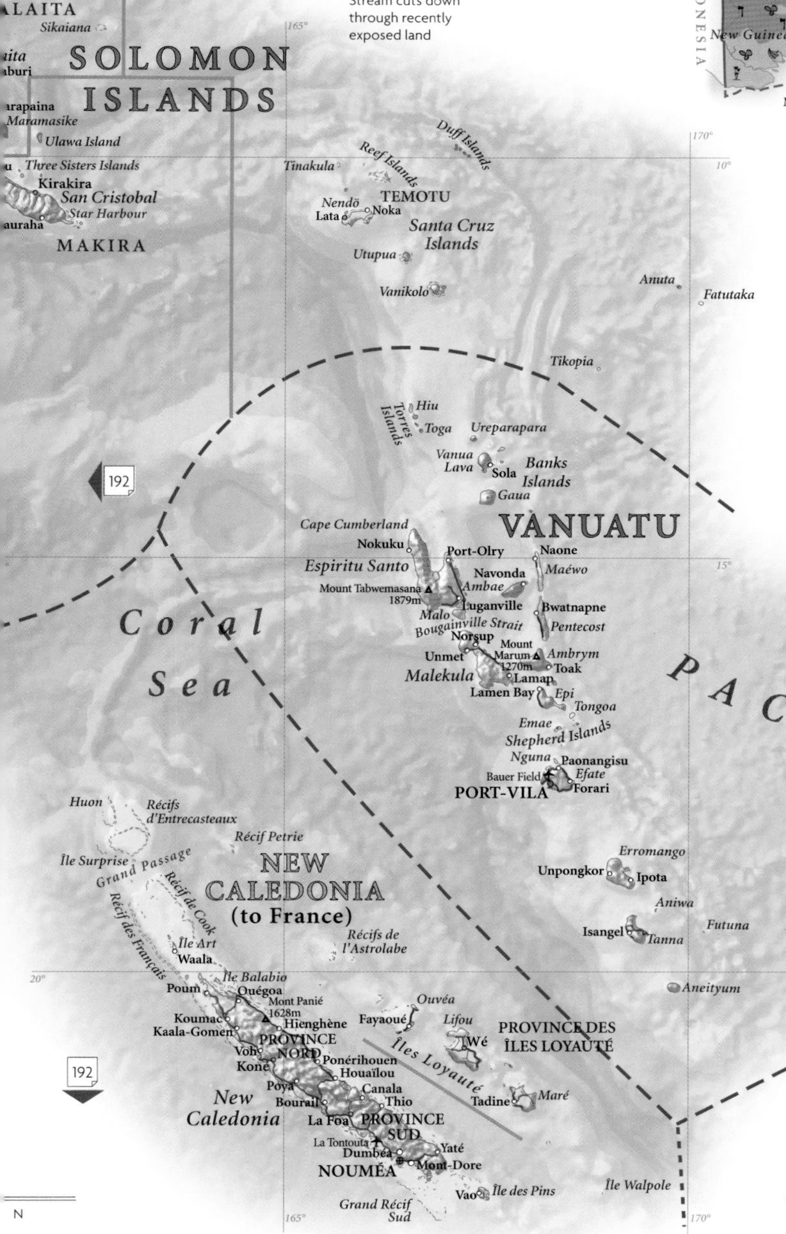

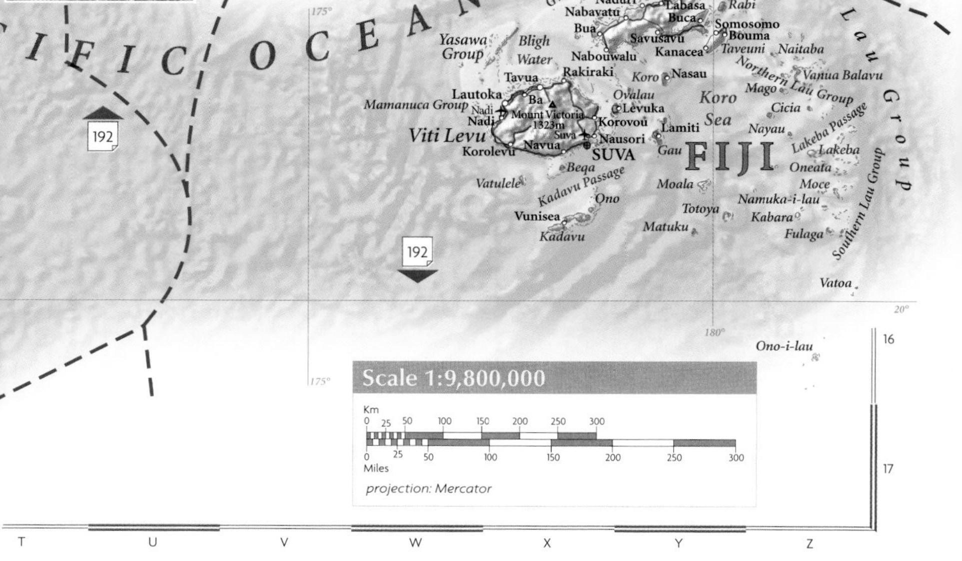

Land use and agricultural distribution

- bananas
- cocoa
- coconuts
- fishing
- oil palms
- rubber
- timber
- capital cities
- major towns
- cropland
- forest
- wetland

Map labels

SOLOMON ISLANDS
MALAITA
Sikaiana
Matamasike
Ulawa Island
Three Sisters Islands
Kirakira
San Cristobal
Star Harbour
MAKIRA
Maraha

Reef Islands
Duff Islands
Tinakula
Nendö
Lata
Noka
TEMOTU
Santa Cruz Islands
Utupua
Vanikolo
Anuta
Fatutaka
Tikopia

Torres Islands
Hiu
Toga
Ureparapara
Vanua Lava
Sola
Gaua
Banks Islands
Cape Cumberland
Nokuku
Port-Olry
Naone
VANUATU
Espiritu Santo
Navonda
Maéwo
Mount Tabwemasana 1879m
Ambae
Luganville
Malo
Bwatnapne
Bougainville Strait
Pentecost
Norsup
Mount Maruma 1270m
Ambrym
Unmet
Toak
Malekula
Laman
Lamen Bay
Epi
Tongoa
Emae
Shepherd Islands
Nguna
Paonangisu
Bauer Field
Efate
PORT-VILA
Forari

Coral Sea

PACIFIC OCEAN

Huon
Récifs d'Entrecasteaux
Récif Petrie
Ile Surprise
Grand Passage
Récifs des Français
Récif du Cook
NEW CALEDONIA (to France)
Récifs de l'Astrolabe
Ile Art
Waala
Poum
Ile Balabio
Ouégoa
Mont Panié 1628m
Koumac
Kaala-Gomen
Hienghène
Ouvéa
Fayaoué
Lifou
Wé
PROVINCE DES ÎLES LOYAUTÉ
Voh
PROVINCE NORD
Pônérihouen
Houaïlou
Poya
Canala
Bourail
Thio
La Foa
PROVINCE SUD
Maré
Tadine
New Caledonia
La Tontouta
Dumbéa
Yaté
NOUMÉA
Mont-Dore
Ile Walpole
Vao
Île des Pins
Grand Récif Sud

Erromango
Unpongkor
Ipota
Aniwa
Futuna
Isangel
Tanna
Aneityum

Cikobia
Qelelevu Lagoon
Vanua Levu
Nabuna
Great Sea Reef
Naduri
Labasa
Rabi
Nabavatu
Bua
Buca
Somosomo
Bouma
Yasawa Group
Bligh Water
Nabouwalu
Savusavu
Taveuni
Naitaba
Tavua
Rakiraki
Kanacea
Northern Lau Group
Vanua Balavu
Mago
Lautoka
Ovalau
Levuka
Nasau
Cicia
Mamanuca Group
Nadi
Mount Victoria
Korovou
Lamiti
Nayau
Viti Levu
Navua
Nausori
Koro Sea
Lakeba Passage
Korolevu
SUVA
Gau
FIJI
Lakeba
Oneata
Beqa
Moala
Moce
Vatulele
Kadavu Passage
Ono
Tötoya
Namuka-i-lau
Kabara
Vunisea
Matuku
Fulaga
Kadavu
Vatoa
Ono-i-lau
Southern Lau Group
Lau Group

Scale 1:9,800,000

Km
0 25 50   100   150   200   250   300
Miles
0 25 50   100   150   200   250   300

projection: Mercator

Micronesia

MARSHALL ISLANDS, MICRONESIA, NAURU, PALAU, Guam, Northern Mariana Islands, Wake Island

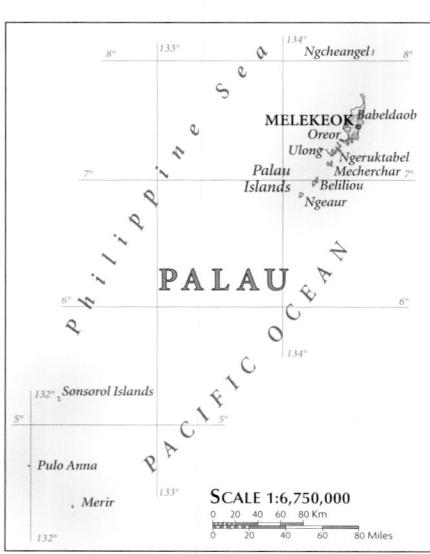

The Micronesian islands lie in the western reaches of the Pacific Ocean and are all part of the same volcanic zone. The Federated States of Micronesia is the largest group, with more than 600 atolls and forested volcanic islands in an area of more than 1120 sq miles (2900 sq km). Micronesia is a mixture of former colonies, overseas territories and dependencies. Most of the region still relies on aid and subsidies to sustain economies limited by resources, isolation, and an emigrating population, drawn to New Zealand and Australia by the attractions of a western lifestyle.

Palau

Palau is an archipelago of over 200 islands, only eight of which are inhabited. It was the last remaining UN trust territory in the Pacific, controlled by the USA until 1994, when it became independent. The economy operates on a subsistence level, with coconuts and cassava the principal crops. Fishing licences and tourism provide foreign currency.

SCALE 1:825,000

SCALE 1:6,750,000

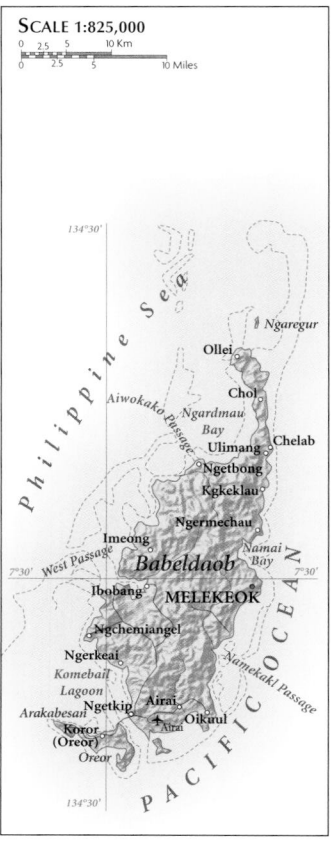

Guam (to US)

Lying at the southern end of the Mariana Islands, Guam is an important US military base and tourist destination. Social and political life is dominated by the indigenous Chamorro, who make up just under half the population, although the increasing prevalence of western culture threatens Guam's traditional social stability.

◀ The tranquillity of these coastal lagoons, at Inarajan in southern Guam, belies the fact that the island lies in a region where typhoons are common.

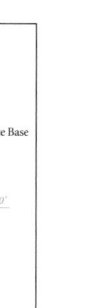

GUAM (to US)

SCALE 1:925,000

SCALE 1:925,000

Northern Mariana Islands (to US)

A US Commonwealth territory, the Northern Marianas comprise the whole of the Mariana archipelago except for Guam. The islands retain their close links with the United States and continue to receive US aid. Tourism, though bringing in much-needed revenue, has speeded the decline of the traditional subsistence economy. Most of the population lives on Saipan.

SCALE 1:550,000

Northern Mariana Islands: capital cities

CAPITOL HILL – executive & legislative capital
SUSUPE – judicial capital

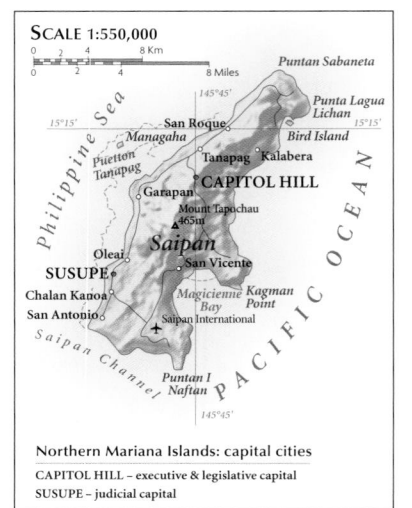

▲ The Palau Islands have numerous hidden lakes and lagoons. These sustain their own ecosystems which have developed in isolation. This has produced adaptations in the animals and plants which are often unique to each lake.

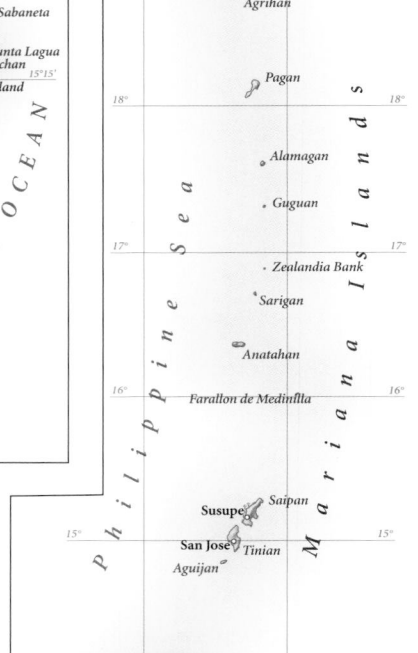

NORTHERN MARIANA ISLANDS (to US)

GUAM (to US)
HAGÅTÑA

SCALE 1:5,500,000

Micronesia

A mixture of high volcanic islands and low-lying coral atolls, the Federated States of Micronesia include all the Caroline Islands except Palau. Pohnpei, Kosrae, Chuuk and Yap are the four main island cluster states, each of which has its own language, with English remaining the official language. Nearly half the population is concentrated on Pohnpei, the largest island. Independent since 1986, the islands continue to receive considerable aid from the USA which supplements an economy based primarily on fishing and copra processing.

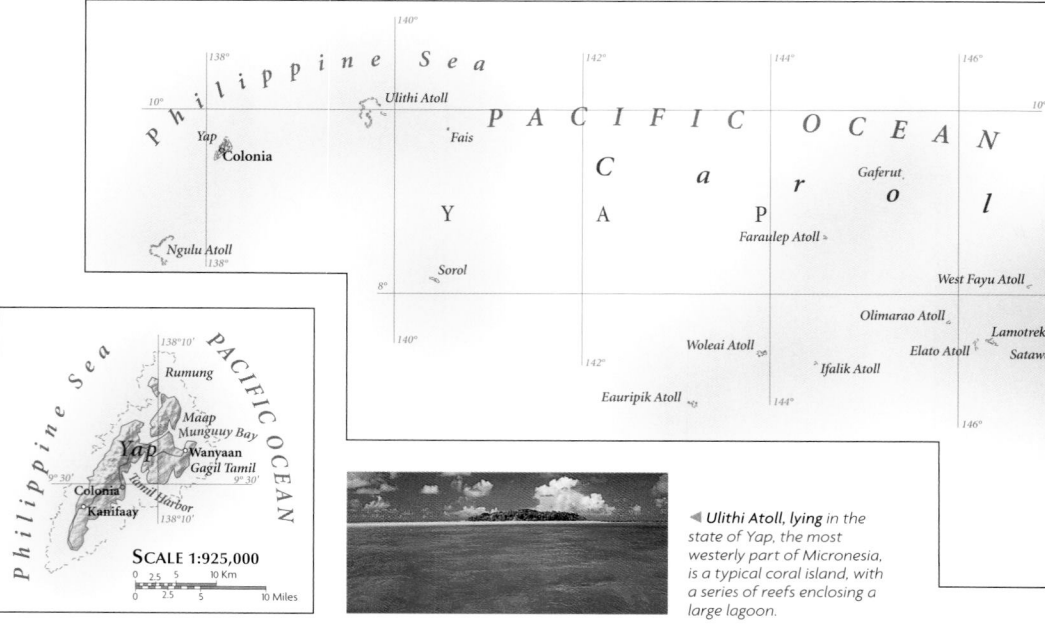

◀ Ulithi Atoll, lying in the state of Yap, the most westerly part of Micronesia, is a typical coral island, with a series of reefs enclosing a large lagoon.

Marshall Islands

A group of 34 widely-scattered atolls in the central Pacific Ocean, the Marshall Islands include some of the largest atolls in the world, formed from low coral islands with sandy beaches and enclosing vast lagoons. Formerly under US protection as part of the UN Trust Territory of the Pacific Islands, and including the former US nuclear testing sites of Bikini atoll and Enewetak Atoll, the Marshall Islands became self-governing in 1979. The economy is reliant on US aid and on the rent paid by the USA for its missile base on Kwajalein atoll.

SCALE 1:1,100,000

Nauru

A former British colony, the tiny island of Nauru, with an area of only 8.2 sq miles (21.2 sq km), has been exploited for its substantial phosphate deposits by the UK, Australia and New Zealand. Since independence in 1968, the phosphate industry has made its citizens some of the wealthiest in the world, and scars from the vast mining operation pit the island's landscape. Phosphate reserves are now virtually exhausted and investment overseas will in future form the bulk of Nauru's income.

▲ Majuro Atoll is the Marshall Islands' capital and commercial center. Almost half the population live on the narrow islands, often in overcrowded conditions.

SCALE 1:7,250,000

SCALE 1:250,000

◀ A series of coral pinnacles stand exposed in the shallow water off the coast of Nauru. Much of the island has an extraordinary 'lunar' landscape, created by years of phosphate extraction.

Wake Island (to US)

An unincorporated territory of the USA with a tiny population, Wake Island remains strategically important to US forces, and has been used as a base in several conflicts. Formed by the rim of an extinct underwater volcano, it is now used as an emergency airstrip for trans-Pacific flights, and as a stop-over for cargo planes.

SCALE 1:725,000

▲ Traditionally built canoes are still important in Micronesia, used for transport and for fishing. This large canoe, on Satawal, in the state of Yap, needs nearly 20 people to return it to the boathouse.

SCALE 1:1,750,000

WAKE ISLAND (to US)

SCALE 1:275,000

SCALE 1:550,000

SCALE 1:9,000,000

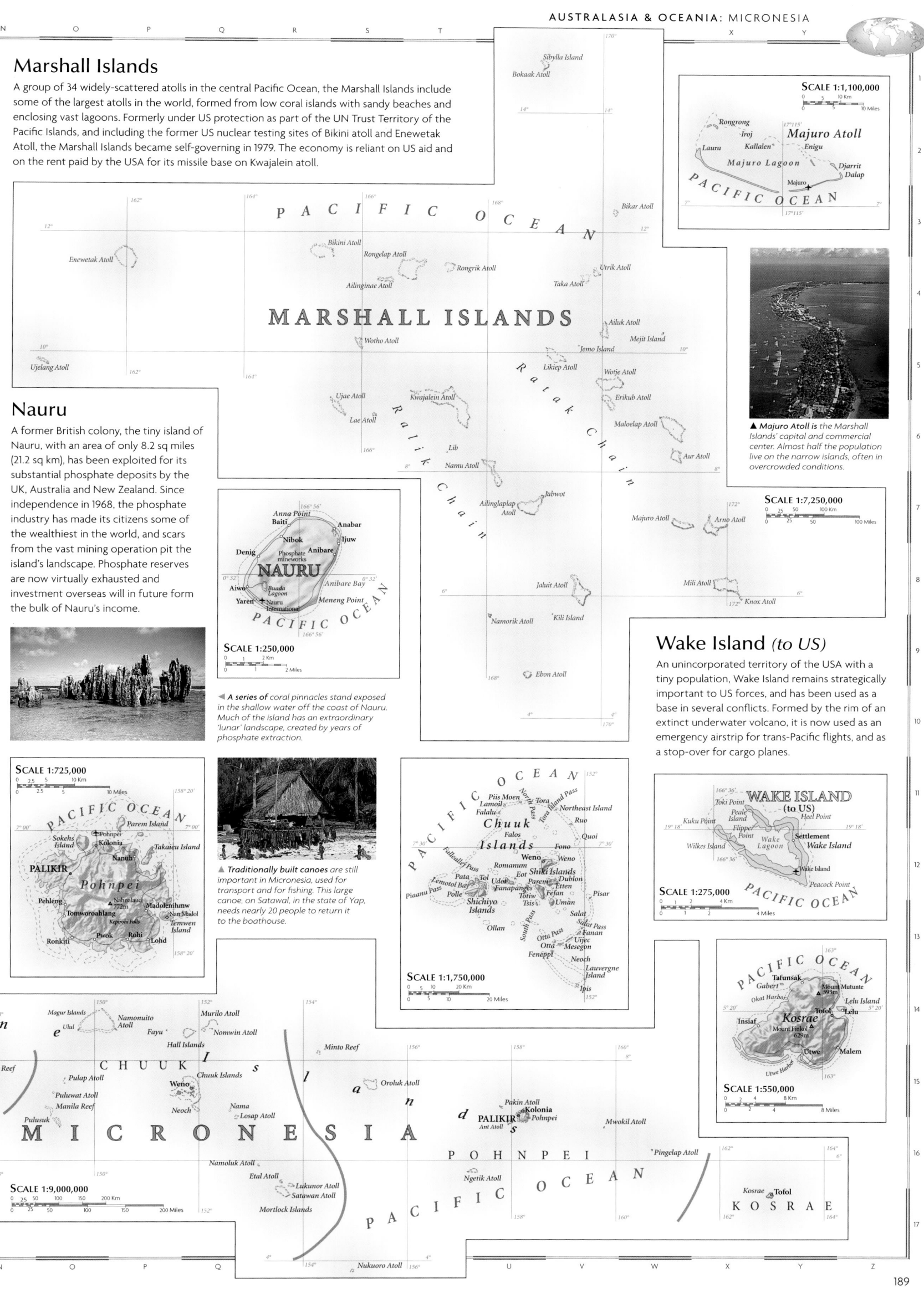

Polynesia

KIRIBATI, TUVALU, Cook Islands, Easter Island, French Polynesia, Niue, Pitcairn Islands, Tokelau, Wallis & Futuna

The numerous island groups of Polynesia lie to the east of Australia, scattered over a vast area in the south Pacific. The islands are a mixture of low-lying coral atolls, some of which enclose lagoons, and the tips of great underwater volcanoes. The populations on the islands are small, and most people are of Polynesian origin, as are the Maori of New Zealand. Local economies remain simple, relying mainly on subsistence crops, mineral deposits – many now exhausted – fishing and tourism.

Kiribati

A former British colony, Kiribati became independent in 1979. Banaba's phosphate deposits ran out in 1980, following decades of exploitation by the British. Economic development remains slow and most agriculture is at a subsistence level, though coconuts provide export income, and underwater agriculture is being developed.

▶ With the exception of Banaba all the islands in Kiribati's three groups are low-lying, coral atolls. This aerial view shows the sparsely vegetated islands, intercut by many small lagoons.

Tuvalu

A chain of nine coral atolls, 360 miles (579 km) long with a land area of just over 9 sq miles (23 sq km), Tuvalu is one of the world's smallest and most isolated states. As the Ellice Islands, Tuvalu was linked to the Gilbert Islands (now part of Kiribati) as a British colony until independence in 1978. Politically and socially conservative, Tuvaluans live by fishing and subsistence farming.

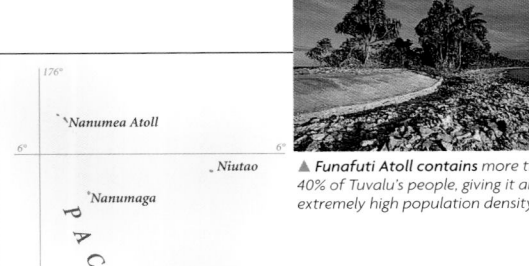

▲ Funafuti Atoll contains more than 40% of Tuvalu's people, giving it an extremely high population density.

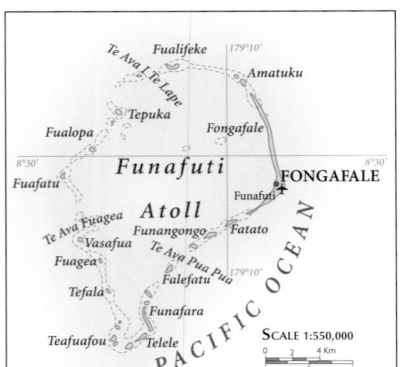

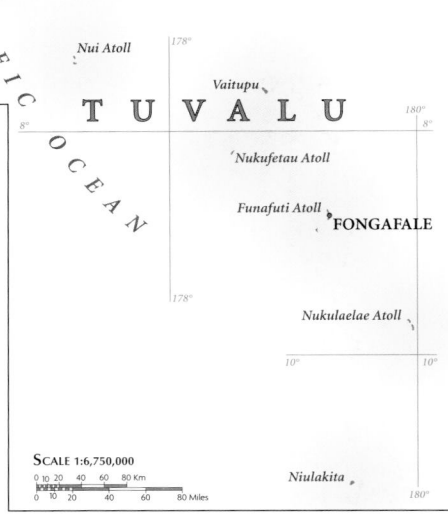

Tokelau (to New Zealand)

A low-lying coral atoll, Tokelau is a dependent territory of New Zealand with few natural resources. Although a 1990 cyclone destroyed crops and infrastructure, a tuna cannery and the sale of fishing licences have raised revenue and a catamaran link between the islands has increased their tourism potential. Tokelau's small size and economic weakness makes independence from New Zealand unlikely.

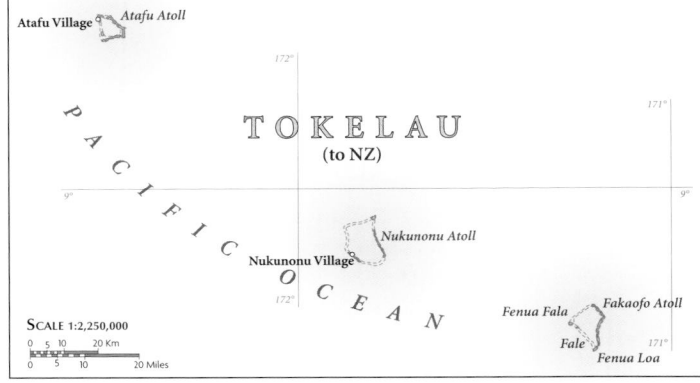

▲ Fishermen cast their nets to catch small fish in the shallow waters off Atafu Atoll, the most westerly island in Tokelau.

Wallis & Futuna (to France)

In contrast to other French overseas territories in the south Pacific, the inhabitants of Wallis and Futuna have shown little desire for greater autonomy. A subsistence economy produces a variety of tropical crops, while foreign currency remittances come from expatriates and from the sale of licences to Japanese and Korean fishing fleets.

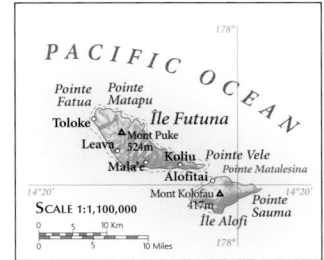

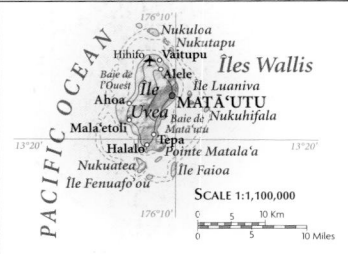

Cook Islands (to New Zealand)

A mixture of coral atolls and volcanic peaks, the Cook Islands achieved self-government in 1965 but exist in free association with New Zealand. A diverse economy includes pearl and giant clam farming, and an ostrich farm, plus tourism and banking. A 1991 friendship treaty with France provides for French surveillance of territorial waters.

Niue (to New Zealand)

Niue, the world's largest coral island, is self-governing but exists in free association with New Zealand. Tropical fruits are grown for local consumption; tourism and the sale of postage stamps provide foreign currency. The lack of local job prospects has led more than 10,000 Niueans to emigrate to New Zealand, which has now invested heavily in Niue's economy in the hope of reversing this trend.

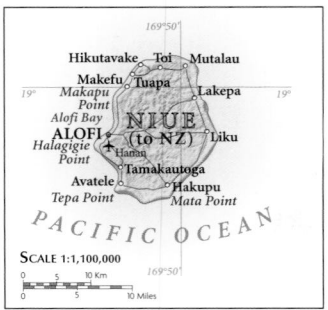

▲ Palm trees fringe the white sands of a beach on Aitutaki in the Southern Cook Islands, where tourism is of increasing economic importance.

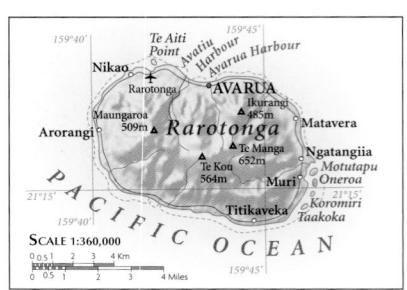

▲ Waves have cut back the original coastline, exposing a sandy beach, near Mutalau in the northeast corner of Niue.

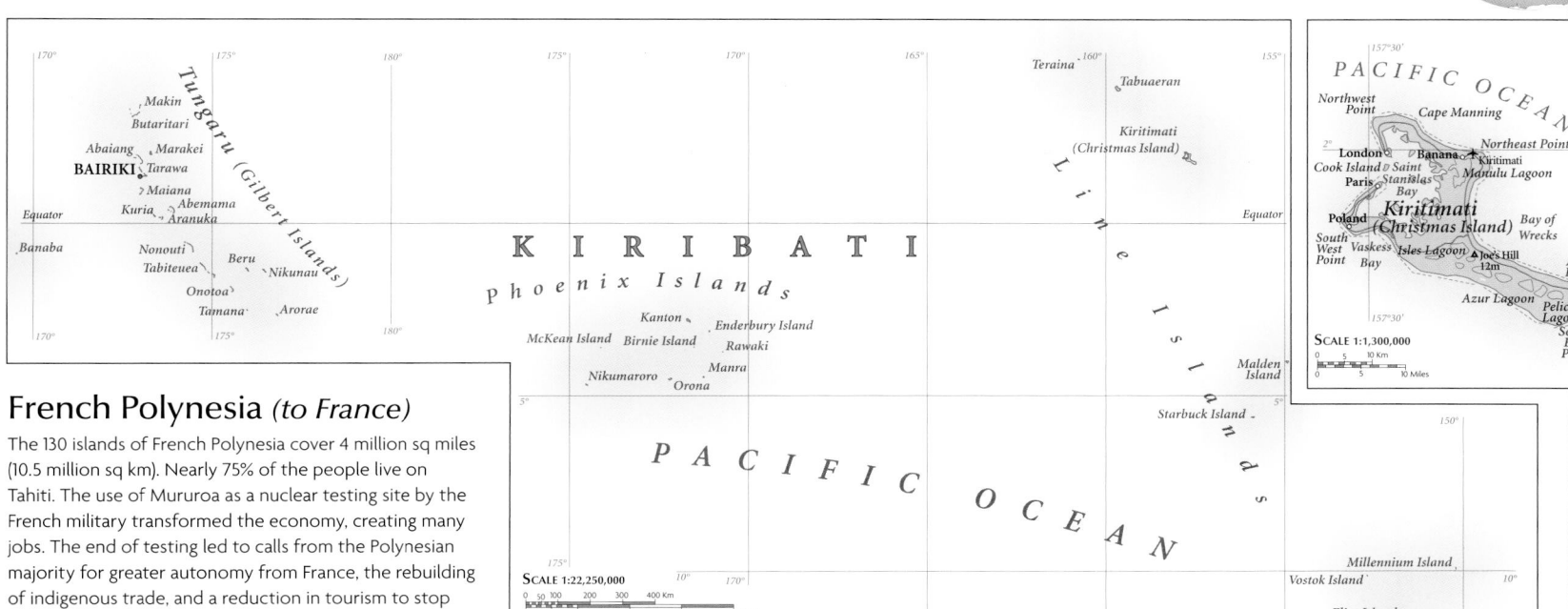

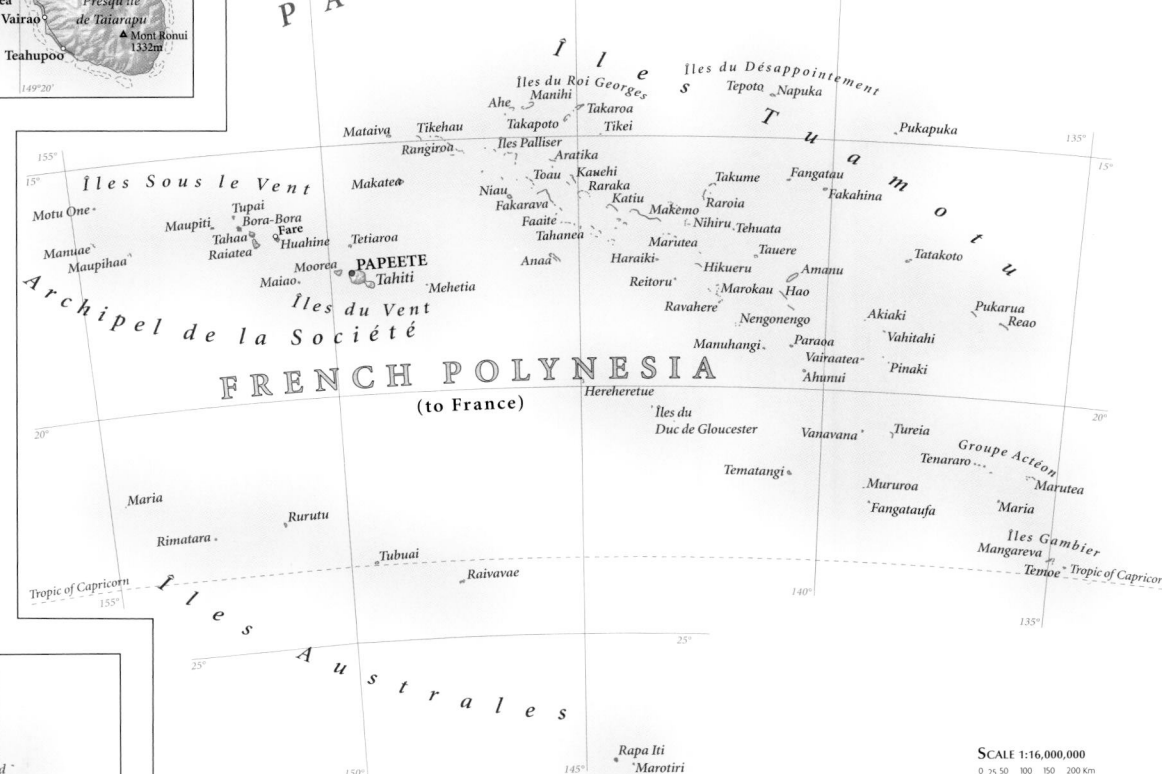

French Polynesia *(to France)*

The 130 islands of French Polynesia cover 4 million sq miles (10.5 million sq km). Nearly 75% of the people live on Tahiti. The use of Mururoa as a nuclear testing site by the French military transformed the economy, creating many jobs. The end of testing led to calls from the Polynesian majority for greater autonomy from France, the rebuilding of indigenous trade, and a reduction in tourism to stop the erosion of the islands' traditional culture.

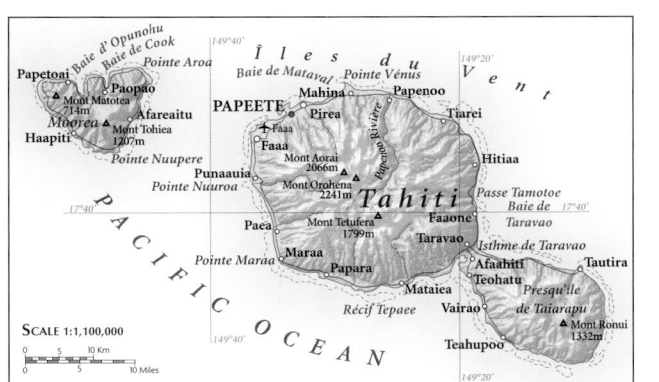

SCALE 1:1,100,000

◀ *The traditional Tahitian welcome for visitors, who are greeted by parties of canoes, has become a major tourist attraction.*

Pitcairn Islands *(to UK)*

Britain's most isolated dependency, Pitcairn Island was first populated by mutineers from the HMS *Bounty* in 1790. Emigration is further depleting the already limited gene pool of the island's inhabitants, with associated social and health problems. Barter, fishing and subsistence farming form the basis of the economy although postage stamp sales provide foreign currency earnings, and offshore mineral exploitation may boost the economy in future.

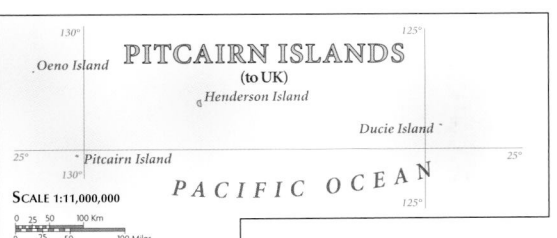

PITCAIRN ISLANDS
(to UK)

SCALE 1:11,000,000

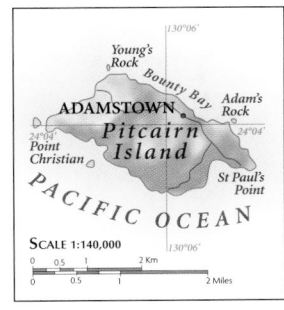

◀ *The Pitcairn Islanders rely on regular airdrops from New Zealand and periodic visits by supply vessels to provide them with basic commodities.*

ADAMSTOWN
Pitcairn Island

SCALE 1:140,000

Easter Island *(to Chile)*

One of the most easterly islands in Polynesia, Easter Island *(Isla de Pascua)* – also known as Rapa Nui, is part of Chile. The mainly Polynesian inhabitants support themselves by farming, which is mainly of a subsistence nature, and includes cattle rearing and crops such as sugar cane, bananas, corn, gourds and potatoes. In recent years, tourism has become the most important source of income and the island sustains a small commercial airport.

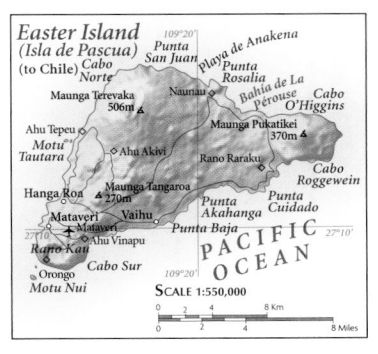

Easter Island (Isla de Pascua) (to Chile)

SCALE 1:550,000

▲ *The Naunau, a series of huge stone statues overlook Playa de Anakena, on Easter Island. Carved from a soft volcanic rock, they were erected between 400 and 900 years ago.*

The Pacific Ocean

The Pacific is the world's largest and deepest ocean. It is nearly twice the area of the Atlantic and contains almost three times as much water. The ocean is dotted with islands and surrounded by some of the world's most populous states; over half the world's population lives on its shores. The Pacific is bordered by active plate margins known as the 'Ring of Fire', causing earthquakes and tsunamis, and creating volcanic islands and subterranean mountain chains. The largest underwater mountains break the surface as island arcs. The fisheries of the Pacific are some of the most productive in the world and provide a vital resource for many of the Pacific islands. Since the Second World War there has been a shift in trading patterns, with a considerable growth in trade between the United States and the countries of the Pacific Rim.

The Ring of Fire

The active plate margins surrounding the Pacific have created numerous land and island volcanoes along its border. The actual basin of the Pacific is made up of a number of separate tectonic plates which move away from each other, colliding with other plates. When they collide, the oceanic plates, being thinner, are forced beneath the thicker continental plates, forming deep ocean trenches and high ridges. These collision zones are known as subduction zones and are characterized by intense seismic and volcanic activity.

◀ *Mayon Volcano* in the Philippines is one of many active volcanoes on the Pacific 'Ring of Fire'. It is noted for its perfect conical shape; the base of the cone is 80 miles (130 km) in circumference.

Ring of Fire

— plate boundaries
● major volcanoes

◀ *The Hawaiian volcanoes* lie in the centre of a plate, not on a plate margin, and are known as intraplate volcanoes. They are associated with hot spots, whereby a plume of hot molten rock rises to the surface as the plate moves over it.

American Samoa and Samoa

American Samoa and Samoa are part of the island archipelago of Polynesia. The two most populous islands are Tutuila in American Samoa and 'Upolu in Samoa. Although the economies of both these states remain predominantly resource-based, both are expanding their light manufacturing sectors, and the US administration is the primary employer in American Samoa. Tuna fishing is particularly important: 25% of all tuna consumed in the USA is processed and canned in Pago Pago.

▶ *Many of the* buildings in Samoa reflect the country's colonial past. Once a colony of New Zealand, Samoa is now an independent state; American Samoa remains an unincorporated territory of the United States.

SCALE 1:3,350,000

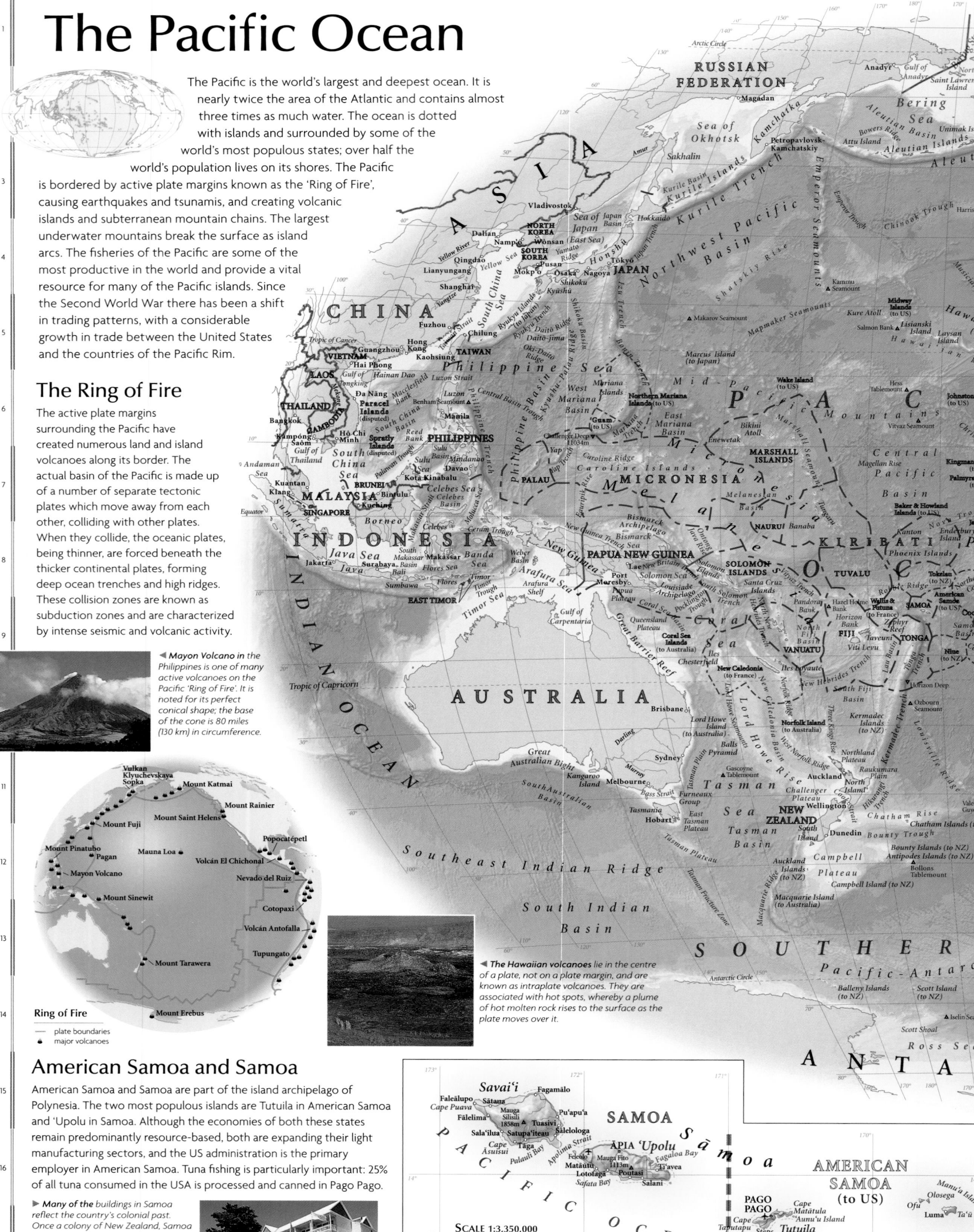

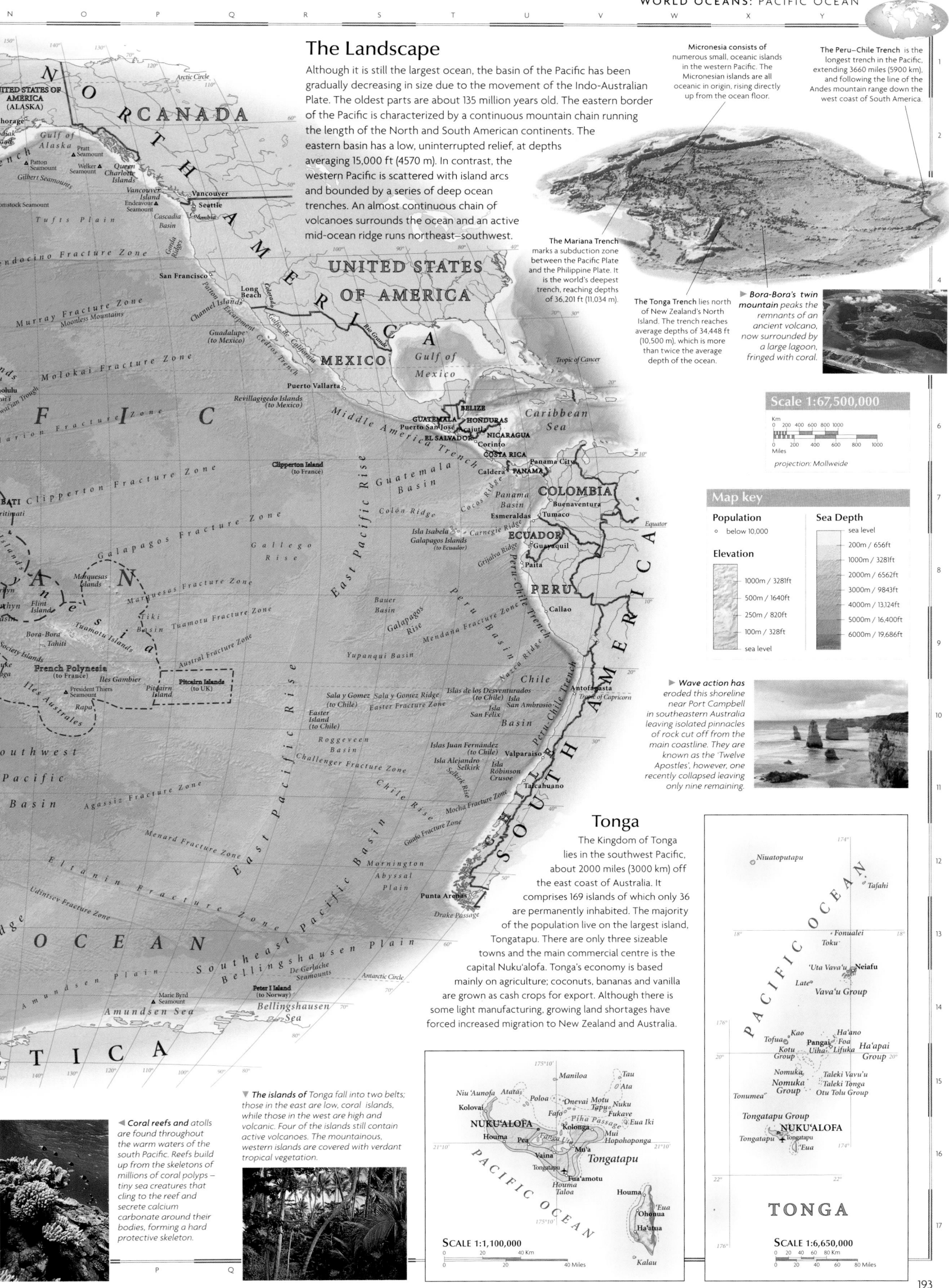

The Landscape

Although it is still the largest ocean, the basin of the Pacific has been gradually decreasing in size due to the movement of the Indo-Australian Plate. The oldest parts are about 135 million years old. The eastern border of the Pacific is characterized by a continuous mountain chain running the length of the North and South American continents. The eastern basin has a low, uninterrupted relief, at depths averaging 15,000 ft (4570 m). In contrast, the western Pacific is scattered with island arcs and bounded by a series of deep ocean trenches. An almost continuous chain of volcanoes surrounds the ocean and an active mid-ocean ridge runs northeast–southwest.

Micronesia consists of numerous small, oceanic islands in the western Pacific. The Micronesian islands are all oceanic in origin, rising directly up from the ocean floor.

▶ **The Peru–Chile Trench** is the longest trench in the Pacific, extending 3660 miles (5900 km), and following the line of the Andes mountain range down the west coast of South America.

The Mariana Trench marks a subduction zone between the Pacific Plate and the Philippine Plate. It is the world's deepest trench, reaching depths of 36,201 ft (11,034 m).

The Tonga Trench lies north of New Zealand's North Island. The trench reaches average depths of 34,448 ft (10,500 m), which is more than twice the average depth of the ocean.

▶ **Bora-Bora's twin mountain** peaks the remnants of an ancient volcano, now surrounded by a large lagoon, fringed with coral.

Scale 1:67,500,000

projection: Mollweide

Map key

Population
○ below 10,000

Elevation
- 1000m / 3281ft
- 500m / 1640ft
- 250m / 820ft
- 100m / 328ft
- sea level

Sea Depth
- sea level
- 200m / 656ft
- 1000m / 3281ft
- 2000m / 6562ft
- 3000m / 9843ft
- 4000m / 13,124ft
- 5000m / 16,400ft
- 6000m / 19,686ft

▶ **Wave action has** eroded this shoreline near Port Campbell in southeastern Australia leaving isolated pinnacles of rock cut off from the main coastline. They are known as the 'Twelve Apostles', however, one recently collapsed leaving only nine remaining.

Tonga

The Kingdom of Tonga lies in the southwest Pacific, about 2000 miles (3000 km) off the east coast of Australia. It comprises 169 islands of which only 36 are permanently inhabited. The majority of the population live on the largest island, Tongatapu. There are only three sizeable towns and the main commercial centre is the capital Nuku'alofa. Tonga's economy is based mainly on agriculture; coconuts, bananas and vanilla are grown as cash crops for export. Although there is some light manufacturing, growing land shortages have forced increased migration to New Zealand and Australia.

◀ **Coral reefs and** atolls are found throughout the warm waters of the south Pacific. Reefs build up from the skeletons of millions of coral polyps — tiny sea creatures that cling to the reef and secrete calcium carbonate around their bodies, forming a hard protective skeleton.

▼ **The islands of** Tonga fall into two belts; those in the east are low, coral islands, while those in the west are high and volcanic. Four of the islands still contain active volcanoes. The mountainous, western islands are covered with verdant tropical vegetation.

TONGATAPU
SCALE 1:1,100,000

TONGA
SCALE 1:6,650,000

Antarctica

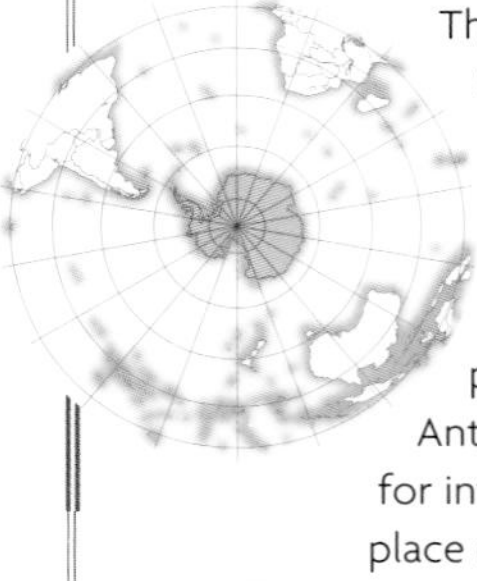

The ice-covered continent of Antarctica, which is the Earth's most southerly region, has for over 200 years drawn explorers and entrepreneurs seeking challenge and riches in its wintry lands. The extreme climate has deterred any large-scale settlement of the continent, and though commercial hunters built outposts in the past, habitation is now limited to scientific bases. The Antarctic Treaty, which came into force in 1961, provides for international governance and scientific co-operation in place of potential territorial conflict.

Resources

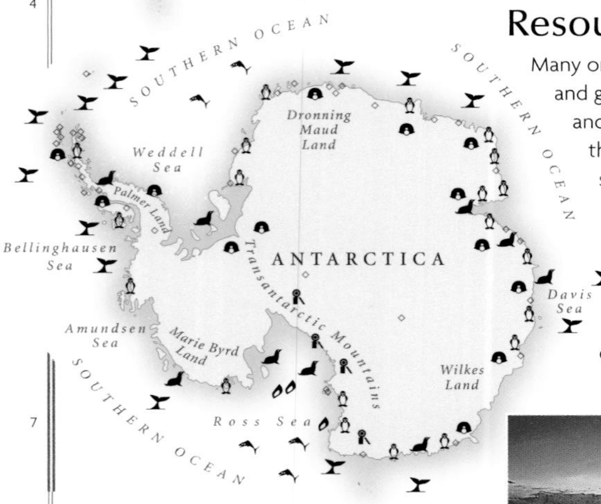

Many ore minerals, including iron and gold, are found in the Antarctic, and there are also coal reserves in the Transantarctic Mountains. The severe conditions and environmental importance of the region mean that exploitation of potential mineral resources is both uneconomic and undesirable. The unique wildlife and landscape draw a small number of tourists annually.

Resources (including wildlife)

- coal
- fish
- minerals
- oil & gas
- penguins
- seals
- whales
- polar research base

◀ **Most settlements in** Antarctica are research bases such as this one at Rothera on Adelaide Island, although there is a small Chilean settlement on King George Island.

The landscape

There are two distinct parts to Antarctica: West Antarctica, a series of ice-covered, mountainous islands, joined together by the ice; and the high plateau of East Antarctica. The Ross Sea and the Weddell Sea are outliers of the Southern Ocean – deep bays partially covered by thick ice shelves.

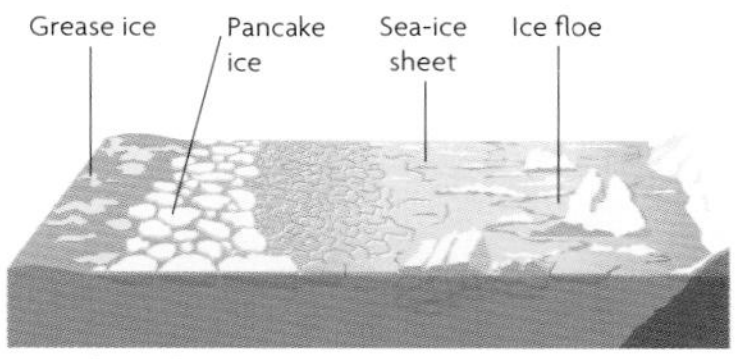

◀ **On Elephant Island,** the coast is edged by glaciers, although the land is not permanently covered by ice.

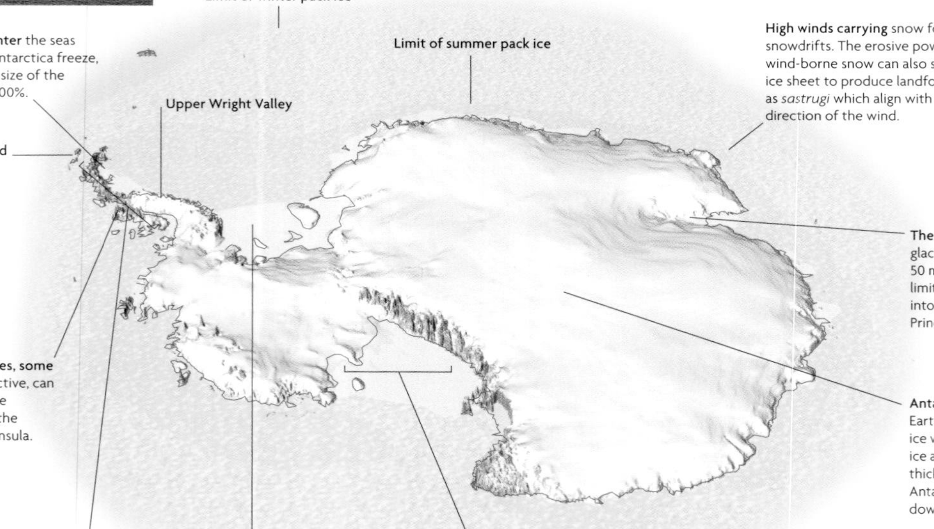

Grease ice   Pancake ice   Sea-ice sheet   Ice floe

▲ **Pack ice forms** out at sea in freezing temperatures. At the outer limits, grease ice congeals on the surface of the ocean. This is then spun around by wind and waves into irregular 'pancakes', freezing and breaking up several times before bonding together again to form sea-ice sheets, which finally cement into enormous ice floes.

During the winter the seas surrounding Antarctica freeze, increasing the size of the continent by 100%.

Limit of winter pack ice

Limit of summer pack ice

Upper Wright Valley

Elephant Island

High winds carrying snow form huge snowdrifts. The erosive power of the wind-borne snow can also sculpt the ice sheet to produce landforms known as *sastrugi* which align with the direction of the wind.

Many volcanoes, some of them still active, can be found in the mountains of the Antarctic Peninsula.

The **Lambert Glacier** is the largest glacier system in the world, up to 50 miles (80 km) wide at its seaward limit, and reaching 180 miles (300 km) into the interior by way of the Prince Charles Mountains.

Antarctica is the highest continent on Earth, because of the great thickness of ice which overlays the land. In places the ice alone can reach up to 15,700 ft (4800 m) thick. Much of the basement rock of west Antarctica lies below sea level, pushed down by the weight of the ice.

The mountainous **Antarctic Peninsula** is formed of rocks 65–225 million years old, overlain by more recent rocks and glacial deposits. It is connected to the Andes in South America by a submarine ridge.

Nearly half – 44% – of the Antarctic coastline is bounded by ice shelves, like the Ronne Ice Shelf, which float on the Ocean. These are joined to the inland ice sheet by dome-shaped ice 'rises'.

More than 30% of Antarctic ice is contained in the Ross Ice Shelf.

◀ **The barren, flat-bottomed** Upper Wright Valley was once filled by a glacier, but is now dry, strewn with boulders and pebbles. In some dry valleys, there has been no rain for over 2 million years.

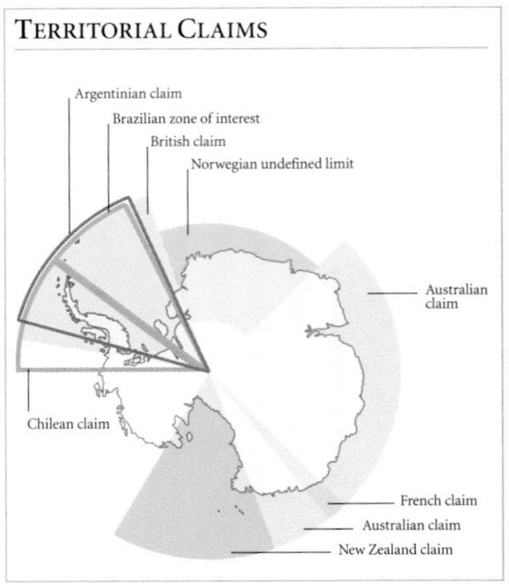

▲ **Large colonies of** seabirds live in the extremely harsh Antarctic climate. The Emperor penguins seen here, the smaller Adélie penguin, the Antarctic petrel and the South Polar skua are the only birds which breed exclusively on the continent.

Territorial Claims

- Argentinian claim
- Brazilian zone of interest
- British claim
- Norwegian undefined limit
- Australian claim
- Chilean claim
- French claim
- Australian claim
- New Zealand claim

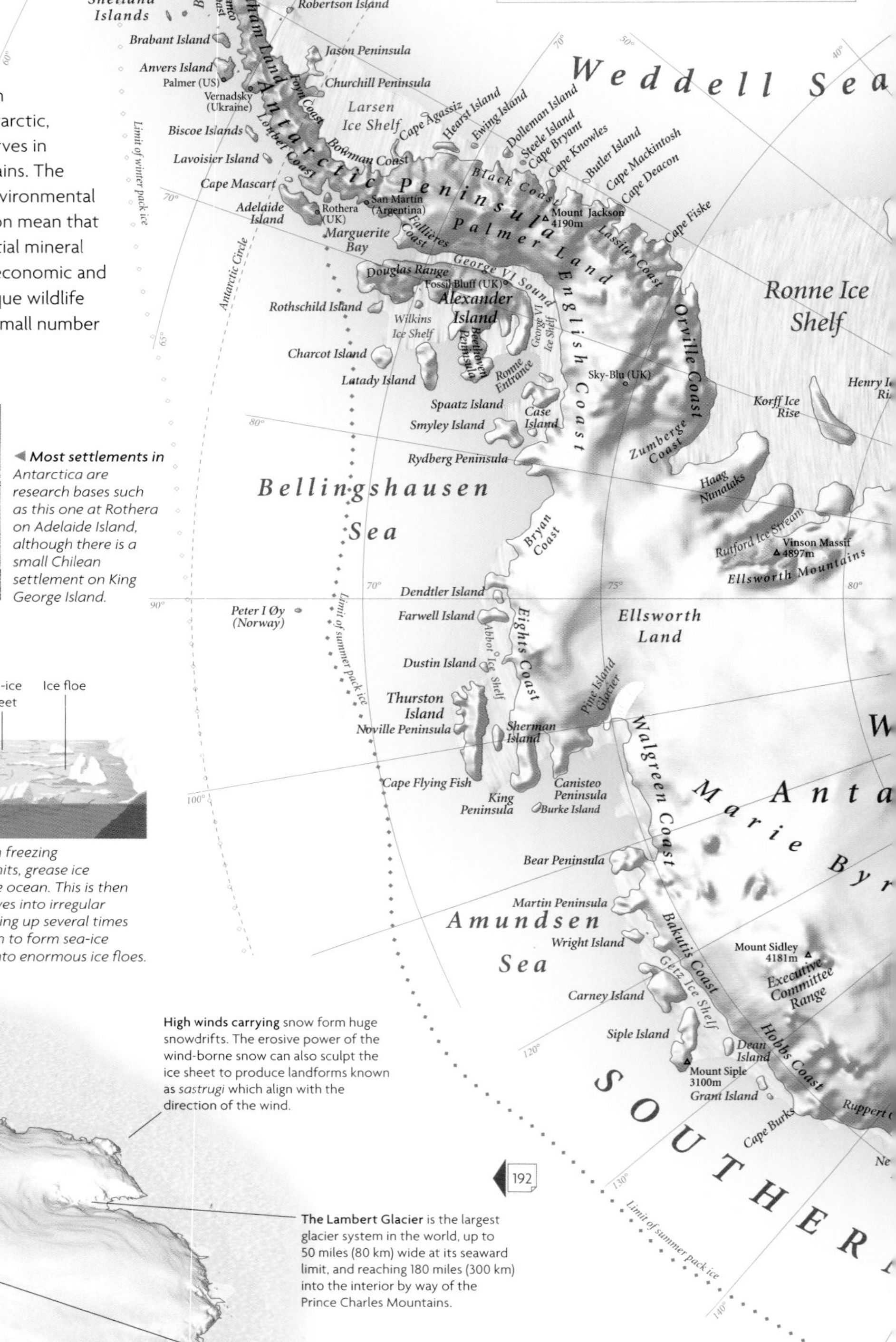

Research Stations on King George Island

- Arctowski (Poland)
- Artigas (Uruguay)
- Bellingshausen (Russian Federation)
- Comandante Ferraz (Brazil)
- Great Wall (China)
- Jubany (Argentina)
- King Sejong (South Korea)
- Teniente Rodolfo Marsh (Chile)

Map labels:
South Orkney Islands, Laurie Island, Orcadas (Argentina), Coronation Island, Signy (UK), Scotia Sea, Clarence Island, Elephant Island, Drake Passage, King George Island, Capitán Arturo Prat (Chile), Livingston Island, South Shetland Islands, Joinville Island, Dundee Island, General Bernardo O'Higgins (Chile), Esperanza (Argentina), Marambio (Argentina), Snowhill Island, James Ross Island, Bransfield Strait, Davis Coast, Robertson Island, Brabant Island, Jason Peninsula, Anvers Island, Palmer (US), Vernadsky (Ukraine), Graham Land, Churchill Peninsula, Larsen Ice Shelf, Cape Agassiz, Hearst Island, Ewing Island, Dolleman Island, Steele Island, Biscoe Islands, Bowman Coast, Black Coast, Cape Bryant, Butler Island, Cape Mackintosh, Lavoisier Island, Cape Knowles, Cape Mascart, Rothera (UK), San Martín (Argentina), Mount Jackson 4190m, Adelaide Island, Palmer Land, English Coast, Cape Fiske, Marguerite Bay, George VI Sound, Ronne Ice Shelf, Douglas Range, Fossil Bluff (UK), Rothschild Island, Alexander Island, Sky-Blu (UK), Orville Coast, Korff Ice Rise, Charcot Island, Wilkins Ice Shelf, Ronne Entrance, Latady Island, Spaatz Island, Case Island, Zumberge Coast, Haag Nunataks, Smyley Island, Rutford Ice Stream, Vinson Massif 4897m, Rydberg Peninsula, Ellsworth Mountains, Bellingshausen Sea, Bryan Coast, Ellsworth Land, Peter I Øy (Norway), Dendtler Island, Farwell Island, Eights Coast, Dustin Island, Abbot Ice Shelf, Thurston Island, Sherman Island, Pine Island Glacier, Noville Peninsula, Walgreen Coast, Cape Flying Fish, King Peninsula, Canisteo Peninsula, Burke Island, Marie Byrd Land, Bear Peninsula, Bakutis Coast, Martin Peninsula, Amundsen Sea, Wright Island, Getz Ice Shelf, Mount Sidley 4181m, Executive Committee Range, Carney Island, Hobbs Coast, Siple Island, Dean Island, Mount Siple 3100m, Grant Island, Cape Burks, Ruppert Coast, Southern Ocean, Weddell Sea, Antarctic Circle, Limit of winter pack ice, Limit of summer pack ice

Resources map labels: Southern Ocean, Dronning Maud Land, Weddell Sea, Palmer Land, Bellingshausen Sea, ANTARCTICA, Transantarctic Mountains, Davis Sea, Amundsen Sea, Marie Byrd Land, Ross Sea, Wilkes Land

192

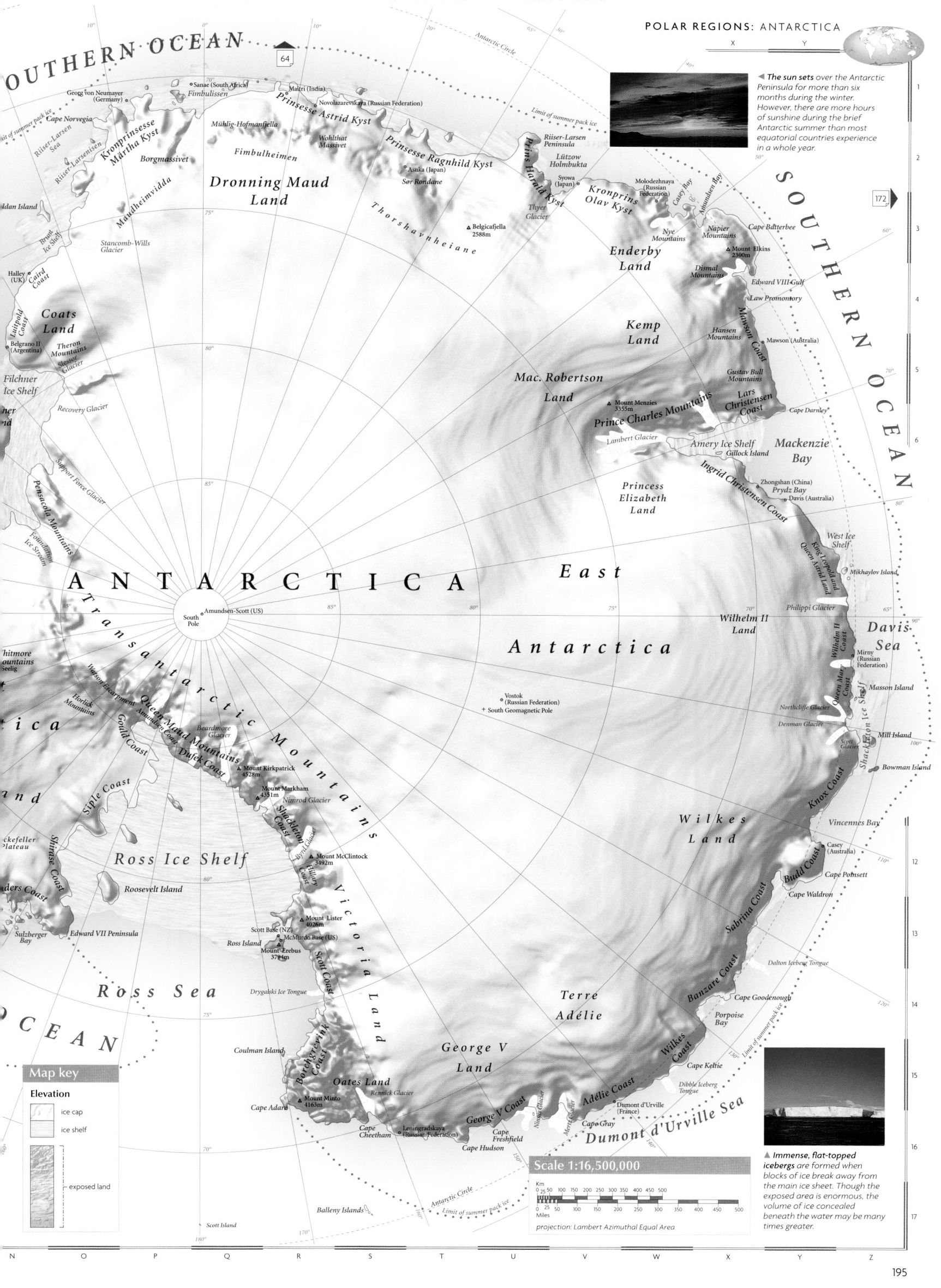

◀ *The sun sets* over the Antarctic Peninsula for more than six months during the winter. However, there are more hours of sunshine during the brief Antarctic summer than most equatorial countries experience in a whole year.

▲ *Immense, flat-topped icebergs* are formed when blocks of ice break away from the main ice sheet. Though the exposed area is enormous, the volume of ice concealed beneath the water may be many times greater.

Scale 1:16,500,000

projection: Lambert Azimuthal Equal Area

A B C D E F G H I J K L M

The Arctic

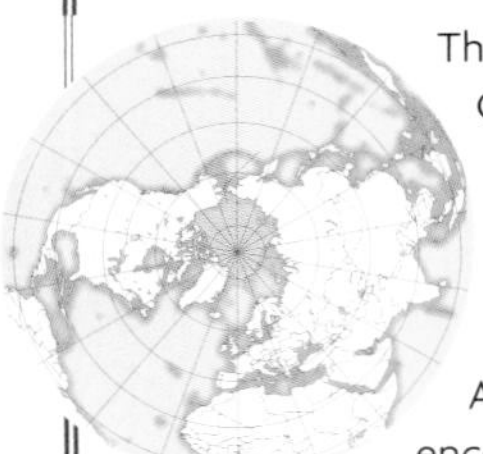

Three continents, Asia, North America and Europe, reach into the Arctic Circle at their northernmost limits, almost entirely encircling the Arctic Ocean. Despite the region's extraordinarily harsh climate, it has been inhabited for thousands of years by peoples such as the European Lapps, the Russian Nenet, and the North American Inuit, who draw a living from fishing, herding and hunting. More recently, particularly in the Russian Arctic, opportunities to exploit oil and other mineral reserves have encouraged immigration. Pollution of the Arctic's unique ecology and damage to the traditional lifestyles of many native peoples have been the unfortunate results of this activity, and international co-operation is needed to safeguard the future of the region.

192

Map key

Population
- ■ above 5 million
- ◉ 1 million to 5 million
- ◎ 500,000 to 1 million
- ⊚ 100,000 to 500,000
- ⊕ 50,000 to 100,000
- ○ 10,000 to 50,000
- ∘ below 10,000

Sea depth
Sea level
- 200m / 656ft
- 1000m / 3281ft
- 2000m / 6562ft
- 3000m / 9843ft
- 4000m / 13,124ft
- 5000m / 16,400ft
- 6000m / 19,686ft

Scale 1:23,500,000

Km 0 100 200 300 400 500 600
Miles 0 100 200 300 400 500 600

projection: Lambert Azimuthal Equal Area

▲ *Wind-blown snow etches deep patterns in the ice sheet known as sastrugi. They align with the direction of the wind.*

8

Resources

Large quantities of coal, oil and natural gas are to be found in the basins of the Arctic Ocean, and in northern Canada, Alaska and the Russian Federation. The cost and difficulty of extraction and, more recently, awareness of damage to the environment, have limited exploitation to coastal regions. The unfrozen waters have stocks of fish including cod, plaice and haddock. Quotas have now been put in place to restrict the number of fish caught annually. Reindeer are herded in large numbers by many of the native Arctic peoples. Most grain and vegetables are imported from elsewhere.

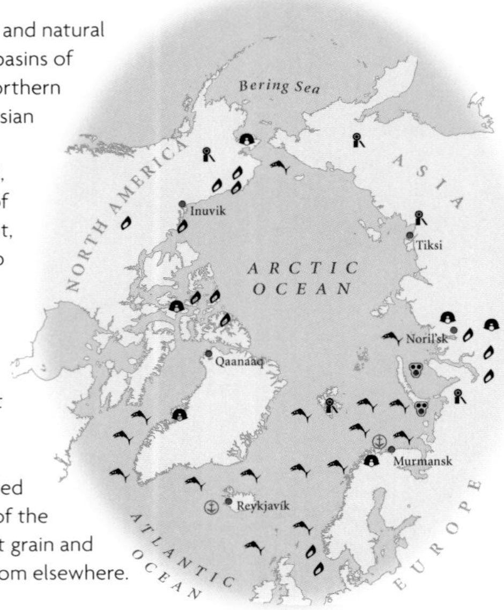

Bering Sea

NORTH AMERICA • ASIA
Inuvik
Tiksi
ARCTIC OCEAN
Noril'sk
Qaanaaq
Murmansk
Reykjavík
ATLANTIC OCEAN • EUROPE

▲ *Icebreakers, ships with* specially strengthened hulls, designed to break a path through the ice, are used to keep important routes open during the winter, when falling temperatures cause much of the Arctic Ocean to freeze over.

Resources
- ⚒ coal
- ⌐ fish
- ⚒ mining
- ◗ oil & gas
- ☢ radioactive contamination
- ● major towns
- ⊕ major ports

8

The landscape

The Arctic Ocean comprises two large ocean basins divided by three submarine ridges, the greatest of which, the Lomonosov Ridge, is a huge underwater mountain range which has an average height of more than 10,000 ft (3000 m). The lands which encircle the Arctic Ocean are underlain by great shield areas of ancient rocks, which were heavily glaciated during the last Ice Age.

◀ *Icebergs are constantly* broken up and re-shaped by wind and the oceans. This flat-topped iceberg has been undercut, leaving a craggy ice cliff.

The Canadian Shield underlies almost all of the Canadian Arctic. It is a very stable plateau of ancient rock, now covered by glacial lakes and sediment, which supports tundra vegetation.

The Arctic Ocean is the world's smallest ocean with a total area of 5,440,000 sq miles (15,100,000 sq km).

At a latitude of more than 75° N, the Arctic Ocean is almost permanently covered by pack-ice, though high winds and the movement of the seas may cause the ice to crack and break up.

In the more southerly reaches of the Arctic, like Siberia, much of the land is covered by permafrost. In the summer, higher temperatures warm the frozen ground, causing a number of typical phenomena. These include solifluction, the fast downhill movement of top soil layers; freeze/thaw activity, which patterns the ground into regular polygonal shapes, and the formation of large domes with a frozen ice core, known as pingos.

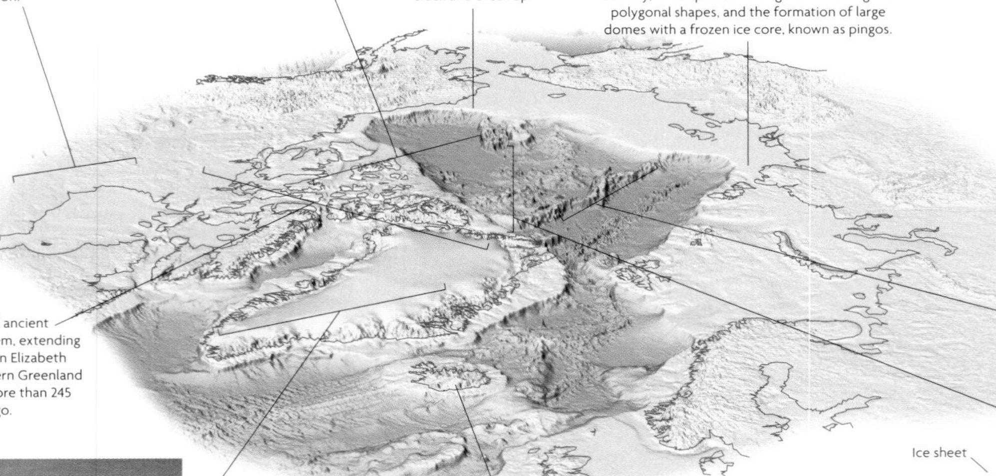

A complex and ancient mountain system, extending from the Queen Elizabeth Islands to eastern Greenland was formed more than 245 million years ago.

Lomonosov Ridge

Arctic ice shelf

Ice sheet — Iceberg

Crevasses occur at the edge of the ice sheet

Sea water melts the edge of the ice sheet

▲ *At the boundary* of the Arctic ice shelves, sea water flows under the ice causing melting and forming crevasses on the surface. This eventually weakens blocks of ice which break away as icebergs. This process is known as calving.

◀ *Much of Greenland* is covered by a massive ice sheet more than 650,000 sq miles (1,683,400 sq km) in extent. The weight of the ice has depressed the central land area to form a basin lying more than 1000 ft (300 m) below sea level. Only at the edges of the island is bare rock visible.

Iceland has five major glaciers, sustained by heavy snowfall. Parts of the ice cap cover active volcanoes, such as Bárdharbunga, which periodically erupt causing the melted ice to form a great lake at the glacier margins.

Map place names (right panel)

NORTH AMERICA
CANADA
Great Bear Lake
Great Slave Lake
Kugluktuk
Bathurst Inlet
Cambridge Bay
Queen Maud Gulf
Back
Nelson
Churchill
Southampton Island
Repulse Bay
Melville Peninsula
Hudson Bay
Coats Island
Mansel Island
Foxe Basin
Prince Charles Island
Ivujivik
Inukjuak
Foxe Peninsula
Hudson Strait
Lake Harbour
Baffin Island
Ungava Bay
Cumberland Sound
Cape Chidley
Davis Strait
Nain
Maniit...
Labrador Sea
NUUK
Labrador Basin
Paamiut
Ivittu...
Qaqortoq
Nanortalik
Numap Isua (Kap Farvel)
Eirik Ridge
ATLANTIC

64

The aurora borealis or Northern Lights are coloured bands of light which appear in northern latitudes. Light is emitted when dust particles from the Sun react with gases in the Earth's atmosphere.

Aleutian Basin
Bering Sea
Bristol Bay
Kodiak Island
Alaska Peninsula
Nunivak Island
Saint Matthew Island
Saint Lawrence Island
Kuskokwim Bay
Norton Sound
Nome
Cape Prince of Wales
Bering Strait
Seward Peninsula
Kotzebue Sound
Vankarem
Point Hope
Providentya
Anadyrskiy Zaliv
Anadyr'
Uelen
Chukotskiy Poluostrov
Arctic Circle
Pevek
Ambarchik
Kolyma
Chukchi Sea
Proliv Longa
Ostrov Vrangelya
Barrow
Limit of summer pack ice
East Siberian Sea
Indigirka
Yana
Limit of permanent ice cap
Prudhoe Bay
Beaufort Sea
Northwind Plain
Chukchi Plain
Chukchi Plateau
Wrangel Plain
Proliv Dmitriya Lapteva
Ostrov Novaya Sibir'
Novosibirskiye Ostrova
Buorkhaya Guba
Tiksi
Lena
Olenëk
Ust'-Olenëk
Laptev Sea
Mendeleyev Ridge
ARCTIC OCEAN
Makarov Basin
Alpha Cordillera
North Pole
Pole Plain
Lomonosov Ridge
Fram Basin
Nansen Cordillera
Nansen Basin
Khatangskiy Zaliv
Khatanga
Ozero Taymyr
Poluostrov Taymyr
Severnaya Zemlya
Ostrov Bol'shevik
Ostrov Oktyabr'skoy Revolyutsii
Ostrov Komsomolets
Svyataya Anna Trough
Noril'sk
Yenisey
Dikson
Kara Sea
Yeniseyskiy Zaliv
Gydanskiy Poluostrov
RUSSIAN FEDERATION
Siberia
Sea of Okhotsk
Komandorskaya Basin
Poluostrov Kamchatka
Karaginskiy Zaliv
Mys Olyutorskiy
Pakhachi
Zaliv Shelikhova
Mys Navarin
Manily
Magadan
Mys Tolstoy
Okhotsk

Polar bears range for great distances over the Arctic pack ice in search of food. They are formidable hunters who live mainly on seals. In December and January, mother bears give birth to their cubs in dens dug deep beneath the snow.

UNITED STATES OF AMERICA
ALASKA
Yukon
Gulf of Alaska
Anchorage
Cook Inlet
Inuvik
Tuktoyaktuk
Cape Bathurst
Amundsen Gulf
Banks Island
Victoria Island
McClure Strait
Melville Island
Prince Patrick Island
Mackenzie King Island
Prince Gustaf Adolf Sea
Ellef Ringnes Island
Axel Heiberg Island
Viscount Melville Sound
Bathurst Island
Prince of Wales Island
North Geomagnetic Pole
Somerset Island
Resolute (Qausuittuq)
Lancaster Sound
Devon Island
Canada Basin
Canada Plain
Queen Elizabeth Islands
Ellesmere Island
Cape Columbia
Nares Strait
Alert
Lincoln Sea
Pond Inlet
Baffin Bay
Innaanganeq
Savissivik
Qimusseriarsuaq
Baffin Bay
Upernavik
Knud Rasmussen Land
Qaanaaq
AVANNAARSUA
Kap Morris Jesup
Wandel Sea
Independence Fjord
Nord
SVALBARD (to Norway)
Franz Josef Land
Barents Plain
Novaya Zemlya
East Novaya Zemlya Trough
Ostrov Belyy
Obskaya Guba
Poluostrov Yamal
Baydaratskaya Guba
Vorkuta
Kara Strait
Ob'
Nar'yan-Mar
Pechora
GREENLAND (to Denmark)
TUNU
Kong Frederik VIII Land
Kong Christian X Land
Daneborg
Petermann Bjerg 2940m
Kong Oscar Fjord
Kangerlussuaq
Ittoqqortoormiit
Kangikajik
Kong Christian IX Land
Mont Forel 3360m
Gunnbjørn Fjeld 3700m
Ammassalik
Greenland Plain
Greenland Sea
Mohns Ridge
Spitsbergen
Longyearbyen
Hopen
Bjørnøya
Barents Sea
Barents Trough
Chëshskaya Guba
Poluostrov Kanin
North Cape
Murmansk Rise
Murmansk
Kola Peninsula
Archangel
Northern Dvina
White Sea
JAN MAYEN (to Norway)
Jan Mayen Fracture Zone
Jan Mayen Ridge
Norwegian Sea
Voring Plateau
Norwegian Basin
Hammerfest
Tromsø
Lapland
NORWAY
SWEDEN
FINLAND
EUROPE
Ummannaq
Qeqertarsuaq
Qasigiannguit
Kangerlussuaq
Kolbeinsey Ridge
Iceland Plateau
Akureyri
Arctic Circle
REYKJAVÍK
ICELAND
Reykjanes Basin
Reykjanes Ridge
Iceland Basin
Hatton Ridge
Denmark Strait
Faeroe-Iceland Ridge
FAEROE ISLANDS (to Denmark)
Bill Baileys Bank
Faeroe-Shetland Trough
Shetland Islands
Orkney Islands
Norwegian Trench
Fugløya Bank
Gulf of Bothnia
HELSINKI
Gulf of Finland
TALLINN
ESTONIA
RIGA
LATVIA
OSLO
STOCKHOLM
MOSCOW
Onezhskoye Ozero
Ladozhskoye Ozero
Baltic Sea
Skagerrak

OCEAN
ATLANTIC OCEAN

Geographical comparisons

Largest countries

Russian Federation	6,592,735 sq miles	(17,075,200 sq km)
Canada	3,854,085 sq miles	(9,984,670 sq km)
USA	3,717,792 sq miles	(9,629,091 sq km)
China	3,705,386 sq miles	(9,596,960 sq km)
Brazil	3,286,470 sq miles	(8,511,965 sq km)
Australia	2,967,893 sq miles	(7,686,850 sq km)
India	1,269,339 sq miles	(3,287,590 sq km)
Argentina	1,068,296 sq miles	(2,766,890 sq km)
Kazakhstan	1,049,150 sq miles	(2,717,300 sq km)
Sudan	967,493 sq miles	(2,505,815 sq km)

Smallest countries

Vatican City	0.17 sq miles	(0.44 sq km)
Monaco	0.75 sq miles	(1.95 sq km)
Nauru	8.2 sq miles	(21.2 sq km)
Tuvalu	10 sq miles	(26 sq km)
San Marino	24 sq miles	(61 sq km)
Liechtenstein	62 sq miles	(160 sq km)
Marshall Islands	70 sq miles	(181 sq km)
St. Kitts & Nevis	101 sq miles	(261 sq km)
Maldives	116 sq miles	(300 sq km)
Malta	124 sq miles	(320 sq km)

Largest islands

	To the nearest 1000 – or 100,000 for the largest	
Greenland	849,400 sq miles	(2,200,000 sq km)
New Guinea	312,000 sq miles	(808,000 sq km)
Borneo	292,222 sq miles	(757,050 sq km)
Madagascar	229,300 sq miles	(594,000 sq km)
Sumatra	202,300 sq miles	(524,000 sq km)
Baffin Island	183,800 sq miles	(476,000 sq km)
Honshu	88,800 sq miles	(230,000 sq km)
Britain	88,700 sq miles	(229,800 sq km)
Victoria Island	81,900 sq miles	(212,000 sq km)
Ellesmere Island	75,700 sq miles	(196,000 sq km)

Richest countries

	GNI per capita, in US$
Luxembourg	65,630
Norway	59,590
Switzerland	54,930
Liechtenstein	50,000
Denmark	47,390
Iceland	46,320
USA	43,740
Sweden	41,060
Ireland	40,150
Japan	38,980

Poorest countries

	GNI per capita, in US$
Burundi	100
Somalia	120
Dem. Rep. Congo	120
Liberia	130
Malawi	160
Ethiopia	160
Guinea-Bissau	180
Sierra Leone	220
Eritrea	220
Afghanistan	222
Rwanda	230
Niger	240

Most populous countries

China	1,331,400,000
India	1,135,600,000
USA	303,900,000
Indonesia	228,100,000
Brazil	191,300,000
Pakistan	164,600,000
Bangladesh	147,100,000
Russian Federation	141,900,000
Nigeria	137,200,000
Japan	128,300,000

Least populous countries

Vatican City	821
Tuvalu	11,992
Nauru	13,528
Palau	20,842
San Marino	29,615
Monaco	32,671
Liechtenstein	34,247
St Kitts & Nevis	39,349
Marshall Islands	61,815
Antigua & Barbuda	69,481
Andorra	71,822
Dominica	72,386

Most densely populated countries

Monaco	43,212 people per sq mile	(16,620 per sq km)
Singapore	18,220 people per sq mile	(7049 per sq km)
Vatican City	5418 people per sq mile	(2093 per sq km)
Malta	3242 people per sq mile	(1256 per sq km)
Maldives	2836 people per sq mile	(1097 per sq km)
Bangladesh	2743 people per sq mile	(1059 per sq km)
Bahrain	2663 people per sq mile	(1030 per sq km)
China	1838 people per sq mile	(710 per sq km)
Mauritius	1671 people per sq mile	(645 per sq km)
Barbados	1627 people per sq mile	(628 per sq km)

Most sparsely populated countries

Mongolia	4 people per sq mile	(2 per sq km)
Namibia	6 people per sq mile	(2 per sq km)
Australia	7 people per sq mile	(3 per sq km)
Mauritania	8 people per sq mile	(3 per sq km)
Surinam	8 people per sq mile	(3 per sq km)
Botswana	8 people per sq mile	(3 per sq km)
Iceland	8 people per sq mile	(3 per sq km)
Canada	9 people per sq mile	(4 per sq km)
Libya	9 people per sq mile	(4 per sq km)
Guyana	10 people per sq mile	(4 per sq km)

Most widely spoken languages

1. Chinese (Mandarin)	6. Arabic
2. English	7. Bengali
3. Hindi	8. Portuguese
4. Spanish	9. Malay-Indonesian
5. Russian	10. French

Largest conurbations

	Population
Tokyo	34,200,000
Mexico City	22,800,000
Seoul	22,300,000
New York	21,900,000
São Paulo	20,200,000
Mumbai	19,850,000
Delhi	19,700,000
Shanghai	18,150,000
Los Angeles	18,000,000
Osaka	16,800,000
Jakarta	16,550,000
Kolkata	15,650,000
Cairo	15,600,000
Manila	14,950,000
Karachi	14,300,000
Moscow	13,750,000
Buenos Aires	13,450,000
Dacca	13,250,000
Rio de Janeiro	12,150,000
Beijing	12,100,000
London	12,000,000
Tehran	11,850,000
Istanbul	11,500,000
Lagos	11,100,000
Shenzhen	10,700,000

Countries with the most land borders

14: China	(Afghanistan, Bhutan, Burma, India, Kazakhstan, Kyrgyzstan, Laos, Mongolia, Nepal, North Korea, Pakistan, Russian Federation, Tajikistan, Vietnam)	
14: Russian Federation	(Azerbaijan, Belarus, China, Estonia, Finland, Georgia, Kazakhstan, Latvia, Lithuania, Mongolia, North Korea, Norway, Poland, Ukraine)	
10: Brazil	(Argentina, Bolivia, Colombia, French Guiana, Guyana, Paraguay, Peru, Surinam, Uruguay, Venezuela)	
9: Congo, Dem. Rep.	(Angola, Burundi, Central African Republic, Congo, Rwanda, Sudan, Tanzania, Uganda, Zambia)	
9: Germany	(Austria, Belgium, Czech Republic, Denmark, France, Luxembourg, Netherlands, Poland, Switzerland)	
9: Sudan	(Central African Republic, Chad, Dem. Rep.Congo, Egypt, Eritrea, Ethiopia, Kenya, Libya, Uganda)	
8: Austria	(Czech Republic, Germany, Hungary, Italy, Liechtenstein, Slovakia, Slovenia, Switzerland)	
8: France	(Andorra, Belgium, Germany, Italy, Luxembourg, Monaco, Spain, Switzerland)	
8: Tanzania	(Burundi, Dem. Rep.Congo, Kenya, Malawi, Mozambique, Rwanda, Uganda, Zambia)	
8: Turkey	(Armenia, Azerbaijan, Bulgaria, Georgia, Greece, Iran, Iraq, Syria)	
8: Zambia	(Angola, Botswana, Dem. Rep.Congo, Malawi, Mozambique, Namibia, Tanzania, Zimbabwe)	

Longest rivers

Nile (NE Africa)	4160 miles	(6695 km)
Amazon (South America)	4049 miles	(6516 km)
Yangtze (China)	3915 miles	(6299 km)
Mississippi/Missouri (USA)	3710 miles	(5969 km)
Ob'-Irtysh (Russian Federation)	3461 miles	(5570 km)
Yellow River (China)	3395 miles	(5464 km)
Congo (Central Africa)	2900 miles	(4667 km)
Mekong (Southeast Asia)	2749 miles	(4425 km)
Lena (Russian Federation)	2734 miles	(4400 km)
Mackenzie (Canada)	2640 miles	(4250 km)
Yenisey (Russian Federation)	2541 miles	(4090km)

Highest mountains

		Height above sea level
Everest	29,035 ft	(8850 m)
K2	28,253 ft	(8611 m)
Kanchenjunga I	28,210 ft	(8598 m)
Makalu I	27,767 ft	(8463 m)
Cho Oyu	26,907 ft	(8201 m)
Dhaulagiri I	26,796 ft	(8167 m)
Manaslu I	26,783 ft	(8163 m)
Nanga Parbat I	26,661 ft	(8126 m)
Annapurna I	26,547 ft	(8091 m)
Gasherbrum I	26,471 ft	(8068 m)

Largest bodies of inland water

	With area and depth	
Caspian Sea	143,243 sq miles (371,000 sq km)	3215 ft (980 m)
Lake Superior	31,151 sq miles (83,270 sq km)	1289 ft (393 m)
Lake Victoria	26,828 sq miles (69,484 sq km)	328 ft (100 m)
Lake Huron	23,436 sq miles (60,700 sq km)	751 ft (229 m)
Lake Michigan	22,402 sq miles (58,020 sq km)	922 ft (281 m)
Lake Tanganyika	12,703 sq miles (32,900 sq km)	4700 ft (1435 m)
Great Bear Lake	12,274 sq miles (31,790 sq km)	1047 ft (319 m)
Lake Baikal	11,776 sq miles (30,500 sq km)	5712 ft (1741 m)
Great Slave Lake	10,981 sq miles (28,440 sq km)	459 ft (140 m)
Lake Erie	9,915 sq miles (25,680 sq km)	197 ft (60 m)

Deepest ocean features

Challenger Deep, Mariana Trench (Pacific)	36,201 ft	(11,034 m)
Vityaz III Depth, Tonga Trench (Pacific)	35,704 ft	(10,882 m)
Vityaz Depth, Kurile-Kamchatka Trench (Pacific)	34,588 ft	(10,542 m)
Cape Johnson Deep, Philippine Trench (Pacific)	34,441 ft	(10,497 m)
Kermadec Trench (Pacific)	32,964 ft	(10,047 m)
Ramapo Deep, Japan Trench (Pacific)	32,758 ft	(9984 m)
Milwaukee Deep, Puerto Rico Trench (Atlantic)	30,185 ft	(9200 m)
Argo Deep, Torres Trench (Pacific)	30,070 ft	(9165 m)
Meteor Depth, South Sandwich Trench (Atlantic)	30,000 ft	(9144 m)
Planet Deep, New Britain Trench (Pacific)	29,988 ft	(9140 m)

Greatest waterfalls

	Mean flow of water	
Boyoma (Dem. Rep. Congo)	600,400 cu. ft/sec	(17,000 cu.m/sec)
Khône (Laos/Cambodia)	410,000 cu. ft/sec	(11,600 cu.m/sec)
Niagara (USA/Canada)	195,000 cu. ft/sec	(5500 cu.m/sec)
Grande (Uruguay)	160,000 cu. ft/sec	(4500 cu.m/sec)
Paulo Afonso (Brazil)	100,000 cu. ft/sec	(2800 cu.m/sec)
Urubupunga (Brazil)	97,000 cu. ft/sec	(2750 cu.m/sec)
Iguaçu (Argentina/Brazil)	62,000 cu. ft/sec	(1700 cu.m/sec)
Maribondo (Brazil)	53,000 cu. ft/sec	(1500 cu.m/sec)
Victoria (Zimbabwe)	39,000 cu. ft/sec	(1100 cu.m/sec)
Kabalega (Uganda)	42,000 cu. ft/sec	(1200 cu.m/sec)
Churchill (Canada)	35,000 cu. ft/sec	(1000 cu.m/sec)
Cauvery (India)	33,000 cu. ft/sec	(900 cu.m/sec)

Highest waterfalls

	* Indicates that the total height is a single leap	
Angel (Venezuela)	3212 ft	(979 m)
Tugela (South Africa)	3110 ft	(948 m)
Utigard (Norway)	2625 ft	(800 m)
Mongefossen (Norway)	2539 ft	(774 m)
Mtarazi (Zimbabwe)	2500 ft	(762 m)
Yosemite (USA)	2425 ft	(739 m)
Ostre Mardola Foss (Norway)	2156 ft	(657 m)
Tyssestrengane (Norway)	2119 ft	(646 m)
*Cuquenan (Venezuela)	2001 ft	(610 m)
Sutherland (New Zealand)	1903 ft	(580 m)
*Kjellfossen (Norway)	1841 ft	(561 m)

Largest deserts

NB – Most of Antarctica is a polar desert, with only 50mm of precipitation annually

Sahara	3,450,000 sq miles	(9,065,000 sq km)
Gobi	500,000 sq miles	(1,295,000 sq km)
Ar Rub al Khali	289,600 sq miles	(750,000 sq km)
Great Victorian	249,800 sq miles	(647,000 sq km)
Sonoran	120,000 sq miles	(311,000 sq km)
Kalahari	120,000 sq miles	(310,800 sq km)
Kara Kum	115,800 sq miles	(300,000 sq km)
Takla Makan	100,400 sq miles	(260,000 sq km)
Namib	52,100 sq miles	(135,000 sq km)
Thar	33,670 sq miles	(130,000 sq km)

Hottest inhabited places

Djibouti (Djibouti)	86° F	(30 °C)
Timbouctou (Mali)	84.7° F	(29.3 °C)
Tirunelveli (India)		
Tuticorin (India)		
Nellore (India)	84.5° F	(29.2 °C)
Santa Marta (Colombia)		
Aden (Yemen)	84° F	(28.9 °C)
Madurai (India)		
Niamey (Niger)		
Hodeida (Yemen)	83.8° F	(28.8 °C)
Ouagadougou (Burkina)		
Thanjavur (India)		
Tiruchchirappalli (India)		

Driest inhabited places

Aswân (Egypt)	0.02 in	(0.5 mm)
Luxor (Egypt)	0.03 in	(0.7 mm)
Arica (Chile)	0.04 in	(1.1 mm)
Ica (Peru)	0.1 in	(2.3 mm)
Antofagasta (Chile)	0.2 in	(4.9 mm)
El Minya (Egypt)	0.2 in	(5.1 mm)
Asyût (Egypt)	0.2 in	(5.2 mm)
Callao (Peru)	0.5 in	(12.0 mm)
Trujillo (Peru)	0.55 in	(14.0 mm)
El Faiyûm (Egypt)	0.8 in	(19.0 mm)

Wettest inhabited places

Buenaventura (Colombia)	265 in	(6743 mm)
Monrovia (Liberia)	202 in	(5131 mm)
Pago Pago (American Samoa)	196 in	(4990 mm)
Moulmein (Burma)	191 in	(4852 mm)
Lae (Papua New Guinea)	183 in	(4645 mm)
Baguio (Luzon Island, Philippines)	180 in	(4573 mm)
Sylhet (Bangladesh)	176 in	(4457 mm)
Padang (Sumatra, Indonesia)	166 in	(4225 mm)
Bogor (Java, Indonesia)	166 in	(4225 mm)
Conakry (Guinea)	171 in	(4341 mm)

The time zones

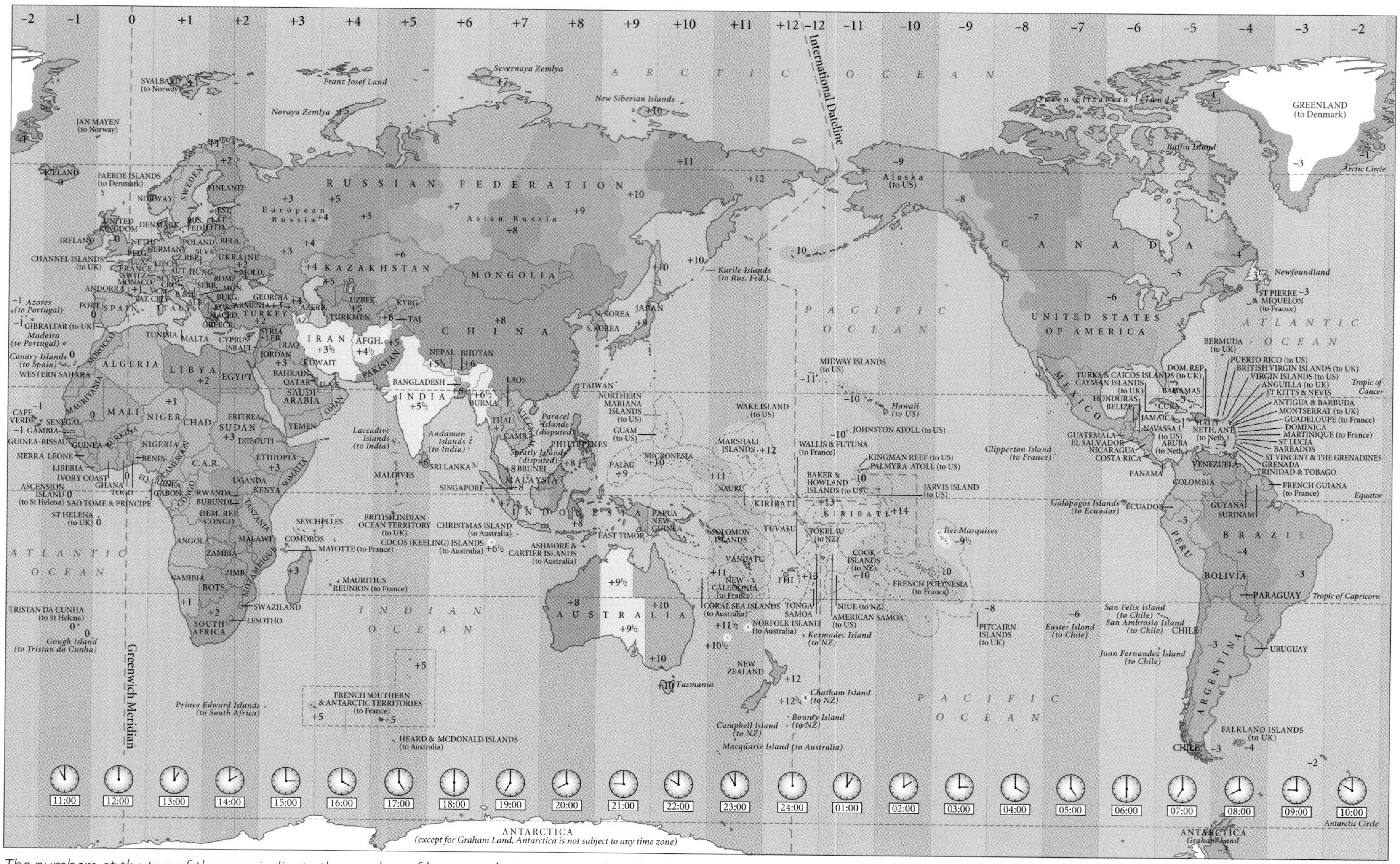

The numbers at the top of the map indicate the number of hours each time zone is ahead or behind Coordinated Universal Time (UTC).
The clocks and 24-hour times given at the bottom of the map show the time in each time zone when it is 12:00 hours noon (UTC)

Time Zones

Because Earth is a rotating sphere, the Sun shines on only half of its surface at any one time. Thus, it is simultaneously morning, evening and night time in different parts of the world (see diagram below). Because of these disparities, each country or part of a country adheres to a local time.

A region of Earth's surface within which a single local time is used is called a time zone. There are 24 one hour time zones around the world, arranged roughly in longitudinal bands.

Standard Time

Standard time is the official local time in a particular country or part of a country. It is defined by the

Day and night around the world

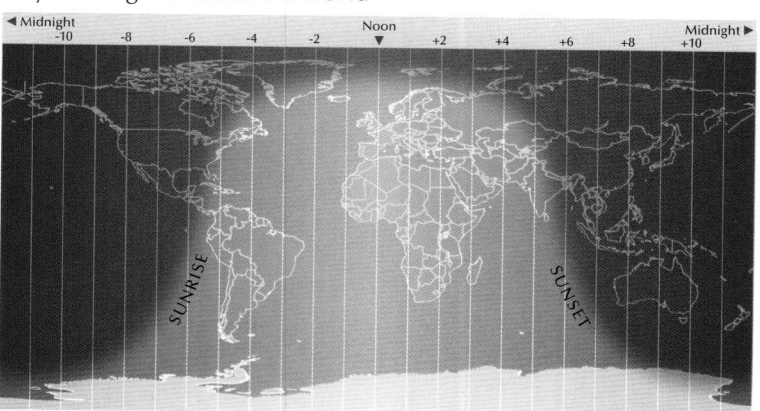

time zone or zones associated with that country or region. Although time zones are arranged roughly in longitudinal bands, in many places the borders of a zone do not fall exactly on longitudinal meridians, as can be seen on the map (above), but are determined by geographical factors or by borders between countries or parts of countries. Most countries have just one time zone and one standard time, but some large countries (such as the USA, Canada and Russia) are split between several time zones, so standard time varies across those countries. For example, the coterminous United States straddles four time zones and so has four standard times, called the Eastern, Central, Mountain and Pacific standard times. China is unusual in that just one standard time is used for the whole country, even though it extends across 60° of longitude from west to east.

Coordinated Universal Time (UTC)

Coordinated Universal Time (UTC) is a reference by which the local time in each time zone is set. For example, Australian Western Standard Time (the local time in Western Australia) is set 8 hours ahead of UTC (it is

UTC+8) whereas Eastern Standard Time in the United States is set 5 hours behind UTC (it is UTC-5). UTC is a successor to, and closely approximates, Greenwich Mean Time (GMT). However, UTC is based on an atomic clock, whereas GMT is determined by the Sun's position in the sky relative to the 0° longitudinal meridian, which runs through Greenwich, UK.

The International Dateline

The International Dateline is an imaginary line from pole to pole that roughly corresponds to the 180° longitudinal meridian. It is an arbitrary marker between calendar days. The dateline is needed because of the use of local times around the world rather than a single universal time. When moving from west to east across the dateline, travellers have to set their watches back one day. Those travelling in the opposite direction, from east to west, must add a day.

Daylight Saving Time

Daylight saving is a summertime adjustment to the local time in a country or region, designed to cause a higher proportion of its citizens' waking hours to pass during daylight. To follow the system, timepieces are advanced by an hour on a pre-decided date in spring and reverted back in autumn. About half of the world's nations use daylight saving.

Countries of the World

There are currently 195 independent countries in the world – more than at any previous time – and 59 dependencies. Antarctica is the only land area on Earth that is not officially part of, and does not belong to, any single country.

In 1950, the world comprised 82 countries. In the decades following, many more states came into being as they achieved independence from their former colonial rulers. Most recent additions were caused by the breakup of the former Soviet Union in 1991, and the former Yugoslavia in 1992, which swelled the ranks of independent states. In February 2008, Kosovo became the latest country to be formed by controversially declaring independence from Serbia.

Country factfile key

Formation Date of independence / date current borders were established

Population Total population / population density – based on total *land* area / percentage of urban-based population

Languages An asterisk (*) denotes the official language(s)

Calorie consumption Average number of calories consumed daily per person

AFGHANISTAN
Central Asia

Official name The Islamic Republic of Afghanistan
Formation 1919 / 1919
Capital Kabul
Population 32.3 million / 128 people per sq mile (50 people per sq km) / 24%
Total area 250,000 sq. miles (647,500 sq. km)
Languages Pashtu*, Tajik, Dari*, Farsi, Uzbek, Turkmen
Religions Sunni Muslim 84%, Shi'a Muslim 15%, Other 1%
Ethnic mix Pashtun 38%, Tajik 25%, Hazara 19%, Uzbek and Turkmen 15%, Other 3%
Government Presidential system
Currency Afghani = 100 puls
Literacy rate 28%
Calorie consumption 1539 calories

ALBANIA
Southeast Europe

Official name Republic of Albania
Formation 1912 / 1921
Capital Tirana
Population 3.2 million / 302 people per sq mile (117 people per sq km) / 44%
Total area 11,100 sq. miles (28,748 sq. km)
Languages Albanian*, Greek
Religions Sunni Muslim 70%, Orthodox Christian 20%, Roman Catholic 10%
Ethnic mix Albanian 93%, Greek 5%, Other 2%
Government Parliamentary system
Currency Lek = 100 qindarka (qintars)
Literacy rate 99%
Calorie consumption 2848 calories

ALGERIA
North Africa

Official name People's Democratic Republic of Algeria
Formation 1962 / 1962
Capital Algiers
Population 33.9 million / 37 people per sq mile (14 people per sq km) / 59%
Total area 919,590 sq. miles (2,381,740 sq. km)
Languages Arabic*, Tamazight (Kabyle, Shawia, Tamashek), French
Religions Sunni Muslim 99%, Christian and Jewish 1%
Ethnic mix Arab 75%, Berber 24%, European and Jewish 1%
Government Presidential system
Currency Algerian dinar = 100 centimes
Literacy rate 70%
Calorie consumption 3022 calories

ANDORRA
Southwest Europe

Official name Principality of Andorra
Formation 1278 / 1278
Capital Andorra la Vella
Population 71,822 / 399 people per sq mile (154 people per sq km) / 91%
Total area 181 sq. miles (468 sq. km)
Languages Spanish, Catalan*, French, Portuguese
Religions Roman Catholic 94%, Other 6%
Ethnic mix Spanish 46%, Andorran 28%, Other 18%, French 8%
Government Parliamentary system
Currency Euro = 100 cents
Literacy rate 99%
Calorie consumption Not available

ANGOLA
Southern Africa

Official name Republic of Angola
Formation 1975 / 1975
Capital Luanda
Population 16.9 million / 35 people per sq mile (14 people per sq km) / 36%
Total area 481,351 sq. miles (1,246,700 sq. km)
Languages Portuguese*, Umbundu, Kimbundu, Kikongo
Religions Roman Catholic 50%, Other 30%, Protestant 20%
Ethnic mix Ovimbundu 37%, Other 25%, Kimbundu 25%, Bakongo 13%
Government Presidential system
Currency Readjusted kwanza = 100 lwei
Literacy rate 67%
Calorie consumption 2083 calories

ANTIGUA & BARBUDA
West Indies

Official name Antigua and Barbuda
Formation 1981 / 1981
Capital St. John's
Population 69,481 / 409 people per sq mile (158 people per sq km) / 38%
Total area 170 sq. miles (442 sq. km)
Languages English*, English patois
Religions Anglican 45%, Other Protestant 42%, Roman Catholic 10%, Other 2%, Rastafarian 1%
Ethnic mix Black African 95%, Other 5%
Government Parliamentary system
Currency Eastern Caribbean dollar = 100 cents
Literacy rate 86%
Calorie consumption 2349 calories

ARGENTINA
South America

Official name The Argentine Republic
Formation 1816 / 1816
Capital Buenos Aires
Population 39.5 million / 37 people per sq mile (14 people per sq km) / 90%
Total area 1,068,296 sq. miles (2,766,890 sq. km)
Languages Spanish*, Italian, Amerindian languages
Religions Roman Catholic 90%, Other 6%, Protestant 2%, Jewish 2%
Ethnic mix Indo-European 83%, Mestizo 14%, Jewish 2%, Amerindian 1%
Government Presidential system
Currency new Argentine peso = 100 centavos
Literacy rate 97%
Calorie consumption 2992 calories

ARMENIA
Southwest Asia

Official name Republic of Armenia
Formation 1991 / 1991
Capital Yerevan
Population 3 million / 261 people per sq mile (101 people per sq km) / 64%
Total area 11,506 sq. miles (29,800 sq. km)
Languages Armenian*, Azeri, Russian
Religions Armenian Apostolic Church (Orthodox) 88%, Other 6%, Armenian Catholic Church 6%
Ethnic mix Armenian 98%, Other 1%, Yezidi 1%
Government Parliamentary system
Currency Dram = 100 luma
Literacy rate 99%
Calorie consumption 2268 calories

AUSTRALIA
Australasia & Oceania

Official name Commonwealth of Australia
Formation 1901 / 1901
Capital Canberra
Population 20.9 million / 7 people per sq mile (3 people per sq km) / 92%
Total area 2,967,893 sq. miles (7,686,850 sq. km)
Languages English*, Italian, Cantonese, Greek, Arabic, Vietnamese, Aboriginal languages
Religions Roman Catholic 26%, Anglican 24%, Other 23%, Nonreligious 13%, United Church 8%, Other Protestant 6%
Ethnic mix European 92%, Asian 5%, Aboriginal 2%, Other 1%
Government Parliamentary system
Currency Australian dollar = 100 cents
Literacy rate 99%
Calorie consumption 3054 calories

AUSTRIA
Central Europe

Official name Republic of Austria
Formation 1918 / 1919
Capital Vienna
Population 8.2 million / 257 people per sq mile (99 people per sq km) / 66%
Total area 32,378 sq. miles (83,858 sq. km)
Languages German*, Croatian, Slovenian, Hungarian (Magyar)
Religions Roman Catholic 78%, Nonreligious 9%, Other (including Jewish and Muslim) 8%, Protestant 5%
Ethnic mix Austrian 93%, Croat, Slovene, and Hungarian 6%, Other 1%
Government Parliamentary system
Currency Euro = 100 cents
Literacy rate 99%
Calorie consumption 3673 calories

AZERBAIJAN
Southwest Asia

Official name Republic of Azerbaijan
Formation 1991 / 1991
Capital Baku
Population 8.5 million / 254 people per sq mile (98 people per sq km) / 50%
Total area 33,436 sq. miles (86,600 sq. km)
Languages Azeri*, Russian
Religions Shi'a Muslim 68%, Sunni Muslim 26%, Russian Orthodox 3%, Armenian Apostolic Church (Orthodox) 2%, Other 1%
Ethnic mix Azeri 91%, Other 3%, Lazs 2%, Armenian 2%, Russian 2%
Government Presidential system
Currency New manat = 100 gopik
Literacy rate 99%
Calorie consumption 2575 calories

BAHAMAS
West Indies

Official name Commonwealth of the Bahamas
Formation 1973 / 1973
Capital Nassau
Population 305,655 / 79 people per sq mile (31 people per sq km) / 90%
Total area 5382 sq. miles (13,940 sq. km)
Languages English*, English Creole, French Creole
Religions Baptist 32%, Anglican 20%, Roman Catholic 19%, Other 17%, Methodist 6%, Church of God 6%
Ethnic mix Black African 85%, Other 15%
Government Parliamentary system
Currency Bahamian dollar = 100 cents
Literacy rate 96%
Calorie consumption 2755 calories

BAHRAIN
Southwest Asia

Official name Kingdom of Bahrain
Formation 1971 / 1971
Capital Manama
Population 708,573 / 2596 people per sq mile (1004 people per sq km) / 90%
Total area 239 sq. miles (620 sq. km)
Languages Arabic
Religions Muslim (mainly Shi'a) 99%, Other 1%
Ethnic mix Bahraini 70%, Iranian, Indian, and Pakistani 24%, Other Arab 4%, European 2%
Government Mixed monarchical–parliamentary system
Currency Bahraini dinar = 1000 fils
Literacy rate 87%
Calorie consumption Not available

BANGLADESH
South Asia

Official name People's Republic of Bangladesh
Formation 1971 / 1971
Capital Dhaka
Population 147 million / 2845 people per sq mile (1098 people per sq km) / 25%
Total area 55,598 sq. miles (144,000 sq. km)
Languages Bengali*, Urdu, Chakma, Marma (Magh), Garo, Khasi, Santhali, Tripuri, Mro
Religions Muslim (mainly Sunni) 87%, Hindu 12%, Other 1%
Ethnic mix Bengali 98%, Other 2%
Government Transitional regime
Currency Taka = 100 poisha
Literacy rate 41%
Calorie consumption 2205 calories

BARBADOS
West Indies

Official name Barbados
Formation 1966 / 1966
Capital Bridgetown
Population 280,946 / 1692 people per sq mile (653 people per sq km) / 52%
Total area 166 sq. miles (430 sq. km)
Languages English*, Bajan (Barbadian English)
Religions Anglican 40%, Other 24%, Nonreligious 17%, Pentecostal 8%, Methodist 7%, Roman Catholic 4%
Ethnic mix Black African 92%, White 3%, Other 3%, Mixed race 2%
Government Parliamentary system
Currency Barbados dollar = 100 cents
Literacy rate 99%
Calorie consumption 3091 calories

BELARUS
Eastern Europe

Official name Republic of Belarus
Formation 1991 / 1991
Capital Minsk
Population 9.6 million / 120 people per sq mile (46 people per sq km) / 71%
Total area 80,154 sq. miles (207,600 sq. km)
Languages Belorussian*, Russian*
Religions Orthodox Christian 60%, Other 32%, Roman Catholic 8%
Ethnic mix Belorussian 81%, Russian 11%, Polish 4%, Other 2%, Ukrainian 2%
Government Presidential system
Currency Belorussian rouble = 100 kopeks
Literacy rate 99%
Calorie consumption 3000 calories

BELGIUM
Northwest Europe

Official name Kingdom of Belgium
Formation 1830 / 1919
Capital Brussels
Population 10.5 million / 829 people per sq mile (320 people per sq km) / 97%
Total area 11,780 sq. miles (30,510 sq. km)
Languages Dutch*, French*, German*
Religions Roman Catholic 88%, Other 10%, Muslim 2%
Ethnic mix Fleming 58%, Walloon 33%, Other 6%, Italian 2%, Moroccan 1%
Government Parliamentary system
Currency Euro = 100 cents
Literacy rate 99%
Calorie consumption 3584 calories

BELIZE
Central America

Official name Belize
Formation 1981 / 1981
Capital Belmopan
Population 294,385 / 33 people per sq mile (13 people per sq km) / 48%
Total area 8867 sq. miles (22,966 sq. km)
Languages English*, English Creole, Spanish, Mayan, Garifuna (Carib)
Religions Roman Catholic 62%, Other 13%, Anglican 12%, Methodist 6%, Mennonite 4%, Seventh-day Adventist 3%
Ethnic mix Mestizo 49%, Creole 25%, Maya 11%, Other 6%, Garifuna 6%, Asian Indian 3%
Government Parliamentary system
Currency Belizean dollar = 100 cents
Literacy rate 75%
Calorie consumption 2869 calories

BENIN
West Africa

Official name Republic of Benin
Formation 1960 / 1960
Capital Porto-Novo
Population 9 million / 211 people per sq mile (81 people per sq km) / 45%
Total area 43,483 sq. miles (112,620 sq. km)
Languages French*, Fon, Bariba, Yoruba, Adja, Houeda, Somba
Religions Voodoo 50%, Muslim 30%, Christian 20%
Ethnic mix Fon 41%, Other 21%, Adja 16%, Yoruba 12%, Bariba 10%
Government Presidential system
Currency CFA franc = 100 centimes
Literacy rate 35%
Calorie consumption 2548 calories

BHUTAN
South Asia

Official name Kingdom of Bhutan
Formation 1656 / 1865
Capital Thimphu
Population 2.3 million / 127 people per sq mile (49 people per sq km) / 9%
Total area 18,147 sq. miles (47,000 sq. km)
Languages Dzongkha*, Nepali, Assamese
Religions Mahayana Buddhist 70%, Hindu 24%, Other 6%
Ethnic mix Bhute 50%, Other 25%, Nepalese 25%
Government Mixed monarchical–parliamentary system
Currency Ngultrum = 100 chetrum
Literacy rate 47%
Calorie consumption Not available

BOLIVIA
South America

Official name Republic of Bolivia
Formation 1825 / 1938
Capital La Paz (administrative); Sucre (judicial)
Population 9.5 million / 23 people per sq mile (9 people per sq km) / 64%
Total area 424,162 sq. miles (1,098,580 sq. km)
Languages Aymara*, Quechua*, Spanish*
Religions Roman Catholic 93%, Other 7%
Ethnic mix Quechua 37%, Aymara 32%, Mixed race 13%, European 10%, Other 8%
Government Presidential system
Currency Boliviano = 100 centavos
Literacy rate 87%
Calorie consumption 2235 calories

BOSNIA & HERZEGOVINA
Southeast Europe

Official name Bosnia and Herzegovina
Formation 1992 / 1992
Capital Sarajevo
Population 3.9 million / 198 people per sq mile (76 people per sq km) / 45%
Total area 19,741 sq. miles (51,129 sq. km)
Languages Bosnian*, Croatian*, Serbian*
Religions Muslim (mainly Sunni) 40%, Orthodox Christian 31%, Roman Catholic 15%, Other 10%, Protestant 4%
Ethnic mix Bosniak 44%, Serb 31%, Croat 17%, Other 8%
Government Parliamentary system
Currency Marka = 100 pfeninga
Literacy rate 97%
Calorie consumption 2894 calories

BOTSWANA
Southern Africa

Official name Republic of Botswana
Formation 1966 / 1966
Capital Gaborone
Population 1.8 million / 8 people per sq mile (3 people per sq km) / 52%
Total area 231,803 sq. miles (600,370 sq. km)
Languages English*, Setswana, Shona, San, Khoikhoi, isiNdebele
Religions Traditional beliefs 50%, Christian (mainly Protestant) 30%, Other (including Muslim) 20%
Ethnic mix Tswana 98%, Other 2%
Government Presidential system
Currency Pula = 100 thebe
Literacy rate 81%
Calorie consumption 2151 calories

BRAZIL
South America

Official name Federative Republic of Brazil
Formation 1822 / 1828
Capital Brasília
Population 191 million / 59 people per sq mile (23 people per sq km) / 84%
Total area 3,286,470 sq. miles (8,511,965 sq. km)
Languages Portuguese*, German, Italian, Spanish, Polish, Japanese, Amerindian languages
Religions Roman Catholic 74%, Protestant 15%, Atheist 7%, Other 4%
Ethnic mix White 54%, Mixed race 38%, Black 6%, Other 2%
Government Presidential system
Currency Real = 100 centavos
Literacy rate 89%
Calorie consumption 3049 calories

BRUNEI
Southeast Asia

Official name Brunei Darussalam
Formation 1984 / 1984
Capital Bandar Seri Begawan
Population 374,577 / 184 people per sq mile (71 people per sq km) / 77%
Total area 2228 sq. miles (5770 sq. km)
Languages Malay*, English, Chinese
Religions Muslim (mainly Sunni) 66%, Buddhist 14%, Other 10%, Christian 10%
Ethnic mix Malay 67%, Chinese 16%, Other 11%, Indigenous 6%
Government Monarchy
Currency Brunei dollar = 100 cents
Literacy rate 93%
Calorie consumption 2855 calories

BULGARIA
Southeast Europe

Official name Republic of Bulgaria
Formation 1908 / 1947
Capital Sofia
Population 7.6 million / 178 people per sq mile (69 people per sq km) / 70%
Total area 42,822 sq. miles (110,910 sq. km)
Languages Bulgarian*, Turkish, Romani
Religions Orthodox Christian 83%, Muslim 12%, Other 4%, Roman Catholic 1%
Ethnic mix Bulgarian 84%, Turkish 9%, Roma 5%, Other 2%
Government Parliamentary system
Currency Lev = 100 stotinki
Literacy rate 98%
Calorie consumption 2848 calories

BURKINA
West Africa

Official name Burkina Faso
Formation 1960 / 1960
Capital Ouagadougou
Population 14 million / 132 people per sq mile (51 people per sq km) / 18%
Total area 105,869 sq. miles (274,200 sq. km)
Languages French*, Mossi, Fulani, Tuareg, Dyula, Songhai
Religions Muslim 55%, Traditional beliefs 35%, Roman Catholic 9%, Other Christian 1%
Ethnic mix Mossi 48%, Other 21%, Peul 10%, Lobi 7%, Bobo 7%, Mandé 7%
Government Presidential system
Currency CFA franc = 100 centimes
Literacy rate 22%
Calorie consumption 2462 calories

BURMA (MYANMAR)
Southeast Asia

Official name Union of Myanmar
Formation 1948 / 1948
Capital Nay Pyi Taw
Population 51.5 million / 203 people per sq mile (78 people per sq km) / 30%
Total area 261,969 sq. miles (678,500 sq. km)
Languages Burmese*, Shan, Karen, Rakhine, Chin, Yangbye, Kachin, Mon
Religions Buddhist 87%, Christian 6%, Muslim 4%, Other 2%, Hindu 1%
Ethnic mix Burman (Bamah) 68%, Other 13%, Shan 9%, Karen 6%, Rakhine 4%
Government Military-based regime
Currency Kyat = 100 pyas
Literacy rate 90%
Calorie consumption 2937 calories

BURUNDI
Central Africa

Official name Republic of Burundi
Formation 1962 / 1962
Capital Bujumbura
Population 8.1 million / 818 people per sq mile (316 people per sq km) / 10%
Total area 10,745 sq. miles (27,830 sq. km)
Languages Kirundi*, French*, Kiswahili
Religions Christian (mainly Roman Catholic) 60%, Traditional beliefs 39%, Muslim 1%
Ethnic mix Hutu 85%, Tutsi 14%, Twa 1%
Government Presidential system
Currency Burundian franc = 100 centimes
Literacy rate 59%
Calorie consumption 1649 calories

CAMBODIA
Southeast Asia

Official name Kingdom of Cambodia
Formation 1953 / 1953
Capital Phnom Penh
Population 14.6 million / 214 people per sq mile (83 people per sq km) / 19%
Total area 69,900 sq. miles (181,040 sq. km)
Languages Khmer*, French, Chinese, Vietnamese, Cham
Religions Buddhist 93%, Muslim 6%, Christian 1%
Ethnic mix Khmer 90%, Other 5%, Vietnamese 4%, Chinese 1%
Government Parliamentary system
Currency Riel = 100 sen
Literacy rate 74%
Calorie consumption 2046 calories

CAMEROON
Central Africa

Official name Republic of Cameroon
Formation 1960 / 1961
Capital Yaoundé
Population 16.3 million / 94 people per sq mile (36 people per sq km) / 52%
Total area 183,567 sq. miles (475,400 sq. km)
Languages English*, French*, Bamileke, Fang, Fulani
Religions Roman Catholic 35%, Traditional beliefs 25%, Muslim 22%, Protestant 18%
Ethnic mix Cameroon highlanders 31%, Other 21%, Equatorial Bantu 19%, Kirdi 11%, Fulani 10%, Northwestern Bantu 8%
Government Presidential system
Currency CFA franc = 100 centimes
Literacy rate 68%
Calorie consumption 2273 calories

CANADA
North America

Official name Canada
Formation 1867 / 1949
Capital Ottawa
Population 32.9 million / 9 people per sq mile (4 people per sq km) / 81%
Total area 3,854,085 sq. miles (9,984,670 sq. km)
Languages English*, French*, Chinese, Italian, German, Ukrainian, Portuguese, Inuktitut, Cree
Religions Roman Catholic 44%, Protestant 29%, Other and nonreligious 27%
Government Parliamentary system
Currency Canadian dollar = 100 cents
Literacy rate 99%
Calorie consumption 3589 calories

CAPE VERDE
Atlantic Ocean

Official name Republic of Cape Verde
Formation 1975 / 1975
Capital Praia
Population 423,613 / 272 people per sq mile (105 people per sq km) / 57%
Total area 1557 sq. miles (4033 sq. km)
Languages Portuguese*, Portuguese Creole
Religions Roman Catholic 97%, Other 2%, Protestant (Church of the Nazarene) 1%
Ethnic mix Mestiço 60%, African 30%, Other 10%
Government Mixed presidential–parliamentary system
Currency Cape Verde escudo = 100 centavos
Literacy rate 76%
Calorie consumption 3243 calories

CENTRAL AFRICAN REPUBLIC
Central Africa

Official name Central African Republic
Formation 1960 / 1960
Capital Bangui
Population 4.2 million / 17 people per sq mile (7 people per sq km) / 43%
Total area 240,534 sq. miles (622,984 sq. km)
Languages French*, Sango, Banda, Gbaya
Religions Traditional beliefs 60%, Christian (mainly Roman Catholic) 35%, Muslim 5%
Ethnic mix Baya 34%, Banda 27%, Mandjia 21%, Sara 10%, Other 8%
Government Presidential system
Currency CFA franc = 100 centimes
Literacy rate 49%
Calorie consumption 1980 calories

CHAD
Central Africa

Official name Republic of Chad
Formation 1960 / 1960
Capital N'Djamena
Population 10.3 million / 21 people per sq mile (8 people per sq km) / 25%
Total area 495,752 sq. miles (1,284,000 sq. km)
Languages Arabic*, French*, Sara, Maba
Religions Muslim 55%, Traditional beliefs 35%, Christian 10%
Ethnic mix Other 30%, Sara 28%, Mayo-Kebbi 12%, Arab 12%, Ouaddai 9%, Kanem-Bornou 9%
Government Presidential system
Currency CFA franc = 100 centimes
Literacy rate 26%
Calorie consumption 2114 calories

CHILE
South America

Official name Republic of Chile
Formation 1818 / 1883
Capital Santiago
Population 16.6 million / 57 people per sq mile (22 people per sq km) / 87%
Total area 292,258 sq. miles (756,950 sq. km)
Languages Spanish*, Amerindian languages
Religions Roman Catholic 80%, Other and nonreligious 20%
Ethnic mix Mixed race and European 90%, Other Amerindian 9%, Mapuche 1%
Government Presidential system
Currency Chilean peso = 100 centavos
Literacy rate 96%
Calorie consumption 2863 calories

CHINA
East Asia

Official name People's Republic of China
Formation 960 / 1999
Capital Beijing
Population 1.33 billion / 370 people per sq mile (143 people per sq km) / 40%
Total area 3,705,386 sq. miles (9,596,960 sq. km)
Languages Mandarin*, Wu, Cantonese, Hsiang, Min, Hakka, Kan
Religions Nonreligious 59%, Traditional beliefs 20%, Other 13%, Buddhist 6%, Muslim 2%
Ethnic mix Han 92%, Other 4%, Hui 1%, Miao 1%, Manchu 1%, Zhuang 1%
Government One-party state
Currency Renminbi (known as yuan) = 10 jiao = 100 fen
Literacy rate 91%
Calorie consumption 2951 calories

COLOMBIA
South America

Official name Republic of Colombia
Formation 1819 / 1903
Capital Bogotá
Population 47 million / 117 people per sq mile (45 people per sq km) / 77%
Total area 439,733 sq. miles (1,138,910 sq. km)
Languages Spanish*, Wayuu, Páez, and other Amerindian languages
Religions Roman Catholic 95%, Other 5%
Ethnic mix Mestizo 58%, White 20%, European–African 14%, African 4%, African–Amerindian 3%, Amerindian 1%
Government Presidential system
Currency Colombian peso = 100 centavos
Literacy rate 93%
Calorie consumption 2585 calories

COMOROS
Indian Ocean

Official name Union of the Comoros
Formation 1975 / 1975
Capital Moroni
Population 711,417 / 826 people per sq mile (319 people per sq km) / 36%
Total area 838 sq. miles (2170 sq. km)
Languages Arabic*, Comoran*, French*
Religions Muslim (mainly Sunni) 98%, Other 1%, Roman Catholic 1%
Ethnic mix Comoran 97%, Other 3%
Government Presidential system
Currency Comoros franc = 100 centimes
Literacy rate 56%
Calorie consumption 1754 calories

CONGO
Central Africa

Official name Republic of the Congo
Formation 1960 / 1960
Capital Brazzaville
Population 4.2 million / 32 people per sq mile (12 people per sq km) / 54%
Total area 132,046 sq. miles (342,000 sq. km)
Languages French*, Kongo, Teke, Lingala
Religions Traditional beliefs 50%, Roman Catholic 25%, Protestant 23%, Muslim 2%
Ethnic mix Bakongo 51%, Teke 17%, Other 16%, Mbochi 11%, Mbédé 5%
Government Presidential system
Currency CFA franc = 100 centimes
Literacy rate 83%
Calorie consumption 2162 calories

CONGO, DEM. REP.
Central Africa

Official name Democratic Republic of the Congo
Formation 1960 / 1960
Capital Kinshasa
Population 61.2 million / 70 people per sq mile (27 people per sq km) / 33%
Total area 905,563 sq. miles (2,345,410 sq. km)
Languages French*, Kiswahili, Tshiluba, Kikongo, Lingala
Religions Roman Catholic 50%, Protestant 20%, Traditional beliefs and other 10%, Muslim 10%, Kimbanguist 10%
Ethnic mix Other 55%, Mongo, Luba, Kongo, and Mangbetu-Azande 45%
Government Presidential system
Currency Congolese franc = 100 centimes
Literacy rate 67%
Calorie consumption 1599 calories

COSTA RICA
Central America

Official name Republic of Costa Rica
Formation 1838 / 1838
Capital San José
Population 4.5 million / 228 people per sq mile (88 people per sq km) / 61%
Total area 19,730 sq. miles (51,100 sq. km)
Languages Spanish*, English Creole, Bribri, Cabecar
Religions Roman Catholic 76%, Other (including Protestant) 24%
Ethnic mix Mestizo and European 96%, Black 2%, Chinese 1%, Amerindian 1%
Government Presidential system
Currency Costa Rican colón = 100 céntimos
Literacy rate 95%
Calorie consumption 2876 calories

CROATIA
Southeast Europe

Official name Republic of Croatia
Formation 1991 / 1991
Capital Zagreb
Population 4.6 million / 211 people per sq mile (81 people per sq km) / 59%
Total area 21,831 sq. miles (56,542 sq. km)
Languages Croatian*
Religions Roman Catholic 88%, Other 7%, Orthodox Christian 4%, Muslim 1%
Ethnic mix Croat 90%, Other 5%, Serb 5%
Government Parliamentary system
Currency Kuna = 100 lipa
Literacy rate 98%
Calorie consumption 2799 calories

CUBA
West Indies

Official name Republic of Cuba
Formation 1902 / 1902
Capital Havana
Population 11.3 million / 264 people per sq mile (102 people per sq km) / 76%
Total area 42,803 sq. miles (110,860 sq. km)
Languages Spanish
Religions Nonreligious 49%, Roman Catholic 40%, Atheist 6%, Other 4%, Protestant 1%
Ethnic mix White 66%, European–African 22%, Black 12%
Government One-party state
Currency Cuban peso = 100 centavos
Literacy rate 99%
Calorie consumption 3152 calories

CYPRUS
Southeast Europe

Official name Republic of Cyprus
Formation 1960 / 1960
Capital Nicosia
Population 788,457 / 221 people per sq mile (85 people per sq km) / 69%
Total area 3571 sq. miles (9250 sq. km)
Languages Greek*, Turkish*
Religions Orthodox Christian 78%, Muslim 18%, Other 4%
Ethnic mix Greek 81%, Turkish 11%, Other 8%
Government Presidential system
Currency Euro (Turkish lira in TRNC) = 100 cents (euro); 100 kurus (Turkish lira)
Literacy rate 97%
Calorie consumption 3255 calories

CZECH REPUBLIC
Central Europe

Official name Czech Republic
Formation 1993 / 1993
Capital Prague
Population 10.2 million / 335 people per sq mile (129 people per sq km) / 74%
Total area 30,450 sq. miles (78,866 sq. km)
Languages Czech*, Slovak, Hungarian (Magyar)
Religions Roman Catholic 39%, Atheist 38%, Other 18%, Protestant 3%, Hussite 2%
Ethnic mix Czech 90%, Other 4%, Moravian 4%, Slovak 2%
Government Parliamentary system
Currency Czech koruna = 100 haleru
Literacy rate 99%
Calorie consumption 3171 calories

DENMARK
Northern Europe

Official name Kingdom of Denmark
Formation 950 / 1944
Capital Copenhagen
Population 5.5 million / 336 people per sq mile (130 people per sq km) / 85%
Total area 16,639 sq. miles (43,094 sq. km)
Languages Danish
Religions Evangelical Lutheran 89%, Other 10%, Roman Catholic 1%
Ethnic mix Danish 96%, Other (including Scandinavian and Turkish) 3%, Faeroese and Inuit 1%
Government Parliamentary system
Currency Danish krone = 100 øre
Literacy rate 99%
Calorie consumption 3439 calories

DJIBOUTI
East Africa

Official name Republic of Djibouti
Formation 1977 / 1977
Capital Djibouti
Population 496,374 / 55 people per sq mile (21 people per sq km) / 84%
Total area 8494 sq. miles (22,000 sq. km)
Languages Arabic*, French*, Somali, Afar
Religions Muslim (mainly Sunni) 94%, Christian 6%
Ethnic mix Issa 60%, Afar 35%, Other 5%
Government Presidential system
Currency Djibouti franc = 100 centimes
Literacy rate 66%
Calorie consumption 2220 calories

DOMINICA
West Indies

Official name Commonwealth of Dominica
Formation 1978 / 1978
Capital Roseau
Population 72,386 / 250 people per sq mile (97 people per sq km) / 72%
Total area 291 sq. miles (754 sq. km)
Languages English*, French Creole
Religions Roman Catholic 77%, Protestant 15%, Other 8%
Ethnic mix Black 87%, Mixed race 9%, Carib 3%, Other 1%
Government Parliamentary system
Currency Eastern Caribbean dollar = 100 cents
Literacy rate 88%
Calorie consumption 2763 calories

DOMINICAN REPUBLIC
West Indies

Official name Dominican Republic
Formation 1865 / 1865
Capital Santo Domingo
Population 9.1 million / 487 people per sq mile (188 people per sq km) / 60%
Total area 18,679 sq. miles (48,380 sq. km)
Languages Spanish*, French Creole
Religions Roman Catholic 92%, Other and nonreligious 8%
Ethnic mix Mixed race 75%, White 15%, Black 10%
Government Presidential system
Currency Dominican Republic peso = 100 centavos
Literacy rate 87%
Calorie consumption 2347 calories

EAST TIMOR
Southeast Asia

Official name Democratic Republic of Timor-Leste
Formation 2002 / 2002
Capital Dili
Population 1.1 million / 192 people per sq mile (74 people per sq km) / 8%
Total area 5756 sq. miles (14,874 sq. km)
Languages Tetum (Portuguese/Austronesian)*, Bahasa Indonesia, and Portuguese*
Religions Roman Catholic 95%, Other (including Muslim and Protestant) 5%
Government Parliamentary system
Currency US dollar = 100 cents
Literacy rate 59%
Calorie consumption 2806 calories

ECUADOR
South America

Official name Republic of Ecuador
Formation 1830 / 1942
Capital Quito
Population 13.6 million / 127 people per sq mile (49 people per sq km) / 62%
Total area 109,483 sq. miles (283,560 sq. km)
Languages Spanish*, Quechua, other Amerindian languages
Religions Roman Catholic 93%, Protestant, Jewish, and other 7%
Ethnic mix Mestizo 55%, Amerindian 25%, White 10%, Black 10%
Government Presidential system
Currency US dollar = 100 cents
Literacy rate 91%
Calorie consumption 2754 calories

EGYPT
North Africa

Official name Arab Republic of Egypt
Formation 1936 / 1982
Capital Cairo
Population 76.9 million / 200 people per sq mile (77 people per sq km) / 42%
Total area 386,660 sq. miles (1,001,450 sq. km)
Languages Arabic*, French, English, Berber
Religions Muslim (mainly Sunni) 94%, Coptic Christian and other 6%
Ethnic mix Egyptian 99%, Nubian, Armenian, Greek, and Berber 1%
Government Presidential system
Currency Egyptian pound = 100 piastres
Literacy rate 71%
Calorie consumption 3338 calories

EL SALVADOR
Central America

Official name Republic of El Salvador
Formation 1841 / 1841
Capital San Salvador
Population 7.1 million / 888 people per sq mile (343 people per sq km) / 60%
Total area 8124 sq. miles (21,040 sq. km)
Languages Spanish
Religions Roman Catholic 80%, Evangelical 18%, Other 2%
Ethnic mix Mestizo 94%, Amerindian 5%, White 1%
Government Presidential system
Currency Salvadorean colón & US dollar = 100 centavos (colón); 100 cents (US dollar)
Literacy rate 80%
Calorie consumption 2584 calories

EQUATORIAL GUINEA
Central Africa

Official name Republic of Equatorial Guinea
Formation 1968 / 1968
Capital Malabo
Population 551,201 / 51 people per sq mile (20 people per sq km) / 49%
Total area 10,830 sq. miles (28,051 sq. km)
Languages French*, Spanish*, Fang, Bubi
Religions Roman Catholic 90%, Other 10%
Ethnic mix Fang 85%, Other 11%, Bubi 4%
Government Presidential system
Currency CFA franc = 100 centimes
Literacy rate 87%
Calorie consumption Not available

ERITREA
East Africa

Official name State of Eritrea
Formation 1993 / 2002
Capital Asmera
Population 4.7 million / 104 people per sq mile (40 people per sq km) / 20%
Total area 46,842 sq. miles (121,320 sq. km)
Languages Tigrinya*, English*, Tigre, Afar, Arabic*, Bilen, Kunama, Nara, Saho, Hadareb
Religions Christian 45%, Muslim 45%, Other 10%
Ethnic mix Tigray 50%, Tigray and Kunama 40%, Afar 4%, Other 3%, Saho 3%
Government Transitional regime
Currency Nakfa = 100 cents
Literacy rate 57%
Calorie consumption 1513 calories

ESTONIA
Northeast Europe

Official name Republic of Estonia
Formation 1991 / 1991
Capital Tallinn
Population 1.3 million / 75 people per sq mile (29 people per sq km) / 70%
Total area 17,462 sq. miles (45,226 sq. km)
Languages Estonian*, Russian
Religions Evangelical Lutheran 56%, Orthodox Christian 25%, Other 19%
Ethnic mix Estonian 68%, Russian 26%, Other 4%, Ukrainian 2%
Government Parliamentary system
Currency Kroon = 100 senti
Literacy rate 99%
Calorie consumption 3002 calories

ETHIOPIA
East Africa

Official name Federal Democratic Republic of Ethiopia
Formation 1896 / 2002
Capital Addis Ababa
Population 81.2 million / 189 people per sq mile (73 people per sq km) / 16%
Total area 435,184 sq. miles (1,127,127 sq. km)
Languages Amharic*, Tigrinya, Galla, Sidamo, Somali, English, Arabic
Religions Orthodox Christian 40%, Muslim 40%, Traditional beliefs 15%, Other 5%
Ethnic mix Oromo 32%, Amhara 30%, Other 22%, Tigrean 6%, Somali 6%, Guragie 4%
Government Parliamentary system
Currency Ethiopian birr = 100 cents
Literacy rate 42%
Calorie consumption 1857 calories

FIJI
Australasia & Oceania

Official name Republic of the Fiji Islands
Formation 1970 / 1970
Capital Suva
Population 918,675 / 130 people per sq mile (50 people per sq km) / 52%
Total area 7054 sq. miles (18,270 sq. km)
Languages Fijian, English*, Hindi, Urdu, Tamil, Telugu
Religions Hindu 38%, Methodist 37%, Roman Catholic 9%, Other 8%, Muslim 8%
Ethnic mix Melanesian 51%, Indian 44%, Other 5%
Government Transitional regime
Currency Fiji dollar = 100 cents
Literacy rate 93%
Calorie consumption 2894 calories

FINLAND
Northern Europe

Official name Republic of Finland
Formation 1917 / 1947
Capital Helsinki
Population 5.3 million / 45 people per sq mile (17 people per sq km) / 61%
Total area 130,127 sq. miles (337,030 sq. km)
Languages Finnish*, Swedish*, Sámi
Religions Evangelical Lutheran 89%, Other 9%, Orthodox Christian 1%, Roman Catholic 1%
Ethnic mix Finnish 93%, Other (including Sámi) 7%
Government Parliamentary system
Currency Euro = 100 cents
Literacy rate 99%
Calorie consumption 3100 calories

FRANCE
Western Europe

Official name French Republic
Formation 987 / 1919
Capital Paris
Population 60.9 million / 287 people per sq mile (111 people per sq km) / 76%
Total area 211,208 sq. miles (547,030 sq. km)
Languages French*, Provençal, German, Breton, Catalan, Basque
Religions Roman Catholic 88%, Muslim 8%, Protestant 2%, Buddhist 1%, Jewish 1%
Ethnic mix French 90%, North African (mainly Algerian) 6%, German (Alsace) 2%, Breton 1%, Other (including Corsicans) 1%
Government Mixed presidential–parliamentary system
Currency Euro = 100 cents
Literacy rate 99%
Calorie consumption 3654 calories

GABON
Central Africa

Official name Gabonese Republic
Formation 1960 / 1960
Capital Libreville
Population 1.4 million / 14 people per sq mile (5 people per sq km) / 84%
Total area 103,346 sq. miles (267,667 sq. km)
Languages Fang, French*, Punu, Sira, Nzebi, Mpongwe
Religions Christian (mainly Roman Catholic) 55%, Traditional beliefs 40%, Other 4%, Muslim 1%
Ethnic mix Fang 26%, Shira-punu 24%, Other 16%, Foreign residents 15%, Nzabi-duma 11%, Mbédé-Teke 8%
Government Presidential system
Currency CFA franc = 100 centimes
Literacy rate 71%
Calorie consumption 2637 calories

GAMBIA
West Africa

Official name Republic of the Gambia
Formation 1965 / 1965
Capital Banjul
Population 1.6 million / 414 people per sq mile (160 people per sq km) / 26%
Total area 4363 sq. miles (11,300 sq. km)
Languages English*, Mandinka, Fulani, Wolof, Jola, Soninke
Religions Sunni Muslim 90%, Christian 9%, Traditional beliefs 1%
Ethnic mix Mandinka 40%, Fulani 19%, Wolof 15%, Jola 11%, Serahuli 9%, Other 6%
Government Presidential system
Currency Dalasi = 100 butut
Literacy rate 38%
Calorie consumption 2273 calories

GEORGIA
Southwest Asia

Official name Georgia
Formation 1991 / 1991
Capital Tbilisi
Population 4.4 million / 164 people per sq mile (63 people per sq km) / 52%
Total area 26,911 sq. miles (69,700 sq. km)
Languages Georgian*, Russian, Azeri, Armenian, Mingrelian, Ossetian, Abkhazian* *(in Abkhazia)*
Religions Georgian Orthodox 65%, Muslim 11%, Russian Orthodox 10%, Armenian Apostolic Church (Orthodox) 8%, Other 6%
Ethnic mix Georgian 84%, Armenian 6%, Azeri 6%, Russian 2%, Other 1%, Ossetian 1%
Government Presidential system
Currency Lari = 100 tetri
Literacy rate 99%
Calorie consumption 2354 calories

GERMANY
Northern Europe

Official name Federal Republic of Germany
Formation 1871 / 1990
Capital Berlin
Population 82.7 million / 613 people per sq mile (237 people per sq km) / 88%
Total area 137,846 sq. miles (357,021 sq. km)
Languages German*, Turkish
Religions Protestant 34%, Roman Catholic 33%, Other 30%, Muslim 3%
Ethnic mix German 92%, Other European 3%, Other 3%, Turkish 2%
Government Parliamentary system
Currency Euro = 100 cents
Literacy rate 99%
Calorie consumption 3496 calories

GHANA
West Africa

Official name Republic of Ghana
Formation 1957 / 1957
Capital Accra
Population 23 million / 259 people per sq mile (100 people per sq km) / 46%
Total area 92,100 sq. miles (238,540 sq. km)
Languages English*, Twi, Fanti, Ewe, Ga, Adangbe, Gurma, Dagomba (Dagbani)
Religions Christian 69%, Muslim 16%, Traditional beliefs 9%, Other 6%
Ethnic mix Akan 49%, Mole-Dagbani 17%, Ewe 13%, Other 9%, Ga and Ga-Adangbe 8%, Guan 4%
Government Presidential system
Currency Cedi = 100 pesewas
Literacy rate 58%
Calorie consumption 2667 calories

GREECE
Southeast Europe

Official name Hellenic Republic
Formation 1829 / 1947
Capital Athens
Population 11.2 million / 222 people per sq mile (86 people per sq km) / 61%
Total area 50,942 sq. miles (131,940 sq. km)
Languages Greek*, Turkish, Macedonian, Albanian
Religions Orthodox Christian 98%, Other 1%, Muslim 1%
Ethnic mix Greek 98%, Other 2%
Government Parliamentary system
Currency Euro = 100 cents
Literacy rate 96%
Calorie consumption 3721 calories

GRENADA
West Indies

Official name Grenada
Formation 1974 / 1974
Capital St. George's
Population 89,971 / 687 people per sq mile (265 people per sq km) / 41%
Total area 131 sq. miles (340 sq. km)
Languages English*, English Creole
Religions Roman Catholic 68%, Anglican 17%, Other 15%
Ethnic mix Black African 82%, Mulatto (mixed race) 13%, East Indian 3%, Other 2%
Government Parliamentary system
Currency Eastern Caribbean dollar = 100 cents
Literacy rate 96%
Calorie consumption 2932 calories

GUATEMALA
Central America

Official name Republic of Guatemala
Formation 1838 / 1838
Capital Guatemala City
Population 13.2 million / 315 people per sq mile (122 people per sq km) / 47%
Total area 42,042 sq. miles (108,890 sq. km)
Languages Spanish*, Quiché, Mam, Cakchiquel, Kekchí
Religions Roman Catholic 65%, Protestant 33%, Other and nonreligious 2%
Ethnic mix Amerindian 60%, Mestizo 30%, Other 10%
Government Presidential system
Currency Quetzal = 100 centavos
Literacy rate 69%
Calorie consumption 2219 calories

GUINEA
West Africa

Official name Republic of Guinea
Formation 1958 / 1958
Capital Conakry
Population 9.8 million / 103 people per sq mile (40 people per sq km) / 36%
Total area 94,925 sq. miles (245,857 sq. km)
Languages French*, Pulaar, Malinke, Soussou
Religions Muslim 65%, Traditional beliefs 33%, Christian 2%
Ethnic mix Peul 39%, Malinké 23%, Other 16%, Soussou 11%, Kissi 6%, Kpellé 5%
Government Presidential system
Currency Guinea franc = 100 centimes
Literacy rate 30%
Calorie consumption 2409 calories

GUINEA-BISSAU
West Africa

Official name Republic of Guinea-Bissau
Formation 1974 / 1974
Capital Bissau
Population 1.7 million / 157 people per sq mile (60 people per sq km) / 35%
Total area 13,946 sq. miles (36,120 sq. km)
Languages Portuguese*, Portuguese Creole, Balante, Fulani, Malinke
Religions Traditional beliefs 52%, Muslim 40%, Christian 8%
Ethnic mix Balante 30%, Fulani 20%, Other 17%, Mandyako 14%, Mandinka 12%, Papel 7%
Government Presidential system
Currency CFA franc = 100 centimes
Literacy rate 40%
Calorie consumption 2024 calories

GUYANA
South America

Official name The Co-operative Republic of Guyana
Formation 1966 / 1966
Capital Georgetown
Population 769,095 / 10 people per sq mile (4 people per sq km) / 38%
Total area 83,000 sq. miles (214,970 sq. km)
Languages English*, English Creole, Hindi, Tamil, Amerindian languages
Religions Christian 57%, Hindu 33%, Muslim 9%, Other 1%
Ethnic mix East Indian 43%, Black African 30%, Mixed race 17%, Amerindian 9%, Other 1%
Government Presidential system
Currency Guyanese dollar = 100 cents
Literacy rate 97%
Calorie consumption 2692 calories

HAITI
West Indies

Official name Republic of Haiti
Formation 1804 / 1844
Capital Port-au-Prince
Population 8.8 million / 827 people per sq mile (319 people per sq km) / 38%
Total area 10,714 sq. miles (27,750 sq. km)
Languages French*, French Creole*
Religions Roman Catholic 80%, Protestant 16%, Other (including Voodoo) 3%, Nonreligious 1%
Ethnic mix Black African 95%, Mulatto (mixed race) and European 5%
Government Presidential system
Currency Gourde = 100 centimes
Literacy rate 52%
Calorie consumption 2086 calories

HONDURAS
Central America

Official name Republic of Honduras
Formation 1838 / 1838
Capital Tegucigalpa
Population 7.5 million / 174 people per sq mile (67 people per sq km) / 46%
Total area 43,278 sq. miles (112,090 sq. km)
Languages Spanish*, Garifuna (Carib), English Creole
Religions Roman Catholic 97%, Protestant 3%
Ethnic mix Mestizo 90%, Black African 5%, Amerindian 4%, White 1%
Government Presidential system
Currency Lempira = 100 centavos
Literacy rate 80%
Calorie consumption 2356 calories

HUNGARY
Central Europe

Official name Republic of Hungary
Formation 1918 / 1947
Capital Budapest
Population 10 million / 280 people per sq mile (108 people per sq km) / 66%
Total area 35,919 sq. miles (93,030 sq. km)
Languages Hungarian (Magyar)*
Religions Roman Catholic 52%, Calvinist 16%, Other 15%, Nonreligious 14%, Lutheran 3%
Ethnic mix Magyar 94%, Other 5%, Roma 1%
Government Parliamentary system
Currency Forint = 100 fillér
Literacy rate 99%
Calorie consumption 3483 calories

ICELAND
Northwest Europe

Official name Republic of Iceland
Formation 1944 / 1944
Capital Reykjavík
Population 301,931 / 8 people per sq mile (3 people per sq km) / 93%
Total area 39,768 sq. miles (103,000 sq. km)
Languages Icelandic*
Religions Evangelical Lutheran 93%, Nonreligious 6%, Other (mostly Christian) 1%
Ethnic mix Icelandic 94%, Other 5%, Danish 1%
Government Parliamentary system
Currency Icelandic króna = 100 aurar
Literacy rate 99%
Calorie consumption 3249 calories

INDIA
South Asia

Official name Republic of India
Formation 1947 / 1947
Capital New Delhi
Population 1.14 billion / 989 people per sq mile (382 people per sq km) / 29%
Total area 1,269,338 sq. miles (3,287,590 sq. km)
Languages Hindi*, English*, Urdu, Bengali, Marathi, Telugu, Tamil, Bihari, Gujarati, Kanarese
Religions Hindu 81%, Muslim 13%, Christian 2%, Sikh 2%, Other 1%, Buddhist 1%
Ethnic mix Indo-Aryan 72%, Dravidian 25%, Mongoloid and other 3%
Government Parliamentary system
Currency Indian rupee = 100 paise
Literacy rate 61%
Calorie consumption 2459 calories

INDONESIA
Southeast Asia

Official name Republic of Indonesia
Formation 1949 / 1999
Capital Jakarta
Population 228 million / 329 people per sq mile (127 people per sq km) / 47%
Total area 741,096 sq. miles (1,919,440 sq. km)
Languages Bahasa Indonesia*, Javanese, Sundanese, Madurese, Dutch
Religions Sunni Muslim 87%, Protestant 6%, Roman Catholic 3%, Hindu 2%, Other 1%, Buddhist 1%
Ethnic mix Javanese 42%, Sundanese 15%, Coastal Malays 12%, Madurese 3%, Other 28%
Government Presidential system
Currency Rupiah = 100 sen
Literacy rate 90%
Calorie consumption 2904 calories

IRAN
Southwest Asia

Official name Islamic Republic of Iran
Formation 1502 / 1990
Capital Tehran
Population 71.2 million / 113 people per sq mile (44 people per sq km) / 67%
Total area 636,293 sq. miles (1,648,000 sq. km)
Languages Farsi*, Azeri, Luri, Gilaki, Kurdish, Mazanderani, Turkmen, Arabic, Baluchi
Religions Shi'a Muslim 93%, Sunni Muslim 6%, Other 1%
Ethnic mix Persian 50%, Azari 24%, Other 10%, Kurdish 8%, Lur and Bakhtiari 8%
Government Islamic theocracy
Currency Iranian rial = 100 dinars
Literacy rate 77%
Calorie consumption 3085 calories

IRAQ
Southwest Asia

Official name Republic of Iraq
Formation 1932 / 1990
Capital Baghdad
Population 30.3 million / 179 people per sq mile (69 people per sq km) / 67%
Total area 168,753 sq. miles (437,072 sq. km)
Languages Arabic*, Kurdish*, Turkic languages, Armenian, Assyrian
Religions Shi'a Muslim 60%, Sunni Muslim 35%, Other (including Christian) 5%
Ethnic mix Arab 80%, Kurdish 15%, Turkmen 3%, Other 2%
Government Parliamentary system
Currency New Iraqi dinar = 1000 fils
Literacy rate 74%
Calorie consumption 2197 calories

IRELAND
Northwest Europe

Official name Ireland
Formation 1922 / 1922
Capital Dublin
Population 4.3 million / 162 people per sq mile (62 people per sq km) / 60%
Total area 27,135 sq. miles (70,280 sq. km)
Languages English*, Irish Gaelic*
Religions Roman Catholic 88%, Other and nonreligious 9%, Anglican 3%
Ethnic mix Irish 99%, Other 1%
Government Parliamentary system
Currency Euro = 100 cents
Literacy rate 99%
Calorie consumption 3656 calories

ISRAEL
Southwest Asia

Official name State of Israel
Formation 1948 / 1994
Capital Jerusalem (not internationally recognized)
Population 7 million / 892 people per sq mile (344 people per sq km) / 92%
Total area 8019 sq. miles (20,770 sq. km)
Languages Hebrew*, Arabic*, Yiddish, German, Russian, Polish, Romanian, Persian
Religions Jewish 76%, Muslim (mainly Sunni) 16%, Other 4%, Druze 2%, Christian 2%
Ethnic mix Jewish 76%, Other (mostly Arab) 24%
Government Parliamentary system
Currency Shekel = 100 agorot
Literacy rate 97%
Calorie consumption 3666 calories

ITALY
Southern Europe

Official name Italian Republic
Formation 1861 / 1947
Capital Rome
Population 58.2 million / 513 people per sq mile (198 people per sq km) / 67%
Total area 116,305 sq. miles (301,230 sq. km)
Languages Italian*, German, French, Rhaeto-Romanic, Sardinian
Religions Roman Catholic 85%, Other and nonreligious 13%, Muslim 2%
Ethnic mix Italian 94%, Other 4%, Sardinian 2%
Government Parliamentary system
Currency Euro = 100 cents
Literacy rate 98%
Calorie consumption 3671 calories

IVORY COAST
West Africa

Official name Republic of Côte d'Ivoire
Formation 1960 / 1960
Capital Yamoussoukro
Population 18.8 million / 153 people per sq mile (59 people per sq km) / 45%
Total area 124,502 sq. miles (322,460 sq. km)
Languages Akan, French*, Krou, Voltaique
Religions Muslim 38%, Traditional beliefs 25%, Roman Catholic 25%, Other 6%, Protestant 6%
Ethnic mix Akan 42%, Voltaique 18%, Mandé du Nord 17%, Krou 11%, Mandé du Sud 10%, Other 2%
Government Presidential system
Currency CFA franc = 100 centimes
Literacy rate 49%
Calorie consumption 2631 calories

JAMAICA
West Indies

Official name Jamaica
Formation 1962 / 1962
Capital Kingston
Population 2.7 million / 646 people per sq mile (249 people per sq km) / 52%
Total area 4243 sq. miles (10,990 sq. km)
Languages English*, English Creole
Religions Other and nonreligious 45%, Other Protestant 20%, Church of God 18%, Baptist 10%, Anglican 7%
Ethnic mix Black African 92%, Mulatto (mixed race) 6%, East Indian 1%, European and Chinese 1%
Government Parliamentary system
Currency Jamaican dollar = 100 cents
Literacy rate 80%
Calorie consumption 2685 calories

JAPAN
East Asia

Official name Japan
Formation 1590 / 1972
Capital Tokyo
Population 128 million / 883 people per sq mile (341 people per sq km) / 66%
Total area 145,882 sq. miles (377,835 sq. km)
Languages Japanese*, Korean, Chinese
Religions Shinto and Buddhist 76%, Buddhist 16%, Other (including Christian) 8%
Ethnic mix Japanese 99%, Other (mainly Korean) 1%
Government Parliamentary system
Currency Yen = 100 sen
Literacy rate 99%
Calorie consumption 2761 calories

JORDAN
Southwest Asia

Official name Hashemite Kingdom of Jordan
Formation 1946 / 1967
Capital Amman
Population 6 million / 175 people per sq mile (67 people per sq km) / 79%
Total area 35,637 sq. miles (92,300 sq. km)
Languages Arabic*
Religions Muslim (mainly Sunni) 92%, Other (mostly Christian) 8%
Ethnic mix Arab 98%, Circassian 1%, Armenian 1%
Government Monarchy
Currency Jordanian dinar = 1000 fils
Literacy rate 90%
Calorie consumption 2673 calories

KAZAKHSTAN
Central Asia

Official name Republic of Kazakhstan
Formation 1991 / 1991
Capital Astana
Population 14.8 million / 14 people per sq mile (5 people per sq km) / 56%
Total area 1,049,150 sq. miles (2,717,300 sq. km)
Languages Kazakh*, Russian, Ukrainian, German, Uzbek, Tatar, Uighur
Religions Muslim (mainly Sunni) 47%, Orthodox Christian 44%, Other 9%
Ethnic mix Kazakh 57%, Russian 27%, Other 8%, Uzbek 3%, Ukrainian 3%, German 2%
Government Presidential system
Currency Tenge = 100 tiyn
Literacy rate 99%
Calorie consumption 2677 calories

KENYA
East Africa

Official name Republic of Kenya
Formation 1963 / 1963
Capital Nairobi
Population 36 million / 164 people per sq mile (63 people per sq km) / 40%
Total area 224,961 sq. miles (582,650 sq. km)
Languages Kiswahili*, English*, Kikuyu, Luo, Kalenjin, Kamba
Religions Christian 60%, Traditional beliefs 25%, Other 9%, Muslim 6%
Ethnic mix Other 31%, Kikuyu 20%, Luhya 14%, Luo 13%, Kalenjin 11%, Kamba 11%
Government Mixed Presidential–Parliamentary system
Currency Kenya shilling = 100 cents
Literacy rate 74%
Calorie consumption 2090 calories

KIRIBATI
Australasia & Oceania

Official name Republic of Kiribati
Formation 1979 / 1979
Capital Bairiki (Tarawa Atoll)
Population 107,817 / 393 people per sq mile (152 people per sq km) / 49%
Total area 277 sq. miles (717 sq. km)
Languages English*, Kiribati
Religions Roman Catholic 53%, Kiribati Protestant Church 39%, Other 8%
Ethnic mix Micronesian 99%, Other 1%
Government Nonparty system
Currency Australian dollar = 100 cents
Literacy rate 99%
Calorie consumption 2859 calories

KOSOVO (not yet fully recognized)
Southeast Europe

Official name Republic of Kosovo
Formation 2008 / 2008
Capital Pristina
Population 2.1 million / 499 people per sq mile (193 people per sq km) / 40%
Total area 4212 sq miles (10,908 sq km)
Languages Albanian*, Serbian*, Bosniak, Gorani, Roma, Turkish
Religions Muslim 92%, Roman Catholic 4%, Orthodox Christian 4%
Ethnic mix Albanian 92%, Serb 4%, Bosniak and Gorani 2%, Turkish 1%, Roma 1%
Government Parliamentary system
Currency Euro = 100 cents
Literacy rate 92%
Calorie consumption Not available

KUWAIT
Southwest Asia

Official name State of Kuwait
Formation 1961 / 1961
Capital Kuwait City
Population 2.8 million / 407 people per sq mile (157 people per sq km) / 96%
Total area 6880 sq. miles (17,820 sq. km)
Languages Arabic*, English
Religions Sunni Muslim 45%, Shi'a Muslim 40%, Christian, Hindu, and other 15%
Ethnic mix Kuwaiti 45%, Other Arab 35%, South Asian 9%, Other 7%, Iranian 4%
Government Monarchy
Currency Kuwaiti dinar = 1000 fils
Literacy rate 93%
Calorie consumption 3010 calories

KYRGYZSTAN
Central Asia

Official name Kyrgyz Republic
Formation 1991 / 1991
Capital Bishkek
Population 5.4 million / 70 people per sq mile (27 people per sq km) / 34%
Total area 76,641 sq. miles (198,500 sq. km)
Languages Kyrgyz*, Russian*, Uzbek, Tatar, Ukrainian
Religions Muslim (mainly Sunni) 70%, Orthodox Christian 30%
Ethnic mix Kyrgyz 65%, Uzbek 14%, Russian 13%, Other 6%, Dungan 1%Ukrainian 1%
Government Presidential system
Currency Som = 100 tyiyn
Literacy rate 99%
Calorie consumption 2999 calories

LAOS
Southeast Asia

Official name Lao People's Democratic Republic
Formation 1953 / 1953
Capital Vientiane
Population 6.2 million / 70 people per sq mile (27 people per sq km) / 21%
Total area 91,428 sq. miles (236,800 sq. km)
Languages Lao*, Mon-Khmer, Yao, Vietnamese, Chinese, French
Religions Buddhist 85%, Other (including animist) 15%
Ethnic mix Lao Loum 66%, Lao Theung 30%, Other 2%, Lao Soung 2%
Government One-party state
Currency New kip = 100 at
Literacy rate 69%
Calorie consumption 2312 calories

LATVIA
Northeast Europe

Official name Republic of Latvia
Formation 1991 / 1991
Capital Riga
Population 2.3 million / 92 people per sq mile (36 people per sq km) / 66%
Total area 24,938 sq. miles (64,589 sq. km)
Languages Latvian*, Russian
Religions Lutheran 55%, Roman Catholic 24%, Other 12%, Orthodox Christian 9%
Ethnic mix Latvian 59%, Russian 29%, Belarussian 4%, Polish 3%, Ukrainian 3%, Other 2%
Government Parliamentary system
Currency Lats = 100 santimi
Literacy rate 99%
Calorie consumption 2938 calories

LEBANON
Southwest Asia

Official name The Lebanese Republic
Formation 1941 / 1941
Capital Beirut
Population 3.7 million / 937 people per sq mile (362 people per sq km) / 88%
Total area 4015 sq. miles (10,400 sq. km)
Languages Arabic*, French, Armenian, Assyrian
Religions Muslim 70%, Christian 30%
Ethnic mix Arab 94%, Armenian 4%, Other 2%
Government Parliamentary system
Currency Lebanese pound = 100 piastres
Literacy rate 86%
Calorie consumption 3196 calories

LESOTHO
Southern Africa

Official name Kingdom of Lesotho
Formation 1966 / 1966
Capital Maseru
Population 1.8 million / 154 people per sq mile (59 people per sq km) / 18%
Total area 11,720 sq. miles (30,355 sq. km)
Languages English*, Sesotho*, isiZulu
Religions Christian 90%, Traditional beliefs 10%
Ethnic mix Sotho 97%, European and Asian 3%
Government Parliamentary system
Currency Loti = 100 lisente
Literacy rate 82%
Calorie consumption 2638 calories

LIBERIA
West Africa

Official name Republic of Liberia
Formation 1847 / 1847
Capital Monrovia
Population 3.5 million / 94 people per sq mile (36 people per sq km) / 47%
Total area 43,000 sq. miles (111,370 sq. km)
Languages English*, Kpelle, Vai, Bassa, Kru, Grebo, Kissi, Gola, Loma
Religions Christian 68%, Traditional beliefs 18%, Muslim 14%
Ethnic mix Indigenous tribes (16 main groups) 95%, Americo-Liberians 5%
Government Presidential system
Currency Liberian dollar = 100 cents
Literacy rate 58%
Calorie consumption 1900 calories

LIBYA
North Africa

Official name The Great Socialist People's Libyan Arab Jamahiriyah
Formation 1951 / 1951
Capital Tripoli
Population 6.1 million / 9 people per sq mile (3 people per sq km) / 87%
Total area 679,358 sq. miles (1,759,540 sq. km)
Languages Arabic*, Tuareg
Religions Muslim (mainly Sunni) 97%, Other 3%
Ethnic mix Arab and Berber 95%, Other 5%
Government One-party state
Currency Libyan dinar = 1000 dirhams
Literacy rate 82%
Calorie consumption 3320 calories

LIECHTENSTEIN
Central Europe

Official name Principality of Liechtenstein
Formation 1719 / 1719
Capital Vaduz
Population 34,247 / 552 people per sq mile (214 people per sq km) / 22%
Total area 62 sq. miles (160 sq. km)
Languages German*, Alemannish dialect, Italian
Religions Roman Catholic 81%, Other 12%, Protestant 7%
Ethnic mix Liechtensteiner 66%, Other 12%, Swiss 10%, Austrian 6%, German 3%, Italian 3%
Government Parliamentary system
Currency Swiss franc = 100 rappen/centimes
Literacy rate 99%
Calorie consumption Not available

LITHUANIA
Northeast Europe

Official name Republic of Lithuania
Formation 1991 / 1991
Capital Vilnius
Population 3.4 million / 135 people per sq mile (52 people per sq km) / 67%
Total area 25,174 sq. miles (65,200 sq. km)
Languages Lithuanian*, Russian
Religions Roman Catholic 83%, Other 12%, Protestant 5%
Ethnic mix Lithuanian 83%, Polish 7%, Russian 6%, Other 3%, Belorussian 1%
Government Parliamentary system
Currency Litas = 100 centu
Literacy rate 99%
Calorie consumption 3324 calories

LUXEMBOURG
Northwest Europe

Official name Grand Duchy of Luxembourg
Formation 1867 / 1867
Capital Luxembourg-Ville
Population 480,222 / 481 people per sq mile (186 people per sq km) / 92%
Total area 998 sq. miles (2586 sq. km)
Languages French*, German*, Luxembourgish*
Religions Roman Catholic 97%, Protestant, Orthodox Christian, and Jewish 3%
Ethnic mix Luxembourger 62%, Foreign residents 38%
Government Parliamentary system
Currency Euro = 100 cents
Literacy rate 99%
Calorie consumption 3701 calories

MACEDONIA
Southeast Europe

Official name Republic of Macedonia
Formation 1991 / 1991
Capital Skopje
Population 2 million / 201 people per sq mile (78 people per sq km) / 60%
Total area 9781 sq. miles (25,333 sq. km)
Languages Macedonian*, Albanian*, Turkish, Romani, Serbian
Religions Orthodox Christian 59%, Muslim 26%, Other 10%, Roman Catholic 4%, Protestant 1%
Ethnic mix Macedonian 64%, Albanian 25%, Turkish 4%, Roma 3%, Other 2%, Serb 2%
Government Mixed presidential–parliamentary system
Currency Macedonian denar = 100 deni
Literacy rate 96%
Calorie consumption 2655 calories

MADAGASCAR
Indian Ocean

Official name Republic of Madagascar
Formation 1960 / 1960
Capital Antananarivo
Population 19.6 million / 87 people per sq mile (34 people per sq km) / 27%
Total area 226,656 sq. miles (587,040 sq. km)
Languages French*, Malagasy*, English*
Religions Traditional beliefs 52%, Christian (mainly Roman Catholic) 41%, Muslim 7%
Ethnic mix Other Malay 46%, Merina 26%, Betsimisaraka 15%, Betsileo 12%, Other 1%
Government Presidential system
Currency Ariary = 5 iraimbilanja
Literacy rate 71%
Calorie consumption 2005 calories

MALAWI
Southern Africa

Official name Republic of Malawi
Formation 1964 / 1964
Capital Lilongwe
Population 13.5 million / 372 people per sq mile (143 people per sq km) / 17%
Total area 45,745 sq. miles (118,480 sq. km)
Languages English*, Chewa, Lomwe, Yao, Ngoni
Religions Protestant 55%, Roman Catholic 20%, Muslim 20%, Traditional beliefs 5%
Ethnic mix Bantu 99%, Other 1%
Government Presidential system
Currency Malawi kwacha = 100 tambala
Literacy rate 64%
Calorie consumption 2155 calories

MALAYSIA
Southeast Asia

Official name Malaysia
Formation 1963 / 1965
Capital Kuala Lumpur; Putrajaya (administrative)
Population 26.2 million / 207 people per sq mile (80 people per sq km) / 64%
Total area 127,316 sq. miles (329,750 sq. km)
Languages Bahasa Malaysia*, Malay, Chinese, Tamil, English
Religions Muslim (mainly Sunni) 53%, Buddhist 19%, Chinese faiths 12%, Other 7%, Christian 7%, Traditional beliefs 2%
Ethnic mix Malay 50%, Chinese 25%, Indigenous tribes 11%, Other 7%, Indian 7%
Government Parliamentary system
Currency Ringgit = 100 sen
Literacy rate 89%
Calorie consumption 2881 calories

MALDIVES
Indian Ocean

Official name Republic of Maldives
Formation 1965 / 1965
Capital Male'
Population 369,031 / 3181 people per sq mile (1230 people per sq km) / 29%
Total area 116 sq. miles (300 sq. km)
Languages Dhivehi (Maldivian)*, Sinhala, Tamil, Arabic
Religions Sunni Muslim 100%
Ethnic mix Arab–Sinhalese–Malay 100%
Government Presidential system
Currency Rufiyaa = 100 laari
Literacy rate 96%
Calorie consumption 2548 calories

MALI
West Africa

Official name Republic of Mali
Formation 1960 / 1960
Capital Bamako
Population 14.3 million / 30 people per sq mile (12 people per sq km) / 33%
Total area 478,764 sq. miles (1,240,000 sq. km)
Languages French*, Bambara, Fulani, Senufo, Soninke
Religions Muslim (mainly Sunni) 80%, Traditional beliefs 18%, Christian 1%, Other 1%
Ethnic mix Bambara 32%, Other 26%, Fulani 14%, Senufu 12%, Soninka 9%, Tuareg 7%
Government Presidential system
Currency CFA franc = 100 centimes
Literacy rate 19%
Calorie consumption 2174 calories

MALTA
Southern Europe

Official name Republic of Malta
Formation 1964 / 1964
Capital Valletta
Population 401,880 / 3241 people per sq mile (1256 people per sq km) / 92%
Total area 122 sq. miles (316 sq. km)
Languages Maltese*, English*
Religions Roman Catholic 98%, Other and nonreligious 2%
Ethnic mix Maltese 96%, Other 4%
Government Parliamentary system
Currency Euro = 100 cents
Literacy rate 88%
Calorie consumption 3587 calories

MARSHALL ISLANDS
Australasia & Oceania

Official name Republic of the Marshall Islands
Formation 1986 / 1986
Capital Majuro
Population 61,815 / 883 people per sq mile (342 people per sq km) / 67%
Total area 70 sq. miles (181 sq. km)
Languages Marshallese*, English*, Japanese, German
Religions Protestant 90%, Roman Catholic 8%, Other 2%
Ethnic mix Micronesian 97%, Other 3%
Government Presidential system
Currency US dollar = 100 cents
Literacy rate 91%
Calorie consumption Not available

MAURITANIA
West Africa

Official name Islamic Republic of Mauritania
Formation 1960 / 1960
Capital Nouakchott
Population 3.2 million / 8 people per sq mile (3 people per sq km) / 63%
Total area 397,953 sq. miles (1,030,700 sq. km)
Languages Hassaniyah Arabic*, Wolof, French
Religions Sunni Muslim 100%
Ethnic mix Maure 81%, Wolof 7%, Tukolor 5%, Other 4%, Soninka 3%
Government Presidential system
Currency Ouguiya = 5 khoums
Literacy rate 51%
Calorie consumption 2772 calories

MAURITIUS
Indian Ocean

Official name Republic of Mauritius
Formation 1968 / 1968
Capital Port Louis
Population 1.3 million / 1811 people per sq mile (699 people per sq km) / 44%
Total area 718 sq. miles (1860 sq. km)
Languages English*, French Creole, Hindi, Urdu, Tamil, Chinese, French
Religions Hindu 52%, Roman Catholic 26%, Muslim 17%, Other 3%, Protestant 2%
Ethnic mix Indo-Mauritian 68%, Creole 27%, Sino-Mauritian 3%, Franco-Mauritian 2%
Government Parliamentary system
Currency Mauritian rupee = 100 cents
Literacy rate 84%
Calorie consumption 2955 calories

MEXICO
North America

Official name United Mexican States
Formation 1836 / 1848
Capital Mexico City
Population 110 million / 149 people per sq mile (57 people per sq km) / 76%
Total area 761,602 sq. miles (1,972,550 sq. km)
Languages Spanish*, Nahuatl, Mayan, Zapotec, Mixtec, Otomi, Totonac, Tzotzil, Tzeltal
Religions Roman Catholic 88%, Other 7%, Protestant 5%
Ethnic mix Mestizo 60%, Amerindian 30%, European 9%, Other 1%
Government Presidential system
Currency Mexican peso = 100 centavos
Literacy rate 91%
Calorie consumption 3145 calories

MICRONESIA
Australasia & Oceania

Official name Federated States of Micronesia
Formation 1986 / 1986
Capital Palikir (Pohnpei Island)
Population 107,862 / 398 people per sq mile (154 people per sq km) / 30%
Total area 271 sq. miles (702 sq. km)
Languages English*, Trukese, Pohnpeian, Mortlockese, Kosraean
Religions Roman Catholic 50%, Protestant 48%, Other 2%
Ethnic mix Chuukese 49%, Pohnpeian 24%, Other 14%, Kosraean 6%, Yapese 5%, Asian 2%
Government Nonparty system
Currency US dollar = 100 cents
Literacy rate 81%
Calorie consumption Not available

MOLDOVA
Southeast Europe

Official name Republic of Moldova
Formation 1991 / 1991
Capital Chisinau
Population 4.2 million / 323 people per sq mile (125 people per sq km) / 46%
Total area 13,067 sq. miles (33,843 sq. km)
Languages Moldovan*, Ukrainian, Russian
Religions Orthodox Christian 98%, Jewish 2%
Ethnic mix Moldovan 64%, Ukrainian 14%, Russian 13%, Gagauz 4%, Other 3%, Bulgarian 2%
Government Parliamentary system
Currency Moldovan leu = 100 bani
Literacy rate 98%
Calorie consumption 2806 calories

MONACO
Southern Europe

Official name Principality of Monaco
Formation 1861 / 1861
Capital Monaco-Ville
Population 32,671 / 43,561 people per sq mile (16,754 people per sq km) / 100%
Total area 0.75 sq. miles (1.95 sq. km)
Languages French*, Italian, Monégasque, English
Religions Roman Catholic 89%, Protestant 6%, Other 5%
Ethnic mix French 32%, Other 29%, Italian 20%, Monégasque 19%
Government Mixed monarchical–parliamentary system
Currency Euro = 100 cents
Literacy rate 99%
Calorie consumption Not available

MONGOLIA
East Asia

Official name Mongolia
Formation 1924 / 1924
Capital Ulan Bator
Population 2.7 million / 4 people per sq mile (2 people per sq km) / 57%
Total area 604,247 sq. miles (1,565,000 sq. km)
Languages Khalkha Mongolian*, Kazakh, Chinese, Russian
Religions Tibetan Buddhist 96%, Muslim 4%
Ethnic mix Khalkh 82%, Other 9%, Kazakh 4%, Dorvod 3%, Bayad 2%
Government Mixed presidential–parliamentary system
Currency Tugrik (tögrög) = 100 möngo
Literacy rate 98%
Calorie consumption 2249 calories

MONTENEGRO
Southeast Europe

Official name Republic of Montenegro
Formation 2006 / 2006
Capital Podgorica
Population 684,736 / 128 people per sq mile (50 people per sq km) / 62%
Total area 5332 sq. miles (13,812 sq. km)
Languages Montenegrin*, Serbian, Albanian, Bosniak, Croatian
Religions Orthodox Christian 74%, Muslim 18%, Other 4%Roman Catholic 4%
Ethnic mix Montenegrin 43%, Serb 32%, Other 12%, Bosniak 8%, Albanian 5%
Government Parliamentary system
Currency Euro = 100 cents
Literacy rate 98%
Calorie consumption Not available

MOROCCO
North Africa

Official name Kingdom of Morocco
Formation 1956 / 1969
Capital Rabat
Population 32.4 million / 188 people per sq mile (73 people per sq km) / 58%
Total area 172,316 sq. miles (446,300 sq. km)
Languages Arabic*, Tamazight (Berber), French, Spanish
Religions Muslim (mainly Sunni) 99%, Other (mostly Christian) 1%
Ethnic mix Arab 70%, Berber 29%, European 1%
Government Mixed monarchical–parliamentary system
Currency Moroccan dirham = 100 centimes
Literacy rate 52%
Calorie consumption 3052 calories

MOZAMBIQUE
Southern Africa

Official name Republic of Mozambique
Formation 1975 / 1975
Capital Maputo
Population 20.5 million / 68 people per sq mile (26 people per sq km) / 37%
Total area 309,494 sq. miles (801,590 sq. km)
Languages Portuguese*, Makua, Xitsonga, Sena, Lomwe
Religions Traditional beliefs 56%, Christian 30%, Muslim 14%
Ethnic mix Makua Lomwe 47%, Tsonga 23%, Malawi 12%, Shona 11%, Yao 4%, Other 3%
Government Presidential system
Currency New metical = 100 centavos
Literacy rate 46%
Calorie consumption 2079 calories

NAMIBIA
Southern Africa

Official name Republic of Namibia
Formation 1990 / 1994
Capital Windhoek
Population 2.1 million / 7 people per sq mile (3 people per sq km) / 33%
Total area 318,694 sq. miles (825,418 sq. km)
Languages English*, Ovambo, Kavango, Bergdama, German, Afrikaans
Religions Christian 90%, Traditional beliefs 10%
Ethnic mix Ovambo 50%, Other tribes 24%, Kavango 9%, Damara 8%, Herero 8%, Other 1%
Government Presidential system
Currency Namibian dollar = 100 cents
Literacy rate 85%
Calorie consumption 2278 calories

NAURU
Australasia & Oceania

Official name Republic of Nauru
Formation 1968 / 1968
Capital None
Population 13,528 / 1670 people per sq mile (644 people per sq km)
Total area 8.1 sq. miles (21 sq. km)
Languages Nauruan*, Kiribati, Chinese, Tuvaluan, English
Religions Nauruan Congregational Church 60%, Roman Catholic 35%, Other 5%
Ethnic mix Nauruan 62%, Other Pacific islanders 27%, Asian 8%, European 3%
Government Nonparty system
Currency Australian dollar = 100 cents
Literacy rate 95%
Calorie consumption Not available

NEPAL
South Asia

Official name Nepal
Formation 1769 / 1769
Capital Kathmandu
Population 28.2 million / 534 people per sq mile (206 people per sq km) / 15%
Total area 54,363 sq. miles (140,800 sq. km)
Languages Nepali*, Maithili, Bhojpuri
Religions Hindu 90%, Buddhist 5%, Muslim 3%, Other (including Christian) 2%
Ethnic mix Other 52%, Chhetri 16%, Hill Brahman 13%, Tharu 7%, Magar 7%, Tamang 5%
Government Parliamentary system
Currency Nepalese rupee = 100 paisa
Literacy rate 49%
Calorie consumption 2453 calories

NETHERLANDS
Northwest Europe

Official name Kingdom of the Netherlands
Formation 1648 / 1839
Capital Amsterdam; The Hague (administrative)
Population 16.4 million / 1252 people per sq mile (483 people per sq km) / 66%
Total area 16,033 sq. miles (41,526 sq. km)
Languages Dutch*, Frisian
Religions Roman Catholic 36%, Other 34%, Protestant 27%, Muslim 3%
Ethnic mix Dutch 82%, Other 12%, Surinamese 2%, Turkish 2%, Moroccan 2%
Government Parliamentary system
Currency Euro = 100 cents
Literacy rate 99%
Calorie consumption 3362 calories

NEW ZEALAND
Australasia & Oceania

Official name New Zealand
Formation 1947 / 1947
Capital Wellington
Population 4.1 million / 40 people per sq mile (15 people per sq km) / 86%
Total area 103,737 sq. miles (268,680 sq. km)
Languages English*, Maori*
Religions Anglican 24%, Other 22%, Presbyterian 18%, Nonreligious 16%, Roman Catholic 15%, Methodist 5%
Ethnic mix European 75%, Maori 15%, Other 7%, Samoan 3%
Government Parliamentary system
Currency New Zealand dollar = 100 cents
Literacy rate 99%
Calorie consumption 3219 calories

NICARAGUA
Central America

Official name Republic of Nicaragua
Formation 1838 / 1838
Capital Managua
Population 5.7 million / 124 people per sq mile (48 people per sq km) / 58%
Total area 49,998 sq. miles (129,494 sq. km)
Languages Spanish*, English Creole, Miskito
Religions Roman Catholic 80%, Protestant Evangelical 17%, Other 3%
Ethnic mix Mestizo 69%, White 14%, Black 8%, Amerindian 5%, Zambo 4%
Government Presidential system
Currency Córdoba oro = 100 centavos
Literacy rate 77%
Calorie consumption 2298 calories

NIGER
West Africa

Official name Republic of Niger
Formation 1960 / 1960
Capital Niamey
Population 14.9 million / 30 people per sq mile (12 people per sq km) / 23%
Total area 489,188 sq. miles (1,267,000 sq. km)
Languages French*, Hausa, Djerma, Fulani, Tuareg, Teda
Religions Muslim 85%, Traditional beliefs 14%, Other (including Christian) 1%
Ethnic mix Hausa 55%, Djerma and Songhai 21%, Peul 9%, Tuareg 9%, Other 6%
Government Presidential system
Currency CFA franc = 100 centimes
Literacy rate 29%
Calorie consumption 2130 calories

NIGERIA
West Africa

Official name Federal Republic of Nigeria
Formation 1960 / 1961
Capital Abuja
Population 137 million / 390 people per sq mile (151 people per sq km) / 47%
Total area 356,667 sq. miles (923,768 sq. km)
Languages English*, Hausa, Yoruba, Ibo
Religions Muslim 50%, Christian 40%, Traditional beliefs 10%
Ethnic mix Other 29%, Hausa 21%, Yoruba 21%, Ibo 18%, Fulani 11%
Government Presidential system
Currency Naira = 100 kobo
Literacy rate 67%
Calorie consumption 2726 calories

NORTH KOREA
East Asia

Official name Democratic People's Republic of Korea
Formation 1948 / 1953
Capital Pyongyang
Population 22.7 million / 488 people per sq mile (189 people per sq km) / 61%
Total area 46,540 sq. miles (120,540 sq. km)
Languages Korean*
Religions Atheist 100%
Ethnic mix Korean 100%
Government One-party state
Currency North Korean won = 100 chon
Literacy rate 98%
Calorie consumption 2142 calories

NORWAY
Northern Europe

Official name Kingdom of Norway
Formation 1905 / 1905
Capital Oslo
Population 4.7 million / 40 people per sq mile (15 people per sq km) / 80%
Total area 125,181 sq. miles (324,220 sq. km)
Languages Norwegian* (Bokmål "book language" and Nynorsk "new Norsk"), Sámi
Religions Evangelical Lutheran 89%, Other and nonreligious 10%, Roman Catholic 1%
Ethnic mix Norwegian 93%, Other 6%, Sámi 1%
Government Parliamentary system
Currency Norwegian krone = 100 øre
Literacy rate 99%
Calorie consumption 3484 calories

OMAN
Southwest Asia

Official name Sultanate of Oman
Formation 1951 / 1951
Capital Muscat
Population 2.7 million / 33 people per sq mile (13 people per sq km) / 78%
Total area 82,031 sq. miles (212,460 sq. km)
Languages Arabic*, Baluchi, Farsi, Hindi, Punjabi
Religions Ibadi Muslim 75%, Other Muslim and Hindu 25%
Ethnic mix Arab 88%, Baluchi 4%, Persian 3%, Indian and Pakistani 3%, African 2%
Government Monarchy
Currency Omani rial = 1000 baisa
Literacy rate 81%
Calorie consumption Not available

PAKISTAN
South Asia

Official name Islamic Republic of Pakistan
Formation 1947 / 1971
Capital Islamabad
Population 165 million / 553 people per sq mile (214 people per sq km) / 34%
Total area 310,401 sq. miles (803,940 sq. km)
Languages Urdu*, Punjabi, Sindhi, Pashtu, Baluchi, Brahui
Religions Sunni Muslim 77%, Shi'a Muslim 20%, Hindu 2%, Christian 1%
Ethnic mix Punjabi 56%, Pathan (Pashtun) 15%, Sindhi 14%, Mohajir 7%, Other 4%, Baluchi 4%
Government Presidential system
Currency Pakistani rupee = 100 paisa
Literacy rate 50%
Calorie consumption 2419 calories

PALAU
Australasia & Oceania

Official name Republic of Palau
Formation 1994 / 1994
Capital Melekeok
Population 20,842 / 106 people per sq mile (41 people per sq km) / 68%
Total area 177 sq. miles (458 sq. km)
Languages Palauan*, English*, Japanese, Angaur, Tobi, Sonsorolese
Religions Christian 66%, Modekngei 34%
Ethnic mix Palauan 74%, Filipino 16%, Other 6%, Chinese and other Asian 4%
Government Nonparty system
Currency US dollar = 100 cents
Literacy rate 98%
Calorie consumption Not available

PANAMA
Central America

Official name Republic of Panama
Formation 1903 / 1903
Capital Panama City
Population 3.3 million / 112 people per sq mile (43 people per sq km) / 57%
Total area 30,193 sq. miles (78,200 sq. km)
Languages English Creole, Spanish*, Amerindian languages, Chibchan languages
Religions Roman Catholic 86%, Other 8%, Protestant 6%
Ethnic mix Mestizo 60%, White 14%, Black 12%, Amerindian 8%, Asian 4%, Other 2%
Government Presidential system
Currency Balboa = 100 centésimos
Literacy rate 92%
Calorie consumption 2272 calories

PAPUA NEW GUINEA
Australasia & Oceania

Official name Independent State of Papua New Guinea
Formation 1975 / 1975
Capital Port Moresby
Population 6.1 million / 35 people per sq mile (13 people per sq km) / 13%
Total area 178,703 sq. miles (462,840 sq. km)
Languages English*, Pidgin English, Papuan, Motu, 750 (est.) native languages
Religions Protestant 60%, Roman Catholic 37%, Other 3%
Ethnic mix Melanesian and mixed race 100%
Government Parliamentary system
Currency Kina = 100 toea
Literacy rate 57%
Calorie consumption 2193 calories

PARAGUAY
South America

Official name Republic of Paraguay
Formation 1811 / 1938
Capital Asunción
Population 6.4 million / 42 people per sq mile (16 people per sq km) / 58%
Total area 157,046 sq. miles (406,750 sq. km)
Languages Spanish*, Guaraní, German
Religions Roman Catholic 96%, Protestant (including Mennonite) 4%
Ethnic mix Mestizo 91%, Other 7%, Amerindian 2%
Government Presidential system
Currency Guaraní = 100 céntimos
Literacy rate 93%
Calorie consumption 2565 calories

PERU
South America

Official name Republic of Peru
Formation 1824 / 1941
Capital Lima
Population 28.8 million / 58 people per sq mile (22 people per sq km) / 74%
Total area 496,223 sq. miles (1,285,200 sq. km)
Languages Spanish*, Quechua*, Aymara
Religions Roman Catholic 95%, Other 5%
Ethnic mix Amerindian 50%, Mestizo 40%, White 7%, Other 3%
Government Presidential system
Currency New sol = 100 céntimos
Literacy rate 88%
Calorie consumption 2571 calories

PHILIPPINES
Southeast Asia

Official name Republic of the Philippines
Formation 1946 / 1946
Capital Manila
Population 85.9 million / 746 people per sq mile (288 people per sq km) / 62%
Total area 115,830 sq. miles (300,000 sq. km)
Languages English*, Filipino*, Tagalog, Cebuano, Ilocano, Hiligaynon, many other local languages
Religions Roman Catholic 83%, Protestant 9%, Muslim 5%, Other (including Buddhist) 3%
Ethnic mix Other 34%, Tagalog 28%, Cebuano 13%, Ilocano 9%, Hiligaynon 8%, Bisaya 8%
Government Presidential system
Currency Philippine peso = 100 centavos
Literacy rate 93%
Calorie consumption 2379 calories

POLAND
Northern Europe

Official name Republic of Poland
Formation 1918 / 1945
Capital Warsaw
Population 38.5 million / 328 people per sq mile (126 people per sq km) / 62%
Total area 120,728 sq. miles (312,685 sq. km)
Languages Polish*
Religions Roman Catholic 93%, Other and nonreligious 5%, Orthodox Christian 2%
Ethnic mix Polish 97%, Other 3%
Government Parliamentary system
Currency Zloty = 100 groszy
Literacy rate 99%
Calorie consumption 3374 calories

PORTUGAL
Southwest Europe

Official name The Portuguese Republic
Formation 1139 / 1640
Capital Lisbon
Population 10.6 million / 299 people per sq mile (115 people per sq km) / 55%
Total area 35,672 sq. miles (92,391 sq. km)
Languages Portuguese*
Religions Roman Catholic 97%, Other 2%, Protestant 1%
Ethnic mix Portuguese 98%, African and other 2%
Government Parliamentary system
Currency Euro = 100 cents
Literacy rate 92%
Calorie consumption 3741 calories

QATAR
Southwest Asia

Official name State of Qatar
Formation 1971 / 1971
Capital Doha
Population 907,229 / 214 people per sq mile (82 people per sq km) / 92%
Total area 4416 sq. miles (11,437 sq. km)
Languages Arabic*
Religions Muslim (mainly Sunni) 95%, Other 5%
Ethnic mix Arab 40%, Indian 18%, Pakistani 18%, Other 14%, Iranian 10%
Government Monarchy
Currency Qatar riyal = 100 dirhams
Literacy rate 89%
Calorie consumption Not available

ROMANIA
Southeast Europe

Official name Romania
Formation 1878 / 1947
Capital Bucharest
Population 21.5 million / 242 people per sq mile (93 people per sq km) / 55%
Total area 91,699 sq. miles (237,500 sq. km)
Languages Romanian*, Hungarian (Magyar), Romani, German
Religions Romanian Orthodox 87%, Roman Catholic 5%, Protestant 4%, Other 2%, Greek Orthodox 1%, Greek Catholic (Uniate) 1%
Ethnic mix Romanian 89%, Magyar 7%, Roma 2%, Other 2%
Government Presidential system
Currency New Romanian leu = 100 bani
Literacy rate 97%
Calorie consumption 3455 calories

RUSSIAN FEDERATION
Europe / Asia

Official name Russian Federation
Formation 1480 / 1991
Capital Moscow
Population 142 million / 22 people per sq mile (8 people per sq km) / 73%
Total area 6,592,735 sq. miles (17,075,200 sq. km)
Languages Russian*, Tatar, Ukrainian, Chavash, various other national languages
Religions Orthodox Christian 75%, Muslim 14%, Other 11%
Ethnic mix Russian 80%, Other 12%, Tatar 4%, Ukrainian 2%, Bashkir 1%, Chavash 1%
Government Mixed Presidential–Parliamentary system
Currency Russian rouble = 100 kopeks
Literacy rate 99%
Calorie consumption 3072 calories

RWANDA
Central Africa

Official name Republic of Rwanda
Formation 1962 / 1962
Capital Kigali
Population 9.4 million / 976 people per sq mile (377 people per sq km) / 20%
Total area 10,169 sq. miles (26,338 sq. km)
Languages Kinyarwanda*, French*, English*, Kiswahili
Religions Roman Catholic 56%, Traditional beliefs 25%, Muslim 10%, Protestant 9%
Ethnic mix Hutu 90%, Tutsi 9%, Other (including Twa) 1%
Government Presidential system
Currency Rwanda franc = 100 centimes
Literacy rate 65%
Calorie consumption 2084 calories

SAINT KITTS & NEVIS
West Indies

Official name Federation of Saint Christopher and Nevis
Formation 1983 / 1983
Capital Basseterre
Population 39,349 / 283 people per sq mile (109 people per sq km) / 32%
Total area 101 sq. miles (261 sq. km)
Languages English*, English Creole
Religions Anglican 33%, Methodist 29%, Other 22%, Moravian 9%, Roman Catholic 7%
Ethnic mix Black 95%, Mixed race 3%, White 1%, Other and Amerindian 1%
Government Parliamentary system
Currency Eastern Caribbean dollar = 100 cents
Literacy rate 98%
Calorie consumption 2609 calories

SAINT LUCIA
West Indies

Official name Saint Lucia
Formation 1979 / 1979
Capital Castries
Population 170,649 / 723 people per sq mile (280 people per sq km) / 31%
Total area 239 sq. miles (620 sq. km)
Languages English*, French Creole
Religions Roman Catholic 90%, Other 10%
Ethnic mix Black 83%, Mulatto (mixed race) 13%, Asian 3%, Other 1%
Government Parliamentary system
Currency Eastern Caribbean dollar = 100 cents
Literacy rate 95%
Calorie consumption 2988 calories

SAINT VINCENT & THE GRENADINES
West Indies

Official name Saint Vincent and the Grenadines
Formation 1979 / 1979
Capital Kingstown
Population 118,149 / 902 people per sq mile (347 people per sq km) / 59%
Total area 150 sq. miles (389 sq. km)
Languages English*, English Creole
Religions Anglican 47%, Methodist 28%, Roman Catholic 13%, Other 12%
Ethnic mix Black 77%, Mulatto (mixed race) 16%, Other 3%, Carib 3%, Asian 1%
Government Parliamentary system
Currency Eastern Caribbean dollar = 100 cents
Literacy rate 88%
Calorie consumption 2599 calories

SAMOA
Australasia & Oceania

Official name Independent State of Samoa
Formation 1962 / 1962
Capital Apia
Population 214,265 / 196 people per sq mile (76 people per sq km) / 22%
Total area 1104 sq. miles (2860 sq. km)
Languages Samoan*, English*
Religions Christian 99%, Other 1%
Ethnic mix Polynesian 90%, Euronesian 9%, Other 1%
Government Parliamentary system
Currency Tala = 100 sene
Literacy rate 99%
Calorie consumption 2945 calories

SAN MARINO
Southern Europe

Official name Republic of San Marino
Formation 1631 / 1631
Capital San Marino
Population 29,615 / 1234 people per sq mile (485 people per sq km) / 89%
Total area 23.6 sq. miles (61 sq. km)
Languages Italian*
Religions Roman Catholic 93%, Other and nonreligious 7%
Ethnic mix Sammarinese 88%, Italian 10%, Other 2%
Government Parliamentary system
Currency Euro = 100 cents
Literacy rate 99%
Calorie consumption Not available

SÃO TOMÉ & PRÍNCIPE
West Africa

Official name The Democratic Republic of Sao Tome and Principe
Formation 1975 / 1975
Capital São Tomé
Population 199,579 / 538 people per sq mile (208 people per sq km) / 38%
Total area 386 sq. miles (1001 sq. km)
Languages Portuguese*, Portuguese Creole
Religions Roman Catholic 84%, Other 16%
Ethnic mix Black 90%, Portuguese and Creole 10%
Government Presidential system
Currency Dobra = 100 céntimos
Literacy rate 83%
Calorie consumption 2460 calories

SAUDI ARABIA
Southwest Asia

Official name Kingdom of Saudi Arabia
Formation 1932 / 1932
Capital Riyadh
Population 25.8 million / 32 people per sq mile (12 people per sq km) / 88%
Total area 756,981 sq. miles (1,960,582 sq. km)
Languages Arabic*
Religions Sunni Muslim 85%, Shi'a Muslim 15%
Ethnic mix Arab 90%, Afro-Asian 10%
Government Monarchy
Currency Saudi riyal = 100 halalat
Literacy rate 79%
Calorie consumption 2844 calories

SENEGAL
West Africa

Official name Republic of Senegal
Formation 1960 / 1960
Capital Dakar
Population 12.2 million / 164 people per sq mile (63 people per sq km) / 50%
Total area 75,749 sq. miles (196,190 sq. km)
Languages French*, Wolof, Pulaar, Serer, Diola, Mandinka, Malinke, Soninke
Religions Sunni Muslim 90%, Christian (mainly Roman Catholic) 5%, Traditional beliefs 5%
Ethnic mix Wolof 43%, Serer 15%, Other 14%, Peul 14%, Toucouleur 9%, Diola 5%
Government Presidential system
Currency CFA franc = 100 centimes
Literacy rate 39%
Calorie consumption 2279 calories

SERBIA
Southeast Europe

Official name Republic of Serbia
Formation 2006 / 2008
Capital Belgrade
Population 8.1 million / 271 people per sq mile (105 people per sq km) / 52%
Total area 29,905 sq miles (77,453 sq km)
Languages Serbian*, Hungarian (Magyar)
Religions Orthodox Christian 85%, Other 6%, Roman Catholic 6%, Muslim 3%
Ethnic mix Serb 83%, Other 10%, Magyar 4%, Bosniak 2%, Roma 1%
Government Parliamentary system
Currency Dinar = 100 para
Literacy rate 96%
Calorie consumption 2678 calories

SEYCHELLES
Indian Ocean

Official name Republic of Seychelles
Formation 1976 / 1976
Capital Victoria
Population 81,895 / 787 people per sq mile (303 people per sq km) / 53%
Total area 176 sq. miles (455 sq. km)
Languages French Creole*, English*, French*
Religions Roman Catholic 90%, Anglican 8%, Other (including Muslim) 2%
Ethnic mix Creole 89%, Indian 5%, Other 4%, Chinese 2%
Government Presidential system
Currency Seychelles rupee = 100 cents
Literacy rate 92%
Calorie consumption 2465 calories

SIERRA LEONE
West Africa

Official name Republic of Sierra Leone
Formation 1961 / 1961
Capital Freetown
Population 5.8 million / 210 people per sq mile (81 people per sq km) / 40%
Total area 27,698 sq. miles (71,740 sq. km)
Languages English*, Mende, Temne, Krio
Religions Muslim 30%, Traditional beliefs 30%, Other 30%, Christian 10%
Ethnic mix Mende 35%, Temne 32%, Other 21%, Limba 8%, Kuranko 4%
Government Presidential system
Currency Leone = 100 cents
Literacy rate 35%
Calorie consumption 1936 calories

SINGAPORE
Southeast Asia

Official name Republic of Singapore
Formation 1965 / 1965
Capital Singapore
Population 4.4 million / 18644 people per sq mile (7213 people per sq km) / 100%
Total area 250 sq. miles (648 sq. km)
Languages Mandarin*, Malay*, Tamil*, English*
Religions Buddhist 55%, Taoist 22%, Muslim 16%, Hindu, Christian, and Sikh 7%
Ethnic mix Chinese 77%, Malay 14%, Indian 8%, Other 1%
Government Parliamentary system
Currency Singapore dollar = 100 cents
Literacy rate 93%
Calorie consumption Not available

SLOVAKIA
Central Europe

Official name Slovak Republic
Formation 1993 / 1993
Capital Bratislava
Population 5.4 million / 285 people per sq mile (110 people per sq km) / 58%
Total area 18,859 sq. miles (48,845 sq. km)
Languages Slovak*, Hungarian (Magyar), Czech
Religions Roman Catholic 60%, Other 18%, Atheist 10%, Protestant 8%, Orthodox Christian 4%
Ethnic mix Slovak 86%, Magyar 10%, Roma 2%, Other 1%, Czech 1%
Government Parliamentary system
Currency Euro = 100 cents
Literacy rate 99%
Calorie consumption 2889 calories

SLOVENIA
Central Europe

Official name Republic of Slovenia
Formation 1991 / 1991
Capital Ljubljana
Population 2 million / 256 people per sq mile (99 people per sq km) / 51%
Total area 7820 sq. miles (20,253 sq. km)
Languages Slovenian*
Religions Roman Catholic 96%, Other 3%, Muslim 1%
Ethnic mix Slovene 83%, Other 12%, Serb 2%, Croat 2%, Bosniak 1%
Government Parliamentary system
Currency Euro = 100 cents
Literacy rate 99%
Calorie consumption 3001 calories

SOLOMON ISLANDS
Australasia & Oceania

Official name Solomon Islands
Formation 1978 / 1978
Capital Honiara
Population 566,842 / 52 people per sq mile (20 people per sq km) / 17%
Total area 10,985 sq. miles (28,450 sq. km)
Languages English*, Pidgin English, Melanesian Pidgin
Religions Church of Melanesia (Anglican) 34%, Roman Catholic 19%, South Seas Evangelical Church 17%, Methodist 11%, Seventh-day Adventist 10%, Other 9%
Ethnic mix Melanesian 94%, Polynesian 4%, Other 2%
Government Parliamentary system
Currency Solomon Islands dollar = 100 cents
Literacy rate 77%
Calorie consumption 2265 calories

SOMALIA
East Africa

Official name The Somali Democratic Republic
Formation 1960 / 1960
Capital Mogadishu
Population 8.8 million / 36 people per sq mile (14 people per sq km) / 35%
Total area 246,199 sq. miles (637,657 sq. km)
Languages Somali*, Arabic*, English, Italian
Religions Sunni Muslim 98%, Christian 2%
Ethnic mix Somali 85%, Other 15%
Government Transitional regime
Currency Somali shilin = 100 senti
Literacy rate 24%
Calorie consumption 1628 calories

SOUTH AFRICA
Southern Africa

Official name Republic of South Africa
Formation 1934 / 1994
Capital Pretoria; Cape Town; Bloemfontein
Population 47.7 million / 101 people per sq mile (39 people per sq km) / 57%
Total area 471,008 sq. miles (1,219,912 sq. km)
Languages English, isiZulu, isiXhosa, Afrikaans, Sepedi, Setswana, Sesotho, Xitsonga, siSwati, Tshivenda, isiNdebele
Religions Christian 68%, Traditional beliefs and animist 29%, Muslim 2%, Hindu 1%
Ethnic mix Black 79%, Colored 10%, White 9%, Asian 2%
Government Presidential system
Currency Rand = 100 cents
Literacy rate 82%
Calorie consumption 2956 calories

SOUTH KOREA
East Asia

Official name Republic of Korea
Formation 1948 / 1953
Capital Seoul
Population 48.1 million / 1262 people per sq mile (487 people per sq km) / 81%
Total area 38,023 sq. miles (98,480 sq. km)
Languages Korean*
Religions Mahayana Buddhist 47%, Protestant 38%, Roman Catholic 11%, Confucianist 3%, Other 1%
Ethnic mix Korean 100%
Government Presidential system
Currency South Korean won = 100 chon
Literacy rate 98%
Calorie consumption 3058 calories

SPAIN
Southwest Europe

Official name Kingdom of Spain
Formation 1492 / 1713
Capital Madrid
Population 43.6 million / 226 people per sq mile (87 people per sq km) / 77%
Total area 194,896 sq. miles (504,782 sq. km)
Languages Spanish*, Catalan*, Galician*, Basque*
Religions Roman Catholic 96%, Other 4%
Ethnic mix Castilian Spanish 72%, Catalan 17%, Galician 6%, Basque 2%, Other 2%, Roma 1%
Government Parliamentary system
Currency Euro = 100 cents
Literacy rate 98%
Calorie consumption 3371 calories

SRI LANKA
South Asia

Official name Democratic Socialist Republic of Sri Lanka
Formation 1948 / 1948
Capital Colombo
Population 21.1 million / 844 people per sq mile (326 people per sq km) / 21%
Total area 25,332 sq. miles (65,610 sq. km)
Languages Sinhala*, Tamil*, Sinhala-Tamil, English
Religions Buddhist 69%, Hindu 15%, Muslim 8%, Christian 8%
Ethnic mix Sinhalese 82%, Tamil 9%, Moor 8%, Other 1%
Government Mixed presidential–parliamentary system
Currency Sri Lanka rupee = 100 cents
Literacy rate 91%
Calorie consumption 2385 calories

SUDAN
East Africa

Official name Republic of the Sudan
Formation 1956 / 1956
Capital Khartoum
Population 37.8 million / 39 people per sq mile (15 people per sq km) / 40%
Total area 967,493 sq. miles (2,505,810 sq. km)
Languages Arabic / Arabic, Dinka, Nuer, Nubian, Beja, Zande, Bari, Fur, Shilluk, Lotuko
Religions Muslim (mainly Sunni) 70%, Traditional beliefs 20%, Christian 9%, Other 1%
Ethnic mix Other Black 52%, Arab 40%, Dinka and Beja 7%, Other 1%
Government Presidential system
Currency new Sudanese pound or dinar = 100 piastres
Literacy rate 61%
Calorie consumption 2228 calories

SURINAM
South America

Official name Republic of Suriname
Formation 1975 / 1975
Capital Paramaribo
Population 470,784 / 8 people per sq mile (3 people per sq km) / 77%
Total area 63,039 sq. miles (163,270 sq. km)
Languages Sranan (Creole), Dutch*, Javanese, Sarnami Hindi, Saramaccan, Chinese, Carib
Religions Hindu 27%, Protestant 25%, Roman Catholic 23%, Muslim 20%, Traditional beliefs 5%
Ethnic mix Creole 34%, South Asian 34%, Javanese 18%, Black 9%, Other 5%
Government Parliamentary system
Currency Surinamese dollar = 100 cents
Literacy rate 90%
Calorie consumption 2652 calories

SWAZILAND
Southern Africa

Official name Kingdom of Swaziland
Formation 1968 / 1968
Capital Mbabane
Population 1 million / 151 people per sq mile (58 people per sq km) / 24%
Total area 6704 sq. miles (17,363 sq. km)
Languages English*, siSwati*, isiZulu, Xitsonga
Religions Christian 60%, Traditional beliefs 40%
Ethnic mix Swazi 97%, Other 3%
Government Monarchy
Currency Lilangeni = 100 cents
Literacy rate 80%
Calorie consumption 2322 calories

SWEDEN
Northern Europe

Official name Kingdom of Sweden
Formation 1523 / 1921
Capital Stockholm
Population 9.1 million / 57 people per sq mile (22 people per sq km) / 83%
Total area 173,731 sq. miles (449,964 sq. km)
Languages Swedish*, Finnish, Sámi
Religions Evangelical Lutheran 82%, Other 13%, Roman Catholic 2%, Muslim 2%, Orthodox Christian 1%
Ethnic mix Swedish 86%, Foreign-born or first-generation immigrant 12%, Finnish and Sámi 2%
Government Parliamentary system
Currency Swedish krona = 100 ore
Literacy rate 99%
Calorie consumption 3185 calories

SWITZERLAND
Central Europe

Official name Swiss Confederation
Formation 1291 / 1857
Capital Bern
Population 7.3 million / 475 people per sq mile (184 people per sq km) / 68%
Total area 15,942 sq. miles (41,290 sq. km)
Languages German*, Swiss-German, French*, Italian*, Romansch
Religions Roman Catholic 42%, Protestant 35%, Other and nonreligious 19%, Muslim 4%
Ethnic mix German 64%, French 20%, Other 9%, Italian 6%, Romansch 1%
Government Parliamentary system
Currency Swiss franc = 100 rappen/centimes
Literacy rate 99%
Calorie consumption 3526 calories

SYRIA
Southwest Asia

Official name Syrian Arab Republic
Formation 1941 / 1967
Capital Damascus
Population 20 million / 281 people per sq mile (109 people per sq km) / 50%
Total area 71,498 sq. miles (184,180 sq. km)
Languages Arabic*, French, Kurdish, Armenian, Circassian, Turkic languages, Assyrian, Aramaic
Religions Sunni Muslim 74%, Other Muslim 16%, Christian 10%
Ethnic mix Arab 89%, Kurdish 6%, Other 3%, Armenian, Turkmen, and Circassian 2%
Government One-party state
Currency Syrian pound = 100 piastres
Literacy rate 80%
Calorie consumption 3038 calories

TAIWAN
East Asia

Official name Republic of China (ROC)
Formation 1949 / 1949
Capital Taipei
Population 22.9 million / 1835 people per sq mile (709 people per sq km) / 80%
Total area 13,892 sq. miles (35,980 sq. km)
Languages Amoy Chinese, Mandarin Chinese*, Hakka Chinese
Religions Buddhist, Confucianist, and Taoist 93%, Christian 5%, Other 2%
Ethnic mix Han (pre-20th-century migration) 84%, Han (20th-century migration) 14%, Aboriginal 2%
Government Presidential system
Currency Taiwan dollar = 100 cents
Literacy rate 97%
Calorie consumption Not available

TAJIKISTAN
Central Asia

Official name Republic of Tajikistan
Formation 1991 / 1991
Capital Dushanbe
Population 6.7 million / 121 people per sq mile (47 people per sq km) / 25%
Total area 55,251 sq. miles (143,100 sq. km)
Languages Tajik*, Uzbek, Russian
Religions Sunni Muslim 80%, Other 15%, Shi'a Muslim 5%
Ethnic mix Tajik 80%, Uzbek 15%, Other 3%, Russian 1%, Kyrgyz 1%
Government Presidential system
Currency Somoni = 100 diram
Literacy rate 99%
Calorie consumption 1828 calories

TANZANIA
East Africa

Official name United Republic of Tanzania
Formation 1964 / 1964
Capital Dodoma
Population 39.7 million / 116 people per sq mile (45 people per sq km) / 36%
Total area 364,898 sq. miles (945,087 sq. km)
Languages Kiswahili*, Sukuma, Chagga, Nyamwezi, Hehe, Makonde, Yao, Sandawe, English*
Religions Muslim 33%, Christian 33%, Traditional beliefs 30%, Other 4%
Ethnic mix Native African (over 120 tribes) 99%, European, Asian, and Arab 1%
Government Presidential system
Currency Tanzanian shilling = 100 cents
Literacy rate 69%
Calorie consumption 1975 calories

THAILAND
Southeast Asia

Official name Kingdom of Thailand
Formation 1238 / 1907
Capital Bangkok
Population 68.3 million / 346 people per sq mile (134 people per sq km) / 32%
Total area 198,455 sq. miles (514,000 sq. km)
Languages Thai*, Chinese, Malay, Khmer, Mon, Karen, Miao
Religions Buddhist 95%, Muslim 4%, Other (including Christian) 1%
Ethnic mix Thai 83%, Chinese 12%, Malay 3%, Khmer and Other 2%
Government Parliamentary system
Currency Baht = 100 satang
Literacy rate 93%
Calorie consumption 2467 calories

TOGO
West Africa

Official name The Togolese Republic
Formation 1960 / 1960
Capital Lomé
Population 6.5 million / 310 people per sq mile (120 people per sq km) / 36%
Total area 21,924 sq. miles (56,785 sq. km)
Languages French*, Ewe, Kabye, Gurma
Religions Traditional beliefs 50%, Christian 35%, Muslim 15%
Ethnic mix Ewe 46%, Other African 41%, Kabye 12%, European 1%
Government Presidential system
Currency CFA franc = 100 centimes
Literacy rate 53%
Calorie consumption 2345 calories

TONGA
Australasia & Oceania

Official name Kingdom of Tonga
Formation 1970 / 1970
Capital Nuku'alofa
Population 116,921 / 421 people per sq mile (162 people per sq km) / 34%
Total area 289 sq. miles (748 sq. km)
Languages English*, Tongan*
Religions Free Wesleyan 41%, Other 17%, Roman Catholic 16%, Church of Jesus Christ of Latter-day Saints 14%, Free Church of Tonga 12%
Ethnic mix Tongan 98%, Other 2%
Government Monarchy
Currency Pa'anga (Tongan dollar) = 100 seniti
Literacy rate 99%
Calorie consumption Not available

TRINIDAD & TOBAGO
West Indies

Official name Republic of Trinidad and Tobago
Formation 1962 / 1962
Capital Port-of-Spain
Population 1.3 million / 656 people per sq mile (253 people per sq km) / 76%
Total area 1980 sq. miles (5128 sq. km)
Languages English Creole, English*, Hindi, French, Spanish
Religions Roman Catholic 32%, Hindu 24%, Protestant 14%, Anglican 14%, Other and nonreligious 9%, Muslim 7%
Ethnic mix East Indian 40%, Black 40%, Mixed race 18%, Other 1%, White and Chinese 1%
Government Parliamentary system
Currency Trinidad and Tobago dollar = 100 cents
Literacy rate 99%
Calorie consumption 2732 calories

TUNISIA
North Africa

Official name The Tunisian Republic
Formation 1956 / 1956
Capital Tunis
Population 10.3 million / 172 people per sq mile (66 people per sq km) / 64%
Total area 63,169 sq. miles (163,610 sq. km)
Languages Arabic*, French
Religions Muslim (mainly Sunni) 98%, Christian 1%, Jewish 1%
Ethnic mix Arab and Berber 98%, Jewish 1%, European 1%
Government Presidential system
Currency Tunisian dinar = 1000 millimes
Literacy rate 74%
Calorie consumption 3238 calories

TURKEY
Asia / Europe

Official name Republic of Turkey
Formation 1923 / 1939
Capital Ankara
Population 75.2 million / 253 people per sq mile (98 people per sq km) / 67%
Total area 301,382 sq. miles (780,580 sq. km)
Languages Turkish*, Kurdish, Arabic, Circassian, Armenian, Greek, Georgian, Ladino
Religions Muslim (mainly Sunni) 99%, Other 1%
Ethnic mix Turkish 70%, Kurdish 20%, Other 8%, Arab 2%
Government Parliamentary system
Currency new Turkish lira = 100 kurus
Literacy rate 98%
Calorie consumption 3357 calories

TURKMENISTAN
Central Asia

Official name Turkmenistan
Formation 1991 / 1991
Capital Ashgabat
Population 5 million / 27 people per sq mile (10 people per sq km) / 46%
Total area 188,455 sq. miles (488,100 sq. km)
Languages Turkmen*, Uzbek, Russian, Kazakh, Tatar
Religions Sunni Muslim 87%, Orthodox Christian 11%, Other 2%
Ethnic mix Turkmen 77%, Uzbek 9%, Russian 7%, Other 4%, Kazakh 2%, Tatar 1%
Government One-party state
Currency Manat = 100 tenge
Literacy rate 99%
Calorie consumption 2742 calories

TUVALU
Australasia & Oceania

Official name Tuvalu
Formation 1978 / 1978
Capital Fongafale, on Funafuti Atoll
Population 11,992 / 1199 people per sq mile (461 people per sq km) / 57%
Total area 10 sq. miles (26 sq. km)
Languages English*, Tuvaluan, Kiribati
Religions Church of Tuvalu 97%, Baha'i 1%, Seventh-day Adventist 1%, Other 1%
Ethnic mix Polynesian 92%, Other 6%, Kiribati 2%
Government Nonparty system
Currency Australian dollar and Tuvaluan dollar = 100 cents
Literacy rate 98%
Calorie consumption Not available

UGANDA
East Africa

Official name Republic of Uganda
Formation 1962 / 1962
Capital Kampala
Population 30.9 million / 401 people per sq mile (155 people per sq km) / 12%
Total area 91,135 sq. miles (236,040 sq. km)
Languages English*, Luganda, Nkole, Chiga, Lango, Acholi, Teso, Lugbara
Religions Roman Catholic 38%, Protestant 33%, Traditional beliefs 13%, Muslim (mainly Sunni) 8%, Other 8%
Ethnic mix Other 50%, Baganda 17%, Banyakole 10%, Basoga 9%, Iteso 7%, Bakiga 7%
Government Presidential system
Currency New Uganda shilling = 100 cents
Literacy rate 67%
Calorie consumption 2410 calories

UKRAINE
Eastern Europe

Official name Ukraine
Formation 1991 / 1991
Capital Kiev
Population 45.5 million / 195 people per sq mile (75 people per sq km) / 67%
Total area 233,089 sq. miles (603,700 sq. km)
Languages Ukrainian*, Russian, Tatar
Religions Christian (mainly Orthodox) 95%, Other 5%
Ethnic mix Ukrainian 78%, Russian 17%, Other 5%
Government Presidential system
Currency Hryvna = 100 kopiykas
Literacy rate 99%
Calorie consumption 3054 calories

UNITED ARAB EMIRATES
Southwest Asia

Official name United Arab Emirates
Formation 1971 / 1972
Capital Abu Dhabi
Population 4.8 million / 149 people per sq mile (57 people per sq km) / 85%
Total area 32,000 sq. miles (82,880 sq. km)
Languages Arabic*, Farsi, Indian and Pakistani languages, English
Religions Muslim (mainly Sunni) 96%, Christian, Hindu, and other 4%
Ethnic mix Asian 60%, Emirian 25%, Other Arab 12%, European 3%
Government Monarchy
Currency UAE dirham = 100 fils
Literacy rate 77%
Calorie consumption 3225 calories

UNITED KINGDOM
Northwest Europe

Official name United Kingdom of Great Britain and Northern Ireland
Formation 1707 / 1922
Capital London
Population 60 million / 643 people per sq mile (248 people per sq km) / 89%
Total area 94,525 sq. miles (244,820 sq. km)
Languages English*, Welsh* (in Wales), Scottish Gaelic, Irish Gaelic
Religions Anglican 45%, Roman Catholic 9%, Presbyterian 4%, Other 42%
Ethnic mix English 80%, Scottish 9%, West Indian, Asian, and other 5%, Northern Irish 3%, Welsh 3%
Government Parliamentary system
Currency Pound sterling = 100 pence
Literacy rate 99%
Calorie consumption 3412 calories

UNITED STATES
North America

Official name United States of America
Formation 1776 / 1959
Capital Washington D.C.
Population 304 million / 86 people per sq mile (33 people per sq km) / 81%
Total area 3,717,792 sq. miles (9,626,091 sq. km)
Languages English*, Spanish, Chinese, French, German, Tagalog, Vietnamese, Italian, Korean, Russian, Polish
Religions Protestant 52%, Roman Catholic 25%, Muslim 2%, Jewish 2%, Other 19%
Ethnic mix White 62%, Hispanic 13%, Black American/African 13%, Other 7%, Asian 4%, Native American 1%
Government Presidential system
Currency US dollar = 100 cents
Literacy rate 99%
Calorie consumption 3774 calories

UZBEKISTAN
Central Asia

Official name Republic of Uzbekistan
Formation 1991 / 1991
Capital Tashkent
Population 27.4 million / 159 people per sq mile (61 people per sq km) / 37%
Total area 172,741 sq. miles (447,400 sq. km)
Languages Uzbek*, Russian, Tajik, Kazakh
Religions Sunni Muslim 88%, Orthodox Christian 9%, Other 3%
Ethnic mix Uzbek 80%, Other 6%, Russian 6%, Tajik 5%, Kazakh 3%
Government Presidential system
Currency Som = 100 tiyin
Literacy rate 99%
Calorie consumption 2241 calories

VANUATU
Australasia & Oceania

Official name Republic of Vanuatu
Formation 1980 / 1980
Capital Port Vila
Population 211,971 / 45 people per sq mile (17 people per sq km) / 23%
Total area 4710 sq. miles (12,200 sq. km)
Languages Bislama* (Melanesian pidgin), English*, French*, other indigenous languages
Religions Presbyterian 37%, Other 19%, Anglican 15%, Roman Catholic 15%, Traditional beliefs 8%, Seventh-day Adventist 6%
Ethnic mix Melanesian 98%, Other 1%, European 1%
Government Parliamentary system
Currency Vatu = 100 centimes
Literacy rate 74%
Calorie consumption 2587 calories

VATICAN CITY
Southern Europe

Official name The Vatican City
Formation 1929 / 1929
Capital Vatican City
Population 821 / 4829 people per sq mile (1866 people per sq km) / 100%
Total area 0.17 sq. miles (0.44 sq. km)
Languages Italian*, Latin*
Religions Roman Catholic 100%
Government Papal state
Currency Euro = 100 cents
Literacy rate 99%
Calorie consumption Not available

VENEZUELA
South America

Official name Bolivarian Republic of Venezuela
Formation 1830 / 1830
Capital Caracas
Population 27.7 million / 81 people per sq mile (31 people per sq km) / 88%
Total area 352,143 sq. miles (912,050 sq. km)
Languages Spanish*, Amerindian languages
Religions Roman Catholic 89%, Protestant and other 11%
Ethnic mix Mestizo 69%, White 20%, Black 9%, Amerindian 2%
Government Presidential system
Currency Bolívar = 100 céntimos
Literacy rate 93%
Calorie consumption 2336 calories

VIETNAM
Southeast Asia

Official name Socialist Republic of Vietnam
Formation 1976 / 1976
Capital Hanoi
Population 86.4 million / 688 people per sq mile (266 people per sq km) / 26%
Total area 127,243 sq. miles (329,560 sq. km)
Languages Vietnamese*, Chinese, Thai, Khmer, Muong, Nung, Miao, Yao, Jarai
Religions Nonreligious 81%, Buddhist 9%, Christian 7%, Other 3%
Ethnic mix Vietnamese 86%, Other 10%, Tay 2%, Thai 2%
Government One-party state
Currency Dông = 10 hao = 100 xu
Literacy rate 90%
Calorie consumption 2566 calories

YEMEN
Southwest Asia

Official name Republic of Yemen
Formation 1990 / 1990
Capital Sana
Population 22.3 million / 103 people per sq mile (40 people per sq km) / 26%
Total area 203,849 sq. miles (527,970 sq. km)
Languages Arabic*
Religions Sunni Muslim 55%, Shi'a Muslim 42%, Christian, Hindu, and Jewish 3%
Ethnic mix Arab 99%, Other 1%
Government Presidential system
Currency Yemeni rial = 100 fils
Literacy rate 49%
Calorie consumption 2038 calories

ZAMBIA
Southern Africa

Official name Republic of Zambia
Formation 1964 / 1964
Capital Lusaka
Population 12.1 million / 42 people per sq mile (16 people per sq km) / 36%
Total area 290,584 sq. miles (752,614 sq. km)
Languages English*, Bemba, Tonga, Nyanja, Lozi, Lala-Bisa, Nsenga
Religions Christian 63%, Traditional beliefs 36%, Muslim and Hindu 1%
Ethnic mix Bemba 34%, Other African 26%, Tonga 16%, Nyanja 14%, Lozi 9%, European 1%
Government Presidential system
Currency Zambian kwacha = 100 ngwee
Literacy rate 68%
Calorie consumption 1927 calories

ZIMBABWE
Southern Africa

Official name Republic of Zimbabwe
Formation 1980 / 1980
Capital Harare
Population 13.2 million / 88 people per sq mile (34 people per sq km) / 35%
Total area 150,803 sq. miles (390,580 sq. km)
Languages English*, Shona, isiNdebele
Religions Syncretic (Christian/traditional beliefs) 50%, Christian 25%, Traditional beliefs 24%, Other (including Muslim) 1%
Ethnic mix Shona 71%, Ndebele 16%, Other African 11%, White 1%, Asian 1%
Government Presidential system
Currency Zimbabwe dollar = 100 cents
Literacy rate 90%
Calorie consumption 1943 calories

URUGUAY
South America

Official name The Oriental Republic of Uruguay
Formation 1828 / 1828
Capital Montevideo
Population 3.5 million / 52 people per sq mile (20 people per sq km) / 93%
Total area 68,039 sq. miles (176,220 sq. km)
Languages Spanish*
Religions Roman Catholic 66%, Other and nonreligious 30%, Jewish 2%, Protestant 2%
Ethnic mix White 90%, Mestizo 6%, Black 4%
Government Presidential system
Currency Uruguayan peso = 100 centésimos
Literacy rate 98%
Calorie consumption 2828 calories

GLOSSARY

This glossary lists all geographical, technical and foreign language terms which appear in the text, followed by a brief definition of the term. Any acronyms used in the text are also listed in full. Terms in italics are for cross-reference and indicate that the word is separately defined in the glossary.

A

Aboriginal The original (indigenous) inhabitants of a country or continent. Especially used with reference to Australia.

Abyssal plain A broad plain found in the depths of the ocean, more than 10,000 ft (3000 m) below sea level.

Acid rain Rain, sleet, snow or mist which has absorbed waste gases from fossil-fuelled power stations and vehicle exhausts, becoming more acid. It causes severe environmental damage.

Adaptation The gradual evolution of plants and animals so that they become better suited to survive and reproduce in their *environment*.

Afforestation The planting of new forest in areas which were once forested but have been cleared.

Agribusiness A term applied to activities such as the growing of crops, rearing of animals or the manufacture of farm machinery, which eventually leads to the supply of agricultural produce at market.

Air mass A huge, homogeneous mass of air, within which horizontal patterns of temperature and *humidity* are consistent. Air masses are separated by *fronts*.

Alliance An agreement between two or more states, to work together to achieve common purposes.

Alluvial fan A large fan-shaped deposit of fine sediments deposited by a river as it emerges from a narrow, mountain valley onto a broad, open *plain*.

Alluvium Material deposited by rivers. Nowadays usually only applied to finer particles of silt and clay.

Alpine Mountain *environment*, between the *treeline* and the level of permanent snow cover.

Alpine mountains Ranges of mountains formed between 30 and 65 million years ago, by *folding*, in west and central Europe.

Amerindian A term applied to people *indigenous* to North, Central and South America.

Animal husbandry The business of rearing animals.

Antarctic circle The parallel which lies at *latitude* of 66° 32′ S.

Anticline A geological *fold* that forms an arch shape, curving upwards in the rock *strata*.

Anticyclone An area of relatively high atmospheric pressure.

Aquaculture Collective term for the farming of produce derived from the sea, including fish-farming, the cultivation of shellfish, and plants such as seaweed.

Aquifer A body of rock which can absorb water. Also applied to any rock strata that have sufficient porosity to yield *groundwater* through wells or springs.

Arable Land which has been ploughed and is being used, or is suitable, for growing crops.

Archipelago A group or chain of islands.

Arctic Circle The parallel which lies at a *latitude* of 66° 32′ N.

Arête A thin, jagged mountain ridge which divides two adjacent *cirques*, found in regions where *glaciation* has occurred.

Arid Dry. An area of low rainfall, where the rate of *evaporation* may be greater than that of *precipitation*. Often defined as those areas that receive less than one inch (25 mm) of rain a year. In these areas only drought-resistant plants can survive.

Artesian well A naturally occurring source of underground water, stored in an *aquifer*.

Artisanal Small-scale, manual operation, such as fishing, using little or no machinery.

ASEAN Association of Southeast Asian Nations. Established in 1967 to promote economic, social and cultural co-operation. Its members include Brunei, Indonesia, Malaysia, Philippines, Singapore and Thailand.

Aseismic A region where *earthquake* activity has ceased.

Asteroid A minor planet circling the Sun, mainly between the orbits of Mars and Jupiter.

Asthenosphere A zone of hot, partially melted rock, which underlies the *lithosphere*, within the Earth's *crust*.

Atmosphere The envelope of odourless, colourless and tasteless gases surrounding the Earth, consisting of *oxygen* (23%), *nitrogen* (75%), argon (1%), *carbon dioxide* (0.03%), as well as tiny proportions of other gases.

Atmospheric pressure The pressure created by the action of gravity on the gases surrounding the Earth.

Atoll A ring-shaped island or *coral reef* often enclosing a *lagoon* of sea water.

Avalanche The rapid movement of a mass of snow and ice down a steep slope. Similar movements of other materials are described as *rock avalanches* or *landslides* and *sand avalanches*.

B

Badlands A landscape that has been heavily eroded and dissected by rainwater, and which has little or no vegetation.

Back slope The gentler windward slope of a sand *dune* or gentler slope of a *cuesta*.

Bajos An *alluvial fan* deposited by a river at the base of mountains and hills which encircle *desert* areas.

Bar, coastal An offshore strip of sand or shingle, either above or below the water. Usually parallel to the shore but sometimes crescent-shaped or at an oblique angle.

Barchan A crescent-shaped sand *dune*, formed where wind direction is very consistent. The horns of the crescent point downwind and where there is enough sand the barchan is mobile.

Barrio A Spanish term for the shanty towns – self-built settlements – which are clustered around many South and Central American cities (*see also Favela*).

Basalt Dark, fine-grained *igneous rock*. Formed near the Earth's surface from fast-cooling *lava*.

Base level The level below which flowing water cannot erode the land.

Basement rock A mass of ancient rock often of *Pre-Cambrian age*, covered by a layer of more recent *sedimentary rocks*. Commonly associated with *shield* areas.

Beach Lake or sea shore where waves break and there is an accumulation of loose material – mud, sand, shingle or pebbles.

Bedrock Solid, consolidated and relatively unweathered rock, found on the surface of the land or just below a layer of soil or *weathered* rock.

Biodiversity The quantity of animal or plant species in a given area.

Biomass The total mass of organic matter – plants and animals – in a given area. It is usually measured in kilogrammes per square metre. Plant biomass is proportionally greater than that of animals, except in cities.

Biosphere The zone just above and below the Earth's surface, where all plants and animals live.

Blizzard A severe windstorm with snow and sleet. Visibility is often severely restricted.

Bluff The steep bank of a *meander*, formed by the erosive action of a river.

Boreal forest Tracts of mainly coniferous forest found in northern *latitudes*.

Breccia A type of rock composed of sharp fragments, cemented by a fine-grained material such as clay.

Butte An isolated, flat-topped hill with steep or vertical sides, buttes are the eroded remnants of a former land surface.

C

Caatinga Portuguese (Brazilian) term for thorny woodland growing in areas of pale granitic soils.

CACM Central American Common Market. Established in 1960 to further economic ties between its members, which are Costa Rica, El Salvador, Guatemala, Honduras and Nicaragua.

Calcite Hexagonal crystals of calcium carbonate.

Caldera A huge volcanic vent, often containing a number of smaller vents, and sometimes a crater lake.

Carbon cycle The transfer of carbon to and from the *atmosphere*. This occurs on land through *photosynthesis*. In the sea, *carbon dioxide* is absorbed, some returning to the air and some taken up into the bodies of sea creatures.

Carbon dioxide A colourless, odourless gas (CO_2) which makes up 0.03% of the *atmosphere*.

Carbonation The process whereby rocks are broken down by carbonic acid. Carbon dioxide in the air dissolves in rainwater, forming carbonic acid. *Limestone* terrain can be rapidly eaten away.

Cash crop A single crop grown specifically for export sale, rather than for local use. Typical examples include coffee, tea and citrus fruits.

Cassava A type of grain meal, used to produce tapioca. A staple crop in many parts of Africa.

Castle kopje Hill or rock outcrop, especially in southern Africa, where steep sides, and a summit composed of blocks, give a castle-like appearance.

Cataracts A series of stepped waterfalls created as a river flows over a band of hard, resistant rock.

Causeway A raised route through marshland or a body of water.

CEEAC Economic Community of Central African States. Established in 1983 to promote regional co-operation and if possible, establish a common market between 16 Central African nations.

Chemical weathering The chemical reactions leading to the decomposition of rocks. Types of chemical weathering include *carbonation*, *hydrolysis* and *oxidation*.

Chernozem A fertile soil, also known as 'black earth' consisting of a layer of dark topsoil, rich in decaying vegetation, overlying a lighter chalky layer.

Cirque Armchair-shaped basin, found in mountain regions, with a steep back, or rear, wall and a raised rock lip, often containing a lake (or *tarn*). The cirque floor has been eroded by a *glacier*, while the back wall is eroded both by the *glacier* and by *weathering*.

Climate The average weather conditions in a given area over a period of years, sometimes defined as 30 years or more.

Cold War A period of hostile relations between the USA and the Soviet Union and their allies after the Second World War.

Composite volcano Also known as a strato-volcano, the volcanic cone is composed of alternating deposits of *lava* and *pyroclastic* material.

Compound A substance made up of *elements* chemically combined in a consistent way.

Condensation The process whereby a gas changes into a liquid. For example, water vapour in the *atmosphere* condenses around tiny airborne particles to form droplets of water.

Confluence The point at which two rivers meet.

Conglomerate Rock composed of large, water-worn or rounded pebbles, held together by a natural cement.

Coniferous forest A forest type containing trees which are generally, but not necessarily, *evergreen* and have slender, needle-like leaves and which reproduce by means of seeds contained in a cone.

Continental drift The theory that the continents of today are fragments of one or more prehistoric *supercontinents* which have moved across the Earth's surface, creating ocean basins. The theory has been superseded by a more sophisticated one – *plate tectonics*.

Continental shelf An area of the continental crust, below sea level, which slopes gently. It is separated from the deep ocean by a much more steeply inclined *continental slope*.

Continental slope A steep slope running from the edge of the *continental shelf* to the ocean floor.

Conurbation A vast metropolitan area created by the expansion of towns and cities into a virtually continuous urban area.

Cool continental A rainy *climate* with warm summers [warmest month below 76°F (22°C)] and often severe winters [coldest month below 32°F (0°C)].

Copra The dried, white kernel of a coconut, from which coconut oil is extracted.

Coral reef An underwater barrier created by colonies of the coral polyp. Polyps secrete a protective skeleton of calcium carbonate, and reefs develop as live polyps build on the skeletons of dead generations.

Core The centre of the Earth, consisting of a dense mass of iron and nickel. It is thought that the outer core is molten or liquid, and that the hot inner core is solid due to extremely high pressures.

Coriolis effect A deflecting force caused by the rotation of the Earth. In the northern hemisphere a body, such as an *air mass* or ocean current, is deflected to the right, and in the southern hemisphere to the left. This prevents winds from blowing straight from areas of high to low pressure.

Coulées A US / Canadian term for a ravine formed by river *erosion*.

Craton A large block of the Earth's *crust* which has remained stable for a long period of *geological time*. It is made up of ancient *shield* rocks.

Cretaceous A period of *geological time* beginning about 145 million years ago and lasting until about 65 million years ago.

Crevasse A deep crack in a *glacier*.

Crust The hard, thin outer shell of the Earth. The crust floats on the *mantle*, which is softer and more dense. Under the oceans (oceanic crust) the crust is 3.7–6.8 miles (6–11 km) thick. Continental crust averages 18–24 miles (30–40 km).

Crystalline rock Rocks formed when molten *magma* crystallizes (*igneous rocks*) or when heat or pressure cause re-crystallization (*metamorphic rocks*). Crystalline rocks are distinct from *sedimentary rocks*.

Cuesta A hill which rises into a steep slope on one side but has a gentler gradient on its other slope.

Cyclone An area of low *atmospheric pressure*, occurring where the air is warm and relatively low in density, causing low level winds to spiral. *Hurricanes* and *typhoons* are tropical cyclones.

D

De facto
1 Government or other activity that takes place, or exists in actuality if not by right.
2 A border, which exists in practice, but which is not officially recognized by all the countries it adjoins.

Deciduous forest A forest of trees which shed their leaves annually at a particular time or season. In *temperate* climates the fall of leaves occurs in the Autumn. Some *coniferous* trees, such as the larch, are deciduous. Deciduous vegetation contrasts with *evergreen*, which keeps its leaves for more than a year.

Defoliant Chemical spray used to remove foliage (leaves) from trees.

Deforestation The act of cutting down and clearing large areas of forest for human activities, such as agricultural land or urban development.

Delta Low-lying, fan-shaped area at a river mouth, formed by the *deposition* of successive layers of *sediment*. Slowing as it enters the sea, a river deposits sediment and may, as a result, split into numerous smaller channels, known as *distributaries*.

Denudation The combined effect of *weathering*, *erosion* and *mass movement*, which, over long periods, exposes underlying rocks.

Deposition The laying down of material that has accumulated:
(1) after being *eroded* and then transported by physical forces such as wind, ice or water;
(2) as organic remains, such as coal and coral;
(3) as the result of *evaporation* and chemical *precipitation*.

Depression
1 In climatic terms it is a large low pressure system.
2 A complex *fold*, producing a large valley, which incorporates both a *syncline* and an *anticline*.

Desert An *arid* region of low rainfall, with little vegetation or animal life, which is adapted to the dry conditions. The term is now applied not only to hot tropical and subtropical regions, but to arid areas of the continental interiors and to the ice deserts of the *Arctic* and *Antarctic*.

Desertification The gradual extension of *desert* conditions in *arid* or *semi-arid* regions, as a result of climatic change or human activity, such as over-grazing and *deforestation*.

Despot A ruler with absolute power. Despots are often associated with oppressive regimes.

Detritus Piles of rock deposited by an erosive agent such as a river or *glacier*.

Distributary A minor branch of a river, which does not rejoin the main stream, common at *deltas*.

Diurnal Daily, something that occurs each day. Diurnal temperature refers to the variation in temperature over the course of a full day and night.

Divide A US term describing the area of high ground separating two *drainage basins*.

Donga A steep-sided *gully*, resulting from *erosion* by a river or by floods.

Dormant A term used to describe a *volcano* which is not currently erupting. They differ from extinct volcanoes as dormant volcanoes are still considered likely to erupt in the future.

Drainage basin The area drained by a single river system, its boundary is marked by a *watershed* or *divide*.

Drought A long period of continuously low rainfall.

Drumlin A long, streamlined hillock composed of material deposited by a *glacier*. They often occur in groups known as swarms.

Dune A mound or ridge of sand, shaped, and often moved, by the wind. They are found in hot *deserts* and on low-lying coasts where onshore winds blow across sandy beaches.

Dyke A wall constructed in low-lying areas to contain floodwaters or protect from high tides.

E

Earthflow The rapid movement of soil and other loose surface material down a slope, when saturated by water. Similar to a mudflow but not as fast-flowing, due to a lower percentage of water.

Earthquake Sudden movements of the Earth's *crust*, causing the ground to shake. Frequently occurring at *tectonic plate* margins. The shock, or series of shocks, spreads out from an *epicentre*.

EC The European Community (*see* EU).

Ecosystem A system of living organisms – plants and animals – interacting with their *environment*.

ECOWAS Economic Community of West African States. Established in 1975, it incorporates 16 West African states and aims to promote closer regional and economic co-operation.

Element
1 A constituent of the *climate* – *precipitation*, *humidity*, temperature, *atmospheric pressure* or wind.
2 A substance that cannot be separated into simpler substances by chemical means.

El Niño A climatic phenomenon, the El Niño effect occurs about 14 times each century and leads to major shifts in global air circulation. It is associated with unusually warm currents off the coasts of Peru, Ecuador and Chile. The anomaly can last for up to two years.

Environment The conditions created by the surroundings (both natural and artificial) within which an organism lives. In human geography the word includes the surrounding economic, cultural and social conditions.

Eon (aeon) Traditionally a long, but indefinite, period of *geological time*.

Ephemeral A non-permanent feature, often used in connection with seasonal rivers or lakes in dry areas.

Epicentre The point on the Earth's surface directly above the underground origin – or focus – of an *earthquake*.

Equator The line of *latitude* which lies equidistant between the North and South Poles.

Erg An extensive area of sand *dunes*, particularly in the Sahara Desert.

Erosion The processes which wear away the surface of the land. *Glaciers*, wind, rivers, waves and currents all carry debris which causes *erosion*. Some definitions also include *mass movement* due to gravity as an agent of erosion.

Escarpment A steep slope at the margin of a level, upland surface. In a landscape created by *folding*, escarpments (or scarps) frequently lie behind a more gentle backward slope.

Esker A narrow, winding ridge of sand and gravel deposited by streams of water flowing beneath or at the edge of a *glacier*.

Erratic A rock transported by a *glacier* and deposited some distance from its place of origin.

Eustacy A world-wide fall or rise in ocean levels.

EU The European Union. Established in 1965, it was formerly known as the EEC (European Economic Community) and then the EC (European Community). Its members are Austria, Belgium, Denmark, Finland, France, Germany, Greece, Ireland, Italy, Luxembourg, Netherlands, Portugal, Spain, Sweden and UK. It seeks to establish an integrated European common market and eventual federation.

Evaporation The process whereby a liquid or solid is turned into a gas or vapour. Also refers to the diffusion of water vapour into the *atmosphere* from exposed water surfaces such as lakes and seas.

Evapotranspiration The loss of moisture from the Earth's surface through a combination of *evaporation*, and *transpiration* from the leaves of plants.

Evergreen Plants with long-lasting leaves, which are not shed annually or seasonally.

Exfoliation A kind of *weathering* whereby scale-like flakes of rock are peeled or broken off by the development of salt crystals in water within the rocks. *Groundwater*, which contains dissolved salts, seeps to the surface and evaporates, precipitating a film of salt crystals, which expands causing fine cracks. As these grow, flakes of rock break off.

Extrusive rock *Igneous* rock formed when molten material (*magma*) pours forth at the Earth's surface and cools rapidly. It usually has a glassy texture.

F

Factionalism The actions of one or more minority political group acting against the interests of the majority government.

Fault A fracture or crack in rock, where strains (*tectonic* movement) have caused blocks to move, vertically or laterally, relative to each other.

Fauna Collective name for the animals of a particular period of time, or region.

Favela Brazilian term for the shanty towns or self-built, temporary dwellings which have grown up around the edge of many South and Central American cities.

Ferrel cell A component in the global pattern of air circulation, which rises in the colder *latitudes* (60° N and S) and descends in warmer *latitudes* (30° N and S). The Ferrel cell forms part of the world's three-cell air circulation pattern, with the *Hadley* and Polar cells.

Fissure A deep crack in a rock or a *glacier*.

Fjord A deep, narrow inlet, created when the sea inundates the *U-shaped valley* created by a *glacier*.

Flash flood A sudden, short-lived rise in the water level of a river or stream, or surge of water down a dry river channel, or *wadi*, caused by heavy rainfall.

Flax A plant used to make linen.

Flood plain The broad, flat part of a river valley, adjacent to the river itself, formed by *sediment* deposited during flooding.

Flora The collective name for the plants of a particular period of time or region.

Flow The movement of a river within its banks, particularly in terms of the speed and volume of water.

Fold A bend in the rock *strata* of the Earth's *crust*, resulting from compression.

Fossil The remains, or traces, of a dead organism preserved in the Earth's *crust*.

Fossil dune A *dune* formed in a once-*arid* region which is now wetter. *Dunes* normally move with the wind, but in these cases vegetation makes them stable.

Fossil fuel Fuel – coal, natural gas or oil – composed of the fossilized remains of plants and animals.

Front The boundary between two *air masses*, which contrast sharply in temperature and *humidity*.

Frontal depression An area of low pressure caused by rising warm air. They are generally 600–1200 miles (1000–2000 km) in diameter. Within *depressions* there are both warm and cold fronts.

Frost shattering A form of *weathering* where water freezes in cracks, causing expansion. As temperatures fluctuate and the ice melts and refreezes, it eventually causes the rocks to shatter and fragments of rock to break off.

G

Gaucho South American term for a stock herder or cowboy who works on the grassy *plains* of Paraguay, Uruguay and Argentina.

Geological time-scale The chronology of the Earth's history as revealed in its rocks. Geological time is divided into a number of periods: *eon*, era, period, epoch, age and chron (the shortest). These units are not of uniform length.

Geosyncline A concave fold (*syncline*) or large depression in the Earth's *crust*, extending hundreds of kilometres. This basin contains a deep layer of sediment, especially at its centre, from the land masses around it.

Geothermal energy Heat derived from hot rocks within the Earth's *crust* and resulting in hot springs, steam or hot rocks at the surface. The energy is generated by rock movements, and from the breakdown of radioactive elements occurring under intense pressure.

GDP Gross Domestic Product. The total value of goods and services produced by a country excluding income from foreign countries.

Geyser A jet of steam and hot water that intermittently erupts from vents in the ground in areas that are, or were, *volcanic*. Some geysers occasionally reach heights of 196 ft (60 m).

Ghetto An area of a city or region occupied by an overwhelming majority of people from one racial or religious group, who may be subject to persecution or containment.

Glaciation The growth of *glaciers* and *ice sheets*, and their impact on the landscape.

Glacier A body of ice moving downslope under the influence of gravity and consisting of compacted and frozen snow. A glacier is distinct from an *ice sheet*, which is wider and less confined by features of the landscape.

Glacio-eustacy A world-wide change in the level of the oceans, caused when the formation of *ice sheets* takes up water or when their melting returns water to the ocean. The formation of ice sheets in the *Pleistocene* epoch, for example, caused sea level to drop by about 320 ft (100 m).

Glaciofluvial To do with glacial *meltwater*, the landforms it creates and its processes; *erosion*, transportation and *deposition*. Glaciofluvial effects are more powerful and rapid where they occur within or beneath the *glacier*, rather than beyond its edge.

Glacis A gentle slope or *pediment*.

Global warming An increase in the average temperature of the Earth. At present the *greenhouse effect* is thought to contribute to this.

GNP Gross National Product. The total value of goods and services produced by a country.

Gondwanaland The *supercontinent* thought to have existed over 200 million years ago in the southern hemisphere. Gondwanaland is believed to have comprised today's Africa, Madagascar, Australia, parts of South America, *Antarctica* and the Indian subcontinent.

Graben A block of rock let down between two parallel *faults*. Where the graben occurs within a valley, the structure is known as a *rift valley*.

Grease ice Slicks of ice which form in *Antarctic* seas, when ice crystals are bonded together by wind and wave action.

Greenhouse effect A change in the temperature of the *atmosphere*. Short-wave solar radiation travels through the *atmosphere* unimpeded to the Earth's surface, whereas outgoing, long-wave terrestrial radiation is absorbed by materials that re-radiate it back to the Earth. Radiation trapped in this way, by water vapour, carbon dioxide and other 'greenhouse gases', keeps the Earth warm. As more *carbon dioxide* is released into the atmosphere by the burning of *fossil fuels*, the greenhouse effect may cause a global increase in temperature.

Groundwater Water that has seeped into the pores, cavities and cracks of rocks or into soil and water held in an *aquifer*.

Gully A deep, narrow channel eroded in the landscape by *ephemeral* streams.

Guyot A small, flat-topped submarine mountain, formed as a result of subsidence which occurs during *sea-floor spreading*.

Gypsum A soft mineral *compound* (hydrated calcium sulphate), used as the basis of many forms of plaster, including plaster of Paris.

H

Hadley cell A large-scale component in the global pattern of air circulation. Warm air rises over the *Equator* and blows at high altitude towards the poles, sinking in subtropical regions (30° N and 30° S) and creating high pressure. The air then flows at the surface towards the *Equator* in the form of trade winds. There is one cell in each hemisphere. Named after G Hadley, who published his theory in 1735.

Hamada An Arabic word for a plateau of bare rock in a *desert*.

Hanging valley A tributary valley which ends suddenly, high above the bed of the main valley. The effect is found where the main valley has been more deeply eroded by a *glacier*, than has the tributary valley. A stream in a hanging valley will descend to the floor of the main valley as a waterfall or *cataract*.

Headwards The action of a river eroding back upstream, as opposed to the normal process of downstream *erosion*. Headwards erosion is often associated with *gullying*.

Hoodos Pinnacles of rock which have been worn away by *weathering* in *semi-arid* regions.

Horst A block of the Earth's *crust* which has been left upstanding by the sinking of adjoining blocks along fault lines.

Hot spot A region of the Earth's *crust* where high thermal activity occurs, often leading to volcanic eruptions. Hot spots often occur far from plate boundaries, but their movement is associated with *plate tectonics*.

Humid equatorial Rainy *climate* with no winter, where the coolest month is generally above 64°F (18°C).

Humidity The relative amount of moisture held in the Earth's *atmosphere*.

Hurricane
1 A tropical *cyclone* occurring in the Caribbean and western North Atlantic.
2 A wind of more than 65 knots (75 kmph).

Hydro-electric power Energy produced by harnessing the rapid movement of water down steep mountain slopes to drive turbines to generate electricity.

Hydrolysis The chemical breakdown of rocks in reaction with water, forming new compounds.

I

Ice Age A period in the Earth's history when surface temperatures in the temperate *latitudes* were much lower and *ice sheets* expanded considerably. There have been *ice ages* from *Pre-Cambrian* times onwards. The most recent began two million years ago and ended 10,000 years ago.

Ice cap A permanent dome of ice in highland areas. The term ice cap is often seen as distinct from *ice sheet*, which denotes a much wider covering of ice; and is also used refer to the extensive polar and Greenland ice caps.

Ice floe A large, flat mass of ice floating free on the ocean surface. It is usually formed after the break-up of winter ice by heavy storms.

Ice sheet A continuous, very thick layer of ice and snow. The term is usually used of ice masses which are continental in extent.

Ice shelf A floating mass of ice attached to the edge of a coast. The seaward edge is usually a sheer cliff up to 100 ft (30 m) high.

Ice wedge Massive blocks of ice up to 6.5 ft (2 m) wide at the top and extending 32 ft (10 m) deep. They are found in cracks in *polygonally-patterned* ground in *periglacial* regions.

Iceberg A large mass of ice in a lake or a sea, which has broken off from a floating *ice sheet* (an *ice shelf*) or from a *glacier*.

Igneous rock Rock formed when molten material, *magma*, from the hot, lower layers of the Earth's *crust*, cools, solidifies and crystallizes, either within the Earth's *crust* (*intrusive*) or on the surface (*extrusive*).

IMF International Monetary Fund. Established in 1944 as a UN agency, it contains 182 members around the world and is concerned with world monetary stability and economic development.

Incised meander A *meander* where the river, following its original course, cuts deeply into *bedrock*. This may occur when a mature, meandering river begins to erode its bed much more vigorously after the surrounding land has been uplifted.

Indigenous People, plants or animals native to a particular region.

Infrastructure The communications and services – roads, railways and telecommunications – necessary for the functioning of a country or region.

Inselberg An isolated, steep-sided hill, rising from a low *plain* in *semi-arid* and *savannah* landscapes. Inselbergs are usually composed of a rock, such as granite, which resists *erosion*.

Interglacial A period of global *climate*, between two *ice ages*, when temperatures rise and *ice sheets* and *glaciers* retreat.

Intraplate volcano A *volcano* which lies in the centre of one of the Earth's *tectonic plates*, rather than, as is more common, at its edge. They are thought to have been formed by a *hot spot*.

Intrusion (intrusive igneous rock) Rock formed when molten material, *magma*, penetrates existing rocks below the Earth's surface before cooling and solidifying. These rocks cool more slowly than extrusive rock and therefore tend to have coarser grains.

Irrigation The artificial supply of agricultural water to dry areas, often involving the creation of canals and the diversion of natural watercourses.

Island arc A curved chain of islands. Typically, such an arc fringes an ocean trench, formed at the margin between two *tectonic plates*. As one plate overrides another, *earthquakes* and volcanic activity are common and the islands themselves are often volcanic cones.

Isostasy The state of equilibrium which the Earth's *crust* maintains as its lighter and heavier parts float on the denser underlying mantle.

Isthmus A narrow strip of land connecting two larger landmasses or islands.

J

Jet stream A narrow belt of westerly winds in the *troposphere*, at altitudes above 39,000 ft (12,000 m). Jet streams tend to blow more strongly in winter and include: the subtropical jet stream; the *polar* front jet stream in mid-*latitudes*; the *Arctic* jet stream; and the polar-night jet stream.

Joint A crack in a rock, formed where blocks of rock have not shifted relative to each other, as is the case with a *fault*. Joints are created by *folding*; by shrinkage in *igneous rock* as it cools or *sedimentary rock* as it dries out; and by the release of pressure in a rock mass when overlying materials are removed by *erosion*.

Jute A plant fibre used to make coarse ropes, sacks and matting.

K

Kame A mound of stratified sand and gravel with steep sides, deposited in a *crevasse* by *meltwater* running over a *glacier*. When the ice retreats, this forms an undulating terrain of hummocks.

Karst A barren *limestone* landscape created by carbonic acid in streams and rainwater, in areas where *limestone* is close to the surface. Typical features include caverns, tower-like hills, *sinkholes* and flat limestone pavements.

Kettle hole A round hollow formed in a glacial deposit by a detached block of glacial ice, which later melted. They can fill with water to form kettle-lakes.

L

Lagoon A shallow stretch of coastal salt-water behind a partial barrier such as a sandbank or *coral reef*. Lagoon is also used to describe the water encircled by an *atoll*.

LAIA Latin American Integration Association. Established in 1980, its members are Argentina, Bolivia, Brazil, Chile, Colombia, Ecuador, Mexico, Paraguay, Peru, Uruguay and Venezuela. It aims to promote economic co-operation between member states.

Landslide The sudden downslope movement of a mass of rock or earth on a slope, caused either by heavy rain; the impact of waves; an *earthquake* or human activity.

Laterite A hard red deposit left by *chemical weathering* in tropical conditions, and consisting mainly of oxides of iron and aluminium.

Latitude The angular distance from the *Equator*, to a given point on the Earth's surface. Imaginary lines of *latitude* running parallel to the Equator encircle the Earth, and are measured in degrees north or south of the Equator. The Equator is 0°, the poles 90° South and North respectively. Also called parallels.

Laurasia In the theory of *continental drift*, the northern part of the great *supercontinent* of *Pangaea*. Laurasia is said to consist of N America, Greenland and all of Eurasia north of the Indian subcontinent.

Lava The molten rock, *magma*, which erupts onto the Earth's surface through a *volcano*, or through a *fault* or crack in the Earth's *crust*. Lava refers to the rock both in its molten and in its later, solidified form.

Leaching The process whereby water dissolves minerals and moves them down through layers of soil or rock.

Levée A raised bank alongside the channel of a river. Levées are either human-made or formed in times of flood when the river overflows its channel, slows and deposits much of its *sediment* load.

Lichen An organism which is the symbiotic product of an algae and a fungus. Lichens form in tight crusts on stones and trees, and are resistant to extreme cold. They are often found in tundra regions.

Lignite Low-grade coal, also known as brown coal. Found in large deposits in eastern Europe.

Limestone A porous *sedimentary* rock formed from carbonate materials.

Lingua franca The language adopted as the common language between speakers whose native languages are different. This is common in former colonial states.

Lithosphere The rigid upper layer of the Earth, comprising the *crust* and the upper part of the *mantle*.

Llanos Vast grassland *plains* of northern South America.

Loess Fine-grained, yellow deposits of unstratified silts and sands. Loess is believed to be wind-carried *sediment* created in the last *Ice Age*. Some deposits may later have been redistributed by rivers. Loess-derived soils are of high quality, fertile and easy to work.

Longitude A division of the Earth which pinpoints how far east or west a given place is from the Prime Meridian (0°) which runs through the Royal Observatory at Greenwich, England (UK). Imaginary lines of longitude are drawn around the world from pole to pole. The world is divided into 360 degrees.

Longshore drift The transport of sand and silt along the coast, carried by waves hitting the beach at an angle.

M

Magma Underground, molten rock, which is very hot and highly charged with gas. It is generated at great pressure, at depths 10 miles (16 km) or more below the Earth's surface. It can issue as *lava* at the Earth's surface or, more often, solidify below the surface as *intrusive igneous rock*.

Mantle The layer of the Earth between the *crust* and the *core*. It is about 1800 miles (2900 km) thick. The uppermost layer of the mantle is the soft, 125 mile (200 km) thick *asthenosphere* on which the more rigid *lithosphere* floats.

Maquiladoras Factories on the Mexico side of the Mexico/US border, which are allowed to import raw materials and components duty-free and use low-cost labour to assemble the goods, finally exporting them for sale in the US.

Market gardening The intensive growing of fruit and vegetables close to large local markets.

Mass movement Downslope movement of weathered materials such as rock, often helped by rainfall or glacial *meltwater*. Mass movement may be a gradual process or rapid, as in a *landslide* or rockfall.

Massif A single very large mountain or an area of mountains with uniform characteristics and clearly-defined boundaries.

Meander A loop-like bend in a river, which is found typically in the lower, mature reaches of a river but can form wherever the valley is wide and the slope gentle.

Mediterranean climate A temperate *climate* of hot, dry summers and warm, damp winters. This is typical of the western fringes of the world's continents in the warm temperate regions between *latitudes* of 30° and 40° (north and south).

Meltwater Water resulting from the melting of a *glacier* or *ice sheet*.

Mesa A broad, flat-topped hill, characteristic of *arid* regions.

Mesosphere A layer of the Earth's *atmosphere*, between the *stratosphere* and the *thermosphere*. Extending from about 25–50 miles (40–80 km) above the surface of the Earth.

Mestizo A person of mixed *Amerindian* and European origin.

Metallurgy The refining and working of metals.

Metamorphic rocks Rocks which have been altered from their original form, in terms of texture, composition and structure by intense heat, pressure, or by the introduction of new chemical substances – or a combination of more than one of these.

Meteor A body of rock, metal or other material, which travels through space at great speeds. Meteors are visible as they enter the Earth's *atmosphere* as shooting stars and fireballs.

Meteorite The remains of a *meteor* that has fallen to Earth.

Meteoroid A *meteor* which is still travelling in space, outside the Earth's *atmosphere*.

Mezzogiorno A term applied to the southern portion of Italy.

Milankovitch hypothesis A theory suggesting that there are a series of cycles which slightly alter the Earth's position when rotating about the Sun. The cycles identified all affect the amount of *radiation* the Earth receives at different *latitudes*. The theory is seen as a key factor in the cause of *ice ages*.

Millet A grain-crop, forming part of the staple diet in much of Africa.

Mistral A strong, dry, cold northerly or north-westerly wind, which blows from the Massif Central of France to the Mediterranean Sea. It is common in winter and its cold blasts can cause crop damage in the Rhône Delta, in France.

Mohorovicic discontinuity (Moho) The structural divide at the margin between the Earth's *crust* and the *mantle*. On average it is 20 miles (35 km) below the continents and 6 miles (10 km) below the oceans. The different densities of the *crust* and the mantle cause *earthquake* waves to accelerate at this point.

Monarchy A form of government in which the head of state is a single hereditary monarch. The monarch may be a mere figurehead, or may retain significant authority.

Monsoon A wind which changes direction bi-annually. The change is caused by the reversal of pressure over landmasses and the adjacent oceans. Because the inflowing moist winds bring rain, the term monsoon is also used to refer to the rains themselves. The term is derived from and most commonly refers to the seasonal winds of south and east Asia.

Montaña Mountain areas along the west coast of South America.

Moraine Debris, transported and deposited by a *glacier* or *ice sheet* in unstratified, mixed, piles of rock, boulders, pebbles and clay.

Mountain-building The formation of *fold* mountains by tectonic activity. Also known as orogeny, mountain-building often occurs on the margin where two *tectonic plates* collide. The periods when most mountain-building occurred are known as orogenic phases and lasted many millions of years.

Mudflow An *avalanche* of mud which occurs when a mass of soil is drenched by rain or melting snow. It is a type of *mass movement*, faster than an *earthflow* because it is lubricated by water.

N

Nappe A mass of rocks which has been overfolded by repeated thrust *faulting*.

NAFTA The North American Free Trade Association. Established in 1994 between Canada, Mexico and the US to set up a free-trade zone.

NASA The North American Space Agency. It is a government body, established in 1958 to develop manned and unmanned space programmes.

NATO The North Atlantic Treaty Organization. Established in 1949 to promote mutual defence and co-operation between its members, which are Belgium, Canada, Czech Republic, Denmark, France, Germany, Greece, Iceland, Italy, Luxembourg, the Netherlands, Norway, Portugal, Poland, Spain, Turkey, UK, and US.

Nitrogen The odourless, colourless gas which makes up 78% of the atmosphere. Within the soil, it is a vital nutrient for plants.

Nomads (nomadic) Wandering communities who move around in search of suitable pasture for their herds of animals.

Nuclear fusion A technique used to create a new nucleus by the merging of two lighter ones, resulting in the release of large quantities of energy.

O

Oasis A fertile area in the midst of a *desert*, usually watered by an underground *aquifer*.

Oceanic ridge A mid-ocean ridge formed, according to the theory of *plate tectonics*, when plates drift apart and hot *magma* pours through to form new oceanic *crust*.

Oligarchy The government of a state by a small, exclusive group of people – such as an elite class or a family group.

Onion-skin weathering The *weathering* away or *exfoliation* of a rock or outcrop by the peeling off of surface layers.

Oriente A flatter region lying to the east of the Andes in South America.

Outwash plain *Glaciofluvial* material (typically clay, sand and gravel) carried beyond an ice sheet by *meltwater* streams, forming a broad, flat deposit.

Oxbow lake A crescent-shaped lake formed on a river *flood plain* when a river erodes the outside bend of a *meander*, making the neck of the *meander* narrower until the river cuts across the neck. The meander is cut off and is dammed off with sediment, creating an oxbow lake. Also known as a cut-off or mortlake.

Oxidation A form of *chemical weathering* where *oxygen* dissolved in water reacts with minerals in rocks – particularly iron – to form oxides. Oxidation causes brown or yellow staining on rocks, and eventually leads to the break down of the rock.

Oxygen A colourless, odourless gas which is one of the main constituents of the Earth's *atmosphere* and is essential to life on Earth.

Ozone layer A layer of enriched *oxygen* (O_3) within the stratosphere, mostly between 18–50 miles (30–80 km) above the Earth's surface. It is vital to the existence of life on Earth because it absorbs harmful shortwave ultraviolet radiation, while allowing beneficial longer wave ultraviolet radiation to penetrate to the Earth's surface.

P

Pacific Rim The name given to the economically-dynamic countries bordering the Pacific Ocean.

Pack ice Ice masses more than 10 ft (3 m) thick which form on the sea surface and are not attached to a landmass.

Pancake ice Thin discs of ice, up to 8 ft (2.4 m) wide which form when slicks of *grease ice* are tossed together by winds and stormy seas.

Pangaea In the theory of continental drift, Pangaea is the original great land mass which, about 190 million years ago, began to split into Gondwanaland in the south and Laurasia in the north, separated by the Tethys Sea.

Pastoralism Grazing of livestock– usually sheep, goats or cattle. Pastoralists in many drier areas have traditionally been *nomadic*.

Parallel *see Latitude.*

Peat Ancient, partially-decomposed vegetation found in wet, boggy conditions where there is little *oxygen*. It is the first stage in the development of coal and is often dried for use as fuel. It is also used to improve soil quality.

Pediment A gently-sloping ramp of *bedrock* below a steeper slope, often found at mountain edges in *desert* areas, but also in other climatic zones. Pediments may include depositional elements such as *alluvial fans*.

Peninsula A thin strip of land surrounded on three of its sides by water. Large examples include Florida and Korea.

Per capita Latin term meaning 'for each person'.

Periglacial Regions on the edges of *ice sheets* or *glaciers* or, more commonly, cold regions experiencing intense frost action, *permafrost* or both. Periglacial climates bring long, freezing winters and short, mild summers.

Permafrost Permanently frozen ground, typical of *Arctic* regions. Although a layer of soil above the permafrost melts in summer, the melted water does not drain through the permafrost.

Permeable rocks Rocks through which water can seep, because they are either porous or cracked.

Pharmaceuticals The manufacture of medicinal drugs.

Phreatic eruption A volcanic eruption which occurs when *lava* combines with *groundwater*, superheating the water and causing a sudden emission of steam at the surface.

Physical weathering (mechanical weathering) The breakdown of rocks by physical, as opposed to chemical, processes. Examples include: changes in pressure or temperature; the effect of windblown sand; the pressure of growing salt crystals in cracks within rock; and the expansion and contraction of water within rock as it freezes and thaws.

Pingo A dome of earth with a core of ice, found in *tundra* regions. Pingos are formed either when *groundwater* freezes and expands, pushing up the land surface, or when trapped, freezing water in a lake expands and pushes up lake *sediments* to form the pingo dome.

Placer A belt of mineral-bearing rock *strata* lying at or close to the Earth's surface, from which minerals can be easily extracted.

Plain A flat, level region of land, often relatively low-lying.

Plateau A highland tract of flat land.

Plate *see Tectonic plates.*

Plate tectonics The study of *tectonic plates*, which helps to explain *continental drift*, mountain formation and volcanic activity. The movement of tectonic plates may be explained by the currents of rock rising and falling from within the Earth's *mantle*, as it heats up and then cools. The boundaries of the plates are known as plate margins and most mountains, *earthquakes* and *volcanoes* occur at these margins. Constructive margins are moving apart; destructive margins are crunching together and conservative margins are sliding past one another.

Pleistocene A period of *geological time* spanning from about 5.2 million years ago to 1.6 million years ago.

Plutonic rock *Igneous* rocks found deep below the surface. They are coarse-grained because they cooled and solidified slowly.

Polar The zones within the *Arctic* and *Antarctic* circles.

Polje A long, broad *depression* found in *karst* (*limestone*) regions.

Polygonal patterning Typical ground patterning, found in areas where the soil is subject to severe frost action, often in *periglacial* regions.

Porosity A measure of how much water can be held within a rock or a soil. Porosity is measured as the percentage of holes or pores in a material, compared to its total volume. For example, the porosity of slate is less than 1%, whereas that of gravel is 25–35%.

Prairies Originally a French word for grassy *plains* with few or no trees.

Pre-Cambrian The earliest period of *geological time* dating from over 570 million years ago.

Precipitation The fall of moisture from the *atmosphere* onto the surface of the Earth, whether as dew, hail, rain, sleet or snow.

Pyramidal peak A steep, isolated mountain summit, formed when the back walls of three or more *cirques* are cut back and move towards each other. The cliffs around such a horned peak, or horn, are divided by sharp *arêtes*. The Matterhorn in the Swiss Alps is an example.

Pyroclasts Fragments of rock ejected during volcanic eruptions.

Q

Quaternary The current period of *geological time*, which started about 1.6 million years ago.

R

Radiation The emission of energy in the form of particles or waves. Radiation from the sun includes heat, light, ultraviolet rays, gamma rays and X-rays. Only some of the solar energy radiated into space reaches the Earth.

Rainforest Dense forests in tropical zones with high rainfall, temperature and *humidity*. Strictly, the term applies to the equatorial rainforest in tropical lowlands with constant rainfall and no seasonal change. The Congo and Amazon basins are examples. The term is applied more loosely to lush forest in other climates. Within rainforests organic life is dense and varied: at least 40% of all plant and animal species are found here and there may be as many as 100 tree species per hectare.

Rainshadow An area which experiences low rainfall, because of its position on the leeward side of a mountain range.

Reg A large area of stony *desert*, where tightly-packed gravel lies on top of clayey sand. A reg is formed where the wind blows away the finer sand.

Remote-sensing Method of obtaining information about the *environment* using unmanned equipment, such as a satellite, which relays the information to a point where it is collected and used.

Resistance The capacity of a rock to resist *denudation*, by processes such as *weathering* and *erosion*.

Ria A flooded *V-shaped river valley* or estuary, flooded by a rise in sea level (*eustacy*) or sinking land. It is shorter than a *fjord* and gets deeper as it meets the sea.

Rift valley A long, narrow depression in the Earth's *crust*, formed by the sinking of rocks between two *faults*.

River channel The trough which contains a river and is moulded by the flow of water within it.

Roche moutonée A rock found in a glaciated valley. The side facing the flow of the *glacier* has been smoothed and rounded, while the other side has been left more rugged because the *glacier*, as it flows over it, has plucked out frozen fragments and carried them away.

Runoff Water draining from a land surface by flowing across it.

S

Sabkha The floor of an isolated *depression* which occurs in an *arid environment* – usually covered by salt deposits and devoid of vegetation.

SADC Southern African Development Community. Established in 1992 to promote economic integration between its member states, which are Angola, Botswana, Lesotho, Malawi, Mauritius, Mozambique, Namibia, South Africa, Swaziland, Tanzania, Zambia and Zimbabwe.

Salt plug A rounded hill produced by the upward doming of rock *strata* caused by the movement of salt or other evaporite deposits under intense pressure.

Sastrugi Ice ridges formed by wind action. They lie parallel to the direction of the wind.

Savannah Open grassland found between the zone of *deserts*, and that of tropical *rainforests* in the tropics and subtropics. Scattered trees and shrubs are found in some kinds of savannah. A savannah *climate* usually has wet and dry seasons.

Scarp *see Escarpment.*

Scree Piles of rock fragments beneath a cliff or rock face, caused by mechanical *weathering*, especially *frost shattering*, where the expansion and contraction of freezing and thawing water within the rock, gradually breaks it up.

Sea-floor spreading The process whereby *tectonic plates* move apart, allowing hot *magma* to erupt and solidify. This forms a new sea floor and, ultimately, widens the ocean.

Seamount An isolated, submarine mountain or hill, probably of volcanic origin.

Season A period of time linked to regular changes in the weather, especially the intensity of solar *radiation*.

Sediment Grains of rock transported and deposited by rivers, sea, ice or wind.

Sedimentary rocks Rocks formed from the debris of pre-existing rocks or of organic material. They are found in many *environments* – on the ocean floor, on beaches, rivers and *deserts*. Organically-formed sedimentary rocks include coal and chalk. Other sedimentary rocks, such as flint, are formed by chemical processes. Most of these rocks contain *fossils*, which can be used to date them.

Seif A sand *dune* which lies parallel to the direction of the prevailing wind. Seifs form steep-sided ridges, sometimes extending for miles.

Seismic activity Movement within the Earth, such as an *earthquake* or *tremor*.

Selva A region of wet forest found in the Amazon Basin.

Semi-arid, semi-desert The *climate* and landscape which lies between *savannah* and *desert* or between savannah and a *mediterranean* climate. In semi-arid conditions there is a little more moisture than in a true *desert*; and more patches of drought-resistant vegetation can survive.

Shale (marine shale) A compacted *sedimentary rock*, with fine-grained particles. Marine shale is formed on the seabed. Fuel such as oil may be extracted from it.

Sheetwash Water which runs downhill in thin sheets without forming channels. It can cause *sheet erosion*.

Sheet erosion The washing away of soil by a thin film or sheet of water, known as *sheetwash*.

Shield A vast stable block of the Earth's *crust*, which has experienced little or no *mountain-building*.

Sierra The Spanish word for mountains.

Sinkhole A circular *depression* in a *limestone* region. They are formed by the collapse of an underground cave system or the *chemical weathering* of the *limestone*.

Sisal A plant-fibre used to make matting.

Slash and burn A farming technique involving the cutting down and burning of scrub forest, to create agricultural land. After a number of seasons this land is abandoned and the process is repeated. This practice is common in Africa and South America.

Slip face The steep leeward side of a sand *dune* or slope. Opposite side to a *back slope*.

Soil A thin layer of rock particles mixed with the remains of dead plants and animals. This occurs naturally on the surface of the Earth and provides a medium for plants to grow.

Soil creep The very gradual downslope movement of rock debris and soil, under the influence of gravity. This is a type of *mass movement*.

Soil erosion The wearing away of soil more quickly than it is replaced by natural processes. Soil can be carried away by wind as well as by water. Human activities, such as over-grazing and the clearing of land for farming, accelerate the process in many areas.

Solar energy Energy derived from the Sun. Solar energy is converted into other forms of energy. For example, the wind and waves, as well as the creation of plant material in photosynthesis, depend on solar energy.

Solifluction A kind of *soil creep*, where water in the surface layer has saturated the soil and rock debris which slips slowly downhill. It often happens where frozen top-layer deposits thaw, leaving frozen layers below them.

Sorghum A type of grass found in South America, similar to sugar cane. When refined it is used to make molasses.

Spit A thin linear deposit of sand or shingle extending from the sea shore. Spits are formed as angled waves shift sand along the beach, eventually extending a ridge of sand beyond a change in the angle of the coast. Spits are common where the coastline bends, especially at estuaries.

Squash A type of edible gourd.

Stack A tall, isolated pillar of rock near a coastline, created as wave action erodes away the adjacent rock.

Stalactite A tapering cylinder of mineral deposit, hanging from the roof of a cave in a *karst* area. It is formed by calcium carbonate, dissolved in water, which drips through the roof of a *limestone* cavern.

Stalagmite A cone of calcium carbonate, similar to a *stalactite*, rising from the floor of a *limestone* cavern and formed when drops of water fall from the roof of a *limestone* cave. If the water has dripped from a *stalactite* above the stalagmite, the two may join to form a continuous pillar.

Staple crop The main crop on which a country is economically and or physically reliant. For example, the major crop grown for large-scale local consumption in South Asia is rice.

Steppe Large areas of dry grassland in the northern hemisphere – particularly found in southeast Europe and central Asia.

Strata The plural of stratum, a distinct, virtually horizontal layer of deposited material, lying parallel to other layers.

Stratosphere A layer of the *atmosphere*, above the *troposphere*, extending from about 7–30 miles (11–50 km) above the Earth's surface. In the lower part of the stratosphere, the temperature is relatively stable and there is little moisture.

Strike-slip fault Occurs where plates move sideways past each other and blocks of rocks move horizontally in relation to each other, not up or down as in normal *faults*.

Subduction zone A region where two *tectonic plates* collide, forcing one beneath the other. Typically, a dense oceanic plate dips below a lighter continental plate, melting in the heat of the *asthenosphere*. This is why the zone is also called a destructive margin (*see Plate tectonics*). These zones are characterized by *earthquakes*, volcanoes, *mountain–building* and the development of oceanic trenches and *island arcs*.

Submarine canyon A steep-sided valley, which extends along the *continental shelf* to the ocean floor. Often formed by *turbidity currents*.

Submarine fan Deposits of silt and *alluvium*, carried by large rivers forming great fan-shaped deposits on the ocean floor.

Subsistence agriculture An agricultural practice, whereby enough food is produced to support the farmer and his dependents, but not providing any surplus to generate an income.

Subtropical A term applied loosely to *climates* which are nearly tropical or tropical for a part of the year – areas north or south of the *tropics* but outside the *temperate zone*.

Supercontinent A large continent that breaks up to form smaller continents or which forms when smaller continents merge. In the theory of *continental drift*, the supercontinents are *Pangaea*, *Gondwanaland* and *Laurasia*.

Sustainable development An approach to development, applied to economies across the world which exploit natural resources without destroying them or the *environment*.

Syncline A basin-shaped downfold in rock *strata*, created when the *strata* are compressed, for example where *tectonic plates* collide.

T

Tableland A highland area with a flat or gently undulating surface.

Taiga The belt of *coniferous* forest found in the north of Asia and North America. The conifers are adapted to survive low temperatures and long periods of snowfall.

Tarn A Scottish term for a small mountain lake, usually found at the head of a *glacier*.

Tectonic plates Plates, or tectonic plates, are the rigid slabs which form the Earth's outer shell, the *lithosphere*. Eight big plates and several smaller ones have been identified.

Temperate A moderate *climate* without extremes of temperature, typical of the mid-*latitudes* between the *tropics* and the *polar* circles.

Theocracy A state governed by religious laws – today Iran is the world's largest theocracy.

Thermokarst Subsidence created by the thawing of ground ice in *periglacial* areas, creating depressions.

Thermosphere A layer of the Earth's *atmosphere* which lies above the *mesophere*, about 60–300 miles (100–500 km) above the Earth

Terraces Steps cut into steep slopes to create flat surfaces for cultivating crops. They also help reduce soil *erosion* on unconsolidated slopes. They are most common in heavily-populated parts of Southeast Asia.

Till Unstratified glacial deposits or drift left by a *glacier* or *ice sheet*. Till includes mixtures of clay, sand, gravel and boulders.

Topography The typical shape and features of a given area such as land height and terrain.

Tombolo A large sand *spit* which attaches part of the mainland to an island.

Tornado A violent, spiralling windstorm, with a centre of very low pressure. Wind speeds reach 200 mph (320 kmph) and there is often thunder and heavy rain.

Transform fault In *plate tectonics*, a *fault* of continental scale, occurring where two plates slide past each other, staying close together for example, the San Andreas Fault, USA. The jerky, uneven movement creates *earthquakes* but does not destroy or add to the Earth's *crust*

Transpiration The loss of water vapour through the pores (or stomata) of plants. The process helps to return moisture to the *atmosphere*.

Trap An area of fine-grained *igneous rock* which has been extruded and cooled on the Earth's surface in stages, forming a series of steps or terraces.

Treeline The line beyond which trees cannot grow, dependent on *latitude* and altitude, as well as local factors such as soil.

Tremor A slight *earthquake*.

Trench (oceanic trench) A long, deep trough in the ocean floor, formed, according to the theory of *plate tectonics*, when two plates collide and one dives under the other, creating a *subduction zone*.

Tropics The zone between the *Tropic of Cancer* and the *Tropic of Capricorn* where the *climate* is hot. Tropical climate is also applied to areas rather further north and south of the *Equator* where the climate is similar to that of the true tropics.

Tropic of Cancer A line of *latitude* or imaginary circle round the Earth, lying at 23° 28' N.

Tropic of Capricorn A line of *latitude* or imaginary circle round the Earth, lying at 23° 28' S.

Troposphere The lowest layer of the Earth's *atmosphere*. From the surface, it reaches a height of between 4–10 miles (7–16 km). It is the most turbulent zone of the atmosphere and accounts for the generation of most of the world's weather. The layer above it is called the *stratosphere*.

Tsunami A huge wave created by shock waves from an *earthquake* under the sea. Reaching speeds of up to 600 mph (960 kmph), the wave may increase to heights of 50 ft (15 m) on entering coastal waters; and it can cause great damage.

Tundra The treeless *plains* of the *Arctic Circle*, found south of the *polar* region of permanent ice and snow, and north of the belt of *coniferous* forests known as *taiga*. In this region of long, very cold winters, vegetation is usually limited to mosses, *lichens*, sedges and rushes, although flowers and dwarf shrubs blossom in the brief summer.

Turbidity current An oceanic feature. A turbidity current is a mass of *sediment*-laden water which has substantial erosive power. Turbidity currents are thought to contribute to the formation of *submarine canyons*.

Typhoon A kind of *hurricane* (or tropical cyclone) bringing violent winds and heavy rain, a typhoon can do great damage. They occur in the South China Sea, especially around the Philippines.

U

U-shaped valley A river valley that has been deepened and widened by a *glacier*. They are characteristically flat-bottomed and steep-sided and generally much deeper than river valleys.

UN United Nations. Established in 1945, it contains 188 nations and aims to maintain international peace and security, and promote co-operation over economic, social, cultural and humanitarian problems.

UNICEF United Nations Children's Fund. A UN organization set up to promote family and child related programmes.

Urstromtäler A German word used to describe *meltwater* channels which flowed along the front edge of the advancing *ice sheet* during the last Ice Age, 18,000–20,000 years ago.

V

V-shaped valley A typical valley eroded by a river in its upper course.

Virgin rainforest Tropical *rainforest* in its original state, untouched by human activity such as logging, clearance for agriculture, settlement or road building.

Viticulture The cultivation of grapes for wine.

Volcano An opening or vent in the Earth's *crust* where molten rock, *magma*, erupts. Volcanoes tend to be conical but may also be a crack in the Earth's surface or a hole blasted through a mountain. The magma is accompanied by other materials such as gas, steam and fragments of rock, or *pyroclasts*. They tend to occur on destructive or constructive *tectonic plate* margins.

W-Z

Wadi The dry bed left by a torrent of water. Also classified as a *ephemeral* stream, found in *arid* and *semi-arid* regions, which are subject to sudden and often severe flash flooding.

Warm humid climate A rainy climate with warm summers and mild winters.

Water cycle The continuous circulation of water between the Earth's surface and the *atmosphere*. The processes include *evaporation* and *transpiration* of moisture into the atmosphere, and its return as *precipitation*, some of which flows into lakes and oceans.

Water table The upper level of *groundwater* saturation in permeable rock *strata*.

Watershed The dividing line between one *drainage basin* – an area where all streams flow into a single river system – and another. In the US, watershed also means the whole drainage basin of a single river system – its catchment area.

Waterspout A rotating column of water in the form of cloud, mist and spray which form on open water. Often has the appearance of a small *tornado*.

Weathering The decay and break-up of rocks at or near the Earth's surface, caused by water, wind, heat or ice, organic material or the *atmosphere*. *Physical weathering* includes the effects of frost and temperature changes. Biological weathering includes the effects of plant roots, burrowing animals and the acids produced by animals, especially as they decay after death. *Carbonation* and *hydrolysis* are among many kinds of *chemical weathering*.

Geographical names

The following glossary lists all geographical terms occurring on the maps and in main-entry names in the Index-Gazetteer. These terms may precede, follow or be run together with the proper element of the name; where they precede it the term is reversed for indexing purposes - thus Poluostrov Yamal is indexed as Yamal, Poluostrov.

Key

Geographical term
Language, Term

A

Å *Danish, Norwegian*, River
Āb *Persian*, River
Adrar *Berber*, Mountains
Agía, Ágios *Greek*, Saint
Air *Indonesian*, River
Ákra *Greek*, Cape, point
Alpen *German*, Alps
Alt- *German*, Old
Altiplanicie *Spanish*, Plateau
Älve(en) *Swedish*, River
-ån *Swedish*, River
Anse *French*, Bay
'Aqabat *Arabic*, Pass
Archipiélago *Spanish*, Archipelago
Arcipelago *Italian*, Archipelago
Arquipélago *Portuguese*, Archipelago
Arrecife(s) *Spanish*, Reef(s)
Aru *Tamil*, River
Augstiene *Latvian*, Upland
Aukštuma *Lithuanian*, Upland
Aust- *Norwegian*, Eastern
Avtonomnyy Okrug *Russian*, Autonomous district
Āw *Kurdish*, River
'Ayn *Arabic*, Spring, well
'Ayoûn *Arabic*, Wells

B

Baelt *Danish*, Strait
Bahía *Spanish*, Bay
Baḩr *Arabic*, River
Baía *Portuguese*, Bay
Baie *French*, Bay
Bañado *Spanish*, Marshy land
Bandao *Chinese*, Peninsula
Banjaran *Malay*, Mountain range
Baraji *Turkish*, Dam
Barragem *Portuguese*, Reservoir
Bassin *French*, Basin
Batang *Malay*, Stream
Beinn, Ben *Gaelic*, Mountain
-berg *Afrikaans, Norwegian*, Mountain
Besar *Indonesian, Malay*, Big
Birkat, Birket *Arabic*, Lake, well, cistern
Boğazi *Turkish*, Strait, defile
Boka *Serbo-Croatian*, Bay
Bol'sh-aya, -iye, -oy, -oye *Russian*, Big
Botigh(i) *Uzbek*, Depression basin
-bre(en) *Norwegian*, Glacier
Bredning *Danish*, Bay
Bucht *German*, Bay
Bugt(en) *Danish*, Bay
Buḩayrat *Arabic*, Lake, reservoir
Buḩeiret *Arabic*, Lake
Bukit *Malay*, Mountain
-bukta *Norwegian*, Bay
bukten *Swedish*, Bay
Bulag *Mongolian*, Spring
Bulak *Uighur*, Spring
Burnu *Turkish*, Cape, point
Buuraha *Somali*, Mountains

C

Cabo *Portuguese*, Cape
Caka *Tibetan*, Salt lake
Canal *Spanish*, Channel
Cap *French*, Cape
Capo *Italian*, Cape, headland
Cascada *Portuguese*, Waterfall
Cayo(s) *Spanish*, Islet(s), rock(s)
Cerro *Spanish*, Mountain
Chaîne *French*, Mountain range
Chapada *Portuguese*, Hills, upland
Chau *Cantonese*, Island
Chāy *Turkish*, River
Chhâk *Cambodian*, Bay
Chhu *Tibetan*, River
-chŏsuji *Korean*, Reservoir
Chott *Arabic*, Depression, salt lake
Chŭli *Uzbek*, Grassland, steppe
Ch'ün-tao *Chinese*, Island group
Chuŏr Phnum *Cambodian*, Mountains
Ciudad *Spanish*, City, town
Co *Tibetan*, Lake
Colline(s) *French*, Hill(s)
Cordillera *Spanish*, Mountain range
Costa *Spanish*, Coast
Côte *French*, Coast
Coxilha *Portuguese*, Mountains
Cuchilla *Spanish*, Mountains

D

Daban *Mongolian, Uighur*, Pass
Daği *Azerbaijani, Turkish*, Mountain
Dağlari *Azerbaijani, Turkish*, Mountains
-dake *Japanese*, Peak
-dal(en) *Norwegian*, Valley
Danau *Indonesian*, Lake
Dao *Chinese*, Island
Đao *Vietnamese*, Island
Daryā *Persian*, River
Daryācheh *Persian*, Lake
Dasht *Persian*, Desert, plain
Dawḩat *Arabic*, Bay
Denizi *Turkish*, Sea
Dere *Turkish*, Stream
Desierto *Spanish*, Desert
Dili *Azerbaijani*, Spit
-do *Korean*, Island
Dooxo *Somali*, Valley
Düzü *Azerbaijani*, Steppe
-dwīp *Bengali*, Island

E

-eilanden *Dutch*, Islands
Embalse *Spanish*, Reservoir
Ensenada *Spanish*, Bay
Erg *Arabic*, Dunes
Estany *Catalan*, Lake
Estero *Spanish*, Inlet
Estrecho *Spanish*, Strait
Étang *French*, Lagoon, lake
-ey *Icelandic*, Island
Ezero *Bulgarian, Macedonian*, Lake
Ezers *Latvian*, Lake

F

Feng *Chinese*, Peak
-fjella *Norwegian*, Mountain
Fjord *Danish*, Fjord
-fjord(en) *Danish, Norwegian, Swedish*, fjord
-fjørdhur *Faeroese*, Fjord
Fleuve *French*, River
Fliegu *Maltese*, Channel
-fljór *Icelandic*, River
-flói *Icelandic*, Bay
Forêt *French*, Forest

G

-gan *Japanese*, Rock
-gang *Korean*, River
Ganga *Hindi, Nepali, Sinhala*, River
Gaoyuan *Chinese*, Plateau
Garagumy *Turkmen*, Sands
-gawa *Japanese*, River
Gebel *Arabic*, Mountain
-gebirge *German*, Mountain range
Ghadīr *Arabic*, Well
Ghubbat *Arabic*, Bay
Gjiri *Albanian*, Bay
Gol *Mongolian*, River
Golfe *French*, Gulf
Golfo *Italian, Spanish*, Gulf
Göl(ü) *Turkish*, Lake
Golyam, -a *Bulgarian*, Big
Gora *Russian, Serbo-Croatian*, Mountain
Góra *Polish*, mountain
Gory *Russian*, Mountain
Gryada *Russian*, ridge
Guba *Russian*, Bay
-gundo *Korean*, island group
Gunung *Malay*, Mountain

H

Ḩadd *Arabic*, Spit
-haehyŏp *Korean*, Strait
Haff *German*, Lagoon
Hai *Chinese*, Bay, lake, sea
Haixia *Chinese*, Strait
Ḩammādah *Arabic*, Desert
Ḩammādat *Arabic*, Rocky plateau
Hāmūn *Persian*, Lake
-hantō *Japanese*, Peninsula
Har, Haré *Hebrew*, Mountain
Ḩarrat *Arabic*, Lava-field
Hav(et) *Danish*, Swedish, Sea
Hawr *Arabic*, Lake
Hāyk' *Amharic*, Lake
He *Chinese*, River
-hegység *Hungarian*, Mountain range
Heide *German*, Heath, moorland
Helodrano *Malagasy*, Bay
Higashi- *Japanese*, East(ern)
Ḩişā' *Arabic*, Well
Hka *Burmese*, River
-ho *Korean*, Lake
Hô *Korean*, Reservoir
Ḩolot *Hebrew*, Dunes
Hora *Belarussian, Czech*, Mountain
Hrada *Belarussian*, Mountain, ridge
Hsi *Chinese*, River
Hu *Chinese*, Lake
Huk *Danish*, Point

I

Île(s) *French*, Island(s)
Ilha(s) *Portuguese*, Island(s)
Ilhéu(s) *Portuguese*, Islet(s)
-isen *Norwegian*, Ice shelf
Imeni *Russian*, In the name of
Inish- *Gaelic*, Island
Insel(n) *German*, Island(s)
Irmağı, Irmak *Turkish*, River
Isla(s) *Spanish*, Island(s)
Isola (Isole) *Italian*, Island(s)

J

Jabal *Arabic*, Mountain
Jāl *Arabic*, Ridge
-järv *Estonian*, Lake
-järvi *Finnish*, Lake
Jazā'ir *Arabic*, Islands
Jazīrat *Arabic*, Island
Jazīreh *Persian*, Island
Jebel *Arabic*, Mountain
Jezero *Serbo-Croatian*, Lake
Jezioro *Polish*, Lake
Jiang *Chinese*, River
-jima *Japanese*, Island
Jižní *Czech*, Southern
-jõgi *Estonian*, River
-joki *Finnish*, River
-jökull *Icelandic*, Glacier
Jūn *Arabic*, Bay
Juzur *Arabic*, Islands

K

Kaikyō *Japanese*, Strait
-kaise *Lappish*, Mountain
Kali *Nepali*, River
Kalnas *Lithuanian*, Mountain
Kalns *Latvian*, Mountain
Kang *Chinese*, Harbour
Kangri *Tibetan*, Mountain(s)
Kaôh *Cambodian*, Island
Kapp *Norwegian*, Cape
Káto *Greek*, Lower
Kavīr *Persian*, Desert
K'edi *Georgian*, Mountain range
Kediet *Arabic*, Mountain
Kepi *Albanian*, Cape, point
Kepulauan *Indonesian, Malay*, Island group
Khalig, Khalīj *Arabic*, Gulf
Khawr *Arabic*, Inlet
Khola *Nepali*, River
Khrebet *Russian*, Mountain range
Ko *Thai*, Island
-ko *Japanese*, Inlet, lake
Kólpos *Greek*, Bay
-kopf *German*, Peak
Körfäzi *Azerbaijani*, Bay
Körfezi *Turkish*, Bay
Kõrgustik *Estonian*, Upland
Kosa *Russian, Ukrainian*, Spit
Koshi *Nepali*, River
Kou *Chinese*, River-mouth
Kowtal *Persian*, Pass
Kray *Russian*, Region, territory
Kryazh *Russian*, Ridge
Kuduk *Uighur*, Well
Kūh(hā) *Persian*, Mountain(s)
-kul' *Russian*, Lake
Kŭl(i) *Tajik, Uzbek*, Lake
-kundo *Korean*, Island group
-kysten *Norwegian*, Coast
Kyun *Burmese*, Island

L

Laaq *Somali*, Watercourse
Lac *French*, Lake
Lacul *Romanian*, Lake
Lagh *Somali*, Stream
Lago *Italian, Portuguese, Spanish*, Lake
Lagoa *Portuguese*, Lagoon
Laguna *Italian, Spanish*, Lagoon, lake
Laht *Estonian*, Bay
Laut *Indonesian*, Bay
Lembalemba *Malagasy*, Plateau
Lerr *Armenian*, Mountain
Lernnashghtt'a *Armenian*, Mountain range
Les *Czech*, Forest
Lich *Armenian*, Lake
Liehtao *Chinese*, Island group
Liqeni *Albanian*, Lake
Límni *Greek*, Lake
Ling *Chinese*, Mountain range
Llano *Spanish*, Plain, prairie
Lumi *Albanian*, River
Lyman *Ukrainian*, Estuary

M

Madīnat *Arabic*, City, town
Mae Nam *Thai*, River
-mägi *Estonian*, Hill
Maja *Albanian*, Mountain
Mal *Albanian*, Mountains
Mal-aya, -oye, -yy, *Russian*, Small
-man *Korean*, Bay
Mar *Spanish*, Lake
Marios *Lithuanian*, Lake
Massif *French*, Mountains
Meer *German*, Lake
-meer *Dutch*, Lake
Melkosopochnik *Russian*, Plain
-meri *Estonian*, Sea
Mifraz *Hebrew*, Bay
Minami- *Japanese*, South(ern)
-misaki *Japanese*, Cape, point
Monkhafad *Arabic*, Depression
Montagne(s) *French*, Mountain(s)
Montañas *Spanish*, Mountains
Mont(s) *French*, Mountain(s)
Monte *Italian, Portuguese*, Mountain
More *Russian*, Sea
Mörön *Mongolian*, River
Mys *Russian*, Cape, point

N

-nada *Japanese*, Open stretch of water
Nadi *Bengali*, River
Nagor'ye *Russian*, Upland
Naḩal *Hebrew*, River
Nahr *Arabic*, River
Nam *Laotian*, River
Namakzār *Persian*, Salt desert
Né-a, -on, -os *Greek*, New
Nedre- *Norwegian*, Lower
-neem *Estonian*, Cape, point
Nehri *Turkish*, River
-nes *Norwegian*, Cape, point
Nevado *Spanish*, Mountain (snow-capped)
Nieder- *German*, Lower
Nishi- *Japanese*, West(ern)
-nísi *Greek*, Island
Nisoi *Greek*, Islands
Nizhn-eye, -iy, -iye, -yaya *Russian*, Lower
Nizmennost' *Russian*, Lowland, plain
Nord *Danish, French, German*, North
Norte *Portuguese, Spanish*, North
Nos *Bulgarian*, Point, spit
Nosy *Malagasy*, Island
Nov-a, -i, *Bulgarian, Serbo-Croatian*, New
Nov-aya, -o, -oye, -yy, -yye *Russian*, New
Now-a, -e, -y *Polish*, New
Nur *Mongolian*, Lake
Nuruu *Mongolian*, Mountains
Nuur *Mongolian*, Lake
Nyzovyna *Ukrainian*, Lowland, plain

O

-ø *Danish*, Island
Ober- *German*, Upper
Oblast' *Russian*, Province
Órmos *Greek*, Bay
Orol(i) *Uzbek*, Island
Øster- *Norwegian*, Eastern
Ostrov(a) *Russian*, Island(s)
Otok *Serbo-Croatian*, Island
Oued *Arabic*, Watercourse
-oy *Faeroese*, Island
-øy(a) *Norwegian*, Island
Oya *Sinhala*, River
Ozero *Russian, Ukrainian*, Lake

P

Passo *Italian*, Pass
Pegunungan *Indonesian, Malay*, Mountain range
Pélagos *Greek*, Sea
Pendi *Chinese*, Basin
Penisola *Italian*, Peninsula
Pertuis *French*, Strait
Peski *Russian*, Sands
Phanom *Thai*, Mountain
Phou *Laotian*, Mountain
Pi *Chinese*, Point
Pic *Catalan, French*, Peak
Pico *Portuguese, Spanish*, Peak
-piggen *Danish*, Peak
Pik *Russian*, Peak
Pivostriv *Ukrainian*, Peninsula
Planalto *Portuguese*, Plateau
Planina, Planini *Bulgarian, Macedonian, Serbo-Croatian*, Mountain range
Plato *Russian*, Plateau
Ploskogor'ye *Russian*, Upland
Poluostrov *Russian*, Peninsula
Ponta *Portuguese*, Point
Porthmós *Greek*, Strait
Pótamos *Greek*, River
Presa *Spanish*, Dam
Prokhod *Bulgarian*, Pass
Proliv *Russian*, Strait
Pulau *Indonesian Malay*, Island
Pulu *Malay*, Island
Punta *Spanish*, Point
Pushcha *Belorussian*, Forest
Puszcza *Polish*, Forest

Q

Qā' *Arabic*, Depression
Qalamat *Arabic*, Well
Qatorkŭh(i) *Tajik*, Mountain
Qiuling *Chinese*, Hills
Qolleh *Persian*, Mountain
Qu *Tibetan*, Stream
Quan *Chinese*, Well
Qulla(i) *Tajik*, Peak
Qundao *Chinese*, Island group

R

Raas *Somali*, Cape
-rags *Latvian*, Cape
Ramlat *Arabic*, Sands
Ra's *Arabic*, Cape, headland, point
Ravnina *Bulgarian, Russian*, Plain
Récif *French*, Reef
Recife *Portuguese*, Reef
Reka *Bulgarian*, River
Represa (Rep.) *Portuguese, Spanish*, Reservoir
Reshteh *Persian*, Mountain range
Respublika *Russian*, Republic, first-order administrative division
Respublika(si) *Uzbek*, Republic, first-order administrative division
-retsugan *Japanese*, Chain of rocks
-rettō *Japanese*, Island chain
Riacho *Spanish*, Stream
Riban' *Malagasy*, Mountains
Rio *Portuguese*, River
Río *Spanish*, River
Riu *Catalan*, River
Rivier *Dutch*, River
Rivière *French*, River
Rowd *Pashtu*, River
Rt *Serbo-Croatian*, Point
Rūd *Persian*, River
Rūdkhāneh *Persian*, River
Rudohorie *Slovak*, Mountains
Ruisseau *French*, Stream

S

-saar *Estonian*, Island
-saari *Finnish*, Island
Sabkhat *Arabic*, Salt marsh
Sāgar(a) *Hindi*, Lake, reservoir
Şaḩrā' *Arabic*, Desert
Saint, Sainte *French*, Saint
Salar *Spanish*, Salt-pan
Salto *Portuguese, Spanish*, Waterfall
Samudra *Sinhala*, Reservoir
-san *Japanese, Korean*, Mountain
-sanchi *Japanese*, Mountains
-sandur *Icelandic*, Beach
Sankt *German, Swedish*, Saint
-sanmaek *Korean*, Mountain range
-sanmyaku *Japanese*, Mountain range
San, Santa, Santo *Italian, Portuguese, Spanish*, Saint
São *Portuguese*, Saint
Sarīr *Arabic*, Desert
Sebkha, Sebkhet *Arabic*, Depression, salt marsh
Sedlo *Czech*, Pass
See *German*, Lake
Selat *Indonesian*, Strait
Selatan *Indonesian*, Southern
-selkä *Finnish*, Lake, ridge
Selseleh *Persian*, Mountain range
Serra *Portuguese*, Mountain
Serranía *Spanish*, Mountain
-seto *Japanese*, Channel, strait
Sever-naya, -noye, -nyy, -o *Russian*, Northern
Sha'īb *Arabic*, Watercourse
Shākh *Kurdish*, Mountain
Shamo *Chinese*, Desert
Shan *Chinese*, Mountain(s)
Shankou *Chinese*, Pass
Shanmo *Chinese*, Mountain range
Shaţţ *Arabic*, Distributary
Shet' *Amharic*, River
Shi *Chinese*, Municipality
-shima *Japanese*, Island
Shiqqat *Arabic*, Depression
-shotō *Japanese*, Group of islands
Shuiku *Chinese*, Reservoir
Shŭrkhog(i) *Uzbek*, Salt marsh
Sierra *Spanish*, Mountains
Sint *Dutch*, Saint
-sjø(en) *Norwegian*, Lake
-sjön *Swedish*, Lake
Solonchak *Russian*, Salt lake
Solonchakovyye Vpadiny *Russian*, Salt basin, wetlands
Son *Vietnamese*, Mountain
Sông *Vietnamese*, River
Sør- *Norwegian*, Southern
-spitze *German*, Peak
Star-á, -é *Czech*, Old
Star-aya, -oye, -yy, -yye *Russian*, Old
Stenó *Greek*, Strait
Step' *Russian*, Steppe
Štít *Slovak*, Peak
Stœng *Cambodian*, River
Stolovaya Strana *Russian*, Plateau
Stredné *Slovak*, Middle
Střední *Czech*, Middle
Stretto *Italian*, Strait
Su Anbari *Azerbaijani*, Reservoir
-suidō *Japanese*, Channel, strait
Sund *Swedish*, Sound, strait
Sungai *Indonesian, Malay*, River
Suu *Turkish*, River

T

Tal *Mongolian*, Plain
Tandavan' *Malagasy*, Mountain range
Tangorombohitr' *Malagasy*, Mountain massif
Tanjung *Indonesian, Malay*, Cape, point
Tao *Chinese*, Island
Ţaraq *Arabic*, Hills
Tassili *Berber*, Mountain, plateau
Tau *Russian*, Mountain(s)
Taungdan *Burmese*, Mountain range
Techníti Límni *Greek*, Reservoir
Tekojärvi *Finnish*, Reservoir
Teluk *Indonesian, Malay*, Bay
Tengah *Indonesian*, Middle
Terara *Amharic*, Mountain
Timur *Indonesian*, Eastern
-tind(an) *Norwegian*, Peak
Tizma(si) *Uzbek*, Mountain range, ridge
-tō *Japanese*, island
Tog *Somali*, Valley
-tōge *Japanese*, pass
Togh(i) *Uzbek*, mountain
Tônlé *Cambodian*, Lake
Top *Dutch*, Peak
-tunturi *Finnish*, Mountain
Ţuraq *Arabic*, hills
Tur'at *Arabic*, Channel

U

Udde(n) *Swedish*, Cape, point
'Uqlat *Arabic*, Well
Utara *Indonesian*, Northern
Uul *Mongolian*, Mountains

V

Väin *Estonian*, Strait
Vallée *French*, Valley
-vatn *Icelandic*, Lake
-vatnet *Norwegian*, Lake
Velayat *Turkmen*, Province
-vesi *Finnish*, Lake
Vestre- *Norwegian*, Western
-vidda *Norwegian*, Plateau
-vík *Icelandic*, Bay
-viken *Swedish*, Bay, inlet
Vinh *Vietnamese*, Bay
Víztárloló *Hungarian*, Reservoir
Vodaskhovishcha *Belarussian*, Reservoir
Vodokhranilishche (Vdkhr.) *Russian*, Reservoir
Vodoskhovyshche (Vdskh.) *Ukrainian*, Reservoir
Volcán *Spanish*, Volcano
Vostochn-o, yy *Russian*, Eastern
Vozvyshennost' *Russian*, Upland, plateau
Vozyera *Belarussian*, Lake
Vpadina *Russian*, Depression
Vrchovina *Czech*, Mountains
Vrha *Macedonian*, Peak
Vychodné *Slovak*, Eastern
Vysochyna *Ukrainian*, Upland
Vysočina *Czech*, Upland

W

Waadi *Somali*, Watercourse
Wādī *Arabic* Watercourse
Wāḩat, Wâhat *Arabic*, Oasis
Wald *German*, Forest
Wan *Chinese*, Bay
Way *Indonesian*, River
Webi *Somali*, River
Wenz *Amharic*, River
Wiloyat(i) *Uzbek*, Province
Wyżyna *Polish*, Upland
Wzgórza *Polish*, Upland
Wzvyshsha *Belarussian*, Upland

X

Xé *Laotian*, River
Xi *Chinese*, Stream

Y

-yama *Japanese*, Mountain
Yanchi *Chinese*, Salt lake
Yang *Chinese*, Bay
Yanhu *Chinese*, Salt lake
Yarımadası *Azerbaijani, Turkish*, Peninsula
Yaylası *Turkish*, Plateau
Yazovir *Bulgarian*, Reservoir
Yoma *Burmese*, Mountains
Ytre- *Norwegian*, Outer
Yü *Chinese*, Island
Yunhe *Chinese*, Canal
Yuzhn-o, -yy *Russian*, Southern

Z

-zaki *Japanese*, Cape, point
Zaliv *Bulgarian, Russian*, Bay
-zan *Japanese*, Mountain
Zangbo *Tibetan*, River
Zapadn-aya, -o, -yy *Russian*, Western
Západné *Slovak*, Western
Západní *Czech*, Western
Zatoka *Polish, Ukrainian*, Bay
-zee *Dutch*, Sea
Zemlya *Russian*, Earth, land
Zizhiqu *Chinese*, Autonomous region

Index

Glossary of Abbreviations

This glossary provides a comprehensive guide to the abbreviations used in this Atlas, and in the Index.

A
abbrev. abbreviated
AD Anno Domini
Afr. Afrikaans
Alb. Albanian
Amh. Amharic
anc. ancient
approx. approximately
Ar. Arabic
Arm. Armenian
ASEAN Association of South East Asian Nations
ASSR Autonomous Soviet Socialist Republic
Aust. Australian
Az. Azerbaijani
Azerb. Azerbaijan

B
Basq. Basque
BC before Christ
Bel. Belorussian
Ben. Bengali
Ber. Berber
B–H Bosnia-Herzegovina
bn billion (one thousand million)
BP British Petroleum
Bret. Breton
Brit. British
Bul. Bulgarian
Bur. Burmese

C
C central
C. Cape
°C degrees Centigrade
CACM Central America Common Market
Cam. Cambodian
Cant. Cantonese
CAR Central African Republic
Cast. Castilian
Cat. Catalan
CEEAC Central America Common Market
Chin. Chinese
CIS Commonwealth of Independent States
cm centimetre(s)
Cro. Croat
Cz. Czech
Czech Rep. Czech Republic

D
Dan. Danish
Div. Divehi
Dom. Rep. Dominican Republic
Dut. Dutch

E
E east
EC see EU
EEC see EU
ECOWAS Economic Community of West African States
ECU European Currency Unit
EMS European Monetary System
Eng. English
est estimated
Est. Estonian
EU European Union (previously European Community [EC], European Economic Community [EEC])

F
°F degrees Fahrenheit
Faer. Faeroese
Fij. Fijian
Fin. Finnish
Fr. French
Fris. Frisian
ft foot/feet
FYROM Former Yugoslav Republic of Macedonia

G
g gram(s)
Gael. Gaelic
Gal. Galician
GDP Gross Domestic Product (the total value of goods and services produced by a country excluding income from foreign countries)
Geor. Georgian
Ger. German
Gk Greek
GNP Gross National Product (the total value of goods and services produced by a country)

H
Heb. Hebrew
HEP hydro-electric power
Hind. Hindi
hist. historical
Hung. Hungarian

I
I. Island
Icel. Icelandic
in inch(es)
In. Inuit (Eskimo)
Ind. Indonesian
Intl International
Ir. Irish
Is Islands
It. Italian

J
Jap. Japanese

K
Kaz. Kazakh
kg kilogram(s)
Kir. Kirghiz
km kilometre(s)
km² square kilometre (singular)
Kor. Korean
Kurd. Kurdish

L
L. Lake
LAIA Latin American Integration Association
Lao. Laotian
Lapp. Lappish
Lat. Latin
Latv. Latvian
Liech. Liechtenstein
Lith. Lithuanian
Lus. Lusatian
Lux. Luxembourg

M
m million/metre(s)
Mac. Macedonian
Maced. Macedonia
Mal. Malay
Malg. Malagasy
Malt. Maltese
mi. mile(s)
Mong. Mongolian
Mt. Mountain
Mts Mountains

N
N north
NAFTA North American Free Trade Agreement
Nep. Nepali
Neth. Netherlands
Nic. Nicaraguan
Nor. Norwegian
NZ New Zealand

P
Pash. Pashtu
PNG Papua New Guinea
Pol. Polish
Poly. Polynesian
Port. Portuguese
prev. previously

R
Rep. Republic
Res. Reservoir
Rmsch Romansch
Rom. Romanian
Rus. Russian
Russ. Fed. Russian Federation

S
S south
SADC Southern Africa Development Community
SCr. Serbian, Croatian
Sinh. Sinhala
Slvk Slovak
Slvn. Slovene
Som. Somali
Sp. Spanish
St., St Saint
Strs Straits
Swa. Swahili
Swe. Swedish
Switz. Switzerland

T
Taj. Tajik
Th. Thai
Thai. Thailand
Tib. Tibetan
Turk. Turkish
Turkm. Turkmenistan

U
UAE United Arab Emirates
Uigh. Uighur
UK United Kingdom
Ukr. Ukrainian
UN United Nations
Urd. Urdu
US/USA United States of America
USSR Union of Soviet Socialist Republics
Uzb. Uzbek

V
var. variant
Vdkhr. Vodokhranilishche (Russian for reservoir)
Vdskh. Vodoskhovyshche (Ukrainian for reservoir)
Vtn. Vietnamese

W
W west
Wel. Welsh

This index lists all the placenames and features shown on the regional and continental maps in this Atlas. Placenames are referenced to the largest scale map on which they appear. The policy followed throughout the Atlas is to use the local spelling or local name at regional level; commonly-used English language names may occasionally be added (in parentheses) where this is an aid to identification e.g. Firenze (Florence). English names, where they exist, have been used for all international features e.g. oceans and country names; they are also used on the continental maps and in the introductory World Today section; these are then fully cross-referenced to the local names found on the regional maps. The index also contains commonly-found alternative names and variant spellings, which are also fully cross-referenced.

All main entry names are those of settlements unless otherwise indicated by the use of italicized definitions or representative symbols, which are keyed at the foot of each page.

ABUT HEAD – AIGEN IM MÜLKREIS

185 E18 **Abut Head** *headland* South Island, New Zealand 43°06′S 170°16′E
80 E9 **Abu ʻUrug** Northern Kordofan, C Sudan 15°52′N 30°25′E
80 K12 **Ābuyē Mēda** ▲ C Ethiopia 10°28′N 39°44′E
80 D11 **Abu Zabad** Western Kordofan, C Sudan 12°21′N 29°16′E
143 P16 **Abū Ẓabī** *var.* Abū Ẓabī, *Eng.* Abu Dhabi. ● (United Arab Emirates) Abū Ẓaby, C United Arab Emirates 24°30′N 54°20′E
Abū Ẓabī *see* Abū Ẓabī
75 X8 **Abu Zenīma** E Egypt 29°01′N 33°08′E
95 N17 **Åby** Östergötland, S Sweden 58°40′N 16°10′E
Abyaḑ, Al Baḩr al *see* White Nile
Åbybro *see* Aabybro
80 D13 **Abyei** Western Kordofan, S Sudan 09°35′N 28°28′E
Abyla *see* Ávila
Abymes *see* les Abymes
Abyssinia *see* Ethiopia
Açaba *see* Assaba
54 F11 **Acacías** Meta, C Colombia 03°59′N 73°46′W
58 L13 **Açailandia** Maranhão, E Brazil 04°51′S 47°26′W
Acaill *see* Achill Island
42 E8 **Acajutla** Sonsonate, W El Salvador 13°34′N 89°50′W
79 D17 **Acalayong** SW Equatorial Guinea 01°05′N 09°34′E
41 N13 **Acámbaro** Guanajuato, C Mexico 20°01′N 100°42′W
54 C6 **Acandí** Chocó, NW Colombia 08°32′N 77°20′W
104 H4 **A Cañiza** *var.* La Cañiza. Galicia, NW Spain 42°13′N 08°16′W
40 J11 **Acaponeta** Nayarit, C Mexico 22°30′N 105°21′W
40 J11 **Acaponeta, Río de** ≈ C Mexico
41 O16 **Acapulco** *var.* Acapulco de Juárez. Guerrero, S Mexico 16°51′N 99°53′W
Acapulco de Juárez *see* Acapulco
55 T13 **Acarai Mountains** *Sp.* Serra Acaraí. ▲▲ Brazil/Guyana
Acaraí, Serra *see* Acarai Mountains
58 O13 **Acaraú** Ceará, NE Brazil 04°35′S 37°37′W
54 J6 **Acarigua** Portuguesa, N Venezuela 09°35′N 69°12′W
42 C6 **Acatenango, Volcán de** ☒ S Guatemala 14°30′N 90°52′W
41 Q15 **Acatlán** *var.* Acatlán de Osorio. Puebla, S Mexico 18°12′N 98°02′W
Acatlán de Osorio *see* Acatlán
41 S15 **Acayucan** *var.* Acayucán. Veracruz-Llave, E Mexico 17°59′N 94°58′W
Accho *see* Akko
21 Y5 **Accomac** Virginia, NE USA 37°43′N 75°41′W
77 Q17 **Accra** ● (Ghana)SE Ghana 05°33′N 00°15′W
97 L17 **Accrington** NW England, United Kingdom 53°46′N 02°21′W
61 B19 **Acebal** Santa Fe, C Argentina 33°14′S 60°50′W
168 H8 **Aceh** *off.* Daerah Istimewa Aceh, *var.* Acheen, Achin, Atchin, Atjeh. ◈ *autonomous district* NW Indonesia
107 M18 **Acerenza** Basilicata, S Italy 40°46′N 15°51′E
107 K17 **Acerra** *anc.* Acerrae. Campania, S Italy 40°56′N 14°22′E
Acerrae *see* Acerra
57 J17 **Achacachi** La Paz, W Bolivia 16°01′S 68°44′W
54 K7 **Achaguas** Apure, C Venezuela 07°46′N 68°14′W
154 H12 **Achalpur** *prev.* Elichpur, Ellichpur. Mahārāshtra, C India 21°19′N 77°30′E
61 F18 **Achar** Tacuarembó, C Uruguay 32°20′S 56°15′W
137 R10 **Achara** *var.* Ajaria. ◈ *autonomous republic* SW Georgia
115 H19 **Acharnés** *var.* Aharnes; *prev.* Akharnaí. Attikí, C Greece 38°09′N 23°58′E
Ach'asar Lerr *see* Achkasar
Acheen *see* Aceh
99 K16 **Achel** Limburg, NE Belgium 51°15′N 05°31′E
115 D16 **Achelóos** *var.* Akhelóös, Aspropótamos; *anc.* Achelous. ≈ W Greece
Achelous *see* Achelóos
163 W8 **Acheng** Heilongjiang, NE China 45°32′N 126°56′E
109 N6 **Achenkirch** Tirol, W Austria 47°31′N 11°42′E
101 L24 **Achenpass** *pass* Austria/Germany
109 N7 **Achensee** ◎ W Austria
101 F22 **Achern** Baden-Württemberg, SW Germany 48°37′N 08°04′E
115 C16 **Acherón** ≈ W Greece
77 W11 **Achétinamou** ≈ S Niger
152 J12 **Achhnera** Uttar Pradesh, N India 27°10′N 77°45′E
42 C7 **Achiguate, Río** ≈ S Guatemala
97 A16 **Achill Head** *Ir.* Ceann Acla. *headland* W Ireland 53°58′N 10°14′W
97 A16 **Achill Island** *Ir.* Acaill. *island* W Ireland
100 H11 **Achim** Niedersachsen, NW Germany 53°01′N 09°01′E
149 S5 **Achin** Nangarhār, E Afghanistan 34°04′N 70°41′E
Achin *see* Aceh
122 K12 **Achinsk** Krasnoyarskiy Kray, S Russian Federation 56°21′N 90°25′E
162 E5 **Achit Nuur** ◎ NW Mongolia
137 T11 **Achkasar** *Arm.* Ach'asar Lerr. ▲ Armenia/Georgia 41°09′N 43°55′E
126 K13 **Achuyevo** Krasnodarskiy Kray, SW Russian Federation 46°00′N 38°01′E
81 F16 **Achwa** *var.* Aswa. ≈ N Uganda
136 E15 **Acıgöl** *salt lake* SW Turkey
107 L24 **Acireale** Sicilia, Italy, C Mediterranean Sea 37°36′N 15°10′E
Aciris *see* Agri
25 N7 **Ackerly** Texas, SW USA 32°31′N 101°43′W
22 M4 **Ackerman** Mississippi, S USA 33°18′N 89°10′W
29 W13 **Ackley** Iowa, C USA 42°33′N 93°03′W
44 J5 **Acklins Island** *island* SE Bahamas
Acla, Ceann *see* Achill Head
62 H11 **Aconcagua, Cerro** ▲ W Argentina 32°36′S 69°53′W
Açores/Açores, Arquipélago dos/Açores, Ilhas dos *see* Azores
104 H2 **A Coruña** *Cast.* La Coruña, *Eng.* Corunna; *anc.* Caronium. Galicia, NW Spain 43°22′N 08°24′W
104 G2 **A Coruña** *Cast.* La Coruña. ◈ *province* Galicia, NW Spain
42 L10 **Acoyapa** Chontales, S Nicaragua 11°58′N 85°10′W
106 H13 **Acquapendente** Lazio, C Italy 42°44′N 11°52′E
106 J13 **Acquasanta Terme** Marche, C Italy 42°46′N 13°24′E
106 I13 **Acquasparta** Lazio, C Italy 42°41′N 12°31′E
106 C9 **Acqui Terme** Piemonte, NW Italy 44°41′N 08°28′E
Acrae *see* Palazzola Acreide
182 F7 **Acraman, Lake** *salt lake* South Australia
59 A15 **Acre** *off.* Estado do Acre. ◈ *state* W Brazil
Acre *see* Akko
59 C16 **Acre, Rio** ≈ W Brazil
107 N20 **Acri** Calabria, SW Italy 39°30′N 16°22′E
Acte *see* Ágion Óros
191 Y12 **Actéon, Groupe** *island group* Îles Tuamotu, SE French Polynesia
15 P12 **Acton-Vale** Québec, SE Canada 45°39′N 72°31′W
41 P13 **Actopan** *var.* Actopán. Hidalgo, C Mexico 20°19′N 98°59′W
59 P14 **Açu** *var.* Assu. Rio Grande do Norte, E Brazil 05°33′S 36°55′W
Acunum Acusio *see* Montélimar
77 Q17 **Ada** SE Ghana 05°47′N 00°42′E
112 L8 **Ada** Vojvodina, N Serbia 45°48′N 20°08′E
29 R5 **Ada** Minnesota, N USA 47°18′N 96°31′W
31 R12 **Ada** Ohio, N USA 40°46′N 83°49′W
27 O12 **Ada** Oklahoma, C USA 34°47′N 96°41′W
162 L8 **Adaatsag** *var.* Tavin. Dundgovĭ, C Mongolia 46°27′N 105°43′E
Ada Bazar *see* Adapazarı
40 D3 **Adair, Bahía de** *bay* NW Mexico
104 M7 **Adaja** ≈ N Spain
38 H17 **Adak Island** *island* Aleutian Islands, Alaska, USA
Adalia *see* Antalya
Adalia, Gulf of *see* Antalya Körfezi
141 X9 **Adam** N Oman 22°22′N 57°30′E
Adama *see* Nazrēt
60 I8 **Adamantina** São Paulo, S Brazil 21°41′S 51°04′W
79 E14 **Adamaoua** *Eng.* Adamawa. ◈ *province* N Cameroon
68 F11 **Adamaoua, Massif d'** *Eng.* Adamawa Highlands. *plateau* NW Cameroon
77 Y14 **Adamawa** ◈ *state* E Nigeria
Adamawa *see* Adamaoua
Adamawa Highlands *see* Adamaoua, Massif d'
106 F6 **Adamello** ▲ N Italy 46°09′N 10°33′E
81 J14 **Ādamī Tulu** Oromīya, C Ethiopia 07°52′N 38°39′E
63 M23 **Adam, Mount** *var.* Monte Independencia. ▲ West Falkland, Falkland Islands 51°36′S 60°00′W
29 R16 **Adams** Nebraska, C USA 40°25′N 96°30′W
18 H8 **Adams** New York, NE USA 43°48′N 75°57′W
29 Q3 **Adams** North Dakota, N USA 48°23′N 98°01′W
155 I23 **Adam's Bridge** *chain of shoals* NW Sri Lanka
32 H10 **Adams, Mount** ▲ Washington, NW USA 46°12′N 121°29′W
Adam's Peak *see* Sri Pada
191 R16 **Adam's Rock** *island* Pitcairn Island, Pitcairn Islands
191 P16 **Adamstown** ○ (Pitcairn Islands)Pitcairn Island, Pitcairn Islands 25°04′S 130°05′W
20 G10 **Adamsville** Tennessee, S USA 35°14′N 88°23′W
25 S9 **Adamsville** Texas, SW USA 31°15′N 98°09′W
141 O17 **ʻAdan** *Eng.* Aden. SW Yemen 12°51′N 45°05′E
136 K16 **Adana** *var.* Seyhan. Adana, S Turkey 37°N 35°19′E
136 K16 **Adana** *var.* Seyhan. ◈ *province* S Turkey
Adâncata *see* Horlivka
169 V12 **Adang, Teluk** *bay* Borneo, C Indonesia
136 F11 **Adapazarı** *prev.* Ada Bazar. Sakarya, NW Turkey 40°49′N 30°24′E
80 H8 **Adarama** River Nile, NE Sudan 17°04′N 34°57′E
195 Q16 **Adare, Cape** *cape* Antarctica
Ādavāni *see* Ādoni
106 E6 **Adda** *anc.* Addua. ≈ N Italy
80 A13 **Adda** ≈ W Sudan
143 Q17 **Aḑ Ḑab'īyah** Abū Ẓaby, C United Arab Emirates 24°17′N 54°08′E
143 O18 **Aḑ Ḑafrah** *desert* S United Arab Emirates
141 Q6 **Ad Dahnā'** *desert* E Saudi Arabia
74 A11 **Ad Dakhla** *var.* Dakhla. SW Western Sahara 23°46′N 15°56′W
Ad Dalanj *see* Dilling
Ad Damar *see* Ed Damer
Ad Damazīn *see* Ed Damazin
Ad Dāmir *see* Ed Damer
173 N2 **Ad Dammām** *desert* NE Saudi Arabia
141 R6 **Ad Dammān** *var.* Dammām. Ash Sharqīyah, NE Saudi Arabia 26°23′N 50°05′E
Ad Dāmūr *see* Damoûr
140 K5 **Ad Dār al Ḩamrā'** Tabūk, NW Saudi Arabia 27°22′N 37°46′E
140 M13 **Ad Darb** Jīzān, SW Saudi Arabia 17°45′N 42°15′E
141 O8 **Ad Dawādimī** Ar Riyāḑ, C Saudi Arabia 24°32′N 44°21′E
143 N16 **Ad Dawḩah** *Eng.* Doha. ● (Qatar) C Qatar 25°15′N 51°36′E
143 N16 **Ad Dawḩah** *Eng.* Doha. ✈ C Qatar 25°11′N 51°37′E
139 S6 **Ad Dawr** Şalāḩ ad Dīn, N Iraq 34°30′N 43°49′E
139 Y12 **Ad Dayr** *var.* Dayr, Shahbān. Al Başrah, E Iraq 30°45′N 47°36′E
Addi Arkay *see* Ādī Ārk'ay
139 X15 **Ad Dibdibah** *physical region* Iraq/Kuwait
Aḑ Ḑiffah *see* Libyan Plateau
Addis Ababa *see* Ādīs Ābeba
Addison *see* Webster Springs
139 U10 **Ad Dīwānīyah** *var.* Diwaniyah. C Iraq 32°00′N 44°57′E
Addoo Atoll *see* Addu Atoll
Addua *see* Adda
151 K22 **Addu Atoll** *var.* Addoo Atoll, Seenu Atoll. *atoll* S Maldives
Ad Dujail *see* Ad Dujayl
139 T7 **Ad Dujayl** *var.* Ad Dujail. Şalāḩ ad Dīn, N Iraq 33°49′N 44°16′E
Ad Duwaym/Ad Duwēm *see* Ed Dueim
99 D16 **Adegem** Oost-Vlaanderen, NW Belgium 51°12′N 03°31′E
23 U7 **Adel** Georgia, SE USA 31°08′N 83°25′W
29 U14 **Adel** Iowa, C USA 41°36′N 94°01′W
182 I9 **Adelaide** *state capital* South Australia 34°56′S 138°36′E
44 H2 **Adelaide** New Providence, N Bahamas 24°59′N 77°30′W
182 I9 **Adelaide** ✈ South Australia 34°55′S 138°31′E
194 H6 **Adelaide Island** *island* Antarctica
181 P2 **Adelaide River** Northern Territory, N Australia 13°12′S 131°06′E
76 M10 **ʻAdel Bagrou** Hodh ech Chargui, SE Mauritania 15°33′N 07°04′W
186 D6 **Adelbert Range** ▲▲ N Papua New Guinea
180 K3 **Adele Island** *island* Western Australia
107 O17 **Adelfia** Puglia, SE Italy 41°01′N 16°52′E
195 V16 **Adélie Coast** *physical region* Antarctica
195 V14 **Adélie, Terre** *physical region* Antarctica
Adelnau *see* Odolanów
Adelsberg *see* Postojna
Aden *see* Khormaksar
Aden *see* ʻAdan
141 Q17 **Aden, Gulf of** *gulf* SW Arabian Sea
77 V10 **Aderbissinat** Agadez, C Niger 15°30′N 07°57′E
Adhaim *see* Al ʻUẓaym
143 R16 **Adh Dhayd** *var.* Al Dhaid. Ash Shāriqah, NE United Arab Emirates 25°19′N 55°51′E
140 M4 **ʻAdhfā'** *spring/well* NW Saudi Arabia 29°15′N 41°24′E
138 I13 **ʻĀdhriyāt, Jabāl al** ▲ S Jordan
80 I10 **Ādī Ārk'ay** *var.* Addi Arkay. Āmara, N Ethiopia 13°18′N 37°56′E
182 C7 **Adieu, Cape** *headland* South Australia 32°01′S 132°12′E
106 H8 **Adige** *Ger.* Etsch. ≈ N Italy
80 J10 **Ādīgrat** Tigray, N Ethiopia 14°17′N 39°27′E
80 J10 **ʻAdi Kh'eyih** C Eritrea 19°58′N 39°06′E
154 I13 **Ādilābād** *var.* Ādilābād. Andhra Pradesh, C India 19°40′N 78°31′E
35 P2 **Adin** California, W USA 41°10′N 120°57′W
171 V14 **Adi, Pulau** *island* E Indonesia
18 K8 **Adirondack Mountains** ▲▲ New York, NE USA
80 J13 **Ādīs Ābeba** *Eng.* Addis Ababa. ● (Ethiopia) Ādīs Ābeba, C Ethiopia 8°59′N 38°43′E
80 J13 **Ādīs Ābeba** ✈ Ādīs Ābeba, C Ethiopia 08°58′N 38°53′E
80 I11 **Ādīs Zemen** Āmara, N Ethiopia 12°00′N 37°43′E
Adi Ugri *see* Mendefera
137 N15 **Adıyaman** Adıyaman, SE Turkey 37°46′N 38°15′E
137 N15 **Adıyaman** ◈ *province* S Turkey
116 L11 **Adjud** Vrancea, E Romania 46°07′N 27°10′E
45 T6 **Adjuntas** C Puerto Rico 18°10′N 66°42′W
Adjuntas, Presa de las *see* Vicente Guerrero, Presa
Ādkup *see* Erikub Atoll
126 L15 **Adler** Krasnodarskiy Kray, SW Russian Federation 43°25′N 39°58′E
Adler *see* Orlice
108 G7 **Adliswil** Zürich, NW Switzerland 47°19′N 08°32′E
32 G7 **Admiralty Inlet** *inlet* Washington, NW USA
39 X13 **Admiralty Island** *island* Alexander Archipelago, Alaska, USA
186 E5 **Admiralty Islands** *island group* N Papua New Guinea
136 B14 **Adnan Menderes** ✈ (İzmir) İzmir, W Turkey 38°16′N 27°09′E
37 V6 **Adobe Creek Reservoir** ⊠ Colorado, C USA
77 T16 **Ado-Ekiti** Ekiti, SW Nigeria 07°42′N 05°13′E
Adola *see* Kibre Mengist
61 C23 **Adolfo González Chaues** Buenos Aires, E Argentina 38°13′S 60°07′W
155 H17 **Ādoni** *var.* Ādavāni. Andhra Pradesh, C India 15°38′N 77°16′E
102 K15 **Adour** *anc.* Aturus. ≈ SW France
Adowa *see* Ādwa
105 O15 **Adra** Andalucía, S Spain 36°45′N 03°01′W
107 L24 **Adrano** Sicilia, Italy, C Mediterranean Sea 37°39′N 14°49′E
74 I9 **Adrar** C Algeria 27°56′N 00°12′W
76 K7 **Adrar** ◈ *region* C Mauritania
74 L11 **Adrar** ▲▲ SE Algeria
74 A12 **Adrar Souttouf** ▲▲ SW Western Sahara
Adrasman *see* Adrasmon
147 Q10 **Adrasmon** *Rus.* Adrasman. NW Tajikistan 40°38′N 69°56′E
78 K10 **Adré** Ouaddaï, E Chad 13°26′N 22°14′E
106 H9 **Adria** *anc.* Atria, Hadria, Hatria. Veneto, NE Italy 45°03′N 12°04′E
31 R10 **Adrian** Michigan, N USA 41°54′N 84°02′W
29 S11 **Adrian** Minnesota, N USA 43°38′N 95°55′W
27 R5 **Adrian** Missouri, C USA 38°24′N 94°21′W
24 M2 **Adrian** Texas, SW USA 35°16′N 102°39′W
21 S4 **Adrian** West Virginia, NE USA 38°53′N 80°14′W
Adrianople/Adrianopolis *see* Edirne
121 P7 **Adriatic Basin** *undersea feature* Adriatic Sea, N Mediterranean Sea 42°00′N 17°30′E
Adriatico, Mare *see* Adriatic Sea
106 L13 **Adriatic Sea** *Alb.* Deti Adriatik, *It.* Mare Adriatico, *SCr.* Jadransko More, *Slvn.* Jadransko Morje. *sea* N Mediterranean Sea
Adriatik, Deti *see* Adriatic Sea
Adua *see* Ādwa
Aduana del Sásabe *see* El Sásabe
79 O17 **Adusa** Orientale, NE Dem. Rep. Congo 01°25′N 28°05′E
118 J13 **Adutiškis** Vilnius, E Lithuania 55°09′N 26°34′E
27 Y7 **Advance** Missouri, C USA 37°06′N 89°54′W
65 D25 **Adventure Sound** *bay* East Falkland, Falkland Islands
80 J10 **Ādwa** *var.* Adowa, *It.* Adua. Tigray, N Ethiopia 14°08′N 38°51′E
123 Q8 **Adycha** ≈ NE Russian Federation
126 L14 **Adygeya, Respublika** ◈ *autonomous republic* SW Russian Federation
Adzhikui *see* Ajyguýy
77 N17 **Adzopé** SE Ivory Coast 06°07′N 03°49′W
125 U4 **Adz'va** ≈ NW Russian Federation
125 U5 **Adz'vavom** Respublika Komi, NW Russian Federation 66°35′N 59°13′E
Ædua *see* Autun
115 K19 **Aegean Islands** *island group* Greece/Turkey
Aegean North *see* Vóreion Aigaíon
115 I17 **Aegean Sea** *Gk.* Aigaíon Pelagos, Aigaío Pélagos, *Turk.* Ege Denizi. *sea* NE Mediterranean Sea
Aegean South *see* Nótion Aigaíon
118 H3 **Aegviidu** *Ger.* Charlottenhof. Harjumaa, NW Estonia 59°17′N 25°37′E
Aegyptus *see* Egypt
Aelana *see* Al ʻAqabah
Aelok *see* Ailuk Atoll
Aelōninae *see* Ailinginae Atoll
Aelōnlaplap *see* Ailinglaplap Atoll
Æmilia *see* Emilia-Romagna
Æmilianum *see* Millau
Aemona *see* Ljubljana
Aenaria *see* Ischia
Aeolian Islands *see* Eolie, Isole
191 Z3 **Aeon Point** *headland* Kiritimati, NE Kiribati 01°46′N 157°11′W
Æsernia *see* Isernia
104 G3 **A Estrada** Galicia, NW Spain 42°41′N 08°29′W
115 C18 **Aetós** Itháki, Iónia Nísoi, Greece, C Mediterranean Sea 38°21′N 20°40′E
191 Q8 **Afaahiti** Tahiti, W French Polynesia 17°43′S 149°18′W
139 U10 **ʻAfak** Al Qādisīyah, C Iraq 32°04′N 45°17′E
Afanasjevo *see* Afanas'yevo
125 T14 **Afanas'yevo** *var.* Afanasjevo. Kirovskaya Oblast', NW Russian Federation 58°55′N 53°13′E
Afándou *see* Afántou
115 O23 **Afántou** *var.* Afándou. Ródos, Dodekánisa, Greece, Aegean Sea 36°17′N 28°10′E
80 K11 **Āfar** ◈ *region* NE Ethiopia
Afar Depression *see* Danakil Desert
191 O7 **Afareaitu** Moorea, W French Polynesia 17°33′S 149°47′W
140 L7 **ʻAfarīyah, Bi'r al** *well* NW Saudi Arabia
Afars et des Issas, Territoire Français des *see* Djibouti
83 D22 **Affenrücken** Karas, SW Namibia 28°05′S 15°49′E
Afghānestān, Dowlat-e Eslāmī-ye *see* Afghanistan
148 M6 **Afghanistan** *off.* Islamic Republic of Afghanistan, *Per.* Dowlat-e Eslāmī-ye Afghānestān; *prev.* Republic of Afghanistan. ◆ *islamic state* C Asia
Afgoi *see* Afgooye
81 N17 **Afgooye** *It.* Afgoi. Shabeellaha Hoose, S Somalia 02°09′N 45°07′E
141 N8 **ʻAfīf** Ar Riyāḑ, C Saudi Arabia 23°57′N 42°57′E
77 V17 **Afikpo** Ebonyi, S Nigeria 05°52′N 07°58′E
Afiun Karahissar *see* Afyon
Åfjord *see* Åi Åfjord
109 V6 **Aflenz Kurort** Steiermark, E Austria 47°33′N 15°14′E
74 J6 **Aflou** N Algeria 34°09′N 02°06′E
81 L18 **Afmadow** Jubbada Hoose, S Somalia 0°24′N 42°04′E
39 Q14 **Afognak Island** *island* Alaska, USA
104 J2 **A Fonsagrada** Galicia, NW Spain 43°09′N 07°03′W
186 E9 **Afore** Northern, S Papua New Guinea 09°10′S 148°30′E
59 O15 **Afrânio** Pernambuco, E Brazil 08°32′S 40°54′W
66-67 **Africa** *continent*
68 L11 **Africa, Horn of** *physical region* Ethiopia/Somalia
172 K11 **Africana Seamount** *undersea feature* SW Indian Ocean 37°10′S 29°10′E
86 A14 **African Plate** *tectonic plate*
138 I2 **ʻAfrīn** Ḩalab, N Syria 36°31′N 36°51′E
136 M15 **Afşin** Kahramanmaraş, C Turkey 38°14′N 36°54′E
98 J7 **Afsluitdijk** *dam* N Netherlands
29 U15 **Afton** Iowa, C USA 41°01′N 94°12′W
29 W9 **Afton** Minnesota, N USA 44°54′N 92°46′W
27 R8 **Afton** Oklahoma, C USA 36°41′N 94°57′W
136 F14 **Afyon** *prev.* Afyonkarahisar. Afyon, W Turkey 38°46′N 30°32′E
136 F14 **Afyon** *var.* Afiun Karahissar, Afyonkarahisar. ◈ *province* W Turkey
Afyonkarahisar *see* Afyon
Agadès *see* Agadez
77 V10 **Agadez** *prev.* Agadès. Agadez, C Niger 16°57′N 07°56′E
77 W8 **Agadez** ◈ *department* N Niger
74 E8 **Agadir** SW Morocco 30°30′N 09°37′W
64 M9 **Agadir Canyon** *undersea feature* SE Atlantic Ocean 32°30′N 12°50′W
145 R12 **Agadyr'** Karaganda, C Kazakhstan 48°15′N 72°55′E
173 O7 **Agalega Islands** *island group* N Mauritius
42 K6 **Agalta, Sierra de** ▲▲ E Honduras
122 I10 **Agan** ≈ C Russian Federation
Agana/Agaña *see* Hagåtña
188 B15 **Agana Bay** *bay* NW Guam
188 C15 **Aganafield** *bay* NW Guam
171 Kk13 **Agano-gawa** ≈ Honshū, C Japan
188 B17 **Aga Point** *headland* S Guam
154 G9 **Agar** Madhya Pradesh, C India 23°44′N 76°01′E
81 I14 **Āgaro** Oromīya, C Ethiopia 07°52′N 36°36′E
153 V15 **Agartala** *state capital* Tripura, NE India 23°49′N 91°15′E
194 I5 **Agassiz, Cape** *headland* Antarctica 68°29′S 62°59′W
175 V13 **Agassiz Fracture Zone** *tectonic feature* S Pacific Ocean
9 N2 **Agassiz Ice Cap** *ice feature* Nunavut, N Canada
188 B16 **Agat** W Guam 13°20′N 144°38′E
188 B16 **Agat Bay** *bay* W Guam
145 P13 **Agat, Gory** *hill* C Kazakhstan
Agatha *see* Agde
115 M20 **Agathónisi** *island* Dodekánisa, Greece, Aegean Sea
171 X14 **Agats** Papua, E Indonesia 05°33′S 138°07′E
155 C21 **Agatti Island** *island* Lakshadweep, India, N Indian Ocean
38 D16 **Agattu Island** *island* Aleutian Islands, Alaska, USA
38 D16 **Agattu Strait** *strait* Aleutian Islands, Alaska, USA
14 B8 **Agawa** ≈ Ontario, S Canada
14 B8 **Agawa Bay** *lake bay* Ontario, S Canada
77 N17 **Agboville** SE Ivory Coast 05°55′N 04°15′W
137 V12 **Ağdam** *Rus.* Agdam. SW Azerbaijan 40°04′N 46°00′E
Agdam *see* Ağdam
103 P16 **Agde** *anc.* Agatha. Hérault, S France 43°19′N 03°29′E
103 P16 **Agde, Cap d'** *headland* S France 43°17′N 03°30′E
Agedabia *see* Ajdābiyā
102 L14 **Agen** *anc.* Aginnum. Lot-et-Garonne, SW France 44°12′N 00°37′E
Agendicum *see* Sens
165 O13 **Ageo** Saitama, Honshū, S Japan 35°58′N 139°36′E
109 R5 **Ager** ≈ N Austria
Agere Hiywet *see* Hāgere Hiywet
108 G8 **Ägerisee** ◎ W Switzerland
142 M10 **Āghā Jārī** Khūzestān, SW Iran 30°48′N 49°45′E
39 P15 **Aghiyuk Island** *island* Alaska, USA
74 B12 **Aghouinit** SE Western Sahara 22°14′N 13°10′W
Aghri Dagh *see* Büyükağrı Dağı
74 B10 **Aghzoumal, Sebkhet** *var.* Sebjet Agsumal. *salt lake* E Western Sahara
115 F15 **Agiá** *var.* Ayiá. Thessalía, C Greece 39°43′N 22°45′E
40 G7 **Agiabampo, Estero de** *estuary* NW Mexico
121 P3 **Agía Fýlaxis** *var.* Ayia Phyla. S Cyprus 34°43′N 33°02′E
Agialoúsa *see* Yenierenköy
115 M21 **Agía Marína** Léros, Dodekánisa, Greece, Aegean Sea 37°09′N 26°51′E
121 Q2 **Agía Nápa** *var.* Ayia Napa. E Cyprus 34°59′N 34°00′E
115 L16 **Agía Paraskeví** Lésvos, E Greece 39°13′N 26°19′E
115 J15 **Agías Eirínis, Akrotírio** *headland* Límnos, E Greece 39°47′N 25°21′E
Agiasós *see* Agiassós
115 L17 **Agiassós** *var.* Agiasós, Ayiásos, Ayiásos. Lésvos, E Greece 39°05′N 26°23′E
127 T3 **Agidel'** Respublika Bashkortostan, W Russian Federation 55°54′N 53°57′E
Aginnum *see* Agen
123 O14 **Aginskiy Buryatskiy Avtonomnyy Okrug** ◈ *autonomous district* S Russian Federation
123 O14 **Aginskoye** Aginskiy Buryatskiy Avtonomnyy Okrug, S Russian Federation 51°10′N 114°32′E
115 I14 **Ágion Óros** *Eng.* Mount Athos. ◈ *monastic republic* NE Greece
115 H14 **Ágion Óros** *var.* Akte, Aktí; *anc.* Acte. *peninsula* NE Greece
114 D13 **Ágios Achílleios** *religious building* Dytikí Makedonía, N Greece
115 J16 **Ágios Efstrátios** *var.* Áyios Evstrátios, Hagios Evstrátios. *island* E Greece 39°34′N 25°00′E
115 H20 **Ágios Geórgios** *island* Kykládes, Greece, Aegean Sea
Ágios Geórgios *see* Ro
115 E21 **Ágios Ilías** ▲ S Greece 36°57′N 22°19′E
115 K25 **Ágios Ioánnis, Akrotírio** *headland* Kríti, Greece, E Mediterranean Sea
115 L20 **Ágios Kírykos** *var.* Áyios Kírikos. Ikaría, Dodekánisa, Greece, Aegean Sea 37°34′N 26°15′E
115 K25 **Ágios Nikólaos** *var.* Áyios Nikólaos. Kríti, Greece, E Mediterranean Sea 35°12′N 25°43′E
115 D16 **Ágios Nikolaos** Thessalía, C Greece 39°33′N 21°21′E
115 H14 **Ágiou Órous, Kólpos** *gulf* N Greece
107 K24 **Agira** *anc.* Agyrium. Sicilia, Italy, C Mediterranean Sea 37°39′N 14°32′E
115 G20 **Agkístri** *island* S Greece
114 G12 **Agkístro** *var.* Angistro. ▲ NE Greece 41°21′N 23°29′E
103 O17 **Agly** ≈ S France
Agnetheln *see* Agnita
14 E10 **Agnew Lake** ◎ Ontario, S Canada
77 O16 **Agnibilékrou** E Ivory Coast 07°10′N 03°11′W
116 I11 **Agnita** *Ger.* Agnetheln, *Hung.* Szentágota. Sibiu, SW Romania 45°59′N 24°40′E
107 K15 **Agnone** Molise, C Italy 41°49′N 14°21′E
164 K14 **Ago** Mie, Honshū, SW Japan 34°18′N 136°50′E
106 C8 **Agogna** ≈ N Italy
Agoitz *see* Agoiz
105 R3 **Agoiz** *var.* Agoitz, Aoiz. Navarra, N Spain 42°47′N 01°23′W
77 P17 **Agona Swedru** *var.* Swedru. SE Ghana 05°31′N 00°42′W
Agordat *see* Ak'ordat
Agosta *see* Augusta
103 N15 **Agout** ≈ S France
152 J12 **Āgra** Uttar Pradesh, N India 27°09′N 78°E
Agra and Oudh, United Provinces of *see* Uttar Pradesh
Agram *see* Zagreb
105 U5 **Agramunt** Cataluña, NE Spain 41°48′N 01°07′E
105 Q5 **Agreda** Castilla-León, N Spain 41°51′N 01°55′W
137 S13 **Ağrı** *var.* Karaköse; *prev.* Karakılısse. Ağrı, NE Turkey 39°44′N 43°04′E
137 S13 **Ağrı** ◈ *province* NE Turkey
107 N19 **Agri** *anc.* Aciris. ≈ S Italy
Agri Dagi *see* Büyükağrı Dağı
107 J24 **Agrigento** *Gk.* Akragas; *prev.* Girgenti. Sicilia, Italy, C Mediterranean Sea 37°19′N 13°33′E
188 K4 **Agrihan** *island* N Northern Mariana Islands
115 L17 **Agriliá, Akrotírio** *prev.* Ákra Maléas. *cape* Lésvos, E Greece
115 D18 **Agrínio** *prev.* Agrinion. Dytikí Ellás, W Greece 38°38′N 21°25′E
Agrinion *see* Agrínio
115 G17 **Agriovótano** Évvoia, C Greece 39°00′N 23°18′E
107 L18 **Agropoli** Campania, S Italy 40°22′N 14°59′E
127 T3 **Agryz** Udmurtskaya Respublika, NW Russian Federation 56°27′N 52°58′E
137 U11 **Ağstafa** *Rus.* Akstafa. NW Azerbaijan 41°06′N 45°28′E
137 X11 **Ağsu** *Rus.* Akhsu. C Azerbaijan
Agsumal, Sebjet *see* Aghzoumal, Sebkhet
40 J11 **Agua Brava, Laguna** *lagoon* W Mexico
54 F7 **Aguachica** Cesar, N Colombia 08°16′N 73°35′W
59 J20 **Água Clara** Mato Grosso do Sul, SW Brazil 20°21′S 52°58′W
44 D5 **Aguada de Pasajeros** Cienfuegos, C Cuba 22°23′N 80°51′W
54 J5 **Aguada Grande** Lara, N Venezuela 10°38′N 69°29′W
45 S5 **Aguadilla** W Puerto Rico 18°27′N 67°08′W
43 S16 **Aguadulce** Coclé, S Panama 08°16′N 80°31′W
104 L14 **Aguadulce** Andalucía, S Spain 37°15′N 04°59′W
41 O8 **Agualeguas** Nuevo León, NE Mexico 26°17′N 99°30′W
40 L9 **Aguanaval, Río** ≈ C Mexico
42 J5 **Aguán, Río** ≈ N Honduras
25 R16 **Agua Nueva** Texas, SW USA 26°57′N 98°34′W
60 J8 **Aguapeí, Rio** ≈ S Brazil
61 E14 **Aguapey, Río** ≈ NE Argentina
40 G3 **Agua Prieta** Sonora, NW Mexico 31°16′N 109°33′W
104 G5 **A Guarda** *var.* A Guardia, Laguardia, La Guardia. Galicia, NW Spain 41°54′N 08°53′W
A Guardia *see* A Guarda
56 E6 **Aguarico, Río** ≈ Ecuador/Peru
55 O6 **Aguasay** Monagas, NE Venezuela 09°25′N 63°44′W
40 M12 **Aguascalientes** Aguascalientes, C Mexico 21°54′N 102°17′W
40 L12 **Aguascalientes** ◈ *state* C Mexico
57 I18 **Aguas Calientes, Río** ≈ S Peru
105 R7 **Aguasvivas** ≈ NE Spain
60 J7 **Água Vermelha, Represa de** ⊠ S Brazil
56 E12 **Aguaytía** Ucayali, C Peru 09°02′S 75°30′W
104 I5 **A Gudiña** *var.* La Gudiña. Galicia, NW Spain 42°04′N 07°08′W
104 G7 **Águeda** Aveiro, N Portugal 40°34′N 08°28′W
104 J8 **Águeda** ≈ Portugal/Spain
77 Q8 **Aguelhok** Kidal, NE Mali 19°18′N 00°50′E
77 V12 **Aguié** Maradi, S Niger 13°28′N 07°43′E
188 K8 **Aguijan** *island* S Northern Mariana Islands
104 M14 **Aguilar** *var.* Aguilar de la Frontera. Andalucía, S Spain 37°31′N 04°40′W
104 M3 **Aguilar de Campóo** Castilla-León, N Spain 42°47′N 04°15′W
Aguilar de la Frontera *see* Aguilar
42 F7 **Aguilares** San Salvador, C El Salvador 13°56′N 89°09′W
105 Q14 **Aguilas** Murcia, SE Spain 37°24′N 01°36′W
40 L15 **Aguililla** Michoacán, SW Mexico 18°43′N 102°45′W
Agulhas *see* L'Agulhas
172 J11 **Agulhas Bank** *undersea feature* SW Indian Ocean 35°30′S 21°00′E
172 K11 **Agulhas Basin** *undersea feature* SW Indian Ocean 47°00′S 27°00′E
83 F26 **Agulhas, Cape** *Afr.* Kaap Agulhas. *headland* SW South Africa 34°51′S 19°59′E
Agulhas, Kaap *see* Agulhas, Cape
60 O9 **Agulhas Negras, Pico das** ▲ SE Brazil 22°21′S 44°39′W
172 K11 **Agulhas Plateau** *undersea feature* SW Indian Ocean 40°00′S 26°00′E
165 S16 **Aguni-jima** *island* Nansei-shotō, SW Japan
Agurain *see* Salvatierra
54 G5 **Agustín Codazzi** *var.* Codazzi. Cesar, N Colombia 10°02′N 73°15′W
Agyrium *see* Agira
74 L12 **Ahaggar** *high plateau region* SE Algeria
146 E12 **Ahal Welaýaty** *Rus.* Akhalskiy Velayat. ◈ *province* C Turkmenistan
142 K2 **Ahar** Āżarbāyjān-e Sharqī, NW Iran 38°25′N 47°07′E
Aharnes *see* Acharnés
138 J3 **Aḩaş, Jabal** ▲ NW Syria
138 J3 **Aḩaş, Jebal** ▲ W Syria
185 G16 **Ahaura** ≈ South Island, New Zealand
100 E13 **Ahaus** Nordrhein-Westfalen, NW Germany 52°04′N 07°01′E
191 U9 **Ahe** *atoll* Îles Tuamotu, C French Polynesia
184 N10 **Ahimanawa Range** ▲▲ North Island, New Zealand
119 I19 **Ahinski Kanal** *Rus.* Oginskiy Kanal. *canal* SW Belarus
186 G10 **Ahioma** SE Papua New Guinea 10°20′S 150°35′E
184 I2 **Ahipara** Northland, North Island, New Zealand 35°11′S 173°07′E
184 I2 **Ahipara Bay** *bay* SE Tasman Sea
Áhkká *see* Akka
39 N13 **Ahklun Mountains** ▲▲ Alaska, USA
137 R14 **Ahlat** Bitlis, E Turkey 38°45′N 42°28′E
101 F14 **Ahlen** Nordrhein-Westfalen, W Germany 51°46′N 07°53′E
154 D10 **Ahmadābād** *var.* Ahmedabad. Gujarāt, W India 23°03′N 72°40′E
143 R10 **Ahmadābād** Kermān, C Iran 35°51′N 59°36′E
Ahmadi *see* Al Aḩmadī
Ahmad Khel *see* Ḩasan Khēl
155 F14 **Ahmadnagar** *var.* Ahmednagar. Mahārāshtra, W India 19°08′N 74°48′E
149 T9 **Ahmadpur Siāl** Punjab, E Pakistan 30°40′N 71°52′E
77 N5 **Aḩmar, ʻErg el** *desert* N Mali
80 K13 **Ahmar Mountains** ▲▲ C Ethiopia
Ahmedabad *see* Ahmadābād
Ahmednagar *see* Ahmadnagar
114 N12 **Ahmetbey** Kırklareli, NW Turkey 41°26′N 27°35′E
14 H12 **Ahmic Lake** ◎ Ontario, S Canada
190 G12 **Ahoa** Île Uvea, E Wallis and Futuna 13°17′S 176°12′W
40 G8 **Ahomé** Sinaloa, C Mexico 25°55′N 109°10′W
21 X8 **Ahoskie** North Carolina, SE USA 36°17′N 76°59′W
101 D17 **Ahr** ≈ W Germany
143 N12 **Ahram** *var.* Ahrom. Būshehr, S Iran 28°52′N 51°18′E
100 J9 **Ahrensburg** Schleswig-Holstein, N Germany 53°41′N 10°14′E
Ahrom *see* Ahram
93 L17 **Ähtäri** Länsi-Suomi, W Finland 62°34′N 24°08′E
40 K12 **Ahuacatlán** Nayarit, C Mexico 21°02′N 104°30′W
42 E7 **Ahuachapán** Ahuachapán, W El Salvador 13°55′N 89°51′W
42 A9 **Ahuachapán** ◈ *department* W El Salvador
191 V16 **Ahu Akivi** *var.* Siete Moai. *ancient monument* Easter Island, Chile, E Pacific Ocean
191 W11 **Ahunui** *atoll* Îles Tuamotu, C French Polynesia
185 E20 **Ahuriri** ≈ South Island, New Zealand
95 L22 **Åhus** Skåne, S Sweden 55°55′N 14°18′E
Ahu Tahira *see* Ahu Vinapu
191 V16 **Ahu Tepeu** *ancient monument* Easter Island, Chile, E Pacific Ocean
191 V17 **Ahu Vinapu** *var.* Ahu Tahira. *ancient monument* Easter Island, Chile, E Pacific Ocean
142 L9 **Ahvāz** *var.* Ahwāz; *prev.* Nāsiri. Khūzestān, SW Iran 31°20′N 48°38′E
Ahvenanmaa *see* Åland
154 E12 **Ahwa** Gujarāt, W India 20°44′N 73°41′E
141 Q16 **Ahwar** SW Yemen 13°34′N 46°41′E
Ahwāz *see* Ahvāz
94 H7 **Åi Åfjord** *var.* Åfjord, Årnes. Sør-Trøndelag, C Norway 63°57′N 10°12′E
Aibak *see* Āybak
101 K22 **Aichach** Bayern, SE Germany 48°26′N 11°06′E
164 L14 **Aichi** *off.* Aichi-ken, *var.* Aiti. ◈ *prefecture* Honshū, SW Japan
Aïdin *see* Aydın
Aidussina *see* Ajdovščina
Aifir, Clochán an *see* Giant's Causeway
Aigaíon Pelagos/Aigaío Pélagos *see* Aegean Sea
109 S3 **Aigen im Mülkreis** Oberösterreich, N Austria 48°39′N 13°57′E

◆ Country ● Country Capital ◇ Dependent Territory ○ Dependent Territory Capital ◈ Administrative Regions ✈ International Airport ▲ Mountain ▲▲ Mountain Range ☒ Volcano ≈ River ◎ Lake ⊠ Reservoir

115 G20 **Aígina** var. Aíyina, Egína. Aígina, C Greece 37°45´N 23°26´E
115 G20 **Aígina** island S Greece
115 E18 **Aígio** var. Egio; prev. Aíyion. Dytikí Ellás, S Greece 38°15´N 22°05´E
108 C10 **Aigle** Vaud, SW Switzerland 46°20´N 06°58´E
103 P14 **Aigoual, Mont** ▲ S France 44°09´N 03°34´E
173 O16 **Aigrettes, Pointe des** headland W Réunion 21°02´S 55°14´E
61 G19 **Aiguá** var. Aigua. Maldonado, S Uruguay 34°13´S 54°46´W
103 S13 **Aigues** ✎ SE France
103 N10 **Aigurande** Indre, C France 46°26´N 01°49´E
Ai-hun see Heihe
163 N10 **Aikawa** Niigata, Sado, C Japan 38°04´N 138°15´E
21 Q13 **Aiken** South Carolina, SE USA 33°34´N 81°44´W
25 N4 **Aiken** Texas, USA 34°06´N 101°31´W
160 F13 **Ailao Shan** ▲ SW China
189 R4 **Ailinginae Atoll** var. Aelöninae. atoll Ralik Chain, SW Marshall Islands
189 T7 **Ailinglaplap Atoll** var. Aelönlaplap. atoll Ralik Chain, S Marshall Islands
Aillionn, Loch see Allen, Lough
96 H13 **Ailsa Craig** island SW Scotland, United Kingdom
189 V5 **Ailuk Atoll** var. Aelok. atoll Ratak Chain, NE Marshall Islands
123 R11 **Aim** Khabarovskiy Kray, E Russian Federation 58°45´N 134°08´E
103 R11 **Ain** ◆ department E France
103 S10 **Ain** ✎ E France
118 G7 **Ainaži** Est. Heinaste, Ger. Hainasch. Limbaži, N Latvia 57°51´N 24°24´E
74 L6 **Aïn Beïda** NE Algeria 35°52´N 07°25´E
76 K4 **'Aïn Ben Tili** Tiris Zemmour, N Mauritania 25°58´N 09°30´W
74 J5 **Aïn Defla** var. Aïn Eddefla. N Algeria 36°16´N 01°58´E
74 J5 **Aïn Eddefla** see Aïn Defla
74 L5 **Aïn El Bey** ✈ (Constantine) NE Algeria 36°15´N 06°30´E
115 C19 **Aínos** ▲ Kefallonía, Iónia Nísoi, Greece, C Mediterranean Sea 38°08´N 20°39´E
105 T4 **Ainsa** Aragón, NE Spain
74 I7 **Aïn Sefra** NW Algeria 32°45´N 00°32´W
29 N13 **Ainsworth** Nebraska, C USA 42°33´N 99°51´W
Aintab see Gaziantep
74 H5 **Aïn Témouchent** N Algeria 35°18´N 01°09´W
186 C6 **Aiome** Madang, N Papua New Guinea 05°08´S 144°45´E
Aïoun el Atrous/Aïoun el Atroûss see 'Ayoûn el 'Atroûs
54 E11 **Aipe** Huila, C Colombia 03°15´N 75°17´W
56 D9 **Aipena, Río** ✎ N Peru
57 L19 **Aiquile** Cochabamba, C Bolivia 18°10´S 65°10´W
Aïr see Aïr, Massif de l'
188 E10 **Airai** Babeldaob, C Palau
188 E10 **Airai** ✈ (Oreor) Babeldaob, N Palau 07°22´N 134°34´E
168 I11 **Airbangis** Sumatera, NW Indonesia 0°12´N 99°22´E
11 Q16 **Airdrie** Alberta, SW Canada 51°20´N 114°00´W
96 I12 **Airdrie** S Scotland, United Kingdom 55°52´N 03°59´W
Air du Azbine see Aïr, Massif de l'
97 M17 **Aire** ✎ N England, United Kingdom
102 K15 **Aire-sur-l'Adour** Landes, SW France 43°43´N 00°16´W
103 O1 **Aire-sur-la-Lys** Pas-de-Calais, N France 50°39´N 02°24´E
9 Q6 **Air Force Island** island Baffin Island, Nunavut, NE Canada
169 Q13 **Airhitam, Teluk** bay Borneo, C Indonesia
171 Q11 **Airmadidi** Sulawesi, N Indonesia 01°25´N 124°59´E
77 V8 **Aïr, Massif de l'** var. Aïr, Aïr du Azbine, Asben. ▲ NC Niger
108 G10 **Airolo** Ticino, S Switzerland 46°30´N 08°38´E
102 K9 **Airvault** Deux-Sèvres, W France 46°51´N 00°07´W
101 K19 **Aisch** ✎ SE Germany
63 G20 **Aisén** off. Región Aisén del General Carlos Ibañez del Campo, var. Aysen. ◆ region S Chile
10 H7 **Aishihik Lake** ◎ Yukon Territory, W Canada
103 P3 **Aisne** ◆ department N France
103 R4 **Aisne** ✎ NE France
109 T4 **Aist** ✎ N Austria
114 K13 **Aisými** Anatolikí Makedonía kai Thráki, NE Greece 41°00´N 25°55´E
105 S11 **Aitana** ▲ E Spain 38°39´N 00°15´E
186 B5 **Aitape** var. Eitape. Sandaun, NW Papua New Guinea 03°10´S 142°17´E
Aiti see Aichi
29 V6 **Aitkin** Minnesota, N USA 46°31´N 93°42´W
115 D18 **Aitolikó** var. Etolíko; prev. Aitolikón. Dytikí Ellás, C Greece 38°26´N 21°21´E
Aitolikón see Aitolikó
190 L15 **Aitutaki** island S Cook Islands
116 H11 **Aiud** Ger. Strassburg, Hung. Nagyenyed; prev. Engeten. Alba, SW Romania 46°19´N 23°43´E
118 I9 **Aiviekste** ✎ C Latvia
189 Q8 **Aiwo** SW Nauru 0°32´S 166°54´E
188 D4 **Aiwokako Passage** passage Babeldaob, N Palau
Aix see Aix-en-Provence
103 S15 **Aix-en-Provence** var. Aix; anc. Aquae Sextiae. Bouches-du-Rhône, SE France 43°31´N 05°27´E
Aix-la-Chapelle see Aachen
103 T11 **Aix-les-Bains** Savoie, E France 45°40´N 05°55´E

186 A6 **Aiyang, Mount** ▲ NW Papua New Guinea 05°03´S 141°15´E
Aíyina see Aígina
153 W15 **Aizawl** state capital Mizoram, NE India 23°41´N 92°45´E
118 H9 **Aizkraukle** Aizkraukle, S Latvia 56°39´N 25°07´E
118 C9 **Aizpute** Liepāja, W Latvia 56°43´N 21°32´E
165 O11 **Aizu-Wakamatsu** var. Aizuwakamatu. Fukushima, Honshū, C Japan 37°30´N 139°58´E
127 P11 **Aizuwakamatu** see Aizu-Wakamatsu
127 P11 **Akhtubinsk** Astrakhanskaya Oblast', SW Russian Federation 48°17´N 46°14´E
164 H14 **Aki** Kōchi, Shikoku, SW Japan 33°30´N 133°53´E
39 N12 **Akiachak** Alaska, USA 60°54´N 161°25´W
39 N12 **Akiak** Alaska, USA 60°54´N 161°12´W
191 X11 **Akiaki** atoll Îles Tuamotu, E French Polynesia
12 H9 **Akimiski Island** island Nunavut, C Canada
136 K17 **Akıncı Burnu** headland S Turkey 36°21´N 35°47´E
Akıncılar see Selçuk
117 U10 **Akinovka** Zaporiz'ka Oblast', S Ukraine
165 P8 **Akita** Akita, Honshū, C Japan 39°44´N 140°06´E
165 Q8 **Akita** off. Akita-ken. ◆ prefecture Honshū, C Japan
76 H8 **Akjoujt** prev. Fort-Repoux. Inchiri, W Mauritania 19°42´N 14°28´W
92 H11 **Akka** Lapp. Áhkká. ▲ N Sweden 67°33´N 17°27´E
92 H11 **Akkajaure** ☒ N Sweden
Akkala see Oqqal'a
155 L25 **Akkaraipattu** Eastern Province, E Sri Lanka 07°13´N 81°51´E
145 P13 **Akkense** Kaz. Aqkengse. Karaganda, C Kazakhstan 46°39´N 68°06´E
Akkerman see Bilhorod-Dnistrovs'kyy
127 W8 **Akkermanovka** Orenburgskaya Oblast', W Russian Federation 51°11´N 58°03´E
165 V4 **Akkeshi** Hokkaidō, NE Japan 43°00´N 144°49´E
165 V4 **Akkeshi-ko** ◎ Hokkaidō, NE Japan
165 V3 **Akkeshi-wan** bay NW Pacific Ocean
138 F8 **Akko** Eng. Acre, Fr. Saint-Jean-d'Acre, Bibl. Accho, Ptolemaïs. Northern, N Israel 32°55´N 35°05´E
165 T3 **Akabira** Hokkaidō, NE Japan 43°30´N 142°04´E
165 N10 **Akadomari** Niigata, Sado, C Japan 37°54´N 138°24´E
81 E20 **Akagera** var. Kagera. ✎ Rwanda/Tanzania see also Kagera
191 W16 **Akahanga, Punta** headland Easter Island, Chile, E Pacific Ocean
80 J13 **Ak'ak'i** Oromiya, C Ethiopia 08°50´N 38°51´E
155 G15 **Akalkot** Mahārāshtra, W India 17°36´N 76°10´E
Akamagaseki see Shimonoseki
98 L6 **Akkrum** Friesland, N Netherlands 53°01´N 05°52´E
145 U8 **Akköl** Kaz. Aqköl; prev. Lebyazh'ye. Pavlodar, NE Kazakhstan 51°29´N 77°48´E
165 U4 **Akan** Hokkaidō, NE Japan 43°09´N 144°03´E
Akanthoú see Tatlısu
185 I19 **Akaroa** Canterbury, South Island, New Zealand 43°48´S 172°58´E
80 E6 **Akasha** Northern, N Sudan 21°03´N 30°46´E
164 H12 **Akashi** var. Akasi. Hyōgo, Honshū, SW Japan 34°39´N 135°00´E
139 N7 **'Akāsh, Wādī** var. Wādī 'Ukásh. dry watercourse W Iraq
Akasi see Akashi
92 K11 **Ääksjokisuu** Lappi, N Finland 67°28´N 23°44´E
137 S11 **Akbaba Dağı** ▲ Armenia/Turkey 41°00´N 43°28´E
Akbük Limanı see Güllük Körfezi
127 V8 **Akbulak** Orenburgskaya Oblast', W Russian Federation 51°01´N 55°35´E
137 O11 **Akçaabat** Trabzon, NE Turkey 41°00´N 39°36´E
137 N15 **Akçadağ** Malatya, C Turkey 38°21´N 37°59´E
136 H13 **Akçakoca** Düzce, NW Turkey 41°05´N 31°07´E
Akchakaya, Vpadina see Akdzhakaya, Vpadina
76 H7 **Akchar** desert W Mauritania
145 S12 **Akchatau** Kaz. Aqshataū. Karaganda, C Kazakhstan 47°59´N 74°02´E
136 L13 **Akdağ** ▲ C Turkey
136 E17 **Akdağları** ▲ SW Turkey 36°30´N 30°01´E
146 G8 **Akdepe** prev. Ak-Tepe, Leninsk, Turkm. Lenin. Daşoguz Welaýaty, N Turkmenistan 42°10´N 59°17´E
Ak-Dere see Byala
121 J14 **Akdoğan** Gk. Lýsi. C Cyprus 35°08´N 33°45´E
122 J14 **Ak-Dovurak** Respublika Tyva, S Russian Federation 51°09´N 90°58´E
146 F9 **Akdzhakaya, Vpadina** var. Vpadina Akchakaya. depression N Turkmenistan
171 S11 **Akelamo** Pulau Halmahera, E Indonesia 01°27´N 128°39´E
95 I14 **Åkers Styckebruk** Södermanland, C Sweden 59°12´N 17°10´E
95 P15 **Åkersberga** Stockholm, C Sweden 59°28´N 18°19´E
Åketi see Aketi
79 L16 **Aketi** Orientale, N Dem. Rep. Congo 02°44´N 23°52´E
146 C10 **Akgyr Erezi** Rus. Gryada Akkyr. hill range NW Turkmenistan

Akheloós see Achelóos
39 Q15 **Akhiok** Kodiak Island, Alaska, USA 56°57´N 154°12´W
136 C13 **Akhisar** Manisa, W Turkey 38°54´N 27°50´E
75 X10 **Akhmîm** var. Akhmim; anc. Panopolis. C Egypt 26°35´N 31°48´E
152 H6 **Akhnûr** Jammu and Kashmir, NW India 32°53´N 74°46´E
Akhsu see Ağsu
114 N10 **Akhtopol** Burgas, E Bulgaria 42°06´N 27°57´E
127 P11 **Akhtuba** ✎ SW Russian Federation 50°05´N 46°18´E
127 O11 **Akhtyrka** see Okhtyrka
164 H14 **Aki** Kōchi, Shikoku, SW Japan 33°30´N 133°53´E
39 N12 **Akiachak** Alaska, USA 60°57´N 161°25´W
39 N12 **Akiak** Alaska, USA 60°54´N 161°12´W
191 X11 **Akiaki** atoll Îles Tuamotu, E French Polynesia
12 H9 **Akimiski Island** island Nunavut, C Canada
136 K17 **Akıncı Burnu** S Turkey 36°21´N 35°47´E
165 P8 **Akita** Akita, Honshū, C Japan 39°44´N 140°06´E
165 Q8 **Akita** off. Akita-ken. ◆ prefecture Honshū, C Japan
76 H8 **Akjoujt** prev. Fort-Repoux. Inchiri, W Mauritania 19°42´N 14°28´W
92 H11 **Akkajaure** ☒ N Sweden
155 L25 **Akkaraipattu** Eastern Province, E Sri Lanka 07°13´N 81°51´E
145 P13 **Akkense** Kaz. Aqkengse. Karaganda, C Kazakhstan 46°39´N 68°06´E
127 W8 **Akkermanovka** Orenburgskaya Oblast', W Russian Federation 51°11´N 58°03´E
165 V3 **Akkeshi** Hokkaidō, NE Japan
165 U4 **Akkeshi-ko** ◎ Hokkaidō, NE Japan
165 U4 **Akkeshi-wan** bay NW Pacific Ocean
80 J13 **Āksum** Tigray, N Ethiopia 14°06´N 38°42´E
145 O12 **Aktas** Kaz. Aqtas. Karaganda, C Kazakhstan 48°03´N 66°21´E
147 V9 **Ak-Tash, Gora** ▲ C Kyrgyzstan 40°53´N 74°39´E
145 R10 **Aktau** Kaz. Aqtaū. Karaganda, C Kazakhstan 51°53´N 73°06´E
144 E11 **Aktau** Kaz. Aqtaū; prev. Shevchenko. Mangistau, W Kazakhstan 43°37´N 51°14´E
Aktau, Khrebet see Oqtogh, Qatorkŭhi. SW Tajikistan
147 X7 **Ak-Terek** Issyk-Kul'skaya Oblast', E Kyrgyzstan 42°14´N 77°46´E
Akti see Ágion Óros
158 E8 **Akto** Xinjiang Uygur Zizhiqu, NW China 39°07´N 75°43´E
144 I10 **Aktobe** Kaz. Aqtöbe; prev. Aktyubinsk, Aktyubinsk. Aktyubinsk, NW Kazakhstan 50°18´N 57°10´E
145 V12 **Aktogay** Kaz. Aqtoghay. Vostochnyy Kazakhstan 46°58´N 79°40´E
146 J14 **Akmeydan** Mary Welaýaty, C Turkmenistan
145 P9 **Akmola** off. Akmolinskaya Oblast', Kaz. Aqmola Oblysy; prev. Tselinogradskaya Voblasts', SE Belarus 52°38´N 71°28´E
Aktyubinsk see Aktobe
147 W7 **Ak-Tyuz** var. Aktyuz. Chuyskaya Oblast', N Kyrgyzstan 42°50´N 76°05´E
79 J20 **Akula** Equateur, NW Dem. Rep. Congo 02°21´N 20°16´E
164 C15 **Akune** Kagoshima, Kyūshū, SW Japan 32°00´N 130°12´E
92 G14 **Åkrehamn** Rogaland, S Norway 59°15´N 05°13´E
94 F13 **Akrån** Aust-Agder, S Norway 60°37´N 08°13´E
134 I3 **Ala** Rus. Ola. ✎ SE Belarus
23 P5 **Alabama** off. State of Alabama, also known as Camellia State, Heart of Dixie, The Cotton State, Yellowhammer State. ◆ state S USA
23 P6 **Alabama River** ✎ Alabama, S USA
23 P4 **Alabaster** Alabama, S USA 33°14´N 86°49´W
138 I9 **'Abdallāh** var. Al Qādisīyah. S Cyprus 34°58´N 32°57´E

121 P3 **Akrotírion, Kólpos** var. Akrotiri Bay. bay S Cyprus
121 O3 **Akrotiri Sovereign Base Area** UK military installation S Cyprus 34°54´N 32°57´E
158 F11 **Aksai Chin** Chin. Aksayqin. disputed region China/India
136 I15 **Aksaray** Aksaray, C Turkey 38°23´N 33°50´E
136 I15 **Aksaray** ◆ province C Turkey
136 G11 **Aksayqin Hu** ◎ W China
136 G14 **Akşehir** Konya, W Turkey 38°22´N 31°24´E
136 G14 **Akşehir Gölü** ◎ C Turkey
136 G16 **Akseki** Antalya, SW Turkey 37°03´N 31°44´E
123 P13 **Aksenovo-Zilovskoye** Chitinskaya Oblast', S Russian Federation 53°10´N 117°26´E
145 X8 **Akshatau, Khrebet** ▲ SE Kazakhstan
147 Y8 **Ak-Shyyrak** Issyk-Kul'skaya Oblast', E Kyrgyzstan 41°46´N 78°34´E
158 H7 **Aksu** Xinjiang Uygur Zizhiqu, NW China 41°17´N 80°15´E
145 R8 **Aksu** Kaz. Aqsū. Akmola, N Kazakhstan 52°31´N 72°00´E
145 W13 **Aksu** Kaz. Aqsū. Almaty, SE Kazakhstan 45°31´N 79°28´E
145 T8 **Aksu** var. Jermak, Kaz. Ermak; prev. Yermak. Pavlodar, N Kazakhstan 52°03´N 76°55´E
145 V13 **Aksu** Kaz. Aqsū. SE Kazakhstan
145 X11 **Aksu** Kaz. Aqsū. Vostochnyy Kazakhstan, E Kazakhstan 47°48´N 82°51´E
145 Y11 **Aksu** Kaz. Aqsū. Vostochnyy Kazakhstan, SE Kazakhstan
145 X11 **Aksu** Kaz. Aqsū. Vostochnyy Kazakhstan 48°16´N 83°39´E
158 H7 **Aksubayevo** Respublika Tatarstan, W Russian Federation 54°52´N 50°50´E
Aksu He Rus. Sary-Dzhaz. ✎ China/Kyrgyzstan see also Sary-Dzhaz
80 J11 **Āksum** Tigray, N Ethiopia 14°06´N 38°42´E
37 V3 **Akron** Colorado, C USA 40°09´N 103°12´W
29 R12 **Akron** Iowa, C USA 42°49´N 96°33´W
31 U12 **Akron** Ohio, N USA 41°05´N 81°31´W
139 W14 **Akrotírion** var. Akrotiri. UK air base S Cyprus 34°36´N 32°57´E
Akrotiri see Akrotírion
121 P3 **Akrotírion var.** Akrotiri, UK air base S Cyprus 34°37´N 32°57´E

147 S9 **Ala-Buka** Dzhalal-Abadskaya Oblast', W Kyrgyzstan 41°22´N 71°27´E
136 J12 **Alaca** Çorum, N Turkey 40°10´N 34°52´E
136 K10 **Alaçam** Samsun, N Turkey 41°36´N 35°36´E
23 V9 **Alachua** Florida, SE USA 29°48´N 82°29´W
136 J13 **Aladağ** ▲ W Turkey
144 G8 **Alag-Erdene** var. Manhan. Hövsgöl, N Mongolia 51°11´N 53°00´E
127 O16 **Alagir** Respublika Severnaya Osetiya, SW Russian Federation 43°02´N 44°10´E
106 B6 **Alagna Valsesia** Valle d'Aosta, NW Italy 45°51´N 07°50´E
59 P16 **Alagoas** off. Estado de Alagoas. ◆ state E Brazil
59 P17 **Alagoinhas** Bahia, E Brazil 12°09´S 38°21´W
105 R5 **Alagón** Aragón, NE Spain 41°46´N 01°07´W
93 K16 **Alahärmä** Länsi-Suomi, W Finland 63°15´N 22°50´E
al Ahdar see Al Akhdar
142 K12 **Al Aḥmadī** var. Ahmadi. E Kuwait 29°02´N 48°01´E
105 Z8 **Alaior** prev. Alayor. Menorca, Spain, W Mediterranean Sea 39°56´N 04°08´E
147 T11 **Alai Range** Rus. Alayskiy Khrebet. ▲ Kyrgyzstan/Tajikistan
145 R8 **Alais** see Alès
140 K5 **Al Akhḍar** var. al Ahdar. Tabūk, NW Saudi Arabia 28°04´N 37°13´E
Alakol' see Alakol', Ozero. Alakol'
145 X13 **Alakol', Ozero** Kaz. Alakol'. ◎ SE Kazakhstan
124 I5 **Alakurtti** Murmanskaya Oblast', NW Russian Federation 66°57´N 30°27´E
38 F10 **Alalakeiki Channel** var. Alalakeiki Channel. channel Hawaii, USA, C Pacific Ocean
75 U12 **Al 'Alamayn** var. El 'Alamein. N Egypt 30°50´N 28°57´E
139 R1 **Al 'Amādīyah** Dahūk, N Iraq 37°09´N 43°27´E
188 K5 **Alamagan** island C Northern Mariana Islands
139 X10 **Al 'Amārah** var. Amara. Maysān, E Iraq 31°51´N 47°10´E
80 J11 **Ālamaṭ'ā** Tigray, N Ethiopia 12°22´N 39°52´E
121 T3 **'Alam el Rûm, Râs** headland N Egypt 31°21´N 27°23´E
Alamicamba see Alamikamba
42 M8 **Alamikamba** var. Alamicamba. Región Autónoma Atlántico Norte, NE Nicaragua 13°26´N 84°09´W
24 M8 **Alamito Creek** ✎ Texas, SW USA
40 M8 **Alamitos, Sierra de los** ▲ NE Mexico 26°15´N 102°14´W
37 S9 **Alamo** Nevada, W USA 37°21´N 115°08´W
20 A6 **Alamo** Tennessee, S USA 35°47´N 89°09´W
37 N13 **Alamogordo** New Mexico, SW USA 32°52´N 105°57´W
36 J12 **Alamo Lake** ☒ Arizona, SW USA
40 F5 **Alamos** Sonora, NW Mexico 26°59´N 108°53´W
37 S7 **Alamosa** Colorado, C USA 37°28´N 105°51´W
139 P10 **Al Anbār** ◆ governorate W Iraq
93 J20 **Åland** var. Aland Islands, Fin. Ahvenanmaa. ◆ province SW Finland
Åland see Ahvenanmaa. island group SW Finland
92 G14 **Åland Islands** see Åland
Åland Sea see Ålands Hav
43 N7 **Alanje** Chiriquí, SW Panama 08°26´N 82°33´W
25 O2 **Alanreed** Texas, SW USA 35°12´N 100°45´W
136 H16 **Alanya** Antalya, S Turkey 36°32´N 32°02´E
23 U7 **Alapaha River** ✎ Florida/Georgia, SE USA
122 G10 **Alapayevsk** Sverdlovskaya Oblast', C Russian Federation 57°48´N 61°50´E
155 G23 **Alappuzha** var. Alleppey. Kerala, SW India 09°30´N 76°22´E see also Alleppey
42 F4 **Al 'Aqabah** var. Akaba, Aqaba, 'Aqaba; anc. Aelana, Elath. Al 'Aqabah, SW Jordan 29°32´N 35°00´E
138 G11 **Al 'Aqabah** off. Muḥāfaẓat al 'Aqabah. ◆ governorate SW Jordan
119 M18 **Alarcón, Embalse de** ☒ C Spain
43 J2 **Al 'Arīmah** Fr. Arime. Halab, N Syria 36°37´N 37°41´E
75 X7 **Al 'Arīsh** var. El 'Arish. NE Egypt 33°00´N 31°00´E
140 P6 **Al Arṭāwīyah** N Saudi Arabia 26°34´N 45°20´E
20 L8 **Albany** Kentucky, S USA 36°42´N 85°09´W

29 U7 **Albany** Minnesota, N USA 38°19´N 28°30´E
27 R2 **Albany** Missouri, C USA 40°15´N 94°33´W
18 L10 **Albany** state capital New York, NE USA 42°39´N 73°45´W
32 F12 **Albany** Oregon, NW USA 44°38´N 123°06´W
25 Q6 **Albany** Texas, SW USA 32°44´N 99°18´W
12 J12 **Albany** ✎ Ontario, S Canada
Alba Pompeia see Alba
Alba Regia see Székesfehérvár
138 J6 **Al Bāridah** var. Bāridah. Ḥimṣ, C Syria 34°15´N 37°39´E
139 Q11 **Al Baṣrah** var. Basra, hist. Busora, Al Başrah, SE Iraq 30°30´N 47°50´E
139 V11 **Al Baṭḥā'** Dhī Qār, SE Iraq 31°06´N 45°54´E
141 X8 **Al Bāṭinah** var. Batinah. coastal region N Oman
0 H16 **Albatross Plateau** undersea feature C Pacific Ocean 10°00´N 103°00´W
39 T13 **Alaska, Gulf of** var. Golfo de Alasca. gulf Canada/USA
39 S10 **Alaska Peninsula** peninsula Alaska, USA
39 Q11 **Alaska Range** ▲ Alaska, USA
Al-Asnam see Chlef
106 B10 **Alassio** Liguria, NW Italy 44°01´N 08°12´E
137 Y12 **Alāt** Rus. Alyat; prev. Alyaty-Pristan'. SE Azerbaijan 39°57´N 49°24´E
139 S13 **Al 'Athmānī** An Najaf, S Iraq 30°27´N 43°41´E
39 P7 **Alatna River** ✎ Alaska, USA
107 J15 **Alatri** Lazio, C Italy 41°43´N 13°21´E
127 P5 **Alatyr'** Chuvashskaya Respublika, W Russian Federation 54°51´N 46°28´E
56 C7 **Alausí** Chimborazo, C Ecuador 02°11´S 78°52´W
105 O3 **Álava** Basq. Araba. ◆ province País Vasco, N Spain
137 T11 **Alaverdi** N Armenia 41°06´N 44°37´E
93 N14 **Ala-Vuokki** Oulu, E Finland 64°46´N 29°29´E
93 K17 **Alavus** Swe. Alavo. Länsi-Suomi, W Finland 62°33´N 23°38´E
182 F2 **Albacutya, Lake** ◎ Victoria, SE Australia
105 P11 **Albacete** Castilla-La Mancha, C Spain 39°00´N 01°52´W
105 P11 **Albacete** ◆ province Castilla-La Mancha, C Spain
29 W5 **Albia** Iowa, C USA 41°01´N 92°48´W
25 X9 **Albia** Marowijne, NE Suriname
140 A15 **Albina, Ponta** headland SW Angola 15°52´S 11°45´E
30 M16 **Albion** Illinois, N USA 38°22´N 88°03´W
31 P11 **Albion** Indiana, N USA 41°23´N 85°26´W
28 P16 **Albion** Nebraska, C USA 41°41´N 98°00´W
18 E9 **Albion** New York, NE USA 43°13´N 78°09´W
18 B12 **Albion** Pennsylvania, NE USA 41°53´N 80°22´W
Al Biqā' see El Beqaa
141 N4 **Al Bi'r** var. Bi'r Ibn Hirmās. Tabūk, NW Saudi Arabia 28°52´N 36°16´E
140 M12 **Al Birk** Makkah, SW Saudi Arabia 18°13´N 41°36´E
141 Q9 **Al Biyāḍ** desert C Saudi Arabia
98 H13 **Alblasserdam** Zuid-Holland, SW Netherlands 51°52´N 04°40´E
105 T8 **Albocàsser** Cast. Albocácer. País Valenciano, E Spain 40°21´N 00°01´E
Alboácer see Albocàsser
Albona see Labin
105 O17 **Alborán, Isla de** island S Spain
Alborán, Mar de see Alboran Sea
105 N17 **Alboran Sea** Sp. Mar de Alborán. SW Mediterranean Sea
95 H21 **Ålborg** var. Aalborg. Nordjylland, N Denmark 57°03´N 09°56´E
Ålborg Bugt bay N Denmark
Ålborg-Nørresundby see Ålborg
143 O5 **Alborz, Reshteh-ye Kūhhā-ye** Eng. Elburz Mountains. ▲ N Iran
105 Q14 **Albox** Andalucía, S Spain 37°22´N 02°08´W
101 H23 **Albstadt** Baden-Württemberg, SW Germany 48°13´N 09°01´E
104 G14 **Albufeira** Beja, S Portugal 37°05´N 08°15´W
37 Q11 **Albuquerque** New Mexico, SW USA 35°05´N 106°39´W
43 Q7 **Albuquerque, Cayos de** island group NW Colombia, Caribbean Sea
141 W8 **Al Buraymī** var. Buraimi. N Oman 24°16´N 55°48´E

◆ Country   ◇ Dependent Territory   ◆ Administrative Regions   ▲ Mountain   ☒ Volcano   ◎ Lake
● Country Capital   ○ Dependent Territory Capital   ✈ International Airport   ▲ Mountain Range   ✎ River   ☒ Reservoir

Al Buraymī – Alme

143 R17 **Al Buraymī** *var.* Buraimi. *spring/well* Oman/United Arab Emirates 24°27′N 55°33′E
Al Burayqah *see* Marsá al Burayqah
Alburgum *see* Aalborg
104 I10 **Alburquerque** Extremadura, W Spain 39°12′N 07°00′W
181 V14 **Albury** New South Wales, SE Australia 36°03′S 146°53′E
141 T14 **Al Buzūn** SE Yemen 15°40′N 50°53′E
93 G17 **Alby** Västernorrland, C Sweden 62°30′N 15°25′E
Albyn, Glen *see* Mor, Glen
104 G12 **Alcácer do Sal** Setúbal, W Portugal 38°22′N 08°29′W
Alcalá de Chisvert/Alcalá de Chivert *see* Alcalà de Xivert
104 K14 **Alcalá de Guadaira** Andalucía, S Spain 37°20′N 05°50′W
105 O8 **Alcalá de Henares** *Ar.* Alkal'a; *anc.* Complutum. Madrid, C Spain 40°28′N 03°22′W
104 K16 **Alcalá de los Gazules** Andalucía, S Spain 36°29′N 05°43′W
105 T8 **Alcalà de Xivert** *var.* Alcalá de Chisvert, *Cast.* Alcalá de Chivert. País Valenciano, E Spain 40°19′N 00°13′E
105 N14 **Alcalá La Real** Andalucía, S Spain 37°28′N 03°55′W
107 I23 **Alcamo** Sicilia, Italy, C Mediterranean Sea 37°58′N 12°58′E
105 T4 **Alcanadre** ≈ NE Spain
105 P12 **Alcanar** Cataluña, NE Spain 40°33′N 00°28′E
104 J5 **Alcañices** Castilla-León, N Spain 41°41′N 06°21′W
105 T7 **Alcañiz** Aragón, NE Spain 41°03′N 00°09′W
104 I9 **Alcántara** Extremadura, W Spain 39°42′N 06°54′W
104 J9 **Alcántara, Embalse de** ⊠ W Spain
105 R13 **Alcantarilla** Murcia, SE Spain 37°59′N 01°12′W
105 P11 **Alcaraz** Castilla-La Mancha, C Spain 38°40′N 02°29′W
105 P12 **Alcaraz, Sierra de** ▲▲ C Spain
104 I12 **Alcarrache** ≈ SW Spain
105 T6 **Alcarràs** Cataluña, NE Spain 41°34′N 00°31′E
105 N14 **Alcaudete** Andalucía, S Spain 37°35′N 04°05′W
Alcázar *see* Ksar-el-Kebir
105 O10 **Alcázar de San Juan** *anc.* Alce. Castilla-La Mancha, C Spain 39°24′N 03°12′W
Alcazarquivir *see* Ksar-el-Kebir
Alce *see* Alcázar de San Juan
57 B17 **Alcebo, Volcán** ✺ Galapagos Islands, Ecuador, E Pacific Ocean 00°25′S 91°06′W
139 X12 **Al Chabā'ish** *var.* Al Kaba'ish. Dhī Qār, SE Iraq 30°58′N 47°02′E
117 Y7 **Alchevs'k** *prev.* Kommunarsk, Voroshilovsk. Luhans'ka Oblast', E Ukraine 48°29′N 38°52′E
Alcira *see* Alzira
21 N9 **Alcoa** Tennessee, S USA 35°47′N 83°58′W
104 F9 **Alcobaça** Leiria, C Portugal 39°32′N 08°59′W
105 N8 **Alcobendas** Madrid, C Spain 40°32′N 03°38′W
Alcoi *see* Alcoy
105 P7 **Alcolea del Pinar** Castilla-La Mancha, C Spain 41°02′N 02°28′W
104 I11 **Alconchel** Extremadura, W Spain 38°31′N 07°04′W
Alcora *see* L'Alcora
105 N8 **Alcorcón** Madrid, C Spain 40°20′N 03°52′W
105 S7 **Alcorisa** Aragón, NE Spain 40°53′N 00°23′W
61 B19 **Alcorta** Santa Fe, C Argentina 33°32′S 61°07′W
104 H14 **Alcoutim** Faro, S Portugal 37°28′N 07°29′W
33 W15 **Alcova** Wyoming, C USA 42°33′N 106°40′W
105 S11 **Alcoy** *Cat.* Alcoi. País Valenciano, E Spain 38°42′N 00°29′W
105 Y9 **Alcúdia** Mallorca, Spain, W Mediterranean Sea 39°51′N 03°06′E
105 Y9 **Alcúdia, Badia d'** *bay* Mallorca, Spain, W Mediterranean Sea
172 M7 **Aldabra Group** *island group* SW Seychelles
139 U10 **Al Daghghārah** Bābil, C Iraq 32°10′N 44°57′E
40 J5 **Aldama** Chihuahua, N Mexico 28°50′N 105°52′W
41 P11 **Aldama** Tamaulipas, C Mexico 22°54′N 98°05′W
123 Q11 **Aldan** Respublika Sakha (Yakutiya), NE Russian Federation 58°31′N 125°15′E
123 Q10 **Aldan** ≈ NE Russian Federation
Aldar *see* Aldarhaan
al Dar al Baida *see* Rabat
162 G7 **Aldarhaan** *var.* Aldar. Dzavhan, W Mongolia 47°43′N 96°36′E
97 Q20 **Aldeburgh** E England, United Kingdom 52°12′N 01°36′E
105 P5 **Aldehuela de Calatañazor** Castilla-León, N Spain 41°42′N 02°46′W
Aldeia Nova *see* Aldeia Nova de São Bento
104 H13 **Aldeia Nova de São Bento** *var.* Aldeia Nova. Beja, S Portugal 37°55′N 07°24′W
29 V11 **Alden** Minnesota, N USA 43°40′N 93°34′W
184 N6 **Aldermen Islands, The** *island group* N New Zealand
97 L25 **Alderney** *island* Channel Islands
97 N22 **Aldershot** S England, United Kingdom 51°15′N 00°47′W
21 R6 **Alderson** West Virginia, NE USA 37°43′N 80°38′W
Al Dhaid *see* Adh Dhayd
30 J11 **Aledo** Illinois, N USA 41°12′N 90°45′W
76 H9 **Aleg** Brakna, SW Mauritania 17°03′N 13°53′W
64 Q10 **Alegranza** *island* Islas Canarias, Spain, NE Atlantic Ocean
37 P12 **Alegres Mountain** ▲ New Mexico, SW USA 34°09′N 108°11′W
61 F15 **Alegrete** Rio Grande do Sul, S Brazil 29°46′S 55°46′W
61 C16 **Alejandra** Santa Fe, C Argentina 29°54′S 59°50′W
193 T11 **Alejandro Selkirk, Isla** *island* Islas Juan Fernández, Chile, E Pacific Ocean
124 I12 **Alekhovshchina** Leningradskaya Oblast', NW Russian Federation 60°22′N 33°57′E
39 O13 **Aleknagik** Alaska, USA 59°16′N 158°37′W
Aleksandriya *see* Oleksandriya
Aleksandropol' *see* Gyumri
126 L3 **Aleksandrov** Vladimirskaya Oblast', W Russian Federation 56°24′N 38°42′E
113 N14 **Aleksandrovac** Serbia, C Serbia 43°28′N 21°05′E
127 R9 **Aleksandrov Gay** Saratovskaya Oblast', W Russian Federation 50°08′N 48°34′E
127 U6 **Aleksandrovka** Orenburgskaya Oblast', W Russian Federation 52°47′N 54°14′E
Aleksandrovka *see* Oleksandrivka
125 V13 **Aleksandrovsk** Permskaya Oblast', NW Russian Federation 59°12′N 57°27′E
Aleksandrovsk *see* Zaporizhzhya
127 N14 **Aleksandrovskoye** Stavropol'skiy Kray, SW Russian Federation 44°43′N 42°56′E
123 T12 **Aleksandrovsk-Sakhalinskiy** Ostrov Sakhalin, Sakhalinskaya Oblast', SE Russian Federation 50°55′N 142°12′E
110 J10 **Aleksandrów Kujawski** Kujawsko-pormorskie, C Poland 52°52′N 18°40′E
110 K12 **Aleksandrów Łódzki** Łódzkie, C Poland 51°49′N 19°19′E
Alekseevka *see* Akkol', Akmola, Kazakhstan
Alekseevka *see* Terekty
145 P7 **Alekseyevka** *Kaz.* Alekseevka. Akmola, N Kazakhstan 53°32′N 69°30′E
126 L9 **Alekseyevka** Belgorodskaya, W Russian Federation 50°35′N 38°41′E
127 S7 **Alekseyevka** Samarskaya Oblast', W Russian Federation 52°37′N 51°20′E
Alekseyevka *see* Akkol', Akmola, Kazakhstan
Alekseyevka *see* Terekty, Vostochnyy Kazakhstan, Kazakhstan
127 R4 **Alekseyevskoye** Respublika Tatarstan, W Russian Federation 55°18′N 50°11′E
126 K5 **Aleksin** Tul'skaya Oblast', W Russian Federation 54°30′N 37°08′E
113 O14 **Aleksinac** Serbia, SE Serbia 43°33′N 21°43′E
190 G11 **Alele** Île Uvea, E Wallis and Futuna 13°14′S 176°09′W
95 N20 **Ålem** Kalmar, S Sweden 56°57′N 16°25′E
102 L6 **Alençon** Orne, N France 48°26′N 00°04′E
58 I12 **Alenquer** Pará, NE Brazil 01°58′S 54°45′W
38 G10 **'Alenuihaha Channel** *var.* Alenuihaha Channel. *channel* Hawai'i, USA, C Pacific Ocean
Alep/Aleppo *see* Ḥalab
103 Y15 **Aléria** Corse, France, C Mediterranean Sea 42°06′N 09°29′E
197 Q11 **Alert** Ellesmere Island, Nunavut, N Canada 82°28′N 62°13′W
103 Q14 **Alès** *prev.* Alais. Gard, S France 44°08′N 04°05′E
116 G9 **Aleşd** *Hung.* Élesd. Bihor, SW Romania 47°03′N 22°22′E
106 C9 **Alessandria** *Fr.* Alexandrie. Piemonte, N Italy 44°54′N 08°37′E
Ålestrup *see* Aalestrup
94 D9 **Ålesund** Møre og Romsdal, S Norway 62°28′N 06°11′E
108 E10 **Aletschhorn** ▲ SW Switzerland 46°33′N 08°01′E
197 S1 **Aleutian Basin** *undersea feature* Bering Sea 57°00′N 177°00′E
38 H17 **Aleutian Islands** *island group* Alaska, USA
39 P14 **Aleutian Range** ▲▲ Alaska, USA
0 B5 **Aleutian Trench** *undersea feature* S Bering Sea 57°00′N 177°00′W
123 T10 **Alevina, Mys** *cape* E Russian Federation
15 Q6 **Alex** ≈ Québec, SE Canada
26 J3 **Alexander** North Dakota, N USA 47°48′N 103°38′W
39 W14 **Alexander Archipelago** *island group* Alaska, USA
Alexanderbaai *see* Alexander Bay
83 D23 **Alexander Bay** *Afr.* Alexanderbaai. Northern Cape, W South Africa 28°40′S 16°30′E
23 Q5 **Alexander City** Alabama, S USA 32°56′N 85°57′W
194 J6 **Alexander Island** *island* Antarctica
Alexander Range *see* Kirghiz Range
183 O12 **Alexandra** Victoria, SE Australia 37°12′S 145°43′E
185 D22 **Alexandra** Otago, South Island, New Zealand 45°15′S 169°25′E
115 F14 **Alexándreia** *var.* Alexándria. Kentrikí Makedonía, N Greece 40°38′N 22°27′E
Alexandretta *see* İskenderun
Alexandretta, Gulf of *see* İskenderun Körfezi
15 N13 **Alexandria** Ontario, SE Canada 45°19′N 74°37′W
121 U13 **Alexandria** *Ar.* Al Iskandarīyah. N Egypt 31°07′N 29°51′E
44 J12 **Alexandria** C Jamaica 18°18′N 77°21′W
116 J15 **Alexandria** Teleorman, S Romania 43°58′N 25°18′E
31 P13 **Alexandria** Indiana, N USA 40°15′N 85°40′W
20 M4 **Alexandria** Kentucky, S USA 38°59′N 84°22′W
22 H7 **Alexandria** Louisiana, S USA 31°19′N 92°27′W
29 T7 **Alexandria** Minnesota, N USA 45°54′N 95°22′W
29 Q11 **Alexandria** South Dakota, N USA 43°39′N 97°46′W
21 W4 **Alexandria** Virginia, NE USA 38°49′N 77°06′W
Alexándria *see* Alexándreia
18 I7 **Alexandria Bay** New York, NE USA 44°20′N 75°54′W
Alexandrie *see* Alessandria
182 J10 **Alexandrina, Lake** ◎ South Australia
114 K13 **Alexandroúpoli** *var.* Alexandroúpolis, *Turk.* Dedeagaç, Dedeagach. Anatolikí Makedonía kai Thráki, NE Greece 40°52′N 25°53′E
Alexandroúpolis *see* Alexandroúpoli
10 L15 **Alexis Creek** British Columbia, SW Canada 52°06′N 123°25′W
122 I13 **Aleysk** Altayskiy Kray, S Russian Federation 52°32′N 82°46′E
139 S8 **Al Fallūjah** *var.* Falluja. Al Anbār, C Iraq 33°21′N 43°46′E
105 R8 **Alfambra** ≈ E Spain
Al Faqa *see* Faq'
141 R15 **Al Farḍah** C Yemen 14°51′N 48°33′E
105 Q4 **Alfaro** La Rioja, N Spain 42°13′N 01°45′W
105 U5 **Alfarràs** Cataluña, NE Spain 41°50′N 00°34′E
Al Fāshir *see* El Fasher
75 W8 **Al Fashn** *var.* El Fashn. C Egypt 28°49′N 30°54′E
114 M7 **Alfatar** Silistra, NE Bulgaria 43°56′N 27°17′E
139 S5 **Al Fatḥah** Ṣalāḥ ad Dīn, C Iraq 35°06′N 43°34′E
139 Q3 **Al Fatsī** Nīnawá, N Iraq 36°04′N 42°39′E
139 Z13 **Al Fāw** *var.* Fao. Al Baṣrah, SE Iraq 29°55′N 48°26′E
75 W8 **Al Fayyūm** *var.* El Faiyûm. N Egypt 29°19′N 30°50′E
El Faiyûm *see* Al Fayyūm
115 D20 **Alfeiós** *prev.* Alfiós; *anc.* Alpheius, Alpheus. ≈ S Greece
100 I13 **Alfeld** Niedersachsen, C Germany 51°58′N 09°49′E
Alfiós *see* Alfeiós
Alföld *see* Great Hungarian Plain
94 C11 **Ålfotbreen** *glacier* S Norway
19 P9 **Alfred** Maine, NE USA 43°29′N 70°44′W
18 F11 **Alfred** New York, NE USA 42°15′N 77°47′W
61 K14 **Alfredo Vagner** Santa Catarina, S Brazil 27°40′S 49°22′W
94 M12 **Alfta** Gävleborg, C Sweden 61°20′N 16°05′E
140 K12 **Al Fuḥayḥīl** *var.* Fahaheel. SE Kuwait 29°01′N 48°05′E
139 Q6 **Al Fuḥaymī** Al Anbār, C Iraq 34°18′N 42°09′E
143 S16 **Al Fujayrah** *Eng.* Fujairah. Al Fujayrah, NE United Arab Emirates 25°09′N 56°18′E
143 S16 **Al Fujayrah** *Eng.* Fujairah. ✈ Al Fujayrah, NE United Arab Emirates 25°04′N 56°12′E
Al-Furāt *see* Euphrates
144 I10 **Alga** *Kaz.* Algha. Aktyubinsk, NW Kazakhstan 49°56′N 57°19′E
144 G9 **Algabas** *Kaz.* Alghabas. Zapadnyy Kazakhstan, NW Kazakhstan 50°43′N 52°09′E
95 C17 **Ålgård** Rogaland, S Norway 58°45′N 05°52′E
104 G14 **Algarve** *cultural region* S Portugal
182 G3 **Algebuckina Bridge** South Australia 28°03′S 135°48′E
104 K16 **Algeciras** Andalucía, SW Spain 36°08′N 05°27′W
105 S10 **Algemesí** País Valenciano, E Spain 39°11′N 00°27′W
Al-Genain *see* El Geneina
120 F9 **Alger** *var.* Algiers, El Djazaïr, Al Jazair. ● (Algeria) N Algeria 36°47′N 02°58′E
74 H9 **Algeria** *off.* Democratic and Popular Republic of Algeria. ◆ *republic* N Africa
Algeria, Democratic and Popular Republic of *see* Algeria
120 J8 **Algerian Basin** *var.* Balearic Plain. *undersea feature* W Mediterranean Sea
Algha *see* Alga
138 I4 **Al Ghāb** *Valley* NW Syria
141 X10 **Al Ghābah** *var.* Ghaba. C Oman 21°22′N 57°14′E
Alghabas *see* Algabas
141 U14 **Al Ghayḍah** E Yemen 16°15′N 52°13′E
140 M6 **Al Ghazālah** Ḥā'il, NW Saudi Arabia 26°55′N 41°23′E
107 B17 **Alghero** Sardegna, Italy, C Mediterranean Sea 40°34′N 08°19′E
95 M20 **Älghult** Kronoberg, S Sweden 57°00′N 15°34′E
Al Ghurdaqah *see* Hurghada
Algiers *see* Alger
105 S10 **Alginet** País Valenciano, E Spain 39°16′N 00°28′W
83 I26 **Algoa Bay** *bay* S South Africa
104 L15 **Algodonales** Andalucía, S Spain 36°54′N 05°24′W
105 N9 **Algodor** ≈ C Spain
Al Golea *see* El Goléa
31 N6 **Algoma** Wisconsin, N USA 44°41′N 87°24′W
29 U12 **Algona** Iowa, C USA 43°04′N 94°13′W
20 L8 **Algood** Tennessee, S USA 36°12′N 85°27′W
105 O2 **Algorta** País Vasco, N Spain 43°20′N 03°00′W
61 E18 **Algorta** Río Negro, W Uruguay 32°26′S 57°18′W
Al Haba *see* Haba
139 Q10 **Al Habbārīyah** Al Anbār, S Iraq 32°16′N 42°12′E
Al Hadhar *see* Al Ḥaḍr
139 Q4 **Al Ḥaḍr** *var.* Al Hadhar; *anc.* Hatra. Nīnawá, NW Iraq 35°34′N 42°44′E
139 T13 **Al Ḥajarah** *desert* S Iraq
141 W8 **Al Ḥajar al Gharbī** ▲▲ N Oman
141 Y8 **Al Ḥajar ash Sharqī** ▲▲ NE Oman
141 R15 **Al Ḥajarayn** C Yemen 15°29′N 48°24′E
138 L10 **Al Ḥamād** *desert* Jordan/Saudi Arabia
Al Hamad *see* Syrian Desert
75 N9 **Al Ḥamādah al Ḥamrā'** *var.* Al Ḥamrā'. *desert* NW Libya
105 N15 **Alhama de Granada** Andalucía, S Spain 37°00′N 03°59′W
105 R13 **Alhama de Murcia** Murcia, SE Spain 37°51′N 01°25′W
35 T15 **Alhambra** California, W USA 34°08′N 118°06′W
139 T12 **Al Ḥammām** An Najaf, S Iraq 31°09′N 44°04′E
141 X8 **Al Ḥamrā'** NE Oman 23°07′N 57°23′E
Al Ḥamrā' *see* Al Ḥamādah al Ḥamrā'
141 O6 **Al Ḥamūdīyah** *spring/well* N Saudi Arabia 27°05′N 44°24′E
140 M7 **Al Ḥanākīyah** Al Madīnah, W Saudi Arabia 24°55′N 40°31′E
139 W14 **Al Ḥanīyah** *escarpment* Iraq/Saudi Arabia
139 Y12 **Al Ḥārithah** Al Baṣrah, SE Iraq 30°43′N 47°44′E
140 L3 **Al Ḥarrah** *desert* NW Saudi Arabia
75 Q10 **Al Harūj al Aswad** *desert* C Libya
Al Hasaifin *see* Al Ḥusayfīn
139 N2 **Al Ḥasakah** *var.* Al Hasijah, El Haseke, *Fr.* Hassetché. Al Ḥasakah, NE Syria 36°22′N 40°44′E
139 O2 **Al Ḥasakah** *off.* Muḥāfaẓat al Ḥasakah, *var.* Al Hasakah, Al Hasakah, Hasakah, Hassakeh. ◈ *governorate* NE Syria
Al Hasakah *see* 'Āmūdah
Al Hasakah *see* Al Ḥasakah
139 T9 **Al Hāshimīyah** Bābil, C Iraq 32°24′N 44°39′E
138 G13 **Al Hāshimīyah** Ma'ān, S Jordan 30°31′N 35°46′E
Al Hasijah *see* Al Ḥasakah
104 M15 **Alhaurín el Grande** Andalucía, S Spain 36°39′N 04°41′W
141 Q16 **Al Ḥawrā** S Yemen 13°54′N 47°36′E
139 V10 **Al Ḥayy** *var.* Kut al Hai, Kūt al Ḥayy. Wāsiṭ, E Iraq 32°11′N 46°03′E
141 U11 **Al Hibāk** *desert* E Saudi Arabia
138 H8 **Al Hījānah** *var.* Hejanah, Hijanah. Dimashq, W Syria 33°23′N 36°34′E
140 K7 **Al Ḥijāz** *Eng.* Hejaz. *physical region* NW Saudi Arabia
Al Hilbeh *see* 'Ulayyānīyah, Bi'r al
139 T9 **Al Ḥillah** *var.* Hilla. Bābil, C Iraq 32°28′N 44°29′E
139 T9 **Al Hindīyah** *var.* Hindiya. Bābil, C Iraq 32°32′N 44°14′E
138 G12 **Al Ḥisā** Aṭ Ṭafīlah, W Jordan 30°49′N 35°58′E
74 G5 **Al-Hoceïma** *var.* al Hoceima, Al-Hoceima, Alhucemas; *prev.* Villa Sanjurjo. N Morocco 35°14′N 03°56′W
Alhucemas *see* Al-Hoceïma
105 N17 **Alhucemas, Peñon de** *island group* S Spain
141 N15 **Al Ḥudaydah** *Eng.* Hodeida. W Yemen 15°N 42°50′E
141 N15 **Al Ḥudaydah** *var.* Hodeida. ✈ W Yemen 14°45′N 43°01′E
140 M4 **Al Ḥudūd ash Shamālīyah** *var.* Minṭaqat al Ḥudūd ash Shamālīyah, *Eng.* Northern Border Region. ◈ *province* N Saudi Arabia
141 S7 **Al Hufūf** *var.* Hofuf. Ash Sharqīyah, NE Saudi Arabia 25°21′N 49°34′E
al-Hurma *see* Al Khurmah
141 X7 **Al Ḥusayfīn** *var.* Al Hasaifin. N Oman 24°33′N 56°33′E
138 G9 **Al Ḥuṣn** *var.* Husn. Irbid, N Jordan 32°29′N 35°53′E
139 U9 **'Alī** Wāsiṭ, E Iraq 32°43′N 45°21′E
104 L10 **Alia** Extremadura, W Spain 39°25′N 05°12′W
143 P9 **'Alīābād** Yazd, C Iran 36°55′N 54°33′E
'Alīābād *see* Qā'emshahr
105 S7 **Aliaga** Aragón, NE Spain 40°40′N 00°42′W
136 B13 **Aliağa** İzmir, W Turkey 38°49′N 26°59′E
Aliákmon *see* Aliákmonas
115 F14 **Aliákmonas** *prev.* Aliákmon; *anc.* Haliacmon. ≈ N Greece
139 W9 **'Alī al Gharbī** Maysān, E Iraq 32°28′N 46°42′E
139 U11 **'Alī al Ḥassūnī** Al Qādisīyah, S Iraq 31°25′N 44°50′E
115 G18 **Alíartos** Stereá Elláda, C Greece 38°23′N 23°06′E
137 Y12 **Äli-Bayramlı** *Rus.* Ali-Bayramly. SE Azerbaijan 39°57′N 48°54′E
Ali-Bayramly *see* Äli-Bayramlı
114 P12 **Alibey Barajı** ⊠ NW Turkey
77 S13 **Alibori** ≈ N Benin
112 M10 **Alibunar** Vojvodina, NE Serbia 45°06′N 20°59′E
105 S12 **Alicante** *Cat.* Alacant, *Lat.* Lucentum. País Valenciano, SE Spain 38°21′N 00°29′W
105 S12 **Alicante** ◈ *province* País Valenciano, SE Spain
105 S12 **Alicante** ✈ Murcia, E Spain 38°21′N 00°29′W
83 I25 **Alice** Eastern Cape, S South Africa 32°47′S 26°50′E
25 S14 **Alice** Texas, SW USA 27°45′N 98°06′W
83 I25 **Alicedale** Eastern Cape, S South Africa 33°19′S 26°05′E
65 B25 **Alice, Mount** *hill* West Falkland, Falkland Islands
107 P20 **Alice, Punta** *headland* S Italy
181 Q7 **Alice Springs** Northern Territory, C Australia 23°42′S 133°52′E
23 N4 **Aliceville** Alabama, S USA 33°07′N 88°09′W
147 U13 **Alichur** SE Tajikistan 37°49′N 73°45′E
147 U14 **Alichuri Janubí, Qatorkŭhi** *Rus.* Yuzhno-Alichurskiy Khrebet. ▲▲ SE Tajikistan
147 U13 **Alichuri Shimolí, Qatorkŭhi** *Rus.* Severo-Alichurskiy Khrebet. ▲▲ SE Tajikistan
107 K22 **Alicudi, Isola** *island* Isole Eolie, S Italy
Alifu Atoll *see* Ari Atoll
43 W14 **Aligandí** Kuna Yala, NE Panama 09°15′N 78°05′W
152 J11 **Alīgarh** Uttar Pradesh, N India 27°54′N 78°04′E
142 M7 **Alīgūdarz** Lorestān, W Iran 33°24′N 49°19′E
163 U5 **Alihe** *var.* Oroqen Zizhiqi. Nei Mongol Zizhiqu, N China 50°34′N 123°40′E
0 F12 **Alijos, Islas** *islets* California, SW USA
149 R6 **'Alī Kbel** *Pash.* 'Alī Khēl. Paktīkā, E Afghanistan 33°55′N 69°49′E
Ali Khel *see* 'Alī Kheyl, Paktīā, Afghanistan
'Alī Khēl *see* 'Alī Kbel, Paktīkā, Afghanistan
149 R6 **'Alī Kheyl** *var.* Ali Khel, Jaji. Paktīā, SE Afghanistan 33°55′N 69°46′E
141 V17 **Al Ikhwān** *island group* SE Yemen
Aliki *see* Alykí
79 H19 **Alima** ≈ C Congo
Al Imārāt al 'Arabīyah al Muttaḥidah *see* United Arab Emirates
115 N23 **Alimía** *island* Dodekánisa, Greece, Aegean Sea
55 V12 **Alimimuni Piek** ▲ S Surinam 02°26′N 55°46′W
79 K15 **Alindao** Basse-Kotto, S Central African Republic 04°58′N 21°16′E
95 J18 **Alingsås** Västra Götaland, S Sweden 57°55′N 12°30′E
81 K18 **Alinjugul** *spring/well* E Kenya 0°03′S 40°31′E
153 S16 **Alīpur** West Bengal, NE India 22°32′N 88°20′E
149 S11 **Alīpur** Punjab, E Pakistan 29°22′N 70°59′E
153 T12 **Alīpur Duār** West Bengal, NE India 26°28′N 89°25′E
18 B14 **Aliquippa** Pennsylvania, NE USA 40°36′N 80°15′W
80 L12 **'Ali Sabieh** *var.* 'Alī Sabīḥ. S Djibouti 11°07′N 42°44′E
'Alī Sabīḥ *see* 'Ali Sabieh
140 K3 **Al 'Īsāwīyah** Al Jawf, NW Saudi Arabia 30°41′N 37°58′E
104 J10 **Aliseda** Extremadura, W Spain 39°25′N 06°42′W
139 T8 **Al Iskandarīyah** Bābil, C Iraq 32°53′N 44°22′E
Al Iskandarīyah *see* Alexandria
123 T6 **Aliskerovo** Chukotskiy Avtonomnyy Okrug, NE Russian Federation 67°40′N 167°37′E
75 W7 **Al Ismā'īlīya** *var.* Ismailia, Ismâ'ilîya. N Egypt 30°32′N 32°13′E
114 H13 **Alistráti** Kentrikí Makedonía, NE Greece 41°03′N 23°58′E
39 P15 **Alitak Bay** *bay* Kodiak Island, Alaska, USA
Al Ittiḥād *see* Madīnat ash Sha'b
115 H18 **Alivéri** *var.* Alivérion. Évvoia, C Greece 38°24′N 24°02′E
Alivérion *see* Alivéri
Aliwal-Noord *see* Aliwal North
83 I24 **Aliwal North** *Afr.* Aliwal-Noord. Eastern Cape, SE South Africa 30°42′S 26°43′E
121 Q13 **Al Jabal al Akhḍar** ▲▲ NE Libya
138 H13 **Al Jafr** Ma'ān, S Jordan 30°18′N 36°13′E
75 T8 **Al Jaghbūb** NE Libya 29°45′N 24°31′E
142 K11 **Al Jahrā'** *var.* Al Jahrah, Jahra. C Kuwait 29°18′N 47°36′E
Al Jahrah *see* Al Jahrā'
Al Jamāhīrīyah al 'Arabīyah al Lībīyah ash Sha'bīyah al Ishtirākīy *see* Libya
140 K3 **Al Jarāwī** *spring/well* NW Saudi Arabia 30°12′N 38°48′E
141 X11 **Al Jawārah** *oasis* SE Oman
140 L3 **Al Jawf** *off.* Jauf. Al Jawf, NW Saudi Arabia 29°51′N 39°49′E
140 L4 **Al Jawf** *var.* Minṭaqat al Jawf. ◈ *province* N Saudi Arabia
Al Jawlān *see* Golan Heights
Al Jazair *see* Alger
139 N4 **Al Jazīrah** *physical region* Iraq/Syria
104 F14 **Aljezur** Faro, S Portugal 37°18′N 08°49′W
139 S13 **Al Jil** An Najaf, S Iraq 30°28′N 43°57′E
138 G11 **Al Jīzah** *var.* Jiza. 'Ammān, N Jordan 31°42′N 35°57′E
Al Jīzah *see* Gîza
Al Jubail *see* Al Jubayl
141 S6 **Al Jubayl** *var.* Al Jubail. Ash Sharqīyah, NE Saudi Arabia 27°N 49°36′E
141 T10 **Āl Juḥaysh, Qalamat** *well* SE Saudi Arabia
143 N15 **Al Jumaylīyah** N Qatar 25°37′N 51°05′E
Al Junaynah *see* El Geneina
104 G13 **Aljustrel** Beja, S Portugal 37°52′N 08°10′W
Al Kaba'ish *see* Al Chabā'ish
Al-Kadhimain *see* Al Kāẓimīyah
Al Kāf *see* El Kef
Alkal'a *see* Alcalá de Henares
35 W4 **Alkali Flat** *salt flat* Nevada, W USA
35 Q1 **Alkali Lake** ◎ Nevada, W USA
141 Z9 **Al Kāmil** NE Oman 22°14′N 58°15′E
138 G11 **Al Karak** *var.* El Kerak, Karak, Kerak; *anc.* Kir Moab, Kir of Moab. Al Karak, W Jordan 31°11′N 35°42′E
138 G12 **Al Karak** *off.* Muḥāfaẓat al Karak. ◈ *governorate* W Jordan
139 W8 **Al Karmashīyah** Wāsiṭ, E Iraq 32°57′N 46°10′E
Al-Kashaniya *see* Al Qash'ānīyah
Al-Kasr al-Kebir *see* Ksar-el-Kebir
139 T8 **Al Kāẓimīyah** *var.* Al-Kadhimain, Kadhimain. Baghdād, C Iraq 33°22′N 44°20′E
99 J18 **Alken** Limburg, NE Belgium 50°52′N 05°19′E
141 X8 **Al Khābūrah** *var.* Khabura. N Oman 23°57′N 57°06′E
Al Khalīl *see* Hebron
139 T7 **Al Khāliṣ** Diyālá, C Iraq 33°51′N 44°33′E
Al Khaluf *see* Khalūf
75 W10 **Al Khārijah** *var.* El Khârga. C Egypt 25°31′N 30°36′E
141 Q8 **Al Kharj** Ar Riyāḍ, C Saudi Arabia 24°12′N 47°12′E
141 W6 **Al Khaṣab** *var.* Khasab. N Oman 26°11′N 56°18′E
Al Khaur *see* Al Khawr
143 N15 **Al Khawr** *var.* Al Khaur, Al Khor. N Qatar 25°40′N 51°33′E
142 K12 **Al Khīrān** *var.* Al Khiran. SE Kuwait 28°34′N 48°21′E
141 W9 **Al Khīrān** *spring/well* NW Oman 22°31′N 55°42′E
Al Khiyām *see* El Khiyam
Al-Khobar *see* Al Khubar
Al Khor *see* Al Khawr
141 S6 **Al Khubar** *var.* Al-Khobar. Ash Sharqīyah, NE Saudi Arabia 26°00′N 50°00′E
120 M12 **Al Khums** *var.* Homs, Khoms, Khums. NW Libya 32°39′N 14°16′E
141 R15 **Al Khuraybah** C Yemen 15°05′N 48°17′E
140 M9 **Al Khurmah** *var.* al-Hurma. Makkah, W Saudi Arabia 21°59′N 42°00′E
141 V9 **Al Kidan** *desert* NE Saudi Arabia
127 V4 **Alkino-2** Respublika Bashkortostan, W Russian Federation 54°30′N 55°40′E
98 H9 **Alkmaar** Noord-Holland, NW Netherlands 52°37′N 04°45′E
139 T10 **Al Kūfah** *var.* Kufa. An Najaf, S Iraq 32°02′N 44°25′E
75 T11 **Al Kufrah** SE Libya 24°11′N 23°19′E
141 T10 **Al Kursū'** *desert* E Saudi Arabia
139 V9 **Al Kūt** *var.* Kūt al 'Amārah, Kut al Imara. Wāsiṭ, E Iraq 32°30′N 45°51′E
Al-Kuwait *see* Al Kuwayt
Al Kuwayr *see* Guwēr
142 K11 **Al Kuwayt** *var.* Al-Kuwait, *Eng.* Kuwait, Kuwait City; *prev.* Qurein. ● (Kuwait) E Kuwait 29°23′N 48°00′E
142 K11 **Al Kuwayt** ✈ C Kuwait 29°13′N 47°57′E
115 G19 **Alkyonídon, Kólpos** *gulf* C Greece
141 N4 **Al Labbah** *physical region* N Saudi Arabia
138 G4 **Al Lādhiqīyah** *Eng.* Latakia, *Fr.* Lattaquié; *anc.* Laodicea, Laodicea ad Mare. Al Lādhiqīyah, W Syria 35°31′N 35°47′E
138 H4 **Al Lādhiqīyah** *off.* Muḥāfaẓat al Lādhiqīyah, *var.* Al Lathqiyah, Latakia, Lattakia. ◈ *governorate* W Syria
19 R2 **Allagash River** ≈ Maine, NE USA
152 M13 **Allahābād** Uttar Pradesh, N India 25°27′N 81°50′E
143 S3 **Allāh Dāgh, Reshteh-ye** ▲▲ NE Iran
39 Q8 **Allakaket** Alaska, USA 66°34′N 152°39′W
141 X12 **Al Lakbī** S Oman 18°27′N 56°37′E
11 T15 **Allan** Saskatchewan, S Canada 51°50′N 105°59′W
83 I22 **Allanridge** Free State, C South Africa 27°45′S 26°40′E
104 H4 **Allariz** Galicia, NW Spain 42°11′N 07°48′W
139 R11 **Al Laṣaf** *var.* Al Lussuf. An Najaf, S Iraq 31°38′N 43°16′E
Al Lathqiyah *see* Al Lādhiqīyah
23 S2 **Allatoona Lake** ⊠ Georgia, SE USA
83 J19 **Alldays** Limpopo, NE South Africa 22°39′S 29°04′E
Alle *see* Łyna
31 P10 **Allegan** Michigan, N USA 42°31′N 85°51′W
18 E14 **Allegheny Mountains** ▲▲ NE USA
18 E12 **Allegheny Plateau** ▲▲ New York/Pennsylvania, NE USA
18 D11 **Allegheny Reservoir** ⊠ New York/Pennsylvania, NE USA
18 E12 **Allegheny River** ≈ New York/Pennsylvania, NE USA
22 K9 **Allemands, Lac des** ◎ Louisiana, S USA
25 U6 **Allen** Texas, SW USA 33°06′N 96°40′W
21 R14 **Allendale** South Carolina, SE USA 33°01′N 81°19′W
41 N6 **Allende** Coahuila, NE Mexico 28°22′N 100°50′W
41 O9 **Allende** Nuevo León, NE Mexico 25°20′N 100°01′W
97 D16 **Allen, Lough** *Ir.* Loch Aillionn. ◎ NW Ireland
185 B26 **Allen, Mount** ▲ Stewart Island, Southland, SW New Zealand 47°05′S 167°49′E
109 V2 **Allensteig** Niederösterreich, N Austria 48°40′N 15°24′E
Allenstein *see* Olsztyn
18 I14 **Allentown** Pennsylvania, NE USA 40°37′N 75°30′W
155 G23 **Alleppey** *var.* Alappuzha. Kerala, SW India 09°30′N 76°22′E *see also* Alappuzha
100 J12 **Aller** ≈ NW Germany
29 V16 **Allerton** Iowa, C USA 40°42′N 93°22′W
99 K19 **Alleur** Liège, E Belgium 50°40′N 05°33′E
101 J25 **Allgäuer Alpen** ▲▲ Austria/Germany
28 J13 **Alliance** Nebraska, C USA 42°08′N 102°54′W
31 U12 **Alliance** Ohio, N USA 40°55′N 81°06′W
103 O10 **Allier** ◈ *department* N France
139 R13 **Al Lifiyah** *well* An Najaf, S Iraq
44 J13 **Alligator Pond** C Jamaica 17°52′N 77°34′W
21 Y9 **Alligator River** ≈ North Carolina, SE USA
29 W12 **Allison** Iowa, C USA 42°45′N 92°48′W
14 G14 **Alliston** Ontario, S Canada 44°09′N 79°51′W
140 L11 **Al Līth** Makkah, SW Saudi Arabia 21°N 41°E
Al Liwā' *see* Līwā
96 J12 **Alloa** C Scotland, United Kingdom 56°07′N 03°49′W
103 U14 **Allos** Alpes-de-Haute-Provence, SE France 44°16′N 06°37′E
108 D6 **Allschwil** Basel-Land, NW Switzerland 47°34′N 07°32′E
Al Lubnān *see* Lebanon
141 N14 **Al Luḥayyah** W Yemen 15°44′N 42°45′E
14 K12 **Allumettes, Île des** *island* Québec, SE Canada
Al Lussuf *see* Al Laṣaf
109 S5 **Alm** ≈ N Austria
15 Q7 **Alma** Québec, SE Canada 48°32′N 71°41′W
27 S10 **Alma** Arkansas, C USA 35°28′N 94°13′W
23 V7 **Alma** Georgia, SE USA 31°32′N 82°27′W
27 P4 **Alma** Kansas, C USA 39°01′N 96°17′W
31 Q8 **Alma** Michigan, N USA 43°22′N 84°39′W
29 O17 **Alma** Nebraska, C USA 40°06′N 99°21′W
30 I7 **Alma** Wisconsin, N USA 44°21′N 91°54′W
139 R12 **Al Ma'ānīyah** *well* An Najaf, S Iraq
Alma-Ata *see* Almaty
Alma-Atinskaya Oblast' *see* Almaty
Almacellas *see* Almacelles
105 T5 **Almacelles** *var.* Almacellas. Cataluña, NE Spain 41°44′N 00°26′E
104 F11 **Almada** Setúbal, W Portugal 38°40′N 09°09′W
104 L11 **Almadén** Castilla-La Mancha, C Spain 38°47′N 04°50′W
66 L6 **Almadies, Pointe des** *headland* W Senegal 14°44′N 17°31′W
140 L7 **Al Madīnah** *Eng.* Medina. Al Madīnah, W Saudi Arabia 24°25′N 39°29′E
140 L7 **Al Madīnah** *off.* Minṭaqat al Madīnah. ◈ *province* W Saudi Arabia
138 H9 **Al Mafraq** *var.* Mafraq. Al Mafraq, N Jordan 32°20′N 36°12′E
138 J10 **Al Mafraq** *off.* Muḥāfaẓat al Mafraq. ◈ *governorate* NW Jordan
141 R15 **Al Maghārim** C Yemen 15°00′N 47°49′E
105 N11 **Almagro** Castilla-La Mancha, C Spain 38°54′N 03°43′W
Al Maḥallah al Kubrá *see* El Maḥalla el Kubra
139 T9 **Al Maḥāwīl** *var.* Khān al Maḥāwīl. Bābil, C Iraq 32°39′N 44°28′E
Al Mahdīyah *see* Mahdia
139 T8 **Al Maḥmūdīyah** *var.* Mahmudiya. Baghdād, C Iraq 33°04′N 44°22′E
141 T14 **Al Mahrah** ▲▲ E Yemen
141 P7 **Al Majma'ah** Ar Riyāḍ, C Saudi Arabia 25°55′N 45°19′E
139 Q11 **Al Makmīn** *well* S Iraq
139 Q1 **Al Mālikīyah** *var.* Malkiye. Al Ḥasakah, N Syria 37°12′N 42°13′E
Almalyk *see* Olmaliq
Al Mamlakah *see* Morocco
Al Mamlaka al Urdunīya al Hashemīyah *see* Jordan
143 Q18 **Al Manādir** *var.* Al Manadir. *desert* Oman/United Arab Emirates
142 L15 **Al Manāmah** *Eng.* Manama. ● (Bahrain) N Bahrain 26°13′N 50°33′E
139 O5 **Al Manāṣif** ▲▲ E Syria
35 O4 **Almanor, Lake** ⊠ California, W USA
105 R11 **Almansa** Castilla-La Mancha, C Spain 38°52′N 01°06′W
75 W7 **Al Manṣūrah** *var.* Manṣūra, El Manṣûra. N Egypt 31°03′N 31°23′E
104 L3 **Almanza** Castilla-León, N Spain 42°40′N 05°01′W
104 L8 **Almanzor** ▲ W Spain 40°13′N 05°18′W
105 P14 **Almanzora** ≈ SE Spain
139 S9 **Al Mardah** Karbalā', C Iraq 32°35′N 43°30′E
Al-Mariyya *see* Almería
75 R7 **Al Marj** *var.* Barka, *It.* Barce. NE Libya 32°30′N 20°54′E
138 L2 **Al Mashrafah** Ar Raqqah, N Syria 36°25′N 39°07′E
141 X8 **Al Maṣna'ah** *var.* Al Muṣana'a. NE Oman 23°45′N 57°38′E
Almassora *see* Almazora
Almatinskaya Oblast' *see* Almaty
145 U15 **Almaty** *var.* Alma-Ata. Almaty, SE Kazakhstan 43°19′N 76°55′E
145 S14 **Almaty** *off.* Almatinskaya Oblast', *Kaz.* Almaty Oblysy; *prev.* Alma-Atinskaya Oblast'. ◈ *province* SE Kazakhstan
145 U15 **Almaty** ✈ Almaty, SE Kazakhstan 43°15′N 76°57′E
Almaty Oblysy *see* Almaty
al-Mawailih *see* Al Muwayliḥ
139 R3 **Al Mawṣil** *Eng.* Mosul. Nīnawá, N Iraq 36°21′N 43°08′E
139 N5 **Al Mayādīn** *var.* Mayadin, *Fr.* Meyadine. Dayr az Zawr, E Syria 35°00′N 40°31′E
139 X10 **Al Maymūnah** *var.* Maimuna. Maysān, SE Iraq 31°43′N 46°55′E
141 N5 **Al Mayyāh** Ḥā'il, N Saudi Arabia 27°57′N 42°53′E
Al Ma'zam *see* Al Ma'zim
105 P6 **Almazán** Castilla-León, N Spain 41°29′N 02°31′W
141 W8 **Al Ma'zim** *var.* Al Ma'zam. NW Oman 23°22′N 56°16′E
123 N11 **Almaznyy** Respublika Sakha (Yakutiya), NE Russian Federation 62°19′N 114°14′E
105 T9 **Almazora** *Cat.* Almassora. País Valenciano, E Spain 39°55′N 00°02′W
Al Mazra' *see* Al Mazra'ah
138 G11 **Al Mazra'ah** *var.* Al Mazra', Mazra'a. Al Karak, W Jordan 31°18′N 35°32′E
101 G15 **Alme** ≈ W Germany

◆ Country ● Country Capital ◇ Dependent Territory ○ Dependent Territory Capital ◈ Administrative Regions ✈ International Airport ▲ Mountain ▲▲ Mountain Range ✺ Volcano ≈ River ◎ Lake ⊠ Reservoir

215

◆ Country   ◇ Dependent Territory   ◆ Administrative Regions   ▲ Mountain   ▼ Volcano   ⊙ Lake
● Country Capital   ○ Dependent Territory Capital   ✕ International Airport   ▲ Mountain Range   ✍ River   ⊠ Reservoir

AMMARNÄS – ANTHONY

92 H13 Ammarnäs Västerbotten, N Sweden 65°58′N 16°10′E
197 O15 Ammassalik var. Angmagssalik. Tunu, S Greenland 65°51′N 37°30′W
101 K24 Ammer ⇝ SE Germany
101 K24 Ammersee ◎ SE Germany
98 J13 Ammerzoden Gelderland, C Netherlands 51°46′N 05°07′E
Ammóchostos see Gazimağusa
Ammóchostos, Kólpos see Gazimağusa Körfezi
Amnok-kang see Yalu
Amoea see Portalegre
Amoentai see Amuntai
Amoerang see Amurang
143 O4 Āmol var. Amul. Māzandarān, N Iran 36°31′N 52°24′E
115 K21 Amorgós Amorgós, Kykládes, Greece, Aegean Sea 36°49′N 25°54′E
115 K22 Amorgós island Kykládes, Greece, Aegean Sea
23 N3 Amory Mississippi, S USA 33°58′N 88°29′W
12 I13 Amos Québec, SE Canada 48°34′N 78°08′W
95 G15 Åmot Buskerud, S Norway 59°52′N 09°55′E
95 E15 Åmot Telemark, S Norway 59°34′N 07°59′E
95 J15 Åmotfors Värmland, C Sweden 59°46′N 12°24′E
76 L10 Amourj Hodh ech Chargui, SE Mauritania 16°04′N 07°12′W
Amoy see Xiamen
172 H7 Ampanihy Toliara, SW Madagascar 24°40′S 44°45′E
155 L25 Ampara var. Amparai. Eastern Province, E Sri Lanka 07°17′N 81°41′E
172 J4 Amparafaravola Toamasina, E Madagascar 17°33′S 48°13′E
Amparai see Ampara
60 M9 Amparo São Paulo, S Brazil 22°40′S 46°49′W
172 J5 Ampasimanolotra Toamasina, E Madagascar 18°49′S 49°04′E
57 H17 Ampato, Nevado ▲ S Peru 15°52′S 71°51′W
101 L23 Amper ⇝ SE Germany
64 M9 Ampère Seamount undersea feature E Atlantic Ocean 35°05′N 13°00′W
Amphipolis see Amfípoli
167 X10 Amphitrite Group island group N Paracel Islands
171 T16 Amplawas var. Emplawas. Pulau Babar, E Indonesia 08°01′S 129°42′E
105 U7 Amposta Cataluña, NE Spain 40°43′N 00°34′E
15 V7 Amqui Québec, SE Canada 48°28′N 67°27′W
141 O14 'Amrān W Yemen 15°39′N 43°59′E
Amraoti see Amrāvati
154 H12 Amrāvati prev. Amraoti. Mahārāshtra, C India 20°56′N 77°45′E
154 C11 Amreli Gujarāt, W India 21°36′N 71°20′E
108 H6 Amriswil Thurgau, NE Switzerland 47°33′N 09°18′E
138 H5 'Amrīt ruins Ṭarṭūs, W Syria
152 H7 Amritsar Punjab, N India 31°38′N 74°55′E
152 J10 Amroha Uttar Pradesh, N India 28°54′N 78°29′E
100 G7 Amrum island NW Germany
93 I15 Åmsele Västerbotten, N Sweden 64°31′N 19°24′E
98 I10 Amstelveen Noord-Holland, C Netherlands 52°18′N 04°50′E
98 I10 Amsterdam ● (Netherlands) Noord-Holland, C Netherlands 52°22′N 04°54′E
18 K10 Amsterdam New York, NE USA 42°56′N 74°11′W
173 Q11 Amsterdam Fracture Zone tectonic feature S Indian Ocean
173 R11 Amsterdam Island island NE French Southern and Antarctic Territories
109 U4 Amstetten Niederösterreich, N Austria 48°08′N 14°52′E
78 J11 Am Timan Salamat, SE Chad 11°02′N 20°17′E
146 L12 Amu-Buxoro Kanali var. Aral-Bukhorskiy Kanal. canal C Uzbekistan
139 O1 'Āmūdah var. Amude. Al Ḥasakah, N Syria 37°06′N 40°56′E
147 O15 Amu Darya Rus. Amudar'ya, Taj. Dar"yoi Amu, Turkm. Amyderya, Uzb. Amudaryo; anc. Oxus. ⇝ C Asia
Amu-Dar'ya see Amyderya
Amudar'ya/Amudaryo/ Amu, Dar"yoi see Amu Darya
Amude see 'Āmūdah
140 L3 'Amūd, Jabal al ▲ NW Saudi Arabia 30°59′N 39°17′E
38 J17 Amukta Island island Aleutian Islands, Alaska, USA
38 I17 Amukta Pass strait Aleutian Islands, Alaska, USA
Amul see Āmol
Amulla see Amla
Amundsen Basin see Fram Basin
195 X3 Amundsen Bay bay Antarctica
195 P10 Amundsen Coast physical region Antarctica
193 O14 Amundsen Plain undersea feature S Pacific Ocean
195 Q9 Amundsen-Scott US research station Antarctica 89°59′S 10°00′E
194 J11 Amundsen Sea sea S Pacific Ocean
94 M12 Amungen ◎ C Sweden
169 U13 Amuntai prev. Amoentai. Borneo, C Indonesia 02°24′S 115°14′E
129 W6 Amur Chin. Heilong Jiang. ⇝ China/Russian Federation
171 Q11 Amurang prev. Amoerang. Sulawesi, C Indonesia 01°12′N 124°37′E
105 O3 Amurrio País Vasco, N Spain 43°03′N 03°00′W
123 S13 Amursk Khabarovskiy Kray, SE Russian Federation 50°13′N 136°34′E
123 Q12 Amurskaya Oblast' ◈ province SE Russian Federation
80 G7 'Amur, Wadi ⇝ NE Sudan
115 C17 Amvrakikós Kólpos gulf W Greece
Amvrosiyevka see Amvrosiyivka
117 X8 Amvrosiyivka Rus. Amvrosiyevka. Donets'ka Oblast', SE Ukraine 47°46′N 38°30′E
146 M14 Amyderýa Rus. Amu-Dar'ya. Lebap Welaýaty, NE Turkmenistan 37°58′N 65°14′E
Amyderya see Amu Darya
114 E13 Amýntaio var. Amindeo; prev. Amíndaion. Dytikí Makedonía, N Greece 40°42′N 21°42′E
14 B6 Amyot Ontario, S Canada 48°28′N 84°58′W
191 U10 Anaa atoll Îles Tuamotu, C French Polynesia
Anabanoea see Anabanua
171 N14 Anabanua prev. Anabanoea. Sulawesi, C Indonesia 03°58′S 120°07′E
189 R8 Anabar NE Nauru 0°30′S 166°56′E
123 N8 Anabar ⇝ NE Russian Federation
An Abhainn Mhór see Blackwater
55 O6 Anaco Anzoátegui, NE Venezuela 09°30′N 64°28′W
33 Q10 Anaconda Montana, NW USA 46°09′N 112°56′W
32 H7 Anacortes Washington, NW USA 48°30′N 122°36′W
26 M11 Anadarko Oklahoma, C USA 35°04′N 98°16′W
114 N12 Ana Dere ⇝ NW Turkey
104 G8 Anadia Aveiro, N Portugal 40°26′N 08°27′W
Anadolu Dağları see Doğu Karadeniz Dağları
123 V6 Anadyr' Chukotskiy Avtonomnyy Okrug, NE Russian Federation 64°41′N 177°22′E
123 V6 Anadyr' ⇝ NE Russian Federation
Anadyr, Gulf of see Anadyrskiy Zaliv
129 X4 Anadyrskiy Khrebet var. Chukot Range. ▲▲ NE Russian Federation
123 W6 Anadyrskiy Zaliv Eng. Gulf of Anadyr. gulf NE Russian Federation
115 K22 Anáfi anc. Anaphe. island Kykládes, Greece, Aegean Sea
107 J15 Anagni Lazio, C Italy 41°43′N 13°12′E
'Ānah see 'Annah
35 T15 Anaheim California, W USA 33°50′N 117°54′W
10 L15 Anahim Lake British Columbia, SW Canada 52°26′N 125°13′W
38 B8 Anahola Kaua'i, Hawai'i, USA, C Pacific Ocean 22°09′N 159°19′W
41 O7 Anáhuac Nuevo León, NE Mexico 27°13′N 100°09′W
25 X11 Anahuac Texas, SW USA 29°44′N 94°41′W
155 G22 Anai Mudi ▲ S India 10°16′N 77°08′E
Anaiza see 'Unayzah
155 M15 Anakāpalle Andhra Pradesh, E India 17°42′N 83°06′E
191 W15 Anakena, Playa de beach Easter Island, Chile, E Pacific Ocean
39 Q7 Anaktuvuk Pass Alaska, USA 68°08′N 151°44′W
39 Q6 Anaktuvuk River ⇝ Alaska, USA
172 J3 Analalava Mahajanga, NW Madagascar 14°38′S 47°46′E
44 F6 Ana María, Golfo de gulf N Caribbean Sea
Anambas Islands see Anambas, Kepulauan
169 N8 Anambas, Kepulauan var. Anambas Islands. island group W Indonesia
77 U17 Anambra ◈ state SE Nigeria
29 N4 Anamoose North Dakota, N USA 47°50′N 100°14′W
29 Y13 Anamosa Iowa, C USA 42°06′N 91°17′W
136 H17 Anamur İçel, S Turkey 36°06′N 32°49′E
136 H17 Anamur Burnu headland S Turkey 36°03′N 32°49′E
154 D11 Ānand Gujarāt, India 22°34′N 73°01′E
154 O12 Anandadur Orissa, E India 21°14′N 86°10′E
155 H18 Anantapur Andhra Pradesh, S India 14°41′N 77°36′E
152 H5 Anantnāg var. Islamabad. Jammu and Kashmir, NW India 33°44′N 75°11′E
Ananyev see Anan'yiv
117 O9 Anan'yiv Rus. Ananyev. Odes'ka Oblast', SW Ukraine 47°43′N 29°51′E
126 J14 Anapa Krasnodarskiy Kray, SW Russian Federation 44°55′N 37°20′E
Anaphe see Anáfi
59 K18 Anápolis Goiás, C Brazil 16°19′S 48°58′W
143 R10 Anār Kermān, C Iran 30°49′N 55°18′E
Anār see Inari
143 P7 Anārak Eşfahān, C Iran 33°21′N 53°43′E
Anar Dara see Anār Darreh
148 J7 Anār Darreh var. Anar Dara. Farāh, W Afghanistan 32°45′N 61°38′E
Anárjohka see Inarijoki
23 X9 Anastasia Island island Florida, SE USA
188 K7 Anatahan island C Northern Mariana Islands
128 M6 Anatolia plateau C Turkey
86 F14 Anatolian Plate tectonic feature Asia/Europe
114 H13 Anatolikí Makedonía kai Thrákí Eng. Macedonia East and Thrace. ◈ region NE Greece
Anatom see Aneityum
62 L8 Añatuya Santiago del Estero, N Argentina 28°28′S 62°52′W
An Baile Meánach see Ballymena
An Bhearú see Barrow
An Bhóinn see Boyne
An Blascaod Mór see Great Blasket Island
An Cabhán see Cavan
An Caisleán Nua see Newcastle
An Caisleán Riabhach see Castlerea, Ireland
An Caisleán Riabhach see Castlereagh
56 C13 Ancash off. Departamento de Ancash. ◈ department W Peru
Ancash, Departamento de see Ancash
An Cathair see Caher
102 J8 Ancenis Loire-Atlantique, NW France 47°23′N 01°10′W
An Chanáil Ríoga see Royal Canal
An Cheacha see Caha Mountains
39 R11 Anchorage Alaska, USA 61°13′N 149°52′W
39 R12 Anchorage ✈ Alaska, USA 61°08′N 150°00′W
39 Q13 Anchor Point Alaska, USA 59°46′N 151°49′W
An Chorr Chríochach see Cookstown
65 M24 Anchorstock Point headland W Tristan da Cunha 37°07′S 12°21′W
An Clár see Clare
An Clochán see Clifden
An Clochán Liath see Dunglow
23 U12 Anclote Keys island group Florida, SE USA
An Cóbh see Cobh
57 J17 Ancohuma, Nevado de ▲ W Bolivia 15°51′S 68°33′W
An Comar see Comber
57 D14 Ancón Lima, W Peru 11°45′S 77°08′W
106 J12 Ancona Marche, C Italy 43°38′N 13°30′E
Ancuabe see Ancuabi
82 Q13 Ancuabi var. Ancuabe. Cabo Delgado, NE Mozambique 13°00′S 39°50′E
63 F17 Ancud prev. San Carlos de Ancud. Los Lagos, S Chile 41°53′S 73°50′W
63 G17 Ancud, Golfo de gulf S Chile
Ancyra see Ankara
163 V8 Anda Heilongjiang, NE China 46°25′N 125°20′E
57 G16 Andahuaylas Apurímac, S Peru 13°39′S 73°24′W
An Daingean see Dingle
153 R15 Āndāl West Bengal, NE India 23°35′N 87°14′E
94 E9 Åndalsnes Møre og Romsdal, S Norway 62°33′N 07°42′E
104 K13 Andalucía Eng. Andalusia. ◈ autonomous community S Spain
23 P7 Andalusia Alabama, S USA 31°18′N 86°29′W
Andalusia see Andalucía
151 Q21 Andaman and Nicobar Islands var. Andamans and Nicobars. ◈ union territory India, NE Indian Ocean
173 T4 Andaman Basin undersea feature NE Indian Ocean 10°00′N 94°00′E
151 P19 Andaman Islands island group India, NE Indian Ocean
Andamans and Nicobars see Andaman and Nicobar Islands
173 T4 Andaman Sea sea NE Indian Ocean
57 K19 Andamarca Oruro, C Bolivia 18°46′S 67°31′W
182 H5 Andamooka South Australia 30°26′S 137°12′E
141 Y9 'Andām, Wādī seasonal river NE Oman
172 J3 Andapa Antsirañana, NE Madagascar 14°39′S 49°40′E
149 R4 Andarāb var. Banow. Baghlān, NE Afghanistan 35°36′N 69°18′E
Andarbag see Andarbogh
147 S13 Andarbogh Rus. Andarbag, Anderbak. S Tajikistan 37°51′N 71°45′E
109 Z5 Andau Burgenland, E Austria 47°47′N 17°02′E
108 I10 Andeer Graubünden, S Switzerland 46°36′N 09°24′E
92 H9 Andenes Nordland, C Norway 69°18′N 16°10′E
99 J20 Andenne Namur, SE Belgium 50°29′N 05°06′E
77 S11 Andéramboukane Gao, E Mali 15°24′N 03°03′E
Anderbak see Andarbogh
99 G18 Anderlecht Brussels, C Belgium 50°50′N 04°18′E
99 G21 Anderlues Hainaut, S Belgium 50°24′N 04°16′E
108 G9 Andermatt Uri, C Switzerland 46°39′N 08°36′E
101 E17 Andernach anc. Antunnacum. Rheinland-Pfalz, SW Germany 50°26′N 07°24′E
188 D15 Andersen Air Force Base air base NE Guam 13°34′N 144°55′E
39 R9 Anderson Alaska, USA 64°20′N 149°11′W
35 N4 Anderson California, W USA 40°26′N 122°21′W
31 P13 Anderson Indiana, N USA 40°06′N 85°40′W
27 R8 Anderson Missouri, C USA 36°39′N 94°26′W
21 P11 Anderson South Carolina, SE USA 34°30′N 82°39′W
25 V10 Anderson Texas, SW USA 30°29′N 96°00′W
95 K20 Anderstorp Jönköping, S Sweden 57°17′N 13°38′E
54 D9 Andes Antioquia, W Colombia 05°40′N 75°56′W
47 P7 Andes ▲▲ W South America
29 P12 Andes, Lake ◎ South Dakota, N USA
92 H9 Andfjorden fjord E Norwegian Sea
155 H16 Andhra Pradesh ◈ state E India
98 J8 Andijk Noord-Holland, NW Netherlands 52°38′N 05°00′E
147 S10 Andijon Rus. Andizhan. Andijon Viloyati, E Uzbekistan 40°46′N 72°19′E
147 S10 Andijon Viloyati Rus. Andizhanskaya Oblast'. ◈ province E Uzbekistan
Andikíthira see Antikýthira
172 J4 Andilamena Toamasina, C Madagascar 17°00′S 48°35′E
142 L8 Andīmeshk var. Andimishk; prev. Salehābād. Khūzestān, SW Iran 32°30′N 48°26′E
Andimishk see Andīmeshk
Andipáros see Antíparos
Andípaxi see Antípaxoi
Andípsara see Antípsara
136 L16 Andırın Kahramanmaraş, S Turkey 37°33′N 36°18′E
158 J8 Andirlangar Xinjiang Uygur Zizhiqu, NW China 37°38′N 83°40′E
Andírrion see Antírrio
Ándissa see Ántissa
Andizhan see Andijon
Andizhanskaya Oblast' see Andijon Viloyati
149 N2 Andkhvoy Fāryāb, N Afghanistan 36°56′N 65°08′E
105 Q2 Andoain País Vasco, N Spain 43°13′N 02°02′W
163 Y15 Andong Jap. Antō. E South Korea 36°34′N 128°44′E
109 R4 Andorf Oberösterreich, N Austria 48°22′N 13°33′E
105 S7 Andorra Aragón, NE Spain 40°59′N 00°27′W
105 V4 Andorra off. Principality of Andorra, Cat. Valls d'Andorra, Fr. Vallée d'Andorre. ◆ monarchy SW Europe
Andorra see Andorra la Vella
105 V4 Andorra la Vella var. Andorra, Fr. Andorre la Vielle, Sp. Andorra la Vieja. ● (Andorra) C Andorra 42°30′N 01°30′E
Andorra la Vieja see Andorra la Vella
Andorra, Principality of see Andorra
Andorra, Valls d'/Andorra, Vallée d' see Andorra
Andorre la Vielle see Andorra la Vella
97 M22 Andover S England, United Kingdom 51°13′N 01°28′W
27 N6 Andover Kansas, C USA 37°42′N 97°08′W
92 G10 Andøya island C Norway
60 I8 Andradina São Paulo, S Brazil 20°54′S 51°19′W
105 X9 Andratx Mallorca, Spain, W Mediterranean Sea 39°35′N 02°25′E
39 N10 Andreafsky River ⇝ Alaska, USA
38 H17 Andreanof Islands island group Aleutian Islands, Alaska, USA
124 H16 Andreapol' Tverskaya Oblast', W Russian Federation 56°38′N 32°17′E
Andreas, Cape see Zafer Burnu
Andreevka see Kabanbay
21 N10 Andrews North Carolina, SE USA 35°19′N 84°01′W
21 T13 Andrews South Carolina, SE USA 33°27′N 79°33′W
24 M7 Andrews Texas, SW USA 32°19′N 102°34′W
173 N5 Andrew Tablemount var. Gora Andryu. undersea feature W Indian Ocean 06°45′S 50°30′E
Andreyevka see Kabanbay
107 N17 Andria Puglia, SE Italy 41°13′N 16°17′E
113 K16 Andrijevica E Montenegro 42°45′N 19°45′E
115 E20 Andrítsaina Pelopónnisos, S Greece 37°29′N 21°52′E
An Droichead Nua see Newbridge
Andropov see Rybinsk
115 J19 Ándros Ándros, Kykládes, Greece, Aegean Sea 37°49′N 24°54′E
115 J20 Ándros island Kykládes, Greece, Aegean Sea
19 O7 Androscoggin River ⇝ Maine/New Hampshire, NE USA
44 F3 Andros Island island NW Bahamas
127 R7 Androsovka Samarskaya Oblast', W Russian Federation 52°41′N 49°34′E
44 G3 Andros Town Andros Island, NW Bahamas 24°40′N 77°47′W
155 D21 Āndrott Island island Lakshadweep, India, N Indian Ocean
117 N5 Andrushivka Zhytomyrs'ka Oblast', N Ukraine 50°01′N 29°02′E
111 K17 Andrychów Małopolskie, S Poland 49°51′N 19°18′E
Andryu, Gora see Andrew Tablemount
92 I10 Andselv Troms, N Norway 69°05′N 18°30′E
79 O17 Andudu Orientale, NE Dem. Rep. Congo 02°26′N 28°39′E
105 N13 Andújar anc. Illiturgis. Andalucía, SW Spain 38°02′N 04°03′W
82 C12 Andulo Bié, W Angola 11°29′S 16°43′E
103 Q14 Anduze Gard, S France 44°03′N 03°59′E
An Earagail see Errigal Mountain
95 L19 Aneby Jönköping, S Sweden 57°50′N 14°45′E
Anécho see Aného
77 Q9 Anéfis Kidal, NE Mali 18°05′N 00°38′E
45 U8 Anegada island NE British Virgin Islands
61 B25 Anegada, Bahía bay E Argentina
45 U9 Anegada Passage passage Anguilla/British Virgin Islands
77 R17 Aného var. Anécho; prev. Petit-Popo. S Togo 06°14′N 01°36′E
197 D17 Aneityum var. Anatom; prev. Kéamu. island S Vanuatu
117 N10 Anenii Noi Rus. Novyye Aneny. C Moldova 46°52′N 29°10′E
186 F7 Anepmete New Britain, E Papua New Guinea 05°47′S 148°37′E
105 U4 Aneto ▲ NE Spain 42°36′N 00°37′E
146 F13 Änew Rus. Annau. Ahal Welaýaty, C Turkmenistan 37°51′N 58°22′E
Änewetak see Enewetak Atoll
77 Y8 Aney Agadez, NE Niger 19°22′N 13°00′E
An Fheoir see Nore
122 L12 Angara ⇝ C Russian Federation
122 M13 Angarsk Irkutskaya Oblast', S Russian Federation 52°31′N 103°55′E
Angaur see Ngeaur
93 G17 Ånge Västernorrland, C Sweden 62°31′N 15°40′E
Angel see Úhlava
40 D4 Ángel de la Guarda, Isla island NW Mexico
171 O3 Angeles off. Angeles City. Luzon, N Philippines 15°16′N 120°37′E
Angeles City see Angeles
Angel Falls see Ángel, Salto
95 J22 Ängelholm Skåne, S Sweden 56°14′N 12°52′E
61 A17 Angélica Santa Fe, C Argentina 31°33′S 61°33′W
25 W8 Angelina River ⇝ Texas, SW USA
55 Q9 Ángel, Salto Eng. Angel Falls. waterfall E Venezuela
95 M15 Ängelsberg Västmanland, C Sweden 59°57′N 16°01′E
35 P8 Angels Camp California, W USA 38°03′N 120°31′W
109 W7 Anger Steiermark, SE Austria 47°16′N 15°41′E
Angerapp see Ozersk
Angerburg see Węgorzewo
93 H15 Ångermanälven ⇝ N Sweden
100 P11 Angermünde Brandenburg, NE Germany 53°02′N 13°59′E
102 K7 Angers anc. Juliomagus. Maine-et-Loire, NW France 47°30′N 00°33′W
15 W7 Angers ⇝ Québec, SE Canada
93 J16 Ängesön island N Sweden
Angistro see Ágkistro
114 H13 Angítis ⇝ NE Greece
167 R13 Ângk Tasaôm prev. Angtassom. Takêv, S Cambodia
185 C25 Anglem, Mount ▲ Stewart Island, Southland, SW New Zealand 46°44′S 167°56′E
97 I18 Anglesey cultural region NW Wales, United Kingdom
97 I18 Anglesey island NW Wales, United Kingdom
102 I15 Anglet Pyrénées-Atlantiques, SW France 43°29′N 01°30′W
25 W12 Angleton Texas, SW USA 29°10′N 95°27′W
Anglia see England
14 H9 Angliers Québec, SE Canada 47°33′N 79°17′W
Anglo-Egyptian Sudan see Sudan
Angmagssalik see Ammassalik
167 Q7 Ang Nam Ngum ◎ C Laos
79 N16 Ango Orientale, N Dem. Rep. Congo 04°01′N 25°52′E
83 Q15 Angoche Nampula, E Mozambique 16°10′S 39°58′E
63 G14 Angol Araucanía, C Chile 37°47′S 72°45′W
31 Q11 Angola Indiana, N USA 41°37′N 85°00′W
82 A9 Angola off. Republic of Angola; prev. People's Republic of Angola, Portuguese West Africa. ◆ republic SW Africa
65 P15 Angola Basin undersea feature E Atlantic Ocean 15°00′S 03°00′E
Angola, People's Republic of see Angola
Angola, Republic of see Angola
39 X13 Angoon Admiralty Island, Alaska, USA 57°33′N 134°30′W
147 O14 Angor Surkhondaryo Viloyati, S Uzbekistan 37°30′N 67°06′E
Angora see Ankara
186 C6 Angoram East Sepik, NW Papua New Guinea 04°04′S 144°04′E
40 H8 Angostura Sinaloa, C Mexico 25°18′N 108°10′W
Angostura see Ciudad Bolívar
41 U17 Angostura, Presa de la ⊠ SE Mexico
28 J11 Angostura Reservoir ⊠ South Dakota, N USA
102 L11 Angoulême anc. Iculisma. Charente, W France 45°39′N 00°10′E
102 K11 Angoumois cultural region W France
64 O2 Angra do Heroísmo Terceira, Azores, Portugal, NE Atlantic Ocean 38°40′N 27°14′W
60 O10 Angra dos Reis Rio de Janeiro, SE Brazil 22°59′S 44°17′W
Angra Pequena see Lüderitz
147 Q10 Angren Toshkent Viloyati, E Uzbekistan 41°05′N 70°18′E
Angtassom see Ângk Tasaôm
167 O10 Ang Thong var. Angthong. Ang Thong, C Thailand 14°35′N 100°25′E
Angthong see Ang Thong
79 M16 Angu Orientale, N Dem. Rep. Congo 03°38′N 24°14′E
105 S5 Angüés Aragón, NE Spain 42°07′N 00°10′W
45 U9 Anguilla ◇ UK dependent territory E West Indies
45 V9 Anguilla island E West Indies
44 F4 Anguilla Cays islets SW Bahamas
Anguli see Anugul
161 N1 Anguli Nur ◎ E China
79 O18 Angumu Orientale, E Dem. Rep. Congo 0°10′S 27°42′E
14 G14 Angus Ontario, S Canada 44°19′N 79°52′W
96 J10 Angus cultural region E Scotland, United Kingdom
59 K19 Anhanguera Goiás, S Brazil 18°12′S 48°19′W
99 I21 Anhée Namur, S Belgium 50°18′N 04°52′E
95 I21 Anholt island C Denmark
160 M11 Anhua var. Dongping. Hunan, S China 28°25′N 111°10′E
161 P8 Anhui var. Anhui Sheng, Anhwei, Wan. ◈ province E China
AnhuiSheng/Anhwei Wan see Anhui
39 O11 Aniak Alaska, USA 61°34′N 159°31′W
39 O12 Aniak River ⇝ Alaska, USA
An Iarmhí see Westmeath
189 R8 Anibare E Nauru 0°31′S 166°56′E
189 R8 Anibare Bay bay E Nauru, W Pacific Ocean
Anicium see le Puy
115 K22 Ánidro island Kykládes, Greece, Aegean Sea
77 R15 Anié C Togo 07°48′N 01°12′E
77 Q15 Anié ⇝ C Togo
102 J16 Anie, Pic d' ▲ SW France 42°56′N 00°44′W
127 Y7 Anikhovka Orenburgskaya Oblast', W Russian Federation 51°27′N 60°17′E
14 G9 Anima Nipissing Lake ◎ Ontario, S Canada
37 O16 Animas New Mexico, SW USA 31°55′N 108°49′W
37 P16 Animas Peak ▲ New Mexico, SW USA 31°34′N 108°46′W
37 P16 Animas Valley valley New Mexico, SW USA
116 F13 Anina Ger. Steierdorf, Hung. Stájerlakanina; prev. Ştaierdorf-Anina, Steierdorf-Anina, Steyerlak-Anina. Caraş-Severin, SW Romania 45°05′N 21°51′E
153 Y9 Anini Arunāchal Pradesh, NE India 28°48′N 95°54′E
29 U14 Anita Iowa, C USA 41°27′N 94°45′W
123 U14 Aniva, Mys headland Ostrov Sakhalin, SE Russian Federation 46°02′N 143°25′E
187 S15 Aniwa island S Vanuatu
93 M19 Anjalankoski Etelä-Suomi, S Finland 60°39′N 26°54′E
'Anjar see Aanjar
Anjiangying see Luanping
14 B8 Anjigami Lake ◎ Ontario, S Canada
149 N13 Anjīra Baluchistān, SW Pakistan 28°19′N 66°19′E
164 K14 Anjō var. Anzyô. Aichi, Honshū, SW Japan 34°56′N 137°05′E
102 J8 Anjou cultural region NW France
172 I13 Anjouan var. Ndzouani, Nzwani. island SE Comoros
172 J4 Anjozorobe Antananarivo, C Madagascar 18°22′S 47°52′E
163 W13 Anju W North Korea 39°36′N 125°44′E
98 M5 Anjum Fris. Eanjum. Friesland, N Netherlands 53°22′N 06°09′E
172 G6 Ankaboa, Tanjona Fr. Cap Saint-Vincent. headland W Madagascar 21°57′S 43°16′E
160 L7 Ankang prev. Xing'an. Shaanxi, C China 32°45′N 109°00′E
136 I12 Ankara prev. Angora; anc. Ancyra. ● (Turkey) Ankara, C Turkey 39°55′N 32°50′E
136 H12 Ankara ◈ province C Turkey
95 N19 Ankarsrum Kalmar, S Sweden 57°40′N 16°19′E
172 H6 Ankazoabo Toliara, SW Madagascar 22°18′S 44°30′E
172 I4 Ankazobe Antananarivo, C Madagascar 18°20′S 47°07′E
29 V14 Ankeny Iowa, C USA 41°43′N 93°37′W
167 V11 An Khê Gia Lai, C Vietnam 13°57′N 108°39′E
100 O9 Anklam Mecklenburg-Vorpommern, NE Germany 53°51′N 13°42′E
80 K13 Ānkober Āmara, N Ethiopia 09°36′N 39°44′E
77 O17 Ankobra ⇝ S Ghana
79 N22 Ankoro Katanga, SE Dem. Rep. Congo 06°45′S 26°58′E
99 L24 Anlier, Forêt d' forest SE Belgium
160 I13 Anlong var. Xin'an. Guizhou, S China 25°05′N 105°29′E
An Longfort see Longford
167 R11 Ânlong Vêng Siĕmréab, NW Cambodia 14°16′N 104°08′E
An Lorgain see Lurgan
161 N8 Anlu Hubei, C China 31°15′N 113°41′E
An Mhí see Meath
An Mhuir Cheilteach see Celtic Sea
An Muileann gCearr see Mullingar
93 F16 Ånn Jämtland, C Sweden 63°19′N 12°34′E
126 M8 Anna Voronezhskaya Oblast', W Russian Federation 51°31′N 40°23′E
30 L17 Anna Illinois, N USA 37°27′N 89°15′W
25 U5 Anna Texas, SW USA 33°21′N 96°33′W
74 L5 Annaba prev. Bône. NE Algeria 36°55′N 07°47′E
An Nabatīyah at Taḥtā see Nabatîyé
101 N17 Annaberg-Buchholz Sachsen, E Germany 50°35′N 13°01′E
109 T9 Annabichl ✈ (Klagenfurt) Kärnten, S Austria 46°39′N 14°21′E
140 M5 An Nafūd desert NW Saudi Arabia
139 P6 'Annah var. 'Ānah. Al Anbār, NW Iraq 34°50′N 42°00′E
139 P6 An Nāḥiyah Al Anbār, W Iraq 34°24′N 41°33′E
139 S11 An Najaf ◈ governorate S Iraq
139 T10 An Najaf var. Najaf. An Najaf, S Iraq 31°59′N 44°19′E
21 V5 Anna, Lake ◎ Virginia, NE USA
97 F16 Annalee ⇝ N Ireland
167 S9 Annamitique, Chaîne ▲▲ C Laos
97 J14 Annan S Scotland, United Kingdom 55°N 03°20′W
29 U8 Annandale Minnesota, N USA 45°15′N 94°07′W
21 W4 Annandale Virginia, NE USA 38°48′N 77°10′W
189 Q7 Anna Point headland N Nauru 0°30′S 166°56′E
21 X3 Annapolis state capital Maryland, NE USA 38°59′N 76°30′W
188 A10 Anna, Pulo island S Palau
153 O10 Annapurṇa ▲ C Nepal 28°30′N 83°50′E
An Nāqūrah see En Nâqoûra
31 R10 Ann Arbor Michigan, N USA 42°17′N 83°45′W
An Nás see Naas
139 W12 An Nāṣirīyah var. Nasiriya. Dhī Qār, SE Iraq 31°04′N 46°17′E
139 W11 An Naṣr Dhī Qār, E Iraq 31°34′N 46°08′E
Annau see Änew
121 O13 An Nawfalīyah var. Al Nūwfalīyah. N Libya 30°46′N 17°48′E
19 P10 Ann, Cape headland Massachusetts, NE USA 42°39′N 70°37′W
180 I10 Annean, Lake ◎ Western Australia
Anneciacum see Annecy
103 T11 Annecy anc. Anneciacum. Haute-Savoie, E France 45°53′N 06°09′E
103 T11 Annecy, Lac d' ◎ E France
103 T10 Annemasse Haute-Savoie, E France 46°10′N 06°13′E
39 Z14 Annette Island island Alexander Archipelago, Alaska, USA
An Nhon see Binh Đinh
An Nîl al Abyaḍ see White Nile
An Nîl al Azraq see Blue Nile
23 Q3 Anniston Alabama, S USA 33°39′N 85°49′W
79 A19 Annobón island W Equatorial Guinea
103 R12 Annonay Ardèche, E France 45°15′N 04°40′E
44 K12 Annotto Bay C Jamaica 18°16′N 76°47′W
141 R5 An Nu'ayrīyah var. Nariya. Ash Sharqīyah, NE Saudi Arabia 27°30′N 48°30′E
182 M9 Annuello Victoria, SE Australia 34°54′S 142°50′E
139 Q10 An Nukhayb Al Anbār, S Iraq 32°02′N 42°15′E
139 U9 An Nu'mānīyah Wāsiṭ, E Iraq 32°34′N 45°23′E
Áno Arkhánai see Archánes
115 J25 Anógeia var. Anogia, Anóyia. Kríti, Greece, E Mediterranean Sea 35°17′N 24°53′E
Anogia see Anógeia
29 V8 Anoka Minnesota, N USA 45°15′N 93°26′W
An Ómaigh see Omagh
172 I1 Anorontany, Tanjona Fr. Cap Saint-Sébastien. headland N Madagascar
172 J5 Anosibe An'Ala Toamasina, E Madagascar 19°24′S 48°11′E
Anóyia see Anógeia
An Pointe see Warrenpoint
161 P9 Anqing Anhui, E China 30°32′N 116°59′E
161 Q5 Anqiu Shandong, E China 36°25′N 119°10′E
An Ráth see Ráth Luirc
An Ribhéar see Kenmare River
An Ros see Rush
99 K19 Ans Liège, E Belgium 50°39′N 05°32′E
Anṣāb see Nişāb
171 W12 Ansas Papua, E Indonesia 01°44′S 135°52′E
101 J20 Ansbach Bayern, SE Germany 49°18′N 10°36′E
An Sciobairín see Skibbereen
An Scoil see Skull
An Seancheann see Old Head of Kinsale
45 Y5 Anse-Bertrand Grande Terre, N Guadeloupe 16°28′N 61°31′W
172 H17 Anse Boileau Mahé, NE Seychelles 04°43′S 55°29′E
45 S11 Anse La Raye NW Saint Lucia 13°57′N 61°01′W
54 D9 Anserma Caldas, W Colombia 05°15′N 75°47′W
109 T4 Ansfelden Oberösterreich, N Austria 48°12′N 14°17′E
163 U12 Anshan Liaoning, NE China 41°06′N 122°55′E
160 J12 Anshun Guizhou, S China 26°15′N 105°58′E
61 F17 Ansina Tacuarembó, C Uruguay 31°58′S 55°28′W
29 O15 Ansley Nebraska, C USA 41°16′N 99°22′W
25 P6 Anson Texas, SW USA 32°45′N 99°55′W
77 Q10 Ansongo Gao, E Mali 15°39′N 00°33′E
An Srath Bán see Strabane
21 R5 Ansted West Virginia, NE USA 38°08′N 81°06′W
171 Y13 Ansudu Papua, E Indonesia 02°09′S 139°19′E
57 G15 Anta Cusco, S Peru 13°30′S 72°08′W
57 G16 Antabamba Apurímac, C Peru 14°23′S 72°54′W
Antafalva see Kovačica
136 L17 Antakya anc. Antioch, Antiochia. Hatay, S Turkey 36°12′N 36°10′E
172 K3 Antalaha Antsirañana, NE Madagascar 14°53′S 50°16′E
136 F17 Antalya prev. Adalia; anc. Attaleia, Bibl. Attalia. Antalya, SW Turkey 36°53′N 30°42′E
136 F17 Antalya ◈ province SW Turkey
136 F16 Antalya ✈ Antalya, SW Turkey 36°53′N 30°45′E
121 U10 Antalya Basin undersea feature E Mediterranean Sea
Antalya, Gulf of see Antalya Körfezi
136 F16 Antalya Körfezi var. Gulf of Adalia, Eng. Gulf of Antalya. gulf SW Turkey
172 J5 Antanambao Manampotsy Toamasina, E Madagascar 19°30′S 48°36′E
172 I5 Antananarivo prev. Tananarive. ● (Madagascar) Antananarivo, C Madagascar 18°52′S 47°30′E
172 I4 Antananarivo ◈ province C Madagascar
172 J5 Antananarivo ✈ Antananarivo, C Madagascar 18°52′S 47°30′E
An tAonach see Nenagh
194-195 Antarctica continent
194 I5 Antarctic Peninsula peninsula Antarctica
174 L13 Antarctic Plate tectonic feature Africa/Antarctica/Australia/South America Atlantic Ocean/Indian Ocean/Pacific Ocean
61 J15 Antas, Rio das ⇝ S Brazil
189 U16 Ant Atoll atoll Caroline Islands, E Micronesia
An Teampall Mór see Templemore
Antep see Gaziantep
104 M15 Antequera anc. Anticaria, Antiquaria. Andalucía, S Spain 37°01′N 04°34′W
Antequera see Oaxaca
37 S5 Antero Reservoir ⊠ Colorado, C USA
26 M7 Anthony Kansas, C USA 37°10′N 98°02′W
37 R16 Anthony New Mexico, SW USA 32°00′N 106°36′W

◆ Country
● Country Capital
◇ Dependent Territory
○ Dependent Territory Capital
◈ Administrative Regions
✈ International Airport
▲ Mountain
▲▲ Mountain Range
⩙ Volcano
⇝ River
◎ Lake
⊠ Reservoir

ANTHONY, LAKE – ARÉVALO

182 D5 **Anthony, Lake** *salt lake* South Australia
74 E8 **Anti-Atlas** ▲▲ SW Morocco
103 U15 **Antibes** *anc.* Antipolis. Alpes-Maritimes, SE France 43°35′N 07°07′E
103 U15 **Antibes, Cap d'** *headland* SE France 43°33′N 07°08′E
Anticaria *see* Antequera
13 Q11 **Anticosti, Île d'** *Eng.* Anticosti Island. *island* Québec, E Canada
Anticosti Island *see* Anticosti, Île d'
102 K3 **Antifer, Cap d'** *headland* N France 49°43′N 00°10′E
30 L6 **Antigo** Wisconsin, N USA 45°10′N 89°10′W
13 Q15 **Antigonish** Nova Scotia, SE Canada 45°39′N 62°00′W
64 P11 **Antigua** Fuerteventura, Islas Canarias, NE Atlantic Ocean
45 X10 **Antigua** *island* S Antigua and Barbuda, Leeward Islands
Antigua *see* Antigua Guatemala
45 W9 **Antigua and Barbuda** ◆ *commonwealth republic* E West Indies
42 C6 **Antigua Guatemala** *var.* Antigua. Sacatepéquez, SW Guatemala 14°33′N 90°42′W
41 P11 **Antiguo Morelos** *var.* Antiguo-Morelos. Tamaulipas, C Mexico 22°35′N 99°08′W
115 F19 **Antíkyras, Kólpos** *gulf* C Greece
115 G24 **Antikýthira** *var.* Andikíthira. *island* S Greece
138 I7 **Anti-Lebanon** *var.* Jebel esh Sharqi, *Ar.* Al Jabal ash Sharqī, *Fr.* Anti-Liban. ▲▲ Lebanon/Syria
Anti-Liban *see* Anti-Lebanon
115 M22 **Antimácheia** Kos, Dodekánisa, Greece 47°19′N 07°54′E
115 I22 **Antímilos** *island* Kykládes, Greece, Aegean Sea
36 L6 **Antimony** Utah, W USA 38°07′N 112°00′W
An tInbhear Mór *see* Arklow
30 M10 **Antioch** Illinois, N USA 42°28′N 88°06′W
Antioch *see* Antakya
102 I10 **Antioche, Pertuis d'** *inlet* W France
Antiochia *see* Antakya
54 D8 **Antioquia** Antioquia, C Colombia 06°36′N 75°53′W
54 E8 **Antioquia** *off.* Departamento de Antioquia. ◈ *province* C Colombia
Antioquia, Departamento de *see* Antioquia
115 J21 **Antíparos** *var.* Andipáros. *island* Kykládes, Greece, Aegean Sea
115 B17 **Antípaxoi** *var.* Andipaxi. *island* Iónia Nísiá, Greece, C Mediterranean Sea
122 J8 **Antipayuta** Yamalo-Nenetskiy Avtonomnyy Okrug, N Russian Federation 69°08′N 76°43′E
192 L12 **Antipodes Islands** *island group* S New Zealand
Antipolis *see* Antibes
115 J18 **Antípsara** *var.* Andípsara. *island* E Greece
Antiquaria *see* Antequera
15 N10 **Antique, Lac** ◎ Québec, SE Canada
115 E18 **Antírrio** *var.* Andírrion. Dytikí Ellás, C Greece 38°20′N 21°46′E
115 K16 **Ántissa** *var.* Ándissa. Lésvos, E Greece 39°15′N 26°00′E
An tIúr *see* Newry
Antivari *see* Bar
56 C6 **Antizana** ▲ N Ecuador 0°29′S 78°08′W
27 Q13 **Antlers** Oklahoma, C USA 34°15′N 95°38′W
93 J14 **Antnäs** Norrbotten, N Sweden 65°32′N 21°53′E
Antō *see* Andong
62 G5 **Antofagasta** Antofagasta, N Chile 23°40′S 70°23′W
62 G6 **Antofagasta** *off.* Región de Antofagasta. ◈ *region* N Chile
Antofagasta, Región de *see* Antofagasta
62 I7 **Antofalla, Salar de** *salt lake* NW Argentina
99 D20 **Antoing** Hainaut, SW Belgium 50°34′N 03°26′E
43 S16 **Antón** Coclé, C Panama 08°23′N 80°15′W
24 M5 **Anton** Texas, SW USA 33°48′N 102°09′W
37 T11 **Anton Chico** New Mexico, SW USA 35°12′N 105°09′W
60 K12 **Antonina** Paraná, S Brazil 25°28′S 48°43′W
188 C16 **Antonio B. Won Pat International** ✈ (Agana) C Guam 13°28′N 144°48′E
103 O5 **Antony** Hauts-de-Seine, N France 48°45′N 02°17′E
Antratsit *see* Antratsyt
117 Y8 **Antratsyt** *Rus.* Antratsit. Luhans'ka Oblast', E Ukraine 48°07′N 39°05′E
97 G15 **Antrim** *Ir.* Aontroim. NE Northern Ireland, United Kingdom 54°43′N 06°13′W
97 G14 **Antrim** *Ir.* Aontroim. *cultural region* NE Northern Ireland, United Kingdom
97 G14 **Antrim Mountains** ▲▲ NE Northern Ireland, United Kingdom
172 H5 **Antsalova** Mahajanga, W Madagascar 18°40′S 44°37′E
Antserana *see* Antsirañana
An tSionainn *see* Shannon
172 J2 **Antsirañana** *var.* Antserana; *prev.* Antsirane, Diégo-Suarez. Antsirañana, N Madagascar 12°19′S 49°17′E
172 J2 **Antsirañana** ◈ *province* N Madagascar
Antsirane *see* Antsirañana
An tSiúir *see* Suir
118 I7 **Antsla** *Ger.* Anzen. Võrumaa, SE Estonia 57°52′N 26°33′E
An tSláine *see* Slaney
172 J3 **Antsohihy** Mahajanga, NW Madagascar 14°50′S 47°58′E
63 G14 **Antuco, Volcán** ⛰ C Chile 37°29′S 71°25′W
169 W10 **Antu, Gunung** ▲ Borneo, N Indonesia 0°57′N 118°51′E
An Tullach *see* Tullow
An-tung *see* Dandong
Antunnacum *see* Andernach
Antwerp *see* Antwerpen
99 G16 **Antwerpen** *Eng.* Antwerp, *Fr.* Anvers. Antwerpen, N Belgium 51°13′N 04°25′E
99 H16 **Antwerpen** *Eng.* Antwerp. ◈ *province* N Belgium
An Uaimh *see* Navan
154 N12 **Anugul** *var.* Angul. Orissa, E India 20°51′N 84°59′E
152 F9 **Anūpgarh** Rājasthān, NW India 29°10′N 73°14′E
154 K10 **Anūppur** Madhya Pradesh, C India 23°05′N 81°45′E
155 K24 **Anuradhapura** North Central Province, C Sri Lanka 08°20′N 80°25′E
Anvers *see* Antwerpen
194 G4 **Anvers Island** *island* Antarctica
39 N11 **Anvik** Alaska, USA 62°39′N 160°12′W
39 N10 **Anvik River** ≈ Alaska, USA
38 F17 **Anvil Peak** ▲ Semisopochnoi Island, Alaska, USA 51°59′N 179°36′E
159 P7 **Anxi** *var.* Yuanquan. Gansu, N China 40°32′N 95°50′E
182 F8 **Anxious Bay** *bay* South Australia
161 O5 **Anyang** Henan, C China 36°11′N 114°18′E
159 S11 **A'nyêmaqên Shan** ▲▲ C China
118 H12 **Anykščiai** Utena, E Lithuania 55°30′N 25°34′E
161 P13 **Anyuan** *var.* Xinshan. Jiangxi, S China 25°10′N 115°25′E
123 T7 **Anyuysk** Chukotskiy Avtonomnyy Okrug, NE Russian Federation 68°22′N 161°33′E
123 T7 **Anyuyskiy Khrebet** ▲▲ NE Russian Federation
54 D8 **Anza** Antioquia, C Colombia 06°18′N 75°54′W
Anzen *see* Antsla
107 I16 **Anzio** Lazio, C Italy 41°28′N 12°38′E
55 O6 **Anzoátegui** *off.* Estado Anzoátegui. ◈ *state* NE Venezuela
Anzoátegui, Estado *see* Anzoátegui
147 P12 **Anzob** W Tajikistan 39°24′N 68°55′E
Anzyô *see* Anjō
Aoba *see* Ambae
165 X13 **Aoga-shima** *island* Izu-shotō, SE Japan
Aohan Qi *see* Xinhui
Aoiz *see* Agoiz
167 O11 **Ao Krung Thep** *var.* Krung Thep Mahanakhon, *Eng.* Bangkok. ● (Thailand) Bangkok, C Thailand 13°44′N 100°30′E
186 M9 **Aola** *var.* Tenaghau. Guadalcanal, C Solomon Islands 09°32′S 160°28′E
166 M15 **Ao Luk Nua** Krabi, SW Thailand 08°21′N 98°43′E
Aomen *see* Macao
172 N8 **Aomori** Aomori, Honshū, C Japan 40°50′N 140°43′E
172 N8 **Aomori** *off.* Aomori-ken. ◈ *prefecture* Honshū, C Japan
Aomori-ken *see* Aomori
Aontroim *see* Antrim
115 C15 **Aóos** *var.* Vijosa, Vijosë, *Alb.* Lumi i Vjosës. ≈ Albania/Greece *see also* Vjosës, Lumi i
Aóos *see* Vjosës, Lumi i
191 Q7 **Aorai, Mont** ⛰ Tahiti, W French Polynesia 17°36′S 149°29′W
185 E19 **Aoraki** *prev.* Aorangi, Mount Cook. ▲ South Island, New Zealand 43°38′S 170°05′E
167 R13 **Aôral, Phnum** *prev.* Phnom Aural. ▲ W Cambodia 12°01′N 104°10′E
Aorangi *see* Aoraki
185 L15 **Aorangi Mountains** ▲▲ North Island, New Zealand
184 H13 **Aorere** ≈ South Island, New Zealand
106 A7 **Aosta** *anc.* Augusta Praetoria. Valle d'Aosta, NW Italy 45°43′N 07°20′E
77 O11 **Aougoundou, Lac** ◎ S Mali
76 K9 **Aoukâr** *var.* Aouker. *plateau* C Mauritania
78 J13 **Aouk, Bahr** ≈ Central African Republic/Chad
Aouker *see* Aoukâr
74 B11 **Aousard** SE Western Sahara 22°42′N 14°22′W
164 H12 **Aoya** Tottori, Honshū, SW Japan 35°31′N 134°01′E
Aoyang *see* Shanggao
78 H5 **Aozou** Borkou-Ennedi-Tibesti, N Chad 22°01′N 17°11′E
26 M11 **Apache** Oklahoma, C USA 34°57′N 98°21′W
36 L14 **Apache Junction** Arizona, SW USA 33°25′N 111°33′W
24 J9 **Apache Mountains** ▲▲ Texas, SW USA
36 M16 **Apache Peak** ▲ Arizona, SW USA 31°50′N 110°25′W
116 H10 **Apahida** Cluj, NW Romania 46°49′N 23°45′E
23 T9 **Apalachee Bay** *bay* Florida, SE USA
23 T3 **Apalachee River** ≈ Georgia, SE USA
23 S10 **Apalachicola** Florida, SE USA 29°43′N 84°58′W
23 S10 **Apalachicola Bay** *bay* Florida, SE USA
23 R9 **Apalachicola River** ≈ Florida, SE USA
Apam *see* Apan
Apamama *see* Abemama
41 P14 **Apan** *var.* Apam. Hidalgo, C Mexico 19°48′N 98°25′W
42 J8 **Apanás, Lago de** ◎ NW Nicaragua
54 H14 **Apaporis, Río** ≈ Brazil/Colombia
185 C23 **Aparima** ≈ South Island, New Zealand
171 O1 **Aparri** Luzon, N Philippines 18°16′N 121°42′E
112 J9 **Apatin** Vojvodina, NW Serbia 45°40′N 19°01′E
124 J4 **Apatity** Murmanskaya Oblast', NW Russian Federation 67°34′N 33°26′E
55 X9 **Apatou** NW French Guiana 05°10′N 54°22′W
40 M14 **Apatzingán** *var.* Apatzingán de la Constitución. Michoacán, SW Mexico 19°05′N 102°20′W
Apatzingán de la Constitución *see* Apatzingán
171 X12 **Apauwar** Papua, E Indonesia 01°36′S 138°10′E
Apaxtla *see* Apaxtla de Castrejón
41 O15 **Apaxtla de Castrejón** *var.* Apaxtla. Guerrero, S Mexico 18°06′N 99°55′W
118 J7 **Ape** Alūksne, NE Latvia 57°32′N 26°42′E
98 L11 **Apeldoorn** Gelderland, E Netherlands 52°13′N 05°57′E
Apennines *see* Appennino
Apenrade *see* Aabenraa
57 L17 **Apere, Río** ≈ C Bolivia
55 W11 **Apetina** Sipaliwini, SE Surinam 03°30′N 55°03′W
21 U9 **Apex** North Carolina, SE USA 35°43′N 78°51′W
79 M16 **Api** Orientale, N Dem. Rep. Congo 03°40′N 25°26′E
152 M9 **Api** ▲ NW Nepal 30°07′N 80°57′E
192 H16 **Āpia** ● (Samoa) Upolu, SE Samoa 13°50′S 171°47′W
Apia *see* Abaiang
60 K11 **Apiaí** São Paulo, S Brazil 24°29′S 48°51′W
170 M16 **Api, Gunung** ▲ Pulau Sangeang, S Indonesia 08°09′S 119°03′E
187 N9 **Apio** Maramasike Island, N Solomon Islands 09°36′S 161°25′E
41 O15 **Apipilulco** Guerrero, S Mexico 18°11′N 99°40′W
41 P14 **Apizaco** Tlaxcala, S Mexico 19°26′N 98°09′W
137 Q8 **Ap'khazet'i** *var.* Abkhazia. ◈ *autonomous republic* NW Georgia
104 I4 **A Pobla de Trives** *Cast.* Puebla de Trives. Galicia, NW Spain 42°21′N 07°16′W
55 U9 **Apoera** Sipaliwini, NW Surinam 05°12′N 57°13′W
115 O23 **Apolakkiá** Ródos, Dodekánisa, Greece, Aegean Sea 36°02′N 27°48′E
101 L16 **Apolda** Thüringen, C Germany 51°02′N 11°31′E
192 H16 **Apolima Strait** *strait* C Pacific Ocean
182 M13 **Apollo Bay** Victoria, SE Australia 38°40′S 143°44′E
Apollonia *see* Sozopol
57 J16 **Apolo** La Paz, W Bolivia 14°48′S 68°31′W
57 J16 **Apolobamba, Cordillera** ▲▲ Bolivia/Peru
171 Q8 **Apo, Mount** ⛰ Mindanao, S Philippines 06°54′N 125°16′E
23 W11 **Apopka** Florida, SE USA 28°40′N 81°30′W
23 W11 **Apopka, Lake** ◎ Florida, SE USA
59 J19 **Aporé, Rio** ≈ SW Brazil
30 K2 **Apostle Islands** *island group* Wisconsin, N USA
Apostolas Andreas, Cape *see* Zafer Burnu
61 F14 **Apóstoles** Misiones, NE Argentina 27°54′S 55°45′W
Apostólou Andréa, Akrotíri *see* Zafer Burnu
117 S9 **Apostolove** *Rus.* Apostolovo. Dnipropetrovs'ka Oblast', E Ukraine 47°40′N 33°45′E
Apostolovo *see* Apostolove
17 S10 **Appalachian Mountains** ▲▲ E USA
95 K14 **Äppelbo** Dalarna, C Sweden 60°30′N 14°00′E
98 N7 **Appelscha** *Fris.* Appelskea. Friesland, N Netherlands 52°57′N 06°19′E
Appelskea *see* Appelscha
106 G11 **Appennino** *Eng.* Apennines. ▲▲ Italy/San Marino
107 L17 **Appennino Campano** ▲▲ C Italy
108 I7 **Appenzell** Appenzell, NW Switzerland 47°20′N 09°25′E
108 H7 **Appenzell** ◈ *canton* NE Switzerland
55 V12 **Appikalo** Sipaliwini, S Surinam 02°07′N 56°16′W
98 O5 **Appingedam** Groningen, NE Netherlands 53°18′N 06°52′E
25 X8 **Appleby** Texas, SW USA 31°43′N 94°36′W
97 L15 **Appleby-in-Westmorland** Cumbria, NW England, United Kingdom 54°35′N 02°26′W
30 K10 **Apple River** ≈ Illinois, N USA
30 I5 **Apple River** ≈ Wisconsin, N USA
25 W9 **Apple Springs** Texas, SW USA 31°13′N 94°57′W
29 S8 **Appleton** Minnesota, N USA 45°12′N 96°01′W
30 M7 **Appleton** Wisconsin, N USA 44°17′N 88°24′W
27 S5 **Appleton City** Missouri, C USA 38°11′N 94°01′W
35 U14 **Apple Valley** California, W USA 34°30′N 117°11′W
29 V9 **Apple Valley** Minnesota, N USA 44°43′N 93°13′W
21 U6 **Appomattox** Virginia, NE USA 37°21′N 78°51′W
188 B16 **Apra Harbor** *harbour* W Guam
188 B16 **Apra Heights** W Guam
106 F6 **Aprica, Passo dell'** *pass* N Italy
107 M15 **Apricena** *anc.* Hadria Picena. Puglia, SE Italy 41°47′N 15°27′E
114 I9 **Apriltsi** Lovech, N Bulgaria 42°50′N 24°54′E
126 L14 **Apsheronsk** Krasnodarskiy Kray, SW Russian Federation 44°27′N 39°45′E
Apsheronskiy Poluostrov *see* Abşeron Yarımadası
103 S15 **Apt** *anc.* Apta Julia. Vaucluse, SE France 43°54′N 05°24′E
Apta Julia *see* Apt
38 H12 **'Āpua Point** *var.* Apua Point. *headland* Hawai'i, USA, C Pacific Ocean 19°15′N 155°13′W
60 I10 **Apucarana** Paraná, S Brazil 23°34′S 51°28′W
Apulia *see* Puglia
54 K8 **Apure** *off.* Estado Apure. ◈ *state* C Venezuela
Apure, Estado *see* Apure
54 J7 **Apure, Río** ≈ W Venezuela
57 F16 **Apurímac** *off.* Departamento de Apurímac. ◈ *department* C Peru
Apurímac, Departamento de *see* Apurímac
57 F15 **Apurímac, Río** ≈ S Peru
116 G10 **Apuseni, Munții** ▲▲ W Romania
Aqaba/'Aqaba *see* Al 'Aqabah
138 F15 **Aqaba, Gulf of** *var.* Gulf of Elat, *Ar.* Khalīj al 'Aqabah; *anc.* Sinus Aelaniticus. *gulf* NE Red Sea
139 R7 **'Aqabah** Al Anbār, C Iraq 33°33′N 42°55′E
'Aqabah, Khalīj al *see* Aqaba, Gulf of
149 O2 **Āqchah** *var.* Āqcheh. Jowzjān, N Afghanistan 37°N 66°07′E
Āqcheh *see* Āqchah
Aqkengse *see* Akkense
Aqköl *see* Akkol'
Aqmola *see* Astana
Aqmola Oblysy *see* Akmola
158 L10 **Aqqikkol Hu** ◎ NW China
Aqqū *see* Akku
Aqqystaū *see* Akkystau
'Aqrah *see* Ākrē
Aqsay *see* Aksay
Aqshataū *see* Akchatau
Aqsū *see* Aksu
Aqsūat *see* Aksuat
Aqtas *see* Aktas
Aqtaū *see* Aktau
Aqtöbe *see* Aktobe
Aqtöbe Oblysy *see* Aktyubinsk
Aqtoghay *see* Aktogay
Aquae Augustae *see* Dax
Aquae Calidae *see* Bath
Aquae Flaviae *see* Chaves
Aquae Grani *see* Aachen
Aquae Panoniae *see* Baden
Aquae Sextiae *see* Aix-en-Provence
Aquae Solis *see* Bath
Aquae Tarbelicae *see* Dax
36 J11 **Aquarius Mountains** ▲▲ Arizona, SW USA
62 O5 **Aquidabán, Río** ≈ E Paraguay
59 H20 **Aquidauana** Mato Grosso do Sul, S Brazil 20°27′S 55°45′W
40 L15 **Aquila** Michoacán, S Mexico 18°36′N 103°32′W
Aquila/Aquila degli Abruzzi *see* L'Aquila
25 T8 **Aquilla** Texas, SW USA 31°51′N 97°13′W
44 L9 **Aquin** S Haiti 18°16′N 73°24′W
Aquisgranum *see* Aachen
102 J13 **Aquitaine** ◈ *region* SW France
Aqzhar *see* Akzhar
153 P13 **Āra** *prev.* Arrah. Bihār, N India 25°34′N 84°40′E
105 S4 **Ara** ≈ NE Spain
23 P2 **Arab** Alabama, S USA 34°19′N 86°30′W
Araba *see* Álava
138 G12 **'Arabah, Wādī al** *Heb.* Ha'Arava. *dry watercourse* Israel/Jordan
117 U12 **Arabats'ka Strilka, Kosa** *spit* S Ukraine
117 U12 **Arabats'ka Zatoka** *gulf* S Ukraine
'Arab, Baḩr al *see* Arab, Bahr el
80 C12 **Arab, Bahr el** *var.* Baḩr al 'Arab. ≈ S Sudan
56 E7 **Arabela, Río** ≈ N Peru
173 O4 **Arabian Basin** *undersea feature* N Arabian Sea 11°30′N 65°00′E
Arabian Desert *see* Sahara el Sharqîya
141 N9 **Arabian Peninsula** *peninsula* SW Asia
85 P15 **Arabian Plate** *tectonic feature* Africa/Asia/Europe
141 W14 **Arabian Sea** *sea* NW Indian Ocean
Arabicus, Sinus *see* Red Sea
'Arabī, Khalīj al *see* Gulf, The
Arabistan *see* Khūzestān
'Arabīyah as Su'ūdīyah, Al Mamlakah al *see* Saudi Arabia
'Arabīyah Jumhūrīyah, Mişr al *see* Egypt
138 I9 **'Arab, Jabal al** ▲▲ S Syria
Arab Republic of Egypt *see* Egypt
139 Y12 **'Arab, Shaţţ al** *Eng.* Shatt al Arab, *Per.* Arvand Rūd. ≈ Iran/Iraq
136 I11 **Araç** Kastamonu, N Turkey 41°14′N 33°20′E
59 P16 **Aracaju** *state capital* Sergipe, E Brazil 10°45′S 37°07′W
54 F5 **Aracataca** Magdalena, N Colombia 10°38′N 74°09′W
58 P13 **Aracati** Ceará, E Brazil 04°32′S 37°45′W
60 J8 **Araçatuba** São Paulo, S Brazil 21°12′S 50°24′W
136 I11 **Araç Çayı** ≈ N Turkey
104 J13 **Aracena** Andalucía, S Spain 37°54′N 06°33′W
115 F20 **Arachnaío** ▲▲ S Greece
115 D16 **Árachthos** *var.* Arta, *prev.* Árakhthos; *anc.* Arachthus. ≈ W Greece
Arachthus *see* Árachthos
59 N19 **Araçuai** Minas Gerais, SE Brazil 16°52′S 42°03′W
138 F11 **Arad** Southern, S Israel 31°16′N 35°09′E
116 F11 **Arad** Arad, W Romania 46°12′N 21°20′E
116 F11 **Arad** ◈ *county* W Romania
78 J9 **Arada** Biltine, NE Chad 15°00′N 20°38′E
143 P18 **'Arādah** Abū Z̧aby, S United Arab Emirates 22°57′N 53°24′E
Aradhippou *see* Aradíppou
121 Q3 **Aradíppou** *var.* Aradhippou. SE Cyprus 34°57′N 33°37′E
174 K6 **Arafura Sea** *Ind.* Laut Arafuru. *sea* W Pacific Ocean
174 L6 **Arafura Shelf** *undersea feature* C Arafura Sea
Arafuru, Laut *see* Arafura Sea
59 J18 **Aragarças** Goiás, C Brazil 15°55′S 52°12′W
Aragats, Gora *see* Aragats Lerr
137 T12 **Aragats Lerr** *Rus.* Gora Aragats. ▲ W Armenia 40°31′N 44°06′E
32 E14 **Arago, Cape** *headland* Oregon, NW USA 43°17′N 124°25′W
105 R6 **Aragón** *autonomous community* E Spain
105 Q4 **Aragón** ≈ NE Spain
107 I24 **Aragona** Sicilia, Italy, C Mediterranean Sea 37°25′N 13°37′E
105 Q7 **Aragoncillo** ▲ C Spain 40°59′N 02°01′W
54 L5 **Aragua** *off.* Estado Aragua. ◈ *state* N Venezuela
55 N6 **Aragua de Barcelona** Anzoátegui, NE Venezuela 09°30′N 64°51′W
55 O5 **Aragua de Maturín** Monagas, NE Venezuela 09°58′N 63°30′W
Aragua, Estado *see* Aragua
59 K15 **Araguaia, Río** *var.* Araguaya. ≈ C Brazil
59 K19 **Araguari** Minas Gerais, SE Brazil 18°38′S 48°13′W
58 J11 **Araguari, Rio** ≈ SW Brazil
Araguaya *see* Araguaia, Río
104 K14 **Arahal** Andalucía, S Spain 37°15′N 05°33′W
165 N11 **Arai** Niigata, Honshū, C Japan 37°02′N 138°17′E
Árainn *see* Inishmore
Árainn Mhór *see* Aran Island
Ara Jovis *see* Aranjuez
74 J11 **Arak** C Algeria 25°17′N 03°45′E
171 Y15 **Arak** Papua, E Indonesia 07°14′S 139°40′E
142 M7 **Arāk** *prev.* Sultānābād. Markazī, W Iran 34°07′N 49°39′E
188 D10 **Arakabesan** *island* Palau Islands, N Palau
55 S7 **Arakaka** NW Guyana 07°37′N 59°58′W
166 K6 **Arakan State** *var.* Rakhine State. ◈ *state* W Burma (Myanmar)
166 K5 **Arakan Yoma** ▲▲ W Burma (Myanmar)
165 O10 **Arakawa** Niigata, Honshū, C Japan 38°06′N 139°25′E
Árakhthos *see* Árachthos
Araks/Arak's *see* Aras
158 H7 **Aral** Xinjiang Uygur Zizhiqu, NW China 40°40′N 81°19′E
Aral *see* Aralsk, Kazakhstan
Aral *see* Vose', Tajikistan
Aral-Bukhorskiy Kanal *see* Amu-Buxoro Kanali
137 T12 **Aralik** Iğdır, E Turkey 39°54′N 44°28′E
146 H5 **Aral Sea** *Kaz.* Aral Tengizi, *Rus.* Aral'skoye More, *Uzb.* Orol Dengizi. *inland sea* Kazakhstan/Uzbekistan
144 L13 **Aral'sk** *Kaz.* Aral. Kzylorda, SW Kazakhstan 46°48′N 61°40′E
Aral'skoye More/Aral Tengizi *see* Aral Sea
41 O10 **Aramberri** Nuevo León, NE Mexico 24°05′N 99°52′W
186 B8 **Aramia** ≈ SW Papua New Guinea
143 N6 **Ārān** *var.* Golārā. Eşfahān, C Iran 34°03′N 51°30′E
105 N5 **Aranda de Duero** Castilla-León, N Spain 41°40′N 03°41′W
112 M12 **Aranđelovac** *prev.* Arandjelovac. Serbia, C Serbia 44°18′N 20°32′E
Arandjelovac *see* Aranđelovac
97 J19 **Aran Fawddwy** ▲ NW Wales, United Kingdom 52°48′N 03°42′W
97 C14 **Aran Island** *Ir.* Árainn Mhór. *island* NW Ireland
97 A18 **Aran Islands** *island group* W Ireland
105 N9 **Aranjuez** *anc.* Ara Jovis. Madrid, C Spain 40°02′N 03°37′W
83 E20 **Aranos** Hardap, SE Namibia 24°10′S 19°08′E
25 U14 **Aransas Bay** *inlet* Texas, SW USA
25 T14 **Aransas Pass** Texas, SW USA 27°54′N 97°09′W
191 O3 **Aranuka** *prev.* Nanouki. *atoll* Tungaru, W Kiribati
167 Q11 **Aranyaprathet** Prachin Buri, S Thailand 13°42′N 102°32′E
Aranyosasztal *see* Zlatý Stôl
Aranyosgyéres *see* Câmpia Turzii
Aranyosmarót *see* Zlaté Moravce
164 C14 **Arao** Kumamoto, Kyūshū, SW Japan 32°58′N 130°26′E
77 O8 **Araouane** Tombouctou, N Mali 18°53′N 03°31′W
26 L10 **Arapaho** Oklahoma, C USA 35°34′N 98°57′W
29 N16 **Arapahoe** Nebraska, C USA 40°18′N 99°54′W
57 I16 **Arapa, Laguna** ◎ SE Peru
185 K14 **Arapawa Island** *island* C New Zealand
61 E17 **Arapey Grande, Río** ≈ N Uruguay
59 P16 **Arapiraca** Alagoas, E Brazil 09°45′S 36°40′W
140 M3 **'Ar'ar** Al Ḩudūd ash Shamālīyah, NW Saudi Arabia 31°N 41°E
54 G15 **Araracuara** Caquetá, S Colombia 0°36′S 72°24′W
61 K15 **Araranguá** Santa Catarina, S Brazil 28°56′S 49°30′W
60 L8 **Araraquara** São Paulo, S Brazil 21°46′S 48°08′W
59 O13 **Araras** Ceará, E Brazil 04°08′S 40°30′W
58 I14 **Araras** Pará, N Brazil 06°04′S 54°34′W
60 L9 **Araras** São Paulo, S Brazil 22°21′S 47°21′W
60 H11 **Araras, Serra das** ▲▲ S Brazil
137 U12 **Ararat** S Armenia 39°49′N 44°45′E
182 M12 **Ararat** Victoria, SE Australia 37°20′S 143°00′E
Ararat, Mount *see* Büyükağrı Dağı
140 M3 **'Ar'ar, Wādī** *dry watercourse* Iraq/Saudi Arabia
129 N7 **Aras** *Arm.* Arak's, *Az.* Araz Nehri, *Per.* Rūd-e Aras, *Rus.* Araks; *prev.* Araxes. ≈ SW Asia
Aras de Alpuente *see* Aras de los Olmos
105 R9 **Aras de los Olmos** *prev.* Aras de Alpuente. País Valenciano, E Spain 39°55′N 01°09′W
137 S13 **Aras Güneyi Dağları** ▲▲ NE Turkey
Aras, Rūd-e *see* Aras
191 U9 **Aratika** *atoll* Îles Tuamotu, C French Polynesia
Aratürük *see* Yiwu
54 I8 **Arauca** Arauca, NE Colombia 07°03′N 70°47′W
54 I8 **Arauca** *off.* Intendencia de Arauca. ◈ *province* NE Colombia
Arauca, Intendencia de *see* Arauca
63 G15 **Araucanía** *off.* Regíon de la Araucanía. ◈ *region* C Chile
Araucanía, Regíon de la *see* Araucanía
54 L7 **Arauca, Río** ≈ Colombia/Venezuela
63 F14 **Arauco** Bío Bío, C Chile 37°15′S 73°22′W
63 F14 **Arauco, Golfo de** *gulf* S Chile
54 H8 **Arauquita** Arauca, C Colombia 06°57′N 71°19′W
Arausio *see* Orange
152 F13 **Arāvali Range** ▲▲ N India
186 J7 **Arawa** Bougainville Island, NE Papua New Guinea 06°15′S 155°35′E
185 C20 **Arawata** ≈ South Island, New Zealand
186 F7 **Arawe Islands** *island group* E Papua New Guinea
59 L20 **Araxá** Minas Gerais, SE Brazil 19°37′S 46°50′W
Araxes *see* Aras
55 O5 **Araya** Sucre, N Venezuela 10°34′N 64°15′W
Araz Nehri *see* Aras
105 R4 **Arba** ≈ N Spain
81 I15 **Ārba Minch'** Southern Nationalities, S Ethiopia 06°02′N 37°34′E
139 U4 **Arbat** As Sulaymānīyah, NE Iraq 35°26′N 45°34′E
107 D19 **Arbatax** Sardegna, Italy, C Mediterranean Sea 39°57′N 09°42′E
Arbe *see* Rab
Arbela *see* Arbīl
139 S3 **Arbīl** ◈ *governorate* N Iraq
139 S3 **Arbīl** *var.* Erbil, Irbīl, *Kurd.* Hawlēr; *anc.* Arbela. Arbīl, N Iraq 36°12′N 44°01′E
95 M16 **Arboga** Västmanland, C Sweden 59°24′N 15°50′E
95 M16 **Arbogaån** ≈ C Sweden
103 S9 **Arbois** Jura, E France 46°54′N 05°45′E
54 D6 **Arboletes** Antioquia, NW Colombia 08°52′N 76°25′W
11 X15 **Arborg** Manitoba, S Canada 50°52′N 97°20′W
94 N12 **Arbrå** Gävleborg, C Sweden 61°27′N 16°21′E
96 K10 **Arbroath** *anc.* Aberbrothock. E Scotland, United Kingdom 56°34′N 02°35′W
35 N6 **Arbuckle** California, W USA 39°00′N 122°05′W
27 N12 **Arbuckle Mountains** ▲▲ Oklahoma, C USA
162 I5 **Arbulag** *var.* Mandal. Hövsgöl, N Mongolia 49°55′N 99°21′E
Arbuzinka *see* Arbuzynka
117 Q8 **Arbuzynka** *Rus.* Arbuzinka. Mykolayivs'ka Oblast', S Ukraine 47°54′N 31°19′E
103 U12 **Arc** ≈ E France
102 J13 **Arcachon** Gironde, SW France 44°40′N 01°11′W
102 J13 **Arcachon, Bassin d'** *inlet* SW France
18 E10 **Arcade** New York, NE USA 42°32′N 78°19′W
23 W14 **Arcadia** Florida, SE USA 27°13′N 81°51′W
22 H5 **Arcadia** Louisiana, S USA 32°33′N 92°55′W
30 J7 **Arcadia** Wisconsin, N USA 44°15′N 91°30′W
Arcae Remorum *see* Châlons-en-Champagne
44 L9 **Arcahaie** C Haiti 18°46′N 72°32′W
34 K3 **Arcata** California, W USA 40°51′N 124°06′W
35 U6 **Arc Dome** ▲ Nevada, W USA 38°52′N 117°20′W
107 J16 **Arce** Lazio, C Italy 41°35′N 13°34′E
41 O15 **Arcelia** Guerrero, S Mexico 18°20′N 100°16′W
99 M15 **Arcen** Limburg, SE Netherlands 51°28′N 06°10′E
115 J25 **Archánes** *var.* Áno Arkhánai, Epáno Archánes; *prev.* Epáno Arkhánai. Kríti, Greece, E Mediterranean Sea 35°12′N 25°10′E
Archangel *see* Arkhangel'sk
Archangel Bay *see* Chëshskaya Guba
115 O23 **Archángelos** *var.* Arhangelos, Arkhángelos. Ródos, Dodekánisa, Greece, Aegean Sea 36°13′N 28°07′E
114 F7 **Archar** ≈ NW Bulgaria
31 R11 **Archbold** Ohio, N USA 41°31′N 84°18′W
105 R12 **Archena** Murcia, SE Spain 38°07′N 01°17′W
25 R5 **Archer City** Texas, SW USA 33°36′N 98°37′W
104 M14 **Archidona** Andalucía, S Spain 37°06′N 04°23′W
106 G13 **Arcidosso** Toscana, C Italy 42°52′N 11°30′E
103 Q5 **Arcis-sur-Aube** Aube, N France 48°32′N 04°09′E
182 F3 **Arckaringa Creek** *seasonal river* South Australia
106 G7 **Arco** Trentino-Alto Adige, N Italy 45°53′N 10°52′E
33 Q14 **Arco** Idaho, NW USA 43°38′N 113°18′W
30 M14 **Arcola** Illinois, N USA 39°39′N 88°19′W
105 P6 **Arcos de Jalón** Castilla-León, N Spain 41°12′N 02°13′W
104 K15 **Arcos de la Frontera** Andalucía, S Spain 36°45′N 05°49′W
104 G5 **Arcos de Valdevez** Viana do Castelo, N Portugal 41°51′N 08°25′W
59 P15 **Arcoverde** Pernambuco, E Brazil 08°23′S 37°W
102 H5 **Arcovest, Pointe de l'** *headland* NW France 48°49′N 02°58′W
Arctic Mid Oceanic Ridge *see* Nansen Cordillera
197 R8 **Arctic Ocean** *ocean*
8 G7 **Arctic Red River** ≈ Northwest Territories/Yukon Territory, NW Canada
Arctic Red River *see* Tsiigehtchic
39 S6 **Arctic Village** Alaska, USA 68°07′N 145°32′W
194 H1 **Arctowski** *Polish research station* South Shetland Islands, Antarctica 61°57′S 58°23′W
114 I12 **Arda** *var.* Ardhas, *Gk.* Ardas. ≈ Bulgaria/Greece *see also* Ardas
142 L2 **Ardabīl** *var.* Ardebil. Ardabīl, NW Iran 38°15′N 48°18′E
142 L2 **Ardabīl** *off.* Ostān-e Ardabīl. ◈ *province* NW Iran
Ardabīl, Ostān-e *see* Ardabīl
137 R11 **Ardahan** Ardahan, NE Turkey 41°08′N 42°41′E
137 S11 **Ardahan** ◈ *province* Ardahan, Turkey
143 O10 **Ardakān** Fārs, SE Iran 30°16′N 52°01′E
143 P8 **Ardakān** Yazd, C Iran 32°20′N 53°59′E
94 E12 **Årdalstangen** Sogn Og Fjordane, S Norway 61°14′N 07°45′E
137 R11 **Ardanuç** Artvin, NE Turkey 41°07′N 42°04′E
114 L12 **Ardas** *var.* Ardhas, *Bul.* Arda. ≈ Bulgaria/Greece *see also* Arda
138 I13 **Arḑ aş Şawwān** *var.* Ardh es Suwwān. *plain* S Jordan
127 N4 **Ardatov** Nizhegorodskaya Oblast', W Russian Federation 55°14′N 43°06′E
127 P5 **Ardatov** Respublika Mordoviya, W Russian Federation 54°49′N 46°13′E
14 G12 **Ardbeg** Ontario, S Canada 45°38′N 80°05′W
Ardeal *see* Transylvania
Ardebil *see* Ardabīl
103 Q13 **Ardèche** ◈ *department* E France
103 Q13 **Ardèche** ≈ C France
97 F17 **Ardee** *Ir.* Baile Átha Fhirdhia. Louth, NE Ireland 53°52′N 06°33′W
103 Q3 **Ardennes** ◈ *department* NE France
99 J23 **Ardennes** *physical region* Belgium/France
137 Q11 **Ardeşen** Rize, NE Turkey 41°14′N 41°00′E
143 O7 **Ardestān** *var.* Ardistan. Eşfahān, C Iran 33°29′N 52°17′E
108 J9 **Ardez** Graubünden, SE Switzerland 46°47′N 10°09′E
Ardhas *see* Arda/Ardas
Ardh es Suwwān *see* Arḑ aş Şawwān
Ardila *see* Ardila, Ribeira de
104 I12 **Ardila, Ribeira de** *Sp.* Ardilla. ≈ Portugal/Spain *see also* Ardilla
Ardila, Ribeira de *see* Ardilla
11 T17 **Ardill** Saskatchewan, S Canada 49°56′N 105°49′W
104 I12 **Ardilla** *Port.* Ribeira de Ardila. ≈ Portugal/Spain *see also* Ardila, Ribeira de
40 M11 **Ardilla, Cerro la** ▲ C Mexico 22°15′N 102°33′W
114 J12 **Ardino** Kŭrdzhali, S Bulgaria 41°38′N 25°22′E
Ardistan *see* Ardestān
183 P9 **Ardlethan** New South Wales, SE Australia 34°24′S 146°52′E
Ard Mhacha *see* Armagh
23 P1 **Ardmore** Alabama, S USA 34°59′N 86°51′W
27 N13 **Ardmore** Oklahoma, C USA 34°11′N 97°08′W
20 J10 **Ardmore** Tennessee, S USA 35°00′N 86°48′W
96 G10 **Ardnamurchan, Point of** *headland* N Scotland, United Kingdom 56°42′N 06°15′W
Árdni *see* Arnøya
99 C17 **Ardooie** West-Vlaanderen, W Belgium 50°59′N 03°10′E
182 I9 **Ardrossan** South Australia 34°27′S 137°54′E
116 H9 **Ardusat** *Hung.* Erdőszáda. Maramureş, N Romania 47°36′N 23°25′E
93 F16 **Åre** Jämtland, C Sweden 63°25′N 13°04′E
79 P16 **Arebi** Orientale, NE Dem. Rep. Congo 02°47′N 29°35′E
45 T5 **Arecibo** C Puerto Rico 18°29′N 66°44′W′N
171 V13 **Aredo** Papua, E Indonesia 02°27′S 133°59′E
59 P14 **Areia Branca** Rio Grande do Norte, E Brazil 04°53′S 37°03′W
119 O14 **Arekhawsk** *Rus.* Orekhovsk. Vitsyebskaya Voblasts', N Belarus 54°42′N 30°30′E
Arel *see* Arlon
Arelas/Arelate *see* Arles
Arenal, Embalse de *see* Arenal Laguna
42 L12 **Arenal Laguna** *var.* Embalse de Arenal. ◎ NW Costa Rica
42 L13 **Arenal, Volcán** ⛰ NW Costa Rica 10°21′N 84°42′W
34 K6 **Arena, Point** *headland* California, W USA 38°57′N 123°44′W
59 H17 **Arenápolis** Mato Grosso, W Brazil 14°25′S 56°52′W
40 G10 **Arena, Punta** *headland* NW Mexico 23°28′N 109°24′W
104 L8 **Arenas de San Pedro** Castilla-León, N Spain 40°12′N 05°05′W
63 I24 **Arenas, Punta de** *headland* S Argentina 53°10′S 68°15′W
61 B20 **Arenaza** Buenos Aires, E Argentina 34°55′S 61°45′W
95 F17 **Arendal** Aust-Agder, S Norway 58°27′N 08°45′E
99 J16 **Arendonk** Antwerpen, N Belgium 51°18′N 05°06′E
43 T15 **Arenosa** Panamá, N Panama 09°02′N 79°57′W
Arensburg *see* Kuressaare
105 W5 **Arenys de Mar** Cataluña, NE Spain 41°35′N 02°33′E
106 C9 **Arenzano** Liguria, NW Italy 44°25′N 08°43′E
115 F22 **Areópoli** *prev.* Areópolis. Pelopónnisos, S Greece 36°40′N 22°24′E
Areópolis *see* Areópoli
57 H18 **Arequipa** Arequipa, SE Peru 16°24′S 71°33′W
57 G17 **Arequipa** *off.* Departamento de Arequipa. ◈ *department* Arequia SW Peru
Arequipa, Departamento de *see* Arequipa
61 B19 **Arequito** Santa Fe, C Argentina 33°09′S 61°28′W
104 M7 **Arévalo** Castilla-León, N Spain 41°04′N 04°44′W

◆ Country
● Country Capital
◇ Dependent Territory
○ Dependent Territory Capital
◈ Administrative Regions
✈ International Airport
▲ Mountain
▲▲ Mountain Range
⛰ Volcano
≈ River
◎ Lake
⊠ Reservoir

Arezzo – Asino

106 H12 **Arezzo** *anc.* Arretium. Toscana, C Italy 43°28′N 11°50′E
105 Q4 **Arga** ≈ N Spain
Argaeus *see* Erciyes Dağı
115 G17 **Argalastí** Thessalía, C Greece 39°13′N 23°13′E
105 O10 **Argamasilla de Alba** Castilla-La Mancha, C Spain 39°08′N 03°05′W
158 L8 **Argan** Xinjiang Uygur Zizhiqu, NW China 40°09′N 88°16′E
105 O8 **Arganda** Madrid, C Spain 40°19′N 03°26′W
104 H8 **Arganil** Coimbra, N Portugal 40°13′N 08°03′W
171 P6 **Argao** Cebu, C Philippines 09°52′N 123°33′E
153 V15 **Argartala** Tripura, NE India
123 N9 **Arga-Sala** ≈ Respublika Sakha (Yakutiya),NE Russian Federation
103 P17 **Argelès-sur-Mer** Pyrénées-Orientales, S France 42°33′N 03°01′E
103 T15 **Argens** ≈ SE France
106 H9 **Argenta** Emilia-Romagna, N Italy 44°37′N 11°49′E
102 K5 **Argentan** Orne, N France 48°45′N 00°01′W
103 N12 **Argentat** Corrèze, C France 45°06′N 01°57′E
106 A9 **Argentera** Piemonte, NE Italy 44°25′N 06°57′E
103 N5 **Argenteuil** Val-d'Oise, N France 48°57′N 02°13′E
62 K13 **Argentina** *off.* Argentine Republic. ◆ *republic* S South America
Argentina Basin *see* Argentine Basin
Argentine Abyssal Plain *see* Argentine Plain
65 I19 **Argentine Basin** *var.* Argentina Basin. *undersea feature* SW Atlantic Ocean 45°00′S 45°00′W
65 I20 **Argentine Plain** *var.* Argentine Abyssal Plain. *undersea feature* SW Atlantic Ocean 47°31′S 50°00′W
Argentine Republic *see* Argentina
Argentine Rise *see* Falkland Plateau
63 H22 **Argentino, Lago** ◎ S Argentina
102 K8 **Argenton-Château** Deux-Sèvres, W France 46°59′N 00°22′W
102 M9 **Argenton-sur-Creuse** Indre, C France 46°34′N 01°32′E
Argentoratum *see* Strasbourg
116 I12 **Argeș** ◆ *county* S Romania
116 K14 **Argeș** ≈ S Romania
149 O8 **Arghandāb, Daryā-ye** ≈ SE Afghanistan
Arghastān *see* Arghestān
149 O8 **Arghestān** *Pash.* Arghastān. ≈ SE Afghanistan
Argirocastro *see* Gjirokastër
80 E7 **Argo** Northern, N Sudan 19°31′N 30°25′E
173 P7 **Argo Fracture Zone** *tectonic feature* C Indian Ocean
115 F20 **Argolikós Kólpos** *gulf* S Greece
Argonne *physical region* NE France
115 F20 **Árgos** Pelopónnisos, S Greece 37°38′N 22°43′E
139 S1 **Argōsh** Dahūk, N Iraq 37°07′N 44°13′E
115 D14 **Árgos Orestikó** Dytikí Makedonía, N Greece 40°27′N 21°15′E
115 B19 **Argostóli** *var.* Argostólion. Kefallonía, Iónia Nisiá, Greece, C Mediterranean Sea 38°13′N 20°29′E
Argostólion *see* Argostóli
Argovie *see* Aargau
35 O14 **Arguello, Point** *headland* California, W USA 34°34′N 120°39′W
127 P16 **Argun** Chechenskaya Respublika, SW Russian Federation 43°16′N 45°53′E
157 T2 **Argun** *Chin.* Ergun He, *Rus.* Argun'. ≈ China/Russian Federation
77 T12 **Argungu** Kebbi, NW Nigeria 12°45′N 04°24′E
Arguut *see* Guchin-Us
181 N3 **Argyle, Lake** *salt lake* Western Australia
96 G12 **Argyll** *cultural region* W Scotland, United Kingdom
Argyrokastron *see* Gjirokastër
162 I7 **Arhangay** ◆ *province* C Mongolia
Arhangelos *see* Archángelos
95 P14 **Arholma** Stockholm, C Sweden 59°51′N 19°01′E
95 G22 **Århus** *var.* Aarhus. Århus, C Denmark 56°09′N 10°11′E
95 G22 **Århus** ◆ *county* C Denmark
139 T1 **Ārī** Arbīl, E Iraq 37°07′N 44°34′E
Aria *see* Herāt
83 F22 **Ariamsvlei** Karas, SE Namibia 28°08′S 19°50′E
107 L17 **Ariano Irpino** Campania, S Italy 41°08′N 15°00′E
54 F11 **Ariari, Río** ≈ C Colombia
151 K19 **Ari Atoll** *var.* Alifu Atoll. *atoll* C Maldives
77 P11 **Aribinda** N Burkina 14°12′N 00°50′W
62 G2 **Arica** *hist.* San Marcos de Arica. Tarapacá, N Chile 18°31′S 70°18′W
54 H16 **Arica** Amazonas, S Colombia 02°09′S 71°48′W
62 G2 **Arica** ✈ Tarapacá, N Chile 18°30′S 70°20′W
114 E13 **Aridaía** *var.* Aridea, Aridhaía. Dytikí Makedonía, N Greece 40°59′N 22°04′E
Aridea *see* Aridaía
172 I15 **Aride, Île** *island* Inner Islands, NE Seychelles
Aridhaía *see* Aridaía
103 N17 **Ariège** ◆ *department* S France
102 M16 **Ariège** *var.* la Riege. ≈ Andorra/France
116 H11 **Arieș** ≈ W Romania
149 U10 **Ārifwāla** Punjab, E Pakistan 30°15′N 73°08′E
Ariguaní *see* El Difícil
138 G11 **Arīhā** Al Karak, W Jordan 31°25′N 35°47′E
138 I3 **Arīḥā** *var.* Arīhā. Idlib, W Syria 35°50′N 36°36′E
Arīhā *see* Arīḥā
Arīhā *see* Jericho
37 W4 **Arikaree River** ≈ Colorado/Nebraska, C USA
112 L13 **Arilje** Serbia, W Serbia 43°45′N 20°06′E
45 U14 **Arima** Trinidad, Trinidad and Tobago 10°38′N 61°17′W
Arime *see* Al 'Arīmah
Ariminum *see* Rimini
59 H16 **Arinos, Rio** ≈ W Brazil
40 M14 **Ario de Rosales** *var.* Ario de Rosáles. Michoacán, SW Mexico 19°12′N 101°42′W
Ario de Rosáles *see* Ario de Rosales
118 F12 **Ariogala** Kaunas, C Lithuania 55°16′N 23°30′E
47 T7 **Aripuanã** ≈ W Brazil
59 E15 **Ariquemes** Rondônia, W Brazil 09°55′S 63°06′W
121 W13 **'Arīsh, Wādi el** ≈ NE Egypt
54 K6 **Arismendi** Barinas, C Venezuela 08°29′N 68°22′W
10 J14 **Aristazabal Island** *island* SW Canada
60 F13 **Aristóbulo del Valle** Misiones, NE Argentina 27°09′S 54°54′W
172 I5 **Arivonimamo** ✈ (Antananarivo) Antananarivo, C Madagascar 19°00′S 47°11′E
Arixang *see* Wenquan
105 Q6 **Ariza** Aragón, NE Spain 41°19′N 02°03′W
62 I6 **Arizaro, Salar de** *salt lake* NW Argentina
105 O2 **Arizgoiti** *var.* Basauri. País Vasco, N Spain 43°13′N 02°54′W
62 K13 **Arizona** San Luis, C Argentina 35°44′S 65°16′W
36 J12 **Arizona** *off.* State of Arizona, *also known as* Copper State, Grand Canyon State. ◆ *state* SW USA
40 G4 **Arizpe** Sonora, NW Mexico 30°20′N 110°11′W
95 J16 **Årjäng** Värmland, C Sweden 59°24′N 12°09′E
143 P8 **Arjenān** Yazd, C Iran 32°19′N 53°48′E
92 I13 **Arjeplog** Norrbotten, N Sweden 66°04′N 18°E
54 E5 **Arjona** Bolívar, N Colombia 10°14′N 75°22′W
105 N13 **Arjona** Andalucía, S Spain 37°56′N 04°04′W
123 S10 **Arka** Khabarovskiy Kray, E Russian Federation 60°04′N 142°17′E
22 L2 **Arkabutla Lake** ⊠ Mississippi, S USA
127 O7 **Arkadak** Saratovskaya Oblast', W Russian Federation 51°55′N 43°29′E
27 T13 **Arkadelphia** Arkansas, C USA 34°07′N 93°06′W
115 J25 **Arkalochóri**; *prev.* Arkalokhórion. Kríti, Greece, E Mediterranean Sea 35°09′N 25°15′E
Arkalohori/Arkalokhórion *see* Arkalochóri
145 O10 **Arkalyk** *Kaz.* Arqalyq. Kostanay, N Kazakhstan 50°17′N 66°51′E
27 U10 **Arkansas** *off.* State of Arkansas, *also known as* The Land of Opportunity. ◆ *state* S USA
27 W14 **Arkansas City** Arkansas, C USA 33°36′N 91°12′W
27 O7 **Arkansas City** Kansas, C USA 37°03′N 97°02′W
16 K11 **Arkansas River** ≈ C USA
182 J5 **Arkaroola** South Australia 30°21′S 139°20′E
Arkhángelos *see* Archángelos
124 L8 **Arkhangel'sk** *Eng.* Archangel. Arkhangel'skaya Oblast', NW Russian Federation 64°32′N 40°40′E
124 L9 **Arkhangel'skaya Oblast'** ◆ *province* NW Russian Federation
127 O14 **Arkhangel'skoye** Stavropol'skiy Kray, SW Russian Federation 44°37′N 44°03′E
123 R14 **Arkhara** Amurskaya Oblast', S Russian Federation 49°20′N 130°04′E
97 G19 **Arklow** *Ir.* An tInbhear Mór. SE Ireland 52°48′N 06°09′W
115 M20 **Arkoí** *island* Dodekánisa, Greece, Aegean Sea
27 R11 **Arkoma** Oklahoma, C USA 35°19′N 94°27′W
100 O7 **Arkona, Kap** *headland* NE Germany 54°40′N 13°24′E
95 N17 **Arkösund** Östergötland, S Sweden 58°28′N 16°55′E
122 J6 **Arkticheskogo Instituta, Ostrova** *island* N Russian Federation
95 O15 **Arlanda** ✈ (Stockholm) Stockholm, C Sweden 59°40′N 17°58′E
146 C11 **Arlandag** *Rus.* Gora Arlan. ▲ W Turkmenistan 39°39′N 54°28′E
Arlan, Gora *see* Arlandag
105 O5 **Arlanza** ≈ N Spain
105 N5 **Arlanzón** ≈ N Spain
103 R15 **Arles** *var.* Arles-sur-Rhône; *anc.* Arelas, Arelate. Bouches-du-Rhône, SE France 43°41′N 04°38′E
Arles-sur-Rhône *see* Arles
103 O17 **Arles-sur-Tech** Pyrénées-Orientales, S France 42°27′N 02°37′E
29 U9 **Arlington** Minnesota, N USA 44°36′N 94°04′W
29 R15 **Arlington** Nebraska, C USA 41°27′N 96°21′W
32 J11 **Arlington** Oregon, NW USA 45°43′N 120°10′W
29 R10 **Arlington** South Dakota, N USA 44°21′N 97°07′W
20 E10 **Arlington** Tennessee, S USA 35°17′N 89°40′W
25 T6 **Arlington** Texas, SW USA 32°44′N 97°05′W
21 W4 **Arlington** Virginia, NE USA 38°54′N 77°09′W
32 H7 **Arlington** Washington, NW USA 48°12′N 122°07′W
30 M10 **Arlington Heights** Illinois, N USA 42°08′N 88°03′W
77 U8 **Arlit** Agadez, C Niger 18°54′N 07°25′E
99 L24 **Arlon** *Dut.* Aarlen, *Ger.* Arel, *Lat.* Orolaunum. Luxembourg, SE Belgium 49°41′N 05°49′E
27 R7 **Arma** Kansas, C USA 37°32′N 94°42′W
97 F16 **Armagh** *Ir.* Ard Mhacha. S Northern Ireland, United Kingdom 54°15′N 06°33′W
97 F16 **Armagh** *cultural region* S Northern Ireland, United Kingdom
102 K15 **Armagnac** *cultural region* S France
103 Q7 **Armançon** ≈ C France
60 K10 **Armando Laydner, Represa** ⊠ S Brazil
115 M24 **Armathía** *island* SE Greece
137 T12 **Armavir** *prev.* Hoktemberyan, *Rus.* Oktemberyan. SW Armenia 40°09′N 43°58′E
126 M14 **Armavir** Krasnodarskiy Kray, SW Russian Federation 44°59′N 41°07′E
54 E10 **Armenia** Quindío, W Colombia 04°32′N 75°40′W
137 T12 **Armenia** *off.* Republic of Armenia, *var.* Ajastan, *Arm.* Hayastani Hanrapetut'yun; *prev.* Armenian Soviet Socialist Republic. ◆ *republic* SW Asia
Armenian Soviet Socialist Republic *see* Armenia
Armenia, Republic of *see* Armenia
Armenierstadt *see* Gherla
103 O1 **Armentières** Nord, N France 50°41′N 02°53′E
40 K14 **Armería** Colima, SW Mexico 18°55′N 103°59′W
183 T5 **Armidale** New South Wales, SE Australia 30°32′S 151°40′E
29 P11 **Armour** South Dakota, N USA 43°19′N 98°21′W
61 B18 **Armstrong** Santa Fe, C Argentina 32°46′S 61°39′W
11 N16 **Armstrong** British Columbia, SW Canada 50°27′N 119°14′W
12 D11 **Armstrong** Ontario, S Canada 50°20′N 89°02′W
29 U11 **Armstrong** Iowa, C USA 43°24′N 94°28′W
25 S16 **Armstrong** Texas, SW USA 26°55′N 97°47′W
117 S11 **Armyans'k** *Rus.* Armyansk. Respublika Krym, S Ukraine 46°05′N 33°43′E
115 H14 **Arnaía** *Cont.* Arnea. Kentrikí Makedonía, N Greece 40°30′N 23°36′E
121 N2 **Arnaoúti, Akrotíri** *var.* Arnaoútis, Cape Arnaouti. *headland* W Cyprus 35°06′N 32°16′E
Arnaouti, Cape/Arnaoútis *see* Arnaoúti, Akrotíri
12 L4 **Arnaud** ≈ Québec, E Canada
103 Q8 **Arnay-le-Duc** Côte d'Or, C France 47°08′N 04°27′E
Arnea *see* Arnaía
105 Q4 **Arnedo** La Rioja, N Spain 42°14′N 02°05′W
95 I14 **Årnes** Akershus, S Norway 60°07′N 11°28′E
Årnes *see* Åi Åfjord
26 K9 **Arnett** Oklahoma, C USA 36°08′N 99°46′W
98 L12 **Arnhem** Gelderland, SE Netherlands 51°59′N 05°54′E
181 Q2 **Arnhem Land** *physical region* Northern Territory, N Australia
106 F11 **Arno** ≈ C Italy
Arno *see* Arno Atoll
189 W7 **Arno Atoll** *var.* Arno. *atoll* Ratak Chain, NE Marshall Islands
182 H8 **Arno Bay** South Australia 33°55′S 136°31′E
35 Q8 **Arnold** California, W USA 38°15′N 120°19′W
27 X5 **Arnold** Missouri, C USA 38°25′N 90°22′W
29 N15 **Arnold** Nebraska, C USA 41°25′N 100°11′W
109 R10 **Arnoldstein** *Slvn.* Pod Klošter. Kärnten, S Austria 46°34′N 13°43′E
103 N9 **Arnon** ≈ C France
45 P14 **Arnos Vale** ✈ (Kingstown) Saint Vincent, SE Saint Vincent and the Grenadines 13°08′N 61°13′W
92 I8 **Arnøya** *Lapp.* Árdni. *island* N Norway
14 L12 **Arnprior** Ontario, SE Canada 45°31′N 76°11′W
101 G15 **Arnsberg** Nordrhein-Westfalen, W Germany 51°24′N 08°04′E
101 K16 **Arnstadt** Thüringen, C Germany 50°50′N 10°57′E
Arnswalde *see* Choszczno
54 K5 **Aroa** Yaracuy, N Venezuela 10°26′N 68°54′W
83 E21 **Aroab** Karas, SE Namibia 26°47′S 19°40′E
Ároania *see* Chelmós
191 O6 **Aroa, Pointe** *headland* Moorea, W French Polynesia 17°27′S 149°45′W
Aroe Islands *see* Aru, Kepulauan
101 H15 **Arolsen** Niedersachsen, C Germany 51°23′N 09°00′E
106 C7 **Arona** Piemonte, NE Italy 45°45′N 08°33′E
19 R3 **Aroostook River** ≈ Canada/USA
Arop Island *see* Long Island
38 M12 **Aropuk Lake** ◎ Alaska, USA
191 P4 **Arorae** *atoll* Tungaru, W Kiribati
190 G16 **Arorangi** Rarotonga, S Cook Islands 21°13′S 159°49′W
108 I9 **Arosa** Graubünden, S Switzerland 46°48′N 09°42′E
104 F4 **Arousa, Ría de** *estuary* E Atlantic Ocean
184 P8 **Arowhana** ▲ North Island, New Zealand 38°07′S 177°52′E
137 V12 **Arp'a** *Az.* Arpaçay. ≈ Armenia/Azerbaijan
137 S11 **Arpaçay** Kars, NE Turkey 40°51′N 43°20′E
Arpaçay *see* Arp'a
Arqalyq *see* Arkalyk
149 N14 **Arra** ≈ SW Pakistan
Arrabona *see* Győr
Arrah *see* Āra
Ar Rahad *see* Er Rahad
139 R9 **Ar Raḥḥālīyah** Al Anbār, C Iraq 32°53′N 43°21′E
60 Q10 **Arraial do Cabo** Rio de Janeiro, SE Brazil 22°57′S 42°00′W
104 H11 **Arraiolos** Évora, S Portugal 38°44′N 07°59′W
139 R8 **Ar Ramādī** *var.* Ramadi, Rumadiya. Al Anbār, SW Iraq 33°27′N 43°19′E
138 J6 **Ar Rāmī** Ḥimṣ, C Syria 34°32′N 37°54′E
Ar Rams *see* Rams
138 H9 **Ar Ramthā** *var.* Ramtha. Irbid, N Jordan 32°34′N 36°00′E
96 H13 **Arran, Isle of** *island* SW Scotland, United Kingdom
138 L3 **Ar Raqqah** *var.* Rakka; *anc.* Nicephorium. Ar Raqqah, N Syria 35°57′N 39°03′E
138 L3 **Ar Raqqah** *off.* Muḥāfaẓat al Raqqah, *var.* Raqqah, *Fr.* Rakka. ◆ *governorate* N Syria
103 O2 **Arras** *anc.* Nemetocenna. Pas-de-Calais, N France 50°17′N 02°46′E
105 P3 **Arrasate** *Cast.* Mondragón. País Vasco, N Spain 43°04′N 02°30′W
138 G12 **Ar Rashādīyah** Aṭ ṭafilah, W Jordan 30°42′N 35°38′E
138 I5 **Ar Rastān** *var.* Rastâne. Ḥimṣ, W Syria 34°57′N 36°43′E
139 X12 **Ar Raṭāwī** Al Baṣrah, E Iraq 30°37′N 47°12′E
102 L15 **Arrats** ≈ S France
141 N10 **Ar Rawḍah** Makkah, S Saudi Arabia 21°19′N 42°48′E
141 Q15 **Ar Rawḍah** S Yemen 14°26′N 47°14′E
142 K11 **Ar Rawḍatayn** *var.* Raudhatain. N Kuwait 29°80′N 47°50′E
143 N16 **Ar Rayyān** *var.* Al Rayyan. C Qatar 25°18′N 51°29′E
102 L17 **Arreau** Hautes-Pyrénées, S France 42°55′N 00°21′E
64 Q11 **Arrecife** *var.* Arrecife de Lanzarote, Puerto Arrecife. Lanzarote, Islas Canarias, NE Atlantic Ocean 28°57′N 13°33′W
Arrecife de Lanzarote *see* Arrecife
43 P6 **Arrecife Edinburgh** *reef* NE Nicaragua
61 C19 **Arrecifes** Buenos Aires, E Argentina 34°06′S 60°09′W
102 F6 **Arrée, Monts d'** ▲▲ NW France
Ar Refā'ī *see* Ar Rifā'ī
Arretium *see* Arezzo
Arriaca *see* Guadalajara
109 S9 **Arriach** Kärnten, S Austria 46°43′N 13°52′E
41 T16 **Arriaga** Chiapas, SE Mexico 16°14′N 93°54′W
41 N12 **Arriaga** San Luis Potosí, C Mexico 21°55′N 101°23′W
139 W10 **Ar Rifā'ī** *var.* Ar Refā'ī. Dhī Qār, SE Iraq 31°47′N 46°07′E
139 V12 **Ar Riḥāb** *salt flat* S Iraq
104 L2 **Arriondas** Asturias, N Spain 43°23′N 05°11′W
141 Q7 **Ar Riyāḍ** *Eng.* Riyadh. ● (Saudi Arabia) Ar Riyāḍ, C Saudi Arabia 24°50′N 46°50′E
141 O8 **Ar Riyāḍ** *off.* Minṭaqat ar Riyāḍ. ◆ *province* C Saudi Arabia
141 S15 **Ar Riyān** S Yemen 14°43′N 49°18′E
Arrö *see* Ærø
61 H18 **Arroio Grande** Rio Grande do Sul, S Brazil 32°15′S 53°02′W
102 K15 **Arros** ≈ S France
103 Q9 **Arroux** ≈ C France
25 R5 **Arrowhead, Lake** ⊠ Texas, SW USA
182 L5 **Arrowsmith, Mount** *hill* New South Wales, SE Australia
185 D21 **Arrowtown** Otago, South Island, New Zealand 44°57′S 168°51′E
61 D17 **Arroyo Barú** Entre Ríos, E Argentina 31°52′S 58°26′W
104 J10 **Arroyo de la Luz** Extremadura, W Spain 39°28′N 06°36′W
63 J16 **Arroyo de la Ventana** Río Negro, SE Argentina 41°41′S 66°03′W
35 P13 **Arroyo Grande** California, W USA 35°07′N 120°35′W
Ar Ru'ays *see* Ar Ruways
141 R11 **Ar Rub 'al Khālī** *Eng.* Empty Quarter, Great Sandy Desert. *desert* SW Asia
139 V13 **Ar Ruḍaymah** Al Muthannā, S Iraq 30°20′N 45°26′E
61 A16 **Arrufó** Santa Fe, C Argentina 30°15′S 61°45′W
138 I7 **Ar Ruḥaybah** *var.* Ruhaybeh, *Fr.* Rouhaïbé. Dimashq, W Syria 33°45′N 36°40′E
139 V15 **Ar Rukhaymīyah** *well* S Iraq
139 U11 **Ar Rumaythah** *var.* Rumaitha. Al Muthannā, S Iraq 31°31′N 45°15′E
141 X8 **Ar Rustāq** *var.* Rostak, Rustaq. N Oman 23°34′N 57°25′E
139 N8 **Ar Ruṭbah** *var.* Rutba. Al Anbār, SW Iraq 33°03′N 40°16′E
140 M3 **Ar Rūthīyah** *spring/well* NW Saudi Arabia 31°18′N 41°23′E
ar-Ruwaida *see* Ar Ruwayḍah
141 O8 **Ar Ruwayḍah** *var.* ar-Ruwaida. Jīzān, C Saudi Arabia 23°48′N 44°44′E
143 N15 **Ar Ruways** *var.* Al Ruweis, Ar Ru'ays, Ruwais. N Qatar 26°08′N 51°13′E
143 O17 **Ar Ruways** *var.* Ar Ru'ays. Abū Ẓaby, W United Arab Emirates 24°09′N 52°57′E
Års *see* Aars
Arsanias *see* Murat Nehri
123 S15 **Arsen'yev** Primorskiy Kray, SE Russian Federation 44°09′N 133°28′E
155 G19 **Arsikere** Karnātaka, W India 13°20′N 76°13′E
127 R3 **Arsk** Respublika Tatarstan, W Russian Federation 56°07′N 49°54′E
94 N10 **Årskogen** Gävleborg, C Sweden 62°07′N 17°19′E
121 O3 **Ársos** C Cyprus 34°51′N 32°46′E
94 N13 **Årsunda** Gävleborg, C Sweden 60°31′N 16°45′E
115 C17 **Árta** *anc.* Ambracia. Ípeiros, W Greece 39°08′N 20°59′E
105 Y9 **Artà** Mallorca, Spain, W Mediterranean Sea 39°42′N 03°20′E
Arta *see* Árachthos
137 T12 **Artashat** S Armenia 39°57′N 44°34′E
40 M15 **Arteaga** Michoacán, SW Mexico 18°22′N 102°18′W
123 S15 **Artem** Primorskiy Kray, SE Russian Federation 43°24′N 132°20′E
44 C4 **Artemisa** La Habana, W Cuba 22°49′N 82°47′W
117 W7 **Artemivs'k** Donets'ka Oblast', E Ukraine 48°35′N 37°58′E
122 K13 **Artemovsk** Krasnoyarskiy Kray, S Russian Federation 54°22′N 93°24′E
105 U5 **Artesa de Segre** Cataluña, NE Spain 41°54′N 01°03′E
37 U14 **Artesia** New Mexico, SW USA 32°50′N 104°24′W
25 Q14 **Artesia Wells** Texas, SW USA 28°13′N 99°18′W
108 G8 **Arth** Schwyz, C Switzerland 47°05′N 08°39′E
14 F15 **Arthur** Ontario, S Canada 43°49′N 80°31′W
30 M14 **Arthur** Illinois, N USA 39°42′N 88°28′W
28 L14 **Arthur** Nebraska, C USA 41°35′N 101°42′W
29 Q5 **Arthur** North Dakota, N USA 47°03′N 97°12′W
185 B21 **Arthur** ≈ South Island, New Zealand
18 B13 **Arthur, Lake** ⊠ Pennsylvania, NE USA
183 N15 **Arthur River** ≈ Tasmania, SE Australia
185 G18 **Arthur's Pass** Canterbury, South Island, New Zealand 42°59′S 171°33′E
185 G17 **Arthur's Pass** *pass* South Island, New Zealand
44 I3 **Arthur's Town** Cat Island, C Bahamas 24°34′N 75°39′W
44 M9 **Artibonite, Rivière de l'** ≈ C Haiti
61 E16 **Artigas** *prev.* San Eugenio, San Eugenio del Cuareim. Artigas, N Uruguay 30°25′S 56°28′W
61 E16 **Artigas** ◆ *department* N Uruguay
194 H1 **Artigas** *Uruguayan research station* Antarctica 61°57′S 58°23′W
137 T11 **Art'ik** W Armenia 40°38′N 43°58′E
187 O16 **Art, Île** *island* Îles Belep, W New Caledonia
103 O2 **Artois** *cultural region* N France
136 L12 **Artova** Tokat, N Turkey 40°04′N 36°17′E
105 Y9 **Artrutx, Cap d'** *var.* Cabo Dartuch. *cape* Menorca, Spain, W Mediterranean Sea
Artsiz *see* Artsyz
117 N11 **Artsyz** *Rus.* Artsiz. Odes'ka Oblast', SW Ukraine 45°59′N 29°26′E
158 E7 **Artux** Xinjiang Uygur Zizhiqu, NW China 39°40′N 76°10′E
137 R11 **Artvin** Artvin, NE Turkey 41°12′N 41°48′E
137 R11 **Artvin** ◆ *province* NE Turkey
146 G14 **Artyk** Ahal Welaýaty, C Turkmenistan 37°32′N 59°16′E
79 Q16 **Aru** Orientale, NE Dem. Rep. Congo 02°53′N 30°50′E
81 E17 **Arua** NW Uganda 03°02′N 30°56′E
104 I4 **A Rúa de Valdeorras** *var.* La Rúa. Galicia, NW Spain 42°22′N 07°12′W
Aruângua *see* Luangwa
45 O15 **Aruba** *var.* Oruba. ◇ *Dutch autonomous region* S West Indies
47 Q4 **Aruba** *island* Aruba, Lesser Antilles
Aru Islands *see* Aru, Kepulauan
171 W15 **Aru, Kepulauan** *Eng.* Aru Islands; *prev.* Aroe Islands. *island group* E Indonesia
153 W10 **Arunāchal Pradesh** *prev.* North East Frontier Agency, North East Frontier Agency of Assam. ◆ *state* NE India
Arun Qi *see* Naji
155 H23 **Aruppukkottai** Tamil Nādu, SE India 09°31′N 78°03′E
81 I20 **Arusha** Arusha, N Tanzania 03°23′S 36°40′E
81 I21 **Arusha** ◆ *region* E Tanzania
81 I20 **Arusha** ✈ Arusha, N Tanzania 03°26′S 37°07′E
54 C9 **Arusí, Punta** *headland* NW Colombia 05°36′N 77°30′W
155 J23 **Aruvi Aru** ≈ NW Sri Lanka
79 M17 **Aruwimi** *var.* Ituri (upper course). ≈ NE Dem. Rep. Congo
Árva *see* Orava
37 T4 **Arvada** Colorado, C USA 39°48′N 105°06′W
Arvand Rūd *see* 'Arab, Shaṭṭ al
162 J8 **Arvayheer** Övörhangay, C Mongolia 46°13′N 102°47′E
9 O10 **Arviat** *prev.* Eskimo Point. Nunavut, C Canada 61°10′N 94°15′W
93 I14 **Arvidsjaur** Norrbotten, N Sweden 65°34′N 19°12′E
95 J15 **Arvika** Värmland, C Sweden 59°41′N 12°38′E
92 J8 **Årviksand** Troms, N Norway 70°10′N 20°30′E
35 S13 **Arvin** California, W USA 35°12′N 118°52′W
163 S8 **Arxan** Nei Mongol Zizhiqu, N China 47.11N 119.58′E
145 P7 **Arykbalyk** *Kaz.* Aryqbalyq. Severnyy Kazakhstan, N Kazakhstan 53°00′N 68°11′E
Aryqbalyq *see* Arykbalyk
145 P17 **Arys'** *Kaz.* Arys. Yuzhnyy Kazakhstan, S Kazakhstan 42°26′N 68°49′E
Arys *see* Arys'
Arys *see* Orzysz
Arys Köli *see* Arys, Ozero
145 O14 **Arys, Ozero** *Kaz.* Arys Köli. ◎ C Kazakhstan
107 D16 **Arzachena** Sardegna, Italy, C Mediterranean Sea 41°05′N 09°21′E
127 O4 **Arzamas** Nizhegorodskaya Oblast', W Russian Federation 55°25′N 43°51′E
141 V13 **Arzāt** S Oman 17°00′N 54°18′E
104 H3 **Arzúa** Galicia, NW Spain 42°55′N 08°10′W
111 A16 **Aš** *Ger.* Asch. Karlovarský Kraj, W Czech Republic 50°18′N 12°12′E
95 H15 **Ås** Akershus, S Norway 59°40′N 10°50′E
Åsa *see* Asaa
95 H20 **Asaa** *var.* Åsa. Nordjylland, N Denmark 57°07′N 10°24′E
83 E21 **Asab** Karas, S Namibia 25°29′S 17°59′E
77 U16 **Asaba** Delta, S Nigeria 06°10′N 06°44′E
76 J10 **Assaba** *var.* Açâba. ◆ *region* S Mauritania
149 S4 **Asadābād** *var.* Asadābād; *prev.* Chaghasarāy. Konar, E Afghanistan 34°52′N 71°09′E
Asadābād *see* Asadābād
138 K3 **Asad, Buḥayrat al** *Eng.* Lake Assad. ◎ N Syria
63 H20 **Asador, Pampa del** *plain* S Argentina
165 P14 **Asahi** Chiba, Honshū, S Japan 35°43′N 140°38′E
164 M11 **Asahi** Toyama, Honshū, SW Japan 36°56′N 137°34′E
165 T13 **Asahi-dake** ▲ Hokkaidō, N Japan 43°42′N 142°50′E
165 T3 **Asahikawa** Hokkaidō, N Japan 43°46′N 142°23′E
147 S10 **Asaka** *Rus.* Assake; *prev.* Leninsk. Andijon Viloyati, E Uzbekistan 40°39′N 72°16′E
77 P17 **Asamankese** SE Ghana 05°47′N 00°41′W
188 B15 **Asan** W Guam 13°28′N 144°43′E
188 B15 **Asan Point** *headland* W Guam
153 R15 **Āsānsol** West Bengal, NE India 23°40′N 86°59′E
80 K12 **Āsayita** Āfar, NE Ethiopia 11°35′S 41°23′E
171 T12 **Asbakin** Papua, E Indonesia 0°45′S 131°40′E
Asben *see* Aïr, Massif de l'
15 Q12 **Asbestos** Québec, SE Canada 45°46′N 71°56′W
29 Y13 **Asbury** Iowa, C USA 42°30′N 90°45′W
18 K15 **Asbury Park** New Jersey, NE USA 40°13′N 74°00′W
41 Z12 **Ascención, Bahiá de la** *bay* NW Caribbean Sea
40 I3 **Ascensión** Chihuahua, N Mexico 31°07′N 107°59′W
65 M14 **Ascension Fracture Zone** *tectonic feature* C Atlantic Ocean
65 G14 **Ascension Island** ◇ *dependency of St.Helena* C Atlantic Ocean
65 N16 **Ascension Island** *island* C Atlantic Ocean
Asch *see* Aš
109 S3 **Aschach an der Donau** Oberösterreich, N Austria 48°22′N 14°00′E
101 H18 **Aschaffenburg** Bayern, SW Germany 49°58′N 09°10′E
101 F14 **Ascheberg** Nordrhein-Westfalen, W Germany 51°46′N 07°36′E
101 L14 **Aschersleben** Sachsen-Anhalt, C Germany 51°46′N 11°28′E
106 G12 **Asciano** Toscana, C Italy 43°15′N 11°32′E
106 J13 **Ascoli Piceno** *anc.* Asculum Picenum. Marche, C Italy 42°51′N 13°34′E
107 M17 **Ascoli Satriano** *anc.* Asculub, Ausculum Apulum. Puglia, SE Italy 41°13′N 15°32′E
108 G11 **Ascona** Ticino, S Switzerland 46°10′N 08°45′E
Asculub *see* Ascoli Satriano
Asculum Picenum *see* Ascoli Piceno
80 L11 **'Aseb** *var.* Assab, *Amh.* Āseb. SE Eritrea 13°04′N 42°36′E
95 M20 **Åseda** Kronoberg, S Sweden 57°10′N 15°20′E
127 T6 **Asekeyevo** Orenburgskaya Oblast', W Russian Federation 53°36′N 52°53′E
81 J14 **Āsela** *var.* Asella, Aselle, Asselle. Oromīya, C Ethiopia 07°55′N 39°08′E
93 H15 **Åsele** Västerbotten, N Sweden 64°10′N 17°20′E
Asella/Aselle *see* Āsela
98 N7 **Assen** Drenthe, NE Netherlands 53°00′N 06°34′E
94 K12 **Åsen** Dalarna, C Sweden 61°18′N 13°49′E
114 J11 **Asenovgrad** *prev.* Stanimaka. Plovdiv, C Bulgaria 42°00′N 24°53′E
171 O13 **Asera** Sulawesi, C Indonesia 03°24′S 121°42′E
95 E17 **Åseral** Vest-Agder, S Norway 58°37′N 07°27′E
118 J3 **Aseri** *Ger.* Asserin. Ida-Virumaa, NE Estonia 59°29′N 26°51′E
40 J10 **Aserradero** Durango, W Mexico
146 F13 **Aşgabat** *prev.* Ashgabat, Ashkhabad, Poltoratsk. ● (Turkmenistan) Ahal Welaýaty, C Turkmenistan 37°58′N 58°22′E
146 F13 **Aşgabat** ✈ Ahal Welaýaty, C Turkmenistan 38°06′N 58°10′E
95 H16 **Åsgårdstrand** Vestfold, S Norway 59°22′N 10°27′E
Ashara *see* Al 'Ashārah
23 T6 **Ashburn** Georgia, SE USA 31°42′N 83°39′W
185 G19 **Ashburton** Canterbury, South Island, New Zealand 43°55′S 171°47′E
185 G19 **Ashburton** ≈ South Island, New Zealand
180 H8 **Ashburton River** ≈ Western Australia
145 V10 **Ashchysu** ≈ E Kazakhstan
10 M16 **Ashcroft** British Columbia, SW Canada 50°41′N 121°17′W
138 E10 **Ashdod** *anc.* Azotos, *Lat.* Azotus. Central, W Israel 31°48′N 34°38′E
27 S14 **Ashdown** Arkansas, C USA 33°40′N 94°09′W
21 T9 **Asheboro** North Carolina, SE USA 35°42′N 79°50′W
11 X15 **Ashern** Manitoba, S Canada 51°10′N 98°22′W
21 P10 **Asheville** North Carolina, SE USA 35°36′N 82°33′W
12 E8 **Asheweig** ≈ Ontario, C Canada
27 V9 **Ash Flat** Arkansas, C USA 36°13′N 91°36′W
183 T4 **Ashford** New South Wales, SE Australia 29°18′S 151°09′E
97 P22 **Ashford** SE England, United Kingdom 51°09′N 00°52′E
36 K11 **Ash Fork** Arizona, SW USA 35°12′N 112°31′W
Ashgabat *see* Aşgabat
27 T7 **Ash Grove** Missouri, C USA 37°19′N 93°35′W
165 O12 **Ashikaga** *var.* Asikaga. Tochigi, Honshū, S Japan 36°21′N 139°26′E
165 Q8 **Ashiro** Iwate, Honshū, C Japan 40°04′N 141°00′E
164 F15 **Ashizuri-misaki** Shikoku, SW Japan
138 E10 **Ashkelon** *prev.* Ashqelon. Southern, C Israel 31°40′N 34°35′E
143 P9 **Ashkeẓar** Yazd, C Iran 31°56′N 54°16′E
Ashkhabad *see* Aşgabat
23 Q4 **Ashland** Alabama, S USA 33°16′N 85°50′W
26 K7 **Ashland** Kansas, C USA 37°12′N 99°47′W
21 P5 **Ashland** Kentucky, S USA 38°28′N 82°40′W
19 S2 **Ashland** Maine, NE USA 46°36′N 68°24′W
22 M1 **Ashland** Mississippi, S USA 34°51′N 89°10′W
27 U4 **Ashland** Missouri, C USA 38°46′N 92°15′W
29 S15 **Ashland** Nebraska, C USA 41°01′N 96°21′W
31 T12 **Ashland** Ohio, N USA 40°52′N 82°19′W
32 G15 **Ashland** Oregon, NW USA 42°11′N 122°42′W
21 W6 **Ashland** Virginia, NE USA 37°45′N 77°28′W
30 K3 **Ashland** Wisconsin, N USA 46°34′N 90°54′W
20 I8 **Ashland City** Tennessee, S USA 36°16′N 87°05′W
183 S4 **Ashley** New South Wales, SE Australia 29°21′S 149°49′E
29 O7 **Ashley** North Dakota, N USA 46°00′N 99°22′W
173 W7 **Ashmore and Cartier Islands** ◇ *Australian external territory* E Indian Ocean
119 I14 **Ashmyany** *Rus.* Oshmyany. Hrodzyenskaya Voblasts', W Belarus 54°24′N 25°57′E
18 K12 **Ashokan Reservoir** ⊠ New York, NE USA
165 U4 **Ashoro** Hokkaidō, NE Japan 43°16′N 143°33′E
Ashqelon *see* Ashkelon
Ashraf *see* Behshahr
139 O3 **Ash Shadādah** *var.* Ash Shadadah, Jisr ash Shadadi, Shaddādī, Shedadi, Tell Shedadi. Al Ḥasakah, NE Syria 36°00′N 40°42′E
Ash Shaddādah *see* Ash Shadādah
139 Y12 **Ash Shāfī** Al Baṣrah, E Iraq 30°49′N 47°30′E
139 R4 **Ash Shakk** *var.* Shaykh. Ṣalāḥ ad Dīn, C Iraq 35°15′N 43°27′E
Ash Sham/Ash Shām *see* Dimashq
139 T10 **Ash Shāmīyah** *var.* Shamiya. Al Qādisīyah, C Iraq 31°56′N 44°37′E
139 Y13 **Ash Shāmīyah** *var.* Al Bādiyah al Janūbīyah. *desert* S Iraq
139 T11 **Ash Shanāfīyah** *var.* Ash Shināfīyah. Al Qādisīyah, S Iraq 31°35′N 44°38′E
138 G13 **Ash Sharāh** *var.* Esh Sharā. ▲▲ W Jordan
143 R16 **Ash Shāriqah** *Eng.* Sharjah. Ash Shāriqah, NE United Arab Emirates 25°22′N 55°28′E
143 R16 **Ash Shāriqah** *var.* Sharjah. ✈ Ash Shāriqah, NE United Arab Emirates 25°19′N 55°37′E
140 I4 **Ash Sharmah** *var.* Šarma. Tabūk, NW Saudi Arabia 28°02′N 35°16′E
139 R4 **Ash Sharqāṭ** Nīnawýa, NW Iraq 35°31′N 43°15′E
141 S10 **Ash Sharqīyah** *off.* Al Minṭaqah ash Sharqīyah, *Eng.* Eastern Region. ◆ *province* E Saudi Arabia
Ash Sharqīyah *see* Al 'Ubaylah
139 W11 **Ash Shaṭrah** *var.* Shatra. Dhī Qār, SE Iraq 31°26′N 46°10′E
138 G13 **Ash Shawbak** Ma'ān, W Jordan 30°32′N 35°34′E
138 L5 **Ash Shaykh Ibrāhīm** Ḥimṣ, C Syria 35°03′N 38°50′E
141 O17 **Ash Shaykh 'Uthmān** SW Yemen 12°53′N 45°00′E
141 S15 **Ash Shiḥr** SE Yemen 14°45′N 49°24′E
Ash Shināfīyah *see* Ash Shanāfīyah
141 V12 **Ash Shiṣar** *var.* Shisur. SW Oman 18°13′N 53°35′E
139 S13 **Ash Shubrūm** *well* S Iraq
141 R10 **Ash Shuqqān** *desert* E Saudi Arabia
75 O9 **Ash Shuwayrif** *var.* Ash Shwayrif. N Libya 29°54′N 14°16′E
Ash Shwayrif *see* Ash Shuwayrif
31 U10 **Ashtabula** Ohio, N USA 41°54′N 80°46′W
29 Q5 **Ashtabula, Lake** ⊠ North Dakota, N USA
137 T12 **Ashtarak** W Armenia 40°18′N 44°22′E
142 M6 **Āshtīān** *var.* Āshtiyān. Markazī, W Iran 34°23′N 49°55′E
Āshtiyān *see* Āshtīān
33 R13 **Ashton** Idaho, NW USA 44°04′N 111°27′W
13 O10 **Ashuanipi Lake** ◎ Newfoundland and Labrador, E Canada
15 P6 **Ashuapmushuan** ≈ Québec, SE Canada
23 Q3 **Ashville** Alabama, S USA 33°50′N 86°15′W
31 S14 **Ashville** Ohio, N USA 39°43′N 82°57′W
30 K3 **Ashwabay, Mount** *hill* Wisconsin, N USA
128-129 **Asia** *continent*
171 T11 **Asia, Kepulauan** *island group* E Indonesia
154 N13 **Āsika** Orissa, E India 19°38′N 84°41′E
Asikaga *see* Ashikaga
93 M18 **Asikkala** *var.* Vääksy. Etelä-Suomi, S Finland 61°09′N 25°36′E
74 G5 **Asilah** N Morocco 35°32′N 06°04′W
'Aṣī, Nahr al *see* Orontes
107 B16 **Asinara, Isola** *island* W Italy
122 J12 **Asino** Tomskaya Oblast', C Russian Federation 56°56′N 86°02′E

◆ Country ● Country Capital ◇ Dependent Territory ○ Dependent Territory Capital ◆ Administrative Regions ✈ International Airport ▲ Mountain ▲▲ Mountain Range 𝕍 Volcano ≈ River ◎ Lake ⊠ Reservoir
219

ASINTORF – AVARUA HARBOUR

119 O14 Asintorf Rus. Osintorf. N Belarus 54°43′N 30°35′E
119 L17 Asipovichy Rus. Osipovichi. Mahilyowskaya Voblasts', C Belarus 53°18′N 28°40′E
141 N12 'Asīr off. Mintaqat 'Asīr. ◈ province SW Saudi Arabia
140 M11 'Asīr Eng. Asir. ▲▲ SW Saudi Arabia
'Asīr, Mintaqat see 'Asīr
139 X10 Askal Maysān, E Iraq 31°45′N 47°07′E
137 P13 Aşkale Erzurum, NE Turkey 39°56′N 40°39′E
117 T11 Askaniya-Nova Khersons'ka Oblast', S Ukraine 46°27′N 33°54′E
95 H15 Asker Akershus, S Norway 59°52′N 10°26′E
95 L17 Askersund Örebro, C Sweden 58°55′N 14°55′E
Askī Kalak see Eski Kaļak
95 I15 Askim Østfold, S Norway 59°15′N 11°10′E
127 V3 Askino Respublika Bashkortostan, W Russian Federation 56°07′N 56°39′E
115 D14 Áskio ▲▲ N Greece
152 L9 Askot Uttarakhand, N India 29°44′N 80°20′E
94 C12 Askvoll Sogn Og Fjordane, S Norway 61°21′N 05°04′E
136 A13 Aslan Burnu headland W Turkey 38°44′N 26°43′E
136 L16 Aslantaş Barajı ⊠ S Turkey
149 S4 Asmār var. Bar Kunar. Kunar, E Afghanistan 34°59′N 71°29′E
Asmara see Asmera
80 I9 Asmera var. Asmara. ● (Eritrea) C Eritrea 15°15′N 38°58′E
95 L21 Åsnen ◎ S Sweden
115 F19 Asopós ≈ S Greece
171 W13 Asori Papua, E Indonesia 02°37′S 136°06′E
80 G12 Āsosa Binishangul Gumuz, W Ethiopia 10°06′N 34°27′E
32 M10 Asotin Washington, NW USA 46°18′N 117°03′W
Aspadana see Eşfahān
Aspang see Aspang Markt
109 X6 Aspang Markt var. Aspang. Niederösterreich, E Austria 47°34′N 16°06′E
105 S12 Aspe País Valenciano, E Spain 38°21′N 00°43′W
37 R5 Aspen Colorado, C USA 39°12′N 106°49′W
25 P6 Aspermont Texas, SW USA 33°08′N 100°14′W
Asphaltites, Lacus see Dead Sea
Aspinwall see Colón
185 C20 Aspiring, Mount ▲ South Island, New Zealand 44°21′S 168°47′E
115 B16 Asprókavos, Akrotírio headland Kérkyra, Iónia Nisiá, Greece, C Mediterranean Sea 39°22′N 20°07′E
Aspropótamos see Achelóos
Assab see 'Aseb
138 L4 As Sabkhah var. Sabkha. Ar Raqqah, NE Syria 35°30′N 35°54′E
139 U6 As Sa'dīyah Diyālá, E Iraq 34°11′N 45°09′E
Assad, Lake see Asad, Buḩayrat al
138 I8 Aş Şafā ▲ S Syria 33°03′N 37°07′E
138 I10 Aş Şafāwī Al Mafraq, N Jordan 32°12′N 32°30′E
75 W8 Aş Şaff var. El Şaff. N Egypt 29°34′N 31°16′E
139 N2 Aş Şafiḩ Al Ḩasakah, N Syria 36°42′N 40°12′E
Aş Şaḩrā' ash Sharqīyah see Sahara el Sharqîya
Assake see Asaka
As Salamīyah see Salamīyah
141 Q4 As Sālimī var. Salemy. SW Kuwait 29°07′N 46°41′E
67 W7 'Assal, Lac ◎ C Djibouti
139 T13 As Salmān Al Muthannā, S Iraq 30°29′N 44°34′E
138 G10 As Salt var. Salt. Al Balqā', NW Jordan 32°03′N 35°44′E
75 T7 As Sallūm var. Salûm. NW Egypt 31°31′N 25°09′E
142 M16 As Salwā var. Salwa, Salwah. S Qatar 24°44′N 50°52′E
153 V12 Assam ◈ state NE India
Assamaka see Assamakka
77 T8 Assamakka var. Assamaka. Agadez, NW Niger 19°24′N 05°53′E
139 U11 As Samāwah var. Samawa. Al Muthannā, S Iraq 31°17′N 45°06′E
As Saqia al Hamra see Saguia al Hamra
138 J4 Aş Şa'rān Ḩamāh, C Syria 35°15′N 37°28′E
138 G9 Aş Şarīḩ Irbid, N Jordan 32°31′N 35°54′E
21 Z5 Assateague Island island Maryland, NE USA
139 O6 As Sayyāl var. Sayyāl. Dayr az Zawr, E Syria 34°37′N 40°52′E
99 G18 Asse Vlaams Brabant, C Belgium 50°55′N 04°12′E
99 D16 Assebroek West-Vlaanderen, NW Belgium 51°12′N 03°16′E
Asselle see Āsela
107 C20 Assemini Sardegna, Italy, C Mediterranean Sea 39°16′N 08°58′E
99 E16 Assenede Oost-Vlaanderen, NW Belgium 51°15′N 03°43′E
95 G24 Assens Fyn, C Denmark 55°16′N 09°54′N
Asserien/Asserin see Aseri
99 I21 Assesse Namur, SE Belgium 50°22′N 05°01′E
141 Y8 As Sib var. Seeb. NE Oman 23°40′N 58°03′E
139 Z13 As Sibah var. Sibah. Al Başrah, SE Iraq 30°13′N 47°24′E
11 T17 Assiniboia Saskatchewan, S Canada 49°39′N 105°59′W
11 V15 Assiniboine ≈ Manitoba, S Canada
11 P16 Assiniboine, Mount ▲ Alberta/British Columbia, SW Canada 50°54′N 115°43′W
Assiout see Asyūţ
60 J9 Assis São Paulo, S Brazil 22°37′S 50°25′W
106 I13 Assisi Umbria, C Italy 43°04′N 12°36′E
Assiut see Asyūţ
Assling see Jesenice
Assouan see Aswân
Assu see Açu
Assuan see Aswân
142 K12 As Şubayḩīyah var. Subiyah. S Kuwait 28°55′N 47°57′E
141 R16 As Sufāl S Yemen 14°06′N 48°42′E
138 L5 As Sukhnah var. Sukhne, Fr. Soukhné. Ḩimş, C Syria 34°56′N 38°52′E
139 U4 As Sulaymānīyah off. Muḩāfaz̧at as Sulaymānīyah. ◈ governorate NE Iraq
139 U4 As Sulaymānīyah var. Sulaimaniya, Kurd. Slēmānī. As Sulaymānīyah, NE Iraq 35°32′N 45°27′E
141 P11 As Sulayyil Ar Riyāḑ, S Saudi Arabia 20°29′N 45°33′E
121 O13 As Sulţān N Libya 31°01′N 17°21′E
141 Q5 Aş Şummān desert N Saudi Arabia
141 Q16 Aş Şurrah SW Yemen 13°56′N 46°23′E
139 N4 Aş Şuwār var. Şuwār. Dayr az Zawr, E Syria 35°31′N 40°37′E
138 H9 As Suwaydā' var. El Suweida, Es Suweida, Suweida, Fr. Soueida. As Suwaydā', SW Syria 32°43′N 36°33′E
138 H9 As Suwaydā' off. Muḩāfaz̧at as Suwaydā', var. As Suwaydā, Suwaydá, Suweida. ◈ governorate S Syria
141 Z9 As Suwayḩ NE Oman 22°07′N 59°42′E
141 X8 As Suwayq var. Suwaik. N Oman 23°49′N 57°30′E
139 T8 Aş Şuwayrah var. Suwaira. Wāsiţ, E Iraq 32°57′N 44°47′E
As Suways see Suez
Asta Colonia see Asti
Astacus see İzmit
115 M23 Astakída island SE Greece
145 Q9 Astana prev. Akmola, Akmolinsk, Tselinograd, Aqmola. ● (Kazakhstan) Akmola, N Kazakhstan 51°13′N 71°25′E
142 M3 Āstāneh Gīlān, NW Iran 37°17′N 49°58′E
Asta Pompeia see Asti
137 Y14 Astara S Azerbaijan 38°28′N 48°51′E
Astarabad see Gorgān
99 L15 Asten Noord-Brabant, SE Netherlands 51°24′N 05°45′E
Asterābād see Gorgān
106 C8 Asti anc. Asta Colonia, Asta Pompeia, Hasta Colonia, Hasta Pompeia. Piemonte, NW Italy 44°54′N 08°11′E
Astigi see Ecija
Astipálaia see Astypálaia
148 L16 Astola Island island SW Pakistan
152 H4 Astor Jammu and Kashmir, NW India 35°21′N 74°52′E
104 K4 Astorga anc. Asturica Augusta. Castilla-León, N Spain 42°27′N 06°04′W
32 F10 Astoria Oregon, NW USA 46°12′N 123°50′W
0 F8 Astoria Fan undersea feature E Pacific Ocean 45°15′N 126°15′W
95 J22 Åstorp Skåne, S Sweden 56°09′N 12°57′E
Astrabad see Gorgān
127 Q13 Astrakhan' Astrakhanskaya Oblast', SW Russian Federation 46°20′N 48°01′E
Astrakhan-Bazar see Cälilabad
127 Q11 Astrakhanskaya Oblast' ◈ province SW Russian Federation
93 J15 Åsträsk Västerbotten, N Sweden 64°38′N 20°00′E
Astrida see Butare
65 O22 Astrid Ridge undersea feature S Atlantic Ocean
187 P15 Astrolabe, Récifs de l' reef C New Caledonia
121 P2 Astromerítis N Cyprus 35°09′N 33°02′E
115 F20 Ástros Pelopónnisos, S Greece 37°24′N 22°43′E
119 G16 Astryna Rus. Ostryna. Hrodzyenskaya Voblasts', W Belarus 53°44′N 24°33′E
104 J2 Asturias ◈ autonomous community NW Spain
Asturias see Oviedo
Asturica Augusta see Astorga
115 L22 Astypálaia var. Astipálaia, It. Stampalia. island Kykládes, Greece, Aegean Sea
192 G16 Āsuisui, Cape headland Savai'i, W Samoa 13°44′S 172°29′W
195 S2 Asuka Japanese research station Antarctica 71°49′S 23°52′E
62 O6 Asunción ● (Paraguay) Central, S Paraguay 25°17′S 57°36′W
62 O6 Asunción ✈ Central, S Paraguay 25°15′S 57°40′W
188 K3 Asuncion Island island N Northern Mariana Islands
42 E6 Asunción Mita Jutiapa, SE Guatemala 14°20′N 89°42′W
Asunción Nochixtlán see Nochixtlán
40 E3 Asunción, Río ≈ NW Mexico
95 M18 Åsunden ◎ S Sweden
118 K11 Asvyeya Rus. Osveya. Vitsyebskaya Voblasts', N Belarus 56°00′N 28°05′E
Aswa see Achwa
75 X11 Aswân var. Assouan, Assuan, Aswān; anc. Syene. SE Egypt 24°03′N 32°59′E
Aswān see Aswân
Aswân Dam see Khazzân Aswân
75 W9 Asyûţ var. Assiout, Assiut, Asyûţ, Siut; anc. Lycopolis. C Egypt 27°06′N 31°11′E
Asyûţ see Asyûţ
193 W15 Ata island Tongatapu Group, SW Tonga
62 G8 Atacama off. Región de Atacama. ◈ region C Chile
Atacama Desert see Atacama, Desierto de
62 H4 Atacama, Desierto de Eng. Atacama Desert. desert N Chile
62 I6 Atacama, Puna de ▲▲ NW Argentina
Atacama, Región de see Atacama
62 I5 Atacama, Salar de salt lake N Chile
54 E11 Ataco Tolima, C Colombia 03°36′N 75°23′W
190 H8 Atafu Atoll island NW Tokelau
190 H8 Atafu Village Atafu Atoll, NW Tokelau 08°40′S 172°40′W
74 K12 Atakor ▲▲ SE Algeria
77 R14 Atakora, Chaîne de l' var. Atakora Mountains. ▲▲ N Benin
Atakora Mountains see Atakora, Chaîne de l'
77 R16 Atakpamé C Togo 07°32′N 01°08′E
146 F11 Atakui Ahal Welaýaty, C Turkmenistan 40°04′N 58°03′E
58 B13 Atalaia do Norte Amazonas, N Brazil 04°22′S 70°10′W
146 M14 Atamyrat prev. Kerki. Lebap Welaýaty, E Turkmenistan 37°52′N 65°06′E
76 I7 Atâr Adrar, W Mauritania 20°30′N 13°03′W
162 G10 Atas Bogd ▲ SW Mongolia 43°17′N 96°47′E
35 P12 Atascadero California, W USA 35°28′N 120°40′W
25 S13 Atascosa River ≈ Texas, SW USA
145 R11 Atasu Karaganda, C Kazakhstan 48°42′N 71°38′E
145 R12 Atasu ≈ Karaganda, C Kazakhstan
193 V15 Atata island Tongatapu Group, S Tonga
136 H10 Atatürk ✈ (İstanbul) İstanbul, NW Turkey 40°58′N 28°50′E
137 N16 Atatürk Barajı ⊠ S Turkey
115 O23 Atavýros prev. Attavyros. Ródos, Dodekánisa, Aegean Sea 36°10′N 27°50′E
115 O23 Atavýros prev. Attávyros. ▲ Ródos, Dodekánisa, Greece, Aegean Sea 36°10′N 27°50′E
Atax see Aude
80 G8 Atbara var. 'Aṭbāra. River Nile, NE Sudan 17°42′N 34°E
80 H8 Atbara var. Nahr 'Aṭbarah. ≈ Eritrea/Sudan
'Aṭbārah/'Aṭbarah, Nahr see Atbara
145 P9 Atbasar Akmola, N Kazakhstan 51°49′N 68°18′E
At-Bashi see At-Bashy
147 W9 At-Bashy var. At-Bashi. Narynskaya Oblast', C Kyrgyzstan 41°07′N 75°48′E
22 I10 Atchafalaya Bay bay Louisiana, S USA
22 I8 Atchafalaya River ≈ Louisiana, S USA
Atchin see Aceh
27 Q3 Atchison Kansas, C USA 39°31′N 95°07′W
77 P16 Atebubu C Ghana 07°47′N 01°00′W
105 Q6 Ateca Aragón, NE Spain 41°20′N 01°49′W
40 K11 Atengo, Río ≈ C Mexico
Aternum see Pescara
107 K15 Atessa Abruzzo, C Italy 42°03′N 14°25′E
Ateste see Este
99 E19 Ath var. Aat. Hainaut, SW Belgium 50°38′N 03°47′E
11 Q13 Athabasca Alberta, SW Canada 54°44′N 113°15′W
11 Q12 Athabasca var. Athabaska. ≈ Alberta, SW Canada
11 R10 Athabasca, Lake ◎ Alberta/Saskatchewan, SW Canada
Athabaska see Athabasca
115 C16 Athamánon ▲▲ C Greece
97 F17 Athboy Ir. Baile Átha Buí. E Ireland 53°38′N 06°55′W
Athenae see Athína
97 C18 Athenry Ir. Baile Átha an Rí. W Ireland 53°19′N 08°49′W
23 P2 Athens Alabama, S USA 34°48′N 86°58′W
23 T3 Athens Georgia, SE USA 33°57′N 83°24′W
31 T14 Athens Ohio, N USA 39°20′N 82°06′W
20 M10 Athens Tennessee, S USA 35°27′N 84°38′W
25 V7 Athens Texas, SW USA 32°12′N 95°51′W
Athens see Athína
115 B18 Athéras, Akrotírio headland Kefalloniá, Iónia Nisiá, Greece, C Mediterranean Sea 38°20′N 20°24′E
181 W4 Atherton Queensland, NE Australia 17°18′S 145°29′E
81 I19 Athi ≈ S Kenya
121 Q2 Athíenou SE Cyprus 35°01′N 33°31′E
115 H19 Athína Eng. Athens, prev. Athínai; anc. Athenae. ● (Greece) Attikí, C Greece 37°59′N 23°44′E
Athínai see Athína
139 S10 Athīyah An Najaf, C Iraq 32°01′N 44°04′E
97 D18 Athlone Ir. Baile Átha Luain. C Ireland 53°25′N 07°56′W
155 F16 Athni Karnātaka, W India 16°43′N 75°04′E
185 C23 Athol Southland, South Island, New Zealand 45°30′S 168°35′E
19 N11 Athol Massachusetts, NE USA 42°35′N 72°11′W
115 I15 Áthos ▲ NE Greece 40°10′N 24°21′E
Athos, Mount see Ágion Óros
Ath Thawrah see Madīnat ath Thawrah
141 P5 Ath Thumāmī spring/well N Saudi Arabia 27°56′N 45°06′E
99 L25 Athus Luxembourg, SE Belgium 49°34′N 05°50′E
97 E19 Athy Ir. Baile Átha I. C Ireland 52°59′N 06°59′W
78 I10 Ati Batha, C Chad 13°11′N 18°20′E
81 F16 Atiak NW Uganda 03°14′N 32°05′E
57 G17 Atico Arequipa, SW Peru 16°13′S 73°13′W
105 O6 Atienza Castilla-La Mancha, C Spain 41°12′N 02°52′W
39 Q6 Atigun Pass pass Alaska, USA
12 B12 Atikokan Ontario, S Canada 48°45′N 91°38′W
13 O9 Atikonak Lac ◎ Newfoundland and Labrador, E Canada
42 C6 Atitlán, Lago de ◎ W Guatemala
190 L16 Atiu island S Cook Islands
Atjeh see Aceh
123 T9 Atka Magadanskaya Oblast', E Russian Federation 60°45′N 151°35′E
38 H17 Atka Atka Island, Alaska, USA 52°12′N 174°14′W
38 H17 Atka Island island Aleutian Islands, Alaska, USA
127 O7 Atkarsk Saratovskaya Oblast', W Russian Federation 52°15′N 43°48′E
27 U11 Atkins Arkansas, C USA 35°15′N 92°56′W
29 O13 Atkinson Nebraska, C USA 42°31′N 98°57′W
171 T12 Atkri Papua, E Indonesia 01°45′S 130°04′E
41 O13 Atlacomulco var. Atlacomulco de Fabela. México, C Mexico 19°49′N 99°54′W
Atlacomulco de Fabela see Atlacomulco
23 S3 Atlanta state capital Georgia, SE USA 33°45′N 84°23′W
31 R6 Atlanta Michigan, N USA 45°01′N 84°07′W
25 X6 Atlanta Texas, SW USA 33°06′N 94°09′W
29 T15 Atlantic Iowa, C USA 41°24′N 95°00′W
21 Y10 Atlantic North Carolina, SE USA 34°52′N 76°20′W
23 W8 Atlantic Beach Florida, SE USA 30°19′N 81°24′W
18 J17 Atlantic City New Jersey, NE USA 39°23′N 74°27′W
172 L14 Atlantic-Indian Basin undersea feature SW Indian Ocean 60°00′S 15°00′E
172 K13 Atlantic-Indian Ridge undersea feature SW Indian Ocean 53°00′S 15°00′E
54 E4 Atlántico off. Departamento del Atlántico. ◈ province NW Colombia
64-65 Atlantic Ocean ocean
Atlántico, Departamento del see Atlántico
42 K7 Atlántico Norte, Región Autónoma prev. Zelaya Norte. ◈ autonomous region NE Nicaragua
42 L10 Atlántico Sur, Región Autónoma prev. Zelaya Sur. ◈ autonomous region SE Nicaragua
42 I5 Atlántida ◈ department N Honduras
77 Y15 Atlantika Mountains ▲▲ E Nigeria
64 J10 Atlantis Fracture Zone tectonic feature NW Atlantic Ocean
74 H7 Atlas Mountains ▲▲ NW Africa
123 V11 Atlasova, Ostrov island SE Russian Federation
123 V10 Atlasovo Kamchatskaya Oblast', E Russian Federation 55°42′N 159°35′E
120 G11 Atlas Saharien var. Saharan Atlas. ▲▲ Algeria/Morocco
Atlas, Tell see Atlas Tellien
120 H10 Atlas Tellien Eng. Tell Atlas. ▲▲ N Algeria
10 I9 Atlin British Columbia, W Canada 59°31′N 133°41′W
10 I9 Atlin Lake ◎ British Columbia, W Canada
41 P14 Atlixco Puebla, S Mexico 18°55′N 98°26′W
94 B11 Atløyna island S Norway
155 I17 Ātmakūr Andhra Pradesh, C India 15°52′N 78°42′E
23 O8 Atmore Alabama, S USA 31°01′N 87°29′W
101 J20 Atmühl ≈ S Germany
94 H11 Atna ≈ S Norway
164 E13 Atō Yamaguchi, Honshū, SW Japan 34°24′N 131°42′E
57 L21 Atocha Potosí, S Bolivia 20°55′S 66°14′W
27 P12 Atoka Oklahoma, C USA 34°22′N 96°08′W
27 O12 Atoka Lake var. Atoka Reservoir. ⊠ Oklahoma, C USA
Atoka Reservoir see Atoka Lake
33 Q14 Atomic City Idaho, NW USA 43°26′N 112°48′W
40 L10 Atotonilco Zacatecas, C Mexico 24°12′N 102°46′W
Atotonilco see Atotonilco el Alto
40 M13 Atotonilco el Alto var. Atotonilco. Jalisco, SW Mexico 20°35′N 102°30′W
77 N7 Atouila, 'Erg desert N Mali
41 N16 Atoyac var. Atoyac de Alvarez. Guerrero, S Mexico 17°12′N 100°28′W
Atoyac de Alvarez see Atoyac
41 P15 Atoyac, Río ≈ S Mexico
39 O5 Atqasuk Alaska, USA 70°28′N 157°24′W
Atrak/Atrak, Rūd-e see Etrek
95 J20 Ätran ≈ S Sweden
54 C7 Atrato, Río ≈ NW Colombia
Atrek see Etrek
107 K14 Atri Abruzzo, C Italy 42°35′N 13°59′E
Atria see Adria
165 P9 Atsumi Yamagata, Honshū, C Japan 38°38′N 139°36′E
165 S3 Atsuta Hokkaidō, NE Japan 43°28′N 141°24′E
143 Q17 Aţ Ţaff desert C United Arab Emirates
138 G12 Aţ Ţafīlah var. Et Tafila, Tafila. Aţ Ţafīlah, W Jordan 30°52′N 35°36′E
138 G12 Aţ Ţafīlah off. Muḩāfaz̧at aţ Ţafīlah. ◈ governorate W Jordan
140 L10 Aţ Ţā'if Makkah, W Saudi Arabia 21°50′N 40°50′E
Attaleia/Attalia see Antalya
23 Q3 Attalla Alabama, S USA 34°01′N 86°05′W
138 L2 At Tall al Abyaḑ var. Tall al Abyad, Tell Abyad, Fr. Tell Abiad. Ar Raqqah, N Syria 36°36′N 34°00′E
139 S5 At Ta'mīm off. Muḩāfaz̧at at Ta'mīm. ◈ governorate N Iraq
138 L7 Aţ Ţanf Ḩimş, S Syria 33°29′N 38°39′E
163 N9 Attanshiree Dornogovĭ, SE Mongolia 45°36′N 110°30′E
Attapu see Samakhixai
139 S10 At Taqtaqānah An Najaf, C Iraq 32°03′N 43°54′E
Attávyros see Atavýros
139 V15 At Tawal desert Iraq/Saudi Arabia
12 G9 Attawapiskat Ontario, C Canada 52°55′N 82°26′W
12 F9 Attawapiskat ≈ Ontario, S Canada
12 D9 Attawapiskat Lake ◎ Ontario, C Canada
At Taybé see Ţayyibah
101 F16 Attendorn Nordrhein-Westfalen, W Germany 51°07′N 07°54′E
109 R5 Attersee Salzburg, NW Austria 47°55′N 13°31′E
109 R5 Attersee ◎ N Austria
99 L24 Attert Luxembourg, SE Belgium 49°45′N 05°47′E
138 M4 At Tibnī var. Tibnī. Dayr az Zawr, NE Syria 35°30′N 39°48′E
31 N13 Attica Indiana, N USA 40°17′N 87°15′W
18 E10 Attica New York, NE USA 42°51′N 78°13′W
Attica see Attikí
13 N7 Attikamagen Lake ◎ Newfoundland and Labrador, E Canada
115 H20 Attikí Eng. Attica. ◈ region C Greece
19 O12 Attleboro Massachusetts, NE USA 41°55′N 71°15′W
109 R5 Attnang Oberösterreich, N Austria 48°02′N 13°44′E
149 U6 Attock City Punjab, E Pakistan 33°52′N 72°20′E
Attopeu see Samakhixai
25 X8 Attoyac River ≈ Texas, SW USA
38 D16 Attu Attu Island, Alaska, USA 52°53′N 173°18′E
139 Y12 Aţ Ţubah Al Başrah, E Iraq 30°29′N 47°28′E
140 K4 Aţ Ţubayq plain Jordan/Saudi Arabia
38 C16 Attu Island island Aleutian Islands, Alaska, USA
75 X8 Aţ Ţūr var. El Ţûr. NE Egypt 28°14′N 33°36′E
155 I21 Āttūr Tamil Nādu, SE India 11°34′N 78°39′E
141 N17 At Turbah SW Yemen 12°42′N 43°31′E
62 I12 Atuel, Río ≈ C Argentina
191 X7 Atuona Hiva Oa, NE French Polynesia 09°47′S 139°03′W
Aturus see Adour
95 M18 Åtvidaberg Östergötland, S Sweden 58°12′N 16°00′E
35 P9 Atwater California, W USA 37°19′N 120°33′W
29 T8 Atwater Minnesota, N USA 45°08′N 94°48′W
26 I2 Atwood Kansas, C USA 39°48′N 101°03′W
31 U12 Atwood Lake ⊠ Ohio, N USA
127 P5 Atyashevo Respublika Mordoviya, W Russian Federation 54°36′N 46°04′E
144 F12 Atyrau prev. Gur'yev. Atyrau, W Kazakhstan 47°07′N 51°56′E
144 E11 Atyrau off. Atyrauskaya Oblast', var.Kaz. Atyraū Oblysy; prev. Gur'yevskaya Oblast'. ◈ province W Kazakhstan
Atyraū Oblysy/Atyrauskaya Oblast' see Atyrau
Atyrauskaya Oblast' see Atyrau
108 J7 Au Vorarlberg, NW Austria 47°19′N 10°01′E
186 B4 Aua Island island NW Papua New Guinea
103 S16 Aubagne anc. Albania. Bouches-du-Rhône, SE France 43°17′N 05°35′E
99 L25 Aubange Luxembourg, SE Belgium 49°35′N 05°49′E
103 Q6 Aube ◈ department N France
103 R6 Aube ≈ N France
99 L19 Aubel Liège, E Belgium 50°45′N 05°49′E
103 Q13 Aubenas Ardèche, E France 44°37′N 04°24′E
103 O8 Aubigny-sur-Nère Cher, C France 47°30′N 02°27′E
103 O13 Aubin Aveyron, S France 44°30′N 02°18′E
103 O13 Aubrac, Monts d' ▲▲ S France
36 J10 Aubrey Cliffs cliff Arizona, SW USA
23 R5 Auburn Alabama, S USA 32°37′N 85°30′W
35 P6 Auburn California, W USA 38°53′N 121°03′W
30 K14 Auburn Illinois, N USA 39°35′N 89°45′W
31 Q11 Auburn Indiana, N USA 41°22′N 85°03′W
20 J7 Auburn Kentucky, S USA 36°52′N 86°42′W
19 P8 Auburn Maine, NE USA 44°05′N 70°15′W
19 N11 Auburn Massachusetts, NE USA 42°11′N 71°47′W
29 S16 Auburn Nebraska, C USA 40°23′N 95°50′W
18 H10 Auburn New York, NE USA 42°55′N 76°31′W
32 H8 Auburn Washington, NW USA 47°18′N 122°13′W
103 N11 Aubusson Creuse, C France 45°58′N 02°10′E
118 E10 Auce Ger. Autz. Dobele, SW Latvia 56°28′N 22°54′E
102 L15 Auch Lat. Augusta Auscorum, Elimberrum. Gers, S France 43°40′N 00°37′E
77 U16 Auchi Edo, S Nigeria 07°01′N 06°17′E
23 T9 Aucilla River ≈ Florida/Georgia, SE USA
184 L6 Auckland Auckland, North Island, New Zealand 36°53′S 174°46′E
184 K5 Auckland off. Auckland Region. ◈ region North Island, New Zealand
184 L6 Auckland ✈ Auckland, North Island, New Zealand 37°01′S 174°49′E
192 J12 Auckland Islands island group S New Zealand
Auckland Region see Auckland
103 O16 Aude ◈ department S France
103 N16 Aude anc. Atax. ≈ S France
Audenarde see Oudenaarde
Audern see Audru
102 E6 Audierne Finistère, NW France 48°01′N 04°30′W
102 E6 Audierne, Baie d' bay NW France
103 U7 Audincourt Doubs, E France 47°29′N 06°50′E
118 G5 Audru Ger. Audern. Pärnumaa, SW Estonia 58°24′N 24°22′E
29 T14 Audubon Iowa, C USA 41°44′N 94°56′W
101 N17 Aue Sachsen, E Germany 50°35′N 12°42′E
100 H12 Aue ≈ NW Germany
100 L9 Auerbach Bayern, SE Germany 49°41′N 11°41′E
101 M17 Auerbach Sachsen, E Germany 50°30′N 12°24′E
108 I10 Auererrhein ≈ SW Switzerland
101 N17 Auersberg ▲ E Germany 50°30′N 12°42′E
181 W9 Augathella Queensland, E Australia 25°54′S 146°38′E
31 Q12 Auglaize River ≈ Ohio, N USA
83 F22 Augrabies Falls waterfall W South Africa
31 R7 Au Gres River ≈ Michigan, N USA
Augsbourg see Augsburg
101 K22 Augsburg Fr. Augsbourg; anc. Augusta Vindelicorum. Bayern, S Germany 48°22′N 10°54′E
180 I14 Augusta Western Australia 34°18′S 115°10′E
107 L25 Augusta It. Agosta. Sicilia, Italy, C Mediterranean Sea 37°14′N 15°14′E
27 W11 Augusta Arkansas, C USA 35°16′N 91°21′W
23 V3 Augusta Georgia, SE USA 33°29′N 81°58′W
27 O6 Augusta Kansas, C USA 37°40′N 96°59′W
19 Q7 Augusta state capital Maine, NE USA 44°20′N 69°44′W
33 Q8 Augusta Montana, NW USA 47°28′N 112°23′W
Augusta see London
Augusta Auscorum see Auch
Augusta Emerita see Mérida
Augusta Praetoria see Aosta
Augusta Suessionum see Soissons
Augusta Trajana see Stara Zagora
Augusta Treverorum see Trier
Augusta Vangionum see Worms
Augusta Vindelicorum see Augsburg
95 G24 Augustenborg Ger. Augustenburg. Sønderjylland, SW Denmark 54°57′N 09°53′E
Augustenburg see Augustenborg
39 Q13 Augustine Island island Alaska, USA
14 L9 Augustines, Lac des ◎ Québec, SE Canada
Augustobona Tricassium see Troyes
Augustodunum see Autun
Augustodurum see Bayeux
Augustoritum Lemovicensium see Limoges
110 O8 Augustów Rus. Avgustov. Podlaskie, NE Poland 53°52′N 22°58′E
Augustow Canal see Augustowski, Kanał
110 O8 Augustowski, Kanał Eng. Augustow Canal, Rus. Avgustovskiy Kanal. canal NE Poland
180 I9 Augustus, Mount ▲ Western Australia 24°42′S 117°42′E
186 M9 Auki Malaita, N Solomon Islands 08°48′S 160°45′E
21 W8 Aulander North Carolina, SE USA 36°15′N 77°16′W
180 L7 Auld, Lake salt lake C Western Australia
Aulie Ata/Auliye-Ata see Taraz
Äülieköl see Auliyekol'
144 M8 Auliyekol' Kaz. Äülieköl; prev. Semiozernoye. Kostanay, N Kazakhstan 52°22′N 64°06′E
106 E10 Aulla Toscana, C Italy 44°15′N 10°00′E
102 F6 Aulne ≈ NW France
Aulong see Ulong
37 T3 Ault Colorado, C USA 40°34′N 104°43′W
95 F22 Aulum var. avlum. Ringkøbing, C Denmark 56°16′N 08°48′E
103 N3 Aumale Seine-Maritime, N France 49°45′N 01°43′E
Aumintzatau, Gory see Ovminzatovo Togʻlari
77 T14 Auna Niger, W Nigeria 10°13′N 04°43′E
166 L6 Aunglan var. Allanmyo, Myaydo. Magway, C Burma (Myanmar) 19°25′N 95°13′E
95 H21 Auning Århus, C Denmark 56°26′N 10°23′E
192 K17 'Aunu'u Island island W American Samoa
83 E20 Auob var. Oup. ≈ Namibia/South Africa
93 K19 Aura Länsi-Suomi, SW Finland 60°37′N 22°35′E
109 R5 Aurach ≈ N Austria
Aural, Phnom see Aôral, Phnum
153 O14 Aurangābād Bihār, N India 24°46′N 84°23′E
154 F13 Aurangābād Mahārāshtra, C India 19°52′N 75°22′E
189 V7 Aur Atoll atoll E Marshall Islands
102 G7 Auray Morbihan, NW France 47°40′N 02°59′W
94 G13 Aurdal Oppland, S Norway 60°51′N 09°25′E
94 F8 Aure Møre og Romsdal, S Norway 63°16′N 08°31′E
29 T12 Aurelia Iowa, C USA 42°42′N 95°26′W
Aurelia Aquensis see Baden-Baden
Aurelianum see Orléans
120 J10 Aurès, Massif de l' ▲▲ NE Algeria
100 F10 Aurich Niedersachsen, NW Germany 53°28′N 07°28′E
103 O13 Aurillac Cantal, C France 44°56′N 02°26′E
Aurine, Alpi see Zillertaler Alpen
Aurium see Ourense
14 H15 Aurora Ontario, S Canada 44°00′N 79°26′W
55 S8 Aurora NW Guyana 06°46′N 59°45′W
37 T4 Aurora Colorado, C USA 39°42′N 104°51′W
30 M11 Aurora Illinois, N USA 41°46′N 88°19′W
31 Q15 Aurora Indiana, N USA 39°01′N 84°55′W
29 W4 Aurora Minnesota, N USA 47°31′N 92°14′W
27 S8 Aurora Missouri, C USA 36°58′N 93°43′W
29 P16 Aurora Nebraska, C USA 40°52′N 98°00′W
36 J5 Aurora Utah, W USA 38°55′N 111°55′W
Aurora see San Francisco, Philippines
Aurora see Maéwo, Vanuatu
94 F10 Aursjøen ◎ S Norway
94 I9 Aursunden ◎ S Norway
83 D21 Aus Karas, SW Namibia 26°38′S 16°19′E
Ausa see Vic
14 E16 Ausable ≈ Ontario, S Canada
31 S7 Au Sable Point headland Michigan, N USA 44°19′N 83°20′W
31 O3 Au Sable Point headland Michigan, N USA 46°40′N 86°08′W
31 R6 Au Sable River ≈ Michigan, N USA
57 H16 Ausangate, Nevado ▲ C Peru 13°47′S 71°13′W
Auschwitz see Oświęcim
Ausculum Apulum see Ascoli Satriano
105 Q4 Ausejo La Rioja, N Spain 42°21′N 02°10′W
Aussig see Ústí nad Labem
95 F17 Aust-Agder ◈ county S Norway
92 P2 Austfonna glacier NE Svalbard
31 P15 Austin Indiana, N USA 38°45′N 85°48′W
29 W11 Austin Minnesota, N USA 43°40′N 92°58′W
35 U5 Austin Nevada, W USA 39°30′N 117°05′W
25 S10 Austin state capital Texas, SW USA 30°16′N 97°45′W
180 J10 Austin, Lake salt lake Western Australia
31 V11 Austintown Ohio, N USA 41°06′N 80°45′W
25 V9 Austonio Texas, SW USA 31°09′N 95°39′W
Australes, Archipel des see Australes, Îles
Australes et Antarctiques Françaises, Terres see French Southern and Antarctic Territories
191 T14 Australes, Îles var. Archipel des Australes, Îles Tubuai, Tubuai Islands, Eng. Austral Islands. island group SW French Polynesia
175 Y11 Austral Fracture Zone tectonic feature S Pacific Ocean
174 M8 Australia continent
181 O7 Australia off. Commonwealth of Australia. ◆ commonwealth republic
Australia, Commonwealth of see Australia
183 Q12 Australian Alps ▲▲ SE Australia
183 R11 Australian Capital Territory prev. Federal Capital Territory. ◈ territory SE Australia
Australie, Bassin Nord de l' see North Australian Basin
Austral Islands see Australes, Îles
Austrava see Ostrov
109 T6 Austria off. Republic of Austria, Ger. Österreich. ◆ republic C Europe
Austria, Republic of see Austria
92 K3 Austurland ◈ region SE Iceland
92 G10 Austvågøya island C Norway
58 G13 Autazes Amazonas, N Brazil 03°37′S 59°08′W
102 M16 Auterive Haute-Garonne, S France 43°22′N 01°28′E
Autesiodorum see Auxerre
103 N2 Authie ≈ N France
Autissiodorum see Auxerre
40 K14 Autlán var. Autlán de Navarro. Jalisco, SW Mexico 19°48′N 104°20′W
Autlán de Navarro see Autlán
Autricum see Chartres
103 Q9 Autun anc. Ædua, Augustodunum. Saône-et-Loire, C France 46°58′N 04°18′E
Autz see Auce
99 H20 Auvelais Namur, S Belgium 50°27′N 04°38′E
103 P11 Auvergne ◈ region C France
102 M12 Auvézère ≈ W France
103 P7 Auxerre anc. Autesiodorum, Autissiodorum. Yonne, C France 47°48′N 03°35′E
103 N2 Auxi-le-Château Pas-de-Calais, N France 50°14′N 02°06′E
103 S8 Auxonne Côte d'Or, C France 47°12′N 05°22′E
55 P9 Auyan Tebuy ▲ SE Venezuela 05°48′N 62°27′W
103 O10 Auzances Creuse, C France 46°01′N 02°29′E
27 U8 Ava Missouri, C USA 36°57′N 92°39′W
142 M5 Āvaj Qazvīn, N Iran
95 C15 Avaldsnes Rogaland, S Norway 59°21′N 05°16′E
103 Q8 Avallon Yonne, C France 47°30′N 03°54′E
102 K6 Avaloirs, Mont des ▲ NW France 48°27′N 00°11′W
35 S16 Avalon Santa Catalina Island, California, W USA 33°20′N 118°19′W
18 J17 Avalon New Jersey, NE USA 39°04′N 74°42′W
13 V13 Avalon Peninsula peninsula Newfoundland and Labrador, E Canada
197 Q11 Avannaarsua ◈ province N Greenland
60 K10 Avaré São Paulo, S Brazil 23°06′S 48°57′W
Avaricum see Bourges
190 H16 Avarua ○ (Cook Islands) Rarotonga, S Cook Islands 21°12′S 159°46′E
190 H16 Avarua Harbour harbour Rarotonga, S Cook Islands

◆ Country ● Country Capital ◇ Dependent Territory ○ Dependent Territory Capital ◈ Administrative Regions ✈ International Airport ▲ Mountain ▲▲ Mountain Range Volcano ≈ River ◎ Lake ⊠ Reservoir

Avasfelsőfalu *see* Negreşti-Oaş
38 L17 **Avatanak Island** *island* Aleutian Islands, Alaska, USA
190 B16 **Avatele** S Niue 19°06′S 169°55′E
190 H15 **Avatiu Harbour** *harbour* Rarotonga, S Cook Islands
Avdeyevka *see* Avdiyivka
114 J13 **Ávdira** Anatolikí Makedonía kai Thráki, NE Greece 40°58′N 24°58′E
117 X8 **Avdiyivka** *Rus.* Avdeyevka. Donets'ka Oblast', SE Ukraine 48°06′N 37°46′E
Avdzaga *see* Gurvanbulag
104 G6 **Ave** ≈ N Portugal
104 G7 **Aveiro** *anc.* Talabriga. Aveiro, W Portugal 40°38′N 08°40′W
104 G7 **Aveiro** ◈ *district* N Portugal
Avela *see* Ávila
99 D18 **Avelgem** West-Vlaanderen, W Belgium 50°46′N 03°25′E
61 D20 **Avellaneda** Buenos Aires, E Argentina 34°43′S 58°23′W
107 L17 **Avellino** *anc.* Abellinum. Campania, S Italy 40°54′N 14°46′E
35 Q12 **Avenal** California, W USA 36°00′N 120°07′W
Avenio *see* Avignon
94 E8 **Averoya** *island* S Norway
107 K17 **Aversa** Campania, S Italy 40°58′N 14°13′E
33 N9 **Avery** Idaho, NW USA 47°14′N 115°48′W
25 W5 **Avery** Texas, SW USA 33°33′N 94°46′W
Aves, Islas de *see* Las Aves, Islas
Avesnes *see* Avesnes-sur-Helpe
103 Q2 **Avesnes-sur-Helpe** *var.* Avesnes. Nord, N France 50°08′N 03°57′E
64 G12 **Aves Ridge** *undersea feature* SE Caribbean Sea 14°00′N 63°30′W
95 M14 **Avesta** Dalarna, C Sweden 60°09′N 16°10′E
103 O14 **Aveyron** ◈ *department* S France
103 N14 **Aveyron** ≈ S France
107 J15 **Avezzano** Abruzzo, C Italy 42°02′N 13°26′E
115 D16 **Avgó** ▲ C Greece 39°31′N 21°24′E
Avgustov *see* Augustów
Avgustovskiy Kanal *see* Augustowski, Kanał
96 J9 **Aviemore** N Scotland, United Kingdom 57°06′N 04°01′W
185 F21 **Aviemore, Lake** ◎ South Island, New Zealand
103 R15 **Avignon** *anc.* Avenio. Vaucluse, SE France 43°57′N 04°49′E
104 M7 **Ávila** *var.* Avila; *anc.* Abela, Abula, Abyla, Avela. Castilla-León, C Spain 40°39′N 04°42′W
104 L8 **Ávila** ◈ *province* Castilla-León, C Spain
104 K2 **Avilés** Asturias, NW Spain 43°33′N 05°55′W
118 J4 **Avinurme** *Ger.* Awwinorm. Ida-Virumaa, NE Estonia 58°58′N 26°53′E
104 H10 **Avis** Portalegre, C Portugal 39°03′N 07°53′W
Avlum *see* Aulum
182 M11 **Avoca** Victoria, SE Australia 37°09′S 143°34′E
29 T14 **Avoca** Iowa, C USA 41°27′N 95°20′W
182 M11 **Avoca River** ≈ Victoria, SE Australia
107 L25 **Avola** Sicilia, Italy, C Mediterranean Sea 36°54′N 15°08′E
18 F10 **Avon** New York, NE USA 42°53′N 77°41′W
29 P12 **Avon** South Dakota, N USA 43°00′N 98°03′W
97 M23 **Avon** ≈ S England, United Kingdom
97 L20 **Avon** ≈ C England, United Kingdom
36 K13 **Avondale** Arizona, SW USA 33°25′N 112°20′W
23 X13 **Avon Park** Florida, SE USA 27°36′N 81°30′W
102 J5 **Avranches** Manche, N France 48°42′N 01°21′W
Avveel *see* Ivalojoki, Finland
186 M6 **Avuavu** *var.* Kolotambu. Guadalcanal, C Solomon Islands 09°52′S 160°25′E
103 O3 **Avure** ≈ N France
Avveel *see* Ivalo, Finland
Avvil *see* Ivalo
77 O17 **Awaaso** *var.* Awaso. SW Ghana 06°10′N 02°18′W
141 X8 **Awābī** *var.* Al 'Awābī. NE Oman 23°20′N 57°35′E
184 L9 **Awakino** Waikato, North Island, New Zealand 38°40′S 174°37′E
142 M15 **'Awālī** C Bahrain 26°07′N 50°33′E
99 K19 **Awans** Liège, E Belgium 50°39′N 05°30′E
184 I2 **Awanui** Northland, North Island, New Zealand 35°01′S 173°16′E
148 M14 **Awārān** Baluchistān, SW Pakistan 26°31′N 65°10′E
81 K16 **Awara Plain** *plain* NE Kenya
80 M13 **Āwarē** Sumalē, E Ethiopia 08°12′N 44°09′E
138 M6 **'Awāriḍ, Wādī** *dry watercourse* E Syria
185 B20 **Awarua Point** *headland* South Island, New Zealand 44°15′S 168°03′E
81 J14 **Āwasa** Southern Nationalities, S Ethiopia 06°54′N 38°26′E
80 K13 **Āwash** Āfar, NE Ethiopia 08°59′N 40°16′E
80 K12 **Āwash** *var.* Hawash. ≈ C Ethiopia
Awaso *see* Awaaso
158 H7 **Awat** Xinjiang Uygur Zizhiqu, NW China 40°36′N 80°22′E
185 J15 **Awatere** ≈ South Island, New Zealand
75 O10 **Awbārī** SW Libya 26°35′N 12°46′E
75 N9 **Awbāri, Idhān** *var.* Edeyen d'Oubari. *desert* Algeria/Libya
80 M12 **Awdal** *off.* Gobolka Awdal. ◈ N Somalia
80 C13 **Aweil** Northern Bahr el Ghazal, SW Sudan 08°42′N 27°20′E
96 H11 **Awe, Loch** ◎ W Scotland, United Kingdom
77 U16 **Awka** Anambra, SW Nigeria 06°12′N 07°04′E
39 O6 **Awuna River** ≈ Alaska, USA
Awwinorm *see* Avinurme
Ax *see* Dax
Axarfjördhur *see* Öxarfjördhur
103 N17 **Axat** Aude, S France 42°47′N 02°14′E
99 F16 **Axel** Zeeland, SW Netherlands 51°16′N 03°55′E
197 P9 **Axel Heiberg Island** *var.* Axel Heiburg. *island* Nunavut, N Canada
Axel Heiburg *see* Axel Heiberg Island
77 O17 **Axim** S Ghana 04°53′N 02°14′W
114 F13 **Axiós** *var.* Vardar. ≈ Greece/FYR Macedonia *see also* Vardar
Axiós *see* Vardar
103 N17 **Ax-les-Thermes** Ariège, S France 42°43′N 01°49′E
120 D11 **Ayachi, Jbel** ▲ C Morocco 32°30′N 05°00′W
61 D22 **Ayacucho** Buenos Aires, E Argentina 37°09′S 58°30′W
57 F15 **Ayacucho** Ayacucho, S Peru 13°10′S 74°15′W
57 E16 **Ayacucho** *off.* Departamento de Ayacucho. ◈ *department* SW Peru
Ayacucho, Departamento de *see* Ayacucho
145 W11 **Ayagoz** *var.* Ayaguz, *Kaz.* Ayaköz; *prev.* Sergiopol. Vostochnyy Kazakhstan, E Kazakhstan 47°54′N 80°25′E
145 V12 **Ayagoz** *var.* Ayaguz, *Kaz.* Ayakoz. ≈ E Kazakhstan
Ayaguz *see* Ayagoz
Ayakagytma *see* Oyoqog'itma
Ayakkuduk *see* Oyoqquduq
158 L10 **Ayakkum Hu** ◎ NW China
Ayaköz *see* Ayagoz
104 H14 **Ayamonte** Andalucía, S Spain 37°13′N 07°24′W
123 S11 **Ayan** Khabarovskiy Kray, E Russian Federation 56°27′N 138°09′E
136 J10 **Ayancık** Sinop, N Turkey 41°56′N 34°35′E
55 S9 **Ayanganna Mountain** ▲ C Guyana 05°21′N 59°54′W
77 U16 **Ayangba** Kogi, C Nigeria 07°36′N 07°10′E
123 U7 **Ayanka** Koryakskiy Avtonomnyy Okrug, E Russian Federation 63°42′N 167°31′E
54 E7 **Ayapel** Córdoba, NW Colombia 08°16′N 75°10′W
136 H12 **Ayaş** Ankara, N Turkey 40°02′N 32°21′E
57 I16 **Ayaviri** Puno, S Peru 14°53′S 70°35′W
149 P3 **Āybak** *var.* Aibak, Haibak; *prev.* Samangān. Samangān, NE Afghanistan 36°16′N 68°04′E
147 N10 **Aydarko'l Ko'li** *Rus.* Ozero Aydarkul'. ◎ C Uzbekistan
Aydarkul', Ozero *see* Aydarko'l Ko'li
21 W10 **Ayden** North Carolina, SE USA 35°28′N 77°25′W
136 C15 **Aydın** *var.* Aïdin; *anc.* Tralles Aydin. Aydın, SW Turkey 37°51′N 27°51′E
136 C15 **Aydın** *var.* Aïdin. ◈ *province* SW Turkey
136 I17 **Aydıncık** İçel, S Turkey 36°08′N 33°17′E
136 C15 **Aydın Dağları** ▲▲ W Turkey
158 L6 **Aydingkol Hu** ◎ NW China
127 X7 **Aydyrlinskiy** Orenburgskaya Oblast', W Russian Federation 52°03′N 59°54′E
105 S4 **Ayerbe** Aragón, NE Spain 42°16′N 00°41′W
Ayers Rock *see* Uluru
Ayeyarwady *see* Irrawaddy
Ayiá *see* Agiá
Ayia Napa *see* Agía Nápa
Ayia Phyla *see* Agía Fýlaxis
Ayiásos/Ayiássos *see* Agiassós
Áyios Evstrátios *see* Ágios Efstrátios
Áyios Kírikos *see* Ágios Kírykos
Áyios Nikólaos *see* Ágios Nikólaos
80 I11 **Āykel** Āmara, N Ethiopia 12°33′N 37°01′E
123 N9 **Aykhal** Respublika Sakha (Yakutiya), NE Russian Federation 66°07′N 110°25′E
14 J12 **Aylen Lake** ◎ Ontario, SE Canada
97 N21 **Aylesbury** SE England, United Kingdom 51°50′N 00°50′W
105 O6 **Ayllón** Castilla-León, N Spain 41°25′N 03°23′W
14 F17 **Aylmer** Ontario, S Canada 42°46′N 80°57′W
14 L12 **Aylmer** Québec, SE Canada 45°23′N 75°51′W
15 R12 **Aylmer, Lac** ◎ Québec, SE Canada
8 L9 **Aylmer Lake** ◎ Northwest Territories, NW Canada
145 V14 **Aynabulak** *Kaz.* Aynabulaq. Almaty, SE Kazakhstan 44°37′N 77°59′E
Aynabulaq *see* Aynabulak
138 K2 **'Ayn al 'Arab** Ḥalab, N Syria 36°55′N 38°21′E
Aynayn *see* 'Aynīn
139 V12 **'Ayn Ḥamūd** Dhī Qār, S Iraq 30°51′N 45°37′E
147 P12 **Ayní** *prev.* Varzimanor Ayni. W Tajikistan 39°24′N 68°30′E
140 M10 **'Aynīn** *var.* Aynayn. *spring/well* SW Saudi Arabia 20°52′N 41°41′E
21 U12 **Aynor** South Carolina, SE USA 33°59′N 79°11′W
139 Q7 **'Ayn Zāzūh** Al Anbār, C Iraq 33°29′N 42°34′E
153 N12 **Ayodhya** Uttar Pradesh, N India 26°47′N 82°12′E
123 S6 **Ayon, Ostrov** *island* NE Russian Federation
105 R11 **Ayora** País Valenciano, E Spain 39°04′N 01°04′W
77 Q11 **Ayorou** Tillabéri, W Niger 14°45′N 00°54′E
79 E16 **Ayos** Centre, S Cameroon 03°53′N 12°31′E
76 L5 **'Ayoûn 'Abd el Mâlek** *well* N Mauritania
76 K10 **'Ayoûn el 'Atroûs** *var.* Aïoun el Atrous, Aïoun el Atroûss. Hodh el Gharbi, SE Mauritania 16°38′N 09°36′W
96 I13 **Ayr** W Scotland, United Kingdom 55°28′N 04°38′W
96 I13 **Ayr** ≈ W Scotland, United Kingdom
96 I13 **Ayrshire** *cultural region* SW Scotland, United Kingdom
Aysen *see* Aisén
80 L12 **Āysha** Sumalē, E Ethiopia 10°36′N 42°31′E
144 L14 **Ayteke Bi** *Kaz.* Zhangaqazaly; *prev.* Novokazalinsk. Kzylorda, SW Kazakhstan 45°53′N 62°10′E
146 K8 **Aytim** Navoiy Viloyati, N Uzbekistan 42°15′N 63°25′E
181 W4 **Ayton** Queensland, NE Australia 15°54′S 145°19′E
114 M9 **Aytos** Burgas, E Bulgaria 42°43′N 27°14′E
171 T11 **Ayu, Kepulauan** *island group* E Indonesia
A Yun Pa *see* Cheo Reo
169 V11 **Ayu, Tanjung** *headland* Borneo, N Indonesia 0°25′N 117°34′E
41 P16 **Ayutlá** *var.* Ayutla de los Libres. Guerrero, S Mexico 16°51′N 99°16′W
40 K13 **Ayutla** Jalisco, C Mexico 20°07′N 104°18′W
Ayutla de los Libres *see* Ayutlá
167 O11 **Ayutthaya** *var.* Phra Nakhon Si Ayutthaya. Phra Nakhon Si Ayutthaya, C Thailand 14°20′N 100°35′E
136 B13 **Ayvalık** Balıkesir, W Turkey 39°18′N 26°42′E
99 L20 **Aywaille** Liège, E Belgium 50°28′N 05°40′E
141 R13 **'Aywat aş Şay'ar, Wādī** *seasonal river* N Yemen
Azaffal *see* Azeffâl
105 T9 **Azahar, Costa del** *coastal region* E Spain
105 S6 **Azaila** Aragón, NE Spain 41°17′N 00°20′W
104 F10 **Azambuja** Lisboa, C Portugal 39°04′N 08°52′W
153 N13 **Āzamgarh** Uttar Pradesh, N India 26°03′N 83°10′E
77 O9 **Azaouâd** *desert* C Mali
77 S10 **Azaouagh, Vallée de l'** *var.* Azaouak. ≈ W Niger
Azaouak *see* Azaouagh, Vallée de l'
61 F14 **Azara** Misiones, NE Argentina 28°03′S 55°42′W
Azaran *see* Hashtrūd
Azärbaycan/Azärbaycan Respublikasī *see* Azerbaijan
Āz̄arbāyjān-e Bākhtarī *see* Āz̄arbāyjān-e Gharbī
142 I4 **Āz̄arbāyjān-e Gharbī** *off.* Ostān-e Āz̄arbāyjān-e Gharbī, *Eng.* West Azerbaijan; *prev.* Āz̄arbāyjān-e Bākhtarī. NW Iran
Āz̄arbāyjān-e Gharbī, Ostān-e *see* Āz̄arbāyjān-e Gharbī
Āz̄arbāyjān-e Khāvarī *see* Āz̄arbāyjān-e Sharqī
142 J3 **Āz̄arbāyjān-e Sharqī** *off.* Ostān-e Azarbāyjān-e Sharqī, *Eng.* East Azerbaijan; *prev.* Āz̄arbāyjān-e Khāvarī. ◈ *province* NW Iran
Āz̄arbāyjān-e Sharqī, Ostān-e *see* Āz̄arbāyjān-e Sharqī
77 W13 **Azare** Bauchi, N Nigeria 11°41′N 10°09′E
119 M19 **Azarychy** *Rus.* Ozarichi. Homyel'skaya Voblasts', SE Belarus 52°31′N 29°19′E
102 L8 **Azay-le-Rideau** Indre-et-Loire, C France 47°16′N 00°25′E
138 I2 **A'zāz** Ḥalab, NW Syria 36°35′N 37°03′E
76 H7 **Azeffâl** *var.* Azaffal. *desert* Mauritania/Western Sahara
137 V12 **Azerbaijan** *off.* Azerbaijani Republic, *Az.* Azärbaycan, Azärbaycan Respublikasī; *prev.* Azerbaijan SSR. ◆ *republic* SE Asia
Azerbaijani Republic *see* Azerbaijan
Azerbaijan SSR *see* Azerbaijan
145 T7 **Azhbulat, Ozero** ◎ NE Kazakhstan
74 F7 **Azilal** C Morocco 31°58′N 06°53′W
Azimabad *see* Patna
19 O6 **Aziscohos Lake** ▣ Maine, NE USA
Azizbekov *see* Vayk'
Azizie *see* Telish
Aziziya *see* Al 'Azīzīyah
127 T4 **Aznakayevo** Respublika Tatarstan, W Russian Federation 54°55′N 53°15′E
56 C8 **Azogues** Cañar, S Ecuador 02°44′S 78°48′W
64 N2 **Azores** *var.* Açores, Ilhas dos Açores, *Port.* Arquipélago dos Açores. *island group* Portugal, NE Atlantic Ocean
64 L8 **Azores-Biscay Rise** *undersea feature* E Atlantic Ocean 19°00′W 42°40′N
Azotos/Azotus *see* Ashdod
78 K11 **Azoum, Bahr** *seasonal river* SE Chad
126 L12 **Azov** Rostovskaya Oblast', SW Russian Federation 47°07′N 39°26′E
126 J13 **Azov, Sea of** *Rus.* Azovskoye More, *Ukr.* Azovs'ke More. *sea* NE Black Sea
Azovs'ke More/Azovskoye More *see* Azov, Sea of
138 I10 **Azraq, Wāḥat al** *oasis* N Jordan
Āzro *see* Āzrow
74 G6 **Azrou** C Morocco 33°30′N 05°12′W
149 R5 **Āzrow** *var.* Āzro. Lowgar, E Afghanistan 34°11′N 69°39′E
37 P8 **Aztec** New Mexico, SW USA 36°49′N 107°59′W
36 M13 **Aztec Peak** ▲ Arizona, SW USA 33°48′N 110°54′W
45 N9 **Azua** *var.* Azua de Compostela. S Dominican Republic 18°29′N 70°44′W
Azua de Compostela *see* Azua
104 K12 **Azuaga** Extremadura, W Spain 38°16′N 05°40′W
56 B8 **Azuay** ◈ *province* W Ecuador
164 C13 **Azuchi-Ō-shima** *island* SW Japan
105 O11 **Azuer** ≈ C Spain
43 S17 **Azuero, Península de** *peninsula* S Panama
62 I6 **Azufre, Volcán** *var.* Volcán Lastarria. ⛰ N Chile 25°16′S 68°35′W
116 J12 **Azuga** Prahova, SE Romania 45°27′N 25°34′E
61 C22 **Azul** Buenos Aires, E Argentina 36°46′S 59°50′W
62 I8 **Azul, Cerro** ▲ NW Argentina 28°28′S 68°43′W
56 E12 **Azul, Cordillera** ▲▲ C Peru
165 P11 **Azuma-san** ▲ Honshū, C Japan 37°44′N 140°05′E
103 V15 **Azur, Côte d'** *coastal region* SE France
191 Z3 **Azur Lagoon** ◎ Kiritimati, E Kiribati
'Azza *see* Gaza
Az Zāb al Kabīr *see* Great Zab
138 H7 **Az Zabdānī** *var.* Zabadani. Dimashq, W Syria 33°45′N 36°07′E
141 W8 **Az̧ Z̧āhirah** *desert* NW Oman
141 S6 **Az̧ Z̧ahrān** *Eng.* Dhahran. Ash Sharqīyah, NE Saudi Arabia 26°18′N 50°02′E
141 R6 **Az̧ Z̧ahrān al Khubar** *var.* Dhahran Al Khobar. ✈ Ash Sharqīyah, NE Saudi Arabia 26°28′N 49°42′E
75 W7 **Az Zaqāzīq** *var.* Az Zaqāzīq *var.* Zagazig. N Egypt 30°36′N 31°32′E
Az Zaqāzīq *see* Az Zaqāzīq
138 H10 **Az Zarqā'** *var.* Zarqa. Az Zarqā', NW Jordan 32°04′N 36°06′E
138 I11 **Az Zarqā'** *off.* Muḩāfazat az Zarqā', *var.* Zarqa. ◈ *governorate* N Jordan
75 O7 **Az Zāwiyah** *var.* Zawia. NW Libya 32°45′N 12°44′E
141 N15 **Az Zaydīyah** W Yemen 15°20′N 43°03′E
74 I11 **Azzel Matti, Sebkha** *var.* Sebkra Azz el Matti. *salt flat* C Algeria
141 P6 **Az Zilfī** Ar Riyāḑ, N Saudi Arabia 26°17′N 44°48′E
139 Y13 **Az Zubayr** *var.* Al Zubair. Al Başrah, SE Iraq 30°24′N 47°45′E
Az Zuqur *see* Jabal Zuqar, Jazīrat

B

187 X15 **Ba** *prev.* Mba. Viti Levu, W Fiji 17°35′S 177°40′E
Ba *see* Da Răng, Sông
171 P17 **Baa** Pulau Rote, C Indonesia 10°44′S 123°06′E
138 H7 **Baalbek** *var.* Ba'labakk; *anc.* Heliopolis. E Lebanon 34°00′N 36°15′E
108 G8 **Baar** Zug, N Switzerland 47°12′N 08°32′E
81 L17 **Baardheere** *var.* Bardere, *It.* Bardera. Gedo, SW Somalia 02°13′N 42°19′E
80 Q12 **Baargaal** Bari, NE Somalia 11°12′N 51°04′E
99 I15 **Baarle-Hertog** Antwerpen, N Belgium 51°26′N 04°56′E
99 I15 **Baarle-Nassau** Noord-Brabant, S Netherlands 51°27′N 04°56′E
98 J11 **Baarn** Utrecht, C Netherlands 52°13′N 05°16′E
162 H9 **Baatsagaan** *var.* Bayansayr. Bayanhongor, C Mongolia 45°36′N 99°27′E
114 D13 **Baba** *var.* Buševa, *Gk.* Varnoús. ▲▲ FYR Macedonia/Greece
76 H10 **Bababé** Brakna, W Mauritania 16°22′N 13°57′W
136 G10 **Baba Burnu** *headland* NW Turkey 41°18′N 31°24′E
117 N13 **Babadag** Tulcea, SE Romania 44°53′N 28°47′E
137 X10 **Babadağ Dağı** ▲ NE Azerbaijan 41°02′N 48°04′E
146 H14 **Babadaýhan** *Rus.* Babadaykhan; *prev.* Kirovsk. Ahal Welaýaty, C Turkmenistan 37°39′N 60°17′E
Babadaykhan *see* Babadaýhan
146 G14 **Babadurmaz** Ahal Welaýaty, C Turkmenistan 37°39′N 59°03′E
114 M12 **Babaeski** Kırklareli, NW Turkey 41°26′N 27°06′E
139 T4 **Bāba Gurgur** At Ta'mīn, N Iraq 35°34′N 44°18′E
56 B7 **Babahoyo** *prev.* Bodegas. Los Ríos, C Ecuador 01°53′S 79°31′W
149 P5 **Bābā, Kūh-e** ▲▲ C Afghanistan
171 N12 **Babana** Sulawesi, C Indonesia 02°03′S 119°13′E
Babao *see* Qilian
171 Q12 **Babar, Kepulauan** *island group* E Indonesia
171 T12 **Babar, Pulau** *island* Kepulauan Babar, E Indonesia
152 G4 **Bābāsar Pass** *pass* India/Pakistan
Babashy, Gory *see* Babaşy
146 C9 **Babaşy** *Rus.* Gory Babashy. ▲▲ W Turkmenistan
168 M13 **Babat** Sumatera, W Indonesia 02°45′S 104°01′E
Babatag, Khrebet *see* Bototog', Tizmasi
81 H21 **Babati** Manyara, NE Tanzania 04°12′S 35°45′E
124 J13 **Babayevo** Vologodskaya Oblast', NW Russian Federation 59°23′N 35°52′E
127 Q15 **Babayurt** Respublika Dagestan, SW Russian Federation 43°38′N 46°49′E
33 P6 **Babb** Montana, NW USA 48°51′N 113°26′W
29 X4 **Babbitt** Minnesota, N USA 47°42′N 91°56′W
188 E9 **Babeldaob** *var.* Babeldaop, Babelthuap. *island* N Palau
Babeldaop *see* Babeldaob
141 N17 **Bab el Mandeb** *strait* Gulf of Aden/Red Sea
Babelthuap *see* Babeldaob
111 K17 **Babia Góra** *var.* Babia Hora. ▲ Poland/Slovakia 49°33′N 19°32′E
Babia Hora *see* Babia Góra
Babian Jiang *see* Black River
Babichi *see* Babichy
119 N19 **Babichy** *Rus.* Babichi. Homyel'skaya Voblasts', SE Belarus 52°17′N 30°00′E
139 U9 **Bābil** ◈ *governorate* S Iraq
112 I10 **Babina Greda** Vukovar-Srijem, E Croatia 45°09′N 18°33′E
10 K13 **Babine Lake** ◎ British Columbia, SW Canada
143 O4 **Bābol** *var.* Babul, Balfrush, Barfrush; *prev.* Barfurush. Māzandarān, N Iran 36°34′N 52°39′E
143 O4 **Bābolsar** *var.* Babulsar; *prev.* Meshed-i-Sar. Māzandarān, N Iran 36°41′N 52°39′E
36 L16 **Baboquivari Peak** ▲ Arizona, SW USA 31°46′N 111°36′W
79 G15 **Baboua** Nana-Mambéré, W Central African Republic 05°46′N 14°47′E
119 M17 **Babruysk** *Rus.* Bobruysk. Mahilyowskaya Voblasts', E Belarus 53°07′N 29°13′E
Babu *see* Hezhou
Babul *see* Bābol
Babulsar *see* Bābolsar
113 O19 **Babuna** ▲▲ C FYR Macedonia
113 O19 **Babuna** ≈ C FYR Macedonia
148 K7 **Bābūs, Dasht-e** *Pash.* Bebas, Dasht-i. ▲▲ W Afghanistan
171 O1 **Babuyan Channel** *channel* N Philippines
171 O1 **Babuyan Islands** *island* N Philippines
139 T9 **Babylon** *site of ancient city* C Iraq
112 J9 **Bač** *Ger.* Batsch. Vojvodina, NW Serbia 45°24′N 19°17′E
58 M13 **Bacabal** Maranhão, E Brazil 04°15′S 44°45′W
41 Y14 **Bacalar** Quintana Roo, SE Mexico 18°38′N 88°17′W
41 Y14 **Bacalar Chico, Boca** *strait* SE Mexico
171 Q12 **Bacan, Kepulauan** *island group* E Indonesia
171 S12 **Bacan, Pulau** *prev.* Batjan. *island* Maluku, E Indonesia
116 L10 **Bacău** *Hung.* Bákó. Bacău, NE Romania 46°36′N 26°56′E
116 K11 **Bacău** ◈ *county* E Romania
Băc Bô, Vinh *see* Tongking, Gulf of
167 T5 **Băc Can** *var.* Bach Thong. Băc Thai, N Vietnam 22°07′N 105°50′E
103 T5 **Baccarat** Meurthe-et-Moselle, NE France 48°27′N 06°46′E
183 N12 **Bacchus Marsh** Victoria, SE Australia 37°41′S 144°30′E
40 H4 **Bacerac** Sonora, NW Mexico 30°27′N 108°55′W
116 L10 **Băceşti** Vaslui, E Romania 46°50′N 27°14′E
167 T6 **Băc Giang** Ha Băc, N Vietnam 21°17′N 106°12′E
54 I5 **Bachaquero** Zulia, NW Venezuela 09°57′N 71°09′W
Bacher *see* Pohorje
118 M13 **Bacheykava** *Rus.* Bocheykovo. Vitsyebskaya Voblasts', N Belarus 55°01′N 29°09′E
40 I5 **Bachíniva** Chihuahua, N Mexico 28°41′N 107°13′W
Bach Thong *see* Băc Can
158 G8 **Bachu** Xinjiang Uygur Zizhiqu, NW China 39°46′N 78°30′E
9 N8 **Back** ≈ Nunavut, N Canada
112 K10 **Bačka Palanka** *prev.* Palanka. Serbia, NW Serbia 44°22′N 20°57′E
112 K8 **Bačka Topola** *Hung.* Topolya; *prev. Hung.* Bácstopolya. Vojvodina, N Serbia 45°48′N 19°39′E
95 J17 **Bäckefors** Västra Götaland, S Sweden 58°49′N 12°07′E
Bäckermühle Schulzenmühle *see* Żywiec
95 L16 **Bäckhammar** Värmland, C Sweden 59°09′N 14°13′E
112 K9 **Bački Petrovac** *Hung.* Petrőcz; *prev.* Petrovac, Petrovácz. Vojvodina, NW Serbia 45°22′N 19°34′E
101 I21 **Backnang** Baden-Württemberg, SW Germany 48°57′N 09°26′E
167 S15 **Bac Liêu** *var.* Vinh Loi. Minh Hai, S Vietnam 09°17′N 105°44′E
167 T6 **Băc Ninh** Ha Băc, N Vietnam 21°10′N 106°04′E
40 G4 **Bacoachi** Sonora, NW Mexico 30°36′N 110°00′W
171 P6 **Bacolod** *off.* Bacolod City. Negros, C Philippines 10°43′N 122°58′E
Bacolod City *see* Bacolod
171 O4 **Baco, Mount** ▲ Mindoro, N Philippines 12°50′N 121°08′E
111 K25 **Bácsalmás** Bács-Kiskun, S Hungary 46°07′N 19°20′E
Bácsjózseffalva *see* Žednik
111 J24 **Bács-Kiskun** *off.* Bács-Kiskun Megye. ◈ *county* S Hungary
Bács-Kiskun Megye *see* Bács-Kiskun
Bácsszenttamás *see* Srbobran
Bácstopolya *see* Bačka Topola
Bactra *see* Balkh
Bada *see* Xilin
155 F21 **Badagara** *var.* Vadakara. Kerala, SW India 11°36′N 75°34′E *see also* Vadakara
101 M24 **Bad Aibling** Bayern, SE Germany 47°52′N 12°00′E
162 I13 **Badain Jaran Shamo** *desert* N China
104 I11 **Badajoz** *anc.* Pax Augusta. Extremadura, W Spain 38°53′N 06°58′W
104 J11 **Badajoz** ◈ *province* Extremadura, W Spain
149 S2 **Badakhshān** ◈ *province* NE Afghanistan
105 W6 **Badalona** *anc.* Baetulo. Cataluña, E Spain 41°27′N 02°15′E
154 O11 **Bādāmapāhārh** Orissa, E India 22°04′N 86°06′E
152 K8 **Badarīnāth** ▲ N India 30°44′N 79°29′E
169 O10 **Badas, Kepulauan** *island group* W Indonesia
109 S6 **Bad Aussee** Salzburg, E Austria 47°35′N 13°44′E
31 S8 **Bad Axe** Michigan, N USA 43°48′N 83°00′W
101 G16 **Bad Berleburg** Nordrhein-Westfalen, W Germany 51°03′N 08°24′E
101 L17 **Bad Blankenburg** Thüringen, C Germany 50°43′N 11°19′E
Bad Borseck *see* Borsec
101 G18 **Bad Camberg** Hessen, W Germany 50°18′N 08°15′E
100 L8 **Bad Doberan** Mecklenburg-Vorpommern, N Germany 54°06′N 11°55′E
101 N14 **Bad Düben** Sachsen, E Germany 51°35′N 12°34′E
109 X4 **Baden** *var.* Baden bei Wien; *anc.* Aquae Panoniae, Thermae Pannonicae. Niederösterreich, NE Austria 48°01′N 16°14′E
108 F9 **Baden** Aargau, N Switzerland 47°28′N 08°19′E
101 G21 **Baden-Baden** *anc.* Aurelia Aquensis. Baden-Württemberg, SW Germany 48°46′N 08°14′E
Baden bei Wien *see* Baden
101 G22 **Baden-Württemberg** *Fr.* Bade-Wurtemberg. ◈ *state* SW Germany
112 A10 **Baderna** Istra, NW Croatia 45°12′N 13°45′E
Bade-Wurtemberg *see* Baden-Württemberg
101 H20 **Bad Fredrichshall** Baden-Württemberg, S Germany 49°13′N 09°15′E
100 P11 **Bad Freienwalde** Brandenburg, NE Germany 52°47′N 14°04′E
109 Q8 **Badgastein** *var.* Gastein. Salzburg, NW Austria 47°07′N 13°09′E
Badger State *see* Wisconsin
148 L4 **Bādghīs** ◈ *province* NW Afghanistan
109 T5 **Bad Hall** Oberösterreich, N Austria 48°03′N 14°13′E
101 J14 **Bad Harzburg** Niedersachsen, C Germany 51°52′N 10°34′E
101 I16 **Bad Hersfeld** Hessen, C Germany 50°52′N 09°42′E
98 I10 **Badhoevedorp** Noord-Holland, C Netherlands 52°21′N 04°46′E
109 Q8 **Bad Hofgastein** Salzburg, NW Austria 47°11′N 13°07′E
Bad Homburg *see* Bad Homburg vor der Höhe
101 G18 **Bad Homburg vor der Höhe** *var.* Bad Homburg. Hessen, W Germany 50°14′N 08°37′E
101 E17 **Bad Honnef** Nordrhein-Westfalen, W Germany 50°39′N 07°13′E
149 Q17 **Badīn** Sind, SE Pakistan 24°38′N 68°53′E
21 S10 **Badin Lake** ▣ North Carolina, SE USA
40 I8 **Badiraguato** Sinaloa, C Mexico 25°21′N 107°31′W
109 R6 **Bad Ischl** Oberösterreich, N Austria 47°43′N 13°36′E
Badjawa *see* Bajawa
Badje-Sohppar *see* Övre Soppero
101 J18 **Bad Kissingen** Bayern, SE Germany 50°12′N 10°04′E
Bad Königswart *see* Lázně Kynžvart
101 F19 **Bad Kreuznach** Rheinland-Pfalz, SW Germany 49°51′N 07°52′E
101 F24 **Bad Krozingen** Baden-Württemberg, SW Germany 47°55′N 07°43′E
101 G16 **Bad Laasphe** Nordrhein-Westfalen, W Germany 50°57′N 08°24′E
28 J6 **Badlands** *physical region* North Dakota/South Dakota, N USA
101 K16 **Bad Langensalza** Thüringen, C Germany 51°05′N 10°40′E
109 T3 **Bad Leonfelden** Oberösterreich, N Austria 48°31′N 14°17′E
101 I20 **Bad Mergentheim** Baden-Württemberg, SW Germany 49°30′N 09°46′E
101 H17 **Bad Nauheim** Hessen, W Germany 50°22′N 08°45′E
101 E17 **Bad Neuenahr-Arhweiler** Rheinland-Pfalz, W Germany 50°33′N 07°07′E
Bad Neustadt *see* Bad Neustadt an der Saale
101 J18 **Bad Neustadt an der Saale** *var.* Bad Neustadt. Berlin, C Germany 50°21′N 10°13′E
Badnur *see* Betūl
100 H13 **Bad Oeynhausen** Nordrhein-Westfalen, NW Germany 52°12′N 08°48′E
100 J9 **Bad Oldesloe** Schleswig-Holstein, N Germany 53°49′N 10°22′E
77 Q16 **Badou** C Togo 07°37′N 00°37′E
Bad Polzin *see* Połczyn-Zdrój
100 H13 **Bad Pyrmont** Niedersachsen, C Germany 51°58′N 09°16′E
109 X9 **Bad Radkersburg** Steiermark, SE Austria 46°40′N 16°02′E
139 V8 **Badrah** Wāsiţ, E Iraq 33°06′N 45°58′E
Badrah *see* Tarialan
101 N24 **Bad Reichenhall** Bayern, SE Germany 47°43′N 12°52′E
140 K8 **Badr Ḩunayn** Al Madīnah, W Saudi Arabia 23°46′N 38°45′E
28 M10 **Bad River** ≈ South Dakota, N USA
30 K4 **Bad River** ≈ Wisconsin, N USA
100 H13 **Bad Salzuflen** Nordrhein-Westfalen, NW Germany 52°06′N 08°45′E
101 J16 **Bad Salzungen** Thüringen, C Germany 50°48′N 10°15′E
109 V8 **Bad Sankt Leonhard im Lavanttal** Kärnten, S Austria 46°55′N 14°51′E
100 K9 **Bad Schwartau** Schleswig-Holstein, N Germany 53°55′N 10°42′E
101 L24 **Bad Tölz** Bayern, SE Germany 47°44′N 11°34′E
181 U1 **Badu Island** *island* Queensland, NE Australia
155 K25 **Badulla** Uva Province, C Sri Lanka 06°59′N 81°03′E
109 X5 **Bad Vöslau** Niederösterreich, NE Austria 47°58′N 16°13′E
101 I24 **Bad Waldsee** Baden-Württemberg, S Germany 47°54′N 09°44′E
35 U11 **Badwater Basin** *depression* California, W USA
101 J20 **Bad Windsheim** Bayern, C Germany 49°30′N 10°25′E
101 J23 **Bad Wörishofen** Bayern, S Germany 48°00′N 10°36′E
100 G10 **Bad Zwischenahn** Niedersachsen, NW Germany 53°10′N 08°01′E
104 M13 **Baena** Andalucía, S Spain 36°37′N 04°20′W
Baeterrae/Baeterrae Septimanorum *see* Béziers
Baetic Cordillera/Baetic Mountains *see* Béticos, Sistemas
Baetulo *see* Badalona
57 K18 **Baeza** Napo, NE Ecuador 0°30′S 77°52′W
105 N13 **Baeza** Andalucía, S Spain 38°00′N 03°28′W
79 D15 **Bafang** Ouest, W Cameroon 05°10′N 10°11′E
76 H12 **Bafatá** C Guinea-Bissau 12°09′N 14°38′W
149 U5 **Baffa** North-West Frontier Province, NW Pakistan 34°30′N 73°18′E
197 O11 **Baffin Basin** *undersea feature* N Labrador Sea
197 N12 **Baffin Bay** *bay* Canada/Greenland
25 T15 **Baffin Bay** *inlet* Texas, SW USA
196 M12 **Baffin Island** *island* Nunavut, NE Canada
79 E15 **Bafia** Centre, C Cameroon 04°49′N 11°14′E
77 R14 **Bafilo** NE Togo 09°23′N 01°20′E
76 J12 **Bafing** ≈ W Africa
76 J12 **Bafoulabé** Kayes, W Mali 13°43′N 10°49′W
79 D15 **Bafoussam** Ouest, W Cameroon 05°31′N 10°25′E
143 R9 **Bāfq** Yazd, C Iran 31°35′N 55°21′E
136 L10 **Bafra** Samsun, N Turkey 41°34′N 35°56′E
136 L10 **Bafra Burnu** *headland* N Turkey 41°42′N 36°02′E
143 S12 **Bāft** Kermān, S Iran 29°12′N 56°36′E
79 N18 **Bafwabalinga** Orientale, NE Dem. Rep. Congo 0°52′N 26°55′E
79 N18 **Bafwaboli** Orientale, NE Dem. Rep. Congo 0°36′N 26°08′E
79 N17 **Bafwasende** Orientale, NE Dem. Rep. Congo 01°00′N 27°09′E
42 K13 **Bagaces** Guanacaste, NW Costa Rica 10°31′N 85°18′W
153 O12 **Bagaha** Bihār, N India 27°08′N 84°04′E
155 F16 **Bāgalkot** Karnātaka, W India 16°11′N 75°42′E
81 J22 **Bagamoyo** Pwani, E Tanzania 06°26′S 38°55′E
Bagan Datok *see* Bagan Datuk
168 J8 **Bagan Datuk** *var.* Bagan Datok. Perak, Peninsular Malaysia 03°58′N 100°47′E
171 R7 **Baganga** Mindanao, S Philippines 07°31′N 126°34′E
168 J9 **Bagansiapiapi** *var.* Pasirpangarayan. Sumatera, W Indonesia 02°06′N 100°52′E
162 M8 **Baganuur** *var.* Nüürst. Töv, C Mongolia 47°44′N 108°22′E
Bagaria *see* Bagheria
77 T11 **Bagaroua** Tahoua, W Niger 14°34′N 04°24′E
79 I20 **Bagata** Bandundu, W Dem. Rep. Congo 03°47′S 17°57′E
Bagdad *see* Baghdād
123 O13 **Bagdarin** Respublika Buryatiya, S Russian Federation 54°27′N 113°34′E
61 G17 **Bagé** Rio Grande do Sul, S Brazil 31°22′S 54°06′W
Bagenalstown *see* Muine Bheag
153 T16 **Bagerhat** *var.* Bagherhat. Khulna, S Bangladesh 22°40′N 89°48′E
103 P16 **Bages et de Sigean, Étang de** ◎ S France
152 K10 **Bāgeshwar** Uttarakhand, N India 29°50′N 79°46′E
33 W17 **Baggs** Wyoming, C USA 41°02′N 107°39′W
154 F11 **Bāgh** Madhya Pradesh, C India 22°22′N 74°49′E
139 T8 **Baghdād** *off.* Muḩāfaz̧at Baghdād. ◈ *governorate* C Iraq
139 T8 **Baghdād** *var.* Bagdad, *Eng.* Baghdad. ● Baghdād, C Iraq 33°20′N 44°26′E
139 T8 **Baghdād** ✈ (Baghdād) Baghdād, C Iraq 33°20′N 44°26′E
Baghdad *see* Baghdād
Baghdād, Muḩāfaz̧at *see* Baghdād
Bagherhat *see* Bagerhat
107 J23 **Bagheria** *var.* Bagaria. Sicilia, Italy, C Mediterranean Sea 38°05′N 13°31′E
143 S10 **Bāghīn** Kermān, C Iran 30°50′N 57°00′E
149 Q3 **Baghlān** Baghlān, NE Afghanistan 36°11′N 68°44′E
149 Q3 **Baghlān** *var.* Bāghlān. ◈ *province* NE Afghanistan
Bāghlān *see* Baghlān
148 M7 **Bāghrān** Helmand, S Afghanistan 32°55′N 64°57′E
29 T4 **Bagley** Minnesota, N USA 47°31′N 95°24′W
106 H10 **Bagnacavallo** Emilia-Romagna, C Italy 44°00′N 12°59′E
102 K16 **Bagnères-de-Bigorre** Hautes-Pyrénées, S France 43°04′N 00°09′E
102 L17 **Bagnères-de-Luchon** Hautes-Pyrénées, S France 42°46′N 00°34′E
106 F11 **Bagni di Lucca** Toscana, C Italy 44°01′N 10°38′E

◆ Country
● Country Capital
◇ Dependent Territory
○ Dependent Territory Capital
◈ Administrative Regions
✈ International Airport
▲ Mountain
▲▲ Mountain Range
⛰ Volcano
≈ River
◎ Lake
▣ Reservoir

Bagno di Romagna – Bandar-e Dayyer

106 H11 **Bagno di Romagna** Emilia-Romagna, C Italy 43°51′N 11°57′E
103 R14 **Bagnols-sur-Cèze** Gard, S France 44°10′N 04°37′E
162 M14 **Bag Nur** ◎ N China
166 L8 **Bago** *var.* Pegu. Bago, SW Burma (Myanmar) 17°18′N 96°31′E
171 P6 **Bago** *off.* Bago City. Negros, C Philippines 10°30′N 122°49′E
166 L7 **Bago** *var.* Pegu. ⬖ *division* S Burma (Myanmar)
Bago City *see* Bago
76 M13 **Bagoé** 〰 Ivory Coast/Mali
Bagrāmē *see* Bagrāmī
149 R5 **Bagrāmī** *var.* Bagrāmē. Kâbōl, E Afghanistan 34°29′N 69°16′E
119 B14 **Bagrationovsk** *Ger.* Preussisch Eylau. Kaliningradskaya Oblast', W Russian Federation 54°24′N 20°39′E
Bagrax *see* Bohu
Bagrax Hu *see* Bosten Hu
56 C10 **Bagua** Amazonas, NE Peru 05°37′S 78°36′W
171 O2 **Baguio** *off.* Baguio City. Luzon, N Philippines 16°25′N 120°36′E
Baguio City *see* Baguio
77 V9 **Bagzane, Monts** ▲ N Niger 17°48′N 08°43′E
Bāḩah, Minţaqat al *see* Al Bāḩah
Bahama Islands *see* Bahamas
44 H3 **Bahamas** *off.* Commonwealth of the Bahamas. ◆ *commonwealth republic* N West Indies
0 L13 **Bahamas** *var.* Bahama Islands. *island group* N West Indies
Bahamas, Commonwealth of the *see* Bahamas
153 S15 **Baharampur** *prev.* Berhampore. West Bengal, NE India 24°06′N 88°19′E
146 E12 **Baharly** *var.* Bäherden, *Rus.* Bakharden; *prev.* Bakherden. Ahal Welaýaty, C Turkmenistan 38°30′N 57°18′E
149 U10 **Bahāwalnagar** Punjab, E Pakistan 30°00′N 73°03′E
149 T11 **Bahāwalpur** Punjab, E Pakistan 29°25′N 71°40′E
136 L16 **Bahçe** Osmaniye, S Turkey 37°14′N 36°34′E
160 J8 **Ba He** 〰 C China
Bäherden *see* Baharly
59 N16 **Bahia** *off.* Estado da Bahia. ⬖ *state* E Brazil
61 B24 **Bahía Blanca** Buenos Aires, E Argentina 38°43′S 62°19′W
40 L15 **Bahía Bufadero** Michoacán, SW Mexico
63 J19 **Bahía Bustamante** Chubut, SE Argentina 45°06′S 66°30′W
40 D5 **Bahía de los Ángeles** Baja California Norte, NW Mexico
40 C6 **Bahía de Tortugas** Baja California Sur, NW Mexico 27°42′N 114°54′W
Bahia, Estado da *see* Bahia
42 J4 **Bahía, Islas de la** *Eng.* Bay Islands. *island group* N Honduras
40 E5 **Bahía Kino** Sonora, NW Mexico 28°48′N 111°55′W
40 E9 **Bahía Magdalena** *var.* Puerto Magdalena. Baja California Sur, NW Mexico 24°34′N 112°07′W
54 C8 **Bahía Solano** *var.* Ciudad Mutis, Solano. Chocó, W Colombia 06°13′N 77°27′W
80 I11 **Bahir Dar** *var.* Bahr Dar, Bahrdar Giyorgis. Āmara, N Ethiopia 11°34′N 37°23′E
141 X8 **Bahlā'** *var.* Bahlah, Bahlat. NW Oman 22°58′N 57°16′E
Bāhla *see* Bālān
Bahlah/Bahlat *see* Bahlā'
152 M11 **Bahraich** Uttar Pradesh, N India 27°35′N 81°36′E
143 M14 **Bahrain** *off.* State of Bahrain, Dawlat al Bahrayn, *Ar.* Al Baḩrayn, *prev.* Bahrein; *anc.* Tylos, Tyros. ◆ *monarchy* SW Asia
142 M14 **Bahrain** ✈ C Bahrain 26°15′N 50°39′E
142 M15 **Bahrain, Gulf of** *gulf* Persian Gulf, NW Arabian Sea
Bahrain, State of *see* Bahrain
138 I7 **Baḩrat Mallāḩah** ◎ W Syria
Bahrayn, Dawlat al *see* Bahrain
Bahr Dar/Bahrdar Giyorgis *see* Bahir Dar
Bahrein *see* Bahrain
Bahr el, Azraq *see* Blue Nile
Bahr el Gebel *see* Central Equatoria
Bahr el Jebel *see* Central Equatoria
80 E13 **Bahr ez Zaref** 〰 C Sudan
67 R8 **Bahr Kameur** 〰 N Central African Republic
Bahr Tabariya, Sea of *see* Tiberias, Lake
143 W15 **Bāhū Kalāt** Sīstān va Balūchestān, SE Iran 25°42′N 61°28′E
118 N13 **Bahushewsk** *Rus.* Bogushëvsk. Vitsyebskaya Voblasts', NE Belarus 54°51′N 30°13′E
Bai *see* Tagow Bāy
116 G13 **Baia de Aramă** Mehedinţi, SW Romania 45°00′N 22°43′E
116 G11 **Baia de Criş** *Ger.* Altenburg, *Hung.* Körösbánya. Hunedoara, SW Romania 46°10′N 22°41′E
83 A16 **Baia dos Tigres** Namibe, SW Angola 16°36′S 11°44′E
82 A13 **Baia Farta** Benguela, W Angola 12°38′S 13°12′E
116 H9 **Baia Mare** *Ger.* Frauenbach, *Hung.* Nagybánya; *prev.* Neustadt. Maramureş, NW Romania 47°40′N 23°35′E
116 H8 **Baia Sprie** *Ger.* Mittelstadt, *Hung.* Felsőbánya. Maramureş, NW Romania 47°40′N 23°42′E
78 G13 **Baïbokoum** Logone-Oriental, SW Chad 07°46′N 15°43′E
160 F12 **Baicao Ling** ▲▲ SW China
163 U9 **Baicheng** *var.* Pai-ch'eng; *prev.* T'aon-an. Jilin, NE China 45°32′N 122°51′E
158 I6 **Baicheng** *var.* Bay. Xinjiang Uygur Zizhiqu, NW China 41°49′N 81°45′E
116 J13 **Băicoi** Prahova, SE Romania 45°02′N 25°51′E
Baidoa *see* Baydhabo
15 U6 **Baie-Comeau** Québec, SE Canada 49°12′N 68°10′W
15 U6 **Baie-des-Sables** Québec, SE Canada 48°41′N 67°55′W
15 T7 **Baie-des-Bacon** Québec, SE Canada 48°31′N 69°17′W
15 S8 **Baie-des-Rochers** Québec, SE Canada 47°57′N 69°50′W
12 K11 **Baie-du-Poste** Québec, SE Canada 50°20′N 73°50′W
172 H17 **Baie Lazare** Mahé, NE Seychelles 04°45′S 55°29′E
45 Y5 **Baie-Mahault** Basse Terre, C Guadeloupe 16°16′N 61°35′W
15 R9 **Baie-St-Paul** Québec, SE Canada 47°27′N 70°30′W
15 V5 **Baie-Trinité** Québec, SE Canada 49°25′N 67°20′W
13 T11 **Baie Verte** Newfoundland and Labrador, SE Canada 49°55′N 56°12′W
Baiguan *see* Shangyu
Baihe *see* Erdaobaihe
139 U11 **Bā'ij al Mahdī** Al Muthanná, S Iraq 31°21′N 44°57′E
Baiji *see* Bayjī
158 K4 **Baijiantan** *var.* Uxin Qi. Xinjiang Uygur Zizhiqu, NW China 45°38′N 85°11′E
Baikal, Lake *see* Baykal, Ozero
154 L11 **Baikunthpur** Chhattīsgarh, SW India 23°18′N 82°32′E
Bailādila *see* Kirandul
Baile an Chaistil *see* Ballycastle
Baile an Róba *see* Ballinrobe
Baile an tSratha *see* Ballintra
Baile Átha an Rí *see* Athenry
Baile Átha Buí *see* Athboy
Baile Átha Cliath *see* Dublin
Baile Átha Fhirdhia *see* Ardee
Baile Átha Í *see* Athy
Baile Átha Luain *see* Athlone
Baile Átha Troim *see* Trim
Baile Brigín *see* Balbriggan
Baile Easa Dara *see* Ballysadare
116 I13 **Băile Govora** Vâlcea, SW Romania 45°00′N 24°08′E
116 F13 **Băile Herculane** *Ger.* Herkulesbad, *Hung.* Herkulesfürdő. Caraş-Severin, SW Romania 44°51′N 22°24′E
Baile Locha Riach *see* Loughrea
Baile Mhistéala *see* Mitchelstown
Baile Monaidh *see* Ballymoney
105 N12 **Bailén** Andalucía, S Spain 38°06′N 03°46′W
Baile na hInse *see* Ballynahinch
Baile na Lorgan *see* Castleblayney
Baile na Mainistreach *see* Newtownabbey
Baile Nua na hArda *see* Newtownards
116 I12 **Băile Olăneşti** Vâlcea, SW Romania 45°14′N 24°18′E
116 H14 **Băileşti** Dolj, SW Romania 44°01′N 23°20′E
163 N12 **Bailingmiao** *var.* Darhan Muminggan Lianheqi. Nei Mongol Zizhiqu, N China 41°41′N 110°25′E
58 K11 **Bailique, Ilha** *island* NE Brazil
103 O1 **Bailleul** Nord, N France 50°43′N 02°43′E
78 H12 **Ba Illi** Chari-Baguirmi, SW Chad 10°31′N 16°29′E
159 V12 **Bailong Jiang** 〰 C China
82 C13 **Bailundo** *Port.* Vila Teixeira da Silva. Huambo, C Angola 12°12′S 15°52′E
159 T13 **Baima** *var.* Sêraitang. Qinghai, C China 32°55′N 100°44′E
Baima *see* Baxoi
186 C8 **Baimuru** Gulf, S Papua New Guinea 07°34′S 144°49′E
158 M16 **Bainang** Xizang Zizhiqu, W China 28°57′N 89°31′E
23 S8 **Bainbridge** Georgia, SE USA 30°54′N 84°33′W
171 O17 **Baing** Pulau Sumba, SE Indonesia 10°09′S 120°34′E
158 M14 **Baingoin** *var.* Pubao. Xizang Zizhiqu, W China 31°22′N 90°00′E
104 G2 **Baio Grande** Galicia, NW Spain 43°08′N 08°58′W
104 G4 **Baiona** Galicia, NW Spain 42°06′N 08°49′W
163 V7 **Baiquan** Heilongjiang, NE China 47°37′N 126°04′E
Bā'ir *see* Bāyir
158 I11 **Bairab Co** ◎ W China
25 Q7 **Baird** Texas, SW USA 32°23′N 99°24′W
39 N7 **Baird Mountains** ▲▲ Alaska, USA
Baireuth *see* Bayreuth
190 H3 **Bairiki** ● (Kiribati) Tarawa, NW Kiribati 01°20′N 173°01′E
Bairin Youqi *see* Daban
Bairin Zuoqi *see* Lindong
145 P17 **Bairkum** *Kaz.* Bayyrqum. Yuzhnyy Kazakhstan, S Kazakhstan 41°57′N 68°05′E
183 P12 **Bairnsdale** Victoria, SE Australia 37°51′S 147°38′E
171 P6 **Bais** Negros, S Philippines 09°36′N 123°07′E
102 L15 **Baïse** *var.* Baise. 〰 S France
Baise *see* Baïse
163 W11 **Baishan** *prev.* Hunjiang. Jilin, NE China 41°57′N 126°31′E
Baishan *see* Mashan
118 F12 **Baisogala** Šiauliai, C Lithuania 55°38′N 23°44′E
189 Q7 **Baiti** N Nauru 0°30′S 166°55′E
Baitou Shan *see* Paektu-san
104 G13 **Baixo Alentejo** *physical region* S Portugal
64 P5 **Baixo, Ilhéu de** *island* Madeira, Portugal, NE Atlantic Ocean
83 E15 **Baixo Longa** Cuando Cubango, SE Angola 15°39′S 18°39′E
159 V10 **Baiyin** Gansu, C China 36°33′N 104°11′E
160 E8 **Baiyü** *var.* Jianshe. Sichuan, C China 30°37′N 97°15′E
161 N14 **Baiyun** ✈ (Guangzhou) Guangdong, S China 23°12′N 113°19′E
160 K4 **Baiyu Shan** ▲▲ C China
111 J25 **Baja** Bács-Kiskun, S Hungary 46°13′N 18°56′E
40 C4 **Baja California** *Eng.* Lower California. *peninsula* NW Mexico
40 C4 **Baja California Norte** ⬖ *state* NW Mexico
40 E9 **Baja California Sur** ⬖ *state* NW Mexico
Bājah *see* Béja
Bajan *see* Bayan
191 V16 **Baja, Punta** *headland* Easter Island, Chile, E Pacific Ocean 27°10′S 109°21′W
40 B4 **Baja, Punta** *headland* NW Mexico 29°57′N 115°48′W
55 R5 **Baja, Punta** *headland* NE Venezuela
42 D5 **Baja Verapaz** *off.* Departamento de Baja Verapaz. ⬖ *department* C Guatemala
Baja Verapaz, Departamento de *see* Baja Verapaz
171 N16 **Bajawa** *prev.* Badjawa. Flores, S Indonesia 08°46′S 120°59′E
153 S16 **Baj Baj** *prev.* Budge-Budge. West Bengal, E India 22°29′N 88°11′E
141 N15 **Bājil** W Yemen 15°05′N 43°16′E
183 U4 **Bajimba, Mount** ▲ New South Wales, SE Australia 29°19′S 152°04′E
112 K13 **Bajina Bašta** Serbia, W Serbia 43°58′N 19°33′E
153 U14 **Bajitpur** Dhaka, E Bangladesh 24°12′N 90°57′E
112 K8 **Bajmok** Vojvodina, NW Serbia 45°59′N 19°25′E
Bajo Boquete *see* Boquete
113 L17 **Bajram Curri** Kukës, N Albania 42°23′N 20°06′E
79 J14 **Bakala** Ouaka, C Central African Republic 06°03′N 20°31′E
127 T4 **Bakaly** Respublika Bashkortostan, W Russian Federation 55°10′N 53°46′E
Bakan *see* Shimonoseki
145 U14 **Bakanas** *Kaz.* Baqanas. Almaty, SE Kazakhstan 44°50′N 76°13′E
145 V12 **Bakanas** *Kaz.* Baqanas. 〰 E Kazakhstan
149 R4 **Bākārak** Panjshīr, NE Afghanistan 35°16′N 69°28′E
145 U14 **Bakbakty** *Kaz.* Baqbaqty. Almaty, SE Kazakhstan 44°36′N 76°41′E
122 J12 **Bakchar** Tomskaya Oblast', C Russian Federation 56°58′N 81°59′E
76 I11 **Bakel** E Senegal 14°54′N 12°26′W
35 W13 **Baker** California, W USA 35°15′N 116°04′W
22 J8 **Baker** Louisiana, S USA 30°35′N 91°10′W
33 Y9 **Baker** Montana, NW USA 46°22′N 104°16′W
32 L12 **Baker** Oregon, NW USA 44°46′N 117°50′W
192 L7 **Baker and Howland Islands** ◇ *US unincorporated territory* W Polynesia
36 L12 **Baker Butte** ▲ Arizona, SW USA 34°24′N 111°22′W
39 X15 **Baker Island** *island* Alexander Archipelago, Alaska, USA
9 N9 **Baker Lake** Nunavut, N Canada 64°20′N 96°10′W
9 N9 **Baker Lake** ◎ Nunavut, N Canada
32 H6 **Baker, Mount** ▲ Washington, NW USA 48°46′N 121°48′W
35 R13 **Bakersfield** California, W USA 35°22′N 119°01′W
24 M9 **Bakersfield** Texas, SW USA 30°54′N 102°21′W
21 P9 **Bakersville** North Carolina, SE USA 36°01′N 82°09′W
Bakhābī *see* Bū Khābī
Bakharden *see* Baharly
Bakhardok *see* Bokurdak
143 U5 **Bākharz, Kuhhā-ye** ▲▲ NE Iran
152 D13 **Bākhāsar** Rājasthān, NW India 24°42′N 71°11′E
Bakhchisaray *see* Bakhchysaray
117 T13 **Bakhchysaray** *Rus.* Bakhchisaray. Respublika Krym, S Ukraine 44°44′N 33°53′E
Bakherden *see* Baharly
117 R3 **Bakhmach** Chernihivs'ka Oblast', N Ukraine 51°10′N 32°48′E
Bākhtarān *see* Kermānshāh
143 Q11 **Bakhtegān, Daryācheh-ye** ◎ C Iran
145 X12 **Bakhty** Vostochnyy Kazakhstan, E Kazakhstan 46°41′N 82°45′E
137 Z11 **Bakı** *Eng.* Baku. ● (Azerbaijan) E Azerbaijan 40°24′N 49°51′E
80 M12 **Baki** Awdal, N Somalia 10°10′N 43°45′E
137 Z11 **Bakı** ✈ E Azerbaijan 40°26′N 49°55′E
136 C13 **Bakır Çayı** 〰 W Turkey
92 L1 **Bakkafjördhur** Austurland, NE Iceland 66°01′N 14°49′W
92 L1 **Bakkaflói** *sea area* W Norwegian Sea
81 I15 **Bako** Southern Nationalities, S Ethiopia 05°45′N 36°39′E
76 L15 **Bako** NW Ivory Coast 09°08′N 07°40′W
Bákó *see* Bacău
111 H23 **Bakony** *Eng.* Bakony Mountains, *Ger.* Bakonywald. ▲▲ W Hungary
Bakony Mountains/Bakonywald *see* Bakony
81 M16 **Bakool** *off.* Gobolka Bakool. ⬖ *region* W Somalia
Bakool, Gobolka *see* Bakool
79 L15 **Bakouma** Mbomou, SE Central African Republic 05°42′N 22°43′E
127 N15 **Baksan** Kabardino-Balkarskaya Respublika, SW Russian Federation 43°43′N 43°31′E
119 I16 **Bakshty** Hrodzyenskaya Voblasts', W Belarus 53°56′N 26°11′E
Baku *see* Bakı
194 K12 **Bakutis Coast** *physical region* Antarctica
Bakwanga *see* Mbuji-Mayi
145 O15 **Bakyrly** Yuzhnyy Kazakhstan, S Kazakhstan 44°30′N 67°41′E
14 H13 **Bala** Ontario, S Canada 45°01′N 79°37′W
136 I13 **Balâ** Ankara, C Turkey 39°34′N 33°07′E
97 J19 **Bala** NW Wales, United Kingdom 52°54′N 03°31′W
170 L7 **Balabac Island** *island* W Philippines
Balabac, Selat *see* Balabac Strait
169 V5 **Balabac Strait** *var.* Selat Balabac. *strait* Malaysia/Philippines
Ba'labakk *see* Baalbek
187 P16 **Balabio, Île** *island* Province Nord, W New Caledonia
116 I14 **Balaci** Teleorman, S Romania 44°21′N 24°55′E
139 S7 **Balad** Şalāḩ ad Dīn, N Iraq 34°00′N 44°07′E
139 U7 **Balad Rūz** Diyālá, E Iraq 33°42′N 45°04′E
154 J11 **Bālāghāt** Madhya Pradesh, C India 21°48′N 80°11′E
155 F14 **Bālāghāt Range** ▲▲ W India
103 X14 **Balagne** *physical region* Corse, France, C Mediterranean Sea
105 U5 **Balaguer** Cataluña, NE Spain 41°48′N 00°48′E
105 S3 **Balaïtous** *var.* Pic de Balaitous. ▲ France/Spain 42°51′N 00°17′W
Balaitous, Pic de *see* Balaïtous
Bálák *see* Ballangen
127 O3 **Balakhna** Nizhegorodskaya Oblast', W Russian Federation 56°26′N 43°43′E
122 L12 **Balakhta** Krasnoyarskiy Kray, S Russian Federation 55°22′N 91°24′E
182 I9 **Balaklava** South Australia 34°10′S 138°22′E
Balakleya *see* Balakliya
117 V6 **Balakliya** *Rus.* Balakleya. Kharkivs'ka Oblast', E Ukraine 49°27′N 36°53′E
127 Q7 **Balakovo** Saratovskaya Oblast', W Russian Federation 52°03′N 47°47′E
83 P14 **Balama** Cabo Delgado, N Mozambique 13°18′S 38°39′E
169 U6 **Balambangan, Pulau** *island* East Malaysia
148 L3 **Bālā Morghāb** Laghmān, NW Afghanistan 35°38′N 63°21′E
152 E11 **Bālān** *prev.* Bāhla. Rājasthān, NW India 27°45′N 71°32′E
116 J10 **Bălan** *Hung.* Balánbánya. Harghita, C Romania 46°39′N 25°47′E
Balánbánya *see* Bălan
171 O3 **Balanga** Luzon, N Philippines 14°40′N 120°32′E
154 M12 **Balāngīr** *prev.* Bolangir. Orissa, E India 20°41′N 83°30′E
127 N8 **Balashov** Saratovskaya Oblast', W Russian Federation 51°32′N 43°14′E
Balasore *see* Bāleshwar
111 K21 **Balassagyarmat** Nógrád, N Hungary 48°06′N 19°17′E
29 S10 **Balaton** Minnesota, N USA 44°13′N 95°52′W
111 H24 **Balaton** *var.* Lake Balaton, *Ger.* Plattensee. ◎ W Hungary
111 I23 **Balatonfüred** *var.* Füred. Veszprém, W Hungary 46°59′N 17°53′E
Balaton, Lake *see* Balaton
116 I11 **Bălăuşeri** *Ger.* Bladenmarkt, *Hung.* Balavásár. Mureş, C Romania 46°24′N 24°41′E
Balavásár *see* Bălăuşeri
105 Q11 **Balazote** Castilla-La Mancha, C Spain 38°54′N 02°09′W
Balázsfalva *see* Blaj
119 F14 **Balbieriškis** Kaunas, S Lithuania 54°29′N 23°52′E
186 J7 **Balbi, Mount** ▲ Bougainville Island, NE Papua New Guinea 05°51′S 154°58′E
58 F11 **Balbina, Represa** ⊠ NW Brazil
43 T15 **Balboa** Panamá, C Panama 08°55′N 79°36′W
97 G17 **Balbriggan** *Ir.* Baile Brigín. E Ireland 53°37′N 06°11′W
Balbunar *see* Kubrat
81 N17 **Balcad** Shabeellaha Dhexe, C Somalia 02°19′N 45°19′E
61 D23 **Balcarce** Buenos Aires, E Argentina 37°51′S 58°16′W
11 U16 **Balcarres** Saskatchewan, S Canada 50°49′N 103°31′W
114 O8 **Balchik** Dobrich, NE Bulgaria 43°25′N 28°11′E
185 E24 **Balclutha** Otago, South Island, New Zealand 46°15′S 169°45′E
25 Q12 **Balcones Escarpment** *escarpment* Texas, SW USA
18 F14 **Bald Eagle Creek** 〰 Pennsylvania, NE USA
Baldenburg *see* Biały Bór
21 V12 **Bald Head Island** *island* North Carolina, SE USA
27 W10 **Bald Knob** Arkansas, C USA 35°18′N 91°34′W
30 K17 **Bald Knob** *hill* Illinois, N USA
Baldohn *see* Baldone
118 G9 **Baldone** *Ger.* Baldohn. Rīga, W Latvia 56°46′N 24°18′E
22 I9 **Baldwin** Louisiana, S USA 29°50′N 91°32′W
31 P7 **Baldwin** Michigan, N USA 43°54′N 85°50′W
27 Q4 **Baldwin City** Kansas, C USA 38°43′N 95°12′W
39 N8 **Baldwin Peninsula** *headland* Alaska, USA 66°45′N 162°19′W
18 H9 **Baldwinsville** New York, NE USA 43°09′N 76°19′W
23 N2 **Baldwyn** Mississippi, S USA 34°30′N 88°38′W
11 W15 **Baldy Mountain** ▲ Manitoba, S Canada 51°29′N 100°46′W
33 T7 **Baldy Mountain** ▲ Montana, NW USA 48°09′N 109°39′W
37 O13 **Baldy Peak** ▲ Arizona, SW USA 33°56′N 109°37′W
Bâle *see* Basel
Balearic Plain *see* Algerian Basin
Baleares *see* Illes Baleares
105 X11 **Baleares, Islas** *Eng.* Balearic Islands. *island group* Spain, W Mediterranean Sea
Baleares Major *see* Mallorca
Balearic Islands *see* Baleares, Islas
Balearis Minor *see* Menorca
169 S9 **Baleh, Batang** 〰 East Malaysia
12 J8 **Baleine, Grande Rivière de la** 〰 Québec, E Canada
12 K7 **Baleine, Petite Rivière de la** 〰 Québec, NE Canada
12 K7 **Baleine, Petite Rivière de la** 〰 Québec, SE Canada
13 N6 **Baleine, Rivière à la** 〰 Québec, E Canada
99 J16 **Balen** Antwerpen, N Belgium 51°12′N 05°12′E
171 O3 **Baler** Luzon, N Philippines 15°47′N 121°30′E
154 P11 **Bāleshwar** *prev.* Balasore. Orissa, E India 21°31′N 86°59′E
77 S12 **Baléyara** Tillabéri, W Niger 13°48′N 02°57′E
127 T1 **Balezino** Udmurtskaya Respublika, NW Russian Federation 57°57′N 53°03′E
42 J4 **Balfate** Colón, N Honduras 15°47′N 86°24′W
11 O17 **Balfour** British Columbia, SW Canada 49°39′N 116°57′W
29 N3 **Balfour** North Dakota, N USA 47°55′N 100°34′W
Balfrush *see* Bābol
122 L14 **Balgazyn** Respublika Tyva, S Russian Federation 50°53′N 95°12′E
11 U16 **Balgonie** Saskatchewan, S Canada 50°30′N 104°12′W
Bălgrad *see* Alba Iulia
81 J19 **Balguda** *spring/well* S Kenya 01°28′S 39°50′E
158 K6 **Balguntay** Xinjiang Uygur Zizhiqu, NW China 42°45′N 86°18′E
141 R16 **Balḩāf** S Yemen 14°02′N 48°16′E
152 F13 **Bāli** Rājasthān, N India 25°10′N 73°20′E
169 U17 **Bali** ⬖ *province* S Indonesia
169 T17 **Bali** *island* C Indonesia
111 K16 **Balice** ✈ (Kraków) Małopolskie, S Poland 49°57′N 19°49′E
171 Y14 **Baliem, Sungai** 〰 Papua, E Indonesia
136 C12 **Balıkesir** Balıkesir, W Turkey 39°38′N 27°52′E
136 C12 **Balıkesir** ⬖ *province* NW Turkey
138 L3 **Balīkh, Nahr** 〰 N Syria
169 V12 **Balikpapan** Borneo, C Indonesia 01°15′S 116°50′E
Bali Laut *see* Bali Sea
171 N9 **Balimbing** Tawitawi, SW Philippines 05°10′N 120°00′E
186 B8 **Balimo** Western, SW Papua New Guinea 08°00′S 143°00′E
Bálinc *see* Balinţ
101 H23 **Balingen** Baden-Württemberg, SW Germany 48°16′N 08°51′E
116 F11 **Balinţ** *Hung.* Bálinc. Timiş, W Romania 45°48′N 21°54′E
171 O1 **Balintang Channel** *channel* N Philippines
138 K3 **Bālis** Ḩalab, N Syria 36°01′N 38°03′E
169 T16 **Bali Sea** *Ind.* Bali Laut. *sea* C Indonesia
98 K7 **Balk** Friesland, N Netherlands 52°54′N 05°34′E
146 B11 **Balkanabat** *Rus.* Nebitdag. Balkan Welaýaty, W Turkmenistan 39°33′N 54°19′E
121 R6 **Balkan Mountains** *Bul./SCr.* Stara Planina. ▲▲ Bulgaria/Serbia
Balkanskiy Welayat *see* Balkan Welaýaty
146 B9 **Balkan Welaýaty** *Rus.* Balkanskiy Velayat. ⬖ *province* W Turkmenistan
145 P8 **Balkashino** Akmola, N Kazakhstan 52°36′N 68°46′E
149 O2 **Balkh** *anc.* Bactra. Balkh, N Afghanistan 36°46′N 66°54′E
149 P2 **Balkh** ⬖ *province* N Afghanistan
145 T13 **Balkhash** *Kaz.* Balqash. Karaganda, SE Kazakhstan 46°52′N 74°55′E
Balkhash, Lake *see* Balkhash, Ozero
145 T13 **Balkhash, Ozero** *Eng.* Lake Balkhash, *Kaz.* Balqash. ◎ SE Kazakhstan
Balla Balla *see* Mbalabala
96 H10 **Ballachulish** N Scotland, United Kingdom 56°40′N 05°10′W
180 M12 **Balladonia** Western Australia 32°21′S 123°32′E
97 C16 **Ballaghaderreen** *Ir.* Bealach an Doirín. C Ireland 53°51′N 08°29′W
92 H10 **Ballangen** *Lapp.* Bálák. Nordland, NW Norway 68°18′N 16°48′E
97 H14 **Ballantrae** W Scotland, United Kingdom 55°05′N 05°W
183 N12 **Ballarat** Victoria, SE Australia 37°36′S 143°51′E
180 K11 **Ballard, Lake** *salt lake* Western Australia
Ballari *see* Bellary
76 L11 **Ballé** Koulikoro, W Mali 15°18′N 08°31′W
40 D7 **Ballenas, Bahía de** *bay* NW Mexico
40 D5 **Ballenas, Canal de** *channel* NW Mexico
195 R17 **Balleny Islands** *island group* Antarctica
40 J7 **Balleza** *var.* San Pablo Balleza. Chihuahua, N Mexico 26°55′N 106°21′W
114 M13 **Ballı** Tekirdağ, NW Turkey 40°48′N 27°03′E
153 O13 **Ballia** Uttar Pradesh, N India 25°45′N 84°09′E
183 V4 **Ballina** New South Wales, SE Australia 28°50′S 153°37′E
97 C16 **Ballina** *Ir.* Béal an Átha. W Ireland 54°07′N 09°09′W
97 D16 **Ballinamore** *Ir.* Béal an Átha Móir. NW Ireland 54°03′N 07°47′W
97 D18 **Ballinasloe** *Ir.* Béal Átha na Sluaighe. W Ireland 53°20′N 08°13′W
25 P8 **Ballinger** Texas, SW USA 31°44′N 99°57′W
97 C17 **Ballinrobe** *Ir.* Baile an Róba. W Ireland 53°37′N 09°14′W
97 A21 **Ballinskelligs Bay** *Ir.* Bá na Scealg. *inlet* SW Ireland
97 D15 **Ballintra** *Ir.* Baile an tSratha. NW Ireland 54°35′N 08°07′W
103 T7 **Ballon d'Alsace** ▲ NE France 47°50′N 06°54′E
Ballon de Guebwiller *see* Grand Ballon
113 K21 **Ballsh** *var.* Ballshi. Fier, SW Albania 40°35′N 19°45′E
Ballshi *see* Ballsh
98 K4 **Ballum** Friesland, N Netherlands 53°27′N 05°40′E
97 F16 **Ballybay** *Ir.* Béal Átha Beithe. N Ireland 54°08′N 06°54′W
97 E14 **Ballybofey** *Ir.* Bealach Féich. NW Ireland 54°49′N 07°47′W
97 G14 **Ballycastle** *Ir.* Baile an Chaistil. N Northern Ireland, United Kingdom 55°12′N 06°14′W
97 G15 **Ballyclare** *Ir.* Bealach Cláir. E Northern Ireland, United Kingdom 54°45′N 06°W
97 E16 **Ballyconnell** *Ir.* Béal Átha Conaill. N Ireland 54°07′N 07°35′W
97 C17 **Ballyhaunis** *Ir.* Beál Átha hAmhnais. W Ireland 53°45′N 08°45′W
97 G14 **Ballymena** *Ir.* An Baile Meánach. NE Northern Ireland, United Kingdom 54°52′N 06°17′W
97 F14 **Ballymoney** *Ir.* Baile Monaidh. NE Northern Ireland, United Kingdom 55°10′N 06°30′W
97 G15 **Ballynahinch** *Ir.* Baile na hInse. SE Northern Ireland, United Kingdom 54°24′N 05°54′W
97 D16 **Ballysadare** *Ir.* Baile Easa Dara. NW Ireland 54°13′N 08°30′W
97 D15 **Ballyshannon** *Ir.* Béal Átha Seanaidh. NW Ireland 54°30′N 08°11′W
63 H19 **Balmaceda** Aisén, S Chile 45°52′S 72°43′W
63 G23 **Balmaceda, Cerro** ▲ S Chile 51°27′S 73°26′W
111 N22 **Balmazújváros** Hajdú-Bihar, E Hungary 47°36′N 21°18′E
108 E10 **Balmhorn** ▲ SW Switzerland 46°27′N 07°41′E
182 L12 **Balmoral** Victoria, SE Australia 37°16′S 141°38′E
24 K9 **Balmorhea** Texas, SW USA 30°58′N 103°44′W
Balneario Claromecó *see* Claromecó
Balochistān *see* Baluchistān
82 B13 **Balombo** *Port.* Norton de Matos, Vila Norton de Matos. Benguela, W Angola 12°21′S 14°46′E
82 B13 **Balombo** 〰 W Angola
181 X10 **Balonne River** 〰 Queensland, E Australia
152 E13 **Bālotra** Rājasthān, N India 25°50′N 72°21′E
145 V14 **Balpyk Bi** *prev.* Kirovskiy, *Kaz.* Kīrov. Almaty, SE Kazakhstan 44°54′N 78°13′E
Balqā'/Balqā', Muḩāfaẓat al *see* Al Balqā'
Balqash *see* Balkhash/Balkhash, Ozero
152 M12 **Balrāmpur** Uttar Pradesh, N India 27°25′N 82°10′E
182 M9 **Balranald** New South Wales, SE Australia 34°39′S 143°33′E
116 H14 **Balş** Olt, S Romania 44°20′N 24°06′E
14 H11 **Balsam Creek** Ontario, S Canada 46°26′N 79°10′W
30 I5 **Balsam Lake** Wisconsin, N USA 45°27′N 92°28′W
14 I14 **Balsam Lake** ◎ Ontario, SE Canada
59 M14 **Balsas** Maranhão, E Brazil 07°30′S 46°W
40 M15 **Balsas, Río** *var.* Río Mexcala. 〰 S Mexico
43 W16 **Balsas, Río** 〰 SE Panama
119 O18 **Bal'shavik** *Rus.* Bol'shevik. Homyel'skaya Voblasts', SE Belarus 52°34′N 30°53′E
95 O15 **Bålsta** Uppsala, C Sweden 59°31′N 17°32′E
108 E7 **Balsthal** Solothurn, NW Switzerland 47°18′N 07°42′E
117 O8 **Balta** Odes'ka Oblast', SW Ukraine 47°58′N 29°39′E
105 N5 **Baltanás** Castilla-León, N Spain 41°56′N 04°12′W
61 E16 **Baltasar Brum** Artigas, N Uruguay 30°44′S 57°19′W
116 M9 **Bălţi** *Rus.* Bel'tsy. N Moldova 47°45′N 27°57′E
Baltic Port *see* Paldiski
118 B10 **Baltic Sea** *Ger.* Ostee, *Rus.* Baltiskoye More. *sea* N Europe
21 X3 **Baltimore** Maryland, NE USA 39°17′N 76°37′W
31 T13 **Baltimore** Ohio, N USA 39°48′N 82°33′W
21 X3 **Baltimore-Washington** ✈ Maryland, E USA 39°10′N 76°40′W
Baltischport/Baltiski *see* Paldiski
Baltiskoye More *see* Baltic Sea
119 A14 **Baltiysk** *Ger.* Pillau. Kaliningradskaya Oblast', W Russian Federation 54°39′N 19°54′E
Baltkrievija *see* Belarus
119 H14 **Baltoji Voke** Vilnius, SE Lithuania 54°35′N 25°13′E
Balūchestān va Sīstān *see* Sīstān va Balūchestān
148 M12 **Baluchistān** *var.* Balochistān, Beluchistan. ⬖ *province* SW Pakistan
171. P5 **Balud** Masbate, N Philippines 12°03′N 123°12′E
169 T9 **Balui, Batang** 〰 East Malaysia
153 S13 **Bālurghat** West Bengal, NE India 25°12′N 88°50′E
118 J8 **Balvi** Balvi, NE Latvia 57°07′N 27°14′E
147 W7 **Balykchy** *Kir.* Ysyk-Köl; *prev.* Issyk-Kul', Rybach'ye. Issyk-Kul'skaya Oblast', NE Kyrgyzstan 42°29′N 76°08′E
56 B7 **Balzar** Guayas, W Ecuador 01°25′S 79°54′W
108 I8 **Balzers** S Liechtenstein 47°04′N 09°32′E
143 T12 **Bam** Kermān, SE Iran 29°08′N 58°27′E
77 Y13 **Bama** Borno, NE Nigeria 11°28′N 13°46′E
76 L12 **Bamako** ● (Mali) Capital District, SW Mali 12°39′N 08°02′W
77 P10 **Bamba** Gao, C Mali 17°03′N 01°19′W
42 M8 **Bambana, Río** 〰 NE Nicaragua
79 J15 **Bambari** Ouaka, C Central African Republic 05°45′N 20°37′E
181 W5 **Bambaroo** Queensland, NE Australia 19°00′S 146°16′E
101 K19 **Bamberg** Bayern, SE Germany 49°54′N 10°53′E
21 R14 **Bamberg** South Carolina, SE USA 33°16′N 81°02′W
79 M16 **Bambesa** Orientale, N Dem. Rep. Congo 03°25′N 25°43′E
76 G11 **Bambey** W Senegal 14°43′N 16°26′W
79 H16 **Bambio** Sangha-Mbaéré, SW Central African Republic 03°57′N 16°54′E
83 I24 **Bamboesberge** ▲ S South Africa 31°24′S 26°10′E
79 D14 **Bamenda** Nord-Ouest, W Cameroon 05°55′N 10°09′E
10 K17 **Bamfield** Vancouver Island, British Columbia, SW Canada 48°48′N 125°05′W
Bami *see* Bamy
149 P4 **Bāmīān** *var.* Bāmiān. Bāmīān, NE Afghanistan 34°50′N 67°50′E
149 O4 **Bāmīān** ⬖ *province* C Afghanistan
79 J14 **Bamingui** Bamingui-Bangoran, C Central African Republic 07°38′N 20°06′E
78 J13 **Bamingui** 〰 N Central African Republic
78 J13 **Bamingui-Bangoran** ⬖ *prefecture* N Central African Republic
143 V13 **Bampūr** Sīstān va Balūchestān, SE Iran 27°13′N 60°28′E
186 C8 **Bamu** 〰 SW Papua New Guinea
146 E12 **Bamy** *Rus.* Bami. Ahal Welaýaty, C Turkmenistan 38°42′N 56°47′E
Bán *see* Bánovce nad Bebravou
81 N17 **Banaadir** *off.* Gobolka Banaadir. ⬖ *region* S Somalia
Banaadir, Gobolka *see* Banaadir
191 N3 **Banaba** *var.* Ocean Island. *island* Tungaru, W Kiribati
59 O14 **Banabuiú, Açude** ⊠ NE Brazil
57 O19 **Bañados del Izozog** *salt lake* SE Bolivia
97 D18 **Banagher** *Ir.* Beannchar. C Ireland 53°12′N 07°56′W
79 M17 **Banalia** Orientale, N Dem. Rep. Congo 01°33′N 25°23′E
76 L12 **Banamba** Koulikoro, W Mali 13°29′N 07°22′W
40 G4 **Banámichi** Sonora, NW Mexico 30°00′N 110°14′W
181 Y9 **Banana** Queensland, E Australia 24°33′S 150°07′E
191 Z2 **Banana** *prev.* Main Camp. Kiritimati, E Kiribati 02°00′N 157°25′W
59 K16 **Bananal, Ilha do** *island* C Brazil
23 Y12 **Banana River** *lagoon* Florida, SE USA
151 Q22 **Bananga** Andaman and Nicobar Islands, India, NE Indian Ocean 06°57′N 93°54′E
Banaras *see* Vārānasi
114 N13 **Banarlı** Tekirdağ, NW Turkey 41°04′N 27°21′E
152 H12 **Banās** 〰 N India
75 Z11 **Banās, Rās** *headland* E Egypt 23°55′N 35°47′E
112 N10 **Banatski Karlovac** Vojvodina, NE Serbia 45°03′N 21°02′E
141 P16 **Banā, Wādī** *dry watercourse* SW Yemen
136 E14 **Banaz** Uşak, W Turkey 38°47′N 29°46′E
136 E14 **Banaz Çayı** 〰 W Turkey
159 P14 **Banbar** *var.* Coka. Xizang Zizhiqu, W China 31°01′N 94°43′E
97 G15 **Banbridge** *Ir.* Droichead na Banna. SE Northern Ireland, United Kingdom 54°21′N 06°16′W
Ban Bua Yai *see* Bua Yai
97 M21 **Banbury** S England, United Kingdom 52°04′N 01°20′W
167 O7 **Ban Chiang Dao** Chiang Mai, NW Thailand 19°22′N 98°59′E
96 K9 **Banchory** NE Scotland, United Kingdom 58°05′N 00°35′W
14 J13 **Bancroft** Ontario, SE Canada 45°03′N 77°52′W
33 R15 **Bancroft** Idaho, NW USA 42°43′N 111°54′W
29 U11 **Bancroft** Iowa, C USA 43°17′N 94°13′W
154 I9 **Bānda** Madhya Pradesh, C India 24°01′N 78°59′E
152 L13 **Bānda** Uttar Pradesh, N India 25°28′N 80°20′E
168 F7 **Bandaaceh** *var.* Banda Atjeh; *prev.* Koetaradja, Kutaradja, Kutaraja. Sumatera, W Indonesia 05°30′N 95°20′E
Banda Atjeh *see* Bandaaceh
171 S14 **Banda, Kepulauan** *island group* E Indonesia
Banda, Laut *see* Banda Sea
77 N17 **Bandama** *var.* Bandama Fleuve. 〰 S Ivory Coast
77 N15 **Bandama Blanc** 〰 C Ivory Coast
Bandama Fleuve *see* Bandama
Bandar 'Abbās *see* Bandar-e 'Abbās
153 W16 **Bandarban** Chittagong, SE Bangladesh 22°13′N 92°13′E
80 Q13 **Bandarbeyla** *var.* Bender Beila, Bender Beyla. Bari, NE Somalia 09°28′N 50°48′E
143 R14 **Bandar-e 'Abbās** *var.* Bandar 'Abbās; *prev.* Gombroon. Hormozgān, S Iran 27°11′N 56°11′E
142 M3 **Bandar-e Anzalī** Gīlān, NW Iran 37°26′N 49°29′E
143 N12 **Bandar-e Būshehr** *var.* Būshehr, *Eng.* Bushire. Būshehr, S Iran 28°59′N 50°50′E
143 O13 **Bandar-e Dayyer** *var.* Deyyer. Būshehr, SE Iran 27°50′N 51°55′E

◆ Country
● Country Capital
◇ Dependent Territory
○ Dependent Territory Capital
⬖ Administrative Regions
✈ International Airport
▲ Mountain
▲▲ Mountain Range
Volcano
〰 River
◎ Lake
⊠ Reservoir

BANDAR-E GONĀVEH – BARTANG

142 M11 **Bandar-e Gonāveh** *var.* Ganāveh; *prev.* Gonāveh. Būshehr, SW Iran 29°33´N 50°39´E
143 T15 **Bandar-e Jāsk** *var.* Jāsk. Hormozgān, SE Iran 25°35´N 58°06´E
143 O13 **Bandar-e Kangān** *var.* Kangān. Būshehr, S Iran 25°50´N 57°30´E
143 R14 **Bandar-e Khamīr** Hormozgān, S Iran 27°00´N 55°50´E
Bandar-e Langeh *see* Bandar-e Lengeh
143 Q14 **Bandar-e Lengeh** *var.* Bandar-e Langeh, Lingeh. Hormozgān, S Iran 26°34´N 54°52´E
142 L10 **Bandar-e Māhshahr** *var.* Māh-Shahr; *prev.* Bandar-e Ma'shūr. Khūzestān, SW Iran 30°34´N 49°10´E
Bandar-e Ma'shūr *see* Bandar-e Māhshahr
143 O14 **Bandar-e Nakhīlū** Hormozgān, S Iran 26°58´N 53°30´E
Bandar-e Shāh *see* Bandar-e Torkaman
143 P4 **Bandar-e Torkaman** *var.* Bandar-e Torkeman, Bandar-e Torkman; *prev.* Bandar-e Shāh. Golestān, N Iran 36°55´N 54°05´E
Bandar-e Torkeman/Bandar-e Torkman *see* Bandar-e Torkaman
Bandar Kassim *see* Boosaaso
168 M15 **Bandar Lampung** *var.* Bandarlampung, Tanjungkarang-Telukbetung; *prev.* Tandjoengkarang, Tanjungkarang, Teloekbetoeng, Telukbetung. Sumatera, W Indonesia 05°28´S 105°16´E
Bandarlampung *see* Bandar Lampung
Bandar Maharani *see* Muar
Bandar Masulipatnam *see* Machilīpatnam
Bandar Penggaram *see* Batu Pahat
169 T7 **Bandar Seri Begawan** *prev.* Brunei Town. ● (Brunei) N Brunei 04°56´N 114°58´E
169 T7 **Bandar Seri Begawan** ✈ N Brunei 04°56´N 114°58´E
171 R15 **Banda Sea** *var.* Laut Banda. *sea* E Indonesia
104 H5 **Bande** Galicia, NW Spain 42°01´N 07°58´W
59 G15 **Bandeirantes** Mato Grosso, W Brazil 09°04´S 57°53´W
59 N20 **Bandeira, Pico da** ▲ SE Brazil 20°25´S 41°45´W
83 K19 **Bandelierkop** Limpopo, South Africa 23°21´S 29°46´E
62 L8 **Banderas** Santiago del Estero, N Argentina 28°53´S 62°15´W
25 Q11 **Bandera** Texas, SW USA 29°44´N 99°06´W
40 J13 **Banderas, Bahía de** *bay* W Mexico
77 O11 **Bandiagara** Mopti, C Mali 14°20´N 03°37´W
152 I12 **Bāndīkūī** Rājasthān, N India 27°01´N 76°33´E
136 C11 **Bandırma** *var.* Penderma. Balıkesir, NW Turkey 40°21´N 27°58´E
Bandjarmasin *see* Banjarmasin
Bandoeng *see* Bandung
97 C21 **Bandon** *Ir.* Droicheadna Bandan. SW Ireland 51°44´N 08°44´W
32 E14 **Bandon** Oregon, NW USA 43°07´N 124°24´W
167 R8 **Ban Dong Bang** Nong Khai, E Thailand 18°00´N 104°08´E
167 Q6 **Ban Donkon** Oudômxai, N Laos 20°20´N 101°37´E
172 J14 **Bandrélé** SE Mayotte
79 H20 **Bandundu** *prev.* Banningville. Bandundu, W Dem. Rep. Congo 03°19´S 17°24´E
79 I21 **Bandundu** *off.* Région de Bandundu. ⬖ *region* W Dem. Rep. Congo
Bandundu, Région de *see* Bandundu
169 O16 **Bandung** *prev.* Bandoeng. Jawa, C Indonesia 06°47´S 107°28´E
116 L15 **Băneasa** Constanța, SW Romania 45°56´N 27°55´E
142 J4 **Bāneh** Kordestān, N Iran 35°58´N 45°54´E
44 I7 **Banes** Holguín, E Cuba 20°58´N 75°43´W
11 P16 **Banff** Alberta, SW Canada 51°10´N 115°34´W
96 K8 **Banff** NE Scotland, United Kingdom 57°39´N 02°33´W
96 K8 **Banff** *cultural region* NE Scotland, United Kingdom
Bánffyhunyad *see* Huedin
77 N14 **Banfora** SW Burkina 10°36´N 04°45´W
155 H19 **Bangalore** *var.* Bengalooru. *state capital* Karnātaka, S India 12°58´N 77°35´E
153 S16 **Bangaon** West Bengal, NE India 23°01´N 88°50´E
79 L15 **Bangassou** Mbomou, SE Central African Republic 04°51´N 22°55´E
186 D7 **Bangeta, Mount** ▲ C Papua New Guinea 06°11´S 147°02´E
171 P12 **Banggai, Kepulauan** *island group* C Indonesia
171 Q12 **Banggai, Pulau** *island* Kepulauan Banggai, N Indonesia
171 X13 **Banggelapa** Papua, E Indonesia 03°47´S 136°53´E
Banggi *see* Banggi, Pulau
169 V6 **Banggi, Pulau** *var.* Banggi. *island* East Malaysia
152 K5 **Banggong Co** *var.* Pangong Tso. ◎ China/India *see also* Pangong Tso
121 P13 **Banghāzī** *Eng.* Bengazi, Benghazi, *It.* Bengasi. NE Libya 32°07´N 20°04´E
Bang Hieng *see* Xé Banghiang
169 O13 **Bangka-Belitung** *off.* Propinsi Bangka-Belitung. ◆ *province* W Indonesia
169 P11 **Bangkai, Tanjung** *var.* Bankai. *headland* Borneo, N Indonesia 0°21´N 108°53´E
169 S16 **Bangkalan** Pulau Madura, C Indonesia 07°05´S 112°44´E
169 N12 **Bangka, Pulau** *island* W Indonesia
169 N13 **Bangka, Selat** *strait* Sumatera, W Indonesia
169 N13 **Bangka, Selat** *var.* Selat Likupang. *strait* Sulawesi, N Indonesia
168 J11 **Bangkinang** Sumatera, W Indonesia 0°21´N 100°52´E
168 K12 **Bangko** Sumatera, W Indonesia 02°05´S 102°20´E
Bangkok *see* Ao Krung Thep
Bangkok, Bight of *see* Krung Thep, Ao
153 T14 **Bangladesh** *off.* People's Republic of Bangladesh; *prev.* East Pakistan. ◆ *republic* S Asia
Bangladesh, People's Republic of *see* Bangladesh
167 V13 **Ba Ngoi** Khanh Hoa, S Vietnam 11°56´N 109°07´E
Bangong Co *see* Pangong Tso
97 I18 **Bangor** NW Wales, United Kingdom 53°13´N 04°08´W
97 G15 **Bangor** *Ir.* Beannchar. E Northern Ireland, United Kingdom 54°40´N 05°40´W
19 R6 **Bangor** Maine, NE USA 44°48´N 68°47´W
18 I14 **Bangor** Pennsylvania, NE USA 40°52´N 75°12´W
67 R8 **Bangoran** ≈ S Central African Republic
Bang Phra *see* Trat
Bang Pla Soi *see* Chon Buri
25 Q8 **Bangs** Texas, SW USA 31°43´N 99°07´W
167 N13 **Bang Saphan** *var.* Bang Saphan Yai. Prachuap Khiri Khan, SW Thailand 11°10´N 99°33´E
Bang Saphan Yai *see* Bang Saphan
36 I8 **Bangs, Mount** ▲ Arizona, SW USA 36°47´N 113°51´W
93 E15 **Bangsund** Nord-Trøndelag, C Norway 64°22´N 11°22´E
171 O2 **Bangued** Luzon, N Philippines 17°36´N 120°40´E
79 I15 **Bangui** ● (Central African Republic) Ombella-Mpoko, SW Central African Republic 04°21´N 18°32´E
79 I15 **Bangui** ✈ Ombella-Mpoko, SW Central African Republic 04°19´N 18°34´E
83 N16 **Bangula** Southern, S Malawi 16°38´S 35°04´E
Bangwaketse *see* Southern
82 K12 **Bangweulu, Lake** *var.* Lake Bengweulu. ◎ N Zambia
121 V13 **Banhā** *var.* Benha. N Egypt 30°28´N 31°11´E
Ban Hat Yai *see* Hat Yai
167 Q7 **Ban Hin Heup** Viangchan, C Laos 18°37´N 102°19´E
Ban Houayxay/Ban Houei Sai *see* Houayxay
167 O12 **Ban Hua Hin** *var.* Hua Hin. Prachuap Khiri Khan, SW Thailand 12°34´N 99°58´E
79 L14 **Bani** Haute-Kotto, E Central African Republic 07°06´N 22°51´E
45 O9 **Baní** S Dominican Republic 18°19´N 70°21´W
77 N12 **Bani** ≈ S Mali
Banias *see* Bāniyās
77 S11 **Bani Bangou** Tillabéri, SW Niger 15°04´N 02°40´E
76 M12 **Banifing** *var.* Ngorolaka. ≈ Burkina/Mali
Banijska Palanka *see* Glina
77 R13 **Banikoara** N Benin 11°18´N 02°26´E
75 W9 **Banī Mazār** *var.* Beni Mazâr. C Egypt 28°29´N 30°48´E
114 K8 **Baniski Lom** ≈ N Bulgaria
21 U7 **Banister River** ≈ Virginia, NE USA
121 V14 **Banī Suwayf** *var.* Beni Suef. N Egypt 29°09´N 31°04´E
75 O8 **Banī Walīd** NW Libya 31°46´N 13°59´E
138 H5 **Bāniyās** *var.* Banias, Baniyas, Paneas. Tarṭūs, W Syria 35°12´N 35°57´E
113 K14 **Banja** Serbia, W Serbia 43°33´N 19°35´E
Banjak, Kepulauan *see* Banyak, Kepulauan
112 J12 **Banja Koviljača** Serbia, W Serbia 44°31´N 19°11´E
112 G11 **Banja Luka** ⬖ Republika Srpska, NW Bosnia and Herzegovina
169 T13 **Banjarmasin** *prev.* Bandjarmasin. Borneo, C Indonesia 03°22´S 114°33´E
76 F11 **Banjul** *prev.* Bathurst. ● (Gambia) W Gambia 13°26´N 16°43´W
76 F11 **Banjul** ✈ W Gambia 13°18´N 16°39´W
Bank *see* Bankā
137 Y13 **Bankā** *Rus.* Bank. SE Azerbaijan 39°25´N 49°13´E
167 S11 **Ban Kadian** *var.* Ban Kadiene. Champasak, S Laos 14°25´N 105°42´E
Ban Kadiene *see* Ban Kadian
Bankai *see* Bangkai, Tanjung
166 M14 **Ban Kam Phuam** Phangnga, SW Thailand 09°16´N 98°24´E
Ban Kantang *see* Kantang
77 O11 **Bankass** Mopti, S Mali 14°05´N 03°30´W
95 L19 **Bankeryd** Jönköping, S Sweden 57°51´N 14°07´E
83 K16 **Banket** Mashonaland West, N Zimbabwe 17°23´S 30°24´E
167 T11 **Ban Khamphô** Attapu, S Laos 14°35´N 106°18´E
23 O4 **Bankhead Lake** ⊠ Alabama, S USA
77 Q11 **Bankilaré** Tillabéri, SW Niger 14°34´N 00°41´E
Banks, Îles *see* Banks Islands
10 I14 **Banks Island** *island* British Columbia, SW Canada
187 R12 **Banks Islands** *Fr.* Îles Banks. *island group* N Vanuatu
23 U8 **Banks Lake** ◎ Georgia, SE USA
32 K8 **Banks Lake** ⊠ Washington, NW USA
185 I19 **Banks Peninsula** *peninsula* South Island, New Zealand
183 Q15 **Banks Strait** *strait* SW Tasman Sea
Ban Kui Nua *see* Kui Buri
153 R16 **Bānkura** West Bengal, NE India 23°14´N 87°05´E
167 S8 **Ban Lakxao** *var.* Lak Sao. Bolikhamxai, C Laos 18°10´N 104°58´E
167 O16 **Ban Lam Phai** Songkhla, SW Thailand 06°43´N 100°57´E
Ban Mae Sot *see* Mae Sot
Ban Mae Suai *see* Mae Suai
Ban Mak Khaeng *see* Udon Thani
166 M3 **Banmauk** Sagaing, N Burma (Myanmar) 24°26´N 95°54´E
Banmo *see* Bhamo
167 T10 **Ban Mun-Houamuang** S Laos 15°11´N 106°44´E
97 F14 **Bann** *var.* Lower Bann, Upper Bann. ≈ N Northern Ireland, United Kingdom
167 S10 **Ban Nadou** Salavan, S Laos 15°51´N 105°38´E
167 S9 **Ban Nakala** Savannakhét, S Laos 16°14´N 105°09´E
167 Q8 **Ban Nakha** Viangchan, C Laos 18°13´N 102°29´E
167 S9 **Ban Nakham** Khammouan, S Laos 17°10´N 105°25´E
167 P7 **Ban Namoun** Xaignabouli, N Laos 18°40´N 101°34´E
167 O17 **Ban Nang Sata** Yala, SW Thailand 06°15´N 101°13´E
167 N15 **Ban Na San** Surat Thani, SW Thailand 08°53´N 99°17´E
167 R7 **Ban Nasi** Xiangkhoang, N Laos 19°37´N 103°33´E
44 I3 **Bannerman Town** Eleuthera Island, C Bahamas 24°38´N 76°09´W
35 V15 **Banning** California, W USA 33°55´N 116°52´W
Banningville *see* Bandundu
167 S11 **Ban Nongsim** Champasak, S Laos 14°45´N 106°00´E
149 S7 **Bannu** *prev.* Edwardesabad. North-West Frontier Province, NW Pakistan 33°00´N 70°36´E
Bañolas *see* Banyoles
56 C7 **Baños** Tungurahua, C Ecuador 01°26´S 78°24´W
Bánovce *see* Bánovce nad Bebravou
111 I19 **Bánovce nad Bebravou** *var.* Bánovce, *Hung.* Bán. Trenčiansky Kraj, W Slovakia 48°43´N 18°15´E
112 I12 **Banovići** ⬖ Federacija Bosna I Hercegovina, E Bosnia and Herzegovina
Banow *see* Andarāb
Ban Pak Phanang *see* Pak Phanang
167 O7 **Ban Pan Nua** Lampang, NW Thailand 18°51´N 99°57´E
167 Q9 **Ban Phai** Khon Kaen, E Thailand 16°00´N 102°42´E
167 T9 **Ban Phou A Douk** Khammouan, C Laos 17°12´N 106°07´E
167 Q8 **Ban Phu** Uthai Thani, W Thailand
167 O11 **Ban Pong** Ratchaburi, W Thailand 13°49´N 99°53´E
190 I3 **Banraeaba** Tarawa, W Kiribati 01°20´N 173°02´E
167 N10 **Ban Sai Yok** Kanchanaburi, W Thailand 14°24´N 98°54´E
Ban Sattahip/Ban Sattahipp *see* Sattahip
Ban Sichon *see* Sichon
Ban Si Racha *see* Siracha
111 J19 **Banská Bystrica** *Ger.* Neusohl, *Hung.* Besztercebánya. Banskobystricky Kraj, C Slovakia 48°46´N 19°08´E
111 K20 **Banskobystrický Kraj** ⬖ *region* C Slovakia
167 R8 **Ban Sôppheung** Bolikhamxai, C Laos 18°33´N 104°18´E
Ban Sop Prap *see* Sop Prap
152 G15 **Bānswāra** Rājasthān, N India 23°32´N 74°28´E
167 N15 **Ban Ta Khun** Surat Thani, SW Thailand 08°53´N 98°52´E
Ban Takua Pa *see* Takua Pa
167 S8 **Ban Talak** Khammouan, C Laos 17°33´N 105°40´E
77 R15 **Bantè** W Benin 08°25´N 01°58´E
167 N16 **Banten** *off.* Propinsi Banten. ◆ *province* W Indonesia
Propinsi Banten *see* Banten
167 Q8 **Ban Thabôk** Bolikhamxai, C Laos 18°21´N 103°12´E
167 T9 **Ban Tôp** Savannakhét, S Laos 16°07´N 106°07´E
97 B21 **Bantry** *Ir.* Beanntraí. Cork, SW Ireland 51°41´N 09°27´W
97 A21 **Bantry Bay** *Ir.* Bá Bheanntraí. *bay* SW Ireland
155 F19 **Bantvāl** *var.* Bantwāl. Karnātaka, E India 12°57´N 75°04´E
Bantwāl *see* Bantvāl
114 N9 **Banya** Burgas, E Bulgaria 42°46´N 27°49´E
168 G10 **Banyak, Kepulauan** *prev.* Kepulauan Banjak. *island group* NW Indonesia
105 U8 **Banya, La** *headland* E Spain 40°34´N 00°37´E
79 E14 **Banyo** Adamaoua, NW Cameroon 06°47´N 11°50´E
105 X4 **Banyoles** *var.* Bañolas. Cataluña, NE Spain 42°07´N 02°46´E
167 N16 **Ban Yong Sata** Trang, SW Thailand 07°09´N 99°42´E
195 X14 **Banzare Coast** *physical region* Antarctica
173 Q14 **Banzare Seamounts** *undersea feature* S Indian Ocean
Banzart *see* Bizerte
163 Q12 **Baochang** *var.* Taibus Qi. Nei Mongol Zizhiqu, N China 41°55´N 115°22´E
161 O3 **Baoding** *var.* Pao-ting; *prev.* Tsingyuan. Hebei, E China 38°47´N 115°30´E
Baoebaoe *see* Baubau
Baoi, Oileán *see* Dursey Island
160 J6 **Baoji** *var.* Pao-chi, Paoki. Shaanxi, C China 34°23´N 107°16´E
163 U9 **Baokang** *var.* Hoqin Zuoyi Zhongji. Nei Mongol Zizhiqu, N China 44°08´N 123°18´E
186 L8 **Baolo** Santa Isabel, N Solomon Islands 07°41´S 158°47´E
167 U13 **Bao Lôc** Lâm Đông, S Vietnam 11°33´N 107°48´E
163 Z7 **Baoqing** Heilongjiang, NE China 46°15´N 132°12´E
Baoqing *see* Shaoyang
79 H15 **Baoro** Nana-Mambéré, W Central African Republic 05°40´N 16°00´E
160 E12 **Baoshan** *var.* Pao-shan. Yunnan, SW China 25°05´N 99°07´E
163 N13 **Baotou** *var.* Pao-t'ou, Paotow. Nei Mongol Zizhiqu, N China 40°38´N 109°59´E
76 L14 **Baoulé** ≈ S Mali
76 K12 **Baoulé** ≈ W Mali
Bao Yèn *see* Phô Rang
103 O2 **Bapaume** Pas-de-Calais, N France 50°06´N 02°50´E
14 J13 **Baptiste Lake** ◎ Ontario, SE Canada
Bapu *see* Meigu
Baqanas *see* Bakanas
Baqbaqty *see* Bakbakty
159 P14 **Baqên** *var.* Dartang. Xizang Zizhiqu, W China 31°50´N 94°08´E
138 F14 **Bāqir, Jabal** ▲ S Jordan
139 T7 **Ba'qūbah** *var.* Qubba. Diyālá, C Iraq 33°45´N 44°40´E
62 H5 **Baquedano** Antofagasta, N Chile 23°20´S 69°50´W
Baquerizo Moreno *see* Puerto Baquerizo Moreno
113 J18 **Bar** *It.* Antivari. S Montenegro 42°02´N 19°09´E
116 M6 **Bar** Vinnyts'ka Oblast', C Ukraine 49°05´N 27°40´E
80 E10 **Bara** Northern Kordofan, C Sudan 13°42´N 30°21´E
81 M18 **Baraawe** *It.* Brava. Shabeellaha Hoose, S Somalia 01°10´N 43°59´E
152 M12 **Bāra Banki** Uttar Pradesh, N India 26°56´N 81°11´E
30 L8 **Baraboo** Wisconsin, N USA 43°27´N 89°45´W
30 K8 **Baraboo Range** *hill range* Wisconsin, N USA
Baracaldo *see* San Vicente de Barakaldo
15 Y6 **Barachois** Québec, SE Canada 48°37´N 64°14´W
44 J7 **Baracoa** Guantánamo, E Cuba 20°23´N 74°31´W
61 C19 **Baradero** Buenos Aires, E Argentina 33°50´S 59°30´W
183 R6 **Baradine** New South Wales, SE Australia 30°55´S 149°03´E
Baraf Daja Islands *see* Damar, Kepulauan
154 M12 **Baragarh** *var.* Bargarh. Orissa, E India 21°25´N 83°35´E
81 I17 **Baragoi** Rift Valley, W Kenya 01°39´N 36°46´E
45 N9 **Barahona** SW Dominican Republic 18°13´N 71°07´W
153 W13 **Barail Range** ▲▲ NE India
Baraka *see* Barka
80 G10 **Barakat** Gezira, C Sudan 14°18´N 33°32´E
Barakī *see* Barakī Barak
149 Q6 **Barakī Barak** *var.* Barakī, Baraki Rajan. Lowgar, E Afghanistan 33°58´N 68°58´E
Baraki Rajan *see* Barakī Barak
154 N11 **Bārākot** Orissa, E India 21°35´N 85°00´E
55 S7 **Barama River** ≈ N Guyana
155 E14 **Bārāmati** Mahārāshtra, W India 18°12´N 74°39´E
152 H5 **Bāramūla** Jammu and Kashmir, NW India 34°15´N 74°24´E
119 N14 **Baran'** Vitsyebskaya Voblasts', NE Belarus 54°29´N 30°18´E
152 I14 **Bārān** Rājasthān, N India 25°08´N 76°32´E
139 U4 **Barānān, Shākh-i** ▲▲ E Iraq
119 I17 **Baranavichy** *Pol.* Baranowicze, *Rus.* Baranovichi. Brestskaya Voblasts', SW Belarus 53°08´N 26°02´E
75 Y11 **Baranīs** *var.* Berenice, Minâ Baranîs. SE Egypt 23°58´N 35°29´E
123 T6 **Baranikha** Chukotskiy Avtonomnyy Okrug, NE Russian Federation 68°29´N 168°13´E
116 M4 **Baranivka** Zhytomyrs'ka Oblast', N Ukraine 50°16´N 27°40´E
39 W14 **Baranof Island** *island* Alexander Archipelago, Alaska, USA
Baranovichi/Baranowicze *see* Baranavichy
111 N15 **Baranów Sandomierski** Podkarpackie, SE Poland 50°28´N 21°31´E
111 I26 **Baranya** *off.* Baranya Megye. ⬖ *county* S Hungary
Baranya Megye *see* Baranya
153 R13 **Barāri** Bihār, NE India 25°31´N 87°23´E
22 L10 **Barataria Bay** *bay* Louisiana, S USA
Barat Daya, Kepulauan *see* Damar, Kepulauan
118 L12 **Baravukha** *Rus.* Borovukha. Vitsyebskaya Voblasts', N Belarus 55°34´N 28°36´E
54 E11 **Baraya** Huila, C Colombia 03°11´N 75°04´W
59 M21 **Barbacena** Minas Gerais, SE Brazil 21°13´S 43°47´W
54 B13 **Barbacoas** Nariño, SW Colombia 01°38´N 78°08´W
54 L6 **Barbacoas** Aragua, N Venezuela 09°29´N 66°58´W
45 Z13 **Barbados** ◆ *commonwealth republic* SE West Indies
47 S3 **Barbados** *island* Barbados
105 U11 **Barbaria, Cap de** *var.* Cabo de Berberia. *headland* Formentera, E Spain 38°39´N 01°24´E
114 N13 **Barbaros** Tekirdağ, NW Turkey 40°55´N 27°28´E
74 A11 **Barbas, Cap** *headland* S Western Sahara 22°14´N 16°45´W
105 T5 **Barbastro** Aragón, NE Spain 42°02´N 00°07´E
104 K16 **Barbate** ≈ SW Spain
104 K16 **Barbate de Franco** Andalucía, S Spain 36°11´N 05°55´W
83 K21 **Barberton** Mpumalanga, NE South Africa 25°48´S 31°03´E
31 U12 **Barberton** Ohio, N USA 41°02´N 81°37´W
102 K12 **Barbezieux-St-Hilaire** Charente, W France 45°28´N 00°09´W
54 G9 **Barbosa** Boyaca, C Colombia 05°57´N 73°37´W
21 N7 **Barbourville** Kentucky, S USA 36°52´N 83°54´W
45 W9 **Barbuda** *island* N Antigua and Barbuda
181 W8 **Barcaldine** Queensland, E Australia 23°33´S 145°21´E
Barcarozsnyó *see* Râşnov
104 I11 **Barcarrota** Extremadura, W Spain 38°31´N 06°51´W
Barcău *see* Berettyó
Barce *see* Al Marj
107 L23 **Barcellona** *var.* Barcellona Pozzo di Gotto. Sicilia, Italy, C Mediterranean Sea 38°10´N 15°15´E
Barcellona Pozzo di Gotto *see* Barcellona
105 W6 **Barcelona** *anc.* Barcino, Barcinona. Cataluña, E Spain 41°25´N 02°10´E
55 N5 **Barcelona** Anzoátegui, NE Venezuela 10°08´N 64°43´W
105 S5 **Barcelona** ⬖ *province* Cataluña, NE Spain
105 W6 **Barcelona** ✈ Cataluña, E Spain 41°25´N 02°10´E
103 U14 **Barcelonnette** Alpes-de-Haute-Provence, SE France 44°24´N 06°37´E
58 E12 **Barcelos** Amazonas, N Brazil 0°59´S 62°58´W
104 G5 **Barcelos** Braga, N Portugal 41°32´N 08°37´W
110 I10 **Barcin** *Ger.* Bartschin. Kujawski-pomorskie, C Poland 52°51´N 17°55´E
Barcino/Barcinona *see* Barcelona
Barcoo *see* Cooper Creek
111 H26 **Barcs** Somogy, SW Hungary 45°58´N 17°26´E
137 W11 **Bärdä** *Rus.* Barda. C Azerbaijan 40°25´N 47°07´E
Barda *see* Bärdä
78 H5 **Bardaï** Borkou-Ennedi-Tibesti, N Chad 21°21´N 16°56´E
139 R2 **Bardaṛash** Dahūk, N Iraq 36°32´N 43°36´E
139 Q7 **Bardasah** Al Anbār, SW Iraq 34°02´N 42°28´E
153 S16 **Barddhamān** West Bengal, NE India 23°10´N 88°03´E
111 N18 **Bardejov** *Ger.* Bartfeld, *Hung.* Bártfa. Presovský Kraj, E Slovakia 49°17´N 21°18´E
105 R4 **Bárdenas Reales** *physical region* N Spain
Bardera/Bardere *see* Baardheere
Bardesīr *see* Bardsīr
92 K3 **Bárdharbunga** ▲ C Iceland 64°39´N 17°30´W
Bardhë, Drini i *see* Beli Drim
106 E9 **Bardi** Emilia-Romagna, C Italy 44°39´N 09°44´E
106 A8 **Bardonecchia** Piemonte, W Italy 45°04´N 06°40´E
97 H19 **Bardsey Island** *island* NW Wales, United Kingdom
143 S11 **Bardsīr** *var.* Bardesīr, Mashīz. Kermān, C Iran 29°58´N 56°29´E
20 L6 **Bardstown** Kentucky, S USA 37°49´N 85°29´W
Barduli *see* Barletta
20 G7 **Bardwell** Kentucky, S USA 36°52´N 89°01´W
152 K11 **Bareilly** *var.* Bareli. Uttar Pradesh, N India 28°20´N 79°24´E
Bareli *see* Bareilly
Baren *see* Jiashi
98 H13 **Barendrecht** Zuid-Holland, SW Netherlands 51°52´N 04°31´E
102 M3 **Barentin** Seine-Maritime, N France 49°33´N 00°57´E
92 N3 **Barentsburg** Spitsbergen, W Svalbard 78°01´N 14°19´E
Barentsevo More/Barents Havet *see* Barents Sea
92 O3 **Barentsøya** *island* E Svalbard
197 T11 **Barents Plain** *undersea feature* N Barents Sea
125 P3 **Barents Sea** *Nor.* Barents Havet, *Rus.* Barentsevo More. *sea* Arctic Ocean
197 U14 **Barents Trough** *undersea feature* SW Barents Sea 75°00´N 29°00´E
80 I9 **Barentu** W Eritrea 15°08´N 37°35´E
102 J3 **Barfleur** Manche, N France 49°41´N 01°18´W
102 J3 **Barfleur, Pointe de** *headland* N France 49°46´N 01°09´W
Barfrush/Barfurush *see* Bābol
158 H14 **Barga** Xizang Zizhiqu, W China 30°51´N 81°20´E
Bargarh *see* Baragarh
105 N9 **Bargas** Castilla-La Mancha, C Spain 39°56´N 04°00´W
81 I15 **Bargē** Southern Nationalities, S Ethiopia 06°11´N 37°04´E
106 A9 **Barge** Piemonte, NE Italy 44°49´N 07°21´E
153 U16 **Barguna** Barisal, S Bangladesh 22°09´N 90°07´E
Bärgüşad *see* Vorotan
123 N13 **Barguzin** Respublika Buryatiya, S Russian Federation 53°37´N 109°47´E
153 O13 **Barhaj** Uttar Pradesh, N India 26°16´N 83°44´E
183 N10 **Barham** New South Wales, SE Australia 35°39´S 144°09´E
152 J12 **Barhan** Uttar Pradesh, N India 27°21´N 78°11´E
19 S7 **Bar Harbor** Mount Desert Island, Maine, NE USA 44°23´N 68°14´W
153 R14 **Barharwa** Jhārkhand, NE India 24°52´N 87°47´E
153 P15 **Barhi** Jhārkhand, N India 24°19´N 85°25´E
107 O17 **Bari** *var.* Bari delle Puglie; *anc.* Barium. Puglia, SE Italy 41°06´N 16°52´E
80 P12 **Bari** *Off.* Gobolka Bari. ⬖ *region* NE Somalia
167 T14 **Ba Ria** *var.* Châu Thanh. Ba Ria-Vung Tau, S Vietnam 10°30´N 107°10´E
Bāridah *see* Al Bāridah
Bari delle Puglie *see* Bari
Bari, Gobolka *see* Bari
Barikot *see* Barīkowṭ
149 T4 **Barīkowṭ** *var.* Barikot. Konar, NE Afghanistan 35°18´N 71°36´E
42 C4 **Barillas** *var.* Santa Cruz Barillas. Huehuetenango, NW Guatemala 15°50´N 91°20´W
54 J6 **Barinas** Barinas, W Venezuela 08°36´N 70°15´W
54 I7 **Barinas** *off.* Estado Barinas; *prev.* Zamora. ⬖ *state* C Venezuela
Barinas, Estado *see* Barinas
54 I6 **Barinitas** Barinas, NW Venezuela 08°45´N 70°26´W
154 P11 **Bāripada** Orissa, E India 21°56´N 86°43´E
60 K9 **Bariri** São Paulo, S Brazil 22°04´S 48°46´W
75 W11 **Bārīs** *var.* Bâris. S Egypt 24°28´N 30°39´E
152 G14 **Bari Sādri** Rājasthān, N India 24°25´N 74°28´E
153 U16 **Barisal** Barisal, S Bangladesh 22°41´N 90°20´E
153 U16 **Barisal** ⬖ *division* S Bangladesh
168 I10 **Barisan, Pegunungan** ▲▲ Sumatera, W Indonesia
169 T12 **Barito, Sungai** ≈ Borneo, C Indonesia
Barium *see* Bari
Bårjås *see* Porjus
80 I9 **Barka** *var.* Baraka, *Ar.* Khawr Barakah. *seasonal river* Eritrea/Sudan
Barka *see* Al Marj
160 H8 **Barkam** Sichuan, C China 31°56´N 102°22´E
118 J9 **Barkava** Madona, C Latvia 56°43´N 26°34´E
10 M15 **Barkerville** British Columbia, SW Canada 53°06´N 121°35´W
149 R11 **Bārkhān** Baluchistān, SW Pakistan 29°54´N 69°31´E
14 J12 **Bark Lake** ◎ Ontario, SE Canada
20 H7 **Barkley, Lake** ⊠ Kentucky/Tennessee, S USA
10 K17 **Barkley Sound** *inlet* British Columbia, W Canada
83 J24 **Barkly East** *Afr.* Barkly-Oos. Eastern Cape, SE South Africa 30°58´S 27°35´E
Barkly-Oos *see* Barkly East
181 S4 **Barkly Tableland** *plateau* Northern Territory/Queensland, N Australia
Barkly-Wes *see* Barkly West
83 H22 **Barkly West** *Afr.* Barkly-Wes. Northern Cape, N South Africa 28°32´S 24°32´E
159 O5 **Barkol** *var.* Barkol Kazak Zizhixian. Xinjiang Uygur Zizhiqu, NW China 43°37´N 93°01´E
159 O5 **Barkol Hu** ◎ NW China
Barkol Kazak Zizhixian *see* Barkol
30 J3 **Bark Point** *headland* Wisconsin, N USA 46°53´N 91°11´W
25 P11 **Barksdale** Texas, SW USA 29°43´N 100°03´W
Bar Kunar *see* Asmār
116 L11 **Bârlad** *prev.* Bîrlad. Vaslui, E Romania 46°12´N 27°39´E
116 M11 **Bârlad** *prev.* Bîrlad. ≈ E Romania
76 D9 **Barlavento, Ilhas de** *var.* Windward Islands. *island group* N Cape Verde
103 R5 **Bar-le-Duc** *var.* Bar-sur-Ornain. Meuse, NE France 48°46´N 05°10´E
180 K11 **Barlee, Lake** ◎ Western Australia
180 H8 **Barlee Range** ▲▲ Western Australia
107 N16 **Barletta** *anc.* Barduli. Puglia, SE Italy 41°20´N 16°17´E
110 E10 **Barlinek** *Ger.* Berlinchen. Zachodnio-pomorskie, NW Poland 53°N 15°11´E
27 S11 **Barling** Arkansas, C USA 35°19´N 94°18´W
171 U12 **Barma** Papua, E Indonesia 01°55´S 132°57´E
183 Q9 **Barmedman** New South Wales, SE Australia 34°09´S 147°21´E
Barmen-Elberfeld *see* Wuppertal
152 D12 **Bārmer** Rājasthān, NW India 25°43´N 71°25´E
182 K9 **Barmera** South Australia 34°14´S 140°26´E
97 I19 **Barmouth** NW Wales, United Kingdom 52°44´N 04°04´W
154 F10 **Barnagar** Madhya Pradesh, C India 23°01´N 75°28´E
152 H9 **Barnāla** Punjab, NW India 30°26´N 75°33´E
97 L15 **Barnard Castle** N England, United Kingdom 54°35´N 01°55´W
183 O6 **Barnato** New South Wales, SE Australia 31°39´S 145°01´E
122 I13 **Barnaul** Altayskiy Kray, C Russian Federation 53°21´N 83°45´E
109 V8 **Bärnbach** Steiermark, SE Austria 47°05´N 15°07´E
18 K16 **Barnegat** New Jersey, NE USA 39°43´N 74°12´W
23 S4 **Barnesville** Georgia, SE USA 33°03´N 84°09´W
29 R6 **Barnesville** Minnesota, N USA 46°39´N 96°25´W
31 U13 **Barnesville** Ohio, N USA 39°59´N 81°10´W
98 K11 **Barneveld** *var.* Barnveld. Gelderland, C Netherlands 52°08´N 05°34´E
25 O9 **Barnhart** Texas, SW USA 31°07´N 101°09´W
27 P8 **Barnsdall** Oklahoma, C USA 36°33´N 96°09´W
97 M17 **Barnsley** N England, United Kingdom 53°34´N 01°28´W
19 Q12 **Barnstable** Massachusetts, NE USA 41°42´N 70°17´W
97 I23 **Barnstaple** SW England, United Kingdom 51°05´N 04°04´W
Barnveld *see* Barneveld
21 Q14 **Barnwell** South Carolina, SE USA 33°14´N 81°21´W
77 U15 **Baro** Niger, C Nigeria 08°35´N 06°28´E
67 U8 **Baro** *var.* Baro Wenz. ≈ Ethiopia/Sudan
Baro *see* Baro Wenz
Baroda *see* Vadodara
149 U2 **Baroghil Pass** *var.* Kowtal-e Barowghīl. *pass* Afghanistan/Pakistan
119 Q17 **Baron'ki** *Rus.* Boron'ki. Mahilyowskaya Voblasts', E Belarus 53°09´N 32°08´E
182 J9 **Barossa Valley** *valley* South Australia
Baroui *see* Salisbury
81 H14 **Baro Wenz** *var.* Baro, Nahr Barū. ≈ Ethiopia/Sudan
Baro Wenz *see* Baro
Barowghīl, Kowtal-e *see* Baroghil Pass
153 U12 **Barpeta** Assam, NE India 26°19´N 91°05´E
31 S7 **Barques, Pointe Aux** *headland* Michigan, N USA 44°04´N 82°57´W
54 I5 **Barquisimeto** Lara, NW Venezuela 10°03´N 69°18´W
59 N16 **Barra** Bahia, E Brazil 11°06´S 43°15´W
96 E9 **Barra** *island* NW Scotland, United Kingdom
183 T5 **Barraba** New South Wales, SE Australia 30°24´S 150°37´E
60 L9 **Barra Bonita** São Paulo, S Brazil 22°30´S 48°35´W
64 J12 **Barracuda Fracture Zone** *var.* Fifteen Twenty Fracture Zone. *tectonic feature* SW Atlantic Ocean
64 G11 **Barracuda Ridge** *undersea feature* N Atlantic Ocean
43 N12 **Barra del Colorado** Limón, NE Costa Rica 10°44´N 83°35´W
43 N9 **Barra de Río Grande** Región Autónoma Atlántico Sur, E Nicaragua 12°56´N 83°30´W
82 A11 **Barra do Cuanza** Luanda, NW Angola 09°12´S 13°08´E
60 O9 **Barra do Piraí** Rio de Janeiro, SE Brazil 22°30´S 43°47´W
61 D16 **Barra do Quaraí** Rio Grande do Sul, SE Brazil 31°03´S 58°10´W
59 G14 **Barra do São Manuel** Pará, N Brazil 07°12´S 58°03´W
83 N19 **Barra Falsa, Ponta da** *headland* S Mozambique 22°57´S 35°36´E
96 E10 **Barra Head** *headland* NW Scotland, United Kingdom 56°46´N 07°37´W
60 O9 **Barra Mansa** Rio de Janeiro, SE Brazil 22°25´S 44°03´W
57 D14 **Barranca** Lima, W Peru 10°46´S 77°46´W
54 F8 **Barrancabermeja** Santander, N Colombia 07°01´N 73°51´W
54 H4 **Barrancas** La Guajira, N Colombia 10°59´N 72°46´W
54 J6 **Barrancas** Barinas, NW Venezuela 08°47´N 70°07´W
55 Q6 **Barrancas** Monagas, NE Venezuela 08°45´N 62°12´W
54 F6 **Barranco de Loba** Bolívar, N Colombia 08°56´N 74°07´W
104 I12 **Barrancos** Beja, S Portugal 38°08´N 06°59´W
62 N7 **Barranqueras** Chaco, N Argentina 27°29´S 58°54´W
54 E4 **Barranquilla** Atlántico, N Colombia 10°59´N 74°48´W
83 N20 **Barra, Ponta da** *headland* S Mozambique 23°46´S 35°33´E
105 P11 **Barrax** Castilla-La Mancha, C Spain 39°04´N 02°12´W
19 N11 **Barre** Massachusetts, NE USA 42°24´N 72°06´W
18 M7 **Barre** Vermont, NE USA 44°09´N 72°25´W
59 M17 **Barreiras** Bahia, E Brazil 12°09´S 44°58´W
104 F11 **Barreiro** Setúbal, W Portugal 38°40´N 09°05´W
20 K7 **Barren River Lake** ⊠ Kentucky, S USA
60 L7 **Barretos** São Paulo, S Brazil 20°33´S 48°33´W
11 P14 **Barrhead** Alberta, SW Canada 54°10´N 114°22´W
14 G14 **Barrie** Ontario, S Canada 44°22´N 79°42´W
11 N16 **Barrière** British Columbia, SW Canada 51°10´N 120°06´W
14 H8 **Barrière, Lac** ◎ Québec, SE Canada
182 L6 **Barrier Range** *hill range* New South Wales, SE Australia
42 G3 **Barrier Reef** *reef* E Belize
188 C16 **Barrigada** C Guam 13°27´N 144°48´E
Barrington Island *see* Santa Fe, Isla
183 T7 **Barrington Tops** ▲ New South Wales, SE Australia 32°06´S 151°18´E
183 O4 **Barringun** New South Wales, SE Australia 29°02´S 145°45´E
59 K18 **Barro Alto** Goiás, S Brazil 15°07´S 48°56´W
59 N14 **Barro Duro** Piauí, NE Brazil 05°49´S 42°30´W
30 I5 **Barron** Wisconsin, N USA 45°24´N 91°50´W
14 J12 **Barron** ≈ Ontario, SE Canada
61 H15 **Barros Cassal** Rio Grande do Sul, S Brazil 29°12´S 52°33´W
45 P14 **Barrouallie** Saint Vincent, W Saint Vincent and the Grenadines 13°14´N 61°17´W
39 O4 **Barrow** Alaska, USA 71°17´N 156°47´W
97 E20 **Barrow** *Ir.* An Bhearú. ≈ SE Ireland
181 Q6 **Barrow Creek Roadhouse** Northern Territory, N Australia 21°30´S 133°52´E
97 J16 **Barrow-in-Furness** NW England, United Kingdom 54°07´N 03°14´W
180 G7 **Barrow Island** *island* Western Australia
39 O4 **Barrow, Point** *headland* Alaska, USA 71°23´N 156°28´W
11 V14 **Barrows** Manitoba, S Canada 52°49´N 101°36´W
97 J22 **Barry** S Wales, United Kingdom 51°24´N 03°18´W
14 J12 **Barry's Bay** Ontario, SE Canada 45°30´N 77°41´W
144 K14 **Barsakel'mes, Ostrov** *island* SW Kazakhstan
Barść Łużyca *see* Forst
147 S14 **Barsem** S Tajikistan 37°36´N 71°43´E
145 V11 **Barshatas** Vostochnyy Kazakhstan, E Kazakhstan 48°13´N 78°33´E
155 F14 **Bārsi** Mahārāshtra, W India 18°14´N 75°42´E
100 I13 **Barsinghausen** Niedersachsen, C Germany 52°19´N 09°30´E
147 X8 **Barskoon** Issyk-Kul'skaya Oblast', E Kyrgyzstan 42°07´N 77°34´E
100 F10 **Barssel** Niedersachsen, NW Germany 53°10´N 07°46´E
35 U14 **Barstow** California, W USA 34°52´N 117°00´W
24 L8 **Barstow** Texas, SW USA 31°27´N 103°23´W
103 R6 **Bar-sur-Aube** Aube, NE France 48°13´N 04°43´E
Bar-sur-Ornain *see* Bar-le-Duc
103 Q6 **Bar-sur-Seine** Aube, N France 48°06´N 04°22´E
147 S13 **Bartang** S Tajikistan 38°06´N 71°48´E
147 T13 **Bartang** ≈ SE Tajikistan

◆ Country ● Country Capital ◇ Dependent Territory ○ Dependent Territory Capital ⬖ Administrative Regions ✈ International Airport ▲ Mountain ▲▲ Mountain Range ▲ Volcano ≈ River ◎ Lake ⊠ Reservoir

BARTENSTEIN – BEČEJ

Bartenstein see Bartoszyce
Bártfa/Bartfeld see Bardejov
100 N7 **Barth** Mecklenburg-Vorpommern, NE Germany 54°21′N 12°43′E
27 W13 **Bartholomew, Bayou** ≈ Arkansas/Louisiana, S USA
55 T8 **Bartica** N Guyana 06°24′N 58°36′W
136 H10 **Bartın** Bartın, NW Turkey 41°37′N 32°20′E
136 H10 **Bartın** ⬖ province NW Turkey
181 W4 **Bartle Frere** ▲ Queensland, E Australia 17°15′S 145°43′E
27 P8 **Bartlesville** Oklahoma, C USA 36°44′N 95°59′W
29 P14 **Bartlett** Nebraska, C USA 41°51′N 98°32′W
20 E10 **Bartlett** Tennessee, S USA 35°12′N 89°52′W
25 T9 **Bartlett** Texas, SW USA 30°47′N 97°25′W
36 L13 **Bartlett Reservoir** ⊠ Arizona, SW USA
19 N6 **Barton** Vermont, NE USA 44°44′N 72°09′W
110 L7 **Bartoszyce** Ger. Bartenstein. Warmińsko-mazurskie, NE Poland 54°16′N 20°49′E
23 W12 **Bartow** Florida, SE USA 27°54′N 81°50′W
Bartschin see Barcin
168 J10 **Barumun, Sungai** ≈ Sumatera, W Indonesia
Barū, Nahr see Baro Wenz
169 S17 **Barung, Nusa** island S Indonesia
168 H9 **Barus** Sumatera, NW Indonesia 02°02′N 98°20′E
162 I9 **Baruunbayan-Ulaan** var. Höövör. Övörhangay, C Mongolia 45°10′N 101°19′E
Baruunsuu see Tsogttsetsiy
163 P8 **Baruun-Urt** Sühbaatar, E Mongolia 46°40′N 113°17′E
43 P15 **Barú, Volcán** var. Volcán de Chiriquí. ⛰ W Panama 08°49′N 82°32′W
99 K21 **Barvaux** Luxembourg, SE Belgium 50°21′N 05°30′E
42 M13 **Barva, Volcán** ⛰ NW Costa Rica 10°07′N 84°08′W
117 W6 **Barvinkove** Kharkivs'ka Oblast', E Ukraine 48°54′N 37°03′E
154 G11 **Barwāh** Madhya Pradesh, C India 22°17′N 76°01′E
Bärwalde Neumark see Mieszkowice
154 F11 **Barwāni** Madhya Pradesh, C India 22°02′N 74°56′E
183 P5 **Barwon River** ≈ New South Wales, SE Australia
119 L15 **Barysaw** Rus. Borisov. Minskaya Voblasts', NE Belarus 54°14′N 28°30′E
127 Q6 **Barysh** Ul'yanovskaya Oblast', W Russian Federation 53°32′N 47°06′E
117 Q4 **Baryshivka** Kyyivs'ka Oblast', N Ukraine 50°21′N 31°21′E
79 J17 **Basankusu** Equateur, NW Dem. Rep. Congo 01°12′N 19°50′E
117 N11 **Basarabeasca** Rus. Bessarabka. SE Moldova 46°22′N 28°56′E
116 M14 **Basarabi** Constanţa, SW Romania 44°10′N 28°26′E
40 H6 **Basaseachic** Chihuahua, NW Mexico 28°18′N 108°13′W
Basauri see Arizgoiti
61 D18 **Basavilbaso** Entre Ríos, E Argentina 32°23′S 58°55′W
79 F21 **Bas-Congo** off. Région du Bas-Congo; prev. Bas-Zaïre. ⬖ region SW Dem. Rep. Congo
108 E6 **Basel** Eng. Basle, Fr. Bâle. Basel-Stadt, NW Switzerland 47°33′N 07°36′E
108 E7 **Basel** Eng. Basle, Fr. Bâle. ⬖ canton NW Switzerland
143 T14 **Bashākerd, Kūhhā-ye** ▲▲ SE Iran
11 Q15 **Bashaw** Alberta, SW Canada 52°40′N 112°53′W
146 K16 **Bashbedeng** Mary Welaýaty, S Turkmenistan 35°44′N 63°07′E
161 T15 **Bashi Channel** Chin. Pa-shih Hai-hsia. channel Philippines/Taiwan
Bashkiria see Bashkortostan, Respublika
122 F11 **Bashkortostan, Respublika** prev. Bashkiria. ⬖ autonomous republic W Russian Federation
127 N6 **Bashmakovo** Penzenskaya Oblast', W Russian Federation 53°13′N 43°00′E
146 J10 **Bashsakarba** Lebap Welaýaty, NE Turkmenistan 40°25′N 62°16′E
117 R9 **Bashtanka** Mykolayivs'ka Oblast', S Ukraine 47°24′N 32°27′E
22 H8 **Basile** Louisiana, S USA 30°29′N 92°36′W
107 M18 **Basilicata** ⬖ region S Italy
33 V13 **Basin** Wyoming, C USA 44°22′N 108°02′W
97 N22 **Basingstoke** S England, United Kingdom 51°16′N 01°08′W
143 U8 **Başīrān** Khorāsān-e Janūbī, E Iran 31°57′N 59°07′E
112 B10 **Baška** It. Bescanuova. Primorje-Gorski Kotar, NW Croatia 44°58′N 14°46′E
137 T15 **Başkale** Van, SE Turkey 38°03′N 43°59′E
14 L10 **Baskatong, Réservoir** ⊠ Québec, SE Canada
137 O14 **Baskil** Elazığ, E Turkey 38°38′N 38°47′E
Basle see Basel
154 H9 **Bāsoda** Madhya Pradesh, C India 23°54′N 77°58′E
79 L17 **Basoko** Orientale, N Dem. Rep. Congo 01°14′N 23°26′E
Basque Country, The see País Vasco
Basra see Al Başrah
103 U5 **Bas-Rhin** ⬖ department NE France
Bassam see Grand-Bassam
11 Q16 **Bassano** Alberta, SW Canada 50°48′N 112°28′W
106 H7 **Bassano del Grappa** Veneto, NE Italy 45°45′N 11°45′E
77 Q15 **Bassar** var. Bassari. NW Togo 09°15′N 00°47′E
Bassari see Bassar
172 L9 **Bassas da India** island group W Madagascar
108 D7 **Bassecourt** Jura, W Switzerland 47°20′N 07°16′E
Bassein see Pathein
79 J15 **Basse-Kotto** ⬖ prefecture S Central African Republic
105 V5 **Bassella** Cataluña, NE Spain 42°01′N 01°17′E
102 J5 **Basse-Normandie** Eng. Lower Normandy. ⬖ region N France
45 Q11 **Basse-Pointe** N Martinique 14°52′N 61°07′W
76 H12 **Basse Santa Su** E Gambia 13°18′N 14°10′W
Basse-Saxe see Niedersachsen
45 X6 **Basse-Terre** ○ (Guadeloupe) Basse Terre, SW Guadeloupe 16°08′N 61°40′W
45 V10 **Basseterre** ● (Saint Kitts and Nevis) Saint Kitts, Saint Kitts and Nevis 17°16′N 62°45′W
45 X6 **Basse Terre** island W Guadeloupe
29 O13 **Bassett** Nebraska, C USA 42°34′N 99°32′W
21 S7 **Bassett** Virginia, NE USA 36°45′N 79°59′W
37 N15 **Bassett Peak** ▲ Arizona, SW USA 32°30′N 110°16′W
76 M10 **Bassikounou** Hodh ech Chargui, SE Mauritania 15°55′N 05°59′W
77 R15 **Bassila** W Benin 08°25′N 01°58′E
Bass, Îlots de see Marotiri
31 O11 **Bass Lake** Indiana, N USA 41°12′N 86°35′W
183 O14 **Bass Strait** strait SE Australia
100 H11 **Bassum** Niedersachsen, NW Germany 52°52′N 08°44′E
29 X3 **Basswood Lake** ◎ Canada/USA
95 J21 **Båstad** Skåne, S Sweden 56°25′N 12°50′E
139 U2 **Baştah** As Sulaymānīyah, E Iraq 36°20′N 45°14′E
143 Q14 **Bastak** Fārs, SW Iran 27°14′N 54°27′E
153 N12 **Basti** Uttar Pradesh, N India 26°48′N 82°44′E
103 X14 **Bastia** Corse, France, C Mediterranean Sea 42°42′N 09°27′E
99 L23 **Bastogne** Luxembourg, SE Belgium 50°N 05°43′E
22 I5 **Bastrop** Louisiana, S USA 32°46′N 91°54′W
25 T11 **Bastrop** Texas, SW USA 30°07′N 97°21′W
93 J15 **Bastuträsk** Västerbotten, N Sweden 64°47′N 20°05′E
119 J19 **Bastyn'** Rus. Bostyn'. Brestskaya Voblasts', SW Belarus 52°23′N 26°45′E
Basuo see Dongfang
Basutoland see Lesotho
119 O15 **Basya** ≈ E Belarus
117 V8 **Basyl'kivka** Dnipropetrovs'ka Oblast', E Ukraine 48°12′N 36°00′E
Bas-Zaïre see Bas-Congo
79 D17 **Bata** NW Equatorial Guinea 01°51′N 09°48′E
79 D17 **Bata** ✈ S Equatorial Guinea 01°55′N 09°48′E
Batae Coritanorum see Leicester
123 Q8 **Batagay** Respublika Sakha (Yakutiya), NE Russian Federation 67°36′N 134°44′E
123 P8 **Batagay-Alyta** Respublika Sakha (Yakutiya), NE Russian Federation 67°48′N 130°15′E
112 L10 **Batajnica** Vojvodina, N Serbia 44°55′N 20°17′E
136 H15 **Batakłak Gölü** ◎ S Turkey
114 H11 **Batak, Yazovir** ⊠ SW Bulgaria
152 H7 **Batāla** Punjab, N India 31°48′N 75°12′E
104 F9 **Batalha** Leiria, C Portugal 39°40′N 08°50′W
79 N17 **Batama** Orientale, NE Dem. Rep. Congo 00°54′N 26°25′E
123 Q10 **Batamay** Respublika Sakha (Yakutiya), NE Russian Federation 63°28′N 129°33′E
160 F9 **Batang** var. Bazhong. Sichuan, C China 30°04′N 99°10′E
79 I14 **Batangafo** Ouham, NW Central African Republic 07°19′N 18°22′E
171 P8 **Batangas** off. Batangas City. Luzon, N Philippines 13°47′N 121°03′E
Batangas City see Batangas
Bâtania see Battonya
171 Q10 **Batan Islands** island group N Philippines
60 L8 **Batatais** São Paulo, S Brazil 20°54′S 47°37′W
18 E10 **Batavia** New York, NE USA 43°00′N 78°11′W
Batavia see Jakarta
173 T9 **Batavia Seamount** undersea feature E Indian Ocean 27°42′S 100°36′E
126 L12 **Bataysk** Rostovskaya Oblast', SW Russian Federation 47°10′N 39°46′E
14 B9 **Batchawana** ≈ Ontario, S Canada
14 B9 **Batchawana Bay** Ontario, S Canada 46°55′N 84°36′W
167 Q12 **Bătdâmbâng** prev. Battambang. Bătdâmbâng, NW Cambodia 13°06′N 103°13′E
79 G20 **Batéké, Plateaux** plateau S Congo
183 S11 **Batemans Bay** New South Wales, SE Australia 35°45′S 150°09′E
21 Q13 **Batesburg** South Carolina, SE USA 33°54′N 81°33′W
28 K12 **Batesland** South Dakota, N USA 43°05′N 102°07′W
27 V10 **Batesville** Arkansas, C USA 35°45′N 91°39′W
31 Q14 **Batesville** Indiana, N USA 39°18′N 85°13′W
22 L2 **Batesville** Mississippi, S USA 34°18′N 89°56′W
25 Q13 **Batesville** Texas, SW USA 28°56′N 99°38′W
149 V5 **Batgrām** North-West Frontier Province, N Pakistan 34°40′N 73°03′E
44 L13 **Bath** E Jamaica 17°57′N 76°22′W
97 L22 **Bath** hist. Akermanceaster; anc. Aquae Calidae, Aquae Solis. SW England, United Kingdom 51°23′N 02°22′W
19 Q8 **Bath** Maine, NE USA 43°54′N 69°49′W
18 F11 **Bath** New York, NE USA 42°20′N 77°16′W
Bath see Berkeley Springs
78 I10 **Batha** off. Préfecture du Batha. ⬖ prefecture C Chad
78 I10 **Batha** seasonal river C Chad
Batha, Préfecture du see Batha
141 Y8 **Baṭḥā', Wādī al** dry watercourse NE Oman
152 H9 **Bathinda** Punjab, NW India 30°14′N 74°54′E
98 M11 **Bathmen** Overijssel, E Netherlands 52°15′N 06°16′E
45 Z14 **Bathsheba** E Barbados 13°13′N 59°31′W
183 R8 **Bathurst** New South Wales, SE Australia 33°32′S 149°35′E
13 O13 **Bathurst** New Brunswick, SE Canada 47°37′N 65°40′W
Bathurst see Banjul
8 H6 **Bathurst, Cape** headland Northwest Territories, NW Canada 70°33′N 128°00′W
196 L8 **Bathurst Inlet** Nunavut, N Canada 66°23′N 107°00′W
196 L8 **Bathurst Inlet** inlet Nunavut, N Canada
181 N1 **Bathurst Island** island Northern Territory, N Australia
197 O9 **Bathurst Island** island Parry Islands, Nunavut, N Canada
77 O14 **Batié** SW Burkina 09°53′N 02°53′W
Batinah see Al Bāṭinah
141 Y9 **Bāṭin, Wādī al** dry watercourse SW Asia
15 P9 **Batiscan** ≈ Québec, SE Canada
136 F16 **BatıToroslar** ▲▲ SW Turkey
Batjan see Bacan, Pulau
147 R11 **Batken** Batenskaya Oblast', SW Kyrgyzstan 40°03′N 70°50′E
Batken Oblasty see Batkenskaya Oblast'
147 Q11 **Batkenskaya Oblast'** Kir. Batken Oblasty. ⬖ province SW Kyrgyzstan
Batlle y Ordóñez see José Batlle y Ordóñez
183 Q10 **Batlow** New South Wales, SE Australia 35°32′S 148°09′E
137 Q15 **Batman** var. Iluh. Batman, SE Turkey 37°52′N 41°06′E
137 Q15 **Batman** ⬖ province SE Turkey
74 L6 **Batna** NE Algeria 35°34′N 06°10′E
163 O7 **Batnorov** var. Dundbürd. Hentiy, E Mongolia 47°55′N 111°37′E
Batoe see Batu, Kepulauan
162 K7 **Bat-Öldziy** var. Övt. Övörhangay, C Mongolia 46°50′N 102°15′E
Bat-Öldziyt see Dzaamar
22 J8 **Baton Rouge** state capital Louisiana, S USA 30°28′N 91°09′W
79 G15 **Batouri** Est, E Cameroon 04°26′N 14°27′E
138 G14 **Baṭrā', Jibāl al** ▲▲ S Jordan
138 G6 **Batroûn** var. Al Batrūn. N Lebanon 34°15′N 35°42′E
Batsch see Bač
Batsevichi see Batsevichy
119 M17 **Batsevichy** Rus. Batsevichi. Mahilyowskaya Voblasts', E Belarus 53°24′N 29°14′E
92 M7 **Båtsfjord** Finnmark, N Norway 70°37′N 29°42′E
Batshireet see Hentiy
162 L7 **Batsümber** var. Mandal. Töv, C Mongolia 48°24′N 106°47′E
Battambang see Bătdâmbâng
195 X3 **Batterbee, Cape** headland Antarctica
155 L24 **Batticaloa** Eastern Province, E Sri Lanka 07°44′N 81°43′E
99 L19 **Battice** Liège, E Belgium 50°39′N 05°50′E
107 L18 **Battipaglia** Campania, S Italy 40°36′N 14°59′E
11 R15 **Battle** ≈ Alberta/ Saskatchewan, SW Canada
Battle Born State see Nevada
31 Q10 **Battle Creek** Michigan, N USA 42°20′N 85°10′W
27 T7 **Battlefield** Missouri, C USA 37°07′N 93°22′W
11 S15 **Battleford** Saskatchewan, S Canada 52°45′N 108°20′W
29 S6 **Battle Lake** Minnesota, N USA 46°16′N 95°42′W
35 U3 **Battle Mountain** Nevada, W USA 40°37′N 116°55′W
111 M25 **Battonya** Rom. Bătania. Békés, SE Hungary 46°16′N 21°00′E
162 J7 **Battsengel** var. Jargalant. Arhangay, C Mongolia 47°46′N 101°56′E
168 D11 **Batu, Kepulauan** prev. Batoe. island group W Indonesia
137 Q10 **Bat'umi** W Georgia 41°39′N 41°38′E
168 K10 **Batu Pahat** prev. Bandar Penggaram. Johor, Peninsular Malaysia 01°51′N 102°56′E
171 O12 **Baturebe** Sulawesi, N Indonesia 01°43′S 121°43′E
122 J12 **Baturino** Tomskaya Oblast', C Russian Federation 57°46′N 85°08′E
117 R3 **Baturyn** Chernihivs'ka Oblast', N Ukraine 51°20′N 32°54′E
138 F10 **Bat Yam** Tel Aviv, C Israel 32°01′N 34°45′E
127 Q4 **Batyrevo** Chuvashskaya Respublika, W Russian Federation 55°04′N 47°34′E
Batys Qazaqstan Oblysy see Zapadnyy Kazakhstan
102 F5 **Batz, Île de** island NW France
169 Q10 **Bau** Sarawak, East Malaysia 01°25′N 110°10′E
171 N2 **Bauang** Luzon, N Philippines 16°33′N 120°19′E
171 P14 **Baubau** var. Baoebaoe. Pulau Buton, C Indonesia 05°30′S 122°37′E
77 W14 **Bauchi** Bauchi, NE Nigeria 10°18′N 09°46′E
77 W14 **Bauchi** ⬖ state C Nigeria
102 H7 **Baud** Morbihan, NW France 47°52′N 02°59′W
154 N13 **Bauda** var. Baudh. Orissa, SW India 20°50′N 84°19′E
29 T2 **Baudette** Minnesota, N USA 48°42′N 94°36′W
Baudh see Bauda
193 S9 **Bauer Basin** undersea feature E Pacific Ocean 10°00′S 101°45′W
187 R14 **Bauer Field** var. Port Vila. ✈ (Port-Vila) Éfaté, C Vanuatu 17°42′S 168°21′E
13 T9 **Bauld, Cape** headland Newfoundland and Labrador, E Canada 51°35′N 55°22′W
103 T8 **Baume-les-Dames** Doubs, E France 47°22′N 06°20′E
101 I15 **Baunatal** Hessen, C Germany 51°15′N 09°25′E
107 D18 **Baunei** Sardegna, Italy, C Mediterranean Sea 40°04′N 09°36′E
57 M15 **Baures, Río** ≈ N Bolivia
60 K9 **Bauru** São Paulo, S Brazil 22°19′S 49°07′W
Baushar see Bawshar
118 G10 **Bauska** Ger. Bauske. Bauska, S Latvia 56°25′N 24°11′E
Bauske see Bauska
101 Q15 **Bautzen** Lus. Budyšin. Sachsen, E Germany 51°11′N 14°29′E
145 Q16 **Bauyrzhan Momyshuly** Kaz. Baüyrzhan Momyshuly; prev. Burnoye. Zhambyl, S Kazakhstan 42°36′N 70°46′E
Bauzanum see Bolzano
Bavaria see Bayern
109 N7 **Bavarian Alps** Ger. Bayrische Alpen. ▲▲ Austria/ Germany
Bavière see Bayern
40 H4 **Bavispe, Río** ≈ NW Mexico
127 T5 **Bavly** Respublika Tatarstan, W Russian Federation 54°20′N 53°21′E
169 P13 **Bawal, Pulau** island N Indonesia
169 T12 **Bawan** Borneo, C Indonesia 01°36′S 113°55′E
183 O12 **Baw Baw, Mount** ▲ Victoria, SE Australia 37°49′S 146°16′E
169 S15 **Bawean, Pulau** island S Indonesia
75 V9 **Bawīṭī** var. Bawīṭī. N Egypt 28°19′N 28°53′E
Bawīṭī see Bawīṭī
77 Q13 **Bawku** N Ghana 11°00′N 00°12′W
167 N7 **Bawlakè** Kayah State, C Burma (Myanmar) 19°10′N 97°19′E
169 H11 **Bawo Ofuloa** Pulau Tanahmasa, W Indonesia 0°10′S 98°24′E
141 Y8 **Bawshar** var. Baushar. NE Oman 23°32′N 58°24′E
Baxian see Bazhou
Ba Xian see Bazhou
158 M8 **Baxkorgan** Xinjiang Uygur Zizhiqu, W China 39°05′N 90°00′E
23 V6 **Baxley** Georgia, SE USA 31°46′N 82°21′W
159 R15 **Baxoi** var. Baima. Xizang Zizhiqu, W China 30°01′N 96°53′E
29 W14 **Baxter** Iowa, C USA 41°49′N 93°09′W
29 U6 **Baxter** Minnesota, N USA 46°21′N 94°18′W
27 R8 **Baxter Springs** Kansas, C USA 37°01′N 94°45′W
81 M17 **Bay** off. Gobolka Bay. ⬖ region SW Somalia
Bay see Baicheng
44 H7 **Bayamo** Granma, E Cuba 20°21′N 76°38′W
45 U5 **Bayamón** E Puerto Rico 18°24′N 66°09′W
163 W8 **Bayan** Heilongjiang, NE China 46°05′N 127°24′E
170 L16 **Bayan** prev. Bajan. Pulau Lombok, C Indonesia 08°16′S 116°28′E
162 M8 **Bayan** var. Maanit. Töv, C Mongolia 47°14′N 107°34′E
Bayan see Hölönbuyr, Dornod, Mongolia
Bayan see Ihhet, Dornogovĭ, Mongolia
Bayan see Bayan-Uul, Govĭ-Altay, Mongolia
Bayan see Bayanhutag, Hentiy, Mongolia
Bayan see Bürentogtoh, Hövsgol, Mongolia
152 I12 **Bayāna** Rājasthān, N India 26°55′N 77°18′E
149 N5 **Bāyān, Band-e** ▲▲ C Afghanistan
162 H8 **Bayanbulag** Bayanhongor, C Mongolia 46°46′N 98°07′E
Bayanbulag see Ömnödelger
158 J5 **Bayanbulak** Xinjiang Uygur Zizhiqu, W China 43°05′N 84°05′E
162 L7 **Bayanchandmanĭ** var. Ihsüüj. Töv, C Mongolia 48°12′N 106°23′E
162 J11 **Bayandalay** var. Dalay. Ömnögovĭ, S Mongolia 43°27′N 103°30′E
163 O9 **Bayandelger** var. Shireet. Sühbaatar, SE Mongolia 45°33′N 112°19′E
162 I5 **Bayandzürh** var. Altraga. Hövsgöl, N Mongolia 50°08′N 98°54′E
Bayan Gol see Dengkou, China
Bayangol see Bugat, Mongolia
162 I9 **Bayangovĭ** var. Örgön. Bayanhongor, C Mongolia 44°43′N 100°23′E
159 R12 **Bayan Har Shan** var. Bayan Khar. ▲▲ C China
162 G6 **Bayanhayrhan** var. Altanbulag. Dzavhan, N Mongolia 49°16′N 96°22′E
162 I8 **Bayanhongor** Bayanhongor, C Mongolia 46°08′N 100°42′E
162 H9 **Bayanhongor** ⬖ province C Mongolia
162 K14 **Bayan Hot** var. Alxa Zuoqi. Nei Mongol Zizhiqu, N China 38°49′N 105°40′E
163 O8 **Bayanhutag** var. Bayan. Hentiy, C Mongolia 47°13′N 110°57′E
163 T9 **Bayan Huxu** var. Horqin Zuoyi Zhongqi. Nei Mongol Zizhiqu, N China 45°02′N 121°28′E
Bayan Khar see Bayan Har Shan
163 N12 **Bayan Kuang** prev. Bayan Obo. Nei Mongol Zizhiqu, N China 41°45′N 109°58′E
168 J7 **Bayan Lepas** ✈ (George Town) Pinang, Peninsular Malaysia 05°18′N 100°15′E
162 I10 **Bayanlig** var. Hatansuudal. Bayanhongor, C Mongolia 44°34′N 100°41′E
162 K13 **Bayan Mod** Nei Mongol Zizhiqu, N China 40°45′N 104°29′E
163 N8 **Bayanmönh** var. Ulaan-Ereg. Hentiy, E Mongolia 46°50′N 109°39′E
162 L12 **Bayannur** var. Linhe. Nei Mongol Zizhiqu, N China 40°46′N 107°27′E
Bayan Nuru see Xar Burd
162 E5 **Bayannuur** var. Tsul-Ulaan. Bayan-Ölgiy, W Mongolia 48°51′N 91°13′E
Bayan Obo see Bayan Kuang
43 V15 **Bayano, Lago** ◎ E Panama
162 C5 **Bayan-Ölgiy** ⬖ province NW Mongolia
162 H9 **Bayan-Öndör** var. Bulgan. Bayanhongor, C Mongolia 44°48′N 98°39′E
162 K8 **Bayan-Öndör** var. Bumbat. Övörhangay, C Mongolia 46°30′N 104°08′E
162 L8 **Bayan-Önjüül** var. Ihhayrhan. Töv, C Mongolia 46°57′N 105°51′E
163 O7 **Bayan-Ovoo** var. Javhlant. Hentiy, E Mongolia 47°46′N 112°06′E
162 L11 **Bayan-Ovoo** var. Erdenetsogt. Ömnögovĭ, S Mongolia 42°54′N 106°16′E
Bayansayr see Baatsagaan
159 Q9 **Bayan Shan** ▲ C China 37°36′N 96°23′E
162 J9 **Bayanteeg** Övörhangay, C Mongolia 45°39′N 101°30′E
162 G5 **Bayantes** var. Altay. Dzavhan, N Mongolia 49°40′N 96°21′E
Bayantöhöm see Büren
162 M8 **Bayantsagaan** var. Dzogsool. Töv, C Mongolia 46°46′N 107°18′E
163 P7 **Bayantümen** var. Tsagaanders. Dornod, NE Mongolia 48°03′N 114°16′E
Bayan-Uhaa see Ih-Uul
163 R10 **Bayan Ul** var. Xi Ujimqin Qi. Nei Mongol Zizhiqu, N China 44°31′N 117°36′E
Bayan-Ulaan see Dzüünbayan-Ulaan
163 O7 **Bayan-Uul** var. Javarthushuu. Dornod, NE Mongolia 49°05′N 112°40′E
162 F7 **Bayan-Uul** var. Bayan. Govĭ-Altay, W Mongolia 47°05′N 95°13′E
162 M8 **Bayanuur** var. Tsul-Ulaan. Töv, C Mongolia 47°44′N 108°22′E
28 J14 **Bayard** Nebraska, C USA 41°45′N 103°19′W
37 P15 **Bayard** New Mexico, SW USA 32°45′N 108°07′W
103 T13 **Bayard, Col** pass SE France
Bayasgalant see Mönhhaan
136 J12 **Bayat** Çorum, N Turkey 40°34′N 34°07′E
171 P6 **Bayawan** Negros, C Philippines 09°22′N 122°50′E
143 R10 **Bayāẓ** Kermān, C Iran 30°41′N 55°29′E
171 Q6 **Baybay** Leyte, C Philippines 10°41′N 124°49′E
21 X10 **Bayboro** North Carolina, SE USA 35°08′N 76°49′W
137 P12 **Bayburt** Bayburt, NE Turkey 40°15′N 40°16′E
137 P12 **Bayburt** ⬖ province NE Turkey
31 R8 **Bay City** Michigan, N USA 43°35′N 83°52′W
25 V12 **Bay City** Texas, SW USA 28°59′N 96°00′W
Baydarata Bay see Baydaratskaya Guba
122 J7 **Baydaratskaya Guba** var. Baydarata Bay. bay N Russian Federation
81 M16 **Baydhabo** var. Baydhowa, Isha Baydhabo, It. Baidoa. Bay, SW Somalia 03°08′N 43°39′E
Baydhowa see Baydhabo
77 U17 **Bayelsa** ⬖ state S Nigeria
101 N21 **Bayerischer Wald** ▲▲ SE Germany
101 K21 **Bayern** Eng. Bavaria, Fr. Bavière. ⬖ state SE Germany
147 V9 **Bayetovo** Narynskaya Oblast', C Kyrgyzstan 41°14′N 74°55′E
102 K4 **Bayeux** anc. Augustodurum. Calvados, N France 49°16′N 00°42′W
14 E15 **Bayfield** ≈ Ontario, S Canada
145 O15 **Baygekum** Kaz. Bäygequm. Kzylorda, S Kazakhstan 44°15′N 66°34′E
Bäygequm see Baygekum
136 C14 **Bayındır** İzmir, SW Turkey 38°12′N 27°40′E
138 H12 **Bāyir** var. Bā'ir. Ma'ān, S Jordan 30°46′N 36°40′E
Bay Islands see Bahía, Islas de la
Bayizhen see Nyingchi
139 R5 **Bayjī** var. Baiji. Şalāḩ ad Dīn, N Iraq 34°56′N 43°29′E
Baykadam see Saudakent
123 N13 **Baykal, Ozero** Eng. Lake Baikal. ◎ S Russian Federation
123 M14 **Baykal'sk** Irkutskaya Oblast', S Russian Federation 51°30′N 104°03′E
137 R15 **Baykan** Siirt, SE Turkey 38°08′N 41°43′E
123 L11 **Baykit** Evenkiyskiy Avtonomnyy Okrug, C Russian Federation 61°37′N 96°23′E
145 N12 **Baykonur** var. Baykonyr. Karaganda, C Kazakhstan 47°50′N 75°33′E
Baykonur see Baykonyr
144 M14 **Baykonyr** var. Baykonur, Kaz. Bayqongyr; prev. Leninsk. Kyzylorda, S Kazakhstan 45°38′N 63°20′E
Baykonyr see Baykonur
158 E7 **Baykurt** Xinjiang Uygur Zizhiqu, W China 39°56′N 75°33′E
14 I9 **Bay, Lac** ◎ Québec, SE Canada
127 W6 **Baymak** Respublika Bashkortostan, W Russian Federation 52°34′N 58°20′E
23 O8 **Bay Minette** Alabama, S USA 30°52′N 87°46′W
143 O17 **Baynūnah** desert W United Arab Emirates
184 O8 **Bay of Plenty** off. Bay of Plenty Region. ⬖ region North Island, New Zealand
Bay of Plenty Region see Bay of Plenty
191 Z3 **Bay of Wrecks** bay Kiritimati, E Kiribati
Bayonnaise Rocks see Beyonēsu-retsugan
102 I15 **Bayonne** anc. Lapurdum. Pyrénées-Atlantiques, SW France 43°30′N 01°28′W
22 H4 **Bayou D'Arbonne Lake** ⊠ Louisiana, S USA
23 N9 **Bayou La Batre** Alabama, S USA 30°24′N 88°15′W
Bayou State see Mississippi
Bayqadam see Saudakent
Bayqongyr see Baykonyr
Bayram-Ali see Baýramaly
146 J14 **Baýramaly** var. Bayramaly; prev. Bayram-Ali. Mary Welaýaty, S Turkmenistan 37°33′N 62°08′E
101 L19 **Bayreuth** var. Baireuth. Bayern, SE Germany 49°57′N 11°34′E
Bayrische Alpen see Bavarian Alps
Bayrūt see Beyrouth
22 L9 **Bay Saint Louis** Mississippi, S USA 30°18′N 89°19′W
Baysān see Beit She'an
Bayshint see Öndörshireet
14 H13 **Bays, Lake of** ◎ Ontario, S Canada
22 M6 **Bay Springs** Mississippi, S USA 31°58′N 89°17′W
Bay State see Massachusetts
Baysun see Boysun
14 H13 **Baysville** Ontario, S Canada 45°10′N 79°03′W
141 N15 **Bayt al Faqīh** W Yemen 14°30′N 43°20′E
158 M4 **Baytik Shan** ▲▲ China/ Mongolia
Bayt Laḩm see Bethlehem
25 W11 **Baytown** Texas, SW USA 29°43′N 94°59′W
169 V11 **Bayur, Tanjung** headland Borneo, N Indonesia 0°43′S 117°32′E
121 N14 **Bayy al Kabīr, Wādī** dry watercourse NW Libya
Bayyrqum see Bairkum
105 P14 **Baza** Andalucía, S Spain 37°30′N 02°45′W
137 X10 **Bazardüzü Dağı** Rus. Gora Bazardyuzyu. ▲ N Azerbaijan 41°13′N 47°50′E
Bazardyuzyu, Gora see Bazardüzü Dağı
Bazargic see Dobrich
83 N18 **Bazaruto, Ilha do** island SE Mozambique
102 K14 **Bazas** Gironde, SW France 44°27′N 00°11′W
105 O14 **Baza, Sierra de** ▲▲ S Spain
160 J8 **Bazhong** var. Bazhou. Sichuan, C China 31°55′N 106°44′E
Bazhong see Batang
161 P3 **Bazhou** prev. Baxian, Ba Xian. Hebei, E China 39°05′N 116°24′E
Bazhou see Bazhong
14 M9 **Bazin** ≈ Québec, SE Canada
Bazin see Pezinok
139 Q7 **Bāzīyah** Al Anbār, C Iraq 33°50′N 42°41′E
138 H6 **Bcharré** var. Bcharreh, Bsharrī, Bsherri. NE Lebanon 34°16′N 36°01′E
Bcharreh see Bcharré
28 J5 **Beach** North Dakota, N USA 46°55′N 104°00′W
182 K12 **Beachport** South Australia 37°29′S 140°03′E
97 O23 **Beachy Head** headland SE England, United Kingdom 50°44′N 00°16′E
18 K13 **Beacon** New York, NE USA 41°30′N 73°54′W
63 J25 **Beagle Channel** channel Argentina/Chile
181 O1 **Beagle Gulf** gulf Northern Territory, N Australia
Bealach an Doirín see Ballaghaderreen
Bealach Cláir see Ballyclare
Bealach Féich see Ballybofey
172 J3 **Bealanana** Mahajanga, NE Madagascar 14°33′S 48°44′E
Béal an Átha see Ballina
Béal an Átha Móir see Ballinamore
Béal an Mhuirhead see Belmullet
Béal Átha Beithe see Ballybay
Béal Átha Conaill see Ballyconnell
Beál Átha hAmhnais see Ballyhaunis
Béal Átha na Sluaighe see Ballinasloe
Béal Átha Seanaidh see Ballyshannon
Bealdovuopmi see Peltovuoma
Béal Feirste see Belfast
Béal Tairbirt see Belturbet
Beanna Boirche see Mourne Mountains
Beannchar see Banagher, Ireland
Beannchar see Bangor, Northern Ireland, UK
Beanntraí see Bantry
Bearalváhki see Berlevåg
23 N2 **Bear Creek** ≈ Alabama/ Mississippi, S USA
30 J13 **Bear Creek** ≈ Illinois, N USA
27 U13 **Bearden** Arkansas, C USA 33°43′N 92°37′W
195 Q10 **Beardmore Glacier** glacier Antarctica
30 K13 **Beardstown** Illinois, N USA 40°01′N 90°25′W
28 L14 **Bear Hill** ▲ Nebraska, C USA 41°24′N 101°49′W
Bear Island see Bjørnøya
14 H12 **Bear Lake** Ontario, S Canada 45°28′N 79°31′W
36 M1 **Bear Lake** ◎ Idaho/Utah, NW USA
39 U11 **Bear, Mount** ▲ Alaska, USA 61°16′N 141°09′W
102 J16 **Béarn** cultural region SW France
194 J11 **Bear Peninsula** peninsula Antarctica
152 I7 **Beās** ≈ India/Pakistan
105 P3 **Beasain** País Vasco, N Spain 43°03′N 02°11′W
105 O12 **Beas de Segura** Andalucía, S Spain 38°16′N 02°54′W
45 N10 **Beata, Cabo** headland SW Dominican Republic 17°34′N 71°25′W
45 N10 **Beata, Isla** island SW Dominican Republic
64 F11 **Beata Ridge** undersea feature N Caribbean Sea 16°00′N 72°30′W
29 R17 **Beatrice** Nebraska, C USA 40°14′N 96°43′W
83 L16 **Beatrice** Mashonaland East, NE Zimbabwe 18°15′S 30°55′E
11 N11 **Beatton** ≈ British Columbia, W Canada
11 N11 **Beatton River** British Columbia, W Canada 57°35′N 121°45′W
35 V10 **Beatty** Nevada, W USA 36°53′N 116°44′W
21 N6 **Beattyville** Kentucky, S USA 37°33′N 83°44′W
173 X16 **Beau Bassin** W Mauritius 20°13′S 57°27′E
103 R15 **Beaucaire** Gard, S France 43°49′N 04°37′E
14 I8 **Beauchastel, Lac** ◎ Québec, SE Canada
14 I10 **Beauchêne, Lac** ◎ Québec, SE Canada
183 V3 **Beaudesert** Queensland, E Australia 28°00′S 152°27′E
182 M12 **Beaufort** Victoria, SE Australia 37°27′S 143°24′E
21 X11 **Beaufort** North Carolina, SE USA 34°44′N 76°41′W
21 R15 **Beaufort** South Carolina, SE USA 32°23′N 80°40′W
38 M11 **Beaufort Sea** sea Arctic Ocean
Beaufort-Wes see Beaufort West
83 G25 **Beaufort West** Afr. Beaufort-Wes. Western Cape, SW South Africa 32°21′S 22°35′E
103 N7 **Beaugency** Loiret, C France 47°46′N 01°38′E
19 R1 **Beau Lake** ⊠ Maine, NE USA
96 I8 **Beauly** N Scotland, United Kingdom 57°29′N 04°29′W
99 G21 **Beaumont** Hainaut, S Belgium 50°12′N 04°13′E
185 E23 **Beaumont** Otago, South Island, New Zealand 45°48′S 169°32′E
22 M7 **Beaumont** Mississippi, S USA 31°10′N 88°55′W
25 X10 **Beaumont** Texas, SW USA 30°05′N 94°06′W
102 M15 **Beaumont-de-Lomagne** Tarn-et-Garonne, S France 43°54′N 01°00′E
102 L6 **Beaumont-sur-Sarthe** Sarthe, NW France 48°15′N 00°07′E
103 R8 **Beaune** Côte d'Or, C France 47°02′N 04°50′E
15 R9 **Beaupré** Québec, SE Canada 47°03′N 70°52′W
102 J8 **Beaupréau** Maine-et-Loire, NW France 47°13′N 00°57′W
99 I22 **Beauraing** Namur, SE Belgium 50°07′N 04°57′E
103 R12 **Beaurepaire** Isère, E France 45°20′N 05°03′E
11 Y16 **Beausejour** Manitoba, S Canada 50°04′N 96°30′W
103 N4 **Beauvais** anc. Bellovacum, Caesaromagus. Oise, N France 49°27′N 02°04′E
11 S13 **Beauval** Saskatchewan, C Canada 55°10′N 107°37′W
102 I9 **Beauvoir-sur-Mer** Vendée, NW France 46°54′N 02°03′W
39 R8 **Beaver** Alaska, USA 66°22′N 147°31′W
26 J8 **Beaver** Oklahoma, C USA 36°48′N 100°32′W
18 B14 **Beaver** Pennsylvania, NE USA 40°39′N 80°19′W
36 K6 **Beaver** Utah, W USA 38°16′N 112°38′W
10 L9 **Beaver** ≈ British Columbia/ Yukon Territory, W Canada
11 S13 **Beaver** ≈ Saskatchewan, C Canada
29 N17 **Beaver City** Nebraska, C USA 40°08′N 99°49′W
10 G6 **Beaver Creek** Yukon Territory, W Canada 62°20′N 140°45′W
31 R14 **Beavercreek** Ohio, N USA 39°42′N 83°58′W
39 S8 **Beaver Creek** ≈ Alaska, USA
26 H3 **Beaver Creek** ≈ Kansas/ Nebraska, C USA
28 J5 **Beaver Creek** ≈ Montana/ North Dakota, N USA
29 Q14 **Beaver Creek** ≈ Nebraska, C USA
25 Q4 **Beaver Creek** ≈ Texas, SW USA
30 M8 **Beaver Dam** Wisconsin, N USA 43°28′N 88°49′W
30 M8 **Beaver Dam Lake** ◎ Wisconsin, N USA
18 B14 **Beaver Falls** Pennsylvania, NE USA 40°45′N 80°20′W
33 P12 **Beaverhead Mountains** ▲▲ Idaho/Montana, NW USA
33 Q12 **Beaverhead River** ≈ Montana, NW USA
65 A25 **Beaver Island** island W Falkland Islands
31 P5 **Beaver Island** island Michigan, N USA
27 S9 **Beaver Lake** ⊠ Arkansas, C USA
11 N13 **Beaverlodge** Alberta, W Canada 55°11′N 119°29′W
18 I8 **Beaver River** ≈ New York, NE USA
26 J8 **Beaver River** ≈ Oklahoma, C USA
18 B13 **Beaver River** ≈ Pennsylvania, NE USA
65 A25 **Beaver Settlement** Beaver Island, W Falkland Islands 51°30′S 61°15′W
Beaver State see Oregon
14 H14 **Beaverton** Ontario, S Canada 44°24′N 79°07′W
32 G11 **Beaverton** Oregon, NW USA 45°29′N 122°49′W
152 G12 **Beāwar** Rājasthān, N India 26°08′N 74°22′E
Bebas, Dasht-i see Bābūs, Dasht-e
60 L8 **Bebedouro** São Paulo, S Brazil 20°58′S 48°28′W
101 I16 **Bebra** Hessen, C Germany 50°59′N 09°46′E
41 W12 **Becal** Campeche, SE Mexico 19°49′N 90°28′W
15 Q11 **Bécancour** ≈ Québec, SE Canada
97 Q19 **Beccles** E England, United Kingdom 52°27′N 01°32′E
112 L9 **Bečej** Ger. Altbetsche, Hung. Óbecse, Rácz-Becse; prev. Magyar-Becse, Stari Bečej. Vojvodina, N Serbia 45°36′N 20°02′E

224
◆ Country ● Country Capital ◇ Dependent Territory ○ Dependent Territory Capital ⬖ Administrative Regions ✈ International Airport ▲ Mountain ▲▲ Mountain Range ⛰ Volcano ≈ River ◎ Lake ⊠ Reservoir

Becerréa – Berberia, Cabo de

104 I3 **Becerréa** Galicia, NW Spain 42°51′N 07°10′W
74 H7 **Béchar** *prev.* Colomb-Béchar. W Algeria 31°38′N 02°11′W
39 O14 **Becharof Lake** ◎ Alaska, USA
116 H15 **Bechet** *var.* Bechetu. Dolj, SW Romania 43°45′N 23°57′E
Bechetu *see* Bechet
21 R6 **Beckley** West Virginia, NE USA 37°46′N 81°12′W
101 G14 **Beckum** Nordrhein-Westfalen, W Germany 51°45′N 08°03′E
25 X7 **Beckville** Texas, SW USA 32°14′N 94°27′W
35 X4 **Becky Peak** ▲ Nevada, W USA 39°59′N 114°33′W
116 I9 **Beclean** *Hung.* Bethlen; *prev.* Betlen. Bistriţa-Năsăud, N Romania 47°10′N 24°11′E
Bécs *see* Wien
111 H18 **Bečva** *Ger.* Betschau, *Pol.* Beczwa. ⤳ E Czech Republic
Beczwa *see* Bečva
103 P15 **Bédarieux** Hérault, S France 43°37′N 03°10′E
120 B10 **Beddouza, Cap** *headland* W Morocco 32°35′N 09°16′W
80 I13 **Bedelē** Oromīya, C Ethiopia 08°25′N 36°21′E
147 Y8 **Bedel Pass** *Rus.* Pereval Bedel. *pass* China/Kyrgyzstan
Bedel, Pereval *see* Bedel Pass
95 H22 **Beder** Århus, C Denmark 56°03′N 10°13′E
97 N20 **Bedford** E England, United Kingdom 52°08′N 00°29′W
31 O15 **Bedford** Indiana, N USA 38°51′N 86°29′W
29 U16 **Bedford** Iowa, C USA 40°40′N 94°43′W
20 L4 **Bedford** Kentucky, S USA 38°36′N 85°18′W
18 D15 **Bedford** Pennsylvania, NE USA 40°00′N 78°29′W
21 T6 **Bedford** Virginia, NE USA 37°20′N 79°31′W
97 N20 **Bedfordshire** *cultural region* E England, United Kingdom
127 N5 **Bednodem'yanovsk** Penzenskaya Oblast', W Russian Federation 53°55′N 43°14′E
98 N5 **Bedum** Groningen, NE Netherlands 53°18′N 06°36′E
27 V11 **Beebe** Arkansas, C USA 35°04′N 91°52′W
Beechy Group *see* Chichijima-rettō
45 T9 **Beef Island** ✈ (Road Town) Tortola, E British Virgin Islands 18°25′N 64°31′W
Beehive State *see* Utah
99 L18 **Beek** Limburg, SE Netherlands 50°56′N 05°47′E
99 L18 **Beek** ✈ (Maastricht) Limburg, SE Netherlands 50°55′N 05°47′E
99 K14 **Beek-en-Donk** Noord-Brabant, S Netherlands 51°31′N 05°37′E
138 F13 **Be'er Menuha** *prev.* Be'ér Menuḥa. Southern, S Israel 30°22′N 35°09′E
Be'ér Menuḥa *see* Be'er Menuha
99 D16 **Beernem** West-Vlaanderen, NW Belgium 51°09′N 03°18′E
99 I16 **Beerse** Antwerpen, N Belgium 51°20′N 04°52′E
Beersheba *see* Be'er Sheva
138 E11 **Be'er Sheva** *var.* Beersheba, *Ar.* Bir es Saba; *prev.* Be'ér Sheva'. Southern, S Israel 31°15′N 34°47′E
Be'ér Sheva' *see* Be'er Sheva
98 J13 **Beesd** Gelderland, C Netherlands 51°52′N 05°12′E
99 M16 **Beesel** Limburg, SE Netherlands 51°16′N 06°02′E
83 J21 **Beestekraal** North-West, N South Africa 25°21′S 27°40′E
194 J7 **Beethoven Peninsula** *peninsula* Alexander Island, Antarctica
Beetstersweach *see* Beetsterzwaag
98 M6 **Beetsterzwaag** *Fris.* Beetstersweach. Friesland, N Netherlands 53°03′N 06°04′E
25 S13 **Beeville** Texas, SW USA 28°25′N 97°47′W
79 J18 **Befale** Equateur, NW Dem. Rep. Congo 0°25′N 20°48′E
Befandriana *see* Befandriana Avaratra
172 J3 **Befandriana Avaratra** *var.* Befandriana, Befandriana Nord. Mahajanga, NW Madagascar 15°14′S 48°33′E
Befandriana Nord *see* Befandriana Avaratra
79 K18 **Befori** Equateur, N Dem. Rep. Congo 0°09′N 22°18′E
172 I7 **Befotaka** Fianarantsoa, S Madagascar 23°49′S 47°00′E
183 R11 **Bega** New South Wales, SE Australia 36°43′S 149°50′E
102 G5 **Bégard** Côtes d'Armor, NW France 48°37′N 03°18′W
112 M9 **Begejski Kanal** *canal* Vojvodina, NE Serbia
94 G13 **Begna** ⤳ S Norway
Begoml' *see* Byahoml'
Begovat *see* Bekobod
153 Q13 **Begusarai** Bihār, NE India 25°25′N 86°08′E
143 R9 **Behābād** Yazd, C Iran 32°23′N 59°50′E
Behagle *see* Laï
55 Z10 **Béhague, Pointe** *headland* E French Guiana 04°38′N 51°52′W
Behar *see* Bihār
142 M10 **Behbahān** *var.* Behbehān. Khūzestān, SW Iran 30°38′N 50°07′E
Behbehān *see* Behbahān
44 G3 **Behring Point** Andros Island, W Bahamas 24°28′N 77°44′W
143 P4 **Behshahr** *prev.* Ashraf. Māzandarān, N Iran 36°42′N 53°36′E
163 V6 **Bei'an** Heilongjiang, NE China 48°16′N 126°29′E
Beibunar *see* Sredishte
Beibu Wan *see* Tongking, Gulf of
Beida *see* Al Bayḍā'
80 H13 **Beigi** Oromīya, C Ethiopia 09°13′N 34°48′E
160 L16 **Beihai** Guangxi Zhuangzu Zizhiqu, S China 21°29′N 109°10′E
159 Q10 **Bei Hulsan Hu** ◎ C China
161 N13 **Bei Jiang** ⤳ S China
161 O2 **Beijing** *var.* Pei-ching, *Eng.* Peking; *prev.* Pei-p'ing. ● (China) Beijing Shi, E China 39°58′N 116°23′E
161 P2 **Beijing** ✈ Beijing Shi, N China 39°54′N 116°22′E
Beijing *see* Beijing Shi, China
161 O2 **Beijing Shi** *var.* Beijing, Jing, Pei-ching, *Eng.* Peking; *prev.* Pei-p'ing. ◆ *municipality* E China
76 G8 **Beïla** Trarza, W Mauritania 18°07′N 15°56′W
98 N7 **Beilen** Drenthe, NE Netherlands 52°52′N 06°27′E
160 L15 **Beiliu** *var.* Lingcheng. Guangxi Zhuangzu Zizhiqu, S China 22°50′N 110°22′E
159 O12 **Beilu He** ⤳ W China
Beilul *see* Beylul
163 U12 **Beining** *prev.* Beizhen. Liaoning, NE China 41°34′N 121°51′E
96 H8 **Beinn Dearg** ▲ N Scotland, United Kingdom 57°47′N 04°52′W
Beinn MacDuibh *see* Ben Macdui
160 I12 **Beipan Jiang** ⤳ S China
163 T12 **Beipiao** Liaoning, NE China 41°49′N 120°45′E
83 N17 **Beira** Sofala, C Mozambique 19°45′S 34°56′E
83 N17 **Beira** ✈ Sofala, C Mozambique 19°39′S 35°05′E
104 I7 **Beira Alta** *former province* N Portugal
104 H9 **Beira Baixa** *former province* C Portugal
104 G8 **Beira Litoral** *former province* N Portugal
Beirut *see* Beyrouth
Beisān *see* Beit She'an
11 Q16 **Beiseker** Alberta, SW Canada 51°20′N 113°34′W
Beitai Ding *see* Wutai Shan
83 K19 **Beitbridge** Matabeleland South, S Zimbabwe 22°10′S 30°02′E
Beit Lekhem *see* Bethlehem
138 G9 **Beit She'an** *Ar.* Baysān, Beisān; *anc.* Scythopolis, *prev.* Bet She'an. Northern, N Israel 32°30′N 35°30′E
116 G10 **Beiuş** *Hung.* Belényes. Bihor, NW Romania 46°40′N 22°21′E
Beizhen *see* Beining
104 H12 **Beja** *anc.* Pax Julia. Beja, SE Portugal 38°01′N 07°52′W
74 M5 **Béja** *var.* Bājah. N Tunisia 36°45′N 09°04′E
104 G13 **Beja** ◆ *district* S Portugal
120 I9 **Béjaïa** *var.* Bejaïa, *Fr.* Bougie; *anc.* Saldae. NE Algeria 36°49′N 05°03′E
Bejaïa *see* Béjaïa
104 K8 **Béjar** Castilla-León, N Spain 40°24′N 05°45′W
Bejraburi *see* Phetchaburi
Bekaa Valley *see* El Beqaa
Bekabad *see* Bekobod
Békás *see* Bicaz
169 O15 **Bekasi** Jawa, C Indonesia 06°14′S 106°595′E
Bek-Budi *see* Qarshi
Bekdaş/Bekdash *see* Garabogaz
147 T10 **Bek-Dzhar** Oshskaya Oblast', SW Kyrgyzstan 40°22′N 73°08′E
111 N24 **Békés** *Rom.* Bichiş. Békés, SE Hungary 46°45′N 21°09′E
111 M24 **Békés** *off.* Békés Megye. ◆ *county* SE Hungary
111 M24 **Békéscsaba** *Rom.* Bichiş-Ciaba. Békés, SE Hungary 46°40′N 21°05′E
Békés Megye *see* Békés
139 S2 **Bēkhma** Arbīl, E Iraq 36°40′N 44°15′E
172 H7 **Bekily** Toliara, S Madagascar 24°12′S 45°20′E
165 W4 **Bekkai** *var.* Betsukai. Hokkaidō, NE Japan 43°23′N 145°07′E
147 Q11 **Bekobod** *Rus.* Bekabad; *prev.* Begovat. Toshkent Viloyati, E Uzbekistan 40°17′N 69°11′E
127 O7 **Bekovo** Penzenskaya Oblast', W Russian Federation 52°27′N 43°41′E
Bel *see* Beliu
152 M13 **Bela** Uttar Pradesh, N India 25°55′N 82°00′E
149 N15 **Bela** Baluchistān, SW Pakistan 26°12′N 66°20′E
79 F15 **Bélabo** Est, C Cameroon 04°54′N 13°10′E
112 N10 **Bela Crkva** *Ger.* Weisskirchen, *Hung.* Fehértemplom. Vojvodina, W Serbia 44°55′N 21°28′E
173 Y16 **Bel Air** *var.* Rivière Sèche. E Mauritius
104 L12 **Belalcázar** Andalucía, S Spain 38°33′N 05°07′W
113 P15 **Bela Palanka** Serbia, SE Serbia 43°13′N 22°19′E
119 H16 **Belarus** *off.* Republic of Belarus, *var.* Belorussia, *Latv.* Baltkrievija; *prev.* Belorussian SSR, *Rus.* Belorusskaya SSR. ◆ *republic* E Europe
Belarus, Republic of *see* Belarus
Belau *see* Palau
59 H21 **Bela Vista** Mato Grosso do Sul, SW Brazil 22°04′S 56°25′W
83 L21 **Bela Vista** Maputo, S Mozambique 26°20′S 32°40′E
168 I8 **Belawan** Sumatera, W Indonesia 03°46′N 98°44′E
Běla Woda *see* Weisswasser
127 U4 **Belaya** ⤳ W Russian Federation
123 R7 **Belaya Gora** Respublika Sakha (Yakutiya), NE Russian Federation 68°25′N 146°12′E
126 M11 **Belaya Kalitiva** Rostovskaya Oblast', SW Russian Federation 48°09′N 40°43′E
125 R14 **Belaya Kholunitsa** Kirovskaya Oblast', NW Russian Federation 58°54′N 50°52′E
Belaya Tserkov' *see* Bila Tserkva
77 V11 **Belbédji** Zinder, S Niger 14°35′N 08°00′E
111 K14 **Bełchatów** *var.* Belchatow. Łódzki, C Poland 51°23′N 19°20′E
Belchatow *see* Bełchatów
Belcher, Îles *see* Belcher Islands
12 H7 **Belcher Islands** *Fr.* Îles Belcher. *island group* Nunavut, SE Canada
105 S6 **Belchite** Aragón, NE Spain 41°18′N 00°45′W
29 O2 **Belcourt** North Dakota, N USA 48°50′N 99°44′W
31 P9 **Belding** Michigan, N USA 43°06′N 85°13′W
127 U5 **Belebey** Respublika Bashkortostan, W Russian Federation 54°04′N 54°13′E
81 N16 **Beledweyne** *var.* Belet Huen, *It.* Belet Uen. Hiiraan, C Somalia 04°39′N 45°12′E
146 B10 **Belek** Balkan Welaýaty, W Turkmenistan 39°57′N 53°51′E
58 L12 **Belém** *var.* Pará. *state capital* Pará, N Brazil 01°27′S 48°29′W
65 I14 **Belém Ridge** *undersea feature* C Atlantic Ocean
62 I7 **Belén** Catamarca, NW Argentina 27°36′N 67°00′W
54 G9 **Belén** Boyacá, C Colombia 06°01′N 72°55′W
42 J11 **Belén** Rivas, SW Nicaragua 11°30′N 85°55′W
62 O5 **Belén** Concepción, C Paraguay 23°25′S 57°14′W
61 D16 **Belén** Salto, N Uruguay 30°47′S 57°47′W
37 R12 **Belen** New Mexico, SW USA 34°37′N 106°46′W
61 D20 **Belén de Escobar** Buenos Aires, E Argentina 34°21′S 58°47′W
114 J7 **Belene** Pleven, N Bulgaria 43°39′N 25°09′E
114 J7 **Belene, Ostrov** *island* N Bulgaria
43 R15 **Belén, Río** ⤳ C Panama
Belényes *see* Beiuş
Embalse de Belesar *see* Belesar, Encoro de
104 H3 **Belesar, Encoro de** *Sp.* Embalse de Belesar. ⊠ NW Spain
Belet Huen/Belet Uen *see* Beledweyne
126 J5 **Belëv** Tul'skaya Oblast', W Russian Federation 53°48′N 36°07′E
19 R7 **Belfast** Maine, NE USA 44°25′N 69°02′W
97 G15 **Belfast** *Ir.* Béal Feirste. ◐ E Northern Ireland, United Kingdom 54°35′N 05°55′W
97 G15 **Belfast Aldergrove** ✈ E Northern Ireland, United Kingdom 54°37′N 06°11′W
97 G15 **Belfast Lough** *Ir.* Loch Lao. *inlet* E Northern Ireland, United Kingdom
28 K5 **Belfield** North Dakota, N USA 46°53′N 103°12′W
103 U7 **Belfort** Territoire-de-Belfort, E France 47°38′N 06°52′E
Belgard *see* Białogard
155 E17 **Belgaum** Karnātaka, W India 15°52′N 74°30′E
Belgian Congo *see* Congo (Democratic Republic of)
195 T3 **Belgicafjella** *var.* Mount Victor. ▲ Antarctica 72°49′S 33°01′E
België/Belgique *see* Belgium
99 F20 **Belgium** *off.* Kingdom of Belgium, *Dut.* België, *Fr.* Belgique. ◆ *monarchy* NW Europe
Belgium, Kingdom of *see* Belgium
126 J8 **Belgorod** Belgorodskaya Oblast', W Russian Federation 50°38′N 36°37′E
Belgorod-Dnestrovskiy *see* Bilhorod-Dnistrovs'kyy
126 J8 **Belgorodskaya Oblast'** ◐ *province* W Russian Federation
Belgrad *see* Beograd
29 T8 **Belgrade** Minnesota, N USA 45°27′N 94°59′W
33 S11 **Belgrade** Montana, NW USA 45°46′N 111°10′W
Belgrade *see* Beograd
Belgrano, Cabo *see* Meredith, Cape
195 N5 **Belgrano II** *Argentinian research station* Antarctica 77°50′S 35°25′W
21 X9 **Belhaven** North Carolina, SE USA 35°36′N 76°50′W
107 I23 **Belice** *anc.* Hypsas. ⤳ Sicilia, Italy, C Mediterranean Sea
Belice *see* Belize/Belize City
113 M16 **Beli Drim** *Alb.* Drini i Bardhë. ⤳ Albania/Serbia
127 R17 **Belidzhi** Respublika Dagestan, SW Russian Federation 41°53′N 48°24′E
Beligrad *see* Berat
188 C8 **Beliliou** *prev.* Peleliu. *island* S Palau
114 L8 **Beli Lom, Yazovir** ⊠ NE Bulgaria
112 I8 **Beli Manastir** *Hung.* Pélmonostor; *prev.* Monostor. Osijek-Baranja, NE Croatia 45°46′N 16°38′E
102 J13 **Bélin-Béliet** Gironde, SW France 44°30′N 00°48′W
79 F17 **Bélinga** Ogooué-Ivindo, NE Gabon 01°05′N 13°12′E
21 S4 **Belington** West Virginia, NE USA 39°01′N 79°57′W
127 O6 **Belinskiy** Penzenskaya Oblast', W Russian Federation 52°58′N 43°25′E
169 N12 **Belinyu** Pulau Bangka, W Indonesia 01°37′S 105°45′E
169 O13 **Belitung, Pulau** *island* W Indonesia
116 F10 **Beliu** *Hung.* Bel. Arad, W Romania 46°31′N 21°57′E
114 I9 **Beli Vit** ⤳ NW Bulgaria
42 G2 **Belize** *Sp.* Belice; *prev.* British Honduras, Colony of Belize. ◆ *commonwealth republic* Central America
42 F2 **Belize** *Sp.* Belice. ◆ *district* NE Belize
42 G2 **Belize** ⤳ Belize/Guatemala
Belize *see* Belize City
42 G2 **Belize City** *var.* Belize, *Sp.* Belice. Belize, NE Belize 17°29′N 88°10′W
42 G2 **Belize City** ✈ Belize, NE Belize 17°31′N 88°15′W
Belize, Colony of *see* Belize
Beljak *see* Villach
39 N16 **Belkofski** Alaska, USA 55°07′N 162°04′W
123 O6 **Bel'kovskiy, Ostrov** *island* Novosibirskiye Ostrova, NE Russian Federation
14 J8 **Bell** ⤳ Québec, SE Canada
10 J15 **Bella Bella** British Columbia, SW Canada 52°04′N 128°07′W
102 M10 **Bellac** Haute-Vienne, C France 46°07′N 01°04′E
10 K15 **Bella Coola** British Columbia, SW Canada 52°23′N 126°46′W
106 D6 **Bellagio** Lombardia, N Italy 45°58′N 09°15′E
31 P6 **Bellaire** Michigan, N USA 44°59′N 85°12′W
106 D6 **Bellano** Lombardia, N Italy 46°06′N 09°21′E
155 G17 **Bellary** *var.* Ballari. Karnātaka, S India 15°11′N 76°54′E
183 S5 **Bellata** New South Wales, SE Australia 29°58′S 149°49′E
61 D16 **Bella Unión** Artigas, N Uruguay 30°18′S 57°35′W
61 C14 **Bella Vista** Corrientes, NE Argentina 28°30′S 59°03′W
62 J7 **Bella Vista** Tucumán, N Argentina 27°05′S 65°19′W
62 P4 **Bella Vista** Amambay, C Paraguay 22°08′S 56°20′W
56 B10 **Bellavista** Cajamarca, N Peru 05°43′S 78°48′W
56 D11 **Bellavista** San Martín, N Peru 07°04′S 76°35′W
183 U6 **Bellbrook** New South Wales, SE Australia 30°48′S 152°32′E
27 V5 **Belle** Missouri, C USA 38°17′N 91°43′W
21 Q5 **Belle** West Virginia, NE USA 38°13′N 81°32′W
31 R13 **Bellefontaine** Ohio, N USA 40°22′N 83°45′W
18 F14 **Bellefonte** Pennsylvania, NE USA 40°54′N 77°43′W
28 J9 **Belle Fourche** South Dakota, N USA 44°40′N 103°50′W
28 J9 **Belle Fourche Reservoir** ⊠ South Dakota, N USA
28 K9 **Belle Fourche River** ⤳ South Dakota/Wyoming, N USA
103 S10 **Bellegarde-sur-Valserine** Ain, E France 46°06′N 05°49′E
23 Y14 **Belle Glade** Florida, SE USA 26°40′N 80°40′W
102 G8 **Belle Île** *island* NW France
13 T9 **Belle Isle** *island* Belle Isle, Newfoundland and Labrador, E Canada
13 S10 **Belle Isle, Strait of** *strait* Newfoundland and Labrador, E Canada
Bellenz *see* Bellinzona
29 W14 **Belle Plaine** Iowa, C USA 41°54′N 92°16′W
29 V9 **Belle Plaine** Minnesota, N USA 44°39′N 93°47′W
14 I9 **Belleterre** Québec, SE Canada 47°24′N 78°40′W
14 J15 **Belleville** Ontario, SE Canada 44°10′N 77°22′W
103 R10 **Belleville** Rhône, E France 46°09′N 04°42′E
30 K15 **Belleville** Illinois, N USA 38°31′N 89°58′W
27 N3 **Belleville** Kansas, C USA 39°51′N 97°38′W
29 Z13 **Bellevue** Iowa, C USA 42°15′N 90°25′W
29 S15 **Bellevue** Nebraska, C USA 41°08′N 95°53′W
31 S11 **Bellevue** Ohio, N USA 41°16′N 82°50′W
25 S5 **Bellevue** Texas, SW USA 33°38′N 98°00′W
32 H8 **Bellevue** Washington, NW USA 47°36′N 122°12′W
55 Y11 **Bellevue de l'Inini, Montagnes** ▲ S French Guiana
103 S11 **Belley** Ain, E France 45°46′N 05°41′E
Bellin *see* Kangirsuk
183 V6 **Bellingen** New South Wales, SE Australia 30°27′S 152°53′E
97 L14 **Bellingham** N England, United Kingdom 55°09′N 02°16′W
32 H6 **Bellingham** Washington, NW USA 48°46′N 122°29′W
Belling Hausen Mulde *see* Southeast Pacific Basin
194 H2 **Bellingshausen** *Russian research station* South Shetland Islands, Antarctica 61°57′S 58°23′W
Bellingshausen *see* Motu One
Bellingshausen Abyssal Plain *see* Bellingshausen Plain
196 R14 **Bellingshausen Plain** *var.* Bellingshausen Abyssal Plain. *undersea feature* SE Pacific Ocean 64°00′S 90°00′W
194 I8 **Bellingshausen Sea** *sea* Antarctica
98 P6 **Bellingwolde** Groningen, NE Netherlands 53°07′N 07°10′E
108 H11 **Bellinzona** *Ger.* Bellenz. Ticino, S Switzerland 46°12′N 09°02′E
25 T8 **Bellmead** Texas, SW USA 31°36′N 97°02′W
54 E8 **Bello** Antioquia, W Colombia 06°19′N 75°34′W
61 B21 **Bellocq** Buenos Aires, E Argentina 35°55′S 61°32′W
Bello Horizonte *see* Belo Horizonte
186 L10 **Bellona** *var.* Mungiki. *island* S Solomon Islands
Bellovacum *see* Beauvais
182 D7 **Bell, Point** *headland* South Australia 32°13′S 133°08′E
20 F9 **Bells** Tennessee, S USA 35°42′N 89°05′W
25 U5 **Bells** Texas, SW USA 33°36′N 96°24′W
92 N3 **Bellsund** *inlet* SW Svalbard
106 H6 **Belluno** Veneto, NE Italy 46°08′N 12°13′E
62 L11 **Bell Ville** Córdoba, C Argentina 32°35′S 62°41′W
83 E26 **Bellville** Western Cape, SW South Africa 33°50′S 18°43′E
25 U11 **Bellville** Texas, SW USA 29°57′N 96°15′W
104 L12 **Belmez** Andalucía, S Spain 38°16′N 05°12′W
29 V12 **Belmond** Iowa, C USA 42°51′N 93°36′W
18 E11 **Belmont** New York, NE USA 42°14′N 78°02′W
21 R10 **Belmont** North Carolina, SE USA 35°13′N 81°01′W
59 O18 **Belmonte** Bahia, E Brazil 15°53′S 38°54′W
104 I8 **Belmonte** Castelo Branco, C Portugal 40°21′N 07°20′W
105 P10 **Belmonte** Castilla-La Mancha, C Spain 39°34′N 02°43′W
42 G2 **Belmopan** ● (Belize) Cayo, C Belize 17°13′N 88°48′W
97 B16 **Belmullet** *Ir.* Béal an Mhuirhead. Mayo, W Ireland 54°14′N 09°59′W
99 E20 **Belœil** Hainaut, SW Belgium 50°33′N 03°45′E
123 R13 **Belogorsk** Amurskaya Oblast', SE Russian Federation 50°53′N 128°24′E
Belogorsk *see* Bilohirs'k
114 F7 **Belogradchik** Vidin, NW Bulgaria 43°37′N 22°42′E
172 H8 **Beloha** Toliara, S Madagascar 25°09′S 45°04′E
59 M20 **Belo Horizonte** *prev.* Bello Horizonte. *state capital* Minas Gerais, SE Brazil 19°54′S 43°54′W
26 M3 **Beloit** Kansas, C USA 39°27′N 98°06′W
30 L9 **Beloit** Wisconsin, N USA 42°31′N 89°01′W
Belokorovichi *see* Novi Bilokorovychi
124 J8 **Belomorsk** Respublika Kareliya, NW Russian Federation 64°30′N 34°43′E
124 J8 **Belomorsko-Baltiyskiy Kanal** *Eng.* White Sea-Baltic Canal, White Sea Canal. *canal* NW Russian Federation
153 V15 **Belonia** Tripura, NE India 23°15′N 91°25′E
Beloozersk *see* Byelaazyorsk
Belopol'ye *see* Bilopillya
105 O4 **Belorado** Castilla-León, N Spain 42°25′N 03°11′W
126 L14 **Belorechensk** Krasnodarskiy Kray, SW Russian Federation 44°46′N 39°53′E
127 W5 **Beloretsk** Respublika Bashkortostan, W Russian Federation 53°56′N 58°26′E
Belorussia/Belorussian SSR *see* Belarus
Belorusskaya Gryada *see* Byelaruskaya Hrada
Belorusskaya SSR *see* Belarus
Beloshchel'ye *see* Nar'yan-Mar
114 N8 **Beloslav** Varna, E Bulgaria 43°13′N 27°42′E
Belostok *see* Białystok
Belo-sur-Tsiribihina *see* Belo Tsiribihina
172 H5 **Belo Tsiribihina** *var.* Belo-sur-Tsiribihina. Toliara, W Madagascar 19°40′S 44°30′E
Belovár *see* Bjelovar
Belovezhskaya, Pushcha *see* Białowieska, Puszcza/Byelavyezhskaya, Pushcha
114 H10 **Belovo** Pazardzhik, C Bulgaria 42°10′N 24°01′E
Belovodsk *see* Bilovods'k
122 H9 **Beloyarskiy** Khanty-Mansiyskiy Avtonomnyy Okrug-Yugra, N Russian Federation 63°40′N 66°31′E
124 K7 **Beloye More** *Eng.* White Sea. *sea* NW Russian Federation
124 K13 **Beloye, Ozero** ◎ NW Russian Federation
114 J10 **Belozem** Plovdiv, C Bulgaria 42°11′N 25°00′E
124 K13 **Belozërsk** Vologodskaya Oblast', NW Russian Federation 59°59′N 37°49′E
108 D8 **Belp** Bern, W Switzerland 46°54′N 07°31′E
108 D8 **Belp** ✈ (Bern) Bern, C Switzerland 46°55′N 07°29′E
107 L24 **Belpasso** Sicilia, Italy, C Mediterranean Sea 37°35′N 14°59′E
31 U14 **Belpre** Ohio, N USA 39°14′N 81°34′W
98 M8 **Belterwijde** ◎ N Netherlands
27 R4 **Belton** Missouri, C USA 38°48′N 94°31′W
21 P11 **Belton** South Carolina, SE USA 34°31′N 82°29′W
25 T9 **Belton** Texas, SW USA 31°04′N 97°30′W
25 S9 **Belton Lake** ⊠ Texas, SW USA
Bel'tsy *see* Bălţi
97 E16 **Belturbet** *Ir.* Béal Tairbirt. Cavan, N Ireland 54°06′N 07°26′W
Beluchistan *see* Baluchistān
145 Z9 **Belukha, Gora** ▲ Kazakhstan/Russian Federation 49°50′N 86°44′E
107 M20 **Belvedere Marittimo** Calabria, SW Italy 39°37′N 15°52′E
30 L10 **Belvidere** Illinois, N USA 42°15′N 88°50′W
18 J14 **Belvidere** New Jersey, NE USA 40°50′N 75°05′W
Bely *see* Belyy
127 V8 **Belyayevka** Orenburgskaya Oblast', W Russian Federation 51°25′N 56°26′E
Belynichi *see* Byalynichy
124 H17 **Belyy** *var.* Bely, Beyj. Tverskaya Oblast', W Russian Federation 55°51′N 32°57′E
126 I6 **Belyye Berega** Bryanskaya Oblast', W Russian Federation 53°11′N 34°42′E
122 J6 **Belyy, Ostrov** *island* N Russian Federation
122 J11 **Belyy Yar** Tomskaya Oblast', C Russian Federation 58°26′N 84°57′E
100 N13 **Belzig** Brandenburg, NE Germany 52°09′N 12°37′E
22 K4 **Belzoni** Mississippi, S USA 33°10′N 90°29′W
172 H4 **Bemaraha** *var.* Plateau du Bemaraha. ▲ W Madagascar
Bemaraha, Plateau du *see* Bemaraha
82 B10 **Bembe** Uíge, NW Angola 07°03′S 14°25′E
77 S14 **Bembèrèkè** *var.* Bimbéréké. N Benin 10°10′N 02°41′E
104 K12 **Bembézar** ⤳ SW Spain
104 J3 **Bembibre** Castilla-León, N Spain 42°37′N 06°25′W
29 T4 **Bemidji** Minnesota, N USA 47°27′N 94°53′W
98 L12 **Bemmel** Gelderland, SE Netherlands 51°53′N 05°54′E
171 T13 **Bemu** Pulau Seram, E Indonesia 03°21′S 129°58′E
Benāb *see* Bonāb
105 T5 **Benabarre** *var.* Benavarn. Aragón, NE Spain 42°06′N 00°28′E
Benaco *see* Garda, Lago di
79 L20 **Bena-Dibele** Kasai-Oriental, C Dem. Rep. Congo 04°01′S 22°50′E
105 R9 **Benagéber, Embalse de** ⊠ E Spain
183 O11 **Benalla** Victoria, SE Australia 36°33′S 146°00′E
104 M14 **Benamejí** Andalucía, S Spain 37°16′N 04°33′W
Benares *see* Vārānasi
Benavarn *see* Benabarre
104 F10 **Benavente** Santarém, C Portugal 38°59′N 08°49′W
104 K5 **Benavente** Castilla-León, N Spain 42°N 05°40′W
25 S15 **Benavides** Texas, SW USA 27°36′N 98°24′W
96 F8 **Benbecula** *island* NW Scotland, United Kingdom
Benbicovazzo *see* Benkovac
32 H13 **Bend** Oregon, NW USA 44°04′N 121°19′W
182 K7 **Benda Range** ▲ South Australia
183 T6 **Bendemeer** New South Wales, SE Australia 30°54′S 151°12′E
Bender *see* Tighina
Bender Beila/Bender Beyla *see* Bandarbeyla
Bender Cassim/Bender Qaasim *see* Boosaaso
Bendery *see* Tighina
183 N11 **Bendigo** Victoria, SE Australia 36°46′S 144°19′E
118 E10 **Bēne** Dobele, SW Latvia 56°30′N 23°04′E
98 K13 **Beneden-Leeuwen** Gelderland, C Netherlands 51°52′N 05°32′E
101 L24 **Benediktenwand** ▲ S Germany 47°39′N 11°28′E
Benemérita de San Cristóbal *see* San Cristóbal
77 N12 **Bénéna** Ségou, S Mali 13°04′N 04°20′W
172 I7 **Benenitra** Toliara, S Madagascar 23°25′S 45°06′E
Beneschau *see* Benešov
Beneški Zaliv *see* Venice, Gulf of
111 D17 **Benešov** *Ger.* Beneschau. Středočeský Kraj, W Czech Republic 49°48′N 14°41′E
123 Q5 **Benetta, Ostrov** *island* Novosibirskiye Ostrova, NE Russian Federation
107 L17 **Benevento** *anc.* Beneventum, Malventum. Campania, S Italy 41°07′N 14°45′E
Beneventum *see* Benevento
173 S3 **Bengal, Bay of** *bay* N Indian Ocean
Bengalooru *see* Bangalore
79 M17 **Bengamisa** Orientale, N Dem. Rep. Congo 0°58′N 25°11′E
Bengasi *see* Banghāzī
Bengazi *see* Banghāzī
161 P7 **Bengbu** *var.* Peng-pu. Anhui, E China 32°57′N 117°17′E
32 L9 **Benge** Washington, NW USA 46°55′N 118°01′W
Benghazi *see* Banghāzī
168 K10 **Bengkalis** Pulau Bengkalis, W Indonesia 01°27′N 102°10′E
168 K10 **Bengkalis, Pulau** *island* W Indonesia
169 Q10 **Bengkayang** Borneo, C Indonesia 0°45′N 109°28′E
168 K14 **Bengkulu** *prev.* Bengkoeloe, Benkoelen, Benkulen. Sumatera, W Indonesia 03°46′S 102°16′E
168 K13 **Bengkulu** *off.* Propinsi Bengkulu; *prev.* Bengkoeloe, Benkoelen, Benkulen. ◐ *province* W Indonesia
Bengkulu, Propinsi *see* Bengkulu
82 A11 **Bengo** ◐ *province* W Angola
95 J16 **Bengtsfors** Västra Götaland, S Sweden 59°03′N 12°14′E
82 B13 **Benguela** *var.* Benguella. Benguela, W Angola 12°35′S 13°30′E
83 A14 **Benguela** ◐ *province* W Angola
Benguella *see* Benguela
138 F10 **Ben Gurion** ✈ Tel Aviv, C Israel 32°04′N 34°45′E
Bengweulu, Lake *see* Bangweulu, Lake
Benha *see* Banhā
192 F6 **Benham Seamount** *undersea feature* W Philippine Sea 15°48′N 124°15′E
96 H6 **Ben Hope** ▲ N Scotland, United Kingdom 58°25′N 04°36′W
79 P18 **Beni** Nord-Kivu, NE Dem. Rep. Congo 0°31′N 29°30′E
57 L15 **Beni** *var.* El Beni. ◐ *department* N Bolivia
74 H8 **Beni Abbès** W Algeria 30°07′N 02°09′W
105 T8 **Benicarló** País Valenciano, E Spain 40°25′N 00°25′E
105 T9 **Benicàssim** *Cat.* Benicàssim. País Valenciano, E Spain 40°03′N 00°03′E
Benicàssim *see* Benicàssim
105 T12 **Benidorm** País Valenciano, SE Spain 38°33′N 00°09′W
Beni Mazâr *see* Banī Mazār
121 C11 **Beni-Mellal** C Morocco 32°20′N 06°21′W
77 R14 **Benin** *off.* Republic of Benin; *prev.* Dahomey. ◆ *republic* W Africa
77 S17 **Benin, Bight of** *gulf* W Africa
77 U16 **Benin City** Edo, SW Nigeria 06°23′N 05°40′E
Benin, Republic of *see* Benin
57 K16 **Beni, Río** ⤳ N Bolivia
120 F10 **Beni Saf** *var.* Beni-Saf. NW Algeria 35°19′N 01°23′W
Beni-Saf *see* Beni Saf
105 T11 **Benissa** País Valenciano, E Spain 38°43′N 00°03′E
Beni Suef *see* Banī Suwayf
11 V15 **Benito** Manitoba, S Canada 51°57′N 101°24′W
Benito *see* Uolo, Río
61 C23 **Benito Juárez** Buenos Aires, E Argentina 37°43′S 59°48′W
41 P14 **Benito Juaréz Internacional** ✈ (México) México, S Mexico 19°24′N 99°02′W
25 P5 **Benjamin** Texas, SW USA 33°35′N 99°49′W
58 B13 **Benjamin Constant** Amazonas, N Brazil 04°22′S 70°02′W
40 F4 **Benjamín Hill** Sonora, NW Mexico 30°13′N 111°08′W
63 F19 **Benjamín, Isla** *island* Archipiélago de los Chonos, S Chile
164 Q4 **Benkei-misaki** *headland* Hokkaidō, NE Japan 42°49′N 140°10′E
28 L17 **Benkelman** Nebraska, C USA 40°04′N 101°30′W
96 I7 **Ben Klibreck** ▲ N Scotland, United Kingdom 58°15′N 04°23′W
Benkoelen/Bengkoeloe *see* Bengkulu
112 D13 **Benkovac** *It.* Bencovazzo. Zadar, SW Croatia 44°02′N 15°36′E
Benkulen *see* Bengkulu
96 I11 **Ben Lawers** ▲ C Scotland, United Kingdom 56°33′N 04°13′W
96 J9 **Ben Macdui** *var.* Beinn MacDuibh. ▲ C Scotland, United Kingdom 57°02′N 03°42′W
96 G11 **Ben More** ▲ W Scotland, United Kingdom 56°26′N 06°00′W
96 I11 **Ben More** ▲ C Scotland, United Kingdom 56°22′N 04°31′W
96 H7 **Ben More Assynt** ▲ N Scotland, United Kingdom 58°09′N 04°51′W
185 E20 **Benmore, Lake** ◎ South Island, New Zealand
98 L12 **Bennekom** Gelderland, SE Netherlands 52°00′N 05°40′E
21 T11 **Bennettsville** South Carolina, SE USA 34°36′N 79°40′W
96 H10 **Ben Nevis** ▲ N Scotland, United Kingdom 56°80′N 05°00′W
184 M9 **Benneydale** Waikato, North Island, New Zealand 38°31′S 175°22′E
Bennichab *see* Bennichchâb
76 H8 **Bennichchâb** *var.* Bennichab. Inchiri, W Mauritania 19°26′N 15°21′W
18 L10 **Bennington** Vermont, NE USA 42°51′N 73°09′W
185 E20 **Ben Ohau Range** ▲ South Island, New Zealand
83 J21 **Benoni** Gauteng, NE South Africa 26°04′S 28°18′E
172 J2 **Be, Nosy** *var.* Nossi-Bé. *island* NW Madagascar
Bénoué *see* Benue
42 F2 **Benque Viejo del Carmen** Cayo, W Belize 17°04′N 89°08′W
101 G19 **Bensheim** Hessen, W Germany 49°41′N 08°38′E
37 N16 **Benson** Arizona, SW USA 31°55′N 110°16′W
29 S8 **Benson** Minnesota, N USA 45°19′N 95°36′W
21 U10 **Benson** North Carolina, SE USA 35°22′N 78°33′W
171 N15 **Benteng** Pulau Selayar, C Indonesia 06°07′S 120°28′E
83 A14 **Bentiaba** Namibe, SW Angola 14°18′S 12°27′E
181 T4 **Bentinck Island** *island* Wellesley Islands, Queensland, N Australia
80 E13 **Bentiu** Wahda, S Sudan 09°14′N 29°49′E
138 G8 **Bent Jbaïl** *var.* Bint Jubayl. S Lebanon 33°07′N 35°26′E
11 Q15 **Bentley** Alberta, SW Canada 52°27′N 114°02′W
61 I15 **Bento Gonçalves** Rio Grande do Sul, S Brazil 29°12′S 51°34′W
27 U12 **Benton** Arkansas, C USA 34°34′N 92°35′W
30 L16 **Benton** Illinois, N USA 38°00′N 88°55′W
20 H7 **Benton** Kentucky, S USA 36°51′N 88°21′W
22 G5 **Benton** Louisiana, S USA 32°41′N 93°44′W
27 Y7 **Benton** Missouri, C USA 37°05′N 89°34′W
20 M10 **Benton** Tennessee, S USA 35°10′N 84°39′W
31 O10 **Benton Harbor** Michigan, N USA 42°07′N 86°27′W
27 S9 **Bentonville** Arkansas, C USA 36°23′N 94°13′W
77 V16 **Benue** ◐ *state* SE Nigeria
78 F13 **Benue** *Fr.* Bénoué. ⤳ Cameroon/Nigeria
163 V12 **Benxi** *prev.* Pen-ch'i, Penhsihu, Penki. Liaoning, NE China 41°20′N 123°45′E
Benyakoni *see* Byenyakoni
112 K10 **Beočin** Vojvodina, N Serbia 45°13′N 19°43′E
Beodericsworth *see* Bury St Edmunds
112 M11 **Beograd** *Eng.* Belgrade, *Ger.* Belgrad; *anc.* Singidunum. ● (Serbia) Serbia, N Serbia 44°48′N 20°27′E
112 L11 **Beograd** *Eng.* Belgrade. ✈ Serbia, N Serbia 44°45′N 20°21′E
76 M16 **Béoumi** C Ivory Coast 07°40′N 05°34′W
35 V3 **Beowawe** Nevada, W USA 40°33′N 116°31′W
164 E14 **Beppu** Ōita, Kyūshū, SW Japan 33°18′N 131°30′E
187 X15 **Beqa** *prev.* Mbengga. *island* W Fiji
45 Y14 **Bequia** *island* C Saint Vincent and the Grenadines
113 L16 **Berane** *prev.* Ivangrad. E Montenegro 42°51′N 19°51′E
113 L21 **Berat** *var.* Berati, *SCr.* Beligrad. Berat, C Albania 40°43′N 19°58′E
113 L21 **Berat** ◐ *district* C Albania
Berătău *see* Berettyó
Berati *see* Berat
Beraun *see* Berounka, Czech Republic
Beraun *see* Beroun, Czech Republic
171 U13 **Berau, Teluk** *var.* MacCluer Gulf. *bay* Papua, E Indonesia
80 G8 **Berber** River Nile, NE Sudan 18°01′N 34°00′E
80 N12 **Berbera** Sahil, NW Somalia 10°24′N 45°02′E
79 H16 **Berbérati** Mambéré-Kadéï, SW Central African Republic 04°14′N 15°50′E
Berberia, Cabo de *see* Barbaria, Cap de

◆ Country ● Country Capital ◇ Dependent Territory ○ Dependent Territory Capital ◐ Administrative Regions ✈ International Airport ▲ Mountain ▲ Mountain Range ⛰ Volcano ⤳ River ◎ Lake ⊠ Reservoir

BERBICE RIVER – BĪJĀR

55 T9 **Berbice River** NE Guyana
Berchid *see* Berrechid
103 N2 **Berck-Plage** Pas-de-Calais, N France 50°24′N 01°35′E
25 T13 **Berclair** Texas, SW USA 28°33′N 97°32′W
117 W10 **Berda** SE Ukraine
Berdichev *see* Berdychiv
123 P10 **Berdigestyakh** Respublika Sakha (Yakutiya), NE Russian Federation 62°02′N 127°03′E
122 J12 **Berdsk** Novosibirskaya Oblast', C Russian Federation 54°42′N 82°56′E
117 W10 **Berdyans'k** *Rus.* Berdyansk; *prev.* Osipenko. Zaporiz'ka Oblast', SE Ukraine 46°46′N 36°49′E
117 W10 **Berdyans'ka Kosa** *spit* SE Ukraine
117 V10 **Berdyans'ka Zatoka** *gulf* S Ukraine
117 N5 **Berdychiv** *Rus.* Berdichev. Zhytomyrs'ka Oblast', N Ukraine 49°54′N 28°39′E
20 M6 **Berea** Kentucky, S USA 37°34′N 84°18′W
Beregovo/Beregszász *see* Berehove
116 G8 **Berehove** *Cz.* Berehovo, *Hung.* Beregszász, *Rus.* Beregovo. Zakarpats'ka Oblast', W Ukraine 48°13′N 22°39′E
Berehovo *see* Berehove
186 D9 **Bereina** Central, S Papua New Guinea 08°29′S 146°30′E
146 C11 **Bereket** *prev. Rus.* Gazandzhyk, Kazandzhik, *Turkm.* Gazanjyk. Balkan Welaýaty, W Turkmenistan 39°17′N 55°27′E
45 O12 **Berekua** S Dominica 15°14′N 61°19′W
77 O16 **Berekum** W Ghana 07°27′N 02°35′W
Berenice *see* Baranīce
11 O14 **Berens** Manitoba/Ontario, C Canada
11 X14 **Berens River** Manitoba, C Canada 52°22′N 97°00′W
29 R12 **Beresford** South Dakota, N USA 43°02′N 96°45′W
116 J4 **Berestechko** Volyns'ka Oblast', NW Ukraine 50°21′N 25°06′E
116 M11 **Bereşti** Galaţi, E Romania 46°04′N 27°54′E
117 U6 **Berestova** E Ukraine
Beretău *see* Berettyó
111 N23 **Berettyó** *Rom.* Barcău; *prev.* Berătău, Beretău. Hungary/Romania
111 N23 **Berettyóújfalu** Hajdú-Bihar, E Hungary 47°15′N 21°33′E
Berëza/Bereza Kartuska *see* Byaroza
117 Q4 **Berezan'** Kyyivs'ka Oblast', N Ukraine 50°18′N 31°30′E
117 Q10 **Berezanka** Mykolayivs'ka Oblast', S Ukraine 46°51′N 31°24′E
116 J6 **Berezhany** *Pol.* Brzeżany. Ternopil's'ka Oblast', W Ukraine 49°29′N 25°00′E
Berezina *see* Byerezino
Berezino *see* Byerazino
117 P10 **Berezivka** *Rus.* Berezovka. Odes'ka Oblast', SW Ukraine 47°12′N 30°56′E
117 Q2 **Berezna** Chernihivs'ka Oblast', NE Ukraine 51°35′N 31°50′E
116 L3 **Berezne** Rivnens'ka Oblast', NW Ukraine 51°00′N 26°46′E
117 R9 **Bereznehuvate** Mykolayivs'ka Oblast', S Ukraine 47°18′N 32°52′E
125 N10 **Bereznik** Arkhangel'skaya Oblast', NW Russian Federation 62°50′N 42°40′E
125 U13 **Berezniki** Permskaya Oblast', NW Russian Federation 59°26′N 56°49′E
Berëzovka *see* Byarozawka, Belarus
Berezovka *see* Berezivka, Ukraine
122 H9 **Berezovo** Khanty-Mansiyskiy Avtonomnyy Okrug-Yugra, N Russian Federation 63°48′N 64°38′E
127 O9 **Berezovskaya** Volgogradskaya Oblast', SW Russian Federation 50°17′N 43°58′E
123 S13 **Berezovyy** Khabarovskiy Kray, E Russian Federation 51°42′N 135°39′E
83 E25 **Berg** W South Africa
Berg *see* Berg bei Rohrbach
105 V4 **Berga** Cataluña, NE Spain 42°06′N 01°41′E
95 N20 **Berga** Kalmar, S Sweden 57°13′N 16°03′E
136 B13 **Bergama** İzmir, W Turkey 39°08′N 27°10′E
106 E7 **Bergamo** *anc.* Bergomum. Lombardia, N Italy 45°42′N 09°40′E
105 P3 **Bergara** País Vasco, N Spain 43°05′N 02°25′W
109 S3 **Berg bei Rohrbach** *var.* Berg. Oberösterreich, N Austria 48°34′N 14°02′E
100 O6 **Bergen** Mecklenburg-Vorpommern, NE Germany 54°25′N 13°25′E
101 I11 **Bergen** Niedersachsen, NW Germany 52°49′N 09°57′E
98 H8 **Bergen** Noord-Holland, NW Netherlands 52°40′N 04°42′E
94 C13 **Bergen** Hordaland, S Norway 60°24′N 05°19′E
Bergen *see* Mons
55 W9 **Berg en Dal** Brokopondo, C Surinam 05°15′N 55°20′W
99 G15 **Bergen op Zoom** Noord-Brabant, S Netherlands 51°30′N 04°17′E
102 L13 **Bergerac** Dordogne, SW France 44°51′N 00°30′E
99 J16 **Bergeyk** Noord-Brabant, S Netherlands 51°19′N 05°21′E
101 D16 **Bergheim** Nordrhein-Westfalen, W Germany 50°57′N 06°39′E
55 X10 **Bergi** Sipaliwini, E Surinam 04°36′N 54°24′W
101 E16 **Bergisch Gladbach** Nordrhein-Westfalen, W Germany 50°59′N 07°09′E
101 F14 **Bergkamen** Nordrhein-Westfalen, W Germany 51°32′N 07°41′E
95 N21 **Bergkvara** Kalmar, S Sweden 56°22′N 16°04′E
Bergomum *see* Bergamo
98 K13 **Bergse Maas** S Netherlands
95 P15 **Bergshamra** Stockholm, C Sweden 59°37′N 18°40′E
94 N10 **Bergsjö** Gävleborg, C Sweden 62°00′N 17°10′E
93 J14 **Bergsviken** Norrbotten, N Sweden 65°16′N 21°24′E
98 L6 **Bergum** *Fris.* Burgum. Friesland, N Netherlands 53°12′N 05°59′E
98 M6 **Bergumer Meer** ◎ N Netherlands
94 N12 **Bergviken** ◎ C Sweden
168 M11 **Berhala, Selat** *strait* Sumatera, W Indonesia
Berhampore *see* Baharampur
99 J17 **Beringen** Limburg, NE Belgium 51°04′N 05°14′E
39 T12 **Bering Glacier** *glacier* Alaska, USA
Beringov Proliv *see* Bering Strait
192 L2 **Bering Sea** *sea* N Pacific Ocean
38 L9 **Bering Strait** *Rus.* Beringov Proliv. *strait* Bering Sea/Chukchi Sea
Berislav *see* Beryslav
105 O15 **Berja** Andalucía, S Spain 36°51′N 02°56′W
94 H9 **Berkåk** Sør-Trøndelag, S Norway 62°50′N 10°01′E
98 N11 **Berkel** Germany/Netherlands
35 N8 **Berkeley** California, W USA 37°52′N 122°16′W
65 E24 **Berkeley Sound** *sound* NE Falkland Islands
21 V2 **Berkeley Springs** *var.* Bath. West Virginia, NE USA 39°38′N 78°14′W
195 N6 **Berkner Island** *island* Antarctica
114 G8 **Berkovitsa** Montana, NW Bulgaria 43°15′N 23°05′E
97 M22 **Berkshire** *former county* S England, United Kingdom
99 H17 **Berlaar** Antwerpen, N Belgium 51°08′N 04°39′E
Berlanga *see* Berlanga de Duero
105 P6 **Berlanga de Duero** *var.* Berlanga. Castilla-León, N Spain 41°28′N 02°51′W
0 I16 **Berlanga Rise** *undersea feature* E Pacific Ocean 08°30′N 93°30′W
99 F17 **Berlare** Oost-Vlaanderen, NW Belgium 51°02′N 04°01′E
104 E9 **Berlenga, Ilha da** *island* C Portugal
92 M7 **Berlevåg** *Lapp.* Bearalváhki. Finnmark, N Norway 70°51′N 29°04′E
100 O12 **Berlin** ● (Germany) Berlin, NE Germany 52°31′N 13°26′E
21 Z4 **Berlin** Maryland, NE USA 38°19′N 75°13′W
19 O7 **Berlin** New Hampshire, NE USA 44°27′N 71°13′W
18 D16 **Berlin** Pennsylvania, NE USA 39°54′N 78°57′W
30 L7 **Berlin** Wisconsin, N USA 43°57′N 88°59′W
100 O12 **Berlin** ◆ *state* NE Germany
Berlinchen *see* Barlinek
31 U12 **Berlin Lake** ⊠ Ohio, N USA
183 R11 **Bermagui** New South Wales, SE Australia 36°26′S 150°01′E
40 L8 **Bermejillo** Durango, C Mexico 25°55′N 103°39′W
62 L5 **Bermejo, Río** N Argentina
62 I10 **Bermejo, Río** W Argentina
62 M6 **Bermejo viejo, Río** N Argentina
105 P2 **Bermeo** País Vasco, N Spain 43°25′N 02°44′W
104 K6 **Bermillo de Sayago** Castilla-León, N Spain 41°22′N 06°08′W
106 E6 **Bermina, Pizzo** *Rmsch.* Piz Bernina. ▲ Italy/Switzerland 46°22′N 09°52′E *see also* Bernina, Piz
Bermina, Pizzo *see* Bernina, Piz
64 A12 **Bermuda** *var.* Bermuda Islands, Bermudas; *prev.* Somers Islands. ◇ *UK crown colony* NW Atlantic Ocean
1 N11 **Bermuda** *var.* Great Bermuda, Long Island, Main Island. *island* Bermuda
Bermuda Islands *see* Bermuda
Bermuda-New England Seamount Arc *see* New England Seamounts
1 N11 **Bermuda Rise** *undersea feature* C Sargasso Sea 32°30′N 65°00′W
Bermudas *see* Bermuda
108 D8 **Bern** *Fr.* Berne. ● (Switzerland) Bern, W Switzerland 46°57′N 07°26′E
108 D9 **Bern** *Fr.* Berne. ◆ *canton* W Switzerland
37 R11 **Bernalillo** New Mexico, SW USA 35°18′N 106°33′W
14 H12 **Bernard Lake** ◎ Ontario, S Canada
61 B18 **Bernardo de Irigoyen** Santa Fe, NE Argentina 32°09′S 61°06′W
18 J14 **Bernardsville** New Jersey, NE USA 40°43′N 74°34′W
63 K14 **Bernasconi** La Pampa, C Argentina 37°55′S 63°44′W
100 O12 **Bernau** Brandenburg, NE Germany 52°41′N 13°36′E
102 L4 **Bernay** Eure, N France 49°05′N 00°36′E
101 L14 **Bernburg** Sachsen-Anhalt, C Germany 51°47′N 11°45′E
109 X5 **Berndorf** Niederösterreich, NE Austria 47°58′N 16°08′E
31 Q12 **Berne** Indiana, N USA 40°39′N 84°57′W
Berne *see* Bern
108 D10 **Berner Alpen** *var.* Berner Oberland, *Eng.* Bernese Oberland. ▲ SW Switzerland
Berner Oberland/Bernese Oberland *see* Berner Alpen
109 Y2 **Bernhardsthal** Niederösterreich, N Austria 48°40′N 16°51′E
22 H4 **Bernice** Louisiana, S USA 32°49′N 92°39′W
27 Y8 **Bernie** Missouri, C USA 36°40′N 89°58′W
180 G9 **Bernier Island** *island* Western Australia
Bernina Pass *see* Bernina, Passo del
108 J10 **Bernina, Passo del** *Eng.* Bernina Pass. *pass* SE Switzerland
108 J10 **Bernina, Piz** *It.* Pizzo Bermina. ▲ Italy/Switzerland 46°22′N 09°55′E *see also* Bermina, Pizzo
Bernina, Piz *see* Bermina, Pizzo
99 E20 **Bernissart** Hainaut, SW Belgium 50°29′N 03°37′E
101 E18 **Bernkastel-Kues** Rheinland-Pfalz, W Germany 49°55′N 07°04′E
Beroea *see* Ḩalab
172 H6 **Beroroha** Toliara, SW Madagascar 21°40′S 45°10′E
Béroubouay *see* Gbéroubouè
111 C17 **Beroun** *Ger.* Beraun. Středočeský Kraj, W Czech Republic 49°58′N 14°05′E
111 C16 **Berounka** *Ger.* Beraun. W Czech Republic
113 Q18 **Berovo** E FYR Macedonia 41°45′N 22°50′E
74 F6 **Berrechid** *var.* Berchid. W Morocco 33°16′N 07°32′W
103 R15 **Berre, Étang de** ◎ SE France
103 S15 **Berre-l'Étang** Bouches-du-Rhône, SE France 43°28′N 05°10′E
182 K9 **Berri** South Australia 34°16′S 140°35′E
31 O10 **Berrien Springs** Michigan, N USA 41°57′N 86°20′W
183 O10 **Berrigan** New South Wales, SE Australia 35°41′S 145°50′E
103 N9 **Berry** *cultural region* C France
35 N7 **Berryessa, Lake** ◎ California, W USA
44 G2 **Berry Islands** *island group* N Bahamas
27 T9 **Berryville** Arkansas, C USA 36°22′N 93°35′W
21 V3 **Berryville** Virginia, NE USA 39°08′N 77°59′W
83 D21 **Berseba** Karas, S Namibia 26°00′S 17°46′E
117 O8 **Bershad'** Vinnyts'ka Oblast', C Ukraine 48°20′N 29°30′E
28 L3 **Berthold** North Dakota, N USA 48°16′N 101°48′W
37 T3 **Berthoud** Colorado, C USA 40°18′N 105°04′W
37 S4 **Berthoud Pass** *pass* Colorado, C USA
79 F15 **Bertoua** Est, E Cameroon 04°34′N 13°42′E
25 S10 **Bertram** Texas, SW USA 30°44′N 98°03′W
63 G22 **Bertrand, Cerro** ▲ S Argentina 50°00′S 73°27′W
99 J23 **Bertrix** Luxembourg, SE Belgium 49°52′N 05°15′E
191 P3 **Beru** *var.* Peru. *atoll* Tungaru, W Kiribati
Beruni *see* Beruniy
146 I9 **Beruniy** *var.* Biruni, *Rus.* Beruni. Qoraqalpog'iston Respublikasi, W Uzbekistan 41°48′N 60°39′E
58 F13 **Beruri** Amazonas, NW Brazil 03°44′S 61°13′W
18 H14 **Berwick** Pennsylvania, NE USA 41°03′N 76°13′W
96 K12 **Berwick** *cultural region* SE Scotland, United Kingdom
96 L12 **Berwick-upon-Tweed** N England, United Kingdom 55°46′N 02°W
117 S10 **Beryslav** *Rus.* Berislav. Khersons'ka Oblast', S Ukraine 46°51′N 33°26′E
Berytus *see* Beyrouth
172 H4 **Besalampy** Mahajanga, W Madagascar 16°43′S 44°29′E
103 T8 **Besançon** *anc.* Besontium, Vesontio. Doubs, E France 47°14′N 06°01′E
103 P10 **Besbre** C France
Bescanuova *see* Baška
Besdan *see* Bezdan
Besed' *see* Byesyedz'
147 R10 **Beshariq** *Rus.* Besharyk; *prev.* Kirovo. Farg'ona Viloyati, E Uzbekistan 40°26′N 70°33′E
Besharyk *see* Beshariq
146 L9 **Beshbuloq** *Rus.* Beshulak. Navoiy Viloyati, N Uzbekistan 41°55′N 64°13′E
Beshenkovichi *see* Byeshankovichy
146 M13 **Beshkent** Qashqadaryo Viloyati, S Uzbekistan 38°47′N 65°42′E
Beshulak *see* Beshbuloq
112 L10 **Beška** Vojvodina, N Serbia 45°09′N 20°04′E
Beskra *see* Biskra
127 O16 **Beslan** Respublika Severnaya Osetiya, SW Russian Federation 43°12′N 44°33′E
113 P16 **Besna Kobila** ▲ SE Serbia 42°30′N 22°16′E
137 N16 **Besni** Adıyaman, S Turkey 37°42′N 37°53′E
Besontium *see* Besançon
121 Q2 **Beşparmak Dağları** *Eng.* Kyrenia Mountains. ▲ N Cyprus
Bessarabka *see* Basarabeasca
92 O2 **Bessels, Kapp** *headland* C Svalbard 78°36′N 21°43′E
23 P4 **Bessemer** Alabama, S USA 33°24′N 86°57′W
30 K3 **Bessemer** Michigan, N USA 46°28′N 90°03′W
21 Q10 **Bessemer City** North Carolina, SE USA 35°16′N 81°16′W
102 M10 **Bessines-sur-Gartempe** Haute-Vienne, C France 46°06′N 01°22′E
99 K15 **Best** Noord-Brabant, S Netherlands 51°31′N 05°24′E
25 N9 **Best** Texas, SW USA 31°13′N 101°34′W
125 O11 **Bestuzhevo** Arkhangel'skaya Oblast', NW Russian Federation 61°36′N 43°54′E
123 M11 **Bestyakh** Respublika Sakha (Yakutiya), NE Russian Federation 61°25′N 129°05′E
Besztercze *see* Bistriţa
Besztercebánya *see* Banská Bystrica
172 I5 **Betafo** Antananarivo, C Madagascar 19°50′S 46°50′E
104 H2 **Betanzos** Galicia, NW Spain 43°17′N 08°17′W
104 G2 **Betanzos, Ría de** *estuary* NW Spain
79 G15 **Bétaré Oya** Est, E Cameroon 05°34′N 14°09′E
105 S9 **Bétera** País Valenciano, E Spain 39°35′N 00°28′W
77 R15 **Bétérou** C Benin 09°13′N 02°18′E
83 K21 **Bethal** Mpumalanga, NE South Africa 26°27′S 29°28′E
30 K15 **Bethalto** Illinois, N USA 38°54′N 90°02′W
83 D21 **Bethanie** *var.* Bethanien, Bethany. Karas, S Namibia 26°32′S 17°11′E
Bethanien *see* Bethanie
27 S2 **Bethany** Missouri, C USA 40°15′N 94°03′W
27 N10 **Bethany** Oklahoma, C USA 35°31′N 97°37′W
Bethany *see* Bethanie
39 N12 **Bethel** Alaska, USA 60°47′N 161°45′W
19 P7 **Bethel** Maine, NE USA 44°24′N 70°47′W
21 W9 **Bethel** North Carolina, SE USA 35°46′N 77°21′W
18 B15 **Bethel Park** Pennsylvania, NE USA 40°21′N 80°03′W
21 W3 **Bethesda** Maryland, NE USA 39°00′N 77°05′W
83 J22 **Bethlehem** Free State, C South Africa 28°12′S 28°16′E
18 I14 **Bethlehem** Pennsylvania, NE USA 40°36′N 75°22′W
138 F10 **Bethlehem** *var.* Beit Lekhem, *Ar.* Bayt Laḩm, *Heb.* Bet Leḩem. C West Bank 31°43′N 35°12′E
Bethlen *see* Beclean
83 I24 **Bethulie** Free State, C South Africa 30°30′S 25°59′E
103 O1 **Béthune** Pas-de-Calais, N France 50°32′N 02°38′E
102 M3 **Béthune** N France
104 M14 **Béticos, Sistemas** *var.* Sistema Penibético, *Eng.* Baetic Cordillera, Baetic Mountains. ▲ S Spain
54 I6 **Betijoque** Trujillo, NW Venezuela 09°25′N 70°45′W
59 M20 **Betim** Minas Gerais, SE Brazil 19°56′S 44°10′W
190 H3 **Betio** Tarawa, W Kiribati 01°21′N 172°56′E
172 H7 **Betioky** Toliara, S Madagascar 23°42′S 44°22′E
Bet Leḩem *see* Bethlehem
Betlen *see* Beclean
167 O17 **Betong** Yala, SW Thailand 05°45′N 101°05′E
79 I16 **Bétou** Likouala, N Congo 03°08′N 18°31′E
145 P14 **Betpak-Dala** *Kaz.* Betpaqdala. *plateau* S Kazakhstan
Betpaqdala *see* Betpak-Dala
172 H7 **Betroka** Toliara, S Madagascar 23°15′S 46°07′E
Betschau *see* Bečva
Bet She'an *see* Beit She'an
15 T6 **Betsiamites** Québec, SE Canada 48°56′N 68°40′W
15 T6 **Betsiamites** Québec, SE Canada
172 I4 **Betsiboka** N Madagascar
Betsukai *see* Bekkai
99 M25 **Bettembourg** Luxembourg, S Luxembourg 49°31′N 06°06′E
99 M23 **Bettendorf** Diekirch, NE Luxembourg 49°53′N 06°13′E
29 Z14 **Bettendorf** Iowa, C USA 41°31′N 90°31′W
75 R13 **Bette, Picco** *var.* Bikkū Bittī, *It.* Picco Bette. ▲ S Libya 22°02′N 19°07′E
Bette, Picco *see* Bette, Picco
153 P12 **Bettiah** Bihār, N India 26°49′N 84°30′E
39 Q7 **Bettles** Alaska, USA 66°54′N 151°40′W
95 N17 **Bettna** Södermanland, C Sweden 58°52′N 16°40′E
154 H11 **Betūl** *prev.* Badnur. Madhya Pradesh, C India 21°55′N 77°54′E
154 H9 **Betwa** C India
101 F16 **Betzdorf** Rheinland-Pfalz, W Germany 50°47′N 07°50′E
82 C9 **Béu** Uíge, NW Angola 06°15′S 15°32′E
31 P6 **Beulah** Michigan, N USA 43°35′N 83°52′W
28 L5 **Beulah** North Dakota, N USA 47°16′N 101°48′W
98 M8 **Beulakerwijde** ◎ N Netherlands
98 L13 **Beuningen** Gelderland, SE Netherlands 51°52′N 05°47′E
Beuthen *see* Bytom
103 N7 **Beuvron** C France
99 F16 **Beveren** Oost-Vlaanderen, N Belgium 51°13′N 04°15′E
21 T9 **B. Everett Jordan Reservoir** *var.* Jordan Lake. ⊠ North Carolina, SE USA
97 N17 **Beverley** E England, United Kingdom 53°51′N 00°26′W
Beverley *see* Beverly
99 J17 **Beverlo** Limburg, NE Belgium 51°06′N 05°14′E
19 P11 **Beverly** Massachusetts, NE USA 42°33′N 70°49′W
32 J9 **Beverly** *var.* Beverley. Washington, NW USA 46°50′N 119°57′W
35 S15 **Beverly Hills** California, W USA 34°02′N 118°25′W
101 I14 **Beverungen** Nordrhein-Westfalen, C Germany 51°39′N 09°22′E
98 H9 **Beverwijk** Noord-Holland, W Netherlands 52°29′N 04°40′E
108 C10 **Bex** Vaud, W Switzerland 46°15′N 07°00′E
97 P23 **Bexhill** *var.* Bexhill-on-Sea. SE England, United Kingdom 50°50′N 00°28′E
Bexhill-on-Sea *see* Bexhill
136 E17 **Bey Dağları** ▲ SW Turkey
Beyj *see* Belyy
136 E10 **Beykoz** İstanbul, NW Turkey 41°09′N 29°06′E
76 K15 **Beyla** SE Guinea 08°43′N 08°41′W
137 X12 **Beyläqan** *prev.* Zhdanov. SW Azerbaijan 39°43′N 47°38′E
80 L10 **Beylul** *var.* Beilul. SE Eritrea 13°10′N 42°27′E
144 H14 **Beyneu** *Kaz.* Beyneū. Mangistau, SW Kazakhstan 45°20′N 55°11′E
Beyneū *see* Beyneu
165 X14 **Beyonēsu-retsugan** *Eng.* Bayonnaise Rocks. *island group* SE Japan
136 G12 **Beypazarı** Ankara, NW Turkey 40°10′N 31°56′E
155 F21 **Beypore** Kerala, SW India 11°10′N 75°49′E
138 G7 **Beyrouth** *var.* Bayrūt, *Eng.* Beirut; *anc.* Berytus. ● (Lebanon) W Lebanon 33°55′N 35°31′E
138 G7 **Beyrouth** ✕ W Lebanon 33°52′N 35°30′E
136 G15 **Beyşehir** Konya, SW Turkey 37°40′N 31°43′E
136 G15 **Beyşehir Gölü** ◎ C Turkey
108 J7 **Bezau** Vorarlberg, NW Austria 47°24′N 09°55′E
112 J8 **Bezdan** *Ger.* Besdan, *Hung.* Bezdán. Vojvodina, NW Serbia 45°51′N 19°00′E
Bezdezh *see* Byezdzyezh
124 G15 **Bezhanitsy** Pskovskaya Oblast', W Russian Federation 56°57′N 29°53′E
124 K15 **Bezhetsk** Tverskaya Oblast', W Russian Federation 57°47′N 36°42′E
103 P16 **Béziers** *anc.* Baeterrae, Baeterrae Septimanorum, Julia Beterrae. Hérault, S France 43°21′N 03°13′E
Bezmein *see* Abadan
Bezwada *see* Vijayawāda
154 P12 **Bhadrak** *var.* Bhadrakh. Orissa, E India 21°04′N 86°30′N
Bhadrakh *see* Bhadrak
155 F19 **Bhadra Reservoir** ⊠ SW India
155 F18 **Bhadrāvati** Karnātaka, SW India 13°52′N 75°43′E
153 R14 **Bhāgalpur** Bihār, NE India 25°14′N 86°59′E
Bhairab *see* Bhairab Bazar
153 U14 **Bhairab Bazar** *var.* Bhairab. Dhaka, C Bangladesh 24°04′N 91°00′E
153 O11 **Bhairahawā** Western, S Nepal 27°31′N 83°27′E
149 S8 **Bhakkar** Punjab, E Pakistan 31°40′N 71°08′E
153 P11 **Bhaktapur** Central, C Nepal 27°47′N 85°21′E
167 N3 **Bhamo** *var.* Banmo. Kachin State, N Burma (Myanmar) 24°15′N 97°15′E
Bhāmragad *see* Bhāmragarh
154 K13 **Bhāmragarh** *var.* Bhāmragad. Mahārāshtra, C India 19°28′N 80°39′E
154 J12 **Bhandāra** Mahārāshtra, C India 21°10′N 79°41′E
Bhārat *see* India
152 J12 **Bharatpur** *prev.* Bhurtpore. Rājasthān, N India 27°14′N 77°29′E
154 D11 **Bharūch** Gujarāt, W India 21°48′N 72°55′E
155 E18 **Bhatkal** Karnātaka, W India 13°59′N 74°34′E
153 O13 **Bhatni** *var.* Bhatni Junction. Uttar Pradesh, N India 26°23′N 83°56′E
Bhatni Junction *see* Bhatni
153 S16 **Bhātpāra** West Bengal, NE India 22°55′N 88°30′E
149 U7 **Bhaun** Punjab, E Pakistan 32°53′N 72°48′E
Bhaunagar *see* Bhāvnagar
154 M13 **Bhavānipātna** *var.* Bhawanipatna. Orissa, E India 19°56′N 83°09′E
155 H21 **Bhavānisāgar** ⊠ S India
154 D11 **Bhāvnagar** *prev.* Bhaunagar. Gujarāt, W India 21°46′N 72°14′E
Bhawanipatna *see* Bhavānipātna
Bheanntraí, Bá *see* Bantry Bay
Bheara, Béal an *see* Gweebarra Bay
154 K12 **Bhilai** Chhattīsgarh, C India 21°12′N 81°26′E
152 G13 **Bhīlwāra** Rājasthān, N India 25°23′N 74°39′E
155 E14 **Bhīma** S India
155 K16 **Bhīmavaram** Andhra Pradesh, E India 16°34′N 81°35′E
154 I7 **Bhind** Madhya Pradesh, C India 26°33′N 78°47′E
152 E13 **Bhīnmāl** Rājasthān, N India 25°01′N 72°22′E
Bhir *see* Bīd
154 D13 **Bhiwandi** Mahārāshtra, W India 19°21′N 73°08′E
152 H10 **Bhiwāni** Haryāna, N India 28°50′N 76°10′E
152 L13 **Bhognīpur** Uttar Pradesh, N India 26°12′N 79°48′E
153 U16 **Bhola** Barisal, S Bangladesh 22°40′N 91°36′E
154 H10 **Bhopāl** *state capital* Madhya Pradesh, C India 23°17′N 77°25′E
155 J14 **Bhopālpatnam** Chhattīsgarh, C India 18°51′N 80°22′E
155 E14 **Bhor** Mahārāshtra, W India 18°10′N 73°55′E
154 O12 **Bhubaneshwar** *prev.* Bhubaneswar, Bhuvaneshwar. *state capital* Orissa, E India 20°16′N 85°51′E
Bhubaneswar *see* Bhubaneshwar
154 B9 **Bhuj** Gujarāt, W India 23°16′N 69°40′E
Bhuket *see* Phuket
Bhurtpore *see* Bharatpur
Bhusaval *see* Bhusāwal
154 G12 **Bhusāwal** *prev.* Bhusaval. Mahārāshtra, C India 21°01′N 75°50′E
153 T12 **Bhutan** *off.* Kingdom of Bhutan, *var.* Druk-yul. ◆ *monarchy* S Asia
Bhutan, Kingdom of *see* Bhutan
Bhuvaneshwar *see* Bhubaneshwar
143 T15 **Bīābān, Kūh-e** ▲ S Iran
77 V18 **Biafra, Bight of** *var.* Bight of Bonny. *bay* W Africa
171 W12 **Biak** Papua, E Indonesia 01°10′S 136°05′E
171 W12 **Biak, Pulau** *island* E Indonesia
110 P12 **Biała Podlaska** Lubelskie, E Poland 52°03′N 23°08′E
110 F7 **Białogard** *Ger.* Belgard. Zachodnio-pomorskie, NW Poland 54°01′N 15°59′E
110 P10 **Białowieska, Puszcza** *Bel.* Byelavyezhskaya Pushcha, *Rus.* Belovezhskaya Pushcha. *physical region* Belarus/Poland *see also* Byelavyezhskaya Pushcha
Białowieska, Puszcza *see* Byelavyezhskaya Pushcha
110 G8 **Biały Bór** *Ger.* Baldenburg. Zachodnio-pomorskie, NW Poland 53°53′N 16°49′E
110 P9 **Białystok** *Rus.* Belostok, Bielostok. Podlaskie, NE Poland 53°08′N 23°09′E
107 L24 **Biancavilla** *prev.* Inessa. Sicilia, Italy, C Mediterranean Sea 37°38′N 14°52′E
Bianco, Monte *see* Blanc, Mont
Bianjing *see* Xunke
76 L15 **Biankouma** W Ivory Coast 07°44′N 07°37′W
167 R7 **Bia, Phou** *var.* Pou Bia. ▲ C Laos 18°59′N 103°09′E
Bia, Pou *see* Bia, Phou
143 R5 **Biārjmand** Semnān, N Iran 36°05′N 55°50′E
105 P4 **Biarra** NE Spain
102 I15 **Biarritz** Pyrénées-Atlantiques, SW France 43°25′N 01°40′W
108 H10 **Biasca** Ticino, S Switzerland 46°22′N 08°59′E
61 E17 **Biassini** Salto, N Uruguay 31°18′S 57°05′W
Biasteri *see* Laguardia
165 S3 **Bibai** Hokkaidō, NE Japan 43°21′N 141°53′E
83 B15 **Bibala** *Port.* Vila Arriaga. Namibe, SW Angola 14°46′S 13°21′E
104 I4 **Bibéi** NW Spain
Biberach *see* Biberach an der Riss
101 I23 **Biberach an der Riss** *var.* Biberach, *Ger.* Biberach an der Riß. Baden-Württemberg, S Germany 48°06′N 09°48′E
108 E7 **Biberist** Solothurn, NW Switzerland 47°11′N 07°34′E
77 O16 **Bibiani** SW Ghana 06°28′N 02°20′W
112 C13 **Bibinje** Zadar, SW Croatia 44°04′N 15°17′E
Biblical Gebal *see* Jbail
116 I5 **Bibrka** *Pol.* Bóbrka, *Rus.* Bobrka. L'vivs'ka Oblast', NW Ukraine 49°39′N 24°16′E
117 N10 **Bic** S Moldova
113 M18 **Bicaj** Kukës, NE Albania 42°00′N 20°24′E
116 K10 **Bicaz** *Hung.* Békás. Neamţ, NE Romania 46°53′N 26°05′E
183 Q16 **Bicheno** Tasmania, SE Australia 41°56′S 148°15′E
Bichiş *see* Békés
Bichiş-Ciaba *see* Békéscsaba
Bichitra *see* Phichit
137 P8 **Bichvint'a** *Rus.* Pitsunda. NW Georgia 43°12′N 40°21′E
15 T7 **Bic, Île du** *island* Québec, SE Canada
32 J10 **Bickleton** Washington, NW USA 46°00′N 120°16′W
36 L6 **Bicknell** Utah, W USA 38°20′N 111°32′W
171 S11 **Bicoli** Pulau Halmahera, E Indonesia 0°34′N 128°33′E
111 J22 **Bicske** Fejér, C Hungary 47°30′N 18°36′E
155 F14 **Bīd** *prev.* Bhir. Mahārāshtra, W India 19°17′N 75°22′E
77 U15 **Bida** Niger, C Nigeria 09°06′N 06°02′E
155 H15 **Bīdar** Karnātaka, C India 17°56′N 77°35′E
141 Y8 **Bidbid** NE Oman 23°25′N 58°08′E
19 P9 **Biddeford** Maine, NE USA 43°29′N 70°27′W
98 L9 **Biddinghuizen** Flevoland, C Netherlands 52°28′N 05°41′E
33 X11 **Biddle** Montana, NW USA 45°04′N 105°21′W
97 J23 **Bideford** SW England, United Kingdom 51°01′N 04°12′W
82 D13 **Bié** ◆ *province* C Angola
35 O2 **Bieber** California, W USA 41°07′N 121°09′W
110 O9 **Biebrza** NE Poland
165 T3 **Biei** Hokkaidō, NE Japan 43°33′N 142°28′E
108 D8 **Biel** *Fr.* Bienne. Bern, W Switzerland 47°09′N 07°16′E
100 G13 **Bielefeld** Nordrhein-Westfalen, NW Germany 52°01′N 08°32′E
108 D8 **Bieler See** *Fr.* Lac de Bienne. ◎ W Switzerland
Bielitz/Bielitz-Biala *see* Bielsko-Biała
106 C7 **Biella** Piemonte, N Italy 45°34′N 08°04′E
Bielostok *see* Białystok
111 J17 **Bielsko-Biała** *Ger.* Bielitz, Bielitz-Biala. Śląskie, S Poland 49°49′N 19°01′E
110 P10 **Bielsk Podlaski** Białystok, E Poland 52°45′N 23°11′E
Bien Bien *see* Điên Biên
Biên Đông *see* South China Sea
11 V17 **Bienfait** Saskatchewan, S Canada 49°06′N 102°47′W
167 T14 **Biên Hoa** Đông Nai, S Vietnam 10°58′N 106°50′E
Bienne *see* Biel
Bienne, Lac de *see* Bieler See
12 K8 **Bienville, Lac** ◎ Québec, C Canada
82 D13 **Bié, Planalto do** *var.* Bié Plateau. *plateau* C Angola
Bié Plateau *see* Bié, Planalto do
108 B9 **Bière** Vaud, W Switzerland 46°32′N 06°19′E
98 O4 **Bierum** Groningen, NE Netherlands 53°25′N 06°51′E
98 I13 **Biesbos** *var.* Biesbosch. *wetland* S Netherlands
Biesbosch *see* Biesbos
99 H21 **Biesme** Namur, S Belgium 50°19′N 04°43′E
101 H21 **Bietigheim-Bissingen** Baden-Württemberg, SW Germany 48°57′N 09°07′E
99 I23 **Bièvre** Namur, SE Belgium 49°56′N 05°01′E
79 D18 **Bifoun** Moyen-Ogooué, NW Gabon 0°15′S 10°24′E
165 T2 **Bifuka** Hokkaidō, NE Japan 44°28′N 142°20′E
136 C11 **Biga** Çanakkale, NW Turkey 40°13′N 27°14′E
136 C13 **Bigadiç** Balıkesir, W Turkey 39°24′N 28°08′E
26 J7 **Big Basin** *basin* Kansas, C USA
185 B20 **Big Bay** *bay* South Island, New Zealand
31 O5 **Big Bay de Noc** ◎ Michigan, N USA
31 N3 **Big Bay Point** *headland* Michigan, N USA 46°51′N 87°40′W
33 R10 **Big Belt Mountains** ▲ Montana, NW USA
29 N10 **Big Bend Dam** *dam* South Dakota, N USA
24 K12 **Big Bend National Park** *national park* Texas, S USA
22 K5 **Big Black River** Mississippi, S USA
27 O3 **Big Blue River** Kansas/Nebraska, C USA
24 M10 **Big Canyon** Texas, SW USA
33 N12 **Big Creek** Idaho, NW USA 45°05′N 115°20′W
23 N8 **Big Creek Lake** ⊠ Alabama, S USA
23 X15 **Big Cypress Swamp** *wetland* Florida, SE USA
39 S9 **Big Delta** Alaska, USA 64°09′N 145°50′W
30 K6 **Big Eau Pleine Reservoir** ⊠ Wisconsin, N USA
19 P5 **Bigelow Mountain** ▲ Maine, NE USA 45°09′N 70°17′W
162 G9 **Biger** *var.* Jargalant. Govĭ-Altay, W Mongolia 45°39′N 97°10′E
29 U3 **Big Falls** Minnesota, N USA 48°13′N 93°48′W
33 P8 **Bigfork** Montana, NW USA 48°03′N 114°04′W
29 U3 **Big Fork River** Minnesota, N USA
11 S15 **Biggar** Saskatchewan, S Canada 52°03′N 107°59′W
180 L3 **Bigge Island** *island* Western Australia
35 O5 **Biggs** California, W USA 39°24′N 121°44′W
32 I11 **Biggs** Oregon, NW USA 45°39′N 120°49′W
14 K13 **Big Gull Lake** ◎ Ontario, SE Canada
37 P16 **Big Hachet Peak** ▲ New Mexico, SW USA 31°38′N 108°24′W
33 P11 **Big Hole River** Montana, NW USA
33 V13 **Bighorn Basin** *basin* Wyoming, C USA
33 U11 **Bighorn Lake** ◎ Montana/Wyoming, N USA
33 W13 **Bighorn Mountains** ▲ Wyoming, C USA
36 J13 **Big Horn Peak** ▲ Arizona, SW USA 33°40′N 113°01′W
33 V11 **Bighorn River** Montana/Wyoming, NW USA
9 S7 **Big Island** *island* Nunavut, NE Canada
39 O16 **Big Koniuji Island** *island* Shumagin Islands, Alaska, USA
25 N9 **Big Lake** Texas, SW USA 31°12′N 101°29′W
19 T5 **Big Lake** ◎ Maine, NE USA
30 I3 **Big Manitou Falls** *waterfall* Wisconsin, N USA
35 R2 **Big Mountain** ▲ Nevada, W USA 41°18′N 119°03′W
108 G10 **Bignasco** Ticino, S Switzerland 46°21′N 08°37′E
29 R16 **Big Nemaha River** Nebraska, C USA
76 G12 **Bignona** SW Senegal 12°49′N 16°16′W
Bigorra *see* Tarbes
Bigosovo *see* Bihosava
35 S10 **Big Pine** California, W USA 37°09′N 118°18′W
35 Q14 **Big Pine Mountain** ▲ California, W USA 34°41′N 119°37′W
27 V6 **Big Piney Creek** Missouri, C USA
65 M24 **Big Point** *headland* N Tristan da Cunha 37°10′S 12°18′W
31 P8 **Big Rapids** Michigan, N USA 43°42′N 85°28′W
30 K6 **Big Rib River** Wisconsin, N USA
14 L14 **Big Rideau Lake** ◎ Ontario, SE Canada
11 T14 **Big River** Saskatchewan, C Canada 53°48′N 106°55′W
27 X5 **Big River** Missouri, C USA
31 N7 **Big Sable Point** *headland* Michigan, N USA 44°03′N 86°30′W
33 S7 **Big Sandy** Montana, NW USA 48°08′N 110°09′W
25 W6 **Big Sandy** Texas, SW USA 32°34′N 95°06′W
37 V5 **Big Sandy Creek** Colorado, C USA
29 Q16 **Big Sandy Creek** Nebraska, C USA
29 V5 **Big Sandy Lake** ◎ Minnesota, N USA
36 J11 **Big Sandy River** Arizona, SW USA
21 P5 **Big Sandy River** S USA
23 V6 **Big Satilla Creek** Georgia, SE USA
29 R12 **Big Sioux River** Iowa/South Dakota, N USA
35 U7 **Big Smoky Valley** *valley* Nevada, W USA
25 N7 **Big Spring** Texas, SW USA 32°15′N 101°30′W
19 Q5 **Big Squaw Mountain** ▲ Maine, NE USA 45°28′N 69°42′W
21 O7 **Big Stone Gap** Virginia, NE USA 36°52′N 82°45′W
29 Q8 **Big Stone Lake** ◎ Minnesota/South Dakota, N USA
22 K4 **Big Sunflower River** Mississippi, S USA
33 T11 **Big Timber** Montana, NW USA 45°50′N 109°57′W
12 D8 **Big Trout Lake** Ontario, C Canada 53°40′N 90°00′W
14 I12 **Big Trout Lake** ◎ Ontario, SE Canada
35 O2 **Big Valley Mountains** ▲ California, W USA
25 Q13 **Big Wells** Texas, SW USA 28°34′N 99°34′W
14 F11 **Bigwood** Ontario, S Canada 46°03′N 80°37′W
112 D11 **Bihać** ◆ Federacija Bosna I Hercegovina, NW Bosnia and Herzegovina
153 P14 **Bihār** *prev.* Behar. ◆ *state* N India
Bihār *see* Bihār Sharīf
81 F20 **Biharamulo** Kagera, NW Tanzania 02°37′S 31°20′E
153 R13 **Bihārīganj** Bihār, NE India 25°44′N 86°59′E
153 P14 **Bihār Sharīf** *var.* Bihār. Bihār, N India 25°13′N 85°31′E
116 F10 **Bihor** ◆ *county* NW Romania
165 V3 **Bihoro** Hokkaidō, NE Japan 43°50′N 144°05′E
118 K11 **Bihosava** *Rus.* Bigosovo. Vitsyebskaya Voblasts', NW Belarus 55°50′N 27°46′E
Bijagos Archipelago *see* Bijagós, Arquipélago dos
76 G13 **Bijagós, Arquipélago dos** *var.* Bijagos Archipelago. *island group* W Guinea-Bissau
155 F16 **Bijāpur** Karnātaka, C India 16°50′N 75°42′E
142 K5 **Bījār** Kordestān, W Iran 35°52′N 47°39′E

◆ Country ● Country Capital ◇ Dependent Territory ○ Dependent Territory Capital ◆ Administrative Regions ✕ International Airport ▲ Mountain ▲ Mountain Range Volcano River ◎ Lake ⊠ Reservoir

Bijeljina – Blue Mountain

112 J11 **Bijeljina** Republika Srpska, NE Bosnia and Herzegovina *44°46′N 19°13′E*
113 K15 **Bijelo Polje** E Montenegro *43°03′N 19°44′E*
160 I11 **Bijie** Guizhou, S China *27°15′N 105°16′E*
152 J10 **Bijnor** Uttar Pradesh, N India *29°22′N 78°09′E*
152 F11 **Bīkāner** Rājasthān, NW India *28°01′N 73°22′E*
189 V3 **Bikar Atoll** *var.* Pikaar. *atoll* Ratak Chain, N Marshall Islands
190 H3 **Bikeman** *atoll* Tungaru, W Kiribati
190 I3 **Bikenebu** Tarawa, W Kiribati
123 S14 **Bikin** Khabarovskiy Kray, SE Russian Federation *46°45′N 134°06′E*
123 S14 **Bikin** ≈ SE Russian Federation
189 R3 **Bikini Atoll** *var.* Pikinni. *atoll* Ralik Chain, NW Marshall Islands
83 L17 **Bikita** Masvingo, E Zimbabwe *20°06′S 31°41′E*
Bikkū Bītti *see* Bette, Picco
79 I19 **Bikoro** Equateur, W Dem. Rep. Congo *0°45′S 18°09′E*
141 Z9 **Bilād Banī Bū 'Alī** NE Oman *22°02′N 59°18′E*
141 Z9 **Bilād Banī Bū Ḩasan** NE Oman *22°09′N 59°14′E*
141 X9 **Bilād Manaḩ** *var.* Manaḩ. NE Oman *22°44′N 57°36′E*
77 Q12 **Bilanga** C Burkina *12°35′N 00°08′W*
152 F12 **Bilāra** Rājasthān, N India *26°10′N 73°48′E*
152 K10 **Bilāri** Uttar Pradesh, N India *28°37′N 78°48′E*
138 J5 **Bil'ās, Jabal al** ▲▲ C Syria
154 L11 **Bilāspur** Chhattīsgarh, C India *22°06′N 82°08′E*
152 I8 **Bilāspur** Himāchal Pradesh, N India *31°18′N 76°48′E*
168 J9 **Bila, Sungai** ≈ Sumatera, W Indonesia
137 Y13 **Biläsuvar** *Rus.* Bilyasuvar; *prev.* Pushkino. SE Azerbaijan *39°26′N 48°34′E*
117 O5 **Bila Tserkva** *Rus.* Belaya Tserkov'. Kyyivs'ka Oblast', N Ukraine *49°49′N 30°08′E*
167 N11 **Bilauktaung Range** *var.* Thanintari Taungdan. ▲▲ Burma (Myanmar)/ Thailand
105 O2 **Bilbao** *Basq.* Bilbo. País Vasco, N Spain *43°15′N 02°56′W*
Bilbo *see* Bilbao
92 H2 **Bíldudalur** Vestfirdhir, NW Iceland *65°40′N 23°35′W*
113 I16 **Bileća** ◆ Republika Srpska, S Bosnia and Herzegovina
136 E12 **Bilecik** Bilecik, NW Turkey *39°59′N 29°54′E*
136 F12 **Bilecik** ◆ *province* NW Turkey
116 E11 **Biled** *Ger.* Billed, *Hung.* Billéd. Timiş, W Romania *45°55′N 20°55′E*
111 O15 **Biłgoraj** Lubelskie, E Poland *50°31′N 22°41′E*
117 P11 **Bilhorod-Dnistrovs'kyy** *Rus.* Belgorod-Dnestrovskiy, *Rom.* Cetatea Albă, *prev.* Akkerman; *anc.* Tyras. Odes'ka Oblast', SW Ukraine *46°10′N 30°19′E*
79 M16 **Bili** Orientale, N Dem. Rep. Congo *04°07′N 25°09′E*
123 T6 **Bilibino** Chukotskiy Avtonomnyy Okrug, NE Russian Federation *67°56′N 166°45′E*
166 M8 **Bilin** Mon State, S Burma (Myanmar) *17°14′N 97°12′E*
113 N21 **Bilisht** *var.* Bilishti. Korçë, SE Albania *40°36′N 21°00′E*
Bilishti *see* Bilisht
183 N10 **Billabong Creek** *var.* Moulamein Creek. *seasonal river* New South Wales, SE Australia
182 G4 **Billa Kalina** South Australia *29°57′S 136°13′E*
197 Q17 **Bill Baileys Bank** *undersea feature* N Atlantic Ocean *60°35′N 10°15′W*
Billed/Billéd *see* Biled
153 N14 **Billi** Uttar Pradesh, N India *24°30′N 82°59′E*
97 M15 **Billingham** N England, United Kingdom *54°36′N 01°17′W*
33 U11 **Billings** Montana, NW USA *45°47′N 108°32′W*
95 J16 **Billingsfors** Västra Götaland, S Sweden *58°57′N 12°14′E*
Bill of Cape Clear, The *see* Clear, Cape
28 L9 **Billsburg** South Dakota, N USA *44°22′N 101°40′W*
95 F23 **Billund** Ribe, W Denmark *55°44′N 09°07′E*
36 L11 **Bill Williams Mountain** ▲ Arizona, SW USA *35°12′N 112°12′W*
36 I12 **Bill Williams River** ≈ Arizona, SW USA
77 Y8 **Bilma** Agadez, NE Niger *18°22′N 13°01′E*
77 Y8 **Bilma, Grand Erg de** *desert* NE Niger
181 Y9 **Biloela** Queensland, E Australia *24°27′S 150°31′E*
112 G8 **Bilo Gora** ▲▲ N Croatia
117 U13 **Bilohirs'k** *Rus.* Belogorsk; *prev.* Karasubazar. Respublika Krym, S Ukraine *45°04′N 34°35′E*
Bilokurakine *see* Bilokurakyne
117 X5 **Bilokurakyne** *var.* Bilokurakine. Luhans'ka Oblast', E Ukraine *49°32′N 38°44′E*
117 T3 **Bilopillya** *Rus.* Belopol'ye. Sums'ka Oblast', NE Ukraine *51°09′N 34°17′E*
117 Y6 **Bilovods'k** *Rus.* Belovodsk. Luhans'ka Oblast', E Ukraine *49°11′N 39°34′E*
22 M9 **Biloxi** Mississippi, S USA *30°24′N 88°53′W*
117 R10 **Bilozerka** Khersons'ka Oblast', S Ukraine *46°36′N 32°23′E*
117 W7 **Bilozers'ke** Donets'ka Oblast', E Ukraine *48°29′N 37°03′E*
98 J11 **Bilthoven** Utrecht, C Netherlands *52°07′N 05°12′E*
78 K9 **Biltine** Biltine, E Chad *14°30′N 20°53′E*
78 J9 **Biltine** *off.* Préfecture de Biltine. ◆ *prefecture* E Chad
Biltine, Préfecture de *see* Biltine
Bilüü *see* Ulaanhus
Bilwi *see* Puerto Cabezas
Bilyasuvar *see* Biläsuvar
117 O11 **Bilyayivka** Odes'ka Oblast', SW Ukraine *46°28′N 30°11′E*
99 K18 **Bilzen** Limburg, NE Belgium *50°52′N 05°31′E*
Bimbéréké *see* Bembèrèkè
183 R10 **Bimberi Peak** ▲ New South Wales, SE Australia *35°42′S 148°46′E*
77 Q15 **Bimbila** E Ghana *08°54′N 00°05′E*
79 I15 **Bimbo** Ombella-Mpoko, SW Central African Republic *04°19′N 18°27′E*
44 F2 **Bimini Islands** *island group* W Bahamas
154 I9 **Bīna** Madhya Pradesh, C India *24°09′N 78°10′E*
143 T4 **Bīnālūd, Kūh-e** ▲▲ NE Iran
99 F20 **Binche** Hainaut, S Belgium *50°25′N 04°10′E*
Bindloe Island *see* Marchena, Isla
83 L16 **Bindura** Mashonaland Central, NE Zimbabwe *17°20′S 31°21′E*
105 T5 **Binefar** Aragón, NE Spain *41°51′N 00°17′E*
83 J16 **Binga** Matabeleland North, W Zimbabwe *17°40′S 27°22′E*
183 T5 **Bingara** New South Wales, SE Australia *29°54′S 150°36′E*
101 F18 **Bingen am Rhein** Rheinland-Pfalz, SW Germany *49°58′N 07°54′E*
26 M11 **Binger** Oklahoma, C USA *35°19′N 98°19′W*
Bingerau *see* Węgrów
Bin Ghalfān, Jazā'ir *see* Ḩalāniyāt, Juzur al
19 Q6 **Bingham** Maine, NE USA *45°01′N 69°51′W*
18 H11 **Binghamton** New York, NE USA *42°06′N 75°55′W*
Bin Ghanimah, Jabal *see* Bin Ghunaymah, Jabal
75 P11 **Bin Ghunaymah, Jabal** *var.* Jabal Bin Ghanīmah. ▲▲ C Libya
139 U3 **Bingird** As Sulaymānīyah, NE Iraq *36°03′N 45°03′E*
Bingmei *see* Congjiang
137 P14 **Bingöl** Bingöl, E Turkey *38°54′N 40°29′E*
137 P14 **Bingöl** ◆ *province* E Turkey
161 R6 **Binhai** *var.* Dongkan. Jiangsu, E China *34°00′N 119°51′E*
167 V11 **Binh Đinh** *var.* An Nhon. Binh Đinh, C Vietnam *13°53′N 109°07′E*
167 U10 **Binh Sơn** *var.* Châu Ô. Quang Ngai, C Vietnam *15°18′N 108°45′E*
Binimani *see* Bintimani
168 I8 **Binjai** Sumatera, W Indonesia *03°37′N 98°30′E*
183 R6 **Binnaway** New South Wales, SE Australia *31°34′S 149°24′E*
108 E6 **Binningen** Basel-Land, NW Switzerland *47°32′N 07°35′E*
80 H12 **Binshangul Gumuz** ◆ *federal region* W Ethiopia
168 J8 **Bintang, Banjaran** ▲▲ Peninsular Malaysia
168 M10 **Bintan, Pulau** *island* Kepulauan Riau, W Indonesia
76 J14 **Bintimani** *var.* Binimani. ▲ NE Sierra Leone *09°21′N 11°09′W*
Bint Jubayl *see* Bent Jbaïl
169 S9 **Bintulu** Sarawak, East Malaysia *03°12′N 113°01′E*
169 S9 **Bintuni** *prev.* Steenkool. Papua, E Indonesia *02°03′S 133°45′E*
163 W8 **Binxian** Heilongjiang, NE China *45°44′N 127°28′E*
160 K14 **Binyang** *var.* Binzhou. Guangxi Zhuangzu Zizhiqu, S China *23°15′N 108°40′E*
161 Q4 **Binzhou** Shandong, E China *37°23′N 118°03′E*
Binzhou *see* Binyang
63 G14 **Bío Bío** *var.* Región del Bío Bío. ◆ *region* C Chile
Bío Bío, Región del *see* Bío Bío
63 G14 **Bío Bío, Río** ≈ C Chile
79 C16 **Bioco, Isla de** *var.* Bioko, *Eng.* Fernando Po, *Sp.* Fernando Póo; *prev.* Macías Nguema Biyogo. *island* NW Equatorial Guinea
112 D13 **Biograd na Moru** *It.* Zaravecchia. Zadar, SW Croatia *43°57′N 15°27′E*
Bioko *see* Bioco, Isla de
113 F14 **Biokovo** ▲▲ S Croatia
Biorra *see* Birr
Bipontium *see* Zweibrücken
143 W13 **Birag, Kūh-e** ▲▲ SE Iran
75 O10 **Birāk** *var.* Brak. C Libya *27°32′N 14°17′E*
139 S10 **Bi'r al Islām** Karbalā', C Iraq *32°15′N 43°40′E*
154 N11 **Biramitrapur** *var.* Birmitrapur. Orissa, E India *22°24′N 84°42′E*
139 T11 **Bi'r an Nişf** An Najaf, S Iraq *31°22′N 44°07′E*
78 L12 **Birao** Vakaga, NE Central African Republic *10°14′N 22°49′E*
146 J10 **Birata** *Rus.* Darganata, Dargan-Ata. Lebap Welaýaty, NE Turkmenistan *40°30′N 62°09′E*
158 M6 **Biratar Bulak** *well* NW China
153 R12 **Birātnagar** Eastern, SE Nepal *26°28′N 87°16′E*
165 R5 **Biratori** Hokkaidō, NE Japan *42°35′N 142°07′E*
39 S8 **Birch Creek** Alaska, USA *66°17′N 145°54′W*
38 M11 **Birch Creek** ≈ Alaska, USA
11 T14 **Birch Hills** Saskatchewan, S Canada *52°58′N 105°22′W*
182 M10 **Birchip** Victoria, SE Australia *36°01′S 142°55′E*
29 X4 **Birch Lake** ◎ Minnesota, N USA
11 Q11 **Birch Mountains** ▲▲ Alberta, W Canada
11 V15 **Birch River** Manitoba, S Canada *52°22′N 101°03′W*
44 H12 **Birchs Hill** *hill* W Jamaica
39 R11 **Birchwood** Alaska, USA *61°24′N 149°28′W*
188 I5 **Bird Island** *island* S Northern Mariana Islands
137 N16 **Birecik** Şanlıurfa, S Turkey *37°03′N 37°59′E*
152 M10 **Birendranagar** *var.* Surkhet. Mid Western, W Nepal *28°35′N 81°36′E*
Bir es Saba *see* Be'er Sheva
74 A12 **Bir-Gandouz** SW Western Sahara *21°35′N 16°27′W*
153 P12 **Birganj** Central, C Nepal *27°03′N 84°53′E*
81 B14 **Biri** ≈ W Sudan
Bi'r Ibn Hirmās *see* Al Bi'r
143 U8 **Bīrjand** Khorāsān-e Janūbī, E Iran *32°54′N 59°14′E*
139 T11 **Birkat Ḩāmid** *well* S Iraq
95 F18 **Birkeland** Aust-Agder, S Norway *58°18′N 08°13′E*
101 E19 **Birkenfeld** Rheinland-Pfalz, SW Germany *49°39′N 07°10′E*
97 K18 **Birkenhead** NW England, United Kingdom *53°24′N 03°02′W*
109 W7 **Birkfeld** Steiermark, SE Austria *47°21′N 15°40′E*
182 A2 **Birksgate Range** ▲▲ South Australia
Bîrlad *see* Bârlad
97 K20 **Birmingham** C England, United Kingdom *52°30′N 01°50′W*
23 P4 **Birmingham** Alabama, S USA *33°30′N 86°47′W*
97 M20 **Birmingham** ✈ C England, United Kingdom *52°27′N 01°46′W*
Birmitrapur *see* Biramitrapur
Bir Moghrein *see* Bîr Mogreïn
76 J4 **Bîr Mogreïn** *var.* Bir Moghrein; *prev.* Fort-Trinquet. Tiris Zemmour, N Mauritania *25°10′N 11°35′W*
191 S4 **Birnie Island** *atoll* Phoenix Islands, C Kiribati
77 S12 **Birnin Gaouré** *var.* Birni-Ngaouré. Dosso, SW Niger *12°59′N 03°02′E*
Birni-Ngaouré *see* Birnin Gaouré
77 S12 **Birnin Kebbi** Kebbi, NW Nigeria *12°28′N 04°08′E*
77 T12 **Birnin Konni** *var.* Birni-Nkonni. Tahoua, SW Niger *13°51′N 05°15′E*
Birni-Nkonni *see* Birnin Konni
77 W13 **Birnin Kudu** Jigawa, N Nigeria *11°28′N 09°29′E*
123 S16 **Birobidzhan** Yevreyskaya Avtonomnaya Oblast', SE Russian Federation *48°42′N 132°55′E*
97 D18 **Birr** *var.* Parsonstown, *Ir.* Biorra. C Ireland *53°06′N 07°55′W*
183 P4 **Birrie River** ≈ New South Wales/Queensland, SE Australia
108 D7 **Birse** ≈ NW Switzerland
Birsen *see* Biržai
108 E6 **Birsfelden** Basel-Land, NW Switzerland *47°33′N 07°37′E*
127 U4 **Birsk** Respublika Bashkortostan, W Russian Federation *55°24′N 55°33′E*
119 F14 **Birštonas** Kaunas, C Lithuania *54°37′N 24°00′E*
159 P14 **Biru** Xinjiang Uygur Zizhiqu, W China *31°30′N 93°56′E*
Biruni *see* Beruniy
122 L12 **Biryusa** ≈ C Russian Federation
122 L12 **Biryusinsk** Irkutskaya Oblast', C Russian Federation *55°52′N 97°48′E*
118 G10 **Biržai** *Ger.* Birsen. Panevėžys, NE Lithuania *56°12′N 24°47′E*
121 P16 **Birżebbuġa** SE Malta *35°50′N 14°32′E*
Bisanthe *see* Tekirdağ
171 R12 **Bisa, Pulau** *island* Maluku, E Indonesia
37 N17 **Bisbee** Arizona, SW USA *31°27′N 109°55′W*
29 O2 **Bisbee** North Dakota, N USA *48°36′N 99°21′W*
Biscaia, Baía de *see* Biscay, Bay of
102 I13 **Biscarrosse et de Parentis, Étang de** ◎ SW France
104 M1 **Biscay, Bay of** *Sp.* Golfo de Vizcaya, *Port.* Baía de Biscaia. *bay* France/Spain
23 Z16 **Biscayne Bay** *bay* Florida, SE USA
64 M7 **Biscay Plain** *undersea feature* SE Bay of Biscay *07°15′W 45°00′N*
107 N17 **Bisceglie** Puglia, SE Italy *41°14′N 16°31′E*
Bischoflack *see* Škofja Loka
Bischofsburg *see* Biskupiec
109 Q7 **Bischofshofen** Salzburg, NW Austria *47°25′N 13°13′E*
101 P15 **Bischofswerda** Sachsen, E Germany *51°07′N 14°13′E*
103 V5 **Bischwiller** Bas-Rhin, NE France *48°46′N 07°52′E*
21 T10 **Biscoe** North Carolina, SE USA *35°20′N 79°46′W*
194 G5 **Biscoe Islands** *island group* Antarctica
14 E9 **Biscotasi Lake** ◎ Ontario, S Canada
14 E9 **Biscotasing** Ontario, S Canada *47°16′N 82°04′W*
54 J6 **Biscucuy** Portuguesa, NW Venezuela *09°22′N 69°59′W*
99 M24 **Bissen** Luxembourg, C Luxembourg *49°47′N 06°04′E*
114 K11 **Biser** Khaskovo, S Bulgaria *41°52′N 25°59′E*
113 D15 **Biševo** *It.* Busi. *island* SW Croatia
141 N12 **Bishah, Wādī** *dry watercourse* C Saudi Arabia
147 U7 **Bishkek** *var.* Pishpek; *prev.* Frunze. ● (Kyrgyzstan) Chuyskaya Oblast', N Kyrgyzstan *42°54′N 74°27′E*
147 U7 **Bishkek** ✈ Chuyskaya Oblast', N Kyrgyzstan *42°55′N 74°37′E*
153 R16 **Bishnupur** West Bengal, NE India *23°05′N 87°20′E*
83 J25 **Bisho** Eastern Cape, S South Africa *32°46′S 27°21′E*
35 S9 **Bishop** California, W USA *37°22′N 118°24′W*
25 S15 **Bishop** Texas, SW USA *27°36′N 97°49′W*
97 L15 **Bishop Auckland** N England, United Kingdom *54°41′N 01°41′W*
Bishop's Lynn *see* King's Lynn
97 O21 **Bishop's Stortford** E England, United Kingdom *51°45′N 00°11′E*
21 S12 **Bishopville** South Carolina, SE USA *34°18′N 80°15′W*
138 M5 **Bishrī, Jabal** ▲▲ E Syria
163 U4 **Bishui** Heilongjiang, NE China *52°06′N 123°42′E*
81 G17 **Bisina, Lake** *prev.* Lake Salisbury. ◎ E Uganda
Biskara *see* Biskra
74 L6 **Biskra** *var.* Beskra, Biskara. NE Algeria *34°51′N 05°44′E*
110 M8 **Biskupiec** *Ger.* Bischofsburg. Warmińsko-Mazurskie, NE Poland *53°52′N 20°57′E*
171 R7 **Bislig** Mindanao, S Philippines *08°10′N 126°19′E*
27 X6 **Bismarck** Missouri, C USA *37°46′N 90°37′W*
28 M5 **Bismarck** *state capital* North Dakota, N USA *46°49′N 100°47′W*
186 D5 **Bismarck Archipelago** *island group* NE Papua New Guinea
129 Z16 **Bismarck Plate** *tectonic feature* W Pacific Ocean
186 D7 **Bismarck Range** ▲▲ N Papua New Guinea
186 E6 **Bismarck Sea** *sea* W Pacific Ocean
137 P15 **Bismil** Diyarbakır, SE Turkey *37°53′N 40°38′E*
43 N6 **Bismuna, Laguna** *lagoon* NE Nicaragua
Bisnulok *see* Phitsanulok
171 R10 **Bisoa, Tanjung** *headland* Pulau Halmahera, N Indonesia *02°15′N 127°57′E*
28 K7 **Bison** South Dakota, N USA *45°31′N 102°27′W*
93 H17 **Bispgården** Jämtland, C Sweden *63°00′N 16°40′E*
76 G13 **Bissau** ● (Guinea-Bissau) W Guinea-Bissau *11°52′N 15°39′W*
76 G13 **Bissau** ✈ W Guinea-Bissau *11°53′N 15°41′W*
Bissojohka *see* Børselv
76 G12 **Bissorã** W Guinea-Bissau *12°16′N 15°35′W*
11 O10 **Bistcho Lake** ◎ Alberta, W Canada
22 G5 **Bistineau, Lake** ⊠ Louisiana, S USA
Bistrica *see* Ilirska Bistrica
116 I9 **Bistriţa** *Ger.* Bistritz, *Hung.* Beszterce; *prev.* Nösen. Bistriţa-Năsăud, N Romania *47°10′N 24°31′E*
116 K10 **Bistriţa** *Ger.* Bistritz. ≈ NE Romania
116 I9 **Bistriţa-Năsăud** ◆ *county* N Romania
Bistritz *see* Bistriţa
Bistritz ober Pernstein *see* Bystřice nad Pernštejnem
152 L11 **Biswān** Uttar Pradesh, N India *27°30′N 81°00′E*
110 M7 **Bisztynek** Warmińsko-Mazurskie, NE Poland *54°05′N 20°53′E*
79 E17 **Bitam** Woleu-Ntem, N Gabon *02°05′N 11°30′E*
101 D18 **Bitburg** Rheinland-Pfalz, SW Germany *49°58′N 06°31′E*
103 U4 **Bitche** Moselle, NE France *49°01′N 07°27′E*
78 I11 **Bitkine** Guéra, C Chad *11°59′N 18°13′E*
137 R15 **Bitlis** Bitlis, SE Turkey *38°23′N 42°04′E*
137 R14 **Bitlis** ◆ *province* E Turkey
Bitoeng *see* Bitung
113 N20 **Bitola** *Turk.* Monastir; *prev.* Bitolj. S FYR Macedonia *41°01′N 21°22′E*
Bitolj *see* Bitola
107 O17 **Bitonto** *anc.* Butuntum. Puglia, SE Italy *41°07′N 16°41′E*
77 Q13 **Bitou** *var.* Bittou. SE Burkina *11°19′N 00°17′W*
155 C20 **Bitra Island** *island* Lakshadweep, India, N Indian Ocean
101 M14 **Bitterfeld** Sachsen-Anhalt, E Germany *51°37′N 12°18′E*
32 O9 **Bitterroot Range** ▲▲ Idaho/ Montana, NW USA
33 P10 **Bitterroot River** ≈ Montana, NW USA
107 D18 **Bitti** Sardegna, Italy, C Mediterranean Sea *40°30′N 09°31′E*
Bittou *see* Bitou
171 Q11 **Bitung** *prev.* Bitoeng. Sulawesi, C Indonesia *01°28′N 125°13′E*
60 I12 **Bituruna** Paraná, S Brazil *26°11′S 51°34′W*
77 Y13 **Biu** Borno, E Nigeria *10°35′N 12°13′E*
Biumba *see* Byumba
164 J13 **Biwa-ko** ◎ Honshū, SW Japan
171 X14 **Biwarlaut** Papua, E Indonesia *05°44′S 138°14′E*
27 P10 **Bixby** Oklahoma, C USA *35°56′N 95°52′W*
122 J13 **Biya** ≈ S Russian Federation
122 J13 **Biysk** Altayskiy Kray, S Russian Federation *52°34′N 85°09′E*
164 H13 **Bizen** Okayama, Honshū, SW Japan *34°45′N 134°10′E*
Bizerta *see* Bizerte
120 K10 **Bizerte** *Ar.* Banzart, *Eng.* Bizerta. N Tunisia *37°18′N 09°48′E*
Bizkaia *see* Vizcaya
92 G2 **Bjargtangar** *headland* W Iceland *63°30′N 24°29′W*
Bjärnå *see* Perniö
95 K22 **Bjärnum** Skåne, S Sweden *56°15′N 13°45′E*
93 I16 **Bjästa** Västernorrland, C Sweden *63°12′N 18°30′E*
113 I14 **Bjelašnica** ▲ SE Bosnia and Herzegovina *43°13′N 18°18′E*
112 C10 **Bjelolasica** ▲ NW Croatia *45°13′N 14°56′E*
112 F8 **Bjelovar** *Hung.* Belovár. Bjelovar-Bilogora, N Croatia *45°54′N 16°49′E*
112 F8 **Bjelovar-Bilogora** *off.* Bjelovarsko-Bilogorska Županija. ◆ *province* NE Croatia
Bjelovarsko-Bilogorska Županija *see* Bjelovar-Bilogora
92 H10 **Bjerkvik** Nordland, C Norway *68°31′N 16°08′E*
95 G21 **Bjerringbro** Viborg, NW Denmark *56°23′N 09°40′E*
Bjeshkët e Namuna *see* North Albanian Alps
95 L14 **Björbo** Dalarna, C Sweden *60°28′N 14°44′E*
95 I15 **Bjørkelangen** Akershus, S Norway *59°54′N 11°33′E*
95 O14 **Björklinge** Uppsala, C Sweden *60°03′N 17°33′E*
93 I14 **Björksele** Västerbotten, N Sweden *64°58′N 18°30′E*
93 I16 **Björna** Västernorrland, C Sweden *63°33′N 18°38′E*
95 C14 **Bjørnafjorden** *fjord* S Norway
95 L16 **Björneborg** Värmland, C Sweden *59°13′N 14°15′E*
Björneborg *see* Pori
95 E14 **Bjornesfjorden** ◎ S Norway
92 M9 **Bjørnevatn** Finnmark, N Norway *69°40′N 29°57′E*
197 T13 **Bjørnøya** *Eng.* Bear Island. *island* N Norway
93 I15 **Bjurholm** Västerbotten, N Sweden *63°57′N 19°16′E*
95 J22 **Bjuv** Skåne, S Sweden *56°05′N 12°57′E*
76 M12 **Bla** Ségou, W Mali *12°58′N 05°45′W*
181 W8 **Blackall** Queensland, E Australia *24°26′S 145°32′E*
29 V2 **Black Bay** *lake bay* Minnesota, N USA
27 N9 **Black Bear Creek** ≈ Oklahoma, C USA
97 K17 **Blackburn** NW England, United Kingdom *53°45′N 02°29′W*
45 W10 **Blackburne** ✈ (Plymouth) E Montserrat *16°45′N 62°09′W*
39 T11 **Blackburn, Mount** ▲ Alaska, USA *61°43′N 143°25′W*
35 N5 **Black Butte Lake** ⊠ California, W USA
194 J5 **Black Coast** *physical region* Antarctica
11 Q16 **Black Diamond** Alberta, SW Canada *50°42′N 114°09′W*
18 K11 **Black Dome** ▲ New York, NE USA *42°16′N 74°07′W*
113 L18 **Black Drin** *Alb.* Lumi i Drinit të Zi, *SCr.* Crni Drim. ≈ Albania/FYR Macedonia
29 U4 **Blackduck** Minnesota, N USA *47°45′N 94°33′W*
12 D6 **Black Duck** ≈ Ontario, C Canada
33 R14 **Blackfoot** Idaho, NW USA *43°11′N 112°20′W*
33 P9 **Blackfoot River** ≈ Montana, NW USA
Black Forest *see* Schwarzwald
28 J10 **Blackhawk** South Dakota, N USA *44°09′N 103°18′W*
28 I10 **Black Hills** ▲▲ South Dakota/ Wyoming, N USA
11 T10 **Black Lake** ◎ Saskatchewan, C Canada
22 G6 **Black Lake** ⊠ Louisiana, S USA
31 Q5 **Black Lake** ◎ Michigan, N USA
18 I7 **Black Lake** ◎ New York, NE USA
26 F7 **Black Mesa** ▲ Oklahoma, C USA *37°00′N 103°07′W*
21 P10 **Black Mountain** North Carolina, SE USA *35°37′N 82°19′W*
35 P13 **Black Mountain** ▲ California, W USA *35°22′N 120°21′W*
37 Q2 **Black Mountain** ▲ Colorado, C USA *40°47′N 107°23′W*
96 K1 **Black Mountains** ▲▲ SE Wales, United Kingdom
36 H10 **Black Mountains** ▲▲ Arizona, SW USA
21 O7 **Black Mountains** ▲ Kentucky, E USA *36°54′N 82°53′W*
33 Q16 **Black Pine Peak** ▲ Idaho, NW USA *42°07′N 113°07′W*
97 K17 **Blackpool** NW England, United Kingdom *53°50′N 03°03′W*
37 Q14 **Black Range** ▲▲ New Mexico, SW USA
44 I12 **Black River** W Jamaica *18°02′N 77°52′W*
14 J14 **Black River** ≈ Ontario, SE Canada
129 U12 **Black River** *Chin.* Babian Jiang, Lixian Jiang, *Fr.* Rivière Noire, *Vtn.* Sông Đa. ≈ China/Vietnam
44 I12 **Black River** ≈ W Jamaica
39 T7 **Black River** ≈ Alaska, USA
37 N13 **Black River** ≈ Arizona, SW USA
27 X7 **Black River** ≈ Arkansas/ Missouri, C USA
22 I7 **Black River** ≈ Louisiana, S USA
31 Q5 **Black River** ≈ Michigan, N USA
31 S8 **Black River** ≈ Michigan, N USA
18 I8 **Black River** ≈ New York, NE USA
21 T13 **Black River** ≈ South Carolina, SE USA
30 J7 **Black River** ≈ Wisconsin, N USA
30 J7 **Black River Falls** Wisconsin, N USA *44°18′N 90°51′W*
35 R3 **Black Rock Desert** *desert* Nevada, W USA
Black Sand Desert *see* Garagum
21 S7 **Blacksburg** Virginia, NE USA *37°15′N 80°25′W*
136 H10 **Black Sea** *var.* Euxine Sea, *Bul.* Cherno More, *Rom.* Marea Neagră, *Rus.* Chernoye More, *Turk.* Karadeniz, *Ukr.* Chorne More. *sea* Asia/ Europe
117 Q10 **Black Sea Lowland** *Ukr.* Prychornomor'ska Nyzovyna. *depression* SE Europe
33 S17 **Blacks Fork** ≈ Wyoming, C USA
23 V7 **Blackshear** Georgia, SE USA *31°18′N 82°14′W*
23 S6 **Blackshear, Lake** ⊠ Georgia, SE USA
97 A16 **Blacksod Bay** *Ir.* Cuan an Fhóid Duibh. *inlet* W Ireland
21 V7 **Blackstone** Virginia, NE USA *37°04′N 78°00′W*
77 O14 **Black Volta** *var.* Borongo, Mouhoun, Moun Hou, *Fr.* Volta Noire. ≈ W Africa
23 O5 **Black Warrior River** ≈ Alabama, S USA
181 X8 **Blackwater** Queensland, E Australia *23°34′S 148°51′E*
97 D20 **Blackwater** *Ir.* An Abhainn Mhór. ≈ S Ireland
27 T4 **Blackwater River** ≈ Missouri, C USA
21 W7 **Blackwater River** ≈ Virginia, NE USA
Blackwater State *see* Nebraska
27 N8 **Blackwell** Oklahoma, C USA *36°48′N 97°16′W*
25 P7 **Blackwell** Texas, SW USA *32°05′N 100°19′W*
99 J15 **Bladel** Noord-Brabant, S Netherlands *51°22′N 05°13′E*
Bladenmarkt *see* Bălăuşeri
127 O14 **Blagodarnyy** Stavropol'skiy Kray, SW Russian Federation *45°06′N 43°26′E*
114 G11 **Blagoevgrad** *prev.* Gorna Dzhumaya. Blagoevgrad, W Bulgaria *42°01′N 23°05′E*
114 G11 **Blagoevgrad** ◆ *province* SW Bulgaria
123 Q14 **Blagoveshchensk** Amurskaya Oblast', SE Russian Federation *50°19′N 127°30′E*
127 V4 **Blagoveshchensk** Respublika Bashkortostan, W Russian Federation *55°03′N 56°01′E*
102 I7 **Blain** Loire-Atlantique, NW France *47°26′N 01°47′W*
29 V8 **Blaine** Minnesota, N USA *45°09′N 93°13′W*
32 H6 **Blaine** Washington, NW USA *48°59′N 122°45′W*
11 T15 **Blaine Lake** Saskatchewan, S Canada *52°49′N 106°48′W*
29 S14 **Blair** Nebraska, C USA *41°32′N 96°07′W*
96 J10 **Blairgowrie** C Scotland, United Kingdom *56°19′N 03°25′W*
18 C15 **Blairsville** Pennsylvania, NE USA *40°25′N 79°12′W*
116 H11 **Blaj** *Ger.* Blasendorf, *Hung.* Balázsfalva. Alba, SW Romania *46°10′N 23°57′E*
64 F9 **Blake-Bahama Ridge** *undersea feature* W Atlantic Ocean *29°00′N 73°30′W*
23 S7 **Blakely** Georgia, SE USA *31°22′N 84°55′W*
64 E10 **Blake Plateau** *var.* Blake Terrace. *undersea feature* W Atlantic Ocean *31°00′N 79°00′W*
30 M1 **Blake Point** *headland* Michigan, N USA *48°11′N 88°25′W*
Blake Terrace *see* Blake Plateau
61 B24 **Blanca, Bahía** *bay* E Argentina
56 C12 **Blanca, Cordillera** ▲▲ W Peru
105 T12 **Blanca, Costa** *physical region* SE Spain
37 S7 **Blanca Peak** ▲ Colorado, C USA *37°34′N 105°29′W*
24 I9 **Blanca, Sierra** ▲ Texas, SW USA *31°15′N 105°26′W*
120 K9 **Blanc, Cap** *headland* N Tunisia *37°20′N 09°41′E*
Blanc, Cap *see* Nouâdhibou, Râs
31 R12 **Blanchard River** ≈ Ohio, N USA
182 E8 **Blanche, Cape** *headland* South Australia *33°03′S 134°10′E*
182 J4 **Blanche, Lake** ◎ South Australia
31 R14 **Blanchester** Ohio, N USA *39°17′N 83°59′W*
182 J9 **Blanchetown** South Australia *34°21′S 139°36′E*
45 U13 **Blanchisseuse** Trinidad, Trinidad and Tobago *10°47′N 61°18′W*
103 T11 **Blanc, Mont** *It.* Monte Bianco. ▲ France/Italy *45°45′N 06°51′E*
25 R11 **Blanco** Texas, SW USA *30°06′N 98°25′W*
42 K14 **Blanco, Cabo** *headland* NW Costa Rica *09°34′N 85°06′W*
32 D14 **Blanco, Cape** *headland* Oregon, NW USA *42°49′N 124°33′W*
62 H10 **Blanco, Río** ≈ W Argentina
56 F10 **Blanco, Río** ≈ NE Peru
15 O9 **Blanc, Réservoir** ⊠ Québec, SE Canada
21 R7 **Bland** Virginia, NE USA *37°06′N 81°08′W*
92 I2 **Blanda** ≈ N Iceland
37 O7 **Blanding** Utah, W USA *37°37′N 109°28′W*
105 X5 **Blanes** Cataluña, NE Spain *41°41′N 02°48′E*
103 N3 **Blangy-sur-Bresle** Seine-Maritime, N France *49°55′N 01°37′E*
111 C18 **Blanice** *Ger.* Blanitz. ≈ SE Czech Republic
Blanitz *see* Blanice
99 C16 **Blankenberge** West-Vlaanderen, NW Belgium *51°19′N 03°08′E*
101 D17 **Blankenheim** Nordrhein-Westfalen, W Germany *50°26′N 06°41′E*
25 R8 **Blanket** Texas, SW USA *31°49′N 98°47′W*
55 O3 **Blanquilla, Isla** *var.* La Blanquilla. *island* N Venezuela
Blanquilla, La *see* Blanquilla, Isla
61 F18 **Blanquillo** Durazno, C Uruguay *32°53′S 55°37′W*
111 G18 **Blansko** *Ger.* Blanz. Jihomoravský Kraj, SE Czech Republic *49°22′N 16°39′E*
83 N15 **Blantyre** *var.* Blantyre-Limbe. Southern, S Malawi *15°45′S 35°04′E*
83 N15 **Blantyre** ✈ Southern, S Malawi *15°34′S 35°03′E*
Blantyre-Limbe *see* Blantyre
Blanz *see* Blansko
98 I10 **Blaricum** Noord-Holland, C Netherlands *52°16′N 05°15′E*
Blasendorf *see* Blaj
Blatnitsa *see* Durankulak
113 F15 **Blato** *It.* Blatta. Dubrovnik-Neretva, S Croatia *42°57′N 16°47′E*
Blatta *see* Blato
108 E10 **Blatten** Valais, SW Switzerland *46°22′N 08°00′E*
101 J20 **Blaufelden** Baden-Württemberg, SW Germany *49°21′N 10°01′E*
95 E23 **Blåvands Huk** *headland* W Denmark *55°33′N 08°04′E*
102 G6 **Blavet** ≈ NW France
102 J12 **Blaye** Gironde, SW France *45°08′N 00°40′W*
183 R8 **Blayney** New South Wales, SE Australia *33°33′S 149°13′E*
65 D25 **Bleaker Island** *island* SE Falkland Islands
109 T10 **Bled** *Ger.* Veldes. NW Slovenia *46°23′N 14°06′E*
99 D20 **Bléharies** Hainaut, SW Belgium *50°31′N 03°25′E*
109 U9 **Bleiburg** *Slvn.* Pliberk. Kärnten, S Austria *46°36′N 14°49′E*
101 L17 **Bleiloch-stausee** ⊠ C Germany
98 H12 **Bleiswijk** Zuid-Holland, W Netherlands *52°01′N 04°32′E*
95 L22 **Blekinge** ◆ *county* S Sweden
14 D17 **Blenheim** Ontario, S Canada *42°20′N 81°59′W*
185 K15 **Blenheim** Marlborough, South Island, New Zealand *41°32′S 174°E*
99 M15 **Blerick** Limburg, SE Netherlands *51°22′N 06°10′E*
Blesae *see* Blois
25 V13 **Blessing** Texas, SW USA *28°52′N 96°12′W*
14 I10 **Bleu, Lac** ◎ Québec, SE Canada
Blibba *see* Blitta
120 H10 **Blida** *var.* El Boulaida, El Boulaïda. N Algeria *36°30′N 02°50′E*
95 P15 **Blidö** Stockholm, C Sweden *59°37′N 18°55′E*
95 K18 **Blidsberg** Västra Götaland, S Sweden *57°55′N 13°30′E*
185 A21 **Bligh Sound** *sound* South Island, New Zealand
187 X14 **Bligh Water** *strait* NW Fiji
14 D11 **Blind River** Ontario, S Canada *46°12′N 82°59′W*
31 R11 **Blissfield** Michigan, N USA *41°49′N 83°51′W*
77 R15 **Blitta** *prev.* Blibba. C Togo *08°19′N 00°59′E*
19 O13 **Block Island** *island* Rhode Island, NE USA
19 O13 **Block Island Sound** *sound* Rhode Island, NE USA
98 H10 **Bloemendaal** Noord-Holland, W Netherlands *52°23′N 04°39′E*
83 H23 **Bloemfontein** *var.* Mangaung. ● (South Africa-judicial capital) Free State, C South Africa *29°07′S 26°14′E*
83 I22 **Bloemhof** North-West, NW South Africa *27°39′S 25°37′E*
102 M7 **Blois** *anc.* Blesae. Loir-et-Cher, C France *47°36′N 01°20′E*
98 L8 **Blokzijl** Overijssel, N Netherlands *52°46′N 05°58′E*
95 N20 **Blomstermåla** Kalmar, S Sweden *56°58′N 16°19′E*
92 I2 **Blönduós** Nordhurland Vestra, N Iceland *65°39′N 20°15′W*
110 L11 **Błonie** Mazowieckie, C Poland *52°13′N 20°36′E*
97 C14 **Bloody Foreland** *Ir.* Cnoc Fola. *headland* NW Ireland *55°09′N 08°18′W*
31 N15 **Bloomfield** Indiana, N USA *39°01′N 86°58′W*
29 X16 **Bloomfield** Iowa, C USA *40°45′N 92°24′W*
27 Y8 **Bloomfield** Missouri, C USA *36°54′N 89°58′W*
37 P9 **Bloomfield** New Mexico, SW USA *36°42′N 108°00′W*
25 U7 **Blooming Grove** Texas, SW USA *32°05′N 96°43′W*
29 W10 **Blooming Prairie** Minnesota, N USA *43°52′N 93°03′W*
30 L13 **Bloomington** Illinois, N USA *40°28′N 88°59′W*
31 O15 **Bloomington** Indiana, N USA *39°10′N 86°31′W*
29 V9 **Bloomington** Minnesota, N USA *44°50′N 93°18′W*
25 U13 **Bloomington** Texas, SW USA *28°39′N 96°53′W*
18 H14 **Bloomsburg** Pennsylvania, NE USA *40°59′N 76°27′W*
181 X7 **Bloomsbury** Queensland, NE Australia *20°47′S 148°35′E*
169 R16 **Blora** Jawa, C Indonesia *06°55′S 111°29′E*
18 G12 **Blossburg** Pennsylvania, NE USA *41°38′N 77°00′W*
25 V5 **Blossom** Texas, SW USA *33°39′N 95°23′W*
123 T5 **Blossom, Mys** *headland* Ostrov Vrangelya, NE Russian Federation *70°49′N 178°49′E*
23 R8 **Blountstown** Florida, SE USA *30°26′N 85°03′W*
21 P8 **Blountville** Tennessee, S USA *36°31′N 82°19′W*
21 Q9 **Blowing Rock** North Carolina, SE USA *36°15′N 81°53′W*
108 J8 **Bludenz** Vorarlberg, W Austria *47°10′N 09°50′E*
36 L6 **Blue Bell Knoll** ▲ Utah, W USA *38°11′N 111°31′W*
23 Y12 **Blue Cypress Lake** ◎ Florida, SE USA
29 U11 **Blue Earth** Minnesota, N USA *43°38′N 94°06′W*
21 Q7 **Bluefield** Virginia, NE USA *37°15′N 81°16′W*
21 R7 **Bluefield** West Virginia, NE USA *37°16′N 81°13′W*
43 N10 **Bluefields** Región Autónoma Atlántico Sur, SE Nicaragua *12°01′N 83°47′W*
43 N10 **Bluefields, Bahía de** *bay* W Caribbean Sea
29 Z14 **Blue Grass** Iowa, C USA *41°30′N 90°46′W*
Bluegrass State *see* Kentucky
Blue Hen State *see* Delaware
19 S7 **Blue Hill** Maine, NE USA *44°25′N 68°36′W*
29 P16 **Blue Hill** Nebraska, C USA *40°19′N 98°27′W*
30 J5 **Blue Hills** *hill range* Wisconsin, N USA
34 L3 **Blue Lake** California, W USA *40°52′N 124°00′W*
Blue Law State *see* Connecticut
37 Q6 **Blue Mesa Reservoir** ⊠ Colorado, C USA
27 S12 **Blue Mountain** ▲ Arkansas, C USA *34°42′N 94°04′W*
19 O6 **Blue Mountain** ▲ New Hampshire, NE USA *44°48′N 71°26′W*
18 K8 **Blue Mountain** ▲ New York, NE USA *43°52′N 74°24′W*

◆ Country ● Country Capital ◇ Dependent Territory ○ Dependent Territory Capital ◆ Administrative Regions ✈ International Airport ▲ Mountain ▲▲ Mountain Range Volcano ≈ River ◎ Lake ⊠ Reservoir

BLUE MOUNTAIN – BORBA

18 H15 **Blue Mountain** *ridge* Pennsylvania, NE USA
44 H10 **Blue Mountain Peak** ▲ E Jamaica 18°02′N 76°34′W
183 S8 **Blue Mountains** ▲ New South Wales, SE Australia
32 L11 **Blue Mountains** ▲ Oregon/ Washington, NW USA
80 G12 **Blue Nile** ◆ *state* E Sudan
80 H12 **Blue Nile** *var.* Abai, Bahr el, Azraq, *Amh.* Ābay Wenz, *Ar.* An Nīl al Azraq. River Ethiopia/ Sudan
8 J7 **Bluenose Lake** ◎ Nunavut, NW Canada
27 O3 **Blue Rapids** Kansas, C USA 39°39′N 96°38′W
23 S1 **Blue Ridge** Georgia, SE USA 34°51′N 84°19′W
17 S11 **Blue Ridge** *var.* Blue Ridge Mountains. ▲ North Carolina/Virginia, USA
23 S1 **Blue Ridge Lake** ⊠ Georgia, SE USA
Blue Ridge Mountains *see* Blue Ridge
11 N15 **Blue River** British Columbia, SW Canada 52°03′N 119°21′W
27 O12 **Blue River** River Oklahoma, C USA
27 R4 **Blue Springs** Missouri, C USA 39°01′N 94°16′W
21 R6 **Bluestone Lake** ⊠ West Virginia, NE USA
185 C25 **Bluff** Southland, South Island, New Zealand 46°36′S 168°22′E
37 O8 **Bluff** Utah, W USA 37°15′N 109°36′W
21 P8 **Bluff City** Tennessee, S USA 36°28′N 82°15′W
65 E24 **Bluff Cove** East Falkland, Falkland Islands 51°45′S 58°11′W
25 S7 **Bluff Dale** Texas, SW USA 32°18′N 98°01′W
183 N15 **Bluff Hill Point** *headland* Tasmania, SE Australia 41°03′S 144°35′E
31 Q12 **Bluffton** Indiana, N USA 40°44′N 85°10′W
31 R12 **Bluffton** Ohio, N USA 40°54′N 83°53′W
25 T7 **Blum** Texas, SW USA 32°08′N 97°24′W
101 G24 **Blumberg** Baden-Württemberg, SW Germany 47°48′N 08°31′E
60 K13 **Blumenau** Santa Catarina, S Brazil 26°55′S 49°07′W
29 N9 **Blunt** South Dakota, N USA 44°30′N 99°58′E
32 H15 **Bly** Oregon, NW USA 42°22′N 121°04′W
39 R13 **Blying Sound** *sound* Alaska, USA
97 M14 **Blyth** N England, United Kingdom 55°07′N 01°30′W
35 Y16 **Blythe** California, W USA 33°35′N 114°36′W
27 Y9 **Blytheville** Arkansas, C USA 35°56′N 89°55′W
117 V7 **Blyznyuky** Kharkivs'ka Oblast', E Ukraine 48°51′N 36°32′E
95 G16 **Bø** Telemark, S Norway 59°24′N 09°04′E
76 I15 **Bo** S Sierra Leone 07°58′N 11°45′W
171 O4 **Boac** Marinduque, N Philippines 13°26′N 121°50′E
42 K10 **Boaco** Boaco, S Nicaragua 12°28′N 85°45′W
42 J10 **Boaco** ◆ *department* C Nicaragua
79 I15 **Boali** Ombella-Mpoko, SW Central African Republic 04°52′N 18°00′E
Boalsert *see* Bolsward
31 V12 **Boardman** Ohio, N USA 41°01′N 80°39′W
32 J11 **Boardman** Oregon, NW USA 45°50′N 119°42′W
14 F13 **Boat Lake** ◎ Ontario, S Canada
58 F10 **Boa Vista** *state capital* Roraima, NW Brazil 02°51′N 60°43′W
76 D9 **Boa Vista** *island* Ilhas de Barlavento, E Cape Verde
23 Q2 **Boaz** Alabama, S USA 34°12′N 86°10′W
160 L15 **Bobai** Guangxi Zhuangzu Zizhiqu, S China 22°09′N 109°57′E
172 J1 **Bobaomby, Tanjona** *Fr.* Cap d'Ambre. *headland* N Madagascar 11°58′S 49°13′E
155 M14 **Bobbili** Andhra Pradesh, E India 18°32′N 83°29′E
106 D9 **Bobbio** Emilia-Romagna, C Italy 44°48′N 09°27′E
14 I14 **Bobcaygeon** Ontario, SE Canada 44°32′N 78°33′W
Bober *see* Bóbr
103 O5 **Bobigny** Seine-St-Denis, N France 48°55′N 02°27′E
77 N13 **Bobo-Dioulasso** SW Burkina 11°12′N 04°21′W
110 G8 **Bobolice** *Ger.* Bublitz. Zachodnio-pomorskie, NW Poland 53°56′N 16°37′E
83 J19 **Bobonong** Central, E Botswana 21°58′S 28°26′E
171 R11 **Bobopayo** Pulau Halmahera, E Indonesia 01°07′N 127°26′E
113 J15 **Bobotov Kuk** ▲ N Montenegro 43°06′N 19°00′E
114 G10 **Bobovdol** Kyustendil, W Bulgaria 42°21′N 22°59′E
119 M15 **Bobr** Minskaya Voblasts', NW Belarus 54°20′N 29°16′E
119 M15 **Bobr** River C Belarus
111 E14 **Bóbr** *Eng.* Bobrawa, *Ger.* Bober. River SW Poland
Bobrawa *see* Bóbr
Bobrik *see* Bobryk
Bobrinets *see* Bobrynets'
Bobrka/Bóbrka *see* Bibrka
126 L8 **Bobrov** Voronezhskaya Oblast', W Russian Federation 51°10′N 40°03′E
117 Q4 **Bobrovytsya** Chernihivs'ka Oblast', N Ukraine 50°43′N 31°24′E
Bobruysk *see* Babruysk
119 J19 **Bobryk** *Rus.* Bobrik. River SW Belarus
117 Q8 **Bobrynets'** *Rus.* Bobrinets. Kirovohrads'ka Oblast', C Ukraine 48°02′N 32°10′E
14 K14 **Bobs Lake** ◎ Ontario, SE Canada
54 I6 **Bobures** Zulia, NW Venezuela 09°15′N 71°10′W
42 H1 **Boca Bacalar Chico** *headland* N Belize 15°05′N 82°12′W
112 G11 **Bočac** ◆ Republika Srpska, NW Bosnia and Herzegovina
41 R14 **Boca del Río** Veracruz-Llave, S Mexico 19°08′N 96°08′W
55 O4 **Boca de Pozo** Nueva Esparta, NE Venezuela 11°00′N 64°23′W
59 C15 **Boca do Acre** Amazonas, N Brazil 08°45′S 67°23′W
55 N12 **Boca Mavaca** Amazonas, S Venezuela 02°30′N 65°11′W
79 G14 **Bocaranga** Ouham-Pendé, W Central African Republic 07°07′N 15°40′E
23 Z15 **Boca Raton** Florida, SE USA 26°22′N 80°05′W
43 P14 **Bocas del Toro** Bocas del Toro, NW Panama 09°20′N 82°15′W
43 P15 **Bocas del Toro** *off.* Provincia de Bocas del Toro. ◆ *province* NW Panama
43 P15 **Bocas del Toro, Archipiélago de** *island group* NW Panama
Bocas del Toro, Provincia de *see* Bocas del Toro
42 L7 **Bocay** Jinotega, N Nicaragua 14°19′N 85°08′W
105 N6 **Boceguillas** Castilla-León, N Spain 41°20′N 03°39′W
Bocheykovo *see* Bacheykava
111 L17 **Bochnia** Małopolskie, SE Poland 49°58′N 20°27′E
99 K16 **Bocholt** Limburg, NE Belgium 51°10′N 05°37′E
101 D14 **Bocholt** Nordrhein-Westfalen, W Germany 51°50′N 06°37′E
101 E15 **Bochum** Nordrhein-Westfalen, W Germany 51°29′N 07°13′E
103 Y15 **Bocognano** Corse, France, C Mediterranean Sea 42°04′N 09°03′E
54 I6 **Boconó** Trujillo, NW Venezuela 09°17′N 70°17′W
116 F12 **Bocşa** *Ger.* Bokschen, *Hung.* Boksánbánya. Caraş-Severin, SW Romania 45°23′N 21°47′E
79 H15 **Boda** Lobaye, SW Central African Republic 04°17′N 17°25′E
94 L12 **Böda** Dalarna, C Sweden 61°00′N 15°15′E
95 O20 **Böda** Kalmar, S Sweden 57°16′N 17°04′E
95 L19 **Bodafors** Jönköping, S Sweden 57°30′N 14°40′E
123 O12 **Bodaybo** Irkutskaya Oblast', E Russian Federation 57°52′N 114°05′E
22 G5 **Bodcau, Bayou** *var.* Bodcau Creek. River Louisiana, S USA
Bodcau Creek *see* Bodcau, Bayou
44 D8 **Bodden Town** *var.* Boddentown. Grand Cayman, SW Cayman Islands 19°20′N 81°14′W
Boddentown *see* Bodden Town
101 K14 **Bode** River C Germany
34 L7 **Bodega Head** *headland* California, W USA 38°16′N 123°04′W
Bodegas *see* Babahoyo
98 H11 **Bodegraven** Zuid-Holland, C Netherlands 52°05′N 04°45′E
78 H8 **Bodélé** *depression* W Chad
92 J13 **Boden** Norrbotten, N Sweden 65°50′N 21°44′E
Bodensee *see* Constance, Lake, C Europe
65 M15 **Bode Verde Fracture Zone** *tectonic feature* E Atlantic Ocean
155 H14 **Bodhan** Andhra Pradesh, C India 18°40′N 77°51′E
Bodī *see* Jinst
155 H22 **Bodināyakkanūr** Tamil Nādu, SE India 10°02′N 77°18′E
108 H10 **Bodio** Ticino, S Switzerland 46°23′N 08°55′E
Bodjonegoro *see* Bojonegoro
97 I24 **Bodmin** SW England, United Kingdom 50°29′N 04°43′W
97 I24 **Bodmin Moor** *moorland* SW England, United Kingdom
92 G12 **Bodø** Nordland, C Norway 67°17′N 14°22′E
59 H20 **Bodoquena, Serra da** ▲ SW Brazil
136 B16 **Bodrum** Muğla, SW Turkey 37°01′N 27°28′E
Bodzafordulő *see* Întorsura Buzăului
99 L14 **Boekel** Noord-Brabant, SE Netherlands 51°35′N 05°42′E
Boeloekoemba *see* Bulukumba
103 Q11 **Boën** Loire, E France 45°45′N 04°01′E
79 K18 **Boende** Equateur, C Dem. Rep. Congo 0°12′S 20°54′E
25 R11 **Boerne** Texas, SW USA 29°47′N 98°44′W
Boeroe *see* Buru, Pulau
Boetoeng *see* Buton, Pulau
22 I5 **Boeuf River** River Arkansas/ Louisiana, S USA
76 H14 **Boffa** W Guinea 10°12′N 14°02′W
Bó Finne, Inis *see* Inishbofin
Boga *see* Bogë
166 L9 **Bogale** Ayeyarwady, SW Burma (Myanmar) 16°16′N 95°21′E
22 L8 **Bogalusa** Louisiana, S USA 30°47′N 89°51′W
77 Q12 **Bogandé** C Burkina 13°02′N 00°08′W
79 I15 **Bogangolo** Ombella-Mpoko, C Central African Republic 05°36′N 18°17′E
183 Q7 **Bogan River** River New South Wales, SE Australia
25 W5 **Bogata** Texas, SW USA 33°28′N 95°12′W
111 D14 **Bogatynia** *Ger.* Reichenau. Dolnośląskie, SW Poland 50°53′N 14°55′E
136 K13 **Boğazlıyan** Yozgat, C Turkey 39°13′N 35°17′E
79 J17 **Bogbonga** Equateur, NW Dem. Rep. Congo 01°36′N 19°24′E
158 J14 **Bogcang Zangbo** River W China
162 I9 **Bogd** *var.* Horiult. Bayanhongor, C Mongolia 45°09′N 100°50′E
162 J10 **Bogd** *var.* Hovd. Övörhangay, C Mongolia 44°43′N 102°08′E
158 L5 **Bogda Feng** ▲ NW China 43°51′N 88°14′E
114 I9 **Bogdan** ▲ C Bulgaria 42°37′N 24°28′E
113 Q20 **Bogdanci** SE FYR Macedonia 41°12′N 22°34′E
158 M5 **Bogda Shan** *var.* Po-ko-to Shan. ▲ NW China
113 K17 **Bogë** *var.* Boga. Shkodër, N Albania 42°25′N 19°38′E
Bogeda'er *see* Wenquan
Bogendorf *see* Łuków
95 G23 **Bogense** Fyn, C Denmark 55°34′N 10°06′E
183 T3 **Boggabilla** New South Wales, SE Australia 28°37′S 150°21′E
183 S6 **Boggabri** New South Wales, SE Australia 30°44′S 150°00′E
186 D6 **Bogia** Madang, N Papua New Guinea 04°16′S 144°56′E
97 N23 **Bognor Regis** SE England, United Kingdom 50°47′N 00°41′W
Bogodukhov *see* Bohodukhiv
181 V15 **Bogong, Mount** ▲ Victoria, SE Australia 36°43′S 147°19′E
169 O16 **Bogor** *Dut.* Buitenzorg. Jawa, C Indonesia 06°34′S 106°45′E
126 L5 **Bogoroditsk** Tul'skaya Oblast', W Russian Federation 53°46′N 38°09′E
127 O3 **Bogorodsk** Nizhegorodskaya Oblast', W Russian Federation 56°06′N 43°29′E
Bogorodskoje *see* Bogorodskoye
123 S12 **Bogorodskoye** Khabarovskiy Kray, SE Russian Federation 52°22′N 140°33′E
125 R15 **Bogorodskoye** *var.* Bogorodskoje. Kirovskaya Oblast', NW Russian Federation 57°50′N 50°41′E
54 F10 **Bogotá** *prev.* Santa Fe, Santa Fe de Bogotá. ● (Colombia) Cundinamarca, C Colombia 04°38′N 74°05′W
153 T14 **Bogra** Rajshahi, N Bangladesh 24°52′N 89°28′E
Bogschan *see* Boldu
122 L12 **Boguchany** Krasnoyarskiy Kray, C Russian Federation 58°20′N 97°20′E
126 M9 **Boguchar** Voronezhskaya Oblast', W Russian Federation 49°57′N 40°34′E
76 H10 **Bogué** Brakna, SW Mauritania 16°36′N 14°15′W
22 K8 **Bogue Chitto** River Louisiana/ Mississippi, S USA
Bogushëvsk *see* Bahushewsk
Boguslav *see* Bohuslav
44 K12 **Bog Walk** C Jamaica 18°06′N 77°01′W
161 Q3 **Bo Hai** *var.* Gulf of Chihli. *gulf* NE China
161 R3 **Bohai Haixia** *strait* NE China
161 Q3 **Bohai Wan** *bay* NE China
111 C17 **Bohemia** *Cz.* Čechy, *Ger.* Böhmen. W Czech Republic
111 B18 **Bohemian Forest** *Cz.* Ceský Les, Šumava, *Ger.* Böhmerwald. ▲ C Europe
Bohemian-Moravian Highlands *see* Českomoravská Vrchovina
77 R16 **Bohicon** S Benin 07°14′N 02°04′E
109 S11 **Bohinjska Bistrica** *Ger.* Wocheiner Feistritz. NW Slovenia 46°16′N 13°55′E
Bohkká *see* Pokka
Böhmen *see* Bohemia
Böhmerwald *see* Bohemian Forest
Böhmisch-Krumau *see* Český Krumlov
Böhmisch-Leipa *see* Česká Lípa
Böhmisch-Mährische Höhe *see* Českomoravská Vrchovina
Böhmisch-Trübau *see* Česká Třebová
117 U5 **Bohodukhiv** *Rus.* Bogodukhov. Kharkivs'ka Oblast', E Ukraine 50°10′N 35°32′E
171 Q6 **Bohol** *island* C Philippines
171 Q7 **Bohol Sea** *var.* Mindanao Sea. *sea* S Philippines
116 I7 **Bohorodchany** Ivano-Frankivs'ka Oblast', W Ukraine 48°46′N 24°31′E
Böhöt *see* Öndörshil
158 K6 **Bohu** *var.* Bagrax. Xinjiang Uygur Zizhiqu, NW China 42°00′N 86°28′E
111 I17 **Bohumín** *Ger.* Oderberg; *prev.* Neuoderberg, Nový Bohumín. Moravskoslezský Kraj, E Czech Republic 49°55′N 18°20′E
117 P6 **Bohuslav** *Rus.* Boguslav. Kyyivs'ka Oblast', N Ukraine 49°33′N 30°53′E
58 F11 **Boiaçu** Roraima, N Brazil 0°27′S 61°46′W
107 K16 **Boiano** Molise, C Italy 41°28′N 14°28′E
15 R8 **Boilleau** Québec, SE Canada 48°06′N 70°49′W
59 O17 **Boipeba, Ilha de** *island* SE Brazil
104 G3 **Boiro** Galicia, NW Spain 42°39′N 08°53′W
31 Q5 **Bois Blanc Island** *island* Michigan, N USA
29 R7 **Bois de Sioux River** River Minnesota, N USA
33 N14 **Boise** *var.* Boise City. *state capital* Idaho, NW USA 43°39′N 116°14′W
26 G8 **Boise City** Oklahoma, C USA 36°44′N 102°31′W
Boise City *see* Boise
33 N14 **Boise River, Middle Fork** River Idaho, NW USA
Bois, Lac des *see* Woods, Lake of the
Bois-le-Duc *see* 's-Hertogenbosch
11 W17 **Boissevain** Manitoba, S Canada 49°14′N 100°02′W
15 T7 **Boisvert, Pointe au** *headland* Québec, SE Canada 48°34′N 69°07′W
100 K10 **Boizenburg** Mecklenburg-Vorpommern, N Germany 53°23′N 10°43′E
Bojador *see* Boujdour
113 K18 **Bojana** *Alb.* Bunë. River Albania/Montenegro *see also* Bunë
Bojana *see* Bunë
143 S3 **Bojnūrd** *var.* Bujnurd. Khorāsān-e Shemālī, N Iran 37°31′N 57°24′E
169 R16 **Bojonegoro** *prev.* Bodjonegoro. Jawa, C Indonesia 07°06′S 111°50′E
189 T1 **Bokaak Atoll** *var.* Bokak, Taongi. *atoll* Ratak Chain, NE Marshall Islands
Bokak *see* Bokaak Atoll
146 K8 **Bo'kantov Tog'lari** *Rus.* Gory Bukantau. ▲ N Uzbekistan
153 Q15 **Bokāro** Jhārkhand, N India 23°46′N 85°55′E
79 I18 **Bokatola** Equateur, NW Dem. Rep. Congo 0°37′S 18°45′E
76 H13 **Boké** W Guinea 10°56′N 14°18′W
Bokhara *see* Buxoro
183 Q4 **Bokharra River** River New South Wales/Queensland, SE Australia
95 C16 **Boknafjorden** *fjord* S Norway
78 H11 **Bokoro** Chari-Baguirmi, W Chad 12°23′N 17°03′E
79 K19 **Bokota** Equateur, NW Dem. Rep. Congo 0°56′S 22°24′E
167 N13 **Bokpyin** Tanintharyi, S Burma (Myanmar) 11°16′N 98°47′E
Boksánbánya/Bokschen *see* Bocşa
124 I13 **Boksitogorsk** Leningradskaya Oblast', NW Russian Federation 59°27′N 33°51′E
83 F21 **Bokspits** Kgalagadi, SW Botswana 26°50′S 20°41′E
79 K18 **Bokungu** Equateur, C Dem. Rep. Congo 0°41′S 22°19′E
146 F12 **Bokurdak** *Rus.* Bakhardok. Ahal Welaýaty, C Turkmenistan 38°51′N 58°34′E
78 G10 **Bol** Lac, W Chad 13°27′N 14°40′E
76 G13 **Bolama** SW Guinea-Bissau 11°35′N 15°30′W
Bolangir *see* Balāngīr
Bolanos *see* Bolanos, Mount, Guam
Bolaños *see* Bolaños de Calatrava, Spain
105 N11 **Bolaños de Calatrava** *var.* Bolaños. Castilla-La Mancha, C Spain 38°55′N 03°39′W
188 B17 **Bolanos, Mount** *var.* Bolanos. ▲ S Guam 13°18′N 144°41′E
40 L12 **Bolaños, Río** River C Mexico
115 M14 **Bolayır** Çanakkale, NW Turkey 40°31′N 26°46′E
102 L3 **Bolbec** Seine-Maritime, N France 49°34′N 00°31′E
116 L13 **Boldu** *var.* Bogschan. Buzău, SE Romania 45°18′N 27°15′E
146 H8 **Boldumsaz** *prev.* Kalinin, Kalininsk, Porsy. Daşoguz Welaýaty, N Turkmenistan 42°12′N 59°33′E
158 I4 **Bole** *var.* Bortala. Xinjiang Uygur Zizhiqu, NW China 44°52′N 82°06′E
77 O15 **Bole** NW Ghana 09°02′N 02°29′W
79 J19 **Boleko** Equateur, W Dem. Rep. Congo 01°27′S 19°52′E
111 E14 **Bolesławiec** *Ger.* Bunzlau. Dolnośląskie, SW Poland 51°16′N 15°34′E
127 R4 **Bolgar** *prev.* Kuybyshev. Respublika Tatarstan, W Russian Federation 54°58′N 49°03′E
77 P14 **Bolgatanga** N Ghana 10°45′N 00°52′W
Bolgrad *see* Bolhrad
117 N12 **Bolhrad** *Rus.* Bolgrad. Odes'ka Oblast', SW Ukraine 45°42′N 28°35′E
163 Y8 **Boli** Heilongjiang, NE China 45°45′N 130°32′E
79 I19 **Bolia** Bandundu, W Dem. Rep. Congo 01°34′S 18°24′E
93 J14 **Boliden** Västerbotten, N Sweden 64°52′N 20°20′E
171 T13 **Bolifar** Pulau Seram, E Indonesia 03°08′S 130°34′E
171 N2 **Bolinao** Luzon, N Philippines 16°22′N 119°52′E
54 C12 **Bolívar** Cauca, SW Colombia 01°52′N 76°56′W
27 T6 **Bolivar** Missouri, C USA 37°37′N 93°25′W
20 F10 **Bolivar** Tennessee, S USA 35°17′N 88°59′W
54 F7 **Bolívar** *off.* Departmento de Bolívar. ◆ *province* N Colombia
56 A13 **Bolívar** ◆ *province* C Ecuador
55 N9 **Bolívar** *off.* Estado Bolívar. ◆ *state* SE Venezuela
Bolívar, Departmento de *see* Bolívar
Bolívar, Estado *see* Bolívar
25 X12 **Bolivar Peninsula** *headland* Texas, SW USA 29°26′N 94°41′W
54 I6 **Bolívar, Pico** ▲ W Venezuela 08°33′N 71°05′W
57 K17 **Bolivia** *off.* Republic of Bolivia. ◆ *republic* W South America
Bolivia, Republic of *see* Bolivia
112 O13 **Boljevac** Serbia, E Serbia 43°50′N 21°57′E
Bolkenhain *see* Bolków
126 J5 **Bolkhov** Orlovskaya Oblast', W Russian Federation 53°28′N 36°00′E
111 F14 **Bolków** *Ger.* Bolkenhain. Dolnośląskie, SW Poland 50°55′N 15°49′E
182 K3 **Bollards Lagoon** South Australia 28°58′S 140°52′E
103 R14 **Bollène** Vaucluse, SE France 44°16′N 04°45′E
94 N12 **Bollnäs** Gävleborg, C Sweden 61°18′N 16°27′E
181 W10 **Bollon** Queensland, C Australia 28°07′S 147°28′E
192 L12 **Bollons Tablemount** *undersea feature* S Pacific Ocean 49°40′S 176°10′W
93 H17 **Bollstabruk** Västernorrland, C Sweden 63°00′N 17°41′E
Bolluilos de Par del Condado *see* Bollulos Par del Condado
104 J14 **Bollulos Par del Condado** *var.* Bolluilos de Par del Condado. Andalucía, S Spain 37°20′N 06°32′W
95 K21 **Bolmen** ◎ S Sweden
137 T10 **Bolnisi** S Georgia 41°28′N 44°34′E
79 H19 **Bolobo** Bandundu, W Dem. Rep. Congo 02°10′S 16°17′E
106 G10 **Bologna** Emilia-Romagna, N Italy 44°30′N 11°20′E
124 I15 **Bologoye** Tverskaya Oblast', W Russian Federation 57°54′N 34°04′E
79 J18 **Bolomba** Equateur, NW Dem. Rep. Congo 0°27′N 19°13′E
41 X13 **Bolonchén de Rejón** *var.* Bolonchén de Rejón. Campeche, SE Mexico 20°00′N 89°34′W
114 J13 **Bolоústra, Akrotírio** *headland* NE Greece 40°56′N 24°58′E
167 L8 **Bolovens, Plateau des** *plateau* S Laos
106 H13 **Bolsena** Lazio, C Italy 42°39′N 11°59′E
107 G14 **Bolsena, Lago di** ◎ C Italy
126 B3 **Bol'shakovo** *Ger.* Kreuzingen; *prev.* Gross-Skaisgirren. Kaliningradskaya Oblast', W Russian Federation 54°53′N 21°38′E
Bol'shaya Berëstovitsa *see* Vyalikaya Byerastavitsa
127 S7 **Bol'shaya Chernigovka** Samarskaya Oblast', W Russian Federation 52°07′N 50°49′E
127 S7 **Bol'shaya Glushitsa** Samarskaya Oblast', W Russian Federation 52°22′N 50°29′E
124 J4 **Bol'shaya Imandra, Ozero** ◎ NW Russian Federation
144 H9 **Bol'shaya Khobda** *Kaz.* Ülkenqobda. River Kazakhstan/ Russian Federation
126 M12 **Bol'shaya Martynovka** Rostovskaya Oblast', SW Russian Federation 47°19′N 41°40′E
122 K12 **Bol'shaya Murta** Krasnoyarskiy Kray, C Russian Federation 56°51′N 93°10′E
125 V4 **Bol'shaya Rogovaya** River NW Russian Federation
125 U7 **Bol'shaya Synya** River NW Russian Federation
145 V9 **Bol'shaya Vladimirovka** Vostochnyy Kazakhstan, E Kazakhstan 50°53′N 79°29′E
123 V11 **Bol'sheretsk** Kamchatskaya Oblast', E Russian Federation 52°20′N 156°24′E
127 W3 **Bol'sheust'ikinskoye** Respublika Bashkortostan, W Russian Federation 56°00′N 58°13′E
Bol'shevik *see* Bal'shavik
122 L5 **Bol'shevik, Ostrov** *island* Severnaya Zemlya, N Russian Federation
125 U4 **Bol'shezemel'skaya Tundra** *physical region* NW Russian Federation
144 J13 **Bol'shiye Barsuki, Peski** *desert* SW Kazakhstan
123 T7 **Bol'shoy Anyuy** River NE Russian Federation
123 N7 **Bol'shoy Begichev, Ostrov** *island* NE Russian Federation
123 S15 **Bol'shoye Kamen'** Primorskiy Kray, SE Russian Federation 43°06′N 132°21′E
127 O4 **Bol'shoye Murashkino** Nizhegorodskaya Oblast', W Russian Federation 55°46′N 44°48′E
127 W4 **Bol'shoy Iremel'** ▲ W Russian Federation 54°31′N 58°47′E
127 R7 **Bol'shoy Irgiz** River W Russian Federation
123 Q6 **Bol'shoy Lyakhovskiy, Ostrov** *island* NE Russian Federation
123 Q11 **Bol'shoy Nimnyr** Respublika Sakha (Yakutiya), NE Russian Federation 57°55′N 125°34′E
Bol'shoy Rozhan *see* Vyaliki Rozhan
144 E10 **Bol'shoy Uzen'** *Kaz.* Ülkenözen. River Kazakhstan/ Russian Federation
40 K6 **Bolson de Mapimi** ▲ NW Mexico
98 K6 **Bolsward** *Fris.* Boalsert. Friesland, N Netherlands 53°04′N 05°31′E
105 T4 **Boltaña** Aragón, NE Spain 42°28′N 00°02′E
14 G15 **Bolton** Ontario, S Canada 43°52′N 79°45′W
97 K17 **Bolton** *prev.* Bolton-le-Moors. NW England, United Kingdom 53°35′N 02°26′W
21 V12 **Bolton** North Carolina, SE USA 34°22′N 78°26′W
Bolton-le-Moors *see* Bolton
136 G11 **Bolu** Bolu, NW Turkey 40°45′N 31°38′E
136 G11 **Bolu** ◆ *province* NW Turkey
186 G9 **Bolubolu** Goodenough Island, S Papua New Guinea 09°22′S 150°22′E
92 H1 **Bolungarvík** Vestfirdhir, NW Iceland 66°09′N 23°17′W
159 O10 **Boluntay** Qinghai, W China 36°30′N 92°11′E
159 P8 **Boluozhuanjing**, Aksay Kazakzu Zizhixian. Gansu, N China 39°25′N 94°09′E
136 F14 **Bolvadin** Afyon, W Turkey 38°43′N 31°02′E
114 M10 **Bolyarovo** *prev.* Pashkeni. Yambol, E Bulgaria 42°09′N 26°49′E
106 G6 **Bolzano** *Ger.* Bozen; *anc.* Bauzanum. Trentino-Alto Adige, N Italy 46°30′N 11°22′E
79 F22 **Boma** Bas-Congo, W Dem. Rep. Congo 05°42′S 13°05′E
183 R12 **Bombala** New South Wales, SE Australia 36°54′S 149°15′E
104 F10 **Bombarral** Leiria, C Portugal 39°15′N 09°09′W
Bombay *see* Mumbai
171 U13 **Bomberai, Semenanjung** *cape* Papua, E Indonesia
81 F18 **Bombo** S Uganda 0°36′N 32°33′E
162 I8 **Bömbögör** *var.* Dzadgay. Bayanhongor, C Mongolia 46°12′N 99°29′E
79 I17 **Bomboma** Equateur, NW Dem. Rep. Congo 02°23′N 19°03′E
59 I14 **Bom Futuro** Pará, N Brazil 06°27′S 54°44′W
159 Q15 **Bomi** *var.* Bowo, Zhamo. Xizang Zizhiqu, W China 29°43′N 96°12′E
79 N17 **Bomili** Orientale, NE Dem. Rep. Congo 01°45′N 27°01′E
59 N17 **Bom Jesus da Lapa** Bahia, E Brazil 13°16′S 43°23′W
60 Q8 **Bom Jesus do Itabapoana** Rio de Janeiro, SE Brazil 21°07′S 41°43′W
95 C15 **Bømlafjorden** *fjord* S Norway
95 B15 **Bømlo** *island* S Norway
12 Q12 **Bomnak** Amurskaya Oblast', SE Russian Federation 54°43′N 128°50′E
79 I17 **Bomongo** Equateur, NW Dem. Rep. Congo 01°22′N 18°21′E
61 K14 **Bom Retiro** Santa Catarina, S Brazil 27°45′S 49°31′W
79 L15 **Bomu** *var.* Mbomou, Mbomu, M'Bomu. River Central African Republic/ Dem. Rep. Congo
142 J3 **Bonāb** *var.* Benāb, Bunab. Āžarbāyjān-e Sharqī, N Iran 37°30′N 46°03′E
45 Q16 **Bonaire** *island* E Netherlands Antilles
39 U11 **Bona, Mount** ▲ Alaska, USA 61°22′N 141°45′W
183 Q12 **Bonang** Victoria, SE Australia 37°13′S 148°43′E
42 L7 **Bonanza** Región Autónoma Atlántico Norte, NE Nicaragua 13°59′N 84°30′W
37 O4 **Bonanza** Utah, W USA 40°01′N 109°12′W
45 O9 **Bonao** C Dominican Republic 18°55′N 70°25′W
180 L3 **Bonaparte Archipelago** *island group* Western Australia
32 K6 **Bonaparte, Mount** ▲ Washington, NW USA 48°47′N 119°07′W
39 N11 **Bonasila Dome** ▲ Alaska, USA 62°24′N 160°28′W
45 T15 **Bonasse** Trinidad, Trinidad and Tobago 10°02′N 61°48′W
15 X7 **Bonaventure** Québec, SE Canada 48°03′N 65°30′W
15 X7 **Bonaventure** River Québec, SE Canada
13 V11 **Bonavista** Newfoundland, Newfoundland and Labrador, SE Canada 48°38′N 53°08′W
13 U11 **Bonavista Bay** *inlet* NW Atlantic Ocean
79 E19 **Bonda** Ogooué-Lolo, C Gabon 0°50′S 12°28′E
127 N6 **Bondari** Tambovskaya Oblast', W Russian Federation 52°58′N 42°02′E
106 G9 **Bondeno** Emilia-Romagna, C Italy 44°53′N 11°24′E
30 L4 **Bond Falls Flowage** ◎ Michigan, N USA
79 L16 **Bondo** Orientale, N Dem. Rep. Congo 03°52′N 23°41′E
171 N17 **Bondokodi** Pulau Sumba, S Indonesia 09°36′S 119°01′E
77 O15 **Bondoukou** E Ivory Coast 08°03′N 02°45′W
Bondoukoui/Bondoukuy *see* Boundoukui
169 T17 **Bondowoso** Jawa, C Indonesia 07°54′S 113°50′E
33 S14 **Bondurant** Wyoming, C USA 43°14′N 110°26′W
Bône *see* Annaba, Algeria
Bone *see* Watampone, Indonesia
30 I5 **Bone Lake** ◎ Wisconsin, N USA
171 P14 **Bonelipu** Pulau Buton, C Indonesia 04°42′S 123°09′E
171 O15 **Bonerate, Kepulauan** *var.* Macan. *island group* C Indonesia
29 O12 **Bonesteel** South Dakota, N USA 43°01′N 98°55′W
62 I8 **Bonete, Cerro** ▲ N Argentina 27°58′S 68°22′W
171 O14 **Bone, Teluk** *bay* Sulawesi, C Indonesia
108 D6 **Bonfol** Jura, NW Switzerland 47°28′N 07°08′E
153 U12 **Bongaigaon** Assam, NE India 26°30′N 90°31′E
79 K17 **Bongandanga** Equateur, NW Dem. Rep. Congo 01°28′N 21°03′E
78 L13 **Bongo, Massif des** *var.* Chaîne des Mongos. ▲ NE Central African Republic
78 G12 **Bongor** Mayo-Kébbi, SW Chad 10°18′N 15°20′E
77 N16 **Bongouanou** E Ivory Coast 06°39′N 04°12′W
167 V11 **Bông Sơn** *var.* Hoai Nhơn. Bình Định, C Vietnam 14°28′N 109°00′E
25 U5 **Bonham** Texas, SW USA 33°36′N 96°12′W
Bonhard *see* Bonyhád
103 U6 **Bonhomme, Col du** *pass* NE France
103 Y16 **Bonifacio** Corse, France, C Mediterranean Sea 41°24′N 09°09′E
Bonifacio, Bocche de/ Bonifacio, Bouches de *see* Bonifacio, Strait of
103 Y16 **Bonifacio, Strait of** *Fr.* Bouches de Bonifacio, *It.* Bocche di Bonifacio. *strait* C Mediterranean Sea
23 Q8 **Bonifay** Florida, SE USA 30°49′N 85°42′W
Bonin Islands *see* Ogasawara-shotō
192 H5 **Bonin Trench** *undersea feature* NW Pacific Ocean
23 W15 **Bonita Springs** Florida, SE USA 26°19′N 81°48′W
42 I5 **Bonito, Pico** ▲ N Honduras 15°33′N 86°55′W
101 E17 **Bonn** Nordrhein-Westfalen, W Germany 50°44′N 07°06′E
92 H11 **Bonnåsjøen** Nordland, C Norway 67°35′N 15°39′E
14 J12 **Bonnechere** Ontario, SE Canada 45°39′N 77°36′W
14 J12 **Bonnechere** River Ontario, SE Canada
33 N7 **Bonners Ferry** Idaho, NW USA 48°41′N 116°19′W
27 R4 **Bonner Springs** Kansas, C USA 39°03′N 94°52′W
102 L6 **Bonnétable** Sarthe, NW France 48°09′N 00°24′E
27 X6 **Bonne Terre** Missouri, C USA 37°55′N 90°33′W
10 J5 **Bonnet Plume** River Yukon Territory, NW Canada
102 M6 **Bonneval** Eure-et-Loir, C France 48°12′N 01°23′E
103 T10 **Bonneville** Haute-Savoie, E France 46°05′N 06°25′E
36 J3 **Bonneville Salt Flats** *salt flat* Utah, W USA
77 U18 **Bonny** Rivers, S Nigeria 04°25′N 07°13′E
Bonny, Bight of *see* Biafra, Bight of
37 W4 **Bonny Reservoir** ⊠ Colorado, C USA
11 R14 **Bonnyville** Alberta, SW Canada 54°16′N 110°46′W
107 C18 **Bono** Sardegna, Italy, C Mediterranean Sea 40°24′N 09°01′E
Bononia *see* Vidin, Bulgaria
Bononia *see* Boulogne-sur-Mer, France
107 B18 **Bonorva** Sardegna, Italy, C Mediterranean Sea 40°27′N 08°46′E
30 M15 **Bonpas Creek** River Illinois, N USA
190 I3 **Bonriki** Tarawa, W Kiribati 01°23′N 173°09′E
183 T4 **Bonshaw** New South Wales, SE Australia 29°06′S 151°15′E
76 I16 **Bonthe** SW Sierra Leone 07°32′N 12°30′W
171 N2 **Bontoc** Luzon, N Philippines 17°04′N 120°58′E
25 Y9 **Bon Wier** Texas, SW USA 30°43′N 93°40′W
111 J25 **Bonyhád** *Ger.* Bonhard. Tolna, S Hungary 46°20′N 18°31′E
Bonzabaai *see* Bonza Bay
83 J25 **Bonza Bay** *Afr.* Bonzabaai. Eastern Cape, S South Africa 32°58′S 27°58′E
182 D7 **Bookabie** South Australia 31°49′S 132°41′E
182 H6 **Bookaloo** South Australia 31°56′S 137°21′E
37 P5 **Book Cliffs** *cliff* Colorado/ Utah, W USA
25 P1 **Booker** Texas, SW USA 36°27′N 100°32′W
76 K15 **Boola** SE Guinea 08°22′N 08°41′W
183 O8 **Booligal** New South Wales, SE Australia 33°56′S 144°54′E
99 G17 **Boom** Antwerpen, N Belgium 51°05′N 04°24′E
43 N6 **Boom** *var.* Boon. Región Autónoma Atlántico Norte, NE Nicaragua 14°52′N 83°36′W
183 S3 **Boomi** New South Wales, SE Australia 28°43′S 149°35′E
Boon *see* Boom
162 H9 **Bööncagaan Nuur** ◎ S Mongolia
29 V13 **Boone** Iowa, C USA 42°04′N 93°52′W
21 Q8 **Boone** North Carolina, SE USA 36°13′N 81°41′W
27 S11 **Booneville** Arkansas, C USA 35°09′N 93°57′W
21 N6 **Booneville** Kentucky, S USA 37°26′N 83°45′W
23 N2 **Booneville** Mississippi, S USA 34°39′N 88°34′W
21 V3 **Boonsboro** Maryland, NE USA 39°30′N 77°39′W
34 L6 **Boonville** California, W USA 38°58′N 123°21′W
31 N16 **Boonville** Indiana, N USA 38°03′N 87°16′W
27 U4 **Boonville** Missouri, C USA 38°58′N 92°43′W
18 I9 **Boonville** New York, NE USA 43°28′N 75°17′W
80 M12 **Booraama** Awdal, NW Somalia 09°58′N 43°15′E
183 O6 **Booroondarra, Mount** *hill* New South Wales, SE Australia
183 N9 **Booroorban** New South Wales, SE Australia 34°55′S 144°45′E
183 R9 **Boorowa** New South Wales, SE Australia 34°26′S 148°42′E
99 H17 **Boortmeerbeek** Vlaams Brabant, C Belgium 50°58′N 04°27′E
80 P11 **Boosaaso** *var.* Bandar Kassim, Bender Qaasim, Bosaso, *It.* Bender Cassim. Bari, N Somalia 11°26′N 49°37′E
19 Q8 **Boothbay Harbor** Maine, NE USA 43°52′N 69°35′W
Boothia Felix *see* Boothia Peninsula
9 N6 **Boothia, Gulf of** *gulf* Nunavut, NE Canada
9 N6 **Boothia Peninsula** *prev.* Boothia Felix. *peninsula* Nunavut, NE Canada
79 E18 **Booué** Ogooué-Ivindo, NE Gabon 0°03′S 11°58′E
101 J21 **Bopfingen** Baden-Württemberg, S Germany 48°51′N 10°21′E
101 F18 **Boppard** Rheinland-Pfalz, W Germany 50°13′N 07°36′E
62 M4 **Boquerón** *off.* Departamento de Boquerón. ◆ *department* W Paraguay
Boquerón, Departamento de *see* Boquerón
43 P15 **Boquete** *var.* Bajo Boquete. Chiriquí, W Panama 08°45′N 82°26′W
40 J6 **Boquilla, Presa de la** ⊠ N Mexico
40 L5 **Boquillas** *var.* Boquillas del Carmen. Coahuila, NE Mexico 29°10′N 102°55′W
Boquillas del Carmen *see* Boquillas
127 O3 **Bor** Nizhegorodskaya Oblast', W Russian Federation 56°21′N 44°03′E
112 P12 **Bor** Serbia, E Serbia 44°05′N 22°07′E
81 F15 **Bor** Jonglei, S Sudan 06°12′N 31°33′E
95 L20 **Bor** Jönköping, S Sweden 57°04′N 14°10′E
136 J15 **Bor** Niğde, S Turkey 37°49′N 35°00′E
191 S10 **Bora-Bora** *island* Îles Sous le Vent, W French Polynesia
167 Q9 **Borabu** Maha Sarakham, E Thailand 16°01′N 103°06′E
172 K4 **Boraha, Nosy** *island* E Madagascar
33 P13 **Borah Peak** ▲ Idaho, NW USA 44°21′N 113°53′W
145 U16 **Boralday** *prev.* Burunday. Almaty, SE Kazakhstan 43°21′N 76°48′E
144 G13 **Borankul** *prev.* Opornyy. Mangistau, SW Kazakhstan 46°09′N 54°32′E
95 J19 **Borås** Västra Götaland, S Sweden 57°44′N 12°55′E
143 N11 **Borāzjān** *var.* Borazjān. Būshehr, S Iran 29°19′N 51°12′E
Borazjān *see* Borāzjān
58 G13 **Borba** Amazonas, N Brazil 04°39′S 59°40′W
104 H11 **Borba** Évora, S Portugal 38°48′N 07°28′W

◆ Country
● Country Capital
◇ Dependent Territory
○ Dependent Territory Capital
◆ Administrative Regions
✈ International Airport
▲ Mountain
▲ Mountain Range
Volcano
River
◎ Lake
⊠ Reservoir

Borbetomagus see Worms
55 O7 Borbón Bolívar, E Venezuela 07°55'N 64°03'W
59 Q15 Borborema, Planalto da plateau NE Brazil
116 M14 Borcea, Braţul ≈ S Romania
Borchalo see Marneuli
195 R15 Borchgrevink Coast physical region Antarctica
137 Q11 Borçka Artvin, NE Turkey 41°24'N 41°38'E
98 N11 Borculo Gelderland, E Netherlands 52°07'N 06°31'E
182 G10 Borda, Cape headland South Australia 35°45'S 136°34'E
102 K13 Bordeaux anc. Burdigala. Gironde, SW France 44°49'N 00°33'W
11 T15 Borden Saskatchewan, S Canada 52°23'N 107°10'W
14 D8 Borden Lake ◎ Ontario, S Canada
9 N4 Borden Peninsula peninsula Baffin Island, Nunavut, NE Canada
182 K11 Bordertown South Australia 36°21'S 140°48'E
92 H2 Bordheyri Vestfirdhir, NW Iceland 65°12'N 21°09'W
95 B18 Bordhoy Dan. Bordø. island NE Faeroe Islands
106 B11 Bordighera Liguria, NW Italy 43°48'N 07°40'E
74 K5 Bordj-Bou-Arreridj var. Bordj Bou Arreridj, Bordj Bou Arréridj. N Algeria 36°02'N 04°49'E
74 L10 Bordj Omar Driss E Algeria 28°09'N 06°52'E
143 N13 Bord Khūn Hormozgān, S Iran
Bordø see Bordhoy
147 V7 Bordunskiy Chuyskaya Oblast', N Kyrgyzstan 42°37'N 75°31'E
95 M17 Borensberg Östergötland, S Sweden 58°33'N 15°15'E
Borgå see Porvoo
92 L2 Borgarfjördhur Austurland, NE Iceland 65°32'N 13°46'W
92 H3 Borgarnes Vesturland, W Iceland 64°33'N 21°55'W
93 G14 Børgefjellet ▲ C Norway
98 O7 Borger Drenthe, NE Netherlands 52°54'N 06°48'E
25 N2 Borger Texas, SW USA 35°40'N 101°24'W
95 N20 Borgholm Kalmar, S Sweden 56°50'N 16°41'E
107 N22 Borgia Calabria, SW Italy 38°48'N 16°28'E
99 J18 Borgloon Limburg, NE Belgium 50°48'N 05°21'E
195 P2 Borgmassivet ▲▲ Antarctica
22 L9 Borgne, Lake ◎ Louisiana, S USA
106 C7 Borgomanero Piemonte, NE Italy 45°42'N 08°33'E
106 G10 Borgo Panigale ✈ (Bologna) Emilia-Romagna, N Italy 44°33'N 11°16'E
107 J15 Borgorose Lazio, C Italy 42°10'N 13°15'E
106 A9 Borgo San Dalmazzo Piemonte, N Italy 44°19'N 07°29'E
106 G11 Borgo San Lorenzo Toscana, C Italy 43°58'N 11°22'E
106 C7 Borgosesia Piemonte, NE Italy 45°41'N 08°21'E
106 E9 Borgo Val di Taro Emilia-Romagna, C Italy 44°29'N 09°48'E
106 G6 Borgo Valsugana Trentino-Alto Adige, N Italy 46°04'N 11°31'E
Borhoyn Tal see Dzamïn-Üüd
167 R8 Borikhan var. Borikhane. Bolikhamxai, C Laos 18°36'N 103°43'E
Borikhane see Borikhan
Borislav see Boryslav
127 N8 Borisoglebsk Voronezhskaya Oblast', W Russian Federation 51°23'N 42°00'E
Borisov see Barysaw
Borisovgrad see Pŭrvomay
Borispol' see Boryspil'
172 I3 Boriziny Fr. Port-Bergé. Mahajanga, NW Madagascar 15°31'S 47°40'E
105 Q5 Borja Aragón, NE Spain 41°50'N 01°32'W
Borjas Blancas see Les Borges Blanques
137 S10 Borjomi Rus. Borzhomi. C Georgia 41°50'N 43°24'E
118 L12 Borkavichy Rus. Borkovichi. Vitsyebskaya Voblasts', N Belarus 55°40'N 28°20'E
101 H16 Borken Hessen, C Germany 51°01'N 09°16'E
101 E14 Borken Nordrhein-Westfalen, W Germany 51°51'N 06°51'E
92 H10 Borkenes Troms, N Norway 68°46'N 16°10'E
78 H7 Borkou-Ennedi-Tibesti off. Préfecture du Borkou-Ennedi-Tibesti. ✦ prefecture N Chad
Borkou-Ennedi-Tibesti, Préfecture du see Borkou-Ennedi-Tibesti
Borkovichi see Borkavichy
100 E9 Borkum island NW Germany
81 K17 Bor, Lagh var. Lak Bor. dry watercourse NE Kenya
Bor, Lak see Bor, Lagh
95 M14 Borlänge Dalarna, C Sweden 60°29'N 15°25'E
106 C9 Bormida ≈ NW Italy
106 F6 Bormio Lombardia, N Italy 46°27'N 10°24'E
101 M16 Borna Sachsen, E Germany 51°07'N 12°30'E
98 O10 Borne Overijssel, E Netherlands 52°18'N 06°45'E
99 F17 Bornem Antwerpen, N Belgium 51°06'N 04°14'E
169 S10 Borneo island Brunei/Indonesia/Malaysia
101 E16 Bornheim Nordrhein-Westfalen, W Germany 50°46'N 06°58'E
95 L24 Bornholm ✦ county E Denmark
95 L24 Bornholm island E Denmark
77 Y13 Borno ✦ state NE Nigeria
104 K15 Bornos Andalucía, S Spain 36°50'N 05°42'W
162 L7 Bornuur Töv, C Mongolia 48°28'N 106°15'E
117 O4 Borodyanka Kyyivs'ka Oblast', N Ukraine 50°40'N 29°54'E
158 I5 Borohoro Shan ▲▲ NW China
77 O13 Boromo SW Burkina 11°47'N 02°54'W
35 T13 Boron California, W USA 35°00'N 117°42'W
Borongo see Black Volta
Boron'ki see Baron'ki
Borosjenő see Ineu
Borossebes see Sebiş
76 L15 Borotou NW Ivory Coast 08°46'N 07°30'W
117 W6 Borova Kharkivs'ka Oblast', E Ukraine 49°22'N 37°39'E
114 H8 Borovan Vratsa, NW Bulgaria 43°25'N 23°45'E
124 I14 Borovichi Novgorodskaya Oblast', W Russian Federation 58°24'N 33°56'E
Borovlje see Ferlach
114 K8 Borovo Ruse, N Bulgaria 43°28'N 25°46'E
112 J9 Borovo Vukovar-Srijem, NE Croatia 45°22'N 18°57'E
145 Q7 Borovoye Kaz. Būrabay. Akmola, N Kazakhstan 53°07'N 70°20'E
126 K4 Borovsk Kaluzhskaya Oblast', W Russian Federation 55°12'N 36°22'E
145 N7 Borovskoy Kostanay, N Kazakhstan 53°48'N 64°17'E
Borovukha see Baravukha
95 L23 Borrby Skåne, S Sweden 55°27'N 14°10'E
181 R3 Borroloola Northern Territory, N Australia 16°09'S 136°18'E
116 F9 Borş Bihor, NW Romania 47°07'N 21°49'E
116 I9 Borşa Hung. Borsa. Maramureş, N Romania 47°40'N 24°37'E
116 J10 Borsec Ger. Bad Borseck, Hung. Borszék. Harghita, C Romania 46°58'N 25°32'E
92 K8 Børselv Lapp. Bissojohka. Finnmark, N Norway 70°18'N 25°35'E
113 L23 Borsh var. Borshi. Vlorë, S Albania 40°04'N 19°51'E
Borshchev see Borshchiv
116 K7 Borshchiv Pol. Borszczów, Rus. Borshchev. Ternopil's'ka Oblast', W Ukraine 48°48'N 26°00'E
Borshi see Borsh
111 L20 Borsod-Abaúj-Zemplén off. Borsod-Abaúj-Zemplén Megye. ✦ county NE Hungary
Borsod-Abaúj-Zemplén Megye see Borsod-Abaúj-Zemplén
99 E15 Borssele Zeeland, SW Netherlands 51°26'N 03°45'E
Borszczów see Borshchiv
Borszék see Borsec
Bortala see Bole
103 O12 Bort-les-Orgues Corrèze, C France 45°28'N 02°31'E
Bor u České Lípy see Nový Bor
Bor-Üdzüür see Altay
143 N9 Borūjen Chahār Maḩāll va Bakhtiārī, C Iran 32°N 51°09'E
142 L7 Borūjerd var. Burujird. Lorestān, W Iran 33°55'N 48°46'E
116 H6 Boryslav Pol. Borysław, Rus. Borislav. L'vivs'ka Oblast', NW Ukraine 49°18'N 23°28'E
Borysław see Boryslav
117 P4 Boryspil' Rus. Borispol'. Kyyivs'ka Oblast', N Ukraine 50°21'N 30°59'E
117 P4 Boryspil' Rus. Borispol'. ✈ (Kyyiv) Kyyivs'ka Oblast', N Ukraine 50°21'N 30°46'E
Borzhomi see Borjomi
117 R3 Borzna Chernihivs'ka Oblast', NE Ukraine 51°15'N 32°25'E
123 O14 Borzya Chitinskaya Oblast', S Russian Federation 50°18'N 116°24'E
107 B18 Bosa Sardegna, Italy, C Mediterranean Sea 40°18'N 08°28'E
112 F10 Bosanska Dubica var. Kozarska Dubica. ✦ Republika Srpska, NW Bosnia and Herzegovina
112 G10 Bosanska Gradiška var. Gradiška. ✦ Republika Srpska, N Bosnia and Herzegovina
112 F10 Bosanska Kostajnica var. Srpska Kostajnica. ✦ Republika Srpska, NW Bosnia and Herzegovina
112 E11 Bosanska Krupa var. Krupa, Krupa na Uni. ✦ Federacija Bosna I Hercegovina, NW Bosnia and Herzegovina
112 H10 Bosanski Brod var. Srpski Brod. ✦ Republika Srpska, N Bosnia and Herzegovina
112 E10 Bosanski Novi var. Novi Grad. Republika Srpska, NW Bosnia and Herzegovina 45°03'N 16°23'E
112 E11 Bosanski Petrovac var. Petrovac. Federacija Bosna I Hercegovina, NW Bosnia and Herzegovina 44°34'N 16°21'E
112 I10 Bosanski Šamac var. Šamac. Republika Srpska, N Bosnia and Herzegovina 45°03'N 18°27'E
112 E12 Bosansko Grahovo var. Grahovo, Hrvatsko Grahovi. Federacija Bosna I Hercegovina, W Bosnia and Herzegovina 44°10'N 16°22'E
Bosaso see Boosaaso
186 B7 Bosavi, Mount ▲ W Papua New Guinea 06°33'S 142°50'E
160 J14 Bose Guangxi Zhuangzu Zizhiqu, S China 23°55'N 106°32'E
161 Q5 Boshan Shandong, E China 36°32'N 117°47'E
113 P16 Bosilegrad prev. Bosiljgrad. Serbia, SE Serbia 42°30'N 22°30'E
Bosiljgrad see Bosilegrad
Bösing see Pezinok
98 H12 Boskoop Zuid-Holland, C Netherlands 52°04'N 04°40'E
111 G18 Boskovice Ger. Boskowitz. Jihomoravský Kraj, SE Czech Republic 49°30'N 16°39'E
Boskowitz see Boskovice
112 I10 Bosna ≈ N Bosnia and Herzegovina
113 G14 Bosna I Hercegovina, Federacija ✦ republic Bosnia and Herzegovina
112 H12 Bosnia and Herzegovina off. Republic of Bosnia and Herzegovina. ◆ republic SE Europe
Bosnia and Herzegovina, Republic of see Bosnia and Herzegovina
79 J16 Bosobolo Equateur, NW Dem. Rep. Congo 04°11'N 19°55'E
165 O14 Bōsō-hantō peninsula Honshū, S Japan
Bosora see Buşrá ash Shām
Bosphorus/Bosporus see İstanbul Boğazi
Bosporus Cimmerius see Kerch Strait
Bosporus Thracius see İstanbul Boğazi
Bosra see Buşrá ash Shām
79 H14 Bossangoa Ouham, C Central African Republic 06°32'N 17°25'E
Bossé Bangou see Bossey Bangou
79 I15 Bossembélé Ombella-Mpoko, C Central African Republic 05°13'N 17°39'E
79 H15 Bossentélé Ouham-Pendé, W Central African Republic 05°36'N 16°37'E
77 R12 Bossey Bangou var. Bossé Bangou. Tillabéri, SW Niger 13°22'N 01°18'E
22 G5 Bossier City Louisiana, S USA 32°31'N 93°43'W
83 D20 Bossiesvlei Hardap, S Namibia 25°02'S 16°48'E
77 Y11 Bosso Diffa, SE Niger 13°42'N 13°18'E
61 F15 Bossoroca Rio Grande do Sul, S Brazil 28°45'S 54°54'W
158 J10 Bostan Xinjiang Uygur Zizhiqu, W China 41°20'N 83°15'E
142 K3 Bostānābād Āžarbāyjān-e Sharqī, N Iran 37°52'N 46°51'E
158 K6 Bosten Hu var. Bagrax Hu. ◎ NW China
97 O18 Boston prev. St.Botolph's Town. E England, United Kingdom 52°59'N 00°01'W
19 O11 Boston state capital Massachusetts, NE USA 42°22'N 71°04'W
146 I9 Bo'ston Rus. Bustan. Qoraqalpog'iston Respublikasi, W Uzbekistan 41°49'N 60°51'E
10 M17 Boston Bar British Columbia, SW Canada 49°54'N 121°22'W
27 T10 Boston Mountains ▲▲ Arkansas, C USA
15 P8 Bostonnais ≈ Québec, SE Canada
Bostyn' see Bastyn'
112 I10 Bosut ≈ E Croatia
154 C11 Botād Gujarāt, W India 22°12'N 71°44'E
183 T9 Botany Bay inlet New South Wales, SE Australia
83 G18 Boteti var. Botletle. ≈ N Botswana
114 J9 Botev ▲ C Bulgaria 42°45'N 24°57'E
114 H9 Botevgrad prev. Orkhaniye. Sofiya, W Bulgaria 42°55'N 23°47'E
93 J16 Bothnia, Gulf of Fin. Pohjanlahti, Swe. Bottniska Viken. gulf N Baltic Sea
183 P17 Bothwell Tasmania, SE Australia 42°24'S 147°01'E
104 H5 Boticas Vila Real, N Portugal 41°41'N 07°40'W
55 W10 Boti-Pasi Sipaliwini, C Surinam 04°15'N 55°27'W
Botletle see Boteti
127 P16 Botlikh Chechenskaya Respublika, SW Russian Federation 42°39'N 46°12'E
117 N10 Botna ≈ E Moldova
116 J9 Botoşani Hung. Botosány. Botoşani, NE Romania 47°44'N 26°41'E
116 K8 Botoşani ✦ county NE Romania
Botosány see Botoşani
147 P12 Bototog', Tizmasi Rus. Khrebet Babatag. ▲▲ Tajikistan/Uzbekistan
161 P4 Botou prev. Bozhen. Hebei, E China 38°09'N 116°37'E
99 M20 Botrange ▲ E Belgium 50°30'N 06°03'E
107 O21 Botricello Calabria, SW Italy 38°56'N 16°51'E
83 J23 Botshabelo Free State, C South Africa 29°15'S 26°51'E
93 J15 Botsmark Västerbotten, N Sweden 64°15'N 20°15'E
83 G19 Botswana off. Republic of Botswana. ◆ republic S Africa
Botswana, Republic of see Botswana
29 N2 Bottineau North Dakota, N USA 48°50'N 100°28'W
Bottniska Viken see Bothnia, Gulf of
60 L9 Botucatu São Paulo, S Brazil 22°52'S 48°30'W
76 M16 Bouaflé C Ivory Coast 06°59'N 05°45'W
77 N16 Bouaké var. Bwake. C Ivory Coast 07°42'N 05°00'W
79 G14 Bouar Nana-Mambéré, W Central African Republic 05°58'N 15°38'E
74 H7 Bouarfa NE Morocco 32°33'N 01°54'W
111 B19 Boubín ▲ SW Czech Republic 49°00'N 13°51'E
79 I14 Bouca Ouham, W Central African Republic 06°57'N 18°18'E
15 T5 Boucher ≈ Québec, SE Canada
103 R15 Bouches-du-Rhône ✦ department SE France
74 C9 Bou Craa var. Bu Craa. NW Western Sahara 26°32'N 12°52'W
77 O9 Boû Djébéha oasis C Mali
108 C8 Boudry Neuchâtel, W Switzerland 46°57'N 06°46'E
79 F21 Bouenza ✦ province S Congo
180 L2 Bougainville, Cape cape Western Australia
Bougainville, Détroit de see Bougainville Strait
186 J7 Bougainville Island island NE Papua New Guinea
186 I8 Bougainville Strait strait N Solomon Islands
187 Q13 Bougainville Strait Fr. Détroit de Bougainville. strait C Vanuatu
120 I9 Bougarou, Cap headland NE Algeria 37°07'N 06°18'E
77 R8 Boughessa Kidal, NE Mali 20°05'N 02°13'E
Bougie see Béjaïa
76 L13 Bougouni Sikasso, SW Mali 11°25'N 07°28'W
99 J24 Bouillon Luxembourg, SE Belgium 49°47'N 05°04'E
74 K5 Bouira var. Bouïra. N Algeria 36°22'N 03°55'E
74 D8 Bou-Izakarn SW Morocco 29°12'N 09°43'W
74 B9 Boujdour var. Bojador. W Western Sahara 26°06'N 14°29'W
74 G5 Boukhalef ✈ (Tanger) N Morocco 35°45'N 05°53'W
Boukombé see Boukoumbé
77 R14 Boukoumbé var. Boukombé. C Benin 10°13'N 01°09'E
76 G6 Boû Lanouâr Dakhlet Nouâdhibou, W Mauritania 21°17'N 16°29'W
37 T4 Boulder Colorado, C USA 40°02'N 105°18'W
33 R10 Boulder Montana, NW USA 46°14'N 112°07'W
35 X12 Boulder City Nevada, W USA 35°58'N 114°49'W
181 T7 Boulia Queensland, C Australia 23°02'S 139°58'E
15 N10 Boullé ≈ Québec, SE Canada
102 J9 Boulogne ≈ NW France
Boulogne see Boulogne-sur-Mer
102 L16 Boulogne-sur-Gesse Haute-Garonne, S France 43°18'N 00°38'E
103 N1 Boulogne-sur-Mer var. Boulogne; anc. Bononia, Gesoriacum, Gessoriacum. Pas-de-Calais, N France 50°43'N 01°36'E
77 Q12 Boulsa C Burkina 12°41'N 00°29'W
77 W11 Boultoum Zinder, C Niger 14°43'N 10°22'E
187 Y14 Bouma Taveuni, N Fiji 16°49'S 179°50'W
79 G16 Boumba ≈ SE Cameroon
76 J9 Boûmdeïd var. Boumdeït. Assaba, S Mauritania 17°26'N 11°21'W
Boumdeït see Boûmdeïd
115 C17 Boumistós ▲ W Greece 38°48'N 20°59'E
77 O15 Bouna NE Ivory Coast 09°16'N 03°00'W
19 P4 Boundary Bald Mountain ▲ Maine, NE USA 45°45'N 70°10'W
35 S8 Boundary Peak ▲ Nevada, W USA 37°50'N 118°21'W
76 M14 Boundiali N Ivory Coast 09°30'N 06°31'W
79 G19 Boundji Cuvette, C Congo 01°05'S 15°18'E
77 O13 Boundoukui var. Bondoukui, Bondoukuy. W Burkina 11°51'N 03°47'W
36 L2 Bountiful Utah, W USA 40°53'N 111°52'W
Bounty Basin see Bounty Trough
191 Q16 Bounty Bay bay Pitcairn Island, C Pacific Ocean
192 L12 Bounty Islands island group S New Zealand
175 Q13 Bounty Trough var. Bounty Basin. undersea feature S Pacific Ocean
187 P17 Bourail Province Sud, C New Caledonia 21°35'S 165°29'E
27 V5 Bourbeuse River ≈ Missouri, C USA
103 Q9 Bourbon-Lancy Saône-et-Loire, C France 46°39'N 03°48'E
31 N11 Bourbonnais Illinois, N USA 41°08'N 87°52'W
103 O10 Bourbonnais cultural region C France
103 S7 Bourbonne-les-Bains Haute-Marne, N France 48°00'N 05°43'E
Bourbon Vendée see la Roche-sur-Yon
74 M8 Bourdj Messaouda E Algeria 30°18'N 09°19'E
77 Q10 Bourem Gao, C Mali 16°56'N 00°21'W
Bourg see Bourg-en-Bresse
103 N11 Bourganeuf Creuse, C France 45°57'N 01°47'E
Bourgas see Burgas
Bourge-en-Bresse see Bourg-en-Bresse
103 S10 Bourg-en-Bresse var. Bourg, Bourge-en-Bresse. Ain, E France 46°12'N 05°13'E
103 O8 Bourges anc. Avaricum. Cher, C France 47°06'N 02°24'E
103 T11 Bourget, Lac du ◎ E France
103 P8 Bourgogne Eng. Burgundy. ✦ region E France
103 S11 Bourgoin-Jallieu Isère, E France 45°34'N 05°16'E
103 R14 Bourg-St-Andéol Ardèche, E France 44°24'N 04°36'E
103 U11 Bourg-St-Maurice Savoie, E France 45°37'N 06°49'E
108 C11 Bourg St. Pierre Valais, SW Switzerland 45°54'N 07°10'E
76 H8 Boû Rjeïmât well W Mauritania
183 P5 Bourke New South Wales, SE Australia 30°08'S 145°57'E
97 M24 Bournemouth S England, United Kingdom 50°43'N 01°54'W
99 M23 Bourscheid Diekirch, NE Luxembourg 49°55'N 06°04'E
74 K6 Bou Saâda var. Bou Saada. N Algeria 35°10'N 04°09'E
36 I13 Bouse Wash ≈ Arizona, SW USA
103 N10 Boussac Creuse, C France 46°20'N 02°12'E
102 M16 Boussens Haute-Garonne, S France 43°11'N 00°58'E
78 H12 Bousso prev. Fort-Bretonnet. Chari-Baguirmi, S Chad 10°32'N 16°45'E
76 H9 Boutilimit Trarza, SW Mauritania 17°33'N 14°42'W
65 D21 Bouvet Island ◇ Norwegian dependency S Atlantic Ocean
77 U11 Bouza Tahoua, SW Niger 14°25'N 06°09'E
109 R10 Bovec Ger. Flitsch, It. Plezzo. NW Slovenia 46°21'N 13°33'E
98 J8 Bovenkarspel Noord-Holland, NW Netherlands 52°33'N 05°03'E
29 V5 Bovey Minnesota, N USA 47°18'N 93°25'W
32 M9 Bovill Idaho, NW USA 46°50'N 116°24'W
24 L4 Bovina Texas, SW USA 34°30'N 102°52'W
107 M17 Bovino Puglia, SE Italy 41°14'N 15°19'E
61 C17 Bovril Entre Ríos, E Argentina 31°24'S 59°25'W
28 L2 Bowbells North Dakota, N USA 48°48'N 102°15'W
11 Q16 Bow City Alberta, SW Canada 50°27'N 112°16'W
29 O8 Bowdle South Dakota, N USA 45°27'N 99°39'W
181 X6 Bowen Queensland, NE Australia 20°S 148°10'E
192 L2 Bowers Ridge undersea feature S Bering Sea 50°00'N 180°00'W
25 S5 Bowie Texas, SW USA 33°33'N 97°51'W
11 R17 Bow Island Alberta, SW Canada 49°53'N 111°24'W
Bowkān see Būkān
20 J7 Bowling Green Kentucky, S USA 37°00'N 86°29'W
27 V3 Bowling Green Missouri, C USA 39°21'N 91°11'W
31 R11 Bowling Green Ohio, N USA 41°22'N 83°40'W
21 W5 Bowling Green Virginia, NE USA 38°02'N 77°22'W
28 J6 Bowman North Dakota, N USA 46°11'N 103°26'W
9 Q7 Bowman Bay bay NW Atlantic Ocean
194 I5 Bowman Coast physical region Antarctica
28 J7 Bowman-Haley Lake ⊠ North Dakota, N USA
195 Z11 Bowman Island island Antarctica
Bowo see Bomi
183 S9 Bowral New South Wales, SE Australia 34°28'S 150°52'E
186 E8 Bowutu Mountains ▲▲ C Papua New Guinea
83 I16 Bowwood Southern, S Zambia 17°09'S 26°16'E
28 I12 Box Butte Reservoir ⊠ Nebraska, C USA
28 J10 Box Elder South Dakota, N USA 44°06'N 103°04'W
95 M18 Boxholm Östergötland, S Sweden 58°12'N 15°05'E
Bo Xian/Boxian see Bozhou
161 Q4 Boxing Shandong, E China 37°06'N 118°05'E
99 L14 Boxmeer Noord-Brabant, SE Netherlands 51°39'N 05°57'E
99 J14 Boxtel Noord-Brabant, S Netherlands 51°36'N 05°20'E
136 J10 Boyabat Sinop, N Turkey 41°27'N 34°45'E
54 F9 Boyacá off. Departamento de Boyacá. ✦ province C Colombia
Boyacá, Departamento de see Boyacá
117 O4 Boyarka Kyyivs'ka Oblast', N Ukraine 50°19'N 30°20'E
22 H7 Boyce Louisiana, S USA 31°23'N 92°40'W
114 H8 Boychinovtsi Montana, NW Bulgaria 43°28'N 23°20'E
33 U11 Boyd Montana, NW USA 45°27'N 109°03'W
25 S6 Boyd Texas, SW USA 33°01'N 97°33'W
21 V8 Boydton Virginia, NE USA 36°40'N 78°26'W
Boyer Ahmadī va Kohkīlūyeh see Kohgīlūyeh va Būyer Aḩmad
29 T13 Boyer River ≈ Iowa, C USA
21 W8 Boykins Virginia, NE USA 36°35'N 77°11'W
11 Q13 Boyle Alberta, SW Canada 54°38'N 112°45'W
97 D16 Boyle Ir. Mainistirna Búille. C Ireland 53°58'N 08°18'W
97 F17 Boyne Ir. An Bhóinn. ≈ E Ireland
31 Q5 Boyne City Michigan, N USA 45°13'N 85°00'W
23 Z14 Boynton Beach Florida, SE USA 26°31'N 80°04'W
147 O13 Boysun Rus. Baysun. Surkhondaryo Viloyati, S Uzbekistan 38°14'N 67°08'E
Bozau see Întorsura Buzăului
136 B12 Bozcaada Island Çanakkale, NW Turkey
136 C14 Boz Dağlari ▲▲ W Turkey
33 S11 Bozeman Montana, NW USA 45°40'N 111°02'W
Bozen see Bolzano
79 J16 Bozene Equateur, NW Dem. Rep. Congo 02°56'N 19°15'E
Bozhen see Botou
161 P7 Bozhou var. Boxian, Bo Xian. Anhui, E China 33°46'N 115°44'E
136 H16 Bozkır Konya, S Turkey 37°10'N 32°15'E
136 K13 Bozok Yaylasi plateau C Turkey
79 H14 Bozoum Ouham-Pendé, W Central African Republic 06°17'N 16°26'E
137 N16 Bozova Sanlıurfa, S Turkey 37°23'N 38°33'E
Bozrah see Buşrá ash Shām
136 E12 Bozüyük Bilecik, NW Turkey 39°55'N 30°02'E
106 B9 Bra Piemonte, NW Italy 44°42'N 07°51'E
194 G4 Brabant Island island Antarctica
99 I20 Brabant Walloon ✦ province C Belgium
113 F15 Brač var. Brach, It. Brazza; anc. Brattia. island S Croatia
Bracara Augusta see Braga
107 H15 Bracciano Lazio, C Italy 42°04'N 12°12'E
107 H14 Bracciano, Lago di ◎ C Italy
14 H13 Bracebridge Ontario, S Canada 45°02'N 79°19'W
Brach see Brač
93 G17 Bräcke Jämtland, C Sweden 62°43'N 15°30'E
25 P12 Brackettville Texas, SW USA 29°19'N 100°27'W
97 N22 Bracknell S England, United Kingdom 51°26'N 00°46'W
61 K14 Braço do Norte Santa Catarina, S Brazil 28°16'S 49°11'W
116 G11 Brad Hung. Brád. Hunedoara, SW Romania 46°52'N 23°00'E
107 N18 Bradano ≈ S Italy
23 V13 Bradenton Florida, SE USA 27°30'N 82°34'W
14 H14 Bradford Ontario, S Canada 44°09'N 79°34'W
97 L17 Bradford N England, United Kingdom 53°48'N 01°45'W
27 W10 Bradford Arkansas, C USA 35°25'N 91°27'W
18 D12 Bradford Pennsylvania, NE USA 41°57'N 78°38'W
27 T15 Bradley Arkansas, C USA 33°06'N 93°39'W
25 P7 Bradshaw Texas, SW USA 32°06'N 99°52'W
25 Q9 Brady Texas, SW USA 31°08'N 99°22'W
25 Q9 Brady Creek ≈ Texas, SW USA
95 G22 Brædstrup Vejle, C Denmark 55°58'N 09°38'E
96 J10 Braemar NE Scotland, United Kingdom 57°12'N 02°52'W
116 K8 Brăeşti Botoşani, NW Romania 47°50'N 26°26'E
104 G5 Braga anc. Bracara Augusta. Braga, NW Portugal 41°32'N 08°26'W
104 G5 Braga ✦ district N Portugal
116 J15 Bragadiru Teleorman, S Romania 43°43'N 25°32'E
61 C20 Bragado Buenos Aires, E Argentina 35°10'S 60°29'W
104 J5 Bragança Eng. Braganza; anc. Julio Briga. Bragança, NE Portugal 41°47'N 06°46'W
104 I5 Bragança ✦ district N Portugal
60 N9 Bragança Paulista São Paulo, S Brazil 22°55'S 46°30'W
Braganza see Bragança
Bragin see Brahin
29 V7 Braham Minnesota, N USA 45°43'N 93°10'W
Brahe see Brda
Brahestad see Raahe
119 O20 Brahin Rus. Bragin. Homyel'skaya Voblasts', SE Belarus 51°47'N 30°16'E
153 U15 Brahmanbaria Chittagong, E Bangladesh 23°58'N 91°04'E
154 O12 Brāhmani ≈ E India
154 N13 Brahmapur Orissa, E India 19°21'N 84°51'E
129 S10 Brahmaputra var. Padma, Tsangpo, Ben. Jamuna, Chin. Yarlung Zangbo Jiang, Ind. Bramaputra, Dihang, Siang. ≈ S Asia
97 H19 Braich y Pwll headland NW Wales, United Kingdom 52°47'N 04°46'W
183 R10 Braidwood New South Wales, SE Australia 35°26'S 149°48'E
30 M11 Braidwood Illinois, N USA 41°16'N 88°12'W
116 M13 Brăila Brăila, E Romania 45°17'N 27°57'E
116 L13 Brăila ✦ county SE Romania
99 G19 Braine-l'Alleud Brabant Walloon, C Belgium 50°41'N 04°22'E
99 F19 Braine-le-Comte Hainaut, SW Belgium 50°37'N 04°08'E
29 U6 Brainerd Minnesota, N USA 46°22'N 94°10'W
99 J19 Braives Liège, E Belgium 50°37'N 05°09'E
83 H23 Brak ≈ C South Africa
Brak see Birāk
99 E18 Brakel Oost-Vlaanderen, SW Belgium 50°50'N 03°48'E
98 J13 Brakel Gelderland, C Netherlands 51°49'N 05°05'E
76 H9 Brakna ✦ region S Mauritania
95 J17 Brålanda Västra Götaland, S Sweden 58°32'N 12°18'E
Bramaputra see Brahmaputra
95 F23 Bramming Ribe, W Denmark 55°28'N 08°42'E
14 G15 Brampton Ontario, S Canada 43°42'N 79°46'W
100 F12 Bramsche Niedersachsen, NW Germany 52°25'N 07°58'E
116 J12 Bran Ger. Törzburg, Hung. Törcsvár. Braşov, S Romania 45°31'N 25°23'E
29 W8 Branch Minnesota, N USA 45°29'N 92°57'W
21 R14 Branchville South Carolina, SE USA 33°15'N 80°49'W
47 Y6 Branco, Cabo headland E Brazil 07°08'S 34°45'W
58 F11 Branco, Rio ≈ N Brazil
108 J8 Brand Vorarlberg, W Austria 47°07'N 09°45'E
83 B18 Brandberg ▲ NW Namibia 21°20'S 14°22'E
95 H14 Brandbu Oppland, S Norway 60°24'N 10°30'E
95 F22 Brande Ringkøbing, W Denmark 55°57'N 09°08'E
Brandebourg see Brandenburg
100 M12 Brandenburg var. Brandenburg an der Havel. Brandenburg, NE Germany 52°25'N 12°34'E
20 K5 Brandenburg Kentucky, S USA 38°00'N 86°11'W
100 N12 Brandenburg off. Freie und Hansestadt Hamburg, Fr. Brandebourg. ✦ state NE Germany
Brandenburg an der Havel see Brandenburg
83 I23 Brandfort Free State, C South Africa 28°42'S 26°28'E
11 W16 Brandon Manitoba, S Canada 49°50'N 99°57'W
23 V12 Brandon Florida, SE USA 27°56'N 82°17'W
22 L6 Brandon Mississippi, S USA 32°16'N 90°01'W
97 A20 Brandon Mountain Ir. Cnoc Bréanainn. ▲ SW Ireland 52°13'N 10°16'W
Brandsen see Coronel Brandsen
95 I14 Brandval Hedmark, S Norway 60°18'N 12°01'E
83 F24 Brandvlei Northern Cape, W South Africa 30°27'S 20°29'E
23 U9 Branford Florida, SE USA 29°57'N 82°54'W
110 K7 Braniewo Ger. Braunsberg. Warmińsko-mazurskie, N Poland 54°24'N 19°50'E
194 H3 Bransfield Strait strait Antarctica
37 U8 Branson Colorado, C USA 37°01'N 103°52'W
27 T8 Branson Missouri, C USA 36°38'N 93°13'W
14 G16 Brantford Ontario, S Canada 43°09'N 80°17'W
102 L12 Brantôme Dordogne, SW France 45°21'N 00°37'E
182 L12 Branxholme Victoria, SE Australia 37°51'S 141°48'E
Brasil see Brazil
59 C16 Brasiléia Acre, W Brazil 10°59'S 48°45'W
59 K18 Brasília ● (Brazil) Distrito Federal, C Brazil 15°45'S 47°57'W
Brasil, República Federativa do see Brazil
Braslav see Braslaw
118 J12 Braslaw Pol. Brasław, Rus. Braslav. Vitsyebskaya Voblasts', N Belarus 55°38'N 27°02'E
116 J12 Braşov Ger. Kronstadt, Hung. Brassó; prev. Oraşul Stalin. Braşov, C Romania 45°40'N 25°35'E
116 I12 Braşov ✦ county C Romania
77 U18 Brass Bayelsa, S Nigeria 04°19'N 06°21'E
99 H16 Brasschaat var. Brasschaet. Antwerpen, N Belgium 51°17'N 04°30'E
Brasschaet see Brasschaat
169 V8 Brassey, Banjaran var. Brassey Range. ▲▲ East Malaysia
Brassey Range see Brassey, Banjaran
Brassó see Braşov
23 T1 Brasstown Bald ▲ Georgia, SE USA 34°52'N 83°48'W
113 K22 Brataj Vlorë, SW Albania 40°18'N 19°37'E
114 J10 Bratan var. Morozov. ▲ C Bulgaria 42°31'N 25°08'E
111 F21 Bratislava Ger. Pressburg, Hung. Pozsony. ● (Slovakia) Bratislavský Kraj, W Slovakia 48°10'N 17°10'E
111 H21 Bratislavský Kraj ✦ region W Slovakia
114 H10 Bratiya ▲ C Bulgaria 42°36'N 24°08'E
122 M12 Bratsk Irkutskaya Oblast', C Russian Federation 56°20'N 101°50'E
117 Q8 Brats'ke Mykolayivs'ka Oblast', S Ukraine 47°52'N 31°34'E
122 M13 Bratskoye Vodokhranilishche Eng. Bratsk Reservoir. ⊠ S Russian Federation
Bratsk Reservoir see Bratskoye Vodokhranilishche
Brattia see Brač
94 D9 Brattvåg Møre og Romsdal, S Norway 62°36'N 06°21'E
112 K12 Bratunac ✦ Republika Srpska, E Bosnia and Herzegovina
114 J10 Bratya Daskalovi prev. Grozdovo. Stara Zagora, C Bulgaria 42°13'N 25°21'E
109 U2 Braunau ≈ N Austria
Braunau see Braunau am Inn
109 Q4 Braunau am Inn var. Braunau. Oberösterreich, N Austria 48°16'N 13°03'E
Braunsberg see Braniewo
100 J13 Braunschweig Eng./Fr. Brunswick. Niedersachsen, N Germany 52°16'N 10°32'E
Brava see Baraawe
105 Y6 Brava, Costa coastal region NE Spain
43 V16 Brava, Punta headland E Panama 08°21'N 78°22'W
95 N17 Bråviken inlet S Sweden
56 B10 Bravo, Cerro ▲ N Peru 05°33'S 79°10'W
Bravo del Norte, Río/Bravo, Río see Grande, Rio
35 X17 Brawley California, W USA 32°58'N 115°31'W
97 G18 Bray Ir. Bré. E Ireland 53°12'N 06°06'W
59 G16 Brazil off. Federative Republic of Brazil, Port. República Federativa do Brasil, Sp. Brasil; prev. United States of Brazil. ◆ federal republic South America
65 K15 Brazil Basin var. Brazilian Basin, Brazil'skaya Kotlovina. undersea feature W Atlantic Ocean 15°00'S 25°00'W
Brazil, Federative Republic of see Brazil
Brazilian Basin see Brazil Basin
Brazilian Highlands see Central, Planalto
Brazil'skaya Kotlovina see Brazil Basin
Brazil, United States of see Brazil
25 U10 Brazos River ≈ Texas, SW USA
Brazza see Brač
79 G21 Brazzaville ● (Congo) Capital District, S Congo 04°14'S 15°14'E
79 G21 Brazzaville ✈ Pool, S Congo 04°15'S 15°15'E
112 J11 Brčko ✦ Republika Srpska, NE Bosnia and Herzegovina
110 H8 Brda Ger. Brahe. ≈ N Poland
Bré see Bray
185 A23 Breaksea Sound sound South Island, New Zealand
184 L4 Bream Bay bay North Island, New Zealand
184 L4 Bream Head headland North Island, New Zealand 35°51'S 174°35'E
Bréanainn, Cnoc see Brandon Mountain
45 S6 Brea, Punta headland W Puerto Rico 17°56'N 66°55'W
22 I9 Breaux Bridge Louisiana, S USA 30°16'N 91°54'W
116 J13 Breaza Prahova, SE Romania 45°13'N 25°38'E
169 P16 Brebes Jawa, C Indonesia 06°54'S 109°00'E
96 K10 Brechin E Scotland, United Kingdom 56°45'N 02°38'W
99 H15 Brecht Antwerpen, N Belgium 51°21'N 04°33'E
37 S4 Breckenridge Colorado, C USA 39°28'N 106°02'W
29 R6 Breckenridge Minnesota, N USA 46°15'N 96°35'W
25 R6 Breckenridge Texas, SW USA 32°45'N 98°56'W
97 J21 Brecknock cultural region SE Wales, United Kingdom
63 G25 Brecknock, Península headland S Chile 54°39'S 71°48'W
111 G19 Břeclav Ger. Lundenburg. Jihomoravský Kraj, SE Czech Republic 49°05'N 16°51'E
97 J21 Brecon E Wales, United Kingdom 51°58'N 03°26'W

◆ Country
● Country Capital
◇ Dependent Territory
○ Dependent Territory Capital
✦ Administrative Regions
✈ International Airport
▲ Mountain
▲▲ Mountain Range
Volcano
≈ River
◎ Lake
⊠ Reservoir

BRECON BEACONS – BUFORD

97 J21 **Brecon Beacons** ▲▲ S Wales, United Kingdom
99 I14 **Breda** Noord-Brabant, S Netherlands *51°35′N 04°46′E*
95 K20 **Bredaryd** Jönköping, S Sweden *57°10′N 13°45′E*
83 F26 **Bredasdorp** Western Cape, SW South Africa *34°32′S 20°02′E*
93 H16 **Bredbyn** Västernorrland, N Sweden *63°28′N 18°04′E*
122 F11 **Bredy** Chelyabinskaya Oblast', C Russian Federation *52°23′N 60°24′E*
99 K17 **Bree** Limburg, NE Belgium *51°08′N 05°36′E*
67 T15 **Breede** ≈ S South Africa
98 I7 **Breezand** Noord-Holland, NW Netherlands *52°52′N 04°47′E*
113 P18 **Bregalnica** ≈ E FYR Macedonia
108 I6 **Bregenz** *anc.* Brigantium. Vorarlberg, W Austria *47°31′N 09°46′E*
108 J7 **Bregenzer Wald** ▲▲ W Austria
114 F6 **Bregovo** Vidin, NW Bulgaria *44°07′N 22°40′E*
102 H5 **Bréhat, Île de** *island* NW France
92 H2 **Breidhafjördhur** *bay* W Iceland
92 L3 **Breidhdalsvík** Austurland, E Iceland *64°48′N 14°02′W*
108 H9 **Breil** *Ger.* Brigels. Graubünden, S Switzerland *46°46′N 09°04′E*
92 J8 **Breivikbotn** Finnmark, N Norway *70°36′N 22°19′E*
94 I9 **Brekken** Sør-Trøndelag, S Norway *62°39′N 11°49′E*
94 G7 **Brekstad** Sør-Trøndelag, S Norway *63°42′N 09°40′E*
94 B10 **Bremangerlandet** *island* S Norway
Brême *see* Bremen
100 H11 **Bremen** *Fr.* Brême. Bremen, NW Germany *53°06′N 08°48′E*
23 R3 **Bremen** Georgia, SE USA *33°43′N 85°09′W*
31 O11 **Bremen** Indiana, N USA *41°24′N 86°07′W*
100 H10 **Bremen** *off.* Freie Hansestadt Bremen, *Fr.* Brême. ⬖ *state* N Germany
100 G9 **Bremerhaven** Bremen, NW Germany *53°33′N 08°35′E*
Bremersdorp *see* Manzini
32 G8 **Bremerton** Washington, NW USA *47°34′N 122°37′W*
100 H10 **Bremervörde** Niedersachsen, NW Germany *53°29′N 09°06′E*
25 U9 **Bremond** Texas, SW USA *31°10′N 96°40′W*
25 U10 **Brenham** Texas, SW USA *30°09′N 96°24′W*
108 M8 **Brenner** Tirol, W Austria *47°10′N 11°51′E*
Brenner, Col du/Brennero, Passo del *see* Brenner Pass
108 M8 **Brenner Pass** *var.* Brenner Sattel, *Fr.* Col du Brenner, *Ger.* Brennerpass, *It.* Passo del Brennero. *pass* Austria/Italy
Brennerpass *see* Brenner Pass
Brenner Sattel *see* Brenner Pass
108 G10 **Brenno** ≈ SW Switzerland
106 F7 **Breno** Lombardia, N Italy *45°58′N 10°18′E*
23 O5 **Brent** Alabama, S USA *32°54′N 87°10′W*
106 H7 **Brenta** ≈ NE Italy
97 P21 **Brentwood** E England, United Kingdom *51°38′N 00°21′E*
18 L14 **Brentwood** Long Island, New York, NE USA *40°46′N 73°12′W*
106 F7 **Brescia** *anc.* Brixia. Lombardia, N Italy *45°33′N 10°13′E*
99 D15 **Breskens** Zeeland, SW Netherlands *51°24′N 03°33′E*
Breslau *see* Wrocław
106 H5 **Bressanone** *Ger.* Brixen. Trentino-Alto Adige, N Italy *46°44′N 11°41′E*
96 M2 **Bressay** *island* NE Scotland, United Kingdom
102 K9 **Bressuire** Deux-Sèvres, W France *46°50′N 00°29′W*
119 F20 **Brest** *Pol.* Brześć nad Bugiem, *Rus.* Brest-Litovsk; *prev.* Brześć Litewski. Brestskaya Voblasts', SW Belarus *52°06′N 23°42′E*
102 F5 **Brest** Finistère, NW France *48°24′N 04°31′W*
Brest-Litovsk *see* Brest
112 A10 **Brestova** Istra, NW Croatia *45°09′N 14°13′E*
Brestskaya Oblast' *see* Brestskaya Voblasts'
119 G19 **Brestskaya Voblasts'** *prev. Rus.* Brestskaya Oblast'. ⬖ *province* SW Belarus
102 G6 **Bretagne** *Eng.* Brittany, *Lat.* Britannia Minor. ⬖ *region* NW France
116 G12 **Bretea-Română** *Hung.* Oláhbrettye; *prev.* Bretea-Romînă. Hunedoara, W Romania *45°39′N 23°00′E*
Bretea-Romînă *see* Bretea-Română
103 O3 **Breteuil** Oise, N France *49°37′N 02°18′E*
102 I10 **Breton, Pertuis** *inlet* W France
22 L10 **Breton Sound** *sound* Louisiana, S USA
184 K2 **Brett, Cape** *headland* North Island, New Zealand *35°11′S 174°21′E*
101 G21 **Bretten** Baden-Württemberg, SW Germany *49°01′N 08°42′E*
99 K15 **Breugel** Noord-Brabant, S Netherlands *51°30′N 05°30′E*
106 B6 **Breuil-Cervinia** *It.* Cervinia. Valle d'Aosta, NW Italy *45°57′N 07°37′E*
98 I11 **Breukelen** Utrecht, C Netherlands *52°11′N 05°01′E*
21 P10 **Brevard** North Carolina, SE USA *35°13′N 82°46′W*
38 L9 **Brevig Mission** Alaska, USA *65°19′N 166°29′W*
95 G16 **Brevik** Telemark, S Norway *59°05′N 09°42′E*
183 P5 **Brewarrina** New South Wales, SE Australia *30°01′S 146°50′E*
19 R6 **Brewer** Maine, NE USA *44°46′N 68°44′W*
29 T11 **Brewster** Minnesota, N USA *43°43′N 95°28′W*
29 N14 **Brewster** Nebraska, C USA *41°57′N 99°52′W*
31 U12 **Brewster** Ohio, N USA *40°42′N 81°36′W*
Brewster, Kap *see* Kangikajik
183 O8 **Brewster, Lake** ◎ New South Wales, SE Australia
23 P7 **Brewton** Alabama, S USA *31°06′N 87°04′W*
Brezhnev *see* Naberezhnyye Chelny
109 W12 **Brežice** *Ger.* Rann. E Slovenia *45°54′N 15°35′E*
114 G9 **Breznik** Pernik, W Bulgaria *42°45′N 22°54′E*
111 K19 **Brezno** *Ger.* Bries, Briesen, *Hung.* Breznóbánya; *prev.* Brezno nad Hronom. Banskobystrický Kraj, C Slovakia *48°49′N 19°40′E*
Breznóbánya/Brezno nad Hronom *see* Brezno
116 I12 **Brezoi** Vâlcea, SW Romania *45°18′N 24°15′E*
114 J10 **Brezovo** *prev.* Abrashlare. Plovdiv, C Bulgaria *42°19′N 25°05′E*
79 K14 **Bria** Haute-Kotto, C Central African Republic *06°30′N 22°00′E*
103 U13 **Briançon** *anc.* Brigantio. Hautes-Alpes, SE France *44°55′N 06°37′E*
36 K7 **Brian Head** ▲ Utah, W USA *37°40′N 112°49′W*
103 O7 **Briare** Loiret, C France *47°35′N 02°46′E*
183 V2 **Bribie Island** *island* Queensland, E Australia
43 O14 **Bribrí** Limón, E Costa Rica *09°37′N 82°51′W*
116 L8 **Briceni** *var.* Brinceni, *Rus.* Brichany. N Moldova *48°21′N 27°02′E*
Bricgstow *see* Bristol
Brichany *see* Briceni
99 M24 **Bridel** Luxembourg, C Luxembourg *49°40′N 06°03′E*
97 J22 **Bridgend** S Wales, United Kingdom *51°30′N 03°37′W*
14 I14 **Bridgenorth** Ontario, SE Canada *44°21′N 78°22′W*
23 Q1 **Bridgeport** Alabama, S USA *34°57′N 85°42′W*
35 R8 **Bridgeport** California, W USA *38°14′N 119°15′W*
18 L13 **Bridgeport** Connecticut, NE USA *41°10′N 73°12′W*
31 N15 **Bridgeport** Illinois, N USA *38°42′N 87°45′W*
28 J14 **Bridgeport** Nebraska, C USA *41°37′N 103°07′W*
25 S6 **Bridgeport** Texas, SW USA *33°12′N 97°45′W*
21 S3 **Bridgeport** West Virginia, NE USA *39°17′N 80°15′W*
25 S5 **Bridgeport, Lake** ⊠ Texas, SW USA
33 U11 **Bridger** Montana, NW USA *45°16′N 108°55′W*
18 I17 **Bridgeton** New Jersey, NE USA *39°24′N 75°10′W*
180 J14 **Bridgetown** Western Australia *34°01′S 116°07′E*
45 Y14 **Bridgetown** ● (Barbados) SW Barbados *13°05′N 59°36′W*
183 P17 **Bridgewater** Tasmania, SE Australia *42°47′S 147°15′E*
13 P16 **Bridgewater** Nova Scotia, SE Canada *44°19′N 64°30′W*
19 P12 **Bridgewater** Massachusetts, NE USA *41°59′N 70°58′W*
29 Q11 **Bridgewater** South Dakota, N USA *43°33′N 97°30′W*
21 U5 **Bridgewater** Virginia, NE USA *38°22′N 78°58′W*
19 P8 **Bridgton** Maine, NE USA *44°04′N 70°43′W*
97 K23 **Bridgwater** SW England, United Kingdom *51°08′N 03°W*
97 K22 **Bridgwater Bay** *bay* SW England, United Kingdom
97 O16 **Bridlington** E England, United Kingdom *54°05′N 00°12′W*
97 O16 **Bridlington Bay** *bay* E England, United Kingdom
183 P15 **Bridport** Tasmania, SE Australia *41°03′S 147°26′E*
97 K24 **Bridport** S England, United Kingdom *50°44′N 02°43′W*
103 O5 **Brie** *cultural region* N France
Brieg *see* Brzeg
Briel *see* Brielle
98 G12 **Brielle** *var.* Briel, Bril, *Eng.* The Brill. Zuid-Holland, SW Netherlands *51°54′N 04°10′E*
108 E9 **Brienz** Bern, C Switzerland *46°45′N 08°00′E*
108 E9 **Brienzer See** ◎ SW Switzerland
Bries/Briesen *see* Brezno
Brietzig *see* Brzesko
103 S4 **Briey** Meurthe-et-Moselle, NE France *49°15′N 05°57′E*
108 E10 **Brig** *Fr.* Brigue, *It.* Briga. Valais, SW Switzerland *46°19′N 08°E*
Briga *see* Brig
101 G24 **Brigach** ≈ S Germany
18 K17 **Brigantine** New Jersey, NE USA *39°23′N 74°21′W*
Brigantio *see* Briançon
Brigantium *see* Bregenz
Brigels *see* Breil
25 S9 **Briggs** Texas, SW USA *30°52′N 97°55′W*
36 L1 **Brigham City** Utah, W USA *41°30′N 112°00′W*
14 J15 **Brighton** Ontario, SE Canada *44°01′N 77°44′W*
97 O23 **Brighton** SE England, United Kingdom *50°50′N 00°10′W*
37 T4 **Brighton** Colorado, C USA *39°58′N 104°46′W*
30 K15 **Brighton** Illinois, N USA *39°01′N 90°09′W*
103 T16 **Brignoles** Var, W France *43°25′N 06°03′E*
Brigue *see* Brig
105 O7 **Brihuega** Castilla-La Mancha, C Spain *40°45′N 02°52′W*
112 A10 **Brijuni** *It.* Brioni. *island group* NW Croatia
76 G12 **Brikama** W Gambia *13°13′N 16°37′W*
Bril *see* Brielle
Brill, The *see* Brielle
101 G15 **Brilon** Nordrhein-Westfalen, W Germany *51°24′N 08°34′E*
Brinceni *see* Briceni
107 Q18 **Brindisi** *anc.* Brundisium, Brundusium. Puglia, SE Italy *40°39′N 17°55′E*
27 W11 **Brinkley** Arkansas, C USA *34°53′N 91°11′W*
Brioni *see* Brijuni
103 P12 **Brioude** *anc.* Brivas. Haute-Loire, C France *45°18′N 03°23′E*
Briovera *see* St-Lô
183 U2 **Brisbane** *state capital* Queensland, E Australia *27°30′S 153°E*
183 V2 **Brisbane** ✈ Queensland, E Australia *27°30′S 153°00′E*
25 P2 **Briscoe** Texas, SW USA *35°34′N 100°17′W*
106 H10 **Brisighella** Emilia-Romagna, C Italy *44°12′N 11°45′E*
108 G11 **Brissago** Ticino, S Switzerland *46°07′N 08°40′E*
97 K22 **Bristol** *anc.* Bricgstow. SW England, United Kingdom *51°27′N 02°35′W*
18 M12 **Bristol** Connecticut, NE USA *41°40′N 72°56′W*
23 R9 **Bristol** Florida, SE USA *30°25′N 84°58′W*
19 N9 **Bristol** New Hampshire, NE USA *43°34′N 71°42′W*
29 Q8 **Bristol** South Dakota, N USA *45°18′N 97°45′W*
21 P8 **Bristol** Tennessee, S USA *36°36′N 82°11′W*
18 M8 **Bristol** Vermont, NE USA *44°07′N 73°00′W*
39 N14 **Bristol Bay** *bay* Alaska, USA
97 I22 **Bristol Channel** *inlet* England/Wales, United Kingdom
35 W14 **Bristol Lake** ◎ California, W USA
27 P10 **Bristow** Oklahoma, C USA *35°49′N 96°23′W*
86 C10 **Britain** *var.* Great Britain. *island* United Kingdom
Britannia Minor *see* Bretagne
10 L12 **British Columbia** *Fr.* Colombie-Britannique. ⬖ *province* SW Canada
British Guiana *see* Guyana
British Honduras *see* Belize
173 Q7 **British Indian Ocean Territory** ◇ *UK dependent territory* C Indian Ocean
86 B9 **British Isles** *island group* NW Europe
10 I1 **British Mountains** ▲▲ Yukon Territory, NW Canada
British North Borneo *see* Sabah
British Solomon Islands Protectorate *see* Solomon Islands
45 S8 **British Virgin Islands** *var.* Virgin Islands. ◇ *UK dependent territory* E West Indies
83 J21 **Brits** North-West, N South Africa *25°39′S 27°47′E*
83 H24 **Britstown** Northern Cape, W South Africa *30°36′S 23°30′E*
14 F12 **Britt** Ontario, S Canada *45°46′N 80°34′W*
29 V12 **Britt** Iowa, C USA *43°06′N 93°48′W*
Brittany *see* Bretagne
29 Q7 **Britton** South Dakota, N USA *45°47′N 97°45′W*
Briva Curretia *see* Brive-la-Gaillarde
Briva Isarae *see* Pontoise
Brivas *see* Brioude
Brive *see* Brive-la-Gaillarde
102 M12 **Brive-la-Gaillarde** *prev.* Brive; *anc.* Briva Curretia. Corrèze, C France *45°09′N 01°31′E*
105 O4 **Briviesca** Castilla-León, N Spain *42°33′N 03°19′W*
Brixen *see* Bressanone
Brixia *see* Brescia
145 S15 **Brlik** *var.* Novotroickoje, Novotroitskoye. Zhambyl, SE Kazakhstan *43°39′N 73°45′E*
Brněnský Kraj *see* Jihomoravský Kraj
111 G18 **Brno** *Ger.* Brünn. Jihomoravský Kraj, SE Czech Republic *49°11′N 16°35′E*
96 G7 **Broad Bay** *bay* NW Scotland, United Kingdom
25 X8 **Broaddus** Texas, SW USA *31°18′N 94°16′W*
183 O12 **Broadford** Victoria, SE Australia *37°07′S 145°04′E*
96 G9 **Broadford** N Scotland, United Kingdom *57°14′N 05°54′W*
96 J13 **Broad Law** ▲ S Scotland, United Kingdom *55°30′N 03°22′W*
23 U3 **Broad River** ≈ Georgia, SE USA
21 N8 **Broad River** ≈ North Carolina/South Carolina, SE USA
181 Y8 **Broadsound Range** ▲▲ Queensland, E Australia
33 X11 **Broadus** Montana, NW USA *45°28′N 105°22′W*
21 U4 **Broadway** Virginia, NE USA *38°36′N 78°48′W*
118 E9 **Brocēni** Saldus, SW Latvia *56°41′N 22°31′E*
11 U11 **Brochet** Manitoba, C Canada *57°55′N 101°40′W*
11 U10 **Brochet, Lac** ◎ Manitoba, C Canada
15 S5 **Brochet, Lac au** ◎ Québec, SE Canada
101 K14 **Brocken** ▲ C Germany *51°48′N 10°38′E*
19 O12 **Brockton** Massachusetts, NE USA *42°04′N 71°01′W*
14 L14 **Brockville** Ontario, SE Canada *44°35′N 75°44′W*
18 D13 **Brockway** Pennsylvania, NE USA *41°14′N 78°45′W*
Brod/Bród *see* Slavonski Brod
9 N5 **Brodeur Peninsula** *peninsula* Baffin Island, Nunavut, NE Canada
96 H13 **Brodick** W Scotland, United Kingdom *55°34′N 05°10′W*
Brod na Savi *see* Slavonski Brod
110 K9 **Brodnica** *Ger.* Buddenbrock. Kujawski-pomorskie, C Poland *53°15′N 19°23′E*
112 G10 **Brod-Posavina** *off.* Brodsko-Posavska Županija, *var.* Slavonski Brod-Posavina. ⬖ *province* NE Croatia
Brodsko-Posavska Županija *see* Brod-Posavina
116 J5 **Brody** L'vivs'ka Oblast', NW Ukraine *50°05′N 25°08′E*
98 I10 **Broek-in-Waterland** Noord-Holland, C Netherlands *52°27′N 04°59′E*
32 L13 **Brogan** Oregon, NW USA *44°15′N 117°34′W*
110 N10 **Brok** Mazowieckie, C Poland *52°42′N 21°53′E*
27 P9 **Broken Arrow** Oklahoma, C USA *36°03′N 95°47′W*
183 T9 **Broken Bay** *bay* New South Wales, SE Australia
29 N15 **Broken Bow** Nebraska, C USA *41°24′N 99°38′W*
27 R13 **Broken Bow** Oklahoma, C USA *34°01′N 94°44′W*
27 R12 **Broken Bow Lake** ⊠ Oklahoma, C USA
182 L6 **Broken Hill** New South Wales, SE Australia *31°58′S 141°27′E*
173 S10 **Broken Ridge** *undersea feature* S Indian Ocean *31°30′S 95°00′E*
186 C6 **Broken Water Bay** *bay* W Bismarck Sea
55 W10 **Brokopondo** Brokopondo, NE Surinam *05°04′N 55°00′W*
55 W10 **Brokopondo** ⬖ *district* C Surinam
Bromberg *see* Bydgoszcz
95 L22 **Bromölla** Skåne, S Sweden *56°04′N 14°28′E*
97 L20 **Bromsgrove** W England, United Kingdom *52°20′N 02°03′W*
95 G20 **Brønderslev** Nordjylland, N Denmark *57°16′N 09°58′E*
106 D8 **Broni** Lombardia, N Italy *45°04′N 09°18′E*
10 K11 **Bronlund Peak** ▲ British Columbia, W Canada *57°27′N 126°43′W*
93 F14 **Brønnøysund** Nordland, C Norway *65°38′N 12°15′E*
23 V10 **Bronson** Florida, SE USA *29°25′N 82°38′W*
31 Q11 **Bronson** Michigan, N USA *41°52′N 85°11′W*
25 X8 **Bronson** Texas, SW USA *31°20′N 94°00′W*
107 L24 **Bronte** Sicilia, Italy, C Mediterranean Sea *37°47′N 14°50′E*
25 P8 **Bronte** Texas, SW USA *31°53′N 100°17′W*
25 Y9 **Brookeland** Texas, SW USA *31°05′N 93°57′W*
170 M7 **Brooke's Point** Palawan, W Philippines *08°54′N 117°54′E*
27 T3 **Brookfield** Missouri, C USA *39°46′N 93°04′W*
22 K7 **Brookhaven** Mississippi, S USA *31°34′N 90°26′W*
32 E16 **Brookings** Oregon, NW USA *42°03′N 124°16′W*
29 R10 **Brookings** South Dakota, N USA *44°15′N 96°46′W*
29 W14 **Brooklyn** Iowa, C USA *41°43′N 92°27′W*
29 U8 **Brooklyn Park** Minnesota, N USA *45°06′N 93°18′W*
21 U7 **Brookneal** Virginia, NE USA *37°03′N 78°56′W*
11 R16 **Brooks** Alberta, SW Canada *50°35′N 111°54′W*
25 V11 **Brookshire** Texas, SW USA *29°47′N 95°57′W*
38 L8 **Brooks Mountain** ▲ Alaska, USA *65°31′N 167°24′W*
38 M11 **Brooks Range** ▲▲ Alaska, USA
31 O12 **Brookston** Indiana, N USA *40°34′N 86°53′W*
23 V11 **Brooksville** Florida, SE USA *28°33′N 82°23′W*
23 N4 **Brooksville** Mississippi, S USA *33°13′N 88°34′W*
180 J13 **Brookton** Western Australia *32°24′S 117°04′E*
31 Q14 **Brookville** Indiana, N USA *39°25′N 85°00′W*
18 D13 **Brookville** Pennsylvania, NE USA *41°07′N 79°05′W*
31 Q14 **Brookville Lake** ⊠ Indiana, N USA
180 K5 **Broome** Western Australia *17°58′S 122°15′E*
37 S4 **Broomfield** Colorado, C USA *39°55′N 105°05′W*
Broos *see* Orăștie
96 J7 **Brora** N Scotland, United Kingdom *57°59′N 04°00′W*
96 I7 **Brora** ≈ N Scotland, United Kingdom
95 F23 **Brørup** Ribe, W Denmark *55°29′N 09°01′E*
95 L23 **Brösarp** Skåne, S Sweden *55°43′N 14°10′E*
116 J9 **Broșteni** Suceava, NE Romania *47°14′N 25°43′E*
102 M6 **Brou** Eure-et-Loir, C France *48°12′N 01°10′E*
Broucsella *see* Brussel/Bruxelles
Broughton Bay *see* Tongjosŏn-man
Broughton Island *see* Qikiqtarjuaq
138 G7 **Broummâna** C Lebanon *33°53′N 35°39′E*
22 I9 **Broussard** Louisiana, S USA *30°09′N 91°57′W*
98 E13 **Brouwersdam** *dam* SW Netherlands
98 E13 **Brouwershaven** Zeeland, SW Netherlands *51°44′N 03°50′E*
117 P4 **Brovary** Kyyivs'ka Oblast', N Ukraine *50°30′N 30°45′E*
95 G20 **Brovst** Nordjylland, N Denmark *57°06′N 09°32′E*
31 S8 **Brown City** Michigan, N USA *43°12′N 82°50′W*
24 M6 **Brownfield** Texas, SW USA *33°11′N 102°16′W*
33 Q7 **Browning** Montana, NW USA *48°33′N 113°00′W*
33 R6 **Brown, Mount** ▲ Montana, NW USA *48°52′N 111°08′W*
0 M9 **Browns Bank** *undersea feature* NW Atlantic Ocean *42°40′N 66°05′W*
31 O14 **Brownsburg** Indiana, N USA *39°50′N 86°24′W*
18 J16 **Browns Mills** New Jersey, NE USA *39°58′N 74°33′W*
44 J12 **Browns Town** C Jamaica *18°28′N 77°22′W*
31 P15 **Brownstown** Indiana, N USA *38°52′N 86°02′W*
29 R8 **Browns Valley** Minnesota, N USA *45°36′N 96°49′W*
20 K7 **Brownsville** Kentucky, S USA *37°10′N 86°18′W*
20 F9 **Brownsville** Tennessee, S USA *35°35′N 89°15′W*
25 T17 **Brownsville** Texas, SW USA *25°56′N 97°28′W*
55 W10 **Brownsweg** Brokopondo, C Surinam
29 U9 **Brownton** Minnesota, N USA *44°43′N 94°21′W*
19 R5 **Brownville Junction** Maine, NE USA *45°20′N 69°04′W*
25 R8 **Brownwood** Texas, SW USA *31°42′N 98°59′W*
25 R8 **Brownwood Lake** ⊠ Texas, SW USA
104 I9 **Brozas** Extremadura, W Spain *39°37′N 06°48′W*
119 M18 **Brozha** Mahilyowskaya Voblasts', E Belarus *52°57′N 29°07′E*
103 O2 **Bruay-en-Artois** Pas-de-Calais, N France *50°31′N 02°30′E*
103 P2 **Bruay-sur-l'Escaut** Nord, N France *50°24′N 03°33′E*
14 F13 **Bruce Peninsula** *peninsula* Ontario, S Canada
20 H9 **Bruceton** Tennessee, S USA *36°02′N 88°14′W*
25 T9 **Bruceville** Texas, SW USA *31°17′N 97°15′W*
101 G21 **Bruchsal** Baden-Württemberg, SW Germany *49°07′N 08°35′E*
109 Q7 **Bruck** Salzburg, NW Austria *47°18′N 12°51′E*
Bruck *see* Bruck an der Mur
109 Y4 **Bruck an der Leitha** Niederösterreich, NE Austria *48°02′N 16°47′E*
109 V7 **Bruck an der Mur** *var.* Bruck. Steiermark, C Austria *47°25′N 15°17′E*
101 M24 **Bruckmühl** Bayern, SE Germany *47°52′N 11°54′E*
168 E7 **Brueuh, Pulau** *island* NW Indonesia
Bruges *see* Brugge
108 F6 **Brugg** Aargau, NW Switzerland *47°29′N 08°13′E*
99 C16 **Brugge** *Fr.* Bruges. West-Vlaanderen, NW Belgium *51°13′N 03°14′E*
109 R9 **Bruggen** Kärnten, S Austria *46°46′N 13°13′E*
101 E16 **Brühl** Nordrhein-Westfalen, W Germany *50°50′N 06°55′E*
99 F14 **Bruinisse** Zeeland, SW Netherlands *51°40′N 04°04′E*
169 R9 **Bruit, Pulau** *island* East Malaysia
14 K10 **Brûlé, Lac** ◎ Québec, SE Canada
30 M4 **Brule River** ≈ Michigan/Wisconsin, N USA
99 H23 **Brûly** Namur, S Belgium *49°55′N 04°31′E*
59 N17 **Brumado** Bahia, E Brazil *14°14′S 41°38′W*
98 M11 **Brummen** Gelderland, E Netherlands *52°05′N 06°10′E*
94 H13 **Brumunddal** Hedmark, S Norway *60°54′N 11°00′E*
23 Q6 **Brundidge** Alabama, S USA *31°43′N 85°49′W*
Brundisium/Brundusium *see* Brindisi
33 N15 **Bruneau River** ≈ Idaho, NW USA
Bruneck *see* Brunico
169 T8 **Brunei** *off.* Brunei Darussalam, *Mal.* Negara Brunei Darussalam. ◆ *monarchy* SE Asia
169 T7 **Brunei Bay** *var.* Teluk Brunei. *bay* N Brunei
Brunei Darussalam *see* Brunei
Brunei, Teluk *see* Brunei Bay
Brunei Town *see* Bandar Seri Begawan
106 H5 **Brunico** *Ger.* Bruneck. Trentino-Alto Adige, N Italy *46°49′N 11°57′E*
Brünn *see* Brno
185 G17 **Brunner, Lake** ◎ South Island, New Zealand
99 M18 **Brunssum** Limburg, SE Netherlands *50°57′N 05°59′E*
23 W7 **Brunswick** Georgia, SE USA *31°09′N 81°30′W*
19 Q8 **Brunswick** Maine, NE USA *43°54′N 69°58′W*
21 V3 **Brunswick** Maryland, NE USA *39°18′N 77°37′W*
27 T3 **Brunswick** Missouri, C USA *39°25′N 93°07′W*
31 T11 **Brunswick** Ohio, N USA *41°14′N 81°50′W*
Brunswick *see* Braunschweig
63 H24 **Brunswick, Península** *headland* S Chile *53°30′S 71°27′W*
111 H17 **Bruntál** *Ger.* Freudenthal. Moravskoslezský Kraj, E Czech Republic *50°00′N 17°27′E*
195 N3 **Brunt Ice Shelf** *ice shelf* Antarctica
Brusa *see* Bursa
114 G7 **Brusartsi** Montana, NW Bulgaria *43°39′N 23°04′E*
37 U3 **Brush** Colorado, C USA *40°15′N 103°37′W*
42 M5 **Brus Laguna** Gracias a Dios, E Honduras *15°46′N 84°32′W*
60 K13 **Brusque** Santa Catarina, S Brazil *27°07′S 48°54′W*
Brussa *see* Bursa
99 E18 **Brussel** *var.* Brussels, *Fr.* Bruxelles, *Ger.* Brüssel; *anc.* Broucsella. ● (Belgium) Brussels, C Belgium *50°52′N 04°21′E* ***see also*** Bruxelles
Brussel *see* Bruxelles
Brüssel/Brussels *see* Brussel/Bruxelles
117 O5 **Brusyliv** Zhytomyrs'ka Oblast', N Ukraine *50°16′N 29°31′E*
183 Q12 **Bruthen** Victoria, SE Australia *37°43′S 147°49′E*
Bruttium *see* Calabria
Brüx *see* Most
99 E18 **Bruxelles** *var.* Brussels, *Dut.* Brussel, *Ger.* Brüssel; *anc.* Broucsella. ● Brussels, C Belgium *50°52′N 04°21′E* ***see also*** Brussel
Bruxelles *see* Brussel
54 J7 **Bruzual** Apure, W Venezuela *07°59′N 69°18′W*
31 Q11 **Bryan** Ohio, N USA *41°30′N 84°34′W*
25 U10 **Bryan** Texas, SW USA *30°40′N 96°23′W*
194 J4 **Bryan Coast** *physical region* Antarctica
122 L11 **Bryanka** Krasnoyarskiy Kray, C Russian Federation *59°01′N 93°13′E*
117 Y7 **Bryanka** Luhans'ka Oblast', E Ukraine *48°30′N 38°45′E*
182 J8 **Bryan, Mount** ▲ South Australia *33°25′S 138°59′E*
126 I6 **Bryansk** Bryanskaya Oblast', W Russian Federation *53°16′N 34°07′E*
126 H6 **Bryanskaya Oblast'** ⬖ *province* W Russian Federation
194 J5 **Bryant, Cape** *headland* Antarctica
27 U8 **Bryant Creek** ≈ Missouri, C USA
36 K8 **Bryce Canyon** *canyon* Utah, W USA
119 O15 **Bryli** Mahilyowskaya Voblasts', E Belarus *53°54′N 30°33′E*
95 C17 **Bryne** Rogaland, S Norway *58°43′N 05°40′E*
25 R6 **Bryson** Texas, SW USA *33°09′N 98°23′W*
21 N10 **Bryson City** North Carolina, SE USA *35°26′N 83°27′W*
14 K11 **Bryson, Lac** ◎ Québec, SE Canada
126 K13 **Bryukhovetskaya** Krasnodarskiy Kray, SW Russian Federation *45°49′N 38°01′E*
111 H15 **Brzeg** *Ger.* Brieg; *anc.* Civitas Altae Ripae. Opolskie, S Poland *50°52′N 17°27′E*
111 G14 **Brzeg Dolny** *Ger.* Dyhernfurth. Dolnośląskie, SW Poland *51°15′N 16°40′E*
Brześć Litewski/Brześć nad Bugiem *see* Brest
111 L17 **Brzesko** *Ger.* Brietzig. Małopolskie, SE Poland *49°59′N 20°34′E*
Brzeżany *see* Berezhany
110 K12 **Brzeziny** Łódzkie, C Poland *51°49′N 19°41′E*
Brzostowica Wielka *see* Vyalikaya Byerastavitsa
111 O17 **Brzozów** Podkarpackie, SE Poland *49°38′N 22°00′E*
Bsharrī/Bsherri *see* Bcharré
187 X14 **Bua** Vanua Levu, N Fiji *16°48′S 178°36′E*
95 J20 **Bua** Halland, S Sweden *57°14′N 12°07′E*
82 M13 **Bua** ≈ C Malawi
Bua *see* Čiovo
81 L18 **Bu'aale** *It.* Buale. Jubbada Dhexe, SW Somalia *0°52′N 42°37′E*
Buache, Mount *see* Mutunte, Mount
189 Q8 **Buada Lagoon** *lagoon* Nauru, C Pacific Ocean
186 M8 **Buala** Santa Isabel, E Solomon Islands *08°06′S 159°31′E*
Buale *see* Bu'aale
190 H1 **Buariki** *atoll* Tungaru, W Kiribati
167 Q10 **Bua Yai** *var.* Ban Bua Yai. Nakhon Ratchasima, E Thailand *15°35′N 102°25′E*
75 P8 **Bu'ayrāt al Ḩasūn** *var.* Buwayrāt al Hasūn. C Libya *31°22′N 15°41′E*
76 H13 **Buba** S Guinea-Bissau *11°36′N 14°55′W*
171 P11 **Bubaa** Sulawesi, N Indonesia *0°32′N 122°27′E*
81 D20 **Bubanza** NW Burundi *03°04′S 29°22′E*
83 K18 **Bubi** *prev.* Bubye. ≈ S Zimbabwe
142 L11 **Būbīyan, Jazīrat** *island* E Kuwait
Bublitz *see* Bobolice
Bubye *see* Bubi
187 Y13 **Buca** *prev.* Mbutha. Vanua Levu, N Fiji *16°39′S 179°51′E*
136 F16 **Bucak** Burdur, SW Turkey *37°28′N 30°37′E*
54 G8 **Bucaramanga** Santander, N Colombia *07°08′N 73°10′W*
107 M18 **Buccino** Campania, S Italy *40°37′N 15°25′E*
116 K9 **Bucecea** Botoșani, NE Romania *47°45′N 26°30′E*
116 J6 **Buchach** *Pol.* Buczacz. Ternopil's'ka Oblast', W Ukraine *49°04′N 25°23′E*
183 Q12 **Buchan** Victoria, SE Australia *37°26′S 148°11′E*
76 J17 **Buchanan** *prev.* Grand Bassa. SW Liberia *05°53′N 10°03′W*
23 R3 **Buchanan** Georgia, SE USA *33°48′N 85°11′W*
31 O11 **Buchanan** Michigan, N USA *41°49′N 86°21′W*
21 T6 **Buchanan** Virginia, NE USA *37°31′N 79°40′W*
25 R10 **Buchanan Dam** Texas, SW USA *30°42′N 98°24′W*
25 R10 **Buchanan, Lake** ⊠ Texas, SW USA
96 L8 **Buchan Ness** *headland* NE Scotland, United Kingdom *57°28′N 01°46′W*
13 T12 **Buchans** Newfoundland and Labrador, SE Canada *48°49′N 56°53′W*
Bucharest *see* București
101 H20 **Buchen** Baden-Württemberg, SW Germany *49°31′N 09°18′E*
100 I10 **Buchholz in der Nordheide** Niedersachsen, NW Germany *53°19′N 09°52′E*
108 F7 **Buchs** Aargau, N Switzerland *47°24′N 08°04′E*
108 I8 **Buchs** Sankt Gallen, NE Switzerland *47°10′N 09°28′E*
100 H13 **Bückeburg** Niedersachsen, NW Germany *52°16′N 09°03′E*
36 K14 **Buckeye** Arizona, SW USA *33°22′N 112°34′W*
Buckeye State *see* Ohio
21 S4 **Buckhannon** West Virginia, NE USA *38°59′N 80°14′W*
25 T9 **Buckholts** Texas, SW USA *30°52′N 97°07′W*
96 K8 **Buckie** NE Scotland, United Kingdom *57°39′N 02°56′W*
14 M12 **Buckingham** Québec, SE Canada *45°35′N 75°25′W*
21 U6 **Buckingham** Virginia, NE USA *37°33′N 78°34′W*
97 N21 **Buckinghamshire** *cultural region* SE England, United Kingdom
39 N8 **Buckland** Alaska, USA *65°58′N 161°07′W*
182 G7 **Buckleboo** South Australia *32°55′S 136°11′E*
26 K7 **Bucklin** Kansas, C USA *37°33′N 99°37′W*
27 T3 **Bucklin** Missouri, C USA *39°46′N 92°53′W*
36 I12 **Buckskin Mountains** ▲▲ Arizona, SW USA
19 R7 **Bucksport** Maine, NE USA *44°34′N 68°46′W*
82 A9 **Buco Zau** Cabinda, NW Angola *04°45′S 12°34′E*
Bu Craa *see* Bou Craa
116 K14 **București** *Eng.* Bucharest, *Ger.* Bukarest, *prev.* Altenburg; *anc.* Cetatea Damboviței. ● (Romania) București, S Romania *44°27′N 26°06′E*
31 S12 **Bucyrus** Ohio, N USA *40°47′N 82°57′W*
Buczacz *see* Buchach
94 E9 **Bud** Møre og Romsdal, S Norway *62°55′N 06°55′E*
25 S11 **Buda** Texas, SW USA *30°05′N 97°50′W*
119 O18 **Buda-Kashalyova** *Rus.* Buda-Koshelëvo. Homyel'skaya Voblasts', SE Belarus *52°43′N 30°34′E*
Buda-Koshelëvo *see* Buda-Kashalyova
166 L4 **Budalin** Sagaing, C Burma (Myanmar) *22°24′N 95°08′E*
111 J22 **Budapest** *off.* Budapest Főváros, *SCr.* Budimpešta. ● (Hungary) Pest, N Hungary *47°30′N 19°03′E*
Budapest Főváros *see* Budapest
152 K11 **Budaun** Uttar Pradesh, N India *28°02′N 79°07′E*
141 O9 **Budayyi'ah** *oasis* C Saudi Arabia
195 Y12 **Budd Coast** *physical region* Antarctica
Buddenbrock *see* Brodnica
107 C17 **Budduso** Sardegna, Italy, C Mediterranean Sea *40°37′N 09°19′E*
97 I23 **Bude** SW England, United Kingdom *50°50′N 04°33′W*
22 J7 **Bude** Mississippi, S USA *31°27′N 90°51′W*
Budějovický Kraj *see* Jihočeský Kraj
99 K16 **Budel** Noord-Brabant, SE Netherlands *51°17′N 05°35′E*
100 I8 **Büdelsdorf** Schleswig-Holstein, N Germany *54°20′N 09°40′E*
127 O14 **Budënnovsk** Stavropol'skiy Kray, SW Russian Federation *44°46′N 44°07′E*
116 K14 **Budești** Călărași, SE Romania *44°13′N 26°30′E*
Budge-Budge *see* Baj Baj
Budgewoi *see* Budgewoi Lake
183 T8 **Budgewoi Lake** *var.* Budgewoi. New South Wales, SE Australia *33°14′S 151°34′E*
92 I2 **Búdhardalur** Vesturland, W Iceland *65°07′N 21°45′W*
Budimpešta *see* Budapest
79 J16 **Budjala** Equateur, NW Dem. Rep. Congo *02°39′N 19°42′E*
106 G10 **Budrio** Emilia-Romagna, C Italy *44°33′N 11°34′E*
Budslav *see* Budslaw
119 K14 **Budslaw** *Rus.* Budslav. Minskaya Voblasts', N Belarus *54°47′N 27°27′E*
Budua *see* Budva
169 R9 **Budu, Tanjung** *headland* East Malaysia *02°51′N 111°42′E*
113 J17 **Budva** *It.* Budua. W Montenegro *42°17′N 18°49′E*
Budweis *see* České Budějovice
Budyšin *see* Bautzen
79 D16 **Buea** Sud-Ouest, SW Cameroon *04°09′N 09°13′E*
103 S13 **Buëch** ≈ SE France
18 J17 **Buena** New Jersey, NE USA *39°30′N 74°55′W*
62 K12 **Buena Esperanza** San Luis, C Argentina *34°45′S 65°15′W*
54 C11 **Buenaventura** Valle del Cauca, W Colombia *03°54′N 77°02′W*
40 I4 **Buenaventura** Chihuahua, N Mexico *29°50′N 107°30′W*
57 M18 **Buena Vista** Santa Cruz, C Bolivia *17°28′S 63°37′W*
40 G10 **Buenavista** Baja California Sur, NW Mexico *23°39′N 109°41′W*
37 S5 **Buena Vista** Colorado, C USA *38°50′N 106°07′W*
23 S5 **Buena Vista** Georgia, SE USA *32°19′N 84°31′W*
21 T6 **Buena Vista** Virginia, NE USA *37°44′N 79°22′W*
44 F5 **Buena Vista, Bahia de** *bay* N Cuba
35 R13 **Buena Vista Lake Bed** ◎ California, W USA
105 P8 **Buendía, Embalse de** ⊠ C Spain
63 F16 **Bueno, Río** ≈ S Chile
62 N12 **Buenos Aires** *hist.* Santa Maria del Buen Aire. ● (Argentina) Buenos Aires, E Argentina *34°40′S 58°30′W*
43 O15 **Buenos Aires** Puntarenas, SE Costa Rica *09°10′N 83°23′W*
61 C20 **Buenos Aires** *off.* Provincia de Buenos Aires. ⬖ *province* E Argentina
63 H19 **Buenos Aires, Lago** *var.* Lago General Carrera. ◎ Argentina/Chile
Buenos Aires, Provincia de *see* Buenos Aires
54 C13 **Buesaco** Nariño, SW Colombia *01°22′N 77°07′W*
29 U8 **Buffalo** Minnesota, N USA *45°11′N 93°50′W*
26 T6 **Buffalo** Missouri, C USA *37°38′N 93°05′W*
18 D10 **Buffalo** New York, NE USA *42°53′N 78°53′W*
27 K8 **Buffalo** Oklahoma, C USA *36°51′N 99°38′W*
28 J7 **Buffalo** South Dakota, N USA *45°25′N 103°35′W*
25 V8 **Buffalo** Texas, SW USA *31°25′N 96°04′W*
33 W12 **Buffalo** Wyoming, C USA *44°21′N 106°40′W*
29 U11 **Buffalo Center** Iowa, C USA *43°23′N 93°57′W*
24 M3 **Buffalo Lake** ⊠ Texas, SW USA
30 K7 **Buffalo Lake** ⊠ Wisconsin, N USA
11 S12 **Buffalo Narrows** Saskatchewan, C Canada *55°52′N 108°28′W*
27 U9 **Buffalo River** ≈ Arkansas, C USA
29 R5 **Buffalo River** ≈ Minnesota, N USA
20 I10 **Buffalo River** ≈ Tennessee, S USA
30 J6 **Buffalo River** ≈ Wisconsin, N USA
44 L12 **Buff Bay** E Jamaica *18°18′N 76°40′W*
23 T3 **Buford** Georgia, SE USA *34°07′N 84°00′W*

◆ Country
● Country Capital
◇ Dependent Territory
○ Dependent Territory Capital
⬖ Administrative Regions
✈ International Airport
▲ Mountain
▲▲ Mountain Range
Volcano
≈ River
◎ Lake
⊠ Reservoir

BUFORD – CAÁLA

28 J3 **Buford** North Dakota, N USA 48°00′N 103°58′W
33 Y17 **Buford** Wyoming, C USA 41°05′N 105°17′W
116 J14 **Buftea** Ilfov, S Romania 44°34′N 25°58′E
84 I9 **Bug** *Bel.* Zakhodni Buh, *Eng.* Western Bug, *Rus.* Zapadnyy Bug, *Ukr.* Zakhidnyy Buh. ≋ E Europe
54 D11 **Buga** Valle del Cauca, W Colombia 03°53′N 76°17′W
Buga *see* Dörvöljin
103 O17 **Bugarach, Pic du** ▲ S France 42°52′N 02°23′E
162 F8 **Bugat** *var.* Bayangol. Govĭ-Altay, SW Mongolia 45°33′N 94°22′E
146 B12 **Bugdaýly** *Rus.* Bugdayly. Balkan Welaýaty, W Turkmenistan 38°42′N 54°14′E
Bugdayly *see* Bugdaýly
Buggs Island Lake *see* John H. Kerr Reservoir
Bughotu *see* Santa Isabel
171 O14 **Bugingkalo** Sulawesi, C Indonesia 04°49′S 121°42′E
64 P6 **Bugio** *island* Madeira, Portugal, NE Atlantic Ocean
92 M8 **Bugøynes** Finnmark, N Norway 69°57′N 29°34′E
125 Q3 **Bugrino** Nenetskiy Avtonomnyy Okrug, NW Russian Federation 68°48′N 49°12′E
127 T5 **Bugul'ma** Respublika Tatarstan, W Russian Federation 54°31′N 52°45′E
Bügür *see* Luntai
127 T6 **Buguruslan** Orenburgskaya Oblast', W Russian Federation 53°38′N 52°30′E
159 R9 **Buh He** ≋ C China
101 F22 **Bühl** Baden-Württemberg, SW Germany 48°42′N 08°07′E
33 O15 **Buhl** Idaho, NW USA 42°36′N 114°45′W
116 K10 **Buhuşi** Bacău, E Romania 46°41′N 26°45′E
Buie d'Istria *see* Buje
97 J20 **Builth Wells** E Wales, United Kingdom 52°07′N 03°28′W
186 J8 **Buin** Bougainville Island, NE Papua New Guinea 06°52′S 155°42′E
108 J9 **Buin, Piz** ▲ Austria/Switzerland 46°51′N 10°07′E
127 Q4 **Buinsk** Chuvashskaya Respublika, W Russian Federation 55°09′N 47°00′E
127 Q4 **Buinsk** Respublika Tatarstan, W Russian Federation 54°58′N 48°16′E
163 R8 **Buir Nur** *Mong.* Buyr Nuur. ◎ China/Mongolia *see also* Buyr Nuur
Buir Nur *see* Buyr Nuur
98 M5 **Buitenpost** *Fris.* Bûtenpost. Friesland, N Netherlands 53°15′N 06°09′E
Buitenzorg *see* Bogor
83 F19 **Buitepos** Omaheke, E Namibia 22°17′S 19°59′E
105 N7 **Buitrago del Lozoya** Madrid, C Spain 41°00′N 03°38′W
Buj *see* Buy
104 M13 **Bujalance** Andalucía, S Spain 37°54′N 04°23′W
113 O17 **Bujanovac** SE Serbia 42°29′N 21°44′E
105 S6 **Bujaraloz** Aragón, NE Spain 41°29′N 00°10′W
112 A9 **Buje** *It.* Buie d'Istria. Istra, NW Croatia 45°23′N 13°40′E
Bujnurd *see* Bojnūrd
81 D21 **Bujumbura** *prev.* Usumbura. ● (Burundi) W Burundi 03°25′S 29°24′E
81 D20 **Bujumbura** ✈ W Burundi 03°21′S 29°19′E
159 N11 **Buka Daban** *var.* Bukadaban Feng. ▲ C China 36°09′N 90°52′E
Bukadaban Feng *see* Buka Daban
186 J6 **Buka Island** *island* NE Papua New Guinea
81 F18 **Bukakata** S Uganda 0°18′S 31°57′E
79 N24 **Bukama** Katanga, SE Dem. Rep. Congo 09°13′S 25°52′E
142 J4 **Būkān** *var.* Bowkān. Āžarbāyjān-e Gharbī, NW Iran 36°31′N 46°10′E
Bukantau, Gory *see* Bo'kantov Tog'lari
Bukarest *see* Bucureşti
79 O19 **Bukavu** *prev.* Costermansville. Sud-Kivu, E Dem. Rep. Congo 02°19′S 28°49′E
81 F21 **Bukene** Tabora, NW Tanzania 04°15′S 32°51′E
141 W8 **Bū Khābī** *var.* Bakhābī. NW Oman 23°29′N 56°06′E
Bukhara *see* Buxoro
Bukharskaya Oblast' *see* Buxoro Viloyati
168 M14 **Bukitkemuning** Sumatera, W Indonesia 04°43′S 104°27′E
168 I11 **Bukittinggi** *prev.* Fort de Kock. Sumatera, W Indonesia 0°18′S 100°20′E
111 L21 **Bükk** ▲▲ NE Hungary
81 F19 **Bukoba** Kagera, NW Tanzania 01°19′S 31°49′E
113 N20 **Bukovo** S FYR Macedonia 40°59′N 21°20′E
108 G6 **Bülach** Zürich, NW Switzerland 47°31′N 08°30′E
Bŭlaevo *see* Bulayevo
Bulag *see* Tünel, Hövsgöl, Mongolia
Bulag *see* Möngönmorĭt, Töv, Mongolia
Bulagiyn Denj *see* Bulgan
183 U7 **Bulahdelah** New South Wales, SE Australia 32°24′S 152°13′E
171 P4 **Bulan** Luzon, N Philippines 12°40′N 123°55′E
137 N11 **Bulancak** Giresun, N Turkey 40°57′N 38°14′E
152 J10 **Bulandshahr** Uttar Pradesh, N India 28°30′N 77°49′E
137 R14 **Bulanık** Muş, E Turkey 39°04′N 42°16′E
127 V7 **Bulanovo** Orenburgskaya Oblast', W Russian Federation 52°27′N 55°08′E
83 J17 **Bulawayo** *var.* Buluwayo. Bulawayo, SW Zimbabwe 20°08′S 28°37′E
83 J17 **Bulawayo** ✈ Matabeleland North, SW Zimbabwe 20°00′S 28°36′E
145 Q6 **Bulayevo** *Kaz.* Bŭlaevo. Severnyy Kazakhstan, N Kazakhstan 54°55′N 70°29′E
136 D15 **Buldan** Denizli, SW Turkey 38°03′N 28°50′E
154 G12 **Buldāna** Mahārāshtra, C India 20°31′N 76°18′E
38 E16 **Buldir Island** *island* Aleutian Islands, Alaska, USA
Buldur *see* Burdur
162 I8 **Bulgan** *var.* Bulagiyn Denj. Arhangay, C Mongolia 47°14′N 100°56′E
162 D7 **Bulgan** *var.* Jargalant. Bayan-Ölgiy, W Mongolia 46°56′N 91°07′E
162 K6 **Bulgan** Bulgan, N Mongolia 50°31′N 101°30′E
162 F7 **Bulgan** *var.* Bürenhayrhan. Hovd, W Mongolia 46°04′N 91°34′E
162 J10 **Bulgan** Ömnögovĭ, S Mongolia 44°07′N 103°28′E
162 J7 **Bulgan** ◈ *province* N Mongolia
Bulgan *see* Bayan-Öndör, Bayanhongor, C Mongolia
Bulgan *see* Darvi, Hovd, Mongolia
Bulgan *see* Tsagaan-Üür, Hövsgöl, Mongolia
114 H10 **Bulgaria** *off.* Republic of Bulgaria, *Bul.* Bŭlgariya; *prev.* People's Republic of Bulgaria. ◆ *republic* SE Europe
Bulgaria, People's Republic of *see* Bulgaria
Bulgaria, Republic of *see* Bulgaria
Bŭlgariya *see* Bulgaria
114 L9 **Bŭlgarka** ▲ E Bulgaria 42°43′N 26°19′E
171 S11 **Buli** Pulau Halmahera, E Indonesia 0°56′N 128°17′E
171 S11 **Buli, Teluk** *bay* Pulau Halmahera, E Indonesia
160 J13 **Buliu He** ≋ S China
Bullange *see* Büllingen
Bulla, Ostrov *see* Xärä Zirä Adası
104 M11 **Bullaque** ≋ C Spain
105 Q13 **Bullas** Murcia, SE Spain 38°02′N 01°40′W
80 M12 **Bullaxaar** Woqooyi Galbeed, NW Somalia 10°28′N 44°15′E
108 C9 **Bulle** Fribourg, SW Switzerland 46°37′N 07°04′E
185 G15 **Buller** ≋ South Island, New Zealand
183 P12 **Buller, Mount** ▲ Victoria, SE Australia 37°10′S 146°31′E
36 H11 **Bullhead City** Arizona, SW USA 35°07′N 114°32′W
99 N21 **Büllingen** *Fr.* Bullange. Liège, E Belgium 50°23′N 06°15′E
Bullion State *see* Missouri
21 T14 **Bull Island** *island* South Carolina, SE USA
182 M4 **Bulloo River Overflow** *wetland* New South Wales, SE Australia
184 M12 **Bulls** Manawatu-Wanganui, North Island, New Zealand 40°10′S 175°22′E
21 T14 **Bulls Bay** *bay* South Carolina, SE USA
27 U9 **Bull Shoals Lake** ⊠ Arkansas/Missouri, C USA
181 Q2 **Bulman** Northern Territory, N Australia 13°39′S 134°21′E
162 I6 **Bulnayn Nuruu** ▲▲ N Mongolia
171 O11 **Bulowa, Gunung** ▲ Sulawesi, N Indonesia 0°33′N 123°39′E
Bulqiza *see* Bulqizë
113 L19 **Bulqizë** *var.* Bulqiza. Dibër, C Albania 41°30′N 20°16′E
Bulsar *see* Valsād
171 N14 **Bulukumba** *prev.* Boeloekoemba. Sulawesi, C Indonesia 05°35′S 120°13′E
147 O11 **Bulungh'ur** *Rus.* Bulungur; *prev.* Krasnogvardeysk. Samarqand Viloyati, C Uzbekistan 39°46′N 67°18′E
79 I21 **Bulungu** Bandundu, SW Dem. Rep. Congo 04°36′S 18°34′E
Bulungur *see* Bulungh'ur
Buluwayo *see* Bulawayo
79 K17 **Bumba** Equateur, N Dem. Rep. Congo 02°14′N 22°25′E
121 R12 **Bumbah, Khalīj al** *gulf* N Libya
Bumbat *see* Bayan-Öndör
81 F19 **Bumbire Island** *island* N Tanzania
169 V8 **Bum Bun, Pulau** *island* East Malaysia
81 J17 **Buna** North Eastern, NE Kenya 02°40′N 39°34′E
25 Y10 **Buna** Texas, SW USA 30°25′N 94°00′W
Bunab *see* Bonāb
Bunai *see* M'bunai
147 S13 **Bunay** S Tajikistan 38°29′N 71°41′E
180 I13 **Bunbury** Western Australia 33°24′S 115°44′E
97 E14 **Buncrana** *Ir.* Bun Cranncha. NW Ireland 55°08′N 07°27′W
Bun Cranncha *see* Buncrana
181 Z9 **Bundaberg** Queensland, E Australia 24°50′S 152°16′E
183 T5 **Bundarra** New South Wales, SE Australia 30°12′S 151°06′E
100 G13 **Bünde** Nordrhein-Westfalen, NW Germany 52°12′N 08°34′E
152 H13 **Būndi** Rājasthān, N India 25°28′N 75°42′E
Bun Dobhráin *see* Bundoran
97 D15 **Bundoran** *Ir.* Bun Dobhráin. NW Ireland 54°30′N 08°11′W
113 K18 **Bunë** *SCr.* Bojana. ≋ Albania/Montenegro *see also* Bojana
Bunë *see* Bojana
171 Q8 **Bunga** ≋ Mindanao, S Philippines
168 I12 **Bungalaut, Selat** *strait* W Indonesia
167 R8 **Bung Kan** Nong Khai, E Thailand 18°19′N 103°39′E
181 N4 **Bungle Bungle Range** ▲▲ Western Australia
82 C10 **Bungo** Uíge, NW Angola 07°30′S 15°24′E
81 G18 **Bungoma** Western, W Kenya 0°34′N 34°34′E
164 F15 **Bungo-suidō** *strait* SW Japan
164 E14 **Bungo-Takada** Ōita, Kyūshū, SW Japan 33°34′N 131°28′E
100 K8 **Bungsberg** *hill* N Germany
Bungur *see* Bunyu
79 P17 **Bunia** Orientale, NE Dem. Rep. Congo 01°33′N 30°16′E
35 U6 **Bunker Hill** ▲ Nevada, W USA 39°16′N 117°06′W
22 I7 **Bunkie** Louisiana, S USA 30°58′N 92°12′W
23 X10 **Bunnell** Florida, SE USA 29°28′N 81°15′W
105 S10 **Buñol** País Valenciano, E Spain 39°25′N 00°47′W
98 K11 **Bunschoten** Utrecht, C Netherlands 52°15′N 05°23′E
136 K14 **Bünyan** Kayseri, C Turkey 38°51′N 35°50′E
169 W8 **Bunyu** *var.* Bungur. Borneo, N Indonesia 03°33′N 117°50′E
169 W8 **Bunyu, Pulau** *island* N Indonesia
Bunzlau *see* Bolesławiec
Buoddobohki *see* Patoniva
123 P7 **Buor-Khaya, Guba** *bay* N Russian Federation
123 P7 **Buor-Khaya, Guba** *bay* N Russian Federation
171 Z15 **Bupul** Papua, E Indonesia 07°24′S 140°57′E
81 K19 **Bura** Coast, SE Kenya 01°06′S 40°01′E
80 P12 **Buraan** Bari, N Somalia 10°03′N 49°08′E
Būrabay *see* Borovoye
Buraida *see* Buraydah
Buraimi *see* Al Buraymī
145 Y11 **Buran** Vostochnyy Kazakhstan, E Kazakhstan 48°00′N 85°09′E
158 G15 **Burang** Xizang Zizhiqu, W China 30°28′N 81°13′E
Burao *see* Burco
138 H8 **Burāq** Dar'ā, S Syria 33°11′N 36°28′E
141 O6 **Buraydah** *var.* Buraida. Al Qaşīm, N Saudi Arabia 26°50′N 44°E
35 S15 **Burbank** California, W USA 34°10′N 118°25′W
31 N11 **Burbank** Illinois, N USA 41°45′N 87°48′W
183 Q8 **Burcher** New South Wales, SE Australia 33°29′S 147°16′E
80 N13 **Burco** *var.* Burao, Bur'o. Togdheer, NW Somalia 09°29′N 45°31′E
162 K8 **Bürd** *var.* Ongon. Övörhangay, C Mongolia 46°58′N 103°45′E
146 L13 **Burdalyk** Lebap Welaýaty, E Turkmenistan 38°31′N 64°21′E
181 W6 **Burdekin River** ≋ Queensland, NE Australia
27 O7 **Burden** Kansas, C USA 37°18′N 96°45′W
Burdigala *see* Bordeaux
136 E15 **Burdur** *var.* Buldur. Burdur, SW Turkey 37°44′N 30°17′E
136 E15 **Burdur** *var.* Buldur. ◈ *province* SW Turkey
136 E15 **Burdur Gölü** *salt lake* SW Turkey
65 H21 **Burdwood Bank** *undersea feature* SW Atlantic Ocean
80 I12 **Burē** Āmara, N Ethiopia 10°43′N 37°09′E
80 H13 **Burē** Oromīya, C Ethiopia 08°13′N 35°09′E
93 J15 **Bureå** Västerbotten, N Sweden 64°36′N 21°15′E
162 K7 **Büreghangay** *var.* Darhan. Bulgan, C Mongolia 48°07′N 103°54′E
101 G14 **Büren** Nordrhein-Westfalen, W Germany 51°34′N 08°34′E
162 L8 **Büren** *var.* Bayantöhöm. Töv, C Mongolia 46°57′N 105°09′E
162 K6 **Bürengiyn Nuruu** ▲▲ N Mongolia
Bürenhayrhan *see* Bulgan
162 I6 **Bürentogtoh** *var.* Bayan. Hövsgol, C Mongolia 49°36′N 99°36′E
Būrewāla *see* Mandi Būrewāla
92 J9 **Burfjord** Troms, N Norway 69°55′N 21°54′E
100 L13 **Burg** *var.* Burg an der Ihle, Burg bei Magdeburg. Sachsen-Anhalt, C Germany 52°17′N 11°51′E
Burg an der Ihle *see* Burg
114 N10 **Burgas** *var.* Bourgas. Burgas, E Bulgaria 42°31′N 27°30′E
114 M10 **Burgas** ◈ *province* E Bulgaria
114 N9 **Burgas** ✈ Burgas, E Bulgaria 42°35′N 27°33′E
114 N10 **Burgaski Zaliv** *gulf* E Bulgaria
114 M10 **Burgasko Ezero** *lagoon* E Bulgaria
21 V11 **Burgaw** North Carolina, SE USA 34°33′N 77°56′W
Burg bei Magdeburg *see* Burg
108 E8 **Burgdorf** Bern, NW Switzerland 47°03′N 07°38′E
109 Y7 **Burgenland** *off.* Land Burgenland. ◈ *state* SE Austria
13 S13 **Burgeo** Newfoundland, Newfoundland and Labrador, SE Canada 47°37′N 57°38′W
83 I24 **Burgersdorp** Eastern Cape, SE South Africa 31°00′S 26°20′E
83 K20 **Burgersfort** Mpumalanga, NE South Africa 24°39′S 30°18′E
101 N23 **Burghausen** Bayern, SE Germany 48°10′N 12°48′E
139 O5 **Burghūth, Sabkhat al** ◎ E Syria
101 M20 **Burglengenfeld** Bayern, SE Germany 49°11′N 12°01′E
41 P9 **Burgos** Tamaulipas, C Mexico 24°55′N 98°46′W
105 N4 **Burgos** Castilla-León, N Spain 42°21′N 03°41′W
105 N4 **Burgos** ◈ *province* Castilla-León, N Spain
Burgstadlberg *see* Hradiště
95 P20 **Burgsvik** Gotland, SE Sweden 57°01′N 18°18′E
Burgum *see* Bergum
Burgundy *see* Bourgogne
159 Q11 **Burhan Budai Shan** ▲▲ C China
136 B12 **Burhaniye** Balıkesir, W Turkey 39°29′N 26°59′E
154 G12 **Burhānpur** Madhya Pradesh, C India 21°18′N 76°14′E
127 W7 **Buribay** Respublika Bashkortostan, W Russian Federation 51°57′N 58°11′E
43 O17 **Burica, Punta** *headland* Costa Rica/Panama 08°02′N 82°53′W
167 Q10 **Buriram** *var.* Buri Ram, Puriramya. Buri Ram, E Thailand 15°01′N 103°06′E
Buri Ram *see* Buriram
105 S10 **Burjassot** País Valenciano, E Spain 39°33′N 00°26′W
81 N16 **Burka Giibi** Hiiraan, C Somalia 03°52′N 45°07′E
147 X8 **Burkan** ≋ E Kyrgyzstan
25 R4 **Burkburnett** Texas, SW USA 34°06′N 98°34′W
29 O12 **Burke** South Dakota, N USA 43°09′N 99°18′W
10 K15 **Burke Channel** *channel* British Columbia, W Canada
194 J10 **Burke Island** *island* Antarctica
20 L7 **Burkesville** Kentucky, S USA 36°48′N 85°21′W
181 T4 **Burketown** Queensland, NE Australia 17°49′S 139°28′E
25 Q8 **Burkett** Texas, SW USA 32°01′N 99°17′W
25 Y9 **Burkeville** Texas, SW USA 30°58′N 93°41′W
21 V7 **Burkeville** Virginia, NE USA 37°11′N 78°12′W
77 O12 **Burkina** *off.* Burkina Faso; *prev.* Upper Volta. ◆ *republic* W Africa
Burkina *see* Burkina
Burkina Faso *see* Burkina
194 L13 **Burks, Cape** *headland* Antarctica
14 H12 **Burk's Falls** Ontario, S Canada 45°38′N 79°25′W
101 H23 **Burladingen** Baden-Württemberg, S Germany 48°18′N 09°05′E
25 T7 **Burleson** Texas, SW USA 32°32′N 97°19′W
33 P15 **Burley** Idaho, NW USA 42°32′N 113°47′W
144 G8 **Burlin** Zapadnyy Kazakhstan, NW Kazakhstan 51°25′N 52°42′E
14 G16 **Burlington** Ontario, S Canada 42°19′N 79°48′W
37 W4 **Burlington** Colorado, C USA 39°17′N 102°17′W
29 Y15 **Burlington** Iowa, C USA 40°48′N 91°05′W
27 P5 **Burlington** Kansas, C USA 38°11′N 95°46′W
21 T9 **Burlington** North Carolina, SE USA 36°05′N 79°27′W
28 M3 **Burlington** North Dakota, N USA 48°16′N 101°25′W
18 L7 **Burlington** Vermont, NE USA 44°28′N 73°14′W
30 M9 **Burlington** Wisconsin, N USA 42°38′N 88°12′W
27 Q1 **Burlington Junction** Missouri, C USA 40°27′N 95°04′W
166 M4 **Burma** *off.* Union of Myanmar, Myanmar. ◆ *military dictatorship* SE Asia
10 L17 **Burnaby** British Columbia, SW Canada 49°16′N 122°58′W
117 O12 **Burnas, Ozero** ◎ SW Ukraine
25 S10 **Burnet** Texas, SW USA 30°46′N 98°14′W
35 O3 **Burney** California, W USA 40°52′N 121°42′W
183 O16 **Burnie** Tasmania, SE Australia 41°07′S 145°52′E
97 L17 **Burnley** NW England, United Kingdom 53°48′N 02°14′W
Burnoye *see* Bauyrzhan Momyshuly
153 R15 **Burnpur** West Bengal, NE India 23°39′N 86°55′E
32 K14 **Burns** Oregon, NW USA 43°35′N 119°03′W
26 K11 **Burns Flat** Oklahoma, C USA 35°21′N 99°10′W
20 M7 **Burnside** Kentucky, S USA 36°55′N 84°34′W
8 K8 **Burnside** ≋ Nunavut, NW Canada
32 L15 **Burns Junction** Oregon, NW USA 42°46′N 117°51′W
10 L13 **Burns Lake** British Columbia, SW Canada 54°14′N 125°45′W
29 V9 **Burnsville** Minnesota, N USA 44°49′N 93°14′W
21 P9 **Burnsville** North Carolina, SE USA 35°56′N 82°18′W
21 R4 **Burnsville** West Virginia, NE USA 38°50′N 80°39′W
14 I13 **Burnt River** ≋ Ontario, SE Canada
14 I11 **Burntroot Lake** ◎ Ontario, SE Canada
11 W12 **Burntwood** ≋ Manitoba, C Canada
Bur'o *see* Burco
158 L2 **Burqin** Xinjiang Uygur Zizhiqu, NW China 47°42′N 86°50′E
182 J8 **Burra** South Australia 33°41′S 138°54′E
183 S9 **Burragorang, Lake** ⊠ New South Wales, SE Australia
96 K5 **Burray** *island* NE Scotland, United Kingdom
113 L19 **Burrel** *var.* Burreli. Dibër, C Albania 41°36′N 20°00′E
Burreli *see* Burrel
183 R8 **Burrendong Reservoir** ⊠ New South Wales, SE Australia
183 R5 **Burren Junction** New South Wales, SE Australia 30°06′S 149°01′E
105 T9 **Burriana** País Valenciano, E Spain 39°54′N 00°05′W
183 R10 **Burrinjuck Reservoir** ⊠ New South Wales, SE Australia
36 J12 **Burro Creek** ≋ Arizona, SW USA
40 M5 **Burro, Serranías del** ▲▲ NW Mexico
62 K7 **Burruyacú** Tucumán, N Argentina 26°30′S 64°45′W
136 E12 **Bursa** *var.* Brussa, *prev.* Brusa; *anc.* Prusa. Bursa, NW Turkey 40°12′N 29°04′E
136 D12 **Bursa** *var.* Brussa. ◈ *province* NW Turkey
75 Y9 **Būr Safāga** *var.* Būr Safājah. E Egypt 26°43′N 33°55′E
Būr Safājah *see* Būr Safāga
75 W7 **Būr Saʻīd** *var.* Port Said. N Egypt 31°17′N 32°18′E
81 O14 **Bur Tinle** Nugaal, C Somalia 07°50′N 48°01′E
31 Q5 **Burt Lake** ◎ Michigan, N USA
118 H7 **Burtnieks** *var.* Burtnieks Ezers. ◎ N Latvia
Burtnieks Ezers *see* Burtnieks
31 Q9 **Burton** Michigan, N USA 43°00′N 84°16′W
Burton on Trent *see* Burton upon Trent
97 M19 **Burton upon Trent** *var.* Burton on Trent, Burton-upon-Trent. C England, United Kingdom 52°48′N 01°36′W
93 J15 **Burträsk** Västerbotten, N Sweden 64°31′N 20°40′E
145 S14 **Burubaytal** *prev.* Burylbaytal. Zhambyl, SE Kazakhstan 44°56′N 73°59′E
Burujird *see* Borūjerd
Burultokay *see* Fuhai
141 R15 **Burūm** SE Yemen 14°22′N 48°53′E
Burunday *see* Boralday
81 D21 **Burundi** *off.* Republic of Burundi; *prev.* Kingdom of Burundi, Urundi. ◆ *republic* C Africa
Burundi, Kingdom of *see* Burundi
Burundi, Republic of *see* Burundi
171 R13 **Buru, Pulau** *prev.* Boeroe. *island* E Indonesia
77 T17 **Burutu** Delta, S Nigeria 05°18′N 05°32′E
10 G7 **Burwash Landing** Yukon Territory, W Canada 61°26′N 139°12′W
29 O14 **Burwell** Nebraska, C USA 41°46′N 99°04′W
97 L17 **Bury** NW England, United Kingdom 53°36′N 02°17′W
123 N13 **Buryatiya, Respublika** *prev.* Buryatskaya ASSR. ◈ *autonomous republic* S Russian Federation
Buryatskaya ASSR *see* Buryatiya, Respublika
Burylbaytal *see* Burubaytal
117 S3 **Buryn'** Sums'ka Oblast', NE Ukraine 51°13′N 33°50′E
97 P20 **Bury St Edmunds** *hist.* Beodericsworth. E England, United Kingdom 52°15′N 00°43′E
114 G8 **Bŭrziya** ≋ NW Bulgaria
106 D9 **Busalla** Liguria, NW Italy 44°35′N 08°55′E
Busan *see* Pusan
139 N5 **Buşayrah** Dayr az Zawr, E Syria 35°10′N 40°25′E
Buševa *see* Baba
143 N12 **Būshehr** *off.* Ostān-e Būshehr. ◈ *province* SW Iran
Būshehr/Bushire *see* Bandar-e Būshehr
Būshehr, Ostān-e *see* Būshehr
25 N2 **Bushland** Texas, SW USA 35°11′N 102°04′W
30 J12 **Bushnell** Illinois, N USA 40°33′N 90°30′W
Busi *see* Biševo
81 G18 **Busia** SE Uganda 01°20′N 34°48′E
Busiasch *see* Buziaş
79 K16 **Businga** Equateur, NW Dem. Rep. Congo 03°20′N 20°53′E
79 J18 **Busira** ≋ NW Dem. Rep. Congo
116 I5 **Bus'k** *Rus.* Busk. L'vivs'ka Oblast', W Ukraine 49°59′N 24°34′E
95 E14 **Buskerud** ◈ *county* S Norway
113 F14 **Buško Jezero** ⊠ SW Bosnia and Herzegovina
111 M15 **Busko-Zdrój** Świętokrzyskie, C Poland 50°28′N 20°44′E
Busra *see* Al Başrah, Iraq
Buşrá *see* Buşrá ash Shām, Syria
138 H9 **Buşrá ash Shām** *var.* Bosora, Bosra, Bozrah, Buşrá. Dar'ā, S Syria 32°31′N 36°29′E
180 I13 **Busselton** Western Australia 33°43′S 115°15′E
81 C14 **Busseri** ≋ W Sudan
106 E9 **Busseto** Emilia-Romagna, C Italy 45°00′N 10°06′E
106 A8 **Bussoleno** Piemonte, NE Italy 45°11′N 07°07′E
Bussora *see* Al Başrah
41 N7 **Bustamante** Nuevo León, NE Mexico 26°29′N 100°30′W
63 I23 **Bustamante, Punta** *headland* S Argentina 51°35′S 68°58′W
Bustan *see* Bo'ston
116 J12 **Buşteni** Prahova, SE Romania 45°23′N 25°32′E
106 D7 **Busto Arsizio** Lombardia, N Italy 45°37′N 08°51′E
147 Q10 **Büston** *Rus.* Buston. NW Tajikistan 40°31′N 69°21′E
100 H8 **Büsum** Schleswig-Holstein, N Germany 54°08′N 08°52′E
98 J10 **Bussum** Noord-Holland, C Netherlands 52°17′N 05°10′E
79 M16 **Buta** Orientale, N Dem. Rep. Congo 02°50′N 24°41′E
81 E20 **Butare** *prev.* Astrida. S Rwanda 02°39′S 29°44′E
191 O2 **Butaritari** *atoll* Tungaru, W Kiribati
Butawal *see* Butwal
96 H13 **Bute** *cultural region* SW Scotland, United Kingdom
162 K6 **Büteeliyn Nuruu** ▲▲ N Mongolia
10 L16 **Bute Inlet** *fjord* British Columbia, W Canada
96 H12 **Bute, Island of** *island* SW Scotland, United Kingdom
79 P18 **Butembo** Nord-Kivu, NE Dem. Rep. Congo 0°09′N 29°17′E
Bûtenpost *see* Buitenpost
107 K25 **Butera** Sicilia, Italy, C Mediterranean Sea 37°12′N 14°12′E
99 M20 **Bütgenbach** Liège, E Belgium 50°25′N 06°12′E
Butha Qi *see* Zalantun
166 J5 **Buthidaung** Rakhine State, W Burma (Myanmar) 20°50′N 92°25′E
61 I16 **Butiá** Rio Grande do Sul, S Brazil 30°09′S 51°55′W
81 F17 **Butiaba** NW Uganda 01°48′N 31°21′E
23 N6 **Butler** Alabama, S USA 32°05′N 88°13′W
23 S5 **Butler** Georgia, SE USA 32°33′N 84°14′W
31 Q11 **Butler** Indiana, N USA 41°25′N 84°52′W
27 R5 **Butler** Missouri, C USA 38°17′N 94°21′W
18 B14 **Butler** Pennsylvania, NE USA 40°51′N 79°52′W
194 K5 **Butler Island** *island* Antarctica
21 U8 **Butner** North Carolina, SE USA 36°07′N 78°45′W
171 P14 **Buton, Pulau** *var.* Pulau Butung; *prev.* Boetoeng. *island* C Indonesia
Bütow *see* Bytów
113 L23 **Butrintit, Liqeni i** ◎ S Albania
23 N3 **Buttahatchee River** ≋ Alabama/Mississippi, S USA
33 Q10 **Butte** Montana, NW USA 46°01′N 112°33′W
29 O12 **Butte** Nebraska, C USA 42°54′N 98°51′W
168 J7 **Butterworth** Pinang, Peninsular Malaysia 05°24′N 100°22′E
83 J25 **Butterworth** *var.* Gcuwa. Eastern Cape, SE South Africa 32°20′S 28°09′E
13 O3 **Button Islands** *island group* Nunavut, NE Canada
35 R13 **Buttonwillow** California, W USA 35°24′N 119°26′W
171 Q7 **Butuan** *off.* Butuan City. Mindanao, S Philippines 08°57′N 125°33′E
Butuan City *see* Butuan
Butung, Pulau *see* Buton, Pulau
Butuntum *see* Bitonto
126 M8 **Buturlinovka** Voronezhskaya Oblast', W Russian Federation 50°48′N 40°33′E
153 O11 **Butwal** *var.* Butawal. Western, C Nepal 27°41′N 83°28′E
101 G17 **Butzbach** Hessen, W Germany 50°26′N 08°40′E
100 L9 **Bützow** Mecklenburg-Vorpommern, N Germany 53°49′N 11°58′E
80 N13 **Buuhoodle** Togdheer, N Somalia 08°18′N 46°15′E
81 N16 **Buulobarde** *var.* Buulo Berde. Hiiraan, C Somalia 03°52′N 45°37′E
Buulo Berde *see* Buulobarde
80 P12 **Buuraha Cal Miskaat** ▲▲ NE Somalia
81 L19 **Buur Gaabo** Jubbada Hoose, S Somalia 01°14′S 41°48′E
99 M22 **Buurgplaatz** ▲ N Luxembourg 50°09′N 06°02′E
162 H8 **Buutsagaan** *var.* Buyant. Bayanhongor, C Mongolia 46°07′N 98°45′E
Buwayrāt al Hasūn *see* Bu'ayrāt al Ḩasūn
146 L11 **Buxoro** *var.* Bokhara, *Rus.* Bukhara. Buxoro Viloyati, C Uzbekistan 39°51′N 64°23′E
146 J11 **Buxoro Viloyati** *Rus.* Bukharskaya Oblast'. ◈ *province* C Uzbekistan
100 I10 **Buxtehude** Niedersachsen, NW Germany 53°29′N 09°42′E
97 L18 **Buxton** C England, United Kingdom 53°18′N 01°52′W
124 M14 **Buy** *var.* Buj. Kostromskaya Oblast', NW Russian Federation 58°27′N 41°31′E
Buyanbat *see* Jargalant
162 D6 **Buyant** Bayan-Ölgiy, W Mongolia 48°31′N 89°36′E
Buyant *see* Buutsagaan, Bayanhongor, Mongolia
Buyant *see* Otgon, Dzavhan, Mongolia
Buyant *see* Galshar, Hentiy, Mongolia
163 N10 **Buyant-Uhaa** Dornogovĭ, SE Mongolia 44°52′N 110°12′E
162 M7 **Buyant Ukha** ✈ (Ulaanbaatar) Töv, N Mongolia
127 Q16 **Buynaksk** Respublika Dagestan, SW Russian Federation 42°53′N 47°03′E
119 L20 **Buynavichy** *Rus.* Buynovichi. Homyel'skaya Voblasts', SE Belarus 51°52′N 28°33′E
Buynovichi *see* Buynavichy
76 L16 **Buyo** SW Ivory Coast 06°16′N 07°03′W
76 L16 **Buyo, Lac de** ⊠ W Ivory Coast
163 R7 **Buyr Nuur** *var.* Buir Nur. ◎ China/Mongolia *see also* Buir Nur
Buyr Nuur *see* Buir Nur
137 T13 **Büyükağrı Dağı** *var.* Aghri Dagh, Agri Dagi, Koh I Noh, Masis, *Eng.* Great Ararat, Mount Ararat. ▲ E Turkey 39°43′N 44°19′E
137 R15 **Büyük Çayı** ≋ NE Turkey
114 O13 **Büyük Çekmece** İstanbul, NW Turkey 41°02′N 28°35′E
114 N12 **Büyükkarıştıran** Kırklareli, NW Turkey 41°17′N 27°33′E
115 L14 **Büyükkemikli Burnu** *cape* NW Turkey
136 E15 **Büyükmenderes Nehri** ≋ SW Turkey
Büyükzap Suyu *see* Great Zab
102 M9 **Buzançais** Indre, C France 46°53′N 01°25′E
116 K13 **Buzău** Buzău, SE Romania 45°08′N 26°51′E
116 K13 **Buzău** ◈ *county* SE Romania
116 L12 **Buzău** ≋ E Romania
75 S11 **Buzaymah** *var.* Bzīmah. SE Libya 24°53′N 22°01′E
164 E13 **Buzen** Fukuoka, Kyūshū, SW Japan 33°37′N 131°06′E
116 F12 **Buziaş** *Ger.* Busiasch, *Hung.* Buziásfürdő; *prev.* Buziás. Timiş, W Romania 45°38′N 21°36′E
Buziás *see* Buziaş
Buziásfürdő *see* Buziaş
83 M18 **Búzi, Rio** ≋ C Mozambique
117 Q10 **Buz'kyy Lyman** *bay* S Ukraine
Būzmeyīn *see* Abadan
145 O8 **Buzuluk** Akmola, C Kazakhstan 51°53′N 66°09′E
127 T6 **Buzuluk** Orenburgskaya Oblast', W Russian Federation 52°47′N 52°16′E
127 N8 **Buzuluk** ≋ SW Russian Federation
19 P12 **Buzzards Bay** Massachusetts, NE USA 41°45′N 70°37′W
19 P13 **Buzzards Bay** *bay* Massachusetts, NE USA
83 G16 **Bwabata** Caprivi, NE Namibia 17°52′S 22°39′E
186 H10 **Bwagaoia** Misima Island, SE Papua New Guinea 10°39′S 152°48′E
Bwake *see* Bouaké
187 R13 **Bwatnapne** Pentecost, C Vanuatu 15°42′S 168°07′E
119 K14 **Byahoml'** *Rus.* Begoml'. Vitsyebskaya Voblasts', N Belarus 54°44′N 28°04′E
114 K8 **Byala** Ruse, N Bulgaria 43°27′N 25°44′E
114 N9 **Byala** *prev.* Ak-Dere. Varna, E Bulgaria 42°52′N 27°53′E
Byala Reka *see* Erythropótamos
114 H8 **Byala Slatina** Vratsa, NW Bulgaria 43°28′N 23°56′E
119 N15 **Byalynichy** *Rus.* Belynichi. Mahilyowskaya Voblasts', E Belarus 54°00′N 29°42′E
Byan Tumen *see* Choybalsan
119 G19 **Byaroza** *Pol.* Bereza Kartuska, *Rus.* Berëza. Brestskaya Voblasts', SW Belarus 52°32′N 24°59′E
119 H16 **Byarozavka** *Rus.* Berëzovka. Hrodzyenskaya Voblasts', W Belarus 53°45′N 25°30′E
Byblos *see* Jbail
111 O14 **Bychawa** Lubelskie, SE Poland 51°06′N 22°34′E
Bychikha *see* Bychykha
118 N11 **Bychykha** *Rus.* Bychikha. Vitsyebskaya Voblasts', NE Belarus 55°41′N 29°59′E
111 I14 **Byczyna** *Ger.* Pitschen. Opolskie, S Poland 51°06′N 18°13′E
110 I10 **Bydgoszcz** *Ger.* Bromberg. Kujawski-pomorskie, C Poland 53°06′N 18°00′E
119 H19 **Byelaazyorsk** *Rus.* Beloozersk. Brestskaya Voblasts', SW Belarus 52°28′N 25°10′E
119 I17 **Byelaruskaya Hrada** *Rus.* Belorusskaya Gryada. *ridge* N Belarus
119 G18 **Byelavyezhskaya Pushcha** *Pol.* Puszcza Białowieska, *Rus.* Belovezhskaya Pushcha. *forest* Belarus/Poland *see also* Białowieska, Puszcza
Byelavyezhskaya, Pushcha *see* Białowieska, Puszcza
119 H15 **Byenyakoni** *Rus.* Benyakoni. Hrodzyenskaya Voblasts', W Belarus 54°15′N 25°22′E
119 M16 **Byerazino** *Rus.* Berezino. Minskaya Voblasts', C Belarus 53°50′N 29°00′E
118 L13 **Byerazino** *Rus.* Berezino. Vitsyebskaya Voblasts', N Belarus 54°54′N 28°12′E
119 L14 **Byerezino** *Rus.* Berezina. ≋ C Belarus
118 M13 **Byeshankovichy** *Rus.* Beshenkovichi. Vitsyebskaya Voblasts', N Belarus 55°04′N 29°27′E
31 U13 **Byesville** Ohio, N USA 39°58′N 81°32′W
119 P18 **Byesyedz'** *Rus.* Besed'. ≋ SE Belarus
119 H19 **Byezdzyezh** *Rus.* Bezdezh. Brestskaya Voblasts', SW Belarus 52°19′N 25°18′E
93 J15 **Bygdeå** Västerbotten, N Sweden 64°03′N 20°49′E
94 F12 **Bygdin** ◎ S Norway
93 J15 **Bygdsiljum** Västerbotten, N Sweden 64°20′N 20°31′E
95 E17 **Bygland** Aust-Agder, S Norway 58°46′N 07°50′E
95 E17 **Byglandsfjord** Aust-Agder, S Norway 58°42′N 07°51′E
119 N16 **Bykhaw** *Rus.* Bykhov. Mahilyowskaya Voblasts', E Belarus 53°31′N 30°15′E
Bykhov *see* Bykhaw
127 P9 **Bykovo** Volgogradskaya Oblast', SW Russian Federation 49°52′N 45°24′E
123 P7 **Bykovskiy** Respublika Sakha (Yakutiya), NE Russian Federation 71°57′N 129°07′E
195 R12 **Byrd Glacier** *glacier* Antarctica
14 K10 **Byrd, Lac** ◎ Québec, SE Canada
183 P5 **Byrock** New South Wales, SE Australia 30°40′S 146°24′E
30 L10 **Byron** Illinois, N USA 42°06′N 89°15′W
183 V4 **Byron Bay** New South Wales, SE Australia 28°39′S 153°34′E
183 V4 **Byron, Cape** *headland* New South Wales, E Australia 28°37′S 153°40′E
63 F21 **Byron, Isla** *island* S Chile
Byron Island *see* Nikunau
65 B24 **Byron Sound** *sound* NW Falkland Islands
122 M6 **Byrranga, Gora** ▲▲ N Russian Federation
93 J14 **Byske** Västerbotten, N Sweden 64°58′N 21°10′E
111 K18 **Bystrá** ▲ N Slovakia 49°10′N 19°49′E
111 F18 **Bystřice nad Pernštejnem** *Ger.* Bistritz ober Pernstein. Vysočina, C Czech Republic 49°32′N 16°16′E
Bystrovka *see* Kemin
111 G16 **Bystrzyca Kłodzka** *Ger.* Habelschwerdt. Wałbrzych, SW Poland 50°19′N 16°39′E
111 I18 **Bytča** Žilinský Kraj, N Slovakia 49°15′N 18°32′E
119 L15 **Bytcha** Minskaya Voblasts', NE Belarus 54°19′N 28°24′E
Byteń/Byten' *see* Bytsyen'
111 J16 **Bytom** *Ger.* Beuthen. Śląskie, S Poland 50°21′N 18°51′E
110 H7 **Bytów** *Ger.* Bütow. Pomorskie, N Poland 54°10′N 17°30′E
119 H18 **Bytsyen'** *Pol.* Byteń, *Rus.* Byten'. Brestskaya Voblasts', SW Belarus 52°53′N 25°30′E
81 E19 **Byumba** *var.* Biumba. N Rwanda 01°37′S 30°05′E
Byuzmeyin *see* Abadan
119 O20 **Byval'ki** Homyel'skaya Voblasts', SE Belarus 51°51′N 30°38′E
95 O20 **Byxelkrok** Kalmar, S Sweden 57°18′N 17°01′E
Byzantium *see* İstanbul
Bzīmah *see* Buzaymah

C

62 O6 **Caacupé** Cordillera, S Paraguay 25°23′S 57°05′W
62 P6 **Caaguazú** *off.* Departamento de Caaguazú. ◈ *department* C Paraguay
Caaguazú, Departamento de *see* Caaguazú
82 C13 **Caála** *var.* Kaala, Robert Williams, *Port.* Vila Robert Williams. Huambo, C Angola 12°51′S 15°33′E

◆ Country ● Country Capital ◇ Dependent Territory ○ Dependent Territory Capital ◈ Administrative Regions ✈ International Airport ▲ Mountain ▲▲ Mountain Range Volcano ≋ River ◎ Lake ⊠ Reservoir
231

Caazapá – Canandaigua

62 P7 **Caazapá** Caazapá, S Paraguay 26°09′S 56°21′W
62 P7 **Caazapá** *off.* Departamento de Caazapá. ◈ *department* SE Paraguay
Caazapá, Departamento de *see* Caazapá
81 P15 **Cabaad, Raas** *headland* C Somalia 06°13′N 49°01′E
55 N10 **Cabadisocaña** Amazonas, S Venezuela 04°28′N 64°45′W
44 F5 **Cabaiguán** Sancti Spíritus, C Cuba 22°04′N 79°32′W
Caballeria, Cabo *see* Cavalleria, Cap de
37 Q14 **Caballo Reservoir** ☒ New Mexico, SW USA
40 L6 **Caballos Mesteños, Llano de los** *plain* N Mexico
104 L2 **Cabañaquinta** Asturias, N Spain 43°10′N 05°37′W
42 B9 **Cabañas** ◈ *department* E El Salvador
171 O3 **Cabanatuan** *off.* Cabanatuan City. Luzon, N Philippines 15°27′N 120°57′E
Cabanatuan City *see* Cabanatuan
15 T8 **Cabano** Québec, SE Canada 47°40′N 68°56′W
104 L11 **Cabeza del Buey** Extremadura, W Spain 38°44′N 05°13′W
45 V5 **Cabezas de San Juan** *headland* E Puerto Rico 18°23′N 65°37′W
105 N2 **Cabezón de la Sal** Cantabria, N Spain 43°19′N 04°14′W
Cabhán *see* Cavan
61 B23 **Cabildo** Buenos Aires, E Argentina 38°28′S 61°50′W
Cabillonum *see* Chalon-sur-Saône
54 H5 **Cabimas** Zulia, NW Venezuela 10°26′N 71°27′W
82 A9 **Cabinda** *var.* Kabinda. Cabinda, NW Angola 05°34′S 12°12′E
82 A9 **Cabinda** *var.* Kabinda. ◈ *province* NW Angola
33 N7 **Cabinet Mountains** ▲▲ Idaho/Montana, NW USA
82 B11 **Cabiri** Bengo, NW Angola 08°50′S 13°42′E
63 J20 **Cabo Blanco** Santa Cruz, SE Argentina 47°13′S 65°43′W
82 P13 **Cabo Delgado** *off.* Província de Cabo Delgado. ◈ *province* NE Mozambique
14 L9 **Cabonga, Réservoir** ☒ Québec, SE Canada
27 V7 **Cabool** Missouri, C USA 37°07′N 92°06′W
183 V2 **Caboolture** Queensland, E Australia 27°05′S 152°50′E
Cabora Bassa, Lake *see* Cahora Bassa, Albufeira de
40 F3 **Caborca** Sonora, NW Mexico 30°44′N 112°06′W
Cabo San Lucas *see* San Lucas
27 V11 **Cabot** Arkansas, C USA 34°58′N 92°01′W
14 F12 **Cabot Head** *headland* Ontario, S Canada 45°13′N 81°17′W
13 R13 **Cabot Strait** *strait* E Canada
Cabo Verde, Ilhas do *see* Cape Verde
104 M14 **Cabra** Andalucía, S Spain 37°28′N 04°28′W
107 B19 **Cabras** Sardegna, Italy, C Mediterranean Sea 39°55′N 08°30′E
188 A15 **Cabras Island** *island* W Guam
45 O8 **Cabrera** N Dominican Republic 19°40′N 69°54′W
104 J4 **Cabrera** ≈ NW Spain
105 X10 **Cabrera, Illa de** *anc.* Capraria. *island* Islas Baleares, Spain, W Mediterranean Sea
105 Q15 **Cabrera, Sierra** ▲▲ S Spain
11 S16 **Cabri** Saskatchewan, S Canada 50°38′N 108°28′W
105 R10 **Cabriel** ≈ E Spain
54 M7 **Cabruta** Guárico, C Venezuela 07°39′N 66°19′W
171 N2 **Cabugao** Luzon, N Philippines 17°55′N 120°29′E
54 G10 **Cabuyaro** Meta, C Colombia 04°21′N 72°47′W
60 I13 **Caçador** Santa Catarina, S Brazil 26°47′S 51°00′W
42 G8 **Cacaguatique, Cordillera** *var.* Cordillera. ▲▲ NE El Salvador
112 L13 **Čačak** Serbia, C Serbia 43°52′N 20°23′E
55 Y10 **Cacao** NE French Guiana 04°37′N 52°29′W
61 H16 **Caçapava do Sul** Rio Grande do Sul, S Brazil 30°28′S 53°29′W
21 U3 **Cacapon River** ≈ West Virginia, NE USA
107 J23 **Caccamo** Sicilia, Italy, C Mediterranean Sea 37°56′N 13°40′E
107 A17 **Caccia, Capo** *headland* Sardegna, Italy, C Mediterranean Sea 40°34′N 08°09′E
146 H15 **Çäçe** *var.* Chäche, *Rus.* Chaacha. Ahal Welaýaty, S Turkmenistan 36°49′N 60°33′E
59 G18 **Cáceres** Mato Grosso, W Brazil 16°05′S 57°40′W
104 J10 **Cáceres** *Ar.* Qazris. Extremadura, W Spain 39°29′N 06°23′W
104 J9 **Cáceres** ◈ *province* Extremadura, W Spain
Cachacrou *see* Scotts Head Village
61 C21 **Cacharí** Buenos Aires, E Argentina 36°24′S 59°32′W
26 L12 **Cache** Oklahoma, C USA 34°37′N 98°37′W
10 M16 **Cache Creek** British Columbia, SW Canada 50°49′N 121°20′W
35 N6 **Cache Creek** ≈ California, W USA
37 S3 **Cache La Poudre River** ≈ Colorado, C USA
Cacheo *see* Cacheu
27 W11 **Cache River** ≈ Arkansas, C USA
30 L17 **Cache River** ≈ Illinois, N USA
76 G12 **Cacheu** *var.* Cacheo. W Guinea-Bissau 12°12′N 16°10′W
59 I15 **Cachimbo** Pará, NE Brazil 09°21′S 54°58′W
59 H15 **Cachimbo, Serra do** ▲▲ C Brazil
82 D13 **Cachingues** Bié, C Angola 13°05′S 16°48′E
54 G7 **Cáchira** Norte de Santander, N Colombia 07°44′N 73°07′W
61 H16 **Cachoeira do Sul** Rio Grande do Sul, S Brazil 29°58′S 52°54′W
59 O20 **Cachoeiro de Itapemirim** Espírito Santo, SE Brazil 20°51′S 41°07′W
82 E12 **Cacolo** Lunda Sul, NE Angola 10°09′S 19°21′E
83 C14 **Caconda** Huíla, C Angola 13°43′S 15°03′E
82 A9 **Cacongo** Cabinda, NW Angola 05°13′S 12°08′E
35 U9 **Cactus Peak** ▲ Nevada, W USA 37°42′N 116°51′W
82 B11 **Cacuaco** Luanda, NW Angola 08°47′S 13°21′E
83 B14 **Cacula** Huíla, SW Angola 14°33′S 14°04′E
67 R12 **Caculuvar** ≈ SW Angola
59 O19 **Caçumba, Ilha** *island* SE Brazil
55 N10 **Cacuri** Amazonas, S Venezuela
81 N17 **Cadale** Shabeellaha Dhexe, E Somalia 02°48′N 46°19′E
105 X4 **Cadaqués** Cataluña, NE Spain 42°17′N 03°16′E
111 J18 **Čadca** *Hung.* Csaca. Žilinský Kraj, N Slovakia 49°27′N 18°46′E
27 P13 **Caddo** Oklahoma, C USA 34°07′N 96°15′W
25 R6 **Caddo** Texas, SW USA 32°42′N 98°40′W
25 X6 **Caddo Lake** ☒ Louisiana/Texas, SW USA
27 S12 **Caddo Mountains** ▲▲ Arkansas, C USA
41 O8 **Cadereyta** Nuevo León, NE Mexico 25°35′N 99°54′W
97 J19 **Cader Idris** ▲ NW Wales, United Kingdom 52°43′N 03°57′W
182 F3 **Cadibarrawirracanna, Lake** *salt lake* South Australia
14 I7 **Cadillac** Québec, SE Canada 48°12′N 78°23′W
11 T17 **Cadillac** Saskatchewan, S Canada 49°43′N 107°41′W
102 K13 **Cadillac** Gironde, SW France 44°37′N 00°16′W
31 P7 **Cadillac** Michigan, N USA 44°15′N 85°23′W
105 V4 **Cadí, Torre de** ▲ NE Spain 42°16′N 01°38′E
171 P5 **Cadiz** *off.* Cadiz City. Negros, C Philippines 10°58′N 123°18′E
104 J15 **Cádiz** *anc.* Gades, Gadier, Gadir, Gadire. Andalucía, SW Spain 36°32′N 06°18′W
20 H7 **Cadiz** Kentucky, S USA 36°52′N 87°50′W
31 U13 **Cadiz** Ohio, N USA 40°16′N 81°00′W
104 K15 **Cádiz** ◈ *province* Andalucía, SW Spain
104 I15 **Cádiz, Bahía de** *bay* SW Spain
Cadiz City *see* Cadiz
104 H15 **Cádiz, Golfo de** *Eng.* Gulf of Cádiz. *gulf* Portugal/Spain
Cadiz, Gulf of *see* Cádiz, Golfo de
35 X14 **Cadiz Lake** ◎ California, W USA
182 E2 **Cadney Homestead** South Australia 27°52′S 134°03′E
Cadurcum *see* Cahors
Caecae *see* Xaixai
102 K4 **Caen** Calvados, N France 49°10′N 00°20′W
Caene/Caenepolis *see* Qinā
Caerdydd *see* Cardiff
Caer Glou *see* Gloucester
Caer Gybi *see* Holyhead
Caerleon *see* Chester
Caer Luel *see* Carlisle
97 I18 **Caernarfon** *var.* Caernarvon, Carnarvon. NW Wales, United Kingdom 53°08′N 04°16′W
97 H18 **Caernarfon Bay** *bay* NW Wales, United Kingdom
97 I19 **Caernarvon** *cultural region* NW Wales, United Kingdom
Caernarvon *see* Caernarfon
Caesaraugusta *see* Zaragoza
Caesarea Mazaca *see* Kayseri
Caesarobriga *see* Talavera de la Reina
Caesarodunum *see* Tours
Caesaromagus *see* Beauvais
Caesena *see* Cesena
59 N17 **Caetité** Bahia, E Brazil 14°04′S 42°29′W
62 J6 **Cafayate** Salta, N Argentina 26°02′S 66°00′W
171 O2 **Cagayan** ≈ Luzon, N Philippines
171 Q7 **Cagayan de Oro** *off.* Cagayan de Oro City. Mindanao, S Philippines 08°29′N 124°38′E
Cagayan de Oro City *see* Cagayan de Oro
170 M8 **Cagayan de Tawi Tawi** *island* S Philippines
171 N6 **Cagayan Islands** *island group* C Philippines
31 O14 **Cagles Mill Lake** ☒ Indiana, N USA
106 I12 **Cagli** Marche, C Italy 43°33′N 12°39′E
107 C20 **Cagliari** *anc.* Caralis. Sardegna, Italy, C Mediterranean Sea 39°15′N 09°06′E
107 C20 **Cagliari, Golfo di** *gulf* Sardegna, Italy, C Mediterranean Sea
103 U15 **Cagnes-sur-Mer** Alpes-Maritimes, SE France 43°40′N 07°09′E
54 L5 **Cagua** Aragua, N Venezuela 10°09′N 67°27′W
171 O1 **Cagua, Mount** ▲ Luzon, N Philippines 18°10′N 122°03′E
54 F13 **Caguán, Río** ≈ SW Colombia
45 U6 **Caguas** E Puerto Rico 18°14′N 66°02′W
146 C9 **Çagyl** *Rus.* Chagyl. Balkan Welaýaty, NW Turkmenistan 40°48′N 55°21′E
23 P5 **Cahaba River** ≈ Alabama, S USA
42 E5 **Cahabón, Río** ≈ C Guatemala
83 B15 **Cahama** Cunene, SW Angola 16°16′S 14°23′E
97 B21 **Caha Mountains** *Ir.* An Cheacha. ▲▲ SW Ireland
97 D20 **Caher** *Ir.* An Cathair. S Ireland 52°21′N 07°58′W
97 A21 **Cahirciveen** *Ir.* Cathair Saidhbhín. SW Ireland 51°56′N 10°12′W
30 K15 **Cahokia** Illinois, N USA 38°34′N 90°11′W
83 L15 **Cahora Bassa, Albufeira de** *var.* Lake Cabora Bassa. ☒ NW Mozambique
97 G20 **Cahore Point** *Ir.* Rinn Chathóir. *headland* SE Ireland 52°33′N 06°11′W
102 M14 **Cahors** *anc.* Cadurcum. Lot, S France 44°26′N 01°27′E
56 D9 **Cahuapanas, Río** ≈ N Peru
116 M12 **Cahul** *Rus.* Kagul. S Moldova 45°53′N 28°13′E
Cahul, Lacul *see* Kahul, Ozero
83 N16 **Caia** Sofala, C Mozambique 17°50′S 35°21′E
59 J19 **Caiapó, Serra do** ▲▲ C Brazil
44 F5 **Caibarién** Villa Clara, C Cuba 22°31′N 79°29′W
55 O5 **Caicara** Monagas, NE Venezuela 09°52′N 63°38′W
54 L5 **Caicara del Orinoco** Bolívar, C Venezuela 07°38′N 66°10′W
59 P14 **Caicó** Rio Grande do Norte, E Brazil 06°25′S 37°04′W
44 M6 **Caicos Islands** *island group* W Turks and Caicos Islands
44 L5 **Caicos Passage** *strait* Bahamas/Turks and Caicos Islands
161 O9 **Caidian** *prev.* Hanyang. Hubei, C China 30°37′N 114°02′E
Caiffa *see* Hefa
180 M12 **Caiguna** Western Australia 32°14′S 125°33′E
Caillí, Ceann *see* Hag's Head
40 J11 **Caimanero, Laguna del** *var.* Laguna del Camaronero. *lagoon* E Pacific Ocean
117 N10 **Căinari** *Rus.* Kaynary. C Moldova 46°43′N 29°00′E
57 L19 **Caine, Río** ≈ C Bolivia
Caiphas *see* Hefa
195 N4 **Caird Coast** *physical region* Antarctica
96 J9 **Cairn Gorm** ▲ C Scotland, United Kingdom 57°07′N 03°38′W
96 J9 **Cairngorm Mountains** ▲▲ C Scotland, United Kingdom
39 P12 **Cairn Mountain** ▲ Alaska, USA 61°07′N 155°23′W
181 W4 **Cairns** Queensland, NE Australia 16°51′S 145°43′E
121 V13 **Cairo** *var.* El Qâhira, *Ar.* Al Qāhirah. ● (Egypt) N Egypt 30°01′N 31°18′E
23 T8 **Cairo** Georgia, SE USA 30°52′N 84°12′W
30 L17 **Cairo** Illinois, N USA 37°00′N 89°10′W
75 V8 **Cairo** ✕ C Egypt 30°06′N 31°36′E
Caiseal *see* Cashel
Caisleán an Bharraigh *see* Castlebar
Caisleán na Finne *see* Castlefinn
96 J6 **Caithness** *cultural region* N Scotland, United Kingdom
83 D15 **Caiundo** Cuando Cubango, S Angola 15°41′S 17°28′E
56 C11 **Cajamarca** *prev.* Caxamarca. Cajamarca, NW Peru 07°09′S 78°32′W
56 B11 **Cajamarca** *off.* Departamento de Cajamarca. ◈ *department* N Peru
Cajamarca, Departamento de *see* Cajamarca
103 N14 **Cajarc** Lot, S France 44°28′N 01°51′E
42 G6 **Cajón, Represa El** ☒ NW Honduras
58 N12 **Caju, Ilha do** *island* NE Brazil
159 R10 **Caka Yanhu** ◎ C China
112 E7 **Čakovec** *Ger.* Csakathurn, *Hung.* Csáktornya; *prev. Ger.* Tschakathurn. Medimurje, N Croatia 46°24′N 16°29′E
77 V17 **Calabar** Cross River, S Nigeria 04°56′N 08°25′E
14 K13 **Calabogie** Ontario, SE Canada 45°18′N 76°46′W
54 L6 **Calabozo** Guárico, C Venezuela 08°58′N 67°28′W
107 N20 **Calabria** *anc.* Bruttium. ◈ *region* SW Italy
104 M16 **Calaburra, Punta de** *headland* S Spain 36°30′N 04°38′W
116 G14 **Calafat** Dolj, SW Romania 43°59′N 22°57′E
Calafate *see* El Calafate
105 Q4 **Calahorra** La Rioja, N Spain 42°19′N 01°58′W
103 N1 **Calais** Pas-de-Calais, N France 51°N 01°54′E
19 T5 **Calais** Maine, NE USA 45°09′N 67°15′W
Calais, Pas de *see* Dover, Strait of
Calalen *see* Kallalen
62 H4 **Calama** Antofagasta, N Chile 22°26′S 68°54′W
Calamianes *see* Calamian Group
170 M5 **Calamian Group** *var.* Calamianes. *island group* W Philippines
105 R7 **Calamocha** Aragón, NE Spain 40°54′N 01°18′W
29 N14 **Calamus River** ≈ Nebraska, C USA
116 G12 **Călan** *Ger.* Kalan, *Hung.* Pusztakalán. Hunedoara, SW Romania 45°45′N 22°59′E
105 S7 **Calanda** Aragón, NE Spain 40°56′N 00°15′W
168 F9 **Calang** Sumatera, W Indonesia 04°37′N 95°37′E
171 N4 **Calapan** Mindoro, N Philippines 13°24′N 121°08′E
Călăras *see* Călărași
116 M9 **Călărași** *var.* Călăras, *Rus.* Kalarash. C Moldova 47°19′N 28°13′E
116 L14 **Călărași** Călărași, SE Romania 44°18′N 26°52′E
116 K14 **Călărași** ◈ *county* SE Romania
54 E10 **Calarca** Quindío, W Colombia 04°31′N 75°38′W
105 Q12 **Calasparra** Murcia, SE Spain 38°14′N 01°41′W
107 I23 **Calatafimi** Sicilia, Italy, C Mediterranean Sea 37°54′N 12°52′E
105 Q6 **Calatayud** Aragón, NE Spain 41°21′N 01°39′W
171 O4 **Calauag** Luzon, N Philippines 13°57′N 122°18′E
35 P8 **Calaveras River** ≈ California, W USA
171 N4 **Calavite, Cape** *headland* Mindoro, N Philippines 13°25′N 120°16′E
171 Q8 **Calbayog** *off.* Calbayog City. Samar, C Philippines 12°08′N 124°36′E
Calbayog City *see* Calbayog
22 G9 **Calcasieu Lake** ◎ Louisiana, S USA
22 H8 **Calcasieu River** ≈ Louisiana, S USA
56 B6 **Calceta** Manabí, W Ecuador 0°51′S 80°07′W
61 B16 **Calchaquí** Santa Fe, C Argentina 29°56′S 60°14′W
62 J6 **Calchaquí, Río** ≈ NW Argentina
58 J10 **Calçoene** Amapá, NE Brazil 02°29′N 51°01′W
153 S16 **Calcutta** ✕ West Bengal, N India 22°30′N 88°20′E
Calcutta *see* Kolkata
54 E9 **Caldas** *off.* Departamento de Caldas. ◈ *province* W Colombia
104 F10 **Caldas da Rainha** Leiria, W Portugal 39°24′N 09°08′W
Caldas, Departamento de *see* Caldas
104 G3 **Caldas de Reis** *var.* Caldas de Reyes. Galicia, NW Spain 42°36′N 08°39′W
Caldas de Reyes *see* Caldas de Reis
58 F13 **Caldeirão** Amazonas, NW Brazil 03°18′S 60°22′W
62 G7 **Caldera** Atacama, N Chile 27°05′S 70°48′W
42 L14 **Caldera** Puntarenas, W Costa Rica 09°55′N 84°51′W
105 N10 **Calderina** ▲ C Spain 39°18′N 03°49′W
137 T13 **Çaldıran** Van, E Turkey 39°10′N 43°52′E
32 M14 **Caldwell** Idaho, NW USA 43°39′N 116°41′W
27 N8 **Caldwell** Kansas, C USA 37°01′N 97°36′W
14 G15 **Caledon** Ontario, S Canada 43°51′N 79°58′W
83 I23 **Caledon** *var.* Mohokare. ≈ Lesotho/South Africa
42 G1 **Caledonia** Corozal, N Belize 18°14′N 88°29′W
14 G16 **Caledonia** Ontario, S Canada 43°04′N 79°57′W
29 X11 **Caledonia** Minnesota, N USA 43°37′N 91°30′W
105 X5 **Calella** *var.* Calella de la Costa. Cataluña, NE Spain 41°37′N 02°40′E
Calella de la Costa *see* Calella
23 P4 **Calera** Alabama, S USA 33°06′N 86°45′W
63 I19 **Caleta Olivia** Santa Cruz, SE Argentina 46°21′S 67°37′W
35 X17 **Calexico** California, W USA 32°39′N 115°28′W
97 H16 **Calf of Man** *island* SW Isle of Man
11 Q16 **Calgary** Alberta, SW Canada 51°05′N 114°05′W
11 Q16 **Calgary** ✕ Alberta, SW Canada 51°15′N 114°03′W
37 U5 **Calhan** Colorado, C USA 39°00′N 104°18′W
64 O5 **Calheta** Madeira, Portugal, NE Atlantic Ocean 32°42′N 17°12′W
23 R2 **Calhoun** Georgia, SE USA 34°30′N 84°57′W
20 I6 **Calhoun** Kentucky, S USA 37°32′N 87°15′W
22 M3 **Calhoun City** Mississippi, S USA 33°51′N 89°18′W
21 P12 **Calhoun Falls** South Carolina, SE USA 34°05′N 82°36′W
54 D11 **Cali** Valle del Cauca, W Colombia 03°24′N 76°30′W
27 V9 **Calico Rock** Arkansas, C USA 36°07′N 92°08′W
155 F21 **Calicut** *var.* Kozhikode. Kerala, SW India 11°17′N 75°49′E *see also* Kozhikode
35 Y9 **Caliente** Nevada, W USA 37°37′N 114°30′W
27 U5 **California** Missouri, C USA 38°39′N 92°35′W
18 B15 **California** Pennsylvania, NE USA 40°02′N 79°52′W
35 Q12 **California** *off.* State of California, *also known as* El Dorado, The Golden State. ◈ *state* W USA
35 P11 **California Aqueduct** *aqueduct* California, W USA
35 T13 **California City** California, W USA 35°06′N 117°55′W
40 F6 **California, Golfo de** *Eng.* Gulf of California; *prev.* Sea of Cortez. *gulf* W Mexico
California, Gulf of *see* California, Golfo de
137 Y13 **Călilabad** *Rus.* Dzhalilabad; *prev.* Astrakhan-Bazar. S Azerbaijan 39°15′N 48°30′E
116 I12 **Călimănești** Vâlcea, SW Romania 45°14′N 24°20′E
116 J9 **Călimani, Munții** ▲▲ N Romania
Calinisc *see* Cupcina
35 X17 **Calipatria** California, W USA 33°07′N 115°30′W
Calisia *see* Kalisz
34 M7 **Calistoga** California, W USA 38°34′N 122°37′W
83 G25 **Calitzdorp** Western Cape, SW South Africa 33°32′S 21°41′E
41 W12 **Calkiní** Campeche, E Mexico 20°21′N 90°03′W
182 K4 **Callabonna Creek** *var.* Tilcha Creek. *seasonal river* New South Wales/South Australia
182 J4 **Callabonna, Lake** ◎ South Australia
102 G5 **Callac** Côtes d'Armor, NW France 48°28′N 03°22′W
35 U5 **Callaghan, Mount** ▲ Nevada, W USA 39°38′N 116°57′W
Callain *see* Callan
97 E19 **Callan** *Ir.* Callain. S Ireland 52°33′N 07°23′W
14 H11 **Callander** Ontario, S Canada 46°14′N 79°21′W
96 I11 **Callander** C Scotland, United Kingdom 56°15′N 04°16′W
98 H7 **Callantsoog** Noord-Holland, NW Netherlands 52°51′N 04°41′E
57 D14 **Callao** Callao, W Peru 12°03′S 77°10′W
57 D15 **Callao** *off.* Departamento del Callao. ◈ *constitutional province* W Peru
Callao, Departamento del *see* Callao
56 F11 **Callaria, Río** ≈ E Peru
Callatis *see* Mangalia
11 Q13 **Calling Lake** Alberta, W Canada 55°12′N 113°07′W
Callosa de Ensarriá *see* Callosa d'En Sarrià
105 T11 **Callosa d'En Sarrià** *var.* Callosa de Ensarriá. País Valenciano, E Spain 38°40′N 00°08′W
105 S12 **Callosa de Segura** País Valenciano, E Spain 38°07′N 00°53′W
29 X11 **Calmar** Iowa, C USA 43°10′N 91°51′W
Calmar *see* Kalmar
43 R16 **Calobre** Veraguas, C Panama 08°18′N 80°49′W
23 X14 **Caloosahatchee River** ≈ Florida, SE USA
183 V2 **Caloundra** Queensland, E Australia 26°48′S 153°08′E
Calp *see* Calpe
105 T11 **Calpe** *Cat.* Calp. País Valenciano, E Spain 38°39′N 00°03′E
41 P14 **Calpulalpan** Tlaxcala, S Mexico 19°36′N 98°26′W
107 K25 **Caltagirone** Sicilia, Italy, C Mediterranean Sea 37°14′N 14°31′E
107 J24 **Caltanissetta** Sicilia, Italy, C Mediterranean Sea 37°30′N 14°01′E
82 E11 **Caluango** Lunda Norte, NE Angola 08°16′S 19°36′E
82 C12 **Calucinga** Bié, W Angola 11°18′S 16°12′E
82 B12 **Calulo** Cuanza Sul, NW Angola 09°58′S 14°56′E
83 B14 **Caluquembe** Huíla, W Angola 13°47′S 14°40′E
80 Q11 **Caluula** Bari, NE Somalia 11°55′N 50°51′E
102 K4 **Calvados** ◈ *department* N France
186 I10 **Calvados Chain, The** *island group* SE Papua New Guinea
25 U9 **Calvert** Texas, SW USA 30°58′N 96°40′W
20 H7 **Calvert City** Kentucky, S USA 37°01′N 88°21′W
103 X14 **Calvi** Corse, France, C Mediterranean Sea 42°34′N 08°44′E
40 L12 **Calvillo** Aguascalientes, C Mexico 21°51′N 102°18′W
83 F24 **Calvinia** Northern Cape, W South Africa 31°25′S 19°47′E
104 K8 **Calvitero** ▲ W Spain 40°16′N 05°48′W
101 G22 **Calw** Baden-Württemberg, SW Germany 48°43′N 08°43′E
Calydon *see* Kalydón
105 N11 **Calzada de Calatrava** Castilla-La Mancha, C Spain 38°42′N 03°46′W
Cama *see* Kama
82 C11 **Camabatela** Cuanza Norte, NW Angola 08°13′S 15°23′E
64 Q5 **Camacha** Porto Santo, Madeira, Portugal, NE Atlantic Ocean 32°41′N 16°52′W
14 L8 **Camachigama, Lac** ◎ Québec, SE Canada
40 M9 **Camacho** Zacatecas, C Mexico 24°23′N 102°20′W
82 D13 **Camacupa** *var.* General Machado, *Port.* Vila General Machado. Bié, C Angola 12°S 17°31′E
54 L7 **Camaguán** Guárico, C Venezuela 08°09′N 67°37′W
44 G6 **Camagüey** *prev.* Puerto Príncipe. Camagüey, C Cuba 21°24′N 77°55′W
44 G5 **Camagüey, Archipiélago de** *island group* C Cuba
40 D5 **Camalli, Sierra de** ▲ NW Mexico 28°21′N 113°26′W
57 G18 **Camana** *var.* Camaná. Arequipa, SW Peru 16°37′S 72°42′W
29 Z14 **Camanche** Iowa, C USA 41°47′N 90°15′W
35 P8 **Camanche Reservoir** ☒ California, W USA
61 I16 **Camaquã** Rio Grande do Sul, S Brazil 30°50′S 51°47′W
61 H16 **Camaquã, Rio** ≈ S Brazil
64 P6 **Câmara de Lobos** Madeira, Portugal, NE Atlantic Ocean 32°38′N 16°59′W
103 U16 **Camarat, Cap** *headland* SE France 43°12′N 06°42′E
41 O8 **Camargo** Tamaulipas, C Mexico 26°16′N 98°49′W
103 R15 **Camargue** *physical region* SE France
104 F2 **Camariñas** Galicia, NW Spain 43°07′N 09°10′W
Camaronero, Laguna del *see* Caimanero, Laguna del
63 J18 **Camarones** Chubut, S Argentina 44°48′S 65°42′W
63 J18 **Camarones, Bahía** *bay* S Argentina
104 J14 **Camas** Andalucía, S Spain 37°24′N 06°01′W
167 S15 **Ca Mau** *var.* Quan Long. Minh Hai, S Vietnam 09°11′N 105°09′E
82 E11 **Camaxilo** Lunda Norte, NE Angola 08°19′S 18°53′E
104 G3 **Cambados** Galicia, NW Spain 42°31′N 08°49′W
Cambay, Gulf of *see* Khambhāt, Gulf of
Camberia *see* Chambéry
97 N22 **Camberley** SE England, United Kingdom 51°21′N 00°45′W
167 R12 **Cambodia** *off.* Kingdom of Cambodia, *var.* Democratic Kampuchea, Roat Kampuchea, *Cam.* Kampuchea; *prev.* People's Democratic Republic of Kampuchea. ◆ *republic* SE Asia
Cambodia, Kingdom of *see* Cambodia
102 I16 **Cambo-les-Bains** Pyrénées-Atlantiques, SW France 43°22′N 01°24′W
103 P2 **Cambrai** *Flem.* Kambryk, *prev.* Cambray; *anc.* Cameracum. Nord, N France 50°10′N 03°14′E
Cambray *see* Cambrai
104 H2 **Cambre** Galicia, NW Spain 43°18′N 08°21′W
35 O12 **Cambria** California, W USA 35°33′N 121°04′W
97 J20 **Cambrian Mountains** ▲▲ C Wales, United Kingdom
14 G16 **Cambridge** Ontario, S Canada 43°22′N 80°20′W
44 I12 **Cambridge** W Jamaica 18°18′N 77°54′W
184 M8 **Cambridge** Waikato, North Island, New Zealand 37°53′S 175°28′E
97 O20 **Cambridge** *Lat.* Cantabrigia. E England, United Kingdom 52°12′N 00°07′E
32 M12 **Cambridge** Idaho, NW USA 44°34′N 116°42′W
30 K11 **Cambridge** Illinois, N USA 41°18′N 90°11′W
21 Y4 **Cambridge** Maryland, NE USA 38°34′N 76°04′W
19 O11 **Cambridge** Massachusetts, NE USA 42°21′N 71°05′W
29 V7 **Cambridge** Minnesota, N USA 45°34′N 93°13′W
29 N16 **Cambridge** Nebraska, C USA 40°18′N 100°10′W
31 U13 **Cambridge** Ohio, NE USA 40°00′N 81°34′W
8 L7 **Cambridge Bay** *var.* Ikaluktutiak. Victoria Island, Nunavut, NW Canada 68°56′N 105°09′W
97 O20 **Cambridgeshire** *cultural region* E England, United Kingdom
105 U6 **Cambrils de Mar** Cataluña, NE Spain 41°06′N 01°02′E
Cambundi-Catembo *see* Nova Gaia
137 N11 **Çam Burnu** *headland* N Turkey 41°07′N 37°48′E
183 S9 **Camden** New South Wales, SE Australia 34°04′S 150°40′E
23 O6 **Camden** Alabama, S USA 31°59′N 87°17′W
27 U14 **Camden** Arkansas, C USA 33°32′N 92°49′W
21 Y3 **Camden** Delaware, NE USA 39°06′N 75°30′W
19 R7 **Camden** Maine, NE USA 44°12′N 69°04′W
18 I16 **Camden** New Jersey, NE USA 39°55′N 75°07′W
18 I9 **Camden** New York, NE USA 43°21′N 75°45′W
21 R12 **Camden** South Carolina, SE USA 34°16′N 80°36′W
20 H8 **Camden** Tennessee, S USA 36°03′N 88°07′W
25 X9 **Camden** Texas, SW USA 30°55′N 94°43′W
39 S5 **Camden Bay** *bay* S Beaufort Sea
27 U6 **Camdenton** Missouri, C USA 38°01′N 92°44′W
Camellia State *see* Alabama
18 M7 **Camels Hump** ▲ Vermont, NE USA 44°18′N 72°50′W
117 N8 **Camenca** *Rus.* Kamenka. N Moldova 48°01′N 28°43′E
Cameracum *see* Cambrai
22 G9 **Cameron** Louisiana, S USA 29°48′N 93°19′W
25 T9 **Cameron** Texas, SW USA 30°51′N 96°58′W
30 J5 **Cameron** Wisconsin, N USA 45°25′N 91°42′W
10 M12 **Cameron** ≈ British Columbia, W Canada
185 A24 **Cameron Mountains** ▲▲ South Island, New Zealand
79 D15 **Cameroon** *off.* Republic of Cameroon, *Fr.* Cameroun. ◆ *republic* W Africa
79 D15 **Cameroon Mountain** ▲ SW Cameroon 04°12′N 09°00′E
Cameroon, Republic of *see* Cameroon
Cameroon Ridge *see* Camerounaise, Dorsale
Cameroun *see* Cameroon
79 E14 **Camerounaise, Dorsale** *Eng.* Cameroon Ridge. *ridge* NW Cameroon
136 B15 **Çamiçi Gölü** ◎ SW Turkey
171 N3 **Camiling** Luzon, N Philippines 15°41′N 120°22′E
23 T7 **Camilla** Georgia, SE USA 31°13′N 84°12′W
104 G5 **Caminha** Viana do Castelo, N Portugal 41°52′N 08°50′W
35 P7 **Camino** California, W USA 38°43′N 120°39′W
107 J24 **Cammarata** Sicilia, Italy, C Mediterranean Sea 37°36′N 13°39′E
42 K10 **Camoapa** Boaco, S Nicaragua 12°25′N 85°30′W
58 O13 **Camocim** Ceará, E Brazil 02°55′S 40°50′W
106 D10 **Camogli** Liguria, NW Italy 44°21′N 09°10′E
181 S5 **Camooweal** Queensland, C Australia 19°57′S 138°14′E
55 Y11 **Camopi** E French Guiana 03°12′N 52°19′W
151 Q22 **Camorta** *island* Nicobar Islands, India, NE Indian Ocean
42 I6 **Campamento** Olancho, C Honduras 14°36′N 86°38′W
61 D19 **Campana** Buenos Aires, E Argentina 34°10′S 58°57′W
63 F21 **Campana, Isla** *island* S Chile
104 K11 **Campanario** Extremadura, W Spain 38°52′N 05°36′W
107 L17 **Campania** *Eng.* Champagne. ◈ *region* S Italy
27 Y8 **Campbell** Missouri, C USA 36°29′N 90°04′W
185 K15 **Campbell, Cape** *headland* South Island, New Zealand 41°44′S 174°16′E
14 J14 **Campbellford** Ontario, SE Canada 44°18′N 77°48′W
31 R13 **Campbell Hill** *hill* Ohio, N USA
192 K13 **Campbell Island** *island* S New Zealand
175 P13 **Campbell Plateau** *undersea feature* SW Pacific Ocean 51°00′S 170°00′E
10 K17 **Campbell River** Vancouver Island, British Columbia, SW Canada 49°59′N 125°18′W
20 L6 **Campbellsville** Kentucky, S USA 37°20′N 85°21′W
13 O13 **Campbellton** New Brunswick, SE Canada 48°00′N 66°41′W
183 S9 **Campbelltown** New South Wales, SE Australia 34°04′S 150°46′E
183 P16 **Campbell Town** Tasmania, SE Australia 41°57′S 147°30′E
96 G13 **Campbeltown** W Scotland, United Kingdom 55°26′N 05°38′W
41 W13 **Campeche** Campeche, SE Mexico 19°47′N 90°29′W
41 W14 **Campeche** ◈ *state* SE Mexico
41 T14 **Campeche, Bahía de** *Eng.* Bay of Campeche. *bay* E Mexico
Campeche, Banco de *see* Campeche Bank
64 C11 **Campeche Bank** *Sp.* Banco de Campeche, Sonda de Campeche. *undersea feature* S Gulf of Mexico 22°00′N 90°00′W
Campeche, Bay of *see* Campeche, Bahía de
Campeche, Sonda de *see* Campeche Bank
44 H7 **Campechuela** Granma, E Cuba 20°15′N 77°17′W
182 M13 **Camperdown** Victoria, SE Australia 38°16′S 143°10′E
167 U6 **Cẩm Phả** Quang Ninh, N Vietnam 21°04′N 107°20′E
116 H10 **Câmpia Turzii** *Ger.* Jerischmarkt, *Hung.* Aranyosgyéres; *prev.* Cîmpia Turzii, Ghiriș, Gyéres. Cluj, NW Romania 46°33′N 23°53′E
104 K12 **Campillo de Llerena** Extremadura, W Spain 38°30′N 05°48′W
104 L15 **Campillos** Andalucía, S Spain 37°04′N 04°51′W
116 J13 **Câmpina** *prev.* Cîmpina. Prahova, SE Romania 45°08′N 25°44′E
59 Q15 **Campina Grande** Paraíba, E Brazil 07°15′S 35°50′W
60 L9 **Campinas** São Paulo, S Brazil 22°54′S 47°06′W
38 L10 **Camp Kulowiye** Saint Lawrence Island, Alaska, USA 63°15′N 168°45′W
79 D17 **Campo** *var.* Kampo. Sud, SW Cameroon 02°22′N 09°50′E
Campo *see* Ntem
59 N15 **Campo Alegre de Lourdes** Bahia, E Brazil 09°28′S 43°01′W
107 L16 **Campobasso** Molise, C Italy 41°34′N 14°40′E
107 H24 **Campobello di Mazara** Sicilia, Italy, C Mediterranean Sea 37°38′N 12°45′E
Campo Criptana *see* Campo de Criptana
105 O10 **Campo de Criptana** *var.* Campo Criptana. Castilla-La Mancha, C Spain 39°25′N 03°07′W
59 I16 **Campo de Diauarum** *var.* Pôsto Diuarum. Mato Grosso, W Brazil 11°08′S 53°16′W
54 E5 **Campo de la Cruz** Atlántico, N Colombia 10°23′N 74°52′W
105 P11 **Campo de Montiel** *physical region* C Spain
Campo dos Goitacazes *see* Campos
60 H12 **Campo Erê** Santa Catarina, S Brazil 26°24′S 53°04′W
62 L7 **Campo Gallo** Santiago del Estero, N Argentina 26°32′S 62°51′W
59 I20 **Campo Grande** *state capital* Mato Grosso do Sul, SW Brazil 20°24′S 54°35′W
60 K12 **Campo Largo** Paraná, S Brazil 25°27′S 49°29′W
58 N13 **Campo Maior** Piauí, E Brazil 04°50′S 42°12′W
104 I10 **Campo Maior** Portalegre, C Portugal 39°01′N 07°04′W
60 H10 **Campo Mourão** Paraná, S Brazil 24°01′S 52°24′W
60 Q9 **Campos** *var.* Campo dos Goitacazes. Rio de Janeiro, SE Brazil 21°46′S 41°21′W
59 L17 **Campos Belos** Goiás, S Brazil 13°11′S 46°47′W
60 N9 **Campos do Jordão** São Paulo, S Brazil 22°45′S 45°36′W
60 I13 **Campos Novos** Santa Catarina, S Brazil 27°22′S 51°11′W
59 O14 **Campos Sales** Ceará, E Brazil 07°01′S 40°21′W
25 Q9 **Camp San Saba** Texas, SW USA 30°57′N 99°16′W
21 N6 **Campton** Kentucky, S USA 37°44′N 83°35′W
116 I13 **Câmpulung** *prev.* Câmpulung-Mușcel, Cîmpulung. Argeș, S Romania 45°16′N 25°03′E
116 J9 **Câmpulung Moldovenesc** *var.* Cîmpulung Moldovenesc, *Ger.* Kimpolung, *Hung.* Hosszúmezjő. Suceava, NE Romania 47°32′N 25°34′E
Câmpulung-Mușcel *see* Câmpulung
Campus Stellae *see* Santiago
36 L12 **Camp Verde** Arizona, SW USA 34°33′N 111°52′W
25 P11 **Camp Wood** Texas, SW USA 29°40′N 100°00′W
167 V13 **Cam Ranh** Khanh Hoa, S Vietnam 11°54′N 109°14′E
11 Q15 **Camrose** Alberta, SW Canada 53°01′N 112°48′W
Camulodunum *see* Colchester
136 B12 **Çan** Çanakkale, NW Turkey 40°03′N 27°03′E
18 L12 **Canaan** Connecticut, NE USA 42°00′N 73°17′W
11 O13 **Canada** ◆ *commonwealth republic* N North America
197 P6 **Canada Basin** *undersea feature* Arctic Ocean 80°00′N 145°00′W
61 B18 **Cañada de Gómez** Santa Fe, C Argentina 32°50′S 61°23′W
197 P6 **Canada Plain** *undersea feature* Arctic Ocean
61 A18 **Cañada Rosquín** Santa Fe, C Argentina 32°04′S 61°35′W
25 P1 **Canadian** Texas, SW USA 35°54′N 100°23′W
16 K12 **Canadian River** ≈ SW USA
8 L12 **Canadian Shield** *physical region* Canada
63 I18 **Cañadón Grande, Sierra** ▲▲ S Argentina
55 P9 **Canaima** Bolívar, SE Venezuela 09°41′N 72°33′W
136 B11 **Çanakkale** *var.* Dardanelli; *prev.* Chanak, Kale Sultanie. Çanakkale, W Turkey 40°09′N 26°25′E
136 B12 **Çanakkale** ◈ *province* NW Turkey
136 B11 **Çanakkale Boğazı** *Eng.* Dardanelles. *strait* NW Turkey
187 Q17 **Canala** Province Nord, C New Caledonia 21°31′S 165°57′E
59 A15 **Canamari** Amazonas, W Brazil 07°37′S 72°33′W
18 G10 **Canandaigua** New York, NE USA 42°52′N 77°14′W

232

◆ Country ● Country Capital ◇ Dependent Territory ○ Dependent Territory Capital ◈ Administrative Regions ✕ International Airport ▲ Mountain ▲▲ Mountain Range ⛰ Volcano ≈ River ◎ Lake ☒ Reservoir

CANANDAIGUA LAKE – CARTHAGE

18 F10 **Canandaigua Lake** ◎ New York, NE USA
40 G3 **Cananea** Sonora, NW Mexico 30°59′N 110°20′W
56 B8 **Cañar** ◈ *province* C Ecuador
64 N10 **Canarias, Islas** *Eng.* Canary Islands. ◈ *autonomous community* Spain, NE Atlantic Ocean
Canaries Basin *see* Canary Basin
44 C6 **Canarreos, Archipiélago de los** *island group* W Cuba
Canary Islands *see* Canarias, Islas
66 K3 **Canary Basin** *var.* Canaries Basin, Monaco Basin. *undersea feature* E Atlantic Ocean 30°00′N 25°00′W
42 L13 **Cañas** Guanacaste, NW Costa Rica 10°25′N 85°07′W
18 I10 **Canastota** New York, NE USA 43°04′N 75°45′W
40 K9 **Canatlán** Durango, C Mexico 24°33′N 104°45′W
104 J9 **Cañaveral** Extremadura, W Spain 39°47′N 06°24′W
23 Y11 **Canaveral, Cape** *headland* Florida, SE USA 28°27′N 80°31′W
59 O18 **Canavieiras** Bahia, E Brazil 15°44′S 38°58′W
43 R16 **Cañazas** Veraguas, W Panama 08°25′N 81°10′W
106 H6 **Canazei** Trentino-Alto Adige, N Italy 46°29′N 11°50′E
183 P6 **Canbelego** New South Wales, SE Australia 31°36′S 146°20′E
183 R10 **Canberra** ● (Australia) Australian Capital Territory, SE Australia 35°21′S 149°08′E
183 R10 **Canberra** ✈ Australian Capital Territory, SE Australia 35°19′S 149°12′E
35 P2 **Canby** California, W USA 41°27′N 120°51′W
29 S9 **Canby** Minnesota, N USA 44°42′N 96°17′W
103 N2 **Canche** ~ N France
102 L13 **Cancon** Lot-et-Garonne, SW France 44°33′N 00°37′E
41 Z11 **Cancún** Quintana Roo, SE Mexico 21°05′N 86°48′W
104 K2 **Candás** Asturias, N Spain 43°35′N 05°45′W
102 J7 **Cande** Maine-et-Loire, NW France 47°33′N 01°03′W
41 W14 **Candelaria** Campeche, SE Mexico 18°10′N 91°00′W
24 J11 **Candelaria** Texas, SW USA 30°05′N 104°40′W
41 W15 **Candelaria, Río** ~ Guatemala/Mexico
104 L8 **Candeleda** Castilla-León, N Spain 40°10′N 05°14′W
Candia *see* Irákleio
41 P8 **Cándido Aguilar** Tamaulipas, C Mexico 25°30′N 97°57′W
39 N8 **Candle** Alaska, USA 65°54′N 161°55′W
11 T14 **Candle Lake** Saskatchewan, C Canada 53°43′N 105°09′W
18 L13 **Candlewood, Lake** ⊠ Connecticut, NE USA
29 O3 **Cando** North Dakota, N USA 48°29′N 99°12′W
Canea *see* Chaniá
45 O12 **Canefield** ✈ (Roseau) SW Dominica 15°20′N 61°24′W
61 F20 **Canelones** *prev.* Guadalupe. Canelones, S Uruguay 34°32′S 56°17′W
61 E20 **Canelones** ◈ *department* S Uruguay
Canendiyú *see* Canindeyú
63 F14 **Cañete** Bío Bío, C Chile 37°48′S 73°25′W
105 Q9 **Cañete** Castilla-La Mancha, C Spain 40°03′N 01°39′W
Cañete *see* San Vicente de Cañete
27 P8 **Caney** Kansas, C USA 37°00′N 95°56′W
27 P8 **Caney River** ~ Kansas/Oklahoma, C USA
105 S3 **Canfranc-Estación** Aragón, NE Spain 42°42′N 00°31′W
83 E14 **Cangamba** *Port.* Vila de Aljustrel. Moxico, E Angola 13°40′S 19°47′E
82 C12 **Cangandala** Malanje, NW Angola 09°47′S 16°27′E
104 G4 **Cangas** Galicia, NW Spain 42°16′N 08°46′W
104 J2 **Cangas del Narcea** Asturias, N Spain 43°10′N 06°32′W
104 L2 **Cangas de Onís** Asturias, N Spain 43°21′N 05°08′W
161 S11 **Cangnan** *var.* Lingxi. Zhejiang, SE China 27°29′N 120°23′E
82 C10 **Cangola** Uíge, NW Angola 07°54′S 15°57′E
83 E14 **Cangombe** Moxico, E Angola 14°27′S 20°05′E
63 H21 **Cangrejo, Cerro** ▲ S Argentina 49°19′S 72°18′W
61 H17 **Canguçu** Rio Grande do Sul, S Brazil 31°25′S 52°37′W
161 P3 **Cangzhou** Hebei, E China 38°19′N 116°54′E
12 M7 **Caniapiscau** ~ Québec, E Canada
12 M8 **Caniapiscau, Réservoir de** ⊠ Québec, C Canada
107 J24 **Canicattì** Sicilia, Italy, C Mediterranean Sea 37°22′N 13°51′E
136 L11 **Canik Dağları** ▲▲ N Turkey
105 P14 **Caniles** Andalucía, S Spain 37°24′N 02°41′W
59 B16 **Canindé** Acre, W Brazil 10°55′S 69°45′W
62 P6 **Canindeyú** *var.* Canendiyú, Canindiyú. ◈ *department* E Paraguay
Canindiyú *see* Canindeyú
194 J10 **Canisteo Peninsula** *peninsula* Antarctica
18 F11 **Canisteo River** ~ New York, NE USA
40 M10 **Cañitas** *var.* Cañitas de Felipe Pescador. Zacatecas, C Mexico 23°35′N 102°39′W
Cañitas de Felipe Pescador *see* Cañitas
105 P15 **Canjáyar** Andalucía, S Spain 37°00′N 02°45′W
136 I12 **Çankırı** *var.* Chankiri; *anc.* Gangra, Germanicopolis. Çankın, N Turkey 40°36′N 33°35′E
136 I11 **Çankırı** *var.* Chankiri. ◈ *province* N Turkey
171 P6 **Canlaon Volcano** ⩕ Negros, C Philippines 10°24′N 123°05′E
11 P16 **Canmore** Alberta, SW Canada 51°07′N 115°18′W
96 F9 **Canna** *island* NW Scotland, United Kingdom
155 F20 **Cannanore** *var.* Kannur. Kerala, SW India 11°53′N 75°23′E *see also* Kannur
31 O17 **Cannelton** Indiana, N USA 37°54′N 86°44′W
103 U15 **Cannes** Alpes-Maritimes, SE France 43°33′N 06°59′E
39 R5 **Canning River** ~ Alaska, USA
106 C6 **Cannobio** Piemonte, NE Italy 46°04′N 08°39′E
97 L19 **Cannock** C England, United Kingdom 52°41′N 02°03′W
28 M6 **Cannonball River** ~ North Dakota, N USA
29 W9 **Cannon Falls** Minnesota, N USA 44°30′N 92°54′W
18 I11 **Cannonsville Reservoir** ⊠ New York, NE USA
183 R12 **Cann River** Victoria, SE Australia 37°34′S 149°11′E
61 I16 **Canoas** Rio Grande do Sul, S Brazil 29°42′S 51°07′W
61 I14 **Canoas, Rio** ~ S Brazil
14 J12 **Canoe Lake** ◎ Ontario, SE Canada
60 J12 **Canoinhas** Santa Catarina, S Brazil 26°12′S 50°24′W
37 T6 **Canon City** Colorado, C USA 38°25′N 105°14′W
55 P8 **Caño Negro** Bolívar, SE Venezuela
173 X15 **Canonniers Point** *headland* N Mauritius
23 W6 **Canoochee River** ~ Georgia, SE USA
11 V15 **Canora** Saskatchewan, S Canada 51°38′N 102°28′W
45 Y14 **Canouan** *island* S Saint Vincent and the Grenadines
13 R15 **Canso** Nova Scotia, SE Canada 45°20′N 61°00′W
104 M3 **Cantabria** ◈ *autonomous community* N Spain
104 K3 **Cantábrica, Cordillera** ▲▲ N Spain
Cantabrigia *see* Cambridge
103 O12 **Cantal** ◈ *department* C France
105 N6 **Cantalejo** Castilla-León, N Spain 41°15′N 03°57′W
103 O12 **Cantal, Monts du** ▲▲ C France
104 G8 **Cantanhede** Coimbra, C Portugal 40°21′N 08°37′W
Cantaño *see* Cataño
55 O6 **Cantaura** Anzoátegui, NE Venezuela 09°22′N 64°24′W
116 M11 **Cantemir** *Rus.* Kantemir. S Moldova 46°17′N 28°12′E
97 Q22 **Canterbury** *hist.* Cantwaraburh; *anc.* Durovernum, *Lat.* Cantuaria. SE England, United Kingdom 51°17′N 01°05′E
185 F19 **Canterbury** *off.* Canterbury Region. ◈ *region* South Island, New Zealand
185 H20 **Canterbury Bight** *bight* South Island, New Zealand
185 H19 **Canterbury Plains** *plain* South Island, New Zealand
Canterbury Region *see* Canterbury
167 S14 **Cần Thơ** Cần Thơ, S Vietnam 10°03′N 105°46′E
104 K13 **Cantillana** Andalucía, S Spain 37°34′N 05°48′W
59 N15 **Canto do Buriti** Piauí, NE Brazil 08°07′S 43°00′W
23 S2 **Canton** Georgia, SE USA 34°14′N 84°29′W
30 K12 **Canton** Illinois, N USA 40°33′N 90°02′W
22 L5 **Canton** Mississippi, S USA 32°36′N 90°02′W
27 V2 **Canton** Missouri, C USA 40°07′N 91°31′W
18 J7 **Canton** New York, NE USA 44°36′N 75°10′W
21 O10 **Canton** North Carolina, SE USA 35°31′N 82°50′W
31 U12 **Canton** Ohio, N USA 40°48′N 81°23′W
26 L9 **Canton** Oklahoma, C USA 36°03′N 98°35′W
18 G12 **Canton** Pennsylvania, NE USA 41°38′N 76°49′W
29 R11 **Canton** South Dakota, N USA 43°19′N 96°33′W
25 V7 **Canton** Texas, SW USA 32°33′N 95°51′W
Canton *see* Guangzhou
Canton Island *see* Kanton
26 L9 **Canton Lake** ⊠ Oklahoma, C USA
106 D7 **Cantù** Lombardia, N Italy 45°44′N 09°08′E
Cantuaria/Cantwaraburh *see* Canterbury
39 R10 **Cantwell** Alaska, USA 63°23′N 148°57′W
59 O16 **Canudos** Bahia, E Brazil 09°51′S 39°08′W
47 T7 **Canumã, Rio** ~ N Brazil
Canusium *see* Puglia, Canosa di
24 G7 **Canutillo** Texas, SW USA 31°53′N 106°34′W
25 N3 **Canyon** Texas, SW USA 34°58′N 101°56′W
33 S12 **Canyon** Wyoming, C USA 44°44′N 110°30′W
32 K13 **Canyon City** Oregon, NW USA 44°24′N 118°58′W
33 R10 **Canyon Ferry Lake** ◎ Montana, NW USA
25 S11 **Canyon Lake** ⊠ Texas, SW USA
167 T5 **Cao Bằng** *var.* Caobang. Cao Bằng, N Vietnam 22°40′N 106°16′E
Caobang *see* Cao Bằng
160 J12 **Caodu He** ~ S China
Caohai *see* Weining
167 S14 **Cao Lanh** Đông Thap, S Vietnam 10°35′N 105°25′E
82 C11 **Caombo** Malanje, NW Angola 08°42′S 16°33′E
Caorach, Cuan na g *see* Sheep Haven
Caozhou *see* Heze
171 Q12 **Capalulu** Pulau Mangole, E Indonesia 01°51′S 125°53′E
54 K8 **Capanaparo, Río** ~ Colombia/Venezuela
58 L12 **Capanema** Pará, NE Brazil 01°08′S 47°07′W
60 L10 **Capão Bonito** São Paulo, S Brazil 24°01′S 48°23′W
60 I13 **Capão Doce, Morro do** ▲ S Brazil 26°37′S 51°28′W
54 I4 **Capatárida** Falcón, N Venezuela 11°11′N 70°37′W
102 I15 **Capbreton** Landes, SW France 43°40′N 01°25′W
Cap-Breton, Île du *see* Cape Breton Island
15 W6 **Cap-Chat** Québec, SE Canada 49°04′N 66°43′W
15 P11 **Cap-de-la-Madeleine** Québec, SE Canada 46°22′N 72°31′W
103 N13 **Capdenac** Aveyron, S France 44°35′N 02°06′E
Cap des Palmès *see* Palmas, Cape
183 Q15 **Cape Barren Island** *island* Furneaux Group, Tasmania, SE Australia
65 O18 **Cape Basin** *undersea feature* S Atlantic Ocean 37°00′S 07°00′E
13 R14 **Cape Breton Island** *Fr.* Île du Cap-Breton. *island* Nova Scotia, SE Canada
23 Y11 **Cape Canaveral** Florida, SE USA 28°24′N 80°36′W
21 Y6 **Cape Charles** Virginia, NE USA 37°16′N 76°01′W
77 P17 **Cape Coast** *prev.* Cape Coast Castle. S Ghana 05°10′N 01°13′W
Cape Coast Castle *see* Cape Coast
19 Q12 **Cape Cod Bay** *bay* Massachusetts, NE USA
23 W15 **Cape Coral** Florida, SE USA 26°33′N 81°57′W
181 R4 **Cape Crawford Roadhouse** Northern Territory, N Australia 16°39′S 135°44′E
9 Q7 **Cape Dorset** Baffin Island, Nunavut, NE Canada 76°14′N 76°32′W
21 N8 **Cape Fear River** ~ North Carolina, SE USA
27 Y7 **Cape Girardeau** Missouri, C USA 37°19′N 89°31′W
21 T14 **Cape Island** *island* South Carolina, SE USA
186 A6 **Capella** ▲ NW Papua New Guinea 05°00′S 141°09′E
98 H12 **Capelle aan den IJssel** Zuid-Holland, SW Netherlands 51°56′N 04°36′E
83 C15 **Capelongo** Huíla, C Angola 14°45′S 15°02′E
18 J17 **Cape May** New Jersey, NE USA 38°54′N 74°54′W
18 J17 **Cape May Court House** New Jersey, NE USA 39°03′N 74°46′W
Cape Palmas *see* Harper
8 I16 **Cape Parry** Northwest Territories, N Canada 70°10′N 124°33′W
65 P19 **Cape Rise** *undersea feature* SW Indian Ocean 42°00′S 15°00′E
Cape Saint Jacques *see* Vung Tau
Capesterre *see* Capesterre-Belle-Eau
45 Y6 **Capesterre-Belle-Eau** *var.* Capesterre. Basse Terre, S Guadeloupe 16°03′N 61°34′W
83 D26 **Cape Town** *var.* Ekapa, *Afr.* Kaapstad, Kapstad. ● (South Africa-legislative capital) Western Cape, SW South Africa 33°56′S 18°28′E
83 E26 **Cape Town** ✈ Western Cape, SW South Africa 31°51′S 21°06′E
76 D9 **Cape Verde** *off.* Republic of Cape Verde, *Port.* Cabo Verde, Ilhas do Cabo Verde. ◆ *republic* E Atlantic Ocean
64 L11 **Cape Verde Basin** *undersea feature* E Atlantic Ocean 15°00′N 30°00′W
66 K5 **Cape Verde Islands** *island group* E Atlantic Ocean
64 L10 **Cape Verde Plain** *undersea feature* E Atlantic Ocean 23°00′N 26°00′W
Cape Verde Plateau/Cape Verde Rise *see* Cape Verde Terrace
Cape Verde, Republic of *see* Cape Verde
64 L11 **Cape Verde Terrace** *var.* Cape Verde Plateau, Cape Verde Rise. *undersea feature* E Atlantic Ocean 18°00′N 20°00′W
181 V2 **Cape York Peninsula** *peninsula* Queensland, N Australia
44 M8 **Cap-Haïtien** *var.* Le Cap. N Haiti 19°44′N 72°12′W
43 T15 **Capira** Panamá, C Panama 08°48′N 79°51′W
14 K8 **Capitachouane** ~ Québec, SE Canada
14 L8 **Capitachouane, Lac** ◎ Québec, SE Canada
37 T13 **Capitan** New Mexico, SW USA 33°33′N 105°34′W
194 G3 **Capitán Arturo Prat** *Chilean research station* South Shetland Islands, Antarctica 62°24′S 59°42′W
37 S13 **Capitan Mountains** ▲▲ New Mexico, SW USA
62 M3 **Capitán Pablo Lagerenza** *var.* Mayor Pablo Lagerenza. Chaco, N Paraguay 19°55′S 60°46′W
37 T13 **Capitan Peak** ▲ New Mexico, SW USA 33°35′N 105°15′W
188 H5 **Capitol Hill** ● (Northern Mariana Islands-legislative capital) Saipan, S Northern Mariana Islands
60 I9 **Capivara, Represa** ⊠ S Brazil
61 J16 **Capivari** Rio Grande do Sul, S Brazil 30°08′S 50°32′W
113 H15 **Čapljina** Federicija Bosna I Hercegovina, S Bosnia and Herzegovina 43°07′N 17°42′E
83 M15 **Capoche** *var.* Kapoche. ~ Mozambique/Zambia
Capo Delgado, Província de *see* Cabo Delgado
107 K17 **Capodichino** ✈ (Napoli) Campania, S Italy 40°53′N 14°15′E
Capodistria *see* Koper
106 E12 **Capraia, Isola di** *island* Arcipelago Toscano, C Italy
107 B16 **Caprara, Punta** *var.* Punta dello Scorno. *headland* Isola Asinara, W Italy 41°07′N 08°19′E
Capraria *see* Cabrera, Illa de
14 F10 **Capreol** Ontario, S Canada 46°43′N 80°56′W
107 K18 **Capri** Campania, S Italy 40°33′N 14°14′E
175 S9 **Capricorn Tablemount** *undersea feature* W Pacific Ocean 18°34′S 172°12′W
107 J18 **Capri, Isola di** *island* S Italy
83 G16 **Caprivi** ◈ *district* NE Namibia
Caprivi Concession *see* Caprivi Strip
83 F16 **Caprivi Strip** *Ger.* Caprivizipfel; *prev.* Caprivi Concession. *cultural region* NE Namibia
Caprivizipfel *see* Caprivi Strip
25 O5 **Cap Rock Escarpment** *cliffs* Texas, SW USA
15 R10 **Cap-Rouge** Québec, SE Canada 46°45′N 71°18′W
Cap Saint-Jacques *see* Vung Tau
38 F12 **Captain Cook** Hawaii, USA, C Pacific Ocean 19°30′N 155°55′W
183 R10 **Captains Flat** New South Wales, SE Australia 35°37′S 149°28′E
102 K14 **Captieux** Gironde, SW France 44°16′N 00°15′W
107 K17 **Capua** Campania, S Italy 41°06′N 14°13′E
54 F14 **Caquetá** *off.* Departamento del Caquetá. ◈ *province* S Colombia
Caquetá, Departamento del *see* Caquetá
54 E13 **Caquetá, Río** *var.* Rio Japurá, Yapurá. ~ Brazil/Colombia *see also* Japurá, Rio
Caquetá, Río *see* Japurá, Rio
CAR *see* Central African Republic
Cara *see* Kara
57 I16 **Carabaya, Cordillera** ▲▲ E Peru
54 K5 **Carabobo** *off.* Estado Carabobo. ◈ *state* N Venezuela
Carabobo, Estado *see* Carabobo
116 I14 **Caracal** Olt, S Romania 44°07′N 24°18′E
58 F10 **Caracaraí** Rondônia, W Brazil 01°47′N 61°11′W
54 L5 **Caracas** ● (Venezuela) Distrito Federal, N Venezuela 10°29′N 66°54′W
54 I5 **Carache** Trujillo, N Venezuela 09°40′N 70°15′W
60 N10 **Caraguatatuba** São Paulo, S Brazil 23°37′S 45°24′W
48 I7 **Carajás, Serra dos** ▲▲ N Brazil
Caralis *see* Cagliari
54 E9 **Caramanta** Antioquia, W Colombia 05°36′N 75°38′W
171 P4 **Caramoan** Catanduanes Island, N Philippines 13°47′N 123°49′E
Caramurat *see* Mihail Kogălniceanu
116 F12 **Caransebeș** *Ger.* Karansebesch, *Hung.* Karánsebes. Caraș-Severin, SW Romania 45°23′N 22°13′E
Carapella *see* Carapelle
107 M16 **Carapelle** *var.* Carapella. ~ SE Italy
55 O9 **Carapo** Bolívar, SE Venezuela
13 P13 **Caraquet** New Brunswick, SE Canada 47°48′N 64°59′W
Caras *see* Caraz
116 F12 **Carașova** *Hung.* Krassóvár. Caraș-Severin, SW Romania 45°11′N 21°51′E
116 F12 **Caraș-Severin** ◈ *county* SW Romania
42 M5 **Caratasca, Laguna de** *lagoon* NE Honduras
58 C13 **Carauari** Amazonas, NW Brazil 04°55′S 66°57′W
Caravaca *see* Caravaca de la Cruz
105 Q12 **Caravaca de la Cruz** *var.* Caravaca. Murcia, SE Spain 38°06′N 01°51′W
106 E7 **Caravaggio** Lombardia, N Italy 45°31′N 09°39′E
107 C18 **Caravai, Passo di** *pass* Sardegna, Italy, C Mediterranean Sea
59 O19 **Caravelas** Bahia, E Brazil 17°45′S 39°15′W
56 C12 **Caraz** *var.* Caras. Ancash, W Peru 09°03′S 77°47′W
61 H14 **Carazinho** Rio Grande do Sul, S Brazil 28°16′S 52°46′W
42 J11 **Carazo** ◈ *department* SW Nicaragua
Carballiño *see* O Carballiño
104 G2 **Carballo** Galicia, NW Spain 43°13′N 08°41′W
11 W16 **Carberry** Manitoba, S Canada 49°52′N 99°20′W
40 F4 **Carbó** Sonora, NW Mexico 29°41′N 111°00′W
107 C20 **Carbonara, Capo** *headland* Sardegna, Italy, C Mediterranean Sea 39°06′N 09°31′E
37 Q5 **Carbondale** Colorado, C USA 39°24′N 107°12′W
30 L17 **Carbondale** Illinois, N USA 37°43′N 89°13′W
27 Q4 **Carbondale** Kansas, C USA 38°49′N 95°41′W
18 I13 **Carbondale** Pennsylvania, NE USA 41°34′N 75°30′W
13 V12 **Carbonear** Newfoundland, Newfoundland and Labrador, SE Canada 47°45′N 53°16′W
105 Q9 **Carboneras de Guadazaón** *var.* Carboneras de Guadazón. Castilla-La Mancha, C Spain 39°54′N 01°50′W
Carboneras de Guadazón *see* Carboneras de Guadazaón
23 O3 **Carbon Hill** Alabama, S USA 33°53′N 87°31′W
107 B20 **Carbonia** *var.* Carbonia Centro. Sardegna, Italy, C Mediterranean Sea 39°11′N 08°31′E
Carbonia Centro *see* Carbonia
105 S10 **Carcaixent** País Valenciano, E Spain 39°08′N 00°28′W
Carcaso *see* Carcassonne
65 B24 **Carcass Island** *island* NW Falkland Islands
103 O16 **Carcassonne** *anc.* Carcaso. Aude, S France 43°13′N 02°21′E
105 R12 **Carche** ▲ S Spain 38°24′N 01°11′W
56 A13 **Carchi** ◈ *province* N Ecuador
10 I8 **Carcross** Yukon Territory, W Canada 60°11′N 134°41′W
Cardamomes, Chaîne des *see* Krâvanh, Chuŏr Phnum
155 G22 **Cardamom Hills** ▲▲ SW India
Cardamom Mountains *see* Krâvanh, Chuŏr Phnum
104 M12 **Cardeña** Andalucía, S Spain 38°16′N 04°20′W
44 D4 **Cárdenas** Matanzas, W Cuba 23°02′N 81°12′W
41 O11 **Cárdenas** San Luis Potosí, C Mexico 22°03′N 99°30′W
41 U15 **Cárdenas** Tabasco, SE Mexico 18°00′N 93°21′W
63 H21 **Cardiel, Lago** ◎ S Argentina
97 K22 **Cardiff** *Wel.* Caerdydd. ◐ S Wales, United Kingdom 51°30′N 03°13′W
97 J22 **Cardiff-Wales** ✈ S Wales, United Kingdom 51°24′N 03°22′W
97 I21 **Cardigan** *Wel.* Aberteifi. SW Wales, United Kingdom 52°06′N 04°40′W
97 I20 **Cardigan** *cultural region* W Wales, United Kingdom
97 I20 **Cardigan Bay** *bay* W Wales, United Kingdom
19 N8 **Cardigan, Mount** ▲ New Hampshire, NE USA 43°39′N 71°52′W
14 M13 **Cardinal** Ontario, SE Canada 44°48′N 75°22′W
105 V5 **Cardona** Cataluña, NE Spain 41°55′N 01°41′E
61 E19 **Cardona** Soriano, SW Uruguay 33°53′S 57°18′W
105 V4 **Cardoner** ~ NE Spain
11 Q17 **Cardston** Alberta, SW Canada 49°14′N 113°19′W
181 W5 **Cardwell** Queensland, NE Australia 18°24′S 146°06′E
116 G8 **Carei** *Ger.* Gross-Karol, Karol, *Hung.* Nagykároly; *prev.* Careii-Mari. Satu Mare, NW Romania 47°40′N 22°28′E
Careii-Mari *see* Carei
58 F13 **Careiro** Amazonas, NW Brazil 03°40′S 60°23′W
102 J4 **Carentan** Manche, N France 49°18′N 01°15′W
104 M2 **Cares** ~ N Spain
33 P14 **Carey** Idaho, NW USA 43°17′N 113°58′W
31 S12 **Carey** Ohio, N USA 40°57′N 83°22′W
25 P4 **Carey** Texas, SW USA 34°28′N 100°18′W
180 L11 **Carey, Lake** ◎ Western Australia
173 O8 **Cargados Carajos Bank** *undersea feature* C Indian Ocean
102 G6 **Carhaix-Plouguer** Finistère, NW France 48°16′N 03°35′W
61 A22 **Carhué** Buenos Aires, E Argentina 37°10′S 62°45′W
55 O5 **Cariaco** Sucre, NE Venezuela 10°33′N 63°37′W
107 O20 **Cariati** Calabria, SW Italy 39°30′N 16°57′E
2 H17 **Caribbean Plate** *tectonic feature*
44 I11 **Caribbean Sea** *sea* W Atlantic Ocean
11 N15 **Cariboo Mountains** ▲▲ British Columbia, SW Canada
11 W9 **Caribou** Manitoba, C Canada 59°27′N 97°43′W
19 S2 **Caribou** Maine, NE USA 46°51′N 68°00′W
11 P10 **Caribou Mountains** ▲▲ Alberta, SW Canada
Caribrod *see* Dimitrovgrad
40 I6 **Carichic** Chihuahua, N Mexico 27°57′N 107°01′W
103 R3 **Carignan** Ardennes, N France 49°38′N 05°08′E
183 Q5 **Carinda** New South Wales, SE Australia 30°26′S 147°45′E
105 R6 **Cariñena** Aragón, NE Spain 41°20′N 01°13′W
107 I23 **Carini** Sicilia, Italy, C Mediterranean Sea 38°06′N 13°09′E
107 K17 **Carinola** Campania, S Italy 41°14′N 14°03′E
Carinthi *see* Kärnten
55 O5 **Caripe** Monagas, NE Venezuela 10°13′N 63°30′W
55 P5 **Caripito** Monagas, NE Venezuela 10°03′N 63°05′W
15 W7 **Carleton** Québec, SE Canada 48°07′N 66°07′W
31 S10 **Carleton** Michigan, N USA 42°03′N 83°23′W
13 O14 **Carleton, Mount** ▲ New Brunswick, SE Canada 47°10′N 66°54′W
14 L13 **Carleton Place** Ontario, SE Canada 45°08′N 76°09′W
35 V3 **Carlin** Nevada, W USA 40°40′N 116°09′W
30 K14 **Carlinville** Illinois, N USA 39°16′N 89°52′W
97 K14 **Carlisle** *anc.* Caer Luel, Luguvallium, Luguvallum. NW England, United Kingdom 54°54′N 02°55′W
27 V11 **Carlisle** Arkansas, C USA 34°46′N 91°45′W
31 N15 **Carlisle** Indiana, N USA 38°57′N 87°23′W
29 V14 **Carlisle** Iowa, C USA 41°30′N 93°29′W
21 N5 **Carlisle** Kentucky, S USA 38°19′N 84°02′W
18 F15 **Carlisle** Pennsylvania, NE USA 40°10′N 77°10′W
21 Q11 **Carlisle** South Carolina, SE USA 34°35′N 81°27′W
38 J17 **Carlisle Island** *island* Aleutian Islands, Alaska, USA
27 R7 **Carl Junction** Missouri, C USA 37°10′N 94°34′W
107 A20 **Carloforte** Sardegna, Italy, C Mediterranean Sea 39°10′N 08°17′E
Carlopago *see* Karlobag
61 B21 **Carlos Casares** Buenos Aires, E Argentina 35°39′S 61°28′W
61 E18 **Carlos Reyles** Durazno, C Uruguay 33°00′S 56°30′W
61 A21 **Carlos Tejedor** Buenos Aires, E Argentina 35°25′S 62°25′W
97 F19 **Carlow** *Ir.* Ceatharlach. SE Ireland 52°50′N 06°55′W
97 F19 **Carlow** *Ir.* Cheatharlach. *cultural region* SE Ireland
96 F7 **Carloway** NW Scotland, United Kingdom 58°17′N 06°48′W
35 U17 **Carlsbad** California, W USA 33°09′N 117°21′W
37 U15 **Carlsbad** New Mexico, SW USA 32°24′N 104°15′W
Carlsbad *see* Karlovy Vary
129 N13 **Carlsberg Ridge** *undersea feature* S Arabian Sea 06°00′N 61°00′E
Carlsruhe *see* Karlsruhe
29 W6 **Carlton** Minnesota, N USA 46°39′N 92°25′W
11 V17 **Carlyle** Saskatchewan, S Canada 49°39′N 102°18′W
30 L15 **Carlyle** Illinois, N USA 38°36′N 89°22′W
30 L15 **Carlyle Lake** ⊠ Illinois, N USA
10 H7 **Carmacks** Yukon Territory, W Canada 62°04′N 136°21′W
106 B9 **Carmagnola** Piemonte, NW Italy 44°50′N 07°43′E
11 X16 **Carman** Manitoba, S Canada 49°32′N 97°59′W
Carmana/Carmania *see* Kermān
97 I21 **Carmarthen** SW Wales, United Kingdom 51°52′N 04°19′W
97 I21 **Carmarthen** *cultural region* SW Wales, United Kingdom
97 I22 **Carmarthen Bay** *inlet* SW Wales, United Kingdom
103 N14 **Carmaux** Tarn, S France 44°03′N 02°09′E
35 N11 **Carmel** California, W USA 36°32′N 121°54′W
31 O13 **Carmel** Indiana, N USA 39°58′N 86°07′W
18 L13 **Carmel** New York, NE USA 41°25′N 73°40′W
97 H18 **Carmel Head** *headland* NW Wales, United Kingdom 53°24′N 04°35′W
42 E2 **Carmelita** Petén, N Guatemala 17°33′N 90°11′W
61 D19 **Carmelo** Colonia, SW Uruguay 34°00′S 58°20′W
41 V14 **Carmen** *var.* Ciudad del Carmen. Campeche, SE Mexico 18°38′N 91°50′W
61 A25 **Carmen de Patagones** Buenos Aires, E Argentina 40°45′S 63°00′W
40 F8 **Carmen, Isla** *island* NW Mexico
40 M5 **Carmen, Sierra del** ▲▲ NW Mexico
30 M16 **Carmi** Illinois, N USA 38°05′N 88°09′W
35 O7 **Carmichael** California, W USA 38°36′N 121°21′W
Carmiel *see* Karmi'el
25 U11 **Carmine** Texas, SW USA 30°07′N 96°40′W
104 K14 **Carmona** Andalucía, S Spain 37°28′N 05°38′W
Carmona *see* Uíge
Carnaro *see* Kvarner
180 G9 **Carnarvon** Western Australia 24°57′S 113°38′E
14 I13 **Carnarvon** Ontario, SE Canada 45°03′N 78°41′W
83 G24 **Carnarvon** Northern Cape, W South Africa 30°59′S 22°08′E
Carnarvon *see* Caernarfon
180 K9 **Carnarvon Range** ▲▲ Western Australia
Carn Domhnach *see* Carndonagh
96 E13 **Carndonagh** *Ir.* Carn Domhnach. NW Ireland 55°15′N 07°15′W
11 V17 **Carnduff** Saskatchewan, S Canada 49°11′N 101°50′W
26 L11 **Carnegie** Oklahoma, C USA 35°06′N 98°36′W
180 L9 **Carnegie, Lake** *salt lake* Western Australia
193 U8 **Carnegie Ridge** *undersea feature* E Pacific Ocean 01°00′S 85°00′W
96 H9 **Carn Eige** ▲ N Scotland, United Kingdom 57°18′N 05°04′W
182 F5 **Carnes** South Australia 30°12′S 134°31′E
194 J12 **Carney Island** *island* Antarctica
18 H16 **Carneys Point** New Jersey, NE USA 39°38′N 75°29′W
Carniche, Alpi *see* Karnische Alpen
151 Q21 **Car Nicobar** *island* Nicobar Islands, India, NE Indian Ocean
79 H15 **Carnot** Mambéré-Kadéï, W Central African Republic 04°58′N 15°55′E
182 F10 **Carnot, Cape** *headland* South Australia 34°57′S 135°39′E
96 K11 **Carnoustie** E Scotland, United Kingdom 56°30′N 02°42′W
97 F20 **Carnsore Point** *Ir.* Ceann an Chairn. *headland* SE Ireland 52°10′N 06°22′W
8 H7 **Carnwath** ~ Northwest Territories, NW Canada
31 R8 **Caro** Michigan, N USA 43°29′N 83°24′W
23 Z15 **Carol City** Florida, SE USA 25°56′N 80°15′W
59 L14 **Carolina** Maranhão, E Brazil 07°20′S 47°25′W
45 U5 **Carolina** E Puerto Rico 18°22′N 65°57′W
21 V12 **Carolina Beach** North Carolina, SE USA 34°02′N 77°53′W
Caroline Island *see* Millennium Island
189 N15 **Caroline Islands** *island group* C Micronesia
129 Z14 **Caroline Plate** *tectonic feature*
192 H7 **Caroline Ridge** *undersea feature* E Philippine Sea 08°00′N 150°00′E
Carolopois *see* Châlons-en-Champagne
45 V14 **Caroni Arena Dam** ⊠ Trinidad, Trinidad and Tobago
Caronie, Monti *see* Nebrodi, Monti
55 P7 **Caroní, Río** ~ E Venezuela
45 U14 **Caroni River** ~ Trinidad, Trinidad and Tobago
Caronium *see* A Coruña
54 J5 **Carora** Lara, N Venezuela 10°12′N 70°07′W
86 F12 **Carpathian Mountains** *var.* Carpathians, *Cz./Pol.* Karpaty, *Ger.* Karpaten. ▲▲ E Europe
Carpathians *see* Carpathian Mountains
Carpathos/Carpathus *see* Kárpathos
116 H12 **Carpații Meridionalii** *var.* Alpi Transilvaniei, Carpații Sudici, *Eng.* South Carpathians, Transylvanian Alps, *Ger.* Südkarpaten, Transsylvanische Alpen, *Hung.* Déli-Kárpátok, Erdélyi-Havasok. ▲▲ C Romania
Carpații Sudici *see* Carpații Meridionalii
174 L7 **Carpentaria, Gulf of** *gulf* N Australia
Carpentoracte *see* Carpentras
103 R14 **Carpentras** *anc.* Carpentoracte. Vaucluse, SE France 44°03′N 05°03′E
106 F9 **Carpi** Emilia-Romagna, N Italy 44°47′N 10°53′E
116 E11 **Cărpiniș** *Hung.* Gyertyámos. Timiș, W Romania 45°46′N 20°53′E
35 R14 **Carpinteria** California, W USA 34°24′N 119°30′W
23 S9 **Carrabelle** Florida, SE USA 29°51′N 84°39′W
Carraig Aonair *see* Fastnet Rock
Carraig Fhearghais *see* Carrickfergus
Carraig Mhachaire Rois *see* Carrickmacross
Carraig na Siúire *see* Carrick-on-Suir
Carrantual *see* Carrauntoohil
106 E10 **Carrara** Toscana, C Italy 44°05′N 10°07′E
61 F20 **Carrasco** ✈ (Montevideo) Canelones, S Uruguay 34°51′S 56°00′W
105 P9 **Carrascosa del Campo** Castilla-La Mancha, C Spain 40°02′N 02°35′W
54 H4 **Carrasquero** Zulia, NW Venezuela 11°00′N 72°01′W
183 O9 **Carrathool** New South Wales, SE Australia 34°25′S 145°30′E
Carrauntohil *see* Carrauntoohil
97 B21 **Carrauntoohil** *Ir.* Carrantual, Carrauntohil, Corrán Tuathail. ▲ SW Ireland 51°98′N 09°53′W
45 Y15 **Carriacou** *island* N Grenada
97 G15 **Carrickfergus** *Ir.* Carraig Fhearghais. NE Northern Ireland, United Kingdom 54°43′N 05°49′W
97 F16 **Carrickmacross** *Ir.* Carraig Mhachaire Rois. N Ireland 53°58′N 06°43′W
97 D16 **Carrick-on-Shannon** *Ir.* Cora Droma Rúisc. NW Ireland 53°57′N 08°05′W
97 E20 **Carrick-on-Suir** *Ir.* Carraig na Siúire. S Ireland 52°21′N 07°25′W
182 I7 **Carrieton** South Australia 32°27′S 138°33′E
40 L7 **Carrillo** Chihuahua, N Mexico 25°53′N 103°54′W
29 O4 **Carrington** North Dakota, N USA 47°27′N 99°07′W
104 M4 **Carrión** ~ N Spain
104 M4 **Carrión de los Condes** Castilla-León, N Spain 42°20′N 04°37′W
25 P13 **Carrizo Springs** Texas, SW USA 28°33′N 99°54′W
37 S13 **Carrizozo** New Mexico, SW USA 33°38′N 105°52′W
29 T13 **Carroll** Iowa, C USA 42°04′N 94°52′W
23 N4 **Carrollton** Alabama, S USA 33°13′N 88°05′W
23 R3 **Carrollton** Georgia, SE USA 33°33′N 85°04′W
30 K14 **Carrollton** Illinois, N USA 39°18′N 90°24′W
20 L4 **Carrollton** Kentucky, S USA 38°41′N 85°09′W
31 R8 **Carrollton** Michigan, N USA 43°27′N 83°55′W
27 T3 **Carrollton** Missouri, C USA 39°20′N 93°30′W
31 U12 **Carrollton** Ohio, N USA 40°34′N 81°05′W
25 T6 **Carrollton** Texas, SW USA 32°57′N 96°53′W
11 U14 **Carrot** ~ Saskatchewan, S Canada
11 U14 **Carrot River** Saskatchewan, C Canada 53°18′N 103°32′W
18 J7 **Carry Falls Reservoir** ⊠ New York, NE USA
136 L11 **Çarşamba** Samsun, N Turkey 41°13′N 36°43′E
28 L6 **Carson** North Dakota, N USA 46°26′N 101°34′W
35 Q6 **Carson City** *state capital* Nevada, W USA 39°10′N 119°46′W
35 R6 **Carson River** ~ Nevada, W USA
35 S5 **Carson Sink** *salt flat* Nevada, W USA
11 Q16 **Carstairs** Alberta, SW Canada 51°35′N 114°02′W
Carstensz, Puntjak *see* Jaya, Puncak
54 E5 **Cartagena** *var.* Cartagena de los Indes. Bolívar, NW Colombia 10°24′N 75°33′W
105 R13 **Cartagena** *anc.* Carthago Nova. Murcia, SE Spain 37°36′N 00°59′W
54 E13 **Cartagena de Chaira** Caquetá, S Colombia 01°19′N 74°52′W
Cartagena de los Indes *see* Cartagena
54 D10 **Cartago** Valle del Cauca, W Colombia 04°45′N 75°55′W
43 N14 **Cartago** Cartago, C Costa Rica 09°50′N 83°54′W
42 M14 **Cartago** *off.* Provincia de Cartago. ◈ *province* C Costa Rica
Cartago, Provincia de *see* Cartago
25 O11 **Carta Valley** Texas, SW USA 29°46′N 100°37′W
104 F10 **Cartaxo** Santarém, C Portugal 39°10′N 08°47′W
104 I14 **Cartaya** Andalucía, S Spain 37°16′N 07°09′W
Carteret Islands *see* Tulun Islands
29 S15 **Carter Lake** Iowa, C USA 41°17′N 95°55′W
23 S3 **Cartersville** Georgia, SE USA 34°10′N 84°48′W
185 M14 **Carterton** Wellington, North Island, New Zealand 41°01′S 175°30′E
30 J13 **Carthage** Illinois, N USA 40°25′N 91°09′W
22 L5 **Carthage** Mississippi, S USA 32°43′N 89°31′W
27 R7 **Carthage** Missouri, C USA 37°10′N 94°20′W
18 I8 **Carthage** New York, NE USA 43°58′N 75°36′W
21 T10 **Carthage** North Carolina, SE USA 35°21′N 79°27′W
20 K8 **Carthage** Tennessee, S USA 36°14′N 85°59′W
25 X7 **Carthage** Texas, SW USA 32°10′N 94°21′W

◆ Country
● Country Capital
◇ Dependent Territory
○ Dependent Territory Capital
◈ Administrative Regions
✈ International Airport
▲ Mountain
▲▲ Mountain Range
⩕ Volcano
~ River
◎ Lake
⊠ Reservoir

CARTHAGE – CERMEI

74 M5 **Carthage** ✈ (Tunis) N Tunisia 36°51′N 10°12′E
Carthago Nova *see* Cartagena
14 E10 **Cartier** Ontario, S Canada 46°40′N 81°31′W
13 S8 **Cartwright** Newfoundland and Labrador, E Canada 53°40′N 57°W
55 P9 **Caruana de Montaña** Bolívar, SE Venezuela 05°16′N 63°12′W
59 Q15 **Caruaru** Pernambuco, E Brazil 08°15′S 35°55′W
55 P5 **Carúpano** Sucre, NE Venezuela 10°39′N 63°14′W
Carusbur *see* Cherbourg
58 M12 **Carutapera** Maranhão, E Brazil 01°12′S 45°57′W
27 Y9 **Caruthersville** Missouri, C USA 36°11′N 89°40′W
103 O1 **Carvin** Pas-de-Calais, N France 50°31′N 03°00′E
58 E12 **Carvoeiro** Amazonas, NW Brazil 01°24′S 61°59′W
104 E10 **Carvoeiro, Cabo** *headland* C Portugal 39°19′N 09°27′W
21 U9 **Cary** North Carolina, SE USA 35°47′N 78°46′W
182 M3 **Caryapundy Swamp** *wetland* New South Wales/ Queensland, SE Australia
74 F6 **Casablanca** *Ar.* Dar-el-Beida. NW Morocco 33°39′N 07°31′W
60 M8 **Casa Branca** São Paulo, S Brazil 21°47′S 47°05′W
36 L14 **Casa Grande** Arizona, SW USA 32°52′N 111°45′W
106 C8 **Casale Monferrato** Piemonte, NW Italy 45°08′N 08°27′E
106 E8 **Casalpusterlengo** Lombardia, N Italy 45°10′N 09°37′E
54 H10 **Casanare** *off.* Intendencia de Casanare. ◈ *province* C Colombia
Casanare, Intendencia de *see* Casanare
55 P5 **Casanay** Sucre, NE Venezuela 10°30′N 63°25′W
24 K11 **Casa Piedra** Texas, SW USA 29°43′N 104°03′W
107 Q19 **Casarano** Puglia, SE Italy 40°01′N 18°10′E
42 J11 **Casares** Carazo, W Nicaragua 11°37′N 86°19′W
105 R10 **Casas Ibáñez** Castilla-La Mancha, C Spain 39°17′N 01°28′W
61 I14 **Casca** Rio Grande do Sul, S Brazil 28°39′S 51°55′W
172 I17 **Cascade** Mahé, NE Seychelles 04°39′S 55°29′E
33 N13 **Cascade** Idaho, NW USA 44°31′N 116°02′W
29 Y13 **Cascade** Iowa, C USA 42°18′N 91°00′W
33 R9 **Cascade** Montana, NW USA 47°15′N 111°46′W
185 B20 **Cascade Point** *headland* South Island, New Zealand 44°00′S 168°23′E
32 G13 **Cascade Range** ▲▲ Oregon/ Washington, NW USA
33 N12 **Cascade Reservoir** ⊠ Idaho, NW USA
0 E8 **Cascadia Basin** *undersea feature* NE Pacific Ocean 47°00′N 127°30′W
104 E11 **Cascais** Lisboa, C Portugal 38°41′N 09°25′W
15 W7 **Cascapédia** ~ Québec, SE Canada
59 I22 **Cascavel** Ceará, E Brazil 04°10′S 38°15′W
60 G11 **Cascavel** Paraná, S Brazil 24°56′S 53°28′W
106 I13 **Cascia** Umbria, C Italy 42°45′N 13°01′E
106 F11 **Cascina** Toscana, C Italy 43°40′N 10°33′E
19 Q8 **Casco Bay** *bay* Maine, NE USA
194 J7 **Case Island** *island* Antarctica
106 B8 **Caselle** ✈ (Torino) Piemonte, NW Italy 45°06′N 07°41′E
107 K17 **Caserta** Campania, S Italy 41°05′N 14°20′E
15 N8 **Casey** Québec, SE Canada 47°50′N 74°09′W
30 M14 **Casey** Illinois, N USA 39°18′N 87°59′W
195 Y12 **Casey** *Australian research station* Antarctica 65°58′S 111°04′E
195 W3 **Casey Bay** *bay* Antarctica
80 Q11 **Caseyr, Raas** *headland* NE Somalia 11°51′S 51°16′E
97 D20 **Cashel** *Ir.* Caiseal. S Ireland 52°31′N 07°53′W
54 G6 **Casigua** Zulia, W Venezuela 08°46′N 72°30′W
61 B19 **Casilda** Santa Fe, C Argentina 33°05′S 61°10′W
Casim *see* General Toshevo
183 V4 **Casino** New South Wales, SE Australia 28°50′S 153°02′E
107 J16 **Cassino** *prev.* San Germano; *anc.* Casinum. Lazio, C Italy 41°29′N 13°50′E
Casinum *see* Cassino
111 E17 **Čáslav** *Ger.* Tschaslau. Střední Čechy, C Czech Republic 49°54′N 15°23′E
56 C13 **Casma** Ancash, C Peru 09°30′S 78°18′W
167 S7 **Ca, Sông** ~ N Vietnam
107 K17 **Casoria** Campania, S Italy 40°54′N 14°28′E
105 T6 **Caspe** Aragón, NE Spain 41°14′N 00°03′W
33 X15 **Casper** Wyoming, C USA 42°48′N 106°22′W
84 M10 **Caspian Depression** *Kaz.* Kaspīy Mangy Oypaty, *Rus.* Prikaspiyskaya Nizmennost'. *depression* Kazakhstan/Russian Federation
130 D10 **Caspian Sea** *Az.* Xäzär Dänizi, *Kaz.* Kaspiy Tengizi, *Per.* Baḩr-e Khazar, Daryā-ye Khazar, *Rus.* Kaspiyskoye More. *inland sea* Asia/Europe
83 L14 **Cassacatiza** Tete, NW Mozambique 14°20′S 32°24′E
Cassai *see* Kasai
82 F13 **Cassamba** Moxico, E Angola 13°07′S 20°22′E
107 N20 **Cassano allo Ionio** Calabria, SE Italy 39°46′N 16°16′E
31 S8 **Cass City** Michigan, N USA 43°36′N 83°10′W
Cassel *see* Kassel
14 M13 **Casselman** Ontario, SE Canada 45°18′N 75°05′W
29 R5 **Casselton** North Dakota, N USA 46°53′N 97°10′W
59 M16 **Cássia** *var.* Santa Rita de Cassia. Bahia, E Brazil 11°03′S 44°16′W
10 J9 **Cassiar** British Columbia, W Canada 59°16′N 129°40′W
10 K10 **Cassiar Mountains** ▲▲ British Columbia, W Canada
83 C15 **Cassinga** Huíla, SW Angola 15°08′S 16°05′E
29 T4 **Cass Lake** Minnesota, N USA 47°22′N 94°36′W
29 T4 **Cass Lake** ◎ Minnesota, N USA
31 P10 **Cassopolis** Michigan, N USA 41°56′N 86°00′W
31 S8 **Cass River** ~ Michigan, N USA
27 S8 **Cassville** Missouri, C USA 36°42′N 93°52′W
Castamoni *see* Kastamonu
58 L12 **Castanhal** Pará, NE Brazil 01°16′S 47°55′W
104 G8 **Castanheira de Pêra** Leiria, C Portugal 40°01′N 08°12′W
41 N7 **Castaños** Coahuila, NE Mexico 26°48′N 101°26′W
108 I10 **Castasegna** Graubünden, SE Switzerland 46°21′N 09°30′E
106 D8 **Casteggio** Lombardia, N Italy 45°02′N 09°10′E
107 K23 **Castelbuono** Sicilia, Italy, C Mediterranean Sea 37°56′N 14°05′E
107 K15 **Castel di Sangro** Abruzzo, C Italy 41°46′N 14°03′E
106 H7 **Castelfranco Veneto** Veneto, NE Italy 45°40′N 11°55′E
102 K14 **Casteljaloux** Lot-et-Garonne, SW France 44°19′N 00°03′E
107 L18 **Castellabate** *var.* Santa Maria di Castellabate. Campania, S Italy 40°16′N 14°57′E
107 I23 **Castellammare del Golfo** Sicilia, Italy, C Mediterranean Sea 38°02′N 12°53′E
107 H22 **Castellammare, Golfo di** *gulf* Sicilia, Italy, C Mediterranean Sea
103 U15 **Castellane** Alpes-de-Haute-Provence, SE France 43°49′N 06°34′E
107 O18 **Castellaneta** Puglia, SE Italy 40°38′N 16°57′E
106 E9 **Castel l'Arquato** Emilia-Romagna, C Italy 44°52′N 09°51′E
61 E21 **Castelli** Buenos Aires, E Argentina 36°07′S 57°47′W
Castelló de la Plana *see* Castellón de la Plana
105 S8 **Castellón** ◈ *province* País Valenciano, E Spain
Castellón *see* Castellón de la Plana
105 T9 **Castellón de la Plana** *var.* Castellón, *Cat.* Castelló de la Plana. País Valenciano, E Spain 39°59′N 00°03′W
105 S7 **Castellote** Aragón, NE Spain 40°46′N 00°18′W
103 N16 **Castelnaudary** Aude, S France 43°18′N 01°57′E
102 L16 **Castelnau-Magnoac** Hautes-Pyrénées, S France 43°18′N 00°30′E
106 F10 **Castelnovo ne' Monti** Emilia-Romagna, C Italy 44°26′N 10°24′E
Castelnuovo *see* Herceg-Novi
104 H9 **Castelo Branco** Castelo Branco, C Portugal 39°50′N 07°30′W
104 H8 **Castelo Branco** ◈ *district* C Portugal
104 I10 **Castelo de Vide** Portalegre, C Portugal 39°25′N 07°27′W
104 G9 **Castelo do Bode, Barragem do** ⊠ C Portugal
106 G10 **Castel San Pietro Terme** Emilia-Romagna, C Italy 44°22′N 11°34′E
107 B17 **Castelsardo** Sardegna, Italy, C Mediterranean Sea 40°54′N 08°42′E
102 M14 **Castelsarrasin** Tarn-et-Garonne, S France 44°02′N 01°06′E
107 I24 **Casteltermini** Sicilia, Italy, C Mediterranean Sea 37°33′N 13°38′E
107 H24 **Castelvetrano** Sicilia, Italy, C Mediterranean Sea 37°40′N 12°46′E
182 L12 **Casterton** Victoria, SE Australia 37°37′S 141°22′E
102 J15 **Castets** Landes, SW France 43°55′N 01°08′W
106 H12 **Castiglione del Lago** Umbria, C Italy 43°07′N 12°02′E
106 F13 **Castiglione della Pescaia** Toscana, C Italy 42°46′N 10°53′E
106 F8 **Castiglione delle Stiviere** Lombardia, N Italy 45°24′N 10°31′E
104 M9 **Castilla-La Mancha** ◈ *autonomous community* NE Spain
104 L5 **Castilla-León** *var.* Castillia y Leon. ◈ *autonomous community* NW Spain
105 N10 **Castilla Nueva** *cultural region* C Spain
105 N6 **Castilla Vieja** ◈ *cultural region* N Spain
Castillia y Leon *see* Castilla-León
Castillo de Locubim *see* Castillo de Locubín
105 N14 **Castillo de Locubín** *var.* Castillo de Locubim. Andalucía, S Spain 37°32′N 03°56′W
102 K13 **Castillon-la-Bataille** Gironde, SW France 44°51′N 00°01′W
63 I19 **Castillo, Pampa del** *plain* S Argentina
61 G19 **Castillos** Rocha, SE Uruguay 34°12′S 53°52′W
97 B16 **Castlebar** *Ir.* Caisleán an Bharraigh. W Ireland 53°52′N 09°17′W
97 F16 **Castleblayney** *Ir.* Baile na Lorgan. N Ireland 54°07′N 06°44′W
45 O11 **Castle Bruce** E Dominica 15°24′N 61°26′W
36 M5 **Castle Dale** Utah, W USA 39°10′N 111°02′W
36 I14 **Castle Dome Peak** ▲ Arizona, SW USA 33°04′N 114°08′W
97 J14 **Castle Douglas** S Scotland, United Kingdom 54°56′N 03°56′W
97 E14 **Castlefinn** *Ir.* Caisleán na Finne. NW Ireland 54°47′N 07°35′W
97 M17 **Castleford** N England, United Kingdom 53°44′N 01°21′W
11 O17 **Castlegar** British Columbia, SW Canada 49°18′N 117°48′W
64 B12 **Castle Harbour** *inlet* Bermuda, NW Atlantic Ocean
21 V12 **Castle Hayne** North Carolina, SE USA 34°23′N 78°07′W
97 B20 **Castleisland** *Ir.* Oileán Ciarral. SW Ireland 52°12′N 09°30′W
183 N12 **Castlemaine** Victoria, SE Australia 37°06′S 144°13′E
37 R5 **Castle Peak** ▲ Colorado, C USA 39°00′N 106°51′W
33 O13 **Castle Peak** ▲ Idaho, NW USA 44°02′N 114°42′W
184 N13 **Castlepoint** Wellington, North Island, New Zealand 40°54′S 176°13′E
97 D17 **Castlerea** *Ir.* An Caisleán Riabhach. W Ireland 53°45′N 08°32′W
97 G15 **Castlereagh** *Ir.* An Caisleán Riabhach. N Northern Ireland, United Kingdom 54°33′N 05°53′W
183 R6 **Castlereagh River** ~ New South Wales, SE Australia
37 T5 **Castle Rock** Colorado, C USA 39°22′N 104°51′W
30 K7 **Castle Rock Lake** ⊠ Wisconsin, N USA
65 G25 **Castle Rock Point** *headland* S Saint Helena 16°02′S 05°45′W
97 I16 **Castletown** SE Isle of Man 54°05′N 04°39′W
29 R9 **Castlewood** South Dakota, N USA 44°43′N 97°01′W
11 R15 **Castor** Alberta, SW Canada 52°14′N 111°54′W
14 M13 **Castor** ~ Ontario, SE Canada
27 X7 **Castor River** ~ Missouri, C USA
Castra Albiensium *see* Castres
Castra Regina *see* Regensburg
103 N15 **Castres** *anc.* Castra Albiensium. Tarn, S France 43°36′N 02°15′E
98 H9 **Castricum** Noord-Holland, W Netherlands 52°33′N 04°40′E
45 S11 **Castries** ● (Saint Lucia) N Saint Lucia 14°01′N 60°59′W
60 J11 **Castro** Paraná, S Brazil 24°46′S 50°03′W
63 F17 **Castro** Los Lagos, W Chile 42°27′S 73°48′W
104 H7 **Castro Daire** Viseu, N Portugal 40°54′N 07°55′W
104 M13 **Castro del Río** Andalucía, S Spain 37°41′N 04°29′W
Castrogiovanni *see* Enna
104 H14 **Castro Marim** Faro, S Portugal 37°13′N 07°26′W
104 J2 **Castropol** Asturias, N Spain 43°30′N 07°01′W
105 O2 **Castro-Urdiales** *var.* Castro Urdiales. Cantabria, N Spain 43°23′N 03°11′W
104 G13 **Castro Verde** Beja, S Portugal 37°42′N 08°05′W
107 N19 **Castrovillari** Calabria, SW Italy 39°48′N 16°12′E
35 N10 **Castroville** California, W USA 36°46′N 121°46′W
25 R12 **Castroville** Texas, SW USA 29°21′N 98°52′W
104 K11 **Castuera** Extremadura, W Spain 38°44′N 05°33′W
61 F19 **Casupá** Florida, S Uruguay 34°09′S 55°38′W
185 A22 **Caswell Sound** *sound* South Island, New Zealand
137 Q13 **Çat** Erzurum, NE Turkey 39°40′N 41°03′E
42 K6 **Catacamas** Olancho, C Honduras 14°55′N 85°54′W
56 A10 **Catacaos** Piura, NW Peru 05°22′S 80°40′W
22 I7 **Catahoula Lake** ◎ Louisiana, S USA
137 S15 **Çatak** Van, SE Turkey 38°02′N 43°05′E
137 S15 **Çatak Çayi** ~ SE Turkey
114 O12 **Çatalca** İstanbul, NW Turkey 41°09′N 28°28′E
114 O12 **Çatalca Yarimadasi** *physical region* NW Turkey
62 H6 **Catalina** Antofagasta, N Chile 25°19′S 69°37′W
Catalonia *see* Cataluña
105 U5 **Cataluña** *Cat.* Catalunya, *Eng.* Catalonia. ◈ *autonomous community* N Spain
Catalunya *see* Cataluña
62 I7 **Catamarca** *off.* Provincia de Catamarca. ◈ *province* NW Argentina
Catamarca *see* San Fernando del Valle de Catamarca
Catamarca, Provincia de *see* Catamarca
83 M16 **Catandica** Manica, C Mozambique 18°05′S 33°10′E
171 P4 **Catanduanes Island** *island* N Philippines
60 K8 **Catanduva** São Paulo, S Brazil 21°05′S 49°00′W
107 L24 **Catania** Sicilia, Italy, C Mediterranean Sea 37°31′N 15°04′E
107 M24 **Catania, Golfo di** *gulf* Sicilia, Italy, C Mediterranean Sea
45 U5 **Cataño** *var.* Cantaño. E Puerto Rico 18°26′N 66°06′W
107 O21 **Catanzaro** Calabria, SW Italy 38°53′N 16°36′E
107 O22 **Catanzaro Marina** *var.* Marina di Catanzaro. Calabria, S Italy 38°48′N 16°33′E
Marina di Catanzaro *see* Catanzaro Marina
25 Q14 **Catarina** Texas, SW USA 28°19′N 99°36′W
171 Q5 **Catarman** Samar, C Philippines 12°29′N 124°34′E
105 S10 **Catarroja** País Valenciano, E Spain 39°24′N 00°24′W
21 R11 **Catawba River** ~ North Carolina/South Carolina, SE USA
171 Q5 **Catbalogan** Samar, C Philippines 11°49′N 124°55′E
14 I14 **Catchacoma** Ontario, SE Canada 44°43′N 78°19′W
41 S15 **Catemaco** Veracruz-Llave, SE Mexico 18°28′N 95°10′W
Cathair na Mart *see* Westport
Cathair Saidhbhín *see* Caherciveen
31 P5 **Cat Head Point** *headland* Michigan, N USA 45°11′N 85°37′W
23 Q2 **Cathedral Caverns** *cave* Alabama, S USA
35 V16 **Cathedral City** California, W USA 33°45′N 116°27′W
24 K10 **Cathedral Mountain** ▲ Texas, SW USA 30°10′N 103°39′W
32 G10 **Cathlamet** Washington, NW USA 46°12′N 123°24′W
76 G13 **Catió** S Guinea-Bissau 11°13′N 15°10′W
55 O10 **Catisimiña** Bolívar, SE Venezuela 04°07′N 63°40′W
44 J3 **Cat Island** *island* C Bahamas
12 B9 **Cat Lake** Ontario, S Canada 51°47′N 91°52′W
21 P5 **Catlettsburg** Kentucky, S USA 38°24′N 82°37′W
185 D24 **Catlins** ~ South Island, New Zealand
35 R1 **Catnip Mountain** ▲ Nevada, W USA 41°53′N 119°19′W
41 Z11 **Catoche, Cabo** *headland* SE Mexico 21°36′N 87°04′W
27 P9 **Catoosa** Oklahoma, C USA 36°11′N 95°45′W
41 N10 **Catorce** San Luis Potosí, C Mexico 23°42′N 100°49′W
63 I14 **Catriel** Río Negro, C Argentina 37°54′S 67°52′W
62 K13 **Catriló** La Pampa, C Argentina 36°28′S 63°20′W
58 F11 **Catrimani** Roraima, N Brazil 0°24′N 61°30′W
58 E10 **Catrimani, Rio** ~ N Brazil
18 K11 **Catskill** New York, NE USA 42°13′N 73°52′W
18 K11 **Catskill Creek** ~ New York, NE USA
18 J11 **Catskill Mountains** ▲▲ New York, NE USA
18 D11 **Cattaraugus Creek** ~ New York, NE USA
Cattaro *see* Kotor
Cattaro, Bocche di *see* Kotorska, Boka
107 I24 **Cattolica Eraclea** Sicilia, Italy, C Mediterranean Sea 37°27′N 13°24′E
83 B14 **Catumbela** ~ W Angola
83 N14 **Catur** Niassa, N Mozambique 13°50′S 35°43′E
82 C10 **Cauale** ~ NE Angola
171 O2 **Cauayan** Luzon, N Philippines 16°55′N 121°46′E
54 C12 **Cauca** *off.* Departamento del Cauca. ◈ *province* SW Colombia
47 P5 **Cauca** ~ SE Venezuela
Cauca, Departamento del *see* Cauca
58 P13 **Caucaia** Ceará, E Brazil 03°44′S 38°45′W
54 E7 **Cauca, Río** ~ N Colombia
54 E7 **Caucasia** Antioquia, NW Colombia 07°59′N 75°13′W
137 Q8 **Caucasus** *Rus.* Kavkaz. ▲▲ Georgia/Russian Federation
62 I10 **Caucete** San Juan, W Argentina 31°38′S 68°16′W
105 R11 **Caudete** Castilla-La Mancha, C Spain 38°42′N 01°00′W
103 P2 **Caudry** Nord, N France 50°07′N 03°24′E
82 D11 **Caungula** Lunda Norte, NE Angola 08°22′S 18°37′E
62 G13 **Cauquenes** Maule, C Chile 35°58′S 72°22′W
55 N8 **Caura, Río** ~ C Venezuela
15 V7 **Causapscal** Québec, SE Canada 48°22′N 67°14′W
117 N10 **Căuşeni** *Rus.* Kaushany. E Moldova 46°37′N 29°21′E
102 M14 **Caussade** Tarn-et-Garonne, S France 44°10′N 01°31′E
102 K17 **Cauterets** Hautes-Pyrénées, S France 42°53′N 00°08′W
10 J15 **Caution, Cape** *headland* British Columbia, SW Canada 51°10′N 127°43′W
44 H7 **Cauto** ~ E Cuba
Cauvery *see* Kāveri
102 L3 **Caux, Pays de** *physical region* N France
107 L18 **Cava de' Tirreni** Campania, S Italy 40°42′N 14°42′E
104 G6 **Cávado** ~ N Portugal
Cavaia *see* Kavajë
103 R15 **Cavaillon** Vaucluse, SE France 43°51′N 05°01′E
103 U16 **Cavalaire-sur-Mer** Var, SE France 43°10′N 06°31′E
106 G6 **Cavalese** *Ger.* Gablös. Trentino-Alto Adige, N Italy 46°18′N 11°29′E
29 Q2 **Cavalier** North Dakota, N USA 48°47′N 97°37′W
76 L17 **Cavalla** *var.* Cavally, Cavally Fleuve. ~ Ivory Coast/ Liberia
105 Y8 **Cavalleria, Cap de** *var.* Cabo Caballeria. *headland* Menorca, Spain, W Mediterranean Sea 40°04′N 04°06′E
184 K2 **Cavalli Islands** *island group* N New Zealand
Cavally/Cavally Fleuve *see* Cavalla
97 E16 **Cavan** *Ir.* Cabhán. N Ireland 54°N 07°21′W
97 E16 **Cavan** *Ir.* An Cabhán. *cultural region* N Ireland
106 H8 **Cavarzare** Veneto, NE Italy 45°08′N 12°05′E
27 W9 **Cave City** Arkansas, C USA 35°56′N 91°33′W
20 K7 **Cave City** Kentucky, S USA 37°08′N 85°57′W
65 M25 **Cave Point** *headland* S Tristan da Cunha
21 N5 **Cave Run Lake** ⊠ Kentucky, S USA
58 K11 **Caviana de Fora, Ilha** *var.* Ilha Caviana. *island* N Brazil
Caviana, Ilha *see* Caviana de Fora, Ilha
113 I16 **Cavtat** *It.* Ragusavecchia. Dubrovnik-Neretva, SE Croatia 42°36′N 18°13′E
Cawnpore *see* Kānpur
Caxamarca *see* Cajamarca
58 A13 **Caxias** Amazonas, W Brazil 04°27′S 71°27′W
58 N13 **Caxias** Maranhão, E Brazil 04°53′S 43°20′W
61 I15 **Caxias do Sul** Rio Grande do Sul, S Brazil 29°14′S 51°10′W
42 J4 **Caxinas, Punta** *headland* N Honduras 16°01′N 86°02′W
82 B11 **Caxito** Bengo, NW Angola 08°34′S 13°38′E
136 F14 **Çay** Afyon, W Turkey 38°35′N 31°01′E
40 L15 **Cayacal, Punta** *var.* Punta Mongrove. *headland* S Mexico 17°55′N 102°09′W
56 C6 **Cayambe** Pichincha, N Ecuador 0°02′N 78°08′W
56 C6 **Cayambe** ▲ N Ecuador 0°00′S 77°58′W
21 R12 **Cayce** South Carolina, SE USA 33°58′N 81°04′W
55 Y10 **Cayenne** ○ (French Guiana) NE French Guiana 04°55′N 52°18′W
55 Y10 **Cayenne** ✈ NE French Guiana 04°55′N 52°18′W
44 K10 **Cayes** *var.* Les Cayes. SW Haiti 18°10′N 73°48′W
45 U6 **Cayey** C Puerto Rico 18°06′N 66°11′W
45 U6 **Cayey, Sierra de** ▲▲ E Puerto Rico
103 N14 **Caylus** Tarn-et-Garonne, S France 44°13′N 01°42′E
44 E8 **Cayman Brac** *island* E Cayman Islands
44 D8 **Cayman Islands** ◇ *UK dependent territory* W West Indies
64 D11 **Cayman Trench** *undersea feature* NW Caribbean Sea 19°00′N 80°00′W
47 O3 **Cayman Trough** *undersea feature* NW Caribbean Sea 18°00′N 81°00′W
80 O13 **Caynabo** Sool, N Somalia 08°55′N 46°28′E
42 F3 **Cayo** ◈ *district* SW Belize
Cayo *see* San Ignacio
43 N9 **Cayos Guerrero** *reef* E Nicaragua
43 O9 **Cayos King** *reef* E Nicaragua
44 E4 **Cay Sal** *islet* SW Bahamas
14 G16 **Cayuga** Ontario, S Canada 42°57′N 79°49′W
25 V8 **Cayuga** Texas, SW USA 31°55′N 95°57′W
18 G10 **Cayuga Lake** ◎ New York, NE USA
104 K13 **Cazalla de la Sierra** Andalucía, S Spain 37°56′N 05°46′W
116 L14 **Căzăneşti** Ialomiţa, SE Romania 44°36′N 27°03′E
102 M16 **Cazères** Haute-Garonne, S France 43°15′N 01°11′E
112 E10 **Cazin** ◈ Federacija Bosna I Hercegovina, NW Bosnia and Herzegovina
82 G13 **Cazombo** Moxico, E Angola 11°54′S 22°56′E
105 O13 **Cazorla** Andalucía, S Spain 37°55′N 03°W
Cazza *see* Sušac
104 L4 **Cea** ~ NW Spain
Ceadâr-Lunga *see* Ciadîr-Lunga
Ceanannas *see* Kells
Ceann Toirc *see* Kanturk
58 O13 **Ceará** *off.* Estado do Ceará. ◈ *state* C Brazil
Ceará *see* Fortaleza
Ceara Abyssal Plain *see* Ceará Plain
Ceará, Estado do *see* Ceará
59 Q14 **Ceará Mirim** Rio Grande do Norte, E Brazil 05°30′S 35°51′W
64 J13 **Ceará Plain** *var.* Ceara Abyssal Plain. *undersea feature* W Atlantic Ocean 0°00 36°30′W
64 I13 **Ceará Ridge** *undersea feature* C Atlantic Ocean
Ceatharlach *see* Carlow
43 Q17 **Cébaco, Isla** *island* SW Panama
40 K7 **Ceballos** Durango, C Mexico 26°33′N 104°07′W
61 G19 **Cebollatí** Rocha, E Uruguay 33°15′S 53°46′W
61 G19 **Cebollatí, Río** ~ E Uruguay
105 P5 **Cebollera** ▲ N Spain 42°01′N 02°40′W
104 M8 **Cebreros** Castilla-León, N Spain 40°27′N 04°28′W
171 P6 **Cebu** *off.* Cebu City. Cebu, C Philippines 10°17′N 123°46′E
171 P6 **Cebu** *island* C Philippines
Cebu City *see* Cebu
107 J16 **Ceccano** Lazio, C Italy 41°34′N 13°20′E
Čechy *see* Bohemia
106 F12 **Cecina** Toscana, C Italy 43°19′N 10°31′E
26 K4 **Cedar Bluff Reservoir** ⊠ Kansas, C USA
30 M8 **Cedarburg** Wisconsin, N USA 43°18′N 87°58′W
36 J7 **Cedar City** Utah, W USA 37°40′N 113°03′W
25 T11 **Cedar Creek** Texas, SW USA 30°04′N 97°30′W
28 L7 **Cedar Creek** ~ North Dakota, N USA
25 U7 **Cedar Creek Reservoir** ⊠ Texas, SW USA
29 W13 **Cedar Falls** Iowa, C USA 42°31′N 92°27′W
31 N8 **Cedar Grove** Wisconsin, N USA 43°31′N 87°48′W
21 Y6 **Cedar Island** *island* Virginia, NE USA
23 U11 **Cedar Key** Cedar Keys, Florida, SE USA 29°08′N 83°03′W
23 U11 **Cedar Keys** *island group* Florida, SE USA
11 V14 **Cedar Lake** ◎ Manitoba, C Canada
14 I11 **Cedar Lake** ◎ Ontario, SE Canada
24 M6 **Cedar Lake** ◎ Texas, SW USA
29 X13 **Cedar Rapids** Iowa, C USA 41°58′N 91°40′W
29 X14 **Cedar River** ~ Iowa/ Minnesota, C USA
29 O14 **Cedar River** ~ Nebraska, C USA
31 P8 **Cedar Springs** Michigan, N USA 43°13′N 85°33′W
23 R3 **Cedartown** Georgia, SE USA 34°00′N 85°16′W
27 O7 **Cedar Vale** Kansas, C USA 37°06′N 96°30′W
35 Q2 **Cedarville** California, W USA 41°30′N 120°10′W
104 H1 **Cedeira** Galicia, NW Spain 43°40′N 08°03′W
42 H8 **Cedeño** Choluteca, S Honduras 13°10′N 87°25′W
41 N10 **Cedral** San Luis Potosí, C Mexico 23°47′N 100°40′W
42 I6 **Cedros** Francisco Morazán, C Honduras 14°38′N 86°42′W
40 M9 **Cedros** Zacatecas, C Mexico 24°39′N 101°47′W
40 B5 **Cedros, Isla** *island* W Mexico
193 R5 **Cedros Trench** *undersea feature* E Pacific Ocean 27°45′N 115°45′W
182 E7 **Ceduna** South Australia 32°09′S 133°43′E
110 D10 **Cedynia** *Ger.* Zehden. Zachodnio-pomorskie, W Poland 52°54′N 14°15′E
80 P12 **Ceelaayo** Sanaag, N Somalia 11°18′N 49°20′E
81 O16 **Ceel Buur** *It.* El Bur. Galguduud, C Somalia 04°36′N 46°33′E
81 N15 **Ceel Dheere** *var.* Ceel Dher, *It.* El Dere. Galguduud, C Somalia 05°18′N 46°07′E
Ceel Dher *see* Ceel Dheere
81 P14 **Ceel Xamure** Mudug, E Somalia 07°15′N 48°55′E
80 O12 **Ceerigaabo** *var.* Erigabo, Erigavo. Sanaag, N Somalia 10°34′N 47°22′E
107 J23 **Cefalù** *anc.* Cephaloedium. Sicilia, Italy, C Mediterranean Sea 38°02′N 14°02′E
105 N6 **Cega** ~ N Spain
111 K23 **Cegléd** *prev.* Czegléd. Pest, C Hungary 47°10′N 19°47′E
113 N18 **Čegrane** W FYR Macedonia 41°50′N 20°59′E
105 Q13 **Cehegín** Murcia, SE Spain 38°04′N 01°48′W
136 K12 **Çekerek** Yozgat, N Turkey 40°04′N 35°30′E
146 B13 **Çekiçler** *Rus.* Chekishlyar, *Turkm.* Chekichler. Balkan Welaýaty, W Turkmenistan 37°35′N 53°52′E
107 J15 **Celano** Abruzzo, C Italy 42°06′N 13°33′E
104 H4 **Celanova** Galicia, NW Spain 42°09′N 07°58′W
42 F6 **Celaque, Cordillera de** ▲▲ W Honduras
41 N13 **Celaya** Guanajuato, C Mexico 20°32′N 100°48′W
Celebes *see* Sulawesi
192 F7 **Celebes Basin** *undersea feature* SE South China Sea 04°00′N 122°00′E
192 F7 **Celebes Sea** *Ind.* Laut Sulawesi. *sea* Indonesia/ Philippines
41 W12 **Celestún** Yucatán, E Mexico 20°50′N 90°22′W
31 Q12 **Celina** Ohio, N USA 40°34′N 84°35′W
20 L8 **Celina** Tennessee, S USA 36°32′N 85°30′W
25 U5 **Celina** Texas, SW USA 33°19′N 96°46′W
112 G11 **Čelinac Donji** Republika Srpska, N Bosnia and Herzegovina 44°43′N 17°19′E
109 V10 **Celje** *Ger.* Cilli. C Slovenia 46°16′N 15°14′E
111 G23 **Celldömölk** Vas, W Hungary 47°16′N 17°10′E
100 J12 **Celle** *var.* Zelle. Niedersachsen, N Germany 52°38′N 10°05′E
99 D19 **Celles** Hainaut, SW Belgium 50°42′N 03°25′E
104 I7 **Celorico da Beira** Guarda, N Portugal 40°38′N 07°24′W
Celovec *see* Klagenfurt
64 M7 **Celtic Sea** *Ir.* An Mhuir Cheilteach. *sea* SW British Isles
64 N7 **Celtic Shelf** *undersea feature* E Atlantic Ocean 07°00′W 49°15′N
114 L13 **Çeltik Gölu** ◎ NW Turkey
146 J17 **Çemenibit** *prev. Rus.* Chemenibit. Mary Welaýaty, S Turkmenistan 35°27′N 62°19′E
113 M14 **Čemerno** ▲▲ C Serbia
105 Q12 **Cenajo, Embalse del** ⊠ S Spain
171 V13 **Cenderawasih, Teluk** *var.* Teluk Irian, Teluk Sarera. *bay* W Pacific Ocean
105 P4 **Cenicero** La Rioja, N Spain 42°29′N 02°38′W
106 E9 **Ceno** ~ NW Italy
102 K13 **Cenon** Gironde, SW France 44°51′N 00°33′W
14 K13 **Centennial Lake** ◎ Ontario, SE Canada
Centennial State *see* Colorado
37 S7 **Center** Colorado, C USA 37°45′N 106°06′W
29 Q13 **Center** Nebraska, C USA 42°33′N 97°51′W
28 M5 **Center** North Dakota, N USA 47°07′N 101°18′W
25 X8 **Center** Texas, SW USA 31°49′N 94°10′W
29 W8 **Center City** Minnesota, N USA 45°25′N 92°48′W
36 L5 **Centerfield** Utah, W USA 39°07′N 111°49′W
20 K9 **Center Hill Lake** ⊠ Tennessee, S USA
29 X13 **Center Point** Iowa, C USA 42°11′N 91°47′W
25 R11 **Center Point** Texas, SW USA 29°56′N 99°01′W
29 W16 **Centerville** Iowa, C USA 40°47′N 92°51′W
27 W7 **Centerville** Missouri, C USA 37°27′N 91°01′W
29 R12 **Centerville** South Dakota, N USA 43°07′N 96°57′W
20 I9 **Centerville** Tennessee, S USA 35°45′N 87°29′W
25 V9 **Centerville** Texas, SW USA 31°17′N 95°59′W
40 M5 **Centinela, Picacho del** ▲ NE Mexico 29°07′N 102°40′W
106 G9 **Cento** Emilia-Romagna, N Italy 44°43′N 11°16′E
Centrafricaine, République *see* Central African Republic
39 S8 **Central** Alaska, USA 65°34′N 144°48′W
37 P15 **Central** New Mexico, SW USA 32°46′N 108°09′W
83 H18 **Central** ◈ *district* E Botswana
138 E10 **Central** ◈ *district* C Israel
81 I19 **Central** ◈ *province* C Kenya
82 M13 **Central** ◈ *region* C Malawi
153 P12 **Central** ◈ *zone* C Nepal
186 E9 **Central** ◈ *province* S Papua New Guinea
63 I21 **Central** ◈ *department* C Paraguay
186 E9 **Central** *off.* Central Province. ◈ *province* S Solomon Islands
155 K25 **Central** ◈ *province* C Sri Lanka
83 J14 **Central** ◈ *province* C Zambia
117 P11 **Central** ✈ (Odesa) Odes'ka Oblast', SW Ukraine 46°26′N 30°41′E
Central *see* Centre
79 H14 **Central African Republic** *var.* République Centrafricaine, *abbrev.* CAR; *prev.* Ubangi-Shari, Oubangui-Chari, Territoire de l'Oubangui-Chari. ◆ *republic* C Africa
192 C6 **Central Basin Trough** *undersea feature* W Pacific Ocean 16°45′N 130°00′E
Central Borneo *see* Kalimantan Tengah
149 P12 **Central Brāhui Range** ▲▲ W Pakistan
Central Celebes *see* Sulawesi Tengah
29 Y13 **Central City** Iowa, C USA 42°12′N 91°31′W
20 I6 **Central City** Kentucky, S USA 37°17′N 87°07′W
29 P15 **Central City** Nebraska, C USA 41°04′N 97°59′W
48 D6 **Central, Cordillera** ▲▲ W Bolivia
54 D11 **Central, Cordillera** ▲▲ W Colombia
42 M13 **Central, Cordillera** ▲▲ C Costa Rica
45 N9 **Central, Cordillera** ▲▲ C Dominican Republic
43 R16 **Central, Cordillera** ▲▲ C Panama
45 S6 **Central, Cordillera** ▲▲ Puerto Rico
42 H7 **Central District** *var.* Tegucigalpa. ◈ *district* C Honduras
81 E16 **Central Equatoria** *var.* Bahr el Gebel, Bahr el Jebel. ◈ *state* S Sudan
Central Group *see* Inner Islands
30 L15 **Centralia** Illinois, N USA 38°31′N 89°07′W
27 U4 **Centralia** Missouri, C USA 39°12′N 92°08′W
32 G9 **Centralia** Washington, NW USA 46°43′N 122°57′W
Central Indian Ridge *see* Mid-Indian Ridge
Central Java *see* Jawa Tengah
Central Kalimantan *see* Kalimantan Tengah
148 L14 **Central Makrān Range** ▲▲ W Pakistan
192 K7 **Central Pacific Basin** *undersea feature* C Pacific Ocean 05°00′N 175°00′W
59 M19 **Central, Planalto** *var.* Brazilian Highlands. ▲▲ E Brazil
32 F15 **Central Point** Oregon, NW USA 42°22′N 122°55′W
Central Province *see* Central
Central Provinces and Berar *see* Madhya Pradesh
186 B6 **Central Range** ▲▲ NW Papua New Guinea
Central Russian Upland *see* Srednerusskaya Vozvyshennost'
Central Siberian Plateau/ Central Siberian Uplands *see* Srednesibirskoye Ploskogor'ye
104 K8 **Central, Sistema** ▲▲ C Spain
Central Sulawesi *see* Sulawesi Tengah
35 N3 **Central Valley** California, W USA 40°39′N 122°21′W
35 P8 **Central Valley** *valley* California, W USA
23 Q3 **Centre** Alabama, S USA 34°09′N 85°40′W
79 E15 **Centre** *Eng.* Central. ◈ *province* C Cameroon
102 M8 **Centre** ◈ *region* N France
173 Y16 **Centre de Flacq** E Mauritius 20°12′S 57°43′E
55 Y9 **Centre Spatial Guyanais** *space station* N French Guiana
23 O5 **Centreville** Alabama, S USA 32°58′N 87°08′W
21 X3 **Centreville** Maryland, NE USA 39°03′N 76°04′W
22 J7 **Centreville** Mississippi, S USA 31°05′N 91°04′W
Centum Cellae *see* Civitavecchia
160 M14 **Cenxi** Guangxi Zhuangzu Zizhiqu, S China 22°58′N 111°00′E
Ceos *see* Tziá
Cephaloedium *see* Cefalù
112 I9 **Čepin** *Hung.* Csepén. Osijek-Baranja, E Croatia 45°32′N 18°33′E
Ceram *see* Seram, Pulau
171 R13 **Ceram Sea** *Ind.* Laut Seram. *sea* E Indonesia
192 G8 **Ceram Trough** *undersea feature* W Pacific Ocean
Cerasus *see* Giresun
36 I10 **Cerbat Mountains** ▲▲ Arizona, SW USA
103 P17 **Cerbère, Cap** *headland* S France 42°28′N 03°15′E
104 F13 **Cercal do Alentejo** Setúbal, S Portugal 37°48′N 08°40′W
111 A18 **Čerchov** *Ger.* Czerkow. ▲ W Czech Republic 49°24′N 12°47′E
103 O13 **Cère** ~ C France
61 A16 **Ceres** Santa Fe, C Argentina 29°55′S 61°55′W
59 K18 **Ceres** Goiás, C Brazil 15°21′S 49°34′W
Ceresio *see* Lugano, Lago di
103 O17 **Céret** Pyrénées-Orientales, S France 42°30′N 02°44′E
54 E6 **Cereté** Córdoba, NW Colombia 08°54′N 75°51′W
172 I17 **Cerf, Île au** *island* Inner Islands, NE Seychelles
99 G22 **Cerfontaine** Namur, S Belgium 50°08′N 04°25′E
Cergy-Pontoise *see* Pontoise
107 N16 **Cerignola** Puglia, SE Italy 41°17′N 15°53′E
Cerigo *see* Kýthira
103 O9 **Cérilly** Allier, C France 46°38′N 02°51′E
136 I11 **Çerkeş** Çankin, N Turkey 40°51′N 32°52′E
136 D10 **Çerkezköy** Tekirdağ, NW Turkey 41°17′N 28°00′E
109 T12 **Cerknica** *Ger.* Zirknitz. SW Slovenia 45°48′N 14°21′E
109 S11 **Cerkno** W Slovenia 46°07′N 13°58′E
116 F10 **Cermei** *Hung.* Csermő. Arad, W Romania 46°33′N 21°51′E

◆ Country ● Country Capital ◇ Dependent Territory ○ Dependent Territory Capital ◈ Administrative Regions ✈ International Airport ▲ Mountain ▲▲ Mountain Range Volcano ~ River ◎ Lake ⊠ Reservoir

Çermik – Chatham Strait

137 O15 **Çermik** Dıyarbakır, SE Turkey 38°09′N 39°27′E
112 I10 **Cerna** Vukovar-Srijem, E Croatia 45°10′N 18°36′E
Cernăuţi *see* Chernivtsi
116 M14 **Cernavodă** Constanţa, SW Romania 44°20′N 28°03′E
103 U7 **Cernay** Haut-Rhin, NE France 47°49′N 07°11′E
Černice *see* Schwarzach
41 O8 **Cerralvo** Nuevo León, NE Mexico 26°10′N 99°40′W
40 G9 **Cerralvo, Isla** *island* NW Mexico
107 L16 **Cerreto Sannita** Campania, S Italy 41°17′N 14°39′E
113 L20 **Cërrik** *var.* Cerriku. Elbasan, C Albania 41°01′N 19°55′E
Cerriku *see* Cërrik
41 O11 **Cerritos** San Luis Potosí, C Mexico 22°25′N 100°16′W
60 K11 **Cerro Azul** Paraná, S Brazil 24°48′S 49°14′W
61 F18 **Cerro Chato** Treinta y Tres, E Uruguay 33°04′S 55°08′W
61 F19 **Cerro Colorado** Florida, S Uruguay 33°52′S 55°33′W
56 E13 **Cerro de Pasco** Pasco, C Peru 10°43′S 76°15′W
61 G14 **Cêrro Largo** Rio Grande do Sul, S Brazil 28°10′S 54°43′W
61 G18 **Cerro Largo** ◈ *department* NE Uruguay
42 E7 **Cerrón Grande, Embalse** ▣ N El Salvador
63 I14 **Cerros Colorados, Embalse** ◎ W Argentina
105 V5 **Cervera** Cataluña, NE Spain 41°40′N 01°16′E
104 M3 **Cervera del Pisuerga** Castilla-León, N Spain 42°51′N 04°30′W
105 Q5 **Cervera del Río Alhama** La Rioja, N Spain 42°01′N 01°58′W
107 H15 **Cerveteri** Lazio, C Italy 42°00′N 12°06′E
106 H10 **Cervia** Emilia-Romagna, N Italy 44°14′N 12°22′E
106 J7 **Cervignano del Friuli** Friuli-Venezia Giulia, NE Italy 45°49′N 13°18′E
107 L17 **Cervinara** Campania, S Italy 41°02′N 14°36′E
Cervinia *see* Breuil-Cervinia
106 B6 **Cervino, Monte** *var.* Matterhorn. ▲ Italy/Switzerland 46°00′N 07°39′E *see also* Matterhorn
Cervino, Monte *see* Matterhorn
103 Y14 **Cervione** Corse, France, C Mediterranean Sea 42°22′N 09°28′E
104 I1 **Cervo** Galicia, NW Spain 43°39′N 07°25′W
54 F5 **Cesar** *off.* Departamento del Cesar. ◈ *province* N Colombia
Cesar, Departamento del *see* Cesar
106 H10 **Cesena** *anc.* Caesena. Emilia-Romagna, N Italy 44°09′N 12°14′E
106 I10 **Cesenatico** Emilia-Romagna, N Italy 44°12′N 12°24′E
118 H8 **Cēsis** *Ger.* Wenden. Cēsis, C Latvia 57°19′N 25°17′E
111 D15 **Česká Lípa** *Ger.* Böhmisch-Leipa. Liberecký Kraj, N Czech Republic 50°43′N 14°35′E
Česká Republika *see* Czech Republic
111 F17 **Česká Třebová** *Ger.* Böhmisch-Trübau. Pardubický Kraj, C Czech Republic 49°54′N 16°27′E
111 D19 **České Budějovice** *Ger.* Budweis. Jihočeský Kraj, S Czech Republic 48°58′N 14°29′E
111 D19 **České Velenice** Jihočeský Kraj, S Czech Republic 48°49′N 14°57′E
111 E18 **Českomoravská Vrchovina** *var.* Českomoravská Vysočina, *Eng.* Bohemian-Moravian Highlands, *Ger.* Böhmisch-Mährische Höhe. ▲▲ S Czech Republic
Českomoravská Vysočina *see* Českomoravská Vrchovina
111 C19 **Český Krumlov** *var.* Böhmisch-Krumau, *Ger.* Krummau. Jihočeský Kraj, S Czech Republic 48°48′N 14°18′E
Ceský Les *see* Bohemian Forest
112 F8 **Česma** ≈ N Croatia
136 A14 **Çeşme** İzmir, W Turkey 38°19′N 26°20′E
Cess *see* Cestos
183 T8 **Cessnock** New South Wales, SE Australia 32°51′S 151°21′E
76 K17 **Cestos** *var.* Cess. ≈ S Liberia
118 I9 **Cesvaine** Madona, E Latvia 56°58′N 26°15′E
116 G14 **Cetate** Dolj, SW Romania 44°06′N 23°01′E
Cetatea Albă *see* Bilhorod-Dnistrovs'kyy
Cetatea Damboviţei *see* Bucureşti
113 J17 **Cetinje** *It.* Cettigne. S Montenegro 42°23′N 18°55′E
107 N20 **Cetraro** Calabria, S Italy 39°30′N 15°59′E
Cette *see* Sète
188 A17 **Cetti Bay** *bay* SW Guam
Cettigne *see* Cetinje
104 L17 **Ceuta** *var.* Sebta. Ceuta, Spain, N Africa 35°53′N 05°19′W
88 C16 **Ceuta** *enclave* Spain, N Africa
106 B9 **Ceva** Piemonte, NE Italy 44°24′N 08°01′E
103 P14 **Cévennes** ▲▲ S France
108 G10 **Cevio** Ticino, S Switzerland 46°18′N 08°36′E
136 K16 **Ceyhan** Adana, S Turkey 37°02′N 35°48′E
136 K17 **Ceyhan Nehri** ≈ S Turkey
137 P17 **Ceylanpınar** Şanlıurfa, SE Turkey 36°53′N 40°02′E
Ceylon *see* Sri Lanka
173 R6 **Ceylon Plain** *undersea feature* N Indian Ocean 04°00′S 82°00′E
Ceyre to the Caribs *see* Marie-Galante
103 Q14 **Cèze** ≈ S France
Chaacha *see* Çäçe
127 P6 **Chaadayevka** Penzenskaya Oblast', W Russian Federation 53°07′N 45°55′E
167 O12 **Cha-Am** Phetchaburi, SW Thailand 12°48′N 99°58′E
143 W15 **Chābahār** *var.* Chāh Bahār, Chahbar. Sīstān va Balūchestān, SE Iran 25°21′N 60°38′E
Chabaricha *see* Khabarikha
61 B19 **Chabas** Santa Fe, C Argentina 33°16′S 61°23′W
103 T10 **Chablais** *physical region* E France
61 B20 **Chacabuco** Buenos Aires, E Argentina 34°40′S 60°27′W
42 K8 **Chachagón, Cerro** ▲ N Nicaragua 13°18′N 85°39′W
56 C10 **Chachapoyas** Amazonas, NW Peru 06°13′S 77°54′W
Chäche *see* Çäçe
119 O18 **Chachersk** *Rus.* Chechersk. Homyel'skaya Voblasts', SE Belarus 52°54′N 30°54′E
119 N16 **Chachevichy** *Rus.* Chechevichi. Mahilyowskaya Voblasts', E Belarus 53°31′N 29°51′E
61 B14 **Chaco** *off.* Provincia de Chaco. ◈ *province* NE Argentina
Chaco *see* Gran Chaco
62 M6 **Chaco Austral** *physical region* N Argentina
62 M3 **Chaco Boreal** *physical region* N Paraguay
62 M6 **Chaco Central** *physical region* N Argentina
39 Y15 **Chacon, Cape** *headland* Prince of Wales Island, Alaska, USA 54°41′N 132°00′W
Chaco, Provincia de *see* Chaco
78 H9 **Chad** *off.* Republic of Chad, *Fr.* Tchad. ◆ *republic* C Africa
122 K14 **Chadan** Respublika Tyva, S Russian Federation 51°16′N 91°25′E
21 U12 **Chadbourn** North Carolina, SE USA 34°19′N 78°49′W
83 L14 **Chadiza** Eastern, E Zambia 14°04′S 32°27′E
67 Q7 **Chad, Lake** *Fr.* Lac Tchad. ◎ C Africa
Chad, Republic of *see* Chad
28 J12 **Chadron** Nebraska, C USA 42°48′N 102°57′W
Chadyr-Lunga *see* Ciadîr-Lunga
163 W14 **Chaeryŏng** SW North Korea 38°22′N 125°35′E
105 P17 **Chafarinas, Islas** *island group* S Spain
27 Y7 **Chaffee** Missouri, C USA 37°10′N 89°39′W
148 L12 **Chāgai Hills** *var.* Chāh Gay. ▲▲ Afghanistan/Pakistan
123 Q11 **Chagda** Respublika Sakha (Yakutiya), NE Russian Federation 58°43′N 130°38′E
Chaghasarāy *see* Asadābād
149 N5 **Chaghcharān** *var.* Chakhcharan, Cheghcheran, Qala Āhangarān. Ghowr, C Afghanistan 34°28′N 65°18′E
103 R9 **Chagny** Saône-et-Loire, C France 46°54′N 04°45′E
173 Q7 **Chagos Archipelago** *var.* Oil Islands. *island group* British Indian Ocean Territory
129 O15 **Chagos Bank** *undersea feature* C Indian Ocean 06°15′S 72°00′E
129 O14 **Chagos-Laccadive Plateau** *undersea feature* N Indian Ocean 03°00′S 73°00′E
173 Q7 **Chagos Trench** *undersea feature* N Indian Ocean 07°00′S 73°30′E
43 T14 **Chagres, Río** ≈ C Panama
45 U14 **Chaguanas** Trinidad, Trinidad and Tobago 10°31′N 61°25′W
54 M6 **Chaguaramas** Guárico, N Venezuela 09°23′N 66°18′W
Chagyl *see* Çagyl
Chahārmahāl and Bakhtiyārī *see* Chahār Maḩall va Bakhtīārī
142 M9 **Chahār Maḩall va Bakhtīārī** *off.* Ostān-e Chahār Maḩall va Bakhtīārī, *var.* Chahārmahāl and Bakhtiyārī. ◈ *province* SW Iran
Chahār Maḩall va Bakhtīārī, Ostān-e *see* Chahār Maḩall va Bakhtīārī
Chāh Bahār/Chahbar *see* Chābahār
143 V13 **Chāh Derāz** Sīstān va Balūchestān, SE Iran 27°07′N 60°01′E
Chāh Gay *see* Chāgai Hills
167 P10 **Chai Badan** Lop Buri, C Thailand 15°08′N 101°03′E
153 Q16 **Chāībāsa** Jhārkhand, N India 22°31′N 85°50′E
79 E19 **Chaillu, Massif du** ▲▲ C Gabon
167 O10 **Chai Nat** *var.* Chainat, Jainat, Jayanath. Chai Nat, C Thailand 15°10′N 100°10′E
Chainat *see* Chai Nat
65 M14 **Chain Fracture Zone** *tectonic feature* E Atlantic Ocean
173 N5 **Chain Ridge** *undersea feature* W Indian Ocean 06°00′N 54°00′E
Chairn, Ceann an *see* Carnsore Point
158 L5 **Chaiwopu** Xinjiang Uygur Zizhiqu, W China 43°32′N 87°55′E
167 Q10 **Chaiyaphum** *var.* Jayabum. Chaiyaphum, C Thailand 15°46′N 101°55′E
62 N10 **Chajarí** Entre Ríos, E Argentina 30°45′S 57°57′W
42 C5 **Chajul** Quiché, W Guatemala 15°28′N 91°02′W
83 K16 **Chakari** Mashonaland West, N Zimbabwe 18°05′S 29°51′E
81 K22 **Chake Chake** Pemba South, E Tanzania 05°12′S 39°44′E
148 J9 **Chakhānsūr** Nīmrūz, SW Afghanistan 31°11′N 62°06′E
Chakhānsūr *see* Nīmrūz
Chakhcharan *see* Chaghcharān
149 V8 **Chak Jhumra** *var.* Jhumra. Punjab, E Pakistan 31°33′N 73°14′E
146 I16 **Chaknakdysonga** Ahal Welaýaty, S Turkmenistan 35°39′N 61°24′E
153 P16 **Chakradharpur** Jhāarkhand, N India 22°42′N 85°38′E
152 J8 **Chakrāta** Uttarakhand, N India 30°42′N 77°52′E
149 U7 **Chakwāl** Punjab, NE Pakistan 32°56′N 72°53′E
57 F17 **Chala** Arequipa, SW Peru 15°52′S 74°13′W
102 K12 **Chalais** Charente, W France 45°16′N 00°02′E
108 D10 **Chalais** Valais, SW Switzerland 46°18′N 07°37′E
115 J20 **Chalándri** *var.* Halandri; *prev.* Khalándrion. *prehistoric site* Sýros, Kykládes, Greece, Aegean Sea
188 H6 **Chalan Kanoa** Saipan, S Northern Mariana Islands 15°08′S 145°43′E
188 C16 **Chalan Pago** C Guam
Chalap Dalam/Chalap Dalan *see* Chehel Abdālān, Kūh-e
42 F7 **Chalatenango** Chalatenango, N El Salvador 14°04′N 88°53′W
42 A9 **Chalatenango** ◈ *department* NW El Salvador
83 P15 **Chalaua** Nampula, NE Mozambique 16°04′S 39°08′E
81 I16 **Chalbi Desert** *desert* N Kenya
42 D7 **Chalchuapa** Santa Ana, W El Salvador 13°59′N 89°41′W
Chalcidice *see* Chalkidikí
Chalcis *see* Chalkída
Chālderān *see* Sīāh Chashmeh
103 N6 **Châlette-sur-Loing** Loiret, C France 48°01′N 02°45′E
15 X8 **Chaleur Bay** *Fr.* Baie des Chaleurs. *bay* New Brunswick/Québec, E Canada
Chaleurs, Baie des *see* Chaleur Bay
57 G16 **Chalhuanca** Apurímac, S Peru 14°17′S 73°15′W
154 F12 **Chālisgaon** Mahārāshtra, C India 20°29′N 75°10′E
115 N23 **Chálki** *island* Dodekánisa, Greece, Aegean Sea
115 F16 **Chalkiádes** Thessalía, C Greece 39°24′N 22°25′E
115 H18 **Chalkída** *var.* Halkida, *prev.* Khalkís; *anc.* Chalcis. Evvoia, E Greece 38°27′N 23°38′E
115 G14 **Chalkidikí** *var.* Khalkidhikí; *anc.* Chalcidice. *peninsula* NE Greece
185 A24 **Chalky Inlet** *inlet* South Island, New Zealand
39 S7 **Chalkyitsik** Alaska, USA 66°39′N 143°43′W
102 I9 **Challans** Vendée, NW France 46°51′N 01°52′W
57 K19 **Challapata** Oruro, SW Bolivia 18°50′S 66°45′W
192 H6 **Challenger Deep** *undersea feature* W Pacific Ocean 11°20′N 142°12′E
Challenger Deep *see* Mariana Trench
193 S11 **Challenger Fracture Zone** *tectonic feature* SE Pacific Ocean
192 K11 **Challenger Plateau** *undersea feature* E Tasman Sea
33 P13 **Challis** Idaho, NW USA 44°31′N 114°14′W
22 L9 **Chalmette** Louisiana, S USA 29°56′N 89°57′W
124 J11 **Chalna** Respublika Kareliya, NW Russian Federation 61°53′N 33°59′E
103 Q5 **Châlons-en-Champagne** *prev.* Châlons-sur-Marne, *hist.* Arcae Remorum; *anc.* Carolopois. Marne, NE France 48°58′N 04°22′E
Châlons-sur-Marne *see* Châlons-en-Champagne
103 R9 **Chalon-sur-Saône** *anc.* Cabillonum. Saône-et-Loire, C France 46°47′N 04°51′E
Chaltel, Cerro *see* Fitzroy, Monte
102 M11 **Châlus** Haute-Vienne, C France 45°38′N 01°00′E
143 N4 **Chālūs** Māzandarān, N Iran 36°40′N 51°25′E
101 N20 **Cham** Bayern, SE Germany 49°13′N 12°40′E
108 F7 **Cham** Zug, N Switzerland 47°11′N 08°28′E
37 R8 **Chama** New Mexico, SW USA 36°54′N 106°34′W
Cha Mai *see* Thung Song
83 E22 **Chamaites** Karas, S Namibia 27°15′S 17°52′E
149 O9 **Chaman** Baluchistān, SW Pakistan 30°55′N 66°27′E
37 R9 **Chama, Rio** ≈ New Mexico, SW USA
152 I6 **Chamba** Himāchal Pradesh, N India 32°33′N 76°10′E
81 I25 **Chamba** Ruvuma, S Tanzania 11°33′S 37°01′E
150 H12 **Chambal** ≈ C India
11 U16 **Chamberlain** Saskatchewan, S Canada 50°49′N 105°29′W
29 O11 **Chamberlain** South Dakota, N USA 43°48′N 99°19′W
19 R3 **Chamberlain Lake** ◎ Maine, NE USA
39 S5 **Chamberlin, Mount** ▲ Alaska, USA 69°16′N 144°54′W
37 O11 **Chambers** Arizona, SW USA 35°11′N 109°25′W
18 F16 **Chambersburg** Pennsylvania, NE USA 39°54′N 77°39′W
31 N5 **Chambers Island** *island* Wisconsin, N USA
103 T11 **Chambéry** *anc.* Camberia. Savoie, E France 45°34′N 05°56′E
82 L12 **Chambeshi** Northern, NE Zambia 10°55′S 31°07′E
82 L12 **Chambeshi** ≈ NE Zambia
74 M6 **Chambi, Jebel** *var.* Jabal ash Sha'nabī. ▲ W Tunisia 35°16′N 08°39′E
15 Q7 **Chambord** Québec, SE Canada 48°25′N 72°02′W
139 U11 **Chamcham** Al Muthanná, S Iraq 31°17′N 45°05′E
139 T4 **Chamchamāl** At Ta'mīn, N Iraq 35°32′N 44°50′E
Chamdmanī *see* Altanshiree
40 J14 **Chamela** Jalisco, SW Mexico 19°31′N 105°02′W
42 G5 **Chamelecón, Río** ≈ NW Honduras
62 J9 **Chamical** La Rioja, C Argentina 30°21′S 66°19′W
115 L23 **Chamilí** *island* Kykládes, Greece, Aegean Sea
167 Q13 **Châmnar** Kaôh Kông, SW Cambodia 11°45′N 103°32′E
152 K9 **Chamoli** Uttarakhand, N India 30°22′N 79°19′E
103 U11 **Chamonix-Mont-Blanc** Haute-Savoie, E France 45°55′N 06°52′E
154 L11 **Chāmpa** Chhattīsgarh, C India 22°02′N 82°42′E
10 H8 **Champagne** Yukon Territory, W Canada 60°48′N 136°22′W
103 Q5 **Champagne** *cultural region* N France
Champagne *see* Campania
103 Q5 **Champagne-Ardenne** ◈ *region* N France
103 S9 **Champagnole** Jura, E France 46°44′N 05°55′E
30 M13 **Champaign** Illinois, N USA 40°07′N 88°15′W
167 S10 **Champasak** Champasak, S Laos 14°50′N 105°51′E
152 L9 **Champāwat** Uttarakhand, N India 29°20′N 80°06′E
103 U6 **Champ de Feu** ▲ NE France 48°24′N 07°15′E
13 O7 **Champdoré, Lac** ◎ Québec, NE Canada
42 B6 **Champerico** Retalhuleu, SW Guatemala 14°18′N 91°54′W
108 C11 **Champéry** Valais, SW Switzerland 46°12′N 06°52′E
18 L6 **Champlain** New York, NE USA 44°58′N 73°25′W
18 L9 **Champlain Canal** *canal* New York, NE USA
15 P13 **Champlain, Lac** ◎ Québec, Canada/USA *see also* Champlain, Lake
18 L7 **Champlain, Lake** ◎ Canada/USA *see also* Champlain, Lac
103 S7 **Champlitte** Haute-Saône, E France 47°36′N 05°31′E
41 W13 **Champotón** Campeche, SE Mexico 19°18′N 90°43′W
155 G21 **Chāmrājnagar** *var.* Chamrajnagar. Karnātaka, SW India 11°58′N 76°54′E
Chamrajnagar *see* Chāmrājnagar
104 G10 **Chamusca** Santarém, C Portugal 39°21′N 08°29′W
119 O20 **Chamyarysy** *Rus.* Chemerisy. Homyel'skaya Voblasts', SE Belarus 51°42′N 30°27′E
127 P5 **Chamzinka** Respublika Mordoviya, W Russian Federation 54°22′N 45°22′E
Chanáil Mhór, An *see* Grand Canal
Chanak *see* Çanakkale
62 G7 **Chañaral** Atacama, N Chile 26°19′S 70°34′W
104 H13 **Chança, Rio** *var.* Chanza. ≈ Portugal/Spain
57 D14 **Chancay** Lima, W Peru 11°36′S 77°14′W
Chan-chiang/Chanchiang *see* Zhanjiang
62 G13 **Chanco** Maule, C Chile 35°43′S 72°35′W
39 R7 **Chandalar** Alaska, USA 67°30′N 148°29′W
39 R6 **Chandalar River** ≈ Alaska, USA
152 L10 **Chandan Chauki** Uttar Pradesh, N India 28°32′N 80°43′E
153 S16 **Chandannagar** *prev.* Chandernagore. West Bengal, E India 22°52′N 88°21′E
152 K10 **Chandausi** Uttar Pradesh, N India 28°27′N 78°43′E
22 M10 **Chandeleur Islands** *island group* Louisiana, S USA
22 M9 **Chandeleur Sound** *sound* N Gulf of Mexico
Chandernagore *see* Chandannagar
152 I8 **Chandīgarh** *state capital* Punjab, N India 30°41′N 76°51′E
153 Q16 **Chāndil** Jhārkhand, NE India 22°58′N 86°04′E
182 D2 **Chandler** South Australia 26°59′S 133°22′E
15 Y7 **Chandler** Québec, SE Canada 48°21′N 64°41′W
36 L14 **Chandler** Arizona, SW USA 33°18′N 111°50′W
27 O10 **Chandler** Oklahoma, C USA 35°43′N 96°54′W
25 V7 **Chandler** Texas, SW USA 32°18′N 95°28′W
39 Q6 **Chandler River** ≈ Alaska, USA
56 H13 **Chandles, Río** ≈ E Peru
162 H9 **Chandmanĭ** *var.* Talshand. Govĭ-Altayĭ, C Mongolia 45°21′N 98°00′E
162 E7 **Chandmanĭ** *var.* Urdgol. Hovd, W Mongolia 47°39′N 92°46′E
14 J13 **Chandos Lake** ◎ Ontario, SE Canada
153 U15 **Chandpur** Chittagong, C Bangladesh 23°13′N 90°43′E
154 I13 **Chandrapur** Mahārāshtra, C India 19°58′N 79°21′E
83 J15 **Changa** Southern, S Zambia 16°24′S 28°27′E
Chang'an *see* Rong'an, Guangxi Zhuangzu Zizhiqu, S China
Changan *see* Xi'an, Shaanxi, C China
155 G23 **Changanācheri** *var.* Changannassery. Kerala, SW India 09°26′N 76°31′E *see also* Changannassery
83 M19 **Changane** ≈ S Mozambique
155 G23 **Changannassery** *var.* Changanācheri. Kerala, SW India 09°26′N 76°31′E *see also* Changanācheri
83 M16 **Changara** Tete, NW Mozambique 16°54′S 33°15′E
163 X11 **Changbai** *var.* Changbai Chosenzu Zizhixian. Jilin, NE China 41°25′N 128°08′E
Changbai Chosenzu Zizhixian *see* Changbai
163 X11 **Changbai Shan** ▲▲ NE China
163 V10 **Changchun** *var.* Ch'angch'un, Ch'ang-ch'un; *prev.* Hsinking. *province capital* Jilin, NE China 43°53′N 125°18′E
Ch'angch'un/Ch'ang-ch'un *see* Changchun
160 M10 **Changde** Hunan, S China 29°04′N 111°42′E
161 S13 **Changhua** *Jap.* Shōka. C Taiwan 24°06′N 120°31′E
168 L10 **Changi** ✕ (Singapore) E Singapore 01°22′N 103°58′E
158 L5 **Changji** Xinjiang Uygur Zizhiqu, NW China 44°02′N 87°12′E
160 L17 **Changjiang** *var.* Changjiang Lizu Zizhixian, Shiliu. Hainan, S China 19°16′N 109°09′E
157 R11 **Chang Jiang** *var.* Yangtze Kiang, *Eng.* Yangtze. ≈ C China
161 S8 **Changjiang Kou** *delta* E China
Changjiang Lizu Zizhixian *see* Changjiang
Changkiakow *see* Zhangjiakou
167 F12 **Chang, Ko** *island* S Thailand
161 Q2 **Changli** Hebei, E China 39°44′N 119°13′E
163 V10 **Changling** Jilin, NE China 44°15′N 124°03′E
Changning *see* Xunwu
161 N11 **Changsha** *var.* Ch'angsha, Ch'ang-sha. *province capital* Hunan, S China 28°10′N 113°E
Ch'angsha/Ch'ang-sha *see* Changsha
161 Q10 **Changshan** Zhejiang, SE China 28°54′N 118°30′E
163 V14 **Changshan Qundao** *island group* NE China
161 S8 **Changshu** *var.* Ch'ang-shu. Jiangsu, E China 31°39′N 120°45′E
Ch'ang-shu *see* Changshu
163 V11 **Changtu** Liaoning, NE China 42°50′N 123°59′E
43 P14 **Changuinola** Bocas del Toro, NW Panama 09°28′N 82°31′W
159 N9 **Changweiliang** Qinghai, W China 38°24′N 92°08′E
160 K6 **Changwu** *var.* Zhaoren. Shaanxi, C China 35°12′N 107°46′E
163 U13 **Changxing Dao** *island* N China
160 M9 **Changyang** *var.* Longzhouping. Hubei, C China 30°45′N 111°13′E
163 W14 **Changyŏn** SW North Korea 38°19′N 125°15′E
161 N5 **Changzhi** Shanxi, C China 36°10′N 113°02′E
161 R8 **Changzhou** Jiangsu, E China 31°45′N 119°58′E
115 H24 **Chaniá** *var.* Hania, Khaniá, *Eng.* Canea; *anc.* Cydonia. Kríti, Greece, E Mediterranean Sea 35°31′N 24°00′E
62 J5 **Chañi, Nevado de** ▲ NW Argentina 24°09′S 65°44′W
115 H24 **Chanión, Kólpos** *gulf* Kríti, Greece, E Mediterranean Sea
Chankiri *see* Çankırı
30 M11 **Channahon** Illinois, N USA 41°25′N 88°13′W
155 H20 **Channapatna** Karnātaka, E India 12°43′N 77°14′E
97 K26 **Channel Islands** *Fr.* Iles Normandes. *island group* S English Channel
35 R16 **Channel Islands** *island group* California, W USA
13 S13 **Channel-Port aux Basques** Newfoundland and Labrador, SE Canada 47°35′N 59°02′W
Channel, The *see* English Channel
97 Q23 **Channel Tunnel** *tunnel* France/United Kingdom
24 M2 **Channing** Texas, SW USA 35°41′N 102°21′W
Chantabun/Chantaburi *see* Chanthaburi
104 H3 **Chantada** Galicia, NW Spain 42°36′N 07°46′W
167 P12 **Chanthaburi** *var.* Chantabun, Chantaburi. Chantaburi, S Thailand 12°35′N 102°08′E
103 O4 **Chantilly** Oise, N France 49°12′N 02°28′E
139 V12 **Chanūn as Sa'ūdī** Dhī Qār, S Iraq 31°04′N 46°00′E
27 Q6 **Chanute** Kansas, C USA 37°40′N 95°27′W
Chanza *see* Chança, Rio
Ch'ao-an/Chaochow *see* Chaozhou
161 Q8 **Chaohu** Anhui, E China 31°36′N 117°55′E
161 P8 **Chao Hu** ◎ E China
167 P11 **Chao Phraya, Mae Nam** ≈ C Thailand
Chaor He *see* Qulin Gol
Chaouèn *see* Chefchaouen
161 P14 **Chaoyang** Guangdong, S China 23°17′N 116°33′E
163 T12 **Chaoyang** Liaoning, NE China 41°34′N 120°29′E
Chaoyang *see* Jiayin, Heilongjiang, China
Chaoyang *see* Huinan, Jilin China
161 Q14 **Chaozhou** *var.* Chaoan, Chao'an, Ch'ao-an; *prev.* Chaochow. Guangdong, SE China 23°42′N 116°36′E
58 N13 **Chapadinha** Maranhão, E Brazil 03°45′S 43°23′W
12 K12 **Chapais** Québec, SE Canada 49°47′N 74°54′W
40 L13 **Chapala** Jalisco, SW Mexico 20°20′N 103°10′W
40 L13 **Chapala, Lago de** ◎ C Mexico
146 F13 **Chapan, Gora** ▲ C Turkmenistan 37°48′N 58°03′E
57 M18 **Chapare, Río** ≈ C Bolivia
54 E11 **Chaparral** Tolima, C Colombia 03°45′N 75°30′W
144 F9 **Chapayev** Zapadnyy Kazakhstan, NW Kazakhstan 50°12′N 51°09′E
123 O11 **Chapayevo** Respublika Sakha (Yakutiya), NE Russian Federation 60°03′N 117°19′E
127 R6 **Chapayevsk** Samarskaya Oblast', W Russian Federation 52°57′N 49°42′E
60 H13 **Chapecó** Santa Catarina, S Brazil 27°14′S 52°41′W
60 I13 **Chapecó, Rio** ≈ S Brazil
20 J9 **Chapel Hill** Tennessee, S USA 35°38′N 86°40′W
44 J12 **Chapelton** C Jamaica 18°05′N 77°16′W
14 C8 **Chapleau** Ontario, SE Canada 47°50′N 83°24′W
14 D7 **Chapleau** ≈ Ontario, S Canada
11 T16 **Chaplin** Saskatchewan, S Canada 50°27′N 106°37′W
126 M6 **Chaplygin** Lipetskaya Oblast', W Russian Federation 53°13′N 39°58′E
117 S11 **Chaplynka** Khersons'ka Oblast', S Ukraine 46°20′N 33°34′E
9 O6 **Chapman, Cape** *headland* Nunavut, NE Canada 69°15′N 89°09′W
25 T15 **Chapman Ranch** Texas, SW USA 27°32′N 97°25′W
Chapman's *see* Okwa
21 P5 **Chapmanville** West Virginia, NE USA 37°58′N 82°01′W
28 K15 **Chappell** Nebraska, C USA 41°05′N 102°28′W
Chapra *see* Chhapra
56 D9 **Chapuli, Río** ≈ N Peru
76 I6 **Châr** *well* N Mauritania
123 P12 **Chara** Chitinskaya Oblast', S Russian Federation 56°57′N 118°05′E
123 O11 **Chara** ≈ C Russian Federation
54 G8 **Charala** Santander, C Colombia 06°17′N 73°09′W
41 N10 **Charcas** San Luis Potosí, C Mexico 23°09′N 101°10′W
25 T13 **Charco** Texas, SW USA 28°42′N 97°35′E
194 H7 **Charcot Island** *island* Antarctica
64 M8 **Charcot Seamounts** *undersea feature* E Atlantic Ocean 11°30′W 45°00′N
Chardara *see* Shardara
145 P17 **Chardarinskoye Vodokhranilishche** ▣ S Kazakhstan
31 U11 **Chardon** Ohio, N USA 41°34′N 81°12′W
44 K9 **Chardonnières** SW Haiti 18°16′N 74°10′W
Chardzhev *see* Türkmenabat
Chardzhevskaya Oblast *see* Lebap Welaýaty
Chardzhou/Chardzhui *see* Türkmenabat
102 L11 **Charente** ◈ *department* W France
102 J11 **Charente** ≈ W France
102 J10 **Charente-Maritime** ◈ *department* W France
137 U12 **Ch'arents'avan** C Armenia 40°23′N 44°41′E
78 I12 **Chari** *var.* Shari. ≈ Central African Republic/Chad
78 G11 **Chari-Baguirmi** *off.* Préfecture du Chari-Baguirmi. ◈ *prefecture* SW Chad
Chari-Baguirmi, Préfecture du *see* Chari-Baguirmi
149 Q4 **Chārīkār** Parvān, NE Afghanistan 35°01′N 69°11′E
29 V15 **Chariton** Iowa, C USA 41°00′N 93°18′W
27 U3 **Chariton River** ≈ Missouri, C USA
55 T7 **Charity** NW Guyana 07°22′N 58°34′W
31 R7 **Charity Island** *island* Michigan, N USA
Chärjew *see* Türkmenabat
Chärjew Oblasty *see* Lebap Welaýaty
Charkhlik/Charkhliq *see* Ruoqiang
99 G20 **Charleroi** Hainaut, S Belgium 50°25′N 04°27′E
11 V12 **Charles** Manitoba, C Canada 55°27′N 100°58′W
15 R10 **Charlesbourg** Québec, SE Canada 46°50′N 71°15′W
21 Y7 **Charles, Cape** *headland* Virginia, NE USA 37°09′N 75°57′W
29 W12 **Charles City** Iowa, C USA 43°04′N 92°40′W
21 W6 **Charles City** Virginia, NE USA 37°21′N 77°05′W
103 O5 **Charles de Gaulle** ✕ (Paris) Seine-et-Marne, N France 49°04′N 02°36′E
12 K1 **Charles Island** *island* Nunavut, NE Canada
Charles Island *see* Santa María, Isla
30 K9 **Charles Mound** *hill* Illinois, N USA
185 A22 **Charles Sound** *sound* South Island, New Zealand
185 G15 **Charleston** West Coast, South Island, New Zealand 41°54′S 171°25′E
27 S11 **Charleston** Arkansas, C USA 35°19′N 94°02′W
30 M14 **Charleston** Illinois, N USA 39°30′N 88°10′W
22 L3 **Charleston** Mississippi, S USA 34°00′N 90°03′W
27 Z7 **Charleston** Missouri, C USA 36°54′N 89°22′W
21 T15 **Charleston** South Carolina, SE USA 32°48′N 79°57′W
21 Q5 **Charleston** *state capital* West Virginia, NE USA 38°21′N 81°38′W
14 L14 **Charleston Lake** ◎ Ontario, SE Canada
35 W11 **Charleston Peak** ▲ Nevada, W USA 36°16′N 115°40′W
45 W10 **Charlestown** Nevis, Saint Kitts and Nevis 17°08′N 62°37′W
31 P16 **Charlestown** Indiana, N USA 38°27′N 85°40′W
18 M9 **Charlestown** New Hampshire, NE USA 43°14′N 72°23′W
21 V3 **Charles Town** West Virginia, NE USA 39°18′N 77°54′W
181 W9 **Charleville** Queensland, E Australia 26°25′S 146°18′E
103 R3 **Charleville-Mézières** Ardennes, N France 49°45′N 04°43′E
31 P5 **Charlevoix** Michigan, N USA 45°19′N 85°15′W
31 Q6 **Charlevoix, Lake** ◎ Michigan, N USA
39 T9 **Charley River** ≈ Alaska, USA
64 J6 **Charlie-Gibbs Fracture Zone** *tectonic feature* N Atlantic Ocean
103 Q10 **Charlieu** Loire, E France 46°11′N 04°10′E
31 Q9 **Charlotte** Michigan, N USA 42°33′N 84°50′W
21 R10 **Charlotte** North Carolina, SE USA 35°14′N 80°51′W
20 I8 **Charlotte** Tennessee, S USA 36°11′N 87°18′W
25 R13 **Charlotte** Texas, SW USA 28°51′N 98°42′W
21 R10 **Charlotte** ✕ North Carolina, SE USA 35°12′N 80°54′W
45 T9 **Charlotte Amalie** *prev.* Saint Thomas. ○ (Virgin Islands (US)) Saint Thomas, N Virgin Islands (US) 18°22′N 64°56′W
21 U7 **Charlotte Court House** Virginia, NE USA 37°04′N 78°37′W
23 W14 **Charlotte Harbor** *inlet* Florida, SE USA
Charlotte Island *see* Abaiang
95 J15 **Charlottenberg** Värmland, C Sweden 59°53′N 12°17′E
Charlottenhof *see* Aegviidu
21 U5 **Charlottesville** Virginia, NE USA 38°02′N 78°29′W
13 Q14 **Charlottetown** *province capital* Prince Edward Island, Prince Edward Island, SE Canada 46°14′N 63°09′W
Charlotte Town *see* Roseau, Dominica
Charlotte Town *see* Gouyave, Grenada
45 Z16 **Charlotteville** Tobago, Trinidad and Tobago 11°16′N 60°33′W
182 M11 **Charlton** Victoria, SE Australia 36°18′S 143°19′E
12 H10 **Charlton Island** *island* Northwest Territories, C Canada
103 T6 **Charmes** Vosges, NE France 48°19′N 06°19′E
119 F19 **Charnawchytsy** *Rus.* Chernavchitsy. Brestskaya Voblasts', SW Belarus 52°13′N 23°44′E
15 R10 **Charny** Québec, SE Canada 46°43′N 71°15′W
149 T5 **Chārsadda** North-West Frontier Province, NW Pakistan 34°12′N 71°46′E
Charshanga/Charshangngy/Charshangy *see* Köýtendag
Charsk *see* Shar
181 W6 **Charters Towers** Queensland, NE Australia 20°02′S 146°20′E
15 R12 **Chartierville** Québec, SE Canada 45°19′N 71°13′W
102 M6 **Chartres** *anc.* Autricum, Civitas Carnutum. Eure-et-Loir, C France 48°27′N 01°27′E
145 W15 **Charyn** *Kaz.* Sharyn. Almaty, SE Kazakhstan 43°48′N 79°22′E
Charyn *see* Sharyn
61 D21 **Chascomús** Buenos Aires, E Argentina 35°34′S 58°01′W
11 N16 **Chase** British Columbia, SW Canada 50°49′N 119°41′W
21 U7 **Chase City** Virginia, NE USA 36°48′N 78°27′W
19 S4 **Chase, Mount** ▲ Maine, NE USA 46°06′N 68°30′W
118 M13 **Chashniki** Vitsyebskaya Voblasts', N Belarus 54°52′N 29°10′E
115 D15 **Chásia** ▲▲ C Greece
29 V9 **Chaska** Minnesota, N USA 44°47′N 93°36′W
185 D25 **Chaslands Mistake** *headland* South Island, New Zealand 46°37′S 169°21′E
125 R11 **Chasovo** Respublika Komi, NW Russian Federation 61°58′N 50°34′E
Chasovo *see* Vazhgort
124 H14 **Chastova** Novgorodskaya Oblast', NW Russian Federation 58°37′N 32°05′E
143 R3 **Chāt** Golestān, N Iran 37°52′N 55°27′E
Chatak *see* Chhatak
Chatang *see* Zhanang
39 R9 **Chatanika** Alaska, USA 65°06′N 147°28′W
39 R9 **Chatanika River** ≈ Alaska, USA
147 T8 **Chat-Bazar** Talasskaya Oblast', NW Kyrgyzstan 42°29′N 72°37′E
45 Y14 **Chateaubelair** Saint Vincent, W Saint Vincent and the Grenadines 13°15′N 61°05′W
102 J7 **Châteaubriant** Loire-Atlantique, NW France 47°43′N 01°22′W
103 Q8 **Château-Chinon** Nièvre, C France 47°04′N 03°50′E
108 C10 **Château d'Oex** Vaud, W Switzerland 46°28′N 07°09′E
102 L7 **Château-du-Loir** Sarthe, NW France 47°40′N 00°25′E
102 M6 **Châteaudun** Eure-et-Loir, C France 48°04′N 01°20′E
102 K7 **Château-Gontier** Mayenne, NW France 47°49′N 00°42′W
15 O13 **Châteauguay** Québec, SE Canada 45°22′N 73°44′W
102 F6 **Châteaulin** Finistère, NW France 48°12′N 04°07′W
103 N9 **Châteaumeillant** Cher, C France 46°33′N 02°10′E
102 K11 **Châteauneuf-sur-Charente** Charente, W France 45°34′N 00°33′W
102 M7 **Château-Renault** Indre-et-Loire, C France 47°34′N 00°52′E
103 N9 **Châteauroux** *prev.* Indreville. Indre, C France 46°50′N 01°43′E
103 T5 **Château-Salins** Moselle, NE France 48°50′N 06°29′E
103 P4 **Château-Thierry** Aisne, N France 49°03′N 03°24′E
99 H21 **Châtelet** Hainaut, S Belgium 50°24′N 04°32′E
Châtelherault *see* Châtellerault
102 L9 **Châtellerault** *var.* Châtelherault. Vienne, W France 46°49′N 00°33′E
29 X10 **Chatfield** Minnesota, N USA 43°51′N 92°11′W
13 O14 **Chatham** New Brunswick, SE Canada 47°02′N 65°30′W
14 D17 **Chatham** Ontario, S Canada 42°24′N 82°11′W
97 P22 **Chatham** SE England, United Kingdom 51°23′N 00°31′E
30 K14 **Chatham** Illinois, N USA 39°40′N 89°42′W
21 T7 **Chatham** Virginia, NE USA 36°49′N 79°26′W
63 F22 **Chatham, Isla** *island* S Chile
175 R12 **Chatham Island** *island* Chatham Islands, New Zealand
Chatham Island *see* San Cristóbal, Isla
Chatham Island Rise *see* Chatham Rise
175 R12 **Chatham Islands** *island group* New Zealand, SW Pacific Ocean
175 Q12 **Chatham Rise** *var.* Chatham Island Rise. *undersea feature* S Pacific Ocean
39 X13 **Chatham Strait** *strait* Alaska, USA

◆ Country
● Country Capital
◇ Dependent Territory
○ Dependent Territory Capital
◈ Administrative Regions
✕ International Airport
▲ Mountain
▲▲ Mountain Range
Volcano
≈ River
◎ Lake
▣ Reservoir

CHATHÓIR, RINN – CHINGUETȚI

Chathóir, Rinn *see* Cahore Point
102 M9 **Châtillon-sur-Indre** Indre, C France 46°58′N 01°10′E
103 Q7 **Châtillon-sur-Seine** Côte d'Or, C France 47°51′N 04°30′E
147 S8 **Chatkal** *Uzb.* Chotqol. ∽ Kyrgyzstan/Uzbekistan
147 R9 **Chatkal Range** *Rus.* Chatkal'skiy Khrebet. ▲▲ Kyrgyzstan/Uzbekistan
Chatkal'skiy Khrebet *see* Chatkal Range
23 N7 **Chatom** Alabama, S USA 31°28′N 88°15′W
153 P14 **Chatra** Jhārkhand, N India 24°12′N 84°52′E
Chatrapur *see* Chhatrapur
143 S10 **Chatrūd** Kermān, C Iran 30°39′N 56°57′E
23 S2 **Chatsworth** Georgia, SE USA 34°46′N 84°46′W
Chāttagām *see* Chittagong
23 S8 **Chattahoochee** Florida, SE USA 30°40′N 84°51′W
23 R8 **Chattahoochee River** ∽ SE USA
20 L10 **Chattanooga** Tennessee, S USA 35°05′N 85°16′W
147 V10 **Chatyr-Kël', Ozero** ◎ C Kyrgyzstan
147 W9 **Chatyr-Tash** Narynskaya Oblast', C Kyrgyzstan 40°54′N 76°22′E
15 R12 **Chaudière** ∽ Québec, SE Canada
167 S14 **Châu Đôc** *var.* Chauphu, Chau Phu. An Giang, S Vietnam 10°53′N 105°07′E
152 D13 **Chauhtan** *prev.* Chohtan. Rājasthān, NW India 25°27′N 71°08′E
166 L5 **Chauk** Magway, W Burma (Myanmar) 20°52′N 94°50′E
103 R6 **Chaumont** *prev.* Chaumont-en-Bassigny. Haute-Marne, N France 48°07′N 05°08′E
Chaumont-en-Bassigny *see* Chaumont
123 T5 **Chaunskaya Guba** *bay* NE Russian Federation
103 P3 **Chauny** Aisne, N France 49°37′N 03°13′E
Châu Ô *see* Binh Sơn
Chau Phu *see* Châu Đôc
102 I5 **Chausey, Îles** *island group* N France
Chausy *see* Chavusy
18 C11 **Chautauqua Lake** ◎ New York, NE USA
ChâuThanh *see* Ba Ria
102 L9 **Chauvigny** Vienne, W France 46°35′N 00°37′E
124 L6 **Chavan'ga** Murmanskaya Oblast', NW Russian Federation 66°07′N 37°44′E
14 K10 **Chavannes, Lac** ◎ Québec, SE Canada
Chavantes, Represa de *see* Xavantes, Represa de
61 D15 **Chavarría** Corrientes, NE Argentina 28°57′S 58°35′W
Chavash Respubliki *see* Chuvashskaya Respublika
104 I5 **Chaves** *anc.* Aquae Flaviae. Vila Real, N Portugal 41°44′N 07°28′W
Chávez, Isla *see* Santa Cruz, Isla
82 G13 **Chavuma** North Western, NW Zambia 13°04′S 22°43′E
119 O16 **Chavusy** *Rus.* Chausy. Mahilyowskaya Voblasts', E Belarus 53°48′N 30°58′E
Chayan *see* Shayan
147 U8 **Chayek** Narynskaya Oblast', C Kyrgyzstan 41°54′N 74°28′E
139 T6 **Chāy Khānah** Diyālá, E Iraq 34°19′N 44°33′E
125 T16 **Chaykovskiy** Permskaya Oblast', NW Russian Federation 56°45′N 54°09′E
167 T12 **Chbar** Môndól Kiri, E Cambodia 12°46′N 107°10′E
23 Q4 **Cheaha Mountain** ▲ Alabama, S USA 33°29′N 85°48′W
Cheatharlach *see* Carlow
21 S2 **Cheat River** ∽ NE USA
111 A16 **Cheb** *Ger.* Eger. Karlovarský Kraj, W Czech Republic 50°05′N 12°23′E
127 Q3 **Cheboksary** Chuvashskaya Respublika, W Russian Federation 56°06′N 47°15′E
31 Q5 **Cheboygan** Michigan, N USA 45°40′N 84°28′W
Chechaouèn *see* Chefchaouen
Chechenia *see* Chechenskaya Respublika
127 O15 **Chechenskaya Respublika** *Eng.* Chechenia, Chechnia, *Rus.* Chechnya. ◈ *autonomous republic* SW Russian Federation
67 N4 **Chech, Erg** *desert* Algeria/Mali
Chechevichi *see* Chachevichy
Che-chiang *see* Zhejiang
Chechnia/Chechnya *see* Chechenskaya Respublika
163 Y15 **Chech'ŏn** *Jap.* Teisen. N South Korea 37°06′N 128°15′E
111 L15 **Chęciny** Świętokrzyskie, S Poland 50°51′N 20°31′E
27 Q10 **Checotah** Oklahoma, C USA 35°28′N 95°31′W
13 R15 **Chedabucto Bay** *inlet* Nova Scotia, E Canada
166 J7 **Cheduba Island** *island* W Burma (Myanmar)
37 T5 **Cheesman Lake** ⊠ Colorado, C USA
195 S16 **Cheetham, Cape** *headland* Antarctica 70°26′S 162°40′E
74 G5 **Chefchaouen** *var.* Chaouèn, Chechaouèn, *Sp.* Xauen. N Morocco 35°10′N 05°16′W
Chefoo *see* Yantai
38 M12 **Chefornak** Alaska, USA 60°09′N 164°09′W
123 R13 **Chegdomyn** Khabarovskiy Kray, SE Russian Federation 51°09′N 132°58′E
76 M4 **Chegga** Tiris Zemmour, NE Mauritania 25°27′N 05°49′W
Cheghcheran *see* Chaghcharān
32 G9 **Chehalis** Washington, NW USA 46°39′N 122°57′W
32 G9 **Chehalis River** ∽ Washington, NW USA
148 M6 **Chehel Abdālān, Kūh-e** *var.* Chalap Dalam, *Pash.* Chalap Dalan. ▲▲ C Afghanistan
115 D14 **Cheimadítis, Límni** *var.* Límni Cheimadítis. ◎ N Greece
Cheimadítis, Límni *see* Cheimadítis, Límni
103 U15 **Cheiron, Mont** ▲ SE France 43°49′N 07°00′E
163 X17 **Cheju** *Jap.* Saishū. S South Korea 33°31′N 126°34′E
163 Y17 **Cheju** ✕ S South Korea 33°31′N 126°29′E
163 Y17 **Cheju-do** *Jap.* Saishū; *prev.* Quelpart. *island* S South Korea
163 Y17 **Cheju-haehyŏp** *Eng.* Cheju Strait. *strait* S South Korea
Cheju Strait *see* Cheju-haehyŏp
Chekiang *see* Zhejiang
Chekichler/Chekishlyar *see* Çekiçler
188 F8 **Chelab** Babeldaob, N Palau
147 N11 **Chelak** *Rus.* Chelek. Samarqand Viloyati, C Uzbekistan 39°55′N 66°45′E
32 J7 **Chelan, Lake** ⊠ Washington, NW USA
Chelek *see* Chelak
Cheleken *see* Hazar
Chélif/Chéliff *see* Chelif, Oued
74 J5 **Chelif, Oued** *var.* Chélif, Chéliff, Chellif, Shellif. ∽ N Algeria
Chelkar *see* Shalkar
Chelkar Ozero *see* Shalkar, Ozero
Chellif *see* Chelif, Oued
111 P14 **Chełm** *Rus.* Kholm. Lubelskie, SE Poland 51°08′N 23°29′E
110 I9 **Chełmno** *Ger.* Culm, Kulm. Kujawski-pomorskie, C Poland 53°21′N 18°27′E
115 E19 **Chelmós** *var.* Ároania. ▲▲ S Greece
14 F10 **Chelmsford** Ontario, S Canada 46°33′N 81°16′W
97 P21 **Chelmsford** E England, United Kingdom 51°44′N 00°28′E
110 J9 **Chełmża** *Ger.* Culmsee, Kulmsee. Kujawski-pomorskie, C Poland 53°11′N 18°34′E
27 Q8 **Chelsea** Oklahoma, C USA 36°32′N 95°25′W
18 M8 **Chelsea** Vermont, NE USA 43°58′N 72°29′W
97 L21 **Cheltenham** C England, United Kingdom 51°54′N 02°04′W
105 R9 **Chelva** País Valenciano, E Spain 39°45′N 01°00′W
122 G11 **Chelyabinsk** Chelyabinskaya Oblast', C Russian Federation 55°12′N 61°25′E
122 F1 **Chelyabinskaya Oblast'** ◈ *province* C Russian Federation
123 N5 **Chelyuskin, Mys** *headland* N Russian Federation 77°42′N 104°13′E
41 Y12 **Chemax** Yucatán, SE Mexico 20°41′N 87°54′W
83 N16 **Chemba** Sofala, C Mozambique 17°11′S 34°53′E
82 J13 **Chembe** Luapula, NE Zambia 11°58′S 28°45′E
Chemenibit *see* Çemenibit
Chemerisy *see* Chamyarysy
116 K7 **Chemerivtsi** Khmel'nyts'ka Oblast', W Ukraine 49°00′N 26°21′E
102 J8 **Chemillé** Maine-et-Loire, NW France 47°15′N 00°42′W
173 X17 **Chemin Grenier** S Mauritius 20°29′S 57°28′E
101 N16 **Chemnitz** *prev.* Karl-Marx-Stadt. Sachsen, E Germany 50°50′N 12°55′E
Chemulpo *see* Inch'ŏn
32 H14 **Chemult** Oregon, NW USA 43°14′N 121°48′W
18 G12 **Chemung River** ∽ New York/Pennsylvania, NE USA
149 U8 **Chenāb** ∽ India/Pakistan
39 S9 **Chena Hot Springs** Alaska, USA 65°06′N 146°02′W
18 I11 **Chenango River** ∽ New York, NE USA
168 J7 **Chenderoh, Tasik** ◎ Peninsular Malaysia
15 Q11 **Chêne, Rivière du** ∽ Québec, SE Canada
32 L8 **Cheney** Washington, NW USA 47°29′N 117°34′W
26 M6 **Cheney Reservoir** ⊠ Kansas, C USA
Chengchiatun *see* Liaoyuan
Ch'eng-chou/Chengchow *see* Zhengzhou
161 P1 **Chengde** *var.* Jehol. Hebei, E China 41°N 117°57′E
160 I9 **Chengdu** *var.* Chengtu, Ch'eng-tu. *province capital* Sichuan, C China 30°41′N 104°03′E
161 Q14 **Chenghai** Guangdong, S China 23°30′N 116°42′E
Chenghsien *see* Zhengzhou
160 H13 **Chengjiang** Yunnan, SW China 24°40′N 102°55′E
Chengjiang *see* Taihe
160 L17 **Chengmai** *var.* Jinjiang. Hainan, S China 19°45′N 109°56′E
Chengtu/Ch'eng-tu *see* Chengdu
Chengwen *see* Chindu
159 W12 **Chengxian** *var.* Cheng Xiang. Gansu, C China 33°42′N 105°45′E
Cheng Xiang *see* Chengxian
Chengyang *see* Juxian
Chengzhong *see* Ningming
Chenkiang *see* Zhenjiang
155 J19 **Chennai** *prev.* Madras. *state capital* Tamil Nādu, S India 13°05′N 80°18′E
155 J19 **Chennai** ✕ Tamil Nādu, S India 13°07′N 80°13′E
103 R8 **Chenôve** Côte d'Or, C France 47°16′N 05°00′E
Chenstokhov *see* Częstochowa
160 L11 **Chenxi** *var.* Chenyang. Hunan, S China 28°02′N 110°15′E
Chen Xian/Chenxian/Chen Xiang *see* Chenzhou
Chenyang *see* Chenxi
161 N12 **Chenzhou** *var.* Chenxian, Chen Xian, Chen Xiang. Hunan, S China 25°51′N 113°01′E
167 U12 **Cheo Reo** *var.* A Yun Pa. Gia Lai, S Vietnam 13°19′N 108°27′E
114 I11 **Chepelare** Smolyan, S Bulgaria 41°44′N 24°41′E
114 I11 **Chepelarska Reka** ∽ S Bulgaria
56 B11 **Chepén** La Libertad, C Peru 07°15′S 79°23′W
62 J10 **Chepes** La Rioja, C Argentina 31°19′S 66°40′W
161 O15 **Chep Lap Kok** ✕ S China 22°23′N 114°11′E
43 U14 **Chepo** Panamá, C Panama 09°09′N 79°03′W
Chepping Wycombe *see* High Wycombe
125 R14 **Cheptsa** ∽ NW Russian Federation
30 K3 **Chequamegon Point** *headland* Wisconsin, N USA 46°42′N 90°45′W
103 O8 **Cher** ◈ *department* C France
102 M8 **Cher** ∽ C France
Cherangani Hills *see* Cherangany Hills
81 H17 **Cherangany Hills** *var.* Cherangani Hills. ▲▲ W Kenya
21 S11 **Cheraw** South Carolina, SE USA 34°42′N 79°52′W
102 I3 **Cherbourg** *anc.* Carusbur. Manche, N France 49°40′N 01°36′W
127 R5 **Cherdakly** Ul'yanovskaya Oblast', W Russian Federation 54°21′N 48°54′E
125 U12 **Cherdyn'** Permskaya Oblast', NW Russian Federation 60°21′N 56°39′E
124 J14 **Cherekha** ∽ W Russian Federation
122 M13 **Cheremkhovo** Irkutskaya Oblast', S Russian Federation 53°16′N 102°44′E
Cheren *see* Keren
124 K14 **Cherepovets** Vologodskaya Oblast', NW Russian Federation 59°09′N 37°50′E
125 O11 **Cherevkovo** Arkhangel'skaya Oblast', NW Russian Federation 61°45′N 45°16′E
74 I6 **Chergui, Chott ech** *salt lake* NW Algeria
Cherikov *see* Cherykaw
117 P6 **Cherkas'ka Oblast'** *var.* Cherkasy, *Rus.* Cherkasskaya Oblast'. ◈ *province* C Ukraine
Cherkasskaya Oblast' *see* Cherkas'ka Oblast'
Cherkassy *see* Cherkasy
117 Q6 **Cherkasy** *Rus.* Cherkassy. Cherkas'ka Oblast', C Ukraine 49°26′N 32°05′E
Cherkasy *see* Cherkas'ka Oblast'
126 M15 **Cherkessk** Karachayevo-Cherkesskaya Respublika, SW Russian Federation 44°12′N 42°06′E
122 H12 **Cherlak** Omskaya Oblast', C Russian Federation 54°06′N 74°59′E
122 H12 **Cherlakskoye** Omskaya Oblast', C Russian Federation 53°42′N 74°23′E
125 U13 **Chermoz** Permskaya Oblast', NW Russian Federation 58°49′N 56°07′E
Chernavchitsy *see* Charnawchytsy
125 T3 **Chernaya** Nenetskiy Avtonomnyy Okrug, NW Russian Federation 68°36′N 56°34′E
125 T4 **Chernaya** ∽ NW Russian Federation
Chernigov *see* Chernihiv
Chernigovskaya Oblast' *see* Chernihivs'ka Oblast'
117 Q2 **Chernihiv** *Rus.* Chernigov. Chernihivs'ka Oblast', NE Ukraine 51°28′N 31°19′E
Chernihiv *see* Chernihivs'ka Oblast'
117 V9 **Chernihivka** Zaporiz'ka Oblast', SE Ukraine 47°11′N 36°10′E
117 P2 **Chernihivs'ka Oblast'** *var.* Chernihiv, *Rus.* Chernigovskaya Oblast'. ◈ *province* NE Ukraine
114 I9 **Cherni Osŭm** ∽ N Bulgaria
116 J8 **Chernivets'ka Oblast'** *var.* Chernivtsi, *Rus.* Chernovitskaya Oblast'. ◈ *province* W Ukraine
114 I9 **Cherni Vit** ∽ NW Bulgaria
114 G10 **Cherni Vrŭkh** ▲ W Bulgaria 42°33′N 23°18′E
116 K8 **Chernivtsi** *Ger.* Czernowitz, *Rom.* Cernăuţi, *Rus.* Chernovtsy. Chernivets'ka Oblast', W Ukraine 48°18′N 25°55′E
116 M7 **Chernivtsi** Vinnyts'ka Oblast', C Ukraine 48°33′N 28°06′E
Chernivtsi *see* Chernivets'ka Oblast'
Chernobyl' *see* Chornobyl'
Cherno More *see* Black Sea
Chernomorskoye *see* Chornomors'ke
145 T7 **Chernoretskoye** Pavlodar, NE Kazakhstan 52°51′N 76°37′E
Chernovitskaya Oblast' *see* Chernivets'ka Oblast'
Chernovtsy *see* Chernivtsi
145 U8 **Chernoye** Pavlodar, NE Kazakhstan 51°40′N 77°33′E
Chernoye More *see* Black Sea
125 U16 **Chernushka** Permskaya Oblast', NW Russian Federation 56°30′N 56°07′E
117 N4 **Chernyakhiv** *Rus.* Chernyakhov. Zhytomyrs'ka Oblast', N Ukraine 50°30′N 28°38′E
Chernyakhov *see* Chernyakhiv
119 C14 **Chernyakhovsk** *Ger.* Insterburg. Kaliningradskaya Oblast', W Russian Federation 54°36′N 21°49′E
126 K8 **Chernyanka** Belgorodskaya Oblast', W Russian Federation 50°59′N 37°54′E
125 V5 **Chernyshëva, Gryada** ▲▲ NW Russian Federation
144 J14 **Chernyshëva, Zaliv** *gulf* SW Kazakhstan
123 O10 **Chernyshevskiy** Respublika Sakha (Yakutiya), NE Russian Federation 62°57′N 112°29′E
127 P13 **Chernyye Zemli** *plain* SW Russian Federation
Chërnyy Irtysh *see* Ertix He, China/Kazakhstan
Chërnyy Irtysh *see* Kara Irtysh, Kazakhstan
127 V7 **Chernyy Otrog** Orenburgskaya Oblast', W Russian Federation 52°03′N 56°09′E
29 T12 **Cherokee** Iowa, C USA 42°45′N 95°33′W
26 M8 **Cherokee** Oklahoma, C USA 36°45′N 98°22′W
25 R9 **Cherokee** Texas, SW USA 30°56′N 98°42′W
21 O8 **Cherokee Lake** ⊠ Tennessee, S USA
Cherokees, Lake O' The *see* Grand Lake O' The Cherokees
44 H1 **Cherokee Sound** Great Abaco, N Bahamas 26°16′N 77°03′W
153 V13 **Cherrapunji** Meghālaya, NE India 25°16′N 91°42′E
28 L9 **Cherry Creek** ∽ South Dakota, N USA
18 J16 **Cherry Hill** New Jersey, NE USA 39°55′N 75°01′W
27 Q7 **Cherryvale** Kansas, C USA 37°16′N 95°33′W
21 Q10 **Cherryville** North Carolina, SE USA 35°22′N 81°22′W
Cherski Range *see* Cherskogo, Khrebet
123 T6 **Cherskiy** Respublika Sakha (Yakutiya), NE Russian Federation 68°45′N 161°15′E
123 R8 **Cherskogo, Khrebet** *var.* Cherski Range. ▲▲ NE Russian Federation
Cherso *see* Cres
126 L10 **Chertkovo** Rostovskaya Oblast', SW Russian Federation 49°22′N 40°10′E
Cherven' *see* Chervyen'
114 H8 **Cherven Bryag** Pleven, N Bulgaria 43°16′N 24°06′E
116 M4 **Chervonoarmiys'k** Zhytomyrs'ka Oblast', N Ukraine 50°27′N 28°15′E
Chervonograd *see* Chervonohrad
116 I4 **Chervonohrad** *Rus.* Chervonograd. L'vivs'ka Oblast', NW Ukraine 50°25′N 24°10′E
117 W6 **Chervonooskil's'ke Vodoskhovyshche** *Rus.* Krasnoosol'skoye Vodokhranilishche. ⊠ NE Ukraine
Chervonoye, Ozero *see* Chyrvonaye, Vozyera
117 S4 **Chervonozavods'ke** Poltavs'ka Oblast', C Ukraine 50°24′N 33°22′E
119 L16 **Chervyen'** *Rus.* Cherven'. Minskaya Voblasts', C Belarus 53°42′N 28°26′E
119 P16 **Cherykaw** *Rus.* Cherikov. Mahilyowskaya Voblasts', E Belarus 53°34′N 31°23′E
31 R9 **Chesaning** Michigan, N USA 43°10′N 84°07′W
21 X5 **Chesapeake Bay** *inlet* NE USA
Chesha Bay *see* Chëshskaya Guba
Cheshevlya *see* Tsyeshawlya
97 K18 **Cheshire** *cultural region* C England, United Kingdom
125 P5 **Chëshskaya Guba** *var.* Archangel Bay, Chesha Bay, Dvina Bay. *bay* NW Russian Federation
14 F14 **Chesley** Ontario, S Canada 44°17′N 81°06′W
21 Q10 **Chesnee** South Carolina, SE USA 35°09′N 81°51′W
97 K18 **Chester** *Wel.* Caerleon, *hist.* Legaceaster, *Lat.* Deva, Devana Castra. C England, United Kingdom 53°12′N 02°54′W
35 O4 **Chester** California, W USA 40°18′N 121°14′W
30 K16 **Chester** Illinois, N USA 37°54′N 89°49′W
33 S7 **Chester** Montana, NW USA 48°30′N 110°59′W
18 I16 **Chester** Pennsylvania, NE USA 39°51′N 75°21′W
21 R1 **Chester** South Carolina, SE USA 34°43′N 81°14′W
25 X9 **Chester** Texas, SW USA 30°55′N 94°36′W
21 W6 **Chester** Virginia, NE USA 37°22′N 77°27′W
21 R11 **Chester** West Virginia, NE USA 40°34′N 80°33′W
97 M18 **Chesterfield** C England, United Kingdom 53°15′N 01°25′W
21 S11 **Chesterfield** South Carolina, SE USA 34°44′N 80°04′W
21 W6 **Chesterfield** Virginia, NE USA 37°22′N 77°31′W
192 J9 **Chesterfield, Îles** *island group* NW New Caledonia
9 O9 **Chesterfield Inlet** Nunavut, NW Canada 63°19′N 90°57′W
9 O9 **Chesterfield Inlet** *inlet* Nunavut, N Canada
21 Y3 **Chester River** ∽ Delaware/Maryland, NE USA
21 X3 **Chestertown** Maryland, NE USA 39°13′N 76°04′W
19 R4 **Chesuncook Lake** ◎ Maine, NE USA
30 J5 **Chetek** Wisconsin, N USA 45°19′N 91°37′W
13 R14 **Chéticamp** Nova Scotia, SE Canada 46°14′N 61°19′W
27 Q8 **Chetopa** Kansas, C USA 37°02′N 95°05′W
41 Y14 **Chetumal** *var.* Payo Obispo. Quintana Roo, SE Mexico 18°32′N 88°16′W
Chetumal, Bahia/Chetumal, Bahía de *see* Chetumal Bay
42 G1 **Chetumal Bay** *var.* Bahia Chetumal, Bahía de Chetumal. *bay* Belize/Mexico
10 M13 **Chetwynd** British Columbia, W Canada 55°42′N 121°36′W
38 M11 **Chevak** Alaska, USA 61°31′N 165°35′W
36 M12 **Chevelon Creek** ∽ Arizona, SW USA
185 J17 **Cheviot** Canterbury, South Island, New Zealand 42°48′S 173°17′E
96 L13 **Cheviot Hills** *hill range* England/Scotland, United Kingdom
96 L13 **Cheviot, The** ▲ NE England, United Kingdom 55°28′N 02°10′W
14 M11 **Chevreuil, Lac du** ◎ Québec, SE Canada
81 I16 **Ch'ew Bahir** *var.* Lake Stefanie. ◎ Ethiopia/Kenya
32 L7 **Chewelah** Washington, NW USA 48°16′N 117°42′W
26 K10 **Cheyenne** Oklahoma, C USA 35°37′N 99°43′W
33 Z17 **Cheyenne** *state capital* Wyoming, C USA 41°08′N 104°46′W
26 L5 **Cheyenne Bottoms** ◎ Kansas, C USA
16 J8 **Cheyenne River** ∽ South Dakota/Wyoming, N USA
37 W5 **Cheyenne Wells** Colorado, C USA 38°49′N 102°21′W
108 C9 **Cheyres** Vaud, W Switzerland 46°48′N 06°48′E
Chezdi-Oşorheiu *see* Târgu Secuiesc
153 P13 **Chhapra** *prev.* Chapra. Bihār, N India 25°50′N 84°42′E
153 V13 **Chhatak** *var.* Chatak. Sylhet, NE Bangladesh 25°02′N 91°33′E
154 J9 **Chhatarpur** Madhya Pradesh, C India 24°54′N 79°35′E
154 N13 **Chhatrapur** *prev.* Chatrapur. Orissa, E India 19°26′N 85°02′E
154 K2 **Chhattīsgarh** ◈ *state* E India
154 L12 **Chhattīsgarh** *plain* C India
154 I11 **Chhindwāra** Madhya Pradesh, C India 22°04′N 78°58′E
153 T12 **Chhukha** SW Bhutan 27°02′N 89°36′E
161 S14 **Chiai** *var.* Chia-i, Chiayi, Kiayi, Jiayi, *Jap.* Kagi. C Taiwan 23°29′N 120°27′E
Chia-i *see* Chiai
Chia-mu-ssu *see* Jiamusi
83 B15 **Chiange** *Port.* Vila de Almoster. Huíla, SW Angola 15°44′S 13°54′E
Chiang-hsi *see* Jiangxi
161 S12 **Chiang Kai-shek** ✕ (T'aipei) N Taiwan 25°09′N 121°20′E
167 P8 **Chiang Khan** Loei, E Thailand 17°51′N 101°43′E
167 O7 **Chiang Mai** *var.* Chiangmai, Chiengmai, Kiangmai. Chiang Mai, NW Thailand 18°48′N 98°59′E
167 O7 **Chiang Mai** ✕ Chiang Mai, NW Thailand 18°44′N 98°53′E
Chiangmai *see* Chiang Mai
167 O6 **Chiang Rai** *var.* Chianpai, Chienrai, Muang Chiang Rai. Chiang Rai, NW Thailand 19°56′N 99°51′E
Chiang-su *see* Jiangsu
Chianning/Chian-ning *see* Nanjing
Chianpai *see* Chiang Rai
106 G12 **Chianti** *cultural region* C Italy
Chiapa *see* Chiapa de Corzo
41 U16 **Chiapa de Corzo** *var.* Chiapa. Chiapas, SE Mexico 16°42′N 92°59′W
41 V16 **Chiapas** ◈ *state* SE Mexico
106 J12 **Chiaravalle** Marche, C Italy 43°36′N 13°19′E
107 N22 **Chiaravalle Centrale** Calabria, SW Italy 38°40′N 16°25′E
106 E7 **Chiari** Lombardia, N Italy 45°33′N 10°00′E
108 H12 **Chiasso** Ticino, S Switzerland 45°51′N 09°02′E
137 S9 **Chiat'ura** C Georgia 42°13′N 43°11′E
41 P15 **Chiautla** *var.* Chiautla de Tapia. Puebla, S Mexico 18°16′N 98°31′W
Chiautla de Tapia *see* Chiautla
106 D10 **Chiavari** Liguria, NW Italy 44°19′N 09°19′E
106 E6 **Chiavenna** Lombardia, N Italy 46°19′N 09°22′E
Chiayi *see* Chiai
Chiazza *see* Piazza Armerina
165 O14 **Chiba** *var.* Tiba. Chiba, Honshū, S Japan 35°37′N 140°06′E
165 O13 **Chiba** *off.* Chiba-ken, *var.* Tiba. ◈ *prefecture* Honshū, S Japan
83 M18 **Chibabava** Sofala, C Mozambique 20°17′S 33°39′E
Chiba-ken *see* Chiba
161 O10 **Chibi** *prev.* Puqi. Hubei, C China 29°45′N 113°55′E
83 B15 **Chibia** *Port.* João de Almeida, Vila João de Almeida. Huíla, SW Angola 15°11′S 13°41′E
83 M18 **Chiboma** Sofala, C Mozambique 20°06′S 33°54′E
82 J12 **Chibondo** Luapula, N Zambia 10°42′S 28°42′E
82 K11 **Chibote** Luapula, NE Zambia 09°52′S 29°33′E
12 K12 **Chibougamau** Québec, SE Canada 49°56′N 74°24′W
164 H11 **Chiburi-jima** *island* Oki-shotō, SW Japan
83 M20 **Chibuto** Gaza, S Mozambique 24°40′S 33°33′E
31 N11 **Chicago** Illinois, N USA 41°51′N 87°39′W
31 N11 **Chicago Heights** Illinois, N USA 41°30′N 87°38′W
15 W6 **Chic-Chocs, Monts** *Eng.* Shickshock Mountains. ▲▲ Québec, SE Canada
39 W13 **Chichagof Island** *island* Alexander Archipelago, Alaska, USA
57 K20 **Chichas, Cordillera de** ▲▲ SW Bolivia
41 X12 **Chichén-Itzá, Ruinas** *ruins* Yucatán, SE Mexico
97 N23 **Chichester** SE England, United Kingdom 50°50′N 00°48′W
42 C5 **Chichicastenango** Quiché, W Guatemala 14°55′N 91°06′W
42 I9 **Chichigalpa** Chinandega, NW Nicaragua 12°35′N 87°04′W
Ch'i-ch'i-ha-erh *see* Qiqihar
165 X16 **Chichijima-rettō** *Eng.* Beechy Group. *island group* SE Japan
54 K4 **Chichiriviche** Falcón, N Venezuela 10°58′N 68°17′W
39 R11 **Chickaloon** Alaska, USA 61°48′N 148°27′W
20 L10 **Chickamauga Lake** ⊠ Tennessee, S USA
23 N7 **Chickasawhay River** ∽ Mississippi, S USA
26 M11 **Chickasha** Oklahoma, C USA 35°03′N 97°57′W
39 T9 **Chicken** Alaska, USA 64°04′N 141°56′W
104 J16 **Chiclana de la Frontera** Andalucía, S Spain 36°26′N 06°09′W
56 B11 **Chiclayo** Lambayeque, NW Peru 06°47′S 79°47′W
35 N5 **Chico** California, W USA 39°42′N 121°51′W
83 L15 **Chicoa** Tete, NW Mozambique 15°45′S 32°25′E
83 M20 **Chicomo** Gaza, S Mozambique 24°29′S 34°15′E
18 M11 **Chicopee** Massachusetts, NE USA 42°08′N 72°34′W
63 I19 **Chico, Río** ∽ SE Argentina
63 I21 **Chico, Río** ∽ S Argentina
27 W14 **Chicot, Lake** ◎ Arkansas, C USA
15 R7 **Chicoutimi** Québec, SE Canada 48°24′N 71°04′W
15 Q8 **Chicoutimi** ∽ Québec, SE Canada
83 L19 **Chicualacuala** Gaza, SW Mozambique 22°06′S 31°42′E
83 B14 **Chicuma** Benguela, C Angola 13°33′S 14°41′E
155 J21 **Chidambaram** Tamil Nādu, SE India 11°25′N 79°42′E
196 K13 **Chidley, Cape** *headland* Newfoundland and Labrador, E Canada 60°25′N 64°39′W
101 N24 **Chiemsee** ◎ SE Germany
Chiengmai *see* Chiang Mai
Chienrai *see* Chiang Rai
106 B8 **Chieri** Piemonte, NW Italy 45°01′N 07°49′E
106 F8 **Chiese** ∽ N Italy
107 K14 **Chieti** *var.* Teate. Abruzzo, C Italy 42°22′N 14°10′E
99 E19 **Chièvres** Hainaut, SW Belgium 50°34′N 03°49′E
163 S12 **Chifeng** *var.* Ulanhad. Nei Mongol Zizhiqu, N China 42°17′N 118°56′E
82 F13 **Chifumage** ∽ E Angola
82 M13 **Chifunda** Eastern, NE Zambia 11°57′S 32°36′E
145 S14 **Chiganak** *var.* Čiganak, *Kaz.* Shyghanaq. Zhambyl, SE Kazakhstan 45°10′N 73°55′E
39 P15 **Chiginagak, Mount** ▲ Alaska, USA 57°10′N 157°00′W
Chigirin *see* Chyhyryn
41 P13 **Chignahuapan** Puebla, S Mexico 19°52′N 98°03′W
39 O15 **Chignik** Alaska, USA 56°18′N 158°24′W
83 M19 **Chigombe** ∽ S Mozambique
54 D7 **Chigorodó** Antioquia, NW Colombia 07°42′N 76°45′W
83 M19 **Chigubo** Gaza, S Mozambique 22°50′S 33°30′E
Chihertey *see* Altay
Chih-fu *see* Yantai
Chihli *see* Hebei
Chihli, Gulf of *see* Bo Hai
40 J6 **Chihuahua** Chihuahua, NW Mexico 28°40′N 106°06′W
40 I6 **Chihuahua** ◈ *state* N Mexico
145 O15 **Chiili** *Kaz.* Shīeli. Kzylorda, S Kazakhstan 44°13′N 66°46′E
26 M7 **Chikaskia River** ∽ Kansas/Oklahoma, C USA
155 H19 **Chik Ballāpur** Karnātaka, W India 13°28′N 77°42′E
124 G15 **Chikhachevo** Pskovskaya Oblast', W Russian Federation 57°17′N 29°51′E
155 F19 **Chikmagalūr** Karnātaka, W India 13°20′N 75°46′E
129 V7 **Chikoy** ∽ C Russian Federation
83 J15 **Chikumbi** Lusaka, C Zambia 15°11′S 28°20′E
82 M13 **Chikwa** Eastern, NE Zambia 11°39′S 32°45′E
Chikwana *see* Chikwawa
83 N15 **Chikwawa** *var.* Chikwana. Southern, S Malawi 16°03′S 34°48′E
155 J16 **Chilakalūrupet** Andhra Pradesh, E India 16°09′N 80°13′E
146 L14 **Chilan** Lebap Welaýaty, E Turkmenistan 37°57′N 64°58′E
Chilapa *see* Chilapa de Alvarez
41 P16 **Chilapa de Alvarez** *var.* Chilapa. Guerrero, S Mexico 17°38′N 99°11′W
155 J25 **Chilaw** North Western Province, W Sri Lanka 07°34′N 79°48′E
57 D15 **Chilca** Lima, W Peru 12°35′S 76°41′W
23 Q4 **Childersburg** Alabama, S USA 33°16′N 86°21′W
25 P4 **Childress** Texas, SW USA 34°25′N 100°14′W
63 G14 **Chile** *off.* Republic of Chile. ◆ *republic* SW South America
47 R10 **Chile Basin** *undersea feature* E Pacific Ocean 33°00′S 80°00′W
63 H20 **Chile Chico** Aisén, W Chile 46°34′S 71°44′W
62 I9 **Chilecito** La Rioja, NW Argentina 29°10′S 67°30′W
62 H12 **Chilecito** Mendoza, W Argentina 33°53′S 69°03′W
83 L14 **Chilembwe** Eastern, E Zambia 13°54′S 31°38′E
Chile, Republic of *see* Chile
193 S11 **Chile Rise** *undersea feature* SE Pacific Ocean 40°00′S 90°00′W
117 N13 **Chilia, Braţul** ∽ SE Romania
Chilia-Nouă *see* Kiliya
145 V15 **Chilik** *Kaz.* Shelek. Almaty, SE Kazakhstan 43°35′N 78°12′E
145 V15 **Chilik** ∽ SE Kazakhstan
154 O13 **Chilika Lake** *var.* Chilka Lake. ◎ E India
82 J13 **Chililabombwe** Copperbelt, C Zambia 12°20′S 27°52′E
Chi-lin *see* Jilin
Chilka Lake *see* Chilika Lake
10 H9 **Chilkoot Pass** *pass* British Columbia, W Canada
Chill Ala, Cuan *see* Killala Bay
62 G13 **Chillán** Bío Bío, C Chile 36°37′S 72°10′W
61 C22 **Chillar** Buenos Aires, E Argentina 37°16′S 59°58′W
Chill Chiaráin, Cuan *see* Kilkieran Bay
30 K12 **Chillicothe** Illinois, N USA 40°55′N 89°29′W
27 S3 **Chillicothe** Missouri, C USA 39°47′N 93°33′W
31 S14 **Chillicothe** Ohio, N USA 39°20′N 83°00′W
25 Q4 **Chillicothe** Texas, SW USA 34°15′N 99°31′W
10 M17 **Chilliwack** British Columbia, SW Canada 49°09′N 121°54′W
Chill Mhantáin, Ceann *see* Wicklow Head
Chill Mhantáin, Sléibhte *see* Wicklow Mountains
108 C10 **Chillon** Vaud, W Switzerland 46°24′N 06°56′E
Chil'mamedkum, Peski/Chilmämetgum *see* Çilmämmetgum
63 F17 **Chiloé, Isla de** *var.* Isla Grande de Chiloé. *island* W Chile
32 H15 **Chiloquin** Oregon, NW USA 42°33′N 121°33′W
41 O16 **Chilpancingo** *var.* Chilpancingo de los Bravos. Guerrero, S Mexico 17°33′N 99°30′W
Chilpancingo de los Bravos *see* Chilpancingo
97 N21 **Chiltern Hills** *hill range* S England, United Kingdom
30 M7 **Chilton** Wisconsin, N USA 44°04′N 88°10′W
82 F11 **Chiluage** Lunda Sul, NE Angola 09°32′S 21°48′E
82 N12 **Chilumba** *prev.* Deep Bay. Northern, N Malawi 10°27′S 34°12′E
161 T12 **Chilung** *var.* Keelung, *Jap.* Kirun, Kirun'; *prev.* *Sp.* Santissima Trinidad. N Taiwan 25°10′N 121°43′E
83 N15 **Chilwa, Lake** *var.* Lago Chirua, Lake Shirwa. ◎ SE Malawi
167 R10 **Chi, Mae Nam** ∽ E Thailand
42 C6 **Chimaltenango** Chimaltenango, C Guatemala 14°40′N 90°48′W
42 A2 **Chimaltenango** *off.* Departamento de Chimaltenango. ◈ *department* S Guatemala
Chimaltenango, Departamento de *see* Chimaltenango
43 V15 **Chimán** Panamá, E Panama 08°42′N 78°35′W
83 M17 **Chimanimani** *prev.* Mandidzudzure, Melsetter. Manicaland, E Zimbabwe 19°48′S 32°52′E
99 G22 **Chimay** Hainaut, S Belgium 50°03′N 04°20′E
37 S10 **Chimayo** New Mexico, SW USA 36°00′N 105°55′W
Chimbay *see* Chimboy
56 A13 **Chimborazo** ◈ *province* C Ecuador
56 C7 **Chimborazo** Ѫ C Ecuador 01°29′S 78°50′W
56 C12 **Chimbote** Ancash, W Peru 09°04′S 78°34′W
146 H7 **Chimboy** *Rus.* Chimbay. Qoraqalpog'iston Respublikasi, NW Uzbekistan 43°03′N 59°52′E
186 D7 **Chimbu** ◈ *province* C Papua New Guinea
54 F6 **Chimichagua** Cesar, N Colombia 09°19′N 73°51′W
Chimishliya *see* Cimişlia
Chimkent *see* Shymkent
Chimkentskaya Oblast' *see* Yuzhnyy Kazakhstan
28 I14 **Chimney Rock** *rock* Nebraska, C USA
83 M17 **Chimoio** Manica, C Mozambique 19°08′S 33°29′E
82 K11 **Chimpembe** Northern, NE Zambia 09°31′S 29°33′E
41 O8 **China** Nuevo León, NE Mexico 25°42′N 99°15′W
156 M9 **China** *off.* People's Republic of China, *Chin.* Chung-hua Jen-min Kung-ho-kuo, Zhonghua Renmin Gongheguo; *prev.* Chinese Empire. ◆ *republic* E Asia
19 Q7 **China Lake** ◎ Maine, NE USA
42 F8 **Chinameca** San Miguel, E El Salvador 13°30′N 88°20′W*
Chi-nan/Chinan *see* Jinan
42 H9 **Chinandega** Chinandega, NW Nicaragua 12°37′N 87°08′W
42 H9 **Chinandega** ◈ *department* NW Nicaragua
China, People's Republic of *see* China
China, Republic of *see* Taiwan
24 J11 **Chinati Mountains** ▲▲ Texas, SW USA
Chinaz *see* Chinoz
57 E15 **Chincha Alta** Ica, SW Peru 13°25′S 76°07′W
11 N11 **Chinchaga** ∽ Alberta, SW Canada
Chin-chiang *see* Quanzhou
Chinchilla *see* Chinchilla de Monte Aragón
105 Q11 **Chinchilla de Monte Aragón** *var.* Chinchilla. Castilla-La Mancha, C Spain 38°56′N 01°44′W
54 D10 **Chinchiná** Caldas, W Colombia 04°59′N 75°37′W
105 O8 **Chinchón** Madrid, C Spain 40°08′N 03°26′W
41 Z14 **Chinchorro, Banco** *island* SE Mexico
Chin-chou/Chinchow *see* Jinzhou
21 Z5 **Chincoteague** Assateague Island, Virginia, NE USA 37°55′N 75°22′W
83 O17 **Chinde** Zambézia, NE Mozambique 18°35′S 36°28′E
163 X17 **Chin-do** *Jap.* Chin-tō. *island* SW South Korea
159 R13 **Chindu** *var.* Chengwen; *prev.* Chuqung. Qinghai, C China 33°19′N 97°08′E
Chindwin *see* Chindwinn
166 M2 **Chindwinn** *var.* Chindwin. ∽ N Burma (Myanmar)
Chinese Empire *see* China
Chinghai *see* Qinghai
Ch'ing Hai *see* Qinghai Hu, China
Chingildi *see* Shengeldi
144 H9 **Chingirlau** *Kaz.* Shyngghyrlaū. Zapadnyy Kazakhstan, W Kazakhstan 51°10′N 53°44′E
82 J13 **Chingola** Copperbelt, C Zambia 12°31′S 27°53′E
Ching-Tao/Ch'ing-tao *see* Qingdao
82 C13 **Chinguar** Huambo, C Angola 12°33′S 16°25′E
76 I7 **Chinguețți** *var.* Chinguetti. Adrar, C Mauritania 20°25′N 12°24′W

◆ Country
● Country Capital
◇ Dependent Territory
○ Dependent Territory Capital
◈ Administrative Regions
✕ International Airport
▲ Mountain
▲▲ Mountain Range
Ѫ Volcano
∽ River
◎ Lake
⊠ Reservoir

CHINHAE – CIRO MARINO

163 Z16 **Chinhae** *Jap.* Chinkai. S South Korea 35°06′N 128°48′E
166 K4 **Chin Hills** ▲▲ W Burma (Myanmar)
83 K16 **Chinhoyi** *prev.* Sinoia. Mashonaland West, N Zimbabwe 17°22′S 30°12′E
Chinhsien *see* Jinzhou
39 Q14 **Chiniak, Cape** *headland* Kodiak Island, Alaska, USA 57°37′N 152°10′W
14 G10 **Chiniguchi Lake** ◎ Ontario, S Canada
149 U8 **Chiniot** Punjab, NE Pakistan 31°40′N 73°00′E
163 Y16 **Chinju** *Jap.* Shinshū. S South Korea 35°12′N 128°06′E
Chinkai *see* Chinhae
78 M13 **Chinko** ≈ E Central African Republic
37 O9 **Chinle** Arizona, SW USA 36°09′N 109°33′W
161 R13 **Chinmen Tao** *var.* Jinmen Dao, Quemoy. *island* W Taiwan
Chinnchâr *see* Shinshār
Chinnereth *see* Tiberias, Lake
164 C12 **Chino** *var.* Tino. Nagano, Honshū, S Japan 36°00′N 138°10′E
102 L8 **Chinon** Indre-et-Loire, C France 47°10′N 00°15′E
33 T7 **Chinook** Montana, NW USA 48°35′N 109°13′W
Chinook State *see* Washington
192 L4 **Chinook Trough** *undersea feature* N Pacific Ocean
36 K11 **Chino Valley** Arizona, SW USA 34°45′N 112°27′W
147 P10 **Chinoz** *Rus.* Chinaz. Toshkent Viloyati, E Uzbekistan 40°58′N 68°46′E
82 L12 **Chinsali** Northern, NE Zambia 10°33′S 32°05′E
166 K5 **Chin State** ◈ *state* W Burma (Myanmar)
Chinsura *see* Chunchura
Chin-tō *see* Chin-do
54 E6 **Chinú** Córdoba, NW Colombia 09°07′N 75°25′W
99 K24 **Chiny, Forêt de** *forest* SE Belgium
83 M15 **Chioco** Tete, NW Mozambique 16°22′S 32°50′E
106 H8 **Chioggia** *anc.* Fossa Claudia. Veneto, NE Italy 45°14′N 12°17′E
114 H12 **Chionótrypa** ▲ NE Greece 41°16′N 24°06′E
115 L18 **Chíos** *var.* Hios, Khíos, *It.* Scio, *Turk.* Sakiz-Adasi. Chíos, E Greece 38°23′N 26°07′E
115 K18 **Chíos** *var.* Khíos. *island* E Greece
83 M14 **Chipata** *prev.* Fort Jameson. Eastern, E Zambia 13°40′S 32°42′E
83 C14 **Chipindo** Huíla, C Angola 13°53′S 15°47′E
23 R8 **Chipley** Florida, SE USA 30°46′N 85°32′W
155 D15 **Chiplūn** Mahārāshtra, W India 17°32′N 73°32′E
81 H22 **Chipogolo** Dodoma, C Tanzania 06°52′S 36°03′E
23 R8 **Chipola River** ≈ Florida, SE USA
97 L22 **Chippenham** S England, United Kingdom 51°28′N 02°07′W
30 J6 **Chippewa Falls** Wisconsin, N USA 44°56′N 91°25′W
30 J4 **Chippewa, Lake** ⊠ Wisconsin, N USA
31 Q8 **Chippewa River** ≈ Michigan, N USA
30 I6 **Chippewa River** ≈ Wisconsin, N USA
Chipping Wycombe *see* High Wycombe
114 G8 **Chiprovtsi** Montana, NW Bulgaria 43°23′N 22°53′E
19 T4 **Chiputneticook Lakes** *lakes* Canada/USA
56 D13 **Chiquián** Ancash, W Peru 10°09′S 77°08′W
41 Y11 **Chiquilá** Quintana Roo, SE Mexico 21°25′N 87°20′W
42 E6 **Chiquimula** Chiquimula, SE Guatemala 14°46′N 89°32′W
42 A3 **Chiquimula** *off.* Departamento de Chiquimula. ◈ *department* SE Guatemala
Chiquimula, Departamento de *see* Chiquimula
42 D7 **Chiquimulilla** Santa Rosa, S Guatemala 14°06′N 90°23′W
54 F9 **Chiquinquirá** Boyacá, C Colombia 05°37′N 73°51′W
155 J17 **Chīrāla** Andhra Pradesh, E India 15°49′N 80°21′E
149 N4 **Chīras** Ghowr, N Afghanistan 35°15′N 65°39′E
152 H11 **Chirāwa** Rājasthān, N India 28°12′N 75°42′E
Chirchik *see* Chirchiq
147 Q9 **Chirchiq** *Rus.* Chirchik. Toshkent Viloyati, E Uzbekistan 41°30′N 69°32′E
147 P10 **Chirchiq** ≈ E Uzbekistan
Chire *see* Shire
83 L18 **Chiredzi** Masvingo, SE Zimbabwe 21°00′S 31°38′E
25 X8 **Chireno** Texas, SW USA 31°30′N 94°21′W
77 X7 **Chirfa** Agadez, NE Niger 21°01′N 12°41′E
37 O16 **Chiricahua Mountains** ▲▲ Arizona, SW USA
37 O16 **Chiricahua Peak** ▲ Arizona, SW USA 31°51′N 109°17′W
54 F6 **Chiriguaná** Cesar, N Colombia 09°24′N 73°38′W
39 P15 **Chirikof Island** *island* Alaska, USA
43 P16 **Chiriquí** *off.* Provincia de Chiriquí. ◈ *province* SW Panama
43 P17 **Chiriquí, Golfo de** *Eng.* Chiriqui Gulf. *gulf* SW Panama
43 P15 **Chiriquí Grande** Bocas del Toro, W Panama 08°58′N 82°08′W
Chiriqui Gulf *see* Chiriquí, Golfo de
43 P15 **Chiriquí, Laguna de** *lagoon* NW Panama
Chiriquí, Provincia de *see* Chiriquí
43 O16 **Chiriquí Viejo, Río** ≈ W Panama
Chiriquí, Volcán de *see* Barú, Volcán
83 N15 **Chiromo** Southern, S Malawi 16°32′S 35°07′E
114 J10 **Chirpan** Stara Zagora, C Bulgaria 42°12′N 25°20′E
43 N14 **Chirripó Atlántico, Río** ≈ E Costa Rica
Chirripó, Cerro *see* Chirripó Grande, Cerro
Chirripó del Pacífico, Río *see* Chirripó, Río
43 N14 **Chirripó Grande, Cerro** *var.* Cerro Chirripó. ▲ SE Costa Rica 09°31′N 83°28′W
43 N13 **Chirripó, Río** *var.* Río Chirripó del Pacífico. ≈ NE Costa Rica
Chirua, Lago *see* Chilwa, Lake
83 J15 **Chirundu** Southern, S Zambia 16°03′S 28°50′E
29 W8 **Chisago City** Minnesota, N USA 45°22′N 92°53′W
83 J14 **Chisamba** Central, C Zambia 15°00′S 28°22′E
39 T10 **Chisana** Alaska, USA 62°09′N 142°07′W
82 I13 **Chisasa** North Western, NW Zambia 12°09′S 25°30′E
12 I9 **Chisasibi** *prev.* Fort George. Québec, C Canada 53°50′N 79°01′W
42 D4 **Chisec** Alta Verapaz, C Guatemala 15°50′N 90°18′W
127 U5 **Chishmy** Respublika Bashkortostan, W Russian Federation 54°33′N 55°21′E
29 V4 **Chisholm** Minnesota, N USA 47°29′N 92°52′W
149 U10 **Chishtiān Mandi** Punjab, E Pakistan 29°44′N 72°54′E
160 I11 **Chishui He** ≈ C China
Chisimaio/Chisimayu *see* Kismaayo
117 N10 **Chişinău** *Rus.* Kishinev. ● (Moldova) C Moldova 47°N 28°51′E
117 N10 **Chişinău** ✈ S Moldova 46°54′N 28°56′E
Chişinău-Criş *see* Chişineu-Criş
116 F10 **Chişineu-Criş** *Hung.* Kisjenő; *prev.* Chişinău-Criş. Arad, W Romania 46°33′N 21°30′E
83 K14 **Chisomo** Central, C Zambia 13°30′S 30°37′E
106 A8 **Chisone** ≈ NW Italy
24 K12 **Chisos Mountains** ▲▲ Texas, SW USA
39 T10 **Chistochina** Alaska, USA 62°34′N 144°39′W
127 R4 **Chistopol'** Respublika Tatarstan, W Russian Federation 55°20′N 50°39′E
145 O8 **Chistopol'ye** Severnyy Kazakhstan, N Kazakhstan 52°37′N 67°14′E
123 O13 **Chita** Chitinskaya Oblast', S Russian Federation 52°03′N 113°35′E
83 B16 **Chitado** Cunene, SW Angola 17°16′S 13°54′E
Chitaldroog/Chitaldrug *see* Chitradurga
83 C15 **Chitanda** ≈ S Angola
Chitangwiza *see* Chitungwiza
82 F10 **Chitato** Lunda Norte, NE Angola 07°23′S 20°46′E
83 C14 **Chitembo** Bié, C Angola 13°33′S 16°47′E
39 T11 **Chitina** Alaska, USA 61°31′N 144°26′W
39 T11 **Chitina River** ≈ Alaska, USA
123 O12 **Chitinskaya Oblast'** ◈ *province* S Russian Federation
82 M11 **Chitipa** Northern, NW Malawi 09°41′S 33°19′E
165 S4 **Chitose** *var.* Titose. Hokkaidō, NE Japan 42°51′N 141°40′E
155 G18 **Chitradurga** *prev.* Chitaldroog, Chitaldrug. Karnātaka, W India 14°16′N 76°23′E
149 T3 **Chitrāl** North-West Frontier Province, NW Pakistan 35°51′N 71°47′E
43 S16 **Chitré** Herrera, S Panama 07°57′N 80°26′W
153 V16 **Chittagong** *Ben.* Chāttagām. Chittagong, SE Bangladesh 22°20′N 91°48′E
153 U16 **Chittagong** ◈ *division* E Bangladesh
153 Q15 **Chittaranjan** West Bengal, NE India 23°52′N 86°40′E
152 G14 **Chittaurgarh** *var.* Chittorgarh. Rājasthān, N India 24°54′N 74°42′E
155 I19 **Chittoor** Andhra Pradesh, E India 13°13′N 79°06′E
Chittorgarh *see* Chittaurgarh
155 G21 **Chittūr** Kerala, SW India 10°42′N 76°46′E
83 K16 **Chitungwiza** *prev.* Chitangwiza. Mashonaland East, NE Zimbabwe 18°S 31°06′E
62 H4 **Chiuchiu** Antofagasta, N Chile 22°13′S 68°34′W
82 F12 **Chiumbe** *var.* Tshiumbe. ≈ Angola/Dem. Rep. Congo
83 F15 **Chiume** Moxico, E Angola 15°08′S 21°09′E
82 K13 **Chiundaponde** Northern, NE Zambia 12°14′S 30°40′E
106 H13 **Chiusi** Toscana, C Italy 43°00′N 11°56′E
54 J5 **Chivacoa** Yaracuy, N Venezuela 10°10′N 68°54′W
106 B8 **Chivasso** Piemonte, NW Italy 45°13′N 07°54′E
83 L17 **Chivhu** *prev.* Enkeldoorn. Midlands, C Zimbabwe 19°01′S 30°54′E
61 C20 **Chivilcoy** Buenos Aires, E Argentina 34°55′S 60°00′W
82 N12 **Chiweta** Northern, N Malawi 10°36′S 34°09′E
42 D4 **Chixoy, Río** *var.* Río Negro, Río Salinas. ≈ Guatemala/Mexico
82 H13 **Chizela** North Western, NW Zambia 13°11′S 24°59′E
125 O5 **Chizha** Nenetskiy Avtonomnyy Okrug, NW Russian Federation 67°04′N 44°19′E
161 Q9 **Chizhou** *var.* Guichi. Anhui, E China 30°39′N 117°29′E
164 I12 **Chizu** Tottori, Honshū, SW Japan 35°15′N 134°14′E
Chkalov *see* Orenburg
127 N3 **Chkalovsk** Nizhegorodskaya Oblast', W Russian Federation 56°45′N 43°15′E
74 J5 **Chlef** *var.* Ech Cheliff, Ech Chleff; *prev.* Al-Asnam, El Asnam, Orléansville. NW Algeria 36°11′N 01°21′E
115 G18 **Chlómo** ▲ C Greece 38°36′N 22°57′E
111 M15 **Chmielnik** Świętokrzyskie, C Poland 50°37′N 20°43′E
167 S11 **Chŏâm Khsant** Preăh Vihéar, N Cambodia 14°13′N 104°56′E
62 G10 **Choapa, Río** *var.* Choapo. ≈ C Chile
Choapas *see* Las Choapas
Choapo *see* Choapa, Río
Choarta *see* Chwārtā
67 T13 **Chobe** ≈ N Botswana
14 K8 **Chochocouane** ≈ Québec, SE Canada
110 E13 **Chocianów** *Ger.* Kotzenan. Dolnośląskie, SW Poland 51°23′N 15°55′E
54 C9 **Chocó** *off.* Departamento del Chocó. ◈ *province* W Colombia
Chocó, Departamento del *see* Chocó
35 X16 **Chocolate Mountains** ▲▲ California, W USA
21 W9 **Chocowinity** North Carolina, SE USA 35°33′N 77°03′W
27 N10 **Choctaw** Oklahoma, C USA 35°30′N 97°16′W
23 Q8 **Choctawhatchee Bay** *bay* Florida, SE USA
23 Q8 **Choctawhatchee River** ≈ Florida, SE USA
Chodau *see* Chodov
163 V14 **Ch'o-do** *island* SW North Korea
Chodorów *see* Khodoriv
111 A16 **Chodov** *Ger.* Chodau. Karlovarský Kraj, W Czech Republic 50°15′N 12°45′E
110 G10 **Chodzież** Wielkopolskie, C Poland 53°N 16°55′E
63 J15 **Choele Choel** Río Negro, C Argentina 39°19′S 65°42′W
83 L14 **Chofombo** Tete, NW Mozambique 14°43′S 31°48′E
Chohtan *see* Chauhtan
11 U14 **Choiceland** Saskatchewan, C Canada 53°28′N 104°26′W
186 K8 **Choiseul** *var.* Lauru. *island* NW Solomon Islands
63 M23 **Choiseul Sound** *sound* East Falkland, Falkland Islands
40 H7 **Choix** Sinaloa, C Mexico 26°43′N 108°20′W
110 D10 **Chojna** Zachodnio-pomorskie, W Poland 52°56′N 14°25′E
110 H8 **Chojnice** *Ger.* Konitz. Pomorskie, N Poland 53°41′N 17°34′E
111 F14 **Chojnów** *Ger.* Hainau, Haynau. Dolnośląskie, SW Poland 51°16′N 15°55′E
167 Q10 **Chok Chai** Nakhon Ratchasima, C Thailand 14°45′N 102°10′E
80 I12 **Ch'ok'ē** *var.* Choke Mountains. ▲▲ NW Ethiopia
25 R13 **Choke Canyon Lake** ⊠ Texas, SW USA
Choke Mountains *see* Ch'ok'ē
145 T15 **Chokpar** *Kaz.* Shoqpar. Zhambyl, S Kazakhstan 43°49′N 74°25′E
147 W7 **Chok-Tal** *var.* Choktal. Issyk-Kul'skaya Oblast', E Kyrgyzstan 42°37′N 76°45′E
Choktal *see* Chok-Tal
Chókué *see* Chokwè
123 R7 **Chokurdakh** Respublika Sakha (Yakutiya), NE Russian Federation 70°38′N 148°18′E
83 L20 **Chokwè** *var.* Chókué. Gaza, S Mozambique 24°27′S 32°55′E
188 F8 **Chol** Babeldaob, N Palau
160 E8 **Chola Shan** ▲▲ C China
102 J8 **Cholet** Maine-et-Loire, NW France 47°03′N 00°52′W
63 H17 **Cholila** Chubut, W Argentina 42°33′S 71°28′W
Cholo *see* Thyolo
147 V8 **Cholpon** Narynskaya Oblast', C Kyrgyzstan 42°07′N 75°25′E
147 X7 **Cholpon-Ata** Issyk-Kul'skaya Oblast', E Kyrgyzstan 42°39′N 77°05′E
41 P14 **Cholula** Puebla, S Mexico 19°03′N 98°19′W
42 I8 **Choluteca** Choluteca, S Honduras 13°15′N 87°10′W
42 H8 **Choluteca** ◈ *department* S Honduras
42 H8 **Choluteca, Río** ≈ SW Honduras
83 I15 **Choma** Southern, S Zambia 16°48′S 26°58′E
158 L17 **Chomo** *var.* Xarsingma. Xizang Zizhiqu, W China 27°31′N 88°58′E *see also* Yadong
153 T11 **Chomo Lhari** ▲ NW Bhutan 27°59′N 89°24′E
167 N7 **Chom Thong** Chiang Mai, NW Thailand 18°25′N 98°44′E
111 B15 **Chomutov** *Ger.* Komotau. Ústecký Kraj, NW Czech Republic 50°28′N 13°24′E
123 N11 **Chona** ≈ C Russian Federation
163 X15 **Ch'ŏnan** *Jap.* Tenan. W South Korea 36°51′N 127°11′E
167 P11 **Chon Buri** *prev.* Bang Pla Soi. Chon Buri, S Thailand 13°24′N 100°59′E
56 B6 **Chone** Manabí, W Ecuador 0°44′S 80°04′W
Chong'an *see* Wuyishan
163 W13 **Ch'ŏngch'ŏn-gang** ≈ W North Korea
163 Y11 **Ch'ŏngjin** NE North Korea 41°48′N 129°44′E
163 W13 **Chŏngju** W North Korea 39°44′N 125°13′E
161 S8 **Chongming Dao** *island* E China
160 J10 **Chongqing** *var.* Ch'ung-ching, Ch'ung-ch'ing, Chungking, Pahsien, Tchongking, Yuzhou. Chongqing Shi, C China 29°34′N 106°27′E
160 K10 **Chongqing Shi** ◈ *municipality* Chongqing Shi, C China
Chŏngup *see* Chŏnju
161 O10 **Chongyang** *var.* Tiancheng. Hubei, C China 29°35′N 114°03′E
160 J15 **Chongzuo** *prev.* Taiping. Guangxi Zhuangzu Zizhiqu, S China 22°18′N 107°23′E
163 Y16 **Chŏnju** *prev.* Chŏngup, *Jap.* Seiyu. SW South Korea 35°51′N 127°08′E
163 Y15 **Chŏnju** *Jap.* Zenshū. SW South Korea 35°51′N 127°08′E
Chonnacht *see* Connaught
Chonogol *see* Erdenetsagaan
63 F19 **Chonos, Archipiélago de los** *island group* S Chile
42 K10 **Chontales** ◈ *department* S Nicaragua
167 T13 **Chơn Thanh** Sông Be, S Vietnam 11°25′N 106°38′E
158 K17 **Cho Oyu** *var.* Qowowuyag. ▲ China/Nepal 28°07′N 86°37′E
116 G7 **Chop** *Cz.* Čop, *Hung.* Csap. Zakarpats'ka Oblast', W Ukraine 48°26′N 22°13′E
21 Y3 **Choptank River** ≈ Maryland, NE USA
115 J22 **Chóra** *prev.* Íos. Íos, Kykládes, Greece, Aegean Sea 36°42′N 25°16′E
115 H25 **Chóra Sfakíon** *var.* Sfákia. Kríti, Greece, E Mediterranean Sea 35°12′N 24°05′E
Chorcaí, Cuan *see* Cork Harbour
43 P15 **Chorcha, Cerro** ▲ W Panama 08°39′N 82°07′W
Chorku *see* Chorkŭh
147 R11 **Chorkŭh** *Rus.* Chorku. N Tajikistan 40°04′N 70°30′E
97 K17 **Chorley** NW England, United Kingdom 53°40′N 02°38′W
Chorne More *see* Black Sea
117 R5 **Chornobay** Cherkas'ka Oblast', C Ukraine 49°40′N 32°20′E
117 O3 **Chornobyl'** *Rus.* Chernobyl'. Kyyivs'ka Oblast', N Ukraine 51°17′N 30°15′E
117 R12 **Chornomors'ke** *Rus.* Chernomorskoye. Respublika Krym, S Ukraine 45°29′N 32°45′E
117 R4 **Chornukhy** Poltavs'ka Oblast', C Ukraine 50°15′N 32°57′E
Chorokh/Chorokhi *see* Çoruh Nehri
110 O9 **Choroszcz** Podlaskie, NE Poland 53°10′N 23°E
116 K6 **Chortkiv** *Rus.* Chortkov. Ternopil's'ka Oblast', W Ukraine 49°01′N 25°46′E
Chortkov *see* Chortkiv
Chorum *see* Çorum
110 M9 **Chorzele** Mazowieckie, C Poland 53°16′N 20°53′E
111 J16 **Chorzów** *Ger.* Königshütte; *prev.* Królewska Huta. Śląskie, S Poland 50°17′N 18°58′E
163 W12 **Ch'osan** N North Korea 40°45′N 125°52′E
Chōsebuz *see* Cottbus
Chōsen-kaikyō *see* Korea Strait
164 P14 **Chōshi** *var.* Tyôsi. Chiba, Honshū, S Japan 35°44′N 140°48′E
63 H14 **Chos Malal** Neuquén, W Argentina 37°23′S 70°16′W
Chosŏn-minjujuŭi-inmin-kanghwaguk *see* North Korea
110 E9 **Choszczno** *Ger.* Arnswalde. Zachodnio-pomorskie, NW Poland 53°10′N 15°24′E
153 O15 **Chota Nāgpur** *plateau* N India
33 R8 **Choteau** Montana, NW USA 47°48′N 112°40′W
Chotqol *see* Chatkal
14 M8 **Chouart** ≈ Québec, SE Canada
76 I7 **Choûm** Adrar, C Mauritania 21°19′N 12°59′W
27 Q9 **Chouteau** Oklahoma, C USA 36°11′N 95°20′W
21 X8 **Chowan River** ≈ North Carolina, SE USA
35 Q10 **Chowchilla** California, W USA 37°06′N 120°15′W
163 P7 **Choybalsan** *prev.* Byan Tumen. Dornod, E Mongolia 48°03′N 114°32′E
163 Q7 **Choybalsan** *var.* Hulstay. Dornod, NE Mongolia 48°25′N 114°56′E
162 M9 **Choyr** Govĭ Sumber, C Mongolia 46°20′N 108°21′E
185 I19 **Christchurch** Canterbury, South Island, New Zealand 43°31′S 172°39′E
97 M24 **Christchurch** S England, United Kingdom 50°44′N 01°45′W
185 I18 **Christchurch** ✈ Canterbury, South Island, New Zealand 43°28′S 172°33′E
44 J12 **Christiana** C Jamaica 18°13′N 77°29′W
83 H22 **Christiana** Free State, C South Africa 27°55′S 25°10′E
115 J23 **Christiáni** *var.* Christiani. *island* Kykládes, Greece, Aegean Sea
Christiania *see* Oslo
14 G13 **Christian Island** *island* Ontario, S Canada
191 P16 **Christian, Point** *headland* Pitcairn Island, Pitcairn Islands 25°04′S 130°08′E
38 M11 **Christian River** ≈ Alaska, USA
Christiansand *see* Kristiansand
21 S7 **Christiansburg** Virginia, NE USA 37°07′N 80°26′W
95 G23 **Christiansfeld** Sønderjylland, SW Denmark 55°21′N 09°30′E
Christianshåb *see* Qasigiannguit
39 X14 **Christian Sound** *inlet* Alaska, USA
45 T9 **Christiansted** Saint Croix, S Virgin Islands (US) 17°43′N 64°42′W
Christiansund *see* Kristiansund
25 R13 **Christine** Texas, SW USA 28°47′N 98°30′W
173 U7 **Christmas Island** ◇ *Australian external territory* E Indian Ocean
129 T17 **Christmas Island** *island* E Indian Ocean
Christmas Island *see* Kiritimati
192 M7 **Christmas Ridge** *undersea feature* C Pacific Ocean
30 L16 **Christopher** Illinois, N USA 37°58′N 89°03′W
25 P9 **Christoval** Texas, SW USA 31°09′N 100°30′W
111 F17 **Chrudim** Pardubický Kraj, C Czech Republic 49°58′N 15°49′E
115 K25 **Chrýsi** *island* SE Greece
121 N2 **Chrysochoú, Kólpos** *var.* Khrysokhou Bay. *bay* E Mediterranean Sea
114 I13 **Chrysoúpoli** *var.* Hrisoupoli; *prev.* Khrisoúpolis. Anatolikí Makedonía kai Thráki, NE Greece 40°59′N 24°42′E
111 K16 **Chrzanów** *var.* Chrzanow, *Ger.* Zaumgarten. Śląskie, S Poland 50°10′N 19°21′E
129 Q7 **Chu** *Kaz.* Shū. ≈ Kazakhstan/Kyrgyzstan
42 C5 **Chuacús, Sierra de** ▲▲ W Guatemala
153 S15 **Chuadanga** Khulna, W Bangladesh 23°38′N 88°52′E
Chuan *see* Sichuan
Ch'uan-chou *see* Quanzhou
Chuankou *see* Minhe
39 O11 **Chuathbaluk** Alaska, USA 61°36′N 159°14′W
Chubek *see* Moskva
63 I17 **Chubut** *off.* Provincia de Chubut. ◈ *province* S Argentina
Chubut, Provincia de *see* Chubut
63 I17 **Chubut, Río** ≈ SE Argentina
43 V15 **Chucanti, Cerro** ▲ E Panama 08°48′N 78°27′W
Ch'u-chiang *see* Shaoguan
43 W15 **Chucunaque, Río** ≈ E Panama
Chudin *see* Chudzin
116 M5 **Chudniv** Zhytomyrs'ka Oblast', N Ukraine 50°02′N 28°06′E
124 H13 **Chudovo** Novgorodskaya Oblast', W Russian Federation 59°07′N 31°42′E
Chudskoye Ozero *see* Peipus, Lake
119 J18 **Chudzin** *Rus.* Chudin. Brestskaya Voblasts', SW Belarus 52°44′N 26°59′E
39 Q13 **Chugach Islands** *island group* Alaska, USA
39 S11 **Chugach Mountains** ▲▲ Alaska, USA
164 G12 **Chūgoku-sanchi** ▲▲ Honshū, SW Japan
Chugqênsumdo *see* Jigzhi
Chuguyev *see* Chuhuyiv
117 V5 **Chuhuyiv** *var.* Chuguyev. Kharkivs'ka Oblast', E Ukraine 49°51′N 36°44′E
61 H19 **Chuí** Rio Grande do Sul, S Brazil 33°45′S 53°23′W
Chuí *see* Chuy
145 S15 **Chu-Iliyskiye Gory** *Kaz.* Shū-Ile Taūlary. ▲▲ S Kazakhstan
Chukai *see* Cukai
Chukchi Avtonomnyy Okrug *see* Chukotskiy Avtonomnyy Okrug
Chukchi Peninsula *see* Chukotskiy Poluostrov
197 R6 **Chukchi Plain** *undersea feature* Arctic Ocean
197 R6 **Chukchi Plateau** *undersea feature* Arctic Ocean
197 R4 **Chukchi Sea** *Rus.* Chukotskoye More. *sea* Arctic Ocean
125 N14 **Chukhloma** Kostromskaya Oblast', NW Russian Federation 58°42′N 42°39′E
Chukotka *see* Chukotskiy Avtonomnyy Okrug
Chukot Range *see* Anadyrskiy Khrebet
123 V6 **Chukotskiy Avtonomnyy Okrug** *var.* Chukchi Avtonomnyy Okrug, Chukotka. ◈ *autonomous district* NE Russian Federation
123 W5 **Chukotskiy, Mys** *headland* NE Russian Federation 64°15′N 173°03′W
123 V5 **Chukotskiy Poluostrov** *Eng.* Chukchi Peninsula. *peninsula* NE Russian Federation
Chukotskoye More *see* Chukchi Sea
Chukurkak *see* Chuqurqoq
Chulakkurgan *see* Sholakkorgan
35 U17 **Chula Vista** California, W USA 32°38′N 117°04′W
123 Q12 **Chul'man** Respublika Sakha (Yakutiya), NE Russian Federation 56°50′N 124°47′E
56 B9 **Chulucanas** Piura, NW Peru 05°08′S 80°10′W
122 J12 **Chulym** ≈ C Russian Federation
152 K6 **Chumar** Jammu and Kashmir, N India 32°38′N 78°36′E
114 K9 **Chumerna** ▲ C Bulgaria 42°45′N 25°58′E
123 R12 **Chumikan** Khabarovskiy Kray, E Russian Federation 54°41′N 135°12′E
167 Q9 **Chum Phae** Khon Kaen, C Thailand 16°31′N 102°09′E
167 N13 **Chumphon** *var.* Jumporn. Chumphon, SW Thailand 10°30′N 99°11′E
167 O9 **Chumsaeng** *var.* Chum Saeng. Nakhon Sawan, C Thailand 15°52′N 100°18′E
Chum Saeng *see* Chumsaeng
122 L12 **Chuna** ≈ C Russian Federation
161 R9 **Chun'an** *var.* Qiandaohu; *prev.* Pailing. Zhejiang, SE China 29°37′N 118°59′E
161 S13 **Chunan** N Taiwan 24°44′N 120°51′E
Chuncheng *see* Yangchun
163 Y14 **Ch'unch'ŏn** *Jap.* Shunsen. N South Korea 37°52′N 127°48′E
153 S16 **Chunchura** *prev.* Chinsura. West Bengal, NE India 22°54′N 88°20′E
145 W15 **Chundzha** *Kaz.* Shonzhy. Almaty, SE Kazakhstan 43°32′N 79°28′E
Ch'ung-ch'ing/Ch'ung-ching *see* Chongqing
Chung-hua Jen-min Kung-ho-kuo *see* China
163 Y15 **Ch'ungju** *Jap.* Chūshū. C South Korea 36°57′N 127°50′E
Chungking *see* Chongqing
161 T14 **Chungyang Shanmo** *Chin.* Taiwan Shan. ▲▲ C Taiwan
149 V9 **Chūniān** Punjab, E Pakistan 30°57′N 74°01′E
122 L12 **Chunskiy** Irkutskaya Oblast', S Russian Federation 56°10′N 99°15′E
122 M11 **Chunya** ≈ C Russian Federation
124 J6 **Chupa** Respublika Kareliya, NW Russian Federation 66°15′N 33°02′E
125 P8 **Chuprovo** Respublika Komi, NW Russian Federation 64°16′N 46°27′E
57 G17 **Chuquibamba** Arequipa, SW Peru 15°47′S 72°44′W
62 H4 **Chuquicamata** Antofagasta, N Chile 22°20′S 68°56′W
57 L21 **Chuquisaca** ◈ *department* S Bolivia
Chuquisaca *see* Sucre
Chuquung *see* Chindu
146 I8 **Chuqurqoq** *Rus.* Chukurkak. Qoraqalpog'iston Respublikasi, NW Uzbekistan 42°44′N 61°33′E
127 T2 **Chur** Udmurtskaya Respublika, NW Russian Federation 57°06′N 52°57′E
108 I9 **Chur** *Fr.* Coire, *It.* Coira, *Rmsch.* Cuera, Quera; *anc.* Curia Rhaetorum. Graubünden, E Switzerland 46°52′N 09°32′E
123 Q10 **Churapcha** Respublika Sakha (Yakutiya), NE Russian Federation 61°59′N 132°06′E
11 V16 **Churchbridge** Saskatchewan, S Canada 50°55′N 101°53′W
21 O8 **Church Hill** Tennessee, S USA 36°31′N 82°42′W
11 X9 **Churchill** Manitoba, C Canada 58°46′N 94°10′W
11 X10 **Churchill** ≈ Manitoba/Saskatchewan, C Canada
13 P9 **Churchill** ≈ Newfoundland and Labrador, E Canada
11 Y9 **Churchill, Cape** *headland* Manitoba, C Canada 58°42′N 93°12′W
13 P9 **Churchill Falls** Newfoundland and Labrador, E Canada 53°38′N 64°00′W
11 S12 **Churchill Lake** ◎ Saskatchewan, C Canada
19 Q3 **Churchill Lake** ⊠ Maine, NE USA
194 I5 **Churchill Peninsula** *peninsula* Antarctica
22 H8 **Church Point** Louisiana, S USA 30°24′N 92°13′W
29 O3 **Churchs Ferry** North Dakota, N USA 48°15′N 99°12′W
146 G12 **Churchuri** Ahal Welaýaty, C Turkmenistan 38°55′N 59°13′E
21 T5 **Churchville** Virginia, NE USA 38°13′N 79°10′W
152 G10 **Chūru** Rājasthān, NW India 28°18′N 75°00′E
54 J4 **Churuguara** Falcón, N Venezuela 10°52′N 69°35′W
167 U11 **Chư Sê** Gia Lai, C Vietnam 13°38′N 108°06′E
144 J12 **Chushkakul, Gory** ▲▲ SW Kazakhstan
Chūshū *see* Ch'ungju
37 O9 **Chuska Mountains** ▲▲ Arizona/New Mexico, SW USA
Chu, Sông *see* Sam, Nam
125 V14 **Chusovoy** Permskaya Oblast', NW Russian Federation 58°17′N 57°54′E
147 R10 **Chust** Namangan Viloyati, E Uzbekistan 40°58′N 71°12′E
Chust *see* Khust
15 U6 **Chute-aux-Outardes** Québec, SE Canada 49°07′N 68°25′W
117 U5 **Chutove** Poltavs'ka Oblast', C Ukraine 49°45′N 35°11′E
189 O15 **Chuuk** *var.* Truk. ◈ *state* C Micronesia
189 P15 **Chuuk Islands** *var.* Hogoley Islands; *prev.* Truk Islands. *island group* Caroline Islands, C Micronesia
Chuvashia *see* Chuvashskaya Respublika
Chuvashiya *see* Chuvashskaya Respublika
127 P4 **Chuvashskaya Respublika** *var.* Chuvashiya, *Eng.* Chuvashia. ◈ *autonomous republic* W Russian Federation
Chuwārtah *see* Chwārtā
Chu Xian/Chuxian *see* Chuzhou
160 G13 **Chuxiong** Yunnan, SW China 25°02′N 101°32′E
147 V7 **Chuy** Chuyskaya Oblast', N Kyrgyzstan 42°45′N 75°11′E
61 H19 **Chuy** *var.* Chuí. Rocha, E Uruguay 33°42′S 53°27′W
123 O11 **Chuya** Respublika Sakha (Yakutiya), NE Russian Federation 59°30′N 112°26′E
Chüy Oblasty *see* Chuyskaya Oblast'
147 U8 **Chuyskaya Oblast'** *Kir.* Chüy Oblasty. ◈ *province* N Kyrgyzstan
161 Q7 **Chuzhou** *var.* Chuxian. Chu Xian. Anhui, E China 32°20′N 118°18′E
139 U3 **Chwārtā** *var.* Choarta, Chuwārtah. As Sulaymānīyah, NE Iraq 35°11′N 45°59′E
119 N16 **Chyhirynskaye Vodaskhovishcha** ⊠ E Belarus
117 R6 **Chyhyryn** *Rus.* Chigirin. Cherkas'ka Oblast', N Ukraine 49°03′N 32°40′E
119 J18 **Chyrvonaya Slabada** *Rus.* Krasnaya Slabada, Krasnaya Sloboda. Minskaya Voblasts', S Belarus 52°51′N 27°10′E
119 L19 **Chyrvonaya, Vozyera** *Rus.* Ozero Chervonoye. ◎ SE Belarus
117 N11 **Ciadîr-Lunga** *var.* Ceadâr-Lunga, *Rus.* Chadyr-Lunga. S Moldova 46°03′N 28°50′E
169 P16 **Ciamis** *prev.* Tjiamis. Jawa, C Indonesia 07°20′S 108°21′E
107 I16 **Ciampino** ✈ Lazio, C Italy 41°48′N 12°36′E
169 N16 **Cianjur** *prev.* Tjiandjoer. Jawa, C Indonesia 06°50′S 107°09′E
60 H10 **Cianorte** Paraná, S Brazil 23°42′S 52°31′W
Ciarraí *see* Kerry
112 N13 **Čićevac** Serbia, E Serbia 43°44′N 21°25′E
187 Z14 **Cicia** *prev.* Thithia. *island* Lau Group, E Fiji
105 P4 **Cidacos** ≈ N Spain
136 I10 **Cide** Kastamonu, N Turkey 41°53′N 33°01′E
110 L10 **Ciechanów** *prev.* Zichenau. Mazowieckie, C Poland 52°53′N 20°37′E
110 O10 **Ciechanowiec** *Ger.* Rudelstadt. Podlaskie, E Poland 52°43′N 22°30′E
110 J10 **Ciechocinek** Kujawsko-pomorskie, C Poland 52°53′N 18°49′E
44 F6 **Ciego de Ávila** Ciego de Ávila, C Cuba 21°50′N 78°44′W
54 F4 **Ciénaga** Magdalena, N Colombia 11°01′N 74°15′W
54 E6 **Ciénaga de Oro** Córdoba, NW Colombia 08°54′N 75°39′W
44 E5 **Cienfuegos** Cienfuegos, C Cuba 22°10′N 80°27′W
104 F4 **Cíes, Illas** *island group* NW Spain
111 P16 **Cieszanów** Podkarpackie, SE Poland 50°15′N 23°09′E
111 J17 **Cieszyn** *Cz.* Těšín, *Ger.* Teschen. Śląskie, S Poland 49°45′N 18°35′E
105 R12 **Cieza** Murcia, SE Spain 38°14′N 01°25′W
136 F13 **Çifteler** Eskişehir, W Turkey 39°25′N 31°00′E
105 P7 **Cifuentes** Castilla-La Mancha, C Spain 40°47′N 02°37′W
Çiganak *see* Chiganak
105 P9 **Cigüela** ≈ C Spain
136 H14 **Cihanbeyli** Konya, C Turkey 38°40′N 32°55′E
136 H14 **Cihanbeyli Yaylası** *plateau* C Turkey
104 L10 **Cíjara, Embalse de** ⊠ C Spain
169 P16 **Cikalong** Jawa, S Indonesia 07°46′S 108°13′E
169 N16 **Cikawung** Jawa, S Indonesia 06°49′S 105°29′E
187 Y13 **Cikobia** *prev.* Thikombia. *island* N Fiji
169 P17 **Cilacap** *prev.* Tjilatjap. Jawa, C Indonesia 07°44′S 109°E
173 O16 **Cilaos** C Réunion 21°08′S 55°28′E
137 S11 **Çıldır** Ardahan, NE Turkey 41°08′N 43°08′E
137 S11 **Çıldır Gölü** ◎ NE Turkey
160 M10 **Cili** Hunan, S China 29°24′N 110°59′E
Cilician Gates *see* Gülek Boğazı
121 V10 **Cilicia Trough** *undersea feature* E Mediterranean Sea
Cill Airne *see* Killarney
Cill Chainnigh *see* Kilkenny
Cill Chaoi *see* Kilkee
Cill Choca *see* Kilcock
Cill Dara *see* Kildare
105 N3 **Cilleruelo de Bezana** Castilla-León, N Spain 42°58′N 03°50′W
Cilli *see* Celje
Cill Mhantáin *see* Wicklow
Cill Rois *see* Kilrush
146 C11 **Çilmämmetgum** *Rus.* Peski Chil'mamedkum, *Turkm.* Chilmämetgum. *desert* Balkan Welaýaty, W Turkmenistan
137 Z11 **Çiloy Adası** *Rus.* Ostrov Zhiloy. *island* E Azerbaijan
26 J6 **Cimarron** Kansas, C USA 37°49′N 100°20′W
37 T9 **Cimarron** New Mexico, SW USA 36°30′N 104°55′W
26 M9 **Cimarron River** ≈ Kansas/Oklahoma, C USA
117 N11 **Cimişlia** *Rus.* Chimishliya. S Moldova 46°31′N 28°45′E
Cîmpia Turzii *see* Câmpia Turzii
Cîmpina *see* Câmpina
Cîmpulung *see* Câmpulung
Cîmpulung Moldovenesc *see* Câmpulung Moldovenesc
137 P15 **Çınar** Diyarbakır, SE Turkey 37°45′N 40°22′E
54 J8 **Cinaruco, Río** ≈ Colombia/Venezuela
Cina Selatan, Laut *see* South China Sea
105 T5 **Cinca** ≈ NE Spain
112 G13 **Cincar** ▲ SW Bosnia and Herzegovina 43°55′N 17°05′E
31 Q15 **Cincinnati** Ohio, N USA 39°04′N 84°34′W
21 M4 **Cincinnati** ✈ Kentucky, S USA 39°03′N 84°39′W
Cinco de Outubro *see* Xá-Muteba
136 C15 **Çine** Aydın, SW Turkey 37°37′N 28°03′E
99 J21 **Ciney** Namur, SE Belgium 50°17′N 05°06′E
104 H6 **Cinfães** Viseu, N Portugal 41°04′N 08°06′W
106 J12 **Cingoli** Marche, C Italy 43°25′N 13°09′E
41 U16 **Cintalapa** *var.* Cintalapa de Figueroa. Chiapas, SE Mexico 16°42′N 93°40′W
Cintalapa de Figueroa *see* Cintalapa
103 X14 **Cinto, Monte** ▲ Corse, France, C Mediterranean Sea 42°22′N 08°57′E
Cintra *see* Sintra
105 Q5 **Cintruénigo** Navarra, N Spain 42°05′N 01°50′W
Cionn tSáile *see* Kinsale
116 K13 **Ciorani** Prahova, SE Romania 44°49′N 26°25′E
113 E14 **Čiovo** *It.* Bua. *island* S Croatia
Cipiúr *see* Kippure
63 I15 **Cipolletti** Río Negro, C Argentina 38°55′S 68°W
120 L7 **Circeo, Capo** *headland* C Italy 41°15′N 13°03′E
39 S8 **Circle** *var.* Circle City. Alaska, USA 65°51′N 144°04′W
33 X8 **Circle** Montana, NW USA 47°25′N 105°32′W
Circle City *see* Circle
31 S14 **Circleville** Ohio, N USA 39°36′N 82°57′W
36 K6 **Circleville** Utah, W USA 38°10′N 112°16′W
169 P16 **Cirebon** *prev.* Tjirebon. Jawa, S Indonesia 06°46′S 108°33′E
97 L21 **Cirencester** *anc.* Corinium, Corinium Dobunorum. C England, United Kingdom 51°44′N 01°59′W
Cirkvenica *see* Crikvenica
107 O20 **Cirò** Calabria, SW Italy 39°22′N 17°02′E
107 O20 **Cirò Marino** Calabria, S Italy 39°21′N 17°07′E

◆ Country ● Country Capital ◇ Dependent Territory ○ Dependent Territory Capital ◈ Administrative Regions ✈ International Airport ▲ Mountain ▲▲ Mountain Range ☖ Volcano ≈ River ◎ Lake ⊠ Reservoir
237

◆ Country   ◇ Dependent Territory   ◇ Administrative Regions   ▲ Mountain   ☒ Volcano   ⊙ Lake
● Country Capital   ○ Dependent Territory Capital   ✕ International Airport   ▲ Mountain Range   ♒ River   ⊟ Reservoir

COLMENAR VIEJO – CORONEL OVIEDO

105 N7 **Colmenar Viejo** Madrid, C Spain 40°39′N 03°46′W
25 X9 **Colmesneil** Texas, SW USA 30°54′N 94°25′W
Cöln *see* Köln
Colneceaste *see* Colchester
59 G15 **Colniza** Mato Grosso, W Brazil 09°16′S 59°25′W
Cologne *see* Köln
42 B6 **Colomba** Quezaltenango, SW Guatemala 14°45′N 91°39′W
Colomb-Béchar *see* Béchar
54 E11 **Colombia** Huila, C Colombia 03°24′N 74°49′W
54 G10 **Colombia** *off.* Republic of Colombia. ◆ *republic* N South America
64 E12 **Colombian Basin** *undersea feature* SW Caribbean Sea 13°00′N 76°00′W
Colombia, Republic of *see* Colombia
Colombie-Britannique *see* British Columbia
15 T6 **Colombier** Québec, SE Canada 48°51′N 68°52′W
155 J25 **Colombo** ● (Sri Lanka) Western Province, W Sri Lanka 06°55′N 79°52′E
155 J25 **Colombo** ✈ Western Province, SW Sri Lanka 06°50′N 79°59′E
29 N11 **Colome** South Dakota, N USA 43°13′N 99°42′W
61 B19 **Colón** Buenos Aires, E Argentina 33°53′S 61°06′W
61 D18 **Colón** Entre Ríos, E Argentina 32°10′S 58°16′W
44 D5 **Colón** Matanzas, C Cuba 22°43′N 80°54′W
43 T14 **Colón** *prev.* Aspinwall. Colón, C Panama 09°04′N 80°33′W
42 K5 **Colón** ◆ *department* NE Honduras
43 S15 **Colón** *off.* Provincia de Colón. ◆ *province* N Panama
57 A16 **Colón, Archipiélago de** *var.* Islas de los Galápagos, *Eng.* Galapagos Islands, Tortoise Islands. *island group* Ecuador, E Pacific Ocean
44 K5 **Colonel Hill** Crooked Island, SE Bahamas 22°43′N 74°12′W
40 C3 **Colonet** Baja California Norte, NW Mexico 31°00′N 116°1′W
40 B3 **Colonet, Cabo** *headland* NW Mexico 30°57′N 116°19′W
188 G14 **Colonia** Yap, W Micronesia 09°29′N 138°06′E
61 D19 **Colonia** ◆ *department* SW Uruguay
Colonia *see* Kolonia, Micronesia
Colonia *see* Colonia del Sacramento, Uruguay
Colonia Agrippina *see* Köln
61 D20 **Colonia del Sacramento** *var.* Colonia. Colonia, SW Uruguay 34°29′S 57°48′W
62 L8 **Colonia Dora** Santiago del Estero, N Argentina 28°34′S 62°59′W
Colonia Julia Fanestris *see* Fano
21 W5 **Colonial Beach** Virginia, NE USA 38°15′N 76°57′W
21 V6 **Colonial Heights** Virginia, NE USA 37°15′N 77°24′W
Colón, Provincia de *see* Colón
193 S7 **Colón Ridge** *undersea feature* E Pacific Ocean 02°00′N 96°00′W
96 F12 **Colonsay** *island* W Scotland, United Kingdom
57 K22 **Colorada, Laguna** ◎ SW Bolivia
37 R6 **Colorado** *off.* State of Colorado, *also known as* Centennial State, Silver State. ◆ *state* C USA
63 H22 **Colorado, Cerro** ▲ S Argentina 49°58′S 71°38′W
25 O7 **Colorado City** Texas, SW USA 32°24′N 100°51′W
36 M7 **Colorado Plateau** *plateau* W USA
61 A24 **Colorado, Río** ⛴ E Argentina
43 N12 **Colorado, Río** ⛴ NE Costa Rica
Colorado, Río *see* Colorado River
16 F12 **Colorado River** *var.* Río Colorado. ⛴ Mexico/USA
16 K14 **Colorado River** ⛴ Texas, SW USA
35 W15 **Colorado River Aqueduct** *aqueduct* California, W USA
44 A4 **Colorados, Archipiélago de los** *island group* NW Cuba
62 J9 **Colorados, Desagües de los** ◎ W Argentina
37 T5 **Colorado Springs** Colorado, C USA 38°50′N 104°47′W
40 L11 **Colotlán** Jalisco, SW Mexico 22°08′N 103°15′W
57 L19 **Colquechaca** Potosí, C Bolivia 18°40′S 66°00′W
23 S7 **Colquitt** Georgia, SE USA 31°10′N 84°43′W
29 R11 **Colton** South Dakota, N USA 43°47′N 96°55′W
32 M10 **Colton** Washington, NW USA 46°34′N 117°10′W
35 P8 **Columbia** California, W USA 38°01′N 120°22′W
30 K16 **Columbia** Illinois, N USA 38°26′N 90°12′W
20 L7 **Columbia** Kentucky, S USA 37°05′N 85°19′W
22 I6 **Columbia** Louisiana, S USA 32°05′N 92°03′W
21 W3 **Columbia** Maryland, NE USA 39°13′N 76°51′W
22 L7 **Columbia** Mississippi, S USA 31°15′N 89°50′W
27 U4 **Columbia** Missouri, C USA 38°56′N 92°19′W
21 Y9 **Columbia** North Carolina, SE USA 35°55′N 76°15′W
18 G16 **Columbia** Pennsylvania, NE USA 40°01′N 76°30′W
21 Q12 **Columbia** *state capital* South Carolina, SE USA 34°00′N 81°02′W
20 I9 **Columbia** Tennessee, S USA 35°37′N 87°02′W
0 F9 **Columbia** ⛴ Canada/USA
32 K9 **Columbia Basin** *basin* Washington, NW USA
197 Q10 **Columbia, Cape** *headland* Ellesmere Island, Nunavut, NE Canada
31 Q12 **Columbia City** Indiana, N USA 41°09′N 85°29′W
21 W3 **Columbia, District of** ◆ *federal district* NE USA
33 P7 **Columbia Falls** Montana, NW USA 48°22′N 114°10′W
11 O15 **Columbia Icefield** *ice field* Alberta/British Columbia, S Canada
11 O15 **Columbia, Mount** ▲ Alberta/British Columbia, SW Canada 52°07′N 117°30′W
11 N15 **Columbia Mountains** ▲ British Columbia, SW Canada
23 P4 **Columbiana** Alabama, S USA 33°10′N 86°36′W
31 V12 **Columbiana** Ohio, N USA 40°53′N 80°41′W
32 M14 **Columbia Plateau** *plateau* Idaho/Oregon, NW USA
29 P7 **Columbia Road Reservoir** ⊠ South Dakota, N USA
65 K16 **Columbia Seamount** *undersea feature* C Atlantic Ocean 20°30′S 32°00′W
83 D25 **Columbine, Cape** *headland* SW South Africa 32°50′S 17°39′E
105 U9 **Columbretes, Islas** *island group* E Spain
23 R5 **Columbus** Georgia, SE USA 32°29′N 84°58′W
31 P14 **Columbus** Indiana, N USA 39°12′N 85°55′W
27 R7 **Columbus** Kansas, C USA 37°09′N 94°52′W
23 N4 **Columbus** Mississippi, S USA 33°30′N 88°25′W
33 U11 **Columbus** Montana, NW USA 45°38′N 109°15′W
29 Q15 **Columbus** Nebraska, C USA 41°25′N 97°22′W
37 Q16 **Columbus** New Mexico, SW USA 31°49′N 107°38′W
21 P10 **Columbus** North Carolina, SE USA 35°15′N 82°09′W
28 K2 **Columbus** North Dakota, N USA 48°52′N 102°47′W
31 S13 **Columbus** *state capital* Ohio, N USA 39°58′N 83°W
25 U11 **Columbus** Texas, SW USA 29°42′N 96°35′W
30 L8 **Columbus** Wisconsin, N USA 43°21′N 89°00′W
31 R12 **Columbus Grove** Ohio, N USA 40°55′N 84°03′W
29 Y15 **Columbus Junction** Iowa, C USA 41°16′N 91°21′W
44 J3 **Columbus Point** *headland* Cat Island, C Bahamas 24°07′N 75°19′W
35 T8 **Columbus Salt Marsh** *salt marsh* Nevada, W USA
35 N6 **Colusa** California, W USA 39°10′N 122°03′W
32 L7 **Colville** Washington, NW USA 48°33′N 117°54′W
184 M5 **Colville, Cape** *headland* North Island, New Zealand 36°28′S 175°20′E
184 M5 **Colville Channel** *channel* North Island, New Zealand
39 P6 **Colville River** ⛴ Alaska, USA
97 J18 **Colwyn Bay** N Wales, United Kingdom 53°18′N 03°43′W
106 H9 **Comacchio** *var.* Commachio; *anc.* Comactium. Emilia-Romagna, N Italy 44°41′N 12°10′E
106 H9 **Comacchio, Valli di** *lagoon* Adriatic Sea, N Mediterranean Sea
Comactium *see* Comacchio
159 N16 **Comai** *var.* Damxoi. Xizang Zizhiqu, W China 28°29′N 91°25′E
41 V17 **Comalapa** Chiapas, SE Mexico 15°42′N 92°06′W
41 U15 **Comalcalco** Tabasco, SE Mexico 18°16′N 93°05′W
63 H16 **Comallo** Río Negro, SW Argentina 40°58′S 70°13′W
26 M12 **Comanche** Oklahoma, C USA 34°22′N 97°57′W
25 R8 **Comanche** Texas, SW USA 31°55′N 98°36′W
194 H2 **Comandante Ferraz** *Brazilian research station* Antarctica 61°57′S 58°23′W
62 N6 **Comandante Fontana** Formosa, N Argentina 25°19′S 59°42′W
63 I22 **Comandante Luis Peidra Buena** Santa Cruz, S Argentina 50°04′S 68°55′W
59 O18 **Comandatuba** Bahia, SE Brazil 15°13′S 39°00′W
116 K11 **Comănești** *Hung.* Kománfalva. Bacău, SW Romania 46°25′N 26°29′E
57 M19 **Comarapa** Santa Cruz, C Bolivia 17°53′S 64°30′W
116 J13 **Comarnic** Prahova, SE Romania 45°18′N 25°37′E
42 H6 **Comayagua** Comayagua, W Honduras 14°30′N 87°39′W
42 H6 **Comayagua** ◆ *department* W Honduras
42 I6 **Comayagua, Montañas de** ▲ C Honduras
21 R15 **Combahee River** ⛴ South Carolina, SE USA
62 G10 **Combarbalá** Coquimbo, C Chile 31°15′S 71°03′W
103 S7 **Combeaufontaine** Haute-Saône, E France 47°43′N 05°52′E
97 G15 **Comber** *Ir.* An Comar. E Northern Ireland, United Kingdom 54°33′N 05°45′W
99 K20 **Comblain-au-Pont** Liège, E Belgium 50°29′N 05°36′E
102 I6 **Combourg** Ille-et-Vilaine, NW France 48°21′N 01°44′W
44 M9 **Comendador** *prev.* Elías Piña. W Dominican Republic 18°53′N 71°42′W
Comer See *see* Como, Lago di
25 R11 **Comfort** Texas, SW USA 29°58′N 98°54′W
153 V15 **Comilla** *Ben.* Kumillā. Chittagong, E Bangladesh 23°28′N 91°10′E
99 B18 **Comines** Hainaut, W Belgium 50°46′N 02°58′E
121 O15 **Comino** *Malt.* Kemmuna. *island* C Malta
107 D18 **Comino, Capo** *headland* Sardegna, Italy, C Mediterranean Sea 40°32′N 09°49′E
107 K25 **Comiso** Sicilia, Italy, C Mediterranean Sea 36°57′N 14°37′E
41 V16 **Comitán** *var.* Comitán de Domínguez. Chiapas, SE Mexico 16°15′N 92°06′W
Comitán de Domínguez *see* Comitán
Commachio *see* Comacchio
Commander Islands *see* Komandorskiye Ostrova
103 O10 **Commentry** Allier, C France 46°18′N 02°46′E
23 T2 **Commerce** Georgia, SE USA 34°12′N 83°27′W
27 R8 **Commerce** Oklahoma, C USA 36°55′N 94°52′W
25 V5 **Commerce** Texas, SW USA 33°16′N 95°52′W
37 T4 **Commerce City** Colorado, C USA 39°45′N 104°54′W
103 S5 **Commercy** Meuse, NE France 48°46′N 05°36′E
55 W9 **Commewijne** *var.* Commewyne. ◆ *district* NE Surinam
Commewyne *see* Commewijne
15 P8 **Commissaires, Lac des** ◎ Québec, SE Canada
64 A12 **Commissioner's Point** *headland* W Bermuda
9 O7 **Committee Bay** *bay* Nunavut, N Canada
106 D7 **Como** *anc.* Comum. Lombardia, N Italy 45°48′N 09°05′E
63 J19 **Comodoro Rivadavia** Chubut, SE Argentina 45°50′S 67°30′W
106 D6 **Como, Lago di** *var.* Lario, *Eng.* Lake Como, *Ger.* Comer See. ◎ N Italy
Como, Lake *see* Como, Lago di
40 E7 **Comondú** Baja California Sur, NW Mexico 26°01′N 111°50′W
116 F12 **Comorâşte** *Hung.* Komornok. Caraș-Severin, SW Romania 45°13′N 21°34′E
Comores, République Fédérale Islamique des *see* Comoros
155 G24 **Comorin, Cape** *headland* SE India 08°00′N 77°10′E
172 M8 **Comoro Basin** *undersea feature* SW Indian Ocean 14°00′S 44°00′E
172 K14 **Comoro Islands** *island group* W Indian Ocean
172 H13 **Comoros** *off.* Federal Islamic Republic of the Comoros, *Fr.* République Fédérale Islamique des Comores. ◆ *republic* W Indian Ocean
Comoros, Federal Islamic Republic of the *see* Comoros
10 L17 **Comox** Vancouver Island, British Columbia, SW Canada 49°40′N 124°55′W
103 O4 **Compiègne** Oise, N France 49°25′N 02°50′E
Complutum *see* Alcalá de Henares
Compniacum *see* Cognac
40 K12 **Compostela** Nayarit, C Mexico 21°12′N 104°52′W
Compostella *see* Santiago
60 L11 **Comprida, Ilha** *island* S Brazil
117 N11 **Comrat** *Rus.* Komrat. S Moldova 46°18′N 28°40′E
25 O11 **Comstock** Texas, SW USA 29°39′N 101°10′W
31 P9 **Comstock Park** Michigan, N USA 43°00′N 85°40′W
193 N3 **Comstock Seamount** *undersea feature* N Pacific Ocean 48°15′N 156°55′W
Comum *see* Como
159 N17 **Cona** Xizang Zizhiqu, W China 27°59′N 91°54′E
76 H14 **Conakry** ● (Guinea) SW Guinea 09°31′N 13°43′W
76 H14 **Conakry** ✈ SW Guinea 09°37′N 13°32′W
Conamara *see* Connemara
Conca *see* Cuenca
25 Q12 **Concan** Texas, SW USA 29°27′N 99°43′W
102 F6 **Concarneau** Finistère, NW France 47°53′N 03°55′W
83 O17 **Conceição** Sofala, C Mozambique 18°47′S 36°18′E
59 K15 **Conceição do Araguaia** Pará, NE Brazil 08°15′S 49°15′W
58 F10 **Conceição do Maú** Roraima, W Brazil 03°35′N 59°52′W
61 D14 **Concepción** *var.* Concepcion. Corrientes, NE Argentina 28°25′S 57°54′W
62 J8 **Concepción** Tucumán, N Argentina 27°20′S 65°35′W
57 O17 **Concepción** Santa Cruz, E Bolivia 16°15′S 62°08′W
62 G13 **Concepción** Bío Bío, C Chile 36°47′S 73°01′W
54 E14 **Concepción** Putumayo, S Colombia 0°03′N 75°35′W
62 O5 **Concepción** *var.* Villa Concepción. Concepción, C Paraguay 23°26′S 57°24′W
62 O5 **Concepción** *off.* Departamento de Concepción. ◆ *department* E Paraguay
Concepción *see* La Concepción
Concepción de la Vega *see* La Vega
41 N9 **Concepción del Oro** Zacatecas, C Mexico 24°38′N 101°25′W
61 D18 **Concepción del Uruguay** Entre Ríos, E Argentina 32°30′S 58°15′W
Concepción, Departamento de *see* Concepción
42 K11 **Concepción, Volcán** ⛰ SW Nicaragua 11°31′N 85°37′W
44 J4 **Conception Island** *island* C Bahamas
35 P14 **Conception, Point** *headland* California, W USA 34°27′N 120°28′W
54 H6 **Concha** Zulia, W Venezuela 09°02′N 71°45′W
60 L9 **Conchas** São Paulo, S Brazil 23°00′S 47°58′W
37 U11 **Conchas Dam** New Mexico, SW USA 35°21′N 104°11′W
37 U10 **Conchas Lake** ⊠ New Mexico, SW USA
102 M5 **Conches-en-Ouche** Eure, N France 49°00′N 01°00′E
37 N12 **Concho** Arizona, SW USA 34°28′N 109°33′W
40 J5 **Conchos, Río** ⛴ NW Mexico
41 O8 **Conchos, Río** ⛴ C Mexico
108 C8 **Concise** Vaud, W Switzerland 46°52′N 06°40′E
35 N8 **Concord** California, W USA 37°58′N 122°01′W
19 O9 **Concord** *state capital* New Hampshire, NE USA 43°10′N 71°32′W
21 R10 **Concord** North Carolina, SE USA 35°25′N 80°34′W
61 D17 **Concordia** Entre Ríos, E Argentina 31°25′S 58°W
60 I13 **Concórdia** Santa Catarina, S Brazil 27°14′S 52°01′W
54 D9 **Concordia** Antioquia, W Colombia 06°03′N 75°57′W
40 J10 **Concordia** Sinaloa, C Mexico 23°18′N 106°02′W
57 I19 **Concordia** Tacna, SW Peru 18°12′S 70°19′W
27 N3 **Concordia** Kansas, C USA 39°35′N 97°39′W
27 S4 **Concordia** Missouri, C USA 38°58′N 93°34′W
167 S7 **Con Cuông** Nghê An, N Vietnam 19°02′N 104°54′E
167 T15 **Côn Đao** *var.* Con Son. *island* S Vietnam
Condate *see* Rennes, Ille-et-Vilaine, France
Condate *see* St-Claude, Jura, France
Condate *see* Montereau-Faut-Yonne, Seine-St-Denis, France
29 P8 **Conde** South Dakota, N USA 45°08′N 98°07′W
42 J8 **Condega** Estelí, NW Nicaragua 13°19′N 86°26′W
103 P2 **Condé-sur-l'Escaut** Nord, N France 50°27′N 03°36′E
102 K5 **Condé-sur-Noireau** Calvados, N France 48°52′N 00°31′W
Condivincum *see* Nantes
183 P8 **Condobolin** New South Wales, SE Australia 33°04′S 147°08′E
102 L15 **Condom** Gers, S France 43°56′N 00°23′E
32 J11 **Condon** Oregon, NW USA 45°15′N 120°10′W
54 D9 **Condoto** Chocó, W Colombia 05°06′N 76°37′W
23 P7 **Conecuh River** ⛴ Alabama/Florida, SE USA
106 H7 **Conegliano** Veneto, NE Italy 45°53′N 12°18′E
61 C19 **Conesa** Buenos Aires, E Argentina 33°36′S 60°21′W
14 F15 **Conestogo** ⛴ Ontario, S Canada
Confluentes *see* Koblenz
102 L10 **Confolens** Charente, W France 46°00′N 00°40′E
36 J4 **Confusion Range** ▲ Utah, W USA
62 N6 **Confuso, Río** ⛴ C Paraguay
21 R12 **Congaree River** ⛴ South Carolina, SE USA
Công Hoa Xa Hôi Chu Nghia Viêt Nam *see* Vietnam
160 K12 **Congjiang** *var.* Bingmei. Guizhou, S China 25°48′N 108°55′E
79 G18 **Congo** *off.* Republic of the Congo, *Fr.* Moyen-Congo; *prev.* Middle Congo. ◆ *republic* C Africa
79 K19 **Congo** *off.* Democratic Republic of Congo; *prev.* Zaire, Belgian Congo, Congo (Kinshasa). ◆ *republic* C Africa
67 T11 **Congo** *var.* Kongo, *Fr.* Zaire. ⛴ C Africa
Congo *see* Zaire (province) Angola
68 G12 **Congo Basin** *drainage basin* W Dem. Rep. Congo
67 Q11 **Congo Canyon** *var.* Congo Seavalley, Congo Submarine Canyon. *undersea feature* E Atlantic Ocean 06°00′S 11°50′E
Congo Cone *see* Congo Fan
Congo/Congo (Kinshasa) *see* Congo (Democratic Republic of)
65 P15 **Congo Fan** *var.* Congo Cone. *undersea feature* E Atlantic Ocean 06°00′S 09°00′E
Congo Seavalley *see* Congo Canyon
Congo Submarine Canyon *see* Congo Canyon
Coni *see* Cuneo
63 H18 **Cónico, Cerro** ▲ SW Argentina 43°12′S 71°42′W
Conimbria/Conimbriga *see* Coimbra
Conjeeveram *see* Kānchīpuram
11 R13 **Conklin** Alberta, C Canada 55°36′N 111°06′W
24 M1 **Conlen** Texas, SW USA 36°16′N 102°10′W
Con, Loch *see* Conn, Lough
Connacht *see* Connaught
97 B17 **Connaught** *var.* Connacht, *Ir.* Chonnacht, Cúige. *cultural region* W Ireland
31 V10 **Conneaut** Ohio, N USA 41°56′N 80°32′W
18 L13 **Connecticut** *off.* State of Connecticut, *also known as* Blue Law State, Constitution State, Land of Steady Habits, Nutmeg State. ◆ *state* NE USA
19 N8 **Connecticut** ⛴ Canada/USA
19 O6 **Connecticut Lakes** *lakes* New Hampshire, NE USA
32 K9 **Connell** Washington, NW USA 46°39′N 118°51′W
97 B17 **Connemara** *Ir.* Conamara. *physical region* W Ireland
31 Q14 **Connersville** Indiana, N USA 39°38′N 85°15′W
97 B16 **Conn, Lough** *Ir.* Loch Con. ◎ W Ireland
35 X6 **Connors Pass** *pass* Nevada, W USA
181 X7 **Connors Range** ▲ Queensland, E Australia
56 E7 **Cononaco, Río** ⛴ E Ecuador
29 W13 **Conrad** Iowa, C USA 42°13′N 92°52′W
33 R7 **Conrad** Montana, NW USA 48°10′N 111°58′W
25 W10 **Conroe** Texas, SW USA 30°19′N 95°28′W
25 V10 **Conroe, Lake** ⊠ Texas, SW USA
61 C17 **Conscripto Bernardi** Entre Ríos, E Argentina 31°03′S 59°05′W
59 M20 **Conselheiro Lafaiete** Minas Gerais, SE Brazil 20°40′S 43°48′W
Consentia *see* Cosenza
97 L14 **Consett** N England, United Kingdom 54°50′N 01°53′W
44 B5 **Consolación del Sur** Pinar del Río, W Cuba 22°32′N 83°32′W
Con Son *see* Côn Đao
11 R15 **Consort** Alberta, SW Canada 51°58′N 110°44′W
Constance *see* Konstanz
108 I6 **Constance, Lake** *Ger.* Bodensee. ◎ C Europe
104 G9 **Constância** Santarém, C Portugal 39°29′N 08°22′W
117 N14 **Constanța** *var.* Küstendje, *Eng.* Constanza, *Ger.* Konstanza, *Turk.* Küstence. Constanța, SE Romania 44°09′N 28°37′E
116 L14 **Constanța** ◆ *county* SE Romania
Constantia *see* Coutances
Constantia *see* Konstanz
104 K13 **Constantina** Andalucía, S Spain 37°54′N 05°36′W
74 L5 **Constantine** *var.* Qacentina, *Ar.* Qoussantîna. NE Algeria 36°23′N 06°44′E
39 O14 **Constantine, Cape** *headland* Alaska, USA 58°23′N 158°53′W
Constantinople *see* İstanbul
Constantiola *see* Oltenița
Constanz *see* Konstanz
Constanza *see* Constanța
62 G13 **Constitución** Maule, C Chile 35°20′S 72°28′W
61 D17 **Constitución** Salto, N Uruguay 31°05′S 57°51′W
Constitution State *see* Connecticut
105 N10 **Consuegra** Castilla-La Mancha, C Spain 39°28′N 03°36′W
181 X9 **Consuelo Peak** ▲ Queensland, E Australia 24°45′S 148°01′E
56 E11 **Contamana** Loreto, N Peru 07°19′S 75°04′W
Contrasto, Colle del *see* Contrasto, Portella del
107 K23 **Contrasto, Portella del** *var.* Colle del Contrasto. *pass* Sicilia, Italy, C Mediterranean Sea
54 G8 **Contratación** Santander, C Colombia 06°18′N 73°27′W
102 M8 **Contres** Loir-et-Cher, C France 47°24′N 01°30′E
107 O17 **Conversano** Puglia, SE Italy 40°58′N 17°07′E
27 U11 **Conway** Arkansas, C USA 35°05′N 92°27′W
19 O8 **Conway** New Hampshire, NE USA 43°58′N 71°05′W
21 U13 **Conway** South Carolina, SE USA 33°51′N 79°04′W
25 N2 **Conway** Texas, SW USA 35°10′N 101°23′W
27 U11 **Conway, Lake** ⊠ Arkansas, C USA
27 N7 **Conway Springs** Kansas, C USA 37°23′N 97°38′W
97 J18 **Conwy** N Wales, United Kingdom 53°17′N 03°51′W
23 T3 **Conyers** Georgia, SE USA 33°40′N 84°01′W
Coo *see* Kos
182 F4 **Coober Pedy** South Australia 29°01′S 134°47′E
181 P2 **Cooinda** Northern Territory, N Australia 12°54′S 132°31′E
182 B6 **Cook** South Australia 30°37′S 130°26′E
29 W4 **Cook** Minnesota, N USA 47°51′N 92°41′W
191 N6 **Cook, Baie de** *bay* Moorea, W French Polynesia
10 J16 **Cook, Cape** *headland* Vancouver Island, British Columbia, SW Canada 50°04′N 127°52′W
37 Q15 **Cookes Peak** ▲ New Mexico, SW USA 32°32′N 107°43′W
20 L8 **Cookeville** Tennessee, S USA 36°10′N 85°30′W
175 P9 **Cook Fracture Zone** *tectonic feature* S Pacific Ocean
Cook, Grand Récif de *see* Cook, Récif de
39 Q12 **Cook Inlet** *inlet* Alaska, USA
191 X2 **Cook Island** *island* Line Islands, E Kiribati
190 J14 **Cook Islands** ◇ *territory in free association with New Zealand* S Pacific Ocean
Cook, Mount *see* Aoraki
187 O15 **Cook, Récif de** *var.* Grand Récif de Cook. *reef* S New Caledonia
14 G14 **Cookstown** Ontario, S Canada 44°12′N 79°39′W
97 F15 **Cookstown** *Ir.* An Chorr Chríochach. C Northern Ireland, United Kingdom 54°39′N 06°45′W
185 K14 **Cook Strait** *var.* Raukawa. *strait* New Zealand
181 W3 **Cooktown** Queensland, NE Australia 15°28′S 145°15′E
183 P6 **Coolabah** New South Wales, SE Australia 31°03′S 146°42′E
182 J11 **Coola Coola Swamp** *wetland* South Australia
183 S7 **Coolah** New South Wales, SE Australia 31°49′S 149°43′E
183 P9 **Coolamon** New South Wales, SE Australia 34°49′S 147°13′E
183 T4 **Coolatai** New South Wales, SE Australia 29°16′S 150°45′E
180 K12 **Coolgardie** Western Australia 31°01′S 121°12′E
36 L14 **Coolidge** Arizona, SW USA 32°58′N 111°29′W
25 U8 **Coolidge** Texas, SW USA 31°45′N 96°39′W
183 Q11 **Cooma** New South Wales, SE Australia 36°16′S 149°09′E
Coomassie *see* Kumasi
183 R6 **Coonabarabran** New South Wales, SE Australia 31°19′S 149°18′E
182 I10 **Coonalpyn** South Australia 35°43′S 139°50′E
183 R6 **Coonamble** New South Wales, SE Australia 30°56′S 148°22′E
Coondapoor *see* Kundāpura
155 G21 **Coonoor** Tamil Nādu, SE India 11°21′N 76°46′E
29 U14 **Coon Rapids** Iowa, C USA 41°52′N 94°40′W
29 V8 **Coon Rapids** Minnesota, N USA 45°12′N 93°18′W
25 V5 **Cooper** Texas, SW USA 33°23′N 95°42′W
181 U9 **Cooper Creek** *var.* Barcoo, Cooper's Creek. *seasonal river* Queensland/South Australia
39 R12 **Cooper Landing** Alaska, USA 60°27′N 149°59′W
21 T14 **Cooper River** ⛴ South Carolina, SE USA
Cooper's Creek *see* Cooper Creek
44 H1 **Coopers Town** Great Abaco, N Bahamas 26°46′N 77°27′W
18 J10 **Cooperstown** New York, NE USA 42°43′N 74°56′W
29 P4 **Cooperstown** North Dakota, N USA 47°26′N 98°07′W
31 P9 **Coopersville** Michigan, N USA 43°03′N 85°55′W
182 D7 **Coorabie** South Australia 31°57′S 132°18′E
23 Q3 **Coosa River** ⛴ Alabama/Georgia, S USA
32 E14 **Coos Bay** Oregon, NW USA 43°22′N 124°13′W
183 Q9 **Cootamundra** New South Wales, SE Australia 34°41′S 148°03′E
97 E16 **Cootehill** *Ir.* Muinchille. N Ireland 54°04′N 07°05′W
Čop *see* Chop
57 J17 **Copacabana** La Paz, W Bolivia 16°11′S 69°02′W
63 H14 **Copahué, Volcán** ⛰ C Chile 37°56′S 71°04′W
41 U16 **Copainalá** Chiapas, SE Mexico 17°04′N 93°13′W
32 F8 **Copalis Beach** Washington, NW USA 47°05′N 124°11′W
42 F6 **Copán** ◆ *department* W Honduras
Copán *see* Copán Ruinas
25 T14 **Copano Bay** *bay* NW Gulf of Mexico
42 F6 **Copán Ruinas** *var.* Copán. Copán, W Honduras 14°52′N 89°10′W
Copenhagen *see* København
107 Q19 **Copertino** Puglia, SE Italy 40°16′N 18°03′E
62 H7 **Copiapó** Atacama, N Chile 27°17′S 70°25′W
62 G8 **Copiapó, Bahía** *bay* N Chile
62 G7 **Copiapó, Río** ⛴ N Chile
114 M12 **Çöpköy** Edirne, NW Turkey 41°14′N 26°51′E
182 I5 **Copley** South Australia 30°36′S 138°26′E
106 H9 **Copparo** Emilia-Romagna, C Italy 44°53′N 11°53′E
55 V10 **Coppename Rivier** *var.* Koppename. ⛴ C Surinam
25 S9 **Copperas Cove** Texas, SW USA 31°07′N 97°54′W
82 J13 **Copperbelt** ◆ *province* C Zambia
39 S11 **Copper Center** Alaska, USA 61°57′N 145°21′W
8 K8 **Coppermine** ⛴ Northwest Territories/Nunavut, N Canada
Coppermine *see* Kugluktuk
39 T11 **Copper River** ⛴ Alaska, USA
Copper State *see* Arizona
116 I11 **Copșa Mică** *Ger.* Kleinkopisch, *Hung.* Kiskapus. Sibiu, C Romania 46°06′N 24°15′E
158 J14 **Coqên** Xizang Zizhiqu, W China 31°13′N 85°12′E
Coquilhatville *see* Mbandaka
32 E14 **Coquille** Oregon, NW USA 43°11′N 124°12′W
62 G9 **Coquimbo** Coquimbo, N Chile 30°S 71°18′W
62 G9 **Coquimbo** *off.* Región de Coquimbo. ◆ *region* C Chile
Coquimbo, Región de *see* Coquimbo
116 I15 **Corabia** Olt, S Romania 43°46′N 24°31′E
57 F17 **Coracora** Ayacucho, SW Peru 15°03′S 73°45′W
Cora Droma Rúisc *see* Carrick-on-Shannon
44 K9 **Corail** SW Haiti 18°34′N 73°53′W
183 V4 **Coraki** New South Wales, SE Australia 29°01′S 153°15′E
180 G8 **Coral Bay** Western Australia 23°02′S 113°51′E
23 Y16 **Coral Gables** Florida, SE USA 25°43′N 80°16′W
9 P8 **Coral Harbour** Southampton Island, Nunavut, NE Canada 64°10′N 83°15′W
192 I9 **Coral Sea** *sea* SW Pacific Ocean
174 M7 **Coral Sea Basin** *undersea feature* N Coral Sea
192 H9 **Coral Sea Islands** ◇ *Australian external territory* SW Pacific Ocean
182 M12 **Corangamite, Lake** ◎ Victoria, SE Australia
Corantijn Rivier *see* Courantyne River
18 B14 **Coraopolis** Pennsylvania, NE USA 40°28′N 80°08′W
107 N17 **Corato** Puglia, SE Italy 41°09′N 16°25′E
103 O17 **Corbières** ▲ S France
103 P8 **Corbigny** Nièvre, C France 47°15′N 03°42′E
21 N7 **Corbin** Kentucky, S USA 36°57′N 84°06′W
104 L14 **Corbones** ⛴ SW Spain
Corcaigh *see* Cork
35 R11 **Corcoran** California, W USA 36°06′N 119°33′W
47 T14 **Corcovado, Golfo** *gulf* S Chile
63 G18 **Corcovado, Volcán** ⛰ S Chile 43°13′S 72°45′W
104 F3 **Corcubión** Galicia, NW Spain 42°56′N 09°12′W
Corcyra Nigra *see* Korčula
60 Q9 **Cordeiro** Rio de Janeiro, SE Brazil 22°01′S 42°20′W
23 T6 **Cordele** Georgia, SE USA 31°59′N 83°49′W
26 L11 **Cordell** Oklahoma, C USA 35°17′N 98°59′W
103 N14 **Cordes** Tarn, S France 44°03′N 01°57′E
62 O6 **Cordillera** *off.* Departamento de la Cordillera. ◆ *department* C Paraguay
Cordillera *see* Cacaguatique, Cordillera
Cordillera, Departamento de la *see* Cordillera
182 K1 **Cordillo Downs** South Australia 26°44′S 140°37′E
62 K10 **Córdoba** Córdoba, C Argentina 31°25′S 64°11′W
41 R14 **Córdoba** Veracruz-Llave, E Mexico 18°55′N 96°55′W
104 M13 **Córdoba** *var.* Cordoba, *Eng.* Cordova; *anc.* Corduba. Andalucía, SW Spain 37°53′N 04°46′W
62 K11 **Córdoba** *off.* Provincia de Córdoba. ◆ *province* C Argentina
54 D7 **Córdoba** *off.* Departamento de Córdoba. ◆ *province* NW Colombia
104 L13 **Córdoba** ◆ *province* Andalucía, S Spain
Córdoba, Departamento de *see* Córdoba
Córdoba, Provincia de *see* Córdoba
62 K10 **Córdoba, Sierras de** ▲ C Argentina
23 O3 **Cordova** Alabama, S USA 33°45′N 87°10′W
39 S12 **Cordova** Alaska, USA 60°32′N 145°45′W
Cordova/Cordoba *see* Córdoba
Corduba *see* Córdoba
Corentyne River *see* Courantyne River
Corfu *see* Kérkyra
104 J9 **Coria** Extremadura, W Spain 39°59′N 06°32′W
104 J14 **Coria del Río** Andalucía, S Spain 37°18′N 06°04′W
183 S8 **Coricudgy, Mount** ▲ New South Wales, SE Australia 32°49′S 150°28′E
107 N20 **Corigliano Calabro** Calabria, SW Italy 39°36′N 16°32′E
Corinium/Corinium Dobunorum *see* Cirencester
23 N1 **Corinth** Mississippi, S USA 34°56′N 88°29′W
Corinth *see* Kórinthos
Corinth Canal *see* Dióryga Korinthou
Corinth, Gulf of/Corinthiacus Sinus *see* Korinthiakós Kólpos
Corinthus *see* Kórinthos
42 I9 **Corinto** Chinandega, NW Nicaragua 12°29′N 87°14′W
97 C21 **Cork** *Ir.* Corcaigh. S Ireland 51°54′N 07°06′W
97 C21 **Cork** *Ir.* Corcaigh. *cultural region* SW Ireland
97 C21 **Cork** ✈ Cork, SW Ireland 51°52′N 08°25′W
97 D21 **Cork Harbour** *Ir.* Cuan Chorcaí. *inlet* SW Ireland
107 I23 **Corleone** Sicilia, Italy, C Mediterranean Sea 37°49′N 13°18′E
114 N13 **Çorlu** Tekirdağ, NW Turkey 41°11′N 27°48′E
114 N12 **Çorlu Çayı** ⛴ NW Turkey
Cormaiore *see* Courmayeur
11 V13 **Cormorant** Manitoba, C Canada 54°12′N 100°33′W
23 T2 **Cornelia** Georgia, SE USA 34°30′N 83°31′W
60 J10 **Cornélio Procópio** Paraná, S Brazil 23°07′S 50°40′W
55 V9 **Corneliskondre** Sipaliwini, N Surinam 05°21′N 56°10′W
30 J5 **Cornell** Wisconsin, N USA 45°09′N 91°10′W
13 S12 **Corner Brook** Newfoundland, Newfoundland and Labrador, E Canada 48°58′N 57°58′W
Corner Rise Seamounts *see* Corner Seamounts
64 I9 **Corner Seamounts** *var.* Corner Rise Seamounts. *undersea feature* NW Atlantic Ocean 35°30′N 51°30′W
116 M9 **Cornești** *Rus.* Korneshty. C Moldova 47°23′N 28°00′E
Corneto *see* Tarquinia
Cornhusker State *see* Nebraska
27 X8 **Corning** Arkansas, C USA 36°26′N 90°35′W
35 N5 **Corning** California, W USA 39°54′N 122°12′W
29 U15 **Corning** Iowa, C USA 40°58′N 94°46′W
18 G11 **Corning** New York, NE USA 42°08′N 77°03′W
Corn Islands *see* Maíz, Islas del
107 J14 **Corno Grande** ▲ C Italy 42°26′N 13°29′E
15 N13 **Cornwall** Ontario, SE Canada 45°02′N 74°45′W
97 H25 **Cornwall** *cultural region* SW England, United Kingdom
97 G25 **Cornwall, Cape** *headland* SW England, United Kingdom 50°11′N 05°39′W
54 J4 **Coro** *prev.* Santa Ana de Coro. Falcón, NW Venezuela 11°27′N 69°41′W
57 J18 **Corocoro** La Paz, W Bolivia 17°10′S 68°28′W
57 K17 **Coroico** La Paz, W Bolivia 16°09′S 67°45′W
184 M5 **Coromandel** Waikato, North Island, New Zealand 36°47′S 175°30′E
155 K20 **Coromandel Coast** *coast* E India
184 M5 **Coromandel Peninsula** *peninsula* North Island, New Zealand
184 M6 **Coromandel Range** ▲ North Island, New Zealand
171 N5 **Coron** Busuanga Island, W Philippines 12°02′N 120°10′E
35 T15 **Corona** California, W USA 33°52′N 117°34′W
37 T12 **Corona** New Mexico, SW USA 34°15′N 105°36′W
11 U17 **Coronach** Saskatchewan, S Canada 49°07′N 105°33′W
35 U17 **Coronado** California, W USA 32°41′N 117°10′W
43 N15 **Coronado, Bahía de** *bay* S Costa Rica
11 R15 **Coronation** Alberta, SW Canada 52°06′N 111°25′W
8 K7 **Coronation Gulf** *gulf* Nunavut, N Canada
194 I1 **Coronation Island** *island* Antarctica
39 X14 **Coronation Island** *island* Alexander Archipelago, Alaska, USA
61 B18 **Coronda** Santa Fe, C Argentina 31°58′S 60°56′W
63 F14 **Coronel** Bío Bío, C Chile 37°01′S 73°08′W
61 D20 **Coronel Brandsen** *var.* Brandsen. Buenos Aires, E Argentina 35°08′S 58°15′W
62 K4 **Coronel Cornejo** Salta, N Argentina 22°46′S 63°49′W
61 B24 **Coronel Dorrego** Buenos Aires, E Argentina 38°38′S 61°15′W
62 P6 **Coronel Oviedo** Caaguazú, SE Paraguay 25°24′S 56°30′W

◆ Country ● Country Capital ◇ Dependent Territory ○ Dependent Territory Capital ◆ Administrative Regions ✈ International Airport ▲ Mountain ▲ Mountain Range ⛰ Volcano ⛴ River ◎ Lake ⊠ Reservoir

CORONEL PRINGLES – CULGOA RIVER

61 B23 **Coronel Pringles** Buenos Aires, E Argentina 37°56′S 61°25′W
61 B23 **Coronel Suárez** Buenos Aires, E Argentina 37°30′S 61°52′W
61 E22 **Coronel Vidal** Buenos Aires, E Argentina 37°28′S 57°45′W
55 V9 **Coronie** ◐ *district* NW Surinam
57 G17 **Coropuna, Nevado** ▲ S Peru 15°31′S 72°31′W
Çorovoda *see* Çorovodë
113 L22 **Çorovodë** *var.* Çorovoda. Berat, S Albania 40°29′N 20°15′E
183 P11 **Corowa** New South Wales, SE Australia 36°01′S 146°22′E
42 G1 **Corozal** Corozal, N Belize 18°23′N 88°23′W
54 E6 **Corozal** Sucre, NW Colombia 09°18′N 75°19′W
42 G1 **Corozal** ◐ *district* N Belize
25 T14 **Corpus Christi** Texas, SW USA 27°48′N 97°24′W
25 T14 **Corpus Christi Bay** *inlet* Texas, SW USA
25 R14 **Corpus Christi, Lake** ⊠ Texas, SW USA
63 F16 **Corral** Los Lagos, C Chile 39°55′S 73°30′W
105 O9 **Corral de Almaguer** Castilla-La Mancha, C Spain 39°45′N 03°10′W
104 K6 **Corrales** Castilla-León, N Spain 41°22′N 05°44′W
37 R11 **Corrales** New Mexico, SW USA 35°11′N 106°37′W
Corrán Tuathail *see* Carrauntoohil
106 F9 **Correggio** Emilia-Romagna, C Italy 44°47′N 10°46′E
59 M16 **Corrente** Piauí, E Brazil 10°29′S 45°11′W
59 I19 **Correntes, Rio** ≈ SW Brazil
103 N12 **Corrèze** ◐ *department* C France
97 C17 **Corrib, Lough** *Ir.* Loch Coirib. ◎ W Ireland
61 C14 **Corrientes** Corrientes, NE Argentina 27°29′S 58°42′W
61 D15 **Corrientes** *off.* Provincia de Corrientes. ◐ *province* NE Argentina
44 A5 **Corrientes, Cabo** *headland* W Cuba 21°48′N 84°30′W
40 I13 **Corrientes, Cabo** *headland* SW Mexico 20°25′N 105°42′W
Corrientes, Provincia de *see* Corrientes
61 C16 **Corrientes, Río** ≈ NE Argentina
56 E8 **Corrientes, Río** ≈ Ecuador/Peru
25 W9 **Corrigan** Texas, SW USA 31°00′N 94°49′W
55 U9 **Corriverton** E Guyana 05°55′N 57°09′W
Corriza *see* Korçë
183 Q11 **Corryong** Victoria, SE Australia 36°14′S 147°54′E
103 F2 **Corse** *Eng.* Corsica. ◐ *region* France, C Mediterranean Sea
101 X13 **Corse** *Eng.* Corsica. *island* France, C Mediterranean Sea
103 Y12 **Corse, Cap** *headland* Corse, France, C Mediterranean Sea 43°01′N 09°25′E
103 X15 **Corse-du-Sud** ◐ *department* Corse, France, C Mediterranean Sea
29 P11 **Corsica** South Dakota, N USA 43°25′N 98°24′W
Corsica *see* Corse
25 U7 **Corsicana** Texas, SW USA 32°05′N 96°27′W
103 Y15 **Corte** Corse, France, C Mediterranean Sea 42°18′N 09°08′E
63 G16 **Corte Alto** Los Lagos, S Chile 40°58′S 73°04′W
104 I13 **Cortegana** Andalucía, S Spain 37°55′N 06°49′W
43 N15 **Cortés** *var.* Ciudad Cortés. Puntarenas, SE Costa Rica 08°59′N 83°32′W
42 G5 **Cortés** ◐ *department* NW Honduras
37 P8 **Cortez** Colorado, C USA 37°22′N 108°36′W
Cortez, Sea of *see* California, Golfo de
106 H6 **Cortina d'Ampezzo** Veneto, NE Italy 46°33′N 12°09′E
18 H11 **Cortland** New York, NE USA 42°34′N 76°09′W
31 V11 **Cortland** Ohio, N USA 41°19′N 80°43′W
106 H12 **Cortona** Toscana, C Italy 43°15′N 12°01′E
76 H13 **Corubal, Rio** ≈ E Guinea-Bissau
104 G10 **Coruche** Santarém, C Portugal 38°58′N 08°31′W
Çoruh *see* Rize
137 R11 **Çoruh Nehri** *Geor.* Chorokh, *Rus.* Chorokhi. ≈ Georgia/Turkey
136 K12 **Çorum** *var.* Chorum. Çorum, N Turkey 40°31′N 34°57′E
136 J12 **Çorum** *var.* Chorum. ◐ *province* N Turkey
59 H19 **Corumbá** Mato Grosso do Sul, S Brazil 19°S 57°35′W
14 D16 **Corunna** Ontario, S Canada 42°49′N 82°25′W
Corunna *see* A Coruña
32 F12 **Corvallis** Oregon, NW USA 44°35′N 122°36′W
64 M1 **Corvo** *var.* Ilha do Corvo. *island* Azores, Portugal, NE Atlantic Ocean
Corvo, Ilha do *see* Corvo
31 O16 **Corydon** Indiana, N USA 38°12′N 86°07′W
29 V16 **Corydon** Iowa, C USA 40°45′N 93°19′W
Cos *see* Kos
40 I9 **Cosalá** Sinaloa, C Mexico 24°25′N 106°39′W
41 R15 **Cosamaloapan** *var.* Cosamaloapan de Carpio. Veracruz-Llave, E Mexico 18°23′N 95°50′W
Cosamaloapan de Carpio *see* Cosamaloapan
107 N21 **Cosenza** *anc.* Consentia. Calabria, SW Italy 39°17′N 16°15′E
31 T13 **Coshocton** Ohio, N USA 40°16′N 81°53′W
42 H9 **Cosigüina, Punta** *headland* NW Nicaragua 12°53′N 87°42′W
29 T9 **Cosmos** Minnesota, N USA 44°56′N 94°42′W
103 O8 **Cosne-Cours-sur-Loire** Nièvre, C France 47°25′N 02°56′E
108 B9 **Cossonay** Vaud, W Switzerland 46°37′N 06°28′E
Cossyra *see* Pantelleria
47 R4 **Costa, Cordillera de la** *var.* Cordillera de Venezuela. ▲▲ N Venezuela
42 K13 **Costa Rica** *off.* Republic of Costa Rica. ◆ *republic* Central America
Costa Rica, Republic of *see* Costa Rica
43 N15 **Costeña, Fila** ▲▲ S Costa Rica
Costermansville *see* Bukavu
116 I14 **Costeşti** Argeş, SW Romania 44°40′N 24°53′E
37 S8 **Costilla** New Mexico, SW USA 36°58′N 105°31′W
35 O7 **Cosumnes River** ≈ California, W USA
101 O16 **Coswig** Sachsen, E Germany 51°07′N 13°36′E
101 M14 **Coswig** Sachsen-Anhalt, E Germany 51°53′N 12°26′E
Cosyra *see* Pantelleria
171 Q7 **Cotabato** Mindanao, S Philippines 07°13′N 124°12′E
56 C5 **Cotacachi** ▲ N Ecuador 0°29′N 78°17′W
57 L21 **Cotagaita** Potosí, S Bolivia 20°47′S 65°40′W
103 V15 **Côte d'Azur** *prev.* Nice. ✈ (Nice) Alpes-Maritimes, SE France 43°40′N 07°12′E
Côte d'Ivoire *see* Ivory Coast
Côte d'Ivoire, République de la *see* Ivory Coast
103 R7 **Côte d'Or** ◐ *department* E France
103 R8 **Côte d'Or** *cultural region* C France
Côte Française des Somalis *see* Djibouti
102 J4 **Cotentin** *peninsula* N France
102 G6 **Côtes d'Armor** *prev.* Côtes-du-Nord. ◐ *department* NW France
Côtes-du-Nord *see* Côtes d'Armor
Cöthen *see* Köthen
Côtière, Chaine *see* Coast Mountains
40 M13 **Cotija** *var.* Cotija de la Paz. Michoacán, SW Mexico 19°49′N 102°39′W
Cotija de la Paz *see* Cotija
77 R16 **Cotonou** *var.* Kotonu. S Benin 06°24′N 02°26′E
77 R16 **Cotonou** ✈ S Benin 06°31′N 02°18′E
56 B6 **Cotopaxi** *prev.* León. ◐ *province* C Ecuador
56 C6 **Cotopaxi** ∧ N Ecuador 0°42′S 78°24′W
Cotrone *see* Crotone
97 L21 **Cotswold Hills** *var.* Cotswolds. *hill range* S England, United Kingdom
Cotswolds *see* Cotswold Hills
32 F13 **Cottage Grove** Oregon, NW USA 43°48′N 123°03′W
21 S14 **Cottageville** South Carolina, SE USA 32°55′N 80°28′W
101 P14 **Cottbus** *Lus.* Chośebuz; *prev.* Kottbus. Brandenburg, E Germany 51°42′N 14°22′E
27 U9 **Cotter** Arkansas, C USA 36°16′N 92°30′W
106 A9 **Cottian Alps** *Fr.* Alpes Cottiennes, *It.* Alpi Cozie. ▲▲ France/Italy
Cottiennes, Alpes *see* Cottian Alps
Cotton State, The *see* Alabama
22 G4 **Cotton Valley** Louisiana, S USA 32°49′N 93°25′W
36 L12 **Cottonwood** Arizona, SW USA 34°43′N 112°00′W
32 M10 **Cottonwood** Idaho, NW USA 46°01′N 116°20′W
29 S9 **Cottonwood** Minnesota, N USA 44°37′N 95°41′W
25 Q7 **Cottonwood** Texas, SW USA 32°12′N 99°14′W
27 O5 **Cottonwood Falls** Kansas, C USA 38°21′N 96°33′W
36 L3 **Cottonwood Heights** Utah, W USA 40°37′N 111°48′W
29 S10 **Cottonwood River** ≈ Minnesota, N USA
45 O9 **Cotuí** C Dominican Republic 19°04′N 70°10′W
25 Q13 **Cotulla** Texas, SW USA 28°27′N 99°15′W
Cotyora *see* Ordu
102 I11 **Coubre, Pointe de la** *headland* W France 45°39′N 01°23′W
18 E12 **Coudersport** Pennsylvania, NE USA 41°45′N 78°00′W
15 S9 **Coudres, Île aux** *island* Québec, SE Canada
182 G11 **Couedic, Cape de** *headland* South Australia 36°04′S 136°43′E
Couentrey *see* Coventry
102 I6 **Couesnon** ≈ NW France
32 H10 **Cougar** Washington, NW USA 46°03′N 122°18′W
102 L10 **Couhé** Vienne, W France 46°18′N 00°10′E
32 K8 **Coulee City** Washington, NW USA 47°36′N 119°18′W
195 Q15 **Coulman Island** *island* Antarctica
103 P5 **Coulommiers** Seine-et-Marne, N France 48°49′N 03°04′E
14 K11 **Coulonge** ≈ Québec, SE Canada
14 K11 **Coulonge Est** ≈ Québec, SE Canada
35 Q9 **Coulterville** California, W USA 37°41′N 120°10′W
38 M9 **Council** Alaska, USA 64°54′N 163°40′W
32 M12 **Council** Idaho, NW USA 44°45′N 116°26′W
29 S15 **Council Bluffs** Iowa, C USA 41°16′N 95°52′W
27 O5 **Council Grove** Kansas, C USA 38°41′N 96°29′W
27 O5 **Council Grove Lake** ⊠ Kansas, C USA
32 G7 **Coupeville** Washington, NW USA 48°13′N 122°41′W
55 U12 **Courantyne River** *var.* Corantijn Rivier, Corentyne River. ≈ Guyana/Surinam
99 G21 **Courcelles** Hainaut, S Belgium 50°28′N 04°23′E
108 C7 **Courgenay** Jura, NW Switzerland 47°24′N 07°09′E
126 B2 **Courland Lagoon** *Ger.* Kurisches Haff, *Rus.* Kurskiy Zaliv. *lagoon* Lithuania/Russian Federation
118 B12 **Courland Spit** *Lith.* Kuršių Nerija, *Rus.* Kurshskaya Kosa. *spit* Lithuania/Russian Federation
106 A6 **Courmayeur** *prev.* Cormaiore. Valle d'Aosta, NW Italy 45°48′N 07°00′E
108 D7 **Courroux** Jura, NW Switzerland 47°22′N 07°23′E
10 K17 **Courtenay** Vancouver Island, British Columbia, SW Canada 49°40′N 124°58′W
21 W7 **Courtland** Virginia, NE USA 36°44′N 77°06′W
25 V10 **Courtney** Texas, SW USA 30°16′N 96°04′W
30 J4 **Court Oreilles, Lac** ◎ Wisconsin, N USA
Courtrai *see* Kortrijk
99 H19 **Court-Saint-Étienne** Walloon Brabant, C Belgium 50°38′N 04°34′E
22 G6 **Coushatta** Louisiana, S USA 32°00′N 93°20′W
172 I16 **Cousin** *island* Inner Islands, NE Seychelles
172 I16 **Cousine** *island* Inner Islands, NE Seychelles
102 J4 **Coutances** *anc.* Constantia. Manche, N France 49°04′N 01°27′W
102 K12 **Coutras** Gironde, SW France 45°01′N 00°07′W
45 U14 **Couva** Trinidad, Trinidad and Tobago 10°25′N 61°27′W
108 B8 **Couvet** Neuchâtel, W Switzerland 46°57′N 06°41′E
99 H22 **Couvin** Namur, S Belgium 50°03′N 04°30′E
116 K12 **Covasna** *Ger.* Kowasna, *Hung.* Kovászna. Covasna, E Romania 45°51′N 26°11′E
116 J11 **Covasna** ◐ *county* E Romania
14 E12 **Cove Island** *island* Ontario, S Canada
34 M5 **Covelo** California, W USA 39°46′N 123°16′W
97 M20 **Coventry** *anc.* Couentrey. C England, United Kingdom 52°25′N 01°30′W
Cove of Cork *see* Cobh
21 U5 **Covesville** Virginia, NE USA 37°52′N 78°41′W
104 I8 **Covilhã** Castelo Branco, E Portugal 40°17′N 07°30′W
23 T3 **Covington** Georgia, SE USA 33°34′N 83°52′W
31 N13 **Covington** Indiana, N USA 40°08′N 87°23′W
20 M3 **Covington** Kentucky, S USA 39°04′N 84°30′W
22 K8 **Covington** Louisiana, S USA 30°28′N 90°06′W
31 Q13 **Covington** Ohio, N USA 40°07′N 84°21′W
20 F9 **Covington** Tennessee, S USA 35°32′N 89°40′W
21 S6 **Covington** Virginia, NE USA 37°48′N 80°01′W
183 Q8 **Cowal, Lake** *seasonal lake* New South Wales, SE Australia
11 W15 **Cowan** Manitoba, S Canada 51°59′N 100°36′W
18 F12 **Cowanesque River** ≈ New York/Pennsylvania, NE USA
180 L12 **Cowan, Lake** ◎ Western Australia
15 P13 **Cowansville** Québec, SE Canada 45°13′N 72°44′W
182 H8 **Cowell** South Australia 33°43′S 136°53′E
97 M23 **Cowes** S England, United Kingdom 50°45′N 01°19′W
27 Q10 **Coweta** Oklahoma, C USA 35°57′N 95°39′W
0 D6 **Cowie Seamount** *undersea feature* NE Pacific Ocean 54°15′N 149°30′W
32 G10 **Cowlitz River** ≈ Washington, NW USA
21 Q11 **Cowpens** South Carolina, SE USA 35°01′N 81°48′W
183 R8 **Cowra** New South Wales, SE Australia 33°50′S 148°45′E
Coxen Hole *see* Roatán
59 I19 **Coxim** Mato Grosso do Sul, S Brazil 18°28′S 54°45′W
59 I19 **Coxim, Rio** ≈ SW Brazil
Coxin Hole *see* Roatán
153 V17 **Cox's Bazar** Chittagong, S Bangladesh 21°25′N 91°59′E
76 H14 **Coyah** Conakry, W Guinea 09°45′N 13°26′W
40 K5 **Coyame** Chihuahua, N Mexico 29°29′N 105°07′W
24 L9 **Coyanosa Draw** ≈ Texas, SW USA
Coyhaique *see* Coihaique
42 C7 **Coyolate, Río** ≈ S Guatemala
Coyote State, The *see* South Dakota
40 I10 **Coyotitán** Sinaloa, C Mexico 23°48′N 106°37′W
41 N15 **Coyuca** *var.* Coyuca de Catalán. Guerrero, S Mexico 18°21′N 100°39′W
41 O16 **Coyuca** *var.* Coyuca de Benítez. Guerrero, S Mexico 17°01′N 100°08′W
Coyuca de Benítez/Coyuca de Catalán *see* Coyuca
29 N15 **Cozad** Nebraska, C USA 40°52′N 99°58′W
158 L14 **Cozhê** Xizang Zizhiqu, W China 31°53′N 87°51′E
Cozie, Alpi *see* Cottian Alps
Cozmeni *see* Kitsman'
40 E3 **Cozón, Cerro** ▲ NW Mexico 31°16′N 112°29′W
41 Z12 **Cozumel** Quintana Roo, E Mexico 20°29′N 86°54′W
41 Z12 **Cozumel, Isla** *island* SE Mexico
32 K8 **Crab Creek** ≈ Washington, NW USA
44 H12 **Crab Pond Point** *headland* W Jamaica 18°07′N 78°01′W
Cracovia/Cracow *see* Kraków
83 I25 **Cradock** Eastern Cape, S South Africa 32°07′S 25°38′E
39 Y14 **Craig** Prince of Wales Island, Alaska, USA 55°29′N 133°04′W
37 Q3 **Craig** Colorado, C USA 40°31′N 107°33′W
97 F15 **Craigavon** C Northern Ireland, United Kingdom 54°28′N 06°25′W
21 T5 **Craigsville** Virginia, NE USA 38°07′N 79°21′W
101 J21 **Crailsheim** Baden-Württemberg, S Germany 49°07′N 10°04′E
116 H14 **Craiova** Dolj, SW Romania 44°19′N 23°49′E
10 K12 **Cranberry Junction** British Columbia, SW Canada 55°35′N 128°21′W
18 J8 **Cranberry Lake** ◎ New York, NE USA
11 V13 **Cranberry Portage** Manitoba, C Canada 54°34′N 101°22′W
11 P17 **Cranbrook** British Columbia, SW Canada 49°29′N 115°48′W
30 M5 **Crandon** Wisconsin, N USA 45°34′N 88°54′W
32 K14 **Crane** Oregon, NW USA 43°24′N 118°35′W
24 M9 **Crane** Texas, SW USA 31°23′N 102°22′W
Crane *see* The Crane
25 S8 **Cranfills Gap** Texas, SW USA 31°46′N 97°49′W
19 O12 **Cranston** Rhode Island, NE USA 41°46′N 71°26′W
Cranz *see* Zelenogradsk
59 L15 **Craolândia** Tocantins, E Brazil 07°17′S 47°23′W
102 J7 **Craon** Mayenne, NW France 47°52′N 00°57′W
195 V16 **Crary, Cape** *headland* Antarctica
Crasna *see* Kraszna
32 G14 **Crater Lake** ◎ Oregon, NW USA
33 P14 **Craters of the Moon National Monument** *national park* Idaho, NW USA
59 O14 **Crateús** Ceará, E Brazil 05°10′S 40°39′W
Crathis *see* Crati
107 N20 **Crati** *anc.* Crathis. ≈ S Italy
11 U16 **Craven** Saskatchewan, S Canada 50°44′N 104°50′W
54 I8 **Cravo Norte** Arauca, E Colombia 06°17′N 70°15′W
28 J12 **Crawford** Nebraska, C USA 42°40′N 103°24′W
25 T8 **Crawford** Texas, SW USA 31°31′N 97°26′W
11 O17 **Crawford Bay** British Columbia, SW Canada 49°39′N 116°44′W
65 M19 **Crawford Seamount** *undersea feature* S Atlantic Ocean 40°30′S 10°00′W
31 O13 **Crawfordsville** Indiana, N USA 40°02′N 86°52′W
23 S9 **Crawfordville** Florida, SE USA 30°10′N 84°22′W
97 O23 **Crawley** SE England, United Kingdom 51°07′N 00°12′W
33 S10 **Crazy Mountains** ▲▲ Montana, NW USA
11 T11 **Cree** ≈ Saskatchewan, C Canada
37 R7 **Creede** Colorado, C USA 37°51′N 106°55′W
40 I6 **Creel** Chihuahua, N Mexico 27°45′N 107°36′W
11 S11 **Cree Lake** ◎ Saskatchewan, C Canada
11 V13 **Creighton** Saskatchewan, C Canada 54°46′N 101°54′W
29 Q13 **Creighton** Nebraska, C USA 42°28′N 97°54′W
103 O4 **Creil** Oise, N France 49°16′N 02°29′E
106 E8 **Crema** Lombardia, N Italy 45°22′N 09°40′E
106 E8 **Cremona** Lombardia, N Italy 45°08′N 10°02′E
Creole State *see* Louisiana
112 M10 **Crepaja** *Hung.* Cserépalja. Vojvodina, N Serbia 45°02′N 20°36′E
103 O4 **Crépy-en-Valois** Oise, N France 49°13′N 02°54′E
112 B10 **Cres** *It.* Cherso. Primorje-Gorski Kotar, NW Croatia 44°57′N 14°24′E
112 A11 **Cres** *It.* Cherso; *anc.* Crexa. *island* W Croatia
32 H14 **Crescent** Oregon, NW USA 43°27′N 121°40′W
34 K1 **Crescent City** California, W USA 41°45′N 124°14′W
23 W10 **Crescent City** Florida, SE USA 29°25′N 81°30′W
167 X10 **Crescent Group** *island group* C Paracel Islands
23 W10 **Crescent Lake** ◎ Florida, SE USA
29 X11 **Cresco** Iowa, C USA 43°22′N 92°06′W
61 B18 **Crespo** Entre Ríos, E Argentina 32°05′S 60°20′W
54 E5 **Crespo** ✈ (Cartagena) Bolívar, NW Colombia 10°27′N 75°31′W
103 R13 **Crest** Drôme, E France 44°45′N 05°00′E
37 R5 **Crested Butte** Colorado, C USA 38°52′N 106°59′W
31 S12 **Crestline** Ohio, N USA 40°47′N 82°44′W
11 O17 **Creston** British Columbia, SW Canada 49°05′N 116°32′W
29 U15 **Creston** Iowa, C USA 41°03′N 94°21′W
33 V16 **Creston** Wyoming, C USA 41°40′N 107°43′W
37 S7 **Crestone Peak** ▲ Colorado, C USA 37°58′N 105°34′W
23 P8 **Crestview** Florida, SE USA 30°44′N 86°34′W
121 R10 **Cretan Trough** *undersea feature* Aegean Sea, C Mediterranean Sea
29 R16 **Crete** Nebraska, C USA 40°36′N 96°58′W
Crete *see* Kriti
103 O5 **Créteil** Val-de-Marne, N France 48°47′N 02°28′E
Crete, Sea of/Creticum, Mare *see* Kritikó Pélagos
105 X4 **Creus, Cap de** *headland* NE Spain 42°18′N 03°18′E
103 N10 **Creuse** ◐ *department* C France
102 L9 **Creuse** ≈ C France
103 T4 **Creutzwald** Moselle, NE France 49°13′N 06°41′E
105 S12 **Crevillente** País Valenciano, E Spain 38°15′N 00°48′W
97 L18 **Crewe** C England, United Kingdom 53°05′N 02°27′W
21 V7 **Crewe** Virginia, NE USA 37°10′N 78°07′W
Crexa *see* Cres
43 Q15 **Cricamola, Río** ≈ NW Panama
61 K14 **Criciúma** Santa Catarina, S Brazil 28°39′S 49°23′W
96 J11 **Crieff** C Scotland, United Kingdom 56°22′N 03°49′W
112 B10 **Crikvenica** *It.* Cirquenizza; *prev.* Cirkvenica, Crjkvenica. Primorje-Gorski Kotar, NW Croatia 45°12′N 14°40′E
Crimea/Crimean Oblast *see* Krym, Avtonomna Respublika
101 M16 **Crimmitschau** *var.* Krimmitzschau. Sachsen, E Germany 50°48′N 12°23′E
116 G11 **Crişcior** *Hung.* Kristyor. Hunedoara, W Romania 46°09′N 22°54′E
21 Y5 **Crisfield** Maryland, NE USA 37°58′N 75°51′W
31 P3 **Crisp Point** *headland* Michigan, N USA 46°45′N 85°15′W
59 L19 **Cristalina** Goiás, C Brazil 16°43′S 47°37′W
44 J7 **Cristal, Sierra del** ▲▲ E Cuba
43 T14 **Cristóbal** Colón, C Panama 09°18′N 79°52′W
54 F4 **Cristóbal Colón, Pico** ▲ N Colombia 10°52′N 73°46′W
106 C10 **Cristoforo Colombo** ✈ Liguria, NW Italy
Cristur/Cristuru Săcuiesc *see* Cristuru Secuiesc
116 I11 **Cristuru Secuiesc** *prev.* Cristur, Cristuru Săcuiesc, Sitaş Cristuru, *Ger.* Kreutz, *Hung.* Székelykeresztúr, Szitás-Keresztúr. Harghita, C Romania 46°17′N 25°02′E
116 F10 **Crişul Alb** *var.* Weisse Kreisch, *Ger.* Weisse Körös, *Hung.* Fehér-Körös. ≈ Hungary/Romania
116 F10 **Crişul Negru** *Ger.* Schwarze Körös, *Hung.* Fekete-Körös. ≈ Hungary/Romania
116 G10 **Crişul Repede** *var.* Schnelle Kreisch, *Ger.* Schnelle Körös, *Hung.* Sebes-Körös. ≈ Hungary/Romania
117 N10 **Criuleni** *Rus.* Kriulyany. C Moldova 47°12′N 29°09′E
Crivadia Vulcanului *see* Vulcan
Crjkvenica *see* Crikvenica
113 O17 **Crna Gora** ▲▲ FYR Macedonia/Serbia
Crna Gora *see* Montenegro
113 O20 **Crna Reka** ≈ S FYR Macedonia
Crni Drim *see* Black Drin
109 V10 **Črni vrh** ▲ NE Slovenia 46°28′N 15°14′E
109 V13 **Črnomelj** *Ger.* Tschernembl. SE Slovenia 45°32′N 15°12′E
97 A17 **Croagh Patrick** *Ir.* Cruach Phádraig. ▲ W Ireland 53°45′N 09°39′W
112 D9 **Croatia** *off.* Republic of Croatia, *Ger.* Kroatien, *SCr.* Hrvatska. ◆ *republic* SE Europe
Croatia, Republic of *see* Croatia
Croce, Picco di *see* Wilde Kreuzspitze
15 P8 **Croche** ≈ Québec, SE Canada
169 V7 **Crocker, Banjaran** *var.* Crocker Range. ▲▲ East Malaysia
Crocker Range *see* Crocker, Banjaran
25 V9 **Crockett** Texas, SW USA 31°21′N 95°30′W
67 V14 **Crocodile** *var.* Krokodil. ≈ N South Africa
Crocodile *see* Limpopo
20 I7 **Crofton** Kentucky, S USA 37°01′N 87°25′W
29 Q12 **Crofton** Nebraska, C USA 42°43′N 97°30′W
Croia *see* Krujë
103 R16 **Croisette, Cap** *headland* SE France 43°12′N 05°21′E
102 G8 **Croisic, Pointe du** *headland* NW France 47°16′N 02°42′W
103 S13 **Croix Haute, Col de la** *pass* E France
15 U5 **Croix, Pointe à la** *headland* Québec, SE Canada 49°16′N 67°46′W
14 F13 **Croker, Cape** *headland* Ontario, S Canada 44°56′N 80°57′W
181 P1 **Croker Island** *island* Northern Territory, N Australia
96 I8 **Cromarty** N Scotland, United Kingdom 57°40′N 04°02′W
99 M21 **Crombach** Liège, E Belgium 50°14′N 06°07′E
97 Q18 **Cromer** E England, United Kingdom 52°56′N 01°06′E
185 D22 **Cromwell** Otago, South Island, New Zealand 45°03′S 169°14′E
185 H16 **Cronadun** West Coast, South Island, New Zealand 42°03′S 171°52′E
39 O11 **Crooked Creek** Alaska, USA 61°52′N 158°06′W
44 K5 **Crooked Island** *island* SE Bahamas
44 J5 **Crooked Island Passage** *channel* SE Bahamas
32 I13 **Crooked River** ≈ Oregon, NW USA
29 R4 **Crookston** Minnesota, N USA 47°47′N 96°36′W
28 I10 **Crooks Tower** ▲ South Dakota, N USA 44°09′N 103°55′W
31 T14 **Crooksville** Ohio, N USA 39°46′N 82°05′W
183 R9 **Crookwell** New South Wales, SE Australia 34°28′S 149°27′E
14 L14 **Crosby** Ontario, SE Canada 44°39′N 76°13′W
97 K17 **Crosby** *var.* Great Crosby. NW England, United Kingdom 53°30′N 03°02′W
29 U6 **Crosby** Minnesota, N USA 46°30′N 93°58′W
28 K2 **Crosby** North Dakota, N USA 48°54′N 103°17′W
25 O5 **Crosbyton** Texas, SW USA 33°40′N 101°16′W
77 V16 **Cross** ≈ Cameroon/Nigeria
23 U10 **Cross City** Florida, SE USA 29°37′N 83°08′W
Crossen *see* Krosno Odrzańskie
27 V14 **Crossett** Arkansas, C USA 33°08′N 91°58′W
97 K15 **Cross Fell** ▲ N England, United Kingdom 54°42′N 02°30′W
11 P16 **Crossfield** Alberta, SW Canada 51°24′N 114°03′W
21 Q12 **Cross Hill** South Carolina, SE USA 34°18′N 81°58′W
19 U6 **Cross Island** *island* Maine, NE USA
11 X13 **Cross Lake** Manitoba, C Canada 54°38′N 97°35′W
22 F5 **Cross Lake** ⊠ Louisiana, S USA
36 I12 **Crossman Peak** ▲ Arizona, SW USA 34°33′N 114°09′W
25 Q7 **Cross Plains** Texas, SW USA 32°07′N 99°10′W
77 V17 **Cross River** ◐ *state* SE Nigeria
20 L9 **Crossville** Tennessee, S USA 35°57′N 85°02′W
31 S8 **Croswell** Michigan, N USA 43°16′N 82°37′W
14 K13 **Crotch Lake** ◎ Ontario, SE Canada
Croton/Crotona *see* Crotone
107 O21 **Crotone** *var.* Cotrone; *anc.* Croton, Crotona. Calabria, SW Italy 39°05′N 17°07′E
33 V11 **Crow Agency** Montana, NW USA 45°35′N 107°28′W
183 U7 **Crowdy Head** *headland* New South Wales, SE Australia 31°52′S 152°45′E
25 Q4 **Crowell** Texas, SW USA 33°59′N 99°45′W
183 O6 **Crowl Creek** *seasonal river* New South Wales, SE Australia
22 H9 **Crowley** Louisiana, S USA 30°11′N 92°21′W
35 S9 **Crowley, Lake** ⊠ California, W USA
27 X10 **Crowleys Ridge** *hill range* Arkansas, C USA
31 N11 **Crown Point** Indiana, N USA 41°25′N 87°22′W
37 P10 **Crownpoint** New Mexico, SW USA 35°40′N 108°09′W
33 R10 **Crow Peak** ▲ Montana, NW USA 46°17′N 111°54′W
11 P17 **Crowsnest Pass** *pass* Alberta/British Columbia, SW Canada
29 T6 **Crow Wing River** ≈ Minnesota, N USA
97 O22 **Croydon** SE England, United Kingdom 51°21′N 00°06′W
Crozer, Mount *see* Finkol, Mount
173 P11 **Crozet Basin** *undersea feature* S Indian Ocean 39°00′S 60°00′E
173 O12 **Crozet Islands** *island group* French Southern and Antarctic Territories
173 N12 **Crozet Plateau** *var.* Crozet Plateaus. *undersea feature* SW Indian Ocean 46°00′S 51°00′E
Crozet Plateaus *see* Crozet Plateau
102 E6 **Crozon** Finistère, NW France 48°14′N 04°31′W
Cruacha Dubha, Na *see* Macgillycuddy's Reeks
Cruach Phádraig *see* Croagh Patrick
116 M14 **Crucea** Constanţa, SE Romania 44°30′N 28°18′E
44 E5 **Cruces** Cienfuegos, C Cuba 22°20′N 80°17′W
107 O20 **Crucoli Torretta** Calabria, SW Italy 39°26′N 17°03′E
41 P9 **Cruillas** Tamaulipas, C Mexico 24°43′N 98°26′W
64 K9 **Cruiser Tablemount** *undersea feature* E Atlantic Ocean 32°00′N 28°00′W
61 G14 **Cruz Alta** Rio Grande do Sul, S Brazil 28°38′S 53°38′W
44 G8 **Cruz, Cabo** *headland* S Cuba 19°50′N 77°43′W
60 N9 **Cruzeiro** São Paulo, S Brazil 22°33′S 44°59′W
60 H10 **Cruzeiro do Oeste** Paraná, S Brazil 23°45′S 53°03′W
59 A15 **Cruzeiro do Sul** Acre, W Brazil 07°40′S 72°39′W
23 U11 **Crystal Bay** *bay* Florida, SE USA NE Gulf of Mexico Atlantic Ocean
182 I8 **Crystal Brook** South Australia 33°24′S 138°10′E
11 X17 **Crystal City** Manitoba, S Canada 49°07′N 98°54′W
27 X5 **Crystal City** Missouri, C USA 38°13′N 90°22′W
25 P13 **Crystal City** Texas, SW USA 28°43′N 99°51′W
30 M4 **Crystal Falls** Michigan, N USA 46°06′N 88°20′W
23 Q8 **Crystal Lake** Florida, SE USA 30°26′N 85°41′W
31 O6 **Crystal Lake** ◎ Michigan, N USA
23 V11 **Crystal River** Florida, SE USA 28°54′N 82°35′W
37 Q5 **Crystal River** ≈ Colorado, C USA
22 K6 **Crystal Springs** Mississippi, S USA 31°59′N 90°21′W
Csaca *see* Čadca
Csakathurn/Csáktornya *see* Čakovec
Csap *see* Chop
Csepén *see* Čepin
Cserépalja *see* Crepaja
Csermő *see* Cermei
Csíkszereda *see* Miercurea-Ciuc
111 L24 **Csongrád** Csongrád, SE Hungary 46°42′N 20°09′E
111 L24 **Csongrád** *off.* Csongrád Megye. ◐ *county* SE Hungary
Csongrád Megye *see* Csongrád
111 H22 **Csorna** Győr-Moson-Sopron, NW Hungary 47°37′N 17°14′E
Csucsa *see* Ciucea
111 G25 **Csurgó** Somogy, SW Hungary 46°16′N 17°09′E
Csurog *see* Čurug
54 L5 **Cúa** Miranda, N Venezuela 10°14′N 66°58′W
82 C11 **Cuale** Malanje, NW Angola 08°22′S 16°10′E
67 T12 **Cuando** *var.* Kwando. ≈ S Africa
83 E15 **Cuando Cubango** *var.* Kuando-Kubango. ◐ *province* SE Angola
83 E16 **Cuangar** Cuando Cubango, S Angola 17°34′S 18°39′E
82 D11 **Cuango** Lunda Norte, NE Angola 09°10′S 17°59′E
82 C10 **Cuango** Uíge, NW Angola 06°20′S 16°42′E
82 C10 **Cuango** *var.* Kwango. ≈ Angola/Dem. Rep. Congo *see also* Kwango
Cuango *see* Kwango
Cuan, Loch *see* Strangford Lough
82 C12 **Cuanza** *var.* Kwanza. ≈ C Angola
82 B11 **Cuanza Norte** *var.* Kuanza Norte. ◐ *province* NE Angola
82 B12 **Cuanza Sul** *var.* Kuanza Sul. ◐ *province* NE Angola
61 E16 **Cuareim, Río** *var.* Rio Quaraí. ≈ Brazil/Uruguay *see also* Quaraí, Rio
Cuareim, Río *see* Quaraí, Rio
83 D15 **Cuatir** ≈ S Angola
40 M7 **Cuatro Ciénegas** *var.* Cuatro Ciénegas de Carranza. Coahuila, NE Mexico 27°00′N 102°03′W
Cuatro Ciénegas de Carranza *see* Cuatro Ciénegas
40 I6 **Cuauhtémoc** Chihuahua, N Mexico 28°22′N 106°52′W
41 P14 **Cuautla** Morelos, S Mexico 18°48′N 98°56′W
104 H12 **Cuba** Beja, S Portugal 38°10′N 07°54′W
27 W6 **Cuba** Missouri, C USA 38°03′N 91°24′W
37 R10 **Cuba** New Mexico, SW USA 36°01′N 107°04′W
44 E6 **Cuba** *off.* Republic of Cuba. ◆ *republic* W West Indies
47 O2 **Cuba** *island* W West Indies
82 B13 **Cubal** Benguela, W Angola 12°58′S 14°16′E
83 C15 **Cubango** *var.* Kuvango, *Port.* Vila Artur de Paiva, Vila da Ponte. Huíla, SW Angola 14°27′S 16°18′E
83 D16 **Cubango** *var.* Kavango, Kavengo, Kubango, Okavango, Okavanggo. ≈ S Africa *see also* Okavango
Cubango *see* Okavango
54 H8 **Cubará** Boyacá, N Colombia 07°01′N 72°07′W
Cuba, Republic of *see* Cuba
136 I12 **Çubuk** Ankara, N Turkey 40°13′N 33°02′E
83 D14 **Cuchi** Cuando Cubango, C Angola 14°40′S 16°58′E
42 C5 **Cuchumatanes, Sierra de los** ▲▲ W Guatemala
Cuculaya, Rio *see* Kukalaya, Rio
82 E12 **Cucumbi** *prev.* Trás-os-Montes. Lunda Sul, NE Angola 10°13′S 19°04′E
54 G7 **Cúcuta** *var.* San José de Cúcuta. Norte de Santander, N Colombia 07°55′N 72°31′W
31 N9 **Cudahy** Wisconsin, N USA 42°54′N 87°51′W
155 J21 **Cuddalore** Tamil Nādu, SE India 11°43′N 79°46′E
155 I18 **Cuddapah** Andhra Pradesh, S India 14°30′N 78°50′E
104 M6 **Cuéllar** Castilla-León, N Spain 41°24′N 04°19′W
82 D13 **Cuemba** *var.* Coemba. Bié, C Angola 12°09′S 18°07′E
56 B8 **Cuenca** Azuay, S Ecuador 02°54′S 79°W
105 Q9 **Cuenca** *anc.* Conca. Castilla-La Mancha, C Spain 40°04′N 02°07′W
105 P9 **Cuenca** ◐ *province* Castilla-La Mancha, C Spain
40 L9 **Cuencamé** *var.* Cuencamé de Ceniceros. Durango, C Mexico 24°53′N 103°41′W
Cuencamé de Ceniceros *see* Cuencamé
105 Q8 **Cuenca, Serranía de** ▲ C Spain
Cuera *see* Chur
105 P5 **Cuerda del Pozo, Embalse de la** ⊠ N Spain
41 O14 **Cuernavaca** Morelos, S Mexico 18°57′N 99°15′W
25 T12 **Cuero** Texas, SW USA 29°06′N 97°19′W
44 I7 **Cueto** Holguín, E Cuba 20°43′N 75°54′W
41 Q13 **Cuetzalán** *var.* Cuetzalán del Progreso. Puebla, S Mexico 20°00′N 97°27′W
Cuetzalán del Progreso *see* Cuetzalán
105 Q14 **Cuevas de Almanzora** Andalucía, S Spain 37°19′N 01°52′W
Cuevas de Vinromá *see* Les Coves de Vinromà
116 H12 **Cugir** *Hung.* Kudzsir. Alba, SW Romania 45°48′N 23°25′E
59 H18 **Cuiabá** *prev.* Cuyabá. *state capital* Mato Grosso, SW Brazil 15°32′S 56°05′W
59 H19 **Cuiabá, Rio** ≈ SW Brazil
41 R15 **Cuicatlán** *var.* San Juan Bautista Cuicatlán. Oaxaca, SE Mexico 17°49′N 96°59′W
191 W16 **Cuidado, Punta** *headland* Easter Island, Chile, E Pacific Ocean 27°08′S 109°18′W
Cúige *see* Connaught
Cúige Laighean *see* Leinster
Cúige Mumhan *see* Munster
Cuihua *see* Daguan
98 L13 **Cuijck** Noord-Brabant, SE Netherlands 51°41′N 05°56′E
Cúil an tSúdaire *see* Portarlington
42 D7 **Cuilapa** Santa Rosa, S Guatemala 14°16′N 90°18′W
42 B5 **Cuilco, Río** ≈ W Guatemala
Cúil Mhuine *see* Collooney
Cúil Raithin *see* Coleraine
83 C14 **Cuima** Huambo, C Angola 13°16′S 15°39′E
83 E16 **Cuito** *var.* Kwito. ≈ SE Angola
83 E15 **Cuito Cuanavale** Cuando Cubango, E Angola 15°01′S 19°07′E
41 N14 **Cuitzeo, Lago de** ◎ C Mexico
27 W4 **Cuivre River** ≈ Missouri, C USA
Çuka *see* Çukë
168 L8 **Cukai** *var.* Chukai, Kemaman. Terengganu, Peninsular Malaysia 04°15′N 103°25′E
113 L23 **Çukë** *var.* Çuka. Vlorë, S Albania 39°50′N 20°01′E
Cularo *see* Grenoble
33 Y7 **Culbertson** Montana, NW USA 48°09′N 104°30′W
28 M16 **Culbertson** Nebraska, C USA 40°13′N 100°50′W
183 P10 **Culcairn** New South Wales, SE Australia 35°41′S 147°01′E
45 W5 **Culebra** *var.* Dewey. E Puerto Rico 18°19′N 65°17′W
45 W6 **Culebra, Isla de** *island* E Puerto Rico
37 T8 **Culebra Peak** ▲ Colorado, C USA 37°07′N 105°11′W
104 J5 **Culebra, Sierra de la** ▲▲ NW Spain
98 J12 **Culemborg** Gelderland, C Netherlands 51°57′N 05°17′E
137 V14 **Çulfa** *Rus.* Dzhul'fa. SW Azerbaijan 38°58′N 45°37′E
183 P4 **Culgoa River** ≈ New South Wales/Queensland, SE Australia

◆ Country
● Country Capital
◇ Dependent Territory
○ Dependent Territory Capital
◐ Administrative Regions
✈ International Airport
▲ Mountain
▲▲ Mountain Range
∧ Volcano
≈ River
◎ Lake
⊠ Reservoir

CULIACÁN – DARENDE

40 I9 **Culiacán** var. Culiacán Rosales, Culiacán-Rosales. Sinaloa, C Mexico 24°48′N 107°25′W

Culiacán-Rosales/Culiacán Rosales see Culiacán

105 P14 **Cúllar-Baza** Andalucía, S Spain 37°35′N 02°34′W

105 S10 **Cullera** País Valenciano, E Spain 39°10′N 00°15′W

23 P3 **Cullman** Alabama, S USA 34°10′N 86°50′W

108 B10 **Cully** Vaud, W Switzerland 46°58′N 06°46′E

Culm see Chełmno

Culmsee see Chełmża

21 V4 **Culpeper** Virginia, NE USA 38°28′N 78°00′W

185 I17 **Culverden** Canterbury, South Island, New Zealand 42°46′S 172°51′E

83 H18 **Cum** var. Xhumo. Central, C Botswana 21°13′S 24°38′E

55 N5 **Cumaná** Sucre, NE Venezuela 10°29′N 64°12′W

55 O5 **Cumanacoa** Sucre, NE Venezuela 10°17′N 63°58′W

54 C13 **Cumbal, Nevado de** elevation S Colombia

21 O7 **Cumberland** Kentucky, S USA 36°55′N 83°00′W

21 U2 **Cumberland** Maryland, NE USA 39°40′N 78°47′W

21 V6 **Cumberland** Virginia, NE USA 37°31′N 78°16′W

187 P12 **Cumberland, Cape** var. Cape Nahoi. headland Espiritu Santo, N Vanuatu 14°39′S 166°35′E

11 V14 **Cumberland House** Saskatchewan, C Canada 53°57′N 102°21′W

23 W8 **Cumberland Island** island Georgia, SE USA

20 L7 **Cumberland, Lake** ⊠ Kentucky, S USA

9 R5 **Cumberland Peninsula** peninsula Baffin Island, Nunavut, NE Canada

2 N9 **Cumberland Plateau** plateau E USA

30 L1 **Cumberland Point** headland Michigan, N USA 47°51′N 89°14′W

21 O7 **Cumberland River** ≈ Kentucky/Tennessee, S USA

9 S6 **Cumberland Sound** inlet Baffin Island, Nunavut, NE Canada

96 I12 **Cumbernauld** S Scotland, United Kingdom 55°57′N 04°W

97 K15 **Cumbria** cultural region NW England, United Kingdom

97 K15 **Cumbrian Mountains** ▲▲ NW England, United Kingdom

23 S2 **Cumming** Georgia, SE USA 34°12′N 84°08′W

Cummin in Pommern see Kamień Pomorski

182 G9 **Cummins** South Australia 34°17′S 135°43′E

96 I13 **Cumnock** W Scotland, United Kingdom 55°32′N 04°28′W

40 G4 **Cumpas** Sonora, NW Mexico 30°N 109°48′W

136 H16 **Çumra** Konya, C Turkey 37°34′N 32°38′E

63 G15 **Cunco** Araucanía, C Chile 38°55′S 72°02′W

54 E9 **Cundinamarca** off. Departamento de Cundinamarca. ⬖ province C Colombia

Cundinamarca, Departamento de see Cundinamarca

41 U15 **Cunduacán** Tabasco, SE Mexico 18°00′N 93°07′W

83 C16 **Cunene** ⬖ province S Angola

83 A16 **Cunene** var. Kunene. ≈ Angola/Namibia see also Kunene

Cunene see Kunene

106 A9 **Cuneo** Fr. Coni. Piemonte, NW Italy 44°23′N 07°32′E

83 E15 **Cunjamba** Cuando Cubango, E Angola 15°22′S 20°07′E

181 V10 **Cunnamulla** Queensland, E Australia 28°09′S 145°44′E

Čunusavvon see Junosuando

Cuokkarašša see Čohkarášša

106 B7 **Cuorgne** Piemonte, NE Italy 45°23′N 07°34′E

96 K11 **Cupar** E Scotland, United Kingdom 56°19′N 03°01′W

116 L8 **Cupcina** Rus. Kupchino; prev. Calinisc, Kalinisk. N Moldova 48°07′N 27°22′E

54 C8 **Cupica** Chocó, W Colombia 06°43′N 77°31′W

54 C8 **Cupica, Golfo de** gulf W Colombia

112 N13 **Ćuprija** Serbia, E Serbia 43°57′N 21°21′E

Cura see Villa de Cura

45 P16 **Curaçao** island Netherlands Antilles

56 H13 **Curanja, Río** ≈ E Peru

56 F7 **Curaray, Rio** ≈ Ecuador/Peru

116 K14 **Curcani** Călăraşi, SE Romania 44°11′N 26°39′E

182 H4 **Curdimurka** South Australia 29°27′S 136°56′E

103 P7 **Cure** ≈ C France

173 Y16 **Curepipe** C Mauritius 20°19′S 57°31′E

55 R6 **Curiapo** Delta Amacuro, NE Venezuela 10°03′N 63°05′W

Curia Rhaetorum see Chur

62 G12 **Curicó** Maule, C Chile 35°00′S 71°15′W

Curieta see Krk

172 I15 **Curieuse** island Inner Islands, NE Seychelles

59 C16 **Curitiba** Acre, W Brazil 10°08′S 69°00′W

60 K12 **Curitiba** prev. Curytiba. state capital Paraná, S Brazil 25°25′S 49°25′W

60 J13 **Curitibanos** Santa Catarina, S Brazil 27°18′S 50°35′W

183 S6 **Curlewis** New South Wales, SE Australia 31°09′S 150°18′E

182 J6 **Curnamona** South Australia 31°39′S 139°35′E

83 A15 **Curoca** ≈ SW Angola

183 T6 **Currabubula** New South Wales, SE Australia 31°17′S 150°43′E

59 Q14 **Currais Novos** Rio Grande do Norte, E Brazil 06°12′S 36°30′W

35 W7 **Currant** Nevada, W USA 38°43′N 115°27′W

35 W6 **Currant Mountain** ▲ Nevada, W USA 38°56′N 115°19′W

44 H2 **Current** Eleuthera Island, C Bahamas 25°24′N 76°44′W

27 W8 **Current River** ≈ Arkansas/Missouri, C USA

182 M14 **Currie** Tasmania, SE Australia 39°59′S 143°51′E

21 Y8 **Currituck** North Carolina, SE USA 36°29′N 76°02′W

21 Y8 **Currituck Sound** sound North Carolina, SE USA

39 R11 **Curry** Alaska, USA 62°36′N 150°00′W

Curtbunar see Tervel

116 I13 **Curtea de Argeş** var. Curtea-de-Arges. Argeş, S Romania 45°06′N 24°40′E

Curtea-de-Arges see Curtea de Argeş

116 E10 **Curtici** Ger. Kurtitsch, Hung. Kürtös. Arad, W Romania 46°21′N 21°17′E

28 M16 **Curtis** Nebraska, C USA 40°36′N 100°27′W

104 H2 **Curtis-Estación** Galicia, NW Spain 43°09′N 08°10′W

183 O14 **Curtis Group** island group Tasmania, SE Australia

181 Y8 **Curtis Island** island Queensland, SE Australia

58 K11 **Curuá, Ilha do** island NE Brazil

47 U7 **Curuá, Rio** ≈ N Brazil

59 A14 **Curuçá, Rio** ≈ NW Brazil

112 L9 **Čurug** Hung. Csurog. Vojvodina, N Serbia 45°30′N 20°02′E

61 D16 **Curuzú Cuatiá** Corrientes, NE Argentina 29°50′S 58°05′W

59 M19 **Curvelo** Minas Gerais, SE Brazil 18°45′S 44°27′W

18 E14 **Curwensville** Pennsylvania, NE USA 40°57′N 78°29′W

30 M3 **Curwood, Mount** ▲ Michigan, N USA 46°42′N 88°14′W

Curytiba see Curitiba

Curzola see Korčula

42 A10 **Cuscatlán** ⬖ department C El Salvador

57 H15 **Cusco** var. Cuzco. Cusco, C Peru 13°35′S 72°02′W

57 H15 **Cusco** off. Departamento de Cusco, var. Cuzco. ⬖ department C Peru

Cusco, Departamento de see Cusco

27 O9 **Cushing** Oklahoma, C USA 36°01′N 96°46′W

25 W8 **Cushing** Texas, SW USA 31°48′N 94°50′W

40 I6 **Cusihuiriachic** Chihuahua, N Mexico 28°16′N 106°46′W

103 P10 **Cusset** Allier, C France 46°08′N 03°27′E

23 S6 **Cusseta** Georgia, SE USA 32°18′N 84°46′W

28 J10 **Custer** South Dakota, N USA 43°46′N 103°36′W

Cüstrin see Kostrzyn

33 Q7 **Cut Bank** Montana, NW USA 48°38′N 112°20′W

Cutch, Gulf of see Kachchh, Gulf of

23 S6 **Cuthbert** Georgia, SE USA 31°46′N 84°47′W

11 S15 **Cut Knife** Saskatchewan, S Canada 52°40′N 108°54′W

23 Y16 **Cutler Ridge** Florida, SE USA 25°34′N 80°21′W

22 K10 **Cut Off** Louisiana, S USA 29°32′N 90°20′W

63 I15 **Cutral-Có** Neuquén, C Argentina 38°56′S 69°13′W

107 O21 **Cutro** Calabria, SW Italy 39°01′N 16°59′E

183 O4 **Cuttaburra Channels** seasonal river New South Wales, SE Australia

154 O12 **Cuttack** Orissa, E India 20°28′N 85°53′E

83 C15 **Cuvelai** Cunene, SW Angola 15°40′S 15°48′E

79 G18 **Cuvette** var. Région de la Cuvette. ⬖ province C Congo

79 G18 **Cuvette-Ouest** ⬖ province C Congo

Cuvette, Région de la see Cuvette

173 V9 **Cuvier Basin** undersea feature E Indian Ocean

173 U9 **Cuvier Plateau** undersea feature E Indian Ocean

82 B12 **Cuvo** ≈ W Angola

100 H9 **Cuxhaven** Niedersachsen, NW Germany 53°51′N 08°43′E

Cuyabá see Cuiabá

Cuyuni, Río see Cuyuni River

55 S8 **Cuyuni River** var. Río Cuyuni. ≈ Guyana/Venezuela

Cuzco see Cusco

97 K22 **Cwmbran** Wel. Cwmbrân. SW Wales, United Kingdom 51°39′N 03°W

Cwmbrân see Cwmbran

28 K15 **C. W. McConaughy, Lake** ⊠ Nebraska, C USA

81 D20 **Cyangugu** SW Rwanda 02°27′S 29°00′E

110 D11 **Cybinka** Ger. Ziebingen. Lubuskie, W Poland 52°11′N 14°46′E

Cyclades see Kykládes

Cydonia see Chaniá

Cymru see Wales

20 M5 **Cynthiana** Kentucky, S USA 38°22′N 84°18′W

11 S17 **Cypress Hills** ▲▲ Alberta/Saskatchewan, SW Canada

Cypro-Syrian Basin see Cyprus Basin

121 U11 **Cyprus** off. Republic of Cyprus, Gk. Kypros, Turk. Kıbrıs, Kıbrıs Cumhuriyeti. ◆ republic E Mediterranean Sea

84 L14 **Cyprus** Gk. Kypros, Turk. Kıbrıs. island E Mediterranean Sea

121 W11 **Cyprus Basin** var. Cypro-Syrian Basin. undersea feature E Mediterranean Sea 34°00′N 34°00′E

Cyprus, Republic of see Cyprus

75 S8 **Cyrenaica** ⬖ cultural region NE Libya

Cythera see Kýthira

Cythnos see Kýthnos

110 F9 **Czaplinek** Ger. Tempelburg. Zachodnio-pomorskie, NW Poland 53°33′N 16°14′E

Czarna Woda see Wda

110 G8 **Czarne** Pomorskie, N Poland 53°40′N 17°00′E

110 G10 **Czarnków** Wielkopolskie, C Poland 52°53′N 16°32′E

111 E17 **Czech Republic** Cz. Česká Republika. ◆ republic C Europe

Czegléd see Cegléd

110 G12 **Czempiń** Wielkopolskie, C Poland 52°10′N 16°46′E

Czenstochau see Częstochowa

Czerkow see Čerchov

Czernowitz see Chernivtsi

110 I8 **Czersk** Pomorskie, N Poland 53°48′N 17°58′E

111 J15 **Częstochowa** Ger. Czenstochau, Tschenstochau, Rus. Chenstokhov. Śląskie, S Poland 50°49′N 19°07′E

110 F10 **Człopa** Ger. Schloppe. Zachodnio-pomorskie, NW Poland 53°05′N 16°05′E

110 H8 **Człuchów** Ger. Schlochau. Pomorskie, NW Poland 53°41′N 17°20′E

D

163 V9 **Da'an** var. Dalai. Jilin, NE China 45°28′N 124°18′E

15 S10 **Daaquam** Québec, SE Canada 46°36′N 70°03′W

Daawo, Webi see Dawa Wenz

54 I4 **Dabajuro** Falcón, NW Venezuela 11°00′N 70°41′W

77 N15 **Dabakala** NE Ivory Coast 08°19′N 04°24′W

163 S11 **Daban** var. Bairin Youqi. Nei Mongol Zizhiqu, N China 43°33′N 118°40′E

158 L5 **Dabancheng** Xinjiang Uygur Zizhiqu, W China 43°21′N 88°19′E

111 K23 **Dabas** Pest, C Hungary 47°36′N 18°22′E

160 L8 **Daba Shan** ▲▲ C China

Dabba see Daocheng

140 J5 **Dabbāgh, Jabal** ▲ NW Saudi Arabia 27°52′N 35°48′E

54 D8 **Dabeiba** Antioquia, NW Colombia 07°01′N 76°18′W

149 P11 **Dādhar** Baluchistān, SW Pakistan 29°28′N 67°39′E

154 E11 **Dabhoi** Gujarāt, W India 22°08′N 73°28′E

161 P8 **Dabie Shan** ▲▲ C China

76 J13 **Dabola** C Guinea 10°48′N 11°02′W

77 N17 **Dabou** S Ivory Coast 05°20′N 04°23′W

162 M15 **Dabqig** prev. Uxin Qi. Nei Mongol Zizhiqu, N China 38°29′N 108°48′E

110 P8 **Dąbrowa Białostocka** Podlaskie, NE Poland 53°38′N 23°18′E

111 M16 **Dąbrowa Tarnowska** Małopolskie, S Poland 50°10′N 21°E

119 M20 **Dabryn'** Rus. Dobryn'. Homyel'skaya Voblasts', SE Belarus 51°46′N 29°12′E

159 P10 **Dabsan Hu** ◎ C China

161 Q13 **Dabu** var. Huliao. Guangdong, S China 24°19′N 116°07′E

116 H15 **Dăbuleni** Dolj, SW Romania 43°48′N 24°05′E

Dacca see Dhaka

101 L23 **Dachau** Bayern, SE Germany 48°15′N 11°26′E

Dachuan see Dazhou

Dacia Bank see Dacia Seamount

64 M10 **Dacia Seamount** var. Dacia Bank. undersea feature E Atlantic Ocean 31°10′N 13°42′W

37 T3 **Dacono** Colorado, C USA 40°04′N 104°56′W

Đăc Tô see Đak Tô

Dacura see Dákura

23 W12 **Dade City** Florida, SE USA 28°21′N 82°12′W

152 L10 **Ḍaḍeldhurā** var. Dandeldhura. Far Western, W Nepal 29°12′N 80°31′E

23 Q5 **Dadeville** Alabama, S USA 32°49′N 85°45′W

Dadong see Donggang

103 N15 **Dadou** ≈ S France

154 D12 **Dādra and Nagar Haveli** ⬖ union territory W India

149 P14 **Dādu** Sind, SE Pakistan 26°42′N 67°48′E

167 U11 **Da Du Boloc** Kon Tum, C Vietnam 14°06′N 107°40′E

160 G9 **Dadu He** ≈ C China

Daegu see Taegu

Daerah Istimewa Aceh see Aceh

171 P4 **Daet** Luzon, N Philippines 14°06′N 122°57′E

160 I11 **Dafang** Guizhou, S China 27°07′N 105°40′E

Dafeng see Shanglin

153 W11 **Dafla Hills** ▲▲ NE India

11 U15 **Dafoe** Saskatchewan, S Canada 51°46′N 104°11′W

76 G10 **Dagana** N Senegal 16°28′N 15°35′W

Dagana see Massakory, Chad

Dagana see Dahana, Tajikistan

Dagcagoin see Zoigê

118 K11 **Dagda** Krāslava, SE Latvia 56°06′N 27°36′E

Dagden see Hiiumaa

Dagden-Sund see Soela Väin

127 P16 **Dagestan, Respublika** prev. Dagestanskaya ASSR, Eng. Daghestan. ⬖ autonomous republic SW Russian Federation

Dagestanskaya ASSR see Dagestan, Respublika

127 R17 **Dagestanskiye Ogni** Respublika Dagestan, SW Russian Federation 42°09′N 48°08′E

Dagezhen see Fengning

149 U5 **Daggar** North-West Frontier Province, N Pakistan 34°30′N 72°28′E

185 A23 **Dagg Sound** sound South Island, New Zealand

Daghestan see Dagestan, Respublika

141 Y8 **Daghmar** NE Oman 23°09′N 59°01′E

Dağliq Quarabağ see Nagorno-Karabakh

Dagö see Hiiumaa

54 D11 **Dagua** Valle del Cauca, W Colombia 03°39′N 76°40′W

160 H11 **Daguan** var. Cuihua. Yunnan, SW China 27°42′N 103°51′E

171 N3 **Dagupan** off. Dagupan City. Luzon, N Philippines 16°05′N 120°21′E

Dagupan City see Dagupan

159 N16 **Dagzê** var. Dêqên. Xizang Zizhiqu, W China 29°38′N 91°15′E

147 Q13 **Dahana** Rus. Dagana, Dakhana. SW Tajikistan 38°03′N 69°51′E

163 V10 **Dahei Shan** ▲▲ N China

163 T7 **Da Hinggan Ling** Eng. Great Khingan Range. ▲▲ NE China

Dahlac Archipelago see Dahlak Archipelago

80 K9 **Dahlak Archipelago** var. Dahlac Archipelago. island group E Eritrea

23 T2 **Dahlonega** Georgia, SE USA 34°31′N 83°59′W

101 O14 **Dahme** Brandenburg, E Germany 52°10′N 13°47′E

100 O13 **Dahme** ≈ E Germany

141 O14 **Dahm, Ramlat** desert NW Yemen

154 E10 **Dāhod** prev. Dohad. Gujarāt, W India 22°48′N 74°18′E

Dahomey see Benin

158 G10 **Dahongliutan** Xinjiang Uygur Zizhiqu, NW China 35°59′N 79°12′E

Dahra see Dara

Dahuaishu see Hongtong

139 R2 **Dahūk** var. Dohuk, Kurd. Dihōk. ⬖ governorate N Iraq

139 R2 **Dahūk** var. Dohuk, Kurd. Dihōk. Dahūk, N Iraq 36°52′N 43°01′E

116 J15 **Daia** Giurgiu, S Romania 44°00′N 25°59′E

165 P12 **Daigo** Ibaraki, Honshū, S Japan 36°43′N 140°22′E

163 O13 **Dai Hai** ◎ N China

Daihoku see T'aipei

186 M8 **Dai Island** island N Solomon Islands

166 M8 **Daik-u** Bago, SW Burma (Myanmar) 17°46′N 96°40′E

138 H9 **Dā'īl** Dar'ā, S Syria 32°45′N 36°08′E

167 U12 **Đai Lanh** Khanh Hoa, S Vietnam 12°49′N 109°20′E

161 Q13 **Daimao Shan** ▲▲ SE China

105 N11 **Daimiel** Castilla-La Mancha, C Spain 39°04′N 03°37′W

115 F22 **Daimoniá** Pelopónnisos, S Greece 36°38′N 22°54′E

Dainan see T'ainan

25 W6 **Daingerfield** Texas, SW USA 33°03′N 94°42′W

Daingin, Bá an see Dingle Bay

159 R13 **Dainkognubma** Xizang Zizhiqu, W China 32°26′N 97°58′E

164 K14 **Daiō-zaki** headland Honshū, SW Japan 34°15′N 136°50′E

Dairbhre see Valencia Island

61 B22 **Daireaux** Buenos Aires, E Argentina 36°34′S 61°40′W

Dairen see Dalian

Dairûṭ see Dayrūṭ

25 X10 **Daisetta** Texas, SW USA 30°06′N 94°38′W

192 G5 **Daitō-jima** island group SW Japan

192 G5 **Daitō Ridge** undersea feature N Philippine Sea 25°30′N 133°00′E

161 N3 **Daixian** var. Dai Xian, Shangguan. Shanxi, C China 39°10′N 112°57′E

Dai Xian see Daixian

Daiyue see Shanyin

161 Q12 **Daiyun Shan** ▲▲ SE China

44 M8 **Dajabón** NW Dominican Republic 19°35′N 71°41′W

160 G8 **Dajin Chuan** ≈ C China

148 J6 **Dak** ◎ W Afghanistan

76 F11 **Dakar** ● (Senegal) W Senegal 14°44′N 17°27′W

76 F11 **Dakar** ✕ W Senegal 14°42′N 17°27′W

167 U10 **Đak Glây** Kon Tum, C Vietnam 15°05′N 107°42′E

Dakhana see Dahana

153 U16 **Dakhin Shahbazpur Island** island S Bangladesh

Dakhla see Ad Dakhla

76 F7 **Dakhlet Nouâdhibou** ⬖ region NW Mauritania

Đak Lap see Kiên Đưc

Đak Nông see Gia Nghia

77 U11 **Dakoro** Maradi, S Niger 14°29′N 06°45′E

29 U12 **Dakota City** Iowa, C USA 42°42′N 94°13′W

29 R13 **Dakota City** Nebraska, C USA 42°25′N 96°25′W

Đakovica see Gjakovë

112 I10 **Đakovo** var. Djakovo, Hung. Diakovár. Osijek-Baranja, E Croatia 45°18′N 18°24′E

Dakshin see Deccan

167 U11 **Đak Tô** var. Đăc Tô. Kon Tum, C Vietnam 14°35′N 107°55′E

43 N7 **Dákura** var. Dacura. Región Autónoma Atlántico Norte, NE Nicaragua 14°22′N 83°13′W

95 I14 **Dal** Akershus, S Norway 60°19′N 11°16′E

82 E12 **Dala** Lunda Sul, E Angola 11°04′S 20°15′E

108 J8 **Dalaas** Vorarlberg, W Austria 47°08′N 10°03′E

76 I13 **Dalaba** W Guinea 10°47′N 12°12′W

Dalai see Da'an

162 I12 **Dalain Hob** var. Ejin Qi. Nei Mongol Zizhiqu, N China 41°59′N 101°04′E

Dalai Nor see Hulun Nur

163 Q11 **Dalai Nur** salt lake N China

Dala-Jarna see Järna

95 M14 **Dalälven** ≈ C Sweden

136 C16 **Dalaman** Muğla, SW Turkey 36°47′N 28°47′E

136 C16 **Dalaman** ✕ Muğla, SW Turkey 36°37′N 28°51′E

136 D16 **Dalaman Çayı** ≈ SW Turkey

162 K11 **Dalandzadgad** Ömnögovĭ, S Mongolia 43°35′N 104°23′E

95 D17 **Dalane** physical region S Norway

189 Z2 **Dalap-Uliga-Djarrit** var. Delap-Uliga-Darrit, D-U-D. island group Ratak Chain, SE Marshall Islands

94 J12 **Dalarna** prev. Kopparberg. ⬖ county C Sweden

94 L13 **Dalarna** prev. Eng. Dalecarlia. cultural region C Sweden

95 P16 **Dalarö** Stockholm, C Sweden 59°07′N 18°25′E

167 U13 **Đa Lat** Lâm Đông, S Vietnam 11°56′N 108°25′E

Dalay see Bayandalay

148 L12 **Dālbandīn** var. Dāl Bandin. Baluchistān, SW Pakistan 28°48′N 64°08′E

95 J17 **Dalbosjön** lake bay S Sweden

181 Y10 **Dalby** Queensland, E Australia 27°11′S 151°12′E

94 D13 **Dale** Hordaland, S Norway 60°35′N 05°48′E

94 C12 **Dale** Sogn Og Fjordane, S Norway 61°22′N 05°24′E

32 K12 **Dale** Oregon, NW USA 44°58′N 118°56′W

25 T11 **Dale** Texas, SW USA 29°56′N 97°34′W

Dalecarlia see Dalarna

21 W4 **Dale City** Virginia, NE USA 38°38′N 77°18′W

20 L8 **Dale Hollow Lake** ⊠ Kentucky/Tennessee, S USA

98 O8 **Dalen** Drenthe, NE Netherlands 52°42′N 06°45′E

95 E15 **Dalen** Telemark, S Norway 59°25′N 07°58′E

166 K14 **Daletme** Chin State, W Burma (Myanmar) 21°44′N 92°48′E

23 Q7 **Daleville** Alabama, S USA 31°18′N 85°42′W

98 M9 **Dalfsen** Overijssel, E Netherlands 52°31′N 06°16′E

24 M1 **Dalhart** Texas, SW USA 36°05′N 102°31′W

13 O13 **Dalhousie** New Brunswick, SE Canada 48°03′N 66°22′W

152 I6 **Dalhousie** Himāchal Pradesh, N India 32°32′N 76°01′E

160 F12 **Dali** var. Xiaguan. Yunnan, SW China 25°34′N 100°11′E

Dali see Idálion

163 U14 **Dalian** var. Dairen, Dalien, Jay Dairen, Lüda, Ta-lien, Rus. Dalny. Liaoning, NE China 38°53′N 121°37′E

105 O15 **Dalías** Andalucía, S Spain 36°49′N 02°50′W

Dalien see Dalian

Dalijan see Delījān

112 J9 **Dalj** Hung. Dalja. Osijek-Baranja, E Croatia 45°29′N 19°00′E

Dalja see Dalj

32 F12 **Dallas** Oregon, NW USA 44°56′N 123°20′W

25 U6 **Dallas** Texas, SW USA 32°47′N 96°48′W

25 T7 **Dallas-Fort Worth** ✕ Texas, SW USA 32°37′N 97°16′W

154 K12 **Dalli Rājhara** var. Dhalli Rajhara. Chhattīsgarh, C India 20°32′N 81°10′E

39 X15 **Dall Island** island Alexander Archipelago, Alaska, USA

38 M12 **Dall Lake** ◎ Alaska, USA

Dállogilli see Korpilombolo

77 S12 **Dallol Bosso** seasonal river W Niger

141 U7 **Dalmā** island W United Arab Emirates

113 E14 **Dalmacija** Eng. Dalmatia, Ger. Dalmatien, It. Dalmazia. cultural region S Croatia

Dalmatia/Dalmatien/Dalmazia see Dalmacija

123 S15 **Dal'negorsk** Primorskiy Kray, SE Russian Federation 44°27′N 135°30′E

Dalny see Dalian

76 M16 **Daloa** C Ivory Coast 06°56′N 06°28′W

160 J11 **Dalou Shan** ▲▲ S China

181 X7 **Dalrymple Lake** ◎ Queensland, E Australia

14 H14 **Dalrymple Lake** ◎ Ontario, S Canada

181 X7 **Dalrymple, Mount** ▲ Queensland, E Australia 21°01′S 148°34′E

93 K20 **Dalsbruk** Fin. Taalintehdas. Länsi-Suomi, W Finland 60°02′N 22°31′E

95 K19 **Dalsjöfors** Västra Götaland, S Sweden 57°43′N 13°05′E

95 J17 **Dals Långed** var. Långed. Västra Götaland, S Sweden 58°54′N 12°20′E

153 O15 **Dāltenganj** prev. Daltonganj. Jhārkhand, N India 24°02′N 84°07′E

23 R2 **Dalton** Georgia, SE USA 34°46′N 84°58′W

Daltonganj see Dāltenganj

195 X14 **Dalton Iceberg Tongue** ice feature Antarctica

92 J1 **Dalvík** Nordhurland Eystra, N Iceland 65°58′N 18°31′W

Dálvvadis see Jokkmokk

35 N8 **Daly City** California, W USA 37°44′N 122°27′W

181 P2 **Daly River** ≈ Northern Territory, N Australia

181 Q3 **Daly Waters** Northern Territory, N Australia 16°21′S 133°22′E

119 F20 **Damachava** var. Damachova, Pol. Domaczewo, Rus. Domachëvo. Brestskaya Voblasts', SW Belarus 51°45′N 23°36′E

Damachova see Damachava

77 W11 **Damagaram Takaya** Zinder, S Niger 14°02′N 09°28′E

154 D12 **Damān** Damān and Diu, W India 20°25′N 72°58′E

154 B12 **Damān and Diu** ⬖ union territory W India

75 V7 **Damanhûr** anc. Hermopolis Parva. N Egypt 31°03′N 30°28′E

161 O1 **Damaqun Shan** ▲▲ E China

79 I15 **Damara** Ombella-Mpoko, S Central African Republic 05°00′N 18°45′E

83 D18 **Damaraland** physical region C Namibia

171 S15 **Damar, Kepulauan** var. Baraf Daja Islands, Kepulauan Barat Daya. island group C Indonesia

168 J8 **Damar Laut** Perak, Peninsular Malaysia 04°13′N 100°36′E

171 S15 **Damar, Pulau** island Maluku, E Indonesia

Damas see Dimashq

77 Y12 **Damasak** Borno, NE Nigeria 13°10′N 12°40′E

Damasco see Dimashq

21 Q8 **Damascus** Virginia, NE USA 36°37′N 81°46′W

Damascus see Dimashq

77 X13 **Damaturu** Yobe, NE Nigeria 11°44′N 11°58′E

171 R9 **Damau** Pulau Kaburuang, N Indonesia 03°46′N 126°49′E

143 O5 **Damāvand, Qolleh-ye** ▲ N Iran 35°56′N 52°08′E

82 B10 **Damba** Uíge, NW Angola 06°44′S 15°20′E

114 M12 **Dambaslar** Tekirdağ, NW Turkey 41°13′N 27°13′E

116 J13 **Dâmboviţa** prev. Dîmboviţa. ⬖ county SE Romania

116 J13 **Dâmboviţa** prev. Dîmboviţa. ≈ S Romania

173 Y15 **D'Ambre, Île** island NE Mauritius

155 K24 **Dambulla** Central Province, C Sri Lanka 07°51′N 80°40′E

44 K9 **Dame-Marie** SW Haiti 18°36′N 74°26′W

44 J9 **Dame Marie, Cap** headland SW Haiti 18°37′N 74°24′W

143 Q4 **Dāmghān** Semnān, N Iran 36°13′N 54°22′E

Damietta see Dumyāt

138 G10 **Dāmiyā** Al Balqā', NW Jordan 32°07′N 35°33′E

146 G11 **Damla** Daşoguz Welaýaty, N Turkmenistan 40°05′N 59°15′E

Dammām see Ad Dammān

100 G12 **Damme** Niedersachsen, NW Germany 52°31′N 08°12′E

153 R15 **Dāmodar** ≈ NE India

154 J9 **Damoh** Madhya Pradesh, C India 23°50′N 79°30′N

77 P15 **Damongo** NW Ghana 09°05′N 01°49′W

138 G7 **Damoûr** var. Ad Dāmūr. W Lebanon 33°36′N 35°30′E

171 N11 **Dampal, Teluk** bay Sulawesi, C Indonesia

180 H7 **Dampier** Western Australia 20°40′S 116°40′E

180 H6 **Dampier Archipelago** island group Western Australia

141 U14 **Damqawt** var. Damqut. E Yemen 16°35′N 52°39′E

159 O13 **Dam Qu** ≈ C China

Damqut see Damqawt

167 R13 **Dâmrei, Chuŏr Phmun** Fr. Chaîne de l'Éléphant. ▲▲ SW Cambodia

108 C7 **Damvant** Jura, NW Switzerland 47°22′N 06°55′E

Damwâld see Damwoude

98 L5 **Damwoude** Fris. Damwâld. Friesland, N Netherlands 53°18′N 05°59′E

Damxoi see Comai

159 N15 **Damxung** var. Gongtang. Xizang Zizhiqu, W China 30°29′N 91°02′E

80 K11 **Danakil Desert** var. Afar Depression, Danakil Plain. desert E Africa

Danakil Plain see Danakil Desert

35 R8 **Dana, Mount** ▲ California, W USA 37°54′N 119°13′W

76 L16 **Danané** W Ivory Coast 07°16′N 08°09′W

167 U10 **Đă Năng** prev. Tourane. Quang Nam-Đa Năng, C Vietnam 16°04′N 108°14′E

160 G9 **Danba** var. Zhanggu, Tib. Rongzhag. Sichuan, C China 30°54′N 101°49′E

Danborg see Daneborg

18 L13 **Danbury** Connecticut, NE USA 41°21′N 73°27′W

25 W12 **Danbury** Texas, SW USA 29°13′N 95°20′W

35 X15 **Danby Lake** ◎ California, W USA

194 H4 **Danco Coast** physical region Antarctica

82 B11 **Dande** ≈ NW Angola

Dandeldhura see Ḍaḍeldhurā

155 E17 **Dandeli** Karnātaka, W India 15°18′N 74°42′E

183 O12 **Dandenong** Victoria, SE Australia 38°01′S 145°13′E

163 V13 **Dandong** var. Tan-tung; prev. An-tung. Liaoning, NE China 40°10′N 124°23′E

197 Q14 **Daneborg** var. Danborg. ⬖ Tunu, N Greenland

25 V12 **Danevang** Texas, SW USA 29°03′N 96°11′W

Dänew see Galkynyş

Danfeng see Shizong

14 L12 **Danford Lake** Québec, SE Canada 45°55′N 76°12′W

19 T4 **Danforth** Maine, NE USA 45°39′N 67°54′W

37 P3 **Danforth Hills** ▲▲ Colorado, C USA

Dangara see Danghara

159 V12 **Dangchang** Gansu, C China 34°01′N 104°19′E

159 P8 **Dangchengwan** var. Subei, Subei Mongolzu Zizhixian. Gansu, N China 39°33′N 94°50′E

82 B10 **Dange** Uíge, NW Angola 07°55′S 15°01′E

Dangerous Archipelago see Tuamotu, Îles

83 E26 **Danger Point** headland SW South Africa 34°37′S 19°20′E

147 Q13 **Danghara** Rus. Dangara. SW Tajikistan 38°05′N 69°14′E

159 P8 **Danghe Nanshan** ▲▲ W China

80 I12 **Dangila** var. Dānglā. Āmara, NW Ethiopia 11°08′N 36°51′E

159 P8 **Dangjin Shankou** pass N China

Dangla see Tanggula Shan, China

Dang La see Tanggula Shankou, China

Dānglā see Dangila, Ethiopia

Dangme Chu see Manās

153 Y11 **Dāngori** Assam, NE India 27°40′N 95°35′E

159 N14 **Dangqên** Xizang Zizhiqu, W China 31°43′N 91°52′E

Dang Raek, Phanom/Dangrek, Chaîne des see Dângrêk, Chuŏr Phnum

167 S11 **Dângrêk, Chuŏr Phnum** var. Phanom Dang Raek, Phanom Dong Rak, Fr. Chaîne des Dangrek. ▲▲ Cambodia/Thailand

42 G3 **Dangriga** prev. Stann Creek. Stann Creek, E Belize 16°59′N 88°13′W

161 P6 **Dangshan** Anhui, E China 34°22′N 116°21′E

33 T15 **Daniel** Wyoming, C USA 42°49′N 110°04′W

83 H22 **Daniëlskuil** Northern Cape, N South Africa 28°11′S 23°33′E

19 N12 **Danielson** Connecticut, NE USA 41°48′N 71°53′W

124 M15 **Danilov** Yaroslavskaya Oblast', W Russian Federation 58°11′N 40°11′E

127 O9 **Danilovka** Volgogradskaya Oblast', SW Russian Federation 50°21′N 44°03′E

Danish West Indies see Virgin Islands (US)

160 L7 **Dan Jiang** ≈ C China

160 M7 **Danjiangkou Shuiku** ⊠ C China

141 W8 **Ḍank** var. Dhank. NW Oman 23°34′N 56°16′E

152 J7 **Dankhar** Himāchal Pradesh, N India 32°08′N 78°12′E

126 L6 **Dankov** Lipetskaya Oblast', W Russian Federation 53°17′N 39°07′E

42 J7 **Danlí** El Paraíso, S Honduras 14°02′N 86°34′W

Danmark see Denmark

Danmarksstraedet see Denmark Strait

95 O14 **Dannemora** Uppsala, C Sweden 60°13′N 17°49′E

18 L6 **Dannemora** New York, NE USA 44°42′N 73°42′W

100 K11 **Dannenberg** Niedersachsen, N Germany 53°05′N 11°06′E

184 N12 **Dannevirke** Manawatu-Wanganui, North Island, New Zealand 40°14′S 176°05′E

21 U8 **Dan River** ≈ Virginia, NE USA

167 P8 **Dan Sai** Loei, C Thailand 17°15′N 101°04′E

18 F10 **Dansville** New York, NE USA 42°34′N 77°40′W

155 K14 **Dantewāra** Chhattīsgarh, E India 18°53′N 81°20′E

Dantzig see Gdańsk

86 E12 **Danube** Bul. Dunav, Cz. Dunaj, Ger. Donau, Hung. Duna, Rom. Dunărea. ≈ C Europe

Danubian Plain see Dunavska Ravnina

166 L8 **Danubyu** Ayeyarwady, SW Burma (Myanmar) 17°15′N 95°35′E

Danum see Doncaster

19 P11 **Danvers** Massachusetts, NE USA 42°34′N 70°54′W

27 T11 **Danville** Arkansas, C USA 35°03′N 93°22′W

31 N13 **Danville** Illinois, N USA 40°10′N 87°37′W

31 O14 **Danville** Indiana, N USA 39°45′N 86°31′W

29 Y15 **Danville** Iowa, C USA 40°52′N 91°18′W

20 M6 **Danville** Kentucky, S USA 37°40′N 84°49′W

18 G14 **Danville** Pennsylvania, NE USA 40°57′N 76°36′W

21 T6 **Danville** Virginia, NE USA 36°34′N 79°25′W

Danxian/Dan Xian see Danzhou

160 L17 **Danzhou** prev. Danxian, Dan Xian, Nada. Hainan, S China 19°31′N 109°31′E

Danzhou see Yichuan

Danzig see Gdańsk

Danziger Bucht see Danzig, Gulf of

110 J6 **Danzig, Gulf of** var. Gulf of Gdańsk, Ger. Danziger Bucht, Pol. Zakota Gdańska, Rus. Gdan'skaya Bukhta. gulf N Poland

160 F10 **Daocheng** var. Jinzhu, Tib. Dabba. Sichuan, C China 29°05′N 100°14′E

Daojiang see Daoxian

Daokou see Huaxian

104 H7 **Dão, Rio** ≈ N Portugal

Daosa see Dausa

77 Y7 **Dao Timmi** Agadez, NE Niger 20°31′N 13°34′E

160 M13 **Daoxian** var. Daojiang. Hunan, S China 25°30′N 111°37′E

77 Q14 **Dapaong** N Togo 10°52′N 00°12′E

23 N8 **Daphne** Alabama, S USA 30°36′N 87°54′W

171 P7 **Dapitan** Mindanao, S Philippines 08°39′N 123°26′E

159 P9 **Da Qaidam** Qinghai, C China 37°50′N 95°18′E

163 V8 **Daqing** var. Sartu. Heilongjiang, NE China 46°29′N 125°07′E

163 O13 **Daqing Shan** ▲▲ N China

163 T11 **Daqin Tal** var. Naiman Qi. Nei Mongol Zizhiqu, N China 42°51′N 120°41′E

Daqm see Duqm

160 G8 **Da Qu** var. Do Qu. ≈ C China

139 T5 **Dāqūq** var. Tāwūq. At Ta'mīn, N Iraq 35°08′N 44°27′E

76 G10 **Dara** var. Dahra. NW Senegal 15°20′N 15°28′W

138 H9 **Dar'ā** var. Der'a, Fr. Déraa. Dar'ā, SW Syria 32°37′N 36°06′E

138 H8 **Dar'ā** off. Muḥāfaẓat Dar'ā, var. Dará, Der'a, Derrá. ⬖ governorate S Syria

143 Q12 **Dārāb** Fārs, S Iran 28°52′N 54°25′E

116 K8 **Darabani** Botoşani, NW Romania 48°10′N 26°39′E

Daraj see Dirj

Dar'ā, Muḥāfaẓat see Dar'ā

142 M8 **Dārān** Eşfahān, W Iran 33°00′N 50°27′E

167 U12 **Da Răng, Sông** var. Ba. ≈ S Vietnam

Daraut-Kurgan see Daroot-Korgon

77 W13 **Darazo** Bauchi, E Nigeria 11°01′N 10°27′E

139 S3 **Darband** Arbīl, N Iraq 36°15′N 44°17′E

139 V4 **Darband-i Khān, Sadd** dam NE Iraq

139 N1 **Darbāsīyah** var. Derbisīye. Al Ḥasakah, N Syria 37°06′N 40°42′E

118 C11 **Darbėnai** Klaipėda, NW Lithuania 56°02′N 21°16′E

153 Q13 **Darbhanga** Bihār, N India 26°10′N 85°54′E

38 M9 **Darby, Cape** headland Alaska, USA 64°19′N 162°46′W

112 I9 **Darda** Hung. Dárda. Osijek-Baranja, E Croatia 45°37′N 18°41′E

Dárda see Darda

27 T11 **Dardanelle** Arkansas, C USA 35°11′N 93°09′W

27 S11 **Dardanelle, Lake** ⊠ Arkansas, C USA

Dardanelles see Çanakkale Boğazı

Dardanelli see Çanakkale

Dardo see Kangding

Dar-el-Beida see Casablanca

136 M14 **Darende** Malatya, C Turkey 38°34′N 37°29′E

◆ Country
● Country Capital
◇ Dependent Territory
○ Dependent Territory Capital
⬖ Administrative Regions
✕ International Airport
▲ Mountain
▲▲ Mountain Range
Volcano
≈ River
◎ Lake
⊠ Reservoir

Dar es Salaam – Den Haag

81 J22 **Dar es Salaam** Dar es Salaam, E Tanzania *06°51′S 39°18′E*
81 J22 **Dar es Salaam** ✈ Pwani, E Tanzania *06°50′S 39°17′E*
185 H18 **Darfield** Canterbury, South Island, New Zealand *43°29′S 172°07′E*
106 F7 **Darfo** Lombardia, N Italy *45°54′N 10°12′E*
80 B10 **Darfur** *var.* Darfur Massif. *cultural region* W Sudan
Darfur Massif *see* Darfur
Darganata/Dargan-Ata *see* Birata
143 T3 **Dargaz** *var.* Darreh Gaz; *prev.* Moḩammadābād. Khorāsān-Razavī, NE Iran *37°28′N 59°08′E*
139 U4 **Dargazayn** As Sulaymānīyah, NE Iraq *35°39′N 45°00′E*
183 P12 **Dargo** Victoria, SE Australia *37°29′S 147°15′E*
162 L6 **Darhan** Darhan Uul, N Mongolia *49°24′N 105°57′E*
163 N8 **Darhan** Hentiy, C Mongolia *46°38′N 109°25′E*
Darhan *see* Büreghangay
Darhan Muminggan Lianheqi *see* Bailingmiao
162 L6 **Darhan Uul** ◈ *province* N Mongolia
23 W7 **Darien** Georgia, SE USA *31°22′N 81°25′W*
43 W16 **Darién** *off.* Provincia del Darién. ◈ *province* SE Panama
Darién, Golfo del *see* Darien, Gulf of
43 X14 **Darien, Gulf of** *Sp.* Golfo del Darién. *gulf* S Caribbean Sea
Darien, Isthmus of *see* Panama, Istmo de
Darién, Provincia del *see* Darién
42 K9 **Dariense, Cordillera** ▲▲ C Nicaragua
43 W15 **Darién, Serranía del** ▲▲ Colombia/Panama
163 P10 **Dariganga** *var.* Ovoot. Sühbaatar, SE Mongolia *45°08′N 113°51′E*
Dario *see* Ciudad Darío
Dariorigum *see* Vannes
Dariv *see* Darvi
Darj *see* Dirj
Darjeeling *see* Dārjiling
153 S12 **Dārjiling** *prev.* Darjeeling. West Bengal, NE India *27°00′N 88°13′E*
Darkehnen *see* Ozersk
159 S12 **Darlag** *var.* Gümai. Qinghai, C China *33°43′N 99°42′E*
183 T3 **Darling Downs** *hill range* Queensland, E Australia
28 M2 **Darling, Lake** ⊠ North Dakota, N USA
180 I12 **Darling Range** ▲▲ Western Australia
182 L8 **Darling River** ≈ New South Wales, SE Australia
97 M15 **Darlington** N England, United Kingdom *54°31′N 01°34′W*
21 T12 **Darlington** South Carolina, SE USA *34°19′N 79°53′W*
30 K9 **Darlington** Wisconsin, N USA *42°41′N 90°08′W*
110 G7 **Darłowo** Zachodnio-pomorskie, NW Poland *54°24′N 16°21′E*
101 G19 **Darmstadt** Hessen, SW Germany *49°52′N 08°39′E*
75 S7 **Darnah** *var.* Dérna. NE Libya *32°46′N 22°39′E*
103 S6 **Darney** Vosges, NE France *48°06′N 05°58′E*
182 M7 **Darnick** New South Wales, SE Australia *32°52′S 143°38′E*
195 Y6 **Darnley, Cape** *cape* Antarctica
105 R7 **Daroca** Aragón, NE Spain *41°07′N 01°25′W*
147 S11 **Daroot-Korgon** *var.* Daraut-Kurgan. Oshskaya Oblast', SW Kyrgyzstan *39°35′N 72°13′E*
61 A23 **Darragueira** *var.* Darregueira. Buenos Aires, E Argentina *37°40′S 63°12′W*
Darregueira *see* Darragueira
Darreh Gaz *see* Dargaz
142 K7 **Darreh Shahr** *var.* Darreh-ye Shahr. Īlām, W Iran *33°10′N 47°18′E*
Darreh-ye Shahr *see* Darreh Shahr
32 I7 **Darrington** Washington, NW USA *48°15′N 121°36′W*
25 P1 **Darrouzett** Texas, SW USA *36°27′N 100°19′W*
153 S15 **Darsana** *var.* Darshana. Khulna, N Bangladesh *23°32′N 88°49′E*
Darshana *see* Darsana
100 M7 **Darss** *peninsula* NE Germany
100 M7 **Darsser Ort** *headland* NE Germany *54°28′N 12°31′E*
97 J24 **Dart** ≈ SW England, United Kingdom
Dartang *see* Baqên
97 P22 **Dartford** SE England, United Kingdom *51°27′N 00°13′E*
182 L12 **Dartmoor** Victoria, SE Australia *37°56′S 141°18′E*
97 I24 **Dartmoor** *moorland* SW England, United Kingdom
13 Q15 **Dartmouth** Nova Scotia, SE Canada *44°40′N 63°35′W*
97 J24 **Dartmouth** SW England, United Kingdom *50°21′N 03°34′W*
15 Y6 **Dartmouth** ≈ Québec, SE Canada
183 Q11 **Dartmouth Reservoir** ◎ Victoria, SE Australia
Dartuch, Cabo *see* Artrutx, Cap d'
186 C9 **Daru** Western, SW Papua New Guinea *09°05′S 143°10′E*
112 G9 **Daruvar** *Hung.* Daruvár. Bjelovar-Bilogora, NE Croatia *45°34′N 17°12′E*
Daruvár *see* Daruvar
Darvaza *see* Derweze, Turkmenistan
Darvaza *see* Darvoza, Uzbekistan
Darvazskiy Khrebet *see* Darvoz, Qatorkŭhi
Darvel Bay *see* Lahad Datu, Teluk
Darvel, Teluk *see* Lahad Datu, Teluk
162 F8 **Darvi** *var.* Dariv. Govĭ-Altay, W Mongolia *46°20′N 94°11′E*
162 F7 **Darvi** *var.* Bulgan. Hovd, W Mongolia *46°57′N 93°40′E*
148 L9 **Darvīshān** *var.* Darweshan, Garmser. Helmand, S Afghanistan *31°02′N 64°12′E*
147 O10 **Darvoza** *Rus.* Darvaza. Jizzax Viloyati, C Uzbekistan *40°59′N 67°19′E*
147 R13 **Darvoz, Qatorkŭhi** *Rus.* Darvazskiy Khrebet. ▲▲ C Tajikistan
Darweshan *see* Darvīshān
63 J15 **Darwin** Río Negro, S Argentina *39°13′S 65°41′W*
181 O1 **Darwin** *prev.* Palmerston, Port Darwin. *territory capital* Northern Territory, N Australia *12°28′S 130°52′E*
65 D24 **Darwin** *var.* Darwin Settlement. East Falkland, Falkland Islands *51°51′S 58°55′W*
62 H8 **Darwin, Cordillera** ▲▲ N Chile
Darwin Settlement *see* Darwin
57 B17 **Darwin, Volcán** ⛰ Galapagos Islands, Ecuador, E Pacific Ocean *0°12′S 91°17′W*
149 S8 **Darya Khān** Punjab, E Pakistan *31°47′N 71°10′E*
145 O15 **Dar'yalyktakyr, Ravnina** *plain* S Kazakhstan
143 T11 **Dārzīn** Kermān, S Iran *29°11′N 58°09′E*
Dashhowuz *see* Daşoguz
Dashhowuz Welayaty *see* Daşoguz Welaýaty
162 K7 **Dashinchilen** *var.* Süüj. Bulgan, C Mongolia *47°49′N 104°06′E*
119 O16 **Dashkawka** *Rus.* Dashkovka. Mahilyowskaya Voblasts', E Belarus *53°44′N 30°16′E*
Dashkhovuz *see* Daşoguz Welaýaty
Dashkhovuzskiy Velayat *see* Daşoguz Welaýaty
Dashköpri *see* Daşköpri
Dashkovka *see* Dashkawka
148 J15 **Dasht** ≈ SW Pakistan
Dasht-i *see* Bābūs, Dasht-e
Dashtidzhum *see* Dashtijum
147 R13 **Dashtijum** *Rus.* Dashtidzhum. SW Tajikistan *38°06′N 70°11′E*
149 W7 **Daska** Punjab, NE Pakistan *32°15′N 74°23′E*
146 J16 **Daşköpri** *var.* Dashköpri, *Rus.* Tashkepri. Mary Welaýaty, S Turkmenistan *36°15′N 62°37′E*
146 H8 **Daşoguz** *Rus.* Dashkhovuz, *Turkm.* Dashhowuz; *prev.* Tashauz. Daşoguz Welaýaty, N Turkmenistan *41°51′N 59°53′E*
146 E9 **Daşoguz Welaýaty** *var.* Dashhowuz Welayaty, *Rus.* Dashkhovuz, Dashkhovuzskiy Velayat. ◈ *province* N Turkmenistan
Đa, Sông *see* Black River
77 R15 **Dassa** *var.* Dassa-Zoumé. S Benin *07°46′N 02°15′E*
Dassa-Zoumé *see* Dassa
29 U8 **Dassel** Minnesota, N USA *45°06′N 94°18′W*
152 H3 **Dastegil Sar** ▲ N India
149 U4 **Dasu** North-West Frontier Province, N Pakistan *35°18′N 73°2′E*
136 C16 **Datça** Muğla, SW Turkey *36°46′N 27°40′E*
165 R4 **Date** Hokkaidō, NE Japan *42°28′N 140°51′E*
154 I8 **Datia** *prev.* Duttia. Madhya Pradesh, C India *25°41′N 78°28′E*
Dåtnejaevrie *see* Tunnsjøen
159 T10 **Datong** *var.* Datong Huizu Tuzu Zizhixian, Qiaotou. Qinghai, C China *37°01′N 101°33′E*
161 N2 **Datong** *var.* Tatung, Ta-t'ung. Shanxi, C China *40°09′N 113°17′E*
Datong *see* Tong'an
159 S8 **Datong He** ≈ C China
Datong Huizu Tuzu Zizhixian *see* Datong
159 S9 **Datong Shan** ▲▲ C China
169 O10 **Datu, Tanjung** *headland* Indonesia/Malaysia *02°01′N 109°37′E*
Datu, Teluk *see* Lahad Datu, Teluk
Daua *see* Dawa Wenz
172 H16 **Dauban, Mount** ▲ Silhouette, NE Seychelles
149 T7 **Dāūd Khel** Punjab, E Pakistan *32°52′N 71°35′E*
119 G15 **Daugai** Alytus, S Lithuania *54°22′N 24°20′E*
Daugava *see* Western Dvina
118 J11 **Daugavpils** *Ger.* Dünaburg; *prev. Rus.* Dvinsk. Daugvapils, SE Latvia *55°53′N 26°34′E*
Dauka *see* Dawkah
Daulatabad *see* Malāyer
Daulpur *see* Dhaulpur
101 D18 **Daun** Rheinland-Pfalz, W Germany *50°13′N 06°50′E*
155 E14 **Daund** *prev.* Dhond. Mahārāshtra, W India *18°28′N 74°38′E*
166 M12 **Daung Kyun** *island* S Burma (Myanmar)
11 W15 **Dauphin** Manitoba, S Canada *51°09′N 100°05′W*
103 S13 **Dauphiné** *cultural region* E France
23 N9 **Dauphin Island** *island* Alabama, S USA
11 X15 **Dauphin River** Manitoba, S Canada *51°55′N 98°03′W*
77 V12 **Daura** Katsina, N Nigeria *13°03′N 08°18′E*
152 H12 **Dausa** *prev.* Daosa. Rājasthān, N India *26°51′N 76°21′E*
Dauwa *see* Dawwah
137 Y10 **Däväçi** *Rus.* Divichi. NE Azerbaijan *41°15′N 48°58′E*
155 F18 **Dāvangere** Karnātaka, W India *14°30′N 75°52′E*
171 Q8 **Davao** *off.* Davao City. Mindanao, S Philippines *07°06′N 125°36′E*
Davao City *see* Davao
171 Q8 **Davao Gulf** *gulf* Mindanao, S Philippines
15 Q11 **Daveluyville** Québec, SE Canada *46°12′N 72°07′W*
29 Z14 **Davenport** Iowa, C USA *41°31′N 90°35′W*
32 L8 **Davenport** Washington, NW USA *47°39′N 118°09′W*
43 P16 **David** Chiriquí, W Panama *08°26′N 82°26′W*
15 O11 **David** ≈ Québec, SE Canada
29 R15 **David City** Nebraska, C USA *41°15′N 97°07′W*
David-Gorodok *see* Davyd-Haradok
11 T16 **Davidson** Saskatchewan, S Canada *51°15′N 105°59′W*
21 R10 **Davidson** North Carolina, SE USA *35°29′N 80°49′W*
26 K12 **Davidson** Oklahoma, C USA *34°15′N 99°06′W*
39 S6 **Davidson Mountains** ▲▲ Alaska, USA
172 M8 **Davie Ridge** *undersea feature* W Indian Ocean *17°10′S 41°45′E*
182 A1 **Davies, Mount** ▲ South Australia *26°14′S 129°14′E*
35 O7 **Davis** California, W USA *38°31′N 121°46′W*
27 N12 **Davis** Oklahoma, C USA *34°30′N 97°07′W*
195 Y7 **Davis** *Australian research station* Antarctica *68°30′S 78°15′E*
194 H3 **Davis Coast** *physical region* Antarctica
18 C16 **Davis, Mount** ▲ Pennsylvania, NE USA *39°47′N 79°10′W*
24 K9 **Davis Mountains** ▲▲ Texas, SW USA
195 Z9 **Davis Sea** *sea* Antarctica
65 O20 **Davis Seamounts** *undersea feature* S Atlantic Ocean
196 M13 **Davis Strait** *strait* Baffin Bay/Labrador Sea
127 U5 **Davlekanovo** Respublika Bashkortostan, W Russian Federation *54°13′N 55°06′E*
108 J9 **Davos** *Rmsch.* Tavau. Graubünden, E Switzerland *46°48′N 09°50′E*
119 J20 **Davyd-Haradok** *Pol.* Dawidgródek, *Rus.* David-Gorodok. Brestskaya Voblasts', SW Belarus *52°03′N 27°13′E*
163 U12 **Dawa** Liaoning, NE China *40°55′N 122°02′E*
141 O11 **Dawāsir, Wādī ad** *dry watercourse* S Saudi Arabia
81 K15 **Dawa Wenz** *var.* Daua, Webi Daawo. ≈ E Africa
Dawaymah, Birkat ad *see also* Umm al Baqar, Hawr
167 N10 **Dawei** *var.* Tavoy, Htawei. Tanintharyi, S Burma (Myanmar) *14°02′N 98°12′E*
119 K14 **Dawhinava** *Rus.* Dolginovo. Minskaya Voblasts', N Belarus *54°39′N 27°29′E*
Dawidgródek *see* Davyd-Haradok
141 V12 **Dawkah** *var.* Dauka. SW Oman *18°32′N 54°03′E*
Dawlat Qaṭar *see* Qatar
24 M3 **Dawn** Texas, SW USA *34°54′N 102°10′W*
Dawo *see* Maqên
140 M11 **Daws** Al Bāḩah, SW Saudi Arabia *20°19′N 41°12′E*
10 H5 **Dawson** *var.* Dawson City. Yukon Territory, NW Canada *64°04′N 139°24′W*
23 S6 **Dawson** Georgia, SE USA *31°46′N 84°27′W*
29 S9 **Dawson** Minnesota, N USA *44°55′N 96°03′W*
Dawson City *see* Dawson
11 N13 **Dawson Creek** British Columbia, W Canada *55°45′N 120°07′W*
10 H7 **Dawson Range** ▲▲ Yukon Territory, W Canada
181 Y9 **Dawson River** ≈ Queensland, E Australia
10 J15 **Dawsons Landing** British Columbia, SW Canada *51°33′N 127°38′W*
20 I7 **Dawson Springs** Kentucky, S USA *37°10′N 87°41′W*
23 S2 **Dawsonville** Georgia, SE USA *34°28′N 84°07′W*
160 G8 **Dawu** *var.* Xianshui. Sichuan, C China *30°55′N 101°08′E*
Dawu *see* Maqên
Dawukou *see* Shizuishan
141 Y10 **Dawwah** *var.* Dauwa. W Oman *20°36′N 58°52′E*
102 J15 **Dax** *var.* Ax; *anc.* Aquae Augustae, Aquae Tarbelicae. Landes, SW France *43°43′N 01°03′W*
Daxian *see* Dazhou
Daxiangshan *see* Gangu
Daxue *see* Wencheng
160 G9 **Daxue Shan** ▲▲ C China
Dayan *see* Lijiang
160 G12 **Dayao** *var.* Jinbi. Yunnan, SW China *25°41′N 101°23′E*
Dayishan *see* Gaoyou
149 O6 **Dāykondī** *province* C Afghanistan
183 N12 **Daylesford** Victoria, SE Australia *37°24′S 144°07′E*
35 U10 **Daylight Pass** *pass* California, W USA
61 D17 **Daymán, Río** ≈ N Uruguay
Dayong *see* Zhangjiajie
Dayr *see* Ad Dayr
138 G10 **Dayr 'Allā** *var.* Deir 'Alla. Al Balqā', N Jordan *32°39′N 36°06′E*
139 N4 **Dayr az Zawr** *var.* Deir ez Zor. Dayr az Zawr, E Syria *35°12′N 40°12′E*
138 M5 **Dayr az Zawr** *off.* Muḩāfaẓat Dayr az Zawr, *var.* Dayr Az-Zor. ◈ *governorate* E Syria
Dayr az Zawr, Muḩāfaẓat *see* Dayr az Zawr
Dayr Az-Zor *see* Dayr az Zawr
75 W9 **Dayrūṭ** *var.* Dairûṭ. C Egypt *27°34′N 30°48′E*
11 Q15 **Daysland** Alberta, SW Canada *52°53′N 112°19′W*
31 R14 **Dayton** Ohio, N USA *39°46′N 84°12′W*
20 L10 **Dayton** Tennessee, S USA *35°30′N 85°01′W*
25 W11 **Dayton** Texas, SW USA *30°03′N 94°53′W*
32 L10 **Dayton** Washington, NW USA *46°19′N 117°58′W*
23 X10 **Daytona Beach** Florida, SE USA *29°12′N 81°03′W*
169 U12 **Dayu** Borneo, C Indonesia *01°59′S 115°04′E*
161 O13 **Dayu Ling** ▲▲ S China
161 R7 **Da Yunhe** *Eng.* Grand Canal. *canal* E China
161 S11 **Dayu Shan** *island* SE China
160 K8 **Dazhou** *prev.* Dachuan, Daxian. Sichuan, C China *31°16′N 107°31′E*
160 J9 **Dazhu** *var.* Zhuyang. Sichuan, C China *30°45′N 107°11′E*
160 J9 **Dazu** *var.* Longgang. Chongqing Shi, C China *29°47′N 106°30′E*
83 H24 **De Aar** Northern Cape, C South Africa *30°40′S 24°01′E*
194 K5 **Deacon, Cape** *headland* Antarctica
39 R5 **Deadhorse** Alaska, USA *70°15′N 148°28′W*
33 T12 **Dead Indian Peak** ▲ Wyoming, C USA *44°36′N 109°45′W*
23 R9 **Dead Lake** ◎ Florida, SE USA
44 J4 **Deadman's Cay** Long Island, C Bahamas *23°09′N 75°06′W*
138 G11 **Dead Sea** *var.* Bahret Lut, Lacus Asphaltites, *Ar.* Al Baḩr al Mayyit, Baḩrat Lūt, *Heb.* Yam HaMelaḩ. *salt lake* Israel/Jordan
28 J9 **Deadwood** South Dakota, N USA *44°22′N 103°43′W*
97 Q22 **Deal** SE England, United Kingdom *51°14′N 01°23′E*
83 I22 **Dealesville** Free State, C South Africa *28°40′S 25°46′E*
161 P10 **De'an** *var.* Puting. Jiangxi, S China *29°24′N 115°46′E*
62 K9 **Deán Funes** Córdoba, C Argentina *30°25′S 64°22′W*
194 L12 **Dean Island** *island* Antarctica
Deanuvuotna *see* Tanafjorden
31 S10 **Dearborn** Michigan, N USA *42°16′N 83°13′W*
27 R3 **Dearborn** Missouri, C USA *39°31′N 94°46′W*
Deargget *see* Tärendö
32 K9 **Deary** Idaho, NW USA *46°46′N 116°33′W*
32 M9 **Deary** Washington, NW USA *46°42′N 116°36′W*
10 J10 **Dease** ≈ British Columbia, W Canada
10 J10 **Dease Lake** British Columbia, W Canada *58°28′N 130°04′W*
35 U11 **Death Valley** California, W USA *36°25′N 116°50′W*
35 U11 **Death Valley** *valley* California, W USA
92 M8 **Deatnu** *Fin.* Tenojoki, *Nor.* Tana. ≈ Finland/Norway *see also* Tenojoki
102 L4 **Deauville** Calvados, N France *49°21′N 00°06′E*
117 X7 **Debal'tseve** *Rus.* Debal'tsevo. Donets'ka Oblast', SE Ukraine *48°21′N 38°26′E*
Debal'tsevo *see* Debal'tseve
113 M19 **Debar** *Ger.* Dibra, *Turk.* Debre. W FYR Macedonia *41°32′N 20°33′E*
39 O9 **Debauch Mountain** ▲ Alaska, USA *64°31′N 159°52′W*
De Behagle *see* Laï
25 X7 **De Berry** Texas, SW USA *32°18′N 94°09′W*
127 T2 **Debessy** Udmurtskaya Respublika, NW Russian Federation *57°41′N 53°56′E*
111 N16 **Dębica** Podkarpackie, SE Poland *50°04′N 21°24′E*
De Bildt *see* De Bilt
98 J11 **De Bilt** *var.* De Bildt. Utrecht, C Netherlands *52°06′N 05°11′E*
123 T9 **Debin** Magadanskaya Oblast', E Russian Federation *62°18′N 150°42′E*
110 N13 **Dęblin** *Rus.* Ivangorod. Lubelskie, E Poland *51°34′N 21°50′E*
110 D10 **Dębno** Zachodnio-pomorskie, NW Poland *52°43′N 14°42′E*
39 S10 **Deborah, Mount** ▲ Alaska, USA *63°38′N 147°13′W*
33 N8 **De Borgia** Montana, NW USA *47°23′N 115°24′W*
Debra Birhan *see* Debre Birhan
Debra Marcos *see* Debre Mark'os
Debra Tabor *see* Debre Tabor
Debre *see* Debar
80 J13 **Debre Birhan** *var.* Debra Birhan. Āmara, N Ethiopia *09°45′N 39°40′E*
111 N22 **Debrecen** *Ger.* Debreczin, *Rom.* Debrețin; *prev.* Debreczen. Hajdú-Bihar, E Hungary *47°32′N 21°38′E*
Debreczen/Debreczin *see* Debrecen
80 I12 **Debre Mark'os** *var.* Debra Marcos. Āmara, N Ethiopia *10°18′N 37°48′E*
113 N19 **Debrešte** SW FYR Macedonia *41°29′N 21°20′E*
80 J11 **Debre Tabor** *var.* Debra Tabor. Āmara, N Ethiopia *11°46′N 38°06′E*
Debrețin *see* Debrecen
80 J13 **Debre Zeyt** Oromīya, C Ethiopia *08°41′N 39°00′E*
113 L16 **Deçan** *Serb.* Dečane; *prev.* Dečani. W Kosovo *42°33′N 20°18′E*
Dečane *see* Deçan
Dečani *see* Deçan
23 P2 **Decatur** Alabama, S USA *34°36′N 86°58′W*
23 S3 **Decatur** Georgia, SE USA *33°46′N 84°18′W*
30 L13 **Decatur** Illinois, N USA *39°50′N 88°57′W*
31 Q12 **Decatur** Indiana, N USA *40°50′N 84°57′W*
22 M5 **Decatur** Mississippi, S USA *32°26′N 89°06′W*
29 S14 **Decatur** Nebraska, C USA *42°00′N 96°19′W*
25 S6 **Decatur** Texas, SW USA *33°14′N 97°35′W*
20 H9 **Decaturville** Tennessee, S USA *35°35′N 88°08′W*
103 O13 **Decazeville** Aveyron, S France *44°34′N 02°18′E*
155 H17 **Deccan** *Hind.* Dakshin. *plateau* C India
14 J8 **Decelles, Réservoir** ⊠ Québec, SE Canada
12 K2 **Déception** Québec, NE Canada *62°06′N 74°36′W*
160 G11 **Dechang** *var.* Dezhou. Sichuan, C China *27°24′N 102°09′E*
111 C15 **Děčín** *Ger.* Tetschen. Ústecký Kraj, NW Czech Republic *50°48′N 14°15′E*
103 P9 **Decize** Nièvre, C France *46°51′N 03°25′E*
98 I6 **De Cocksdorp** Noord-Holland, NW Netherlands *53°09′N 04°52′E*
29 X11 **Decorah** Iowa, C USA *43°18′N 91°47′W*
Dedeagaç/Dedeagach *see* Alexandroúpoli
188 C15 **Dededo** N Guam *13°30′N 144°51′E*
98 N9 **Dedemsvaart** Overijssel, E Netherlands *52°36′N 06°28′E*
19 O11 **Dedham** Massachusetts, NE USA *42°14′N 71°10′W*
63 H19 **Dedo, Cerro** ▲ SW Argentina *44°46′S 71°48′W*
77 O13 **Dédougou** W Burkina *12°29′N 03°25′W*
124 G15 **Dedovichi** Pskovskaya Oblast', W Russian Federation *57°31′N 29°53′E*
Dedu *see* Wudalianchi
155 J24 **Deduru Oya** ≈ W Sri Lanka
83 N14 **Dedza** Central, S Malawi *14°20′S 34°24′E*
83 N14 **Dedza Mountain** ▲ C Malawi *14°22′S 34°16′E*
96 K9 **Dee** ≈ NE Scotland, United Kingdom
97 J19 **Dee** *Wel.* Afon Dyfrdwy. ≈ England/Wales, United Kingdom
Deep Bay *see* Chilumba
21 T3 **Deep Creek Lake** ⊠ Maryland, NE USA
36 J4 **Deep Creek Range** ▲▲ Utah, W USA
27 P10 **Deep Fork River** ≈ Oklahoma, C USA
14 J11 **Deep River** Ontario, SE Canada *46°04′N 77°29′W*
21 T10 **Deep River** ≈ North Carolina, SE USA
183 U4 **Deepwater** New South Wales, SE Australia *29°27′S 151°52′E*
31 S14 **Deer Creek Lake** ◎ Ohio, N USA
23 Z15 **Deerfield Beach** Florida, SE USA *26°19′N 80°06′W*
39 N8 **Deering** Alaska, USA *66°04′N 162°43′W*
38 M16 **Deer Island** *island* Alaska, USA
19 S7 **Deer Isle** *island* Maine, NE USA
13 S11 **Deer Lake** Newfoundland and Labrador, SE Canada *49°11′N 57°27′W*
99 D18 **Deerlijk** West-Vlaanderen, W Belgium *50°52′N 03°21′E*
33 Q10 **Deer Lodge** Montana, NW USA *46°24′N 112°43′W*
32 L8 **Deer Park** Washington, NW USA *47°55′N 117°28′W*
29 U5 **Deer River** Minnesota, N USA *47°19′N 93°47′W*
Deés *see* Dej
Defeng *see* Liping
31 R11 **Defiance** Ohio, N USA *41°17′N 84°21′W*
23 Q8 **De Funiak Springs** Florida, SE USA *30°43′N 86°07′W*
95 L23 **Degeberga** Skåne, S Sweden *55°48′N 14°06′E*
104 H12 **Degebe, Ribeira** ≈ S Portugal
80 M13 **Degeh Bur** Sumalē, E Ethiopia *08°08′N 43°35′E*
15 U9 **Dégelis** Québec, SE Canada *47°30′N 68°38′W*
77 U17 **Degema** Rivers, S Nigeria *04°46′N 06°47′E*
95 L16 **Degerfors** Örebro, C Sweden *59°14′N 14°26′E*
193 R14 **De Gerlache Seamounts** *undersea feature* SE Pacific Ocean
101 N21 **Deggendorf** Bayern, SE Germany *48°50′N 12°58′E*
80 I11 **Degoma** Āmara, N Ethiopia *12°22′N 37°36′E*
De Gordyk *see* Gorredijk
27 T12 **De Gray Lake** ⊠ Arkansas, C USA
180 J6 **De Grey River** ≈ Western Australia
126 M10 **Degtevo** Rostovskaya Oblast', SW Russian Federation *49°12′N 40°39′E*
Dehbārez *see* Rūdān
Deh Bīd *see* Şafāshahr
142 M10 **Deh Dasht** Kohkīlūyeh va Būyer AHmad, SW Iran *30°49′N 50°36′E*
75 N8 **Dehibat** SE Tunisia *31°58′N 10°43′E*
Dehli *see* Delhi
142 K8 **Dehlorān** Īlām, W Iran *32°41′N 47°18′E*
147 N13 **Dehqonobod** *Rus.* Dekhkanabad. Qashqadaryo Viloyati, S Uzbekistan *38°24′N 66°31′E*
152 J9 **Dehra Dūn** Uttaranchal, N India *30°19′N 78°04′E*
153 O14 **Dehri** Bihār, N India *24°55′N 84°11′E*
148 K10 **Deh Shū** *var.* Deshu. Helmand, S Afghanistan *30°28′N 63°21′E*
163 W9 **Dehui** Jilin, NE China *44°23′N 125°42′E*
99 D17 **Deinze** Oost-Vlaanderen, NW Belgium *50°59′N 03°32′E*
Deir 'Alla *see* Dayr 'Allā
Deir ez Zor *see* Dayr az Zawr
Deirgeirt, Loch *see* Derg, Lough
116 H9 **Dej** *Hung.* Dés; *prev.* Deés. Cluj, NW Romania *47°08′N 23°55′E*
95 K15 **Deje** Värmland, C Sweden *59°35′N 13°29′E*
171 Y15 **De Jongs, Tanjung** *headland* Papua, SE Indonesia *06°56′S 138°32′E*
De Jouwer *see* Joure
30 M10 **De Kalb** Illinois, N USA *41°55′N 88°45′W*
22 M5 **De Kalb** Mississippi, S USA *32°46′N 88°39′W*
25 W5 **De Kalb** Texas, SW USA *33°30′N 94°34′W*
83 G18 **Dekar** *var.* D'Kar. Ghanzi, NW Botswana *21°31′S 21°55′E*
Dekéleia *see* Dhekéleia
79 K20 **Dekese** Kasai-Occidental, C Dem. Rep. Congo *03°28′S 21°24′E*
Dekhkanabad *see* Dehqonobod
79 I14 **Dékoa** Kémo, C Central African Republic *06°17′N 19°07′E*
98 H6 **De Koog** Noord-Holland, NW Netherlands *53°06′N 04°43′E*
30 M9 **Delafield** Wisconsin, N USA *43°03′N 88°22′W*
61 C23 **De La Garma** Buenos Aires, E Argentina *37°58′S 60°25′W*
14 K10 **Delahey, Lac** ◎ Québec, SE Canada
80 E11 **Delami** Southern Kordofan, C Sudan *11°51′N 30°30′E*
23 X11 **De Land** Florida, SE USA *29°01′N 81°18′W*
35 R12 **Delano** California, W USA *35°46′N 119°15′W*
29 V8 **Delano** Minnesota, N USA *45°03′N 93°46′W*
36 K6 **Delano Peak** ▲ Utah, W USA *38°22′N 112°21′W*
Delap-Uliga-Darrit *see* Dalap-Uliga-Djarrit
148 L7 **Delārām** Nīmrūz, SW Afghanistan *32°11′N 63°27′E*
38 F17 **Delarof Islands** *island group* Aleutian Islands, Alaska, USA
30 M9 **Delavan** Wisconsin, N USA *42°37′N 88°37′W*
31 S13 **Delaware** Ohio, N USA *40°18′N 83°06′W*
18 I17 **Delaware** *off.* State of Delaware, *also known as* Blue Hen State, Diamond State, First State. ◈ *state* NE USA
18 I17 **Delaware Bay** *bay* NE USA
24 J8 **Delaware Mountains** ▲▲ Texas, SW USA
18 I12 **Delaware River** ≈ NE USA
27 Q3 **Delaware River** ≈ Kansas, C USA
18 J14 **Delaware Water Gap** *valley* New Jersey/Pennsylvania, NE USA
101 G14 **Delbrück** Nordrhein-Westfalen, W Germany *51°46′N 08°34′E*
11 Q15 **Delburne** Alberta, SW Canada *52°09′N 113°11′W*
172 M12 **Del Cano Rise** *undersea feature* SW Indian Ocean *45°15′S 44°15′E*
113 Q18 **Delčevo** NE FYR Macedonia *41°57′N 22°45′E*
Delcommune, Lac *see* Nzilo, Lac
98 O10 **Delden** Overijssel, E Netherlands *52°16′N 06°41′E*
183 R12 **Delegate** New South Wales, SE Australia *37°04′S 148°57′E*
De Lemmer *see* Lemmer
108 D7 **Delémont** *Ger.* Delsberg. Jura, NW Switzerland *47°22′N 07°21′E*
25 R7 **De Leon** Texas, SW USA *32°06′N 98°33′W*
115 F18 **Delfoi** Stereá Elláda, C Greece *38°28′N 22°31′E*
98 G12 **Delft** Zuid-Holland, W Netherlands *52°01′N 04°22′E*
155 J23 **Delft** *island* NW Sri Lanka
98 O5 **Delfzijl** Groningen, NE Netherlands *53°20′N 06°55′E*
0 E9 **Delgada Fan** *undersea feature* NE Pacific Ocean *39°15′N 126°00′W*
42 F7 **Delgado** San Salvador, SW El Salvador *13°44′N 89°07′W*
82 Q12 **Delgado, Cabo** *headland* N Mozambique *10°41′S 40°40′E*
162 G8 **Delger** *var.* Taygan. Govĭ-Altay, C Mongolia *46°20′N 97°22′E*
163 O9 **Delgereh** *var.* Hongor. Dornogovĭ, SE Mongolia *45°49′N 111°20′E*
162 J8 **Delgerhaan** *var.* Hujirt. Töv, C Mongolia *46°41′N 104°40′E*
162 K9 **Delgerhangay** *var.* Hashaat. Dundgovĭ, C Mongolia *45°09′N 104°51′E*
162 L9 **Delgertsogt** *var.* Amardalay. Dundgovĭ, C Mongolia *46°09′N 106°24′E*
80 E6 **Delgo** Northern, N Sudan *20°08′N 30°35′E*
159 R10 **Delhi** *var.* Delingha. Qinghai, C China *37°19′N 97°22′E*
152 I10 **Delhi** *var.* Dehli, *Hind.* Dilli, *hist.* Shahjahanabad. *union territory capital* Delhi, N India *28°40′N 77°11′E*
22 J5 **Delhi** Louisiana, S USA *32°28′N 91°29′W*
18 J11 **Delhi** New York, NE USA *42°16′N 74°55′W*
152 I10 **Delhi** ◈ *union territory* NW India
136 J17 **Deli Burnu** *headland* S Turkey *36°43′N 34°55′E*
14 F16 **Delice Çayı** ≈ C Turkey
55 X10 **Délices** C French Guiana *04°45′N 53°45′W*
40 J6 **Delicias** *var.* Ciudad Delicias. Chihuahua, N Mexico *28°09′N 105°22′W*
143 N7 **Delījān** *var.* Dalijan, Diliján. Markazī, W Iran *34°02′N 50°39′E*
112 P12 **Deli Jovan** ▲▲ E Serbia
Déli-Kárpátok *see* Carpații Meridionali
8 I8 **Déline** *prev.* Fort Franklin. Northwest Territories, NW Canada *65°10′N 123°30′W*
Delingha *see* Delhi
15 Q7 **Delisle** Québec, SE Canada *48°39′N 71°42′W*
11 T15 **Delisle** Saskatchewan, S Canada *51°54′N 107°01′W*
101 M15 **Delitzsch** Sachsen, E Germany *51°31′N 12°19′E*
33 Q12 **Dell** Montana, NW USA *44°41′N 112°42′W*
24 I7 **Dell City** Texas, SW USA *31°56′N 105°12′W*
103 U7 **Delle** Territoire-de-Belfort, E France *47°30′N 07°00′E*
36 J9 **Dellenbaugh, Mount** ▲ Arizona, SW USA *36°06′N 113°32′W*
29 R11 **Dell Rapids** South Dakota, N USA *43°50′N 96°42′W*
21 Y4 **Delmar** Maryland, NE USA *38°26′N 75°32′W*
18 K11 **Delmar** New York, NE USA *42°37′N 73°49′W*
100 G11 **Delmenhorst** Niedersachsen, NW Germany *53°03′N 08°38′E*
112 C9 **Delnice** Primorje-Gorski Kotar, NW Croatia *45°24′N 14°49′E*
37 R7 **Del Norte** Colorado, C USA *37°40′N 106°21′W*
39 N6 **De Long Mountains** ▲▲ Alaska, USA
183 P16 **Deloraine** Tasmania, SE Australia *41°34′S 146°43′E*
11 W17 **Deloraine** Manitoba, S Canada *49°12′N 100°28′W*
31 O12 **Delphi** Indiana, N USA *40°35′N 86°40′W*
31 Q12 **Delphos** Ohio, N USA *40°49′N 84°20′W*
23 Z15 **Delray Beach** Florida, SE USA *26°27′N 80°04′W*
25 O12 **Del Rio** Texas, SW USA *29°23′N 100°56′W*
Delsberg *see* Delémont
94 N11 **Delsbo** Gävleborg, C Sweden *61°49′N 16°34′E*
37 P6 **Delta** Colorado, C USA *38°44′N 108°04′W*
36 K5 **Delta** Utah, W USA *39°21′N 112°34′W*
77 T17 **Delta** ◈ *state* S Nigeria
55 Q6 **Delta Amacuro** *off.* Territorio Delta Amacuro. ◈ *federal district* NE Venezuela
Delta Amacuro, Territorio *see* Delta Amacuro
39 S9 **Delta Junction** Alaska, USA *64°02′N 145°43′W*
23 X11 **Deltona** Florida, SE USA *28°54′N 81°15′W*
183 T5 **Delungra** New South Wales, SE Australia *29°40′S 150°49′E*
162 D6 **Delüün** *var.* Rashaant. Bayan-Ölgiy, W Mongolia *47°48′N 90°45′E*
154 C12 **Delvāda** Gujarāt, W India *20°46′N 71°02′E*
61 B21 **Del Valle** Buenos Aires, E Argentina *35°55′S 60°42′W*
Delvina *see* Delvinë
115 C15 **Delvináki** *var.* Dhelvinákion; *prev.* Pogónion. Ípeiros, W Greece *39°57′N 20°28′E*
113 L23 **Delvinë** *var.* Delvina, *It.* Delvino. Vlorë, S Albania *39°56′N 20°07′E*
Delvino *see* Delvinë
116 I7 **Delyatyn** Ivano-Frankivs'ka Oblast', W Ukraine *48°32′N 24°38′E*
127 U5 **Dëma** ≈ W Russian Federation
105 O5 **Demanda, Sierra de la** ▲▲ W Spain
39 T5 **Demarcation Point** *headland* Alaska, USA *69°40′N 141°19′W*
79 K21 **Demba** Kasai-Occidental, C Dem. Rep. Congo *05°24′S 22°16′E*
172 H13 **Dembéni** Grande Comore, NW Comoros *11°50′S 43°25′E*
79 M15 **Dembia** Mbomou, SE Central African Republic *05°08′N 24°25′E*
Dembidollo *see* Dembī Dolo
80 H13 **Dembī Dolo** *var.* Dembidollo. Oromīya, C Ethiopia *08°33′N 34°49′E*
152 K6 **Demchok** *var.* Dêmqog. China/India *32°30′N 79°42′E* *see also* Dêmqog
152 L6 **Demchok** *var.* Dêmqog. *disputed region* China/India *see also* Dêmqog
99 I12 **De Meern** Utrecht, C Netherlands *52°06′N 05°00′E*
99 I17 **Demer** ≈ C Belgium
64 H12 **Demerara Plain** *undersea feature* W Atlantic Ocean *10°00′N 48°00′W*
64 H12 **Demerara Plateau** *undersea feature* W Atlantic Ocean
55 T9 **Demerara River** ≈ NE Guyana
126 H3 **Demidov** Smolenskaya Oblast', W Russian Federation *55°15′N 31°30′E*
37 Q15 **Deming** New Mexico, SW USA *32°17′N 107°46′W*
32 H6 **Deming** Washington, NW USA *48°49′N 122°13′W*
58 E10 **Demini, Rio** ≈ NW Brazil
136 D13 **Demirci** Manisa, W Turkey *39°03′N 28°40′E*
113 P19 **Demir Kapija** *prev.* Železna Vrata. SE FYR Macedonia *41°25′N 22°15′E*
114 N11 **Demirköy** Kırklareli, NW Turkey *41°48′N 27°49′E*
100 N9 **Demmin** Mecklenburg-Vorpommern, NE Germany *53°53′N 13°03′E*
23 O5 **Demopolis** Alabama, S USA *32°31′N 87°50′W*
31 N11 **Demotte** Indiana, N USA *41°13′N 87°07′W*
158 F13 **Dêmqog** *var.* Demchok. China/India *32°36′N 79°29′E* *see also* Demchok
152 L6 **Dêmqog** *var.* Demchok. *disputed region* China/India *see also* Demchok
171 Y13 **Demta** Papua, E Indonesia *02°19′S 140°06′E*
121 K11 **Dem'yanka** ≈ C Russian Federation
124 H15 **Demyansk** Novgorodskaya Oblast', W Russian Federation *57°39′N 32°31′E*
122 H10 **Dem'yanskoye** Tyumenskaya Oblast', C Russian Federation *59°39′N 69°15′E*
103 P2 **Denain** Nord, N France *50°19′N 03°24′E*
39 S10 **Denali** Alaska, USA *63°08′N 147°33′W*
Denali *see* McKinley, Mount
81 M14 **Denan** Sumalē, E Ethiopia *06°40′N 43°31′E*
Denau *see* Denov
97 J18 **Denbigh** *Wel.* Dinbych. NE Wales, United Kingdom *53°11′N 03°25′W*
97 J18 **Denbigh** *cultural region* N Wales, United Kingdom
98 I6 **Den Burg** Noord-Holland, NW Netherlands *53°03′N 04°47′E*
99 F18 **Dender** *Fr.* Dendre. ≈ W Belgium
99 F18 **Denderleeuw** Oost-Vlaanderen, NW Belgium *50°53′N 04°05′E*
99 F17 **Dendermonde** *Fr.* Termonde. Oost-Vlaanderen, NW Belgium *51°02′N 04°08′E*
Dendre *see* Dender
194 I9 **Dendtler Island** *island* Antarctica
98 P10 **Denekamp** Overijssel, E Netherlands *52°23′N 07°E*
77 W12 **Dengas** Zinder, S Niger *13°15′N 09°43′E*
Dêngka *see* Têwo
Dêngkagoin *see* Têwo
162 L13 **Dengkou** *var.* Bayan Gol. Nei Mongol Zizhiqu, N China *40°15′N 106°59′E*
159 Q14 **Dêngqên** *var.* Gyamotang. Xizang Zizhiqu, W China *31°28′N 95°28′E*
Deng Xian *see* Dengzhou
160 M7 **Dengzhou** *prev.* Deng Xian. Henan, C China *32°48′N 111°59′E*
Dengzhou *see* Penglai
Den Haag *see* 's-Gravenhage

◆ Country ● Country Capital ◇ Dependent Territory ○ Dependent Territory Capital ◈ Administrative Regions ✈ International Airport ▲ Mountain ▲▲ Mountain Range ⛰ Volcano ≈ River ◎ Lake ⊠ Reservoir

DENHAM – DIU

180 H10 Denham Western Australia 25°56′S 113°35′E
98 N9 Den Ham Overijssel, E Netherlands 52°30′N 06°31′E
44 J12 Denham, Mount ▲ C Jamaica 18°13′N 77°33′W
22 J8 Denham Springs Louisiana, S USA 30°29′N 90°57′W
98 I7 Den Helder Noord-Holland, NW Netherlands 52°54′N 04°45′E
105 T11 Dénia País Valenciano, E Spain 38°51′N 00°07′E
189 Q8 Denig W Nauru
183 N10 Deniliquin New South Wales, SE Australia 35°33′S 144°58′E
29 T14 Denison Iowa, C USA 42°00′N 95°22′W
25 U5 Denison Texas, SW USA 33°45′N 96°32′W
144 L8 Denisovka prev. Ordzhonikidze. Kostanay, N Kazakhstan 52°27′N 61°42′E
136 D15 Denizli Denizli, SW Turkey 37°46′N 29°05′E
136 D15 Denizli ◆ province SW Turkey
Denjong see Sikkim
183 S7 Denman New South Wales, SE Australia 32°24′S 150°43′E
195 Y10 Denman Glacier glacier Antarctica
21 R14 Denmark South Carolina, SE USA 33°19′N 81°08′W
95 G23 Denmark off. Kingdom of Denmark, Dan. Danmark; anc. Hafnia. ◆ monarchy N Europe
Denmark, Kingdom of see Denmark
92 H1 Denmark Strait var. Danmarksstraedet. strait Greenland/Iceland
45 T11 Dennery E Saint Lucia 13°55′N 60°53′W
98 I7 Den Oever Noord-Holland, NW Netherlands 52°56′N 05°01′E
147 O13 Denov Rus. Denau. Surkhondaryo Viloyati, S Uzbekistan 38°20′N 67°48′E
169 U17 Denpasar prev. Paloe. Bali, C Indonesia 08°40′S 115°14′E
116 E12 Denta Timiş, W Romania 45°20′N 21°15′E
21 Y3 Denton Maryland, NE USA 38°53′N 75°50′W
25 T6 Denton Texas, SW USA 33°11′N 97°08′W
186 G9 D'Entrecasteaux Islands island group SE Papua New Guinea
37 T4 Denver state capital Colorado, C USA 39°45′N 105°W
37 T4 Denver ✈ Colorado, C USA 39°57′N 104°38′W
24 L6 Denver City Texas, SW USA 32°57′N 102°49′W
152 J9 Deoband Uttar Pradesh, N India 29°41′N 77°40′E
154 N12 Deogarh Orissa, SW India 21°32′N 84°44′E
Deoghar see Devghar
154 E13 Deolāli Mahārāshtra, W India 19°55′N 73°49′E
154 I10 Deori Madhya Pradesh, C India 23°09′N 78°39′E
153 O12 Deoria Uttar Pradesh, N India 26°31′N 83°48′E
99 A17 De Panne West-Vlaanderen, W Belgium 51°06′N 02°35′E
Departamento del Quindío see Quindío
Departamento de Nariño, see Nariño
54 M5 Dependencia Federal off. Territorio Dependencia Federal. ◆ federal dependency N Venezuela
Dependencia Federal, Territorio see Dependencia Federal
30 M7 De Pere Wisconsin, N USA 44°26′N 88°03′W
18 D10 Depew New York, NE USA 42°54′N 78°41′W
99 E17 De Pinte Oost-Vlaanderen, NW Belgium 51°00′N 03°37′E
25 V5 Deport Texas, SW USA 33°31′N 95°19′W
123 Q8 Deputatskiy Respublika Sakha (Yakutiya), NE Russian Federation 69°18′N 139°48′E
Dêqên see Dagzê
27 S13 De Queen Arkansas, C USA 34°02′N 94°20′W
22 G8 De Quincy Louisiana, S USA 30°27′N 93°25′W
81 J20 Dera spring/well S Kenya 02°39′S 39°52′E
149 V11 Dera Bugti Baluchistān, SW Pakistan 28°35′N 65°25′E
Der'a/Derá/Déraa see Dar'ā
149 S10 Dera Ghāzi Khān var. Dera Ghāzikhān. Punjab, C Pakistan 30°01′N 70°37′E
Dera Ghāzikhān see Dera Ghāzi Khān
149 S8 Dera Ismāīl Khān North-West Frontier Province, C Pakistan 31°51′N 70°56′E
149 Q12 Dera Murād Jamāli Baluchistān, SW Pakistan 28°34′N 68°12′E
113 L16 Đeravica ▲ S Serbia 42°33′N 20°08′E
116 L6 Derazhnya Khmel'nyts'ka Oblast', W Ukraine 49°16′N 27°24′E
127 R17 Derbent Respublika Dagestan, SW Russian Federation 42°01′N 48°16′E
147 N13 Derbent Surkhondaryo Viloyati, S Uzbekistan 38°15′N 66°59′E
Derbisīye see Darbāsīyah
79 M15 Derbissaka Mbomou, SE Central African Republic 05°43′N 24°48′E
180 L4 Derby Western Australia 17°18′S 123°37′E
97 M19 Derby C England, United Kingdom 52°55′N 01°30′W
27 N7 Derby Kansas, C USA 37°33′N 97°16′W
97 L18 Derbyshire cultural region C England, United Kingdom
112 O11 Đerdap physical region E Serbia
Derelí see Gónnoi
162 L9 Deren var. Tsant. Dundgovĭ, C Mongolia 46°16′N 106°55′E
171 W13 Derew ≈ Papua, E Indonesia
127 R8 Dergachi Saratovskaya Oblast', W Russian Federation 51°15′N 48°58′E
Dergachi see Derhachi
97 C19 Derg, Lough Ir. Loch Deirgeirt. ◎ W Ireland
117 V5 Derhachi Rus. Dergachi. Kharkivs'ka Oblast', E Ukraine 50°09′N 36°11′E
22 G8 De Ridder Louisiana, S USA 30°51′N 93°18′W
137 P16 Derik Mardin, SE Turkey 37°22′N 40°16′E
83 E20 Derm Hardap, C Namibia 23°38′S 18°12′E
144 M14 Dermentobe prev. Dyurment'yube. Kzyl-Orda, S Kazakhstan 45°46′N 63°42′E
27 W14 Dermott Arkansas, C USA 33°31′N 91°26′W
Dérna see Darnah
Dernberg, Cape see Dolphin Head
22 J11 Dernieres, Isles island group Louisiana, S USA
102 I4 Déroute, Passage de la strait Channel Islands/France
Derrá see Dar'ā
Derry see Londonderry
Dertona see Tortona
Dertosa see Tortosa
80 H8 Derudeb Red Sea, NE Sudan 17°31′N 36°07′E
112 H10 Derventa Republika Srpska, N Bosnia and Herzegovina 44°57′N 17°55′E
183 O16 Derwent Bridge Tasmania, SE Australia 42°10′S 146°13′E
183 O17 Derwent, River ≈ Tasmania, SE Australia
146 F10 Derweze Rus. Darvaza. Ahal Welaýaty, C Turkmenistan 40°10′N 58°27′E
Deržavinsk see Derzhavinsk
145 O9 Derzhavinsk var. Deržavinsk. ◆ Akmola, C Kazakhstan
Dés see Dej
57 J18 Desaguadero Puno, S Peru 16°35′S 69°05′W
57 J18 Desaguadero, Río ≈ Bolivia/Peru
191 W9 Désappointement, Îles du island group Îles Tuamotu, C French Polynesia
27 W11 Des Arc Arkansas, C USA 34°58′N 91°30′W
14 C10 Desbarats Ontario, S Canada 46°20′N 83°52′W
62 H13 Descabezado Grande, Volcán Ж C Chile 35°34′S 70°40′W
40 B2 Descanso Baja California Norte, NW Mexico 32°08′N 116°51′W
102 L9 Descartes Indre-et-Loire, C France 46°58′N 00°40′E
11 T13 Deschambault Lake ◎ Saskatchewan, C Canada
Deschnaer Koppe see Velká Deštná
32 I11 Deschutes River ≈ Oregon, NW USA
80 J12 Desē var. Desse, It. Dessie. Āmara, N Ethiopia 11°02′N 39°39′E
63 I20 Deseado, Río ≈ S Argentina
106 F8 Desenzano del Garda Lombardia, N Italy 45°28′N 10°31′E
36 K3 Deseret Peak ▲ Utah, W USA 40°27′N 112°37′W
64 P6 Deserta Grande island Madeira, Portugal, NE Atlantic Ocean
64 P6 Desertas, Ilhas island group Madeira, Portugal, NE Atlantic Ocean
35 X16 Desert Center California, W USA 33°42′N 115°22′W
35 V15 Desert Hot Springs California, W USA 33°57′N 116°33′W
14 K10 Désert, Lac ◎ Québec, SE Canada
36 J2 Desert Peak ▲ Utah, W USA 41°03′N 113°22′W
31 R11 Deshler Ohio, N USA 41°12′N 83°55′W
Deshu see Deh Shū
Desiderii Fanum see St-Dizier
106 D7 Desio Lombardia, N Italy 45°37′N 09°12′E
115 E15 Deskáti var. Dheskáti. Dytikí Makedonía, N Greece 39°55′N 21°49′E
28 L2 Des Lacs River ≈ North Dakota, N USA
27 X6 Desloge Missouri, C USA 37°52′N 90°31′W
11 Q12 Desmarais Alberta, W Canada 55°58′N 113°56′W
29 Q10 De Smet South Dakota, N USA 44°23′N 97°33′W
29 V14 Des Moines state capital Iowa, C USA 41°36′N 93°37′W
17 N9 Des Moines River ≈ C USA
117 P4 Desna ≈ Russian Federation/Ukraine
116 G14 Desnăţui ≈ S Romania
63 F24 Desolación, Isla island S Chile
29 V14 De Soto Iowa, C USA 41°31′N 94°00′W
27 X5 De Soto Falls waterfall Alabama, S USA
83 I25 Despatch Eastern Cape, S South Africa 33°48′S 25°28′E
105 N12 Despeñaperros, Desfiladero de pass S Spain
31 N10 Des Plaines Illinois, N USA 42°01′N 87°52′W
115 J21 Despotikó island Kykládes, Greece, Aegean Sea
112 N12 Despotovac Serbia, E Serbia 44°06′N 21°25′E
101 M14 Dessau Sachsen-Anhalt, E Germany 51°51′N 12°15′E
Desse see Desē
99 J16 Dessel Antwerpen, N Belgium 51°15′N 05°07′E
Dessie see Desē
Destêrro see Florianópolis
23 P9 Destin Florida, SE USA 30°23′N 86°30′W
Deštná see Velká Deštná
193 T10 Desventurados, Islas de los island group W Chile
103 N1 Desvres Pas-de-Calais, N France 50°41′N 01°48′E
116 E12 Deta Ger. Detta. Timiş, W Romania 45°24′N 21°14′E
101 H14 Detmold Nordrhein-Westfalen, W Germany 51°55′N 08°52′E
31 S10 Detroit Michigan, N USA 42°20′N 83°03′W
25 W5 Detroit Texas, SW USA 33°39′N 95°16′W
31 S10 Detroit ≈ Canada/USA
29 S6 Detroit Lakes Minnesota, N USA 46°49′N 95°49′W
31 S10 Detroit Metropolitan ✈ Michigan, N USA 42°12′N 83°16′W
Detta see Deta
167 S10 Det Udom Ubon Ratchathani, E Thailand 14°54′N 105°03′E
111 K20 Detva Hung. Gyeva. Bankobýstricky Kraj, C Slovakia 48°35′N 19°25′E
154 G13 Deūlgaon Rāja Mahārāshtra, C India 20°04′N 76°08′E
99 L15 Deurne Noord-Brabant, SE Netherlands 51°28′N 05°47′E
99 H16 Deurne ✈ (Antwerpen) Antwerpen, N Belgium 51°10′N 04°28′E
Deutsch-Brod see Havlíčkův Brod
Deutschendorf see Poprad
Deutsch-Eylau see Iława
109 Y6 Deutschkreutz Burgenland, E Austria 47°37′N 16°37′E
Deutsch Krone see Wałcz
Deutschland/Deutschland, Bundesrepublik see Germany
109 V9 Deutschlandsberg Steiermark, SE Austria 46°52′N 15°13′E
Deutsch-Südwestafrika see Namibia
109 Y3 Deutsch-Wagram Niederösterreich, E Austria 48°19′N 16°33′E
Deux-Ponts see Zweibrücken
14 I11 Deux Rivieres Ontario, SE Canada 46°13′N 78°16′W
102 K9 Deux-Sèvres ◆ department W France
116 G11 Deva Ger. Diemrich, Hung. Déva. Hunedoara, W Romania 45°55′N 22°55′E
Déva see Deva
Deva see Chester
Devana see Aberdeen
Devana Castra see Chester
Đevđelija see Gevgelija
136 L12 Deveci Dağları ▲▲ N Turkey
137 P15 Devegeçidi Barajı ⊠ SE Turkey
136 K15 Develi Kayseri, C Turkey 38°22′N 35°28′E
98 M11 Deventer Overijssel, E Netherlands 52°15′N 06°10′E
15 O10 Devenyns, Lac ◎ Québec, SE Canada
96 K8 Deveron ≈ NE Scotland, United Kingdom
153 R14 Devghar prev. Deoghar. Jhārkhand, NE India
27 R10 Devil's Den plateau Arkansas, C USA
35 R7 Devils Gate pass California, W USA
30 J2 Devils Island island Apostle Islands, Wisconsin, N USA
Devil's Island see Diable, Île du
29 P3 Devils Lake North Dakota, N USA 48°08′N 98°50′W
31 R10 Devils Lake ◎ Michigan, N USA
29 O3 Devils Lake ◎ North Dakota, N USA
35 W13 Devils Playground desert California, W USA
25 O11 Devils River ≈ Texas, SW USA
33 Y12 Devils Tower ▲ Wyoming, C USA 44°33′N 104°45′W
114 I11 Devin prev. Dovlen. Smolyan, S Bulgaria 41°45′N 24°24′E
25 R12 Devine Texas, SW USA 29°08′N 98°54′W
152 H13 Devli Rājasthān, N India 25°47′N 75°23′E
Devne see Devnya
114 N8 Devnya prev. Devne. Varna, E Bulgaria 43°15′N 27°35′E
31 U14 Devola Ohio, N USA 39°28′N 81°28′W
Devoll see Devollit, Lumi i
113 M21 Devollit, Lumi i var. Devoll. ≈ SE Albania
11 Q14 Devon Alberta, SW Canada 53°21′N 113°47′W
97 I23 Devon cultural region SW England, United Kingdom
197 N10 Devon Island prev. North Devon Island. island Parry Islands, Nunavut, NE Canada
183 O16 Devonport Tasmania, SE Australia 41°14′S 146°21′E
136 H11 Devrek Zonguldak, N Turkey 41°14′N 31°57′E
154 G10 Dewās Madhya Pradesh, C India 22°59′N 76°03′E
De Westerein see Zwaagwesteinde
27 P8 Dewey Oklahoma, C USA 36°48′N 95°56′W
Dewey see Culebra
98 M8 De Wijk Drenthe, NE Netherlands 52°41′N 06°13′E
27 W12 De Witt Arkansas, C USA 34°17′N 91°21′W
29 Z14 De Witt Iowa, C USA 41°49′N 90°32′W
29 R16 De Witt Nebraska, C USA 40°23′N 96°55′W
97 M17 Dewsbury N England, United Kingdom 53°42′N 01°37′W
161 Q10 Dexing Jiangxi, S China 28°51′N 117°36′E
27 Y8 Dexter Missouri, C USA 36°48′N 89°57′W
37 U14 Dexter New Mexico, SW USA 33°12′N 104°25′W
160 I8 Deyang Sichuan, C China 31°08′N 104°23′E
182 C4 Dey-Dey, Lake salt lake South Australia
143 S7 Deyhūk Yazd, E Iran 33°18′N 57°30′E
Deynau see Galkynyş
Deyyer see Bandar-e Dayyer
142 L8 Dezfūl var. Dizful. Khūzestān, SW Iran 32°23′N 48°28′E
129 X4 Dezhneva, Mys headland NE Russian Federation 66°08′N 169°40′W
161 P4 Dezhou Shandong, E China 37°28′N 116°18′E
Dezhou see Dechang
Dezh Shāhpūr see Marīvān
Dhaalu Atoll see South Nilandhe Atoll
Dhahran see Az Zahrān
Dhahran Al Khobar see Az Zahrān al Khubar
153 U14 Dhaka prev. Dacca. ● (Bangladesh) Dhaka, C Bangladesh 23°42′N 90°22′E
153 T15 Dhaka ◆ division C Bangladesh
Dhali see Idálion
Dhalli Rajhara see Dalli Rājhara
141 O15 Dhamār W Yemen 14°31′N 44°25′E
154 K12 Dhamtari Chhattīsgarh, C India 20°43′N 81°36′E
153 Q15 Dhanbād Jhārkhand, NE India 23°48′N 86°27′E
152 L10 Dhangaḍhi var. Dhangarhi. Far Western, W Nepal 28°45′N 80°38′E
Dhangarhi see Dhangaḍhi
Dhank see Dank
153 R12 Dhankuṭā Eastern, E Nepal 27°06′N 87°21′E
152 I6 Dhaola Dhār ▲▲ NE India
154 F10 Dhār Madhya Pradesh, C India 22°32′N 75°24′E
153 R12 Dharān var. Dharan Bazar. Eastern, E Nepal 26°51′N 87°18′E
Dharan Bazar see Dharān
155 H21 Dhārāpuram Tamil Nādu, SE India 10°45′N 77°33′E
155 H20 Dharmapuri Tamil Nādu, SE India 12°11′N 78°07′E
155 H18 Dharmavaram Andhra Pradesh, E India 14°27′N 77°44′E
154 M11 Dharmjaygarh Chhattīsgarh, C India 22°27′N 83°16′E
Dharmsāla see Dharmshāla
152 I7 Dharmshāla prev. Dharmsāla. Himāchal Pradesh, N India 32°14′N 76°24′E
155 F17 Dhārwād prev. Dharwar. Karnātaka, SW India 15°30′N 75°04′E
Dharwar see Dhārwād
Dhaulagiri see Dhawalāgiri
152 J12 Dhaulpur var. Daulpur, Dholpur. Rājasthān, N India 26°43′N 77°54′E
153 O10 Dhawalāgiri var. Dhaulagiri. ▲ C Nepal 28°45′N 83°27′E
81 L18 Dheere Laaq var. Lak Dera, It. Lach Dera. seasonal river Kenya/Somalia
121 Q3 Dhekelia Sovereign Base Area UK military installation E Cyprus34°59′N 33°45′E
121 Q3 Dhekélia Eng. Dhekelia, Gk. Dekéleia. UK air base SE Cyprus35°00′N 33°45′E
see Dhekélia
Dhelvinákion see Delvináki
113 M22 Dhëmbelit, Majae ▲ S Albania 40°10′N 20°22′E
154 O12 Dhenkānāl Orissa, E India 20°40′N 85°36′E
Dheskáti see Deskáti
138 G11 Dhībān Ma'dabā, NW Jordan 31°30′N 35°47′E
Dhidhimótikhon see Didymóteicho
Dhíkti Ori see Díkti
153 V12 Dhing Assam, NE India 26°26′N 92°29′E
139 W12 Dhī Qār ◆ governorate SE Iraq
138 I12 Dhirwah, Wādī adh dry watercourse C Jordan
Dhístomon see Dístomo
Dhodhekánisos see Dodekánisa
Dhodhóni see Dodóni
Dhofar see Ẓufār
Dholpur see Dhaulpur
Dhomokós see Domokós
Dhond see Daund
155 H17 Dhone Andhra Pradesh, C India 15°25′N 77°52′E
154 B11 Dhorāji Gujarāt, W India 21°44′N 70°27′E
Dhráma see Dráma
154 C10 Dhrāngadhra Gujarāt, W India 22°59′N 71°32′E
Dhrepanon, Akrotírio see Drépano, Akrotírio
153 T13 Dhuburi Assam, NE India 26°06′N 89°55′E
154 F12 Dhule prev. Dhulia. Mahārāshtra, C India 20°54′N 74°47′E
Dhulia see Dhule
Dhún Dealgan, Cuan see Dundalk Bay
Dhún Droma, Cuan see Dundrum Bay
Dhún na nGall, Bá see Donegal Bay
Dhū Shaykh see Qazānīyah
80 Q13 Dhuudo Bari, NE Somalia 09°21′N 50°19′E
81 N15 Dhuusa Marreeb var. Dusa Marreb, It. Dusa Mareb. Galguduud, C Somalia 05°33′N 46°24′E
115 J24 Día island SE Greece
55 Y9 Diable, Île du var. Devil's Island. island N French Guiana
15 N12 Diable, Rivière du ≈ Québec, SE Canada
35 N8 Diablo, Mount ▲ California, W USA 37°52′N 121°57′W
35 O9 Diablo Range ▲▲ California, W USA
24 I8 Diablo, Sierra ▲▲ Texas, SW USA
45 O11 Diablotins, Morne ▲ N Dominica 15°30′N 61°23′W
77 N11 Diafarabé Mopti, C Mali 14°09′N 05°01′W
77 N11 Diaka ≈ SW Mali
Diakovár see Đakovo
76 I12 Dialakoto S Senegal 13°21′N 13°19′W
61 B18 Diamante Entre Ríos, E Argentina 32°05′S 60°40′W
62 I12 Diamante, Río ≈ C Argentina
59 M19 Diamantina Minas Gerais, SE Brazil 18°17′S 43°37′W
59 N17 Diamantina, Chapada ▲ E Brazil
173 U11 Diamantina Fracture Zone tectonic feature E Indian Ocean
181 T8 Diamantina River ≈ Queensland/South Australia
38 D9 Diamond Head headland O'ahu, Hawai'i, USA 21°15′N 157°48′W
37 P2 Diamond Peak ▲ Colorado, C USA 40°56′N 108°56′W
35 W5 Diamond Peak ▲ Nevada, W USA 39°34′N 115°46′W
Diamond State see Delaware
76 J11 Diamou Kayes, SW Mali 14°04′N 11°16′W
95 I23 Dianalund Vestsjælland, C Denmark 55°32′N 11°30′E
65 G25 Diana's Peak ▲ C Saint Helena
160 M16 Dianbai var. Shuidong. Guangdong, S China 21°30′N 111°05′E
160 G13 Dian Chi ⊠ SW China
106 B10 Diano Marina Liguria, NW Italy 43°55′N 08°06′E
163 V11 Diaobingshan var. Tiefa. Liaoning, NE China 42°25′N 123°39′E
77 R13 Diapaga E Burkina 12°09′N 01°48′E
Diarbekr see Diyarbakır
107 J15 Diavolo, Passo del pass C Italy
61 B18 Díaz Santa Fe, C Argentina 32°22′S 61°05′W
141 W6 Dibā al Ḥiṣn var. Dibāh, Dibba. Ash Shāriqah, NE United Arab Emirates 25°35′N 56°16′E
139 S3 Dibaga Arbīl, N Iraq 35°51′N 43°49′E
Dibāh see Dibā al Ḥiṣn
79 L22 Dibaya Kasai-Occidental, S Dem. Rep. Congo 06°31′S 22°57′E
Dibba see Dibā al Ḥiṣn
195 W15 Dibble Iceberg Tongue ice feature Antarctica
113 L19 Dibër ◆ district E Albania
83 I20 Dibete Central, SE Botswana 23°45′S 26°26′E
Dibio see Dijon
25 W9 Diboll Texas, SW USA 31°11′N 94°46′W
Dibra see Debar
153 X11 Dibrugarh Assam, NE India 27°29′N 94°49′E
54 G4 Dibulla La Guajira, N Colombia 11°14′N 73°22′W
25 O5 Dickens Texas, SW USA 33°38′N 100°51′W
19 R2 Dickey Maine, NE USA 47°04′N 69°05′W
30 K9 Dickeyville Wisconsin, N USA 42°37′N 90°36′W
28 K5 Dickinson North Dakota, N USA 46°54′N 102°48′W
0 E6 Dickins Seamount undersea feature NE Pacific Ocean 54°30′N 137°00′W
27 O13 Dickson Oklahoma, C USA 34°11′N 96°58′W
20 I9 Dickson Tennessee, S USA 36°04′N 87°23′W
Dicle see Tigris
Dicsőszentmárton see Târnăveni
98 M12 Didam Gelderland, E Netherlands 51°56′N 06°08′E
163 Y8 Didao Heilongjiang, NE China 45°22′N 130°48′E
76 L12 Didiéni Koulikoro, W Mali 13°48′N 08°01′W
Didimo see Dídymo
Didimotiho see Didymóteicho
81 K17 Didimtu spring/well NE Kenya 02°58′N 40°07′E
67 U9 Didinga Hills ▲▲ S Sudan
11 Q16 Didsbury Alberta, SW Canada 51°39′N 114°09′W
152 G11 Dīdwāna Rājasthān, N India 27°23′N 74°36′E
115 G20 Dídymo var. Didimo. ▲ S Greece 37°28′N 23°12′E
114 L12 Didymóteicho var. Dhidhimótikhon, Didimotiho. Anatolikí Makedonía kai Thráki, NE Greece 41°22′N 26°29′E
103 S13 Die Drôme, E France 44°46′N 05°21′E
77 O13 Diébougou SW Burkina 11°00′N 03°12′W
Diedenhofen see Thionville
11 S16 Diefenbaker, Lake ⊠ Saskatchewan, S Canada
62 H7 Diego de Almagro Atacama, N Chile 26°24′S 70°10′W
63 F23 Diego de Almagro, Isla island S Chile
61 A20 Diego de Alvear Santa Fe, C Argentina 34°25′S 62°10′W
173 Q7 Diego Garcia island S British Indian Ocean Territory
Diégo-Suarez see Antsirañana
99 M23 Diekirch Diekirch, C Luxembourg 49°52′N 06°10′E
99 L23 Diekirch ◆ district N Luxembourg
76 K11 Diéma Kayes, W Mali 14°30′N 09°12′W
101 H15 Diemel ≈ W Germany
98 I10 Diemen Noord-Holland, C Netherlands 52°21′N 04°58′E
Diemrich see Deva
167 R6 Điện Biên var. Bien Bien, Dien Bien Phu. Lai Châu, N Vietnam 21°23′N 103°02′E
Dien Bien Phu see Điện Biên
167 S7 Diễn Châu Nghê An, N Vietnam 18°54′N 105°35′E
99 K18 Diepenbeek Limburg, NE Belgium 50°54′N 05°25′E
98 N11 Diepenheim Overijssel, E Netherlands 52°10′N 06°37′E
98 M10 Diepenveen Overijssel, E Netherlands 52°18′N 06°09′E
100 G12 Diepholz Niedersachsen, NW Germany 52°36′N 08°23′E
102 M3 Dieppe Seine-Maritime, N France 49°55′N 01°05′E
98 M12 Dieren Gelderland, E Netherlands 52°03′N 06°06′E
27 S13 Dierks Arkansas, C USA 34°07′N 94°01′W
99 J17 Diest Vlaams Brabant, C Belgium 50°58′N 05°03′E
108 F7 Dietikon Zürich, NW Switzerland 47°24′N 08°25′E
103 R13 Dieulefit Drôme, E France 44°30′N 05°01′E
103 T5 Dieuze Moselle, NE France 48°49′N 06°41′E
119 H15 Dieveniškės Vilnius, SE Lithuania 54°12′N 25°38′E
98 N7 Diever Drenthe, NE Netherlands 52°49′N 06°19′E
101 F17 Diez Rheinland-Pfalz, W Germany 50°22′N 08°01′E
77 Y12 Diffa Diffa, SE Niger 13°19′N 12°37′E
77 Y10 Diffa ◆ department SE Niger
99 L25 Differdange Luxembourg, SW Luxembourg 49°32′N 05°53′E
13 O16 Digby Nova Scotia, SE Canada 44°37′N 65°47′W
26 J5 Dighton Kansas, C USA 38°28′N 100°28′W
Dignano d'Istria see Vodnjan
103 T14 Digne var. Digne-les-Bains. Alpes-de-Haute-Provence, SE France 44°05′N 06°14′E
Digne-les-Bains see Digne
Digoel see Digul, Sungai
103 Q10 Digoin Saône-et-Loire, C France 46°30′N 04°E
171 Q8 Digos Mindanao, S Philippines 06°46′N 125°21′E
149 Q16 Digri Sind, SE Pakistan 25°11′N 69°10′E
171 Y14 Digul Barat, Sungai ≈ Papua, E Indonesia
171 Y15 Digul, Sungai prev. Digoel. ≈ Papua, E Indonesia
171 Z14 Digul Timur, Sungai ≈ Papua, E Indonesia
153 X10 Dihāng ≈ NE India
Dihang see Brahmaputra
Dihōk see Dahūk
81 L17 Diinsoor Bay, S Somalia 02°28′N 43°00′E
Dijlah see Tigris
99 H17 Dijle ≈ C Belgium
103 R8 Dijon anc. Dibio. Côte d'Or, C France 47°21′N 05°04′E
93 H14 Dikanäs Västerbotten, N Sweden 65°15′N 16°00′E
80 L12 Dikhil SW Djibouti 11°08′N 42°19′E
136 B13 Dikili İzmir, W Turkey 39°05′N 26°52′E
99 B17 Diksmuide var. Dixmuide, Fr. Dixmude. West-Vlaanderen, W Belgium 51°02′N 02°52′E
122 K7 Dikson Taymyrskiy (Dolgano-Nenetskiy) Avtonomnyy Okrug, N Russian Federation 73°30′N 80°35′E
115 K25 Díkti var. Dhíkti Ori. ▲▲ Kríti, Greece, E Mediterranean Sea
77 Z13 Dikwa Borno, NE Nigeria 12°00′N 13°57′E
81 J15 Dīla Southern Nationalities, S Ethiopia 06°19′N 38°16′E
99 G18 Dilbeek Vlaams Brabant, C Belgium 50°51′N 04°16′E
171 Q16 Dili var. Dilli, Dilly. ● (East Timor) N East Timor 08°33′S 125°34′E
77 Y11 Dilia var. Dillia. ≈ SE Niger
Dilijan see Delijan
167 U13 Di Linh Lâm Đông, S Vietnam 11°38′N 108°07′E
101 G16 Dillenburg Hessen, W Germany 50°45′N 08°16′E
25 Q13 Dilley Texas, SW USA 28°40′N 99°10′W
Dilli see Dili, East Timor
Dilli see Delhi, India
Dillia see Dilia
80 E11 Dilling var. Ad Dalanj. Southern Kordofan, C Sudan 12°02′N 29°41′E
101 D20 Dillingen Saarland, SW Germany 49°20′N 06°43′E
Dillingen see Dillingen an der Donau
101 J22 Dillingen an der Donau var. Dillingen. Bayern, S Germany 48°34′N 10°29′E
39 O13 Dillingham Alaska, USA 59°03′N 158°30′W
33 Q12 Dillon Montana, NW USA 45°14′N 112°38′W
21 T12 Dillon South Carolina, SE USA 34°25′N 79°22′W
31 T13 Dillon Lake ⊠ Ohio, N USA
Dilly see Dili
Dilman see Salmās
79 K24 Dilolo Katanga, S Dem. Rep. Congo 10°42′S 22°21′E
115 J20 Dílos island Kykládes, Greece, Aegean Sea
141 Y11 Dil', Ra's ad headland E Oman 19°12′N 57°53′E
29 R5 Dilworth Minnesota, N USA 46°53′N 96°38′W
138 H7 Dimashq var. Ash Shām, Esh Sham, Eng. Damascus, Fr. Damas, It. Damasco. ● Dimashq, SW Syria 33°30′N 36°19′E
138 I8 Dimashq off. Muḥāfaẓat Dimashq, var. Damascus, Ar. Ash Sham, Ash Shām, Damasco, Esh Sham, Fr. Damas. ◆ governorate S Syria
138 I7 Dimashq ✈ Dimashq, S Syria 33°30′N 36°19′E
Dimashq, Muḥāfaẓat see Dimashq
79 L21 Dimbelenge Kasai-Occidental, C Dem. Rep. Congo 05°36′S 23°04′E
77 N16 Dimbokro E Ivory Coast 06°43′N 04°46′W
182 L11 Dimboola Victoria, SE Australia 36°29′S 142°03′E
Dimboviţa see Dâmboviţa
Dimitrov see Dymytrov
114 K11 Dimitrovgrad Khaskovo, S Bulgaria 42°03′N 25°36′E
127 R5 Dimitrovgrad Ul'yanovskaya Oblast', W Russian Federation 54°14′N 49°37′E
113 Q15 Dimitrovgrad prev. Caribrod. Serbia, SE Serbia 43°01′N 22°46′E
Dimitrovo see Pernik
Dimlang see Vogel Peak
24 M3 Dimmitt Texas, SW USA 34°32′N 102°20′W
114 F7 Dimovo Vidin, NW Bulgaria 43°46′N 22°47′E
59 A16 Dimpolis Acre, W Brazil 09°52′S 71°51′W
115 O23 Dimyliá Ródos, Dodekánisa, Greece, Aegean Sea 36°17′N 27°59′E
171 Q6 Dinagat Island island S Philippines
153 S13 Dinajpur Rajshahi, NW Bangladesh 25°38′N 88°40′E
102 I6 Dinan Côtes d'Armor, NW France 48°27′N 02°02′W
99 I21 Dinant Namur, S Belgium 50°16′N 04°55′E
136 E15 Dinar Afyon, SW Turkey 38°05′N 30°09′E
112 F13 Dinara ▲ W Croatia 43°49′N 16°42′E
Dinara see Dinaric Alps
102 I5 Dinard Ille-et-Vilaine, NW France 48°38′N 02°04′W
112 F13 Dinaric Alps var. Dinara. ▲▲ Bosnia and Herzegovina/Croatia
143 N10 Dīnār, Kūh-e ▲ C Iran 30°51′N 51°36′E
Dinbych see Denbigh
155 H22 Dindigul Tamil Nādu, SE India 10°23′N 78°E
83 M19 Dindiza Gaza, S Mozambique 23°22′S 33°28′E
79 H21 Dinga Bandundu, SW Dem. Rep. Congo 05°00′S 16°29′E
149 V7 Dinga Punjab, E Pakistan 32°38′N 73°45′E
Dingchang see Qinxian
158 L16 Dinggyê var. Gyangkar. Xizang Zizhiqu, W China 28°18′N 88°06′E
97 A20 Dingle Ir. An Daingean. SW Ireland 52°09′N 10°16′W
97 A20 Dingle Bay Ir. Bá an Daingin. bay SW Ireland
18 I13 Dingmans Ferry Pennsylvania, NE USA 41°12′N 74°51′W
101 N22 Dingolfing Bayern, SE Germany 48°37′N 12°28′E
171 O1 Dingras Luzon, N Philippines 18°06′N 120°43′E
76 J13 Dinguiraye N Guinea 11°19′N 10°49′W
96 I8 Dingwall N Scotland, United Kingdom 57°36′N 04°26′W
159 V10 Dingxi Gansu, C China 35°36′N 104°33′E
Ding Xian see Dingzhou
161 Q7 Dingyuan Anhui, E China 32°30′N 117°40′E
161 O3 Dingzhou prev. Ding Xian. Hebei, E China 38°31′N 114°52′E
167 U6 Đinh Lâp Lang Sơn, N Vietnam 21°33′N 107°03′E
167 T13 Đinh Quan var. Tân Phu. Đông Nai, S Vietnam 11°11′N 107°20′E
100 E13 Dinkel ≈ Germany/Netherlands
101 J21 Dinkelsbühl Bayern, S Germany 49°06′N 10°18′E
101 D14 Dinslaken Nordrhein-Westfalen, W Germany 51°34′N 06°43′E
35 R11 Dinuba California, W USA 36°32′N 119°23′W
21 W7 Dinwiddie Virginia, NE USA 37°02′N 77°40′W
98 N13 Dinxperlo Gelderland, E Netherlands 51°51′N 06°30′E
Dío see Díon
Diófás see Nucet
76 M12 Dioïla Koulikoro, W Mali 12°28′N 06°43′W
115 F14 Díon var. Dio; anc. Dium. site of ancient city Kentrikí Makedonía, N Greece
115 G19 Dióryga Korinthou Eng. Corinth Canal. canal S Greece
76 G12 Diouloulou SW Senegal 13°00′N 16°34′W
77 N11 Dioura Mopti, W Mali 14°48′N 05°20′W
76 G11 Diourbel W Senegal 14°39′N 16°12′W
152 L10 Dipāyal Far Western, W Nepal 29°09′N 80°46′E
121 R1 Dipkarpaz Gk. Rizokarpaso, Rizokárpason. NE Cyprus 35°36′N 34°23′E
149 R17 Diplo Sind, SE Pakistan 24°29′N 69°36′E
171 P7 Dipolog var. Dipolog City. Mindanao, S Philippines 08°31′N 123°20′E
Dipolog City see Dipolog
185 C23 Dipton Southland, South Island, New Zealand 45°55′S 168°21′E
149 T4 Dīr North-West Frontier Province, N Pakistan 35°12′N 71°53′E
77 O10 Diré Tombouctou, C Mali 16°12′N 03°31′W
80 L13 Dirē Dawa Dirē Dawa, E Ethiopia 09°35′N 41°53′E
Dirfis see Dírfys
115 H18 Dírfys var. Dírfis. ▲▲ Évvioa, C Greece
75 N9 Dirj var. Daraj, Darj. W Libya 30°09′N 10°26′E
180 G10 Dirk Hartog Island island Western Australia
77 Y8 Dirkou Agadez, NE Niger 18°45′N 13°00′E
181 X11 Dirranbandi Queensland, E Australia 28°37′S 148°13′E
81 O16 Dirri Galguduud, C Somalia 04°15′N 46°31′E
Dirschau see Tczew
37 N6 Dirty Devil River ≈ Utah, W USA
32 E10 Disappointment, Cape headland Washington, NW USA 46°16′N 124°06′W
180 L8 Disappointment, Lake salt lake Western Australia
183 R12 Disaster Bay bay New South Wales, SE Australia
44 J11 Discovery Bay C Jamaica 18°27′N 77°24′W
182 K13 Discovery Bay inlet SE Australia
67 Y15 Discovery II Fracture Zone tectonic feature SW Indian Ocean
Discovery Seamount/Discovery Seamounts see Discovery Tablemounts
65 O19 Discovery Tablemounts var. Discovery Seamount, Discovery Seamounts. undersea feature SW Atlantic Ocean 42°00′S 00°10′E
108 G9 Disentis Rmsch. Mustér. Graubünden, S Switzerland 46°43′N 08°52′E
39 O10 Dishna River ≈ Alaska, USA
Disko Bugt see Qeqertarsuup Tunua
195 X4 Dismal Mountains ▲▲ Antarctica
28 M14 Dismal River ≈ Nebraska, C USA
Disna see Dzisna
99 L19 Dison Liège, E Belgium 50°37′N 05°52′E
153 V12 Dispur state capital Assam, NE India 26°03′N 91°52′E
15 R11 Disraeli Québec, SE Canada 45°58′N 71°21′W
115 F18 Dístomo prev. Dhístomon. Stereá Ellás, C Greece 38°25′N 22°40′E
Dístos, Límni see Dýstos, Límni
59 L18 Distrito Federal Eng. Federal District. ◆ federal district C Brazil
41 P14 Distrito Federal ◆ federal district S Mexico
54 L4 Distrito Federal off. Territorio Distrito Federal. ◆ federal district N Venezuela
Distrito Federal, Territorio see Distrito Federal
116 J10 Ditrău Hung. Ditró. Harghita, C Romania 46°49′N 25°31′E
Ditró see Ditrău
154 B12 Diu Damān and Diu, W India 20°42′N 70°59′E

◆ Country
● Country Capital
◇ Dependent Territory
○ Dependent Territory Capital
◆ Administrative Regions
✈ International Airport
▲ Mountain
▲▲ Mountain Range
Ж Volcano
≈ River
◎ Lake
⊠ Reservoir

Dium – Drâa, Hammada du

Dium see Díon
109 S13 **Divača** SW Slovenia 45°40′N 13°58′E
142 J5 **Dīvāndarreh** Kordestān, NW Iran 35°55′N 47°02′E
102 K5 **Dives** ≈ N France
Divichi see Däväçi
33 Q11 **Divide** Montana, NW USA 45°44′N 112°47′W
Divin see Dzivin
83 N18 **Divinhe** Sofala, E Mozambique 20°41′S 34°46′E
59 L20 **Divinópolis** Minas Gerais, SE Brazil 20°08′S 44°55′W
127 N13 **Divnoye** Stavropol'skiy Kray, SW Russian Federation 45°54′N 43°18′E
76 M17 **Divo** S Ivory Coast 05°50′N 05°22′W
Divodurum Mediomatricum see Metz
137 N13 **Divriği** Sivas, C Turkey 39°23′N 38°06′E
Diwaniyah see Ad Dīwānīyah
14 J10 **Dix Milles, Lac** ◎ Québec, SE Canada
14 M8 **Dix Milles, Lac des** ◎ Québec, SE Canada
Dixmude/Dixmuide see Diksmuide
35 N7 **Dixon** California, W USA 38°19′N 121°49′W
30 L10 **Dixon** Illinois, N USA 41°51′N 89°26′W
20 I6 **Dixon** Kentucky, S USA 37°30′N 87°39′W
27 V6 **Dixon** Missouri, C USA 37°59′N 92°05′W
37 S9 **Dixon** New Mexico, SW USA 36°10′N 105°49′W
39 Y15 **Dixon Entrance** *strait* Canada/USA
18 D14 **Dixonville** Pennsylvania, NE USA 40°43′N 79°01′W
137 T13 **Diyadin** Ağrı, E Turkey 39°33′N 43°41′E
Diyālá, Nahr see Sīrvān, Rūdkhāneh-ye
139 V5 **Diyālá, Sirwan Nahr** *var.* Rudkhaneh-ye Sīrvān, Sīrwān. ≈ Iran/Iraq *see also* Sīrvān, Rudkhaneh-ye
137 P15 **Diyarbakır** *var.* Diarbekr; *anc.* Amida. Diyarbakır, SE Turkey 37°55′N 40°14′E
137 P15 **Diyarbakır** *var.* Diarbekr. ◐ *province* SE Turkey
Dizful see Dezfūl
79 F16 **Dja** ≈ SE Cameroon
Djadié see Zadié
77 X7 **Djado** Agadez, NE Niger 21°00′N 12°11′E
77 X6 **Djado, Plateau du** ▲ NE Niger
Djailolo see Halmahera, Pulau
Djajapura see Jayapura
Djakarta see Jakarta
Djakovo see Đakovo
79 G20 **Djambala** Plateaux, C Congo 02°32′S 14°43′E
Djambi see Jambi
Djambi see Hari, Batang
74 M9 **Djanet** E Algeria 24°43′N 08°57′E
74 M11 **Djanet** *prev.* Fort Charlet. SE Algeria 24°34′N 09°33′E
Djaul see Dyaul Island
Djawa see Jawa
Djéblé see Jablah
78 I10 **Djédaa** Batha, C Chad 13°31′N 18°34′E
74 J6 **Djelfa** *var.* El Djelfa. N Algeria 34°43′N 03°14′E
79 M14 **Djéma** Haut-Mbomou, E Central African Republic 06°04′N 25°20′E
Djember see Jember
Djeneponto see Jeneponto
77 N12 **Djenné** *var.* Jenné. Mopti, C Mali 13°55′N 04°31′W
Djérablous see Jarābulus
Djerba see Jerba, Île de
79 F15 **Djérem** ≈ C Cameroon
Djevdjelija see Gevgelija
77 P11 **Djibo** N Burkina 14°09′N 01°38′W
80 L12 **Djibouti** *var.* Jibuti. ● (Djibouti) E Djibouti 11°33′N 42°55′E
80 L12 **Djibouti** *off.* Republic of Djibouti, *var.* Jibuti; *prev.* French Somaliland, French Territory of the Afars and Issas, *Fr.* Côte Française des Somalis, Territoire Français des Afars et des Issas. ◆ *republic* E Africa
80 L12 **Djibouti** ✈ C Djibouti 11°29′N 42°54′E
Djibouti, Republic of see Djibouti
Djidjel/Djidjelli see Jijel
55 W10 **Djoemoe** Sipaliwini, C Surinam 04°00′N 55°27′W
Djokjakarta see Yogyakarta
79 K21 **Djoku-Punda** Kasai-Occidental, S Dem. Rep. Congo 05°27′S 20°58′E
79 K18 **Djolu** Equateur, N Dem. Rep. Congo 00°35′N 22°30′E
Djombang see Jombang
Djorče Petrov see Đorče Petrov
79 F17 **Djoua** ≈ Congo/Gabon
77 R14 **Djougou** W Benin 09°42′N 01°38′E
79 F16 **Djoum** Sud, S Cameroon 02°38′N 12°51′E
78 I8 **Djourab, Erg du** *desert* N Chad
79 P17 **Djugu** Orientale, NE Dem. Rep. Congo 01°55′N 30°31′E
Djumbir see Ďumbier
92 L3 **Djúpivogur** Austurland, SE Iceland 64°40′N 14°18′W
94 L13 **Djura** Dalarna, C Sweden 60°37′N 15°00′E
Djurdjevac see Đurđevac
D'Kar see Dekar
197 U6 **Dmitriya Lapteva, Proliv** *strait* N Russian Federation
126 J7 **Dmitriyev-L'govskiy** Kurskaya Oblast', W Russian Federation 52°08′N 35°09′E
Dmitriyevsk see Makiyivka
126 K3 **Dmitrov** Moskovskaya Oblast', W Russian Federation 56°23′N 37°30′E
Dmitrovichi see Dzmitravichy
126 J6 **Dmitrovsk-Orlovskiy** Orlovskaya Oblast', W Russian Federation 52°28′N 35°01′E
117 R3 **Dmytrivka** Chernihivs'ka Oblast', N Ukraine 50°56′N 32°57′E
Dnepr see Dnieper
Dneprodzerzhinsk see Romaniv
Dneprodzerzhinskoye Vodokhranilishche see Dniprodzerzhyns'ke Vodoskhovyshche
Dnepropetrovsk see Dnipropetrovs'k
Dnepropetrovskaya Oblast' see Dnipropetrovs'ka Oblast'
Dneprorudnoye see Dniprorudne
Dneprovskiy Liman see Dniprovs'kyy Lyman
Dneprovsko-Bugskiy Kanal see Dnyaprowska-Buhski Kanal
Dnestr see Dniester
Dnestrovskiy Liman see Dnistrovs'kyy Lyman
86 H11 **Dnieper** *Bel.* Dnyapro, *Rus.* Dnepr, *Ukr.* Dnipro. ≈ E Europe
117 P3 **Dnieper Lowland** *Bel.* Prydnyaprowskaya Nizina, *Ukr.* Prydniprovs'ka Nyzovyna. *lowlands* Belarus/Ukraine
116 M8 **Dniester** *Rom.* Nistru, *Rus.* Dnestr, *Ukr.* Dnister; *anc.* Tyras. ≈ Moldova/Ukraine
Dnipro see Dnieper
Dniprodzerzhyns'k see Romaniv
117 T7 **Dniprodzerzhyns'ke Vodoskhovyshche** *Rus.* Dneprodzerzhinskoye Vodokhranilishche. ⊠ C Ukraine
117 U7 **Dnipropetrovs'k** *Rus.* Dnepropetrovsk; *prev.* Yekaterinoslav. Dnipropetrovs'ka Oblast', E Ukraine 48°28′N 35°E
117 U8 **Dnipropetrovs'k** ✈ Dnipropetrovs'ka Oblast', S Ukraine 48°20′N 35°04′E
Dnipropetrovs'k see Dnipropetrovs'ka Oblast'
117 T7 **Dnipropetrovs'ka Oblast'** *var.* Dnipropetrovs'k, *Rus.* Dnepropetrovskaya Oblast'. ◐ *province* E Ukraine
117 U9 **Dniprorudne** *Rus.* Dneprorudnoye. Zaporiz'ka Oblast', SE Ukraine 47°21′N 35°00′E
117 Q11 **Dniprovs'kyy Lyman** *Rus.* Dneprovskiy Liman. *bay* S Ukraine
Dnister see Dniester
117 O11 **Dnistrovs'kyy Lyman** *Rus.* Dnestrovskiy Liman. *inlet* S Ukraine
124 G14 **Dno** Pskovskaya Oblast', W Russian Federation 57°48′N 29°58′E
Dnyapro see Dnieper
119 H20 **Dnyaprowska-Buhski Kanal** *Rus.* Dneprovsko-Bugskiy Kanal. *canal* SW Belarus
13 O14 **Doaktown** New Brunswick, SE Canada 46°34′N 66°06′W
78 H13 **Doba** Logone-Oriental, S Chad 08°40′N 16°50′E
118 E9 **Dobele** *Ger.* Doblen. Dobele, W Latvia 56°36′N 23°14′E
101 N16 **Döbeln** Sachsen, E Germany 51°07′N 13°07′E
171 U12 **Doberai, Jazirah** *Dut.* Vogelkop. *peninsula* Papua, E Indonesia
110 F10 **Dobiegniew** *Ger.* Lubuskie, Woldenberg Neumark. Lubuskie, W Poland 52°58′N 15°43′E
Doblen see Dobele
81 K18 **Dobli** *spring/well* SW Somalia 0°24′N 41°18′E
112 H11 **Doboj** Republiks Srpska, N Bosnia and Herzegovina 44°45′N 18°03′E
143 R12 **Doborji** *var.* Fūrg. Fārs, S Iran 28°16′N 55°13′E
110 L8 **Dobre Miasto** *Ger.* Guttstadt. Warmińsko-mazurskie, NE Poland 53°59′N 20°25′E
114 N7 **Dobrich** *Rom.* Bazargic; *prev.* Tolbukhin. Dobrich, NE Bulgaria 43°35′N 27°49′E
114 N7 **Dobrich** ◐ *province* NE Bulgaria
126 M8 **Dobrinka** Lipetskaya Oblast', W Russian Federation 52°10′N 40°30′E
126 M7 **Dobrinka** Volgogradskaya Oblast', SW Russian Federation 50°52′N 41°48′E
Dobrla Vas see Eberndorf
111 I15 **Dobrodzień** *Ger.* Guttentag. Opolskie, S Poland 50°43′N 18°24′E
Dobrogea see Dobruja
117 W7 **Dobropillya** *Rus.* Dobropol'ye. Donets'ka Oblast', SE Ukraine 48°25′N 37°02′E
Dobropol'ye see Dobropillya
117 P8 **Dobrovelychkivka** Kirovohrads'ka Oblast', C Ukraine 48°22′N 31°12′E
Dobrudja/Dobrudzha see Dobruja
114 O7 **Dobruja** *var.* Dobrudja, *Bul.* Dobrudzha, *Rom.* Dobrogea. *physical region* Bulgaria/Romania
119 P19 **Dobrush** Homyel'skaya Voblasts', SE Belarus 52°25′N 31°19′E
125 U14 **Dobryanka** Permskaya Oblast', NW Russian Federation 58°28′N 56°27′E
117 P2 **Dobryanka** Chernihivs'ka Oblast', N Ukraine 52°03′N 31°09′E
Dobryn' see Dabryn'
21 R8 **Dobson** North Carolina, SE USA 36°25′N 80°45′W
59 N20 **Doce, Rio** ≈ SE Brazil
93 I16 **Docksta** Västernorrland, C Sweden 63°06′N 18°22′E
41 N10 **Doctor Arroyo** Nuevo León, NE Mexico 23°40′N 100°09′W
62 L4 **Doctor Pedro P. Peña** Boquerón, W Paraguay 22°22′S 62°23′W
171 S11 **Dodaga** Pulau Halmahera, E Indonesia 01°06′N 128°10′E
155 G21 **Dodda Betta** ▲ S India 11°28′N 76°44′E
Dodecanese see Dodekánisa
115 M22 **Dodekánisa** *var.* Nóties Sporádes, *Eng.* Dodecanese; *prev.* Dhodhekánisos, Dodekanisos. *island group* SE Greece
Dodekanisos see Dodekánisa
26 J6 **Dodge City** Kansas, C USA 37°45′N 100°01′W
30 K9 **Dodgeville** Wisconsin, N USA 42°57′N 90°08′W
97 H25 **Dodman Point** *headland* SW England, United Kingdom 50°13′N 04°47′W
81 J14 **Dodola** Oromīya, C Ethiopia 07°00′N 39°15′E
81 H22 **Dodoma** ● (Tanzania) Dodoma, C Tanzania 06°11′S 35°45′E
81 H22 **Dodoma** ◐ *region* C Tanzania
115 C16 **Dodóni** *var.* Dhodhóni. *site of ancient city* Ípeiros, W Greece
33 U7 **Dodson** Montana, NW USA 48°25′N 108°18′W
25 P3 **Dodson** Texas, SW USA 34°46′N 100°01′W
98 M12 **Doesburg** Gelderland, E Netherlands 52°01′N 06°08′E
98 N12 **Doetinchem** Gelderland, E Netherlands 51°58′N 06°17′E
158 L12 **Dogai Coring** *var.* Lake Montcalm. ◎ W China
137 N15 **Doğanşehir** Malatya, C Turkey 38°07′N 37°54′E
84 E9 **Dogger Bank** *undersea feature* C North Sea 55°00′N 03°00′E
23 S10 **Dog Island** *island* Florida, SE USA
14 C7 **Dog Lake** ◎ Ontario, S Canada
106 B9 **Dogliani** Piemonte, NE Italy 44°33′N 07°55′E
164 H11 **Dōgo** *island* Oki-shotō, SW Japan
143 N10 **Do Gonbadān** *var.* Dow Gonbadān, Gonbadān. Kohkīlūyeh va Būyer AHmad, SW Iran 30°12′N 50°48′E
77 S12 **Dogondoutchi** Dosso, SW Niger 13°36′N 04°03′E
137 T13 **Doğubayazıt** Ağrı, E Turkey 39°33′N 44°07′E
137 P12 **Doğu Karadeniz Dağları** *var.* Anadolu Dağları. ▲ NE Turkey
158 K16 **Dogxung Zangbo** ≈ W China
Doha see Ad Dawḩah
Doha see Ad Dawḩah
Dohad see Dāhod
Dohuk see Dahūk
159 N16 **Doilungdêqên** *var.* Namka. Xizang Zizhiqu, W China 29°41′N 90°58′E
114 F12 **Doïrani, Límnis** *var.* Limni Doïranis, *Bul.* Ezero Doyransko. ◎ N Greece
Doire see Londonderry
99 H22 **Doische** Namur, S Belgium 50°09′N 04°43′E
59 P17 **Dois de Julho** ✈ (Salvador) Bahia, NE Brazil 12°04′S 38°58′W
60 H12 **Dois Vizinhos** Paraná, S Brazil 25°47′S 53°03′W
80 H10 **Doka** Gedaref, E Sudan 13°30′N 35°47′E
Doka see Kéita, Bahr
139 T3 **Dokan** *var.* Dūkān. As Sulaymānīyah, E Iraq 35°55′N 44°58′E
94 H13 **Dokka** Oppland, S Norway 60°49′N 10°04′E
98 L5 **Dokkum** Friesland, N Netherlands 53°20′N 06°E
98 L5 **Dokkumer Ee** ≈ N Netherlands
76 K13 **Doko** NE Guinea 11°46′N 08°58′W
Dokshitsy see Dokshytsy
118 K13 **Dokshytsy** *Rus.* Dokshitsy. Vitsyebskaya Voblasts', N Belarus 54°54′N 27°46′E
117 X8 **Dokuchayevs'k** *var.* Dokuchayevsk. Donets'ka Oblast', SE Ukraine 47°43′N 37°41′E
Dokuchayevsk see Dokuchayevs'k
Dolak, Pulau see Yos Sudarso, Pulau
29 P9 **Doland** South Dakota, N USA 44°51′N 98°06′W
63 J18 **Dolavón** Chaco, S Argentina 43°16′S 65°44′W
15 P6 **Dolbeau** Québec, SE Canada 48°52′N 72°15′W
102 I5 **Dol-de-Bretagne** Ille-et-Vilaine, NW France 48°33′N 01°45′W
64 J13 **Doldrums Fracture Zone** *tectonic feature* W Atlantic Ocean
103 S8 **Dôle** Jura, E France 47°05′N 05°30′E
97 J19 **Dolgellau** NW Wales, United Kingdom 52°45′N 03°54′W
Dolginovo see Dawhinava
Dolgi, Ostrov see Dolgiy, Ostrov
125 U2 **Dolgiy, Ostrov** *var.* Ostrov Dolgi. *island* NW Russian Federation
162 J9 **Dölgöön** Övörhangay, C Mongolia 45°57′N 103°14′E
107 C20 **Dolianova** Sardegna, Italy, C Mediterranean Sea 39°23′N 09°08′E
Dolina see Dolyna
123 T13 **Dolinsk** Ostrov Sakhalin, Sakhalinskaya Oblast', SE Russian Federation 47°20′N 142°52′E
Dolinskaya see Dolyns'ka
79 F21 **Dolisie** *prev.* Loubomo. Niari, S Congo 04°12′S 12°41′E
116 G14 **Dolj** ◐ *county* SW Romania
98 P5 **Dollard** *bay* NW Germany
194 J5 **Dolleman Island** *island* Antarctica
114 K8 **Dolna Oryakhovitsa** Veliko Tŭrnovo, N Bulgaria 43°09′N 25°44′E
114 N9 **Dolni Chiflik** Varna, E Bulgaria 42°59′N 27°43′E
114 I8 **Dolni Dŭbnik** Pleven, N Bulgaria 43°24′N 24°25′E
114 F8 **Dolni Lom** Vidin, NW Bulgaria 43°31′N 22°46′E
Dolnja Lendava see Lendava
129 F14 **Dolnośląskie** ◐ *province* SW Poland
111 K18 **Dolný Kubín** *Hung.* Alsókubin. Žilinský Kraj, N Slovakia 49°12′N 19°17′E
106 H8 **Dolo** Veneto, NE Italy 45°25′N 12°06′E
Dolomites/Dolomiti see Dolomitiche, Alpi
106 H6 **Dolomitiche, Alpi** *var.* Dolomiti, *Eng.* Dolomites. ▲ NE Italy
Dolonnur see Duolun
Doloon see Tsogt-Ovoo
61 E21 **Dolores** Buenos Aires, E Argentina 36°21′S 57°39′W
42 E3 **Dolores** Petén, N Guatemala 16°33′N 89°26′W
171 Q5 **Dolores** Samar, C Philippines 12°01′N 125°27′E
105 S12 **Dolores** País Valenciano, E Spain 38°09′N 00°45′W
61 D19 **Dolores** Soriano, SW Uruguay 33°34′S 58°15′W
41 N12 **Dolores Hidalgo** *var.* Ciudad de Dolores Hidalgo. Guanajuato, C Mexico 21°10′N 100°55′W
8 J7 **Dolphin and Union Strait** *strait* Northwest Territories/Nunavut, N Canada
65 D23 **Dolphin, Cape** *headland* East Falkland, Falkland Islands 51°15′S 58°57′W
44 H12 **Dolphin Head** *hill* W Jamaica
83 B21 **Dolphin Head** *var.* Cape Dernberg. *headland* SW Namibia 25°33′S 14°36′E
110 G12 **Dolsk** *Ger.* Dolzig. Weilkopolskie, C Poland 51°59′N 17°03′E
167 S8 **Đô Lương** Nghê An, N Vietnam 18°51′N 105°19′E
116 I6 **Dolyna** *Rus.* Dolina. Ivano-Frankivs'ka Oblast', W Ukraine 48°58′N 24°01′E
117 R8 **Dolyns'ka** *Rus.* Dolinskaya. Kirovohrads'ka Oblast', S Ukraine 48°06′N 32°46′E
Dolzig see Dolsk
Domachëvo/Domaczewo see Damachava
117 P9 **Domanivka** Mykolayivs'ka Oblast', S Ukraine 47°40′N 30°56′E
153 S13 **Domar** Rajshahi, N Bangladesh 26°08′N 88°57′E
158 G12 **Domar** *prev.* Zangkaxa. Xizang Zizhiqu, W China 33°42′N 80°21′E
108 I9 **Domat/Ems** Graubünden, SE Switzerland 46°50′N 09°28′E
111 A18 **Domažlice** *Ger.* Taus. Plzeňský Kraj, W Czech Republic 49°26′N 12°54′E
127 X8 **Dombarovskiy** Orenburgskaya Oblast', W Russian Federation 50°53′N 59°18′E
94 G10 **Dombås** Oppland, S Norway 62°04′N 09°07′E
83 M17 **Dombe** Manica, C Mozambique 19°59′S 33°24′E
82 A13 **Dombe Grande** Benguela, C Angola 12°57′S 13°07′E
103 R10 **Dombes** *physical region* E France
111 I25 **Dombóvár** Tolna, S Hungary 46°24′N 18°09′E
99 D14 **Domburg** Zeeland, SW Netherlands 51°34′N 03°30′E
58 L13 **Dom Eliseu** Pará, NE Brazil 04°02′S 47°31′W
Domel Island see Letsôk-aw Kyun
103 O11 **Dôme, Puy de** ▲ C France 45°46′N 03°00′E
36 H13 **Dome Rock Mountains** ▲ Arizona, SW USA
Domesnes, Cape see Kolkasrags
62 G8 **Domeyko** Atacama, N Chile 28°58′S 70°54′W
62 H5 **Domeyko, Cordillera** ▲ N Chile
102 K5 **Domfront** Orne, N France 48°35′N 00°39′W
171 X13 **Dom, Gunung** ▲ Papua, E Indonesia 02°41′S 137°00′E
45 X11 **Dominica** *off.* Commonwealth of Dominica. ◆ *republic* E West Indies
47 S3 **Dominica** *island* Dominica
Dominica Channel see Martinique Passage
Dominica, Commonwealth of see Dominica
43 N15 **Dominical** Puntarenas, SE Costa Rica 09°16′N 83°52′W
45 Q8 **Dominican Republic** ◆ *republic* C West Indies
45 X11 **Dominica Passage** *passage* E Caribbean Sea
99 K14 **Dommel** ≈ S Netherlands
81 O14 **Domo** Sumalē, E Ethiopia 07°53′N 46°55′E
126 L4 **Domodedovo** ✈ (Moskva) Moskovskaya Oblast', W Russian Federation 55°19′N 37°55′E
106 C6 **Domodossola** Piemonte, NE Italy 46°07′N 08°20′E
115 F17 **Domokós** *var.* Dhomokós. Stereá Ellás, C Greece 39°07′N 22°18′E
172 I14 **Domoni** Anjouan, SE Comoros 12°15′S 44°39′E
61 G16 **Dom Pedrito** Rio Grande do Sul, S Brazil 31°00′S 54°40′W
Dompoe see Dompu
170 M16 **Dompu** *prev.* Dompoe. Sumbawa, C Indonesia 08°30′S 118°28′E
Domschale see Domžale
62 H13 **Domuyo, Volcán** ☒ W Argentina 36°36′S 70°22′W
109 U11 **Domžale** *Ger.* Domschale. C Slovenia 46°09′N 14°33′E
127 O10 **Don** *var.* Duna, Tanais. ≈ SW Russian Federation
96 K9 **Don** ≈ NE Scotland, United Kingdom
182 M11 **Donald** Victoria, SE Australia 36°27′S 143°03′E
22 J9 **Donaldsonville** Louisiana, S USA 30°06′N 90°59′W
23 S8 **Donalsonville** Georgia, SE USA 31°02′N 84°52′W
Donau see Danube
101 G23 **Donaueschingen** Baden-Württemberg, SW Germany 47°57′N 08°30′E
101 K22 **Donaumoos** *wetland* S Germany
101 K22 **Donauwörth** Bayern, S Germany 48°43′N 10°46′E
109 U7 **Donawitz** Steiermark, SE Austria 47°23′N 15°00′E
117 X7 **Donbass** *industrial region* Russian Federation/Ukraine
104 K11 **Don Benito** Extremadura, W Spain 38°57′N 05°52′W
97 M17 **Doncaster** *anc.* Danum. N England, United Kingdom 53°32′N 01°07′W
44 K12 **Don Christophers Point** *headland* C Jamaica 18°19′N 76°48′W
55 V9 **Donderkamp** Sipaliwini, NW Surinam 05°18′N 56°22′W
82 B12 **Dondo** Cuanza Norte, NW Angola 09°40′S 14°24′E
171 O12 **Dondo** Sulawesi, N Indonesia 0°54′S 121°33′E
83 N17 **Dondo** Sofala, C Mozambique 19°41′S 34°45′E
155 K26 **Dondra Head** *headland* S Sri Lanka 05°57′N 80°33′E
Donduşani see Donduşeni
116 M8 **Donduşeni** *var.* Donduşani, *Rus.* Dondyushany. N Moldova 48°13′N 27°38′E
Dondyushany see Donduşeni
97 D15 **Donegal** *Ir.* Dún na nGall. Donegal, NW Ireland 54°39′N 08°06′W
97 D14 **Donegal** *Ir.* Dún na nGall. *cultural region* NW Ireland
97 C15 **Donegal Bay** *Ir.* Bá Dhún na nGall. *bay* NW Ireland
84 K10 **Donets** ≈ Russian Federation/Ukraine
117 X8 **Donets'k** *Rus.* Donetsk; *prev.* Stalino. Donets'ka Oblast', E Ukraine 47°58′N 37°50′E
117 W8 **Donets'k** ✈ Donets'ka Oblast', E Ukraine 48°03′N 37°44′E
Donets'k see Donets'ka Oblast'
117 W8 **Donets'ka Oblast'** *var.* Donets'k, *Rus.* Donetskaya Oblast'; *prev. Rus.* Stalins'kaya Oblast'. ◐ *province* SE Ukraine
Donetskaya Oblast' see Donets'ka Oblast'
67 P8 **Donga** ≈ Cameroon/Nigeria
157 O13 **Dongchuan** Yunnan, SW China 26°09′N 103°10′E
99 I14 **Dongen** Noord-Brabant, S Netherlands 51°38′N 04°56′E
160 K17 **Dongfang** *var.* Basuo. Hainan, S China 19°05′N 108°40′E
163 Z7 **Dongfanghong** Heilongjiang, NE China 46°13′N 133°13′E
163 W11 **Dongfeng** Jilin, NE China 42°39′N 125°33′E
171 N12 **Donggala** Sulawesi, C Indonesia 0°40′S 119°44′E
163 V13 **Donggang** *var.* Dadong; *prev.* Donggou. Liaoning, NE China 39°52′N 124°08′E
Donggou see Donggang
161 O14 **Dongguan** Guangdong, S China 23°03′N 113°43′E
167 T9 **Đông Ha** Quang Tri, C Vietnam 16°45′N 107°10′E
Dong Hai see East China Sea
160 M16 **Donghai Dao** *island* S China
162 I12 **Dong He** *Mong.* Narin Gol. ≈ N China
Donghe see Wangcang
167 T9 **Đông Hơi** Quang Binh, C Vietnam 17°32′N 106°35′E
Donghua see Huating
Donghuang see Xishui
108 H10 **Dongio** Ticino, S Switzerland 46°27′N 08°58′E
159 P15 **Dongjug** Xizang Zizhiqu, W China 29°58′N 94°51′E
Dongkan see Binhai
160 L11 **Dongkou** Hunan, S China 27°06′N 110°35′E
Dongliao see Liaoyuan
Dong-nai see Đông Nai, Sông
167 U13 **Đông Nai, Sông** *var.* Dong-nai, Dong Noi, Donnai. ≈ S Vietnam
161 N14 **Dongnan Qiuling** *plateau* SE China
163 Y9 **Dongning** Heilongjiang, NE China 44°01′N 131°03′E
Dong Noi see Đông Nai, Sông
83 C14 **Dongo** Huíla, C Angola 14°35′S 15°51′E
80 E7 **Dongola** *var.* Donqola, Dunqulah. Northern, N Sudan 19°10′N 30°27′E
79 I17 **Dongou** Likouala, NE Congo 02°05′N 18°00′E
Đông Phu see Đông Xoai
Dongping see Anhua
Dong Rak, Phanom see Dângrêk, Chuŏr Phnum
161 Q14 **Dongshan Dao** *island* SE China
Dongsha Qundao see Tungsha Tao
Dongsheng see Ordos
161 R7 **Dongtai** Jiangsu, E China 32°50′N 120°22′E
161 N10 **Dongting Hu** *var.* Tung-t'ing Hu. ◎ S China
161 P10 **Dongxiang** *var.* Xiaogang. Jiangxi, S China 28°16′N 116°32′E
167 T13 **Đông Xoai** *var.* Đông Phu. Sông Be, S Vietnam 11°31′N 106°55′E
161 Q4 **Dongying** Shandong, E China 37°27′N 118°01′E
27 X8 **Doniphan** Missouri, C USA 36°39′N 90°51′W
Donja Łužica see Niederlausitz
10 G7 **Donjek** ≈ Yukon Territory, W Canada
112 E11 **Donji Lapac** Lika-Senj, W Croatia 44°33′N 15°58′E
112 H8 **Donji Miholjac** Osijek-Baranja, NE Croatia 45°45′N 18°10′E
112 P12 **Donji Milanovac** Serbia, E Serbia 44°27′N 22°06′E
112 G12 **Donji Vakuf** *var.* Srbobran. ◆ Federacija Bosna I Hercegovina, C Bosnia and Herzegovina
98 M6 **Donkerbroek** Friesland, N Netherlands 52°58′N 05°15′E
167 P11 **Don Muang** ✈ (Krung Thep) Nonthaburi, C Thailand 13°51′N 100°40′E
25 S17 **Donna** Texas, SW USA 26°10′N 98°03′W
15 Q10 **Donnacona** Québec, SE Canada 46°41′N 71°46′W
Donnai see Đông Nai, Sông
29 Y16 **Donnellson** Iowa, C USA 40°38′N 91°33′W
11 O13 **Donnelly** Alberta, W Canada 55°42′N 117°06′W
35 P6 **Donner Pass** *Pass* California, W USA
101 F19 **Donnersberg** ▲ W Germany 49°37′N 07°54′E
Donoso see Miguel de la Borda
105 P2 **Donostia-San Sebastián** País Vasco, N Spain 43°19′N 01°59′W
115 K21 **Donoúsa** *var.* Donoússa. *island* Kykládes, Greece, Aegean Sea
Donoússa see Donoúsa
35 P8 **Don Pedro Reservoir** ⊠ California, W USA
Donqola see Dongola
126 L5 **Donskoy** Tul'skaya Oblast', W Russian Federation 54°02′N 38°27′E
81 L16 **Doolow** Sumalē, E Ethiopia 04°10′N 42°05′E
39 Q7 **Doonerak, Mount** ▲ Alaska, USA 67°54′N 150°33′W
98 J12 **Doorn** Utrecht, C Netherlands 52°02′N 05°21′E
Doornik see Tournai
31 N6 **Door Peninsula** *peninsula* Wisconsin, N USA
80 P13 **Dooxo Nugaaleed** *var.* Nogal Valley. *valley* E Somalia
Do Qu see Da Qu
106 B7 **Dora Baltea** *anc.* Duria Major. ≈ NW Italy
180 K7 **Dora, Lake** *salt lake* Western Australia
106 A8 **Dora Riparia** *anc.* Duria Minor. ≈ NW Italy
Dorbiljin see Emin
Dorbod/Dorbod Mongolzu Zizhixian see Taikang
Dorbod Mongolzu Zizhixian see Taikang
113 N18 **Dorče Petrov** *var.* Djorče Petrov, Gorče Petrov. N Macedonia 42°01′N 21°21′E
14 F16 **Dorchester** Ontario, S Canada 43°00′N 81°04′W
97 L24 **Dorchester** *anc.* Durnovaria. S England, United Kingdom 50°43′N 02°26′W
9 P7 **Dorchester, Cape** *headland* Baffin Island, Nunavut, NE Canada 65°25′N 77°25′W
83 D19 **Dordabis** Khomas, C Namibia 22°57′S 17°39′E
102 L12 **Dordogne** ◐ *department* SW France
103 N12 **Dordogne** ≈ W France
98 H13 **Dordrecht** *var.* Dordt, Dort. Zuid-Holland, SW Netherlands 51°48′N 04°40′E
Dordt see Dordrecht
103 P11 **Dore** ≈ C France
11 S13 **Doré Lake** Saskatchewan, C Canada 54°37′N 107°36′W
103 O12 **Dore, Monts** ▲ C France
101 M23 **Dorfen** Bayern, SE Germany 48°16′N 12°06′E
107 D18 **Dorgali** Sardegna, Italy, C Mediterranean Sea 40°18′N 09°34′E
159 N11 **Dorgê Co** *var.* Elsen Nur. ◎ C China
162 E6 **Dörgön** *var.* Seer. Hovd, W Mongolia 48°18′N 92°37′E
162 F7 **Dörgön Nuur** ◎ NW Mongolia
77 Q12 **Dori** N Burkina 14°03′N 00°02′W
83 E24 **Doring** ≈ S South Africa
101 E16 **Dormagen** Nordrhein-Westfalen, W Germany 51°06′N 06°49′E
103 P4 **Dormans** Marne, N France 49°03′N 03°44′E
108 E6 **Dornach** Solothurn, NW Switzerland 47°29′N 07°37′E
Dorna Watra see Vatra Dornei
108 J7 **Dornbirn** Vorarlberg, W Austria 47°25′N 09°46′E
96 I7 **Dornoch** N Scotland, United Kingdom 57°52′N 04°01′W
96 J7 **Dornoch Firth** *inlet* N Scotland, United Kingdom
163 P7 **Dornod** ◐ *province* E Mongolia
163 N10 **Dornogovĭ** ◐ *province* SE Mongolia
77 P10 **Doro** Tombouctou, S Mali 16°07′N 00°57′W
116 L14 **Dorobanţu** Călăraşi, S Romania 44°15′N 26°55′E
111 J22 **Dorog** Komárom-Esztergom, N Hungary 47°43′N 18°42′E
126 I4 **Dorogobuzh** Smolenskaya Oblast', W Russian Federation 54°56′N 33°16′E
116 K8 **Dorohoi** Botoşani, NE Romania 47°57′N 26°24′E
93 H15 **Dorotea** Västerbotten, N Sweden 64°17′N 16°30′E
Dorpat see Tartu
180 G10 **Dorre Island** *island* Western Australia
183 U5 **Dorrigo** New South Wales, SE Australia 30°22′S 152°43′E
35 N1 **Dorris** California, W USA 41°58′N 121°54′W
14 H13 **Dorset** Ontario, SE Canada 45°12′N 78°52′W
97 K23 **Dorset** *cultural region* S England, United Kingdom
101 E14 **Dorsten** Nordrhein-Westfalen, W Germany 51°38′N 06°58′E
Dort see Dordrecht
101 F15 **Dortmund** Nordrhein-Westfalen, W Germany 51°31′N 07°28′E
100 F12 **Dortmund-Ems-Kanal** *canal* W Germany
136 L17 **Dörtyol** Hatay, S Turkey 36°51′N 36°11′E
142 L7 **Do Rūd** *var.* Dow Rūd, Durud. Lorestān, W Iran 33°28′N 49°04′E
79 O15 **Doruma** Orientale, N Dem. Rep. Congo 04°35′N 27°43′E
15 O12 **Dorval** ✈ (Montréal) Québec, SE Canada 45°27′N 73°46′W
162 F7 **Dörvöljin** *var.* Buga. Dzavhan, W Mongolia 47°42′N 94°53′E
45 T5 **Dos Bocas, Lago** ◎ C Puerto Rico
104 K14 **Dos Hermanas** Andalucía, S Spain 37°16′N 05°55′W
Dospad Dagh see Rhodope Mountains
35 P10 **Dos Palos** California, W USA 37°00′N 120°39′W
114 I11 **Dospat** Smolyan, S Bulgaria 41°39′N 24°10′E
114 H11 **Dospat, Yazovir** ⊠ SW Bulgaria
100 M11 **Dosse** ≈ NE Germany
77 S12 **Dosso** Dosso, SW Niger 13°03′N 03°10′E
77 S12 **Dosso** ◐ *department* SW Niger
144 G12 **Dossor** Atyrau, SW Kazakhstan 47°31′N 53°01′E
147 O10 **Do'stlik** Jizzax Viloyati, C Uzbekistan 40°37′N 67°59′E
147 V9 **Dostuk** Narynskaya Oblast', C Kyrgyzstan 41°19′N 75°40′E
145 X13 **Dostyk** *prev.* Druzhba. Almaty, SE Kazakhstan 45°15′N 82°29′E
23 R7 **Dothan** Alabama, S USA 31°13′N 85°23′W
39 T9 **Dot Lake** Alaska, USA 63°39′N 144°10′W
118 F12 **Dotnuva** Kaunas, C Lithuania 55°23′N 23°53′E
99 D19 **Dottignies** Hainaut, W Belgium 50°43′N 03°16′E
103 P2 **Douai** *prev.* Douay; *anc.* Duacum. Nord, N France 50°22′N 03°04′E
14 L9 **Douaire, Lac** ◎ Québec, SE Canada
79 D16 **Douala** *var.* Duala. Littoral, W Cameroon 04°04′N 09°43′E
79 D16 **Douala** ✈ Littoral, W Cameroon 03°57′N 09°48′E
102 F6 **Douarnenez** Finistère, NW France 48°05′N 04°20′W
102 E6 **Douarnenez, Baie de** *bay* NW France
Douay see Douai
25 O6 **Double Mountain Fork Brazos River** ≈ Texas, SW USA
23 O3 **Double Springs** Alabama, S USA 34°09′N 87°24′W
103 T8 **Doubs** ◐ *department* E France
108 C8 **Doubs** ≈ France/Switzerland
185 A22 **Doubtful Sound** *sound* South Island, New Zealand
184 J2 **Doubtless Bay** *bay* North Island, New Zealand
25 X9 **Doucette** Texas, SW USA 30°48′N 94°25′W
102 K8 **Doué-la-Fontaine** Maine-et-Loire, NW France 47°12′N 00°16′W
77 O11 **Douentza** Mopti, S Mali 14°59′N 02°57′W
97 I16 **Douglas** ○ (Isle of Man) E Isle of Man 54°09′N 04°28′W
83 H23 **Douglas** Northern Cape, C South Africa 29°04′S 23°47′E
39 X13 **Douglas** Alexander Archipelago, Alaska, USA 58°12′N 134°18′W
37 O17 **Douglas** Arizona, SW USA 31°20′N 109°32′W
23 U7 **Douglas** Georgia, SE USA 31°30′N 82°51′W
33 Y15 **Douglas** Wyoming, C USA 42°48′N 105°23′W
21 O7 **Douglas Cape** *headland* Alaska, N USA 64°59′N 166°41′W
10 J14 **Douglas Channel** *channel* British Columbia, W Canada
182 G3 **Douglas Creek** *seasonal river* South Australia
31 P5 **Douglas Lake** ◎ Michigan, N USA
21 O9 **Douglas Lake** ⊠ Tennessee, S USA
39 Q13 **Douglas, Mount** ▲ Alaska, USA 58°51′N 153°31′W
194 I6 **Douglas Range** ▲ Alexander Island, Antarctica
103 O2 **Doullens** Somme, N France 50°09′N 02°21′E
Douma see Dūmā
79 F15 **Doumé** Est, E Cameroon 04°14′N 13°27′E
99 E21 **Dour** Hainaut, S Belgium 50°24′N 03°47′E
59 K18 **Dourada, Serra** ▲ S Brazil
59 I21 **Dourados** Mato Grosso do Sul, S Brazil 22°09′S 54°52′W
103 N5 **Dourdan** Essonne, N France 48°33′N 01°58′E
104 I6 **Douro** *Sp.* Duero. ≈ Portugal/Spain *see also* Duero
Douro see Duero
104 G6 **Douro Litoral** *former province* N Portugal
Douvres see Dover
102 K15 **Douze** ≈ SW France
183 P17 **Dover** Tasmania, SE Australia 43°19′S 147°01′E
97 Q22 **Dover** *Fr.* Douvres, *Lat.* Dubris Portus. SE England, United Kingdom 51°08′N 03°E
21 Y3 **Dover** *state capital* Delaware, NE USA 39°09′N 75°31′W
19 P9 **Dover** New Hampshire, NE USA 43°10′N 70°50′W
18 J14 **Dover** New Jersey, NE USA 40°51′N 74°33′W
31 U12 **Dover** Ohio, N USA 40°31′N 81°28′W
20 H8 **Dover** Tennessee, S USA 36°30′N 87°50′W
97 Q23 **Dover, Strait of** *var.* Straits of Dover, *Fr.* Pas de Calais. *strait* England, United Kingdom/France
Dover, Straits of see Dover, Strait of
Dovlen see Devin
94 G11 **Dovre** Oppland, S Norway 61°59′N 09°16′E
94 G10 **Dovrefjell** *plateau* S Norway
Dovsk see Dowsk
83 M14 **Dowa** Central, C Malawi 13°40′S 33°55′E
31 O10 **Dowagiac** Michigan, N USA 41°58′N 86°06′W
Dow Gonbadān see Do Gonbadān
148 M2 **Dowlatābād** Fāryāb, N Afghanistan 36°30′N 64°51′E
97 G16 **Down** *cultural region* SE Northern Ireland, United Kingdom
33 R16 **Downey** Idaho, NW USA 42°25′N 112°06′W
35 P5 **Downieville** California, W USA 39°34′N 120°49′W
97 G16 **Downpatrick** *Ir.* Dún Pádraig. SE Northern Ireland, United Kingdom 54°20′N 05°43′W
26 M3 **Downs** Kansas, C USA 39°30′N 98°33′W
18 J12 **Downsville** New York, NE USA 42°03′N 74°59′W
Dow Rūd see Do Rūd
29 V12 **Dows** Iowa, C USA 42°39′N 93°30′W
119 O17 **Dowsk** *Rus.* Dovsk. Homyel'skaya Voblasts', SE Belarus 53°09′N 30°28′E
35 Q4 **Doyle** California, W USA 40°00′N 120°06′W
18 I15 **Doylestown** Pennsylvania, NE USA 40°18′N 75°08′W
Doyransko, Ezero see Doïrani, Límnis
114 I8 **Doyrentsi** Lovech, N Bulgaria 43°13′N 24°46′E
164 G11 **Dōzen** *island* Oki-shotō, SW Japan
14 K9 **Dozois, Réservoir** ⊠ Québec, SE Canada
74 D9 **Drâa** *seasonal river* S Morocco
Drâa, Hammada du see Dra, Hamada du

◆ Country ● Country Capital ◇ Dependent Territory ○ Dependent Territory Capital ◐ Administrative Regions ✈ International Airport ▲ Mountain ▲ Mountain Range ☒ Volcano ≈ River ◎ Lake ⊠ Reservoir

DRABBLE – DYHERNFURTH

Drabble see José Enrique Rodó
117 Q5 **Drabiv** Cherkas'ka Oblast', C Ukraine 49°57′N 32°10′E
Drable see José Enrique Rodó
103 S13 **Drac** ≈ E France
Drač/Draç see Durrës
60 I8 **Dracena** São Paulo, S Brazil 21°27′S 51°30′W
98 M6 **Drachten** Friesland, N Netherlands 53°07′N 06°06′E
92 H11 **Drag** Lapp. Ájluokta. Nordland, C Norway 68°02′N 16°E
116 L14 **Dragalina** Călărași, SE Romania 44°26′N 27°19′E
116 I14 **Draganesti-Olt** Olt, S Romania 44°06′N 25°00′E
116 J14 **Drăgănești-Vlașca** Teleorman, S Romania 44°05′N 25°39′E
116 I13 **Drăgășani** Vâlcea, SW Romania 44°40′N 24°16′E
114 G9 **Dragoman** Sofiya, W Bulgaria 42°32′N 22°56′E
115 L25 **Dragonáda** island SE Greece
Dragonera, Isla see Sa Dragonera
45 T14 **Dragon's Mouths, The** strait Trinidad and Tobago/Venezuela
95 J23 **Dragør** København, E Denmark 55°36′N 12°42′E
114 F10 **Dragovishtitsa** Kysutendil, W Bulgaria 42°22′N 22°39′E
103 U15 **Draguignan** Var, SE France 43°31′N 06°31′E
74 E9 **Dra, Hamada du** var. Hammada du Drâa, Haut Plateau du Dra. plateau W Algeria
Dra, Haut Plateau du see Dra, Hamada du
119 H19 **Drahichyn** Pol. Drohiczyn Poleski, Rus. Drogichin. Brestskaya Voblasts', SW Belarus 52°11′N 25°10′E
29 N4 **Drake** North Dakota, N USA 47°54′N 100°23′W
83 K23 **Drakensberg** ▲▲ Lesotho/South Africa
194 F3 **Drake Passage** passage Atlantic Ocean/Pacific Ocean
114 L8 **Dralfa** Tŭrgovishte, N Bulgaria 43°17′N 26°25′E
114 I12 **Dráma** var. Dhráma. Anatolikí Makedonía kai Thráki, NE Greece 41°09′N 24°10′E
Dramburg see Drawsko Pomorskie
95 H15 **Drammen** Buskerud, S Norway 59°44′N 10°12′E
95 H15 **Drammensfjorden** fjord S Norway
92 H1 **Drangajökull** ▲ NW Iceland 66°13′N 22°18′W
95 F16 **Drangedal** Telemark, S Norway 59°05′N 09°05′E
92 I2 **Drangsnes** Vestfirdhir, NW Iceland 65°42′N 21°27′W
Drann see Dravinja
109 T10 **Drau** var. Drava, Eng. Drave, Hung. Dráva. ≈ C Europe see also Drava
Drau see Drava
84 I11 **Drava** var. Drau, Eng. Drave, Hung. Dráva. ≈ C Europe see also Drau
Dráva/Drave see Drau/Drava
109 W10 **Dravinja** Ger. Drann. ≈ NE Slovenia
109 V9 **Dravograd** Ger. Unterdrauburg; prev. Spodnji Dravograd. N Slovenia 46°36′N 15°00′E
110 F10 **Drawa** ≈ NW Poland
110 F9 **Drawno** Zachodnio-pomorskie, NW Poland 53°12′N 15°44′E
110 F9 **Drawsko Pomorskie** Ger. Dramburg. Zachodnio-pomorskie, NW Poland 53°32′N 15°48′E
29 R3 **Drayton** North Dakota, N USA 48°34′N 97°10′W
11 P14 **Drayton Valley** Alberta, SW Canada 53°15′N 115°00′W
186 B6 **Dreikikir** East Sepik, NW Papua New Guinea 03°42′S 142°46′E
Dreikirchen see Teiuș
98 N7 **Drenthe** ◈ province NE Netherlands
115 H15 **Drépano, Akrotírio** var. Akrotírio Dhrepanon. headland N Greece 39°56′N 23°57′E
Drepanum see Trapani
14 D17 **Dresden** Ontario, S Canada 42°34′N 82°09′W
101 O16 **Dresden** Sachsen, E Germany 51°03′N 13°43′E
20 G8 **Dresden** Tennessee, S USA 36°17′N 88°42′W
118 M11 **Dretun'** Vitsyebskaya Voblasts', N Belarus 55°41′N 29°13′E
102 M5 **Dreux** anc. Drocae, Durocasses. Eure-et-Loir, C France 48°44′N 01°23′E
94 I11 **Drevsjø** Hedmark, S Norway 61°52′N 12°01′E
22 K3 **Drew** Mississippi, S USA 33°48′N 90°31′W
110 F10 **Drezdenko** Ger. Driesen. Lubuskie, W Poland 52°51′N 15°50′E
98 J12 **Driebergen** var. Driebergen-Rijsenburg. Utrecht, C Netherlands 52°03′N 05°17′E
Driebergen-Rijsenburg see Driebergen
Driesen see Drezdenko
97 N16 **Driffield** E England, United Kingdom 54°00′N 00°28′W
33 S14 **Driggs** Idaho, NW USA 43°44′N 111°06′W
Drin see Drinit, Lumi i
112 K12 **Drina** ≈ Bosnia and Herzegovina/Serbia
Drin, Gulf of see Drinit, Gjiri i
113 K18 **Drinit, Gjiri i** var. Pellg i Drinit, Eng. Gulf of Drin. gulf NW Albania
113 L17 **Drinit, Lumi i** var. Drin. ≈ NW Albania
Drinit, Pellg i see Drinit, Gjiri i
Drinit të Zi, Lumi i see Black Drin
113 L22 **Drino** var. Drino, Drínos Pótamos, Alb. Lumi i Drinos. ≈ Albania/Greece
Drinos, Lumi i/Drínos Pótamos see Drino
25 S11 **Dripping Springs** Texas, SW USA 30°11′N 98°04′W
25 S15 **Driscoll** Texas, SW USA 27°40′N 97°45′W
22 H5 **Driskill Mountain** ▲ Louisiana, S USA 32°25′N 92°54′W
Drissa see Drysa
94 G10 **Driva** ≈ S Norway
112 E13 **Drniš** It. Šibenik-Knin. Šibenik-Knin, S Croatia 43°51′N 16°10′E
95 H15 **Drøbak** Akershus, S Norway 59°40′N 10°40′E
116 G13 **Drobeta-Turnu Severin** prev. Turnu Severin. Mehedinți, SW Romania 44°39′N 22°40′E
Drocae see Dreux
116 M8 **Drochia** Rus. Drokiya. N Moldova 48°02′N 27°46′E
97 F17 **Drogheda** Ir. Droichead Átha. NE Ireland 53°43′N 06°21′W
Drogichin see Drahichyn
Drogobych see Drohobych
Drohiczyn Poleski see Drahichyn
116 H6 **Drohobych** Pol. Drohobycz, Rus. Drogobych. L'vivs'ka Oblast', NW Ukraine 49°22′N 23°33′E
Drohobycz see Drohobych
Droichead Átha see Drogheda
Droicheadna Bandan see Bandon
Droichead na Banna see Banbridge
97 F18 **Droichead Nua** E Ireland 52°12′N 06°40′W
Droim Mór see Dromore
Drokiya see Drochia
103 R13 **Drôme** ◈ department E France
103 S13 **Drôme** ≈ E France
97 G15 **Dromore** Ir. Droim Mór. SE Northern Ireland, United Kingdom 54°25′N 06°09′W
106 A9 **Dronero** Piemonte, NE Italy 44°28′N 07°25′E
102 L12 **Dronne** ≈ SW France
195 Q3 **Dronning Maud Land** physical region Antarctica
98 K6 **Dronrijp** Fris. Dronryp. Friesland, N Netherlands 53°12′N 05°37′E
Dronryp see Dronrijp
98 L9 **Dronten** Flevoland, C Netherlands 52°31′N 05°41′E
Drontheim see Trondheim
102 L13 **Dropt** ≈ SW France
149 T4 **Drosh** North-West Frontier Province, NW Pakistan 35°33′N 71°48′E
Drossen see Ośno Lubuskie
Drug see Durg
Drujba see Pitnak
118 I12 **Drūkšiai** ◎ NE Lithuania
Druk-yul see Bhutan
11 Q16 **Drumheller** Alberta, SW Canada 51°28′N 112°42′W
33 Q10 **Drummond** Montana, NW USA 46°39′N 113°12′W
31 R4 **Drummond Island** island Michigan, N USA
Drummond Island see Tabiteuea
21 X7 **Drummond, Lake** ◎ Virginia, NE USA
15 P12 **Drummondville** Québec, SE Canada 45°52′N 72°28′W
39 T11 **Drum, Mount** ▲ Alaska, USA 62°11′N 144°37′W
27 O9 **Drumright** Oklahoma, C USA 35°59′N 96°36′W
99 J14 **Drunen** Noord-Brabant, S Netherlands 51°41′N 05°08′E
Druskienniki see Druskininkai
119 F15 **Druskininkai** Pol. Druskieniki. Alytus, S Lithuania 54°00′N 24°00′E
98 K13 **Druten** Gelderland, SE Netherlands 51°53′N 05°37′E
118 K11 **Druya** Vitsyebskaya Voblasts', NW Belarus 55°47′N 27°27′E
117 S2 **Druzhba** Sums'ka Oblast', NE Ukraine 52°01′N 33°56′E
Druzhba see Dostyk, Kazakhstan
Druzhba see Pitnak, Uzbekistan
123 R7 **Druzhina** Respublika Sakha (Yakutiya), NE Russian Federation 68°01′N 144°58′E
117 X7 **Druzhkivka** Donets'ka Oblast', E Ukraine 48°38′N 37°31′E
112 E12 **Drvar** Federacija Bosna I Hercegovina, W Bosnia and Herzegovina 44°21′N 16°24′E
113 G15 **Drvenik** Split-Dalmacija, SE Croatia 43°10′N 17°13′E
114 K9 **Dryanovo** Gabrovo, N Bulgaria 42°58′N 25°28′E
26 G7 **Dry Cimarron River** ≈ Kansas/Oklahoma, C USA
12 B11 **Dryden** Ontario, C Canada 49°48′N 92°48′W
24 M11 **Dryden** Texas, SW USA 30°01′N 102°06′W
195 Q14 **Drygalski Ice Tongue** ice feature Antarctica
118 L11 **Drysa** Rus. Drissa. ≈ N Belarus
23 V17 **Dry Tortugas** island Florida, SE USA
79 D15 **Dschang** Ouest, W Cameroon 05°28′N 10°02′E
54 J5 **Duaca** Lara, N Venezuela 10°22′N 69°08′W
Duacum see Douai
Duala see Douala
45 N9 **Duarte, Pico** ▲ C Dominican Republic 19°02′N 70°57′W
140 J5 **Ḑubā** Tabūk, NW Saudi Arabia 27°26′N 35°42′E
Dubai see Dubayy
117 N9 **Dubăsari** Rus. Dubossary. NE Moldova 47°16′N 29°07′E
117 N9 **Dubăsari Reservoir** ⊠ NE Moldova
8 M10 **Dubawnt** ≈ Nunavut, NW Canada
8 L9 **Dubawnt Lake** ◎ Northwest Territories/Nunavut, N Canada
30 L6 **Du Bay, Lake** ⊠ Wisconsin, N USA
141 U7 **Dubayy** Eng. Dubai. Dubayy, NE United Arab Emirates 25°11′N 55°18′E
141 W7 **Dubayy** Eng. Dubai. ✕ Dubayy, NE United Arab Emirates 25°15′N 55°22′E
183 R7 **Dubbo** New South Wales, SE Australia 32°16′S 148°41′E
108 G7 **Dübendorf** Zürich, NW Switzerland 47°23′N 08°37′E
97 F18 **Dublin** Ir. Baile Átha Cliath; anc. Eblana. ● (Ireland) Dublin, E Ireland 53°20′N 06°15′W
23 U5 **Dublin** Georgia, SE USA 32°32′N 82°54′W
25 R7 **Dublin** Texas, SW USA 32°05′N 98°20′W
97 G18 **Dublin** Ir. Baile Átha Cliath; anc. Eblana. cultural region E Ireland
97 G18 **Dublin Airport** ✕ Dublin, E Ireland 53°25′N 06°18′W
189 V12 **Dublon** var. Tonoas. island Chuuk Islands, C Micronesia
126 K2 **Dubna** Moskovskaya Oblast', W Russian Federation 56°45′N 37°09′E
111 G19 **Dubňany** Ger. Dubnian. Jihomoravský Kraj, SE Czech Republic 48°54′N 17°00′E
Dubnian see Dubňany
111 I19 **Dubnica nad Váhom** Hung. Máriatölgyes; prev. Dubnicz. Trenčiansky Kraj, W Slovakia 48°58′N 18°10′E
Dubnicz see Dubnica nad Váhom
116 K4 **Dubno** Rivnens'ka Oblast', NW Ukraine 50°28′N 25°40′E
33 R13 **Dubois** Idaho, NW USA 44°10′N 112°13′W
18 D13 **Du Bois** Pennsylvania, NE USA 41°07′N 78°45′W
33 T14 **Dubois** Wyoming, C USA 43°31′N 109°37′W
Dubossary see Dubăsari
127 O10 **Dubovka** Volgogradskaya Oblast', SW Russian Federation 49°10′N 48°49′E
76 H14 **Dubréka** SW Guinea 09°48′N 13°31′W
14 B7 **Dubreuilville** Ontario, S Canada 48°21′N 84°31′W
Dubris Portus see Dover
119 L20 **Dubrova** Homyel'skaya Voblasts', SE Belarus 51°47′N 28°13′E
Dubrovačko-Neretvanska Županija see Dubrovnik-Neretva
126 I5 **Dubrovka** Bryanskaya Oblast', W Russian Federation 53°44′N 33°27′E
113 H16 **Dubrovnik** It. Ragusa. Dubrovnik-Neretva, SE Croatia 42°40′N 18°06′E
113 I16 **Dubrovnik** ✕ Dubrovnik-Neretva, SE Croatia 42°34′N 18°17′E
113 F16 **Dubrovnik-Neretva** off. Dubrovačko-Neretvanska Županija. ◈ province SE Croatia
Dubrovno see Dubrowna
116 L2 **Dubrovytsya** Rivnens'ka Oblast', NW Ukraine 51°34′N 26°37′E
119 O14 **Dubrowna** Rus. Dubrovno. Vitsyebskaya Voblasts', N Belarus 54°35′N 30°41′E
29 Z13 **Dubuque** Iowa, C USA 42°30′N 90°40′W
118 E12 **Dubysa** ≈ C Lithuania
167 U11 **Đức Cơ** Gia Lai, C Vietnam 13°48′N 107°41′E
191 V12 **Duc de Gloucester, Îles du** Eng. Duke of Gloucester Islands. island group C French Polynesia
111 C15 **Duchcov** Ger. Dux. Ústecký Kraj, NW Czech Republic 50°37′N 13°45′E
37 N3 **Duchesne** Utah, W USA 40°09′N 110°24′W
191 P17 **Ducie Island** atoll E Pitcairn Islands
11 W15 **Duck Bay** Manitoba, S Canada 52°11′N 100°08′W
23 X17 **Duck Key** island Florida Keys, Florida, SE USA
11 T14 **Duck Lake** Saskatchewan, S Canada 52°52′N 106°12′W
11 V15 **Duck Mountain** ▲ Manitoba, S Canada
20 I9 **Duck River** ≈ Tennessee, S USA
20 M10 **Ducktown** Tennessee, S USA 35°01′N 84°24′W
167 U10 **Đức Phô** Quang Ngai, C Vietnam 14°56′N 108°55′E
Đức Tho see Lin Camh
167 U13 **Đức Trong** var. Liên Nghia. Lâm Đông, S Vietnam 11°45′N 108°24′E
D-U-D see Dalap-Uliga-Djarrit
99 M25 **Dudelange** var. Forge du Sud, Ger. Dudelingen. Luxembourg, S Luxembourg 49°28′N 06°05′E
Dudelingen see Dudelange
101 J15 **Duderstadt** Niedersachsen, C Germany 51°31′N 10°16′E
153 N15 **Dūdhi** Uttar Pradesh, N India 24°09′N 83°16′E
122 K8 **Dudinka** Taymyrskiy (Dolgano-Nenetskiy) Avtonomnyy Okrug, N Russian Federation 69°27′N 86°13′E
97 L20 **Dudley** C England, United Kingdom 52°30′N 02°05′W
154 G13 **Dudna** ≈ C India
76 L16 **Duékoué** W Ivory Coast 06°50′N 05°22′W
104 M5 **Dueñas** Castilla-León, N Spain 41°52′N 04°33′W
104 K4 **Duerna** ≈ NW Spain
105 O6 **Duero** Port. Douro. ≈ Portugal/Spain see also Douro
Duero see Douro
Duesseldorf see Düsseldorf
21 P12 **Due West** South Carolina, SE USA 34°19′N 82°23′W
195 P11 **Dufek Coast** physical region Antarctica
99 H17 **Duffel** Antwerpen, C Belgium 51°06′N 04°30′E
35 S2 **Duffer Peak** ▲ Nevada, W USA 41°40′N 118°45′W
187 Q9 **Duff Islands** island group E Solomon Islands
Dufour, Pizzo/Dufour, Punta see Dufour Spitze
108 E12 **Dufour Spitze** It. Pizzo Dufour, Punta Dufour. ▲ Italy/Switzerland 45°54′N 07°50′E
112 D9 **Duga Resa** Karlovac, C Croatia 45°25′N 15°30′E
22 H5 **Dugdemona River** ≈ Louisiana, S USA
154 J12 **Duggīpar** Mahārāshtra, C India 21°06′N 80°10′E
112 B13 **Dugi Otok** var. Isola Grossa, It. Isola Lunga. island W Croatia
113 F14 **Dugopolje** Split-Dalmacija, S Croatia 43°35′N 16°35′E
160 L8 **Du He** ≈ C China
54 M11 **Duida, Cerro** ▲ S Venezuela 03°21′N 65°45′W
Duinekerke see Dunkerque
101 E15 **Duisburg** prev. Duisburg-Hamborn. Nordrhein-Westfalen, W Germany 51°25′N 06°47′E
Duisburg-Hamborn see Duisburg
99 F14 **Duiveland** island SW Netherlands
98 M12 **Duiven** Gelderland, E Netherlands 51°57′N 06°02′E
139 W10 **Dujaylah, Hawr ad** ◎ S Iraq
160 H9 **Dujiangyan** var. Guanxian, Guan Xian. Sichuan, C China 31°01′N 103°40′E
81 L18 **Dujuuma** Shabeellaha Hoose, S Somalia 01°04′N 42°37′E
Dūkān see Dokan
39 Z14 **Duke Island** island Alexander Archipelago, Alaska, USA
Dukelský Priesmy/Dukelský Průsmyk see Dukla Pass
Duke of Gloucester Islands see Duc de Gloucester, Îles du
81 F14 **Duk Faiwil** Jonglei, SE Sudan 07°30′N 31°27′E
141 T7 **Dukhān** C Qatar 25°29′N 50°48′E
Dukhan Heights see Dukhān, Jabal
143 N16 **Dukhān, Jabal** var. Dukhan Heights. hill range S Qatar
127 Q7 **Dukhovnitskoye** Saratovskaya Oblast', W Russian Federation 52°31′N 48°32′E
126 H4 **Dukhovshchina** Smolenskaya Oblast', W Russian Federation 55°15′N 32°22′E
Dukielska, Przełęcz see Dukla Pass
111 N17 **Dukla** Podkarpackie, SE Poland 49°33′N 21°40′E
Duklai Hág see Dukla Pass
111 N18 **Dukla Pass** Cz. Dukelský Průsmyk, Ger. Dukla-Pass, Hung. Duklai Hág, Pol. Przełęcz Dukielska, Slvk. Dukelský Priesmy. pass Poland/Slovakia
Dukla-Pass see Dukla Pass
Dukou see Panzhihua
118 I12 **Dūkštas** Utena, E Lithuania 55°32′N 26°21′E
Dulaan see Herlenbayan-Ulaan
159 R10 **Dulan** var. Qagan Us. Qinghai, C China 36°11′N 97°51′E
37 R8 **Dulce** New Mexico, SW USA 36°55′N 107°00′W
43 N16 **Dulce, Golfo** gulf S Costa Rica
Dulce, Golfo see Izabal, Lago de
42 K6 **Dulce Nombre de Culmí** Olancho, C Honduras 15°09′N 85°37′W
62 L9 **Dulce, Río** ≈ C Argentina
123 Q9 **Dulgalakh** ≈ NE Russian Federation
114 M8 **Dŭlgopol** Varna, E Bulgaria 43°05′N 27°24′E
153 V14 **Dullabchara** Assam, NE India 24°25′N 92°22′E
20 D3 **Dulles** ✕ (Washington DC) Virginia, NE USA 39°00′N 77°27′W
101 E14 **Dülmen** Nordrhein-Westfalen, W Germany 51°51′N 07°17′E
114 M7 **Dulovo** Silistra, NE Bulgaria 43°51′N 27°10′E
29 W5 **Duluth** Minnesota, N USA 46°47′N 92°06′W
138 H7 **Dūmā** Fr. Douma. Dimashq, SW Syria 33°33′N 36°24′E
171 O8 **Dumagasa Point** headland Mindanao, S Philippines 07°01′N 121°54′E
171 P6 **Dumaguete** var. Dumaguete City. Negros, C Philippines 09°16′N 123°17′E
Dumaguete City see Dumaguete
168 J10 **Dumai** Sumatera, W Indonesia 01°39′N 101°28′E
183 T4 **Dumaresq River** ≈ New South Wales/Queensland, SE Australia
27 W13 **Dumas** Arkansas, C USA 33°53′N 91°29′W
25 N1 **Dumas** Texas, SW USA 35°51′N 101°57′W
138 I7 **Ḑumayr** Dimashq, W Syria 33°36′N 36°28′E
96 I12 **Dumbarton** W Scotland, United Kingdom 55°57′N 04°35′W
96 I12 **Dumbarton** cultural region C Scotland, United Kingdom
187 Q17 **Dumbéa** Province Sud, S New Caledonia 22°11′S 166°27′E
111 K19 **Ďumbier** Ger. Djumbir, Hung. Gyömbér. ▲ C Slovakia 48°54′N 19°36′E
116 I11 **Dumbrăveni** Ger. Elisabethstedt, Hung. Erzsébetváros; prev. Ebesfalva, Eppeschdorf, Ibașfalău. Sibiu, C Romania 46°14′N 24°34′E
116 L12 **Dumbrăveni** Vrancea, E Romania 45°31′N 27°09′E
97 J14 **Dumfries** S Scotland, United Kingdom 55°04′N 03°37′W
97 J14 **Dumfries** cultural region SW Scotland, United Kingdom
153 R15 **Dumka** Jhārkhand, NE India 24°17′N 87°15′E
Dümmer see Dümmersee
100 G12 **Dümmersee** var. Dümmer. ◎ NW Germany
14 J11 **Dumoine** ≈ Québec, SE Canada
14 J10 **Dumoine, Lac** ◎ Québec, SE Canada
195 V16 **Dumont d'Urville** French research station Antarctica 66°24′S 139°38′E
195 W15 **Dumont d'Urville Sea** sea S Pacific Ocean
14 K11 **Dumont, Lac** ◎ Québec, SE Canada
75 W7 **Dumyāt** var. Dumyât, Eng. Damietta. N Egypt 31°26′N 31°48′E
Duna see Danube, C Europe
Düna see Western Dvina
Duna see Don, Russian Federation
Dünaburg see Daugavpils
111 J24 **Dunaföldvár** Tolna, C Hungary 46°48′N 18°55′E
Dunaj see Wien, Austria
Dunaj see Danube, C Europe
111 L18 **Dunajec** ≈ S Poland
111 H21 **Dunajská Streda** Hung. Dunaszerdahely. Trnavský Kraj, W Slovakia 48°N 17°28′E
Dunapentele see Dunaújváros
Dunărea see Danube
116 M13 **Dunărea Veche, Braţul** ≈ SE Romania
117 N13 **Dunării, Delta** delta SE Romania
Dunaszerdahely see Dunajská Streda
111 J23 **Dunaújváros** prev. Dunapentele, Sztálinváros. Fejér, C Hungary 47°N 18°55′E
Dunav see Danube
114 J8 **Dunavska Ravnina** Eng. Danubian Plain. lowlands N Bulgaria
114 G7 **Dunavtsi** Vidin, NW Bulgaria 43°54′N 22°49′E
123 S15 **Dunay** Primorskiy Kray, SE Russian Federation 42°53′N 132°20′E
Dunayevtsy see Dunayivtsi
116 L7 **Dunayivtsi** Rus. Dunayevtsy. Khmel'nyts'ka Oblast', NW Ukraine 48°56′N 26°50′E
185 F22 **Dunback** Otago, South Island, New Zealand 45°22′S 170°37′E
10 L17 **Duncan** Vancouver Island, British Columbia, SW Canada 48°46′N 123°10′W
37 O15 **Duncan** Arizona, SW USA 32°43′N 109°06′W
26 M12 **Duncan** Oklahoma, C USA 34°30′N 97°57′W
Duncan Island see Pinzón, Isla
151 Q20 **Duncan Passage** strait Andaman Sea/Bay of Bengal
96 K6 **Duncansby Head** headland N Scotland, United Kingdom 58°37′N 03°01′W
14 G12 **Dunchurch** Ontario, S Canada 45°36′N 79°54′W
118 D7 **Dundaga** Talsi, NW Latvia 57°29′N 22°19′E
14 G14 **Dundalk** Ontario, S Canada 44°11′N 80°22′W
97 F16 **Dundalk** Ir. Dún Dealgan. Louth, NE Ireland 54°01′N 06°25′W
21 X3 **Dundalk** Maryland, NE USA 39°15′N 76°31′W
97 F16 **Dundalk Bay** Ir. Cuan Dhún Dealgan. bay NE Ireland
14 G16 **Dundas** Ontario, S Canada 43°16′N 79°55′W
180 L12 **Dundas, Lake** salt lake Western Australia
Dundbürd see Batnorov
Dún Dealgan see Dundalk
15 N13 **Dundee** Québec, SE Canada 45°01′N 74°27′W
83 K22 **Dundee** KwaZulu/Natal, E South Africa 28°09′S 30°12′E
96 K11 **Dundee** E Scotland, United Kingdom 56°28′N 03°W
31 R10 **Dundee** Michigan, N USA 41°57′N 83°39′W
25 R5 **Dundee** Texas, SW USA 33°43′N 98°52′W
194 H3 **Dundee Island** island Antarctica
162 L9 **Dundgovĭ** ◈ province C Mongolia
97 G16 **Dundrum Bay** Ir. Cuan Dhún Droma. inlet NW Irish Sea
11 T15 **Dundurn** Saskatchewan, S Canada 51°43′N 106°27′W
Dund-Us see Hovd
Dund-Us see Hovd
185 F23 **Dunedin** Otago, South Island, New Zealand 45°52′S 170°31′E
183 R7 **Dunedoo** New South Wales, SE Australia 32°04′S 149°23′E
97 D14 **Dunfanaghy** Ir. Dún Fionnachaidh. NW Ireland 55°11′N 07°59′W
96 J12 **Dunfermline** C Scotland, United Kingdom 56°04′N 03°29′W
Dún Fionnachaidh see Dunfanaghy
149 V10 **Dunga Bunga** Punjab, E Pakistan 29°51′N 73°19′E
97 F15 **Dungannon** Ir. Dún Geanainn. C Northern Ireland, United Kingdom 54°31′N 06°46′W
Dun Garbháin see Dungarvan
152 F15 **Dūngarpur** Rājasthān, N India 23°50′N 73°43′E
97 E21 **Dungarvan** Ir. Dun Garbháin. Waterford, S Ireland 52°05′N 07°37′W
101 N21 **Dungau** cultural region SE Germany
Dún Geanainn see Dungannon
97 P23 **Dungeness** headland SE England, United Kingdom 50°55′N 00°58′E
63 I23 **Dungeness, Punta** headland S Argentina 52°25′S 68°25′W
Dungloe see Dunglow
97 D14 **Dunglow** var. Dungloe, Ir. An Clochán Liath. Donegal, NW Ireland 54°57′N 08°22′W
183 T7 **Dungog** New South Wales, SE Australia 32°24′S 151°45′E
79 O16 **Dungu** Orientale, NE Dem. Rep. Congo 03°40′N 28°32′E
168 L8 **Dungun** var. Kuala Dungun. Terengganu, Peninsular Malaysia 04°47′N 103°26′E
80 I6 **Dungûnab** Red Sea, NE Sudan 21°10′N 37°09′E
15 P13 **Dunham** Québec, SE Canada 45°08′N 72°48′W
Dunheved see Launceston
Dunholme see Durham
163 X10 **Dunhua** Jilin, NE China 43°22′N 128°12′E
159 P8 **Dunhuang** Gansu, N China 40°10′N 94°40′E
182 L12 **Dunkeld** Victoria, SE Australia 37°41′S 142°19′E
103 O1 **Dunkerque** Eng. Dunkirk, Flem. Duinekerke; prev. Dunquerque. Nord, N France 51°06′N 02°34′E
97 K23 **Dunkery Beacon** ▲ SW England, United Kingdom 51°10′N 03°36′W
18 C11 **Dunkirk** New York, NE USA 42°28′N 79°19′W
Dunkirk see Dunkerque
77 P17 **Dunkwa** SW Ghana 05°59′N 01°45′W
97 G18 **Dún Laoghaire** Eng. Dunleary; prev. Kingstown. E Ireland 53°17′N 06°08′W
29 S14 **Dunlap** Iowa, C USA 41°51′N 95°36′W
20 L10 **Dunlap** Tennessee, S USA 35°22′N 85°23′W
Dunleary see Dún Laoghaire
Dún Mánmhaí see Dunmanway
97 B21 **Dunmanway** Ir. Dún Mánmhaí. Cork, SW Ireland 51°43′N 09°07′W
18 I13 **Dunmore** Pennsylvania, NE USA 41°25′N 75°37′W
21 U10 **Dunn** North Carolina, SE USA 35°18′N 78°36′W
Dún na nGall see Donegal
23 V11 **Dunnellon** Florida, SE USA 29°03′N 82°27′W
96 J6 **Dunnet Head** headland N Scotland, United Kingdom 58°40′N 03°27′W
29 N14 **Dunning** Nebraska, C USA 41°49′N 100°04′W
14 G17 **Dunnville** Ontario, S Canada 42°54′N 79°36′W
Dún Pádraig see Downpatrick
Dunquerque see Dunkerque
Dunqulah see Dongola
96 L12 **Duns** SE Scotland, United Kingdom 55°46′N 02°13′W
29 N2 **Dunseith** North Dakota, N USA 48°48′N 100°03′W
35 N2 **Dunsmuir** California, W USA 41°12′N 122°19′W
97 N21 **Dunstable** Lat. Durocobrivae. E England, United Kingdom 51°53′N 00°32′W
185 D21 **Dunstan Mountains** ▲▲ South Island, New Zealand
103 O9 **Dun-sur-Auron** Cher, C France 46°52′N 02°40′E
185 F21 **Duntroon** Canterbury, South Island, New Zealand 44°52′S 170°40′E
149 T10 **Dunyāpur** Punjab, E Pakistan 29°48′N 71°48′E
163 U5 **Duobukur He** ≈ NE China
163 R12 **Duolun** var. Dolonnur. Nei Mongol Zizhiqu, N China 42°11′N 116°30′E
167 R14 **Dương Đông** Kiên Giang, S Vietnam 10°15′N 103°58′E
114 G10 **Dupnitsa** prev. Marek, Stanke Dimitrov. Kyustendil, W Bulgaria 42°16′N 23°07′E
28 L8 **Dupree** South Dakota, N USA 45°03′N 101°36′W
33 Q7 **Dupuyer** Montana, NW USA 48°13′N 112°34′W
141 Y11 **Duqm** var. Daqm. E Oman 19°42′N 57°40′E
63 F23 **Duque de York, Isla** island S Chile
181 N4 **Durack Range** ▲▲ Western Australia
136 K10 **Durağan** Sinop, N Turkey 41°26′N 35°03′E
103 S15 **Durance** ≈ SE France
31 R9 **Durand** Michigan, N USA 42°54′N 83°58′W
30 I6 **Durand** Wisconsin, N USA 44°37′N 91°56′W
40 K10 **Durango** var. Victoria de Durango. Durango, W Mexico 24°03′N 104°38′W
105 P3 **Durango** País Vasco, N Spain 43°10′N 02°38′W
37 Q8 **Durango** Colorado, C USA 37°13′N 107°51′W
40 J9 **Durango** ◈ state C Mexico
114 O7 **Durankulak** Rom. Răcari; prev. Blatnitsa, Duranulac. Dobrich, NE Bulgaria 43°41′N 28°31′E
22 L4 **Durant** Mississippi, S USA 33°04′N 89°51′W
27 P13 **Durant** Oklahoma, C USA 33°59′N 96°24′W
Duranulac see Durankulak
105 N6 **Duratón** ≈ N Spain
61 E19 **Durazno** var. San Pedro de Durazno. Durazno, C Uruguay 33°22′S 56°31′W
61 E19 **Durazno** ◈ department C Uruguay
Durazzo see Durrës
83 K23 **Durban** var. Port Natal. KwaZulu/Natal, E South Africa 29°51′S 31°E
83 K23 **Durban** ✕ KwaZulu/Natal, E South Africa 29°55′S 31°01′E
118 C9 **Durbe** Ger. Durben. Liepāja, W Latvia 56°34′N 21°22′E
Durben see Durbe
99 K21 **Durbuy** Luxembourg, SE Belgium 50°21′N 05°27′E
105 N15 **Dúrcal** Andalucía, S Spain 37°00′N 03°24′W
112 F8 **Đurđevac** Ger. Sankt Georgen, Hung. Szentgyörgy; prev. Djurdjevac, Gjurgjevac. Koprivnica-Kri»zevci, N Croatia 46°02′N 17°03′E
113 K15 **Đurđevica Tara** N Montenegro 43°09′N 19°18′E
97 L24 **Durdle Door** natural arch S England, United Kingdom 50°37′N 02°16′W
158 L3 **Düre** Xinjiang Uygur Zizhiqu, W China 46°30′N 88°26′E
101 D16 **Düren** anc. Marcodurum. Nordrhein-Westfalen, W Germany 50°48′N 06°30′E
154 K12 **Durg** prev. Drug. Chhattīsgarh, C India 21°12′N 81°20′E
153 U13 **Durgapur** Dhaka, N Bangladesh 25°10′N 90°41′E
153 R15 **Durgāpur** West Bengal, NE India 23°30′N 87°20′E
14 F14 **Durham** Ontario, S Canada 44°10′N 80°48′W
97 M14 **Durham** hist. Dunholme. N England, United Kingdom 54°47′N 01°34′W
21 U9 **Durham** North Carolina, SE USA 36°N 78°54′W
97 L15 **Durham** cultural region N England, United Kingdom
168 J10 **Duri** Sumatera, W Indonesia 01°13′N 101°13′E
Duria Major see Dora Baltea
Duria Minor see Dora Riparia
Durlas see Thurles
141 P8 **Ḑurmā** Ar Riyāḑ, C Saudi Arabia 24°37′N 46°06′E
113 J15 **Durmitor** ▲ N Montenegro
96 H6 **Durness** N Scotland, United Kingdom 58°34′N 04°46′W
109 Y3 **Dürnkrut** Niederösterreich, E Austria 48°28′N 16°50′E
Durnovaria see Dorchester
Durobrivae see Rochester
Durocasses see Dreux
Durocobrivae see Dunstable
Durocortorum see Reims
Durostorum see Silistra
Durovernum see Canterbury
113 K20 **Durrës** var. Durrësi, Dursi, It. Durazzo, SCr. Drač, Turk. Draç. Durrës, W Albania 41°20′N 19°26′E
113 K19 **Durrës** ◈ district W Albania
Durrësi see Durrës
97 A21 **Dursey Island** Ir. Oileán Baoi. island SW Ireland
Dursi see Durrës
Duru see Wuchuan
Durud see Do Rūd
114 P12 **Durusu** İstanbul, NW Turkey 41°18′N 28°41′E
114 O12 **Durusu Gölü** ◎ NW Turkey
138 I9 **Durūz, Jabal ad** ▲ SW Syria 37°00′N 32°30′E
184 K13 **D'Urville Island** island C New Zealand
171 X12 **D'Urville, Tanjung** headland Papua, E Indonesia 01°26′S 137°52′E
146 H14 **Duşak** Rus. Dushak. Ahal Welaýaty, S Turkmenistan 37°15′N 59°57′E
Dusa Mareb/Dusa Marreb see Dhuusa Marreeb
118 I11 **Dusetos** Utena, NE Lithuania 55°44′N 25°49′E
Dushak see Duşak
160 K12 **Dushan** Guizhou, S China 25°50′N 107°36′E
147 P13 **Dushanbe** var. Dyushambe; prev. Stalinabad, Taj. Stalinobod. ● (Tajikistan) W Tajikistan 38°35′N 68°44′E
147 P13 **Dushanbe** ✕ W Tajikistan 38°31′N 68°49′E
158 J5 **Dushanzi** Xinjiang Uygur Zizhiqu, NW China 44°20′N 84°51′E
137 T9 **Dushet'i** E Georgia 42°07′N 44°44′E
18 H13 **Dushore** Pennsylvania, NE USA 41°30′N 76°23′W
185 A23 **Dusky Sound** sound South Island, New Zealand
101 E15 **Düsseldorf** var. Duesseldorf. Nordrhein-Westfalen, W Germany 51°14′N 06°49′E
147 P14 **Dŭsti** Rus. Dusti. SW Tajikistan 37°22′N 68°41′E
194 I9 **Dustin Island** island Antarctica
Dutch East Indies see Indonesia
Dutch Guiana see Surinam
38 L17 **Dutch Harbor** Unalaska Island, Alaska, USA 53°51′N 166°33′W
36 J3 **Dutch Mount** ▲ Utah, W USA 40°16′N 113°56′W
Dutch New Guinea see Papua
Dutch West Indies see Netherlands Antilles
83 H20 **Dutlwe** Kweneng, S Botswana 23°58′S 23°56′E
67 V16 **Du Toit Fracture Zone** tectonic feature SW Indian Ocean
125 U8 **Dutovo** Respublika Komi, NW Russian Federation 63°45′N 56°38′E
77 V13 **Dutsan Wai** var. Dutsen Wai. Kaduna, C Nigeria 10°49′N 08°15′E
77 W13 **Dutse** Jigawa, N Nigeria 11°43′N 09°25′E
Dutsen Wai see Dutsan Wai
Duttia see Datia
14 E17 **Dutton** Ontario, S Canada 42°40′N 81°28′W
36 L7 **Dutton, Mount** ▲ Utah, W USA 38°00′N 112°10′W
162 E7 **Duut** Hovd, W Mongolia 47°28′N 91°52′E
14 K11 **Duval, Lac** ◎ Québec, SE Canada
127 W3 **Duvan** Respublika Bashkortostan, W Russian Federation 55°42′N 57°56′E
138 L9 **Duwaykhilat Satīḩ ar Ruwayshid** seasonal river SE Jordan
Dux see Duchcov
160 J13 **Duyang Shan** ▲ S China
167 T14 **Duyên Hai** Tra Vinh, S Vietnam 09°39′N 106°28′E
160 K12 **Duyun** Guizhou, S China 26°16′N 107°29′E
136 G11 **Düzce** Düzce, NW Turkey 40°51′N 31°09′E
136 K14 **Düzce** ◈ province NW Turkey
Duzdab see Zāhedān
Duzenkyr, Khrebet see Duzkyr, Khrebet
146 I16 **Duzkyr, Khrebet** prev. Khrebet Duzenkyr. ▲▲ S Turkmenistan
114 K8 **Dve Mogili** Ruse, N Bulgaria 43°35′N 25°51′E
Dvina Bay see Chëshskaya Guba
Dvinsk see Daugavpils
124 L7 **Dvinskaya Guba** bay NW Russian Federation
112 E10 **Dvor** Sisak-Moslavina, C Croatia 45°05′N 16°22′E
117 W5 **Dvorichna** Kharkivs'ka Oblast', E Ukraine 49°52′N 37°43′E
111 F16 **Dvůr Králové nad Labem** Ger. Königinhof an der Elbe. Královéhradecký Kraj, N Czech Republic 50°27′N 15°50′E
154 A10 **Dwārka** Gujarāt, W India 22°14′N 68°58′E
30 M12 **Dwight** Illinois, N USA 41°05′N 88°25′W
98 N8 **Dwingeloo** Drenthe, NE Netherlands 52°49′N 06°20′E
33 N10 **Dworshak Reservoir** ⊠ Idaho, NW USA
Dyal see Dyaul Island
Dyanev see Galkynyş
Dyatlovo see Dzyatlava
186 G5 **Dyaul Island** var. Djaul, Dyal. island NE Papua New Guinea
20 G8 **Dyer** Tennessee, S USA 36°04′N 88°59′W
9 S5 **Dyer, Cape** headland Baffin Island, Nunavut, NE Canada 66°37′N 61°13′W
20 F8 **Dyersburg** Tennessee, S USA 36°02′N 89°21′W
29 Y13 **Dyersville** Iowa, C USA 42°29′N 91°07′W
97 I21 **Dyfed** cultural region SW Wales, United Kingdom
Dyfrdwy, Afon see Dee
Dyhernfurth see Brzeg Dolny

◆ Country ● Country Capital ◇ Dependent Territory ○ Dependent Territory Capital ◈ Administrative Regions ✕ International Airport ▲ Mountain ▲▲ Mountain Range Ʌ Volcano ≈ River ◎ Lake ⊠ Reservoir
245

DYJE – EIŠIŠKES

111 E19 **Dyje** *var.* Thaya. ≈ Austria/Czech Republic *see also* Thaya
Dyje *see* Thaya
117 T5 **Dykan'ka** Poltavs'ka Oblast', C Ukraine 49°48′N 34°33′E
127 N16 **Dykhtau** ▲ SW Russian Federation 43°01′N 42°56′E
111 A16 **Dyleń** *Ger.* Tillenberg. ▲ NW Czech Republic 49°58′N 12°31′E
110 K9 **Dylewska Góra** ▲ N Poland 53°33′N 19°57′E
117 O4 **Dymer** Kyyivs'ka Oblast', N Ukraine 50°50′N 30°20′E
117 W7 **Dymytrov** *Rus.* Dimitrov. Donets'ka Oblast', SE Ukraine 48°18′N 37°19′E
111 O17 **Dynów** Podkarpackie, SE Poland 49°49′N 22°14′E
29 X13 **Dysart** Iowa, C USA 42°10′N 92°18′W
Dysna *see* Dzisna
115 H18 **Dýstos, Límni** *var.* Límni Dístos. ◎ Évvoia, C Greece
115 D18 **Dytikí Ellás** *Eng.* Greece West. ◈ *region* C Greece
115 C14 **Dytikí Makedonía** *Eng.* Macedonia West. ◈ *region* N Greece
Dyurment'yube *see* Dermentobe
127 U4 **Dyurtyuli** Respublika Bashkortostan, W Russian Federation 55°31′N 54°49′E
Dyushambe *see* Dushanbe
162 K7 **Dzaamar** *var.* Bat-Öldziyt. Töv, C Mongolia 48°10′N 104°49′E
Dzaanhushuu *see* Ihtamir
Dza Chu *see* Mekong
Dzadgay *see* Bömbögör
162 H8 **Dzag** Bayanhongor, C Mongolia 46°54′N 99°11′E
Dzalaa *see* Shinejinst
163 O11 **Dzamïn-Üüd** *var.* Borhoyn Tal. Dornogovĭ, SE Mongolia 43°43′N 111°53′E
172 J14 **Dzaoudzi** E Mayotte 12°48′S 45°18′E
Dzaudzhikau *see* Vladikavkaz
162 G7 **Dzavhan** ◈ *province* NW Mongolia
162 G7 **Dzavhan Gol** ≈ NW Mongolia
162 G6 **Dzavhanmandal** *var.* Nuga. Dzavhan, W Mongolia 48°17′N 95°07′E
Dzegstey *see* Ögiynuur
162 E7 **Dzereg** *var.* Altanteel. Hovd, W Mongolia 47°05′N 92°57′E
127 O3 **Dzerzhinsk** Nizhegorodskaya Oblast', W Russian Federation 56°20′N 43°22′E
Dzerzhinsk *see* Dzyarzhynsk Belarus
Dzerzhinsk *see* Dzerzhyns'k
Dzerzhinskiy *see* Nar'yan-Mar
Dzerzhinskoye *see* Tokzhaylau
Dzerzhinskoye *see* Tokzhaylau
117 X7 **Dzerzhyns'k** *Rus.* Dzerzhinsk. Donets'ka Oblast', SE Ukraine 48°21′N 37°50′E
116 M5 **Dzerzhyns'k** Zhytomyrs'ka Oblast', N Ukraine 50°07′N 27°56′E
Dzetygara *see* Zhitikara
Dzhailgan *see* Jayilgan
145 N14 **Dzhalagash** *Kaz.* Zhalaghash. Kzylorda, S Kazakhstan 45°06′N 64°40′E
147 T10 **Dzhalal-Abad** *Kir.* Jalal-Abad. Dzhalal-Abadskaya Oblast', W Kyrgyzstan 40°56′N 73°00′E
147 S9 **Dzhalal-Abadskaya Oblast'** *Kir.* Jalal-Abad Oblasty. ◈ *province* W Kyrgyzstan
Dzhalilabad *see* Cälilabad
Dzhambeyty *see* Zhympity
Dzhambul *see* Taraz
Dzhambulskaya Oblast' *see* Zhambyl
144 D9 **Dzhanibek** *var.* Dzhanybek, *Kaz.* Zhänibek. Zapadnyy Kazakhstan, W Kazakhstan 49°27′N 46°51′E
Dzhankel'dy *see* Jongeldi
117 T12 **Dzhankoy** Respublika Krym, S Ukraine 45°40′N 34°20′E
145 V14 **Dzhansugurov** *Kaz.* Zhansügirov. Almaty, SE Kazakhstan 45°23′N 79°29′E
147 R9 **Dzhany-Bazar** *var.* Yangibazar. Dzhalal-Abadskaya Oblast', W Kyrgyzstan 41°40′N 70°49′E
Dzhanybek *see* Dzhanibek
123 P8 **Dzhardzhan** Respublika Sakha (Yakutiya), NE Russian Federation 68°47′N 123°51′E
Dzharkurgan *see* Jarqo'rg'on
117 S11 **Dzharylhats'ka Zatoka** *gulf* S Ukraine
Dzhayilgan *see* Jayilgan
Dzhebel *see* Jebel
147 T14 **Dzhelandy** SE Tajikistan 37°34′N 72°35′E
147 Y7 **Dzhergalan** *Kir.* Jyrgalan. Issyk-Kul'skaya Oblast', NE Kyrgyzstan 42°37′N 78°56′E
Dzhetysay *see* Zhetysay
Dzhezkazgan *see* Zhezkazgan
Dzhigirbent *see* Jigerbent
Dzhirgatal' *see* Jirgatol
Dzhizak *see* Jizzax
Dzhizakskaya Oblast' *see* Jizzax Viloyati
123 P8 **Dzhugdzhur, Khrebet** ▲▲ E Russian Federation
Dzhul'fa *see* Culfa
Dzhuma *see* Juma
145 W14 **Dzhungarskiy Alatau** ▲▲ China/Kazakhstan
144 M14 **Dzhusaly** *Kaz.* Zhosaly. Kzylorda, SW Kazakhstan 45°29′N 64°04′E
146 J12 **Dzhynlykum, Peski** *desert* E Turkmenistan
110 L9 **Działdowo** Warmińsko-Mazurskie, C Poland 53°13′N 20°12′E
111 L16 **Działoszyce** Świętokrzyskie, C Poland 50°21′N 20°19′E
41 X11 **Dzidzantún** Yucatán, E Mexico
111 G15 **Dzierżoniów** *Ger.* Reichenbach. Dolnośląskie, SW Poland 50°43′N 16°40′E
41 X11 **Dzilam de Bravo** Yucatán, E Mexico 21°24′N 88°52′W
118 L12 **Dzisna** *Rus.* Disna. Vitsyebskaya Voblasts', N Belarus 55°33′N 28°13′E
118 K12 **Dzisna** *Lith.* Dysna, *Rus.* Disna. ≈ Belarus/Lithuania
119 G20 **Dzivin** *Rus.* Divin. Brestskaya Voblasts', SW Belarus 51°58′N 24°33′E
119 M15 **Dzmitravichy** *Rus.* Dmitrovichi. Minskaya Voblasts', C Belarus 53°58′N 29°14′E
Dzogsool *see* Bayantsagaan
162 I5 **Dzöölön** *var.* Rinchinlhumbe. Hövsgöl, N Mongolia 51°06′N 99°40′E
129 S8 **Dzungaria** *var.* Sungaria, Zungaria. *physical region* W China
Dzungarian Basin *see* Junggar Pendi
Dzür *see* Tes
162 J8 **Dzüünbayan-Ulaan** *var.* Bayan-Ulaan. Övörhangay, C Mongolia 46°38′N 102°30′E
Dzüünbulag *see* Matad, Dornod, Mongolia
Dzüünbulag *see* Uulbayan, Sühbaatar, Mongolia
162 L8 **Dzuunmod** Töv, C Mongolia 47°45′N 107°00′E
Dzuunmod *see* Ider
Dzüün Soyonĭ Nuruu *see* Eastern Sayans
Dzüyl *see* Tonhil
Dzvina *see* Western Dvina
119 J16 **Dzyarzhynsk Belarus** *Rus.* Dzerzhinsk; *prev.* Kaydanovo. Minskaya Voblasts', C Belarus 53°41′N 27°09′E
119 H17 **Dzyatlava** *Pol.* Zdzięcioł, *Rus.* Dyatlovo. Hrodzyenskaya Voblasts', W Belarus 53°27′N 25°23′E

E

E *see* Hubei
Éadan Doire *see* Edenderry
37 W6 **Eads** Colorado, C USA 38°28′N 102°46′W
37 O13 **Eagar** Arizona, SW USA 34°05′N 109°17′W
39 T8 **Eagle** Alaska, USA 64°47′N 141°12′W
13 S8 **Eagle** ≈ Newfoundland and Labrador, E Canada
10 I3 **Eagle** ≈ Yukon Territory, NW Canada
29 T7 **Eagle Bend** Minnesota, N USA 46°10′N 95°02′W
28 M8 **Eagle Butte** South Dakota, N USA 45°00′N 101°13′W
29 V12 **Eagle Grove** Iowa, C USA 42°39′N 93°54′W
19 R2 **Eagle Lake** Maine, NE USA 47°01′N 68°35′W
25 U11 **Eagle Lake** Texas, SW USA 29°35′N 96°19′W
12 A11 **Eagle Lake** ◎ Ontario, S Canada
35 P3 **Eagle Lake** ◎ California, W USA
19 R3 **Eagle Lake** ◎ Maine, NE USA
29 Y3 **Eagle Mountain** ▲ Minnesota, N USA 47°54′N 90°33′W
25 T6 **Eagle Mountain Lake** ⊞ Texas, SW USA
37 S9 **Eagle Nest Lake** ⊞ New Mexico, SW USA
25 P13 **Eagle Pass** Texas, SW USA 28°44′N 100°31′W
65 C25 **Eagle Passage** *passage* SW Atlantic Ocean
35 R8 **Eagle Peak** ▲ California, W USA 38°11′N 119°22′W
35 Q2 **Eagle Peak** ▲ California, W USA 41°16′N 120°12′W
37 P13 **Eagle Peak** ▲ New Mexico, SW USA 33°39′N 109°36′W
10 I4 **Eagle Plain** Yukon Territory, NW Canada 66°23′N 136°42′W
32 G15 **Eagle Point** Oregon, NW USA 42°28′N 122°48′W
186 P10 **Eagle Point** *headland* SE Papua New Guinea 10°31′S 149°53′E
39 R11 **Eagle River** Alaska, USA 61°18′N 149°38′W
30 M2 **Eagle River** Michigan, N USA 47°24′N 88°18′W
30 L4 **Eagle River** Wisconsin, N USA 45°56′N 89°15′W
21 S6 **Eagle Rock** Virginia, NE USA 37°40′N 79°46′W
36 J13 **Eagletail Mountains** ▲▲ Arizona, SW USA
167 U12 **Ea Hleo** Đắc Lắc, S Vietnam 13°09′N 108°14′E
167 U12 **Ea Kar** Đắc Lắc, S Vietnam 12°47′N 108°26′E
Eanjum *see* Anjum
Eanodat *see* Enontekiö
12 B10 **Ear Falls** Ontario, C Canada 50°38′N 93°13′W
27 X10 **Earle** Arkansas, C USA 35°16′N 90°28′W
35 R12 **Earlimart** California, W USA 35°52′N 119°17′W
20 I6 **Earlington** Kentucky, S USA 37°16′N 87°30′W
14 H8 **Earlton** Ontario, S Canada 47°41′N 79°46′W
29 T13 **Early** Iowa, C USA 42°27′N 95°09′W
96 J11 **Earn** ≈ N Scotland, United Kingdom
185 C21 **Earnslaw, Mount** ▲ South Island, New Zealand 44°34′S 168°26′E
24 M4 **Earth** Texas, SW USA 34°13′N 102°24′W
21 P11 **Easley** South Carolina, SE USA 34°49′N 82°36′W
East *see* Est
East Açores Fracture Zone *see* East Azores Fracture Zone
97 P19 **East Anglia** *physical region* E England, United Kingdom
15 Q12 **East Angus** Québec, SE Canada 45°29′N 71°39′W
195 V8 **East Antarctica** *var.* Greater Antarctica. *physical region* Antarctica
18 E10 **East Aurora** New York, NE USA 42°44′N 78°36′W
East Australian Basin *see* Tasman Basin
East Azerbaijan *see* Āžarbāyjān-e Sharqī
64 L9 **East Azores Fracture Zone** *var.* East Açores Fracture Zone. *tectonic feature* E Atlantic Ocean
22 M11 **East Bay** *bay* Louisiana, S USA
25 V11 **East Bernard** Texas, SW USA 29°32′N 96°04′W
29 V8 **East Bethel** Minnesota, N USA 45°24′N 93°14′W
East Borneo *see* Kalimantan Timur
97 P23 **Eastbourne** SE England, United Kingdom 50°46′N 00°16′E
15 R11 **East-Broughton** Québec, SE Canada 46°14′N 71°05′W
44 M6 **East Caicos** *island* E Turks and Caicos Islands
184 R7 **East Cape** *headland* North Island, New Zealand 37°40′S 178°31′E
174 M4 **East Caroline Basin** *undersea feature* SW Pacific Ocean 04°00′N 146°45′E
192 P4 **East China Sea** *Chin.* Dong Hai. *sea* W Pacific Ocean
97 P19 **East Dereham** E England, United Kingdom 52°41′N 00°55′E
30 J9 **East Dubuque** Illinois, N USA 42°29′N 90°38′W
11 S17 **Eastend** Saskatchewan, S Canada 49°29′N 108°48′W
193 S10 **Easter Fracture Zone** *tectonic feature* E Pacific Ocean
Easter Island *see* Pascua, Isla de
81 J18 **Eastern** ◈ *province* Kenya
153 Q12 **Eastern** ◈ *zone* E Nepal
155 K25 **Eastern** ◈ *province* E Sri Lanka
83 L13 **Eastern** ◈ *province* E Zambia
83 H24 **Eastern Cape** *off.* Eastern Cape Province, *Afr.* Oos-Kaap. ◈ *province* SE South Africa
Eastern Cape Province *see* Eastern Cape
Eastern Desert *see* Sahara el Sharqîya
81 F15 **Eastern Equatoria** ◈ *state* SE Sudan
Eastern Euphrates *see* Murat Nehri
155 J17 **Eastern Ghats** ▲▲ SE India
186 E7 **Eastern Highlands** ◈ *province* C Papua New Guinea
Eastern Region *see* Ash Sharqīyah
122 L13 **Eastern Sayans** *Mong.* Dzüün Soyonĭ Nuruu, *Rus.* Vostochnyy Sayan. ▲▲ Mongolia/Russian Federation
Eastern Scheldt *see* Oosterschelde
Eastern Sierra Madre *see* Madre Oriental, Sierra
Eastern Transvaal *see* Mpumalanga
11 W14 **Easterville** Manitoba, C Canada 53°06′N 99°53′W
Easterwâlde *see* Oosterwolde
63 M23 **East Falkland** *var.* Isla Soledad. *island* E Falkland Islands
19 P12 **East Falmouth** Massachusetts, NE USA 41°34′N 70°31′W
East Fayu *see* Fayu
East Flanders *see* Oost-Vlaanderen
39 S6 **East Fork Chandalar River** ≈ Alaska, USA
29 U12 **East Fork Des Moines River** ≈ Iowa/Minnesota, C USA
East Frisian Islands *see* Ostfriesische Inseln
18 K10 **East Glenville** New York, NE USA 42°53′N 73°55′W
29 R4 **East Grand Forks** Minnesota, N USA 47°54′N 97°59′W
97 O23 **East Grinstead** SE England, United Kingdom 51°08′N 00°00′W
18 M12 **East Hartford** Connecticut, NE USA 41°45′N 72°36′W
18 M13 **East Haven** Connecticut, NE USA 41°16′N 72°52′W
173 T9 **East Indiaman Ridge** *undersea feature* E Indian Ocean
129 V16 **East Indies** *island group* SE Asia
East Java *see* Jawa Timur
31 Q6 **East Jordan** Michigan, N USA 45°09′N 85°07′W
East Kalimantan *see* Kalimantan Timur
East Kazakhstan *see* Vostochnyy Kazakhstan
96 I12 **East Kilbride** S Scotland, United Kingdom 55°46′N 04°10′W
25 R7 **Eastland** Texas, SW USA 32°23′N 98°50′W
31 Q9 **East Lansing** Michigan, N USA 42°44′N 84°28′W
35 X11 **East Las Vegas** Nevada, W USA 36°05′N 115°02′W
97 M23 **Eastleigh** S England, United Kingdom 50°58′N 01°22′W
31 V12 **East Liverpool** Ohio, N USA 40°37′N 80°34′W
83 J25 **East London** *Afr.* Oos-Londen; *prev.* Emonti, Port Rex. Eastern Cape, S South Africa 33°S 27°54′E
96 K12 **East Lothian** *cultural region* SE Scotland, United Kingdom
12 I10 **Eastmain** Québec, E Canada 52°11′N 78°27′W
12 J10 **Eastmain** ≈ Québec, C Canada
15 P13 **Eastman** Québec, SE Canada 45°19′N 72°18′W
23 U6 **Eastman** Georgia, SE USA 32°12′N 83°10′W
175 O3 **East Mariana Basin** *undersea feature* W Pacific Ocean
30 K11 **East Moline** Illinois, N USA 41°30′N 90°26′W
186 H7 **East New Britain** ◈ *province* E Papua New Guinea
29 T15 **East Nishnabotna River** ≈ Iowa, C USA
197 V12 **East Novaya Zemlya Trough** *var.* Novaya Zemlya Trough. *undersea feature* W Kara Sea
East Nusa Tenggara *see* Nusa Tenggara Timur
21 X4 **Easton** Maryland, NE USA 38°46′N 76°04′W
18 I14 **Easton** Pennsylvania, NE USA 40°41′N 75°13′W
193 R16 **East Pacific Rise** *undersea feature* E Pacific Ocean 20°00′S 115°00′W
East Pakistan *see* Bangladesh
31 V12 **East Palestine** Ohio, N USA 40°49′N 80°32′W
30 L12 **East Peoria** Illinois, N USA 40°40′N 89°34′W
23 S3 **East Point** Georgia, SE USA 33°40′N 84°26′W
19 U6 **Eastport** Maine, NE USA 44°54′N 66°59′W
27 Z8 **East Prairie** Missouri, C USA 36°46′N 89°23′W
19 O12 **East Providence** Rhode Island, NE USA 41°48′N 71°20′W
20 L11 **East Ridge** Tennessee, S USA 35°00′N 85°15′W
97 N16 **East Riding** *cultural region* N England, United Kingdom
18 F9 **East Rochester** New York, NE USA 43°06′N 77°29′W
30 K15 **East Saint Louis** Illinois, N USA 38°35′N 90°07′W
65 K21 **East Scotia Basin** *undersea feature* SE Scotia Sea
129 Y8 **East Sea** *var.* Sea of Japan, *Rus.* Yapanskoye More. *Sea* NW Pacific Ocean *see also* Japan, Sea of
186 B6 **East Sepik** ◈ *province* NW Papua New Guinea
173 N4 **East Sheba Ridge** *undersea feature* W Arabian Sea 14°30′N 56°15′E
East Siberian Sea *see* Vostochno-Sibirskoye More
18 I14 **East Stroudsburg** Pennsylvania, NE USA 41°00′N 75°10′W
East Tasmanian Rise/ East Tasmania Plateau/ East Tasmania Rise *see* East Tasman Plateau
192 I12 **East Tasman Plateau** *var.* East Tasmanian Rise, East Tasmania Plateau, East Tasmania Rise. *undersea feature* SW Tasman Sea
64 L7 **East Thulean Rise** *undersea feature* N Atlantic Ocean
171 R16 **East Timor** *var.* Loro Sae; *prev.* Portuguese Timor, Timor Timur. ◆ *country* S Indonesia
21 Y6 **Eastville** Virginia, NE USA 37°22′N 75°58′W
35 R7 **East Walker River** ≈ California/Nevada, W USA
182 D1 **Eateringinna Creek** ≈ South Australia
37 T3 **Eaton** Colorado, C USA 40°31′N 104°42′W
15 Q12 **Eaton** ≈ Québec, SE Canada
11 S16 **Eatonia** Saskatchewan, S Canada 51°13′N 109°22′W
31 Q10 **Eaton Rapids** Michigan, N USA 42°30′N 84°39′W
23 U4 **Eatonton** Georgia, SE USA 33°19′N 83°23′W
32 H9 **Eatonville** Washington, NW USA 46°51′N 122°19′W
30 J6 **Eau Claire** Wisconsin, N USA 44°50′N 91°30′W
12 J7 **Eau Claire, Lac à l'** ◎ Québec, SE Canada
Eau Claire, Lac à L' *see* St. Clair, Lake
30 L6 **Eau Claire River** ≈ Wisconsin, N USA
188 J16 **Eauripik Atoll** *atoll* Caroline Islands, C Micronesia
192 H7 **Eauripik Rise** *undersea feature* W Pacific Ocean 03°00′N 142°00′E
102 K15 **Eauze** Gers, S France 43°52′N 00°06′E
41 P11 **Ébano** San Luis Potosí, C Mexico 22°16′N 98°26′W
97 K21 **Ebbw Vale** SE Wales, United Kingdom 51°48′N 03°13′W
79 E17 **Ebebiyin** NE Equatorial Guinea 02°08′N 11°15′E
95 H22 **Ebeltoft** Århus, C Denmark 56°11′N 10°42′E
109 X5 **Ebenfurth** Niederösterreich, E Austria 47°53′N 16°22′E
18 D14 **Ebensburg** Pennsylvania, NE USA 40°28′N 78°44′W
109 S5 **Ebensee** Oberösterreich, N Austria 47°48′N 13°46′E
101 H20 **Eberbach** Baden-Württemberg, SW Germany 49°28′N 08°58′E
121 U8 **Eber Gölü** *salt lake* C Turkey
109 U9 **Eberndorf** *Slvn.* Dobrla Vas. Kärnten, S Austria 46°33′N 14°35′E
109 R4 **Eberschwang** Oberösterreich, N Austria 48°09′N 13°37′E
100 O11 **Eberswalde-Finow** Brandenburg, E Germany 52°50′N 13°48′E
Ebesfalva *see* Dumbrăveni
165 T4 **Ebetsu** *var.* Ebetu. Hokkaidō, NE Japan 43°08′N 141°37′E
Ebetu *see* Ebetsu
Ebinayon *see* Evinayong
158 I4 **Ebinur Hu** ◎ NW China
138 I3 **Ebla** *Ar.* Tell Mardīkh. *site of ancient city* Idlib, NW Syria
Eblana *see* Dublin
108 H7 **Ebnat** Sankt Gallen, NE Switzerland 47°16′N 09°07′E
107 L18 **Eboli** Campania, S Italy 40°37′N 15°03′E
79 E16 **Ebolowa** Sud, S Cameroon 02°56′N 11°11′E
79 N21 **Ebombo** Kasai-Oriental, C Dem. Rep. Congo 05°42′S 26°07′E
189 T9 **Ebon Atoll** *var.* Epoon. *atoll* Ralik Chain, S Marshall Islands
77 U16 **Ebonyi** ◈ *state* SE Nigeria
Ebora *see* Évora
Eboracum *see* York
Eborodunum *see* Yverdon
101 J19 **Ebrach** Bayern, C Germany 49°49′N 10°30′E
109 X5 **Ebreichsdorf** Niederösterreich, E Austria 47°58′N 16°24′E
105 S6 **Ebro** ≈ NE Spain
105 N3 **Ebro, Embalse del** ⊞ N Spain
120 G7 **Ebro Fan** *undersea feature* W Mediterranean Sea
Eburacum *see* York
Ebusus *see* Ibiza
Ebusus *see* Eivissa
99 F20 **Écaussinnes-d'Enghien** Hainaut, SW Belgium 50°34′N 04°10′E
Ecbatana *see* Hamadān
21 Q6 **Eccles** West Virginia, NE USA 37°46′N 81°16′W
115 L14 **Eceabat** Çanakkale, NW Turkey 40°12′N 26°22′E
171 O2 **Echague** Luzon, N Philippines 16°42′N 121°37′E
Ech Cheliff/Ech Chleff *see* Chlef
Echeng *see* Ezhou
115 C18 **Echinádes** *island group* W Greece
114 J12 **Echínos** *var.* Ehinos, Ekhínos. Anatolikí Makedonía kai Thráki, NE Greece 41°16′N 25°00′E
Echizen *see* Takefu
164 J12 **Echizen-misaki** *headland* Honshū, SW Japan 35°59′N 135°57′E
Echmiadzin *see* Vagharshapat
8 J8 **Echo Bay** Northwest Territories, NW Canada 66°04′N 118°W
35 Y11 **Echo Bay** Nevada, W USA 36°19′N 114°27′W
36 L9 **Echo Cliffs** *cliff* Arizona, SW USA
14 C10 **Echo Lake** ◎ Ontario, S Canada
35 Q7 **Echo Summit** ▲ California, W USA 38°47′N 120°06′W
14 L8 **Échouani, Lac** ◎ Québec, SE Canada
99 L17 **Echt** Limburg, SE Netherlands 51°07′N 05°52′E
101 H22 **Echterdingen** ✈ (Stuttgart) Baden-Württemberg, SW Germany 48°40′N 09°13′E
99 N24 **Echternach** Grevenmacher, E Luxembourg 49°49′N 06°25′E
183 N11 **Echuca** Victoria, SE Australia 36°10′S 144°20′E
104 L14 **Écija** *anc.* Astigi. Andalucía, SW Spain 37°33′N 05°04′W
Eckengraf *see* Viesīte
100 I7 **Eckernförde** Schleswig-Holstein, N Germany 54°28′N 09°49′E
100 J7 **Eckernförder Bucht** *inlet* N Germany
102 L7 **Écommoy** Sarthe, NW France 47°51′N 00°15′E
14 L10 **Écorce, Lac de l'** ◎ Québec, SE Canada
15 Q8 **Écorces, Rivière aux** ≈ Québec, SE Canada
56 C7 **Ecuador** *off.* Republic of Ecuador. ◆ *republic* NW South America
Ecuador, Republic of *see* Ecuador
95 I17 **Ed** Västra Götaland, S Sweden 58°55′N 11°55′E
Ed *see* 'Idi
98 I9 **Edam** Noord-Holland, C Netherlands 52°30′N 05°02′E
96 K4 **Eday** *island* NE Scotland, United Kingdom
25 S17 **Edcouch** Texas, SW USA 26°17′N 97°57′W
80 C11 **Ed Da'ein** Southern Darfur, W Sudan 11°25′N 26°08′E
80 G11 **Ed Damazin** *var.* Ad Damazīn. Blue Nile, E Sudan 11°45′N 34°20′E
80 G8 **Ed Damer** *var.* Ad Dāmir, Ad Damar. River Nile, NE Sudan 17°37′N 33°59′E
80 E8 **Ed Debba** Northern, N Sudan 18°02′N 30°56′E
80 F10 **Ed Dueim** *var.* Ad Duwaym, Ad Duwēm. White Nile, C Sudan 13°38′N 32°36′E
183 Q16 **Eddystone Point** *headland* Tasmania, SE Australia 41°01′S 148°18′E
97 I25 **Eddystone Rocks** *rocks* SW England, United Kingdom
29 W15 **Eddyville** Iowa, C USA 41°09′N 92°37′W
20 H7 **Eddyville** Kentucky, S USA 37°03′N 88°02′W
98 L12 **Ede** Gelderland, C Netherlands 52°03′N 05°40′E
77 T16 **Ede** Osun, SW Nigeria 07°40′N 04°21′E
79 D16 **Edéa** Littoral, SW Cameroon 03°47′N 10°08′E
111 M20 **Edelény** Borsod-Abaúj-Zemplén, NE Hungary 48°18′N 20°40′E
183 R12 **Eden** New South Wales, SE Australia 37°04′S 149°51′E
21 T8 **Eden** North Carolina, SE USA 36°29′N 79°46′W
25 P9 **Eden** Texas, SW USA 31°13′N 99°51′W
97 K14 **Eden** ≈ NW England, United Kingdom
83 I23 **Edenburg** Free State, C South Africa 29°45′S 25°57′E
185 D24 **Edendale** Southland, South Island, New Zealand 46°18′S 168°48′E
97 E18 **Edenderry** *Ir.* Éadan Doire. Offaly, C Ireland 53°21′N 07°03′W
182 L11 **Edenhope** Victoria, SE Australia 37°04′S 141°15′E
21 X8 **Edenton** North Carolina, SE USA 36°04′N 76°39′W
101 G16 **Eder** ≈ NW Germany
101 H15 **Edersee** ◎ W Germany
114 E13 **Édessa** *var.* Édhessa. Kentrikí Makedonía, N Greece 40°48′N 22°03′E
Edessa *see* Şanlıurfa
Edfu *see* Idfū
29 P16 **Edgar** Nebraska, C USA 40°22′N 97°58′W
19 P13 **Edgartown** Martha's Vineyard, Massachusetts, NE USA 41°23′N 70°30′W
39 X13 **Edgecumbe, Mount** ▲ Baranof Island, Alaska, USA 57°03′N 135°45′W
21 Q13 **Edgefield** South Carolina, SE USA 33°50′N 81°57′W
29 P6 **Edgeley** North Dakota, N USA 46°19′N 98°42′W
28 I11 **Edgemont** South Dakota, N USA 43°18′N 103°49′W
92 O3 **Edgeøya** *island* S Svalbard
27 Q4 **Edgerton** Kansas, C USA 38°45′N 95°00′W
29 S10 **Edgerton** Minnesota, N USA 43°52′N 96°07′W
21 X3 **Edgewood** Maryland, NE USA 39°20′N 76°21′W
25 V6 **Edgewood** Texas, SW USA 32°42′N 95°53′W
Édhessa *see* Edessa
29 V9 **Edina** Minnesota, N USA 44°53′N 93°21′W
27 U2 **Edina** Missouri, C USA 40°10′N 92°10′W
25 S17 **Edinburg** Texas, SW USA 26°18′N 98°10′W
65 M24 **Edinburgh** *var.* Settlement of Edinburgh. ○ (Tristan da Cunha) NW Tristan da Cunha 37°03′S 12°18′W
96 J12 **Edinburgh** ● S Scotland, United Kingdom 55°57′N 03°13′W
31 P14 **Edinburgh** Indiana, N USA 39°19′N 86°00′W
96 J12 **Edinburgh** ✈ S Scotland, United Kingdom 55°57′N 03°22′W
116 L8 **Edineţ** *var.* Edineţi, *Rus.* Yedintsy. NW Moldova 48°10′N 27°18′E
Edineţi *see* Edineţ
Edingen *see* Enghien
136 B9 **Edirne** *Eng.* Adrianople; *anc.* Adrianopolis, Hadrianopolis. Edirne, NW Turkey 41°40′N 26°34′E
136 B11 **Edirne** ◈ *province* NW Turkey
18 K15 **Edison** New Jersey, NE USA 40°31′N 74°24′W
21 S15 **Edisto Island** South Carolina, SE USA 32°34′N 80°17′W
21 R14 **Edisto River** ≈ South Carolina, SE USA
33 S10 **Edith, Mount** ▲ Montana, NW USA 46°25′N 111°10′W
27 N10 **Edmond** Oklahoma, C USA 35°40′N 97°30′W
32 H8 **Edmonds** Washington, NW USA 47°48′N 122°22′W
11 Q14 **Edmonton** *province capital* Alberta, SW Canada 53°34′N 113°25′W
20 K7 **Edmonton** Kentucky, S USA 36°59′N 85°39′W
11 Q14 **Edmonton** ✈ Alberta, SW Canada 53°22′N 113°43′W
29 P3 **Edmore** North Dakota, N USA 48°22′N 98°26′W
13 N13 **Edmundston** New Brunswick, SE Canada 47°22′N 68°20′W
25 U12 **Edna** Texas, SW USA 29°00′N 96°41′W
39 X14 **Edna Bay** Kosciusko Island, Alaska, USA 55°54′N 133°40′W
77 U16 **Edo** ◈ *state* S Nigeria
106 F6 **Edolo** Lombardia, N Italy 46°13′N 10°20′E
64 L6 **Edoras Bank** *undersea feature* C Atlantic Ocean
96 G7 **Edrachillis Bay** *bay* NW Scotland, United Kingdom
136 B12 **Edremit** Balıkesir, NW Turkey 39°34′N 27°01′E
136 B12 **Edremit Körfezi** *gulf* NW Turkey
95 P14 **Edsbro** Stockholm, C Sweden 59°54′N 18°30′E
95 N18 **Edsbruk** Kalmar, S Sweden 58°01′N 16°30′E
94 M12 **Edsbyn** Gävleborg, C Sweden 61°22′N 15°45′E
11 O14 **Edson** Alberta, SW Canada 53°36′N 116°28′W
62 K13 **Eduardo Castex** La Pampa, C Argentina 35°55′S 64°18′W
58 F12 **Eduardo Gomes** ✈ (Manaus) Amazonas, NW Brazil 05°55′S 35°15′W
Edwardesabad *see* Bannu
67 U9 **Edward, Lake** *var.* Albert Edward Nyanza, Edward Nyanza, Lac Idi Amin, Lake Rutanzige. ◎ Uganda/Dem. Rep. Congo
Edward Nyanza *see* Edward, Lake
22 K5 **Edwards** Mississippi, S USA 32°19′N 90°36′W
25 O10 **Edwards Plateau** *plain* Texas, SW USA
30 J11 **Edwards River** ≈ Illinois, N USA
30 K15 **Edwardsville** Illinois, N USA 38°48′N 89°57′W
195 X4 **Edward VIII Gulf** *bay* Antarctica
195 O13 **Edward VII Peninsula** *peninsula* Antarctica
10 J11 **Edziza, Mount** ▲ British Columbia, W Canada 57°43′N 130°39′W
23 H16 **Edzo** *prev.* Rae-Edzo. Northwest Territories, NW Canada 62°44′N 115°55′W
39 N12 **Eek** Alaska, USA 60°13′N 162°01′W
99 D16 **Eeklo** *var.* Eekloo. Oost-Vlaanderen, NW Belgium 51°11′N 03°34′E
Eekloo *see* Eeklo
39 N12 **Eek River** ≈ Alaska, USA
98 N6 **Eelde** Drenthe, NE Netherlands 53°07′N 06°30′E
34 L5 **Eel River** ≈ California, W USA
31 P12 **Eel River** ≈ Indiana, N USA
Eems *see* Ems
98 O4 **Eemshaven** Groningen, NE Netherlands 53°28′N 06°50′E
98 O5 **Eems Kanaal** *canal* NE Netherlands
98 M11 **Eerbeek** Gelderland, E Netherlands 52°07′N 06°04′E
99 C17 **Eernegem** West-Vlaanderen, W Belgium 51°08′N 03°03′E
99 J15 **Eersel** Noord-Brabant, S Netherlands 51°22′N 05°19′E
Eesti Vabariik *see* Estonia
187 R14 **Efate** *var.* Efate, *Fr.* Vaté; *prev.* Sandwich Island. *island* C Vanuatu
Efate *see* Efate
109 S4 **Eferding** Oberösterreich, N Austria 48°18′N 14°00′E
30 M15 **Effingham** Illinois, N USA 39°07′N 88°32′W
117 N15 **Eforie-Nord** Constanţa, SE Romania 44°04′N 28°37′E
117 N15 **Eforie Sud** Constanţa, E Romania 44°00′N 28°38′E
Efyrnwy, Afon *see* Vyrnwy
Eg *see* Hentiy
107 G23 **Egadi, Isole** *island group* S Italy
35 X6 **Egan Range** ▲▲ Nevada, W USA
14 K12 **Eganville** Ontario, SE Canada 45°33′N 77°03′W
Ege Denizi *see* Aegean Sea
39 O14 **Egegik** Alaska, USA 58°13′N 157°22′W
111 L21 **Eger** *Ger.* Erlau. Heves, NE Hungary 47°54′N 20°22′E
Eger *see* Cheb, Czech Republic
Eger *see* Ohre, Czech Republic/Germany
173 P8 **Egeria Fracture Zone** *tectonic feature* W Indian Ocean
95 C17 **Egersund** Rogaland, S Norway 58°27′N 06°01′E
108 J7 **Egg** Vorarlberg, NW Austria 47°27′N 09°55′E
101 H14 **Egge-gebirge** ▲▲ C Germany
109 Q4 **Eggelsberg** Oberösterreich, N Austria 48°04′N 13°00′E
109 W2 **Eggenburg** Niederösterreich, NE Austria 48°29′N 15°49′E
101 N22 **Eggenfelden** Bayern, SE Germany 48°24′N 12°45′E
18 J17 **Egg Harbor City** New Jersey, NE USA 39°31′N 74°39′W
65 G25 **Egg Island** *island* W Saint Helena
183 N14 **Egg Lagoon** Tasmania, SE Australia 39°42′S 143°57′E
99 I20 **Éghezée** Namur, C Belgium 50°36′N 04°55′E
92 L2 **Egilsstadhir** Austurland, E Iceland 65°14′N 14°21′W
Egina *see* Aígina
Egindibulaq *see* Yegindybulak
Egio *see* Aígio
103 N12 **Égletons** Corrèze, C France 45°24′N 02°01′E
98 H9 **Egmond aan Zee** Noord-Holland, NW Netherlands 52°37′N 04°37′E
Egmont *see* Taranaki, Mount
184 J10 **Egmont, Cape** *headland* North Island, New Zealand 39°18′S 173°44′E
Egoli *see* Johannesburg
136 I15 **Eğridir Gölü** ◎ W Turkey
Egri Palanka *see* Kriva Palanka
95 G23 **Egtved** Vejle, C Denmark 55°34′N 09°18′E
123 U5 **Egvekinot** Chukotskiy Avtonomnyy Okrug, NE Russian Federation 66°13′N 178°55′W
75 V9 **Egypt** *off.* Arab Republic of Egypt, *Ar.* Jumhūrīyah Miṣr al 'Arabīyah, *prev.* United Arab Republic; *anc.* Aegyptus. ◆ *republic* NE Africa
30 L17 **Egypt, Lake Of** ⊞ Illinois, N USA
162 I14 **Ehen Hudag** *var.* Alx Youqi. Nei Mongol Zizhiqu, N China 39°12′N 101°40′E
164 F14 **Ehime** *off.* Ehime-ken. ◈ *prefecture* Shikoku, SW Japan
Ehime-ken *see* Ehime
101 I23 **Ehingen** Baden-Württemberg, S Germany 48°16′N 09°43′E
Ehinos *see* Echínos
21 R14 **Ehrhardt** South Carolina, SE USA 33°06′N 81°00′W
108 L7 **Ehrwald** Tirol, W Austria 47°24′N 10°52′E
191 W6 **Eiao** *island* Îles Marquises, NE French Polynesia
105 P2 **Eibar** País Vasco, N Spain 43°11′N 02°28′W
98 O11 **Eibergen** Gelderland, E Netherlands 52°06′N 06°39′E
109 V9 **Eibiswald** Steiermark, SE Austria 46°40′N 15°15′E
109 P8 **Eichham** ▲ SW Austria 47°04′N 12°24′E
101 J15 **Eichsfeld** *hill range* C Germany
101 K21 **Eichstätt** Bayern, SE Germany 48°53′N 11°11′E
100 H8 **Eider** ≈ N Germany
94 E13 **Eidfjord** Hordaland, S Norway 60°26′N 07°05′E
94 D13 **Eidfjorden** *fjord* S Norway
94 F9 **Eidsvåg** Møre og Romsdal, S Norway 62°46′N 08°00′E
95 I14 **Eidsvoll** Akershus, S Norway 60°19′N 11°14′E
92 N2 **Eidsvollfjellet** ▲ NW Svalbard 79°13′N 13°23′E
Eier-Berg *see* Suur Munamägi
101 D18 **Eifel** *plateau* W Germany
108 E9 **Eiger** ▲ C Switzerland 46°33′N 08°02′E
96 G10 **Eigg** *island* W Scotland, United Kingdom
155 D24 **Eight Degree Channel** *channel* India/Maldives
44 G1 **Eight Mile Rock** Grand Bahama Island, N Bahamas 26°28′N 78°43′W
194 J9 **Eights Coast** *physical region* Antarctica
180 K6 **Eighty Mile Beach** *beach* Western Australia
99 L18 **Eijsden** Limburg, SE Netherlands 50°47′N 05°41′E
95 G15 **Eikeren** ◎ S Norway
Eil *see* Eyl
Eilat *see* Elat
183 O12 **Eildon** Victoria, SE Australia 37°17′S 145°57′E
183 O12 **Eildon, Lake** ◎ Victoria, SE Australia
80 E8 **Eilei** Northern Kordofan, C Sudan 16°33′N 30°54′E
101 N15 **Eilenburg** Sachsen, E Germany 51°28′N 12°37′E
Eil Malk *see* Mecherchar
94 H13 **Eina** Oppland, S Norway 60°37′N 10°37′E
138 E12 **Ein Avdat** *prev.* En 'Avedat. *well* S Israel
101 I14 **Einbeck** Niedersachsen, C Germany 51°49′N 09°52′E
99 K15 **Eindhoven** Noord-Brabant, S Netherlands 51°26′N 05°30′E
138 F11 **Ein Gedi** *prev.* 'En Gedi. Southern, E Israel 31°23′N 35°21′E
108 G8 **Einsiedeln** Schwyz, NE Switzerland 47°07′N 08°45′E
Eipel *see* Ipel'
Éire *see* Ireland
Éireann, Muir *see* Irish Sea
Eirik Outer Ridge *see* Eirik Ridge
64 I6 **Eirik Ridge** *var.* Eirik Outer Ridge. *undersea feature* E Labrador Sea
92 I3 **Eiríksjökull** ▲ C Iceland 64°47′N 20°23′W
59 B14 **Eirunepé** Amazonas, N Brazil 06°38′S 69°53′W
99 L17 **Eisden** Limburg, NE Belgium 51°05′N 05°42′E
83 F18 **Eiseb** ≈ Botswana/Namibia
Eisen *see* Yŏngch'ŏn
101 J16 **Eisenach** Thüringen, C Germany 50°59′N 10°19′E
Eisenburg *see* Vasvár
109 U6 **Eisenerz** Steiermark, SE Austria 47°33′N 14°53′E
100 Q13 **Eisenhüttenstadt** Brandenburg, E Germany 52°09′N 14°36′E
109 U10 **Eisenkappel** *Slvn.* Železna Kapela. Kärnten, S Austria 46°27′N 14°33′E
Eisenmarkt *see* Hunedoara
109 Y5 **Eisenstadt** Burgenland, E Austria 47°50′N 16°32′E
Eishū *see* Yŏngju
119 H15 **Eišiškės** Vilnius, SE Lithuania 54°10′N 24°59′E

◆ Country
● Country Capital
◇ Dependent Territory
○ Dependent Territory Capital
◈ Administrative Regions
✈ International Airport
▲ Mountain
▲▲ Mountain Range
Volcano
≈ River
◎ Lake
⊞ Reservoir

EISLEBEN – ENÅNGER

101 L15 **Eisleben** Sachsen-Anhalt, C Germany 51°32′N 11°33′E
190 I3 **Eita** Tarawa, W Kiribati 01°21′N 173°05′E
Eitape see Aitape
105 V11 **Eivissa** var. Iviza, Cast. Ibiza; anc. Ebusus. Ibiza, Spain, W Mediterranean Sea 38°54′N 01°26′E
Eivissa see Ibiza
105 R4 **Ejea de los Caballeros** Aragón, NE Spain 42°07′N 01°09′W
40 E8 **Ejido Insurgentes** Baja California Sur, NW Mexico 25°18′N 111°51′W
Ejin Qi see Dalain Hob
Ejmiadzin/Ejmiatsin see Vagharshapat
77 P16 **Ejura** C Ghana 07°23′N 01°22′W
41 R16 **Ejutla** var. Ejutla de Crespo. Oaxaca, SE Mexico 16°33′N 96°40′W
Ejutla de Crespo see Ejutla
33 Y10 **Ekalaka** Montana, NW USA 45°52′N 104°32′W
Ekapa see Cape Town
Ekaterinodar see Krasnodar
93 L20 **Ekenäs** Fin. Tammisaari. Etelä-Suomi, SW Finland 60°00′N 23°30′E
146 B13 **Ekerem** Rus. Okarem. Balkan Welaýaty, W Turkmenistan 38°06′N 53°52′E
184 M13 **Eketahuna** Manawatu-Wanganui, North Island, New Zealand 40°41′S 175°40′E
Ekhínos see Echinos
145 T8 **Ekibastuz** Pavlodar, NE Kazakhstan 51°42′N 75°22′E
123 R13 **Ekimchan** Amurskaya Oblast', SE Russian Federation 53°04′N 132°56′E
77 T15 **Ekiti** ⬖ state S Nigeria
95 O15 **Ekoln** ◎ C Sweden
80 I7 **Ekowit** Red Sea, NE Sudan 18°46′N 37°07′E
95 L19 **Eksjö** Jönköping, S Sweden 57°40′N 15°00′E
93 I15 **Ekträsk** Västerbotten, N Sweden 64°28′N 19°49′E
39 O13 **Ekuk** Alaska, USA 58°48′N 158°25′W
123 U5 **Ekvyvatapskiy Khrebet** ▲▲ NE Russian Federation
12 F9 **Ekwan** ⁓ Ontario, C Canada
39 O13 **Ekwok** Alaska, USA 59°21′N 157°28′W
166 M6 **Ela** Mandalay, C Burma (Myanmar) 19°37′N 96°15′E
El Aaiun see El Ayoun
81 N15 **El Ābrēd** Sumalē, E Ethiopia 05°33′N 45°12′E
115 F22 **Elafónisos** island S Greece
115 F22 **Elafonísou, Porthmós** strait S Greece
El-Aïoun see El Ayoun
El 'Alamein see Al 'Alamayn
41 Q12 **El Alazán** Veracruz-Llave, C Mexico 21°06′N 97°43′W
57 J18 **El Alto** var. La Paz. ✈ (La Paz) La Paz, W Bolivia 16°31′S 68°07′W
Elam see Īlām
El Amparo see El Amparo de Apure
54 I8 **El Amparo de Apure** var. El Amparo. Apure, C Venezuela 07°07′N 70°47′W
171 R13 **Elara** Pulau Ambelau, E Indonesia 03°49′S 127°10′E
El Araïch/El Araïche see Larache
40 D6 **El Arco** Baja California Norte, NW Mexico 28°03′N 113°25′W
El 'Arîsh see Al 'Arīsh
115 L25 **Elása** island SE Greece
El Asnam see Chlef
Elassón see Elassóna
115 E15 **Elassóna** prev. Elassón. Thessalía, C Greece 39°53′N 22°10′E
105 N2 **El Astillero** Cantabria, N Spain 43°23′N 03°45′W
138 F14 **Elat** var. Eilat, Elath. Southern, S Israel 29°33′N 34°57′E
Elat, Gulf of see Aqaba, Gulf of
Elath see Elat, Israel
Elath see Al 'Aqabah, Jordan
115 C17 **Eláti** ▲ Lefkáda, Iónia Nisiá, Greece, C Mediterranean Sea 38°43′N 20°38′E
188 L16 **Elato Atoll** atoll Caroline Islands, C Micronesia
80 C7 **El'Atrun** Northern Darfur, NW Sudan 18°11′N 26°40′E
74 H6 **El Ayoun** var. El Aaiun, El-Aïoun, La Youne. NE Morocco 34°39′N 02°29′W
137 N14 **Elâzığ** var. Elâzig, Elâziz. Elâzığ, E Turkey 38°41′N 39°14′E
137 O14 **Elâzığ** var. Elâzig, Elâziz. ⬖ province C Turkey
Elâzig/Elâziz see Elâzığ
23 Q7 **Elba** Alabama, S USA 31°24′N 86°04′W
106 E13 **Elba, Isola d'** island Archipelago Toscano, C Italy
123 S13 **El'ban** Khabarovskiy Kray, E Russian Federation 50°03′N 136°34′E
54 F6 **El Banco** Magdalena, N Colombia 09°00′N 74°01′W
El Barco see O Barco
104 L8 **El Barco de Ávila** Castilla-León, N Spain 40°21′N 05°31′W
El Barco de Valdeorras see O Barco
138 H7 **El Barouk, Jabal** ▲▲ C Lebanon
113 L20 **Elbasan** var. Elbasani. Elbasan, C Albania 41°07′N 20°04′E
113 L20 **Elbasan** ⬖ district C Albania
Elbasani see Elbasan
54 K6 **El Baúl** Cojedes, C Venezuela 08°59′N 68°16′W
86 D11 **Elbe** Cz. Labe. ⁓ Czech Republic/Germany
100 L13 **Elbe-Havel-Kanal** canal E Germany
100 K9 **Elbe-Lübeck-Kanal** canal N Germany
El Beni see Beni
138 H7 **El Beqaa** var. Al Biqā', Bekaa Valley. valley E Lebanon
25 R6 **Elbert** Texas, SW USA 33°15′N 98°58′W
37 R5 **Elbert, Mount** ▲ Colorado, C USA 39°07′N 106°26′W
23 U3 **Elberton** Georgia, SE USA 34°06′N 82°52′W
100 K11 **Elbe-Seiten-Kanal** canal N Germany
102 M4 **Elbeuf** Seine-Maritime, N France 49°16′N 01°01′E
Elbing see Elbląg
136 M15 **Elbistan** Kahramanmaraş, S Turkey 38°14′N 37°11′E
110 K7 **Elbląg** var. Elblag, Ger. Elbing. Warmińsko-Mazurskie, NE Poland 54°10′N 19°25′E
43 N10 **El Bluff** Región Autónoma Atlántico Sur, SE Nicaragua 12°00′N 83°40′W
63 H17 **El Bolsón** Río Negro, W Argentina 41°59′S 71°35′W
105 P11 **El Bonillo** Castilla-La Mancha, C Spain 38°57′N 02°32′W
El Bordo see Patía
El Boulaida/El Boulaïda see Blida
11 T16 **Elbow** Saskatchewan, S Canada 51°07′N 106°30′W
29 S7 **Elbow Lake** Minnesota, N USA 45°59′N 95°58′W
127 N16 **El'brus** var. Gora El'brus. ▲ SW Russian Federation 42°29′E 43°21′N
El'brus, Gora see El'brus
126 M15 **El'brusskiy** Karachayevo-Cherkesskaya Respublika, SW Russian Federation 43°36′N 42°06′E
81 D14 **El Buhayrat** var. Lakes State. ⬖ state S Sudan
El Bur see Ceel Buur
98 L10 **Elburg** Gelderland, E Netherlands 52°27′N 05°46′E
105 O6 **El Burgo de Osma** Castilla-León, C Spain 41°36′N 03°04′W
Elburz Mountains see Alborz, Reshteh-ye Kūhhā-ye
35 V17 **El Cajon** California, W USA 32°46′N 116°52′W
63 H22 **El Calafate** var. Calafate. Santa Cruz, S Argentina 50°20′S 72°13′W
55 Q8 **El Callao** Bolívar, E Venezuela 07°18′N 61°48′W
25 U12 **El Campo** Texas, SW USA 29°12′N 96°16′W
54 I7 **El Cantón** Barinas, W Venezuela 07°23′N 71°10′W
35 Q8 **El Capitan** ▲ California, W USA 37°46′N 119°39′W
54 H5 **El Carmelo** Zulia, NW Venezuela 10°20′N 71°48′W
62 J5 **El Carmen** Jujuy, NW Argentina 24°24′S 65°16′W
54 E5 **El Carmen de Bolívar** Bolívar, NW Colombia 09°43′N 75°07′W
55 O8 **El Casabe** Bolívar, SE Venezuela 06°26′N 63°35′W
42 M12 **El Castillo de La Concepción** Río San Juan, SE Nicaragua 11°01′N 84°24′W
El Cayo see San Ignacio
35 X17 **El Centro** California, W USA 32°47′N 115°33′W
55 N6 **El Chaparro** Anzoátegui, NE Venezuela 09°12′N 65°03′W
105 S12 **Elche** Cat. Elx; anc. Ilici, Lat. Illicis. País Valenciano, E Spain 38°16′N 00°41′W
105 Q12 **Elche de la Sierra** Castilla-La Mancha, C Spain 38°27′N 02°03′W
41 U15 **El Chichónal, Volcán** ⛰ SE Mexico 17°20′N 93°12′W
40 C2 **El Chinero** Baja California Norte, NW Mexico
181 R1 **Elcho Island** island Wessel Islands, Northern Territory, N Australia
63 H18 **El Corcovado** Chubut, SW Argentina 43°31′S 71°30′W
105 R12 **Elda** País Valenciano, E Spain 38°29′N 00°47′W
100 M10 **Elde** ⁓ NE Germany
98 L12 **Elden** Gelderland, E Netherlands 51°57′N 05°53′E
81 J16 **El Der** spring/well S Ethiopia 03°55′N 39°48′E
El Dere see Ceel Dheere
40 E3 **El Desemboque** Sonora, NW Mexico 30°33′N 112°59′W
54 F5 **El Difícil** var. Ariguaní. Magdalena, N Colombia 09°55′N 74°12′W
123 R10 **El'dikan** Respublika Sakha (Yakutiya), NE Russian Federation 60°46′N 135°04′E
El Djazaïr see Alger
El Djelfa see Djelfa
29 X15 **Eldon** Iowa, C USA 40°55′N 92°13′W
27 U5 **Eldon** Missouri, C USA 38°21′N 92°34′W
54 E13 **El Doncello** Caquetá, S Colombia 01°43′N 75°17′W
29 W13 **Eldora** Iowa, C USA 42°21′N 93°06′W
60 G12 **Eldorado** Misiones, NE Argentina 26°24′S 54°38′W
40 I9 **El Dorado** Sinaloa, C Mexico 24°19′N 107°23′W
27 U14 **El Dorado** Arkansas, C USA 33°12′N 92°40′W
30 M17 **Eldorado** Illinois, N USA 37°48′N 88°26′W
27 O6 **El Dorado** Kansas, C USA 37°51′N 96°52′W
26 K12 **Eldorado** Oklahoma, C USA 34°28′N 99°39′W
25 O9 **Eldorado** Texas, SW USA 30°53′N 100°37′W
55 Q8 **El Dorado** Bolívar, E Venezuela 06°45′N 61°37′W
54 F10 **El Dorado** ✈ (Bogotá) Cundinamarca, C Colombia 01°15′N 71°52′W
El Dorado see California
27 O6 **El Dorado Lake** ⊠ Kansas, C USA
27 S6 **El Dorado Springs** Missouri, C USA 37°53′N 94°01′W
81 H18 **Eldoret** Rift Valley, W Kenya 0°31′N 35°17′E
29 Z14 **Eldridge** Iowa, C USA 41°39′N 90°34′W
95 J21 **Eldsberga** Halland, S Sweden 56°36′N 13°00′E
25 R4 **Electra** Texas, SW USA 34°01′N 98°55′W
37 Q7 **Electra Lake** ⊠ Colorado, C USA
38 B8 **'Ele'ele** var. Eleele. Kaua'i, Hawaii, USA, C Pacific Ocean 21°54′N 159°35′W
Eleele see 'Ele'ele
Elefantes see Olifants
115 H19 **Elefsína** prev. Elevsís. Attikí, C Greece 38°02′N 23°33′E
115 G19 **Eléftheres** anc. Eleutherae. site of ancient city Attikí/Stereá Ellás, C Greece
114 I13 **Eleftheroúpoli** prev. Elevtheroúpolis. Anatolikí Makedonía kai Thráki, NE Greece 40°55′N 24°15′E
74 F10 **El Eglab** ▲▲ SW Algeria
118 F10 **Eleja** Jelgava, C Latvia 56°24′N 23°41′E
Elek see Ilek
119 G14 **Elektrėnai** Vilnius, SE Lithuania 54°47′N 24°35′E
126 L3 **Elektrostal'** Moskovskaya Oblast', W Russian Federation 55°47′N 38°24′E
81 H15 **Elemi Triangle** disputed region Kenya/Sudan
114 K9 **Elena** Veliko Tŭrnovo, N Bulgaria 42°55′N 25°53′E
54 G16 **El Encanto** Amazonas, S Colombia 01°45′S 73°12′W
37 R14 **Elephant Butte Reservoir** ⊠ New Mexico, SW USA
Éléphant, Chaîne de l' see Dâmrei, Chuŏr Phmun
194 G2 **Elephant Island** island South Shetland Islands, Antarctica
Elephant River see Olifants
El Escorial see San Lorenzo de El Escorial
Élesd see Aleşd
114 F11 **Eleshnitsa** ⁓ W Bulgaria
137 S13 **Eleşkirt** Ağrı, E Turkey 39°22′N 42°48′E
42 F5 **El Estor** Izabal, E Guatemala 15°37′N 89°22′W
Eleutherae see Eléftheres
44 I2 **Eleuthera Island** island N Bahamas
37 S5 **Elevenmile Canyon Reservoir** ⊠ Colorado, C USA
27 W8 **Eleven Point River** ⁓ Arkansas/Missouri, C USA
Elevsís see Elefsína
Elevtheroúpolis see Eleftheroúpoli
80 B10 **El Fasher** var. Al Fāshir. Northern Darfur, W Sudan 13°37′N 25°22′E
El Fashn see Al Fashn
El Ferrol/El Ferrol del Caudillo see Ferrol
39 W13 **Elfin Cove** Chichagof Island, Alaska, USA 58°09′N 136°16′W
105 W4 **El Fluvià** ⁓ NE Spain
40 H7 **El Fuerte** Sinaloa, W Mexico 26°28′N 108°35′W
80 D11 **El Fula** Western Kordofan, C Sudan 11°44′N 28°20′E
El Gedaref see Gedaref
80 A10 **El Geneina** var. Ajjinena, Al-Genain, Al Junaynah. Western Darfur, W Sudan 13°27′N 22°30′E
96 J8 **Elgin** NE Scotland, United Kingdom 57°39′N 03°20′W
30 M10 **Elgin** Illinois, N USA 42°02′N 88°16′W
29 P14 **Elgin** Nebraska, C USA 41°58′N 98°04′W
35 Y9 **Elgin** Nevada, W USA 37°19′N 114°30′W
28 L6 **Elgin** North Dakota, N USA 46°24′N 101°51′W
26 M12 **Elgin** Oklahoma, C USA 34°46′N 98°17′W
25 T10 **Elgin** Texas, SW USA 30°21′N 97°22′W
123 R9 **El'ginskiy** Respublika Sakha (Yakutiya), NE Russian Federation 64°27′N 141°57′E
El Giza see Giza
74 J8 **El Goléa** var. Al Golea. C Algeria 30°35′N 02°59′E
40 D2 **El Golfo de Santa Clara** Sonora, NW Mexico 31°48′N 114°40′W
81 G18 **Elgon, Mount** ▲ E Uganda 01°07′N 34°29′E
94 I10 **Elgpiggen** ▲ S Norway 62°13′N 11°18′E
105 T4 **El Grado** Aragón, NE Spain 42°09′N 00°13′E
40 L6 **El Guaje, Laguna** ⊠ NE Mexico
54 H6 **El Guayabo** Zulia, W Venezuela 08°37′N 72°20′W
77 O6 **El Guettâra** oasis N Mali
76 J6 **El Ḥammâmi** desert N Mauritania
76 M5 **El Hank** cliff N Mauritania
El Haseke see Al Ḥasakah
80 H10 **El Hawata** Gedaref, E Sudan 13°25′N 34°42′E
El Higo see Higos
171 T16 **Eliase** Pulau Selaru, E Indonesia 08°16′S 130°49′E
Elías Piña see Comendador
25 R6 **Eliasville** Texas, SW USA 32°55′N 98°46′W
Elichpur see Achalpur
37 V13 **Elida** New Mexico, SW USA 33°57′N 103°39′W
115 F18 **Elikónas** ▲ C Greece
67 T10 **Elila** ⁓ W Dem. Rep. Congo
39 N9 **Elim** Alaska, USA 64°37′N 162°15′W
Elimberrum see Auch
Eliocroca see Lorca
61 B16 **Elisa** Santa Fe, C Argentina 30°42′S 61°04′W
Elisabethstedt see Dumbrăveni
Élisabethville see Lubumbashi
127 O13 **Elista** Respublika Kalmykiya, SW Russian Federation 46°18′N 44°09′E
182 I9 **Elizabeth** South Australia 34°44′S 138°39′E
21 Q3 **Elizabeth** West Virginia, NE USA 39°04′N 81°24′W
19 J9 **Elizabeth, Cape** headland Maine, NE USA 43°34′N 70°12′W
21 Y8 **Elizabeth City** North Carolina, SE USA 36°18′N 76°16′W
21 P8 **Elizabethton** Tennessee, S USA 36°22′N 82°15′W
30 M17 **Elizabethtown** Illinois, N USA 37°24′N 88°21′W
20 K6 **Elizabethtown** Kentucky, S USA 37°41′N 85°51′W
18 L7 **Elizabethtown** New York, NE USA 44°13′N 73°38′W
21 U11 **Elizabethtown** North Carolina, SE USA 34°36′N 78°36′W
18 G15 **Elizabethtown** Pennsylvania, NE USA 40°08′N 76°36′W
74 E6 **El-Jadida** prev. Mazagan. W Morocco 33°15′N 08°27′W
El Jafr see Jafr, Qā' al
80 F11 **El Jebelein** White Nile, E Sudan 12°38′N 32°51′E
110 N8 **Ełk** Ger. Lyck. Warmińsko-mazurskie, NE Poland 53°51′N 22°20′E
110 O8 **Ełk** ⁓ NE Poland
29 Y12 **Elkader** Iowa, C USA 42°51′N 91°24′W
80 G9 **El Kamlin** Gezira, C Sudan 15°03′N 33°11′E
33 N11 **Elk City** Idaho, NW USA 45°50′N 115°28′W
26 K10 **Elk City** Oklahoma, C USA 35°24′N 99°24′W
27 P7 **Elk City Lake** ⊠ Kansas, C USA
34 M5 **Elk Creek** California, W USA 39°34′N 122°34′W
28 J10 **Elk Creek** ⁓ South Dakota, N USA
74 M5 **El Kef** var. Al Kāf, Le Kef. NW Tunisia 36°13′N 08°44′E
74 F7 **El Kelâa Srarhna** var. Kal al Sraghna. C Morocco 32°05′N 07°20′W
El Kerak see Al Karak
11 P17 **Elkford** British Columbia, SW Canada 49°58′N 114°57′W
El Khalil see Hebron
80 E7 **El Khandaq** Northern, N Sudan 18°34′N 30°34′E
El Khârga see Al Khārijah
31 P11 **Elkhart** Indiana, N USA 41°40′N 85°58′W
26 H7 **Elkhart** Kansas, C USA 37°00′N 101°51′W
25 V8 **Elkhart** Texas, SW USA 31°37′N 95°34′W
30 M7 **Elkhart Lake** ◎ Wisconsin, N USA
El Khartûm see Khartoum
37 Q3 **Elkhead Mountains** ▲▲ Colorado, C USA
18 I12 **Elk Hill** ▲ Pennsylvania, NE USA 41°42′N 75°33′W
138 G8 **El Khiyam** var. Al Khiyām, Khiam. S Lebanon 33°12′N 35°42′E
29 S15 **Elkhorn** Nebraska, C USA 41°17′N 96°13′W
30 M9 **Elkhorn** Wisconsin, N USA 42°40′N 88°34′W
29 R14 **Elkhorn River** ⁓ Nebraska, C USA
127 O16 **El'khotovo** Respublika Severnaya Osetiya, SW Russian Federation 43°18′N 44°17′E
114 L10 **Elkhovo** prev. Kizilagach. Yambol, E Bulgaria 42°10′N 26°34′E
21 R8 **Elkin** North Carolina, SE USA 36°14′N 80°51′W
21 S4 **Elkins** West Virginia, NE USA 38°56′N 79°53′W
195 X3 **Elkins, Mount** ▲ Antarctica 66°25′S 53°54′E
14 G8 **Elk Lake** Ontario, S Canada 47°44′N 80°19′W
31 P6 **Elk Lake** ◎ Michigan, N USA
18 F12 **Elkland** Pennsylvania, NE USA 41°59′N 77°16′W
35 W3 **Elko** Nevada, W USA 40°48′N 115°46′W
11 R14 **Elk Point** Alberta, SW Canada 53°52′N 110°49′W
29 R12 **Elk Point** South Dakota, N USA 42°42′N 96°37′W
29 V8 **Elk River** Minnesota, N USA 45°18′N 93°34′W
20 J10 **Elk River** ⁓ Alabama/Tennessee, S USA
21 R4 **Elk River** ⁓ West Virginia, NE USA
20 I7 **Elkton** Kentucky, S USA 36°49′N 87°11′W
21 Y2 **Elkton** Maryland, NE USA 39°37′N 75°50′W
29 R10 **Elkton** South Dakota, N USA 44°14′N 96°28′W
20 I10 **Elkton** Tennessee, S USA 35°01′N 86°51′W
21 U5 **Elkton** Virginia, NE USA 38°22′N 78°35′W
El Kuneitra see Al Qunayṭirah
81 L15 **El Kure** Somali, E Ethiopia 05°37′N 42°05′E
80 D12 **El Lagowa** Western Kordofan, C Sudan 11°23′N 29°10′E
39 S12 **Ellamar** Alaska, USA 60°54′N 146°37′W
Ellás see Greece
23 S6 **Ellaville** Georgia, SE USA 32°14′N 84°18′W
197 P9 **Ellef Ringnes Island** island Nunavut, N Canada
29 V10 **Ellendale** Minnesota, N USA 43°53′N 93°19′W
29 P7 **Ellendale** North Dakota, N USA 45°57′N 98°33′W
36 M6 **Ellen, Mount** ▲ Utah, W USA 38°06′N 110°48′W
32 I9 **Ellensburg** Washington, NW USA 47°00′N 120°34′W
18 K12 **Ellenville** New York, NE USA 41°43′N 74°24′W
Ellep see Lib
21 T10 **Ellerbe** North Carolina, SE USA 35°04′N 79°45′W
197 P10 **Ellesmere Island** island Queen Elizabeth Islands, Nunavut, N Canada
185 H19 **Ellesmere, Lake** ◎ South Island, New Zealand
97 K18 **Ellesmere Port** C England, United Kingdom 53°17′N 02°54′W
31 O14 **Ellettsville** Indiana, N USA 39°13′N 86°37′W
99 E19 **Ellezelles** Hainaut, SW Belgium 50°44′N 03°40′E
8 L7 **Ellice** ⁓ Nunavut, NE Canada
Ellice Islands see Tuvalu
Ellichpur see Achalpur
21 W3 **Ellicott City** Maryland, NE USA 39°16′N 76°48′W
23 S2 **Ellijay** Georgia, SE USA 34°42′N 84°28′W
27 W7 **Ellington** Missouri, C USA 37°14′N 90°58′W
26 L5 **Ellinwood** Kansas, C USA 38°21′N 98°34′W
83 J24 **Elliot** Eastern Cape, SE South Africa 31°20′S 27°51′E
14 D10 **Elliot Lake** Ontario, S Canada 46°24′N 82°38′W
181 X6 **Elliot, Mount** ▲ Queensland, E Australia 19°36′S 147°02′E
21 T5 **Elliott Knob** ▲ Virginia, NE USA 38°10′N 79°18′W
26 K4 **Ellis** Kansas, C USA 38°56′N 99°33′W
182 F8 **Elliston** South Australia 33°40′S 134°56′E
22 M7 **Ellisville** Mississippi, S USA 31°36′N 89°12′W
105 V5 **El Llobregat** ⁓ NE Spain
96 L9 **Ellon** NE Scotland, United Kingdom 57°22′N 02°06′W
Ellore see Elūru
21 S13 **Elloree** South Carolina, SE USA 33°34′N 80°37′W
26 M4 **Ellsworth** Kansas, C USA 38°45′N 98°15′W
19 S7 **Ellsworth** Maine, NE USA 44°32′N 68°25′W
30 I6 **Ellsworth** Wisconsin, N USA 44°44′N 92°29′W
26 M11 **Ellsworth, Lake** ⊠ Oklahoma, C USA
194 K9 **Ellsworth Land** physical region Antarctica
194 L9 **Ellsworth Mountains** ▲▲ Antarctica
101 J21 **Ellwangen** Baden-Württemberg, S Germany 48°58′N 10°07′E
18 B14 **Ellwood City** Pennsylvania, NE USA 40°49′N 80°15′W
108 H8 **Elm** Glarus, NE Switzerland 46°55′N 09°09′E
32 G9 **Elma** Washington, NW USA 47°00′N 123°24′W
121 V13 **El Maḥalla el Kubra** var. Al Maḥallah al Kubrá, Mahalla el Kubra. N Egypt 30°59′N 31°10′E
74 E9 **El Mahbas** var. Mahbés. SW Western Sahara 27°26′N 09°09′W
63 H17 **El Maitén** Chubut, W Argentina 42°03′S 71°10′W
136 E16 **Elmalı** Antalya, SW Turkey 36°43′N 29°19′E
80 G10 **El Manaqil** Gezira, C Sudan 14°12′N 33°01′E
54 M12 **El Mango** Amazonas, S Venezuela 01°55′N 66°35′W
El Manṣûra see Al Manṣūrah
55 P8 **El Manteco** Bolívar, E Venezuela 07°27′N 62°32′W
29 O16 **Elm Creek** Nebraska, C USA 40°43′N 99°22′W
El Mediyya see Médéa
77 V9 **Elméki** Agadez, C Niger 17°52′N 08°07′E
108 K7 **Elmen** Tirol, W Austria 47°22′N 10°34′E
18 I16 **Elmer** New Jersey, NE USA 39°34′N 75°09′W
138 G6 **El Mina** var. Al Mīnā'. N Lebanon 34°28′N 35°49′E
El Minya see Al Minyā
14 F15 **Elmira** Ontario, S Canada 43°35′N 80°34′W
18 G11 **Elmira** New York, NE USA 42°06′N 76°50′W
36 K13 **El Mirage** Arizona, SW USA 33°36′N 112°19′W
29 O7 **Elm Lake** ⊠ South Dakota, N USA
El Mojân see San Rafael
105 N7 **El Molar** Madrid, C Spain 40°43′N 03°35′W
76 L7 **El Mrâyer** well C Mauritania
76 L5 **El Mreiti** well N Mauritania
76 L8 **El Mreyyé** desert E Mauritania
29 P8 **Elm River** ⁓ North Dakota/South Dakota, N USA
100 I9 **Elmshorn** Schleswig-Holstein, N Germany 53°45′N 09°39′E
80 D12 **El Muglad** Western Kordofan, C Sudan 11°02′N 27°44′E
El Muwaqqar see Al Muwaqqar
14 G14 **Elmvale** Ontario, S Canada 44°34′N 79°53′W
30 K12 **Elmwood** Illinois, N USA 40°46′N 89°58′W
26 J8 **Elmwood** Oklahoma, C USA 36°37′N 100°31′W
103 P17 **Elne** anc. Illiberis. Pyrénées-Orientales, S France 42°36′N 02°58′E
54 F11 **El Nevado, Cerro** elevation C Colombia
171 N5 **El Nido** Palawan, W Philippines 11°10′N 119°25′E
62 I12 **El Nihuil** Mendoza, W Argentina 34°58′S 68°40′W
75 W7 **El Nouzha** ✈ (Alexandria) N Egypt 31°06′N 29°58′E
80 E10 **El Obeid** var. Al Obayyid, Al Ubayyiḍ. Northern Kordofan, C Sudan 13°11′N 30°10′E
41 O13 **El Oro** México, S Mexico 19°51′N 100°07′W
56 B8 **El Oro** ⬖ province SW Ecuador
61 B19 **Elortondo** Santa Fe, C Argentina 33°42′S 61°37′W
54 J8 **Elorza** Apure, C Venezuela 07°02′N 69°30′W
El Ouâdi see El Oued
74 L7 **El Oued** var. Al Oued, El Ouâdi, El Wad. NE Algeria 33°20′N 06°53′E
36 L15 **Eloy** Arizona, SW USA 32°47′N 111°33′W
55 Q7 **El Palmar** Bolívar, E Venezuela 08°01′N 61°53′W
40 K8 **El Palmito** Durango, W Mexico 25°40′N 104°59′W
55 P7 **El Pao** Bolívar, E Venezuela 08°03′N 62°40′W
54 K5 **El Pao** Cojedes, N Venezuela 09°40′N 68°08′W
42 J7 **El Paraíso** El Paraíso, S Honduras 13°51′N 86°31′W
42 I7 **El Paraíso** ⬖ department SE Honduras
30 L12 **El Paso** Illinois, N USA 40°44′N 89°01′W
24 G8 **El Paso** Texas, SW USA 31°45′N 106°30′W
24 G8 **El Paso** ✈ Texas, SW USA 31°48′N 106°24′W
105 U7 **El Perello** Cataluña, NE Spain 40°53′N 00°43′E
55 P5 **El Pilar** Sucre, NE Venezuela 10°31′N 63°12′W
42 F7 **El Pital, Cerro** ▲ El Salvador/Honduras 14°19′N 89°06′W
35 Q9 **El Portal** California, W USA 37°40′N 119°46′W
40 J3 **El Porvenir** Chihuahua, N Mexico 31°15′N 105°48′W
43 U14 **El Porvenir** Kuna Yala, N Panama 09°33′N 78°56′W
105 W6 **El Prat de Llobregat** Cataluña, NE Spain 41°20′N 02°05′E
42 H5 **El Progreso** Yoro, NW Honduras 15°25′N 87°49′W
42 A2 **El Progreso** off. Departamento de El Progreso. ⬖ department C Guatemala
El Progreso see Guastatoya
El Progreso, Departamento de see El Progreso
104 L9 **El Puente del Arzobispo** Castilla-La Mancha, C Spain 39°48′N 05°10′W
104 J15 **El Puerto de Santa María** Andalucía, S Spain 36°36′N 06°13′W
62 I8 **El Puesto** Catamarca, NW Argentina 27°57′S 67°37′W
El Qâhira see Cairo
El Qaṣr see Al Qaṣr
El Qatrani see Al Qaṭrānah
40 I10 **El Quelite** Sinaloa, C Mexico 23°37′N 106°26′W
62 G9 **Elqui, Río** ⁓ N Chile
El Q'unaytirah see Al Qunayṭirah
El Quneitra see Al Qunayṭirah
El Quseir see Al Quṣayr
El Quweira see Al Quwayrah
141 O15 **El-Rahaba** ✈ (Şan'ā') W Yemen 15°28′N 44°12′E
42 M10 **El Rama** Región Autónoma Atlántico Sur, SE Nicaragua 12°09′N 84°15′W
43 W16 **El Real** var. El Real de Santa María. Darién, SE Panama 08°06′N 77°42′W
El Real de Santa María see El Real
26 M10 **El Reno** Oklahoma, C USA 35°32′N 95°57′W
40 K9 **El Rodeo** Durango, C Mexico 25°12′N 104°35′W
104 J13 **El Ronquillo** Andalucía, S Spain 37°43′N 06°09′W
11 S16 **Elrose** Saskatchewan, S Canada 51°07′N 107°59′W
30 K8 **Elroy** Wisconsin, N USA 43°43′N 90°16′W
25 S17 **Elsa** Texas, SW USA 26°17′N 97°59′W
El Ṣaff see Aş Şaff
40 J10 **El Salto** Durango, C Mexico 23°47′N 105°22′W
42 D8 **El Salvador** off. Republica de El Salvador. ◆ republic Central America
El Salvador, Republica de see El Salvador
54 K7 **El Samán de Apure** Apure, C Venezuela 07°54′N 68°44′W
14 D7 **Elsas** Ontario, S Canada 48°31′N 82°53′W
40 F3 **El Sásabe** var. Aduana del Sásabe. Sonora, NW Mexico 31°27′N 111°31′W
Elsass see Alsace
40 J5 **El Sáuz** Chihuahua, N Mexico 29°03′N 106°15′W
27 W4 **Elsberry** Missouri, C USA 39°10′N 90°46′W
45 P9 **El Seibo** var. Santa Cruz de El Seibo, Santa Cruz del Seibo. E Dominican Republic 18°45′N 69°04′W
42 B7 **El Semillero Barra Nahualate** Escuintla, SW Guatemala 14°01′N 91°28′W
Elsene see Ixelles
Elsen Nur see Dorgê Co
36 L6 **Elsinore** Utah, W USA 38°40′N 112°09′W
Elsinore see Helsingør
99 L18 **Elsloo** Limburg, SE Netherlands 50°57′N 05°46′E
60 G13 **El Soberbio** Misiones, NE Argentina 27°15′S 54°05′W
55 N6 **El Socorro** Guárico, C Venezuela 09°00′N 65°42′W
54 L6 **El Sombrero** Guárico, N Venezuela 09°25′N 67°06′W
98 L10 **Elspeet** Gelderland, E Netherlands 52°19′N 05°47′E
98 L12 **Elst** Gelderland, E Netherlands 51°55′N 05°51′E
101 O15 **Elsterwerda** Brandenburg, E Germany 51°27′N 13°32′E
40 J4 **El Sueco** Chihuahua, N Mexico 29°53′N 106°24′W
El Suweida see As Suwaydā'
El Suweis see Suez
54 D12 **El Tambo** Cauca, SW Colombia 02°25′N 76°50′W
175 T13 **Eltanin Fracture Zone** tectonic feature SE Pacific Ocean
105 X5 **El Ter** ⁓ NE Spain
184 K11 **Eltham** Taranaki, North Island, New Zealand 39°26′S 174°25′E
55 O6 **El Tigre** Anzoátegui, NE Venezuela 08°55′N 64°15′W
El Tigrito see San José de Guanipa
54 J5 **El Tocuyo** Lara, N Venezuela 09°48′N 69°51′W
127 Q10 **El'ton** Volgogradskaya Oblast', SW Russian Federation 49°07′N 46°50′E
32 K10 **Eltopia** Washington, NW USA 46°33′N 118°59′W
El Toro see Mare de Déu del Toro
61 A18 **El Trébol** Santa Fe, C Argentina 32°12′S 61°40′W
40 J13 **El Tuito** Jalisco, SW Mexico 20°19′N 105°22′W
El Ṭûr see Aṭ Ṭūr
155 K16 **Elūru** prev. Ellore. Andhra Pradesh, E India 16°45′N 81°10′E
118 H13 **Elva** Ger. Elwa. Tartumaa, SE Estonia 58°13′N 26°25′E
37 R9 **El Vado Reservoir** ⊠ New Mexico, SW USA
43 S15 **El Valle** Coclé, C Panama 08°39′N 80°08′W
104 I11 **Elvas** Portalegre, C Portugal 38°53′N 07°10′W
54 K7 **El Venado** Apure, C Venezuela 07°25′N 68°46′W
105 V6 **El Vendrell** Cataluña, NE Spain 41°13′N 01°32′E
94 I13 **Elverum** Hedmark, S Norway 60°54′N 11°33′E
42 I9 **El Viejo** Chinandega, NW Nicaragua 12°39′N 87°11′W
54 G7 **El Viejo, Cerro** ▲ C Colombia 07°31′N 72°56′W
54 H6 **El Vigía** Mérida, NW Venezuela 08°38′N 71°39′W
105 Q4 **El Villar de Arnedo** La Rioja, N Spain 42°19′N 02°05′W
59 A14 **Elvira** Amazonas, W Brazil 07°12′S 69°56′W
Elwa see Elva
El Wad see El Oued
81 K17 **El Wak** North Eastern, NE Kenya 02°46′N 40°57′E
33 R7 **Elwell, Lake** ⊠ Montana, NW USA
31 P13 **Elwood** Indiana, N USA 40°16′N 85°50′W
27 R3 **Elwood** Kansas, C USA 39°43′N 94°52′W
29 N16 **Elwood** Nebraska, C USA 40°35′N 99°51′W
Elx see Elche
97 O20 **Ely** E England, United Kingdom 52°24′N 00°15′E
29 X4 **Ely** Minnesota, N USA 47°54′N 91°52′W
35 X6 **Ely** Nevada, W USA 39°15′N 114°53′W
El Yopal see Yopal
31 T11 **Elyria** Ohio, N USA 41°22′N 82°06′W
45 S9 **El Yunque** ▲ E Puerto Rico 18°15′N 65°46′W
101 F23 **Elz** ⁓ SW Germany
187 R14 **Emae** island Shepherd Islands, C Vanuatu
118 I5 **Emajõgi** Ger. Embach. ⁓ SE Estonia
Emāmrūd see Shāhrūd
149 Q2 **Emām Şāḩeb** var. Emam Saheb, Hazarat Imam. Kunduz, NE Afghanistan 37°11′N 68°55′E
Emam Saheb see Emām Şāḩeb
Emāmshahr see Shāhrūd
95 M20 **Emån** ⁓ S Sweden
144 J11 **Emba** Kaz. Embi. Aktyubinsk, W Kazakhstan 48°50′N 58°10′E
144 H12 **Emba** Kaz. Zhem. ⁓ W Kazakhstan
Embach see Emajõgi
62 K5 **Embarcación** Salta, N Argentina 23°15′S 64°05′W
30 M15 **Embarras River** ⁓ Illinois, N USA
Embi see Emba
81 I19 **Embu** Eastern, C Kenya 0°32′N 37°28′E
100 E10 **Emden** Niedersachsen, NW Germany 53°22′N 07°12′E
160 H9 **Emei Shan** ▲ Sichuan, C China 29°32′N 103°21′E
29 Q4 **Emerado** North Dakota, N USA 47°55′N 97°21′W
181 X8 **Emerald** Queensland, E Australia 23°33′S 148°11′E
Emerald Isle see Montserrat
57 J15 **Emero, Río** ⁓ W Bolivia
11 Y17 **Emerson** Manitoba, S Canada 49°01′N 97°07′W
29 T15 **Emerson** Iowa, C USA 41°00′N 95°22′W
29 R13 **Emerson** Nebraska, C USA 42°16′N 96°43′W
36 M5 **Emery** Utah, W USA 38°54′N 111°16′W
Emesa see Ḩimş
136 E13 **Emet** Kütahya, W Turkey 39°22′N 29°15′E
186 B8 **Emeti** Western, SW Papua New Guinea 07°54′S 143°18′E
35 V3 **Emigrant Pass** pass Nevada, W USA
78 I6 **Emi Koussi** ▲ N Chad 19°52′N 18°34′E
Emilia see Emilia-Romagna
41 V15 **Emiliano Zapata** Chiapas, SE Mexico 17°42′N 91°46′W
106 E9 **Emilia-Romagna** prev. Emilia; anc. Æmilia. ⬖ region N Italy
158 J3 **Emin** var. Dorbiljin. Xinjiang Uygur Zizhiqu, NW China 46°30′N 83°42′E
149 W8 **Eminābād** Punjab, E Pakistan 32°02′N 73°51′E
21 L5 **Eminence** Kentucky, S USA 38°22′N 85°10′W
27 W7 **Eminence** Missouri, C USA 37°09′N 91°22′W
114 N9 **Emine, Nos** headland E Bulgaria 42°43′N 27°53′E
158 I3 **Emin He** ⁓ NW China
186 G4 **Emirau Island** island N Papua New Guinea
136 F13 **Emirdağ** Afyon, W Turkey 39°01′N 31°09′E
95 M21 **Emmaboda** Kalmar, S Sweden 56°36′N 15°30′E
118 E5 **Emmaste** Hiiumaa, W Estonia 58°43′N 22°36′E
18 I15 **Emmaus** Pennsylvania, NE USA 40°32′N 75°28′W
183 U4 **Emmaville** New South Wales, SE Australia 29°26′S 151°38′E
108 E9 **Emme** ⁓ W Switzerland
98 L8 **Emmeloord** Flevoland, N Netherlands 52°43′N 05°46′E
98 O8 **Emmen** Drenthe, NE Netherlands 52°48′N 06°57′E
108 F8 **Emmen** Luzern, C Switzerland 47°03′N 08°14′E
101 F23 **Emmendingen** Baden-Württemberg, SW Germany 48°07′N 07°51′E
98 P8 **Emmer-Compascuum** Drenthe, NE Netherlands 52°47′N 07°03′E
101 D14 **Emmerich** Nordrhein-Westfalen, W Germany 51°49′N 06°16′E
29 U12 **Emmetsburg** Iowa, C USA 43°06′N 94°40′W
32 M14 **Emmett** Idaho, NW USA 43°52′N 116°30′W
38 M10 **Emmonak** Alaska, USA 62°46′N 164°31′W
Emona see Ljubljana
Emonti see East London
24 L12 **Emory Peak** ▲ Texas, SW USA 29°15′N 103°18′W
40 F6 **Empalme** Sonora, NW Mexico 27°57′N 110°49′W
83 L23 **Empangeni** KwaZulu/Natal, E South Africa 28°45′S 31°54′E
61 C14 **Empedrado** Corrientes, NE Argentina 27°59′S 58°47′W
192 K3 **Emperor Seamounts** undersea feature NW Pacific Ocean 42°00′N 170°00′E
192 L3 **Emperor Trough** undersea feature N Pacific Ocean
35 R4 **Empire** Nevada, W USA 40°26′N 119°21′W
Empire State of the South see Georgia
Emplawas see Amplawas
106 F11 **Empoli** Toscana, C Italy 43°43′N 10°57′E
27 P5 **Emporia** Kansas, C USA 38°24′N 96°10′W
21 W7 **Emporia** Virginia, NE USA 36°42′N 77°33′W
18 E13 **Emporium** Pennsylvania, NE USA 41°31′N 78°14′W
Empty Quarter see Ar Rub 'al Khali
100 E10 **Ems** Dut. Eems. ⁓ NW Germany
100 F13 **Emsdetten** Nordrhein-Westfalen, NW Germany 52°11′N 07°32′E
Ems-Hunte Canal see Küstenkanal
100 F10 **Ems-Jade-Kanal** canal NW Germany
100 F11 **Emsland** cultural region NW Germany
182 D3 **Emu Junction** South Australia 28°39′S 132°13′E
163 T3 **Emur He** ⁓ NE China
55 R8 **Enachu Landing** NW Guyana 06°09′N 60°02′W
93 F16 **Enafors** Jämtland, C Sweden 63°17′N 12°24′E
94 N11 **Enånger** Gävleborg, C Sweden 61°30′N 17°10′E

◆ Country ● Country Capital ◇ Dependent Territory ○ Dependent Territory Capital ⬖ Administrative Regions ✈ International Airport ▲ Mountain ▲▲ Mountain Range ⛰ Volcano ⁓ River ◎ Lake ⊠ Reservoir
247

ENARD BAY – ETNA, MOUNT

96 G7 **Enard Bay** *bay* NW Scotland, United Kingdom
Enaretäsk *see* Inarijärvi
171 X14 **Enarotali** Papua, E Indonesia 03°55´S 136°21´E
En 'Avedat *see* Ein Avdat
165 T2 **Enbetsu** Hokkaidō, NE Japan 44°44´N 141°47´E
61 H16 **Encantadas, Serra das** ▲▲ S Brazil
40 E7 **Encantado, Cerro** ▲ NW Mexico 26°46´N 112°33´W
62 P7 **Encarnación** Itapúa, S Paraguay 27°20´S 55°50´W
40 M12 **Encarnación de Díaz** Jalisco, SW Mexico 21°33´N 102°13´W
77 O17 **Enchi** SW Ghana 05°53´N 02°48´W
25 Q14 **Encinal** Texas, SW USA 28°02´N 99°21´W
35 U17 **Encinitas** California, W USA 33°02´N 117°17´W
25 S16 **Encino** Texas, SW USA 26°58´N 98°06´W
54 H6 **Encontrados** Zulia, NW Venezuela 09°04´N 72°16´W
182 I10 **Encounter Bay** *inlet* South Australia
61 F15 **Encruzilhada** Rio Grande do Sul, S Brazil 28°58´S 55°31´W
61 H16 **Encruzilhada do Sul** Rio Grande do Sul, S Brazil 30°30´S 52°32´W
111 M20 **Encs** Borsod-Abaúj-Zemplén, NE Hungary 48°21´N 21°09´E
193 P3 **Endeavour Seamount** *undersea feature* N Pacific Ocean 48°15´N 129°04´W
181 V1 **Endeavour Strait** *strait* Queensland, NE Australia
171 O16 **Endeh** Flores, S Indonesia 08°48´S 121°37´E
95 G23 **Endelave** *island* C Denmark
191 T4 **Enderbury Island** *atoll* Phoenix Islands, C Kiribati
11 N16 **Enderby** British Columbia, SW Canada 50°34´N 119°09´W
195 W4 **Enderby Land** *physical region* Antarctica
173 N14 **Enderby Plain** *undersea feature* S Indian Ocean
29 Q6 **Enderlin** North Dakota, N USA 46°37´N 97°36´W
Endersdorf *see* Jędrzejów
28 K16 **Enders Reservoir** ⊠ Nebraska, C USA
18 H11 **Endicott** New York, NE USA 42°06´N 76°03´W
39 P7 **Endicott Mountains** ▲▲ Alaska, USA
118 I5 **Endla Raba** *wetland* C Estonia
127 X7 **Energetik** Orenburgskaya Oblast', W Russian Federation 51°37´N 58°44´E
117 T9 **Enerhodar** Zaporiz'ka Oblast', SE Ukraine 47°30´N 34°40´E
57 F14 **Ene, Río** ~ C Peru
189 N4 **Enewetak Atoll** *var.* Ānewetak, Eniwetok. *atoll* Ralik Chain, W Marshall Islands
114 L13 **Enez** Edirne, NW Turkey 40°44´N 26°05´E
21 W8 **Enfield** North Carolina, SE USA 36°10´N 77°40´W
186 B7 **Enga** ⬖ *province* W Papua New Guinea
45 Q9 **Engaño, Cabo** *headland* E Dominican Republic 18°36´N 68°19´W
164 U3 **Engaru** Hokkaidō, NE Japan 44°06´N 143°30´E
'En Gedi *see* Ein Gedi
108 F9 **Engelberg** Unterwalden, C Switzerland 46°51´N 08°25´E
21 Y9 **Engelhard** North Carolina, SE USA 35°30´N 76°00´W
127 P8 **Engel's** Saratovskaya Oblast', W Russian Federation 51°27´N 46°09´E
101 G24 **Engen** Baden-Württemberg, SW Germany 47°52´N 08°46´E
Engeten *see* Aiud
168 K15 **Enggano, Pulau** *island* W Indonesia
80 J8 **Enghershatu** ▲ N Eritrea 16°41´N 38°21´E
99 F19 **Enghien** *Dut.* Edingen. Hainaut, SW Belgium 50°42´N 04°03´E
27 V12 **England** Arkansas, C USA 34°32´N 91°58´W
97 M20 **England** *Lat.* Anglia. ⬖ *national region* England, United Kingdom
14 H8 **Englehart** Ontario, S Canada 47°50´N 79°52´W
37 T4 **Englewood** Colorado, C USA 39°39´N 104°59´W
31 O16 **English** Indiana, N USA 38°20´N 86°28´W
39 Q13 **English Bay** Alaska, USA 59°21´N 151°55´W
English Bazar *see* Ingrāj Bāzār
97 N25 **English Channel** *var.* The Channel, *Fr.* la Manche. *channel* NW Europe
194 J7 **English Coast** *physical region* Antarctica
105 S11 **Enguera** País Valenciano, E Spain 38°58´N 00°42´W
118 E8 **Engure** Tukums, W Latvia 57°09´N 23°13´E
118 E8 **Engures Ezers** ◎ NW Latvia
137 R9 **Enguri** *Rus.* Inguri. ~ NW Georgia
Engyum *see* Gangi
26 M9 **Enid** Oklahoma, C USA 36°25´N 97°53´W
22 L3 **Enid Lake** ⊠ Mississippi, S USA
189 Y2 **Enigu** *island* Ratak Chain, SE Marshall Islands
Enikale Strait *see* Kerch Strait
147 Z8 **Enil'chek** Issyk-Kul'skaya Oblast', E Kyrgyzstan 42°04´N 79°01´E
115 F17 **Enipéfs** ~ C Greece
165 S4 **Eniwa** Hokkaidō, NE Japan 42°53´N 141°14´E
Eniwetok *see* Enewetak Atoll
Enjiang *see* Yongfeng
Enkeldoorn *see* Chivhu
98 J8 **Enkhuizen** Noord-Holland, NW Netherlands 52°34´N 05°03´E
109 Q4 **Enknach** ~ N Austria
95 N15 **Enköping** Uppsala, C Sweden 59°38´N 17°07´E
107 K24 **Enna** *var.* Castrogiovanni, Henna. Sicilia, Italy, C Mediterranean Sea 37°34´N 14°16´E
80 D11 **En Nahud** Western Kordofan, C Sudan 12°41´N 28°28´E
138 F8 **En Nâqoûra** *var.* An Nāqūrah. SW Lebanon 33°06´N 33°30´E
En Nazira *see* Natzrat
78 K8 **Ennedi** *plateau* E Chad
101 E15 **Ennepetal** Nordrhein-Westfalen, W Germany 51°18´N 07°23´E
183 P4 **Enngonia** New South Wales, SE Australia 29°19´S 145°52´E
97 C19 **Ennis** *Ir.* Inis. Clare, W Ireland 52°50´N 08°59´W
33 R11 **Ennis** Montana, NW USA 45°21´N 111°45´W
25 U7 **Ennis** Texas, SW USA 32°19´N 96°37´W
97 F20 **Enniscorthy** *Ir.* Inis Córthaidh. SE Ireland 52°30´N 06°34´W
97 E15 **Enniskillen** *var.* Inniskilling, *Ir.* Inis Ceithleann. SW Northern Ireland, United Kingdom 54°21´N 07°38´W
97 B19 **Ennistimon** *Ir.* Inis Díomáin. Clare, W Ireland 52°57´N 09°17´W
109 T4 **Enns** Oberösterreich, N Austria 48°13´N 14°28´E
109 T4 **Enns** ~ C Austria
93 O16 **Eno** Itä-Suomi, SE Finland 62°45´N 30°15´E
24 M5 **Enochs** Texas, SW USA 33°51´N 102°46´W
93 N17 **Enonkoski** Itä-Suomi, E Finland 62°04´N 28°53´E
92 K10 **Enontekiö** *Lapp.* Eanodat. Lappi, N Finland 68°25´N 23°40´E
21 Q11 **Enoree** South Carolina, SE USA 34°39´N 81°58´W
21 P11 **Enoree River** ~ South Carolina, SE USA
18 M6 **Enosburg Falls** Vermont, NE USA 44°54´N 72°50´W
171 N13 **Enrekang** Sulawesi, C Indonesia 03°33´S 119°46´E
45 N10 **Enriquillo** SW Dominican Republic 17°57´N 71°13´W
45 N9 **Enriquillo, Lago** ◎ SW Dominican Republic
98 L9 **Ens** Flevoland, N Netherlands 52°39´N 05°49´E
98 P11 **Enschede** Overijssel, E Netherlands 52°13´N 06°55´E
40 B2 **Ensenada** Baja California Norte, NW Mexico 31°52´N 116°32´W
101 E20 **Ensheim** ✈ (Saarbrücken) Saarland, W Germany 49°13´N 07°09´E
160 L9 **Enshi** Hubei, C China 30°16´N 109°26´E
164 L14 **Enshū-nada** *gulf* SW Japan
23 O8 **Ensley** Florida, SE USA 30°31´N 87°16´W
Enso *see* Svetogorsk
81 F18 **Entebbe** S Uganda 0°07´N 32°30´E
81 F18 **Entebbe** ✈ C Uganda 0°04´N 32°29´E
101 M18 **Entenbühl** ▲ Czech Republic/Germany 50°09´N 12°10´E
98 N10 **Enter** Overijssel, E Netherlands 52°19´N 06°34´E
23 Q7 **Enterprise** Alabama, S USA 31°19´N 85°50´W
32 L11 **Enterprise** Oregon, NW USA 45°25´N 117°18´W
36 J7 **Enterprise** Utah, W USA 37°33´N 113°42´W
32 J8 **Entiat** Washington, NW USA 47°39´N 120°15´W
105 P15 **Entinas, Punta de las** *headland* S Spain 36°40´N 02°44´W
108 F8 **Entlebuch** Luzern, W Switzerland 47°02´N 08°04´E
108 F8 **Entlebuch** *valley* C Switzerland
63 I22 **Entrada, Punta** *headland* S Argentina
103 O13 **Entraygues-sur-Truyère** Aveyron, S France 44°39´N 02°36´E
187 O14 **Entrecasteaux, Récifs d'** *reef* N New Caledonia
61 C17 **Entre Ríos** *off.* Provincia de Entre Ríos. ⬖ *province* NE Argentina
42 K7 **Entre Ríos, Cordillera** ▲▲ Honduras/Nicaragua
Entre Ríos, Provincia de *see* Entre Ríos
104 G9 **Entroncamento** Santarém, C Portugal 39°28´N 08°28´W
77 V16 **Enugu** Enugu, S Nigeria 06°24´N 07°24´E
77 U16 **Enugu** ⬖ *state* SE Nigeria
123 V5 **Enurmino** Chukotskiy Avtonomnyy Okrug, NE Russian Federation 66°46´N 171°40´W
54 E9 **Envigado** Antioquia, W Colombia 06°09´N 75°38´W
59 B15 **Envira** Amazonas, W Brazil 07°12´S 69°59´W
Enyélé *see* Enyellé
79 I16 **Enyellé** *var.* Enyélé. Likouala, NE Congo 02°49´N 18°02´E
101 H21 **Enz** ~ SW Germany
165 N13 **Enzan** *var.* Kōshū. Yamanashi, Honshū, S Japan 35°44´N 138°43´E
104 I2 **Eo** ~ NW Spain
Eochaill *see* Youghal
Eochaille, Cuan *see* Youghal Bay
107 K22 **Eolie, Isole** *var.* Isole Lipari, *Eng.* Aeolian Islands, Lipari Islands. *island group* S Italy
189 U12 **Eot** *island* Chuuk, C Micronesia
Epáno Archánes/Epáno Arkhánai *see* Archánes
115 G14 **Epanomí** Kentrikí Makedonía, N Greece 40°25´N 22°57´E
98 M10 **Epe** Gelderland, E Netherlands 52°21´N 05°59´E
77 S16 **Epe** Lagos, S Nigeria 06°37´N 04°01´E
79 I17 **Epéna** Likouala, NE Congo 01°28´N 17°29´E
Eperies/Eperjes *see* Prešov
103 Q4 **Épernay** *anc.* Sparnacum. Marne, N France 49°02´N 03°58´E
36 L5 **Ephraim** Utah, W USA 39°21´N 111°35´W
18 H15 **Ephrata** Pennsylvania, NE USA 40°09´N 76°08´W
32 J8 **Ephrata** Washington, NW USA 47°19´N 119°33´W
187 R14 **Epi** *var.* Épi. *island* C Vanuatu
Épi *see* Epi
105 R6 **Épila** Aragón, NE Spain 41°34´N 01°19´W
103 T6 **Épinal** Vosges, NE France 48°10´N 06°28´E
Epiphania *see* Ḥamāh
Epirus *see* Ípeiros
121 P3 **Episkopí** SW Cyprus 34°37´N 32°53´E
Episkopi Bay *see* Episkopí, Kólpos
121 P3 **Episkopí, Kólpos** *var.* Episkopi Bay. *bay* SE Cyprus
Epitoli *see* Tshwane
Epoon *see* Ebon Atoll
Eporedia *see* Ivrea
Eppeschdorf *see* Dumbrăveni
101 H21 **Eppingen** Baden-Württemberg, SW Germany 49°09´N 08°54´E
83 E18 **Epukiro** Omaheke, E Namibia 21°40´S 19°09´E
29 Y13 **Epworth** Iowa, C USA 42°27´N 90°55´W
143 O10 **Eqlīd** *var.* Iqlid. Fārs, C Iran 30°54´N 52°40´E
Equality State *see* Wyoming
79 J18 **Equateur** *off.* Région de l' Equateur. ⬖ *region* N Dem. Rep. Congo
Equateur, Région de l' *see* Equateur
151 K22 **Equatorial Channel** *channel* S Maldives
79 B17 **Equatorial Guinea** *off.* Equatorial Guinea, Republic of. ◆ *republic* C Africa
Equatorial Guinea, Republic of *see* Equatorial Guinea
121 V11 **Eratosthenes Tablemount** *undersea feature* E Mediterranean Sea 33°48´N 32°53´E
Erautini *see* Johannesburg
136 L12 **Erbaa** Tokat, N Turkey 40°42´N 36°37´E
101 E19 **Erbeskopf** ▲ W Germany 49°43´N 07°04´E
Erbil *see* Arbīl
121 P2 **Ercan** ✈ (Nicosia) N Cyprus 35°07´N 33°30´E
Ercegnovi *see* Herceg-Novi
137 T14 **Erçek Gölü** ◎ E Turkey
137 S14 **Erciş** Van, E Turkey 39°02´N 43°21´E
136 K14 **Erciyes Dağı** *anc.* Argaeus. ▲ C Turkey 38°32´N 35°28´E
111 J22 **Érd** *Ger.* Hanselbeck. Pest, C Hungary 47°22´N 18°56´E
163 X11 **Erdaobaihe** *prev.* Baihe. Jilin, NE China 42°24´N 128°09´E
159 O12 **Erdaogou** Qinghai, W China 34°30´N 92°50´E
163 X11 **Erdao Jiang** ~ NE China
Erdăt-Sângeorz *see* Sângeorgiu de Pădure
136 C11 **Erdek** Balıkesir, NW Turkey 40°24´N 27°47´E
Erdély *see* Transylvania
Erdélyi-Havasok *see* Carpaţii Meridionalii
136 J17 **Erdemli** İçel, S Turkey 36°35´N 34°19´E
163 O10 **Erdene** *var.* Ulaan-Uul. Dornogovĭ, SE Mongolia 44°21´N 111°06´E
162 H9 **Erdene** *var.* Sangiyn Dalay. Govĭ-Altay, C Mongolia 45°12´N 97°51´E
162 E6 **Erdenebüren** *var.* Har-Us. Hovd, W Mongolia 48°30´N 91°25´E
162 K9 **Erdenedalay** *var.* Sangiyn Dalay. Dundgovĭ, C Mongolia 45°59´N 104°58´E
162 G7 **Erdenehayrhan** *var.* Altan. Dzavhan, W Mongolia 48°05´N 95°48´E
162 J7 **Erdenemandal** *var.* Öldziyt. Arhangay, C Mongolia 48°30´N 101°25´E
162 K6 **Erdenet** Orhon, N Mongolia 49°01´N 104°07´E
163 Q9 **Erdenetsagaan** *var.* Chonogol. Sühbaatar, E Mongolia 45°55´N 115°19´E
162 I8 **Erdenetsogt** Bayanhongor, C Mongolia 46°27´N 100°53´E
Erdenetsogt *see* Bayan-Ovoo
78 K7 **Erdi** *plateau* NE Chad
78 L7 **Erdi Ma** *desert* NE Chad
101 M23 **Erding** Bayern, SE Germany 48°18´N 11°54´E
Erdőszáda *see* Ardusat
Erdőszentgyörgy *see* Sângeorgiu de Pădure
102 I7 **Erdre** ~ NW France
195 R13 **Erebus, Mount** ⛰ Ross Island, Antarctica 78°11´S 165°09´E
61 H14 **Erechim** Rio Grande do Sul, S Brazil 27°35´S 52°15´W
163 O7 **Ereen Davaanĭ Nuruu** ▲▲ NE Mongolia
163 Q6 **Ereentsav** Dornod, NE Mongolia 49°51´N 115°41´E
136 I16 **Ereğli** Konya, S Turkey 37°30´N 34°02´E
115 A15 **Ereíkoussa** *island* Iónia Nisiá, Greece, C Mediterranean Sea
163 O11 **Erenhot** *var.* Erlian. Nei Mongol Zizhiqu, NE China 43°35´N 112°E
104 M6 **Eresma** ~ N Spain
115 K17 **Eresós** *var.* Eressós. Lésvos, E Greece 39°11´N 25°57´E
Eressós *see* Eresós
Ereymentaū *see* Yereymentau
99 K21 **Érezée** Luxembourg, SE Belgium 50°16´N 05°34´E
74 G7 **Erfoud** SE Morocco 31°29´N 04°18´W
101 D16 **Erft** ~ W Germany
101 K16 **Erfurt** Thüringen, C Germany 50°59´N 11°02´E
137 P15 **Ergani** Diyarbakır, SE Turkey 38°17´N 39°44´E
Ergel *see* Hatanbulag
Ergene Çayı *see* Ergene Irmağı
136 C10 **Ergene Irmağı** *var.* Ergene Çayı. ~ NW Turkey
118 I9 **Ērgļi** Madona, C Latvia 56°55´N 25°38´E
78 H11 **Erguig, Bahr** ~ SW Chad
163 S5 **Ergun** *var.* Labudalin; *prev.* Ergun Youqi. Nei Mongol Zizhiqu, N China 50°13´N 120°09´E
Ergun He *see* Argun
Ergun Youqi *see* Ergun
Ergun Zuoqi *see* Genhe
160 F12 **Er Hai** ◎ SW China
104 K4 **Ería** ~ NW Spain
80 H8 **Eriba** Kassala, NE Sudan 16°37´N 36°04´E
96 I6 **Eriboll, Loch** *inlet* NW Scotland, United Kingdom
65 Q18 **Erica Seamount** *undersea feature* SW Indian Ocean 38°15´S 14°30´E
107 H23 **Erice** Sicilia, Italy, C Mediterranean Sea 38°02´N 12°35´E
104 E10 **Ericeira** Lisboa, C Portugal 38°58´N 09°25´W
96 H10 **Ericht, Loch** ◎ C Scotland, United Kingdom
26 J11 **Erick** Oklahoma, C USA 35°13´N 99°52´W
18 B11 **Erie** Pennsylvania, NE USA 42°07´N 80°04´W
18 E9 **Erie Canal** *canal* New York, NE USA
Érié, Lac *see* Erie, Lake
31 T10 **Erie, Lake** *Fr.* Lac Érié. ◎ Canada/USA
Erigabo *see* Ceerigaabo
77 N8 **'Erîgât** *desert* N Mali
Erigavo *see* Ceerigaabo
92 P2 **Erik Eriksenstretet** *strait* E Svalbard
11 X15 **Eriksdale** Manitoba, S Canada 50°52´N 98°07´W
189 V6 **Erikub Atoll** *var.* Ādkup. *atoll* Ratak Chain, C Marshall Islands
102 G4 **Er, Îles d'** *Island group* NW France
Erimanthos *see* Erýmanthos
165 T6 **Erimo** Hokkaidō, NE Japan 42°01´N 143°07´E
165 T6 **Erimo-misaki** *headland* Hokkaidō, NE Japan 41°57´N 143°12´E
20 H8 **Erin** Tennessee, S USA 36°19´N 87°42´W
96 E9 **Eriskay** *island* NW Scotland, United Kingdom
Erithraí *see* Erythrés
80 I9 **Eritrea** *off.* State of Eritrea, Ērtra. ◆ *transitional government* E Africa
Eritrea, State of *see* Eritrea
Erivan *see* Yerevan
101 D16 **Erkelenz** Nordrhein-Westfalen, W Germany 51°04´N 06°19´E
95 P15 **Erken** ◎ C Sweden
101 K19 **Erlangen** Bayern, S Germany 49°36´N 11°E
160 G9 **Erlang Shan** ▲ C China 29°56´N 102°24´E
Erlau *see* Eger
109 V5 **Erlauf** ~ NE Austria
181 Q8 **Erldunda Roadhouse** Northern Territory, N Australia 25°13´S 133°13´E
Erlian *see* Erenhot
27 T15 **Erling, Lake** ⊠ Arkansas, USA
109 O8 **Erlsbach** Tirol, W Austria 46°54´N 12°15´E
Ermak *see* Aksu
98 K10 **Ermelo** Gelderland, C Netherlands 52°18´N 05°38´E
83 K21 **Ermelo** Mpumalanga, NE South Africa 26°32´S 29°59´E
136 H17 **Ermenek** Karaman, S Turkey 36°38´N 32°55´E
Érmihályfalva *see* Valea lui Mihai
115 G20 **Ermióni** Pelopónnisos, S Greece 37°24´N 23°15´E
115 J20 **Ermoúpoli** *var.* Hermoupolis; *prev.* Ermoúpolis. Sýyros, Kykládes, Greece, Aegean Sea 37°26´N 24°55´E
Ermoúpolis *see* Ermoúpoli
Ernabella *see* Pukatja
155 G22 **Ernākulam** Kerala, SW India 10°04´N 76°18´E
102 J6 **Ernée** Mayenne, NW France 48°18´N 00°54´W
61 H14 **Ernestina, Barragem** ⊠ S Brazil
54 E4 **Ernesto Cortissoz** ✈ (Barranquilla) Atlántico, N Colombia
155 H21 **Erode** Tamil Nādu, SE India 11°21´N 77°43´E
Eroj *see* Iroj
83 C19 **Erongo** ⬖ *district* W Namibia
99 F21 **Erquelinnes** Hainaut, S Belgium 50°18´N 04°08´E
74 G7 **Er-Rachidia** *var.* Ksar al Soule. E Morocco 31°58´N 04°22´W
80 E11 **Er Rahad** *var.* Ar Rahad. Northern Kordofan, C Sudan 12°43´N 30°39´E
Er Ramle *see* Ramla
83 O15 **Errego** Zambézia, NE Mozambique 16°02´S 37°11´E
105 Q2 **Errenteria** *Cast.* Rentería. País Vasco, N Spain 43°17´N 01°54´W
Er Rif/Er Riff *see* Rif
97 D14 **Errigal Mountain** *Ir.* An Earagail. ▲ N Ireland 55°03´N 08°09´W
97 A15 **Erris Head** *Ir.* Ceann Iorrais. *headland* W Ireland 54°18´N 10°01´W
187 S15 **Erromango** *island* S Vanuatu
Error Guyot *see* Error Tablemount
173 O4 **Error Tablemount** *var.* Error Guyot. *undersea feature* W Indian Ocean 10°20´N 56°05´E
80 G11 **Er Roseires** Blue Nile, E Sudan 11°52´N 34°23´E
Erseka *see* Ersekë
113 M22 **Ersekë** *var.* Erseka, Kolonjë. Korçë, SE Albania 40°19´N 20°39´E
Érsekújvár *see* Nové Zámky
29 S4 **Erskine** Minnesota, N USA 47°42´N 96°00´W
103 V6 **Erstein** Bas-Rhin, NE France 48°24´N 07°39´E
108 G9 **Erstfeld** Uri, C Switzerland 46°49´N 08°41´E
158 M3 **Ertai** Xinjiang Uygur Zizhiqu, NW China 46°04´N 90°06´E
126 M7 **Ertil'** Voronezhskaya Oblast', W Russian Federation 51°51´N 40°46´E
Ertis *see* Irtysh, C Asia
Ertis *see* Irtyshsk, Kazakhstan
158 K2 **Ertix He** *Rus.* Chërnyy Irtysh. ~ China/Kazakhstan
Ērtra *see* Eritrea
21 P9 **Erwin** North Carolina, SE USA 35°19´N 78°40´W
Erydropótamos *see* Erythropótamos
115 E19 **Erýmanthos** *var.* Erimanthos. ▲ S Greece 37°57´N 21°51´E
115 G19 **Erythrés** *prev.* Erithraí. Stereá Ellás, C Greece 38°18´N 23°20´E
114 L12 **Erythropótamos** *Bul.* Byala Reka, *var.* Erydropótamos. ~ Bulgaria/Greece
160 F12 **Eryuan** *var.* Yuhu. Yunnan, SW China 26°09´N 100°01´E
109 U6 **Erzbach** ~ W Austria
Erzerum *see* Erzurum
101 N17 **Erzgebirge** *Cz.* Krušné Hory, *Eng.* Ore Mountains. ▲ Czech Republic/Germany *see also* Krušné Hory
Erzgebirge *see* Krušné Hory
122 L14 **Erzin** Respublika Tyva, S Russian Federation 50°17´N 95°03´E
137 O13 **Erzincan** *var.* Erzinjan. Erzincan, E Turkey 39°44´N 39°30´E
137 N13 **Erzincan** *var.* Erzinjan. ⬖ *province* NE Turkey
Erzinjan *see* Erzincan
Erzsébetváros *see* Dumbrăveni
137 Q13 **Erzurum** *prev.* Erzerum. Erzurum, NE Turkey 39°57´N 41°17´E
137 Q12 **Erzurum** *prev.* Erzerum. ⬖ *province* NE Turkey
186 G9 **Esa'ala** Normanby Island, SE Papua New Guinea 09°45´S 150°47´E
165 T2 **Esashi** Hokkaidō, NE Japan 44°57´N 142°32´E
165 Q9 **Esashi** *var.* Esasi. Iwate, Honshū, C Japan 39°13´N 141°11´E
165 Q5 **Esasho** Hokkaidō, N Japan 41°52´N 140°07´E
Esasi *see* Esashi
95 F23 **Esbjerg** Ribe, W Denmark 55°28´N 08°28´E
Esbo *see* Espoo
36 L7 **Escalante** Utah, W USA 37°46´N 111°36´W
36 M7 **Escalante River** ~ Utah, W USA
14 L12 **Escalier, Réservoir l'** ⊠ Québec, SE Canada
40 K7 **Escalón** Chihuahua, N Mexico 26°43´N 104°20´W
104 M8 **Escalona** Castilla-La Mancha, C Spain 40°10´N 04°24´W
23 O8 **Escambia River** ~ Florida, SE USA
31 N5 **Escanaba** Michigan, N USA 45°45´N 87°03´W
31 N4 **Escanaba River** ~ Michigan, N USA
105 R8 **Escandón, Puerto de** *pass* E Spain
41 W14 **Escárcega** Campeche, SE Mexico 18°33´N 90°41´W
171 O1 **Escarpada Point** *headland* Luzon, N Philippines 18°28´N 122°10´E
23 N8 **Escatawpa River** ~ Alabama/Mississippi, S USA
103 P2 **Escaut** ~ N France
Escaut *see* Scheldt
99 M25 **Esch-sur-Alzette** Luxembourg, S Luxembourg 49°30´N 05°59´E
101 J15 **Eschwege** Hessen, C Germany 51°10´N 10°03´E
101 D16 **Eschweiler** Nordrhein-Westfalen, W Germany 50°49´N 06°16´E
Esclaves, Grand Lac des *see* Great Slave Lake
45 O8 **Escocesa, Bahía** *bay* N Dominican Republic
43 W15 **Escocés, Punta** *headland* NE Panama 08°50´N 77°37´W
35 U17 **Escondido** California, W USA 33°07´N 117°05´W
42 M10 **Escondido, Río** ~ SE Nicaragua
15 S7 **Escoumins, Rivière des** ~ Québec, SE Canada
37 O13 **Escudilla Mountain** ▲ Arizona, SW USA 33°57´N 109°07´W
40 J11 **Escuinapa** *var.* Escuinapa de Hidalgo. Sinaloa, C Mexico 22°50´N 105°46´W
Escuinapa de Hidalgo *see* Escuinapa
42 C6 **Escuintla** Escuintla, S Guatemala 14°17´N 90°46´W
41 V17 **Escuintla** Chiapas, SE Mexico 15°20´N 92°40´W
42 A2 **Escuintla** *off.* Departamento de Escuintla. ⬖ *department* S Guatemala
Escuintla, Departamento de *see* Escuintla
15 W7 **Escuminac** ~ Québec, SE Canada
79 D16 **Eséka** Centre, SW Cameroon 03°40´N 10°48´E
136 I12 **Esenboğa** ✈ (Ankara) Ankara, C Turkey 40°05´N 33°01´E
136 D17 **Eşen Çayı** ~ SW Turkey
146 B13 **Esenguly** *Rus.* Gasan-Kuli. Balkan Welaýaty, W Turkmenistan 37°29´N 53°57´E
105 T4 **Ésera** ~ NE Spain
143 N8 **Eşfahān** *Eng.* Isfahan; *anc.* Aspadana. Eşfahān, C Iran 32°41´N 51°41´E
143 O7 **Eşfahān** *off.* Ostān-e Eşfahān. ⬖ *province* C Iran
Eşfahān, Ostān-e *see* Eşfahān
105 N5 **Esgueva** ~ N Spain
149 Q3 **Eshkamesh** Takhār, NE Afghanistan 36°25´N 69°11´E
149 T2 **Eshkāshem** Badakhshān, NE Afghanistan 36°43´N 71°34´E
83 L23 **Eshowe** KwaZulu/Natal, E South Africa 28°58´S 31°28´E
143 T5 **'Eshqābād** Khorāsān, NE Iran 36°00´N 59°01´E
Esh Sham *see* Dimashq
Esh Sharā *see* Ash Sharāh
Esik *see* Yesik
Esil *see* Yesil'
Esil *see* Ishim, Kazakhstan/Russian Federation
183 V2 **Esk** Queensland, E Australia 27°15´S 152°23´E
184 O11 **Eskdale** Hawke's Bay, North Island, New Zealand 39°24´S 176°51´E
Eski Dzhumaya *see* Türgovishte
92 L2 **Eskifjördhur** Austurland, E Iceland 65°04´N 14°01´W
139 S3 **Eski Kalak** *var.* Askī Kalak, Kalak. Arbīl, N Iraq 36°16´N 43°40´E
95 N16 **Eskilstuna** Södermanland, C Sweden 59°22´N 16°31´E
8 H6 **Eskimo Lakes** ◎ Northwest Territories, NW Canada
9 O10 **Eskimo Point** *headland* Nunavut, E Canada 61°19´N 93°49´W
Eskimo Point *see* Arviat
139 Q2 **Eski Mosul** Nīnawá, N Iraq 36°31´N 42°45´E
147 T10 **Eski-Nookat** *var.* Iski-Nauket. Oshskaya Oblast', SW Kyrgyzstan 40°18´N 72°29´E
136 F12 **Eskişehir** *var.* Eskishehr. Eskişehir, W Turkey 39°46´N 30°30´E
136 F13 **Eskişehir** *var.* Eski shehr. ⬖ *province* NW Turkey
Eskishehr *see* Eskişehir
104 K5 **Esla** ~ NW Spain
142 J6 **Eslāmābād** *var.* Eslāmābād-e Gharb; *prev.* Harunabad, Shāhābād. Kermānshāhān, W Iran 34°08´N 46°35´E
Eslāmābād-e Gharb *see* Eslāmābād
148 J4 **Eslām Qal'eh** *Pash.* Islam Qala. Herāt, W Afghanistan 34°41´N 61°03´E
95 K23 **Eslöv** Skåne, S Sweden 55°50´N 13°20´E
143 S12 **Esmā'īlābād** Kermān, S Iran 28°48´N 56°39´E
143 U8 **Esmā'īlābād** Khorāsān, E Iran 35°20´N 60°30´E
136 D14 **Eşme** Uşak, W Turkey 38°26´N 28°59´E
44 G6 **Esmeralda** Camagüey, E Cuba 21°51´N 78°10´W
63 F21 **Esmeralda, Isla** *island* S Chile
56 B5 **Esmeraldas** Esmeraldas, N Ecuador 0°55´N 79°40´W
56 B5 **Esmeraldas** ⬖ *province* NW Ecuador
Esna *see* Isnā
14 B6 **Esnagi Lake** ◎ Ontario, S Canada
143 V14 **Espakeh** Sīstān va Balūchestān, SE Iran 26°54´N 60°09´E
103 O13 **Espalion** Aveyron, S France 44°31´N 02°45´E
España *see* Spain
14 E11 **Espanola** Ontario, S Canada 46°15´N 81°46´W
37 S10 **Espanola** New Mexico, SW USA 35°59´N 106°04´W
57 C18 **Española, Isla** *var.* Hood Island. *island* Galapagos Islands, Ecuador, E Pacific Ocean
104 M13 **Espejo** Andalucía, S Spain 37°40´N 04°34´W
94 C13 **Espeland** Hordaland, S Norway 60°22´N 05°27´E
100 G12 **Espelkamp** Nordrhein-Westfalen, NW Germany 52°22´N 08°37´E
38 M8 **Espenberg, Cape** *headland* Alaska, USA 66°33´N 163°36´W
180 L13 **Esperance** Western Australia 33°49´S 121°52´E
186 L9 **Esperance, Cape** *headland* Guadalcanal, C Solomon Islands 09°09´S 159°38´E
57 P18 **Esperancita** Santa Cruz, E Bolivia
61 B17 **Esperanza** Santa Fe, C Argentina 31°29´S 61°00´W
40 G6 **Esperanza** Sonora, NW Mexico 27°37´N 109°51´W
24 H9 **Esperanza** Texas, SW USA 31°09´N 105°40´W
194 H3 **Esperanza** *Argentinian research station* Antarctica 63°29´S 56°53´W
104 E12 **Espichel, Cabo** *headland* S Portugal 38°25´N 09°15´W
54 E10 **Espinal** Tolima, C Colombia 04°08´N 74°53´W
48 K10 **Espinhaço, Serra do** ▲▲ SE Brazil
104 G6 **Espinho** Aveiro, N Portugal 41°01´N 08°38´W
59 N18 **Espinosa** Minas Gerais, SE Brazil 14°58´S 42°49´W
103 O15 **Espinouse** ▲ S France
60 Q8 **Espírito Santo** *off.* Estado do Espírito Santo. ⬖ *state* E Brazil
Espírito Santo, Estado do *see* Espírito Santo
187 P13 **Espiritu Santo** *var.* Santo. *island* W Vanuatu
41 Z13 **Espíritu Santo, Bahía del** *bay* SE Mexico
40 F9 **Espíritu Santo, Isla del** *island* NW Mexico
41 Y12 **Espita** Yucatán, SE Mexico 21°00´N 88°17´W
15 Y7 **Espoir, Cap d'** *headland* Québec, SE Canada 48°24´N 64°21´W
Esponsede/Esponsende *see* Esposende
93 L20 **Espoo** *Swe.* Esbo. Etelä-Suomi, S Finland 60°10´N 24°42´E
104 G5 **Esposende** *var.* Esponsede, Esponsende. Braga, N Portugal 41°32´N 08°47´W
83 M18 **Espungabera** Manica, SW Mozambique 20°29´S 32°48´E
63 H17 **Esquel** Chubut, SW Argentina 42°55´S 71°20´W
10 L17 **Esquimalt** Vancouver Island, British Columbia, SW Canada 48°26´N 123°27´W
61 C16 **Esquina** Corrientes, NE Argentina 30°00´S 59°30´W
42 E6 **Esquipulas** Chiquimula, SE Guatemala 14°36´N 89°22´W
42 K9 **Esquipulas** Matagalpa, C Nicaragua 12°30´N 85°55´W
94 I8 **Essandjøen** ◎ S Norway
74 E7 **Essaouira** *prev.* Mogador. W Morocco 31°33´N 09°40´W
Esseg *see* Osijek
Es Semara *see* Smara
99 G15 **Essen** Antwerpen, N Belgium 51°28´N 04°28´E
101 E15 **Essen** *var.* Essen an der Ruhr. Nordrhein-Westfalen, W Germany 51°28´N 07°01´E
Essen an der Ruhr *see* Essen
74 I5 **Es Senia** ✈ (Oran) NW Algeria 35°34´N 00°42´W
55 T8 **Essequibo Islands** *island group* N Guyana
55 T11 **Essequibo River** ~ C Guyana
14 C18 **Essex** Ontario, S Canada 42°10´N 82°50´W
29 T16 **Essex** Iowa, C USA 40°49´N 95°18´W
97 P21 **Essex** *cultural region* E England, United Kingdom
31 R8 **Essexville** Michigan, N USA 43°37´N 83°50´W
101 H22 **Esslingen** *var.* Esslingen am Neckar. Baden-Württemberg, SW Germany 48°45´N 09°19´E
Esslingen am Neckar *see* Esslingen
103 N6 **Essonne** ⬖ *department* N France
Es Suweida *see* As Suwaydā'
79 F16 **Est** *Eng.* East. ⬖ *province* SE Cameroon
104 I1 **Estaca de Bares, Punta da** *point* NW Spain
24 M5 **Estacado, Llano** *plain* New Mexico/Texas, SW USA
63 K25 **Estados, Isla de los** *prev. Eng.* Staten Island. *island* S Argentina
Estado Vargas *see* Vargas
143 P12 **Eşţahbān** Fārs, S Iran
14 F11 **Estaire** Ontario, S Canada 46°19´N 80°47´W
59 P16 **Estância** Sergipe, E Brazil 11°15´S 37°28´W
37 S12 **Estancia** New Mexico, SW USA 34°45´N 106°03´W
104 G7 **Estarreja** Aveiro, N Portugal 40°45´N 08°35´W
102 M17 **Estats, Pic d'** *Sp.* Pico d'Estats. ▲ France/Spain 42°39´N 01°24´E
Estats, Pico d' *see* Estats, Pic d'
83 K23 **Estcourt** KwaZulu/Natal, E South Africa 29°00´S 29°53´E
106 H8 **Este** *anc.* Ateste. Veneto, NE Italy 45°14´N 11°40´E
42 J9 **Estelí** Estelí, NW Nicaragua 13°05´N 86°21´W
42 J9 **Estelí** ⬖ *department* NW Nicaragua
105 Q4 **Estella** *Bas.* Lizarra. Navarra, N Spain 42°41´N 02°02´W
29 R9 **Estelline** South Dakota, N USA 44°34´N 96°54´W
25 P4 **Estelline** Texas, SW USA 34°33´N 100°26´W
104 L14 **Estepa** Andalucía, S Spain 37°17´N 04°52´W
104 L16 **Estepona** Andalucía, S Spain 36°26´N 05°09´W
39 R9 **Ester** Alaska, USA 64°49´N 148°03´W
11 V16 **Esterhazy** Saskatchewan, S Canada 50°40´N 102°02´W
37 S3 **Estes Park** Colorado, C USA 40°22´N 105°31´W
43 Q7 **Este Sudeste, Cayos del** *island* NW Colombia, Caribbean Sea
11 V17 **Estevan** Saskatchewan, S Canada 49°07´N 103°05´W
29 T11 **Estherville** Iowa, C USA 43°24´N 94°49´W
21 R15 **Estill** South Carolina, SE USA 32°45´N 81°14´W
103 Q6 **Estissac** Aube, N France 48°17´N 03°51´E
15 T9 **Est, Lac de l'** ◎ Québec, SE Canada
Estland *see* Estonia
11 S16 **Eston** Saskatchewan, S Canada 51°09´N 108°42´W
118 G5 **Estonia** *off.* Republic of Estonia, *Est.* Eesti Vabariik, *Ger.* Estland, *Latv.* Igaunija; *prev.* Estonian SSR, *Rus.* Estonskaya SSR. ◆ *republic* NE Europe
Estonian SSR *see* Estonia
Estonia, Republic of *see* Estonia
Estonskaya SSR *see* Estonia
104 E11 **Estoril** Lisboa, W Portugal 38°42´N 09°23´W
59 L14 **Estreito** Maranhão, E Brazil 06°34´S 47°22´W
104 I8 **Estrela, Serra da** ▲▲ C Portugal
40 D3 **Estrella, Punta** *headland* NW Mexico 30°53´N 114°45´W
104 F10 **Estremadura** *cultural and historical region* W Portugal
Estremadura *see* Extremadura
104 H11 **Estremoz** Évora, S Portugal 38°50´N 07°35´W
79 D18 **Estuaire** *off.* Province de l'Estuaire, *var.* L'Estuaire. ⬖ *province* NW Gabon
Estuaire, Province de l' *see* Estuaire
Eszék *see* Osijek
111 I22 **Esztergom** *Ger.* Gran; *anc.* Strigonium. Komárom-Esztergom, N Hungary 47°47´N 18°44´E
152 K11 **Etah** Uttar Pradesh, N India 27°33´N 78°39´E
189 R17 **Etal Atoll** *atoll* Mortlock Islands, C Micronesia
99 K24 **Étalle** Luxembourg, SE Belgium 49°41´N 05°36´E
103 N6 **Étampes** Essonne, N France 48°26´N 02°10´E
182 J1 **Etamunbanie, Lake** *salt lake* South Australia
103 N1 **Étaples** Pas-de-Calais, N France 50°31´N 01°39´E
152 K12 **Etāwah** Uttar Pradesh, N India 26°46´N 79°01´E
15 R10 **Etchemin** ~ Québec, SE Canada
Etchmiadzin *see* Vagharshapat
40 G7 **Etchojoa** Sonora, NW Mexico 26°54´N 109°37´W
93 L19 **Etelä-Suomi** ⬖ *province* S Finland
83 B16 **Etengua** Kunene, NW Namibia 17°24´S 13°05´E
99 K25 **Ëthe** Luxembourg, SE Belgium 49°34´N 05°32´E
11 W15 **Ethelbert** Manitoba, S Canada 51°30´N 100°22´W
80 H12 **Ethiopia** *off.* Federal Democratic Republic of Ethiopia; *prev.* Abyssinia, People's Democratic Republic of Ethiopia. ◆ *republic* E Africa
Ethiopia, Federal Democratic Republic of *see* Ethiopia
80 I13 **Ethiopian Highlands** *var.* Ethiopian Plateau. *plateau* N Ethiopia
Ethiopian Plateau *see* Ethiopian Highlands
Ethiopia, People's Democratic Republic of *see* Ethiopia
34 M2 **Etna** California, W USA 41°25´N 122°53´W
18 B14 **Etna** Pennsylvania, NE USA 40°29´N 79°55´W
94 G12 **Etna** ~ S Norway
107 L24 **Etna, Monte** *Eng.* Mount Etna. ⛰ Sicilia, Italy, C Mediterranean Sea 37°46´N 15°00´E
Etna, Mount *see* Etna, Monte

◆ Country ● Country Capital ◇ Dependent Territory ○ Dependent Territory Capital ⬖ Administrative Regions ✈ International Airport ▲ Mountain ▲▲ Mountain Range ⛰ Volcano ~ River ◎ Lake ⊠ Reservoir

Etne – Featherston

95 C15 **Etne** Hordaland, S Norway 59°40′N 05°55′E
Etoliko *see* Aitolikó
39 Y14 **Etolin Island** *island* Alexander Archipelago, Alaska, USA
38 L12 **Etolin Strait** *strait* Alaska, USA
83 C17 **Etosha Pan** *salt lake* N Namibia
79 G18 **Etoumbi** Cuvette Ouest, NW Congo 0°01′N 14°57′E
20 M10 **Etowah** Tennessee, S USA 35°19′N 84°31′W
23 S2 **Etowah River** ♂ Georgia, SE USA
146 B13 **Etrek** *var.* Gyzyletrek, *Rus.* Kizyl-Atrek. Balkan Welaýaty, W Turkmenistan 37°40′N 54°44′E
146 C13 **Etrek** *Per.* Rūd-e Atrak, *Rus.* Atrak, Atrek. ♂ Iran/Turkmenistan
102 L3 **Étretat** Seine-Maritime, N France 49°46′N 00°23′E
114 H9 **Etropole** Sofiya, W Bulgaria 42°50′N 24°00′E
Etsch *see* Adige
Et Tafila *see* Aṭ Ṭafilah
99 M23 **Ettelbrück** Diekirch, C Luxembourg 49°51′N 06°06′E
189 V12 **Etten** *atoll* Chuuk Islands, C Micronesia
99 H14 **Etten-Leur** Noord-Brabant, S Netherlands 51°34′N 04°37′E
76 G7 **Et Tîdra** *var.* Ile Tîdra. *island* Dakhlet Nouâdhibou, NW Mauritania
101 G21 **Ettlingen** Baden-Württemberg, SW Germany 48°57′N 08°25′E
102 M2 **Eu** Seine-Maritime, N France 50°01′N 01°24′E
193 W16 **'Eua** *prev.* Middleburg Island. *island* Tongatapu Group, SE Tonga
193 W15 **Eua Iki** *island* Tongatapu Group, S Tonga
Euboea *see* Évvoia
181 O12 **Eucla** Western Australia 31°41′S 128°51′E
31 U11 **Euclid** Ohio, N USA 41°34′N 81°33′W
27 W14 **Eudora** Arkansas, C USA 33°06′N 91°15′W
27 Q4 **Eudora** Kansas, C USA 38°56′N 95°06′W
182 J9 **Eudunda** South Australia 34°11′S 139°03′E
23 R6 **Eufaula** Alabama, S USA 31°53′N 85°09′W
27 Q11 **Eufaula** Oklahoma, C USA 35°16′N 95°36′W
27 Q11 **Eufaula Lake** *var.* Eufaula Reservoir. ⊠ Oklahoma, C USA
Eufaula Reservoir *see* Eufaula Lake
32 F13 **Eugene** Oregon, NW USA 44°03′N 123°05′W
40 B6 **Eugenia, Punta** *headland* NW Mexico 27°48′N 115°03′W
183 Q8 **Eugowra** New South Wales, SE Australia 33°28′S 148°21′E
104 I2 **Eume** ♂ NW Spain
104 H2 **Eume, Embalse do** ⊠ NW Spain
Eumolpias *see* Plovdiv
59 O18 **Eunápolis** Bahia, SE Brazil 16°20′S 39°36′W
22 H8 **Eunice** Louisiana, S USA 30°29′N 92°25′W
37 W15 **Eunice** New Mexico, SW USA 32°26′N 103°09′W
99 M19 **Eupen** Liège, E Belgium 50°38′N 06°02′E
130 B10 **Euphrates** *Ar.* Al-Furāt, *Turk.* Firat Nehri. ♂ SW Asia
138 L3 **Euphrates Dam** *dam* N Syria
22 M4 **Eupora** Mississippi, S USA 33°32′N 89°16′W
93 K19 **Eura** Länsi-Suomi, SW Finland 61°07′N 22°12′E
93 K19 **Eurajoki** Länsi-Suomi, SW Finland 61°13′N 21°45′E
0-1 **Eurasian Plate** *tectonic feature*
102 L4 **Eure** ◆ *department* N France
102 M4 **Eure** ♂ N France
102 M6 **Eure-et-Loir** ◆ *department* C France
34 K3 **Eureka** California, W USA 40°47′N 124°12′W
27 P6 **Eureka** Kansas, C USA 37°51′N 96°17′W
33 O6 **Eureka** Montana, NW USA 48°52′N 115°03′W
35 V5 **Eureka** Nevada, W USA 39°31′N 115°58′W
29 O7 **Eureka** South Dakota, N USA 45°46′N 99°37′W
36 L4 **Eureka** Utah, W USA 39°57′N 112°07′W
32 K10 **Eureka** Washington, NW USA 46°21′N 118°41′W
27 S9 **Eureka Springs** Arkansas, C USA 36°25′N 93°45′W
182 K6 **Eurinilla Creek** *seasonal river* South Australia
183 O11 **Euroa** Victoria, SE Australia 36°46′S 145°35′E
172 M9 **Europa, Île** *island* W Madagascar
104 L3 **Europa, Picos de** ▲ N Spain
104 L16 **Europa Point** *headland* S Gibraltar 36°07′N 05°20′W
84-85 **Europe** *continent*
98 F12 **Europoort** Zuid-Holland, W Netherlands 51°59′N 04°08′E
Euskadi *see* País Vasco
101 D17 **Euskirchen** Nordrhein-Westfalen, W Germany 50°40′N 06°47′E
23 W11 **Eustis** Florida, SE USA 28°51′N 81°41′W
182 M9 **Euston** New South Wales, SE Australia 34°34′S 142°45′E
23 N5 **Eutaw** Alabama, S USA 32°50′N 87°53′W
100 K8 **Eutin** Schleswig-Holstein, N Germany 54°08′N 10°38′E
10 K14 **Eutsuk Lake** ⊠ British Columbia, SW Canada
Euxine Sea *see* Black Sea
83 C16 **Evale** Cunene, SW Angola 16°36′S 15°46′E
37 T3 **Evans** Colorado, C USA 40°22′N 104°41′W
11 P14 **Evansburg** Alberta, SW Canada 53°34′N 114°57′W
29 X13 **Evansdale** Iowa, C USA 42°28′N 92°16′W
183 V4 **Evans Head** New South Wales, SE Australia 29°07′S 153°27′E
12 J11 **Evans, Lac** ◎ Québec, SE Canada
37 S5 **Evans, Mount** ▲ Colorado, C USA 39°15′N 106°10′W
9 Q6 **Evans Strait** *strait* Nunavut, N Canada
31 N10 **Evanston** Illinois, N USA 42°02′N 87°41′W
33 S17 **Evanston** Wyoming, C USA 41°16′N 110°57′W
14 D11 **Evansville** Manitoulin Island, Ontario, S Canada 45°48′N 82°34′W
31 N16 **Evansville** Indiana, N USA 37°58′N 87°33′W
30 L9 **Evansville** Wisconsin, N USA 42°46′N 89°16′W
25 S8 **Evant** Texas, SW USA 31°28′N 98°09′W
143 P13 **Evaz** Fārs, S Iran 27°48′N 53°58′E
29 W4 **Eveleth** Minnesota, N USA 47°27′N 92°32′W
182 E3 **Evelyn Creek** *seasonal river* South Australia
181 Q2 **Evelyn, Mount** ▲ Northern Territory, N Australia 13°28′S 132°50′E
122 K10 **Evenkiyskiy Avtonomnyy Okrug** ◆ *autonomous district* Krasnoyarskiy Kray, N Russian Federation
183 R13 **Everard, Cape** *headland* Victoria, SE Australia 37°48′S 149°21′E
182 F6 **Everard, Lake** *salt lake* South Australia
182 C2 **Everard Ranges** ▲ South Australia
153 R11 **Everest, Mount** *Chin.* Qomolangma Feng, *Nep.* Sagarmāthā. ▲ China/Nepal 27°59′N 86°57′E
18 E15 **Everett** Pennsylvania, NE USA 40°00′N 78°22′W
32 H7 **Everett** Washington, NW USA 47°59′N 122°12′W
99 E17 **Evergem** Oost-Vlaanderen, NW Belgium 51°07′N 03°43′E
23 X16 **Everglades City** Florida, SE USA 25°51′N 81°22′W
23 Y16 **Everglades, The** *wetland* Florida, SE USA
23 P7 **Evergreen** Alabama, S USA 31°25′N 86°55′W
37 T4 **Evergreen** Colorado, C USA 39°37′N 105°19′W
Evergreen State *see* Washington
97 L21 **Evesham** C England, United Kingdom 52°06′N 01°57′W
103 T10 **Évian-les-Bains** Haute-Savoie, E France 46°22′N 06°34′E
93 K16 **Evijärvi** Länsi-Suomi, W Finland 63°22′N 23°30′E
79 D17 **Evinayong** *var.* Ebinayon, Evinayoung. C Equatorial Guinea 01°28′N 10°17′E
Evinayoung *see* Evinayong
115 E18 **Évinos** ♂ C Greece
95 E17 **Evje** Aust-Agder, S Norway 58°35′N 07°49′E
Evmolpia *see* Plovdiv
104 H11 **Évora** *anc.* Ebora, *Lat.* Liberalitas Julia. Évora, C Portugal 38°34′N 07°54′W
104 G11 **Évora** ◆ *district* S Portugal
102 M4 **Évreux** *anc.* Civitas Eburovicum. Eure, N France 49°02′N 01°10′E
102 K6 **Évron** Mayenne, NW France 48°10′N 00°24′W
114 L13 **Évros** *Bul.* Maritsa, *Turk.* Meriç; *anc.* Hebrus. ♂ SE Europe *see also* Maritsa/Meriç
Évros *see* Meriç
Évros *see* Maritsa
115 F21 **Evrótas** ♂ S Greece
103 O5 **Évry** Essonne, N France 48°38′N 02°34′E
25 O8 **E. V. Spence Reservoir** ⊠ Texas, SW USA
115 I18 **Évvoia** *Lat.* Euboea. *island* C Greece
38 D9 **'Ewa Beach** *var.* Ewa Beach. O'ahu, Hawaii, USA, C Pacific Ocean 21°19′N 158°00′W
Ewa Beach *see* 'Ewa Beach
32 L9 **Ewan** Washington, NW USA 47°06′N 117°46′W
44 K12 **Ewarton** C Jamaica 18°11′N 77°06′W
81 J18 **Ewaso Ng'iro** *var.* Nyiro. ♂ C Kenya
29 P13 **Ewing** Nebraska, C USA 42°13′N 98°20′W
194 J5 **Ewing Island** *island* Antarctica
65 P17 **Ewing Seamount** *undersea feature* E Atlantic Ocean 23°20′S 08°45′E
158 L6 **Ewirgol** Xinjiang Uygur Zizhiqu, W China 42°56′N 87°39′E
79 G19 **Ewo** Cuvette, W Congo 0°55′S 14°49′E
27 S3 **Excelsior Springs** Missouri, C USA 39°20′N 94°13′W
97 J23 **Exe** ♂ SW England, United Kingdom
194 L12 **Executive Committee Range** ▲ Antarctica
14 E16 **Exeter** Ontario, S Canada 43°19′N 81°26′W
97 J24 **Exeter** *anc.* Isca Damnoniorum. SW England, United Kingdom 50°43′N 03°31′W
35 R11 **Exeter** California, W USA 36°17′N 119°08′W
19 P10 **Exeter** New Hampshire, NE USA 42°57′N 70°55′W
Exin *see* Kcynia
29 T14 **Exira** Iowa, C USA 41°36′N 94°55′W
97 J23 **Exmoor** *moorland* SW England, United Kingdom
21 Y6 **Exmore** Virginia, NE USA 37°31′N 75°48′W
180 G8 **Exmouth** Western Australia 22°01′S 114°06′E
97 J24 **Exmouth** SW England, United Kingdom 50°36′N 03°25′W
180 G8 **Exmouth Gulf** *gulf* Western Australia
173 V8 **Exmouth Plateau** *undersea feature* E Indian Ocean
115 J20 **Exompourgo** *ancient monument* Tínos, Kykládes, Greece, Aegean Sea
104 I10 **Extremadura** *var.* Estremadura. ◆ *autonomous community* W Spain
78 F12 **Extrême-Nord** *Eng.* Extreme North. ◆ *province* N Cameroon
Extreme North *see* Extrême-Nord
44 I3 **Exuma Cays** *islets* C Bahamas
44 I3 **Exuma Sound** *sound* C Bahamas
81 H20 **Eyasi, Lake** ◎ N Tanzania
95 F17 **Eydehavn** Aust-Agder, S Norway 58°31′N 08°53′E
96 L12 **Eyemouth** SE Scotland, United Kingdom 55°52′N 02°07′W
96 G7 **Eye Peninsula** *peninsula* NW Scotland, United Kingdom
80 Q13 **Eyl** *It.* Eil. Nugaal, E Somalia 08°03′N 49°49′E
103 N11 **Eymoutiers** Haute-Vienne, C France 45°45′N 01°43′E
Eyo (lower course) *see* Uolo, Río
29 X10 **Eyota** Minnesota, N USA 44°00′N 92°13′W
182 H2 **Eyre Basin, Lake** *salt lake* South Australia
182 I1 **Eyre Creek** *seasonal river* South Australia
174 L9 **Eyre, Lake** *salt lake* South Australia
185 C22 **Eyre Mountains** ▲ South Island, New Zealand
182 H3 **Eyre North, Lake** *salt lake* South Australia
182 G7 **Eyre Peninsula** *peninsula* South Australia
182 H4 **Eyre South, Lake** *salt lake* South Australia
95 B18 **Eysturoy** *Dan.* Østerø. *island* N Faeroe Islands
142 J7 **Eyvān** Īlām, W Iran 33°51′N 46°18′E
61 D20 **Ezeiza** ✈ (Buenos Aires) Buenos Aires, E Argentina 34°49′S 58°30′W
Ezeres *see* Ezeriş
116 F12 **Ezeriş** *Hung.* Ezeres. Caraş-Severin, W Romania 45°21′N 21°55′E
161 O9 **Ezhou** *prev.* Echeng. Hubei, C China 30°23′N 114°52′E
125 R11 **Ezhva** Respublika Komi, NW Russian Federation 61°45′N 50°43′E
136 B12 **Ezine** Çanakkale, NW Turkey 39°46′N 26°20′E
Ezo *see* Hokkaidō
Ezra/Ezraa *see* Izra'

F

191 P7 **Faaa** Tahiti, W French Polynesia 17°32′S 149°36′W
191 P7 **Faaa** ✈ (Papeete) Tahiti, W French Polynesia 17°31′S 149°36′W
95 H24 **Faaborg** *var.* Fåborg. Fyn, C Denmark 55°06′N 10°10′E
151 K19 **Faadhippolhu Atoll** *var.* Fadiffolu, Lhaviyani Atoll. *atoll* N Maldives
191 U10 **Faaite** *atoll* Îles Tuamotu, C French Polynesia
191 Q8 **Faaone** Tahiti, W French Polynesia 17°39′S 149°18′W
24 H8 **Fabens** Texas, SW USA 31°30′N 106°09′W
94 H12 **Fåberg** Oppland, S Norway 61°15′N 10°21′E
Fåborg *see* Faaborg
106 I12 **Fabriano** Marche, C Italy 43°20′N 12°54′E
145 U16 **Fabrichnyy** Almaty, SE Kazakhstan 43°12′N 76°19′E
54 F10 **Facatativá** Cundinamarca, C Colombia 04°49′N 74°22′W
77 X9 **Fachi** Agadez, C Niger 18°01′N 11°36′E
188 B16 **Facpi Point** *headland* W Guam
18 I13 **Factoryville** Pennsylvania, NE USA 41°34′N 75°45′W
78 K8 **Fada** Borkou-Ennedi-Tibesti, E Chad 17°14′N 21°32′E
77 Q13 **Fada-Ngourma** E Burkina 12°05′N 00°26′E
123 N6 **Faddeya, Zaliv** *bay* N Russian Federation
123 Q5 **Faddeyevskiy, Ostrov** *island* Novosibirskiye Ostrova, NE Russian Federation
141 W12 **Fadhī** S Oman 17°54′N 55°30′E
Fadiffolu *see* Faadhippolhu Atoll
106 H10 **Faenza** *anc.* Faventia. Emilia-Romagna, N Italy 44°17′N 11°53′E
64 M5 **Faeroe-Iceland Ridge** *undersea feature* NW Norwegian Sea 64°00′N 10°00′W
64 M5 **Faeroe Islands** *Dan.* Færøerne, *Faer.* Føroyar. ◇ Danish external territory N Atlantic Ocean
86 C8 **Faeroe Islands** *island group* N Atlantic Ocean
Færøerne *see* Faeroe Islands
64 N6 **Faeroe-Shetland Trough** *undersea feature* NE Atlantic Ocean
104 H6 **Fafe** Braga, N Portugal 41°27′N 08°11′W
80 K13 **Fafen Shet'** ♂ E Ethiopia
193 V15 **Fafo** *island* Tongatapu Group, S Tonga
192 I16 **Fagaloa Bay** *bay* Upolu, E Samoa
192 H15 **Fagamālo** Savai'i, N Samoa 13°27′S 172°22′W
116 I12 **Făgăraş** *Ger.* Fogarasch, *Hung.* Fogaras. Braşov, C Romania 45°50′N 24°59′E
95 M20 **Fagerhult** Kalmar, S Sweden 57°07′N 15°40′E
94 G13 **Fagernes** Oppland, S Norway 60°59′N 09°14′E
92 I9 **Fagernes** Troms, N Norway 69°31′N 19°16′E
95 M14 **Fagersta** Västmanland, C Sweden 59°59′N 15°49′E
77 W13 **Faggo** *var.* Foggo. Bauchi, N Nigeria 11°22′N 09°55′E
Faghman *see* Fughmah
Fagibina, Lake *see* Faguibine, Lac
63 J25 **Fagnano, Lago** ◎ S Argentina
99 G22 **Fagne** *hill range* S Belgium
77 N10 **Faguibine, Lac** *var.* Lake Fagibina. ◎ NW Mali
Fahaheel *see* Al Fuḩayḩīl
Fahlun *see* Falun
143 U12 **Fahraj** Kermān, SE Iran 29°00′N 59°00′E
64 P5 **Faial** Madeira, Portugal, NE Atlantic Ocean 32°47′N 16°53′W
64 N2 **Faial** *var.* Ilha do Faial. *island* Azores, Portugal, NE Atlantic Ocean
Faial, Ilha do *see* Faial
108 G10 **Faido** Ticino, S Switzerland 46°30′N 08°48′E
Faifo *see* Hôi An
Failaka Island *see* Faylakah
190 G12 **Faioa, Île** *island* N Wallis and Futuna
181 W8 **Fairbairn Reservoir** ⊠ Queensland, E Australia
39 R9 **Fairbanks** Alaska, USA 64°48′N 147°47′W
21 U12 **Fair Bluff** North Carolina, SE USA 34°18′N 79°02′W
31 R14 **Fairborn** Ohio, N USA 39°48′N 84°03′W
23 S3 **Fairburn** Georgia, SE USA 33°34′N 84°34′W
30 M12 **Fairbury** Illinois, N USA 40°45′N 88°30′W
29 Q17 **Fairbury** Nebraska, C USA 40°08′N 97°10′W
29 T9 **Fairfax** Minnesota, N USA 44°31′N 94°43′W
27 O8 **Fairfax** Oklahoma, C USA 36°34′N 96°42′W
21 R14 **Fairfax** South Carolina, SE USA 32°57′N 81°14′W
35 N8 **Fairfield** California, W USA 38°14′N 122°03′W
33 O14 **Fairfield** Idaho, NW USA 43°20′N 114°45′W
30 M16 **Fairfield** Illinois, N USA 38°22′N 88°23′W
29 X15 **Fairfield** Iowa, C USA 41°00′N 91°57′W
33 R8 **Fairfield** Montana, NW USA 47°36′N 111°59′W
31 Q14 **Fairfield** Ohio, N USA 39°21′N 84°34′W
25 U8 **Fairfield** Texas, SW USA 31°43′N 96°10′W
27 T7 **Fair Grove** Missouri, C USA 37°22′N 93°09′W
19 P12 **Fairhaven** Massachusetts, NE USA 41°38′N 70°51′W
23 N8 **Fairhope** Alabama, S USA 30°31′N 87°54′W
96 L4 **Fair Isle** *island* NE Scotland, United Kingdom
185 F20 **Fairlie** Canterbury, South Island, New Zealand 44°06′S 170°50′E
29 U11 **Fairmont** Minnesota, N USA 43°40′N 94°27′W
29 Q16 **Fairmont** Nebraska, C USA 40°37′N 97°36′W
21 S3 **Fairmont** West Virginia, NE USA 39°28′N 80°08′W
31 P13 **Fairmount** Indiana, N USA 40°25′N 85°39′W
18 H10 **Fairmount** New York, NE USA 43°03′N 76°14′W
29 R7 **Fairmount** North Dakota, N USA 46°02′N 96°36′W
37 S5 **Fairplay** Colorado, C USA 39°13′N 106°00′W
18 F9 **Fairport** New York, NE USA 43°06′N 77°26′W
11 O12 **Fairview** Alberta, W Canada 56°03′N 118°28′W
26 L9 **Fairview** Oklahoma, C USA 36°16′N 98°29′W
36 L4 **Fairview** Utah, W USA 39°37′N 111°26′W
35 T6 **Fairview Peak** ▲ Nevada, W USA 39°13′N 118°09′W
188 H14 **Fais** *atoll* Caroline Islands, W Micronesia
149 U8 **Faisalābād** *prev.* Lyallpur. Punjab, NE Pakistan 31°26′N 73°06′E
Faisaliya *see* Fayşaliyah
28 L8 **Faith** South Dakota, N USA 45°01′N 102°02′W
153 N12 **Faizābād** Uttar Pradesh, N India 26°46′N 82°08′E
Faizabad/Faizābād *see* Feyẕābād
45 S9 **Fajardo** E Puerto Rico 18°20′N 65°39′W
139 R9 **Fajj, Wādī al** *dry watercourse* S Iraq
140 K4 **Fajr, Bi'r** *well* NW Saudi Arabia
191 W10 **Fakahina** *atoll* Îles Tuamotu, C French Polynesia
190 L10 **Fakaofo Atoll** *island* SE Tokelau
191 U10 **Fakarava** *atoll* Îles Tuamotu, C French Polynesia
127 T2 **Fakel** Udmurtskaya Respublika, NW Russian Federation 57°35′N 53°00′E
97 P19 **Fakenham** E England, United Kingdom 52°50′N 00°51′E
171 U13 **Fakfak** Papua, E Indonesia 02°55′S 132°17′E
153 T12 **Fakirāgrām** Assam, NE India 26°22′N 90°15′E
114 M10 **Fakiyska Reka** ♂ SE Bulgaria
95 J24 **Fakse** Storstrøm, SE Denmark 55°16′N 12°08′E
95 J24 **Fakse Bugt** *bay* SE Denmark
95 J24 **Fakse Ladeplads** Storstrøm, SE Denmark 55°14′N 12°11′E
163 V11 **Faku** Liaoning, NE China 42°30′N 123°27′E
76 J14 **Falaba** N Sierra Leone 09°54′N 11°22′W
102 K5 **Falaise** Calvados, N France 48°52′N 00°12′W
114 H12 **Falakró** ▲ NE Greece
189 T12 **Falalu** *island* Chuuk, C Micronesia
166 L4 **Falam** Chin State, W Burma 22°58′N 93°45′E
143 N8 **Falāvarjān** Eşfahān, C Iran 32°33′N 51°28′E
116 M11 **Fălciu** Vaslui, E Romania 46°19′N 28°10′E
54 I4 **Falcón** *off.* Estado Falcón. ◆ *state* NW Venezuela
106 J12 **Falconara Marittima** Marche, C Italy 43°37′N 13°23′E
Falcone, Capo del *see* Falcone, Punta del
107 A16 **Falcone, Punta del** *var.* Capo del Falcone. *headland* Sardegna, Italy, C Mediterranean Sea 40°57′N 8°12′E
Falcón, Estado *see* Falcón
11 Y16 **Falcon Lake** Manitoba, S Canada 49°44′N 95°18′W
Falcon Lake *see* Falcón, Presa/Falcon Reservoir
41 O7 **Falcón, Presa** *var.* Falcon Lake, Falcon Reservoir. ⊠ Mexico/USA *see also* Falcon Reservoir
Falcón, Presa *see* Falcon Reservoir
25 Q16 **Falcon Reservoir** *var.* Falcon Lake, Presa Falcón. ⊠ Mexico/USA *see also* Falcón, Presa
Falcon Reservoir *see* Falcón, Presa
190 L10 **Fale** *island* Fakaofo Atoll, SE Tokelau
192 F15 **Faleālupo** Savai'i, NW Samoa 13°30′S 172°46′W
190 B10 **Falefatu** *island* Funafuti Atoll, C Tuvalu
192 G15 **Fālelima** Savai'i, NW Samoa 13°30′S 172°41′W
95 N18 **Falerum** Östergötland, S Sweden 58°07′N 16°15′E
Faleshty *see* Făleşti
116 M9 **Făleşti** *Rus.* Faleshty. NW Moldova 47°33′N 27°43′E
25 S15 **Falfurrias** Texas, SW USA 27°17′N 98°10′W
11 O13 **Falher** Alberta, W Canada 55°45′N 117°18′W
Falkenau an der Eger *see* Sokolov
95 J21 **Falkenberg** Halland, S Sweden 56°55′N 12°30′E
Falkenberg *see* Niemodlin
Falkenburg in Pommern *see* Złocieniec
100 N12 **Falkensee** Brandenburg, NE Germany 52°34′N 13°04′E
96 J12 **Falkirk** C Scotland, United Kingdom 56°N 03°48′W
65 I20 **Falkland Escarpment** *undersea feature* SW Atlantic Ocean 50°00′S 45°00′W
63 K24 **Falkland Islands** *var.* Falklands, Islas Malvinas. ◇ *UK dependent territory* SW Atlantic Ocean
47 W14 **Falkland Islands** *island group* SW Atlantic Ocean
65 I20 **Falkland Plateau** *var.* Argentine Rise. *undersea feature* SW Atlantic Ocean 51°00′S 50°00′W
Falklands *see* Falkland Islands
63 M23 **Falkland Sound** *var.* Estrecho de San Carlos. *strait* C Falkland Islands
Falknov nad Ohří *see* Sokolov
115 H21 **Falkonéra** *island* S Greece
95 K18 **Falköping** Västra Götaland, S Sweden 58°10′N 13°31′E
139 U8 **Fallāḩ** Wāsiţ, E Iraq 32°58′N 45°09′E
35 U16 **Fallbrook** California, W USA 33°22′N 117°15′W
189 U12 **Falleallej Pass** *passage* Chuuk Islands, C Micronesia
93 J14 **Fällfors** Västerbotten, N Sweden 65°07′N 20°46′E
194 I6 **Fallières Coast** *physical region* Antarctica
100 I11 **Fallingbostel** Niedersachsen, NW Germany 52°52′N 09°42′E
33 X9 **Fallon** Montana, NW USA 46°49′N 105°07′W
35 S5 **Fallon** Nevada, W USA 39°29′N 118°47′W
19 O12 **Fall River** Massachusetts, NE USA 41°42′N 71°09′W
27 P6 **Fall River Lake** ⊠ Kansas, C USA
35 O3 **Fall River Mills** California, W USA 41°00′N 121°28′W
21 W4 **Falls Church** Virginia, NE USA 38°53′N 77°11′W
29 S17 **Falls City** Nebraska, C USA 40°03′N 95°36′W
25 S12 **Falls City** Texas, SW USA 28°58′N 98°01′W
Falluja *see* Al Fallūjah
77 S12 **Falmey** Dosso, SW Niger 12°29′N 02°58′E
45 W10 **Falmouth** Antigua, Antigua and Barbuda 17°02′N 61°47′W
44 J11 **Falmouth** W Jamaica 18°28′N 77°39′W
97 H25 **Falmouth** SW England, United Kingdom 50°08′N 05°04′W
20 M4 **Falmouth** Kentucky, S USA 38°40′N 84°20′W
19 P13 **Falmouth** Massachusetts, NE USA 41°31′N 70°36′W
21 W5 **Falmouth** Virginia, NE USA 38°19′N 77°28′W
189 U12 **Falos** *island* Chuuk, C Micronesia
83 E26 **False Bay** *Afr.* Valsbaai. *bay* SW South Africa
155 K17 **False Divi Point** *headland* E India 15°46′N 80°43′E
38 M16 **False Pass** Unimak Island, Alaska, USA 54°52′N 163°15′W
154 P12 **False Point** *headland* E India 20°23′N 86°52′E
105 U6 **Falset** Cataluña, NE Spain 41°08′N 00°49′E
95 I25 **Falster** *island* SE Denmark
116 K9 **Fălticeni** *Hung.* Falticsén. Suceava, NE Romania 47°27′N 26°20′E
Falticsén *see* Fălticeni
94 M13 **Falun** *var.* Fahlun. Kopparberg, C Sweden 60°36′N 15°36′E
Famagusta *see* Gazimağusa
Famagusta Bay *see* Gazimağusa Körfezi
62 I8 **Famatina** La Rioja, NW Argentina 28°58′S 67°46′W
99 J21 **Famenne** *physical region* SE Belgium
113 D22 **Fan** *var.* Fani. ♂ N Albania
77 X15 **Fan** ♂ E Nigeria
76 M12 **Fana** Koulikoro, SW Mali 12°45′N 06°55′W
115 K19 **Fána** *ancient harbour* Chíos, SE Greece
189 V13 **Fanan** *island* Chuuk, C Micronesia
189 U12 **Fanapanges** *island* Chuuk, C Micronesia
115 L20 **Fanári, Akrotírio** *headland* Ikaría, Dodekánisa, Greece, Aegean Sea 37°40′N 26°21′E
45 Q13 **Fancy** Saint Vincent, Saint Vincent and the Grenadines 13°22′N 61°10′W
172 I5 **Fandriana** Fianarantsoa, SE Madagascar 20°14′S 47°21′E
167 O6 **Fang** Chiang Mai, NW Thailand 19°56′N 99°14′E
80 E13 **Fangak** Jonglei, SE Sudan 09°05′N 30°52′E
191 W10 **Fangatau** *atoll* Îles Tuamotu, C French Polynesia
191 X12 **Fangataufa** *island* Îles Tuamotu, SE French Polynesia
193 V15 **Fanga Uta** *bay* S Tonga
161 N7 **Fangcheng** Henan, C China 33°18′N 113°03′E
Fangcheng *see* Fangchenggang
160 K15 **Fangchenggang** *var.* Fangcheng Gezu Zizhixian; *prev.* Fangcheng. Guangxi Zhuangzu Zizhiqu, S China 21°49′N 108°21′E
Fangcheng Gezu Zizhixian *see* Fangchenggang
161 S15 **Fangshan** S Taiwan 22°19′N 120°41′E
163 X8 **Fangzheng** Heilongjiang, NE China 45°50′N 128°50′E
Fani *see* Fan
119 K16 **Fanipal'** *Rus.* Fanipol'. Minskaya Voblasts', C Belarus 53°45′N 27°20′E
Fanipol' *see* Fanipal'
25 T13 **Fannin** Texas, SW USA 28°41′N 97°13′W
Fanning Island *see* Tabuaeran
94 G8 **Fannrem** Sør-Trøndelag, S Norway 63°16′N 09°48′E
106 I11 **Fano** *anc.* Colonia Julia Fanestris, Fanum Fortunae. Marche, C Italy 43°50′N 13°E
95 E23 **Fanø** *island* W Denmark
167 R5 **Fan Si Pan** ▲ N Vietnam 22°18′N 103°36′E
Fanum Fortunae *see* Fano
Fao *see* Al Fāw
141 W7 **Faq'** *var.* Al Faqa. Dubayy, E United Arab Emirates 24°42′N 55°37′E
Farab *see* Farap
185 G16 **Faraday, Mount** ▲ South Island, New Zealand 42°01′S 171°37′E
79 P16 **Faradje** Orientale, NE Dem. Rep. Congo 03°45′N 29°43′E
Faradofay *see* Tôlañaro
172 I7 **Farafangana** Fianarantsoa, SE Madagascar 22°50′S 47°50′E
148 J7 **Farāh** *var.* Farah, Fararud. Farāh, W Afghanistan 32°22′N 62°07′E
148 K7 **Farāh** ◆ *province* W Afghanistan
148 J7 **Farāh Rūd** ♂ W Afghanistan
188 K7 **Farallon de Medinilla** *island* C Northern Mariana Islands
188 J2 **Farallon de Pajaros** *var.* Uracas. *island* N Northern Mariana Islands
76 J14 **Faranah** Haute-Guinée, S Guinea 10°02′N 10°44′W
146 K12 **Farap** *Rus.* Farab. Lebap Welaýaty, NE Turkmenistan 39°15′N 63°32′E
Fararud *see* Farāh
140 M13 **Farasān, Jazā'ir** *island group* SW Saudi Arabia
172 I5 **Faratsiho** Antananarivo, C Madagascar 19°24′S 46°57′E
188 K15 **Faraulep Atoll** *atoll* Caroline Islands, C Micronesia
99 H20 **Farciennes** Hainaut, S Belgium 50°26′N 04°33′E
105 O14 **Fardes** ♂ S Spain
191 S10 **Fare** Huahine, W French Polynesia 16°42′S 151°01′W
97 M23 **Fareham** S England, United Kingdom 50°51′N 01°10′W
39 P11 **Farewell** Alaska, USA 62°35′N 153°59′W
184 H13 **Farewell, Cape** *headland* South Island, New Zealand 40°30′S 172°39′E
Farewell, Cape *see* Nunap Isua
184 I13 **Farewell Spit** *spit* South Island, New Zealand
95 I17 **Färgelanda** Västra Götaland, S Sweden 58°34′N 11°59′E
Farghona, Wodii/ Farghona Valley *see* Fergana Valley
Farghona Wodiysi *see* Fergana Valley
23 V8 **Fargo** Georgia, SE USA 30°42′N 82°33′W
29 R5 **Fargo** North Dakota, N USA 46°53′N 96°47′W
147 S10 **Farg'ona** *Rus.* Fergana; *prev.* Novyy Margilan. Farg'ona Viloyati, E Uzbekistan 40°28′N 71°44′E
147 R10 **Farg'ona Viloyati** *Rus.* Ferganskaya Oblast'. ◆ *province* E Uzbekistan
29 V10 **Faribault** Minnesota, N USA 44°18′N 93°16′W
152 J11 **Farīdābād** Haryāna, N India 28°26′N 77°19′E
152 H8 **Farīdkot** Punjab, NW India 30°42′N 74°47′E
153 T15 **Faridpur** Dhaka, C Bangladesh 23°29′N 89°50′E
121 P14 **Fārigh, Wādī al** ♂ N Libya
172 I4 **Farihy Alaotra** ◎ C Madagascar
94 M11 **Färila** Gävleborg, C Sweden 61°48′N 15°55′E
104 E9 **Farilhões** *island* C Portugal
76 G12 **Farim** NW Guinea-Bissau 12°30′N 15°09′W
Farish *see* Forish
141 T11 **Fāris, Qalamat** *well* SE Saudi Arabia
95 N21 **Färjestaden** Kalmar, S Sweden 56°38′N 16°30′E
149 R2 **Farkhār** Takhār, NE Afghanistan 36°39′N 69°43′E
147 Q14 **Farkhor** *Rus.* Parkhar. SW Tajikistan 37°32′N 69°22′E
116 F12 **Fârliug** *prev.* Fîrliug, *Hung.* Furluk. Caraş-Severin, SW Romania 45°21′N 21°55′E
115 M21 **Farmakonísi** *island* Dodekánisa, Greece, Aegean Sea
30 M13 **Farmer City** Illinois, N USA 40°14′N 88°38′W
31 N14 **Farmersburg** Indiana, N USA 39°14′N 87°21′W
25 U6 **Farmersville** Texas, SW USA 33°09′N 96°21′W
22 H5 **Farmerville** Louisiana, S USA 32°46′N 92°24′W
29 X16 **Farmington** Iowa, C USA 40°37′N 91°43′W
19 Q6 **Farmington** Maine, NE USA 44°40′N 70°09′W
29 V9 **Farmington** Minnesota, N USA 44°39′N 93°09′W
27 X6 **Farmington** Missouri, C USA 37°46′N 90°26′W
19 O9 **Farmington** New Hampshire, NE USA 43°23′N 71°04′W
37 P9 **Farmington** New Mexico, SW USA 36°44′N 108°13′W
36 L2 **Farmington** Utah, W USA 40°58′N 111°53′W
21 W9 **Farmville** North Carolina, SE USA 35°37′N 77°36′W
21 U6 **Farmville** Virginia, NE USA 37°17′N 78°25′W
97 N22 **Farnborough** S England, United Kingdom 51°17′N 00°46′W
97 N22 **Farnham** S England, United Kingdom 51°13′N 00°49′W
10 J7 **Faro** Yukon Territory, W Canada 62°15′N 133°30′W
104 G14 **Faro** Faro, S Portugal 37°01′N 07°56′W
95 Q18 **Fårö** Gotland, SE Sweden 57°55′N 19°10′E
104 G14 **Faro** ◆ *district* S Portugal
78 F13 **Faro** ♂ Cameroon/Nigeria
104 G14 **Faro** ✈ Faro, S Portugal 37°02′N 08°01′W
Faro, Punta del *see* Peloro, Capo
95 Q18 **Fårösund** Gotland, SE Sweden 57°51′N 19°02′E
173 N7 **Farquhar Group** *island group* S Seychelles
18 B13 **Farrell** Pennsylvania, NE USA 41°12′N 80°28′W
152 K11 **Farrukhābād** Uttar Pradesh, N India 27°24′N 79°34′E
143 P11 **Fārs** *off.* Ostān-e Fārs; *anc.* Persis. ◆ *province* S Iran
115 F16 **Fársala** Thessalía, C Greece 39°17′N 22°23′E
143 R4 **Fārsīān** Golestān, N Iran
Fars, Khalīj-e *see* Gulf, The
95 G21 **Farsø** Nordjylland, N Denmark 56°47′N 09°21′E
Fārs, Ostān-e *see* Fārs
95 D18 **Farsund** Vest-Agder, S Norway 58°05′N 06°49′E
141 U14 **Fartak, Ra's** *headland* E Yemen 15°34′N 52°19′E
60 H13 **Fartura, Serra da** ▲ S Brazil
Farvel, Kap *see* Nunap Isua
24 L4 **Farwell** Texas, SW USA 34°23′N 103°03′W
194 I9 **Farwell Island** *island* Antarctica
152 L9 **Far Western** ◆ *zone* W Nepal
148 M3 **Fāryāb** ◆ *province* N Afghanistan
143 P12 **Fasā** Fārs, S Iran 28°55′N 53°39′E
141 U12 **Fasad, Ramlat** *desert* SW Oman
107 P17 **Fasano** Puglia, SE Italy 40°50′N 17°21′E
92 L3 **Fáskrúdhsfjördhur** Austurland, E Iceland 64°55′N 14°01′W
117 O5 **Fastiv** *Rus.* Fastov. Kyyivs'ka Oblast', NW Ukraine 50°08′N 29°59′E
97 B22 **Fastnet Rock** *Ir.* Carraig Aonair. *island* SW Ireland
Fastov *see* Fastiv
190 C9 **Fatato** *island* Funafuti Atoll, C Tuvalu
152 H10 **Fatehābād** Haryāna, N India 29°31′N 75°27′E
152 K12 **Fatehgarh** Uttar Pradesh, N India 27°22′N 79°38′E
149 U6 **Fatehjang** Punjab, E Pakistan 33°33′N 72°43′E
152 G11 **Fatehpur** Rājasthān, N India 27°59′N 74°58′E
152 L13 **Fatehpur** Uttar Pradesh, N India 25°56′N 80°55′E
126 J7 **Fatezh** Kurskaya Oblast', W Russian Federation 52°01′N 35°51′E
76 G11 **Fatick** W Senegal 14°19′N 16°27′W
104 G9 **Fátima** Santarém, W Portugal 39°37′N 08°39′W
136 M11 **Fatsa** Ordu, N Turkey 41°02′N 37°31′E
Fatshan *see* Foshan
190 D12 **Fatua, Pointe** *var.* Pointe Nord. *headland* Île Futuna, S Wallis and Futuna
191 X7 **Fatu Hiva** *island* Îles Marquises, NE French Polynesia
Fatunda *see* Fatundu
79 H21 **Fatundu** *var.* Fatunda. Bandundu, W Dem. Rep. Congo 04°08′S 17°13′E
29 O8 **Faulkton** South Dakota, N USA 45°02′N 99°07′W
116 L13 **Făurei** *prev.* Filimon Sîrbu. Brăila, SE Romania 45°05′N 27°15′E
92 G12 **Fauske** Nordland, C Norway 67°15′N 15°27′E
11 P13 **Faust** Alberta, W Canada 55°19′N 115°33′W
99 L23 **Fauvillers** Luxembourg, SE Belgium 49°52′N 05°40′E
107 J24 **Favara** Sicilia, Italy, C Mediterranean Sea 37°19′N 13°40′E
Faventia *see* Faenza
107 G23 **Favignana, Isola** *island* Isole Egadi, S Italy
12 D8 **Fawn** ♂ Ontario, SE Canada
Faxa Bay *see* Faxaflói
92 H3 **Faxaflói** *Eng.* Faxa Bay. *bay* W Iceland
78 I7 **Faya** *prev.* Faya-Largeau, Largeau. Borkou-Ennedi-Tibesti, N Chad 17°58′N 19°06′E
Faya-Largeau *see* Faya
187 Q16 **Fayaoué** Province des Îles Loyauté, C New Caledonia 20°41′S 166°31′E
138 M5 **Fayḑat** *hill range* E Syria
23 O3 **Fayette** Alabama, S USA 33°40′N 87°49′W
29 X12 **Fayette** Iowa, C USA 42°50′N 91°48′W
22 J6 **Fayette** Mississippi, S USA 31°42′N 91°03′W
27 U4 **Fayette** Missouri, C USA 39°09′N 92°40′W
27 S9 **Fayetteville** Arkansas, C USA 36°04′N 94°10′W
21 U10 **Fayetteville** North Carolina, SE USA 35°03′N 78°53′W
20 J10 **Fayetteville** Tennessee, S USA 35°08′N 86°33′W
25 U11 **Fayetteville** Texas, SW USA 29°52′N 96°40′W
21 R5 **Fayetteville** West Virginia, NE USA 38°03′N 81°09′W
141 R4 **Faylakah** *var.* Failaka Island. *island* E Kuwait
139 T10 **Fayşalīyah** *var.* Faisaliya. Al Qādisīyah, S Iraq 31°48′N 44°36′E
189 P15 **Fayu** *var.* East Fayu. *island* Hall Islands, C Micronesia
152 G8 **Fāzilka** Punjab, NW India 30°26′N 74°04′E
Fdérick *see* Fdérik
76 I6 **Fdérik** *var.* Fdérick, *Fr.* Fort Gouraud. Tiris Zemmour, NW Mauritania 22°40′N 12°41′W
Feabhail, Loch *see* Foyle, Lough
97 B20 **Feale** ♂ SW Ireland
21 V12 **Fear, Cape** *headland* Bald Head Island, North Carolina, SE USA 33°50′N 77°57′W
35 O6 **Feather River** ♂ California, W USA
185 M14 **Featherston** Wellington, North Island, New Zealand 41°07′S 175°28′E

◆ Country
● Country Capital
◇ Dependent Territory
○ Dependent Territory Capital
◆ Administrative Regions
✈ International Airport
▲ Mountain
▲ Mountain Range
⚲ Volcano
♂ River
◎ Lake
⊠ Reservoir

FÉCAMP – FOREST GROVE

102 L3 **Fécamp** Seine-Maritime, N France 49°45′N 00°22′E
Fédala see Mohammedia
61 D17 **Federación** Entre Ríos, E Argentina 31°00′S 57°55′W
61 D17 **Federal** Entre Ríos, E Argentina 30°55′S 58°45′W
77 T15 **Federal Capital District** ◈ capital territory C Nigeria
Federal Capital Territory see Australian Capital Territory
Federal District see Distrito Federal
21 Y4 **Federalsburg** Maryland, NE USA 38°41′N 75°46′W
74 M6 **Fedjaj, Chott el** var. Chott el Fejaj, Shaṭṭ al Fijāj. salt lake C Tunisia
94 B13 **Fedje** island S Norway
144 M7 **Fedorovka** Kostanay, N Kazakhstan 51°12′N 52°00′E
127 U6 **Fedorovka** Respublika Bashkortostan, W Russian Federation 53°09′N 55°07′E
Fëdory see Fyadory
117 U11 **Fedotova Kosa** spit SE Ukraine
189 V13 **Fefan** atoll Chuuk Islands, C Micronesia
111 O21 **Fehérgyarmat** Szabolcs-Szatmár-Bereg, E Hungary 47°59′N 22°29′E
Fehér-Körös see Crişul Alb
Fehértemplom see Bela Crkva
Fehérvölgy see Albac
100 L7 **Fehmarn** island N Germany
95 H25 **Fehmarn Belt** Dan. Femern Bælt, Ger. Fehmarnbelt. strait Denmark/Germany see also Femern Bælt
Fehmarnbelt see Fehmarn Belt/Femer Bælt
109 X8 **Fehring** Steiermark, SE Austria 46°56′N 16°00′E
59 B15 **Feijó** Acre, W Brazil 08°07′S 70°27′W
184 M12 **Feilding** Manawatu-Wanganui, North Island, New Zealand 40°15′S 175°34′E
Feira see Feira de Santana
59 O17 **Feira de Santana** var. Feira. Bahia, E Brazil 12°17′S 38°53′W
109 X7 **Feistritz** ≈ SE Austria
Feistritz see Ilirska Bistrica
161 P8 **Feixi** var. Shangpai; prev. Shangpaihe. Anhui, E China 31°40′N 117°08′E
Fejaj, Chott el see Fedjaj, Chott el
111 I23 **Fejér** off. Fejér Megye. ◈ county W Hungary
Fejér Megye see Fejér
95 I24 **Fejø** island SE Denmark
136 K15 **Feke** Adana, S Turkey 37°49′N 35°55′E
Feketehalom see Codlea
Fekete-Körös see Crişul Negru
105 Y9 **Felanitx** Mallorca, Spain, W Mediterranean Sea 39°28′N 03°08′E
109 T3 **Feldaist** ≈ N Austria
109 W8 **Feldbach** Steiermark, SE Austria 46°58′N 15°53′E
101 F24 **Feldberg** ▲ SW Germany 47°52′N 08°01′E
116 J12 **Feldioara** Ger. Marienburg, Hung. Földvár. Braşov, C Romania 45°49′N 25°36′E
108 I7 **Feldkirch** anc. Clunia. Vorarlberg, W Austria 47°15′N 09°38′E
109 S9 **Feldkirchen in Kärnten** Slvn. Trg. Kärnten, S Austria 46°42′N 14°01′E
Félegyháza see Kiskunfélegyháza
192 H16 **Feleolo** ✈ (Āpia) Upolu, C Samoa 13°49′S 171°59′W
104 H6 **Felgueiras** Porto, N Portugal 41°22′N 08°12′W
Felicitas Julia see Lisboa
172 J16 **Félicité** island Inner Islands, NE Seychelles
151 K20 **Felidhu Atoll** atoll C Maldives
41 Y13 **Felipe Carrillo Puerto** Quintana Roo, SE Mexico 19°34′N 88°02′W
97 Q21 **Felixstowe** E England, United Kingdom 51°58′N 01°20′E
103 N11 **Felletin** Creuse, C France 45°53′N 02°12′E
Fellin see Viljandi
Felsőbánya see Baia Sprie
Felsőmuzslya see Mužlja
Felsővisó see Vişeu de Sus
35 N10 **Felton** California, W USA 37°03′N 122°04′W
106 H7 **Feltre** Veneto, NE Italy 46°01′N 11°55′E
95 H25 **Femer Bælt** Dan. Fehmarn Belt, Ger. Fehmarnbelt. strait Denmark/Germany see also Fehmarn Belt
95 I24 **Femø** island SE Denmark
94 I10 **Femunden** ◎ S Norway
104 H2 **Fene** Galicia, NW Spain 43°28′N 08°10′W
14 I14 **Fenelon Falls** Ontario, SE Canada 44°34′N 78°43′W
189 U13 **Feneppi** atoll Chuuk Islands, C Micronesia
137 O11 **Fener Burnu** headland N Turkey 41°07′N 39°26′E
Fénérive see Fenoarivo Atsinanana
115 J14 **Fengári** ▲ Samothráki, E Greece 40°27′N 25°37′E
163 V13 **Fengcheng** var. Feng-cheng, Fenghwangcheng. Liaoning, NE China 40°28′N 124°01′E
Fengcheng see Lianjiang
Feng-cheng see Fengcheng
160 K11 **Fenggang** var. Longquan. Guizhou, S China 27°57′N 107°42′E
161 S9 **Fenghua** Zhejiang, SE China 29°40′N 121°25′E
Fenghwangcheng see Fengcheng
Fengjiaba see Wangcang
160 L9 **Fengjie** var. Yong'an. Sichuan, C China 31°06′N 109°30′E
160 M14 **Fengkai** var. Jiangkou. Guangdong, S China 23°26′N 111°28′E
161 T13 **Fenglin** Jap. Hōrin. C Taiwan 23°52′N 121°30′E
161 P1 **Fengning** prev. Dagezhen. Hebei, E China 41°12′N 116°37′E
160 E13 **Fengqing** var. Fengshan. Yunnan, SW China 24°38′N 99°54′E
161 O6 **Fengqiu** Henan, C China 35°02′N 114°24′E
161 Q2 **Fengrun** Hebei, E China 39°50′N 118°10′E
Fengshan see Luoyuan, Fujian, China
Fengshan see Fengqing, Yunnan, China
163 T4 **Fengshui Shan** ▲ NE China
161 P14 **Fengshun** Guangdong, S China 23°51′N 116°11′E
Fengtien see Liaoning, China
Fengtien see Shenyang, China
160 J7 **Fengxian** var. Feng Xian; prev. Shuangshipu. Shaanxi, C China 33°50′N 106°33′E
Feng Xian see Fengxian
Fengxiang see Luobei
Fengyizhen see Maoxian
163 P13 **Fengzhen** Nei Mongol Zizhiqu, N China 40°25′N 113°09′E
160 M6 **Fen He** ≈ C China
153 V15 **Feni** Chittagong, E Bangladesh 23°00′N 91°24′E
186 I6 **Feni Islands** island group NE Papua New Guinea
38 H17 **Fenimore Pass** strait Aleutian Islands, Alaska, USA
84 B9 **Feni Ridge** undersea feature N Atlantic Ocean 53°45′N 18°00′W
Fennern see Vändra
30 J9 **Fennimore** Wisconsin, N USA 42°58′N 90°39′W
172 J4 **Fenoarivo Atsinanana** Fr. Fénérive. Toamasina, E Madagascar 20°52′S 46°52′E
95 I24 **Fensmark** Storstrøm, SE Denmark 55°17′N 11°48′E
97 O19 **Fens, The** wetland E England, United Kingdom
31 R9 **Fenton** Michigan, N USA 42°48′N 83°42′W
190 K10 **Fenua Fala** island SE Tokelau
190 F12 **Fenuafo'ou, Île** island E Wallis and Futuna
190 L10 **Fenua Loa** island Fakaofo Atoll, E Tokelau
160 M4 **Fenyang** Shanxi, C China 37°14′N 111°40′E
117 U13 **Feodosiya** var. Kefe, It. Kaffa; anc. Theodosia. Respublika Krym, S Ukraine 45°03′N 35°24′E
94 I10 **Feragen** ◎ S Norway
74 L5 **Fer, Cap de** headland NE Algeria 37°05′N 07°10′E
31 O16 **Ferdinand** Indiana, N USA 38°13′N 86°51′W
Ferdinand see Montana, Bulgaria
Ferdinand see Mihail Kogălniceanu, Romania
Ferdinandsberg see Oţelu Roşu
143 T7 **Ferdows** var. Firdaus; prev. Tūn. Khorāsān-Razavī, E Iran 34°00′N 58°09′E
103 Q5 **Fère-Champenoise** Marne, N France 48°45′N 03°59′E
Ferencz-József Csúcs see Gerlachovský štít
107 J16 **Ferentino** Lazio, C Italy 41°40′N 13°16′E
114 L13 **Féres** Anatolikí Makedonía kai Thráki, NE Greece 40°54′N 26°12′E
Fergana see Farg'ona
147 S10 **Fergana Valley** var. Farghona Valley, Rus. Ferganskaya Dolina, Taj. Wodii Farghona, Uzb. Farghona Wodiysi. basin Tajikistan/Uzbekistan
Ferganskaya Dolina see Fergana Valley
Ferganskaya Oblast' see Farg'ona Viloyati
147 U9 **Ferganskiy Khrebet** ▲▲ C Kyrgyzstan
14 F15 **Fergus** Ontario, S Canada 43°42′N 80°22′W
29 S6 **Fergus Falls** Minnesota, N USA 46°15′N 96°02′W
186 G9 **Fergusson Island** var. Kaluwawa. island SE Papua New Guinea
111 K22 **Ferihegy** ✈ (Budapest) Budapest, C Hungary 47°25′N 19°13′E
113 N17 **Ferizaj** Serb. Uroševac. C Kosovo 42°23′N 21°09′E
77 N14 **Ferkessédougou** N Ivory Coast 09°36′N 05°12′W
109 T10 **Ferlach** Slvn. Borovlje. Kärnten, S Austria 46°31′N 14°18′E
97 E16 **Fermanagh** cultural region SW Northern Ireland, United Kingdom
106 J13 **Fermo** anc. Firmum Picenum. Marche, C Italy 43°09′N 13°44′E
104 J6 **Fermoselle** Castilla-León, N Spain 41°19′N 06°24′W
97 D20 **Fermoy** Ir. Mainistir Fhear Maí. SW Ireland 52°08′N 08°16′W
23 W8 **Fernandina Beach** Amelia Island, Florida, SE USA 30°40′N 81°27′W
57 A17 **Fernandina, Isla** var. Narborough Island. island Galapagos Islands, Ecuador, E Pacific Ocean
47 Y5 **Fernando de Noronha** island E Brazil
Fernando Po/Fernando Póo see Bioco, Isla de
60 J7 **Fernandópolis** São Paulo, S Brazil 20°18′S 50°13′W
104 M13 **Fernán Núñez** Andalucía, S Spain 37°40′N 04°44′W
83 Q14 **Fernão Veloso, Baia de** bay NE Mozambique
34 K3 **Ferndale** California, W USA 40°34′N 124°16′W
32 H6 **Ferndale** Washington, NW USA 48°51′N 122°35′W
11 P17 **Fernie** British Columbia, SW Canada 49°30′N 115°00′W
35 R5 **Fernley** Nevada, W USA 39°35′N 119°15′W
Ferozepore see Firozpur
107 N18 **Ferrandina** Basilicata, S Italy 40°30′N 16°25′E
106 G9 **Ferrara** anc. Forum Alieni. Emilia-Romagna, N Italy 44°50′N 11°36′E
120 F9 **Ferrat, Cap** headland NW Algeria 35°52′N 00°24′W
107 D20 **Ferrato, Capo** headland Sardegna, Italy, C Mediterranean Sea 39°18′N 09°37′E
104 G12 **Ferreira do Alentejo** Beja, S Portugal 38°04′N 08°06′W
56 B11 **Ferreñafe** Lambayeque, W Peru 06°42′S 79°45′W
108 C12 **Ferret** Valais, SW Switzerland 45°57′N 07°01′E
102 I13 **Ferret, Cap** headland W France 44°37′N 01°15′W
22 I6 **Ferriday** Louisiana, S USA 31°37′N 91°33′W
Ferro see Hierro
107 D16 **Ferro, Capo** headland Sardegna, Italy, C Mediterranean Sea 41°09′N 09°31′E
104 H2 **Ferrol** var. El Ferrol; prev. El Ferrol del Caudillo. Galicia, NW Spain 43°29′N 08°14′W
56 B12 **Ferrol, Península de** peninsula W Peru
36 M5 **Ferron** Utah, W USA 39°05′N 111°07′W
21 S7 **Ferrum** Virginia, NE USA 36°54′N 80°01′W
23 O8 **Ferry Pass** Florida, SE USA 30°30′N 87°12′W
Ferryville see Menzel Bourguiba
29 S4 **Fertile** Minnesota, N USA 47°32′N 96°16′W
Fertő see Neusiedler See
98 L5 **Ferwerd** Fris. Ferwert. Friesland, N Netherlands 53°21′N 05°47′E
Ferwert see Ferwerd
74 G6 **Fès** Eng. Fez. N Morocco 34°06′N 04°57′W
79 I22 **Feshi** Bandundu, SW Dem. Rep. Congo 06°08′S 18°12′E
29 O4 **Fessenden** North Dakota, N USA 47°36′N 99°37′W
Festenberg see Twardogóra
27 X5 **Festus** Missouri, C USA 38°13′N 90°24′W
116 M14 **Feteşti** Ialomiţa, SE Romania 44°22′N 27°51′E
136 D17 **Fethiye** Muğla, SW Turkey 36°37′N 29°08′E
96 M1 **Fetlar** island NE Scotland, United Kingdom
95 I15 **Fetsund** Akershus, S Norway 59°55′N 11°03′E
12 L5 **Feuilles, Lac aux** ◎ Québec, E Canada
12 L5 **Feuilles, Rivière aux** ≈ Québec, E Canada
99 M23 **Feulen** Diekirch, C Luxembourg 49°52′N 06°03′E
103 Q11 **Feurs** Loire, E France 45°44′N 04°14′E
95 F18 **Fevik** Aust-Agder, S Norway 58°22′N 08°40′E
123 R13 **Fevral'sk** Amurskaya Oblast', SE Russian Federation 52°25′N 131°06′E
149 S2 **Feyzābād** var. Faizabad, Faizābād, Feyzābād, Fyzabad. Badakhshān, NE Afghanistan 37°06′N 70°34′E
Feyzābād see Feyzābād
Fez see Fès
75 Q10 **Fezzan** ◈ cultural region C Libya
97 J19 **Ffestiniog** NW Wales, United Kingdom 52°55′N 03°54′W
Fhóid Duibh, Cuan an see Blacksod Bay
62 I8 **Fiambalá** Catamarca, NW Argentina 27°45′S 67°37′W
172 I6 **Fianarantsoa** Fianarantsoa, C Madagascar 21°27′S 47°05′E
172 H6 **Fianarantsoa** ◈ province SE Madagascar
78 G12 **Fianga** Mayo-Kébbi, SW Chad 09°57′N 15°09′E
Ficce see Fichē
80 J12 **Fichē** It. Ficce. Oromīya, C Ethiopia 09°48′N 38°43′E
101 N17 **Fichtelberg** ▲ Czech Republic/Germany 50°26′N 12°57′E
101 M18 **Fichtelgebirge** ▲▲ SE Germany
101 M19 **Fichtelnaab** ≈ SE Germany
106 E9 **Fidenza** Emilia-Romagna, N Italy 44°52′N 10°04′E
113 K21 **Fier** var. Fieri. Fier, SW Albania 40°44′N 19°34′E
113 K21 **Fier** ◈ district W Albania
Fieri see Fier
Fierza see Fierzë
113 L17 **Fierzë** var. Fierza. Shkodër, N Albania 42°15′N 20°02′E
113 L17 **Fierzës, Liqeni i** ◎ N Albania
108 F10 **Fiesch** Valais, SW Switzerland 46°25′N 08°09′E
106 G11 **Fiesole** Toscana, C Italy 43°50′N 11°18′E
138 G12 **Fīfah** Aṭ Ṭafīlah, W Jordan 30°55′N 35°25′E
96 K11 **Fife** var. Kingdom of Fife. cultural region E Scotland, United Kingdom
Fife, Kingdom of see Fife
96 K11 **Fife Ness** headland E Scotland, United Kingdom 56°16′N 02°35′W
Fifteen Twenty Fracture Zone see Barracuda Fracture Zone
103 N13 **Figeac** Lot, S France 44°37′N 02°01′E
95 N19 **Figeholm** Kalmar, SE Sweden 57°12′N 16°34′E
Figig see Figuig
83 J18 **Figtree** Matabeleland South, SW Zimbabwe 20°24′S 28°21′E
104 F8 **Figueira da Foz** Coimbra, W Portugal 40°09′N 08°51′W
105 X4 **Figueres** Cataluña, E Spain 42°16′N 02°57′E
74 H7 **Figuig** var. Figig. E Morocco 32°09′N 01°13′W
Fijājj, Shaṭṭ al see Fedjaj, Chott el
187 Y15 **Fiji** off. Sovereign Democratic Republic of Fiji, Fij. Viti. ◆ republic SW Pacific Ocean
192 K9 **Fiji** island group SW Pacific Ocean
175 Q8 **Fiji Plate** tectonic feature
Fiji, Sovereign Democratic Republic of see Fiji
105 P14 **Filabres, Sierra de los** ▲▲ SE Spain
83 K18 **Filabusi** Matabeleland South, S Zimbabwe 20°34′S 29°20′E
42 K13 **Filadelfia** Guanacaste, W Costa Rica 10°28′N 85°33′W
111 K20 **Fil'akovo** Hung. Fülek. Banskobystrický Kraj, C Slovakia 48°15′N 19°53′E
195 N5 **Filchner Ice Shelf** ice shelf Antarctica
14 J11 **Fildegrand** ≈ Québec, SE Canada
33 O15 **Filer** Idaho, NW USA 42°34′N 114°36′W
Filevo see Vŭrbitsa
116 H14 **Filiaşi** Dolj, SW Romania 44°32′N 23°31′E
115 B16 **Filiátes** Ípeiros, W Greece 39°38′N 20°16′E
115 D21 **Filiatrá** Pelopónnisos, S Greece 37°09′N 21°35′E
107 K22 **Filicudi, Isola** island Isole Eolie, S Italy
141 Y10 **Filim** E Oman 20°37′N 58°11′E
Filimon Sîrbu see Făurei
77 S11 **Filingué** Tillabéri, W Niger 14°21′N 03°22′E
Filiouri see Lissos
114 I13 **Fílippoi** anc. Philippi. site of ancient city Anatolikí Makedonía kai Thráki, NE Greece
95 L15 **Filipstad** Värmland, C Sweden 59°44′N 14°10′E
108 I9 **Filisur** Graubünden, S Switzerland 46°40′N 09°43′E
94 E12 **Fillefjell** ▲▲ S Norway
35 R14 **Fillmore** California, W USA 34°23′N 118°56′W
36 K5 **Fillmore** Utah, W USA 38°57′N 112°19′W
14 J10 **Fils, Lac du** ◎ Québec, SE Canada
Filyos Çayı see Yenice Çayı
195 Q1 **Fimbulisen** ice shelf Antarctica
195 Q2 **Fimbutheimen** physical region Antarctica
106 G9 **Finale Emilia** Emilia-Romagna, C Italy 44°50′N 11°17′E
106 C10 **Finale Ligure** Liguria, NW Italy 44°11′N 08°22′E
105 P14 **Fiñana** Andalucía, S Spain 37°09′N 02°47′W
21 S6 **Fincastle** Virginia, NE USA 37°30′N 79°54′W
99 M25 **Findel** ✈ (Luxembourg) Luxembourg, C Luxembourg 49°39′N 06°16′E
96 J9 **Findhorn** ≈ N Scotland, United Kingdom
31 R12 **Findlay** Ohio, N USA 41°02′N 83°40′W
18 G11 **Finger Lakes** ◎ New York, NE USA
83 L14 **Fingoè** Tete, NW Mozambique 15°10′S 31°51′E
136 E17 **Finike** Antalya, SW Turkey 36°18′N 30°08′E
102 F6 **Finistère** ◈ department NW France
186 D7 **Finisterre Range** ▲▲ N Papua New Guinea
181 Q8 **Finke** Northern Territory, N Australia 25°37′S 134°35′E
109 S10 **Finkenstein** Kärnten, S Austria 46°34′N 13°53′E
189 Y15 **Finkol, Mount** var. Mount Crozer. ▲ Kosrae, E Micronesia 05°18′N 163°00′E
93 L17 **Finland** off. Republic of Finland, Fin. Suomen Tasavalta, Suomi. ◆ republic N Europe
124 F12 **Finland, Gulf of** Est. Soome Laht, Fin. Suomenlahti, Ger. Finnischer Meerbusen, Rus. Finskiy Zaliv, Swe. Finska Viken. gulf E Baltic Sea
Finland, Republic of see Finland
10 L11 **Finlay** ≈ British Columbia, W Canada
183 O10 **Finley** New South Wales, SE Australia 35°41′S 145°33′E
29 Q4 **Finley** North Dakota, N USA 47°30′N 97°50′W
Finnischer Meerbusen see Finland, Gulf of
92 K9 **Finnmark** ◈ county N Norway
92 K9 **Finnmarksvidda** physical region N Norway
92 I9 **Finnsnes** Troms, N Norway 69°16′N 18°00′E
186 E7 **Finschhafen** Morobe, C Papua New Guinea 06°35′S 147°51′E
94 E13 **Finse** Hordaland, S Norway 60°35′N 07°33′E
Finska Viken/Finskiy Zaliv see Finland, Gulf of
95 M17 **Finspång** Östergötland, S Sweden 58°42′N 15°45′E
108 F10 **Finsteraarhorn** ▲ S Switzerland 46°33′N 08°07′E
101 O14 **Finsterwalde** Brandenburg, E Germany 51°38′N 13°43′E
185 A23 **Fiordland** physical region South Island, New Zealand
106 E9 **Fiorenzuola d'Arda** Emilia-Romagna, C Italy 44°57′N 09°53′E
Firat Nehri see Euphrates
Firdaus see Ferdows
18 M14 **Fire Island** island New York, NE USA
106 G11 **Firenze** Eng. Florence; anc. Florentia. Toscana, C Italy 43°47′N 11°15′E
106 G10 **Firenzuola** Toscana, C Italy 44°07′N 11°22′E
14 C6 **Fire River** Ontario, S Canada 48°46′N 83°34′W
Firlīng see Fârliug
61 B19 **Firmat** Santa Fe, C Argentina 33°29′S 61°29′W
103 Q12 **Firminy** Loire, E France 45°22′N 04°18′E
Firmum Picenum see Fermo
152 J12 **Firozābād** Uttar Pradesh, N India 27°09′N 78°24′E
152 G8 **Firozpur** var. Ferozepore. Punjab, NW India 30°55′N 74°38′E
First State see Delaware
143 O12 **Fīrūzābād** Fārs, S Iran 28°51′N 52°35′E
Fischamend see Fischamend Markt
109 Y4 **Fischamend Markt** var. Fischamend. Niederösterreich, NE Austria 48°08′N 16°37′E
109 W6 **Fischbacher Alpen** ▲ E Austria
Fischhausen see Primorsk
83 D21 **Fish** var. Vis. ≈ S Namibia
83 F24 **Fish** Afr. Vis. ≈ SW South Africa
11 X15 **Fisher Branch** Manitoba, S Canada 51°09′N 97°34′W
11 X15 **Fisher River** Manitoba, S Canada 51°25′N 97°23′W
19 N13 **Fishers Island** island New York, NE USA
37 U8 **Fishers Peak** ▲ Colorado, C USA 37°06′N 104°27′W
9 P9 **Fisher Strait** strait Nunavut, N Canada
97 H21 **Fishguard** Wel. Abergwaun. SW Wales, United Kingdom 51°59′N 04°49′W
19 R2 **Fish River Lake** ◎ Maine, NE USA
194 K6 **Fiske, Cape** headland Antarctica 74°27′S 60°28′W
103 P4 **Fismes** Marne, N France 49°19′N 03°41′E
104 F3 **Fisterra, Cabo** headland NW Spain 42°53′N 09°16′W
19 N11 **Fitchburg** Massachusetts, NE USA 42°34′N 71°48′W
96 L3 **Fitful Head** headland NE Scotland, United Kingdom 59°57′N 01°24′W
95 C14 **Fitjar** Hordaland, S Norway 59°55′N 05°19′E
192 H16 **Fito, Mauga** ▲ Upolu, C Samoa 13°57′S 171°42′W
23 U6 **Fitzgerald** Georgia, SE USA 31°42′N 83°15′W
180 M5 **Fitzroy Crossing** Western Australia 18°10′S 125°40′E
63 G21 **Fitzroy, Monte** var. Cerro Chaltel. ▲ S Argentina 49°18′S 73°06′W
181 Y8 **Fitzroy River** ≈ Queensland, E Australia
180 L5 **Fitzroy River** ≈ Western Australia
14 E12 **Fitzwilliam Island** island Ontario, S Canada
107 J15 **Fiuggi** Lazio, C Italy 41°47′N 13°16′E
Fiume see Rijeka
107 H15 **Fiumicino** Lazio, C Italy 41°46′N 12°13′E
Fiumicino see Leonardo da Vinci
106 E10 **Fivizzano** Toscana, C Italy 44°13′N 10°06′E
79 O21 **Fizi** Sud-Kivu, E Dem. Rep. Congo 04°15′S 28°57′E
Fizuli see Füzuli
92 I11 **Fjällåsen** Norrbotten, N Sweden 67°31′N 20°08′E
95 G20 **Fjerritslev** Nordjylland, N Denmark 57°06′N 09°17′E
F.J.S. see Franz Josef Strauss
95 L16 **Fjugesta** Örebro, C Sweden 59°10′N 14°50′E
Fladstrand see Frederikshavn
37 V5 **Flagler** Colorado, C USA 39°17′N 103°04′W
23 X10 **Flagler Beach** Florida, SE USA 29°28′N 81°07′W
36 L11 **Flagstaff** Arizona, SW USA 35°12′N 111°39′W
65 H24 **Flagstaff Bay** bay N Saint Helena, C Atlantic Ocean
19 P5 **Flagstaff Lake** ◎ Maine, NE USA
94 E13 **Flåm** Sogn Og Fjordane, S Norway 60°51′N 07°06′E
15 O8 **Flamand** ≈ Québec, SE Canada
30 J5 **Flambeau River** ≈ Wisconsin, N USA
97 O16 **Flamborough Head** headland E England, United Kingdom 54°06′N 00°03′W
100 N13 **Fläming** hill range NE Germany
16 H8 **Flaming Gorge Reservoir** ▣ Utah/Wyoming, NW USA
99 B18 **Flanders** Dut. Vlaanderen, Fr. Flandre. cultural region Belgium/France
Flandre see Flanders
29 R10 **Flandreau** South Dakota, N USA 44°03′N 96°36′W
96 D6 **Flannan Isles** island group NW Scotland, United Kingdom
28 M6 **Flasher** North Dakota, N USA 46°25′N 101°12′W
93 G15 **Flåsjön** ◎ N Sweden
39 O11 **Flat** Alaska, USA 62°27′N 158°00′W
92 H1 **Flateyri** Vestfirdhir, NW Iceland 66°03′N 23°28′W
33 P8 **Flathead Lake** ◎ Montana, NW USA
173 Y15 **Flat Island** Fr. Île Plate. island N Mauritius
25 T11 **Flatonia** Texas, SW USA 29°41′N 97°06′W
185 M14 **Flat Point** headland North Island, New Zealand 41°12′S 176°03′E
27 X6 **Flat River** Missouri, C USA 37°51′N 90°31′W
31 P8 **Flat River** ≈ Michigan, N USA
31 P14 **Flatrock River** ≈ Indiana, N USA
32 E6 **Flattery, Cape** headland Washington, NW USA 48°22′N 124°43′W
64 B12 **Flatts Village** var. The Flatts Village. C Bermuda 32°19′N 64°44′W
108 H7 **Flawil** Sankt Gallen, NE Switzerland 47°25′N 09°12′E
97 N22 **Fleet** S England, United Kingdom 51°16′N 00°50′W
97 K16 **Fleetwood** NW England, United Kingdom 53°55′N 03°02′W
18 H15 **Fleetwood** Pennsylvania, NE USA 40°27′N 75°49′W
95 D18 **Flekkefjord** Vest-Agder, S Norway 58°17′N 06°40′E
21 N5 **Flemingsburg** Kentucky, S USA 38°26′N 83°43′W
18 J15 **Flemington** New Jersey, NE USA 40°30′N 74°51′W
64 I7 **Flemish Cap** undersea feature NW Atlantic Ocean 47°00′N 45°00′W
95 N16 **Flen** Södermanland, C Sweden 59°04′N 16°39′E
100 I6 **Flensburg** Schleswig-Holstein, N Germany 54°47′N 09°26′E
100 J6 **Flensburger Förde** inlet Denmark/Germany
102 K5 **Flers** Orne, N France 48°45′N 00°34′W
95 C14 **Flesland** ✈ (Bergen) Hordaland, S Norway 60°18′N 05°15′E
Flessingue see Vlissingen
21 P10 **Fletcher** North Carolina, SE USA 35°24′N 82°29′W
31 R6 **Fletcher Pond** ◎ Michigan, N USA
102 L15 **Fleurance** Gers, S France 43°50′N 00°39′E
108 B8 **Fleurier** Neuchâtel, W Switzerland 46°55′N 06°37′E
99 H20 **Fleurus** Hainaut, S Belgium 50°28′N 04°33′E
103 N7 **Fleury-les-Aubrais** Loiret, C France 47°55′N 01°55′E
98 K10 **Flevoland** ◈ province C Netherlands
Flickertail State see North Dakota
108 H9 **Flims** Glarus, NE Switzerland 46°50′N 09°16′E
182 F8 **Flinders Island** island Investigator Group, South Australia
183 P14 **Flinders Island** island Furneaux Group, Tasmania, SE Australia
182 I6 **Flinders Ranges** ▲▲ South Australia
181 U5 **Flinders River** ≈ Queensland, NE Australia
11 V13 **Flin Flon** Manitoba, C Canada 54°47′N 101°51′W
97 K18 **Flint** NE Wales, United Kingdom 53°15′N 03°10′W
31 R9 **Flint** Michigan, N USA 43°01′N 83°41′W
97 J18 **Flint** cultural region NE Wales, United Kingdom
27 O7 **Flint Hills** hill range Kansas, C USA
191 Y6 **Flint Island** island Line Islands, E Kiribati
23 S4 **Flint River** ≈ Georgia, SE USA
31 R9 **Flint River** ≈ Michigan, N USA
189 X12 **Flipper Point** headland C Wake Island 19°18′N 166°37′E
94 I13 **Flisa** Hedmark, S Norway 60°36′N 12°02′E
94 J13 **Flisa** ≈ S Norway
122 J5 **Flissingskiy, Mys** headland Novaya Zemlya, NW Russian Federation 76°43′N 69°01′E
Flitsch see Bovec
105 U6 **Flix** Cataluña, NE Spain 41°13′N 00°32′E
95 J19 **Floda** Västra Götaland, S Sweden 57°47′N 12°20′E
101 O16 **Flöha** ≈ E Germany
25 O4 **Flomot** Texas, SW USA 34°13′N 100°58′W
29 V5 **Floodwood** Minnesota, N USA 46°55′N 92°55′W
30 M15 **Flora** Illinois, N USA 38°40′N 88°29′W
103 P14 **Florac** Lozère, S France 44°18′N 03°35′E
23 Q8 **Florala** Alabama, S USA 31°00′N 86°19′W
103 S4 **Florange** Moselle, NE France 49°21′N 06°06′E
Floreana, Isla see Santa María, Isla
23 O2 **Florence** Alabama, S USA 34°48′N 87°40′W
36 L14 **Florence** Arizona, SW USA 33°01′N 111°23′W
37 T6 **Florence** Colorado, C USA 38°20′N 105°06′W
27 O5 **Florence** Kansas, C USA 38°13′N 96°56′W
20 M4 **Florence** Kentucky, S USA 39°00′N 84°37′W
32 E13 **Florence** Oregon, NW USA 43°58′N 124°06′W
21 T12 **Florence** South Carolina, SE USA 34°12′N 79°44′W
25 S9 **Florence** Texas, SW USA 30°50′N 97°47′W
Florence see Firenze
54 E13 **Florencia** Caquetá, S Colombia 01°37′N 75°37′W
99 H21 **Florennes** Namur, S Belgium 50°15′N 04°36′E
Florentia see Firenze
63 J18 **Florentino Ameghino, Embalse** ◎ S Argentina
99 J24 **Florenville** Luxembourg, SE Belgium 49°42′N 05°19′E
42 E3 **Flores** Petén, N Guatemala 16°55′N 89°56′W
61 E19 **Flores** ◈ department S Uruguay
171 O16 **Flores** island Nusa Tenggara, C Indonesia
64 M1 **Flores** island Azores, Portugal, NE Atlantic Ocean
Floreshty see Floreşti
Flores, Lago de see Petén Itzá, Lago
Flores, Laut see Flores Sea
171 N15 **Flores Sea** Ind. Laut Flores. sea C Indonesia
116 M8 **Floreşti** Rus. Floreshty. N Moldova 47°52′N 28°19′E
25 S12 **Floresville** Texas, SW USA 29°09′N 98°10′W
59 N14 **Floriano** Piauí, E Brazil 06°45′S 43°00′W
61 K14 **Florianópolis** prev. Destêrro. state capital Santa Catarina, S Brazil 27°35′S 48°32′W
44 G6 **Florida** Camagüey, C Cuba 21°32′N 78°14′W
61 F19 **Florida** Florida, S Uruguay 34°04′S 56°14′W
61 F19 **Florida** ◈ department S Uruguay
23 U9 **Florida** off. State of Florida, also known as Peninsular State, Sunshine State. ◈ state SE USA
23 Y17 **Florida Bay** bay Florida, SE USA
54 G8 **Floridablanca** Santander, N Colombia 07°04′N 73°06′W
23 Y17 **Florida Keys** island group Florida, SE USA
37 Q16 **Florida Mountains** ▲▲ New Mexico, SW USA
64 D10 **Florida, Straits of** strait Atlantic Ocean/Gulf of Mexico
114 D13 **Flórina** var. Phlórina. Dytikí Makedonía, N Greece 40°48′N 21°26′E
27 X4 **Florissant** Missouri, C USA 38°48′N 90°20′W
94 C11 **Florø** Sogn Og Fjordane, S Norway 61°36′N 05°04′E
115 L22 **Floúda, Akrotírio** headland Astypálaia, Kykládes, Greece, Aegean Sea 36°38′N 26°23′E
21 S7 **Floyd** Virginia, NE USA 36°55′N 80°22′W
25 N4 **Floydada** Texas, SW USA 33°58′N 101°20′W
Flüela Wisshorn see Weisshorn
98 K7 **Fluessen** ◎ N Netherlands
105 S5 **Flúmen** ≈ NE Spain
107 C20 **Flumendosa** ≈ Sardegna, Italy, C Mediterranean Sea
31 R9 **Flushing** Michigan, N USA 43°03′N 83°51′W
Flushing see Vlissingen
25 O6 **Fluvanna** Texas, SW USA 32°54′N 101°06′W
186 B8 **Fly** ≈ Indonesia/Papua New Guinea
194 I10 **Flying Fish, Cape** headland Thurston Island, Antarctica 72°00′S 102°25′W
Flylân see Vlieland
193 Y15 **Foa** island Ha'apai Group, C Tonga
11 U15 **Foam Lake** Saskatchewan, S Canada 51°38′N 103°31′W
113 J14 **Foča** var. Srbinje. SE Bosnia and Herzegovina 43°32′N 18°46′E
116 L12 **Focşani** Vrancea, E Romania 45°45′N 27°13′E
Fogaras/Fogarasch see Făgăraş
107 M16 **Foggia** Puglia, SE Italy 41°28′N 15°31′E
Foggo see Faggo
76 D10 **Fogo** island Ilhas de Sotavento, SW Cape Verde
13 U11 **Fogo Island** island Newfoundland and Labrador, E Canada
109 U7 **Fohnsdorf** Steiermark, SE Austria 47°13′N 14°40′E
100 G7 **Föhr** island NW Germany
104 F14 **Fóia** ▲ S Portugal 37°19′N 08°39′W
14 I10 **Foins, Lac aux** ◎ Québec, SE Canada
103 N17 **Foix** Ariège, S France 42°58′N 01°39′E
126 I5 **Fokino** Bryanskaya Oblast', W Russian Federation 53°22′N 34°22′E
123 S15 **Fokino** Primorskiy Kray, SE Russian Federation 42°58′N 132°25′E
Fola, Cnoc see Bloody Foreland
94 E13 **Folarskardnuten** ▲ S Norway 60°34′N 07°18′E
92 G11 **Folda** fjord C Norway
93 F14 **Foldereid** Nord-Trøndelag, C Norway 64°58′N 12°09′E
Földvár see Feldioara
115 J22 **Folégandros** island Kykládes, Greece, Aegean Sea
23 O9 **Foley** Alabama, S USA 30°24′N 87°40′W
29 U7 **Foley** Minnesota, N USA 45°39′N 93°54′W
14 E7 **Foleyet** Ontario, S Canada 48°15′N 82°26′W
95 D14 **Folgefonni** glacier S Norway
106 I13 **Foligno** Umbria, C Italy 42°58′N 12°40′E
97 Q23 **Folkestone** SE England, United Kingdom 51°05′N 01°11′E
23 W8 **Folkston** Georgia, SE USA 30°49′N 82°00′W
94 H10 **Folldal** Hedmark, S Norway 62°08′N 10°00′E
25 P1 **Follett** Texas, SW USA 36°25′N 100°08′W
106 F13 **Follonica** Toscana, C Italy 42°55′N 10°45′E
21 T15 **Folly Beach** South Carolina, SE USA 32°39′N 79°56′W
35 O7 **Folsom** California, W USA 38°40′N 121°11′W
116 M12 **Folteşti** Galaţi, E Romania 45°45′N 28°00′E
172 H14 **Fomboni** Mohéli, S Comoros 12°18′S 43°46′E
18 K10 **Fonda** New York, NE USA 42°57′N 74°24′W
11 S10 **Fond-du-Lac** Saskatchewan, C Canada 59°20′N 107°09′W
30 M8 **Fond du Lac** Wisconsin, N USA 43°48′N 88°27′W
11 T10 **Fond-du-Lac** ≈ Saskatchewan, C Canada
190 C9 **Fongafale** var. Funafuti. ● (Tuvalu) Funafuti Atoll, SE Tuvalu 08°31′N 179°11′E
190 G8 **Fongafale** atoll C Tuvalu
107 C18 **Fonni** Sardegna, Italy, C Mediterranean Sea 40°07′N 09°17′E
189 V12 **Fono** island Chuuk, C Micronesia
54 G4 **Fonseca** La Guajira, N Colombia 10°53′N 72°51′W
Fonseca, Golfo de see Fonseca, Gulf of
42 H8 **Fonseca, Gulf of** Sp. Golfo de Fonseca. gulf C Central America
103 O6 **Fontainebleau** Seine-et-Marne, N France 48°24′N 02°42′E
63 G19 **Fontana, Lago** ◎ W Argentina
21 N10 **Fontana Lake** ▣ North Carolina, SE USA
107 L24 **Fontanarossa** ✈ (Catania) Sicilia, Italy, C Mediterranean Sea 37°28′N 15°04′E
11 N11 **Fontas** ≈ British Columbia, W Canada
58 D12 **Fonte Boa** Amazonas, N Brazil 02°32′S 66°01′W
102 J10 **Fontenay-le-Comte** Vendée, NW France 46°28′N 00°48′W
33 T16 **Fontenelle Reservoir** ▣ Wyoming, C USA
193 Y14 **Fonualei** island Vava'u Group, N Tonga
111 H24 **Fonyód** Somogy, W Hungary 46°43′N 17°32′E
Foochow see Fuzhou
39 Q10 **Foraker, Mount** ▲ Alaska, USA 62°57′N 151°24′W
187 R14 **Forari** Éfaté, C Vanuatu 17°42′S 168°33′E
103 U4 **Forbach** Moselle, NE France 49°11′N 06°54′E
183 Q8 **Forbes** New South Wales, SE Australia 33°24′S 148°00′E
77 T17 **Forcados** Delta, S Nigeria 05°16′N 05°25′E
103 S14 **Forcalquier** Alpes-de-Haute-Provence, SE France 43°57′N 05°46′E
101 K19 **Forchheim** Bayern, SE Germany 49°43′N 11°07′E
35 R13 **Ford City** California, W USA 35°09′N 119°27′W
94 D11 **Førde** Sogn Og Fjordane, S Norway 61°27′N 05°51′E
31 N4 **Ford River** ≈ Michigan, N USA
183 O4 **Fords Bridge** New South Wales, SE Australia 29°44′S 145°25′E
20 J6 **Fordsville** Kentucky, S USA 37°36′N 86°39′W
27 U13 **Fordyce** Arkansas, C USA 33°49′N 92°23′W
76 I14 **Forécariah** SW Guinea 09°28′N 13°06′W
197 O14 **Forel, Mont** ▲ SE Greenland 66°55′N 36°45′W
11 R17 **Foremost** Alberta, SW Canada 49°30′N 111°34′W
14 D16 **Forest** Ontario, S Canada 43°05′N 82°00′W
22 L5 **Forest** Mississippi, S USA 32°22′N 89°30′W
31 S12 **Forest** Ohio, N USA 40°47′N 83°26′W
29 V11 **Forest City** Iowa, C USA 43°15′N 93°38′W
21 Q10 **Forest City** North Carolina, SE USA 35°19′N 81°52′W
32 G11 **Forest Grove** Oregon, NW USA 45°31′N 123°06′W

◆ Country
● Country Capital
◇ Dependent Territory
○ Dependent Territory Capital
◈ Administrative Regions
✈ International Airport
▲ Mountain
▲▲ Mountain Range
Ж Volcano
≈ River
◎ Lake
▣ Reservoir

FORESTIER PENINSULA – FROST

183 P17 **Forestier Peninsula** *peninsula* Tasmania, SE Australia
29 V8 **Forest Lake** Minnesota, N USA 45°16′N 92°59′W
23 S3 **Forest Park** Georgia, SE USA 33°37′N 84°22′W
29 Q3 **Forest River** ≈ North Dakota, N USA
15 T6 **Forestville** Québec, SE Canada 48°45′N 69°04′W
103 Q11 **Forez, Monts du** ▲▲ C France
96 K10 **Forfar** E Scotland, United Kingdom 56°38′N 02°54′W
26 J8 **Forgan** Oklahoma, C USA 36°54′N 100°32′W
Forge du Sud *see* Dudelange
101 J24 **Forggensee** ◎ S Germany
147 N10 **Forish** *Rus.* Farish. Jizzax Viloyati, C Uzbekistan 40°33′N 66°52′E
20 F9 **Forked Deer River** ≈ Tennessee, S USA
32 F7 **Forks** Washington, NW USA 47°57′N 124°22′W
92 N2 **Forlandsundet** *sound* W Svalbard
106 H10 **Forlì** *anc.* Forum Livii. Emilia-Romagna, N Italy 44°14′N 12°02′E
29 Q7 **Forman** North Dakota, N USA 46°07′N 97°39′W
97 K17 **Formby** NW England, United Kingdom 53°34′N 03°05′W
105 V11 **Formentera** *anc.* Ophiusa, *Lat.* Frumentum. *island* Islas Baleares, Spain, W Mediterranean Sea
Formentor, Cabo de *see* Formentor, Cap de
105 Y9 **Formentor, Cap de** *var.* Cabo de Formentor, Cape Formentor. *headland* Mallorca, Spain, W Mediterranean Sea 39°57′N 03°12′E
Formentor, Cape *see* Formentor, Cap de
107 J16 **Formia** Lazio, C Italy 41°16′N 13°37′E
62 O7 **Formosa** Formosa, NE Argentina 26°07′S 58°14′W
62 M6 **Formosa** *off.* Provincia de Formosa. ◈ *province* NE Argentina
Formosa/Formo'sa *see* Taiwan
Formosa, Provincia de *see* Formosa
59 I17 **Formosa, Serra** ▲▲ C Brazil
Formosa Strait *see* Taiwan Strait
95 H21 **Fornæs** *headland* C Denmark 56°26′N 10°57′E
25 U6 **Forney** Texas, SW USA 32°45′N 96°28′W
106 E9 **Fornovo di Taro** Emilia-Romagna, C Italy 44°42′N 10°07′E
117 T14 **Foros** Respublika Krym, S Ukraine 44°24′N 33°47′E
Føroyar *see* Faeroe Islands
96 J8 **Forres** NE Scotland, United Kingdom 57°32′N 03°38′W
27 X11 **Forrest City** Arkansas, C USA 35°01′N 90°48′W
39 Y15 **Forrester Island** *island* Alexander Archipelago, Alaska, USA
25 N7 **Forsan** Texas, SW USA 32°06′N 101°22′W
181 V5 **Forsayth** Queensland, NE Australia 18°31′S 143°37′E
95 L19 **Forserum** Jönköping, S Sweden 57°42′N 14°28′E
95 K15 **Forshaga** Värmland, C Sweden 59°33′N 13°29′E
93 L19 **Forssa** Etelä-Suomi, S Finland 60°49′N 23°40′E
101 Q14 **Forst** *Lus.* Baršć Łužyca. Brandenburg, E Germany 51°43′N 14°38′E
183 U7 **Forster-Tuncurry** New South Wales, SE Australia 32°11′S 152°30′E
23 T4 **Forsyth** Georgia, SE USA 33°00′N 83°57′W
27 T8 **Forsyth** Missouri, C USA 36°41′N 93°07′W
33 W10 **Forsyth** Montana, NW USA 46°16′N 106°40′W
149 U11 **Fort Abbās** Punjab, E Pakistan 29°12′N 73°00′E
12 G10 **Fort Albany** Ontario, C Canada 52°15′N 81°35′W
56 L13 **Fortaleza** Pando, N Bolivia 09°48′S 65°29′W
58 P13 **Fortaleza** *prev.* Ceará. *state capital* Ceará, NE Brazil 03°45′S 38°35′W
59 D16 **Fortaleza** Rondônia, W Brazil 08°45′S 64°06′W
56 C13 **Fortaleza, Río** ≈ W Peru
Fort-Archambault *see* Sarh
21 U3 **Fort Ashby** West Virginia, NE USA 39°30′N 78°46′W
96 I9 **Fort Augustus** N Scotland, United Kingdom 57°14′N 04°38′W
Fort-Bayard *see* Zhanjiang
33 S8 **Fort Benton** Montana, NW USA 47°49′N 110°40′W
35 Q1 **Fort Bidwell** California, W USA 41°50′N 120°07′W
34 L5 **Fort Bragg** California, W USA 39°25′N 123°48′W
31 N16 **Fort Branch** Indiana, N USA 38°15′N 87°34′W
Fort-Bretonnet *see* Bousso
33 T17 **Fort Bridger** Wyoming, C USA 41°18′N 110°19′W
Fort-Cappolani *see* Tidjikja
Fort-Carnot *see* Ikongo
Fort Charlet *see* Djanet
Fort-Chimo *see* Kuujjuaq
11 R10 **Fort Chipewyan** Alberta, C Canada 58°42′N 111°08′W
Fort Cobb Lake *see* Fort Cobb Reservoir
26 L11 **Fort Cobb Reservoir** *var.* Fort Cobb Lake. ⊠ Oklahoma, C USA
37 T3 **Fort Collins** Colorado, C USA 40°35′N 105°05′W
14 K12 **Fort-Coulonge** Québec, SE Canada 45°50′N 76°45′W
Fort-Crampel *see* Kaga Bandoro
Fort-Dauphin *see* Tôlañaro
24 K10 **Fort Davis** Texas, SW USA 30°35′N 103°54′W
37 O10 **Fort Defiance** Arizona, SW USA 35°44′N 109°04′W
45 Q12 **Fort-de-France** *prev.* Fort-Royal. ○ (Martinique) W Martinique 14°36′N 61°05′W
45 P12 **Fort-de-France, Baie de** *bay* W Martinique
Fort de Kock *see* Bukittinggi
23 P6 **Fort Deposit** Alabama, S USA 31°58′N 86°34′W
29 U13 **Fort Dodge** Iowa, C USA 42°30′N 94°10′W
13 S10 **Forteau** Québec, E Canada 51°30′N 56°55′W
106 E11 **Forte dei Marmi** Toscana, C Italy 43°59′N 10°10′E
14 H17 **Fort Erie** Ontario, S Canada 42°55′N 78°56′W
180 H7 **Fortescue River** ≈ Western Australia
19 S2 **Fort Fairfield** Maine, NE USA 46°45′N 67°51′W
Fort-Foureau *see* Kousséri
12 A11 **Fort Frances** Ontario, S Canada 48°37′N 93°23′W
Fort Franklin *see* Déline
23 R7 **Fort Gaines** Georgia, SE USA 31°36′N 85°03′W
37 T8 **Fort Garland** Colorado, C USA 37°22′N 105°24′W
21 P5 **Fort Gay** West Virginia, NE USA 38°06′N 82°35′W
Fort George *see* La Grande Rivière
Fort George *see* Chisasibi
27 Q10 **Fort Gibson** Oklahoma, C USA 35°48′N 95°15′W
27 Q9 **Fort Gibson Lake** ⊠ Oklahoma, C USA
8 H7 **Fort Good Hope** *var.* Rádeyilikóé. Northwest Territories, NW Canada 66°16′N 128°37′W
23 V4 **Fort Gordon** Georgia, SE USA 33°25′N 82°09′W
Fort Gouraud *see* Fdérik
96 I11 **Forth** ≈ C Scotland, United Kingdom
Fort Hall *see* Murang'a
24 H8 **Fort Hancock** Texas, SW USA 31°18′N 105°49′W
Fort Hertz *see* Putao
96 K12 **Forth, Firth of** *estuary* E Scotland, United Kingdom
14 L14 **Forthton** Ontario, SE Canada 44°43′N 75°31′W
14 M8 **Fortier** ≈ Québec, SE Canada
Fortín General Eugenio Garay *see* General Eugenio A. Garay
Fort Jameson *see* Chipata
Fort Johnston *see* Mangochi
19 R1 **Fort Kent** Maine, NE USA 47°15′N 68°33′W
Fort-Lamy *see* Ndjamena
23 Z15 **Fort Lauderdale** Florida, SE USA 26°07′N 80°09′W
21 R11 **Fort Lawn** South Carolina, SE USA 34°43′N 80°46′W
8 H10 **Fort Liard** *var.* Liard. Northwest Territories, W Canada 60°14′N 123°28′W
44 M8 **Fort-Liberté** NE Haiti 19°42′N 71°51′W
21 N9 **Fort Loudoun Lake** ⊠ Tennessee, S USA
37 T3 **Fort Lupton** Colorado, C USA 40°04′N 104°48′W
11 R12 **Fort MacKay** Alberta, C Canada 57°12′N 111°41′W
11 Q17 **Fort Macleod** *var.* MacLeod. Alberta, SW Canada 49°44′N 113°24′W
29 Y16 **Fort Madison** Iowa, C USA 40°37′N 91°15′W
Fort Manning *see* Mchinji
25 P9 **Fort McKavett** Texas, SW USA 30°50′N 100°07′W
11 R12 **Fort McMurray** Alberta, C Canada 56°44′N 111°23′W
8 G7 **Fort McPherson** *var.* McPherson. Northwest Territories, NW Canada 67°29′N 134°50′W
21 R11 **Fort Mill** South Carolina, SE USA 35°00′N 80°57′W
Fort-Millot *see* Ngouri
37 U3 **Fort Morgan** Colorado, C USA 40°14′N 103°48′W
23 W14 **Fort Myers** Florida, SE USA 26°39′N 81°52′W
23 W15 **Fort Myers Beach** Florida, SE USA 26°27′N 81°57′W
10 M10 **Fort Nelson** British Columbia, W Canada 58°48′N 122°44′W
10 M10 **Fort Nelson** ≈ British Columbia, W Canada
Fort Norman *see* Tulita
23 Q2 **Fort Payne** Alabama, S USA 34°23′N 85°43′W
33 W7 **Fort Peck** Montana, NW USA 48°00′N 106°28′W
33 V8 **Fort Peck Lake** ⊠ Montana, NW USA
23 Y13 **Fort Pierce** Florida, SE USA 27°28′N 80°20′W
29 N10 **Fort Pierre** South Dakota, N USA 44°21′N 100°22′W
81 E18 **Fort Portal** SW Uganda 0°39′N 30°17′E
8 J10 **Fort Providence** *var.* Providence. Northwest Territories, W Canada 61°21′N 117°39′W
11 U16 **Fort Qu'Appelle** Saskatchewan, S Canada 50°50′N 103°52′W
Fort-Repoux *see* Akjoujt
8 K10 **Fort Resolution** *var.* Resolution. Northwest Territories, W Canada 61°10′N 113°39′W
33 T13 **Fortress Mountain** ▲ Wyoming, C USA 44°20′N 109°51′W
Fort Rosebery *see* Mansa
Fort Rousset *see* Owando
Fort-Royal *see* Fort-de-France
Fort Rupert *see* Waskaganish
8 H13 **Fort St. James** British Columbia, SW Canada 54°26′N 124°15′W
11 N12 **Fort St. John** British Columbia, W Canada 56°16′N 120°52′W
Fort Sandeman *see* Zhob
11 Q14 **Fort Saskatchewan** Alberta, SW Canada 53°42′N 113°12′W
27 R6 **Fort Scott** Kansas, C USA 37°52′N 94°43′W
12 E6 **Fort Severn** Ontario, C Canada 56°N 87°40′W
31 R12 **Fort Shawnee** Ohio, N USA 40°41′N 84°08′W
144 E14 **Fort-Shevchenko** Mangistau, W Kazakhstan 44°29′N 50°16′E
Fort-Sibut *see* Sibut
8 I10 **Fort Simpson** *var.* Simpson. Northwest Territories, W Canada 61°52′N 121°23′W
8 I10 **Fort Smith** Northwest Territories, W Canada 60°01′N 111°55′W
27 R10 **Fort Smith** Arkansas, C USA 35°23′N 94°24′W
37 T13 **Fort Stanton** New Mexico, SW USA 33°28′N 105°31′W
24 L9 **Fort Stockton** Texas, SW USA 30°54′N 102°54′W
37 U12 **Fort Sumner** New Mexico, SW USA 34°28′N 104°15′W
26 K8 **Fort Supply** Oklahoma, C USA 36°34′N 99°34′W
26 K8 **Fort Supply Lake** ⊠ Oklahoma, C USA
29 O10 **Fort Thompson** South Dakota, N USA 44°01′N 99°22′W
Fort-Trinquet *see* Bîr Mogreïn
105 R12 **Fortuna** Murcia, SE Spain 38°11′N 01°07′W
34 K3 **Fortuna** California, W USA 40°35′N 124°07′W
28 J2 **Fortuna** North Dakota, N USA 48°53′N 103°46′W
23 T5 **Fort Valley** Georgia, SE USA 32°33′N 83°53′W
11 P11 **Fort Vermilion** Alberta, W Canada 58°22′N 115°59′W
Fort Victoria *see* Masvingo
31 P13 **Fortville** Indiana, N USA 39°55′N 85°51′W
23 P9 **Fort Walton Beach** Florida, SE USA 30°24′N 86°37′W
31 P12 **Fort Wayne** Indiana, N USA 41°08′N 85°08′W
96 H10 **Fort William** N Scotland, United Kingdom 56°49′N 05°07′W
25 T6 **Fort Worth** Texas, SW USA 32°44′N 97°19′W
28 M7 **Fort Yates** North Dakota, N USA 46°05′N 100°37′W
39 S7 **Fort Yukon** Alaska, USA 66°35′N 145°05′W
Forum Alieni *see* Ferrara
Forum Julii *see* Fréjus
Forum Livii *see* Forlì
143 Q15 **Forūr-e Bozorg, Jazīreh-ye** *island* S Iran
94 H7 **Fosen** *physical region* S Norway
161 N14 **Foshan** *var.* Fatshan, Fo-shan, Namhoi. Guangdong, S China 23°03′N 113°08′E
Fo-shan *see* Foshan
194 J6 **Fossil Bluff** *UK research station* Antarctica 71°30′S 68°30′W
Fossa Claudia *see* Chioggia
106 B9 **Fossano** Piemonte, NW Italy 44°33′N 07°43′E
99 H21 **Fosses-la-Ville** Namur, S Belgium 50°24′N 04°42′E
32 J12 **Fossil** Oregon, NW USA 45°01′N 120°14′W
Foss Lake *see* Foss Reservoir
106 I11 **Fossombrone** Marche, C Italy 43°42′N 12°48′E
26 K10 **Foss Reservoir** *var.* Foss Lake. ⊠ Oklahoma, C USA
29 S4 **Fosston** Minnesota, N USA 47°34′N 95°45′W
183 O13 **Foster** Victoria, SE Australia 38°40′S 146°15′E
11 T12 **Foster Lakes** ◎ Saskatchewan, C Canada
31 S12 **Fostoria** Ohio, N USA 41°09′N 83°25′W
79 D19 **Fougamou** Ngounié, C Gabon 01°16′S 10°30′E
102 J6 **Fougères** Ille-et-Vilaine, NW France 48°21′N 01°12′W
Fou-hsin *see* Fuxin
27 S14 **Fouke** Arkansas, C USA 33°15′N 93°53′W
96 K2 **Foula** *island* NE Scotland, United Kingdom
65 D24 **Foul Bay** *bay* East Falkland, Falkland Islands
97 P21 **Foulness Island** *island* SE England, United Kingdom
185 F15 **Foulwind, Cape** *headland* South Island, New Zealand 41°45′S 171°28′E
79 E15 **Foumban** Ouest, NW Cameroon 05°43′N 10°50′E
172 H13 **Foumbouni** Grande Comore, NW Comoros 11°49′S 43°30′E
195 N8 **Foundation Ice Stream** *glacier* Antarctica
37 T6 **Fountain** Colorado, C USA 38°40′N 104°42′W
36 L4 **Fountain Green** Utah, W USA 39°37′N 111°37′W
21 P11 **Fountain Inn** South Carolina, SE USA 34°41′N 82°12′W
27 S11 **Fourche LaFave River** ≈ Arkansas, C USA
33 Z13 **Four Corners** Wyoming, C USA 44°04′N 104°08′W
103 Q2 **Fourmies** Nord, N France 50°01′N 04°03′E
38 J17 **Four Mountains, Islands of** *island group* Aleutian Islands, Alaska, USA
173 P17 **Fournaise, Piton de la** ⛰ SE Réunion 21°14′S 55°43′E
14 J8 **Fournière, Lac** ◎ Québec, SE Canada
115 L20 **Foúrnoi** *island* Dodekánisa, Greece, Aegean Sea
64 K13 **Four North Fracture Zone** *tectonic feature* W Atlantic Ocean
Fouron-Saint-Martin *see* Sint-Martens-Voeren
30 L3 **Fourteen Mile Point** *headland* Michigan, N USA 46°59′N 89°07′W
Fou-shan *see* Fushun
76 I13 **Fouta Djallon** *var.* Futa Jallon. ▲▲ W Guinea
185 C25 **Foveaux Strait** *strait* S New Zealand
35 Q11 **Fowler** California, W USA 36°35′N 119°40′W
37 U6 **Fowler** Colorado, C USA 38°07′N 104°01′W
31 N12 **Fowler** Indiana, N USA 40°36′N 87°20′W
182 D7 **Fowlers Bay** *bay* South Australia
25 R13 **Fowlerton** Texas, SW USA 28°27′N 98°48′W
142 M3 **Fowman** *var.* Fuman, Fumen. Gīlān, NW Iran 37°15′N 49°19′E
65 C25 **Fox Bay East** West Falkland, Falkland Islands
14 J14 **Foxboro** Ontario, SE Canada 44°16′N 77°23′W
11 O14 **Fox Creek** Alberta, W Canada 54°25′N 116°57′W
64 G5 **Foxe Basin** *sea* Nunavut, N Canada
64 G5 **Foxe Channel** *channel* Nunavut, N Canada
95 I16 **Foxen** ◎ C Sweden
9 Q7 **Foxe Peninsula** *peninsula* Baffin Island, Nunavut, NE Canada
185 E19 **Fox Glacier** West Coast, South Island, New Zealand 43°28′S 170°00′E
38 L17 **Fox Islands** *island* Aleutian Islands, Alaska, USA
30 M10 **Fox Lake** Illinois, N USA 42°24′N 88°10′W
9 V12 **Fox Mine** Manitoba, C Canada 56°36′N 101°48′W
35 R3 **Fox Mountain** ▲ Nevada, W USA 41°01′N 119°30′W
65 E25 **Fox Point** *headland* East Falkland, Falkland Islands 51°55′S 58°24′W
30 M11 **Fox River** ≈ Illinois/Wisconsin, N USA
30 L7 **Fox River** ≈ Wisconsin, N USA
184 L13 **Foxton** Manawatu-Wanganui, North Island, New Zealand 40°27′S 175°18′E
11 S16 **Fox Valley** Saskatchewan, S Canada 50°29′N 109°29′W
11 W16 **Foxwarren** Manitoba, S Canada 50°30′N 101°09′W
97 E14 **Foyle, Lough** *Ir.* Loch Feabhail. *inlet* N Ireland
194 H5 **Foyn Coast** *physical region* Antarctica
104 I2 **Foz** Galicia, NW Spain 43°33′N 07°16′W
60 I12 **Foz do Areia, Represa de** ⊠ S Brazil
59 A16 **Foz do Breu** Acre, W Brazil 09°21′S 72°41′W
83 A16 **Foz do Cunene** Namibe, SW Angola 17°11′S 11°52′E
60 G12 **Foz do Iguaçu** Paraná, S Brazil 25°33′S 54°31′W
58 C12 **Foz do Mamoriá** Amazonas, NW Brazil 02°28′S 66°06′W
105 T6 **Fraga** Aragón, NE Spain 41°32′N 00°21′E
44 F5 **Fragoso, Cayo** *island* C Cuba
61 G18 **Fraile Muerto** Cerro Largo, NE Uruguay 32°30′S 54°30′W
99 H21 **Fraire** Namur, S Belgium 50°16′N 04°30′E
99 L21 **Fraiture, Baraque de** *hill* SE Belgium
Frakštát *see* Hlohovec
197 S10 **Fram Basin** *var.* Amundsen Basin. *undersea feature* Arctic Ocean 88°00′N 90°00′E
99 F20 **Frameries** Hainaut, S Belgium 50°25′N 03°41′E
19 O11 **Framingham** Massachusetts, NE USA 42°15′N 71°24′W
60 L7 **Franca** São Paulo, S Brazil 20°33′S 47°27′W
187 O15 **Français, Récif des** *reef* W New Caledonia
107 K14 **Francavilla al Mare** Abruzzo, C Italy 42°25′N 14°16′E
107 P18 **Francavilla Fontana** Puglia, SE Italy 40°32′N 17°35′E
102 M8 **France** *off.* French Republic, *It./Sp.* Francia; *prev.* Gaul, Gaule, *Lat.* Gallia. ◆ *republic* W Europe
45 O8 **Francés Viejo, Cabo** *headland* NE Dominican Republic 19°39′N 69°57′W
79 F19 **Franceville** *var.* Massoukou, Masuku. Haut-Ogooué, E Gabon 01°40′S 13°31′E
79 F19 **Franceville** ✈ Haut-Ogooué, E Gabon 01°38′S 13°24′E
Francfort *see* Frankfurt am Main
103 T8 **Franche-Comté** ◈ *region* E France
Francia *see* France
29 O11 **Francis Case, Lake** ⊠ South Dakota, N USA
60 H12 **Francisco Beltrão** Paraná, S Brazil 26°05′S 53°04′W
Francisco l. Madero *see* Villa Madero
61 A21 **Francisco Madero** Buenos Aires, E Argentina 35°52′S 62°03′W
42 H6 **Francisco Morazán** *prev.* Tegucigalpa. ◈ *department* C Honduras
83 J18 **Francistown** North East, NE Botswana 21°08′S 27°31′E
Franconian Forest *see* Frankenwald
Franconian Jura *see* Fränkische Alb
98 K6 **Franeker** *Fris.* Frjentsjer. Friesland, N Netherlands 53°11′N 05°33′E
Frankenalb *see* Fränkische Alb
101 H16 **Frankenberg** Hessen, C Germany 51°04′N 08°49′E
101 J20 **Frankenhöhe** *hill range* C Germany
31 R8 **Frankenmuth** Michigan, N USA 43°19′N 83°44′W
101 F20 **Frankenstein** *hill* W Germany
Frankenstein/Frankenstein in Schlesien *see* Ząbkowice Śląskie
101 G20 **Frankenthal** Rheinland-Pfalz, W Germany 49°32′N 08°22′E
101 L18 **Frankenwald** *Eng.* Franconian Forest. ▲▲ C Germany
44 J12 **Frankfield** C Jamaica 18°08′N 77°22′W
14 J14 **Frankford** Ontario, SE Canada 44°12′N 77°36′W
31 O13 **Frankfort** Indiana, N USA 40°16′N 86°30′W
27 O3 **Frankfort** Kansas, C USA 39°42′N 96°25′W
20 L5 **Frankfort** *state capital* Kentucky, S USA 38°12′N 84°52′W
Frankfort on the Main *see* Frankfurt am Main
Frankfurt *see* Frankfurt am Main, Germany
Frankfurt *see* Słubice, Poland
101 G18 **Frankfurt am Main** *var.* Frankfurt, *Fr.* Francfort; *prev. Eng.* Frankfort on the Main. Hessen, SW Germany 50°07′N 08°41′E
100 Q12 **Frankfurt an der Oder** Brandenburg, E Germany 52°20′N 14°32′E
101 L21 **Fränkische Alb** *var.* Frankenalb, *Eng.* Franconian Jura. ▲▲ S Germany
101 I18 **Fränkische Saale** ≈ C Germany
101 L19 **Fränkische Schweiz** *hill range* C Germany
23 R4 **Franklin** Georgia, SE USA 33°15′N 85°06′W
31 P14 **Franklin** Indiana, N USA 39°29′N 86°02′W
20 J7 **Franklin** Kentucky, S USA 36°42′N 86°35′W
22 I9 **Franklin** Louisiana, S USA 29°48′N 91°30′W
29 O17 **Franklin** Nebraska, C USA 40°06′N 98°57′W
21 N10 **Franklin** North Carolina, SE USA 35°12′N 83°23′W
18 C13 **Franklin** Pennsylvania, NE USA 41°24′N 79°49′W
20 J9 **Franklin** Tennessee, S USA 35°55′N 86°52′W
25 U9 **Franklin** Texas, SW USA 31°02′N 96°30′W
21 X7 **Franklin** Virginia, NE USA 36°41′N 76°58′W
21 T4 **Franklin** West Virginia, NE USA 38°39′N 79°21′W
30 M9 **Franklin** Wisconsin, N USA 42°53′N 88°00′W
8 I6 **Franklin Bay** *inlet* Northwest Territories, N Canada
32 K7 **Franklin D. Roosevelt Lake** ⊠ Washington, NW USA
35 W4 **Franklin Lake** ◎ Nevada, W USA
185 B22 **Franklin Mountains** ▲▲ South Island, New Zealand
39 R5 **Franklin Mountains** ▲▲ Alaska, USA
39 N4 **Franklin, Point** *headland* Alaska, USA 70°54′N 158°48′W
183 O17 **Franklin River** ≈ Tasmania, SE Australia
22 K8 **Franklinton** Louisiana, S USA 30°51′N 90°09′W
21 U9 **Franklinton** North Carolina, SE USA 36°06′N 78°27′W
Frankstadt *see* Frenštát pod Radhoštěm
25 V7 **Frankston** Texas, SW USA 32°03′N 95°30′W
33 U12 **Frannie** Wyoming, C USA 44°57′N 108°37′W
15 U5 **Franquelin** Québec, SE Canada 49°17′N 67°52′W
15 U5 **Franquelin** ≈ Québec, SE Canada
83 C18 **Fransfontein** Kunene, NW Namibia 20°12′S 15°01′E
93 H17 **Fränsta** Västernorrland, C Sweden 62°30′N 16°06′E
122 J3 **Frantsa-Iosifa, Zemlya** *Eng.* Franz Josef Land. *island group* N Russian Federation
185 E18 **Franz Josef Glacier** West Coast, South Island, New Zealand 43°22′S 170°11′E
Franz Josef Land *see* Frantsa-Iosifa, Zemlya
Franz-Josef Spitze *see* Gerlachovský štít
101 L23 **Franz Josef Strauss** *abbrev.* F.J.S.. ✈ (München) Bayern, SE Germany 48°07′N 11°43′E
107 A19 **Frasca, Capo della** *headland* Sardegna, Italy, C Mediterranean Sea 39°46′N 08°27′E
107 I15 **Frascati** Lazio, C Italy 41°48′N 12°41′E
11 N14 **Fraser** ≈ British Columbia, SW Canada
83 G24 **Fraserburg** Western Cape, SW South Africa 31°55′S 21°31′E
96 L8 **Fraserburgh** NE Scotland, United Kingdom 57°42′N 02°20′W
181 Z9 **Fraser Island** *var.* Great Sandy Island. *island* Queensland, E Australia
10 L14 **Fraser Lake** British Columbia, SW Canada 54°00′N 124°45′W
10 L15 **Fraser Plateau** *plateau* British Columbia, SW Canada
184 P10 **Frasertown** Hawke's Bay, North Island, New Zealand 38°58′S 177°25′E
99 E19 **Frasnes-lez-Buissenal** Hainaut, SW Belgium 50°40′N 03°37′E
108 I7 **Frastanz** Vorarlberg, NW Austria 47°13′N 09°38′E
14 B8 **Frater** Ontario, S Canada 47°19′N 84°28′W
Frauenbach *see* Baia Mare
Frauenburg *see* Saldus, Latvia
Frauenburg *see* Frombork, Poland
108 H6 **Frauenfeld** Thurgau, NE Switzerland 47°34′N 08°54′E
109 Z5 **Frauenkirchen** Burgenland, E Austria 47°50′N 16°57′E
61 D19 **Fray Bentos** Río Negro, W Uruguay 33°09′S 58°14′W
61 F19 **Fray Marcos** Florida, S Uruguay 34°13′S 55°43′W
29 S6 **Frazee** Minnesota, N USA 46°42′N 95°40′W
104 M5 **Frechilla** Castilla-León, N Spain 42°08′N 04°50′W
30 I4 **Frederic** Wisconsin, N USA 45°42′N 92°30′W
95 G23 **Fredericia** Vejle, C Denmark 55°34′N 09°47′E
21 W3 **Frederick** Maryland, NE USA 39°25′N 77°25′W
26 L12 **Frederick** Oklahoma, C USA 34°24′N 99°03′W
29 P7 **Frederick** South Dakota, N USA 45°49′N 98°31′W
29 X12 **Fredericksburg** Iowa, C USA 42°58′N 92°12′W
25 R10 **Fredericksburg** Texas, SW USA 30°17′N 98°52′W
21 W5 **Fredericksburg** Virginia, NE USA 38°16′N 77°27′W
39 X13 **Frederick Sound** *sound* Alaska, USA
27 X6 **Fredericktown** Missouri, C USA 37°33′N 90°19′W
60 H13 **Frederico Westphalen** Rio Grande do Sul, S Brazil 27°22′S 53°20′W
13 O15 **Fredericton** *province capital* New Brunswick, SE Canada 45°57′N 66°40′W
95 I22 **Frederiksborg** *off.* Frederiksborgs Amt. ◈ *county* E Denmark
Frederiksborgs Amt *see* Frederiksborg
Frederikshåb *see* Paamiut
95 H19 **Frederikshavn** *prev.* Fladstrand. Nordjylland, N Denmark 57°28′N 10°33′E
95 J22 **Frederikssund** Frederiksborg, E Denmark 55°51′N 12°05′E
45 T9 **Frederiksted** Saint Croix, S Virgin Islands (US) 17°41′N 64°51′W
95 I22 **Frederiksværk** *var.* Frederiksværk og Hanehoved. Frederiksborg, E Denmark 55°58′N 12°02′E
Frederiksværk og Hanehoved *see* Frederiksværk
54 E9 **Fredonia** Antioquia, W Colombia 05°57′N 75°42′W
36 K8 **Fredonia** Arizona, SW USA 36°57′N 112°31′W
27 P7 **Fredonia** Kansas, C USA 37°32′N 95°50′W
18 C11 **Fredonia** New York, NE USA 42°26′N 79°19′W
35 P4 **Fredonyer Pass** *pass* California, W USA
93 I15 **Fredrika** Västerbotten, N Sweden 64°03′N 18°25′E
95 L14 **Fredriksberg** Dalarna, C Sweden 60°07′N 14°23′E
Fredrikshald *see* Halden
Fredrikshamn *see* Hamina
95 H16 **Fredrikstad** Østfold, S Norway 59°12′N 10°57′E
30 K16 **Freeburg** Illinois, N USA 38°25′N 89°54′W
18 K15 **Freehold** New Jersey, NE USA 40°14′N 74°14′W
18 H14 **Freeland** Pennsylvania, NE USA 41°01′N 75°54′W
182 J5 **Freeling Heights** ▲ South Australia 30°09′S 139°24′E
35 Q7 **Freel Peak** ▲ California, W USA 38°52′N 119°52′W
11 Z9 **Freels, Cape** *headland* Newfoundland and Labrador, E Canada 49°16′N 53°30′W
29 Q11 **Freeman** South Dakota, N USA 43°21′N 97°26′W
44 G1 **Freeport** Grand Bahama Island, N Bahamas 26°28′N 78°43′W
30 L10 **Freeport** Illinois, N USA 42°18′N 89°37′W
25 W12 **Freeport** Texas, SW USA 28°57′N 95°21′W
44 G1 **Freeport** ✈ Grand Bahama Island, N Bahamas 26°31′N 78°48′W
25 R14 **Freer** Texas, SW USA 27°52′N 98°37′W
83 I22 **Free State** *off.* Free State Province; *prev.* Orange Free State, *Afr.* Oranje Vrystaat. ◈ *province* C South Africa
Free State *see* Maryland
Free State Province *see* Free State
76 G15 **Freetown** ● (Sierra Leone) W Sierra Leone 08°27′N 13°16′W
172 J16 **Frégate** *island* Inner Islands, NE Seychelles
104 J12 **Fregenal de la Sierra** Extremadura, W Spain 38°10′N 06°39′W
182 C2 **Fregon** South Australia 26°44′S 132°03′E
102 H5 **Fréhel, Cap** *headland* NW France 48°41′N 02°21′W
94 F8 **Frei** Møre og Romsdal, S Norway 63°02′N 07°47′E
101 O16 **Freiberg** Sachsen, E Germany 50°55′N 13°21′E
101 O16 **Freiberger Mulde** ≈ E Germany
Freiburg *see* Freiburg im Breisgau, Germany
Freiburg *see* Fribourg, Switzerland
101 F23 **Freiburg im Breisgau** *var.* Freiburg, *Fr.* Fribourg-en-Brisgau. Baden-Württemberg, SW Germany 48°N 07°52′E
Freiburg in Schlesien *see* Świebodzice
Freie Hansestadt Bremen *see* Bremen
Freie und Hansestadt Hamburg *see* Brandenburg
101 L22 **Freising** Bayern, SE Germany 48°24′N 11°45′E
109 T3 **Freistadt** Oberösterreich, N Austria 48°31′N 14°31′E
Freistadtl *see* Hlohovec
101 O16 **Freital** Sachsen, E Germany 51°00′N 13°40′E
Freiwaldau *see* Jeseník
104 J6 **Freixo de Espada à Cinta** Bragança, N Portugal 41°05′N 06°49′W
103 U15 **Fréjus** *anc.* Forum Julii. Var, SE France 43°26′N 06°44′E
180 I13 **Fremantle** Western Australia 32°07′S 115°44′E
35 N9 **Fremont** California, W USA 37°34′N 122°01′W
31 Q11 **Fremont** Indiana, N USA 41°43′N 84°54′W
29 W15 **Fremont** Iowa, C USA 41°12′N 92°26′W
31 P8 **Fremont** Michigan, N USA 43°28′N 85°56′W
29 R15 **Fremont** Nebraska, C USA 41°25′N 96°30′W
31 S11 **Fremont** Ohio, N USA 41°21′N 83°08′W
33 T14 **Fremont Peak** ▲ Wyoming, C USA 43°07′N 109°37′W
36 M6 **Fremont River** ≈ Utah, W USA
21 O9 **French Broad River** ≈ Tennessee, S USA
21 N5 **Frenchburg** Kentucky, S USA 37°58′N 83°37′W
18 C12 **French Creek** ≈ Pennsylvania, NE USA
32 K15 **Frenchglen** Oregon, NW USA 42°49′N 118°55′W
55 Y10 **French Guiana** *var.* Guiana, Guyane. ◇ *French overseas department* N South America
French Guinea *see* Guinea
31 O15 **French Lick** Indiana, N USA 38°33′N 86°37′W
185 J14 **French Pass** Marlborough, South Island, New Zealand 40°57′S 173°49′E
191 T11 **French Polynesia** ◇ *French overseas territory* S Pacific Ocean
French Republic *see* France
14 F11 **French River** ≈ Ontario, S Canada
French Somaliland *see* Djibouti
173 P12 **French Southern and Antarctic Territories** *Fr.* Terres Australes et Antarctiques Françaises. ◇ *French overseas territory* S Indian Ocean
French Sudan *see* Mali
French Territory of the Afars and Issas *see* Djibouti
French Togoland *see* Togo
74 J6 **Frenda** NW Algeria 35°04′N 01°03′E
111 I18 **Frenštát pod Radhoštěm** *Ger.* Frankstadt. Moravskoslezský Kraj, E Czech Republic 49°33′N 18°10′E
76 M17 **Fresco** S Ivory Coast 05°03′N 05°31′W
195 U16 **Freshfield, Cape** *headland* Antarctica
40 L10 **Fresnillo** *var.* Fresnillo de González Echeverría. Zacatecas, C Mexico 23°11′N 102°53′W
Fresnillo de González Echeverría *see* Fresnillo
35 Q10 **Fresno** California, W USA 36°45′N 119°48′W
Freu, Cabo del *see* Freu, Cap des
105 Y9 **Freu, Cap des** *var.* Cabo del Freu. *cape* Mallorca, Spain, W Mediterranean Sea
101 G22 **Freudenstadt** Baden-Württemberg, SW Germany 48°28′N 08°25′E
Freudenthal *see* Bruntál
183 Q17 **Freycinet Peninsula** *peninsula* Tasmania, SE Australia
76 H14 **Fria** W Guinea 10°27′N 13°38′W
83 A17 **Fria, Cape** *headland* NW Namibia 18°32′S 12°00′E
35 Q10 **Friant** California, W USA 36°56′N 119°44′W
62 K8 **Frías** Catamarca, N Argentina 28°41′S 65°00′W
108 D9 **Fribourg** *Ger.* Freiburg. Fribourg, W Switzerland 46°50′N 07°10′E
108 C9 **Fribourg** *Ger.* Freiburg. ◈ *canton* W Switzerland
Fribourg-en-Brisgau *see* Freiburg im Breisgau
32 G7 **Friday Harbor** San Juan Islands, Washington, NW USA 48°31′N 123°01′W
Friedau *see* Ormož
101 K23 **Friedberg** Bayern, S Germany 48°21′N 10°58′E
101 H18 **Friedberg** Hessen, W Germany 50°19′N 08°46′E
Friedeberg Neumark *see* Strzelce Krajeńskie
Friedek-Mistek *see* Frýdek-Místek
Friedland *see* Pravdinsk
101 I24 **Friedrichshafen** Baden-Württemberg, S Germany 47°39′N 09°29′E
Friedrichstadt *see* Jaunjelgava
29 Q16 **Friend** Nebraska, C USA 40°37′N 97°16′W
Friendly Islands *see* Tonga
55 V9 **Friendship** Coronie, N Surinam 05°50′N 56°16′W
30 L7 **Friendship** Wisconsin, N USA 43°58′N 89°48′W
109 T8 **Friesach** Kärnten, S Austria 46°58′N 14°24′E
Friesche Eilanden *see* Frisian Islands
101 F22 **Friesenheim** Baden-Württemberg, SW Germany 48°27′N 07°56′E
Friesische Inseln *see* Frisian Islands
98 K6 **Friesland** ◈ *province* N Netherlands
60 Q10 **Frio, Cabo** *headland* SE Brazil 23°01′S 41°59′W
24 M3 **Friona** Texas, SW USA 34°38′N 102°43′W
42 L12 **Frío, Río** ≈ N Costa Rica
25 R13 **Frio River** ≈ Texas, SW USA
99 M25 **Frisange** Luxembourg, S Luxembourg 49°31′N 06°12′E
Frisches Haff *see* Vistula Lagoon
36 J6 **Frisco Peak** ▲ Utah, W USA 38°31′N 113°17′W
84 F9 **Frisian Islands** *Dut.* Friesche Eilanden, *Ger.* Friesische Inseln. *island group* N Europe
18 L12 **Frissell, Mount** ▲ Connecticut, NE USA 42°01′N 73°25′W
95 J19 **Fristad** Västra Götaland, S Sweden 57°50′N 13°01′E
25 N2 **Fritch** Texas, SW USA 35°38′N 101°36′W
95 J19 **Fritsla** Västra Götaland, S Sweden 57°33′N 12°47′E
101 H16 **Fritzlar** Hessen, C Germany 51°09′N 09°16′E
106 H6 **Friuli-Venezia Giulia** ◈ *region* NE Italy
Frjentsjer *see* Franeker
196 L13 **Frobisher Bay** *inlet* Baffin Island, Nunavut, NE Canada
Frobisher Bay *see* Iqaluit
11 S12 **Frobisher Lake** ◎ Saskatchewan, C Canada
94 G7 **Frohavet** *sound* C Norway
Frohenbruck *see* Veselí nad Lužnicí
109 V7 **Frohnleiten** Steiermark, SE Austria 47°17′N 15°20′E
99 G22 **Froidchapelle** Hainaut, S Belgium 50°10′N 04°18′E
127 O9 **Frolovo** Volgogradskaya Oblast', SW Russian Federation 49°46′N 43°38′E
110 K7 **Frombork** *Ger.* Frauenburg. Warmińsko-Mazurkskie, NE Poland 54°21′N 19°40′E
97 L22 **Frome** SW England, United Kingdom 51°15′N 02°22′W
182 I4 **Frome Creek** *seasonal river* South Australia
182 J6 **Frome Downs** South Australia 31°17′S 139°48′E
182 J5 **Frome, Lake** *salt lake* South Australia
Fronicken *see* Wronki
104 H10 **Fronteira** Portalegre, C Portugal 39°03′N 07°39′W
40 M7 **Frontera** Coahuila, NE Mexico 26°55′N 101°27′W
41 U14 **Frontera** Tabasco, SE Mexico 18°32′N 92°39′W
40 G3 **Fronteras** Sonora, NW Mexico 30°51′N 109°33′W
103 Q16 **Frontignan** Hérault, S France 43°27′N 03°45′E
54 D8 **Frontino** Antioquia, NW Colombia 06°46′N 76°10′W
21 V4 **Front Royal** Virginia, NE USA 38°56′N 78°13′W
107 J16 **Frosinone** *anc.* Frusino. Lazio, C Italy 41°38′N 13°22′E
107 K16 **Frosolone** Molise, C Italy 41°34′N 14°25′E
25 U7 **Frost** Texas, SW USA 32°04′N 96°48′W

◆ Country
● Country Capital
◇ Dependent Territory
○ Dependent Territory Capital
◈ Administrative Regions
✈ International Airport
▲ Mountain
▲▲ Mountain Range
⛰ Volcano
≈ River
◎ Lake
⊠ Reservoir

FROSTBURG – GARDELEGEN

21 U2 **Frostburg** Maryland, NE USA 39°39′N 78°55′W
23 X13 **Frostproof** Florida, SE USA 27°45′N 81°31′W
Frostviken see Kvarnbergsvattnet
95 M15 **Frövi** Örebro, C Sweden 59°28′N 15°24′E
94 F7 **Frøya** island W Norway
37 P5 **Fruita** Colorado, C USA 39°10′N 108°42′W
28 J9 **Fruitdale** South Dakota, N USA 44°39′N 103°38′W
23 W11 **Fruitland Park** Florida, SE USA 28°51′N 81°54′W
Frumentum see Formentera
147 S11 **Frunze** Batkenskaya Oblast', SW Kyrgyzstan 40°07′N 71°40′E
Frunze see Bishkek
117 O9 **Frunzivka** Odes'ka Oblast', SW Ukraine 47°19′N 29°46′E
Frusino see Frosinone
108 E9 **Frutigen** Bern, W Switzerland 46°35′N 07°38′E
111 I17 **Frýdek-Místek** Ger. Friedek-Mistek. Moravskoslezský Kraj, E Czech Republic 49°40′N 18°22′E
193 V16 **Fua'amotu** Tongatapu, S Tonga 21°15′S 175°08′W
190 A9 **Fuafatu** island Funafuti Atoll, C Tuvalu
190 A9 **Fuagea** island Funafuti Atoll, C Tuvalu
190 B8 **Fualifeke** atoll C Tuvalu
190 A8 **Fualopa** island Funafuti Atoll, C Tuvalu
151 K22 **Fuammulah** var. Fuammulah, Gnaviyani. atoll S Maldives
Fuammulah see Fuammulah
161 R11 **Fu'an** Fujian, SE China 27°11′N 119°42′E
Fu-chien see Fujian
Fu-chou see Fuzhou
164 G13 **Fuchū** var. Hutyû. Hiroshima, Honshū, SW Japan 34°35′N 133°12′E
160 M13 **Fuchuan** var. Fuyang. Guangxi Zhuangzu Zizhiqu, S China 24°56′N 111°15′E
165 R8 **Fudai** Iwate, Honshū, C Japan 39°59′N 141°50′E
161 S11 **Fuding** var. Tongshan. Fujian, SE China 27°21′N 120°10′E
81 J20 **Fudua** spring/well S Kenya 02°13′S 39°43′E
104 M16 **Fuengirola** Andalucía, S Spain 36°32′N 04°38′W
104 J12 **Fuente de Cantos** Extremadura, W Spain 38°15′N 06°18′W
104 J11 **Fuente del Maestre** Extremadura, W Spain 38°31′N 06°26′W
104 L12 **Fuente Obejuna** Andalucía, S Spain 38°15′N 05°25′W
104 L6 **Fuentesaúco** Castilla-León, N Spain 41°14′N 05°30′W
62 O3 **Fuerte Olimpo** var. Olimpo. Alto Paraguay, NE Paraguay 21°02′S 57°51′W
40 H8 **Fuerte, Río** ⇝ C Mexico
64 Q11 **Fuerteventura** island Islas Canarias, Spain, NE Atlantic Ocean
141 S14 **Fughmah** var. Faghman, Fugma. C Yemen 16°08′N 49°23′E
92 M2 **Fuglehuken** headland W Svalbard 78°54′N 10°30′E
Fuglø see Fugloy
95 B18 **Fugloy** Dan. Fuglø. island NE Faeroe Islands
197 T15 **Fugløya Bank** undersea feature E Norwegian Sea 71°00′N 19°20′E
Fugma see Fughmah
160 E11 **Fugong** Yunnan, SW China 27°00′N 98°48′E
81 K16 **Fugugo** spring/well NE Kenya 03°19′N 39°39′E
158 L2 **Fuhai** var. Burultokay. Xinjiang Uygur Zizhiqu, NW China 47°15′N 87°39′E
161 P10 **Fu He** ⇝ S China
Fuhkien see Fujian
100 J9 **Fuhlsbüttel** ✈ (Hamburg) Hamburg, N Germany 53°37′N 09°57′E
101 L14 **Fuhne** ⇝ C Germany
Fu-hsin see Fuxin
Fujairah see Al Fujayrah
164 M14 **Fuji** var. Huzi. Shizuoka, Honshū, S Japan 35°08′N 138°39′E
161 Q12 **Fujian** var. Fu-chien, Fuhkien, Fukien, Min, Fujian Sheng. ◈ province SE China
160 I9 **Fu Jiang** ⇝ C China
Fujian Sheng see Fujian
164 M14 **Fujieda** var. Huzieda. Shizuoka, Honshū, S Japan 34°54′N 138°15′E
Fuji, Mount/Fujiyama see Fuji-san
163 Y7 **Fujin** Heilongjiang, NE China 47°12′N 132°01′E
164 M13 **Fujinomiya** var. Huzinomiya. Shizuoka, Honshū, S Japan 35°16′N 138°33′E
164 N13 **Fuji-san** var. Fujiyama, Eng. Mount Fuji. ▲ Honshū, SE Japan 35°23′N 138°44′E
165 N14 **Fujisawa** var. Huzisawa. Kanagawa, Honshū, S Japan 35°22′N 139°29′E
165 T3 **Fukagawa** var. Hukagawa. Hokkaidō, NE Japan 43°44′N 142°03′E
158 L5 **Fukang** Xinjiang Uygur Zizhiqu, W China 44°07′N 87°55′E
165 P7 **Fukaura** Aomori, Honshū, C Japan 40°38′N 139°55′E
193 W15 **Fukave** island Tongatapu Group, S Tonga
Fukien see Fujian
164 J13 **Fukuchiyama** var. Hukutiyama. Kyōto, Honshū, SW Japan 35°19′N 135°08′E
164 A14 **Fukue** var. Hukue. Nagasaki, Fukue-jima, SW Japan 32°41′N 128°52′E
164 A13 **Fukue-jima** island Gotō-rettō, SW Japan
164 K12 **Fukui** var. Hukui. Fukui, Honshū, SW Japan 36°03′N 136°12′E
164 K12 **Fukui** off. Fukui-ken, var. Hukui. ◈ prefecture Honshū, SW Japan
Fukui-ken see Fukui
164 D13 **Fukuoka** var. Hukuoka, hist. Najima. Fukuoka, Kyūshū, SW Japan 33°36′N 130°24′E
164 D13 **Fukuoka** off. Fukuoka-ken, var. Hukuoka. ◈ prefecture Kyūshū, SW Japan
Fukuoka-ken see Fukuoka
165 Q6 **Fukushima** Hokkaidō, NE Japan 41°27′N 140°14′E
165 Q12 **Fukushima** off. Fukushima-ken, var. Hukusima. ◈ prefecture Honshū, C Japan
Fukushima-ken see Fukushima
164 G13 **Fukuyama** var. Hukuyama. Hiroshima, Honshū, SW Japan 34°29′N 133°21′E
76 G13 **Fulacunda** C Guinea-Bissau 11°44′N 15°03′W
129 P8 **Fūlādī, Kūh-e** ▲ E Afghanistan 34°38′N 67°32′E
187 Z15 **Fulaga** island Lau Group, E Fiji
101 I17 **Fulda** Hessen, C Germany 50°33′N 09°41′E
29 S10 **Fulda** Minnesota, N USA 43°52′N 95°36′W
101 I16 **Fulda** ⇝ C Germany
Fülek see Fil'akovo
Fulin see Hanyuan
160 K10 **Fuling** Chongqing Shi, C China 29°45′N 107°23′E
35 T15 **Fullerton** California, W USA 33°53′N 117°55′W
29 P15 **Fullerton** Nebraska, C USA 41°21′N 97°58′W
108 M8 **Fulpmes** Tirol, W Austria 47°11′N 11°22′E
20 G8 **Fulton** Kentucky, S USA 36°31′N 88°52′W
23 N2 **Fulton** Mississippi, S USA 34°16′N 88°24′W
27 V4 **Fulton** Missouri, C USA 38°50′N 91°57′W
18 H9 **Fulton** New York, NE USA 43°18′N 76°22′W
Fuman/Fumen see Fowman
103 R3 **Fumay** Ardennes, N France 49°58′N 04°42′E
102 M13 **Fumel** Lot-et-Garonne, SW France 44°31′N 00°58′E
190 B10 **Funafara** atoll C Tuvalu
190 C9 **Funafuti** ✈ Funafuti Atoll, C Tuvalu 08°30′S 179°12′E
Funafuti see Fongafale
190 F8 **Funafuti Atoll** atoll C Tuvalu
Funan see Fusui
190 B9 **Funangongo** atoll C Tuvalu
93 F17 **Funäsdalen** Jämtland, C Sweden 62°33′N 12°33′E
64 O6 **Funchal** Madeira, Portugal, NE Atlantic Ocean 32°40′N 16°55′W
64 P5 **Funchal** ✈ Madeira, Portugal, NE Atlantic Ocean 32°38′N 16°53′W
54 F5 **Fundación** Magdalena, N Colombia 10°31′N 74°09′W
104 I8 **Fundão** var. Fundão. Castelo Branco, C Portugal 40°08′N 07°30′W
Fundão see Fundão
13 O16 **Fundy, Bay of** bay Canada/USA
Fünen see Fyn
54 C13 **Fúnes** Nariño, SW Colombia 0°59′N 77°27′W
Fünfkirchen see Pécs
83 M19 **Funhalouro** Inhambane, S Mozambique 23°04′S 34°24′E
161 R6 **Funing** Jiangsu, E China 33°43′N 119°47′E
160 I14 **Funing** var. Xinhua. Yunnan, SW China 23°39′N 105°41′E
160 M7 **Funiu Shan** ▲▲ C China
77 U13 **Funtua** Katsina, N Nigeria 11°31′N 07°19′E
161 R12 **Fuqing** Fujian, SE China 25°40′N 119°23′E
83 M14 **Furancungo** Tete, NW Mozambique 14°51′S 33°39′E
116 J15 **Furculeşti** Teleorman, S Romania 43°51′N 25°07′E
Füred see Balatonfüred
165 W4 **Füren-ko** ◎ Hokkaidō, NE Japan
Fürg see Doborjī
Furluk see Fârliug
Fürmanov/Furmanovka see Moyynkum
Furmanovo see Zhalpaktal
59 L20 **Furnas, Represa de** ☒ SE Brazil
183 Q14 **Furneaux Group** island group Tasmania, SE Australia
Furnes see Veurne
160 J10 **Furong Jiang** ⇝ S China
138 I5 **Furqlus** Ḥimṣ, W Syria 34°40′N 37°02′E
100 F12 **Fürstenau** Niedersachsen, NW Germany 52°30′N 07°40′E
109 X8 **Fürstenfeld** Steiermark, SE Austria 47°03′N 16°05′E
101 L23 **Fürstenfeldbruck** Bayern, S Germany 48°10′N 11°16′E
100 P12 **Fürstenwalde** Brandenburg, NE Germany 52°22′N 14°04′E
101 K20 **Fürth** Bayern, S Germany 49°29′N 10°59′E
109 W3 **Furth bei Göttweig** Niederösterreich, NW Austria 48°22′N 15°33′E
165 R3 **Furubira** Hokkaidō, NE Japan 43°14′N 140°38′E
94 L12 **Furudal** Dalarna, C Sweden 61°10′N 15°07′E
164 L12 **Furukawa** var. Hida. Gifu, Honshū, SW Japan 36°13′N 137°11′E
165 Q10 **Furukawa** var. Hurukawa. Ōsaki. Miyagi, Honshū, C Japan 38°36′N 140°57′E
54 F10 **Fusagasugá** Cundinamarca, C Colombia 04°22′N 74°21′W
Fusan see Pusan
Fushë-Arëzi/Fushë-Arrësi see Fushë-Arrëz
113 L18 **Fushë-Arrëz** var. Fushë-Arëzi, Fushë-Arrësi. Shkodër, N Albania 42°05′N 20°01′E
113 N16 **Fushë Kosovë** Serb. Kosovo Polje. C Kosovo 42°40′N 21°07′E
Fushë-Kruja see Fushë-Krujë
113 K19 **Fushë-Krujë** var. Fushë-Kruja. Durrës, C Albania 41°30′N 19°43′E
163 V12 **Fushun** var. Fou-shan, Fu-shun. Liaoning, NE China 41°50′N 123°54′E
Fu-shun see Fushun
Fusin see Fuxin
108 G10 **Fusio** Ticino, S Switzerland 46°27′N 08°39′E
163 X11 **Fusong** Jilin, NE China 42°20′N 127°17′E
101 K24 **Füssen** Bayern, S Germany 47°34′N 10°43′E
160 K15 **Fusui** var. Xinning; prev. Funan. Guangxi Zhuangzu Zizhiqu, S China 22°39′N 107°49′E
Futa Jallon see Fouta Djallon
63 G18 **Futaleufú** Los Lagos, S Chile 43°14′S 71°50′W
112 K10 **Futog** Vojvodina, NW Serbia 45°15′N 19°43′E
165 O14 **Futtsu** var. Huttu. Chiba, Honshū, S Japan 35°11′N 139°52′E
187 S15 **Futuna** island S Vanuatu
190 D12 **Futuna, Île** island S Wallis and Futuna
161 Q11 **Futun Xi** ⇝ SE China
160 L5 **Fuxian** var. Fu Xian. Shaanxi, C China 36°03′N 109°19′E
Fuxian see Wafangdian
Fu Xian see Fuxian
160 G13 **Fuxian Hu** ☒ SW China
163 U12 **Fuxin** var. Fou-hsin, Fu-hsin, Fusin. Liaoning, NE China 41°59′N 121°40′E
Fuxing see Wangmo
161 P7 **Fuyang** Anhui, E China 32°52′N 115°51′E
Fuyang see Fuchuan
161 O4 **Fuyang He** ⇝ E China
163 U7 **Fuyu** Heilongjiang, NE China 47°48′N 124°26′E
163 Z6 **Fuyuan** Heilongjiang, NE China 48°20′N 134°22′E
Fuyu/Fu-yü see Songyuan
158 M3 **Fuyun** var. Koktokay. Xinjiang Uygur Zizhiqu, NW China 46°58′N 89°30′E
111 L22 **Füzesabony** Heves, E Hungary 47°46′N 20°25′E
161 R12 **Fuzhou** var. Foochow, Fu-chou. province capital Fujian, SE China 26°09′N 119°17′E
161 P11 **Fuzhou** Jiangxi, S China 27°58′N 116°20′E
137 W13 **Füzuli** Rus. Fizuli. SW Azerbaijan 39°33′N 47°09′E
119 I20 **Fyadory** Rus. Fëdory. Brestskaya Voblasts', SW Belarus 51°57′N 26°24′E
95 G24 **Fyn** off. Fyns Amt, var. Fünen. ◈ county C Denmark
95 G23 **Fyn** Ger. Fünen. island C Denmark
96 H12 **Fyne, Loch** inlet W Scotland, United Kingdom
Fyns Amt see Fyn
95 E16 **Fyresvatnet** ◎ S Norway
FYR Macedonia/FYROM see Macedonia, FYR
Fyzabad see Feyzābād

G

Gaafu Alifu Atoll see North Huvadhu Atoll
81 O14 **Gaalkacyo** var. Galka'yo, It. Galcaio. Mudug, C Somalia 06°42′N 47°24′E
146 J11 **Gabakly** Rus. Kabakly. Lebap Welaýaty, NE Turkmenistan 39°45′N 62°30′E
114 H8 **Gabare** Vratsa, NW Bulgaria 43°20′N 23°57′E
102 K15 **Gabas** ⇝ SW France
Gabasumdo see Tongde
35 T7 **Gabbs** Nevada, W USA 38°51′N 117°55′W
82 B12 **Gabela** Cuanza Sul, W Angola 10°50′S 14°21′E
Gaberones see Gaborone
189 X14 **Gabert** island Caroline Islands, E Micronesia
74 M7 **Gabès** var. Qābis. E Tunisia 33°53′N 10°03′E
74 M6 **Gabès, Golfe de** Ar. Khalīj Qābis. gulf E Tunisia
Gablonz an der Neisse see Jablonec nad Nisou
Gablös see Cavalese
79 E18 **Gabon** off. Gabonese Republic. ◆ republic C Africa
Gabonese Republic see Gabon
83 I20 **Gaborone** prev. Gaberones. ● (Botswana) South East, SE Botswana 24°42′S 25°50′E
83 I20 **Gaborone** ✈ South East, SE Botswana 24°45′S 25°49′E
104 K8 **Gabriel y Galán, Embalse de** ☒ W Spain
143 U15 **Gābrīk, Rūd-e** ⇝ SE Iran
114 J9 **Gabrovo** Gabrovo, N Bulgaria 42°54′N 25°19′E
114 J9 **Gabrovo** ◈ province N Bulgaria
76 H12 **Gabú** prev. Nova Lamego. E Guinea-Bissau 12°16′N 14°09′W
29 O6 **Gackle** North Dakota, N USA 46°34′N 99°07′W
113 I15 **Gacko** Republika Srpska, S Bosnia and Herzegovina 43°08′N 18°29′E
155 F17 **Gadag** Karnātaka, W India 15°25′N 75°37′E
93 G15 **Gäddede** Jämtland, C Sweden 64°30′N 14°15′E
159 S12 **Gadê** var. Kequ; prev. Pagqên. Qinghai, C China 33°56′N 99°49′E
Gades/Gadier/Gadir/Gadire see Cádiz
105 P15 **Gádor, Sierra de** ▲ S Spain
149 S15 **Gadra** Sind, SE Pakistan 25°39′N 70°28′E
23 Q3 **Gadsden** Alabama, S USA 34°00′N 86°00′W
36 H15 **Gadsden** Arizona, SW USA 32°33′N 114°45′W
Gadyach see Hadyach
124 J3 **Gadzhiyevo** Murmanskaya Oblast', NW Russian Federation 69°16′N 33°20′E
79 H15 **Gadzi** Mambéré-Kadéï, SW Central African Republic 04°46′N 16°42′E
116 J13 **Găeşti** Dâmboviţa, S Romania 44°42′N 25°19′E
107 J17 **Gaeta** Lazio, C Italy 41°12′N 13°35′E
107 J17 **Gaeta, Golfo di** var. Gulf of Gaeta. gulf C Italy
Gaeta, Gulf of see Gaeta, Golfo di
188 L14 **Gaferut** atoll Caroline Islands, W Micronesia
21 Q10 **Gaffney** South Carolina, SE USA 35°03′N 81°40′W
Gäfle see Gävle
Gäfleborg see Gävleborg
74 M6 **Gafsa** var. Qafşah. W Tunisia 34°25′N 08°52′E
Gafurov see Ghafurov
126 J3 **Gagarin** prev. Gzhatsk. Smolenskaya Oblast', W Russian Federation 55°33′N 35°00′E
147 O10 **Gagarin** Jizzax Viloyati, C Uzbekistan 40°40′N 68°04′E
101 G21 **Gaggenau** Baden-Württemberg, SW Germany 48°48′N 08°19′E
188 F16 **Gagil Tamil** var. Gagil-Tomil. island Caroline Islands, W Micronesia
Gagil-Tomil see Gagil Tamil
127 O4 **Gagino** Nizhegorodskaya Oblast', W Russian Federation 55°18′N 45°01′E
107 Q19 **Gagliano del Capo** Puglia, SE Italy 39°49′N 18°22′E
94 L13 **Gagnef** Dalarna, C Sweden 60°34′N 15°04′E
76 M17 **Gagnoa** C Ivory Coast 06°11′N 05°56′W
13 N10 **Gagnon** Québec, E Canada 51°56′N 68°16′W
Gago Coutinho see Lumbala N'Guimbo
137 P8 **Gagra** NW Georgia 43°17′N 40°18′E
31 S13 **Gahanna** Ohio, N USA 40°01′N 82°52′W
143 R13 **Gahkom** Hormozgān, S Iran 28°14′N 55°48′E
Gahnpa see Ganta
57 Q19 **Gaíba, Laguna** ◎ E Bolivia
153 T13 **Gaibandha** var. Gaibanda. Rajshahi, NW Bangladesh 25°21′N 89°36′E
Gaibhlte, Cnoc Mór na n see Galtymore Mountain
109 R9 **Gail** ⇝ S Austria
101 I21 **Gaildorf** Baden-Württemberg, S Germany 48°41′N 10°08′E
103 N15 **Gaillac** var. Gaillac-sur-Tarn. Tarn, S France 43°54′N 01°54′E
Gaillac-sur-Tarn see Gaillac
Gaillimh see Galway
Gaillimhe, Cuan na see Galway Bay
109 Q9 **Gailtaler Alpen** ▲▲ S Austria
63 J17 **Gaimán** Chaco, S Argentina 43°15′S 65°30′W
20 K8 **Gainesboro** Tennessee, S USA 36°20′N 85°41′W
23 V10 **Gainesville** Florida, SE USA 29°39′N 82°19′W
23 T2 **Gainesville** Georgia, SE USA 34°18′N 83°49′W
27 U8 **Gainesville** Missouri, C USA 36°37′N 92°28′W
25 T5 **Gainesville** Texas, SW USA 33°39′N 97°08′W
109 X5 **Gainfarn** Niederösterreich, NE Austria 47°59′N 16°11′E
97 N18 **Gainsborough** E England, United Kingdom 53°24′N 00°48′W
182 G6 **Gairdner, Lake** salt lake South Australia
Gaissane see Gáissát
92 L8 **Gáissát** var. Gaissane. ▲ N Norway
43 T15 **Gaital, Cerro** ▲ C Panama 08°37′N 80°04′W
21 W3 **Gaithersburg** Maryland, NE USA 39°08′N 77°13′W
163 U13 **Gaizhou** Liaoning, NE China 40°24′N 122°17′E
Gaizina Kalns see Gaiziņkalns
118 H7 **Gaiziņkalns** var. Gaizina Kalns. ▲ E Latvia 56°51′N 25°58′E
Gajac see Villeneuve-sur-Lot
39 S10 **Gakona** Alaska, USA 62°21′N 145°16′W
158 M16 **Gala** Xizang Zizhiqu, China 28°17′N 89°21′E
Galaassiya see Galaosiyo
Galāģil see Jalājil
Galam, Pulau see Gelam, Pulau
62 J6 **Galán, Cerro** ▲ NW Argentina 25°54′S 66°45′W
111 H21 **Galanta** Hung. Galánta. Trnavský Kraj, W Slovakia 48°12′N 17°45′E
146 L11 **Galaosiyo** Rus. Galaassiya. Buxoro Viloyati, C Uzbekistan 39°53′N 64°25′E
57 B17 **Galápagos** off. Provincia de Galápagos. ◈ province W Ecuador, E Pacific Ocean
193 P8 **Galapagos Fracture Zone** tectonic feature E Pacific Ocean
Galapagos Islands see Colón, Archipiélago de
Galápagos, Islas de los see Colón, Archipiélago de
Galápagos, Provincia de see Galápagos
193 S9 **Galapagos Rise** undersea feature E Pacific Ocean 15°00′S 97°00′W
96 K13 **Galashiels** SE Scotland, United Kingdom 55°37′N 02°49′W
116 M12 **Galaţi** Ger. Galatz. Galaţi, E Romania 45°27′N 28°00′E
116 L12 **Galaţi** ◈ county E Romania
107 Q19 **Galatina** Puglia, SE Italy 40°10′N 18°10′E
107 Q19 **Galatone** Puglia, SE Italy 40°09′N 18°05′E
Galatz see Galaţi
21 R8 **Galax** Virginia, NE USA 36°40′N 80°56′W
146 J16 **Galaýmor** Rus. Kala-i-Mor. Mary Welaýaty, S Turkmenistan 35°40′N 62°28′E
Galcaio see Gaalkacyo
64 P11 **Gáldar** Gran Canaria, Islas Canarias, NE Atlantic Ocean 28°09′N 15°40′W
94 F11 **Galdhøpiggen** ▲ S Norway 61°30′N 08°08′E
40 I4 **Galeana** Chihuahua, N Mexico 30°08′N 107°38′W
41 O9 **Galeana** Nuevo León, NE Mexico 24°45′N 100°04′W
60 P9 **Galeão** ✈ (Rio de Janeiro) Rio de Janeiro, SE Brazil 22°48′S 43°16′W
171 R10 **Galela** Pulau Halmahera, E Indonesia 01°52′N 127°48′E
39 O9 **Galena** Alaska, USA 64°43′N 156°55′W
30 K10 **Galena** Illinois, N USA 42°25′N 90°25′W
27 R7 **Galena** Kansas, C USA 37°04′N 94°38′W
27 T8 **Galena** Missouri, C USA 36°45′N 93°30′W
45 V15 **Galeota Point** headland Trinidad, Trinidad and Tobago 10°07′N 60°59′W
105 P13 **Galera** Andalucía, S Spain 37°45′N 02°33′W
45 Y16 **Galera Point** headland Trinidad, Trinidad and Tobago 10°49′N 60°54′W
56 A5 **Galera, Punta** headland NW Ecuador 00°49′N 80°03′W
30 K12 **Galesburg** Illinois, N USA 40°57′N 90°22′W
30 J7 **Galesville** Wisconsin, N USA 44°04′N 91°21′W
18 F12 **Galeton** Pennsylvania, NE USA 41°43′N 77°38′W
116 H9 **Gâlgău** Hung. Galgó; prev. Gilgău. Sălaj, NW Romania 47°17′N 23°43′E
Galgó see Gâlgău
Galgóc see Hlohovec
81 N15 **Galguduud** off. Gobolka Galguduud. ◈ region E Somalia
Galguduud, Gobolka see Galguduud
137 Q9 **Gali** W Georgia 42°40′N 41°39′E
125 N14 **Galich** Kostromskaya Oblast', NW Russian Federation 58°21′N 42°21′E
114 H7 **Galiche** Vratsa, NW Bulgaria 43°36′N 23°53′E
104 H3 **Galicia** anc. Gallaecia. ◈ autonomous community NW Spain
64 M8 **Galicia Bank** undersea feature E Atlantic Ocean 11°45′W 42°40′N
Galilee see HaGalil
181 W7 **Galilee, Lake** ◎ Queensland, NE Australia
Galilee, Sea of see Tiberias, Lake
106 E11 **Galileo Galilei** ✈ (Pisa) Toscana, C Italy 43°40′N 10°22′E
31 S12 **Galion** Ohio, N USA 40°43′N 82°47′W
Galka'yo see Gaalkacyo
146 K12 **Galkynyş** prev. Rus. Deynau, Dyanev, Turkm. Dänew. Lebap Welaýaty, NE Turkmenistan 39°16′N 63°10′E
80 H11 **Gallabat** Gedaref, E Sudan 12°57′N 36°10′E
Gallaecia see Galicia
147 O11 **G'allaorol** Jizzax Viloyati, C Uzbekistan 40°01′N 67°30′E
106 C7 **Gallarate** Lombardia, NW Italy 45°39′N 08°47′E
27 S2 **Gallatin** Missouri, C USA 39°54′N 93°57′W
20 J8 **Gallatin** Tennessee, S USA 36°22′N 86°28′W
33 R11 **Gallatin Peak** ▲ Montana, NW USA 45°22′N 111°21′W
33 R12 **Gallatin River** ⇝ Montana/Wyoming, NW USA
155 J26 **Galle** prev. Point de Galle. Southern Province, SW Sri Lanka 06°04′N 80°12′E
105 S5 **Gállego** ⇝ NE Spain
193 Q8 **Gallego Rise** undersea feature E Pacific Ocean 02°00′S 115°00′W
Gallegos see Río Gallegos
63 H23 **Gallegos, Río** ⇝ Argentina/Chile
Gallia see France
22 K10 **Galliano** Louisiana, S USA 29°26′N 90°18′W
114 G13 **Gallikós** ⇝ N Greece
37 S12 **Gallinas Peak** ▲ New Mexico, SW USA 34°14′N 105°47′W
54 H3 **Gallinas, Punta** headland NE Colombia 12°27′N 71°44′W
37 T11 **Gallinas River** ⇝ New Mexico, SW USA
107 Q19 **Gallipoli** Puglia, SE Italy 40°08′N 18°E
Gallipoli see Gelibolu
Gallipoli Peninsula see Gelibolu Yarımadası
31 T15 **Gallipolis** Ohio, N USA 38°49′N 82°14′W
92 J12 **Gällivare** Lapp. Váhtjer. Norrbotten, N Sweden 67°08′N 20°39′E
109 T4 **Gallneukirchen** Oberösterreich, N Austria 48°22′N 14°25′E
93 G17 **Gällö** Jämtland, C Sweden 62°57′N 15°15′E
105 Q7 **Gallo** ⇝ C Spain
107 I23 **Gallo, Capo** headland Sicilia, Italy, C Mediterranean Sea 38°13′N 13°18′E
37 P13 **Gallo Mountains** ▲▲ New Mexico, SW USA
18 G8 **Galloo Island** island New York, NE USA
97 H15 **Galloway, Mull of** headland S Scotland, United Kingdom 54°37′N 04°54′W
37 P10 **Gallup** New Mexico, SW USA 35°32′N 108°45′W
105 R5 **Gallur** Aragón, NE Spain 41°51′N 01°21′W
Gâlma see Guelma
163 N9 **Galshar** var. Buyant. Hentiy, C Mongolia 46°15′N 110°50′E
162 I6 **Galt** var. Ider. Hövsgöl, C Mongolia 48°45′N 99°52′E
35 O8 **Galt** California, W USA 38°15′N 121°19′W
74 C10 **Galtat-Zemmour** C Western Sahara 25°07′N 12°21′W
95 G22 **Galten** Århus, C Denmark 56°09′N 09°54′E
97 D20 **Galtymore Mountain** Ir. Cnoc Mór na nGaibhlte. ▲ S Ireland 52°21′N 08°09′W
97 D20 **Galty Mountains** Ir. Na Gaibhlte. ▲▲ S Ireland
30 K11 **Galva** Illinois, N USA 41°10′N 90°02′W
25 X12 **Galveston** Texas, SW USA 29°17′N 94°48′W
25 W11 **Galveston Bay** inlet Texas, SW USA
25 W12 **Galveston Island** island Texas, SW USA
61 B18 **Gálvez** Santa Fe, C Argentina 32°03′S 61°14′W
97 C18 **Galway** Ir. Gaillimh. W Ireland 53°16′N 09°03′W
97 B18 **Galway** Ir. Gaillimh. cultural region W Ireland
97 B18 **Galway Bay** Ir. Cuan na Gaillimhe. bay W Ireland
83 F18 **Gam** Otjozondjupa, NE Namibia 20°10′S 20°51′E
164 L14 **Gamagōri** Aichi, Honshū, SW Japan 34°49′N 137°15′E
54 F7 **Gamarra** Cesar, N Colombia 08°21′N 73°46′W
Gámas see Kaamanen
158 L17 **Gamba** Xizang Zizhiqu, W China 28°13′N 88°32′E
Gamba see Zamtang
77 F14 **Gambaga** NE Ghana 10°32′N 00°28′W
80 G13 **Gambēla** Gambēla Hizboch, W Ethiopia 08°09′N 34°15′E
81 H14 **Gambēla** ◈ federal region W Ethiopia
38 K10 **Gambell** Saint Lawrence Island, Alaska, USA 63°44′N 171°41′W
76 E12 **Gambia** off. Republic of The Gambia, The Gambia. ◆ republic W Africa
76 I12 **Gambia** Fr. Gambie. ⇝ W Africa
64 K12 **Gambia Plain** undersea feature E Atlantic Ocean
Gambia, Republic of The see Gambia
Gambia, The see Gambia
Gambie see Gambia
31 T13 **Gambier** Ohio, N USA 40°22′N 82°24′W
191 Y13 **Gambier, Îles** island group E French Polynesia
182 G10 **Gambier Islands** island group South Australia
79 H19 **Gamboma** Plateaux, E Congo 01°53′S 15°51′E
79 G16 **Gamboula** Mambéré-Kadéï, SW Central African Republic 04°09′N 15°12′E
37 P10 **Gamerco** New Mexico, SW USA 35°34′N 108°45′W
137 V12 **Gamış Dağı** ▲ W Azerbaijan 40°18′N 46°15′E
Gamlakarleby see Kokkola
95 N18 **Gamleby** Kalmar, S Sweden 57°54′N 16°25′E
Gammelstad see Gammelstaden
93 J14 **Gammelstaden** var. Gammelstad. Norrbotten, N Sweden 65°38′N 22°05′E
Gammouda see Sidi Bouzid
155 J25 **Gampaha** Western Province, W Sri Lanka 07°05′N 80°00′E
155 K25 **Gampola** Central Province, C Sri Lanka 07°10′N 80°34′E
167 S5 **Gâm, Sông** ⇝ N Vietnam
92 L7 **Gamvik** Finnmark, N Norway 71°04′N 28°08′E
150 H13 **Gan** Addu Atoll, C Maldives
Gan see Gansu, China
Gan see Jiangxi, China
Ganaane see Juba
37 O10 **Ganado** Arizona, SW USA 35°42′N 109°31′W
25 U12 **Ganado** Texas, SW USA 29°02′N 96°30′W
14 L14 **Gananoque** Ontario, SE Canada 44°21′N 76°11′W
Ganāveh see Bandar-e Gonāveh
137 V11 **Gäncä** Rus. Gyandzha; prev. Kirovabad, Yelisavetpol. W Azerbaijan 40°42′N 46°23′E
Ganchi see Ghonchí
Gand see Gent
82 B13 **Ganda** var. Mariano Machado, Port. Vila Mariano Machado. Benguela, W Angola 13°02′S 14°40′E
79 L22 **Gandajika** Kasai-Oriental, S Dem. Rep. Congo 06°42′S 24°01′E
153 O12 **Gandak** Nep. Nārāyāni. ⇝ India/Nepal
149 P12 **Gandāva** Baluchistān, SW Pakistan 28°37′N 67°29′E
13 U11 **Gander** Newfoundland and Labrador, SE Canada 48°56′N 54°33′W
13 U11 **Gander** ✈ Newfoundland and Labrador, E Canada 49°03′N 54°49′W
100 G11 **Ganderkesee** Niedersachsen, NW Germany 53°01′N 08°33′E
105 T7 **Gandesa** Cataluña, NE Spain 41°03′N 00°26′E
154 B10 **Gāndhīdhām** Gujarāt, W India 23°08′N 70°05′E
154 D10 **Gāndhīnagar** state capital Gujarāt, W India 23°12′N 72°37′E
154 F9 **Gāndhi Sāgar** ◎ C India
105 T11 **Gandía** País Valenciano, E Spain 38°59′N 00°11′W
159 O10 **Gang** Qinghai, W China
152 G9 **Gangānagar** Rājasthān, N India 29°54′N 73°56′E
152 I12 **Gangāpur** Rājasthān, N India 26°30′N 76°49′E
153 S17 **Ganga Sāgar** West Bengal, NE India 21°39′N 88°05′E
Gangavathi see Gangāwati
155 G17 **Gangāwati** var. Gangavathi. Karnātaka, C India 15°26′N 76°35′E
159 S9 **Gangca** var. Shaliuhe. Qinghai, C China 37°21′N 100°09′E
158 H14 **Gangdisê Shan** Eng. Kailas Range. ▲▲ W China
103 Q15 **Ganges** Hérault, S France 43°57′N 03°42′E
153 P13 **Ganges** Ben. Padma. ⇝ Bangladesh/India see also Padma
Ganges see Padma
Ganges Cone see Ganges Fan
173 S3 **Ganges Fan** var. Ganges Cone. undersea feature N Bay of Bengal 12°00′N 87°00′E
153 U17 **Ganges, Mouths of the** delta Bangladesh/India
107 K23 **Gangi** anc. Engyum. Sicilia, Italy, C Mediterranean Sea 37°48′N 14°13′E
152 K8 **Gangotri** Uttarakhand, N India 30°56′N 79°02′E
Gangra see Çankırı
153 S11 **Gangtok** state capital Sikkim, N India 27°20′N 88°39′E
159 W11 **Gangu** var. Daxiangshan. Gansu, C China 34°38′N 105°18′E
163 U5 **Gan He** ⇝ NE China
171 S12 **Gani** Pulau Halmahera, E Indonesia 0°45′S 128°13′E
161 O12 **Gan Jiang** ⇝ S China
163 U11 **Ganjig** var. Horqin Zuoyi Houqi. Nei Mongol Zizhiqu, N China 42°53′N 122°22′E
146 H15 **Gannaly** Ahal Welaýaty, S Turkmenistan 37°02′N 60°43′E
163 U7 **Gannan** Heilongjiang, NE China 47°58′N 123°36′E
103 P10 **Gannat** Allier, C France 46°06′N 03°12′E
33 T14 **Gannett Peak** ▲ Wyoming, C USA 43°10′N 109°39′W
29 O10 **Gannvalley** South Dakota, N USA 44°01′N 98°59′W
Ganqu see Lhünzhub
109 Y3 **Gänserndorf** Niederösterreich, NE Austria 48°21′N 16°43′E
Gansos, Lago dos see Goose Lake
159 T9 **Gansu** var. Gan, Gansu Sheng, Kansu. ◈ province N China
Gansu Sheng see Gansu
76 K16 **Ganta** var. Gahnpa. NE Liberia 07°15′N 08°59′W
182 H11 **Gantheaume, Cape** headland South Australia 36°04′S 137°28′E
Gantsevichi see Hantsavichy
161 Q6 **Ganyu** var. Qingkou. Jiangsu, E China 34°52′N 119°11′E
144 D12 **Ganyushkino** Atyrau, SW Kazakhstan 46°38′N 49°12′E
161 O12 **Ganzhou** Jiangxi, S China 25°51′N 114°59′E
Ganzhou see Zhangye
77 Q10 **Gao** Gao, E Mali 16°16′N 00°03′E
77 R10 **Gao** ◈ region SE Mali
161 O10 **Gao'an** Jiangxi, S China 28°24′N 115°27′E
Gaocheng see Litang
Gaoleshan see Xianfeng
161 R5 **Gaomi** Shandong, C China 36°23′N 119°45′E
161 N5 **Gaoping** Shanxi, C China 35°51′N 112°55′E
159 S8 **Gaotai** Gansu, N China 39°22′N 99°44′E
Gaoth Dobhair see Gweedore
77 O14 **Gaoua** SW Burkina 10°18′N 03°12′W
76 I13 **Gaoual** N Guinea 11°44′N 13°14′W
Gaoxiong see Kaohsiung
161 R7 **Gaoyou** var. Dayishan. Jiangsu, E China 32°48′N 119°26′E
161 R7 **Gaoyou Hu** ◎ E China
160 M15 **Gaozhou** Guangdong, S China 21°56′N 110°49′E
103 T13 **Gap** anc. Vapincum. Hautes-Alpes, SE France 44°33′N 06°05′E
146 E9 **Gaplaňgyr Platosy** Rus. Plato Kaplangky. ridge Turkmenistan/Uzbekistan
158 G13 **Gar** Xizang Zizhiqu, W China 32°50′N 79°46′E
Gar see Gar Xincun
Garabekevyul see Garabekewül
146 L13 **Garabekewül** Rus. Garabekevyul, Karabekaul. Lebap Welaýaty, E Turkmenistan 38°31′N 64°04′E
146 K15 **Garabil Belentligi** Rus. Vozvyshennost' Karabil'. ▲ S Turkmenistan
146 A8 **Garabogaz** Rus. Bekdash. Balkan Welaýaty, NW Turkmenistan 41°33′N 52°33′E
146 B9 **Garabogaz Aylagy** Rus. Zaliv Kara-Bogaz-Gol. bay NW Turkmenistan
146 A9 **Garabogazköl** Rus. Kara-Bogaz-Gol. Balkan Welaýaty, NW Turkmenistan 41°03′N 52°52′E
43 V16 **Garachiné** Darién, SE Panama 08°03′N 78°22′W
43 V16 **Garachiné, Punta** headland SE Panama 08°05′N 78°23′W
146 K12 **Garagan** Rus. Karagan. Ahal Welaýaty, C Turkmenistan 38°16′N 57°34′E
54 G10 **Garagoa** Boyacá, C Colombia 05°05′N 73°20′W
146 A11 **Garagöl'** Rus. Karagel'. Balkan Welaýaty, W Turkmenistan 39°24′N 53°13′E
146 F12 **Garagum** var. Garagumy, Qara Qum, Eng. Black Sand Desert, Kara Kum; prev. Peski Karakumy. desert C Turkmenistan
146 E12 **Garagum Kanaly** var. Kara Kum Canal, Rus. Karagumskiy Kanal, Karakumskiy Kanal. canal C Turkmenistan
Garagumy see Garagum
183 S4 **Garah** New South Wales, SE Australia 29°07′S 149°37′E
64 O11 **Garajonay** ▲ Gomera, Islas Canarias, NE Atlantic Ocean 28°07′N 17°14′W
114 M8 **Gara Khitrino** Shumen, NE Bulgaria 43°26′N 26°55′E
76 L13 **Garalo** Sikasso, SW Mali 10°58′N 07°26′W
Garam see Hron, Slovakia
146 L14 **Garamätnyýaz** Rus. Karamet-Niyaz. Lebap Welaýaty, E Turkmenistan 37°45′N 64°28′E
Garamszentkereszt see Žiar nad Hronom
77 Q13 **Garango** S Burkina 11°45′N 00°30′W
59 Q15 **Garanhuns** Pernambuco, E Brazil 08°53′S 36°28′W
188 H5 **Garapan** Saipan, S Northern Mariana Islands 15°12′S 145°43′E
Gárasavvon see Kaaresuvanto
Gárassavon see Kaaresuvanto
78 J13 **Garba** Bamingui-Bangoran, N Central African Republic 09°09′N 20°24′E
Garba see Jiulong
81 L16 **Garbahaarrey** It. Garba Harre. Gedo, SW Somalia 03°14′N 42°18′E
Garba Harre see Garbahaarrey
81 J18 **Garba Tula** Eastern, C Kenya 0°31′N 38°35′E
27 N9 **Garber** Oklahoma, C USA 36°26′N 97°35′W
34 L4 **Garberville** California, W USA 40°07′N 123°48′W
Garbo see Lhozhag
100 I12 **Garbsen** Niedersachsen, N Germany 52°25′N 09°36′E
60 K9 **Garça** São Paulo, S Brazil 22°14′S 49°36′W
104 L10 **García de Solá, Embalse de** ☒ C Spain
103 Q14 **Gard** ◈ department S France
103 Q14 **Gard** ⇝ S France
106 F7 **Garda, Lago di** var. Benaco, Eng. Lake Garda, Ger. Gardasee. ◎ NE Italy
Garda, Lake see Garda, Lago di
Gardan Divāl see Gardan Diwāl
149 Q5 **Gardan Diwāl** var. Gardan Divāl. Vardak, C Afghanistan 34°30′N 68°15′E
103 S15 **Gardanne** Bouches-du-Rhône, SE France 43°27′N 05°28′E
Gardasee see Garda, Lago di
100 L12 **Gardelegen** Sachsen-Anhalt, C Germany 52°31′N 11°25′E

◆ Country
● Country Capital
◇ Dependent Territory
○ Dependent Territory Capital
◈ Administrative Regions
✈ International Airport
▲ Mountain
▲▲ Mountain Range
Volcano
⇝ River
◎ Lake
☒ Reservoir

GARDEN – GHUGRI

14 B10 **Garden** Ontario, S Canada
23 X6 **Garden City** Georgia, SE USA 32°06´N 81°09´W
26 I6 **Garden City** Kansas, C USA 37°57´N 100°54´W
27 S5 **Garden City** Missouri, C USA 38°34´N 94°12´W
25 N8 **Garden City** Texas, SW USA 31°51´N 101°30´W
23 P3 **Gardendale** Alabama, S USA 33°39´N 86°48´W
31 P5 **Garden Island** *island* Michigan, N USA
22 M11 **Garden Island Bay** *bay* Louisiana, S USA
31 O5 **Garden Peninsula** *peninsula* Michigan, N USA
Garden State, The *see* New Jersey
95 I14 **Gardermoen** Akershus, S Norway 60°10´N 11°04´E
95 I14 **Gardermoen** ✈ (Oslo) Akershus, S Norway 60°12´N 11°05´E
Gardeyz/Gardez *see* Gardīz
93 G14 **Gardiken** ◎ N Sweden
19 Q7 **Gardiner** Maine, NE USA 44°13´N 69°46´W
33 S12 **Gardiner** Montana, NW USA 45°02´N 110°42´W
19 N13 **Gardiners Island** *island* New York, NE USA
149 Q6 **Gardīz** *var.* Gardeyz, Gardez, Gordiaz. Paktīā, E Afghanistan 33°35´N 69°14´E
Gardner Island *see* Nikumaroro
19 T6 **Gardner Lake** ◎ Maine, NE USA
35 Q6 **Gardnerville** Nevada, W USA 38°55´N 119°44´W
Gardo *see* Qardho
106 F7 **Gardone Val Trompia** Lombardia, N Italy 45°40´N 10°11´E
Garegegasnjárga *see* Karigasniemi
38 F17 **Gareloi Island** *island* Aleutian Islands, Alaska, USA
Gares *see* Puente la Reina
106 B10 **Garessio** Piemonte, NE Italy 44°14´N 08°01´E
32 M9 **Garfield** Washington, NW USA 47°00´N 117°07´W
31 U11 **Garfield Heights** Ohio, N USA 41°25´N 81°36´W
Gargaliani *see* Gargaliánoi
115 D21 **Gargaliánoi** *var.* Gargaliani. Pelopónnisos, S Greece 37°04´N 21°38´E
107 N15 **Gargàno, Promontorio del** *headland* SE Italy 41°51´N 16°11´E
108 J8 **Gargellen** Graubünden, W Switzerland 46°57´N 09°55´E
93 I14 **Gargnäs** Västerbotten, N Sweden 65°19´N 18°00´E
118 C11 **Gargždai** Klaipėda, W Lithuania 55°42´N 21°24´E
154 J13 **Garhchiroli** Mahārāshtra, C India 20°14´N 79°58´E
155 O15 **Garhwa** Jhārkhand, N India 24°07´N 83°52´E
171 V13 **Gariau** Papua, E Indonesia 03°43´S 134°54´E
83 E24 **Garies** Northern Cape, W South Africa 30°30´S 18°00´E
107 K17 **Garigliano** C Italy
81 K19 **Garissa** Coast, E Kenya 0°27´S 39°39´E
21 V11 **Garland** North Carolina, SE USA 34°45´N 78°25´W
25 T6 **Garland** Texas, SW USA 32°50´N 96°37´W
36 L1 **Garland** Utah, W USA 41°43´N 112°07´W
106 D8 **Garlasco** Lombardia, N Italy 45°12´N 08°59´E
119 F14 **Garliava** Kaunas, S Lithuania 54°49´N 23°52´E
Garm *see* Gharm
142 M9 **Garm, Āb-e** *var.* Rūd-e Kharsān. SW Iran
101 K25 **Garmisch-Partenkirchen** Bayern, S Germany 47°30´N 11°05´E
143 O5 **Garmsār** *prev.* Qishlaq. Semnān, N Iran 35°18´N 52°22´E
Garmser *see* Darvīshān
29 V12 **Garner** Iowa, C USA 43°06´N 93°36´W
21 U9 **Garner** North Carolina, SE USA 35°42´N 78°36´W
27 Q5 **Garnett** Kansas, C USA 38°16´N 95°15´W
99 M25 **Garnich** Luxembourg, SW Luxembourg 49°37´N 05°57´E
182 M8 **Garnpung, Lake** *salt lake* New South Wales, SE Australia
Garoe *see* Garoowe
Garoet *see* Garut
153 U13 **Gāro Hills** *hill range* NE India
102 K13 **Garonne** *anc.* Garumna. S France
80 P13 **Garoowe** *var.* Garoe. Nugaal, N Somalia 08°24´N 48°29´E
78 F12 **Garoua** *var.* Garua. Nord, N Cameroon 09°17´N 13°22´E
79 G14 **Garoua Boulaï** Est, E Cameroon 05°54´N 14°33´E
77 O10 **Garou, Lac** ◎ C Mali
95 L16 **Garphyttan** Örebro, C Sweden 59°18´N 14°54´E
29 R11 **Garretson** South Dakota, N USA 43°43´N 96°30´W
31 Q11 **Garrett** Indiana, N USA 41°21´N 85°08´W
33 Q10 **Garrison** Montana, NW USA 46°32´N 112°46´W
28 M4 **Garrison** North Dakota, N USA 47°36´N 101°25´W
25 X8 **Garrison** Texas, SW USA 31°49´N 94°29´W
28 L4 **Garrison Dam** *dam* North Dakota, N USA
104 J9 **Garrovillas** Extremadura, W Spain 39°43´N 06°33´W
Garrygala *see* Magtymguly
8 L8 **Garry Lake** ◎ Nunavut, N Canada
Gars *see* Gars am Kamp
109 W3 **Gars am Kamp** *var.* Gars. Niederösterreich, NE Austria 48°35´N 15°40´E
81 K20 **Garsen** Coast, S Kenya 02°16´S 40°07´E
Garshy *see* Garşy
14 F10 **Garson** Ontario, S Canada 46°33´N 80°51´W
109 T5 **Garsten** Oberösterreich, N Austria 48°00´N 14°24´E
146 A9 **Garşy** *var.* Garshy, *Rus.* Karshi. Balkan Welaýaty, NW Turkmenistan 40°45´N 52°50´E
Gartar *see* Qianning
102 M10 **Gartempe** C France
Gartog *see* Markam
Garua *see* Garoua
83 D21 **Garub** Karas, SW Namibia 26°33´S 16°00´E
Garumna *see* Garonne
169 P16 **Garut** *prev.* Garoet. Jawa, C Indonesia 07°15´S 107°55´E
185 C20 **Garvie Mountains** ▲▲ South Island, New Zealand
110 N12 **Garwolin** Mazowieckie, E Poland 51°54´N 21°36´E
25 U12 **Garwood** Texas, SW USA 29°25´N 96°26´W
158 G13 **Gar Xincun** *prev.* Gar. Xizang Zizhiqu, W China 32°04´N 80°01´E
31 N11 **Gary** Indiana, N USA 41°36´N 87°21´W
25 X7 **Gary** Texas, SW USA 32°00´N 94°21´W
158 G13 **Garyarsa** Xizang Zizhiqu, SW China 31°44´N 80°20´E
158 G13 **Gar Zangbo** W China
160 F8 **Garzê** Sichuan, C China 31°40´N 99°58´E
54 E12 **Garzón** Huila, S Colombia 02°14´N 75°37´W
Gasan-Kuli *see* Esenguly
31 P13 **Gas City** Indiana, N USA 40°29´N 85°36´W
102 K15 **Gascogne** *Eng.* Gascony. *cultural region* S France
26 V5 **Gasconade River** Missouri, C USA
Gascony *see* Gascogne
180 H9 **Gascoyne Junction** Western Australia 25°06´S 115°10´E
173 V8 **Gascoyne Plain** *undersea feature* E Indian Ocean
180 H9 **Gascoyne River** Western Australia
192 J11 **Gascoyne Tablemount** *undersea feature* N Tasman Sea 36°30´S 156°30´E
Gash *see* Nahr al Qāsh
67 U6 **Gash** *var.* Nahr al Qāsh. W Sudan
149 X3 **Gasherbrum** ▲ NE Pakistan 35°39´N 76°34´E
Gas Hu *see* Gas Hure Hu
77 X12 **Gashua** Yobe, NE Nigeria 12°55´N 11°10´E
159 N9 **Gas Hure Hu** *var.* Gas Hu. ◎ C China
186 G7 **Gasmata** New Britain, E Papua New Guinea 06°12´S 150°25´E
23 V14 **Gasparilla Island** *island* Florida, SE USA
169 O13 **Gaspar, Selat** *strait* W Indonesia
15 Y6 **Gaspé** Québec, SE Canada 48°50´N 64°33´W
15 Z6 **Gaspé, Cap de** *headland* Québec, SE Canada 48°45´N 64°10´W
15 X6 **Gaspé, Péninsule de** *var.* Péninsule de la Gaspésie. *peninsula* Québec, SE Canada
Gaspésie, Péninsule de la *see* Gaspé, Péninsule de
77 W15 **Gassol** Taraba, E Nigeria 08°28´N 10°24´E
Gastein *see* Badgastein
21 R10 **Gastonia** North Carolina, SE USA 35°14´N 81°12´W
21 V8 **Gaston, Lake** ▣ North Carolina/Virginia, SE USA
115 D19 **Gastoúni** Dytikí Ellás, S Greece 37°51´N 21°15´E
63 I17 **Gastre** Chubut, S Argentina 42°20´S 69°10´W
Gat *see* Ghāt
105 P15 **Gata, Cabo de** *cape* S Spain
Gata, Cape *see* Gátas, Akrotíri
105 T11 **Gata de Gorgos** País Valenciano, E Spain 38°45´N 00°06´E
116 E12 **Gătaia** *Ger.* Gataja, *Hung.* Gátalja; *prev.* Gáttája. Timiş, W Romania 45°24´N 21°26´E
Gataja/Gátalja *see* Gătaia
121 P3 **Gátas, Akrotíri** *var.* Cape Gata. *headland* S Cyprus 34°34´N 33°03´E
104 J8 **Gata, Sierra de** ▲▲ W Spain
124 G13 **Gatchina** Leningradskaya Oblast', NW Russian Federation 59°34´N 30°06´E
21 P8 **Gate City** Virginia, NE USA 36°38´N 82°37´W
97 M14 **Gateshead** NE England, United Kingdom 54°57´N 01°37´W
21 X8 **Gatesville** North Carolina, SE USA 36°24´N 76°46´W
25 S8 **Gatesville** Texas, SW USA 31°26´N 97°46´W
14 L12 **Gatineau** Québec, SE Canada 45°29´N 75°40´W
14 L11 **Gatineau** Ontario/Québec, SE Canada
21 N9 **Gatlinburg** Tennessee, S USA 35°42´N 83°30´W
Gatooma *see* Kadoma
Gáttája *see* Gătaia
43 T14 **Gatún, Lago** ▣ C Panama
59 N14 **Gaturiano** Piauí, NE Brazil 06°53´S 41°45´W
97 O22 **Gatwick** ✈ (London) SE England, United Kingdom 51°10´N 00°12´W
187 Y14 **Gau** *prev.* Ngau. *island* C Fiji
187 R12 **Gaua** *var.* Santa Maria. *Island* Banks Island, N Vanuatu
104 L16 **Gaucín** Andalucía, S Spain 36°31´N 05°19´W
Gauhāti *see* Guwāhāti
118 I8 **Gauja** *Ger.* Aa. Estonia/Latvia
118 I7 **Gaujiena** Alūksne, NE Latvia 57°31´N 26°24´E
94 H9 **Gauldalen** *valley* S Norway
21 R5 **Gauley River** West Virginia, NE USA
Gaul/Gaule *see* France
99 D19 **Gaurain-Ramecroix** Hainaut, SW Belgium 50°35´N 03°31´E
95 F15 **Gaustatoppen** ▲ S Norway 59°50´N 08°39´E
83 J21 **Gauteng** *off.* Gauteng Province; *prev.* Pretoria-Witwatersrand-Vereeniging. ◆ *province* NE South Africa
Gauteng *see* Johannesburg, South Africa
Gauteng *see* Germiston, South Africa
Gauteng Province *see* Gauteng
137 U11 **Gavarr** *prev.* Kamo. C Armenia 40°21´N 45°07´E
143 P14 **Gāvbandī** Hormozgān, S Iran 27°07´N 53°21´E
115 H25 **Gavdopoúla** *island* SE Greece
115 H26 **Gávdos** *island* SE Greece
102 K16 **Gave de Pau** *var.* Gave-de-Pay. SW France
Gave-de-Pay *see* Gave de Pau
102 J16 **Gave d'Oloron** SW France
99 E18 **Gavere** Oost-Vlaanderen, NW Belgium 50°56´N 03°41´E
94 N13 **Gävle** *var.* Gäfle; *prev.* Gefle. Gävleborg, C Sweden 60°41´N 17°09´E
94 M11 **Gävleborg** *var.* Gäfleborg, Gefleborg. ◆ *county* C Sweden
94 O13 **Gävlebukten** *bay* C Sweden
124 L16 **Gavrilov-Yam** Yaroslavskaya Oblast', W Russian Federation 57°19´N 39°52´E
182 I9 **Gawler** South Australia 34°38´S 138°44´E
182 G7 **Gawler Ranges** *hill range* South Australia
Gawso *see* Goaso
162 H11 **Gaxun Nur** ◎ N China
127 W7 **Gay** Orenburgskaya Oblast', W Russian Federation 51°31´N 58°31´E
153 P14 **Gaya** Bihār, N India 24°48´N 85°00´E
77 S13 **Gaya** Dosso, SW Niger 11°52´N 03°28´E
Gaya *see* Kyjov
31 Q6 **Gaylord** Michigan, N USA 45°01´N 84°40´W
29 U9 **Gaylord** Minnesota, N USA 44°33´N 94°13´W
181 Y9 **Gayndah** Queensland, E Australia 25°37´S 151°31´E
125 T12 **Gayny** Komi-Permyatskiy Avtonomnyy Okrug, NW Russian Federation 60°19´N 54°15´E
Gaysin *see* Haysyn
Gayvorno *see* Hayvoron
138 E11 **Gaza** *Ar.* Ghazzah, *Heb.* 'Azza. NE Gaza Strip 31°30´N 34°28´E
83 L20 **Gaza** *off.* Província de Gaza. ◆ *province* SW Mozambique
Gaz-Achak *see* Gazojak
147 Q9 **G'azalkent** *Rus.* Gazalkent. Toshkent Viloyati, E Uzbekistan 41°30´N 69°46´E
Gazalkent *see* G'azalkent
Gazandzhyk/Gazanjyk *see* Bereket
77 V12 **Gazaoua** Maradi, S Niger 13°28´N 07°54´E
Gaza, Província de *see* Gaza
138 E11 **Gaza Strip** *Ar.* Qita Ghazzah. *disputed region* SW Asia
136 M16 **Gaziantep** *var.* Gazi Antep; *prev.* Aintab, Antep. Gaziantep, S Turkey 37°04´N 37°21´E
136 M17 **Gaziantep** *var.* Gazi Antep. ◆ *province* S Turkey
Gazi Antep *see* Gaziantep
114 M13 **Gaziköy** Tekirdağ, NW Turkey 40°45´N 27°18´E
121 Q2 **Gazimağusa** *var.* Famagusta, *Gk.* Ammóchostos. E Cyprus 35°07´N 33°57´E
121 Q2 **Gazimağusa Körfezi** *var.* Famagusta Bay, *Gk.* Kólpos Ammóchostos. *bay* E Cyprus
146 K11 **Gazli** Buxoro Viloyati, C Uzbekistan 40°09´N 63°28´E
146 I9 **Gazojak** *Rus.* Gaz-Achak. Lebap Welaýaty, NE Turkmenistan 41°12´N 61°24´E
79 K15 **Gbadolite** Equateur, NW Dem. Rep. Congo 04°14´N 20°59´E
76 K16 **Gbanga** *var.* Gbarnga. N Liberia 07°02´N 09°30´W
Gbarnga *see* Gbanga
77 S14 **Gbéroubouè** *var.* Gbérouboué. N Benin 10°35´N 02°47´E
77 W16 **Gboko** Benue, S Nigeria 07°21´N 08°57´E
Gcuwa *see* Butterworth
110 J7 **Gdańsk** *Fr.* Dantzig, *Ger.* Danzig. Pomorskie, N Poland 54°22´N 18°35´E
Gdan'skaya Bukhta/Gdańsk, Gulf of *see* Danzig, Gulf of
Gdańska, Zatoka *see* Danzig, Gulf of
Gdingen *see* Gdynia
124 F13 **Gdov** Pskovskaya Oblast', W Russian Federation 58°43´N 27°51´E
110 I6 **Gdynia** *Ger.* Gdingen. Pomorskie, N Poland 54°31´N 18°30´E
26 M10 **Geary** Oklahoma, C USA 35°37´N 98°19´W
Geavvú *see* Kevo
76 H12 **Gêba, Rio** C Guinea-Bissau
136 E11 **Gebze** Kocaeli, NW Turkey 40°48´N 29°26´E
80 H10 **Gedaref** *var.* Al Qaḍārif, El Gedaref. Gedaref, E Sudan 14°03´N 35°24´E
80 H10 **Gedaref** ◆ *state* E Sudan
80 B11 **Gedid Ras el Fil** Southern Darfur, W Sudan 12°45´N 25°45´E
99 I23 **Gedinne** Namur, SE Belgium 49°57´N 04°55´E
136 E13 **Gediz** Kütahya, W Turkey 39°04´N 29°25´E
136 C14 **Gediz Nehri** W Turkey
81 N14 **Gedlegubē** Sumalē, E Ethiopia 06°53´N 45°08´E
81 L17 **Gedo** *off.* Gobolka Gedo. ◆ *region* SW Somalia
Gedo, Gobolka *see* Gedo
95 I25 **Gedser** Storstrøm, SE Denmark 54°34´N 11°57´E
99 I16 **Geel** *var.* Gheel. Antwerpen, N Belgium 51°10´N 04°59´E
183 N13 **Geelong** Victoria, SE Australia 38°10´S 144°21´E
Ge'e'mu *see* Golmud
99 I14 **Geertruidenberg** Noord-Brabant, S Netherlands 51°43´N 04°52´E
100 H10 **Geeste** NW Germany
100 J10 **Geesthacht** Schleswig-Holstein, N Germany 53°25´N 10°22´E
183 P17 **Geeveston** Tasmania, SE Australia 43°12´S 146°54´E
Gefle *see* Gävle
Gefleborg *see* Gävleborg
158 G13 **Ge'gyai** Xizang Zizhiqu, W China 32°29´N 81°04´E
77 X12 **Geidam** Yobe, NE Nigeria 12°52´N 11°55´E
11 T11 **Geikie** Saskatchewan, C Canada
94 F13 **Geilo** Buskerud, S Norway 60°32´N 08°13´E
94 E10 **Geiranger** Møre og Romsdal, S Norway 62°07´N 07°12´E
101 I22 **Geislingen** *var.* Geislingen an der Steige. Baden-Württemberg, SW Germany 48°37´N 09°50´E
Geislingen an der Steige *see* Geislingen
81 F20 **Geita** Mwanza, NW Tanzania 02°52´S 32°12´E
95 G15 **Geithus** Buskerud, S Norway 59°56´N 09°58´E
160 H14 **Gejiu** *var.* Kochiu. Yunnan, S China 23°22´N 103°07´E
Gëkdepe *see* Gökdepe
146 E9 **Gekdengkui, Solonchak** *var.* Solonchak Goklenkuy. *salt marsh* NW Turkmenistan
81 D14 **Gel** W Sudan
107 K25 **Gela** *prev.* Terranova di Sicilia. Sicilia, Italy, C Mediterranean Sea 37°05´N 14°15´E
159 N13 **Gêladaindong** ▲ C China 33°24´N 91°00´E
81 N14 **Geladī** SE Ethiopia 06°58´N 46°24´E
169 P13 **Gelam, Pulau** *var.* Pulau Galam. *island* N Indonesia
Gelaozu Miaozu Zhizhixian *see* Wuchuan
98 L11 **Gelderland** *prev. Eng.* Guelders. ◆ *province* E Netherlands
98 J13 **Geldermalsen** Gelderland, C Netherlands 51°53´N 05°17´E
101 D14 **Geldern** Nordrhein-Westfalen, W Germany 51°31´N 06°19´E
99 K15 **Geldrop** Noord-Brabant, SE Netherlands 51°25´N 05°34´E
99 L17 **Geleen** Limburg, SE Netherlands 50°57´N 05°49´E
126 K14 **Gelendzhik** Krasnodarskiy Kray, SW Russian Federation 44°34´N 38°06´E
Gelib *see* Jilib
136 B11 **Gelibolu** *Eng.* Gallipoli. Çanakkale, NW Turkey 40°25´N 26°41´E
115 L14 **Gelibolu Yarımadası** *Eng.* Gallipoli Peninsula. *peninsula* NW Turkey
81 O14 **Gellinsor** Mudug, C Somalia 06°25´N 46°44´E
101 H18 **Gelnhausen** Hessen, C Germany 50°12´N 09°12´E
101 E14 **Gelsenkirchen** Nordrhein-Westfalen, W Germany 51°30´N 07°05´E
83 C20 **Geluk** Hardap, SW Namibia 24°35´S 15°48´E
99 H20 **Gembloux** Namur, Belgium 50°34´N 04°42´E
79 J16 **Gemena** Equateur, NW Dem. Rep. Congo 03°13´N 19°49´E
99 L14 **Gemert** Noord-Brabant, SE Netherlands 51°33´N 05°41´E
136 E11 **Gemlik** Bursa, NW Turkey 40°26´N 29°10´E
Gem of the Mountains *see* Idaho
106 J6 **Gemona del Friuli** Friuli-Venezia Giulia, NE Italy 46°18´N 13°12´E
Gem State *see* Idaho
Genalē Wenz *see* Juba
169 R10 **Genali, Danau** ◎ Borneo, N Indonesia
99 G19 **Genappe** Walloon Brabant, C Belgium 50°39´N 04°27´E
137 P14 **Genç** Bingöl, E Turkey 38°44´N 40°35´E
Genck *see* Genk
98 M9 **Genemuiden** Overijssel, E Netherlands 52°38´N 06°03´E
63 K14 **General Acha** La Pampa, C Argentina 37°25´S 64°38´W
61 C21 **General Alvear** Buenos Aires, E Argentina 36°03´S 60°01´W
62 I12 **General Alvear** Mendoza, W Argentina 34°59´S 67°40´W
61 B20 **General Arenales** Buenos Aires, E Argentina 34°21´S 61°20´W
61 D21 **General Belgrano** Buenos Aires, E Argentina 35°47´S 58°30´W
194 H3 **General Bernardo O'Higgins** *Chilean research station* Antarctica 63°09´S 57°13´W
41 O8 **General Bravo** Nuevo León, NE Mexico 25°47´N 99°04´W
62 M7 **General Capdevila** Chaco, N Argentina 27°25´S 61°30´W
General Carrera, Lago *see* Buenos Aires, Lago
41 N9 **General Cepeda** Coahuila, NE Mexico 25°18´N 101°24´W
63 K15 **General Conesa** Río Negro, E Argentina 40°06´S 64°26´W
61 G18 **General Enrique Martínez** Treinta y Tres, E Uruguay 33°13´S 53°47´W
62 L3 **General Eugenio A. Garay** *var.* Fortín General Eugenio Garay; *prev.* Yrendagüé. Nueva Asunción, NW Paraguay 20°30´S 61°56´W
61 C18 **General Galarza** Entre Ríos, E Argentina 32°43´S 59°24´W
61 E22 **General Guido** Buenos Aires, E Argentina 36°36´S 57°45´W
General José F.Uriburu *see* Zárate
61 E22 **General Juan Madariaga** Buenos Aires, E Argentina 37°00´S 57°09´W
41 O16 **General Juan N Alvarez** ✈ (Acapulco) Guerrero, S Mexico 16°47´N 99°47´W
61 B22 **General La Madrid** Buenos Aires, E Argentina 37°17´S 61°20´W
61 E21 **General Lavalle** Buenos Aires, E Argentina 36°25´S 56°56´W
General Machado *see* Camacupa
62 I8 **General Manuel Belgrano, Cerro** ▲ W Argentina 29°05´S 67°05´W
41 O8 **General Mariano Escobero** ✈ (Monterrey) Nuevo León, NE Mexico 25°47´N 100°00´W
61 B20 **General O'Brien** Buenos Aires, E Argentina 34°54´S 60°45´W
62 K13 **General Pico** La Pampa, C Argentina 35°43´S 63°45´W
62 M7 **General Pinedo** Chaco, N Argentina 27°17´S 61°20´W
61 B20 **General Pinto** Buenos Aires, E Argentina 34°45´S 61°50´W
61 E22 **General Pirán** Buenos Aires, E Argentina 37°16´S 57°46´W
43 N15 **General, Río** S Costa Rica
63 I15 **General Roca** Río Negro, C Argentina 39°00´S 67°35´W
171 Q8 **General Santos** *off.* General Santos City. Mindanao, S Philippines 06°10´N 125°10´E
General Santos City *see* General Santos
41 O9 **General Terán** Nuevo León, NE Mexico 25°18´N 99°40´W
114 N7 **General Toshevo** *Rom.* I.G.Duca; *prev.* Casim, Kasimköj. Dobrich, NE Bulgaria 43°43´N 28°04´E
61 B20 **General Viamonte** Buenos Aires, E Argentina 35°01´S 61°00´W
61 A20 **General Villegas** Buenos Aires, E Argentina 35°02´S 63°01´W
Gênes *see* Genova
18 E11 **Genesee River** New York/Pennsylvania, NE USA
30 K11 **Geneseo** Illinois, N USA 41°27´N 90°08´W
18 F10 **Geneseo** New York, NE USA 42°48´N 77°46´W
57 L14 **Geneshuaya, Río** N Bolivia
23 Q8 **Geneva** Alabama, S USA 31°01´N 85°51´W
30 M10 **Geneva** Illinois, N USA 41°53´N 88°18´W
29 Q16 **Geneva** Nebraska, C USA 40°31´N 97°36´W
18 G10 **Geneva** New York, NE USA 42°52´N 76°58´W
31 U10 **Geneva** Ohio, NE USA 41°48´N 80°53´W
Geneva *see* Genève
108 B10 **Geneva, Lake** *Fr.* Lac de Genève, Lac Léman, le Léman, *Ger.* Genfer See. ◎ France/Switzerland
108 A10 **Genève** *Eng.* Geneva, *Ger.* Genf, *It.* Ginevra. Genève, SW Switzerland 46°13´N 06°09´E
108 A11 **Genève** *Eng.* Geneva, *Ger.* Genf, *It.* Ginevra. ◆ *canton* SW Switzerland
108 A10 **Genève** *var.* Geneva. ✈ Vaud, SW Switzerland 46°13´N 06°06´E
Genève, Lac de *see* Geneva, Lake
Genf *see* Genève
Genfer See *see* Geneva, Lake
163 T5 **Genhe** *prev.* Ergun Zuoqi. Nei Mongol Zizhiqu, N China 50°48´N 121°30´E
163 S5 **Gen He** NE China
Genichesk *see* Heniches'k
104 L14 **Genil** S Spain
99 K18 **Genk** *var.* Genck. Limburg, NE Belgium 50°58´N 05°30´E
164 C13 **Genkai-nada** *gulf* Kyūshū, SW Japan
107 C19 **Gennargentu, Monti del** ▲▲ Sardegna, Italy, C Mediterranean Sea
99 M14 **Gennep** Limburg, SE Netherlands 51°43´N 05°58´E
30 M10 **Genoa** Illinois, N USA 42°06´N 88°41´W
29 Q15 **Genoa** Nebraska, C USA 41°27´N 97°43´W
Genoa *see* Genova
Genoa, Gulf of *see* Genova, Golfo di
106 D10 **Genova** *Eng.* Genoa; *anc.* Genua, *Fr.* Gênes. Liguria, NW Italy 44°28´N 09°E
106 D10 **Genova, Golfo di** *Eng.* Gulf of Genoa. *gulf* NW Italy
57 C17 **Genovesa, Isla** *var.* Tower Island. *island* Galapagos Islands, Ecuador, E Pacific Ocean
Genshū *see* Wŏnju
99 E17 **Gent** *Eng.* Ghent, *Fr.* Gand. Oost-Vlaanderen, NW Belgium 51°02´N 03°42´E
169 N16 **Genteng** Jawa, C Indonesia 07°21´S 106°20´E
100 M12 **Genthin** Sachsen-Anhalt, E Germany 52°24´N 12°10´E
27 R9 **Gentry** Arkansas, C USA 36°16´N 94°28´W
Genua *see* Genova
107 I15 **Genzano di Roma** Lazio, C Italy 41°42´N 12°42´E
Geokchay *see* Göyçay
Geok-Tepe *see* Gökdepe
122 I3 **Georga, Zemlya** *Eng.* George Land. *island* Zemlya Frantsa-Iosifa, N Russian Federation
83 G26 **George** Western Cape, S South Africa 33°57´S 22°28´E
29 S11 **George** Iowa, C USA 43°20´N 96°00´W
13 O5 **George** Newfoundland and Labrador/Québec, E Canada
George F L Charles *see* Vigie
65 C25 **George Island** *island* S Falkland Islands
183 R10 **George, Lake** ◎ New South Wales, SE Australia
81 E18 **George, Lake** ◎ SW Uganda
23 W10 **George, Lake** ◎ Florida, SE USA
18 L8 **George, Lake** ▣ New York, NE USA
George Land *see* Georga, Zemlya
Georgenburg *see* Jurbarkas
George River *see* Kangiqsualujjuaq
64 G8 **Georges Bank** *undersea feature* W Atlantic Ocean 41°15´N 67°30´W
185 A21 **George Sound** *sound* South Island, New Zealand
65 F15 **Georgetown** O (Ascension Island) NW Ascension Island 17°56´S 14°25´W
181 V5 **Georgetown** Queensland, NE Australia 18°17´S 143°37´E
183 P15 **George Town** Tasmania, SE Australia 41°04´S 146°48´E
44 I4 **George Town** Great Exuma Island, C Bahamas 23°28´N 75°47´W
44 D8 **George Town** *var.* Georgetown. O (Cayman Islands) Grand Cayman, SW Cayman Islands 19°16´N 81°23´W
76 H12 **Georgetown** E Gambia 13°33´N 14°49´W
55 T8 **Georgetown** ● (Guyana) N Guyana 06°46´N 58°10´W
168 I7 **George Town** *var.* Penang, Pinang. Pinang, Peninsular Malaysia 05°28´N 100°20´E
45 Y14 **Georgetown** Saint Vincent, Saint Vincent and the Grenadines 13°19´N 61°09´W
21 Y4 **Georgetown** Delaware, NE USA 38°39´N 75°22´W
23 R6 **Georgetown** Georgia, SE USA 31°52´N 85°04´W
20 M5 **Georgetown** Kentucky, S USA 38°13´N 84°30´W
21 T13 **Georgetown** South Carolina, SE USA 33°23´N 79°18´W
25 S10 **Georgetown** Texas, SW USA 30°39´N 97°42´W
55 T8 **Georgetown** ✈ N Guyana 06°46´N 58°10´W
Georgetown *see* George Town
195 U16 **George V Coast** *physical region* Antarctica
194 J7 **George VI Ice Shelf** *ice shelf* Antarctica
194 J6 **George VI Sound** *sound* Antarctica
195 T15 **George V Land** *physical region* Antarctica
25 S14 **George West** Texas, SW USA 28°21´N 98°08´W
137 R9 **Georgia** *off.* Republic of Georgia, *Geor.* Sak'art'velo, *Rus.* Gruzinskaya SSR, Gruziya. ◆ *republic* SW Asia
23 S5 **Georgia** *off.* State of Georgia, *also known as* Empire State of the South, Peach State. ◆ *state* SE USA
14 F12 **Georgian Bay** *lake bay* Ontario, S Canada
Georgia, Republic of *see* Georgia
10 L17 **Georgia, Strait of** *strait* British Columbia, W Canada
Georgi Dimitrov *see* Kostenets
Georgi Dimitrov, Yazovir *see* Koprinka, Yazovir
114 M9 **Georgi Traykov, Yazovir** ▣ NE Bulgaria
Georgiu-Dezh *see* Liski
145 W10 **Georgiyevka** Vostochnyy Kazakhstan, E Kazakhstan 49°19´N 81°35´E
Georgiyevka *see* Korday
127 N15 **Georgiyevsk** Stavropol'skiy Kray, SW Russian Federation 44°07´N 43°22´E
100 G13 **Georgsmarienhütte** Niedersachsen, NW Germany 52°13´N 08°02´E
195 O1 **Georg von Neumayer** *German research station* Antarctica 70°41´S 08°18´W
101 M16 **Gera** Thüringen, E Germany 50°51´N 12°13´E
101 K16 **Gera** C Germany
99 E19 **Geraardsbergen** Oost-Vlaanderen, SW Belgium 50°47´N 03°53´E
115 F21 **Geráki** Pelopónnisos, S Greece 36°56´N 22°46´E
27 W5 **Gerald** Missouri, C USA 38°24´N 91°20´W
47 V8 **Geral de Goiás, Serra** ▲▲ E Brazil
185 G20 **Geraldine** Canterbury, South Island, New Zealand 44°06´S 171°14´E
180 H11 **Geraldton** Western Australia 28°48´S 114°40´E
12 E11 **Geraldton** Ontario, S Canada 49°44´N 86°59´W
60 J12 **Geral, Serra** ▲▲ S Brazil
103 U6 **Gérardmer** Vosges, NE France 48°05´N 06°54´E
Gerasa *see* Jarash
Gerdauen *see* Zheleznodorozhnyy
39 Q11 **Gerdine, Mount** ▲ Alaska, USA 61°40´N 152°21´W
136 H11 **Gerede** Bolu, N Turkey 40°48´N 32°13´E
136 H11 **Gerede Çayı** N Turkey
148 M8 **Gereshk** Helmand, SW Afghanistan 31°50´N 64°32´E
101 L24 **Geretsried** Bayern, S Germany 47°51´N 11°28´E
105 P14 **Gérgal** Andalucía, S Spain 37°07´N 02°34´W
28 I14 **Gering** Nebraska, C USA 41°49´N 103°39´W
35 R3 **Gerlach** Nevada, W USA 40°38´N 119°21´W
Gerlachfalvi Csúcs/Gerlachovka *see* Gerlachovský štít
111 L18 **Gerlachovský štít** *var.* Gerlachovka, *Ger.* Gerlsdorfer Spitze, *Hung.* Gerlachfalvi Csúcs; *prev.* Stalinov Štít, *Ger.* Franz-Josef Spitze, *Hung.* Ferencz-Jósef Csúcs. ▲ N Slovakia 49°12´N 20°09´E
108 E8 **Gerlafingen** Solothurn, NW Switzerland 47°10´N 07°35´E
Gerlsdorfer Spitze *see* Gerlachovský štít
139 V3 **Germak** As Sulaymānīyah, E Iraq 35°49´N 46°09´E
German East Africa *see* Tanzania
Germanicopolis *see* Çankırı
Germanicum, Mare/German Ocean *see* North Sea
Germanovichi *see* Hyermanavichy
German Southwest Africa *see* Namibia
20 E10 **Germantown** Tennessee, S USA 35°06´N 89°51´W
101 I15 **Germany** *off.* Federal Republic of Germany, Bundesrepublik Deutschland, *Ger.* Deutschland. ◆ *federal republic* N Europe
Germany, Federal Republic of *see* Germany
101 L23 **Germering** Bayern, SE Germany 48°07´N 11°22´E
83 J21 **Germiston** *var.* Gauteng. Gauteng, NE South Africa 26°15´S 28°10´E
Gernika *see* Gernika-Lumo
105 P2 **Gernika-Lumo** *var.* Gernika, Guernica, Guernica y Lumo. País Vasco, N Spain 43°19´N 02°40´W
164 L12 **Gero** Gifu, Honshū, SW Japan 35°48´N 137°15´E
115 F22 **Geroliménas** Pelopónnisos, S Greece 36°28´N 22°25´E
Gerona *see* Girona
99 H21 **Gerpinnes** Hainaut, S Belgium 50°20´N 04°38´E
102 L15 **Gers** ◆ *department* S France
102 L14 **Gers** S France
Gerunda *see* Girona
158 I13 **Gêrzê** *var.* Luring. Xizang Zizhiqu, W China 32°19´N 84°05´E
136 K10 **Gerze** Sinop, N Turkey 41°48´N 35°13´E
Gesoriacum *see* Boulogne-sur-Mer
Gessoriacum *see* Boulogne-sur-Mer
99 J21 **Gesves** Namur, SE Belgium 50°24´N 05°04´E
93 J20 **Geta** Åland, SW Finland 60°22´N 19°49´E
105 N8 **Getafe** Madrid, C Spain 40°18´N 03°44´W
95 J21 **Getinge** Halland, S Sweden 56°46´N 12°42´E
18 F16 **Gettysburg** Pennsylvania, NE USA 39°49´N 77°13´W
29 N8 **Gettysburg** South Dakota, N USA 45°00´N 99°57´W
194 K12 **Getz Ice Shelf** *ice shelf* Antarctica
137 S15 **Gevaş** Van, SE Turkey 38°16´N 43°05´E
Gevgeli *see* Gevgelija
113 Q20 **Gevgelija** *var.* Đevđelija, Djevdjelija, *Turk.* Gevgeli. SE Macedonia 41°09´N 22°30´E
103 T10 **Gex** Ain, E France 46°21´N 06°02´E
92 I3 **Geysir** *physical region* SW Iceland
136 F11 **Geyve** Sakarya, NW Turkey 40°32´N 30°18´E
80 G10 **Gezira** ◆ *state* E Sudan
109 V3 **Gföhl** Niederösterreich, N Austria 48°30´N 15°27´E
83 H22 **Ghaap Plateau** *Afr.* Ghaapplato. *plateau* C South Africa
Ghaapplato *see* Ghaap Plateau
Ghaba *see* Al Ghābah
138 J8 **Ghāb, Tall** ▲ SE Syria 33°09´N 37°48´E
139 Q9 **Ghadaf, Wādī al** *dry watercourse* C Iraq
Ghadamès *see* Ghadāmis
74 M9 **Ghadāmis** *var.* Ghadamès, Rhadames. W Libya 30°08´N 09°30´E
141 Y10 **Ghadan** E Oman 20°20´N 57°58´E
75 O10 **Ghaddūwah** C Libya 26°36´N 14°26´E
147 Q11 **Ghafurov** *Rus.* Gafurov; *prev.* Sovetabad. NW Tajikistan 40°13´N 69°42´E
153 R12 **Ghāghara** S Asia
149 P13 **Ghaibi Dero** Sind, SE Pakistan 27°35´N 67°42´E
141 Y10 **Ghalat** E Oman 21°06´N 58°51´E
139 W11 **Ghamūkah, Hawr** ◎ S Iraq
77 P15 **Ghana** *off.* Republic of Ghana. ◆ *republic* W Africa
141 X12 **Ghānah** *spring/well* S Oman 18°35´N 56°34´E
Ghanongga *see* Ranongga
Ghansi/Ghansiland *see* Ghanzi
83 F18 **Ghanzi** *var.* Khanzi. Ghanzi, W Botswana 21°39´S 21°38´E
83 G19 **Ghanzi** *var.* Ghansi, Ghansiland, Khanzi. ◆ *district* C Botswana
67 T14 **Ghanzi** *var.* Knanzi. Botswana/South Africa
Ghap'an *see* Kapan
138 F13 **Gharandal** Al'Aqabah, SW Jordan 30°12´N 35°18´E
139 U14 **Gharbīyah, Sha'īb al** S Iraq
Gharbt, Jabal al *see* Liban, Jebel
74 K7 **Ghardaïa** N Algeria 32°30´N 03°44´E
147 R12 **Gharm** *Rus.* Garm. C Tajikistan 39°03´N 70°25´E
149 P17 **Gharo** Sind, SE Pakistan 24°44´N 67°35´E
139 W10 **Gharrāf, Shaṭṭ al** S Iraq
Gharvān *see* Gharyān
75 O7 **Gharyān** *var.* Gharvān. NW Libya 32°10´N 13°01´E
74 M11 **Ghāt** *var.* Gat. SW Libya 24°58´N 10°11´E
Ghawdex *see* Gozo
141 U8 **Ghayathi** Abū Ẓaby, W United Arab Emirates 23°51´N 53°01´E
Ghazāl, Baḥr al *see* Ghazal, Bahr el
78 H9 **Ghazal, Bahr el** *var.* Soro. *seasonal river* C Chad
80 E13 **Ghazal, Bahr el** *var.* Baḥr al Ghazāl. S Sudan
74 H6 **Ghazaouet** NW Algeria 35°08´N 01°50´W
152 J10 **Ghāziābād** Uttar Pradesh, N India 28°42´N 77°28´E
153 O13 **Ghāzīpur** Uttar Pradesh, N India 25°36´N 83°36´E
149 Q6 **Ghaznī** *var.* Ghazni. Ghaznī, E Afghanistan 33°31´N 68°24´E
149 P7 **Ghaznī** ◆ *province* SE Afghanistan
Ghazzah *see* Gaza
Gheel *see* Geel
Ghelīzāne *see* Relizane
Ghent *see* Gent
Gheorghe Braţul *see* Sfântu Gheorghe, Braţul
Gheorghe Gheorghiu-Dej *see* Oneşti
116 J10 **Gheorgheni** *prev.* Gheorghieni, Sîn-Miclăuş, *Ger.* Niklasmarkt, *Hung.* Gyergyószentmiklós. Harghita, C Romania 46°43´N 25°36´E
Gheorghieni *see* Gheorgheni
116 H10 **Gherla** *Ger.* Neuschliss, *Hung.* Szamosújvár; *prev.* Armenierstadt. Cluj, NW Romania 47°02´N 23°55´E
Gheweifat *see* Ghuwayfāt
Ghilan *see* Gīlān
107 C18 **Ghilarza** Sardegna, Italy, C Mediterranean Sea 40°09´N 08°50´E
Ghilizane *see* Relizane
Ghimbi *see* Gīmbī
Ghiriş *see* Câmpia Turzii
103 Y15 **Ghisonaccia** Corse, France, C Mediterranean Sea 42°00´N 09°25´E
147 Q11 **Ghonchí** *Rus.* Ganchi. NW Tajikistan 39°57´N 69°10´E
Ghor *see* Ghowr
153 T13 **Ghoraghat** Rajshahi, NW Bangladesh 25°18´N 89°20´E
149 R13 **Ghotki** Sind, SE Pakistan 28°00´N 69°21´E
148 M5 **Ghowr** *var.* Ghor. ◆ *province* C Afghanistan
147 T13 **Ghŭdara** *var.* Gudara, *Rus.* Kudara. SE Tajikistan 38°28´N 72°39´E
153 R13 **Ghugri** N India

◆ Country
● Country Capital
◇ Dependent Territory
O Dependent Territory Capital
◆ Administrative Regions
✈ International Airport
▲ Mountain
▲▲ Mountain Range
Volcano
River
◎ Lake
▣ Reservoir

GHUND – GOODHOPE BAY

147 S14 **Ghund** *Rus.* Gunt. ≈ SE Tajikistan
Ghurābīyah, Sha'īb al *see* Gharbīyah, Sha'īb al
Ghurdaqah *see* Hurghada
148 J5 **Ghūriān** Herāt, W Afghanistan *34°20′N 61°26′E*
141 T8 **Ghuwayfāt** *var.* Gheweifat. Abū Ẓaby, W United Arab Emirates *24°06′N 51°40′E*
121 O14 **Ghuzayyil, Sabkhat** *salt lake* N Libya
126 J3 **Ghzatsk** Smolenskaya Oblast', W Russian Federation *55°33′N 35°00′E*
115 G17 **Giáltra** Évvoia, C Greece *38°21′N 22°58′E*
Giamame *see* Jamaame
167 U13 **Gia Nghia** *var.* Đak Nông. Đăc Lăc, S Vietnam *11°58′N 107°42′E*
114 F13 **Giannitsá** *var.* Yiannitsá. Kentrikí Makedonía, N Greece *40°49′N 22°24′E*
107 F14 **Giannutri, Isola di** *island* Archipelago Toscano, C Italy
96 F13 **Giant's Causeway** *Ir.* Clochán an Aifir. *lava flow* N Northern Ireland, United Kingdom
167 S15 **Gia Rai** Minh Hai, S Vietnam *09°14′N 105°28′E*
107 L24 **Giarre** Sicilia, Italy, C Mediterranean Sea *37°44′N 15°12′E*
44 I7 **Gibara** Holguín, E Cuba *21°09′N 76°11′W*
29 O16 **Gibbon** Nebraska, C USA *40°45′N 98°50′W*
32 K11 **Gibbon** Oregon, NW USA *45°40′N 118°22′W*
33 P11 **Gibbonsville** Idaho, NW USA *45°33′N 113°55′W*
62 A13 **Gibbs Hill** *hill* S Bermuda
92 I9 **Gibostad** Troms, N Norway *69°21′N 18°01′E*
104 I14 **Gibraleón** Andalucía, S Spain *37°23′N 06°58′W*
104 L16 **Gibraltar** ○ (Gibraltar) S Gibraltar *36°08′N 05°21′W*
104 L16 **Gibraltar** ◇ *UK dependent territory* SW Europe
Gibraltar, Détroit de/ Gibraltar, Estrecho de *see* Gibraltar, Strait of
104 J17 **Gibraltar, Strait of** *Fr.* Détroit de Gibraltar, *Sp.* Estrecho de Gibraltar. *strait* Atlantic Ocean/ Mediterranean Sea
31 S11 **Gibsonburg** Ohio, N USA *41°22′N 83°19′W*
30 M13 **Gibson City** Illinois, N USA *40°27′N 88°24′W*
180 L8 **Gibson Desert** *desert* Western Australia
10 L17 **Gibsons** British Columbia, SW Canada *49°24′N 123°32′W*
149 N12 **Gidār** Baluchistān, SW Pakistan *28°16′N 66°00′E*
155 I17 **Giddalūr** Andhra Pradesh, E India *15°24′N 78°54′E*
25 U10 **Giddings** Texas, SW USA *30°12′N 96°59′W*
27 Y8 **Gideon** Missouri, C USA *36°27′N 89°55′W*
81 I15 **Gīdolē** Southern Nationalities, S Ethiopia *05°31′N 37°26′E*
118 H13 **Giedraičiai** Utena, E Lithuania *55°05′N 25°16′E*
103 O7 **Gien** Loiret, C France *47°40′N 02°37′E*
101 G17 **Giessen** Hessen, W Germany *50°35′N 08°41′E*
98 O6 **Gieten** Drenthe, NE Netherlands *53°00′N 06°43′E*
23 Y13 **Gifford** Florida, SE USA *27°40′N 80°24′W*
9 O5 **Gifford** ≈ Baffin Island, Nunavut, NE Canada
100 J12 **Gifhorn** Niedersachsen, N Germany *52°28′N 10°33′E*
11 P13 **Gift Lake** Alberta, W Canada *55°49′N 115°57′W*
164 L13 **Gifu** *var.* Gihu. Gifu, Honshū, SW Japan *35°24′N 136°46′E*
164 K13 **Gifu** *off.* Gifu-ken, *var.* Gihu. ◈ *prefecture* Honshū, SW Japan
Gifu-ken *see* Gifu
126 M13 **Gigant** Rostovskaya Oblast', SW Russian Federation *46°29′N 41°18′E*
40 E8 **Giganta, Sierra de la** ▲▲ NW Mexico
54 E12 **Gigante** Huila, S Colombia *02°24′N 75°34′W*
114 I7 **Gigen** Pleven, N Bulgaria *43°40′N 24°31′E*
Giggiga *see* Jijiga
96 G12 **Gigha Island** *island* SW Scotland, United Kingdom
107 E14 **Giglio, Isola del** *island* Archipelago Toscano, C Italy
Gihu *see* Gifu
146 L11 **G'ijduvon** *Rus.* Gizhduvon. Buxoro Viloyati, C Uzbekistan *40°06′N 64°38′E*
104 L2 **Gijón** *var.* Xixón. Asturias, NW Spain *43°32′N 05°40′W*
81 D20 **Gikongoro** SW Rwanda *02°30′S 29°32′E*
36 K14 **Gila Bend** Arizona, SW USA *32°57′N 112°43′W*
36 J14 **Gila Bend Mountains** ▲▲ Arizona, SW USA
37 N14 **Gila Mountains** ▲▲ Arizona, SW USA
36 I15 **Gila Mountains** ▲▲ Arizona, SW USA
142 M4 **Gīlān** *off.* Ostān-e Gīlān, *var.* Ghilan, Guilan. ◈ *province* NW Iran
Gīlān, Ostān-e *see* Gīlān
36 L14 **Gila River** ≈ Arizona, SW USA
29 W4 **Gilbert** Minnesota, N USA *47°29′N 92°27′W*
Gilbert Islands *see* Tungaru
10 L16 **Gilbert, Mount** ▲ British Columbia, SW Canada *50°49′N 124°03′W*
181 U4 **Gilbert River** ≈ Queensland, NE Australia
0 C6 **Gilbert Seamounts** *undersea feature* NE Pacific Ocean *52°50′N 150°10′W*
33 S7 **Gildford** Montana, NW USA *48°34′N 110°21′W*
83 P15 **Gilé** Zambézia, NE Mozambique *16°10′S 38°17′E*
30 K4 **Gile Flowage** ◎ Wisconsin, N USA
182 G7 **Giles, Lake** *salt lake* South Australia
Gilf Kebir Plateau *see* Haḍabat al Jilf al Kabīr
183 R6 **Gilgandra** New South Wales, SE Australia *31°43′S 148°39′E*
Gilgău *see* Gâlgău
81 I19 **Gilgil** Rift Valley, SW Kenya *0°29′S 36°19′E*
183 S4 **Gil Gil Creek** ≈ New South Wales, SE Australia
149 V3 **Gilgit** Jammu and Kashmir, NE Pakistan *35°54′N 74°20′E*
149 V3 **Gilgit** ≈ N Pakistan
11 X11 **Gillam** Manitoba, C Canada *56°25′N 94°45′W*
95 J22 **Gilleleje** Frederiksborg, E Denmark *56°05′N 12°17′E*
30 K14 **Gillespie** Illinois, N USA *39°07′N 89°49′W*
27 W13 **Gillett** Arkansas, C USA *34°07′N 91°22′W*
33 X12 **Gillette** Wyoming, C USA *44°17′N 105°30′W*
97 P22 **Gillingham** SE England, United Kingdom *51°24′N 00°33′E*
195 X6 **Gillock Island** *island* Antarctica
173 O16 **Gillot** ✈ (St-Denis) N Réunion *20°53′S 55°31′E*
65 H25 **Gill Point** *headland* E Saint Helena *15°59′S 05°38′W*
30 M12 **Gilman** Illinois, N USA *40°44′N 87°58′W*
25 W6 **Gilmer** Texas, SW USA *32°44′N 94°58′W*
Gilolo *see* Halmahera, Pulau
81 G14 **Gīlo Wenz** ≈ SW Ethiopia
35 O10 **Gilroy** California, W USA *37°00′N 121°34′W*
123 Q12 **Gilyuy** ≈ SE Russian Federation
99 I14 **Gilze** Noord-Brabant, S Netherlands *51°33′N 04°56′E*
165 R16 **Gima** Okinawa, Kume-jima, SW Japan
80 H13 **Gīmbī** *It.* Ghimbi. Oromīya, C Ethiopia *09°13′N 35°39′E*
45 T12 **Gimie, Mount** ▲ C Saint Lucia *13°51′N 61°00′W*
11 X16 **Gimli** Manitoba, S Canada *50°39′N 97°00′W*
Gimma *see* Jīma
95 O14 **Gimo** Uppsala, C Sweden *60°11′N 18°12′E*
102 L15 **Gimone** ≈ S France
Gimpoe *see* Gimpu
171 N12 **Gimpu** *prev.* Gimpoe. Sulawesi, C Indonesia *01°38′S 120°00′E*
182 F5 **Gina** South Australia *29°56′S 134°33′E*
Ginevra *see* Genève
99 J19 **Gingelom** Limburg, NE Belgium *50°46′N 05°09′E*
180 I12 **Gingin** Western Australia *31°22′S 115°51′E*
171 Q7 **Gingoog** Mindanao, S Philippines *08°47′N 125°05′E*
81 K14 **Gīnīr** Oromīya, C Ethiopia *07°12′N 40°43′E*
Giohar *see* Jawhar
107 O17 **Gióia del Colle** Puglia, SE Italy *40°47′N 16°56′E*
107 M22 **Gioia, Golfo di** *gulf* S Italy
Giona *see* Gkióna
115 I16 **Gioúra** *island* Vóreies Sporádes, Greece, Aegean Sea
107 O17 **Giovinazzo** Puglia, SE Italy *41°11′N 16°40′E*
Gipeswic *see* Ipswich
Gipuzkoa *see* Guipúzcoa
Giran *see* Ilan
30 K14 **Girard** Illinois, N USA *39°27′N 89°46′W*
27 R7 **Girard** Kansas, C USA *37°30′N 94°50′W*
25 O6 **Girard** Texas, SW USA *33°18′N 100°38′W*
54 E10 **Girardot** Cundinamarca, C Colombia *04°19′N 74°47′W*
172 M7 **Giraud Seamount** *undersea feature* SW Indian Ocean *09°57′S 46°55′E*
83 A15 **Giraul** ≈ SW Angola
96 L9 **Girdle Ness** *headland* NE Scotland, United Kingdom *57°09′N 02°04′W*
137 N11 **Giresun** *var.* Kerasunt; *anc.* Cerasus, Pharnacia. Giresun, NE Turkey *40°55′N 38°35′E*
137 N12 **Giresun** *var.* Kerasunt. ◈ *province* NE Turkey
137 N12 **Giresun Dağları** ▲▲ N Turkey
Girga *see* Jirjā
Girgeh *see* Jirjā
Girgenti *see* Agrigento
153 Q15 **Girīdīh** Jhārkhand, NE India *24°10′N 86°20′E*
183 P6 **Girilambone** New South Wales, SE Australia *31°19′S 146°57′E*
Girin *see* Jilin
121 W10 **Girne** *Gk.* Kerýneia, Kyrenia. N Cyprus *35°20′N 33°20′E*
Giron *see* Kiruna
105 X5 **Girona** *var.* Gerona; *anc.* Gerunda. Cataluña, NE Spain *41°59′N 02°49′E*
105 W5 **Girona** *var.* Gerona. ◈ *province* Cataluña, NE Spain
102 J12 **Gironde** ◈ *department* SW France
102 J11 **Gironde** *estuary* SW France
105 V5 **Gironella** Cataluña, NE Spain *42°02′N 01°53′E*
103 N15 **Girou** ≈ S France
97 H14 **Girvan** W Scotland, United Kingdom *55°14′N 04°53′W*
24 M9 **Girvin** Texas, SW USA *31°05′N 102°24′W*
184 Q9 **Gisborne** Gisborne, North Island, New Zealand *38°41′S 178°01′E*
184 P9 **Gisborne** *off.* Gisborne District. ◈ *unitary authority* North Island, New Zealand
Gisborne District *see* Gisborne
Giseifu *see* Uijŏngbu
Gisenye *see* Gisenyi
81 D19 **Gisenyi** *var.* Gisenye. NW Rwanda *01°42′S 29°18′E*
95 K20 **Gislaved** Jönköping, S Sweden *57°19′N 13°30′E*
103 N4 **Gisors** Eure, N France *49°18′N 01°46′E*
Gissar *see* Hisor
147 P12 **Gissar Range** *Rus.* Gissarskiy Khrebet. ▲▲ Tajikistan/Uzbekistan
Gissarskiy Khrebet *see* Gissar Range
99 B16 **Gistel** West-Vlaanderen, W Belgium *51°09′N 02°58′E*
108 F9 **Giswil** Unterwalden, C Switzerland *46°49′N 08°11′E*
115 B16 **Gitánes** *ancient monument* Ípeiros, W Greece
81 E20 **Gitarama** C Rwanda *02°05′S 29°45′E*
81 E20 **Gitega** C Burundi *03°20′S 29°56′E*
Githio *see* Gýtheio
108 H11 **Giubiasco** Ticino, S Switzerland *46°11′N 09°01′E*
106 K13 **Giulianova** Abruzzi, C Italy *42°45′N 13°58′E*
Giulie, Alpi *see* Julian Alps
Giumri *see* Gyumri
116 M13 **Giurgeni** Ialomiţa, SE Romania *44°45′N 27°48′E*
116 J15 **Giurgiu** Giurgiu, S Romania *43°54′N 25°58′E*
116 J14 **Giurgiu** ◈ *county* SE Romania
95 F22 **Give** Vejle, C Denmark *55°51′N 09°15′E*
103 R2 **Givet** Ardennes, N France *50°08′N 04°50′E*
103 R11 **Givors** Rhône, E France *45°35′N 04°47′E*
83 K19 **Giyani** Limpopo, NE South Africa *23°20′S 30°37′E*
80 I13 **Giyon** Oromīya, C Ethiopia *08°31′N 37°56′E*
75 W8 **Gîza** *var.* Al Jīzah, El Gîza, Gizeh. N Egypt *30°01′N 31°13′E*
75 V8 **Giza, Pyramids of** *ancient monument* N Egypt
Gizhduvon *see* G'ijduvon
123 U8 **Gizhiga** Magadanskaya Oblast', E Russian Federation *61°58′N 160°16′E*
123 T9 **Gizhiginskaya Guba** *bay* E Russian Federation
186 K8 **Gizo** Gizo, NW Solomon Islands *08°03′S 156°49′E*
110 N7 **Giżycko** *Ger.* Lötzen. Warmińsko-Mazurskie, NE Poland *54°03′N 21°48′E*
Gízymałów *see* Hrymayliv
113 M17 **Gjakovë** *Serb.* Đakovica. W Kosovo *42°22′N 20°30′E*
94 F12 **Gjende** ◎ S Norway
95 F17 **Gjerstad** Aust-Agder, S Norway *58°54′N 09°03′E*
113 O17 **Gjilan** *Serb.* Gnjilane. E Kosovo *42°27′N 21°28′E*
Gjinokastër *see* Gjirokastër
113 L23 **Gjirokastër** *var.* Gjirokastra; *prev.* Gjinokastër, *Gk.* Argyrokastron, *It.* Argirocastro. Gjirokastër, S Albania *40°04′N 20°09′E*
113 L22 **Gjirokastër** ◈ *district* S Albania
Gjirokastra *see* Gjirokastër
9 N7 **Gjoa Haven** *var.* Uqsuqtuuq. King William Island, Nunavut, NW Canada *68°38′N 95°57′W*
94 H13 **Gjøvik** Oppland, S Norway *60°47′N 10°40′E*
113 J22 **Gjuhëzës, Kepi i** *headland* SW Albania *40°25′N 19°19′E*
Gjurgjevac *see* Đurđevac
115 E18 **Gkióna** *var.* Giona. ▲▲ C Greece
121 R3 **Gkréko, Akrotíri** *var.* Cape Greco, Pidálion. *cape* E Cyprus
99 I18 **Glabbeek-Zuurbemde** Vlaams Brabant, C Belgium *50°54′N 04°58′E*
13 R14 **Glace Bay** Cape Breton Island, Nova Scotia, SE Canada *46°12′N 59°57′W*
11 O16 **Glacier** British Columbia, SW Canada *51°12′N 117°33′W*
39 W12 **Glacier Bay** *inlet* Alaska, USA
32 I7 **Glacier Peak** ▲ Washington, NW USA *48°06′N 121°06′W*
21 Q7 **Glade Spring** Virginia, NE USA *36°47′N 81°46′W*
43 W7 **Gladewater** Texas, SW USA *32°32′N 94°57′W*
181 Y8 **Gladstone** Queensland, E Australia *23°52′S 151°16′E*
182 I8 **Gladstone** South Australia *33°16′S 138°21′E*
11 X16 **Gladstone** Manitoba, S Canada *50°12′N 98°56′W*
31 O5 **Gladstone** Michigan, N USA *45°51′N 87°01′W*
27 R4 **Gladstone** Missouri, C USA *39°12′N 94°33′W*
31 Q7 **Gladwin** Michigan, N USA *43°58′N 84°29′W*
95 J15 **Glafsfjorden** ◎ C Sweden
92 H2 **Gláma** *physical region* NW Iceland
94 I12 **Gláma** *var.* Glommen. ≈ S Norway
112 F13 **Glamoč** Federacija Bosna I Hercegovina, NE Boznia and Herzegovina *44°01′N 16°51′E*
97 J22 **Glamorgan** *cultural region* S Wales, United Kingdom
95 G24 **Glamsbjerg** Fyn, C Denmark *55°17′N 10°07′E*
171 Q8 **Glan** Mindanao, S Philippines *05°49′N 125°11′E*
109 T9 **Glan** ≈ SE Austria
101 F19 **Glan** ≈ W Germany
95 M17 **Glan** ◎ S Sweden
Glaris *see* Glarus
108 H9 **Glarner Alpen** *Eng.* Glarus Alps. ▲▲ E Switzerland
108 H8 **Glarus** Glarus, E Switzerland *47°03′N 09°04′E*
108 H9 **Glarus** *Fr.* Glaris. ◈ *canton* C Switzerland
Glarus Alps *see* Glarner Alpen
27 N3 **Glasco** Kansas, C USA *39°21′N 97°50′W*
96 I12 **Glasgow** S Scotland, United Kingdom *55°53′N 04°15′W*
20 K7 **Glasgow** Kentucky, S USA *37°00′N 85°54′W*
27 T4 **Glasgow** Missouri, C USA *39°13′N 92°51′W*
33 W7 **Glasgow** Montana, NW USA *48°12′N 106°37′W*
21 T6 **Glasgow** Virginia, NE USA *37°37′N 79°27′W*
96 I12 **Glasgow** ✈ W Scotland, United Kingdom *55°52′N 04°27′W*
11 S14 **Glaslyn** Saskatchewan, S Canada *53°20′N 108°18′W*
18 I16 **Glassboro** New Jersey, NE USA *39°40′N 75°05′W*
24 L10 **Glass Mountains** ▲▲ Texas, SW USA
97 K23 **Glastonbury** SW England, United Kingdom *51°09′N 02°43′W*
Glatz *see* Kłodzko
101 N16 **Glauchau** Sachsen, E Germany *50°48′N 12°32′E*
114 M7 **Glavinitsa** Silistra, NE Bulgaria *43°55′N 26°50′E*
Glavn'a Morava *see* Velika Morava
Glavnik *see* Gllamnik
127 T1 **Glazov** Udmurtskaya Respublika, NW Russian Federation *58°06′N 52°38′E*
Glda *see* Gwda
109 U8 **Gleinalpe** ▲▲ SE Austria
109 W8 **Gleisdorf** Steiermark, SE Austria *47°07′N 15°43′E*
Gleiwitz *see* Gliwice
39 S11 **Glenallen** Alaska, USA *62°06′N 145°33′W*
102 F7 **Glénan, Îles** *island group* NW France
185 G21 **Glenavy** Canterbury, South Island, New Zealand *44°53′S 171°04′E*
10 H5 **Glenboyle** Yukon Territory, NW Canada *63°55′N 138°43′W*
21 X3 **Glen Burnie** Maryland, NE USA *39°09′N 76°37′W*
36 L8 **Glen Canyon** *canyon* Utah, W USA
36 L8 **Glen Canyon Dam** *dam* Arizona, SW USA
30 K15 **Glen Carbon** Illinois, N USA *38°45′N 89°58′W*
14 E17 **Glencoe** Ontario, S Canada *42°44′N 81°42′W*
83 K22 **Glencoe** KwaZulu/Natal, E South Africa *28°10′S 30°15′E*
29 U9 **Glencoe** Minnesota, N USA *44°46′N 94°09′W*
96 H10 **Glen Coe** *valley* N Scotland, United Kingdom
36 K13 **Glendale** Arizona, SW USA *33°32′N 112°11′W*
35 S15 **Glendale** California, W USA *34°09′N 118°20′W*
182 G5 **Glendambo** South Australia *30°59′S 135°45′E*
33 Y8 **Glendive** Montana, NW USA *47°08′N 104°42′W*
33 Y15 **Glendo** Wyoming, C USA *42°27′N 105°01′W*
55 S10 **Glendor Mountains** ▲▲ C Guyana
182 K12 **Glenelg River** ≈ South Australia/Victoria, SE Australia
29 P4 **Glenfield** North Dakota, N USA *47°25′N 98°33′W*
25 V12 **Glen Flora** Texas, SW USA *29°22′N 96°12′W*
181 P7 **Glen Helen** Northern Territory, N Australia *23°45′S 132°46′E*
183 U5 **Glen Innes** New South Wales, SE Australia *29°42′S 151°45′E*
31 P6 **Glen Lake** ◎ Michigan, N USA
10 I7 **Glenlyon Peak** ▲ Yukon Territory, W Canada *62°32′N 134°51′W*
37 N16 **Glenn, Mount** ▲ Arizona, SW USA *31°55′N 110°00′W*
33 N15 **Glenns Ferry** Idaho, NW USA *42°57′N 115°18′W*
23 W6 **Glennville** Georgia, SE USA *31°56′N 81°55′W*
10 J10 **Glenora** British Columbia, W Canada *57°52′N 131°16′W*
182 M11 **Glenorchy** Victoria, SE Australia *36°56′S 142°39′E*
183 V5 **Glenreagh** New South Wales, SE Australia *30°04′S 153°00′E*
33 X15 **Glenrock** Wyoming, C USA *42°51′N 105°52′W*
96 K11 **Glenrothes** E Scotland, United Kingdom *56°11′N 03°09′W*
18 L9 **Glens Falls** New York, NE USA *43°18′N 73°38′W*
97 D14 **Glenties** *Ir.* Na Gleannta. Donegal, NW Ireland *54°47′N 08°17′W*
28 L5 **Glen Ullin** North Dakota, N USA *46°49′N 101°49′W*
21 R4 **Glenville** West Virginia, NE USA *38°57′N 80°51′W*
27 T12 **Glenwood** Arkansas, C USA *34°19′N 93°33′W*
29 S15 **Glenwood** Iowa, C USA *41°03′N 95°44′W*
29 T7 **Glenwood** Minnesota, N USA *45°39′N 95°23′W*
36 L5 **Glenwood** Utah, W USA *38°45′N 111°59′W*
30 I5 **Glenwood City** Wisconsin, N USA *45°04′N 92°11′W*
37 Q4 **Glenwood Springs** Colorado, C USA *39°33′N 107°21′W*
108 F10 **Gletsch** Valais, S Switzerland *46°34′N 08°21′E*
Glevum *see* Gloucester
29 U14 **Glidden** Iowa, C USA *42°03′N 94°43′W*
112 E9 **Glina** *var.* Banijska Palanka. Sisak-Moslavina, NE Croatia *45°19′N 16°07′E*
94 F11 **Glittertind** ▲ S Norway *61°24′N 08°19′E*
111 J16 **Gliwice** *Ger.* Gleiwitz. Śląskie, S Poland *50°19′N 18°49′E*
113 N16 **Gllamnik** *Serb.* Glavnik. N Kosovo *42°53′N 21°10′E*
36 M14 **Globe** Arizona, SW USA *33°24′N 110°47′W*
Globino *see* Hlobyne
108 L9 **Glockturm** ▲ SW Austria *46°54′N 10°42′E*
116 L9 **Glodeni** *Rus.* Glodyany. N Moldova *47°47′N 27°33′E*
109 S9 **Glödnitz** Kärnten, S Austria *46°57′N 14°03′E*
Glodyany *see* Glodeni
Glogau *see* Głogów
109 W6 **Gloggnitz** Niederösterreich, E Austria *47°41′N 15°57′E*
110 F13 **Głogów** *Ger.* Glogau, Glogow. Dolnośląskie, SW Poland *51°40′N 16°04′E*
Glogow *see* Głogów
111 I16 **Głogówek** *Ger.* Oberglogau. Opolskie, S Poland *50°21′N 17°51′E*
92 G12 **Glomfjord** Nordland, C Norway *66°49′N 14°00′E*
Glomma *see* Gláma
Glommen *see* Gláma
93 I14 **Glommersträsk** Norrbotten, N Sweden *65°17′N 19°40′E*
172 I1 **Glorieuses, Îles** *Eng.* Glorioso Islands. *island* (to France) N Madagascar
Glorioso Islands *see* Glorieuses, Îles
38 J12 **Glory of Russia Cape** *headland* Saint Matthew Island, Alaska, USA *60°36′N 172°57′W*
22 J7 **Gloster** Mississippi, S USA *31°12′N 91°01′W*
183 U7 **Gloucester** New South Wales, SE Australia *32°01′S 152°00′E*
186 F7 **Gloucester** New Britain, E Papua New Guinea *05°30′S 148°30′E*
97 L21 **Gloucester** *hist.* Caer Glou, *Lat.* Glevum. C England, United Kingdom *51°53′N 02°14′W*
19 P10 **Gloucester** Massachusetts, NE USA *42°36′N 70°36′W*
21 X6 **Gloucester** Virginia, NE USA *37°26′N 76°33′W*
97 K21 **Gloucestershire** *cultural region* C England, United Kingdom
31 T14 **Glouster** Ohio, N USA *39°30′N 82°04′W*
42 H3 **Glovers Reef** *reef* E Belize
18 K10 **Gloversville** New York, NE USA *43°03′N 74°20′W*
110 K12 **Głowno** Łódź, C Poland *51°58′N 19°43′E*
111 H16 **Głubczyce** *Ger.* Leobschütz. Opolskie, S Poland *50°13′N 17°50′E*
126 L11 **Glubokiy** Rostovskaya Oblast', SW Russian Federation *48°34′N 40°16′E*
145 W9 **Glubokoye** Vostochnyy Kazakhstan, E Kazakhstan *50°08′N 82°16′E*
Glubokoye *see* Hlybokaye
111 H16 **Głuchołazy** *Ger.* Ziegenhais. Opolskie, S Poland *50°20′N 17°23′E*
100 I9 **Glückstadt** Schleswig-Holstein, N Germany *53°47′N 09°26′E*
Glukhov *see* Hlukhiv
Glushkevichi *see* Hlushkavichy
Glusk/Glussk *see* Hlusk
Glybokaya *see* Hlyboka
95 F21 **Glyngøre** Viborg, NW Denmark *56°45′N 08°55′E*
127 Q9 **Gmelinka** Volgogradskaya Oblast', SW Russian Federation *50°50′N 46°51′E*
109 R8 **Gmünd** Kärnten, S Austria *46°56′N 13°32′E*
109 U2 **Gmünd** Niederösterreich, N Austria *48°47′N 14°59′E*
Gmünd *see* Schwäbisch Gmünd
109 S5 **Gmunden** Oberösterreich, N Austria *47°56′N 13°48′E*
Gmundner See *see* Traunsee
94 N10 **Gnarp** Gävleborg, C Sweden *62°03′N 17°19′E*
109 W8 **Gnas** Steiermark, SE Austria *46°53′N 15°48′E*
Gnaviyani *see* Fuammulah
Gnesen *see* Gniezno
95 O16 **Gnesta** Södermanland, C Sweden *59°05′N 17°20′E*
110 H11 **Gniezno** *Ger.* Gnesen. Weilkopolskie, C Poland *52°33′N 17°35′E*
Gnjilane *see* Gjilan
95 K20 **Gnosjö** Jönköping, S Sweden *57°22′N 13°44′E*
155 E17 **Goa** *prev.* Old Goa, Vela Goa, Velha Goa. W India *15°31′N 73°56′E*
155 E17 **Goa** *var.* Old Goa. ◈ *state* W India
Goabddális *see* Kåbdalis
153 U12 **Goalpāra** Assam, NE India *26°11′N 90°37′E*
42 H7 **Goascorán, Río** ≈ El Salvador/Honduras
77 O16 **Goaso** *var.* Gawso. W Ghana *06°49′N 02°27′W*
81 K14 **Goba** *It.* Oromo. Bīnishangul Gumuz, C Ethiopia *07°02′N 39°58′E*
83 C20 **Gobabed** Erongo, W Namibia *23°36′S 15°03′E*
83 E19 **Gobabis** Omaheke, E Namibia *22°25′S 18°58′E*
Gobannium *see* Abergavenny
64 M7 **Goban Spur** *undersea feature* NW Atlantic Ocean
63 H21 **Gobernador Gregores** Santa Cruz, S Argentina *48°43′S 70°21′W*
61 F14 **Gobernador Ingeniero Virasoro** Corrientes, NE Argentina *28°06′S 56°00′W*
162 L12 **Gobi** *desert* China/Mongolia
164 I14 **Gobō** Wakayama, Honshū, SW Japan *33°52′N 135°09′E*
Gobolka Awdal *see* Awdal
Gobolka Sahil *see* Sahil
Gobolka Sool *see* Sool
101 D14 **Goch** Nordrhein-Westfalen, W Germany *51°41′N 06°10′E*
83 E20 **Gochas** Hardap, S Namibia *24°54′S 18°43′E*
155 I14 **Godāvari** *var.* Godavari. ≈ C India
Godavari *see* Godāvari
155 L16 **Godāvari, Mouths of the** *delta* E India
15 V5 **Godbout** Québec, SE Canada *49°19′N 67°37′W*
15 U5 **Godbout** ≈ Québec, SE Canada
15 U5 **Godbout Est** ≈ Québec, SE Canada
153 R14 **Godda** Jharkhand, India *24°50′N 87°13′E*
27 N6 **Goddard** Kansas, C USA *37°39′N 97°34′W*
14 E15 **Goderich** Ontario, S Canada *43°43′N 81°43′W*
Godhavn *see* Qeqertarsuaq
154 E10 **Godhra** Gujarāt, W India *22°49′N 73°40′E*
Göding *see* Hodonín
111 K22 **Gödöllő** Pest, N Hungary *47°36′N 19°20′E*
62 H11 **Godoy Cruz** Mendoza, W Argentina *32°59′S 68°49′W*
11 Y11 **Gods** ≈ Manitoba, C Canada
11 Y13 **Gods Lake** Manitoba, C Canada *54°29′N 94°21′W*
11 X13 **Gods Lake** ◎ Manitoba, C Canada
Godthaab/Godthåb *see* Nuuk
Godwin Austen, Mount *see* K2
Goede Hoop, Kaap de *see* Good Hope, Cape of
Goedgegun *see* Nhlangano
Goeie Hoop, Kaap die *see* Good Hope, Cape of
13 O7 **Goéland, Lac au** ◎ Québec, SE Canada
98 E13 **Goeree** *island* SW Netherlands
99 F15 **Goes** Zeeland, SW Netherlands *51°30′N 03°55′E*
Goettingen *see* Göttingen
19 O10 **Goffstown** New Hampshire, NE USA *43°01′N 71°34′W*
14 E8 **Gogama** Ontario, S Canada *47°42′N 81°44′W*
30 L3 **Gogebic, Lake** ◎ Michigan, N USA
30 K3 **Gogebic Range** *hill range* Michigan/Wisconsin, N USA
Gogi Lerr *see* Gogi, Mount
137 V13 **Gogi, Mount** *Arm.* Gogi Lerr, *Az.* Küküdağ. ▲ Armenia/Azerbaijan *39°33′N 45°35′E*
124 F12 **Gogland, Ostrov** *island* NW Russian Federation
111 I15 **Gogolin** Opolskie, S Poland *50°28′N 18°04′E*
Gogonou *see* Gogounou
77 S14 **Gogounou** *var.* Gogonou. N Benin *10°50′N 02°50′E*
152 I10 **Gohāna** Haryāna, N India *29°06′N 76°43′E*
59 K18 **Goianésia** Goiás, C Brazil *15°21′S 49°02′W*
59 K18 **Goiânia** *prev.* Goyania. *state capital* Goiás, C Brazil *16°43′S 49°18′W*
59 K18 **Goiás** Goiás, C Brazil *15°57′S 50°07′W*
59 J18 **Goiás** *off.* Estado de Goiás; *prev.* Goiaz, Goyaz. ◈ *state* C Brazil
Goiás, Estado de *see* Goiás
Goiaz *see* Goiás
Goidhoo Atoll *see* Horsburgh Atoll
159 R14 **Goinsargoin** Xizang Zizhiqu, W China *31°56′N 98°04′E*
60 H10 **Goio-Erê** Paraná, SW Brazil *24°08′S 53°07′W*
99 I15 **Goirle** Noord-Brabant, S Netherlands *51°31′N 05°04′E*
104 H8 **Góis** Coimbra, N Portugal *40°10′N 08°06′W*
165 Q8 **Gojōme** Akita, Honshū, NW Japan *39°55′N 140°07′E*
149 U9 **Gojra** Punjab, E Pakistan *31°10′N 72°43′E*
136 A11 **Gökçeada** *var.* Imroz Adasī, *Gk.* Imbros. *island* NW Turkey
Gökçeada *see* Imroz
146 F13 **Gökdepe** *Rus.* Gëkdepe, Geok-Tepe. Ahal Welaýaty, C Turkmenistan *38°05′N 58°08′E*
136 I10 **Gökırmak** ≈ N Turkey
Goklenkuy, Solonchak *see* Geklengkui, Solonchak
136 C16 **Gökova Körfezi** *gulf* SW Turkey
136 K15 **Göksu** ≈ S Turkey
136 L15 **Göksun** Kahramanmaraş, C Turkey *38°03′N 36°30′E*
136 I17 **Göksu Nehri** ≈ S Turkey
83 J16 **Gokwe** Midlands, NW Zimbabwe *18°13′S 28°55′E*
94 F13 **Gol** Buskerud, S Norway *60°42′N 08°57′E*
153 X12 **Golāghāt** Assam, NE India *26°31′N 93°54′E*
110 H10 **Gołańcz** Wielkopolskie, C Poland *52°57′N 17°17′E*
138 G8 **Golan Heights** *Ar.* Al Jawlān, *Heb.* HaGolan. ▲▲ SW Syria
Golārā *see* Ārān
Golaya Pristan *see* Hola Prystan'
143 T11 **Golbāf** Kermān, C Iran *29°51′N 57°44′E*
136 M15 **Gölbaşı** Adıyaman, S Turkey *37°46′N 37°40′E*
109 P9 **Gölbner** ▲ SW Austria *46°51′N 12°31′E*
30 M17 **Golconda** Illinois, N USA *37°20′N 88°29′W*
35 T3 **Golconda** Nevada, W USA *40°56′N 117°29′W*
136 E11 **Gölcük** Kocaeli, NW Turkey *40°44′N 29°50′E*
108 I7 **Goldach** Sankt Gallen, NE Switzerland *47°28′N 09°28′E*
110 N7 **Gołdap** *Ger.* Goldap. Warmińsko-Mazurskie, NE Poland *54°19′N 22°23′E*
32 E15 **Gold Beach** Oregon, NW USA *42°25′N 124°27′W*
Goldberg *see* Złotoryja
183 V3 **Gold Coast** *cultural region* Queensland, E Australia
68 D12 **Gold Coast** *coastal region* S Ghana
39 R10 **Gold Creek** Alaska, USA *62°48′N 149°40′W*
11 O16 **Golden** British Columbia, SW Canada *51°19′N 116°58′W*
37 T4 **Golden** Colorado, C USA *39°40′N 105°12′W*
184 I13 **Golden Bay** *bay* South Island, New Zealand
27 R7 **Golden City** Missouri, C USA *37°23′N 94°05′W*
32 I11 **Goldendale** Washington, NW USA *45°49′N 120°49′W*
Goldener Tisch *see* Zlatý Stôl
44 L13 **Golden Grove** E Jamaica *17°56′N 76°17′W*
14 J12 **Golden Lake** ◎ Ontario, SE Canada
22 K10 **Golden Meadow** Louisiana, S USA *29°22′N 90°15′W*
45 V10 **Golden Rock** ✈ (Basseterre) Saint Kitts, Saint Kitts and Nevis *17°16′N 62°43′W*
Golden State, The *see* California
83 K16 **Golden Valley** Mashonaland West, N Zimbabwe *18°11′S 29°50′E*
35 U9 **Goldfield** Nevada, W USA *37°42′N 117°15′W*
Goldingen *see* Kuldīga
Goldmarkt *see* Zlatna
10 K17 **Gold River** Vancouver Island, British Columbia, SW Canada *49°41′N 126°05′W*
21 V10 **Goldsboro** North Carolina, SE USA *35°23′N 78°00′W*
24 M8 **Goldsmith** Texas, SW USA *31°58′N 102°36′W*
25 R8 **Goldthwaite** Texas, SW USA *31°28′N 98°35′W*
137 R11 **Göle** Ardahan, NE Turkey *40°47′N 42°36′E*
Golema Ada *see* Ostrovo
114 H9 **Golema Planina** ▲▲ W Bulgaria
114 F9 **Golemi Vrŭkh** ▲ W Bulgaria *42°41′N 22°38′E*
110 D8 **Goleniów** *Ger.* Gollnow. Zachodnio-pomorskie, NW Poland *53°34′N 14°48′E*
143 R3 **Golestān** ◈ *province* N Iran
35 Q14 **Goleta** California, W USA *34°26′N 119°50′W*
43 O16 **Golfito** Puntarenas, SE Costa Rica *08°42′N 83°10′W*
25 T13 **Goliad** Texas, SW USA *28°40′N 97°26′W*
113 L14 **Golija** ▲▲ SW Serbia
Golinka *see* Gongbo'gyamda
113 O16 **Goljak** ▲▲ SE Serbia
136 M12 **Gölköy** Ordu, N Turkey *40°42′N 37°37′E*
Gollel *see* Lavumisa
109 X3 **Göllersbach** ≈ NE Austria
Gollnow *see* Goleniów
Golmo *see* Golmud
159 P10 **Golmud** *var.* Ge'e'mu, Golmo, *Chin.* Ko-erh-mu. Qinghai, C China *36°23′N 94°56′E*
103 Y14 **Golo** ≈ Corse, France, C Mediterranean Sea
Golovanevsk *see* Holovanivs'k
Golovchin *see* Halowchyn
39 N9 **Golovin** Alaska, USA *64°33′N 162°54′W*
142 M7 **Golpāyegān** *var.* Gulpaigan. Eşfahān, W Iran *33°23′N 50°18′E*
Golshan *see* Ṭabas
Gol'shany *see* Hal'shany
96 J7 **Golspie** N Scotland, United Kingdom *57°59′N 03°56′W*
112 O11 **Golubac** Serbia, NE Serbia *44°38′N 21°36′E*
110 J9 **Golub-Dobrzyń** Kujawski-pomorskie, C Poland *53°07′N 19°03′E*
145 S7 **Golubovka** Pavlodar, N Kazakhstan *53°07′N 74°11′E*
82 B11 **Golungo Alto** Cuanza Norte, NW Angola *09°10′S 14°45′E*
114 M8 **Golyama Kamchiya** ≈ E Bulgaria
114 L8 **Golyama Reka** ≈ N Bulgaria
114 H11 **Golyama Syutkya** ▲ SW Bulgaria *41°55′N 24°03′E*
114 I12 **Golyam Perelik** ▲ S Bulgaria *41°37′N 24°34′E*
114 I11 **Golyam Persenk** ▲ S Bulgaria *41°50′N 24°33′E*
79 P19 **Goma** Nord-Kivu, NE Dem. Rep. Congo *01°36′S 29°08′E*
153 N13 **Gomati** *var.* Gumti. ≈ N India
77 X14 **Gombe** Gombe, E Nigeria *10°19′N 11°02′E*
67 U10 **Gombe** *var.* Igombe. ≈ E Tanzania
77 Y14 **Gombi** Adamawa, E Nigeria *10°07′N 12°45′E*
Gombroon *see* Bandar-e 'Abbās
Gomel' *see* Homyel'
Gomel'skaya Oblast' *see* Homyel'skaya Voblasts'
64 N11 **Gomera** *island* Islas Canarias, Spain, NE Atlantic Ocean
40 I5 **Gómez Farias** Chihuahua, N Mexico *29°25′N 107°46′W*
40 L8 **Gómez Palacio** Durango, C Mexico *25°39′N 103°30′W*
158 J13 **Gomo** Xizang Zizhiqu, W China *33°37′N 86°40′E*
143 T6 **Gonābād** *var.* Gunabad. Khorāsān-Razavī, NE Iran *36°30′N 59°18′E*
44 L8 **Gonaïves** *var.* Les Gonaïves. N Haiti *19°26′N 72°41′W*
123 Q12 **Gonam** ≈ NE Russian Federation
44 L9 **Gonâve, Canal de la** *var.* Canal de Sud. *channel* N Caribbean Sea
44 K9 **Gonâve, Golfe de la** *gulf* N Caribbean Sea
Gonāveh *see* Bandar-e Gonāveh
44 K9 **Gonâve, Île de la** *island* C Haiti
Gonbadān *see* Do Gonbadān
143 Q3 **Gonbad-e Kāvūs** *var.* Gunbad-i-Qawus. Golestān, N Iran *37°15′N 55°11′E*
152 M12 **Gonda** Uttar Pradesh, N India *27°08′N 81°58′E*
Gondar *see* Gonder
80 I11 **Gonder** *var.* Gondar. Āmara, NW Ethiopia *12°36′N 37°27′E*
78 J13 **Gondey** Moyen-Chari, S Chad *09°07′N 19°10′E*
154 J12 **Gondia** Mahārāshtra, C India *21°27′N 80°12′E*
104 G6 **Gondomar** Porto, NW Portugal *41°10′N 08°35′W*
136 C12 **Gönen** Balıkesir, W Turkey *40°06′N 27°39′E*
136 C12 **Gönen Çayı** ≈ NW Turkey
159 O15 **Gongbo'gyamda** *var.* Golinka. Xizang Zizhiqu, W China *30°03′N 93°10′E*
Gongchang *see* Longxi
159 N16 **Gonggar** *var.* Gyixong. Xizang Zizhiqu, W China *29°18′N 90°56′E*
160 G9 **Gongga Shan** ▲ C China *29°50′N 101°55′E*
159 T10 **Gonghe** *var.* Qabqa. Qinghai, C China *36°20′N 100°46′E*
Gongjiang *see* Yudu
158 I5 **Gongliu** *var.* Tokkuztara. Xinjiang Uygur Zizhiqu, NW China *43°29′N 82°16′E*
77 W14 **Gongola** ≈ E Nigeria
Gongoleh State *see* Jonglei
183 P5 **Gongolgon** New South Wales, SE Australia *30°19′S 146°57′E*
159 Q6 **Gongpoquan** Gansu, N China *41°45′N 100°27′E*
Gongquan *see* Gongxian
Gongtang *see* Damxung
160 I10 **Gongxian** *var.* Gongquan, Gong Xian. Sichuan, C China *28°25′N 104°51′E*
Gong Xian *see* Gongxian
157 V10 **Gongzhuling** *prev.* Huaide. Jilin, NE China *43°30′N 124°48′E*
159 S14 **Gonjo** Xizang Zizhiqu, W China *30°51′N 98°16′E*
107 B20 **Gonnesa** Sardegna, Italy, C Mediterranean Sea *39°15′N 08°27′E*
Gonni/Gónnos *see* Gónnoi
115 F15 **Gónnoi** *var.* Gonni, Gónnos; *prev.* Dereli. Thessalía, C Greece *39°52′N 22°27′E*
164 C13 **Gōnoura** Nagasaki, Iki, SW Japan *33°44′N 129°41′E*
35 O11 **Gonzales** California, W USA *36°30′N 121°26′W*
22 J9 **Gonzales** Louisiana, S USA *30°14′N 90°55′W*
25 T12 **Gonzales** Texas, SW USA *29°31′N 97°29′W*
41 P11 **González** Tamaulipas, C Mexico *22°50′N 98°25′W*
21 V6 **Goochland** Virginia, NE USA *37°42′N 77°54′W*
195 X14 **Goodenough, Cape** *headland* Antarctica *66°15′S 126°35′E*
186 F9 **Goodenough Island** *var.* Morata. *island* SE Papua New Guinea
39 N8 **Goodhope Bay** *bay* Alaska, USA

◆ Country ● Country Capital ◇ Dependent Territory ○ Dependent Territory Capital ◈ Administrative Regions ✈ International Airport ▲ Mountain ▲▲ Mountain Range Volcano ≈ River ◎ Lake ⊠ Reservoir

GOOD HOPE, CAPE OF – GRAYLAND

83 D26 **Good Hope, Cape of** *Afr.* Kaap de Goede Hoop, Kaap die Goeie Hoop. *headland* SW South Africa 34°19′S 18°25′E
10 K10 **Good Hope Lake** British Columbia, W Canada 59°15′N 129°18′W
83 E23 **Goodhouse** Northern Cape, W South Africa 28°54′S 18°13′E
33 O15 **Gooding** Idaho, NW USA 42°56′N 114°42′W
26 H3 **Goodland** Kansas, C USA 39°20′N 101°43′W
173 Y15 **Goodlands** NW Mauritius 20°02′S 57°39′E
20 J8 **Goodlettsville** Tennessee, S USA 36°19′N 86°42′W
39 N13 **Goodnews** Alaska, USA 59°07′N 161°35′W
25 O3 **Goodnight** Texas, SW USA 35°00′N 101°07′W
183 Q4 **Goodooga** New South Wales, SE Australia 29°09′S 147°30′E
29 N4 **Goodrich** North Dakota, N USA 47°24′N 100°07′W
25 W10 **Goodrich** Texas, SW USA 30°36′N 94°57′W
29 X10 **Goodview** Minnesota, N USA 44°04′N 91°42′W
26 H8 **Goodwell** Oklahoma, C USA 36°36′N 101°38′W
97 N17 **Goole** E England, United Kingdom 53°43′N 00°46′W
183 O8 **Goolgowi** New South Wales, SE Australia 34°00′S 145°43′E
182 I10 **Goolwa** South Australia 35°31′S 138°43′E
181 Y11 **Goondiwindi** Queensland, E Australia 28°33′S 150°22′E
98 O11 **Goor** Overijssel, E Netherlands 52°13′N 06°33′E
Goose Bay *see* Happy Valley-Goose Bay
33 V13 **Gooseberry Creek** ≋ Wyoming, C USA
21 S14 **Goose Creek** South Carolina, SE USA 32°58′N 80°01′W
63 M23 **Goose Green** *var.* Prado del Ganso. East Falkland, Falkland Islands 51°52′S 59°W
16 D8 **Goose Lake** *var.* Lago dos Gansos. ◎ California/Oregon, W USA
29 Q4 **Goose River** ≋ North Dakota, N USA
153 T16 **Gopalganj** Dhaka, S Bangladesh 23°00′N 89°48′E
153 O12 **Gopālganj** Bihār, N India 26°28′N 84°26′E
Gopher State *see* Minnesota
101 I22 **Göppingen** Baden-Württemberg, SW Germany 48°42′N 09°39′E
110 G13 **Góra** *Ger.* Guhrau. Dolnośląskie, SW Poland 51°40′N 16°03′E
110 M12 **Góra Kalwaria** Mazowieckie, C Poland 52°00′N 21°14′E
153 O12 **Gorakhpur** Uttar Pradesh, N India 26°45′N 83°23′E
Gora Kyuren *see* Kürendag
Gorany *see* Harany
113 J14 **Goražde** Federacija Bosna I Hercegovina, SE Bosnia and Herzegovina 43°39′N 18°58′E
Gorbovichi *see* Harbavichy
Gorče Petrov *see* Đorče Petrov
0 E9 **Gorda Ridges** *undersea feature* NE Pacific Ocean 41°30′N 128°00′W
Gordiaz *see* Gardīz
78 K12 **Gordil** Vakaga, N Central African Republic 09°37′N 21°42′E
23 U5 **Gordon** Georgia, SE USA 32°52′N 83°19′W
28 K12 **Gordon** Nebraska, C USA 42°48′N 102°12′W
25 R7 **Gordon** Texas, SW USA 32°32′N 98°21′W
28 L13 **Gordon Creek** ≋ Nebraska, C USA
63 I25 **Gordon, Isla** *island* S Chile
183 O17 **Gordon, Lake** ◎ Tasmania, SE Australia
183 O17 **Gordon River** ≋ Tasmania, SE Australia
21 V5 **Gordonsville** Virginia, NE USA 38°08′N 78°11′W
78 H13 **Goré** Logone-Oriental, S Chad 07°55′N 16°38′E
80 H13 **Gorē** Oromīya, C Ethiopia 08°08′N 35°33′E
185 D24 **Gore** Southland, South Island, New Zealand 46°06′S 168°58′E
14 D11 **Gore Bay** Manitoulin Island, Ontario, S Canada 45°54′N 82°28′W
25 Q5 **Goree** Texas, SW USA 33°28′N 99°31′W
137 O11 **Görele** Giresun, NE Turkey 41°00′N 39°00′E
19 N6 **Gore Mountain** ▲ Vermont, NE USA 44°55′N 71°47′W
39 R13 **Gore Point** *headland* Alaska, USA 59°12′N 150°57′W
37 R4 **Gore Range** ▲▲ Colorado, C USA
97 F19 **Gorey** *Ir.* Guaire. Wexford, SE Ireland 52°40′N 06°18′W
143 R12 **Gorgāb** Kermān, S Iran
143 Q4 **Gorgān** *var.* Astarabad, Astrabad, Gurgan, *prev.* Asterābād; *anc.* Hyrcania. Golestán, N Iran 36°53′N 54°28′E
143 Q4 **Gorgān, Rūd-e** ≋ N Iran
76 I10 **Gorgol** ◆ *region* S Mauritania
106 D12 **Gorgona, Isola di** *island* Archipelago Toscano, C Italy
19 P8 **Gorham** Maine, NE USA 43°41′N 70°27′W
137 T10 **Gori** C Georgia 42°00′N 44°07′E
98 I13 **Gorinchem** *var.* Gorkum. Zuid-Holland, C Netherlands 51°50′N 04°59′E
137 V13 **Goris** SE Armenia 39°31′N 46°20′E
124 K16 **Goritsy** Tverskaya Oblast', W Russian Federation 57°09′N 36°44′E
106 J7 **Gorizia** *Ger.* Görz. Friuli-Venezia Giulia, NE Italy 45°57′N 13°37′E
116 G13 **Gorj** ◆ *county* SW Romania
109 W12 **Gorjanci** *var.* Uskočke Planine, Žumberak, Žumberačko Gorje, *Ger.* Uskokengebirge; *prev.* Sichelburger Gerbirge. ▲ Croatia/Slovenia Europe *see also* Žumberačko Gorje
Görkau *see* Jirkov
Gorki *see* Horki
Gor'kiy *see* Nizhniy Novgorod
127 O11 **Gor'kovskiy** Volgogradskaya Oblast', SW Russian Federation 48°41′N 44°20′E
Gorkum *see* Gorinchem
95 I23 **Gørlev** Vestsjælland, E Denmark 55°33′N 11°14′E
111 M17 **Gorlice** Małopolskie, S Poland 49°40′N 21°09′E
101 Q15 **Görlitz** Sachsen, E Germany 51°09′N 14°58′E
Görlitz *see* Zgorzelec
Gorlovka *see* Horlivka
25 R7 **Gorman** Texas, SW USA 32°12′N 98°40′W
21 T3 **Gormania** West Virginia, NE USA 39°16′N 79°18′W
Gorna Dzhumaya *see* Blagoevgrad
114 K8 **Gorna Oryakhovitsa** Veliko Tŭrnovo, N Bulgaria 43°07′N 25°40′E
114 J8 **Gorna Studena** Veliko Tŭrnovo, N Bulgaria 43°26′N 25°21′E
Gornja Mužlja *see* Mužlja
109 X9 **Gornja Radgona** *Ger.* Oberradkersburg. NE Slovenia 46°39′N 16°00′E
112 M13 **Gornji Milanovac** Serbia, C Serbia 44°01′N 20°26′E
112 G13 **Gornji Vakuf** *var.* Uskoplje. Federacija Bosna I Hercegovina, SW Bosnia and Herzegovina 43°55′N 17°34′E
122 J13 **Gorno-Altaysk** Respublika Altay, S Russian Federation 51°59′N 85°56′E
Gorno-Altayskaya Respublika *see* Altay, Respublika
123 N12 **Gorno-Chuyskiy** Irkutskaya Oblast', C Russian Federation 57°33′N 111°38′E
125 V14 **Gornozavodsk** Permskaya Oblast', NW Russian Federation 58°21′N 58°24′E
125 V14 **Gornozavodsk** Ostrov Sakhalin, Sakhalinskaya Oblast', SE Russian Federation 46°34′N 141°52′E
122 I13 **Gornyak** Altayskiy Kray, S Russian Federation 50°58′N 81°24′E
123 O14 **Gornyy** Chitunskaya Oblast', Russian Federation 51°42′N 114°16′E
127 R8 **Gornyy** Saratovskaya Oblast', W Russian Federation 51°42′N 48°26′E
Gornyy Altay *see* Altay, Respublika
127 O10 **Gornyy Balykley** Volgogradskaya Oblast', SW Russian Federation 49°37′N 45°03′E
80 I13 **Goroch'an** ▲ W Ethiopia 09°09′N 37°16′E
116 J7 **Gorodenka** *var.* Horodenka. Ivano-Frankivs'ka Oblast', W Ukraine 48°41′N 25°28′E
127 O3 **Gorodets** Nizhegorodskaya Oblast', W Russian Federation 56°36′N 43°27′E
Gorodets *see* Haradzyets
Gorodeya *see* Haradzyeya
127 P6 **Gorodishche** Penzenskaya Oblast', W Russian Federation 53°17′N 45°39′E
Gorodishche *see* Horodyshche
Gorodnya *see* Horodnya
Gorodok *see* Haradok
Gorodok/Gorodok Yagellonski *see* Horodok
126 M13 **Gorodovikovsk** Respublika Kalmykiya, SW Russian Federation 46°07′N 41°56′E
186 D7 **Goroka** Eastern Highlands, C Papua New Guinea 06°02′S 145°22′E
Gorokhov *see* Horokhiv
127 N3 **Gorokhovets** Vladimirskaya Oblast', W Russian Federation 56°12′N 42°40′E
77 Q11 **Gorom-Gorom** NE Burkina 14°27′N 00°14′W
171 U13 **Gorong, Kepulauan** *island group* E Indonesia
83 M17 **Gorongosa** Sofala, C Mozambique 18°40′S 34°03′E
171 P11 **Gorontalo** Sulawesi, C Indonesia 0°33′N 123°05′E
171 O11 **Gorontalo** *off.* Propinsi Gorontalo. ◆ *province* N Indonesia
Propinsi Gorontalo *see* Gorontalo
Gorontalo, Teluk *see* Tomini, Gulf of
110 L7 **Górowo Iławeckie** *Ger.* Landsberg. Warmińsko-Mazurskie, NE Poland 54°18′N 20°30′E
98 M7 **Gorredijk** *Fris.* De Gordyk. Friesland, N Netherlands 53°00′N 06°04′E
84 C14 **Gorringe Ridge** *undersea feature* E Atlantic Ocean 36°40′N 11°35′W
98 M11 **Gorssel** Gelderland, E Netherlands 52°12′N 06°13′E
109 T8 **Görtschitz** ≋ S Austria
Goryn *see* Horyn'
Görz *see* Gorizia
110 E10 **Gorzów Wielkopolski** *Ger.* Landsberg, Landsberg an der Warthe. Lubuskie, W Poland 52°44′N 15°12′E
146 B10 **Goşabo** *var.* Goshoba, *Rus.* Koshoba. Balkan Welaýaty, NW Turkmenistan 40°28′N 54°11′E
108 G9 **Göschenen** Uri, C Switzerland 46°40′N 08°36′E
165 O11 **Gosen** Niigata, Honshū, C Japan 37°45′N 139°11′E
183 T8 **Gosford** New South Wales, SE Australia 33°25′S 151°18′E
31 P11 **Goshen** Indiana, N USA 41°34′N 85°49′W
18 K13 **Goshen** New York, NE USA 41°24′N 74°17′W
Goshoba *see* Goşabo
Goshoba *see* Goşoba
165 Q7 **Goshogawara** *var.* Gosyogawara. Aomori, Honshū, C Japan 40°47′N 140°24′E
Goshquduq Qum *see* Tosquduq Qumlari
101 J14 **Goslar** Niedersachsen, C Germany 51°55′N 10°25′E
27 Y9 **Gosnell** Arkansas, C USA 35°57′N 89°58′W
146 B10 **Goşoba** *var.* Goshoba, *Rus.* Koshoba. Balkanskiy Velayat, NW Turkmenistan 40°28′N 54°11′E
112 C11 **Gospić** Lika-Senj, C Croatia 44°32′N 15°21′E
97 N23 **Gosport** S England, United Kingdom 50°48′N 01°08′W
94 D9 **Gossa** *island* S Norway
108 H7 **Gossau** Sankt Gallen, NE Switzerland 47°25′N 09°16′E
99 G20 **Gosselies** *var.* Goss'lies. Hainaut, S Belgium 50°28′N 04°26′E
77 P10 **Gossi** Tombouctou, C Mali 15°44′N 01°19′W
Goss'lies *see* Gosselies
113 N18 **Gostivar** W FYR Macedonia 41°48′N 20°55′E
Gostomel' *see* Hostomel'
110 G12 **Gostyń** *var.* Gostyn. Wielkopolskie, C Poland 51°52′N 17°00′E
Gostyn *see* Gostyń
110 K11 **Gostynin** Mazowiesckie, C Poland 52°25′N 19°27′E
Gosyogawara *see* Goshogawara
95 J18 **Göta Älv** ≋ S Sweden
95 N17 **Göta kanal** *canal* S Sweden
95 K18 **Götaland** *cultural region* S Sweden
95 H17 **Göteborg** *Eng.* Gothenburg. Västra Götaland, S Sweden 57°43′N 11°58′E
77 X16 **Gotel Mountains** ▲▲ E Nigeria
95 K17 **Götene** Västra Götaland, S Sweden 58°32′N 13°29′E
Gotera *see* San Francisco
101 K16 **Gotha** Thüringen, C Germany 50°57′N 10°43′E
29 N15 **Gothenburg** Nebraska, C USA 40°57′N 100°09′W
Gothenburg *see* Göteborg
77 R12 **Gothèye** Tillabéri, SW Niger 13°52′N 01°27′E
Gothland *see* Gotland
95 P19 **Gotland** *var.* Gothland, Gottland. ◆ *county* SE Sweden
95 O18 **Gotland** *island* SE Sweden
164 B13 **Gotō-rettō** *island group* SW Japan
114 H12 **Gotse Delchev** *prev.* Nevrokop. Blagoevgrad, SW Bulgaria 41°33′N 23°42′E
95 P17 **Gotska Sandön** *island* SE Sweden
101 I15 **Göttingen** *var.* Goettingen. Niedersachsen, C Germany 51°33′N 09°55′E
Gottland *see* Gotland
93 I16 **Gottne** Västernorrland, C Sweden 63°27′N 18°25′E
Gottschee *see* Kočevje
Gottwaldov *see* Zlín
146 B11 **Goturdepe** *Rus.* Koturdepe. Balkan Welaýaty, W Turkmenistan 39°32′N 53°39′E
108 I7 **Götzis** Vorarlberg, NW Austria 47°21′N 09°40′E
98 H12 **Gouda** Zuid-Holland, C Netherlands 52°01′N 04°42′E
76 I11 **Goudiri** *var.* Goudiry. E Senegal 14°12′N 12°41′W
Goudiry *see* Goudiri
77 X12 **Goudoumaria** Diffa, S Niger 13°28′N 11°15′E
15 R9 **Gouffre, Rivière du** ≋ Québec, SE Canada
65 M19 **Gough Fracture Zone** *tectonic feature* S Atlantic Ocean
65 M19 **Gough Island** *island* Tristan da Cunha, S Atlantic Ocean
15 N8 **Gouin, Réservoir** ⊠ Québec, SE Canada
14 B10 **Goulais River** Ontario, S Canada 46°41′N 84°22′W
183 R9 **Goulburn** New South Wales, SE Australia 34°45′S 149°44′E
183 O11 **Goulburn River** ≋ Victoria, SE Australia
195 O10 **Gould Coast** *physical region* Antarctica
Goulimime *see* Guelmime
114 F13 **Gouménissa** Kentrikí Makedonía, N Greece 40°56′N 22°27′E
77 O10 **Goundam** Tombouctou, NW Mali 16°27′N 03°39′W
78 H12 **Goundi** Moyen-Chari, S Chad 09°22′N 17°21′E
78 G12 **Gounou-Gaya** Mayo-Kébbi, SW Chad 09°37′N 15°30′E
Gourci *see* Goursi
Gourcy *see* Goursi
102 M13 **Gourdon** Lot, S France 44°45′N 01°22′E
77 W11 **Gouré** Zinder, SE Niger 13°59′N 10°16′E
102 G6 **Gourin** Morbihan, NW France 48°07′N 03°37′W
77 P10 **Gourma-Rharous** Tombouctou, C Mali 16°54′N 01°55′W
103 N4 **Gournay-en-Bray** Seine-Maritime, N France 49°29′N 01°42′E
78 J6 **Gouro** Borkou-Ennedi-Tibesti, N Chad 19°26′N 19°36′E
77 O12 **Goursi** *var.* Gourci, Gourcy. NW Burkina 13°13′N 02°20′W
104 H8 **Gouveia** Guarda, N Portugal 40°29′N 07°35′W
18 I7 **Gouverneur** New York, NE USA 44°20′N 75°27′W
99 L21 **Gouvy** Luxembourg, E Belgium 50°10′N 05°55′E
45 R14 **Gouyave** *var.* Charlotte Town. NW Grenada 12°10′N 61°44′W
Goverla, Gora *see* Hoverla, Hora
59 N20 **Governador Valadares** Minas Gerais, SE Brazil 18°51′S 41°57′W
171 R8 **Governor Generoso** Mindanao, S Philippines 06°36′N 126°06′E
44 I2 **Governor's Harbour** Eleuthera Island, C Bahamas 25°11′N 76°15′W
162 F9 **Govĭ-Altay** ◆ *province* SW Mongolia
162 I10 **Govĭ Altayn Nuruu** ▲▲ S Mongolia
154 L9 **Govind Ballabh Pant Sāgar** ⊠ C India
152 I7 **Govind Sāgar** ⊠ NE India
162 M8 **Govĭ-Sumber** ◆ *province* C Mongolia
Govurdak *see* Magdanly
18 D11 **Gowanda** New York, NE USA 42°25′N 78°55′W
148 J10 **Gowd-e Zereh, Dasht-e** *var.* Guad-i-Zirreh. *marsh* SW Afghanistan
14 F8 **Gowganda** Ontario, S Canada 47°41′N 80°46′W
14 G8 **Gowganda Lake** ◎ Ontario, S Canada
29 U13 **Gowrie** Iowa, C USA 42°16′N 94°17′W
Gowurdak *see* Magdanly
61 C15 **Goya** Corrientes, NE Argentina 29°10′S 59°15′W
Goyania *see* Goiânia
Goyaz *see* Goiás
137 X11 **Göyçay** *Rus.* Geokchay. C Azerbaijan 40°38′N 47°44′E
146 D10 **Goymat** *Rus.* Koymat. Balkan Welaýaty, NW Turkmenistan 40°23′N 55°45′E
146 D10 **Goymatdag, Gory** *Rus.* Gory Koymatdag. *hill range* Balkan Welaýaty, NW Turkmenistan
136 F12 **Göynük** Bolu, NW Turkey 40°24′N 30°45′E
165 R9 **Goyō-san** ▲ Honshū, C Japan 39°12′N 141°40′E
78 K11 **Goz Beïda** Ouaddaï, SE Chad 12°06′N 21°22′E
146 M10 **G'ozg'on** *Rus.* Gazgan. Navoiy Viloyati, C Uzbekistan 40°36′N 65°29′E
158 H11 **Gozha Co** ◎ W China
121 O15 **Gozo** *var.* Ghawdex. *island* N Malta
80 H9 **Gōz Regeb** Kassala, NE Sudan 16°03′N 35°33′E
83 H25 **Graaff-Reinet** Eastern Cape, S South Africa 32°15′S 24°32′E
Graasten *see* Gråsten
76 L17 **Grabo** SW Ivory Coast 04°57′N 07°30′W
112 P11 **Grabovica** Serbia, E Serbia 44°30′N 22°29′E
110 I13 **Grabów nad Prosną** Wielkopolskie, C Poland 51°30′N 18°06′E
108 I8 **Grabs** Sankt Gallen, NE Switzerland 47°10′N 09°27′E
112 D12 **Gračac** Zadar, SW Croatia 44°18′N 15°52′E
112 I11 **Gračanica** Federacija Bosna I Hercegovina, NE Bosnia and Herzegovina 44°41′N 18°20′E
14 L11 **Gracefield** Québec, SE Canada 46°06′N 76°03′W
99 K19 **Grâce-Hollogne** Liège, E Belgium 50°38′N 05°30′E
23 R8 **Graceville** Florida, SE USA 30°57′N 85°31′W
29 R8 **Graceville** Minnesota, N USA 45°34′N 96°25′W
42 G6 **Gracias** Lempira, W Honduras 14°35′N 88°35′W
Gracias *see* Lempira
42 L5 **Gracias a Dios** ◆ *department* E Honduras
43 O6 **Gracias a Dios, Cabo de** *headland* Honduras/Nicaragua 15°00′N 83°10′W
64 O2 **Graciosa** *var.* Ilha Graciosa. *island* Azores, Portugal, NE Atlantic Ocean
64 Q11 **Graciosa** *island* Islas Canarias, Spain, NE Atlantic Ocean
Graciosa, Ilha *see* Graciosa
112 I11 **Gradačac** Federacija Bosna I Hercegovina, N Bosnia and Herzegovina 44°51′N 18°24′E
59 J15 **Gradaús, Serra dos** ▲▲ C Brazil
104 L3 **Gradefes** Castilla-León, N Spain 42°37′N 05°14′W
Gradiška *see* Bosanska Gradiška
Gradizhsk *see* Hradyz'k
106 J7 **Grado** Friuli-Venezia Giulia, NE Italy 45°41′N 13°24′E
104 K2 **Grado** Asturias, N Spain 43°23′N 06°04′W
113 P19 **Gradsko** C FYR Macedonia 41°34′N 21°56′E
37 V11 **Grady** New Mexico, SW USA 34°49′N 103°19′W
Grad Zagreb *see* Zagreb
29 T12 **Graettinger** Iowa, C USA 43°14′N 94°45′W
101 M23 **Grafing** Bayern, SE Germany 48°01′N 11°57′E
25 S6 **Graford** Texas, SW USA 32°56′N 98°15′W
183 V5 **Grafton** New South Wales, SE Australia 29°41′S 152°55′E
29 Q3 **Grafton** North Dakota, N USA 48°24′N 97°24′W
21 S3 **Grafton** West Virginia, NE USA 39°21′N 80°03′W
21 T9 **Graham** North Carolina, SE USA 36°05′N 79°25′W
25 R6 **Graham** Texas, SW USA 33°07′N 98°36′W
Graham Bell Island *see* Greem-Bell, Ostrov
10 I13 **Graham Island** *island* Queen Charlotte Islands, British Columbia, SW Canada
19 S6 **Graham Lake** ◎ Maine, NE USA
194 H4 **Graham Land** *physical region* Antarctica
37 N15 **Graham, Mount** ▲ Arizona, SW USA 32°42′N 109°52′W
Grahamstad *see* Grahamstown
83 I25 **Grahamstown** *Afr.* Grahamstad. Eastern Cape, S South Africa 33°18′S 26°32′E
Grahovo *see* Bosansko Grahovo
68 C12 **Grain Coast** *coastal region* S Liberia
169 S17 **Grajagan, Teluk** *bay* Jawa, S Indonesia
59 L14 **Grajaú** Maranhão, E Brazil 05°50′S 45°12′W
58 M13 **Grajaú, Rio** ≋ NE Brazil
110 O8 **Grajewo** Podlaskie, NE Poland 53°38′N 22°26′E
95 F24 **Gram** Sønderjylland, SW Denmark 55°18′N 09°03′E
103 N13 **Gramat** Lot, S France 44°45′N 01°45′E
22 H5 **Grambling** Louisiana, S USA 32°31′N 92°43′W
115 C14 **Grámmos** ▲▲ Albania/Greece
96 I9 **Grampian Mountains** ▲▲ C Scotland, United Kingdom
182 L12 **Grampians, The** ▲▲ Victoria, SE Australia
98 O9 **Gramsbergen** Overijssel, E Netherlands 52°37′N 06°39′E
113 L21 **Gramsh** *var.* Gramshi. Elbasan, C Albania 40°52′N 20°12′E
Gramshi *see* Gramsh
Gran *see* Esztergom, Hungary
Gran *see* Hron
54 F11 **Granada** Meta, C Colombia 03°33′N 73°44′W
42 J10 **Granada** Granada, SW Nicaragua 11°55′N 85°58′W
105 N14 **Granada** Andalucía, S Spain 37°13′N 03°41′W
37 W6 **Granada** Colorado, C USA 38°00′N 102°18′W
42 J11 **Granada** ◆ *department* SW Nicaragua
105 N14 **Granada** ◆ *province* Andalucía, S Spain
63 I21 **Gran Antiplanicie Central** *plain* S Argentina
97 E17 **Granard** *Ir.* Gránard. C Ireland 53°47′N 07°30′W
Gránard *see* Granard
63 J20 **Gran Bajo** *basin* S Argentina
63 J15 **Gran Bajo del Gualicho** *basin* E Argentina
63 I21 **Gran Bajo de San Julián** *basin* SE Argentina
25 S7 **Granbury** Texas, SW USA 32°27′N 97°47′W
15 P12 **Granby** Québec, SE Canada 45°23′N 72°44′W
27 S8 **Granby** Missouri, C USA 36°55′N 94°14′W
37 S3 **Granby, Lake** ⊠ Colorado, C USA
64 O12 **Gran Canaria** *var.* Grand Canary. *island* Islas Canarias, Spain, NE Atlantic Ocean
47 T11 **Gran Chaco** *var.* Chaco. *lowland plain* South America
45 R14 **Grand Anse** SW Grenada 12°01′N 61°45′W
Grand-Anse *see* Portsmouth
44 G1 **Grand Bahama Island** *island* N Bahamas
Grand Balé *see* Tui
103 U7 **Grand Ballon** *Ger.* Ballon de Guebwiller. ▲ NE France 47°53′N 07°06′E
13 T13 **Grand Bank** Newfoundland, Newfoundland and Labrador, SE Canada 47°06′N 55°48′W
64 I7 **Grand Banks of Newfoundland** *undersea feature* NW Atlantic Ocean 45°00′N 40°00′W
Grand Bassa *see* Buchanan
77 N17 **Grand-Bassam** *var.* Bassam. SE Ivory Coast 05°14′N 03°45′W
14 E16 **Grand Bend** Ontario, S Canada 43°17′N 81°46′W
76 L17 **Grand-Bérébi** *var.* Grand-Béréby. SW Ivory Coast 04°38′N 06°55′W
Grand-Béréby *see* Grand-Bérébi
45 X11 **Grand-Bourg** Marie-Galante, SE Guadeloupe 15°53′N 61°19′W
44 M6 **Grand Caicos** *var.* Middle Caicos. *island* C Turks and Caicos Islands
14 K12 **Grand Calumet, Île du** *island* Québec, SE Canada
97 E18 **Grand Canal** *Ir.* An Chanáil Mhór. *canal* C Ireland
Grand Canal *see* Da Yunhe
Grand Canary *see* Gran Canaria
36 K10 **Grand Canyon** Arizona, SW USA 36°01′N 112°10′W
36 J9 **Grand Canyon** *canyon* Arizona, SW USA
Grand Canyon State *see* Arizona
44 D8 **Grand Cayman** *island* SW Cayman Islands
11 R14 **Grand Centre** Alberta, SW Canada 54°25′N 110°13′W
76 L17 **Grand Cess** SE Liberia 04°36′N 08°12′W
108 D12 **Grand Combin** ▲ S Switzerland 45°58′N 07°27′E
32 K8 **Grand Coulee** Washington, NW USA 47°56′N 119°00′W
32 J8 **Grand Coulee** *valley* Washington, NW USA
45 X5 **Grand Cul-de-Sac Marin** *bay* N Guadeloupe
Grand Duchy of Luxembourg *see* Luxembourg
63 I22 **Grande, Bahía** *bay* S Argentina
11 N14 **Grande Cache** Alberta, W Canada 53°53′N 119°07′W
103 U12 **Grande Casse** ▲ E France 45°22′N 06°50′E
Grande-Comor *see* Ngazidja
61 G18 **Grande, Cuchilla** *hill range* E Uruguay
45 S5 **Grande de Añasco, Río** ≋ W Puerto Rico
Grande de Chiloé, Isla *see* Chiloé, Isla de
58 J12 **Grande de Gurupá, Ilha** *river island* NE Brazil
57 K21 **Grande de Lipez, Río** ≋ SW Bolivia
45 U6 **Grande de Loíza, Río** ≋ E Puerto Rico
45 T5 **Grande de Manatí, Río** ≋ C Puerto Rico
42 L9 **Grande de Matagalpa, Río** ≋ C Nicaragua
40 K12 **Grande de Santiago, Río** *var.* Santiago. ≋ C Mexico
43 O15 **Grande de Térraba, Río** *var.* Río Térraba. ≋ SE Costa Rica
12 J9 **Grande Deux, Réservoir la** ⊠ Québec, E Canada
60 O10 **Grande, Ilha** *island* SE Brazil
11 O13 **Grande Prairie** Alberta, W Canada 55°10′N 118°52′W
74 I8 **Grand Erg Occidental** *desert* W Algeria
74 L9 **Grand Erg Oriental** *desert* Algeria/Tunisia
57 M18 **Grande, Río** ≋ C Bolivia
59 J20 **Grande, Rio** ≋ S Brazil
2 F15 **Grande, Rio** *var.* Río Bravo, *Sp.* Río Bravo del Norte, Bravo del Norte. ≋ Mexico/USA
15 Y7 **Grande-Rivière** Québec, SE Canada 48°27′N 64°37′W
15 Y6 **Grande Rivière** ≋ Québec, SE Canada
44 M8 **Grande-Rivière-du-Nord** N Haiti 19°36′N 72°10′W
62 K9 **Grande, Salina** *var.* Gran Salitral. *salt lake* C Argentina
15 S7 **Grandes-Bergeronnes** Québec, SE Canada 48°16′N 69°32′W
47 W6 **Grande, Serra** ▲▲ W Brazil
40 K4 **Grande, Sierra** ▲▲ N Mexico
103 S12 **Grandes Rousses** ▲▲ E France
63 K17 **Grandes, Salinas** *salt lake* E Argentina
45 Y5 **Grande Terre** *island* E West Indies
15 X5 **Grande-Vallée** Québec, SE Canada 49°14′N 65°08′W
45 Y5 **Grande Vigie, Pointe de la** *headland* Grande Terre, N Guadeloupe 16°31′N 61°27′W
13 N14 **Grand Falls** New Brunswick, SE Canada 47°02′N 67°46′W
13 T11 **Grand Falls** Newfoundland, Newfoundland and Labrador, SE Canada 48°57′N 55°48′W
24 L9 **Grandfalls** Texas, SW USA 31°20′N 102°51′W
21 P9 **Grandfather Mountain** ▲ North Carolina, SE USA 36°06′N 81°48′W
26 L13 **Grandfield** Oklahoma, C USA 34°15′N 98°40′W
11 N17 **Grand Forks** British Columbia, SW Canada 49°02′N 118°30′W
29 R4 **Grand Forks** North Dakota, N USA 47°54′N 97°03′W
31 O9 **Grand Haven** Michigan, N USA 43°03′N 86°13′W
Grandichi *see* Hrandzichy
29 P15 **Grand Island** Nebraska, C USA 40°55′N 98°20′W
31 O3 **Grand Island** *island* Michigan, N USA
22 K10 **Grand Isle** Louisiana, S USA 29°12′N 90°00′W
65 A23 **Grand Jason** *island* Jason Islands, NW Falkland Islands
37 P5 **Grand Junction** Colorado, C USA 39°03′N 108°33′W
20 F10 **Grand Junction** Tennessee, S USA 35°03′N 89°11′W
14 J9 **Grand-Lac-Victoria** Québec, SE Canada 47°33′N 77°28′W
14 J9 **Grand lac Victoria** ◎ Québec, SE Canada
77 N17 **Grand-Lahou** *var.* Grand Lahu. S Ivory Coast 05°09′N 05°01′W
Grand Lahu *see* Grand-Lahou
37 S3 **Grand Lake** Colorado, C USA 40°15′N 105°49′W
13 S11 **Grand Lake** ◎ Newfoundland and Labrador, E Canada
22 G9 **Grand Lake** ◎ Louisiana, S USA
31 R5 **Grand Lake** ◎ Michigan, N USA
31 Q13 **Grand Lake** ⊠ Ohio, N USA
27 R9 **Grand Lake O' The Cherokees** *var.* Lake O' The Cherokees. ⊠ Oklahoma, C USA
31 Q9 **Grand Ledge** Michigan, N USA 42°45′N 84°45′W
102 I8 **Grand-Lieu, Lac de** ◎ NW France
19 U6 **Grand Manan Channel** *channel* Canada/USA
13 O15 **Grand Manan Island** *island* New Brunswick, SE Canada
29 Y4 **Grand Marais** Minnesota, N USA 47°45′N 90°19′W
15 P10 **Grand-Mère** Québec, SE Canada 46°36′N 72°41′W
37 P5 **Grand Mesa** ▲▲ Colorado, C USA
108 C10 **Grand Muveran** ▲ W Switzerland 46°16′N 07°12′E
104 G12 **Grândola** Setúbal, S Portugal 38°10′N 08°34′W
Grand Paradis *see* Gran Paradiso
187 O15 **Grand Passage** *passage* N New Caledonia
77 R16 **Grand-Popo** S Benin 06°19′N 01°50′E
29 Z3 **Grand Portage** Minnesota, N USA 48°00′N 89°36′W
25 T6 **Grand Prairie** Texas, SW USA 32°45′N 97°00′W
11 W14 **Grand Rapids** Manitoba, C Canada 53°12′N 99°19′W
31 P9 **Grand Rapids** Michigan, N USA 42°57′N 86°40′W
29 V5 **Grand Rapids** Minnesota, N USA 47°14′N 93°31′W
14 L10 **Grand-Remous** Québec, SE Canada 46°36′N 75°53′W
14 F15 **Grand River** ≋ Ontario, S Canada
31 P9 **Grand River** ≋ Michigan, N USA
27 T3 **Grand River** ≋ Missouri, C USA
28 M7 **Grand River** ≋ South Dakota, N USA
45 Q11 **Grand' Rivière** N Martinique 14°52′N 61°11′W
32 F11 **Grand Ronde** Oregon, NW USA 45°03′N 123°43′W
32 L11 **Grand Ronde River** ≋ Oregon/Washington, NW USA
Grand-Saint-Bernard, Col du *see* Great Saint Bernard Pass
25 V6 **Grand Saline** Texas, SW USA 32°40′N 95°42′W
55 X10 **Grand-Santi** W French Guiana 04°19′N 54°24′W
Grandsee *see* Grandson
172 J16 **Grand Sœur** *island* Les Sœurs, NE Seychelles
108 B9 **Grandson** *prev.* Grandsee. Vaud, W Switzerland 46°49′N 06°39′E
33 S14 **Grand Teton** ▲ Wyoming, C USA 43°44′N 110°48′W
31 P5 **Grand Traverse Bay** *lake bay* Michigan, N USA
45 N6 **Grand Turk** O (Turks and Caicos Islands) Grand Turk Island, S Turks and Caicos Islands 21°24′N 71°08′W
45 N6 **Grand Turk Island** *island* SE Turks and Caicos Islands
103 S13 **Grand Veymont** ▲ E France 44°51′N 05°32′E
11 W15 **Grandview** Manitoba, S Canada 51°11′N 100°41′W
27 R4 **Grandview** Missouri, C USA 38°53′N 94°31′W
36 I10 **Grand Wash Cliffs** *cliff* Arizona, SW USA
14 J8 **Granet, Lac** ◎ Québec, SE Canada
95 L14 **Grangärde** Dalarna, C Sweden 60°15′N 15°00′E
44 H12 **Grange Hill** W Jamaica 18°19′N 78°11′W
96 J12 **Grangemouth** C Scotland, United Kingdom 56°01′N 03°44′W
25 T10 **Granger** Texas, SW USA 30°43′N 97°26′W
32 J10 **Granger** Washington, NW USA 46°20′N 120°11′W
33 T17 **Granger** Wyoming, C USA 41°37′N 109°58′W
Granges *see* Grenchen
95 L14 **Grängesberg** Dalarna, C Sweden 60°06′N 15°00′E
33 N11 **Grangeville** Idaho, NW USA 45°55′N 116°07′W
10 K13 **Granisle** British Columbia, SW Canada 54°55′N 126°14′W
30 K15 **Granite City** Illinois, N USA 38°42′N 90°09′W
29 S9 **Granite Falls** Minnesota, N USA 44°48′N 95°33′W
21 Q9 **Granite Falls** North Carolina, SE USA 35°48′N 81°25′W
36 K12 **Granite Mountain** ▲ Arizona, SW USA 34°38′N 112°34′W
33 T12 **Granite Peak** ▲ Montana, NW USA 45°09′N 109°48′W
35 T2 **Granite Peak** ▲ Nevada, W USA 41°40′N 117°35′W
36 J3 **Granite Peak** ▲ Utah, W USA 40°09′N 113°18′W
Granite State *see* New Hampshire
107 H24 **Granitola, Capo** *headland* Sicilia, Italy, C Mediterranean Sea 37°33′N 12°39′E
185 H15 **Granity** West Coast, South Island, New Zealand 41°37′S 171°53′E
Gran Lago *see* Nicaragua, Lago de
63 J18 **Gran Laguna Salada** ◎ S Argentina
Gran Malvina *see* West Falkland
95 L18 **Gränna** Jönköping, S Sweden 58°02′N 14°30′E
105 W5 **Granollers** *var.* Granollérs. Cataluña, NE Spain 41°37′N 02°18′E
Granollérs *see* Granollers
106 A7 **Gran Paradiso** *Fr.* Grand Paradis. ▲ NW Italy 45°31′N 07°13′E
Gran Pilastro *see* Hochfeiler
Gran Salitral *see* Grande, Salina
Gran San Bernardo, Passo di *see* Great Saint Bernard Pass
Gran Santiago *see* Santiago
107 J14 **Gran Sasso d'Italia** ▲▲ C Italy
100 N11 **Gransee** Brandenburg, NE Germany 53°00′N 13°10′E
28 L15 **Grant** Nebraska, C USA 40°50′N 101°43′W
27 R1 **Grant City** Missouri, C USA 40°29′N 94°25′W
97 N19 **Grantham** E England, United Kingdom 52°55′N 00°39′W
194 K13 **Grant Island** *island* Antarctica
45 Z14 **Grantley Adams** ✈ (Bridgetown) SE Barbados 13°04′N 59°29′W
35 S7 **Grant, Mount** ▲ Nevada, W USA 38°34′N 118°47′W
96 J9 **Grantown-on-Spey** N Scotland, United Kingdom 57°11′N 03°53′W
35 W8 **Grant Range** ▲▲ Nevada, W USA
37 Q11 **Grants** New Mexico, SW USA 35°09′N 107°50′W
30 I4 **Grantsburg** Wisconsin, N USA 45°47′N 92°40′W
32 F15 **Grants Pass** Oregon, NW USA 42°26′N 123°20′W
36 K3 **Grantsville** Utah, W USA 40°36′N 112°27′W
21 R4 **Grantsville** West Virginia, NE USA 38°55′N 81°07′W
102 I5 **Granville** Manche, N France 48°50′N 01°35′W
11 V12 **Granville Lake** ◎ Manitoba, C Canada
25 V8 **Grapeland** Texas, SW USA 31°29′N 95°28′W
25 T6 **Grapevine** Texas, SW USA 32°55′N 97°04′W
83 K20 **Graskop** Mpumalanga, NE South Africa 24°58′S 30°49′E
95 P14 **Gräsö** Uppsala, C Sweden 60°22′N 18°30′E
93 I19 **Gräsö** *island* C Sweden
103 U15 **Grasse** Alpes-Maritimes, SE France 43°42′N 06°52′E
18 E14 **Grassflat** Pennsylvania, NE USA 41°00′N 78°04′W
33 U9 **Grassrange** Montana, NW USA 47°02′N 108°48′W
18 J6 **Grass River** ≋ New York, NE USA
35 P6 **Grass Valley** California, W USA 39°12′N 121°04′W
183 N14 **Grassy** Tasmania, SE Australia 40°03′S 144°04′E
28 K4 **Grassy Butte** North Dakota, N USA 47°20′N 103°13′W
21 R5 **Grassy Knob** ▲ West Virginia, NE USA 38°04′N 80°31′W
95 G24 **Gråsten** *var.* Graasten. Sønderjylland, SW Denmark 54°55′N 09°37′E
95 J18 **Grästorp** Västra Götaland, S Sweden 58°20′N 12°40′E
Gratianopolis *see* Grenoble
109 V8 **Gratwein** Steiermark, SE Austria 47°08′N 15°20′E
Gratz *see* Graz
108 I9 **Graubünden** *Fr.* Grisons, *It.* Grigioni. ◆ *canton* SE Switzerland
Graudenz *see* Grudziądz
103 N15 **Graulhet** Tarn, S France 43°45′N 01°58′E
105 T4 **Graus** Aragón, NE Spain 42°11′N 00°21′E
61 I16 **Gravataí** Rio Grande do Sul, S Brazil 29°55′S 51°00′W
98 L13 **Grave** Noord-Brabant, SE Netherlands 51°45′N 05°45′E
11 T17 **Gravelbourg** Saskatchewan, S Canada 49°53′N 106°33′W
103 N1 **Gravelines** Nord, N France 51°00′N 02°07′E
Graven *see* Grez-Doiceau
14 H13 **Gravenhurst** Ontario, S Canada 44°55′N 79°22′W
33 O10 **Grave Peak** ▲ Idaho, NW USA 46°24′N 114°43′W
102 I11 **Grave, Pointe de** *headland* W France 45°33′N 01°24′W
183 S4 **Gravesend** New South Wales, SE Australia 29°37′S 150°15′E
97 P22 **Gravesend** SE England, United Kingdom 51°27′N 00°24′E
107 N17 **Gravina in Puglia** Puglia, SE Italy 40°48′N 16°25′E
103 S8 **Gray** Haute-Saône, E France 47°28′N 05°34′E
23 T4 **Gray** Georgia, SE USA 33°00′N 83°31′W
195 V16 **Gray, Cape** *headland* Antarctica 67°30′N 143°30′E
32 F9 **Grayland** Washington, NW USA 46°46′N 124°07′W

◆ Country
● Country Capital
◇ Dependent Territory
O Dependent Territory Capital
◆ Administrative Regions
✈ International Airport
▲ Mountain
▲▲ Mountain Range
Volcano
≋ River
◎ Lake
⊠ Reservoir

GRAYLING – GUANGSHUI

39 N10 **Grayling** Alaska, USA 62°55′N 160°07′W
31 Q6 **Grayling** Michigan, N USA 44°40′N 84°43′W
32 F9 **Grays Harbor** inlet Washington, NW USA
21 O5 **Grayson** Kentucky, S USA 38°21′N 82°59′W
37 S4 **Grays Peak** ▲ Colorado, C USA 39°37′N 105°49′W
30 M16 **Grayville** Illinois, N USA 38°15′N 87°59′W
109 V8 **Graz** prev. Gratz. Steiermark, SE Austria 47°05′N 15°23′E
104 L15 **Grazalema** Andalucía, S Spain 36°46′N 05°23′W
113 P15 **Grdelica** Serbia, SE Serbia 42°54′N 22°05′E
44 H1 **Great Abaco** var. Abaco Island. island N Bahamas
Great Admiralty Island see Manus Island
Great Alfold see Great Hungarian Plain
Great Ararat see Büyükağrı Dağı
181 U8 **Great Artesian Basin** lowlands Queensland, C Australia
181 O12 **Great Australian Bight** bight S Australia
64 E11 **Great Bahama Bank** undersea feature E Gulf of Mexico 23°15′N 78°00′W
184 M4 **Great Barrier Island** island N New Zealand
181 X4 **Great Barrier Reef** reef Queensland, NE Australia
18 L11 **Great Barrington** Massachusetts, NE USA 42°11′N 73°20′W
0 F10 **Great Basin** basin W USA
8 I8 **Great Bear Lake** Fr. Grand Lac de l'Ours. ◎ Northwest Territories, NW Canada
Great Belt see Storebælt
26 L5 **Great Bend** Kansas, C USA 38°22′N 98°47′W
Great Bermuda see Bermuda
97 A20 **Great Blasket Island** Ir. An Blascaod Mór. island SW Ireland
Great Britain see Britain
151 Q23 **Great Channel** channel Andaman Sea/Indian Ocean
166 J10 **Great Coco Island** island SW Burma (Myanmar)
Great Crosby see Crosby
21 X7 **Great Dismal Swamp** wetland North Carolina/Virginia, SE USA
33 V16 **Great Divide Basin** basin Wyoming, C USA
181 W7 **Great Dividing Range** ▲▲ NE Australia
14 D12 **Great Duck Island** island Ontario, S Canada
Great Elder Reservoir see Waconda Lake
44 G8 **Greater Antilles** island group West Indies
129 V16 **Greater Sunda Islands** var. Sunda Islands. island group Indonesia
184 I1 **Great Exhibition Bay** inlet North Island, New Zealand
44 H4 **Great Exuma Island** island C Bahamas
33 R8 **Great Falls** Montana, NW USA 47°30′N 111°18′W
21 R11 **Great Falls** South Carolina, SE USA 34°34′N 80°54′W
84 F9 **Great Fisher Bank** undersea feature C North Sea 57°00′N 04°00′E
Great Glen see Mor, Glen
Great Grimsby see Grimsby
44 I4 **Great Guana Cay** island C Bahamas
64 I5 **Great Hellefiske Bank** undersea feature N Atlantic Ocean
111 L24 **Great Hungarian Plain** var. Great Alfold, Plain of Hungary, Hung. Alföld. plain SE Europe
44 L7 **Great Inagua** var. Inagua Islands. island S Bahamas
Great Indian Desert see Thar Desert
83 G25 **Great Karoo** var. Great Karroo, High Veld, Afr. Groot Karoo, Hoë Karoo. plateau region S South Africa
Great Karroo see Great Karoo
Great Kei see Nciba
Great Khingan Range see Da Hinggan Ling
14 E11 **Great La Cloche Island** island Ontario, S Canada
183 P16 **Great Lake** ◎ Tasmania, SE Australia
Great Lake see Tônlé Sap
11 R15 **Great Lakes** lakes Ontario, Canada/USA
Great Lakes State see Michigan
97 L20 **Great Malvern** W England, United Kingdom 52°07′N 02°19′W
184 M5 **Great Mercury Island** island N New Zealand
Great Meteor Seamount see Great Meteor Tablemount
64 K10 **Great Meteor Tablemount** var. Great Meteor Seamount. undersea feature E Atlantic Ocean 30°00′N 28°30′W
31 Q14 **Great Miami River** ≈ Ohio, N USA
151 Q24 **Great Nicobar** island Nicobar Islands, India, NE Indian Ocean
97 O19 **Great Ouse** var. Ouse. ≈ E England, United Kingdom
183 Q17 **Great Oyster Bay** bay Tasmania, SE Australia
44 I13 **Great Pedro Bluff** headland W Jamaica 17°51′N 77°44′W
21 T12 **Great Pee Dee River** ≈ North Carolina/South Carolina, SE USA
129 W9 **Great Plain of China** plain E China
0 F12 **Great Plains** var. High Plains. plains Canada/USA
37 W6 **Great Plains Reservoirs** ⊞ Colorado, C USA
19 Q13 **Great Point** headland Nantucket Island, Massachusetts, NE USA 41°23′N 70°03′W
68 I13 **Great Rift Valley** var. Rift Valley. depression Asia/Africa
81 I23 **Great Ruaha** ≈ S Tanzania
18 K10 **Great Sacandaga Lake** ⊞ New York, NE USA
108 C12 **Great Saint Bernard Pass** Fr. Col du Grand-Saint-Bernard, It. Passo del Gran San Bernardo. pass Italy/Switzerland
44 F1 **Great Sale Cay** island N Bahamas
Great Salt Desert see Kavīr, Dasht-e
36 K1 **Great Salt Lake** salt lake Utah, W USA
36 J3 **Great Salt Lake Desert** plain Utah, W USA
26 M8 **Great Salt Plains Lake** ⊞ Oklahoma, C USA
75 T9 **Great Sand Sea** desert Egypt/Libya
180 L6 **Great Sandy Desert** desert Western Australia
Great Sandy Desert see Ar Rub 'al Khali
Great Sandy Island see Fraser Island
187 Y13 **Great Sea Reef** reef Vanua Levu, N Fiji
38 H17 **Great Sitkin Island** island Aleutian Islands, Alaska, USA
8 J10 **Great Slave Lake** Fr. Grand Lac des Esclaves. ◎ Northwest Territories, NW Canada
21 O10 **Great Smoky Mountains** ▲▲ North Carolina/Tennessee, SE USA
10 L11 **Great Snow Mountain** ▲ British Columbia, W Canada 57°22′N 124°08′W
Great Socialist People's Libyan Arab Jamahiriya see Libya
64 A12 **Great Sound** sound Bermuda, NW Atlantic Ocean
180 M10 **Great Victoria Desert** desert South Australia/Western Australia
194 H2 **Great Wall** Chinese research station South Shetland Islands, Antarctica 61°57′S 58°23′W
19 T7 **Great Wass Island** island Maine, NE USA
97 Q19 **Great Yarmouth** var. Yarmouth. E England, United Kingdom 52°37′N 01°44′E
139 S1 **Great Zab** Ar. Az Zāb al Kabīr, Kurd. Zē-i Bādīnān, Turk. Büyükzap Suyu. ≈ Iraq/Turkey
95 I17 **Grebbestad** Västra Götaland, S Sweden 58°42′N 11°15′E
Grebenka see Hrebinka
42 M13 **Grecia** Alajuela, C Costa Rica 10°04′N 84°19′W
61 E18 **Greco** Río Negro, W Uruguay 32°49′S 57°03′W
Greco, Cape see Gkréko, Akrotíri
104 L8 **Gredos, Sierra de** ▲▲ W Spain
18 F9 **Greece** New York, NE USA 43°12′N 77°41′W
115 E17 **Greece** off. Hellenic Republic, Gk. Ellás; anc. Hellas. ◆ republic SE Europe
Greece Central see Stereá Elláda
Greece West see Dytikí Elláda
37 T3 **Greeley** Colorado, C USA 40°21′N 104°41′W
29 P14 **Greeley** Nebraska, C USA 41°33′N 98°31′W
122 K3 **Greem-Bell, Ostrov** Eng. Graham Bell Island. island Zemlya Frantsa-Iosifa, N Russian Federation
30 M6 **Green Bay** Wisconsin, N USA 44°32′N 88°W
31 N6 **Green Bay** lake bay Michigan/Wisconsin, N USA
21 S5 **Greenbrier River** ≈ West Virginia, NE USA
29 S2 **Greenbush** Minnesota, N USA 48°42′N 96°10′W
183 R12 **Green Cape** headland New South Wales, SE Australia 37°15′S 150°03′E
31 O14 **Greencastle** Indiana, N USA 39°38′N 86°51′W
18 F16 **Greencastle** Pennsylvania, NE USA 39°47′N 77°43′W
27 T2 **Green City** Missouri, C USA 40°16′N 92°57′W
21 O9 **Greeneville** Tennessee, S USA 36°10′N 82°50′W
35 O11 **Greenfield** California, W USA 36°19′N 121°15′W
31 P14 **Greenfield** Indiana, N USA 39°47′N 85°46′W
29 U15 **Greenfield** Iowa, C USA 41°18′N 94°27′W
18 M11 **Greenfield** Massachusetts, NE USA 42°33′N 72°34′W
27 S7 **Greenfield** Missouri, C USA 37°25′N 93°50′W
31 S14 **Greenfield** Ohio, N USA 39°21′N 83°22′W
20 G8 **Greenfield** Tennessee, S USA 36°09′N 88°48′W
30 M9 **Greenfield** Wisconsin, N USA 42°55′N 87°59′W
27 T9 **Green Forest** Arkansas, C USA 36°19′N 93°24′W
37 T7 **Greenhorn Mountain** ▲ Colorado, C USA 37°50′N 104°59′W
Green Island see Lü Tao
186 I6 **Green Islands** var. Nissan Islands. island group NE Papua New Guinea
11 S14 **Green Lake** Saskatchewan, C Canada 54°15′N 107°51′W
30 L8 **Green Lake** ◎ Wisconsin, N USA
197 O14 **Greenland** Dan. Grønland, Inuit Kalaallit Nunaat. ◇ Danish external territory NE North America
84 D4 **Greenland** island NE North America
197 R13 **Greenland Plain** undersea feature N Greenland Sea
197 R14 **Greenland Sea** sea Arctic Ocean
37 R4 **Green Mountain Reservoir** ⊞ Colorado, C USA
18 M8 **Green Mountains** ▲▲ Vermont, NE USA
Green Mountain State see Vermont
96 H12 **Greenock** W Scotland, United Kingdom 55°57′N 04°45′W
39 T5 **Greenough, Mount** ▲ Alaska, USA 69°15′N 141°37′W
186 A6 **Green River** Sandaun, NW Papua New Guinea 03°54′S 141°08′E
37 N5 **Green River** Utah, W USA 39°00′N 110°07′W
33 U17 **Green River** Wyoming, C USA 41°33′N 109°27′W
16 H9 **Green River** ≈ W USA
30 K11 **Green River** ≈ Illinois, N USA
20 J7 **Green River** ≈ Kentucky, C USA
28 K5 **Green River** ≈ North Dakota, N USA
37 N6 **Green River** ≈ Utah, W USA
33 T16 **Green River** ≈ Wyoming, C USA
20 L7 **Green River Lake** ⊞ Kentucky, S USA
23 O5 **Greensboro** Alabama, S USA 32°42′N 87°36′W
23 U3 **Greensboro** Georgia, SE USA 33°34′N 83°10′W
21 T9 **Greensboro** North Carolina, SE USA 36°04′N 79°48′W
31 P14 **Greensburg** Indiana, N USA 39°20′N 85°28′W
26 K6 **Greensburg** Kansas, C USA 37°36′N 99°17′W
20 L7 **Greensburg** Kentucky, S USA 37°14′N 85°30′W
18 C15 **Greensburg** Pennsylvania, NE USA 40°18′N 79°33′W
37 O13 **Greens Peak** ▲ Arizona, SW USA 34°06′N 109°34′W
21 V12 **Green Swamp** wetland North Carolina, SE USA
21 O4 **Greenup** Kentucky, S USA 38°34′N 82°49′W
36 M16 **Green Valley** Arizona, SW USA 31°49′N 111°00′W
76 K17 **Greenville** var. Sino, Sinoe. SE Liberia 05°01′N 09°03′W
23 P6 **Greenville** Alabama, S USA 31°49′N 86°37′W
23 T8 **Greenville** Florida, SE USA 30°28′N 83°37′W
23 S4 **Greenville** Georgia, SE USA 33°03′N 84°42′W
30 L15 **Greenville** Illinois, N USA 38°53′N 89°24′W
20 I7 **Greenville** Kentucky, S USA 37°11′N 87°11′W
19 Q5 **Greenville** Maine, NE USA 45°26′N 69°36′W
31 P9 **Greenville** Michigan, N USA 43°10′N 85°15′W
22 J4 **Greenville** Mississippi, S USA 33°24′N 91°03′W
21 W9 **Greenville** North Carolina, SE USA 35°36′N 77°23′W
31 Q13 **Greenville** Ohio, N USA 40°06′N 84°37′W
19 O12 **Greenville** Rhode Island, NE USA 41°52′N 71°33′W
21 P11 **Greenville** South Carolina, SE USA 34°51′N 82°24′W
25 U6 **Greenville** Texas, SW USA 33°09′N 96°07′W
31 T12 **Greenwich** Ohio, N USA 41°01′N 82°31′W
27 S11 **Greenwood** Arkansas, C USA 35°13′N 94°15′W
31 O14 **Greenwood** Indiana, N USA 39°38′N 86°06′W
22 K4 **Greenwood** Mississippi, S USA 33°30′N 90°11′W
21 P12 **Greenwood** South Carolina, SE USA 34°11′N 82°10′W
21 Q12 **Greenwood, Lake** ⊞ South Carolina, SE USA
21 P11 **Greer** South Carolina, SE USA 34°56′N 82°13′W
27 V10 **Greers Ferry Lake** ⊞ Arkansas, C USA
27 S13 **Greeson, Lake** ⊞ Arkansas, C USA
29 O12 **Gregory** South Dakota, N USA 43°11′N 99°26′W
182 J3 **Gregory, Lake** salt lake South Australia
180 J9 **Gregory Lake** ◎ Western Australia
181 V5 **Gregory Range** ▲▲ Queensland, E Australia
Greifenberg/Greifenberg in Pommern see Gryfice
Greifenhagen see Gryfino
100 O8 **Greifswald** Mecklenburg-Vorpommern, NE Germany 54°04′N 13°24′E
100 O8 **Greifswalder Bodden** bay NE Germany
109 U4 **Grein** Oberösterreich, N Austria 48°14′N 14°50′E
101 M17 **Greiz** Thüringen, C Germany 50°40′N 12°11′E
125 V14 **Gremyachinsk** Permskaya Oblast', NW Russian Federation 58°33′N 57°52′E
Grenå see Grenaa
95 H21 **Grenaa** var. Grenå. Århus, C Denmark 56°25′N 10°53′E
22 L3 **Grenada** Mississippi, S USA 33°46′N 89°48′W
45 W15 **Grenada** ◆ commonwealth republic SE West Indies
47 S4 **Grenada** island Grenada
47 R4 **Grenada Basin** undersea feature W Atlantic Ocean 13°30′N 62°00′W
22 L3 **Grenada Lake** ⊞ Mississippi, S USA
45 Y14 **Grenadines, The** island group Grenada/St Vincent and the Grenadines
108 D7 **Grenchen** Fr. Granges. Solothurn, NW Switzerland 47°13′N 07°24′E
183 Q9 **Grenfell** New South Wales, SE Australia 33°54′S 148°09′E
11 V16 **Grenfell** Saskatchewan, S Canada 50°24′N 102°56′W
92 J1 **Grenivík** Nordhurland Eystra, N Iceland 65°57′N 18°10′W
103 S12 **Grenoble** anc. Cularo, Gratianopolis. Isère, E France 45°11′N 05°42′E
28 J2 **Grenora** North Dakota, N USA 48°36′N 103°57′W
92 N8 **Grense-Jakobselv** Finnmark, N Norway 69°46′N 30°39′E
45 S14 **Grenville** E Grenada 12°07′N 61°37′W
32 G11 **Gresham** Oregon, NW USA 45°30′N 122°25′W
Gresk see Hresk
106 B7 **Gressoney-St-Jean** Valle d'Aosta, NW Italy 45°48′N 07°49′E
22 K9 **Gretna** Louisiana, S USA 29°54′N 90°03′W
21 T7 **Gretna** Virginia, NE USA 36°57′N 79°21′W
98 F13 **Grevelingen** inlet S North Sea
100 F13 **Greven** Nordrhein-Westfalen, NW Germany 52°07′N 07°38′E
115 D15 **Grevená** Dytikí Makedonía, N Greece 40°05′N 21°26′E
101 D16 **Grevenbroich** Nordrhein-Westfalen, W Germany 51°06′N 06°34′E
99 N24 **Grevenmacher** Grevenmacher, E Luxembourg 49°41′N 06°27′E
99 M24 **Grevenmacher** ◈ district E Luxembourg
100 K9 **Grevesmühlen** Mecklenburg-Vorpommern, N Germany 53°52′N 11°12′E
185 H16 **Grey** ≈ South Island, New Zealand
33 V12 **Greybull** Wyoming, C USA 44°29′N 108°03′W
33 U13 **Greybull River** ≈ Wyoming, C USA
65 A24 **Grey Channel** sound Falkland Islands
Greyerzer See see Gruyère, Lac de la
13 T10 **Grey Islands** island group Newfoundland and Labrador, E Canada
18 L10 **Greylock, Mount** ▲ Massachusetts, NE USA 42°38′N 73°09′W
185 G17 **Greymouth** West Coast, South Island, New Zealand 42°29′S 171°14′E
181 U10 **Grey Range** ▲▲ New South Wales/Queensland, E Australia
97 G18 **Greystones** Ir. Na Clocha Liatha. E Ireland 53°08′N 06°05′W
185 M14 **Greytown** Wellington, North Island, New Zealand 41°04′S 175°29′E
83 K23 **Greytown** KwaZulu/Natal, E South Africa 29°04′S 30°35′E
Greytown see San Juan del Norte
99 H19 **Grez-Doiceau** Dut. Graven. Walloon Brabant, C Belgium 50°43′N 04°41′E
115 J19 **Griá, Akrotírio** headland Ándros, Kykládes, Greece, Aegean Sea 37°54′N 24°57′E
127 N8 **Gribanovskiy** Voronezhskaya Oblast', W Russian Federation 51°27′N 41°53′E
78 I13 **Gribingui** ≈ N Central African Republic
35 O6 **Gridley** California, W USA 39°21′N 121°41′W
83 G23 **Griekwastad** Northern Cape, C South Africa 28°50′S 23°16′E
23 S4 **Griffin** Georgia, SE USA 33°15′N 84°17′W
183 O9 **Griffith** New South Wales, SE Australia 34°18′S 146°04′E
14 F13 **Griffith Island** island Ontario, S Canada
21 W10 **Grifton** North Carolina, SE USA 35°22′N 77°26′W
Grigioni see Graubünden
119 H14 **Grigiškes** Vilnius, SE Lithuania 54°42′N 25°00′E
117 N10 **Grigoriopol** C Moldova 47°09′N 29°18′E
147 X7 **Grigor'yevka** Issyk-Kul'skaya Oblast', E Kyrgyzstan 42°43′N 77°27′E
193 U8 **Grijalva Ridge** undersea feature E Pacific Ocean
41 U15 **Grijalva, Río** var. Tabasco. ≈ Guatemala/Mexico
98 N5 **Grijpskerk** Groningen, NE Netherlands 53°15′N 06°18′E
83 C22 **Grillenthal** Karas, SW Namibia 26°55′S 15°24′E
79 J15 **Grimari** Ouaka, C Central African Republic 05°44′N 20°02′E
Grimaylov see Hrymayliv
99 G18 **Grimbergen** Vlaams Brabant, C Belgium 50°56′N 04°22′E
183 N15 **Grim, Cape** headland Tasmania, SE Australia 40°42′S 144°42′E
100 N8 **Grimmen** Mecklenburg-Vorpommern, NE Germany 54°06′N 13°03′E
14 G16 **Grimsby** Ontario, S Canada 43°12′N 79°35′W
97 O17 **Grimsby** prev. Great Grimsby. E England, United Kingdom 53°35′N 00°05′W
92 J1 **Grímsey** var. Grimsey. island N Iceland
Grimsey see Grímsey
11 O12 **Grimshaw** Alberta, W Canada 56°11′N 117°37′W
95 F18 **Grimstad** Aust-Agder, S Norway 58°20′N 08°35′E
92 H4 **Grindavík** Reykjanes, W Iceland 65°57′N 18°10′W
108 F9 **Grindelwald** Bern, S Switzerland 46°37′N 08°04′E
95 F23 **Grindsted** Ribe, W Denmark 55°46′N 08°56′E
29 W14 **Grinnell** Iowa, C USA 41°44′N 92°43′W
109 U10 **Grintovec** ▲ N Slovenia 46°21′N 14°31′E
9 N4 **Grise Fiord** var. Ausuitoq. Northwest Territories, Ellesmere Island, N Canada 76°10′N 83°15′W
182 H1 **Griselda, Lake** salt lake South Australia
Grisons see Graubünden
95 P14 **Grisslehamn** Stockholm, C Sweden 60°04′N 18°50′E
29 T15 **Griswold** Iowa, C USA 41°14′N 95°08′W
102 M1 **Griz Nez, Cap** headland N France 50°51′N 01°34′E
112 P13 **Grljan** Serbia, E Serbia 43°52′N 22°18′E
112 E11 **Grmeč** ▲▲ NW Bosnia and Herzegovina
99 H16 **Grobbendonk** Antwerpen, N Belgium 51°12′N 04°41′E
Grobin see Grobiņa
118 C10 **Grobiņa** Ger. Grobin. Liepāja, W Latvia 56°32′N 21°12′E
83 K20 **Groblersdal** Mpumalanga, NE South Africa 25°15′S 29°25′E
83 G23 **Groblershoop** Northern Cape, W South Africa 28°51′S 22°01′E
Gródek Jagielloński see Horodok
109 Q6 **Grödig** Salzburg, W Austria 47°42′N 13°06′E
111 H15 **Grodków** Opolskie, S Poland 50°42′N 17°23′E
Grodnenskaya Oblast' see Hrodzyenskaya Voblasts'
Grodno see Hrodna
110 L12 **Grodzisk Mazowiecki** Mazowieckie, C Poland 52°09′N 20°38′E
110 F12 **Grodzisk Wielkopolski** Wielkopolskie, C Poland 52°13′N 16°21′E
Grodzyanka see Hradzyanka
98 O12 **Groenlo** Gelderland, E Netherlands 52°02′N 06°36′E
83 E22 **Groenrivier** Karas, SE Namibia 27°27′S 18°52′E
25 U8 **Groesbeck** Texas, SW USA 31°31′N 96°35′W
98 L13 **Groesbeek** Gelderland, SE Netherlands 51°47′N 05°56′E
102 G7 **Groix, Îles de** island group NW France
110 M12 **Grójec** Mazowieckie, C Poland 51°51′N 20°52′E
65 K15 **Gröll Seamount** undersea feature C Atlantic Ocean 12°54′S 33°24′W
100 E13 **Gronau** var. Gronau in Westfalen. Nordrhein-Westfalen, NW Germany 52°13′N 07°02′E
Gronau in Westfalen see Gronau
93 F15 **Grong** Nord-Trøndelag, C Norway 64°29′N 12°19′E
95 N22 **Grönhögen** Kalmar, S Sweden 56°16′N 16°09′E
98 N5 **Groningen** Groningen, NE Netherlands 53°13′N 06°35′E
55 W9 **Groningen** Saramacca, N Surinam 05°45′N 55°31′W
98 N5 **Groningen** ◈ province NE Netherlands
Grønland see Greenland
108 H11 **Grono** Graubünden, S Switzerland 46°15′N 09°07′E
95 M20 **Grönskåra** Kalmar, S Sweden 57°04′N 15°45′E
25 O2 **Groom** Texas, SW USA 35°12′N 101°06′W
35 W9 **Groom Lake** ◎ Nevada, W USA
83 H25 **Groot** ≈ S South Africa
181 S2 **Groote Eylandt** island Northern Territory, N Australia
98 M6 **Grootegast** Groningen, NE Netherlands 53°11′N 06°12′E
83 D17 **Grootfontein** Otjozondjupa, N Namibia 19°32′S 18°05′E
83 E22 **Groot Karasberge** ▲▲ S Namibia
Groot Karoo see Great Karoo
Groot-Kei see Nciba
15 V6 **Grosses-Roches** Québec, SE Canada 48°55′N 67°06′W
109 V2 **Gross-Siegharts** Niederösterreich, N Austria 48°48′N 15°25′E
45 T10 **Gros Islet** N Saint Lucia 14°04′N 60°57′W
44 L8 **Gros-Morne** NW Haiti 19°45′N 72°46′W
13 S11 **Gros Morne** ▲ Newfoundland, Newfoundland and Labrador, E Canada 49°38′N 57°45′W
103 R9 **Grosne** ≈ C France
45 S12 **Gros Piton** ▲ SW Saint Lucia 13°48′N 61°04′W
Grossa, Isola see Dugi Otok
Grossbetschkerek see Zrenjanin
Grosse Isper see Grosse Ysper
Grosse Kokel see Târnava Mare
101 M21 **Grosse Laaber** var. Grosse Laber. ≈ SE Germany
Grosse Laber see Grosse Laaber
Grosse Morava see Velika Morava
101 O15 **Grossenhain** Sachsen, E Germany 51°18′N 13°31′E
109 Y4 **Grossenzersdorf** Niederösterreich, NE Austria 48°12′N 16°33′E
101 O21 **Grosser Arber** ▲ SE Germany 49°07′N 13°10′E
101 K17 **Grosser Beerberg** ▲ C Germany 50°39′N 10°45′E
101 G18 **Grosser Feldberg** ▲ W Germany 50°13′N 08°28′E
109 O8 **Grosser Löffler** It. Monte Lovello. ▲ Austria/Italy 47°02′N 11°56′E
109 N8 **Grosser Möseler** var. Mesule. ▲ Austria/Italy 47°01′N 11°52′E
100 J8 **Grosser Plöner See** ◎ N Germany
101 O21 **Grosser Rachel** ▲ SE Germany 48°59′N 13°23′E
Grosser Sund see Suur Väin
109 P8 **Grosses Wiesbachhorn** var. Wiesbachhorn. ▲ W Austria 47°09′N 12°44′E
106 F13 **Grosseto** Toscana, C Italy 42°45′N 11°07′E
101 M22 **Grosse Vils** ≈ SE Germany
109 U4 **Grosse Ysper** var. Grosse Isper. ≈ N Austria
101 G19 **Gross-Gerau** Hessen, W Germany 49°55′N 08°28′E
109 U3 **Gross Gerungs** Niederösterreich, N Austria 48°33′N 14°58′E
109 P8 **Grossglockner** ▲ W Austria 47°05′N 12°39′E
Grosskanizsa see Nagykanizsa
Gross-Karol see Carei
Grosskikinda see Kikinda
109 W9 **Grossklein** Steiermark, SE Austria 46°43′N 15°24′E
Grosskoppe see Velká Deštná
Grossmeseritsch see Velké Meziříčí
Grossmichel see Michalovce
101 H19 **Grossostheim** Bayern, C Germany 49°54′N 09°03′E
109 X7 **Grosspetersdorf** Burgenland, SE Austria 47°15′N 16°19′E
109 T5 **Grossraming** Oberösterreich, C Austria 47°54′N 14°34′E
101 P14 **Grossräschen** Brandenburg, E Germany 51°34′N 14°00′E
Grossrauschenbach see Revúca
Gross-Sankt-Johannis see Suure-Jaani
Gross-Schlatten see Abrud
Gross-Skaisgirren see Bol'shakovo
Gross-Steffelsdorf see Rimavská Sobota
Gross Strehlitz see Strzelce Opolskie
109 O8 **Grossvenediger** ▲ W Austria 47°07′N 12°19′E
Grosswardein see Oradea
Gross Wartenberg see Syców
109 U11 **Grosuplje** C Slovenia 46°00′N 14°36′E
99 H17 **Grote Nete** ≈ N Belgium
94 E10 **Grotli** Oppland, S Norway 62°02′N 07°36′E
19 N13 **Groton** Connecticut, NE USA 41°20′N 72°03′W
29 P8 **Groton** South Dakota, N USA 45°27′N 98°06′W
107 P18 **Grottaglie** Puglia, SE Italy 40°32′N 17°26′E
107 L17 **Grottaminarda** Campania, S Italy 41°04′N 15°02′E
106 K13 **Grottammare** Marche, C Italy 43°00′N 13°52′E
21 U5 **Grottoes** Virginia, NE USA 38°16′N 78°49′W
Grou see Grouw
13 N10 **Groulx, Monts** ▲▲ Québec, E Canada
14 E7 **Groundhog** ≈ Ontario, S Canada
36 J1 **Grouse Creek** Utah, W USA 41°41′N 113°52′W
36 J1 **Grouse Creek Mountains** ▲▲ Utah, W USA
98 L6 **Grouw** Fris. Grou. Friesland, N Netherlands 53°07′N 05°51′E
27 R8 **Grove** Oklahoma, C USA 36°35′N 94°46′W
31 S13 **Grove City** Ohio, N USA 39°52′N 83°05′W
18 B13 **Grove City** Pennsylvania, NE USA 41°09′N 80°02′W
23 O6 **Grove Hill** Alabama, S USA 31°42′N 87°46′W
33 S15 **Grover** Wyoming, C USA 42°48′N 110°57′W
35 P13 **Grover City** California, W USA 35°08′N 120°37′W
25 Y11 **Groves** Texas, SW USA 29°57′N 93°55′W
19 O7 **Groveton** New Hampshire, NE USA 44°35′N 71°28′W
25 W9 **Groveton** Texas, SW USA 31°04′N 95°08′W
36 J15 **Growler Mountains** ▲▲ Arizona, SW USA
Grozdovo see Bratya Daskalovi
127 P16 **Groznyy** Chechenskaya Respublika, SW Russian Federation 43°20′N 45°43′E
Grubeshov see Hrubieszów
112 G9 **Grubišno Polje** Bjelovar-Bilogora, NE Croatia 45°42′N 17°09′E
Grudovo see Sredets
110 J9 **Grudziądz** Ger. Graudenz. Kujawsko-pomorskie, C Poland 53°29′N 18°45′E
25 R17 **Grulla** var. La Grulla. Texas, SW USA 26°15′N 98°37′W
40 K14 **Grullo** Jalisco, SW Mexico 19°45′N 104°15′W
67 V10 **Grumeti** ≈ N Tanzania
95 K16 **Grums** Värmland, C Sweden 59°22′N 13°11′E
109 S5 **Grünau im Almtal** Oberösterreich, N Austria 47°51′N 13°56′E
101 H17 **Grünberg** Hessen, W Germany 50°36′N 08°57′E
Grünberg/Grünberg in Schlesien see Zielona Góra
92 H3 **Grundarfjördhur** Vestfirdhir, W Iceland 64°55′N 23°15′W
21 P7 **Grundy** Virginia, NE USA 37°17′N 82°06′W
29 W13 **Grundy Center** Iowa, C USA 42°21′N 92°46′W
Grüneberg see Zielona Góra
25 N1 **Gruver** Texas, SW USA 36°16′N 101°24′W
108 C9 **Gruyère, Lac de la** Ger. Greyerzer See. ◎ SW Switzerland
108 C9 **Gruyères** Fribourg, W Switzerland 46°34′N 07°04′E
118 E11 **Gruzdžiai** Šiauliai, N Lithuania 56°06′N 23°15′E
Gruzinskaya SSR/Gruziya see Georgia
Gryada Akkyr see Akgyr Erezi
126 L7 **Gryazi** Lipetskaya Oblast', W Russian Federation 52°27′N 39°56′E
124 M14 **Gryazovets** Vologodskaya Oblast', NW Russian Federation 58°52′N 40°12′E
111 M17 **Grybów** Małopolskie, SE Poland 49°35′N 20°54′E
94 M13 **Grycksbo** Dalarna, C Sweden 60°40′N 15°30′E
110 E8 **Gryfice** Ger. Greifenberg, Greifenberg in Pommern. Zachodnio-pomorskie, NW Poland 53°55′N 15°11′E
110 D9 **Gryfino** Ger. Greifenhagen. Zachodnio-pomorskie, NW Poland 53°15′N 14°30′E
92 H9 **Gryllefjord** Troms, N Norway 69°21′N 17°07′E
95 L15 **Grythyttan** Örebro, C Sweden 59°52′N 14°31′E
108 D10 **Gstaad** Bern, W Switzerland 46°30′N 07°16′E
43 P14 **Guabito** Bocas del Toro, NW Panama 09°30′N 82°35′W
44 G7 **Guacanayabo, Golfo de** gulf S Cuba
40 I7 **Guachochi** Chihuahua, N Mexico
104 I11 **Guadajira** ≈ SW Spain
104 M13 **Guadajoz** ≈ S Spain
40 L13 **Guadalajara** Jalisco, C Mexico 20°43′N 103°24′W
105 O8 **Guadalajara** Ar. Wad Al-Hajarah; anc. Arriaca. Castilla-La Mancha, C Spain 40°37′N 03°10′W
105 O7 **Guadalajara** ◈ province Castilla-La Mancha, C Spain
104 K12 **Guadalcanal** Andalucía, S Spain 38°06′N 05°49′W
186 L10 **Guadalcanal** off. Guadalcanal Province. ◈ province C Solomon Islands
186 M9 **Guadalcanal** island C Solomon Islands
Guadalcanal Province see Guadalcanal
105 O12 **Guadalén** ≈ S Spain
105 R13 **Guadalentín** ≈ SE Spain
104 K15 **Guadalete** ≈ SW Spain
105 O13 **Guadalimar** ≈ S Spain
105 P12 **Guadalmena** ≈ S Spain
104 L11 **Guadalmez** ≈ W Spain
105 S7 **Guadalope** ≈ E Spain
104 K13 **Guadalquivir** ≈ W Spain
104 J14 **Guadalquivir, Marismas del** var. Las Marismas. wetland SW Spain
40 M11 **Guadalupe** Zacatecas, C Mexico 22°47′N 102°30′W
57 E16 **Guadalupe** Ica, W Peru 13°59′S 75°49′W
104 L10 **Guadalupe** Extremadura, W Spain 39°26′N 05°18′W
36 L14 **Guadalupe** Arizona, SW USA 33°20′N 111°57′W
35 P13 **Guadalupe** California, W USA 34°55′N 120°34′W
Guadalupe see Canelones
40 J3 **Guadalupe Bravos** Chihuahua, N Mexico 31°22′N 106°04′W
40 A4 **Guadalupe, Isla** island NW Mexico
37 U15 **Guadalupe Mountains** ▲▲ New Mexico/Texas, SW USA
24 J8 **Guadalupe Peak** ▲ Texas, SW USA 31°53′N 104°51′W
25 R11 **Guadalupe River** ≈ SW USA
104 K10 **Guadalupe, Sierra de** ▲▲ W Spain
40 K9 **Guadalupe Victoria** Durango, C Mexico 24°30′N 104°08′W
40 I8 **Guadalupe y Calvo** Chihuahua, N Mexico 26°04′N 106°58′W
105 N7 **Guadarrama** Madrid, C Spain 40°40′N 04°06′W
105 N7 **Guadarrama** ≈ C Spain
104 M7 **Guadarrama, Puerto de** pass C Spain
105 N9 **Guadarrama, Sierra de** ▲▲ C Spain
105 Q9 **Guadazaón** ≈ C Spain
45 X10 **Guadeloupe** ◇ French overseas department E West Indies
47 S3 **Guadeloupe** island group E West Indies
45 W10 **Guadeloupe Passage** passage E Caribbean Sea
104 H13 **Guadiana** ≈ Portugal/Spain
105 O13 **Guadiana Menor** ≈ S Spain
105 Q8 **Guadiela** ≈ C Spain
105 O14 **Guadix** Andalucía, S Spain 37°19′N 03°08′W
Guad-i-Zirreh see Gowd-e Zereh, Dasht-e
193 T12 **Guafo Fracture Zone** tectonic feature SE Pacific Ocean
63 F18 **Guafo, Isla** island S Chile
42 I6 **Guaimaca** Francisco Morazán, C Honduras 14°34′N 86°49′W
54 J12 **Guainía** off. Comisaría del Guainía. ◈ province E Colombia
Guainía, Comisaría del see Guainía
54 K12 **Guainía, Río** ≈ Colombia/Venezuela
55 O9 **Guaiquinima, Cerro** elevation SE Venezuela
60 G10 **Guaíra** Paraná, S Brazil 24°05′S 54°15′W
60 L7 **Guaíra** São Paulo, S Brazil 20°17′S 48°21′W
62 O7 **Guairá** off. Departamento del Guairá. ◈ department S Paraguay
Guairá, Departamento del see Guairá
Guaire see Gorey
63 F18 **Guaiteca, Isla** island S Chile
44 G6 **Guajaba, Cayo** headland C Cuba 21°50′N 77°33′W
59 D16 **Guajará-Mirim** Rondônia, W Brazil 10°50′S 65°21′W
Guajira see La Guajira
Guajira, Departamento de La see La Guajira
54 H3 **Guajira, Península de la** peninsula N Colombia
42 J6 **Gualaco** Olancho, C Honduras 15°00′N 86°03′W
34 L7 **Gualala** California, W USA 38°45′N 123°33′W
42 E5 **Gualán** Zacapa, C Guatemala 15°06′N 89°22′W
61 C19 **Gualeguay** Entre Ríos, E Argentina 33°09′S 59°20′W
61 D18 **Gualeguaychú** Entre Ríos, E Argentina 33°03′S 58°31′W
61 C18 **Gualeguay, Río** ≈ E Argentina
63 K16 **Gualicho, Salina del** salt lake E Argentina
188 B15 **Guam** ◇ US unincorporated territory W Pacific Ocean
63 F19 **Guamblin, Isla** island Archipiélago de los Chonos, S Chile
61 A22 **Guaminí** Buenos Aires, E Argentina 37°01′S 62°28′W
40 H8 **Guamúchil** Sinaloa, C Mexico 25°23′N 108°01′W
54 H4 **Guana** var. Misión de Guana. Zulia, NW Venezuela 11°07′N 72°17′W
44 C4 **Guanabacoa** La Habana, W Cuba 23°02′N 82°12′W
42 K13 **Guanacaste** off. Provincia de Guanacaste. ◈ province NW Costa Rica
42 K12 **Guanacaste, Cordillera de** ▲▲ NW Costa Rica
Guanacaste, Provincia de see Guanacaste
40 J8 **Guanaceví** Durango, C Mexico 25°55′N 105°51′W
44 A5 **Guanahacabibes, Golfo de** gulf W Cuba
42 K4 **Guanaja, Isla de** island Islas de la Bahía, N Honduras
44 C4 **Guanajay** La Habana, W Cuba 22°56′N 82°42′W
41 N12 **Guanajuato** Guanajuato, C Mexico 21°N 101°19′W
40 M12 **Guanajuato** ◈ state C Mexico
54 J6 **Guanare** Portuguesa, N Venezuela 09°04′N 69°45′W
54 K7 **Guanare, Río** ≈ W Venezuela
54 J6 **Guanarito** Portuguesa, NW Venezuela 08°43′N 69°12′W
160 M3 **Guancen Shan** ▲▲ C China
62 I9 **Guandacol** La Rioja, W Argentina 29°32′S 68°37′W
44 A5 **Guane** Pinar del Río, W Cuba 22°12′N 84°05′W
160 J9 **Guang'an** Sichuan, C China 30°28′N 106°22′E
161 N14 **Guangdong** var. Guangdong Sheng, Kuang-tung, Kwangtung, Yue. ◈ province S China
Guangdong Sheng see Guangdong
Guanghua see Laohekou
Guangju see Kwangju
160 I13 **Guangnan** var. Liancheng. Yunnan, SW China 24°07′N 104°54′E
161 N8 **Guangshui** prev. Yingshan. Hubei, C China 31°41′N 113°53′E

◆ Country
● Country Capital
◇ Dependent Territory
○ Dependent Territory Capital
◈ Administrative Regions
✈ International Airport
▲ Mountain
▲▲ Mountain Range
Volcano
≈ River
◎ Lake
⊞ Reservoir

GUANGXI – HAFNIA

Guangxi see Guangxi Zhuangzu Zizhiqu
160 K14 **Guangxi Zhuangzu Zizhiqu** var. Guangxi, Gui, Kuang-hsi, Kwangsi, Eng. Kwangsi Chuang Autonomous Region. ◈ autonomous region S China
160 J8 **Guangyuan** var. Kuang-yuan, Kwangyuan. Sichuan, C China 32°27′N 105°49′E
161 N14 **Guangzhou** var. Kuang-chou, Kwangchow, Eng. Canton. province capital Guangdong, S China 23°11′N 113°19′E
59 N19 **Guanhães** Minas Gerais, SE Brazil 18°46′S 42°58′W
160 I12 **Guanling** var. Guanling Bouyeizu Miaozu Zizhixian. Guizhou, S China 26°00′N 105°40′E
Guanling Bouyeizu Miaozu Zizhixian see Guanling
55 N5 **Guanta** Anzoátegui, NE Venezuela 10°15′N 64°38′W
44 J8 **Guantánamo** Guantánamo, SE Cuba 20°06′N 75°16′W
44 J8 **Guantánamo, Bahia de** Eng. Guantanamo Bay. US military base SE Cuba 20°06′N 75°16′W
Guantanamo Bay see Guantánamo, Bahia de
Guanxian/Guan Xian see Dujiangyan
161 Q6 **Guanyun** var. Yishan. Jiangsu, E China 34°18′N 119°14′E
54 C12 **Guapí** Cauca, SW Colombia 02°36′N 77°54′W
43 N13 **Guápiles** Limón, NE Costa Rica 10°15′N 83°46′W
61 I15 **Guaporé** Rio Grande do Sul, S Brazil 28°55′S 51°53′W
47 S8 **Guaporé, Rio** var. Río Iténez. ≈ Bolivia/Brazil see also Río Iténez
Guaporé, Rio see Iténez, Río
56 B7 **Guaranda** Bolívar, C Ecuador 01°35′S 78°59′W
60 H11 **Guaraniaçu** Paraná, S Brazil 25°05′S 52°52′W
59 O20 **Guarapari** Espírito Santo, SE Brazil 20°39′S 40°31′W
60 I12 **Guarapuava** Paraná, S Brazil 25°22′S 51°28′W
60 J8 **Guararapes** São Paulo, S Brazil 21°16′S 50°37′W
105 S4 **Guara, Sierra de** ▲▲ NE Spain
60 N10 **Guaratinguetá** São Paulo, S Brazil 22°44′S 45°16′W
104 I7 **Guarda** Guarda, N Portugal 40°32′N 07°17′W
104 I7 **Guarda** ◈ district N Portugal
Guardak see Magdanly
104 M3 **Guardo** Castilla-León, N Spain 42°48′N 04°50′W
104 K11 **Guareña** Extremadura, W Spain 38°51′N 06°06′W
60 J11 **Guaricana, Pico** ▲ S Brazil 25°13′S 48°50′W
54 L6 **Guárico** off. Estado Guárico. ◈ state N Venezuela
Guárico, Estado see Guárico
44 J7 **Guarico, Punta** headland E Cuba 20°36′N 74°43′W
54 L7 **Guárico, Río** ≈ C Venezuela
60 M10 **Guarujá** São Paulo, SE Brazil 23°50′S 46°27′W
61 L22 **Guarulhos** ✈ (São Paulo) São Paulo, S Brazil 23°23′S 46°32′W
43 R17 **Guarumal** Veraguas, S Panama 07°48′N 81°15′W
Guasapa see Guasopa
40 H8 **Guasave** Sinaloa, C Mexico 25°33′N 108°29′W
54 I8 **Guasdualito** Apure, C Venezuela 07°15′N 70°40′W
55 Q7 **Guasipati** Bolívar, E Venezuela 07°28′N 61°58′W
186 I9 **Guasopa** var. Guasapa. Woodlark Island, SE Papua New Guinea 09°12′S 152°58′E
106 F9 **Guastalla** Emilia-Romagna, C Italy 44°54′N 10°38′E
42 D6 **Guastatoya** var. El Progreso. El Progreso, C Guatemala 14°51′N 90°01′W
42 D5 **Guatemala** off. Republic of Guatemala. ◆ republic Central America
42 A2 **Guatemala** off. Departamento de Guatemala. ◈ department S Guatemala
193 S7 **Guatemala Basin** undersea feature E Pacific Ocean 11°00′N 95°00′W
Guatemala City see Ciudad de Guatemala
Guatemala, Departamento de see Guatemala
Guatemala, Republic of see Guatemala
45 V14 **Guatuaro Point** headland Trinidad, Trinidad and Tobago 10°19′N 60°58′W
186 B8 **Guavi** ≈ SW Papua New Guinea
54 G13 **Guaviare** off. Comisaría Guaviare. ◈ province S Colombia
Guaviare, Comisaría see Guaviare
54 J11 **Guaviare, Río** ≈ E Colombia
61 E15 **Guaviravi** Corrientes, NE Argentina 29°20′S 56°50′W
54 I12 **Guayabero, Río** ≈ SW Colombia
45 U6 **Guayama** E Puerto Rico 17°59′N 66°07′W
42 J7 **Guayambre, Río** ≈ S Honduras
Guayanas, Macizo de las see Guiana Highlands
45 V6 **Guayanés, Punta** headland E Puerto Rico 18°03′N 65°48′W
42 J6 **Guayape, Río** ≈ C Honduras
56 B7 **Guayaquil** var. Santiago de Guayaquil. Guayas, SW Ecuador 02°13′S 79°54′W
Guayaquil see Simon Bolivar
56 A8 **Guayaquil, Golfo de** var. Gulf of Guayaquil. gulf SW Ecuador
Guayaquil, Gulf of see Guayaquil, Golfo de
56 A7 **Guayas** ◈ province W Ecuador
62 N7 **Guaycurú, Río** ≈ NE Argentina
40 F6 **Guaymas** Sonora, NW Mexico 27°56′N 110°54′W
45 U5 **Guaynabo** E Puerto Rico 18°19′N 66°05′W
80 H12 **Guba** Binishangul Gumuz, W Ethiopia 11°11′N 35°21′E
146 H8 **Gubadag** Turkm. Tel'man; prev. Tel'mansk. Daşoguz Welaýaty, N Turkmenistan 42°07′N 59°55′E
125 T1 **Guba Dolgaya** Nenetskiy Avtonomnyy Okrug, NW Russian Federation 70°16′N 58°45′E
125 V13 **Gubakha** Permskaya Oblast', NW Russian Federation 58°52′N 57°35′E
106 I12 **Gubbio** Umbria, C Italy 43°27′N 12°34′E
100 Q13 **Guben** var. Wilhelm-Pieck-Stadt. Brandenburg, E Germany 51°59′N 14°42′E
Guben see Gubin
110 D12 **Gubin** Ger. Guben. Lubuskie, W Poland 51°59′N 14°43′E
126 K8 **Gubkin** Belgorodskaya Oblast', W Russian Federation 51°16′N 37°32′E
162 J9 **Guchin-Us** var. Arguut. Övörhangay, C Mongolia 45°27′N 102°25′E
Gudara see Ghŭdara
105 S8 **Gúdar, Sierra de** ▲▲ E Spain
137 P8 **Gudaut'a** NW Georgia 43°07′N 40°35′E
94 G12 **Gudbrandsdalen** valley S Norway
95 G21 **Gudenå** var. Gudenaa. ≈ C Denmark
Gudenaa see Gudenå
127 P16 **Gudermes** Chechenskaya Respublika, SW Russian Federation 43°23′N 46°06′E
155 J18 **Gūdūr** Andhra Pradesh, E India 14°10′N 79°51′E
146 B13 **Gudurolum** Balkan Welaýaty, W Turkmenistan 37°28′N 54°30′E
94 D13 **Gudvangen** Sogn Og Fjordane, S Norway 60°54′N 06°49′E
103 U7 **Guebwiller** Haut-Rhin, NE France 47°55′N 07°13′E
Guéckédou see Guékédou
14 K8 **Guéguen, Lac** ◎ Québec, SE Canada
76 J15 **Guékédou** var. Guéckédou. Guinée-Forestière, S Guinea 08°33′N 10°08′W
41 R16 **Guelatao** Oaxaca, SE Mexico
Guelders see Gelderland
78 G11 **Guélengdeng** Mayo-Kébbi, W Chad 10°55′N 15°31′E
74 L5 **Guelma** var. Gâlma. NE Algeria 36°29′N 07°25′E
74 D8 **Guelmime** var. Goulimime. SW Morocco 28°59′N 10°10′W
14 G15 **Guelph** Ontario, S Canada 43°34′N 80°16′W
102 I7 **Guémené-Penfao** Loire-Atlantique, NW France 47°37′N 01°49′W
102 I7 **Guer** Morbihan, NW France 47°54′N 02°07′W
78 I11 **Guéra** off. Préfecture du Guéra. ◈ prefecture S Chad
102 H8 **Guérande** Loire-Atlantique, NW France 47°20′N 02°25′W
Guéra, Préfecture du see Guéra
78 K9 **Guéréda** Biltine, E Chad 14°30′N 22°05′E
103 N10 **Guéret** Creuse, C France 46°10′N 01°52′E
Guernica/Guernica y Lumo see Gernika-Lumo
33 Z15 **Guernsey** Wyoming, C USA 42°16′N 104°44′W
97 K25 **Guernsey** island Channel Islands, NW Europe
76 J10 **Guérou** Assaba, S Mauritania 16°48′N 11°40′W
25 R16 **Guerra** Texas, SW USA 26°54′N 98°53′W
41 O15 **Guerrero** ◈ state S Mexico
40 D6 **Guerrero Negro** Baja California Sur, NW Mexico 27°56′N 114°04′W
103 P9 **Gueugnon** Saône-et-Loire, C France 46°36′N 04°03′E
76 M17 **Guéyo** S Ivory Coast 05°25′N 06°04′W
107 L15 **Guglionesi** Molise, C Italy 41°54′N 14°54′E
188 K5 **Guguan** island C Northern Mariana Islands
Guhrau see Góra
Gui see Guangxi Zhuangzu Zizhiqu
Guiana see French Guiana
47 V4 **Guiana Basin** undersea feature W Atlantic Ocean 11°00′N 52°00′W
48 G6 **Guiana Highlands** var. Macizo de las Guayanas. ▲▲ N South America
Guiba see Juba
102 I7 **Guichen** Ille-et-Vilaine, NW France 47°57′N 01°47′W
Guichi see Chizhou
61 E18 **Guichón** Paysandú, W Uruguay 32°30′S 57°13′W
77 U12 **Guidan-Roumji** Maradi, S Niger 13°40′N 06°41′E
Guidder see Guider
159 T10 **Guide** var. Heyin. Qinghai, C China 36°06′N 101°25′E
78 F12 **Guider** var. Guidder. Nord, N Cameroon 09°55′N 13°59′E
76 I11 **Guidimaka** ◈ region S Mauritania
77 W12 **Guidimouni** Zinder, S Niger 13°40′N 09°31′E
76 G10 **Guier, Lac de** var. Lac de Guiers. ◎ N Senegal
Guiers, Lac de see Guier, Lac de
160 L14 **Guigang** var. Guixian, Gui Xian. Guangxi Zhuangzu Zizhiqu, S China 23°06′N 109°36′E
76 L16 **Guiglo** W Ivory Coast 06°33′N 07°29′W
54 L5 **Güigüe** Carabobo, N Venezuela 10°05′N 67°48′W
83 M20 **Guijá** Gaza, S Mozambique 24°31′S 33°02′E
42 E7 **Güija, Lago de** ◎ El Salvador/Guatemala
160 L14 **Gui Jiang** var. Gui Shui. ≈ S China
104 K8 **Guijuelo** Castilla-León, N Spain 40°34′N 05°40′W
Guilan see Gīlān
97 N22 **Guildford** SE England, United Kingdom 51°14′N 00°35′W
19 R5 **Guildford** Maine, NE USA 45°10′N 69°22′W
19 O7 **Guildhall** Vermont, NE USA 44°34′N 71°36′W
103 R13 **Guilherand** Ardèche, E France 44°57′N 04°49′E
160 L13 **Guilin** var. Kuei-lin, Kweilin. Guangxi Zhuangzu Zizhiqu, S China 25°15′N 110°16′E
12 J6 **Guillaume-Delisle, Lac** ◎ Québec, NE Canada
103 U13 **Guillestre** Hautes-Alpes, SE France 44°41′N 06°39′E
104 H6 **Guimarães** var. Guimaráes. Braga, N Portugal 41°26′N 08°19′W
Guimarães see Guimarães
58 D11 **Guimarães Rosas, Pico** ▲ NW Brazil
23 N3 **Guin** Alabama, S USA 33°58′N 87°54′W
Güina see Wina
76 I14 **Guinea** off. Republic of Guinea, var. Guinée; prev. French Guinea, People's Revolutionary Republic of Guinea. ◆ republic W Africa
64 N13 **Guinea Basin** undersea feature E Atlantic Ocean 0°00′N 05°00′W
76 E12 **Guinea-Bissau** off. Republic of Guinea-Bissau, Fr. Guinée-Bissau, Port. Guiné-Bissau; prev. Portuguese Guinea. ◆ republic W Africa
Guinea-Bissau, Republic of see Guinea-Bissau
66 K7 **Guinea Fracture Zone** tectonic feature E Atlantic Ocean
64 O13 **Guinea, Gulf of** Fr. Golfe de Guinée. gulf E Atlantic Ocean
Guinea, People's Revolutionary Republic of see Guinea
Guinea, Republic of see Guinea
Guiné-Bissau see Guinea-Bissau
Guinée see Guinea
Guinée-Bissau see Guinea-Bissau
Guinée, Golfe de see Guinea, Gulf of
44 C4 **Güines** La Habana, W Cuba 22°50′N 82°02′W
102 G5 **Guingamp** Côtes d'Armor, NW France 48°34′N 03°09′W
105 P3 **Guipúzcoa** Basq. Gipuzkoa. ◈ province País Vasco, N Spain
44 C5 **Güira de Melena** La Habana, W Cuba 22°47′N 82°33′W
74 G8 **Guir, Hamada du** desert Algeria/Morocco
55 P5 **Güiria** Sucre, NE Venezuela 10°37′N 62°21′W
Gui Shui see Gui Jiang
104 H2 **Guitiriz** Galicia, NW Spain 43°10′N 07°52′W
77 N17 **Guitri** S Ivory Coast 05°31′N 05°14′W
171 Q5 **Guiuan** Samar, C Philippines 11°02′N 125°45′E
Gui Xian/Guixian see Guigang
160 J12 **Guiyang** var. Kuei-Yang, Kuei-yang, Kueyang, Kweiyang; prev. Kweichu. province capital Guizhou, S China 26°33′N 106°45′E
160 J12 **Guizhou** var. Guizhou Sheng, Kuei-chou, Kweichow, Qian. ◈ province S China
Guizhou Sheng see Guizhou
102 J13 **Gujan-Mestras** Gironde, SW France 44°39′N 01°04′W
154 B10 **Gujarāt** var. Gujerat. ◈ state W India
149 V6 **Gūjar Khān** Punjab, E Pakistan 33°19′N 73°23′E
Gujerat see Gujarāt
149 V7 **Gujrānwāla** Punjab, NE Pakistan 32°11′N 74°09′E
149 V7 **Gujrāt** Punjab, E Pakistan 32°34′N 74°04′E
146 B8 **Gulandag** Rus. Gory Kulandag. ▲▲ Balkan Welaýaty, W Turkmenistan
159 U9 **Gulang** Gansu, C China 37°31′N 102°55′E
183 R6 **Gulargambone** New South Wales, SE Australia 31°19′S 148°31′E
155 G15 **Gulbarga** Karnātaka, C India 17°22′N 76°47′E
118 J8 **Gulbene** Ger. Alt-Schwanenburg. Gulbene, NE Latvia 57°10′N 26°44′E
147 U10 **Gul'cha** Kir. Gülchö. Oshskaya Oblast', SW Kyrgyzstan 40°16′N 73°27′E
Gülchö see Gul'cha
173 T10 **Gulden Draak Seamount** undersea feature E Indian Ocean 33°45′S 101°00′E
136 J16 **Gülek Boğazı** var. Cilician Gates. pass S Turkey
186 D8 **Gulf** ◈ province S Papua New Guinea
23 O9 **Gulf Breeze** Florida, SE USA 30°21′N 87°09′W
Gulf of Liaotung see Liaodong Wan
23 V13 **Gulfport** Florida, SE USA 27°45′N 82°42′W
22 M9 **Gulfport** Mississippi, S USA 30°22′N 89°06′W
23 O9 **Gulf Shores** Alabama, S USA 30°15′N 87°40′W
141 T5 **Gulf, The** var. Persian Gulf, Ar. Khalīj al 'Arabī, Per. Khalīj-e Fars. gulf SW Asia see also Persian Gulf
183 R7 **Gulgong** New South Wales, SE Australia 32°22′S 149°31′E
160 I11 **Gulin** Sichuan, C China 28°06′N 105°47′E
171 U14 **Gulir** Pulau Kasiui, E Indonesia 04°27′S 131°41′E
Gulistan see Guliston
147 P10 **Guliston** Rus. Gulistan. Sirdaryo Viloyati, E Uzbekistan 40°29′N 68°46′E
163 T6 **Guliya Shan** ▲ NE China 49°42′N 122°22′E
Gulja see Yining
39 S11 **Gulkana** Alaska, USA 62°17′N 145°25′W
11 S17 **Gull Lake** Saskatchewan, S Canada 50°05′N 108°30′W
31 P10 **Gull Lake** ◎ Michigan, N USA
29 T6 **Gull Lake** ◎ Minnesota, N USA
95 L16 **Gullspång** Västra Götaland, S Sweden 58°58′N 14°04′E
136 B15 **Güllük Körfezi** prev. Akbük Limanı. bay W Turkey
152 H5 **Gulmarg** Jammu and Kashmir, NW India 34°04′N 74°25′E
Gulpaigan see Golpāyegān
99 L18 **Gulpen** Limburg, SE Netherlands 50°48′N 05°53′E
Gul'shad see Gul'shat
145 S13 **Gul'shat** var. Gul'shad. Karaganda, E Kazakhstan 46°37′N 74°22′E
81 F17 **Gulu** N Uganda 02°46′N 32°21′E
114 K10 **Gŭlŭbovo** Stara Zagora, C Bulgaria 42°08′N 25°51′E
114 I7 **Gulyantsi** Pleven, N Bulgaria 43°37′N 24°40′E
Gulyaypole see Hulyaypole
Guma see Pishan
Gümai see Darlag
79 K16 **Gumba** Equateur, NW Dem. Rep. Congo 02°58′N 21°23′E
Gumbinnen see Gusev
81 H24 **Gumbiro** Ruvuma, S Tanzania 10°19′S 35°40′E
146 B11 **Gumdag** prev. Kum-Dag. Balkan Welaýaty, W Turkmenistan 39°13′N 54°35′E
77 W12 **Gumel** Jigawa, N Nigeria 12°37′N 09°23′E
105 N5 **Gumiel de Hizán** Castilla-León, N Spain 41°46′N 03°42′W
153 P16 **Gumla** Jhārkhand, N India 23°03′N 84°36′E
Gumma see Gunma
101 F16 **Gummersbach** Nordrhein-Westfalen, W Germany 51°01′N 07°34′E
77 T13 **Gummi** Zamfara, NW Nigeria 12°07′N 05°07′E
Gumpolds see Humpolec
Gumti see Gomati
Gümülcine/Gümüljina see Komotiní
Gümüşane see Gümüşhane
137 O12 **Gümüşhane** var. Gümüşane, Gumushkhane. Gümüşhane, NE Turkey 40°31′N 39°27′E
137 O12 **Gümüşhane** var. Gümüşane, Gumushkhane. ◈ province NE Turkey
Gumushkhane see Gümüşhane
171 V14 **Gumzai** Pulau Kola, E Indonesia 05°27′S 134°38′E
154 H9 **Guna** Madhya Pradesh, C India 24°39′N 77°18′E
Gunabad see Gonābād
Gunan see Qijiang
Gunbad-i-Qawus see Gonbad-e Kāvūs
183 O9 **Gunbar** New South Wales, SE Australia 34°03′S 145°32′E
183 O9 **Gun Creek** seasonal river New South Wales, SE Australia
183 Q10 **Gundagai** New South Wales, SE Australia 35°06′S 148°03′E
79 K17 **Gundji** Equateur, N Dem. Rep. Congo 02°03′N 21°31′E
155 G20 **Gundlupet** Karnātaka, W India 11°48′N 76°42′E
136 G16 **Gündoğmuş** Antalya, S Turkey 36°50′N 32°07′E
137 O14 **Güney Doğu Toroslar** ▲▲ SE Turkey
79 J21 **Gungu** Bandundu, SW Dem. Rep. Congo 05°43′S 19°20′E
127 P17 **Gunib** Respublika Dagestan, SW Russian Federation 42°24′N 46°55′E
112 J11 **Gunja** Vukovar-Srijem, E Croatia 44°53′N 18°51′E
31 P9 **Gun Lake** ◎ Michigan, N USA
165 N12 **Gunma** off. Gunma-ken, var. Gumma. ◈ prefecture Honshū, S Japan
Gunma-ken see Gunma
197 P15 **Gunnbjørn Fjeld** var. Gunnbjörns Bjerge. ▲ C Greenland 69°03′N 29°36′W
Gunnbjörns Bjerge see Gunnbjørn Fjeld
183 S6 **Gunnedah** New South Wales, SE Australia 30°59′S 150°15′E
173 Y15 **Gunner's Quoin** var. Coin de Mire. island N Mauritius
37 R6 **Gunnison** Colorado, C USA 38°33′N 106°55′W
36 L5 **Gunnison** Utah, W USA 39°09′N 111°49′W
37 P5 **Gunnison River** ≈ Colorado, C USA
21 X2 **Gunpowder River** ≈ Maryland, NE USA
Güns see Kőszeg
Gunsan see Kunsan
109 S4 **Gunskirchen** Oberösterreich, N Austria 48°07′N 13°54′E
Gunt see Ghund
155 H17 **Guntakal** Andhra Pradesh, C India 15°11′N 77°24′E
23 Q2 **Guntersville** Alabama, S USA 34°21′N 86°17′W
23 Q2 **Guntersville Lake** ▣ Alabama, S USA
109 X4 **Guntramsdorf** Niederösterreich, E Austria 48°03′N 16°19′E
155 J16 **Guntūr** var. Guntur. Andhra Pradesh, SE India 16°20′N 80°27′E
168 H10 **Gunungsitoli** Pulau Nias, W Indonesia 01°11′N 97°35′E
155 M14 **Gunupur** Orissa, E India 19°04′N 83°52′E
101 J23 **Günz** ≈ S Germany
Gunzan see Kunsan
101 J22 **Günzburg** Bayern, S Germany 48°26′N 10°18′E
101 K21 **Gunzenhausen** Bayern, S Germany 49°07′N 10°45′E
Guovdageaidnu see Kautokeino
161 P7 **Guoyang** Anhui, E China 33°30′N 116°12′E
116 G11 **Gurahonţ** Hung. Honctő. Arad, W Romania 46°16′N 22°21′E
Gurahumora see Gura Humorului
116 K9 **Gura Humorului** Ger. Gurahumora. Suceava, NE Romania 47°31′N 26°00′E
146 H8 **Gurbansoltan Eje** prev. Ýylanly, Rus. Il'yaly. Daşoguz Welaýaty, N Turkmenistan 41°57′N 59°42′E
158 K4 **Gurbantünggüt Shamo** desert W China
152 H7 **Gurdāspur** Punjab, N India 32°04′N 75°28′E
27 T13 **Gurdon** Arkansas, C USA 33°55′N 93°09′W
Gurdzhaani see Gurjaani
Gurgan see Gorgān
152 I10 **Gurgaon** Haryāna, N India 28°27′N 77°01′E
59 M15 **Gurguéia, Rio** ≈ NE Brazil
55 Q7 **Guri, Embalse de** ▣ E Venezuela
137 V10 **Gurjaani** Rus. Gurdzhaani. E Georgia 41°42′N 45°47′E
109 T8 **Gurk** Kärnten, S Austria 46°52′N 14°17′E
109 T9 **Gurk** Slvn. Krka. ≈ S Austria
Gurkfeld see Krško
114 K9 **Gurkovo** prev. Kolupchii. Stara Zagora, C Bulgaria 42°42′N 25°46′E
109 S9 **Gurktaler Alpen** ▲▲ S Austria
146 H8 **Gurlan** Rus. Gurlen. Xorazm Viloyati, W Uzbekistan 41°54′N 60°18′E
Gurlen see Gurlan
83 M16 **Guro** Manica, C Mozambique 17°28′S 33°18′E
136 M14 **Gürün** Sivas, C Turkey 38°44′N 37°15′E
59 K16 **Gurupi** Tocantins, C Brazil 11°44′S 49°01′W
58 L12 **Gurupi, Rio** ≈ NE Brazil
152 E14 **Guru Sikhar** ▲ NW India 24°45′N 72°51′E
162 H8 **Gurvanbulag** var. Höviyn Am. Bayanhongor, C Mongolia 47°08′N 98°41′E
162 K7 **Gurvanbulag** var. Avdzaga. Bulgan, C Mongolia 47°43′N 103°30′E
162 I11 **Gurvantes** var. Urt. Ömnögovĭ, S Mongolia 43°16′N 101°00′E
Gur'yev/Gur'yevskaya Oblast' see Atyrau
77 U13 **Gusau** Zamfara, NW Nigeria 12°18′N 06°27′E
126 C3 **Gusev** Ger. Gumbinnen. Kaliningradskaya Oblast', W Russian Federation 54°36′N 22°14′E
146 J17 **Gushgy** Rus. Kushka. ≈ Mary Welaýaty, S Turkmenistan
Gushiago see Gushiegu
77 Q14 **Gushiegu** var. Gushiago. NE Ghana 09°54′N 00°12′W
165 S17 **Gushikawa** Okinawa, Okinawa, SW Japan 26°21′N 127°50′E
113 L16 **Gusinje** E Montenegro 42°34′N 19°51′E
126 M4 **Gus'-Khrustal'nyy** Vladimirskaya Oblast', W Russian Federation 55°39′N 40°42′E
107 B19 **Guspini** Sardegna, Italy, C Mediterranean Sea 39°33′N 08°39′E
109 X8 **Güssing** Burgenland, SE Austria 47°03′N 16°19′E
109 V6 **Gusswerk** Steiermark, E Austria 47°43′N 15°18′E
92 O2 **Gustav Adolf Land** physical region NE Svalbard
195 X5 **Gustav Bull Mountains** ▲▲ Antarctica
39 W13 **Gustavus** Alaska, USA 58°24′N 135°44′W
92 O1 **Gustav V Land** physical region NE Svalbard
35 P9 **Gustine** California, W USA 37°14′N 121°00′W
25 R8 **Gustine** Texas, SW USA 31°51′N 98°24′W
100 M9 **Güstrow** Mecklenburg-Vorpommern, NE Germany 53°48′N 12°12′E
95 N18 **Gusum** Östergötland, S Sweden 58°15′N 16°30′E
Guta/Gúta see Kolárovo
Gutenstein see Ravne na Koroškem
101 G14 **Gütersloh** Nordrhein-Westfalen, W Germany 51°54′N 08°23′E
27 N10 **Guthrie** Oklahoma, C USA 35°53′N 97°25′W
25 P5 **Guthrie** Texas, SW USA 33°38′N 100°21′W
29 U14 **Guthrie Center** Iowa, C USA 41°40′N 94°30′W
41 Q13 **Gutiérrez Zamora** Veracruz-Llave, E Mexico 20°29′N 97°07′W
Gutta see Kolárovo
29 Y12 **Guttenberg** Iowa, C USA 42°47′N 91°06′W
Guttentag see Dobrodzień
Guttstadt see Dobre Miasto
162 G8 **Guulin** Govĭ-Altay, C Mongolia 46°33′N 97°21′E
153 V12 **Guwāhāti** prev. Gauhāti. Assam, NE India 26°09′N 91°42′E
139 R3 **Guwēr** var. Al Kuwayr, Al Quwayr, Quwair. Arbīl, N Iraq 36°03′N 43°30′E
146 A10 **Guwlumaýak** Rus. Kuuli-Mayak. Balkan Welaýaty, NW Turkmenistan 40°14′N 52°43′E
55 R9 **Guyana** off. Co-operative Republic of Guyana; prev. British Guiana. ◆ republic N South America
Guyana, Co-operative Republic of see Guyana
21 P5 **Guyandotte River** ≈ West Virginia, NE USA
Guyane see French Guiana
Guyi see Sanjiang
26 H8 **Guymon** Oklahoma, C USA 36°42′N 101°30′W
146 K12 **Guynuk** Lebap Welaýaty, NE Turkmenistan 39°18′N 63°00′E
Guyong see Jiangle
21 O9 **Guyot, Mount** ▲ North Carolina/Tennessee, SE USA 35°42′N 83°15′W
183 U5 **Guyra** New South Wales, SE Australia 30°13′S 151°42′E
159 W10 **Guyuan** Ningxia, N China 35°57′N 106°13′E
Guzar see G'uzor
121 P2 **Güzelyurt** Gk. Kólpos Mórfu, Morphou. W Cyprus 35°12′N 33°E
121 N2 **Güzelyurt Körfezi** var. Morfou Bay, Morphou Bay, Gk. Kólpos Mórfou. bay W Cyprus
Guzhou see Rongjiang
40 I3 **Guzmán** Chihuahua, N Mexico 31°13′N 107°27′W
147 N13 **G'uzor** Rus. Guzar. Qashqadaryo Viloyati, S Uzbekistan 38°41′N 66°12′E
119 B14 **Gvardeysk** Ger. Tapaiu. Kaliningradskaya Oblast', W Russian Federation 54°39′N 21°02′E
Gvardeyskoye see Hvardiys'ke
183 R5 **Gwabegar** New South Wales, SE Australia 30°34′S 148°58′E
148 J16 **Gwādar** var. Gwadur. Baluchistān, SW Pakistan 25°09′N 62°21′E
148 J16 **Gwādar East Bay** bay SW Pakistan
148 J16 **Gwādar West Bay** bay SW Pakistan
Gwadur see Gwādar
83 J17 **Gwai** Matabeleland North, W Zimbabwe 19°17′S 27°37′E
154 I7 **Gwalior** Madhya Pradesh, C India 26°16′N 78°12′E
83 J18 **Gwanda** Matabeleland South, SW Zimbabwe 20°56′S 29°E
79 N15 **Gwane** Orientale, N Dem. Rep. Congo 04°40′N 25°51′E
83 I17 **Gwayi** ≈ W Zimbabwe
110 G8 **Gwda** var. Głda, Ger. Küddow. ≈ NW Poland
97 C14 **Gweebarra Bay** Ir. Béal an Bheara. inlet W Ireland
97 D14 **Gweedore** Ir. Gaoth Dobhair. Donegal, NW Ireland 55°03′N 08°14′W
Gwelo see Gweru
97 K21 **Gwent** cultural region S Wales, United Kingdom
83 K17 **Gweru** prev. Gwelo. Midlands, C Zimbabwe 19°27′S 29°49′E
29 Q7 **Gwinner** North Dakota, N USA 46°10′N 97°42′W
77 Y13 **Gwoza** Borno, NE Nigeria 11°07′N 13°40′E
Gwy see Wye
183 R4 **Gwydir River** ≈ New South Wales, SE Australia
97 I19 **Gwynedd** var. Gwyneth. cultural region NW Wales, United Kingdom
Gwyneth see Gwynedd
159 O16 **Gyaca** var. Ngarrab. Xizang Zizhiqu, W China 29°06′N 92°37′E
Gya'gya see Saga
Gyaijêpozhanggê see Zhidoi
Gyaisi see Jiulong
115 M22 **Gyalí** var. Yialí. island Dodekánisa, Greece, Aegean Sea
Gyamotang see Dêngqên
Gyandzha see Gäncä
Gyangkar see Dinggyê
158 M16 **Gyangzê** Xizang Zizhiqu, W China 28°50′N 89°38′E
158 L14 **Gyaring Co** ◎ W China
159 Q12 **Gyaring Hu** ◎ C China
115 I20 **Gyáros** var. Yioúra. island Kykládes, Greece, Aegean Sea
122 J7 **Gyda** Yamalo-Nenetskiy Avtonomnyy Okrug, N Russian Federation 70°55′N 78°34′E
122 J7 **Gydanskiy Poluostrov** Eng. Gyda Peninsula. peninsula N Russian Federation
Gyda Peninsula see Gydanskiy Poluostrov
Gyêgu see Yushu
Gyéres see Câmpia Turzii
Gyergyószentmiklós see Gheorgheni
Gyergyótölgyes see Tulgheş
Gyertyámos see Cărpiniş
Gyeva see Detva
Gyigang see Zayü
158 J16 **Gyirong** Xizang Zizhiqu, W China 28°55′N 85°16′E
Gyixong see Gonggar
95 I23 **Gyldenløveshøy** hill range C Denmark
181 Z10 **Gympie** Queensland, E Australia 26°05′S 152°40′E
166 L7 **Gyobingauk** Bago, SW Burma (Myanmar) 18°14′N 95°39′E
111 M23 **Gyomaendrőd** Békés, SE Hungary 46°56′N 20°50′E
Gyömbér see Ďumbier
111 L22 **Gyöngyös** Heves, NE Hungary 47°44′N 19°49′E
111 H22 **Győr** Ger. Raab, Lat. Arrabona. Győr-Moson-Sopron, NW Hungary 47°41′N 17°40′E
111 G22 **Győr-Moson-Sopron** off. Győr-Moson-Sopron Megye. ◈ county NW Hungary
Győr-Moson-Sopron Megye see Győr-Moson-Sopron
11 X15 **Gypsumville** Manitoba, S Canada 51°47′N 98°38′W
12 M4 **Gyrfalcon Islands** island group Northwest Territories, NE Canada
95 N14 **Gysinge** Gävleborg, C Sweden 60°16′N 16°55′E
115 F22 **Gýtheio** var. Githio; prev. Yíthion. Pelopónnisos, S Greece 36°46′N 22°34′E
146 L13 **Gyuichbirleshik** Lebap Welaýaty, E Turkmenistan 38°10′N 64°33′E
111 N24 **Gyula** Rom. Jula. Békés, SE Hungary 46°39′N 21°17′E
Gyulafehérvár see Alba Iulia
Gyulovo see Roza
137 T11 **Gyumri** var. Giumri, Rus. Kumayri; prev. Aleksandropol', Leninakan. W Armenia 40°48′N 43°51′E
146 D13 **Gyunuzyndag, Gora** ▲ Balkan Welaýaty, W Turkmenistan 38°15′N 56°25′E
146 J15 **Gyzylbaydak** Rus. Krasnoye Znamya. Mary Welaýaty, S Turkmenistan 36°51′N 62°24′E
Gyzyletrek see Etrek
146 D10 **Gyzylgaýa** Rus. Kizyl-Kaya. Balkan Welaýaty, NW Turkmenistan 40°37′N 55°15′E
146 A10 **Gyzylsuw** Rus. Kizyl-Su. Balkan Welaýaty, W Turkmenistan 39°49′N 53°00′E
Gyzyrlabat see Serdar
Gzhatsk see Gagarin

H

153 T12 **Ha** W Bhutan 27°17′N 89°22′E
Haabai see Ha'apai Group
99 H17 **Haacht** Vlaams Brabant, C Belgium 50°58′N 04°38′E
109 T4 **Haag** Niederösterreich, NE Austria 48°07′N 14°32′E
194 L8 **Haag Nunataks** ▲ Antarctica
92 N2 **Haakon VII Land** physical region NW Svalbard
98 O11 **Haaksbergen** Overijssel, E Netherlands 52°09′N 06°45′E
99 E14 **Haamstede** Zeeland, SW Netherlands 51°43′N 03°45′E
193 Y15 **Ha'ano** island Ha'apai Group, C Tonga
193 Y15 **Ha'apai Group** var. Haabai. island group C Tonga
93 L15 **Haapajärvi** Oulu, C Finland 63°45′N 25°20′E
93 L17 **Haapamäki** Länsi-Suomi, C Finland 62°11′N 24°32′E
93 L15 **Haapavesi** Oulu, C Finland 64°09′N 25°25′E
191 N7 **Haapiti** Moorea, W French Polynesia 17°33′S 149°52′W
118 F4 **Haapsalu** Ger. Hapsal. Läänemaa, W Estonia 58°58′N 23°32′E
Ha'Arava see 'Arabah, Wādī al
95 G24 **Haarby** var. Hårby. Fyn, C Denmark 55°13′N 10°07′E
98 H10 **Haarlem** prev. Harlem. Noord-Holland, W Netherlands 52°23′N 04°39′E
185 D19 **Haast** West Coast, South Island, New Zealand 43°53′S 169°02′E
185 C20 **Haast** ≈ South Island, New Zealand
185 D20 **Haast Pass** pass South Island, New Zealand
193 W16 **Ha'atua** 'Eau, E Tonga
149 P15 **Hab** ≈ SW Pakistan
141 W7 **Haba** var. Al Haba. Dubayy, NE United Arab Emirates 25°01′N 55°37′E
158 K2 **Habahe** var. Kaba. Xinjiang Uygur Zizhiqu, NW China 48°04′N 86°20′E
141 U13 **Ḩabarūt** var. Habrut. SW Oman 17°19′N 52°45′E
81 J18 **Habaswein** North Eastern, NE Kenya 01°01′N 39°27′E
99 L24 **Habay-la-Neuve** Luxembourg, SE Belgium 49°43′N 05°38′E
139 S8 **Ḩabbānīyah, Buḩayrat** ◎ C Iraq
Habelschwerdt see Bystrzyca Kłodzka
153 V14 **Habiganj** Sylhet, NE Bangladesh 24°23′N 91°25′E
163 Q12 **Habirag** Nei Mongol Zizhiqu, N China 42°18′N 115°40′E
95 L19 **Habo** Västra Götaland, S Sweden 57°55′N 14°05′E
123 V14 **Habomai Islands** island group Kuril'skiye Ostrova, SE Russian Federation
165 S2 **Haboro** Hokkaidō, NE Japan 44°19′N 141°42′E
153 S16 **Habra** West Bengal, NE India 22°39′N 88°17′E
Habrut see Ḩabarūt
143 P17 **Ḩabshān** Abū Ẓaby, C United Arab Emirates 23°51′N 53°34′E
54 E14 **Hacha** Putumayo, S Colombia 0°02′S 75°30′W
165 X13 **Hachijō** Tōkyō, Hachijō-jima, SE Japan 35°40′N 139°20′E
165 X13 **Hachijō-jima** island Izu-shotō, SE Japan
164 L12 **Hachiman** Gifu, Honshū, SW Japan 35°46′N 136°57′E
165 P7 **Hachimori** Akita, Honshū, C Japan 40°22′N 139°59′E
165 R7 **Hachinohe** Aomori, Honshū, C Japan 40°30′N 141°29′E
93 G17 **Hackås** Jämtland, C Sweden 62°55′N 14°31′E
18 K14 **Hackensack** New Jersey, NE USA 40°51′N 73°57′W
75 U12 **Hadabat al Jilf al Kabīr** var. Gilf Kebir Plateau. plateau SW Egypt
Hadama see Nazrēt
141 W13 **Ḩadbaram** S Oman 17°27′N 55°13′E
139 U13 **Ḩaddānīyah** well S Iraq
96 K12 **Haddington** SE Scotland, United Kingdom 55°59′N 02°46′W
141 Z8 **Ḩadd, Ra's al** headland NE Oman 22°28′N 59°58′E
Haded see Xadeed
77 W12 **Hadejia** Jigawa, N Nigeria 12°22′N 10°02′E
77 W12 **Hadejia** ≈ N Nigeria
138 F9 **Hadera** var. Khadera; prev. Ḩadera. Haifa, C Israel 32°26′N 34°55′E
Ḩadera see Hadera
Hadersleben see Haderslev
95 G24 **Haderslev** Ger. Hadersleben. Sønderjylland, SW Denmark 55°15′N 09°30′E
151 J21 **Hadhdhunmathi Atoll** atoll S Maldives
141 W17 **Ḩadīboh** Suquṭrā, SE Yemen 12°38′N 54°05′E
158 K9 **Hadilik** Xinjiang Uygur Zizhiqu, W China 37°51′N 86°10′E
136 H16 **Hadım** Konya, S Turkey 36°58′N 32°27′E
140 K7 **Hadīyah** Al Madīnah, W Saudi Arabia 25°36′N 38°31′E
8 L5 **Hadley Bay** bay Victoria Island, Nunavut, N Canada
167 S6 **Ha Đông** var. Hadong. Ha Tây, N Vietnam 20°58′N 105°46′E
Hadong see Ha Đông
Hadramaut see Ḩaḑramawt
141 R15 **Ḩaḑramawt** Eng. Hadramaut. ▲▲ S Yemen
Hadria see Adria
Hadrianopolis see Edirne
Hadria Picena see Apricena
95 G22 **Hadsten** Århus, C Denmark 56°19′N 10°03′E
95 G21 **Hadsund** Nordjylland, N Denmark 56°43′N 10°08′E
117 S4 **Hadyach** Rus. Gadyach. Poltavs'ka Oblast', NE Ukraine 50°21′N 34°00′E
112 I13 **Hadžići** Federacija Bosna I Hercegovina, SE Bosnia and Herzegovina 43°49′N 18°12′E
163 W14 **Haeju** S North Korea 38°04′N 125°40′E
Haerbin/Haerhpin/Ha-erh-pin see Harbin
141 P5 **Ḩafar al Bāṭin** Ash Sharqīyah, N Saudi Arabia 28°25′N 45°59′E
11 T15 **Hafford** Saskatchewan, S Canada 52°43′N 107°19′W
136 M13 **Hafik** Sivas, N Turkey 39°53′N 37°24′E
149 V8 **Ḩāfizābād** Punjab, E Pakistan 32°03′N 73°42′E
153 W13 **Hāflong** Assam, NE India 25°10′N 93°01′E
92 H4 **Hafnarfjördhur** Reykjanes, W Iceland 64°03′N 21°57′W
Hafnia see Denmark
Hafnia see København

◆ Country ● Country Capital ◇ Dependent Territory ○ Dependent Territory Capital ◈ Administrative Regions ✈ International Airport ▲ Mountain ▲▲ Mountain Range ⛰ Volcano ≈ River ◎ Lake ▣ Reservoir

Hafren see Severn
Hafun see Xaafuun
Hafun, Ras see Xaafuun, Raas
80 G10 **Hag 'Abdullah** Sinnar, E Sudan 13°59′N 33°35′E
81 K18 **Hagadera** North Eastern, E Kenya 0°06′N 40°23′E
138 G8 **HaGalil** Eng. Galilee. ▲▲ N Israel
14 G10 **Hagar** Ontario, S Canada 46°27′N 80°22′W
155 G18 **Hagari** var. Vedāvati. ≈ W India
188 B16 **Hagåtña** , var. Agaña. ○ (Guam) NW Guam 13°27′N 144°45′E
100 M13 **Hagelberg** hill NE Germany
39 N14 **Hagemeister Island** island Alaska, USA
101 F15 **Hagen** Nordrhein-Westfalen, W Germany 51°22′N 07°27′E
100 K10 **Hagenow** Mecklenburg-Vorpommern, N Germany 53°27′N 11°10′E
10 K15 **Hagensborg** British Columbia, SW Canada 52°24′N 126°24′W
80 I13 **Hāgere Hiywet** var. Agere Hiywet, Ambo. Oromīya, C Ethiopia 09°00′N 37°55′E
33 O15 **Hagerman** Idaho, NW USA 42°48′N 114°53′W
37 U14 **Hagerman** New Mexico, SW USA 33°07′N 104°19′W
21 V2 **Hagerstown** Maryland, NE USA 39°39′N 77°44′W
14 G16 **Hagersville** Ontario, S Canada 42°58′N 80°03′W
102 J15 **Hagetmau** Landes, SW France 43°40′N 00°36′W
95 K14 **Hagfors** Värmland, C Sweden 60°03′N 13°45′E
93 G16 **Häggenås** Jämtland, C Sweden 63°24′N 14°53′E
164 E12 **Hagi** Yamaguchi, Honshū, SW Japan 34°25′N 131°22′E
167 S5 **Ha Giang** Ha Giang, N Vietnam 22°50′N 104°58′E
Hagios Evstrátios see Ágios Efstrátios
HaGolan see Golan Heights
103 T4 **Hagondange** Moselle, NE France 49°16′N 06°06′E
97 B18 **Hag's Head** Ir. Ceann Caillí. headland W Ireland 52°56′N 09°29′W
102 I3 **Hague, Cap de la** headland N France 49°43′N 01°56′W
103 V5 **Haguenau** Bas-Rhin, NE France 48°49′N 07°47′E
165 X16 **Hahajima-rettō** island group SE Japan
15 R8 **Há Há , Lac** ◎ Québec, SE Canada
172 H13 **Hahaya** ✈ (Moroni) Grande Comore, NW Comoros
22 K9 **Hahnville** Louisiana, S USA 29°58′N 90°24′W
83 E22 **Haib** Karas, S Namibia 28°12′S 18°19′E
Haibak see Āybak
149 N15 **Haibo** ≈ SW Pakistan
Haibowan see Wuhai
163 U12 **Haicheng** Liaoning, NE China 40°53′N 122°45′E
Haicheng see Haifeng
Haicheng see Haiyuan
Haida see Nový Bor
Haidarabad see Hyderābād
Haidenschaft see Ajdovščina
167 T6 **Hai Dương** Hai Hưng, N Vietnam 20°56′N 106°21′E
138 F9 **Haifa** ◐ district NW Israel
Haifa see Hefa
Haifa, Bay of see Mifrats Hefa
161 P14 **Haifeng** var. Haicheng. Guangdong, S China 22°56′N 115°19′E
Haifong see Hai Phong
161 P3 **Hai He** ≈ E China
Haikang see Leizhou
160 L17 **Haikou** var. Hai-k'ou, Hoihow, Fr. Hoï-Hao. province capital Hainan, S China 20°N 110°17′E
Hai-k'ou see Haikou
140 M6 **Ḩā'il** Ḩā'il, NW Saudi Arabia 27°N 42°50′E
141 N5 **Ḩā'il** off. Minţaqah Ḩā'il. ◐ province N Saudi Arabia
163 S6 **Hailar He** ≈ NE China
33 P14 **Hailey** Idaho, NW USA 43°31′N 114°18′W
14 H9 **Haileybury** Ontario, S Canada 47°27′N 79°39′W
163 X9 **Hailin** Heilongjiang, NE China 44°37′N 129°24′E
Ḩā'il, Minţaqah see Ḩā'il
Hailong see Meihekou
93 K14 **Hailuoto** Swe. Karlö. island W Finland
Haima see Haymā'
Haimen see Taizhou
160 M17 **Hainan** var. Hainan Sheng, Qiong. ◐ province S China
160 K17 **Hainan Dao** island S China
Hainan Sheng see Hainan
Hainan Strait see Qiongzhou Haixia
Hainasch see Ainaži
Hainau see Chojnów
99 E20 **Hainaut** ◐ province SW Belgium
Hainburg see Hainburg an der Donau
109 Z4 **Hainburg an der Donau** var. Hainburg. Niederösterreich, NE Austria 48°09′N 16°57′E
39 W12 **Haines** Alaska, USA 59°13′N 135°27′W
32 L12 **Haines** Oregon, NW USA 44°53′N 117°56′W
23 W12 **Haines City** Florida, SE USA 28°06′N 81°37′W
10 H8 **Haines Junction** Yukon Territory, W Canada 60°45′N 137°30′W
109 W4 **Hainfeld** Niederösterreich, NE Austria 48°03′N 15°47′E
101 N16 **Hainichen** Sachsen, E Germany 50°58′N 13°08′E
Hai Ninh see Mong Cai
167 T6 **Hai Phong** var. Haifong, Haiphong. N Vietnam 20°50′N 106°41′E
Haiphong see Hai Phong
161 S12 **Haitan Dao** island SE China
44 K8 **Haiti** off. Republic of Haiti. ◆ republic C West Indies
Haiti, Republic of see Haiti
35 T11 **Haiwee Reservoir** ⊠ California, W USA
80 I7 **Haiya** Red Sea, NE Sudan 18°17′N 36°21′E
159 T10 **Haiyan** var. Sanjiaocheng. Qinghai, W China 36°55′N 100°54′E
160 M13 **Haiyang Shan** ▲▲ S China
159 V10 **Haiyuan** Ningxia, N China 36°32′N 105°31′E
Hajda see Nový Bor
111 M22 **Hajdú-Bihar** off. Hajdú-Bihar Megye. ◐ county E Hungary
Hajdú-Bihar Megye see Hajdú-Bihar
111 N22 **Hajdúböszörmény** Hajdú-Bihar, E Hungary 47°39′N 21°32′E
111 N22 **Hajdúhadház** Hajdú-Bihar, E Hungary 47°40′N 21°40′E
111 N21 **Hajdúnánás** Hajdú-Bihar, E Hungary 47°50′N 21°26′E
111 N22 **Hajdúszoboszló** Hajdú-Bihar, E Hungary 47°27′N 21°24′E
142 I3 **Ḩājī Ebrāhīm, Kūh-e** ▲ Iran/Iraq 36°53′N 44°56′E
165 O9 **Hajiki-zaki** headland Sado, C Japan 38°19′N 138°28′E
Hajîne see Abū Ḩardān
153 P13 **Hājīpur** Bihār, N India 25°41′N 85°13′E
141 N14 **Ḩajjah** W Yemen 15°43′N 43°33′E
139 U11 **Hajjama** Al Muthanná, S Iraq 31°24′N 45°20′E
143 Q13 **Ḩājjīābād** Fārs, S Iran 28°21′N 54°27′E
143 R12 **Ḩājjīābād** Hormozgān, C Iran
139 U14 **Ḩājj, Thaqb al** well S Iraq
113 L16 **Hajla** ▲▲ E Montenegro
110 P10 **Hajnówka** Ger. Hermhausen. Podlaskie, NE Poland 52°45′N 23°32′E
Haka see Hakha
Hakapehi see Punaauia
Hakâri see Hakkâri
138 F12 **HaKatan, HaMakhtesh** prev. HaMakhtesh HaQatan. ▲▲ S Israel
166 K4 **Hakha** var. Haka. Chin State, W Burma (Myanmar) 22°42′N 93°41′E
137 T16 **Hakkâri** var. Çölemerik, Hakâri. Hakkâri, SE Turkey 37°36′N 43°45′E
137 T16 **Hakkâri** var. Hakkari. ◐ province SE Turkey
Hakkari see Hakkâri
92 J12 **Hakkas** Norrbotten, N Sweden 66°53′N 21°36′E
164 J14 **Hakken-zan** ▲ Honshū, SW Japan 34°11′N 135°57′E
165 R7 **Hakkōda-san** ▲ Honshū, C Japan 40°40′N 140°49′E
165 T2 **Hako-dake** ▲ Hokkaidō, NE Japan 44°40′N 142°22′E
165 R5 **Hakodate** Hokkaidō, NE Japan 41°46′N 140°43′E
164 L11 **Hakui** Ishikawa, Honshū, SW Japan 36°55′N 136°46′E
190 B16 **Hakupu** SE Niue 19°06′S 169°50′E
164 L12 **Haku-san** ▲ Honshū, SW Japan 36°07′N 136°45′E
Hakusan see Mattō
Hal see Halle
149 Q15 **Hāla** Sind, SE Pakistan 25°47′N 68°28′E
138 J3 **Ḩalab** Eng. Aleppo, Fr. Alep; anc. Beroea. Ḩalab, NW Syria 36°14′N 37°10′E
138 J3 **Ḩalab** off. Muḩāfaz̧at Ḩalab, var. Aleppo, Halab. ◐ governorate NW Syria
138 J3 **Ḩalab** ✈ Ḩalab, NW Syria 36°12′N 37°10′E
Halab see Ḩalab
141 O8 **Ḩalabān** var. Halibān. Ar Riyāḑ, C Saudi Arabia 23°29′N 44°20′E
139 V4 **Ḩalabja** As Sulaymānīyah, NE Iraq 35°11′N 45°59′E
Ḩalab, Muḩāfaz̧at see Ḩalab
146 L13 **Halaç** Rus. Khalach. Lebap Welaýaty, E Turkmenistan 38°05′N 64°46′E
190 A16 **Halagigie Point** headland W Niue
75 Z11 **Halaib** SE Egypt 22°10′N 36°33′E
190 G12 **Halalo** Île Uvea, N Wallis and Futuna 13°21′S 176°11′W
Halandri see Chalándri
141 X13 **Ḩalānīyāt, Juzur al** var. Jazā'ir Bin Ghalfān, Eng. Kuria Muria Islands. island group S Oman
141 W13 **Ḩalānīyāt, Khalīj al** Eng. Kuria Muria Bay. bay S Oman
Halas see Kiskunhalas
38 G11 **Hālawa** var. Halawa. Hawaii, USA, C Pacific Ocean 20°13′N 155°46′W
Halawa see Hālawa
38 F9 **Hālawa, Cape** var. Cape Halawa. headland Moloka'i, Hawai'i, USA 21°09′N 156°43′W
Cape Halawa see Hālawa, Cape
Halban see Tsetserleg
101 K14 **Halberstadt** Sachsen-Anhalt, C Germany 51°54′N 11°04′E
184 M12 **Halcombe** Manawatu-Wanganui, North Island, New Zealand 40°09′S 175°30′E
95 I16 **Halden** prev. Fredrikshald. Østfold, S Norway 59°08′N 11°20′E
100 L13 **Haldensleben** Sachsen-Anhalt, C Germany 52°18′N 11°25′E
Háldi see Halti
153 S17 **Haldia** West Bengal, NE India 22°04′N 88°02′E
152 K10 **Haldwāni** Uttarakhand, N India 29°13′N 79°31′E
163 P9 **Haldzan** Sühbaatar, E Mongolia 46°10′N 112°57′E
163 P9 **Haldzan** var. Hatavch. Sühbaatar, E Mongolia 46°10′N 112°57′E
38 F10 **Haleakalā** var. Haleakala. crater Maui, Hawai'i, USA
Haleakala see Haleakalā
25 N4 **Hale Center** Texas, SW USA 34°03′N 101°50′W
99 J18 **Halen** Limburg, NE Belgium 50°35′N 05°08′E
23 O2 **Haleyville** Alabama, S USA 34°13′N 87°37′W
77 O17 **Half Assini** SW Ghana 05°03′N 02°57′W
35 R8 **Half Dome** ▲ California, W USA 37°46′N 119°27′W
185 C25 **Halfmoon Bay** var. Oban. Stewart Island, Southland, New Zealand 46°53′S 168°08′E
182 E5 **Half Moon Lake** salt lake South Australia
163 R7 **Halhgol** Dornod, E Mongolia 47°57′N 118°07′E
163 S8 **Halhgol** var. Tsagaannuur. Dornod, E Mongolia 47°30′N 118°45′E
Haliacmon see Aliákmonas
Halibān see Ḩalabān
14 I13 **Haliburton** Ontario, SE Canada 45°03′N 78°20′W
14 I12 **Haliburton Highlands** var. Madawaska Highlands. hill range Ontario, SE Canada
13 Q15 **Halifax** province capital Nova Scotia, SE Canada 44°38′N 63°35′W
97 L17 **Halifax** N England, United Kingdom 53°44′N 01°52′W
21 W8 **Halifax** North Carolina, SE USA 36°19′N 77°37′W
21 U7 **Halifax** Virginia, NE USA 36°46′N 78°55′W
13 Q15 **Halifax** ✈ Nova Scotia, SE Canada 44°33′N 63°48′W
143 T13 **Halīl Rūd** seasonal river SE Iran
138 I6 **Ḩalīmah** ▲ Lebanon/Syria 34°12′N 36°37′E
162 G8 **Haliun** Govĭ-Altay, W Mongolia 45°55′N 96°06′E
118 I3 **Haljala** Ger. Halljal. Lääne-Virumaa, N Estonia 59°25′N 26°18′E
39 Q4 **Halkett, Cape** headland Alaska, USA 70°48′N 152°11′W
Halkida see Chalkída
96 J6 **Halkirk** N Scotland, United Kingdom 58°30′N 03°29′W
15 X7 **Hall** ≈ Québec, SE Canada
Hall see Schwäbisch Hall
93 H15 **Hälla** Västerbotten, N Sweden 63°56′N 17°20′E
96 J6 **Halladale** ≈ N Scotland, United Kingdom
95 J21 **Halland** ◐ county S Sweden
23 Z15 **Hallandale** Florida, SE USA 25°58′N 80°09′W
95 K22 **Hallandsås** physical region S Sweden
9 P6 **Hall Beach** Nunavut, N Canada 68°10′N 81°56′W
99 G19 **Halle** Fr. Hal. Vlaams Brabant, C Belgium 50°44′N 04°14′E
101 M15 **Halle** var. Halle an der Saale. Sachsen-Anhalt, C Germany 51°28′N 11°58′E
Halle an der Saale see Halle
35 W3 **Halleck** Nevada, W USA 40°57′N 115°27′W
95 L15 **Hällefors** Örebro, C Sweden 59°46′N 14°30′E
95 N16 **Hälleforsnäs** Södermanland, C Sweden 59°10′N 16°30′E
109 Q6 **Hallein** Salzburg, N Austria 47°41′N 13°06′E
101 L15 **Halle-Neustadt** Sachsen-Anhalt, C Germany 51°29′N 11°54′E
25 U12 **Hallettsville** Texas, SW USA 29°27′N 96°57′W
195 N4 **Halley** UK research station Antarctica 75°42′S 26°30′W
28 L4 **Halliday** North Dakota, N USA 47°19′N 102°19′W
37 S2 **Halligan Reservoir** ⊠ Colorado, C USA
100 G7 **Halligen** island group N Germany
94 G13 **Hallingdal** valley S Norway
38 J12 **Hall Island** island Alaska, USA
Hall Island see Maiana
189 P15 **Hall Islands** island group C Micronesia
118 H6 **Halliste** ≈ S Estonia
Halljal see Haljala
93 I15 **Hällnäs** Västerbotten, N Sweden 64°20′N 19°41′E
29 R2 **Hallock** Minnesota, N USA 48°47′N 96°56′W
9 S6 **Hall Peninsula** peninsula Baffin Island, Nunavut, NE Canada
20 F9 **Halls** Tennessee, S USA 35°52′N 89°24′W
95 M16 **Hallsberg** Örebro, C Sweden 59°05′N 15°07′E
181 N5 **Halls Creek** Western Australia 18°17′S 127°39′E
182 L12 **Halls Gap** Victoria, SE Australia 37°09′S 142°30′E
95 N15 **Hallstahammar** Västmanland, C Sweden 59°37′N 16°13′E
109 R6 **Hallstatt** Salzburg, W Austria 47°32′N 13°39′E
109 R6 **Hallstätter See** ◎ C Austria
95 P14 **Hallstavik** Stockholm, C Sweden 60°12′N 18°45′E
25 X7 **Hallsville** Texas, SW USA 32°31′N 94°30′W
103 P1 **Halluin** Nord, N France 50°46′N 03°07′E
Halmahera, Laut see Halmahera Sea
171 R11 **Halmahera, Pulau** prev. Djailolo, Gilolo, Jailolo. island E Indonesia
171 S12 **Halmahera Sea** Ind. Laut Halmahera. sea E Indonesia
95 J21 **Halmstad** Halland, S Sweden 56°41′N 12°49′E
119 N15 **Halowchyn** Rus. Golovchin. Mahilyowskaya Voblasts', E Belarus 54°04′N 29°55′E
95 H20 **Hals** Nordjylland, N Denmark 57°00′N 10°19′E
94 F8 **Halsa** Møre og Romsdal, S Norway 63°04′N 08°13′E
119 I15 **Hal'shany** Rus. Gol'shany. Hrodzyenskaya Voblasts', W Belarus 54°15′N 26°01′E
Hälsingborg see Helsingborg
29 R5 **Halstad** Minnesota, N USA 47°21′N 96°49′W
27 N6 **Halstead** Kansas, C USA 38°00′N 97°30′W
99 G15 **Halsteren** Noord-Brabant, S Netherlands 51°32′N 04°16′E
93 L16 **Halsua** Länsi-Suomi, W Finland 63°28′N 24°10′E
101 E14 **Haltern** Nordrhein-Westfalen, W Germany 51°45′N 07°10′E
92 J9 **Halti** var. Haltiatunturi, Lapp. Háldi. ▲ Finland/Norway 69°18′N 21°19′E
Haltiatunturi see Halti
116 J6 **Halych** Ivano-Frankivs'ka Oblast', W Ukraine 49°08′N 24°44′E
Halycus see Platani
103 P3 **Ham** Somme, N France 49°46′N 03°03′E
Hama see Ḩamāh
164 F12 **Hamada** Shimane, Honshū, SW Japan 34°54′N 132°07′E
142 L6 **Hamadān** anc. Ecbatana. Hamadān, W Iran 34°51′N 48°31′E
142 L6 **Hamadān** off. Ostān-e Hamadān. ◐ province W Iran
Hamadān, Ostān-e see Hamadān
138 I5 **Ḩamāh** var. Hama; anc. Epiphania, Bibl. Hamath. Ḩamāh, W Syria 35°09′N 36°44′E
138 I5 **Ḩamāh** off. Muḩāfaz̧at Ḩamāh, var. Hama. ◐ governorate C Syria
Hamāh, Muḩāfaz̧at see Ḩamāh
1665 S3 **Hamamasu** Hokkaidō, NE Japan 43°37′N 141°24′E
164 L14 **Hamamatsu** var. Hamamatu. Shizuoka, Honshū, S Japan 34°43′N 137°46′E
Hamamatu see Hamamatsu
165 W14 **Hamanaka** Hokkaidō, NE Japan 43°05′N 145°05′E
164 L14 **Hamana-ko** ◎ Honshū, S Japan
94 I13 **Hamar** prev. Storhammer. Hedmark, S Norway 60°57′N 10°55′E
141 U10 **Ḩamārīr al Kidan, Qalamat** well E Saudi Arabia
164 I12 **Hamasaka** Hyōgo, Honshū, SW Japan 35°37′N 134°27′E
Hamath see Ḩamāh
165 T1 **Hamatonbetsu** Hokkaidō, NE Japan 45°07′N 142°21′E
155 K26 **Hambantota** Southern Province, SE Sri Lanka 06°07′N 81°07′E
Hambourg see Hamburg
100 J9 **Hamburg** Hamburg, N Germany 53°33′N 10°03′E
27 V14 **Hamburg** Arkansas, C USA 33°13′N 91°50′W
29 S16 **Hamburg** Iowa, C USA 40°36′N 95°39′W
18 D10 **Hamburg** New York, NE USA 42°40′N 78°49′W
100 I10 **Hamburg** Fr. Hambourg. ◐ state N Germany
148 K5 **Hamdam Āb, Dasht-e** Pash. Dasht-i Hamdamab. ▲▲ W Afghanistan
Hamdamab, Dasht-i see Hamdam Āb, Dasht-e
18 M13 **Hamden** Connecticut, NE USA 41°23′N 72°55′W
140 K6 **Ḩamḑ, Wādī al** dry watercourse W Saudi Arabia
93 K18 **Hämeenkyrö** Länsi-Suomi, W Finland 61°39′N 23°10′E
93 L19 **Hämeenlinna** Swe. Tavastehus. Etelä-Suomi, S Finland 61°N 24°25′E
HaMela h, Yam see Dead Sea
Hamelin see Hameln
100 I13 **Hameln** Eng. Hamelin. Niedersachsen, N Germany 52°07′N 09°22′E
180 I8 **Hamersley Range** ▲▲ Western Australia
163 Y12 **Hamgyŏng-sanmaek** ▲▲ N North Korea
163 X13 **Hamhŭng** C North Korea 39°53′N 127°31′E
159 O6 **Hami** var. Ha-mi, Uigh. Kumul, Qomul. Xinjiang Uygur Zizhiqu, NW China 42°48′N 93°27′E
Ha-mi see Hami
139 X10 **Ḩāmid Amīn** Maysān, E Iraq 32°06′N 46°53′E
141 W11 **Hamīdān, Khawr** oasis SE Saudi Arabia
138 H5 **Ḩamīdīyah** var. Hamîdîyé. Tarţūs, W Syria 34°43′N 35°58′E
114 L12 **Hamidiye** Edirne, NW Turkey 41°09′N 26°40′E
Hamîdîyé see Ḩamīdīyah
182 L12 **Hamilton** Victoria, SE Australia 37°45′S 142°04′E
64 B12 **Hamilton** ○ (Bermuda) C Bermuda 32°18′N 64°48′W
14 G16 **Hamilton** Ontario, S Canada 43°15′N 79°50′W
184 M7 **Hamilton** Waikato, North Island, New Zealand 37°49′S 175°16′E
96 I12 **Hamilton** S Scotland, United Kingdom 55°47′N 04°03′W
23 N3 **Hamilton** Alabama, S USA 34°08′N 87°59′W
38 M10 **Hamilton** Alaska, USA 62°54′N 163°53′W
30 J13 **Hamilton** Illinois, N USA 40°24′N 91°20′W
27 S3 **Hamilton** Missouri, C USA 39°44′N 94°00′W
33 P10 **Hamilton** Montana, NW USA 46°15′N 114°09′W
25 S8 **Hamilton** Texas, SW USA 31°42′N 98°08′W
14 G16 **Hamilton** ✈ Ontario, SE Canada 43°12′N 79°54′W
64 I6 **Hamilton Bank** undersea feature SE Labrador Sea
182 E1 **Hamilton Creek** seasonal river South Australia
13 R8 **Hamilton Inlet** inlet Newfoundland and Labrador, E Canada
27 T12 **Hamilton, Lake** ⊠ Arkansas, C USA
35 W6 **Hamilton, Mount** ▲ Nevada, W USA 39°15′N 115°30′W
75 S8 **Ḩamīm, Wādī al** ≈ NE Libya
93 N19 **Hamina** Swe. Fredrikshamn. Kymi, S Finland 60°33′N 27°15′E
11 W16 **Hamiota** Manitoba, S Canada 50°13′N 100°37′W
152 L13 **Hamīrpur** Uttar Pradesh, N India 25°57′N 80°08′E
Hamis Musait see Khamīs Mushayt
21 T11 **Hamlet** North Carolina, SE USA 34°52′N 79°41′W
25 P6 **Hamlin** Texas, SW USA 32°52′N 100°07′W
21 P5 **Hamlin** West Virginia, NE USA 38°16′N 82°07′W
31 O7 **Hamlin Lake** ◎ Michigan, N USA
101 F14 **Hamm** var. Hamm in Westfalen. Nordrhein-Westfalen, W Germany 51°39′N 07°49′E
Ḩammāmāt, Khalīj al see Hammamet, Golfe de
75 N5 **Hammamet, Golfe de** Ar. Khalīj al Ḩammāmāt. gulf NE Tunisia
139 R3 **Ḩammān al 'Alīl** Nīnawé, N Iraq 36°07′N 43°15′E
139 X12 **Ḩammār, Hawr al** ◎ SE Iraq
93 J20 **Hammarland** Åland, SW Finland 60°13′N 19°45′E
93 H16 **Hammarstrand** Jämtland, C Sweden 63°07′N 16°27′E
93 O17 **Hammaslahti** Itä-Suomi, SE Finland 62°26′N 29°58′E
99 F17 **Hamme** Oost-Vlaanderen, NW Belgium 51°06′N 04°08′E
100 H10 **Hamme** ≈ NW Germany
95 G22 **Hammel** Århus, C Denmark 56°15′N 09°53′E
101 I18 **Hammelburg** Bayern, C Germany 50°06′N 09°50′E
99 H18 **Hamme-Mille** Walloon Brabant, C Belgium 50°48′N 04°42′E
100 H10 **Hamme-Oste-Kanal** canal NW Germany
93 G16 **Hammerdal** Jämtland, C Sweden 63°34′N 15°19′E
92 K8 **Hammerfest** Finnmark, N Norway 70°40′N 23°44′E
101 D14 **Hamminkeln** Nordrhein-Westfalen, W Germany 51°43′N 06°36′E
Hamm in Westfalen see Hamm
26 K10 **Hammon** Oklahoma, C USA 35°37′N 99°22′W
31 N11 **Hammond** Indiana, N USA 41°35′N 87°30′W
22 K8 **Hammond** Louisiana, S USA 30°30′N 90°27′W
99 K20 **Hamoir** Liège, E Belgium 50°28′N 05°35′E
99 J21 **Hamois** Namur, SE Belgium 50°21′N 05°09′E
99 K16 **Hamont** Limburg, NE Belgium 51°15′N 05°33′E
185 F22 **Hampden** Otago, South Island, New Zealand 45°18′S 170°49′E
19 R6 **Hampden** Maine, NE USA 44°44′N 68°51′W
97 M23 **Hampshire** cultural region S England, United Kingdom
13 O15 **Hampton** New Brunswick, SE Canada 45°30′N 65°50′W
27 U14 **Hampton** Arkansas, C USA 33°33′N 92°28′W
29 V12 **Hampton** Iowa, C USA 42°44′N 93°12′W
19 P10 **Hampton** New Hampshire, NE USA 42°55′N 70°48′W
21 R14 **Hampton** South Carolina, SE USA 32°52′N 81°06′W
21 P8 **Hampton** Tennessee, S USA 36°16′N 82°10′W
21 X7 **Hampton** Virginia, NE USA 37°02′N 76°23′W
94 L11 **Hamra** Gävleborg, C Sweden 61°40′N 15°00′E
80 D10 **Hamrat esh Sheikh** Northern Kordofan, C Sudan 14°38′N 27°56′E
139 S5 **Ḩamrīn, Jabal** ▲▲ N Iraq
121 P16 **Ħamrun** C Malta 35°53′N 14°28′E
167 U14 **Ham Thuân Nam** Binh Thuân, S Vietnam 10°49′N 107°49′E
Hāmūn, Daryācheh-ye see Şāberī, Hāmūn-e/Sīstān, Daryācheh-ye
Hamwih see Southampton
38 G10 **Hāna** var. Hana. Maui, Hawaii, USA, C Pacific Ocean 20°45′N 155°59′W
Hana see Hāna
21 S14 **Hanahan** South Carolina, SE USA 32°55′N 80°01′W
38 B8 **Hanalei** Kaua'i, Hawaii, USA, C Pacific Ocean 22°12′N 159°30′W
167 U10 **Ha Nam** Quang Nam-Đa Năng, C Vietnam 15°42′N 108°24′E
165 Q9 **Hanamaki** Iwate, Honshū, C Japan 39°25′N 141°04′E
38 F10 **Hanamanioa, Cape** headland Maui, Hawai'i, USA 20°34′N 156°22′W
190 B16 **Hanan** ✈ (Alofi) SW Niue
101 H18 **Hanau** Hessen, W Germany 50°06′N 08°56′E
162 M11 **Hanbogd** var. Ih Bulag. Ömnögovĭ, S Mongolia 43°04′N 107°43′E
8 L9 **Hanbury** ≈ Northwest Territories, NW Canada
Hânceşti see Hînceşti
10 M15 **Hanceville** British Columbia, SW Canada 51°54′N 122°56′W
23 P3 **Hanceville** Alabama, S USA 34°03′N 86°46′W
Hancewicze see Hantsavichy
160 L6 **Hancheng** Shaanxi, C China 35°22′N 110°27′E
21 V2 **Hancock** Maryland, NE USA 39°42′N 78°10′W
30 M3 **Hancock** Michigan, N USA 47°07′N 88°34′W
29 S8 **Hancock** Minnesota, N USA 45°30′N 95°47′W
18 I12 **Hancock** New York, NE USA 41°57′N 75°15′W
80 Q12 **Handa** Bari, NE Somalia 10°35′N 51°09′E
161 O5 **Handan** var. Han-tan. Hebei, E China 36°35′N 114°28′E
95 P16 **Handen** Stockholm, C Sweden 59°12′N 18°09′E
81 J22 **Handeni** Tanga, E Tanzania 05°25′S 38°04′E
37 Q7 **Handies Peak** ▲ Colorado, C USA 37°54′N 107°30′W
111 J19 **Handlová** Ger. Krickerhäu, Hung. Nyitrabánya; prev. Kriegerhaj. Trenčiansky Kraj, C Slovakia 48°45′N 18°45′E
165 O13 **Haneda** ✈ (Tōkyō) Tōkyō, Honshū, S Japan 35°33′N 139°45′E
138 F13 **HaNegev** Eng. Negev. desert S Israel
Hanfeng see Kaixian
35 Q11 **Hanford** California, W USA 36°19′N 119°39′W
191 V16 **Hanga Roa** Easter Island, Chile, E Pacific Ocean 27°09′S 109°26′W
162 I7 **Hangay** var. Hunt. Arhangay, C Mongolia 47°49′N 99°24′E
162 H7 **Hangayn Nuruu** ▲▲ C Mongolia
Hang-chou/Hangchow see Hangzhou
95 K20 **Hånger** Jönköping, S Sweden 57°06′N 13°58′E
Hangö see Hanko
149 T6 **Hangu** North-West Frontier Province, N Pakistan 33°32′N 71°04′E
161 R9 **Hangzhou** var. Hang-chou, Hangchow. province capital Zhejiang, SE China 30°18′N 120°07′E
162 J4 **Hanh** var. Turt. Hövsgöl, N Mongolia 51°30′N 100°40′E
162 F5 **Hanhöhiy Uul** ▲▲ NW Mongolia
162 K10 **Hanhongor** var. Ögöömör. Ömnögovĭ, S Mongolia 43°47′N 104°31′E
146 I14 **Hanhowuz** Rus. Khauz-Khan. Ahal Welaýaty, S Turkmenistan 37°15′N 61°12′E
146 I14 **Hanhowuz Suw Howdany** Rus. Khauzkhanskoye Vodoranilishche. ⊠ S Turkmenistan
137 P15 **Hani** Dıyarbakır, SE Turkey 38°26′N 40°23′E
Hania see Chaniá
141 R11 **Ḩanīsh al Kabīr, Jazīrat al** island SW Yemen
Hanka, Lake see Khanka, Lake
93 M17 **Hankasalmi** Länsi-Suomi, C Finland 62°25′N 26°27′E
29 R7 **Hankinson** North Dakota, N USA 46°04′N 96°54′W
93 K20 **Hanko** Swe. Hangö. Etelä-Suomi, SW Finland 59°50′N 23°E
Han-kou/Han-k'ou/Hankow see Wuhan
36 M6 **Hanksville** Utah, W USA 38°21′N 110°43′W
152 K6 **Hanle** Jammu and Kashmir, NW India 32°46′N 79°01′E
185 I17 **Hanmer Springs** Canterbury, South Island, New Zealand 42°31′S 172°49′E
11 R16 **Hanna** Alberta, SW Canada 51°38′N 111°56′W
27 V3 **Hannibal** Missouri, C USA 39°42′N 91°23′W
180 M3 **Hann, Mount** ▲ Western Australia 15°53′S 125°46′E
100 I12 **Hannover** Eng. Hanover. Niedersachsen, NW Germany 52°23′N 09°43′E
99 J19 **Hannut** Liège, C Belgium 50°40′N 05°05′E
95 L22 **Hanöbukten** bay S Sweden
167 T6 **Ha Nôi** Eng. Hanoi, Fr. Hanoï. ● (Vietnam) N Vietnam 21°01′N 105°52′E
14 F14 **Hanover** Ontario, S Canada 44°10′N 81°03′W
31 P15 **Hanover** Indiana, N USA 38°42′N 85°28′W
18 G16 **Hanover** Pennsylvania, NE USA 39°46′N 76°57′W
21 W6 **Hanover** Virginia, NE USA 37°44′N 77°21′W
Hanover see Hannover
63 G23 **Hanover, Isla** island S Chile
Hanselbeck see Érd
195 X5 **Hansen Mountains** ▲▲ Antarctica
160 M8 **Han Shui** ≈ C China
152 H10 **Hānsi** Haryāna, NW India 29°06′N 76°01′E
95 F20 **Hanstholm** Viborg, NW Denmark 57°05′N 08°39′E
Han-tan see Handan
158 H6 **Hantengri Feng** var. Pik Khan-Tengri. ▲ China/Kazakhstan 42°17′N 80°11′E see also Khan-Tengri, Pik
119 I18 **Hantsavichy** Pol. Hancewicze, Rus. Gantsevichi. Brestskaya Voblasts', SW Belarus 52°45′N 26°27′E
9 Q6 **Hantzsch** ≈ Baffin Island, Nunavut, NE Canada
152 G9 **Hanumāngarh** Rājasthān, NW India 29°33′N 74°21′E
183 O9 **Hanwood** New South Wales, SE Australia 34°19′S 146°03′E
Hanyang see Wuhan
Hanyang see Caidian
160 H10 **Hanyuan** var. Fulin. Sichuan, C China 29°29′N 102°45′E
Hanyuan see Xihe
160 J7 **Hanzhong** Shaanxi, C China 33°12′N 107°E
191 W11 **Hao** atoll Îles Tuamotu, C French Polynesia
153 S16 **Hāora** prev. Howrah. West Bengal, NE India 22°35′N 88°20′E
78 K8 **Haouach, Ouadi** dry watercourse E Chad
92 K13 **Haparanda** Norrbotten, N Sweden 65°49′N 24°05′E
25 N3 **Happy** Texas, SW USA 34°44′N 101°51′W
34 M1 **Happy Camp** California, W USA 41°48′N 123°24′W
13 Q9 **Happy Valley-Goose Bay** prev. Goose Bay. Newfoundland and Labrador, E Canada 53°19′N 60°24′W
Hapsal see Haapsalu
152 J10 **Hāpur** Uttar Pradesh, N India 28°43′N 77°47′E
HaQatan, HaMakhtesh see HaKatan, HaMakhtesh
140 I4 **Ḩaql** Tabūk, NW Saudi Arabia 29°18′N 34°58′E
171 U14 **Har** Pulau Kai Besar, E Indonesia 05°21′S 133°09′E
Haraat see Tsagaandelger
141 R8 **Ḩaraḑ** var. Haradh. Ash Sharqīyah, E Saudi Arabia 24°08′N 49°02′E
Haradh see Ḩaraḑ
118 N12 **Haradok** Rus. Gorodok. Vitsyebskaya Voblasts', N Belarus 55°28′N 30°00′E
92 J13 **Harads** Norrbotten, N Sweden 66°04′N 21°04′E
119 G19 **Haradzyets** Rus. Gorodets. Brestskaya Voblasts', SW Belarus 52°12′N 24°40′E
119 J17 **Haradzyeya** Rus. Gorodeya. Minskaya Voblasts', C Belarus 53°19′N 26°32′E
191 V10 **Haraiki** atoll Îles Tuamotu, C French Polynesia
165 Q11 **Haramachi** Fukushima, Honshū, E Japan 37°40′N 140°55′E
118 M12 **Harany** Rus. Gorany. Vitsyebskaya Voblasts', N Belarus 55°25′N 29°03′E
83 L16 **Harare** prev. Salisbury. ● (Zimbabwe) Mashonaland East, NE Zimbabwe 17°47′S 31°04′E
83 L16 **Harare** ✈ Mashonaland East, NE Zimbabwe 17°51′S 31°06′E
78 J10 **Haraz-Djombo** Batha, C Chad 14°10′N 19°35′E
119 O16 **Harbavichy** Rus. Gorbovichi. Mahilyowskaya Voblasts', E Belarus 53°49′N 30°42′E
76 J16 **Harbel** W Liberia 06°19′N 10°20′W
163 W8 **Harbin** var. Haerbin, Ha-erh-pin, Kharbin; prev. Haerhpin, Pingkiang, Pinkiang. province capital Heilongjiang, NE China 45°45′N 126°41′E
31 S7 **Harbor Beach** Michigan, N USA 43°50′N 82°39′W
13 T13 **Harbour Breton** Newfoundland, Newfoundland and Labrador, E Canada 47°29′N 55°50′W
65 D25 **Harbours, Bay of** bay East Falkland, Falkland Islands
Hårby see Haarby
36 I13 **Harcuvar Mountains** ▲▲ Arizona, SW USA
108 I7 **Hard** Vorarlberg, NW Austria 47°29′N 09°42′E
154 H11 **Harda Khas** Madhya Pradesh, C India 22°22′N 77°06′E
95 D14 **Hardanger** physical region S Norway
95 D14 **Hardangerfjorden** fjord S Norway
94 E13 **Hardangerjøkulen** glacier S Norway
95 E14 **Hardangervidda** plateau S Norway
83 D20 **Hardap** ◐ district S Namibia
21 R15 **Hardeeville** South Carolina, SE USA 32°18′N 81°04′W
98 L5 **Hardegarijp** Fris. Hurdegaryp. Friesland, N Netherlands 53°13′N 05°57′E
98 O9 **Hardenberg** Overijssel, E Netherlands 52°34′N 06°38′E
183 Q9 **Harden-Murrumburrah** New South Wales, SE Australia 34°33′S 148°22′E
98 K10 **Harderwijk** Gelderland, C Netherlands 52°21′N 05°37′E
30 J14 **Hardin** Illinois, N USA 39°10′N 90°38′W
33 V11 **Hardin** Montana, NW USA 45°44′N 107°35′W
23 R5 **Harding, Lake** ⊠ Alabama/Georgia, SE USA
20 J6 **Hardinsburg** Kentucky, S USA 37°46′N 86°29′W
98 I13 **Hardinxveld-Giessendam** Zuid-Holland, C Netherlands 51°52′N 04°49′E
11 R15 **Hardisty** Alberta, SW Canada 52°42′N 111°22′W
152 L12 **Hardoi** Uttar Pradesh, N India 27°23′N 80°06′E
Hardwar see Haridwār
23 U4 **Hardwick** Georgia, SE USA 33°03′N 83°13′W
27 W9 **Hardy** Arkansas, C USA 36°19′N 91°29′W
94 D10 **Hareid** Møre og Romsdal, S Norway 62°22′N 06°02′E
8 H7 **Hare Indian** ≈ Northwest Territories, NW Canada
99 D18 **Harelbeke** var. Harlebeke. West-Vlaanderen, W Belgium 50°51′N 03°19′E
Harem see Ḩārim
100 E11 **Haren** Niedersachsen, NW Germany 52°47′N 07°16′E
98 N6 **Haren** Groningen, NE Netherlands 53°10′N 06°37′E
80 L13 **Hārer** E Ethiopia 09°17′N 42°19′E
95 P14 **Harg** Uppsala, C Sweden 60°13′N 18°25′E
Hargeisa see Hargeysa
80 M13 **Hargeysa** var. Hargeisa. Woqooyi Galbeed, NW Somalia 09°32′N 44°07′E
116 J10 **Harghita** ◐ county NE Romania
25 S17 **Hargill** Texas, SW USA 26°26′N 98°00′W
162 J8 **Harhorin** Övörhangay, C Mongolia 47°13′N 102°48′E
159 Q9 **Har Hu** ◎ C China
Hariana see Haryāna
141 P15 **Ḩarīb** W Yemen 15°08′N 45°35′E
168 M12 **Hari, Batang** prev. Djambi. ≈ Sumatera, W Indonesia
152 J9 **Haridwār** prev. Hardwar. Uttarakhand, N India 29°58′N 78°09′E
155 F18 **Harihar** Karnātaka, W India 14°33′N 75°44′E
185 F18 **Harihari** West Coast, South Island, New Zealand 43°09′S 170°35′E
138 I3 **Ḩārim** var. Harem. Idlib, W Syria 36°30′N 36°30′E
98 F13 **Haringvliet** channel SW Netherlands
98 F13 **Haringvlietdam** dam SW Netherlands
149 U5 **Harīpur** North-West Frontier Province, NW Pakistan 34°00′N 73°01′E
148 J4 **Harīrūd** var. Tedzhen, Turkm. Tejen. ≈ Afghanistan/Iran see also Tejen
Harīrūd see Tejen
94 J11 **Härjåhågnen** Swe. Härjahågnen, var. Härjehågna. ▲ Norway/Sweden 61°43′N 12°07′E
Härjahågnen see Østrehogna
Härjahågnen see Härjåhågnen
93 K18 **Harjavalta** Länsi-Suomi, W Finland 61°19′N 22°10′E
Härjehågna see Østrehogna
Härjehågna see Härjåhågnen
118 G4 **Harjumaa** var. Harju Maakond. ◐ province NW Estonia
Harju Maakond see Harjumaa
21 X11 **Harkers Island** North Carolina, SE USA 34°42′N 76°33′W
139 S1 **Harki** Dahūk, N Iraq 37°03′N 43°39′E
29 T14 **Harlan** Iowa, C USA 41°40′N 95°19′W
21 O7 **Harlan** Kentucky, S USA 36°50′N 83°19′W
29 N17 **Harlan County Lake** ⊠ Nebraska, C USA
116 L9 **Hârlău** var. Hîrlău. Iaşi, NE Romania 47°26′N 26°54′E
Harlebeke see Harelbeke
33 U7 **Harlem** Montana, NW USA 48°31′N 108°46′W
Harlem see Haarlem
95 G22 **Harlev** Århus, C Denmark 56°08′N 10°00′E
98 K6 **Harlingen** Fris. Harns. Friesland, N Netherlands 53°10′N 05°25′E
25 T17 **Harlingen** Texas, SW USA 26°12′N 97°43′W
97 O21 **Harlow** E England, United Kingdom 51°47′N 00°07′E
33 T10 **Harlowton** Montana, NW USA 46°26′N 109°49′W
94 N11 **Harmånger** Gävleborg, C Sweden 61°55′N 17°19′E
98 I11 **Harmelen** Utrecht, C Netherlands 52°06′N 04°58′E
29 X11 **Harmony** Minnesota, N USA 43°33′N 92°00′W

◆ Country
● Country Capital
◇ Dependent Territory
○ Dependent Territory Capital
◐ Administrative Regions
✈ International Airport
▲ Mountain
▲▲ Mountain Range
Volcano
≈ River
◎ Lake
⊠ Reservoir

Harney Basin – Helvecia

32 J14 **Harney Basin** basin Oregon, NW USA
32 J14 **Harney Lake** ◎ Oregon, NW USA
28 J10 **Harney Peak** ▲ South Dakota, N USA 43°52′N 103°31′W
93 H17 **Härnösand** var. Hernösand. Västernorrland, C Sweden 62°37′N 17°55′E
Harns see Harlingen
162 F6 **Har Nuur** ◎ NW Mongolia
105 P4 **Haro** La Rioja, N Spain 42°34′N 02°52′W
40 F6 **Haro, Cabo** headland NW Mexico 27°50′N 110°55′W
94 D9 **Harøy** island S Norway
97 N21 **Harpenden** E England, United Kingdom 51°49′N 00°22′W
76 L18 **Harper** var. Cape Palmas. NE Liberia 04°25′N 07°43′W
26 M7 **Harper** Kansas, C USA 37°17′N 98°01′W
32 L13 **Harper** Oregon, NW USA 43°51′N 117°37′W
25 Q10 **Harper** Texas, SW USA 30°18′N 99°18′W
35 U13 **Harper Lake** salt flat California, W USA
39 T9 **Harper, Mount** ▲ Alaska, USA 64°18′N 143°54′W
95 J21 **Harplinge** Halland, S Sweden 56°45′N 12°45′E
36 J13 **Harquahala Mountains** ▲▲ Arizona, SW USA
141 T15 **Ḩarrah** SE Yemen 15°02′N 50°23′E
12 H11 **Harricana** ≈ Québec, SE Canada
20 M9 **Harriman** Tennessee, S USA 35°57′N 84°33′W
13 R11 **Harrington Harbour** Québec, E Canada 50°34′N 59°29′W
64 B12 **Harrington Sound** bay Bermuda, NW Atlantic Ocean
96 F8 **Harris** physical region NW Scotland, United Kingdom
27 X10 **Harrisburg** Arkansas, C USA 35°33′N 90°43′W
30 M17 **Harrisburg** Illinois, N USA 37°44′N 88°32′W
28 I14 **Harrisburg** Nebraska, C USA 41°33′N 103°46′W
32 F12 **Harrisburg** Oregon, NW USA 44°16′N 123°10′W
18 G15 **Harrisburg** state capital Pennsylvania, NE USA 40°16′N 76°53′W
182 F6 **Harris, Lake** ◎ South Australia
23 W11 **Harris, Lake** ◎ Florida, SE USA
83 J22 **Harrismith** Free State, E South Africa 28°16′S 29°08′E
27 T9 **Harrison** Arkansas, C USA 36°13′N 93°07′W
31 Q7 **Harrison** Michigan, N USA 44°02′N 84°46′W
28 I12 **Harrison** Nebraska, C USA 42°42′N 103°53′W
39 Q5 **Harrison Bay** inlet Alaska, USA
22 I6 **Harrisonburg** Louisiana, S USA 31°44′N 91°51′W
21 U4 **Harrisonburg** Virginia, NE USA 38°27′N 78°54′W
13 R7 **Harrison, Cape** headland Newfoundland and Labrador, E Canada 54°55′N 57°48′W
27 R5 **Harrisonville** Missouri, C USA 38°40′N 94°21′W
Harris Ridge see Lomonosov Ridge
192 M3 **Harris Seamount** undersea feature N Pacific Ocean 46°09′N 161°25′W
96 F8 **Harris, Sound of** strait NW Scotland, United Kingdom
31 R6 **Harrisville** Michigan, N USA 44°41′N 83°19′W
21 R3 **Harrisville** West Virginia, NE USA 39°13′N 81°04′W
20 M6 **Harrodsburg** Kentucky, S USA 37°45′N 84°51′W
97 M16 **Harrogate** N England, United Kingdom 54°N 01°33′W
25 Q4 **Harrold** Texas, SW USA 34°05′N 99°02′W
27 S5 **Harry S. Truman Reservoir** ⊠ Missouri, C USA
100 G13 **Harsewinkel** Nordrhein-Westfalen, W Germany 51°58′N 08°13′E
116 M14 **Hârşova** prev. Hîrşova. Constanţa, SE Romania 44°41′N 27°56′E
92 H10 **Harstad** Troms, N Norway 68°48′N 16°31′E
31 O8 **Hart** Michigan, N USA 43°43′N 86°22′W
24 M4 **Hart** Texas, SW USA 34°23′N 102°07′W
10 I5 **Hart** ≈ Yukon Territory, NW Canada
83 F23 **Hartbees** ≈ C South Africa
109 X7 **Hartberg** Steiermark, SE Austria 47°18′N 15°58′E
182 I10 **Hart, Cape** headland South Australia 35°54′S 138°01′E
95 E14 **Hårteigen** ▲ S Norway 60°11′N 07°01′E
23 Q7 **Hartford** Alabama, S USA 31°06′N 85°42′W
27 R11 **Hartford** Arkansas, C USA 35°01′N 94°22′W
18 M12 **Hartford** state capital Connecticut, NE USA 41°46′N 72°41′W
20 J6 **Hartford** Kentucky, S USA 37°26′N 86°57′W
31 P10 **Hartford** Michigan, N USA 42°12′N 85°54′W
29 R11 **Hartford** South Dakota, N USA 43°37′N 96°56′W
30 M8 **Hartford** Wisconsin, N USA 43°19′N 88°25′W
31 P13 **Hartford City** Indiana, N USA 40°27′N 85°22′W
29 Q13 **Hartington** Nebraska, C USA 42°37′N 97°15′W
13 N14 **Hartland** New Brunswick, SE Canada 46°18′N 67°31′W
97 H23 **Hartland Point** headland SW England, United Kingdom 51°01′N 04°33′W
97 M15 **Hartlepool** N England, United Kingdom 54°41′N 01°13′W
29 T12 **Hartley** Iowa, C USA 43°10′N 95°28′W
24 M1 **Hartley** Texas, SW USA 35°52′N 102°24′W
32 J15 **Hart Mountain** ▲ Oregon, NW USA 42°24′N 119°46′W
173 U10 **Hartog Ridge** undersea feature W Indian Ocean
93 M18 **Hartola** Etelä-Suomi, S Finland 61°34′N 26°04′E
67 U14 **Harts** var. Hartz. ≈ N South Africa
23 P2 **Hartselle** Alabama, S USA 34°26′N 86°56′W
23 S3 **Hartsfield Atlanta** ✈ Georgia, SE USA 33°38′N 84°24′W
27 Q11 **Hartshorne** Oklahoma, C USA 34°51′N 95°33′W
21 S12 **Hartsville** South Carolina, SE USA 34°22′N 80°04′W
20 K8 **Hartsville** Tennessee, S USA 36°23′N 86°11′W
27 U7 **Hartville** Missouri, C USA 37°15′N 92°30′W
23 U2 **Hartwell** Georgia, SE USA 34°21′N 82°55′W
21 O11 **Hartwell Lake** ⊠ Georgia/South Carolina, SE USA
Hartz see Harts
Harunabad see Eslāmābād
Har-Us see Erdenebüren
162 F6 **Har Us Gol** ◎ Hovd, W Mongolia
162 E6 **Har Us Nuur** ◎ NW Mongolia
30 M10 **Harvard** Illinois, N USA 42°25′N 88°36′W
29 P16 **Harvard** Nebraska, C USA 40°37′N 98°06′W
37 R5 **Harvard, Mount** ▲ Colorado, C USA 38°55′N 106°19′W
31 N11 **Harvey** Illinois, N USA 41°36′N 87°39′W
29 N4 **Harvey** North Dakota, N USA 47°43′N 99°55′W
97 Q21 **Harwich** E England, United Kingdom 51°56′N 01°16′E
152 H10 **Haryāna** var. Hariana. ◈ state N India
141 Y9 **Ḩaryān, Ţawī al** spring/well NE Oman 21°56′N 58°33′E
101 J14 **Harz** ▲▲ C Germany
Ḩasakah, Muḩāfaẓat al see Al Ḩasakah
165 Q9 **Hasama** Miyagi, Honshū, C Japan 38°42′N 141°09′E
136 J15 **Hasan Dağı** ▲ C Turkey 38°09′N 34°15′E
139 T9 **Ḩasan Ibn Ḩassūn** An Najaf, C Iraq 32°24′N 44°13′E
149 R6 **Ḩasan Khēl** var. Ahmad Khel. Paktīā, SE Afghanistan 33°46′N 69°37′E
100 F12 **Hase** ≈ NW Germany
Haselberg see Krasnoznamensk
100 F12 **Haselünne** Niedersachsen, NW Germany 52°40′N 07°28′E
Hashaat see Delgerhangay
Hashemite Kingdom of Jordan see Jordan
139 V8 **Hāshimah** Wāsiţ, E Iraq 33°22′N 45°56′E
142 K3 **Hashtrūd** var. Azaran. Āžarbāyjān-e Khāvarī, N Iran 37°34′N 47°10′E
141 W13 **Ḩāsik** S Oman 17°22′N 55°18′E
149 U10 **Hāsilpur** Punjab, E Pakistan 29°42′N 72°40′E
27 Q10 **Haskell** Oklahoma, C USA 35°49′N 95°40′W
25 Q6 **Haskell** Texas, SW USA 33°10′N 99°45′W
114 M11 **Hasköy** Edirne, NW Turkey 41°37′N 26°51′E
95 L24 **Hasle** Bornholm, E Denmark 55°12′N 14°43′E
97 N23 **Haslemere** SE England, United Kingdom 51°06′N 00°45′W
102 I16 **Hasparren** Pyrénées-Atlantiques, SW France 43°23′N 01°18′W
Hassakeh see Al Ḩasakah
155 G19 **Hassan** Karnātaka, W India 13°01′N 76°03′E
36 J13 **Hassayampa River** ≈ Arizona, SW USA
101 J18 **Hassberge** hill range C Germany
94 N10 **Hassela** Gävleborg, C Sweden 62°06′N 16°45′E
99 J18 **Hasselt** Limburg, NE Belgium 50°56′N 05°20′E
98 M9 **Hasselt** Overijssel, E Netherlands 52°36′N 06°06′E
Hassetché see Al Ḩasakah
101 J18 **Hassfurt** Bayern, C Germany 50°02′N 10°32′E
74 L9 **Hassi Bel Guebbour** E Algeria 28°41′N 06°29′E
74 L8 **Hassi Messaoud** E Algeria 31°41′N 06°10′E
95 K22 **Hässleholm** Skåne, S Sweden 56°09′N 13°45′E
Hasta Colonia/Hasta Pompeia see Asti
183 O13 **Hastings** Victoria, SE Australia 38°18′S 145°12′E
184 O11 **Hastings** Hawke's Bay, North Island, New Zealand 39°39′S 176°51′E
97 P23 **Hastings** SE England, United Kingdom 50°51′N 00°36′E
31 P9 **Hastings** Michigan, N USA 42°38′N 85°17′W
29 W9 **Hastings** Minnesota, N USA 44°44′N 92°51′W
29 P16 **Hastings** Nebraska, C USA 40°35′N 98°23′W
95 K22 **Hästveda** Skåne, S Sweden 56°16′N 13°55′E
92 J8 **Hasvik** Finnmark, N Norway 70°29′N 22°08′E
37 V6 **Haswell** Colorado, C USA 38°27′N 103°09′W
163 N11 **Hatanbulag** var. Ergel. Dornogovĭ, SE Mongolia 43°10′N 109°13′E
Hatansuudal see Bayanlig
Hatavch see Haldzan
136 K17 **Hatay** ◈ province S Turkey
37 R15 **Hatch** New Mexico, SW USA 32°40′N 107°10′W
36 K7 **Hatch** Utah, W USA 37°39′N 112°25′W
20 F9 **Hatchie River** ≈ Tennessee, S USA
116 G12 **Haţeg** Ger. Wallenthal, Hung. Hátszeg; prev. Hatzeg, Hötzing. Hunedoara, SW Romania 45°35′N 22°57′E
165 O17 **Hateruma-jima** island Yaeyama-shotō, SW Japan
183 N8 **Hatfield** New South Wales, SE Australia 33°54′S 143°43′E
162 I5 **Hatgal** Hövsgöl, N Mongolia 50°24′N 100°12′E
153 V16 **Hathazari** Chittagong, SE Bangladesh 22°30′N 91°46′E
141 T13 **Hathūt, Hişā'** oasis NE Yemen
167 R14 **Ha Tiên** Kiên Giang, S Vietnam 10°24′N 104°30′E
167 T8 **Ha Tinh** Ha Tinh, N Vietnam 18°21′N 105°55′E
Ḫatira, Haré see Hatira, Harei
138 F12 **Hatira, Harei** prev. Haré Ḫatira. hill range S Israel
167 R6 **Hat Lot** var. Mai Son. Son La, N Vietnam 21°07′N 104°10′E
45 P16 **Hato Airport** ✈ (Willemstad) Curaçao, SW Netherlands Antilles 12°10′N 68°56′W
54 H9 **Hato Corozal** Casanare, C Colombia 06°08′N 71°45′W
Hato del Volcán see Volcán
45 P9 **Hato Mayor** E Dominican Republic 18°49′N 69°16′W
Hatra see Al Ḩaḑr
Hatria see Adria
Hátszeg see Haţeg
143 R16 **Ḩattá** Dubayy, NE United Arab Emirates 24°50′N 56°06′E
182 L9 **Hattah** Victoria, SE Australia 34°49′S 142°18′E
98 M9 **Hattem** Gelderland, E Netherlands 52°29′N 06°04′E
21 Z10 **Hatteras** Hatteras Island, North Carolina, SE USA 35°13′N 75°39′W
21 Rr10 **Hatteras, Cape** headland North Carolina, SE USA 35°29′N 75°33′W
21 Z9 **Hatteras Island** island North Carolina, SE USA
64 F10 **Hatteras Plain** undersea feature W Atlantic Ocean 31°00′N 71°00′W
93 G14 **Hattfjelldal** Troms, N Norway 65°37′N 13°58′E
22 M7 **Hattiesburg** Mississippi, S USA 31°20′N 89°17′W
29 Q4 **Hatton** North Dakota, N USA 47°38′N 97°27′W
Hatton Bank see Hatton Ridge
64 L6 **Hatton Ridge** var. Hatton Bank. undersea feature N Atlantic Ocean 59°00′N 17°30′W
191 W6 **Hatutu** island Îles Marquises, NE French Polynesia
111 K22 **Hatvan** Heves, NE Hungary 47°40′N 19°39′E
167 O16 **Hat Yai** var. Ban Hat Yai. Songkhla, SW Thailand 07°01′N 100°27′E
Hatzeg see Haţeg
Hatzfeld see Jimbolia
80 N13 **Haud** plateau Ethiopia/Somalia
95 D18 **Hauge** Rogaland, S Norway 58°20′N 06°17′E
95 C15 **Haugesund** Rogaland, S Norway 59°24′N 05°17′E
109 X2 **Haugsdorf** Niederösterreich, NE Austria 48°41′N 16°04′E
184 M9 **Hauhungaroa Range** ▲▲ North Island, New Zealand
95 E15 **Haukeligrend** Telemark, S Norway 59°45′N 07°33′E
93 L14 **Haukipudas** Oulu, C Finland 65°11′N 25°21′E
93 M17 **Haukivesi** ◎ SE Finland
93 M17 **Haukivuori** Itä-Suomi, E Finland 62°02′N 27°11′E
Hauptkanal see Havelländ Grosse
187 N10 **Hauraha** San Cristobal, SE Solomon Islands 10°47′S 162°00′E
184 L5 **Hauraki Gulf** gulf North Island, N New Zealand
185 B24 **Hauroko, Lake** ◎ South Island, New Zealand
167 S14 **Hâu, Sông** ≈ S Vietnam
92 N12 **Hautajärvi** Lappi, NE Finland 66°30′N 29°01′E
74 F7 **Haut Atlas** Eng. High Atlas. ▲▲ C Morocco
79 M17 **Haut-Congo** off. Région du Haut-Congo; prev. Haut-Zaïre. ◈ region NE Dem. Rep. Congo
103 Y14 **Haute-Corse** ◈ department Corse, France, C Mediterranean Sea
102 L16 **Haute-Garonne** ◈ department S France
79 K14 **Haute-Kotto** ◈ prefecture E Central African Republic
103 P12 **Haute-Loire** ◈ department C France
103 R6 **Haute-Marne** ◈ department N France
102 M3 **Haute-Normandie** ◈ region N France
15 U6 **Hauterive** Québec, SE Canada 49°11′N 68°16′W
103 T13 **Hautes-Alpes** ◈ department SE France
103 S7 **Haute-Saône** ◈ department E France
103 T10 **Haute-Savoie** ◈ department E France
99 M20 **Hautes Fagnes** Ger. Hohes Venn. ▲▲ E Belgium
102 K16 **Hautes-Pyrénées** ◈ department S France
99 L23 **Haute Sûre, Lac de la** ⊠ NW Luxembourg
102 M11 **Haute-Vienne** ◈ department C France
19 S8 **Haut, Isle au** island Maine, NE USA
79 M14 **Haut-Mbomou** ◈ prefecture SE Central African Republic
103 Q2 **Hautmont** Nord, N France 50°15′N 03°55′E
79 F19 **Haut-Ogooué** off. Province du Haut-Ogooué, var. Le Haut-Ogooué. ◈ province SE Gabon
Haut-Ogooué, Le see Haut-Ogooué
Haut-Ogooué, Province du see Haut-Ogooué
103 U7 **Haut-Rhin** ◈ department NE France
74 I6 **Hauts Plateaux** plateau Algeria/Morocco
Haut-Zaïre see Haut-Congo
38 D9 **Hau'ula** var. Hauula. O'ahu, Hawaii, USA, C Pacific Ocean 21°36′N 157°54′W
Hauula see Hau'ula
101 O22 **Hauzenberg** Bayern, SE Germany 48°39′N 13°37′E
30 K13 **Havana** Illinois, N USA 40°18′N 90°03′W
Havana see La Habana
97 N23 **Havant** S England, United Kingdom 50°51′N 00°59′W
35 Y14 **Havasu, Lake** ⊠ Arizona/California, W USA
95 J23 **Havdrup** Roskilde, E Denmark 55°33′N 12°08′E
100 N10 **Havel** ≈ NE Germany
99 J21 **Havelange** Namur, SE Belgium 50°23′N 05°14′E
100 M11 **Havelberg** Sachsen-Anhalt, NE Germany 52°49′N 12°05′E
149 U5 **Haveliān** North-West Frontier Province, NW Pakistan 34°05′N 73°14′E
100 N12 **Havelländ Grosse** var. Hauptkanal. canal NE Germany
14 J14 **Havelock** Ontario, SE Canada 44°22′N 77°57′W
185 J14 **Havelock** Marlborough, South Island, New Zealand 41°17′S 173°46′E
21 X11 **Havelock** North Carolina, SE USA 34°52′N 76°54′W
184 O11 **Havelock North** Hawke's Bay, North Island, New Zealand 39°40′S 176°53′E
98 M8 **Havelte** Drenthe, NE Netherlands 52°46′N 06°14′E
27 N6 **Haven** Kansas, C USA 37°54′N 97°46′W
97 H21 **Haverfordwest** SW Wales, United Kingdom 51°50′N 04°57′W
97 P20 **Haverhill** E England, United Kingdom 52°05′N 00°26′E
19 O10 **Haverhill** Massachusetts, NE USA 42°46′N 71°02′W
155 F18 **Hāveri** Karnātaka, SW India 14°47′N 75°24′E
93 G17 **Haverö** Västernorrland, C Sweden 62°25′N 15°04′E
111 I17 **Havířov** Moravskoslezský Kraj, E Czech Republic 49°47′N 18°30′E
111 E17 **Havlíčkův Brod** Ger. Deutsch-Brod; prev. Německý Brod. Vysočina, C Czech Republic 49°38′N 15°46′E
92 K7 **Havøysund** Finnmark, N Norway 70°59′N 24°39′E
99 F20 **Havré** Hainaut, S Belgium 50°29′N 04°03′E
33 T7 **Havre** Montana, NW USA 48°33′N 109°41′W
Havre see le Havre
13 P11 **Havre-St-Pierre** Québec, E Canada 50°16′N 63°36′W
136 B10 **Havsa** Edirne, NW Turkey 41°32′N 26°49′E
38 D8 **Hawai'i** off. State of Hawai'i, also known as Aloha State, Paradise of the Pacific, var. Hawaii. ◈ state USA, C Pacific Ocean
38 G12 **Hawai'i** var. Hawaii. island Hawaiian Islands, USA, C Pacific Ocean
192 M5 **Hawaiian Islands** prev. Sandwich Islands. island group Hawaii, USA
192 L5 **Hawaiian Ridge** undersea feature N Pacific Ocean 24°00′N 165°00′W
193 N6 **Hawaiian Trough** undersea feature N Pacific Ocean
29 R12 **Hawarden** Iowa, C USA 43°00′N 96°29′W
Hawash see Āwash
139 P6 **Hawbayn al Gharbīyah** Al Anbār, C Iraq 34°24′N 42°06′E
185 D21 **Hawea, Lake** ◎ South Island, New Zealand
184 K11 **Hawera** Taranaki, North Island, New Zealand 39°36′S 174°16′E
20 J5 **Hawesville** Kentucky, S USA 37°53′N 86°47′W
38 G11 **Hawi** Hawaii, USA, C Pacific Ocean 20°14′N 155°50′W
38 G11 **Hāwī** var. Hawi. Hawaii, USA, C Pacific Ocean 20°13′N 155°49′E
Hawi see Hāwī
96 K13 **Hawick** SE Scotland, United Kingdom 55°24′N 02°49′W
139 S4 **Ḩawījah** At Ta'mīn, C Iraq 35°15′N 43°54′E
139 Y10 **Ḩawīzah, Hawr al** ◎ S Iraq
185 E21 **Hawkdun Range** ▲▲ South Island, New Zealand
184 P10 **Hawke Bay** bay North Island, New Zealand
182 I6 **Hawker** South Australia 31°54′S 138°25′E
184 N11 **Hawke's Bay** off. Hawkes Bay Region. ◈ region North Island, New Zealand
149 O16 **Hawkes Bay** bay SE Pakistan
Hawkes Bay Region see Hawke's Bay
15 N12 **Hawkesbury** Ontario, SE Canada 45°36′N 74°38′W
Hawkeye State see Iowa
23 T5 **Hawkinsville** Georgia, SE USA 32°16′N 83°28′W
14 B7 **Hawk Junction** Ontario, S Canada 48°05′N 84°34′W
21 N10 **Haw Knob** ▲ North Carolina/Tennessee, SE USA 35°18′N 84°01′W
21 Q9 **Hawksbill Mountain** ▲ North Carolina, SE USA 35°54′N 81°53′W
33 Z16 **Hawk Springs** Wyoming, C USA 41°48′N 104°17′W
Hawlēr see Arbīl
29 S5 **Hawley** Minnesota, N USA 46°53′N 96°18′W
25 P7 **Hawley** Texas, SW USA 32°36′N 99°47′W
141 R14 **Ḩawrā'** C Yemen 15°39′N 48°21′E
139 P7 **Ḩawrān, Wadi** dry watercourse W Iraq
21 T9 **Haw River** ≈ North Carolina, SE USA
139 U5 **Hawshqūrah** Diyālá, E Iraq 34°34′N 45°33′E
35 S7 **Hawthorne** Nevada, W USA 38°30′N 118°38′W
37 W3 **Haxtun** Colorado, C USA 40°36′N 102°38′W
183 N9 **Hay** New South Wales, SE Australia 34°31′S 144°51′E
11 O10 **Hay** ≈ W Canada
171 S13 **Haya** Pulau Seram, E Indonesia 03°22′S 129°31′E
165 R9 **Hayachine-san** ▲ Honshū, C Japan 39°31′N 141°28′E
103 S4 **Hayange** Moselle, NE France 49°19′N 06°04′E
HaYarden see Jordan
Hayastani Hanrapetut'yun see Armenia
Hayasui-seto see Hōyo-kaikyō
39 N9 **Haycock** Alaska, USA 65°12′N 161°10′W
36 M14 **Hayden** Arizona, SW USA 33°00′N 110°46′W
37 Q3 **Hayden** Colorado, C USA 40°29′N 107°15′W
28 M10 **Hayes** South Dakota, N USA 44°20′N 101°01′W
9 X13 **Hayes** ≈ Manitoba, C Canada
11 P12 **Hayes** ≈ Nunavut, NE Canada
28 M16 **Hayes Center** Nebraska, C USA 40°30′N 101°02′W
39 S10 **Hayes, Mount** ▲ Alaska, USA 63°37′N 146°43′W
21 N11 **Hayesville** North Carolina, SE USA 35°03′N 83°49′W
35 X10 **Hayford Peak** ▲ Nevada, W USA 36°40′N 115°10′W
34 M3 **Hayfork** California, W USA 40°33′N 123°10′W
Hayir, Qasr al see Ḩayr al Gharbī, Qaşr al
Haylaastay see Sühbaatar
14 I12 **Hay Lake** ◎ Ontario, SE Canada
141 X11 **Haymā'** var. Haima. C Oman 19°59′N 56°20′E
136 H13 **Haymana** Ankara, C Turkey 39°26′N 32°30′E
138 J7 **Ḩaymūr, Jabal** ▲▲ W Syria
Haynau see Chojnów
22 G4 **Haynesville** Louisiana, S USA 32°57′N 93°08′W
23 P6 **Hayneville** Alabama, S USA 32°13′N 86°34′W
114 M12 **Hayrabolu** Tekirdağ, NW Turkey 41°14′N 27°04′E
136 C10 **Hayrabolu Deresi** ≈ NW Turkey
138 J6 **Ḩayr al Gharbī, Qaşr al** var. Qasr al Hayir, Qasr al Hir al Gharbi. ruins Ḩimş, C Syria
138 L5 **Ḩayr ash Sharqī, Qaşr al** var. Qasr al Hir Ash Sharqī. ruins Ḩimş, C Syria
162 J7 **Hayrhan** var. Uubulan. Arhangay, C Mongolia 48°37′N 101°58′E
162 J9 **Hayrhandulaan** var. Mardzad. Övörhangay, C Mongolia 45°58′N 102°06′E
8 J10 **Hay River** Northwest Territories, W Canada 60°51′N 115°42′W
26 K4 **Hays** Kansas, C USA 38°53′N 99°20′W
28 K12 **Hay Springs** Nebraska, C USA 42°40′N 102°41′W
65 H25 **Haystack, The** ▲ NE Saint Helena 15°55′S 05°40′W
27 N7 **Haysville** Kansas, C USA 37°34′N 97°21′W
117 O7 **Haysyn** Rus. Gaysin. Vinnyts'ka Oblast', C Ukraine 48°50′N 29°29′E
27 Y9 **Hayti** Missouri, C USA 36°13′N 89°45′W
29 Q9 **Hayti** South Dakota, N USA 44°40′N 97°22′W
117 O8 **Hayvoron** Rus. Gayvorno. Kirovohrads'ka Oblast', C Ukraine 48°20′S 29°52′E
35 N9 **Hayward** California, W USA 37°40′N 122°07′W
30 J4 **Hayward** Wisconsin, N USA 46°02′N 91°26′W
97 O23 **Haywards Heath** SE England, United Kingdom 51°N 00°06′W
146 A11 **Hazar** prev. Rus. Cheleken. Balkan Welaýaty, W Turkmenistan 39°26′N 53°07′E
143 S11 **Hazārān, Kūh-e** var. Kūh-e ā Hazr. ▲ SE Iran 29°26′N 57°15′E
Hazarat Imam see Emām Şāḩeb
21 O7 **Hazard** Kentucky, S USA 37°14′N 83°11′W
137 O15 **Hazar Gölü** ◎ C Turkey
153 P15 **Hazārībāg** var. Hazāribāgh. Jhārkhand, N India 24°00′N 85°23′E
Hazāribāgh see Hazārībāg
103 O1 **Hazebrouck** Nord, N France 50°43′N 02°33′E
30 K9 **Hazel Green** Wisconsin, N USA 42°33′N 90°26′W
192 K9 **Hazel Holme Bank** undersea feature S Pacific Ocean 12°49′S 174°30′E
10 K13 **Hazelton** British Columbia, SW Canada 55°15′N 127°38′W
29 N6 **Hazelton** North Dakota, N USA 46°27′N 100°17′W
35 R5 **Hazen** Nevada, W USA 39°33′N 119°02′W
28 L5 **Hazen** North Dakota, N USA 47°18′N 101°37′W
38 L12 **Hazen Bay** bay E Bering Sea
9 N1 **Hazen, Lake** ◎ Nunavut, N Canada
139 S5 **Hazīm, Bi'r** well C Iraq
23 V6 **Hazlehurst** Georgia, SE USA 31°51′N 82°35′W
22 K6 **Hazlehurst** Mississippi, S USA 31°51′N 90°24′W
18 K15 **Hazlet** New Jersey, NE USA 40°24′N 74°10′W
146 I9 **Hazorasp** Rus. Khazarosp. Xorazm Viloyati, W Uzbekistan 41°21′N 61°01′E
147 R13 **Hazratishoh, Qatorkŭhi** var. Khrebet Khazretishi, Rus. Khrebet Khozretishi. ▲▲ S Tajikistan
Hazr, Kūh-e ā see Hazārān, Kūh-e
149 U6 **Hazro** Punjab, E Pakistan 33°55′N 72°33′E
23 R7 **Headland** Alabama, S USA 31°21′N 85°20′W
182 C6 **Head of Bight** headland South Australia 31°33′S 131°05′E
33 N10 **Headquarters** Idaho, NW USA 46°38′N 115°52′W
34 M7 **Healdsburg** California, W USA 38°36′N 122°52′W
27 N13 **Healdton** Oklahoma, C USA 34°13′N 97°29′W
183 O12 **Healesville** Victoria, SE Australia 37°41′S 145°31′E
39 R10 **Healy** Alaska, USA 63°51′N 148°58′W
173 R13 **Heard and McDonald Islands** ◇ Australian external territory S Indian Ocean
173 R13 **Heard Island** island Heard and McDonald Islands, S Indian Ocean
25 U9 **Hearne** Texas, SW USA 30°52′N 96°35′W
12 F12 **Hearst** Ontario, S Canada 49°42′N 83°40′W
194 J5 **Hearst Island** island Antarctica
Heart of Dixie see Alabama
28 L5 **Heart River** ≈ North Dakota, N USA
31 T13 **Heath** Ohio, N USA 40°01′N 82°26′W
183 N11 **Heathcote** Victoria, SE Australia 36°57′S 144°43′E
97 N22 **Heathrow** ✈ (London) SE England, United Kingdom 51°28′N 00°27′W
21 X5 **Heathsville** Virginia, NE USA 37°55′N 76°29′W
27 R11 **Heavener** Oklahoma, C USA 34°53′N 94°36′W
25 R15 **Hebbronville** Texas, SW USA 27°19′N 98°41′W
163 Q13 **Hebei** var. Hebei Sheng, Hopeh, Hopei, Ji; prev. Chihli. ◈ province E China
Hebei Sheng see Hebei
36 M3 **Heber City** Utah, W USA 40°31′N 111°25′W
27 V10 **Heber Springs** Arkansas, C USA 35°30′N 92°01′W
161 N5 **Hebi** Henan, C China 35°57′N 114°08′E
32 F11 **Hebo** Oregon, NW USA 45°10′N 123°55′W
96 F9 **Hebrides, Sea of the** sea NW Scotland, United Kingdom
13 P5 **Hebron** Newfoundland and Labrador, E Canada 58°15′N 62°45′W
31 N11 **Hebron** Indiana, N USA 41°19′N 87°12′W
29 Q17 **Hebron** Nebraska, C USA 40°10′N 97°35′W
28 L5 **Hebron** North Dakota, N USA 46°54′N 102°03′W
138 F11 **Hebron** var. Al Khalīl, El Khalil, Heb. Hevron; anc. Kiriath-Arba. S West Bank 31°30′N 35°E
Hebrus see Évros/Maritsa/Meriç
95 N14 **Heby** Västmanland, C Sweden 59°56′N 16°53′E
10 I14 **Hecate Strait** strait British Columbia, W Canada
41 W12 **Hecelchakán** Campeche, SE Mexico 20°09′N 90°04′W
160 K13 **Hechi** var. Jinchengjiang. Guangxi Zhuangzu Zizhiqu, S China 24°39′N 108°02′E
101 H23 **Hechingen** Baden-Württemberg, S Germany 48°20′N 08°58′E
99 K17 **Hechtel** Limburg, NE Belgium 51°07′N 05°24′E
160 J9 **Hechuan** var. Heyang. Chongqing Shi, C China 30°02′N 106°15′E
29 P7 **Hecla** South Dakota, N USA 45°52′N 98°09′W
9 N1 **Hecla, Cape** headland Nunavut, N Canada 82°00′N 64°00′W
29 T9 **Hector** Minnesota, N USA 44°44′N 94°43′W
93 F17 **Hede** Jämtland, C Sweden 62°25′N 13°33′E
Hede see Sheyang
95 M14 **Hedemora** Dalarna, C Sweden 60°18′N 15°58′E
92 K13 **Hedenäset** Norrbotten, N Sweden 66°12′N 23°40′E
95 G23 **Hedensted** Vejle, C Denmark 55°47′N 09°43′E
95 N14 **Hedesunda** Gävleborg, C Sweden 60°25′N 17°00′E
95 N14 **Hedesundafjord** ◎ C Sweden
25 O3 **Hedley** Texas, SW USA 34°52′N 100°39′W
94 I12 **Hedmark** ◈ county S Norway
165 T16 **Hedo-misaki** headland Okinawa, SW Japan 26°55′N 128°15′E
29 X15 **Hedrick** Iowa, C USA 41°10′N 92°18′W
99 L16 **Heel** Limburg, SE Netherlands 51°12′N 06°01′E
189 Y12 **Heel Point** point Wake Island
98 H9 **Heemskerk** Noord-Holland, W Netherlands 52°31′N 04°40′E
98 M10 **Heerde** Gelderland, E Netherlands 52°24′N 06°02′E
98 L7 **Heerenveen** Fris. It Hearrenfean. Friesland, N Netherlands 52°57′N 05°55′E
98 I8 **Heerhugowaard** Noord-Holland, NW Netherlands 52°40′N 04°50′E
92 O3 **Heer Land** physical region C Svalbard
99 M18 **Heerlen** Limburg, SE Netherlands 50°55′N 06°E
99 J19 **Heers** Limburg, NE Belgium 50°46′N 05°17′E
Heerwegen see Polkowice
98 K13 **Heesch** Noord-Brabant, S Netherlands 51°44′N 05°32′E
99 K15 **Heeze** Noord-Brabant, SE Netherlands 51°23′N 05°35′E
138 F8 **Hefa** var. Haifa, hist. Caiffa, Caiphas; anc. Sycaminum. Haifa, N Israel 32°49′N 34°59′E
Ḫefa, Mifraz see Mifrats Hefa
161 Q8 **Hefei** var. Hofei, hist. Luchow. province capital Anhui, E China 31°51′N 117°20′E
23 R3 **Heflin** Alabama, S USA 33°39′N 85°35′W
163 X7 **Hegang** Heilongjiang, NE China 47°18′N 130°16′E
164 L10 **Hegura-jima** island SW Japan
Heguri-jima see Heigun-tō
Hei see Heilongjiang
100 H8 **Heide** Schleswig-Holstein, N Germany 54°12′N 09°06′E
101 G20 **Heidelberg** Baden-Württemberg, SW Germany 49°24′N 08°41′E
83 J21 **Heidelberg** Gauteng, NE South Africa 26°31′S 28°21′E
22 M6 **Heidelberg** Mississippi, S USA 31°53′N 88°58′W
Heidenheim see Heidenheim an der Brenz
101 J22 **Heidenheim an der Brenz** var. Heidenheim. Baden-Württemberg, S Germany 48°41′N 10°09′E
109 U2 **Heidenreichstein** Niederösterreich, N Austria 48°53′N 15°07′E
164 F14 **Heigun-tō** var. Heguri-jima. island SW Japan
163 W5 **Heihe** prev. Ai-hun. Heilongjiang, NE China 50°13′N 127°29′E
162 S8 **Hei He** ≈ C China
Hei-ho see Nagqu
83 J22 **Heilbron** Free State, N South Africa 27°17′S 27°58′E
101 H21 **Heilbronn** Baden-Württemberg, SW Germany 49°09′N 09°13′E
Heiligenbeil see Mamonovo
109 Q8 **Heiligenblut** Tirol, W Austria 47°04′N 12°50′E
100 K7 **Heiligenhafen** Schleswig-Holstein, N Germany 54°22′N 10°57′E
Heiligenkreuz see Žiar nad Hronom
101 J15 **Heiligenstadt** Thüringen, C Germany 51°22′N 10°09′E
163 W8 **Heilongjiang** var. Hei, Heilongjiang Sheng, Hei-lung-chiang, Heilungkiang. ◈ province NE China
Heilong Jiang see Amur
Heilongjiang Sheng see Heilongjiang
98 H9 **Heiloo** Noord-Holland, NW Netherlands 52°36′N 04°43′E
Heilsberg see Lidzbark Warmiński
Hei-lung-chiang/Heilungkiang see Heilongjiang
Heimaæy see Heimaey
92 I4 **Heimaey** var. Heimaæy. island S Iceland
94 H8 **Heimdal** Sør-Trøndelag, S Norway 63°21′N 10°23′E
Heinaste see Ainaži
93 N17 **Heinävesi** Itä-Suomi, E Finland 62°22′N 28°42′E
99 M22 **Heinerscheid** Diekirch, N Luxembourg 50°06′N 06°05′E
98 M10 **Heino** Overijssel, E Netherlands 52°26′N 06°13′E
93 M18 **Heinola** Etelä-Suomi, S Finland 61°13′N 26°05′E
101 C16 **Heinsberg** Nordrhein-Westfalen, W Germany 51°02′N 06°01′E
163 U12 **Heishan** Liaoning, NE China 41°43′N 122°12′E
160 H8 **Heishui** var. Luhua. Sichuan, C China 32°08′N 102°54′E
99 H17 **Heist-op-den-Berg** Antwerpen, C Belgium 51°04′N 04°43′E
Heitō see P'ingtung
171 X15 **Heitske** Papua, E Indonesia 07°02′S 138°45′E
Hejanah see Al Hījānah
Hejaz see Al Ḩijāz
160 M14 **He Jiang** ≈ S China
Hejiayan see Lüeyang
158 K6 **Hejing** Xinjiang Uygur Zizhiqu, NW China 42°21′N 86°19′E
Héjjasfalva see Vânători
Heka see Hoika
137 N14 **Hekimhan** Malatya, C Turkey 38°50′N 37°56′E
92 J4 **Hekla** ▲ S Iceland 63°56′N 19°42′W
Hekou see Yanshan, Jiangxi, China
Hekou see Yajiang, Sichuan, China
110 J6 **Hel** Ger. Hela. Pomorskie, N Poland 54°35′N 18°48′E
Hela see Hel
93 F17 **Helagsfjället** ▲ C Sweden 62°57′N 12°31′E
159 W8 **Helan** var. Xigang. Ningxia, N China 38°33′N 106°21′E
162 K14 **Helan Shan** ▲▲ N China
99 M16 **Helden** Limburg, SE Netherlands 51°20′N 06°00′E
27 X12 **Helena** Arkansas, C USA 34°32′N 90°34′W
33 R10 **Helena** state capital Montana, NW USA 46°36′N 112°02′W
96 H12 **Helensburgh** W Scotland, United Kingdom 56°00′N 04°45′W
184 K5 **Helensville** Auckland, North Island, New Zealand 36°42′S 174°26′E
95 L20 **Helgasjön** ◎ S Sweden
100 G8 **Helgoland** Eng. Heligoland. island NW Germany
Helgoland Bay see Helgoländer Bucht
100 G8 **Helgoländer Bucht** var. Helgoland Bay, Heligoland Bight. bay NW Germany
Heligoland see Helgoland
Heligoland Bight see Helgoländer Bucht
Heliopolis see Baalbek
92 I4 **Hella** Sudhurland, SW Iceland 63°51′N 20°24′W
Hellas see Greece
143 N11 **Ḩelleh, Rūd-e** ≈ S Iran
98 N10 **Hellendoorn** Overijssel, E Netherlands 52°22′N 06°27′E
Hellenic Republic see Greece
121 Q10 **Hellenic Trough** undersea feature Aegean Sea, C Mediterranean Sea 22°00′E 35°30′N
94 E10 **Hellesylt** Møre og Romsdal, S Norway 62°06′N 06°51′E
98 F13 **Hellevoetsluis** Zuid-Holland, SW Netherlands 51°49′N 04°08′E
105 Q12 **Hellín** Castilla-La Mancha, C Spain 38°31′N 01°43′W
115 H19 **Hellinikon** ✈ (Athína) Attikí, C Greece 37°53′N 23°43′E
32 M12 **Hells Canyon** valley Idaho/Oregon, NW USA
148 L9 **Helmand** ◈ province S Afghanistan
148 K10 **Helmand, Daryā-ye** var. Rūd-e Hīrmand. ≈ Afghanistan/Iran see also Hīrmand, Rūd-e
Helmand, Daryā-ye see Hīrmand, Rūd-e
Helmantica see Salamanca
101 K15 **Helme** ≈ C Germany
99 L15 **Helmond** Noord-Brabant, S Netherlands 51°29′N 05°41′E
96 J7 **Helmsdale** N Scotland, United Kingdom 58°06′N 03°36′W
100 K13 **Helmstedt** Niedersachsen, N Germany 52°14′N 11°01′E
163 Y10 **Helong** Jilin, NE China 42°38′N 129°01′E
36 M4 **Helper** Utah, W USA 39°40′N 110°52′W
100 O10 **Helpter Berge** hill NE Germany
95 J22 **Helsingborg** prev. Hälsingborg. Skåne, S Sweden 56°N 12°48′E
Helsingfors see Helsinki
95 J22 **Helsingør** Eng. Elsinore. Frederiksborg, E Denmark 56°03′N 12°38′E
93 M20 **Helsinki** Swe. Helsingfors. ● (Finland) Etelä-Suomi, S Finland 60°18′N 24°58′E
97 H25 **Helston** SW England, United Kingdom 50°04′N 05°17′W
Heltau see Cisnădie
61 C17 **Helvecia** Santa Fe, C Argentina 31°09′S 60°09′W

◆ Country
● Country Capital
◇ Dependent Territory
○ Dependent Territory Capital
◈ Administrative Regions
✈ International Airport
▲ Mountain
▲▲ Mountain Range
Volcano
≈ River
◎ Lake
⊠ Reservoir

97 K15 **Helvellyn** ▲ NW England, United Kingdom *54°31'N 03°00'W*
Helvetia *see* Switzerland
Helwân *see* Hilwān
97 N21 **Hemel Hempstead** E England, United Kingdom *51°46'N 00°28'W*
35 U16 **Hemet** California, W USA *33°45'N 116°58'W*
28 J13 **Hemingford** Nebraska, C USA *42°18'N 103°02'W*
21 T13 **Hemingway** South Carolina, SE USA *33°45'N 79°25'W*
92 G13 **Hemnesberget** Nordland, C Norway *66°14'N 13°40'E*
25 Y8 **Hemphill** Texas, SW USA *31°21'N 93°50'W*
25 V11 **Hempstead** Texas, SW USA *30°06'N 96°06'W*
95 P20 **Hemse** Gotland, SE Sweden *57°12'N 18°22'E*
94 F13 **Hemsedal** *valley* S Norway
161 N6 **Henan** ***var.*** Henan Sheng, Honan, Yu. ◈ *province* C China
184 L4 **Hen and Chickens** *island group* N New Zealand
Henan Mongolzu Zizhixian/Henan Sheng *see* Yêgainnyin
105 O7 **Henares** ≈ C Spain
165 P7 **Henashi-zaki** *headland* Honshū, C Japan *40°37'N 139°51'E*
102 I16 **Hendaye** Pyrénées-Atlantiques, SW France *43°22'N 01°46'W*
136 F11 **Hendek** Sakarya, NW Turkey *40°47'N 30°45'E*
61 B21 **Henderson** Buenos Aires, E Argentina *36°18'S 61°43'W*
20 I5 **Henderson** Kentucky, S USA *37°50'N 87°35'W*
35 X11 **Henderson** Nevada, W USA *36°02'N 114°58'W*
21 V8 **Henderson** North Carolina, SE USA *36°20'N 78°26'W*
20 G10 **Henderson** Tennessee, S USA *35°27'N 88°40'W*
25 W7 **Henderson** Texas, SW USA *32°11'N 94°48'W*
30 J12 **Henderson Creek** ≈ Illinois, N USA
186 M9 **Henderson Field** ✈ (Honiara) Guadalcanal, C Solomon Islands *09°28'S 160°02'E*
191 O17 **Henderson Island** *atoll* N Pitcairn Islands
21 O10 **Hendersonville** North Carolina, SE USA *35°19'N 82°28'W*
20 J8 **Hendersonville** Tennessee, S USA *36°18'N 86°37'W*
143 O14 **Hendorābī, Jazīreh-ye** *island* S Iran
55 V10 **Hendrik Top** ***var.*** Hendriktop. *elevation* C Surinam
Hendriktop *see* Hendrik Top
Hendū Kosh *see* Hindu Kush
14 L12 **Heney, Lac** ◎ Québec, SE Canada
Hengchow *see* Hengyang
161 S15 **Hengchun** S Taiwan *22°09'N 120°43'E*
159 R16 **Hengduan Shan** ▲▲ SW China
98 N12 **Hengelo** Gelderland, E Netherlands *52°03'N 06°19'E*
98 O10 **Hengelo** Overijssel, E Netherlands *52°16'N 06°46'E*
Hengnan *see* Hengyang
161 N11 **Hengshan** Hunan, S China *27°17'N 112°51'E*
160 L4 **Hengshan** Shaanxi, C China *37°57'N 109°17'E*
161 O4 **Hengshui** Hebei, E China *37°42'N 115°39'E*
161 N12 **Hengyang** ***var.*** Hengnan, Heng-yang; ***prev.*** Hengchow. Hunan, S China *26°55'N 112°34'E*
Heng-yang *see* Hengyang
117 U11 **Heniches'k** ***Rus.*** Genichesk. Khersons'ka Oblast', S Ukraine *46°10'N 34°49'E*
21 Z4 **Henlopen, Cape** *headland* Delaware, NE USA *38°48'N 75°06'W*
Henna *see* Enna
94 M10 **Hennan** Gävleborg, C Sweden *62°01'N 15°55'E*
102 G7 **Hennebont** Morbihan, NW France *47°48'N 03°17'W*
30 L11 **Hennepin** Illinois, N USA *41°14'N 89°21'W*
26 M9 **Hennessey** Oklahoma, C USA *36°06'N 97°54'W*
100 N12 **Hennigsdorf** ***var.*** Hennigsdorf bei Berlin. Brandenburg, NE Germany *52°37'N 13°13'E*
Hennigsdorf bei Berlin *see* Hennigsdorf
19 N9 **Henniker** New Hampshire, NE USA *43°10'N 71°47'W*
25 S5 **Henrietta** Texas, SW USA *33°49'N 98°13'W*
Henrique de Carvalho *see* Saurimo
30 L12 **Henry** Illinois, N USA *41°06'N 89°21'W*
21 Y7 **Henry, Cape** *headland* Virginia, NE USA *36°55'N 76°01'W*
27 P10 **Henryetta** Oklahoma, C USA *35°26'N 95°58'W*
194 M7 **Henry Ice Rise** *ice cap* Antarctica
9 R5 **Henry Kater, Cape** *headland* Baffin Island, Nunavut, NE Canada *69°09'N 66°45'W*
33 R13 **Henrys Fork** ≈ Idaho, NW USA
14 E15 **Hensall** Ontario, S Canada *43°25'N 81°28'W*
100 J9 **Henstedt-Ulzburg** Schleswig-Holstein, N Germany *53°45'N 09°59'E*
163 N7 **Hentiy** ***var.*** Batshireet, Eg. ◈ *province* N Mongolia
162 M7 **Hentiyn Nuruu** ▲▲ N Mongolia
183 P10 **Henty** New South Wales, SE Australia *35°33'S 147°03'E*
Henzada *see* Hinthada
Heping *see* Huishui
101 G19 **Heppenheim** Hessen, W Germany *49°39'N 08°38'E*
32 J11 **Heppner** Oregon, NW USA *45°21'N 119°32'W*
160 L15 **Hepu** ***var.*** Lianzhou. Guangxi Zhuangzu Zizhiqu, S China *21°40'N 109°12'E*
Heracleum *see* Irákleio
92 J2 **Heradhsvötn** ≈ C Iceland
Herakleion *see* Irákleio
148 K5 **Herāt** ***var.*** Herat; ***anc.*** Aria. Herāt, W Afghanistan *34°23'N 62°11'E*
148 J5 **Herāt** ◈ *province* W Afghanistan
103 P14 **Hérault** ◈ *department* S France
103 P15 **Hérault** ≈ S France
11 T16 **Herbert** Saskatchewan, S Canada *50°27'N 107°09'W*
185 F22 **Herbert** Otago, South Island, New Zealand *45°14'S 170°48'E*
38 J17 **Herbert Island** *island* Aleutian Islands, Alaska, USA
Herbertshöhe *see* Kokopo
15 Q7 **Hérbertville** Québec, SE Canada *48°23'N 71°42'W*
101 G17 **Herborn** Hessen, W Germany *50°40'N 08°18'E*
113 I17 **Herceg-Novi** ***It.*** Castelnuovo; ***prev.*** Ercegnovi. SW Montenegro *42°28'N 18°35'E*
11 X10 **Herchmer** Manitoba, C Canada *57°25'N 94°12'W*
186 E8 **Hercules Bay** *bay* E Papua New Guinea
92 K2 **Herdhubreidh** ▲ C Iceland *65°12'N 16°26'W*
42 M13 **Heredia** Heredia, C Costa Rica *10°N 84°06'W*
42 M12 **Heredia** ***off.*** Provincia de Heredia. ◈ *province* N Costa Rica
Heredia, Provincia de *see* Heredia
97 K21 **Hereford** W England, United Kingdom *52°04'N 02°43'W*
24 M3 **Hereford** Texas, SW USA *34°49'N 102°25'W*
15 Q13 **Hereford, Mont** ▲ Québec, SE Canada *45°04'N 71°38'W*
97 K21 **Herefordshire** *cultural region* W England, United Kingdom
191 U11 **Hereheretue** *atoll* Îles Tuamotu, C French Polynesia
105 N10 **Herencia** Castilla-La Mancha, C Spain *39°22'N 03°12'W*
99 H18 **Herent** Vlaams Brabant, C Belgium *50°54'N 04°40'E*
99 I16 **Herentals** ***var.*** Herenthals. Antwerpen, N Belgium *51°11'N 04°50'E*
Herenthals *see* Herentals
99 H17 **Herenthout** Antwerpen, N Belgium *51°09'N 04°45'E*
95 J23 **Herfølge** Roskilde, E Denmark *55°25'N 12°09'E*
100 G13 **Herford** Nordrhein-Westfalen, NW Germany *52°07'N 08°41'E*
27 O5 **Herington** Kansas, C USA *38°37'N 96°55'W*
108 H7 **Herisau** ***Fr.*** Hérisau. Appenzell Ausser Rhoden, NE Switzerland *47°23'N 09°17'E*
Hérisau *see* Herisau
Héristal *see* Herstal
99 J18 **Herk-de-Stad** Limburg, NE Belgium *50°57'N 05°12'E*
Herkulesbad/Herkulesfürdő *see* Băile Herculane
162 M8 **Herlenbayan-Ulaan** ***var.*** Dulaan. Hentiy, C Mongolia *47°09'N 108°48'E*
Herlen Gol/Herlen He *see* Kerulen
35 Q4 **Herlong** California, W USA *40°07'N 120°06'W*
97 L26 **Herm** *island* Channel Islands
109 R9 **Hermagor** ***Slvn.*** Šmohor. Kärnten, S Austria *46°37'N 13°24'E*
29 S7 **Herman** Minnesota, N USA *45°49'N 96°08'W*
96 L1 **Herma Ness** *headland* NE Scotland, United Kingdom *60°51'N 00°55'W*
27 V4 **Hermann** Missouri, C USA *38°43'N 91°26'W*
181 Q8 **Hermannsburg** Northern Territory, N Australia *23°59'S 132°55'E*
Hermannstadt *see* Sibiu
94 E12 **Hermansverk** Sogn Og Fjordane, S Norway *61°11'N 06°52'E*
138 H6 **Hermel** ***var.*** Hirmil. NE Lebanon *34°23'N 36°19'E*
Hermhausen *see* Hajnówka
183 P6 **Hermidale** New South Wales, SE Australia *31°36'S 146°42'E*
55 X9 **Herminadorp** Sipaliwini, NE Surinam *05°05'N 54°22'W*
32 K11 **Hermiston** Oregon, NW USA *45°50'N 119°17'W*
27 T6 **Hermitage** Missouri, C USA *37°57'N 93°21'W*
186 D4 **Hermit Islands** *island group* N Papua New Guinea
25 O7 **Hermleigh** Texas, SW USA *32°37'N 100°44'W*
138 G7 **Hermon, Mount** ***Ar.*** Jabal ash Shaykh. ▲ S Syria *35°30'N 33°30'E*
Hermopolis Parva *see* Damanhûr
28 J10 **Hermosa** South Dakota, N USA *43°49'N 103°12'W*
40 F5 **Hermosillo** Sonora, NW Mexico *28°59'N 110°53'W*
Hermoupolis *see* Ermoúpoli
111 N20 **Hernád** ***var.*** Hornád, ***Ger.*** Kundert. ≈ Hungary/Slovakia
61 C18 **Hernández** Entre Ríos, E Argentina *32°21'S 60°02'W*
23 V11 **Hernando** Florida, SE USA *28°54'N 82°22'W*
22 L1 **Hernando** Mississippi, S USA *34°49'N 89°59'W*
105 Q2 **Hernani** País Vasco, N Spain *43°16'N 01°59'W*
99 F19 **Herne** Vlaams Brabant, C Belgium *50°45'N 04°03'E*
101 E14 **Herne** Nordrhein-Westfalen, W Germany *51°32'N 07°12'E*
95 F22 **Herning** Ringkøbing, W Denmark *56°08'N 08°59'E*
Hernösand *see* Härnösand
121 U11 **Herodotus Basin** *undersea feature* E Mediterranean Sea
121 Q12 **Herodotus Trough** *undersea feature* C Mediterranean Sea
29 T11 **Heron Lake** Minnesota, N USA *43°48'N 95°18'W*
Herowābād *see* Khalkhāl
95 G16 **Herre** Telemark, S Norway *59°06'N 09°34'E*
29 N7 **Herreid** South Dakota, N USA *45°49'N 100°04'W*
101 H22 **Herrenberg** Baden-Württemberg, S Germany *48°36'N 08°52'E*
104 L14 **Herrera** Andalucía, S Spain *37°22'N 04°50'W*
43 R17 **Herrera** ***off.*** Provincia de Herrera. ◈ *province* S Panama
104 L10 **Herrera del Duque** Extremadura, W Spain *39°10'N 05°03'W*
104 M4 **Herrera de Pisuerga** Castilla-León, N Spain *42°35'N 04°20'W*
Herrera, Provincia de *see* Herrera
41 Z13 **Herrero, Punta** *headland* SE Mexico *19°15'N 87°28'W*
183 P16 **Herrick** Tasmania, SE Australia *41°07'S 147°53'E*
30 L17 **Herrin** Illinois, N USA *37°48'N 89°01'W*
20 M6 **Herrington Lake** ⊠ Kentucky, S USA
95 K18 **Herrljunga** Västra Götaland, S Sweden *58°05'N 13°02'E*
103 N16 **Hers** ≈ S France
10 I1 **Herschel Island** *island* Yukon Territory, NW Canada
99 I17 **Herselt** Antwerpen, C Belgium *51°04'N 04°53'E*
18 G15 **Hershey** Pennsylvania, NE USA *40°17'N 76°39'W*
99 K19 **Herstal** ***Fr.*** Héristal. Liège, E Belgium *50°40'N 05°38'E*
97 O21 **Hertford** E England, United Kingdom *51°48'N 00°05'W*
21 X8 **Hertford** North Carolina, SE USA *36°11'N 76°30'W*
97 O21 **Hertfordshire** *cultural region* E England, United Kingdom
181 Z9 **Hervey Bay** Queensland, E Australia *25°17'S 152°48'E*
101 O14 **Herzberg** Brandenburg, E Germany *51°42'N 13°15'E*
99 E18 **Herzele** Oost-Vlaanderen, NW Belgium *50°52'N 03°52'E*
101 K20 **Herzogenaurach** Bayern, SE Germany *49°34'N 10°52'E*
109 W4 **Herzogenburg** Niederösterreich, NE Austria *48°18'N 15°43'E*
Herzogenbusch *see* 's-Hertogenbosch
103 N2 **Hesdin** Pas-de-Calais, N France *50°21'N 02°00'E*
160 K14 **Heshan** Guangxi Zhuangzu Zizhiqu, S China *23°45'N 108°58'E*
159 X10 **Heshui** ***var.*** Xihuachi. Gansu, C China *35°42'N 108°06'E*
99 M25 **Hespérange** Luxembourg, SE Luxembourg *49°34'N 06°10'E*
35 U14 **Hesperia** California, W USA *34°25'N 117°17'W*
37 P7 **Hesperus Mountain** ▲ Colorado, C USA *37°27'N 108°05'W*
10 J6 **Hess** ≈ Yukon Territory, NW Canada
Hesse *see* Hessen
101 J21 **Hesselberg** ▲ S Germany *49°04'N 10°32'E*
95 I22 **Hesselo** *island* E Denmark
101 H17 **Hessen** ***Eng./Fr.*** Hesse. ◈ *state* C Germany
192 L6 **Hess Tablemount** *undersea feature* C Pacific Ocean *17°49'N 174°15'W*
27 N6 **Hesston** Kansas, C USA *38°08'N 97°25'W*
93 G15 **Hestkjøltoppen** ▲ C Norway *64°21'N 13°57'E*
97 K18 **Heswall** NW England, United Kingdom *53°20'N 03°06'W*
153 P12 **Hetaudā** Central, C Nepal
Hétfalu *see* Săcele
28 K7 **Hettinger** North Dakota, N USA *46°00'N 102°38'W*
101 L14 **Hettstedt** Sachsen-Anhalt, C Germany *51°39'N 11°31'E*
92 P3 **Heuglin, Kapp** *headland* SE Svalbard *78°15'N 22°49'E*
187 N10 **Heuru** San Cristobal, SE Solomon Islands *10°13'S 161°25'E*
99 J17 **Heusden** Limburg, NE Belgium *51°02'N 05°17'E*
98 J13 **Heusden** Noord-Brabant, S Netherlands *51°43'N 05°05'E*
102 K3 **Hève, Cap de la** *headland* N France *49°28'N 00°13'W*
99 H18 **Heverlee** Vlaams Brabant, C Belgium *50°52'N 04°41'E*
111 L22 **Heves** Heves, NE Hungary *47°36'N 20°17'E*
111 L22 **Heves** ***off.*** Heves Megye. ◈ *county* NE Hungary
Heves Megye *see* Heves
Hevron *see* Hebron
45 Y13 **Hewanorra** ✈ (Saint Lucia) S Saint Lucia *13°44'N 60°57'W*
Hexian *see* Hezhou
160 L6 **Heyang** Shaanxi, C China *35°14'N 110°02'E*
Heyang *see* Hechuan
Heydebrech *see* Kędzierzyn-Kozle
Heydekrug *see* Šilutė
Heyin *see* Guide
97 K16 **Heysham** NW England, United Kingdom *54°02'N 02°54'W*
161 O14 **Heyuan** ***var.*** Yuancheng. Guangdong, S China *23°41'N 114°45'E*
182 L12 **Heywood** Victoria, SE Australia *38°09'S 141°38'E*
180 K3 **Heywood Islands** *island group* Western Australia
161 O6 **Heze** ***var.*** Caozhou. Shandong, E China *35°16'N 115°27'E*
159 U11 **Hezheng** Gansu, C China *35°29'N 103°36'E*
160 M13 **Hezhou** ***var.*** Babu; ***prev.*** Hexian. Guangxi Zhuangzu Zizhiqu, S China *24°33'N 11°30'E*
159 U11 **Hezuo** Gansu, C China *34°55'N 102°49'E*
23 Z16 **Hialeah** Florida, SE USA *25°51'N 80°16'W*
27 Q3 **Hiawatha** Kansas, C USA *39°51'N 95°34'W*
36 M4 **Hiawatha** Utah, W USA *39°28'N 111°00'W*
29 V4 **Hibbing** Minnesota, N USA *47°24'N 92°55'W*
183 N17 **Hibbs, Point** *headland* Tasmania, SE Australia *42°37'S 145°15'E*
Hibernia *see* Ireland
20 F8 **Hickman** Kentucky, S USA *36°33'N 89°11'W*
21 Q9 **Hickory** North Carolina, SE USA *35°44'N 81°20'W*
21 Q9 **Hickory, Lake** ◎ North Carolina, SE USA
184 Q7 **Hicks Bay** Gisborne, North Island, New Zealand *37°36'S 178°18'E*
25 S8 **Hico** Texas, SW USA *31°58'N 98°01'W*
Hida *see* Furukawa
165 T4 **Hidaka** Hokkaidō, NE Japan *42°53'N 142°24'E*
164 I12 **Hidaka** Hyōgo, Honshū, SW Japan *35°27'N 134°43'E*
165 T5 **Hidaka-sanmyaku** ▲▲ Hokkaidō, NE Japan
41 O6 **Hidalgo** ***var.*** Villa Hidalgo. Coahuila, NE Mexico *27°46'N 99°54'W*
41 N8 **Hidalgo** Nuevo León, NE Mexico *29°59'N 100°27'W*
41 O10 **Hidalgo** Tamaulipas, C Mexico *24°16'N 99°28'W*
41 O13 **Hidalgo** ◈ *state* C Mexico
40 J7 **Hidalgo del Parral** ***var.*** Parral. Chihuahua, N Mexico *26°58'N 105°40'W*
100 N7 **Hiddensee** *island* NE Germany
80 G6 **Hidiglib, Wadi** ≈ NE Sudan
109 U6 **Hieflau** Salzburg, E Austria *47°36'N 14°34'E*
187 P16 **Hienghène** Province Nord, C New Caledonia *20°43'S 164°54'E*
Hierosolyma *see* Jerusalem
64 N12 **Hierro** ***var.*** Ferro. *island* Islas Canarias, Spain, NE Atlantic Ocean
164 G13 **Higashi-Hiroshima** ***var.*** Higasihirosima. Hiroshima, Honshū, SW Japan *34°27'N 132°43'E*
164 C12 **Higashi-suidō** *strait* SW Japan
Higasihirosima *see* Higashi-Hiroshima
25 P1 **Higgins** Texas, SW USA *36°06'N 100°01'W*
31 P7 **Higgins Lake** ◎ Michigan, N USA
27 S4 **Higginsville** Missouri, C USA *39°04'N 93°43'W*
High Atlas *see* Haut Atlas
30 M5 **High Falls Reservoir** ⊠ Wisconsin, N USA
44 K12 **Highgate** C Jamaica *18°16'N 76°53'W*
25 X11 **High Island** Texas, SW USA *29°35'N 94°24'W*
31 O5 **High Island** *island* Michigan, N USA
30 K15 **Highland** Illinois, N USA *38°44'N 89°40'W*
31 N10 **Highland Park** Illinois, N USA *42°10'N 87°48'W*
21 O10 **Highlands** North Carolina, SE USA *35°04'N 83°10'W*
11 O11 **High Level** Alberta, W Canada *58°31'N 117°08'W*
29 O9 **Highmore** South Dakota, N USA *44°29'N 99°26'W*
171 N3 **High Peak** ▲ Luzon, N Philippines *15°28'N 120°07'E*
High Plains *see* Great Plains
21 S9 **High Point** North Carolina, SE USA *35°58'N 80°00'W*
18 J13 **High Point** *hill* New Jersey, NE USA
11 P13 **High Prairie** Alberta, W Canada *55°27'N 116°28'W*
11 Q16 **High River** Alberta, SW Canada *50°35'N 113°50'W*
21 S9 **High Rock Lake** ⊠ North Carolina, SE USA
23 V9 **High Springs** Florida, SE USA *29°49'N 82°36'W*
High Veld *see* Great Karoo
97 J24 **High Willhays** ▲ SW England, United Kingdom *50°39'N 03°58'W*
97 N22 **High Wycombe** ***prev.*** Chepping Wycombe, Chipping Wycombe. SE England, United Kingdom *51°38'N 00°46'W*
41 P12 **Higos** ***var.*** El Higo. Veracruz-Llave, E Mexico *21°48'N 98°25'W*
102 I16 **Higuer, Cap** *headland* NE Spain *43°23'N 01°46'W*
45 R5 **Higüero, Punta** *headland* W Puerto Rico *18°21'N 67°15'W*
45 P9 **Higüey** ***var.*** Salvaleón de Higüey. E Dominican Republic *18°40'N 68°43'W*
190 G11 **Hihifo** ✈ (Matā'utu) Île Uvea, N Wallis and Futuna
81 N16 **Hiiraan** ***off.*** Gobolka Hiiraan. ◈ *region* C Somalia
Hiiraan, Gobolka *see* Hiiraan
118 E4 **Hiiumaa** ***var.*** Hiiumaa Maakond. ◈ *province* W Estonia
118 D4 **Hiiumaa** ***Ger.*** Dagden, ***Swe.*** Dagö. *island* W Estonia
Hiiumaa Maakond *see* Hiiumaa
Hijanah *see* Al Hījānah
105 S6 **Híjar** Aragón, NE Spain *41°10'N 00°27'W*
191 V10 **Hikueru** *atoll* Îles Tuamotu, C French Polynesia
184 K3 **Hikurangi** Northland, North Island, New Zealand *35°37'S 174°16'E*
184 Q8 **Hikurangi** ▲ North Island, New Zealand *37°55'S 177°59'E*
192 L11 **Hikurangi Trench** ***var.*** Hikurangi Trough. *undersea feature* SW Pacific Ocean
Hikurangi Trough *see* Hikurangi Trench
190 B15 **Hikutavake** NW Niue
121 Q12 **Hilāl, Ra's al** *headland* N Libya *32°55'N 22°09'E*
61 A24 **Hilario Ascasubi** Buenos Aires, E Argentina *39°22'S 62°39'W*
101 K17 **Hildburghausen** Thüringen, C Germany *50°26'N 10°44'E*
101 E15 **Hilden** Nordrhein-Westfalen, W Germany *51°12'N 06°56'E*
100 I13 **Hildesheim** Niedersachsen, N Germany *52°09'N 09°57'E*
33 T9 **Hilger** Montana, NW USA *47°15'N 109°18'W*
153 S13 **Hili** ***var.*** Hilli. Rajshahi, NW Bangladesh *25°16'N 89°04'E*
Hilla *see* Al Ḥillah
45 O14 **Hillaby, Mount** ▲ N Barbados *13°12'N 59°34'W*
95 K19 **Hillared** Västra Götaland, S Sweden *57°37'N 13°10'E*
195 R12 **Hillary Coast** *physical region* Antarctica
42 G2 **Hill Bank** Orange Walk, N Belize *17°36'N 88°43'W*
33 O14 **Hill City** Idaho, NW USA *43°18'N 115°03'W*
26 K3 **Hill City** Kansas, C USA *39°23'N 99°51'W*
29 V5 **Hill City** Minnesota, N USA *46°59'N 93°36'W*
28 J10 **Hill City** South Dakota, N USA *43°54'N 103°33'W*
98 H10 **Hillegom** Zuid-Holland, W Netherlands *52°18'N 04°35'E*
95 J22 **Hillerød** Frederiksborg, E Denmark *55°56'N 12°19'E*
36 M7 **Hillers, Mount** ▲ Utah, W USA *37°53'N 110°42'W*
Hilli *see* Hili
29 R11 **Hills** Minnesota, N USA *43°31'N 96°21'W*
30 L14 **Hillsboro** Illinois, N USA *39°09'N 89°29'W*
27 N5 **Hillsboro** Kansas, C USA *38°21'N 97°12'W*
27 X5 **Hillsboro** Missouri, C USA *38°13'N 90°33'W*
19 N10 **Hillsboro** New Hampshire, NE USA *43°06'N 71°52'W*
37 Q14 **Hillsboro** New Mexico, SW USA *32°55'N 107°33'W*
29 R4 **Hillsboro** North Dakota, N USA *47°25'N 97°03'W*
31 R14 **Hillsboro** Ohio, N USA *39°12'N 83°36'W*
32 G11 **Hillsboro** Oregon, NW USA *45°32'N 122°59'W*
25 T8 **Hillsboro** Texas, SW USA *32°01'N 97°08'W*
30 K8 **Hillsboro** Wisconsin, N USA *43°40'N 90°21'W*
23 Y14 **Hillsboro Canal** *canal* Florida, SE USA
45 Y15 **Hillsborough** Carriacou, N Grenada *12°28'N 61°28'W*
97 G15 **Hillsborough** E Northern Ireland, United Kingdom *54°27'N 06°06'W*
21 U9 **Hillsborough** North Carolina, SE USA *36°04'N 79°06'W*
31 Q10 **Hillsdale** Michigan, N USA *41°55'N 84°37'W*
183 O8 **Hillston** New South Wales, SE Australia *33°30'S 145°33'E*
21 R7 **Hillsville** Virginia, NE USA *36°46'N 80°44'W*
96 L2 **Hillswick** NE Scotland, United Kingdom *60°28'N 01°37'W*
Hill Tippera *see* Tripura
38 H11 **Hilo** Hawaii, USA, C Pacific Ocean *19°42'N 155°04'W*
18 F9 **Hilton** New York, NE USA *43°17'N 77°47'W*
14 C10 **Hilton Beach** Ontario, S Canada *46°14'N 83°51'W*
21 R16 **Hilton Head Island** South Carolina, SE USA *32°13'N 80°45'W*
21 R16 **Hilton Head Island** *island* South Carolina, SE USA
99 J15 **Hilvarenbeek** Noord-Brabant, S Netherlands *51°29'N 05°08'E*
98 J11 **Hilversum** Noord-Holland, C Netherlands *52°14'N 05°10'E*
75 W8 **Hilwān** ***var.*** Helwân, Hulwan, Hulwân. N Egypt *29°51'N 31°20'E*
Hilwân *see* Hilwān
152 J7 **Himāchal Pradesh** ◈ *state* NW India
Himalaya/Himalaya Shan *see* Himalayas
152 M9 **Himalayas** ***var.*** Himalaya, ***Chin.*** Himalaya Shan. ▲▲ S Asia
171 P6 **Himamaylan** Negros, C Philippines *10°04'N 122°52'E*
93 K15 **Himanka** Länsi-Suomi, W Finland *64°04'N 23°40'E*
Himara *see* Himarë
113 L23 **Himarë** ***var.*** Himara. Vlorë, S Albania *40°06'N 19°45'E*
138 M2 **Ḥimār, Wādī al** *dry watercourse* N Syria
154 D9 **Himatnagar** Gujarāt, W India *23°38'N 73°02'E*
109 Y4 **Himberg** Niederösterreich, E Austria *48°05'N 16°27'E*
164 I13 **Himeji** ***var.*** Himezi. Hyōgo, Honshū, SW Japan *34°47'N 134°32'E*
164 E14 **Hime-jima** *island* SW Japan
Himezi *see* Himeji
164 L13 **Himi** Toyama, Honshū, SW Japan *36°54'N 136°59'E*
109 S9 **Himmelberg** Kärnten, S Austria *46°45'N 14°01'E*
138 I5 **Ḥimş** ***var.*** Homs; ***anc.*** Emesa. Ḥimş, C Syria *34°44'N 36°43'E*
138 K6 **Ḥimş** ***off.*** Muḥāfazat Hims, ***var.*** Homs. ◈ *governorate* C Syria
138 I5 **Ḥimş, Buḥayrat** ***var.*** Buhayrat Qattinah. ◎ W Syria
171 R7 **Hinatuan** Mindanao, S Philippines *08°21'N 126°19'E*
117 N10 **Hînceşti** ***var.*** Hânceşti; ***prev.*** Kotovsk. C Moldova *46°48'N 28°33'E*
44 M9 **Hinche** C Haiti *19°07'N 72°00'W*
181 X5 **Hinchinbrook Island** *island* Queensland, NE Australia
39 S12 **Hinchinbrook Island** *island* Alaska, USA
97 M19 **Hinckley** C England, United Kingdom *52°33'N 01°21'W*
29 V7 **Hinckley** Minnesota, N USA *46°01'N 92°57'W*
36 K5 **Hinckley** Utah, W USA *39°21'N 112°39'W*
18 J9 **Hinckley Reservoir** ⊠ New York, NE USA
152 I12 **Hindaun** Rājasthān, N India *26°44'N 77°02'E*
Hindenburg/Hindenburg in Oberschlesien *see* Zabrze
Hindiya *see* Al Hindīyah
21 O6 **Hindman** Kentucky, S USA *37°20'N 82°58'W*
182 L10 **Hindmarsh, Lake** ◎ Victoria, SE Australia
185 G19 **Hinds** Canterbury, South Island, New Zealand *44°01'S 171°33'E*
185 G19 **Hinds** ≈ South Island, New Zealand
95 H23 **Hindsholm** *island* C Denmark
149 S4 **Hindu Kush** ***Per.*** Hendū Kosh. ▲▲ Afghanistan/Pakistan
155 H19 **Hindupur** Andhra Pradesh, E India *13°46'N 77°33'E*
11 O12 **Hines Creek** Alberta, W Canada *56°14'N 118°36'W*
23 W6 **Hinesville** Georgia, SE USA *31°51'N 81°36'W*
154 I12 **Hinganghāt** Mahārāshtra, C India *20°32'N 78°52'E*
149 N15 **Hingol** ≈ SW Pakistan
154 H13 **Hingoli** Mahārāshtra, C India *19°45'N 77°08'E*
137 R13 **Hınıs** Erzurum, E Turkey *39°22'N 41°44'E*
92 O2 **Hinlopenstretet** *strait* N Svalbard
92 G10 **Hinnøya** ***Lapp.*** Iinnasuolu. *island* C Norway
108 H10 **Hinterrhein** ≈ SW Switzerland
166 L8 **Hinthada** ***var.*** Henzada. Ayeyarwady, SW Burma (Myanmar) *17°36'N 95°26'E*
11 O14 **Hinton** Alberta, SW Canada *53°24'N 117°35'W*
26 M10 **Hinton** Oklahoma, C USA *35°28'N 98°21'W*
21 R6 **Hinton** West Virginia, NE USA *37°42'N 80°54'W*
Hios *see* Chíos
41 N8 **Hipolito** Coahuila, NE Mexico *25°42'N 101°22'W*
Hipponium *see* Vibo Valentia
164 B13 **Hirado** Nagasaki, Hirado-shima, SW Japan *33°22'N 129°31'E*
164 B13 **Hirado-shima** *island* SW Japan
165 P16 **Hirakubo-saki** *headland* Ishigaki-jima, SW Japan *24°36'N 124°19'E*
154 M11 **Hīrākud Reservoir** ⊠ E India
Hir al Gharbi, Qasr al *see* Ḥayr al Gharbī, Qaşr al
165 Q16 **Hirara** Okinawa, Miyako-jima, SW Japan *24°48'N 125°17'E*
Hir Ash Sharqī, Qasr al *see* Ḥayr ash Sharqī, Qaşr al
164 G12 **Hirata** Shimane, Honshū, SW Japan *35°25'N 132°45'E*
136 I13 **Hirfanlı Barajı** ⊠ C Turkey
155 G18 **Hiriyūr** Karnātaka, W India *13°58'N 76°33'E*
Hîrlău *see* Hârlău
148 K10 **Hīrmand, Rūd-e** ***var.*** Daryā-ye Helmand. ≈ Afghanistan/Iran ***see also*** Helmand, Daryā-ye
Hīrmand, Rūd-e *see* Helmand, Daryā-ye
Hirmil *see* Hermel
165 T5 **Hiroo** Hokkaidō, NE Japan *42°16'N 143°16'E*
165 Q7 **Hirosaki** Aomori, Honshū, C Japan *40°34'N 140°28'E*
164 G13 **Hiroshima** ***var.*** Hirosima. Hiroshima, Honshū, SW Japan *34°23'N 132°26'E*
164 F13 **Hiroshima** ***off.*** Hiroshima-ken, ***var.*** Hirosima. ◈ *prefecture* Honshū, SW Japan
Hiroshima-ken *see* Hiroshima
Hirosima *see* Hiroshima
Hirschberg/Hirschberg im Riesengebirge/Hirschberg in Schlesien *see* Jelenia Góra
103 Q3 **Hirson** Aisne, N France *49°56'N 04°05'E*
Hîrşova *see* Hârşova
95 G19 **Hirtshals** Nordjylland, N Denmark *57°34'N 09°58'E*
152 H10 **Hisār** Haryāna, NW India *29°10'N 75°45'E*
162 K7 **Hishig Öndör** ***var.*** Maanĭt. Bulgan, C Mongolia *48°17'N 103°29'E*
186 E9 **Hisiu** Central, SW Papua New Guinea *09°20'S 146°48'E*
147 P13 **Hisor** ***Rus.*** Gissar. W Tajikistan *38°34'N 68°29'E*
Hispalis *see* Sevilla
Hispana/Hispania *see* Spain
44 M7 **Hispaniola** *island* Dominion Republic/Haiti
64 F11 **Hispaniola Basin** ***var.*** Hispaniola Trough. *undersea feature* SW Atlantic Ocean
Hispaniola Trough *see* Hispaniola Basin
Histonium *see* Vasto
139 R7 **Hīt** Al Anbār, SW Iraq *33°38'N 42°50'E*
165 P14 **Hita** Ōita, Kyūshū, SW Japan *33°19'N 130°55'E*
165 P12 **Hitachi** ***var.*** Hitati. Ibaraki, Honshū, S Japan *36°40'N 140°42'E*
165 P12 **Hitachi-Ōta** ***var.*** Hitatiôta. Ibaraki, Honshū, S Japan *36°32'N 140°31'E*
Hitati *see* Hitachi
Hitatiôta *see* Hitachi-Ōta
97 O21 **Hitchin** E England, United Kingdom *51°57'N 00°17'W*
191 Q7 **Hitiaa** Tahiti, W French Polynesia *17°35'S 149°17'W*
164 D15 **Hitoyoshi** ***var.*** Hitoyosi. Kumamoto, Kyūshū, SW Japan *32°12'N 130°48'E*
Hitoyosi *see* Hitoyoshi
94 F7 **Hitra** ***prev.*** Hitteren. *island* S Norway
Hitteren *see* Hitra
187 Q11 **Hiu** *island* Torres Islands, N Vanuatu
165 O11 **Hiuchiga-take** ▲ Honshū, C Japan *36°57'N 139°18'E*
191 X7 **Hiva Oa** *island* Îles Marquises, N French Polynesia
20 M10 **Hiwassee Lake** ⊠ North Carolina, SE USA
20 M10 **Hiwassee River** ≈ SE USA
95 H20 **Hjallerup** Nordjylland, N Denmark *57°10'N 10°10'E*
95 M16 **Hjälmaren** ***Eng.*** Lake Hjalmar. ◎ C Sweden
Hjalmar, Lake *see* Hjälmaren
95 C14 **Hjellestad** Hordaland, S Norway *60°15'N 05°13'E*
95 D16 **Hjelmeland** Rogaland, S Norway *59°12'N 06°07'E*
94 G10 **Hjerkinn** Oppland, S Norway *62°13'N 09°37'E*
95 L18 **Hjo** Västra Götaland, S Sweden *58°18'N 14°17'E*
95 G19 **Hjørring** Nordjylland, N Denmark *57°28'N 09°59'E*
167 O1 **Hkakabo Razi** ▲ Burma (Myanmar)/China *28°17'N 97°28'E*
167 N1 **Hkring Bum** ▲ N Burma (Myanmar) *27°05'N 97°16'E*
83 L21 **Hlathikulu** ***var.*** Hlatikulu. S Swaziland *26°58'S 31°19'E*
Hlatikulu *see* Hlathikulu
Hliboka *see* Hlyboka
111 F17 **Hlinsko** ***var.*** Hlinsko v Čechách. Pardubický Kraj, C Czech Republic *49°46'N 15°54'E*
Hlinsko v Čechách *see* Hlinsko
117 S6 **Hlobyne** ***Rus.*** Globino. Poltavs'ka Oblast', NE Ukraine *49°24'N 33°16'E*
111 H20 **Hlohovec** ***Ger.*** Freistadtl, ***Hung.*** Galgóc; ***prev.*** Frakštát. Trnavský Kraj, W Slovakia *48°26'N 17°49'E*
83 J23 **Hlotse** ***var.*** Leribe. NW Lesotho *28°55'S 28°01'E*
111 I17 **Hlučín** ***Ger.*** Hultschin, ***Pol.*** Hulczyn. Moravskoslezský Kraj, E Czech Republic *49°54'N 18°11'E*
117 S2 **Hlukhiv** ***Rus.*** Glukhov. Sums'ka Oblast', NE Ukraine *51°40'N 33°53'E*
119 K21 **Hlushkavichy** ***Rus.*** Glushkevichi. Homyel'skaya Voblasts', SE Belarus *51°34'N 27°47'E*
119 L18 **Hlusk** ***Rus.*** Glusk, Glussk. Mahilyowskaya Voblasts', E Belarus *52°54'N 28°41'E*
116 K8 **Hlyboka** ***Ger.*** Hliboka, ***Rus.*** Glybokaya. Chernivets'ka Oblast', W Ukraine *48°04'N 25°56'E*
118 K13 **Hlybokaye** ***Rus.*** Glubokoye. Vitsyebskaya Voblasts', N Belarus *55°08'N 27°41'E*
77 Q16 **Ho** SE Ghana *06°36'N 00°28'E*
167 S6 **Hoa Binh** Hoa Binh, N Vietnam *20°49'N 105°20'E*
83 E20 **Hoachanas** Hardap, C Namibia *23°55'S 18°04'E*
Hoai Nhơn *see* Bông Sơn
167 T8 **Hoa Lac** Quang Binh, C Vietnam *17°54'N 106°24'E*
167 S5 **Hoang Liên Sơn** ▲▲ N Vietnam
83 B17 **Hoanib** ≈ NW Namibia
33 S15 **Hoback Peak** ▲ Wyoming, C USA *43°04'N 110°34'W*
183 P17 **Hobart** ***prev.*** Hobarton, Hobart Town. *state capital* Tasmania, SE Australia *42°54'S 147°18'E*
26 L11 **Hobart** Oklahoma, C USA *35°03'N 99°04'W*
183 P17 **Hobart** ✈ Tasmania, SE Australia *42°52'S 147°28'E*
Hobarton/Hobart Town *see* Hobart
37 W14 **Hobbs** New Mexico, SW USA *32°42'N 103°08'W*
194 L12 **Hobbs Coast** *physical region* Antarctica
23 Z14 **Hobe Sound** Florida, SE USA *27°03'N 80°08'W*
Hobicaurikány *see* Uricani
54 E12 **Hobo** Huila, S Colombia *02°34'N 75°28'W*
99 G16 **Hoboken** Antwerpen, N Belgium *51°12'N 04°22'E*
158 K3 **Hoboksar** ***var.*** Hoboksar Mongol Zizhixian. Xinjiang Uygur Zizhiqu, NW China *46°48'N 85°42'E*
Hoboksar Mongol Zizhixian *see* Hoboksar
95 G21 **Hobro** Nordjylland, N Denmark *56°39'N 09°51'E*
21 X10 **Hobucken** North Carolina, SE USA *35°15'N 76°31'W*
95 O20 **Hoburgen** *headland* SE Sweden *56°54'N 18°07'E*
81 P15 **Hobyo** ***It.*** Obbia. Mudug, E Somalia *05°16'N 48°24'E*
109 R8 **Hochalmspitze** ▲ SW Austria *47°00'N 13°19'E*
109 Q4 **Hochburg** Oberösterreich, N Austria *48°10'N 12°57'E*
108 F8 **Hochdorf** Luzern, N Switzerland *47°10'N 08°16'E*
109 N8 **Hochfeiler** ***It.*** Gran Pilastro. ▲ Austria/Italy *46°59'N 11°42'E*
167 T14 **Hô Chi Minh** ***var.*** Ho Chi Minh City; ***prev.*** Saigon. S Vietnam *10°46'N 106°43'E*
Ho Chi Minh City *see* Hô Chi Minh
108 I7 **Höchst** Vorarlberg, NW Austria *47°28'N 09°40'E*
Höchstadt *see* Höchstadt an der Aisch
101 K19 **Höchstadt an der Aisch** ***var.*** Höchstadt. Bayern, C Germany *49°43'N 10°48'E*
108 L9 **Hochwilde** ***It.*** L'Altissima. ▲ Austria/Italy *46°45'N 11°00'E*
109 S7 **Hochwildstelle** ▲ C Austria *47°21'N 13°53'E*
31 T14 **Hocking River** ≈ Ohio, N USA
Hoctúm *see* Hoctún
41 X12 **Hoctún** ***var.*** Hoctúm. Yucatán, E Mexico *20°48'N 89°14'W*
Hodeida *see* Al Ḥudaydah
20 K6 **Hodgenville** Kentucky, S USA *37°34'N 85°45'W*
11 T17 **Hodgeville** Saskatchewan, S Canada *50°06'N 106°55'W*
76 L9 **Hodh ech Chargui** ◈ *region* E Mauritania
Hodh el Garbi *see* Hodh el Gharbi
76 J10 **Hodh el Gharbi** ***var.*** Hodh el Garbi. ◈ *region* S Mauritania
111 L25 **Hódmezővásárhely** Csongrád, SE Hungary *46°27'N 20°18'E*
74 J6 **Hodna, Chott El** ***var.*** Chott el-Hodna, ***Ar.*** Shatt al-Hodna. *salt lake* N Algeria
Hodna, Chott el-/Hodna, Shatt al- *see* Hodna, Chott El
111 G19 **Hodonín** ***Ger.*** Göding. Jihomoravský Kraj, SE Czech Republic *48°52'N 17°07'E*
Hödrögö *see* Nömrög
Hodság/Hodschag *see* Odžaci
39 R7 **Hodzana River** ≈ Alaska, USA
Hoei *see* Huy
99 H19 **Hoeilaart** Vlaams Brabant, C Belgium *50°46'N 04°28'E*
Hoë Karoo *see* Great Karoo
98 F12 **Hoek van Holland** ***Eng.*** Hook of Holland. Zuid-Holland, W Netherlands *52°00'N 04°07'E*
98 L11 **Hoenderloo** Gelderland, E Netherlands *52°08'N 05°46'E*
99 L18 **Hoensbroek** Limburg, SE Netherlands *50°55'N 05°55'E*
163 Y11 **Hoeryŏng** NE North Korea *42°23'N 129°46'E*
99 K18 **Hoeselt** Limburg, NE Belgium *50°50'N 05°30'E*
98 K11 **Hoevelaken** Gelderland, C Netherlands *52°10'N 05°27'E*
Hoey *see* Huy
101 M18 **Hof** Bayern, SE Germany *50°19'N 11°55'E*
Höfdhakaupstadhur *see* Skagaströnd
Hofei *see* Hefei
101 G18 **Hofheim am Taunus** Hessen, W Germany *50°04'N 08°27'E*
Hofmarkt *see* Odorheiu Secuiesc

◆ Country ● Country Capital ◇ Dependent Territory ○ Dependent Territory Capital ◈ Administrative Regions ✈ International Airport ▲ Mountain ▲▲ Mountain Range Volcano ≈ River ◎ Lake ⊠ Reservoir

92 L3 Höfn Austurland, SE Iceland 64°14′N 15°17′W
94 N13 Hofors Gävleborg, C Sweden 60°33′N 16°21′E
92 J6 Hofsjökull glacier C Iceland
92 J1 Hofsós Nordhurland Vestra, N Iceland 65°54′N 19°25′W
164 E13 Hōfu Yamaguchi, Honshū, SW Japan 34°01′N 131°34′E
Hofuf see Al Hufūf
95 J22 Höganäs Skåne, S Sweden 56°11′N 12°39′E
183 P14 Hogan Group island group Tasmania, SE Australia
23 R4 Hogansville Georgia, SE USA 33°10′N 84°55′W
39 P8 Hogatza River ≈ Alaska, USA
28 I14 Hogback Mountain ▲ Nebraska, C USA 41°40′N 103°44′W
95 G14 Høgevarde ▲ S Norway 60°19′N 09°27′E
Högfors see Karkkila
31 P5 Hog Island island Michigan, N USA
21 Y6 Hog Island island Virginia, NE USA
Hogoley Islands see Chuuk Islands
95 N20 Högsby Kalmar, S Sweden 57°10′N 16°03′E
36 K1 Hogup Mountains ▲▲ Utah, W USA
101 E17 Hohe Acht ▲ W Germany 50°23′N 07°00′E
Hohenelbe see Vrchlabí
108 I7 Hohenems Vorarlberg, W Austria 47°23′N 09°43′E
Hohenmauth see Vysoké Mýto
Hohensalza see Inowrocław
Hohenstadt see Zábřeh
Hohenstein in Ostpreussen see Olsztynek
20 I9 Hohenwald Tennessee, S USA 35°33′N 87°31′W
101 L17 Hohenwarte-Stausee ⊠ C Germany
Hohes Venn see Hautes Fagnes
109 Q8 Hohe Tauern ▲▲ W Austria
163 O13 Hohhot var. Huhehot, Huhohaote, Mong. Kukukhoto; prev. Kweisui, Kwesui. Nei Mongol Zizhiqu, N China 40°49′N 111°37′E
162 F7 Hohmorit var. Sayn-Ust. Govĭ-Altay, W Mongolia 47°23′N 94°19′E
103 U6 Hohneck ▲ NE France 48°04′N 07°01′E
77 Q16 Hohoe E Ghana 07°08′N 00°32′E
164 E12 Hōhoku Yamaguchi, Honshū, SW Japan 34°15′N 130°56′E
159 O11 Hoh Sai Hu ◎ C China
159 N11 Hoh Xil Hu ◎ C China
158 L11 Hoh Xil Shan ▲▲ W China
167 U10 Hôi An prev. Faifo. Quang Nam-Đa Năng, C Vietnam 15°54′N 108°19′E
Hoï-Hao/Hoihow see Haikou
159 S11 Hoika prev. Heka. Qinghai, W China 35°49′N 99°50′E
81 F17 Hoima W Uganda 01°25′N 31°22′E
26 L5 Hoisington Kansas, C USA 38°31′N 98°46′W
146 D12 Hojagala Rus. Khodzhakala. Balkan Welaýaty, W Turkmenistan 38°46′N 56°14′E
146 M13 Hojambaz Rus. Khodzhambas. Lebap Welaýaty, E Turkmenistan 38°11′N 64°33′E
95 H23 Højby Fyn, C Denmark 55°20′N 10°27′E
95 F24 Højer Sønderjylland, SW Denmark 54°57′N 08°43′E
164 E14 Hōjō var. Hôzyô. Ehime, Shikoku, SW Japan 33°58′N 132°47′E
184 J3 Hokianga Harbour inlet SE Tasman Sea
185 F17 Hokitika West Coast, South Island, New Zealand 42°44′S 170°58′E
165 U4 Hokkai-dō ◈ territory Hokkaidō, NE Japan
165 T3 Hokkaidō prev. Ezo, Yeso, Yezo. island NE Japan
95 G15 Hokksund Buskerud, S Norway 59°45′N 09°55′E
143 S4 Hokmābād Khorāsān-Razavī, N Iran 36°37′N 57°34′E
Hokō see P'ohang
Hoko-guntō/Hoko-shotō see P'enghu Liehtao
Hoktemberyan see Armavir
94 F13 Hol Buskerud, S Norway 60°36′N 08°18′E
117 R11 Hola Prystan' Rus. Golaya Pristan. Khersons'ka Oblast', S Ukraine 46°31′N 32°31′E
95 I23 Holbæk Vestsjælland, E Denmark 55°42′N 11°42′E
Holboo see Santmargats
183 P10 Holbrook New South Wales, SE Australia 35°45′S 147°18′E
37 N11 Holbrook Arizona, SW USA 34°54′N 110°09′W
27 S5 Holden Missouri, C USA 38°42′N 93°59′W
36 K5 Holden Utah, W USA 39°06′N 112°16′W
27 O11 Holdenville Oklahoma, C USA 35°05′N 96°25′W
29 O16 Holdrege Nebraska, C USA 40°28′N 99°28′W
35 X3 Hole in the Mountain Peak ▲ Nevada, W USA 40°54′N 115°06′W
155 G20 Hole Narsipur Karnātaka, W India 12°46′N 76°14′E
111 H18 Holešov Ger. Holleschau. Zlínský Kraj, E Czech Republic 49°20′N 17°35′E
45 N14 Holetown prev. Jamestown. W Barbados 13°11′N 59°38′W
31 Q12 Holgate Ohio, N USA 41°12′N 84°06′W
44 I7 Holguín Holguín, SE Cuba 20°51′N 76°16′W
23 V12 Holiday Florida, SE USA 28°11′N 82°44′W
39 O12 Holitna River ≈ Alaska, USA
94 J13 Höljes Värmland, C Sweden 60°54′N 12°34′E
109 X3 Hollabrunn Niederösterreich, NE Austria 48°33′N 16°06′E
36 L3 Holladay Utah, W USA 40°39′N 111°49′W
11 X16 Holland Manitoba, S Canada 49°36′N 98°52′W
31 O9 Holland Michigan, N USA 42°47′N 86°06′W
25 T9 Holland Texas, SW USA 30°52′N 97°24′W
Holland see Netherlands
22 K4 Hollandale Mississippi, S USA 33°10′N 90°51′W
Hollandia see Jayapura
Hollandsch Diep see Hollands Diep
99 H14 Hollands Diep var. Hollandsch Diep. channel SW Netherlands
Holleschau see Holešov
25 R5 Holliday Texas, SW USA 33°49′N 98°41′W
18 E15 Hollidaysburg Pennsylvania, NE USA 40°24′N 78°22′W
21 S6 Hollins Virginia, NE USA 37°20′N 79°56′W
26 J12 Hollis Oklahoma, C USA 34°42′N 99°56′W
35 O10 Hollister California, W USA 36°51′N 121°25′W
27 T8 Hollister Missouri, C USA 36°37′N 93°13′W
93 M19 Hollola Etelä-Suomi, S Finland 61°N 25°32′E
98 K4 Hollum Friesland, N Netherlands 53°27′N 05°38′E
95 J23 Höllviksnäs Skåne, S Sweden 55°25′N 12°57′E
37 W6 Holly Colorado, C USA 38°03′N 102°07′W
31 R9 Holly Michigan, N USA 42°47′N 83°37′W
21 S14 Holly Hill South Carolina, SE USA 33°19′N 80°24′W
21 W11 Holly Ridge North Carolina, SE USA 34°31′N 77°31′W
22 L1 Holly Springs Mississippi, S USA 34°47′N 89°25′W
23 Z15 Hollywood Florida, SE USA 26°00′N 80°09′W
8 J6 Holman Victoria Island, Northwest Territories, N Canada 70°42′N 117°45′W
92 I2 Hólmavík Vestfirdhir, NW Iceland 65°42′N 21°43′W
30 J7 Holmen Wisconsin, N USA 43°57′N 91°14′W
23 R8 Holmes Creek ≈ Alabama/Florida, SE USA
95 H16 Holmestrand Vestfold, S Norway 59°29′N 10°20′E
93 J16 Holmön island N Sweden
95 E22 Holmsland Klit beach W Denmark
93 J16 Holmsund Västerbotten, N Sweden 63°42′N 20°26′E
95 Q18 Holmudden headland SE Sweden 57°59′N 19°14′E
138 F10 Holon var. Kholon; prev. Ḥolon. Tel Aviv, C Israel 32°01′N 34°46′E
Ḥolon see Holon
163 P7 Hölönbuyr var. Bayan. Dornod, E Mongolia 47°56′N 112°58′E
117 P8 Holovanivs'k Rus. Golovanevsk. Kirovohrads'ka Oblast', C Ukraine 48°21′N 30°26′E
95 F21 Holstebro Ringkøbing, W Denmark 56°22′N 08°38′E
95 F23 Holsted Ribe, W Denmark 55°30′N 08°54′E
29 T13 Holstein Iowa, C USA 42°29′N 95°32′W
Holsteinborg/Holsteinsborg/Holstenborg/Holstensborg see Sisimiut
21 O8 Holston River ≈ Tennessee, S USA
31 Q9 Holt Michigan, N USA 42°38′N 84°31′W
98 N10 Holten Overijssel, E Netherlands 52°16′N 06°25′E
27 P3 Holton Kansas, C USA 39°27′N 95°44′W
27 U5 Holts Summit Missouri, C USA 38°38′N 92°07′W
35 X17 Holtville California, W USA 32°48′N 115°22′W
98 L5 Holwerd Fris. Holwert. Friesland, N Netherlands 53°22′N 05°51′E
Holwert see Holwerd
39 O11 Holy Cross Alaska, USA 62°12′N 159°46′W
37 R4 Holy Cross, Mount Of The ▲ Colorado, C USA 39°28′N 106°28′W
97 I18 Holyhead Wel. Caer Gybi. NW Wales, United Kingdom 53°19′N 04°38′W
97 H18 Holy Island island NW Wales, United Kingdom
96 L12 Holy Island island NE England, United Kingdom
37 W3 Holyoke Colorado, C USA 40°31′N 102°18′W
18 M11 Holyoke Massachusetts, NE USA 42°12′N 72°37′W
101 I14 Holzminden Niedersachsen, C Germany 51°49′N 09°27′E
81 G19 Homa Bay Nyanza, W Kenya 0°31′S 34°30′E
Homāyūnshahr see Khomeynīshahr
77 P11 Hombori Mopti, S Mali 15°13′N 01°39′W
101 E20 Homburg Saarland, SW Germany 49°20′N 07°20′E
9 R5 Home Bay bay Baffin Bay, Nunavut, NE Canada
Homenau see Humenné
39 Q13 Homer Alaska, USA 59°38′N 151°33′W
22 H4 Homer Louisiana, S USA 32°47′N 93°03′W
18 H10 Homer New York, NE USA 42°38′N 76°10′W
23 V7 Homerville Georgia, SE USA 31°02′N 82°45′W
23 Y16 Homestead Florida, SE USA 25°28′N 80°28′W
27 O9 Hominy Oklahoma, C USA 36°24′N 96°24′W
94 H8 Hommelvik Sør-Trøndelag, S Norway 63°24′N 10°48′E
95 C16 Hommersåk Rogaland, S Norway 58°55′N 05°51′E
155 H15 Homnābād Karnātaka, C India 17°46′N 77°08′E
22 J7 Homochitto River ≈ Mississippi, S USA
83 N20 Homoine Inhambane, SE Mozambique 23°51′S 35°04′E
112 O12 Homoljske Planine ▲ E Serbia
Homonna see Humenné
Homs see Al Khums, Libya
Homs see Ḥimṣ
119 P19 Homyel' Rus. Gomel'. Homyel'skaya Voblasts', SE Belarus 52°25′N 31°E
118 L12 Homyel' Vitsyebskaya Voblasts', N Belarus 55°20′N 28°52′E
119 L19 Homyel'skaya Voblasts' prev. Rus. Gomel'skaya Oblast'. ◈ province SE Belarus
Honan see Luoyang, China
Honan see Henan, China
164 U4 Honbetsu Hokkaidō, NE Japan 43°09′N 143°46′E
Honctō see Gurahonț
54 E9 Honda Tolima, C Colombia 05°12′N 74°45′W
83 D24 Hondeklip Afr. Hondeklipbaai. Northern Cape, W South Africa 30°15′S 17°17′E
Hondeklipbaai see Hondeklip
11 Q13 Hondo Alberta, W Canada 54°43′N 113°14′W
164 C15 Hondo Kumamoto, Shimo-jima, SW Japan 32°28′N 130°12′E
25 Q12 Hondo Texas, SW USA 29°21′N 99°09′W
42 G1 Hondo ≈ Central America
Hondo see Honshū
42 G6 Honduras off. Republic of Honduras. ◆ republic Central America
Honduras, Golfo de see Honduras, Gulf of
42 H4 Honduras, Gulf of Sp. Golfo de Honduras. gulf W Caribbean Sea
Honduras, Republic of see Honduras
11 V12 Hone Manitoba, C Canada 56°13′N 101°12′W
21 P12 Honea Path South Carolina, SE USA 34°27′N 82°23′W
95 H14 Hønefoss Buskerud, S Norway 60°10′N 10°15′E
31 S12 Honey Creek ≈ Ohio, N USA
25 V5 Honey Grove Texas, SW USA 33°34′N 95°54′W
35 Q4 Honey Lake ◎ California, W USA
102 L4 Honfleur Calvados, N France 49°25′N 00°14′E
Hon Gai see Hông Gai
161 O8 Hong'an prev. Huang'an. Hubei, C China 31°20′N 114°43′E
Hongay see Hông Gai
167 T6 Hông Gai var. Hon Gai, Hongay. Quang Ninh, N Vietnam 20°57′N 107°06′E
161 O15 Honghai Wan bay N South China Sea
Hông Hà, Sông see Red River
161 O7 Hong He ≈ C China
161 N9 Hong Hu ◎ C China
160 L11 Hongjiang Hunan, S China 27°09′N 109°58′E
Hongjiang see Wangcang
161 O15 Hong Kong Chin. Xianggang. Hong Kong, S China 22°17′N 114°09′E
160 L4 Hongliu He ≈ C China
160 L4 Hongliu He ≈ C China
159 P8 Hongliuwan var. Aksay, Aksay Kazakzu Zizhixian. Gansu, N China 39°25′N 94°09′E
159 P7 Hongliuyuan Gansu, N China 41°02′N 95°24′E
Hongor see Delgereh
161 S8 Hongqiao ✈ (Shanghai) Shanghai Shi, E China 31°28′N 121°08′E
Hongshui see Minle
160 K14 Hongshui He ≈ S China
160 M5 Hongtong var. Dahuaishu. Shanxi, C China 36°30′N 111°42′E
164 J15 Hongū Wakayama, Honshū, SW Japan 33°50′N 135°42′E
Honguedo, Détroit d' see Honguedo Passage
15 Y5 Honguedo Passage var. Honguedo Strait, Fr. Détroit d'Honguedo. strait Québec, E Canada
Honguedo Strait see Honguedo Passage
Hongwan see Hongwansi
159 S8 Hongwansi var. Sunan, Sunan Yugurzu Zizhixian; prev. Hongwan. Gansu, N China 38°55′N 99°29′E
163 X13 Hongwŏn E North Korea 40°03′N 127°54′E
160 H7 Hongyuan var. Qiongxi; prev. Hurama. Sichuan, C China 32°49′N 102°40′E
161 Q7 Hongze Hu var. Hung-tse Hu. ◎ E China
186 L9 Honiara ● (Solomon Islands) Guadalcanal, C Solomon Islands 09°27′S 159°56′E
165 P8 Honjō var. Honzyô, Yurihonjō. Akita, Honshū, C Japan 39°23′N 140°03′E
93 K18 Honkajoki Länsi-Suomi, SW Finland 62°00′N 22°15′E
92 K7 Honningsvåg Finnmark, N Norway 70°58′N 25°59′E
95 I19 Hönö Västra Götaland, S Sweden 57°42′N 11°39′E
38 G11 Honoka'a Hawaii, USA, C Pacific Ocean 20°04′N 155°27′W
38 G11 Honoka'a var. Honokaa. Hawaii, USA, C Pacific Ocean 20°04′N 155°27′W
Honokaa see Honoka'a
38 D9 Honolulu state capital O'ahu, Hawaii, USA, C Pacific Ocean 21°18′N 157°52′W
38 H11 Honomū var. Honomu. Hawaii, USA, C Pacific Ocean 19°51′N 155°06′W
105 P10 Honrubia Castilla-La Mancha, C Spain 39°36′N 02°17′W
164 M12 Honshū var. Hondo, Honsyû. island SW Japan
Honsyû see Honshū
Honte see Westerschelde
Honzyô see Honjō
8 K8 Hood ≈ Nunavut, NW Canada
Hood Island see Española, Isla
32 H11 Hood, Mount ▲ Oregon, NW USA 45°22′N 121°41′W
32 H11 Hood River Oregon, NW USA 45°44′N 121°31′W
98 H10 Hoofddorp Noord-Holland, W Netherlands 52°18′N 04°41′E
99 G15 Hoogerheide Noord-Brabant, S Netherlands 51°25′N 04°19′E
98 N8 Hoogeveen Drenthe, NE Netherlands 52°44′N 06°30′E
98 O6 Hoogezand-Sappemeer Groningen, NE Netherlands 53°10′N 06°47′E
98 J8 Hoogkarspel Noord-Holland, NW Netherlands 52°42′N 04°59′E
98 N5 Hoogkerk Groningen, NE Netherlands 53°13′N 06°30′E
98 G13 Hoogvliet Zuid-Holland, SW Netherlands 51°51′N 04°23′E
26 I8 Hooker Oklahoma, C USA 36°51′N 101°12′W
97 E21 Hook Head Ir. Rinn Duáin. headland SE Ireland 52°07′N 06°55′W
Hook of Holland see Hoek van Holland
Hoolt see Tögrög
39 W13 Hoonah Chichagof Island, Alaska, USA 58°05′N 135°21′W
38 L11 Hooper Bay Alaska, USA 61°31′N 166°06′W
31 N13 Hoopeston Illinois, N USA 40°28′N 87°40′W
95 K22 Höör Skåne, S Sweden 55°55′N 13°33′E
98 I9 Hoorn Noord-Holland, NW Netherlands 52°38′N 05°04′E
18 L10 Hoosic River ≈ New York, NE USA
Hoosier State see Indiana
35 Y11 Hoover Dam dam Arizona/Nevada, W USA
Höövör see Baruunbayan-Ulaan
137 Q11 Hopa Artvin, NE Turkey 41°23′N 41°28′E
18 J14 Hopatcong New Jersey, NE USA 40°55′N 74°39′W
10 M17 Hope British Columbia, SW Canada 49°21′N 121°28′W
39 R12 Hope Alaska, USA 60°55′N 149°38′W
27 T14 Hope Arkansas, C USA 33°40′N 93°36′W
31 P14 Hope Indiana, N USA 39°18′N 85°46′W
29 Q5 Hope North Dakota, N USA 47°18′N 97°42′W
13 Q7 Hopedale Newfoundland and Labrador, NE Canada 55°26′N 60°14′W
Hopeh/Hopei see Hebei
180 K13 Hope, Lake salt lake Western Australia
41 X13 Hopelchén Campeche, SE Mexico 19°46′N 89°50′W
21 U11 Hope Mills North Carolina, SE USA 34°58′N 78°57′W
183 O7 Hope, Mount New South Wales, SE Australia 32°49′S 145°55′E
92 P4 Hopen island SE Svalbard
197 Q4 Hope, Point headland Alaska, USA
12 M3 Hopes Advance, Cap cape Québec, NE Canada
182 L10 Hopetoun Victoria, SE Australia 35°46′S 142°23′E
83 H23 Hopetown Northern Cape, W South Africa 29°37′S 24°05′E
21 W6 Hopewell Virginia, NE USA 37°16′N 77°15′W
109 O7 Hopfgarten im Brixental Tirol, W Austria 47°28′N 12°14′E
181 N8 Hopkins Lake salt lake Western Australia
182 M12 Hopkins River ≈ Victoria, SE Australia
20 I7 Hopkinsville Kentucky, S USA 36°50′N 87°30′W
34 M6 Hopland California, W USA 38°58′N 123°09′W
95 G24 Hoptrup Sønderjylland, SW Denmark 55°09′N 09°27′E
Hoqin Zuoyi Zhongji see Baokang
32 F9 Hoquiam Washington, NW USA 46°58′N 123°53′W
29 R6 Horace North Dakota, N USA 46°44′N 96°54′W
117 T14 Hora Roman-Kash ▲ S Ukraine 44°37′N 34°13′E
137 R12 Horasan Erzurum, NE Turkey 40°03′N 42°10′E
101 G22 Horb am Neckar Baden-Württemberg, S Germany 48°27′N 08°42′E
95 K23 Hörby Skåne, S Sweden 55°51′N 13°42′E
43 P16 Horconcitos Chiriquí, W Panama 08°20′N 82°10′W
95 C14 Hordaland ◈ county S Norway
116 H13 Horezu Vâlcea, SW Romania 45°06′N 24°00′E
108 G7 Horgen Zürich, N Switzerland 47°16′N 08°36′E
Horgo see Tariat
Hörin see Fenglin
163 O13 Horinger Nei Mongol Zizhiqu, N China 40°23′N 111°48′E
Horiult see Bogd
11 U17 Horizon Saskatchewan, S Canada 49°33′N 105°05′W
192 K9 Horizon Bank undersea feature S Pacific Ocean
192 L10 Horizon Deep undersea feature W Pacific Ocean
95 L14 Hörken Örebro, S Sweden 60°03′N 14°55′E
119 O15 Horki Rus. Gorki. Mahilyowskaya Voblasts', E Belarus 54°18′N 31°E
195 O10 Horlick Mountains ▲▲ Antarctica
117 X7 Horlivka Rom. Adâncata, Rus. Gorlovka. Donets'ka Oblast', E Ukraine 48°19′N 38°04′E
143 V11 Hormak Sīstān va Balūchestān, SE Iran 30°00′N 60°50′E
143 R13 Hormozgān off. Ostān-e Hormozgān. ◈ province S Iran
Hormozgān, Ostān-e see Hormozgān
Hormoz, Tangeh-ye see Hormuz, Strait of
141 W6 Hormuz, Strait of var. Strait of Ormuz, Per. Tangeh-ye Hormoz. strait Iran/Oman
109 W2 Horn Niederösterreich, NE Austria 48°40′N 15°40′E
95 M18 Horn Östergötland, S Sweden 57°54′N 15°49′E
8 J9 Horn ≈ Northwest Territories, NW Canada
Hornád see Hernád
8 I6 Hornaday ≈ Northwest Territories, NW Canada
92 H13 Hornavan ◎ N Sweden
65 C24 Hornby Mountains hill range West Falkland, Falkland Islands
Horn, Cape see Hornos, Cabo de
97 O18 Horncastle E England, United Kingdom 53°12′N 00°07′W
95 N14 Horndal Dalarna, C Sweden 60°16′N 16°25′E
93 I16 Hörnefors Västerbotten, N Sweden 63°37′N 19°54′E
18 F11 Hornell New York, NE USA 42°19′N 77°38′W
Horné Nové Mesto see Kysucké Nové Mesto
12 F12 Hornepayne Ontario, S Canada 49°14′N 84°48′W
94 D10 Hornindalsvatnet ◎ S Norway
101 G22 Hornisgrinde ▲ SW Germany 48°37′N 08°13′E
22 M9 Horn Island island Mississippi, S USA
Hornja Łužica see Oberlausitz
63 J26 Hornos, Cabo de Eng. Cape Horn. headland S Chile 55°52′S 67°00′W
117 S10 Hornostayivka Khersons'ka Oblast', S Ukraine 47°00′N 33°42′E
183 T9 Hornsby New South Wales, SE Australia 33°44′S 151°08′E
97 O16 Hornsea E England, United Kingdom 53°54′N 00°10′W
94 O11 Hornslandet peninsula C Sweden
95 H22 Hornslet Århus, C Denmark 56°19′N 10°20′E
92 O4 Hornsundtind ▲ S Svalbard 76°54′N 16°07′E
Horochów see Horokhiv
Horodenka see Gorodenka
117 Q2 Horodnya Rus. Gorodnya. Chernihivs'ka Oblast', NE Ukraine 51°54′N 31°30′E
116 K6 Horodok Khmel'nyts'ka Oblast', W Ukraine 49°10′N 26°34′E
116 H5 Horodok Pol. Gródek Jagielloński, Rus. Gorodok, Gorodok Yagellonski. L'vivs'ka Oblast', NW Ukraine 49°48′N 23°39′E
117 Q6 Horodyshche Rus. Gorodishche. Cherkas'ka Oblast', C Ukraine 49°19′N 31°27′E
165 T3 Horokanai Hokkaidō, NE Japan 44°02′N 142°08′E
116 J4 Horokhiv Pol. Horochów, Rus. Gorokhov. Volyns'ka Oblast', NW Ukraine 50°31′N 24°50′E
165 T4 Horoshiri-dake var. Horosiri Dake. ▲ Hokkaidō, N Japan 42°43′N 142°41′E
Horosiri Dake see Horoshiri-dake
111 C17 Hořovice Ger. Horowitz. Středni Čechy, W Czech Republic 49°49′N 13°53′E
Horowitz see Hořovice
Horqin Zuoyi Houqi see Ganjig
Horqin Zuoyi Zhongqi see Bayan Huxu
62 O5 Horqueta Concepción, C Paraguay 23°24′S 56°53′W
55 O12 Horqueta Minas Amazonas, S Venezuela 02°20′N 63°32′W
95 J20 Horred Västra Götaland, S Sweden 57°22′N 12°25′E
151 J19 Horsburgh Atoll var. Goidhoo Atoll. atoll N Maldives
20 K7 Horse Cave Kentucky, S USA 37°10′N 85°54′W
37 V6 Horse Creek ≈ Colorado, C USA
27 S6 Horse Creek ≈ Missouri, C USA
18 G11 Horseheads New York, NE USA 42°10′N 76°49′W
37 P13 Horse Mount ▲ New Mexico, SW USA 33°58′N 108°10′W
95 G22 Horsens Vejle, C Denmark 55°53′N 09°53′E
65 F25 Horse Pasture Point headland W Saint Helena 15°57′S 05°46′W
33 N13 Horseshoe Bend Idaho, NW USA 43°55′N 116°11′W
36 L13 Horseshoe Reservoir ⊠ Arizona, SW USA
64 M9 Horseshoe Seamounts undersea feature E Atlantic Ocean 36°30′N 15°00′W
182 L11 Horsham Victoria, SE Australia 36°44′S 142°13′E
97 O23 Horsham SE England, United Kingdom 51°01′N 00°21′W
99 M15 Horst Limburg, SE Netherlands 51°30′N 06°05′E
64 N2 Horta Faial, Azores, Portugal, NE Atlantic Ocean 38°32′N 28°39′W
95 H16 Horten Vestfold, S Norway 59°25′N 10°25′E
111 M23 Hortobágy-Berettyó ≈ E Hungary
27 Q3 Horton Kansas, C USA 39°39′N 95°31′W
8 I7 Horton ≈ Northwest Territories, NW Canada
95 I23 Hørve Vestsjælland, E Denmark 55°46′N 11°28′E
95 L22 Hörvik Blekinge, S Sweden 56°01′N 14°45′E
Horvot Haluza see Horvot Halutsa
14 E7 Horwood Lake ◎ Ontario, S Canada
116 K4 Horyn' Rus. Goryn. ≈ NW Ukraine
81 I14 Hosa'ina var. Hosseina, It. Hosanna. Southern Nationalities, S Ethiopia 07°38′N 37°58′E
Hosanna see Hosa'ina
101 H18 Hösbach Bayern, C Germany 50°00′N 09°12′E
Hose Mountains see Hose, Pegunungan
169 T9 Hose, Pegunungan var. Hose Mountains. ▲▲ East Malaysia
148 L15 Hoshāb Baluchistān, SW Pakistan 26°01′N 63°51′E
154 H10 Hoshangābād Madhya Pradesh, C India 22°44′N 77°45′E
116 L4 Hoshcha Rivnens'ka Oblast', NW Ukraine 50°37′N 26°38′E
152 I7 Hoshiārpur Punjab, NW India 31°30′N 75°59′E
Höshööt see Öldziyt
99 M23 Hosingen Diekirch, NE Luxembourg 50°01′N 06°05′E
186 G7 Hoskins New Britain, E Papua New Guinea 05°28′S 150°25′E
155 G17 Hospet Karnātaka, C India 15°16′N 76°20′E
104 K4 Hospital de Orbigo Castilla-León, N Spain 42°27′N 05°53′W
Hospitalet see L'Hospitalet de Llobregat
92 N13 Hossa Oulu, E Finland 65°28′N 29°36′E
Hosseina see Hosa'ina
Hosszúmezjő see Câmpulung Moldovenesc
63 I25 Hoste, Isla island S Chile
117 O4 Hostomel' Rus. Gostomel'. Kyyivs'ka Oblast', N Ukraine 50°41′N 30°15′E
155 H20 Hosūr Tamil Nādu, SE India 12°45′N 77°51′E
167 N8 Hot Chiang Mai, NW Thailand 18°07′N 98°34′E
158 G10 Hotan var. Khotan, Chin. Ho-t'ien. Xinjiang Uygur Zizhiqu, NW China 37°10′N 79°51′E
158 H9 Hotan He ≈ NW China
83 G22 Hotazel Northern Cape, N South Africa 27°12′S 22°58′E
37 Q5 Hotchkiss Colorado, C USA 38°47′N 107°43′W
35 V7 Hot Creek Range ▲ Nevada, W USA
Hote see Hoti
171 T13 Hoti var. Hote. Pulau Seram, E Indonesia 02°58′S 130°19′E
Ho-t'ien see Hotan
Hotin see Khotyn
93 H15 Hoting Jämtland, C Sweden 64°07′N 16°14′E
162 L14 Hotong Qagan Nur ◎ N China
162 J8 Hotont Arhangay, C Mongolia 47°21′N 102°27′E
27 T12 Hot Springs Arkansas, C USA 34°31′N 93°03′W
28 J11 Hot Springs South Dakota, N USA 43°26′N 103°29′W
21 S5 Hot Springs Virginia, NE USA 38°00′N 79°50′W
35 Q4 Hot Springs Peak ▲ California, W USA 40°23′N 120°06′W
27 T12 Hot Springs Village Arkansas, C USA 34°39′N 93°03′W
Hotspur Bank see Hotspur Seamount
65 J16 Hotspur Seamount var. Hotspur Bank. undersea feature C Atlantic Ocean 18°00′S 35°00′W
8 J8 Hottah Lake ◎ Northwest Territories, NW Canada
44 K9 Hotte, Massif de la ▲ SW Haiti
99 K21 Hotton Luxembourg, SE Belgium 50°18′N 05°25′E
Hötzing see Hațeg
187 P17 Houaïlou Province Nord, C New Caledonia 21°17′S 165°37′E
74 K5 Houari Boumediène ✈ (Alger) N Algeria 36°38′N 03°15′E
167 P6 Houayxay var. Ban Houayxay. Bokèo, N Laos 20°17′N 100°27′E
103 N5 Houdan Yvelines, N France 48°48′N 01°36′E
99 F20 Houdeng-Goegnies var. Houdeng-Gœgnies. Hainaut, S Belgium 50°29′N 04°10′E
102 K14 Houeillès Lot-et-Garonne, SW France 44°15′N 00°02′E
99 L22 Houffalize Luxembourg, SE Belgium 50°08′N 05°47′E
30 M3 Houghton Michigan, N USA 47°07′N 88°34′W
31 Q7 Houghton Lake Michigan, N USA 44°18′N 84°45′W
31 Q7 Houghton Lake ◎ Michigan, N USA
19 T3 Houlton Maine, NE USA 46°09′N 67°50′W
160 M5 Houma Shanxi, C China 35°36′N 111°23′E
193 U16 Houma Tongatapu, S Tonga 21°18′S 174°55′W
22 J10 Houma Louisiana, S USA 29°35′N 90°44′W
196 V16 Houma Taloa headland Tongatapu, S Tonga 21°16′S 175°08′W
77 O13 Houndé SW Burkina 11°34′N 03°31′W
102 J12 Hourtin-Carcans, Lac d' ◎ SW France
36 J5 House Range ▲ Utah, W USA
10 K13 Houston British Columbia, SW Canada 54°24′N 126°39′W
39 R11 Houston Alaska, USA 61°37′N 149°50′W
29 X10 Houston Minnesota, N USA 43°45′N 91°34′W
22 M3 Houston Mississippi, S USA 33°54′N 89°00′W
27 V7 Houston Missouri, C USA 37°19′N 91°59′W
25 W11 Houston Texas, SW USA 29°46′N 95°22′W
25 W11 Houston ✈ Texas, SW USA 30°03′N 95°18′W
98 J12 Houten Utrecht, C Netherlands 52°02′N 05°10′E
99 K17 Houthalen Limburg, NE Belgium 51°02′N 05°22′E
99 I22 Houyet Namur, SE Belgium 50°10′N 05°00′E
95 H22 Hov Århus, C Denmark 55°54′N 10°13′E
95 L17 Hova Västra Götaland, S Sweden 58°52′N 14°13′E
162 E6 Hovd var. Khovd, Kobdo; prev. Jirgalanta. Hovd, W Mongolia 47°59′N 91°41′E
162 J10 Hovd var. Dund-Us. Hovd, W Mongolia 48°06′N 91°22′E
162 E6 Hovd var. Dund-Us. Hovd, W Mongolia 48°06′N 91°22′E
162 E7 Hovd ◈ province W Mongolia
Hovd see Bogd
162 C5 Hovd Gol ≈ NW Mongolia
97 O23 Hove SE England, United Kingdom 50°49′N 00°11′W
29 N8 Hoven South Dakota, N USA 45°12′N 99°47′W
116 I8 Hoverla, Hora Rus. Gora Goverla. ▲ W Ukraine 48°09′N 24°30′E
Höviyn Am see Gurvanbulag
95 M21 Hovmantorp Kronoberg, S Sweden 56°47′N 15°08′E
163 N11 Hövsgöl Dornogovĭ, SE Mongolia 43°35′N 109°40′E
162 I5 Hövsgöl ◈ province N Mongolia
Hovsgol, Lake see Hövsgöl Nuur
162 J5 Hövsgöl Nuur var. Lake Hovsgol. ◎ N Mongolia
78 L9 Howa, Ouadi var. Wādi Howar. ≈ Chad/Sudan see also Howa, Wādi
Howa, Ouadi see Howar, Wādi
27 P7 Howard Kansas, C USA 37°27′N 96°16′W
29 Q10 Howard South Dakota, N USA 43°58′N 97°31′W
25 N10 Howard Draw valley Texas, SW USA
29 U8 Howard Lake Minnesota, N USA 45°03′N 94°03′W
80 B8 Howar, Wādi var. Ouadi Howa. ≈ Chad/Sudan see also Howa, Ouadi
Howar, Wādi see Howa, Ouadi
25 U5 Howe Texas, SW USA 33°29′N 96°38′W
183 R12 Howe, Cape headland New South Wales/Victoria, SE Australia 37°30′S 149°58′E
31 R9 Howell Michigan, N USA 42°36′N 83°55′W
28 L9 Howes South Dakota, N USA 44°34′N 102°03′W
83 K23 Howick KwaZulu/Natal, E South Africa 29°29′S 30°13′E
Howrah see Hāora
27 W9 Hoxie Arkansas, C USA 36°03′N 90°58′W
26 J3 Hoxie Kansas, C USA 39°21′N 100°27′W
101 I14 Höxter Nordrhein-Westfalen, W Germany 51°46′N 09°22′E
158 K6 Hoxud var. Tewulike. Xinjiang Uygur Zizhiqu, NW China 42°18′N 86°51′E
96 J5 Hoy island N Scotland, United Kingdom
43 S17 Hoya, Cerro ▲ S Panama 07°22′N 80°38′W
94 D12 Høyanger Sogn Og Fjordane, S Norway 61°13′N 06°05′E
101 P15 Hoyerswerda Lus. Wojerecy. Sachsen, E Germany 51°27′N 14°18′E
164 R14 Hōyo-kaikyō var. Hayasui-seto. strait SW Japan
104 J8 Hoyos Extremadura, W Spain 40°10′N 06°43′W
29 W4 Hoyt Lakes Minnesota, N USA 47°31′N 92°08′W
87 V2 Hoyvík Streymoy, N Faeroe Islands
137 O14 Hozat Tunceli, E Turkey 39°09′N 39°13′E
Hôzyô see Hōjō
167 N8 Hpa-an var. Pa-an. Kayin State, S Burma (Myanmar) 16°51′N 97°37′E
Hpyu see Phyu
111 F16 Hradec Králové Ger. Königgrätz. Královéhradecký Kraj, N Czech Republic 50°13′N 15°50′E
Hradecký Kraj see Královéhradecký Kraj
111 B16 Hradiště Ger. Burgstadlberg. ▲ NW Czech Republic 50°12′N 13°04′E
117 R6 Hradyz'k Rus. Gradizhsk. Poltavs'ka Oblast', NE Ukraine 49°14′N 33°07′E
119 M16 Hradzyanka Rus. Grodzyanka. Mahilyowskaya Voblasts', E Belarus 53°33′N 28°45′E
119 F16 Hrandzichy Rus. Grandichi. Hrodzyenskaya Voblasts', W Belarus 53°43′N 23°49′E
111 H18 Hranice Ger. Mährisch-Weisskirchen. Olomoucký Kraj, E Czech Republic 49°34′N 17°45′E
112 I13 Hrasnica Federacija Bosna I Hercegovina, SE Bosnia and Herzegovina 43°48′N 18°19′E
109 V11 Hrastnik C Slovenia 46°09′N 15°08′E
137 U12 Hrazdan Rus. Razdan. C Armenia 40°30′N 44°50′E
137 T12 Hrazdan var. Zanga, Rus. Razdan. ≈ C Armenia
117 R5 Hrebinka Rus. Grebenka. Poltavs'ka Oblast', NE Ukraine 50°08′N 32°27′E
119 K17 Hresk Rus. Gresk. Minskaya Voblasts', C Belarus 53°10′N 27°29′E
Hrisoupoli see Chrysoúpoli
119 F16 Hrodna Pol. Grodno. Hrodzyenskaya Voblasts', W Belarus 53°40′N 23°50′E
119 F16 Hrodzyenskaya Voblasts' prev. Rus. Grodnenskaya Oblast'. ◈ province W Belarus
111 J21 Hron Ger. Gran, Hung. Garam. ≈ C Slovakia
111 Q14 Hrubieszów Rus. Grubeshov. Lubelskie, E Poland 50°49′N 23°53′E
112 F13 Hrvace Split-Dalmacija, SE Croatia 43°46′N 16°35′E
Hrvatska see Croatia
112 F10 Hrvatska Kostanjnica var. Kostajnica. Sisak-Moslavina, C Croatia 45°14′N 16°35′E
Hrvatsko Grahovi see Bosansko Grahovo
116 K6 Hrymayliv Pol. Gizymałów, Rus. Grimaylov. Ternopil's'ka Oblast', W Ukraine 49°18′N 26°02′E
167 N4 Hsenwi Shan State, E Burma (Myanmar) 23°20′N 97°59′E
Hsia-men see Xiamen
Hsiang-t'an see Xiangtan
Hsi Chiang see Xi Jiang
167 N6 Hsihseng Shan State, C Burma (Myanmar) 20°07′N 97°17′E
161 S13 Hsinchu N Taiwan 24°48′N 120°59′E
Hsing-K'ai Hu see Khanka, Lake
Hsi-ning/Hsining see Xining
Hsinking see Changchun
Hsin-yang see Xinyang
161 S14 Hsinying var. Sinying, Jap. Shinei. C Taiwan 23°12′N 120°15′E
167 N4 Hsipaw Shan State, C Burma (Myanmar) 22°32′N 97°12′E
Hsu-chou see Xuzhou
161 S13 Hsüeh Shan ▲ N Taiwan

◆ Country
● Country Capital
◇ Dependent Territory
○ Dependent Territory Capital
◈ Administrative Regions
✈ International Airport
▲ Mountain
▲▲ Mountain Range
Ѫ Volcano
≈ River
◎ Lake
⊠ Reservoir

Htawei – Ider

Htawei see Dawei
Hu see Shanghai Shi
83 B18 Huab W Namibia
57 M21 Huacaya Chuquisaca, S Bolivia 20°45′S 63°42′W
57 J19 Huachacalla Oruro, SW Bolivia 18°47′S 68°23′W
159 X9 Huachi var. Rouyuan, Rouyuanchengzi. Gansu, C China 36°24′N 107°58′E
57 N16 Huachi, Laguna N Bolivia
57 D14 Huacho Lima, W Peru 11°05′S 77°36′W
163 Y7 Huachuan Heilongjiang, NE China 46°57′S 130°48′E
162 P12 Huade Nei Mongol Zizhiqu, N China 41°52′N 113°58′E
163 W10 Huadian Jilin, NE China 42°59′N 126°38′E
56 E13 Huagaruncho, Cordillera C Peru
Hua Hin see Ban Hua Hin
191 S10 Huahine island Îles Sous le Vent, W French Polynesia
Huahua, Rio see Wawa, Río
167 R8 Huai E Thailand
161 Q7 Huai'an var. Qingjiang; prev. Huaiyin. Jiangsu, E China 33°33′N 119°03′E
161 P6 Huaibei Anhui, E China 34°00′N 116°48′E
Huaide see Gongzhuling
157 T10 Huai He C China
160 L11 Huaihua Hunan, S China 27°36′N 109°57′E
161 N14 Huaiji Guangdong, S China 23°54′N 112°12′E
161 O2 Huailai var. Shacheng. Hebei, E China 40°22′N 115°34′E
161 P7 Huainan var. Huai-nan, Hwainan. Anhui, E China 32°37′N 116°57′E
Huai-nan see Huainan
161 N2 Huairen var. Yunzhong. Shanxi, C China 35°28′N 110°29′E
161 O7 Huaiyang Henan, C China 33°44′N 114°55′E
161 Q7 Huaiyin Jiangsu, E China 33°31′N 119°03′E
Huaiyin see Huai'an
167 N16 Huai Yot Trang, SW Thailand 07°45′N 99°36′E
41 Q15 Huajuapan var. Huajuapan de León. Oaxaca, SE Mexico 17°50′N 97°48′W
Huajuapan de León see Huajuapan
41 O9 Hualahuises Nuevo León, NE Mexico 24°56′N 99°42′W
36 I11 Hualapai Mountains Arizona, SW USA
36 I11 Hualapai Peak Arizona, SW USA 35°04′N 113°54′W
62 J7 Hualfín Catamarca, N Argentina 27°15′S 66°53′W
161 T13 Hualien var. Hwalien, Jap. Karen. C Taiwan 23°58′N 121°35′E
56 E10 Huallaga, Río N Peru
159 U10 Hualong Qinghai, C China 36°06′N 102°16′E
56 C11 Huamachuco La Libertad, C Peru 07°50′S 78°01′W
41 Q14 Huamantla Tlaxcala, S Mexico 19°18′N 97°57′W
82 C13 Huambo Port. Nova Lisboa. Huambo, C Angola 12°48′S 15°45′E
82 B13 Huambo province C Angola
41 P15 Huamuxtitlán Guerrero, S Mexico 17°49′N 98°34′W
163 Y8 Huanan Heilongjiang, NE China 46°21′N 130°43′E
63 H17 Huancache, Sierra SW Argentina
57 I17 Huancané Puno, SE Peru 15°10′S 69°44′W
57 F16 Huancapi Ayacucho, C Peru 13°40′S 74°05′W
57 E15 Huancavelica Huancavelica, SW Peru 12°45′S 75°03′W
57 E15 Huancavelica off. Departamento de Huancavelica. department W Peru
Huancavelica, Departamento de see Huancavelica
57 E14 Huancayo Junín, C Peru 12°03′S 75°14′W
57 K20 Huanchaca, Cerro S Bolivia 20°12′S 66°35′W
Huancheng see Huanxian
56 C12 Huandoy, Nevado W Peru 08°48′S 77°33′W
Huang'an see Hong'an
161 O8 Huangchuan Henan, C China 32°00′N 115°02′E
161 O9 Huanggang Hubei, C China 30°27′N 114°48′E
Huang Hai see Yellow Sea
157 Q8 Huang He var. Yellow River. C China
Huanghe see Madoi
161 Q4 Huanghe Kou delta E China
Huangheyan see Madoi
160 L5 Huangling Shaanxi, C China 35°40′N 109°14′E
161 O9 Huangpi Hubei, C China 30°53′N 114°22′E
163 P13 Huangqi Hai N China
161 Q9 Huangshan var. Tunxi. Anhui, E China 29°43′N 118°20′E
161 Q9 Huangshan Anhui, China 30°06′N 118°04′E
161 O9 Huangshi var. Huang-shih, Hwangshih. Hubei, C China 30°14′N 115°E
Huang-shih see Huangshi
160 L5 Huangtu Gaoyuan plateau C China
61 B22 Huanguelén Buenos Aires, E Argentina 37°02′S 61°57′W
161 S10 Huangyan Zhejiang, SE China 28°39′N 121°19′E
159 T10 Huangyuan Qinghai, C China 36°40′N 101°12′E
159 T10 Huangzhong var. Lushar. Qinghai, C China 36°31′N 101°32′E
163 W12 Huanren var. Huanren Manzu Zizhixian. Liaoning, NE China 41°16′N 125°25′E
Huanren Manzu Zizhixian see Huanren
57 F15 Huanta Ayacucho, C Peru 12°54′S 74°13′W
56 E13 Huánuco Huánuco, C Peru 09°58′S 76°16′W
56 D13 Huánuco off. Departamento de Huánuco. department C Peru
Huánuco, Departamento de see Huánuco
57 K19 Huanuni Oruro, W Bolivia 18°15′S 66°48′W
159 X9 Huanxian var. Huancheng. Gansu, C China 36°30′N 107°20′E
161 S12 Huap'ing Yu island N Taiwan
62 H3 Huara Tarapacá, N Chile 19°59′S 69°42′W
57 D14 Huaral Lima, W Peru 11°31′S 77°10′W
Huarás see Huaraz
56 D13 Huaraz var. Huarás. Ancash, W Peru 09°31′S 77°32′W
57 I16 Huari Huari, Río S Peru
56 C13 Huarmey Ancash, W Peru 10°03′S 78°08′W
40 H4 Huásabas Sonora, NW Mexico 29°47′N 109°18′W
56 D8 Huasaga, Río Ecuador/Peru
167 O15 Hua Sai Nakhon Si Thammarat, SW Thailand 08°02′N 100°18′E
56 D12 Huascarán, Nevado W Peru 09°01′S 77°27′W
62 G8 Huasco Atacama, N Chile 28°30′S 71°15′W
62 G8 Huasco, Río C Chile
159 S11 Huashikia Qinghai, W China
40 G7 Huatabampo Sonora, NW Mexico 26°49′N 109°40′W
159 W10 Huating var. Donghua. Gansu, C China 35°13′N 106°39′E
167 S7 Huatt, Phou N Vietnam 19°45′N 104°48′E
41 Q14 Huatusco var. Huatusco de Chicuellar. Veracruz-Llave, C Mexico 19°13′N 96°57′W
Huatusco de Chicuellar see Huatusco
41 P13 Huauchinango Puebla, S Mexico 20°11′N 98°04′W
Huaunta see Wounta
41 R15 Huautla var. Huautla de Jiménez. Oaxaca, SE Mexico 18°10′N 96°51′W
Huautla de Jiménez see Huautla
161 O5 Huaxian var. Daokou, Hua Xian. Henan, C China 35°33′N 114°30′E
Hua Xian see Huaxian
Huazangsi see Tianzhu
29 V13 Hubbard Iowa, C USA 42°18′N 93°18′W
25 U8 Hubbard Texas, SW USA 31°52′N 96°43′W
25 Q6 Hubbard Creek Lake Texas, SW USA
31 R6 Hubbard Lake Michigan, N USA
160 M9 Hubei var. E, Hubei Sheng, Hupeh, Hupei. province C China
Hubei Sheng see Hubei
109 P8 Huben Tirol, W Austria 46°55′N 12°35′E
31 R13 Huber Heights Ohio, N USA 39°50′N 84°07′W
155 F17 Hubli Karnātaka, SW India 15°20′N 75°14′E
163 X12 Huch'ang N North Korea 41°25′N 127°04′E
97 M18 Hucknall C England, United Kingdom 53°02′N 01°11′W
97 L17 Huddersfield N England, United Kingdom 53°39′N 01°47′W
95 O16 Huddinge Stockholm, C Sweden 59°15′N 17°57′E
94 N11 Hudiksvall Gävleborg, C Sweden 61°45′N 17°12′E
29 W13 Hudson Iowa, C USA 42°24′N 92°27′W
19 O11 Hudson Massachusetts, NE USA 42°24′N 71°34′W
31 Q11 Hudson Michigan, N USA 41°51′N 84°21′W
30 H6 Hudson Wisconsin, N USA 44°59′N 92°43′W
11 V14 Hudson Bay Saskatchewan, S Canada 52°51′N 102°23′W
12 G6 Hudson Bay bay NE Canada
195 T16 Hudson, Cape headland Antarctica 68°15′S 154°00′E
Hudson, Détroit d' see Hudson Strait
27 Q9 Hudson, Lake Oklahoma, C USA
18 K9 Hudson River New Jersey/New York, NE USA
10 M12 Hudson's Hope British Columbia, W Canada 56°03′N 121°59′W
12 L2 Hudson Strait Fr. Détroit d'Hudson. strait Northwest Territories/Québec, NE Canada
Ḩudūd ash Shamālīyah, Minṭaqat al see Al Ḩudūd ash Shamālīyah
Hudur see Xuddur
167 U9 Huê Th,a Thiên-Huê, C Vietnam 16°28′N 107°35′E
104 J7 Huebra W Spain
24 H8 Hueco Mountains Texas, SW USA
116 G10 Huedin Hung. Bánffyhunyad. Cluj, NW Romania 46°52′N 23°02′E
40 J10 Huehuento, Cerro C Mexico 24°04′N 105°42′W
42 B5 Huehuetenango Huehuetenango, W Guatemala 15°19′N 91°26′W
42 B4 Huehuetenango off. Departamento de Huehuetenango. department W Guatemala
Huehuetenango, Departamento de see Huehuetenango
40 L11 Huejuquilla Jalisco, SW Mexico 22°40′N 103°52′W
41 P12 Huejutla var. Huejutla de Reyes. Hidalgo, C Mexico 21°10′N 98°25′W
Huejutla de Reyes see Huejutla
102 G6 Huelgoat Finistère, NW France 48°22′N 03°45′W
105 O13 Huelma Andalucía, S Spain 37°39′N 03°28′W
104 I14 Huelva anc. Onuba. Andalucía, SW Spain 37°15′N 06°56′W
104 I13 Huelva province Andalucía, SW Spain
104 J13 Huelva SW Spain
105 Q14 Huercal-Overa Andalucía, S Spain 37°23′N 01°56′W
37 Q9 Huerfano Mountain New Mexico, SW USA 36°25′N 107°50′W
37 T7 Huerfano River Colorado, C USA
105 S12 Huertas, Cabo headland SE Spain 38°21′N 00°25′W
105 R6 Huerva N Spain
105 S4 Huesca anc. Osca. Aragón, NE Spain 42°08′N 00°25′W
105 T4 Huesca province Aragón, NE Spain
105 P13 Huéscar Andalucía, S Spain 37°39′N 02°32′W
41 N15 Huetamo var. Huetamo de Núñez. Michoacán, SW Mexico 18°36′N 100°54′W
Huetamo de Núñez see Huetamo
105 P8 Huete Castilla-La Mancha, C Spain 40°09′N 02°42′W
23 P4 Hueytown Alabama, S USA 33°27′N 87°00′W
28 L16 Hugh Butler Lake Nebraska, C USA
181 V6 Hughenden Queensland, NE Australia 20°57′S 144°16′E
182 A6 Hughes South Australia 30°41′S 129°31′E
39 P8 Hughes Alaska, USA 66°03′N 154°15′W
27 X11 Hughes Arkansas, C USA 34°57′N 90°28′W
25 W6 Hughes Springs Texas, SW USA 33°00′N 94°37′W
153 S17 Hugli N India
37 V5 Hugo Colorado, C USA 39°08′N 103°28′W
27 Q13 Hugo Oklahoma, C USA 34°01′N 95°31′W
27 Q13 Hugo Lake Oklahoma, C USA
26 H7 Hugoton Kansas, C USA 37°11′N 101°22′W
Huhehot/Huhohaote see Hohhot
Huhttán see Kvikkjokk
161 R13 Hui'an var. Luocheng. Fujian, SE China 25°06′N 118°45′E
184 O9 Huiarau Range North Island, New Zealand
83 D22 Huib-Hoch Plateau plateau S Namibia
41 O13 Huichapán Hidalgo, C Mexico 20°24′N 99°40′W
Huicheng see Shexian
163 W13 Hŭich'ŏn C North Korea 40°09′N 126°17′E
83 B15 Huíla province SW Angola
54 E12 Huila off. Departamento del Huila. province S Colombia
Huila, Departamento del see Huila
54 D11 Huila, Nevado del elevation C Colombia
83 B15 Huíla Plateau plateau S Angola
160 G12 Huili Sichuan, C China 26°39′N 102°13′E
161 P4 Huimin Shandong, E China 37°29′N 117°30′E
163 W11 Huinan var. Chaoyang. Jilin, NE China 42°40′N 126°03′E
62 K12 Huinca Renancó Córdoba, C Argentina 34°51′S 64°22′W
159 V10 Huining var. Huishi. Gansu, C China 35°42′N 105°01′E
Huishi see Huining
160 J12 Huishui var. Heping. Guizhou, S China 26°07′N 106°39′E
102 L6 Huisne NW France
98 L12 Huissen Gelderland, SE Netherlands 51°57′N 05°57′E
159 N11 Huiten Nur C China
93 K19 Huittinen Länsi-Suomi, SW Finland 61°11′N 22°40′E
41 O15 Huitzuco var. Huitzuco de los Figueroa. Guerrero, S Mexico 18°18′N 99°22′W
Huitzuco de los Figueroa see Huitzuco
159 W11 Huixian var. Hui Xian. Gansu, C China 33°48′N 106°02′E
Hui Xian see Huixian
41 V17 Huixtla Chiapas, SE Mexico 15°09′N 92°30′W
160 H12 Huize var. Zhongping. Yunnan, SW China 26°28′N 103°18′E
98 J10 Huizen Noord-Holland, C Netherlands 52°17′N 05°15′E
161 O14 Huizhou Guangdong, S China 23°02′N 114°28′E
162 J6 Hujirt Arhangay, C Mongolia 48°49′N 101°20′E
Hujirt see Tsetserleg, Övörhangay, Mongolia
Hujirt see Delgerhaan, Töv, Mongolia
Hukagawa see Fukagawa
163 W17 Hŭksan-chedo var. Hŭksan-chedo. island group SW South Korea
Hŭksan-chedo see Hŭksan-chedo
Hukue see Fukue
Hukui see Fukui
83 G20 Hukuntsi Kgalagadi, SW Botswana 23°59′S 21°44′E
Hukuoka see Fukuoka
Hukusima see Fukushima
Hukutiyama see Fukuchiyama
Hukuyama see Fukuyama
163 W8 Hulan Heilongjiang, NE China 45°59′N 126°37′E
163 W8 Hulan He NE China
31 Q4 Hulbert Lake Michigan, N USA
Hulczyn see Hlučín
Huliao see Dabu
163 Z8 Hulin Heilongjiang, NE China 45°48′N 133°06′E
163 S9 Hulingol prev. Huolin Gol. Nei Mongol Zizhiqu, N China 45°36′N 119°54′E
14 L12 Hull Québec, SE Canada 45°26′N 75°45′W
29 S12 Hull Iowa, C USA 43°11′N 96°07′W
Hull see Kingston upon Hull
Hull Island see Orona
99 F16 Hulst Zeeland, SW Netherlands 51°17′N 04°03′E
Hulstay see Choybalsan
Hultschin see Hlučín
95 M19 Hultsfred Kalmar, S Sweden 57°30′N 15°50′E
163 T13 Huludao prev. Jinxi, Lianshan. Liaoning, NE China 40°46′N 120°47′E
Hulun see Hulun Buir
163 S6 Hulun Buir var. Hailar; prev. Hulun. Nei Mongol Zizhiqu, N China 49°15′N 119°41′E
Hu-lun Ch'ih see Hulun Nur
163 Q6 Hulun Nur var. Hu-lun Ch'ih; prev. Dalai Nor. NE China
Hulwan/Hulwân see Hilwān
117 V8 Hulyaypole Rus. Gulyaypole. Zaporiz'ka Oblast', SE Ukraine 47°41′N 36°10′E
163 V4 Huma Heilongjiang, NE China 51°40′N 126°38′E
45 V6 Humacao E Puerto Rico 18°09′N 65°50′W
163 U4 Huma He NE China
62 J5 Humahuaca Jujuy, N Argentina 23°13′S 65°20′W
59 E14 Humaitá Amazonas, N Brazil 07°33′S 63°01′W
62 N7 Humaitá Ñeembucú, S Paraguay 27°02′S 58°31′W
83 H26 Humansdorp Eastern Cape, S South Africa 34°01′S 24°45′E
27 S6 Humansville Missouri, C USA 37°47′N 93°34′W
40 I8 Humaya, Río C Mexico
83 C16 Humbe Cunene, SW Angola 16°37′S 14°52′E
97 N17 Humber estuary E England, United Kingdom
97 N17 Humberside cultural region E England, United Kingdom
Humberto see Umberto
25 W11 Humble Texas, SW USA 29°58′N 95°15′W
11 U15 Humboldt Saskatchewan, S Canada 52°13′N 105°09′W
29 U12 Humboldt Iowa, C USA 42°42′N 94°13′W
27 Q6 Humboldt Kansas, C USA 37°48′N 95°26′W
29 S17 Humboldt Nebraska, C USA 40°09′N 95°56′W
35 S3 Humboldt Nevada, W USA 40°36′N 118°15′W
20 G9 Humboldt Tennessee, S USA 35°49′N 88°55′W
34 K3 Humboldt Bay bay California, W USA
35 S4 Humboldt Lake Nevada, W USA
35 S4 Humboldt River Nevada, W USA
35 T5 Humboldt Salt Marsh wetland Nevada, W USA
183 P11 Hume, Lake New South Wales/Victoria, SE Australia
111 N19 Humenné Ger. Homenau, Hung. Homonna. Prešovský Kraj, E Slovakia 48°57′N 21°54′E
29 V15 Humeston Iowa, C USA 40°51′N 93°30′W
54 J5 Humocaro Bajo Lara, N Venezuela 09°41′N 70°00′W
29 Q14 Humphrey Nebraska, C USA 41°38′N 97°29′W
35 S9 Humphreys, Mount California, W USA 37°11′N 118°39′W
36 L11 Humphreys Peak Arizona, SW USA 35°18′N 111°40′W
111 E17 Humpolec Ger. Gumpolds, Humpoletz. Vysočina, C Czech Republic 49°33′N 15°23′E
Humpoletz see Humpolec
93 K19 Humppila Etelä-Suomi, S Finland 60°54′N 23°21′E
32 F8 Humptulips Washington, NW USA 47°13′N 123°57′W
42 H7 Humuya, Río W Honduras
75 P9 Hūn N Libya 29°06′N 15°56′E
92 I1 Húnaflói bay NW Iceland
160 M11 Hunan var. Hunan Sheng, Xiang. province S China
Hunan Sheng see Hunan
163 Y10 Hunchun Jilin, NE China 42°51′N 130°21′E
95 I22 Hundested Frederiksborg, E Denmark 55°58′N 11°53′E
Hundred Mile House see 100 Mile House
116 G12 Hunedoara Ger. Eisenmarkt, Hung. Vajdahunyad. Hunedoara, SW Romania 45°45′N 22°54′E
116 G12 Hunedoara county W Romania
101 I17 Hünfeld Hessen, C Germany 50°41′N 09°46′E
Hungarian People's Republic see Hungary
111 H23 Hungary off. Republic of Hungary, Ger. Ungarn, Hung. Magyarország, Rom. Ungaria, SCr. Madarska, Ukr. Uhorshchyna; prev. Hungarian People's Republic. republic C Europe
Hungary, Plain of see Great Hungarian Plain
Hungary, Republic of see Hungary
Hungiy see Urgamal
163 X13 Hŭngnam E North Korea 39°50′N 127°36′E
33 P8 Hungry Horse Reservoir Montana, NW USA
Hungt'ou see Lan Yü
Hung-tse Hu see Hongze Hu
167 T6 Hưng Yên Hai Hưng, N Vietnam 20°38′N 106°05′E
Hunjiang see Baishan
95 I18 Hunnebostrand Västra Götaland, S Sweden 58°26′N 11°19′E
101 E19 Hunsrück W Germany
97 P18 Hunstanton E England, United Kingdom 52°57′N 00°27′E
155 G20 Hunsūr Karnātaka, E India 12°18′N 76°15′E
Hunt see Hangay
100 G12 Hunte NW Germany
29 Q5 Hunter North Dakota, N USA 47°10′N 97°11′W
25 S11 Hunter Texas, SW USA 29°47′N 98°01′W
185 D20 Hunter South Island, New Zealand
183 N15 Hunter Island island Tasmania, SE Australia
18 K11 Hunter Mountain New York, NE USA 42°10′N 74°13′W
185 B23 Hunter Mountains South Island, New Zealand
183 S7 Hunter River New South Wales, SE Australia
32 L7 Hunters Washington, NW USA 48°07′N 118°13′W
185 F20 Hunters Hills, The hill range South Island, New Zealand
184 M12 Hunterville Manawatu-Wanganui, North Island, New Zealand 39°55′S 175°34′E
31 N16 Huntingburg Indiana, N USA 38°18′N 86°57′W
97 O20 Huntingdon E England, United Kingdom 52°20′N 00°12′W
18 E15 Huntingdon Pennsylvania, NE USA 40°28′N 78°00′W
20 G9 Huntingdon Tennessee, S USA 36°00′N 88°25′W
97 O20 Huntingdonshire cultural region C England, United Kingdom
31 P12 Huntington Indiana, N USA 40°52′N 85°30′W
32 L13 Huntington Oregon, NW USA 44°22′N 117°18′W
25 X9 Huntington Texas, SW USA 31°16′N 94°34′W
36 M5 Huntington Utah, W USA 39°19′N 110°57′W
21 P5 Huntington West Virginia, NE USA 38°25′N 82°27′W
35 T16 Huntington Beach California, W USA 33°39′N 118°00′W
35 W4 Huntington Creek Nevada, W USA
184 L7 Huntly Waikato, North Island, New Zealand 37°34′S 175°09′E
96 K8 Huntly NE Scotland, United Kingdom 57°25′N 02°48′W
10 K8 Hunt, Mount Yukon Territory, NW Canada 61°29′N 129°10′W
14 H12 Huntsville Ontario, S Canada 45°20′N 79°14′W
23 P2 Huntsville Alabama, S USA 34°44′N 86°35′W
27 S9 Huntsville Arkansas, C USA 36°04′N 93°46′W
27 U3 Huntsville Missouri, C USA 39°27′N 92°31′W
20 M8 Huntsville Tennessee, S USA 36°25′N 84°30′W
25 V10 Huntsville Texas, SW USA 30°43′N 95°34′W
36 L2 Huntsville Utah, W USA 41°16′N 111°47′W
41 W12 Hunucmá Yucatán, SE Mexico 20°59′N 89°55′W
149 W3 Hunza var. Karīmābād. Jammu and Kashmir, NE Pakistan 36°23′N 74°43′E
149 W3 Hunza NE Pakistan
Hunze see Oostermoers Vaart
158 H4 Huocheng var. Shuiding. Xinjiang Uygur Zizhiqu, NW China 44°03′N 80°49′E
161 N6 Huojia Henan, C China 35°14′N 113°38′E
Huolin Gol see Hulingol
186 H14 Huon reef N New Caledonia
186 E7 Huon Peninsula headland C Papua New Guinea 06°24′S 147°50′E
Huoshao Dao see Lü Tao
Huoshao Tao see Lan Yü
Hupeh/Hupei see Hubei
Hurama see Hongyuan
95 H14 Hurdalssjøen S Norway
14 E13 Hurd, Cape headland Ontario, S Canada 45°12′N 81°43′W
Hurdegaryp see Hardegarijp
29 N4 Hurdsfield North Dakota, N USA 47°24′N 99°55′W
Hüremt see Sayhan, Bulgan, Mongolia
Hüremt see Taragt, Övörhangay, Mongolia
75 X9 Hurghada var. Al Ghurdaqah, Ghurdaqah. E Egypt 27°17′N 33°47′E
67 V9 Huri Hills NW Kenya
37 P15 Hurley New Mexico, SW USA 32°42′N 108°07′W
30 K4 Hurley Wisconsin, N USA 46°25′N 90°15′W
21 Y4 Hurlock Maryland, NE USA 38°37′N 75°51′W
162 K11 Hürmen var. Tsoohor. Ömnögovĭ, S Mongolia 43°15′N 104°04′E
29 P10 Huron South Dakota, N USA 44°19′N 98°13′W
31 S6 Huron, Lake Canada/USA
31 N3 Huron Mountains hill range Michigan, N USA
36 J8 Hurricane Utah, W USA 37°10′N 113°18′W
21 P5 Hurricane West Virginia, NE USA 38°25′N 82°01′W
36 J8 Hurricane Cliffs cliff Arizona, SW USA
23 V6 Hurricane Creek Georgia, SE USA
94 E12 Hurrungane S Norway 61°25′N 07°48′E
101 E16 Hürth Nordrhein-Westfalen, W Germany 50°52′N 06°49′E
Hurukawa see Furukawa
185 I17 Hurunui South Island, New Zealand
95 F21 Hurup Viborg, NW Denmark 56°46′N 08°26′E
117 T14 Hurzuf Respublika Krym, S Ukraine 44°33′N 34°18′E
Huş see Huşi
95 B19 Húsavík Dan. Husevig. Sandoy, C Faeroe Islands 65°24′N 06°38′W
92 K1 Húsavík Nordhurland Eystra, NE Iceland 66°03′N 17°20′W
Husevig see Húsavík
116 M10 Huşi var. Huş. Vaslui, E Romania 46°40′N 28°05′E
95 L19 Huskvarna Jönköping, S Sweden 57°47′N 14°15′E
39 P8 Huslia Alaska, USA 65°42′N 156°24′W
Husn see Al Ḩuṣn
95 C15 Husnes Hordaland, S Norway 59°52′N 05°46′E
94 D8 Hustadvika sea area S Norway
Husté see Khust
100 H7 Husum Schleswig-Holstein, N Germany 54°29′N 09°04′E
93 I16 Husum Västernorrland, C Sweden 63°21′N 19°12′E
116 K6 Husyatyn Ternopil's'ka Oblast', W Ukraine 49°04′N 26°10′E
Huszt see Khust
Hutag see Hutag-Öndör
162 K6 Hutag-Öndör var. Hutag. Bulgan, N Mongolia 49°22′N 102°50′E
26 M6 Hutchinson Kansas, C USA 38°03′N 97°56′W
29 U9 Hutchinson Minnesota, N USA 44°53′N 94°22′W
23 Y13 Hutchinson Island island Florida, SE USA
36 L11 Hutch Mountain Arizona, SW USA 34°49′N 111°22′W
141 O14 Ḩūth NW Yemen 16°14′N 44°E
186 I7 Hutjena Buka Island, NE Papua New Guinea 05°19′S 154°40′E
109 T8 Hüttenberg Kärnten, S Austria 46°58′N 14°33′E
25 T10 Hutto Texas, SW USA 30°32′N 97°33′W
Huttu see Futtsu
108 E8 Huttwil Bern, W Switzerland 47°06′N 07°48′E
158 K3 Hutubi Xinjiang Uygur Zizhiqu, NW China 44°10′N 86°51′E
161 N4 Hutuo He C China
Hutyû see Fuchū
185 E20 Huxley, Mount South Island, New Zealand 44°02′S 169°42′E
99 J20 Huy Dut. Hoei, Hoey. Liège, E Belgium 50°32′N 05°14′E
161 R8 Huzhou var. Wuxing. Zhejiang, SE China 30°56′N 120°05′E
159 T10 Huzhu Qinghai, China 36°40′N 101°58′E
Huzi see Fuji
Huzieda see Fujieda
Huzinomiya see Fujinomiya
Huzisawa see Fujisawa
92 I2 Hvammstangi Nordhurland Vestra, N Iceland 65°22′N 20°54′W
92 K4 Hvannadalshnúkur S Iceland 64°01′N 16°39′W
113 E15 Hvar It. Lesina. Split-Dalmacija, S Croatia 43°10′N 16°27′E
113 F15 Hvar It. Lesina; anc. Pharus. island S Croatia
117 T13 Hvardiys'ke Rus. Gvardeyskoye. Respublika Krym, S Ukraine 45°08′N 34°01′E
92 I4 Hveragerdhi Sudhurland, SW Iceland 64°00′N 21°13′W
95 E22 Hvide Sande Ringkøbing, W Denmark 56°00′N 08°08′E
92 I3 Hvítá C Iceland
95 G15 Hvittingfoss Buskerud, S Norway 59°28′N 10°00′E
92 I4 Hvolsvöllur Sudhurland, SW Iceland 63°44′N 20°12′W
Hwach'ŏn-chŏsuji see P'aro-ho
Hwainan see Huainan
Hwalien see Hualien
83 I16 Hwange prev. Wankie. Matabeleland North, W Zimbabwe 18°18′S 26°31′E
Hwang-Hae see Yellow Sea
Hwangshih see Huangshi
83 L17 Hwedza Mashonaland East, E Zimbabwe 18°35′S 31°35′E
63 G20 Hyades, Cerro S Chile 46°57′S 73°09′W
162 K6 Hyalganat var. Selenge. Bulgan, N Mongolia 49°34′N 104°18′E
19 Q12 Hyannis Massachusetts, NE USA 41°38′N 70°15′W
28 L13 Hyannis Nebraska, C USA 42°00′N 101°45′W
162 F6 Hyargas Nuur NW Mongolia
Hybla/Hybla Major see Paternò
39 Y14 Hydaburg Prince of Wales Island, Alaska, USA 55°10′N 132°44′W
185 F22 Hyde Otago, South Island, New Zealand 45°17′S 170°17′E
21 O7 Hyden Kentucky, S USA 37°08′N 83°23′W
18 K12 Hyde Park New York, NE USA 41°46′N 73°52′W
39 Z14 Hyder Alaska, USA 55°55′N 130°01′W
155 I15 Hyderābād var. Haidarabad. state capital Andhra Pradesh, C India 17°22′N 78°26′E
149 Q16 Hyderābād var. Haidarabad. Sind, SE Pakistan 25°26′N 68°22′E
103 T16 Hyères Var, SE France 43°07′N 06°08′E
103 T16 Hyères, Îles d' island group S France
118 K12 Hyermanavichy Rus. Germanovichi. Vitsyebskaya Voblasts', N Belarus 55°24′N 27°48′E
163 X12 Hyesan N North Korea 41°18′N 128°13′E
10 K8 Hyland Yukon Territory, NW Canada
95 K20 Hyltebruk Halland, S Sweden 57°N 13°14′E
18 D16 Hyndman Pennsylvania, NE USA 39°49′N 78°42′W
33 P14 Hyndman Peak Idaho, NW USA 43°45′N 114°07′W
164 I13 Hyōgo off. Hyōgo-ken. prefecture Honshū, SW Japan
Hyōgo-ken see Hyōgo
Hypsas see Belice
Hyrcania see Gorgān
36 L1 Hyrum Utah, W USA 41°37′N 111°51′W
93 N14 Hyrynsalmi Oulu, C Finland 64°41′N 28°30′E
33 V10 Hysham Montana, NW USA 46°16′N 107°14′W
11 N13 Hythe Alberta, W Canada 55°18′N 119°44′W
97 Q23 Hythe SE England, United Kingdom 51°05′N 01°04′E
Hyvinge see Hyvinkää
93 L19 Hyvinkää Swe. Hyvinge. Etelä-Suomi, S Finland 60°37′N 24°50′E

I

116 J9 Iacobeni Ger. Jakobeny. Suceava, NE Romania 47°24′N 25°20′E
Iader see Zadar
172 I7 Iakora Fianarantsoa, SE Madagascar 23°04′S 46°40′E
116 K14 Ialomiţa var. Jalomitsa. county SE Romania
116 K14 Ialomiţa SE Romania
117 N10 Ialoveni Rus. Yaloveny. C Moldova 46°57′N 28°47′E
117 N11 Ialpug var. Ialpugul Mare, Rus. Yalpug. Moldova/Ukraine
Ialpugul Mare see Ialpug
23 T8 Iamonia, Lake Florida, SE USA
116 L13 Ianca Brăila, SE Romania 45°06′N 27°29′E
116 M10 Iaşi Ger. Jassy. Iaşi, NE Romania 47°08′N 27°38′E
116 L9 Iaşi Ger. Jassy, Yassy. county NE Romania
114 J13 Íasmos Anatolikí Makedonía kai Thrákí, NE Greece 41°07′N 25°12′E
22 H6 Iatt, Lake Louisiana, S USA
58 B11 Iauretê Amazonas, NW Brazil 0°37′N 69°10′W
171 N3 Iba Luzon, N Philippines 15°25′N 119°55′E
77 S16 Ibadan Oyo, SW Nigeria 07°22′N 03°58′E
54 E10 Ibagué Tolima, C Colombia 04°27′N 75°14′W
60 J10 Ibaiti Paraná, S Brazil 23°49′S 50°15′W
36 J4 Ibapah Peak Utah, W USA 39°51′N 113°55′W
113 M15 Ibar Alb. Ibër. C Serbia
165 P13 Ibaraki off. Ibaraki-ken. prefecture Honshū, S Japan
Ibaraki-ken see Ibaraki
56 C5 Ibarra var. San Miguel de Ibarra. Imbabura, N Ecuador 0°23′N 78°08′W
Ibaşfalău see Dumbrăveni
141 O16 Ibb W Yemen 13°55′N 44°10′E
100 F13 Ibbenbüren Nordrhein-Westfalen, NW Germany 52°17′N 07°43′E
79 H16 Ibenga N Congo
Ibër see Ibar
57 I14 Iberia Madre de Dios, E Peru 11°21′S 69°36′W
Iberia see Spain
66 M1 Iberian Basin undersea feature E Atlantic Ocean 39°00′N 16°00′W
Iberian Mountains see Ibérico, Sistema
84 D12 Iberian Peninsula physical region Portugal/Spain
64 M8 Iberian Plain undersea feature E Atlantic Ocean 13°30′W 43°45′N
Ibérica, Cordillera see Ibérico, Sistema
105 P6 Ibérico, Sistema var. Cordillera Ibérica, Eng. Iberian Mountains. NE Spain
12 K7 Iberville Lac d' Québec, NE Canada
77 T14 Ibeto Niger, W Nigeria 10°30′N 05°07′E
77 W15 Ibi Taraba, C Nigeria 08°13′N 09°46′E
105 S11 Ibi País Valenciano, E Spain 38°38′N 00°35′W
59 L20 Ibiá Minas Gerais, SE Brazil 19°30′S 46°31′W
61 F15 Ibicuí, Rio S Brazil
61 C19 Ibicuy Entre Ríos, E Argentina 33°44′S 59°10′W
61 F16 Ibirapuitã S Brazil
105 V10 Ibiza var. Iviza, Cast. Eivissa; anc. Ebusus. island Islas Baleares, Spain, W Mediterranean Sea
Ibiza see Eivissa
138 J4 Ibn Wardān, Qaşr ruins Ḩamāh, C Syria
Ibo see Sassandra
188 E9 Ibobang Babeldaob, N Palau
171 V13 Ibonma Papua, E Indonesia 03°27′S 133°30′E
59 N17 Ibotirama Bahia, E Brazil 12°13′S 43°12′W
141 Y8 Ibrā NE Oman 22°45′N 58°30′E
127 Q4 Ibresi Chuvashskaya Respublika, W Russian Federation 55°22′N 47°04′E
141 X8 'Ibrī NW Oman 23°12′N 56°28′E
164 C16 Ibusuki Kagoshima, Kyūshū, SW Japan 31°15′N 130°40′E
57 E16 Ica Ica, SW Peru 14°02′S 75°48′W
57 E16 Ica off. Departamento de Ica. department SW Peru
Ica, Departamento de see Ica
58 C11 Içana Amazonas, NW Brazil 0°22′N 67°25′W
Icaria see Ikaría
58 B13 Içá, Rio var. Río Putumayo. NW South America see also Putumayo, Río
Içá, Rio see Putumayo, Río
136 I17 İçel prev. Ichili; prev. Mersin. province S Turkey
İçel see Mersin
92 I3 Iceland off. Republic of Iceland, Dan. Island, Icel. Ísland. republic N Atlantic Ocean
86 B6 Iceland island N Atlantic Ocean
64 L5 Iceland Basin undersea feature N Atlantic Ocean 61°00′N 19°00′W
Icelandic Plateau see Iceland Plateau
197 Q15 Iceland Plateau var. Icelandic Plateau. undersea feature S Greenland Sea 12°00′W 69°30′N
Iceland, Republic of see Iceland
155 E16 Ichalkaranji Mahārāshtra, W India 16°42′N 74°28′E
164 D15 Ichifusa-yama Kyūshū, SW Japan 32°18′N 131°05′E
Ichili see İçel
164 K13 Ichinomiya var. Itinomiya. Aichi, Honshū, SW Japan 35°18′N 136°48′E
165 Q9 Ichinoseki var. Itinoseki. Iwate, Honshū, C Japan 38°56′N 141°08′E
117 R3 Ichnya Chernihivs'ka Oblast', NE Ukraine 50°52′N 32°24′E
57 L17 Ichoa, Río C Bolivia
Iconium see Konya
Iculisma see Angoulême
39 U12 Icy Bay inlet Alaska, USA
39 N5 Icy Cape headland Alaska, USA 70°19′N 161°52′W
39 W13 Icy Strait strait Alaska, USA
27 R13 Idabel Oklahoma, C USA 33°54′N 94°50′W
29 T13 Ida Grove Iowa, C USA 42°21′N 95°28′W
77 U16 Idah Kogi, S Nigeria 07°06′N 06°45′E
33 N13 Idaho off. State of Idaho, also known as Gem of the Mountains, Gem State. state NW USA
33 N14 Idaho City Idaho, NW USA 43°48′N 115°51′W
33 R14 Idaho Falls Idaho, NW USA 43°28′N 112°01′W
121 P2 Idálion var. Dali, Dhali. C Cyprus 35°00′N 33°25′E
25 N5 Idalou Texas, SW USA 33°40′N 101°40′W
104 I9 Idanha-a-Nova Castelo Branco, C Portugal 39°55′N 07°15′W
101 E19 Idar-Oberstein Rheinland-Pfalz, SW Germany 49°43′N 07°19′E
118 J3 Ida-Virumaa var. Ida-Viru Maakond. province NE Estonia
Ida-Viru Maakond see Ida-Virumaa
124 J8 Idel' Respublika Kareliya, NW Russian Federation 64°08′N 34°12′E
79 C15 Idenao Sud-Ouest, SW Cameroon 04°04′N 09°01′E
Idensalmi see Iisalmi
162 I6 Ider var. Dzuunmod. Hövsgöl, C Mongolia 48°09′N 97°22′E

◆ Country ● Country Capital ◇ Dependent Territory ○ Dependent Territory Capital ◆ Administrative Regions ✕ International Airport ▲ Mountain ▲ Mountain Range Volcano River Lake Reservoir

IDER – INVESTIGATOR RIDGE

Ider *see* Galt
75 X10 **Idfū** *var.* Edfu. SE Egypt 24°55′N 32°52′E
Ídhi Óros *see* Ídi
Ídhra *see* Ýdra
80 L10 **'Īdi** *var.* Ed. SE Eritrea 13°54′N 41°39′E
168 H7 **Idi** Sumatera, W Indonesia 05°00′N 98°00′E
115 I25 **Ídi** *var.* Ídhi Óros. ▲▲ Kríti, Greece, E Mediterranean Sea
Idi Amin, Lac *see* Edward, Lake
106 G10 **Idice** ≈ N Italy
76 G9 **Idîni** Trarza, W Mauritania 17°58′N 15°40′W
79 J21 **Idiofa** Bandundu, SW Dem. Rep. Congo 05°00′S 19°38′E
39 O10 **Iditarod River** ≈ Alaska, USA
95 M14 **Idkerberget** Dalarna, C Sweden 60°22′N 15°15′E
138 I3 **Idlib** Idlib, NW Syria 35°57′N 36°38′E
138 I4 **Idlib** *off.* Muḩāfaẓat Idlib. ◈ *governorate* NW Syria
Idlib, Muḩāfaẓat *see* Idlib
Idra *see* Ýdra
94 J11 **Idre** Dalarna, C Sweden 61°52′N 12°45′E
Idria *see* Idrija
109 S11 **Idrija** *It.* Idria. W Slovenia 46°00′N 14°59′E
101 G18 **Idstein** Hessen, W Germany 50°10′N 08°16′E
83 J25 **Idutywa** Eastern Cape, SE South Africa 32°06′S 28°20′E
Idzhevan *see* Ijevan
118 G9 **Iecava** Bauska, S Latvia 56°36′N 24°10′E
165 T16 **Ie-jima** *var.* Ii-shima. *island* Nansei-shotō, SW Japan
99 B18 **Ieper** *Fr.* Ypres. West-Vlaanderen, W Belgium 50°51′N 02°53′E
115 K25 **Ierápetra** Kríti, Greece, E Mediterranean Sea 35°00′N 25°45′E
115 G22 **Iérax, Akrotírio** *headland* S Greece 36°45′N 23°06′E
Ierisós *see* Ierissós
115 H14 **Ierissós** *var.* Ierisós. Kentrikí Makedonía, N Greece 40°24′N 23°53′E
116 I11 **Iernut** *Hung.* Radnót. Mureş, C Romania 46°27′N 24°15′E
106 J12 **Iesi** *var.* Jesi. Marche, C Italy 43°33′N 13°16′E
92 K9 **Iešjávri** ◎ N Norway
Iesolo *see* Jesolo
188 K16 **Ifalik Atoll** *atoll* Caroline Islands, C Micronesia
172 I6 **Ifanadiana** Fianarantsoa, SE Madagascar 21°19′S 47°39′E
77 T16 **Ife** Osun, SW Nigeria 07°25′N 04°31′E
77 V8 **Iferouâne** Agadez, N Niger 19°05′N 08°24′E
Iferten *see* Yverdon
92 L8 **Ifjord** Finnmark, N Norway 70°27′N 27°06′E
77 R8 **Ifôghas, Adrar des** *var.* Adrar des Iforas. ▲▲ NE Mali
Iforas, Adrar des *see* Ifôghas, Adrar des
182 D6 **Ifould lake** *salt lake* South Australia
74 G6 **Ifrane** C Morocco 33°31′N 05°09′W
171 S11 **Iga** Pulau Halmahera, E Indonesia 01°23′N 128°17′E
81 G18 **Iganga** SE Uganda 0°34′N 33°27′E
60 L7 **Igarapava** São Paulo, S Brazil 20°01′S 47°46′W
122 K9 **Igarka** Krasnoyarskiy Kray, N Russian Federation 67°31′N 86°33′E
Igaunija *see* Estonia
137 T12 **Iğdir** E Turkey 39°50′N 44°00′E
I.G.Duca *see* General Toshevo
Igel *see* Jihlava
94 N11 **Iggesund** Gävleborg, C Sweden 61°38′N 17°04′E
39 P7 **Igikpak, Mount** ▲ Alaska, USA 67°28′N 154°55′W
39 P13 **Igiugig** Alaska, USA 59°19′N 155°53′W
Iglau/Iglawa/Igława *see* Jihlava
107 B20 **Iglesias** Sardegna, Italy, C Mediterranean Sea 39°20′N 08°34′E
127 V4 **Iglino** Respublika Bashkortostan, W Russian Federation 54°51′N 56°29′E
Igló *see* Spišská Nová Ves
9 O6 **Igloolik** Nunavut, N Canada 69°24′N 81°55′W
12 B11 **Ignace** Ontario, S Canada 49°26′N 91°40′W
118 I12 **Ignalina** Utena, E Lithuania 55°20′N 26°10′E
127 Q5 **Ignatovka** Ul'yanovskaya Oblast', W Russian Federation 53°56′N 47°40′E
124 K12 **Ignatovo** Vologodskaya Oblast', NW Russian Federation 60°47′N 37°51′E
114 N11 **İğneada** Kırklareli, NW Turkey 41°54′N 27°58′E
121 S7 **İğneada Burnu** *headland* NW Turkey 41°54′N 28°03′E
Igombe *see* Gombe
115 B16 **Igoumenítsa** Ípeiros, W Greece 39°30′N 20°16′E
127 T2 **Igra** Udmurtskaya Respublika, NW Russian Federation 57°30′N 53°01′E
122 H9 **Igrim** Khanty-Mansiyskiy Avtonomnyy Okrug-Yugra, N Russian Federation 63°09′N 64°33′E
60 G12 **Iguaçu, Rio** *Sp.* Río Iguazú. ≈ Argentina/Brazil *see also* Iguazú, Río
Iguaçu, Río *see* Iguazú, Río
59 I22 **Iguaçu, Salto do** *Sp.* Cataratas del Iguazú; *prev.* Victoria Falls. *waterfall* Argentina/Brazil *see also* Iguazú, Cataratas del
Iguaçu, Salto do *see* Iguazú, Cataratas del
41 O15 **Iguala** *var.* Iguala de la Independencia. Guerrero, S Mexico 18°21′N 99°31′W
105 V5 **Igualada** Cataluña, NE Spain 41°35′N 01°37′E
Iguala de la Independencia *see* Iguala
60 G12 **Iguazú, Cataratas del** *Port.* Salto do Iguaçu; *prev.* Victoria Falls. *waterfall* Argentina/Brazil *see also* Iguaçu, Salto do
Iguazú, Cataratas del *see* Iguaçu, Salto do
62 Q6 **Iguazú, Río** *var.* Río Iguaçu. ≈ Argentina/Brazil *see also* Iguaçu, Río
Iguazú, Río *see* Iguaçu, Rio
79 D19 **Iguéla** Ogooué-Maritime, SW Gabon 02°00′S 09°23′E
Iguid, Erg *see* Iguîdi, 'Erg
67 M5 **Iguîdi, 'Erg** *var.* Erg Iguid. *desert* Algeria/Mauritania
172 K2 **Iharaña** *prev.* Vohémar. Antsiranana, NE Madagascar 13°22′S 50°00′E
151 K18 **Ihavandhippolhu Atoll** *var.* Ihavandiffulu Atoll. *atoll* N Maldives
Ihavandiffulu Atoll *see* Ihavandhippolhu Atoll
Ih Bulag *see* Hanbogd
165 T16 **Iheya-jima** *island* Nansei-shotō, SW Japan
Ihhayrhan *see* Bayan-Önjüül
163 N9 **Ihhet** *var.* Bayan. Dornogovĭ, SE Mongolia 46°15′N 110°16′E
172 I6 **Ihosy** Fianarantsoa, S Madagascar 22°23′S 46°09′E
Ihsüüj *see* Bayanchandmanĭ
162 I7 **Ihtamir** *var.* Dzaanhushuu. Arhangay, C Mongolia 47°36′N 101°06′E
162 H6 **Ih-Uul** *var.* Bayan-Uhaa. Dzavhan, C Mongolia 48°41′N 98°46′E
162 J6 **Ih-Uul** *var.* Selenge. Hövsgöl, N Mongolia 49°25′N 101°30′E
93 L14 **Ii** Oulu, C Finland 65°18′N 25°23′E
164 M13 **Iida** Nagano, Honshū, S Japan 35°32′N 137°48′E
93 M14 **Iijoki** ≈ C Finland
Iinnasuolu *see* Hinnøya
118 J4 **Iisaku** *Ger.* Isaak. Ida-Virumaa, NE Estonia 59°06′N 27°19′E
93 M16 **Iisalmi** *var.* Idensalmi. Itä-Suomi, C Finland 63°32′N 27°10′E
Ii-shima *see* Ie-jima
165 N11 **Iiyama** Nagano, Honshū, S Japan 36°52′N 138°22′E
77 S16 **Ijebu-Ode** Ogun, SW Nigeria 06°46′N 03°57′E
137 U11 **Ijevan** *Rus.* Idzhevan. N Armenia 40°53′N 45°07′E
98 H9 **IJmuiden** Noord-Holland, W Netherlands 52°28′N 04°38′E
98 M12 **IJssel** *var.* Yssel. ≈ Netherlands
98 J8 **IJsselmeer** *prev.* Zuider Zee. ◎ N Netherlands
98 L9 **IJsselmuiden** Overijssel, E Netherlands 52°34′N 05°55′E
98 I12 **IJsselstein** Utrecht, C Netherlands 52°01′N 05°02′E
61 G14 **Ijuí** Rio Grande do Sul, S Brazil 28°23′S 53°55′W
61 G14 **Ijuí, Rio** ≈ S Brazil
189 R8 **Ijuw** NE Nauru 0°30′S 166°57′E
99 E16 **IJzendijke** Zeeland, SW Netherlands 51°20′N 03°36′E
99 A18 **Ijzer** ≈ W Belgium
Ikaahuk *see* Sachs Harbour
93 K18 **Ikaalinen** Länsi-Suomi, W Finland 61°46′N 23°05′E
172 I6 **Ikalamavony** Fianarantsoa, SE Madagascar 21°10′S 46°35′E
Ikaluktutiak *see* Cambridge Bay
185 G16 **Ikamatua** West Coast, South Island, New Zealand 42°16′S 171°42′E
77 U16 **Ikare** Ondo, SW Nigeria 07°36′N 05°52′E
115 L20 **Ikaría** *var.* Kariot, Nicaria, Nikaria; *anc.* Icaria. *island* Dodekánisa, Greece, Aegean Sea
95 F22 **Ikast** Ringkøbing, W Denmark 56°09′N 09°10′E
184 O9 **Ikawhenua Range** ▲▲ North Island, New Zealand
165 U4 **Ikeda** Hokkaidō, NE Japan 42°54′N 143°25′E
164 H14 **Ikeda** Tokushima, Shikoku, SW Japan 34°00′N 133°47′E
77 S16 **Ikeja** Lagos, SW Nigeria 06°36′N 03°16′E
79 L19 **Ikela** Equateur, C Dem. Rep. Congo 01°11′S 23°16′E
114 H10 **Ikhtiman** Sofiya, W Bulgaria 42°26′N 23°49′E
164 C13 **Iki** *island* SW Japan
127 O13 **Iki Burul** Respublika Kalmykiya, SW Russian Federation 45°48′N 44°44′E
137 P11 **İkizdere** Rize, NE Turkey 40°47′N 40°34′E
39 P14 **Ikolik, Cape** *headland* Kodiak Island, Alaska, USA 57°12′N 154°46′W
77 V17 **Ikom** Cross River, SE Nigeria 05°57′N 08°43′E
172 I6 **Ikongo** *prev.* Fort-Carnot. Fianarantsoa, SE Madagascar 21°52′S 47°27′E
39 P5 **Ikpikpuk River** ≈ Alaska, USA
190 H1 **Iku** *prev.* Lone Tree Islet. *atoll* Tungaru, W Kiribati
164 I12 **Ikuno** Hyōgo, Honshū, SW Japan 35°13′N 134°48′E
190 H16 **Ikurangi** ▲ Rarotonga, S Cook Islands 21°12′S 159°45′W
171 X14 **Ilaga** Papua, E Indonesia 03°54′S 137°30′E
171 O2 **Ilagan** Luzon, N Philippines 17°08′N 121°54′E
142 J7 **Īlām** *var.* Elam. Īlām, W Iran 33°37′N 46°27′E
153 R12 **Ilām** Eastern, E Nepal 26°52′N 87°58′E
142 J8 **Īlām** *off.* Ostān-e Īlām. ◈ *province* W Iran
Īlām, Ostān-e *see* Īlām
161 T13 **Ilan** *Jap.* Giran. N Taiwan 24°45′N 121°44′E
146 G9 **Ilanly Obvodnitel'nyy Kanal** *canal* N Turkmenistan
122 L12 **Ilanskiy** Krasnoyarskiy Kray, S Russian Federation 56°16′N 95°59′E
108 H9 **Ilanz** Graubünden, S Switzerland 46°46′N 09°10′E
77 S16 **Ilaro** Ogun, SW Nigeria 06°52′N 03°01′E
57 I17 **Ilave** Puno, S Peru 16°07′S 69°40′W
110 K8 **Iława** *Ger.* Deutsch-Eylau. Warmińsko-Mazurskie, NE Poland 53°36′N 19°35′E
123 P10 **Il'benge** Respublika Sakha (Yakutiya), NE Russian Federation 62°52′N 124°13′E
129 R7 **Ile** *var.* Ili, *Chin.* Ili He, *Rus.* Reka Ili. ≈ China/Kazakhstan *see also* Ili He
Ile *see* Ili He
11 S13 **Ile-à-la-Crosse** Saskatchewan, C Canada 55°29′N 108°00′W
79 J21 **Ilebo** *prev.* Port-Francqui. Kasai-Occidental, W Dem. Rep. Congo 04°19′S 20°32′E
103 N5 **Île-de-France** ◈ *region* N France
144 I9 **Ilek** *Kaz.* Elek. ≈ Kazakhstan/Russian Federation
Ilerda *see* Lleida
77 T16 **Ilesha** Osun, SW Nigeria 07°35′N 04°49′E
187 Q16 **Îles Loyauté, Province des** ◈ *province* E New Caledonia
11 X12 **Ilford** Manitoba, C Canada 56°02′N 95°48′W
116 K14 **Ilfov** ◈ *county* S Romania
97 I23 **Ilfracombe** SW England, United Kingdom 51°12′N 04°10′W
136 I11 **Ilgaz Dağları** ▲▲ N Turkey
136 G15 **Ilgın** Konya, W Turkey 38°16′N 31°57′E
60 I7 **Ilha Solteira** São Paulo, S Brazil 20°28′S 51°19′W
104 G7 **Ílhavo** Aveiro, N Portugal 40°36′N 08°40′W
59 O18 **Ilhéus** Bahia, E Brazil 14°50′S 39°06′W
Ili *see* Ile/Ili He
116 G11 **Ilia** *Hung.* Marosillye. Hunedoara, SW Romania 45°57′N 22°40′E
39 P13 **Iliamna** Alaska, USA 59°42′N 154°49′W
39 P13 **Iliamna Lake** ◎ Alaska, USA
137 N13 **Iliç** Erzincan, C Turkey 39°27′N 38°34′E
Il'ichevsk *see* Şärur, Azerbaijan
Il'ichevsk *see* Illichivs'k, Ukraine
Ilici *see* Elche
37 V2 **Iliff** Colorado, C USA 40°46′N 103°04′W
171 Q7 **Iligan** *off.* Iligan City. Mindanao, S Philippines 08°12′N 124°16′E
171 Q7 **Iligan Bay** *bay* S Philippines
Iligan City *see* Iligan
158 I5 **Ili He** *var.* Ili, *Kaz.* Ile, *Rus.* Reka Ili. ≈ China/Kazakhstan *see also* Ile
Ili He *see* Ile
56 C6 **Iliniza** ▲ N Ecuador 0°37′S 78°41′W
Ilinski *see* Il'inskiy
125 U14 **Il'inskiy** *var.* Ilinski. Permskaya Oblast', NW Russian Federation 58°33′N 55°31′E
125 U14 **Il'inskiy** Ostrov Sakhalin, Sakhalinskaya Oblast', SE Russian Federation 47°59′N 142°14′E
18 I10 **Ilion** New York, NE USA 43°01′N 75°02′W
38 E9 **'Ilio Point** *var.* Ilio Point. *headland* Moloka'i, Hawai'i, USA 21°13′N 157°15′W
Ilio Point *see* 'Ilio Point
109 T13 **Ilirska Bistrica** *prev.* Bistrica, *Ger.* Feistritz, Illyrisch-Feistritz, *It.* Villa del Nevoso. SW Slovenia 45°34′N 14°12′E
137 Q16 **Ilisu Barajı** ⊠ SE Turkey
155 G17 **Ilkal** Karnātaka, C India 15°59′N 76°08′E
97 M19 **Ilkeston** C England, United Kingdom 52°59′N 01°18′W
121 O16 **Il-Kullana** *headland* SW Malta 35°49′N 14°26′E
108 J8 **Ill** ≈ W Austria
103 U6 **Ill** ≈ NE France
62 G10 **Illapel** Coquimbo, C Chile 31°40′S 71°13′W
Illaue Fartak Trench *see* Alula-Fartak Trench
182 C2 **Illbillee, Mount** ▲ South Australia 27°01′S 132°13′E
102 I6 **Ille-et-Vilaine** ◈ *department* NW France
77 T11 **Illéla** Tahoua, SW Niger 14°25′N 05°10′E
101 J24 **Iller** ≈ S Germany
101 J23 **Illertissen** Bayern, S Germany 48°13′N 10°08′E
105 X9 **Illes Baleares** ◈ *autonomous community* E Spain
105 N8 **Illescas** Castilla-La Mancha, C Spain 40°08′N 03°51′W
Ille-sur-la-Têt *see* Ille-sur-Têt
103 O17 **Ille-sur-Têt** *var.* Ille-sur-la-Têt. Pyrénées-Orientales, S France 42°40′N 02°37′E
Illiberis *see* Elne
117 P11 **Illichivs'k** *Rus.* Il'ichevsk. Odes'ka Oblast', SW Ukraine 46°18′N 30°36′E
Illicis *see* Elche
102 M6 **Illiers-Combray** Eure-et-Loir, C France 48°18′N 01°15′E
30 K12 **Illinois** *off.* State of Illinois, *also known as* Prairie State, Sucker State. ◈ *state* C USA
30 J13 **Illinois River** ≈ Illinois, N USA
117 N6 **Illintsi** Vinnyts'ka Oblast', C Ukraine 49°07′N 29°13′E
Illiturgis *see* Andújar
74 M10 **Illizi** SE Algeria 26°30′N 08°28′E
27 Y7 **Illmo** Missouri, C USA 37°13′N 89°30′W
Illurco *see* Lorca
Illuro *see* Mataró
Illyrisch-Feistritz *see* Ilirska Bistrica
101 K16 **Ilm** ≈ C Germany
101 K17 **Ilmenau** Thüringen, C Germany 50°40′N 10°55′E
124 H14 **Il'men', Ozero** ◎ NW Russian Federation
57 H18 **Ilo** Moquegua, SW Peru 17°42′S 71°20′W
171 O6 **Iloilo** *off.* Iloilo City. Panay Island, C Philippines 10°42′N 122°34′E
Iloilo City *see* Iloilo
112 K10 **Ilok** *Hung.* Újlak. Vojvodina, NW Serbia 45°12′N 19°22′E
93 O16 **Ilomantsi** Itä-Suomi, SE Finland 62°40′N 30°55′E
42 F8 **Ilopango, Lago de** *volcanic lake* C El Salvador
77 T15 **Ilorin** Kwara, W Nigeria 08°32′N 04°35′E
117 X8 **Ilovays'k** *Rus.* Ilovaysk. Donets'ka Oblast', SE Ukraine 47°55′N 38°14′E
Ilovaysk *see* Ilovays'k
127 O10 **Ilovlya** Volgogradskaya Oblast', SW Russian Federation 49°45′N 44°19′E
127 O10 **Ilovlya** ≈ SW Russian Federation
126 K14 **Il'skiy** Krasnodarskiy Kray, SW Russian Federation 44°52′N 38°26′E
182 B2 **Iltur** South Australia 27°33′S 130°31′E
171 Y13 **Ilugwa** Papua, E Indonesia 03°42′S 139°09′E
İluh *see* Batman
118 I11 **Ilūkste** Daugvapils, SE Latvia 55°58′N 26°21′E
171 Y13 **Ilur** Pulau Gorong, E Indonesia 04°00′S 131°25′E
32 F10 **Ilwaco** Washington, NW USA 46°19′N 124°03′W
Il'yaly *see* Gurbansoltan Eje
İlyasbaba Burnu *see* Tekke Burnu
125 U9 **Ilych** ≈ NW Russian Federation
101 O21 **Ilz** ≈ SE Germany
111 M14 **Iłża** Radom, SE Poland 51°09′N 21°15′E
164 G13 **Imabari** *var.* Imaharu. Ehime, Shikoku, SW Japan 34°04′N 132°59′E
Imaharu *see* Imabari
165 O12 **Imaichi** *var.* Imaiti. Tochigi, Honshū, S Japan 36°43′N 139°41′E
Imaiti *see* Imaichi
164 K12 **Imajō** Fukui, Honshū, SW Japan 35°45′N 136°10′E
139 R9 **Imām Ibn Hāshim** Karbalā', C Iraq 32°46′N 43°21′E
139 T11 **Imān 'Abd Allāh** Al Qādisīyah, S Iraq 31°36′N 44°34′E
164 F15 **Imano-yama** ▲ Shikoku, SW Japan 32°51′N 132°48′E
164 C13 **Imari** Saga, Kyūshū, SW Japan 33°18′N 129°51′E
Imarssuak Mid-Ocean Seachannel *see* Imarssuak Seachannel
64 J6 **Imarssuak Seachannel** *var.* Imarssuak Mid-Ocean Seachannel. *channel* N Atlantic Ocean
93 N18 **Imatra** Etelä-Suomi, SE Finland 61°14′N 28°50′E
164 K13 **Imazu** Shiga, Honshū, SW Japan 35°25′N 136°00′E
56 C6 **Imbabura** ◈ *province* N Ecuador
55 R9 **Imbaimadai** W Guyana 05°44′N 60°23′W
61 K14 **Imbituba** Santa Catarina, S Brazil 28°15′S 48°44′W
27 W9 **Imboden** Arkansas, C USA 36°12′N 91°10′W
Imbros *see* Gökçeada
Imeni 26 Bakinskikh Komissarov *see* 26 Bakı Komissarı
Imeni 26 Bakinskikh Komissarov *see* Uzboý
125 N13 **Imeni Babushkina** Vologodskaya Oblast', NW Russian Federation 59°40′N 43°04′E
126 J7 **Imeni Karla Libknekhta** Kurskaya Oblast', W Russian Federation 51°36′N 35°28′E
Imeni Mollanepesa *see* Mollanepes Adyndaky
Imeni S. A. Niyazova *see* S. A.Nyýazow Adyndaky
Imeni Sverdlova Rudnik *see* Sverdlovs'k
188 E9 **Imeong** Babeldaob, N Palau
81 L14 **Īmī** Sumalē, E Ethiopia 06°27′N 42°10′E
115 M21 **Imia** *Turk.* Kardak. *island* Dodekánisa, Greece, Aegean Sea
Imishli *see* İmişli
137 X12 **İmişli** *Rus.* Imishli. C Azerbaijan 39°54′N 48°04′E
163 X14 **Imjin-gang** ≈ North Korea/South Korea
35 S3 **Imlay** Nevada, W USA 40°39′N 118°10′W
31 S9 **Imlay City** Michigan, N USA 43°01′N 83°04′W
23 X15 **Immokalee** Florida, SE USA 26°24′N 81°25′W
77 U17 **Imo** ◈ *state* SE Nigeria
106 G10 **Imola** Emilia-Romagna, N Italy 44°22′N 11°43′E
186 A5 **Imonda** Sandaun, NW Papua New Guinea 03°21′S 141°10′E
Imoschi *see* Imotski
113 G14 **Imotski** *It.* Imoschi. Split-Dalmacija, SE Croatia 43°28′N 17°13′E
59 L14 **Imperatriz** Maranhão, NE Brazil 05°32′S 47°28′W
106 B10 **Imperia** Liguria, NW Italy 43°53′N 08°03′E
57 E15 **Imperial** Lima, W Peru 13°04′S 76°21′W
35 X17 **Imperial** California, W USA 32°51′N 115°34′W
28 L16 **Imperial** Nebraska, C USA 40°30′N 101°37′W
24 M9 **Imperial** Texas, SW USA 31°15′N 102°40′W
35 Y17 **Imperial Dam** *dam* California, W USA
79 I17 **Impfondo** Likouala, NE Congo 01°37′N 18°04′E
153 X14 **Imphāl** *state capital* Manipur, NE India 24°47′N 93°55′E
103 P9 **Imphy** Nièvre, C France 46°55′N 03°16′E
106 G11 **Impruneta** Toscana, C Italy 43°42′N 11°16′E
115 K15 **İmroz** *var.* Gökçeada. Çanakkale, NW Turkey 40°06′N 25°50′E
Imroz Adası *see* Gökçeada
108 L7 **Imst** Tirol, W Austria 47°14′N 10°45′E
40 F3 **Imuris** Sonora, NW Mexico 30°48′N 110°52′W
164 M13 **Ina** Nagano, Honshū, S Japan 35°52′N 137°58′E
65 M18 **Inaccessible Island** *island* W Tristan da Cunha
115 F20 **Ínachos** ≈ S Greece
188 H6 **I Naftan, Puntan** *headland* Saipan, S Northern Mariana Islands
Inagua Islands *see* Great Inagua
Inagua Islands *see* Little Inagua
185 H15 **Inangahua** West Coast, South Island, New Zealand 41°51′S 171°58′E
57 I14 **Iñapari** Madre de Dios, E Peru 11°00′S 69°34′W
188 B17 **Inarajan** SE Guam 13°16′N 144°45′E
92 L10 **Inari** *Lapp.* Anár, Aanaar. Lappi, N Finland 68°54′N 27°06′E
92 L10 **Inarijärvi** *Lapp.* Aanaarjävri, *Swe.* Enareträsk. ◎ N Finland
92 L9 **Inarijoki** *Lapp.* Anárjohka. ≈ Finland/Norway
Inău *see* Ineu
165 P11 **Inawashiro-ko** *var.* Inawasiro Ko. ◎ Honshū, C Japan
Inawasiro Ko *see* Inawashiro-ko
105 X9 **Inca** Mallorca, Spain, W Mediterranean Sea 39°43′N 02°54′E
62 H7 **Inca de Oro** Atacama, N Chile 26°45′S 69°54′W
115 J15 **İnce Burnu** *cape* NW Turkey
136 K9 **İnce Burnu** *headland* N Turkey 42°06′N 34°57′E
136 I17 **İncekum Burnu** *headland* S Turkey 36°13′N 33°57′E
76 G7 **Inchiri** ◈ *region* NW Mauritania
163 X15 **Inch'ŏn** *off.* Inch'ŏn-gwangyŏksi, *Jap.* Jinsen; *prev.* Chemulpo. NW South Korea 37°27′N 126°41′E
161 X15 **Inch'on** ✈ (Sŏul) NW South Korea 37°37′N 126°42′E
Inch'ŏn-gwangyŏksi *see* Inch'ŏn
83 M17 **Inchope** Manica, C Mozambique 19°09′S 33°54′E
Incoronata *see* Kornat
103 Y15 **Incudine, Monte** ▲ Corse, France, C Mediterranean Sea 41°52′N 09°13′E
60 M10 **Indaiatuba** São Paulo, S Brazil 23°03′S 47°14′W
93 H17 **Indal** Västernorrland, C Sweden 62°36′N 17°06′E
93 H17 **Indalsälven** ≈ C Sweden
40 K8 **Inde** Durango, C Mexico 25°55′N 105°10′W
Indefatigable Island *see* Santa Cruz, Isla
35 S10 **Independence** California, W USA 36°48′N 118°14′W
29 X13 **Independence** Iowa, C USA 42°28′N 91°42′W
27 P7 **Independence** Kansas, C USA 37°13′N 95°43′W
20 M4 **Independence** Kentucky, S USA 38°56′N 84°32′W
27 R4 **Independence** Missouri, C USA 39°04′N 94°27′W
21 R8 **Independence** Virginia, NE USA 36°38′N 81°11′W
30 J7 **Independence** Wisconsin, N USA 44°21′N 91°25′W
197 R12 **Independence Fjord** *fjord* N Greenland
Independence Island *see* Malden Island
35 W2 **Independence Mountains** ▲▲ Nevada, W USA
57 K18 **Independencia** Cochabamba, C Bolivia 17°08′S 66°52′W
57 E16 **Independencia, Bahía de la** *bay* W Peru
Independencia, Monte *see* Adam, Mount
116 M12 **Independenţa** Galaţi, SE Romania 45°29′N 27°45′E
Inderagiri *see* Indragiri, Sungai
Inderbor *see* Inderborskiy
144 F11 **Inderborskiy** *Kaz.* Inderbor. Atyrau, W Kazakhstan 48°35′N 51°45′E
151 I14 **India** *off.* Republic of India, *var.* Indian Union, Union of India, *Hind.* Bhārat. ◆ *republic* S Asia
India *see* Inđija
18 D14 **Indiana** Pennsylvania, NE USA 40°37′N 79°09′W
31 N13 **Indiana** *off.* State of Indiana, *also known as* Hoosier State. ◈ *state* N USA
31 O14 **Indianapolis** *state capital* Indiana, N USA 39°46′N 86°09′W
11 O10 **Indian Cabins** Alberta, W Canada 59°51′N 117°06′W
42 G1 **Indian Church** Orange Walk, N Belize 17°47′N 88°39′W
Indian Desert *see* Thar Desert
11 U16 **Indian Head** Saskatchewan, S Canada 50°32′N 103°41′W
31 O4 **Indian Lake** ◎ Michigan, N USA
18 K9 **Indian Lake** ◎ New York, NE USA
31 R13 **Indian Lake** ⊠ Ohio, N USA
172-173 **Indian Ocean** *ocean*
29 V15 **Indianola** Iowa, C USA 41°21′N 93°33′W
22 K4 **Indianola** Mississippi, S USA 33°27′N 90°39′W
36 J6 **Indian Peak** ▲ Utah, W USA 38°18′N 113°52′W
23 Y13 **Indian River** *lagoon* Florida, SE USA
35 W10 **Indian Springs** Nevada, W USA 36°33′N 115°40′W
23 Y14 **Indiantown** Florida, SE USA 27°01′N 80°29′W
Indian Union *see* India
59 K19 **Indiara** Goiás, S Brazil 17°12′S 50°09′W
India, Republic of *see* India
India, Union of *see* India
125 Q4 **Indiga** Nenetskiy Avtonomnyy Okrug, NW Russian Federation 67°40′N 49°01′E
123 R9 **Indigirka** ≈ NE Russian Federation
112 L10 **Inđija** *Hung.* India; *prev.* Indjija. Vojvodina, N Serbia 45°03′N 20°04′E
35 V16 **Indio** California, W USA 33°42′N 116°13′W
42 M12 **Indio, Río** ≈ SE Nicaragua
152 I10 **Indira Gandhi** ✈ (Delhi) Delhi, N India
151 Q23 **Indira Point** *headland* Andaman and Nicobar Island, India, NE Indian Ocean 6°54′N 93°54′E
Indjija *see* Inđija
129 Q13 **Indo-Australian Plate** *tectonic feature*
173 N11 **Indomed Fracture Zone** *tectonic feature* SW Indian Ocean
170 L12 **Indonesia** *off.* Republic of Indonesia, *Ind.* Republik Indonesia; *prev.* Dutch East Indies, Netherlands East Indies, United States of Indonesia. ◆ *republic* SE Asia
Indonesian Borneo *see* Kalimantan
Indonesia, Republic of *see* Indonesia
Indonesia, Republik *see* Indonesia
Indonesia, United States of *see* Indonesia
154 G10 **Indore** Madhya Pradesh, C India 22°42′N 75°51′E
168 L11 **Indragiri, Sungai** *var.* Batang Kuantan, Inderagiri. ≈ Sumatera, W Indonesia
Indramajoe/Indramaju *see* Indramayu
169 P15 **Indramayu** *prev.* Indramajoe, Indramaju. Jawa, C Indonesia 06°22′S 108°20′E
155 K14 **Indrāvati** ≈ S India
103 N9 **Indre** ◈ *department* C France
102 M8 **Indre** ≈ C France
94 D13 **Indre Ålvik** Hordaland, S Norway 60°26′N 06°27′E
102 L8 **Indre-et-Loire** ◈ *department* C France
Indreville *see* Châteauroux
152 G3 **Indus** *Chin.* Yindu He; *prev.* Yin-tu Ho. ≈ S Asia
Indus Cone *see* Indus Fan
173 P3 **Indus Fan** *var.* Indus Cone. *undersea feature* N Arabian Sea 16°00′N 66°30′E
149 P17 **Indus, Mouths of the** *delta* S Pakistan
83 I24 **Indwe** Eastern Cape, SE South Africa 31°28′S 27°20′E
136 I10 **İnebolu** Kastamonu, N Turkey 41°57′N 33°45′E
77 P8 **I-n-Échaï** *oasis* C Mali
114 M13 **İnecik** Tekirdağ, NW Turkey 40°55′N 27°16′E
136 E12 **İnegöl** Bursa, NW Turkey 40°06′N 29°31′E
Inessa *see* Biancavilla
116 F10 **Ineu** *Hung.* Borosjenő; *prev.* Inău. Arad, W Romania 46°26′N 21°51′E
Ineul/Ineu, Vîrful *see* Ineu, Vârful
116 J9 **Ineu, Vârful** *var.* Ineul; *prev.* Vîrful Ineu. ▲ N Romania 47°31′N 24°52′E
21 P6 **Inez** Kentucky, S USA 37°53′N 82°33′W
74 E8 **Inezgane** ✈ (Agadir) W Morocco 30°35′N 09°27′W
41 T17 **Inferior, Laguna** *lagoon* S Mexico
40 M15 **Infiernillo, Presa del** ⊠ S Mexico
104 L2 **Infiesto** Asturias, N Spain 43°21′N 05°21′W
93 L20 **Ingå** *Fin.* Inkoo. Etelä-Suomi, S Finland 60°01′N 24°05′E
77 U10 **Ingal** *var.* I-n-Gall. Agadez, C Niger 16°52′N 06°57′E
I-n-Gall *see* Ingal
99 C18 **Ingelmunster** West-Vlaanderen, W Belgium 50°12′N 03°15′E
79 I18 **Ingende** Equateur, W Dem. Rep. Congo 0°15′S 18°58′E
62 L5 **Ingeniero Guillermo Nueva Juárez** Formosa, N Argentina 23°55′S 61°50′W
63 H16 **Ingeniero Jacobacci** Río Negro, C Argentina 41°18′S 69°35′W
14 F16 **Ingersoll** Ontario, S Canada 43°03′N 80°53′W
Ingettolgoy *see* Selenge
181 W5 **Ingham** Queensland, NE Australia 18°35′S 146°12′E
146 M11 **Ingichka** Samarqand Viloyati, C Uzbekistan 39°46′N 65°56′E
97 L16 **Ingleborough** ▲ N England, United Kingdom 54°07′N 02°22′W
25 T14 **Ingleside** Texas, SW USA 27°52′N 97°12′W
184 K10 **Inglewood** Taranaki, North Island, New Zealand 39°07′S 174°13′E
35 S15 **Inglewood** California, W USA 33°57′N 118°21′W
101 L21 **Ingolstadt** Bayern, S Germany 48°46′N 11°26′E
33 V9 **Ingomar** Montana, NW USA 46°34′N 107°21′W
13 R14 **Ingonish Beach** Cape Breton Island, Nova Scotia, SE Canada 46°42′N 60°22′W
153 S14 **Ingrāj Bāzār** *prev.* English Bazar. West Bengal, NE India 25°00′N 88°10′E
25 Q11 **Ingram** Texas, SW USA 30°04′N 99°14′W
195 X7 **Ingrid Christensen Coast** *physical region* Antarctica
74 K14 **I-n-Guezzam** S Algeria 19°35′N 05°49′E
Ingulets *see* Inhulets'
Inguri *see* Enguri
Ingushetia/Ingushetiya, Respublika *see* Ingushetiya, Respublika
127 O15 **Ingushetiya, Respublika** *var.* Respublika Ingushetiya, *Eng.* Ingushetia. ◈ *autonomous republic* SW Russian Federation
83 N20 **Inhambane** Inhambane, SE Mozambique 23°52′S 35°31′E
83 M20 **Inhambane** *off.* Província de Inhambane. ◈ *province* S Mozambique
Inhambane, Província de *see* Inhambane
83 N17 **Inhaminga** Sofala, C Mozambique 18°24′S 35°00′E
83 N20 **Inharrime** Inhambane, SE Mozambique 24°29′S 35°01′E
83 M18 **Inhassoro** Inhambane, E Mozambique 21°32′S 35°13′E
117 S9 **Inhulets'** *Rus.* Ingulets. Dnipropetrovs'ka Oblast', E Ukraine 47°43′N 33°16′E
117 R10 **Inhulets'** *Rus.* Ingulets. ≈ S Ukraine
105 Q10 **Iniesta** Castilla-La Mancha, C Spain 39°27′N 01°45′W
I-ning *see* Yining
54 K11 **Inírida, Río** ≈ E Colombia
Inis *see* Ennis
Inis Ceithleann *see* Enniskillen
Inis Córthaidh *see* Enniscorthy
Inis Díomáin *see* Ennistimon
97 A17 **Inishbofin** *Ir.* Inis Bó Finne. *island* W Ireland
97 B18 **Inisheer** *var.* Inishere, *Ir.* Inis Oírr. *island* W Ireland
Inishere *see* Inisheer
97 B18 **Inishmaan** *Ir.* Inis Meáin. *island* W Ireland
97 A18 **Inishmore** *Ir.* Árainn. *island* W Ireland
96 E13 **Inishtrahull** *Ir.* Inis Trá Tholl. *island* NW Ireland
97 A17 **Inishturk** *Ir.* Inis Toirc. *island* W Ireland
Inkoo *see* Ingå
185 J16 **Inland Kaikoura Range** ▲▲ South Island, New Zealand
Inland Sea *see* Seto-naikai
21 P11 **Inman** South Carolina, SE USA 35°03′N 82°05′W
108 L7 **Inn** ≈ C Europe
197 O11 **Innaanganeq** *var.* Kap York. *headland* NW Greenland 75°54′N 66°27′W
182 K2 **Innamincka** South Australia 27°47′S 140°45′E
92 G12 **Inndyr** Nordland, C Norway 67°01′N 14°00′E
42 G3 **Inner Channel** *inlet* SE Belize
96 F11 **Inner Hebrides** *island group* W Scotland, United Kingdom
172 H15 **Inner Islands** *var.* Central Group. *island group* NE Seychelles
Inner Mongolia/Inner Mongolian Autonomous Region *see* Nei Mongol Zizhiqu
96 G8 **Inner Sound** *strait* NW Scotland, United Kingdom
100 J13 **Innerste** ≈ C Germany
181 W5 **Innisfail** Queensland, NE Australia 17°29′S 146°03′E
11 Q15 **Innisfail** Alberta, SW Canada 52°01′N 113°59′W
Inniskilling *see* Enniskillen
39 O11 **Innoko River** ≈ Alaska, USA
Innsbruch *see* Innsbruck
108 M7 **Innsbruck** *var.* Innsbruch. Tirol, W Austria 47°17′N 11°25′E
79 I19 **Inongo** Bandundu, W Dem. Rep. Congo 01°55′S 18°20′E
Inoucdjouac *see* Inukjuak
Inowrazlaw *see* Inowrocław
110 I10 **Inowrocław** *Ger.* Hohensalza; *prev.* Inowrazlaw. Kujawski-pomorskie, C Poland 52°47′N 18°15′E
57 K18 **Inquisivi** La Paz, W Bolivia 16°55′S 67°10′W
Inrin *see* Yüanlin
77 O8 **I-n-Sâkâne, 'Erg** *desert* N Mali
77 O8 **I-n-Sâkâne, 'Erg** *desert* N Mali
74 J10 **I-n-Salah** *var.* In Salah. C Algeria 27°11′N 02°31′E
127 O5 **Insar** Respublika Mordoviya, W Russian Federation 53°52′N 44°26′E
189 X15 **Insiaf** Kosrae, E Micronesia
94 L13 **Insjön** Dalarna, C Sweden 60°40′N 15°05′E
Insterburg *see* Chernyakhovsk
Insula *see* Lille
116 L13 **Însurăţei** Brăila, SE Romania 44°55′N 27°40′E
125 V6 **Inta** Respublika Komi, NW Russian Federation 66°00′N 60°10′E
77 R9 **I-n-Tebezas** Kidal, E Mali 17°58′N 01°51′E
Interamna *see* Teramo
Interamna Nahars *see* Terni
28 L11 **Interior** South Dakota, N USA 43°42′N 101°57′W
108 E9 **Interlaken** Bern, SW Switzerland 46°41′N 07°51′E
29 V2 **International Falls** Minnesota, N USA 48°38′N 93°26′W
167 O7 **Inthanon, Doi** ▲ NW Thailand 18°33′N 98°29′E
42 G7 **Intibucá** ◈ *department* SW Honduras
42 G8 **Intipucá** La Unión, SE El Salvador 13°10′N 88°03′W
61 B15 **Intiyaco** Santa Fe, C Argentina 28°43′S 60°04′W
116 K12 **Întorsura Buzăului** *Ger.* Bozau, *Hung.* Bodzafordulő. Covasna, E Romania 45°40′N 26°02′E
22 H9 **Intracoastal Waterway** *inland waterway system* Louisiana, S USA
25 V13 **Intracoastal Waterway** *inland waterway system* Texas, SW USA
108 G11 **Intragna** Ticino, S Switzerland 46°12′N 08°42′E
165 P14 **Inubō-zaki** *headland* Honshū, S Japan 35°42′N 140°51′E
164 E14 **Inukai** Ōita, Kyūshū, SW Japan 33°05′N 131°37′E
12 I5 **Inukjuak** *var.* Inoucdjouac; *prev.* Port Harrison. Québec, NE Canada 58°28′N 77°58′W
63 I24 **Inútil, Bahía** *bay* S Chile
Inuuvik *see* Inuvik
11 R8 **Inuvik** *var.* Inuuvik. Northwest Territories, NW Canada 68°25′N 133°35′W
164 L13 **Inuyama** Aichi, Honshū, SW Japan 35°23′N 136°56′E
56 G13 **Inuya, Río** ≈ E Peru
125 U13 **In'va** ≈ NW Russian Federation
96 H11 **Inveraray** W Scotland, United Kingdom 56°13′N 05°05′W
185 C24 **Invercargill** Southland, South Island, New Zealand 46°25′S 168°22′E
183 T5 **Inverell** New South Wales, SE Australia 29°46′S 151°10′E
96 I8 **Invergordon** N Scotland, United Kingdom 57°42′N 04°02′W
11 P16 **Invermere** British Columbia, SW Canada 50°30′N 116°00′W
13 R14 **Inverness** Cape Breton Island, Nova Scotia, SE Canada 46°14′N 61°19′W
96 I8 **Inverness** N Scotland, United Kingdom 57°27′N 04°15′W
23 V11 **Inverness** Florida, SE USA 28°50′N 82°19′W
96 I9 **Inverness** *cultural region* NW Scotland, United Kingdom
96 K9 **Inverurie** NE Scotland, United Kingdom 57°14′N 02°14′W
182 F8 **Investigator Group** *island group* South Australia
173 T7 **Investigator Ridge** *undersea feature* E Indian Ocean 11°30′S 98°10′E

◆ Country
● Country Capital
◇ Dependent Territory
○ Dependent Territory Capital
◈ Administrative Regions
✈ International Airport
▲ Mountain
▲▲ Mountain Range
Volcano
≈ River
◎ Lake
⊠ Reservoir

INVESTIGATOR STRAIT – IZOBIL’NYY

182 H10 **Investigator Strait** strait South Australia
29 R11 **Inwood** Iowa, C USA 43°16´N 96°25´W
123 S10 **Inya** ≈ E Russian Federation
Inyanga see Nyanga
83 M16 **Inyangani** ▲ NE Zimbabwe 18°22´S 32°57´E
83 J17 **Inyathi** Matabeleland North, SW Zimbabwe 19°39´S 28°54´E
35 T12 **Inyokern** California, W USA 35°37´N 117°48´W
35 T10 **Inyo Mountains** ▲▲ California, W USA
127 P6 **Inza** Ul’yanovskaya Oblast’, W Russian Federation 53°51´N 46°21´E
127 W5 **Inzer** Respublika Bashkortostan, W Russian Federation 54°11´N 57°37´E
127 N7 **Inzhavino** Tambovskaya Oblast’, W Russian Federation 52°18´N 42°28´E
115 C16 **Ioánnina** var. Janina, Yannina. Ípeiros, W Greece 39°39´N 20°52´E
164 B17 **Iō-jima** var. Iwojima. island Nansei-shotō, SW Japan
124 L4 **Iokan’ga** ≈ NW Russian Federation
27 Q6 **Iola** Kansas, C USA 37°55´N 95°24´W
Iolcus see Iolkós
115 G16 **Iolkós** anc. Iolcus. site of ancient city Thessalía, C Greece
Iolotan’ see Ýolöten
83 A16 **Iona** Namibe, SW Angola 16°54´S 12°39´E
96 F11 **Iona** island W Scotland, United Kingdom
116 M15 **Ion Corvin** Constanţa, SE Romania 44°07´N 27°50´E
35 P7 **Ione** California, W USA 38°21´N 120°55´W
116 I13 **Ioneşti** Vâlcea, SW Romania 44°52´N 24°12´E
31 Q9 **Ionia** Michigan, N USA 42°59´N 85°04´W
Ionia Basin see Ionian Basin
121 O10 **Ionian Basin** var. Ionia Basin. undersea feature Ionian Sea, C Mediterranean Sea 36°00´N 20°00´E
115 B17 **Iónia Nisiá** var. Iónioi Nísoi, Eng. Ionian Islands. island group W Greece
Ionian Islands see Iónia Nisiá/Iónioi Nísoi
121 O10 **Ionian Sea** Gk. Iónio Pélagos, It. Mar Ionio. sea C Mediterranean Sea
115 B17 **Iónioi Nísoi** Eng. Ionian Islands. ◈ region W Greece
Iónioi Nísoi see Iónia Nisiá
Ionio, Mar/Iónio Pélagos see Ionian Sea
Iordan see Yordon
137 U10 **Iori** var. Qabırrı. ≈ Azerbaijan/Georgia
Iorrais, Ceann see Erris Head
115 J22 **Íos** var. Nio. island Kykládes, Greece, Aegean Sea
Íos see Chóra
115 I20 **Ioulís** prev. Kéa. Tziá, Kykládes, Greece, Aegean Sea 37°40´N 24°19´E
22 G9 **Iowa** Louisiana, S USA 30°12´N 93°00´W
29 V13 **Iowa** off. State of Iowa, also known as Hawkeye State. ◈ state C USA
29 Y14 **Iowa City** Iowa, C USA 41°40´N 91°32´W
29 V13 **Iowa Falls** Iowa, C USA 42°31´N 93°15´W
25 R4 **Iowa Park** Texas, SW USA 33°57´N 98°40´W
29 Y14 **Iowa River** ≈ Iowa, C USA
119 M19 **Ipa** Rus. Ipa. ≈ SE Belaeus
Ipa see Ipa
59 N20 **Ipatinga** Minas Gerais, SE Brazil 19°32´S 42°30´W
127 N13 **Ipatovo** Stavropol’skiy Kray, SW Russian Federation 45°40´N 42°51´E
115 C16 **Ípeiros** Eng. Epirus. ◈ region W Greece
111 J21 **Ipel’** var. Ipoly, Ger. Eipel. ≈ Hungary/Slovakia
54 C13 **Ipiales** Nariño, SW Colombia 0°52´N 77°38´W
189 V14 **Ipis** atoll Chuuk Islands, C Micronesia
59 A14 **Ipixuna** Amazonas, W Brazil 06°57´S 71°42´W
168 J8 **Ipoh** Perak, Peninsular Malaysia 04°36´N 101°02´E
Ipoly see Ipel’
187 S15 **Ipota** Erromango, S Vanuatu 18°54´S 169°19´E
79 K14 **Ippy** Ouaka, C Central African Republic 06°17´N 21°13´E
114 L13 **İpsala** Edirne, NW Turkey 40°56´N 26°23´E
Ipsario see Ypsário
183 V3 **Ipswich** Queensland, E Australia 27°28´S 152°40´E
97 Q20 **Ipswich** hist. Gipeswic. E England, United Kingdom 52°05´N 01°08´E
29 O8 **Ipswich** South Dakota, N USA 45°24´N 99°00´W
Iput’ see Iputs’
119 P18 **Iputs’** Rus. Iput’. ≈ Belarus/Russian Federation
9 R7 **Iqaluit** prev. Frobisher Bay. province capital Baffin Island, Nunavut, NE Canada 63°44´N 68°28´W
159 P9 **Iqe** Qinghai, W China 38°03´N 94°45´E
159 P9 **Iqe He** ≈ C China
Iqlid see Eqlīd
62 G3 **Iquique** Tarapacá, N Chile 20°15´S 70°08´W
56 G8 **Iquitos** Loreto, N Peru 03°51´S 73°13´W
25 N9 **Iraan** Texas, SW USA 30°52´N 101°52´W
79 K14 **Ira Banda** Haute-Kotto, E Central African Republic 05°57´N 22°05´E
165 P16 **Irabu-jima** island Miyako-shotō, SW Japan
55 Y9 **Iracoubo** N French Guiana 05°28´N 53°15´W
60 H13 **Iraí** Rio Grande do Sul, S Brazil 27°15´S 53°17´W
114 G12 **Irákleia** Kentrikí Makedonía, N Greece 41°09´N 23°16´E
115 J21 **Irákleia** island Kykládes, Greece, Aegean Sea
115 J25 **Irákleio** var. Herakleion, Eng. Candia; prev. Iráklion. Kríti, Greece, E Mediterranean Sea 35°20´N 25°08´E
115 F15 **Irákleio** anc. Heracleum. castle Kentrikí Makedonía, N Greece
115 J25 **Irákleio** ✈ Kríti, Greece, E Mediterranean Sea 35°20´N 25°10´E
Iráklion see Irákleio
143 O7 **Iran** off. Islamic Republic of Iran; prev. Persia. ◆ republic SW Asia
58 F13 **Iranduba** Amazonas, NW Brazil 03°19´S 60°09´W
85 P13 **Iranian Plate** tectonic feature
143 Q9 **Iranian Plateau** var. Plateau of Iran. plateau N Iran
Iran, Islamic Republic of see Iran
Iran Mountains see Iran, Pegunungan
169 U9 **Iran, Pegunungan** var. Iran Mountains. ▲▲ Indonesia/Malaysia
Iran, Plateau of see Iranian Plateau
143 W13 **Īrānshahr** Sīstān va Balūchestān, SE Iran 27°14´N 60°40´E
55 P5 **Irapa** Sucre, NE Venezuela 10°37´N 62°35´W
41 N13 **Irapuato** Guanajuato, C Mexico 20°40´N 101°23´W
139 R7 **Iraq** off. Republic of Iraq, Ar. ‘Irāq. ◆ republic SW Asia
‘Irāq see Iraq
Iraq, Republic of see Iraq
60 J12 **Irati** Paraná, S Brazil 25°25´S 50°38´W
105 R3 **Irati** ≈ N Spain
125 T8 **Irayël’** Respublika Komi, NW Russian Federation 64°28´N 55°20´E
43 N13 **Irazú, Volcán** ⩓ C Costa Rica 09°57´N 83°52´W
Irbenskiy Zaliv/Irbes Šaurums see Irbe Strait
118 D7 **Irbe Strait** Est. Kura Kurk, Latv. Irbes Šaurums, Irbenskiy Zaliv; prev. Est. Irbe Väin. strait Estonia/Latvia
Irbe Väin see Irbe Strait
138 G9 **Irbid** Irbid, N Jordan 32°33´N 35°51´E
138 G9 **Irbid** off. Muḩāfaẓat Irbid. ◈ governorate N Jordan
Irbid, Muḩāfaẓat see Irbid
Irbīl see Arbīl
109 S6 **Irdning** Steiermark, SE Austria 47°29´N 14°04´E
79 I18 **Irebu** Equateur, W Dem. Rep. Congo 0°32´S 17°44´E
97 D17 **Ireland** off. Republic of Ireland, Ir. Éire. ◆ republic NW Europe
84 C9 **Ireland** Lat. Hibernia. island Ireland/United Kingdom
64 A12 **Ireland Island North** island W Bermuda
64 A12 **Ireland Island South** island W Bermuda
Ireland, Republic of see Ireland
125 V15 **Iren’** ≈ NW Russian Federation
185 A22 **Irene, Mount** ▲ South Island, New Zealand 45°04´S 167°24´E
Irgalem see Yirga ‘Alem
144 L11 **Irgiz** Kaz. Yrghyz. Aktyubinsk, C Kazakhstan 48°36´N 61°14´E
Irian see New Guinea
Irian Barat see Papua
Irian Jaya see Papua
Irian, Teluk see Cenderawasih, Teluk
78 K9 **Iriba** Biltine, NE Chad 15°10´N 22°11´E
127 X7 **Iriklinskoye Vodokhranilishche** ⊠ W Russian Federation
81 H23 **Iringa** Iringa, C Tanzania 07°49´S 35°39´E
81 H23 **Iringa** ◈ region S Tanzania
165 O16 **Iriomote-jima** island Sakishima-shotō, SW Japan
42 L4 **Iriona** Colón, NE Honduras 15°55´N 85°10´W
47 U7 **Iriri** ≈ N Brazil
58 I13 **Iriri, Rio** ≈ C Brazil
Iris see Yeşilırmak
35 W9 **Irish, Mount** ▲ Nevada, W USA 37°39´N 115°22´W
97 H17 **Irish Sea** Ir. Muir Éireann. sea C British Isles
139 U12 **Irjal ash Shaykhīyah** Al Muthanná, S Iraq 30°49´N 44°58´E
147 U11 **Irkeshtam** Oshskaya Oblast’, SW Kyrgyzstan 39°39´N 73°49´E
122 M13 **Irkutsk** Irkutskaya Oblast’, S Russian Federation 52°18´N 104°15´E
122 M12 **Irkutskaya Oblast’** ◈ province S Russian Federation
Irlir, Gora see Irlir Tog‘i
146 K8 **Irlir Tog‘i** var. Gora Irlir. ▲ N Uzbekistan 42°43´N 63°24´E
Irminger Basin see Reykjanes Basin
21 R12 **Irmo** South Carolina, SE USA 34°05´N 81°10´W
102 E6 **Iroise** sea NW France
189 X2 **Iroj** var. Eroj. island Ratak Chain, SE Marshall Islands
182 H7 **Iron Baron** South Australia 33°01´S 137°13´E
14 C10 **Iron Bridge** Ontario, S Canada 46°16´N 83°12´W
20 H10 **Iron City** Tennessee, S USA 35°01´N 87°34´W
14 I13 **Irondale** ≈ Ontario, SE Canada
182 H7 **Iron Knob** South Australia 32°46´S 137°08´E
30 M5 **Iron Mountain** Michigan, N USA 45°51´N 88°03´W
30 M4 **Iron River** Michigan, N USA 46°05´N 88°38´W
30 J3 **Iron River** Wisconsin, N USA 46°34´N 91°22´W
27 X6 **Ironton** Missouri, C USA 37°37´N 90°40´W
31 S15 **Ironton** Ohio, N USA 38°32´N 82°40´W
30 K4 **Ironwood** Michigan, N USA 46°27´N 90°10´W
12 H12 **Iroquois Falls** Ontario, S Canada 48°47´N 80°41´W
31 N12 **Iroquois River** ≈ Illinois/Indiana, N USA
164 M15 **Irō-zaki** headland Honshū, S Japan 34°36´N 138°49´E
Irpen’ see Irpin’
117 O4 **Irpin’** Rus. Irpen’. Kyyivs’ka Oblast’, N Ukraine 50°31´N 30°16´E
117 O4 **Irpin’** Rus. Irpen’. ≈ N Ukraine
141 Q16 **‘Irqah** SW Yemen 13°42´N 47°21´E
166 K8 **Irrawaddy** var. Ayeyarwady. ◈ division SW Burma (Myanmar)
166 L6 **Irrawaddy** var. Ayeyarwady. ≈ W Burma (Myanmar)
166 K8 **Irrawaddy, Mouths of the** delta SW Burma (Myanmar)
117 N4 **Irsha** ≈ N Ukraine
116 H7 **Irshava** Zakarpats’ka Oblast’, W Ukraine 48°19´N 23°03´E
107 N18 **Irsina** Basilicata, S Italy 40°42´N 16°18´E
Irtish see Irtysh
129 R5 **Irtysh** var. Irtish, Kaz. Ertis. ≈ C Asia
145 S7 **Irtyshsk** Kaz. Ertis. Pavlodar, NE Kazakhstan 53°21´N 75°27´E
79 P17 **Irumu** Orientale, E Dem. Rep. Congo 01°27´N 29°52´E
105 Q2 **Irun** Cast. Irún. País Vasco, N Spain 43°20´N 01°48´W
Irún see Irun
Iruña see Pamplona
105 Q3 **Irurtzun** Navarra, N Spain 42°55´N 01°50´W
96 I13 **Irvine** W Scotland, United Kingdom 55°37´N 04°40´W
21 N6 **Irvine** Kentucky, S USA 37°42´N 83°59´W
25 T6 **Irving** Texas, SW USA 32°47´N 96°57´W
20 K5 **Irvington** Kentucky, S USA 37°52´N 86°16´W
Isaak see Iisaku
28 L8 **Isabel** South Dakota, N USA 45°21´N 101°25´W
186 L8 **Isabel** off. Isabel Province. ◈ province N Solomon Islands
171 O8 **Isabela** Basilan Island, SW Philippines 06°41´N 122°00´E
45 S5 **Isabela** W Puerto Rico 18°30´N 67°02´W
45 N8 **Isabela, Cabo** headland NW Dominican Republic 19°54´N 71°03´W
57 A18 **Isabela, Isla** var. Albemarle Island. island Galapagos Islands, Ecuador, E Pacific Ocean
40 I12 **Isabela, Isla** island C Mexico
42 K9 **Isabella, Cordillera** ▲▲ NW Nicaragua
35 S12 **Isabella Lake** ⊠ California, W USA
31 N2 **Isabelle, Point** headland Michigan, N USA 47°20´N 87°56´W
Isabel Province see Isabel
Isabel Segunda see Vieques
116 M13 **Isaccea** Tulcea, E Romania 45°16´N 28°28´E
92 H1 **Ísafjarðardjúp** inlet NW Iceland
92 H1 **Ísafjördhur** Vestfirdhir, NW Iceland 66°04´N 23°09´W
164 C14 **Isahaya** Nagasaki, Kyūshū, SW Japan 32°51´N 130°02´E
149 S7 **Īsa Khel** Punjab, E Pakistan 32°39´N 71°20´E
172 H7 **Isalo** var. Massif de L’Isalo. ▲▲ SW Madagascar
79 K20 **Isandja** Kasai-Occidental, C Dem. Rep. Congo 03°03´S 21°57´E
187 R15 **Isangel** Tanna, S Vanuatu 19°34´S 169°17´E
79 M18 **Isangi** Orientale, C Dem. Rep. Congo 0°46´N 24°15´E
101 L24 **Isar** ≈ Austria/Germany
101 M23 **Isar-Kanal** canal SE Germany
Isbarta see Isparta
Isca Damnoniorum see Exeter
107 K18 **Ischia** var. Isola d’Ischia; anc. Aenaria. Campania, S Italy 40°44´N 13°57´E
107 J18 **Ischia, Isola d’** island S Italy
54 B12 **Iscuandé** var. Santa Bárbara. Nariño, SW Colombia 02°32´N 78°00´W
164 K14 **Ise** Mie, Honshū, SW Japan 34°29´N 136°43´E
100 J12 **Ise** ≈ N Germany
95 I23 **Isefjord** fjord E Denmark
Iseghem see Izegem
192 M14 **Iselin Seamount** undersea feature S Pacific Ocean 72°30´S 179°00´W
Isenhof see Püssi
106 E7 **Iseo** Lombardia, N Italy 45°40´N 10°03´E
103 U12 **Iseran, Col de l’** pass E France
103 S11 **Isère** ◈ department E France
103 S12 **Isère** ≈ E France
101 F15 **Iserlohn** Nordrhein-Westfalen, W Germany 51°23´N 07°42´E
107 K16 **Isernia** var. Æsernia. Molise, C Italy 41°35´N 14°14´E
165 N12 **Isesaki** Gunma, Honshū, S Japan 36°19´N 139°11´E
129 Q5 **Iset’** ≈ C Russian Federation
77 S15 **Iseyin** Oyo, W Nigeria 07°56´N 03°33´E
Isfahan see Eşfahān
147 Q11 **Isfana** Batkenskaya Oblast’, SW Kyrgyzstan 39°51´N 69°31´E
147 R11 **Isfara** N Tajikistan 40°06´N 70°34´E
149 O4 **Isfi Maidān** Ghowr, N Afghanistan 35°09´N 66°16´E
92 O3 **Isfjorden** fjord W Svalbard
Isgender see Kul’mach
Isha Baydhabo see Baydhabo
125 V11 **Isherim, Gora** ▲ NW Russian Federation 61°06´N 59°09´E
127 Q5 **Isheyevka** Ul’yanovskaya Oblast’, W Russian Federation 54°27´N 48°18´E
165 P16 **Ishigaki** Okinawa, Ishigaki-jima, SW Japan 24°20´N 124°09´E
165 P16 **Ishigaki-jima** island Sakishima-shotō, SW Japan
165 R3 **Ishikari-wan** bay Hokkaidō, NE Japan
165 S16 **Ishikawa** var. Isikawa. Okinawa, Okinawa, SW Japan 26°25´N 127°47´E
164 K11 **Ishikawa** off. Ishikawa-ken, var. Isikawa. ◈ prefecture Honshū, SW Japan
Ishikawa-ken see Ishikawa
122 H11 **Ishim** Tyumenskaya Oblast’, C Russian Federation 56°13´N 69°25´E
129 R6 **Ishim** Kaz. Esil. ≈ Kazakhstan/Russian Federation
127 V6 **Ishimbay** Respublika Bashkortostan, W Russian Federation 53°21´N 56°03´E
145 O9 **Ishimskoye** Akmola, C Kazakhstan 51°23´N 67°07´E
165 Q10 **Ishinomaki** var. Isinomaki. Miyagi, Honshū, C Japan 38°26´N 141°17´E
165 P13 **Ishioka** var. Isioka. Ibaraki, Honshū, S Japan 36°11´N 140°16´E
Ishkashim see Ishkoshim
Ishkashimskiy Khrebet see Ishkoshim, Qatorkŭhi
147 S15 **Ishkoshim** Rus. Ishkashim. S Tajikistan 36°46´N 71°35´E
147 S15 **Ishkoshim, Qatorkŭhi** Rus. Ishkashimskiy Khrebet. ▲▲ SE Tajikistan
31 N4 **Ishpeming** Michigan, N USA 46°29´N 87°40´W
147 N11 **Ishtixon** Rus. Ishtykhan. Samarqand Viloyati, C Uzbekistan 39°59´N 66°28´E
Ishtykhan see Ishtixon
Ishurdi see Iswardi
61 G17 **Isidoro Noblia** Cerro Largo, NE Uruguay 31°58´S 54°09´W
102 J4 **Isigny-sur-Mer** Calvados, N France 49°20´N 01°06´W
Isikawa see Ishikawa
136 C11 **Işıklar Dağı** ▲▲ NW Turkey
107 C19 **Isili** Sardegna, Italy, C Mediterranean Sea 39°46´N 09°06´E
122 H12 **Isil’kul’** Omskaya Oblast’, C Russian Federation 54°52´N 71°07´E
Isinomaki see Ishinomaki
Isioka see Ishioka
81 I18 **Isiolo** Eastern, C Kenya 0°20´N 37°36´E
79 O16 **Isiro** Orientale, NE Dem. Rep. Congo 02°51´N 27°47´E
92 P2 **Isispynten** headland NE Svalbard 79°51´N 26°44´E
123 P11 **Isit** Respublika Sakha (Yakutiya), NE Russian Federation 60°53´N 125°32´E
149 O2 **Iskabad Canal** canal N Afghanistan
147 Q9 **Iskandar** Rus. Iskander. Toshkent Viloyati, E Uzbekistan 41°32´N 69°46´E
Iskander see Iskandar
Iskăr see Iskŭr
121 Q2 **İskele** var. Trikomo, Gk. Tríkomon. E Cyprus 35°16´N 33°54´E
136 K17 **İskenderun** Eng. Alexandretta. Hatay, S Turkey 36°34´N 36°10´E
138 H2 **İskenderun Körfezi** Eng. Gulf of Alexandretta. gulf S Turkey
136 J11 **İskilip** Çorum, N Turkey 40°45´N 34°28´E
Iski-Nauket see Eski-Nookat
114 J11 **Iskra** prev. Popovo. Khaskovo, S Bulgaria 41°55´N 25°12´E
114 G10 **Iskŭr** var. Iskăr. ≈ NW Bulgaria
114 H10 **Iskŭr, Yazovir** prev. Yazovir Stalin. ⊠ W Bulgaria
41 S15 **Isla** Veracruz-Llave, SE Mexico 18°01´N 95°30´W
119 J15 **Islach** Rus. Isloch’. ≈ C Belarus
104 H14 **Isla Cristina** Andalucía, S Spain 37°12´N 07°20´W
Isla de León see San Fernando
149 U6 **Islāmābād** ● (Pakistan) Federal Capital Territory Islāmābād, NE Pakistan 33°40´N 73°08´E
149 V6 **Islāmābād** ✈ Federal Capital Territory Islāmābād, NE Pakistan 33°40´N 73°08´E
Islamabad see Anantnāg
149 R17 **Islāmkot** Sind, SE Pakistan 24°37´N 70°04´E
23 Y17 **Islamorada** Florida Keys, Florida, SE USA 24°55´N 80°37´W
153 P14 **Islāmpur** Bihār, N India 25°09´N 85°13´E
Islam Qala see Eslām Qal‘eh
18 K16 **Island Beach** spit New Jersey, NE USA
19 S4 **Island Falls** Maine, NE USA 45°59´N 68°16´W
Island/Ísland see Iceland
182 H6 **Island Lagoon** ◎ South Australia
11 Y13 **Island Lake** ◎ Manitoba, C Canada
29 W5 **Island Lake Reservoir** ⊠ Minnesota, N USA
33 R13 **Island Park** Idaho, NW USA 44°27´N 111°21´W
19 N6 **Island Pond** Vermont, NE USA 44°48´N 71°51´W
184 K2 **Islands, Bay of** inlet North Island, New Zealand
103 R7 **Is-sur-Tille** Côte d’Or, C France 47°34´N 05°03´E
42 J3 **Islas de la Bahía** ◈ department N Honduras
65 L20 **Islas Orcadas Rise** undersea feature S Atlantic Ocean
96 F12 **Islay** island SW Scotland, United Kingdom
116 I15 **Islaz** Teleorman, S Romania 43°44´N 24°45´E
29 V7 **Isle** Minnesota, N USA 46°08´N 93°28´W
102 M12 **Isle** ≈ W France
97 I16 **Isle of Man** ◇ UK crown dependency NW Europe
21 X7 **Isle of Wight** Virginia, NE USA 36°54´N 76°41´W
97 M24 **Isle of Wight** cultural region S England, United Kingdom
191 Y3 **Isles Lagoon** ◎ Kiritimati, E Kiribati
37 R11 **Isleta Pueblo** New Mexico, SW USA 34°54´N 106°40´W
Isloch’ see Islach
61 E19 **Ismael Cortinas** Flores, S Uruguay 33°57´S 57°05´W
Ismailia see Al Ismā‘īlīya
Ismâ‘ilîya see Al Ismā‘īlīya
Ismailly see İsmayıllı
137 X11 **İsmayıllı** Rus. Ismailly. N Azerbaijan 40°47´N 48°09´E
Ismid see İzmit
147 S12 **Ismoili Somoní, Qullai** prev. Qullai Kommunizm. ▲ E Tajikistan
75 X10 **Isnā** var. Esna. SE Egypt 25°16´N 32°30´E
93 K18 **Isojoki** Länsi-Suomi, W Finland 62°07´N 22°00´E
82 M12 **Isoka** Northern, NE Zambia 10°08´S 32°43´E
Isola d’Ischia see Ischia
Isola d’Istria see Izola
Isonzo see Soča
15 U4 **Isoukustouc** ≈ Québec, SE Canada
136 F15 **Isparta** var. Isbarta. Isparta, SW Turkey 37°46´N 30°32´E
136 F15 **Isparta** var. Isbarta. ◈ province SW Turkey
114 M7 **Isperikh** prev. Kemanlar. Razgrad, N Bulgaria 43°43´N 26°49´E
107 L26 **Ispica** Sicilia, Italy, C Mediterranean Sea 36°47´N 14°55´E
148 J14 **Ispikān** Baluchistān, SW Pakistan 26°21´N 62°15´E
137 Q12 **İspir** Erzurum, NE Turkey 40°29´N 41°02´E
138 E12 **Israel** off. State of Israel, var. Medinat Israel, Heb. Yisrael, Yisra‘el. ◆ republic SW Asia
Israel, State of see Israel
Issa see Vis
55 S9 **Issano** C Guyana 05°49´N 59°28´W
76 M16 **Issia** SW Ivory Coast 06°33´N 06°33´W
Issiq Köl see Issyk-Kul’, Ozero
103 P11 **Issoire** Puy-de-Dôme, C France 45°33´N 03°15´E
103 N9 **Issoudun** anc. Uxellodunum. Indre, C France 46°57´N 01°59´E
81 H22 **Issuna** Singida, C Tanzania 05°24´S 34°48´E
Issyk see Yesik
Issyk-Kul’ see Balykchy
147 X7 **Issyk-Kul’, Ozero** var. Issiq Köl, Kir. Ysyk-Köl. ◎ E Kyrgyzstan
147 X7 **Issyk-Kul’skaya Oblast’** Kir. Ysyk-Köl Oblasty. ◈ province E Kyrgyzstan
149 Q7 **Īstādeh-ye Moqor, Āb-e-** var. Āb-i-Istāda. ◎ SE Afghanistan
136 D11 **İstanbul** Bul. Tsarigrad, Eng. Istanbul, prev. Constantinople; anc. Byzantium. Istanbul, NW Turkey 41°02´N 28°57´E
114 P12 **İstanbul** ◈ province NW Turkey
114 P12 **İstanbul Boğazı** var. Bosporus Thracius, Eng. Bosphorus, Bosporus, Turk. Karadeniz Boğazi. strait NW Turkey
Istarska Županija see Istra
115 G19 **Isthmía** Pelopónnisos, S Greece 37°55´N 23°02´E
115 G17 **Istiaía** Évvoia, C Greece 38°57´N 23°09´E
54 D9 **Istmina** Chocó, W Colombia 05°09´N 76°42´W
23 W13 **Istokpoga, Lake** ◎ Florida, SE USA
112 A9 **Istra** off. Istarska Županija. ◈ province NW Croatia
112 I10 **Istra** Eng. Istria, Ger. Istrien. cultural region NW Croatia
103 R15 **Istres** Bouches-du-Rhône, SE France 43°30´N 04°59´E
Istria/Istrien see Istra
153 T15 **Iswardi** var. Ishurdi. Rajshahi, W Bangladesh 24°10´N 89°04´E
127 V7 **Isyangulovo** Respublika Bashkortostan, W Russian Federation 52°10´N 56°38´E
62 O6 **Itá** Central, S Paraguay 25°29´S 57°21´W
59 O17 **Itaberaba** Bahia, E Brazil 12°34´S 40°21´W
59 M20 **Itabira** prev. Presidente Vargas. Minas Gerais, SE Brazil 19°39´S 43°14´W
59 O18 **Itabuna** Bahia, E Brazil 14°48´S 39°18´W
59 J18 **Itacaiu** Mato Grosso, S Brazil 14°49´S 51°21´W
58 G12 **Itacoatiara** Amazonas, N Brazil 03°06´S 58°22´W
54 D9 **Itagüí** Antioquia, W Colombia 06°12´N 75°40´W
60 D13 **Itá Ibaté** Corrientes, NE Argentina 27°27´S 57°24´W
60 G11 **Itaipú, Represa de** ⊠ Brazil/Paraguay
58 H13 **Itaituba** Pará, NE Brazil 04°15´S 55°56´W
60 K13 **Itajaí** Santa Catarina, S Brazil 26°50´S 48°39´W
Italia/Italiana, Republica/Italian Republic, The see Italy
Italian Somaliland see Somalia
25 T7 **Italy** Texas, SW USA 32°10´N 96°52´W
106 G12 **Italy** off. The Italian Republic, It. Italia, Repubblica Italiana. ◆ republic S Europe
59 O19 **Itamaraju** Bahia, E Brazil 16°58´S 39°32´W
59 C14 **Itamarati** Amazonas, W Brazil 06°13´S 68°17´W
59 M19 **Itambé, Pico de** ▲ SE Brazil 18°23´S 43°21´W
164 J13 **Itami** ✈ (Ōsaka) Ōsaka, Honshū, SW Japan 34°47´N 135°24´E
115 H15 **Ítamos** ▲ N Greece 40°06´N 23°51´E
153 W11 **Itānagar** state capital Arunāchal Pradesh, NE India 27°02´N 93°38´E
Itany see Litani
59 N19 **Itaobim** Minas Gerais, SE Brazil 16°34´S 41°27´W
59 P15 **Itaparica, Represa de** ⊠ E Brazil
58 M13 **Itapecuru-Mirim** Maranhão, E Brazil 03°24´S 44°20´W
60 Q8 **Itaperuna** Rio de Janeiro, SE Brazil 21°14´S 41°51´W
59 O18 **Itapetinga** Bahia, E Brazil 15°17´S 40°16´W
60 L10 **Itapetininga** São Paulo, S Brazil 23°36´S 48°07´W
60 K10 **Itapeva** São Paulo, S Brazil 23°58´S 48°54´W
47 W6 **Itapicuru, Rio** ≈ NE Brazil
58 O13 **Itapipoca** Ceará, E Brazil 03°29´S 39°35´W
60 M9 **Itapira** São Paulo, S Brazil 22°25´S 46°46´W
60 K8 **Itápolis** São Paulo, S Brazil 21°36´S 48°43´W
60 K10 **Itaporanga** São Paulo, S Brazil 23°43´S 49°28´W
62 P7 **Itapúa** off. Departamento de Itapúa. ◈ department SE Paraguay
Itapúa, Departamento de see Itapúa
59 E15 **Itapuã do Oeste** Rondônia, W Brazil 09°21´S 63°07´W
61 E15 **Itaqui** Rio Grande do Sul, S Brazil 29°10´S 56°28´W
60 K10 **Itararé** São Paulo, S Brazil 24°07´S 49°16´W
60 K10 **Itararé, Rio** ≈ S Brazil
154 H11 **Itārsi** Madhya Pradesh, C India 22°39´N 77°48´E
25 T7 **Itasca** Texas, SW USA 32°09´N 97°09´W
Itassi see Vieille Case
93 N17 **Itä-Suomi** ◈ province E Finland
60 D13 **Itatí** Corrientes, NE Argentina 27°16´S 58°15´W
60 K10 **Itatinga** São Paulo, S Brazil 23°08´S 48°36´W
115 F18 **Itéas, Kólpos** gulf C Greece
57 N15 **Iténez, Río** var. Rio Guaporé. ≈ Bolivia/Brazil see also Rio Guaporé
Iténez, Río see Guaporé, Rio
54 H11 **Iteviate, Río** ≈ C Colombia
100 I13 **Ith** hill range C Germany
31 Q8 **Ithaca** Michigan, N USA 43°17´N 84°36´W
18 H11 **Ithaca** New York, NE USA 42°26´N 76°30´W
115 C18 **Itháki** island Iónia Nisiá, Greece, C Mediterranean Sea
Itháki see Vathy
It Hearrenfean see Heerenveen
79 L17 **Itimbiri** ≈ N Dem. Rep. Congo
Itinomiya see Ichinomiya
Itinoseki see Ichinoseki
39 Q5 **Itkilik River** ≈ Alaska, USA
164 M11 **Itoigawa** Niigata, Honshū, C Japan 37°02´N 137°53´E
15 R6 **Itomamo, Lac** ◎ Québec, SE Canada
165 S17 **Itoman** Okinawa, SW Japan 26°05´N 127°40´E
102 M5 **Iton** ≈ N France
57 M16 **Itonamas Río** ≈ NE Bolivia
Itoupé, Mont see Sommet Tabulaire
Itseqqortoormiit see Ittoqqortoormiit
22 K4 **Itta Bena** Mississippi, S USA 33°30´N 90°19´W
107 B17 **Ittiri** Sardegna, Italy, C Mediterranean Sea 40°36´N 08°34´E
197 Q14 **Ittoqqortoormiit** var. Itseqqortoormiit, Dan. Scoresbysund, Eng. Scoresby Sound. Tunu, C Greenland 70°33´N 21°52´W
60 M10 **Itu** São Paulo, S Brazil 23°17´S 47°16´W
54 D8 **Ituango** Antioquia, NW Colombia 07°07´N 75°46´W
59 A14 **Ituí, Rio** ≈ NW Brazil
79 O20 **Itula** Sud-Kivu, E Dem. Rep. Congo 03°30´S 27°50´E
59 K19 **Itumbiara** Goiás, C Brazil 18°25´S 49°15´W
55 T9 **Ituni** E Guyana 05°24´N 58°18´W
41 X13 **Iturbide** Campeche, SE Mexico 19°41´N 89°29´W
Ituri see Aruwimi
123 V13 **Iturup, Ostrov** island Kuril’skiye Ostrova, SE Russian Federation
60 L7 **Ituverava** São Paulo, S Brazil 20°22´S 47°48´W
59 C15 **Ituxi, Rio** ≈ W Brazil
61 E14 **Ituzaingó** Corrientes, NE Argentina 27°34´S 56°44´W
101 K18 **Itz** ≈ C Germany
100 I9 **Itzehoe** Schleswig-Holstein, N Germany 53°56´N 09°31´E
23 N2 **Iuka** Mississippi, S USA 34°48´N 88°11´W
60 I11 **Ivaiporã** Paraná, S Brazil 24°16´S 51°46´W
60 I11 **Ivaí, Rio** ≈ S Brazil
92 L10 **Ivalo** Lapp. Avveel, Avvil. Lappi, N Finland 68°34´N 27°29´E
92 L10 **Ivalojoki** Lapp. Avveel. ≈ N Finland
119 H20 **Ivanava** Pol. Janów, Janów Poleski, Rus. Ivanovo. Brestskaya Voblasts’, SW Belarus 52°09´N 25°32´E
124 F13 **Ivangorod** Est. Jaanilinn. Leningradskaya Oblast’, NW Russian Federation 59°22´N 28°14´E
Ivangorod see Dęblin
Ivangrad see Berane
183 N7 **Ivanhoe** New South Wales, SE Australia 32°55´S 144°21´E
29 S9 **Ivanhoe** Minnesota, N USA 44°27´N 96°15´W
14 D8 **Ivanhoe** ≈ Ontario, S Canada
112 E8 **Ivanić-Grad** Sisak-Moslavina, N Croatia 45°43´N 16°23´E
117 T10 **Ivanivka** Khersons’ka Oblast’, S Ukraine 46°43´N 34°28´E
117 P10 **Ivanivka** Odes’ka Oblast’, SW Ukraine 46°57´N 30°26´E
113 L14 **Ivanjica** Serbia, C Serbia 43°36´N 20°14´E
112 G11 **Ivanjska** var. Potkozarje. Republika Srpska, NW Bosnia and Herzegovina 44°54´N 17°04´E
111 H21 **Ivanka** ✈ (Bratislava) Bratislavský Kraj, W Slovakia 48°10´N 17°13´E
117 O3 **Ivankiv** Rus. Ivankov. Kyyivs’ka Oblast’, N Ukraine 50°55´N 29°53´E
Ivankov see Ivankiv
39 O15 **Ivanof Bay** Alaska, USA 55°55´N 159°28´W
116 J7 **Ivano-Frankivs’k** Ger. Stanislau, Pol. Stanisławów, Rus. Ivano-Frankovsk; prev. Stanislav. Ivano-Frankivs’ka Oblast’, W Ukraine 48°55´N 24°45´E
Ivano-Frankivs’k see Ivano-Frankivs’ka Oblast’
116 I7 **Ivano-Frankivs’ka Oblast’** var. Ivano-Frankivs’k, Rus. Ivano-Frankovskaya Oblast’; prev. Stanislavskaya Oblast’. ◈ province W Ukraine
Ivano-Frankovsk see Ivano-Frankivs’k
Ivano-Frankovskaya Oblast’ see Ivano-Frankivs’ka Oblast’
124 M16 **Ivanovo** Ivanovskaya Oblast’, W Russian Federation 57°02´N 40°58´E
Ivanovo see Ivanava
124 M16 **Ivanovskaya Oblast’** ◈ province W Russian Federation
35 X12 **Ivanpah Lake** ◎ California, W USA
112 E7 **Ivanščica** ▲▲ NE Croatia
127 R7 **Ivanteyevka** Saratovskaya Oblast’, W Russian Federation 52°13´N 49°06´E
Ivantsevichi/Ivatsevichi see Ivatsevichy
116 I4 **Ivanychi** Volyns’ka Oblast’, NW Ukraine 50°37´N 24°22´E
119 H18 **Ivatsevichy** Pol. Iwacewicze, Rus. Ivantsevichi, Ivatsevichi. Brestskaya Voblasts’, SW Belarus 52°43´N 25°21´E
114 L12 **Ivaylovgrad** Khaskovo, S Bulgaria 41°32´N 26°06´E
114 K11 **Ivaylovgrad, Yazovir** ⊠ S Bulgaria
122 G9 **Ivdel’** Sverdlovskaya Oblast’, C Russian Federation 60°42´N 60°07´E
Ivenets see Ivyanyets
116 L12 **Iveşti** Galaţi, E Romania 45°27´N 28°00´E
Ivgovuotna see Lyngen
Ivigtut see Ivittuut
79 F18 **Ivindo** ≈ Congo/Gabon
59 I21 **Ivinheima** Mato Grosso do Sul, SW Brazil 22°16´S 53°52´W
196 M15 **Ivittuut** var. Ivigtut. Kitaa, S Greenland 61°28´N 48°33´W
Iviza see Eivissa\Ibiza
172 I6 **Ivohibe** Fianarantsoa, SE Madagascar 22°28´S 46°53´E
Ivoire, Côte d’ see Ivory Coast
76 L15 **Ivory Coast** off. Republic of the Ivory Coast, Fr. Côte d’Ivoire, République de la Côte d’Ivoire. ◆ republic W Africa
68 C12 **Ivory Coast** Fr. Côte d’Ivoire. coastal region S Ivory Coast
Ivory Coast, Republic of the see Ivory Coast
95 L22 **Ivösjön** ◎ S Sweden
106 B7 **Ivrea** anc. Eporedia. Piemonte, NW Italy 45°28´N 07°52´E
12 J2 **Ivujivik** Québec, NE Canada 62°26´N 77°49´W
119 J16 **Ivyanyets** Rus. Ivenets. Minskaya Voblasts’, C Belarus 53°53´N 26°45´E
Iv’ye see Iwye
Iwacewicze see Ivatsevichy
165 R8 **Iwaizumi** Iwate, Honshū, NE Japan 39°48´N 141°46´E
165 P12 **Iwaki** Fukushima, Honshū, N Japan 37°01´N 140°52´E
164 F13 **Iwakuni** Yamaguchi, Honshū, SW Japan 34°08´N 132°06´E
165 S4 **Iwamizawa** Hokkaidō, NE Japan 43°12´N 141°47´E
165 R4 **Iwanai** Hokkaidō, NE Japan 42°51´N 140°21´E
165 Q10 **Iwanuma** Miyagi, Honshū, C Japan 38°06´N 140°51´E
164 L14 **Iwata** Shizuoka, Honshū, S Japan 34°42´N 137°51´E
165 R8 **Iwate** Iwate, Honshū, N Japan 40°03´N 141°12´E
165 R8 **Iwate** off. Iwate-ken. ◈ prefecture Honshū, C Japan
Iwate-ken see Iwate
77 S16 **Iwo** Oyo, SW Nigeria 07°21´N 03°58´E
Iwojima see Iō-jima
119 I16 **Iwye** Pol. Iwje, Rus. Iv’ye. Hrodzyenskaya Voblasts’, W Belarus 53°56´N 25°46´E
42 C4 **Ixcán, Río** ≈ Guatemala/Mexico
99 G18 **Ixelles** Dut. Elsene. Brussels, C Belgium 50°49´N 04°21´E
57 J16 **Ixiamas** La Paz, NW Bolivia 13°45´S 68°10´W
41 O13 **Ixmiquilpan** var. Ixmiquilpán. Hidalgo, C Mexico 20°30´N 99°15´W
Ixmiquilpán see Ixmiquilpan
83 K23 **Ixopo** KwaZulu/Natal, E South Africa 30°10´S 30°05´E
Ixtaccíhuatal, Volcán see Iztaccíhuati, Volcán
40 M16 **Ixtapa** Guerrero, S Mexico 17°38´N 101°29´W
41 S16 **Ixtepec** Oaxaca, SE Mexico 16°32´N 95°03´W
40 K12 **Ixtlán** var. Ixtlán del Río. Nayarit, C Mexico 21°02´N 104°21´W
Ixtlán del Río see Ixtlán
122 H11 **Iyevlevo** Tyumenskaya Oblast’, C Russian Federation 57°36´N 67°20´E
164 F14 **Iyo** Ehime, Shikoku, SW Japan 33°43´N 132°42´E
164 E14 **Iyo-nada** sea S Japan
42 E4 **Izabal** off. Departamento de Izabal. ◈ department E Guatemala
Izabal, Departamento de see Izabal
42 F5 **Izabal, Lago de** prev. Golfo Dulce. ◎ E Guatemala
143 O9 **Īzad Khvāst** Fārs, C Iran 31°31´N 52°09´E
41 X12 **Izamal** Yucatán, SE Mexico 20°58´N 89°00´W
127 Q16 **Izberbash** Respublika Dagestan, SW Russian Federation 42°32´N 47°51´E
99 C18 **Izegem** prev. Iseghem. West-Vlaanderen, W Belgium 50°55´N 03°13´E
142 M9 **Īzeh** Khūzestān, SW Iran 31°48´N 49°49´E
165 T16 **Izena-jima** island Nansei-shotō, SW Japan
114 N10 **Izgrev** Burgas, E Bulgaria 42°09´N 27°49´E
127 T2 **Izhevsk** prev. Ustinov. Udmurtskaya Respublika, NW Russian Federation 56°48´N 53°12´E
125 S7 **Izhma** Respublika Komi, NW Russian Federation 64°56´N 53°52´E
125 S7 **Izhma** ≈ NW Russian Federation
141 X8 **Izkī** NE Oman 22°45´N 57°36´E
Izmail see Izmayil
117 N13 **Izmayil** Rus. Izmail. Odes’ka Oblast’, SW Ukraine 45°19´N 28°49´E
136 B14 **İzmir** prev. Smyrna. İzmir, W Turkey 38°25´N 27°10´E
136 C14 **İzmir** prev. Smyrna. ◈ province W Turkey
136 E11 **İzmit** var. Ismid; anc. Astacus. Kocaeli, NW Turkey 40°47´N 29°55´E
104 M14 **Iznájar** Andalucía, S Spain 37°17´N 04°16´W
104 M14 **Iznajar, Embalse de** ⊠ S Spain
105 N14 **Iznalloz** Andalucía, S Spain 37°23´N 03°31´W
136 E11 **İznik** Bursa, NW Turkey 40°27´N 29°43´E
136 E12 **İznik Gölü** ◎ NW Turkey
126 M14 **Izobil’nyy** Stavropol’skiy Kray, SW Russian Federation 45°22´N 41°40´E

◆ Country
● Country Capital
◇ Dependent Territory
○ Dependent Territory Capital
◈ Administrative Regions
✈ International Airport
▲ Mountain
▲▲ Mountain Range
⩓ Volcano
≈ River
◎ Lake
⊠ Reservoir

Izola – Jhang/Jhang Sadar

109 S13 Izola It. Isola d'Istria. SW Slovenia 45°31′N 13°40′E
138 H9 Izra' var. Ezra, Ezraa. Dar'ā, S Syria 32°52′N 36°15′E
41 P14 Iztaccíhuatl, Volcán var. Volcán Ixtaccíhuatl. Ѫ S Mexico 19°07′N 98°37′W
42 C7 Iztapa Escuintla, SE Guatemala 13°58′N 90°42′W
Izúcar de Matamoros see Matamoros
165 N14 Izu-hantō peninsula Honshū, S Japan
164 C12 Izuhara Nagasaki, Tsushima, SW Japan 34°11′N 129°16′E
164 J14 Izumiōtsu Ōsaka, Honshū, SW Japan 34°29′N 135°25′E
164 I14 Izumi-Sano Ōsaka, Honshū, SW Japan 34°23′N 135°18′E
164 G12 Izumo Shimane, Honshū, SW Japan 35°22′N 132°46′E
192 H5 Izu Trench undersea feature NW Pacific Ocean
122 K6 Izvestiy TsIK, Ostrova island N Russian Federation
114 G10 Izvor Pernik, W Bulgaria 42°27′N 22°53′E
116 L5 Izyaslav Khmel'nyts'ka Oblast', W Ukraine 50°08′N 26°53′E
117 W6 Izyum Kharkivs'ka Oblast', E Ukraine 49°12′N 37°19′E

J

93 M18 Jaala Etelä-Suomi, S Finland 61°04′N 26°30′E
Jaanilinn see Ivangorod
140 J5 Jabal ash Shifā desert NW Saudi Arabia
141 U8 Jabal aẓ Ẓannah var. Jebel Dhanna. Abū Ẓaby, W United Arab Emirates 24°10′N 52°36′E
138 E11 Jabālīya var. Jabāliyah. NE Gaza Strip 31°32′N 34°29′E
Jabāliyah see Jabālīya
105 N11 Jabalón ≈ C Spain
154 J10 Jabalpur prev. Jubbulpore. Madhya Pradesh, C India 23°10′N 79°59′E
141 N15 Jabal Zuqar, Jazīrat var. Az Zuqur. island SW Yemen
Jabat see Jabwot
138 J3 Jabbūl, Sabkhat al sabkha NW Syria
181 P1 Jabiru Northern Territory, N Australia 12°44′S 132°48′E
138 H4 Jablah var. Jeble, Fr. Djéblé. Al Lādhiqīyah, W Syria 35°00′N 36°00′E
112 C11 Jablanac Lika-Senj, W Croatia 44°43′N 14°54′E
113 H14 Jablanica Federacija Bosna I Hercegovina, SW Bosnia and Herzegovina 43°39′N 17°43′E
113 M20 Jablanica Alb. Mali i Jabllanicës, var. Malet e Jabllanicës. ▲ Albania/ FYR Macedonia see also Jabllanicës, Mali i
Jabllanicës, Malet e see Jablanica/Jabllanicës, Mali i
113 M20 Jabllanicës, Mali i, Mac. Jablanica. ▲ Albania/ FYR Macedonia see also Jablanica
111 E15 Jablonec nad Nisou Ger. Gablonz an der Neisse. Liberecký Kraj, N Czech Republic 50°44′N 15°10′E
Jabłonków/Jablunkau see Jablunkov
110 J9 Jabłonowo Pomorskie Kujawski-pomorskie, C Poland 53°24′N 19°08′E
111 J17 Jablunkov Ger. Jablunkau, Pol. Jabłonków. Moravskoslezský Kraj, E Czech Republic 49°35′N 18°46′E
59 Q15 Jaboatão Pernambuco, E Brazil 08°05′S 35°W
60 L8 Jaboticabal São Paulo, S Brazil 21°15′S 48°17′W
189 U7 Jabwot var. Jabat, Jebat, Jōwat. island Ralik Chain, S Marshall Islands
105 S4 Jaca Aragón, NE Spain 42°34′N 00°33′W
42 B4 Jacaltenango Huehuetenango, W Guatemala 15°39′N 91°46′W
59 G14 Jacaré-a-Canga Pará, NE Brazil 05°59′S 57°32′W
60 N10 Jacareí São Paulo, S Brazil 23°18′S 45°55′W
59 I18 Jaciara Mato Grosso, W Brazil 15°59′S 54°57′W
59 E15 Jaciparaná Rondônia, W Brazil 09°20′S 64°28′W
19 P5 Jackman Maine, NE USA 45°35′N 70°14′W
35 X1 Jackpot Nevada, W USA 41°57′N 114°41′W
20 M8 Jacksboro Tennessee, S USA 36°19′N 84°11′W
25 S6 Jacksboro Texas, SW USA 33°13′N 98°11′W
23 N7 Jackson Alabama, S USA 31°30′N 87°53′W
35 P7 Jackson California, W USA 38°19′N 120°46′W
23 T4 Jackson Georgia, SE USA 33°17′N 83°58′W
21 O6 Jackson Kentucky, S USA 37°32′N 83°24′W
22 J8 Jackson Louisiana, S USA 30°50′N 91°13′W
31 Q10 Jackson Michigan, N USA 42°15′N 84°24′W
29 T11 Jackson Minnesota, N USA 43°38′N 95°00′W
22 K5 Jackson state capital Mississippi, S USA 32°19′N 90°12′W
27 Y7 Jackson Missouri, C USA 37°23′N 89°40′W
21 W8 Jackson North Carolina, SE USA 36°24′N 77°25′W
31 T15 Jackson Ohio, NE USA 39°03′N 82°40′W
20 G9 Jackson Tennessee, S USA 35°37′N 88°50′W
33 S14 Jackson Wyoming, C USA 43°28′N 110°45′W
185 C19 Jackson Bay bay South Island, New Zealand
186 E9 Jackson Field ✈ (Port Moresby) Central/National Capital District, S Papua New Guinea 09°28′S 147°12′E
185 C20 Jackson Head headland South Island, New Zealand 43°57′S 168°38′E
23 S8 Jackson, Lake ◎ Florida, SE USA
33 S13 Jackson Lake ◎ Wyoming, C USA
194 J6 Jackson, Mount ▲ Antarctica 71°43′S 63°45′W
37 U3 Jackson Reservoir ⊠ Colorado, C USA
23 Q3 Jacksonville Alabama, S USA 33°48′N 85°45′W
27 V11 Jacksonville Arkansas, C USA 34°52′N 92°08′W
23 W8 Jacksonville Florida, SE USA 30°20′N 81°39′W
30 K14 Jacksonville Illinois, N USA 39°43′N 90°13′W
21 W11 Jacksonville North Carolina, SE USA 34°45′N 77°26′W
25 W7 Jacksonville Texas, SW USA 31°57′N 95°16′W
23 X9 Jacksonville Beach Florida, SE USA 30°17′N 81°23′W
44 L9 Jacmel var. Jaquemel. S Haiti 18°13′N 72°33′W
Jacob see Nkayi
149 Q12 Jacobābād Sind, SE Pakistan 28°16′N 68°30′E
55 T11 Jacobs Ladder Falls waterfall S Guyana
45 O11 Jaco, Pointe headland N Dominica 15°38′N 61°25′W
15 Q9 Jacques-Cartier ≈ Québec, SE Canada
13 P11 Jacques-Cartier, Détroit de var. Jacques-Cartier Passage. strait Gulf of St. Lawrence/St. Lawrence River, Canada
15 W6 Jacques-Cartier, Mont ▲ Québec, SE Canada 48°58′N 66°00′W
Jacques-Cartier Passage see Jacques-Cartier, Détroit de
61 H16 Jacuí, Rio ≈ S Brazil
60 L11 Jacupiranga São Paulo, S Brazil 24°42′S 48°00′W
100 G10 Jade ≈ NW Germany
100 G10 Jadebusen bay NW Germany
Jadotville see Likasi
Jadransko More/Jadransko Morje see Adriatic Sea
105 O7 Jadraque Castilla-La Mancha, C Spain 40°55′N 02°55′W
95 I22 Jægerspris Frederiksborg, E Denmark 55°52′N 11°59′E
56 C10 Jaén Cajamarca, N Peru 05°45′S 78°51′W
105 N13 Jaén Andalucía, SW Spain 37°46′N 03°48′W
105 N13 Jaén ◈ province Andalucía, S Spain
95 C17 Jæren physical region S Norway
155 J23 Jaffna Northern Province, N Sri Lanka 09°42′N 80°03′E
155 K23 Jaffna Lagoon lagoon N Sri Lanka
19 N10 Jaffrey New Hampshire, NE USA 42°46′N 72°00′W
138 H13 Jafr, Qā' al var. El Jafr. salt pan S Jordan
152 J9 Jagādhri Haryāna, N India 30°11′N 77°18′E
118 H4 Jägala var. Jägala Jõgi, Ger. Jaggowal. ≈ NW Estonia
Jägala Jõgi see Jägala
Jagannath see Puri
154 P13 httt†t Orissa, SE India 20°15′N 86°10′E
155 L14 Jagdalpur Chhattīsgarh, C India 19°07′N 82°04′E
163 U5 Jagdaqi Nei Mongol Zizhiqu, N China 50°26′N 124°03′E
Jägerndorf see Krnov
Jaggowal see Jägala
139 O2 Jaghjaghah, Nahr ≈ N Syria
112 N13 Jagodina prev. Svetozarevo. Serbia, C Serbia 43°59′N 21°15′E
112 K12 Jagodnja ▲▲ W Serbia
101 I20 Jagst ≈ SW Germany
155 I14 Jagtiāl Andhra Pradesh, C India 18°49′N 78°53′E
61 H18 Jaguarão Rio Grande do Sul, S Brazil 32°30′S 53°25′W
61 H18 Jaguarão, Rio var. Río Yaguarón. ≈ Brazil/ Uruguay
60 K11 Jaguariaíva Paraná, S Brazil 24°15′S 49°44′W
44 D5 Jagüey Grande Matanzas, W Cuba 22°31′N 81°07′W
153 P14 Jahānābād Bihār, N India 25°13′N 84°59′E
Jahra see Al Jahrā'
143 P12 Jahrom var. Jahrum. Fārs, S Iran 28°35′N 53°32′E
Jahrum see Jahrom
Jailolo see Halmahera, Pulau
Jainat see Chai Nat
Jainti see Jayanti
152 H12 Jaipur prev. Jeypore. state capital Rājasthān, N India 26°54′N 75°47′E
153 T14 Jaipurhat var. Joypurhat. Rajshahi, NW Bangladesh 25°04′N 89°06′E
152 D11 Jaisalmer Rājasthān, NW India 26°55′N 70°56′E
154 O12 Jājapur var. Jajpur, Panikoilli. Orissa, E India 18°54′N 82°36′E
143 R4 Jājarm Khorāsān-e Shemālī, NE Iran 36°58′N 56°26′E
112 G12 Jajce Federacija Bosna I Hercegovina, W Bosnia and Herzegovina 44°20′N 17°16′E
Jaji see 'Alī Kheyl
Jajpur see Jājapur
83 D17 Jakalsberg Otjozondjupa, N Namibia 19°23′S 17°28′E
169 O15 Jakarta prev. Djakarta, Dut. Batavia. ● (Indonesia) Jawa, C Indonesia 06°08′S 106°45′E
10 I8 Jakes Corner Yukon Territory, W Canada 60°18′N 134°00′W
152 H9 Jākhal Haryāna, NW India 29°46′N 75°51′E
Jakobeny see Iacobeni
93 K16 Jakobstad Fin. Pietarsaari. Länsi-Suomi, W Finland 63°41′N 22°40′E
Jakobstadt see Jēkabpils
113 O18 Jakupica ▲▲ C FYR Macedonia
37 W15 Jal New Mexico, SW USA 32°07′N 103°10′W
141 P7 Jalājil var. Ğalāğil. Ar Riyāḍ, C Saudi Arabia 25°43′N 45°22′E
149 S5 Jalālābād var. Jalalabad, Jelalabad. Nangarhār, E Afghanistan 34°26′N 70°28′E
Jalal-Abad see Dzhalal-Abad, Dzhalal-Abadskaya Oblast', Kyrgyzstan
Jalal-Abad Oblasty see Dzhalal-Abadskaya Oblast'
149 V7 Jalālpur Punjab, E Pakistan 32°39′N 74°11′E
149 T11 Jalālpur Pīrwāla Punjab, E Pakistan 29°30′N 71°20′E
152 H8 Jalandhar prev. Jullundur. Punjab, N India 31°20′N 75°37′E
42 J7 Jalán, Río ≈ S Honduras
42 E6 Jalapa Jalapa, C Guatemala 14°39′N 89°59′W
42 J7 Jalapa Nueva Segovia, NW Nicaragua 13°56′N 86°11′W
42 A3 Jalapa off. Departamento de Jalapa. ◈ department SE Guatemala
Jalapa, Departamento de see Jalapa
42 E6 Jalapa, Río ≈ SE Guatemala
143 X13 Jālaq Sīstān va Balūchestān, SE Iran
93 K17 Jalasjärvi Länsi-Suomi, W Finland 62°30′N 22°50′E
149 O8 Jaldak Zābol, SE Afghanistan 32°00′N 66°45′E
60 J7 Jales São Paulo, S Brazil 20°15′S 50°34′W
154 P11 Jaleshwar var. Jaleswar. Orissa, NE India 21°51′N 87°15′E
Jaleswar see Jaleshwar
154 F12 Jalgaon Mahārāshtra, C India 21°01′N 75°34′E
139 W12 Jalībah Dhī Qār, S Iraq 30°37′N 46°31′E
139 W13 Jalīb Shahāb Al Muthannā, S Iraq 30°26′N 46°09′E
77 X15 Jalingo Taraba, E Nigeria 08°54′N 11°22′E
40 K13 Jalisco ◈ state SW Mexico
154 G13 Jālna Mahārāshtra, W India 19°50′N 75°53′E
Jalomitsa see Ialomiţa
105 R5 Jalón ≈ N Spain
152 E13 Jālor Rājasthān, N India 25°21′N 72°43′E
112 K11 Jalovik Serbia, W Serbia 44°37′N 19°48′E
40 L12 Jalpa Zacatecas, C Mexico 21°40′N 103°W
153 S12 Jalpāiguri West Bengal, NE India 26°43′N 88°24′E
41 O12 Jalpán var. Jalpan. Querétaro de Arteaga, C Mexico 21°13′N 99°28′W
Jalpan see Jalpán
67 P2 Jalta island N Tunisia
75 S9 Jālū var. Jūlā. NE Libya 29°02′N 21°33′E
189 U8 Jaluit Atoll var. Jālwōj. atoll Ralik Chain, S Marshall Islands
Jālwōj see Jaluit Atoll
81 L18 Jamaame It. Giamame; prev. Margherita. Jubbada Hoose, S Somalia 0°00′N 42°43′E
77 W13 Jamaare ≈ NE Nigeria
44 G9 Jamaica ◆ commonwealth republic W West Indies
47 P3 Jamaica island W West Indies
44 I9 Jamaica Channel channel Haiti/Jamaica
153 T14 Jamalpur Dhaka, N Bangladesh 24°54′N 89°57′E
153 Q14 Jamālpur Bihār, NE India 25°19′N 86°30′E
168 L9 Jamaluang var. Jemaluang. Johor, Peninsular Malaysia 02°15′N 103°50′E
59 I14 Jamanxim, Rio ≈ C Brazil
56 B8 Jambeli, Canal de channel S Ecuador
99 I20 Jambes Namur, SE Belgium 50°26′N 04°51′E
168 L12 Jambi var. Telanaipura; prev. Djambi. Sumatera, W Indonesia 01°34′S 103°37′E
168 K12 Jambi off. Propinsi Jambi, var. Djambi. ◈ province W Indonesia
Jambi, Propinsi see Jambi
Jamdena see Yamdena, Pulau
12 H8 James Bay bay Ontario/ Québec, E Canada
63 F19 James, Isla island Archipiélago de los Chonos, S Chile
181 Q8 James Ranges ▲▲ Northern Territory, C Australia
29 P8 James River ≈ North Dakota/South Dakota, N USA
21 X7 James River ≈ Virginia, NE USA
194 H4 James Ross Island island Antarctica
182 I8 Jamestown South Australia 33°13′S 138°36′E
65 G25 Jamestown ○ (Saint Helena) NW Saint Helena 15°56′S 05°44′W
35 P8 Jamestown California, W USA 37°57′N 120°25′W
20 L7 Jamestown Kentucky, S USA 36°58′N 85°03′W
18 D11 Jamestown New York, NE USA 42°05′N 79°15′W
29 P5 Jamestown North Dakota, N USA 46°54′N 98°42′W
20 L8 Jamestown Tennessee, S USA 36°24′N 84°58′W
Jamestown see Holetown
15 N10 Jamet ≈ Québec, SE Canada
41 Q17 Jamiltepec var. Santiago Jamiltepec. Oaxaca, SE Mexico 16°18′N 97°51′W
95 F20 Jammerbugten bay Skagerrak, E North Sea
152 H6 Jammu prev. Jummoo. state capital Jammu and Kashmir, NW India 32°43′N 74°54′E
152 I5 Jammu and Kashmir var. Jammu-Kashmir, Kashmir. ◈ state NW India
149 V4 Jammu and Kashmīr disputed region India/Pakistan
Jammu-Kashmir see Jammu and Kashmir
154 B10 Jāmnagar prev. Navanagar. Gujarāt, W India 22°28′N 70°06′E
149 S11 Jāmpur Punjab, E Pakistan 29°38′N 70°40′E
93 L18 Jämsä Länsi-Suomi, C Finland 61°51′N 25°10′E
93 L18 Jämsänkoski Länsi-Suomi, C Finland 61°54′N 25°10′E
153 Q16 Jamshedpur Jhārkhand, NE India 22°47′N 86°12′E
94 K9 Jämtland ◈ county C Sweden
153 Q14 Jamūi Bihār, NE India 24°57′N 86°14′E
Jamuna see Brahmaputra
153 T14 Jamuna Nadi ≈ N Bangladesh
Jamundá see Nhamundá, Rio
54 D11 Jamundí Valle del Cauca, SW Colombia 03°16′N 76°31′W
153 Q12 Janakpur Central, C Nepal 26°45′N 85°55′E
59 N18 Janaúba Minas Gerais, SE Brazil 15°47′S 43°16′W
58 K11 Janaucu, Ilha island NE Brazil
143 Q7 Jandaq Eşfahān, C Iran 34°04′N 54°26′E
64 Q11 Jandia, Punta de headland Fuerteventura, Islas Canarias, Spain, NE Atlantic Ocean 28°03′N 14°32′W
59 B14 Jandiatuba, Rio ≈ NW Brazil
105 N12 Jándula ≈ S Spain
29 V10 Janesville Minnesota, N USA 44°07′N 93°43′W
30 L9 Janesville Wisconsin, N USA 42°42′N 89°02′W
83 N20 Jangamo Inhambane, SE Mozambique 24°04′S 35°25′E
155 J14 Jangaon Andhra Pradesh, C India 18°47′N 79°25′E
153 S14 Jangīpur West Bengal, NE India 24°31′N 88°03′E
Janina see Ioánnina
Janischken see Joniškis
112 J11 Janja NE Bosnia and Herzegovina 44°40′N 19°15′E
154 L12 Jānjgīr Chhattīsgarh, SW India 22°01′N 82°30′E
Jankovac see Jánoshalma
197 Q15 Jan Mayen ◇ Norwegian dependency N Atlantic Ocean
84 D5 Jan Mayen island N Atlantic Ocean
197 R15 Jan Mayen Fracture Zone tectonic feature Greenland Sea/Norwegian Sea
197 R15 Jan Mayen Ridge undersea feature Greenland Sea/Norwegian Sea 69°00′N 08°00′W
40 H3 Janos Chihuahua, N Mexico 30°50′N 108°10′W
111 K25 Jánoshalma SCr. Jankovac. Bács-Kiskun, S Hungary 46°19′N 19°16′E
Janów see Ivanava, Belarus
110 H10 Janowiec Wielkopolski Ger. Janowitz. Kujawski-pomorskie, C Poland 52°47′N 17°30′E
Janowitz see Janowiec Wielkopolski
Janow/Janów see Jonava, Lithuania
111 O15 Janów Lubelski Lubelski, E Poland 50°42′N 22°24′E
Janów Poleski see Ivanava
83 H25 Jansenville Eastern Cape, S South Africa 32°56′S 24°40′E
59 M18 Januária Minas Gerais, SE Brazil 15°28′S 44°23′W
Janūbīyah, Al Bādiyah al see Ash Shāmīyah
102 I7 Janzé Ille-et-Vilaine, NW France 47°55′N 01°28′W
154 F10 Jaora Madhya Pradesh, C India 23°40′N 75°10′E
131 Y9 Japan var. Nippon, Jap. Nihon. ◆ monarchy E Asia
129 Y9 Japan island group E Asia
192 H4 Japan Basin undersea feature N Sea of Japan 40°00′N 135°00′E
129 Y8 Japan, Sea of var. East Sea, Rus. Yapanskoye More. sea NW Pacific Ocean see also East Sea
192 H4 Japan Trench undersea feature NW Pacific Ocean 37°00′N 143°00′E
Japen see Yapen, Pulau
59 A15 Japiim var. Máncio Lima. Acre, W Brazil 08°00′S 73°39′W
58 D12 Japurá Amazonas, N Brazil 01°43′S 66°14′W
58 C12 Japurá, Rio var. Río Caquetá, Yapurá. ≈ Brazil/ Colombia see also Caquetá, Río
Japurá, Rio see Caquetá, Río
43 W17 Jaqué Darién, SE Panama 07°31′N 78°09′W
Jaquemel see Jacmel
Jarablos see Jarābulus
138 K2 Jarābulus var. Jarablos, Jerablus, Fr. Djérablous. Ḥalab, N Syria 36°51′N 38°02′E
60 K13 Jaraguá do Sul Santa Catarina, S Brazil 26°29′S 49°07′W
104 K9 Jaraicejo Extremadura, W Spain 39°40′N 05°49′W
104 K9 Jaráiz de la Vera Extremadura, W Spain 40°04′N 05°45′W
105 O7 Jarama ≈ C Spain
63 J20 Jaramillo Santa Cruz, SE Argentina 47°10′S 67°07′W
Jarandilla de la Vega see Jarandilla de la Vera
104 K8 Jarandilla de la Vera var. Jarandilla de la Vega. Extremadura, W Spain 40°08′N 05°39′W
149 V9 Jarānwāla Punjab, E Pakistan 31°20′N 73°26′E
138 G9 Jarash var. Jerash; anc. Gerasa. Irbid, NW Jordan 32°17′N 35°54′E
Jarbah, Jazīrat see Jerba, Île de
94 N13 Järbo Gävleborg, C Sweden 60°43′N 16°40′E
Jardan see Yordon
44 F7 Jardines de la Reina, Archipiélago de los island group C Cuba
162 I8 Jargalant Bayanhongor, C Mongolia 47°14′N 99°43′E
162 K6 Jargalant Bulgan, N Mongolia 49°09′N 104°19′E
162 G7 Jargalant var. Buyanbat. Govĭ-Altay, W Mongolia 47°00′N 95°57′E
162 I6 Jargalant var. Orgil. Hövsgöl, C Mongolia 48°31′N 99°19′E
Jargalant see Battsengel
Jargalant see Bulgan, Bayan-Ölgiy, Mongolia
Jargalant see Biger, Govĭ-Altay, Mongolia
Jarīd, Shaṭṭ al see Jerid, Chott el
58 I11 Jari, Rio var. Jary. ≈ N Brazil
141 N7 Jarīr, Wādī al dry watercourse C Saudi Arabia
Jarja see Yur'ya
94 L13 Järna var. Dala-Jarna. Dalarna, C Sweden 60°31′N 14°22′E
95 O16 Järna Stockholm, C Sweden 59°05′N 17°35′E
102 K11 Jarnac Charente, W France 45°41′N 00°10′W
110 H12 Jarocin Wielkopolskie, C Poland 51°59′N 17°30′E
111 F16 Jaroměř Ger. Jermer. Královéhradecký Kraj, N Czech Republic 50°22′N 15°55′E
Jaroslau see Jarosław
111 O16 Jarosław Ger. Jaroslau, Rus. Yaroslav. Podkarpackie, SE Poland 50°01′N 22°41′E
93 F16 Järpen Jämtland, C Sweden 63°21′N 13°30′E
147 O14 Jarqo'rg'on Rus. Dzharkurgan. Surkhondaryo Viloyati, S Uzbekistan 37°31′N 67°20′E
139 P2 Jarrāh, Wadi dry watercourse NE Syria
Jars, Plain of see Xiangkhoang, Plateau de
162 K14 Jartai Yanchi ◎ N China
59 E16 Jaru Rondônia, W Brazil 10°24′S 62°45′W
Jarud Qi see Lubei
118 I4 Järva-Jaani Ger. Sankt-Johannis. Järvamaa, N Estonia 59°03′N 25°54′E
118 G5 Järvakandi Ger. Jerwakant. Raplamaa, NW Estonia 58°45′N 24°49′E
118 H4 Järvamaa var. Järva Maakond. ◈ province N Estonia
Järva Maakond see Järvamaa
93 L19 Järvenpää Etelä-Suomi, S Finland 60°29′N 25°06′E
14 G17 Jarvis Ontario, S Canada 42°53′N 80°06′W
177 R8 Jarvis Island ◇ US unincorporated territory C Pacific Ocean
94 M11 Järvsö Gävleborg, C Sweden 61°43′N 16°25′E
Jary see Jari, Rio
112 M9 Jaša Tomić Vojvodina, NE Serbia 45°27′N 20°51′E
112 D12 Jasenice Zadar, SW Croatia 44°15′N 15°33′E
154 L12 Jashpurnagar Chhattīsgarh, C India 22°53′N 84°09′E
138 I11 Jashshat al 'Adlah, Wādī al dry watercourse C Jordan
77 Q16 Jasikan E Ghana 07°24′N 00°28′E
Jāsk see Bandar-e Jāsk
146 F6 Jasliq Rus. Zhaslyk. Qoraqalpog'iston Respublikasi, NW Uzbekistan 43°57′N 57°30′E
111 N17 Jasło Podkarpackie, SE Poland 49°45′N 21°28′E
11 U16 Jasmin Saskatchewan, S Canada 51°11′N 103°34′W
65 A23 Jason Islands island group NW Falkland Islands
194 I4 Jason Peninsula peninsula Antarctica
31 N15 Jasonville Indiana, N USA 39°09′N 87°12′W
11 O15 Jasper Alberta, SW Canada 52°55′N 118°05′W
14 L13 Jasper Ontario, SE Canada 44°50′N 75°57′W
23 O3 Jasper Alabama, S USA 33°49′N 87°16′W
27 T9 Jasper Arkansas, C USA 36°00′N 93°11′W
23 U8 Jasper Florida, SE USA 30°31′N 82°57′W
31 N16 Jasper Indiana, N USA 38°22′N 86°57′W
29 R11 Jasper Minnesota, N USA 43°51′N 96°24′W
27 S7 Jasper Missouri, C USA 37°20′N 94°18′W
20 K10 Jasper Tennessee, S USA 35°04′N 85°36′W
25 Y9 Jasper Texas, SW USA 30°55′N 94°00′W
11 O15 Jasper National Park national park Alberta/British Columbia, SW Canada
Jassy see Iaşi
113 N14 Jastrebac ▲▲ SE Serbia
112 D9 Jastrebarsko Zagreb, N Croatia 45°40′N 15°40′E
Jastrow see Jastrowie
110 G9 Jastrowie Ger. Jastrow. Wielkopolskie, C Poland 53°25′N 16°48′E
111 J17 Jastrzębie-Zdrój Śląskie, S Poland 49°58′N 18°34′E
111 L22 Jászapáti Jász-Nagykun-Szolnok, E Hungary 47°30′N 20°10′E
111 L22 Jászberény Jász-Nagykun-Szolnok, E Hungary 47°30′N 19°56′E
111 L23 Jász-Nagykun-Szolnok off. Jász-Nagykun-Szolnok Megye. ◈ county E Hungary
Jász-Nagykun-Szolnok Megye see Jász-Nagykun-Szolnok
59 J19 Jataí Goiás, C Brazil 17°58′S 51°45′W
58 G12 Jatapu, Serra do ▲▲ N Brazil
41 W16 Jatate, Río ≈ SE Mexico
149 P17 Jāti Sind, SE Pakistan 24°20′N 68°18′E
44 F6 Jatibonico Sancti Spíritus, C Cuba 21°56′N 79°11′W
169 O16 Jatiluhur, Danau ◎ Jawa, S Indonesia
Jativa see Xàtiva
149 S11 Jatoi Punjab, E Pakistan 29°29′N 70°58′E
60 L9 Jaú São Paulo, S Brazil 22°11′S 48°35′W
58 F11 Jauaperi, Rio ≈ N Brazil
99 I19 Jauche Walloon Brabant, C Belgium 50°42′N 04°55′E
Jauer see Jawor
Jauf see Al Jawf
149 U7 Jauharābād Punjab, E Pakistan 32°16′N 72°17′E
57 E14 Jauja Junín, C Peru 11°48′S 75°30′W
41 O10 Jaumave Tamaulipas, C Mexico 23°28′N 99°22′W
118 H10 Jaunjelgava Ger. Friedrichstadt. Aizkraukle, S Latvia 56°38′N 25°03′E
Jaunlatgale see Pytalovo
118 I8 Jaunpiebalga Gulbene, NE Latvia 57°10′N 26°02′E
118 E9 Jaunpils Tukums, C Latvia 56°45′N 23°03′E
153 N13 Jaunpur Uttar Pradesh, N India 25°44′N 82°41′E
29 N8 Java South Dakota, N USA 45°29′N 99°54′W
Java see Jawa
105 R9 Javalambre ▲ E Spain 40°02′N 01°06′W
173 V7 Java Ridge undersea feature E Indian Ocean
59 A14 Javari, Rio var. Yavarí. ≈ Brazil/Peru
Javarthushuu see Bayan-Uul
169 Q15 Java Sea Ind. Laut Jawa. sea W Indonesia
173 U7 Java Trench var. Sunda Trench. undersea feature E Indian Ocean
143 Q10 Javazm var. Jowzam. Kermān, C Iran 30°31′N 55°01′E
105 T11 Jávea Cat. Xàbia. País Valenciano, E Spain 38°48′N 00°10′E
Javhlant see Bayan-Ovoo
63 G20 Javier, Isla island S Chile
113 L14 Javor ▲▲ Bosnia and Herzegovina/Serbia
111 K20 Javorie Hung. Jávoros. ▲ S Slovakia 48°26′N 19°16′E
Jávoros see Javorie
93 J14 Jävre Norrbotten, N Sweden 65°07′N 21°31′E
192 E8 Jawa Eng. Java; prev. Djawa. island C Indonesia
169 O16 Jawa Barat off. Propinsi Jawa Barat, Eng. West Java. ◈ province S Indonesia
Jawa Barat, Propinsi see Jawa Barat
Jawa, Laut see Java Sea
139 R3 Jawān Nīnawýa, NW Iraq 35°57′N 43°03′E
169 P16 Jawa Tengah off. Propinsi Jawa Tengah, Eng. Central Java. ◈ province S Indonesia
Jawa Tengah, Propinsi see Jawa Tengah
169 R16 Jawa Timur off. Propinsi Jawa Timur, Eng. East Java. ◈ province S Indonesia
Jawa Timur, Propinsi see Jawa Timur
81 N17 Jawhar var. Jowhar, It. Giohar. Shabeellaha Dhexe, S Somalia 02°37′N 45°30′E
111 F14 Jawor Ger. Jauer. Dolnośląskie, SW Poland 51°01′N 16°11′E
Jaworów see Yavoriv
111 J16 Jaworzno Śląskie, S Poland 50°13′N 19°11′E
Jaxartes see Syr Darya
27 R9 Jay Oklahoma, C USA 36°25′N 94°49′W
Jayabum see Chaiyaphum
Jayanath see Chai Nat
153 T12 Jayanti prev. Jainti. West Bengal, NE India 26°45′N 89°40′E
171 X14 Jaya, Puncak prev. Puntjak Carstensz, Puntjak Sukarno. ▲ Papua, E Indonesia 04°00′S 137°10′E
171 Z13 Jayapura var. Djajapura, Dut. Hollandia; prev. Kotabaru, Sukarnapura. Papua, E Indonesia 02°37′S 140°39′E
Jay Dairen see Dalian
Jayhawker State see Kansas
147 S12 Jayilgan Rus. Dzhailgan, Dzhayilgan. C Tajikistan 39°17′N 71°32′E
155 L14 Jaypur var. Jeypore, Jeypur. Orissa, E India 18°54′N 82°36′E
25 O6 Jayton Texas, SW USA 33°16′N 100°35′W
143 U13 Jaz Mūrīān, Hāmūn-e ◎ SE Iran
138 M4 Jazrah Ar Raqqah, C Syria 35°56′N 39°02′E
138 G6 Jbaïl var. Jebeil, Jubayl, Jubeil; anc. Biblical Gebal, Bybles. W Lebanon 34°00′N 35°45′E
25 O7 J. B. Thomas, Lake ⊠ Texas, SW USA
Jdaïdé see Judaydah
35 X12 Jean Nevada, W USA 35°45′N 115°20′W
22 I9 Jeanerette Louisiana, S USA 29°54′N 91°39′W
44 L8 Jean-Rabel NW Haiti 19°48′N 73°05′W
143 T12 Jebāl Bārez, Kūh-e ▲▲ SE Iran
Jebat see Jabwot
77 T15 Jebba Kwara, W Nigeria 09°04′N 04°50′E
Jebeil see Jbaïl
116 E12 Jebel Hung. Széphely; prev. Hung. Zsebely. Timiş, W Romania 45°33′N 21°14′E
146 B11 Jebel Rus. Dzhebel. Balkan Welaýaty, W Turkmenistan 39°42′N 54°10′E
Jebel, Bahr el see White Nile
Jebel Dhanna see Jabal aẓ Ẓannah
Jeble see Jablah
96 K13 Jedburgh SE Scotland, United Kingdom 55°29′N 02°34′W
Jedda see Jiddah
111 L15 Jędrzejów Ger. Endersdorf. Świętokrzyskie, C Poland 50°39′N 20°18′E
100 K12 Jeetze var. Jeetzel. ≈ C Germany
Jeetzel see Jeetze
29 U14 Jefferson Iowa, C USA 42°01′N 94°22′W
21 Q8 Jefferson North Carolina, SE USA 36°24′N 81°33′W
25 X6 Jefferson Texas, SW USA 32°45′N 94°21′W
30 M9 Jefferson Wisconsin, N USA 43°01′N 88°48′W
27 U5 Jefferson City state capital Missouri, C USA 38°33′N 92°13′W
33 R10 Jefferson City Montana, NW USA 46°24′N 112°01′W
21 N9 Jefferson City Tennessee, S USA 36°07′N 83°29′W
35 U7 Jefferson, Mount ▲ Nevada, W USA 38°49′N 116°54′W
32 H12 Jefferson, Mount ▲ Oregon, NW USA 44°40′N 121°48′W
20 L5 Jeffersontown Kentucky, S USA 38°11′N 85°33′W
31 P16 Jeffersonville Indiana, N USA 38°16′N 85°45′W
33 V15 Jeffrey City Wyoming, C USA 42°29′N 107°49′W
77 T13 Jega Kebbi, NW Nigeria 12°15′N 04°21′E
Jehol see Chengde
62 P5 Jejui-Guazú, Río ≈ E Paraguay
118 I10 Jēkabpils Ger. Jakobstadt. Jēkabpils, S Latvia 56°30′N 25°56′E
23 W7 Jekyll Island island Georgia, SE USA
169 R13 Jelai, Sungai ≈ Borneo, N Indonesia
Jelalabad see Jalālābād
111 H14 Jelcz-Laskowice Dolnośląskie, SW Poland 51°01′N 17°24′E
111 E14 Jelenia Góra Ger. Hirschberg, Hirschberg im Riesengebirge, Hirschberg in Riesengebirge, Hirschberg in Schlesien. Dolnośląskie, SW Poland 50°54′N 15°48′E
153 S11 Jelep La pass N India
118 F9 Jelgava Ger. Mitau. Jelgava, C Latvia 56°38′N 23°47′E
112 L13 Jelica ▲▲ C Serbia
20 M8 Jellico Tennessee, S USA 36°33′N 84°06′W
95 G23 Jelling Vejle, C Denmark 55°45′N 09°24′E
169 N9 Jemaja, Pulau island W Indonesia
Jemaluang see Jamaluang
99 E20 Jemappes Hainaut, S Belgium 50°27′N 03°53′E
169 S17 Jember prev. Djember. Jawa, C Indonesia 08°07′S 113°45′E
99 I20 Jemeppe-sur-Sambre Namur, S Belgium 50°27′N 04°41′E
37 R10 Jemez Pueblo New Mexico, SW USA 35°36′N 106°43′W
158 K2 Jeminay var. Tuotiereke. Xinjiang Uygur Zizhiqu, NW China 47°28′N 85°49′E
189 U5 Jemo Island atoll Ratak Chain, C Marshall Islands
169 U11 Jempang, Danau ◎ Borneo, N Indonesia
101 L16 Jena Thüringen, C Germany 50°56′N 11°35′E
22 I6 Jena Louisiana, S USA 31°40′N 92°07′W
108 I8 Jenaz Graubünden, SE Switzerland 46°56′N 09°43′E
109 N7 Jenbach Tirol, W Austria 47°24′N 11°47′E
171 N15 Jeneponto prev. Djeneponto. Sulawesi, C Indonesia 05°41′S 119°42′E
138 F9 Jenin N West Bank 32°28′N 35°17′E
21 P7 Jenkins Kentucky, S USA 37°10′N 82°37′W
27 P9 Jenks Oklahoma, C USA 36°01′N 95°58′W
Jenné see Djenné
109 X8 Jennersdorf Burgenland, SE Austria 46°57′N 16°08′E
22 H9 Jennings Louisiana, S USA 30°13′N 92°39′W
11 N7 Jenny Lind Island island Nunavut, N Canada
23 Y13 Jensen Beach Florida, SE USA 27°15′N 80°13′W
9 P6 Jens Munk Island island Nunavut, NE Canada
59 O17 Jequié Bahia, E Brazil 13°52′S 40°06′W
59 O18 Jequitinhonha, Rio ≈ E Brazil
Jerablus see Jarābulus
74 H6 Jerada NE Morocco 34°16′N 02°07′W
Jerash see Jarash
75 N7 Jerba, Île de var. Djerba, Jazīrat Jarbah. island E Tunisia
44 K9 Jérémie SW Haiti 18°39′N 74°11′W
Jeréz see Jerez de García Salinas, Mexico
Jerez see Jeréz de la Frontera, Spain
40 L11 Jerez de García Salinas var. Jeréz. Zacatecas, C Mexico 22°40′N 103°00′W
104 J15 Jeréz de la Frontera var. Jerez; prev. Xeres. Andalucía, SW Spain 36°41′N 06°08′W
104 I12 Jeréz de los Caballeros Extremadura, W Spain 38°20′N 06°45′W
Jergucati see Jorgucat
138 G10 Jericho Ar. Arīḥā, Heb. Yeriḥo. E West Bank 31°51′N 35°27′E
74 M7 Jerid, Chott el var. Shaṭṭ al Jarīd. salt lake SW Tunisia
183 O10 Jerilderie New South Wales, SE Australia 35°24′S 145°43′E
Jerischmarkt see Câmpia Turzii
92 K11 Jerisjärvi ◎ NW Finland
Jermak see Aksu
Jermentau see Yereymentau
Jermer see Jaroměř
36 K11 Jerome Arizona, SW USA 34°45′N 112°06′W
33 O15 Jerome Idaho, NW USA 42°43′N 114°31′W
97 L26 Jersey island NW Europe
18 K14 Jersey City New Jersey, NE USA 40°42′N 74°01′W
18 F13 Jersey Shore Pennsylvania, NE USA 41°12′N 77°13′W
30 K14 Jerseyville Illinois, N USA 39°07′N 90°19′W
104 K8 Jerte ≈ W Spain
138 F10 Jerusalem Ar. Al Quds, Al Quds ash Sharīf, Heb. Yerushalayim; anc. Hierosolyma. ● (Israel) Jerusalem, NE Israel 31°47′N 35°13′E
138 G10 Jerusalem ◈ district E Israel
183 S10 Jervis Bay New South Wales, SE Australia 35°09′S 150°42′E
183 S10 Jervis Bay Territory ◈ territory SE Australia
Jerwakant see Järvakandi
109 S10 Jesenice Ger. Assling. NW Slovenia 46°26′N 14°01′E
111 H16 Jeseník Ger. Freiwaldau. Olomoucký Kraj, E Czech Republic 50°14′N 17°12′E
Jesi see Iesi
106 I8 Jesolo var. Iesolo. Veneto, NE Italy 45°32′N 12°37′E
Jesselton see Kota Kinabalu
95 I14 Jessheim Akershus, S Norway 60°07′N 11°10′E
153 T15 Jessore Khulna, W Bangladesh 23°10′N 89°12′E
23 W6 Jesup Georgia, SE USA 31°36′N 81°54′W
41 S15 Jesús Carranza Veracruz-Llave, SE Mexico 17°30′N 95°01′W
62 K10 Jesús María Córdoba, C Argentina 30°59′S 64°05′W
26 K6 Jetmore Kansas, C USA 38°05′N 99°55′W
103 Q2 Jeumont Nord, N France 50°18′N 04°06′E
95 H14 Jevnaker Oppland, S Norway 60°15′N 10°25′E
Jewe see Jõhvi
25 V9 Jewett Texas, SW USA 31°21′N 96°08′W
19 N12 Jewett City Connecticut, NE USA 41°36′N 71°58′W
Jeypore see Jaipur, Rājasthān, India
Jeypore/Jeypur see Jaypur, Orissa, India
113 L17 Jezercës, Maja e ▲ N Albania 42°27′N 19°49′E
111 B18 Jezerní Hora ▲ SW Czech Republic 49°10′N 13°11′E
154 F10 Jhābua Madhya Pradesh, C India 22°44′N 74°37′E
152 H10 Jhajjar Haryāna, N India 28°35′N 76°39′E
152 H14 Jhālāwār Rājasthān, N India 24°37′N 76°12′E
Jhang/Jhang Sadar see Jhang Sadr

◆ Country ● Country Capital ◇ Dependent Territory ○ Dependent Territory Capital ◈ Administrative Regions ✈ International Airport ▲ Mountain ▲▲ Mountain Range Ѫ Volcano ≈ River ◎ Lake ⊠ Reservoir

JHANG SADR – KABALEBO RIVIER

149 U9 **Jhang Sadr** *var.* Jhang, Jhang Sadar. Punjab, NE Pakistan 31°16′N 72°19′E
152 J13 **Jhānsi** Uttar Pradesh, N India 25°27′N 78°34′E
153 O16 **Jhārkhand** ◐ *state* NE India
154 M11 **Jhārsuguda** Orissa, E India 21°56′N 84°04′E
149 Q12 **Jhatpat** Baluchistān, SW Pakistan 28°22′N 68°21′E
149 V7 **Jhelum** Punjab, NE Pakistan 32°55′N 73°42′E
129 P9 **Jhelum** ≈ E Pakistan
Jhenaida *see* Jhenaidaha
153 T15 **Jhenaidaha** *var.* Jhenaida, Jhenida. Khulna, Bangladesh 23°32′N 89°09′E
Jhenaidaha *see* Jhenida
153 T15 **Jhenida** *var.* Jhenaidaha. Dhaka, W Bangladesh 23°34′N 89°39′E
Jhenida *see* Jhenaidaha
149 P16 **Jhimpir** Sind, SE Pakistan 25°00′N 68°01′E
Jhind *see* Jīnd
149 R16 **Jhudo** Sind, SE Pakistan 24°58′N 69°18′E
Jhumra *see* Chak Jhumra
152 H11 **Jhunjhunūn** Rājasthān, N India 28°05′N 75°30′E
Ji *see* Hebei, China
Ji *see* Jilin, China
Jiading *see* Xinfeng
153 S14 **Jiāganj** West Bengal, NE India 24°18′N 88°07′E
Jiaji *see* Qionghai
160 J7 **Jialing Jiang** ≈ C China
163 Y7 **Jiamusi** *var.* Chia-mu-ssu, Kiamusze. Heilongjiang, NE China 46°46′N 130°19′E
161 O11 **Ji'an** Jiangxi, S China 27°08′N 115°00′E
163 W12 **Ji'an** Jilin, NE China 41°04′N 126°07′E
163 T13 **Jianchang** Liaoning, NE China 40°48′N 119°51′E
Jianchang *see* Nancheng
Jiancheng *see* Jianyang
160 F11 **Jianchuan** *var.* Jinhuan. Yunnan, SW China 26°28′N 99°49′E
158 M4 **Jiangjunmiao** Xinjiang Uygur Zizhiqu, W China 44°42′N 90°06′E
160 K11 **Jiangkou** *var.* Shuangjiang. Guizhou, S China 27°46′N 108°53′E
Jiangkou *see* Fengkai
161 Q12 **Jiangle** *var.* Guyong. Fujian, SE China 26°44′N 117°26′E
161 N15 **Jiangmen** Guangdong, S China 22°35′N 113°02′E
Jiangna *see* Yanshan
161 Q10 **Jiangshan** Zhejiang, SE China 28°41′N 118°33′E
161 Q7 **Jiangsu** *var.* Chiang-su, Jiangsu Sheng, Kiangsu, Su. ◐ *province* E China
Jiangsu *see* Nanjing
Jiangsu Sheng *see* Jiangsu
161 O11 **Jiangxi** *var.* Chiang-hsi, Gan, Jiangxi Sheng, Kiangsi. ◐ *province* S China
Jiangxi Sheng *see* Jiangxi
160 I8 **Jiangyou** *prev.* Zhongba. Sichuan, C China 31°52′N 104°52′E
161 N9 **Jianli** *var.* Rongcheng. Hubei, C China 29°51′N 112°50′E
161 Q11 **Jian'ou** Fujian, SE China 27°04′N 118°20′E
163 S12 **Jianping** *var.* Yebaishou. Liaoning, NE China 41°13′N 119°37′E
Jianshe *see* Baiyü
160 L9 **Jianshi** *var.* Yezhou. Hubei, C China 30°37′N 109°42′E
129 V11 **Jian Xi** ≈ SE China
161 Q11 **Jianyang** Fujian, SE China 27°20′N 118°01′E
160 I9 **Jianyang** *var.* Jiancheng. Sichuan, C China 30°22′N 104°31′E
163 X10 **Jiaohe** Jilin, NE China 43°41′N 127°20′E
Jiaojiang *see* Taizhou
Jiaoxian *see* Jiaozhou
161 R5 **Jiaozhou** *prev.* Jiaoxian. Shandong, E China 36°17′N 120°00′E
161 N6 **Jiaozuo** Henan, C China 35°14′N 113°13′E
Jiashan *see* Mingguang
158 F8 **Jiashi** *var.* Baren, Payzawat. Xinjiang Uygur Zizhiqu, NW China 39°27′N 76°45′E
154 L9 **Jiāwān** Madhya Pradesh, C India 24°20′N 82°17′E
161 S9 **Jiaxing** Zhejiang, SE China 30°44′N 120°46′E
Jiayi *see* Chiai
163 X6 **Jiayin** *var.* Chaoyang. Heilongjiang, NE China 48°51′N 130°24′E
159 R8 **Jiayuguan** Gansu, N China 39°47′N 98°14′E
Jibhalanta *see* Uliastay
138 M4 **Jibli** Ar Raqqah, C Syria 35°49′N 39°23′E
116 H9 **Jibou** *Hung.* Zsibó. Sălaj, NW Romania 47°15′N 23°17′E
141 Z9 **Jibsh, Ra's al** *headland* E Oman 21°20′N 59°23′E
Jibuti *see* Djibouti
Jichang *see* Jixian
111 E15 **Jičín** *Ger.* Jitschin. Královéhradecký Kraj, N Czech Republic 50°27′N 15°20′E
140 K10 **Jiddah** *Eng.* Jedda. (Saudi Arabia) Makkah, W Saudi Arabia 21°34′N 39°13′E
141 W11 **Jiddat al Ḥarāsīs** *desert* C Oman
Jiesjavrre *see* Iešjávri
160 M4 **Jiexiu** Shanxi, C China 37°00′N 111°50′E
161 P14 **Jieyang** Guangdong, S China 23°32′N 116°20′E
119 F14 **Jieznas** Kaunas, S Lithuania 54°37′N 24°10′E
Jīfa', Bi'r *see* Jif'īyah, Bi'r
141 P15 **Jif'īyah, Bi'r** *var.* Bi'r Jīfa'. *well* C Yemen
77 W13 **Jigawa** ◐ *state* N Nigeria
146 J10 **Jigerbent** *Rus.* Dzhigirbent. Lebap Welaýaty, NE Turkmenistan 40°44′N 61°56′E
44 I7 **Jiguaní** Granma, E Cuba 20°24′N 76°26′W
159 T12 **Jigzhi** *var.* Chugqênsumdo. Qinghai, C China 33°23′N 101°25′E
Jih-k'a-tse *see* Xigazê
111 E18 **Jihlava** *Ger.* Iglau, *Pol.* Igława. Vysocina, S Czech Republic 49°22′N 15°36′E
111 E18 **Jihlava** *var.* Igel, *Ger.* Iglawa. ≈ Vysočina, C Czech Republic
Jihlavský Kraj *see* Vysočina
111 C18 **Jihočeský Kraj** *prev.* Budějovický Kraj. ◐ *region* Czech Republic
111 G19 **Jihomoravský Kraj** *prev.* Brněnský Kraj. ◐ *region* SE Czech Republic
74 L5 **Jijel** *var.* Djidjel; *prev.* Djidjelli. NE Algeria 36°50′N 05°43′E
116 L9 **Jijia** ≈ N Romania
80 L13 **Jijiga** *It.* Giggiga. Sumalē, E Ethiopia 09°21′N 42°53′E
105 S12 **Jijona** *var.* Xixona. País Valenciano, E Spain 38°34′N 00°29′W
81 L18 **Jilib** *It.* Gelib. Jubbada Dhexe, S Somalia 0°18′N 42°48′E
163 W10 **Jilin** *var.* Chi-lin, Girin, Kirin; *prev.* Yungki, Yunki. Jilin, NE China 43°46′N 126°32′E
163 W10 **Jilin** *var.* Chi-lin, Girin, Ji, Jilin Sheng, Kirin. ◐ *province* NE China
163 W11 **Jilin Hada Ling** ▲▲ NE China
Jilin Sheng *see* Jilin
163 S4 **Jilin He** ≈ NE China
105 Q6 **Jiloca** ≈ N Spain
81 I14 **Jīma** *var.* Jimma, *It.* Gimma. Oromīya, C Ethiopia 07°42′N 36°51′E
44 M9 **Jimaní** W Dominican Republic 18°29′N 71°49′W
116 E11 **Jimbolia** *Ger.* Hatzfeld, *Hung.* Zsombolya. Timiş, W Romania 45°47′N 20°43′E
104 K16 **Jimena de la Frontera** Andalucía, S Spain 36°27′N 05°28′W
40 K7 **Jiménez** Chihuahua, N Mexico 27°09′N 104°54′W
41 N5 **Jiménez** Coahuila, NE Mexico 29°05′N 100°40′W
41 P9 **Jiménez** *var.* Santander Jiménez. Tamaulipas, C Mexico 24°11′N 98°29′W
40 L10 **Jiménez del Teul** Zacatecas, C Mexico 23°13′N 103°46′W
77 Y14 **Jimeta** Adamawa, E Nigeria 09°16′N 12°25′E
Jimma *see* Jīma
158 M5 **Jimsar** Xinjiang Uygur Zizhiqu, NW China 44°05′N 88°48′E
18 I14 **Jim Thorpe** Pennsylvania, NE USA 40°51′N 75°43′W
Jin *see* Shanxi
Jin *see* Tianjin Shi
161 P5 **Jinan** *var.* Chinan, Chi-nan, Tsinan. *province capital* Shandong, E China 36°43′N 116°58′E
Jin'an *see* Songpan
Jinbi *see* Dayao
159 T8 **Jinchang** Gansu, N China 38°31′N 102°07′E
161 N5 **Jincheng** Shanxi, C China 35°30′N 112°52′E
Jincheng *see* Wuding
Jinchengjiang *see* Hechi
152 I9 **Jīnd** *prev.* Jhind. Haryāna, NW India 29°29′N 76°22′E
183 Q11 **Jindabyne** New South Wales, SE Australia 36°28′S 148°36′E
111 O18 **Jindřichův Hradec** *Ger.* Neuhaus. Jihočeský Kraj, S Czech Republic 49°09′N 15°01′E
Jing *see* Beijing Shi
Jing *see* Jinghe, China
159 X10 **Jingchuan** Gansu, C China 35°20′N 107°45′E
161 Q10 **Jingdezhen** Jiangxi, S China 29°18′N 117°18′E
161 O12 **Jinggangshan** Jiangxi, S China 26°36′N 114°11′E
161 P3 **Jinghai** Tianjin Shi, E China 38°53′N 116°45′E
158 I4 **Jinghe** *var.* Jing. Xinjiang Uygur Zizhiqu, NW China 44°35′N 82°55′E
160 K6 **Jing He** ≈ C China
160 F15 **Jinghong** *var.* Yunjinghong. Yunnan, SW China 22°03′N 100°56′E
160 M9 **Jingmen** Hubei, C China 30°58′N 112°09′E
163 X10 **Jingpo Hu** ◎ NE China
160 M8 **Jing Shan** ▲ C China
159 V9 **Jingtai** *var.* Yitiaoshan. Gansu, C China 37°12′N 104°06′E
160 J14 **Jingxi** *var.* Xinjing. Guangxi Zhuangzu Zizhiqu, S China 23°10′N 106°22′E
Jing Xian *see* Jingzhou, Hunan, China
163 W11 **Jingyu** Jilin, NE China 42°23′N 126°48′E
159 V10 **Jingyuan** *var.* Wulan. Gansu, C China 36°35′N 104°40′E
160 M9 **Jingzhou** *prev.* Shashi, Shashih, Shasi. Hubei, C China 30°21′N 112°09′E
160 L12 **Jingzhou** *var.* Jing Xian, Jingzhou Miaouzu Dongzu Zizhixian, Quyang. Hunan, S China 26°35′N 109°40′E
Jingzhou Miaouzu Dongzu Zizhixian *see* Jingzhou
Jinhe *see* Jinping
161 R10 **Jinhua** Zhejiang, SE China 29°15′N 119°36′E
Jinhuan *see* Jianchuan
161 P5 **Jining** Shandong, E China 35°25′N 116°35′E
Jining *see* Ulan Qab
81 G18 **Jinja** S Uganda 0°27′N 33°14′E
161 R13 **Jinjiang** *var.* Qingyang. Fujian, SE China 24°53′N 118°36′E
161 O11 **Jin Jiang** ≈ S China
Jinjiang *see* Chengmai
171 V15 **Jin, Kepulauan** *island group* E Indonesia
Jinmen Dao *see* Chinmen Tao
42 J9 **Jinotega** Jinotega, NW Nicaragua 13°03′N 85°59′W
42 K7 **Jinotega** ◐ *department* N Nicaragua
42 J11 **Jinotepe** Carazo, SW Nicaragua 11°50′N 86°10′W
160 L13 **Jinping** *var.* Sanjiang. Guizhou, S China 26°42′N 109°13′E
160 H14 **Jinping** *var.* Jinhe. Yunnan, SW China 22°47′N 103°12′E
Jinsen *see* Inch'ŏn
160 J11 **Jinsha** Guizhou, S China 27°24′N 106°16′E
157 N12 **Jinsha Jiang** *Eng.* Yangtze. ≈ SW China
160 M10 **Jinshi** Hunan, S China 29°42′N 111°46′E
Jinshi *see* Xinning
162 I9 **Jinst** *var.* Bodī. Bayanhongor, C Mongolia 45°25′N 100°33′E
159 R7 **Jinta** Gansu, N China 40°01′N 98°57′E
161 Q12 **Jin Xi** ≈ SE China
Jinxi *see* Huludao
Jinxian *see* Jinzhou
161 P6 **Jinxiang** Shandong, E China 35°08′N 116°19′E
161 P8 **Jinzhai** *var.* Meishan. Anhui, E China 31°42′N 115°47′E
161 N4 **Jinzhong** *var.* Yuci. Shanxi, C China 37°34′N 112°45′E
163 U14 **Jinzhou** *prev.* Jinxian. Liaoning, NE China 39°04′N 121°45′E
163 T12 **Jinzhou** *var.* Chin-chou, Chinchow; *prev.* Chinhsien. Liaoning, NE China 41°07′N 121°06′E
Jinzhu *see* Daocheng
138 H12 **Jinz, Qā' al** ◎ C Jordan
47 S8 **Jiparaná, Rio** ≈ W Brazil
56 A7 **Jipijapa** Manabí, W Ecuador 01°23′S 80°35′W
42 F8 **Jiquilisco** Usulután, S El Salvador 13°19′N 88°35′W
Jirgalanta *see* Hovd
147 S12 **Jirgatol** *Rus.* Dzhirgatal'. C Tajikistan 39°13′N 71°09′E
75 X10 **Jirjā** *var.* Girga, Jirjā, Girgeh. C Egypt 26°17′N 31°58′E
Jirjā *see* Jirjā
111 B15 **Jirkov** *Ger.* Görkau. Ústecký Kraj, NW Czech Republic 50°30′N 13°27′E
143 T12 **Jīroft** *var.* Sabzvārān. Kermān, SE Iran 28°40′N 57°40′E
160 L11 **Jishou** Hunan, S China 28°20′N 109°43′E
Jisr ash Shadadi *see* Ash Shadādah
116 I14 **Jitaru** Olt, S Romania 44°27′N 24°32′E
Jitschin *see* Jičín
116 H14 **Jiu** *Ger.* Schil, Schyl, *Hung.* Zsil, Zsily. ≈ S Romania
161 R11 **Jiufeng Shan** ▲▲ SE China
161 P9 **Jiujiang** Jiangxi, S China 29°45′N 115°59′E
161 O10 **Jiuling Shan** ▲ S China
160 G10 **Jiulong** *var.* Garba, *Tib.* Gyaisi. Sichuan, C China 29°00′N 101°30′E
161 Q13 **Jiulong Jiang** ≈ SE China
161 Q12 **Jiulong Xi** ≈ SE China
159 R8 **Jiuquan** *var.* Suzhou. Gansu, N China 39°47′N 98°30′E
160 K17 **Jiusuo** Hainan, S China 18°25′N 109°55′E
163 W10 **Jiutai** Jilin, NE China 44°01′N 125°51′E
160 K13 **Jiuwan Dashan** ▲▲ S China
160 I7 **Jiuzhaigou** *prev.* Nanping. Sichuan, C China 33°23′N 104°05′E
148 I16 **Jīwani** Baluchistān, SW Pakistan 25°05′N 61°46′E
163 Y8 **Jixi** Heilongjiang, NE China 45°17′N 131°01′E
163 Y7 **Jixian** *var.* Jichang. Heilongjiang, NE China 46°43′N 131°10′E
160 M5 **Jixian** *var.* Ji Xian. Shanxi, C China 36°15′N 110°41′E
Ji Xian *see* Jixian
Jīza *see* Al Jīzah
141 N13 **Jīzān** *var.* Qīzān. Jīzān, SW Saudi Arabia 17°50′N 42°50′E
141 N13 **Jīzān** *var.* Minṭaqat Jīzān. ◐ *province* SW Saudi Arabia
Jīzān, Minṭaqat *see* Jīzān
140 K6 **Jizl, Wādī al** *dry watercourse* W Saudi Arabia
164 H12 **Jizō-zaki** *headland* Honshū, SW Japan 35°34′N 133°16′E
141 U14 **Jiz', Wādī al** *dry watercourse* E Yemen
147 O11 **Jizzax** *Rus.* Dzhizak. Jizzax Viloyati, C Uzbekistan 40°08′N 67°47′E
147 N10 **Jizzax Viloyati** *Rus.* Dzhizakskaya Oblast'. ◐ *province* C Uzbekistan
60 I13 **Joaçaba** Santa Catarina, S Brazil 27°08′S 51°30′W
Joal *see* Joal-Fadiout
76 F11 **Joal-Fadiout** *prev.* Joal. W Senegal 14°09′N 16°50′W
76 E10 **João Barrosa** Boa Vista, E Cape Verde 16°01′N 22°44′W
João Belo *see* Xai-Xai
João de Almeida *see* Chibia
59 Q15 **João Pessoa** *prev.* Paraíba. *state capital* Paraíba, E Brazil 07°06′S 34°53′W
25 X7 **Joaquin** Texas, SW USA 31°58′N 94°03′W
62 K6 **Joaquín V. González** Salta, N Argentina 25°06′S 64°07′W
Joazeiro *see* Juazeiro
Job'urg *see* Johannesburg
109 O7 **Jochberger Ache** ≈ W Austria
Jo-ch'iang *see* Ruoqiang
92 K12 **Jock** Norrbotten, N Sweden 66°40′N 22°45′E
42 I5 **Jocón** Yoro, N Honduras 15°17′N 86°55′W
105 O13 **Jódar** Andalucía, S Spain 37°51′N 03°18′W
152 F12 **Jodhpur** Rājasthān, NW India 26°17′N 73°02′E
99 I19 **Jodoigne** Walloon Brabant, C Belgium 50°43′N 04°52′E
93 O16 **Joensuu** Itä-Suomi, SE Finland 62°36′N 29°45′E
37 W4 **Joes** Colorado, C USA 39°36′N 102°40′W
191 Z3 **Joe's Hill** *hill* Kiritimati, NE Kiribati
165 N11 **Jōetsu** *var.* Zyôetu. Niigata, Honshū, C Japan 37°09′N 138°13′E
83 M18 **Jofane** Inhambane, S Mozambique 21°16′S 34°21′E
153 R12 **Jogbani** Bihār, NE India 26°23′N 87°16′E
118 I5 **Jõgeva** *Ger.* Laisholm. Jõgevamaa, E Estonia 58°48′N 26°28′E
118 I4 **Jõgevamaa** *off.* Jõgeva Maakond. ◐ *province* E Estonia
Jõgeva Maakond *see* Jõgevamaa
155 E18 **Jog Falls** *Waterfall* Karnātaka, W India
143 S4 **Joghatāy** Khorāsān, NE Iran 36°34′N 57°00′E
153 U12 **Jogīghopa** Assam, NE India 26°14′N 90°35′E
152 I7 **Jogindarnagar** Himāchal Pradesh, N India 31°51′N 76°47′E
Jogjakarta *see* Yogyakarta
164 L11 **Jōhana** Toyama, Honshū, SW Japan 36°30′N 136°53′E
83 J21 **Johannesburg** *var.* Egoli, Erautini, Gauteng, *abbrev.* Job'urg. Gauteng, NE South Africa 26°10′S 28°02′E
35 T13 **Johannesburg** California, W USA 35°20′N 117°37′W
Johannisburg *see* Pisz
149 P14 **Johi** Sind, SE Pakistan 26°46′N 67°28′E
55 T13 **Johi Village** S Guyana 01°48′N 58°33′W
32 K13 **John Day** Oregon, NW USA 44°25′N 118°57′W
32 I11 **John Day River** ≈ Oregon, NW USA
18 L14 **John F Kennedy** ✈ (New York) Long Island, New York, NE USA 40°39′N 73°45′W
21 V8 **John H. Kerr Reservoir** *var.* Buggs Island Lake, Kerr Lake. ⊠ North Carolina/Virginia, SE USA
37 V6 **John Martin Reservoir** ⊠ Colorado, C USA
96 K6 **John o'Groats** N Scotland, United Kingdom 58°38′N 03°03′W
27 P5 **John Redmond Reservoir** ⊠ Kansas, C USA
39 Q7 **John River** ≈ Alaska, USA
26 H6 **Johnson** Kansas, C USA 37°33′N 101°46′W
18 M7 **Johnson** Vermont, NE USA 44°39′N 72°40′W
18 D13 **Johnsonburg** Pennsylvania, NE USA 41°28′N 78°37′W
18 H11 **Johnson City** New York, NE USA 42°06′N 75°54′W
21 P8 **Johnson City** Tennessee, S USA 36°18′N 82°21′W
25 R10 **Johnson City** Texas, SW USA 30°17′N 98°27′W
35 S12 **Johnsondale** California, W USA 35°58′N 118°32′W
10 I8 **Johnsons Crossing** Yukon Territory, W Canada 60°30′N 133°15′W
21 T13 **Johnsonville** South Carolina, SE USA 33°50′N 79°26′W
21 Q13 **Johnston** South Carolina, SE USA 33°49′N 81°48′W
192 M6 **Johnston Atoll** ◇ *US unincorporated territory* C Pacific Ocean
175 Q3 **Johnston Atoll** *atoll* C Pacific Ocean
30 L17 **Johnston City** Illinois, N USA 37°49′N 88°55′W
180 K12 **Johnston, Lake** *salt lake* Western Australia
31 S13 **Johnstown** Ohio, N USA 40°08′N 82°39′W
18 D15 **Johnstown** Pennsylvania, NE USA 40°20′N 78°56′W
168 L10 **Johor** *var.* Johore. ◐ *state* Peninsular Malaysia
Johor Baharu *see* Johor Bahru
168 K10 **Johor Bahru** *var.* Johor Baharu, Johore Bahru. Johor, Peninsular Malaysia 01°29′N 103°44′E
Johore *see* Johor
Johore Bahru *see* Johor Bahru
118 K3 **Jõhvi** *Ger.* Jewe. Ida-Virumaa, NE Estonia 59°21′N 27°25′E
103 P7 **Joigny** Yonne, C France 47°58′N 03°24′E
Joinville *see* Joinville
60 K12 **Joinville** *var.* Joinville. Santa Catarina, S Brazil 26°20′S 48°55′W
103 R6 **Joinville** Haute-Marne, N France 48°26′N 05°07′E
194 H3 **Joinville Island** *island* Antarctica
41 O15 **Jojutla** *var.* Jojutla de Juárez. Morelos, S Mexico 18°38′N 99°10′W
Jojutla de Juárez *see* Jojutla
92 I12 **Jokkmokk** *Lapp.* Dálvvadis. Norrbotten, N Sweden 66°35′N 19°57′E
92 L2 **Jökulsá á Dal** ≈ E Iceland
92 K2 **Jökulsá á Fjöllum** ≈ NE Iceland
Jokyakarta *see* Yogyakarta
30 M11 **Joliet** Illinois, N USA 41°33′N 88°05′W
15 O11 **Joliette** Québec, SE Canada 46°02′N 73°27′W
171 O8 **Jolo** Jolo Island, SW Philippines 06°02′N 121°00′E
94 D11 **Jølstervatnet** ◎ S Norway
169 S16 **Jombang** *prev.* Djombang. Jawa, S Indonesia 07°33′S 112°14′E
159 R14 **Jomda** Xizang Zizhiqu, W China 31°26′N 98°09′E
118 G13 **Jonava** *Ger.* Janow, *Pol.* Janów. Kaunas, C Lithuania 55°05′N 24°19′E
146 L11 **Jondor** *Rus.* Zhondor. Buxoro Viloyati, C Uzbekistan 39°46′N 64°11′E
159 V11 **Jonê** *var.* Liulin. Gansu, C China 34°36′N 103°39′E
27 X9 **Jonesboro** Arkansas, C USA 35°50′N 90°42′W
23 S4 **Jonesboro** Georgia, SE USA 33°31′N 84°21′W
30 L17 **Jonesboro** Illinois, N USA 37°25′N 89°19′W
22 H5 **Jonesboro** Louisiana, S USA 32°14′N 92°43′W
21 P8 **Jonesboro** Tennessee, S USA 36°17′N 82°28′W
19 T6 **Jonesport** Maine, NE USA 44°33′N 67°35′W
0 J4 **Jones Sound** *channel* Nunavut, N Canada
22 I6 **Jonesville** Louisiana, S USA 31°37′N 91°49′W
31 Q10 **Jonesville** Michigan, N USA 41°58′N 84°39′W
21 Q11 **Jonesville** South Carolina, SE USA 34°49′N 81°38′W
146 K10 **Jongeldi** *Rus.* Dzhankel'dy. Buxoro Viloyati, C Uzbekistan 40°50′N 63°16′E
81 F14 **Jonglei** Jonglei, SE Sudan 06°54′N 31°19′E
81 F14 **Jonglei** *var.* Gongoleh State. ◐ *state* SE Sudan
81 F14 **Jonglei Canal** *canal* S Sudan
118 F11 **Joniškėlis** Panevėžys, N Lithuania 56°02′N 24°10′E
118 F10 **Joniškis** *Ger.* Janischken. Šiauliai, N Lithuania 56°15′N 23°36′E
95 L19 **Jönköping** Jönköping, S Sweden 57°45′N 14°10′E
95 K20 **Jönköping** ◐ *county* S Sweden
15 Q7 **Jonquière** Québec, SE Canada 48°25′N 71°16′W
41 V15 **Jonuta** Tabasco, SE Mexico 18°04′N 92°03′W
102 K12 **Jonzac** Charente-Maritime, W France 45°26′N 00°25′W
27 R7 **Joplin** Missouri, C USA 37°04′N 94°31′W
33 W8 **Jordan** Montana, NW USA 47°18′N 106°54′W
138 H12 **Jordan** *off.* Hashemite Kingdom of Jordan, *Ar.* Al Mamlaka al Urdunīya al Hashemīyah, Al Urdunn; *prev.* Transjordan. ◆ *monarchy* SW Asia
138 G9 **Jordan** *Ar.* Urdunn, *Heb.* HaYarden. ≈ SW Asia
Jordan Lake *see* B. Everett Jordan Reservoir
111 K17 **Jordanów** Małopolskie, S Poland 49°39′N 19°51′E
32 M15 **Jordan Valley** Oregon, NW USA 42°59′N 117°03′W
138 G9 **Jordan Valley** *valley* N Israel
57 D15 **Jorge Chávez International** *var.* Lima. ✈ (Lima) Lima, W Peru 12°07′S 77°01′W
113 L23 **Jorgucat** *var.* Jergucati, Jorgucati. Gjirokastër, S Albania 39°57′N 20°14′E
Jorgucati *see* Jorgucat
153 X12 **Jorhāt** Assam, NE India 26°45′N 94°09′E
93 J14 **Jörn** Västerbotten, N Sweden 65°03′N 20°04′E
37 R14 **Jornada Del Muerto** *valley* New Mexico, SW USA
93 N17 **Joroinen** Itä-Suomi, E Finland 62°11′N 27°50′E
95 C16 **Jørpeland** Rogaland, S Norway 59°01′N 06°04′E
77 W14 **Jos** Plateau, C Nigeria 09°54′N 08°53′E
171 Q8 **Jose Abad Santos** *var.* Trinidad. Mindanao, S Philippines 05°51′N 125°35′E
61 F19 **José Batlle y Ordóñez** *var.* Batlle y Ordóñez. Florida, C Uruguay 33°28′S 55°08′W
63 H18 **José de San Martín** Chubut, S Argentina 44°04′S 70°29′W
61 E19 **José Enrique Rodó** *var.* Rodó, José E.Rodo; *prev.* Drabble, Drable. Soriano, SW Uruguay 33°43′S 57°33′W
José E.Rodo *see* José Enrique Rodó
Josefsdorf *see* Žabalj
44 C4 **José Martí** ✈ (La Habana) Cuidad de La Habana, N Cuba 23°03′N 82°22′W
61 F19 **José Pedro Varela** *var.* José P.Varela. Lavalleja, S Uruguay 33°30′S 54°28′W
181 N2 **Joseph Bonaparte Gulf** *gulf* N Australia
37 N11 **Joseph City** Arizona, SW USA 34°56′N 110°18′W
13 O9 **Joseph, Lake** ◎ Newfoundland and Labrador, E Canada
14 G13 **Joseph, Lake** ◎ Ontario, S Canada
186 C6 **Josephstaal** Madang, N Papua New Guinea 04°42′S 144°55′E
José P.Varela *see* José Pedro Varela
59 J14 **José Rodrigues** Pará, N Brazil 05°45′S 51°20′W
152 K9 **Joshimath** Uttarakhand, N India 30°33′N 79°35′E
25 T7 **Joshua** Texas, SW USA 32°27′N 97°23′W
35 V15 **Joshua Tree** California, W USA 34°07′N 116°18′W
77 V14 **Jos Plateau** *plateau* C Nigeria
102 H6 **Josselin** Morbihan, NW France 47°57′N 02°35′W
Jos Sudarso *see* Yos Sudarso, Pulau
94 E11 **Jostedalsbreen** *glacier* S Norway
94 F12 **Jotunheimen** ▲▲ S Norway
138 G7 **Joûnié** *var.* Juniyah. W Lebanon 33°54′N 35°36′E
25 R13 **Jourdanton** Texas, SW USA 28°55′N 98°34′W
98 L7 **Joure** *Fris.* De Jouwer. Friesland, N Netherlands 52°58′N 05°48′E
93 M18 **Joutsa** Länsi-Suomi, C Finland 61°46′N 26°09′E
93 N18 **Joutseno** Etelä-Suomi, SE Finland 61°06′N 28°30′E
92 M12 **Joutsijärvi** Lappi, NE Finland 66°40′N 28°00′E
108 A9 **Joux, Lac de** ◎ W Switzerland
143 O12 **Jovakān** Fārs, S Iran
44 D5 **Jovellanos** Matanzas, W Cuba 22°49′N 81°11′W
153 V13 **Jowai** Meghālaya, NE India 25°25′N 92°21′E
Jowat *see* Jabwot
Jowhar *see* Jawhar
Jowzam *see* Javazm
149 N2 **Jowzjān** ◐ *province* N Afghanistan
Joypurhat *see* Jaipurhat
Józseffalva *see* Žabalj
J.Storm Thurmond Reservoir *see* Clark Hill Lake
45 T6 **Juana Díaz** C Puerto Rico 18°03′N 66°30′W
40 L9 **Juan Aldama** Zacatecas, C Mexico 24°20′N 103°23′W
0 E9 **Juan de Fuca Plate** *tectonic feature*
32 F7 **Juan de Fuca, Strait of** *strait* Canada/USA
Juan Fernandez Islands *see* Juan Fernández, Islas
193 S11 **Juan Fernández, Islas** *Eng.* Juan Fernandez Islands. *island group* W Chile
55 O4 **Juangriego** Nueva Esparta, NE Venezuela 11°06′N 63°59′W
56 D11 **Juanjuí** *var.* Juanjuy. San Martín, N Peru 07°10′S 76°44′W
Juanjuy *see* Juanjuí
93 N16 **Juankoski** Itä-Suomi, C Finland 63°01′N 28°24′E
Juan Lacaze *see* Juan L. Lacaze
61 E20 **Juan L. Lacaze** *var.* Juan Lacaze, Puerto Sauce; *prev.* Sauce. Colonia, SW Uruguay 34°26′S 57°25′W
62 L5 **Juan Solá** Salta, N Argentina 23°30′S 62°42′W
63 F21 **Juan Stuven, Isla** *island* S Chile
59 H16 **Juará** Mato Grosso, W Brazil 11°10′S 57°28′W
41 N7 **Juárez** *var.* Villa Juárez. Coahuila, NE Mexico 27°39′N 100°43′W
40 C2 **Juárez, Sierra de** ▲▲ NW Mexico
59 O15 **Juazeiro** *prev.* Joazeiro. Bahia, E Brazil 09°25′S 40°30′W
59 P14 **Juazeiro do Norte** Ceará, E Brazil 07°10′S 39°18′W
81 F15 **Juba** *var.* Jūbā. Bahr el Gabel, S Sudan 04°50′N 31°35′E
81 L17 **Juba** *Amh.* Genalē Wenz, *It.* Guiba, *Som.* Ganaane, Webi Jubba. ≈ Ethiopia/Somalia
194 H2 **Jubany** *Argentinian research station* Antarctica 61°57′S 58°23′W
Jubayl *see* Jbaïl
81 L18 **Jubbada Dhexe** *off.* Gobolka Jubbada Dhexe. ◐ *region* SW Somalia
Jubbada Dhexe, Gobolka *see* Jubbada Dhexe
81 K18 **Jubbada Hoose** ◐ *region* SW Somalia
Jubba, Webi *see* Juba
Jubbulpore *see* Jabalpur
Jubeil *see* Jbaïl
74 B9 **Juby, Cap** *headland* SW Morocco 27°58′N 12°56′W
105 R10 **Júcar** *var.* Jucar. ≈ C Spain
40 L12 **Juchipila** Zacatecas, C Mexico 21°25′N 103°06′W
41 S16 **Juchitán** *var.* Juchitán de Zaragosa. Oaxaca, SE Mexico 16°27′N 95°W
Juchitán de Zaragosa *see* Juchitán
138 G11 **Judaea** *cultural region* Israel/West Bank
138 F11 **Judaean Hills** *Heb.* Haré Yehuda. *hill range* E Israel
138 H8 **Judaydah** *Fr.* Jdaïdé. Dimashq, W Syria 33°17′N 36°15′E
139 P11 **Judayyidat Hāmir** Al Anbār, S Iraq 31°50′N 41°50′E
109 U8 **Judenburg** Steiermark, C Austria 47°09′N 14°43′E
33 T8 **Judith River** ≈ Montana, NW USA
27 V11 **Judsonia** Arkansas, C USA 35°16′N 91°38′W
141 P14 **Jufrah, Wādī al** *dry watercourse* NW Yemen
Jugar *see* Sêrxü
Jugoslavija *see* Serbia
42 K10 **Juigalpa** Chontales, S Nicaragua 12°04′N 85°21′W
161 T13 **Juishui** C Taiwan 23°43′N 121°28′E
100 E9 **Juist** *island* NW Germany
59 M21 **Juiz de Fora** Minas Gerais, SE Brazil 21°47′S 43°23′W
62 J5 **Jujuy** *off.* Provincia de Jujuy. ◐ *province* N Argentina
Jujuy *see* San Salvador de Jujuy
Jujuy, Provincia de *see* Jujuy
92 J11 **Jukkasjärvi** *Lapp.* Čohkkiras. Norrbotten, N Sweden 67°52′N 20°39′E
Jula *see* Gyula, Hungary
Jūlā *see* Jālū, Libya
37 W2 **Julesburg** Colorado, C USA 40°59′N 102°15′W
Julia Beterrae *see* Béziers
57 I17 **Juliaca** Puno, SE Peru 15°32′S 70°10′W
181 U6 **Julia Creek** Queensland, C Australia 20°40′S 141°49′E
35 V17 **Julian** California, W USA 33°04′N 116°36′W
98 H7 **Julianadorp** Noord-Holland, NW Netherlands 52°53′N 04°43′E
109 S11 **Julian Alps** *Ger.* Julische Alpen, *It.* Alpi Giulie, *Slvn.* Julijske Alpe. ▲▲ Italy/Slovenia
55 V11 **Juliana Top** ▲ C Surinam 03°39′N 56°36′W
Julianehåb *see* Qaqortoq
Julijske Alpe *see* Julian Alps
40 J6 **Julimes** Chihuahua, N Mexico 28°29′N 105°21′W
Julio Briga *see* Bragança
Juliobriga *see* Logroño
61 G15 **Júlio de Castilhos** Rio Grande do Sul, S Brazil 29°14′S 53°42′W
Juliomagus *see* Angers
Julische Alpen *see* Julian Alps
Jullundur *see* Jalandhar
147 N11 **Juma** *Rus.* Dzhuma. Samarqand Viloyati, C Uzbekistan 39°43′N 66°37′E
161 O3 **Juma He** ≈ E China
81 L18 **Jumboo** Jubbada Hoose, S Somalia 0°12′S 42°34′E
35 Y11 **Jumbo Peak** ▲ Nevada, W USA 36°12′N 114°09′W
105 R12 **Jumilla** Murcia, SE Spain 38°28′N 01°19′W
153 N10 **Jumla** Mid Western, NW Nepal 29°22′N 82°13′E
Jummoo *see* Jammu
Jumna *see* Yamuna
Jumporn *see* Chumphon
30 K5 **Jump River** ≈ Wisconsin, N USA
154 B11 **Jūnāgadh** *var.* Junagarh. Gujarāt, W India 21°32′N 70°32′E
Junagarh *see* Jūnāgadh
161 Q6 **Junan** *var.* Shizilu. Shandong, E China 35°11′N 118°47′E
62 G11 **Juncal, Cerro** ▲ C Chile 33°03′S 70°02′W
25 Q10 **Junction** Texas, SW USA 30°31′N 99°48′W
36 K6 **Junction** Utah, W USA 38°14′N 112°13′W
27 O4 **Junction City** Kansas, C USA 39°02′N 96°51′W
32 F13 **Junction City** Oregon, NW USA 44°13′N 123°12′W
60 M10 **Jundiaí** São Paulo, S Brazil 23°10′S 46°54′W
39 X12 **Juneau** *state capital* Alaska, USA 58°13′N 134°11′W
30 M8 **Juneau** Wisconsin, N USA 43°23′N 88°42′W
105 U6 **Juneda** Cataluña, NE Spain 41°33′N 00°49′E
183 Q9 **Junee** New South Wales, SE Australia 34°51′S 147°33′E
35 R8 **June Lake** California, W USA 37°46′N 119°04′W
Jungbunzlau *see* Mladá Boleslav
158 L4 **Junggar Pendi** *Eng.* Dzungarian Basin. *basin* NW China
99 N24 **Junglinster** Grevenmacher, C Luxembourg 49°43′N 06°15′E
18 F14 **Juniata River** ≈ Pennsylvania, NE USA
61 B20 **Junín** Buenos Aires, E Argentina 34°36′S 61°02′W
57 E14 **Junín** Junín, C Peru 11°11′S 76°00′W
57 F14 **Junín** *off.* Departamento de Junín. ◐ *department* C Peru
63 H15 **Junín de los Andes** Neuquén, W Argentina 39°57′S 71°05′W
Junín, Departamento de *see* Junín
57 D14 **Junín, Lago de** ◎ C Peru
Junīyah *see* Joûnié
Junkseylon *see* Phuket
160 I11 **Junlian** Sichuan, C China 28°11′N 104°31′E
25 O11 **Juno** Texas, SW USA 30°09′N 101°07′W
92 J11 **Junosuando** *Lapp.* Čunusavvon. Norrbotten, N Sweden 67°25′N 22°28′E
93 H16 **Junsele** Västernorrland, C Sweden 63°42′N 16°54′E
Junten *see* Sunch'ŏn
32 L14 **Juntura** Oregon, NW USA 43°43′N 118°05′W
93 N14 **Juntusranta** Oulu, E Finland 65°12′N 29°30′E
118 H11 **Juodupė** Panevėžys, NE Lithuania 56°07′N 25°37′E
119 H14 **Juozapinės Kalnas** ▲ SE Lithuania 54°29′N 25°27′E
99 K19 **Jupille** Liège, E Belgium 50°43′N 05°31′E
80 D13 **Jur** ≈ C Sudan
103 S9 **Jura** ◐ *department* E France
108 C7 **Jura** ◐ *canton* NW Switzerland
108 B8 **Jura** *var.* Jura Mountains. ▲▲ France/Switzerland
96 G12 **Jura** *island* SW Scotland, United Kingdom
Juraciszki *see* Yuratsishki
54 C8 **Juradó** Chocó, NW Colombia 07°07′N 77°45′W
Jura Mountains *see* Jura
96 G12 **Jura, Sound of** *strait* W Scotland, United Kingdom
139 V15 **Juraybīyāt, Bi'r** *well* S Iraq
118 E13 **Jurbarkas** *Ger.* Georgenburg, Jurburg. Tauragė, W Lithuania 55°04′N 22°45′E
99 F20 **Jurbise** Hainaut, SW Belgium 50°33′N 03°54′E
Jurburg *see* Jurbarkas
118 F9 **Jūrmala** Rīga, C Latvia 56°57′N 23°42′E
58 D13 **Juruá** Amazonas, NW Brazil 03°08′S 65°59′W
48 F7 **Juruá, Rio** *var.* Río Yuruá. ≈ Brazil/Peru
59 G16 **Juruena** Mato Grosso, W Brazil 10°32′S 58°38′W
59 G16 **Juruena, Rio** ≈ W Brazil
165 Q6 **Jūsan-ko** ◎ Honshū, C Japan
25 O6 **Justiceburg** Texas, SW USA 32°57′N 101°07′W
Justinianopolis *see* Kirşehir
62 K11 **Justo Daract** San Luis, C Argentina 33°52′S 65°12′W
59 C14 **Jutaí** Amazonas, W Brazil 05°10′S 68°45′W
58 C13 **Jutaí, Rio** ≈ NW Brazil
100 N13 **Jüterbog** Brandenburg, E Germany 51°58′N 13°06′E
42 E6 **Jutiapa** Jutiapa, S Guatemala 14°18′N 89°52′W
42 A3 **Jutiapa** *off.* Departamento de Jutiapa. ◐ *department* SE Guatemala
Jutiapa, Departamento de *see* Jutiapa
42 J6 **Juticalpa** Olancho, C Honduras 14°39′N 86°12′W
82 I13 **Jutila** North Western, NW Zambia 12°33′S 26°09′E
Jutland *see* Jylland
84 F8 **Jutland Bank** *undersea feature* SE North Sea 56°50′N 07°20′E
93 N16 **Juuka** Itä-Suomi, E Finland 63°12′N 29°17′E
93 N17 **Juva** Itä-Suomi, E Finland 61°55′N 27°54′E
Juvavum *see* Salzburg
44 A6 **Juventud, Isla de la** *var.* Isla de Pinos, *Eng.* Isle of Youth; *prev.* The Isle of the Pines. *island* W Cuba
161 Q5 **Juxian** *var.* Chengyang, Ju Xian. Shandong, E China 35°33′N 118°45′E
Ju Xian *see* Juxian
161 P6 **Juye** Shandong, E China 35°26′N 116°04′E
113 O15 **Južna Morava** *Ger.* Südliche Morava. ≈ SE Serbia
83 H20 **Jwaneng** Southern, S Botswana 24°35′S 24°45′E
95 I23 **Jyderup** Vestsjælland, E Denmark 55°40′N 11°25′E
95 F22 **Jylland** *Eng.* Jutland. *peninsula* W Denmark
Jyrgalan *see* Dzhergalan
93 M17 **Jyväskylä** Länsi-Suomi, C Finland 62°08′N 25°47′E

K

38 D9 **Ka'a'awa** *var.* Kaaawa. O'ahu, Hawaii, USA, C Pacific Ocean 21°33′N 157°47′W
Kaaawa *see* Ka'a'awa
81 G16 **Kaabong** NE Uganda 03°30′N 34°08′E
Kaaden *see* Kadaň
Kaafu Atoll *see* Male' Atoll
55 V9 **Kaaimanston** Sipaliwini, N Surinam 05°06′N 56°04′W
Kaakhka *see* Kaka
Kaala *see* Caála
187 O16 **Kaala-Gomen** Province Nord, W New Caledonia 20°40′S 164°24′E
92 L9 **Kaamanen** *Lapp.* Gámas. Lappi, N Finland 69°05′N 27°16′E
Kaapstad *see* Cape Town
Kaarasjoki *see* Karasjok
Kaaresuanto *see* Karesuando
92 J10 **Kaaresuvanto** *Lapp.* Gárassavon. Lappi, N Finland 68°28′N 22°29′E
93 K19 **Kaarina** Länsi-Suomi, SW Finland 60°24′N 22°25′E
99 I14 **Kaatsheuvel** Noord-Brabant, S Netherlands 51°39′N 05°02′E
93 N16 **Kaavi** Itä-Suomi, C Finland 62°58′N 28°30′E
Kaba *see* Habahe
171 O14 **Kabaena, Pulau** *island* C Indonesia
Kabakly *see* Gabakly
76 J14 **Kabala** N Sierra Leone 09°40′N 11°36′W
81 E19 **Kabale** SW Uganda 01°15′S 29°58′E
55 U10 **Kabalebo Rivier** ≈ W Surinam

◆ Country ● Country Capital ◇ Dependent Territory ○ Dependent Territory Capital ◐ Administrative Regions ✈ International Airport ▲ Mountain ▲▲ Mountain Range Volcano ≈ River ◎ Lake ⊠ Reservoir

79 N22 **Kabalo** Katanga, SE Dem. Rep. Congo 06°02′S 26°55′E
79 O21 **Kabambare** Maniema, E Dem. Rep. Congo 04°40′S 27°41′E
145 W13 **Kabanbay** *Kaz.* Qabanbay; *prev.* Andreyevka, *Kaz.* Andreevka. Almaty, SE Kazakhstan 45°50′N 80°34′E
187 Y15 **Kabara** *prev.* Kambara. *island* Lau Group, E Fiji
Kabardino-Balkaria *see* Kabardino-Balkarskaya Respublika
126 M15 **Kabardino-Balkarskaya Respublika** *Eng.* Kabardino-Balkaria. ◆ *autonomous republic* SW Russian Federation
79 O19 **Kabare** Sud-Kivu, E Dem. Rep. Congo
171 T11 **Kabarei** Papua, E Indonesia 0°01′S 130°58′E
171 P7 **Kabasalan** Mindanao, S Philippines 07°46′N 122°49′E
77 U15 **Kabba** Kogi, S Nigeria 07°48′N 06°07′E
92 I13 **Kåbdalis** *Lapp.* Goabddális. Norrbotten, N Sweden 66°08′N 20°03′E
138 M6 **Kabd aş Şārim** *hill range* E Syria
14 B7 **Kabenung Lake** ◎ Ontario, S Canada
29 W3 **Kabetogama Lake** ◎ Minnesota, N USA
Kabia, Pulau *see* Kabin, Pulau
79 M22 **Kabinda** Kasai-Oriental, SE Dem. Rep. Congo 06°09′S 24°29′E
Kabinda *see* Cabinda
171 O15 **Kabin, Pulau** *var.* Pulau Kabia. *island* W Indonesia
171 P16 **Kabir** Pulau Pantar, S Indonesia 08°15′S 124°12′E
149 T10 **Kabīrwāla** Punjab, E Pakistan 30°24′N 71°51′E
114 M9 **Kableshkovo** Burgas, E Bulgaria 42°65′N 27°34′E
78 I13 **Kabo** Ouham, NW Central African Republic 07°43′N 18°38′E
149 Q5 **Kābol** *var.* Kabul, *Pash.* Kābul. ● (Afghanistan) Kābul, E Afghanistan 34°34′N 69°08′E
149 Q5 **Kābol** *Eng.* Kabul, *Pash.* Kābul. ◆ *province* E Afghanistan
149 Q5 **Kābol** ✕ Kābul, E Afghanistan 34°31′N 69°11′E
83 H14 **Kabompo** North Western, W Zambia 13°36′S 24°10′E
83 H14 **Kabompo** ➶ W Zambia
79 M22 **Kabongo** Katanga, SE Dem. Rep. Congo
120 K11 **Kaboudia, Rass** *headland* E Tunisia 35°13′N 11°09′E
124 J14 **Kabozha** Novgorodskaya Oblast', W Russian Federation 58°48′N 35°00′E
Kabūd Gonbad *see* Kalāt
142 L5 **Kabūd Rāhang** Hamadān, W Iran 35°12′N 48°44′E
82 L12 **Kabwe** Northern, NE Zambia 11°31′S 31°16′E
149 R5 **Kabul** *var.* Daryā-ye Kābul. ➶ Afghanistan/Pakistan *see also* Kābul, Daryā-ye
Kābul *see* Kābol
149 S5 **Kābul, Daryā-ye** *var.* Kabul. ➶ Afghanistan/Pakistan *see also* Kabul
Kābul, Daryā-ye *see* Kabul
79 O25 **Kabunda** Katanga, SE Dem. Rep. Congo 12°21′S 29°14′E
171 R9 **Kaburuang, Pulau** *island* Kepulauan Talaud, N Indonesia
80 G8 **Kabushiya** River Nile, NE Sudan 16°54′N 33°41′E
83 J14 **Kabwe** Central, C Zambia 14°29′S 28°25′E
186 E7 **Kabwum** Morobe, C Papua New Guinea 06°04′S 147°09′E
113 N17 **Kaçanik** *Serb.* Kačanik. S Kosovo 42°13′N 21°16′E
Kačanik *see* Kaçanik
118 F13 **Kačerginė** Kaunas, C Lithuania 54°55′N 23°40′E
117 S13 **Kacha** Respublika Krym, S Ukraine 44°46′N 33°33′E
154 A10 **Kachchh, Gulf of** *var.* Gulf of Cutch, Gulf of Kutch. *gulf* W India
154 I11 **Kachchhidhāna** Madhya Pradesh, C India 21°33′N 78°54′E
149 Q11 **Kachchh, Rann of** *var.* Rann of Kachh, Rann of Kutch. *salt marsh* India/Pakistan
Kachh, Rann of *see* Kachchh, Rann of
39 Q13 **Kachemak Bay** *bay* Alaska, USA
77 V14 **Kachia** Kaduna, C Nigeria 09°52′N 08°00′E
167 N2 **Kachin State** ◆ *state* N Burma (Myanmar)
145 T7 **Kachiry** Pavlodar, NE Kazakhstan 53°07′N 76°08′E
137 Q11 **Kaçkar Dağları** ▲ NE Turkey
155 C21 **Kadamatt Island** *island* Lakshadweep, India, N Indian Ocean
111 B15 **Kadaň** *Ger.* Kaaden. Ústecký Kraj, NW Czech Republic 50°24′N 13°16′E
1667 N11 **Kadan Kyun** *prev.* King Island. *island* Mergui Archipelago, S Burma (Myanmar)
187 X15 **Kadavu** *prev.* Kandavu. *island* S Fiji
187 X15 **Kadavu Passage** *channel* S Fiji
79 G16 **Kadéï** ➶ Cameroon/Central African Republic
Kadhimain *see* Al Kāẓimīyah
114 M13 **Kadıköy Baraji** ◎ NW Turkey
182 I8 **Kadina** South Australia 33°59′S 137°43′E
136 H15 **Kadınhanı** Konya, C Turkey 38°15′N 32°14′E
76 M14 **Kadiolo** Sikasso, S Mali 10°30′N 05°43′W
136 L16 **Kadirli** Osmaniye, S Turkey 37°22′N 36°05′E
114 G11 **Kadiytsa** *Mac.* Kadijica. ▲ Bulgaria/FYR Macedonia 41°48′N 22°58′E
28 L10 **Kadoka** South Dakota, N USA 43°49′N 101°30′W

127 N5 **Kadom** Ryazanskaya Oblast', W Russian Federation 54°35′N 42°27′E
83 K16 **Kadoma** *prev.* Gatooma. Mashonaland West, C Zimbabwe 18°22′S 29°55′E
80 E12 **Kadugli** Southern Kordofan, S Sudan 11°N 29°44′E
77 V14 **Kaduna** Kaduna, C Nigeria 10°32′N 07°26′E
77 V15 **Kaduna** ◆ *state* C Nigeria
77 V15 **Kaduna** ➶ N Nigeria
124 K14 **Kaduy** Vologodskaya Oblast', NW Russian Federation 59°10′N 37°11′E
154 E13 **Kadwa** ➶ W India
123 S9 **Kadykchan** Magadanskaya Oblast', E Russian Federation 62°54′N 146°53′E
125 T7 **Kadzherom** Respublika Komi, NW Russian Federation 64°42′N 55°51′E
147 X8 **Kadzhi-Say** *Kir.* Kajisay. Issyk-Kul'skaya Oblast', NE Kyrgyzstan 42°07′N 77°11′E
76 I10 **Kaédi** Gorgol, S Mauritania 16°12′N 13°32′W
78 G12 **Kaélé** Extrême-Nord, N Cameroon 10°05′N 14°28′E
38 C9 **Ka'ena Point** *var.* Kaena Point. *headland* O'ahu, Hawai'i, USA 21°34′N 158°16′W
184 J2 **Kaeo** Northland, North Island, New Zealand 35°03′S 173°40′E
163 X14 **Kaesŏng** *prev.* Kaesŏng-si. S North Korea 37°58′N 126°31′E
Kaesŏng-si *see* Kaesŏng
Kaewieng *see* Kavieng
79 L24 **Kafakumba** Shaba, S Dem. Rep. Congo 09°39′S 23°43′E
Kafan *see* Kapan
77 V14 **Kafanchan** Kaduna, C Nigeria 09°32′N 08°18′E
Kaffa *see* Feodosiya
76 G11 **Kaffrine** C Senegal 14°07′N 15°27′W
Kafiréas, Akrotírio *see* Ntóro, Kávo
115 I19 **Kafiréos, Stenó** *strait* Évvoia/Kykládes, Greece, Aegean Sea
Kafirnigan *see* Kofarnihon
Kafo *see* Kafu
75 W7 **Kafr ash Shaykh** *var.* Kafr el Sheikh, Kafr el Sheikh. N Egypt 31°07′N 30°56′E
Kafr el Sheikh *see* Kafr ash Shaykh
81 F17 **Kafu** *var.* Kafo. ➶ W Uganda
83 J15 **Kafue** Lusaka, SE Zambia 15°44′S 28°10′E
83 I14 **Kafue** ➶ C Zambia
67 T13 **Kafue Flats** *plain* C Zambia
79 K12 **Kaga** Ishikawa, Honshū, SW Japan 36°18′N 136°19′E
79 J14 **Kaga Bandoro** *prev.* Fort-Crampel. Nana-Grébizi, C Central African Republic 06°54′N 19°10′E
81 E18 **Kagadi** W Uganda 0°57′N 30°52′E
38 H17 **Kagalaska Island** *island* Aleutian Islands, Alaska, USA
Kagan *see* Kogon
Kaganovichabad *see* Kolkhozobod
Kagarlyk *see* Kaharlyk
164 H14 **Kagawa** *off.* Kagawa-ken. ◆ *prefecture* Shikoku, SW Japan
Kagawa-ken *see* Kagawa
154 J13 **Kagaznagar** Andhra Pradesh, C India 19°23′N 79°30′E
93 J14 **Kåge** Västerbotten, N Sweden 64°49′N 21°00′E
81 E19 **Kagera** *var.* Ziwa Magharibi, *Eng.* West Lake. ◆ *region* NW Tanzania
81 E19 **Kagera** *var.* Akagera. ➶ Rwanda/Tanzania *see also* Akagera
76 L5 **Kâghet** *var.* Karet. *physical region* N Mauritania
Kagi *see* Chiai
137 S12 **Kağızman** Kars, NE Turkey 40°08′N 43°07′E
188 I6 **Kagman Point** *headland* Saipan, S Northern Mariana Islands
164 C16 **Kagoshima** *var.* Kagosima. Kagoshima, Kyūshū, SW Japan 31°37′N 130°33′E
164 C16 **Kagoshima** *off.* Kagoshima-ken, *var.* Kagosima. ◆ *prefecture* Kyūshū, SW Japan
Kagoshima-ken *see* Kagoshima
Kagosima *see* Kagoshima
Kagul *see* Cahul
Kagul, Ozero *see* Kahul, Ozero
38 B8 **Kahala Point** *headland* Kaua'i, Hawai'i, USA 22°08′N 159°17′W
81 F21 **Kahama** Shinyanga, NW Tanzania 03°48′S 32°36′E
117 P7 **Kaharlyk** *Rus.* Kagarlyk. Kyyivs'ka Oblast', N Ukraine 49°50′N 30°50′E
169 T13 **Kahayan, Sungai** ➶ Borneo, C Indonesia
79 I22 **Kahemba** Bandundu, SW Dem. Rep. Congo 07°20′S 19°00′E
185 A23 **Kaherekoau Mountains** ▲ South Island, New Zealand
143 W14 **Kahīrī** *var.* Kūhīrī. Sīstān va Balūchestān, SE Iran 26°55′N 61°04′E
101 L16 **Kahla** Thüringen, C Germany 50°49′N 11°33′E
101 G15 **Kahler Asten** ▲ W Germany 51°11′N 08°32′E
149 Q4 **Kahmard, Daryā-ye** *prev.* Darya-i-surkhab. ➶ NE Afghanistan
143 T13 **Kahnūj** Kermān, SE Iran 27°55′N 57°45′E
27 V1 **Kahoka** Missouri, C USA 40°24′N 91°44′W
38 E10 **Kaho'olawe** *var.* Kahoolawe. *island* Hawai'i, USA C Pacific Ocean
Kahoolawe *see* Kaho'olawe
136 M16 **Kahramanmaraş** *var.* Kahraman Maraş, Maraş, Marash. Kahramanmaraş, S Turkey 37°34′N 36°54′E
136 L15 **Kahramanmaraş** *var.* Kahraman Maraş, Maraş, Marash. ◆ *province* C Turkey
Kahraman Maraş *see* Kahramanmaraş

Kahror/Kahror Pakka *see* Karor Pacca
137 N15 **Kâhta** Adıyaman, S Turkey 37°48′N 38°35′E
38 D8 **Kahuku** O'ahu, Hawaii, USA, C Pacific Ocean 21°40′N 157°57′W
38 D8 **Kahuku Point** *headland* O'ahu, Hawai'i, USA 21°42′N 157°26′E
116 M12 **Kahul, Ozero** *var.* Lacul Cahul, *Rus.* Ozero Kagul. ◎ Moldova/Ukraine
143 V11 **Kahūrak** Sīstān va Balūchestān, SE Iran 29°25′N 59°38′E
184 G13 **Kahurangi Point** *headland* South Island, New Zealand 40°41′S 171°57′E
149 N9 **Kahūta** Punjab, E Pakistan 33°37′N 73°26′E
77 S14 **Kaiama** Kwara, W Nigeria 09°37′N 03°58′E
186 C7 **Kaiapit** Morobe, C Papua New Guinea 06°14′S 146°09′E
185 I18 **Kaiapoi** Canterbury, South Island, New Zealand 43°23′S 172°40′E
36 K9 **Kaibab Plateau** *plain* Arizona, SW USA
171 U14 **Kai Besar, Pulau** *island* Kepulauan Kai, E Indonesia
36 L9 **Kaibito Plateau** *plain* Arizona, SW USA
158 K6 **Kaidu He** *var.* Karaxahar. ➶ NW China
55 S10 **Kaieteur Falls** *waterfall* C Guyana
161 O6 **Kaifeng** Henan, C China 34°47′N 114°20′E
184 J2 **Kaihu** Northland, North Island, New Zealand 35°47′S 173°39′E
Kaihua *see* Wenshan
171 U14 **Kai Kecil, Pulau** *island* E Indonesia
169 U16 **Kai, Kepulauan** *prev.* Kei Islands. *island group* Maluku, SE Indonesia
184 J3 **Kaikohe** Northland, North Island, New Zealand 35°25′S 173°48′E
185 J16 **Kaikoura** Canterbury, South Island, New Zealand 42°22′S 173°40′E
185 J16 **Kaikoura Peninsula** *peninsula* South Island, New Zealand
Kailas Range *see* Gangdisê Shan
160 K12 **Kaili** Guizhou, S China 26°34′N 107°58′E
38 F10 **Kailua** Maui, Hawaii, USA, C Pacific Ocean 20°53′N 156°13′W
Kailua *see* Kalaoa
38 G11 **Kailua-Kona** *var.* Kona. Hawaii, USA, C Pacific Ocean 19°43′N 155°58′W
186 B7 **Kaim** ➶ W Papua New Guinea
171 X14 **Kaimana** Papua, E Indonesia 05°36′S 138°39′E
184 M7 **Kaimai Range** ▲ North Island, New Zealand
114 E13 **Kaimakčalan** ▲ Greece/FYR Macedonia 40°57′N 21°48′E *see also* Kajmakčalan
Kaïmaktsalán *see* Kajmakčalan
Kaïmaktsalán *see* Kaïmakčalan
185 C20 **Kaimanawa Mountains** ▲ North Island, New Zealand
118 E4 **Käina** *Ger.* Keinis; *prev.* Keina. Hiiumaa, W Estonia 58°50′N 22°49′E
109 V7 **Kainach** ➶ SE Austria
164 I14 **Kainan** Tokushima, Shikoku, SW Japan 33°36′N 134°20′E
164 H15 **Kainan** Wakayama, Honshū, SW Japan 34°09′N 135°12′E
Kainda *see* Kayyngdy
147 U7 **Kaindy** *Kir.* Kayyngdy. Chuyskaya Oblast', ...
77 T14 **Kainji Dam** *dam* W Nigeria
Kainji Lake *see* Kainji Reservoir
77 T14 **Kainji Reservoir** *var.* Kainji Lake. ◎ W Nigeria
186 D8 **Kaintiba** *var.* Kamina. Gulf, S Papua New Guinea 07°29′S 146°04′E
92 K12 **Kainulasjärvi** Norrbotten, N Sweden 67°00′N 22°31′E
184 K5 **Kaipara Harbour** *harbour* North Island, New Zealand
152 I10 **Kairāna** Uttar Pradesh, N India 29°24′N 77°10′E
74 M6 **Kairouan** *var.* Al Qayrawān. E Tunisia 35°46′N 10°11′E
101 F20 **Kaiserslautern** Rheinland-Pfalz, SW Germany 49°27′N 07°46′E
118 G13 **Kaišiadorys** Kaunas, S Lithuania 54°51′N 24°27′E
184 I2 **Kaitaia** Northland, North Island, New Zealand 35°07′S 173°13′E
185 E24 **Kaitangata** Otago, South Island, New Zealand 46°18′S 169°52′E
152 I9 **Kaithal** Haryana, NW India 29°47′N 76°26′E
169 N13 **Kait, Tanjung** *headland* Sumatera, W Indonesia 03°13′S 106°03′E
38 D9 **Kaiwi Channel** *channel* Hawai'i, USA, C Pacific Ocean
160 K9 **Kaixian** *var.* Hanfeng. Sichuan, C China 31°13′N 108°25′E
163 V11 **Kaiyuan** Liaoning, NE China 42°33′N 124°04′E
160 H14 **Kaiyuan** Yunnan, SW China 23°42′N 103°12′E
Kai-yüan *see* Kaiyuan
39 O9 **Kaiyuh Mountains** ▲ Alaska, USA
93 M15 **Kajaani** *Swe.* Kajana. Oulu, C Finland 64°17′N 27°46′E
149 N7 **Kajaki, Band-e** ◎ C Afghanistan
137 V13 **K'ajaran** *Rus.* Kadzharan. SE Armenia 39°09′N 46°09′E
Kajisay *see* Kadzhi-Say
113 O20 **Kajmakčalan** ▲ S FYR Macedonia 40°57′N 21°48′E *see also* Kaimakčalan
149 Q6 **Kajrān** Dāykondi, C Afghanistan 33°12′N 65°28′E

149 N5 **Kaj Rūd** ➶ C Afghanistan
146 G14 **Kaka** *Rus.* Kaakhka. Ahal Welaýaty, S Turkmenistan 37°20′N 59°37′E
12 C12 **Kakabeka Falls** Ontario, S Canada 48°24′N 89°40′W
83 F23 **Kakamas** Northern Cape, W South Africa 28°45′S 20°33′E
81 H18 **Kakamega** Western, W Kenya 0°17′N 34°47′E
155 Q22 **Kakana** Andaman and Nicobar Islands, SE India 09°08′N 92°48′E
112 H13 **Kakanj** Federacija Bosna I Hercegovina, C Bosnia and Herzegovina 44°06′N 18°07′E
185 F22 **Kakanui Mountains** ▲ South Island, New Zealand
184 K11 **Kakaramea** Taranaki, North Island, New Zealand 39°42′S 174°27′E
76 J16 **Kakata** W Liberia 06°32′N 10°21′W
184 M11 **Kakatahi** Manawatu-Wanganui, North Island, New Zealand 39°40′S 175°20′E
147 O12 **Kakaydi** Surkhondaryo Viloyati, S Uzbekistan 37°32′N 67°30′E
164 F13 **Kake** Hiroshima, Honshū, SW Japan 34°37′N 132°17′E
39 X13 **Kake** Kupreanof Island, Alaska, USA 56°58′N 133°57′W
171 P14 **Kakea** Pulau Wowoni, N Indonesia 03°05′S 123°06′E
164 M14 **Kakegawa** Shizuoka, Honshū, S Japan 34°47′N 138°02′E
81 F18 **Kakoge** C Uganda 01°03′N 32°30′E
145 O7 **Kak, Ozero** ◎ N Kazakhstan
39 S5 **Kaktovik** Alaska, USA 70°08′N 143°37′W
165 Q11 **Kakuda** Miyagi, Honshū, S Japan 37°59′N 140°48′E
165 Q8 **Kakunodate** Akita, Honshū, NE Japan 39°35′N 140°35′E
Kalaallit Nunaat *see* Greenland
149 T7 **Kālābāgh** Punjab, E Pakistan 33°00′N 71°35′E
171 Q16 **Kalabahi** Pulau Alor, S Indonesia 08°14′S 124°32′E
188 I5 **Kalabera** Saipan, S Northern Mariana Islands
83 G14 **Kalabo** Western, W Zambia 15°00′S 22°37′E
126 M3 **Kalach** Voronezhskaya Oblast', W Russian Federation 50°24′N 41°00′E
127 N10 **Kalach-na-Donu** Volgogradskaya Oblast', SW Russian Federation 48°45′N 43°29′E
14 K14 **Kaladar** Ontario, SE Canada 44°38′N 77°06′W
38 G13 **Ka Lae** *var.* South Cape, South Point. *headland* Hawai'i, USA, C Pacific Ocean 18°54′N 155°40′W
83 **Kalahari Desert** *desert* Southern Africa
38 G13 **Kalāheo** *var.* Kalaheo. Kaua'i, Hawaii, USA, C Pacific Ocean 21°55′N 159°31′W
Kalaheo *see* Kalāheo
Kalaikhum *see* Qal'aikhum
Kala-i-Mor *see* Galaýmor
93 K15 **Kalajoki** Oulu, W Finland 64°15′N 24°E
Kalak *see* Eski Kalak
Kal al Sraghna *see* El Kelâa Srarhna
32 G10 **Kalama** Washington, NW USA 46°00′N 122°50′W
115 G14 **Kalamariá** Kentrikí Makedonía, N Greece 40°35′N 22°58′E
115 C15 **Kalamás** *var.* Thiamis; *prev.* Thýamis. ➶ W Greece
115 E21 **Kalámata** *prev.* Kalámai. Pelopónnisos, S Greece 37°02′N 22°07′E
31 P10 **Kalamazoo** Michigan, N USA 42°17′N 85°35′W
31 P9 **Kalamazoo River** ➶ Michigan, N USA
117 S13 **Kalamits'ka Zatoka** *Rus.* Kalamitskiy Zaliv. *gulf* S Ukraine
Kalamitskiy Zaliv *see* Kalamits'ka Zatoka
110 F9 **Kalamos** Attikí, C Greece 38°16′N 23°51′E
115 C18 **Kálamos** *island* Iónioi Nísia, Greece, C Mediterranean Sea 38°37′N 20°55′E
110 F9 **Kalampáka** *var.* Kalambaka. Thessalía, C Greece 39°43′N 21°36′E
Kalan *see* Tunceli, Turkey
81 F22 **Kalang** Tabora, C Tanzania 05°03′S 31°48′E
92 K12 **Kalixälv** ➶ N Sweden
149 U9 **Kamália** Punjab, NE Pakistan

155 J24 **Kala Oya** ➶ NW Sri Lanka
Kalarash *see* Călăraşi
93 V15 **Kälarne** Jämtland, C Sweden 63°00′N 16°10′E
169 R9 **Kalasin** *var.* Muang Kalasin. Kalasin, E Thailand 16°29′N 103°31′E
143 N4 **Kalāt** *var.* Kabūd Gonbad. Khorāsān, NE Iran 37°02′N 59°46′E
149 O11 **Kalāt** *var.* Kelat, Khelat. Baluchistān, SW Pakistan 29°01′N 66°38′E
Kalāt *see* Qalāt
115 J23 **Kalathriá, Ákrotírio** *headland* Kríti, Greece, E Mediterranean Sea 34°24′N 25°34′E
193 W14 **Kalau** *island* Tongatapu Group, SE Tonga
38 E9 **Kalaupapa** Moloka'i, Hawaii, USA, C Pacific Ocean 21°11′N 156°59′W
127 N23 **Kalaus** ➶ SW Russian Federation
Kalávrita *see* Kalávryta
115 E19 **Kalávryta** *var.* Kalávrita. Dytikí Ellás, S Greece 38°55′N 20°19′E
141 Y10 **Kalbān** W Oman
180 H11 **Kalbarri** Western Australia 27°43′S 114°08′E
145 X10 **Kalbinskiy Khrebet** *Kaz.* Qalba Zhotasy. ▲ E Kazakhstan
144 D10 **Kaldygayty** ➶ W Kazakhstan
136 I12 **Kalecik** Ankara, N Turkey 40°08′N 33°27′E
79 O19 **Kalehe** Sud-Kivu, E Dem. Rep. Congo 02°05′S 28°52′E
79 P22 **Kalemie** *prev.* Albertville. Katanga, SE Dem. Rep. Congo 05°55′S 29°09′E
166 L4 **Kalemyo** Sagaing, W Burma (Myanmar) 23°11′N 94°04′E
82 H12 **Kalene Hill** North Western, NW Zambia 11°10′S 24°12′E
79 N20 **Kalima** Maniema, E Dem. Rep. Congo 02°34′S 26°27′E
166 L4 **Kalewa** Sagaing, C Burma (Myanmar) 23°15′N 94°19′E
39 Q12 **Kalgin Island** *island* Alaska, USA
180 L12 **Kalgoorlie** Western Australia 30°51′S 121°27′E
115 E17 **Kalaïdoúda** ▲ C Greece 38°47′N 21°42′E
155 L16 **Kākināda** *prev.* Cocanada. Andhra Pradesh, E India 16°56′N 82°13′E
114 O8 **Kaliakra, Nos** *headland* NE Bulgaria 43°22′N 28°28′E
115 F19 **Kaliánoí** Pelopónnisos, S Greece 37°55′N 22°28′E
81 F18 **Kalinin** *see* Tver'
126 B7 **Kalinin** *see* Boldumsaz
Kalininabad *see* Kalininobod
164 I13 **Kalinin** Saratovskaya Oblast', W Russian Federation 51°31′N 44°25′E
Kalininsk *see* Cupcina
119 M19 **Kalinkavichy** *Rus.* Kalinkovichi. Homyel'skaya Voblasts', SE Belarus 52°08′N 29°19′E
Kalinkovichi *see* Kalinkavichy
115 M22 **Kálymnos** *var.* Kálimnos. Kálymnos, Dodekánisa, Greece, Aegean Sea
165 R5 **Kalispell** Montana, NW USA 48°12′N 114°18′W
110 I13 **Kalisz** *Ger.* Kalisch; *Rus.* Kalish; *anc.* Calisia. C Poland 51°46′N 18°04′E
110 F9 **Kalisz Pomorski** *Ger.* Kallies. Zachodnio-pomorskie, NW Poland 53°55′N 15°02′E
165 M10 **Kalixälven** ➶ N Sweden
92 K12 **Kalixälven** ➶ N Sweden
171 U8 **Kalixälven** ➶ N Sweden

145 T8 **Kalkaman** *Kaz.* Qalqaman. Pavlodar, NE Kazakhstan 51°57′N 75°58′E
Kalkandelen *see* Tetovo
181 O4 **Kalkarindji** Northern Territory, N Australia 17°32′S 130°40′E
31 P6 **Kalkaska** Michigan, N USA 44°44′N 85°11′W
31 F16 **Kall** Jämtland, C Sweden 63°11′N 13°16′E
189 X2 **Kalle** *atoll* Ratak Chain, SE Marshall Islands
93 H15 **Kallavesi** ◎ SE Finland
115 F17 **Kallídromo** ▲ C Greece
95 M22 **Kallinge** Blekinge, S Sweden 56°14′N 15°17′E
115 L16 **Kallóni** Lésvos, E Greece 39°14′N 26°16′E
93 F16 **Kallsjön** ◎ C Sweden
95 N21 **Kalmar** *var.* Calmar. Kalmar, S Sweden 56°40′N 16°22′E
95 M19 **Kalmar** *var.* Calmar. ◆ *county* S Sweden
95 N20 **Kalmarsund** *strait* S Sweden
117 X9 **Kal'mius** ➶ E Ukraine
99 H15 **Kalmthout** Antwerpen, N Belgium 51°24′N 04°27′E
127 O12 **Kalmykiya, Respublika** *var.* Respublika Kalmykiya-Khal'mg Tangch, *Eng.* Kalmykia; *prev.* Kalmytskaya ASSR. ◆ *autonomous republic* SW Russian Federation
Kalmytskaya ASSR *see* Kalmykiya, Respublika
118 F9 **Kalnciems** Jelgava, C Latvia 56°46′N 23°37′E
114 L10 **Kalnitsa** ➶ SE Bulgaria
111 J24 **Kalocsa** Bács-Kiskun, S Hungary 46°31′N 19°00′E
114 J9 **Kalofer** Plovdiv, C Bulgaria 42°36′N 25°00′E
83 J16 **Kalomo** Southern, S Zambia 17°02′S 26°29′E
29 X14 **Kalona** Iowa, C USA 41°28′N 91°42′W
115 M22 **Kalotási, Akrotírio** *cape* Amorgós, Kykládes, Greece, Aegean Sea
152 J8 **Kalpa** Himāchal Pradesh, N India 31°33′N 78°16′E
155 C15 **Kalpáki** Ípeiros, W Greece 39°53′N 20°38′E
155 C22 **Kalpeni Island** *island* Lakshadweep, India, N Indian Ocean
155 F21 **Kalpetta** Kerala, SW India 11°36′N 76°05′E
152 K13 **Kālpi** Uttar Pradesh, N India 26°07′N 79°44′E
158 G7 **Kalpin** Xinjiang Uygur Zizhiqu, NW China 40°31′N 78°54′E
149 P16 **Kalri Lake** ◎ SE Pakistan
143 R5 **Kāl Shūr** ➶ N Iran
39 N11 **Kalskag** Alaska, USA 61°32′N 160°15′W
Kalse *see* Kalsoy
35 B18 **Kalsoy** *Dan.* Kalsø. *island* N Faeroe Islands
36 G14 **Kaltag** Alaska, USA 64°19′N 158°43′W
108 H7 **Kaltbrunn** Sankt Gallen, NE Switzerland 47°11′N 09°00′E
Kaltdorf *see* Pruszków
77 X14 **Kaltungo** Gombe, E Nigeria 09°49′N 11°22′E
126 K4 **Kaluga** Kaluzhskaya Oblast', W Russian Federation 54°31′N 36°16′E
155 J26 **Kalu Ganga** ➶ S Sri Lanka
82 J13 **Kalulushi** Copperbelt, C Zambia 12°50′S 28°03′E
180 M2 **Kalumburu** Western Australia 14°11′S 126°40′E
95 H23 **Kalundborg** Vestsjælland, E Denmark 55°42′N 11°06′E
149 T8 **Kalūr Kot** Punjab, E Pakistan 32°08′N 71°20′E
116 L11 **Kalush** *Pol.* Kałusz. Ivano-Frankivs'ka Oblast', W Ukraine 49°02′N 24°20′E
Kałusz *see* Kalush
118 H11 **Kałuszyn** Mazowieckie, C Poland 52°12′N 21°52′E
155 J25 **Kalutara** Western Province, SW Sri Lanka 06°35′N 79°59′E
126 A3 **Kaliningradskaya Oblast'** *var.* Kaliningrad. ◆ *province and enclave* W Russian Federation
119 E14 **Kalvarija** *Pol.* Kalwaria. Marijampolė, S Lithuania 54°25′N 23°14′E
95 K15 **Kälviä** Länsi-Suomi, W Finland 63°53′N 23°30′E
109 U6 **Kalwang** C Austria 47°25′N 14°48′E
Kalwaria *see* Kalvarija
154 F13 **Kalyān** Mahārāshtra, W India 19°17′N 73°11′E
124 J14 **Kalyazin** Tverskaya Oblast', W Russian Federation 57°15′N 37°52′E
115 M22 **Kálymnos** *var.* Kálimnos. Kálymnos, Dodekánisa, Greece, Aegean Sea
115 M21 **Kálymnos** *var.* Kálimnos. *island* Dodekánisa, Greece, Aegean Sea
117 O5 **Kalynivka** Kyyivs'ka Oblast', N Ukraine 50°16′N 30°16′E
117 N6 **Kalynivka** Vinnyts'ka Oblast', C Ukraine 49°27′N 28°32′E

83 J14 **Kamalondo** North Western, NW Zambia 13°42′S 25°38′E
136 H13 **Kaman** Kırşehir, C Turkey 39°22′N 33°43′E
79 O20 **Kamanyola** Sud-Kivu, E Dem. Rep. Congo 02°54′S 29°04′E
141 N14 **Kamarān** *island* W Yemen
55 R9 **Kamarang** W Guyana 05°49′N 60°38′W
Kāmārēddi/Kamareddy *see* Rāmāreddi
Kama Reservoir *see* Kamskoye Vodokhranilishche
148 K13 **Kamarod** Baluchistān, SW Pakistan 25°34′N 63°36′E
171 P14 **Kamaru** Pulau Buton, C Indonesia 05°15′S 123°03′E
77 S13 **Kamba** Kebbi, NW Nigeria 11°50′N 03°44′E
Kamphaeng Phet *see* Kamphaeng Phet
180 L12 **Kambalda** Western Australia 31°15′S 121°33′E
149 P13 **Kambar** *var.* Qambar. Sind, SE Pakistan 27°35′N 68°03′E
Kambara *see* Kabara
127 X3 **Kambarka** Udmurtskaya Respublika, NW Russian Federation 56°16′N 54°15′E
76 I14 **Kambia** W Sierra Leone 09°09′N 12°53′W
Kambos *see* Kampos
79 N25 **Kambove** Katanga, SE Dem. Rep. Congo 10°50′S 26°39′E
123 V10 **Kamchatka** ➶ E Russian Federation
Kamchatka *see* Kamchatka, Poluostrov
Kamchatka Basin *see* Komandorskaya Basin
123 U10 **Kamchatka, Poluostrov** *Eng.* Kamchatka. *peninsula* E Russian Federation
123 V10 **Kamchatskaya Oblast'** ◆ *province* E Russian Federation
123 V10 **Kamchatskiy Zaliv** *gulf* E Russian Federation
114 N9 **Kamchiya** ➶ E Bulgaria
114 L9 **Kamchiya, Yazovir** ◎ E Bulgaria
154 T4 **Kāmdesh** *var.* Kamdesh. Nūrestān, E Afghanistan
118 M13 **Kamen'** Vitsyebskaya Voblasts', N Belarus 55°01′N 28°53′E
Kamenets *see* Kamyanets
115 K22 **Kamenets-Podol'skaya Oblast'** *see* Khmel'nyts'ka Oblast'
Kamenets-Podil'skiy *see* Kam"yanets'-Podil's'kyy
113 Q18 **Kamenica** NE Macedonia 42°03′N 22°34′E
113 O16 **Kamenica** *var.* Kamenicë; *prev.* Kosovska Kamenica. E Kosovo 42°33′N 21°33′E
112 A11 **Kamenjak, Rt** *headland* NW Croatia
144 F8 **Kamenka** Zapadnyy Kazakhstan, NW Kazakhstan 51°06′N 51°16′E
125 O5 **Kamenka** Arkhangel'skaya Oblast', NW Russian Federation 65°55′N 44°01′E
127 N6 **Kamenka** Penzenskaya Oblast', W Russian Federation 50°44′N 39°31′E
Kamenka *see* Camenca
Kamenka *see* Kam"yanka
Kamenka-Bugskaya *see* Kam"yanka-Buz'ka
Kamenka Dneprovskaya *see* Kam"yanka-Dniprovs'ka
Kamen Kashirskiy *see* Kamin'-Kashyrs'kyy
126 L15 **Kamennomostskiy** Respublika Adygeya, SW Russian Federation 44°13′N 40°12′E
126 L11 **Kamenolomni** Rostovskaya Oblast', SW Russian Federation 47°36′N 40°18′E
127 P8 **Kamenka** Saratovskaya Oblast', W Russian Federation 50°56′N 45°32′E
Kamenskoye *see* Romanov
126 L11 **Kamensk-Shakhtinskiy** Rostovskaya Oblast', SW Russian Federation 48°18′N 40°16′E
101 P15 **Kamenz** Sachsen, E Germany 51°15′N 14°06′E
164 J13 **Kameoka** Kyōto, Honshū, SW Japan 35°02′N 135°35′E
126 M3 **Kameshkovo** Vladimirskaya Oblast', W Russian Federation 56°20′N 40°58′E
164 C11 **Kami-Agata** Nagasaki, Tsushima, SW Japan 34°40′N 129°27′E
33 N10 **Kamiah** Idaho, NW USA 46°13′N 116°01′W
Kamień Koszalski *see* Kamień Koszarski
110 H9 **Kamień Krajeński** *Ger.* Kamin in Westpreussen. Kujawski-pomorskie, C Poland 53°31′N 17°31′E
111 F15 **Kamienna Góra** *Ger.* Landeshut, Landeshut in Schlesien. Dolnośląskie, SW Poland 50°48′N 16°00′E
110 D8 **Kamień Pomorski** *Ger.* Cammin in Pommern. Zachodnio-pomorskie, NW Poland 53°59′N 14°45′E
165 R5 **Kamiiso** Hokkaidō, NE Japan 41°48′N 140°37′E
79 L22 **Kamiji** Kasai-Oriental, S Dem. Rep. Congo 06°39′S 23°27′E
165 R3 **Kamikawa** Hokkaidō, NE Japan 43°51′N 142°47′E
165 S3 **Kami-Koshiki-jima** *island* SW Japan
79 N20 **Kamina** Katanga, S Dem. Rep. Congo 08°42′S 25°01′E
42 C6 **Kaminaljuyú** *ruins* Guatemala, C Guatemala
Kamin in Westpreussen *see* Kamień Krajeński
110 J2 **Kamin'-Kashyrs'kyy** *Pol.* Kamień Koszarski, *Rus.* Kamen Kashirskiy. Volyns'ka Oblast', NW Ukraine
165 Q5 **Kaminokuni** Hokkaidō, NE Japan 41°48′N 140°05′E

◆ Country   ◇ Dependent Territory   ◈ Administrative Regions   ▲ Mountain   ☊ Volcano   ◎ Lake
● Country Capital   ○ Dependent Territory Capital   ✕ International Airport   ▲▲ Mountain Range   ➶ River   ▨ Reservoir

165 P10 **Kaminoyama** Yamagata, Honshū, C Japan 38°10′N 140°16′E

39 Q13 **Kamishak Bay** bay Alaska, USA

165 U4 **Kami-Shihoro** Hokkaidō, NE Japan 43°14′N 143°18′E **Kamishli** see Al Qāmishlī **Kamissar** see Kamsar

164 C11 **Kami-Tsushima** Nagasaki, Tsushima, SW Japan 34°40′N 129°27′E

79 O20 **Kamituga** Sud-Kivu, E Dem. Rep. Congo 03°07′S 28°10′E

164 B17 **Kamiyaku** Kagoshima, Yaku-shima, SW Japan 30°24′N 130°32′E

11 N16 **Kamloops** British Columbia, SW Canada 50°39′N 120°24′W

107 G25 **Kamma** Sicilia, Italy, C Mediterranean Sea 36°46′N 12°03′E

192 K4 **Kammu Seamount** undersea feature N Pacific Ocean 32°09′N 173°00′E

109 U11 **Kamnik** Ger. Stein. C Slovenia 46°13′N 14°34′E **Kamniške Alpe** see **Kamniško-Savinjske Alpe**

109 T10 **Kamniško-Savinjske Alpe** var. Kamniške Alpe, Sanntaler Alpen, Ger. Steiner Alpen. ▲ N Slovenia **Kamo** see Gavarr

165 R3 **Kamoenai** var. Kamuenai. Hokkaidō, NE Japan 43°07′N 140°25′E

165 O14 **Kamogawa** Chiba, Honshū, S Japan 35°05′N 140°04′E

149 W8 **Kāmoke** Punjab, E Pakistan 31°58′N 74°15′E

82 L13 **Kamoto** Eastern, E Zambia 13°16′S 32°04′E

109 V3 **Kamp** ✍ N Austria

81 F18 **Kampala** ● (Uganda) S Uganda 00°20′N 32°28′E

168 K11 **Kampar, Sungai** ✍ Sumatera, W Indonesia

98 L9 **Kampen** Overijssel, E Netherlands 52°33′N 05°55′E

79 N20 **Kampene** Maniema, E Dem. Rep. Congo 03°35′S 26°40′E

29 Q9 **Kamphaeng, Lake** ◙ South Dakota, N USA

167 O9 **Kamphaeng Phet** var. Kamphaeng Petch. Kamphaeng Phet, W Thailand 16°28′N 99°31′E **Kampo** see Campo, Cameroon **Kampo** see Ntem, Cameroon/ Equatorial Guinea

167 S12 **Kâmpóng Cham** prev. Kompong Cham. Kâmpóng Cham, C Cambodia 12°N 105°27′E

167 R12 **Kâmpóng Chhnǎng** prev. Kompong. Kâmpóng Chhnǎng, C Cambodia 12°15′N 104°40′E

167 R12 **Kâmpóng Khleang** prev. Kompong Kleang. Siĕmréab, NW Cambodia 13°04′N 104°07′E

167 Q14 **Kâmpóng Saôm** prev. Kompong Som, Sihanoukville. Kâmpóng Saôm, SW Cambodia 10°38′N 103°30′E

167 R13 **Kâmpóng Spoe** prev. Kompong Speu. Kâmpóng Spœ, S Cambodia 11°28′N 104°29′E

121 O2 **Kámpos** var. Kambos. NW Cyprus 35°03′N 32°44′E

167 R14 **Kâmpôt** Kâmpôt, SW Cambodia 10°37′N 104°11′E **Kamptee** see Kāmthi

77 O14 **Kampti** SW Burkina 10°07′N 03°22′W **Kampuchea** see Cambodia **Kampuchea, Democratic** see Cambodia **Kampuchea, People's Democratic Republic of** see Cambodia

169 Q9 **Kampung Sirik** Sarawak, East Malaysia 02°42′N 111°28′E

11 V15 **Kamsack** Saskatchewan, S Canada 51°34′N 101°51′W

76 H13 **Kamsar** var. Kamissar. Guinée-Maritime, W Guinea 10°33′N 14°34′W

127 R4 **Kamskoye Ust'ye** Respublika Tatarstan, W Russian Federation 55°13′N 49°11′E

125 U14 **Kamskoye Vodokhranilishche** var. Kama Reservoir. ◙ NW Russian Federation

154 I12 **Kāmthi** prev. Kamptee. Mahārāshtra, C India 21°19′N 79°11′E **Kamuela** see Waimea **Kamuenai** see Kamoenai

165 T5 **Kamui-dake** ▲ Hokkaidō, NE Japan 42°24′N 142°57′E

165 R3 **Kamui-misaki** headland Hokkaidō, NE Japan 43°20′N 140°20′E

43 O15 **Kámuk, Cerro** ▲ SE Costa Rica 09°15′N 83°01′W

116 K7 **Kam"yanets'-Podil's'kyy** Rus. Kamenets-Podol'skiy. Khmel'nyts'ka Oblast', W Ukraine 48°43′N 26°36′E

117 Q6 **Kam"yanka** Rus. Kamenka. Cherkas'ka Oblast', C Ukraine 49°03′N 32°06′E

116 I5 **Kam"yanka-Buz'ka** Rus. Kamenka-Bugskaya. L'vivs'ka Oblast', W Ukraine 50°04′N 24°21′E

117 T9 **Kam"yanka-Dniprovs'ka** Rus. Kamenka Dneprovskaya. Zaporiz'ka Oblast', SE Ukraine 47°28′N 34°22′E

119 F19 **Kamyanyets** Rus. Kamenets. Brestskaya Voblasts', SW Belarus 52°24′N 23°49′E

127 P9 **Kamyshin** Volgogradskaya Oblast', SW Russian Federation 50°07′N 45°20′E

127 Q13 **Kamyzyak** Astrakhanskaya Oblast', SW Russian Federation 46°07′N 48°03′E

12 K8 **Kanaaupscow** ✍ Québec, C Canada

36 K8 **Kanab** Utah, W USA 37°03′N 112°31′W

36 K9 **Kanab Creek** ✍ Arizona/ Utah, SW USA

187 Y14 **Kanacea** prev. Kanathea. Taveuni, N Fiji 16°59′S 179°54′E

38 G17 **Kanaga Island** island Aleutian Islands, Alaska, USA

38 G17 **Kanaga Volcano** ▲ Kanaga Island, Alaska, USA 51°55′N 177°09′W

164 N14 **Kanagawa** off. Kanagawa-ken. ◆ prefecture Honshū, S Japan **Kanagawa-ken** see Kanagawa

13 Q8 **Kanairiktok** ✍ Newfoundland and Labrador, E Canada **Kanaky** see New Caledonia

79 K22 **Kananga** prev. Luluabourg. Kasai-Occidental, S Dem. Rep. Congo 05°51′S 22°22′E **Kanara** see Karnātaka

36 J7 **Kanarraville** Utah, W USA 37°32′N 113°10′W

163 X12 **Kanggye** N North Korea 40°58′N 126°37′E

197 P15 **Kangikajik** var. Kap Brewster. headland E Greenland 70°10′N 22°00′W

13 N5 **Kangiqsualujjuaq** prev. George River, Port-Nouveau-Québec. Québec, E Canada 58°35′N 65°59′W

12 L2 **Kangiqsujuaq** prev. Maricourt, Wakeham Bay. Québec, NE Canada 61°35′N 72°00′W

12 M4 **Kangirsuk** prev. Bellin, Payne. Québec, E Canada 60°00′N 70°01′E

159 V11 **Kangle** var. Kangu. C China 35°22′N 103°42′E **Kangle** var Wanzai

158 M16 **Kangmar** Xizang Zizhiqu, W China 28°34′N 89°40′E

163 Y14 **Kangnŭng** Jap. Kōryō. NE South Korea 37°47′N 128°51′E

79 D18 **Kango** Estuaire, NW Gabon 0°17′N 10°00′E

152 I7 **Kāngra** Himāchal Pradesh, NW India 32°04′N 76°16′E

153 Q16 **Kangsabati Reservoir** ◙ E India

159 O17 **Kangto** ▲ China/India 27°51′N 92°31′E

159 W12 **Kangxian** var. Kang Xian, Zuitai, Zuitaizi. Gansu, C China 33°21′N 105°00′E

76 M15 **Kani** NW Ivory Coast 08°29′N 06°36′W

166 L4 **Kani** Sagaing, C Burma (Myanmar) 22°24′N 94°55′E

79 M23 **Kaniama** Katanga, S Dem. Rep. Congo 07°31′S 24°11′E

169 V6 **Kanibongan** Sabah, East Malaysia 06°40′N 117°12′E

185 F17 **Kaniere** West Coast, South Island, New Zealand 42°45′S 171°00′E

185 G17 **Kaniere, Lake** ◙ South Island, New Zealand

188 E17 **Kanifaay** Yap, W Micronesia

125 O4 **Kanin Kamen'** ▲ NW Russian Federation

125 N3 **Kanin Nos** Nenetskiy Avtonomnyy Okrug, NW Russian Federation 68°38′N 43°19′E

125 N3 **Kanin Nos, Mys** cape NW Russian Federation

125 O5 **Kanin, Poluostrov** peninsula NW Russian Federation

139 V8 **Kānī Sakht** Wāsiṭ, E Iraq

139 T3 **Kānī Sulaymān** Arbīl, N Iraq 35°54′N 44°35′E

165 Q6 **Kanita** Aomori, Honshū, C Japan 41°01′N 140°36′E

117 Q5 **Kaniv** Rus. Kanëv. Cherkas'ka Oblast', C Ukraine 49°46′N 31°28′E

182 K11 **Kanivá** Victoria, SE Australia 36°25′S 141°13′E

117 Q5 **Kanivs'ke Vodoskhovyshche** Rus. Kanevskoye Vodokhranilishche.

112 L8 **Kanjiža** Ger. Altkanischa, Hung. Magyarkanizsa, Ókanizsa; prev. Stara Kanjiža. Vojvodina, N Serbia 46°03′N 20°03′E

155 K25 **Kankankanäää** Länsi-Suomi, W Finland 61°47′N 22°25′E

144 I10 **Kandyagash** Kaz. Qandyaghash; prev. Oktyab'rsk. Aktyubinsk, W Kazakhstan 49°25′N 57°24′E

18 D12 **Kane** Pennsylvania, NE USA 41°39′N 78°47′W

64 I11 **Kane Fracture Zone** tectonic feature NW Atlantic Ocean **Kaněka** see Kanēvka

78 G9 **Kanem** off. Préfecture du Kanem. ◆ prefecture W Chad **Kanem, Préfecture du** see Kanem

38 D9 **Kāne'ohe** var. Kaneohe. O'ahu, Hawaii, USA, C Pacific Ocean 21°25′N 157°48′W **Kanestron, Akrotírio** see Palioúri, Akrotírio **Kanëv** see Kaniv

124 M5 **Kanëvka** var. Kaněka. Murmanskaya Oblast', NW Russian Federation 67°01′N 39°43′E

126 K13 **Kanevskaya** Krasnodarskiy Kray, SW Russian Federation 46°07′N 38°57′E **Kanevskoye Vodokhranilishche** see Kanivs'ke Vodoskhovyshche

165 P9 **Kaneyama** Yamagata, Honshū, C Japan 38°54′N 140°20′E

83 G20 **Kang** Kgalagadi, C Botswana 23°41′S 22°50′E

78 L13 **Kangaba** Koulikoro, SW Mali 11°57′N 08°24′W

137 M13 **Kangal** Sivas, C Turkey 39°15′N 37°07′E

143 S15 **Kangān** Hormozgān, SE Iran 27°49′N 52°29′E

168 J6 **Kangar** Perlis, Peninsular Malaysia 06°28′N 100°11′E

76 L13 **Kangaré** Sikasso, S Mali 11°35′N 08°10′W

182 F10 **Kangaroo Island** island South Australia

93 M17 **Kangasniemi** Itä-Suomi, E Finland 61°58′N 26°37′E

142 K6 **Kangāvar** var. Kangāwar. Kermānshāhān, W Iran 34°29′N 47°55′E **Kangāwar** see Kangāvar

153 S11 **Kānchanpur** Kānchenjunga, Nep. Kānchanjanghā. ▲ NE India 27°36′N 88°06′E

160 I9 **Kanging** var. Lucheng, Tib. Dardo. Sichuan, C China 30°01′N 101°56′E

169 U16 **Kangean, Kepulauan** island group S Indonesia

169 T16 **Kangean, Pulau** island Kepulauan Kangean, S Indonesia

67 U8 **Kangen** var. Kengen. ✍ SE Sudan

197 N14 **Kangerlussuaq** Dan. Sondre Stromfjord. ✈ Kitaa, W Greenland 66°59′N 50°28′E

197 Q15 **Kangertittivaq** Dan. Scoresby Sund. fjord E Greenland

167 O2 **Kangfang** Kachin State, N Burma (Myanmar) 26°09′N 98°36′E

115 H25 **Kánggye** N North Korea 40°58′N 126°37′E

27 R3 **Kansas City** ✈ Missouri, C USA 39°18′N 94°45′W

27 P4 **Kansas River** ✍ Kansas, C USA

122 L14 **Kansk** Krasnoyarskiy Kray, S Russian Federation 56°11′N 95°32′E **Kansu** see Gansu

197 N14 **Kangerlussuaq** Dan.

147 V7 **Kant** Chuyskaya Oblast', N Kyrgyzstan 42°54′N 74°47′E **Kantalahti** see Kandalaksha

167 N16 **Kantang** var. Ban Kantang. Trang, SW Thailand 07°25′N 99°30′E

115 H25 **Kántanos** Kríti, Greece, E Mediterranean Sea 35°20′N 23°42′E

77 R12 **Kantchari** E Burkina 12°31′N 01°37′E **Kanté** see Kandé

126 L9 **Kantemirovka** Voronezhskaya Oblast', W Russian Federation 49°44′N 39°53′E

167 R11 **Kantharalak** Si Sa Ket, E Thailand 14°32′N 104°37′E **Kantipur** see Kathmandu

39 Q9 **Kanton** var. Abariringa, Canton Island; prev. Mary Island. atoll Phoenix Islands, C Kiribati

97 C20 **Kanturk** Ir. Ceann Toirc. Cork, SW Ireland 52°11′N 08°54′W

55 T11 **Kanuku Mountains** ▲ S Guyana

165 O12 **Kanuma** Tochigi, Honshū, S Japan 36°34′N 139°44′E

83 H20 **Kanye** Southern, SE Botswana 24°55′S 25°14′E

83 H17 **Kanyu** North-West, C Botswana 20°04′S 24°36′E

166 M7 **Kanyutkwin** Bago, C Burma (Myanmar) 18°19′N 96°30′E

79 M24 **Kanzenze** Katanga, S Dem. Rep. Congo 10°33′S 25°28′E

193 Y15 **Kao** island Kotu group, W Tonga

161 S14 **Kaohsiung** var. Gaoxiong, Jap. Takao, Takow. S Taiwan 22°36′N 120°17′E

161 S14 **Kaohsiung** ✈ S Taiwan 22°26′N 120°32′E

83 B17 **Kaoko Veld** ▲ N Namibia

76 G11 **Kaolack** var. Kaolak. W Senegal 14°09′N 16°08′W **Kaolak** see Kaolack

76 G11 **Kaolan** see Lanzhou

114 M7 **Kaolinovo** Shumen, NE Bulgaria 43°36′N 27°04′E

186 M8 **Kaolo** San Jorge, N Solomon Islands 08°25′S 159°35′E

83 H14 **Kaoma** North-West, W Zambia 14°50′S 24°48′E

136 C17 **Kara Burnu** headland SW Turkey 36°34′N 28°00′E

38 B8 **Kapa'a** var. Kapaa. Kaua'i, Hawaii, USA, C Pacific Ocean 22°04′N 159°19′W

113 J16 **Kapa** var. Kapa'a

137 V13 **Kapan** Rus. Kafan; prev. Ghap'an. SE Armenia 39°13′N 46°25′E

82 L13 **Kapandashila** Northern, NE Zambia 13°45′S 31°00′E

79 L23 **Kapanga** Katanga, S Dem. Rep. Congo 08°22′S 22°37′E

145 U15 **Kapshaghay**. Almaty, SE Kazakhstan

145 V15 **Kapchagayskoye Vodokhranilishche** Kaz. Qapshagay Böyeni. ◙ SE Kazakhstan

99 F15 **Kapelle** Zeeland, SW Netherlands 51°29′N 03°58′E

99 G16 **Kapellen** Antwerpen, N Belgium 51°19′N 04°26′E

95 P15 **Kapellskär** Stockholm, C Sweden 59°43′N 19°03′E

81 H18 **Kapenguria** Rift Valley, W Kenya 01°14′N 35°08′E

109 V6 **Kapfenberg** Steiermark, C Austria 47°27′N 15°18′E

83 J14 **Kapiri Mposhi** Central, C Zambia 13°59′S 28°40′E

149 R4 **Kāpisā** ◆ province E Afghanistan

12 G10 **Kapiskau** ✍ Ontario, C Canada

184 K13 **Kapiti Island** island C New Zealand

78 K9 **Kapka, Massif du** ▲ E Chad **Kaplamadans** see

126 J6 **Kapelle** Zeeland

128 K11 **Kapelle**

12 G12 **Kapuskasing** Ontario, S Canada 49°25′N 82°26′W

14 D6 **Kapuskasing** ✍ Ontario, S Canada

127 P11 **Kapustin Yar** Astrakhanskaya Oblast', SW Russian Federation 48°36′N 45°49′E

82 K11 **Kaputa** Northern, NE Zambia 08°28′S 29°41′E

111 G22 **Kapuvár** Győr-Moson-Sopron, NW Hungary 47°35′N 17°01′E

119 J17 **Kapyl'** Rus. Kopyl'. Minskaya Voblasts', C Belarus 53°09′N 27°05′E

43 N9 **Kara** var. Région Autónoma Atlántico Sur, E Nicaragua 12°50′N 83°35′W

77 R14 **Kara** var. Lama-Kara. ✍ NE Togo 09°33′N 01°12′E

147 U7 **Kara-Balta** Chuyskaya Oblast', N Kyrgyzstan 42°51′N 73°51′E

144 L7 **Karabau** Kaz. Qarabaū. Atyrau, W Kazakhstan 48°29′N 53°53′E

146 E7 **Karabaur', Uval** Kaz. Korabavur Pastligi, Uzb. Qorabowur Kirlari. physical region Kazakhstan/Uzbekistan **Karabekaul** see Garabekewül **Karabil', Vozvyshennost'** see Garabil Belentligi **Kara-Bogaz-Gol** see Garabogazköl **Kara-Bogaz-Gol, Zaliv** see Garabogaz Aylagy

145 R15 **Karaboget** Kaz. Qaraböget. Zhambyl, S Kazakhstan 44°36′N 72°03′E

136 H11 **Karabük** Karabük, NW Turkey 41°12′N 32°36′E

136 H11 **Karabük** ◆ province NW Turkey

122 L12 **Karabula** Krasnoyarskiy Kray, C Russian Federation 58°01′N 97°17′E

145 V14 **Karabulak** Kaz. Qarabulaq. Taldykorgan, SE Kazakhstan 44°53′N 78°29′E

145 Q17 **Karabulak** Kaz. Qarabulaq. Yuzhnyy Kazakhstan, S Kazakhstan 42°31′N 69°47′E

169 T14 **Karamain, Pulau** island N Indonesia

136 I16 **Karaman** Karaman, S Turkey 37°11′N 33°13′E

136 H16 **Karaman** ◆ province S Turkey

114 M8 **Karamandere** ✍ NE Bulgaria

158 J4 **Karamay** var. Karamai, Kelamayi; prev. Chin. K'o-la-ma-i. Xinjiang Uygur Zizhiqu, NW China 45°33′N 84°45′E

169 U14 **Karambu** Borneo, N Indonesia 03°48′S 116°06′E

185 H14 **Karamea** West Coast, South Island, New Zealand 41°15′S 172°07′E

185 H14 **Karamea** ✍ South Island, New Zealand

185 G15 **Karamea Bight** gulf South Island, New Zealand **Karamet-Niyaz** see Garamätnyýaz

158 K10 **Karamiran He** ✍ NW China

147 S11 **Karamyk** Oshskaya Oblast', SW Kyrgyzstan 39°28′N 71°45′E

169 U17 **Karangasem** Bali, S Indonesia 08°24′S 115°40′E

154 F11 **Karanja** Mahārāshtra, C India 20°30′N 77°30′E **Karanpur** see Karanpura

152 F9 **Karanpura** var. Karanpur. Rājasthān, NW India 29°46′N 73°30′E **Karánsebes/Karansebesch** see Caransebeș

114 N7 **Karapınar** Konya, C Turkey 37°43′N 33°34′E

83 D22 **Karas** ◆ district S Namibia

147 Y8 **Kara-Say** Issyk-Kul'skaya Oblast', NE Kyrgyzstan 41°34′N 77°56′E

83 E22 **Karasburg** Karas, S Namibia 27°59′S 18°46′E **Kara Sea** see Karskoye More

92 K9 **Kárášjohka** var. Karašjokk. ✍ Norway **Kárášjohka** var. Karasjok, Lapp. Kárášjoki. Finnmark, N Norway 69°27′N 25°28′E **Kárášjoki** see Kárášjohka

92 L9 **Karasjok** Fin. Kaarasjoki, Lapp. Kárášjoki. Finnmark, N Norway 69°27′N 25°28′E

137 P11 **Karasu** Sakarya, NW Turkey 41°07′N 30°37′E

136 F11 **Karasu** Sakarya, NW Turkey 41°07′N 30°37′E **Kara Su** see Mesta/Néstos **Karasubazar** see Bilohirs'k

122 I12 **Karasuk** Novosibirskaya Oblast', C Russian Federation 53°41′N 78°04′E

145 S14 **Karatal** Kaz. Qaratal. ✍ SE Kazakhstan

136 K17 **Karataş** Adana, S Turkey 36°32′N 35°22′E

145 Q16 **Karatau** Kaz. Qarataū. Zhambyl, S Kazakhstan 43°09′N 70°28′E

145 P16 **Karatau, Khrebet** var. ▲ S Kazakhstan

144 G13 **Karaton** Kaz. Qaraton. Atyrau, W Kazakhstan 46°33′N 53°31′E

164 C13 **Karatsu** Saga, Kyūshū, SW Japan 33°28′N 129°48′E **Karatu** see Karatsu

122 K8 **Karaul** Taymyrskiy (Dolgano-Nenetskiy) Avtonomnyy Okrug, N Russian Federation 70°07′N 83°21′E

(rightmost column)

Karaulbazar see Qorowulbozor

152 I13 **Karauli** Rājasthān, N India 26°29′N 77°01′E **Karauzyak** see Qorao'zak

115 D16 **Kárava** ▲ C Greece 39°19′N 21°23′E

115 F22 **Karavás** Kýthira, S Greece

113 J20 **Karavastasë, Laguna e** var. Kënet' e Karavastasë, Kravasta Lagoon. lagoon W Albania **Karavastasë, Kënet' e** see Karavastasë, Laguna e

118 I5 **Kärevere** Tartumaa, E Estonia 58°25′N 26°18′E

115 L23 **Karavonísia** island Kykládes, Greece, Aegean Sea

169 O15 **Karawang** var. Krawang. Jawa, C Indonesia 06°13′S 107°16′E

109 T10 **Karawanken** Slvn. Karavanke. ▲ Austria/Serbia

137 R13 **Karayazı** Erzurum, NE Turkey 39°40′N 42°09′E

145 Q12 **Karazhal** Kaz. Qarazhal. Karaganda, C Kazakhstan 48°02′N 70°52′E

139 T10 **Karbalā'** var. Kerbala, Kerbela. Karbalā', S Iraq 32°37′N 44°03′E

139 S9 **Karbalā'** var. Kerbala, Kerbela. ◆ governorate S Iraq

94 L11 **Kårböle** Gävleborg, C Sweden 61°59′N 15°16′E

111 M23 **Karcag** Jász-Nagykun-Szolnok, E Hungary 47°22′N 20°51′E

114 N7 **Kardam** Dobrich, NE Bulgaria 43°36′N 28°06′E **Kardak** see Kardámyla

115 L18 **Kardámyla** var. Kardamila, Kardhámila. Chíos, E Greece 38°33′N 26°04′E **Kardeljevo** see Ploče

127 T3 **Kardh** see Qardho **Kardhámila** see Kardámyla

115 E16 **Karditsa** var. Kardhítsa. Thessalía, C Greece 39°22′N 21°56′E

118 E4 **Kärdla** Ger. Kertel. Hiiumaa, W Estonia 59°00′N 22°42′E

123 I10 **Karelia, Respublika** see Kareliya, Respublika

124 I10 **Karel'skaya ASSR**, Eng. Karelia. ◆ autonomous republic NW Russian Federation **Karel'skaya ASSR** see Kareliya, Respublika

81 E22 **Karema** Rukwa, W Tanzania 06°50′S 30°25′E

83 I14 **Karen** see Hualien

167 N8 **Karen State** var. Kawthule State, Kayin State. ◆ state S Burma (Myanmar) **Karesuando** Fin. Kaaresuanto, Lapp. Gárasavvon. Norrbotten, N Sweden 68°25′N 22°28′E **Karet** see Kâghet

92 J10 **Kárez-e-Elyās/Kārez Iliās** see Kârez-e Elyās

122 J5 **Kargasok** Tomskaya Oblast', C Russian Federation 59°01′N 80°34′E

122 J12 **Kargat** Novosibirskaya Oblast', C Russian Federation 55°11′N 80°24′E

136 J11 **Kargı** Çorum, N Turkey 41°09′N 34°32′E

152 J5 **Kargil** Jammu and Kashmir, NW India 34°34′N 76°06′E **Kargilik** see Yecheng

124 L10 **Kargopol'** Arkhangel'skaya Oblast', NW Russian Federation 61°30′N 38°53′E

110 F12 **Kargowa** Ger. Unruhstadt. Lubuskie, W Poland 52°05′N 15°50′E

77 X13 **Kari** Bauchi, E Nigeria 11°13′N 10°34′E

83 J16 **Kariba** Mashonaland West, N Zimbabwe 16°29′S 28°48′E

83 J16 **Kariba, Lake** ◙ Zambia/ Zimbabwe

165 Q4 **Kariba-yama** ▲ Hokkaidō, NE Japan 42°36′N 139°55′E

83 C19 **Karibib** Erongo, C Namibia 21°56′S 15°51′E

155 I14 **Karies** see Karyés

92 K9 **Karigasniemi** Lapp. Garegasnjárga. Lappi, N Finland 69°24′N 25°52′E

184 K3 **Karikari, Cape** headland North Island, New Zealand 34°47′S 173°24′E

152 J4 **Karimābād** see Hunza

169 P12 **Karimata, Kepulauan** island group N Indonesia

169 P12 **Karimata, Pulau** island Kepulauan Karimata, N Indonesia

169 O11 **Karimata, Selat** strait W Indonesia

155 I14 **Karimnagar** Andhra Pradesh, C India 18°28′N 79°09′E

186 C7 **Karimui** Chimbu, C Papua New Guinea 06°19′S 144°48′E

169 U12 **Karimunjawa, Pulau** island S Indonesia

80 N13 **Karin** Sahil, N Somalia 10°48′N 45°46′E **Kariot** see Ikaría

115 J20 **Káristos** see Kárystos

148 J4 **Kárkár** var. Kharkar. Etelä-Suomi, SW Finland 60°05′N 23°39′E **Kârîz-e-Elyâs** var. Kárez-e-Elyâs, Kárez Iliás. Herât, NW Afghanistan 35°26′N 61°24′E

145 R20 **Karkaralinsk** Kaz. Qarqaraly. Karaganda, E Kazakhstan 49°31′N 75°53′E

186 D6 **Karkar Island** island N Papua New Guinea

143 N7 **Karkas, Kūh-e** ▲ C Iran

142 K8 **Karkheh, Rūd-e** ✍ SW Iran

115 L20 **Karkinágri** var. Karkinagrio. Ikaría, Dodekánisa, Greece, Aegean Sea 37°31′N 26°01′E **Karkinagrio** see Karkinágri

117 R12 **Karkinits'ka Zatoka** Rus. Karkinitskiy Zaliv. gulf S Ukraine

KARKINITSKIY ZALIV – KELLETT, CAPE

Karkinitskiy Zaliv see Karkinits'ka Zatoka
93 L19 **Karkkila** Swe. Högfors. Uusimaa, S Finland 60°32′N 24°10′E
93 M19 **Kärkölä** Etelä-Suomi, S Finland 60°52′N 25°17′E
182 G9 **Karkoo** South Australia 34°03′S 135°45′E
Karkūk see Kirkūk
118 D5 **Kärla** Ger. Kergel. Saaremaa, W Estonia 58°20′N 22°15′E
Karleby see Kokkola
110 F7 **Karlino** Ger. Körlin an der Persante. Zachodnio-pomorskie, NW Poland 54°02′N 15°52′E
137 Q13 **Karlıova** Bingöl, E Turkey 39°16′N 41°01′E
117 U6 **Karlivka** Poltavs'ka Oblast', C Ukraine 49°27′N 35°08′E
Karl-Marx-Stadt see Chemnitz
Karlö see Hailuoto
112 C11 **Karlobag** It. Carlopago. Lika-Senj, W Croatia 44°31′N 15°06′E
112 D9 **Karlovac** Ger. Karlstadt, Hung. Károlyváros. Karlovac, C Croatia 45°29′N 15°31′E
112 C10 **Karlovac** off. Karlovačka Županija. ◈ province C Croatia
Karlovačka Županija see Karlovac
111 A16 **Karlovarský Kraj** ◈ W Czech Republic
115 M19 **Karlovási** var. Néon Karlovásion, Néon Karlovasi. Sámos, Dodekánisa, Greece, Aegean Sea 37°47′N 26°40′E
114 J9 **Karlovo** prev. Levskigrad. Plovdiv, C Bulgaria 42°38′N 24°49′E
111 A16 **Karlovy Vary** Ger. Karlsbad; prev. Eng. Carlsbad. Karlovarský Kraj, W Czech Republic 50°13′N 12°51′E
Karlsbad see Karlovy Vary
95 L17 **Karlsborg** Västra Götaland, S Sweden 58°32′N 14°32′E
Karlsburg see Alba Iulia
95 L22 **Karlshamn** Blekinge, S Sweden 56°10′N 14°50′E
95 L16 **Karlskoga** Örebro, C Sweden 59°19′N 14°33′E
95 M22 **Karlskrona** Blekinge, S Sweden 56°11′N 15°39′E
101 G21 **Karlsruhe** var. Carlsruhe. Baden-Württemberg, SW Germany 49°01′N 08°24′E
95 K16 **Karlstad** Värmland, C Sweden 59°22′N 13°36′E
29 R3 **Karlstad** Minnesota, N USA 48°34′N 96°31′W
101 I18 **Karlstadt** Bayern, C Germany 49°58′N 09°46′E
Karlstadt see Karlovac
39 Q14 **Karluk** Kodiak Island, Alaska, USA 57°34′N 154°27′W
Karluk see Qarluq
119 O17 **Karma** Rus. Korma. Homyel'skaya Voblasts', SE Belarus 53°07′N 30°48′E
155 F14 **Karmāla** Mahārāshtra, W India 18°26′N 75°08′E
146 M11 **Karmana** Navoiy Viloyati, C Uzbekistan 40°09′N 65°18′E
138 G8 **Karmi'el** var. Carmiel. Northern, N Israel 32°55′N 35°18′E
95 B16 **Karmøy** island S Norway
152 I9 **Karnāl** Haryāna, N India 29°41′N 76°58′E
153 W15 **Karnaphuli Reservoir** ⊠ NE India
155 F17 **Karnātaka** var. Kanara; prev. Maisur, Mysore. ◈ state W India
25 S13 **Karnes City** Texas, SW USA 28°54′N 97°55′W
109 P9 **Karnische Alpen** It. Alpi Carniche. ▲▲ Austria/Italy
114 M9 **Karnobat** Burgas, E Bulgaria 42°39′N 26°59′E
109 Q9 **Kärnten** off. Land Kärnten, Eng. Carinthia, Slvn. Koroška. ◈ state S Austria
Karnul see Kurnool
83 K16 **Karoi** Mashonaland West, N Zimbabwe 16°50′S 29°40′E
Karol see Carei
Károly-Fehérvár see Alba Iulia
Károlyváros see Karlovac
82 M12 **Karonga** Northern, N Malawi 09°54′S 33°55′E
147 W10 **Karool-Tëbë** Narynskaya Oblast', C Kyrgyzstan 40°33′N 75°52′E
182 J9 **Karoonda** South Australia 35°04′S 139°58′E
149 S9 **Karor Lāl Esan** Punjab, E Pakistan 31°15′N 70°58′E
149 T11 **Karor Pacca** var. Kahror, Kahror Pakka. Punjab, E Pakistan 29°38′N 71°59′E
Karosa see Karossa
171 N12 **Karossa** var. Karosa. Sulawesi, C Indonesia 01°38′S 119°21′E
Karpaten see Carpathian Mountains
115 L22 **Karpáthio Pélagos** sea Dodekánisa, Greece, Aegean Sea
115 N24 **Kárpathos** Kárpathos, SE Greece 35°30′N 27°13′E
115 N24 **Kárpathos** It. Scarpanto; anc. Carpathos, Carpathus. island SE Greece
Karpathos Strait see Karpathou, Stenó
115 N24 **Karpathou, Stenó** var. Karpathos Strait, Scarpanto Strait. strait Dodekánisa, Greece, Aegean Sea
Karpaty see Carpathian Mountains
115 E17 **Karpenísi** prev. Karpenísion. Stereá Ellás, C Greece 38°55′N 21°46′E
Karpenísion see Karpenísi
Karpilovka see Aktsyabrski
125 O8 **Karpogory** Arkhangel'skaya Oblast', NW Russian Federation 64°01′N 44°22′E
180 I7 **Karratha** Western Australia 20°44′S 116°52′E
137 S12 **Kars** var. Qars. Kars, NE Turkey 40°35′N 43°05′E
137 S12 **Kars** var. Qars. ◈ province NE Turkey
145 O12 **Karsakpay** Kaz. Qarsaqbay. Karaganda, C Kazakhstan 47°51′N 66°42′E
93 L15 **Kärsämäki** Oulu, C Finland 63°58′N 25°49′E
Karsau see Kārsava
118 K9 **Kārsava** Ger. Karsau; prev. Rus. Korsovka. Ludza, E Latvia 56°46′N 27°39′E
Karshi see Garşy, Turkmenistan
Karshi see Qarshi, Uzbekistan
Karshinskaya Step see Qarshi Cho'li
Karshinskiy Kanal see Qarshi Kanali
84 I5 **Karskiye Vorota, Proliv** Eng. Kara Strait. strait N Russian Federation
122 J6 **Karskoye More** Eng. Kara Sea. sea Arctic Ocean
93 L17 **Karstula** Länsi-Suomi, C Finland 62°52′N 24°48′E
127 Q5 **Karsun** Ul'yanovskaya Oblast', W Russian Federation 54°12′N 47°00′E
122 F11 **Kartaly** Chelyabinskaya Oblast', C Russian Federation 53°02′N 60°42′E
18 E13 **Karthaus** Pennsylvania, NE USA 41°06′N 78°03′W
110 I7 **Kartuzy** Pomorskie, NW Poland 54°21′N 18°11′E
165 R8 **Karumai** Iwate, Honshū, C Japan 40°19′N 141°27′E
181 U4 **Karumba** Queensland, NE Australia 17°31′S 140°51′E
142 L10 **Kārūn** var. Rūd-e Kārūn. ≈ SW Iran
92 K13 **Karungi** Norrbotten, N Sweden 66°03′N 23°55′E
92 K13 **Karunki** Lappi, N Finland 66°01′N 24°06′E
Kārūn, Rūd-e see Kārūn
155 H21 **Karūr** Tamil Nādu, SE India 10°58′N 78°03′E
93 K17 **Karvia** Länsi-Suomi, SW Finland 62°07′N 22°34′E
111 J17 **Karviná** Ger. Karwin, Pol. Karwina; prev. Nová Karvinná. Moravskoslezský Kraj, E Czech Republic 49°50′N 18°30′E
155 E17 **Kārwār** Karnātaka, W India 14°50′N 74°09′E
108 M7 **Karwendelgebirge** ▲▲ Austria/Germany
Karwin/Karwina see Karviná
115 I14 **Karyés** var. Karies. Ágion Óros, N Greece 40°15′N 24°15′E
115 I19 **Kárystos** var. Káristos. Évvoia, C Greece 38°01′N 24°25′E
136 E17 **Kaş** Antalya, SW Turkey 36°12′N 29°38′E
39 Y14 **Kasaan** Prince of Wales Island, Alaska, USA 55°32′N 132°24′W
164 I13 **Kasai** Hyōgo, Honshū, SW Japan 34°56′N 134°49′E
79 K21 **Kasai** var. Cassai, Kassai. ≈ Angola/Dem. Rep. Congo
79 K22 **Kasai-Occidental** off. Région Kasai Occidental. ◈ region S Dem. Rep. Congo
Kasai Occidental, Région see Kasai-Occidental
79 L21 **Kasai-Oriental** off. Région Kasai Oriental. ◈ region C Dem. Rep. Congo
Kasai Oriental, Région see Kasai-Oriental
79 L24 **Kasaji** Katanga, S Dem. Rep. Congo 10°22′S 23°29′E
82 L12 **Kasama** Northern, N Zambia 10°14′S 31°12′E
Kasan see Koson
83 H16 **Kasane** North-West, NE Botswana 17°48′S 20°06′E
81 E23 **Kasanga** Rukwa, W Tanzania 08°27′S 31°10′E
79 G21 **Kasangulu** Bas-Congo, W Dem. Rep. Congo 04°33′S 15°12′E
Kasansay see Kosonsoy
155 E20 **Kāsaragod** Kerala, SW India 12°30′N 74°59′E
Kasargen see Kasari
118 P13 **Kasari** var. Kasari Jõgi, Ger. Kasargen. ≈ W Estonia
Kasari Jõgi see Kasari
8 L11 **Kasba Lake** ⊗ Northwest Territories, Nunavut C Canada
Kaschau see Košice
164 B16 **Kaseda** var. Minami-Satsuma. Kagoshima, Kyūshū, SW Japan 31°25′N 130°17′E
83 I14 **Kasempa** North Western, NW Zambia 13°27′S 25°49′E
79 O24 **Kasenga** Katanga, SE Dem. Rep. Congo 10°22′S 28°37′E
79 P17 **Kasenye** var. Kasenyi. Orientale, NE Dem. Rep. Congo 01°23′N 30°25′E
Kasenyi see Kasenye
79 O19 **Kasese** Maniema, E Dem. Rep. Congo 01°36′S 27°31′E
81 E18 **Kasese** SW Uganda 0°10′N 30°06′E
152 J11 **Kāsganj** Uttar Pradesh, N India 27°48′N 78°38′E
143 U4 **Kashaf Rūd** ≈ NE Iran
143 N7 **Kāshān** Eşfahān, C Iran 33°57′N 51°31′E
126 M10 **Kashary** Rostovskaya Oblast', SW Russian Federation 49°02′N 40°58′E
39 O12 **Kashegelok** Alaska, USA 60°57′N 157°46′W
Kashgar see Kashi
158 E7 **Kashi** Chin. Kaxgar, K'o-shih, Uigh. Kashgar. Xinjiang Uygur Zizhiqu, NW China 39°32′N 75°58′E
164 J14 **Kashihara** var. Kasihara. Nara, Honshū, SW Japan 34°28′N 135°46′E
165 P13 **Kashima-nada** gulf S Japan
124 K15 **Kashin** Tverskaya Oblast', W Russian Federation 57°20′N 37°34′E
152 K10 **Kāshīpur** Uttarakhand, N India 29°13′N 78°58′E
126 L4 **Kashira** Moskovskaya Oblast', W Russian Federation 54°53′N 38°13′E
165 N11 **Kashiwazaki** var. Kasiwazaki. Niigata, Honshū, C Japan 37°22′N 138°33′E
Kashkadar'inskaya Oblast' see Qashqadaryo Viloyati
143 T5 **Kāshmar** var. Turshiz; prev. Solṭānābād, Torshiz. Khorāsān, NE Iran 35°13′N 58°25′E
Kashmir see Jammu and Kashmir
149 R12 **Kashmor** Sind, SE Pakistan 28°24′N 69°42′E
149 S5 **Kashmūnd Ghar** Eng. Kashmund Range. ▲▲ E Afghanistan
Kashmund Range see Kashmūnd Ghar
Kasi see Vārānasi
153 O12 **Kasia** Uttar Pradesh, N India 26°45′N 83°55′E
39 N12 **Kasigluk** Alaska, USA 60°54′N 162°31′W
Kasihara see Kashihara
39 R12 **Kasilof** Alaska, USA 60°20′N 151°16′W
Kasimköj see General Toshevo
126 M4 **Kasimov** Ryazanskaya Oblast', W Russian Federation 54°59′N 41°22′E
79 P18 **Kasindi** Nord-Kivu, E Dem. Rep. Congo 0°03′N 29°43′E
82 M12 **Kasitu** ≈ N Malawi
Kasiwazaki see Kashiwazaki
30 L14 **Kaskaskia River** ≈ Illinois, N USA
93 J17 **Kaskinen** Swe. Kaskö. Länsi-Suomi, W Finland 62°23′N 21°10′E
Kaskö see Kaskinen
Kas Kong see Kông, Kaôh
11 O17 **Kaslo** British Columbia, SW Canada 49°54′N 116°57′W
Käsmark see Kežmarok
169 T12 **Kasongan** Borneo, C Indonesia 02°01′S 113°21′E
79 N21 **Kasongo** Maniema, E Dem. Rep. Congo 04°22′S 26°42′E
79 H22 **Kasongo-Lunda** Bandundu, SW Dem. Rep. Congo 06°30′S 16°51′E
115 M24 **Kásos** island S Greece
Kasos Strait see Kasou, Stenó
115 M25 **Kasou, Stenó** var. Kasos Strait. strait Dodekánisos/Kríti, Greece, Aegean Sea
137 T10 **Kasp'i** C Georgia 41°54′N 44°25′E
114 M8 **Kaspichan** Shumen, NE Bulgaria 43°18′N 27°09′E
Kaspiy Mangy Oypaty see Caspian Depression
127 Q16 **Kaspiysk** Respublika Dagestan, SW Russian Federation 42°52′N 47°40′E
Kaspiyskiy see Lagan'
Kaspiyskoye More/Kaspiy Tengizi see Caspian Sea
Kassa see Košice
Kassai see Kasai
80 I9 **Kassala** Kassala, E Sudan 15°24′N 36°25′E
80 H9 **Kassala** ◈ state NE Sudan
115 G15 **Kassándra** prev. Pallíni; anc. Pallene. peninsula NE Greece
115 G15 **Kassándra** headland N Greece 39°58′N 23°22′E
115 H15 **Kassándras, Kólpos** var. Kólpos Toronaíos. gulf N Greece
139 Y11 **Kassārah** Maysān, E Iraq 31°21′N 47°25′E
101 I15 **Kassel** prev. Cassel. Hessen, C Germany 51°19′N 09°30′E
74 M6 **Kasserine** var. Al Qaşrayn. W Tunisia 35°15′N 08°52′E
14 J14 **Kasshabog Lake** ⊗ Ontario, SE Canada
139 O5 **Kassīr, Sabkhat al** ⊗ E Syria
29 W10 **Kasson** Minnesota, N USA 44°00′N 92°42′W
115 C17 **Kassópeia** Var. Kassópi. site of ancient city Ípeiros, W Greece
Kassópi see Kassópeia
115 N24 **Kastállou, Akrotírio** headland Kárpathos, SE Greece 35°24′N 27°08′E
136 I11 **Kastamonu** var. Castamoni, Kastamuni. Kastamonu, N Turkey 41°22′N 33°47′E
136 I10 **Kastamonu** var. Kastamuni. ◈ province N Turkey
Kastamuni see Kastamonu
115 E14 **Kastaneá** Kentrikí Makedonía, N Greece 40°25′N 22°09′E
Kastélli see Kíssamos
Kastellórizon see Megísti
95 N21 **Kastlösa** Kalmar, S Sweden 56°25′N 16°25′E
115 D14 **Kastoría** Dytikí Makedonía, N Greece 40°33′N 21°15′E
126 K7 **Kastornoye** Kurskaya Oblast', W Russian Federation 51°49′N 38°07′E
115 I21 **Kástro** Sífnos, Kykládes, Greece, Aegean Sea 36°58′N 24°45′E
95 J23 **Kastrup** ✈ (København) København, E Denmark 55°36′N 12°39′E
119 Q17 **Kastsyukovichy** Rus. Kostyukovichi. Mahilyowskaya Voblasts', E Belarus 53°20′N 32°03′E
119 O18 **Kastsyukowka** Rus. Kostyukovka. Homyel'skaya Voblasts', SE Belarus 52°32′N 30°54′E
164 D13 **Kasuga** Fukuoka, Kyūshū, SW Japan 33°31′N 130°27′E
164 L13 **Kasugai** Aichi, Honshū, SW Japan 35°15′N 136°57′E
81 E21 **Kasulu** Kigoma, W Tanzania 04°33′S 30°06′E
164 I12 **Kasumi** Hyōgo, Honshū, SW Japan 35°36′N 134°37′E
127 R17 **Kasumkent** Respublika Dagestan, SW Russian Federation 41°39′N 48°09′E
82 M13 **Kasungu** Central, C Malawi 13°04′S 33°29′E
149 W9 **Kasūr** Punjab, E Pakistan 31°07′N 74°30′E
83 G15 **Kataba** Western, W Zambia 15°28′S 23°25′E
19 R4 **Katahdin, Mount** ▲ Maine, NE USA 45°55′N 68°52′W
79 M20 **Katako-Kombe** Kasai-Oriental, C Dem. Rep. Congo 03°24′S 24°25′E
39 T12 **Katalla** Alaska, USA 60°12′N 144°31′W
Katana see Qaṭanā
79 L24 **Katanga** off. Région du Katanga; prev. Shaba. ◈ region SE Dem. Rep. Congo
122 M11 **Katanga** ≈ C Russian Federation
Katanga, Région du see Katanga
154 J11 **Katāngi** Madhya Pradesh, C India 21°46′N 79°50′E
180 J13 **Katanning** Western Australia 33°45′S 117°33′E
181 P8 **Kata Tjuta** var. Mount Olga. ▲ Northern Territory, C Australia 25°20′S 130°47′E
Katawaz see Zarghūn Shahr
151 Q22 **Katchall Island** island Nicobar Islands, India, NE Indian Ocean
115 F14 **Kateríni** Kentrikí Makedonía, N Greece 40°15′N 22°30′E
117 P7 **Katerynopil'** Cherkas'ka Oblast', C Ukraine 49°00′N 30°59′E
166 M3 **Katha** Sagaing, N Burma (Myanmar) 24°11′N 96°20′E
181 P2 **Katherine** Northern Territory, N Australia 14°29′S 132°20′E
154 B11 **Kāthiāwār Peninsula** peninsula W India
153 P11 **Kathmandu** prev. Kantipur. ● (Nepal) Central, C Nepal 27°46′N 85°17′E
152 H7 **Kathua** Jammu and Kashmir, NW India 32°23′N 75°34′E
76 L12 **Kati** Koulikoro, SW Mali 12°41′N 08°04′W
153 R13 **Katihār** Bihār, NE India 25°33′N 87°34′E
184 N7 **Katikati** Bay of Plenty, North Island, New Zealand 37°34′S 175°55′E
83 H16 **Katima Mulilo** Caprivi, NE Namibia 17°31′S 24°20′E
77 N15 **Katiola** C Ivory Coast 08°11′N 05°04′W
191 V10 **Katiu** atoll Îles Tuamotu, C French Polynesia
117 N12 **Katlabukh, Ozero** ⊗ SW Ukraine
39 P14 **Katmai, Mount** ▲ Alaska, USA 58°16′N 154°57′W
154 J9 **Katni** Madhya Pradesh, C India 23°47′N 80°29′E
115 D19 **Káto Achaïa** var. Kato Ahaia, Káto Akhaía. Dytikí Ellás, S Greece 38°08′N 21°33′E
Kato Ahaia/Káto Akhaía see Káto Achaïa
121 P2 **Kato Lakatámeia** var. Kato Lakatamia. C Cyprus 35°07′N 33°20′E
Kato Lakatamia see Kato Lakatámeia
79 N22 **Katompi** Katanga, SE Dem. Rep. Congo 06°10′S 26°19′E
83 K14 **Katondwe** Lusaka, C Zambia 15°08′S 30°10′E
114 H12 **Káto Nevrokópi** prev. Káto Nevrokópion. Anatolikí Makedonía kai Thráki, NE Greece 41°21′N 23°51′E
Káto Nevrokópion see Káto Nevrokópi
81 E18 **Katonga** ≈ S Uganda
115 F15 **Káto Ólympos** ▲▲ C Greece
115 D17 **Katoúna** Dytikí Ellás, C Greece 38°47′N 21°07′E
115 E19 **Káto Vlasiá** Dytikí Makedonía, S Greece 38°02′N 21°54′E
111 J16 **Katowice** Ger. Kattowitz. Śląskie, S Poland 50°15′N 19°01′E
153 S15 **Kātoya** West Bengal, NE India 23°39′N 88°11′E
136 E16 **Katrançik Dağı** ▲▲ SW Turkey
95 N16 **Katrineholm** Södermanland, C Sweden 58°59′N 16°15′E
96 I11 **Katrine, Loch** ⊗ C Scotland, United Kingdom
77 V12 **Katsina** Katsina, N Nigeria 12°59′N 07°33′E
77 U12 **Katsina** ◈ state N Nigeria
67 P8 **Katsina Ala** ≈ S Nigeria
164 C13 **Katsumoto** Nagasaki, Iki, SW Japan 33°49′N 129°42′E
165 P13 **Katsuta** var. Katuta. Ibaraki, Honshū, S Japan 36°24′N 140°32′E
165 O14 **Katsuura** var. Katuura. Chiba, Honshū, S Japan 35°09′N 140°16′E
164 K12 **Katsuyama** var. Katuyama. Fukui, Honshū, SW Japan 36°00′N 136°30′E
164 H12 **Katsuyama** Okayama, Honshū, SW Japan 35°06′N 133°43′E
Kattakurgan see Kattaqo'rg'on
147 N11 **Kattaqo'rg'on** Rus. Kattakurgan. Samarqand Viloyati, C Uzbekistan 39°56′N 66°11′E
115 O23 **Kattavía** Ródos, Dodekánisa, Greece, Aegean Sea 35°56′N 27°47′E
95 I21 **Kattegat** Dan. Kattegatt. strait N Europe
Kattegatt see Kattegat
95 P19 **Katthammarsvik** Gotland, SE Sweden 57°27′N 18°54′E
Kattowitz see Katowice
122 J13 **Katun'** ≈ S Russian Federation
Katuta see Katsuta
Katuura see Katsuura
Katuyama see Katsuyama
Katwijk see Katwijk aan Zee
98 G11 **Katwijk aan Zee** var. Katwijk. Zuid-Holland, W Netherlands 52°12′N 04°24′E
38 B8 **Kaua'i** var. Kauai. island Hawaiian Islands, Hawai'i, USA, C Pacific Ocean
Kauai see Kaua'i
38 C8 **Kaua'i Channel** var. Kauai Channel. channel Hawai'i, USA, C Pacific Ocean
Kauai Channel see Kaua'i Channel
171 R13 **Kaubalatmada, Gunung** var. Kaplamada. ▲ Pulau Buru, E Indonesia 03°16′S 126°17′E
191 U10 **Kauehi** atoll Îles Tuamotu, C French Polynesia
Kauen see Kaunas
101 K24 **Kaufbeuren** Bayern, S Germany 47°53′N 10°37′E
25 U7 **Kaufman** Texas, SW USA 32°35′N 96°18′W
101 I15 **Kaufungen** Hessen, C Germany 51°16′N 09°39′E
93 K17 **Kauhajoki** Länsi-Suomi, W Finland 62°26′N 22°10′E
93 K16 **Kauhava** Länsi-Suomi, W Finland 63°06′N 23°08′E
30 M7 **Kaukauna** Wisconsin, N USA 44°18′N 88°18′W
92 L11 **Kaukonen** Lappi, N Finland 67°28′N 24°49′E
38 A8 **Kaulakahi Channel** channel Hawai'i, USA, C Pacific Ocean
38 E9 **Kaunakakai** Moloka'i, Hawaii, USA, C Pacific Ocean 21°05′N 157°01′W
38 F12 **Kaunā Point** var. Kauna Point. headland Hawai'i, USA, C Pacific Ocean 19°02′N 155°52′W
Kauna Point see Kaunā Point
118 F13 **Kaunas** Ger. Kauen, Pol. Kowno; prev. Rus. Kovno. Kaunas, C Lithuania 54°54′N 23°57′E
118 F13 **Kaunas** ◈ province C Lithuania
186 C6 **Kaup** East Sepik, NW Papua New Guinea 03°50′S 144°01′E
77 U12 **Kaura Namoda** Zamfara, NW Nigeria 12°43′N 06°17′E
Kaushany see Căuşeni
93 K16 **Kaustinen** Länsi-Suomi, W Finland 63°33′N 23°40′E
99 M23 **Kautenbach** Diekirch, NE Luxembourg 49°57′N 06°01′E
92 K10 **Kautokeino** Lapp. Guovdageaidnu. Finnmark, N Norway 69°N 23°01′E
Kavadar see Kavadarci
113 P19 **Kavadarci** Turk. Kavadar. C Macedonia 41°25′N 22°00′E
Kavaja see Kavajë
113 K20 **Kavajë** It. Cavaia, Kavaja. Tiranë, W Albania 41°11′N 19°33′E
114 M13 **Kavak Çayı** ≈ NW Turkey
Kavakli see Topolovgrad
114 I13 **Kavála** prev. Kaválla. Anatolikí Makedonía kai Thráki, NE Greece 40°57′N 24°26′E
114 I13 **Kaválas, Kólpos** gulf Aegean Sea, NE Mediterranean Sea
155 J17 **Kāvali** Andhra Pradesh, E India 15°05′N 80°02′E
Kaválla see Kavála
Kavango see Cubango/Okavango
155 C21 **Kavaratti** Lakshadweep, SW India 10°33′N 72°38′E
114 O8 **Kavarna** Dobrich, NE Bulgaria 43°27′N 28°21′E
118 G12 **Kavarskas** Utena, E Lithuania 55°27′N 24°55′E
76 I13 **Kavendou** ▲ C Guinea 10°49′N 12°14′W
Kavengo see Cubango/Okavango
155 F20 **Kāveri** var. Cauvery. ≈ S India
186 G5 **Kavieng** var. Kaewieng. New Ireland, NE Papua New Guinea 02°34′S 152°11′E
83 H16 **Kavimba** North-West, NE Botswana 18°02′S 24°38′E
83 I15 **Kavingu** Southern, S Zambia 15°39′S 26°03′E
143 Q6 **Kavīr, Dasht-e** var. Great Salt Desert. salt pan N Iran
Kavirondo Gulf see Winam Gulf
Kavkaz see Caucasus
95 K23 **Kävlinge** Skåne, S Sweden 55°47′N 13°05′E
82 G12 **Kavungo** Moxico, E Angola 11°31′S 22°59′E
165 Q8 **Kawabe** Akita, Honshū, C Japan 39°39′N 140°14′E
165 R9 **Kawai** Iwate, Honshū, C Japan 39°36′N 141°40′E
38 A8 **Kawaihoa Point** headland Ni'ihau, Hawai'i, USA, C Pacific Ocean 21°47′N 160°12′W
184 K3 **Kawakawa** Northland, North Island, New Zealand 35°23′S 174°06′E
82 I13 **Kawama** North Western, NW Zambia 13°04′S 25°59′E
82 K11 **Kawambwa** Luapula, N Zambia 09°45′S 29°10′E
154 K11 **Kawardha** Chhattisgarh, C India 21°59′N 81°12′E
14 I14 **Kawartha Lakes** ⊗ Ontario, SE Canada
165 O13 **Kawasaki** Kanagawa, Honshū, S Japan 35°32′N 139°41′E
171 R12 **Kawassi** Pulau Obi, E Indonesia 01°32′S 127°25′E
165 R6 **Kawauchi** Aomori, Honshū, C Japan 41°11′N 141°00′E
184 L5 **Kawau Island** island N New Zealand
184 N10 **Kaweka Range** ▲▲ North Island, New Zealand
Kawelecht see Puhja
184 O8 **Kawerau** Bay of Plenty, North Island, New Zealand 38°06′S 176°43′E
184 L8 **Kawhia** Waikato, North Island, New Zealand 38°04′S 174°49′E
184 K8 **Kawhia Harbour** inlet North Island, New Zealand
35 V8 **Kawich Peak** ▲ Nevada, W USA 38°00′N 116°27′W
35 V9 **Kawich Range** ▲▲ Nevada, W USA
14 G12 **Kawigamog Lake** ⊗ Ontario, S Canada
171 P9 **Kawio, Kepulauan** island group N Indonesia
167 N9 **Kawkareik** Kayin State, S Burma (Myanmar) 16°33′N 98°18′E
27 O8 **Kaw Lake** ⊠ Oklahoma, C USA
166 M3 **Kawlin** Sagaing, N Burma (Myanmar) 23°48′N 95°41′E
Kawm Umbū see Kom Ombo
Kawthule State see Karen State
Kaxgar see Kashi
158 D7 **Kaxgar He** ≈ NW China
158 J5 **Kax He** ≈ NW China
77 P12 **Kaya** C Burkina 13°04′N 01°09′W
167 N6 **Kayah State** ◈ state C Burma (Myanmar)
39 T12 **Kayak Island** island Alaska, USA
114 M11 **Kayalıköy Barajı** ⊠ NW Turkey
166 M8 **Kayan** Yangon, SW Burma (Myanmar) 16°54′N 96°35′E
Kayangel Islands see Ngcheangel
155 G23 **Kāyankulam** Kerala, SW India 09°10′N 76°31′E
169 V9 **Kayan, Sungai** prev. Kajan. ≈ Borneo, C Indonesia
144 F14 **Kaydak, Sor** salt flat SW Kazakhstan
Kaydanovo see Dzyarzhynsk Belarus
37 N9 **Kayenta** Arizona, SW USA 36°43′N 110°15′W
76 J11 **Kayes** Kayes, W Mali 14°26′N 11°22′W
76 J11 **Kayes** ◈ region SW Mali
Kayin State see Karen State
145 U10 **Kaynar** Kaz. Qaynar, var. Kajnar. Vostochnyy Kazakhstan, E Kazakhstan 49°13′N 77°27′E
Kaynary see Căinari
83 H15 **Kayoya** Western, W Zambia 16°13′S 24°09′E
Kayrakkum see Qayroqqum
Kayrakkumskoye Vodokhranilishche see Qayroqqum, Obanbori
136 K14 **Kayseri** var. Kaisaria; anc. Caesarea Mazaca, Mazaca. Kayseri, C Turkey 38°42′N 35°28′E
136 K14 **Kayseri** var. Kaisaria. ◈ province C Turkey
36 L2 **Kaysville** Utah, W USA 41°10′N 111°55′W
Kayyngdy see Kaindy
14 L11 **Kazabazua** Québec, SE Canada 45°58′N 76°00′W
14 L12 **Kazabazua** ≈ Québec, SE Canada
123 Q7 **Kazach'ye** Respublika Sakha (Yakutiya), NE Russian Federation 70°38′N 135°54′E
Kazakdar'ya see Qozoqdaryo
146 E9 **Kazakhlyshor, Solonchak** var. Solonchak Shorkazakhly. salt marsh NW Turkmenistan
Kazakhskaya SSR/Kazakh Soviet Socialist Republic see Kazakhstan
145 R9 **Kazakhskiy Melkosopochnik** Eng. Kazakh Uplands, Kirghiz Steppe, Kaz. Saryarqa. uplands C Kazakhstan
144 L12 **Kazakhstan** off. Republic of Kazakhstan, var. Kazakstan, Kaz. Qazaqstan Respublikasy; prev. Kazakh Soviet Socialist Republic, Rus. Kazakhskaya SSR. ◆ republic C Asia
Kazakhstan, Republic of see Kazakhstan
Kazakh Uplands see Kazakhskiy Melkosopochnik
Kazakstan see Kazakhstan
144 L14 **Kazalinsk** Kzyl-Orda, S Kazakhstan 45°45′N 62°01′E
127 R4 **Kazan'** Respublika Tatarstan, W Russian Federation 55°43′N 49°07′E
8 M10 **Kazan** ≈ Nunavut, NW Canada
127 R4 **Kazan'** ✈ Respublika Tatarstan, W Russian Federation 55°46′N 49°21′E
Kazandzhik see Bereket
117 R8 **Kazanka** Mykolayivs'ka Oblast', S Ukraine 47°49′N 32°50′E
Kazanketken see Qozonketkan
Kazanlik see Kazanlŭk
114 J9 **Kazanlŭk** prev. Kazanlik. Stara Zagora, C Bulgaria 42°38′N 25°24′E
165 Y16 **Kazan-rettō** Eng. Volcano Islands. island group SE Japan
117 V12 **Kazantip, Mys** headland S Ukraine 45°27′N 35°50′E
147 U9 **Kazarman** Narynskaya Oblast', C Kyrgyzstan 41°21′N 74°03′E
Kazatin see Kozyatyn
Kazbegi see Qazbegi
Kazbegi see Kazbek
137 T9 **Kazbek** var. Kazbegi, Geor. Mqinvartsveri. ▲ N Georgia 42°43′N 44°28′E
82 M13 **Kazembe** Eastern, NE Zambia 12°06′S 32°45′E
143 N11 **Kāzerūn** Fārs, S Iran 29°41′N 51°38′E
125 R12 **Kazhym** Respublika Komi, NW Russian Federation 60°19′N 51°26′E
Kazi Ahmad see Qāzi Ahmad
Kazi Magomed see Qazimämmäd
136 H16 **Kazımkarabekir** Karaman, S Turkey 37°13′N 32°58′E
111 M20 **Kazincbarcika** Borsod-Abaúj-Zemplén, NE Hungary 48°15′N 20°40′E
119 H17 **Kazlowshchyna** Pol. Kozlowszczyzna, Rus. Kozlovshchina. Hrodzyenskaya Voblasts', W Belarus 53°19′N 25°18′E
119 E14 **Kazlų Rūda** Marijampolė, S Lithuania 54°45′N 23°28′E
144 E9 **Kaztalovka** Zapadnyy Kazakhstan, W Kazakhstan 49°45′N 48°42′E
79 K22 **Kazumba** Kasai-Occidental, S Dem. Rep. Congo 06°25′S 22°02′E
165 Q8 **Kazuno** Akita, Honshū, C Japan 40°14′N 140°48′E
Kazvin see Qazvin
118 J12 **Kaz'yany** Rus. Koz'yany. Vitsyebskaya Voblasts', NW Belarus 55°18′N 26°52′E
122 H9 **Kazym** ≈ N Russian Federation
110 H10 **Kcynia** Ger. Exin. Kujawsko-pomorskie, C Poland 53°00′N 17°29′E
Kéa see Tziá
Kéa see Ioulís
38 H11 **Kea'au** var. Keaau. Hawaii, USA, C Pacific Ocean 19°36′N 155°01′W
Keaau see Kea'au
38 F11 **Keāhole Point** var. Keahole Point. headland Hawai'i, USA, C Pacific Ocean 19°43′N 156°03′W
38 G12 **Kealakekua** Hawaii, USA, C Pacific Ocean 19°31′N 155°56′W
38 H11 **Kea, Mauna** ▲ Hawai'i, USA 19°50′N 155°30′W
37 N10 **Keams** Arizona, SW USA 35°47′N 110°09′W
Kéamu see Aneityum
29 O16 **Kearney** Nebraska, C USA 40°42′N 99°06′W
36 L3 **Kearns** Utah, W USA 40°39′N 112°00′W
115 H20 **Kéas, Stenó** strait SE Greece
137 O14 **Keban Barajı** dam C Turkey
137 O14 **Keban Barajı** ⊠ C Turkey
77 S13 **Kebbi** ◈ state NW Nigeria
76 G10 **Kébémèr** NW Senegal 15°24′N 16°25′W
74 M7 **Kebili** var. Qibilī. C Tunisia 33°42′N 09°06′E
138 H4 **Kebir, Nahr el** ≈ NW Syria
80 A10 **Kebkabiya** Northern Darfur, W Sudan 13°39′N 24°05′E
92 I11 **Kebnekaise** ▲ N Sweden 68°01′N 18°24′E
81 M14 **K'ebrī Dehar** Somalē, E Ethiopia 06°43′N 44°15′E
148 K15 **Kech** ≈ SW Pakistan
10 K10 **Kechika** ≈ British Columbia, W Canada
111 K23 **Kecskemét** Bács-Kiskun, C Hungary 46°54′N 19°42′E
168 J6 **Kedah** ◈ state Peninsular Malaysia
118 F12 **Kėdainiai** Kaunas, C Lithuania 55°19′N 24°00′E
152 K8 **Kedārnāth** Uttarakhand, N India 30°44′N 79°03′E
Kedder see Kehra
13 N13 **Kedgwick** New Brunswick, SE Canada 47°38′N 67°21′W
169 R16 **Kediri** Jawa, C Indonesia 07°45′S 112°01′E
171 Y13 **Kedir Sarmi** Papua, E Indonesia 02°00′S 139°01′E
163 V7 **Kedong** Heilongjiang, NE China 48°00′N 126°15′E
76 I12 **Kédougou** SE Senegal 12°35′N 12°09′W
122 I11 **Kedrovyy** Tomskaya Oblast', C Russian Federation 57°31′N 79°45′E
111 H16 **Kędzierzyn-Kozle** Ger. Heydebrech. Opolskie, S Poland 50°20′N 18°12′E
8 H8 **Keele** ≈ Northwest Territories, NW Canada
10 K6 **Keele Peak** ▲ Yukon Territory, NW Canada 63°31′N 130°21′W
Keelung see Chilung
19 N10 **Keene** New Hampshire, NE USA 42°56′N 72°14′W
99 H17 **Keerbergen** Vlaams Brabant, C Belgium 51°01′N 04°39′E
83 E21 **Keetmanshoop** Karas, S Namibia 26°36′S 18°08′E
12 A11 **Keewatin** Ontario, S Canada 49°47′N 94°30′W
29 V4 **Keewatin** Minnesota, N USA 47°24′N 93°04′W
Kefallinía see Kefallonía
115 B18 **Kefallonía** var. Kefallinía. island Iónia Nisiá, Greece, C Mediterranean Sea
115 M22 **Kéfalos** Kos, Dodekánisa, Greece, Aegean Sea 36°44′N 26°58′E
171 Q17 **Kefamenanu** Timor, C Indonesia 09°31′S 124°29′E
Kefar Sava see Kfar Sava
Kefe see Feodosiya
77 V15 **Keffi** Nassarawa, C Nigeria 08°52′N 07°54′E
92 H4 **Keflavík** Reykjanes, W Iceland 64°01′N 22°35′W
92 H4 **Keflavík** ✈ (Reykjavík) Reykjanes, W Iceland 63°58′N 22°37′W
Kegalee see Kegalla
155 J25 **Kegalla** var. Kegalee, Kegalle. Sabaragamuwa Province, C Sri Lanka 07°14′N 80°21′E
Kegalle see Kegalla
Kegayli see Kegeyli
Kegel see Keila
145 W16 **Kegen** Almaty, SE Kazakhstan 42°58′N 79°12′E
146 H7 **Kegeyli** prev. Kegayli. Qoraqalpog'iston Respublikasi, W Uzbekistan 42°46′N 59°49′E
101 F22 **Kehl** Baden-Württemberg, SW Germany 48°34′N 07°49′E
118 H3 **Kehra** Ger. Kedder. Harjumaa, NW Estonia 59°19′N 25°21′E
117 U6 **Kehychivka** Kharkivs'ka Oblast', E Ukraine 49°18′N 35°46′E
97 L17 **Keighley** N England, United Kingdom 53°51′N 01°58′W
Kei Islands see Kai, Kepulauan
Keijō see Sŏul
118 G3 **Keila** Ger. Kegel. Harjumaa, NW Estonia 59°18′N 24°29′E
Keilberg see Klínovec
83 F23 **Keimoes** Northern Cape, W South Africa 28°41′S 20°59′E
Keina/Keinis see Käina
Keishū see Kyŏngju
77 T11 **Keita** Tahoua, C Niger 14°45′N 05°40′E
78 J12 **Kéita, Bahr** var. Doka. ≈ S Chad
182 K10 **Keith** South Australia 36°01′S 140°22′E
96 K8 **Keith** NE Scotland, United Kingdom 57°33′N 02°57′W
26 K3 **Keith Sebelius Lake** ⊠ Kansas, C USA
32 G11 **Keizer** Oregon, NW USA 44°59′N 123°01′W
38 A8 **Kekaha** Kaua'i, Hawaii, USA, C Pacific Ocean 21°58′N 159°43′W
147 U10 **Këk-Art** prev. Alaykel', Alay-Kuu. Oshskaya Oblast', SW Kyrgyzstan 40°16′N 74°21′E
147 W10 **Këk-Aygyr** var. Keyaygyr. Narynskaya Oblast', C Kyrgyzstan 40°42′N 75°37′E
147 V9 **Këk-Dzhar** Narynskaya Oblast', C Kyrgyzstan 41°28′N 74°48′E
14 L8 **Kekek** ≈ Québec, SE Canada
185 K15 **Kekerengu** Canterbury, South Island, New Zealand 41°55′S 174°05′E
111 L21 **Kékes** ▲ N Hungary 47°53′N 19°59′E
171 P17 **Kekneno, Gunung** ▲ Timor, S Indonesia
147 S9 **Këk-Tash** Kir. Kök-Tash. Dzhalal-Abadskaya Oblast', W Kyrgyzstan 41°08′N 72°25′E
81 M15 **K'elafo** Sumalē, E Ethiopia 05°36′N 44°12′E
169 U10 **Kelai, Sungai** ≈ Borneo, N Indonesia
Kelamayi see Karamay
Kelang see Klang
168 K7 **Kelantan** ◈ state Peninsular Malaysia
Kelantan see Kelantan, Sungai
168 K7 **Kelantan, Sungai** var. Kelantan. ≈ Peninsular Malaysia
Kelat see Kālat
Kelcyra see Këlcyrë
113 L22 **Këlcyrë** var. Kelcyra. Gjirokastër, S Albania 40°19′N 20°10′E
Kelifskiy Uzboy see Kelif Uzboýy
146 L14 **Kelif Uzboýy** Rus. Kelifskiy Uzboy. salt marsh E Turkmenistan
137 O12 **Kelkit** Gümüşhane, NE Turkey 40°07′N 39°28′E
136 M12 **Kelkit Çayı** ≈ N Turkey
79 G18 **Kellé** Cuvette-Ouest, W Congo 0°04′S 14°33′E
77 W11 **Kellé** Zinder, S Niger 14°10′N 10°10′E
145 P7 **Kellerovka** Severnyy Kazakhstan, N Kazakhstan 53°51′N 69°15′E
8 I5 **Kellett, Cape** headland Banks Island, Northwest Territories, NW Canada 71°57′N 125°55′W

◆ Country
● Country Capital
◇ Dependent Territory
○ Dependent Territory Capital
◈ Administrative Regions
✈ International Airport
▲ Mountain
▲▲ Mountain Range
Volcano
≈ River
⊗ Lake
⊠ Reservoir

31 S11 **Kelleys Island** island Ohio, N USA
33 N8 **Kellogg** Idaho, NW USA 47°30′N 116°07′W
92 M12 **Kelloselkä** Lappi, N Finland 66°56′N 28°52′E
97 F17 **Kells** Ir. Ceanannas. Meath, E Ireland 53°44′N 06°53′W
118 E12 **Kelmé** Šiaulai, C Lithuania 55°39′N 22°57′E
99 M19 **Kelmis** var. La Calamine. Liège, E Belgium 50°43′N 06°01′E
78 H12 **Kélo** Tandjilé, SW Chad 09°21′N 15°50′E
83 I14 **Kelongwa** North Western, NW Zambia 13°41′S 26°19′E
11 N17 **Kelowna** British Columbia, SW Canada 49°50′N 119°29′W
11 X12 **Kelsey** Manitoba, C Canada 56°02′N 96°31′W
34 M6 **Kelseyville** California, W USA 38°58′N 122°51′W
96 K13 **Kelso** SE Scotland, United Kingdom 55°36′N 02°27′W
32 G10 **Kelso** Washington, NW USA 46°09′N 122°54′W
195 W15 **Keltie, Cape** headland Antarctica
Keltsy see Kielce
168 L9 **Keluang** var. Kluang. Johor, Peninsular Malaysia 02°01′N 103°18′E
168 M11 **Kelume** Pulau Lingga, W Indonesia 0°12′S 104°27′E
11 U15 **Kelvington** Saskatchewan, S Canada 52°10′N 103°30′W
124 J7 **Kem'** Respublika Kareliya, NW Russian Federation 64°55′N 34°18′E
124 I7 **Kem'** ✍ NW Russian Federation
137 O13 **Kemah** Erzincan, E Turkey 39°35′N 39°02′E
137 N13 **Kemaliye** Erzincan, C Turkey 39°16′N 38°29′E
Kemaman see Cukai
Kemanlar see Isperikh
10 K14 **Kemano** British Columbia, SW Canada 53°39′N 127°58′W
171 P12 **Kembani** Pulau Peleng, N Indonesia 01°32′S 122°57′E
136 F17 **Kemer** Antalya, SW Turkey 36°39′N 30°33′E
122 J12 **Kemerovo** prev. Shcheglovsk. Kemerovskaya Oblast', C Russian Federation 55°25′N 86°05′E
122 K12 **Kemerovskaya Oblast'** ◆ province S Russian Federation
92 L13 **Kemi** Lappi, NW Finland 65°46′N 24°34′E
92 M12 **Kemijärvi** Swe. Kemiträsk. Lappi, N Finland 66°41′N 27°24′E
92 M12 **Kemijärvi** ◎ N Finland
92 L13 **Kemijoki** ✍ NW Finland
147 V7 **Kemin** prev. Bystrovka. Chuyskaya Oblast', N Kyrgyzstan
92 L13 **Keminmaa** Lappi, NW Finland 65°49′N 24°34′E
Kemins Island see Nikumaroro
Kemiö see Kimito
Kemiträsk see Kemijärvi
127 P5 **Kemlya** Respublika Mordoviya, W Russian Federation 54°42′N 45°16′E
99 B18 **Kemmel** West-Vlaanderen, W Belgium 50°42′N 02°51′E
33 S16 **Kemmerer** Wyoming, C USA 41°47′N 110°32′W
Kemmuna see Comino
79 I14 **Kémo** ◆ prefecture S Central African Republic
25 U7 **Kemp** Texas, SW USA 32°26′N 96°13′W
93 L14 **Kempele** Oulu, C Finland 64°56′N 25°26′E
101 D15 **Kempen** Nordrhein-Westfalen, W Germany 51°22′N 06°25′E
25 Q5 **Kemp, Lake** ◎ Texas, SW USA
195 W5 **Kemp Land** physical region Antarctica
25 S9 **Kempner** Texas, SW USA 31°03′S 98°01′W
44 H3 **Kemp's Bay** Andros Island, W Bahamas 24°02′N 77°32′W
183 U6 **Kempsey** New South Wales, SE Australia 31°05′S 152°50′E
101 J24 **Kempten** Bayern, S Germany 47°44′N 10°19′E
15 N9 **Kempt, Lac** ◎ Québec, SE Canada
183 P17 **Kempton** Tasmania, SE Australia 42°34′S 147°13′E
154 J9 **Ken** ✍ C India
39 R12 **Kenai** Alaska, USA 60°33′N 151°15′W
0 D5 **Kenai Mountains** ▲ Alaska, USA
39 R12 **Kenai Peninsula** peninsula Alaska, USA
21 V11 **Kenansville** North Carolina, SE USA 34°57′N 77°54′W
146 A10 **Kenar** prev. Rus. Ufra. Balkan Welaýaty, NW Turkmenistan 40°00′N 53°05′E
121 U13 **Kenâyis, Râs el-** headland N Egypt 31°13′N 27°53′E
97 K16 **Kendal** NW England, United Kingdom 54°20′N 02°45′W
23 Y16 **Kendall** Florida, SE USA 25°33′N 80°18′W
9 O8 **Kendall, Cape** headland Nunavut, E Canada 63°31′N 87°09′W
18 J15 **Kendall Park** New Jersey, NE USA 40°25′N 74°33′W
31 Q11 **Kendallville** Indiana, N USA 41°26′N 85°15′W
171 N12 **Kendari** Sulawesi, C Indonesia 03°57′S 122°36′E
169 Q13 **Kendawangan** Borneo, C Indonesia 02°32′S 110°13′E
154 O12 **Kendrāpara** ◆ Orissa, E India 20°29′N 86°25′E
Kendrāparha see Kendrapara
154 O11 **Kendujhargarh** prev. Keonjihargarh. Orissa, E India 21°38′N 85°40′E
25 S13 **Kenedy** Texas, SW USA 28°49′N 97°51′W
76 J15 **Kenema** SE Sierra Leone 07°51′N 11°12′W
29 P16 **Kenesaw** Nebraska, C USA 40°37′N 98°39′W
Kēneugesenc see Köneürgenç
79 H21 **Kenge** Bandundu, SW Dem. Rep. Congo 04°52′S 16°59′E
Kengen see Kangen

167 O5 **Keng Tung** var. Kentung. Shan State, E Burma (Myanmar) 21°18′N 99°36′E
83 F23 **Kenhardt** Northern Cape, W South Africa 29°19′S 21°08′E
76 J12 **Kéniéba** Kayes, W Mali 12°47′N 11°16′W
Kenimekh see Konimex
169 U7 **Keningau** Sabah, East Malaysia 05°21′N 116°11′E
74 F6 **Kénitra** prev. Port-Lyautey. NW Morocco 34°20′N 06°29′W
21 V9 **Kenly** North Carolina, SE USA 35°39′N 78°16′W
97 B21 **Kenmare** Ir. Neidín. S Ireland 51°53′N 09°35′W
28 L2 **Kenmare** North Dakota, N USA 48°40′N 102°04′W
97 A21 **Kenmare River** Ir. An Ribhéar. inlet NE Atlantic Ocean
18 D10 **Kenmore** New York, NE USA 42°58′N 78°52′W
25 W8 **Kennard** Texas, SW USA 31°21′N 95°10′W
29 N10 **Kennebec** South Dakota, N USA 43°53′N 99°51′W
19 Q7 **Kennebec River** ✍ Maine, NE USA
19 P9 **Kennebunk** Maine, NE USA 43°22′N 70°33′W
39 R13 **Kennedy Entrance** strait Alaska, USA
166 L3 **Kennedy Peak** ▲ W Burma (Myanmar) 23°18′N 93°52′E
22 K9 **Kenner** Louisiana, S USA 29°57′N 90°15′W
180 I8 **Kenneth Range** ▲ Western Australia
27 Y9 **Kennett** Missouri, C USA 36°15′N 90°04′W
18 I16 **Kennett Square** Pennsylvania, NE USA
32 K10 **Kennewick** Washington, NW USA 46°12′N 119°08′W
12 E11 **Kenogami** ✍ Ontario, S Canada
15 Q7 **Kénogami, Lac** ◎ Québec, SE Canada
14 G8 **Kenogami Lake** ◎ Ontario, S Canada 48°04′N 80°10′W
14 F7 **Kenogamissi Lake** ◎ Ontario, S Canada
10 I6 **Keno Hill** Yukon Territory, NW Canada 63°54′N 135°18′W
12 A11 **Kenora** Ontario, S Canada 49°47′N 94°26′W
31 N9 **Kenosha** Wisconsin, N USA 42°34′N 87°50′W
13 P14 **Kensington** Prince Edward Island, SE Canada 46°26′N 63°39′W
26 L3 **Kensington** Kansas, C USA 39°46′N 99°01′W
32 I11 **Kent** Oregon, NW USA 45°13′N 120°43′W
24 J9 **Kent** Texas, SW USA 31°03′N 104°13′W
32 H8 **Kent** Washington, NW USA 47°22′N 122°13′W
97 P22 **Kent** cultural region SE England, United Kingdom
145 P16 **Kentau** Yuzhnyy Kazakhstan, S Kazakhstan 43°28′N 68°41′E
183 P14 **Kent Group** island group Tasmania, SE Australia
31 N12 **Kentland** Indiana, N USA 40°46′N 87°26′W
31 R12 **Kenton** Ohio, N USA 40°39′N 83°43′W
8 K7 **Kent Peninsula** peninsula Nunavut, N Canada
115 F14 **Kentrikí Makedonía** Eng. Macedonia Central. ◆ region N Greece
20 J6 **Kentucky** off. Commonwealth of Kentucky, also known as Bluegrass State. ◆ state C USA
20 H8 **Kentucky Lake** ◎ Kentucky/Tennessee, S USA
Kentung see Keng Tung
13 P15 **Kentville** Nova Scotia, SE Canada 45°04′N 64°30′W
22 K8 **Kentwood** Louisiana, S USA 30°56′N 90°30′W
31 P9 **Kentwood** Michigan, N USA 42°52′N 85°33′W
81 H17 **Kenya** off. Republic of Kenya. ◆ republic E Africa
Kenya, Mount see Kirinyaga
Kenya, Republic of see Kenya
168 L7 **Kenyir, Tasik** var. Tasek Kenyir. ◎ Peninsular Malaysia
29 W10 **Kenyon** Minnesota, N USA 44°16′N 92°59′W
29 Y16 **Keokuk** Iowa, C USA 40°24′N 91°23′W
29 X15 **Keosauqua** Iowa, C USA 40°43′N 91°58′W
21 O11 **Keowee, Lake** ◎ South Carolina, SE USA
124 I7 **Kepa** var. Kepe. Respublika Kareliya, NW Russian Federation 65°09′N 32°15′E
Kepe see Kepa
189 O13 **Kepirohi Falls** waterfall Pohnpei, E Micronesia
185 B22 **Kepler Mountains** ▲ South Island, New Zealand
111 I14 **Kępno** Wielkopolskie, C Poland 51°17′N 17°57′E
65 C24 **Keppel Island** island N Falkland Islands
Keppel Island see Niuatoputapu
65 C23 **Keppel Sound** sound N Falkland Islands
136 D12 **Kepsut** Balıkesir, NW Turkey 39°41′N 28°09′E
168 M11 **Kepulauan Riau** off. Propinsi Kepulauan Riau. ◆ province NW Indonesia
Kequ see Gadê
171 V13 **Kerai** Papua, E Indonesia 03°53′S 134°30′E
155 F22 **Kerala** ◆ state S India
165 R16 **Kerama-rettō** island group SW Japan
183 N10 **Kerang** Victoria, SE Australia 35°46′S 144°01′E
115 H19 **Keratéa** var. Keratea. Attiki, C Greece 37°48′S 23°58′E
Keratea see Keratéa
93 M19 **Kerava** Fin. Kervo. Etelä-Suomi, S Finland 60°24′N 25°07′E
Kerbala/Kerbela see Karbalā'

32 F15 **Kerby** Oregon, NW USA 42°10′N 123°39′W
117 W12 **Kerch** Rus. Kerch'. Respublika Krym, SE Ukraine 45°22′N 36°30′E
Kerch' see Kerch
Kerchens'ka Protska/ Kerchenskiy Proliv see Kerch Strait
117 V13 **Kerchens'kyy Pivostriv** peninsula S Ukraine
121 V4 **Kerch Strait** var. Bosporus Cimmerius, Enikale Strait, Rus. Kerchenskiy Proliv, Ukr. Kerchens'ka Protska. strait Black Sea/Sea of Azov
Kerdilio see Kerdýlio
114 H13 **Kerdýlio** var. Kerdilio. ▲ N Greece 40°46′N 23°37′E
186 D8 **Kerema** Gulf, S Papua New Guinea 07°59′S 145°46′E
Keremitlik see Lyulyakovo
136 I9 **Kerempe Burnu** headland N Turkey 42°01′N 33°20′E
80 J9 **Keren** var. Cheren. C Eritrea 15°45′N 38°22′E
25 U7 **Kerens** Texas, SW USA 32°07′N 96°13′W
184 M6 **Kerepehi** Waikato, North Island, New Zealand 37°18′S 175°33′E
145 P10 **Kerey, Ozero** ◎ C Kazakhstan
Kergel see Kárla
173 Q13 **Kerguelen** island C French Southern and Antarctic Territories
173 Q13 **Kerguelen Plateau** undersea feature S Indian Ocean
115 C20 **Kerí** Zákynthos, Iónia Nisiá, Greece, C Mediterranean Sea 37°40′N 20°48′E
81 H19 **Kericho** Rift Valley, W Kenya 0°22′S 35°19′E
184 K2 **Kerikeri** Northland, North Island, New Zealand 35°14′S 173°58′E
93 O17 **Kerimäki** Itä-Suomi, E Finland 61°56′N 29°18′E
168 K12 **Kerinci, Gunung** ▲ Sumatera, W Indonesia 02°00′S 101°40′E
Keriya see Yutian
158 H9 **Keriya He** ✍ NW China
98 J9 **Kerkbuurt** Noord-Holland, C Netherlands N 05°08′E
98 J13 **Kerkdriel** Gelderland, C Netherlands 51°46′N 05°21′E
75 N6 **Kerkenah, Îles de** var. Kerkenna Islands, Ar. Juzur Qarqannah. island group E Tunisia
Kerkenna Islands/Kerkenah, Îles de see Kerkenah, Îles de
115 M20 **Kerketévs** ▲ Sámos, Dodekánisa, Greece, Aegean Sea 37°34′N 26°43′E
29 T8 **Kerkhoven** Minnesota, N USA 45°12′N 95°18′W
Kerki see Atamyrat
146 M14 **Kerki** Rus. Kerkichi. Lebap Welaýaty, E Turkmenistan 37°46′N 65°18′E
Kerkichi see Kerki
115 F16 **Kerkíneo** prehistoric site Thessalía, C Greece
114 G12 **Kerkíni, Límni** var. Límni Kerkínas. ◎ N Greece
Kerkinítis Límni see Kerkíni, Límni
99 M18 **Kerkrade** Limburg, SE Netherlands 50°53′N 06°04′E
115 B16 **Kérkyra** var. Kérkira, Eng. Corfu. Kérkyra, Iónia Nisiá, Greece, C Mediterranean Sea 39°37′N 19°56′E
115 B16 **Kerkyra** ✈ Kérkyra, Iónia Nisiá, Greece, C Mediterranean Sea 39°35′N 19°55′E
115 A16 **Kérkyra** var. Kérkira, Eng. Corfu. island Iónia Nisiá, Greece, C Mediterranean Sea
192 K10 **Kermadec Islands** island group New Zealand, SW Pacific Ocean
175 R10 **Kermadec Ridge** undersea feature SW Pacific Ocean 30°30′S 178°30′W
175 R11 **Kermadec Trench** undersea feature SW Pacific Ocean
143 S10 **Kermān** var. Kirman; anc. Carmana. Kermān, C Iran 30°18′N 57°05′E
143 R11 **Kermān** off. Ostān-e Kermān; var. Kirman; anc. Carmania. ◆ province SE Iran
143 U12 **Kermān, Bīābān-e** desert SE Iran
142 K6 **Kermānshāh** var. Qahremānshahr; prev. Bākhtarān. Kermānshāhān, W Iran 34°19′N 47°04′E
143 Q9 **Kermānshāh** Yazd, C Iran
142 J6 **Kermānshāh** off. Ostān-e Bākhtarān. ◆ province W Iran
Kermānshāhān, Ostān-e see Kermānshāh
114 L10 **Kermen** Sliven, C Bulgaria 42°30′N 26°12′E
24 L8 **Kermit** Texas, SW USA 31°49′N 103°07′W
21 P6 **Kermit** West Virginia, NE USA 37°50′N 82°24′W
127 O11 **Kern River** ✍ California, USA
35 S12 **Kernville** California, W USA 35°45′N 118°25′W
115 K21 **Kéros** island Kykládes, Greece, Aegean Sea
76 K14 **Kérouané** SE Guinea 09°16′N 09°00′W
101 D16 **Kerpen** Nordrhein-Westfalen, W Germany 50°51′N 06°40′E
146 I11 **Kerpichli** Lebap Welaýaty, NE Turkmenistan 40°12′N 61°09′E
24 M1 **Kerrick** Texas, SW USA 36°29′N 102°14′W
11 S15 **Kerrobert** Saskatchewan, S Canada 51°56′N 109°11′W
25 Q11 **Kerrville** Texas, SW USA 30°03′N 99°08′W
97 B20 **Kerry** Ir. Ciarraí. cultural region SW Ireland
21 S15 **Kershaw** South Carolina, SE USA 34°33′N 80°34′W

Kertel see Kärdla
95 H23 **Kerteminde** Fyn, C Denmark 55°27′N 10°40′E
163 Q7 **Kerulen** Chin. Herlen He, Mong. Herlen Gol. ✍ China/Mongolia
Kerýneia see Girne
12 H11 **Kesagami Lake** ◎ Ontario, C Canada
93 O17 **Kesälahti** Itä-Suomi, SE Finland 61°54′N 29°49′E
136 B11 **Keşan** Edirne, NW Turkey 40°52′N 26°37′E
165 R9 **Kesennuma** Miyagi, Honshū, C Japan 38°55′N 141°35′E
163 V7 **Keshan** Heilongjiang, NE China 48°00′N 125°46′E
30 M6 **Keshena** Wisconsin, N USA 44°54′N 88°37′W
136 I13 **Keskin** Kırıkkale, C Turkey 39°41′N 33°36′E
Kesmárk see Kežmarok
124 I6 **Kesten'ga** var. Kest' Enga. Respublika Kareliya, NW Russian Federation 65°53′N 31°47′E
Kest Enga see Kesten'ga
98 L12 **Kesteren** Gelderland, C Netherlands 51°55′N 05°34′E
14 H14 **Keswick** Ontario, S Canada 44°15′N 79°26′W
97 K15 **Keswick** NW England, United Kingdom 54°30′N 03°04′W
111 H24 **Keszthely** Zala, SW Hungary 46°47′N 17°16′E
77 R17 **Keta** SE Ghana 05°55′N 00°59′E
169 Q12 **Ketapang** Borneo, C Indonesia 01°50′S 109°59′E
127 Q7 **Ketchenery** prev. Sovetskoye. Respublika Kalmykiya, SW Russian Federation 47°18′N 44°31′E
39 Y14 **Ketchikan** Revillagigedo Island, Alaska, USA 55°21′N 131°39′W
33 Q14 **Ketchum** Idaho, NW USA 43°40′N 114°24′W
Kete/Kete Krakye see Kete-Krachi
77 Q15 **Kete-Krachi** var. Kete, Kete Krakye. E Ghana 07°50′N 00°03′W
98 L9 **Ketelmeer** channel E Netherlands
149 P17 **Keti Bandar** Sind, SE Pakistan 23°55′N 67°31′E
145 W16 **Ketmen', Khrebet** ▲ SE Kazakhstan
77 S16 **Kétou** SE Benin 07°25′N 02°36′E
110 M7 **Kętrzyn** Ger. Rastenburg. Warmińsko-Mazurskie, NE Poland 54°05′N 21°24′E
97 N20 **Kettering** C England, United Kingdom 52°N 00°44′W
31 R14 **Kettering** Ohio, N USA 39°41′N 84°10′W
18 F13 **Kettle Creek** ✍ Pennsylvania, NE USA
32 L7 **Kettle Falls** Washington, NW USA 48°36′N 118°03′W
14 D16 **Kettle Point** headland Ontario, S Canada 43°12′N 81°59′W
29 V6 **Kettle River** ✍ Minnesota, N USA
186 B7 **Ketu** ✍ W Papua New Guinea
18 G10 **Keuka Lake** ◎ New York, NE USA
Keupriya see Primorsko
92 L17 **Keuruu** Länsi-Suomi, C Finland 62°15′N 24°34′E
92 L9 **Kevo** Lapp. Geavvú. Lappi, N Finland 69°42′N 27°08′E
44 M6 **Kew** North Caicos, N Turks and Caicos Islands 21°52′N 71°57′W
30 L13 **Kewanee** Illinois, N USA 41°15′N 89°55′W
31 N7 **Kewaunee** Wisconsin, N USA 44°27′N 87°31′W
30 M3 **Keweenaw Bay** ◎ Michigan, N USA
31 N2 **Keweenaw Peninsula** peninsula Michigan, N USA
31 N2 **Keweenaw Point** peninsula Michigan, N USA
29 N12 **Keya Paha River** ✍ Nebraska/South Dakota, N USA
Keyayagyz see Kök-Aygyr
23 Z16 **Key Biscayne** Florida, SE USA 25°41′N 80°09′W
26 G8 **Keyes** Oklahoma, C USA 36°48′N 102°15′W
23 Y17 **Key Largo** Key Largo, Florida, SE USA 25°06′N 80°25′W
21 U3 **Keyser** West Virginia, NE USA 39°26′N 78°59′W
27 O9 **Keystone Lake** ◎ Oklahoma, C USA
36 L16 **Keystone Peak** ▲ Arizona, SW USA 31°52′N 111°12′W
Keystone State see Pennsylvania
21 U7 **Keysville** Virginia, NE USA 37°02′N 78°28′W
27 T3 **Keytesville** Missouri, C USA 39°25′N 92°56′W
23 W17 **Key West** Florida, Keys, SE USA 24°34′N 81°48′W
127 V6 **Kez** Udmurtskaya Respublika, NW Russian Federation 57°55′N 53°42′E
Kezdivásárhely see Târgu Secuiesc
111 L18 **Kežmarok** Ger. Késmark, Hung. Késmárk. Prešovský Kraj, E Slovakia 49°09′N 20°25′E
138 G7 **Kfar Sava** see Kfar Saba; prev. Kefar Sava. Central, C Israel 32°11′N 34°58′E
83 F20 **Kgalagadi** ◆ district SW Botswana
83 I20 **Kgatleng** ◆ district SE Botswana
188 F8 **Kgkelau** Babeldaob, N Palau
125 R6 **Khabarikha** ✍ NW Russian Federation
Khabarovo see Xankändi
122 M13 **Khabarovsk** Khabarovskiy Kray, SE Russian Federation 48°32′N 135°08′E
123 R11 **Khabarovsk Kray** ◆ territory E Russian Federation

141 W7 **Khabb** Abū Ẓaby, E United Arab Emirates 24°39′N 55°43′E
Khabour, Nahr al see Khābūr, Nahr al
139 N2 **Khabura** see Al Khābūrah
141 X12 **Khabbal** var. Khudal. SE Oman 18°48′N 56°48′E
155 E14 **Khadki** var. Kirkee. Mahārāshtra, W India 18°34′N 73°52′E
126 L14 **Khadyzhensk** Krasnodarskiy Kray, SW Russian Federation 44°26′N 39°31′E
114 N9 **Khadzhiyska Reka** ✍ E Bulgaria
117 P10 **Khadzhybey's'kyy Lyman** ◎ SW Ukraine
138 K3 **Khafsah** Ḥalab, N Syria 36°16′N 38°03′E
152 M13 **Khāga** Uttar Pradesh, N India 25°47′N 81°05′E
153 Q13 **Khairpur** Sind, SE Pakistan 27°30′N 68°50′E
122 K13 **Khakasiya, Respublika** ◆ autonomous republic C Russian Federation
Khakassia/Khakasskaya Avtonomnaya Oblast' see Khakasiya, Respublika
Khalach see Halaç
Khalándrion see Chalándri
75 X8 **Khalīj as Sallūm** Ar. Gulf of Salūm. gulf Egypt/Libya
127 W7 **Khalilovo** Orenburgskaya Oblast', W Russian Federation 51°25′N 58°13′E
143 P15 **Khalkhāl** prev. Herowābād. Ardabīl, NW Iran 37°36′N 48°36′E
Khalkidhikí see Chalkidikí
Khalkís see Chalkída
111 H24 **Khalmer-Yu** Respublika Komi, NW Russian Federation 68°00′N 64°45′E
119 M14 **Khalopyenichy** Rus. Kholopenichi. Minskaya Voblasts', NE Belarus 54°31′N 28°58′E
141 Y10 **Khaluf** var. Al Khaluf. E Oman 20°27′N 57°59′E
154 K10 **Khamaria** Madhya Pradesh, C India 23°07′N 80°54′E
154 D11 **Khambhat** Gujarāt, W India 22°19′N 72°39′E
154 G12 **Khambhāt, Gulf of** Eng. Gulf of Cambay. gulf W India
154 G12 **Khāmgaon** Mahārāshtra, C India 20°41′N 76°34′E
141 O14 **Khamir** var. Khamr. W Yemen 16°N 43°56′E
141 N12 **Khamis Mushayt** var. Hamīs Musait. 'Asīr, SW Saudi Arabia 18°19′N 42°41′E
155 I18 **Khammam** Andhra Pradesh, India 17°16′N 80°13′E
123 P10 **Khampa** Respublika Sakha (Yakutiya), NE Russian Federation 63°43′N 123°02′E
Khamr see Khamir
139 T7 **Khān al Baghdādī** see Al Baghdādī
139 T7 **Khān al Maḥāwīl** see Al Maḥāwīl
139 T7 **Khān al Mashāhidah** Baghdād, C Iraq 33°40′N 44°15′E
139 T10 **Khān al Muşallá** An Najaf, S Iraq 32°09′N 44°20′E
139 U6 **Khānaqīn** Diyālá, E Iraq 34°22′N 45°22′E
139 T11 **Khān ar Ruḥbah** An Najaf, S Iraq 31°42′N 44°18′E
139 P2 **Khān as Sūr** Nīnawá, N Iraq 36°28′N 41°36′E
139 T8 **Khān Āzād** Baghdād, C Iraq 33°08′N 44°21′E
154 H13 **Khandaparha** prev. Khandapara. Orissa, E India 20°15′N 85°11′E
149 T2 **Khandūd** var. Khandud, Wakhan. Badakhshān, NE Afghanistan 36°57′N 72°19′E
Khandūd see Khandūd
122 G11 **Khandyga** Respublika Sakha (Yakutiya), NE Russian Federation 62°35′N 135°30′E
149 S10 **Khānewāl** Punjab, NE Pakistan 30°18′N 71°55′E
149 S10 **Khāngarh** Punjab, E Pakistan 29°57′N 71°11′E
149 S16 **Khanh Hung** see Soc Trăng
163 Z8 **Khanka** see Xonqa
138 G7 **Khanka, Lake** var. Hsing-K'ai Hu, Lake Hanka, Chin. Xingkai Hu, Rus. Ozero Khanka. ◎ China/Russian Federation
Khanka, Ozero see Khanka, Lake
149 O9 **Khankendi** see Xankändi
149 S12 **Khanlar** see Xanlar
149 R11 **Khanna** Punjab, E Pakistan 28°31′N 70°30′E
114 K11 **Khānpur** Punjab, E Pakistan 28°39′N 70°41′E
145 S15 **Khantau** Zhambyl, S Kazakhstan 44°13′N 73°47′E
122 G11 **Khatanga** ✍ N Russian Federation
Khatanga, Gulf of see Khatangskiy Zaliv
123 N7 **Khatangskiy Zaliv** var. Gulf of Khatanga. bay N Russian Federation
149 S12 **Khānewāl** Punjab
149 S16 **Khāngarh** Punjab, E Pakistan
143 S16 **Khash** var. Vāsht. Sīstān va Balūchestān, SE Iran 28°15′N 61°11′E
148 J5 **Khāsh, Dasht-e** Eng. Khash Desert. desert SW Afghanistan
Khash Desert see Khāsh, Dasht-e
80 H9 **Khashm el Girba** var. Khashim al Qirba, Khashm al Qirbah. Kassala, E Sudan 15°00′N 35°59′E
138 G12 **Khashsh, Jabal al** ▲ S Jordan
137 S10 **Khashuri** C Georgia 41°59′N 43°36′E
153 V13 **Khāsi Hills** hill range NE India
114 L11 **Khaskovo** Khaskovo, S Bulgaria 41°56′N 25°33′E
114 L11 **Khaskovo** ◆ province S Bulgaria
122 M7 **Khatanga** ✍ N Russian Federation
141 W7 **Khatmat al Malāḩah** N Oman 58°N 56°22′E
143 S16 **Khatmat al Malāḩah** Ash Shāriqah, E United Arab Emirates
123 T9 **Khatyrka** Chukotskiy Avtonomnyy Okrug, NE Russian Federation 62°03′N 175°09′E
123 T9 **Khauz-Khan** see Hanhowuz
Khauzkhanskoye Vodoranilishche see Hanhowuz Suw Howdany
149 N7 **Khavaling** see Khovaling
147 P8 **Khavast** see Xovos
139 W10 **Khawr al Amayā** ✍ S Iraq
Khawr Barakah see Barka
141 W7 **Khawr Fakkān** var. Khor Fakkan. Ash Shāriqah, NE United Arab Emirates 25°22′N 56°19′E
140 L6 **Khaybar** Al Madīnah, NW Saudi Arabia 25°53′N 39°21′E
Khaybar, Kowtal-e see Khyber Pass

145 W16 **Khan Tengri, Pik** ▲ SE Kazakhstan 42°17′N 80°11′E
Khan-Tengri, Pik see Hantengri Feng
167 S9 **Khanthabouli** prev. Savannakhét. Savannakhét, S Laos 16°34′N 104°49′E
127 V8 **Khanty-Mansiysk** prev. Ostyako-Vogul'sk. Khanty-Mansiyskiy Avtonomnyy Okrug-Yugra, C Russian Federation 61°01′N 69°00′E
125 V9 **Khanty-Mansiyskiy Avtonomnyy Okrug-Yugra** ◆ autonomous district
139 R4 **Khānūqah** Nīnawé, C Iraq 35°25′N 43°15′E
138 T7 **Khān Yūnis** var. Khān Yūnus. ◆ Gaza Strip 31°21′N 34°18′E
Khān Yūnus see Khān Yūnis
139 U5 **Khān Zūr** As Sulaymānīyah, E Iraq 35°03′N 45°08′E
139 N8 **Khao Luem Reservoir** ◎ W Thailand
123 O14 **Khapcheranga** Chitinskaya Oblast', S Russian Federation 49°42′N 112°23′E
127 Q12 **Kharabali** Astrakhanskaya Oblast', SW Russian Federation 47°26′N 47°14′E
153 R16 **Kharagpur** West Bengal, NE India 22°30′N 87°19′E
139 V7 **Kharā'ib 'Abd al Karīm** Al Muthanná, S Iraq 31°07′N 45°33′E
149 N12 **Kharān** Baluchistān, SW Pakistan 28°35′N 65°25′E
143 Q8 **Kharānaq** Yazd, C Iran 31°54′N 54°21′E
Kharbin see Harbin
Kharchi see Mārwār
146 H13 **Khardzhagaz** Ahal Welaýaty, C Turkmenistan 37°22′N 59°47′E
154 F11 **Khargon** Madhya Pradesh, C India 21°49′N 75°39′E
149 V7 **Khārian** Punjab, NE Pakistan 32°51′N 73°52′E
117 X8 **Kharisyz'k** Donets'ka Oblast', E Ukraine 48°01′N 38°10′E
117 V5 **Kharkiv** Rus. Khar'kov. Kharkivs'ka Oblast', NE Ukraine 50°N 36°14′E
117 V5 **Kharkiv** ✈ Kharkivs'ka Oblast', E Ukraine 49°54′N 36°20′E
117 U5 **Kharkivs'ka Oblast'** var. Kharkiv, Rus. Khar'kovskaya Oblast'. ◆ province E Ukraine
Khar'kov see Kharkiv
Khar'kovskaya Oblast' see Kharkivs'ka Oblast'
114 M9 **Kharmanli** ✍ S Bulgaria
114 K11 **Kharmanli** S Bulgaria 41°56′N 25°54′E
114 K11 **Kharmanliyska Reka** ✍ S Bulgaria
124 M13 **Kharovsk** Vologodskaya Oblast', NW Russian Federation 59°57′N 40°05′E
141 O14 **Khārtmat al Malāḩah** N Oman
141 N12 **Khartoum** var. El Khartûm, Khartum. ● (Sudan) Khartoum, C Sudan 18°19′N 42°41′E
80 F9 **Khartoum** ◆ state NE Sudan
80 F9 **Khartoum** ✕ Khartoum, C Sudan 15°36′N 32°37′E
80 F9 **Khartoum North** Khartoum, C Sudan 15°38′N 32°33′E
117 X8 **Khartsyz'k** Rus. Khartsyzsk. Donets'ka Oblast', SE Ukraine 48°01′N 38°10′E
Khartsyzsk see Khartsyz'k
Khartum see Khartoum
154 G12 **Khash** Madhya Pradesh, C India 22°12′N 77°30′E
123 S14 **Khasan** Primorskiy Kray, SE Russian Federation 42°24′N 130°45′E
127 P16 **Khasavyurt** Respublika Dagestan, SW Russian Federation 43°16′N 46°33′E
143 W12 **Khash** var. Sīstān va Balūchestān, SE Iran 28°15′N 61°11′E
148 J5 **Khāsh, Dasht-e** Eng. Khash Desert. desert SW Afghanistan
Khash Desert see Khāsh, Dasht-e
80 H9 **Khashm el Girba** var. Khashim al Qirba, Khashm al Qirbah. Kassala, E Sudan 15°00′N 35°59′E
138 G12 **Khashsh, Jabal al** ▲ S Jordan
137 S10 **Khashuri** C Georgia 41°59′N 43°36′E
153 V13 **Khāsi Hills** hill range NE India
114 K11 **Khaskovo** Khaskovo, S Bulgaria 41°56′N 25°33′E
114 K11 **Khaskovo** ◆ province S Bulgaria
122 M7 **Khatanga** ✍ N Russian Federation
Khatanga, Gulf of see Khatangskiy Zaliv
123 N7 **Khatangskiy Zaliv** var. Gulf of Khatanga. bay N Russian Federation
141 W7 **Khatmat al Malāḩah** N Oman 58°N 56°22′E
143 S16 **Khatmat al Malāḩah** Ash Shāriqah, E United Arab Emirates
123 T9 **Khatyrka** Chukotskiy Avtonomnyy Okrug, NE Russian Federation 62°03′N 175°09′E
Khauz-Khan see Hanhowuz
Khauzkhanskoye Vodoranilishche see Hanhowuz Suw Howdany
Khavaling see Khovaling
Khavast see Xovos
139 W10 **Khawr al Amayā** ✍ S Iraq
Khawr Barakah see Barka
141 W7 **Khawr Fakkān** var. Khor Fakkan. Ash Shāriqah, NE United Arab Emirates 25°22′N 56°19′E
140 L6 **Khaybar** Al Madīnah, NW Saudi Arabia 25°53′N 39°21′E
Khaybar, Kowtal-e see Khyber Pass

147 S11 **Khaydarkan** var. Khaydarken. Batkenskaya Oblast', SW Kyrgyzstan 39°56′N 71°17′E
Khaydarken see Khaydarkan
125 U2 **Khaypudyrskaya Guba** bay NW Russian Federation
139 S1 **Khayrūzuk** Arbīl, E Iraq 36°58′N 44°19′E
Khazar, Bahr-e/Khazar, Daryā-ye see Caspian Sea
Khazarasp see Hazorasp
75 X11 **Khazretishi, Khrebet** see
74 F7 **Khemisset** NW Morocco 35°25′N 43°15′E
167 R10 **Khemmarat** var. Kemarat. Ubon Ratchathani, E Thailand 16°03′N 105°11′E
74 L6 **Khenchela** var. Khenchla. NE Algeria 35°22′N 07°09′E
74 G7 **Khénifra** C Morocco
152 L12 **Kheri** Uttar Pradesh, N India 27°54′N 80°47′E
Khērsān, Rūd-e see Garm, Āb-e
117 R10 **Kherson** Khersons'ka Oblast', S Ukraine 46°39′N 32°38′E
117 S14 **Kherson** Khersons'ka
117 S14 **Khersones, Mys** Rus. Mys Khersonesskiy. headland S Ukraine 44°34′N 33°24′E
Khersonesskiy, Mys see Khersones, Mys
117 R10 **Khersons'ka Oblast'** var. Kherson, Rus. Khersonskaya Oblast'. ◆ province S Ukraine
Khersonskaya Oblast' see Khersons'ka Oblast'
122 LE **Kheta** ✍ N Russian Federation
167 S8 **Khe Ve** Quang Binh, C Vietnam 17°52′N 105°49′E
149 V7 **Khewra** Punjab, E Pakistan 32°41′N 73°04′E
124 J7 **Khibiny** ▲ NW Russian Federation
126 K3 **Khimki** Moskovskaya Oblast', W Russian Federation 55°57′N 37°48′E
147 S12 **Khingov** Rus. Obi-Khingou. ✍ C Tajikistan
Khíos see Chíos
149 R15 **Khipro** Sind, SE Pakistan 25°50′N 69°22′E
139 S10 **Khirr, Wādī al** dry watercourse S Iraq
114 I10 **Khisarya** Plovdiv, C Bulgaria 42°33′N 24°43′E
Khiva/Khiwa see Xiva
167 N9 **Khlong Khlung** Kamphaeng Phet, W Thailand 16°15′N 99°41′E
167 N13 **Khlong Thom** Krabi, SW Thailand 07°55′N 99°09′E
167 P12 **Khlung** Chantaburi, S Thailand 12°25′N 102°12′E
Khmel'nik see Khmil'nyk
Khmel'nitskaya Oblast' see Khmel'nyts'ka Oblast'
Khmel'nitskiy see Khmel'nyts'kyy
116 K5 **Khmel'nyts'ka Oblast'** var. Khmel'nyts'kyy, Rus. Khmel'nitskaya Oblast'; prev. Kamenets-Podol'skaya Oblast'. ◆ province W Ukraine
116 L6 **Khmel'nyts'kyy** Rus. Khmel'nitskiy; prev. Proskurov. Khmel'nyts'ka Oblast', W Ukraine 49°24′N 26°59′E
Khmel'nyts'kyy see Khmel'nyts'ka Oblast'
116 M6 **Khmil'nyk** Rus. Khmel'nik. Vinnyts'ka Oblast', C Ukraine 49°36′N 27°59′E
144 I9 **Khobda** prev. Novoalekseyevka. Aktyubinsk, W Kazakhstan 50°09′N 55°39′E
137 R9 **Khobi** NW Georgia 42°20′N 41°54′E
119 P15 **Khodasy** Rus. Khodosy. Mahilyowskaya Voblasts', E Belarus 53°59′N 31°23′E
116 J6 **Khodoriv** Pol. Chodorów, Rus. Khodorov. L'vivs'ka Oblast', NW Ukraine 49°20′N 24°19′E
Khodorov see Khodoriv
Khodosy see Khodasy
Khodzhakala see Hojagala
Khodzhambas see Hojambaz
Khodzhent see Khujand
Khodzheyli see Xo'jayli
Khoi see Khvoy
Khojend see Khujand
Khokand see Qo'qon
Khokhol'skiy Voronezhskaya Oblast', W Russian Federation 51°33′N 38°43′E
167 D19 **Khok Samrong** Lop Buri, C Thailand 15°03′N 100°44′E
149 P2 **Kholm** var. Tashqurghan, Pash. Khulm. Balkh, N Afghanistan 36°42′N 67°41′E
Kholm see Chełm
Kholmech' see Kholmyech
123 H15 **Kholm** Novgorodskaya Oblast', W Russian Federation 57°10′N 31°06′E
Kholm see Chełm
123 S14 **Kholmsk** Ostrov Sakhalin, Sakhalinskaya Oblast', SE Russian Federation 46°57′N 142°02′E
119 O18 **Kholmyech** Rus. Kholmech'. Homyel'skaya Voblasts', SE Belarus 52°09′N 30°37′E
Kholon see Holon
Kholopenichi see Khalopyenichy
83 D19 **Khomas** ◆ district C Namibia
83 D19 **Khomas Hochland** var. Khomasplato. plateau C Namibia
Khomasplato see Khomas Hochland
Khomein see Khomeyn
142 M7 **Khomeyn** var. Khomein, Khumain. Markazī, W Iran 33°38′N 50°03′E
143 N8 **Khomeynīshahr** prev. Homāyūnshahr. Eşfahān, C Iran 32°42′N 51°28′E
Khoms see Al Khums
Khong Sedone see Muang Khôngxédôn

◆ Country   ◇ Dependent Territory   ◈ Administrative Regions   ▲ Mountain   ▼ Volcano   ◎ Lake
● Country Capital   ○ Dependent Territory Capital   ✕ International Airport   ▲ Mountain Range   ✍ River   ▭ Reservoir

KHON KAEN – KISHANGARH

167 Q9 **Khon Kaen** *var.* Muang Khon Kaen. Khon Kaen, E Thailand 16°25′N 102°50′E
Khonqa *see* Xonqa
153 Y11 **Khonsa** Arunāchal Pradesh, NE India 27°01′N 95°35′E
167 Q9 **Khon San** Khon Kaen, E Thailand 16°40′N 101°51′E
123 R8 **Khonuu** Respublika Sakha (Yakutiya), NE Russian Federation 66°24′N 143°15′E
127 N8 **Khopër** *var.* Khoper. ⛐ SW Russian Federation
Khoper *see* Khopër
123 S14 **Khor** Khabarovskiy Kray, SE Russian Federation 47°44′N 134°48′E
143 U9 **Khorāsān-e Janūbī** *off.* Ostan-e Khorāsān-e Janūbī. ◆ *province* E Iran
143 U5 **Khorāsān-e Razavī** *off.* Ostān-e Khorāsān, *var.* Khorassan, Khurasan. ◆ *province* NE Iran
143 S3 **Khorāsān-e Shemālī** *off.* Ostan-e Khorāsān-e Shemālī. ◆ *province* NE Iran
Khorāsān, Ostān-e *see* Khorāsān-e Razavī
Khorassan *see* Khorāsān-e Razavī
Khorat *see* Nakhon Ratchasima
154 O13 **Khordha** *prev.* Khurda. Orissa, E India 20°10′N 85°42′E
125 U4 **Khorey-Ver** Nenetskiy Avtonomnyy Okrug, NW Russian Federation 67°25′N 58°05′E
Khorezmskaya Oblast' *see* Xorazm Viloyati
Khor Fakkan *see* Khawr Fakkān
145 W15 **Khorgos** Almaty, SE Kazakhstan 44°13′N 80°22′E
123 N13 **Khorinsk** Respublika Buryatiya, S Russian Federation 52°13′N 109°52′E
83 C18 **Khorixas** Kunene, NW Namibia 20°23′S 14°55′E
141 O17 **Khormaksar** *var.* Aden. ✈ ('Aden) SW Yemen 12°56′N 45°00′E
Khormal *see* Khurmāl
Khormuj *see* Khvormūj
Khorog *see* Khorugh
117 S5 **Khorol** Poltavs'ka Oblast', NE Ukraine 49°49′N 33°17′E
142 L7 **Khorramābād** *var.* Khurramabad. Lorestān, W Iran 33°29′N 48°21′E
143 R9 **Khorramdasht** Kermān, C Iran 31°41′N 56°10′E
142 K10 **Khorramshahr** *var.* Khurramshahr, Muhammerah; *prev.* Mohammerah. Khūzestān, SW Iran 30°30′N 48°09′E
147 S14 **Khorugh** *Rus.* Khorog. S Tajikistan 37°30′N 71°31′E
Khorvot Khalutsa *see* Horvot Halutsa
127 Q12 **Khosheutovo** Astrakhanskaya Oblast', SW Russian Federation 47°04′N 47°49′E
Khotan *see* Hotan
Khotimsk *see* Khotsimsk
Khotin *see* Khotyn
119 R16 **Khotsimsk** *Rus.* Khotimsk. Mahilyowskaya Voblasts', E Belarus 53°24′N 32°35′E
116 K7 **Khotyn** *Rom.* Hotin, *Rus.* Khotin. Chernivets'ka Oblast', W Ukraine 48°29′N 26°30′E
74 F7 **Khouribga** C Morocco 32°55′N 06°51′W
147 Q13 **Khovaling** *Rus.* Khavaling. SW Tajikistan 38°22′N 69°54′E
Khovd *see* Hovd
149 R6 **Khowst** Khowst, E Afghanistan 33°22′N 69°57′E
149 S6 **Khowst** ◆ *province* E Afghanistan
Khoy *see* Khvoy
119 N20 **Khoyniki** Homyel'skaya Voblasts', SE Belarus 51°54′N 29°58′E
Khozretishi, Khrebet *see* Hazratishoh, Qatorkŭhi
Khrisoúpolis *see* Chrysoúpoli
144 J10 **Khromtau** *Kaz.* Khromtaū. Aktyubinsk, W Kazakhstan 50°14′N 58°22′E
Khromtaū *see* Khromtau
Khrysokhou Bay *see* Chrysochoú, Kólpos
117 O7 **Khrystynivka** Cherkas'ka Oblast', C Ukraine 48°49′N 29°55′E
167 R10 **Khuang Nai** Ubon Ratchathani, E Thailand 15°22′N 104°33′E
Khudal *see* Khādhil
Khudat *see* Xudat
149 W9 **Khudiān** Punjab, E Pakistan 30°59′N 74°19′E
Khudzhand *see* Khujand
83 G21 **Khuis** Kgalagadi, SW Botswana 26°37′S 21°50′E
147 Q11 **Khujand** *var.* Khodzhent, Khojend, *Rus.* Khudzhand; *prev.* Leninabad, *Taj.* Leninobod. N Tajikistan 40°17′N 69°37′E
167 R11 **Khukhan** Si Sa Ket, E Thailand 14°38′N 104°12′E
Khulm *see* Kholm
153 T16 **Khulna** Khulna, SW Bangladesh 22°48′N 89°32′E
153 T16 **Khulna** ◆ *division* SW Bangladesh
Khumain *see* Khomeyn
Khums *see* Al Khums
149 W2 **Khunjerāb Pass** *pass* China/Pakistan
Khūnjerāb Pass *see* Kunjirap Daban
153 P16 **Khunti** Jhārkhand, N India 23°02′N 85°19′E
167 N7 **Khun Yuam** Mae Hong Son, NW Thailand 18°54′N 97°54′E
Khurais *see* Khurayş
Khurasan *see* Khorāsān-e Razavī
141 R7 **Khurays** *var.* Khurais. Ash Sharqīyah, C Saudi Arabia 25°06′N 48°03′E
Khurda *see* Khordha
152 J11 **Khurja** Uttar Pradesh, N India 28°15′N 77°51′E
139 V4 **Khurmāl** *var.* Khormal. As Sulaymānīyah, NE Iraq 35°19′N 46°06′E
Khurramabad *see* Khorramābād
Khurramshahr *see* Khorramshahr
149 U7 **Khushāb** Punjab, NE Pakistan 32°16′N 72°18′E
116 H8 **Khust** *var.* Husté, *Cz.* Chust, *Hung.* Huszt. Zakarpats'ka Oblast', W Ukraine 48°11′N 23°19′E
80 D11 **Khuwei** Western Kordofan, C Sudan 13°02′N 29°13′E
149 O13 **Khuzdār** Baluchistān, SW Pakistan 27°49′N 66°39′E
142 L9 **Khūzestān** *off.* Ostān-e Khūzestān, *var.* Khuzistan, *prev.* Arabistan; *anc.* Susiana. ◆ *province* SW Iran
Khūzestān, Ostān-e *see* Khūzestān
Khuzistan *see* Khūzestān
149 R2 **Khvājeh Ghār** *var.* Khwajaghar, Khwaja-i-Ghar. Takhār, NE Afghanistan 37°08′N 69°24′E
127 Q7 **Khvalynsk** Saratovskaya Oblast', W Russian Federation 52°30′N 48°06′E
143 N12 **Khvormūj** *var.* Khormuj. Būshehr, S Iran 28°32′N 51°22′E
142 I2 **Khvoy** *var.* Khoi, Khoy. Āżarbāyjān-e Bākhtarī, NW Iran 38°36′N 45°04′E
Khwajaghar/Khwaja-i-Ghar *see* Khvājeh Ghār
149 S5 **Khyber Pass** *var.* Kowtal-e Khaybar. *pass* Afghanistan/Pakistan
186 L8 **Kia** Santa Isabel, N Solomon Islands 07°34′S 158°31′E
183 S10 **Kiama** New South Wales, SE Australia 34°41′S 150°49′E
79 O22 **Kiambi** Katanga, SE Dem. Rep. Congo 07°15′S 28°01′E
27 Q12 **Kiamichi Mountains** ▲▲ Oklahoma, C USA
27 Q12 **Kiamichi River** ⛐ Oklahoma, C USA
14 M10 **Kiamika, Réservoir** ▣ Québec, SE Canada
Kiamusze *see* Jiamusi
39 N7 **Kiana** Alaska, USA 66°58′N 160°25′W
Kiangmai *see* Chiang Mai
Kiang-ning *see* Nanjing
Kiangsi *see* Jiangxi
Kiangsu *see* Jiangsu
93 M14 **Kiantajärvi** ◎ E Finland
115 F19 **Kiáto** *prev.* Kiáton. Pelopónnisos, S Greece 38°01′N 22°45′E
Kiáton *see* Kiáto
Kiayi *see* Chiai
95 F22 **Kibæk** Ringkøbing, W Denmark 56°03′N 08°52′E
67 T9 **Kibali** *var.* Uele (upper course). ⛐ NE Dem. Rep. Congo
79 E20 **Kibangou** Niari, SW Congo 03°27′S 12°21′E
Kibarty *see* Kybartai
92 M8 **Kiberg** Finnmark, N Norway 70°17′N 30°47′E
79 N20 **Kibombo** Maniema, E Dem. Rep. Congo 03°52′S 25°59′E
81 E20 **Kibondo** Kigoma, NW Tanzania 03°34′S 30°41′E
81 J15 **Kibre Mengist** *var.* Adola. Oromīya, C Ethiopia 05°50′N 39°06′E
Kıbrıs *see* Cyprus
Kıbrıs/Kıbrıs Cumhuriyeti *see* Cyprus
81 E20 **Kibungo** *var.* Kibungu. SE Rwanda 02°09′S 30°30′E
Kibungu *see* Kibungo
113 N19 **Kičevo** SW FYR Macedonia 41°31′N 20°57′E
125 P13 **Kichmengskiy Gorodok** Vologodskaya Oblast', NW Russian Federation 60°00′N 45°52′E
30 J8 **Kickapoo River** ⛐ Wisconsin, N USA
11 P16 **Kicking Horse Pass** *pass* Alberta/British Columbia, SW Canada
77 R9 **Kidal** Kidal, C Mali 18°22′N 01°21′E
77 Q8 **Kidal** ◆ *region* NE Mali
171 Q7 **Kidapawan** Mindanao, S Philippines 07°02′N 125°04′E
97 L20 **Kidderminster** C England, United Kingdom 52°23′N 02°14′W
76 I11 **Kidira** E Senegal 14°28′N 12°13′W
184 O11 **Kidnappers, Cape** *headland* North Island, New Zealand 41°13′S 175°15′E
100 J8 **Kiel** Schleswig-Holstein, N Germany 54°21′N 10°05′E
111 L15 **Kielce** *Rus.* Keltsy. Świętokrzyskie, C Poland 50°53′N 20°39′E
100 K7 **Kieler Bucht** *bay* N Germany
100 J7 **Kieler Förde** *inlet* N Germany
167 U13 **Kiến Đức** *var.* Đak Lap. Đắc Lắc, S Vietnam 11°59′N 107°30′E
79 N24 **Kienge** Katanga, SE Dem. Rep. Congo 10°33′S 27°33′E
100 Q12 **Kietz** Brandenburg, NE Germany 52°33′N 14°36′E
Kiev *see* Kyyiv
Kiev Reservoir *see* Kyyivs'ke Vodoskhovyshche
76 J10 **Kiffa** Assaba, S Mauritania 16°38′N 11°23′W
115 H19 **Kifisiá** Attikí, C Greece 38°04′N 23°49′E
115 F18 **Kifisós** ⛐ C Greece
139 U5 **Kifrī** At Ta'mīn, N Iraq 34°44′N 44°58′E
81 D20 **Kigali** ● (Rwanda) C Rwanda 01°59′S 30°02′E
81 E20 **Kigali** ✈ C Rwanda 01°43′S 30°01′E
137 P13 **Kiğı** Bingöl, E Turkey 39°19′N 40°20′E
81 E21 **Kigoma** Kigoma, W Tanzania 04°52′S 29°36′E
81 E21 **Kigoma** ◆ *region* W Tanzania
38 F10 **Kīhei** *var.* Kihei. Maui, Hawaii, USA, C Pacific Ocean 20°47′N 156°28′W
93 K17 **Kihniö** Länsi-Suomi, W Finland 62°11′N 23°10′E
118 F6 **Kihnu** *var.* Kihnu Saar, *Ger.* Kühnö. *island* SW Estonia
Kihnu Saar *see* Kihnu
38 A8 **Kii Landing** Ni'ihau, Hawaii, USA, C Pacific Ocean 21°58′N 160°03′W
93 L14 **Kiiminki** Oulu, C Finland 65°05′N 25°47′E
164 J14 **Kii-Nagashima** *var.* Nagashima. Mie, Honshū, SW Japan 34°10′N 136°18′E
164 J14 **Kii-sanchi** ▲▲ Honshū, SW Japan
92 L11 **Kiistala** Lappi, N Finland 67°52′N 25°19′E
164 I15 **Kii-suidō** *strait* S Japan
165 V16 **Kikai-shima** *island* Nansei-shotō, SW Japan
112 M8 **Kikinda** *Ger.* Grosskikinda, *Hung.* Nagykikinda; *prev.* Velika Kikinda. Vojvodina, N Serbia 45°48′N 20°29′E
Kikládhes *see* Kykládes
165 Q5 **Kikonai** Hokkaidō, NE Japan 41°40′N 140°25′E
186 C8 **Kikori** Gulf, S Papua New Guinea 07°25′S 144°13′E
186 C8 **Kikori** ⛐ W Papua New Guinea
165 O14 **Kikuchi** *var.* Kikuti. Kumamoto, Kyūshū, SW Japan 33°00′N 130°49′E
Kikuti *see* Kikuchi
127 N8 **Kikvidze** Volgogradskaya Oblast', SW Russian Federation 50°47′N 42°58′E
14 I10 **Kikwissi, Lac** ◎ Québec, SE Canada
79 I21 **Kikwit** Bandundu, W Dem. Rep. Congo 05°S 18°53′E
95 K15 **Kil** Värmland, C Sweden 59°30′N 13°20′E
94 N12 **Kilafors** Gävleborg, C Sweden 61°13′N 16°34′E
38 B8 **Kīlauea** Kaua'i, Hawaii, USA, C Pacific Ocean 22°12′N 159°24′W
38 H12 **Kīlauea Caldera** *var.* Kilauea Caldera. *crater* Hawai'i, USA, C Pacific Ocean
Kilauea Caldera *see* Kīlauea Caldera
109 V4 **Kilb** Niederösterreich, C Austria 48°06′N 15°21′E
39 O12 **Kilbuck Mountains** ▲▲ Alaska, USA
163 Y12 **Kilchu** NE North Korea 40°58′N 129°22′E
97 F18 **Kilcock** *Ir.* Cill Choca. Kildare, E Ireland 53°25′N 06°40′W
183 V2 **Kilcoy** Queensland, E Australia 26°58′S 152°30′E
97 F18 **Kildare** *Ir.* Cill Dara. E Ireland 53°10′N 06°55′W
97 F18 **Kildare** *Ir.* Cill Dara. *cultural region* E Ireland
124 K2 **Kil'din, Ostrov** *island* NW Russian Federation
25 W7 **Kilgore** Texas, SW USA 32°23′N 94°52′W
Kilien Mountains *see* Qilian Shan
114 K9 **Kilifarevo** Veliko Tŭrnovo, N Bulgaria 43°00′N 25°36′E
81 K20 **Kilifi** Coast, SE Kenya 03°37′S 39°50′E
189 U9 **Kili Island** *var.* Kōle. *island* Ralik Chain, S Marshall Islands
149 V2 **Kilik Pass** *pass* Afghanistan/China
Kilimane *see* Quelimane
81 I21 **Kilimanjaro** ◆ *region* E Tanzania
81 I20 **Kilimanjaro** *var.* Uhuru Peak. ⛰ NE Tanzania 03°01′S 37°14′E
Kilimbangara *see* Kolombangara
Kilinailau Islands *see* Tulun Islands
81 K23 **Kilindoni** Pwani, E Tanzania 07°56′S 39°40′E
118 H6 **Kilingi-Nõmme** *Ger.* Kurkund. Pärnumaa, SW Estonia 58°07′N 24°00′E
136 M17 **Kilis** Kilis, S Turkey 36°43′N 37°07′E
136 M16 **Kilis** ◆ *province* S Turkey
117 N12 **Kiliya** *Rom.* Chilia-Nouă. Odes'ka Oblast', SW Ukraine 45°30′N 29°16′E
97 B19 **Kilkee** *Ir.* Cill Chaoi. Clare, W Ireland 52°41′N 09°38′W
97 E19 **Kilkenny** *Ir.* Cill Chainnigh. Kilkenny, S Ireland 52°39′N 07°15′W
97 E19 **Kilkenny** *Ir.* Cill Chainnigh. *cultural region* S Ireland
97 B18 **Kilkieran Bay** *Ir.* Cuan Chill Chiaráin. *bay* W Ireland
114 G13 **Kilkís** Kentrikí Makedonía, N Greece 40°59′N 22°55′E
97 C15 **Killala Bay** *Ir.* Cuan Chill Ala. *inlet* NW Ireland
11 R15 **Killam** Alberta, SW Canada 52°45′N 111°46′W
183 U3 **Killarney** Queensland, E Australia 28°18′S 152°15′E
11 W17 **Killarney** Manitoba, S Canada 49°12′N 99°40′W
14 E11 **Killarney** Ontario, S Canada 45°58′N 81°27′W
97 B20 **Killarney** *Ir.* Cill Airne. Kerry, SW Ireland 52°03′N 09°30′W
28 K4 **Killdeer** North Dakota, N USA 47°21′N 102°45′W
28 J4 **Killdeer Mountains** ▲▲ North Dakota, N USA
45 V15 **Killdeer River** ⛐ Trinidad, Trinidad and Tobago
25 S9 **Killeen** Texas, SW USA 31°07′N 97°44′W
39 P6 **Killik River** ⛐ Alaska, USA
11 T7 **Killinek Island** *island* Nunavut, NE Canada
Killini *see* Kyllíni
115 C19 **Killinís, Akrotírio** *headland* S Greece 37°55′N 21°07′E
97 D15 **Killybegs** *Ir.* Na Cealla Beaga. NW Ireland 54°38′N 08°27′W
Kilmain *see* Quelimane
96 I13 **Kilmarnock** W Scotland, United Kingdom 55°37′N 04°30′W
21 X6 **Kilmarnock** Virginia, NE USA 37°42′N 76°22′W
125 S16 **Kil'mez'** Kirovskaya Oblast', NW Russian Federation 56°55′N 51°03′E
127 S2 **Kil'mez'** Udmurtskaya Respublika, NW Russian Federation 57°04′N 51°22′E
125 R16 **Kil'mez'** ⛐ NW Russian Federation
67 V11 **Kilombero** ⛐ S Tanzania
92 J10 **Kilpisjarvi** Lappi, N Finland 69°03′N 20°50′E
97 B19 **Kilrush** *Ir.* Cill Rois. Clare, W Ireland 52°39′N 09°29′W
79 O24 **Kilwa** Katanga, SE Dem. Rep. Congo 09°22′S 28°19′E
Kilwa *see* Kilwa Kivinje
81 J24 **Kilwa Kivinje** *var.* Kilwa. Lindi, SE Tanzania 08°45′S 39°21′E
81 J24 **Kilwa Masoko** Lindi, SE Tanzania 08°55′S 39°31′E
171 T13 **Kilwo** Pulau Seram, E Indonesia 03°36′S 130°48′E
114 P12 **Kilyos** İstanbul, NW Turkey 41°15′N 29°01′E
37 V8 **Kim** Colorado, C USA 37°12′N 103°22′W
169 U7 **Kimanis, Teluk** *bay* Sabah, East Malaysia
182 H8 **Kimba** South Australia 33°09′S 136°26′E
28 I15 **Kimball** Nebraska, C USA 41°16′N 103°40′W
29 O11 **Kimball** South Dakota, N USA 43°45′N 98°57′W
79 I21 **Kimbao** Bandundu, SW Dem. Rep. Congo 05°27′S 17°40′E
186 F7 **Kimbe** New Britain, E Papua New Guinea 05°36′S 150°10′E
186 G7 **Kimbe Bay** *inlet* New Britain, E Papua New Guinea
11 P17 **Kimberley** British Columbia, SW Canada 49°40′N 115°58′W
83 H23 **Kimberley** Northern Cape, C South Africa 28°45′S 24°46′E
180 M4 **Kimberley Plateau** *plateau* Western Australia
33 P15 **Kimberly** Idaho, NW USA 42°31′N 114°21′W
163 Y12 **Kimch'aek** *prev.* Sŏngjin. E North Korea 40°42′N 129°13′E
163 Y15 **Kimch'ŏn** C South Korea 36°08′N 128°06′E
163 Z16 **Kim Hae** *var.* Pusan. ✈ (Pusan) SE South Korea 35°10′N 128°57′E
Kimi *see* Kými
93 K20 **Kimito** *Swe.* Kemiö. Länsi-Suomi, SW Finland 60°10′N 22°45′E
9 R7 **Kimmirut** *prev.* Lake Harbour. Baffin Island, Nunavut, NE Canada 62°48′N 69°49′W
165 R4 **Kimobetsu** Hokkaidō, NE Japan 42°47′N 140°55′E
115 I21 **Kímolos** *island* Kykládes, Greece, Aegean Sea
115 I21 **Kímolou Sífnou, Stenó** *strait* Kykládes, Greece, Aegean Sea
126 L5 **Kimovsk** Tul'skaya Oblast', W Russian Federation 53°59′N 38°34′E
Kimpolung *see* Câmpulung Moldovenesc
124 K16 **Kimry** Tverskaya Oblast', W Russian Federation 56°52′N 37°21′E
79 H21 **Kimvula** Bas-Congo, SW Dem. Rep. Congo 05°44′S 15°58′E
169 U6 **Kinabalu, Gunung** ▲ East Malaysia 05°52′N 116°08′E
Kinabatangan *see* Kinabatangan, Sungai
169 V7 **Kinabatangan, Sungai** *var.* Kinabatangan. ⛐ East Malaysia
115 L21 **Kínaros** *island* Kykládes, Greece, Aegean Sea
11 O15 **Kinbasket Lake** ▣ British Columbia, SW Canada
96 I7 **Kinbrace** N Scotland, United Kingdom 58°16′N 02°59′W
14 E14 **Kincardine** Ontario, S Canada 44°11′N 81°38′W
96 K10 **Kincardine** *cultural region* E Scotland, United Kingdom
79 K21 **Kinda** Kasai-Occidental, SE Dem. Rep. Congo 04°48′S 21°50′E
79 M24 **Kinda** Katanga, SE Dem. Rep. Congo 09°20′S 25°06′E
166 L3 **Kindat** Sagaing, N Burma (Myanmar) 23°42′N 94°29′E
109 V6 **Kindberg** Steiermark, C Austria 47°31′N 15°27′E
22 H8 **Kinder** Louisiana, S USA 30°29′N 92°51′W
98 H13 **Kinderdijk** Zuid-Holland, SW Netherlands 51°52′N 04°37′E
97 M17 **Kinder Scout** ▲ C England, United Kingdom 53°25′N 01°52′W
11 S16 **Kindersley** Saskatchewan, S Canada 51°29′N 109°08′W
76 I14 **Kindia** Guinée-Maritime, SW Guinea 10°12′N 12°26′W
64 B11 **Kindley Field** *air base* E Bermuda
29 R6 **Kindred** North Dakota, N USA 46°39′N 97°01′W
79 N20 **Kindu** *prev.* Kindu-Port-Empain. Maniema, C Dem. Rep. Congo 02°57′S 25°54′E
Kindu-Port-Empain *see* Kindu
127 S6 **Kinel'** Samarskaya Oblast', W Russian Federation 53°14′N 50°40′E
125 N15 **Kineshma** Ivanovskaya Oblast', W Russian Federation 57°28′N 42°08′E
King *see* King William's Town
140 K10 **King Abdul Aziz** ✈ (Makkah) Makkah, W Saudi Arabia 21°44′N 39°08′E
21 X6 **King and Queen Court House** Virginia, NE USA 37°40′N 76°49′W
King Charles Islands *see* Kong Karls Land
King Christian IX Land *see* Kong Christian IX Land
King Christian X Land *see* Kong Christian X Land
35 O11 **King City** California, W USA 36°12′N 121°09′W
27 R2 **King City** Missouri, C USA 40°03′N 94°31′W
38 M16 **King Cove** Alaska, USA 55°03′N 162°19′W
26 M10 **Kingfisher** Oklahoma, C USA 35°53′N 97°56′W
King Frederik VI Coast *see* Kong Frederik VI Kyst
King Frederik VIII Land *see* Kong Frederik VIII Land
65 B24 **King George Bay** *bay* West Falkland, Falkland Islands
194 G3 **King George Island** *var.* King George Land. *island* South Shetland Islands, Antarctica
12 I6 **King George Islands** *island group* Northwest Territories, C Canada
King George Land *see* King George Island
124 G13 **Kingisepp** Leningradskaya Oblast', NW Russian Federation 59°23′N 28°37′E
183 N14 **King Island** *island* Tasmania, SE Australia
10 J15 **King Island** *island* British Columbia, SW Canada
King Island *see* Kadan Kyun
Kingissepp *see* Kuressaare
141 Q7 **King Khalid** ✈ (Ar Riyāḍ) Ar Riyāḍ, C Saudi Arabia 25°00′N 46°40′E
35 S2 **King Lear Peak** ▲ Nevada, W USA 41°13′N 118°30′W
195 Y8 **King Leopold and Queen Astrid Land** *physical region* Antarctica
180 M4 **King Leopold Ranges** ▲▲ Western Australia
36 I11 **Kingman** Arizona, SW USA 35°12′N 114°02′W
26 M6 **Kingman** Kansas, C USA 37°39′N 98°07′W
192 L7 **Kingman Reef** ◇ US *territory* C Pacific Ocean
79 N20 **Kingombe** Maniema, E Dem. Rep. Congo 02°37′S 26°39′E
182 F5 **Kingoonya** South Australia 30°56′S 135°20′E
194 J10 **King Peninsula** *peninsula* Antarctica
39 P13 **King Salmon** Alaska, USA 58°41′N 156°39′W
35 Q6 **Kings Beach** California, W USA 39°13′N 120°02′W
35 R11 **Kingsburg** California, W USA 36°30′N 119°33′W
182 I10 **Kingscote** South Australia 35°41′S 137°36′E
King's County *see* Offaly
194 H2 **King Sejong** *South Korean research station* Antarctica 61°57′S 58°23′W
183 T9 **Kingsford Smith** ✈ (Sydney) New South Wales, SE Australia 33°58′S 151°09′E
11 P17 **Kingsgate** British Columbia, SW Canada 48°58′N 116°09′W
23 W8 **Kingsland** Georgia, SE USA 30°48′N 81°41′W
29 S13 **Kingsley** Iowa, C USA 42°35′N 95°58′W
97 O19 **King's Lynn** *var.* Bishop's Lynn, Kings Lynn, Lynn, Lynn Regis. E England, United Kingdom 52°45′N 00°24′E
Kings Lynn *see* King's Lynn
21 Q10 **Kings Mountain** North Carolina, SE USA 35°15′N 81°20′W
180 K4 **King Sound** *sound* Western Australia
37 N2 **Kings Peak** ▲ Utah, W USA 40°43′N 110°27′W
21 O8 **Kingsport** Tennessee, S USA 36°32′N 82°33′W
35 R11 **Kings River** ⛐ California, W USA
183 P17 **Kingston** Tasmania, SE Australia 42°57′S 147°18′E
14 K14 **Kingston** Ontario, SE Canada 44°14′N 76°30′W
44 K13 **Kingston** ● (Jamaica) E Jamaica 17°58′N 76°48′W
185 C22 **Kingston** Otago, South Island, New Zealand 45°20′S 168°45′E
19 P12 **Kingston** Massachusetts, NE USA 41°59′N 70°43′W
27 S3 **Kingston** Missouri, C USA 39°36′N 94°02′W
18 K12 **Kingston** New York, NE USA 41°55′N 74°00′W
31 S14 **Kingston** Ohio, N USA 39°28′N 82°54′W
19 O13 **Kingston** Rhode Island, NE USA 41°28′N 71°31′W
20 M9 **Kingston** Tennessee, S USA 35°52′N 84°30′W
35 W12 **Kingston Peak** ▲ California, W USA 35°43′N 115°54′W
182 J11 **Kingston Southeast** South Australia 36°51′S 139°53′E
97 N17 **Kingston upon Hull** *var.* Hull. E England, United Kingdom 53°45′N 00°20′W
97 N22 **Kingston upon Thames** SE England, United Kingdom 51°26′N 00°18′W
45 P14 **Kingstown** ● (Saint Vincent and the Grenadines) Saint Vincent, Saint Vincent and the Grenadines 13°09′N 61°14′W
Kingstown *see* Dún Laoghaire
21 T13 **Kingstree** South Carolina, SE USA 33°40′N 79°50′W
64 L8 **Kings Trough** *undersea feature* E Atlantic Ocean 22°00′W 43°48′N
14 C18 **Kingsville** Ontario, S Canada 42°03′N 82°43′W
25 S15 **Kingsville** Texas, SW USA 27°32′N 97°53′W
21 W6 **King William** Virginia, NE USA 37°42′N 77°03′W
9 N7 **King William Island** *island* Nunavut, N Canada
83 I25 **King William's Town** *var.* King, Kingwilliamstown. Eastern Cape, S South Africa 32°53′S 27°24′E
Kingwilliamstown *see* King William's Town
21 T3 **Kingwood** West Virginia, NE USA 39°27′N 79°43′W
136 C13 **Kınık** İzmir, W Turkey 39°05′N 27°25′E
79 G21 **Kinkala** Pool, S Congo 04°18′S 14°49′E
165 R10 **Kinka-san** *headland* Honshū, C Japan 38°17′N 141°34′E
184 M8 **Kinleith** Waikato, North Island, New Zealand 38°16′S 175°53′E
95 J19 **Kinna** Västra Götaland, S Sweden 57°32′N 12°42′E
96 L8 **Kinnaird Head** *var.* Kinnairds Head. *headland* NE Scotland, United Kingdom 58°39′N 03°22′W
Kinnairds Head *see* Kinnaird Head
95 K20 **Kinnared** Halland, S Sweden 57°01′N 13°04′E
Kinneret, Yam *see* Tiberias, Lake
155 K24 **Kinniyai** Eastern Province, NE Sri Lanka 08°30′N 81°11′E
93 L16 **Kinnula** Länsi-Suomi, C Finland 63°24′N 25°E
14 I8 **Kinojévis** ⛐ Québec, SE Canada
164 I14 **Kino-kawa** ⛐ Honshū, SW Japan
11 U11 **Kinoosao** Saskatchewan, C Canada 57°06′N 101°02′W
99 L17 **Kinrooi** Limburg, NE Belgium 51°09′N 05°48′E
96 J11 **Kinross** C Scotland, United Kingdom 56°14′N 03°27′W
96 J11 **Kinross** *cultural region* C Scotland, United Kingdom
97 C21 **Kinsale** *Ir.* Cionn tSáile. Cork, SW Ireland 51°42′N 08°32′W
95 D14 **Kinsarvik** Hordaland, S Norway 60°22′N 06°43′E
79 G21 **Kinshasa** *prev.* Léopoldville. ● Kinshasa, W Dem. Rep. Congo 04°21′S 15°16′E
79 G21 **Kinshasa** *off.* Ville de Kinshasa, *var.* Kinshasa City. ◆ *region* (Dem. Rep. Congo) SW Dem. Rep. Congo
79 G21 **Kinshasa** ✈ Kinshasa, SW Dem. Rep. Congo 04°23′S 15°30′E
Kinshasa City *see* Kinshasa
117 U9 **Kins'ka** ⛐ SE Ukraine
26 K6 **Kinsley** Kansas, C USA 37°55′N 99°26′W
21 W10 **Kinston** North Carolina, SE USA 35°16′N 77°35′W
77 P15 **Kintampo** W Ghana 08°06′N 01°40′W
182 B1 **Kintore, Mount** ▲ South Australia 26°30′S 130°24′E
96 G13 **Kintyre** *peninsula* W Scotland, United Kingdom
96 G13 **Kintyre, Mull of** *headland* W Scotland, United Kingdom 55°16′N 05°46′W
166 M4 **Kin-u** Sagaing, C Burma (Myanmar) 22°47′N 95°36′E
12 G8 **Kinushseo** ⛐ Ontario, C Canada
11 P13 **Kinuso** Alberta, W Canada 55°19′N 115°23′W
154 I13 **Kinwat** Mahārāshtra, C India 19°37′N 78°12′E
81 F16 **Kinyeti** ▲ S Sudan 03°56′N 32°52′E
101 I17 **Kinzig** ⛐ SW Germany
Kioga, Lake *see* Kyoga, Lake
26 M8 **Kiowa** Kansas, C USA 37°01′N 98°29′W
27 P12 **Kiowa** Oklahoma, C USA 34°43′N 95°54′W
Kiparissía *see* Kyparissía
14 H10 **Kipawa, Lac** ◎ Québec, SE Canada
81 G24 **Kipengere Range** ▲▲ SW Tanzania
81 E23 **Kipili** Rukwa, W Tanzania 07°30′S 30°39′E
81 K20 **Kipini** Coast, SE Kenya 02°30′S 40°30′E
11 V16 **Kipling** Saskatchewan, S Canada 50°04′N 102°45′W
38 M13 **Kipnuk** Alaska, USA 59°56′N 164°02′W
97 F18 **Kippure** *Ir.* Cipiúr. ▲ E Ireland 53°10′N 06°22′W
79 N25 **Kipushi** Katanga, SE Dem. Rep. Congo 11°45′S 27°20′E
187 N10 **Kirakira** *var.* Kaokaona. San Cristobal, SE Solomon Islands 10°28′S 161°54′E
155 K14 **Kirandul** *var.* Bailādila. Chhattīsgarh, C India 18°46′N 81°18′E
155 I21 **Kīranūr** Tamil Nādu, SE India 11°37′N 79°10′E
119 N21 **Kiraw** *Rus.* Kirovo. Homyel'skaya Voblasts', SE Belarus 51°30′N 29°25′E
119 M17 **Kirawsk** *Rus.* Kirovsk; *prev.* Startsy. Mahilyowskaya Voblasts', E Belarus 53°16′N 29°29′E
118 F5 **Kirbla** Läänemaa, W Estonia 58°45′N 23°57′E
25 Y9 **Kirbyville** Texas, SW USA 30°39′N 93°53′W
114 M12 **Kırcasalih** Edirne, NW Turkey 41°24′N 26°48′E
109 W8 **Kirchbach** *var.* Kirchbach in Steiermark. Steiermark, SE Austria 46°55′N 15°40′E
Kirchbach in Steiermark *see* Kirchbach
108 H7 **Kirchberg** Sankt Gallen, NE Switzerland 47°24′N 09°03′E
109 S5 **Kirchdorf an der Krems** Oberösterreich, N Austria 47°55′N 14°08′E
Kirchheim *see* Kirchheim unter Teck
101 I22 **Kirchheim unter Teck** *var.* Kirchheim. Baden-Württemberg, SW Germany 48°39′N 09°28′E
Kirdzhali *see* Kŭrdzhali
123 N13 **Kirenga** ⛐ S Russian Federation
123 N12 **Kirensk** Irkutskaya Oblast', C Russian Federation 57°37′N 107°54′E
Kirghizia *see* Kyrgyzstan
145 S16 **Kirghiz Range** *Rus.* Kirgizskiy Khrebet; *prev.* Alexander Range. ▲▲ Kazakhstan/Kyrgyzstan
Kirghiz SSR *see* Kyrgyzstan
Kirghiz Steppe *see* Kazakhskiy Melkosopochnik
Kirgizskaya SSR *see* Kyrgyzstan
Kirgizskiy Khrebet *see* Kirghiz Range
79 I19 **Kiri** Bandundu, W Dem. Rep. Congo 01°29′S 19°00′E
Kiriath-Arba *see* Hebron
191 R3 **Kiribati** *off.* Republic of Kiribati. ◆ *republic* C Pacific Ocean
Kiribati, Republic of *see* Kiribati
136 L17 **Kırıkhan** Hatay, S Turkey 36°30′N 36°20′E
136 I13 **Kırıkkale** Kırıkkale, C Turkey 39°50′N 33°31′E
136 C10 **Kırıkkale** ◆ *province* C Turkey
124 L13 **Kirillov** Vologodskaya Oblast', NW Russian Federation 59°52′N 38°24′E
Kirin *see* Jilin
81 I18 **Kirinyaga** *prev.* Mount Kenya. ⛰ C Kenya 0°02′S 37°19′E
124 H13 **Kirishi** *var.* Kirisi. Leningradskaya Oblast', NW Russian Federation 59°28′N 32°02′E
164 C16 **Kirishima-yama** ▲ Kyūshū, SW Japan 31°58′N 130°51′E
Kirisi *see* Kirishi
191 S2 **Kiritimati** ✈ Kiritimati, E Kiribati 02°00′N 157°30′W
191 Y2 **Kiritimati** *prev.* Christmas Island. *atoll* Line Islands, E Kiribati
186 G9 **Kiriwina Island** *Eng.* Trobriand Island. *island* SE Papua New Guinea
186 G9 **Kiriwina Islands** *var.* Trobriand Islands. *island group* S Papua New Guinea
96 K12 **Kirkcaldy** E Scotland, United Kingdom 56°07′N 03°10′W
97 I14 **Kirkcudbright** S Scotland, United Kingdom 54°50′N 04°03′W
97 I14 **Kirkcudbright** *cultural region* S Scotland, United Kingdom
Kirkee *see* Khadki
95 I14 **Kirkenær** Hedmark, S Norway 60°27′N 12°04′E
92 M8 **Kirkenes** *Fin.* Kirkkoniemi. Finnmark, N Norway 69°43′N 30°02′E
92 J4 **Kirkjubæjarklaustur** Sudhurland, S Iceland 63°46′N 18°03′W
Kirk-Kilissa *see* Kırklareli
Kirkkoniemi *see* Kirkenes
93 L20 **Kirkkonummi** *Swe.* Kyrkslätt. Uusimaa, S Finland 60°06′N 24°20′E
14 G7 **Kirkland Lake** Ontario, S Canada 48°10′N 80°02′W
136 C9 **Kırklareli** *prev.* Kirk-Kilissa. Kırklareli, NW Turkey 41°45′N 27°12′E
136 I13 **Kırklareli** ◆ *province* NW Turkey
185 F20 **Kirkliston Range** ▲▲ South Island, New Zealand
14 D10 **Kirkpatrick Lake** ◎ Ontario, S Canada
195 Q11 **Kirkpatrick, Mount** ▲ Antarctica 84°37′S 164°36′E
27 U2 **Kirksville** Missouri, C USA 40°12′N 92°35′W
139 T4 **Kirkūk** *var.* Karkūk, Kerkuk. At Ta'mīn, N Iraq 35°28′N 44°26′E
139 U7 **Kir Kush** Diyālá, E Iraq 33°42′N 45°15′E
96 K5 **Kirkwall** NE Scotland, United Kingdom 58°59′N 02°58′W
83 H25 **Kirkwood** Eastern Cape, S South Africa 33°23′S 25°19′E
27 X5 **Kirkwood** Missouri, C USA 38°35′N 90°24′W
Kirman *see* Kermān
Kir Moab/Kir of Moab *see* Al Karak
126 I5 **Kirov** Kaluzhskaya Oblast', W Russian Federation 54°02′N 34°17′E
125 R14 **Kirov** *prev.* Vyatka. Kirovskaya Oblast', NW Russian Federation 58°35′N 49°39′E
Kirov *see* Balpyk Bi/Ust'yevoye
Kirovabad *see* Gäncä
Kirovabad *see* Panj, Tajikistan
Kirovakan *see* Vanadzor
Kirov/Kirova *see* Kopbirlik, Kazakhstan
Kirovo *see* Kiraw, Belarus
Kirovo *see* Beshariq, Uzbekistan
125 R14 **Kirovo-Chepetsk** Kirovskaya Oblast', NW Russian Federation 58°33′N 50°06′E
Kirovogradskaya Oblast'/Kirovohrad *see* Kirovohrads'ka Oblast'
117 R7 **Kirovohrad** *Rus.* Kirovograd; *prev.* Kirovo, Yelizavetgrad, Zinov'yevsk. Kirovohrads'ka Oblast', C Ukraine 48°30′N 31°17′E
117 P7 **Kirovohrads'ka Oblast'** *var.* Kirovohrad, *Rus.* Kirovogradskaya Oblast'. ◆ *province* C Ukraine
Kirovo/Kirovograd *see* Kirovohrad
124 J4 **Kirovsk** Murmanskaya Oblast', NW Russian Federation 67°37′N 33°38′E
117 X7 **Kirovs'k** Luhans'ka Oblast', E Ukraine 48°40′N 38°39′E
Kirovsk *see* Kirawsk, Belarus
Kirovsk *see* Babadaýhan, Turkmenistan
122 E9 **Kirovskaya Oblast'** ◆ *province* NW Russian Federation
117 X8 **Kirovs'ke** Donets'ka Oblast', E Ukraine 48°12′N 38°20′E
117 U13 **Kirovs'ke** *Rus.* Kirovskoye. Respublika Krym, S Ukraine 45°13′N 35°12′E
Kirovskiy *see* Balpyk Bi
Kirovskiy *see* Ust'yevoye
Kirovskoye *see* Kyzyl-Adyr
Kirovskoye *see* Kirovs'ke
146 E11 **Kirpili** Ahal Welaýaty, C Turkmenistan 39°31′N 57°13′E
96 K10 **Kirriemuir** E Scotland, United Kingdom 56°38′N 03°01′W
125 S13 **Kirs** Kirovskaya Oblast', NW Russian Federation 59°22′N 52°20′E
127 N7 **Kirsanov** Tambovskaya Oblast', W Russian Federation 52°40′N 42°48′E
136 J14 **Kırşehir** *anc.* Justinianopolis. Kırşehir, C Turkey 39°09′N 34°08′E
136 I13 **Kırşehir** ◆ *province* C Turkey
149 P4 **Kirthar Range** ▲▲ S Pakistan
37 P9 **Kirtland** New Mexico, SW USA 36°43′N 108°21′W
92 J11 **Kiruna** *Lapp.* Giron. Norrbotten, N Sweden 67°50′N 20°16′E
79 M18 **Kirundu** Orientale, NE Dem. Rep. Congo 0°45′S 25°28′E
Kirun/Kirun' *see* Chilung
26 L3 **Kirwin Reservoir** ▣ Kansas, C USA
127 Q4 **Kirya** Chuvashskaya Respublika, W Russian Federation 55°04′N 46°50′E
138 G8 **Kiryat Shmona** *prev.* Qiryat Shemona. Northern, N Israel 33°13′N 35°35′E
95 M18 **Kisa** Östergötland, S Sweden 58°N 15°39′E
165 P9 **Kisakata** Akita, Honshū, C Japan 39°12′N 139°55′E
Kisalföld *see* Little Alföld
79 L18 **Kisangani** *prev.* Stanleyville. Orientale, NE Dem. Rep. Congo 0°30′N 25°14′E
39 N12 **Kisaralik River** ⛐ Alaska, USA
165 O14 **Kisarazu** Chiba, Honshū, S Japan 35°23′N 139°57′E
111 I22 **Kisbér** Komárom-Esztergom, NW Hungary 47°30′N 18°00′E
11 V17 **Kisbey** Saskatchewan, S Canada 49°41′N 102°39′W
122 J13 **Kiselevsk** Kemerovskaya Oblast', S Russian Federation 54°00′N 86°38′E
153 R13 **Kishanganj** Bihār, NE India 26°06′N 87°57′E
152 G12 **Kishangarh** Rājasthān, N India 26°33′N 74°52′E

◆ Country
● Country Capital
◇ Dependent Territory
○ Dependent Territory Capital
◆ Administrative Regions
✈ International Airport
▲ Mountain
▲▲ Mountain Range
⛰ Volcano
⛐ River
◎ Lake
▣ Reservoir

KISHEGYES – KOMI-PERMYATSKIY AVTONOMNYY OKRUG

Kishegyes see Mali Iđoš
77 S15 **Kishi** Oyo, W Nigeria 09°01'N 03°53'E
Kishinev see Chişinău
Kishiözen see Malyy Uzen'
164 I14 **Kishiwada** var. Kisiwada. Ōsaka, Honshū, SW Japan 34°28'N 135°22'E
143 P14 **Kish, Jazīreh-ye** var. Qey. island S Iran
145 R7 **Kishkenekol'** prev. Kzyltu, Kaz. Qyzyltū. Kokshetau, N Kazakhstan 53°39'N 72°22'E
138 G9 **Kishon, Nahal** prev. Naḥal Qishon. ≈ N Israel
152 I6 **Kishtwār** Jammu and Kashmir, NW India 33°20'N 75°49'E
81 H19 **Kisii** Nyanza, SW Kenya 0°40'S 34°47'E
81 J23 **Kisiju** Pwani, E Tanzania 07°25'S 39°20'E
Kisiwada see Kishiwada
Kisjenő see Chişineu-Criş
38 E17 **Kiska Island** island Aleutian Islands, Alaska, USA
Kiskapus see Copşa Mică
111 M22 **Kiskörei-víztároló** ⊠ E Hungary
Kis-Küküllo see Târnava Mică
111 L24 **Kiskunfélegyháza** var. Félegyháza. Bács-Kiskun, C Hungary 46°42'N 19°52'E
111 K25 **Kiskunhalas** var. Halas. Bács-Kiskun, S Hungary 46°26'N 19°29'E
111 K24 **Kiskunmajsa** Bács-Kiskun, S Hungary 46°30'N 19°46'E
127 N15 **Kislovodsk** Stavropol'skiy Kray, SW Russian Federation 43°55'N 42°45'E
81 L18 **Kismaayo** var. Chisimayu, Kismayu, It. Chisimaio. Jubbada Hoose, S Somalia 0°05'S 42°35'E
Kismayu see Kismaayo
164 M13 **Kiso-sanmyaku** ▲▲ Honshū, S Japan
115 H24 **Kíssamos** prev. Kastélli. Kríti, Greece, E Mediterranean Sea 35°30'N 23°39'E
Kisseraing see Kanmaw Kyun
76 K14 **Kissidougou** Guinée-Forestière, S Guinea 09°15'N 10°08'W
23 X12 **Kissimmee** Florida, SE USA 28°17'N 81°24'W
23 X12 **Kissimmee, Lake** ◎ Florida, SE USA
23 X13 **Kissimmee River** ≈ Florida, SE USA
11 V13 **Kississing Lake** ◎ Manitoba, C Canada
111 L24 **Kistelek** Csongrád, SE Hungary 46°27'N 19°58'E
Kistna see Krishna
111 M23 **Kisújszállás** Jász-Nagykun-Szolnok, E Hungary 47°14'N 20°45'E
164 G12 **Kisuki** var. Unnan. Shimane, Honshū, SW Japan 35°25'N 133°15'E
81 H18 **Kisumu** prev. Port Florence. Nyanza, W Kenya 0°02'N 34°42'E
Kisutzaneustadtl see Kysucké Nové Mesto
111 O20 **Kisvárda** Ger. Kleinwardein. Szabolcs-Szatmár-Bereg, E Hungary 48°13'N 22°03'E
81 J24 **Kiswere** Lindi, SE Tanzania 09°24'S 39°37'E
Kiszucaújhely see Kysucké Nové Mesto
76 K12 **Kita** Kayes, W Mali 13°00'N 09°28'W
197 N14 **Kitaa** ◆ province W Greenland
Kita-Akita see Takanosu
Kitab see Kitob
165 Q4 **Kitahiyama** Hokkaidō, NE Japan 42°25'N 139°55'E
165 P12 **Kita-Ibaraki** Ibaraki, Honshū, S Japan 36°46'N 140°45'E
165 X16 **Kita-Iō-jima** Eng. San Alessandro. island SE Japan
165 Q9 **Kitakami** Iwate, Honshū, C Japan 39°18'N 141°05'E
165 P11 **Kitakata** Fukushima, Honshū, C Japan 37°38'N 139°52'E
164 D13 **Kitakyūshū** var. Kitakyûsyû. Fukuoka, Kyūshū, SW Japan 33°51'N 130°49'E
Kitakyûsyû see Kitakyūshū
81 H18 **Kitale** Rift Valley, W Kenya 01°01'N 35°01'E
165 U3 **Kitami** Hokkaidō, NE Japan 43°52'N 143°51'E
165 T2 **Kitami-sanchi** ▲▲ Hokkaidō, NE Japan
37 W5 **Kit Carson** Colorado, C USA 38°45'N 102°47'W
180 M12 **Kitchener** Western Australia 31°03'S 124°00'E
14 F16 **Kitchener** Ontario, S Canada 43°28'N 80°27'W
93 O17 **Kitee** Itä-Suomi, SE Finland 62°06'N 30°09'E
81 G16 **Kitgum** N Uganda 03°17'N 32°54'E
Kithareng see Kanmaw Kyun
Kíthira see Kýthira
Kíthnos see Kýthnos
10 J13 **Kitimat** British Columbia, SW Canada 54°05'N 128°38'W
92 L11 **Kitinen** ≈ N Finland
147 O12 **Kitob** Rus. Kitab. Qashqadaryo Viloyati, S Uzbekistan 39°06'N 66°47'E
116 K7 **Kitsman'** Ger. Kotzman, Rom. Cozmeni, Rus. Kitsman. Chernivets'ka Oblast', W Ukraine 48°30'N 25°50'E
164 E14 **Kitsuki** var. Kituki. Ōita, Kyūshū, SW Japan 33°24'N 131°36'E
18 C14 **Kittanning** Pennsylvania, NE USA 40°48'N 79°28'W
19 P10 **Kittery** Maine, NE USA 43°05'N 70°44'W
92 L11 **Kittilä** Lappi, N Finland 67°39'N 24°53'E
109 Z4 **Kittsee** Burgenland, E Austria 48°06'N 17°03'E
81 J19 **Kitui** Eastern, S Kenya 01°25'S 38°00'E
Kituki see Kitsuki
81 G22 **Kitunda** Tabora, C Tanzania 06°47'S 33°13'E
10 K13 **Kitwanga** British Columbia, SW Canada 55°07'N 128°03'W
82 J13 **Kitwe** var. Kitwe-Nkana. Copperbelt, C Zambia 12°48'S 28°13'E
Kitwe-Nkana see Kitwe
109 O7 **Kitzbühel** Tirol, W Austria 47°27'N 12°23'E
109 O7 **Kitzbüheler Alpen** ▲▲ W Austria
101 J19 **Kitzingen** Bayern, SE Germany 49°45'N 10°11'E
153 Q14 **Kiul** Bihār, NE India 25°10'N 86°06'E
186 A7 **Kiunga** Western, SW Papua New Guinea 06°10'S 141°15'E
93 M16 **Kiuruvesi** Itä-Suomi, C Finland 63°38'N 26°40'E
38 M7 **Kivalina** Alaska, USA 67°44'N 164°32'W
92 L13 **Kivalo** ridge C Finland
116 J3 **Kivertsi** Pol. Kiwerce, Rus. Kivertsy. Volyns'ka Oblast', NW Ukraine 50°50'N 25°31'E
Kivertsy see Kivertsi
93 L16 **Kivijärvi** Länsi-Suomi, C Finland 63°09'N 25°04'E
95 L23 **Kivik** Skåne, S Sweden 55°40'N 14°15'E
118 J3 **Kiviõli** Ida-Virumaa, NE Estonia 59°20'N 27°00'E
Kivu, Lac see Kivu, Lake
67 U10 **Kivu, Lake** Fr. Lac Kivu. ◎ Rwanda/Dem. Rep. Congo
186 C9 **Kiwai Island** island SW Papua New Guinea
39 N8 **Kiwalik** Alaska, USA 66°01'N 161°50'W
Kiwerce see Kivertsi
Kiyev see Kyyiv
145 R10 **Kiyevka** Karaganda, C Kazakhstan 50°15'N 71°33'E
Kiyevskaya Oblast' see Kyyivs'ka Oblast'
Kiyevskoye Vodokhranilishche see Kyyivs'ke Vodoskhovyshche
136 D10 **Kıyıköy** Kırklareli, NW Turkey 41°37'N 28°07'E
145 O9 **Kiyma** Akmola, C Kazakhstan 51°37'N 67°31'E
125 V13 **Kizel** Permskaya Oblast', NW Russian Federation 58°59'N 57°37'E
125 O12 **Kizema** var. Kizëma. Arkhangel'skaya Oblast', NW Russian Federation 61°06'N 44°51'E
Kizëma see Kizema
Kizilagach see Elkhovo
136 H12 **Kızılcahamam** Ankara, N Turkey 40°28'N 32°37'E
136 J10 **Kızıl Irmak** ≈ C Turkey
Kizil Kum see Kyzyl Kum
137 P16 **Kızıltepe** Mardin, SE Turkey 37°12'N 40°36'E
Ki Zil Uzen see Qezel Owzan, Rūd-e
127 Q16 **Kizilyurt** Respublika Dagestan, SW Russian Federation 43°13'N 46°54'E
127 Q15 **Kizlyar** Respublika Dagestan, SW Russian Federation 43°51'N 46°39'E
127 S3 **Kizner** Udmurtskaya Respublika, NW Russian Federation 56°19'N 51°37'E
Kizyl-Arvat see Serdar
Kizyl-Atrek see Etrek
Kizyl-Kaya see Gyzylgaya
Kizyl-Su see Gyzylsuw
95 H16 **Kjerkøy** island S Norway
Kjølen see Kölen
92 L7 **Kjøllefjord** Finnmark, N Norway 70°55'N 27°19'E
92 H11 **Kjøpsvik** Nordland, C Norway 68°06'N 16°21'E
169 N12 **Klabat, Teluk** bay Pulau Bangka, W Indonesia
112 I12 **Kladanj** ◆ Federacija Bosna I Hercegovina, E Bosnia and Herzegovina
171 X16 **Kladar** Papua, E Indonesia 08°14'S 137°46'E
111 C16 **Kladno** Středočeský, NW Czech Republic 50°10'N 14°05'E
112 P11 **Kladovo** Serbia, E Serbia 44°37'N 22°36'E
167 P12 **Klaeng** Rayong, S Thailand 12°48'N 101°41'E
109 T9 **Klagenfurt** Slvn. Celovec. Kärnten, S Austria 46°38'N 14°20'E
118 B11 **Klaipėda** Ger. Memel. Klaipeda, NW Lithuania 55°42'N 21°09'E
118 C11 **Klaipėda** ◆ province W Lithuania
Klaksvig see Klaksvík
95 B18 **Klaksvík** Dan. Klaksvig. Faeroe Islands 62°13'N 06°34'W
34 L2 **Klamath** California, W USA 41°31'N 124°02'W
32 H16 **Klamath Falls** Oregon, NW USA 42°14'N 121°47'W
34 M1 **Klamath Mountains** ▲▲ California/Oregon, W USA
34 L2 **Klamath River** ≈ California/Oregon, W USA
168 K9 **Klang** var. Kelang; prev. Port Swettenham. Selangor, Peninsular Malaysia 03°02'N 101°27'E
94 J13 **Klarälven** ≈ Norway/Sweden
111 B15 **Klášterec nad Ohří** Ger. Klösterle an der Eger. Ústecky Kraj, NW Czech Republic 50°24'N 13°10'E
111 B18 **Klatovy** Ger. Klattau. Plzeňský Kraj, W Czech Republic 49°24'N 13°16'E
Klattau see Klatovy
Klausenburg see Cluj-Napoca
39 Y14 **Klawock** Prince of Wales Island, Alaska, USA 55°33'N 133°06'W
98 P8 **Klazienaveen** Drenthe, NE Netherlands 52°43'N 07°E
Kleck see Klyetsk
110 H11 **Klecko** Weilkopolskie, C Poland 52°37'N 17°27'E
110 I11 **Kleczew** Wielkopolskie, C Poland 52°22'N 18°12'E
10 L15 **Kleena Kleene** British Columbia, SW Canada 51°55'N 124°54'W
83 D20 **Klein Aub** Hardap, C Namibia 23°48'S 16°39'E
Kleine Donau see Mosoni-Duna
101 O14 **Kleine Elster** ≈ E Germany
Kleine Kokel see Târnava Mică
99 I16 **Kleine Nete** ≈ N Belgium
Kleines Ungarisches Tiefland see Little Alföld
83 E22 **Klein Karas** Karas, S Namibia 27°36'S 18°05'E
Kleinkopisch see Copşa Mică
Klein-Marien see Väike-Maarja
Kleinschlatten see Zlatna
83 D23 **Kleinsee** Northern Cape, W South Africa 29°43'S 17°03'E
Kleinwardein see Kisvárda
115 C16 **Kleisoúra** Ípeiros, W Greece 39°21'N 20°52'E
95 C17 **Klepp** Rogaland, S Norway 58°46'N 05°39'E
83 I22 **Klerksdorp** North-West, N South Africa 26°52'S 26°39'E
126 I5 **Kletnya** Bryanskaya Oblast', W Russian Federation 53°25'N 32°58'E
Kletsk see Klyetsk
101 D14 **Kleve** Eng. Cleves, Fr. Clèves; prev. Cleve. Nordrhein-Westfalen, W Germany 51°47'N 06°11'E
113 J16 **Kličevo** C Montenegro 42°45'N 18°58'E
119 M16 **Klichaw** Rus. Klichev. Mahilyowskaya Voblasts', E Belarus 53°29'N 29°21'E
Klichev see Klichaw
119 Q16 **Klimavichy** Rus. Klimovichi. Mahilyowskaya Voblasts', E Belarus 53°37'N 31°58'E
114 M7 **Kliment** Shumen, NE Bulgaria 43°37'N 27°00'E
Klimovichi see Klimavichy
93 G14 **Klimpfjäll** Västerbotten, N Sweden 65°05'N 14°50'E
126 K3 **Klin** Moskovskaya Oblast', W Russian Federation 56°19'N 36°45'E
Klina see Klinë
113 M16 **Klinë** Serb. Klina. W Kosovo 42°38'N 20°35'E
111 B15 **Klínovec** Ger. Keilberg. ▲ NW Czech Republic 50°23'N 12°57'E
95 P19 **Klintehamn** Gotland, SE Sweden 57°22'N 18°15'E
127 R8 **Klintsovka** Saratovskaya Oblast', W Russian Federation 51°42'N 49°17'E
126 H6 **Klintsy** Bryanskaya Oblast', W Russian Federation 52°46'N 32°21'E
95 K22 **Klippan** Skåne, S Sweden 56°08'N 13°10'E
92 G13 **Klippen** Västerbotten, N Sweden 65°50'N 15°07'E
121 P2 **Klírou** W Cyprus 35°01'N 33°11'E
114 I9 **Klisura** Plovdiv, C Bulgaria 42°40'N 24°28'E
95 F20 **Klitmøller** Viborg, NW Denmark 57°01'N 08°29'E
112 F11 **Ključ** Federacija Bosna I Hercegovina, NW Bosnia and Herzegovina 44°32'N 16°46'E
111 J14 **Kłobuck** Śląskie, S Poland 50°56'N 18°55'E
110 J11 **Kłodawa** Wielkopolskie, C Poland 52°14'N 18°55'E
111 G16 **Kłodzko** Ger. Glatz. Dolnośląskie, SW Poland 50°27'N 16°37'E
95 I14 **Kløfta** Akershus, S Norway 60°04'N 11°06'E
112 P12 **Klokočevac** Serbia, E Serbia 44°19'N 22°11'E
118 G3 **Klooga** Ger. Lodensee. Harjumaa, NW Estonia 59°18'N 24°10'E
99 F15 **Kloosterzande** Zeeland, SW Netherlands 51°22'N 04°01'E
113 L19 **Klos** var. Klosi. Dibër, C Albania 41°30'N 20°07'E
Klosi see Klos
Klösterle an der Eger see Klášterec nad Ohří
109 X3 **Klosterneuburg** Niederösterreich, NE Austria 48°19'N 16°20'E
108 J9 **Klosters** Graubünden, SE Switzerland 46°54'N 09°52'E
108 G7 **Kloten** Zürich, N Switzerland 47°27'N 08°35'E
108 G7 **Kloten** ✈ (Zürich) Zürich, N Switzerland 47°25'N 08°36'E
100 K12 **Klötze** Sachsen-Anhalt, C Germany 52°37'N 11°09'E
12 K3 **Klotz, Lac** ◎ Québec, NE Canada
101 O15 **Klotzsche** ✈ (Dresden) Sachsen, E Germany 51°06'N 13°44'E
10 H7 **Kluane Lake** ◎ Yukon Territory, W Canada
Kluang see Keluang
111 I14 **Kluczbork** Ger. Kreuzburg, Kreuzburg in Oberschlesien. Opolskie, S Poland 50°59'N 18°13'E
39 W12 **Klukwan** Alaska, USA 59°24'N 135°49'W
Klyastitsy see Klyastsitsy
118 L11 **Klyastsitsy** Rus. Klyastitsy. Vitsyebskaya Voblasts', N Belarus 55°53'N 28°36'E
127 T5 **Klyavlino** Samarskaya Oblast', W Russian Federation 54°21'N 52°12'E
84 K9 **Klyaz'in** ≈ W Russian Federation
127 N3 **Klyaz'ma** ≈ W Russian Federation
119 J17 **Klyetsk** Pol. Kleck, Rus. Kletsk. Minskaya Voblasts', SW Belarus 53°04'N 26°38'E
147 S8 **Klyuchevka** Talasskaya Oblast', NW Kyrgyzstan 42°34'N 71°45'E
123 V10 **Klyuchevskaya Sopka, Vulkan** 🌋 E Russian Federation 56°03'N 160°38'E
95 D17 **Knaben** Vest-Agder, S Norway 58°46'N 07°04'E
95 K21 **Knäred** Halland, S Sweden 56°30'N 13°21'E
97 M16 **Knaresborough** N England, United Kingdom 54°01'N 01°35'W
114 H8 **Knezha** Vratsa, NW Bulgaria 43°29'N 24°04'E
25 O9 **Knickerbocker** Texas, SW USA 31°18'N 100°35'W
28 K5 **Knife River** ≈ North Dakota, N USA
10 K16 **Knight Inlet** inlet British Columbia, W Canada
39 S12 **Knight Island** island Alaska, USA
97 K20 **Knighton** E Wales, United Kingdom 52°20'N 03°01'W
35 O7 **Knights Landing** California, W USA 38°47'N 121°43'W
112 E13 **Knin** Šibenik-Knin, S Croatia 44°03'N 16°12'E
25 Q12 **Knippal** Texas, SW USA 29°01'N 99°38'W
109 U7 **Knittelfeld** Steiermark, C Austria 47°14'N 14°50'E
95 O15 **Knivsta** Uppsala, C Sweden 59°43'N 17°49'E
113 P14 **Knjaževac** Serbia, E Serbia 43°34'N 22°16'E
27 S4 **Knob Noster** Missouri, C USA 38°47'N 93°33'W
99 D15 **Knokke-Heist** West-Vlaanderen, NW Belgium 51°21'N 03°19'E
95 H20 **Knøsen** hill N Denmark
Knosós see Knossos
115 J25 **Knossos** Gk. Knosós. prehistoric site Kríti, Greece, E Mediterranean Sea
25 N7 **Knott** Texas, SW USA 32°21'N 101°35'W
194 K5 **Knowles, Cape** headland Antarctica 71°45'S 60°20'W
31 O11 **Knox** Indiana, N USA 41°17'N 86°37'W
29 O3 **Knox** North Dakota, N USA 48°19'N 99°43'W
18 C13 **Knox** Pennsylvania, NE USA 41°13'N 79°33'W
189 X8 **Knox Atoll** var. Ņadikdik, Narikrik. atoll Ratak Chain, SE Marshall Islands
10 H13 **Knox, Cape** headland Graham Island, British Columbia, SW Canada 54°05'N 133°02'W
25 P5 **Knox City** Texas, SW USA 33°25'N 99°49'W
195 Y11 **Knox Coast** physical region Antarctica
31 T12 **Knox Lake** ◎ Ohio, N USA
23 T5 **Knoxville** Georgia, SE USA 32°44'N 83°58'W
30 K12 **Knoxville** Illinois, N USA 40°54'N 90°16'W
29 W15 **Knoxville** Iowa, C USA 41°19'N 93°06'W
21 N9 **Knoxville** Tennessee, S USA 35°58'N 83°55'W
197 P11 **Knud Rasmussen Land** physical region N Greenland
Knüll see Knüllgebirge
101 I16 **Knüllgebirge** var. Knüll. ▲▲ C Germany
124 I5 **Knyazhegubskoye Vodokhranilishche** ◎ NW Russian Federation
Knyazhevo see Sredishte
Knyazhitsy see Knyazhytsy
119 O15 **Knyazhytsy** Rus. Knyazhitsy. Mahilyowskaya Voblasts', E Belarus 54°10'N 30°28'E
83 G26 **Knysna** Western Cape, SW South Africa 34°03'S 23°03'E
Koartac see Quaqtaq
81 J23 **Koani** Zanzibar South, E Tanzania 06°08'S 39°18'E
169 N13 **Koba** Pulau Bangka, W Indonesia 02°30'S 106°26'E
164 D16 **Kobayashi** var. Kobayasi. Miyazaki, Kyūshū, SW Japan 32°00'N 130°58'E
Kobayasi see Kobayashi
Kobdo see Hovd
164 I13 **Kōbe** Hyōgo, Honshū, SW Japan 34°40'N 135°10'E
Kobelyaki see Kobelyaky
117 T6 **Kobelyaky** Rus. Kobelyaki. Poltavs'ka Oblast', NE Ukraine 49°10'N 34°13'E
95 J22 **København** Eng. Copenhagen; anc. Hafnia. ● (Denmark) Sjælland, København, E Denmark 55°43'N 12°34'E
95 J23 **København** off. Københavns Amt. ◆ county E Denmark
Københavns Amt see København
76 K10 **Kobenni** Hodh el Gharbi, S Mauritania 15°58'N 09°24'W
171 T13 **Kobi** Pulau Seram, E Indonesia 02°56'S 129°53'E
101 F17 **Koblenz** prev. Coblenz, Fr. Coblence; anc. Confluentes. Rheinland-Pfalz, W Germany 50°21'N 07°36'E
108 F6 **Koblenz** Aargau, N Switzerland 47°34'N 08°16'E
Kobrin see Kobryn
171 V15 **Kobroor, Pulau** island Kepulauan Aru, E Indonesia
119 G19 **Kobryn** Rus. Kobrin. Brestskaya Voblasts', SW Belarus 52°13'N 24°21'E
39 O7 **Kobuk** Alaska, USA 66°54'N 156°52'W
39 O7 **Kobuk River** ≈ Alaska, USA
137 Q10 **K'obulet'i** W Georgia 41°47'N 41°47'E
123 P10 **Kobyay** Respublika Sakha (Yakutiya), NE Russian Federation 63°36'N 126°33'E
136 E11 **Kocaeli** ◆ province NW Turkey
113 P18 **Kočani** NE FYR Macedonia 41°55'N 22°25'E
112 K12 **Koceljevo** Serbia, W Serbia 44°28'N 19°49'E
109 U12 **Kočevje** Ger. Gottschee. S Slovenia 45°41'N 14°48'E
153 T12 **Koch Bihār** West Bengal, NE India 26°19'N 89°26'E
Kochchi see Cochin/Kochi
122 M9 **Kochechum** ≈ N Russian Federation
101 I20 **Kocher** ≈ SW Germany
125 T13 **Kochevo** Komi-Permyatskiy Avtonomnyy Okrug, NW Russian Federation 59°37'N 54°16'E
155 G22 **Kochi** var. Cochin, Kochchi. Kerala, SW India 09°56'N 76°15'E see also Cochin
164 G14 **Kōchi** var. Kôti. Kōchi, Shikoku, SW Japan 33°31'N 133°30'E
164 G14 **Kōchi** off. Kōchi-ken, var. Kôti. ◆ prefecture Shikoku, SW Japan
Kōchi-ken see Kōchi
Kochiu see Gejiu
Kochkor see Kochkorka
147 V8 **Kochkorka** Kir. Kochkor. Narynskaya Oblast', C Kyrgyzstan 42°09'N 75°42'E
125 V5 **Kochmes** Respublika Komi, NW Russian Federation 66°10'N 60°46'E
127 P15 **Kochubey** Respublika Dagestan, SW Russian Federation 44°25'N 46°33'E
115 I17 **Kochylas** ▲ Skýros, Vóreies Sporádes, Greece, Aegean Sea 38°50'N 24°35'E
110 O13 **Kock** Lubelskie, E Poland 51°39'N 22°26'E
81 J19 **Kodacho** spring/well S Kenya 01°52'S 39°22'E
153 Q14 **Kodarma** Jharkhand, N India 24°26'N 85°31'E
155 K24 **Koddiyar Bay** bay NE Sri Lanka
39 Q14 **Kodiak** Kodiak Island, Alaska, USA 57°47'N 152°24'W
39 Q14 **Kodiak Island** island Alaska, USA
154 B12 **Kodīnār** Gujarāt, W India 20°44'N 70°46'E
124 M9 **Kodino** Arkhangel'skaya Oblast', NW Russian Federation 63°36'N 39°54'E
122 M12 **Kodinsk** Krasnoyarskiy Kray, C Russian Federation 58°37'N 99°18'E
80 F12 **Kodok** Upper Nile, SE Sudan 09°51'N 32°07'E
117 N8 **Kodyma** Odes'ka Oblast', SW Ukraine 48°05'N 29°09'E
Koedoes see Kudus
99 B17 **Koekelare** West-Vlaanderen, W Belgium 51°07'N 02°58'E
Koeln see Köln
Koepang see Kupang
Ko-erh-mu see Golmud
99 J17 **Koersel** Limburg, NE Belgium 51°04'N 05°17'E
83 E21 **Koës** Karas, SE Namibia 25°59'S 19°08'E
Koetai see Mahakam, Sungai
Koetaradja see Bandaaceh
36 I14 **Kofa Mountains** ▲▲ Arizona, SW USA
171 Y15 **Kofarau** Papua, E Indonesia 07°29'S 140°28'E
147 P13 **Kofarnihon** Rus. Kofarnikhon; prev. Ordzhonikidzeabad, Taj. Orjonikidzeobod, Yangi-Bazar. W Tajikistan 38°32'N 68°56'E
147 P14 **Kofarnihon** Rus. Kafirnigan. ≈ SW Tajikistan
Kofarnikhon see Kofarnihon
114 M11 **Kofçaz** Kırklareli, NW Turkey 41°58'N 27°12'E
115 J25 **Kófinas** ▲ Kríti, Greece, E Mediterranean Sea 34°58'N 25°03'E
121 P3 **Kófinou** var. Kophinou. S Cyprus 34°49'N 33°24'E
109 V8 **Köflach** Steiermark, SE Austria 47°04'N 15°04'E
77 Q17 **Koforidua** SE Ghana 06°01'N 00°12'W
164 H12 **Kōfu** Tottori, Honshū, SW Japan 35°16'N 133°31'E
164 M13 **Kōfu** var. Kôhu. Yamanashi, Honshū, S Japan 35°41'N 138°33'E
81 F22 **Koga** Tabora, C Tanzania 06°08'S 32°20'E
Kogălniceanu see Mihail Kogălniceanu
13 P6 **Kogaluk** ≈ Newfoundland and Labrador, E Canada
12 J4 **Kogaluk** ≈ Québec, NE Canada
122 I10 **Kogalym** Khanty-Mansiyskiy Avtonomnyy Okrug-Yugra, C Russian Federation 62°13'N 74°34'E
95 J23 **Køge** Roskilde, E Denmark 55°28'N 12°12'E
95 J23 **Køge Bugt** bay E Denmark
77 U16 **Kogi** ◆ state C Nigeria
146 L11 **Kogon** Rus. Kagan. Buxoro Viloyati, C Uzbekistan 39°47'N 64°29'E
163 Y17 **Kōgŭm-do** island S South Korea
Kohalom see Rupea
149 T6 **Kohāt** North-West Frontier Province, NW Pakistan 33°37'N 71°30'E
142 L10 **Kohgīlūyeh va Būyer Aḥmad** off. Ostān-e Kohkīlūyeh va Būyer Aḥmadī, var. Boyer Ahmadī va Kohkīlūyeh. ◆ province SW Iran
118 G4 **Kohila** Ger. Koil. Raplamaa, NW Estonia 59°09'N 24°45'E
153 X13 **Kohīma** state capital Nāgāland, E India 25°40'N 94°08'E
Koh I Noh see Büyükağrı Dağı
Kohkīlūyeh va Būyer Aḥmadī, Ostān-e see Kohgīlūyeh va Būyer Aḥmad
149 R10 **Kohlu** Baluchistān, SW Pakistan 29°54'N 69°15'E
Kohsān see Kūhestān
118 J3 **Kohtla-Järve** Ida-Virumaa, NE Estonia 59°22'N 27°21'E
Kôhu see Kōfu
Kohyl'nyk see Cogîlnic
165 N11 **Koide** Niigata, Honshū, C Japan 37°13'N 138°58'E
10 G7 **Koidern** Yukon Territory, W Canada 61°55'N 140°22'W
76 J15 **Koidu** E Sierra Leone 08°40'N 11°01'W
118 I4 **Koigi** Järvamaa, C Estonia 58°51'N 25°45'E
Koil see Kohila
172 H13 **Koimbani** Grande Comore, NW Comoros 11°37'S 43°23'E
139 T3 **Koi Sanjaq** var. Koysanjaq, Kūysanjaq. Arbīl, N Iraq 36°05'N 44°38'E
93 O16 **Koitere** ◎ E Finland
Koivisto see Primorsk
163 Z16 **Kōje-do** Jap. Kyōsai-tō. island S South Korea
80 J13 **K'ok'a Hāyk'** ◎ C Ethiopia
Kokand see Qo'qon
182 F6 **Kokatha** South Australia 31°17'S 135°16'E
146 M10 **Ko'kcha** Rus. Kokcha. Buxoro Viloyati, C Uzbekistan 40°30'N 64°58'E
Kokcha see Ko'kcha
Kokchetav see Kokshetau
93 K18 **Kokemäenjoki** ≈ SW Finland
171 W14 **Kokenau** var. Kokonau. Papua, E Indonesia 04°38'S 136°24'E
83 E22 **Kokerboom** Karas, SE Namibia 28°11'S 19°25'E
119 N14 **Kokhanava** Rus. Kokhanovo. Vitsyebskaya Voblasts', NE Belarus 54°28'N 29°59'E
Kokhanovichi see Kakhanavichy
Kokhanovo see Kokhanava
Kok-Janggak see Kok-Yangak
93 K16 **Kokkola** Swe. Karleby; prev. Swe. Gamlakarleby. Länsi-Suomi, W Finland 63°50'N 23°10'E
158 L3 **Kok Kuduk** spring/well N China 46°03'N 87°34'E
118 H9 **Koknese** Aizkraukle, C Latvia 56°38'N 25°27'E
77 T13 **Koko** Kebbi, W Nigeria 11°25'N 04°33'E
186 E9 **Kokoda** Northern, S Papua New Guinea 08°52'S 147°44'E
76 K12 **Kokofata** Kayes, W Mali 12°48'N 09°56'W
39 N6 **Kokolik River** ≈ Alaska, USA
31 O13 **Kokomo** Indiana, N USA 40°29'N 86°07'W
Kokonau see Kokenau
Koko Nor see Qinghai Hu, China
Koko Nor see Qinghai, China
186 H6 **Kokopo** var. Kopopo; prev. Herbertshöhe. New Britain, E Papua New Guinea 04°18'S 152°17'E
145 X10 **Kokpekti** Kaz. Kökpekti. Vostochnyy Kazakhstan, E Kazakhstan 48°47'N 82°28'E
145 X11 **Kokpekti** ≈ E Kazakhstan
Kökpekti see Kokpekti
153 T12 **Kokrajhar** Assam, NE India 26°24'N 90°16'E
39 P9 **Kokrines** Alaska, USA 64°58'N 154°42'W
39 P9 **Kokrines Hills** ▲▲ Alaska, USA
145 P17 **Koksaray** Yuzhnyy Kazakhstan, S Kazakhstan 42°34'N 68°06'E
147 X9 **Kokshaal-Tau** Rus. Khrebet Kakshaal-Too. ▲▲ China/Kyrgyzstan
145 P7 **Kokshetau** Kaz. Kökshetaū; prev. Kokchetav. Kokshetau, N Kazakhstan 53°18'N 69°25'E
Kökshetaū see Kokshetau
99 A17 **Koksijde** West-Vlaanderen, W Belgium 51°07'N 02°40'E
12 M5 **Koksoak** ≈ Québec, E Canada
83 K24 **Kokstad** KwaZulu/Natal, E South Africa 30°23'S 29°23'E
145 V14 **Koksu** Kaz. Rūdnīchnyy. Almaty, SE Kazakhstan 44°39'N 78°57'E
145 W15 **Koktal** Kaz. Köktal. Almaty, SE Kazakhstan 44°05'N 79°44'E
145 Q12 **Koktas** ≈ C Kazakhstan
Kök-Tash see Këk-Tash
Koktokay see Fuyun
147 T9 **Kok-Yangak** Kir. Kök-Janggak. Dzhalal-Abadskaya Oblast', W Kyrgyzstan 41°02'N 73°11'E
158 F9 **Kokyar** Xinjiang Uygur Zizhiqu, W China 37°24'N 77°15'E
124 J3 **Kola** Murmanskaya Oblast', NW Russian Federation 68°52'N 33°03'E
149 O13 **Kolāchi** var. Kulachi. ≈ SW Pakistan
76 J15 **Kolahun** N Liberia 08°24'N 10°02'W
171 O14 **Kolaka** Sulawesi, C Indonesia 04°04'S 121°38'E
K'o-la-ma-i see Karamay
Kola Peninsula see Kol'skiy Poluostrov
155 H19 **Kolār** Karnātaka, E India 13°10'N 78°10'E
155 H19 **Kolār Gold Fields** Karnātaka, E India 12°56'N 78°16'E
92 K11 **Kolari** Lappi, NW Finland 67°20'N 23°51'E
111 I21 **Kolárovo** Ger. Gutta; prev. Guta, Hung. Gúta. Nitriansky Kraj, SW Slovakia 47°54'N 18°01'E
113 K16 **Kolašin** E Montenegro 42°49'N 19°32'E
152 F11 **Kolāyat** Rājasthān, NW India 27°56'N 73°02'E
95 N15 **Kolbäck** Västmanland, C Sweden 59°33'N 16°15'E
Kolbcha see Kowbcha
197 Q15 **Kolbeinsey Ridge** undersea feature Denmark Strait/Norwegian Sea 69°00'N 17°30'W
Kolberg see Kołobrzeg
95 H15 **Kolbotn** Akershus, S Norway 62°15'N 10°24'E
111 N16 **Kolbuszowa** Podkarpackie, SE Poland 50°12'N 22°07'E
126 L3 **Kol'chugino** Vladimirskaya Oblast', W Russian Federation 56°19'N 39°24'E
76 H12 **Kolda** S Senegal 12°58'N 14°58'W
95 G23 **Kolding** Vejle, C Denmark 55°29'N 09°30'E
79 K20 **Kole** Kasai-Oriental, SW Dem. Rep. Congo 03°30'S 22°28'E
79 M17 **Kole** Orientale, N Dem. Rep. Congo 02°08'N 25°25'E
Kole see Kili Island
84 F6 **Kölen** Nor. Kjølen. ▲▲ Norway/Sweden
Kolepom, Pulau see Yos Sudarso, Pulau
118 H3 **Kolga Laht** Ger. Kolko-Wiek. bay N Estonia
125 Q3 **Kolguyev, Ostrov** island NW Russian Federation
155 E16 **Kolhāpur** Mahārāshtra, SW India 16°42'N 74°13'E
151 K21 **Kolhumadulu** var. Thaa Atoll. atoll S Maldives
93 O16 **Koli** var. Kolinkylä. Itä-Suomi, E Finland 63°06'N 29°46'E
39 O13 **Koliganek** Alaska, USA 59°43'N 157°16'W
111 E16 **Kolín** Ger. Kolin. Střední Čechy, C Czech Republic 50°02'N 15°10'E
Kolinkylä see Koli
190 E12 **Koliu** Île Futuna, W Wallis and Futuna
118 E7 **Kolka** Talsi, NW Latvia 57°44'N 22°34'E
118 E7 **Kolkasrags** prev. Eng. Cape Domesnes. headland NW Latvia 57°45'N 22°35'E
153 S16 **Kolkata** prev. Calcutta. state capital West Bengal, NE India 22°30'N 88°20'E
Kolkhozabad see Kolkhozobod
147 P14 **Kolkhozobod** Rus. Kolkhozabad; prev. Kaganovichabad, Tugalan. SW Tajikistan 37°33'N 68°34'E
Kolki/Kołki see Kolky
Kolko-Wiek see Kolga Laht
116 K3 **Kolky** Pol. Kołki, Rus. Kolki. Volyns'ka Oblast', NW Ukraine 51°05'N 25°40'E
155 G23 **Kollam** var. Quilon. Kerala, SW India 08°57'N 76°37'E see also Quilon
155 G20 **Kollegāl** Karnātaka, W India 12°08'N 77°06'E
98 M5 **Kollum** Friesland, N Netherlands 53°17'N 06°09'E
Kolmar see Colmar
101 E16 **Köln** var. Koeln, Eng./Fr. Cologne, prev. Cöln; anc. Colonia Agrippina, Oppidum Ubiorum. Nordrhein-Westfalen, W Germany 50°57'N 06°57'E
110 N9 **Kolno** Podlaskie, NE Poland 53°24'N 21°57'E
110 J12 **Koło** Wielkopolskie, C Poland 52°11'N 18°39'E
38 B8 **Kōloa** var. Koloa. Kaua'i, Hawaii, USA, C Pacific Ocean 21°54'N 159°28'W
Koloa see Kōloa
110 E7 **Kołobrzeg** Ger. Kolberg. Zachodnio-pomorskie, NW Poland 54°11'N 15°34'E
126 H4 **Kolodnya** Smolenskaya Oblast', W Russian Federation 54°57'N 32°22'E
190 E13 **Kolofau, Mont** 🌋 Île Alofi, S Wallis and Futuna 14°21'S 178°02'W
125 O14 **Kologriv** Kostromskaya Oblast', NW Russian Federation 58°49'N 44°22'E
76 L12 **Kolokani** Koulikoro, W Mali 13°35'N 08°01'W
77 N13 **Koloko** W Burkina 11°06'N 05°18'W
186 K8 **Kolombangara** var. Kilimbangara, Nduke. island New Georgia Islands, NW Solomon Islands
Kolomea see Kolomyya
126 L4 **Kolomna** Moskovskaya Oblast', W Russian Federation 55°03'N 38°52'E
116 J7 **Kolomyya** Ger. Kolomea. Ivano-Frankivs'ka Oblast', W Ukraine 48°31'N 25°00'E
76 M13 **Kolondiéba** Sikasso, SW Mali 11°04'N 06°55'W
193 V15 **Kolonga** Tongatapu, S Tonga 21°07'S 175°05'W
189 U16 **Kolonia** var. Colonia. Pohnpei, E Micronesia 06°57'N 158°12'E
Kolonja see Kolonjë
113 K21 **Kolonjë** var. Kolonja. Fier, C Albania 40°49'N 19°37'E
Kolonjë see Ersekë
Kolosjoki see Nikel'
Kolotambu see Avuavu
193 U15 **Kolovai** Tongatapu, S Tonga 21°05'S 175°20'W
Kolozsvár see Cluj-Napoca
112 C9 **Kolpa** Ger. Kulpa, SCr. Kupa. ≈ Croatia/Slovenia
122 J11 **Kolpashevo** Tomskaya Oblast', C Russian Federation 58°21'N 82°44'E
124 H13 **Kolpino** Leningradskaya Oblast', NW Russian Federation 59°44'N 30°39'E
100 M10 **Kölpinsee** ◎ NE Germany
Kólpos Mórfu see Güzelyurt Körfezi
146 K8 **Ko'lquduq** Rus. Kulkuduk. Navoiy Viloyati, N Uzbekistan 42°36'N 63°24'E
124 K5 **Kol'skiy Poluostrov** Eng. Kola Peninsula. peninsula NW Russian Federation
127 T6 **Koltubanovskiy** Orenburgskaya Oblast', W Russian Federation 53°00'N 52°00'E
112 L11 **Kolubara** ≈ C Serbia
Kolupchii see Gurkovo
110 K13 **Koluszki** Łódźskie, C Poland 51°44'N 19°50'E
125 T6 **Kolva** ≈ NW Russian Federation
93 E14 **Kolvereid** Nord-Trøndelag, W Norway 64°47'N 11°22'E
79 M24 **Kolwezi** Katanga, S Dem. Rep. Congo 10°43'S 25°29'E
123 S7 **Kolyma** ≈ NE Russian Federation
Kolyma Lowland see Kolymskaya Nizmennost'
Kolyma Range/Kolymskiy, Khrebet see Kolymskoye Nagor'ye
123 S7 **Kolymskaya Nizmennost'** Eng. Kolyma Lowland. lowlands NE Russian Federation
123 S7 **Kolymskoye** Respublika Sakha (Yakutiya), NE Russian Federation 68°42'N 158°46'E
123 U8 **Kolymskoye Nagor'ye** var. Khrebet Kolymskiy, Eng. Kolyma Range. ▲▲ E Russian Federation
123 V5 **Kolyuchinskaya Guba** bay NE Russian Federation
145 W15 **Kol'zhat** Kaz. Qalzhat. Almaty, SE Kazakhstan 43°29'N 80°37'E
114 G8 **Kom** ▲ NW Bulgaria 43°10'N 23°02'E
80 I13 **Koma** Oromīya, C Ethiopia 08°19'N 36°48'E
77 X12 **Komadugu Gana** ≈ NE Nigeria
164 M13 **Komagane** Nagano, Honshū, S Japan 35°44'N 137°54'E
79 P17 **Komanda** Orientale, NE Dem. Rep. Congo 01°25'N 29°43'E
197 U1 **Komandorskaya Basin** var. Kamchatka Basin. undersea feature SW Bering Sea 57°00'N 168°00'E
125 Pp9 **Komandorskiye Ostrova** Eng. Commander Islands. island group E Russian Federation
Kománfalva see Comăneşti
111 I22 **Komárno** Ger. Komorn, Hung. Komárom. Nitriansky Kraj, SW Slovakia 47°46'N 18°07'E
111 I22 **Komárom** Komárom-Esztergom, NW Hungary 47°43'N 18°06'E
Komárom see Komárno
111 I22 **Komárom-Esztergom** off. Komárom-Esztergom Megye. ◆ county N Hungary
Komárom-Esztergom Megye see Komárom-Esztergom
164 K11 **Komatsu** var. Komatu. Ishikawa, Honshū, SW Japan 36°25'N 136°27'E
Komatu see Komatsu
83 D17 **Kombat** Otjozondjupa, N Namibia 19°42'S 17°45'E
Kombissiguiri see Kombissiri
77 P13 **Kombissiri** var. Kombissiguiri. C Burkina 12°01'N 01°27'W
188 E10 **Komebail Lagoon** lagoon N Palau
81 F20 **Kome Island** island N Tanzania
Komeyo see Wandai
117 P10 **Kominternivs'ke** Odes'ka Oblast', SW Ukraine 46°52'N 30°56'E
125 S12 **Komi-Permyatskiy Avtonomnyy Okrug** ◆ autonomous district Permskiy Kray, W Russian Federation

◆ Country ● Country Capital ◇ Dependent Territory ○ Dependent Territory Capital ◆ Administrative Regions ✈ International Airport ▲ Mountain ▲▲ Mountain Range 🌋 Volcano ≈ River ◎ Lake ⊠ Reservoir

Komi, Respublika – Kozhikode

125 R8 **Komi, Respublika** ◈ *autonomous republic* NW Russian Federation
111 I25 **Komló** Baranya, SW Hungary 46°11′N 18°15′E
Kommunarsk *see* Alchevs'k
Kommunizm, Qullai *see* Ismoili Somonī, Qullai
186 B7 **Komo** Southern Highlands, W Papua New Guinea 06°06′S 142°52′E
170 M16 **Komodo, Pulau** *island* Nusa Tenggara, S Indonesia
77 N15 **Komoé** *var.* Komoé Fleuve. ≈ E Ivory Coast
Komoé Fleuve *see* Komoé
75 X11 **Kom Ombo** *var.* Kôm Ombo, Kawm Umbū. SE Egypt 24°26′N 32°57′E
79 F20 **Komono** Lékoumou, SW Congo 03°15′S 13°14′E
171 Y16 **Komoran** Papua, E Indonesia 08°14′S 138°51′E
171 Y16 **Komoran, Pulau** *island* E Indonesia
Komorn *see* Komárno
Komornok *see* Comorâşte
Komosolabad *see* Komsomolobod
Komotau *see* Chomutov
114 K13 **Komotiní** *var.* Gümüljina, *Turk.* Gümülcine. Anatolikí Makedonía kai Thráki, NE Greece 41°07′N 25°27′E
113 K16 **Komovi** ▲▲ E Montenegro
117 R8 **Kompaniyivka** Kirovohrads'ka Oblast', C Ukraine 48°16′N 32°12′E
Kompong *see* Kâmpóng Chhnăng
Kompong Cham *see* Kâmpóng Cham
Kompong Kleang *see* Kâmpóng Khleăng
Kompong Som *see* Kâmpóng Saôm
Kompong Speu *see* Kâmpóng Spoe
Komrat *see* Comrat
Komsomol *see* Komsomol'skiy
122 K14 **Komsomolets, Ostrov** *island* Severnaya Zemlya, N Russian Federation
144 F13 **Komsomolets, Zaliv** *lake gulf* SW Kazakhstan
Komsomol/Komsomolets *see* Karabalyk, Kostanay, Kazakhstan
147 Q12 **Komsomolobod** *Rus.* Komosolabad. C Tajikistan 38°51′N 69°54′E
124 M16 **Komsomol'sk** Ivanovskaya Oblast', W Russian Federation 56°58′N 40°15′E
117 S6 **Komsomol's'k** Poltavs'ka Oblast', C Ukraine 49°01′N 33°37′E
146 M11 **Komsomol'sk** Navoiy Viloyati, N Uzbekistan 40°14′N 65°10′E
144 G12 **Komsomol'skiy** *Kaz.* Komsomol. Atyrau, W Kazakhstan 47°18′N 53°37′E
127 P5 **Komsomol'skiy** Respublika Mordoviya, W Russian Federation 54°26′N 45°50′E
125 W4 **Komsomol'skiy** Respublika Komi, NW Russian Federation 67°33′N 64°00′E
123 S13 **Komsomol'sk-na-Amure** Khabarovskiy Kray, SE Russian Federation 50°32′N 136°59′E
Komsomol'sk-na-Ustyurte *see* Kubla-Ustyurt
144 K10 **Komsomol'skoye** Aktyubinsk, NW Kazakhstan
127 Q8 **Komsomol'skoye** Saratovskaya Oblast', W Russian Federation 50°45′N 47°00′E
145 P10 **Kon** ≈ C Kazakhstan
Kona *see* Kailua-Kona
124 K16 **Konakovo** Tverskaya Oblast', W Russian Federation 56°42′N 36°44′E
149 S4 **Konar** *Per.* Konarhā, *Pash.* Kunar. ◈ *province* E Afghanistan
143 V15 **Konārak** Sīstān va Balūchestān, SE Iran 25°26′N 60°23′E
Konarhā *see* Konar
27 O11 **Konawa** Oklahoma, C USA 34°57′N 96°45′W
122 H10 **Konda** ≈ C Russian Federation
154 L13 **Kondagaon** Chhattīsgarh, C India 19°38′N 81°41′E
14 K10 **Kondiaronk, Lac** ◎ Québec, SE Canada
180 J13 **Kondinin** Western Australia 32°31′S 118°15′E
81 H21 **Kondoa** Dodoma, C Tanzania 04°54′S 35°46′E
127 P6 **Kondol'** Penzenskaya Oblast', W Russian Federation 52°49′N 45°03′E
114 N10 **Kondolovo** Burgas, E Bulgaria 42°07′N 27°43′E
171 Z16 **Kondomirat** Papua, E Indonesia 08°57′S 140°55′E
124 J10 **Kondopoga** Respublika Kareliya, NW Russian Federation 62°13′N 34°17′E
149 Q2 **Kondoz** *var.* Kondūz, Qondūz, *Pash.* Kunduz, Kundūz. Kunduz, NE Afghanistan 36°49′N 68°50′E
149 Q2 **Kondoz** *Pash.* Kunduz. ◈ *province* NE Afghanistan
155 J17 **Kondukūr** *var.* Kandukur. Andhra Pradesh, E India 15°17′N 79°49′E
Kondūz *see* Kondoz
187 P16 **Koné** Province Nord, W New Caledonia 21°04′S 164°51′E
Konechnaya *see* Kurchatov
146 E13 **Könekesir** Balkan Welaýaty, W Turkmenistan 38°16′N 56°51′E
146 G8 **Köneürgenç** *var.* Köneürgench, *Rus.* Këneurgench; *prev.* Kunya-Urgench. Daşoguz Welaýaty, N Turkmenistan 42°21′N 59°09′E
77 N15 **Kong** N Ivory Coast 09°10′N 04°33′W
39 S5 **Kongakut River** ≈ Alaska, USA
197 O14 **Kong Christian IX Land** *Eng.* King Christian IX Land. *physical region* SE Greenland
197 P13 **Kong Christian X Land** *Eng.* King Christian X Land. *physical region* E Greenland
197 N13 **Kong Frederik IX Land** *physical region* SW Greenland
197 Q12 **Kong Frederik VIII Land** *Eng.* King Frederik VIII Land. *physical region* NE Greenland
197 N15 **Kong Frederik VI Kyst** *Eng.* King Frederik VI Coast. *physical region* SE Greenland
167 P13 **Kông, Kaôh** *prev.* Kas Kong. *island* SW Cambodia
92 P2 **Kong Karls Land** *Eng.* King Charles Islands. *island group* SE Svalbard
81 G14 **Kong Kong** ≈ SE Sudan
Kongo *see* Congo (river)
83 G16 **Kongola** Caprivi, NE Namibia 17°47′S 23°24′E
79 N21 **Kongolo** Katanga, E Dem. Rep. Congo 05°20′S 26°58′E
81 F14 **Kongor** Jonglei, SE Sudan 07°09′N 31°44′E
197 Q14 **Kong Oscar Fjord** *fjord* E Greenland
77 P12 **Kongoussi** N Burkina 13°19′N 01°31′W
95 G15 **Kongsberg** Buskerud, S Norway 59°39′N 09°38′E
92 Q2 **Kongsøya** *island* Kong Karls Land, E Svalbard
95 I14 **Kongsvinger** Hedmark, S Norway 60°10′N 12°00′E
Kongtong *see* Pingliang
167 T11 **Kông, Tônle** *var.* Xê Kong. ≈ Cambodia/Laos
158 E8 **Kongur Shan** ▲ NW China 38°39′N 75°21′E
81 I22 **Kongwa** Dodoma, C Tanzania 06°13′S 36°28′E
Kong, Xê *see* Kông, Tônle
Konia *see* Konya
147 R11 **Konibodom** *Rus.* Kanibadam. N Tajikistan 40°16′N 70°20′E
111 K15 **Koniecpol nad Pilicą** Śląskie, S Poland 50°47′N 19°45′E
Konieh *see* Konya
Königgrätz *see* Hradec Králové
Königinhof an der Elbe *see* Dvůr Králové nad Labem
101 K23 **Königsbrunn** Bayern, S Germany 48°16′N 10°52′E
101 O24 **Königssee** ◎ SE Germany
Königshütte *see* Chorzów
109 S8 **Königstuhl** ▲ S Austria 46°57′N 13°47′E
109 U3 **Königswiesen** Oberösterreich, N Austria 48°25′N 14°48′E
101 E17 **Königswinter** Nordrhein-Westfalen, W Germany 50°40′N 07°12′E
146 M11 **Konimex** *Rus.* Kenimekh. Navoiy Viloyati, N Uzbekistan 40°14′N 65°10′E
110 I12 **Konin** *Ger.* Kuhnau. Weilkopolskie, C Poland 52°13′N 18°17′E
Koninkrijk der Nederlanden *see* Netherlands
113 L24 **Konispol** *var.* Konispoli. Vlorë, S Albania 39°40′N 20°10′E
Konispoli *see* Konispol
115 C15 **Kónitsa** Ípeiros, W Greece 40°04′N 20°48′E
Konitz *see* Chojnice
108 D8 **Köniz** Bern, W Switzerland 46°56′N 07°25′E
113 H14 **Konjic** ◈ Federacija Bosna I Hercegovina, S Bosnia and Herzegovina
92 J10 **Könkämäälven** ≈ Finland/Sweden
155 D14 **Konkan** *plain* W India
83 D22 **Konkiep** ≈ S Namibia
76 I14 **Konkouré** ≈ W Guinea
77 O11 **Konna** Mopti, S Mali 14°58′N 03°49′W
186 H6 **Konogaiang, Mount** ▲ New Ireland, NE Papua New Guinea 04°05′S 152°43′E
186 H5 **Konogogo** New Ireland, NE Papua New Guinea 03°25′S 152°09′E
108 E9 **Konolfingen** Bern, W Switzerland 46°53′N 07°36′E
77 P16 **Konongo** C Ghana 06°39′N 01°06′W
186 H5 **Konos** New Ireland, NE Papua New Guinea 03°09′S 151°47′E
124 M12 **Konosha** Arkhangel'skaya Oblast', NW Russian Federation 60°58′N 40°09′E
117 R3 **Konotop** Sums'ka Oblast', NE Ukraine 51°15′N 33°14′E
158 L7 **Konqi He** ≈ NW China
111 L14 **Końskie** Siętokrzyskie, C Poland 51°12′N 20°23′E
Konstantinovka *see* Kostyantynivka
126 M11 **Konstantinovsk** Rostovskaya Oblast', SW Russian Federation 47°37′N 41°07′E
101 H24 **Konstanz** *var.* Constanz, *Eng.* Constance, *hist.* Kostnitz; *anc.* Constantia. Baden-Württemberg, S Germany 47°40′N 09°10′E
Konstanza *see* Constanţa
77 T14 **Kontagora** Niger, W Nigeria 10°25′N 05°29′E
78 E13 **Kontcha** Nord, N Cameroon 08°00′N 12°13′E
99 G17 **Kontich** Antwerpen, N Belgium 51°08′N 04°27′E
93 O16 **Kontiolahti** Itä-Suomi, SE Finland 62°46′N 29°51′E
93 M15 **Kontiomäki** Oulu, C Finland 64°20′N 28°09′E
167 U11 **Kon Tum** *var.* Kontum. Kon Tum, C Vietnam 14°23′N 108°00′E
Kontum *see* Kon Tum
Konur *see* Sulakyurt
136 H15 **Konya** *var.* Konieh, *prev.* Konia; *anc.* Iconium. Konya, C Turkey 37°51′N 32°30′E
136 H15 **Konya** *var.* Konia, Konieh. ◈ *province* C Turkey
151 E15 **Konya Reservoir** *prev.* Shivāji Sāgar. ⊠ W India
145 T13 **Konyrat** *var.* Kounradskiy, *Kaz.* Qongyrat. Karaganda, SE Kazakhstan 46°57′N 75°01′E
145 W15 **Konyrolen** Almaty, SE Kazakhstan 44°16′N 79°18′E
81 I19 **Konza** Eastern, S Kenya 01°44′S 37°07′E
98 I9 **Koog aan den Zaan** Noord-Holland, C Netherlands 52°28′N 04°49′E
182 E7 **Koonibba** South Australia 31°55′S 133°23′E
31 O11 **Koontz Lake** Indiana, N USA 41°25′N 86°24′W
171 U12 **Koor** Papua, E Indonesia 0°21′S 132°28′E
183 R9 **Koorawatha** New South Wales, SE Australia 34°03′S 148°33′E
118 J5 **Koosa** Tartumaa, E Estonia 58°31′N 27°06′E
33 N7 **Kootenai** *var.* Kootenay. ≈ Canada/USA *see also* Kootenay
Kootenai *see* Kootenay
11 P17 **Kootenay** *var.* Kootenai. ≈ Canada/USA *see also* Kootenai
Kootenay *see* Kootenai
83 F24 **Kootjieskolk** Northern Cape, W South Africa 31°16′S 20°21′E
Kopal *see* Koppal
113 M15 **Kopaonik** ▲▲ S Serbia
Kopar *see* Koper
92 K1 **Kópasker** Nordhurland Eystra, N Iceland 66°16′N 16°23′W
92 H4 **Kópavogur** Reykjanes, W Iceland 64°06′N 21°47′W
145 U13 **Kopbirlik** *prev.* Kirov, Kirova. Almaty, SE Kazakhstan 46°24′N 77°16′E
109 S13 **Koper** *It.* Capodistria; *prev.* Kopar. SW Slovenia 45°32′N 13°43′E
95 C16 **Kopervik** Rogaland, S Norway 59°17′N 05°20′E
Köpetdag Gershi/Kopetdag, Khrebet *see* Koppeh Dāgh
Kophinou *see* Kofínou
182 G8 **Kopi** South Australia 33°24′S 135°40′E
153 W12 **Kopili** ≈ NE India
95 M15 **Köping** Västmanland, C Sweden 59°31′N 16°00′E
113 K17 **Koplik** *var.* Kopliku. Shkodër, NW Albania 42°12′N 19°26′E
Kopliku *see* Koplik
Kopopo *see* Kokopo
155 G18 **Koppal** *var.* Kopal. Karnātaka, SW India 14°20′N 76°09′E
94 I11 **Koppang** Hedmark, S Norway 61°34′N 11°04′E
Kopparberg *see* Dalarna
143 S3 **Koppeh Dāgh** *Rus.* Khrebet Kopetdag, *Turkm.* Köpetdag Gershi. ▲▲ Iran/Turkmenistan
Koppename *see* Coppename Rivier
95 J15 **Koppom** Värmland, C Sweden 59°42′N 12°07′E
Kopreinitz *see* Koprivnica
114 K9 **Koprinka, Yazovir** *prev.* Yazovir Georgi Dimitrov. ⊠ C Bulgaria
112 F7 **Koprivnica** *Ger.* Kopreinitz, *Hung.* Kaproncza. Koprivnica-Križevci, N Croatia 46°10′N 16°49′E
112 F8 **Koprivnica-Križevci** *off.* Koprivničko-Križevačka Županija. ◈ *province* N Croatia
111 I17 **Kopřivnice** *Ger.* Nesselsdorf. Moravskoslezský Kraj, E Czech Republic 49°36′N 18°09′E
Koprivničko-Križevačka Županija *see* Koprivnica-Križevci
Köprülü *see* Veles
Koptsevichi *see* Kaptsevichy
Kopyl' *see* Kapyl'
119 O14 **Kopys'** Vitsyebskaya Voblasts', NE Belarus 54°19′N 30°18′E
113 M18 **Korab** ▲ Albania/FYR Macedonia 41°48′N 20°33′E
Korabavur Pastligi *see* Karabaur', Uval
81 M14 **K'orahē** Sumalē, E Ethiopia 06°36′N 44°21′E
115 L16 **Kórakas, Akrotírio** *cape* Lésvos, E Greece
112 D9 **Korana** ≈ C Croatia
155 L14 **Korāput** Orissa, E India 18°48′N 82°41′E
Korat *see* Nakhon Ratchasima
167 Q9 **Korat Plateau** *plateau* E Thailand
139 T1 **Kōrāwa, Sar-i** ▲ NE Iraq 37°08′N 44°39′E
154 L11 **Korba** Chhattīsgarh, C India 22°25′N 82°43′E
101 H15 **Korbach** Hessen, C Germany 51°16′N 08°52′E
Korça *see* Korçë
113 M21 **Korçë** *var.* Korça, *Gk.* Korytsa, *It.* Corriza; *prev.* Koritsa. Korçë, SE Albania 40°38′N 20°47′E
113 M21 **Korçë** ◈ *district* SE Albania
113 G15 **Korčula** *It.* Curzola. Dubrovnik-Neretva, S Croatia 42°57′N 17°08′E
113 F15 **Korčula** *It.* Curzola; *anc.* Corcyra Nigra. *island* S Croatia
113 F15 **Korčulanski Kanal** *channel* S Croatia
145 T6 **Korday** *prev.* Georgiyevka. Zhambyl, SE Kazakhstan 43°03′N 74°43′E
142 J5 **Kordestān** *off.* Ostān-e Kordestān, *var.* Kurdestan. ◈ *province* W Iran
Kordestān, Ostān-e *see* Kordestān
143 P4 **Kord Kūy** *var.* Kurd Kui. Golestān, N Iran 36°49′N 54°05′E
163 V13 **Korea Bay** *bay* China/North Korea
Korea, Democratic People's Republic of *see* North Korea
171 T15 **Koreare** Pulau Yamdena, E Indonesia 07°33′S 131°13′E
Korea, Republic of *see* South Korea
163 Z17 **Korea Strait** *Jap.* Chōsen-kaikyō, *Kor.* Taehan-haehyŏp. *channel* Japan/South Korea
Korelichi/Korelicze *see* Karelichy
80 J11 **Korem** Tigrai, N Ethiopia 12°32′N 39°29′E
77 U11 **Korén Adoua** ≈ C Niger
126 J7 **Korenevo** Kurskaya Oblast', W Russian Federation 51°21′N 34°53′E
126 L13 **Korenovsk** Krasnodarskiy Kray, SW Russian Federation 45°28′N 39°25′E
116 L4 **Korets'** *Pol.* Korzec, *Rus.* Korets. Rivnens'ka Oblast', NW Ukraine 50°38′N 27°12′E
Korets *see* Korets'
194 L7 **Korff Ice Rise** *ice cap* Antarctica
145 Q10 **Korgalzhyn** *var.* Kurgal'dzhino, Kurgal'dzhinsky, *Kaz.* Qorghalzhyn. Akmola, C Kazakhstan 50°33′N 69°58′E
92 G13 **Korgen** Troms, N Norway 66°04′N 13°51′E
147 R9 **Korgon-Dēbē** Dzhalal-Abadskaya Oblast', W Kyrgyzstan 41°51′N 70°52′E
76 M14 **Korhogo** N Ivory Coast 09°29′N 05°39′W
115 F19 **Korinthiakós Kólpos** *Eng.* Gulf of Corinth; *anc.* Corinthiacus Sinus. *gulf* C Greece
115 F19 **Kórinthos** *anc.* Corinthus *Eng.* Corinth. Pelopónnisos, S Greece 37°56′N 22°55′E
113 M18 **Koritnik** ▲ S Serbia 42°06′N 20°34′E
Koritsa *see* Korçë
165 P11 **Kōriyama** Fukushima, Honshū, C Japan 37°25′N 140°20′E
136 E16 **Korkuteli** Antalya, SW Turkey 37°07′N 30°11′E
158 K6 **Korla** *Chin.* Ku-erh-lo. Xinjiang Uygur Zizhiqu, NW China 41°48′N 86°10′E
122 J10 **Korliki** Khanty-Mansiyskiy Avtonomnyy Okrug-Yugra, C Russian Federation 61°28′N 82°12′E
Körlin an der Persante *see* Karlino
Korma *see* Karma
14 D8 **Kormak** Ontario, S Canada 47°38′N 83°00′W
Kormakíti, Akrotíri/Kormakiti, Cape/Kormakítis *see* Koruçam Burnu
111 G23 **Körmend** Vas, W Hungary 47°02′N 16°35′E
139 T5 **Kōrmōr** Şalāḩ ad Dīn, E Iraq 35°06′N 44°47′E
112 C13 **Kornat** *It.* Incoronata. *island* W Croatia
Korneshty *see* Corneşti
109 X3 **Korneuburg** Niederösterreich, NE Austria 48°22′N 16°20′E
145 P7 **Korneyevka** Severnyy Kazakhstan, N Kazakhstan 54°01′N 68°30′E
95 I17 **Kornsjø** Østfold, S Norway 58°55′N 11°40′E
77 O11 **Koro** Mopti, S Mali 14°05′N 03°06′W
1873 Y14 **Koro** *island* C Fiji
186 B7 **Koroba** Southern Highlands, W Papua New Guinea 05°46′S 142°48′E
126 K8 **Korocha** Belgorodskaya Oblast', W Russian Federation 50°49′N 37°08′E
136 H12 **Köroğlu Dağları** ▲▲ C Turkey
183 V6 **Korogoro Point** *headland* New South Wales, SE Australia 31°03′S 153°04′E
81 J21 **Korogwe** Tanga, E Tanzania 05°10′S 38°30′E
182 L13 **Koroit** Victoria, SE Australia 38°17′S 142°22′E
187 X15 **Korolevu** Viti Levu, W Fiji 18°12′S 177°44′E
190 I17 **Koromiri** *island* S Cook Islands
171 Q8 **Koronadal** Mindanao, S Philippines 06°23′N 124°54′E
114 G13 **Korónia, Límni** *var.* Límni Korónia. ◎ N Greece
115 E22 **Koróni** Pelopónnisos, S Greece 36°47′N 21°57′E
Korónia, Límni *see* Korónia, Límni
110 I9 **Koronowo** *Ger.* Krone an der Brahe. Kujawski-pomorskie, C Poland 53°18′N 17°56′E
117 R2 **Korop** Chernihivs'ka Oblast', N Ukraine 51°35′N 32°57′E
115 H19 **Koropí** Attikí, C Greece 37°54′N 23°52′E
188 C8 **Koror** (Palau) Oreor, N Palau 07°21′N 134°28′E
Koror *see* Oreor
111 L23 **Kőrös** ≈ E Hungary
Kőrös *see* Križevci
Kőrösbánya *see* Baia de Criş
187 Y14 **Koro Sea** *sea* C Fiji
Koroška *see* Kärnten
117 N3 **Korosten'** Zhytomyrs'ka Oblast', NW Ukraine 50°56′N 28°39′E
Korostyshev *see* Korostyshiv
117 N4 **Korostyshiv** *Rus.* Korostyshev. Zhytomyrs'ka Oblast', N Ukraine 50°18′N 29°05′E
125 V3 **Korotaikha** ≈ NW Russian Federation
122 J9 **Korotchayevo** Yamalo-Nenetskiy Avtonomnyy Okrug, N Russian Federation 66°00′N 78°11′E
78 I8 **Koro Toro** Borkou-Ennedi-Tibesti, N Chad 16°01′N 18°27′E
39 N16 **Korovin Island** *island* Shumagin Islands, Alaska, USA
187 X14 **Korovou** Viti Levu, W Fiji 17°48′S 178°32′E
93 M17 **Korpilahti** Länsi-Suomi, C Finland 62°02′N 25°34′E
92 K12 **Korpilombolo** *Lapp.* Dállogilli. Norrbotten, N Sweden 66°51′N 23°00′E
123 T13 **Korsakov** Ostrov Sakhalin, Sakhalinskaya Oblast', SE Russian Federation 46°41′N 142°45′E
93 J16 **Korsholm** *Fin.* Mustasaari. Länsi-Suomi, W Finland 63°05′N 21°43′E
95 I23 **Korsør** Vestsjælland, E Denmark 55°19′N 11°09′E
Korsovka *see* Kārsava
117 P6 **Korsun'-Shevchenkivs'kyy** *Rus.* Korsun'-Shevchenkovskiy. Cherkas'ka Oblast', C Ukraine 49°26′N 31°15′E
Korsun'-Shevchenkovskiy *see* Korsun'-Shevchenkivs'kyy
99 C17 **Kortemark** West-Vlaanderen, W Belgium 51°03′N 03°03′E
99 H18 **Kortenberg** Vlaams Brabant, C Belgium 50°53′N 04°33′E
99 K18 **Kortessem** Limburg, NE Belgium 50°52′N 05°22′E
99 E14 **Kortgene** Zeeland, SW Netherlands 51°34′N 03°48′E
80 F8 **Korti** Northern, N Sudan 18°06′N 31°33′E
99 C18 **Kortrijk** *Fr.* Courtrai. West-Vlaanderen, W Belgium 50°50′N 03°17′E
121 O2 **Koruçam Burnu** *var.* Cape Kormakiti, Kormakítis, *Gk.* Akrotíri Kormakíti. *headland* N Cyprus 35°24′N 32°55′E
183 O13 **Korumburra** Victoria, SE Australia 38°27′S 145°48′E
Koryak Range *see* Koryakskoye Nagor'ye
123 V8 **Koryakskiy Avtonomnyy Okrug** ◈ *autonomous district* E Russian Federation
Koryakskiy Khrebet *see* Koryakskoye Nagor'ye
123 V7 **Koryakskoye Nagor'ye** *var.* Koryakskiy Khrebet, *Eng.* Koryak Range. ▲▲ NE Russian Federation
125 P11 **Koryazhma** Arkhangel'skaya Oblast', NW Russian Federation 61°16′N 47°07′E
Kōryō *see* Kangnŭng
Korytsa *see* Korçë
117 Q2 **Koryukivka** Chernihivs'ka Oblast', N Ukraine 51°45′N 32°16′E
Korzec *see* Korets'
115 N21 **Kos** Kos, Dodekánisa, Greece, Aegean Sea 36°53′N 27°19′E
115 M21 **Kos** *It.* Coo; *anc.* Cos. *island* Dodekánisa, Greece, Aegean Sea
125 T12 **Kosa** Komi-Permyatskiy Avtonomnyy Okrug, NW Russian Federation 59°55′N 54°54′E
125 T13 **Kosa** ≈ NW Russian Federation
164 B12 **Kō-saki** *headland* Nagasaki, Tsushima, SW Japan 34°06′N 129°13′E
163 X13 **Kosan** SE North Korea 38°50′N 127°26′E
119 H18 **Kosava** *Rus.* Kosovo. Brestskaya Voblasts', SW Belarus 52°45′N 25°16′E
Kosch *see* Kose
144 G12 **Koschagyl** *Kaz.* Qosshaghyl. Atyrau, W Kazakhstan 46°52′N 53°46′E
110 G12 **Kościan** *Ger.* Kosten. Wielkopolskie, C Poland 52°05′N 16°38′E
110 I7 **Kościerzyna** Pomorskie, NW Poland 54°07′N 17°55′E
22 L4 **Kosciusko** Mississippi, S USA 33°03′N 89°35′W
Kosciusko, Mount *see* Kosciuszko, Mount
183 R11 **Kosciuszko, Mount** *prev.* Mount Kosciusko. ▲ New South Wales, SE Australia 36°28′S 148°15′E
118 H4 **Kose** *Ger.* Kosch. Harjumaa, NW Estonia 59°11′N 25°10′E
25 U9 **Kosse** Texas, SW USA 31°16′N 96°38′W
114 G6 **Koshava** Vidin, NW Bulgaria 44°03′N 23°00′E
147 U9 **Kosh-Dēbē** *var.* Koshtebë. Narynskaya Oblast', C Kyrgyzstan 41°03′N 74°08′E
K'o-shih *see* Kashi
164 B12 **Koshikijima-rettō** *var.* Kosikizima Rettô. *island group* SW Japan
145 W13 **Koshkarkol', Ozero** ◎ SE Kazakhstan
30 L9 **Koshkonong, Lake** ◎ Wisconsin, N USA
Koshoba *see* Goşabo
Koshoba *see* Goşoba
164 M12 **Kōshoku** *var.* Kôsyoku. Nagano, Honshū, S Japan 36°33′N 138°09′E
Koshtebë *see* Kosh-Dēbē
Kōshū *see* Enzan
Kōshū *see* Kwangju
111 N19 **Košice** *Ger.* Kaschau, *Hung.* Kassa. Košický Kraj, E Slovakia 48°44′N 21°15′E
111 M20 **Košický Kraj** ◈ *region* E Slovakia
Kosikizima Rettô *see* Koshikijima-rettō
153 R12 **Kosi Reservoir** ⊠ E Nepal
116 J8 **Kosiv** Ivano-Frankivs'ka Oblast', W Ukraine 48°19′N 25°04′E
145 O11 **Koskol'** *Kaz.* Qosqōl. Karaganda, C Kazakhstan 49°32′N 67°08′E
125 Q9 **Koslan** Respublika Komi, NW Russian Federation 63°27′N 48°52′E
Köslin *see* Koszalin
146 M12 **Koson** *Rus.* Kasan. Qashqadaryo Viloyati, S Uzbekistan 39°04′N 65°35′E
163 Y13 **Kosŏng** SE North Korea 38°41′N 128°14′E
147 S9 **Kosonsoy** *Rus.* Kasansay. Namangan Viloyati, E Uzbekistan 41°15′N 71°28′E
113 M16 **Kosovo** *prev.* Autonomous Province of Kosovo and Metohija. ◆ *republic* SE Europe
Kosovo *see* Kosava
Kosovo and Metohija, Autonomous Province of *see* Kosovo
Kosovo Polje *see* Fushë Kosovë
Kosovska Kamenica *see* Kamenicë
Kosovska Mitrovica *see* Mitrovicë
189 X17 **Kosrae** ◈ *state* E Micronesia
189 Y14 **Kosrae** *prev.* Kusaie. *island* Caroline Islands, E Micronesia
109 P6 **Kössen** Tirol, W Austria 47°40′N 12°24′E
76 M16 **Kossou, Lac de** ◎ C Ivory Coast
Kossukavak *see* Krumovgrad
Kostajnica *see* Hrvatska Kostajnica
Kostamus *see* Kostomuksha
144 M7 **Kostanay** *var.* Kustanay, *Kaz.* Qostanay. Kostanay, N Kazakhstan 53°16′N 63°34′E
144 L8 **Kostanay** *var.* Kostanayskaya Oblast', *Kaz.* Qostanay Oblysy. ◈ *province* N Kazakhstan
Kostanayskaya Oblast' *see* Kostanay
Kosten *see* Kościan
114 H10 **Kostenets** *prev.* Georgi Dimitrov. Sofiya, W Bulgaria 42°15′N 23°48′E
80 F10 **Kosti** White Nile, C Sudan 13°11′N 32°38′E
Kostnitz *see* Konstanz
124 H7 **Kostomuksha** *Fin.* Kostamus. Respublika Kareliya, NW Russian Federation 64°33′N 30°28′E
116 K3 **Kostopil'** *Rus.* Kostopol'. Rivnens'ka Oblast', NW Ukraine 50°20′N 26°29′E
Kostopol' *see* Kostopil'
124 M15 **Kostroma** Kostromskaya Oblast', NW Russian Federation 57°46′N 41°E
125 N14 **Kostroma** ≈ NW Russian Federation
125 N14 **Kostromskaya Oblast'** ◈ *province* NW Russian Federation
110 D11 **Kostrzyn** *Ger.* Cüstrin, Küstrin. Lubuskie, W Poland 52°35′N 14°40′E
110 H11 **Kostrzyn** Wielkopolskie, C Poland 52°23′N 17°13′E
117 X7 **Kostyantynivka** *Rus.* Konstantinovka. Donets'ka Oblast', SE Ukraine
Kostyukovichi *see* Kastsyukovichy
Kostyukovka *see* Kastsyukowka
Kôsyoku *see* Kōshoku
125 U6 **Kos'yu** Respublika Komi, NW Russian Federation 65°39′N 59°01′E
125 U6 **Kos'yu** ≈ NW Russian Federation
110 F7 **Koszalin** *Ger.* Köslin. Zachodnio-pomorskie, NW Poland 54°12′N 16°10′E
111 F22 **Kőszeg** *Ger.* Güns. Vas, W Hungary 47°23′N 16°33′E
152 H13 **Kota** *prev.* Kotah. Rājasthān, N India 25°14′N 75°52′E
Kota Baharu *see* Kota Bharu
Kota Bahru *see* Kota Bharu
169 U13 **Kotabaru** Pulau Laut, C Indonesia 03°15′S 116°15′E
168 K12 **Kota Baru** Sumatera, W Indonesia 01°07′S 101°43′E
Kotabaru *see* Jayapura
168 K6 **Kota Bharu** *var.* Kota Baharu, Kota Bahru. Kelantan, Peninsular Malaysia 06°07′N 102°15′E
Kotaboemi *see* Kotabumi
168 M14 **Kotabumi** *prev.* Kotaboemi. Sumatera, W Indonesia 04°50′S 104°54′E
149 S10 **Kot Addu** Punjab, E Pakistan 30°28′N 70°58′E
Kotah *see* Kota
169 U7 **Kota Kinabalu** *prev.* Jesselton. Sabah, East Malaysia 05°59′N 116°04′E
169 U7 **Kota Kinabalu** ✈ Sabah, East Malaysia 05°59′N 116°04′E
92 M12 **Kotala** Lappi, N Finland 67°01′N 29°00′E
Kotamobagoe *see* Kotamobagu
171 Q11 **Kotamobagu** *prev.* Kotamobagoe. Sulawesi, C Indonesia 0°46′N 124°21′E
155 L14 **Kotapad** *var.* Kotapārh. Orissa, E India 19°10′N 82°23′E
Kotapārh *see* Kotapad
166 N17 **Ko Ta Ru Tao** *island* SW Thailand
169 R13 **Kotawaringin, Teluk** *bay* Borneo, C Indonesia
149 Q13 **Kot Dīji** Sind, SE Pakistan 27°16′N 68°44′E
152 K9 **Kotdwāra** Uttarakhand, N India 29°44′N 78°33′E
125 Q14 **Kotel'nich** Kirovskaya Oblast', NW Russian Federation 58°19′N 48°12′E
127 N12 **Kotel'nikovo** Volgogradskaya Oblast', SW Russian Federation 47°37′N 43°07′E
123 Q6 **Kotel'nyy, Ostrov** *island* Novosibirskiye Ostrova, N Russian Federation
117 T5 **Kotel'va** Poltavs'ka Oblast', C Ukraine 50°04′N 34°46′E
101 M14 **Köthen** *var.* Cöthen. Sachsen-Anhalt, C Germany 51°46′N 11°59′E
Kôti *see* Kōchi
81 G17 **Kotido** NE Uganda 03°03′N 34°07′E
93 N19 **Kotka** Etelä-Suomi, S Finland 60°28′N 26°55′E
125 P11 **Kotlas** Arkhangel'skaya Oblast', NW Russian Federation 61°14′N 46°43′E
38 M10 **Kotlik** Alaska, USA 63°01′N 163°33′W
77 Q17 **Kotoka** ✈ (Accra) S Ghana 05°41′N 00°10′W
Kotonu *see* Cotonou
113 J17 **Kotor** *It.* Cattaro. SW Montenegro 42°25′N 18°47′E
Kotor *see* Kotoriba
112 F7 **Kotoriba** *Hung.* Kotor. Medimurje, N Croatia 46°20′N 16°47′E
113 I17 **Kotorska, Boka** *It.* Bocche di Cattaro. *bay* SW Montenegro
112 H11 **Kotorsko** ◈ Republika Srpska, N Bosnia and Herzegovina
112 G11 **Kotor Varoš** ◈ Republika Srpska, N Bosnia and Herzegovina
Koto Sho/Kotosho *see* Lan Yu
126 M7 **Kotovsk** Tambovskaya Oblast', W Russian Federation 52°39′N 41°31′E
117 O9 **Kotovs'k** *Rus.* Kotovsk. Odes'ka Oblast', SW Ukraine 47°42′N 29°30′E
Kotovsk *see* Hînceşti
119 G16 **Kotra** ≈ W Belarus
149 P16 **Kotri** Sind, SE Pakistan 25°22′N 68°18′E
109 Q9 **Kötschach** Kärnten, S Austria 46°41′N 12°57′E
155 K15 **Kottagūdem** Andhra Pradesh, E India 17°36′N 80°40′E
155 F21 **Kottappadi** Kerala, SW India 11°38′N 76°03′E
155 G23 **Kottayam** Kerala, SW India 09°34′N 76°31′E
Kottbus *see* Cottbus
79 K15 **Kotto** ≈ Central African Republic/Dem. Rep. Congo
193 X15 **Kotu Group** *island group* W Tonga
Koturdepe *see* Goturdepe
122 M9 **Kotuy** ≈ N Russian Federation
83 M16 **Kotwa** Mashonaland East, NE Zimbabwe 16°58′S 32°46′E
39 N7 **Kotzebue** Alaska, USA 66°54′N 162°36′W
38 M7 **Kotzebue Sound** *inlet* Alaska, USA
Kotzenan *see* Chocianów
Kotzman *see* Kitsman'
77 R14 **Kouandé** NW Benin 10°20′N 01°42′E
79 J15 **Kouango** Ouaka, S Central African Republic 05°00′N 20°01′E
77 O13 **Koudougou** C Burkina 12°15′N 02°23′W
98 K7 **Koudum** Friesland, N Netherlands 52°55′N 05°26′E
115 L25 **Koufonísi** *island* SE Greece
115 K21 **Koufonísi** *island* Kykládes, Greece, Aegean Sea
38 M8 **Kougarok Mountain** ▲ Alaska, USA 65°41′N 165°29′W
79 E21 **Kouilou** ◈ *province* SW Congo
79 E20 **Kouilou** ≈ S Congo
121 O3 **Koúklia** SW Cyprus 34°42′N 32°35′E
79 E19 **Koulamoutou** Ogooué-Lolo, C Gabon 01°07′S 12°27′E
76 L12 **Koulikoro** Koulikoro, SW Mali 12°55′N 07°31′W
76 L11 **Koulikoro** ◈ *region* SW Mali
187 P16 **Koumac** Province Nord, W New Caledonia 20°34′S 164°18′E
165 N12 **Koumi** Nagano, Honshū, S Japan 36°06′N 138°27′E
78 I13 **Koumra** Moyen-Chari, S Chad 08°56′N 17°32′E
Kounadougou *see* Koundougou
76 M15 **Kounahiri** C Ivory Coast 07°47′N 05°51′W
76 I12 **Koundâra** Moyenne-Guinée, NW Guinea 12°28′N 13°15′W
77 N13 **Koundougou** *var.* Kounadougou. C Burkina 11°43′N 04°40′W
76 H11 **Koungheul** C Senegal 14°00′N 14°48′W
Kounradskiy *see* Konyrat
25 X10 **Kountze** Texas, SW USA 30°22′N 94°20′W
77 Q13 **Koupéla** C Burkina 12°07′N 00°21′W
77 N13 **Kouri** Sikasso, SW Mali 12°09′N 04°46′W
55 Y9 **Kourou** N French Guiana 05°08′N 52°37′W
114 J12 **Kouroú** ≈ NE Greece
76 K14 **Kouroussa** C Guinea 10°40′N 09°50′W
Kousseir *see* Al Quşayr
78 G11 **Kousséri** *prev.* Fort-Foureau. Extrême-Nord, NE Cameroon 12°05′N 14°56′E
Kouteifé *see* Al Quţayfah
76 M13 **Koutiala** Sikasso, S Mali 12°20′N 05°23′W
76 M14 **Kouto** NW Ivory Coast 09°51′N 06°25′W
93 M19 **Kouvola** Etelä-Suomi, S Finland 60°50′N 26°48′E
79 G18 **Kouyou** ≈ C Congo
112 M10 **Kovačica** *Hung.* Antafalva; *prev.* Kovacsicza. Vojvodina, N Serbia 45°08′N 20°36′E
Kovacsicza *see* Kovačica
Kővárhosszúfalu *see* Satulung
Kovászna *see* Covasna
124 I4 **Kovdor** Murmanskaya Oblast', NW Russian Federation 67°32′N 30°27′E
116 J3 **Kovel'** *Pol.* Kowel. Volyns'ka Oblast', NW Ukraine 51°14′N 24°43′E
112 M11 **Kovin** *Hung.* Kevevára; *prev.* Temes-Kubin. Vojvodina, NE Serbia 44°45′N 20°59′E
Kovno *see* Kaunas
127 N3 **Kovrov** Vladimirskaya Oblast', W Russian Federation 56°24′N 41°21′E
127 O5 **Kovylkino** Respublika Mordoviya, W Russian Federation 54°03′N 43°52′E
110 J11 **Kowal** Kujawsko-pomorskie, C Poland 52°31′N 19°09′E
110 J9 **Kowalewo Pomorskie** *Ger.* Schönsee. Kujawsko-pomorskie, N Poland 53°07′N 18°48′E
Kowasna *see* Covasna
119 M16 **Kowbcha** *Rus.* Kolbcha. Mahilyowskaya Voblasts', E Belarus 53°39′N 29°14′E
Koweit *see* Kuwait
Kowel *see* Kovel'
185 F17 **Kowhitirangi** West Coast, South Island, New Zealand 42°54′S 171°01′E
161 O15 **Kowloon** Hong Kong, S China
Kowno *see* Kaunas
159 N7 **Kox Kuduk** *well* NW China
136 D16 **Köyceğiz** Muğla, SW Turkey 36°57′N 28°40′E
125 N6 **Koyda** Arkhangel'skaya Oblast', NW Russian Federation 66°22′N 42°42′E
Koymat *see* Goymat
Koymatdag, Gory *see* Goymatdag, Gory
151 E15 **Koyna Reservoir** ⊠ W India
165 P9 **Koyoshi-gawa** ≈ Honshū, C Japan
Koysanjaq *see* Koi Sanjaq
Koytash *see* Qo'ytosh
146 M14 **Köýtendag** *prev. Rus.* Charshanga, Charshangy, *Turkm.* Charshangngy. Lebap Welaýaty, E Turkmenistan 37°31′N 65°58′E
39 O9 **Koyuk** Alaska, USA 64°55′N 161°09′W
39 N9 **Koyuk River** ≈ Alaska, USA
39 O9 **Koyukuk** Alaska, USA 64°52′N 157°42′W
39 O9 **Koyukuk River** ≈ Alaska, USA
136 J13 **Kozaklı** Nevşehir, C Turkey 39°12′N 34°48′E
136 K16 **Kozan** Adana, S Turkey 37°27′N 35°47′E
115 E14 **Kozáni** Dytikí Makedonía, N Greece 40°19′N 21°48′E
112 F10 **Kozara** ▲▲ NW Bosnia and Herzegovina
Kozarska Dubica *see* Bosanska Dubica
117 P3 **Kozelets'** *Rus.* Kozelets. Chernihivs'ka Oblast', NE Ukraine 50°54′N 31°09′E
Kozelets *see* Kozelets'
117 S6 **Kozel'shchyna** Poltavs'ka Oblast', C Ukraine 49°13′N 33°49′E
126 J5 **Kozel'sk** Kaluzhskaya Oblast', W Russian Federation 54°04′N 35°51′E
151 F21 **Kozhikode** *var.* Calicut. Kerala, SW India 11°17′N 75°49′E *see also* Calicut

◆ Country ● Country Capital ◇ Dependent Territory ○ Dependent Territory Capital ◈ Administrative Regions ✈ International Airport ▲ Mountain ▲▲ Mountain Range ⋀ Volcano ≈ River ◎ Lake ⊠ Reservoir

Kumamoto – Labrador City

164 D15 **Kumamoto** *off.* Kumamoto-ken. ◈ *prefecture* Kyūshū, SW Japan
Kumamoto-ken *see* Kumamoto
164 J15 **Kumano** Mie, Honshū, SW Japan 33°54′N 136°08′E
Kumanova *see* Kumanovo
113 O17 **Kumanovo** *Turk.* Kumanova. N Macedonia 42°08′N 21°43′E
185 G17 **Kumara** West Coast, South Island, New Zealand 42°39′S 171°12′E
180 J8 **Kumarina Roadhouse** Western Australia 24°46′S 119°39′E
153 T15 **Kumarkhali** Khulna, W Bangladesh 23°54′N 89°16′E
77 P16 **Kumasi** *prev.* Coomassie. C Ghana 06°41′N 01°40′W
Kumayri *see* Gyumri
79 D15 **Kumba** Sud-Ouest, W Cameroon 04°39′N 09°26′E
114 N13 **Kumbağ** Tekirdağ, NW Turkey 40°51′N 27°26′E
155 J21 **Kumbakonam** Tamil Nādu, SE India 10°59′N 79°24′E
Kum-Dag *see* Gumdag
165 R16 **Kume-jima** *island* Nansei-shotō, SW Japan
127 V6 **Kumertau** Respublika Bashkortostan, W Russian Federation 52°48′N 55°48′E
Kumillā *see* Comilla
35 R4 **Kumiva Peak** ▲ Nevada, W USA 40°24′N 119°16′W
159 N7 **Kum Kuduk** Xinjiang Uygur Zizhiqu, W China 40°15′N 91°55′E
159 N8 **Kum Kuduk** *well* NW China
Kumkurgan *see* Qumqo'rg'on
95 M16 **Kumla** Örebro, C Sweden 59°08′N 15°09′E
136 F17 **Kumluca** Antalya, SW Turkey 36°23′N 30°17′E
100 N9 **Kummerower See** ◎ NE Germany
77 X14 **Kumo** Gombe, E Nigeria 10°03′N 11°14′E
145 O13 **Kumola** ≈ C Kazakhstan
167 N1 **Kumon Range** ▲▲ N Burma (Myanmar)
83 F22 **Kums** Karas, SE Namibia 28°07′S 19°40′E
124 I7 **Kumskoye Vodokhranilishche** ▣ NW Russian Federation
155 E18 **Kumta** Karnātaka, W India 14°25′N 74°24′E
158 L6 **Kümük** Xinjiang Uygur Zizhiqu, W China
38 H12 **Kumukahi, Cape** *headland* Hawai'i, USA, C Pacific Ocean 19°31′N 154°48′W
127 Q17 **Kumukh** Respublika Dagestan, SW Russian Federation 42°10′N 47°07′E
Kumul *see* Hami
127 N9 **Kumylzhenskaya** Volgogradskaya Oblast', SW Russian Federation 49°54′N 42°35′E
141 W6 **Kumzār** N Oman 26°19′N 56°26′E
43 W15 **Kuna de Madungandí** ◈ *special territory* NE Panama
Kunar *see* Konar
Kunashiri *see* Kunashir, Ostrov
123 U14 **Kunashir, Ostrov** *var.* Kunashiri. *island* Kuril'skiye Ostrova, SE Russian Federation
43 V14 **Kuna Yala** *prev.* San Blas. ◈ *special territory* NE Panama
118 I3 **Kunda** Lääne-Virumaa, NE Estonia 59°31′N 26°33′E
152 M13 **Kunda** Uttar Pradesh, N India 25°43′N 81°31′E
155 E19 **Kundāpura** *var.* Coondapoor. Karnātaka, W India 13°39′N 74°41′E
79 O24 **Kundelungu, Monts** ▲▲ S Dem. Rep. Congo
Kundert *see* Hernád
186 D7 **Kundiawa** Chimbu, W Papua New Guinea 06°00′S 144°57′E
Kundla *see* Sāvarkundla
Kunduk, Ozero *see* Sasyk, Ozero
168 L10 **Kundur, Pulau** *island* W Indonesia
Kunduz *see* Kondoz
Kunduz/Kundūz *see* Kondoz
Kuneitra *see* Al Qunayṭirah
83 B18 **Kunene** ◈ *district* NE Namibia
83 A16 **Kunene** *var.* Cunene. ≈ Angola/Namibia *see also* Cunene
Kunene *see* Cunene
Künes *see* Xinyuan
158 J5 **Künes He** ≈ NW China
95 I19 **Kungälv** Västra Götaland, S Sweden 57°54′N 12°00′E
147 W7 **Kungei Ala-Tau** *Rus.* Khrebet Kyungëy Ala-Too, *Kir.* Küngöy Ala-Too. ▲▲ Kazakhstan/Kyrgyzstan
Küngöy Ala-Too *see* Kungei Ala-Tau
Kungrad *see* Qo'ng'irot
95 J19 **Kungsbacka** Halland, S Sweden 57°30′N 12°05′E
95 I18 **Kungshamn** Västra Götaland, S Sweden 58°21′N 11°15′E
95 M16 **Kungsör** Västmanland, C Sweden 59°25′N 16°05′E
79 J16 **Kungu** Equateur, NW Dem. Rep. Congo 02°47′N 19°12′E
125 V15 **Kungur** Permskaya Oblast', NW Russian Federation 57°24′N 56°56′E
166 L9 **Kungyangon** Yangon, SW Burma (Myanmar) 16°27′N 96°00′E
111 M22 **Kunhegyes** Jász-Nagykun-Szolnok, E Hungary 47°22′N 20°36′E
167 O5 **Kunhing** Shan State, E Burma (Myanmar) 21°17′N 98°26′E
158 D9 **Kunjirap Daban** *var.* Khūnjerāb Pass. *pass* China/Pakistan *see also* Khūnjerāb Pass
Kunjirap Daban *see* Khunjerāb Pass
Kunlun Mountains *see* Kunlun Shan
158 H10 **Kunlun Shan** *Eng.* Kunlun Mountains. ▲▲ NW China
159 P11 **Kunlun Shankou** *pass* C China
160 G13 **Kunming** *var.* K'un-ming; *prev.* Yunnan. *province capital* Yunnan, SW China 25°04′N 102°41′E
K'un-ming *see* Kunming
Kunø *see* Kunoy
95 B18 **Kunoy** *Dan.* Kunø. *island* N Faeroe Islands
163 X16 **Kunsan** *var.* Gunsan, *Jap.* Gunzan. W South Korea 35°58′N 126°42′E
111 L24 **Kunszentmárton** Jász-Nagykun-Szolnok, E Hungary 46°50′N 20°19′E
111 J23 **Kunszentmiklós** Bács-Kiskun, C Hungary 47°00′N 19°07′E
181 N3 **Kununurra** Western Australia 15°50′S 128°44′E
Kunyang *see* Pingyang
Kunya-Urgench *see* Köneürgenç
Kunyé *see* Pins, Île des
169 T11 **Kunyi** Borneo, C Indonesia 03°23′S 119°20′E
101 I20 **Künzelsau** Baden-Württemberg, S Germany 49°22′N 09°43′E
161 S10 **Kuocang Shan** ▲▲ SE China
Kuolajärvi *see* Kuoloyarvi
124 H5 **Kuoloyarvi** *Finn.* Kuolajärvi, *var.* Luolajarvi. Murmanskaya Oblast', NW Russian Federation 66°58′N 29°13′E
93 N16 **Kuopio** Itä-Suomi, C Finland 62°54′N 27°41′E
93 K17 **Kuortane** Länsi-Suomi, W Finland 62°48′N 23°30′E
93 M18 **Kuortti** Itä-Suomi, E Finland 61°25′N 26°25′E
112 E9 **Kupa** ≈ Croatia/Slovenia
Kupa *see* Kolpa
171 P17 **Kupang** *prev.* Koepang. Timor, C Indonesia 10°13′S 123°38′E
39 Q5 **Kuparuk River** ≈ Alaska, USA
Kupchino *see* Cupcina
186 E9 **Kupiano** Central, S Papua New Guinea 10°06′S 148°12′E
180 M4 **Kupingarri** Western Australia 16°46′S 125°57′E
122 I12 **Kupino** Novosibirskaya Oblast', C Russian Federation 54°22′N 77°09′E
118 H11 **Kupiškis** Panevėžys, NE Lithuania 55°51′N 24°58′E
114 L13 **Küplü** Edirne, NW Turkey 41°06′N 26°23′E
39 X13 **Kupreanof Island** *island* Alexander Archipelago, Alaska, USA
39 O16 **Kupreanof Point** *headland* Alaska, USA 55°34′N 159°36′W
112 G13 **Kupres** ◈ Federacija Bosna I Hercegovina, SW Bosnia and Herzegovina
117 W5 **Kup"yans'k** *Rus.* Kupyansk. Kharkivs'ka Oblast', E Ukraine 49°42′N 37°36′E
Kupyansk *see* Kup"yans'k
117 W5 **Kup"yans'k-Vuzlovyy** Kharkivs'ka Oblast', E Ukraine 49°40′N 37°41′E
158 I6 **Kuqa** Xinjiang Uygur Zizhiqu, NW China 41°43′N 82°58′E
Kür *see* Kura
137 W11 **Kura** *Az.* Kür, *Geor.* Mtkvari, *Turk.* Kura Nehri. ≈ SW Asia
55 R8 **Kuracki** NW Guyana 06°52′N 60°13′W
Kura Kurk *see* Irbe Strait
147 Q10 **Kurama Range** *Rus.* Kuraminskiy Khrebet. ▲▲ Tajikistan/Uzbekistan
Kuraminskiy Khrebet *see* Kurama Range
Kura Nehri *see* Kura
119 J14 **Kuranyets** *Rus.* Kurenets. Minskaya Voblasts', C Belarus 54°33′N 26°57′E
164 H13 **Kurashiki** *var.* Kurasiki. Okayama, Honshū, SW Japan 34°35′N 133°44′E
154 L10 **Kurasia** Chhattīsgarh, C India 23°11′N 82°16′E
Kurasiki *see* Kurashiki
164 H12 **Kurayoshi** *var.* Kurayosi. Tottori, Honshū, SW Japan 35°27′N 133°52′E
Kurayosi *see* Kurayoshi
163 X6 **Kurbin He** ≈ NE China
145 U9 **Kurchatov** *prev.* Konechnaya. Pavlodar, NE Kazakhstan 50°45′N 78°32′E
145 X10 **Kurchum** *Kaz.* Kürshim. Vostochnyy Kazakhstan, E Kazakhstan 48°35′N 83°37′E
145 Y10 **Kurchum** ≈ E Kazakhstan
137 X11 **Kürdämir** *Rus.* Kyurdamir. C Azerbaijan 40°21′N 48°08′E
Kurdestan *see* Kordestān
139 S1 **Kurdistan** *cultural region* SW Asia
Kurd Kui *see* Kord Küy
155 F15 **Kurduvādi** Mahārāshtra, W India 18°06′N 75°31′E
114 J11 **Kŭrdzhali** *var.* Kirdzhali. Kŭrdzhali, S Bulgaria 41°39′N 25°23′E
114 K11 **Kŭrdzhali** ◈ *province* S Bulgaria
114 J11 **Kŭrdzhali, Yazovir** ▣ S Bulgaria
164 F13 **Kure** Hiroshima, Honshū, SW Japan 34°15′N 132°33′E
192 K5 **Kure Atoll** *var.* Ocean Island. *atoll* Hawaiian Islands, Hawaii, USA
136 J10 **Küre Dağları** ▲▲ N Turkey
146 C11 **Kürendag** *Rus.* Gora Kyuren. ▲ W Turkmenistan 39°05′N 55°09′E
Kurenets *see* Kuranyets
118 E6 **Kuressaare** *Ger.* Arensburg; *prev.* Kingissepp. Saaremaa, W Estonia 58°17′N 22°29′E
122 K9 **Kureyka** Krasnoyarskiy Kray, N Russian Federation 66°22′N 87°21′E
122 K9 **Kureyka** ≈ N Russian Federation
Kurgal'dzhino/Kurgal'dzhinskiy *see* Korgalzhyn
122 G11 **Kurgan** Kurganskaya Oblast', C Russian Federation 55°30′N 65°20′E
126 L14 **Kurganinsk** Krasnodarskiy Kray, SW Russian Federation 44°55′N 40°45′E
122 G11 **Kurganskaya Oblast'** ◈ *province* C Russian Federation
Kurgan-Tyube *see* Qŭrghonteppa
191 O2 **Kuria** *prev.* Woodle Island. *island* Tungaru, W Kiribati
Kuria Muria Bay *see* Ḩalānīyāt, Khalīj al
Kuria Muria Islands *see* Ḩalānīyāt, Juzur al
153 T13 **Kurigram** Rajshahi, N Bangladesh 25°49′N 89°39′E
93 K17 **Kurikka** Länsi-Suomi, W Finland 62°36′N 22°25′E
192 I3 **Kurile Basin** *undersea feature* NW Pacific Ocean 47°00′N 150°00′E
Kurile Islands *see* Kuril'skiye Ostrova
Kurile-Kamchatka Depression *see* Kurile Trench
192 J3 **Kurile Trench** *var.* Kurile-Kamchatka Depression. *undersea feature* NW Pacific Ocean 47°00′N 155°00′E
127 Q9 **Kurilovka** Saratovskaya Oblast', W Russian Federation 50°39′N 48°02′E
123 U13 **Kuril'sk** *Jap.* Shana. Kuril'skiye Ostrova, Sakhalinskaya Oblats', SE Russian Federation 45°10′N 147°51′E
122 G11 **Kuril'skiye Ostrova** *Eng.* Kurile Islands. *island group* SE Russian Federation
42 M9 **Kurinwas, Río** ≈ E Nicaragua
Kurisches Haff *see* Courland Lagoon
Kurkund *see* Kilingi-Nõmme
126 M4 **Kurlovskiy** Vladimirskaya Oblast', W Russian Federation 55°25′N 40°39′E
80 G12 **Kurmuk** Blue Nile, SE Sudan 10°36′N 34°16′E
Kurna *see* Al Qurnah
155 H17 **Kurnool** *var.* Karnul. Andhra Pradesh, S India 15°51′N 78°01′E
164 M11 **Kurobe** Toyama, Honshū, SW Japan 36°55′N 137°24′E
165 Q7 **Kuroishi** *var.* Kuroisi. Aomori, Honshū, C Japan 40°37′N 140°34′E
Kuroisi *see* Kuroishi
165 O12 **Kuroiso** Tochigi, Honshū, S Japan 36°58′N 140°02′E
165 Q4 **Kuromatsunai** Hokkaidō, NE Japan 42°40′N 140°18′E
164 B17 **Kuro-shima** *island* SW Japan
185 F21 **Kurow** Canterbury, South Island, New Zealand 44°44′S 170°29′E
127 N15 **Kursavka** Stavropol'skiy Kray, SW Russian Federation 44°28′N 42°31′E
118 E11 **Kuršėnai** Šiauliai, N Lithuania 56°00′N 22°56′E
Kürshim *see* Kurchum
Kurshskaya Kosa/Kuršių Nerija *see* Courland Spit
126 J7 **Kursk** Kurskaya Oblast', W Russian Federation 51°44′N 36°47′E
126 I7 **Kurskaya Oblast'** ◈ *province* W Russian Federation
Kurskiy Zaliv *see* Courland Lagoon
113 N15 **Kuršumlija** Serbia, S Serbia 43°09′N 21°16′E
137 R15 **Kurtalan** Siirt, SE Turkey 37°58′N 41°36′E
Kurtbunar *see* Tervel
Kurt-Dere *see* Vŭlchidol
Kurtitsch/Kürtös *see* Curtici
145 U15 **Kurtty** ≈ SE Kazakhstan
93 L18 **Kuru** Länsi-Suomi, W Finland 61°51′N 23°46′E
80 C13 **Kuru** ≈ W Sudan
114 M13 **Kuru Dağı** ▲▲ NW Turkey
158 L7 **Kuruktag** ▲▲ NW China
83 G22 **Kuruman** Northern Cape, N South Africa 27°28′S 23°27′E
67 T14 **Kuruman** ≈ W South Africa
164 D14 **Kurume** Fukuoka, Kyūshū, SW Japan 33°15′N 130°27′E
123 N13 **Kurumkan** Respublika Buryatiya, S Russian Federation 54°13′N 110°21′E
155 J25 **Kurunegala** North Western Province, C Sri Lanka 07°28′N 80°23′E
55 T10 **Kurupukari** C Guyana 04°39′N 58°39′W
125 U10 **Kur"ya** Respublika Komi, NW Russian Federation 61°38′N 57°12′E
144 E15 **Kuryk** *var.* Yeraliyev, *Kaz.* Quryq. Mangistau, SW Kazakhstan 43°12′N 51°43′E
136 B15 **Kuşadası** Aydın, SW Turkey 37°50′N 27°16′E
115 M19 **Kuşadası Körfezi** *gulf* SW Turkey
164 A17 **Kusagaki-guntō** *island* SW Japan
Kusaie *see* Kosrae
145 T12 **Kusak** ≈ C Kazakhstan
Kusary *see* Qusar
167 P7 **Ku Sathan, Doi** ▲ NW Thailand 18°22′N 100°31′E
164 J13 **Kusatsu** *var.* Kusatu. Shiga, Honshū, SW Japan 35°02′N 136°00′E
Kusatu *see* Kusatsu
138 F11 **Kuseifa** Southern, C Israel 31°15′N 35°01′E
136 C12 **Kuş Gölü** ◎ NW Turkey
126 L12 **Kushchevskaya** Krasnodarskiy Kray, SW Russian Federation 46°35′N 39°40′E
164 D16 **Kushima** *var.* Kusima. Miyazaki, Kyūshū, SW Japan 31°28′N 131°14′E
164 I15 **Kushimoto** Wakayama, Honshū, SW Japan 33°28′N 135°45′E
165 V4 **Kushiro** *var.* Kusiro. Hokkaidō, NE Japan 42°58′N 144°24′E
148 K4 **Kushk** Herāt, W Afghanistan 34°55′N 62°20′E
Kushka *see* Serhetabat
Kushka *see* Gushgy/Serhetabat
145 N8 **Kushmurun** *Kaz.* Qusmuryn. Kostanay, N Kazakhstan 52°27′N 64°31′E
145 N8 **Kushmurun, Ozero** *Kaz.* Qusmuryn. ◎ N Kazakhstan
127 U4 **Kushnarenkovo** Respublika Bashkortostan, W Russian Federation 55°07′N 55°24′E
Kushrabat *see* Qo'shrabot
Kushtia *see* Kustia
Kusima *see* Kushima
Kusiro *see* Kushiro
38 M13 **Kuskokwim Bay** *bay* Alaska, USA
39 P11 **Kuskokwim Mountains** ▲▲ Alaska, USA
39 N12 **Kuskokwim River** ≈ Alaska, USA
108 G7 **Küsnacht** Zürich, N Switzerland 47°19′N 08°34′E
165 V4 **Kussharo-ko** *var.* Kussyaro. ◎ Hokkaidō, NE Japan
Küssnacht *see* Küssnacht am Rigi
108 F8 **Küssnacht am Rigi** *var.* Küssnacht. Schwyz, C Switzerland 47°03′N 08°25′E
Kussyaro *see* Kussharo-ko
Kustanay *see* Kostanay
Küstence/Küstendje *see* Constanța
100 F11 **Küstenkanal** *var.* Ems-Hunte Canal. *canal* NW Germany
153 T15 **Kustia** *var.* Kushtia. Khulna, W Bangladesh 23°54′N 89°07′E
Küstrin *see* Kostrzyn
171 R11 **Kusu** Pulau Halmahera, E Indonesia 0°51′N 127°41′E
170 L16 **Kuta** Pulau Lombok, S Indonesia 08°53′S 116°15′E
139 T4 **Kutabān** At Ta'mīn, N Iraq 35°21′N 44°45′E
136 E13 **Kütahya** *prev.* Kutaia. Kütahya, W Turkey 39°25′N 29°56′E
136 E13 **Kütahya** *var.* Kutaia. ◈ *province* W Turkey
Kutai *see* Mahakam, Sungai
Kutaia *see* Kütahya
137 R9 **K'ut'aisi** W Georgia 42°16′N 42°42′E
Kūt al 'Amārah *see* Al Kūt
Kut al Hai/Kūt al Ḩayy *see* Al Ḩayy
Kut al Imara *see* Al Kūt
123 Q11 **Kutana** Respublika Sakha (Yakutiya), NE Russian Federation 59°05′N 131°43′E
Kutaradja/Kutaraja *see* Bandaaceh
165 R4 **Kutchan** Hokkaidō, NE Japan 42°54′N 140°46′E
Kutch, Gulf of *see* Kachchh, Gulf of
Kutch, Rann of *see* Kachchh, Rann of
112 F9 **Kutina** Sisak-Moslavina, NE Croatia 45°29′N 16°45′E
112 H9 **Kutjevo** Požega-Slavonija, NE Croatia 45°26′N 17°54′E
111 E17 **Kutná Hora** *Ger.* Kuttenberg. Střední Čechy, C Czech Republic 49°58′N 15°18′E
110 K12 **Kutno** Łódzkie, C Poland 52°14′N 19°23′E
Kuttenberg *see* Kutná Hora
79 I20 **Kutu** Bandundu, W Dem. Rep. Congo 02°42′S 18°10′E
153 V17 **Kutubdia Island** *island* SE Bangladesh
80 B10 **Kutum** Northern Darfur, W Sudan 14°10′N 24°40′E
147 Y7 **Kuturgu** Issyk-Kul'skaya Oblast', E Kyrgyzstan 42°45′N 78°04′E
12 M5 **Kuujjuaq** *prev.* Fort-Chimo. Québec, E Canada 58°10′N 68°15′W
12 I7 **Kuujjuarapik** Québec, C Canada 55°07′N 78°09′W
Kuuli-Mayak *see* Guwlumaýak
118 I6 **Kuulsemägi** ▲ S Estonia
92 N13 **Kuusamo** Oulu, E Finland 65°57′N 29°15′E
93 M19 **Kuusankoski** Etelä-Suomi, S Finland 60°51′N 26°40′E
127 W7 **Kuvandyk** Orenburgskaya Oblast', W Russian Federation 51°27′N 57°18′E
Kuvango *see* Cubango
Kuvasay *see* Quvasoy
Kuvdlorssuak *see* Kullorsuaq
124 I16 **Kuvshinovo** Tverskaya Oblast', W Russian Federation 57°03′N 34°09′E
141 Q4 **Kuwait** *off.* State of Kuwait, *var.* Dawlat al Kuwait, Koweit, Kuweit. ◆ *monarchy* SW Asia
Kuwait *see* Al Kuwayt
Kuwait Bay *see* Kuwayt, Jūn al
Kuwait City *see* Al Kuwayt
Kuwait, Dawlat al *see* Kuwait
Kuwait, State of *see* Kuwait
Kuwajleen *see* Kwajalein Atoll
164 K13 **Kuwana** Mie, Honshū, SW Japan 35°04′N 136°40′E
139 X9 **Kuwayt** Maysān, E Iraq 32°26′N 47°12′E
142 K11 **Kuwayt, Jūn al** *var.* Kuwait Bay. *bay* E Kuwait
Kuweit *see* Kuwait
117 P10 **Kuyal'nyts'kyy Lyman** ◎ SW Ukraine
122 I12 **Kuybyshev** Novosibirskaya Oblast', C Russian Federation 55°28′N 77°55′E
Kuybyshev *see* Bolgar, Respublika Tatarstan, Russian Federation
Kuybyshev *see* Samara
117 W9 **Kuybysheve** *Rus.* Kuybyshevo. Zaporiz'ka Oblast', SE Ukraine 47°20′N 36°41′E
Kuybyshevo *see* Kuybysheve
Kuybyshev Reservoir *see* Kuybyshevskoye Vodokhranilishche
Kuybyshevskaya Oblast' *see* Samarskaya Oblast'
Kuybyshevskiy *see* Novoishimskiy
127 R4 **Kuybyshevskoye Vodokhranilishche** *var.* Kuibyshev, *Eng.* Kuybyshev Reservoir. ▣ W Russian Federation
123 S9 **Kuydusun** Respublika Sakha (Yakutiya), NE Russian Federation 63°15′N 143°10′E
125 U16 **Kuyeda** Permskaya Oblast', NW Russian Federation 56°23′N 55°19′E
Küysanjaq *see* Koi Sanjaq
158 J4 **Kuytun** Xinjiang Uygur Zizhiqu, NW China 44°25′N 84°55′E
122 M13 **Kuytun** Irkutskaya Oblast', S Russian Federation 54°18′N 101°28′E
55 S12 **Kuyuwini Landing** S Guyana 02°06′N 59°14′W
Kuzi *see* Kuji
38 M9 **Kuzitrin River** ≈ Alaska, USA
127 P6 **Kuznetsk** Penzenskaya Oblast', W Russian Federation 53°06′N 46°27′E
116 K3 **Kuznetsovs'k** Rivnens'ka Oblast', NW Ukraine 51°21′N 25°51′E
165 R8 **Kuzumaki** Iwate, Honshū, C Japan 40°04′N 141°26′E
95 H24 **Kværndrup** Fyn, C Denmark 55°10′N 10°31′E
92 H9 **Kvaløya** *island* N Norway
92 K8 **Kvalsund** Finnmark, N Norway 70°30′N 23°56′E
94 G11 **Kvam** Oppland, S Norway 61°42′N 09°43′E
127 X7 **Kvarkeno** Orenburgskaya Oblast', W Russian Federation 52°09′N 59°44′E
93 G15 **Kvarnbergsvattnet** *var.* Frostviken. ◎ N Sweden
112 A11 **Kvarner** *var.* Carnaro, *It.* Quarnero. *gulf* W Croatia
112 B11 **Kvarnerić** *channel* W Croatia
39 O14 **Kvichak Bay** *bay* Alaska, USA
92 H12 **Kvikkjokk** *Lapp.* Huhttán. Norrbotten, N Sweden 66°58′N 17°45′E
95 D17 **Kvina** ≈ S Norway
92 Q1 **Kvitøya** *island* NE Svalbard
95 F16 **Kvitseid** Telemark, S Norway 59°23′N 08°31′E
79 H20 **Kwa** ≈ W Dem. Rep. Congo
77 Q15 **Kwadwokurom** C Ghana 07°49′N 00°15′W
186 M8 **Kwailibesi** Malaita, N Solomon Islands 08°25′S 160°48′E
189 S6 **Kwajalein Atoll** *var.* Kuwajleen. *atoll* Ralik Chain, C Marshall Islands
55 W9 **Kwakoegron** Brokopondo, N Surinam 05°14′N 55°20′W
81 J21 **Kwale** Coast, S Kenya 04°10′S 39°27′E
77 U17 **Kwale** Delta, S Nigeria 05°51′N 06°29′E
79 H20 **Kwamouth** Bandundu, W Dem. Rep. Congo 03°11′S 16°16′E
Kwando *see* Cuando
Kwangchow *see* Guangzhou
Kwangchu *see* Kwangju
163 X16 **Kwangju** *off.* Kwangju-gwangyŏksi, *var.* Guangju, Kwangchu, *Jap.* Kōshū. SW South Korea 35°09′N 126°53′E
Kwangju-gwangyŏksi *see* Kwangju
79 H20 **Kwango** *Port.* Cuango. ≈ Angola/Dem. Rep. Congo *see also* Cuango
Kwango *see* Cuango
Kwangsi/Kwangsi Chuang Autonomous Region *see* Guangxi Zhuangzu Zizhiqu
Kwangtung *see* Guangdong
Kwangyuan *see* Guangyuan
81 F17 **Kwania, Lake** ◎ C Uganda
Kwanza *see* Cuanza
77 S15 **Kwara** ◈ *state* SW Nigeria
83 K22 **KwaZulu/Natal** *off.* KwaZulu/Natal Province; *prev.* Natal. ◈ *province* E South Africa
KwaZulu/Natal Province *see* KwaZulu/Natal
Kweichow *see* Guizhou
Kweichu *see* Guiyang
Kweilin *see* Guilin
Kweisui *see* Hohhot
Kweiyang *see* Guiyang
83 K17 **Kwekwe** *prev.* Que Que. Midlands, C Zimbabwe 18°56′S 29°49′E
83 G20 **Kweneng** ◈ *district* S Botswana
Kwesui *see* Hohhot
39 N12 **Kwethluk** Alaska, USA 60°48′N 161°26′W
39 N12 **Kwethluk River** ≈ Alaska, USA
110 J8 **Kwidzyń** *Ger.* Marienwerder. Pomorskie, N Poland 53°44′N 18°55′E
38 M13 **Kwigillingok** Alaska, USA 59°52′N 163°08′W
186 E9 **Kwikila** Central, S Papua New Guinea 09°51′S 147°43′E
79 I20 **Kwilu** ≈ W Dem. Rep. Congo
Kwito *see* Cuito
171 U12 **Kwoka, Gunung** ▲ Papua, E Indonesia 0°34′S 132°25′E
78 I12 **Kyabé** Moyen-Chari, S Chad 09°28′N 18°54′E
183 O11 **Kyabram** Victoria, SE Australia 36°21′S 145°05′E
166 M9 **Kyaikkami** *prev.* Amherst. Mon State, S Burma (Myanmar) 16°03′N 97°36′E
166 L9 **Kyaiklat** Ayeyarwady, SW Burma (Myanmar) 16°25′N 95°42′E
166 M8 **Kyaikto** Mon State, S Burma (Myanmar) 17°16′N 97°01′E
123 N14 **Kyakhta** Respublika Buryatiya, S Russian Federation 50°25′N 106°13′E
182 G8 **Kyancutta** South Australia 33°10′S 135°33′E
167 T8 **Ky Anh** Ha Tinh, N Vietnam 18°05′N 106°16′E
166 L5 **Kyaukpadaung** Mandalay, C Burma (Myanmar) 20°50′N 95°08′E
166 J6 **Kyaukpyu** Rakhine State, W Burma (Myanmar) 19°27′N 93°33′E
166 M5 **Kyaukse** Mandalay, C Burma (Myanmar) 21°33′N 96°06′E
166 L8 **Kyaunggon** Ayeyarwady, SW Burma (Myanmar) 17°04′N 95°12′E
119 E14 **Kybartai** *Pol.* Kibarty. Marijampolė, S Lithuania 54°37′N 22°44′E
152 I7 **Kyelang** Himāchal Pradesh, NW India 32°33′N 77°03′E
111 G19 **Kyjov** *Ger.* Gaya. Jihomoravský Kraj, SE Czech Republic 49°00′N 17°07′E
115 J21 **Kykládes** *var.* Kikládhes, *Eng.* Cyclades. *island group* SE Greece
25 S11 **Kyle** Texas, SW USA 29°59′N 97°52′W
96 G9 **Kyle of Lochalsh** N Scotland, United Kingdom 57°18′N 05°39′W
101 D18 **Kyll** ≈ W Germany
115 F19 **Kyllíni** *var.* Killini. ▲ S Greece
115 H18 **Kými** *prev.* Kími. Évvoia, C Greece 38°38′N 24°06′E
93 M19 **Kymijoki** ≈ S Finland
115 H18 **Kýmis, Akrotírio** *headland* Évvoia, C Greece 38°39′N 24°08′E
125 W14 **Kyn** Permskaya Oblast', NW Russian Federation 57°48′N 58°38′E
183 N12 **Kyneton** Victoria, SE Australia 37°14′S 144°28′E
81 G17 **Kyoga, Lake** *var.* Lake Kioga. ◎ C Uganda
164 J12 **Kyōga-misaki** *headland* Honshū, SW Japan 35°46′N 135°13′E
183 V4 **Kyogle** New South Wales, SE Australia 28°37′S 153°00′E
163 W15 **Kyŏnggi-man** *bay* NW South Korea
163 Z16 **Kyŏngju** *Jap.* Keishū. SE South Korea 35°49′N 129°09′E
Kyŏngsŏng *see* Sŏul
Kyōsai-tō *see* Kŏje-do
81 F19 **Kyotera** S Uganda 0°38′S 31°34′E
164 J13 **Kyōto** Kyōto, Honshū, SW Japan 35°01′N 135°46′E
164 J13 **Kyōto** *off.* Kyōto-fu, *var.* Kyōto Hu. ◈ *urban prefecture* Honshū, SW Japan
Kyōto-fu/Kyōto Hu *see* Kyōto
115 D21 **Kyparissía** *var.* Kiparissía. Pelopónnisos, S Greece 37°15′N 21°40′E
115 D20 **Kyparissiakós Kólpos** *gulf* S Greece
Kyperounda *see* Kyperoúnta
121 P3 **Kyperoúnta** *var.* Kyperounda. C Cyprus 34°57′N 33°02′E
Kypros *see* Cyprus
115 H16 **Kyrá Panagía** *island* Vóreies Sporádes, Greece, Aegean Sea
Kyrenia *see* Girne
Kyrenia Mountains *see* Beşparmak Dağları
Kyrgyz Republic *see* Kyrgyzstan
147 U9 **Kyrgyzstan** *off.* Kyrgyz Republic, *var.* Kirghizia; *prev.* Kirgizskaya SSR, Kirghiz SSR, Republic of Kyrgyzstan. ◆ *republic* C Asia
Kyrgyzstan, Republic of *see* Kyrgyzstan
138 F11 **Kyriat Gat** *prev.* Qiryat Gat. Southern, C Israel 31°37′N 34°47′E
100 M11 **Kyritz** Brandenburg, NE Germany 52°56′N 12°24′E
94 G8 **Kyrkseterøra** Sør-Trøndelag, S Norway 63°17′N 09°06′E
Kyrkslätt *see* Kirkkonummi
125 U8 **Kyrta** Respublika Komi, NW Russian Federation 64°03′N 57°41′E
111 J18 **Kysucké Nové Mesto** *prev.* Horné Nové Mesto, *Ger.* Kisutzaneustadtl, Oberneustadtl, *Hung.* Kiszucaújhely. Žilinský Kraj, N Slovakia 49°18′N 18°48′E
117 N12 **Kytay, Ozero** ◎ SW Ukraine
115 F23 **Kýthira** *var.* Kíthira, *It.* Cerigo, *Lat.* Cythera. Kýthira, S Greece 41°39′N 26°30′E
115 F23 **Kýthira** *var.* Kíthira, *It.* Cerigo, *Lat.* Cythera. *island* S Greece
115 I20 **Kýthnos** Kýthnos, Kykládes, Greece, Aegean Sea 37°24′N 24°28′E
115 I20 **Kýthnos** *var.* Kíthnos, Thermiá, *It.* Termia; *anc.* Cythnos. *island* Kykládes, Greece, Aegean Sea
115 I20 **Kýthnou, Stenó** *strait* Kykládes, Greece, Aegean Sea
Kyungëy Ala-Too, Khrebet *see* Kungei Ala-Tau
Kyurdamir *see* Kürdämir
164 D15 **Kyūshū** *var.* Kyûsyû. *island* SW Japan
192 H6 **Kyushu-Palau Ridge** *var.* Kyusyu-Palau Ridge. *undersea feature* W Pacific Ocean 20°00′N 136°00′E
114 F10 **Kyustendil** *anc.* Pautalia. Kyustendil, W Bulgaria 42°17′N 22°42′E
114 G11 **Kyustendil** ◈ *province* W Bulgaria
Kyûsyû *see* Kyūshū
Kyusyu-Palau Ridge *see* Kyushu-Palau Ridge
123 P8 **Kyusyur** Respublika Sakha (Yakutiya), NE Russian Federation 70°36′N 127°19′E
183 P10 **Kywong** New South Wales, SE Australia 34°59′S 146°42′E
117 P4 **Kyyiv** *Eng.* Kiev, *Rus.* Kiyev. ● (Ukraine) Kyyivs'ka Oblast', N Ukraine 50°26′N 30°32′E
Kyyiv *see* Kyyivs'ka Oblast'
117 O4 **Kyyivs'ka Oblast'** *var.* Kyyiv, *Rus.* Kiyevskaya Oblast'. ◈ *province* N Ukraine
117 P3 **Kyyivs'ke Vodoskhovyshche** *Eng.* Kiev Reservoir, *Rus.* Kiyevskoye Vodokhranilishche. ▣ N Ukraine
93 L16 **Kyyjärvi** Länsi-Suomi, C Finland 63°02′N 24°34′E
122 K14 **Kyzyl** Respublika Tyva, C Russian Federation 51°45′N 94°28′E
147 S8 **Kyzyl-Adyr** *var.* Kirovskoye. Talasskaya Oblast', NW Kyrgyzstan 42°37′N 71°34′E
145 V14 **Kyzylagash** *Kaz.* Qyzylaghash. Almaty, SE Kazakhstan 45°20′N 78°45′E
146 C13 **Kyzylbair** Balkan Welaýaty, W Turkmenistan 38°13′N 55°38′E
Kyzyl-Dzhiik, Pereval *see* Uzbel Shankou
145 S7 **Kyzylkak, Ozero** ◎ NE Kazakhstan
145 X11 **Kyzylkesek** Vostochnyy Kazakhstan, E Kazakhstan 47°56′N 82°02′E
147 S10 **Kyzyl-Kiya** *Kir.* Kyzyl-Kyya. Batkenskaya Oblast', SW Kyrgyzstan 40°15′N 72°07′E
144 L11 **Kyzylkol', Ozero** ◎ C Kazakhstan
122 K14 **Kyzyl Kum** *var.* Kizil Kum, Qizil Qum, *Uzb.* Qizilqum. *desert* Kazakhstan/Uzbekistan
Kyzyl-Kyya *see* Kyzyl-Kiya
144 L14 **Kyzylorda** *off.* Kyzylordinskaya Oblast', *Kaz.* Qyzylorda Oblysy. ◈ *province* S Kazakhstan
Kyzylordinskaya Oblast' *see* Kyzylorda
Kyzylrabat *see* Qizilravote
Kyzylrabot *see* Qizilrabot
Kyzylsu *see* Kyzyl-Suu
147 X7 **Kyzyl-Suu** *prev.* Pokrovka. Issyk-Kul'skaya Oblast', NE Kyrgyzstan 42°20′N 77°55′E
147 S12 **Kyzyl-Suu** *var.* Kyzylsu. ≈ Kyrgyzstan/Tajikistan
147 X8 **Kyzyl-Tuu** Issyk-Kul'skaya Oblast', E Kyrgyzstan 42°06′N 76°54′E
145 Q12 **Kyzylzhar** *Kaz.* Qyzylzhar. Karaganda, C Kazakhstan 48°22′N 70°00′E
145 N15 **Kzylorda** *var.* Kzyl-Orda, Qizil Orda, Qyzylorda; *prev.* Perovsk. Kyzylorda, S Kazakhstan 44°54′N 65°31′E
Kzyl-Orda *see* Kzylorda
Kzyltu *see* Kishkenekol'

L

109 X2 **Laa an der Thaya** Niederösterreich, NE Austria 48°44′N 16°23′E
63 K15 **La Adela** La Pampa, SE Argentina 38°57′S 64°02′W
Laagen *see* Numedalslågen
109 S5 **Laakirchen** Oberösterreich, N Austria 47°59′N 13°49′E
Laaland *see* Lolland
104 I11 **La Albuera** Extremadura, W Spain 38°43′N 06°49′W
105 O7 **La Alcarria** *physical region* C Spain
104 K14 **La Algaba** Andalucía, S Spain 37°27′N 06°01′W
105 P9 **La Almarcha** Castilla-La Mancha, C Spain 39°41′N 02°23′W
105 R6 **La Almunia de Doña Godina** Aragón, NE Spain 41°28′N 01°23′W
41 N5 **La Amistad, Presa** ▣ NW Mexico
118 F4 **Läänemaa** *var.* Lääne Maakond. ◈ *province* NW Estonia
Lääne Maakond *see* Läänemaa
118 I3 **Lääne-Virumaa** *off.* Lääne-Viru Maakond. ◈ *province* NE Estonia
Lääne-Viru Maakond *see* Lääne-Virumaa
62 J9 **La Antigua, Salina** *salt lake* W Argentina
99 E17 **Laarne** Oost-Vlaanderen, NW Belgium 51°03′N 03°50′E
80 O13 **Laas Caanood** Sool, N Somalia 08°33′N 47°44′E
41 O9 **La Ascensión** Nuevo León, NE Mexico 24°15′N 99°53′W
80 N12 **Laas Dhaareed** Sanaag, N Somalia 10°12′N 46°09′E
55 O4 **La Asunción** Nueva Esparta, NE Venezuela 11°06′N 63°53′W
Laatokka *see* Ladozhskoye, Ozero
100 I13 **Laatzen** Niedersachsen, NW Germany 52°19′N 09°46′E
38 E9 **La'au Point** *var.* Laau Point. *headland* Moloka'i, Hawai'i, USA 21°06′N 157°18′W
Laau Point *see* La'au Point
42 D6 **La Aurora** ✈ (Ciudad de Guatemala) Guatemala, C Guatemala 14°33′N 90°30′W
74 C9 **Laâyoune** *var.* Aaiún. ● (Western Sahara) NW Western Sahara 27°10′N 13°11′W
126 L14 **Laba** ≈ SW Russian Federation
40 M6 **La Babia** Coahuila, NE Mexico 28°39′N 102°00′W
15 R7 **La Baie** Québec, SE Canada 48°20′N 70°54′W
171 P16 **Labala** Pulau Lomblen, S Indonesia 08°30′S 123°27′E
62 K8 **La Banda** Santiago del Estero, N Argentina 27°44′S 64°14′W
La Banda Oriental *see* Uruguay
104 K4 **La Bañeza** Castilla-León, N Spain 42°18′N 05°54′W
40 M13 **La Barca** Jalisco, SW Mexico 20°20′N 102°33′W
40 K14 **La Barra de Navidad** Jalisco, C Mexico 19°12′N 104°38′W
187 Y13 **Labasa** *prev.* Lambasa. Vanua Levu, N Fiji 16°25′S 179°24′E
102 H8 **la Baule-Escoublac** Loire-Atlantique, NW France 47°17′N 02°24′W
76 I13 **Labé** NW Guinea 11°19′N 12°17′W
Labe *see* Elbe
15 N11 **Labelle** Québec, SE Canada 46°15′N 74°43′W
23 X14 **La Belle** Florida, SE USA 26°45′N 81°26′W
10 H7 **Laberge, Lake** ◎ Yukon Territory, W Canada
Labes *see* Łobez
Labiau *see* Polessk
112 A10 **Labin** *It.* Albona. Istra, NW Croatia 45°05′N 14°10′E
126 L14 **Labinsk** Krasnodarskiy Kray, SW Russian Federation 44°39′N 40°43′E
105 X5 **La Bisbal d'Empordà** Cataluña, NE Spain 41°58′N 03°02′E
119 P16 **Labkovichy** *Rus.* Lobkovichi. Mahilyowskaya Voblasts', E Belarus 53°50′N 31°45′E
15 S4 **La Blache, Lac de** ◎ Québec, SE Canada
171 P4 **Labo** Luzon, N Philippines 14°10′N 122°47′E
Laboehanbadjo *see* Labuhanbajo
Laborca *see* Laborec
111 N18 **Laborec** *Hung.* Laborca. ≈ E Slovakia
108 D11 **La Borgne** ≈ S Switzerland
45 T12 **Laborie** SW Saint Lucia 13°45′N 61°00′W
102 J14 **Labouheyre** Landes, SW France 44°12′N 00°55′W
62 L12 **Laboulaye** Córdoba, C Argentina 34°05′S 63°20′W
13 Q7 **Labrador** *cultural region* Newfoundland and Labrador, SW Canada
64 I6 **Labrador Basin** *var.* Labrador Sea Basin. *undersea feature* Labrador Sea 53°00′N 48°00′W
13 N9 **Labrador City** Newfoundland and Labrador, E Canada 52°56′N 66°52′W

◆ Country ● Country Capital ◇ Dependent Territory ○ Dependent Territory Capital ◈ Administrative Regions ✈ International Airport ▲ Mountain ▲▲ Mountain Range ⛰ Volcano ≈ River ◎ Lake ▣ Reservoir
275

LABRADOR SEA – LANDEN

13 Q5 **Labrador Sea** sea NW Atlantic Ocean
Labrador Sea Basin see Labrador Basin
Labrang see Xiahe
54 G9 **Labranzagrande** Boyacá, C Colombia 05°34′N 72°34′W
59 D14 **Lábrea** Amazonas, N Brazil 07°20′S 64°46′W
45 U15 **La Brea** Trinidad, Trinidad and Tobago 10°14′N 61°37′W
15 S6 **Labrieville** Québec, SE Canada 49°15′N 69°31′W
102 K14 **Labrit** Landes, SW France 44°03′N 00°29′W
108 C9 **La Broye** ≈ SW Switzerland
103 N15 **Labruguière** Tarn, S France 43°32′N 02°15′E
168 M11 **Labu** Pulau Singkep, W Indonesia 0°34′S 104°24′E
169 T7 **Labuan** var. Victoria. Labuan, East Malaysia 05°20′N 115°14′E
169 T7 **Labuan** ◈ federal territory East Malaysia
Labuan see Labuan, Pulau
169 T7 **Labuan, Pulau** var. Labuan. island East Malaysia
Labudalin see Ergun
171 N16 **Labuhanbajo** prev. Laboehanbadjo. Flores, S Indonesia 08°33′S 119°55′E
168 J9 **Labuhanbilik** Sumatera, N Indonesia 02°30′N 100°10′E
168 G8 **Labuhanhaji** Sumatera, W Indonesia 03°31′N 97°00′E
Labuk see Labuk, Sungai
Labuk Bay see Labuk, Teluk
169 V7 **Labuk, Sungai** var. Labuk. ≈ East Malaysia
169 W6 **Labuk, Teluk** var. Labuk Bay, Telukan Labuk. bay S Sulu Sea
Labuk, Telukan see Labuk, Teluk
166 K9 **Labutta** Ayeyarwady, SW Burma (Myanmar) 16°08′N 94°45′E
122 I8 **Labytnangi** Yamalo-Nenetskiy Avtonomnyy Okrug, N Russian Federation 66°39′N 66°26′E
113 K19 **Laç** var. Laci. Lezhë, C Albania 41°37′N 19°37′E
78 F10 **Lac** off. Préfecture du Lac. ◈ prefecture W Chad
57 K19 **Lacajahuira, Rio** ≈ W Bolivia
La Calamine see Kelmis
62 G11 **La Calera** Valparaíso, C Chile 32°47′S 71°16′W
13 P11 **Lac-Allard** Québec, E Canada 50°37′N 63°26′W
104 L13 **La Campana** Andalucía, S Spain 37°35′N 05°24′W
102 J12 **Lacanau** Gironde, SW France 44°59′N 01°04′W
42 C2 **Lacandón, Sierra del** ▲▲ Guatemala/Mexico
La Cañiza see A Cañiza
41 W16 **Lacantún, Río** ≈ SE Mexico
103 Q3 **la Capelle** Aisne, N France 49°58′N 03°55′E
112 K10 **Lačarak** Vojvodina, NW Serbia 45°00′N 19°34′E
62 L11 **La Carlota** Córdoba, C Argentina 33°30′S 63°15′W
104 L13 **La Carlota** Andalucía, S Spain 37°40′N 04°56′W
105 N12 **La Carolina** Andalucía, S Spain 38°15′N 03°37′W
103 O15 **Lacaune** Tarn, S France 43°42′N 02°42′E
15 P7 **Lac-Bouchette** Québec, SE Canada 48°14′N 72°11′W
Laccadive Islands/Laccadive Minicoy and Amindivi Islands, the see Lakshadweep
11 Y16 **Lac du Bonnet** Manitoba, S Canada 50°13′N 96°04′W
30 L4 **Lac du Flambeau** Wisconsin, N USA 45°58′N 89°51′W
15 P8 **Lac-Édouard** Québec, SE Canada 47°39′N 72°16′W
42 I4 **La Ceiba** Atlántida, N Honduras 15°45′N 86°29′W
54 E9 **La Ceja** Antioquia, W Colombia 06°02′N 75°30′W
182 J11 **Lacepede Bay** bay South Australia
32 G9 **Lacey** Washington, NW USA 47°01′N 122°49′W
103 P12 **la Chaise-Dieu** Haute-Loire, C France 45°19′N 03°41′E
114 G13 **Lachanás** Kentrikí Makedonía, N Greece 40°57′N 23°15′E
124 L11 **Lacha, Ozero** ◎ NW Russian Federation
103 O8 **la Charité-sur-Loire** Nièvre, C France 47°10′N 02°59′E
103 N9 **la Châtre** Indre, C France 46°35′N 01°59′E
108 C8 **La Chaux-de-Fonds** Neuchâtel, W Switzerland 47°07′N 06°51′E
Lach Dera see Dheere Laaq
108 G8 **Lachen** Schwyz, C Switzerland 47°12′N 08°51′E
183 Q8 **Lachlan River** ≈ New South Wales, SE Australia
43 T15 **La Chorrera** Panamá, C Panama 08°51′N 79°46′W
15 V7 **Lac-Humqui** Québec, SE Canada 48°21′N 67°32′W
15 N12 **Lachute** Québec, SE Canada 45°39′N 74°21′W
Lachyn see Laçın
Laci see Laç
137 W13 **Laçın** Rus. Lachyn. SW Azerbaijan 39°36′N 46°34′E
103 S16 **la Ciotat** anc. Citharista. Bouches-du-Rhône, SE France 43°10′N 05°36′E
18 D10 **Lackawanna** New York, NE USA 42°49′N 78°49′W
11 Q13 **Lac La Biche** Alberta, SW Canada 54°46′N 111°59′W
Lac la Martre see Wha Ti
15 R12 **Lac-Mégantic** var. Mégantic. Québec, SE Canada 45°35′N 70°53′W
Lacobriga see Lagos
40 G5 **La Colorada** Sonora, NW Mexico 28°49′N 110°32′W
11 Q15 **Lacombe** Alberta, SW Canada 52°30′N 113°42′W
30 L12 **Lacon** Illinois, N USA 41°01′N 89°24′W
43 P16 **La Concepción** var. Concepción. Chiriquí, W Panama 08°31′N 82°39′W
54 H5 **La Concepción** Zulia, NW Venezuela 10°48′N 71°46′W
107 C19 **Laconi** Sardegna, Italy, C Mediterranean Sea 39°52′N 09°02′E
19 O9 **Laconia** New Hampshire, NE USA 43°32′N 71°29′W
61 H19 **La Coronilla** Rocha, E Uruguay 33°44′S 53°31′W
La Coruña see A Coruña
103 O11 **la Courtine** Creuse, C France 45°42′N 02°18′E
Lac, Préfecture du see Lac
102 J16 **Lacq** Pyrénées-Atlantiques, SW France 43°25′N 00°37′W
15 P9 **La Croche** Québec, SE Canada 47°38′N 72°42′W
29 X3 **la Croix, Lac** ◎ Canada/USA
26 K5 **La Crosse** Kansas, C USA 38°32′N 99°19′W
21 V7 **La Crosse** Virginia, NE USA 36°41′N 78°03′W
32 L9 **La Crosse** Washington, NW USA 46°48′N 117°51′W
30 J7 **La Crosse** Wisconsin, N USA 43°46′N 91°12′W
54 C13 **La Cruz** Nariño, SW Colombia 01°33′N 76°58′W
42 K12 **La Cruz** Guanacaste, NW Costa Rica 11°05′N 85°39′W
40 I10 **La Cruz** Sinaloa, W Mexico 23°53′N 106°53′W
61 F19 **La Cruz** Florida, S Uruguay 33°54′S 56°11′W
42 M9 **La Cruz de Río Grande** Región Autónoma Atlántico Sur, E Nicaragua 13°04′N 84°12′W
54 J4 **La Cruz de Taratara** Falcón, N Venezuela 11°03′N 69°44′W
15 Q10 **Lac-St-Charles** Québec, SE Canada 46°56′N 71°24′W
40 M6 **La Cuesta** Coahuila, NE Mexico 28°45′N 102°26′W
57 A17 **La Cumbra, Volcán** ⛰ Galapagos Islands, Ecuador, E Pacific Ocean 0°21′S 91°30′W
152 J5 **Ladākh Range** ▲▲ NE India
26 I5 **Ladder Creek** ≈ Kansas, C USA
45 X10 **la Désirade** atoll E Guadeloupe
Lādhiqīyah, Muḩāfaẓat al see Al Lādhiqīyah
172 J16 **La Digue** island Inner Islands, NE Seychelles
83 F25 **Ladismith** Western Cape, SW South Africa 33°30′S 21°15′E
152 G11 **Lādnūn** Rājasthān, NW India 27°36′N 74°26′E
Ladoga, Lake see Ladozhskoye, Ozero
115 E19 **Ládon** ≈ S Greece
54 E9 **La Dorada** Caldas, C Colombia 05°28′N 74°41′W
124 H11 **Ladozhskoye, Ozero** Eng. Lake Ladoga, Fin. Laatokka. ◎ NW Russian Federation
37 R12 **Ladron Peak** ▲ New Mexico, SW USA 34°25′N 107°04′W
124 J11 **Ladva-Vetka** Respublika Kareliya, NW Russian Federation 61°18′N 34°24′E
183 Q15 **Lady Barron** Tasmania, SE Australia 40°12′S 148°12′E
14 G9 **Lady Evelyn Lake** ◎ Ontario, S Canada
23 W11 **Lady Lake** Florida, SE USA 28°55′N 81°55′W
10 L17 **Ladysmith** Vancouver Island, British Columbia, SW Canada 48°55′N 123°45′W
83 J22 **Ladysmith** KwaZulu/Natal, E South Africa 28°34′S 29°47′E
30 J5 **Ladysmith** Wisconsin, N USA 45°27′N 91°07′W
145 P9 **Ladyzhenka** Akmola, C Kazakhstan 50°58′N 68°44′E
186 E7 **Lae** Morobe, W Papua New Guinea 06°45′S 147°00′E
189 R6 **Lae Atoll** atoll Ralik Chain, W Marshall Islands
40 C3 **La Encantada, Cerro de** ▲ NW Mexico 31°03′N 115°25′W
55 N11 **La Esmeralda** Amazonas, S Venezuela 03°11′N 65°33′W
42 G7 **La Esperanza** Intibucá, SW Honduras 14°19′N 88°09′W
30 K8 **La Farge** Wisconsin, N USA 43°36′N 90°39′W
23 R5 **Lafayette** Alabama, S USA 32°54′N 85°24′W
37 T4 **Lafayette** Colorado, C USA 39°59′N 105°06′W
23 R2 **La Fayette** Georgia, SE USA 34°42′N 85°16′W
31 O13 **Lafayette** Indiana, N USA 40°25′N 86°52′W
22 I9 **Lafayette** Louisiana, S USA 30°13′N 92°01′W
20 K8 **Lafayette** Tennessee, S USA 36°31′N 86°01′W
19 N7 **Lafayette, Mount** ▲ New Hampshire, NE USA 44°09′N 71°37′W
La Fe see Santa Fé
103 P3 **la Fère** Aisne, N France 49°41′N 03°20′E
102 L6 **la Ferté-Bernard** Sarthe, NW France 48°13′N 00°40′E
102 K5 **la Ferté-Macé** Orne, N France 48°35′N 00°21′W
103 N7 **la Ferté-St-Aubin** Loiret, C France 47°42′N 01°57′E
103 P5 **la Ferté-sous-Jouarre** Seine-et-Marne, N France 48°57′N 03°08′E
77 V15 **Lafia** Nassarawa, C Nigeria 08°29′N 08°34′E
77 T15 **Lafiagi** Kwara, W Nigeria 08°52′N 05°25′E
11 T17 **Lafleche** Saskatchewan, S Canada 49°40′N 106°28′W
102 K7 **la Flèche** Sarthe, NW France 47°42′N 00°04′W
109 X7 **Lafnitz** Hung. Lapines. ≈ Austria/Hungary
187 P17 **La Foa** Province Sud, S New Caledonia 21°46′S 165°49′E
20 M8 **La Follette** Tennessee, S USA 36°22′N 84°07′W
15 N12 **Lafontaine** Québec, SE Canada 45°52′N 74°01′W
22 K10 **Lafourche, Bayou** ≈ Louisiana, S USA
62 K6 **La Fragua** Santiago del Estero, N Argentina 26°06′S 64°06′W
54 H7 **La Fría** Táchira, NW Venezuela 08°13′N 72°15′W
104 J7 **La Fuente de San Esteban** Castilla-León, N Spain 40°48′N 06°14′W
186 C7 **Lagaip** ≈ W Papua New Guinea
61 B15 **La Gallareta** Santa Fe, C Argentina 29°34′S 60°23′W
127 Q14 **Lagan′** prev. Kaspiyskiy. Respublika Kalmykiya, SW Russian Federation 45°25′N 47°19′E
95 L20 **Lagan** Kronoberg, S Sweden 56°55′N 14°01′E
95 K21 **Lågan** ≈ S Sweden
92 L2 **Lagarfljót** var. Lögurinn. ◎ E Iceland
37 R7 **La Garita Mountains** ▲▲ Colorado, C USA
171 O2 **Lagawe** Luzon, N Philippines 16°46′N 121°06′E
78 F13 **Lagdo** Nord, N Cameroon 09°12′N 13°43′E
78 F13 **Lagdo, Lac de** ◎ N Cameroon
100 H13 **Lage** Nordrhein-Westfalen, W Germany 52°00′N 08°48′E
94 H12 **Lågen** ≈ S Norway
61 J14 **Lages** Santa Catarina, S Brazil 27°45′S 50°16′W
Lágesvuotna see Laksefjorden
149 R4 **Laghmān** ◈ province E Afghanistan
74 J6 **Laghouat** N Algeria 33°49′N 02°59′E
105 Q10 **La Gineta** Castilla-La Mancha, C Spain 39°08′N 02°00′W
115 E21 **Lagkáda** var. Langada. Pelopónnisos, S Greece 36°49′N 22°19′E
114 G13 **Lagkadás** var. Langades, Langadhás. Kentrikí Makedonía, N Greece 40°45′N 23°04′E
115 E20 **Lagkádia** var. Langádhia, cont. Langadia. Pelopónnisos, S Greece 37°40′N 22°01′E
54 F6 **La Gloria** Cesar, N Colombia 08°37′N 73°51′W
41 O7 **La Gloria** Nuevo León, NE Mexico
92 N3 **Lågneset** headland W Svalbard 77°46′N 13°44′E
104 G14 **Lagoa** Faro, S Portugal 37°07′N 08°27′W
La Goagira see La Guajira
Lago Agrio see Nueva Loja
61 I14 **Lagoa Vermelha** Rio Grande do Sul, S Brazil 28°13′S 51°32′W
137 V10 **Lagodekhi** SE Georgia 41°49′N 46°15′E
42 C7 **La Gomera** Escuintla, S Guatemala 14°05′N 91°03′W
Lagone see Logone
107 M19 **Lagonegro** Basilicata, S Italy 40°06′N 15°42′E
63 G16 **Lago Ranco** Los Lagos, S Chile 40°21′S 72°29′W
77 S16 **Lagos** Lagos, SW Nigeria 06°24′N 03°17′E
104 F14 **Lagos** anc. Lacobriga. Faro, S Portugal 37°05′N 08°40′W
77 S16 **Lagos** ◈ state SW Nigeria
40 M12 **Lagos de Moreno** Jalisco, SW Mexico 21°21′N 101°55′W
Lagosta see Lastovo
74 A12 **Lagouira** SW Western Sahara 20°55′N 17°05′W
92 O1 **Lågøya** island N Svalbard
32 L11 **La Grande** Oregon, NW USA 45°21′N 118°05′W
103 Q14 **la Grande-Combe** Gard, S France 44°13′N 04°01′E
12 K9 **La Grande Rivière** var. Fort George. ≈ Québec, SE Canada
23 R4 **La Grange** Georgia, SE USA 33°02′N 85°02′W
31 P11 **Lagrange** Indiana, N USA 41°38′N 85°25′W
20 L5 **La Grange** Kentucky, S USA 38°24′N 85°23′W
27 V2 **La Grange** Missouri, C USA 40°00′N 91°31′W
21 V10 **La Grange** North Carolina, SE USA 35°18′N 77°47′W
25 U11 **La Grange** Texas, SW USA 29°55′N 96°54′W
105 N7 **La Granja** Castilla-León, N Spain 40°53′N 04°01′W
55 Q9 **La Gran Sabana** grassland E Venezuela
54 H7 **La Grita** Táchira, NW Venezuela 08°09′N 71°58′W
La Grulla see Grulla
15 R11 **La Guadeloupe** Québec, SE Canada 45°57′N 70°56′W
65 L6 **La Guaira** Distrito Federal, N Venezuela 10°35′N 66°52′W
54 G4 **La Guajira** off. Departamento de La Guajira, var. Guajira, La Goagira. ◈ province NE Colombia
188 I4 **Lagua Lichan, Punta** headland Saipan, S Northern Mariana Islands
105 P4 **Laguardia** Basq. Biasteri. País Vasco, N Spain 42°32′N 02°31′W
18 K14 **La Guardia** ✈ (New York) Long Island, New York, NE USA 40°44′N 73°51′W
La Guardia/Laguardia see A Guarda
La Gudiña see A Gudiña
103 O9 **la Guerche-sur-l'Aubois** Cher, C France 46°55′N 03°00′E
103 O13 **Laguiole** Aveyron, S France 44°42′N 02°51′E
83 F26 **L'Agulhas** var. Agulhas. Western Cape, SW South Africa 34°49′S 20°01′E
61 K14 **Laguna** Santa Catarina, S Brazil 28°29′S 48°45′W
37 Q11 **Laguna** New Mexico, SW USA 35°03′N 107°30′W
35 T16 **Laguna Beach** California, W USA 33°32′N 117°46′W
35 Y17 **Laguna Dam** dam Arizona/California, W USA
40 L7 **Laguna El Rey** Coahuila, N Mexico
35 V17 **Laguna Mountains** ▲▲ California, W USA
61 B17 **Laguna Paiva** Santa Fe, C Argentina 31°21′S 60°40′W
62 H3 **Lagunas** Tarapacá, N Chile 21°01′S 69°36′W
56 E9 **Lagunas** Loreto, N Peru 05°15′S 75°24′W
57 M20 **Lagunillas** Santa Cruz, SE Bolivia 19°38′S 63°39′W
54 H6 **Lagunillas** Mérida, NW Venezuela 08°31′N 71°24′W
44 C4 **La Habana** var. Havana. ● (Cuba) Ciudad de La Habana, W Cuba 23°07′N 82°25′W
169 W7 **Lahad Datu** Sabah, East Malaysia 05°01′N 118°20′E
169 W7 **Lahad Datu, Teluk** var. Telukan Lahad Datu, Teluk Darvel, Teluk Datu; prev. Darvel Bay. bay Sabah, East Malaysia, C Pacific Ocean
Lahad Datu, Telukan see Lahad Datu, Teluk
38 F10 **Lahaina** Maui, Hawaii, USA, C Pacific Ocean 20°52′N 156°40′W
168 L14 **Lahat** Sumatera, W Indonesia 03°46′S 103°32′E
La Haye see 's-Gravenhage
Lahej see Laḩij
62 G9 **La Higuera** Coquimbo, N Chile 29°33′S 71°15′W
141 S13 **Lahī, Ḩisā' al** spring/well NE Yemen 17°28′N 50°05′E
141 O16 **Laḩij** var. Laḩj, Eng. Lahej. SW Yemen 13°04′N 44°55′E
142 M3 **Lāhījān** Gīlān, NW Iran 37°12′N 50°00′E
119 I19 **Lahishyn** Pol. Lohiszyn, Rus. Logishin. Brestskaya Voblasts′, SW Belarus 52°20′N 25°59′E
Laḩj see Laḩij
101 F18 **Lahn** ≈ W Germany
Lähn see Wleń
95 J21 **Laholm** Halland, S Sweden 56°30′N 13°05′E
95 J21 **Laholmsbukten** bay S Sweden
35 R6 **Lahontan Reservoir** ▣ Nevada, W USA
149 W8 **Lahore** Punjab, NE Pakistan 31°36′N 74°18′E
149 W8 **Lahore** ✈ Punjab, E Pakistan 31°34′N 74°22′E
55 Q6 **La Horqueta** Delta Amacuro, NE Venezuela 09°13′N 62°02′W
119 K15 **Lahoysk** Rus. Logoysk. Minskaya Voblasts′, C Belarus 54°12′N 27°53′E
101 F22 **Lahr** Baden-Württemberg, S Germany 48°21′N 07°52′E
93 M19 **Lahti** Swe. Lahtis. Etelä-Suomi, S Finland 61°N 25°40′E
Lahtis see Lahti
40 M14 **La Huacana** Michoacán, SW Mexico 18°56′N 101°52′W
40 K14 **La Huerta** Jalisco, SW Mexico 19°29′N 104°40′W
78 H12 **Laï** prev. Behagle, De Behagle. Tandjilé, S Chad 09°22′N 16°14′E
Laibach see Ljubljana
160 K14 **Laibin** Guangxi Zhuangzu Zizhiqu, China 23°26′N 109°06′E
167 Q5 **Lai Châu** Lai Châu, N Vietnam 22°04′N 103°10′E
Laichow Bay see Laizhou Wan
38 D9 **Lā'ie** var. Laie. O'ahu, Hawaii, USA, C Pacific Ocean 21°39′N 157°55′W
Laie see Lā'ie
102 L5 **l'Aigle** Orne, N France 48°46′N 00°37′E
103 Q7 **Laignes** Côte d'Or, C France 47°51′N 04°24′E
93 K17 **Laihia** Länsi-Suomi, W Finland 62°58′N 22°00′E
Laila see Laylā
83 F25 **Laingsburg** Western Cape, SW South Africa 33°12′S 20°51′E
109 U2 **Lainsitz** Cz. Lužnice. ≈ Austria/Czech Republic
96 I7 **Lairg** N Scotland, United Kingdom 58°02′N 04°23′W
81 I17 **Laisamis** Eastern, N Kenya 01°35′N 37°49′E
Laisberg see Leisi
127 R4 **Laishevo** Respublika Tatarstan, W Russian Federation 55°26′N 49°27′E
Laisholm see Jõgeva
92 H13 **Laisvall** Norrbotten, N Sweden 66°07′N 17°10′E
93 K19 **Laitila** Länsi-Suomi, SW Finland 60°52′N 21°40′E
161 P5 **Laiwu** Shandong, E China 36°14′N 117°40′E
161 R4 **Laixi** var. Shuiji. Shandong, E China 36°50′N 120°40′E
161 R4 **Laiyang** Shandong, E China 36°58′N 120°40′E
161 O3 **Laiyuan** Hebei, E China 39°19′N 114°44′E
161 R4 **Laizhou** var. Ye Xian. Shandong, E China 37°12′N 120°01′E
161 Q4 **Laizhou Wan** var. Laichow Bay. bay E China
37 S8 **La Jara** Colorado, C USA 37°16′N 105°57′W
61 I15 **Lajeado** Rio Grande do Sul, S Brazil 29°28′S 52°00′W
112 L12 **Lajkovac** Serbia, C Serbia 44°22′N 20°12′E
111 K23 **Lajosmizse** Bács-Kiskun, C Hungary 47°02′N 19°31′E
Lajta see Leitha
40 I6 **La Junta** Chihuahua, N Mexico 28°30′N 107°20′W
37 V7 **La Junta** Colorado, C USA 37°59′N 103°34′W
92 J13 **Lakaträsk** Norrbotten, N Sweden 66°16′N 21°10′E
Lak Dera see Dheere Laaq
Lakeamu see Lakekamu
29 P12 **Lake Andes** South Dakota, N USA 43°08′N 98°33′W
22 H9 **Lake Arthur** Louisiana, S USA 30°04′N 92°40′W
187 Z15 **Lakeba** prev. Lakemba. island Lau Group, E Fiji
187 Z14 **Lakeba Passage** channel E Fiji
29 S10 **Lake Benton** Minnesota, N USA 44°15′N 96°17′W
23 V9 **Lake Butler** Florida, SE USA 30°01′N 82°20′W
183 P8 **Lake Cargelligo** New South Wales, SE Australia 33°21′S 146°25′E
22 G9 **Lake Charles** Louisiana, S USA 30°14′N 93°13′W
27 X9 **Lake City** Arkansas, C USA 35°50′N 90°28′W
37 Q7 **Lake City** Colorado, C USA 38°01′N 107°18′W
23 V9 **Lake City** Florida, SE USA 30°12′N 82°39′W
29 U13 **Lake City** Iowa, C USA 42°16′N 94°43′W
31 P7 **Lake City** Michigan, N USA 44°22′N 85°12′W
29 W9 **Lake City** Minnesota, N USA 44°27′N 92°16′W
21 T13 **Lake City** South Carolina, SE USA 33°52′N 79°45′W
29 Q7 **Lake City** South Dakota, N USA 45°42′N 97°22′W
20 M8 **Lake City** Tennessee, S USA 36°13′N 84°09′W
10 L17 **Lake Cowichan** Vancouver Island, British Columbia, SW Canada 48°50′N 124°04′W
29 U10 **Lake Crystal** Minnesota, N USA 44°07′N 94°13′W
25 T6 **Lake Dallas** Texas, SW USA 33°06′N 97°01′W
97 K15 **Lake District** physical region NW England, United Kingdom
18 D10 **Lake Erie Beach** New York, NE USA 42°37′N 79°04′W
29 T11 **Lakefield** Minnesota, N USA 43°40′N 95°10′W
25 V6 **Lake Fork Reservoir** ▣ Texas, SW USA
30 M9 **Lake Geneva** Wisconsin, N USA 42°36′N 88°25′W
18 L9 **Lake George** New York, NE USA 43°25′N 73°45′W
Lake Harbour see Kimmirut
36 I12 **Lake Havasu City** Arizona, SW USA 34°26′N 114°20′W
25 W12 **Lake Jackson** Texas, SW USA 29°01′N 95°25′W
186 D8 **Lakekamu** var. Lakeamu. ≈ S Papua New Guinea
180 K13 **Lake King** Western Australia 33°09′S 119°46′E
23 V12 **Lakeland** Florida, SE USA 28°03′N 81°57′W
23 U7 **Lakeland** Georgia, SE USA 31°02′N 83°04′W
181 W4 **Lakeland Downs** Queensland, NE Australia 15°54′S 144°54′E
11 P16 **Lake Louise** Alberta, SW Canada 51°26′N 116°10′W
Lakemba see Lakeba
29 V11 **Lake Mills** Iowa, C USA 43°25′N 93°31′W
39 Q10 **Lake Minchumina** Alaska, USA 63°55′N 152°25′W
Lakemti see Nek'emtē
186 A7 **Lake Murray** Western, SW Papua New Guinea 06°35′S 141°28′E
31 R9 **Lake Orion** Michigan, N USA 42°46′N 83°14′W
190 B16 **Lakepa** NE Niue 18°59′S 169°48′E
29 T11 **Lake Park** Iowa, C USA 43°27′N 95°19′W
18 K7 **Lake Placid** New York, NE USA 44°16′N 73°57′W
18 K9 **Lake Pleasant** New York, NE USA 43°27′N 74°24′W
34 M6 **Lakeport** California, W USA 39°04′N 122°56′W
29 Q10 **Lake Preston** South Dakota, N USA 44°21′N 97°22′W
22 J5 **Lake Providence** Louisiana, S USA 32°48′N 91°10′W
185 E20 **Lake Pukaki** Canterbury, South Island, New Zealand 44°12′S 170°10′E
183 Q12 **Lakes Entrance** Victoria, SE Australia 37°52′S 147°58′E
37 N12 **Lakeside** Arizona, SW USA 34°09′N 109°58′W
35 V17 **Lakeside** California, W USA 32°50′N 116°55′W
23 S9 **Lakeside** Florida, SE USA 30°22′N 84°18′W
28 K13 **Lakeside** Nebraska, C USA 42°01′N 102°27′W
32 E13 **Lakeside** Oregon, NW USA 43°34′N 124°10′W
21 W6 **Lakeside** Virginia, NE USA 37°36′N 77°28′W
Lakes State see El Buhayrat
Lake State see Michigan
185 F20 **Lake Tekapo** Canterbury, South Island, New Zealand 44°01′S 170°29′E
21 O10 **Lake Toxaway** North Carolina, SE USA 35°06′N 82°57′W
29 T13 **Lake View** Iowa, C USA 42°18′N 95°04′W
32 I16 **Lakeview** Oregon, NW USA 42°13′N 120°21′W
25 O3 **Lakeview** Texas, SW USA 34°38′N 100°36′W
27 W14 **Lake Village** Arkansas, C USA 33°20′N 91°19′W
23 W12 **Lake Wales** Florida, SE USA 27°54′N 81°35′W
37 T4 **Lakewood** Colorado, C USA 39°38′N 105°07′W
18 K15 **Lakewood** New Jersey, NE USA 40°04′N 74°11′W
18 C11 **Lakewood** New York, NE USA 42°03′N 79°19′W
31 T11 **Lakewood** Ohio, N USA 41°28′N 81°48′W
23 Y13 **Lakewood Park** Florida, SE USA 27°32′N 80°24′W
23 Z14 **Lake Worth** Florida, SE USA 26°37′N 80°03′W
124 H11 **Lakhdenpokh'ya** Respublika Kareliya, NW Russian Federation 61°25′N 30°05′E
152 L11 **Lakhīmpur** Uttar Pradesh, N India 27°57′N 80°47′E
154 J11 **Lakhnādon** Madhya Pradesh, C India 22°34′N 79°38′E
Lakhnau see Lucknow
154 A9 **Lakhpat** Gujarāt, W India 23°49′N 68°54′E
119 K19 **Lakhva** Brestskaya Voblasts′, SW Belarus 52°13′N 27°06′E
26 I6 **Lakin** Kansas, C USA 37°57′N 101°16′W
149 S7 **Lakki Marwat** North-West Frontier Province, NW Pakistan 32°35′N 70°58′E
115 F21 **Lakonía** historical region S Greece
115 F22 **Lakonikós Kólpos** gulf S Greece
76 M17 **Lakota** S Ivory Coast 05°50′N 05°40′W
29 U11 **Lakota** Iowa, C USA 43°22′N 94°04′W
29 P3 **Lakota** North Dakota, N USA 48°02′N 98°20′W
Lak Sao see Ban Lakxao
92 L8 **Laksefjorden** Lapp. Lágesvuotna. fjord N Norway
92 K8 **Lakselv** Lapp. Leavdnja. Finnmark, N Norway 70°02′N 24°57′E
155 B21 **Lakshadweep** prev. the Laccadive Minicoy and Amindivi Islands. ◈ union territory India, N Indian Ocean
155 C22 **Lakshadweep** Eng. Laccadive Islands. island group India, N Indian Ocean
153 S17 **Lakshmikāntapur** West Bengal, NE India 22°05′N 88°19′E
112 G11 **Laktaši** ◈ Republika Srpska, N Bosnia and Herzegovina
149 V7 **Lāla Mūsa** Punjab, NE Pakistan 32°41′N 74°01′E
la Laon see Laon
114 M11 **Lalapaşa** Edirne, NW Turkey 41°52′N 26°44′E
83 P14 **Lalaua** Nampula, N Mozambique 14°21′S 38°16′E
105 S9 **L'Alcora** var. Alcora. País Valenciano, E Spain 40°05′N 00°14′W
105 S10 **L'Alcúdia** var. L'Alcudia. País Valenciano, E Spain 39°10′N 00°30′W
80 J11 **Lalibela** Āmara, Ethiopia 12°01′N 39°05′E
42 E8 **La Libertad** La Libertad, SW El Salvador 13°28′N 89°20′W*
42 E3 **La Libertad** Petén, N Guatemala 16°49′N 90°08′W
42 H6 **La Libertad** Comayagua, SW Honduras 14°43′N 87°36′W
40 E4 **La Libertad** var. Puerto Libertad. Sonora, NW Mexico 29°52′N 112°39′W
42 K10 **La Libertad** Chontales, S Nicaragua 12°12′N 85°10′W
42 A9 **La Libertad** ◈ department SW El Salvador
56 B11 **La Libertad** off. Departamento de La Libertad. ◈ department W Peru
La Libertad, Departamento de see La Libertad
62 G11 **La Ligua** Valparaíso, C Chile 32°30′S 71°16′W
139 U5 **La'lī Khān** As Sulaymānīyah, E Iraq 34°58′N 45°36′E
104 H3 **Lalín** Galicia, NW Spain 42°40′N 08°06′W
102 L13 **Lalinde** Dordogne, SW France 44°52′N 00°42′E
104 K16 **La Línea** var. La Línea de la Concepción. Andalucía, S Spain 36°10′N 05°21′W
La Línea de la Concepción see La Línea
152 J14 **Lalitpur** Uttar Pradesh, N India 24°42′N 78°24′E
153 P11 **Lalitpur** Central, C Nepal 27°45′N 85°18′E
152 K10 **Lālkua** Uttarachal, N India 29°04′N 79°31′E
153 T12 **Lalmanirhat** Rājshāhi, N Bangladesh 25°51′N 89°34′E
11 R12 **La Loche** Saskatchewan, C Canada 56°31′N 109°27′W
102 M6 **la Loupe** Eure-et-Loir, C France 48°30′N 01°04′E
99 G20 **La Louvière** Hainaut, S Belgium 50°29′N 04°15′E
L'Altissima see Hochwilde
104 L14 **La Luisiana** Andalucía, S Spain 37°30′N 05°14′W
37 S14 **La Luz** New Mexico, SW USA 32°58′N 105°56′W
107 D16 **la Maddalena** Sardegna, Italy, C Mediterranean Sea 41°13′N 09°25′E
62 J7 **La Madrid** Tucumán, N Argentina 27°37′S 65°16′W
Lama-Kara see Kara
15 S8 **La Malbaie** Québec, SE Canada 47°39′N 70°11′W
167 T10 **Lamam** Xékong, S Laos 15°22′N 106°40′E
105 P10 **La Mancha** physical region C Spain
la Manche see English Channel
187 R13 **Lamap** Malekula, C Vanuatu 16°26′S 167°47′E
37 W6 **Lamar** Colorado, C USA 38°40′N 102°37′W
27 S7 **Lamar** Missouri, C USA 37°30′N 94°18′W
21 S12 **Lamar** South Carolina, SE USA 34°10′N 80°03′W
Lamard see Lāmerd
107 C19 **La Marmora, Punta** ▲ Sardegna, Italy, C Mediterranean Sea 39°58′N 09°20′E
8 I9 **La Martre, Lac** ◎ Northwest Territories, NW Canada
56 D10 **Lamas** San Martín, N Peru 06°28′S 76°31′W
42 J5 **La Masica** Atlántida, NW Honduras 15°38′N 87°08′W
103 R12 **Lamastre** Ardèche, E France 45°00′N 04°32′E
La Matepec see Santa Ana, Volcán de
44 I7 **La Maya** Santiago de Cuba, E Cuba 20°11′N 75°40′W
109 S5 **Lambach** Oberösterreich, N Austria 48°06′N 13°52′E
168 I11 **Lambak** Pulau Pini, W Indonesia 0°08′N 98°36′E
102 H5 **Lamballe** Côtes d'Armor, NW France 48°28′N 02°31′W
79 D18 **Lambaréné** Moyen-Ogooué, W Gabon 0°41′S 10°13′E
Lambasa see Labasa
56 B11 **Lambayeque** Lambayeque, W Peru 06°42′S 79°55′W
56 A10 **Lambayeque** off. Departamento de Lambayeque. ◈ department NW Peru
Lambayeque, Departamento de see Lambayeque
97 G17 **Lambay Island** Ir. Reachrainn. island E Ireland
186 G6 **Lambert, Cape** headland New Britain, E Papua New Guinea 04°15′S 151°31′E
195 W6 **Lambert Glacier** glacier Antarctica
29 T10 **Lamberton** Minnesota, N USA 44°14′N 95°15′W
27 X4 **Lambert-Saint Louis** ✈ Missouri, C USA 38°43′N 90°19′W
31 R11 **Lambertville** Michigan, N USA 41°46′N 83°37′W
18 J15 **Lambertville** New Jersey, NE USA 40°20′N 74°55′W
171 N12 **Lambogo** Sulawesi, N Indonesia 0°57′S 120°23′E
106 D8 **Lambro** ≈ N Italy
33 W11 **Lame Deer** Montana, NW USA 45°37′N 106°37′W
104 H6 **Lamego** Viseu, N Portugal 41°05′N 07°49′W
187 Q14 **Lamen Bay** Épi, C Vanuatu 16°36′S 168°10′E
45 X6 **Lamentin** Basse Terre, N Guadeloupe 16°16′N 61°38′W
Lamentin see le Lamentin
143 P14 **Lāmerd** var. Lamard. Fārs, S Iran 27°22′N 53°08′E
182 K10 **Lameroo** South Australia 35°22′S 140°30′E
54 F10 **La Mesa** Cundinamarca, C Colombia 04°37′N 74°30′W
35 U17 **La Mesa** California, W USA 32°44′N 117°00′W
37 R16 **La Mesa** New Mexico, SW USA 32°03′N 106°41′W
25 N6 **Lamesa** Texas, SW USA 32°43′N 101°57′W
107 N21 **Lamezia Terme** Calabria, SE Italy 38°54′N 16°13′E
115 F17 **Lamía** Stereá Ellás, C Greece 38°54′N 22°27′E
171 O8 **Lamitan** Basilan Island, SW Philippines 06°40′N 122°07′E
187 Y14 **Lamiti** Gau, C Fiji 18°00′S 179°20′E
171 T11 **Lamman** Papua, E Indonesia 0°03′S 130°46′E
188 B16 **Lamlam, Mount** ▲ SW Guam 13°20′N 144°40′E
109 Q6 **Lammer** ≈ E Austria
185 E23 **Lammerlaw Range** ▲▲ South Island, New Zealand
95 L20 **Lammhult** Kronoberg, S Sweden 57°09′N 14°35′E
93 L18 **Lammi** Etelä-Suomi, S Finland 61°06′N 25°00′E
189 U11 **Lamoil** island Chuuk, C Micronesia
35 W3 **Lamoille** Nevada, W USA 40°47′N 115°37′W
18 M7 **Lamoille River** ≈ Vermont, NE USA
30 J13 **La Moine River** ≈ Illinois, N USA
171 P4 **Lamon Bay** bay Luzon, N Philippines
29 V16 **Lamoni** Iowa, C USA 40°37′N 93°56′W
35 R13 **Lamont** California, W USA 35°15′N 118°54′W
27 N8 **Lamont** Oklahoma, C USA 36°41′N 97°33′W
54 E13 **La Montañita** var. Montañita. Caquetá, S Colombia 01°22′N 75°25′W
43 N8 **La Mosquitia** var. Miskito Coast, Eng. Mosquito Coast. coastal region E Nicaragua
102 I9 **la Mothe-Achard** Vendée, NW France 46°37′N 01°37′W
188 L15 **Lamotrek Atoll** atoll Caroline Islands, C Micronesia
29 P6 **La Moure** North Dakota, N USA 46°21′N 98°17′W
167 O8 **Lampang** var. Muang Lampang. Lampang, NW Thailand 18°16′N 99°30′E
167 R9 **Lam Pao Reservoir** ▣ E Thailand
25 S9 **Lampasas** Texas, SW USA 31°04′N 98°12′W
25 S9 **Lampasas River** ≈ Texas, SW USA
41 N7 **Lampazos** var. Lampazos de Naranjo. Nuevo León, NE Mexico 27°00′N 100°28′W
Lampazos de Naranjo see Lampazos
115 E19 **Lámpeia** Dytikí Ellás, S Greece 37°51′N 21°48′E
101 G19 **Lampertheim** Hessen, W Germany 49°36′N 08°28′E
97 I20 **Lampeter** SW Wales, United Kingdom 52°08′N 04°04′W
167 O7 **Lamphun** var. Lampun, Muang Lamphun. Lamphun, NW Thailand 18°36′N 99°02′E
11 X10 **Lamprey** Manitoba, C Canada 58°18′N 94°06′W
Lampun see Lamphun
168 M15 **Lampung** off. Propinsi Lampung. ◈ province SW Indonesia
Lampung, Propinsi see Lampung
126 K6 **Lamskoye** Lipetskaya Oblast′, W Russian Federation 52°57′N 38°04′E
81 K20 **Lamu** Coast, SE Kenya 02°17′S 40°54′E
43 N14 **La Muerte, Cerro** ▲ C Costa Rica 09°33′N 83°47′W
103 S13 **la Mure** Isère, E France 44°54′N 05°48′E
37 S10 **Lamy** New Mexico, SW USA 35°27′N 105°52′W
119 J18 **Lan′** Rus. Lan′. ≈ C Belarus
38 E10 **Lāna'i** var. Lanai. island Hawai'i, USA, C Pacific Ocean
38 E10 **Lāna'i City** var. Lanai City. Lanai, Hawaii, USA, C Pacific Ocean 20°49′N 156°55′W
Lanai City see Lāna'i City
99 L18 **Lanaken** Limburg, NE Belgium 50°53′N 05°39′E
171 Q7 **Lanao, Lake** var. Lake Sultan Alonto. ◎ Mindanao, S Philippines
96 J12 **Lanark** S Scotland, United Kingdom 55°38′N 04°25′W
96 I13 **Lanark** cultural region C Scotland, United Kingdom
104 L9 **La Nava de Ricomalillo** Castilla-La Mancha, C Spain 39°40′N 04°59′W
166 M13 **Lanbi Kyun** prev. Sullivan Island. island Mergui Archipelago, S Burma (Myanmar)
Lancang Jiang see Mekong
97 K17 **Lancashire** cultural region N England, United Kingdom
15 N13 **Lancaster** Ontario, SE Canada 45°10′N 74°31′W
97 K16 **Lancaster** NW England, United Kingdom 54°03′N 02°48′W
35 T14 **Lancaster** California, W USA 34°42′N 118°08′W
20 M6 **Lancaster** Kentucky, S USA 37°35′N 84°34′W
27 U1 **Lancaster** Missouri, C USA 40°32′N 92°31′W
19 O7 **Lancaster** New Hampshire, NE USA 44°29′N 71°34′W
18 D10 **Lancaster** New York, NE USA 42°54′N 78°40′W
31 T14 **Lancaster** Ohio, N USA 39°42′N 82°36′W
18 H16 **Lancaster** Pennsylvania, NE USA 40°03′N 76°18′W
21 R11 **Lancaster** South Carolina, SE USA 34°43′N 80°47′W
25 U7 **Lancaster** Texas, SW USA 32°35′N 96°45′W
21 X5 **Lancaster** Virginia, NE USA 37°48′N 76°30′W
30 J9 **Lancaster** Wisconsin, N USA 42°52′N 90°43′W
197 N10 **Lancaster Sound** sound Nunavut, N Canada
Lan-chou/Lan-chow/Lanchow see Lanzhou
107 K14 **Lanciano** Abruzzo, C Italy 42°13′N 14°23′E
111 O16 **Łańcut** Podkarpackie, SE Poland 50°04′N 22°14′E
169 Q11 **Landak, Sungai** ≈ Borneo, N Indonesia
Landao see Lantau Island
Landau see Landau an der Isar
Landau see Landau in der Pfalz
101 N22 **Landau an der Isar** var. Landau. Bayern, SE Germany 48°40′N 12°41′E
101 F20 **Landau in der Pfalz** var. Landau. Rheinland-Pfalz, SW Germany 49°12′N 08°07′E
Land Burgenland see Burgenland
108 K8 **Landeck** Tirol, W Austria 47°09′N 10°35′E
99 J19 **Landen** Vlaams Brabant, C Belgium 50°45′N 05°05′E

◆ Country ● Country Capital ◇ Dependent Territory ○ Dependent Territory Capital ◈ Administrative Regions ✈ International Airport ▲ Mountain ▲▲ Mountain Range ⛰ Volcano ≈ River ◎ Lake ▣ Reservoir

LANDER – LA VALL D'UIXÓ

33 U15 Lander Wyoming, C USA 42°49′N 108°43′W
102 F5 Landerneau Finistère, NW France 48°27′N 04°16′W
95 K20 Landeryd Halland, S Sweden 57°04′N 13°15′E
102 J15 Landes ◈ department SW France
Landeshut/Landeshut in Schlesien see Kamienna Góra
105 R9 Landete Castilla-La Mancha, C Spain 39°54′N 01°22′W
99 M18 Landgraaf Limburg, SE Netherlands 50°55′N 06°04′E
102 F5 Landivisiau Finistère, NW France 48°31′N 04°03′W
Land Kärten see Kärnten
Land of Enchantment see New Mexico
The Land of Opportunity see Arkansas
Land of Steady Habits see Connecticut
Land of the Midnight Sun see Alaska
108 I8 Landquart Graubünden, SE Switzerland 46°58′N 09°35′E
108 J9 Landquart ≈ Austria/Switzerland
21 P10 Landrum South Carolina, SE USA 35°10′N 82°11′W
Landsberg see Gorzów Wielkopolski, Lubuskie, Poland
Landsberg see Górowo Iławeckie, Warmińsko-Mazurskie, NE Poland
101 K23 Landsberg am Lech Bayern, S Germany 48°03′N 10°52′E
Landsberg an der Warthe see Gorzów Wielkopolski
97 G25 Land's End headland SW England, United Kingdom 50°02′N 05°41′W
101 M22 Landshut Bayern, SE Germany 48°32′N 12°09′E
Landskron see Lanškroun
95 J22 Landskrona Skåne, S Sweden 55°52′N 12°52′E
98 I10 Landsmeer Noord-Holland, C Netherlands 52°26′N 04°55′E
95 J19 Landvetter ✈ (Göteborg) Västra Götaland, S Sweden 57°39′N 12°22′E
Landwarów see Lentvaris
23 R5 Lanett Alabama, S USA 32°52′N 85°11′W
108 C8 La Neuveville var. Neuveville, Ger. Neuenstadt. Neuchâtel, W Switzerland 47°05′N 07°03′E
95 G21 Langå var. Langaa. Århus, C Denmark 56°23′N 09°55′E
Langaa see Langå
158 G14 La'nga Co ◎ W China
Langada see Lagkáda
Langades/Langadhás see Lagkadás
Langádhia/ see Lagkádia
147 T14 Langar Rus. Lyangar. SE Tajikistan 37°04′N 72°39′E
146 M10 Langar Rus. Lyangar. Navoiy Viloyati, C Uzbekistan 40°27′N 65°54′E
142 M3 Langarūd Gīlān, NW Iran 37°10′N 50°09′E
11 V16 Langbank Saskatchewan, S Canada 50°01′N 102°16′W
29 P2 Langdon North Dakota, N USA 48°45′N 98°22′W
103 P12 Langeac Haute-Loire, C France 45°06′N 03°31′E
102 L8 Langeais Indre-et-Loire, C France 47°22′N 00°27′E
80 I8 Langeb, Wadi ≈ NE Sudan
Långed see Dals Långed
95 G25 Langeland island S Denmark
99 B18 Langemark West-Vlaanderen, W Belgium 50°55′N 02°55′E
101 G18 Langen Hessen, W Germany 49°58′N 08°40′E
101 J22 Langenau Baden-Württemberg, S Germany 48°30′N 10°08′E
11 V16 Langenburg Saskatchewan, S Canada 50°50′N 101°43′W
108 L8 Längenfeld Tirol, W Austria 47°04′N 10°59′E
101 E16 Langenfeld Nordrhein-Westfalen, W Germany 51°06′N 06°57′E
100 I12 Langenhagen Niedersachsen, N Germany 52°26′N 09°45′E
100 I12 Langenhagen ✈ (Hannover) Niedersachsen, NW Germany 52°28′N 09°40′E
109 W3 Langenlois Niederösterreich, NE Austria 48°29′N 15°42′E
108 E7 Langenthal Bern, NW Switzerland 47°13′N 07°48′E
109 W6 Langenwang Steiermark, E Austria 47°34′N 15°39′E
109 X3 Langenzersdorf Niederösterreich, E Austria 48°20′N 16°22′E
100 F9 Langeoog island NW Germany
95 H23 Langeskov Fyn, C Denmark 55°22′N 10°36′E
95 G16 Langesund Telemark, S Norway 59°00′N 09°43′E
95 G17 Langesundsfjorden fjord S Norway
94 D10 Langevågen Møre og Romsdal, S Norway 62°26′N 06°15′E
161 P3 Langfang Hebei, E China 39°30′N 116°39′E
94 E9 Langfjorden fjord S Norway
29 Q8 Langford South Dakota, N USA 45°36′N 97°48′W
168 I10 Langgapayung Sumatera, W Indonesia 01°42′N 99°57′E
106 E9 Langhirano Emilia-Romagna, C Italy 44°37′N 10°16′E
97 K14 Langholm S Scotland, United Kingdom 55°14′N 03°11′W
92 I3 Langjökull glacier C Iceland
168 I6 Langkawi, Pulau island Peninsular Malaysia
166 M14 Langkha Tuk, Khao ▲ SW Thailand 09°19′N 98°39′E
14 L8 Langlade Québec, SE Canada 48°13′N 75°58′W
10 M17 Langley British Columbia, SW Canada 49°07′N 122°39′W
167 S7 Lang Mô Thanh Hoa, N Vietnam 19°36′N 105°30′E
Langnau see Langnau im Emmental
108 E8 Langnau im Emmental var. Langnau. Bern, W Switzerland 46°57′N 07°47′E
103 Q13 Langogne Lozère, S France 44°40′N 03°52′E
102 K13 Langon Gironde, SW France 44°33′N 00°14′W
La Ngounié see Ngounié
92 G10 Langøya island C Norway
158 G14 Langqên Zangbo ≈ China/India
104 K2 Langreo var. Sama de Langreo. Asturias, N Spain 43°18′N 05°40′W
103 S7 Langres Haute-Marne, N France 47°53′N 05°20′E
103 R8 Langres, Plateau de plateau C France
168 H8 Langsa Sumatera, W Indonesia 04°30′N 97°53′E
93 H16 Långsele Västernorrland, C Sweden 63°11′N 17°05′E
162 L12 Lang Shan ▲▲ N China
95 M14 Långshyttan Dalarna, C Sweden 60°26′N 16°02′E
167 T5 Lang Sơn var. Langson. Lang Sơn, N Vietnam 21°50′N 106°45′E
Langson see Lang Sơn
167 N14 Lang Suan Chumphon, SW Thailand 09°55′N 99°07′E
93 J14 Långträsk Norrbotten, N Sweden 65°22′N 20°19′E
25 N11 Langtry Texas, SW USA 29°46′N 101°25′W
103 P16 Languedoc cultural region S France
103 P15 Languedoc-Roussillon ◈ region S France
27 X10 L'Anguille River ≈ Arkansas, C USA
93 I16 Långviksmon Västernorrland, N Sweden 63°39′N 18°45′E
101 K22 Langweid Bayern, S Germany 48°29′N 10°50′E
160 J8 Langzhong Sichuan, C China 31°46′N 105°55′E
Lan Hsü see Lan Yü
11 U15 Lanigan Saskatchewan, S Canada 51°50′N 105°01′W
116 K5 Lanivtsi Ternopil's'ka Oblast', W Ukraine 49°52′N 26°05′E
137 Y13 Länkäran Rus. Lenkoran'. S Azerbaijan 38°46′N 48°51′E
102 L16 Lannemezan Hautes-Pyrénées, S France 43°08′N 00°22′E
102 G5 Lannion Côtes d'Armor, NW France 48°44′N 03°27′W
14 M11 L'Annonciation Québec, SE Canada 46°22′N 74°51′W
105 V5 L'Anoia ≈ NE Spain
18 I15 Lansdale Pennsylvania, NE USA 40°14′N 75°13′W
14 L14 Lansdowne Ontario, SE Canada 44°25′N 76°00′W
152 K9 Lansdowne Uttarakhand, N India 29°50′N 78°42′E
30 M3 L'Anse Michigan, N USA 46°45′N 88°27′W
15 S7 L'Anse-St-Jean Québec, SE Canada 48°14′N 70°13′W
29 Y11 Lansing Iowa, C USA 43°22′N 91°11′W
27 R4 Lansing Kansas, C USA 39°15′N 94°54′W
31 Q9 Lansing state capital Michigan, N USA 42°44′N 84°33′W
93 K18 Länsi-Suomi ◈ province W Finland
92 J12 Lansjärv Norrbotten, N Sweden 66°39′N 22°10′E
111 G17 Lanškroun Ger. Landskron. Pardubický Kraj, E Czech Republic 49°55′N 16°38′E
167 N16 Lanta, Ko island S Thailand
161 O15 Lantau Island Cant. Tai Yue Shan, Chin. Landao. island Hong Kong, S China
Lantian see Lianyuan
Lan-ts'ang Chiang see Mekong
Lantung, Gulf of see Liaodong Wan
171 O11 Lanu Sulawesi, N Indonesia 01°00′N 121°33′E
107 D19 Lanusei Sardegna, Italy, C Mediterranean Sea 39°55′N 09°31′E
102 H7 Lanvaux, Landes de physical region NW France
163 W8 Lanxi Heilongjiang, NE China 46°18′N 126°15′E
161 R10 Lanxi Zhejiang, SE China 29°12′N 119°27′E
La Nyanga see Nyanga
161 T15 Lan Yü var. Huoshao Tao, Hungt'ou, Lan Hsü, Lanyü, Eng. Orchid Island; prev. Kotosho, Koto Sho. island SE Taiwan
Lanyü see Lan Yü
64 P11 Lanzarote island Islas Canarias, Spain, NE Atlantic Ocean
159 V10 Lanzhou var. Lan-chou, Lanchow, Lan-chow; prev. Kaolan. province capital Gansu, C China 36°01′N 103°52′E
106 B8 Lanzo Torinese Piemonte, NE Italy 45°18′N 07°26′E
171 O11 Laoag Luzon, N Philippines 18°11′N 120°34′E
171 Q5 Laoang Samar, C Philippines 12°29′N 125°01′E
167 R5 Lao Cai Lao Cai, N Vietnam 22°29′N 104°00′E
Laodicea/Laodicea ad Mare see Al Lādhiqīyah
Laoet see Laut, Pulau
163 T11 Laoha He ≈ NE China
160 M8 Laohekou var. Guanghua. Hubei, C China 32°20′N 111°42′E
Laoi, An see Lee
97 E19 Laois prev. Leix, Queen's County. cultural region C Ireland
159 R8 Laojunmiao prev. Yumen. Gansu, N China 39°49′N 97°47′E
163 W12 Lao Ling ▲▲ N China
64 Q11 La Oliva var. Oliva. Fuerteventura, Islas Canarias, Spain, NE Atlantic Ocean 28°36′N 13°53′W
Lao, Loch see Belfast Lough
Laolong see Longchuan
Lao Mangnai see Mangnai
103 P3 Laon var. la Laon; anc. Laudunum. Aisne, N France 49°34′N 03°37′E
Lao People's Democratic Republic see Laos
54 M3 La Orchila, Isla island N Venezuela
64 O11 La Orotava Tenerife, Islas Canarias, Spain, NE Atlantic Ocean 28°23′N 16°32′W
57 E14 La Oroya Junín, C Peru 11°36′S 75°54′W
167 Q7 Laos off. Lao People's Democratic Republic. ◆ republic SE Asia
161 R5 Laoshan Wan bay E China
163 Y10 Laoye Ling ▲▲ NE China
60 J12 Lapa Paraná, S Brazil 25°46′S 49°44′W
103 P10 Lapalisse Allier, C France 46°13′N 03°39′E
54 F9 La Palma Cundinamarca, C Colombia 05°23′N 74°24′W
42 F7 La Palma Chalatenango, N El Salvador 14°19′N 89°10′W
43 W16 La Palma Darién, SE Panama 08°24′N 78°09′W
64 N11 La Palma island Islas Canarias, Spain, NE Atlantic Ocean
104 J14 La Palma del Condado Andalucía, S Spain 37°23′N 06°33′W
61 F18 La Paloma Durazno, C Uruguay 32°54′S 55°36′W
61 G20 La Paloma Rocha, E Uruguay 34°37′S 54°08′W
61 A21 La Pampa off. Provincia de La Pampa. ◈ province C Argentina
La Pampa, Provincia de see La Pampa
55 P8 La Paragua Bolívar, E Venezuela 06°53′N 63°16′W
119 O16 Lapatsichy Rus. Lopatichi. Mahilyowskaya Voblasts', E Belarus 53°34′N 30°53′E
61 C16 La Paz Entre Ríos, E Argentina 30°45′S 59°36′W
62 I11 La Paz Mendoza, C Argentina 33°30′S 67°36′W
57 J18 La Paz var. La Paz de Ayacucho. ● (Bolivia-legislative and administrative capital) La Paz, W Bolivia 16°30′S 68°13′W
42 H6 La Paz La Paz, SW Honduras 14°20′N 87°40′W
40 F9 La Paz Baja California Sur, NW Mexico 24°07′N 110°18′W
61 F20 La Paz Canelones, S Uruguay 34°46′S 56°13′W
57 J16 La Paz ◈ department W Bolivia
42 B9 La Paz ◈ department S El Salvador
42 G7 La Paz ◈ department SW Honduras
La Paz see El Alto, Bolivia
La Paz see Robles, Colombia
La Paz see La Paz Centro
40 F9 La Paz, Bahía de bay NW Mexico
42 I10 La Paz Centro var. La Paz. León, W Nicaragua 12°20′N 86°41′W
La Paz de Ayacucho see La Paz
54 J15 La Pedrera Amazonas, SE Colombia 01°19′S 69°31′W
31 S9 Lapeer Michigan, N USA 43°03′N 83°19′W
40 K6 La Perla Chihuahua, N Mexico 28°18′N 104°34′W
165 T1 La Pérouse Strait Jap. Sōya-kaikyō, Rus. Proliv Laperuza. strait Japan/Russian Federation
63 I14 La Perra, Salitral de salt lake C Argentina
Laperuza, Proliv see La Perouse Strait
41 Q10 La Pesca Tamaulipas, C Mexico 23°49′N 97°45′W
40 M13 La Piedad Cavadas Michoacán, C Mexico 20°20′N 102°01′W
Lapines see Lafnitz
93 M16 Lapinlahti Itä-Suomi, C Finland 63°21′N 27°25′E
Lápithos see Lapta
22 K9 Laplace Louisiana, S USA 30°04′N 90°28′W
45 X12 La Plaine SE Dominica 15°20′N 61°15′W
173 P16 La Plaine-des-Palmistes C Réunion
92 K11 Lapland Fin. Lappi, Swe. Lappland. cultural region N Europe
28 M8 La Plant South Dakota, N USA 45°06′N 100°40′W
61 D20 La Plata Buenos Aires, E Argentina 34°56′S 57°55′W
54 D12 La Plata Huila, SW Colombia 02°33′N 75°55′W
21 W4 La Plata Maryland, NE USA 38°32′N 76°59′W
La Plata see Sucre
45 U6 la Plata, Río de ≈ C Puerto Rico
105 W4 La Pobla de Lillet Cataluña, NE Spain 42°15′N 01°57′E
105 U4 La Pobla de Segur Cataluña, NE Spain 42°15′N 00°58′E
15 S9 La Pocatière Québec, SE Canada 47°21′N 70°04′W
104 L3 La Pola de Gordón Castilla-León, N Spain 42°50′N 05°38′W
31 O11 La Porte Indiana, N USA 41°36′N 86°43′W
18 H13 Laporte Pennsylvania, NE USA 41°25′N 76°29′W
29 X13 La Porte City Iowa, C USA 42°19′N 92°11′W
62 J8 La Posta Catamarca, C Argentina 27°59′S 65°32′W
40 E8 La Poza Grande Baja California Sur, NW Mexico 25°50′N 112°00′W
93 K16 Lappajärvi Länsi-Suomi, W Finland 63°13′N 23°40′E
93 L16 Lappajärvi ◎ W Finland
93 N18 Lappeenranta Swe. Villmanstrand. Etelä-Suomi, SE Finland 61°04′N 28°15′E
93 J17 Lappfjärd Fin. Lapväärtti. Länsi-Suomi, W Finland 62°14′N 21°30′E
92 L12 Lappi Swe. Lappland. ◈ province N Finland
Lappi/Lappland see Lapland
Lappo see Lapua
61 C23 Laprida Buenos Aires, E Argentina 37°34′S 60°45′W
25 P13 La Pryor Texas, SW USA 28°56′N 99°51′W
136 B11 Lâpseki Çanakkale, NW Turkey 40°22′N 26°42′E
121 P2 Lapta Gk. Lápithos. NW Cyprus 35°20′N 33°11′E
Laptev Sea see Laptevykh, More
122 N6 Laptevykh, More Eng. Laptev Sea. sea Arctic Ocean
93 K16 Lapua Swe. Lappo. Länsi-Suomi, W Finland 62°57′N 23°00′E
105 P3 La Puebla de Arganzón País Vasco, N Spain 42°45′N 02°49′W
104 L14 La Puebla de Cazalla Andalucía, S Spain 37°14′N 05°18′W
104 M9 La Puebla de Montalbán Castilla-La Mancha, C Spain 39°52′N 04°22′W
54 I6 La Puerta Trujillo, NW Venezuela 09°08′N 70°46′W
Lapurdum see Bayonne
40 E7 La Purísima Baja California Sur, NW Mexico 26°10′N 112°05′W
Lapväärtti see Lappfjärd
110 O10 Łapy Podlaskie, NE Poland 53°N 22°54′E
80 D6 Laqiya Arba'in Northern, NW Sudan 20°01′N 28°01′E
62 J4 La Quiaca Jujuy, N Argentina 22°12′S 65°36′W
107 J14 L'Aquila var. Aquila, Aquila degli Abruzzi. Abruzzo, C Italy 42°21′N 13°24′E
143 Q13 Lār Fārs, S Iran 27°42′N 54°19′E
54 J5 Lara off. Estado Lara. ◈ state NW Venezuela
104 G2 Laracha Galicia, NW Spain 43°14′N 08°34′W
74 G5 Larache var. al Araïch, El Araïch, prev. El Araïche; anc. Lixus. NW Morocco 35°12′N 06°10′W
Lara, Estado see Lara
103 T14 Laragne-Montéglin Hautes-Alpes, SE France 44°21′N 05°46′E
104 M13 La Rambla Andalucía, S Spain 37°37′N 04°44′W
33 Y17 Laramie Wyoming, C USA 41°18′N 105°35′W
33 X15 Laramie Mountains ▲▲ Wyoming, C USA
33 Y16 Laramie River ≈ Wyoming, C USA
Larang see Zhongdian
60 H12 Laranjeiras do Sul Paraná, S Brazil 25°23′S 52°23′W
Larantoeka see Larantuka
171 P16 Larantuka prev. Larantoeka. Flores, C Indonesia 08°20′S 123°00′E
171 U15 Larat Pulau Larat, E Indonesia 07°07′S 131°46′E
171 U15 Larat, Pulau island Kepulauan Tanimbar, E Indonesia
95 P19 Lärbro Gotland, SE Sweden 57°46′N 18°49′E
106 A9 Larche, Col de pass France/Italy
14 H8 Larder Lake Ontario, S Canada 48°06′N 79°44′W
105 O2 Laredo Cantabria, N Spain 43°23′N 03°22′W
25 Q15 Laredo Texas, SW USA 27°30′N 99°30′W
40 H9 La Reforma Sinaloa, W Mexico 25°05′N 108°03′W
98 N11 Laren Gelderland, E Netherlands 52°12′N 06°22′E
98 J11 Laren Noord-Holland, C Netherlands 52°15′N 05°13′E
102 K13 La Réole Gironde, SW France 44°34′N 00°00′W
La Réunion see Réunion
Largeau see Faya
103 U13 l'Argentière-la-Bessée Hautes-Alpes, SE France 44°49′N 06°34′E
149 O4 Lar Gerd var. Largird. Balkh, N Afghanistan 35°36′N 66°48′E
Largird see Lar Gerd
23 V12 Largo Florida, SE USA 27°55′N 82°47′W
37 Q9 Largo, Canon valley New Mexico, SW USA
44 D6 Largo, Cayo island W Cuba
23 Z17 Largo, Key island Florida Keys, Florida, SE USA
96 H12 Largs W Scotland, United Kingdom 55°48′N 04°50′W
102 I16 la Rhune var. Larrún. ▲ France/Spain 43°19′N 01°36′W see also Larrún
la Rhune see Larrún
la Riege see Ariège
29 Q4 Larimore North Dakota, N USA 47°54′N 97°37′W
107 L15 Larino Molise, C Italy 41°46′N 14°50′E
Lario see Como, Lago di
62 J9 La Rioja La Rioja, NW Argentina 29°26′S 66°50′W
62 I9 La Rioja off. Provincia de La Rioja. ◈ province NW Argentina
105 O4 La Rioja ◈ autonomous community N Spain
La Rioja, Provincia de see La Rioja
115 F16 Lárisa var. Larissa. Thessalía, C Greece 39°38′N 22°27′E
Larissa see Lárisa
149 Q13 Lārkāna var. Larkhana. Sind, SE Pakistan 27°32′N 68°18′E
Larkhana see Lārkāna
Larnaca see Lárnaka
121 Q3 Lárnaka var. Larnaca, Larnax. SE Cyprus 34°55′N 33°39′E
121 Q3 Lárnaka ✈ SE Cyprus 34°52′N 33°38′E
Larnax see Lárnaka
97 G14 Larne Ir. Latharna. E Northern Ireland, United Kingdom 54°51′N 05°49′W
26 L5 Larned Kansas, C USA 38°12′N 99°05′W
104 L3 La Robla Castilla-León, N Spain 42°48′N 05°37′W
104 J10 La Roca de la Sierra Extremadura, W Spain 39°06′N 06°41′W
99 K22 La Roche-en-Ardenne Luxembourg, SE Belgium 50°11′N 05°35′E
102 L11 la Rochefoucauld Charente, W France 45°43′N 00°23′E
102 J10 la Rochelle anc. Rupella. Charente-Maritime, W France 46°09′N 01°07′W
102 I9 la Roche-sur-Yon prev. Bourbon Vendée, Napoléon-Vendée. Vendée, NW France 46°40′N 01°26′W
105 Q10 La Roda Castilla-La Mancha, C Spain 39°13′N 02°10′W
104 L14 La Roda de Andalucía Andalucía, S Spain 37°12′N 04°45′W
45 P9 La Romana E Dominican Republic 18°25′N 69°00′W
11 T13 La Ronge Saskatchewan, C Canada 55°07′N 105°18′W
11 U13 La Ronge, Lac ◎ Saskatchewan, C Canada
22 K10 Larose Louisiana, S USA 29°34′N 90°22′W
42 M7 La Rosita Región Autónoma Atlántico Norte, NE Nicaragua 13°55′N 84°23′W
181 Q3 Larrimah Northern Territory, N Australia 15°30′S 133°12′E
62 N11 Larroque Entre Ríos, E Argentina 33°05′S 59°06′W
105 Q2 Larrún Fr. la Rhune. ▲ France/Spain 43°18′N 01°35′W see also la Rhune
Larrún see la Rhune
195 X6 Lars Christensen Coast physical region Antarctica
39 Q14 Larsen Bay Kodiak Island, Alaska, USA 57°32′N 153°58′W
194 I5 Larsen Ice Shelf ice shelf Antarctica
8 M6 Larsen Sound sound Nunavut, N Canada
La Rúa see A Rúa de Valdeorras
102 K16 Laruns Pyrénées-Atlantiques, SW France 43°00′N 00°25′W
95 G16 Larvik Vestfold, S Norway 59°04′N 10°02′E
La-sa see Lhasa
171 S13 Lasahata Pulau Seram, E Indonesia 02°52′S 128°27′E
Lasahau see Lasihao
37 O6 La Sal Utah, W USA 38°19′N 109°14′W
14 C17 La Salle Ontario, S Canada 42°13′N 83°05′W
30 L11 La Salle Illinois, N USA 41°19′N 89°06′W
45 O9 Las Americas ✈ (Santo Domingo) S Dominican Republic 18°24′N 69°38′W
37 V6 Las Animas Colorado, C USA 38°04′N 103°13′W
108 D10 La Sarine var. Sarine. ≈ SW Switzerland
108 B9 La Sarraz Vaud, W Switzerland 46°40′N 06°32′E
12 H12 La Sarre Québec, SE Canada 48°49′N 79°12′W
54 L3 Las Aves, Islas var. Islas de Aves. island group N Venezuela
55 N7 Las Bonitas Bolívar, C Venezuela 07°50′N 65°40′W
104 K15 Las Cabezas de San Juan Andalucía, S Spain 36°59′N 05°56′W
61 G19 Lascano Rocha, E Uruguay 33°40′S 54°12′W
62 I5 Lascar, Volcán △ N Chile 23°22′S 67°33′W
41 T15 Las Choapas var. Choapas. Veracruz-Llave, SE Mexico 17°51′N 94°00′W
37 R15 Las Cruces New Mexico, SW USA 32°19′N 106°49′W
Lasdehnen see Krasnoznamensk
105 V4 La See d'Urgel var. La Seu d'Urgell, Seo de Urgel. Cataluña, NE Spain 42°22′N 01°27′E
La Selle see Selle, Pic de la
62 G9 La Serena Coquimbo, C Chile 29°54′S 71°18′W
104 K11 La Serena physical region W Spain
La Seu d'Urgell see La See d'Urgel
103 T16 la Seyne-sur-Mer Var, SE France 43°07′N 05°53′E
61 D21 Las Flores Buenos Aires, E Argentina 36°03′S 59°08′W
62 H9 Las Flores San Juan, W Argentina 30°14′S 69°10′W
11 S14 Lashburn Saskatchewan, S Canada 53°09′N 109°37′W
62 J10 Las Heras Mendoza, W Argentina 32°48′S 68°50′W
148 M8 Lashkar Gāh var. Lash-Kar-Gar'. Helmand, S Afghanistan 31°35′N 64°21′E
Lash-Kar-Gar' see Lashkar Gāh
171 P14 Lasihao var. Lasahau. Pulau Muna, C Indonesia 05°01′S 122°23′E
107 N21 La Sila ▲▲ SW Italy
63 H23 La Silueta, Cerro ▲ S Chile 52°22′S 72°09′W
42 L9 La Sirena Región Autónoma Atlántico Sur, E Nicaragua 12°59′N 84°35′W
110 J13 Łask Łódzkie, C Poland 51°36′N 19°06′E
109 V11 Laško Ger. Tüffer. C Slovenia 46°08′N 15°13′E
63 H14 Las Lajas Neuquén, W Argentina 38°31′S 70°22′W
63 H15 Las Lajas, Cerro ▲ W Argentina 38°49′S 70°42′W
62 M6 Las Lomitas Formosa, N Argentina 24°45′S 60°35′W
41 V16 Las Margaritas Chiapas, SE Mexico 16°15′N 91°58′W
Las Marismas see Guadalquivir, Marismas del
54 M6 Las Mercedes Guárico, N Venezuela 09°08′N 66°27′W
42 F6 Las Minas, Cerro ▲ W Honduras 14°33′N 88°41′W
105 O11 La Solana Castilla-La Mancha, C Spain 38°56′N 03°14′W
45 Q14 La Soufrière △ Saint Vincent, Saint Vincent and the Grenadines 13°20′N 61°11′W
102 M10 la Souterraine Creuse, C France 46°15′N 01°28′E
62 N7 Las Palmas Chaco, N Argentina 27°08′S 58°45′W
43 Q16 Las Palmas Veraguas, W Panama 08°09′N 81°28′W
64 P12 Las Palmas var. Las Palmas de Gran Canaria. Gran Canaria, Islas Canarias, Spain, NE Atlantic Ocean 28°08′N 15°27′W
64 P12 Las Palmas ◈ province Islas Canarias, Spain, NE Atlantic Ocean
64 Q12 Las Palmas ✈ Gran Canaria, Islas Canarias, Spain, NE Atlantic Ocean
Las Palmas de Gran Canaria see Las Palmas
40 D6 Las Palomas Baja California Norte, W Mexico 31°44′N 107°37′W
105 P10 Las Pedroñeras Castilla-La Mancha, C Spain 39°27′N 02°41′W
106 E10 La Spezia Liguria, NW Italy 44°08′N 09°50′E
61 F20 Las Piedras Canelones, S Uruguay 34°42′S 56°14′W
63 J18 Las Plumas Chubut, S Argentina 43°46′S 67°15′W
61 B18 Las Rosas Santa Fe, C Argentina 32°27′S 61°30′W
Lassa see Lhasa
35 O4 Lassen Peak ▲ California, W USA 40°27′N 121°28′W
194 K6 Lassiter Coast physical region Antarctica
109 V9 Lassnitz ≈ SE Austria
15 O12 L'Assomption Québec, SE Canada 45°48′N 73°27′W
15 N11 L'Assomption ≈ Québec, SE Canada
43 S17 Las Tablas Los Santos, S Panama 07°45′N 80°17′W
Lastarria, Volcán see Azufre, Volcán
37 V4 Last Chance Colorado, C USA 39°41′N 103°34′W
Last Frontier, The see Alaska
11 U16 Last Mountain Lake ◎ Saskatchewan, S Canada
62 H9 Las Tórtolas, Cerro ▲ W Argentina 29°57′S 69°49′W
61 C14 Las Toscas Santa Fe, C Argentina 28°22′S 59°20′W
79 F19 Lastoursville Ogooué-Lolo, E Gabon 00°50′S 12°43′E
113 F16 Lastovo It. Lagosta. island SW Croatia
113 F16 Lastovski Kanal channel SW Croatia
40 E6 Las Tres Vírgenes, Volcán △ NW Mexico 27°27′N 112°34′W
40 F4 Las Trincheras Sonora, NW Mexico 30°21′N 111°27′W
55 N8 Las Trincheras Bolívar, E Venezuela 06°57′N 64°49′W
44 H7 Las Tunas var. Victoria de las Tunas. Las Tunas, E Cuba 20°58′N 76°59′W
La Suisse see Switzerland
40 I5 Las Varas Chihuahua, N Mexico 29°35′N 108°01′W
40 J12 Las Varas Nayarit, C Mexico 21°12′N 105°10′W
62 L10 Las Varillas Córdoba, E Argentina 31°54′S 62°45′W
35 X11 Las Vegas Nevada, W USA 36°09′N 115°10′W
37 T10 Las Vegas New Mexico, SW USA 35°35′N 105°15′W
187 P10 Lata Nendö, Solomon Islands 10°45′S 165°43′E
13 R10 La Tabatière Québec, E Canada 50°51′N 58°59′W
56 C6 Latacunga Cotopaxi, C Ecuador 00°58′S 78°36′W
194 I7 Latady Island island Antarctica
54 E14 La Tagua Putumayo, S Colombia 0°05′S 74°39′W
Latakia see Al Lādhiqīyah
92 J10 Lätäseno ≈ NW Finland
14 H9 Latchford Ontario, S Canada 47°20′N 79°45′W
14 J13 Latchford Bridge Ontario, SE Canada 45°16′N 77°29′W
193 Y14 Late island Vava'u Group, N Tonga
153 P15 Lātehār Jhārkhand, N India 23°48′N 84°28′E
15 R7 Laterrière Québec, SE Canada 48°17′N 71°10′W
102 J13 la Teste Gironde, SW France 44°38′N 01°04′W
25 V8 Latexo Texas, SW USA 31°24′N 95°28′W
18 L10 Latham New York, NE USA 42°45′N 73°45′W
Latharna see Larne
108 B9 La Thielle var. Thièle. ≈ W Switzerland
27 R3 Lathrop Missouri, C USA 39°33′N 94°19′W
107 I16 Latina prev. Littoria. Lazio, C Italy 41°28′N 12°53′E
41 R14 La Tinaja Veracruz-Llave, S Mexico
106 J7 Latisana Friuli-Venezia Giulia, NE Italy 45°47′N 13°01′E
Latium see Lazio
115 K25 Lató site of ancient city Kríti, Greece, E Mediterranean Sea
187 Q17 La Tontouta ✈ (Noumea) Province Sud, S New Caledonia 22°06′S 166°12′E
55 N4 La Tortuga, Isla var. Isla Tortuga. island N Venezuela
108 C10 La Tour-de-Peilz var. La Tour de Peilz. Vaud, SW Switzerland 46°28′N 06°52′E
La Tour de Peilz see La Tour-de-Peilz
103 S11 la Tour-du-Pin Isère, E France 45°34′N 05°25′E
102 J11 la Tremblade Charente-Maritime, W France 45°45′N 01°07′W
102 L10 la Trimouille Vienne, W France 46°27′N 01°02′E
42 J9 La Trinidad Estelí, NW Nicaragua 12°57′N 86°15′W
41 U16 La Trinitaria Chiapas, SE Mexico 16°02′N 92°00′W
45 Q11 la Trinité E Martinique 14°44′N 60°58′W
15 U7 La Trinité-des-Monts Québec, SE Canada 48°07′N 68°31′W
18 C15 Latrobe Pennsylvania, NE USA 40°18′N 79°19′W
183 P13 La Trobe River ≈ Victoria, SE Australia
Lattakia/Lattaquié see Al Lādhiqīyah
171 S13 Latu Pulau Seram, E Indonesia 03°24′S 128°37′E
15 P9 La Tuque Québec, SE Canada 47°26′N 72°47′W
155 G14 Lātūr Mahārāshtra, C India 18°24′N 76°34′E
118 G8 Latvia off. Republic of Latvia, Ger. Lettland, Latv. Latvija, Latvijas Republika; prev. Latvian SSR, Rus. Latviyskaya SSR. ◆ republic NE Europe
Latvian SSR/Latvija/Latvijas Republika/Latviyskaya SSR see Latvia
Latvia, Republic of see Latvia
186 H7 Lau New Britain, E Papua New Guinea 05°46′S 151°21′E
175 R9 Lau Basin undersea feature S Pacific Ocean
101 O15 Lauchhammer Brandenburg, E Germany 51°30′N 13°48′E
Laudunum see Laon
Laudus see St-Lô
Lauenburg/Lauenburg in Pommern see Lębork
101 L20 Lauf an der Pegnitz Bayern, SE Germany 49°31′N 11°16′E
108 D7 Laufen Basel, NW Switzerland 47°26′N 07°31′E
109 P5 Lauffen Salzburg, NW Austria 47°54′N 12°57′E
92 I2 Laugarbakki Nordhurland Vestra, N Iceland 65°18′N 20°51′W
92 I4 Laugarvatn Sudhurland, SW Iceland 64°09′N 20°43′W
31 O3 Laughing Fish Point headland Michigan, N USA 46°31′N 87°01′W
187 Z14 Lau Group island group E Fiji
Lauis see Lugano
93 M17 Laukaa Länsi-Suomi, C Finland 62°27′N 25°58′E
118 D12 Laukuva Tauragė, W Lithuania 55°37′N 22°12′E
Laun see Louny
183 P16 Launceston Tasmania, SE Australia 41°25′S 147°07′E
97 I24 Launceston anc. Dunheved. SW England, United Kingdom 50°38′N 04°21′W
54 C13 La Unión Nariño, SW Colombia 01°35′N 77°09′W
42 H8 La Unión La Unión, SE El Salvador 13°20′N 87°50′W
42 I6 La Unión Olancho, C Honduras 15°02′N 86°40′W
40 M15 La Unión Guerrero, S Mexico 17°58′N 101°49′W
41 Y14 La Unión Quintana Roo, E Mexico 18°00′N 101°48′W
105 S13 La Unión Murcia, SE Spain 37°37′N 00°54′W
54 L7 La Unión Barinas, C Venezuela 08°15′N 67°46′W
42 B10 La Unión ◈ department E El Salvador
38 H11 Laupāhoehoe var. Laupahoehoe. Hawaii, USA, C Pacific Ocean 20°00′N 155°15′W
Laupahoehoe see Laupāhoehoe
101 I23 Laupheim Baden-Württemberg, S Germany 48°13′N 09°54′E
181 W3 Laura Queensland, NE Australia 15°37′S 144°34′E
189 X2 Laura atoll Majuro Atoll, SE Marshall Islands
Laurana see Lovran
54 L8 La Urbana Bolívar, C Venezuela 07°05′N 66°58′W
21 Y4 Laurel Delaware, NE USA 38°33′N 75°34′W
23 V14 Laurel Florida, SE USA 27°07′N 82°27′W
21 W3 Laurel Maryland, NE USA 39°06′N 76°51′W
22 M6 Laurel Mississippi, S USA 31°41′N 89°10′W
33 U11 Laurel Montana, NW USA 45°40′N 108°46′W
29 R13 Laurel Nebraska, C USA 42°25′N 97°04′W
18 H15 Laureldale Pennsylvania, NE USA 40°24′N 75°52′W
18 C16 Laurel Hill ridge Pennsylvania, NE USA
29 T12 Laurens Iowa, C USA 42°51′N 94°51′W
21 P11 Laurens South Carolina, SE USA 34°29′N 82°01′W
Laurentian Highlands see Laurentian Mountains
15 P10 Laurentian Mountains var. Laurentian Highlands, Fr. Les Laurentides. plateau Newfoundland and Labrador/Québec, Canada
15 O12 Laurentides Québec, SE Canada 45°51′N 73°49′W
Laurentides, Les see Laurentian Mountains
107 M19 Lauria Basilicata, S Italy 40°03′N 15°50′E
194 I1 Laurie Island island Antarctica
21 T11 Laurinburg North Carolina, SE USA 34°46′N 79°29′W
30 M2 Laurium Michigan, N USA 47°14′N 88°26′W
Lauru see Choiseul
108 B9 Lausanne It. Losanna. Vaud, SW Switzerland 46°32′N 06°39′E
101 Q16 Lausche var. Luže. ▲ Czech Republic/Germany 50°52′N 14°39′E see also Luže
Lausche see Luže
101 Q16 Lausitzer Bergland var. Lausitzer Gebirge, Cz. Gory Lužyckie, Lužické Hory', Eng. Lusatian Mountains. ▲▲ E Germany
Lausitzer Gebirge see Lausitzer Bergland
Lausitzer Neisse see Neisse
103 T12 Lautaret, Col du pass SE France
63 G15 Lautaro Araucanía, C Chile 38°30′S 71°30′W
101 F21 Lauter ≈ W Germany
108 I7 Lauterach Vorarlberg, NW Austria 47°29′N 09°44′E
101 I17 Lauterbach Hessen, C Germany 50°37′N 09°24′E
108 E9 Lauterbrunnen Bern, C Switzerland 46°36′N 07°52′E
169 U14 Laut Kecil, Kepulauan island group N Indonesia
187 X14 Lautoka Viti Levu, W Fiji 17°36′S 177°28′E
169 O8 Laut, Pulau prev. Laoet. island Borneo, C Indonesia
169 V14 Laut, Pulau island Kepulauan Natuna, W Indonesia
169 U13 Laut, Selat strait Borneo, C Indonesia
168 H8 Laut Tawar, Danau ◎ Sumatera, NW Indonesia
189 V14 Lauvergne Island island Chuuk, C Micronesia
98 M5 Lauwers Meer ◎ N Netherlands
98 M4 Lauwersoog Groningen, NE Netherlands 53°25′N 06°14′E
102 M14 Lauzerte Tarn-et-Garonne, S France 44°15′N 01°08′E
25 U13 Lavaca Bay bay Texas, SW USA
25 U12 Lavaca River ≈ Texas, SW USA
15 O12 Laval Québec, SE Canada 45°32′N 73°44′W
102 J6 Laval Mayenne, NW France 48°04′N 00°46′W
15 T6 Laval ≈ Québec, SE Canada
105 S9 La Vall d'Uixó var. Vall D'Uxó. País Valenciano, E Spain 39°49′N 00°15′W

◆ Country
● Country Capital
◇ Dependent Territory
○ Dependent Territory Capital
◈ Administrative Regions
✈ International Airport
▲ Mountain
▲▲ Mountain Range
△ Volcano
≈ River
◎ Lake
⊠ Reservoir

◆ Country ◇ Dependent Territory ◆ Administrative Regions ▲ Mountain ☈ Volcano ⊠ Lake
● Country Capital ○ Dependent Territory Capital × International Airport ▲ Mountain Range ≈ River ⊠ Reservoir

LESTER B. PEARSON – LIPIN BOR

14 G15 **Lester B. Pearson** var. Toronto. ✈ (Toronto) Ontario, S Canada 43°59′N 81°30′W
29 U9 **Lester Prairie** Minnesota, N USA 44°52′N 94°02′W
93 L16 **Lestijärvi** Länsi-Suomi, W Finland 63°29′N 24°41′E
L'Estuaire see Estuaire
29 U9 **Le Sueur** Minnesota, N USA 44°27′N 93°53′W
108 B8 **Les Verrières** Neuchâtel, W Switzerland 46°54′N 06°29′E
115 L17 **Lésvos** anc. Lesbos. island E Greece
110 G12 **Leszno** Ger. Lissa. Wielkopolskie, C Poland 51°51′N 16°35′E
83 L20 **Letaba** Northern, NE South Africa 23°44′S 31°29′E
173 P17 **Le Tampon** SW Réunion
97 O21 **Letchworth** E England, United Kingdom 51°58′N 00°14′W
111 G25 **Letenye** Zala, SW Hungary 46°25′N 16°44′E
11 Q17 **Lethbridge** Alberta, SW Canada 49°43′N 112°48′W
55 S11 **Lethem** S Guyana 03°24′N 59°45′W
83 H18 **Letiahau** ≈ W Botswana
54 J18 **Leticia** Amazonas, S Colombia 04°09′N 69°57′W
171 S16 **Leti, Kepulauan** island group E Indonesia
83 I18 **Letlhakane** Central, C Botswana 21°26′S 25°36′E
83 H20 **Letlhakeng** Kweneng, SE Botswana 24°05′S 25°03′E
114 J8 **Letnitsa** Lovech, N Bulgaria 43°19′N 25°02′E
103 N1 **le Touquet-Paris-Plage** Pas-de-Calais, N France 50°31′N 01°36′E
166 L8 **Letpadan** Bago, SW Burma (Myanmar) 17°46′N 94°45′E
166 K6 **Letpan** Rakhine State, W Burma (Myanmar) 19°22′N 94°11′E
102 M2 **le Tréport** Seine-Maritime, N France 50°03′N 01°21′E
166 M12 **Letsôk-aw Kyun** var. Letsutan Island; prev. Domel Island. island Mergui Archipelago, S Burma (Myanmar)
Letsutan Island see Letsôk-aw Kyun
97 E14 **Letterkenny** Ir. Leitir Ceanainn. Donegal, NW Ireland 54°57′N 07°44′W
Lettland see Latvia
116 M6 **Letychiv** Khmel'nyts'ka Oblast', W Ukraine 49°24′N 27°39′E
Lëtzebuerg see Luxembourg
116 H14 **Leu** Dolj, SW Romania 44°10′N 24°01′E
Leucas see Lefkáda
103 P17 **Leucate** Aude, S France 42°55′N 03°03′E
103 P17 **Leucate, Étang de** ☉ S France
108 E10 **Leuk** Valais, SW Switzerland 46°18′N 07°46′E
108 E10 **Leukerbad** Valais, SW Switzerland 46°22′N 07°47′E
Leusden see Leusden-Centrum
98 K11 **Leusden-Centrum** var. Leusden. Utrecht, C Netherlands 52°08′N 05°25′E
Leutensdorf see Litvínov
Leutschau see Levoča
99 H18 **Leuven** Fr. Louvain, Ger. Löwen. Vlaams Brabant, C Belgium 50°53′N 04°42′E
99 I20 **Leuze** Namur, C Belgium 50°33′N 04°55′E
Leuze see Leuze-en-Hainaut
99 E19 **Leuze-en-Hainaut** var. Leuze. Hainaut, SW Belgium 50°36′N 03°37′E
Léva see Levice
Levádia see Livádeia
Levajok see Leavvajohka
36 L4 **Levan** Utah, W USA 39°33′N 111°51′W
93 E16 **Levanger** Nord-Trøndelag, C Norway 63°45′N 11°18′E
106 D10 **Levanto** Liguria, W Italy 44°12′N 09°33′E
107 H23 **Levanzo, Isola di** island Isole Egadi, S Italy
127 Q17 **Levashi** Respublika Dagestan, SW Russian Federation 42°27′N 47°19′E
24 M5 **Levelland** Texas, SW USA 33°35′N 102°23′W
39 P13 **Levelock** Alaska, USA 59°07′N 156°51′W
101 E16 **Leverkusen** Nordrhein-Westfalen, W Germany 51°02′N 07°E
111 J21 **Levice** Ger. Lewentz, Hung. Léva, Lewenz. Nitriansky Kraj, SW Slovakia 48°14′N 18°38′E
106 G6 **Levico Terme** Trentino-Alto Adige, N Italy 46°02′N 11°19′E
115 E20 **Levídi** Pelopónnisos, S Greece 37°39′N 22°13′E
103 P14 **le Vigan** Gard, S France 43°00′N 03°36′E
184 L13 **Levin** Manawatu-Wanganui, North Island, New Zealand 40°38′S 175°17′E
15 R10 **Lévis** var. Levis. Québec, SE Canada 46°47′N 71°12′W
Levis see Lévis
21 P6 **Levisa Fork** ≈ Kentucky/Virginia, S USA
115 L21 **Levítha** island Kykládes, Greece, Aegean Sea
18 L14 **Levittown** Long Island, New York, NE USA 40°42′N 73°29′W
18 J15 **Levittown** Pennsylvania, NE USA 40°09′N 74°50′W
Levkás see Lefkáda
Levkímmi see Lefkímmi
111 L19 **Levoča** Ger. Leutschau, Hung. Lőcse. Prešovský Kraj, E Slovakia 49°01′N 20°34′E
Lévrier, Baie du see Nouâdhibou, Dakhlet
103 N9 **Levroux** Indre, C France 47°00′N 01°37′E
114 J8 **Levski** Pleven, N Bulgaria 43°21′N 25°11′E
Levskigrad see Karlovo
126 L6 **Lev Tolstoy** Lipetskaya Oblast', W Russian Federation 53°12′N 39°28′E
187 X14 **Levuka** Ovalau, C Fiji 17°42′S 178°50′E
166 L6 **Lewe** Mandalay, C Burma (Myanmar) 19°40′N 96°04′E
Lewentz/Lewenz see Levice
97 O23 **Lewes** SE England, United Kingdom 50°52′N 00°01′E
21 Z4 **Lewes** Delaware, NE USA 38°46′N 75°08′W
29 Q12 **Lewis And Clark Lake** ⊠ Nebraska/South Dakota, N USA
18 G14 **Lewisburg** Pennsylvania, NE USA 40°57′N 76°52′W
20 J10 **Lewisburg** Tennessee, S USA 35°29′N 86°49′W
21 S6 **Lewisburg** West Virginia, NE USA 37°49′N 80°28′W
96 F6 **Lewis, Butt of** headland NW Scotland, United Kingdom 58°31′N 06°18′W
96 F7 **Lewis, Isle of** island NW Scotland, United Kingdom
35 U4 **Lewis, Mount** ▲ Nevada, W USA 40°22′N 116°50′W
185 H16 **Lewis Pass** pass South Island, New Zealand
33 P7 **Lewis Range** ▲▲ Montana, NW USA
23 O3 **Lewis Smith Lake** ⊠ Alabama, S USA
32 M10 **Lewiston** Idaho, NW USA 46°25′N 117°01′W
19 P7 **Lewiston** Maine, NE USA 44°08′N 70°14′W
29 X10 **Lewiston** Minnesota, N USA 43°58′N 91°52′W
18 D9 **Lewiston** New York, NE USA 43°10′N 79°02′W
36 L1 **Lewiston** Utah, W USA 41°58′N 111°52′W
30 K13 **Lewistown** Illinois, N USA 40°23′N 90°09′W
33 T9 **Lewistown** Montana, NW USA 47°04′N 109°26′W
27 T14 **Lewisville** Arkansas, C USA 33°21′N 93°38′W
25 T6 **Lewisville** Texas, SW USA 33°00′N 96°57′W
25 T6 **Lewisville, Lake** ⊠ Texas, SW USA
Le Woleu-Ntem see Woleu-Ntem
23 U3 **Lexington** Georgia, SE USA 33°51′N 83°04′W
20 M5 **Lexington** Kentucky, S USA 38°03′N 84°30′W
22 L4 **Lexington** Mississippi, S USA 33°06′N 90°03′W
27 S4 **Lexington** Missouri, C USA 39°11′N 93°52′W
29 N16 **Lexington** Nebraska, C USA 40°46′N 99°44′W
20 S9 **Lexington** North Carolina, SE USA 35°49′N 80°15′W
27 N11 **Lexington** Oklahoma, C USA 35°00′N 97°20′W
21 R12 **Lexington** South Carolina, SE USA 33°59′N 81°15′W
20 G9 **Lexington** Tennessee, S USA 35°39′N 88°24′W
25 T10 **Lexington** Texas, SW USA 30°25′N 97°00′W
21 T6 **Lexington** Virginia, NE USA 37°47′N 79°27′W
21 X5 **Lexington Park** Maryland, NE USA 38°16′N 76°27′W
Leyden see Leiden
102 J14 **Leyre** ≈ SW France
171 Q5 **Leyte** island C Philippines
171 Q6 **Leyte Gulf** gulf E Philippines
111 O16 **Leżajsk** Podkarpackie, SE Poland 50°15′N 22°25′E
Lezha see Lezhë
113 K18 **Lezhë** prev. Lezha; prev. Lesh, Leshi. Lezhë, NW Albania 41°46′N 19°40′E
113 K18 **Lezhë** ◈ district NW Albania
103 O16 **Lézignan-Corbières** Aude, S France 43°12′N 02°46′E
126 J7 **L'gov** Kurskaya Oblast', W Russian Federation 51°38′N 35°17′E
159 P15 **Lhari** Xizang Zizhiqu, W China 30°34′N 93°40′E
159 N16 **Lhasa** var. La-sa, Lassa. Xizang Zizhiqu, W China 29°41′N 91°10′E
159 O15 **Lhasa He** ≈ W China
Lhaviyani Atoll see Faadhippolhu Atoll
158 K16 **Lhazê** var. Quxar. Xizang Zizhiqu, W China 29°07′N 87°32′E
158 K14 **Lhazhong** Xizang Zizhiqu, W China 31°58′N 86°43′E
168 H7 **Lhoksukon** Sumatera, W Indonesia 05°04′N 97°19′E
159 Q15 **Lhorong** var. Zito. Xizang Zizhiqu, W China 30°51′N 95°41′E
105 W6 **L'Hospitalet de Llobregat** var. Hospitalet. Cataluña, NE Spain 41°21′N 02°06′E
153 R11 **Lhotse** ▲ China/Nepal 28°00′N 86°55′E
159 N17 **Lhozhag** var. Garbo. Xizang Zizhiqu, W China 28°21′N 90°47′E
159 O16 **Lhünzê** var. Xingba. Xizang Zizhiqu, W China 28°25′N 92°30′E
159 N15 **Lhünzhub** var. Ganqu. Xizang Zizhiqu, W China 30°14′N 91°20′E
167 N8 **Li** Lamphun, NW Thailand 17°46′N 98°54′E
115 L21 **Liádi** var. Livádi. island Kykládes, Greece, Aegean Sea
Liancheng see Lianjiang, Guangdong, China
Liancheng see Qinglong, Guizhou, China
Liancheng see Guangnan, Yunnan, China
Lianfeng see Liancheng
161 P12 **Liangcheng** var. Lianfeng. Fujian, SE China 25°47′N 116°42′E
160 K9 **Liangping** var. Liangshan. Sichuan, C China 30°40′N 107°46′E
Liangshan see Liangping
Liangzhou see Wuwei
161 O9 **Liang Zi Hu** ☉ C China
161 R12 **Lianjiang** var. Fengcheng. Fujian, SE China 26°14′N 119°33′E
160 L15 **Lianjiang** var. Liancheng. Guangdong, S China 21°41′N 110°12′E
Lianjiang see Xingguo
161 O13 **Lianping** var. Yuanshan. Guangdong, S China 24°18′N 114°27′E
Lianshan see Huludao
Lian Xian see Lianzhou
160 M11 **Lianyuan** prev. Lantian. Hunan, S China 27°51′N 111°44′E
161 Q6 **Lianyungang** var. Xinpu. Jiangsu, E China 34°38′N 119°12′E
161 N13 **Lianzhou** var. Linxian; prev. Lian Xian. Guangdong, S China 24°48′N 112°26′E
Lianzhou see Hepu
Liao see Liaoning
161 P5 **Liaocheng** Shandong, E China 36°31′N 115°59′E
163 U13 **Liaodong Bandao** var. Liaotung Peninsula. peninsula NE China
163 T13 **Liaodong Wan** Eng. Gulf of Lantung, Gulf of Liaotung. gulf NE China
163 U11 **Liao He** ≈ NE China
163 U12 **Liaoning** var. Liao, Liaoning Sheng, Shengking, hist. Fengtien, Shenking. ◈ province NE China
Liaoning Sheng see Liaoning
Liaotung Peninsula see Liaodong Bandao
163 V12 **Liaoyang** var. Liao-yang. Liaoning, NE China 41°16′N 123°12′E
Liao-yang see Liaoyang
163 V11 **Liaoyuan** var. Dongliao, Shuang-liao, Jap. Chengchiatun. Jilin, NE China 42°52′N 125°09′E
163 U12 **Liaozhong** Liaoning, NE China 41°33′N 122°54′E
Liaqatabad see Piplān
10 M10 **Liard** ≈ W Canada
Liard see Fort Liard
10 L10 **Liard River** British Columbia, W Canada 59°23′N 126°05′W
149 O15 **Liāri** Baluchistān, SW Pakistan 25°43′N 66°28′E
Liatroim see Leitrim
189 S6 **Lib** var. Ellep. island Ralik Chain, C Marshall Islands
Liban see Lebanon
138 H6 **Liban, Jebel** Ar. Jabal al Gharbt, Jabal Lubnān, Eng. Mount Lebanon. ▲▲ C Lebanon
Libau see Liepāja
33 N7 **Libby** Montana, NW USA 48°25′N 115°33′W
79 I16 **Libenge** Equateur, NW Dem. Rep. Congo 03°39′N 18°39′E
26 I7 **Liberal** Kansas, C USA 37°03′N 100°56′W
27 R7 **Liberal** Missouri, C USA 37°33′N 94°31′W
Liberalitas Julia see Évora
111 D15 **Liberec** Ger. Reichenberg. Liberecký Kraj, N Czech Republic 50°45′N 15°05′E
111 D15 **Liberecký Kraj** ◈ region N Czech Republic
42 K12 **Liberia** Guanacaste, NW Costa Rica 10°36′N 85°26′W
76 K17 **Liberia** off. Republic of Liberia. ◆ republic W Africa
Liberia, Republic of see Liberia
61 D16 **Libertad** Corrientes, NE Argentina 30°01′S 57°51′W
61 E20 **Libertad** San José, S Uruguay 34°38′S 56°39′W
54 I7 **Libertad** Barinas, NW Venezuela 08°21′N 69°39′W
54 K6 **Libertad** Cojedes, N Venezuela 09°15′N 68°30′W
62 G12 **Libertador** off. Región del Libertador General Bernardo O'Higgins. ◈ region C Chile
Libertador General Bernardo O'Higgins, Región del see Libertador
Libertador General San Martín see Ciudad de Libertador General San Martín
20 L6 **Liberty** Kentucky, S USA 37°19′N 84°58′W
22 J7 **Liberty** Mississippi, S USA 31°09′N 90°49′W
27 R4 **Liberty** Missouri, C USA 39°15′N 94°22′W
18 J12 **Liberty** New York, NE USA 41°48′N 74°45′W
21 T9 **Liberty** North Carolina, SE USA 35°49′N 79°34′W
Libian Desert see Libyan Desert
99 J23 **Libin** Luxembourg, SE Belgium 50°01′N 05°13′E
Lībīyah, Aş Şahrā' al see Libyan Desert
160 K13 **Libo** var. Yuping. Guizhou, S China 25°28′N 107°52′E
Libohova see Libohovë
113 L23 **Libohovë** var. Libohova. Gjirokastër, S Albania 40°03′N 20°13′E
81 K18 **Liboi** North Eastern, E Kenya 0°23′N 40°55′E
102 K13 **Libourne** Gironde, SW France 44°55′N 00°14′W
99 K23 **Libramont** Luxembourg, SE Belgium 49°55′N 05°21′E
113 M20 **Librazhd** var. Librazhdi. Elbasan, E Albania 41°10′N 20°22′E
Librazhdi see Librazhd
79 C18 **Libreville** ● (Gabon) Estuaire, NW Gabon 0°25′N 09°29′E
75 P10 **Libya** off. Great Socialist People's Libyan Arab Jamahiriya, Ar. Al Jamāhīrīyah al 'Arabīyah al Lībīyah ash Sha'bīyah al Ishtirākīy; prev. Libyan Arab Republic. ◆ Islamic state N Africa
Libyan Arab Republic see Libya
75 T11 **Libyan Desert** var. Libian Desert, Ar. Aş Şahrā' al Lībīyah. desert N Africa
75 T8 **Libyan Plateau** var. Aḑ Diffah. plateau Egypt/Libya
62 G12 **Licantén** Maule, C Chile 35°00′S 72°00′W
107 J25 **Licata** anc. Phintias. Sicilia, Italy, C Mediterranean Sea 37°07′N 13°57′E
137 P14 **Lice** Diyarbakır, SE Turkey 38°29′N 40°39′E
Licheng see Lipu
97 L19 **Lichfield** C England, United Kingdom 52°42′N 01°48′W
83 N14 **Lichinga** Niassa, N Mozambique 13°19′S 35°13′E
109 V3 **Lichtenau** Niederösterreich, N Austria 48°29′N 15°24′E
83 I21 **Lichtenburg** North-West, N South Africa 26°09′S 26°11′E
101 K18 **Lichtenfels** Bayern, SE Germany 50°09′N 11°04′E
98 O12 **Lichtenvoorde** Gelderland, E Netherlands 51°59′N 06°34′E
Lichtenwald see Sevnica
99 C17 **Lichtervelde** West-Vlaanderen, W Belgium 51°02′N 03°09′E
160 L9 **Lichuan** Hubei, C China 30°20′N 108°56′E
27 V7 **Licking** Missouri, C USA 37°30′N 91°51′W
20 M4 **Licking River** ≈ Kentucky, S USA
112 C11 **Lički Osik** Lika-Senj, C Croatia 44°36′N 15°24′E
Ličko-Senjska Županija see Lika-Senj
107 K19 **Licosa, Punta** headland S Italy 40°15′N 14°54′E
119 H16 **Lida** Hrodzyenskaya Voblasts', W Belarus 53°53′N 25°20′E
93 H17 **Liden** Västernorrland, C Sweden 62°43′N 16°49′E
29 R7 **Lidgerwood** North Dakota, N USA 46°04′N 97°09′W
Lidhorikion see Lidoríki
95 K21 **Lidhult** Kronoberg, S Sweden 56°49′N 13°25′E
95 P16 **Lidingö** Stockholm, C Sweden 59°22′N 18°10′E
95 K17 **Lidköping** Västra Götaland, S Sweden 58°30′N 13°10′E
Lido di Iesolo see Lido di Jesolo
106 I8 **Lido di Jesolo** var. Lido di Iesolo. Veneto, NE Italy 45°30′N 12°37′E
107 H15 **Lido di Ostia** Lazio, C Italy 41°42′N 12°19′E
Lidokhorikion see Lidoríki
115 E18 **Lidoríki** prev. Lidhorikion, Lidokhorikion. Stereá Ellás, C Greece 38°32′N 22°12′E
110 K9 **Lidzbark** Warmińsko-Mazurskie, NE Poland 53°15′N 19°49′E
110 L7 **Lidzbark Warmiński** Ger. Heilsberg. Olsztyn, N Poland 54°08′N 20°35′E
109 U3 **Liebenau** Oberösterreich, N Austria 48°33′N 14°48′E
181 P7 **Liebig, Mount** ▲ Northern Territory, C Australia 23°19′S 131°30′E
109 V8 **Lieboch** Steiermark, SE Austria 47°00′N 15°21′E
108 I8 **Liechtenstein** off. Principality of Liechtenstein. ◆ principality C Europe
Liechtenstein, Principality of see Liechtenstein
99 F18 **Liedekerke** Vlaams Brabant, C Belgium 50°51′N 04°05′E
99 K19 **Liège** Dut. Luik, Ger. Lüttich. Liège, E Belgium 50°38′N 05°35′E
99 K20 **Liège** Dut. Luik. ◈ province E Belgium
Liegnitz see Legnica
93 O16 **Lieksa** Itä-Suomi, E Finland 63°20′N 30°E
118 F10 **Lielupe** ≈ Latvia/Lithuania
118 G9 **Lielvārde** Ogre, C Latvia 56°45′N 24°48′E
167 U13 **Liên Hương** var. Tuy Phong. Binh Thuân, S Vietnam 11°13′N 108°40′E
Liên Nghia see Đưc Trong
109 P9 **Lienz** Tirol, W Austria 46°50′N 12°45′E
118 B10 **Liepāja** Ger. Libau. Liepāja, W Latvia 56°32′N 21°02′E
99 H17 **Lier** Fr. Lierre. Antwerpen, N Belgium 51°08′N 04°35′E
95 H15 **Lierbyen** Buskerud, S Norway 59°57′N 10°14′E
99 L21 **Lierneux** Liège, E Belgium 50°12′N 05°51′E
Lierre see Lier
101 D18 **Lieser** ≈ W Germany
109 U7 **Liesing** ≈ E Austria
108 E6 **Liestal** Basel-Land, N Switzerland 47°29′N 07°43′E
Lietuva see Lithuania
Lievenhof see Līvāni
103 O2 **Liévin** Pas-de-Calais, N France 50°25′N 02°48′E
14 M9 **Lièvre, Rivière du** ≈ Québec, SE Canada
109 T6 **Liezen** Steiermark, C Austria 47°34′N 14°12′E
97 E14 **Lifford** Ir. Leifear. Donegal, NW Ireland 54°50′N 07°29′W
187 Q16 **Lifou** island Îles Loyauté, E New Caledonia
193 Y15 **Lifuka** island Ha'apai Group, C Tonga
171 P4 **Ligao** Luzon, N Philippines 13°16′N 123°30′E
Liger see Loire
42 H2 **Lighthouse Reef** reef E Belize
183 Q4 **Lightning Ridge** New South Wales, SE Australia 29°29′S 148°00′E
103 N9 **Lignières** Cher, C France 46°45′N 02°10′E
103 S5 **Ligny-en-Barrois** Meuse, NE France 48°42′N 05°22′E
83 P15 **Ligonha** ≈ NE Mozambique
31 P11 **Ligonier** Indiana, N USA 41°25′N 85°33′W
81 I25 **Ligunga** Ruvuma, S Tanzania 10°51′S 37°10′E
106 D9 **Ligure, Appennino** Eng. Ligurian Mountains. ▲▲ NW Italy
Ligure, Mar see Ligurian Sea
106 C9 **Liguria** ◈ region NW Italy
Ligurian Mountains see Ligure, Appennino
120 K6 **Ligurian Sea** Fr. Mer Ligurienne, It. Mar Ligure. sea N Mediterranean Sea
Ligurienne, Mer see Ligurian Sea
186 H5 **Lihir Group** island group NE Papua New Guinea
38 B8 **Līhu'e** var. Lihue. Kaua'i, Hawaii, USA 21°59′N 159°23′W
Lihue see Līhu'e
118 F5 **Lihula** Ger. Leal. Läänemaa, W Estonia 58°44′N 23°49′E
124 I2 **Liinakhamari** var. Linacmamari. Murmanskaya Oblast', NW Russian Federation 69°40′N 31°27′E
Liivi Laht see Riga, Gulf of
160 F11 **Lijiang** var. Dayan, Lijiang Naxizu Zizhixian. Yunnan, SW China 26°52′N 100°10′E
Lijiang Naxizu Zizhixian see Lijiang
112 C11 **Lika-Senj** off. Ličko-Senjska Županija. ◈ province W Croatia
79 N25 **Likasi** prev. Jadotville. Shaba, SE Dem. Rep. Congo 11°02′S 26°51′E
79 L16 **Likati** Orientale, N Dem. Rep. Congo 03°28′N 23°45′E
10 M15 **Likely** British Columbia, SW Canada 52°40′N 121°34′W
153 Y11 **Likhapāni** Assam, NE India 27°19′N 95°54′E
124 J16 **Likhoslavl'** Tverskaya Oblast', W Russian Federation 57°08′N 35°27′E
189 U5 **Likiep Atoll** atoll Ratak Chain, C Marshall Islands
95 D18 **Liknes** Vest-Agder, S Norway 58°20′N 06°58′E
79 H16 **Likouala** ◈ province NE Congo
79 H18 **Likouala** ≈ N Congo
79 H18 **Likouala aux Herbes** ≈ E Congo
190 B16 **Liku** E Niue 19°02′S 169°47′E
Likupang, Selat see Bangka, Selat
27 Y8 **Lilbourn** Missouri, C USA 36°35′N 89°37′W
103 X14 **l'Île-Rousse** Corse, France, C Mediterranean Sea 42°39′N 08°59′E
109 W5 **Lilienfeld** Niederösterreich, NE Austria 48°01′N 15°36′E
161 N11 **Liling** Hunan, S China 27°42′N 113°49′E
95 J18 **Lilla Edet** Västra Götaland, S Sweden 58°08′N 12°08′E
103 P1 **Lille** var. l'Isle, Dut. Rijssel, Flem. Ryssel, prev. Lisle; anc. Insula. Nord, N France 50°38′N 03°04′E
95 G24 **Lillebælt** var. Lille Bælt, Eng. Little Belt. strait S Denmark
Lille Bælt see Lillebælt
102 L3 **Lillebonne** Seine-Maritime, N France 49°30′N 00°34′E
94 H12 **Lillehammer** Oppland, S Norway 61°07′N 10°28′E
103 O1 **Lillers** Pas-de-Calais, N France 50°34′N 02°26′E
95 F18 **Lillesand** Aust-Agder, S Norway 58°15′N 08°23′E
95 I15 **Lillestrøm** Akershus, S Norway 59°58′N 11°05′E
93 F18 **Lillhärdal** Jämtland, C Sweden 61°51′N 14°04′E
21 U10 **Lillington** North Carolina, SE USA 35°25′N 78°50′W
105 O9 **Lillo** Castilla-La Mancha, C Spain 39°43′N 03°19′W
10 M16 **Lillooet** British Columbia, SW Canada 50°41′N 121°59′W
83 M14 **Lilongwe** ● (Malawi) Central, W Malawi 13°58′S 33°48′E
83 M14 **Lilongwe** ✈ Central, W Malawi 13°46′S 33°44′E
83 M14 **Lilongwe** ≈ W Malawi
171 P7 **Liloy** Mindanao, S Philippines 08°04′N 122°42′E
Lilybaeum see Marsala
182 J7 **Lilydale** South Australia 32°57′S 140°00′E
183 P16 **Lilydale** Tasmania, SE Australia 41°17′S 147°13′E
113 J14 **Lim** ≈ SE Europe
57 D15 **Lima** ● (Peru) Lima, W Peru 12°06′S 78°W
94 K13 **Lima** Dalarna, C Sweden 60°55′N 13°19′E
31 R12 **Lima** Ohio, NE USA 40°43′N 84°06′W
57 D14 **Lima** ◈ department W Peru
Lima see Jorge Chávez International
127 R13 **Liman** Astrakhanskaya Oblast', SW Russian Federation 45°48′N 47°17′E
111 L17 **Limanowa** Małopolskie, S Poland 49°43′N 20°25′E
104 G5 **Lima, Rio** Sp. Limia. ≈ Portugal/Spain see also Limia
Lima, Rio see Limia
168 M11 **Limas** Pulau Sebangka, W Indonesia 0°09′N 104°31′E
Limassol see Lemesós
97 F14 **Limavady** Ir. Léim An Mhadaidh. NW Northern Ireland, United Kingdom 55°03′N 06°57′W
63 J14 **Limay Mahuida** La Pampa, C Argentina 37°09′S 66°40′W
63 H15 **Limay, Río** ≈ W Argentina
101 N16 **Limbach-Oberfrohna** Sachsen, E Germany 50°52′N 12°46′E
81 F22 **Limba Limba** ≈ C Tanzania
107 C17 **Limbara, Monte** ▲ Sardegna, Italy, C Mediterranean Sea 40°50′N 09°10′E
118 G7 **Limbaži** Est. Lemsalu. Limbaži, N Latvia 57°33′N 24°46′E
44 M8 **Limbé** N Haiti 19°44′N 72°25′W
99 L19 **Limbourg** Liège, E Belgium 50°37′N 05°56′E
99 K17 **Limburg** ◈ province NE Belgium
99 L16 **Limburg** ◈ province SE Netherlands
101 F17 **Limburg an der Lahn** Hessen, W Germany 50°22′N 08°04′E
94 K13 **Limedsforsen** Dalarna, C Sweden 60°52′N 13°25′E
60 L9 **Limeira** São Paulo, S Brazil 22°34′S 47°25′W
97 C19 **Limerick** Ir. Luimneach. Limerick, SW Ireland 52°40′N 08°38′W
97 C20 **Limerick** Ir. Luimneach. cultural region SW Ireland
19 S2 **Limestone** Maine, NE USA 46°52′N 67°49′W
25 U9 **Limestone, Lake** ☉ Texas, SW USA
39 P12 **Lime Village** Alaska, USA 61°21′N 155°26′W
95 F20 **Limfjorden** fjord N Denmark
95 J23 **Limhamn** Skåne, S Sweden 55°34′N 12°57′E
104 H5 **Limia** Port. Rio Lima. ≈ Portugal/Spain see also Lima, Rio
Limia see Lima, Rio
93 L14 **Liminka** Oulu, C Finland 64°48′N 25°19′E
Límni Vathéos see Sámos
115 G17 **Límni** Évvoia, C Greece 38°46′N 23°20′E
115 J15 **Límnos** anc. Lemnos. island E Greece
102 M11 **Limoges** anc. Augustoritum Lemovicensium, Lemovices. Haute-Vienne, C France 45°51′N 01°16′E
43 O13 **Limón** var. Puerto Limón. Limón, E Costa Rica 09°59′N 83°02′W
42 K4 **Limón** Colón, NE Honduras 15°50′N 85°31′W
37 U5 **Limon** Colorado, C USA 39°15′N 103°41′W
43 N13 **Limón** off. Provincia de Limón. ◈ province E Costa Rica
106 A10 **Limone Piemonte** Piemonte, NE Italy 44°12′N 07°37′E
Limones see Valdéz
Limón, Provincia de see Limón
Limonum see Poitiers
103 N11 **Limousin** ◈ region C France
103 N16 **Limoux** Aude, S France 43°03′N 02°13′E
83 J20 **Limpopo** off. Limpopo Province; prev. Northern, Northern Transvaal. ◈ province NE South Africa
83 L19 **Limpopo** var. Crocodile. ≈ S Africa
Limpopo Province see Limpopo
160 K17 **Limu Ling** ▲ S China
113 M20 **Lin** var. Lini. Elbasan, E Albania 41°03′N 20°37′E
Linacmamari see Liinakhamari
62 G13 **Linares** Maule, C Chile 35°50′S 71°37′W
54 C13 **Linares** Nariño, SW Colombia 01°24′N 77°30′W
41 O9 **Linares** Nuevo León, NE Mexico 24°54′N 99°38′W
105 N12 **Linares** Andalucía, S Spain 38°05′N 03°38′W
107 G15 **Linaro, Capo** headland C Italy 42°01′N 11°49′E
106 D8 **Linate** ✈ (Milano) Lombardia, N Italy 45°27′N 09°18′E
167 T8 **Lin Camh** prev. Đưc Tho. Ha Tinh, N Vietnam 18°30′N 105°36′E
160 F13 **Lincang** Yunnan, SW China 23°55′N 100°03′E
Lincheng see Lingao
61 B20 **Lincoln** Buenos Aires, E Argentina 34°54′S 61°30′W
185 H19 **Lincoln** Canterbury, South Island, New Zealand 43°37′S 172°30′E
97 N18 **Lincoln** anc. Lindum, Lindum Colonia. E England, United Kingdom 53°14′N 00°33′W
35 O6 **Lincoln** California, W USA 38°52′N 121°18′W
30 L13 **Lincoln** Illinois, N USA 40°09′N 89°21′W
26 M4 **Lincoln** Kansas, C USA 39°03′N 98°09′W
19 S5 **Lincoln** Maine, NE USA 45°22′N 68°30′W
27 T5 **Lincoln** Missouri, C USA 38°23′N 93°19′W
29 R16 **Lincoln** state capital Nebraska, C USA 40°46′N 96°43′W
32 F11 **Lincoln City** Oregon, NW USA 44°57′N 124°01′W
167 X10 **Lincoln Island** island E Paracel Islands
197 Q11 **Lincoln Sea** sea Arctic Ocean
97 N18 **Lincolnshire** cultural region E England, United Kingdom
21 R10 **Lincolnton** North Carolina, SE USA 35°27′N 81°16′W
25 V7 **Lindale** Texas, SW USA 32°31′N 95°24′W
101 I25 **Lindau** var. Lindau am Bodensee. Bayern, S Germany 47°33′N 09°41′E
Lindau am Bodensee see Lindau
123 P9 **Linde** ≈ NE Russian Federation
55 T9 **Linden** E Guyana 05°58′N 58°12′W
23 O6 **Linden** Alabama, S USA 32°18′N 87°48′W
20 H9 **Linden** Tennessee, S USA 35°38′N 87°50′W
25 X6 **Linden** Texas, SW USA 33°01′N 94°22′W
18 J16 **Lindenwold** New Jersey, NE USA 39°47′N 74°58′W
95 M15 **Lindesberg** Örebro, C Sweden 59°36′N 15°15′E
95 D18 **Lindesnes** headland S Norway 57°58′N 07°03′E
Líndhos see Líndos
81 K24 **Lindi** Lindi, SE Tanzania 10°S 39°41′E
81 J24 **Lindi** ◈ region SE Tanzania
79 N17 **Lindi** ≈ NE Dem. Rep. Congo
163 V7 **Lindian** Heilongjiang, NE China 47°15′N 124°51′E
185 E21 **Lindis Pass** pass South Island, New Zealand
83 J22 **Lindley** Free State, C South Africa 27°52′S 27°55′E
95 J19 **Lindome** Västra Götaland, S Sweden 57°34′N 12°05′E
163 S10 **Lindong** var. Bairin Zuoqi. Nei Mongol Zizhiqu, N China 43°59′N 119°24′E
115 O23 **Líndos** var. Líndhos. Ródos, Dodekánisa, Greece, Aegean Sea 36°05′N 28°05′E
14 I14 **Lindsay** Ontario, SE Canada 44°21′N 78°44′W
35 R11 **Lindsay** California, W USA 36°11′N 119°06′W
33 X8 **Lindsay** Montana, NW USA 47°13′N 105°10′W
27 N11 **Lindsay** Oklahoma, C USA 34°50′N 97°37′W
27 N5 **Lindsborg** Kansas, C USA 38°34′N 97°39′W
95 N21 **Lindsdal** Kalmar, S Sweden 56°44′N 16°18′E
Lindum/Lindum Colonia see Lincoln
191 W3 **Line Islands** island group E Kiribati
Linëvo see Linova
160 M5 **Linfen** var. Lin-fen. Shanxi, C China 36°08′N 111°34′E
Lin-fen see Linfen
155 F18 **Linganamakki Reservoir** ⊠ SW India
160 L17 **Lingao** var. Lincheng. Hainan, S China 19°44′N 109°23′E
171 N3 **Lingayen** Luzon, N Philippines 16°00′N 120°12′E
160 M6 **Lingbao** var. Guolüezhen. Henan, C China 34°34′N 110°50′E
94 N12 **Lingbo** Gävleborg, C Sweden 61°04′N 16°45′E
Lingcheng see Beiliu, Guangxi, China
Lingcheng see Lingshan, Guangxi, China
Lingeh see Bandar-e Lengeh
100 E12 **Lingen** var. Lingen an der Ems. Niedersachsen, NW Germany 52°31′N 07°19′E
Lingen an der Ems see Lingen
168 M11 **Lingga, Kepulauan** island group W Indonesia
168 L11 **Lingga, Pulau** island Kepulauan Lingga, W Indonesia
14 J14 **Lingham Lake** ☉ Ontario, SE Canada
94 M13 **Linghed** Dalarna, C Sweden 60°48′N 15°55′E
33 Z15 **Lingle** Wyoming, C USA 42°07′N 104°21′W
18 G15 **Linglestown** Pennsylvania, NE USA 40°20′N 76°46′W
79 K18 **Lingomo 11** Equateur, NW Dem. Rep. Congo 0°42′N 21°59′E
160 L15 **Lingshan** var. Lingcheng. Guangxi Zhuangzu Zizhiqu, S China 22°28′N 109°19′E
160 L17 **Lingshui** var. Lingshui Lizu Zizhixian. Hainan, S China 18°35′N 110°03′E
Lingshui Lizu Zizhixian see Lingshui
155 G16 **Lingsugūr** Karnātaka, C India 16°13′N 76°33′E
107 L23 **Linguaglossa** Sicilia, Italy, C Mediterranean Sea 37°51′N 15°06′E
76 H10 **Linguère** N Senegal 15°24′N 15°06′W
159 W8 **Lingwu** Ningxia, N China 38°04′N 106°21′E
Lingxi see Yongshun, Hunan, China
Lingxi see Cangnan, Zhejiang, China
Lingxian/Ling Xian see Yanling
163 S12 **Lingyuan** Liaoning, NE China 41°09′N 119°24′E
163 U4 **Linhai** Heilongjiang, NE China 51°30′N 124°18′E
161 S10 **Linhai** var. Taizhou. Zhejiang, SE China 28°54′N 121°08′E
59 O20 **Linhares** Espírito Santo, SE Brazil 19°22′S 40°04′W
Linhe see Bayannur
Lini see Lin
139 S1 **Līnik, Chiyā-ē** ▲▲ N Iraq
Linjiang see Shanghang
95 M18 **Linköping** Östergötland, S Sweden 58°25′N 15°37′E
163 Y8 **Linkou** Heilongjiang, NE China 45°18′N 130°17′E
118 F11 **Linkuva** Šiauliai, N Lithuania 56°06′N 23°58′E
27 V5 **Linn** Missouri, C USA 38°29′N 91°51′W
25 S16 **Linn** Texas, SW USA 26°32′N 98°06′W
27 T2 **Linneus** Missouri, C USA 39°53′N 93°10′W
96 H10 **Linnhe, Loch** inlet W Scotland, United Kingdom
119 G19 **Linova** Rus. Linëvo. Brestskaya Voblasts', SW Belarus 52°29′N 24°30′E
161 O5 **Linqing** Shandong, E China 36°51′N 115°42′E
60 K8 **Lins** São Paulo, S Brazil 21°40′S 49°44′W
93 F17 **Linsell** Jämtland, C Sweden 62°10′N 14°E
160 J9 **Linshui** Sichuan, C China 30°24′N 106°54′E
44 K12 **Linstead** C Jamaica 18°08′N 77°02′W
159 U11 **Lintan** Gansu, N China 34°43′N 103°27′E
159 V11 **Lintao** var. Taoyang. Gansu, C China 35°23′N 103°54′E
15 S12 **Lintère** ≈ Québec, SE Canada
108 H8 **Linth** ≈ NW Switzerland
108 H8 **Linthal** Glarus, NE Switzerland 46°59′N 08°57′E
31 N15 **Linton** Indiana, N USA 39°01′N 87°10′W
29 N6 **Linton** North Dakota, N USA 46°16′N 100°13′W
163 R11 **Linxi** Nei Mongol Zizhiqu, N China 43°29′N 117°59′E
159 U11 **Linxia** var. Linxia Huizu Zizhizhou. Gansu, C China 35°34′N 103°08′E
Linxia Huizu Zizhizhou see Linxia
Linxian see Lianzhou
161 Q6 **Linyi** Shandong, S China 37°06′N 118°18′E
161 P4 **Linyi** var. Yishi. Shandong, E China 37°12′N 116°54′E
160 M6 **Linyi** Shanxi, C China 35°10′N 118°18′E
109 T4 **Linz** anc. Lentia. Oberösterreich, N Austria 48°19′N 14°18′E
159 S8 **Linze** var. Shahe; prev. Shahepu. Gansu, N China 39°06′N 100°03′E
44 J13 **Lionel Town** C Jamaica 17°49′N 77°14′W
103 Q16 **Lion, Golfe du** Eng. Gulf of Lion, Gulf of Lions; anc. Sinus Gallicus. gulf S France
Lion, Gulf of/Lions, Gulf of see Lion, Golfe du
83 K16 **Lions Den** Mashonaland West, N Zimbabwe 17°16′S 30°00′E
14 F13 **Lion's Head** Ontario, S Canada 44°59′N 81°16′W
Lios Ceannúir, Bá see Liscannor Bay
Lios Mór see Lismore
Lios na gCearrbhach see Lisburn
Lios Tuathail see Listowel
79 G17 **Liouesso** Sangha, N Congo 01°02′N 15°43′E
Liozno see Lyozna
171 O4 **Lipa** off. Lipa City. Luzon, N Philippines 13°57′N 121°10′E
Lipa City see Lipa
25 S7 **Lipan** Texas, SW USA 32°31′N 98°03′W
Lipari Islands/Lipari, Isole see Eolie, Isole
107 L22 **Lipari, Isola** island Isole Eolie, S Italy
116 L8 **Lipcani** Rus. Lipkany. N Moldova 48°16′N 26°47′E
93 N17 **Liperi** Itä-Suomi, SE Finland 62°33′N 29°29′E
126 L7 **Lipetsk** Lipetskaya Oblast', W Russian Federation 52°37′N 39°38′E
126 K6 **Lipetskaya Oblast'** ◈ province W Russian Federation
57 K22 **Lipez, Cordillera de** ▲▲ SW Bolivia
110 E10 **Lipiany** Ger. Lippehne. Zachodnio-pomorskie, W Poland 53°00′N 14°58′E
112 G9 **Lipik** Požega-Slavonija, NE Croatia 45°24′N 17°08′E
124 L12 **Lipin Bor** Vologodskaya Oblast', NW Russian Federation 60°12′N 38°04′E

◆ Country
● Country Capital
◇ Dependent Territory
○ Dependent Territory Capital
◈ Administrative Regions
✈ International Airport
▲ Mountain
▲▲ Mountain Range
Volcano
≈ River
☉ Lake
⊠ Reservoir

LIPING – LONGPING

160 L12 **Liping** *var.* Defeng. Guizhou, S China *26°16′N 109°08′E*
Lipkany *see* Lipcani
119 H15 **Lipnishki** Hrodzyenskaya Voblasts', W Belarus *54°00′N 25°37′E*
110 J10 **Lipno** Kujawsko-pomorskie, C Poland *52°52′N 19°11′E*
116 F11 **Lipova** *Hung.* Lippa. Arad, W Romania *46°05′N 21°42′E*
Lipovets *see* Lypovets'
Lippa *see* Lipova
101 E14 **Lippe** ≈ W Germany
Lippehne *see* Lipiany
101 G14 **Lippstadt** Nordrhein-Westfalen, W Germany *51°41′N 08°20′E*
25 P1 **Lipscomb** Texas, SW USA *36°14′N 100°16′W*
Lipsia/Lipsk *see* Leipzig
Liptau-Sankt-Nikolaus/Liptószentmiklós *see* Liptovský Mikuláš
111 K19 **Liptovský Mikuláš** *Ger.* Liptau-Sankt-Nikolaus, *Hung.* Liptószentmiklós. Žilinský Kraj, N Slovakia *49°06′N 19°36′E*
183 O13 **Liptrap, Cape** *headland* Victoria, SE Australia *38°55′S 145°58′E*
160 L13 **Lipu** *var.* Licheng. Guangxi Zhuangzu Zizhiqu, S China *24°25′N 110°15′E*
81 G17 **Lira** N Uganda *02°15′N 32°55′E*
57 F15 **Lircay** Huancavelica, C Peru *12°59′S 74°44′W*
107 K17 **Liri** ≈ C Italy
144 M8 **Lisakovsk** Kostanay, NW Kazakhstan *52°32′N 62°32′E*
79 K17 **Lisala** Equateur, N Dem. Rep. Congo *02°10′N 21°29′E*
104 F11 **Lisboa** *Eng.* Lisbon; *anc.* Felicitas Julia, Olisipo. ● (Portugal) Lisboa, W Portugal *38°44′N 09°08′W*
104 F10 **Lisboa** *Eng.* Lisbon. ◈ *district* C Portugal
19 N7 **Lisbon** New Hampshire, NE USA *44°11′N 71°52′W*
29 Q6 **Lisbon** North Dakota, N USA *46°27′N 97°42′W*
Lisbon *see* Lisboa
19 Q8 **Lisbon Falls** Maine, NE USA *44°00′N 70°03′W*
97 G15 **Lisburn** *Ir.* Lios na gCearrbhach. E Northern Ireland, United Kingdom *54°31′N 06°03′W*
38 L6 **Lisburne, Cape** *headland* Alaska, USA *68°52′N 166°13′W*
97 B19 **Liscannor Bay** *Ir.* Bá Lios Ceannúir. *inlet* W Ireland
113 Q18 **Lisec** ▲ E FYR Macedonia *41°46′N 22°30′E*
160 F13 **Lishe Jiang** ≈ SW China
Lishi *see* Lüliang
163 V10 **Lishu** Jilin, NE China *43°25′N 124°19′E*
161 R10 **Lishui** Zhejiang, SE China *28°27′N 119°25′E*
192 L5 **Lisianski Island** *island* Hawaiian Islands, Hawai'i, USA
Lisichansk *see* Lysychans'k
102 L4 **Lisieux** *anc.* Noviomagus. Calvados, N France *49°09′N 00°13′E*
126 L8 **Liski** *prev.* Georgiu-Dezh. Voronezhskaya Oblast', W Russian Federation *51°00′N 39°36′E*
103 N4 **l'Isle-Adam** Val-d'Oise, N France *49°07′N 02°13′E*
Lisle/l'Isle *see* Lille
103 R15 **l'Isle-sur-la-Sorgue** Vaucluse, SE France *43°55′N 05°03′E*
15 S9 **L'Islet** Québec, SE Canada *47°07′N 70°18′W*
183 V4 **Lismore** New South Wales, SE Australia *28°48′S 153°12′E*
182 M12 **Lismore** Victoria, SE Australia *37°59′S 143°18′E*
97 D20 **Lismore** *Ir.* Lios Mór. S Ireland *52°10′N 07°10′W*
Lissa *see* Vis, Croatia
Lissa *see* Leszno, Poland
98 H11 **Lisse** Zuid-Holland, W Netherlands *52°15′N 04°33′E*
114 K13 **Líssos** *var.* Filiouri. ≈ NE Greece
95 D18 **Lista** *peninsula* S Norway
95 D18 **Listafjorden** *fjord* S Norway
195 R13 **Lister, Mount** ▲ Antarctica *78°12′S 161°46′E*
126 M8 **Listopadovka** Voronezhskaya Oblast', W Russian Federation *51°54′N 41°08′E*
14 F15 **Listowel** Ontario, S Canada *43°44′N 80°57′W*
97 B20 **Listowel** *Ir.* Lios Tuathail. Kerry, SW Ireland *52°27′N 09°29′W*
160 L14 **Litang** Guangxi Zhuangzu Zizhiqu, S China *23°09′N 109°08′E*
160 F9 **Litang** *var.* Gaocheng. Sichuan, C China *30°03′N 100°12′E*
160 F10 **Litang Qu** ≈ C China
55 X12 **Litani** *var.* Itany. ≈ French Guiana/Surinam
138 G8 **Lītani, Nahr el** *var.* Nahr al Litant. ≈ C Lebanon
Litant, Nahr al *see* Lītani, Nahr el
Litauen *see* Lithuania
30 K14 **Litchfield** Illinois, N USA *39°17′N 89°52′W*
29 U8 **Litchfield** Minnesota, N USA *45°09′N 94°31′W*
36 K13 **Litchfield Park** Arizona, SW USA *33°29′N 112°21′W*
183 S8 **Lithgow** New South Wales, SE Australia *33°30′S 150°09′E*
115 I26 **Líthino, Akrotírio** *headland* Kríti, Greece, E Mediterranean Sea *34°55′N 24°43′E*
118 D12 **Lithuania** *off.* Republic of Lithuania, *Ger.* Litauen, *Lith.* Lietuva, *Pol.* Litwa, *Rus.* Litva; *prev.* Lithuanian SSR, *Rus.* Litovskaya SSR. ◆ *republic* NE Europe
Lithuanian SSR *see* Lithuania
Lithuania, Republic of *see* Lithuania
109 U11 **Litija** *Ger.* Littai. C Slovenia *46°03′N 14°50′E*
18 H15 **Lititz** Pennsylvania, NE USA *40°09′N 76°18′W*
115 F15 **Litóchoro** *var.* Litohoro, Litókhoron. Kentrikí Makedonía, N Greece *40°06′N 22°30′E*
Litohoro/Litókhoron *see* Litóchoro
111 C15 **Litoměřice** *Ger.* Leitmeritz. Ústecký Kraj, NW Czech Republic *50°33′N 14°10′E*
111 F17 **Litomyšl** *Ger.* Leitomischl. Pardubický Kraj, C Czech Republic *49°54′N 16°18′E*
111 G17 **Litovel** *Ger.* Littau. Olomoucký Kraj, E Czech Republic *49°42′N 17°05′E*
123 S13 **Litovko** Khabarovskiy Kray, SE Russian Federation *49°22′N 135°10′E*
Litovskaya SSR *see* Lithuania
Littai *see* Litija
Littau *see* Litovel
44 G1 **Little Abaco** *var.* Abaco Island. *island* N Bahamas
111 I21 **Little Alföld** *Ger.* Kleines Ungarisches Tiefland, *Hung.* Kisalföld, *Slvk.* Podunajská Rovina. *plain* Hungary/Slovakia
151 Q20 **Little Andaman** *island* Andaman Islands, India, NE Indian Ocean
26 M5 **Little Arkansas River** ≈ Kansas, C USA
184 L4 **Little Barrier Island** *island* N New Zealand
Little Belt *see* Lillebælt
38 M11 **Little Black River** ≈ Alaska, USA
27 O2 **Little Blue River** ≈ Kansas/Nebraska, C USA
44 D8 **Little Cayman** *island* E Cayman Islands
11 X11 **Little Churchill** ≈ Manitoba, C Canada
166 J10 **Little Coco Island** *island* SW Burma (Myanmar)
36 L10 **Little Colorado River** ≈ Arizona, SW USA
14 E11 **Little Current** Manitoulin Island, Ontario, S Canada *45°57′N 81°56′W*
12 E11 **Little Current** ≈ Ontario, S Canada
38 L8 **Little Diomede Island** *island* Alaska, USA
44 I4 **Little Exuma** *island* C Bahamas
29 U7 **Little Falls** Minnesota, N USA *45°59′N 94°21′W*
18 J10 **Little Falls** New York, NE USA *43°02′N 74°51′W*
24 M5 **Littlefield** Texas, SW USA *33°56′N 102°20′W*
29 V3 **Littlefork** Minnesota, N USA *48°24′N 93°33′W*
29 V3 **Little Fork River** ≈ Minnesota, N USA
11 N16 **Little Fort** British Columbia, SW Canada *51°27′N 120°15′W*
11 Y14 **Little Grand Rapids** Manitoba, C Canada *52°06′N 95°29′W*
97 N23 **Littlehampton** SE England, United Kingdom *50°48′N 00°33′W*
35 T2 **Little Humboldt River** ≈ Nevada, W USA
44 K6 **Little Inagua** *var.* Inagua Islands. *island* S Bahamas
21 Q4 **Little Kanawha River** ≈ West Virginia, NE USA
83 F25 **Little Karoo** *plateau* S South Africa
39 O16 **Little Koniuji Island** *island* Shumagin Islands, Alaska, USA
44 H12 **Little London** W Jamaica *18°15′N 78°13′W*
13 R10 **Little Mecatina** *Fr.* Rivière du Petit Mécatina. ≈ Newfoundland and Labrador/Québec, E Canada
96 F8 **Little Minch, The** *strait* NW Scotland, United Kingdom
27 T13 **Little Missouri River** ≈ Arkansas, USA
28 J7 **Little Missouri River** ≈ NW USA
28 J3 **Little Muddy River** ≈ North Dakota, N USA
151 Q22 **Little Nicobar** *island* Nicobar Islands, India, NE Indian Ocean
27 R6 **Little Osage River** ≈ Missouri, C USA
97 P20 **Little Ouse** ≈ E England, United Kingdom
149 V2 **Little Pamir** *Pash.* Pāmīr-e Khord, *Rus.* Malyy Pamir. ▲▲ Afghanistan/Tajikistan
21 U12 **Little Pee Dee River** ≈ North Carolina/South Carolina, SE USA
27 V10 **Little Red River** ≈ Arkansas, C USA
Little Rhody *see* Rhode Island
185 I19 **Little River** Canterbury, South Island, New Zealand *43°45′S 172°49′E*
21 U12 **Little River** South Carolina, SE USA *33°52′N 78°36′W*
27 Y9 **Little River** ≈ Arkansas/Missouri, C USA
27 R13 **Little River** ≈ Arkansas/Oklahoma, USA
23 T7 **Little River** ≈ Georgia, SE USA
22 H6 **Little River** ≈ Louisiana, S USA
25 T10 **Little River** ≈ Texas, SW USA
27 V12 **Little Rock** *state capital* Arkansas, C USA *34°45′N 92°17′W*
31 N8 **Little Sable Point** *headland* Michigan, N USA *43°38′N 86°32′W*
103 U11 **Little Saint Bernard Pass** *Fr.* Col du Petit St-Bernard, *It.* Colle del Piccolo San Bernardo. *pass* France/Italy
36 K7 **Little Salt Lake** ◎ Utah, W USA
180 K8 **Little Sandy Desert** *desert* Western Australia
29 S13 **Little Sioux River** ≈ Iowa, C USA
38 E17 **Little Sitkin Island** *island* Aleutian Islands, Alaska, USA
11 O13 **Little Smoky** Alberta, W Canada *54°35′N 117°06′W*
11 O14 **Little Smoky** ≈ Alberta, W Canada
37 P3 **Little Snake River** ≈ Colorado, C USA
64 A12 **Little Sound** *bay* Bermuda, NW Atlantic Ocean
37 T4 **Littleton** Colorado, C USA *39°36′N 105°01′W*
19 N7 **Littleton** New Hampshire, NE USA *44°18′N 71°46′W*
18 D11 **Little Valley** New York, NE USA *42°13′N 78°47′W*
30 M15 **Little Wabash River** ≈ Illinois, N USA
14 D10 **Little White River** ≈ Ontario, S Canada
28 M12 **Little White River** ≈ South Dakota, N USA
25 R5 **Little Wichita River** ≈ Texas, SW USA
142 I4 **Little Zab** *Ar.* Nahraz Zāb aş Şaghīr, *Kurd.* Zē-i Kōya, *Per.* Rūdkhāneh-ye Zāb-e Kūchek. ≈ Iran/Iraq
79 D15 **Littoral** ◈ *province* W Cameroon
Littoria *see* Latina
Litva/Litwa *see* Lithuania
111 B15 **Litvínov** *Ger.* Leutensdorf. Ústecký Kraj, NW Czech Republic *50°38′N 13°30′E*
116 M6 **Lityn** Vinnyts'ka Oblast', C Ukraine *49°19′N 28°06′E*
Liu-chou/Liuchow *see* Liuzhou
163 W11 **Liuhe** Jilin, NE China *42°15′N 125°49′E*
Liujiaxia *see* Yongjing
Liulin *see* Jonê
83 Q15 **Liúpo** Nampula, NE Mozambique *15°36′S 39°57′E*
83 G14 **Liuwa Plain** *plain* W Zambia
160 L13 **Liuzhou** *var.* Liu-chou, Liuchow. Guangxi Zhuangzu Zizhiqu, S China *24°09′N 108°55′E*
116 H8 **Livada** *Hung.* Sárköz. Satu Mare, NW Romania *47°52′N 23°04′E*
115 J20 **Liváda, Akrotírio** *headland* Tínos, Kykládes, Greece, Aegean Sea *37°36′N 25°15′E*
115 F18 **Livádeia** *prev.* Levádia. Stereá Ellás, C Greece *38°24′N 22°51′E*
Livádi *see* Liádi
Livanátai *see* Livanátes
115 G18 **Livanátes** *prev.* Livanátai. Stereá Ellás, C Greece *38°43′N 23°03′E*
118 I10 **Līvāni** *Ger.* Lievenhof. Preiļi, SE Latvia *56°22′N 26°12′E*
65 E25 **Lively Island** *island* SE Falkland Islands
65 D25 **Lively Sound** *sound* SE Falkland Islands
39 R8 **Livengood** Alaska, USA *65°31′N 148°32′W*
106 I7 **Livenza** ≈ NE Italy
35 O6 **Live Oak** California, W USA *39°17′N 121°41′W*
23 U9 **Live Oak** Florida, SE USA *30°18′N 82°59′W*
35 O9 **Livermore** California, W USA *37°40′N 121°46′W*
20 I6 **Livermore** Kentucky, S USA *37°31′N 87°08′W*
19 Q7 **Livermore Falls** Maine, NE USA *44°30′N 70°09′W*
24 J10 **Livermore, Mount** ▲ Texas, SW USA *30°37′N 104°10′W*
13 P16 **Liverpool** Nova Scotia, SE Canada *44°03′N 64°43′W*
97 K17 **Liverpool** NW England, United Kingdom *53°25′N 02°55′W*
183 S7 **Liverpool Range** ▲▲ New South Wales, SE Australia
42 F4 **Livingston** Izabal, E Guatemala *15°50′N 88°44′W*
96 J12 **Livingston** C Scotland, United Kingdom *55°51′N 03°31′W*
23 N5 **Livingston** Alabama, S USA *32°35′N 88°12′W*
35 P9 **Livingston** California, W USA *37°22′N 120°45′W*
22 J8 **Livingston** Louisiana, S USA *30°30′N 90°45′W*
33 S11 **Livingston** Montana, NW USA *45°40′N 110°33′W*
20 L8 **Livingston** Tennessee, S USA *36°22′N 85°20′W*
25 W9 **Livingston** Texas, SW USA *30°42′N 94°58′W*
83 I16 **Livingstone** *var.* Maramba. Southern, S Zambia *17°51′S 25°48′E*
185 B22 **Livingstone Mountains** ▲▲ South Island, New Zealand
80 K13 **Livingstone Mountains** ▲▲ S Tanzania
82 N12 **Livingstonia** Northern, N Malawi *10°29′S 34°06′E*
194 G4 **Livingston Island** *island* Antarctica
25 W9 **Livingston, Lake** ⊠ Texas, SW USA
112 F13 **Livno** ◈ Federicija Bosna I Hercegovina, SW Bosnia and Herzegovina
126 K7 **Livny** Orlovskaya Oblast', W Russian Federation *52°25′N 37°42′E*
93 M14 **Livojoki** ≈ C Finland
31 R10 **Livonia** Michigan, N USA *42°22′N 83°22′W*
106 E11 **Livorno** *Eng.* Leghorn. Toscana, C Italy *43°32′N 10°18′E*
Livramento *see* Santana do Livramento
141 U8 **Līwā** *var.* Al Liwā'. *oasis region* S United Arab Emirates
81 I24 **Liwale** Lindi, SE Tanzania *09°46′S 37°56′E*
159 W9 **Liwangbu** Ningxia, N China *36°42′N 106°05′E*
83 N15 **Liwonde** Southern, S Malawi *15°01′S 35°15′E*
159 V11 **Lixian** *var.* Li Xian. Gansu, C China *34°15′N 105°07′E*
160 H8 **Lixian** *var.* Li Xian, Zagunao. Sichuan, C China *31°27′N 103°06′E*
Li Xian *see* Lixian
Lixian Jiang *see* Black River
115 B18 **Lixoúri** *prev.* Lixoúrion. Kefallinía, Iónia Nisiá, Greece, C Mediterranean Sea *38°14′N 20°24′E*
Lixoúrion *see* Lixoúri
Lixus *see* Larache
33 U15 **Lizard Head Peak** ▲ Wyoming, C USA *42°47′N 109°12′W*
97 H25 **Lizard Point** *headland* SW England, United Kingdom *49°57′N 05°12′W*
Lizarra *see* Estella
112 L12 **Ljig** Serbia, C Serbia *44°14′N 20°16′E*
Ljouwert *see* Leeuwarden
Ljubelj *see* Loibl Pass
109 U11 **Ljubljana** *Ger.* Laibach, *It.* Lubiana; *anc.* Aemona, Emona. ● (Slovenia) C Slovenia *46°03′N 14°29′E*
109 T11 **Ljubljana** ✈ C Slovenia *46°14′N 14°26′E*
113 N17 **Ljuboten** ▲ S Serbia *42°12′N 21°06′E*
95 P19 **Ljugarn** Gotland, SE Sweden *57°23′N 18°45′E*
84 G7 **Ljungan** ≈ N Sweden
93 F17 **Ljungan** ≈ C Sweden
95 K21 **Ljungby** Kronoberg, S Sweden *56°49′N 13°55′E*
95 M17 **Ljungsbro** Östergötland, S Sweden *58°31′N 15°30′E*
95 I18 **Ljungskile** Västra Götaland, S Sweden *58°14′N 11°55′E*
94 M11 **Ljusdal** Gävleborg, C Sweden *61°50′N 16°10′E*
94 M11 **Ljusnan** ≈ C Sweden
94 N12 **Ljusne** Gävleborg, C Sweden *61°11′N 17°07′E*
95 P15 **Ljusterö** Stockholm, C Sweden *59°31′N 18°40′E*
109 X9 **Ljutomer** *Ger.* Luttenberg. NE Slovenia *46°31′N 16°12′E*
63 G15 **Llaima, Volcán** [volcano] S Chile *39°01′S 71°38′W*
105 X4 **Llançà** *var.* Llansá. Cataluña, NE Spain *42°23′N 03°08′E*
97 J21 **Llandovery** C Wales, United Kingdom *52°01′N 03°47′W*
97 J20 **Llandrindod Wells** E Wales, United Kingdom *52°15′N 03°23′W*
97 J18 **Llandudno** N Wales, United Kingdom *53°19′N 03°49′W*
97 I21 **Llanelli** *prev.* Llanelly. SW Wales, United Kingdom *51°41′N 04°12′W*
Llanelly *see* Llanelli
104 M2 **Llanes** Asturias, N Spain *43°25′N 04°46′W*
97 K19 **Llangollen** NE Wales, United Kingdom *52°58′N 03°10′W*
25 R10 **Llano** Texas, SW USA *30°49′N 98°42′W*
25 Q10 **Llano River** ≈ Texas, SW USA
54 I9 **Llanos** *physical region* Colombia/Venezuela
63 G16 **Llanquihue, Lago** ◎ S Chile
Llansá *see* Llançà
105 U5 **Lleida** *Cast.* Lérida; *anc.* Ilerda. Cataluña, NE Spain *41°38′N 00°35′E*
104 K12 **Llerena** Extremadura, W Spain *38°13′N 06°00′W*
105 S9 **Llíria** País Valenciano, E Spain *39°38′N 00°36′W*
105 W4 **Llivia** Cataluña, NE Spain *42°27′N 02°00′E*
105 O3 **Llodio** País Vasco, N Spain *43°08′N 02°59′W*
105 X5 **Lloret de Mar** Cataluña, NE Spain *41°42′N 02°51′E*
Llorri *see* Toretta de l'Orri
10 L11 **Lloyd George, Mount** ▲ British Columbia, W Canada *57°46′N 124°57′W*
11 R14 **Lloydminster** Alberta/Saskatchewan, SW Canada *53°18′N 110°00′W*
105 X9 **Llucmajor** Mallorca, Spain, W Mediterranean Sea *39°29′N 02°53′E*
36 L6 **Loa** Utah, W USA *38°24′N 111°38′W*
169 S8 **Loagan Bunut** ◎ East Malaysia
38 G12 **Loa, Mauna** ▲ Hawai'i, USA *19°28′N 155°39′W*
Loanda *see* Luanda
79 J22 **Loange** ≈ S Dem. Rep. Congo
79 E21 **Loango** Kouilou, S Congo *04°38′S 11°50′E*
106 B10 **Loano** Liguria, NW Italy *44°07′N 08°15′E*
62 H4 **Loa, Río** ≈ N Chile
83 I20 **Lobatse** *var.* Lobatsi. Kgatleng, SE Botswana *25°11′S 25°40′E*
Lobatsi *see* Lobatse
101 Q15 **Löbau** Sachsen, E Germany *51°07′N 14°40′E*
79 H16 **Lobaye** ◈ *prefecture* SW Central African Republic
79 I16 **Lobaye** ≈ SW Central African Republic
99 G21 **Lobbes** Hainaut, S Belgium *50°21′N 04°16′E*
61 D23 **Lobería** Buenos Aires, E Argentina *38°08′S 58°48′W*
110 F8 **Łobez** *Ger.* Labes. Zacodnio-pomorskie, NW Poland *53°38′N 15°39′E*
82 A13 **Lobito** Benguela, W Angola *12°20′S 13°34′E*
Lobkovichi *see* Labkovichy
Lob Nor *see* Lop Nur
171 V13 **Lobo** Papua, E Indonesia *03°41′S 134°06′E*
104 J11 **Lobón** Extremadura, W Spain *38°51′N 06°38′W*
61 D20 **Lobos** Buenos Aires, E Argentina *35°11′S 59°08′W*
40 E4 **Lobos, Cabo** *headland* NW Mexico *29°53′N 112°43′W*
40 F6 **Lobos, Isla** *island* NW Mexico
Lobositz *see* Lovosice
Lobsens *see* Łobżenica
Loburi *see* Lop Buri
110 H9 **Łobżenica** *Ger.* Lobsens. Wielkopolskie, C Poland *53°19′N 17°11′E*
108 G11 **Locarno** *Ger.* Luggarus. Ticino, S Switzerland *46°11′N 08°48′E*
96 E9 **Lochboisdale** NW Scotland, United Kingdom *57°08′N 07°17′W*
98 N11 **Lochem** Gelderland, E Netherlands *52°10′N 06°25′E*
102 M8 **Loches** Indre-et-Loire, C France *47°08′N 01°00′E*
Loch Garman *see* Wexford
96 H12 **Lochgilphead** W Scotland, United Kingdom *56°02′N 05°27′W*
96 H7 **Lochinver** N Scotland, United Kingdom *58°10′N 05°15′W*
96 F8 **Lochmaddy** NW Scotland, United Kingdom *57°35′N 07°10′W*
96 J10 **Lochnagar** ▲ C Scotland, United Kingdom *56°58′N 03°09′W*
99 E17 **Lochristi** Oost-Vlaanderen, NW Belgium *51°07′N 03°49′E*
96 H9 **Lochy, Loch** ◎ N Scotland, United Kingdom
182 G8 **Lock** South Australia *33°37′S 135°45′E*
97 J14 **Lockerbie** S Scotland, United Kingdom *55°11′N 03°27′W*
27 S13 **Lockesburg** Arkansas, C USA *33°58′N 94°10′W*
183 P10 **Lockhart** New South Wales, SE Australia *35°15′S 146°43′E*
25 S11 **Lockhart** Texas, SW USA *29°54′N 97°41′W*
18 F13 **Lock Haven** Pennsylvania, NE USA *41°08′N 77°27′W*
25 N4 **Lockney** Texas, SW USA *34°06′N 101°27′W*
100 O12 **Löcknitz** ≈ NE Germany
18 E9 **Lockport** New York, NE USA *43°09′N 78°40′W*
167 T13 **Lôc Ninh** Sông Be, S Vietnam *11°51′N 106°35′E*
107 N23 **Locri** Calabria, SW Italy *38°16′N 16°16′E*
Locse *see* Levoča
27 T2 **Locust Creek** ≈ Missouri, C USA
23 P3 **Locust Fork** ≈ Alabama, S USA
27 Q9 **Locust Grove** Oklahoma, C USA *36°12′N 95°10′W*
94 E11 **Lodalskåpa** ▲ S Norway *61°47′N 07°10′E*
183 N10 **Loddon River** ≈ Victoria, SE Australia
Lodensee *see* Klooga
103 P15 **Lodève** *anc.* Luteva. Hérault, S France *43°44′N 03°19′E*
124 I12 **Lodeynoye Pole** Leningradskaya Oblast', NW Russian Federation *60°41′N 33°29′E*
33 V11 **Lodge Grass** Montana, NW USA *45°19′N 107°20′W*
28 J15 **Lodgepole Creek** ≈ Nebraska/Wyoming, C USA
149 T11 **Lodhrān** Punjab, E Pakistan *29°32′N 71°40′E*
106 D8 **Lodi** Lombardia, NW Italy *45°19′N 09°30′E*
35 O8 **Lodi** California, W USA *38°07′N 121°17′W*
31 T12 **Lodi** Ohio, N USA *41°00′N 82°01′W*
92 H10 **Lødingen** Nordland, C Norway *68°25′N 16°00′E*
79 L20 **Lodja** Kasai-Oriental, C Dem. Rep. Congo *03°29′S 23°25′E*
37 O3 **Lodore, Canyon of** *canyon* Colorado, C USA
105 Q4 **Lodosa** Navarra, N Spain *42°26′N 02°05′W*
81 H16 **Lodwar** Rift Valley, NW Kenya *03°06′N 35°38′E*
110 K13 **Łódź** *Rus.* Lodz. Łódź, C Poland *51°51′N 19°26′E*
110 E12 **Łódzkie** ◈ *province* C Poland
167 P8 **Loei** *var.* Loey, Muang Loei. Loei, C Thailand *17°32′N 101°40′E*
98 I11 **Loenen** Utrecht, C Netherlands *52°13′N 05°01′E*
167 R9 **Loeng Nok Tha** Yasothon, E Thailand *16°12′N 104°31′E*
83 F24 **Loeriesfontein** Northern Cape, W South Africa *30°59′S 19°29′E*
Loewek *see* Łuków
Loey *see* Loei
76 J16 **Lofa** ≈ N Liberia
109 P6 **Lofer** Salzburg, C Austria *47°37′N 12°42′E*
92 F11 **Lofoten** *var.* Lofoten Islands. *island group* C Norway
Lofoten Islands *see* Lofoten
95 N18 **Loftahammar** Kalmar, S Sweden *57°55′N 16°45′E*
127 O10 **Log** Volgogradskaya Oblast', SW Russian Federation *49°32′N 43°52′E*
77 S12 **Loga** Dosso, SW Niger *13°40′N 03°15′E*
29 S14 **Logan** Iowa, C USA *41°38′N 95°47′W*
26 K3 **Logan** Kansas, C USA *39°39′N 99°34′W*
31 T14 **Logan** Ohio, N USA *39°32′N 82°24′W*
36 L1 **Logan** Utah, W USA *41°45′N 111°50′W*
21 P6 **Logan** West Virginia, NE USA *37°52′N 82°00′W*
35 Y10 **Logandale** Nevada, W USA *36°36′N 114°28′W*
19 O11 **Logan International** ✈ (Boston) Massachusetts, NE USA *42°22′N 71°00′W*
11 N16 **Logan Lake** British Columbia, SW Canada *50°28′N 120°42′W*
23 Q4 **Logan Martin Lake** ⊠ Alabama, S USA
10 G8 **Logan, Mount** ▲ Yukon Territory, W Canada *60°32′N 140°34′W*
32 I7 **Logan, Mount** ▲ Washington, NW USA *48°32′N 120°57′W*
33 P7 **Logan Pass** *pass* Montana, NW USA
31 O12 **Logansport** Indiana, N USA *40°44′N 86°25′W*
22 F6 **Logansport** Louisiana, S USA *31°58′N 94°00′W*
Logar *see* Lowgar
67 R11 **Loge** ≈ NW Angola
Logishin *see* Lahishyn
Log na Coille *see* Lugnaquillia Mountain
78 G11 **Logone** *var.* Lagone. ≈ Cameroon/Chad
78 G13 **Logone-Occidental** *off.* Préfecture du Logone-Occidental. ◈ *prefecture* SW Chad
78 H13 **Logone Occidental** ≈ SW Chad
Logone-Occidental, Préfecture du *see* Logone-Occidental
78 G13 **Logone-Oriental** *off.* Préfecture du Logone-Oriental. ◈ *prefecture* SW Chad
78 H13 **Logone Oriental** ≈ SW Chad
Logone Oriental *see* Pendé
Logone-Oriental, Préfecture du *see* Logone-Oriental
L'Ogooué-Ivindo *see* Ogooué-Ivindo
L'Ogooué-Lolo *see* Ogooué-Lolo
L'Ogooué-Maritime *see* Ogooué-Maritime
Logoysk *see* Lahoysk
105 P4 **Logroño** *anc.* Vareia, *Lat.* Juliobriga. La Rioja, N Spain *42°28′N 02°26′W*
104 L10 **Logrosán** Extremadura, W Spain *39°21′N 05°29′W*
95 G20 **Løgstør** Nordjylland, N Denmark *56°57′N 09°19′E*
95 H22 **Løgten** Århus, C Denmark *56°17′N 10°20′E*
95 F24 **Løgumkloster** Sønderjylland, SW Denmark *55°04′N 08°58′E*
Lögurinn *see* Lagarfljót
153 P15 **Lohārdaga** Jhārkhand, N India *23°27′N 84°42′E*
152 H10 **Lohāru** Haryāna, N India *28°28′N 75°50′E*
101 D15 **Lohausen** ✈ (Düsseldorf) Nordrhein-Westfalen, W Germany *51°18′N 06°51′E*
189 O14 **Lohd** Pohnpei, E Micronesia
92 L12 **Lohiniva** Lappi, N Finland *67°09′N 25°04′E*
Lohiszyn *see* Lahishyn
93 L20 **Lohja** *var.* Lojo. Etelä-Suomi, S Finland *60°14′N 24°07′E*
169 V11 **Lohjanan** Borneo, C Indonesia
25 Q9 **Lohn** Texas, SW USA *31°15′N 99°22′W*
100 G12 **Lohne** Niedersachsen, NW Germany *52°40′N 08°13′E*
Lohr *see* Lohr am Main
101 I18 **Lohr am Main** *var.* Lohr. Bayern, C Germany *50°00′N 09°30′E*
109 T10 **Loibl Pass** *Ger.* Loiblpass, *Slvn.* Ljubelj. *pass* Austria/Slovenia
Loiblpass *see* Loibl Pass
167 N6 **Loikaw** Kayah State, C Burma (Myanmar) *19°40′N 97°17′E*
93 K19 **Loimaa** Länsi-Suomi, SW Finland *60°51′N 23°03′E*
103 O6 **Loing** ≈ C France
167 R6 **Loi, Phou** ▲ N Laos *20°18′N 103°14′E*
102 L7 **Loir** ≈ C France
103 Q11 **Loire** ◈ *department* E France
102 M7 **Loire** *var.* Liger. ≈ C France
102 I7 **Loire-Atlantique** ◈ *department* NW France
103 O7 **Loiret** ◈ *department* C France
102 M8 **Loir-et-Cher** ◈ *department* C France
101 L24 **Loisach** ≈ SE Germany
56 B9 **Loja** Loja, S Ecuador *03°59′S 79°16′W*
104 M14 **Loja** Andalucía, S Spain *37°10′N 04°09′W*
56 B9 **Loja** ◈ *province* S Ecuador
Lojo *see* Lohja
116 J4 **Lokachi** Volyns'ka Oblast', NW Ukraine *50°44′N 24°39′E*
79 M20 **Lokandu** Maniema, C Dem. Rep. Congo *02°34′S 25°44′E*
92 M11 **Lokan Tekojärvi** ◎ NE Finland
137 Z11 **Lökbatan** *Rus.* Lokbatan. E Azerbaijan *40°21′N 49°43′E*
Lokbatan *see* Lökbatan
99 F17 **Lokeren** Oost-Vlaanderen, NW Belgium *51°06′N 03°59′E*
Lokhvitsa *see* Lokhvytsya
117 S4 **Lokhvytsya** *Rus.* Lokhvitsa. Poltavs'ka Oblast', NE Ukraine *50°22′N 33°16′E*
81 H17 **Lokichar** Rift Valley, NW Kenya *02°23′N 35°40′E*
81 G16 **Lokichokio** Rift Valley, NW Kenya *04°16′N 34°22′E*
81 H16 **Lokitaung** Rift Valley, NW Kenya *04°15′N 35°45′E*
92 M11 **Lokka** Lappi, N Finland *67°48′N 27°41′E*
94 G8 **Løkken Verk** Sør-Trøndelag, S Norway *63°06′N 09°43′E*
124 G16 **Loknya** Pskovskaya Oblast', W Russian Federation *56°48′N 30°08′E*
77 V15 **Loko** Nassarawa, C Nigeria *08°00′N 07°48′E*
77 U15 **Lokoja** Kogi, C Nigeria *07°48′N 06°45′E*
81 H17 **Lokori** Rift Valley, W Kenya *01°56′N 36°03′E*
77 R16 **Lokossa** S Benin *06°38′N 01°43′E*
118 I3 **Loksa** *Ger.* Loxa. Harjumaa, NW Estonia *59°32′N 25°42′E*
9 T7 **Loks Land** *island* Nunavut, NE Canada
80 C13 **Lol** ≈ S Sudan
76 K15 **Lola** SE Guinea *07°52′N 08°29′W*
35 Q5 **Lola, Mount** ▲ California, W USA *39°27′N 120°20′W*
81 H20 **Loliondo** Arusha, NE Tanzania *02°03′S 35°46′E*
95 H25 **Lolland** *prev.* Laaland. *island* S Denmark
186 G6 **Lolobau Island** *island* E Papua New Guinea
79 E16 **Lolodorf** Sud, SW Cameroon *03°17′N 10°50′E*
114 G7 **Lom** *prev.* Lom-Palanka. Montana, NW Bulgaria *43°49′N 23°16′E*
114 G7 **Lom** ≈ NW Bulgaria
79 M19 **Lomami** ≈ C Dem. Rep. Congo
57 F17 **Lomas** Arequipa, SW Peru *15°29′S 74°54′W*
63 I23 **Lomas, Bahía** *bay* S Chile
61 D20 **Lomas de Zamora** Buenos Aires, E Argentina *34°53′S 58°26′W*
61 D20 **Loma Verde** Buenos Aires, E Argentina *35°16′S 58°24′W*
180 K4 **Lombadina** Western Australia *16°39′S 122°54′E*
106 E6 **Lombardia** *Eng.* Lombardy. ◈ *region* N Italy
Lombardy *see* Lombardia
102 M15 **Lombez** Gers, S France *43°29′N 00°54′E*
171 Q16 **Lomblen, Pulau** *island* Nusa Tenggara, S Indonesia
173 W7 **Lombok Basin** *undersea feature* E Indian Ocean *09°50′S 116°00′E*
170 L16 **Lombok, Pulau** *island* Nusa Tenggara, C Indonesia
77 Q16 **Lomé** ● (Togo) S Togo *06°08′N 01°13′E*
77 Q16 **Lomé** ✈ S Togo *06°08′N 01°13′E*
79 L19 **Lomela** Kasai-Oriental, C Dem. Rep. Congo *02°19′S 23°15′E*
25 R9 **Lometa** Texas, SW USA *31°13′N 98°23′W*
79 F16 **Lomié** Est, SE Cameroon *03°09′N 13°35′E*
30 M8 **Lomira** Wisconsin, N USA *43°36′N 88°26′W*
95 K23 **Lomma** Skåne, S Sweden *55°41′N 13°05′E*
99 J16 **Lommel** Limburg, N Belgium *51°14′N 05°19′E*
96 I11 **Lomond, Loch** ◎ C Scotland, United Kingdom
197 R9 **Lomonosov Ridge** *var.* Harris Ridge, *Rus.* Khrebet Homonsova. *undersea feature* Arctic Ocean *88°00′N 140°00′E*
Lomonsova, Khrebet *see* Lomonosov Ridge
Lom-Palanka *see* Lom
Lomphat *see* Lumphăt
35 P14 **Lompoc** California, W USA *34°39′N 120°29′W*
167 P9 **Lom Sak** *var.* Muang Lom Sak. Phetchabun, C Thailand *16°45′N 101°12′E*
110 N9 **Łomża** *Rus.* Lomzha. Podlaskie, NE Poland *53°11′N 22°04′E*
Lomzha *see* Łomża
Lonaula *see* Lonāvale
155 D14 **Lonāvale** *prev.* Lonaula. Mahārāshtra, W India *18°45′N 73°27′E*
63 G15 **Loncoche** Araucanía, C Chile *39°22′S 72°34′W*
63 H14 **Loncopue** Neuquén, W Argentina *38°04′S 70°43′W*
99 G17 **Londerzeel** Vlaams Brabant, C Belgium *51°00′N 04°19′E*
Londinium *see* London
14 E16 **London** Ontario, S Canada *42°59′N 81°13′W*
191 Y2 **London** Kiritimati, E Kiribati *02°00′N 157°28′W*
97 O22 **London** *anc.* Augusta, *Lat.* Londinium. ● (United Kingdom) SE England, United Kingdom *51°30′N 00°10′W*
21 N7 **London** Kentucky, S USA *37°07′N 84°05′W*
31 S13 **London** Ohio, NE USA *39°52′N 83°27′W*
25 Q10 **London** Texas, SW USA *30°40′N 99°33′W*
97 O22 **London City** ✈ SE England, United Kingdom *51°31′N 00°07′E*
97 E14 **Londonderry** *var.* Derry, *Ir.* Doire. NW Northern Ireland, United Kingdom *55°N 07°19′W*
97 F14 **Londonderry** *cultural region* NW Northern Ireland, United Kingdom
180 M2 **Londonderry, Cape** *cape* Western Australia
63 H25 **Londonderry, Isla** *island* S Chile
43 O7 **Londres, Cayos** *reef* NE Nicaragua
60 I10 **Londrina** Paraná, S Brazil *23°18′S 51°13′W*
27 N13 **Lone Grove** Oklahoma, C USA *34°11′N 97°15′W*
14 E12 **Lonely Island** *island* Ontario, S Canada
35 T8 **Lone Mountain** ▲ Nevada, W USA *38°01′N 117°28′W*
25 V6 **Lone Oak** Texas, SW USA *33°02′N 95°58′W*
35 T11 **Lone Pine** California, W USA *36°36′N 118°04′W*
Lone Star State *see* Texas
Lone Tree Islet *see* Iku
83 D14 **Longa** Cuando Cubango, C Angola *14°44′S 18°36′E*
82 B12 **Longa** ≈ W Angola
83 E15 **Longa** ≈ SE Angola
Long'an *see* Pingwu
163 W11 **Longang Shan** ▲▲ NE China
197 S4 **Longa, Proliv** *Eng.* Long Strait. *strait* NE Russian Federation
44 J13 **Long Bay** *bay* W Jamaica
21 V13 **Long Bay** *bay* North Carolina/South Carolina, E USA
35 T16 **Long Beach** California, W USA *33°46′N 118°11′W*
22 M9 **Long Beach** Mississippi, S USA *30°21′N 89°09′W*
18 L14 **Long Beach** Long Island, New York, NE USA *40°34′N 73°38′W*
32 F9 **Long Beach** Washington, NW USA *46°21′N 124°03′W*
18 K16 **Long Beach Island** *island* New Jersey, NE USA
65 M25 **Longbluff** *headland* SW Tristan da Cunha
23 U13 **Longboat Key** *island* Florida, SE USA
18 K15 **Long Branch** New Jersey, NE USA *40°18′N 73°59′W*
44 J5 **Long Cay** *island* SE Bahamas
Longcheng *see* Xiaoxian
161 P14 **Longchuan** *var.* Laolong. Guangdong, S China *24°07′N 115°10′E*
Longchuan *see* Nanhua
Longchuan Jiang *see* Shweli
32 K12 **Long Creek** Oregon, NW USA *44°40′N 119°07′W*
159 W10 **Longde** Ningxia, N China *35°37′N 106°07′E*
183 P16 **Longford** Tasmania, SE Australia *41°41′S 147°03′E*
97 D17 **Longford** *Ir.* An Longfort. Longford, C Ireland *53°45′N 07°50′W*
97 E17 **Longford** *Ir.* An Longfort. *cultural region* C Ireland
Longgang *see* Dazu
161 P1 **Longhua** Hebei, E China *41°18′N 117°44′E*
169 U11 **Longiram** Borneo, C Indonesia *0°02′S 115°36′E*
44 J4 **Long Island** *island* C Bahamas
12 H8 **Long Island** *island* Nunavut, C Canada
186 D7 **Long Island** *var.* Arop Island. *island* N Papua New Guinea
18 L14 **Long Island** *island* New York, NE USA
Long Island *see* Bermuda
18 M14 **Long Island Sound** *sound* NE USA
163 U7 **Longjiang** Heilongjiang, NE China *47°20′N 123°09′E*
160 K13 **Long Jiang** ≈ S China
163 Y10 **Longjing** *var.* Yanji. Jilin, NE China *42°48′N 129°26′E*
161 R4 **Longkou** Shandong, E China *37°40′N 120°21′E*
12 E11 **Longlac** Ontario, S Canada *49°47′N 86°34′W*
19 S1 **Long Lake** ◎ Maine, NE USA
31 R5 **Long Lake** ◎ Michigan, N USA
31 O6 **Long Lake** ◎ Michigan, N USA
29 N6 **Long Lake** ◎ North Dakota, N USA
30 J4 **Long Lake** ⊠ Wisconsin, N USA
99 K23 **Longlier** Luxembourg, SE Belgium *49°51′N 05°27′E*
160 I13 **Longlin** *var.* Longlin Gezu Zizhixian, Xinzhou. Guangxi Zhuangzu Zizhiqu, S China *24°46′N 105°19′E*
Longlin Gezu Zizhixian *see* Longlin
37 T3 **Longmont** Colorado, C USA *40°09′N 105°07′W*
157 P10 **Longnan** *var.* Wudu. Gansu, C China *33°27′N 104°57′E*
29 N13 **Long Pine** Nebraska, C USA *42°32′N 99°42′W*
Longping *see* Luodian

◆ Country
● Country Capital
◇ Dependent Territory
○ Dependent Territory Capital
◈ Administrative Regions
✈ International Airport
▲ Mountain
▲▲ Mountain Range
[volcano] Volcano
≈ River
◎ Lake
⊠ Reservoir

LONG POINT – LUKRANSAR

14 F17 **Long Point** headland Ontario, S Canada 42°33′N 80°15′W
14 K15 **Long Point** headland Ontario, SE Canada 43°56′N 76°53′W
184 P10 **Long Point** headland North Island, New Zealand 39°07′S 177°41′E
30 L2 **Long Point** headland Michigan, N USA 47°50′N 89°09′W
14 G17 **Long Point Bay** lake bay Ontario, S Canada
29 T7 **Long Prairie** Minnesota, N USA 45°58′N 94°52′W
Longquan see Fenggang
Longquàn see Yanggao
13 S11 **Long Range Mountains** hill range Newfoundland and Labrador, E Canada
65 H25 **Long Range Point** headland SE Saint Helena 16°00′S 05°41′W
181 V8 **Longreach** Queensland, E Australia 23°31′S 144°18′E
160 H7 **Longriba** Sichuan, C China 32°32′N 102°20′E
160 L10 **Longshan** var. Min'an. Hunan, S China 29°25′N 109°28′E
37 S3 **Longs Peak** ▲ Colorado, C USA 40°15′N 105°37′W
Long Strait see Longa, Proliv
102 K8 **Longué** Maine-et-Loire, NW France 47°23′N 00°07′W
13 P11 **Longue-Pointe** Québec, E Canada 50°20′N 64°13′W
103 S4 **Longuyon** Meurthe-et-Moselle, NE France 49°25′N 05°37′E
25 W7 **Longview** Texas, SW USA 32°30′N 94°45′W
32 G10 **Longview** Washington, NW USA 46°08′N 122°56′W
65 H25 **Longwood** C Saint Helena
25 P7 **Longworth** Texas, SW USA 32°37′N 100°20′W
103 S3 **Longwy** Meurthe-et-Moselle, NE France 49°31′N 05°46′E
159 V11 **Longxi** var. Gongchang. Gansu, C China 35°00′N 104°34′E
Longxian see Wengyuan
167 S14 **Long Xuyên** var. Longxuyen. An Giang, S Vietnam 10°23′N 105°25′E
Longxuyen see Long Xuyên
161 Q13 **Longyan** Fujian, SE China 25°06′N 117°02′E
92 O3 **Longyearbyen** ○ (Svalbard) Spitsbergen, W Svalbard 78°12′N 15°39′E
160 J15 **Longzhou** Guangxi Zhuangzu Zizhiqu, S China 22°22′N 106°46′E
Longzhouping see Changyang
100 F12 **Löningen** Niedersachsen, NW Germany 52°43′N 07°42′E
27 V11 **Lonoke** Arkansas, C USA 34°46′N 91°56′W
95 L21 **Lönsboda** Skåne, S Sweden 56°24′N 14°19′E
103 S9 **Lons-le-Saunier** anc. Ledo Salinarius. Jura, E France 46°41′N 05°32′E
31 O15 **Loogootee** Indiana, N USA 38°40′N 86°54′W
31 Q9 **Looking Glass River** ≈ Michigan, N USA
21 X11 **Lookout, Cape** headland North Carolina, SE USA 34°36′N 76°31′W
39 O6 **Lookout Ridge** ridge Alaska, USA
Lookransar see Lūnkaransar
181 N11 **Loongana** Western Australia 30°53′S 127°15′E
99 I14 **Loon op Zand** Noord-Brabant, S Netherlands 51°38′N 05°05′E
97 A19 **Loop Head** Ir. Ceann Léime. promontory W Ireland
109 V4 **Loosdorf** Niederösterreich, NE Austria 48°13′N 15°25′E
158 G10 **Lop** Xinjiang Uygur Zizhiqu, NW China 37°06′N 80°12′E
112 J11 **Lopare** ◈ Republika Srpska, NE Bosnia and Herzegovina
Lopatichi see Lapatsichy
127 P7 **Lopatino** Penzenskaya Oblast', W Russian Federation 52°38′N 45°46′E
167 P10 **Lop Buri** var. Loburi. Lop Buri, C Thailand 14°49′N 100°37′E
25 R16 **Lopeno** Texas, SW USA 26°42′N 99°06′W
79 C18 **Lopez, Cap** headland W Gabon 0°39′S 08°44′E
98 I12 **Lopik** Utrecht, C Netherlands 51°58′N 04°57′E
Lop Nor see Lop Nur
158 M7 **Lop Nur** var. Lob Nor, Lop Nor, Lo-pu Po. seasonal lake NW China
Lopnur see Yuli
79 K17 **Lopori** ≈ NW Dem. Rep. Congo
98 O5 **Loppersum** Groningen, NE Netherlands 53°20′N 06°45′E
92 I8 **Lopphavet** sound N Norway
Lo-pu Po see Lop Nur
Lora see Lowrah
182 F3 **Lora Creek** seasonal river South Australia
104 K13 **Lora del Río** Andalucía, S Spain 37°39′N 05°32′W
148 M11 **Lora, Hāmūn-i** wetland SW Pakistan
31 T11 **Lorain** Ohio, N USA 41°27′N 82°10′W
25 O7 **Loraine** Texas, SW USA 32°24′N 100°42′W
149 Q10 **Loralai** Baluchistān, SW Pakistan 30°22′N 68°36′E
31 R13 **Loramie, Lake** ⊠ Ohio, N USA
105 Q13 **Lorca** Ar. Lurka; anc. Eliocroca, Lat. Illurco. Murcia, S Spain 37°40′N 01°41′W
143 N11 **Lordegān** Chahār Mahall va Bakhtiārī, C Iran 31°31′N 50°48′E
192 I10 **Lord Howe Island** island E Australia
Lord Howe Island see Ontong Java Atoll
175 O10 **Lord Howe Rise** undersea feature SW Pacific Ocean
192 J10 **Lord Howe Seamounts** undersea feature W Pacific Ocean
37 P15 **Lordsburg** New Mexico, SW USA 32°19′N 108°42′W
186 E5 **Lorengau** var. Lorungau. Manus Island, N Papua New Guinea 02°01′S 147°15′E
25 N5 **Lorenzo** Texas, SW USA 33°40′N 101°31′W
142 K7 **Lorestān** off. Ostān-e Lorestān, var. Luristan. ◈ province W Iran
Lorestān, Ostān-e see Lorestān
57 M17 **Loreto** Beni, N Bolivia 15°13′S 64°44′W
106 J12 **Loreto** Marche, C Italy 43°25′N 13°37′E
40 F8 **Loreto** Baja California Sur, NW Mexico 25°59′N 111°22′W
40 M11 **Loreto** Zacatecas, C Mexico 22°15′N 102°00′W
56 E9 **Loreto** off. Departamento de Loreto. ◈ department NE Peru
Loreto, Departamento de see Loreto
81 K18 **Lorian Swamp** swamp E Kenya
54 E6 **Lorica** Córdoba, NW Colombia 09°14′N 75°50′W
102 G7 **Lorient** prev. l'Orient. Morbihan, NW France 47°45′N 03°22′W
l'Orient see Lorient
111 K22 **Lőrinci** Heves, NE Hungary 47°46′N 19°40′E
14 G11 **Loring** Ontario, S Canada 45°55′N 79°59′W
33 V6 **Loring** Montana, NW USA 48°49′N 107°48′W
103 R13 **Loriol-sur-Drôme** Drôme, E France 44°46′N 04°51′E
21 U12 **Loris** South Carolina, SE USA 34°03′N 78°53′W
57 I18 **Loriscota, Laguna** ◎ S Peru
183 N13 **Lorne** Victoria, SE Australia 38°33′S 143°57′E
96 G11 **Lorn, Firth of** inlet W Scotland, United Kingdom
Loro Sae see East Timor
101 F24 **Lörrach** Baden-Württemberg, S Germany 47°38′N 07°40′E
103 T5 **Lorraine** ◈ region NE France
Lorungau see Lorengau
94 L11 **Los** Gävleborg, C Sweden 61°43′N 15°15′E
35 P14 **Los Alamos** California, W USA 34°44′N 120°16′W
37 S10 **Los Alamos** New Mexico, SW USA 35°52′N 106°17′W
42 F5 **Los Amates** Izabal, E Guatemala 15°14′N 89°06′W
63 G14 **Los Ángeles** Bío Bío, C Chile 37°30′S 72°18′W
35 S15 **Los Angeles** California, W USA 34°03′N 118°15′W
35 S15 **Los Angeles** ✈ California, W USA 33°54′N 118°24′W
35 T13 **Los Angeles Aqueduct** aqueduct California, W USA
Losanna see Lausanne
63 H20 **Los Antiguos** Santa Cruz, SW Argentina 46°36′S 71°31′W
189 Q16 **Losap Atoll** atoll C Micronesia
35 P10 **Los Banos** California, W USA 37°00′N 120°39′W
104 K16 **Los Barrios** Andalucía, S Spain 36°11′N 05°30′W
62 L5 **Los Blancos** Salta, N Argentina 23°36′S 62°35′W
42 L12 **Los Chiles** Alajuela, NW Costa Rica 11°00′N 84°42′W
105 O2 **Los Corrales de Buelna** Cantabria, N Spain 43°15′N 04°04′W
25 T17 **Los Fresnos** Texas, SW USA 26°03′N 97°28′W
35 N9 **Los Gatos** California, W USA 37°13′N 121°58′W
127 P10 **Loshchina** Volgogradskaya Oblast', SW Russian Federation 48°58′N 46°14′E
110 O11 **Łosice** Mazowieckie, C Poland 52°13′N 22°42′E
112 B11 **Lošinj** Ger. Lussin, It. Lussino. island W Croatia
Los Jardines see Ngetik Atoll
63 G15 **Los Lagos** Los Lagos, C Chile 39°50′S 72°50′W
63 F17 **Los Lagos** off. Región de los Lagos. ◈ region C Chile
los Lagos, Región de see Los Lagos
Loslau see Wodzisław Śląski
64 N11 **Los Llanos de Aridane** var. Los Llanos de Aridane. La Palma, Islas Canarias, Spain, NE Atlantic Ocean 28°39′N 17°54′W
Los Llanos de Aridane see Los Llanos de Aridane
37 R11 **Los Lunas** New Mexico, SW USA 34°48′N 106°43′W
63 I16 **Los Menucos** Río Negro, C Argentina 40°52′S 68°07′W
40 H8 **Los Mochis** Sinaloa, C Mexico 25°48′N 108°58′W
35 N4 **Los Molinos** California, W USA 40°00′N 122°05′W
104 M9 **Los Navalmorales** Castilla-La Mancha, C Spain 39°43′N 04°38′W
25 S15 **Los Olmos Creek** ≈ Texas, SW USA
Losonc/Losontz see Lučenec
167 S5 **Lô, Sông** var. Panlong Jiang. ≈ China/Vietnam
44 B5 **Los Palacios** Pinar del Río, W Cuba 22°35′N 83°16′W
104 K14 **Los Palacios y Villafranca** Andalucía, S Spain 37°10′N 05°55′W
37 R12 **Los Pinos Mountains** ▲▲ New Mexico, SW USA
37 R11 **Los Ranchos de Albuquerque** New Mexico, SW USA 35°09′N 106°37′W
40 M14 **Los Reyes** Michoacán, SW Mexico 19°36′N 102°29′W
56 B7 **Los Ríos** ◈ province C Ecuador
64 O11 **Los Rodeos** ✈ (Santa Cruz de Tenerife) Tenerife, Islas Canarias, Spain, NE Atlantic Ocean 28°27′N 16°20′W
54 L4 **Los Roques, Islas** island group N Venezuela
43 S17 **Los Santos** Los Santos, S Panama 07°56′N 80°23′W
43 S17 **Los Santos** off. Provincia de Los Santos. ◈ province S Panama
Los Santos see Los Santos de Maimona
104 J12 **Los Santos de Maimona** var. Los Santos. Extremadura, W Spain 38°27′N 06°22′W
Los Santos, Provincia de see Los Santos
98 P10 **Losser** Overijssel, E Netherlands 52°16′N 06°25′E
96 J8 **Lossiemouth** NE Scotland, United Kingdom 57°43′N 03°18′W
61 B14 **Los Tábanos** Santa Fe, C Argentina 28°27′S 59°57′W
54 J4 **Los Taques** Falcón, N Venezuela 11°50′N 70°16′W
14 G11 **Lost Channel** Ontario, S Canada 45°54′N 80°20′W
54 L5 **Los Teques** Miranda, N Venezuela 10°25′N 67°01′W
35 Q12 **Lost Hills** California, W USA 35°35′N 119°40′W
36 I7 **Lost Peak** ▲ Utah, W USA 37°30′N 113°57′W
33 P11 **Lost Trail Pass** pass Montana, NW USA
186 G9 **Losuia** Kiriwina Island, SE Papua New Guinea 08°29′S 151°03′E
62 G10 **Los Vilos** Coquimbo, C Chile 31°56′S 71°35′W
105 N10 **Los Yébenes** Castilla-La Mancha, C Spain 39°35′N 03°52′W
103 N13 **Lot** ◈ department S France
103 N13 **Lot** ≈ S France
63 F14 **Lota** Bío Bío, C Chile 37°07′S 73°10′W
81 G15 **Lotagipi Swamp** wetland Kenya/Sudan
102 K14 **Lot-et-Garonne** ◈ department SW France
83 K21 **Lothair** Mpumalanga, NE South Africa 26°23′S 30°26′E
33 R7 **Lothair** Montana, NW USA 48°28′N 111°15′W
79 L20 **Loto** Kasai-Oriental, C Dem. Rep. Congo 02°48′S 22°30′E
108 E10 **Lötschbergtunnel** tunnel Valais, SW Switzerland
25 T9 **Lott** Texas, SW USA 31°12′N 97°02′W
124 H3 **Lotta** var. Lutto. ≈ Finland/Russian Federation
184 Q7 **Lottin Point** headland North Island, New Zealand 37°26′S 178°07′E
Lötzen see Giżycko
Loualaba see Lualaba
167 P6 **Louangnamtha** var. Luong Nam Tha. Louang Namtha, N Laos 20°55′N 101°24′E
167 Q7 **Louangphabang** var. Louangphrabang, Luang Prabang. Louangphabang, N Laos 19°51′N 102°08′E
Louangphrabang see Louangphabang
194 H5 **Loubet Coast** physical region Antarctica
Loubomo see Dolisie
Louch see Loukhi
102 H6 **Loudéac** Côtes d'Armor, NW France 48°11′N 02°45′W
160 M11 **Loudi** Hunan, S China 27°51′N 111°59′E
79 F21 **Loudima** Bouenza, S Congo 04°06′S 13°05′E
20 M9 **Loudon** Tennessee, S USA 35°43′N 84°19′W
31 T12 **Loudonville** Ohio, N USA 40°38′N 82°13′W
102 L8 **Loudun** Vienne, W France 47°01′N 00°05′E
102 K7 **Loué** Sarthe, NW France 48°00′N 00°14′W
76 G10 **Louga** NW Senegal 15°36′N 16°15′W
97 M19 **Loughborough** C England, United Kingdom 52°47′N 01°11′W
97 C18 **Loughrea** Ir. Baile Locha Riach. Galway, W Ireland 53°12′N 08°34′W
103 S9 **Louhans** Saône-et-Loire, C France 46°38′N 05°12′E
21 P5 **Louisa** Kentucky, S USA 38°06′N 82°37′W
21 V5 **Louisa** Virginia, NE USA 38°02′N 78°00′W
21 V9 **Louisburg** North Carolina, SE USA 36°05′N 78°18′W
25 U12 **Louise** Texas, SW USA 29°07′N 96°22′W
15 P11 **Louiseville** Québec, SE Canada 46°15′N 72°54′W
27 W3 **Louisiana** Missouri, C USA 39°25′N 91°03′W
22 G8 **Louisiana** off. State of Louisiana, also known as Creole State, Pelican State. ◈ state S USA
Louis Trichardt see Makhado
23 V4 **Louisville** Georgia, SE USA 33°00′N 82°24′W
30 M15 **Louisville** Illinois, N USA 38°46′N 88°32′W
20 K5 **Louisville** Kentucky, S USA 38°15′N 85°46′W
22 M4 **Louisville** Mississippi, S USA 33°07′N 89°03′W
29 S15 **Louisville** Nebraska, C USA 41°00′N 96°09′W
192 L11 **Louisville Ridge** undersea feature S Pacific Ocean
124 J6 **Loukhi** var. Louch. Respublika Kareliya, NW Russian Federation 66°05′N 33°04′E
79 H19 **Loukoléla** Cuvette, E Congo 01°04′S 17°10′E
104 G14 **Loulé** Faro, S Portugal 37°08′N 08°02′W
111 C16 **Louny** Ger. Laun. Ústecký Kraj, NW Czech Republic 50°22′N 13°50′E
29 O15 **Loup City** Nebraska, C USA 41°16′N 98°58′W
29 P15 **Loup River** ≈ Nebraska, C USA
15 S9 **Loup, Rivière du** ≈ Québec, SE Canada
12 K7 **Loups Marins, Lacs des** ◎ Québec, NE Canada
102 K16 **Lourdes** Hautes-Pyrénées, S France 43°06′N 00°03′W
Lourenço Marques see Maputo
104 F11 **Loures** Lisboa, C Portugal 38°50′N 09°10′W
104 F10 **Lourinhã** Lisboa, C Portugal 39°14′N 09°19′W
115 C16 **Loúros** ≈ W Greece
104 G8 **Lousã** Coimbra, N Portugal 40°07′N 08°15′W
Loushanguan see Tongzi
160 M10 **Lou Shui** ≈ C China
183 O5 **Louth** New South Wales, SE Australia 30°34′S 145°07′E
97 O18 **Louth** E England, United Kingdom 53°19′N 00°00′E
97 F17 **Louth** Ir. Lú. cultural region NE Ireland
115 H15 **Loutrá** Kentrikí Makedonía, N Greece 39°55′N 23°37′E
115 G19 **Loutráki** Pelopónnisos, S Greece 37°55′N 22°55′E
Louvain see Leuven
99 H19 **Louvain-la Neuve** Walloon Brabant, C Belgium 50°39′N 04°36′E
14 J8 **Louvicourt** Québec, SE Canada 48°04′N 77°22′W
102 M4 **Louviers** Eure, N France 49°13′N 01°11′E
30 K14 **Lou Yaeger, Lake** ⊠ Illinois, N USA
93 J15 **Lövånger** Västerbotten, N Sweden 64°22′N 21°19′E
124 J14 **Lovat'** ≈ NW Russian Federation
113 J17 **Lovćen** ▲ SW Montenegro 42°22′N 18°49′E
114 I8 **Lovech** Lovech, N Bulgaria 43°08′N 24°45′E
114 I9 **Lovech** ◈ province N Bulgaria
25 V9 **Lovelady** Texas, SW USA 31°07′N 95°27′W
37 T3 **Loveland** Colorado, C USA 40°24′N 105°04′W
33 U12 **Lovell** Wyoming, C USA 44°50′N 108°23′W
Lovello, Monte see Grosser Löffler
35 S4 **Lovelock** Nevada, W USA 40°11′N 118°30′W
106 E7 **Lovere** Lombardia, N Italy 45°51′N 10°06′E
30 L10 **Loves Park** Illinois, N USA 42°19′N 89°03′W
26 M2 **Lovewell Reservoir** ⊠ Kansas, C USA
93 M19 **Loviisa** Swe. Lovisa. Etelä-Suomi, S Finland 60°27′N 26°15′E
37 V15 **Loving** New Mexico, SW USA 32°17′N 104°06′W
21 U6 **Lovingston** Virginia, NE USA 37°46′N 78°54′W
37 V14 **Lovington** New Mexico, SW USA 32°56′N 103°21′W
Lovisa see Loviisa
111 C15 **Lovosice** Ger. Lobositz. Ústecký Kraj, NW Czech Republic 50°30′N 14°02′E
124 K4 **Lovozero** Murmanskaya Oblast', NW Russian Federation 68°00′N 35°03′E
124 K4 **Lovozero, Ozero** ◎ NW Russian Federation
112 B9 **Lovran** It. Laurana. Primorje-Gorski Kotar, NW Croatia 45°16′N 14°15′E
116 E11 **Lovrin** Ger. Lowrin. Timiș, W Romania 45°58′N 20°49′E
82 E10 **Lóvua** Lunda Norte, NE Angola 07°21′S 20°09′E
82 G12 **Lóvua** Moxico, E Angola 11°33′S 23°35′E
65 D25 **Low Bay** bay East Falkland, Falkland Islands
9 P9 **Low, Cape** headland Nunavut, E Canada 63°05′N 85°27′W
33 N10 **Lowell** Idaho, NW USA 46°07′N 115°36′W
19 O10 **Lowell** Massachusetts, NE USA 42°38′N 71°19′W
Löwen see Leuven
Löwenberg in Schlesien see Lwówek Śląski
Lower Austria see Niederösterreich
Lower Bann see Bann
Lower California see Baja California
Lower Danube see Niederösterreich
185 L14 **Lower Hutt** Wellington, North Island, New Zealand 41°13′S 174°51′E
39 N11 **Lower Kalskag** Alaska, USA 61°30′N 160°28′W
35 O1 **Lower Klamath Lake** ◎ California, W USA
35 Q2 **Lower Lake** ◎ California/Nevada, W USA
97 E15 **Lower Lough Erne** ◎ SW Northern Ireland, United Kingdom
Lower Lusatia see Niederlausitz
Lower Normandy see Basse-Normandie
10 K9 **Lower Post** British Columbia, W Canada 59°53′N 128°19′W
29 T4 **Lower Red Lake** ◎ Minnesota, N USA
Lower Rhine see Neder Rijn
Lower Saxony see Niedersachsen
97 Q19 **Lowestoft** E England, United Kingdom 52°29′N 01°45′E
149 Q5 **Lowgar** var. Logar. ◈ province E Afghanistan
182 H7 **Low Hill** South Australia 32°17′S 136°46′E
110 K12 **Łowicz** Łódzkie, C Poland 52°06′N 19°55′E
33 N13 **Lowman** Idaho, NW USA 44°04′N 115°37′W
149 P8 **Lowrah** var. Lora. ≈ SE Afghanistan
Lowrin see Lovrin
183 N17 **Low Rocky Point** headland Tasmania, SE Australia 42°59′S 145°28′E
18 I8 **Lowville** New York, NE USA 43°47′N 75°29′W
Loxa see Loksa
182 K9 **Loxton** South Australia 34°30′S 140°36′E
81 G21 **Loya** Tabora, C Tanzania 04°57′S 33°53′E
30 K6 **Loyal** Wisconsin, N USA 44°45′N 90°30′W
18 G13 **Loyalsock Creek** ≈ Pennsylvania, NE USA
35 Q5 **Loyalton** California, W USA 39°39′N 120°16′W
Lo-yang see Luoyang
187 Q16 **Loyauté, Îles** island group S New Caledonia
Loyev see Loyew
119 O20 **Loyew** Rus. Loyev. Homyel'skaya Voblasts', SE Belarus 51°56′N 30°48′E
125 S13 **Loyno** Kirovskaya Oblast', NW Russian Federation 59°44′N 52°42′E
103 P13 **Lozère** ◈ department S France
103 Q14 **Lozère, Mont** ▲ S France 44°27′N 03°44′E
112 J11 **Loznica** Serbia, W Serbia 44°32′N 19°13′E
114 L8 **Loznitsa** Razgrad, N Bulgaria 43°22′N 26°36′E
117 V7 **Lozova** Rus. Lozovaya. Kharkivs'ka Oblast', E Ukraine 48°54′N 36°23′E
Lozovaya see Lozova
105 N7 **Lozoyuela** Madrid, C Spain 40°55′N 03°36′W
Lu see Shandong, China
Lú see Louth, Ireland
82 F12 **Luacano** Moxico, E Angola 11°19′S 21°30′E
79 N21 **Lualaba** Fr. Loualaba. ≈ SE Dem. Rep. Congo
83 H14 **Luampa** Western, NW Zambia 15°02′S 24°27′E
83 H15 **Luampa Kuta** Western, W Zambia 15°22′S 24°40′E
161 P8 **Lu'an** Anhui, E China 31°46′N 116°31′E
104 K2 **Luanco** Asturias, N Spain 43°36′N 05°48′W
82 A11 **Luanda** var. Loanda, Port. São Paulo de Loanda. ● Luanda, NW Angola 08°48′S 13°17′E
82 A11 **Luanda** ◈ province (Angola) NW Angola
82 A11 **Luanda** ✈ Luanda, NW Angola 08°49′S 13°16′E
82 D12 **Luando** ≈ C Angola
Luang see Tapi, Mae Nam
83 G14 **Luanginga** var. Luanguinga. ≈ Angola/Zambia
167 N15 **Luang, Khao** ▲ SW Thailand 08°21′N 99°46′E
Luang Prabang see Louangphabang
167 P8 **Luang Prabang Range** Th. Thiukhaoluang Phrahang. ▲▲ Laos/Thailand
167 N16 **Luang, Thale** lagoon S Thailand
Luangua, Rio see Luangwa
82 E11 **Luangue** ≈ NE Angola
Luanguinga see Luanginga
83 K15 **Luangwa** var. Aruângua. Lusaka, C Zambia 15°36′S 30°27′E
83 K14 **Luangwa** var. Aruângua, Rio Luangua. ≈ Mozambique/Zambia
161 Q2 **Luan He** ≈ E China
190 G11 **Luaniva, Île** island E Wallis and Futuna
161 P2 **Luanping** var. Anjiangying. Hebei, E China 40°55′N 117°19′E
82 J13 **Luanshya** Copperbelt, C Zambia 13°09′S 28°24′E
62 K13 **Luan Toro** La Pampa, C Argentina 36°14′S 64°15′W
161 Q2 **Luanxian** var. Luan Xian. Hebei, E China 39°46′N 118°46′E
Luan Xian see Luanxian
82 J12 **Luapula** ◈ province N Zambia
79 O25 **Luapula** ≈ Dem. Rep. Congo/Zambia
104 J2 **Luarca** Asturias, N Spain 43°33′N 06°31′W
169 R10 **Luar, Danau** ◎ Borneo, N Indonesia
79 L25 **Luashi** Katanga, S Dem. Rep. Congo 10°54′S 23°55′E
82 G12 **Luau** Port. Vila Teixeira de Sousa. Moxico, NE Angola 10°42′S 22°12′E
79 C16 **Luba** prev. San Carlos. Isla de Bioco, NW Equatorial Guinea 03°26′N 08°36′E
42 F4 **Lubaantun** ruins Toledo, S Belize
111 P16 **Lubaczów** var. Lúbaczów. Podkarpackie, SE Poland 50°10′N 23°08′E
Lubale see Lubalo
82 E11 **Lubalo** Lunda Norte, NE Angola 09°02′S 19°11′E
82 E11 **Lubalo** var. Lubale. ≈ Angola/Dem. Rep. Congo
118 J9 **Lubāna** Madona, E Latvia 56°55′N 26°43′E
Lubānas Ezers see Lubāns
171 N4 **Lubang Island** island N Philippines
83 B15 **Lubango** Port. Sá da Bandeira. Huíla, SW Angola 14°55′S 13°33′E
118 J9 **Lubāns** var. Lubānas Ezers. ◎ E Latvia
79 M21 **Lubao** Kasai-Oriental, C Dem. Rep. Congo 05°21′S 25°42′E
110 O13 **Lubartów** Ger. Qumälisch. Lublin, E Poland 51°29′N 22°38′E
100 G13 **Lübbecke** Nordrhein-Westfalen, NW Germany 52°18′N 08°37′E
100 O13 **Lübben** Brandenburg, E Germany 51°56′N 13°52′E
101 P14 **Lübbenau** Brandenburg, E Germany 51°52′N 13°57′E
25 N5 **Lubbock** Texas, SW USA 33°35′N 101°51′W
19 U6 **Lubec** Maine, NE USA 44°49′N 67°00′W
100 K9 **Lübeck** Schleswig-Holstein, N Germany 53°52′N 10°41′E
100 K8 **Lübecker Bucht** bay N Germany
79 M21 **Lubefu** Kasai-Oriental, C Dem. Rep. Congo 04°43′S 24°25′E
163 T10 **Lubei** var. Jarud Qi. Nei Mongol Zizhiqu, N China 44°25′N 121°12′E
111 O14 **Lubelska, Wyżyna** plateau SE Poland
110 O13 **Lubelskie** ◈ province E Poland
Lubembe see Luembe
Lüben see Lubin
144 H9 **Lubenka** Zapadnyy Kazakhstan, W Kazakhstan 50°27′N 54°07′E
79 P18 **Lubero** Nord-Kivu, E Dem. Rep. Congo 0°10′S 29°12′E
79 L22 **Lubi** ≈ S Dem. Rep. Congo
Lubiana see Ljubljana
110 J11 **Lubień Kujawski** Kujawsko-pomorskie, C Poland 52°25′N 19°10′E
67 T11 **Lubilandji** ≈ S Dem. Rep. Congo
110 F13 **Lubin** Ger. Lüben. Dolnośląskie, SW Poland 51°24′N 16°12′E
111 O14 **Lublin** Rus. Lyublin. Lubelskie, E Poland 51°15′N 22°33′E
111 J15 **Lubliniec** Śląskie, S Poland 50°41′N 18°41′E
Lubnān, Jabal see Liban, Jebel
117 R5 **Lubny** Poltavs'ka Oblast', NE Ukraine 50°00′N 33°00′E
Luboml' see Lyuboml'
110 G11 **Luboń** Ger. Peterhof. Wielkolpolskie, C Poland 52°23′N 16°54′E
110 D12 **Lubsko** Ger. Sommerfeld. Lubuskie, W Poland 51°47′N 14°57′E
79 N24 **Lubudi** Katanga, SE Dem. Rep. Congo 09°57′S 25°59′E
168 L13 **Lubuklinggau** Sumatera, W Indonesia 03°10′S 102°52′E
79 N25 **Lubumbashi** prev. Élisabethville. Shaba, SE Dem. Rep. Congo 11°40′S 27°31′E
83 I14 **Lubungu** Central, C Zambia 14°28′S 26°30′E
110 E12 **Lubuskie** ◈ province W Poland
Lubuskie see Dobiegniew
79 N18 **Lubutu** Maniema, E Dem. Rep. Congo 0°48′S 26°39′E
Luca see Lucca
82 C11 **Lucala** ≈ W Angola
14 E16 **Lucan** Ontario, S Canada 43°10′N 81°22′W
97 F18 **Lucan** Ir. Leamhcán. Dublin, E Ireland 53°22′N 06°27′W
Lucanian Mountains see Lucano, Appennino
107 M18 **Lucano, Appennino** Eng. Lucanian Mountains. ▲▲ S Italy
82 F11 **Lucapa** var. Lukapa. Lunda Norte, NE Angola 08°24′S 20°42′E
29 V15 **Lucas** Iowa, C USA 41°01′N 93°26′W
61 C18 **Lucas González** Entre Ríos, E Argentina 32°25′S 59°33′W
31 S15 **Lucasville** Ohio, N USA 38°52′N 83°00′W
106 F11 **Lucca** anc. Luca. Toscana, C Italy 43°50′N 10°30′E
44 H12 **Lucea** W Jamaica 18°26′N 78°11′W
97 H15 **Luce Bay** inlet SW Scotland, United Kingdom
22 M8 **Lucedale** Mississippi, S USA 30°55′N 88°35′W
171 O4 **Lucena** off. Lucena City. Luzon, N Philippines 13°57′N 121°38′E
104 M14 **Lucena** Andalucía, S Spain 37°25′N 04°29′W
Lucena City see Lucena
105 S8 **Lucena del Cid** País Valenciano, E Spain 40°07′N 00°15′W
111 D15 **Lučenec** Ger. Losontz, Hung. Losonc. Banskobystrický Kraj, C Slovakia 48°21′N 19°37′E
Lucentum see Alicante
107 M16 **Lucera** Puglia, SE Italy 41°30′N 15°19′E
Lucerna/Lucerne see Luzern
Lucerne, Lake of see Vierwaldstätter See
40 J4 **Lucero** Chihuahua, N Mexico 30°50′N 106°30′W
123 S14 **Luchegorsk** Primorskiy Kray, SE Russian Federation 46°26′N 134°10′E
105 Q13 **Luchena** ≈ SE Spain
Lucheng see Kangding
82 N13 **Lucheringo** var. Luchulingo. ≈ N Mozambique
Luchesa see Luchosa
Luchin see Luchyn
118 N13 **Luchosa** Rus. Luchesa. ≈ N Belarus
100 K11 **Lüchow** Mecklenburg-Vorpommern, N Germany 52°57′N 11°10′E
Luchow see Hefei
Luchulingo see Lucheringo
119 N17 **Luchyn** Rus. Luchin. Homyel'skaya Voblasts', SE Belarus 53°01′N 30°01′E
55 U11 **Lucie Rivier** ≈ W Surinam
182 K11 **Lucindale** South Australia 36°57′S 140°20′E
83 A14 **Lucira** Namibe, SW Angola 13°51′S 12°35′E
Luck see Luts'k
101 O14 **Luckau** Brandenburg, E Germany 51°50′N 13°42′E
100 N13 **Luckenwalde** Brandenburg, E Germany 52°05′N 13°11′E
14 E15 **Lucknow** Ontario, S Canada 43°58′N 81°30′W
152 L12 **Lucknow** var. Lakhnau. state capital Uttar Pradesh, N India 26°50′N 80°54′E
102 J10 **Luçon** Vendée, NW France 46°27′N 01°10′W
44 I7 **Lucrecia, Cabo** headland E Cuba 21°00′N 75°34′W
82 F13 **Lucusse** Moxico, E Angola 12°32′S 20°46′E
Lüda see Dalian
114 M9 **Luda Kamchiya** ≈ E Bulgaria
Ludasch see Luduș
114 I10 **Luda Yana** ≈ C Bulgaria
112 F7 **Ludbreg** Varaždin, N Croatia 46°15′N 16°36′E
29 P7 **Ludden** North Dakota, N USA 45°58′N 98°07′W
101 F15 **Lüdenscheid** Nordrhein-Westfalen, W Germany 51°13′N 07°38′E
83 C21 **Lüderitz** prev. Angra Pequena. Karas, SW Namibia 26°38′S 15°10′E
152 H8 **Ludhiāna** Punjab, N India 30°56′N 75°52′E
31 O7 **Ludington** Michigan, N USA 43°58′N 86°27′W
97 K20 **Ludlow** W England, United Kingdom 52°20′N 02°28′W
35 W14 **Ludlow** California, W USA 34°43′N 116°07′W
28 J7 **Ludlow** South Dakota, N USA 45°48′N 103°21′W
18 M9 **Ludlow** Vermont, NE USA 43°24′N 72°39′W
114 L7 **Ludogorie** physical region NE Bulgaria
23 W6 **Ludowici** Georgia, SE USA 31°42′N 81°44′W
Ludsan see Ludza
116 I10 **Luduș** Ger. Ludasch, Hung. Marosludas. Mureș, C Romania 46°28′N 24°05′E
95 M14 **Ludvika** Dalarna, C Sweden 60°08′N 15°14′E
101 H21 **Ludwigsburg** Baden-Württemberg, SW Germany 48°54′N 09°12′E
100 O13 **Ludwigsfelde** Brandenburg, NE Germany 52°17′N 13°15′E
101 G20 **Ludwigshafen** var. Ludwigshafen am Rhein. Rheinland-Pfalz, W Germany 49°29′N 08°24′E
Ludwigshafen am Rhein see Ludwigshafen
101 L20 **Ludwigskanal** canal SE Germany
100 L10 **Ludwigslust** Mecklenburg-Vorpommern, N Germany 53°19′N 11°29′E
118 K10 **Ludza** Ger. Ludsan. Ludza, E Latvia 56°32′N 27°41′E
79 K21 **Luebo** Kasai-Occidental, SW Dem. Rep. Congo 05°19′S 21°21′E
25 Q6 **Lueders** Texas, SW USA 32°46′N 99°38′W
79 N20 **Lueki** Maniema, C Dem. Rep. Congo 03°25′S 25°50′E
82 F10 **Luembe** var. Lubembe. ≈ Angola/Dem. Rep. Congo
82 E13 **Luena** var. Lwena, Port. Luso. Moxico, E Angola 11°47′S 19°52′E
79 M24 **Luena** Katanga, SE Dem. Rep. Congo 09°28′S 25°45′E
82 K12 **Luena** Northern, NE Zambia 10°40′S 30°21′E
82 F13 **Luena** ≈ E Angola
83 F16 **Luengue** ≈ SE Angola
67 V13 **Luenha** ≈ W Mozambique
83 G15 **Lueti** ≈ Angola/Zambia
160 J7 **Lüeyang** var. Hejiayan. Shaanxi, C China 33°12′N 106°31′E
161 P14 **Lufeng** Guangdong, S China 22°59′N 115°40′E
79 N24 **Lufira** ≈ SE Dem. Rep. Congo
79 N25 **Lufira, Lac de Retenue de la** var. Lac Tshangalele. ◎ SE Dem. Rep. Congo
25 W8 **Lufkin** Texas, SW USA 31°21′N 94°47′W
82 L11 **Lufubu** ≈ N Zambia
124 G14 **Luga** Leningradskaya Oblast', NW Russian Federation 58°43′N 29°46′E
124 G13 **Luga** ≈ NW Russian Federation
Luganer See see Lugano, Lago di
108 H11 **Lugano** Ger. Lauis. Ticino, S Switzerland 46°01′N 08°57′E
108 H12 **Lugano, Lago di** var. Ceresio, Ger. Luganer See. ◎ S Switzerland
Lugansk see Luhans'k
187 Q13 **Luganville** Espiritu Santo, C Vanuatu 15°31′S 167°12′E
Lugdunum see Lyon
Lugdunum Batavorum see Leiden
83 O15 **Lugela** Zambézia, NE Mozambique 16°27′S 36°47′E
83 O16 **Lugela** ≈ C Mozambique
82 P13 **Lugenda, Rio** ≈ N Mozambique
Luggarus see Locarno
Lugh Ganana see Luuq
97 G19 **Lugnaquillia Mountain** Ir. Log na Coille. ▲ E Ireland 52°58′N 06°27′W
106 H10 **Lugo** Emilia-Romagna, N Italy 44°25′N 11°53′E
104 I3 **Lugo** anc. Lugus Augusti. Galicia, NW Spain 43°00′N 07°33′W
104 I3 **Lugo** ◈ province Galicia, NW Spain
21 R12 **Lugoff** South Carolina, SE USA 34°13′N 80°41′W
116 F12 **Lugoj** Ger. Lugosch, Hung. Lugos. Timiș, W Romania 45°41′N 21°56′E
Lugos/Lugosch see Lugoj
Lugovoy/Lugovoye see Kulan
158 I13 **Lugu** Xizang Zizhiqu, W China 33°26′N 84°10′E
Lugus Augusti see Lugo
Luguvallium/Luguvallum see Carlisle
117 Y7 **Luhans'k** Rus. Lugansk; prev. Voroshilovgrad. Luhans'ka Oblast', E Ukraine 48°32′N 39°21′E
117 Y7 **Luhans'k** ✈ Luhans'ka Oblast', E Ukraine 48°25′N 39°24′E
Luhans'k see Luhans'ka Oblast'
117 X6 **Luhans'ka Oblast'** var. Luhans'k; prev. Voroshilovgrad, Rus. Voroshilovgradskaya Oblast'. ◈ province E Ukraine
161 Q7 **Luhe** Jiangsu, E China 32°20′N 118°52′E
171 S13 **Luhu** Pulau Seram, E Indonesia 03°20′S 127°58′E
Luhua see Heishui
160 G8 **Luhuo** var. Xindu, Tib. Zhaggo. Sichuan, C China 31°18′N 100°39′E
116 M3 **Luhyny** Zhytomyrs'ka Oblast', N Ukraine 51°06′N 28°24′E
83 G15 **Lui** ≈ W Zambia
83 G16 **Luiana** ≈ SE Angola
83 L15 **Luia, Rio** var. Ruya. ≈ Mozambique/Zimbabwe
Luichow Peninsula see Leizhou Bandao
Luik see Liège
82 C13 **Luimbale** Huambo, C Angola 12°15′S 15°19′E
Luimneach see Limerick
106 D6 **Luino** Lombardia, N Italy 46°00′N 08°45′E
82 E13 **Luio** ≈ E Angola
92 L11 **Luiro** ≈ NE Finland
79 N25 **Luishia** Katanga, SE Dem. Rep. Congo 11°18′S 27°08′E
59 M19 **Luislândia do Oeste** Minas Gerais, SE Brazil 17°59′S 45°35′W
40 K5 **Luis L. León, Presa** ⊠ N Mexico
Luis Muñoz Marin see San Juan
195 N5 **Luitpold Coast** physical region Antarctica
79 K22 **Luiza** Kasai-Occidental, S Dem. Rep. Congo 07°11′S 22°27′E
61 D20 **Luján** Buenos Aires, E Argentina 34°34′S 59°07′W
79 N24 **Lukafu** Katanga, SE Dem. Rep. Congo 10°28′S 27°32′E
Lukapa see Lucapa
112 I11 **Lukavac** ◈ Federacija Bosna I Hercegovina, NE Bosnia and Herzegovina
79 I20 **Lukenie** ≈ C Dem. Rep. Congo
114 J11 **Lŭki** Plovdiv, C Bulgaria 41°50′N 24°49′E
79 H19 **Lukolela** Equateur, W Dem. Rep. Congo 01°10′S 17°11′E
119 M14 **Lukoml'skaye, Vozyera** Rus. Ozero Lukoml'skoye. ◎ N Belarus
Lukoml'skoye, Ozero see Lukoml'skaye, Vozyera
114 I8 **Lukovit** Lovech, N Bulgaria 43°11′N 24°10′E
110 O12 **Łuków** Ger. Bogendorf. Lubelskie, E Poland 51°57′N 22°22′E
127 O4 **Lukoyanov** Nizhegorodskaya Oblast', W Russian Federation 55°02′N 44°26′E
Lukransar see Lūnkaransar

◆ Country ● Country Capital ◇ Dependent Territory ○ Dependent Territory Capital ◈ Administrative Regions ✈ International Airport ▲ Mountain ▲▲ Mountain Range Volcano ≈ River ◎ Lake ⊠ Reservoir

LUKUGA – MADENIYET

79 N22 Lukuga ≈ SE Dem. Rep. Congo
79 F21 Lukula Bas-Congo, SW Dem. Rep. Congo 05°23′S 12°57′E
83 G14 Lukulu Western, NW Zambia 14°24′S 23°12′E
189 R17 Lukunor Atoll atoll Mortlock Islands, C Micronesia
82 J12 Lukwesa Luapula, NE Zambia 10°03′S 28°42′E
93 K14 Luleå Norrbotten, N Sweden 65°35′N 22°10′E
92 J13 Luleälven ≈ N Sweden
136 C10 Lüleburgaz Kırklareli, NW Turkey 41°25′N 27°22′E
160 M4 Lüliang var. Lishi. Shanxi, C China 37°27′N 111°05′E
160 M4 Lüliang Shan ▲▲ C China
79 O21 Lulimba Maniema, E Dem. Rep. Congo 04°42′S 28°38′E
22 K9 Luling Louisiana, S USA 29°55′N 90°22′W
25 T11 Luling Texas, SW USA 29°40′N 97°39′W
79 I18 Lulonga ≈ NW Dem. Rep. Congo
79 K22 Lulua ≈ S Dem. Rep. Congo
Luluabourg see Kananga
192 L17 Luma Ta'ū, E American Samoa 14°15′S 169°30′W
169 S17 Lumajang Jawa, C Indonesia 08°06′S 113°13′E
158 G12 Lumajangdong Co ◎ W China
82 G13 Lumbala Kaquengue Moxico, E Angola 12°40′S 22°34′E
83 F14 Lumbala N'Guimbo var. Nguimbo, Gago Coutinho, Port. Vila Gago Coutinho. Moxico, E Angola 14°08′S 21°25′E
21 T11 Lumber River ≈ North Carolina/South Carolina, SE USA
Lumber State see Maine
22 L8 Lumberton Mississippi, S USA 31°00′N 89°27′W
21 U11 Lumberton North Carolina, SE USA 34°37′N 79°00′W
105 R4 Lumbier Navarra, N Spain 42°39′N 01°19′W
83 Q15 Lumbo Nampula, NE Mozambique 15°S 40°40′E
124 M4 Lumbovka Murmanskaya Oblast', NW Russian Federation 67°41′N 40°31′E
104 J7 Lumbrales Castilla-León, N Spain 40°57′N 06°43′W
153 W13 Lumding Assam, NE India 25°46′N 93°10′E
82 F12 Lumege var. Lumeje. Moxico, E Angola 11°30′S 20°57′E
Lumeje see Lumege
99 J17 Lummen Limburg, NE Belgium 50°58′N 05°12′E
93 J20 Lumparland Åland, SW Finland 60°06′N 20°15′E
167 T11 Lumphăt prev. Lomphat. Rôtânôkiri, NE Cambodia 13°30′N
11 U16 Lumsden Saskatchewan, S Canada 50°39′N 104°52′W
185 C23 Lumsden Southland, South Island, New Zealand 45°43′S 168°26′E
169 N14 Lumut, Tanjung headland Sumatera, W Indonesia 03°47′S 105°55′E
157 P4 Lün Töv, C Mongolia 47°51′N 105°11′E
116 I13 Lunca Corbului Argeş, S Romania 44°41′N 24°46′E
95 K23 Lund Skåne, S Sweden 55°42′N 13°10′E
35 X6 Lund Nevada, W USA 38°50′N 115°00′W
82 D11 Lunda Norte ◈ province NE Angola
82 E12 Lunda Sul ◈ province NE Angola
82 M13 Lundazi Eastern, NE Zambia 12°19′S 33°11′E
95 G16 Lunde Telemark, S Norway 61°31′N 06°38′E
Lundenburg see Břeclav
95 C17 Lundevatnet ◎ S Norway
Lundi see Runde
97 I23 Lundy island SW England, United Kingdom
100 J10 Lüneburg Niedersachsen, N Germany 53°15′N 10°25′E
100 J11 Lüneburger Heide heathland NW Germany
103 Q15 Lunel Hérault, S France 43°40′N 04°08′E
101 F14 Lünen Nordrhein-Westfalen, W Germany 51°37′N 07°31′E
13 P16 Lunenburg Nova Scotia, SE Canada 44°23′N 64°21′W
21 V7 Lunenburg Virginia, NE USA 36°56′N 78°15′W
103 T5 Lunéville Meurthe-et-Moselle, NE France 48°35′N 06°30′E
83 I14 Lunga ≈ C Zambia
Lunga, Isola see Dugi Otok
158 H12 Lungdo Xizang Zizhiqu, W China 33°45′N 82°09′E
158 I14 Lunggar Xizang Zizhiqu, W China 31°10′N 84°01′E
76 I15 Lungi ✈ (Freetown) W Sierra Leone 08°36′N 13°10′W
Lungkiang see Qiqihar
Lungleh see Lunglei
153 W15 Lunglei prev. Lungleh. Mizoram, NE India 22°55′N 92°49′E
158 L15 Lungsang Xizang Zizhiqu, W China 29°50′N 88°27′E
82 E13 Lungué-Bungo var. Lungwebungu. ≈ Angola/Zambia see also Lungwebungu
Lungué-Bungo see Lungwebungu
83 G14 Lungwebungu var. Lungué-Bungo. ≈ Angola/Zambia see also Lungué-Bungo
Lungwebungu see Lungué-Bungo
152 F12 Lūni Rājasthān, N India 26°03′N 73°00′E
152 F12 Lūni ≈ N India
Luninets see Luninyets
35 S7 Luning Nevada, W USA 38°29′N 118°10′W
Łuniniec see Luninyets
127 P6 Lunino Penzenskaya Oblast', W Russian Federation 53°35′N 45°12′E
119 J19 Luninyets Pol. Łuniniec, Rus. Luninets. Brestskaya Voblasts', SW Belarus 52°15′N 26°48′E
152 F10 Lūnkaransar var. Lookransar, Lukransar. Rājasthān, NW India 28°32′N 73°50′E
119 G17 Lunna Pol. Łunna. Hrodzyenskaya Voblasts', W Belarus 53°27′N 24°16′E
76 I15 Lunsar W Sierra Leone 08°41′N 12°32′W
83 K14 Lunsemfwa ≈ C Zambia
158 J6 Luntai var. Bügür. Xinjiang Uygur Zizhiqu, NW China 41°48′N 84°14′E
98 K11 Lunteren Gelderland, C Netherlands 52°05′N 05°38′E
109 U5 Lunz am See Niederösterreich, C Austria 47°54′N 15°01′E
163 Y7 Luobei var. Fengxiang. Heilongjiang, NE China 47°35′N 130°51′E
Luocheng see Hui'an, Fujian, China
Luocheng see Luoding, Guangdong, China
160 J13 Luodian var. Longping. Guizhou, S China 25°25′N 106°49′E
160 M15 Luoding var. Luocheng. Guangdong, S China 22°44′N 111°28′E
161 N7 Luohe Henan, C China 33°37′N 114°00′E
160 M6 Luo He ≈ C China
160 L5 Luo He ≈ C China
Luolajarvi see Kuoloyarvi
Luong Nam Tha see Louangnamtha
160 L13 Luoqing Jiang ≈ S China
161 O8 Luoshan Henan, C China 32°12′N 114°30′E
161 O12 Luoxiao Shan ▲▲ S China
161 N6 Luoyang var. Honan, Lo-yang. Henan, C China 34°41′N 112°25′E
161 R12 Luoyuan var. Fengshan. Fujian, SE China 26°29′N 119°32′E
79 F21 Luozi Bas-Congo, W Dem. Rep. Congo 04°57′S 14°08′E
83 J17 Lupane Matabeleland North, W Zimbabwe 18°54′S 27°44′E
160 I12 Lupanshui prev. Shuicheng. Guizhou, S China 26°38′N 104°49′E
169 R10 Lupar, Batang ≈ East Malaysia
Lupatia see Altamura
116 G12 Lupeni Hung. Lupény. Hunedoara, SW Romania 45°20′N 23°10′E
Lupény see Lupeni
82 N13 Lupiliche Niassa, N Mozambique 11°36′S 35°15′E
83 E14 Lupire Cuando Cubango, E Angola 14°39′S 19°39′E
79 L22 Luputa Kasai-Oriental, S Dem. Rep. Congo 07°07′S 23°43′E
121 P16 Luqa ✈ (Valletta) S Malta 35°53′N 14°27′E
159 U11 Luqu var. Ma'ai. Gansu, C China 34°34′N 102°27′E
45 U5 Luquillo, Sierra de ▲▲ E Puerto Rico
26 L4 Luray Kansas, C USA 39°06′N 98°41′W
21 U4 Luray Virginia, NE USA 38°40′N 78°28′W
103 T7 Lure Haute-Saône, E France 47°42′N 06°30′E
82 D11 Luremo Lunda Norte, NE Angola 08°32′S 17°55′E
97 F15 Lurgan Ir. An Lorgain. S Northern Ireland, United Kingdom 54°28′N 06°20′W
57 K18 Luribay La Paz, W Bolivia 17°05′S 67°37′W
Luring see Gêrzê
83 Q14 Lúrio Nampula, NE Mozambique 13°32′S 40°34′E
83 P14 Lúrio, Rio ≈ NE Mozambique
Luristan see Lorestān
Lurka see Lorca
83 J15 Lusaka ● (Zambia) Lusaka, C Zambia 15°24′S 28°17′E
83 J15 Lusaka ◈ province C Zambia
83 J15 Lusaka ✈ Lusaka, C Zambia 15°10′S 28°22′E
79 L21 Lusambo Kasai-Oriental, C Dem. Rep. Congo 04°59′S 23°26′E
186 F8 Lusancay Islands and Reefs island group SE Papua New Guinea
79 I21 Lusanga Bandundu, SW Dem. Rep. Congo 04°55′S 18°40′E
79 N21 Lusangi Maniema, E Dem. Rep. Congo 04°39′S 27°10′E
Lusatian Mountains see Lausitzer Bergland
Lushar see Huangzhong
Lushnja see Lushnjë
113 K21 Lushnjë var. Lushnja. Fier, C Albania 40°54′N 19°43′E
81 J21 Lushoto Tanga, E Tanzania 04°48′S 38°20′E
102 L10 Lusignan Vienne, W France 46°25′N 00°06′E
33 Z15 Lusk Wyoming, C USA 42°45′N 104°27′W
Luso see Luena
102 L10 Lussac-les-Châteaux Vienne, W France 46°23′N 00°44′E
Lussin/Lussino see Lošinj
Lussinpiccolo see Mali Lošinj
108 I7 Lustenau Vorarlberg, W Austria 47°26′N 09°42′E
161 T14 Lü Tao var. Huoshao Dao, Lütao, Eng. Green Island. island SE Taiwan
Lütao see Lü Tao
Lūt, Baḩrat/Lut, Bahret see Dead Sea
22 K9 Lutcher Louisiana, S USA 30°02′N 90°42′W
143 T9 Lūt, Dasht-e var. Kavīr-e Lūt. desert E Iran
83 F14 Lutembo Moxico, E Angola 13°30′S 21°21′E
Lutetia/Lutetia Parisiorum see Paris
Luteva see Lodève
14 G15 Luther Lake ◎ Ontario, S Canada
186 K8 Luti Choiseul Island, NW Solomon Islands 07°13′S 157°01′E
Lūt, Kavīr-e see Lūt, Dasht-e
97 N21 Luton E England, United Kingdom 51°53′N 00°25′W
97 N21 Luton ✈ (London) SE England, United Kingdom 51°54′N 00°24′W
108 B10 Lutry Vaud, SW Switzerland 46°31′N 06°32′E
8 K10 Łutselk'e prev. Snowdrift. Northwest Territories, W Canada 62°24′N 110°42′W
29 Y4 Lutsen Minnesota, N USA 47°39′N 90°37′W
116 J4 Luts'k Pol. Łuck, Rus. Lutsk. Volyns'ka Oblast', NW Ukraine 50°45′N 25°23′E
Lutsk see Luts'k
Luttenberg see Ljutomer
Lüttich see Liège
83 G25 Luttig Western Cape, SW South Africa 32°33′S 22°13′E
Lutto see Lotta
82 E13 Lutuai Moxico, E Angola 12°38′S 20°06′E
117 Y7 Lutuhyne Luhans'ka Oblast', E Ukraine 48°24′N 39°12′E
171 V14 Lutur, Pulau island Kepulauan Aru, E Indonesia
23 V12 Lutz Florida, SE USA 28°09′N 82°27′W
Lutzow-Holm Bay see Lützow Holmbukta
195 V2 Lützow Holmbukta var. Lutzow-Holm Bay. bay Antarctica
81 L16 Luuq It. Lugh Ganana. Gedo, SW Somalia 03°42′N 42°34′E
92 M12 Luusua Lappi, NE Finland 66°28′N 27°16′E
23 Q6 Luverne Alabama, S USA 31°43′N 86°15′W
29 S11 Luverne Minnesota, N USA 43°39′N 96°12′W
79 O22 Luvua ≈ SE Dem. Rep. Congo
82 F13 Luvuei Moxico, E Angola 13°08′S 21°09′E
81 H24 Luwego ≈ S Tanzania
82 K12 Luwingu Northern, NE Zambia 10°13′S 29°58′E
171 P12 Luwuk prev. Loewoek. Sulawesi, C Indonesia 00°56′S 122°47′E
23 N3 Luxapallila Creek ≈ Alabama/Mississippi, S USA
99 M25 Luxembourg ● (Luxembourg) Luxembourg, S Luxembourg 49°37′N 06°08′E
99 M25 Luxembourg off. Grand Duchy of Luxembourg, var. Lëtzebuerg, Luxemburg. ◆ monarchy NW Europe
99 J23 Luxembourg ◈ province SE Belgium
99 L24 Luxembourg ◈ district S Luxembourg
31 N6 Luxemburg Wisconsin, N USA 44°32′N 87°42′W
Luxemburg see Luxembourg
103 U7 Luxeuil-les-Bains Haute-Saône, E France 47°49′N 06°22′E
160 E13 Luxi prev. Mangshi. Yunnan, SW China 24°27′N 98°31′E
82 E10 Luxico ≈ Angola/Dem. Rep. Congo
75 X10 Luxor Ar. Al Uqşur. E Egypt 25°39′N 32°39′E
75 X10 Luxor ✈ C Egypt 25°39′N 32°48′E
160 M4 Luya Shan ▲▲ C China
102 J15 Luy de Béarn ≈ SW France
102 J15 Luy de France ≈ SW France
125 P12 Luza Kirovskaya Oblast', NW Russian Federation 60°38′N 47°13′E
125 Q12 Luza ≈ NW Russian Federation
104 I16 Luz, Costa de la coastal region SW Spain
111 K20 Luže var. Lausche. ▲ Czech Republic/Germany 50°51′N 14°40′E see also Lausche
Luže see Lausche
108 F8 Luzern Fr. Lucerne, It. Lucerna. Luzern, C Switzerland 47°03′N 08°17′E
108 E8 Luzern Fr. Lucerne. ◈ canton C Switzerland
160 L13 Luzhai Guangxi Zhuangzu Zizhiqu, S China 24°31′N 109°46′E
118 K12 Luzhki Vitsyebskaya Voblasts', N Belarus 55°21′N 27°52′E
160 I10 Luzhou Sichuan, C China 28°55′N 105°25′E
Lužická Nisa see Neisse
Lužické Hory' see Lausitzer Bergland
Lužnice see Lainsitz
171 O2 Luzon island N Philippines
171 N1 Luzon Strait strait Philippines/Taiwan
Lužyckie, Gory see Lausitzer Bergland
116 I5 L'viv Ger. Lemberg, Pol. Lwów, Rus. L'vov. L'vivs'ka Oblast', W Ukraine 49°49′N 24°05′E
L'viv see L'vivs'ka Oblast'
116 I4 L'vivs'ka Oblast' var. L'viv, Rus. L'vovskaya Oblast'. ◈ province NW Ukraine
L'vov see L'viv
L'vovskaya Oblast' see L'vivs'ka Oblast'
Lwena see Luena
Lwów see L'viv
110 F11 Lwówek Ger. Neustadt bei Pinne. Wielkopolskie, C Poland 52°27′N 16°10′E
111 E14 Lwówek Śląski Ger. Löwenberg in Schlesien. Jelenia Góra, SW Poland 51°06′N 15°35′E
119 I18 Lyakhavichy Rus. Lyakhovichi. Brestskaya Voblasts', SW Belarus 53°02′N 26°16′E
Lyakhovichi see Lyakhavichy
185 B22 Lyall, Mount ▲ South Island, New Zealand 45°14′S 167°31′E
Lyallpur see Faisalābād
Lyangar see Langar
124 H11 Lyaskelya Respublika Kareliya, NW Russian Federation 61°42′N 31°06′E
119 I18 Lyasnaya Rus. Lesnaya. Brestskaya Voblasts', SW Belarus 52°59′N 25°46′E
119 F19 Lyasnaya Pol. Leśna, Rus. Lesnaya. ≈ SW Belarus
124 H15 Lychkovo Novgorodskaya Oblast', W Russian Federation 57°55′N 32°24′E
Lyck see Ełk
93 I15 Lycksele Västerbotten, N Sweden 64°34′N 18°40′E
18 G13 Lycoming Creek ≈ Pennsylvania, NE USA
Lycopolis see Asyūţ
195 N3 Lyddan Island island Antarctica
83 K20 Lydenburg Mpumalanga, NE South Africa 25°10′S 30°29′E
119 L20 Lyel'chytsy Rus. Lel'chitsy. Homyel'skaya Voblasts', SE Belarus 51°47′N 28°20′E
119 P14 Lyenina Rus. Lenino. Mahilyowskaya Voblasts', E Belarus 54°25′N 31°08′E
118 L13 Lyepyel' Rus. Lepel'. Vitsyebskaya Voblasts', N Belarus 54°54′N 28°44′E
25 S17 Lyford Texas, SW USA 26°24′N 97°47′W
95 E17 Lygna ≈ S Norway
18 G14 Lykens Pennsylvania, NE USA 40°33′N 76°42′W
115 E21 Lykódimo ▲ S Greece 36°56′N 21°49′E
97 K24 Lyme Bay bay S England, United Kingdom
97 K24 Lyme Regis S England, United Kingdom 50°44′N 02°56′W
110 L7 Łyna Ger. Alle. ≈ N Poland
29 P12 Lynch Nebraska, C USA 42°49′N 98°27′W
20 J10 Lynchburg Tennessee, S USA 35°17′N 86°22′W
21 T6 Lynchburg Virginia, NE USA 37°24′N 79°09′W
21 T12 Lynches River ≈ South Carolina, SE USA
32 H6 Lynden Washington, NW USA 48°57′N 122°27′W
182 I5 Lyndhurst South Australia 30°19′S 138°20′E
27 Q5 Lyndon Kansas, C USA 38°37′N 95°40′W
19 N7 Lyndonville Vermont, NE USA 44°31′N 71°58′W
95 D18 Lyngdal Vest-Agder, S Norway 58°10′N 07°08′E
92 I9 Lyngen Lapp. Ivgovuotna. inlet Arctic Ocean
95 G17 Lyngør Aust-Agder, S Norway 58°38′N 09°05′E
92 I9 Lyngseidet Troms, N Norway 69°36′N 20°07′E
19 P11 Lynn Massachusetts, NE USA 42°28′N 70°57′W
Lynn see King's Lynn
23 R9 Lynn Haven Florida, SE USA 30°15′N 85°39′W
11 V11 Lynn Lake Manitoba, C Canada 56°51′N 101°01′W
Lynn Regis see King's Lynn
118 I13 Lyntupy Vitsyebskaya Voblasts', NW Belarus 55°03′N 26°19′E
103 R11 Lyon Eng. Lyons; anc. Lugdunum. Rhône, E France 45°46′N 04°50′E
8 I6 Lyon, Cape headland Northwest Territories, NW Canada 69°47′N 123°10′W
18 K6 Lyon Mountain ▲ New York, NE USA 44°42′N 73°52′W
103 Q11 Lyonnais, Monts du ▲ C France
65 N25 Lyon Point headland SE Tristan da Cunha 37°06′S 12°13′W
182 E5 Lyons South Australia 30°40′S 133°50′E
37 T3 Lyons Colorado, C USA 40°13′N 105°16′W
23 V6 Lyons Georgia, SE USA 32°12′N 82°19′W
26 M5 Lyons Kansas, C USA 38°22′N 98°13′W
29 R14 Lyons Nebraska, C USA 41°56′N 96°28′W
18 G10 Lyons New York, NE USA 43°03′N 76°58′W
Lyons see Lyon
118 O13 Lyozna Rus. Liozno. Vitsyebskaya Voblasts', NE Belarus 55°02′N 30°48′E
117 S4 Lypova Dolyna Sums'ka Oblast', NE Ukraine 50°36′N 33°50′E
117 N6 Lypovets' Rus. Lipovets. Vinnyts'ka Oblast', C Ukraine 49°13′N 29°06′E
Lys see Leie
111 I18 Lysá Hora ▲ E Czech Republic 49°31′N 18°27′E
95 D16 Lysefjorden fjord S Norway
95 I18 Lysekil Västra Götaland, S Sweden 58°16′N 11°26′E
Lysi see Akdoğan
33 V14 Lysite Wyoming, C USA 43°16′N 107°42′W
127 P3 Lyskovo Nizhegorodskaya Oblast', W Russian Federation 56°04′N 45°01′E
108 D8 Lyss Bern, W Switzerland 47°04′N 07°19′E
95 H22 Lystrup Århus, C Denmark 56°14′N 10°14′E
125 V14 Lys'va Permskaya Oblast', NW Russian Federation 58°04′N 57°48′E
117 P6 Lysyanka Cherkas'ka Oblast', C Ukraine 49°15′N 30°50′E
117 X6 Lysychans'k Rus. Lisichansk. Luhans'ka Oblast', E Ukraine 48°52′N 38°27′E
97 K17 Lytham St Anne's NW England, United Kingdom 53°45′N 03°01′W
185 I19 Lyttelton South Island, New Zealand 43°35′S 172°44′E
10 M17 Lytton British Columbia, SW Canada 50°12′N 121°34′W
119 L18 Lyuban' Minskaya Voblasts', S Belarus 52°48′N 28°00′E
119 L18 Lyubanskaye Vodaskhovishcha ▣ C Belarus
116 M5 Lyubar Zhytomyrs'ka Oblast', N Ukraine 49°54′N 27°48′E
Lyubashëvka see Lyubashivka
117 O8 Lyubashivka Rus. Lyubashëvka. Odes'ka Oblast', SW Ukraine 47°49′N 30°18′E
119 I16 Lyubcha Pol. Lubcz. Hrodzyenskaya Voblasts', W Belarus 53°45′N 26°04′E
126 L4 Lyubertsy Moskovskaya Oblast', W Russian Federation 55°37′N 38°02′E
116 K2 Lyubeshiv Volyns'ka Oblast', NW Ukraine 51°46′N 25°33′E
124 M14 Lyubim Yaroslavskaya Oblast', NW Russian Federation 58°21′N 40°46′E
114 K11 Lyubimets Khaskovo, S Bulgaria 41°51′N 26°03′E
Lyublin see Lublin
116 I3 Lyuboml' Pol. Luboml. Volyns'ka Oblast', NW Ukraine 51°12′N 24°01′E
Lyubotin see Lyubotyn
117 U5 Lyubotyn Rus. Lyubotin. Kharkivs'ka Oblast', E Ukraine 49°57′N 35°57′E
126 I5 Lyudinovo Kaluzhskaya Oblast', W Russian Federation 53°52′N 34°28′E
127 T2 Lyuk Udmurtskaya Respublika, NW Russian Federation 56°55′N 52°45′E
114 M9 Lyulyakovo prev. Keremitlik. Burgas, E Bulgaria 42°53′N 27°05′E
119 I18 Lyusina Rus. Lyusino. Brestskaya Voblasts', SW Belarus 52°38′N 26°31′E
Lyusino see Lyusina

M

138 G9 Ma'ād Irbid, N Jordan 32°37′N 35°36′E
Ma'ai see Luqu
Maalahti see Malax
Maale see Male'
138 G13 Ma'ān Ma'ān, SW Jordan 30°11′N 35°45′E
138 H13 Ma'ān off. Muḩāfaz̧at Ma'ān, var. Ma'an, Ma'ān. ◈ governorate S Jordan
93 M16 Maaninka Itä-Suomi, C Finland 63°10′N 27°19′E
Maanīt see Bayan, Töv, Mongolia
Maanīt see Hishig Öndör, Bulgan, Mongolia
Ma'ān, Muḩāfaz̧at see Ma'ān
93 N15 Maanselkä Oulu, C Finland 63°54′N 28°28′E
161 Q8 Ma'anshan Anhui, E China 31°45′N 118°32′E
188 F16 Maap island Caroline Islands, W Micronesia
118 H3 Maardu Ger. Maart. Harjumaa, NW Estonia 59°28′N 24°56′E
Ma'aret-en-Nu'man see Ma'arrat an Nu'mān
99 K16 Maarheeze Noord-Brabant, SE Netherlands 51°19′N 05°37′E
Maarianhamina see Mariehamn
138 I4 Ma'arrat an Nu'mān var. Ma'aret-en-Nu'man, Fr. Maarret enn Naamâne. Idlib, NW Syria 35°40′N 36°40′E
Maarret enn Naamâne see Ma'arrat an Nu'mān
98 I11 Maarssen Utrecht, C Netherlands 52°08′N 05°03′E
Maart see Maardu
99 L17 Maas Fr. Meuse. ≈ W Europe see also Meuse
Maas see Meuse
99 M15 Maasbree Limburg, SE Netherlands 51°22′N 06°03′E
99 L17 Maaseik prev. Maeseyck. Limburg, NE Belgium 51°05′N 05°48′E
171 Q6 Maasin Leyte, C Philippines 10°10′N 124°55′E
99 L17 Maasmechelen Limburg, NE Belgium 50°58′N 05°42′E
98 G12 Maassluis Zuid-Holland, SW Netherlands 51°55′N 04°15′E
99 L18 Maastricht var. Maestricht; anc. Traiectum ad Mosam, Traiectum Tungorum. Limburg, SE Netherlands 50°51′N 05°42′E
183 N18 Maatsuyker Group island group Tasmania, SE Australia
Maba see Qujiang
83 L20 Mabalane Gaza, S Mozambique 23°43′S 32°37′E
25 V7 Mabank Texas, SW USA 32°22′N 96°06′W
97 O18 Mablethorpe E England, United Kingdom 53°21′N 00°14′E
171 V12 Maboi Papua, E Indonesia 01°00′S 134°02′E
83 M19 Mabote Inhambane, S Mozambique 22°03′S 34°09′E
32 J10 Mabton Washington, NW USA 46°13′N 120°00′W
83 H20 Mabutsane Southern, S Botswana 24°24′S 23°34′E
63 G19 Macá, Cerro ▲ S Chile 45°07′S 73°11′W
60 Q9 Macaé Rio de Janeiro, SE Brazil 22°21′S 41°48′W
82 N13 Macaloge Niassa, N Mozambique 12°27′S 35°25′E
Macan see Bonerate, Kepulauan
161 N15 Macao Chin. Aomen, Port. Macau. Guangdong, SE China 22°06′N 113°30′E
104 H9 Mação Santarém, C Portugal 39°33′N 08°00′W
58 J11 Macapá state capital Amapá, N Brazil 0°04′N 51°04′W
43 S17 Macaracas Los Santos, S Panama 07°46′N 80°31′W
55 P6 Macare, Caño ≈ NE Venezuela
55 Q6 Macareo, Caño ≈ NE Venezuela
Macarsca see Makarska
182 L12 Macarthur Victoria, SE Australia 38°04′S 142°02′E
MacArthur see Ormoc
56 C7 Macas Morona Santiago, SE Ecuador 02°22′S 78°08′W
Macassar see Makassar
59 Q14 Macau Rio Grande do Norte, E Brazil 05°05′S 36°37′W
Macău see Makó, Hungary
Macau see Macao
65 E24 Macbride Head headland East Falkland, Falkland Islands 51°25′S 57°55′W
23 V9 Macclenny Florida, SE USA 30°16′N 82°07′W
97 L18 Macclesfield C England, United Kingdom 53°16′N 02°07′W
192 F6 Macclesfield Bank undersea feature N South China Sea 15°50′N 114°20′E
MacCluer Gulf see Berau, Teluk
181 N7 Macdonald, Lake salt lake Western Australia
181 Q7 Macdonnell Ranges ▲▲ Northern Territory, C Australia
96 K8 Macduff NE Scotland, United Kingdom 57°40′N 02°29′W
104 I6 Macedo de Cavaleiros Bragança, N Portugal 41°31′N 06°57′W
Macedonia see Macedonia, FYR
Macedonia Central see Kentrikí Makedonía
Macedonia East and Thrace see Anatolikí Makedonía kai Thráki
113 O19 Macedonia, FYR off. the Former Yugoslav Republic of Macedonia, var. Macedonia, Mac. Makedonija, abbrev. FYR Macedonia, FYROM. ◆ republic SE Europe
Macedonia, the Former Yugoslav Republic of see Macedonia, FYR
Macedonia West see Dytikí Makedonía
59 Q16 Maceió state capital Alagoas, E Brazil 09°40′S 35°44′W
76 K15 Macenta SE Guinea 08°31′N 09°32′W
106 J12 Macerata Marche, C Italy 43°18′N 13°27′E
11 S11 MacFarlane ≈ Saskatchewan, C Canada
182 H7 Macfarlane, Lake var. Lake Mcfarlane. ◎ South Australia
Macgillicuddy's Reeks Mountains see Macgillycuddy's Reeks
97 B21 Macgillycuddy's Reeks var. Macgillicuddy's Reeks Mountains, Ir. Na Cruacha Dubha. ▲▲ SW Ireland
11 X16 MacGregor Manitoba, S Canada 49°58′N 98°49′W
149 O10 Mach Baluchistān, SW Pakistan 29°52′N 67°20′E
56 C6 Machachi Pichincha, C Ecuador 0°33′S 78°34′W
83 M19 Machaila Gaza, S Mozambique 22°15′S 32°57′E
Machaire Fíolta see Magherafelt
Machaire Rátha see Maghera
81 I19 Machakos Eastern, S Kenya 01°31′S 37°16′E
56 B8 Machala El Oro, SW Ecuador 03°20′S 79°57′W
83 J19 Machaneng Central, SE Botswana 23°12′S 27°30′E
83 M18 Machanga Sofala, E Mozambique 20°56′S 35°04′E
80 G13 Machar Marshes wetland SE Sudan
102 I8 Machecoul Loire-Atlantique, NW France 46°59′N 01°51′W
161 O8 Macheng Hubei, C China 31°10′N 115°00′E
155 J16 Mācherla Andhra Pradesh, C India 16°29′N 79°25′E
153 O11 Māchhāpuchhre ▲ C Nepal 28°30′N 83°57′E
19 T6 Machias Maine, NE USA 44°44′N 67°28′W
19 R3 Machias River ≈ Maine, NE USA
19 T6 Machias River ≈ Maine, NE USA
64 P5 Machico Madeira, Portugal, NE Atlantic Ocean 32°43′N 16°47′W
155 K16 Machilīpatnam var. Bandar Masulipatnam. Andhra Pradesh, E India 16°12′N 81°11′E
54 G5 Machiques Zulia, NW Venezuela 10°04′N 72°37′W
57 G15 Machu Picchu Cusco, C Peru 13°08′S 72°30′W
83 M20 Macia var. Vila de Macia. Gaza, S Mozambique 25°02′S 33°08′E
Macías Nguema Biyogo see Bioco, Isla de
116 M13 Măcin Tulcea, SE Romania 45°15′N 28°09′E
183 T4 Macintyre River ≈ New South Wales/Queensland, SE Australia
181 Y7 Mackay Queensland, NE Australia 21°10′S 149°10′E
181 O7 Mackay, Lake salt lake Northern Territory/Western Australia
10 M13 Mackenzie British Columbia, W Canada 55°18′N 123°09′W
8 I9 Mackenzie ≈ Northwest Territories, NW Canada
195 Y6 Mackenzie Bay bay Antarctica
10 J1 Mackenzie Bay bay NW Canada
2 D9 Mackenzie Delta delta Northwest Territories, NW Canada
197 P8 Mackenzie King Island island Queen Elizabeth Islands, Northwest Territories, N Canada
8 H8 Mackenzie Mountains ▲▲ Northwest Territories, NW Canada
31 Q5 Mackinac, Straits of ◎ Michigan, N USA
194 K5 Mackintosh, Cape headland Antarctica 72°52′S 60°00′W
11 R15 Macklin Saskatchewan, S Canada 52°19′N 109°51′W
183 V6 Macksville New South Wales, SE Australia 30°39′S 152°54′E
183 V5 Maclean New South Wales, SE Australia 29°30′S 153°15′E
83 J24 Maclear Eastern Cape, SE South Africa 31°05′S 28°22′E
183 U6 Macleay River ≈ New South Wales, SE Australia
MacLeod see Fort Macleod
180 G9 Macleod, Lake ◎ Western Australia
10 I6 Macmillan ≈ Yukon Territory, NW Canada
30 J12 Macomb Illinois, N USA 40°27′N 90°40′W
107 B18 Macomer Sardegna, Italy, C Mediterranean Sea 40°15′N 08°47′E
82 Q13 Macomia Cabo Delgado, NE Mozambique 12°15′S 40°06′E
103 R10 Mâcon anc. Matisco, Matisco Ædourum. Saône-et-Loire, C France 46°19′N 04°49′E
23 T5 Macon Georgia, SE USA 32°49′N 83°41′W
23 N4 Macon Mississippi, S USA 33°06′N 88°33′W
27 U3 Macon Missouri, C USA 39°44′N 92°27′W
22 J6 Macon, Bayou ≈ Arkansas/Louisiana, S USA
82 G13 Macondo Moxico, E Angola 12°31′S 23°45′E
83 M16 Macossa Manica, C Mozambique 17°51′S 33°54′E
11 T12 Macoun Lake ◎ Saskatchewan, C Canada
30 K14 Macoupin Creek ≈ Illinois, N USA
Macouria see Tonate
83 N18 Macovane Inhambane, SE Mozambique 21°30′S 35°07′E
183 N17 Macquarie Harbour inlet Tasmania, SE Australia
192 J13 Macquarie Island island New Zealand, SW Pacific Ocean
183 T8 Macquarie, Lake lagoon New South Wales, SE Australia
183 Q6 Macquarie Marshes wetland New South Wales, SE Australia
175 O13 Macquarie Ridge undersea feature SW Pacific Ocean 57°00′S 159°00′E
183 Q6 Macquarie River ≈ New South Wales, SE Australia
183 P17 Macquarie River ≈ Tasmania, SE Australia
195 V5 Mac. Robertson Land physical region Antarctica
97 C21 Macroom Ir. Maigh Chromtha. Cork, SW Ireland 51°54′N 08°57′W
42 G5 Macuelizo Santa Bárbara, NW Honduras 15°21′N 88°31′W
182 G2 Macumba River ≈ South Australia
57 I16 Macusani Puno, S Peru 14°05′S 70°24′W
56 E8 Macusari, Río ≈ N Peru
41 U15 Macuspana Tabasco, SE Mexico 17°43′N 92°36′W
138 G10 Mādabā var. Mādabā, Madeba; anc. Medeba. Ma'dabā, NW Jordan 31°44′N 35°48′E
138 G11 Ma'dabā off. Muḩāfaz̧at Ma'dabā. ◈ governorate C Jordan
Mādabā see Ma'dabā
172 G2 Madagascar off. Democratic Republic of Madagascar, Malg. Madagasikara; prev. Malagasy Republic. ◆ republic W Indian Ocean
172 I5 Madagascar island W Indian Ocean
128 L17 Madagascar Basin undersea feature W Indian Ocean 27°00′S 53°00′E
Madagascar, Democratic Republic of see Madagascar
128 L16 Madagascar Plain undersea feature W Indian Ocean 19°00′S 52°00′E
67 Y14 Madagascar Plateau var. Madagascar Ridge, Madagascar Rise, Rus. Madagaskarskiy Khrebet. undersea feature W Indian Ocean 30°00′S 45°00′E
Madagascar Rise/Madagascar Ridge see Madagascar Plateau
Madagasikara see Madagascar
Madagaskarskiy Khrebet see Madagascar Plateau
64 N2 Madalena Pico, Azores, Portugal, NE Atlantic Ocean 38°32′N 28°15′W
77 Y6 Madama Agadez, NE Niger 21°54′N 13°43′E
114 J12 Madan Smolyan, S Bulgaria 41°29′N 24°56′E
155 I19 Madanapalle Andhra Pradesh, E India 13°33′N 78°31′E
186 D7 Madang Madang, N Papua New Guinea 05°14′S 145°45′E
186 C6 Madang ◈ province N Papua New Guinea
146 G7 Madaniyat Rus. Madeniyet. Qoraqalpog'iston Respublikasi, W Uzbekistan 42°48′N 59°00′E
Madanīyīn see Médenine
77 U11 Madaoua Tahoua, SW Niger 14°06′N 06°01′E
Madaras see Vtáčnik
153 U15 Madaripur Dhaka, C Bangladesh 23°09′N 90°11′E
77 U12 Madarounfa Maradi, S Niger 13°16′N 07°07′E
Mađarska see Hungary
146 B13 Madau Balkan Welaýaty, W Turkmenistan 38°11′N 54°46′E
186 H9 Madau Island island SE Papua New Guinea
19 S1 Madawaska Maine, NE USA 47°19′N 68°19′W
14 J13 Madawaska ≈ Ontario, SE Canada
Madawaska Highlands see Haliburton Highlands
166 M4 Madaya Mandalay, C Burma (Myanmar) 22°12′N 96°05′E
107 K17 Maddaloni Campania, S Italy 41°03′N 14°23′E
29 O3 Maddock North Dakota, N USA 47°57′N 99°31′W
99 I14 Made Noord-Brabant, S Netherlands 51°41′N 04°48′E
Madeba see Ma'dabā
64 L9 Madeira var. Ilha de Madeira. island Madeira, Portugal, NE Atlantic Ocean
Madeira, Ilha de see Madeira
64 O5 Madeira Islands Port. Região Autoónoma da Madeira. ◈ autonomous region Madeira, Portugal, NE Atlantic Ocean
64 L9 Madeira Plain undersea feature E Atlantic Ocean
Madeira, Região Autoónoma da see Madeira Islands
64 L9 Madeira Ridge undersea feature E Atlantic Ocean 35°30′N 15°45′W
59 F14 Madeira, Rio var. Río Madera. ≈ Bolivia/Brazil see also Madera, Río
Madeira, Rio see Madera, Río
101 J25 Mädelegabel ▲ Austria/Germany 47°18′N 10°19′E
15 X6 Madeleine ≈ Québec, SE Canada
15 X5 Madeleine, Cap de la headland Québec, SE Canada 49°13′N 65°20′W
13 Q13 Madeleine, Îles de la Eng. Magdalen Islands. island group Québec, E Canada
29 U10 Madelia Minnesota, N USA 44°03′N 94°26′W
35 P3 Madeline California, W USA 41°02′N 120°28′W
30 K3 Madeline Island island Apostle Islands, Wisconsin, N USA
137 O15 Maden Elazığ, SE Turkey 38°24′N 39°42′E
145 V12 Madeniyet Vostochnyy Kazakhstan, E Kazakhstan 47°51′N 78°37′E

282
◆ Country ● Country Capital ◇ Dependent Territory ○ Dependent Territory Capital ◈ Administrative Regions ✈ International Airport ▲ Mountain ▲▲ Mountain Range Volcano ≈ River ◎ Lake ▣ Reservoir

MADENIYET – MALĀYER

Madeniyet *see* Madaniyat
40 *H5* **Madera** Chihuahua, N Mexico *29°10′N 108°10′W*
35 *Q10* **Madera** California, W USA *36°57′N 120°02′W*
56 *L13* **Madera, Río** ***Port.*** Rio Madeira. ≈ Bolivia/Brazil ***see also*** Madeira, Rio
Madera, Río *see* Madeira, Rio
106 *D6* **Madesimo** Lombardia, N Italy *46°20′N 09°26′E*
141 *O14* **Madhāb, Wādī** *dry watercourse* NW Yemen
153 *R13* **Madhepura** ***prev.*** Madhipure. Bihār, NE India *25°56′N 86°48′E*
Madhipure *see* Madhepura
153 *Q13* **Madhubani** Bihār, N India *26°21′N 86°05′E*
153 *Q15* **Madhupur** Jhārkhand, NE India *24°17′N 86°38′E*
154 *I10* **Madhya Pradesh** ***prev.*** Central Provinces and Berar. ◈ *state* C India
57 *K15* **Madidi, Río** ≈ W Bolivia
155 *F20* **Madikeri** ***prev.*** Mercara. Karnātaka, W India *12°29′N 75°40′E*
27 *O13* **Madill** Oklahoma, C USA *34°06′N 96°46′W*
79 *G21* **Madimba** Bas-Congo, SW Dem. Rep. Congo *04°58′S 15°08′E*
138 *M4* **Ma'din** Ar Raqqah, C Syria *35°45′N 39°36′E*
Madīnah, Minṭaqat al *see* Al Madīnah
76 *M14* **Madinani** NW Ivory Coast *09°37′N 06°57′W*
141 *O17* **Madīnat ash Sha'b** ***prev.*** Al Ittiḥād. SW Yemen *12°52′N 44°55′E*
138 *K3* **Madīnat ath Thawrah** ***var.*** Ath Thawrah. Ar Raqqah, N Syria *35°36′N 39°00′E*
173 *O6* **Madingley Rise** *undersea feature* W Indian Ocean
79 *E21* **Madingo-Kayes** Kouilou, S Congo *04°27′S 11°43′E*
79 *F21* **Madingou** Bouenza, S Congo *04°10′S 13°33′E*
Madioen *see* Madiun
23 *U8* **Madison** Florida, SE USA *30°27′N 83°24′W*
23 *T3* **Madison** Georgia, SE USA *33°37′N 83°28′W*
31 *P15* **Madison** Indiana, N USA *38°44′N 85°22′W*
27 *P6* **Madison** Kansas, C USA *45′01′N 96′11′W*
19 *Q6* **Madison** Maine, NE USA *44°48′N 69°52′W*
29 *S9* **Madison** Minnesota, N USA *45°00′N 96°12′W*
22 *K5* **Madison** Mississippi, S USA *32°27′N 90°07′W*
29 *Q14* **Madison** Nebraska, C USA *41°49′N 97°27′W*
29 *R10* **Madison** South Dakota, N USA *44°00′N 97°06′W*
21 *V5* **Madison** Virginia, NE USA *38°23′N 78°16′W*
21 *Q5* **Madison** West Virginia, NE USA *38°03′N 81°50′W*
30 *L9* **Madison** *state capital* Wisconsin, N USA *43°04′N 89°22′W*
21 *T6* **Madison Heights** Virginia, NE USA *37°25′N 79°07′W*
20 *I6* **Madisonville** Kentucky, S USA *37°20′N 87°30′W*
20 *M10* **Madisonville** Tennessee, S USA *35°31′N 84°21′W*
25 *V9* **Madisonville** Texas, SW USA *30°58′N 95°56′W*
Madisonville *see* Taiohae
169 *R16* **Madiun** ***prev.*** Madioen. Jawa, C Indonesia *07°37′S 111°33′E*
Madjene *see* Majene
14 *J14* **Madoc** Ontario, SE Canada *44°31′N 77°27′W*
Madoera *see* Madura, Pulau
81 *J18* **Mado Gashi** North Eastern, E Kenya *0°40′N 39°09′E*
159 *R11* **Madoi** ***var.*** Huanghe; ***prev.*** Huangheyan. Qinghai, C China *34°53′N 98°07′E*
189 *O13* **Madolenihmw** Pohnpei, E Micronesia
118 *I9* **Madona** ***Ger.*** Modohn. Madona, E Latvia *56°51′N 26°10′E*
107 *J23* **Madonie** ▲▲ Sicilia, Italy, C Mediterranean Sea
141 *Y11* **Madrakah, Ra's** *headland* E Oman *18°56′N 57°54′E*
32 *I12* **Madras** Oregon, NW USA *44°39′N 121°08′W*
Madras *see* Tamil Nādu
Madras *see* Chennai
57 *H14* **Madre de Dios** ***off.*** Departamento de Madre de Dios. ◈ *department* E Peru
Madre de Dios, Departamento de *see* Madre de Dios
63 *F22* **Madre de Dios, Isla** *island* S Chile
57 *J14* **Madre de Dios, Río** ≈ Bolivia/Peru
0 *H15* **Madre del Sur, Sierra** ▲▲ S Mexico
41 *Q9* **Madre, Laguna** *lagoon* NE Mexico
25 *T16* **Madre, Laguna** *lagoon* Texas, SW USA
37 *Q12* **Madre Mount** ▲ New Mexico, SW USA *34°18′N 107°54′W*
0 *H13* **Madre Occidental, Sierra** ***var.*** Western Sierra Madre. ▲▲ C Mexico
0 *H13* **Madre Oriental, Sierra** ***var.*** Eastern Sierra Madre. ▲▲ C Mexico
41 *U17* **Madre, Sierra** ***var.*** Sierra de Soconusco. ▲▲ Guatemala/Mexico
37 *R2* **Madre, Sierra** ▲▲ Colorado/Wyoming, C USA
105 *N8* **Madrid** ● (Spain) Madrid, C Spain *40°25′N 03°43′W*
29 *V14* **Madrid** Iowa, C USA *41°52′N 93°49′W*
105 *N7* **Madrid** ◈ *autonomous community* C Spain
105 *N10* **Madridejos** Castilla-La Mancha, C Spain *39°29′N 03°32′W*
104 *L7* **Madrigal de las Altas Torres** Castilla-León, N Spain *41°05′N 05°00′W*
104 *K10* **Madrigalejo** Extremadura, W Spain *39°08′N 05°36′W*
34 *L3* **Mad River** ≈ California, W USA
42 *J8* **Madriz** ◈ *department* NW Nicaragua
104 *K10* **Madroñera** Extremadura, W Spain *39°25′N 05°46′W*
181 *N12* **Madura** Western Australia *31°52′S 127°01′E*
Madura *see* Madurai
155 *H22* **Madurai** ***prev.*** Madura, Mathurai. Tamil Nādu, S India *09°55′N 78°07′E*
169 *S16* **Madura, Pulau** ***prev.*** Madoera. *island* C Indonesia
169 *S16* **Madura, Selat** *strait* C Indonesia
127 *Q17* **Madzhalis** Respublika Dagestan, SW Russian Federation *42°12′N 47°46′E*
114 *K12* **Madzharovo** Khaskovo, S Bulgaria *41°36′N 25°52′E*
83 *M14* **Madzimoyo** Eastern, E Zambia *13°42′S 32°34′E*
165 *O12* **Maebashi** ***var.*** Maebasi, Mayebashi. Gunma, Honshū, S Japan *36°24′N 139°02′E*
Maebasi *see* Maebashi
167 *O6* **Mae Chan** Chiang Rai, NW Thailand *20°13′N 99°52′E*
167 *N7* **Mae Hong Son** ***var.*** Maehongson, Muai To. Mae Hong Son, NW Thailand *19°16′N 97°56′E*
Maehongson *see* Mae Hong Son
Mae Nam Khong *see* Mekong
167 *Q7* **Mae Nam Nan** ≈ NW Thailand
167 *O10* **Mae Nam Tha Chin** ≈ W Thailand
167 *P7* **Mae Nam Yom** ≈ W Thailand
37 *O3* **Maeser** Utah, W USA *40°28′N 109°35′W*
Maeseyck *see* Maaseik
167 *N9* **Mae Sot** ***var.*** Ban Mae Sot. Tak, W Thailand *16°44′N 98°32′E*
44 *H8* **Maestra, Sierra** ▲▲ E Cuba
Maestricht *see* Maastricht
167 *O7* **Mae Suai** ***var.*** Ban Mae Suai. Chiang Rai, NW Thailand *19°43′N 99°30′E*
167 *O7* **Mae Tho, Doi** ▲ NW Thailand *18°56′N 99°20′E*
172 *I4* **Maevatanana** Mahajanga, C Madagascar *16°57′S 46°50′E*
187 *R13* **Maéwo** ***prev.*** Aurora. *island* C Vanuatu
171 *S11* **Mafa** Pulau Halmahera, E Indonesia *0°01′N 127°50′E*
83 *I23* **Mafeteng** W Lesotho *29°48′S 27°15′E*
99 *J21* **Maffe** Namur, SE Belgium *50°21′N 05°19′E*
183 *P12* **Maffra** Victoria, SE Australia *37°59′S 147°03′E*
81 *K23* **Mafia** *island* E Tanzania
81 *J23* **Mafia Channel** *sea waterway* E Tanzania
83 *I21* **Mafikeng** North-West, N South Africa *25°53′S 25°39′E*
60 *J12* **Mafra** Santa Catarina, S Brazil *26°08′S 49°47′W*
104 *F10* **Mafra** Lisboa, C Portugal *38°57′N 09°19′W*
143 *Q17* **Mafraq** Abū Ẓaby, C United Arab Emirates *24°21′N 54°33′E*
Mafraq/Muḥāfaẓat al Mafraq *see* Al Mafraq
123 *T10* **Magadan** Magadanskaya Oblast', E Russian Federation *59°38′N 150°50′E*
123 *T9* **Magadanskaya Oblast'** ◈ *province* E Russian Federation
108 *G11* **Magadino** Ticino, S Switzerland *46°09′N 08°50′E*
63 *G23* **Magallanes** ***var.*** Región de Magallanes y de la Antártica Chilena. ◈ *region* S Chile
Magallanes *see* Punta Arenas
Magallanes, Estrecho de *see* Magellan, Strait of
Magallanes y de la Antártica Chilena, Región de *see* Magallanes
14 *I10* **Maganasipi, Lac** ◎ Québec, SE Canada
54 *F6* **Magangué** Bolívar, N Colombia *09°14′N 74°46′W*
Magareva *see* Mangareva
77 *V12* **Magaria** Zinder, S Niger *13°00′N 08°55′E*
186 *F10* **Magarida** Central, SW Papua New Guinea *10°10′S 149°21′E*
171 *O2* **Magat** ≈ Luzon, N Philippines
27 *T11* **Magazine Mountain** ▲ Arkansas, C USA *35°10′N 93°38′W*
76 *I15* **Magburaka** C Sierra Leone *08°44′N 11°57′W*
123 *Q13* **Magdagachi** Amurskaya Oblast', SE Russian Federation *53°25′N 125°41′E*
62 *O12* **Magdalena** Buenos Aires, E Argentina *35°05′S 57°30′W*
57 *M15* **Magdalena** Beni, N Bolivia *13°22′S 64°07′W*
40 *F4* **Magdalena** Sonora, NW Mexico *30°38′N 110°59′W*
37 *Q13* **Magdalena** New Mexico, SW USA *34°07′N 107°14′W*
54 *F5* **Magdalena** ***off.*** Departamento del Magdalena. ◈ *province* N Colombia
40 *E9* **Magdalena, Bahía** *bay* W Mexico
Magdalena, Departamento del *see* Magdalena
63 *G19* **Magdalena, Isla** *island* Archipiélago de los Chonos, S Chile
40 *D8* **Magdalena, Isla** *island* NW Mexico
47 *P6* **Magdalena, Río** ≈ C Colombia
40 *F4* **Magdalena, Río** ≈ NW Mexico
Magdalen Islands *see* Madeleine, Îles de la
147 *N14* **Magdanly** ***Rus.*** Govurdak; ***prev.*** gowurdak, Guardak. Lebap Welaýaty, E Turkmenistan *37°50′N 66°06′E*
100 *L13* **Magdeburg** Sachsen-Anhalt, C Germany *52°08′N 11°39′E*
22 *L6* **Magee** Mississippi, S USA *31°52′N 89°43′W*
169 *Q16* **Magelang** Jawa, C Indonesia *07°28′S 110°11′E*
192 *K7* **Magellan Rise** *undersea feature* C Pacific Ocean
63 *H24* **Magellan, Strait of** ***Sp.*** Estrecho de Magallanes. *strait* Argentina/Chile
106 *D7* **Magenta** Lombardia, NW Italy *45°28′N 08°52′E*
Magerøy *see* Magerøya
92 *K7* **Magerøya** ***var.*** Magerøy, ***Lapp.*** Máhkarávju. *island* N Norway
164 *C17* **Mage-shima** *island* Nansei-shotō, SW Japan
108 *G11* **Maggia** Ticino, S Switzerland *46°15′N 08°42′E*
108 *G10* **Maggia** ≈ SW Switzerland
Maggiore, Lago *see* Maggiore, Lake
106 *C6* **Maggiore, Lake** ***It.*** Lago Maggiore. ◎ Italy/Switzerland
44 *I12* **Maggotty** W Jamaica *18°09′N 77°46′W*
76 *I10* **Maghama** Gorgol, S Mauritania *15°31′N 12°50′W*
97 *F14* **Maghera** ***Ir.*** Machaire Rátha. C Northern Ireland, United Kingdom *54°51′N 06°40′W*
97 *F15* **Magherafelt** ***Ir.*** Machaire Fíolta. C Northern Ireland, United Kingdom *54°45′N 06°36′W*
188 *H6* **Magicienne Bay** *bay* Saipan, S Northern Mariana Islands
105 *O13* **Magina** ▲ S Spain *37°43′N 03°24′W*
81 *H24* **Magingo** Ruvuma, S Tanzania *09°57′S 35°23′E*
112 *H11* **Maglaj** ◈ Federacija Bosna I Hercegovina, N Bosnia and Herzegovina
107 *Q19* **Maglie** Puglia, SE Italy *40°07′N 18°18′E*
36 *L2* **Magna** Utah, W USA *40°42′N 112°06′W*
Magnesia *see* Manisa
14 *G12* **Magnetawan** ≈ Ontario, S Canada
27 *T14* **Magnolia** Arkansas, C USA *33°17′N 93°16′W*
22 *K7* **Magnolia** Mississippi, S USA *31°08′N 90°27′W*
25 *V10* **Magnolia** Texas, SW USA *30°12′N 95°46′W*
Magnolia State *see* Mississippi
95 *J15* **Magnor** Hedmark, S Norway *59°57′N 12°14′E*
187 *Y14* **Mago** ***prev.*** Mango. *island* Lau Group, E Fiji
83 *L15* **Màgoé** Tete, NW Mozambique *15°50′S 31°42′E*
15 *Q13* **Magog** Québec, SE Canada *45°16′N 72°09′W*
83 *J15* **Magoye** Southern, S Zambia *16°00′S 27°34′E*
41 *Q12* **Magozal** Veracruz-Llave, C Mexico *21°33′N 97°57′W*
14 *B7* **Magpie** ≈ Ontario, S Canada
11 *Q17* **Magrath** Alberta, SW Canada *49°27′N 112°52′W*
105 *R10* **Magre** ≈ E Spain
76 *I9* **Magṭa' Lahjar** ***var.*** Magta Lahjar, Magta' Lahjar, Magtá Lahjar. Brakna, SW Mauritania *17°27′N 13°07′W*
146 *D12* **Magtymguly** ***prev.*** Garrygala, ***Rus.*** Kara-Kala. Balkan Welaýaty, W Turkmenistan *38°27′N 56°15′E*
83 *L20* **Magude** Maputo, S Mozambique *25°02′S 32°40′E*
77 *Y12* **Magumeri** Borno, NE Nigeria *12°07′N 12°48′E*
189 *O14* **Magur Islands** *island group* Caroline Islands, C Micronesia
166 *L6* **Magway** ***var.*** Magwe. Magway, W Burma (Myanmar) *20°08′N 94°55′E*
Magway *see* Magwe
166 *L6* **Magwe** ***var.*** Magway. ◈ *division* C Burma (Myanmar)
Magyar-Becse *see* Bečej
Magyarkanizsa *see* Kanjiža
Magyarország *see* Hungary
Magyarzsombor *see* Zimbor
142 *J4* **Mahābād** ***var.*** Mehabad; ***prev.*** Sāūjbulāgh. Āżarbāyjān-e Gharbī, NW Iran *36°44′N 45°44′E*
172 *H5* **Mahabo** Toliara, W Madagascar *20°22′S 44°39′E*
Maha Chai *see* Samut Sakhon
155 *D14* **Mahād** Mahārāshtra, W India *18°04′N 73°21′E*
81 *N17* **Mahadday Weyne** Shabeellaha Dhexe, C Somalia *02°55′N 45°30′E*
79 *Q17* **Mahagi** Orientale, NE Dem. Rep. Congo *02°16′N 30°59′E*
Mahāil *see* Muḥāyil
172 *I4* **Mahajamba** *seasonal river* NW Madagascar
152 *G10* **Mahājan** Rājasthān, NW India *28°47′N 73°50′E*
172 *I3* **Mahajanga** ***var.*** Majunga. Mahajanga, NW Madagascar *15°40′S 46°20′E*
172 *I3* **Mahajanga** ◈ *province* W Madagascar
172 *I3* **Mahajanga** ✈ Mahajanga, NW Madagascar *15°40′S 46°20′E*
169 *U10* **Mahakam, Sungai** ***var.*** Koetai, Kutai. ≈ Borneo, C Indonesia
83 *I19* **Mahalapye** ***var.*** Mahalatswe. Central, SE Botswana *23°02′S 26°53′E*
Mahalatswe *see* Mahalapye
Mahalla el Kubra *see* El Maḥalla el Kubra
171 *O13* **Mahalona** Sulawesi, C Indonesia *02°37′S 121°26′E*
Mahameru *see* Semeru, Gunung
143 *S11* **Māhān** Kermān, E Iran *30°00′N 57°00′E*
154 *N12* **Mahanādi** ≈ E India
172 *J5* **Mahanoro** Toamasina, E Madagascar *19°53′S 48°48′E*
153 *P13* **Mahārājganj** Bihār, N India *26°07′N 84°31′E*
153 *O12* **Mahārājganj** Uttar Pradesh, N India *27°08′N 83°34′E*
154 *G13* **Mahārāshtra** ◈ *state* W India
154 *L13* **Mahāsamund** Chhattīsgarh, SW India *21°06′N 82°06′E*
172 *I4* **Mahavavy** *seasonal river* N Madagascar
155 *K24* **Mahaweli Ganga** ≈ C Sri Lanka
Mahbés *see* El Mahbas
155 *J15* **Mahbūbābād** Andhra Pradesh, E India *17°35′N 80°00′E*
155 *H16* **Mahbūbnagar** Andhra Pradesh, C India *16°46′N 78°01′E*
140 *M8* **Mahd adh Dhahab** Al Madīnah, W Saudi Arabia *23°33′N 40°56′E*
55 *S9* **Mahdia** C Guyana *05°16′N 59°08′W*
75 *N6* **Mahdia** ***var.*** Al Mahdīyah, Mehdia. NE Tunisia *35°14′N 11°06′E*
155 *F20* **Mahe** ***Fr.*** Mahé; ***prev.*** Mayyali. Pondicherry, SW India *11°41′N 75°31′E*
172 *I16* **Mahé** ✈ Mahé, NE Seychelles *04°37′S 55°27′E*
172 *H16* **Mahé** *island* Inner Islands, NE Seychelles
Mahé *see* Mahe
173 *Y17* **Mahebourg** SE Mauritius *20°24′S 57°42′E*
152 *L10* **Mahendranagar** Far Western, W Nepal *28°58′N 80°13′E*
81 *I23* **Mahenge** Morogoro, SE Tanzania *08°41′S 36°41′E*
185 *F22* **Maheno** Otago, South Island, New Zealand *45°10′S 170°51′E*
154 *D9* **Mahesāna** Gujarāt, W India *23°37′N 72°28′E*
154 *F11* **Maheshwar** Madhya Pradesh, C India *22°11′N 75°40′E*
153 *V17* **Maheskhali Island** ***var.*** Maiskhal Island. *island* SE Bangladesh
151 *F14* **Mahi** ≈ N India
184 *Q10* **Mahia Peninsula** *peninsula* North Island, New Zealand
119 *O16* **Mahilyow** ***Rus.*** Mogilëv. Mahilyowskaya Voblasts', E Belarus *53°55′N 30°23′E*
119 *M16* **Mahilyowskaya Voblasts'** ***prev. Rus.*** Mogilëvskaya Oblast'. ◈ *province* E Belarus
191 *P7* **Mahina** Tahiti, W French Polynesia *17°29′S 149°27′W*
185 *E23* **Mahinerangi, Lake** ◎ South Island, New Zealand
Máhkarávju *see* Magerøya
83 *L22* **Mahlabatini** KwaZulu/Natal, E South Africa *28°15′S 31°28′E*
166 *L5* **Mahlaing** Mandalay, C Burma (Myanmar) *21°03′N 95°44′E*
109 *X8* **Mahldorf** Steiermark, SE Austria *46°54′N 15°55′E*
Mahmūd-e 'Erāqī *see* Maḥmūd-e Rāqī
149 *R4* **Maḥmūd-e Rāqī** ***var.*** Mahmūd-e 'Erāqī. Kāpīsā, NE Afghanistan *35°01′N 69°20′E*
Mahmudiya *see* Al Maḥmūdīyah
29 *S5* **Mahnomen** Minnesota, N USA *47°19′N 95°58′W*
152 *K14* **Mahoba** Uttar Pradesh, N India *25°18′N 79°53′E*
105 *Z9* **Mahón** ***Cat.*** Maó, ***Eng.*** Port Mahon; ***anc.*** Portus Magonis. Menorca, Spain, W Mediterranean Sea *39°54′N 04°15′E*
81 *J23* **Mahonda** Zanzibar North, E Tanzania *6°00′S 39°14′E*
18 *D14* **Mahoning Creek Lake** ▣ Pennsylvania, NE USA
105 *Q10* **Mahora** Castilla-La Mancha, C Spain *39°13′N 01°44′W*
Mähren *see* Moravia
Mährisch-Budwitz *see* Moravské Budějovice
Mährisch-Kromau *see* Moravský Krumlov
Mährisch-Neustadt *see* Uničov
Mährisch-Schönberg *see* Šumperk
Mährisch-Trübau *see* Moravská Třebová
Mährisch-Weisskirchen *see* Hranice
Māh-Shahr *see* Bandar-e Māhshahr
79 *N19* **Mahulu** Maniema, E Dem. Rep. Congo *01°04′S 27°10′E*
154 *C12* **Mahuva** Gujarāt, W India *21°06′N 71°46′E*
114 *N11* **Mahya Dağı** ▲ NW Turkey *41°47′N 27°34′E*
105 *T6* **Maials** ***var.*** Mayals. Cataluña, NE Spain *41°22′N 00°30′E*
191 *O2* **Maiana** ***prev.*** Hall Island. *atoll* Tungaru, W Kiribati
191 *S11* **Maiao** ***var.*** Tapuaemanu, Tubuai-Manu. *island* Îles du Vent, W French Polynesia
54 *H4* **Maicao** La Guajira, N Colombia *11°23′N 72°16′W*
Mai Ceu/Mai Chio *see* Maych'ew
103 *U8* **Maîche** Doubs, E France *47°15′N 06°43′E*
97 *N22* **Maidenhead** S England, United Kingdom *51°32′N 00°44′W*
11 *S15* **Maidstone** Saskatchewan, S Canada *53°06′N 109°21′W*
97 *P22* **Maidstone** SE England, United Kingdom *51°17′N 00°31′E*
77 *Y13* **Maiduguri** Borno, NE Nigeria *11°51′N 13°10′E*
108 *I8* **Maienfeld** Sankt Gallen, NE Switzerland *47°01′N 09°30′E*
116 *J12* **Măieruș** ***Hung.*** Szászmagyarós. Brașov, C Romania *45°55′N 25°30′E*
Maigh Chromtha *see* Macroom
Maigh Eo *see* Mayo
55 *N9* **Maigualida, Sierra** ▲▲ S Venezuela
154 *K9* **Maihar** Madhya Pradesh, C India *24°18′N 80°46′E*
154 *K11* **Maikala Range** ▲▲ C India
67 *T10* **Maiko** ≈ W Dem. Rep. Congo
Mailand *see* Milano
152 *L11* **Mailāni** Uttar Pradesh, N India *28°17′N 80°20′E*
149 *U10* **Māilsi** Punjab, E Pakistan *29°46′N 72°15′E*
147 *R8* **Maimak** Talasskaya Oblast', NW Kyrgyzstan *42°40′N 71°12′E*
Maimāna *see* Meymaneh
171 *V13* **Maimawa** Papua, E Indonesia *03°21′S 133°36′E*
Maimuna *see* Al Maymūnah
101 *G18* **Main** ≈ C Germany
115 *F22* **Maïna** *ancient monument* Pelopónnisos, S Greece
115 *E20* **Maínalo** ▲▲ S Greece
101 *L22* **Mainburg** Bayern, SE Germany *48°40′N 11°48′E*
Main Camp *see* Banana
14 *E12* **Main Channel** *lake channel* Ontario, S Canada
79 *I20* **Mai-Ndombe, Lac** ***prev.*** Lac Léopold II. ◎ W Dem. Rep. Congo
101 *K20* **Main-Donau-Kanal** *canal* SE Germany
19 *R6* **Maine** ***off.*** State of Maine, ***also known as*** Lumber State, Pine Tree State. ◈ *state* NE USA
102 *K6* **Maine** *cultural region* NW France
102 *J7* **Maine-et-Loire** ◈ *department* NW France
19 *Q9* **Maine, Gulf of** *gulf* NE USA
77 *X12* **Maïné-Soroa** Diffa, SE Niger *13°14′N 12°00′E*
167 *N2* **Maingkwan** ***var.*** Mungkawn. Kachin State, N Burma (Myanmar) *26°20′N 96°37′E*
Main Island *see* Bermuda
Mainistir Fhear Maí *see* Fermoy
Mainistirna Búille *see* Boyle
Mainistir na Corann *see* Midleton
Mainistir na Féile *see* Abbeyfeale
96 *J5* **Mainland** *island* N Scotland, United Kingdom
96 *L2* **Mainland** *island* NE Scotland, United Kingdom
159 *P16* **Mainling** ***var.*** Tungdor. Xizang Zizhiqu, W China *29°12′N 94°06′E*
152 *K12* **Mainpuri** Uttar Pradesh, N India *27°14′N 79°01′E*
103 *N5* **Maintenon** Eure-et-Loir, C France *48°35′N 01°34′E*
172 *H4* **Maintirano** Mahajanga, W Madagascar *18°01′S 44°03′E*
93 *M15* **Mainua** Oulu, C Finland *64°05′N 27°28′E*
101 *G18* **Mainz** ***Fr.*** Mayence. Rheinland-Pfalz, SW Germany *50°00′N 08°16′E*
76 *I9* **Maio** ***var.*** Vila do Maio. Maio, S Cape Verde *15°07′N 23°12′W*
76 *E10* **Maio** ***var.*** Mayo. *island* Ilhas de Sotavento, SE Cape Verde
62 *G12* **Maipo, Río** ≈ C Chile
62 *H12* **Maipo, Volcán** ⛰ W Argentina *34°09′S 69°51′W*
61 *E22* **Maipú** Buenos Aires, E Argentina *36°52′S 57°52′W*
62 *I11* **Maipú** Mendoza, E Argentina *33°00′S 68°46′W*
62 *H11* **Maipú** Santiago, C Chile *33°30′S 70°52′W*
106 *A9* **Maira** ≈ NW Italy
108 *I10* **Maira** ***It.*** Mera. ≈ Italy/Switzerland
153 *V12* **Mairābari** Assam, NE India *26°28′N 92°22′E*
44 *K7* **Maisí** Guantánamo, E Cuba *20°13′N 74°08′W*
118 *H13* **Maišiagala** Vilnius, SE Lithuania *54°52′N 25°03′E*
Maiskhal Island *see* Maheskhali Island
167 *N13* **Mai Sombun** Chumphon, SW Thailand *10°49′N 99°13′E*
Mai Son *see* Hat Lot
Maisur *see* Karnātaka, India
Maisur *see* Mysore, India
183 *T8* **Maitland** New South Wales, SE Australia *32°33′S 151°33′E*
182 *I9* **Maitland** South Australia *34°21′S 137°42′E*
14 *F15* **Maitland** ≈ Ontario, S Canada
195 *R1* **Maitri** *Indian research station* Antarctica *70°03′S 08°59′E*
159 *N15* **Maizhokunggar** Xizang Zizhiqu, W China *29°50′N 91°40′E*
43 *O10* **Maíz, Islas del** ***var.*** Corn Islands. *island group* SE Nicaragua
164 *J12* **Maizuru** Kyōto, Honshū, SW Japan *35°30′N 135°20′E*
54 *F6* **Majagual** Sucre, N Colombia *08°36′N 74°39′W*
41 *Z13* **Majahual** Quintana Roo, E Mexico *18°43′N 87°43′W*
Mājeej *see* Mejit Island
171 *N13* **Majene** ***prev.*** Madjene. Sulawesi, C Indonesia *03°33′S 118°59′E*
43 *V15* **Majé, Serranía de** ▲▲ E Panama
112 *I11* **Majevica** ▲▲ NE Bosnia and Herzegovina
81 *H15* **Majī** Southern Nationalities, S Ethiopia *06°11′N 35°32′E*
141 *X7* **Majīs** NW Oman *24°25′N 56°34′E*
Majorca *see* Mallorca
105 *X9* **Major, Puig** ▲ Mallorca, Spain, W Mediterranean Sea *39°50′N 2°50′E*
Mājro *see* Majuro Atoll
Majunga *see* Mahajanga
189 *Y3* **Majuro** ✈ Majuro Atoll, SE Marshall Islands *07°05′N 171°08′E*
189 *Y2* **Majuro Atoll** ***var.*** Mājro. *atoll* Ratak Chain, SE Marshall Islands
189 *X2* **Majuro Lagoon** *lagoon* Majuro Atoll, SE Marshall Islands
76 *H11* **Maka** C Senegal *13°40′N 14°12′W*
79 *F20* **Makabana** Niari, SW Congo *03°28′S 12°36′E*
38 *D9* **Mākaha** ***var.*** Makaha. O'ahu, Hawaii, USA, C Pacific Ocean *21°28′N 158°13′W*
38 *B8* **Makahū'ena Point** ***var.*** Makahuena Point. *headland* Kaua'i, Hawai'i, USA *21°52′N 159°28′W*
38 *D9* **Makakilo City** O'ahu, Hawaii, USA, C Pacific Ocean *21°21′N 158°05′W*
83 *H18* **Makalamabedi** Central, C Botswana *20°19′S 23°51′E*
Makale *see* Mek'elē
158 *K17* **Makalu** ***Chin.*** Makaru Shan. ▲ China/Nepal *27°53′N 87°09′E*
81 *G23* **Makampi** Mbeya, S Tanzania *08°00′S 33°17′E*
145 *X12* **Makanchi** ***Kaz.*** Maqanshy. Vostochnyy Kazakhstan, E Kazakhstan *46°47′N 82°00′E*
42 *M8* **Makantaka** Región Autónoma Atlántico Norte, NE Nicaragua *13°13′N 84°04′W*
190 *B16* **Makapu Point** *headland* W Niue *18°59′S 169°56′E*
185 *C24* **Makarewa** Southland, South Island, New Zealand *46°17′S 168°16′E*
117 *O4* **Makariv** Kyyivs'ka Oblast', N Ukraine *50°28′N 29°49′E*
185 *D20* **Makarora** ≈ South Island, New Zealand
123 *T13* **Makarov** Ostrov Sakhalin, Sakhalinskaya Oblast', SE Russian Federation *48°24′N 142°37′E*
197 *R9* **Makarov Basin** *undersea feature* Arctic Ocean
192 *I5* **Makarov Seamount** *undersea feature* W Pacific Ocean *29°30′N 153°30′E*
113 *F15* **Makarska** ***It.*** Macarsca. Split-Dalmacija, SE Croatia *43°18′N 17°00′E*
Makaru Shan *see* Makalu
125 *O15* **Makar'yev** Kostromskaya Oblast', NW Russian Federation *57°52′N 43°46′E*
82 *L11* **Makasa** Northern, NE Zambia *09°42′S 31°54′E*
Makasar *see* Makassar
Makasar, Selat *see* Makassar Straits
170 *M14* **Makassar** ***var.*** Macassar, Makasar; ***prev.*** Ujungpandang. Sulawesi, C Indonesia *05°09′S 119°28′E*
192 *F7* **Makassar Straits** ***Ind.*** Makasar Selat. *strait* C Indonesia
144 *G12* **Makat** ***Kaz.*** Maqat. Atyrau, SW Kazakhstan *47°40′N 53°28′E*
191 *T10* **Makatea** *island* Îles Tuamotu, C French Polynesia
139 *U7* **Makātū** Diyālá, E Iraq *33°55′N 45°25′E*
172 *H6* **Makay** ***var.*** Massif du Makay. ▲▲ SW Madagascar
Makay, Massif du *see* Makay
114 *J12* **Makaza** *pass* Bulgaria/Greece
Makedonija *see* Macedonia, FYR
190 *B16* **Makefu** W Niue *18°59′S 169°55′W*
191 *V10* **Makemo** *atoll* Îles Tuamotu, C French Polynesia
76 *I15* **Makeni** C Sierra Leone *08°57′N 12°02′W*
Makenzen *see* Orlyak
Makeyevka *see* Makiyivka
127 *Q16* **Makhachkala** ***prev.*** Petrovsk-Port. Respublika Dagestan, SW Russian Federation *42°58′N 47°30′E*
83 *K19* **Makhado** ***prev.*** Louis Trichardt. Northern, NE South Africa *23°01′S 29°43′E*
144 *F11* **Makhambet** Atyrau, W Kazakhstan *47°35′N 51°35′E*
Makharadze *see* Ozurget'i
139 *W13* **Makhfar Al Buṣayyah** Al Muthanná, S Iraq *30°09′N 46°09′E*
139 *R4* **Makhmūr** Arbīl, N Iraq *35°47′N 43°32′E*
138 *I11* **Makhrūq, Wadi al** *dry watercourse* E Jordan
139 *R4* **Makḥūl, Jabal** ▲▲ C Iraq
141 *R13* **Makhyah, Wādī** *dry watercourse* N Yemen
171 *V13* **Maki** Papua, E Indonesia *03°00′S 134°10′E*
185 *G21* **Makikihi** Canterbury, South Island, New Zealand *44°36′S 171°09′E*
191 *O2* **Makin** ***prev.*** Pitt Island. *atoll* Tungaru, W Kiribati
81 *I20* **Makindu** Eastern, S Kenya *02°15′S 37°49′E*
145 *Q8* **Makinsk** Akmola, N Kazakhstan *52°40′N 70°28′E*
187 *N10* **Makira** ***off.*** Makira Province. ◈ *province* SE Solomon Islands
Makira *see* San Cristobal
Makira Province *see* Makira
117 *X8* **Makiyivka** ***Rus.*** Makeyevka; ***prev.*** Dmitriyevsk. Donets'ka Oblast', E Ukraine *47°57′N 37°47′E*
140 *L10* **Makkah** ***Eng.*** Mecca. Makkah, W Saudi Arabia *21°28′N 39°50′E*
140 *M10* **Makkah** ***var.*** Minṭaqat Makkah. ◈ *province* W Saudi Arabia
Makkah, Minṭaqat *see* Makkah
13 *R7* **Makkovik** Newfoundland and Labrador, NE Canada *55°06′N 59°07′W*
98 *K6* **Makkum** Friesland, N Netherlands *53°03′N 05°25′E*
111 *M25* **Makó** ***Rom.*** Macău. Csongrád, SE Hungary *46°14′N 20°28′E*
Mako *see* Makung
14 *G9* **Makobe Lake** ◎ Ontario, S Canada
79 *F18* **Makokou** Ogooué-Ivindo, NE Gabon *0°38′N 12°47′E*
81 *G23* **Makongolosi** Mbeya, S Tanzania *08°24′S 33°09′E*
81 *E19* **Makota** SW Uganda *0°37′S 30°12′E*
79 *G18* **Makoua** Cuvette, C Congo *0°01′S 15°40′E*
110 *M10* **Maków Mazowiecki** Mazowieckie, C Poland *52°51′N 21°06′E*
111 *K17* **Maków Podhalański** Małopolskie, S Poland *49°43′N 19°40′E*
143 *V14* **Makran** *cultural region* Iran/Pakistan
152 *G12* **Makrāna** Rājasthān, N India *27°02′N 74°44′E*
143 *U15* **Makran Coast** *coastal region* SE Iran
119 *F20* **Makrany** ***Rus.*** Mokrany. Brestskaya Voblasts', SW Belarus *51°50′N 24°15′E*
Makrinoros *see* Makrynóros
115 *H20* **Makrónisosi** *island* Kykládes, Greece, Aegean Sea
115 *D17* **Makrynóros** ***var.*** Makrinoros. ▲▲ C Greece
115 *G19* **Makryplági** ▲ C Greece *38°00′N 23°06′E*
Maksamaa *see* Maxmo
Maksatha *see* Maksatikha
Maksaticha *see* Maksatikha
124 *J15* **Maksatikha** ***var.*** Maksatha, Maksaticha. Tverskaya Oblast', W Russian Federation *57°49′N 35°46′E*
154 *G10* **Maksi** Madhya Pradesh, C India *23°20′N 76°36′E*
142 *I1* **Mākū** Āżarbāyjān-e Gharbī, NW Iran *39°20′N 44°50′E*
153 *Y11* **Mākum** Assam, NE India *27°28′N 95°28′E*
Makun *see* Makung
161 *R14* **Makung** ***prev.*** Mako, Makun. W Taiwan *23°35′N 119°35′E*
164 *B16* **Makurazaki** Kagoshima, Kyūshū, SW Japan *31°16′N 130°18′E*
77 *V15* **Makurdi** Benue, C Nigeria *07°42′N 08°36′E*
38 *L17* **Makushin Volcano** ▲ Unalaska Island, Alaska, USA *53°53′N 166°55′W*
83 *K16* **Makwiro** Mashonaland West, N Zimbabwe *17°58′S 30°25′E*
57 *D15* **Mala** Lima, W Peru *12°40′S 76°36′W*
93 *I14* **Malå** Västerbotten, N Sweden *65°12′N 18°45′E*
Mala *see* Mallow, Ireland
Mala *see* Malaita, Solomon Islands
171 *P8* **Malabang** Mindanao, S Philippines
155 *E21* **Malabār Coast** *coast* SW India
79 *C16* **Malabo** ***prev.*** Santa Isabel. ● (Equatorial Guinea) Isla de Bioco, NW Equatorial Guinea *03°43′N 08°52′E*
79 *C16* **Malabo** ✈ Isla de Bioco, N Equatorial Guinea *03°44′N 08°51′E*
Malaca *see* Málaga
Malacca *see* Melaka
168 *I7* **Malacca, Strait of** ***Ind.*** Selat Malaka. *strait* Indonesia/Malaysia
Malacka *see* Malacky
111 *G20* **Malacky** ***Hung.*** Malacka. Bratislavský Kraj, W Slovakia *48°26′N 17°01′E*
33 *R16* **Malad City** Idaho, NW USA *42°10′N 112°16′W*
117 *Q4* **Mala Divytsya** Chernihivs'ka Oblast', N Ukraine *50°40′N 32°13′E*
119 *J15* **Maladzyechna** ***Pol.*** Molodeczno, ***Rus.*** Molodechno. Minskaya Voblasts', C Belarus *54°19′N 26°51′E*
190 *D12* **Malaee** Île Futuna, N Wallis and Futuna
190 *G12* **Mala'etoli** Île Uvea, E Wallis and Futuna
54 *G8* **Málaga** Santander, C Colombia *06°44′N 72°45′W*
104 *M15* **Málaga** ***anc.*** Malaca. Andalucía, S Spain *36°43′N 04°25′W*
37 *V15* **Malaga** New Mexico, SW USA *32°10′N 104°04′W*
104 *L15* **Málaga** ◈ *province* Andalucía, S Spain
104 *M15* **Málaga** ✈ Andalucía, S Spain *36°38′N 04°36′W*
Malagasy Republic *see* Madagascar
105 *N10* **Malagón** Castilla-La Mancha, C Spain *39°10′N 03°51′W*
97 *G18* **Malahide** ***Ir.*** Mullach Íde. Dublin, E Ireland *53°27′N 06°09′W*
187 *N9* **Malaita** ***off.*** Malaita Province. ◈ *province* N Solomon Islands
187 *N8* **Malaita** ***var.*** Mala. *island* N Solomon Islands
Malaita Province *see* Malaita
80 *F13* **Malakal** Upper Nile, S Sudan *09°31′N 31°40′E*
Malakanagiri *see* Malkangiri
149 *T5* **Malākand** North-West Frontier Province, N Pakistan *34°34′N 71°56′E*
112 *C10* **Mala Kapela** ▲▲ NW Croatia
25 *V7* **Malakoff** Texas, SW USA *32°10′N 96°00′W*
Malakula *see* Malekula
149 *V7* **Malakwāl** ***var.*** Mālikwāla. Punjab, E Pakistan *32°32′N 73°18′E*
186 *E7* **Malalamai** Madang, W Papua New Guinea *05°49′S 146°44′E*
171 *O13* **Malamala** Sulawesi, C Indonesia *03°21′S 120°58′E*
169 *S17* **Malang** Jawa, C Indonesia *07°59′S 112°45′E*
83 *O14* **Malanga** Niassa, N Mozambique *13°27′S 36°05′E*
Malange *see* Malanje
92 *I9* **Malangen** *sound* N Norway
82 *C11* **Malanje** ***var.*** Malange. Malanje, NW Angola *09°34′S 16°25′E*
82 *C11* **Malanje** ***var.*** Malange. ◈ *province* N Angola
148 *M16* **Malān, Rās** *cape* SW Pakistan
77 *S13* **Malanville** NE Benin *11°50′N 03°23′E*
Malapane *see* Ozimek
155 *F21* **Malappuram** Kerala, SW India *11°00′N 76°02′E*
43 *T17* **Mala, Punta** *headland* S Panama *07°28′N 79°58′W*
148 *L15* **Malar** Baluchistān, SW Pakistan *26°19′N 64°55′E*
95 *N16* **Mälaren** ◎ C Sweden
62 *H13* **Malargüe** Mendoza, W Argentina *35°32′S 69°35′W*
14 *J8* **Malartic** Québec, SE Canada *48°09′N 78°09′W*
119 *F20* **Malaryta** ***Pol.*** Maloryta, ***Rus.*** Malorita. Brestskaya Voblasts', SW Belarus *51°47′N 24°05′E*
63 *J19* **Malaspina** Chubut, SE Argentina *44°56′S 66°52′W*
39 *U12* **Malaspina Glacier** *glacier* Alaska, USA
137 *N15* **Malatya** ***anc.*** Melitene. Malatya, SE Turkey *38°22′N 38°18′E*
136 *M14* **Malatya** ◈ *province* C Turkey
Malavate *see* Pédima
117 *Q7* **Mala Vyska** ***Rus.*** Malaya Viska. Kirovohrads'ka Oblast', S Ukraine *48°37′N 31°36′E*
83 *M14* **Malawi** ***off.*** Republic of Malaŵi; ***prev.*** Nyasaland, Nyasaland Protectorate. ◆ *republic* S Africa
Malawi, Lake *see* Nyasa, Lake
Malaŵi, Republic of *see* Malawi
93 *J17* **Malax** ***Fin.*** Maalahti. Länsi-Suomi, W Finland *62°55′N 21°30′E*
124 *H14* **Malaya Vishera** Novgorodskaya Oblast', W Russian Federation *58°52′N 32°12′E*
Malaya Viska *see* Mala Vyska
171 *Q7* **Malaybalay** Mindanao, S Philippines *08°10′N 125°08′E*
142 *L6* **Malāyer** ***prev.*** Daulatabad. Hamadān, W Iran *34°20′N 48°47′E*

◆ Country
● Country Capital
◇ Dependent Territory
○ Dependent Territory Capital
◈ Administrative Regions
✈ International Airport
▲ Mountain
▲▲ Mountain Range
⛰ Volcano
≈ River
◎ Lake
▣ Reservoir

MALAY PENINSULA – MANTORVILLE

168 J7 **Malay Peninsula** *peninsula* Malaysia/Thailand
168 L7 **Malaysia** *off.* Malaysia, *var.* Federation of Malaysia; *prev.* the separate territories of Federation of Malaya, Sarawak and Sabah (North Borneo) and Singapore. ◆ *monarchy* SE Asia
Malaysia, Federation of *see* Malaysia
137 R14 **Malazgirt** Muş, E Turkey 39°09′N 42°30′E
15 R8 **Malbaie** ≈ Québec, SE Canada
77 T12 **Malbaza** Tahoua, S Niger 13°57′N 05°32′E
110 J7 **Malbork** *Ger.* Marienburg, Marienburg in Westpreussen. Pomorskie, N Poland 54°01′N 19°03′E
100 N9 **Malchin** Mecklenburg-Vorpommern, N Germany 53°43′N 12°46′E
100 M9 **Malchiner See** ◎ NE Germany
99 D16 **Maldegem** Oost-Vlaanderen, NW Belgium 51°12′N 03°27′E
98 L13 **Malden** Gelderland, SE Netherlands 51°47′N 05°51′E
19 O11 **Malden** Massachusetts, NE USA 42°25′N 71°04′W
27 Y8 **Malden** Missouri, C USA 36°33′N 89°58′W
191 X4 **Malden Island** *prev.* Independence Island. *atoll* E Kiribati
173 Q6 **Maldives** *off.* Maldivian Divehi, Republic of Maldives. ◆ *republic* N Indian Ocean
Maldives, Republic of *see* Maldives
Maldivian Divehi *see* Maldives
97 P21 **Maldon** E England, United Kingdom 51°44′N 00°40′E
61 G20 **Maldonado** Maldonado, S Uruguay 34°57′S 54°59′W
61 G20 **Maldonado** ◆ *department* S Uruguay
41 P17 **Maldonado, Punta** *headland* S Mexico 16°18′N 98°31′W
106 G6 **Malè** Trentino-Alto Adige, N Italy 46°21′N 10°51′E
151 K19 **Male'** *Div.* Maale. ● (Maldives) Male' Atoll, C Maldives 04°10′N 73°29′E
76 K13 **Maléa** *var.* Maléya. NE Guinea 11°46′N 09°43′W
Maléas, Ákra *see* Agriliá, Akrotírio
115 G22 **Maléas, Akrotírio** *headland* S Greece 36°25′N 23°11′E
151 K19 **Male' Atoll** *var.* Kaafu Atoll. *atoll* C Maldives
Malebo, Pool *see* Stanley Pool
154 E12 **Mālegaon** Mahārāshtra, W India 20°33′N 74°32′E
81 F15 **Malek** Jonglei, S Sudan 06°04′N 31°36′E
187 Q13 **Malekula** *var.* Malakula; *prev.* Mallicolo. *island* W Vanuatu
189 Y15 **Malem** Kosrae, E Micronesia 05°16′N 163°01′E
83 O15 **Malema** Nampula, N Mozambique 14°57′S 37°28′E
79 N23 **Malemba-Nkulu** Katanga, SE Dem. Rep. Congo 08°01′S 26°48′E
124 K9 **Malen'ga** Respublika Kareliya, NW Russian Federation 63°50′N 36°21′E
95 M20 **Målerås** Kalmar, S Sweden 56°55′N 15°34′E
103 O6 **Malesherbes** Loiret, C France 48°18′N 02°25′E
115 G18 **Malesína** Stereá Ellás, E Greece 38°37′N 23°15′E
Maléya *see* Maléa
127 O15 **Malgobek** Respublika Ingushetiya, SW Russian Federation 43°34′N 44°34′E
105 X5 **Malgrat de Mar** Cataluña, NE Spain 41°39′N 02°45′E
80 C9 **Malha** Northern Darfur, W Sudan 15°07′N 26°00′E
139 Q5 **Malḥah** *var.* Malḥāt. Şalāḩ ad Dīn, C Iraq 34°44′N 42°41′E
Malḥāt *see* Malḥah
32 K14 **Malheur Lake** ◎ Oregon, NW USA
32 L14 **Malheur River** ≈ Oregon, NW USA
76 I13 **Mali** NW Guinea 12°08′N 12°29′W
77 O9 **Mali** *off.* Republic of Mali, *Fr.* République du Mali; *prev.* French Sudan, Sudanese Republic. ◆ *republic* W Africa
171 Q16 **Maliana** W East Timor 08°57′S 125°25′E
167 O2 **Mali Hka** ≈ N Burma (Myanmar)
Mali Idjoš *see* Mali Idoš
112 K8 **Mali Idoš** *var.* Mali Idjoš, *Hung.* Kishegyes; *prev.* Krivaja. Vojvodina, N Serbia 45°43′N 19°40′E
112 K9 **Mali Kanal** *canal* N Serbia
171 P12 **Maliku** Sulawesi, N Indonesia 0°36′S 123°13′E
Malik, Wadi al *see* Milk, Wadi el
Mālikwāla *see* Malakwāl
167 N11 **Mali Kyun** *var.* Tavoy Island. *island* Mergui Archipelago, S Burma (Myanmar)
95 M19 **Målilla** Kalmar, S Sweden 57°24′N 15°49′E
112 B11 **Mali Lošinj** *It.* Lussinpiccolo. Primorje-Gorski Kotar, W Croatia 44°31′N 14°28′E
Malin *see* Malyn
171 P7 **Malindang, Mount** ▲ Mindanao, S Philippines 08°12′N 123°37′E
81 K20 **Malindi** Coast, SE Kenya 03°14′S 40°05′E
Malines *see* Mechelen
96 E13 **Malin Head** *Ir.* Cionn Mhálanna. *headland* NW Ireland 55°37′N 07°37′W
171 O11 **Malino, Gunung** ▲ Sulawesi, N Indonesia 0°44′N 120°45′E
113 M21 **Maliq** *var.* Maliqi. Korçë, SE Albania 40°45′N 20°45′E
Maliqi *see* Maliq
149 O16 **Malir** Sind, SE Pakistan 24°52′N 67°11′E
Mali, Republic of *see* Mali
Mali, République du *see* Mali
171 Q8 **Malita** Mindanao, S Philippines 06°13′N 125°39′E
155 L15 **Malkangiri** *var.* Malakanagiri. Orissa, E India 18°21′N 81°53′E
154 G12 **Malkāpur** Mahārāshtra, C India 20°52′N 76°18′E
136 B10 **Malkara** Tekirdağ, NW Turkey 40°54′N 26°54′E
119 J19 **Mal'kavichy** *Rus.* Mal'kovichi. Brestskaya Voblasts', SW Belarus 52°31′N 26°36′E
Malkiye *see* Al Mālikīyah
114 L11 **Malko Sharkovo, Yazovir** ⊠ SE Bulgaria
114 N11 **Malko Tŭrnovo** Burgas, E Bulgaria 42°00′N 27°33′E
Mal'kovichi *see* Mal'kavichy
183 R12 **Mallacoota** Victoria, SE Australia 37°34′S 149°45′E
96 G10 **Mallaig** N Scotland, United Kingdom 57°04′N 05°48′W
182 I9 **Mallala** South Australia 34°29′S 138°30′E
75 W9 **Mallawī** *var.* Mallawi. C Egypt 27°44′N 30°50′E
Mallawi *see* Mallawī
105 R5 **Mallén** Aragón, NE Spain 41°53′N 01°25′W
106 F5 **Malles Venosta** *Ger.* Mals im Vinschgau. Trentino-Alto Adige, N Italy 46°40′N 10°37′E
Mallicolo *see* Malekula
109 Q8 **Mallnitz** Salzburg, S Austria 46°58′N 13°09′E
105 W9 **Mallorca** *Eng.* Majorca; *anc.* Baleares Major. *island* Islas Baleares, Spain, W Mediterranean Sea
97 C20 **Mallow** *Ir.* Mala. SW Ireland 52°08′N 08°39′W
93 E15 **Malm** Nord-Trøndelag, C Norway 64°04′N 11°12′E
95 L19 **Malmbäck** Jönköping, S Sweden 57°34′N 14°30′E
92 J12 **Malmberget** *Lapp.* Malmivaara. Norrbotten, N Sweden 67°09′N 20°39′E
99 M20 **Malmédy** Liège, E Belgium 50°26′N 06°02′E
83 E25 **Malmesbury** Western Cape, SW South Africa 33°28′S 18°43′E
Malmivaara *see* Malmberget
95 N16 **Malmköping** Södermanland, C Sweden 59°08′N 16°49′E
95 K23 **Malmö** Skåne, S Sweden 55°36′N 13°E
95 K23 **Malmo** ✕ Skåne, S Sweden 55°33′N 13°23′E
45 Q16 **Malmok** *headland* Bonaire, S Netherlands Antilles 12°16′N 68°21′W
95 M18 **Malmslätt** Östergötland, S Sweden 58°25′N 15°30′E
125 R16 **Malmyzh** Kirovskaya Oblast', NW Russian Federation 56°30′N 50°37′E
187 Q13 **Malo** *island* W Vanuatu
126 J7 **Maloarkhangel'sk** Orlovskaya Oblast', W Russian Federation 52°25′N 36°37′E
Maloelap *see* Maloelap Atoll
189 V6 **Maloelap Atoll** *var.* Maloelap. *atoll* E Marshall Islands
Maloenda *see* Malunda
108 I10 **Maloja** Graubünden, S Switzerland 46°25′N 09°42′E
82 L12 **Malole** Northern, NE Zambia 10°05′S 31°37′E
171 O3 **Malolos** Luzon, N Philippines 14°51′N 120°49′E
18 K6 **Malone** New York, NE USA 44°51′N 74°18′W
79 K25 **Malonga** Katanga, S Dem. Rep. Congo 10°26′S 23°10′E
111 L17 **Małopolskie** ◆ *province* SE Poland
Malorita/Maloryta *see* Malaryta
124 K9 **Maloshuyka** Arkhangel'skaya Oblast', NW Russian Federation 63°43′N 37°20′E
114 G10 **Mal'ovitsa** ▲ W Bulgaria 42°12′N 23°19′E
145 V15 **Malovodnoye** Almaty, SE Kazakhstan 43°31′N 77°42′E
94 C10 **Måløy** Sogn Og Fjordane, S Norway 61°57′N 05°06′E
126 K4 **Maloyaroslavets** Kaluzhskaya Oblast', W Russian Federation 55°03′N 36°31′E
122 G7 **Malozemel'skaya Tundra** *physical region* NW Russian Federation
104 J10 **Malpartida de Cáceres** Extremadura, W Spain 39°26′N 06°30′W
104 K9 **Malpartida de Plasencia** Extremadura, W Spain 39°59′N 06°03′W
106 C7 **Malpensa** ✕ (Milano) Lombardia, N Italy 45°41′N 08°40′E
76 J6 **Malqteïr** *desert* N Mauritania
Mals im Vinschgau *see* Malles Venosta
118 J10 **Malta** Rēzekne, SE Latvia 56°19′N 27°11′E
33 V7 **Malta** Montana, NW USA 48°21′N 107°52′W
120 M11 **Malta** *off.* Republic of Malta. ◆ *republic* C Mediterranean Sea
109 R8 **Malta** *var.* Maltabach. ≈ S Austria
120 M11 **Malta** *island* Malta, C Mediterranean Sea
Maltabach *see* Malta
Malta, Canale di *see* Malta Channel
120 M11 **Malta Channel** *It.* Canale di Malta. *strait* Italy/Malta
83 D20 **Maltahöhe** Hardap, SW Namibia 24°50′S 17°00′E
Malta, Republic of *see* Malta
97 N16 **Malton** N England, United Kingdom 54°07′N 00°50′W
171 R13 **Maluku** *off.* Propinsi Maluku, *Dut.* Molukken, *Eng.* Moluccas. ◆ *province* E Indonesia
171 R13 **Maluku** *Dut.* Molukken, *Eng.* Moluccas; *prev.* Spice Islands. *island group* E Indonesia
Maluku, Laut *see* Molucca Sea
Maluku, Propinsi *see* Maluku
171 R11 **Maluku Utara** *off.* Propinsi Maluku Utara. ◆ *province* E Indonesia
Maluku Utara, Propinsi *see* Maluku Utara
77 V13 **Malumfashi** Katsina, N Nigeria 11°51′N 07°39′E
171 N13 **Malunda** *prev.* Maloenda. Sulawesi, C Indonesia 02°58′S 118°52′E
94 K13 **Malung** Dalarna, C Sweden 60°40′N 13°45′E
94 K13 **Malungsfors** Dalarna, C Sweden 60°43′N 13°34′E
186 M8 **Maluu** *var.* Malu'u. Malaita, N Solomon Islands 08°22′S 160°39′E
Malu'u *see* Maluu
155 D16 **Mālvan** Mahārāshtra, W India 16°05′N 73°28′E
Malventum *see* Benevento
27 U12 **Malvern** Arkansas, C USA 34°21′N 92°50′W
29 S15 **Malvern** Iowa, C USA 40°59′N 95°36′W
44 I13 **Malvern** ▲ W Jamaica 17°59′N 77°42′W
Malvina, Isla Gran *see* West Falkland
Malvinas, Islas *see* Falkland Islands
117 N4 **Malyn** *Rus.* Malin. Zhytomyrs'ka Oblast', N Ukraine 50°46′N 29°14′E
127 O11 **Malyye Derbety** Respublika Kalmykiya, SW Russian Federation 47°57′N 44°39′E
Malyy Kavkaz *see* Lesser Caucasus
123 Q6 **Malyy Lyakhovskiy, Ostrov** *island* NE Russian Federation
Malyy Pamir *see* Little Pamir
122 N5 **Malyy Taymyr, Ostrov** *island* Severnaya Zemlya, N Russian Federation
144 E10 **Malyy Uzen'** *Kaz.* Kishiözen. ≈ Kazakhstan/Russian Federation
122 L14 **Malyy Yenisey** *var.* Ka-Krem. ≈ S Russian Federation
127 S3 **Mamadysh** Respublika Tatarstan, W Russian Federation 55°46′N 51°22′E
117 N14 **Mamaia** Constanţa, E Romania 44°13′N 28°37′E
187 W14 **Mamanuca Group** *island group* Yasawa Group, W Fiji
146 L13 **Mamash** Lebap Welaýaty, E Turkmenistan 38°24′N 64°12′E
79 O17 **Mambasa** Orientale, NE Dem. Rep. Congo 01°20′N 29°05′E
171 X13 **Mamberamo, Sungai** ≈ Papua, E Indonesia
79 G15 **Mambéré** ≈ SW Central African Republic
79 G15 **Mambéré-Kadéï** ◆ *prefecture* SW Central African Republic
Mambij *see* Manbij
79 H18 **Mambili** ≈ W Congo
83 N18 **Mambone** *var.* Nova Mambone. Inhambane, E Mozambique 20°59′S 35°04′E
171 O4 **Mamburao** Mindoro, N Philippines 13°16′N 120°36′E
172 I16 **Mamelles** *island* Inner Islands, NE Seychelles
99 M25 **Mamer** Luxembourg, SW Luxembourg 49°37′N 06°01′E
102 L6 **Mamers** Sarthe, NW France 48°21′N 00°22′E
79 D15 **Mamfe** Sud-Ouest, W Cameroon 05°46′N 09°18′E
145 P6 **Mamlyutka** Severnyy Kazakhstan, N Kazakhstan 54°54′N 68°36′E
36 M15 **Mammoth** Arizona, SW USA 32°43′N 110°38′W
33 S12 **Mammoth Hot Springs** Wyoming, C USA 44°57′N 110°40′W
Mamoedjoe *see* Mamuju
119 A14 **Mamonovo** *Ger.* Heiligenbeil. Kaliningradskaya Oblast', W Russian Federation 54°28′N 19°57′E
57 L14 **Mamoré, Río** ≈ Bolivia/Brazil
76 I14 **Mamou** W Guinea 10°24′N 12°05′W
22 H8 **Mamou** Louisiana, S USA 30°37′N 92°25′W
172 I14 **Mamoudzou** ○ (Mayotte) C Mayotte 12°48′S 45°E
172 I3 **Mampikony** Mahajanga, N Madagascar 16°03′S 47°39′E
77 P16 **Mampong** C Ghana 07°06′N 01°20′W
110 M7 **Mamry, Jezioro** *Ger.* Mauersee. ◎ NE Poland
171 N13 **Mamuju** *prev.* Mamoedjoe. Sulawesi, S Indonesia 02°41′S 118°55′E
83 F19 **Mamuno** Ghanzi, W Botswana 22°15′S 20°02′E
113 K19 **Mamuras** *var.* Mamurasi, Mamurras. Lezhë, C Albania 41°34′N 19°42′E
Mamurasi/Mamurras *see* Mamuras
76 L16 **Man** W Ivory Coast 07°24′N 07°33′W
55 X9 **Mana** NW French Guiana 05°40′N 53°49′W
56 A6 **Manabí** ◆ *province* W Ecuador
42 G4 **Manabique, Punta** *var.* Cabo Tres Puntas. *headland* E Guatemala 15°57′N 88°37′W
54 G11 **Manacacías, Río** ≈ C Colombia
58 F13 **Manacapuru** Amazonas, N Brazil 03°16′S 60°37′W
105 Y9 **Manacor** Mallorca, Spain, W Mediterranean Sea 39°35′N 03°12′E
171 Q11 **Manado** *prev.* Menado. Sulawesi, C Indonesia 01°32′N 124°55′E
188 H5 **Managaha** *island* S Northern Mariana Islands
99 G20 **Manage** Hainaut, S Belgium 50°30′N 04°14′E
42 J10 **Managua** ● (Nicaragua) Managua, W Nicaragua 12°08′N 86°15′W
42 J10 **Managua** ◆ *department* W Nicaragua
42 J10 **Managua** ✕ Managua, W Nicaragua 12°07′N 86°11′W
42 J10 **Managua, Lago de** *var.* Xolotlán. ◎ W Nicaragua
Manah *see* Bilād Manaḥ
18 K16 **Manahawkin** New Jersey, NE USA 39°39′N 74°12′W
184 K11 **Manaia** Taranaki, North Island, New Zealand 39°33′S 174°07′E
172 J6 **Manakara** Fianarantsoa, SE Madagascar 22°09′S 48°E
152 J7 **Manāli** Himāchal Pradesh, NW India 32°12′N 77°06′E
Ma, Nam *see* Sông Ma
Manama *see* Al Manāmah
186 D6 **Manam Island** *island* N Papua New Guinea
67 Y13 **Mananara Avaratra** ≈ SE Madagascar
182 M9 **Manangatang** Victoria, SE Australia 35°04′S 142°53′E
172 J6 **Mananjary** Fianarantsoa, SE Madagascar 21°13′S 48°20′E
76 L14 **Manankoro** Sikasso, SW Mali 10°33′N 07°25′W
76 J12 **Manantali, Lac de** ⊠ W Mali
Manáos *see* Manaus
185 B23 **Manapouri** Southland, South Island, New Zealand 45°33′S 167°38′E
185 B23 **Manapouri, Lake** ◎ South Island, New Zealand
58 F13 **Manaquiri** Amazonas, NW Brazil 03°27′S 60°37′W
Manar *see* Mannar
158 K5 **Manas** Xinjiang Uygur Zizhiqu, NW China 44°16′N 86°12′E
153 U12 **Manās** *var.* Dangme Chu. ≈ Bhutan/India
153 P10 **Manāslu** *var.* Manaslu. ▲ C Nepal 28°33′N 84°33′E
147 R8 **Manas, Gora** ▲ Kyrgyzstan/Uzbekistan 42°17′N 71°04′E
158 K3 **Manas Hu** ◎ NW China
Manaslu *see* Manāslu
37 S8 **Manassa** Colorado, C USA 37°10′N 105°56′W
21 W4 **Manassas** Virginia, NE USA 38°45′N 77°28′W
45 T5 **Manatí** C Puerto Rico 18°26′N 66°29′W
186 E8 **Manau** Northern, S Papua New Guinea 08°02′S 148°00′E
54 H4 **Manaure** La Guajira, N Colombia 11°46′N 72°28′W
58 F12 **Manaus** *prev.* Manáos. *state capital* Amazonas, NW Brazil 03°06′S 60°W
136 G17 **Manavgat** Antalya, SW Turkey 36°47′N 31°28′E
184 M13 **Manawatu** ≈ North Island, New Zealand
184 L11 **Manawatu-Wanganui** *off.* Manawatu-Wanganui Region. ◆ *region* North Island, New Zealand
Manawatu-Wanganui Region *see* Manawatu-Wanganui
171 R7 **Manay** Mindanao, S Philippines 07°12′N 126°29′E
138 K2 **Manbij** *var.* Mambij, *Fr.* Membidj. Ḩalab, N Syria 36°32′N 37°55′E
105 N13 **Mancha Real** Andalucía, S Spain 37°47′N 03°37′W
102 I4 **Manche** ◆ *department* N France
97 L17 **Manchester** *Lat.* Mancunium. NW England, United Kingdom 53°30′N 02°15′W
23 S5 **Manchester** Georgia, SE USA 32°51′N 84°37′W
29 Y13 **Manchester** Iowa, C USA 42°28′N 91°27′W
21 N7 **Manchester** Kentucky, S USA 37°09′N 83°46′W
19 O10 **Manchester** New Hampshire, NE USA 42°59′N 71°26′W
20 K10 **Manchester** Tennessee, S USA 35°28′N 86°05′W
18 M9 **Manchester** Vermont, NE USA 43°09′N 73°03′W
97 L18 **Manchester** ✕ NW England, United Kingdom 53°21′N 02°16′W
149 P15 **Manchhar Lake** ◎ SE Pakistan
Man-chou-li *see* Manzhouli
129 X7 **Manchurian Plain** *plain* NE China
Máncio Lima *see* Japiim
Mancunium *see* Manchester
148 J15 **Mand** Baluchistān, SW Pakistan 26°06′N 61°58′E
Mand *see* Mand, Rūd-e
81 H25 **Manda** Iringa, SW Tanzania 10°30′S 34°37′E
172 H6 **Mandabe** Toliara, W Madagascar 21°02′S 44°56′E
162 M10 **Mandah** *var.* Töhöm. Dornogovĭ, SE Mongolia 44°25′N 108°18′E
95 E18 **Mandal** Vest-Agder, S Norway 58°02′N 07°30′E
Mandal *see* Arbulag, Hövsgöl, Mongolia
Mandal *see* Batsümber, Töv, Mongolia
166 L5 **Mandalay** Mandalay, C Burma (Myanmar) 21°57′N 96°04′E
166 M6 **Mandalay** ◆ *division* C Burma (Myanmar)
162 L9 **Mandalgovĭ** Dundgovĭ, C Mongolia 45°47′N 106°18′E
139 V7 **Mandalī** Diyālá, E Iraq 33°43′N 45°33′E
162 K10 **Mandal-Ovoo** *var.* Sharhulsan. Ömnögovĭ, S Mongolia 44°43′N 104°06′E
95 E18 **Mandalselva** ≈ S Norway
163 P11 **Mandalt** *var.* Sonid Zuoqi. Nei Mongol Zizhiqu, N China 43°49′N 113°36′E
28 M5 **Mandan** North Dakota, N USA 46°49′N 100°53′W
Mandargiri Hill *see* Mandār Hill
153 R14 **Mandār Hill** *prev.* Mandargiri Hill. Bihār, NE India 24°51′N 87°03′E
170 M13 **Mandar, Teluk** *bay* Sulawesi, C Indonesia
107 C19 **Mandas** Sardegna, Italy, C Mediterranean Sea 39°40′N 09°07′E
Mandasor *see* Mandsaur
81 L16 **Mandera** North Eastern, NE Kenya 03°56′N 41°53′E
33 V13 **Manderson** Wyoming, C USA 44°13′N 107°55′W
44 J12 **Mandeville** C Jamaica 18°02′N 77°31′W
22 K9 **Mandeville** Louisiana, S USA 30°21′N 90°04′W
152 I7 **Mandi** Himāchal Pradesh, NW India 31°40′N 76°59′E
76 K14 **Mandiana** E Guinea 10°37′N 08°39′W
149 U10 **Mandi Būrewāla** *var.* Būrewāla. Punjab, E Pakistan 30°05′N 72°47′E
152 G9 **Mandi Dabwāli** Haryāna, NW India 29°56′N 74°40′E
Mandidzudzure *see* Chimanimani
83 M15 **Mandié** Manica, NW Mozambique 16°27′S 33°28′E
83 N14 **Mandimba** Niassa, N Mozambique 14°21′S 35°40′E
57 Q19 **Mandioré, Laguna** ◎ E Bolivia
154 J10 **Mandla** Madhya Pradesh, C India 22°36′N 80°23′E
83 M20 **Mandlakazi** *var.* Manjacaze. Gaza, S Mozambique 24°47′S 33°50′E
95 E24 **Mandø** *var.* Manø. *island* W Denmark
Mandoúdhion/Mandoudi *see* Mantoúdi
115 G19 **Mándra** Attikí, C Greece 38°04′N 23°30′E
172 I7 **Mandrare** ≈ S Madagascar
114 M10 **Mandra, Yazovir** *salt lake* SE Bulgaria
107 L23 **Mandrazzi, Portella** *pass* Sicilia, Italy, C Mediterranean Sea
172 J3 **Mandritsara** Mahajanga, N Madagascar 15°49′S 48°50′E
143 O13 **Mand, Rūd-e** *var.* Mand. ≈ S Iran
154 F9 **Mandsaur** *prev.* Mandasor. Madhya Pradesh, C India 24°03′N 75°10′E
154 F11 **Māndu** Madhya Pradesh, C India 22°22′N 75°24′E
169 W8 **Mandul, Pulau** *island* N Indonesia
83 G15 **Mandundu** Western, W Zambia 16°34′S 22°18′E
180 I13 **Mandurah** Western Australia 32°31′S 115°41′E
107 P18 **Manduria** Puglia, SE Italy 40°24′N 17°38′E
155 G20 **Mandya** Karnātaka, C India 12°34′N 76°55′E
77 P12 **Mané** C Burkina 12°59′N 01°21′W
106 E8 **Manerbio** Lombardia, NW Italy 45°22′N 10°09′E
Manevichi *see* Manevychi
116 K3 **Manevychi** *Pol.* Maniewicze, *Rus.* Manevichi. Volyns'ka Oblast', NW Ukraine 51°18′N 25°29′E
107 N16 **Manfredonia** Puglia, SE Italy 41°38′N 15°54′E
107 N16 **Manfredonia, Golfo di** *gulf* Adriatic Sea, N Mediterranean Sea
77 P13 **Manga** C Burkina 11°41′N 01°04′W
59 L16 **Mangabeiras, Chapada das** ▲ E Brazil
79 J20 **Mangai** Bandundu, W Dem. Rep. Congo 03°58′S 19°32′E
190 L17 **Mangaia** *island group* S Cook Islands
184 M9 **Mangakino** Waikato, North Island, New Zealand 38°23′S 175°47′E
153 V12 **Mangaldai** Assam, NE India 26°26′N 92°02′E
116 M15 **Mangalia** *anc.* Callatis. Constanţa, SE Romania 43°48′N 28°35′E
78 J11 **Mangalmé** Guéra, SE Chad 12°26′N 19°37′E
155 E19 **Mangalore** Karnātaka, W India 12°54′N 74°51′E
191 Y13 **Mangareva** *var.* Magareva. *island* Îles Tuamotu, SE French Polynesia
83 I23 **Mangaung** Free State, C South Africa 29°10′S 26°19′E
Mangaung *see* Bloemfontein
154 K9 **Mangawān** Madhya Pradesh, C India 24°39′N 81°33′E
184 M11 **Mangaweka** Manawatu-Wanganui, North Island, New Zealand 39°49′S 175°47′E
184 N11 **Mangaweka** ▲ North Island, New Zealand 39°51′S 176°06′E
79 P17 **Mangbwalu** Orientale, NE Dem. Rep. Congo 02°06′N 30°04′E
101 L24 **Mangfall** ≈ SE Germany
169 P13 **Manggar** Pulau Belitung, W Indonesia 02°52′S 108°13′E
166 M2 **Mangin Range** ▲ N Burma (Myanmar)
139 R1 **Mangish** Dahūk, N Iraq 37°03′N 43°04′E
144 F15 **Mangistau** *Kaz.* Mangqystaū Oblysy; *prev.* Mangyshlaskaya. ◆ *province* SW Kazakhstan
146 H8 **Mang'it** *Rus.* Mangit. Qoraqalpog'iston Respublikasi, W Uzbekistan 42°06′N 60°02′E
Mangit *see* Mang'it
54 A13 **Manglares, Cabo** *headland* SW Colombia 01°36′N 79°02′W
149 V6 **Mangla Reservoir** ⊠ NE Pakistan
159 N9 **Mangnai** *var.* Lao Mangnai. Qinghai, C China 37°52′N 91°45′E
Mango *see* Mago, Fiji
Mango *see* Sansanné-Mango, Togo
Mangoche *see* Mangochi
83 N14 **Mangochi** *var.* Mangoche; *prev.* Fort Johnston. Southern, SE Malawi 14°30′S 35°15′E
77 N14 **Mangodara** SW Burkina 09°49′N 04°22′W
172 H6 **Mangoky** ≈ W Madagascar
171 Q12 **Mangole, Pulau** *island* Kepulauan Sula, E Indonesia
184 J2 **Mangonui** Northland, North Island, New Zealand 35°00′S 173°30′E
Mangqystaū Oblysy *see* Mangistau
Mangqystaū Shyghanaghy *see* Mangyshlakskiy Zaliv
Mangshi *see* Luxi
104 H7 **Mangualde** Viseu, N Portugal 40°36′N 07°46′W
61 H18 **Mangueira, Lagoa** ◎ S Brazil
77 X6 **Manguéni, Plateau du** ▲ NE Niger
163 T4 **Mangui** Nei Mongol Zizhiqu, N China 52°02′N 122°13′E
26 K11 **Mangum** Oklahoma, C USA 34°52′N 99°30′W
79 O18 **Manguredjipa** Nord-Kivu, E Dem. Rep. Congo 0°28′N 28°33′E
83 L16 **Mangwendi** Mashonaland East, E Zimbabwe 18°22′S 31°24′E
144 F15 **Mangyshlak, Plato** *plateau* SW Kazakhstan
144 E14 **Mangyshlakskiy Zaliv** *Kaz.* Mangqystaū Shyghanaghy. *gulf* SW Kazakhstan
Mangyshlaskaya *see* Mangistau
162 E7 **Manhan** *var.* Tögrög. Hovd, W Mongolia 47°24′N 92°06′E
Manhan *see* Alag-Erdene
27 O4 **Manhattan** Kansas, C USA 39°11′N 96°35′W
99 L21 **Manhay** Luxembourg, SE Belgium 50°13′N 05°43′E
83 L21 **Manhiça** *prev.* Vila de Manhiça. Maputo, S Mozambique 25°25′S 32°49′E
83 L21 **Manhoca** Maputo, S Mozambique 26°49′S 32°36′E
59 N20 **Manhuaçu** Minas Gerais, SE Brazil 20°16′S 42°01′W
117 W9 **Manhush** *prev.* Pershotravneve. Donets'ka Oblast', E Ukraine 47°03′N 37°20′E
54 H10 **Maní** Casanare, C Colombia 04°50′N 72°15′W
143 R11 **Mānī** Kermān, C Iran
83 M17 **Manica** *var.* Vila de Manica. Manica, W Mozambique 18°56′S 32°52′E
83 M17 **Manica** *off.* Província de Manica. ◆ *province* W Mozambique
83 L17 **Manicaland** ◆ *province* E Zimbabwe
Manica, Província de *see* Manica
15 U5 **Manic Deux, Réservoir** ⊠ Québec, SE Canada
Manich *see* Manych
59 F14 **Manicoré** Amazonas, N Brazil 05°48′S 61°16′W
13 N11 **Manicouagan** Québec, SE Canada 50°40′N 68°46′W
13 N11 **Manicouagan** ≈ Québec, SE Canada
15 U6 **Manicouagan, Péninsule de** *peninsula* Québec, SE Canada
13 N11 **Manicouagan, Réservoir** ◎ Québec, E Canada
15 T4 **Manic Trois, Réservoir** ⊠ Québec, SE Canada
79 M20 **Maniema** *off.* Région du Maniema. ◆ *region* E Dem. Rep. Congo
Maniema, Région du *see* Maniema
Maniewicze *see* Manevychi
160 F8 **Maniganggo** Sichuan, C China 32°01′N 99°04′E
11 Y15 **Manigotagan** Manitoba, S Canada 51°06′N 96°18′W
153 R13 **Manihāri** Bihār, N India 25°21′N 87°37′E
191 U9 **Manihi** *island* Îles Tuamotu, C French Polynesia
190 L13 **Manihiki** *atoll* N Cook Islands
175 U8 **Manihiki Plateau** *undersea feature* C Pacific Ocean
196 M14 **Maniitsoq** *var.* Manitsoq, *Dan.* Sukkertoppen. ◆ Kitaa, S Greenland
153 T15 **Manikganj** Dhaka, C Bangladesh 23°52′N 90°00′E
152 M14 **Mānikpur** Uttar Pradesh, N India 25°04′N 81°06′E
171 N4 **Manila** *off.* City of Manila. ● (Philippines) Luzon, N Philippines 14°34′N 120°59′E
27 Y9 **Manila** Arkansas, C USA 35°52′N 90°10′W
Manila, City of *see* Manila
189 N16 **Manila Reef** *reef* W Micronesia
183 T6 **Manilla** New South Wales, SE Australia 30°44′S 150°43′E
192 P6 **Maniloa** *island* Tongatapu Group, S Tonga
123 U8 **Manily** Koryakskiy Avtonomnyy Okrug, E Russian Federation 62°33′N 165°03′E
171 V12 **Manim, Pulau** *island* E Indonesia
168 I11 **Maninjau, Danau** ◎ Sumatera, W Indonesia
153 W13 **Manipur** ◆ *state* NE India
153 X14 **Manipur Hills** *hill range* E India
136 C14 **Manisa** *var.* Manissa, *prev.* Saruhan; *anc.* Magnesia. Manisa, W Turkey 38°36′N 27°29′E
136 C13 **Manisa** *var.* Manissa. ◆ *province* W Turkey
Manissa *see* Manisa
31 O7 **Manistee** Michigan, N USA 44°14′N 86°19′W
31 P7 **Manistee River** ≈ Michigan, N USA
31 O4 **Manistique** Michigan, N USA 45°57′N 86°15′W
31 P4 **Manistique Lake** ◎ Michigan, N USA
11 W13 **Manitoba** ◆ *province* S Canada
11 X16 **Manitoba, Lake** ◎ Manitoba, S Canada
11 X17 **Manitou** Manitoba, S Canada 49°12′N 98°28′W
31 N2 **Manitou Island** *island* Michigan, N USA
14 H11 **Manitou Lake** ◎ Ontario, SE Canada
12 G15 **Manitoulin Island** *island* Ontario, S Canada
37 T5 **Manitou Springs** Colorado, C USA 38°51′N 104°56′W
14 G12 **Manitouwabing Lake** ◎ Ontario, S Canada
12 E12 **Manitouwadge** Ontario, S Canada 49°14′N 85°51′W
12 G15 **Manitowaning** Manitoulin Island, Ontario, S Canada 45°44′N 81°50′W
14 B7 **Manitowik Lake** ◎ Ontario, S Canada
31 N7 **Manitowoc** Wisconsin, N USA 44°04′N 87°40′W
Manitsoq *see* Maniitsoq
139 O7 **Mānī', Wādī al** *dry watercourse* W Iraq
12 J14 **Maniwaki** Québec, SE Canada 46°22′N 75°58′W
171 W13 **Maniwori** Papua, E Indonesia 02°49′S 136°00′E
54 E10 **Manizales** Caldas, W Colombia 05°03′N 73°52′W
112 F11 **Manjača** ▲ NW Bosnia and Herzegovina
Manjacaze *see* Mandlakazi
180 J14 **Manjimup** Western Australia 34°18′S 116°14′E
109 V4 **Mank** Niederösterreich, C Austria 48°06′N 15°13′E
79 I17 **Mankanza** Equateur, NW Dem. Rep. Congo 01°40′N 19°08′E
152 M12 **Mankāpur** Uttar Pradesh, N India 27°03′N 82°12′E
26 M3 **Mankato** Kansas, C USA 39°48′N 98°13′W
29 U10 **Mankato** Minnesota, N USA 44°10′N 94°00′W
117 O7 **Man'kivka** Cherkas'ka Oblast', C Ukraine 48°58′N 30°10′E
76 M15 **Mankono** C Ivory Coast 08°01′N 06°09′W
11 T17 **Mankota** Saskatchewan, S Canada 49°25′N 107°05′W
155 K23 **Mankulam** Northern Province, N Sri Lanka 09°07′N 80°27′E
162 L10 **Manlay** *var.* Üydzen. Ömnögovĭ, S Mongolia 44°08′N 106°48′E
39 Q9 **Manley Hot Springs** Alaska, USA 65°00′N 150°37′W
18 H10 **Manlius** New York, NE USA 43°00′N 75°58′W
105 W5 **Manlleu** Cataluña, NE Spain 41°59′N 02°17′E
29 V11 **Manly** Iowa, C USA 43°17′N 93°12′W
154 E13 **Manmād** Mahārāshtra, W India 20°15′N 74°29′E
182 J7 **Mannahill** South Australia 32°29′S 139°58′E
155 J23 **Mannar** *var.* Manar. Northern Province, NW Sri Lanka 09°01′N 79°53′E
155 I24 **Mannar, Gulf of** *gulf* India/Sri Lanka
155 J23 **Mannar Island** *island* N Sri Lanka
Mannersdorf *see* Mannersdorf am Leithagebirge
109 Y5 **Mannersdorf am Leithagebirge** *var.* Mannersdorf. Niederösterreich, E Austria 47°59′N 16°36′E
109 Y6 **Mannersdorf an der Rabnitz** Burgenland, E Austria 47°25′N 16°32′E
101 G20 **Mannheim** Baden-Württemberg, SW Germany 49°29′N 08°29′E
11 O12 **Manning** Alberta, W Canada 56°53′N 117°39′W
29 T14 **Manning** Iowa, C USA 41°54′N 95°03′W
28 K5 **Manning** North Dakota, N USA 47°15′N 102°48′W
21 S13 **Manning** South Carolina, SE USA 33°42′N 80°12′W
191 Y2 **Manning, Cape** *headland* Kiritimati, NE Kiribati 02°02′N 157°26′W
21 S3 **Mannington** West Virginia, NE USA 39°31′N 80°20′W
182 A1 **Mann Ranges** ▲ South Australia
107 C19 **Mannu** ≈ Sardegna, Italy, C Mediterranean Sea
11 R14 **Mannville** Alberta, SW Canada 53°19′N 111°08′W
76 J15 **Mano** ≈ Liberia/Sierra Leone
Manø *see* Mandø
39 O13 **Manokotak** Alaska, USA 59°00′N 158°58′W
171 V12 **Manokwari** Papua, E Indonesia 0°53′S 134°05′E
79 N22 **Manono** Shaba, SE Dem. Rep. Congo 07°18′S 27°25′E
25 T10 **Manor** Texas, SW USA 30°20′N 97°33′W
97 D16 **Manorhamilton** *Ir.* Cluainín. Leitrim, NW Ireland 54°18′N 08°10′W
103 S15 **Manosque** Alpes-de-Haute-Provence, SE France 43°50′N 05°47′E
12 L11 **Manouane, Lac** ◎ Québec, SE Canada
163 W12 **Manp'o** *var.* Manp'ojin. NW North Korea 41°10′N 126°24′E
Manp'ojin *see* Manp'o
191 T4 **Manra** *prev.* Sydney Island. *atoll* Phoenix Islands, C Kiribati
105 V5 **Manresa** Cataluña, NE Spain 41°43′N 01°50′E
152 H9 **Mānsa** Punjab, NW India 30°00′N 75°25′E
82 J12 **Mansa** *prev.* Fort Rosebery. Luapula, N Zambia 11°14′S 28°55′E
76 G12 **Mansa Konko** C Gambia 13°26′N 15°29′W
15 Q11 **Manseau** Québec, SE Canada 46°23′N 71°59′W
149 U5 **Mānsehra** North-West Frontier Province, NW Pakistan 34°23′N 73°18′E
9 Q9 **Mansel Island** *island* Nunavut, NE Canada
183 O12 **Mansfield** Victoria, SE Australia 37°04′S 146°06′E
97 M18 **Mansfield** C England, United Kingdom 53°09′N 01°11′W
27 S11 **Mansfield** Arkansas, C USA 35°03′N 94°15′W
22 G6 **Mansfield** Louisiana, S USA 32°02′N 93°42′W
19 O12 **Mansfield** Massachusetts, NE USA 42°00′N 71°11′W
31 T12 **Mansfield** Ohio, N USA 40°45′N 82°31′W
18 G12 **Mansfield** Pennsylvania, NE USA 41°46′N 77°02′W
18 M7 **Mansfield, Mount** ▲ Vermont, NE USA 44°31′N 72°49′W
59 M16 **Mansidão** Bahia, E Brazil 10°46′S 44°04′W
102 L11 **Mansle** Charente, W France 45°52′N 00°11′E
76 G12 **Mansôa** C Guinea-Bissau 12°08′N 15°18′W
47 V8 **Manso, Rio** ≈ C Brazil
Manşūra *see* Al Manşūrah
Mansurabad *see* Mehrān, Rūd-e
56 A6 **Manta** Manabí, W Ecuador 0°59′S 80°44′W
56 A6 **Manta, Bahía de** *bay* W Ecuador
57 F14 **Mantaro, Río** ≈ C Peru
35 O8 **Manteca** California, W USA 37°48′N 121°13′W
54 J7 **Mantecal** Apure, C Venezuela 07°34′N 69°07′W
31 N11 **Manteno** Illinois, N USA 41°15′N 87°49′W
21 Y9 **Manteo** Roanoke Island, North Carolina, SE USA 35°54′N 75°42′W
Mantes-Gassicourt *see* Mantes-la-Jolie
103 N5 **Mantes-la-Jolie** *prev.* Mantes-Gassicourt, Mantes-sur-Seine; *anc.* Medunta. Yvelines, N France 48°59′N 01°43′E
Mantes-sur-Seine *see* Mantes-la-Jolie
36 L5 **Manti** Utah, W USA 39°16′N 111°38′W
Mantinea *see* Mantíneia
115 F20 **Mantíneia** *anc.* Mantinea. *site of ancient city* Pelopónnisos, S Greece
59 M21 **Mantiqueira, Serra da** ▲ S Brazil
29 W10 **Mantorville** Minnesota, N USA 44°04′N 92°45′W

284
◆ Country ● Country Capital ◇ Dependent Territory ○ Dependent Territory Capital ◆ Administrative Regions ✕ International Airport ▲ Mountain ▲ Mountain Range Volcano ◎ Lake ≈ River ⊠ Reservoir

115 G17 **Mantoúdi** *var.* Mandoudi; *prev.* Mandoúdhion. Évvoia, C Greece 38°47′N 23°29′E
Mantoue *see* Mantova
106 F8 **Mantova** *Eng.* Mantua, *Fr.* Mantoue. Lombardia, NW Italy 45°10′N 10°47′E
93 M19 **Mäntsälä** Etelä-Suomi, S Finland 60°38′N 25°21′E
93 L17 **Mänttä** Länsi-Suomi, W Finland 62°00′N 24°36′E
Mantua *see* Mantova
125 O14 **Manturovo** Kostromskaya Oblast', NW Russian Federation 58°19′N 44°42′E
93 M18 **Mäntyharju** Itä-Suomi, SE Finland 61°25′N 26°53′E
92 M13 **Mäntyjärvi** Lappi, N Finland 66°00′N 27°35′E
190 L16 **Manuae** *island* S Cook Islands
191 Q10 **Manuae** *atoll* Îles Sous le Vent, W French Polynesia
192 L16 **Manu'a Islands** *island group* E American Samoa
40 L5 **Manuel Benavides** Chihuahua, N Mexico 29°07′N 103°52′W
61 D21 **Manuel J. Cobo** Buenos Aires, E Argentina 35°49′S 57°54′W
58 M12 **Manuel Luís, Recife** *reef* E Brazil
61 F15 **Manuel Viana** Rio Grande do Sul, S Brazil 29°33′S 55°28′W
59 I14 **Manuel Zinho** Pará, N Brazil 07°21′S 54°47′W
191 V11 **Manuhangi** *atoll* Îles Tuamotu, C French Polynesia
185 E22 **Manuherikia** ≈ South Island, New Zealand
171 P13 **Manui, Pulau** *island* N Indonesia
Manukau *see* Manurewa
184 L6 **Manukau Harbour** *harbour* North Island, New Zealand
191 Z2 **Manulu Lagoon** ◎ Kiritimati, E Kiribati
182 J7 **Manunda Creek** *seasonal river* South Australia
57 K15 **Manupari, Río** ≈ N Bolivia
184 L6 **Manurewa** *var.* Manukau. Auckland, North Island, New Zealand 37°01′S 174°55′E
57 K15 **Manurimi, Río** ≈ NW Bolivia
186 D5 **Manus** ◈ *province* N Papua New Guinea
186 D5 **Manus Island** *var.* Great Admiralty Island. *island* N Papua New Guinea
171 T16 **Manuwui** Pulau Babar, E Indonesia 07°47′S 129°39′E
29 Q3 **Manvel** North Dakota, N USA 48°07′N 97°15′W
33 Z14 **Manville** Wyoming, C USA 42°45′N 104°38′W
22 G6 **Many** Louisiana, S USA 31°34′N 93°28′W
81 I22 **Manyara** ◈ NE Tanzania
81 H21 **Manyara, Lake** ◎ NE Tanzania
126 L12 **Manych** *var.* Manich. ≈ SW Russian Federation
83 H14 **Manyinga** North Western, NW Zambia 13°28′S 24°18′E
105 O11 **Manzanares** Castilla-La Mancha, C Spain 39°N 03°23′W
44 H7 **Manzanillo** Granma, E Cuba 20°21′N 77°07′W
40 K14 **Manzanillo** Colima, SW Mexico 19°00′N 104°19′W
40 K14 **Manzanillo, Bahía** *bay* SW Mexico
37 S11 **Manzano Mountains** ▲▲ New Mexico, SW USA
37 R12 **Manzano Peak** ▲ New Mexico, SW USA 34°35′N 106°27′W
163 R6 **Manzhouli** *var.* Man-chou-li. Nei Mongol Zizhiqu, N China 49°36′N 117°28′E
Manzil Bū Ruqaybah *see* Menzel Bourguiba
139 X9 **Manzilīyah** Maysān, E Iraq 32°26′N 47°01′E
83 L21 **Manzini** *prev.* Bremersdorp. C Swaziland 26°30′S 31°22′E
83 L21 **Manzini** ✈ (Mbabane) C Swaziland 26°36′S 31°25′E
78 G10 **Mao** Kanem, W Chad 14°06′N 15°17′E
45 N8 **Mao** NW Dominican Republic 19°37′N 71°04′W
Maó *see* Mahón
Maoemere *see* Maumere
159 W9 **Maojing** Gansu, N China 36°26′N 106°36′E
171 Y14 **Maoke, Pegunungan** *Dut.* Sneeuw-gebergte, *Eng.* Snow Mountains. ▲▲ Papua, E Indonesia
Maol Réidh, Caoc *see* Mweelrea
160 M15 **Maoming** Guangdong, S China 21°46′N 110°51′E
160 H8 **Maoxian** *var.* Mao Xian; *prev.* Fengyizhen. Sichuan, C China 31°42′N 103°48′E
Mao Xian *see* Maoxian
83 L19 **Mapai** Gaza, SW Mozambique 22°52′S 32°00′E
158 H15 **Mapam Yumco** ◎ W China
83 I15 **Mapanza** Southern, S Zambia 16°16′S 26°54′E
54 J4 **Mapararí** Falcón, N Venezuela 10°52′N 69°27′W
41 U17 **Mapastepec** Chiapas, SE Mexico 15°28′N 93°00′W
169 V9 **Mapat, Pulau** *island* N Indonesia
171 Y15 **Mapi** Papua, E Indonesia 07°02′S 139°24′E
171 V11 **Mapia, Kepulauan** *island group* E Indonesia
40 L8 **Mapimí** Durango, C Mexico 25°50′N 103°50′W
83 N19 **Mapinhane** Inhambane, SE Mozambique 22°14′S 35°07′E
55 N7 **Mapire** Monagas, NE Venezuela 07°48′N 64°40′W
11 S17 **Maple Creek** Saskatchewan, S Canada 49°55′N 109°28′W
31 Q9 **Maple River** ≈ Michigan, N USA
29 P7 **Maple River** ≈ North Dakota/South Dakota, N USA
29 S13 **Mapleton** Iowa, C USA 42°10′N 95°47′W
29 U10 **Mapleton** Minnesota, N USA 43°55′N 93°57′W
29 R5 **Mapleton** North Dakota, N USA 46°51′N 97°04′W
32 F13 **Mapleton** Oregon, NW USA 44°01′N 123°56′W
36 L3 **Mapleton** Utah, W USA 40°07′N 111°37′W
192 K5 **Mapmaker Seamounts** *undersea feature* N Pacific Ocean 25°00′N 165°00′E
186 B6 **Maprik** East Sepik, NW Papua New Guinea 03°38′S 143°02′E
83 L21 **Maputo** *prev.* Lourenço Marques. ● (Mozambique) Maputo, S Mozambique 25°58′S 32°35′E
83 L21 **Maputo** ◈ *province* S Mozambique
67 V14 **Maputo** ≈ S Mozambique
83 L21 **Maputo** ✈ Maputo, S Mozambique 25°47′S 32°36′E
Maqanshy *see* Makanchi
Maqat *see* Makat
113 K19 **Maqë** ≈ NW Albania
113 M19 **Maqellarë** Dibër, C Albania 41°36′N 20°29′E
159 S12 **Maqên** *var.* Dawo; *prev.* Dawu. Qinghai, C China 34°32′N 100°17′E
159 S11 **Maqên Kangri** ▲ C China 34°44′N 99°25′E
141 X7 **Maqiz al Kurbá** N Oman 24°13′N 56°48′E
159 U12 **Maqu** *var.* Nyinma. Gansu, C China 34°02′N 102°00′E
104 M9 **Maqueda** Castilla-La Mancha, C Spain 40°04′N 04°22′W
82 B9 **Maquela do Zombo** Uíge, NW Angola 06°06′S 15°12′E
63 I16 **Maquinchao** Río Negro, C Argentina 41°19′S 68°47′W
29 Z13 **Maquoketa** Iowa, C USA 42°03′N 90°42′W
29 Y13 **Maquoketa River** ≈ Iowa, C USA
14 F13 **Mar** Ontario, S Canada 44°48′N 81°12′W
95 F14 **Mår** ◎ S Norway
81 G19 **Mara** ◈ *region* N Tanzania
58 D12 **Maraã** Amazonas, NW Brazil 01°48′S 65°21′W
191 P8 **Maraa** Tahiti, W French Polynesia 17°44′S 149°34′W
191 O8 **Maraa, Pointe** *headland* Tahiti, W French Polynesia 17°44′S 149°34′W
59 K14 **Marabá** Pará, NE Brazil 05°23′S 49°10′W
54 H5 **Maracaibo** Zulia, NW Venezuela 10°40′N 71°39′W
Maracaibo, Gulf of *see* Venezuela, Golfo de
54 H5 **Maracaibo, Lago de** *var.* Lake Maracaibo. *inlet* NW Venezuela
Maracaibo, Lake *see* Maracaibo, Lago de
58 K10 **Maracá, Ilha de** *island* NE Brazil
59 H20 **Maracaju, Serra de** ▲▲ S Brazil
58 I11 **Maracanaquará, Planalto** ▲▲ NE Brazil
54 L5 **Maracay** Aragua, N Venezuela 10°15′N 67°36′W
Marada *see* Marādah
75 R9 **Marādah** *var.* Marada. N Libya 29°16′N 19°29′E
77 U12 **Maradi** Maradi, S Niger 13°30′N 07°05′E
77 U11 **Maradi** ◈ *department* S Niger
81 E21 **Maragarazi** *var.* Muragarazi. ≈ Burundi/Tanzania
Maragha *see* Marāgheh
142 J3 **Marāgheh** *var.* Maragha. Āžarbāyjān-e Khāvarī, NW Iran 37°21′N 46°14′E
141 P7 **Marāh** *var.* Marrāt. Ar Riyāḍ, C Saudi Arabia 25°04′N 45°30′E
55 N11 **Marahuaca, Cerro** ▲ S Venezuela 03°37′N 65°25′W
27 R5 **Marais des Cygnes River** ≈ Kansas/Missouri, C USA
58 L11 **Marajó, Baía de** *bay* N Brazil
59 K12 **Marajó, Ilha de** *island* N Brazil
191 O2 **Marakei** *atoll* Tungaru, W Kiribati
Marakesh *see* Marrakech
81 I18 **Maralal** Rift Valley, C Kenya 01°05′N 36°42′E
83 G21 **Maralaleng** Kgalagadi, S Botswana 25°42′S 22°39′E
145 U8 **Maraldy, Ozero** ◎ NE Kazakhstan
182 C5 **Maralinga** South Australia 30°16′S 131°35′E
Máramarossziget *see* Sighetu Marmației
187 N9 **Maramasike** *var.* Small Malaita. *island* N Solomon Islands
Maramba *see* Livingstone
194 H3 **Marambio** *Argentinian research station* Antarctica 64°22′S 57°18′W
116 H9 **Maramureș** ◈ *county* NW Romania
36 L15 **Marana** Arizona, SW USA 32°24′N 111°12′W
105 P7 **Maranchón** Castilla-La Mancha, C Spain 41°02′N 02°11′W
142 J2 **Marand** *var.* Merend. Āžarbāyjān-e Sharqī, NW Iran 38°25′N 45°40′E
Marandellas *see* Marondera
58 L13 **Maranhão** *off.* Estado do Maranhão. ◈ *state* E Brazil
104 H10 **Maranhão, Barragem do** ⊞ C Portugal
Maranhão, Estado do *see* Maranhão
149 O11 **Mārān, Koh-i** ▲ SW Pakistan 29°24′N 66°50′E
106 J7 **Marano, Laguna di** *lagoon* NE Italy
56 E9 **Marañón, Río** ≈ N Peru
102 J10 **Marans** Charente-Maritime, W France 46°19′N 00°58′W
83 M20 **Marão** Inhambane, S Mozambique 24°15′S 34°09′E
185 B23 **Mararoa** ≈ South Island, New Zealand
Maraş/Marash *see* Kahramanmaraş
107 M19 **Maratea** Basilicata, S Italy 39°57′N 15°44′E
104 G11 **Marateca** Setúbal, S Portugal 38°34′N 08°40′W
115 B20 **Marathiá, Akrotírio** *headland* Zákynthos, Iónia Nisiá, Greece, C Mediterranean Sea 37°39′N 20°49′E
12 E12 **Marathon** Ontario, S Canada 48°44′N 86°23′W
23 Y17 **Marathon** Florida Keys, Florida, SE USA 24°42′N 81°05′W
24 L10 **Marathon** Texas, SW USA 30°10′N 103°14′W
Marathón *see* Marathónas
115 H19 **Marathónas** *prev.* Marathón. Attikí, C Greece 38°09′N 23°57′E
169 W9 **Maratua, Pulau** *island* N Indonesia
59 O18 **Maraú** Bahia, SE Brazil 14°07′S 39°02′W
143 R3 **Marāveh Tappeh** Golestán, N Iran 37°53′N 55°57′E
24 L11 **Maravillas Creek** ≈ Texas, SW USA
186 D8 **Marawaka** Eastern Highlands, C Papua New Guinea 06°56′S 145°54′E
171 Q7 **Marawi** Mindanao, S Philippines 07°59′N 124°16′E
137 Y11 **Märäzä** *Rus.* Maraza. E Azerbaijan 40°32′N 48°56′E
Maraza *see* Märäzä
Marbat *see* Mirbāṭ
104 L16 **Marbella** Andalucía, S Spain 36°31′N 04°50′W
180 J7 **Marble Bar** Western Australia 21°13′S 119°48′E
36 L9 **Marble Canyon** *canyon* Arizona, SW USA
25 S10 **Marble Falls** Texas, SW USA 30°34′N 98°16′W
27 Y7 **Marble Hill** Missouri, C USA 37°18′N 89°58′W
33 T15 **Marbleton** Wyoming, C USA 42°31′N 110°06′W
Marburg *see* Marburg an der Lahn, Germany
Marburg *see* Maribor, Slovenia
101 H16 **Marburg an der Lahn** *hist.* Marburg. Hessen, W Germany 50°49′N 08°46′E
111 H23 **Marcal** ≈ W Hungary
42 G7 **Marcala** La Paz, SW Honduras 14°11′N 88°00′W
111 H24 **Marcali** Somogy, SW Hungary 46°33′N 17°29′E
83 A16 **Marca, Ponta da** *headland* SW Angola 16°31′S 11°42′E
59 I16 **Marcelândia** Mato Grosso, W Brazil 11°18′S 54°49′W
27 T3 **Marceline** Missouri, C USA 39°42′N 92°57′W
60 I13 **Marcelino Ramos** Rio Grande do Sul, S Brazil 27°31′S 51°57′W
55 Y12 **Marcel, Mont** ▲ S French Guiana 02°32′N 53°00′W
97 O19 **March** E England, United Kingdom 52°37′N 00°13′E
109 Z3 **March** *var.* Morava. ≈ C Europe *see also* Morava
March *see* Morava
106 I12 **Marche** *Eng.* Marches. ◈ *region* C Italy
103 N11 **Marche** *cultural region* C France
99 J21 **Marche-en-Famenne** Luxembourg, SE Belgium 50°13′N 05°21′E
104 K14 **Marchena** Andalucía, S Spain 37°20′N 05°24′W
57 B17 **Marchena, Isla** *var.* Bindloe Island. *island* Galapagos Islands, Ecuador, E Pacific Ocean
Marches *see* Marche
99 J20 **Marchin** Liège, E Belgium 50°30′N 05°17′E
181 S1 **Marchinbar Island** *island* Wessel Islands, Northern Territory, N Australia
62 L9 **Mar Chiquita, Laguna** ◎ C Argentina
103 Q10 **Marcigny** Saône-et-Loire, C France 46°16′N 04°04′E
23 W16 **Marco** Florida, SE USA 25°56′N 81°43′W
Marcodurum *see* Düren
59 O15 **Marcolândia** Pernambuco, E Brazil 07°21′S 40°40′W
106 I8 **Marco Polo** ✈ (Venezia) Veneto, NE Italy 45°30′N 12°21′E
Marcounda *see* Markounda
Marcq *see* Mark
116 M8 **Mărculești** *Rus.* Markuleshty. N Moldova 47°54′N 28°14′E
29 S12 **Marcus** Iowa, C USA 42°49′N 95°48′W
39 S11 **Marcus Baker, Mount** ▲ Alaska, USA 61°26′N 147°45′W
192 I5 **Marcus Island** *var.* Minami Tori Shima. *island* E Japan
18 K8 **Marcy, Mount** ▲ New York, NE USA 44°06′N 73°55′W
149 T5 **Mardān** North-West Frontier Province, N Pakistan 34°14′N 71°59′E
63 N14 **Mar del Plata** Buenos Aires, E Argentina 38°S 57°32′W
137 Q16 **Mardin** Mardin, SE Turkey 37°19′N 40°43′E
137 Q16 **Mardin** ◈ *province* SE Turkey
137 Q16 **Mardin Dağları** ▲▲ SE Turkey
Mardzad *see* Hayrhandulaan
187 R17 **Maré** *island* Îles Loyauté, E New Caledonia
Marea Neagră *see* Black Sea
105 Z8 **Mare de Déu del Toro** *var.* El Toro. ▲ Menorca, Spain, W Mediterranean Sea 39°59′N 04°06′E
181 W4 **Mareeba** Queensland, NE Australia 17°03′S 145°30′E
96 G8 **Maree, Loch** ◎ N Scotland, United Kingdom
Mareeq *see* Mereeg
Marek *see* Dupnitsa
76 J11 **Maréna** Kayes, W Mali 14°36′N 10°57′W
190 I2 **Marenanuka** *atoll* Tungaru, W Kiribati
29 X14 **Marengo** Iowa, C USA 41°48′N 92°04′W
102 J11 **Marennes** Charente-Maritime, W France 45°47′N 01°04′W
107 G23 **Marettimo, Isola** *island* Isole Egadi, S Italy
24 K10 **Marfa** Texas, SW USA 30°19′N 104°03′W
57 P17 **Marfil, Laguna** ◎ E Bolivia
Marganets *see* Marhanets'
25 Q4 **Margaret** Texas, SW USA 34°00′N 99°38′W
180 I14 **Margaret River** Western Australia 33°58′S 115°10′E
186 C7 **Margarima** Southern Highlands, W Papua New Guinea 06°00′S 143°23′E
55 N4 **Margarita, Isla de** *island* N Venezuela
115 I25 **Margarítes** Kríti, Greece, E Mediterranean Sea 35°19′N 24°40′E
97 Q22 **Margate** *prev.* Mergate. SE England, United Kingdom 51°24′N 01°24′E
23 Z15 **Margate** Florida, SE USA 26°14′N 80°12′W
Margelan *see* Marg'ilon
103 P13 **Margeride, Montagnes de la** ▲▲ C France
Margherita *see* Jamaame
107 N16 **Margherita di Savoia** Puglia, SE Italy 41°23′N 16°09′E
Margherita, Lake *see* Ābaya Hāyk'
81 E18 **Margherita Peak** *Fr.* Pic Marguerite. ▲ Uganda/Dem. Rep. Congo 0°28′N 29°58′E
149 O4 **Marghī** Bāmīān, N Afghanistan 35°10′N 66°26′E
116 G9 **Marghita** *Hung.* Margitta. Bihor, NW Romania 47°20′N 22°20′E
Margilan *see* Marg'ilon
147 S10 **Marg'ilon** *var.* Margelan, *Rus.* Margilan. Farg'ona Viloyati, E Uzbekistan 40°29′N 71°43′E
116 K8 **Marginea** Suceava, NE Romania 47°49′N 25°47′E
Margitta *see* Marghita
148 K9 **Māragow, Dasht-e** *desert* SW Afghanistan
99 L18 **Margraten** Limburg, SE Netherlands 50°49′N 05°49′E
10 M15 **Marguerite** British Columbia, SW Canada 52°17′N 122°10′W
15 V3 **Marguerite** ≈ Quebec, SE Canada
194 I6 **Marguerite Bay** *bay* Antarctica
Marguerite, Pic *see* Margherita Peak
117 T9 **Marhanets'** *Rus.* Marganets. Dnipropetrovs'ka Oblast', E Ukraine 47°35′N 34°37′E
186 B9 **Mari** Western, SW Papua New Guinea 09°10′S 141°39′E
191 Y12 **Maria** *atoll* Groupe Actéon, SE French Polynesia
191 R12 **Maria** *island* Îles Australes, SW French Polynesia
40 I12 **María Cleofas, Isla** *island* C Mexico
62 H4 **María Elena** *var.* Oficina María Elena. Antofagasta, N Chile 22°18′S 69°40′W
95 G21 **Mariager** Århus, C Denmark 56°39′N 09°59′E
61 C22 **María Ignacia** Buenos Aires, E Argentina 37°24′S 59°30′W
183 P17 **Maria Island** *island* Tasmania, SE Australia
40 H12 **María Madre, Isla** *island* C Mexico
40 I12 **María Magdalena, Isla** *island* C Mexico
192 H6 **Mariana Islands** *island group* Guam/Northern Mariana Islands
175 N3 **Mariana Trench** *var.* Challenger Deep. *undersea feature* W Pacific Ocean 15°00′N 147°30′E
153 X12 **Mariāni** Assam, NE India 26°39′N 94°18′E
27 X11 **Marianna** Arkansas, C USA 34°46′N 90°49′W
23 R8 **Marianna** Florida, SE USA 30°46′N 85°13′W
172 J16 **Marianne** *island* Inner Islands, NE Seychelles
95 M19 **Mariannelund** Jönköping, S Sweden 57°37′N 15°33′E
61 D15 **Mariano I. Loza** Corrientes, NE Argentina 29°22′S 58°12′W
Mariano Machado *see* Ganda
111 A16 **Mariánské Lázně** *Ger.* Marienbad. Karlovarský Kraj, W Czech Republic 49°57′N 12°43′E
Máriaradna *see* Radna
33 S7 **Marias River** ≈ Montana, NW USA
Maria-Theresiopel *see* Subotica
Máriatölgyes *see* Dubnica nad Váhom
184 H1 **Maria van Diemen, Cape** *headland* North Island, New Zealand 34°27′S 172°38′E
109 V5 **Mariazell** Steiermark, E Austria 47°47′N 15°20′E
141 P15 **Mar'ib** W Yemen 15°28′N 45°25′E
95 I25 **Maribo** Storstrøm, S Denmark 54°47′N 11°30′E
109 W9 **Maribor** *Ger.* Marburg. NE Slovenia 46°34′N 15°40′E
Marica *see* Maritsa
35 R13 **Maricopa** California, W USA 35°03′N 119°24′W
Maricourt *see* Kangiqsujuaq
81 D15 **Maridi** Western Equatoria, SW Sudan 04°55′N 29°30′E
194 M11 **Marie Byrd Land** *physical region* Antarctica
193 P14 **Marie Byrd Seamount** *undersea feature* N Amundsen Sea 70°00′S 118°00′W
45 X11 **Marie-Galante** *var.* Ceyre to the Caribs. *island* SE Guadeloupe
45 Y6 **Marie-Galante, Canal de** *channel* S Guadeloupe
93 J20 **Mariehamn** *Fin.* Maarianhamina. Åland, SW Finland 60°05′N 19°55′E
44 C4 **Mariel** La Habana, W Cuba 23°02′N 82°44′W
99 H22 **Mariembourg** Namur, S Belgium 50°07′N 04°30′E
Marienbad *see* Mariánské Lázně
Marienburg *see* Alūksne, Latvia
Marienburg *see* Malbork, Poland
Marienburg *see* Feldioara, Romania
Marienburg in Westpreussen *see* Malbork
Marienhausen *see* Viļaka
83 D20 **Mariental** Hardap, SW Namibia 24°35′S 17°56′E
18 D13 **Marienville** Pennsylvania, NE USA 41°27′N 79°07′W
Marienwerder *see* Kwidzyń
58 C12 **Marié, Rio** ≈ NW Brazil
95 K17 **Mariestad** Västra Götaland, S Sweden 58°42′N 13°50′E
23 S3 **Marietta** Georgia, SE USA 33°57′N 84°34′W
31 U14 **Marietta** Ohio, N USA 39°25′N 81°27′W
27 N13 **Marietta** Oklahoma, C USA 33°57′N 97°08′W
81 H18 **Marigat** Rift Valley, W Kenya 0°29′S 35°59′E
103 S16 **Marignane** Bouches-du-Rhône, SE France 43°25′N 05°12′E
Marignano *see* Melegnano
45 O11 **Marigot** NE Dominica 15°32′N 61°18′W
122 K12 **Mariinsk** Kemerovskaya Oblast', S Russian Federation 56°13′N 87°27′E
127 Q3 **Mariinskiy Posad** Respublika Mariy El, W Russian Federation 56°07′N 47°44′E
119 E14 **Marijampolė** *prev.* Kapsukas. Marijampolė, S Lithuania 54°33′N 23°21′E
114 G12 **Marikostinovo** Blagoevgrad, SW Bulgaria 41°25′N 23°21′E
60 J9 **Marília** São Paulo, S Brazil 22°13′S 49°58′W
82 D11 **Marimba** Malanje, NW Angola 08°18′S 16°58′E
139 T1 **Marī Mīlā** Arbīl, E Iraq 36°58′N 44°42′E
104 G4 **Marín** Galicia, NW Spain 42°23′N 08°43′W
35 N10 **Marina** California, W USA 36°40′N 121°48′W
Mar'ina Gorka *see* Mar"ina Horka
119 L17 **Mar"ina Horka** *Rus.* Mar'ina Gorka. Minskaya Voblasts', C Belarus 53°31′N 28°09′E
171 O4 **Marinduque** *island* C Philippines
31 S9 **Marine City** Michigan, N USA 42°43′N 82°29′W
31 N6 **Marinette** Wisconsin, N USA 45°06′N 87°38′W
60 I10 **Maringá** Paraná, S Brazil 23°26′S 51°55′W
83 N16 **Maringuè** Sofala, C Mozambique 17°57′S 34°23′E
104 F9 **Marinha Grande** Leiria, C Portugal 39°45′N 08°55′W
107 I15 **Marino** Lazio, C Italy 41°46′N 12°40′E
59 A15 **Mário Lobão** Acre, W Brazil 08°21′S 72°58′W
23 O5 **Marion** Alabama, S USA 32°37′N 87°19′W
27 Y11 **Marion** Arkansas, C USA 35°12′N 90°12′W
30 L17 **Marion** Illinois, N USA 37°43′N 88°55′W
31 P13 **Marion** Indiana, N USA 40°32′N 85°40′W
29 X13 **Marion** Iowa, C USA 42°01′N 91°36′W
27 O5 **Marion** Kansas, C USA 38°22′N 97°02′W
20 H6 **Marion** Kentucky, S USA 37°19′N 88°06′W
21 P9 **Marion** North Carolina, SE USA 35°43′N 82°00′W
31 S12 **Marion** Ohio, N USA 40°35′N 83°08′W
21 T12 **Marion** South Carolina, SE USA 34°11′N 79°23′W
21 Q7 **Marion** Virginia, NE USA 36°51′N 81°30′W
27 O5 **Marion Lake** ⊞ Kansas, C USA
21 S13 **Marion, Lake** ⊞ South Carolina, SE USA
27 S8 **Marionville** Missouri, C USA 37°00′N 93°38′W
55 N7 **Maripa** Bolívar, E Venezuela 07°27′N 65°10′W
55 X11 **Maripasoula** W French Guiana 03°43′N 54°04′W
35 Q9 **Mariposa** California, W USA 37°28′N 119°59′W
61 G19 **Mariscala** Lavalleja, S Uruguay 34°03′S 54°47′W
62 M4 **Mariscal Estigarribia** Boquerón, NW Paraguay 22°03′S 60°39′W
56 C6 **Mariscal Sucre** *var.* Quito. ✈ (Quito) Pichincha, C Ecuador 0°21′S 78°37′W
30 K16 **Marissa** Illinois, N USA 38°15′N 89°45′W
103 U14 **Maritime Alps** *Fr.* Alpes Maritimes, *It.* Alpi Marittime. ▲▲ France/Italy
Maritimes, Alpes *see* Maritime Alps
Maritime Territory *see* Primorskiy Kray
114 K11 **Maritsa** *var.* Marica, *Gk.* Évros, *Turk.* Meriç; *anc.* Hebrus. ≈ SW Europe *see also* Évros/Meriç
Maritsa *see* Simeonovgrad, Bulgaria
Marittime, Alpi *see* Maritime Alps
Maritzburg *see* Pietermaritzburg
117 X9 **Mariupol'** *prev.* Zhdanov. Donets'ka Oblast', SE Ukraine 47°06′N 37°34′E
55 Q6 **Mariusa, Caño** ≈ NE Venezuela
142 J5 **Marīvān** *prev.* Dezh Shāhpūr. Kordestān, W Iran 35°30′N 46°09′E
127 R3 **Mariyets** Respublika Mariy El, W Russian Federation 56°31′N 49°48′E
118 G4 **Märjamaa** *Ger.* Merjama. Raplamaa, NW Estonia 58°54′N 24°21′E
99 I15 **Mark** *Fr.* Marcq. ≈ Belgium/Netherlands
81 N17 **Marka** *var.* Merca. Shabeellaha Hoose, S Somalia 01°43′N 44°45′E
145 Z10 **Markakol', Ozero** *Kaz.* Marqaköl. ◎ E Kazakhstan
76 M12 **Markala** Ségou, W Mali 13°38′N 06°07′W
159 S15 **Markam** *var.* Gartog. Xizang Zizhiqu, W China 29°40′N 98°33′E
95 K21 **Markaryd** Kronoberg, S Sweden 56°26′N 13°35′E
142 L7 **Markazī** *off.* Ostān-e Markazī. ◈ *province* W Iran
Markazī, Ostān-e *see* Markazī
14 F14 **Markdale** Ontario, S Canada 44°19′N 80°37′W
27 X10 **Marked Tree** Arkansas, C USA 35°31′N 90°25′W
98 N11 **Markelo** Overijssel, E Netherlands 52°15′N 06°30′E
98 J9 **Markermeer** ◎ C Netherlands
97 N20 **Market Harborough** C England, United Kingdom 52°30′N 00°57′W
97 N18 **Market Rasen** E England, United Kingdom 53°23′N 00°21′W
123 O10 **Markha** ≈ NE Russian Federation
12 H16 **Markham** Ontario, S Canada 43°54′N 79°16′W
25 V12 **Markham** Texas, SW USA 28°57′N 96°04′W
186 E7 **Markham** ≈ C Papua New Guinea
195 Q11 **Markham, Mount** ▲ Antarctica 82°58′S 163°30′E
110 M11 **Marki** Mazowieckie, C Poland 52°20′N 21°07′E
158 F8 **Markit** Xinjiang Uygur Zizhiqu, NW China 38°55′N 77°40′E
117 Y5 **Markivka** *Rus.* Markovka. Luhans'ka Oblast', E Ukraine 49°34′N 39°35′E
35 Q7 **Markleeville** California, W USA 38°41′N 119°46′W
98 L8 **Marknesse** Flevoland, N Netherlands 52°44′N 05°54′E
79 H14 **Markounda** *var.* Marcounda. Ouham, NW Central African Republic 07°38′N 17°00′E
Markovka *see* Markivka
123 U7 **Markovo** Chukotskiy Avtonomnyy Okrug, NE Russian Federation 64°43′N 170°13′E
127 P8 **Marks** Saratovskaya Oblast', W Russian Federation 51°40′N 46°44′E
22 K2 **Marks** Mississippi, S USA 34°15′N 90°16′W
22 I7 **Marksville** Louisiana, S USA 31°07′N 92°04′W
101 I19 **Marktheidenfeld** Bayern, C Germany 49°50′N 09°36′E
101 J24 **Marktoberdorf** Bayern, S Germany 47°45′N 10°36′E
101 M18 **Marktredwitz** Bayern, E Germany 50°N 12°04′E
Markt-Übelbach *see* Übelbach
27 V3 **Mark Twain Lake** ⊞ Missouri, C USA
Markuleshty *see* Mărculești
101 E14 **Marl** Nordrhein-Westfalen, W Germany 51°38′N 07°06′E
182 E2 **Marla** South Australia 27°19′S 133°35′E
181 Y8 **Marlborough** Queensland, E Australia 22°55′S 150°07′E
97 M22 **Marlborough** S England, United Kingdom 51°25′N 01°45′W
185 I15 **Marlborough** *off.* Marlborough District. ◈ *unitary authority* South Island, New Zealand
Marlborough District *see* Marlborough
103 P3 **Marle** Aisne, N France 49°44′N 03°47′E
31 S8 **Marlette** Michigan, N USA 43°20′N 83°05′W
25 T9 **Marlin** Texas, SW USA 31°20′N 96°55′W
21 S5 **Marlinton** West Virginia, NE USA 38°14′N 80°06′W
26 M12 **Marlow** Oklahoma, C USA 34°39′N 97°57′W
155 E17 **Marmagao** Goa, W India 15°26′N 73°50′E
Marmanda *see* Marmande
102 L13 **Marmande** *anc.* Marmanda. Lot-et-Garonne, SW France 44°30′N 00°10′E
136 C11 **Marmara** Balıkesir, NW Turkey 40°36′N 27°34′E
136 D11 **Marmara Denizi** *Eng.* Sea of Marmara. *sea* NW Turkey
114 N13 **Marmaraereğlisi** Tekirdağ, NW Turkey 40°59′N 27°57′E
Marmara, Sea of *see* Marmara Denizi
136 C16 **Marmaris** Muğla, SW Turkey 36°52′N 28°17′E
28 J6 **Marmarth** North Dakota, N USA 46°17′N 103°55′W
21 Q5 **Marmet** West Virginia, NE USA 38°12′N 81°31′W
106 H5 **Marmolada, Monte** ▲ N Italy 46°36′N 11°58′E
104 M13 **Marmolejo** Andalucía, S Spain 38°03′N 04°10′W
14 J14 **Marmora** Ontario, SE Canada 44°29′N 77°40′W
39 Q14 **Marmot Bay** *bay* Alaska, USA
103 Q4 **Marne** ◈ *department* N France
103 Q4 **Marne** ≈ N France
137 U10 **Marneuli** *prev.* Borchalo, Sarvani. S Georgia 41°28′N 44°45′E
78 I13 **Maro** Moyen-Chari, S Chad 08°25′N 18°46′E
54 L12 **Maroa** Amazonas, S Venezuela 02°40′N 67°33′W
172 J3 **Maroantsetra** Toamasina, NE Madagascar 15°23′S 49°44′E
191 W11 **Marokau** *atoll* Îles Tuamotu, C French Polynesia
172 J5 **Marolambo** Toamasina, E Madagascar 20°03′S 48°08′E
172 J2 **Maromokotro** ▲ N Madagascar
83 L16 **Marondera** *prev.* Marandellas. Mashonaland East, NE Zimbabwe 18°11′S 31°33′E
55 X9 **Maroni** *Dut.* Marowijne. ≈ French Guiana/Surinam
183 V2 **Maroochydore-Mooloolaba** Queensland, E Australia 26°36′S 153°04′E
171 N14 **Maros** Sulawesi, C Indonesia 04°59′S 119°35′E
116 H11 **Maros** *var.* Mureș, Mureșul, *Ger.* Marosch, Mieresch. ≈ Hungary/Romania *see also* Mureś
Marosch *see* Maros/Mureș
Marosheviz *see* Toplița
Marosillye *see* Ilia
Marosludas *see* Luduș
Marosújvár/Marosújvárakna *see* Ocna Mureș
Marosvásárhely *see* Târgu Mureș
191 V14 **Marotiri** *var.* Îlots de Bass, Morotiri. *island group* Îles Australes, SW French Polynesia
78 G12 **Maroua** Extrême-Nord, N Cameroon 10°35′N 14°20′E
55 X12 **Marouini Rivier** ≈ SE Surinam
172 I3 **Marovoay** Mahajanga, NW Madagascar 16°05′S 46°40′E
55 W9 **Marowijne** ◈ *district* NE Surinam
Marowijne *see* Maroni
Marqaköl *see* Markakol', Ozero
193 P8 **Marquesas Fracture Zone** *tectonic feature* E Pacific Ocean
Marquesas Islands *see* Marquises, Îles
23 W17 **Marquesas Keys** *island group* Florida, SE USA
29 Y12 **Marquette** Iowa, C USA 43°02′N 91°10′W
31 N3 **Marquette** Michigan, N USA 46°32′N 87°24′W
103 N1 **Marquise** Pas-de-Calais, N France 50°49′N 01°42′E
191 X7 **Marquises, Îles** *Eng.* Marquesas Islands. *island group* N French Polynesia
183 Q6 **Marra Creek** ≈ New South Wales, SE Australia
80 B10 **Marra Hills** *plateau* W Sudan
80 B11 **Marra, Jebel** ▲ W Sudan 12°59′N 24°16′E
74 E7 **Marrakech** *var.* Marakesh, *Eng.* Marrakesh; *prev.* Morocco. W Morocco 31°39′N 07°58′W
Marrakesh *see* Marrakech
Marrāt *see* Marāh
183 N15 **Marrawah** Tasmania, SE Australia 40°56′S 144°41′E
182 I4 **Marree** South Australia 29°40′S 138°06′E
81 L17 **Marrehan** ▲▲ SW Somalia
83 N17 **Marromeu** Sofala, C Mozambique 18°18′S 35°58′E
104 J17 **Marroquí, Punta** *headland* SW Spain 36°01′N 05°39′W
183 N8 **Marrowie Creek** *seasonal river* New South Wales, SE Australia
83 O14 **Marrupa** Niassa, N Mozambique 13°10′S 37°30′E
182 D1 **Marryat** South Australia 26°22′S 133°22′E
75 Y10 **Marsá al 'Alam** *var.* Marsa 'Alam. SE Egypt 25°03′N 33°44′E
Marsa 'Alam *see* Marsá al 'Alam
75 R8 **Marsá al Burayqah** *var.* Al Burayqah. N Libya 30°21′N 19°37′E
81 J17 **Marsabit** Eastern, N Kenya 02°20′N 37°59′E
107 H23 **Marsala** *anc.* Lilybaeum. Sicilia, Italy, C Mediterranean Sea 37°48′N 12°26′E
121 P16 **Marsaxlokk Bay** *bay* SE Malta
65 G15 **Mars Bay** *bay* Ascension Island, C Atlantic Ocean
101 H15 **Marsberg** Nordrhein-Westfalen, W Germany 51°28′N 08°51′E
11 R15 **Marsden** Saskatchewan, S Canada 52°50′N 109°45′W
98 H7 **Marsdiep** *strait* NW Netherlands
103 R16 **Marseille** *Eng.* Marseilles; *anc.* Massilia. Bouches-du-Rhône, SE France 43°19′N 05°22′E
Marseille-Marigrane *see* Provence
30 M11 **Marseilles** Illinois, N USA 41°19′N 88°42′W
Marseilles *see* Marseille
76 J16 **Marshall** W Liberia 06°10′N 10°23′W
39 N11 **Marshall** Alaska, USA 61°52′N 162°04′W
27 U9 **Marshall** Arkansas, C USA 35°54′N 92°40′W
31 N14 **Marshall** Illinois, N USA 39°23′N 87°41′W
31 Q10 **Marshall** Michigan, N USA 42°16′N 84°57′W
29 S9 **Marshall** Minnesota, N USA 44°26′N 95°48′W
27 T4 **Marshall** Missouri, C USA 39°07′N 93°12′W
21 O9 **Marshall** North Carolina, SE USA 35°48′N 82°43′W
25 X6 **Marshall** Texas, SW USA 32°33′N 94°22′W
189 S4 **Marshall Islands** *off.* Republic of the Marshall Islands. ◆ *republic* W Pacific Ocean
175 Q3 **Marshall Islands** *island group* W Pacific Ocean
Marshall Islands, Republic of the *see* Marshall Islands
192 K6 **Marshall Seamounts** *undersea feature* SW Pacific Ocean 10°00′N 165°00′E
29 W13 **Marshalltown** Iowa, C USA 42°01′N 92°54′W
19 P12 **Marshfield** Massachusetts, NE USA 42°04′N 70°40′W
27 T7 **Marshfield** Missouri, C USA 37°20′N 92°55′W
30 K6 **Marshfield** Wisconsin, N USA 44°41′N 90°12′W
44 H1 **Marsh Harbour** Great Abaco, W Bahamas 26°31′N 77°03′W
19 S3 **Mars Hill** Maine, NE USA 46°31′N 67°51′W
21 P9 **Mars Hill** North Carolina, SE USA 35°49′N 82°33′W
22 H10 **Marsh Island** *island* Louisiana, S USA
21 S11 **Marshville** North Carolina, SE USA 34°59′N 80°22′W
15 W5 **Marsoui** Québec, SE Canada 49°12′N 65°58′W
15 R8 **Mars, Rivière à** ≈ Québec, SE Canada
95 O15 **Märsta** Stockholm, C Sweden 59°37′N 17°52′E
95 H24 **Marstal** Fyn, C Denmark 54°52′N 10°32′E
95 I19 **Marstrand** Västra Götaland, S Sweden 57°54′N 11°31′E
25 U8 **Mart** Texas, SW USA 31°32′N 96°49′W
166 M9 **Martaban** *var.* Moktama. Mon State, S Burma (Myanmar) 16°32′N 97°35′E
166 L9 **Martaban, Gulf of** *gulf* S Burma (Myanmar)
107 Q19 **Martano** Puglia, SE Italy 40°12′N 18°19′E
Martapoera *see* Martapura
169 T13 **Martapura** *prev.* Martapoera. Borneo, C Indonesia 03°25′S 114°51′E
99 L23 **Martelange** Luxembourg, SE Belgium 49°50′N 05°43′E
114 L7 **Marten** Ruse, N Bulgaria 43°57′N 26°08′E
14 H10 **Marten River** Ontario, S Canada 46°43′N 79°45′W
11 T15 **Martensville** Saskatchewan, S Canada 52°15′N 106°42′W
Marteskirch *see* Târnăveni
Martes Tolosane *see* Martres-Tolosane
115 K25 **Mártha** Kríti, Greece, E Mediterranean Sea 35°03′N 25°22′E
183 Q6 **Marthaguy Creek** ≈ New South Wales, SE Australia

◆ Country
● Country Capital
◇ Dependent Territory
○ Dependent Territory Capital
◈ Administrative Regions
✈ International Airport
▲ Mountain
▲▲ Mountain Range
Ѫ Volcano
≈ River
◎ Lake
⊞ Reservoir

MARTHA'S VINEYARD – MAZARRÓN

19 P13 **Martha's Vineyard** *island* Massachusetts, NE USA
108 C11 **Martigny** Valais, SW Switzerland *46°06′N 07°04′E*
103 R16 **Martigues** Bouches-du-Rhône, SE France *43°24′N 05°03′E*
111 J19 **Martin** *Ger.* Sankt Martin, *Hung.* Turócszentmárton; *prev.* Turčiansky Svätý Martin. Žilinský Kraj, N Slovakia *49°03′N 18°54′E*
28 L11 **Martin** South Dakota, N USA *43°10′N 101°43′W*
20 G8 **Martin** Tennessee, S USA *36°20′N 88°51′W*
105 S7 **Martín** ~ E Spain
107 P18 **Martina Franca** Puglia, SE Italy *40°42′N 17°20′E*
185 M14 **Martinborough** Wellington, North Island, New Zealand *41°12′S 175°28′E*
25 S11 **Martindale** Texas, SW USA *29°49′N 97°49′W*
35 N8 **Martinez** California, W USA *38°00′N 122°12′W*
23 V3 **Martinez** Georgia, SE USA *33°31′N 82°04′W*
41 Q13 **Martínez de La Torre** Veracruz-Llave, E Mexico *20°05′N 97°02′W*
45 Y12 **Martinique** ◇ *French overseas department* E West Indies
1 O15 **Martinique** *island* E West Indies
Martinique Channel *see* Martinique Passage
45 X12 **Martinique Passage** *var.* Dominica Channel, Martinique Channel. *channel* Dominica/Martinique
23 Q5 **Martin Lake** ⊠ Alabama, S USA
115 G18 **Martíno** *prev.* Martínon. Štereá Ellás, C Greece *38°34′N 23°13′E*
Martínon *see* Martíno
194 J11 **Martin Peninsula** *peninsula* Antarctica
39 S5 **Martin Point** *headland* Alaska, USA *70°06′N 143°04′W*
109 V3 **Martinsberg** Niederösterreich, NE Austria *48°23′N 15°09′E*
21 V3 **Martinsburg** West Virginia, NE USA *39°28′N 77°59′W*
31 V13 **Martins Ferry** Ohio, N USA *40°06′N 80°43′W*
Martinskirch *see* Târnăveni
31 O14 **Martinsville** Indiana, N USA *39°25′N 86°25′W*
21 S8 **Martinsville** Virginia, NE USA *36°43′N 79°53′W*
65 K16 **Martin Vaz, Ilhas** *island group* E Brazil
Martök *see* Martuk
184 M12 **Marton** Manawatu-Wanganui, North Island, New Zealand *40°05′S 175°22′E*
105 N13 **Martos** Andalucía, S Spain *37°44′N 03°58′W*
102 M16 **Martres-Tolosane** *var.* Martes Tolosane. Haute-Garonne, S France *43°13′N 01°00′E*
92 M11 **Martti** Lappi, NE Finland *67°28′N 28°20′E*
144 I9 **Martuk** *Kaz.* Martök. Aktyubinsk, NW Kazakhstan *50°45′N 56°30′E*
137 U12 **Martuni** E Armenia *40°07′N 45°20′E*
58 L11 **Marudá** Pará, E Brazil *05°25′S 49°04′W*
169 V6 **Marudu, Teluk** *bay* East Malaysia
149 O8 **Ma'rūf** Kandahār, SE Afghanistan *31°34′N 67°06′E*
164 H13 **Marugame** Kagawa, Shikoku, SW Japan *34°17′N 133°46′E*
185 H16 **Maruia** ~ South Island, New Zealand
98 M6 **Marum** Groningen, NE Netherlands *53°07′N 06°16′E*
187 R13 **Marum, Mount** ▲ Ambrym, C Vanuatu *16°15′S 168°07′E*
79 P23 **Marungu** ▲▲ SE Dem. Rep. Congo
191 Y12 **Marutea** *atoll* Groupe Actéon, C French Polynesia
143 O11 **Marv Dasht** *var.* Mervdasht. Fārs, S Iran *29°50′N 52°40′E*
103 P13 **Marvejols** Lozère, S France *44°35′N 03°16′E*
27 X12 **Marvell** Arkansas, C USA *34°33′N 90°52′W*
36 L6 **Marvine, Mount** ▲ Utah, W USA *38°40′N 111°38′W*
139 Q7 **Marwānīyah** Al Anbār, C Iraq *33°58′N 42°31′E*
152 F13 **Mārwār** *var.* Kharchi, Marwar Junction. Rājasthān, N India *25°41′N 73°42′E*
Marwar Junction *see* Mārwār
11 R14 **Marwayne** Alberta, SW Canada *53°30′N 110°25′W*
146 I14 **Mary** *prev.* Merv. Mary Welaýaty, S Turkmenistan *37°25′N 61°48′E*
Mary *see* Mary Welaýaty
181 Z9 **Maryborough** Queensland, E Australia *25°32′S 152°36′E*
182 M11 **Maryborough** Victoria, SE Australia *37°05′S 143°47′E*
Maryborough *see* Port Laoise
83 G23 **Marydale** Northern Cape, W South Africa *29°25′S 22°06′E*
117 W8 **Mar"yinka** Donets'ka Oblast', E Ukraine *47°57′N 37°27′E*
Mary Island *see* Kanton
21 W4 **Maryland** *off.* State of Maryland, *also known as* America in Miniature, Cockade State, Free State, Old Line State. ⬖ *state* NE USA
Maryland, State of *see* Maryland
25 P7 **Maryneal** Texas, SW USA *32°12′N 100°25′W*
97 J15 **Maryport** NW England, United Kingdom *54°45′N 03°28′W*
13 U13 **Marystown** Newfoundland, Newfoundland and Labrador, SE Canada *47°10′N 55°10′W*
36 K6 **Marysvale** Utah, W USA *38°26′N 112°14′W*
35 O6 **Marysville** California, W USA *39°07′N 121°35′W*
27 O3 **Marysville** Kansas, C USA *39°48′N 96°37′W*
31 S13 **Marysville** Michigan, N USA *42°54′N 82°29′W*
31 S9 **Marysville** Ohio, NE USA *40°13′N 83°22′W*
32 H7 **Marysville** Washington, NW USA *48°03′N 122°10′W*
27 R2 **Maryville** Missouri, C USA *40°20′N 94°53′W*
21 N9 **Maryville** Tennessee, S USA *35°45′N 83°59′W*
146 I15 **Mary Welaýaty** *var.* Mary, *Rus.* Maryyskiy Velayat. ⬖ *province* S Turkmenistan
Maryyskiy Velayat *see* Mary Welaýaty
Marzūq *see* Murzuq
42 J11 **Masachapa** *var.* Puerto Masachapa. Managua, W Nicaragua *11°47′N 86°31′W*
81 G19 **Masai Mara National Reserve** *reserve* C Kenya
81 I21 **Masai Steppe** *grassland* NW Tanzania
81 F19 **Masaka** SW Uganda *0°20′S 31°46′E*
169 T15 **Masalembo Besar, Pulau** *island* S Indonesia
137 Y13 **Masallı** *Rus.* Masally. S Azerbaijan *39°03′N 48°39′E*
Masally *see* Masallı
171 N13 **Masamba** Sulawesi, C Indonesia *02°33′S 120°20′E*
Masampo *see* Masan
163 Y16 **Masan** *prev.* Masampo. S South Korea *35°11′N 128°36′E*
Masandam Peninsula *see* Musandam Peninsula
81 J25 **Masasi** Mtwara, SE Tanzania *10°43′S 38°48′E*
Masawa/Massawa *see* Mits'iwa
42 J10 **Masaya** Masaya, W Nicaragua *11°59′N 86°06′W*
42 J10 **Masaya** ⬖ *department* W Nicaragua
171 P5 **Masbate** Masbate, N Philippines *12°21′N 123°34′E*
171 P5 **Masbate** *island* C Philippines
74 J6 **Mascara** *var.* Mouaskar. NW Algeria *35°20′N 00°09′E*
173 O7 **Mascarene Basin** *undersea feature* W Indian Ocean *15°00′S 56°00′E*
173 O9 **Mascarene Islands** *island group* W Indian Ocean
173 N9 **Mascarene Plain** *undersea feature* W Indian Ocean *19°00′S 52°00′E*
173 O7 **Mascarene Plateau** *undersea feature* W Indian Ocean *10°00′S 60°00′E*
194 H5 **Mascart, Cape** *headland* Adelaide Island, Antarctica
62 J10 **Mascasín, Salinas de** *salt lake* C Argentina
40 K13 **Mascota** Jalisco, C Mexico *20°31′N 104°46′W*
15 O12 **Mascouche** Québec, SE Canada *45°46′N 73°37′W*
124 J9 **Masel'gskaya** Respublika Kareliya, NW Russian Federation *63°09′N 34°22′E*
83 J23 **Maseru** ● (Lesotho) W Lesotho *29°21′S 27°35′E*
83 J23 **Maseru** ✈ W Lesotho *29°27′S 27°37′E*
Mashaba *see* Mashava
160 K14 **Mashan** *var.* Baishan. Guangxi Zhuangzu Zizhiqu, S China *23°40′N 108°10′E*
83 K17 **Mashava** *prev.* Mashaba. Masvingo, SE Zimbabwe *20°03′S 30°29′E*
143 U4 **Mashhad** *var.* Meshed. Khorāsān-Razavī, NE Iran *36°16′N 59°34′E*
165 S3 **Mashike** Hokkaidō, NE Japan *43°51′N 141°30′E*
Mashīz *see* Bardsīr
149 N14 **Mashkai** ~ SW Pakistan
143 X13 **Māshkel** *var.* Rūd-i Māshkel, Rūd-e Māshkīd. ~ Iran/Pakistan
148 K12 **Māshkel, Hāmūn-i** *salt marsh* SW Pakistan
Māshkel, Rūd-i/Māshkīd, Rūd-e *see* Māshkel
83 K15 **Mashonaland Central** ⬖ *province* N Zimbabwe
83 K16 **Mashonaland East** ⬖ *province* NE Zimbabwe
83 J16 **Mashonaland West** ⬖ *province* NW Zimbabwe
Mashtagi *see* Maştağa
141 S14 **Masīlah, Wādī al** *dry watercourse* SE Yemen
79 I21 **Masi-Manimba** Bandundu, SW Dem. Rep. Congo *04°47′S 17°54′E*
81 F17 **Masindi** W Uganda *01°41′N 31°45′E*
81 I19 **Masinga Reservoir** ⊠ S Kenya
Masīra *see* Maşīrah, Jazīrat
Masīra, Gulf of *see* Maşīrah, Khalīj
141 Y10 **Maşīrah, Jazīrat** *var.* Masīra. *island* E Oman
141 Y10 **Maşīrah, Khalīj** *var.* Gulf of Masira. *bay* E Oman
Masis *see* Büyükağrı Dağı
79 O19 **Masisi** Nord-Kivu, E Dem. Rep. Congo *01°25′S 28°50′E*
Masjed-e Soleymān *see* Masjed Soleymān
142 L9 **Masjed Soleymān** *var.* Masjed-e Soleymān, Masjid-i Sulaiman. Khūzestān, SW Iran *31°59′N 49°18′E*
Masjid-i Sulaiman *see* Masjed Soleymān
Maskat *see* Masqaţ
139 Q7 **Maskhān** Al Anbār, C Iraq *33°41′N 42°46′E*
141 X8 **Maskin** *var.* Miskin. NW Oman *23°28′N 56°46′E*
97 B17 **Mask, Lough** *Ir.* Loch Measca. ◎ W Ireland
114 N10 **Maslen Nos** *headland* E Bulgaria *42°19′N 27°47′E*
172 K3 **Masoala, Tanjona** *headland* NE Madagascar *15°59′N 50°13′E*
Masohi *see* Amahai
31 Q9 **Mason** Michigan, N USA *42°33′N 84°25′W*
31 R14 **Mason** Ohio, N USA *39°21′N 84°18′W*
25 Q10 **Mason** Texas, SW USA *30°45′N 99°15′W*
21 P4 **Mason** West Virginia, NE USA *39°01′N 82°01′W*
185 B25 **Mason Bay** *bay* Stewart Island, New Zealand
30 K13 **Mason City** Illinois, N USA *40°12′N 89°42′W*
29 V12 **Mason City** Iowa, C USA *43°09′N 93°12′W*
18 B16 **Masontown** Pennsylvania, NE USA *39°49′N 79°53′W*
141 Y8 **Masqaţ** *var.* Maskat, *Eng.* Muscat. ● (Oman) NE Oman *23°35′N 58°36′E*
106 E10 **Massa** Toscana, C Italy *44°02′N 10°07′E*
18 M11 **Massachusetts** *off.* Commonwealth of Massachusetts, *also known as* Bay State, Old Bay State, Old Colony State. ⬖ *state* NE USA
19 P11 **Massachusetts Bay** *bay* Massachusetts, NE USA
35 R2 **Massacre Lake** ◎ Nevada, W USA
107 O18 **Massafra** Puglia, SE Italy *40°35′N 17°08′E*
108 G11 **Massagno** Ticino, S Switzerland *46°01′N 08°55′E*
78 G11 **Massaguet** Chari-Baguirmi, W Chad *12°28′N 15°26′E*
Massakori *see* Massakory
78 G10 **Massakory** *var.* Massakori; *prev.* Dagana. Chari-Baguirmi, W Chad *13°02′N 15°43′E*
78 H11 **Massalassef** Chari-Baguirmi, SW Chad *11°37′N 17°09′E*
106 F13 **Massa Marittima** Toscana, C Italy *43°03′N 10°55′E*
82 B11 **Massangano** Cuanza Norte, NW Angola *09°40′S 14°13′E*
83 M18 **Massangena** Gaza, S Mozambique *21°34′S 32°57′E*
80 K9 **Massawa Channel** *channel* E Eritrea
18 J6 **Massena** New York, NE USA *44°55′N 74°53′W*
78 H11 **Massenya** Chari-Baguirmi, SW Chad *11°21′N 16°09′E*
10 I13 **Masset** Graham Island, British Columbia, SW Canada *54°00′N 132°09′W*
102 L16 **Masseube** Gers, S France *43°26′N 00°33′E*
14 E11 **Massey** Ontario, S Canada *46°13′N 82°06′W*
103 P12 **Massiac** Cantal, C France *45°16′N 03°13′E*
103 P12 **Massif Central** *plateau* C France
Massif de L'Isalo *see* Isalo
Massilia *see* Marseille
31 U12 **Massillon** Ohio, N USA *40°48′N 81°31′W*
77 N12 **Massina** Ségou, W Mali *13°58′N 05°24′W*
83 N19 **Massinga** Inhambane, SE Mozambique *23°20′S 35°25′E*
83 L20 **Massingir** Gaza, SW Mozambique *23°51′S 31°58′E*
195 Z10 **Masson Island** *island* Antarctica
Massoukou *see* Franceville
137 Z11 **Maştağa** *Rus.* Mashtagi, Mastaga. E Azerbaijan *40°31′N 50°01′E*
Mastanli *see* Momchilgrad
184 M13 **Masterton** Wellington, North Island, New Zealand *40°56′S 175°40′E*
18 M14 **Mastic** Long Island, New York, NE USA *40°48′N 72°50′W*
149 O10 **Mastung** Baluchistān, SW Pakistan *29°44′N 66°56′E*
119 J20 **Mastva** *Rus.* Mostva. ~ SW Belarus
119 G17 **Masty** *Rus.* Mosty. Hrodzyenskaya Voblasts', W Belarus *53°25′N 24°32′E*
164 F12 **Masuda** Shimane, Honshū, SW Japan *34°40′N 131°50′E*
92 J11 **Masugnsbyn** Norrbotten, N Sweden *67°28′N 22°01′E*
Masuku *see* Franceville
83 K17 **Masvingo** *prev.* Fort Victoria, Nyanda, Victoria. Masvingo, SE Zimbabwe *20°05′S 30°50′E*
83 K18 **Masvingo** *prev.* Victoria. ⬖ *province* SE Zimbabwe
138 H5 **Maşyāf** *Fr.* Misiaf. Ḩamāh, C Syria *35°04′N 36°21′E*
110 E9 **Maszewo** Zachodniopomorskie, NW Poland *53°29′N 15°01′E*
83 I17 **Matabeleland North** ⬖ *province* W Zimbabwe
83 J18 **Matabeleland South** ⬖ *province* S Zimbabwe
82 O13 **Mataca** Niassa, N Mozambique *12°27′S 36°13′E*
14 G8 **Matachewan** Ontario, S Canada *47°58′N 80°37′W*
163 Q8 **Matad** *var.* Dzüünbulag. Dornod, E Mongolia *46°48′N 115°21′E*
79 F22 **Matadi** Bas-Congo, W Dem. Rep. Congo *05°49′S 13°31′E*
25 O4 **Matador** Texas, SW USA *34°01′N 100°50′W*
42 J9 **Matagalpa** Matagalpa, C Nicaragua *12°53′N 85°56′W*
42 K9 **Matagalpa** ⬖ *department* W Nicaragua
12 I12 **Matagami** Québec, S Canada *49°47′N 77°38′W*
25 U13 **Matagorda** Texas, SW USA *28°40′N 96°57′W*
25 U13 **Matagorda Bay** *inlet* Texas, SW USA
25 U14 **Matagorda Island** *island* Texas, SW USA
25 V13 **Matagorda Peninsula** *headland* Texas, SW USA *28°34′N 96°01′W*
191 Q8 **Mataiea** Tahiti, W French Polynesia *17°46′S 149°25′W*
191 T9 **Mataiva** *atoll* Îles Tuamotu, C French Polynesia
183 O7 **Matakana** New South Wales, SE Australia *32°59′S 145°53′E*
184 N7 **Matakana Island** *island* NE New Zealand
83 C15 **Matala** Huíla, SW Angola *14°45′S 15°02′E*
190 G12 **Matala'a Pointe** *headland* Île Uvea, N Wallis and Futuna *13°20′S 176°08′W*
155 K25 **Matale** Central Province, C Sri Lanka *07°29′N 80°38′E*
190 E12 **Matalesina, Pointe** *headland* Île Alofi, W Wallis and Futuna
76 I10 **Matam** NE Senegal *15°40′N 13°18′W*
184 M8 **Matamata** Waikato, North Island, New Zealand *37°49′S 175°45′E*
77 V12 **Matamey** Zinder, S Niger *13°27′N 08°27′E*
40 L8 **Matamoros** Coahuila, NE Mexico *25°34′N 103°13′W*
41 P15 **Matamoros** *var.* Izúcar de Matamoros. Puebla, S Mexico *18°38′N 98°30′W*
41 Q8 **Matamoros** Tamaulipas, C Mexico *25°50′N 97°31′W*
75 S13 **Ma'ṭan as Sārah** SE Libya *21°45′N 21°55′E*
82 J12 **Matanda** Luapula, N Zambia *11°24′S 28°25′E*
81 J24 **Matandu** ~ S Tanzania
15 V6 **Matane** Québec, SE Canada *48°50′N 67°31′W*
15 V6 **Matane** ~ Québec, SE Canada
77 S12 **Matankari** Dosso, SW Niger *13°39′N 04°03′E*
39 R11 **Matanuska River** ~ Alaska, USA
54 G7 **Matanza** Santander, N Colombia *07°22′N 73°02′W*
44 D4 **Matanzas** Matanzas, NW Cuba *23°N 81°32′W*
15 V7 **Matapédia** ~ Québec, SE Canada
15 V6 **Matapédia, Lac** ◎ Québec, SE Canada
190 B17 **Mata Point** *headland* SE Niue *19°07′S 169°51′E*
190 D12 **Matapu, Pointe** *headland* Île Futuna, W Wallis and Futuna
62 G12 **Mataquito, Río** ~ C Chile
155 K26 **Matara** Southern Province, S Sri Lanka *05°58′N 80°33′E*
115 D18 **Mataránga** *var.* Mataránga. Dytikí Ellás, C Greece *38°32′N 21°28′E*
171 K16 **Mataram** Pulau Lombok, C Indonesia *08°36′S 116°07′E*
Mataránga *see* Matarágka
181 Q3 **Mataranka** Northern Territory, N Australia *14°55′S 133°03′E*
105 W6 **Mataró** *anc.* Illuro. Cataluña, E Spain *41°32′N 02°27′E*
184 O8 **Matata** Bay of Plenty, North Island, New Zealand *37°54′S 176°45′E*
192 K16 **Matātula, Cape** *headland* Tutuila, W American Samoa *14°15′S 170°35′W*
185 D24 **Mataura** Southland, South Island, New Zealand *46°12′S 168°53′E*
185 D24 **Mataura** ~ South Island, New Zealand
Mata Uta *see* Matā'utu
192 H16 **Matāutu** Upolu, C Samoa *13°57′S 171°55′W*
190 G11 **Matā'utu** *var.* Mata Uta. ○ (Wallis and Futuna) Île Uvea, Wallis and Futuna *13°22′S 176°12′W*
190 G12 **Matā'utu, Baie de** *bay* Île Uvea, Wallis and Futuna
191 P7 **Mataval, Baie de** *bay* Tahiti, W French Polynesia
190 I16 **Matavera** Rarotonga, S Cook Islands *21°13′S 159°44′W*
191 V16 **Mataveri** Easter Island, Chile, E Pacific Ocean *27°10′S 109°27′W*
191 V17 **Mataveri** ✈ (Easter Island) Easter Island, Chile, E Pacific Ocean *27°10′S 109°27′W*
184 P9 **Matawai** Gisborne, North Island, New Zealand *38°23′S 177°31′E*
15 O10 **Matawin** ~ Québec, SE Canada
145 V13 **Matay** Almaty, SE Kazakhstan *45°53′N 78°45′E*
14 K8 **Matchi-Manitou, Lac** ◎ Québec, SE Canada
41 O10 **Matehuala** San Luis Potosí, C Mexico *23°40′N 100°40′W*
45 V13 **Matelot** Trinidad, Trinidad and Tobago *10°48′N 61°06′W*
83 M15 **Matenge** Tete, NW Mozambique *15°22′S 33°47′E*
107 O18 **Matera** Basilicata, S Italy *40°39′N 16°35′E*
111 O21 **Mátészalka** Szabolcs-Szatmár-Bereg, E Hungary *47°58′N 22°17′E*
93 H17 **Matfors** Västernorrland, C Sweden *62°21′N 17°02′E*
102 K11 **Matha** Charente-Maritime, W France *45°50′N 00°13′W*
0 F15 **Mathematicians Seamounts** *undersea feature* E Pacific Ocean *15°00′N 111°00′W*
21 X6 **Mathews** Virginia, NE USA *37°26′N 76°20′W*
25 S14 **Mathis** Texas, SW USA *28°05′N 97°49′W*
152 J11 **Mathura** *prev.* Muttra. Uttar Pradesh, N India *27°30′N 77°42′E*
Mathurai *see* Madurai
171 R7 **Mati** Mindanao, S Philippines *06°58′N 126°11′E*
Matianus *see* Orūmīyeh, Daryācheh-ye
Matiara *see* Matiāri
149 Q15 **Matiāri** *var.* Matiara. Sind, SE Pakistan *25°38′N 68°29′E*
41 S16 **Matías Romero** Oaxaca, SE Mexico *16°53′N 95°02′W*
43 O13 **Matina** Limón, E Costa Rica *10°06′N 83°18′W*
14 D10 **Matinenda Lake** ◎ Ontario, S Canada
19 R8 **Matinicus Island** *island* Maine, NE USA
Matisco/Matisco Ædourum *see* Mâcon
190 G12 **Mati'utu, Baie de** E Wallis and Futuna
149 Q16 **Mātli** Sind, SE Pakistan *25°06′N 68°37′E*
97 M18 **Matlock** C England, United Kingdom *53°08′N 01°32′W*
59 F18 **Mato Grosso** *prev.* Vila Bela da Santissima Trindade. Mato Grosso, W Brazil *14°53′S 59°58′W*
59 G17 **Mato Grosso** *off.* Estado de Mato Grosso; *prev.* Matto Grosso. ⬖ *state* W Brazil
60 H8 **Mato Grosso do Sul** *off.* Estado de Mato Grosso do Sul. ⬖ *state* S Brazil
Mato Grosso do Sul, Estado de *see* Mato Grosso do Sul
Mato Grosso, Estado de *see* Mato Grosso
59 I18 **Mato Grosso, Planalto de** *plateau* C Brazil
83 L21 **Matola** Maputo, S Mozambique *25°57′S 32°27′E*
104 G6 **Matosinhos** *prev.* Matozinhos. Porto, NW Portugal *41°11′N 08°42′W*
191 O7 **Matotea, Mont** ▲ Moorea, W French Polynesia *17°31′S 149°52′W*
Matou *see* Pingguo
55 Z10 **Matoury** NE French Guiana *04°49′N 52°17′W*
Matozinhos *see* Matosinhos
111 L21 **Mátra** ▲▲ N Hungary
141 Y8 **Maṭraḥ** *var.* Mutrah. NE Oman *23°35′N 58°31′E*
116 L12 **Mătrăşeşti** Vrancea, E Romania *45°53′N 27°14′E*
108 M8 **Matrei am Brenner** Tirol, W Austria *47°09′N 11°28′E*
109 P8 **Matrei in Osttirol** Tirol, W Austria *47°04′N 12°31′E*
76 I15 **Matru** SW Sierra Leone *07°37′N 12°08′W*
Maṭrūḥ *see* Mersá Maṭrūḥ
165 U16 **Matsubara** *var.* Matubara. Kagoshima, Tokuno-shima, SW Japan *32°58′N 129°56′E*
164 G12 **Matsue** *var.* Matsuye, Matue. Shimane, Honshū, SW Japan *35°27′N 133°04′E*
165 Q6 **Matsumae** Hokkaidō, NE Japan *41°27′N 140°04′E*
164 M12 **Matsumoto** *var.* Matumoto. Nagano, Honshū, S Japan *36°18′N 137°58′E*
164 K14 **Matsusaka** *var.* Matsuzaka, Matusaka. Mie, Honshū, SW Japan *34°33′N 136°31′E*
161 S12 **Matsu Tao** *Chin.* Mazu Dao. *island* NW Taiwan
Matsutō *see* Mattō
164 F14 **Matsuyama** *var.* Matuyama. Ehime, Shikoku, SW Japan *33°50′N 132°47′E*
Matsuye *see* Matsue
Matsuzaka *see* Matsusaka
164 M14 **Matsuzaki** Shizuoka, Honshū, S Japan *34°43′N 138°45′E*
14 F8 **Mattagami** ~ Ontario, S Canada
14 F8 **Mattagami Lake** ◎ Ontario, S Canada
62 K12 **Mattaldi** Córdoba, C Argentina *34°26′S 64°14′W*
21 Y9 **Mattamuskeet, Lake** ◎ North Carolina, SE USA
21 W6 **Mattaponi River** ~ Virginia, NE USA
14 I11 **Mattawa** Ontario, SE Canada *46°19′N 78°42′W*
14 I11 **Mattawa** ~ Ontario, SE Canada
19 S5 **Mattawamkeag** Maine, NE USA *45°30′N 68°20′W*
19 S4 **Mattawamkeag Lake** ◎ Maine, NE USA
108 D11 **Matterhorn** *It.* Monte Cervino. ▲ Italy/Switzerland *45°58′N 07°36′E* *see also* Cervino, Monte
32 L12 **Matterhorn** *var.* Sacajawea Peak. ▲ Oregon, NW USA *45°12′N 117°18′W*
35 W1 **Matterhorn** ▲ Nevada, W USA *41°48′N 115°22′W*
Matterhorn *see* Cervino, Monte
35 R8 **Matterhorn Peak** ▲ California, W USA *38°06′N 119°19′W*
109 Y5 **Mattersburg** Burgenland, E Austria *47°45′N 16°24′E*
108 E11 **Matter Vispa** ~ S Switzerland
55 R7 **Matthews Ridge** N Guyana *07°30′N 60°07′W*
44 K7 **Matthew Town** Great Inagua, S Bahamas *20°56′N 73°41′W*
109 Q4 **Mattighofen** Oberösterreich, NW Austria *48°07′N 13°09′E*
107 N16 **Mattinata** Puglia, SE Italy *41°41′N 16°01′E*
141 T9 **Maṭṭī, Sabkhat** *salt flat* Saudi Arabia/United Arab Emirates
18 M14 **Mattituck** Long Island, New York, NE USA *40°59′N 72°31′W*
164 L11 **Mattō** *var.* Hakusan, Matsutō. Ishikawa, Honshū, SW Japan *36°31′N 136°34′E*
Matto Grosso *see* Mato Grosso
30 M14 **Mattoon** Illinois, N USA *39°28′N 88°22′W*
57 L16 **Mattos, Río** ~ C Bolivia
Mattu *see* Metu
169 R9 **Matu** Sarawak, East Malaysia *02°39′N 111°31′E*
Matubara *see* Matsubara
57 E14 **Matucana** Lima, W Peru *11°54′S 76°25′W*
Matue *see* Matsue
187 Y15 **Matuku** *island* S Fiji
112 B9 **Matulji** Primorje-Gorski Kotar, NW Croatia *45°21′N 14°18′E*
Matumoto *see* Matsumoto
55 P5 **Maturín** Monagas, NE Venezuela *09°45′N 63°10′W*
Matusaka *see* Matsusaka
Matuyama *see* Matsuyama
126 K11 **Matveyev Kurgan** Rostovskaya Oblast', SW Russian Federation *47°31′N 38°55′E*
127 O8 **Matyshevo** Volgogradskaya Oblast', SW Russian Federation *50°53′N 44°09′E*
153 O13 **Mau** *var.* Maunāth Bhanjan. Uttar Pradesh, N India *25°57′N 83°33′E*
83 O14 **Maúa** Niassa, N Mozambique *13°53′S 37°10′E*
102 M17 **Maubermé, Pic de** *var.* Tuc de Moubermé, *Sp.* Pico Mauberme; *prev.* Tuc de Maubermé. ▲ France/Spain *42°48′N 00°54′E* *see also* Moubermé, Tuc de
Maubermé, Pic de *see* Moubermé, Tuc de
Mauberme, Pico *see* Maubermé, Pic de/ Moubermé, Tuc de
Maubermé, Tuc de *see* Maubermé, Pic de/ Moubermé, Tuc de
103 Q2 **Maubeuge** Nord, N France *50°16′N 04°00′E*
166 L8 **Maubin** Ayeyarwady, SW Burma (Myanmar) *16°44′N 95°37′E*
152 L13 **Maudaha** Uttar Pradesh, N India *25°41′N 80°07′E*
183 N9 **Maude** New South Wales, SE Australia *34°30′S 144°20′E*
195 P3 **Maudheimvidda** *physical region* Antarctica
65 N22 **Maud Rise** *undersea feature* S Atlantic Ocean
109 Q4 **Mauerkirchen** Oberösterreich, NW Austria *48°11′N 13°08′E*
Mauersee *see* Mamry, Jezioro
188 K2 **Maug Islands** *island group* N Northern Mariana Islands
103 Q15 **Mauguio** Hérault, S France *43°37′N 04°01′E*
193 N5 **Maui** *island* Hawai'i, USA, C Pacific Ocean
190 M16 **Mauke** *atoll* S Cook Islands
62 G13 **Maule** *var.* Región del Maule. ⬖ *region* C Chile
102 J9 **Mauléon** Deux-Sèvres, W France *46°55′N 00°45′W*
102 J16 **Mauléon-Licharre** Pyrénées-Atlantiques, SW France *43°14′N 00°51′W*
Maule, Región del *see* Maule
62 G13 **Maule, Río** ~ C Chile
63 G17 **Maullín** Los Lagos, S Chile *41°38′S 73°35′W*
31 R11 **Maumee** Ohio, N USA *41°34′N 83°40′W*
31 Q12 **Maumee River** ~ Indiana/Ohio, N USA
27 U11 **Maumelle** Arkansas, C USA *34°51′N 92°24′W*
27 T11 **Maumelle, Lake** ⊠ Arkansas, C USA
171 O16 **Maumere** *prev.* Maoemere. Flores, S Indonesia *08°35′S 122°13′E*
83 G17 **Maun** North-West, C Botswana *20°01′S 23°28′E*
Maunāth Bhanjan *see* Mau
Maunawai *see* Waimea
190 H16 **Maungaroa** ▲ Rarotonga, S Cook Islands *21°13′S 159°48′W*
184 K3 **Maungatapere** Northland, North Island, New Zealand *35°46′S 174°10′E*
184 K4 **Maungaturoto** Northland, North Island, New Zealand *36°06′S 174°21′E*
191 R10 **Maupiti** *var.* Maurua. *island* Îles Sous le Vent, W French Polynesia
152 K14 **Mau Rānīpur** Uttar Pradesh, N India *25°14′N 79°07′E*
22 K9 **Maurepas, Lake** ◎ Louisiana, S USA
103 T16 **Maures** ▲▲ SE France
103 O12 **Mauriac** Cantal, C France *45°13′N 02°21′E*
Maurice *see* Mauritius
65 J20 **Maurice Ewing Bank** *undersea feature* SW Atlantic Ocean *51°00′S 43°00′W*
182 C4 **Maurice, Lake** *salt lake* South Australia
18 I17 **Maurice River** ~ New Jersey, NE USA
25 Y10 **Mauriceville** Texas, SW USA *30°13′N 93°52′W*
98 K12 **Maurik** Gelderland, C Netherlands *51°57′N 05°25′E*
76 H8 **Mauritania** *off.* Islamic Republic of Mauritania, *Ar.* Mūrītānīyah. ◆ *republic* W Africa
Mauritania, Islamic Republic of *see* Mauritania
173 W15 **Mauritius** *off.* Republic of Mauritius, *Fr.* Maurice. ◆ *republic* W Indian Ocean
128 M17 **Mauritius** *island* W Indian Ocean
Mauritius, Republic of *see* Mauritius
173 N9 **Mauritius Trench** *undersea feature* W Indian Ocean
102 H6 **Mauron** Morbihan, NW France *48°06′N 02°16′W*
103 N13 **Maurs** Cantal, C France *44°45′N 02°12′E*
Maurua *see* Maupiti
Maury Mid-Ocean Channel *see* Maury Seachannel
64 L6 **Maury Seachannel** *var.* Maury Mid-Ocean Channel. *undersea feature* N Atlantic Ocean *56°33′N 24°00′W*
30 K8 **Mauston** Wisconsin, N USA *43°46′N 90°06′W*
109 R8 **Mauterndorf** Salzburg, NW Austria *47°09′N 13°39′E*
109 T4 **Mauthausen** Oberösterreich, N Austria *48°13′N 14°30′E*
109 Q9 **Mauthen** Kärnten, S Austria *46°39′N 12°58′E*
83 F15 **Mavinga** Cuando Cubango, SE Angola *15°44′S 20°21′E*
83 M17 **Mavita** Manica, W Mozambique *19°31′S 33°09′E*
115 K22 **Mavrópetra, Akrotírio** *headland* Santoríni, Kykládes, Greece, Aegean Sea *36°28′N 25°22′E*
115 F16 **Mavrovoúni** ▲ C Greece *39°37′N 22°45′E*
184 Q8 **Mawhai Point** *headland* North Island, New Zealand *38°08′S 178°24′E*
166 L3 **Mawlaik** Sagaing, C Burma (Myanmar) *23°40′N 94°26′E*
Mawlamyaing *see* Mawlamyine
166 M9 **Mawlamyine** *var.* Mawlamyaing, Moulmein. Mon State, S Burma (Myanmar) *16°30′N 97°39′E*
141 N14 **Mawr, Wādī** *dry watercourse* NW Yemen
195 X5 **Mawson** *Australian research station* Antarctica *67°24′S 63°16′E*
195 X5 **Mawson Coast** *physical region* Antarctica
28 M4 **Max** North Dakota, N USA *47°48′N 101°18′W*
41 W12 **Maxcanú** Yucatán, SE Mexico *20°35′N 90°00′W*
Maxesibebi *see* Mount Ayliff
109 Q5 **Maxglan** ✈ (Salzburg) Salzburg, W Austria *47°46′N 13°00′E*
93 K16 **Maxmo** *Fin.* Maksamaa. Länsi-Suomi, W Finland *63°13′N 22°04′E*
21 T11 **Maxton** North Carolina, SE USA *34°47′N 79°34′W*
25 R8 **May** Texas, SW USA *31°58′N 98°54′W*
186 B6 **May** ~ NW Papua New Guinea
123 R10 **Maya** ~ E Russian Federation
151 Q19 **Māyābandar** Andaman and Nicobar Islands, India, E Indian Ocean *12°43′N 92°52′E*
Mayadin *see* Al Mayādīn
44 L5 **Mayaguana** *island* SE Bahamas
44 L5 **Mayaguana Passage** *passage* SE Bahamas
45 S6 **Mayagüez** W Puerto Rico *18°12′N 67°08′W*
45 R6 **Mayagüez, Bahía de** *bay* W Puerto Rico
Mayals *see* Maials
79 G20 **Mayama** Pool, SE Congo *03°50′S 14°52′E*
37 V8 **Maya, Mesa De** ▲ Colorado, C USA *37°06′N 103°30′W*
143 R4 **Mayamey** Semnān, N Iran *36°50′N 55°50′E*
42 F3 **Maya Mountains** *Sp.* Montañas Mayas. ▲▲ Belize/Guatemala
44 I7 **Mayarí** Holguín, E Cuba *20°41′N 75°42′W*
Mayas, Montañas *see* Maya Mountains
18 I17 **May, Cape** *headland* New Jersey, NE USA *38°55′N 74°57′W*
80 J11 **Maych'ew** *var.* Mai Chio, *It.* Mai Ceu. Tigray, N Ethiopia *12°55′N 39°30′E*
138 I2 **Maydān Ikbiz** Ḩalab, N Syria *36°51′N 36°40′E*
Maydān Shahr *see* Meydān Shahr
80 O12 **Maydh** Sanaag, N Somalia *10°57′N 47°07′E*
Maydī *see* Mīdī
Mayebashi *see* Maebashi
Mayence *see* Mainz
102 K6 **Mayenne** Mayenne, NW France *48°18′N 00°37′W*
102 J6 **Mayenne** ⬖ *department* NW France
102 J7 **Mayenne** ~ N France
36 K12 **Mayer** Arizona, SW USA *34°25′N 112°15′W*
22 J4 **Mayersville** Mississippi, S USA *32°54′N 91°04′W*
11 P14 **Mayerthorpe** Alberta, SW Canada *53°59′N 115°06′W*
21 S12 **Mayesville** South Carolina, SE USA *34°00′N 80°10′W*
185 G19 **Mayfield** Canterbury, South Island, New Zealand *43°50′S 171°24′E*
33 N14 **Mayfield** Idaho, NW USA *43°24′N 115°56′W*
20 G7 **Mayfield** Kentucky, S USA *36°45′N 88°40′W*
36 L5 **Mayfield** Utah, W USA *39°06′N 111°42′W*
Mayhan *see* Sant
37 T14 **Mayhill** New Mexico, SW USA *32°52′N 105°28′W*
145 T9 **Maykain** *Kaz.* Mayqayyng. Pavlodar, NE Kazakhstan *51°27′N 75°52′E*
126 L14 **Maykop** Respublika Adygeya, SW Russian Federation *44°36′N 40°07′E*
Maylibash *see* Maylybas
Mayli-Say *see* Mayluu-Suu
147 T9 **Mayluu-Suu** *prev.* Mayli-Say, *Kir.* Mayly-Say. Dzhalal-Abadskaya Oblast', W Kyrgyzstan *41°16′N 72°27′E*
144 L14 **Maylybas** *prev.* Maylibash. Kzylorda, S Kazakhstan *45°51′N 62°37′E*
Mayly-Say *see* Mayluu-Suu
Maymana *see* Meymaneh
Maymyo *see* Pyin-Oo-Lwin
123 V7 **Mayn** ~ NE Russian Federation
127 Q5 **Mayna** Ul'yanovskaya Oblast', W Russian Federation *54°04′N 47°20′E*
21 N8 **Maynardville** Tennessee, S USA *36°15′N 83°48′W*
14 J13 **Maynooth** Ontario, SE Canada *45°14′N 77°54′W*
10 I6 **Mayo** Yukon Territory, NW Canada *63°37′N 135°48′W*
23 U9 **Mayo** Florida, SE USA *30°03′N 83°10′W*
97 B16 **Mayo** *Ir.* Maigh Eo. *cultural region* W Ireland
Mayo *see* Maio
78 G12 **Mayo-Kébbi** *off.* Préfecture du Mayo-Kébbu, *var.* Mayo-Kébi. ⬖ *prefecture* SW Chad
Mayo-Kébbu, Préfecture du *see* Mayo-Kébbi
Mayo-Kébi *see* Mayo-Kébbi
79 F19 **Mayoko** Niari, SW Congo *02°19′S 12°47′E*
171 P4 **Mayon Volcano** ⛰ Luzon, N Philippines *13°15′N 123°41′E*
61 A24 **Mayor Buratovich** Buenos Aires, E Argentina *39°15′S 62°35′W*
104 L4 **Mayorga** Castilla-León, N Spain *42°10′N 05°16′W*
184 N6 **Mayor Island** *island* NE New Zealand
Mayor Pablo Lagerenza *see* Capitán Pablo Lagerenza
173 I14 **Mayotte** ◇ *French territorial collectivity* E Africa
Mayoumba *see* Mayumba
44 J13 **May Pen** C Jamaica *17°58′N 77°15′W*
Mayqayyng *see* Maykain
171 O1 **Mayraira Point** *headland* Luzon, N Philippines *18°36′N 120°47′E*
109 N8 **Mayrhofen** Tirol, W Austria *47°09′N 11°52′E*
186 A6 **May River** East Sepik, NW Papua New Guinea *04°24′S 141°52′E*
139 X10 **Maysān** ⬖ *governorate* SE Iraq
123 R13 **Mayskiy** Amurskaya Oblast', SE Russian Federation *52°13′N 129°30′E*
127 O15 **Mayskiy** Kabardino-Balkarskaya Respublika, SW Russian Federation *43°37′N 44°04′E*
145 U9 **Mayskoye** Pavlodar, NE Kazakhstan *50°55′N 78°11′E*
18 J17 **Mays Landing** New Jersey, NE USA *39°27′N 74°44′W*
21 N4 **Maysville** Kentucky, S USA *38°38′N 83°46′W*
27 R2 **Maysville** Missouri, C USA *39°53′N 94°21′W*
79 D20 **Mayumba** *var.* Mayoumba. Nyanga, S Gabon *03°23′S 10°38′E*
31 S8 **Mayville** Michigan, N USA *43°18′N 83°16′W*
18 C11 **Mayville** New York, NE USA *42°15′N 79°32′W*
29 Q4 **Mayville** North Dakota, N USA *47°27′N 97°17′W*
Mayyali *see* Mahe
Mayyit, Al Baḩr al *see* Dead Sea
83 J15 **Mazabuka** Southern, S Zambia *15°52′S 27°46′E*
Mazaca *see* Kayseri
Mazagan *see* El-Jadida
32 J7 **Mazama** Washington, NW USA *48°34′N 120°26′W*
103 O15 **Mazamet** Tarn, S France *43°30′N 02°21′E*
143 O4 **Māzandarān** *off.* Ostān-e Māzandarān. ⬖ *province* N Iran
Māzandarān, Ostān-e *see* Māzandarān
156 F7 **Mazar** Xinjiang Uygur Zizhiqu, NW China *36°28′N 77°00′E*
107 H24 **Mazara del Vallo** Sicilia, Italy, C Mediterranean Sea *37°39′N 12°36′E*
149 O2 **Mazār-e Sharīf** *var.* Mazār-i Sharif. Balkh, N Afghanistan *36°44′N 67°06′E*
Mazār-i Sharif *see* Mazār-e Sharīf
105 R13 **Mazarrón** Murcia, SE Spain *37°36′N 01°19′W*

◆ Country
● Country Capital
◇ Dependent Territory
○ Dependent Territory Capital
⬖ Administrative Regions
✈ International Airport
▲ Mountain
▲▲ Mountain Range
⛰ Volcano
~ River
◎ Lake
⊠ Reservoir

Menešjávri *see* Menesjärvi
107 *I24* **Menfi** Sicilia, Italy, C Mediterranean Sea *37°36′N 12°59′E*
161 *P7* **Mengcheng** Anhui, E China *33°15′N 116°33′E*
160 *F15* **Menghai** Yunnan, SW China *22°02′N 100°18′E*
160 *F15* **Mengla** Yunnan, SW China *21°30′N 101°33′E*
160 *M13* **Mengzhu Ling** ▲▲ S China
160 *H14* **Mengzi** Yunnan, SW China *23°20′N 103°32′E*
114 *H13* **Menīkio** *var.* Menoíkio. ▲ NE Greece *40°50′N 12°40′E*
Menin *see* Menen
182 *L7* **Menindee** New South Wales, SE Australia *32°24′S 142°25′E*
182 *L7* **Menindee Lake** ◎ New South Wales, SE Australia
182 *J10* **Meningie** South Australia *35°43′S 139°20′E*
103 *O5* **Mennecy** Essonne, N France *48°34′N 02°25′E*
29 *Q12* **Menno** South Dakota, N USA *43°14′N 97°34′W*
114 *H13* **Menoíkio** ▲▲ NE Greece
Menoíkio *see* Menīkio
31 *N5* **Menominee** Michigan, N USA *45°06′N 87°36′W*
30 *M5* **Menominee River** ∽ Michigan/Wisconsin, N USA
30 *M8* **Menomonee Falls** Wisconsin, N USA *43°11′N 88°09′W*
30 *I6* **Menomonie** Wisconsin, N USA *44°52′N 91°55′W*
83 *D14* **Menongue** *var.* Vila Serpa Pinto, *Port.* Serpa Pinto. Cuando Cubango, C Angola *14°38′S 17°39′E*
120 *H8* **Menorca** *Eng.* Minorca; *anc.* Balearis Minor. *island* Islas Baleares, Spain, W Mediterranean Sea
105 *S13* **Menor, Mar** *lagoon* SE Spain
39 *S10* **Mentasta Lake** ◎ Alaska, USA
39 *S10* **Mentasta Mountains** ▲▲ Alaska, USA
168 *I13* **Mentawai, Kepulauan** *island group* W Indonesia
168 *I12* **Mentawai, Selat** *strait* W Indonesia
168 *M12* **Mentok** Pulau Bangka, W Indonesia *02°01′S 105°10′E*
103 *V15* **Menton** *It.* Mentone. Alpes-Maritimes, SE France *43°47′N 07°30′E*
24 *K8* **Mentone** Texas, SW USA *31°42′N 103°36′W*
Mentone *see* Menton
31 *U11* **Mentor** Ohio, N USA *41°40′N 81°20′W*
169 *U10* **Menyapa, Gunung** ▲ Borneo, N Indonesia *01°04′N 116°01′E*
159 *T9* **Menyuan** *var.* Menyuan Huizu Zizhixian. Qinghai, C China *37°27′N 101°33′E*
Menyuan Huizu Zizhixian *see* Menyuan
74 *M5* **Menzel Bourguiba** *var.* Manzil Bū Ruqaybah; *prev.* Ferryville. N Tunisia *37°09′N 09°51′E*
136 *M15* **Menzelet Barajı** ▣ C Turkey
127 *T4* **Menzelinsk** Respublika Tatarstan, W Russian Federation *55°44′N 53°00′E*
180 *K11* **Menzies** Western Australia *29°42′S 121°04′E*
195 *V6* **Menzies, Mount** ▲ Antarctica *73°32′S 61°02′E*
40 *J6* **Meoqui** Chihuahua, N Mexico *28°18′N 105°30′W*
83 *N14* **Meponda** Niassa, NE Mozambique *13°20′S 34°53′E*
98 *M8* **Meppel** Drenthe, NE Netherlands *52°42′N 06°12′E*
100 *E12* **Meppen** Niedersachsen, NW Germany *52°42′N 07°18′E*
Meqerghane, Sebkha *see* Mekerrhane, Sebkha
105 *T6* **Mequinenza, Embalse de** ▣ NE Spain
30 *M8* **Mequon** Wisconsin, N USA *43°13′N 87°57′W*
Mera *see* Maira
182 *D3* **Meramangye, Lake** *salt lake* South Australia
27 *W5* **Meramec River** ∽ Missouri, C USA
Meran *see* Merano
168 *K13* **Merangin** ∽ Sumatera, W Indonesia
106 *G5* **Merano** *Ger.* Meran. Trentino-Alto Adige, N Italy *46°40′N 11°10′E*
168 *K8* **Merapuh Lama** Pahang, Peninsular Malaysia *04°37′N 101°58′E*
106 *D7* **Merate** Lombardia, N Italy *45°42′N 09°26′E*
169 *U13* **Meratus, Pegunungan** ▲▲ Borneo, N Indonesia
171 *Y16* **Merauke, Sungai** ∽ Papua, E Indonesia
182 *L9* **Merbein** Victoria, SE Australia *34°11′S 142°03′E*
99 *F21* **Merbes-le-Château** Hainaut, S Belgium *50°19′N 04°09′E*
Merca *see* Marka
54 *C13* **Mercaderes** Cauca, SW Colombia *01°46′N 77°09′W*
Mercara *see* Madikeri
35 *P9* **Merced** California, W USA *37°17′N 120°30′W*
61 *C20* **Mercedes** Buenos Aires, E Argentina *34°42′S 59°30′W*
61 *D15* **Mercedes** Corrientes, NE Argentina *29°09′S 58°05′W*
61 *D19* **Mercedes** Soriano, SW Uruguay *33°16′S 58°01′W*
25 *S17* **Mercedes** Texas, SW USA *26°09′N 97°54′W*
Mercedes *see* Villa Mercedes
35 *R9* **Merced Peak** ▲ California, W USA *37°34′N 119°30′W*
35 *P9* **Merced River** ∽ California, W USA
18 *B13* **Mercer** Pennsylvania, NE USA *41°14′N 80°14′W*
99 *G18* **Merchtem** Vlaams Brabant, C Belgium *50°57′N 04°14′E*
15 *O13* **Mercier** Québec, SE Canada *45°15′N 73°45′W*
25 *Q9* **Mercury** Texas, SW USA *31°23′N 99°09′W*
184 *M5* **Mercury Islands** *island group* N New Zealand
19 *O9* **Meredith** New Hampshire, NE USA *43°36′N 71°28′W*
65 *B25* **Meredith, Cape** *var.* Cabo Belgrano. *headland* West Falkland, Falkland Islands *52°15′S 60°40′W*
37 *V6* **Meredith, Lake** ◎ Colorado, C USA
25 *N2* **Meredith, Lake** ▣ Texas, SW USA
81 *O16* **Mereeg** *var.* Mareeq, *It.* Meregh. Galguduud, E Somalia *03°47′N 47°19′E*
117 *V5* **Merefa** Kharkivs'ka Oblast', E Ukraine *49°49′N 36°05′E*
Meregh *see* Mereeg
99 *E17* **Merelbeke** Oost-Vlaanderen, NW Belgium *51°00′N 03°45′E*
Merend *see* Marand
167 *T12* **Mereuch** Môndól Kiri, E Cambodia *13°01′N 107°26′E*
Mergate *see* Margate
Mergui *see* Myeik
166 *M12* **Mergui Archipelago** *island group* S Burma (Myanmar)
114 *L12* **Meriç** Edirne, NW Turkey *41°12′N 26°24′E*
114 *L12* **Meriç** *Bul.* Maritsa, *Gk.* Évros; *anc.* Hebrus. ∽ SE Europe *see also* Évros/Maritsa
41 *X12* **Mérida** Yucatán, SW Mexico *20°58′N 89°35′W*
104 *J11* **Mérida** *anc.* Augusta Emerita. Extremadura, W Spain *38°55′N 06°20′W*
54 *I6* **Mérida** Mérida, W Venezuela *08°36′N 71°08′W*
54 *H7* **Mérida** *off.* Estado Mérida. ◐ *state* W Venezuela
Mérida, Estado *see* Mérida
18 *M13* **Meriden** Connecticut, NE USA *41°32′N 72°48′W*
22 *M5* **Meridian** Mississippi, S USA *32°24′N 88°43′W*
25 *S8* **Meridian** Texas, SW USA *31°56′N 97°40′W*
102 *J13* **Mérignac** Gironde, SW France *44°50′N 00°40′W*
102 *J13* **Mérignac** ✈ (Bordeaux) Gironde, SW France *44°51′N 00°44′W*
93 *J18* **Merikarvia** Länsi-Suomi, SW Finland *61°51′N 21°30′E*
183 *R12* **Merimbula** New South Wales, SE Australia *36°52′S 149°51′E*
182 *L9* **Meringur** Victoria, SE Australia *34°26′S 141°19′E*
Merín, Laguna *see* Mirim Lagoon
97 *I19* **Merioneth** *cultural region* W Wales, United Kingdom
188 *A11* **Merir** *island* Palau Islands, N Palau
188 *B17* **Merizo** SW Guam *13°15′N 144°40′E*
Merjama *see* Märjamaa
145 *S16* **Merke** Zhambyl, S Kazakhstan *42°48′N 73°10′E*
25 *P7* **Merkel** Texas, SW USA *32°28′N 100°00′W*
146 *E12* **Merkezi Garagumy** *var.* Mencezi Garagum, *Rus.* Tsentral'nyye Nizmennyye Garagumy. *desert* C Turkmenistan
119 *F15* **Merkinė** Alytus, S Lithuania *54°09′N 24°11′E*
99 *G16* **Merksem** Antwerpen, N Belgium *51°17′N 04°26′E*
99 *I15* **Merksplas** Antwerpen, N Belgium *51°22′N 04°54′E*
Merkulovichi *see* Myerkulavichy
119 *G15* **Merkys** ∽ S Lithuania
32 *F15* **Merlin** Oregon, NW USA *42°34′N 123°23′W*
61 *C20* **Merlo** Buenos Aires, E Argentina *34°39′S 58°45′W*
138 *G8* **Meron, Harei** *prev.* Haré Meron. ▲ N Israel *35°06′N 33°00′E*
74 *K6* **Merouane, Chott** *salt lake* NE Algeria
80 *F7* **Merowe** Northern, N Sudan *18°29′N 31°49′E*
180 *J12* **Merredin** Western Australia *31°31′S 118°18′E*
97 *I14* **Merrick** ▲ S Scotland, United Kingdom *55°09′N 04°28′W*
32 *H16* **Merrill** Oregon, NW USA *42°00′N 121°37′W*
30 *L5* **Merrill** Wisconsin, N USA *45°12′N 89°43′W*
31 *N11* **Merrillville** Indiana, N USA *41°28′N 87°19′W*
19 *O10* **Merrimack River** ∽ Massachusetts/New Hampshire, NE USA
28 *L12* **Merriman** Nebraska, C USA *42°54′N 101°42′W*
11 *N17* **Merritt** British Columbia, SW Canada *50°09′N 120°49′W*
23 *Y12* **Merritt Island** Florida, SE USA *28°21′N 80°42′W*
23 *Y11* **Merritt Island** *island* Florida, SE USA
28 *M12* **Merritt Reservoir** ▣ Nebraska, C USA
183 *S7* **Merriwa** New South Wales, SE Australia *32°09′S 150°24′E*
183 *O8* **Merriwagga** New South Wales, SE Australia *33°51′S 145°38′E*
22 *G8* **Merryville** Louisiana, S USA *30°45′N 93°32′W*
80 *K9* **Mersa Fat'ma** E Eritrea *14°52′N 40°16′E*
102 *M7* **Mer St-Aubin** Loir-et-Cher, C France *47°42′N 01°31′E*
75 *U7* **Mersá Maṭrūḥ** *var.* Maṭrūḥ; *anc.* Paraetonium. NW Egypt *31°21′N 27°15′E*
99 *M24* **Mersch** Luxembourg, C Luxembourg *49°45′N 06°06′E*
101 *M15* **Merseburg** Sachsen-Anhalt, C Germany *51°22′N 12°00′E*
Mersen *see* Meerssen
97 *K18* **Mersey** ∽ NW England, United Kingdom
136 *J17* **Mersin** *var.* İçel. İçel, S Turkey *36°50′N 34°39′E*
Mersin *see* İçel
168 *L9* **Mersing** Johor, Peninsular Malaysia *02°25′N 103°50′E*
118 *E8* **Mērsrags** Talsi, NW Latvia *57°21′N 23°05′E*
152 *G12* **Merta** *var.* Merta City. Rājasthān, N India *26°40′N 74°04′E*
Merta City *see* Merta
152 *F12* **Merta Road** Rājasthān, N India *26°42′N 73°54′E*
97 *J21* **Merthyr Tydfil** S Wales, United Kingdom *51°46′N 03°23′W*
104 *H13* **Mértola** Beja, S Portugal *37°38′N 07°40′W*
144 *G14* **Mertvyy Kultuk, Sor** *salt flat* SW Kazakhstan
195 *V16* **Mertz Glacier** *glacier* Antarctica
99 *M24* **Mertzig** Diekirch, C Luxembourg *49°50′N 06°00′E*
25 *O9* **Mertzon** Texas, SW USA *31°16′N 100°50′W*
103 *N4* **Méru** Oise, N France *49°15′N 02°07′E*
81 *I18* **Meru** Eastern, C Kenya *0°03′N 37°38′E*
81 *I20* **Meru, Mount** ▲ NE Tanzania *03°12′S 36°45′E*
Merv *see* Mary
Mervdasht *see* Marv Dasht
136 *K11* **Merzifon** Amasya, N Turkey *40°52′N 35°28′E*
101 *D20* **Merzig** Saarland, SW Germany *49°27′N 06°39′E*
36 *L14* **Mesa** Arizona, SW USA *33°25′N 111°49′W*
29 *V4* **Mesabi Range** ▲▲ Minnesota, N USA
54 *H6* **Mesa Bolívar** Mérida, NW Venezuela *08°30′N 71°38′W*
107 *Q18* **Mesagne** Puglia, SE Italy *40°33′N 17°49′E*
39 *P12* **Mesa Mountain** ▲ Alaska, USA *60°26′N 155°14′W*
115 *J25* **Mesará** *lowland* Kriti, Greece, E Mediterranean Sea
37 *S14* **Mescalero** New Mexico, SW USA *33°09′N 105°46′W*
101 *G15* **Meschede** Nordrhein-Westfalen, W Germany *51°21′N 08°16′E*
137 *Q12* **Mescit Dağları** ▲▲ NE Turkey
189 *V13* **Mesegon** *island* Chuuk, C Micronesia
Meseritz *see* Międzyrzecz
54 *F11* **Mesetas** Meta, C Colombia *03°14′N 74°09′W*
Meshchera Lowland *see* Meshcherskaya Nizmennost'
Meshcherskaya Nizina *see* Meshcherskaya Nizmennost'
126 *M4* **Meshcherskaya Nizmennost'** *var.* Meshcherskaya Nizina, *Eng.* Meshchera Lowland. *basin* W Russian Federation
126 *J5* **Meshchovsk** Kaluzhskaya Oblast', W Russian Federation *54°21′N 35°23′E*
125 *R9* **Meshchura** Respublika Komi, NW Russian Federation *63°18′N 50°56′E*
Meshed *see* Mashhad
Meshed-i-Sar *see* Bābolsar
80 *E13* **Meshra'er Req** Warab, S Sudan *08°30′N 29°27′E*
37 *R15* **Mesilla** New Mexico, SW USA *32°15′N 106°49′W*
108 *H10* **Mesocco** *Ger.* Misox. Ticino, S Switzerland *46°18′N 09°13′E*
115 *D18* **Mesolóngi** *prev.* Mesolóngion. Dytikí Ellás, W Greece *38°21′N 21°26′E*
Mesolóngion *see* Mesolóngi
14 *E8* **Mesomikenda Lake** ◎ Ontario, S Canada
61 *D15* **Mesopotamia** *var.* Mesopotamia Argentina. *physical region* NE Argentina
Mesopotamia Argentina *see* Mesopotamia
35 *Y10* **Mesquite** Nevada, W USA *36°47′N 114°04′W*
82 *Q13* **Messalo, Rio** *var.* Mualo. ∽ NE Mozambique
Messana/Messene *see* Messina
99 *L25* **Messancy** Luxembourg, SE Belgium *49°36′N 05°49′E*
107 *M23* **Messina** *var.* Messana, Messene; *anc.* Zancle. Sicilia, Italy, C Mediterranean Sea *38°12′N 15°33′E*
Messina *see* Musina
Messina, Strait of *see* Messina, Stretto di
107 *M23* **Messina, Stretto di** *Eng.* Strait of Messina. *strait* SW Italy
115 *E21* **Messíni** Pelopónnisos, S Greece *37°03′N 22°00′E*
115 *E21* **Messinía** *peninsula* S Greece
115 *E22* **Messiniakós Kólpos** *gulf* S Greece
122 *J8* **Messoyakha** ∽ N Russian Federation
114 *H11* **Mesta** *Gk.* Néstos, *Turk.* Kara Su. ∽ Bulgaria/Greece *see also* Néstos
Mesta *see* Néstos
Mestghanem *see* Mostaganem
137 *R8* **Mestia** *var.* Mestiya. N Georgia *43°03′N 42°50′E*
Mestiya *see* Mestia
115 *K18* **Mestón, Akrotírio** *cape* Chíos, E Greece
106 *H8* **Mestre** Veneto, NE Italy *45°30′N 12°14′E*
59 *M16* **Mestre, Espigão** ▲▲ E Brazil
169 *N14* **Mesuji** ∽ Sumatera, W Indonesia
Mesule *see* Grosser Möseler
10 *J10* **Meszah Peak** ▲ British Columbia, W Canada *58°31′N 131°28′W*
54 *G11* **Meta** *off.* Departamento del Meta. ◐ *province* C Colombia
15 *Q8* **Metabetchouane** ∽ Québec, SE Canada
Meta, Departamento del *see* Meta
9 *S7* **Meta Incognita Peninsula** *peninsula* Baffin Island, Nunavut, NE Canada
22 *K9* **Metairie** Louisiana, S USA *29°58′N 90°09′W*
32 *M6* **Metaline Falls** Washington, NW USA *48°51′N 117°21′W*
62 *K6* **Metán** Salta, N Argentina *25°29′S 64°57′W*
82 *N13* **Metangula** Niassa, N Mozambique *12°41′S 34°50′E*
42 *E7* **Metapán** Santa Ana, NW El Salvador *14°20′N 89°28′W*
54 *K9* **Meta, Río** ∽ Colombia/Venezuela
106 *I11* **Metauro** ∽ C Italy
80 *H11* **Metema** Āmara, N Ethiopia *12°53′N 36°10′E*
115 *D15* **Metéora** *religious building* Thessalía, C Greece
65 *O20* **Meteor Rise** *undersea feature* SW Indian Ocean *46°00′S 05°30′E*
186 *G5* **Meteran** New Hanover, NE Papua New Guinea *02°40′S 150°12′E*
Meterlam *see* Mehtar Lām
115 *G20* **Methanon** *peninsula* S Greece
Methariam/Metharlam *see* Mehtar Lām
32 *J6* **Methow River** ∽ Washington, NW USA
19 *O10* **Methuen** Massachusetts, NE USA *42°43′N 71°10′W*
185 *G19* **Methven** Canterbury, South Island, New Zealand *43°37′S 171°38′E*
Metis *see* Metz
113 *G15* **Metković** Dubrovnik-Neretva, SE Croatia *43°02′N 17°37′E*
39 *Y14* **Metlakatla** Annette Island, Alaska, USA *55°07′N 131°34′W*
109 *V13* **Metlika** *Ger.* Möttling. SE Slovenia *45°38′N 15°18′E*
109 *T8* **Metnitz** Kärnten, S Austria *46°58′N 14°09′E*
27 *W12* **Meto, Bayou** ∽ Arkansas, C USA
168 *M15* **Metro** Sumatera, W Indonesia *05°05′S 105°20′E*
30 *M17* **Metropolis** Illinois, N USA *37°09′N 88°43′W*
Metropolitan *see* Santiago
35 *N8* **Metropolitan Oakland** ✈ California, W USA *37°42′N 122°13′W*
115 *D15* **Métsovo** *prev.* Métsovon. Ípeiros, C Greece *39°47′N 21°12′E*
Métsovon *see* Métsovo
23 *V5* **Metter** Georgia, SE USA *32°24′N 82°03′W*
99 *H21* **Mettet** Namur, S Belgium *50°19′N 04°43′E*
101 *D20* **Mettlach** Saarland, SW Germany *49°28′N 06°37′E*
Mettu *see* Metu
80 *H13* **Metu** *var.* Mattu, Mettu. Oromīya, C Ethiopia *08°18′N 35°39′E*
138 *G8* **Metula** *prev.* Metulla. Northern, N Israel *33°16′N 35°35′E*
169 *T10* **Metulang** Borneo, N Indonesia *01°28′N 114°40′E*
Metulla *see* Metula
103 *T4* **Metz** *anc.* Divodurum Mediomatricum, Mediomatrica, Metis. Moselle, NE France *49°07′N 06°09′E*
101 *H22* **Metzingen** Baden-Württemberg, S Germany *48°31′N 09°16′E*
168 *G8* **Meulaboh** Sumatera, W Indonesia *04°10′N 96°09′E*
99 *D18* **Meulebeke** West-Vlaanderen, W Belgium *50°57′N 03°18′E*
103 *U6* **Meurthe** ∽ NE France
103 *S5* **Meurthe-et-Moselle** ◐ *department* NE France
103 *S4* **Meuse** ◐ *department* NE France
84 *F10* **Meuse** *Dut.* Maas. ∽ W Europe *see also* Maas
Meuse *see* Maas
Mexcala, Río *see* Balsas, Río
25 *U8* **Mexia** Texas, SW USA *31°40′N 96°28′W*
58 *K11* **Mexiana, Ilha** *island* NE Brazil
40 *C1* **Mexicali** Baja California Norte, NW Mexico *32°34′N 115°26′W*
Mexicanos, Estados Unidos *see* Mexico
41 *O14* **México** *var.* Ciudad de México, *Eng.* Mexico City. ● (Mexico) México, C Mexico *19°26′N 99°08′W*
27 *V4* **Mexico** Missouri, C USA *19°10′N 99°04′W*
18 *H9* **Mexico** New York, NE USA *43°27′N 76°14′W*
40 *L7* **Mexico** *off.* United Mexican States, *var.* Méjico, México, *Sp.* Estados Unidos Mexicanos. ◆ *federal republic* N Central America
41 *O13* **México** ◐ *state* S Mexico
México *see* Mexico
0 *J13* **Mexico Basin** *var.* Sigsbee Deep. *undersea feature* C Gulf of Mexico *25°00′N 92°00′W*
Mexico City *see* México
México, Golfo de *see* Mexico, Gulf of
44 *B4* **Mexico, Gulf of** *Sp.* Golfo de México. *gulf* W Atlantic Ocean
Meyadine *see* Al Mayādīn
143 *Q9* **Meybod** Yazd, C Iran *32°16′N 53°59′E*
149 *Q5* **Meydān Shahr** *var.* Maydān Shahr. Vardak, E Afghanistan *34°27′N 68°48′E*
39 *Y14* **Meyers Chuck** Etolin Island, Alaska, USA *55°44′N 132°15′W*
148 *M3* **Meymaneh** *var.* Maimāna, Maymana. Fāryāb, NW Afghanistan *35°57′N 64°48′E*
143 *N7* **Meymeh** Eşfahān, C Iran *33°29′N 51°09′E*
123 *V7* **Meynypil'gyno** Chukotskiy Avtonomnyy Okrug, NE Russian Federation *62°33′N 177°00′E*
108 *A10* **Meyrin** Genève, SW Switzerland *46°14′N 06°05′E*
166 *L7* **Mezaligon** Ayeyarwady, SW Burma (Myanmar) *17°53′N 95°12′E*
41 *O15* **Mezcala** Guerrero, S Mexico *17°55′N 99°34′W*
114 *H8* **Mezdra** Vratsa, NW Bulgaria *43°08′N 23°42′E*
103 *P16* **Mèze** Hérault, S France *43°26′N 03°37′E*
125 *O6* **Mezen'** Arkhangel'skaya Oblast', NW Russian Federation *65°54′N 44°10′E*
125 *P8* **Mezen'** ∽ NW Russian Federation
Mezen, Bay of *see* Mezenskaya Guba
103 *Q13* **Mézenc, Mont** ▲ C France *44°57′N 04°15′E*
125 *O8* **Mezenskaya Guba** *var.* Bay of Mezen. *bay* NW Russian Federation
Mezha *see* Myazha
122 *H6* **Mezhdusharskiy, Ostrov** *island* Novaya Zemlya, N Russian Federation
Mezhëvo *see* Myezhava
Mezhgor'ye *see* Mizhhir"ya
117 *V8* **Mezhova** Dnipropetrovs'ka Oblast', E Ukraine *48°15′N 36°44′E*
10 *J12* **Meziadin Junction** British Columbia, W Canada *56°06′N 129°15′W*
111 *G16* **Mezileské Sedlo** *var.* Przełęcz Międzyleska. *pass* Czech Republic/Poland
102 *L14* **Mézin** Lot-et-Garonne, SW France *44°03′N 00°16′E*
111 *M24* **Mezőberény** Békés, SE Hungary *46°49′N 21°00′E*
111 *M25* **Mezőhegyes** Békés, SE Hungary *46°20′N 20°48′E*
111 *M25* **Mezőkovácsháza** Békés, SE Hungary *46°24′N 20°52′E*
111 *M21* **Mezőkövesd** Borsod-Abaúj-Zemplén, NE Hungary *47°49′N 20°32′E*
Mezőtelegd *see* Tileagd
111 *M23* **Mezőtúr** Jász-Nagykun-Szolnok, E Hungary *47°N 20°37′E*
40 *K10* **Mezquital** Durango, C Mexico *23°31′N 104°19′W*
106 *G6* **Mezzolombardo** Trentino-Alto Adige, N Italy *46°13′N 11°08′E*
82 *L13* **Mfuwe** Northern, N Zambia *13°00′S 31°45′E*
121 *O15* **Mġarr** Gozo, N Malta *36°01′N 14°18′E*
126 *H6* **Mglin** Bryanskaya Oblast', W Russian Federation *53°01′N 32°54′E*
Mhálanna, Cionn *see* Malin Head
154 *G10* **Mhow** Madhya Pradesh, C India *22°32′N 75°49′E*
Miadzioł Nowy *see* Myadzyel
171 *O6* **Miagao** Panay Island, C Philippines *10°40′N 122°15′E*
41 *R17* **Miahuatlán** *var.* Miahuatlán de Porfirio Díaz. Oaxaca, SE Mexico *16°21′N 96°36′W*
Miahuatlán de Porfirio Díaz *see* Miahuatlán
104 *K10* **Miajadas** Extremadura, W Spain *39°10′N 05°54′W*
Miajlar *see* Myājlār
36 *M14* **Miami** Arizona, SW USA *33°23′N 110°53′W*
23 *Z16* **Miami** Florida, SE USA *25°46′N 80°12′W*
27 *R8* **Miami** Oklahoma, C USA *36°53′N 94°54′W*
25 *O2* **Miami** Texas, SW USA *35°42′N 100°37′W*
23 *Z16* **Miami** ✈ Florida, SE USA *25°47′N 80°16′W*
23 *Z16* **Miami Beach** Florida, SE USA *25°47′N 80°08′W*
23 *Y15* **Miami Canal** *canal* Florida, SE USA
31 *R14* **Miamisburg** Ohio, N USA *39°38′N 84°17′W*
149 *U10* **Miān Channūn** Punjab, E Pakistan *30°24′N 72°27′E*
142 *J4* **Miāndowāb** *var.* Mianduab, Miyāndoāb. Āžarbāyjān-e Gharbī, NW Iran *36°57′N 46°06′E*
172 *H5* **Miandrivazo** Toliara, C Madagascar *19°31′S 45°29′E*
Mianduab *see* Miāndowāb
142 *K3* **Mīāneh** *var.* Miyāneh. Āžarbāyjān-e Sharqī, NW Iran *37°23′N 47°45′E*
149 *O16* **Miāni Hōr** *lagoon* S Pakistan
160 *G10* **Mianning** Sichuan, C China *28°34′N 102°12′E*
149 *T7* **Miānwāli** Punjab, NE Pakistan *32°32′N 71°33′E*
160 *J7* **Mianxian** *var.* Mian Xian. Shaanxi, C China *33°12′N 106°36′E*
Mian Xian *see* Mianxian
160 *I8* **Mianyang** Sichuan, C China *31°29′N 104°43′E*
Mianyang *see* Xiantao
161 *R3* **Miaodao Qundao** *island group* E China
161 *S13* **Miaoli** N Taiwan *24°33′N 120°48′E*
122 *F11* **Miass** Chelyabinskaya Oblast', C Russian Federation *55°00′N 59°55′E*
110 *G8* **Miastko** *Ger.* Rummelsburg in Pommern. Pomorskie, N Poland *54°N 16°58′E*
Miava *see* Myjava
11 *O15* **Mica Creek** British Columbia, SW Canada *51°58′N 118°29′W*
160 *J7* **Micang Shan** ▲▲ C China
Mi Chai *see* Nong Khai
111 *O19* **Michalovce** *Ger.* Grossmichel, *Hung.* Nagymihály. Košický Kraj, E Slovakia *48°46′N 21°55′E*
99 *M20* **Michel, Baraque** *hill* E Belgium
39 *S5* **Michelson, Mount** ▲ Alaska, USA *69°19′N 144°16′W*
45 *P9* **Miches** El Seibo, E Dominican Republic *18°59′N 69°03′W*
30 *M4* **Michigamme, Lake** ◎ Michigan, N USA
30 *M4* **Michigamme Reservoir** ▣ Michigan, N USA
31 *N4* **Michigamme River** ∽ Michigan, N USA
31 *O7* **Michigan** *off.* State of Michigan, *also known as* Great Lakes State, Lake State, Wolverine State. ◐ *state* N USA
31 *O11* **Michigan City** Indiana, N USA *41°43′N 86°52′W*
31 *O8* **Michigan, Lake** ◎ N USA
31 *P2* **Michipicoten Bay** *lake bay* Ontario, N Canada
14 *A8* **Michipicoten Island** *island* Ontario, S Canada
14 *B7* **Michipicoten River** Ontario, S Canada *47°56′N 84°48′W*
Michurin *see* Tsarevo
126 *M6* **Michurinsk** Tambovskaya Oblast', W Russian Federation *52°56′N 40°31′E*
Mico, Punta/Mico, Punto *see* Monkey Point
42 *L10* **Mico, Río** ∽ SE Nicaragua
45 *T12* **Micoud** SE Saint Lucia *13°49′N 60°54′W*
189 *N16* **Micronesia** *off.* Federated States of Micronesia. ◆ *federation* W Pacific Ocean
175 *P4* **Micronesia** *island group* W Pacific Ocean
Micronesia, Federated States of *see* Micronesia
169 *O9* **Midai, Pulau** *island* Kepulauan Natuna, W Indonesia
Mid-Atlantic Cordillera *see* Mid-Atlantic Ridge
65 *M17* **Mid-Atlantic Ridge** *var.* Mid-Atlantic Cordillera, Mid-Atlantic Rise, Mid-Atlantic Swell. *undersea feature* Atlantic Ocean *0°00′N 20°00′W*
Mid-Atlantic Rise/Mid-Atlantic Swell *see* Mid-Atlantic Ridge
99 *E15* **Middelburg** Zeeland, SW Netherlands *51°30′N 03°36′E*
83 *H24* **Middelburg** Eastern Cape, S South Africa *31°28′S 25°01′E*
83 *K21* **Middelburg** Mpumalanga, NE South Africa *25°47′S 29°28′E*
95 *G23* **Middelfart** Fyn, C Denmark *55°30′N 09°44′E*
98 *G13* **Middelharnis** Zuid-Holland, SW Netherlands *51°45′N 04°10′E*
99 *B16* **Middelkerke** West-Vlaanderen, W Belgium *51°12′N 02°51′E*
98 *I9* **Middenbeemster** Noord-Holland, C Netherlands *52°33′N 04°55′E*
98 *I8* **Middenmeer** Noord-Holland, NW Netherlands *52°48′N 04°58′E*
35 *Q2* **Middle Alkali Lake** ◎ California, W USA
193 *S6* **Middle America Trench** *undersea feature* E Pacific Ocean *15°00′N 95°00′W*
151 *P19* **Middle Andaman** *island* Andaman Islands, India, NE Indian Ocean
Middle Atlas *see* Moyen Atlas
21 *R3* **Middlebourne** West Virginia, NE USA *39°30′N 80°53′W*
23 *W9* **Middleburg** Florida, SE USA *30°03′N 81°55′W*
Middleburg Island *see* 'Eua
Middle Caicos *see* Grand Caicos
25 *N8* **Middle Concho River** ∽ Texas, SW USA
Middle Congo *see* Congo (Republic of)
39 *R6* **Middle Fork Chandalar River** ∽ Alaska, USA
39 *Q7* **Middle Fork Koyukuk River** ∽ Alaska, USA
33 *O12* **Middle Fork Salmon River** ∽ Idaho, NW USA
11 *T15* **Middle Lake** Saskatchewan, S Canada *52°31′N 105°16′W*
28 *L13* **Middle Loup River** ∽ Nebraska, C USA
185 *E22* **Middlemarch** Otago, South Island, New Zealand *45°30′S 170°07′E*
31 *T15* **Middleport** Ohio, N USA *39°00′N 82°03′W*
29 *U14* **Middle Raccoon River** ∽ Iowa, C USA
29 *R3* **Middle River** ∽ Minnesota, N USA
21 *N8* **Middlesboro** Kentucky, S USA *36°37′N 83°42′W*
97 *M15* **Middlesbrough** N England, United Kingdom *54°35′N 01°14′W*
42 *G3* **Middlesex** Stann Creek, C Belize *17°00′N 88°31′W*
97 *N22* **Middlesex** *cultural region* SE England, United Kingdom
13 *P15* **Middleton** Nova Scotia, SE Canada *44°56′N 65°04′W*
20 *F10* **Middleton** Tennessee, S USA *35°05′N 88°57′W*
30 *L9* **Middleton** Wisconsin, N USA *43°06′N 89°30′W*
39 *S13* **Middleton Island** *island* Alaska, USA
34 *M7* **Middletown** California, W USA *38°44′N 122°39′W*
21 *Y2* **Middletown** Delaware, NE USA *39°25′N 75°39′W*
18 *K15* **Middletown** New Jersey, NE USA *40°23′N 74°08′W*
18 *K13* **Middletown** New York, NE USA *41°27′N 74°25′W*
31 *R14* **Middletown** Ohio, N USA *39°33′N 84°19′W*
18 *G15* **Middletown** Pennsylvania, NE USA *40°11′N 76°42′W*
141 *N14* **Midī** *var.* Maydī. NW Yemen *16°18′N 42°51′E*
103 *O16* **Midi, Canal du** *canal* S France
102 *K17* **Midi de Bigorre, Pic du** ▲ S France *42°57′N 00°08′E*
102 *K17* **Midi d'Ossau, Pic du** ▲ SW France *42°51′N 00°27′W*
173 *R7* **Mid-Indian Basin** *undersea feature* N Indian Ocean *10°00′S 80°00′E*
173 *P7* **Mid-Indian Ridge** *var.* Central Indian Ridge. *undersea feature* C Indian Ocean *12°00′S 66°00′E*
103 *N14* **Midi-Pyrénées** ◐ *region* S France
25 *N8* **Midkiff** Texas, SW USA *31°35′N 101°51′W*
14 *G13* **Midland** Ontario, S Canada *44°45′N 79°53′W*
31 *R8* **Midland** Michigan, N USA *43°37′N 84°15′W*
28 *M10* **Midland** South Dakota, N USA *44°04′N 101°07′W*
24 *M8* **Midland** Texas, SW USA *32°N 102°05′W*
83 *K17* **Midlands** ◐ *province* C Zimbabwe
97 *D21* **Midleton** *Ir.* Mainistir na Corann. SW Ireland *51°55′N 08°10′W*
25 *T7* **Midlothian** Texas, SW USA *32°28′N 96°59′W*
96 *K12* **Midlothian** *cultural region* S Scotland, United Kingdom
172 *I7* **Midongy Atsimo** Fianarantsoa, S Madagascar *21°58′S 47°47′E*
102 *K15* **Midou** ∽ SW France
192 *J6* **Mid-Pacific Mountains** *var.* Mid-Pacific Seamounts. *undersea feature* NW Pacific Ocean *20°00′N 178°00′W*
Mid-Pacific Seamounts *see* Mid-Pacific Mountains
171 *Q7* **Midsayap** Mindanao, S Philippines *07°12′N 124°31′E*
36 *L3* **Midway** Utah, W USA *40°30′N 111°28′W*
192 *L5* **Midway Islands** ◇ *US territory* C Pacific Ocean
33 *X14* **Midwest** Wyoming, C USA *43°24′N 106°15′W*
27 *N10* **Midwest City** Oklahoma, C USA *35°28′N 98°24′W*
152 *M10* **Mid Western** ◐ *zone* W Nepal
98 *P5* **Midwolda** Groningen, NE Netherlands *53°12′N 07°00′E*
137 *Q16* **Midyat** Mardin, SE Turkey *37°25′N 41°20′E*
114 *F8* **Midzhur** *SCr.* Midžor. ▲ Bulgaria/Serbia *43°24′N 22°41′E* *see also* Midžor
Midzhur *see* Midžor
113 *Q14* **Midžor** *Bul.* Midzhur. ▲ Bulgaria/Serbia *43°24′N 22°40′E* *see also* Midzhur
Midžor *see* Midzhur
164 *K14* **Mie** *off.* Mie-ken. ◐ *prefecture* Honshū, SW Japan
111 *L16* **Miechów** Małopolskie, S Poland *50°21′N 20°01′E*
110 *F11* **Międzychód** *Ger.* Mitteldorf. Wielkopolskie, C Poland *52°36′N 15°53′E*
Międzyleska, Przełęcz *see* Mezileské Sedlo
110 *O12* **Międzyrzec Podlaski** Lubelskie, E Poland *52°N 22°47′E*
110 *E11* **Międzyrzecz** *Ger.* Meseritz. Lubuskie, W Poland *52°26′N 15°33′E*
Mie-ken *see* Mie
102 *L16* **Miélan** Gers, S France *43°26′N 00°19′E*
111 *N16* **Mielec** Podkarpackie, SE Poland *50°18′N 21°27′E*
95 *L21* **Mien** ◎ S Sweden
41 *O8* **Mier** Tamaulipas, C Mexico *26°28′N 99°10′W*
116 *J11* **Miercurea-Ciuc** *Ger.* Szeklerburg, *Hung.* Csíkszereda. Harghita, C Romania *46°24′N 25°48′E*
Mieresch *see* Maros/Mureş
Mieres del Camín *see* Mieres del Camino
104 *K2* **Mieres del Camino** *var.* Mieres del Camín. Asturias, NW Spain *43°15′N 05°46′W*
99 *K15* **Mierlo** Noord-Brabant, SE Netherlands *51°27′N 05°37′E*
41 *O10* **Mier y Noriega** Nuevo León, NE Mexico *23°24′N 100°06′W*
Mies *see* Stříbro
80 *K13* **Mī'ēso** *var.* Meheso, Miesso. Oromīya, C Ethiopia *09°13′N 40°47′E*
Miesso *see* Mī'ēso
110 *D10* **Mieszkowice** *Ger.* Bärwalde Neumark. Zachodnio-pomorskie, W Poland *52°45′N 14°24′E*
18 *G14* **Mifflinburg** Pennsylvania, NE USA *40°55′N 77°03′W*
18 *F14* **Mifflintown** Pennsylvania, NE USA *40°34′N 77°24′W*
138 *F8* **Mifrats Hefa** *Eng.* Bay of Haifa; *prev.* MifrazHefa. *bay* N Israel
41 *R15* **Miguel Alemán, Presa** ▣ SE Mexico
40 *L9* **Miguel Asua** *var.* Miguel Auza. Zacatecas, C Mexico *24°17′N 103°29′W*
Miguel Auza *see* Miguel Asua
43 *S15* **Miguel de la Borda** *var.* Donoso. Colón, C Panama *09°09′N 80°20′W*
41 *N13* **Miguel Hidalgo** ✈ (Guadalajara) Jalisco, SW Mexico *20°52′N 101°09′W*
40 *H7* **Miguel Hidalgo, Presa** ▣ W Mexico
116 *J14* **Mihăileşti** Giurgiu, S Romania *44°20′N 25°54′E*
116 *M14* **Mihail Kogălniceanu** *var.* Kogălniceanu; *prev.* Caramurat, Ferdinand. Constanţa, SE Romania *44°22′N 28°27′E*
117 *N14* **Mihai Viteazu** Constanţa, SE Romania *44°37′N 28°41′E*
136 *G12* **Mihalıççık** Eskişehir, NW Turkey *39°52′N 31°30′E*
164 *G13* **Mihara** Hiroshima, Honshū, SW Japan *34°24′N 133°04′E*
165 *N14* **Mihara-yama** Ѫ Miyako-jima, SE Japan *34°43′N 139°23′E*
105 *S8* **Mijares** ∽ E Spain
98 *I11* **Mijdrecht** Utrecht, C Netherlands *52°12′N 04°52′E*
165 *S4* **Mikasa** Hokkaidō, NE Japan *43°15′N 141°57′E*
Mikashevichi *see* Mikashevichy
119 *K19* **Mikashevichy** *Pol.* Mikaszewicze, *Rus.* Mikashevichi. Brestskaya Voblasts', SW Belarus *52°13′N 27°28′E*
Mikaszewicze *see* Mikashevichy
126 *L5* **Mikhaylov** Ryazanskaya Oblast', W Russian Federation *54°12′N 39°03′E*
Mikhaylovgrad *see* Montana
195 *Z8* **Mikhaylov Island** *island* Antarctica
145 *T6* **Mikhaylovka** Pavlodar, N Kazakhstan *53°49′N 76°31′E*
127 *N9* **Mikhaylovka** Volgogradskaya Oblast', SW Russian Federation *50°06′N 43°17′E*
Mikhaylovka *see* Mykhaylivka
81 *K24* **Mikindani** Mtwara, SE Tanzania *10°16′S 40°05′E*
93 *N18* **Mikkeli** *Swe.* Sankt Michel. Itä-Suomi, SE Finland *61°41′N 27°14′E*
110 *M8* **Mikołajki** *Ger.* Nikolaiken. Warmińsko-Mazurskie, NE Poland *53°49′N 21°31′E*
Míkonos *see* Mýkonos
114 *I9* **Mikre** Lovech, N Bulgaria *43°01′N 24°31′E*
114 *C13* **Mikrí Préspa, Límni** ◎ N Greece
125 *P4* **Mikulkin, Mys** *headland* NW Russian Federation *67°50′N 46°36′E*
81 *I23* **Mikumi** Morogoro, SE Tanzania *07°22′S 37°00′E*
125 *R10* **Mikun'** Respublika Komi, NW Russian Federation *62°20′N 50°02′E*
164 *K13* **Mikuni** Fukui, Honshū, SW Japan *36°12′N 136°09′E*
165 *X13* **Mikura-jima** *island* E Japan
29 *V7* **Milaca** Minnesota, N USA *45°45′N 93°40′W*
62 *J10* **Milagro** La Rioja, C Argentina *31°00′S 66°01′W*
56 *B7* **Milagro** Guayas, SW Ecuador *02°11′S 79°36′W*
31 *P4* **Milakokia Lake** ◎ Michigan, N USA
30 *J1* **Milan** Illinois, N USA *41°27′N 90°33′W*
31 *R10* **Milan** Michigan, N USA *42°05′N 83°40′W*
27 *T2* **Milan** Missouri, C USA *40°12′N 93°08′W*
37 *Q11* **Milan** New Mexico, SW USA *35°10′N 107°53′W*
20 *G9* **Milan** Tennessee, S USA *35°55′N 88°45′W*
Milan *see* Milano
95 *F15* **Miland** Telemark, S Norway *59°57′N 08°48′E*
83 *N15* **Milange** Zambézia, NE Mozambique *16°09′S 35°44′E*

◆ Country
● Country Capital
◇ Dependent Territory
○ Dependent Territory Capital
◐ Administrative Regions
✈ International Airport
▲ Mountain
▲▲ Mountain Range
Ѫ Volcano
∽ River
◎ Lake
▣ Reservoir

MILANO – MOCKSVILLE

106 D8 **Milano** *Eng.* Milan, *Ger.* Mailand; *anc.* Mediolanum. Lombardia, N Italy 45°28′N 09°10′E
25 U10 **Milano** Texas, SW USA 30°42′N 96°51′W
136 C15 **Milas** Muğla, SW Turkey 37°17′N 27°46′E
119 K21 **Milashavichy** *Rus.* Milashevichi. Homyel'skaya Voblasts', SE Belarus 51°39′N 27°56′E
Milashevichi *see* Milashavichy
119 I18 **Milavidy** *Rus.* Milovidy. Brestskaya Voblasts', SW Belarus 52°54′N 25°51′E
107 L23 **Milazzo** *anc.* Mylae. Sicilia, Italy, C Mediterranean Sea 38°13′N 15°15′E
29 R8 **Milbank** South Dakota, N USA 45°12′N 96°36′W
19 T7 **Milbridge** Maine, NE USA 44°31′N 67°55′W
100 L11 **Milde** ≈ C Germany
14 F14 **Mildmay** Ontario, S Canada 44°03′N 81°07′W
182 L9 **Mildura** Victoria, SE Australia 34°13′S 142°09′E
137 X12 **Mil Düzü** *Rus.* Mil'skaya Ravnina, Mil'skaya Step'. *physical region* C Azerbaijan
160 H13 **Mile** *var.* Miyang. Yunnan, SW China 24°28′N 103°26′E
Mile *see* Mili Atoll
181 Y10 **Miles** Queensland, E Australia 26°41′S 150°15′E
25 P8 **Miles** Texas, SW USA 31°36′N 100°10′W
33 X9 **Miles City** Montana, NW USA 46°24′N 105°48′W
11 U17 **Milestone** Saskatchewan, S Canada 50°00′N 104°24′W
107 N22 **Mileto** Calabria, SW Italy 38°35′N 16°03′E
107 K15 **Miletto, Monte** ▲ C Italy 41°28′N 14°21′E
18 M13 **Milford** Connecticut, NE USA 41°12′N 73°01′W
21 Y3 **Milford** *var.* Milford City. Delaware, NE USA 38°54′N 75°25′W
29 T11 **Milford** Iowa, C USA 43°19′N 95°09′W
19 S6 **Milford** Maine, NE USA 44°57′N 68°37′W
29 R16 **Milford** Nebraska, C USA 40°46′N 97°03′W
19 O10 **Milford** New Hampshire, NE USA 42°49′N 71°38′W
18 J13 **Milford** Pennsylvania, NE USA 41°20′N 74°48′W
25 T7 **Milford** Texas, SW USA 32°07′N 96°57′W
36 K6 **Milford** Utah, W USA 38°22′N 112°57′W
Milford *see* Milford Haven
Milford City *see* Milford
97 H21 **Milford Haven** *prev.* Milford. SW Wales, United Kingdom 51°44′N 05°02′W
27 O4 **Milford Lake** ⊠ Kansas, C USA
185 B21 **Milford Sound** Southland, South Island, New Zealand 44°41′S 167°57′E
185 B21 **Milford Sound** *inlet* South Island, New Zealand
Milhau *see* Millau
Milh, Bahr al *see* Razāzah, Buḩayrat ar
139 T10 **Milḩ, Wādī al** *dry watercourse* S Iraq
189 W8 **Mili Atoll** *var.* Mile. *atoll* Ratak Chain, SE Marshall Islands
110 H13 **Milicz** Dolnośląskie, SW Poland 51°32′N 17°15′E
107 L25 **Militello in Val di Catania** Sicilia, Italy, C Mediterranean Sea 37°17′N 14°47′E
11 R17 **Milk River** Alberta, SW Canada 49°10′N 112°06′W
44 J13 **Milk River** ≈ C Jamaica
33 W7 **Milk River** ≈ Montana, NW USA
80 D9 **Milk, Wadi el** *var.* Wadi al Malik. ≈ C Sudan
99 L14 **Mill** Noord-Brabant, SE Netherlands 51°42′N 05°46′E
103 P14 **Millau** *var.* Milhau; *anc.* Æmilianum. Aveyron, S France 44°06′N 03°05′E
14 I14 **Millbrook** Ontario, SE Canada 44°09′N 78°26′W
23 U4 **Milledgeville** Georgia, SE USA 33°04′N 83°13′W
12 C12 **Mille Lacs, Lac des** ◎ Ontario, S Canada
29 V6 **Mille Lacs Lake** ◎ Minnesota, N USA
23 V4 **Millen** Georgia, SE USA 32°50′N 81°56′W
191 Y5 **Millennium Island** *prev.* Caroline Island, Thornton Island. *atoll* Line Islands, E Kiribati
29 O9 **Miller** South Dakota, N USA 44°31′N 98°59′W
30 K5 **Miller Dam Flowage** ◎ Wisconsin, N USA
39 U12 **Miller, Mount** ▲ Alaska, USA 60°29′N 142°16′W
126 L10 **Millerovo** Rostovskaya Oblast', SW Russian Federation 48°57′N 40°26′E
37 N17 **Miller Peak** ▲ Arizona, SW USA 31°23′N 110°17′W
31 T12 **Millersburg** Ohio, N USA 40°33′N 81°55′W
18 G15 **Millersburg** Pennsylvania, NE USA 40°31′N 76°56′W
185 D23 **Millers Flat** Otago, South Island, New Zealand 45°42′S 169°25′E
25 Q8 **Millersview** Texas, SW USA 31°26′N 99°44′W
106 B10 **Millesimo** Piemonte, NE Italy 44°24′N 08°09′E
12 C12 **Milles Lacs, Lac des** ◎ Ontario, SW Canada
25 Q13 **Millett** Texas, SW USA 28°33′N 99°10′W
103 N11 **Millevaches, Plateau de** *plateau* C France
182 K12 **Millicent** South Australia 37°29′S 140°01′E
98 M13 **Millingen aan den Rijn** Gelderland, SE Netherlands 51°52′N 06°02′E
20 E10 **Millington** Tennessee, S USA 35°20′N 89°54′W
19 R4 **Millinocket** Maine, NE USA 45°38′N 68°45′W
19 R4 **Millinocket Lake** ◎ Maine, NE USA
195 Z11 **Mill Island** *island* Antarctica
183 T3 **Millmerran** Queensland, E Australia 27°53′S 151°15′E
109 R9 **Millstatt** Kärnten, S Austria 46°45′N 13°36′E
97 B19 **Milltown Malbay** *Ir.* Sráid na Cathrach. W Ireland 52°51′N 09°23′W
18 J17 **Millville** New Jersey, NE USA 39°24′N 75°01′W
27 S13 **Millwood Lake** ⊠ Arkansas, C USA
Milne Bank *see* Milne Seamounts
186 G10 **Milne Bay** ◐ *province* SE Papua New Guinea
64 J8 **Milne Seamounts** *var.* Milne Bank. *undersea feature* N Atlantic Ocean
29 Q6 **Milnor** North Dakota, N USA 46°15′N 97°27′W
19 R5 **Milo** Maine, NE USA 45°15′N 69°01′W
115 I22 **Mílos** *island* Kykládes, Greece, Aegean Sea
Mílos *see* Pláka
110 H11 **Miłosław** Wielkopolskie, C Poland 52°13′N 17°28′E
113 K19 **Milot** *var.* Miloti. Lezhë, C Albania 41°42′N 19°43′E
Miloti *see* Milot
117 Z5 **Milove** Luhans'ka Oblast', E Ukraine 49°22′N 40°09′E
Milovidy *see* Milavidy
182 L4 **Milparinka** New South Wales, SE Australia 29°48′S 141°57′E
35 N9 **Milpitas** California, W USA 37°25′N 121°54′W
Mil'skaya Ravnina/ Mil'skaya Step' *see* Mil Düzü
14 G15 **Milton** Ontario, S Canada 43°31′N 79°53′W
185 E24 **Milton** Otago, South Island, New Zealand 46°08′S 169°59′E
21 Y4 **Milton** Delaware, NE USA 38°48′N 75°21′W
23 P8 **Milton** Florida, SE USA 30°37′N 87°02′W
18 G14 **Milton** Pennsylvania, NE USA 41°01′N 76°49′W
18 L7 **Milton** Vermont, NE USA 44°37′N 73°04′W
32 K11 **Milton-Freewater** Oregon, NW USA 45°54′N 118°24′W
97 N21 **Milton Keynes** SE England, United Kingdom 52°N 00°43′W
27 N3 **Miltonvale** Kansas, C USA 39°21′N 97°27′W
161 N10 **Miluo** Hunan, S China 28°52′N 113°00′E
30 M9 **Milwaukee** Wisconsin, N USA 43°03′N 87°56′W
Milyang *see* Miryang
Mimatum *see* Mende
37 Q15 **Mimbres Mountains** ▲▲ New Mexico, SW USA
182 D2 **Mimili** South Australia 27°01′S 132°33′E
102 J14 **Mimizan** Landes, SW France 44°12′N 01°12′W
Mimmaya *see* Minmaya
79 E19 **Mimongo** Ngounié, C Gabon 01°36′S 11°44′E
Min *see* Fujian
35 T7 **Mina** Nevada, W USA 38°23′N 118°07′W
143 S14 **Mīnāb** Hormozgān, SE Iran 27°08′N 57°02′E
Mīnā Baranīs *see* Baranice
149 R9 **Mīna Bāzār** Baluchistān, SW Pakistan 30°58′N 69°11′E
Minami-Awaji *see* Nandan
165 X17 **Minami-Iō-jima** *Eng.* San Augustine. *island* SE Japan
165 R5 **Minami-Kayabe** Hokkaidō, NE Japan 41°54′N 140°58′E
Minami-Satsuma *see* Kaseda
164 C17 **Minamitane** Kagoshima, Tanega-shima, SW Japan 30°23′N 130°54′E
Minami Tori Shima *see* Marcus Island
Min'an *see* Longshan
62 J4 **Mina Pirquitas** Jujuy, NW Argentina 22°48′S 66°24′W
173 O3 **Mīnā' Qābūs** NE Oman
61 F19 **Minas** Lavalleja, S Uruguay 34°20′S 55°15′W
13 P15 **Minas Basin** *bay* Nova Scotia, SE Canada
61 F17 **Minas de Corrales** Rivera, NE Uruguay 31°35′S 55°20′W
44 A5 **Minas de Matahambre** Pinar del Río, W Cuba 22°34′N 83°57′W
104 J13 **Minas de Ríotinto** Andalucía, S Spain 37°40′N 06°36′W
60 K7 **Minas Gerais** *off.* Estado de Minas Gerais. ◐ *state* E Brazil
Minas Gerais, Estado de *see* Minas Gerais
42 E5 **Minas, Sierra de las** ▲▲ E Guatemala
41 T15 **Minatitlán** Veracruz-Llave, E Mexico 17°59′N 94°32′W
166 L6 **Minbu** Magway, W Burma (Myanmar) 20°09′N 94°52′E
149 V10 **Minchinābād** Punjab, E Pakistan 30°10′N 73°40′E
63 G17 **Minchinmávida, Volcán** ⛰ S Chile 42°51′S 72°23′W
96 G7 **Minch, The** *var.* North Minch. *strait* NW Scotland, United Kingdom
106 F8 **Mincio** *anc.* Mincius. ≈ N Italy
Mincius *see* Mincio
26 M11 **Minco** Oklahoma, C USA 35°18′N 97°56′W
171 Q7 **Mindanao** *island* S Philippines
Mindanao Sea *see* Bohol Sea
101 J23 **Mindel** ≈ S Germany
101 J23 **Mindelheim** Bayern, S Germany 48°03′N 10°30′E
Mindello *see* Mindelo
76 C9 **Mindelo** *var.* Mindello; *prev.* Porto Grande. São Vicente, N Cape Verde 16°54′N 25°01′W
14 I13 **Minden** Ontario, SE Canada 44°54′N 78°41′W
100 H13 **Minden** *anc.* Minthun. Nordrhein-Westfalen, NW Germany 52°18′N 08°55′E
22 G5 **Minden** Louisiana, S USA 32°37′N 93°17′W
29 O16 **Minden** Nebraska, C USA 40°30′N 98°57′W
35 Q6 **Minden** Nevada, W USA 38°58′N 119°47′W
182 L8 **Mindona Lake** *seasonal lake* New South Wales, SE Australia
171 O4 **Mindoro** *island* N Philippines
171 N5 **Mindoro Strait** *strait* W Philippines
159 S9 **Mine** Gansu, N China
97 J23 **Minehead** SW England, United Kingdom 51°13′N 03°29′W
97 E21 **Mine Head** *Ir.* Mionn Ard. *headland* S Ireland 51°58′N 07°36′W
59 J19 **Mineiros** Goiás, C Brazil 17°34′S 52°33′W
25 V6 **Mineola** Texas, SW USA 32°39′N 95°29′W
25 S13 **Mineral** Texas, SW USA 28°32′N 97°54′W
127 N15 **Mineral'nyye Vody** Stavropol'skiy Kray, SW Russian Federation 44°13′N 43°06′E
30 K9 **Mineral Point** Wisconsin, N USA 42°54′N 90°09′W
25 S6 **Mineral Wells** Texas, SW USA 32°48′N 98°06′W
36 K6 **Minersville** Utah, W USA 38°12′N 112°56′W
31 U12 **Minerva** Ohio, N USA 40°43′N 81°06′W
107 N17 **Minervino Murge** Puglia, SE Italy 41°06′N 16°05′E
103 O16 **Minervois** *physical region* S France
158 I10 **Minfeng** *var.* Niya. Xinjiang Uygur Zizhiqu, NW China 37°07′N 82°43′E
79 O25 **Minga** Katanga, SE Dem. Rep. Congo 11°06′S 27°57′E
137 W11 **Mingäçevir** *Rus.* Mingechaur, Mingechevir. C Azerbaijan 40°46′N 47°02′E
137 W11 **Mingäçevir Su Anbarı** *Rus.* Mingechaurskoye Vodokhranilishche, Mingechevirskoye Vodokhranilishche. ⊠ NW Azerbaijan
166 L8 **Mingaladon** ✈ (Yangon) Yangon, SW Burma (Myanmar) 16°55′N 96°11′E
13 P11 **Mingan** Québec, E Canada 50°19′N 64°02′W
146 K8 **Mingbuloq** *Rus.* Mynbulak. Navoiy Viloyati, N Uzbekistan 42°18′N 62°53′E
146 K9 **Mingbuloq Botig'i** *Rus.* Vpadina Mynbulak. *depression* N Uzbekistan
Mingechaur/Mingechevir *see* Mingäçevir
Mingechaurskoye Vodokhranilishche/ Mingechevirskoye Vodokhranilishche *see* Mingäçevir Su Anbarı
161 Q7 **Mingguang** *prev.* Jiashan. Anhui, SE China 32°45′N 117°59′E
166 L4 **Mingin** Sagaing, C Burma (Myanmar) 22°51′N 94°30′E
105 Q10 **Minglanilla** Castilla-La Mancha, C Spain 39°32′N 01°36′W
31 V13 **Mingo Junction** Ohio, N USA 40°19′N 80°36′W
Mingora *see* Saidu Sharif
163 V7 **Mingshui** Heilongjiang, NE China 47°10′N 125°53′E
Mingtekl Daban *see* Mintaka Pass
Mingu *see* Zhenfeng
83 Q14 **Minguri** Nampula, NE Mozambique 14°30′S 40°37′E
Mingzhou *see* Suide
159 U10 **Minhe** *var.* Chuankou; *prev.* Minhe Huizu Tuzu Zizhixian, Shangchuankou. Qinghai, C China 36°21′N 102°40′E
Minhe Huizu Tuzu Zizhixian *see* Minhe
166 L6 **Minhla** Magway, W Burma (Myanmar) 19°58′N 95°03′E
167 S14 **Minh Lương** Kiên Giang, S Vietnam 09°52′N 105°10′E
104 G5 **Minho** *former province* N Portugal
104 G5 **Minho, Rio** *Sp.* Miño. ≈ Portugal/Spain *see also* Miño
Minho, Rio *see* Miño
155 C24 **Minicoy Island** *island* SW India
33 P15 **Minidoka** Idaho, NW USA 42°45′N 113°29′W
118 C11 **Minija** ≈ W Lithuania
180 G9 **Minilya** Western Australia 23°45′S 114°03′E
14 E8 **Minisinakwa Lake** ◎ Ontario, S Canada
45 T12 **Ministre Point** *headland* S Saint Lucia 13°42′N 60°57′W
11 V15 **Minitonas** Manitoba, S Canada 52°07′N 101°02′W
Minius *see* Miño
161 R12 **Min Jiang** ≈ SE China
160 H10 **Min Jiang** ≈ C China
182 H9 **Minlaton** South Australia 34°52′S 137°33′E
159 S9 **Minle** *var.* Hongshui. Gansu, N China 38°15′N 100°36′E
165 Q6 **Minmaya** *var.* Mimmaya. Aomori, Honshū, C Japan 41°10′N 140°24′E
77 U14 **Minna** Niger, C Nigeria 09°33′N 06°33′E
165 P16 **Minna-jima** *island* Sakishima-shotō, SW Japan
27 N4 **Minneapolis** Kansas, C USA 39°08′N 97°43′W
29 U9 **Minneapolis** Minnesota, N USA 44°59′N 93°16′W
29 V8 **Minneapolis-Saint Paul** ✈ Minnesota, N USA 44°53′N 93°13′W
11 W16 **Minnedosa** Manitoba, S Canada 50°14′N 99°50′W
26 J7 **Minneola** Kansas, C USA 37°26′N 100°00′W
29 S7 **Minnesota** *off.* State of Minnesota, *also known as* Gopher State, New England of the West, North Star State. ◐ *state* N USA
29 S9 **Minnesota River** ≈ Minnesota/South Dakota, N USA
29 V9 **Minnetonka** Minnesota, N USA 44°55′N 93°28′W
29 O3 **Minnewaukan** North Dakota, N USA 48°04′N 99°14′W
182 F7 **Minnipa** South Australia 32°52′S 135°07′E
104 H2 **Miño** Galicia, NW Spain 43°21′N 08°12′W
104 G5 **Miño** *var.* Mino, Minius, *Port.* Rio Minho. ≈ Portugal/Spain *see also* Minho, Rio
Miño *see* Minho, Rio
30 L4 **Minocqua** Wisconsin, N USA 45°53′N 89°42′W
30 L12 **Minonk** Illinois, N USA 40°54′N 89°01′W
Minorca *see* Menorca
28 M3 **Minot** North Dakota, N USA 48°15′N 101°19′W
159 U8 **Minqin** Gansu, N China 38°35′N 103°07′E
119 J16 **Minsk** ● (Belarus) Minskaya Voblasts', C Belarus 53°52′N 27°34′E
119 L16 **Minsk** ✈ Minskaya Voblasts', C Belarus 53°52′N 27°58′E
Minskaya Oblast' *see* Minskaya Voblasts'
119 K16 **Minskaya Voblasts'** *prev. Rus.* Minskaya Oblast'. ◐ *province* C Belarus
119 J16 **Minskaya Wzvyshsha** ▲▲ C Belarus
110 N12 **Mińsk Mazowiecki** *var.* Nowo-Minsk. Mazowieckie, C Poland 52°10′N 21°31′E
31 Q13 **Minster** Ohio, N USA 40°23′N 84°22′W
79 F15 **Minta** Centre, C Cameroon 04°34′N 12°54′E
149 W2 **Mintaka Pass** *Chin.* Mingtekl Daban. *pass* China/ Pakistan
115 D20 **Mínthi** ▲▲ S Greece
Minthun *see* Minden
13 O14 **Minto** New Brunswick, SE Canada 46°05′N 66°05′W
10 H6 **Minto** Yukon Territory, W Canada 62°33′N 136°45′W
39 R9 **Minto** Alaska, USA 65°07′N 149°22′W
29 Q3 **Minto** North Dakota, N USA 48°17′N 97°22′W
12 K6 **Minto, Lac** ◎ Québec, C Canada
195 R16 **Minto, Mount** ▲ Antarctica 71°38′S 169°11′E
11 U17 **Minton** Saskatchewan, S Canada 49°10′N 104°33′W
189 R15 **Minto Reef** *atoll* Caroline Islands, C Micronesia
37 R4 **Minturn** Colorado, C USA 39°34′N 106°21′W
107 J16 **Minturno** Lazio, C Italy 41°15′N 13°47′E
122 K13 **Minusinsk** Krasnoyarskiy Kray, S Russian Federation 53°37′N 91°49′E
108 G11 **Minusio** Ticino, S Switzerland 46°11′N 08°47′E
79 E17 **Minvoul** Woleu-Ntem, N Gabon 02°08′N 12°12′E
141 R13 **Minwakh** N Yemen 16°55′N 48°04′E
159 V11 **Minxian** *var.* Min Xian, Minyang. Gansu, C China 34°20′N 104°09′E
Min Xian *see* Minxian
Minya *see* Al Minyā
Minyang *see* Minxian
31 R6 **Mio** Michigan, N USA 44°40′N 84°09′W
Mionn Ard *see* Mine Head
158 L5 **Miquan** Xinjiang Uygur Zizhiqu, NW China 44°04′N 87°40′E
119 I17 **Mir** Hrodzyenskaya Voblasts', W Belarus 53°25′N 26°28′E
106 H8 **Mira** Veneto, NE Italy 45°25′N 12°07′E
12 K15 **Mirabel** *var.* Montreal. ✈ (Montréal) Québec, SE Canada 45°27′N 73°47′W
60 Q8 **Miracema** Rio de Janeiro, SE Brazil 21°24′S 42°10′W
54 G9 **Miraflores** Boyacá, C Colombia 05°07′N 73°09′W
40 G10 **Miraflores** Baja California Sur, NW Mexico 23°24′N 109°45′W
44 L9 **Miragoâne** S Haiti 18°25′N 73°07′W
155 E16 **Miraj** Mahārāshtra, W India 16°51′N 74°42′E
61 E23 **Miramar** Buenos Aires, E Argentina 38°15′S 57°50′W
103 R15 **Miramas** Bouches-du-Rhône, SE France 43°33′N 05°02′E
102 K12 **Mirambeau** Charente-Maritime, W France 45°23′N 00°33′W
102 L13 **Miramont-de-Guyenne** Lot-et-Garonne, SW France 44°34′N 00°20′E
115 L25 **Mirampéllou Kólpos** *gulf* Kríti, Greece, E Mediterranean Sea
158 L8 **Miran** Xinjiang Uygur Zizhiqu, NW China 39°13′N 88°58′E
54 M5 **Miranda** *off.* Estado Miranda. ◐ *state* N Venezuela
Miranda de Corvo *see* Miranda do Corvo
105 O3 **Miranda de Ebro** La Rioja, N Spain 42°41′N 02°57′W
104 G8 **Miranda do Corvo** *var.* Miranda de Corvo. Coimbra, N Portugal 40°05′N 08°20′W
104 J6 **Miranda do Douro** Bragança, N Portugal 41°30′N 06°16′W
Miranda, Estado *see* Miranda
102 L15 **Mirande** Gers, S France 43°31′N 00°25′E
104 I6 **Mirandela** Bragança, N Portugal 41°28′N 07°10′W
25 R15 **Mirando City** Texas, SW USA 27°24′N 99°00′W
106 G9 **Mirandola** Emilia-Romagna, N Italy 44°52′N 11°04′E
60 I8 **Mirandópolis** São Paulo, S Brazil 21°10′S 51°03′W
104 G13 **Mira, Rio** ≈ S Portugal
60 K8 **Mirassol** São Paulo, S Brazil 20°50′S 49°30′W
104 J3 **Miravalles** ▲ NW Spain 42°52′N 06°45′W
42 L12 **Miravalles, Volcán** ⛰ NW Costa Rica 10°43′N 85°07′W
141 W13 **Mirbāṭ** *var.* Marbat. S Oman 17°03′N 54°44′E
44 M9 **Mirebalais** C Haiti 18°51′N 72°08′W
103 T6 **Mirecourt** Vosges, NE France 48°19′N 06°04′E
103 N16 **Mirepoix** Ariège, S France 43°05′N 01°51′E
Mirgorod *see* Myrhorod
139 W10 **Mīr Ḩājī Khalīl** Wāsiţ, E Iraq 32°11′N 46°19′E
169 T8 **Miri** Sarawak, East Malaysia 04°23′N 113°59′E
77 W12 **Miria** Zinder, S Niger 13°39′N 09°15′E
182 F5 **Mirikata** South Australia 29°56′S 135°13′E
54 K4 **Mirimire** Falcón, N Venezuela 11°14′N 68°39′W
61 H18 **Mirim Lagoon** *var.* Lake Mirim, *Sp.* Laguna Merín. *lagoon* Brazil/Uruguay
Mirim, Lake *see* Mirim Lagoon
Mírina *see* Mýrina
172 H14 **Miringoni** Mohéli, S Comoros 12°17′S 93°39′E
143 W11 **Mīrjāveh** Sīstān va Balūchestān, SE Iran 29°04′N 61°24′E
195 Z9 **Mirny** *Russian research station* Antarctica 66°25′S 93°09′E
124 M10 **Mirnyy** Arkhangel'skaya Oblast', NW Russian Federation 62°50′N 40°20′E
123 O10 **Mirnyy** Respublika Sakha (Yakutiya), NE Russian Federation 62°30′N 113°58′E
Mironovka *see* Myronivka
110 F9 **Mirosławiec** Zachodnio-pomorskie, NW Poland 53°21′N 16°04′E
Mirovo *see* Vrattsa
100 N10 **Mirow** Mecklenburg-Vorpommern, N Germany 53°16′N 12°48′E
152 G6 **Mīrpur** Jammu and Kashmir, NW India 33°06′N 73°49′E
Mīrpur *see* New Mīrpur
149 P17 **Mīrpur Batoro** Sind, SE Pakistan 24°40′N 68°15′E
149 Q16 **Mīrpur Khās** Sind, SE Pakistan 25°31′N 69°01′E
149 P17 **Mīrpur Sakro** Sind, SE Pakistan 24°32′N 67°38′E
143 T14 **Mīr Shahdād** Hormozgān, S Iran 26°15′N 58°29′E
Mirtoan Sea *see* Mirtóo Pélagos
115 G21 **Mirtóo Pélagos** *Eng.* Mirtoan Sea; *anc.* Myrtoum Mare. *sea* S Greece
163 Z16 **Miryang** *var.* Milyang, *Jap.* Mitsuō. SE South Korea 35°30′N 128°46′E
Mirzachirla *see* Murzechirla
164 E14 **Misaki** Ehime, Shikoku, SW Japan 33°22′N 132°04′E
41 Q13 **Misantla** Veracruz-Llave, E Mexico 19°54′N 96°51′W
165 R7 **Misawa** Aomori, Honshū, C Japan 40°42′N 141°26′E
57 G14 **Mishagua, Río** ≈ C Peru
163 Z8 **Mishan** Heilongjiang, NE China 45°30′N 131°53′E
31 O11 **Mishawaka** Indiana, N USA 41°40′N 86°10′W
39 N6 **Misheguk Mountain** ▲ Alaska, USA 68°13′N 161°11′W
165 N14 **Mishima** *var.* Misima. Shizuoka, Honshū, S Japan 35°08′N 138°54′E
164 E12 **Mi-shima** *island* SW Japan
127 V4 **Mishkino** Respublika Bashkortostan, W Russian Federation 55°31′N 55°57′E
153 Y10 **Mishmi Hills** *hill range* NE India
161 N11 **Mi Shui** ≈ S China
Misiaf *see* Maşyāf
107 J23 **Misilmeri** Sicilia, Italy, C Mediterranean Sea 38°03′N 13°27′E
Misima *see* Mishima
14 C7 **Missinaibi Lake** ◎ Ontario, S Canada
Misión de Guana *see* Guana
60 F13 **Misiones** *off.* Provincia de Misiones. ◐ *province* NE Argentina
62 P8 **Misiones** *off.* Departamento de las Misiones. ◐ *department* S Paraguay
Misiones, Departamento de las *see* Misiones
Misiones, Provincia de *see* Misiones
Misión San Fernando *see* San Fernando
Miskin *see* Maskin
Miskito Coast *see* La Mosquitia
43 O7 **Miskitos, Cayos** *island group* NE Nicaragua
111 M21 **Miskolc** Borsod-Abaúj-Zemplén, NE Hungary 48°05′N 20°46′E
171 T12 **Misool, Pulau** *island* Maluku, E Indonesia
Misox *see* Mesocco
29 Y3 **Misquah Hills** *hill range* Minnesota, N USA
75 P7 **Mişrātah** *var.* Misurata. NW Libya 32°23′N 15°06′E
75 P7 **Mişrātah, Râs** *headland* N Libya 32°22′N 15°16′E
14 C7 **Missanabie** Ontario, S Canada 48°18′N 84°04′W
58 E10 **Missão Catrimani** Roraima, N Brazil 01°26′N 62°05′W
14 D6 **Missinaibi** ≈ Ontario, S Canada
11 T13 **Missinipe** Saskatchewan, C Canada 55°36′N 104°45′W
28 M11 **Mission** South Dakota, N USA 43°16′N 100°38′W
25 S17 **Mission** Texas, SW USA 26°13′N 98°19′W
12 F10 **Missisa Lake** ◎ Ontario, C Canada
18 M6 **Missisquoi Bay** *lake bay* Canada/USA
14 C10 **Missisagi** ≈ Ontario, S Canada
14 G15 **Mississauga** Ontario, S Canada 43°38′N 79°36′W
31 P12 **Mississinewa Lake** ⊠ Indiana, N USA
31 P12 **Mississinewa River** ≈ Indiana/Ohio, N USA
22 K4 **Mississippi** *off.* State of Mississippi, *also known as* Bayou State, Magnolia State. ◐ *state* SE USA
14 K13 **Mississippi** ≈ Ontario, SE Canada
47 N1 **Mississippi Fan** *undersea feature* N Gulf of Mexico 26°45′N 88°30′W
14 L13 **Mississippi Lake** ◎ Ontario, SE Canada
22 M10 **Mississippi Delta** *delta* Louisiana, S USA
0 J11 **Mississippi River** ≈ C USA
22 M9 **Mississippi Sound** *sound* Alabama/Mississippi, S USA
33 P9 **Missoula** Montana, NW USA 46°54′N 114°03′W
27 T5 **Missouri** *off.* State of Missouri, *also known as* Bullion State, Show Me State. ◐ *state* C USA
25 V11 **Missouri City** Texas, SW USA 29°37′N 95°32′W
0 J10 **Missouri River** ≈ C USA
15 Q6 **Mistassibi** ≈ Québec, SE Canada
15 P6 **Mistassini** ≈ Québec, SE Canada
15 P6 **Mistassini** Québec, SE Canada 48°54′N 72°13′W
12 J11 **Mistassini, Lac** ◎ Québec, SE Canada
109 Y3 **Mistelbach an der Zaya** Niederösterreich, NE Austria 48°34′N 16°33′E
107 L24 **Misterbianco** Sicilia, Italy, C Mediterranean Sea 37°31′N 15°01′E
95 N19 **Misterhult** Kalmar, S Sweden 57°28′N 16°34′E
57 H17 **Misti, Volcán** ⛰ S Peru 16°20′S 71°22′W
Mistras *see* Mystrás
107 K23 **Mistretta** *anc.* Amestratus. Sicilia, Italy, C Mediterranean Sea 37°56′N 14°22′E
164 F12 **Misumi** Shimane, Honshū, SW Japan 34°47′N 132°00′E
Misurata *see* Mişrātah
83 O14 **Mitande** Niassa, N Mozambique 14°06′S 36°03′E
40 J13 **Mita, Punta de** *headland* C Mexico 20°46′N 105°31′W
55 W12 **Mitaraka, Massif du** ▲ NE South America 02°18′N 54°31′W
Mitau *see* Jelgava
181 X9 **Mitchell** Queensland, E Australia 26°29′S 148°00′E
14 E15 **Mitchell** Ontario, S Canada 43°28′N 81°11′W
28 I13 **Mitchell** Nebraska, C USA 41°56′N 103°48′W
32 J12 **Mitchell** Oregon, NW USA 44°34′N 120°09′W
29 P11 **Mitchell** South Dakota, N USA 43°42′N 98°01′W
23 P5 **Mitchell Lake** ⊠ Alabama, S USA
31 P7 **Mitchell, Lake** ◎ Michigan, N USA
21 P9 **Mitchell, Mount** ▲ North Carolina, SE USA 35°46′N 82°16′W
181 V3 **Mitchell River** ≈ Queensland, NE Australia
97 D20 **Mitchelstown** *Ir.* Baile Mhistéala. SW Ireland 52°20′N 08°16′W
14 M9 **Mitchinamécus, Lac** ◎ Québec, SE Canada
Mitèmboni *see* Mitemele, Río
79 D17 **Mitemele, Río** *var.* Mitèmboni, Temboni, Utamboni. ≈ S Equatorial Guinea
149 S12 **Mithān Kot** Punjab, E Pakistan 28°53′N 70°25′E
149 T7 **Mitha Tiwāna** Punjab, E Pakistan 32°18′N 72°08′E
149 R17 **Mithi** Sind, SE Pakistan 24°43′N 69°53′E
Míthimna *see* Míthymna
Mi Tho *see* My Tho
115 L16 **Míthymna** *var.* Míthimna. Lésvos, E Greece 39°20′N 26°12′E
190 L16 **Mitiaro** *island* S Cook Islands
Mitilíni *see* Mytilíni
15 U7 **Mitis** ≈ Québec, SE Canada
41 R16 **Mitla** Oaxaca, SE Mexico 16°56′N 96°19′W
165 P13 **Mito** Ibaraki, Honshū, S Japan 36°21′N 140°26′E
92 N2 **Mitra, Kapp** *headland* W Svalbard 79°07′N 11°11′E
184 M13 **Mitre** ▲ North Island, New Zealand 40°46′S 175°27′E
185 B21 **Mitre Peak** ▲ South Island, New Zealand 44°37′S 167°45′E
39 O15 **Mitrofania Island** *island* Alaska, USA
Mitrovica/Mitrovicë *see* Kosovska Mitrovica, Serbia
Mitrovica/Mitrowitz *see* Sremska Mitrovica, Serbia
113 M16 **Mitrovicë** *Serb.* Mitrovica, Kosovska Mitrovica, Titova Mitrovica. N Kosovo 42°54′N 20°52′E
172 H12 **Mitsamiouli** Grande Comore, NW Comoros 11°22′S 43°19′E
172 I13 **Mitsinjo** Mahajanga, NW Madagascar 16°00′S 45°52′E
80 J9 **Mits'iwa** *var.* Masawa, Massawa. E Eritrea 15°37′N 39°27′E
172 H13 **Mitsoudjé** Grande Comore, NW Comoros
138 F12 **Mitspe Ramon** *prev.* Mizpe Ramon. Southern, S Israel 30°38′N 34°47′E
165 T5 **Mitsuishi** Hokkaidō, NE Japan 42°12′N 142°40′E
165 O11 **Mitsuke** *var.* Mituke. Niigata, Honshū, C Japan 37°30′N 138°54′E
Mitsuō *see* Miryang
164 C12 **Mitsushima** Nagasaki, Tsushima, SW Japan 34°16′N 129°18′E
100 G12 **Mittellandkanal** *canal* NW Germany
108 J7 **Mittelberg** Vorarlberg, NW Austria 47°19′N 10°09′E
Mitteldorf *see* Międzychód
Mittelstadt *see* Baia Sprie
Mitterburg *see* Pazin
109 P7 **Mittersill** Salzburg, NW Austria 47°16′N 12°27′E
101 N16 **Mittweida** Sachsen, E Germany 50°59′N 12°57′E
54 J13 **Mitú** Vaupés, SE Colombia 01°07′N 70°05′W
Mituke *see* Mitsuke
Mitumba, Chaîne des/ Mitumba Range *see* Mitumba, Monts
79 O22 **Mitumba, Monts** *var.* Chaîne des Mitumba, Mitumba Range. ▲▲ E Dem. Rep. Congo
79 N23 **Mitwaba** Katanga, SE Dem. Rep. Congo 08°37′S 27°20′E
79 E18 **Mitzic** Woleu-Ntem, N Gabon 00°48′N 11°30′E
82 K11 **Miueru Wantipa, Lake** ◎ N Zambia
165 N14 **Miura** Kanagawa, Honshū, S Japan 35°08′N 139°37′E
165 Q10 **Miyagi** *off.* Miyagi-ken. ◐ *prefecture* Honshū, C Japan
Miyagi-ken *see* Miyagi
138 M7 **Miyāh, Wādī al** *dry watercourse* E Syria
165 X13 **Miyake** Tōkyō, Miyako-jima, SE Japan 34°35′N 135°33′E
165 Q16 **Miyake-jima** *island* Sakishima-shotō, SW Japan
165 R8 **Miyako** Iwate, Honshū, C Japan 39°39′N 141°57′E
164 D16 **Miyakonojō** *var.* Miyakonzyô. Miyazaki, Kyūshū, SW Japan 31°42′N 131°04′E
Miyakonzyô *see* Miyakonojō
165 Q16 **Miyako-shotō** *island group* SW Japan
144 G11 **Miyaly** Atyrau, W Kazakhstan 48°52′N 53°55′E
Miyāndoāb *see* Mīāndowāb
Miyāneh *see* Mīāneh
Miyang *see* Mile
164 D16 **Miyazaki** Miyazaki, Kyūshū, SW Japan 31°55′N 131°24′E
164 D16 **Miyazaki** *off.* Miyazaki-ken. ◐ *prefecture* Kyūshū, SW Japan
Miyazaki-ken *see* Miyazaki
164 J12 **Miyazu** Kyōto, Honshū, SW Japan 35°33′N 135°12′E
Miyory *see* Myory
164 G12 **Miyoshi** *var.* Miyosi. Hiroshima, Honshū, SW Japan 34°48′N 132°51′E
Miyosi *see* Miyoshi
Miza *see* Mizë
81 H14 **Mīzan Teferī** Southern Nationalities, S Ethiopia 06°57′N 35°30′E
Mizda *see* Mizdah
75 O8 **Mizdah** *var.* Mizda. NW Libya 31°26′N 12°59′E
113 K20 **Mizë** *var.* Miza. Fier, W Albania 40°58′N 19°32′E
97 A22 **Mizen Head** *Ir.* Carn Uí Néid. *headland* SW Ireland 51°26′N 09°50′W
116 H7 **Mizhhir"ya** *Rus.* Mezhgor'ye. Zakarpats'ka Oblast', W Ukraine 48°30′N 23°30′E
160 L4 **Mizhi** Shaanxi, C China 37°50′N 110°03′E
116 K13 **Mizil** Prahova, SE Romania 45°00′N 26°29′E
114 H7 **Miziya** Vratsa, NW Bulgaria 43°42′N 23°52′E
153 W15 **Mizo Hills** *hill range* E India
153 W15 **Mizoram** ◐ *state* NE India
Mizpe Ramon *see* Mitspe Ramon
57 L19 **Mizque** Cochabamba, C Bolivia 17°57′S 65°10′W
57 M19 **Mizque, Río** ≈ C Bolivia
165 Q9 **Mizusawa** *var.* Ôshû. Iwate, Honshû, C Japan 39°10′N 141°07′E
95 M18 **Mjölby** Östergötland, S Sweden 58°19′N 15°10′E
95 G15 **Mjøndalen** Buskerud, S Norway 59°45′N 09°58′E
95 J19 **Mjörn** ◎ S Sweden
94 I13 **Mjøsa** *var.* Mjøsen. ◎ S Norway
Mjøsen *see* Mjøsa
81 G21 **Mkalama** Singida, C Tanzania 04°09′S 34°35′E
83 K13 **Mkata** ≈ C Tanzania
83 K14 **Mkushi** Central, C Zambia 13°40′S 29°26′E
83 L22 **Mkuze** KwaZulu/Natal, E South Africa 27°37′S 32°03′E
81 J22 **Mkwaja** Tanga, E Tanzania 05°42′S 38°48′E
111 D16 **Mladá Boleslav** *Ger.* Jungbunzlau. Středočeský Kraj, N Czech Republic 50°26′N 14°55′E
112 M12 **Mladenovac** Serbia, C Serbia 44°27′N 20°42′E
114 L11 **Mladinovo** Khaskovo, S Bulgaria 41°57′N 26°13′E
113 O17 **Mlado Nagoričane** N FYR Macedonia 42°11′N 21°49′E
Mlanje *see* Mulanje
112 N12 **Mlava** ≈ E Serbia
110 L9 **Mława** Mazowieckie, C Poland 53°07′N 20°23′E
113 G16 **Mljet** *It.* Meleda; *anc.* Melita. *island* S Croatia
116 K4 **Mlyniv** Rivnens'ka Oblast', NW Ukraine 50°31′N 25°36′E
83 I21 **Mmabatho** North-West, N South Africa 25°51′S 25°37′E
83 I19 **Mmashoro** Central, E Botswana 21°56′S 26°39′E
44 J7 **Moa** Holguín, E Cuba 20°42′N 74°57′W
76 J15 **Moa** ≈ Guinea/Sierra Leone
37 O6 **Moab** Utah, W USA 38°35′N 109°34′W
181 V1 **Moa Island** *island* Queensland, NE Australia
187 Y15 **Moala** *island* S Fiji
83 L21 **Moamba** Maputo, SW Mozambique 25°35′S 32°13′E
79 F19 **Moanda** *var.* Mouanda. Haut-Ogooué, SE Gabon 01°31′S 13°07′E
83 M15 **Moatize** Tete, NW Mozambique 16°04′S 33°43′E
79 P22 **Moba** Katanga, E Dem. Rep. Congo 07°03′S 29°52′E
Mobay *see* Montego Bay
79 K15 **Mobaye** Basse-Kotto, S Central African Republic 04°19′N 21°17′E
79 K15 **Mobayi-Mbongo** Equateur, NW Dem. Rep. Congo 04°21′N 21°10′E
25 P2 **Mobeetie** Texas, SW USA 35°33′N 100°25′W
27 U3 **Moberly** Missouri, C USA 39°25′N 92°26′W
23 N8 **Mobile** Alabama, S USA 30°42′N 88°03′W
23 N9 **Mobile Bay** *bay* Alabama, S USA
23 N8 **Mobile River** ≈ Alabama, S USA
29 N8 **Mobridge** South Dakota, N USA 45°32′N 100°25′W
Mobutu Sese Seko, Lac *see* Albert, Lake
45 N8 **Moca** N Dominican Republic 19°26′N 70°33′W
83 Q15 **Moçambique** Nampula, NE Mozambique 15°00′S 40°44′E
Moçâmedes *see* Namibe
167 S6 **Môc Châu** Sơn La, N Vietnam 20°49′N 104°38′E
187 Z15 **Moce** *island* Lau Group, E Fiji
Mocha *see* Al Mukhā
193 T11 **Mocha Fracture Zone** *tectonic feature* SE Pacific Ocean
63 F14 **Mocha, Isla** *island* C Chile
56 C12 **Moche, Río** ≈ W Peru
167 S14 **Môc Hoa** Long An, S Vietnam 10°46′N 105°56′E
83 I20 **Mochudi** Kgatleng, SE Botswana 24°25′S 26°07′E
82 Q13 **Mocimboa da Praia** *var.* Vila de Mocímboa da Praia. Cabo Delgado, N Mozambique 11°17′S 40°21′E
94 L13 **Mockfjärd** Dalarna, C Sweden 60°30′N 14°57′E
21 R9 **Mocksville** North Carolina, SE USA 35°53′N 80°33′W

◆ Country
● Country Capital
◇ Dependent Territory
○ Dependent Territory Capital
◐ Administrative Regions
✈ International Airport
▲ Mountain
▲▲ Mountain Range
⛰ Volcano
≈ River
◎ Lake
⊠ Reservoir

MOCLIPS – MONTICELLO

32 F8 **Moclips** Washington, NW USA *47°11′N 124°13′W*
82 C13 **Môco** ***var.*** Morro de Môco. ▲ W Angola *12°36′S 15°09′E*
54 D13 **Mocoa** Putumayo, SW Colombia *01°07′N 76°38′W*
60 M8 **Mococa** São Paulo, S Brazil *21°30′S 47°00′W*
Môco, Morro de *see* Môco
40 H8 **Mocorito** Sinaloa, C Mexico *25°24′N 107°55′W*
40 J4 **Moctezuma** Chihuahua, N Mexico *30°10′N 106°28′W*
41 N11 **Moctezuma** San Luis Potosí, C Mexico *22°46′N 101°06′W*
40 G4 **Moctezuma** Sonora, NW Mexico *29°50′N 109°40′W*
41 P12 **Moctezuma, Río** ≈ C Mexico
Mó, Cuan *see* Clew Bay
83 O16 **Mocuba** Zambézia, NE Mozambique *16°50′S 37°02′E*
103 U12 **Modane** Savoie, E France *45°14′N 06°41′E*
106 F9 **Modena** ***anc.*** Mutina. Emilia-Romagna, N Italy *44°39′N 10°55′E*
36 I7 **Modena** Utah, W USA *37°46′N 113°54′W*
35 O9 **Modesto** California, W USA *37°38′N 121°02′W*
107 L25 **Modica** ***anc.*** Motyca. Sicilia, Italy, C Mediterranean Sea *36°52′N 14°45′E*
83 J20 **Modimolle** ***prev.*** Nylstroom. Limpopo, NE South Africa *24°39′N 28°23′E*
79 K17 **Modjamboli** Equateur, N Dem. Rep. Congo *02°27′N 22°03′E*
109 X4 **Mödling** Niederösterreich, NE Austria *48°06′N 16°18′E*
Modohn *see* Madona
Modot *see* Tsenhermandal
171 V14 **Modowi** Papua, E Indonesia *04°05′S 134°39′E*
112 I12 **Modračko Jezero** ⊠ NE Bosnia and Herzegovina
112 I10 **Modriča** Republika Srpska, N Bosnia and Herzegovina *44°57′N 18°17′E*
183 O13 **Moe** Victoria, SE Australia *38°11′S 146°18′E*
Moearatewe *see* Muaratewe
Moei, Mae Nam *see* Thaungyin
94 H13 **Moelv** Hedmark, S Norway *60°55′N 10°47′E*
92 I10 **Moen** Troms, N Norway *69°08′N 18°35′E*
Möen *see* Møn, Denmark
Moen *see* Weno, Micronesia
Moena *see* Muna, Pulau
36 M10 **Moenkopi Wash** ≈ Arizona, SW USA
185 F22 **Moeraki Point** *headland* South Island, New Zealand *45°23′S 170°52′E*
99 F16 **Moerbeke** Oost-Vlaanderen, NW Belgium *51°11′N 03°57′E*
99 H14 **Moerdijk** Noord-Brabant, S Netherlands *51°42′N 04°37′E*
Moero, Lac *see* Mweru, Lake
101 D15 **Moers** ***var.*** Mörs. Nordrhein-Westfalen, W Germany *51°27′N 06°36′E*
Moesi *see* Musi, Air
Moeskroen *see* Mouscron
96 J13 **Moffat** S Scotland, United Kingdom *55°29′N 03°36′W*
185 C22 **Moffat Peak** ▲ South Island, New Zealand *44°57′S 168°10′E*
79 N19 **Moga** Sud-Kivu, E Dem. Rep. Congo *02°16′S 26°54′E*
152 H8 **Moga** Punjab, N India *30°49′N 75°13′E*
Mogadiscio/Mogadishu *see* Muqdisho
Mogador *see* Essaouira
104 J6 **Mogadouro** Bragança, N Portugal *41°20′N 06°43′W*
167 N2 **Mogaung** Kachin State, N Burma (Myanmar) *25°20′N 96°54′E*
110 L13 **Mogielnica** Mazowieckie, C Poland *51°40′N 20°42′E*
Mogilëv *see* Mahilyow
Mogilev-Podol'skiy *see* Mohyliv-Podil's'kyy
Mogilëvskaya Oblast' *see* Mahilyowskaya Voblasts'
110 I11 **Mogilno** Kujawsko-pomorskie, C Poland *52°39′N 17°58′E*
60 L9 **Mogi-Mirim** ***var.*** Moji-Mirim. São Paulo, S Brazil *22°26′S 46°55′W*
83 Q15 **Mogincual** Nampula, NE Mozambique *15°33′S 40°28′E*
114 E13 **Moglenítsas** ≈ N Greece
106 H8 **Mogliano Veneto** Veneto, NE Italy *45°34′N 12°14′E*
113 M21 **Moglicë** Korçë, SE Albania *40°43′N 20°22′E*
123 O13 **Mogocha** Chitinskaya Oblast', S Russian Federation *53°39′N 119°47′E*
122 J11 **Mogochin** Tomskaya Oblast', C Russian Federation *57°42′N 83°24′E*
80 F13 **Mogogh** Jonglei, SE Sudan *08°26′N 31°19′E*
171 U12 **Mogoi** Papua, E Indonesia *01°44′S 133°13′E*
166 M4 **Mogok** Mandalay, C Burma (Myanmar) *22°55′N 96°29′E*
37 P14 **Mogollon Mountains** ⛰ New Mexico, SW USA
36 M12 **Mogollon Rim** *cliff* Arizona, SW USA
61 E23 **Mogotes, Punta** *headland* E Argentina *38°03′S 57°31′W*
42 J8 **Mogotón** ▲ NW Nicaragua *13°45′N 86°22′W*
104 I14 **Moguer** Andalucía, S Spain *37°15′N 06°52′W*
111 J26 **Mohács** Baranya, SW Hungary *46°N 18°40′E*
185 C20 **Mohaka** ≈ North Island, New Zealand
28 M2 **Mohall** North Dakota, N USA *48°45′N 101°30′W*
Moḥammadābād *see* Dargaz
143 U12 **Moḥammadābād-e Rīgān** Kermān, SE Iran *28°39′N 59°01′E*
74 F6 **Mohammedia** ***prev.*** Fédala. NW Morocco *33°46′N 07°16′W*
74 F6 **Mohammed V** ✈ (Casablanca) W Morocco *33°07′N 08°28′W*
Mohammerah *see* Khorramshahr
36 H10 **Mohave, Lake** ⊠ Arizona/Nevada, W USA
36 I12 **Mohave Mountains** ⛰ Arizona, SW USA
36 I15 **Mohawk Mountains** ⛰ Arizona, SW USA
18 J10 **Mohawk River** ≈ New York, NE USA
163 T3 **Mohe** ***var.*** Xilinji. Heilongjiang, NE China *53°00′N 122°34′E*
95 L20 **Moheda** Kronoberg, S Sweden *57°00′N 14°34′E*
Mohéli *see* Mwali
152 I11 **Mohendergarh** Haryāna, N India *28°17′N 76°14′E*
38 K12 **Mohican, Cape** *headland* Nunivak Island, Alaska, USA *60°12′N 167°25′W*
Mohn *see* Muhu
101 G15 **Möhne** ≈ W Germany
101 G15 **Möhne-Stausee** ⊠ W Germany
92 P2 **Mohn, Kapp** *headland* NW Svalbard *79°26′N 25°44′E*
197 S14 **Mohns Ridge** *undersea feature* Greenland Sea/Norwegian Sea *72°30′N 05°00′E*
57 I17 **Moho** Puno, SE Peru *15°21′S 69°32′W*
Mohokare *see* Caledon
95 L17 **Moholm** Västra Götaland, S Sweden *58°37′N 14°04′E*
36 J11 **Mohon Peak** ▲ Arizona, SW USA *34°55′N 113°07′W*
81 J23 **Mohoro** Pwani, E Tanzania *08°09′S 39°10′E*
Mohra *see* Moravice
Mohrungen *see* Morąg
116 M7 **Mohyliv-Podil's'kyy** ***Rus.*** Mogilev-Podol'skiy. Vinnyts'ka Oblast', C Ukraine *48°29′N 27°49′E*
95 D17 **Moi** Rogaland, S Norway *58°27′N 06°32′E*
Moili *see* Mwali
116 K11 **Moineşti** ***Hung.*** Mojnest. Bacău, E Romania *46°27′N 26°31′E*
Móinteach Mílic *see* Mountmellick
14 J14 **Moira** ≈ Ontario, SE Canada
92 G13 **Mo i Rana** Nordland, C Norway *66°19′N 14°10′E*
153 X14 **Moirāng** Manipur, NE India *24°29′N 93°45′E*
115 J25 **Moíres** Kríti, Greece, E Mediterranean Sea *35°03′N 24°51′E*
118 H6 **Mõisaküla** ***Ger.*** Moiseküll. Viljandimaa, S Estonia *58°05′N 25°12′E*
Moiseküll *see* Mõisaküla
15 W4 **Moisie** Québec, E Canada *50°12′N 66°06′W*
15 W3 **Moisie** ≈ Québec, SE Canada
102 M14 **Moissac** Tarn-et-Garonne, S France *44°07′N 01°05′E*
78 I13 **Moïssala** Moyen-Chari, S Chad *08°21′N 17°46′E*
55 O7 **Moitaco** Bolívar, E Venezuela *08°00′N 64°22′W*
95 P15 **Möja** Stockholm, C Sweden *59°25′N 18°55′E*
105 Q14 **Mojácar** Andalucía, S Spain *37°09′N 01°50′W*
35 T13 **Mojave** California, W USA *35°03′N 118°10′W*
35 V13 **Mojave Desert** *plain* California, W USA
35 V13 **Mojave River** ≈ California, W USA
Moji-Mirim *see* Mogi-Mirim
113 K15 **Mojkovac** E Montenegro *42°57′N 19°34′E*
Mojnest *see* Moineşti
Mōka *see* Mooka
153 Q13 **Mokāma** ***prev.*** Mokameh, Mukama. Bihār, N India *25°24′N 85°55′E*
79 O25 **Mokambo** Katanga, SE Dem. Rep. Congo *12°23′S 28°21′E*
Mokameh *see* Mokāma
38 D9 **Mōkapu Point** ***var.*** Mokapu Point. *headland* O'ahu, Hawai'i, USA *21°27′N 157°43′W*
184 L9 **Mokau** Waikato, North Island, New Zealand *38°42′S 174°37′E*
184 L9 **Mokau** ≈ North Island, New Zealand
35 P7 **Mokelumne River** ≈ California, W USA
83 J23 **Mokhotlong** NE Lesotho *29°19′S 29°06′E*
Mokil Atoll *see* Mwokil Atoll
95 N14 **Möklinta** Västmanland, C Sweden *60°04′N 16°34′E*
184 L4 **Mokohinau Islands** *island group* N New Zealand
153 X12 **Mokokchūng** Nāgāland, NE India *26°20′N 94°30′E*
78 F12 **Mokolo** Extrême-Nord, N Cameroon *10°49′N 13°54′E*
83 J20 **Mokopane** ***prev.*** Potgietersrus. Limpopo, NE South Africa *24°09′S 28°58′E*
185 D24 **Mokoreta** ≈ South Island, New Zealand
163 X17 **Mokp'o** ***Jap.*** Moppo. SW South Korea *34°50′N 126°26′E*
113 L16 **Mokra Gora** ⛰ S Serbia
Mokrany *see* Makrany
127 O5 **Moksha** ≈ W Russian Federation
127 O6 **Mokshan** Penzenskaya Oblast', W Russian Federation *53°26′N 44°38′E*
143 X12 **Mok Sukhteh-ye Pāyīn** Sīstān va Balūchestān, SE Iran
Moktama *see* Martaban
77 T14 **Mokwa** Niger, W Nigeria *09°19′N 05°01′E*
99 J16 **Mol** ***prev.*** Moll. Antwerpen, N Belgium *51°11′N 05°07′E*
107 O17 **Mola di Bari** Puglia, SE Italy *41°03′N 17°05′E*
Molai *see* Moláoi
41 P13 **Molango** Hidalgo, C Mexico *20°48′N 98°44′W*
115 F22 **Moláoi** ***var.*** Molai. Pelopónnisos, S Greece *36°48′N 22°51′E*
41 Z12 **Molas del Norte, Punta** ***var.*** Punta Molas. *headland* SE Mexico *20°34′N 86°43′W*
Molas, Punta *see* Molas del Norte, Punta
105 R11 **Molatón** ▲ C Spain *38°58′N 01°19′W*
97 K18 **Mold** NE Wales, United Kingdom *53°10′N 03°08′W*
Moldau *see* Vltava, Czech Republic
Moldau *see* Moldova
Moldavia *see* Moldova
Moldavian SSR/ Moldavskaya SSR *see* Moldova
94 E9 **Molde** Møre og Romsdal, S Norway *62°44′N 07°08′E*
Moldotau, Khrebet *see* Moldo-Too, Khrebet
147 V9 **Moldo-Too, Khrebet** ***prev.*** Khrebet Moldotau. ⛰ C Kyrgyzstan
116 L9 **Moldova** ***off.*** Republic of Moldova, ***var.*** Moldavia; ***prev.*** Moldavian SSR, ***Rus.*** Moldavskaya SSR. ◆ *republic* SE Europe
116 K9 **Moldova** ***Eng.*** Moldavia, ***Ger.*** Moldau. *former province* NE Romania
116 K9 **Moldova** ≈ N Romania
116 F13 **Moldova Nouă** ***Ger.*** Neumoldowa, ***Hung.*** Újmoldova. Caraş-Severin, SW Romania *44°45′N 21°39′E*
Moldova, Republic of *see* Moldova
116 F13 **Moldova Veche** ***Ger.*** Altmoldowa, ***Hung.*** Ómoldova. Caraş-Severin, SW Romania *44°45′N 21°13′E*
Moldoveanul *see* Vârful Moldoveanu
83 I20 **Molepolole** Kweneng, SE Botswana *24°25′S 25°30′E*
44 L8 **Môle-St-Nicolas** NW Haiti *19°46′N 73°19′W*
118 H13 **Molėtai** Utena, E Lithuania *55°14′N 25°25′E*
107 O17 **Molfetta** Puglia, SE Italy *41°12′N 16°35′E*
171 P11 **Molibagu** Sulawesi, N Indonesia *0°25′N 123°57′E*
62 G12 **Molina** Maule, C Chile *35°06′S 71°18′W*
105 Q7 **Molina de Aragón** Castilla-La Mancha, C Spain *40°50′N 01°54′W*
105 R13 **Molina de Segura** Murcia, SE Spain *38°03′N 01°11′W*
30 J11 **Moline** Illinois, N USA *41°30′N 90°31′W*
27 P7 **Moline** Kansas, C USA *37°21′N 96°18′W*
79 P23 **Moliro** Katanga, SE Dem. Rep. Congo *08°11′S 30°31′E*
107 K16 **Molise** ◈ *region* S Italy
95 K15 **Molkom** Värmland, C Sweden *59°36′N 13°43′E*
109 Q9 **Möll** ≈ S Austria
Moll *see* Mol
146 I14 **Mollanepes Adyndaky** ***Rus.*** Imeni Mollanepesa. Mary Welaýaty, S Turkmenistan *37°36′N 61°54′E*
95 J22 **Mölle** Skåne, S Sweden *56°15′N 12°19′E*
57 H18 **Mollendo** Arequipa, SW Peru *17°02′S 72°01′W*
105 U5 **Mollerussa** Cataluña, NE Spain *41°37′N 00°53′E*
108 H8 **Mollis** Glarus, NE Switzerland *47°05′N 09°03′E*
95 J19 **Mölndal** Västra Götaland, S Sweden *57°39′N 12°05′E*
95 J19 **Mölnlycke** Västra Götaland, S Sweden *57°39′N 12°09′E*
117 U9 **Molochans'k** ***Rus.*** Molochansk. Zaporiz'ka Oblast', SE Ukraine *47°10′N 35°38′E*
117 U10 **Molochna** ***Rus.*** Molochnaya. ≈ S Ukraine
Molochnaya *see* Molochna
117 U10 **Molochnyy Lyman** *bay* N Black Sea
Molodechno/Molodeczno *see* Maladzyechna
195 V3 **Molodezhnaya** *Russian research station* Antarctica *67°33′S 46°12′E*
124 J14 **Mologa** ≈ NW Russian Federation
38 E9 **Moloka'i** ***var.*** Molokai. *island* Hawaiian Islands, Hawai'i, USA
175 X3 **Molokai Fracture Zone** *tectonic feature* NE Pacific Ocean
124 K15 **Molokovo** Tverskaya Oblast', W Russian Federation *58°10′N 36°43′E*
125 Q14 **Moloma** ≈ NW Russian Federation
183 R8 **Molong** New South Wales, SE Australia *33°07′S 148°52′E*
83 H21 **Molopo** *seasonal river* Botswana/South Africa
115 F17 **Mólos** Stereá Ellás, C Greece *38°48′N 22°39′E*
171 O11 **Molosipat** Sulawesi, N Indonesia *0°28′N 121°08′E*
Molotov *see* Severodvinsk, Arkhangel'skaya Oblast', Russian Federation
Molotov *see* Perm', Permskaya Oblast', Russian Federation
79 G17 **Moloundou** Est, SE Cameroon *02°03′N 15°14′E*
103 U5 **Molsheim** Bas-Rhin, NE France *48°33′N 07°30′E*
11 X13 **Molson Lake** ◎ Manitoba, C Canada
Moluccas *see* Maluku
171 Q12 **Molucca Sea** ***Ind.*** Laut Maluku. *sea* E Indonesia
Molukken *see* Maluku
83 O15 **Molumbo** Zambézia, N Mozambique *15°33′S 36°19′E*
171 T15 **Molu, Pulau** *island* Maluku, E Indonesia
83 P16 **Moma** Nampula, NE Mozambique *16°42′S 39°12′E*
171 X14 **Momats** ≈ Papua, E Indonesia
42 J11 **Mombacho, Volcán** 🌋 SW Nicaragua *11°49′N 85°58′W*
81 K21 **Mombasa** Coast, SE Kenya *04°04′N 39°40′E*
81 J21 **Mombasa** ✈ Coast, SE Kenya *04°01′S 39°31′E*
Mombetsu *see* Monbetsu
114 J12 **Momchilgrad** ***prev.*** Mastanli. Kŭrdzhali, S Bulgaria *41°33′N 25°25′E*
99 F23 **Momignies** Hainaut, S Belgium *50°02′N 04°10′E*
54 E6 **Momil** Córdoba, NW Colombia *09°15′N 75°40′W*
42 I10 **Momotombo, Volcán** 🌋 W Nicaragua *12°25′N 86°33′W*
56 B5 **Mompiche, Ensenada de** *bay* NW Ecuador
79 K18 **Mompono** Equateur, NW Dem. Rep. Congo *0°11′N 21°31′E*
54 F6 **Mompós** Bolívar, NW Colombia *09°15′N 74°29′W*
95 J24 **Møn** ***prev.*** Möen. *island* SE Denmark
153 Y12 **Mon** Nāgāland, NE India *26°43′N 95°01′E*
36 L4 **Mona** Utah, W USA *39°49′N 111°52′W*
Mona, Canal de la *see* Mona Passage
96 E8 **Monach Islands** *island group* NW Scotland, United Kingdom
103 V14 **Monaco** ***var.*** Monaco-Ville; ***anc.*** Monoecus. ● (Monaco) S Monaco *43°46′N 07°23′E*
103 V14 **Monaco** ***off.*** Principality of Monaco. ◆ *monarchy* W Europe
Monaco *see* München
Monaco Basin *see* Canary Basin
Monaco, Principality of *see* Monaco
Monaco-Ville *see* Monaco
96 I9 **Monadhliath Mountains** ⛰ N Scotland, United Kingdom
55 O6 **Monagas** ***off.*** Estado Monagas. ◈ *state* NE Venezuela
Monagas, Estado *see* Monagas
97 F16 **Monaghan** ***Ir.*** Muineachán. Monaghan, N Ireland *54°15′N 06°58′W*
97 E16 **Monaghan** ***Ir.*** Muineachán. *cultural region* N Ireland
43 S16 **Monagrillo** Herrera, S Panama *08°00′N 80°28′W*
24 L8 **Monahans** Texas, SW USA *31°35′N 102°54′W*
45 Q9 **Mona, Isla** *island* W Puerto Rico
45 Q9 **Mona Passage** ***Sp.*** Canal de la Mona. *channel* Dominican Republic/Puerto Rico
43 O14 **Mona, Punta** *headland* E Costa Rica *09°44′N 82°48′W*
155 K25 **Monaragala** Uva Province, SE Sri Lanka *06°52′N 81°22′E*
33 S9 **Monarch** Montana, NW USA *47°04′N 110°51′W*
10 H14 **Monarch Mountain** ▲ British Columbia, SW Canada *51°59′N 125°56′W*
Monasterio *see* Monesterio
Monasterzyska *see* Monastyrys'ka
Monastir *see* Bitola
Monastyriska *see* Monastyrys'ka
117 O7 **Monastyryshche** Cherkas'ka Oblast', C Ukraine *48°59′N 29°47′E*
116 J6 **Monastyrys'ka** ***Pol.*** Monasterzyska, ***Rus.*** Monastyriska. Ternopil's'ka Oblast', W Ukraine *49°05′N 25°10′E*
79 E15 **Monatélé** Centre, SW Cameroon *04°16′N 11°12′E*
165 U2 **Monbetsu** ***var.*** Mombetsu, Monbetu. Hokkaidō, NE Japan *44°23′N 143°22′E*
Monbetu *see* Monbetsu
106 B8 **Moncalieri** Piemonte, NW Italy *45°N 07°41′E*
104 G4 **Monção** Viana do Castelo, N Portugal *42°03′N 08°29′W*
105 Q5 **Moncayo** ▲ N Spain *41°43′N 01°51′W*
105 Q5 **Moncayo, Sierra del** ⛰ N Spain
124 J4 **Monchegorsk** Murmanskaya Oblast', NW Russian Federation *67°56′N 32°47′E*
101 D15 **Mönchengladbach** ***prev.*** München-Gladbach. Nordrhein-Westfalen, W Germany *51°12′N 06°35′E*
104 F14 **Monchique** Faro, S Portugal *37°19′N 08°33′W*
104 G14 **Monchique, Serra de** ⛰ S Portugal
21 S14 **Moncks Corner** South Carolina, SE USA *33°12′N 80°00′W*
41 N7 **Monclova** Coahuila, NE Mexico *26°55′N 101°25′W*
Moncorvo *see* Torre de Moncorvo
13 P14 **Moncton** New Brunswick, SE Canada *46°04′N 64°50′W*
104 F8 **Mondego, Cabo** *headland* N Portugal *40°10′N 08°58′W*
104 G8 **Mondego, Rio** ≈ N Portugal
104 I2 **Mondoñedo** Galicia, NW Spain *43°25′N 07°22′W*
99 N25 **Mondorf-les-Bains** Grevenmacher, SE Luxembourg *49°30′N 06°16′E*
102 M7 **Mondoubleau** Loir-et-Cher, C France *48°00′N 00°49′E*
106 B9 **Mondovì** Piemonte, NW Italy *44°23′N 07°56′E*
30 J6 **Mondovi** Wisconsin, N USA *44°34′N 91°40′W*
Mondragón *see* Arrasate
107 J17 **Mondragone** Campania, S Italy *41°07′N 13°53′E*
109 R5 **Mondsee** ◎ N Austria
115 G22 **Monemvasiá** ***var.*** Monemvasía. Pelopónnisos, S Greece *36°22′N 23°03′E*
18 B15 **Monessen** Pennsylvania, NE USA *40°07′N 79°51′W*
104 J12 **Monesterio** ***var.*** Monasterio. Extremadura, W Spain *38°05′N 06°16′W*
14 L8 **Monet** Québec, SE Canada *48°09′N 75°37′W*
27 S8 **Monett** Missouri, C USA *36°55′N 93°55′W*
27 X9 **Monette** Arkansas, C USA *35°53′N 90°20′W*
14 G11 **Monetville** Ontario, S Canada *46°08′N 80°24′W*
106 J7 **Monfalcone** Friuli-Venezia Giulia, NE Italy *45°49′N 13°32′E*
104 H10 **Monforte** Portalegre, C Portugal *39°03′N 07°26′W*
104 I4 **Monforte de Lemos** Galicia, NW Spain *42°32′N 07°30′W*
79 L16 **Monga** Orientale, N Dem. Rep. Congo *04°12′N 22°49′E*
81 I24 **Monga** Lindi, SE Tanzania *09°05′S 37°51′E*
81 F15 **Mongalla** Bahr el Gabel, S Sudan *05°12′N 31°42′E*
153 U11 **Mongar** E Bhutan *27°16′N 91°07′E*
167 U6 **Mong Cai** ***var.*** Hai Ninh. Quang Ninh, N Vietnam *21°33′N 107°56′E*
180 I11 **Mongers Lake** *salt lake* Western Australia
186 K8 **Mongga** Kolombangara, NW Solomon Islands *07°51′S 157°00′E*
167 O6 **Möng Hpayak** Shan State, E Burma (Myanmar) *20°56′N 100°00′E*
Monghyr *see* Munger
106 B10 **Mongioie** ▲ NW Italy *44°13′N 07°46′E*
153 T16 **Mongla** ***var.*** Mungla. Khulna, S Bangladesh *22°18′N 89°34′E*
188 C15 **Mongmong** C Guam
167 N6 **Möng Nai** Shan State, E Burma (Myanmar) *20°28′N 97°51′E*
78 I11 **Mongo** Guéra, C Chad *12°12′N 18°40′E*
76 I14 **Mongo** ≈ N Sierra Leone
163 I8 **Mongolia** ***Mong.*** Mongol Uls. ◆ *republic* E Asia
129 V8 **Mongolia, Plateau of** *plateau* E Mongolia
Mongolküre *see* Zhaosu
Mongol Uls *see* Mongolia
79 E17 **Mongomo** E Equatorial Guinea *01°39′N 11°18′E*
162 M7 **Möngönmorīt** ***var.*** Bulag. Töv, C Mongolia *48°09′N 108°33′E*
77 Y12 **Mongonu** ***var.*** Monguno. Borno, NE Nigeria *12°42′N 13°37′E*
Mongora *see* Saidu Sharif
78 K11 **Mongororo** Ouaddaï, SE Chad *12°03′N 22°26′E*
Mongos, Chaîne des *see* Bongo, Massif des
79 I16 **Mongoumba** Lobaye, SW Central African Republic *03°39′N 18°30′E*
Mongrove, Punta *see* Cayacal, Punta
83 G15 **Mongu** Western, W Zambia *15°13′S 23°09′E*
76 I10 **Mônguel** Gorgol, SW Mauritania *16°25′N 13°08′W*
Monguno *see* Mongonu
167 N4 **Möng Yai** Shan State, E Burma (Myanmar) *22°25′N 98°02′E*
167 O5 **Möng Yang** Shan State, E Burma (Myanmar) *21°52′N 99°31′E*
167 N3 **Möng Yu** Shan State, E Burma (Myanmar) *24°00′N 97°57′E*
Mönhbulag *see* Yösöndzüyl
163 O8 **Mönhhaan** ***var.*** Bayasgalant. Sühbaatar, E Mongolia *46°55′N 112°11′E*
162 E7 **Mönhhayrhan** ***var.*** Tsenher. Hovd, W Mongolia *47°07′N 92°04′E*
Mönh Sarĭdag *see* Munku-Sardyk, Gora
186 P9 **Moni** ≈ S Papau New Guinea
115 I15 **Moní Megístis Lávras** *monastery* Kentrikí Makedonía, N Greece
115 F18 **Moní Osíou Loúkas** *monastery* Stereá Ellás, C Greece
54 F9 **Moniquirá** Boyacá, C Colombia *05°54′N 73°35′W*
103 Q12 **Monistrol-sur-Loire** Haute-Loire, C France *45°19′N 04°12′E*
35 V7 **Monitor Range** ⛰ Nevada, W USA
115 I14 **Moní Vatopedíou** *monastery* Kentrikí Makedonía, N Greece
Monkchester *see* Newcastle upon Tyne
83 N14 **Monkey Bay** Southern, SE Malawi *14°09′S 34°53′E*
43 N11 **Monkey Point** ***var.*** Punta Mico, Punte Mono, Punto Mico. *headland* SE Nicaragua *11°37′N 83°39′W*
Monkey River *see* Monkey River Town
42 G3 **Monkey River Town** ***var.*** Monkey River. Toledo, SE Belize *16°22′N 88°29′W*
14 M13 **Monkland** Ontario, SE Canada *45°11′N 74°51′W*
79 J19 **Monkoto** Equateur, NW Dem. Rep. Congo *01°39′S 20°41′E*
97 K21 **Monmouth** ***Wel.*** Trefynwy. SE Wales, United Kingdom *51°50′N 02°43′W*
30 J12 **Monmouth** Illinois, N USA *40°54′N 90°39′W*
32 F12 **Monmouth** Oregon, NW USA *44°51′N 123°13′W*
97 K21 **Monmouth** *cultural region* SE Wales, United Kingdom
98 I10 **Monnickendam** Noord-Holland, C Netherlands *52°28′N 05°02′E*
77 R15 **Mono** ≈ C Togo
Monoecus *see* Monaco
35 R8 **Mono Lake** ◎ California, W USA
115 O23 **Monólithos** Ródos, Dodekánisa, Greece, Aegean Sea *36°08′N 27°45′E*
19 Q12 **Monomoy Island** *island* Massachusetts, NE USA
31 O12 **Monon** Indiana, N USA *40°52′N 86°54′W*
29 Y12 **Monona** Iowa, C USA *43°03′N 91°23′W*
30 L9 **Monona** Wisconsin, N USA *43°03′N 89°18′W*
18 B15 **Monongahela** Pennsylvania, NE USA *40°10′N 79°54′W*
18 B16 **Monongahela River** ≈ NE USA
107 P17 **Monopoli** Puglia, SE Italy *40°57′N 17°18′E*
Mono, Punte *see* Monkey Point
111 K23 **Monor** Pest, C Hungary *47°21′N 18°27′E*
Monostor *see* Beli Manastir
78 K8 **Monou** Borkou-Ennedi-Tibesti, NE Chad *16°22′N 22°15′E*
105 S12 **Monovar** ***Cat.*** Monover. País Valenciano, E Spain *38°26′N 00°50′W*
Monover *see* Monovar
105 R7 **Monreal del Campo** Aragón, NE Spain *40°47′N 01°20′W*
107 I23 **Monreale** Sicilia, Italy, C Mediterranean Sea *38°05′N 13°17′E*
23 T3 **Monroe** Georgia, SE USA *33°47′N 83°42′W*
29 W14 **Monroe** Iowa, C USA *41°31′N 93°06′W*
22 I5 **Monroe** Louisiana, S USA *32°32′N 92°06′W*
31 S10 **Monroe** Michigan, N USA *41°55′N 83°24′W*
18 K13 **Monroe** New York, NE USA *41°18′N 74°09′W*
21 S11 **Monroe** North Carolina, SE USA *35°00′N 80°35′W*
36 L6 **Monroe** Utah, W USA *38°37′N 112°07′W*
32 H7 **Monroe** Washington, NW USA *47°51′N 121°58′W*
30 L9 **Monroe** Wisconsin, N USA *42°35′N 89°39′W*
27 V3 **Monroe City** Missouri, C USA *39°39′N 91°43′W*
31 O15 **Monroe Lake** ⊠ Indiana, N USA
23 O7 **Monroeville** Alabama, S USA *31°31′N 87°19′W*
18 C15 **Monroeville** Pennsylvania, NE USA *40°24′N 79°44′W*
76 J16 **Monrovia** ● (Liberia) W Liberia *06°18′N 10°48′W*
76 J16 **Monrovia** ✈ W Liberia *06°22′N 10°50′W*
105 T7 **Monroyo** Aragón, NE Spain *40°47′N 00°03′W*
99 F20 **Mons** ***Dut.*** Bergen. Hainaut, S Belgium *50°28′N 03°58′E*
104 I8 **Monsanto** Castelo Branco, C Portugal *40°02′N 07°07′W*
106 H8 **Monselice** Veneto, NE Italy *45°15′N 11°47′E*
166 M9 **Mon State** ◈ *state* S Burma (Myanmar)
98 G12 **Monster** Zuid-Holland, W Netherlands *52°01′N 04°10′E*
95 N20 **Mönsterås** Kalmar, S Sweden *57°03′N 16°27′E*
101 F17 **Montabaur** Rheinland-Pfalz, W Germany *50°25′N 07°48′E*
106 G8 **Montagnana** Veneto, NE Italy *45°14′N 11°31′E*
35 N1 **Montague** California, W USA *41°43′N 122°31′W*
25 S5 **Montague** Texas, SW USA *33°40′N 97°44′W*
183 S11 **Montague Island** *island* New South Wales, SE Australia
39 S12 **Montague Island** *island* Alaska, USA
39 S13 **Montague Strait** *strait* N Gulf of Alaska
102 J8 **Montaigu** Vendée, NW France *46°58′N 01°18′W*
Montaigu *see* Scherpenheuvel
105 S7 **Montalbán** Aragón, NE Spain *40°49′N 00°48′W*
106 G13 **Montalcino** Toscana, C Italy *43°01′N 11°34′E*
104 H5 **Montalegre** Vila Real, N Portugal *41°49′N 07°48′W*
114 G8 **Montana** ***prev.*** Ferdinand, Mikhaylovgrad. Montana, NW Bulgaria *43°25′N 23°14′E*
108 D10 **Montana** Valais, SW Switzerland *46°23′N 07°29′E*
39 R11 **Montana** Alaska, USA *62°06′N 150°03′W*
114 G8 **Montana** ◈ *province* NW Bulgaria
33 T9 **Montana** ***off.*** State of Montana, ***also known as*** Mountain State, Treasure State. ◈ *state* NW USA
104 J10 **Montánchez** Extremadura, W Spain *39°15′N 06°07′W*
Montañita *see* La Montañita
15 Q8 **Mont-Apica** Québec, SE Canada *47°57′N 71°24′W*
104 G10 **Montargil** Portalegre, C Portugal *39°05′N 08°10′W*
104 G10 **Montargil, Barragem de** ⊠ C Portugal
103 O7 **Montargis** Loiret, C France *48°N 02°44′E*
103 O4 **Montataire** Oise, N France *49°16′N 02°24′E*
102 M14 **Montauban** Tarn-et-Garonne, S France *44°01′N 01°20′E*
19 N14 **Montauk** Long Island, New York, NE USA *41°01′N 71°58′W*
19 N14 **Montauk Point** *headland* Long Island, New York, NE USA *41°04′N 71°51′W*
103 Q7 **Montbard** Côte d'Or, C France *47°35′N 04°25′E*
103 U7 **Montbéliard** Doubs, E France *47°31′N 06°49′E*
25 W11 **Mont Belvieu** Texas, SW USA *29°51′N 94°53′W*
105 U6 **Montblanc** ***var.*** Montblanch. Cataluña, NE Spain *41°23′N 01°10′E*
Montblanch *see* Montblanc
103 Q11 **Montbrison** Loire, E France *45°37′N 04°04′E*
Montcalm, Lake *see* Dogai Coring
103 Q9 **Montceau-les-Mines** Saône-et-Loire, C France *46°40′N 04°19′E*
103 U12 **Mont Cenis, Col du** *pass* E France
102 K15 **Mont-de-Marsan** Landes, SW France *43°54′N 00°30′W*
103 O3 **Montdidier** Somme, N France *49°39′N 02°35′E*
187 Q17 **Mont-Dore** Province Sud, S New Caledonia *22°18′S 166°34′E*
20 K10 **Monteagle** Tennessee, S USA *35°15′N 85°47′W*
57 M20 **Monteagudo** Chuquisaca, S Bolivia *19°48′S 63°57′W*
41 R16 **Monte Albán** *ruins* Oaxaca, S Mexico
105 R11 **Montealegre del Castillo** Castilla-La Mancha, C Spain *38°48′N 01°18′W*
59 N18 **Monte Azul** Minas Gerais, SE Brazil *15°13′S 42°53′W*
14 M12 **Montebello** Québec, SE Canada *45°40′N 74°56′W*
106 H7 **Montebelluna** Veneto, NE Italy *45°46′N 12°03′E*
60 G13 **Montecarlo** Misiones, NE Argentina *26°38′S 54°45′W*
61 D16 **Monte Caseros** Corrientes, NE Argentina *30°15′S 57°39′W*
60 J13 **Monte Castelo** Santa Catarina, S Brazil *26°34′S 50°12′W*
106 F11 **Montecatini Terme** Toscana, C Italy *43°53′N 10°46′E*
42 H7 **Montecillos, Cordillera de** ⛰ W Honduras
62 I12 **Monte Comén** Mendoza, W Argentina *34°35′S 67°53′W*
44 M8 **Monte Cristi** ***var.*** San Fernando de Monte Cristi. NW Dominican Republic *19°52′N 71°39′W*
58 C13 **Monte Cristo** Amazonas, W Brazil *03°14′S 68°00′W*
107 E14 **Montecristo, Isola di** *island* Archipelago Toscano, C Italy
Monte Croce Carnico, Passo di *see* Plöcken Pass
58 J12 **Monte Dourado** Pará, NE Brazil *0°48′S 52°32′W*
40 L11 **Monte Escobedo** Zacatecas, C Mexico *22°19′N 103°30′W*
106 I13 **Montefalco** Umbria, C Italy *42°54′N 12°40′E*
107 H14 **Montefiascone** Lazio, C Italy *42°33′N 12°01′E*
105 N14 **Montefrío** Andalucía, S Spain *37°19′N 04°00′W*
44 I11 **Montego Bay** ***var.*** Mobay. W Jamaica *18°28′N 77°55′W*
Montego Bay *see* Sangster
104 J8 **Montehermoso** Extremadura, W Spain *40°05′N 06°20′W*
104 F10 **Montejunto, Serra de** ▲ C Portugal *39°10′N 09°01′W*
Monteleone di Calabria *see* Vibo Valentia
54 E7 **Montelíbano** Córdoba, NW Colombia *08°02′N 75°29′W*
103 R13 **Montélimar** ***anc.*** Acunum Acusio, Montilium Adhemari. Drôme, E France *44°33′N 04°45′E*
104 K15 **Montellano** Andalucía, S Spain *37°00′N 05°34′W*
35 Y2 **Montello** Nevada, W USA *41°18′N 114°10′W*
30 L8 **Montello** Wisconsin, N USA *43°47′N 89°20′W*
63 J18 **Montemayor, Meseta de** *plain* SE Argentina
41 O9 **Montemorelos** Nuevo León, NE Mexico *25°10′N 99°52′W*
104 G11 **Montemor-o-Novo** Évora, S Portugal *38°38′N 08°13′W*
104 G8 **Montemor-o-Velho** ***var.*** Montemor-o-Vélho. Coimbra, N Portugal *40°11′N 08°41′W*
Montemor-o-Vélho *see* Montemor-o-Velho
104 H7 **Montemuro, Serra de** ▲ N Portugal *40°59′N 07°59′W*
102 K12 **Montendre** Charente-Maritime, W France *45°17′N 00°24′W*
61 I15 **Montenegro** Rio Grande do Sul, S Brazil *29°40′S 51°32′W*
113 J16 **Montenegro** ***Serb.*** Crna Gora. ◆ *republic* SW Europe
62 G10 **Monte Patria** Coquimbo, N Chile *30°40′S 71°00′W*
45 O9 **Monte Plata** E Dominican Republic *18°50′N 69°47′W*
83 P14 **Montepuez** Cabo Delgado, N Mozambique *13°09′S 39°00′E*
83 P14 **Montepuez** ≈ N Mozambique
106 G13 **Montepulciano** Toscana, C Italy *43°02′N 11°51′E*
62 L6 **Monte Quemado** Santiago del Estero, N Argentina *25°48′S 62°52′W*
103 O6 **Montereau-Faut-Yonne** ***anc.*** Condate. Seine-St-Denis, N France *48°23′N 02°57′E*
35 N11 **Monterey** California, W USA *36°36′N 121°53′W*
20 L9 **Monterey** Tennessee, S USA *36°09′N 85°16′W*
21 T5 **Monterey** Virginia, NE USA *38°24′N 79°36′W*
Monterey *see* Monterrey
35 N10 **Monterey Bay** *bay* California, W USA
54 D6 **Montería** Córdoba, NW Colombia *08°45′N 75°54′W*
57 N18 **Montero** Santa Cruz, C Bolivia *17°20′S 63°15′W*
62 J7 **Monteros** Tucumán, C Argentina *27°12′S 65°30′W*
104 I5 **Monterrei** Galicia, NW Spain *41°56′N 07°27′W*
41 O8 **Monterrey** ***var.*** Monterey. Nuevo León, NE Mexico *25°41′N 100°16′W*
32 F9 **Montesano** Washington, NW USA *46°58′N 123°37′W*
107 M19 **Montesano sulla Marcellana** Campania, S Italy *40°15′N 15°41′E*
107 N16 **Monte Sant' Angelo** Puglia, SE Italy *41°43′N 15°58′E*
59 O16 **Monte Santo** Bahia, E Brazil *10°25′S 39°18′W*
107 D18 **Monte Santu, Capo di** *headland* Sardegna, Italy, C Mediterranean Sea *40°05′N 09°43′E*
59 M19 **Montes Claros** Minas Gerais, SE Brazil *16°45′S 43°52′W*
107 K14 **Montesilvano Marina** Abruzzo, C Italy *42°28′N 14°07′E*
23 P4 **Montevallo** Alabama, S USA *33°06′N 86°51′W*
106 G12 **Montevarchi** Toscana, C Italy *43°32′N 11°34′E*
61 F20 **Montevideo** ● (Uruguay) Montevideo, S Uruguay *34°55′S 56°10′W*
29 S9 **Montevideo** Minnesota, N USA *44°56′N 95°43′W*
37 S7 **Monte Vista** Colorado, C USA *37°33′N 106°08′W*
23 T5 **Montezuma** Georgia, SE USA *32°18′N 84°01′W*
29 W14 **Montezuma** Iowa, C USA *41°35′N 92°31′W*
26 J6 **Montezuma** Kansas, C USA *37°33′N 100°25′W*
103 U12 **Montgenèvre, Col de** *pass* France/Italy
97 K20 **Montgomery** E Wales, United Kingdom *52°38′N 03°05′W*
23 Q5 **Montgomery** *state capital* Alabama, S USA *32°22′N 86°18′W*
29 V9 **Montgomery** Minnesota, N USA *44°26′N 93°34′W*
18 G13 **Montgomery** Pennsylvania, NE USA *41°08′N 76°52′W*
21 Q5 **Montgomery** West Virginia, NE USA *38°07′N 81°19′W*
97 K19 **Montgomery** *cultural region* E Wales, United Kingdom
Montgomery *see* Sāhīwāl
27 V4 **Montgomery City** Missouri, C USA *38°57′N 91°27′W*
35 S8 **Montgomery Pass** *pass* Nevada, W USA
102 K12 **Montguyon** Charente-Maritime, W France *45°12′N 00°13′W*
108 C10 **Monthey** Valais, SW Switzerland *46°15′N 06°56′E*
27 V13 **Monticello** Arkansas, C USA *33°38′N 91°49′W*
23 T4 **Monticello** Florida, SE USA *30°33′N 83°52′W*
23 T8 **Monticello** Georgia, SE USA *33°18′N 83°40′W*
30 M13 **Monticello** Illinois, N USA *40°01′N 88°34′W*
31 O12 **Monticello** Indiana, N USA *40°45′N 86°46′W*

◆ Country
● Country Capital
◇ Dependent Territory
○ Dependent Territory Capital
◈ Administrative Regions
✈ International Airport
▲ Mountain
⛰ Mountain Range
🌋 Volcano
≈ River
◎ Lake
⊠ Reservoir

MONTICELLO – MOUNT PLEASANT

29 Y13 **Monticello** Iowa, C USA *42°14′N 91°11′W*
20 L7 **Monticello** Kentucky, S USA *36°50′N 84°50′W*
29 V8 **Monticello** Minnesota, N USA *45°19′N 93°45′W*
22 K7 **Monticello** Mississippi, S USA *31°33′N 90°06′W*
27 V2 **Monticello** Missouri, C USA *40°07′N 91°42′W*
18 J12 **Monticello** New York, NE USA *41°39′N 74°41′W*
37 O7 **Monticello** Utah, W USA *37°52′N 109°20′W*
106 F8 **Montichiari** Lombardia, N Italy *45°24′N 10°27′E*
102 M12 **Montignac** Dordogne, SW France *45°24′N 00°54′E*
99 G21 **Montignies-le-Tilleul** *var.* Montigny-le-Tilleul. Hainaut, S Belgium *50°22′N 04°23′E*
14 J8 **Montigny, Lac de** ◎ Québec, SE Canada
103 S6 **Montigny-le-Roi** Haute-Marne, N France *48°02′N 05°28′E*
Montigny-le-Tilleul *see* Montignies-le-Tilleul
43 R16 **Montijo** Veraguas, S Panama *07°59′N 80°58′W*
104 F11 **Montijo** Setúbal, W Portugal *38°42′N 08°59′W*
104 J11 **Montijo** Extremadura, W Spain *38°55′N 06°38′W*
Montilium Adhemari *see* Montélimar
104 M13 **Montilla** Andalucía, S Spain *37°36′N 04°39′W*
102 L3 **Montivilliers** Seine-Maritime, N France *49°31′N 00°10′E*
15 U7 **Mont-Joli** Québec, SE Canada *48°36′N 68°14′W*
14 M10 **Mont-Laurier** Québec, SE Canada *46°33′N 75°31′W*
15 X5 **Mont-Louis** Québec, SE Canada *49°15′N 65°46′W*
103 N17 **Mont-Louis** *var.* Mont Louis. Pyrénées-Orientales, S France *42°30′N 02°08′E*
103 O10 **Montluçon** Allier, C France *46°21′N 02°37′E*
15 R10 **Montmagny** Québec, SE Canada *47°00′N 70°31′W*
103 S3 **Montmédy** Meuse, NE France *49°31′N 05°21′E*
103 P5 **Montmirail** Marne, N France *48°53′N 03°31′E*
15 R9 **Montmorency** ~ Québec, SE Canada
102 M10 **Montmorillon** Vienne, W France *46°26′N 00°52′E*
107 J14 **Montorio al Vomano** Abruzzo, C Italy *42°31′N 13°39′E*
104 M13 **Montoro** Andalucía, S Spain *38°00′N 04°21′W*
33 S16 **Montpelier** Idaho, NW USA *42°19′N 111°18′W*
29 P6 **Montpelier** North Dakota, N USA *46°40′N 98°34′W*
18 M7 **Montpelier** *state capital* Vermont, NE USA *44°16′N 72°32′W*
103 Q15 **Montpellier** Hérault, S France *43°37′N 03°52′E*
102 L12 **Montpon-Ménestérol** Dordogne, SW France *45°01′N 00°10′E*
12 K15 **Montréal** *Eng.* Montreal. Québec, SE Canada *45°30′N 73°36′W*
14 G8 **Montreal** ~ Ontario, S Canada
Montreal *see* Mirabel
11 T14 **Montreal Lake** ◎ Saskatchewan, C Canada
14 B9 **Montreal River** Ontario, S Canada *47°13′N 84°36′W*
103 N2 **Montreuil** Pas-de-Calais, N France *50°28′N 01°46′E*
102 K8 **Montreuil-Bellay** Maine-et-Loire, NW France *47°07′N 00°10′W*
108 C10 **Montreux** Vaud, SW Switzerland *46°27′N 06°55′E*
108 B9 **Montricher** Vaud, W Switzerland *46°37′N 06°24′E*
96 K10 **Montrose** E Scotland, United Kingdom *56°43′N 02°29′W*
27 W14 **Montrose** Arkansas, C USA *33°18′N 91°29′W*
37 Q6 **Montrose** Colorado, C USA *38°29′N 107°53′W*
29 Y16 **Montrose** Iowa, C USA *40°31′N 91°24′W*
18 H12 **Montrose** Pennsylvania, NE USA *41°49′N 75°53′W*
21 X5 **Montross** Virginia, NE USA *38°04′N 76°51′W*
15 O12 **Mont-St-Hilaire** Québec, SE Canada *45°34′N 73°10′W*
103 S3 **Mont-St-Martin** Meurthe-et-Moselle, NE France *49°31′N 05°51′E*
45 V10 **Montserrat** *var.* Emerald Isle. ◇ *UK dependent territory* E West Indies
105 V5 **Montserrat** ▲ NE Spain *41°39′N 01°44′E*
104 M7 **Montuenga** Castilla-León, N Spain *41°04′N 04°38′W*
99 M19 **Montzen** Liège, E Belgium *50°42′N 05°59′E*
37 N8 **Monument Valley** *valley* Arizona/Utah, SW USA
166 L4 **Monywa** Sagaing, C Burma (Myanmar) *22°05′N 95°12′E*
106 D7 **Monza** Lombardia, N Italy *45°35′N 09°16′E*
83 J15 **Monze** Southern, S Zambia *16°20′S 27°29′E*
105 T5 **Monzón** Aragón, NE Spain *41°54′N 00°12′E*
25 T9 **Moody** Texas, SW USA *31°18′N 97°21′W*
98 L13 **Mook** Limburg, SE Netherlands *51°45′N 05°52′E*
165 O12 **Mooka** *var.* Môka. Tochigi, Honshū, S Japan *36°27′N 139°59′E*
182 K3 **Moomba** South Australia *28°07′S 140°12′E*
14 G13 **Moon** ~ Ontario, S Canada
Moon *see* Muhu
181 Y10 **Moonie** Queensland, E Australia *27°46′S 150°22′E*
193 O5 **Moonless Mountains** *undersea feature* E Pacific Ocean *30°40′N 140°00′W*
182 L13 **Moonlight Head** *headland* Victoria, SE Australia *38°47′S 143°12′E*
Moon-Sund *see* Väinameri
182 H8 **Moonta** South Australia *34°03′S 137°36′E*
Moor *see* Mór
180 I12 **Moora** Western Australia *30°23′S 116°05′E*
98 H12 **Moordrecht** Zuid-Holland, C Netherlands *51°59′N 04°40′E*
33 T9 **Moore** Montana, NW USA *47°00′N 109°40′W*
27 N11 **Moore** Oklahoma, C USA *35°21′N 97°30′W*
25 R12 **Moore** Texas, SW USA *29°03′N 99°01′W*
191 S10 **Moorea** *island* Îles du Vent, W French Polynesia
21 U3 **Moorefield** West Virginia, NE USA *39°04′N 78°59′W*
23 X14 **Moore Haven** Florida, SE USA *26°49′N 81°05′W*
180 J11 **Moore, Lake** ◎ Western Australia
19 N7 **Moore Reservoir** ⊠ New Hampshire/Vermont, NE USA
44 G1 **Moores Island** *island* N Bahamas
21 R10 **Mooresville** North Carolina, SE USA *35°34′N 80°48′W*
29 R5 **Moorhead** Minnesota, N USA *46°51′N 96°44′W*
22 K4 **Moorhead** Mississippi, S USA *33°27′N 90°30′W*
99 F18 **Moorsel** Oost-Vlaanderen, C Belgium *50°58′N 04°06′E*
99 C18 **Moorslede** West-Vlaanderen, W Belgium *50°53′N 03°03′E*
18 L8 **Moosalamoo, Mount** ▲ Vermont, NE USA *43°55′N 73°03′W*
101 M22 **Moosburg in der Isar** Bayern, SE Germany *48°28′N 11°55′E*
33 S14 **Moose** Wyoming, C USA *43°38′N 110°42′W*
12 H11 **Moose** ~ Ontario, S Canada
12 H10 **Moose Factory** Ontario, S Canada *51°16′N 80°32′W*
19 Q4 **Moosehead Lake** ◎ Maine, NE USA
11 U16 **Moose Jaw** Saskatchewan, S Canada *50°23′N 105°35′W*
11 V14 **Moose Lake** Manitoba, C Canada *53°42′N 100°22′W*
29 W6 **Moose Lake** Minnesota, N USA *46°28′N 92°46′W*
19 P6 **Mooselookmeguntic Lake** ◎ Maine, NE USA
39 R12 **Moose Pass** Alaska, USA *60°28′N 149°21′W*
19 P5 **Moose River** ~ Maine, NE USA
18 J9 **Moose River** ~ New York, NE USA
11 V16 **Moosomin** Saskatchewan, S Canada *50°09′N 101°41′W*
12 H10 **Moosonee** Ontario, SE Canada *51°18′N 80°40′W*
19 N12 **Moosup** Connecticut, NE USA *41°42′N 71°51′W*
83 N16 **Mopeia** Zambézia, NE Mozambique *17°59′S 35°43′E*
83 H18 **Mopipi** Central, C Botswana *21°07′S 24°55′E*
Moppo *see* Mokp'o
77 N11 **Mopti** Mopti, C Mali *14°30′N 04°15′W*
77 O11 **Mopti** ⬖ *region* S Mali
57 H18 **Moquegua** Moquegua, SE Peru *17°07′S 70°55′W*
57 H18 **Moquegua** *off.* Departamento de Moquegua. ⬖ *department* S Peru
Moquegua, Departamento de *see* Moquegua
111 I23 **Mór** *Ger.* Moor. Fejér, C Hungary *47°21′N 18°12′E*
78 G11 **Mora** Extrême-Nord, N Cameroon *11°02′N 14°07′E*
104 G11 **Mora** Évora, S Portugal *38°56′N 08°10′W*
105 N9 **Mora** Castilla-La Mancha, C Spain *39°40′N 03°46′W*
94 L12 **Mora** Dalarna, C Sweden *61°N 14°30′E*
29 V7 **Mora** Minnesota, N USA *45°52′N 93°18′W*
37 T10 **Mora** New Mexico, SW USA *35°56′N 105°16′W*
113 J17 **Morača** ~ S Montenegro
152 K10 **Morādābād** Uttar Pradesh, N India *28°50′N 78°45′E*
105 U6 **Móra d'Ebre** *var.* Mora de Ebro. Cataluña, NE Spain *41°05′N 00°38′E*
Mora de Ebro *see* Móra d'Ebre
105 S8 **Mora de Rubielos** Aragón, NE Spain *40°15′N 00°45′W*
172 H4 **Morafenobe** Mahajanga, W Madagascar *17°49′S 44°54′E*
110 K8 **Morąg** *Ger.* Mohrungen. Warmińsko-Mazurskie, N Poland *53°55′N 19°56′E*
111 L25 **Mórahalom** Csongrád, S Hungary *46°14′N 19°52′E*
105 N11 **Moral de Calatrava** Castilla-La Mancha, C Spain *38°50′N 03°34′W*
63 G19 **Moraleda, Canal** *strait* SE Pacific Ocean
54 J3 **Morales** Bolívar, N Colombia *08°17′N 73°52′W*
54 D12 **Morales** Cauca, SW Colombia *02°46′N 76°44′W*
42 F5 **Morales** Izabal, E Guatemala *15°28′N 88°46′W*
172 J5 **Moramanga** Toamasina, E Madagascar *18°57′S 48°13′E*
27 Q6 **Moran** Kansas, C USA *37°55′N 95°10′W*
25 Q7 **Moran** Texas, SW USA *32°33′N 99°10′W*
181 X7 **Moranbah** Queensland, NE Australia *22°01′S 148°08′E*
44 L13 **Morant Bay** E Jamaica *17°53′N 76°25′W*
96 G10 **Morar, Loch** ◎ N Scotland, United Kingdom
Morata *see* Goodenough Island
105 Q12 **Moratalla** Murcia, SE Spain *38°11′N 01°53′W*
108 C8 **Morat, Lac de** *Ger.* Murtensee. ◎ W Switzerland
84 I11 **Morava** *var.* March. ~ C Europe *see also* March
Morava *see* March
Morava *see* Moravia, Czech Republic
Morava *see* Velika Morava, Serbia
29 W15 **Moravia** Iowa, C USA *40°53′N 92°49′W*
111 F18 **Moravia** *Cz.* Morava, *Ger.* Mähren. *cultural region* E Czech Republic
111 H17 **Moravice** *Ger.* Mohra. ~ NE Czech Republic
116 E12 **Moravița** Timiș, SW Romania *45°15′N 21°17′E*
111 G17 **Moravská Třebová** *Ger.* Mährisch-Trübau. Pardubický Kraj, C Czech Republic *49°47′N 16°40′E*
111 E19 **Moravské Budějovice** *Ger.* Mährisch-Budwitz. Vysočina, C Czech Republic *49°03′N 15°48′E*
111 H17 **Moravskoslezský Kraj** *prev.* Ostravský Kraj. ⬖ *region* E Czech Republic
111 F19 **Moravský Krumlov** *Ger.* Mährisch-Kromau. Jihomoravský Kraj, SE Czech Republic *48°58′N 16°30′E*
96 J8 **Moray** *cultural region* N Scotland, United Kingdom
96 J8 **Moray Firth** *inlet* N Scotland, United Kingdom
42 B10 **Morazán** ⬖ *department* NE El Salvador
154 C10 **Morbi** Gujarāt, W India *22°51′N 70°49′E*
102 G7 **Morbihan** ⬖ *department* NW France
Mörbisch *see* Mörbisch am See
109 Y5 **Mörbisch am See** *var.* Mörbisch. Burgenland, E Austria *47°43′N 16°40′E*
95 N21 **Mörbylånga** Kalmar, S Sweden *56°31′N 16°25′E*
102 J14 **Morcenx** Landes, SW France *44°04′N 00°55′W*
Morcheh Khort *see* Mürcheh Khvort
163 T5 **Mordaga** Nei Mongol Zizhiqu, N China *51°15′N 120°47′E*
11 X17 **Morden** Manitoba, S Canada *49°12′N 98°05′W*
Mordovia *see* Mordoviya, Respublika
127 N5 **Mordoviya, Respublika** *prev.* Mordovskaya ASSR, *Eng.* Mordovia, Mordvinia. ⬖ *autonomous republic* W Russian Federation
126 M7 **Mordovo** Tambovskaya Oblast', W Russian Federation *52°05′N 40°49′E*
Mordovskaya ASSR/ Mordvinia *see* Mordoviya, Respublika
Morea *see* Pelopónnisos
28 K8 **Moreau River** ~ South Dakota, N USA
97 K16 **Morecambe** NW England, United Kingdom *54°04′N 02°53′W*
97 K16 **Morecambe Bay** *inlet* NW England, United Kingdom
183 S4 **Moree** New South Wales, SE Australia *29°29′S 149°53′E*
21 N5 **Morehead** Kentucky, S USA *38°11′N 83°27′W*
21 X11 **Morehead City** North Carolina, SE USA *34°43′N 76°43′W*
27 Y8 **Morehouse** Missouri, C USA *36°51′N 89°41′W*
108 E10 **Mörel** Valais, SW Switzerland *46°22′N 08°03′E*
54 D13 **Morelia** Caquetá, S Colombia *01°30′N 75°43′W*
41 N14 **Morelia** Michoacán, S Mexico *19°40′N 101°11′W*
105 T7 **Morella** País Valenciano, E Spain *40°37′N 00°06′W*
40 I7 **Morelos** Chihuahua, N Mexico *26°37′N 107°37′W*
41 O15 **Morelos** ⬖ *state* S Mexico
154 H7 **Morena** Madhya Pradesh, C India *26°30′N 78°04′E*
104 L12 **Morena, Sierra** ▲▲ S Spain
37 O14 **Morenci** Arizona, SW USA *33°05′N 109°21′W*
31 R11 **Morenci** Michigan, N USA *41°43′N 84°13′W*
116 J13 **Moreni** Dâmbovița, S Romania *44°59′N 25°39′E*
94 D9 **Møre og Romsdal** ⬖ *county* S Norway
10 I14 **Moresby Island** *island* Queen Charlotte Islands, British Columbia, SW Canada
183 W2 **Moreton Island** *island* Queensland, E Australia
103 O3 **Moreuil** Somme, N France *49°47′N 02°28′E*
35 V7 **Morey Peak** ▲ Nevada, W USA *38°40′N 116°16′W*
125 U4 **More-Yu** ~ NW Russian Federation
103 T9 **Morez** Jura, E France *46°33′N 06°01′E*
Morfou Bay/Mórfou, Kólpos *see* Güzelyurt Körfezi
182 J8 **Morgan** South Australia *34°02′S 139°39′E*
23 S7 **Morgan** Georgia, SE USA *31°31′N 84°34′W*
25 S8 **Morgan** Texas, SW USA *32°01′N 97°36′W*
22 J10 **Morgan City** Louisiana, S USA *29°42′N 91°12′W*
20 H6 **Morganfield** Kentucky, S USA *37°41′N 87°55′W*
35 O10 **Morgan Hill** California, W USA *37°05′N 121°38′W*
21 Q9 **Morganton** North Carolina, SE USA *35°44′N 81°43′W*
20 J7 **Morgantown** Kentucky, S USA *37°12′N 86°42′W*
21 S2 **Morgantown** West Virginia, NE USA *39°38′N 79°57′W*
108 B10 **Morges** Vaud, SW Switzerland *46°31′N 06°30′E*
148 M4 **Morghāb, Daryā-ye** *Rus.* Murgab, Murghab, *Turk.* Murgap, Deryasy Murgap. ~ Afghanistan/Turkmenistan *see also* Murgap
Morghāb, Daryā-ye *see* Murgap
96 I9 **Mor, Glen** *var.* Glen Albyn, Great Glen. *valley* N Scotland, United Kingdom
103 T5 **Morhange** Moselle, NE France *48°56′N 06°37′E*
158 M5 **Mori** *var.* Mori Kazak Zizhixian. Xinjiang Uygur Zizhiqu, NW China *43°48′N 90°21′E*
165 R5 **Mori** Hokkaidō, NE Japan *42°04′N 140°36′E*
35 Y6 **Moriah, Mount** ▲ Nevada, W USA *39°16′N 114°10′W*
37 S11 **Moriarty** New Mexico, SW USA *34°59′N 106°03′W*
54 J12 **Morichal** Guaviare, E Colombia *02°09′N 70°35′W*
Mori Kazak Zizhixian *see* Mori
Morin Dawa Daurzu Zizhiqi *see* Nirji
11 Q14 **Morinville** Alberta, SW Canada *53°48′N 113°38′W*
165 R8 **Morioka** Iwate, Honshū, C Japan *39°42′N 141°08′E*
183 T8 **Morisset** New South Wales, SE Australia *33°07′S 151°32′E*
165 Q8 **Moriyoshi-zan** ▲ Honshū, C Japan *39°58′N 140°32′E*
92 K13 **Morjärv** Norrbotten, N Sweden *66°03′N 22°45′E*
127 R3 **Morki** Respublika Mariy El, W Russian Federation *56°27′N 49°01′E*
123 N10 **Morkoka** ~ NE Russian Federation
102 F5 **Morlaix** Finistère, NW France *48°35′N 03°50′W*
95 M20 **Mörlunda** Kalmar, S Sweden *57°19′N 15°52′E*
107 N19 **Mormanno** Calabria, SW Italy *39°54′N 15°58′E*
36 L11 **Mormon Lake** ◎ Arizona, SW USA
35 Y10 **Mormon Peak** ▲ Nevada, W USA *36°59′N 114°25′W*
Mormon State *see* Utah
45 Y5 **Morne-à-l'Eau** Grande Terre, N Guadeloupe *16°20′N 61°31′W*
29 Y15 **Morning Sun** Iowa, C USA *41°06′N 91°15′W*
193 S12 **Mornington Abyssal Plain** *undersea feature* SE Pacific Ocean *50°00′S 90°00′W*
63 F22 **Mornington, Isla** *island* S Chile
181 T4 **Mornington Island** *island* Wellesley Islands, Queensland, N Australia
115 E18 **Mórnos** ~ C Greece
149 P14 **Moro** Sind, SE Pakistan *26°36′N 67°59′E*
32 I11 **Moro** Oregon, NW USA *45°30′N 120°46′W*
186 E8 **Morobe** Morobe, C Papua New Guinea *07°46′S 147°35′E*
186 E8 **Morobe** ⬖ *province* C Papua New Guinea
31 N12 **Morocco** Indiana, N USA *40°57′N 87°27′W*
74 E8 **Morocco** *off.* Kingdom of Morocco, *Ar.* Al Mamlakah. ◆ *monarchy* N Africa
Morocco *see* Marrakech
Morocco, Kingdom of *see* Morocco
81 I22 **Morogoro** Morogoro, E Tanzania *06°49′S 37°40′E*
81 H24 **Morogoro** ⬖ *region* SE Tanzania
171 Q7 **Moro Gulf** *gulf* S Philippines
41 N13 **Moroleón** Guanajuato, C Mexico *20°00′N 101°13′W*
172 H6 **Morombe** Toliara, W Madagascar *21°47′S 43°21′E*
44 G5 **Morón** Ciego de Ávila, C Cuba *22°08′N 78°39′W*
163 N8 **Mörön** Hentiy, C Mongolia *47°21′N 110°21′E*
162 I6 **Mörön** Hövsgöl, N Mongolia *49°39′N 100°08′E*
54 K5 **Morón** Carabobo, N Venezuela *10°29′N 68°11′W*
Morón *see* Morón de la Frontera
56 D8 **Morona, Río** ~ N Peru
56 C8 **Morona Santiago** ⬖ *province* E Ecuador
172 H5 **Morondava** Toliara, W Madagascar *20°19′S 44°17′E*
104 K14 **Morón de la Frontera** *var.* Morón. Andalucía, S Spain *37°07′N 05°27′W*
172 G13 **Moroni** ● (Comoros) Grande Comore, NW Comoros *11°41′S 43°16′E*
171 S10 **Morotai, Pulau** *island* Maluku, E Indonesia
Morotiri *see* Marotiri
81 H17 **Moroto** NE Uganda *02°32′N 34°41′E*
Morozov *see* Bratan
126 M11 **Morozovsk** Rostovskaya Oblast', SW Russian Federation *48°21′N 41°54′E*
97 L14 **Morpeth** N England, United Kingdom *55°10′N 01°41′W*
Morphou *see* Güzelyurt
Morphou Bay *see* Güzelyurt Körfezi
28 I13 **Morrill** Nebraska, C USA *41°57′N 103°55′W*
27 U11 **Morrilton** Arkansas, C USA *35°09′N 92°45′W*
11 Q16 **Morrin** Alberta, SW Canada *51°40′N 112°45′W*
184 M7 **Morrinsville** Waikato, North Island, New Zealand *37°41′S 175°32′E*
11 X16 **Morris** Manitoba, S Canada *49°22′N 97°21′W*
30 M11 **Morris** Illinois, N USA *41°21′N 88°25′W*
29 S8 **Morris** Minnesota, N USA *45°32′N 95°53′W*
14 M13 **Morrisburg** Ontario, SE Canada *44°55′N 75°07′W*
197 R11 **Morris Jesup, Kap** *headland* N Greenland *83°33′N 32°40′W*
182 B1 **Morris, Mount** ▲ South Australia *26°04′S 131°03′E*
30 K10 **Morrison** Illinois, N USA *41°48′N 89°58′W*
36 K13 **Morristown** Arizona, SW USA *33°48′N 112°34′W*
18 J14 **Morristown** New Jersey, NE USA *40°48′N 74°29′W*
21 O8 **Morristown** Tennessee, S USA *36°13′N 83°18′W*
42 L11 **Morrito** Río San Juan, SW Nicaragua *11°37′N 85°05′W*
35 P13 **Morro Bay** California, W USA *35°21′N 120°51′W*
95 L22 **Mörrum** Blekinge, S Sweden *56°11′N 14°45′E*
83 N16 **Morrumbala** Zambézia, NE Mozambique *17°17′S 35°35′E*
83 N20 **Morrumbene** Inhambane, SE Mozambique *23°41′S 35°25′E*
95 F21 **Mors** *island* NW Denmark
Mörs *see* Moers
25 N1 **Morse** Texas, SW USA *36°03′N 101°28′W*
127 N6 **Morshansk** Tambovskaya Oblast', W Russian Federation *53°27′N 41°46′E*
102 L5 **Mortagne-au-Perche** Orne, N France *48°32′N 00°31′E*
102 J8 **Mortagne-sur-Sèvre** Vendée, NW France *47°00′N 00°57′W*
104 G8 **Mortágua** Viseu, N Portugal *40°24′N 08°14′W*
102 J5 **Mortain** Manche, N France *48°39′N 00°51′W*
106 C8 **Mortara** Lombardia, N Italy *45°15′N 08°44′E*
59 J17 **Mortes, Rio das** ~ C Brazil
182 M12 **Mortlake** Victoria, SE Australia *38°06′S 142°48′E*
Mortlock Group *see* Takuu Islands
189 Q17 **Mortlock Islands** *prev.* Nomoi Islands. *island group* C Micronesia
29 T9 **Morton** Minnesota, N USA *44°33′N 94°58′W*
22 L5 **Morton** Mississippi, S USA *32°21′N 89°39′W*
24 M5 **Morton** Texas, SW USA *33°40′N 102°45′W*
32 H9 **Morton** Washington, NW USA *46°33′N 122°16′W*
0 D7 **Morton Seamount** *undersea feature* NE Pacific Ocean *50°15′N 142°45′W*
45 U15 **Moruga** Trinidad, Trinidad and Tobago *10°04′N 61°16′W*
183 P9 **Morundah** New South Wales, SE Australia *34°57′S 146°18′E*
Moruroa *see* Mururoa
183 S11 **Moruya** New South Wales, SE Australia *35°55′S 150°04′E*
103 Q8 **Morvan** *physical region* C France
185 G21 **Morven** Canterbury, South Island, New Zealand *44°51′S 171°07′E*
183 O13 **Morwell** Victoria, SE Australia *38°14′S 146°25′E*
125 N6 **Morzhovets, Ostrov** *island* NW Russian Federation
126 J4 **Mosal'sk** Kaluzhskaya Oblast', W Russian Federation *54°30′N 34°55′E*
101 H20 **Mosbach** Baden-Württemberg, SW Germany *49°21′N 09°06′E*
95 E18 **Mosby** Vest-Agder, S Norway *58°12′N 07°55′E*
33 V9 **Mosby** Montana, NW USA *46°58′N 107°53′W*
32 M9 **Moscow** Idaho, NW USA *46°43′N 117°00′W*
20 F10 **Moscow** Tennessee, S USA *35°04′N 89°27′W*
Moscow *see* Moskva
101 D19 **Mosel** *Fr.* Moselle. ~ W Europe *see also* Moselle
Mosel *see* Moselle
103 T4 **Moselle** ⬖ *department* NE France
103 T6 **Moselle** *Ger.* Mosel. ~ W Europe *see also* Mosel
Moselle *see* Mosel
32 K9 **Moses Lake** ◎ Washington, NW USA
83 I18 **Mosetse** Central, E Botswana *20°40′S 26°38′E*
92 H4 **Mosfellsbær** Sudhurland, SW Iceland *65°09′N 21°43′W*
183 N8 **Mossgiel** New South Wales, SE Australia *33°16′S 144°34′E*
185 F23 **Mosgiel** Otago, South Island, New Zealand *45°51′S 170°22′E*
124 M11 **Mosha** ~ NW Russian Federation
81 I20 **Moshi** Kilimanjaro, NE Tanzania *03°21′S 37°19′E*
110 G12 **Mosina** Wielkolpolskie, C Poland *52°15′N 16°50′E*
30 L6 **Mosinee** Wisconsin, N USA *44°45′N 89°39′W*
92 F13 **Mosjøen** Nordland, C Norway *65°49′N 13°12′E*
123 S12 **Moskal'vo** Ostrov Sakhalin, Sakhalinskaya Oblast', SE Russian Federation *53°36′N 142°31′E*
92 I13 **Moskosel** Norrbotten, N Sweden *65°52′N 19°30′E*
126 K4 **Moskovskaya Oblast'** ⬖ *province* W Russian Federation
Moskovskiy *see* Moskva
126 J3 **Moskva** *Eng.* Moscow. ● (Russian Federation) Gorod Moskva, W Russian Federation *55°45′N 37°42′E*
147 Q14 **Moskva** *Rus.* Moskovskiy; *prev.* Chubek. SW Tajikistan *37°41′N 69°33′E*
126 L4 **Moskva** ~ W Russian Federation
83 I20 **Mosomane** Kgatleng, SE Botswana *24°04′S 26°15′E*
Moson and Magyaróvár *see* Mosonmagyaróvár
111 H21 **Mosoni-Duna** *Ger.* Kleine Donau. ~ NW Hungary
111 H21 **Mosonmagyaróvár** *Ger.* Wieselburg-Ungarisch-Altenburg; *prev.* Moson and Magyaróvár, *Ger.* Wieselburg and Ungarisch-Altenburg. Győr-Moson-Sopron, NW Hungary *47°52′N 17°15′E*
Mospino *see* Mospyne
117 X8 **Mospyne** *Rus.* Mospino. Donets'ka Oblast', E Ukraine *47°53′N 38°03′E*
54 B12 **Mosquera** Nariño, SW Colombia *02°32′N 78°24′W*
37 U10 **Mosquero** New Mexico, SW USA *35°46′N 103°57′W*
Mosquito Coast *see* La Mosquitia
31 U11 **Mosquito Creek Lake** ⊠ Ohio, N USA
Mosquito Gulf *see* Mosquitos, Golfo de los
23 X11 **Mosquito Lagoon** *wetland* Florida, SE USA
43 N10 **Mosquito, Punta** *headland* E Nicaragua *12°18′N 83°38′W*
43 W14 **Mosquito, Punta** *headland* NE Panama *09°06′N 77°52′W*
43 Q15 **Mosquitos, Golfo de los** *Eng.* Mosquito Gulf. *gulf* N Panama
95 H16 **Moss** Østfold, S Norway *59°25′N 10°40′E*
Mossâmedes *see* Namibe
22 G8 **Moss Bluff** Louisiana, S USA *30°18′N 93°11′W*
185 C23 **Mossburn** Southland, South Island, New Zealand *45°40′S 168°15′E*
83 G26 **Mosselbaai** *var.* Mosselbai, *Eng.* Mossel Bay. Western Cape, SW South Africa *34°11′S 22°08′E*
Mosselbai/Mossel Bay *see* Mosselbaai
79 F20 **Mossendjo** Niari, SW Congo *02°57′S 12°40′E*
101 H22 **Mössingen** Baden-Württemberg, S Germany *48°22′N 09°01′E*
181 W4 **Mossman** Queensland, NE Australia *16°34′S 145°27′E*
59 P14 **Mossoró** Rio Grande do Norte, NE Brazil *05°11′S 37°20′W*
23 N9 **Moss Point** Mississippi, S USA *30°24′N 88°31′W*
183 S9 **Moss Vale** New South Wales, SE Australia *34°33′S 150°20′E*
32 G9 **Mossyrock** Washington, NW USA *46°32′N 122°30′W*
111 B15 **Most** *Ger.* Brüx. Ústecký Kraj, NW Czech Republic *50°30′N 13°37′E*
162 E7 **Möst** *var.* Ulaantolgoy. Hovd, W Mongolia *46°39′N 92°50′E*
121 P16 **Mosta** *var.* Musta. C Malta *35°54′N 14°25′E*
74 I5 **Mostaganem** *var.* Mestghanem. NW Algeria *35°54′N 00°05′E*
113 H14 **Mostar** Federacija Bosna I Hercegovina, S Bosnia and Herzegovina *43°21′N 17°47′E*
61 J17 **Mostardas** Rio Grande do Sul, S Brazil *31°02′S 50°51′W*
116 K14 **Mostiștea** ~ S Romania
Mostva *see* Mastva
Mosty *see* Masty
116 H5 **Mostys'ka** L'vivs'ka Oblast', W Ukraine *49°47′N 23°09′E*
Mosul *see* Al Mawșil
95 F15 **Møsvatnet** ◎ S Norway
80 J12 **Mot'a** Āmara, N Ethiopia *11°03′N 38°03′E*
79 H16 **Motaba** ~ N Congo
105 O10 **Mota del Cuervo** Castilla-La Mancha, C Spain *39°30′N 02°52′W*
104 L5 **Mota del Marqués** Castilla-León, N Spain *41°38′N 05°11′W*
42 F5 **Motagua, Río** ~ Guatemala/Honduras
119 H19 **Motal'** Brestskaya Voblasts', SW Belarus *52°13′N 25°34′E*
95 L17 **Motala** Östergötland, S Sweden *58°34′N 15°05′E*
191 X7 **Motane** *island* Îles Marquises, NE French Polynesia
152 K13 **Moth** Uttar Pradesh, N India *25°44′N 78°56′E*
Mother of Presidents/ Mother of States *see* Virginia
96 I12 **Motherwell** C Scotland, United Kingdom *55°48′N 04°W*
153 P12 **Motīhāri** Bihār, N India *26°40′N 84°55′E*
105 Q10 **Motilla del Palancar** Castilla-La Mancha, C Spain *39°34′N 01°55′W*
184 N7 **Motiti Island** *island* NE New Zealand
83 J19 **Motloutse** ~ E Botswana
41 V17 **Motozintla de Mendoza** Chiapas, SE Mexico *15°21′N 92°14′W*
105 N15 **Motril** Andalucía, S Spain *36°45′N 03°30′W*
116 G13 **Motru** Gorj, SW Romania *44°49′N 22°56′E*
165 Q4 **Motsuta-misaki** *headland* Hokkaidō, NE Japan *42°36′N 139°48′E*
28 L6 **Mott** North Dakota, N USA *46°21′N 102°17′W*
Möttling *see* Metlika
107 O18 **Mottola** Puglia, SE Italy *40°38′N 17°02′E*
184 P8 **Motu** ~ North Island, New Zealand
185 I14 **Motueka** Tasman, South Island, New Zealand *41°08′S 173°00′E*
185 I14 **Motueka** ~ South Island, New Zealand
Motu Iti *see* Tupai
41 X12 **Motul** *var.* Motul de Felipe Carrillo Puerto. Yucatán, SE Mexico *21°06′N 89°17′W*
Motul de Felipe Carrillo Puerto *see* Motul
191 U17 **Motu Nui** *island* Easter Island, Chile, E Pacific Ocean
191 Q10 **Motu One** *var.* Bellingshausen. *atoll* Îles Sous le Vent, W French Polynesia
190 I16 **Motutapu** *island* E Cook Islands
193 V15 **Motu Tapu** *island* Tongatapu Group, S Tonga
184 L5 **Motutapu Island** *island* N New Zealand
Motyca *see* Modica
Mouanda *see* Moanda
Mouaskar *see* Mascara
105 U3 **Moubermé, Tuc de** *Fr.* Pic de Maubermé; *Sp.* Pico Mauberme; *prev.* Tuc de Maubermé. ▲ France/Spain *42°48′N 00°57′E* *see also* Maubermé, Pic de
Moubermé, Tuc de *see* Maubermé, Pic de
45 N7 **Mouchoir Passage** *passage* SE Turks and Caicos Islands
76 I9 **Moudjéria** Tagant, SW Mauritania *17°52′N 12°20′W*
108 C9 **Moudon** Vaud, W Switzerland *46°41′N 06°49′E*
Mouhoun *see* Black Volta
79 E19 **Mouila** Ngounié, C Gabon *01°50′S 11°02′E*
79 K14 **Mouka** Haute-Kotto, C Central African Republic *07°12′N 21°52′E*
Moukden *see* Shenyang
183 N10 **Moulamein** New South Wales, SE Australia *35°06′S 144°03′E*
Moulamein Creek *see* Billabong Creek
74 F6 **Moulay-Bousselham** NW Morocco *35°00′N 06°22′W*
Moule *see* le Moule
80 M11 **Moulhoulé** N Djibouti *12°34′N 43°06′E*
103 P9 **Moulins** Allier, C France *46°34′N 03°20′E*
Moulmein *see* Mawlamyine
166 L8 **Moulmeingyun** Ayeyarwady, SW Burma (Myanmar) *16°24′N 95°15′E*
74 G6 **Moulouya** *var.* Mulucha, Muluya, Mulwiya. *seasonal river* NE Morocco
23 O2 **Moulton** Alabama, S USA *34°28′N 87°18′W*
29 W16 **Moulton** Iowa, C USA *40°41′N 92°40′W*
25 T11 **Moulton** Texas, SW USA *29°34′N 97°08′W*
23 T7 **Moultrie** Georgia, SE USA *31°10′N 83°47′W*
21 S14 **Moultrie, Lake** ⊠ South Carolina, SE USA
22 K3 **Mound Bayou** Mississippi, S USA *33°52′N 90°43′W*
30 L17 **Mound City** Illinois, N USA *37°06′N 89°09′W*
27 R6 **Mound City** Kansas, C USA *38°07′N 94°49′W*
27 Q2 **Mound City** Missouri, C USA *40°07′N 95°13′W*
29 N7 **Mound City** South Dakota, N USA *45°44′N 100°03′W*
78 H13 **Moundou** Logone-Occidental, SW Chad *08°35′N 16°01′E*
27 P10 **Mounds** Oklahoma, C USA *35°52′N 96°03′W*
21 R2 **Moundsville** West Virginia, NE USA *39°54′N 80°44′W*
167 Q12 **Moŭng Roessei** Bătdâmbâng, W Cambodia *12°47′N 103°28′E*
Moun Hou *see* Black Volta
8 H8 **Mountain** ~ Northwest Territories, NW Canada
37 S12 **Mountainair** New Mexico, SW USA *34°31′N 106°14′W*
35 V1 **Mountain City** Nevada, W USA *41°48′N 115°58′W*
21 Q8 **Mountain City** Tennessee, S USA *36°28′N 81°48′W*
27 U7 **Mountain Grove** Missouri, C USA *37°07′N 92°15′W*
27 U9 **Mountain Home** Arkansas, C USA *36°19′N 92°24′W*
33 N15 **Mountain Home** Idaho, NW USA *43°07′N 115°42′W*
25 Q11 **Mountain Home** Texas, SW USA *30°11′N 99°19′W*
29 W4 **Mountain Iron** Minnesota, N USA *47°31′N 92°37′W*
29 T10 **Mountain Lake** Minnesota, N USA *43°57′N 94°54′W*
23 S3 **Mountain Park** Georgia, SE USA *34°04′N 84°24′W*
35 W12 **Mountain Pass** *pass* California, W USA
27 T12 **Mountain Pine** Arkansas, C USA *34°34′N 93°10′W*
39 Y14 **Mountain Point** Annette Island, Alaska, USA *55°17′N 131°31′W*
Mountain State *see* Montana
Mountain State *see* West Virginia
27 V7 **Mountain View** Arkansas, C USA *35°52′N 92°07′W*
38 H12 **Mountain View** Hawaii, USA, C Pacific Ocean *19°32′N 155°03′W*
27 V10 **Mountain View** Missouri, C USA *37°00′N 91°42′W*
38 M11 **Mountain Village** Alaska, USA *62°06′N 163°42′W*
21 R8 **Mount Airy** North Carolina, SE USA *36°30′N 80°36′W*
83 K24 **Mount Ayliff** *Xh.* Maxesibebi. Eastern Cape, SE South Africa *30°48′S 29°23′E*
29 U16 **Mount Ayr** Iowa, C USA *40°42′N 94°14′W*
182 J9 **Mount Barker** South Australia *35°06′S 138°52′E*
180 J14 **Mount Barker** Western Australia *34°42′S 117°40′E*
183 P11 **Mount Beauty** Victoria, SE Australia *36°47′S 147°12′E*
14 E16 **Mount Brydges** Ontario, S Canada *42°54′N 81°29′W*
31 N16 **Mount Carmel** Illinois, N USA *38°23′N 87°46′W*
30 K10 **Mount Carroll** Illinois, N USA *42°05′N 89°59′W*
31 S9 **Mount Clemens** Michigan, N USA *42°36′N 82°52′W*
185 E19 **Mount Cook** Canterbury, South Island, New Zealand *43°47′S 170°06′E*
83 L16 **Mount Darwin** Mashonaland Central, NE Zimbabwe *16°45′S 31°39′E*
19 S7 **Mount Desert Island** *island* Maine, NE USA
23 W11 **Mount Dora** Florida, SE USA *28°48′N 81°38′W*
182 G5 **Mount Eba** South Australia *30°11′S 135°40′E*
25 W8 **Mount Enterprise** Texas, SW USA *31°53′N 94°40′W*
182 J4 **Mount Fitton** South Australia *29°55′S 139°26′E*
83 J24 **Mount Fletcher** Eastern Cape, SE South Africa *30°41′S 28°30′E*
14 F15 **Mount Forest** Ontario, S Canada *43°58′N 80°44′W*
182 K12 **Mount Gambier** South Australia *37°47′S 140°49′E*
181 W5 **Mount Garnet** Queensland, NE Australia *17°41′S 145°07′E*
21 P6 **Mount Gay** West Virginia, NE USA *37°49′N 82°00′W*
31 S12 **Mount Gilead** Ohio, N USA *40°33′N 82°49′W*
186 C7 **Mount Hagen** Western Highlands, C Papua New Guinea *05°54′S 144°13′E*
18 J16 **Mount Holly** New Jersey, NE USA *39°59′N 74°46′W*
21 R10 **Mount Holly** North Carolina, SE USA *35°18′N 81°01′W*
27 T12 **Mount Ida** Arkansas, C USA *34°32′N 93°38′W*
181 T6 **Mount Isa** Queensland, C Australia *20°48′S 139°32′E*
21 U4 **Mount Jackson** Virginia, NE USA *38°45′N 78°38′W*
18 D12 **Mount Jewett** Pennsylvania, NE USA *41°43′N 78°37′W*
18 L13 **Mount Kisco** New York, NE USA *41°12′N 73°42′W*
18 B15 **Mount Lebanon** Pennsylvania, NE USA *40°21′N 80°03′W*
182 J8 **Mount Lofty Ranges** ▲▲ South Australia
180 J10 **Mount Magnet** Western Australia *28°09′S 117°52′E*
184 N7 **Mount Maunganui** Bay of Plenty, North Island, New Zealand *37°39′S 176°11′E*
97 E18 **Mountmellick** *Ir.* Móinteach Mílic. Laois, C Ireland *53°07′N 07°20′W*
30 L10 **Mount Morris** Illinois, N USA *42°03′N 89°25′W*
31 R9 **Mount Morris** Michigan, N USA *43°07′N 83°42′W*
18 F10 **Mount Morris** New York, NE USA *42°43′N 77°51′W*
18 B16 **Mount Morris** Pennsylvania, NE USA *39°43′N 80°06′W*
30 K15 **Mount Olive** Illinois, N USA *39°04′N 89°43′W*
21 V10 **Mount Olive** North Carolina, SE USA *35°12′N 78°03′W*
21 N4 **Mount Olivet** Kentucky, S USA *38°32′N 84°01′W*
29 Y15 **Mount Pleasant** Iowa, C USA *40°57′N 91°33′W*
31 Q8 **Mount Pleasant** Michigan, N USA *43°36′N 84°46′W*
18 C15 **Mount Pleasant** Pennsylvania, NE USA *40°07′N 79°33′W*
21 T14 **Mount Pleasant** South Carolina, SE USA *32°47′N 79°51′W*
20 I9 **Mount Pleasant** Tennessee, S USA *35°32′N 87°11′W*
25 W6 **Mount Pleasant** Texas, SW USA *33°10′N 94°49′W*
36 L4 **Mount Pleasant** Utah, W USA *39°33′N 111°27′W*

◆ Country ● Country Capital ◇ Dependent Territory ○ Dependent Territory Capital ⬖ Administrative Regions ✈ International Airport ▲ Mountain ▲▲ Mountain Range Volcano ~ River ◎ Lake ⊠ Reservoir

MOUNT PLEASANT – MURRUPULA

63 N23 Mount Pleasant ✈ (Stanley) East Falkland, Falkland Islands
97 G25 Mount's Bay inlet SW England, United Kingdom
35 N2 Mount Shasta California, W USA 41°18′N 122°19′W
30 J13 Mount Sterling Illinois, N USA 39°59′N 90°44′W
21 N5 Mount Sterling Kentucky, S USA 38°03′N 83°56′W
18 E15 Mount Union Pennsylvania, NE USA 40°21′N 77°51′W
23 V6 Mount Vernon Georgia, SE USA 32°10′N 82°35′W
30 L16 Mount Vernon Illinois, N USA 38°19′N 88°54′W
20 M6 Mount Vernon Kentucky, S USA 37°20′N 84°20′W
27 S7 Mount Vernon Missouri, C USA 37°05′N 93°49′W
31 T13 Mount Vernon Ohio, N USA 40°23′N 82°29′W
32 K13 Mount Vernon Oregon, NW USA 44°22′N 119°07′W
25 W6 Mount Vernon Texas, SW USA 33°11′N 95°13′W
32 H7 Mount Vernon Washington, NW USA 48°25′N 122°19′W
20 L5 Mount Washington Kentucky, S USA 38°03′N 85°33′W
182 F8 Mount Wedge South Australia 33°29′S 135°08′E
30 L14 Mount Zion Illinois, N USA 39°46′N 88°52′W
181 Y9 Moura Queensland, NE Australia 24°34′S 149°57′E
58 F12 Moura Amazonas, NW Brazil 01°32′S 61°43′W
104 H12 Moura Beja, S Portugal 38°08′N 07°27′W
104 I12 Mourão Évora, S Portugal 38°22′N 07°20′W
76 L11 Mourdiah Koulikoro, W Mali 14°28′N 07°31′W
78 K7 Mourdi, Dépression du desert lowland Chad/Sudan
102 J16 Mourenx Pyrénées-Atlantiques, SW France 43°24′N 00°37′W
Mourgana see Mourgkána
115 C15 Mourgkána var. Mourgana. ▲ Albania/Greece 39°48′N 20°24′E
97 G16 Mourne Mountains Ir. Beanna Boirche. ▲▲ SE Northern Ireland, United Kingdom
115 I15 Moúrtzeflos, Akrotírio headland Límnos, E Greece 40°00′N 25°02′E
99 C19 Mouscron Dut. Moeskroen. Hainaut, W Belgium 50°44′N 03°14′E
Mouse River see Souris River
78 H10 Moussoro Kanem, W Chad 13°41′N 16°31′E
103 T11 Moûtiers Savoie, E France 45°28′N 06°31′E
172 J14 Moutsamudou var. Mutsamudu. Anjouan, SE Comoros 12°10′S 44°25′E
74 K11 Mouydir, Monts de ▲▲ S Algeria
79 F20 Mouyondzi Bouenza, S Congo 03°58′S 13°57′E
115 E16 Mouzáki prev. Mouzákion. Thessalía, C Greece 39°25′N 21°40′E
Mouzákion see Mouzáki
29 S13 Moville Iowa, C USA 42°30′N 96°04′W
82 E13 Moxico ◐ province E Angola
172 I14 Moya Anjouan, SE Comoros 12°18′S 44°27′E
40 L12 Moyahua Zacatecas, C Mexico 21°18′N 103°09′W
81 J16 Moyalē Oromīya, C Ethiopia 03°34′N 38°58′E
76 I15 Moyamba W Sierra Leone 08°04′N 12°30′W
74 G7 Moyen Atlas Eng. Middle Atlas. ▲▲ N Morocco
78 H13 Moyen-Chari off. Préfecture du Moyen-Chari. ◐ prefecture S Chad
Moyen-Chari, Préfecture du see Moyen-Chari
Moyen-Congo see Congo (Republic of)
83 J24 Moyeni var. Quthing. SW Lesotho 30°25′S 27°43′E
79 D18 Moyen-Ogooué off. Province du Moyen-Ogooué, var. Le Moyen-Ogooué. ◐ province C Gabon
Moyen-Ogooué, Province du see Moyen-Ogooué
103 S4 Moyeuvre-Grande Moselle, NE France 49°15′N 06°03′E
33 N7 Moyie Springs Idaho, NW USA 48°43′N 116°15′W
146 G6 Mo'ynoq Rus. Muynak. Qoraqalpog'iston Respublikasi, NW Uzbekistan 43°45′N 59°03′E
81 F16 Moyo NW Uganda 03°38′N 31°43′E
56 D10 Moyobamba San Martín, NW Peru 06°04′S 76°56′W
78 H10 Moyto Chari-Baguirmi, W Chad 12°35′N 16°33′E
158 G9 Moyu var. Karakax. Xinjiang Uygur Zizhiqu, NW China 37°16′N 79°39′E
122 M9 Moyyero ≈ N Russian Federation
145 S15 Moyynkum var. Furmanovka, Kaz. Fūrmanov. Zhambyl, S Kazakhstan 44°15′N 72°55′E
145 Q15 Moyynkum, Peski Kaz. Moyynqum. desert S Kazakhstan
Moyynqum see Moyynkum, Peski
145 S12 Moyynty Karaganda, C Kazakhstan 47°10′N 73°24′E
145 S12 Moyynty ≈ Karaganda, C Kazakhstan
Mozambika, Lakandranon' i see Mozambique Channel
83 M18 Mozambique off. Republic of Mozambique; prev. People's Republic of Mozambique, Portuguese East Africa. ◆ republic S Africa
Mozambique Basin see Natal Basin
Mozambique, Canal de see Mozambique Channel
83 P17 Mozambique Channel Fr. Canal de Mozambique, Mal. Lakandranon' i Mozambika. strait W Indian Ocean
172 L11 Mozambique Escarpment var. Mozambique Scarp. undersea feature SW Indian Ocean 33°00′S 36°30′E
Mozambique, People's Republic of see Mozambique
172 L10 Mozambique Plateau var. Mozambique Rise. undersea feature SW Indian Ocean 32°00′S 35°00′E
Mozambique, Republic of see Mozambique
Mozambique Rise see Mozambique Plateau
Mozambique Scarp see Mozambique Escarpment
127 O15 Mozdok Respublika Severnaya Osetiya, SW Russian Federation 43°48′N 44°42′E
57 K17 Mozetenes, Serranías de ▲▲ C Bolivia
126 J4 Mozhaysk Moskovskaya Oblast', W Russian Federation 55°31′N 36°01′E
127 T3 Mozhga Udmurtskaya Respublika, NW Russian Federation 56°24′N 52°13′E
Mozyr' see Mazyr
79 P22 Mpala Katanga, E Dem. Rep. Congo 06°43′S 29°28′E
79 G19 Mpama ≈ C Congo
81 E22 Mpanda Rukwa, W Tanzania 06°21′S 31°01′E
82 L11 Mpande Northern, NE Zambia 09°13′S 31°42′E
83 J18 Mphoengs Matabeleland South, SW Zimbabwe 21°04′S 27°56′E
81 F18 Mpigi S Uganda 00°14′N 32°19′E
82 L13 Mpika Northern, NE Zambia 11°50′S 31°30′E
83 J14 Mpima Central, C Zambia 14°25′S 28°34′E
82 J13 Mpongwe Copperbelt, C Zambia 13°25′S 28°13′E
82 K11 Mporokoso Northern, N Zambia 09°22′S 30°06′E
79 H20 Mpouya Plateaux, SE Congo 02°38′S 16°13′E
77 P16 Mpraeso C Ghana 06°36′N 00°43′W
82 L11 Mpulungu Northern, N Zambia 08°50′S 31°06′E
83 K21 Mpumalanga prev. Eastern Transvaal, Afr. Oos-Transvaal. ◐ province NE South Africa
83 D16 Mpungu Okavango, N Namibia 17°36′S 18°16′E
81 I22 Mpwapwa Dodoma, C Tanzania 06°21′S 36°29′E
Mqinvartsveri see Kazbek
110 M8 Mrągowo Ger. Sensburg. Warmińsko-Mazurskie, NE Poland 53°53′N 21°19′E
127 V6 Mrakovo Respublika Bashkortostan, W Russian Federation 52°43′N 56°36′E
172 I13 Mramani Anjouan, E Comoros 12°18′N 44°39′E
166 K5 Mrauk-oo var. Mrauk U, Myohaung. Rakhine State, W Burma (Myanmar) 20°35′N 93°12′E
Mrauk U see Mrauk-oo
112 F12 Mrkonjić Grad ◐ Republika Srpska, W Bosnia and Herzegovina
110 H9 Mrocza Kujawsko-pomorskie, C Poland 53°15′N 17°38′E
124 I14 Msta ≈ NW Russian Federation
Mstislavl' see Mstsislaw
119 P15 Mstsislaw Rus. Mstislavl'. Mahilyowskaya Voblasts', E Belarus 54°01′N 31°43′E
Mtkvari see Kura
Mtoko see Mutoko
126 K6 Mtsensk Orlovskaya Oblast', W Russian Federation 53°17′N 36°34′E
81 K24 Mtwara Mtwara, SE Tanzania 10°17′S 40°11′E
81 J25 Mtwara ◐ region SE Tanzania
104 G14 Mu ▲ S Portugal 37°24′N 08°04′W
193 V15 Mu'a Tongatapu, S Tonga 21°11′S 175°07′W
Muai To see Mae Hong Son
83 P16 Mualama Zambézia, NE Mozambique 16°51′S 38°21′E
Mualo see Messalo, Rio
79 E22 Muanda Bas-Congo, SW Dem. Rep. Congo 05°53′S 12°17′E
Muang Chiang Rai see Chiang Rai
167 R6 Muang Ham Houaphan, N Laos 20°19′N 104°00′E
167 S8 Muang Hinboun Khammouan, C Laos 17°37′N 104°37′E
Muang Kalasin see Kalasin
Muang Khammouan see Thakhèk
167 S11 Muang Không Champasak, S Laos 14°08′N 105°48′E
167 S10 Muang Khôngxédôn var. Khong Sedone. Salavan, S Laos 15°34′N 105°46′E
Muang Khon Kaen see Khon Kaen
167 Q6 Muang Khoua Phôngsali, N Laos 21°07′N 102°31′E
Muang Krabi see Krabi
Muang Lampang see Lampang
Muang Lamphun see Lamphun
Muang Loei see Loei
Muang Lom Sak see Lom Sak
Muang Nakhon Sawan see Nakhon Sawan
167 Q6 Muang Namo Oudômxai, N Laos 20°58′N 101°46′E
Muang Nan see Nan
167 Q6 Muang Ngoy Louangphabang, N Laos 20°43′N 102°42′E
167 Q5 Muang Ou Tai Phôngsali, N Laos 22°06′N 101°59′E
Muang Pak Lay see Pak Lay
Muang Pakxan see Pakxan
167 T10 Muang Pakxong Champasak, S Laos 15°10′N 106°17′E
167 S9 Muang Phalan var. Muang Phalane. Savannakhét, S Laos 16°40′N 105°33′E
Muang Phalane see Muang Phalan
Muang Phan see Phan
Muang Phayao see Phayao
Muang Phichit see Phichit
167 T9 Muang Phin Savannakhét, S Laos 16°31′N 106°01′E
Muang Phitsanulok see Phitsanulok
Muang Phrae see Phrae
Muang Roi Et see Roi Et
Muang Sakon Nakhon see Sakon Nakhon
Muang Samut Prakan see Samut Prakan
167 P6 Muang Sing Louang Namtha, N Laos 21°12′N 101°09′E
Muang Ubon see Ubon Ratchathani
Muang Uthai Thani see Uthai Thani
167 P7 Muang Vangviang Viangchan, C Laos 18°53′N 102°27′E
Muang Xaignabouri see Xaignabouli
Muang Xay see Xai
167 S9 Muang Xépôn var. Sepone. Savannakhét, S Laos 16°40′N 106°15′E
168 K10 Muar var. Bandar Maharani. Johor, Peninsular Malaysia 02°01′N 102°35′E
168 J9 Muara Sumatera, W Indonesia 02°18′N 98°54′E
168 L13 Muarabeliti Sumatera, W Indonesia 03°13′S 103°00′E
168 K12 Muarabungo Sumatera, W Indonesia 01°28′S 102°06′E
168 L13 Muaraenim Sumatera, W Indonesia 03°40′S 103°48′E
169 T11 Muarajuloi Borneo, C Indonesia 0°12′S 114°03′E
169 U12 Muarakaman Borneo, C Indonesia 0°09′S 116°43′E
168 H12 Muarasigep Pulau Siberut, W Indonesia 01°01′S 98°48′E
168 L12 Muaratembesi Sumatera, W Indonesia 01°40′S 103°08′E
169 T12 Muaratewe var. Muarateweh; prev. Moearatewe. Borneo, C Indonesia 0°58′S 114°52′E
Muarateweh see Muaratewe
169 U10 Muarawahau Borneo, N Indonesia 01°03′N 116°48′E
138 G13 Mubārak, Jabal ▲ S Jordan 29°19′N 35°13′E
153 N13 Mubārakpur Uttar Pradesh, N India 26°05′N 83°19′E
Mubarek see Muborak
81 F18 Mubende SW Uganda 0°35′N 31°24′E
77 Y14 Mubi Adamawa, NE Nigeria 10°15′N 13°18′E
146 M12 Muborak Rus. Mubarek. Qashqadaryo Viloyati, S Uzbekistan 39°17′N 65°10′E
171 U12 Mubrani Papua, E Indonesia 0°42′S 133°25′E
67 U12 Muchinga Escarpment escarpment NE Zambia
127 N7 Muchkapskiy Tambovskaya Oblast', W Russian Federation 51°51′N 42°25′E
96 G10 Muck island W Scotland, United Kingdom
82 Q13 Mucojo Cabo Delgado, N Mozambique 12°05′S 40°30′E
82 F12 Muconda Lunda Sul, NE Angola 10°37′S 21°19′E
54 I10 Muco, Río ≈ E Colombia
83 O16 Mucubela Zambézia, NE Mozambique 16°51′S 37°48′E
42 J5 Mucupina, Monte ▲ N Honduras 15°07′N 86°36′W
136 J14 Mucur Kirşehir, C Turkey 39°05′N 34°25′E
143 U8 Mūd Khorāsān-e Janūbī, E Iran 32°41′N 59°30′E
163 Y9 Mudanjiang var. Mu-tan-chiang. Heilongjiang, NE China 44°33′N 129°40′E
163 Y9 Mudan Jiang ≈ NE China
136 D11 Mudanya Bursa, NW Turkey 40°23′N 28°53′E
28 K8 Mud Butte South Dakota, N USA 45°00′N 102°51′W
155 G16 Muddebihāl Karnātaka, C India 16°26′N 76°07′E
27 P12 Muddy Boggy Creek ≈ Oklahoma, C USA
36 M6 Muddy Creek ≈ Utah, W USA
37 V7 Muddy Creek Reservoir ▣ Colorado, C USA
33 W15 Muddy Gap Wyoming, C USA 42°21′N 107°27′W
35 Y11 Muddy Peak ▲ Nevada, W USA 36°17′N 114°40′W
183 R7 Mudgee New South Wales, SE Australia 32°37′S 149°36′E
29 S3 Mud Lake ◎ Minnesota, N USA
29 P7 Mud Lake Reservoir ▣ South Dakota, N USA
167 N9 Mudon Mon State, S Burma (Myanmar) 16°17′N 97°40′E
80 O14 Mudug off. Gobolka Mudug. ◐ region NE Somalia
81 O14 Mudug var. Mudugh. plain N Somalia
Mudug, Gobolka see Mudug
Mudugh see Mudug
83 Q15 Muecate Nampula, NE Mozambique 14°56′S 39°38′E
82 Q13 Mueda Cabo Delgado, NE Mozambique 11°40′S 39°31′E
42 L10 Muelle de los Bueyes Región Autónoma Atlántico Sur, SE Nicaragua 12°03′N 84°34′W
Muenchen see München
83 M14 Muende Tete, NW Mozambique 14°22′S 33°00′E
25 T5 Muenster Texas, SW USA 33°39′N 97°22′W
Muenster see Münster
43 O6 Muerto, Cayo reef NE Nicaragua
41 T17 Muerto, Mar lagoon SE Mexico
64 F11 Muertos Trough undersea feature N Caribbean Sea
83 H14 Mufaya Kuta Western, NW Zambia 14°30′S 24°18′E
82 J13 Mufulira Copperbelt, C Zambia 12°33′S 28°16′E
161 O10 Mufu Shan ▲▲ C China
Mugalla see Yutian
Mugalzhar Taūlary see Mugodzhary, Gory
137 Y12 Muğan Düzü Rus. Muganskaya Ravnina, Muganskaya Step'. physical region S Azerbaijan
Muganskaya Ravnina/Muganskaya Step' see Muğan Düzü
106 K8 Múggia Friuli-Venezia Giulia, NE Italy 45°36′N 13°48′E
153 N14 Mughal Sarāi Uttar Pradesh, N India 25°18′N 83°07′E
Mughla see Muğla
141 W11 Mughshin var. Muqshin. S Oman 19°26′N 54°38′E
147 S12 Mughsu Rus. Muksu. ≈ C Tajikistan
164 H14 Mugi Tokushima, Shikoku, SW Japan 33°39′N 134°24′E
136 C16 Muğla var. Mughla. Muğla, SW Turkey 37°13′N 28°22′E
136 C16 Muğla var. Mughla. ◐ province SW Turkey
114 K10 Müglizh Stara Zagora, C Bulgaria 42°36′N 25°32′E
144 J11 Mugodzhary, Gory Kaz. Mugalzhar Taūlary. ▲▲ W Kazakhstan
83 O15 Mugulama Zambézia, NE Mozambique 16°01′S 37°33′E
Muḩāfazat Hims see Ḩimş
Muḩāfazat Ma'dabā see Ma'dabā
139 U9 Muḩammad Wāsiţ, E Iraq 32°46′N 45°14′E
139 R8 Muḩammadīyah Al Anbār, C Iraq 33°22′N 42°48′E
80 I6 Muhammad Qol Red Sea, NE Sudan 20°53′N 37°09′E
75 Y9 Muhammad, Râs headland E Egypt 27°45′N 34°18′E
Muhammerah see Khorramshahr
Muḩāfazat Al 'Aqabah see Al 'Aqabah
140 M12 Muḩāyil var. Mahāil. 'Asīr, SW Saudi Arabia 18°34′N 42°01′E
139 O7 Muḩaywīr Al Anbār, W Iraq 33°35′N 41°06′E
101 H21 Mühlacker Baden-Württemberg, SW Germany 48°57′N 08°51′E
Mühlbach see Sebeş
Mühldorf see Mühldorf am Inn
101 N23 Mühldorf am Inn var. Mühldorf. Bayern, SE Germany 48°14′N 12°32′E
101 J15 Mühlhausen var. Mühlhausen in Thüringen. Thüringen, C Germany 51°13′N 10°28′E
Mühlhausen in Thüringen see Mühlhausen
195 Q2 Mühlig-Hofmanfjella ▲▲ Antarctica
93 L14 Muhos Oulu, C Finland 64°48′N 26°00′E
138 K6 Muḩ, Sabkhat al ◎ C Syria
118 E5 Muhu Ger. Mohn, Moon. island W Estonia
81 F19 Muhutwe Kagera, NW Tanzania 01°31′S 31°41′E
Muhu Väin see Väinameri
98 J10 Muiden Noord-Holland, C Netherlands 52°19′N 05°04′E
193 W15 Mui Hopohoponga headland Tongatapu, S Tonga 21°09′S 175°02′W
Muinchille see Cootehill
Muineachán see Monaghan
97 F19 Muine Bheag Eng. Bagenalstown. Carlow, SE Ireland 52°42′N 06°57′W
56 B5 Muisne Esmeraldas, NW Ecuador 0°35′N 79°58′W
83 P14 Muite Nampula, NE Mozambique 14°02′S 39°06′E
41 Z11 Mujeres, Isla island E Mexico
116 G7 Mukacheve Hung. Munkács, Rus. Mukachevo. Zakarpats'ka Oblast', W Ukraine 48°27′N 22°45′E
Mukachevo see Mukacheve
169 R9 Mukah Sarawak, East Malaysia 02°56′N 112°02′E
Mukalla see Al Mukallā
Mukama see Mokāma
Mukāshafa/Mukashshafah see Mukayshīfah
139 S6 Mukayshīfah var. Mukāshafa, Mukashshafah. Şalāḩ ad Dīn, N Iraq 34°24′N 43°44′E
167 R9 Mukdahan Mukdahan, E Thailand 16°31′N 104°43′E
Mukden see Shenyang
165 Y15 Mukojima-rettō Eng. Parry group. island group SE Japan
146 M14 Mukry Lebap Welaýaty, E Turkmenistan 37°39′N 65°37′E
Muksu see Mughsu
Muktagacha see Muktagachha
153 U14 Muktagachha var. Muktagacha. N Bangladesh 24°46′N 90°16′E
82 K13 Mukuku Central, C Zambia 12°10′S 29°50′E
82 K11 Mukupa Kaoma Northern, NE Zambia 09°55′S 30°19′E
81 I18 Mukutan Rift Valley, W Kenya 01°06′N 36°16′E
83 F16 Mukwe Caprivi, NE Namibia 18°01′S 21°24′E
105 R13 Mula Murcia, SE Spain 38°02′N 01°29′W
151 K20 Mulakatholhu var. Meemu Atoll, Mulaku Atoll. atoll C Maldives
Mulaku Atoll see Mulakatholhu
83 J15 Mulalika Lusaka, C Zambia 15°37′S 28°48′E
163 X8 Mulan Heilongjiang, NE China 45°57′N 128°00′E
83 N15 Mulanje var. Mlanje. Southern, S Malawi 16°05′S 35°29′E
40 H5 Mulatos Sonora, NW Mexico 28°42′N 108°44′W
23 P3 Mulberry Fork ≈ Alabama, S USA
39 P12 Mulchatna River ≈ Alaska, USA
125 W4 Mul'da Respublika Komi, NW Russian Federation 67°29′N 63°55′E
101 M14 Mulde ≈ E Germany
27 R10 Muldrow Oklahoma, C USA 35°25′N 94°34′W
40 E7 Mulegé Baja California Sur, NW Mexico 26°54′N 112°00′W
108 I10 Mulegns Graubünden, S Switzerland 46°30′N 09°36′E
79 M21 Mulenda Kasai-Oriental, C Dem. Rep. Congo 04°19′S 24°55′E
24 M4 Muleshoe Texas, SW USA 34°13′N 102°43′W
83 O15 Mulevala Zambézia, NE Mozambique 16°25′S 37°35′E
183 P5 Mulgoa Creek seasonal river New South Wales, SE Australia
105 O15 Mulhacén var. Cerro de Mulhacén. ▲ S Spain 37°07′N 03°11′W
Mulhacén, Cerro de see Mulhacén
Mülhausen see Mulhouse
101 E24 Müllheim Baden-Württemberg, SW Germany 47°50′N 07°37′E
101 E15 Mülheim var. Mulheim an der Ruhr. Nordrhein-Westfalen, W Germany 51°25′N 06°50′E
Mülheim an der Ruhr see Mülheim
103 U7 Mulhouse Ger. Mülhausen. Haut-Rhin, NE France 47°45′N 07°20′E
160 G11 Muli var. Qiaowa. Muli Zangzu Zizhixian. Sichuan, C China 27°49′N 101°10′E
171 X15 Muli channel Papua, E Indonesia
163 Y9 Muling Heilongjiang, NE China 44°54′N 130°35′E
Muli Zangzu Zizhixian see Muli
Mullach Íde see Malahide
Mullaitivu see Mullaittivu
155 K23 Mullaittivu var. Mullaitivu. Northern Province, N Sri Lanka 09°15′N 80°48′E
33 N8 Mullan Idaho, NW USA 47°28′N 115°48′W
28 M13 Mullen Nebraska, C USA 42°02′N 101°01′W
183 Q6 Mullengudgery New South Wales, SE Australia 31°42′S 147°24′E
21 Q6 Mullens West Virginia, NE USA 37°34′N 81°22′W
Müller-gerbergte see Muller, Pegunungan
169 T10 Muller, Pegunungan Dut. Müller-gerbergte. ▲▲ Borneo, C Indonesia
31 Q5 Mullett Lake ◎ Michigan, N USA
18 J16 Mullica River ≈ New Jersey, NE USA
25 R8 Mullin Texas, SW USA 31°33′N 98°40′W
97 E17 Mullingar Ir. An Muileann gCearr. C Ireland 53°32′N 07°20′W
21 T12 Mullins South Carolina, SE USA 34°12′N 79°15′W
96 G11 Mull, Isle of island W Scotland, United Kingdom
127 R5 Mullovka Ul'yanovskaya Oblast', W Russian Federation 54°13′N 49°19′E
95 K19 Mullsjö Västra Götaland, S Sweden 57°56′N 13°55′E
183 V4 Mullumbimby New South Wales, SE Australia 28°34′S 153°28′E
83 H15 Mulobezi Western, SW Zambia 16°48′S 25°11′E
83 C15 Mulondo Huíla, SW Angola 15°41′S 15°09′E
83 G15 Mulonga Plain plain W Zambia
79 N23 Mulongo Katanga, SE Dem. Rep. Congo 07°44′S 26°57′E
149 T10 Multān Punjab, E Pakistan 30°12′N 71°30′E
93 L17 Multia Länsi-Suomi, C Finland 62°27′N 24°49′E
Mulucha see Moulouya
83 J14 Mulungushi Central, C Zambia 14°15′S 28°27′E
83 K14 Mulungwe Central, C Zambia 13°57′S 29°51′E
Muluya see Moulouya
27 N7 Mulvane Kansas, C USA 37°28′N 97°14′W
183 O10 Mulwala New South Wales, SE Australia 35°59′S 146°00′E
Mulwiya see Moulouya
182 K6 Mulyungarie South Australia 31°29′S 140°45′E
154 D13 Mumbai prev. Bombay. state capital Mahārāshtra, W India 18°56′N 72°51′E
154 D13 Mumbai ✈ Mahārāshtra, W India 19°10′N 72°51′E
83 D14 Mumbué Bié, C Angola 13°52′S 17°15′E
186 E8 Mumeng Morobe, C Papua New Guinea 06°57′S 146°34′E
171 V12 Mumi Papua, E Indonesia 01°33′S 134°09′E
Muminabad/Mū'minobod see Leningrad
127 Q13 Mumra Astrakhanskaya Oblast', SW Russian Federation 45°46′N 47°46′E
41 X12 Muna Yucatán, SE Mexico 20°29′N 89°41′W
123 O9 Muna ≈ NE Russian Federation
152 C12 Munābāo Rājasthān, NW India 25°46′N 70°19′E
Munamägi see Suur Munamägi
171 O14 Muna, Pulau prev. Moena. island C Indonesia
101 L18 Münchberg Bayern, E Germany 50°10′N 11°50′E
101 L23 München var. Muenchen, Eng. Munich, It. Monaco. Bayern, SE Germany 48°09′N 11°34′E
München-Gladbach see Mönchengladbach
108 E6 Münchenstein Basel-Land, NW Switzerland 47°31′N 07°38′E
10 L10 Muncho Lake British Columbia, W Canada 58°52′N 125°40′W
31 P13 Muncie Indiana, N USA 40°11′N 85°22′W
18 G13 Muncy Pennsylvania, NE USA 41°10′N 76°46′W
11 Q14 Mundare Alberta, SW Canada 53°34′N 112°20′W
25 Q5 Munday Texas, SW USA 33°27′N 99°37′W
31 N10 Mundelein Illinois, N USA 42°15′N 88°00′W
101 I15 Münden Niedersachsen, C Germany 52°16′N 08°54′E
105 Q12 Mundo ≈ S Spain
82 B12 Munenga Cuanza Sul, NW Angola 10°03′S 14°40′E
105 P11 Munera Castilla-La Mancha, C Spain 39°03′N 02°29′W
20 E9 Munford Tennessee, S USA 35°27′N 89°49′W
20 K7 Munfordville Kentucky, S USA 37°17′N 85°55′W
182 D5 Mungala South Australia 30°36′S 132°57′E
83 M16 Mungári Manica, C Mozambique 17°09′S 33°33′E
79 O16 Mungbere Orientale, NE Dem. Rep. Congo 02°38′N 28°30′E
153 Q13 Munger prev. Monghyr. Bihār, NE India 25°23′N 86°28′E
182 I2 Mungeranie South Australia 28°02′S 138°42′E
Mu Nggava see Rennell
169 O10 Mungguresak, Tanjung headland Borneo, N Indonesia 01°57′N 109°19′E
Mungiki see Bellona
183 R4 Mungindi New South Wales, SE Australia 28°59′S 149°00′E
Mungkawn see Maingkwan
Mungla see Mongla
82 C13 Mungo Huambo, W Angola 11°49′S 16°16′E
188 F16 Munguuy Bay bay Yap, W Micronesia
82 E13 Munhango Bié, C Angola 12°12′S 18°34′E
Munich see München
105 S7 Muniesa Aragón, NE Spain 41°02′N 00°49′W
31 O4 Munising Michigan, N USA 46°24′N 86°39′W
Munkács see Mukacheve
95 I17 Munkedal Västra Götaland, S Sweden 58°28′N 11°38′E
95 K15 Munkfors Värmland, C Sweden 59°50′N 13°35′E
122 M14 Munku-Sardyk, Gora var. Mönh Sarĭdag. ▲ Mongolia/Russian Federation 51°45′N 100°22′E
99 E18 Munkzwalm Oost-Vlaanderen, NW Belgium 50°53′N 03°44′E
167 R10 Mun, Mae Nam ≈ E Thailand
153 U15 Munshiganj Dhaka, C Bangladesh 23°32′N 90°32′E
108 D8 Münsingen Bern, W Switzerland 46°53′N 07°34′E
103 U6 Munster Haut-Rhin, NE France 48°03′N 07°09′E
100 J11 Munster Niedersachsen, NW Germany 52°59′N 10°07′E
100 F13 Münster var. Muenster, Münster in Westfalen. Nordrhein-Westfalen, W Germany 51°58′N 07°38′E
108 F10 Münster Valais, S Switzerland 46°31′N 08°18′E
97 B20 Munster Ir. Cúige Mumhan. cultural region S Ireland
Münsterberg in Schlesien see Ziębice
Münster in Westfalen see Münster
100 E13 Münsterland cultural region NW Germany
100 F13 Münster-Osnabruck ✈ Nordrhein-Westfalen, NW Germany 52°08′N 07°41′E
31 R4 Munuscong Lake ◎ Michigan, N USA
83 K17 Munyati ≈ C Zimbabwe
109 R3 Münzkirchen Oberösterreich, N Austria 48°29′N 13°37′E
92 K11 Muodoslompolo Norrbotten, N Sweden 67°57′N 23°31′E
92 M13 Muojärvi ◎ NE Finland
167 S6 Mường Khên Hoa Binh, N Vietnam 20°34′N 105°18′E
Muong Sai see Xai
167 Q7 Muong Xiang Ngeun var. Xieng Ngeun. Louangphabang, N Laos 19°43′N 102°09′E
92 K11 Muonio Lappi, N Finland 67°58′N 23°40′E
Muonioälv/Muoniojoki see Muonionjoki
92 K11 Muonionjoki var. Muoniojoki, Swe. Muonioälv. ≈ Finland/Sweden
83 N17 Mupa ≈ C Mozambique
83 E16 Mupini Okavango, NE Namibia 17°55′S 19°34′E
80 F8 Muqaddam, Wadi ≈ N Sudan
138 K9 Muqāṭ Al Mafraq, E Jordan 32°28′N 38°04′E
81 N17 Muqdisho Eng. Mogadishu, It. Mogadiscio. ● (Somalia) Banaadir, S Somalia 02°06′N 45°27′E
81 N17 Muqdisho ✈ Banaadir, E Somalia 01°58′N 45°18′E
Muqshin see Mughshin
109 T8 Mur SCr. Mura. ≈ C Europe
109 X9 Mura ≈ NE Slovenia
Mura see Mur
137 T14 Muradiye Van, E Turkey 39°N 43°44′E
Muragarazi see Maragarazi
165 O10 Murakami Niigata, Honshū, C Japan 38°13′N 139°28′E
63 G22 Murallón, Cerro ▲ S Argentina 49°49′S 73°25′W
81 E20 Muramvya C Burundi 03°18′S 29°41′E
81 I19 Murang'a prev. Fort Hall. Central, SW Kenya 0°43′S 37°10′E
81 H16 Murangering Rift Valley, NW Kenya 03°48′N 35°29′E
Murapara see Murupara
140 M5 Murār, Bi'r al well NW Saudi Arabia
125 Q13 Murashi Kirovskaya Oblast', NW Russian Federation 59°27′N 48°02′E
103 O12 Murat Cantal, C France 45°07′N 02°52′E
114 N12 Muratlı Tekirdağ, NW Turkey 41°12′N 27°30′E
137 R14 Murat Nehri var. Eastern Euphrates; anc. Arsanias. ≈ NE Turkey
107 D20 Muravera Sardegna, Italy, C Mediterranean Sea 39°24′N 09°34′E
165 P10 Murayama Yamagata, Honshū, C Japan 38°29′N 140°21′E
121 R13 Muraysah, Ra's al headland N Libya 31°58′N 25°00′E
104 I6 Murça Vila Real, N Portugal 41°24′N 07°28′W
80 Q11 Murcanyo Bari, NE Somalia 11°39′N 50°27′E
143 N8 Mūrcheh Khvort var. Morcheh Khort. Eşfahān, C Iran 33°07′N 51°26′E
185 H15 Murchison Tasman, South Island, New Zealand 41°48′S 172°19′E
185 B22 Murchison Mountains ▲▲ South Island, New Zealand
180 I10 Murchison River ≈ Western Australia
105 R13 Murcia Murcia, SE Spain 37°59′N 01°08′W
105 Q13 Murcia ◐ autonomous community SE Spain
103 O13 Mur-de-Barrez Aveyron, S France 44°48′N 02°39′E
182 G8 Murdinga South Australia 33°46′S 135°46′E
28 M10 Murdo South Dakota, N USA 43°53′N 100°42′W
15 X6 Murdochville Québec, SE Canada 48°57′N 65°30′W
109 W9 Mureck Steiermark, SE Austria 46°42′N 15°46′E
114 M13 Mürefte Tekirdağ, NW Turkey 40°40′N 27°15′E
116 I10 Mureş ◐ county N Romania
84 J11 Mureş ≈ Hungary/Romania
Mureş see Maros
Mureşul see Maros/Mureş
102 M16 Muret Haute-Garonne, S France 43°28′N 01°19′E
27 T13 Murfreesboro Arkansas, C USA 34°04′N 93°42′W
21 W8 Murfreesboro North Carolina, SE USA 36°26′N 77°06′W
20 J9 Murfreesboro Tennessee, S USA 35°50′N 86°25′W
Murgab see Morghāb, Daryā-ye/Murgap
Murgab see Murghob
146 I14 Murgap Mary Welaýaty, S Turkmenistan 37°19′N 61°48′E
146 J16 Murgap var. Deryasy Murgap, Murghab, Pash. Daryā-ye Morghāb, Rus. Murgab. ≈ Afghanistan/Turkmenistan see also Morghāb, Daryā-ye
Murgap see Morghāb, Daryā-ye
Murgap, Deryasy see Morghāb, Daryā-ye/Murgap
114 H9 Murgash ▲ W Bulgaria 42°51′N 23°58′E
Murghab see Morghāb, Daryā-ye/Murgap
147 U13 Murghob Rus. Murgab. SE Tajikistan 38°11′N 74°E
147 U13 Murghob Rus. Murgab. ≈ SE Tajikistan
181 Z10 Murgon Queensland, E Australia 26°08′S 152°04′E
190 I16 Muri Rarotonga, S Cook Islands 21°15′S 159°44′W
108 F7 Muri Aargau, W Switzerland 47°16′N 08°21′E
108 D8 Muri var. Muri bei Bern. Bern, W Switzerland 46°55′N 07°30′E
104 K3 Murias de Paredes Castilla-León, N Spain 42°51′N 06°11′W
Muri bei Bern see Muri
82 F11 Muriege Lunda Sul, NE Angola 09°55′S 21°12′E
189 P14 Murilo Atoll atoll Hall Islands, C Micronesia
Murītānīyah see Mauritania
100 N10 Müritz var. Müritzee. ◎ NE Germany
Müritzee see Müritz
100 L10 Müritz-Elde-Kanal canal N Germany
184 K6 Muriwai Beach Auckland, North Island, New Zealand 36°56′S 174°28′E
92 J13 Murjek Norrbotten, N Sweden 66°27′N 20°54′E
124 J3 Murmansk Murmanskaya Oblast', NW Russian Federation 68°59′N 33°08′E
124 I4 Murmanskaya Oblast' ◐ province NW Russian Federation
197 V14 Murmansk Rise undersea feature SW Barents Sea 71°00′N 37°00′E
124 J3 Murmashi Murmanskaya Oblast', NW Russian Federation 68°49′N 32°43′E
126 M5 Murmino Ryazanskaya Oblast', W Russian Federation 54°31′N 40°01′E
101 K24 Murnau Bayern, SE Germany 47°41′N 11°12′E
103 X16 Muro, Capo di headland Corse, France, C Mediterranean Sea 41°45′N 08°40′E
107 M18 Muro Lucano Basilicata, S Italy 40°48′N 15°33′E
127 N4 Murom Vladimirskaya Oblast', W Russian Federation 55°33′N 42°03′E
122 I11 Muromtsevo Omskaya Oblast', C Russian Federation 56°18′N 75°15′E
165 R5 Muroran Hokkaidō, NE Japan 42°20′N 140°58′E
104 G3 Muros Galicia, NW Spain 42°47′N 09°04′W
104 F3 Muros e Noia, Ría de estuary NW Spain
164 H15 Muroto Kōchi, Shikoku, SW Japan 33°16′N 134°10′E
164 H15 Muroto-zaki Shikoku, SW Japan
116 L7 Murovani Kurylivtsi Vinnyts'ka Oblast', C Ukraine 48°43′N 27°31′E
110 G11 Murowana Goślina Wielkolpolskie, W Poland 52°33′N 16°59′E
32 M14 Murphy Idaho, NW USA 43°14′N 116°36′W
21 N10 Murphy North Carolina, SE USA 35°05′N 84°02′W
35 P8 Murphys California, W USA 38°07′N 120°27′W
30 L17 Murphysboro Illinois, N USA 37°45′N 89°20′W
29 V15 Murray Iowa, C USA 41°03′N 93°56′W
20 H8 Murray Kentucky, S USA 36°35′N 88°20′W
182 J10 Murray Bridge South Australia 35°10′S 139°17′E
175 X2 Murray Fracture Zone tectonic feature NE Pacific Ocean
192 H11 Murray, Lake ◎ SW Papua New Guinea
21 P12 Murray, Lake ▣ South Carolina, SE USA
10 K8 Murray, Mount ▲ Yukon Territory, NW Canada 60°49′N 128°57′W
Murray Range see Murray Ridge
173 O3 Murray Ridge var. Murray Range. undersea feature N Arabian Sea 21°45′N 61°50′E
183 N10 Murray River ≈ SE Australia
182 K10 Murrayville Victoria, SE Australia 35°17′S 141°12′E
149 U5 Murree Punjab, E Pakistan 33°55′N 73°26′E
101 I21 Murrhardt Baden-Württemberg, S Germany 49°00′N 09°34′E
183 O9 Murrumbidgee River ≈ New South Wales, SE Australia
83 P15 Murrupula Nampula, NE Mozambique 15°26′S 38°46′E

◆ Country ● Country Capital ◇ Dependent Territory ○ Dependent Territory Capital ◐ Administrative Regions ✈ International Airport ▲ Mountain ▲▲ Mountain Range Volcano ≈ River ◎ Lake ▣ Reservoir

MURRURUNDI – NAMHAE-DO

183 T7 **Murrurundi** New South Wales, SE Australia 31°47′S 150°51′E
109 X9 **Murska Sobota** *Ger.* Olsnitz. NE Slovenia 46°41′N 16°09′E
154 G12 **Murtajāpur** *prev.* Murtazapur. Mahārāshtra, C India 20°43′N 77°28′E
77 S16 **Murtala Muhammed** ✈ (Lagos) Ogun, SW Nigeria 06°31′N 03°12′E
Murtazapur *see* Murtajāpur
108 C8 **Murten** Neuchâtel, W Switzerland 46°55′N 07°06′E
Murtensee *see* Morat, Lac de
182 L11 **Murtoa** Victoria, SE Australia 36°39′S 142°27′E
92 N13 **Murtovaara** Oulu, E Finland 65°40′N 29°25′E
Murua Island *see* Woodlark Island
155 D14 **Murud** Mahārāshtra, W India 18°27′N 72°56′E
184 O9 **Murupara** *var.* Murapara. Bay of Plenty, North Island, New Zealand 38°27′S 176°41′E
191 X12 **Mururoa** *var.* Moruroa. *atoll* Îles Tuamotu, SE French Polynesia
Murviedro *see* Sagunto
154 J9 **Murwāra** Madhya Pradesh, N India 23°50′N 80°23′E
183 V4 **Murwillumbah** New South Wales, SE Australia 28°20′S 153°24′E
146 H11 **Murzechirla** *prev.* Mirzachirla. Ahal Welaýaty, C Turkmenistan 39°33′N 60°02′E
Murzuk *see* Murzuq
75 O11 **Murzuq** *var.* Marzūq, Murzuk. SW Libya 25°55′N 13°55′E
Murzuq, Edeyin *see* Murzuq, Idhān
75 N11 **Murzuq, Ḩammādat** *plateau* W Libya
75 O11 **Murzuq, Idhān** *var.* Edeyin Murzuq. *desert* SW Libya
109 W6 **Mürzzuschlag** Steiermark, E Austria 47°35′N 15°41′E
137 Q14 **Muş** *var.* Mush. Muş, E Turkey 38°45′N 41°30′E
137 Q14 **Muş** *var.* Mush. ◈ *province* E Turkey
118 G11 **Mūša** ≈ Latvia/Lithuania
186 F9 **Musa** ≈ S Papua New Guinea
Mûsa, Gebel *see* Mūsá, Jabal
Musaiyib *see* Al Musayyib
75 X8 **Mūsá, Jabal** *var.* Gebel Mûsa. ▲ NE Egypt 28°33′N 33°51′E
Musa Khel *see* Mūsa Khel Bāzār
149 R9 **Mūsa Khel Bāzār** *var.* Musa Khel. Baluchistān, SW Pakistan 30°53′N 69°52′E
114 H10 **Musala** ▲ W Bulgaria 42°12′N 23°36′E
168 H10 **Musala, Pulau** *island* W Indonesia
83 J15 **Musale** Southern, S Zambia 15°27′S 26°50′E
141 Y9 **Muşalla** NE Oman 22°20′N 58°03′E
141 W6 **Musandam Peninsula** *Ar.* Masandam Peninsula. *peninsula* N Oman
Musay'id *see* Umm Sa'id
Muscat *see* Masqaț
Muscat and Oman *see* Oman
29 Y14 **Muscatine** Iowa, C USA 41°25′N 91°03′W
Muscat Sīb Airport *see* Seeb
31 O15 **Muscatuck River** ≈ Indiana, N USA
30 K8 **Muscoda** Wisconsin, N USA 43°11′N 90°27′W
185 F19 **Musgrave, Mount** ▲ South Island, New Zealand 43°48′S 170°43′E
181 P9 **Musgrave Ranges** ▲ South Australia
Mush *see* Muş
138 H12 **Mushayyish, Qaşr al** *castle* Ma'ān, C Jordan
79 H20 **Mushie** Bandundu, W Dem. Rep. Congo 03°00′S 16°55′E
168 M13 **Musi, Air** *prev.* Moesi. ≈ Sumatera, W Indonesia
192 M4 **Musicians Seamounts** *undersea feature* N Pacific Ocean
83 K19 **Musina** *prev.* Messina. Limpopo, NE South Africa 22°18′S 30°02′E
54 D8 **Musinga, Alto** ▲ NW Colombia 06°49′N 76°24′W
29 T2 **Muskeg Bay** *lake bay* Minnesota, N USA
31 O8 **Muskegon** Michigan, N USA 43°13′N 86°15′W
31 O8 **Muskegon Heights** Michigan, N USA 43°12′N 86°14′W
31 P8 **Muskegon River** ≈ Michigan, N USA
31 T14 **Muskingum River** ≈ Ohio, N USA
95 P16 **Muskö** Stockholm, C Sweden 58°58′N 18°10′E
Muskogean *see* Tallahassee
27 Q10 **Muskogee** Oklahoma, C USA 35°45′N 95°21′W
14 H13 **Muskoka, Lake** ◎ Ontario, S Canada
80 H8 **Musmar** Red Sea, NE Sudan 18°13′N 35°40′E
83 K14 **Musofu** Central, C Zambia 13°31′S 29°02′E
81 G19 **Musoma** Mara, N Tanzania 01°31′S 33°49′E
82 L13 **Musoro** Central, C Zambia 13°21′S 31°04′E
186 F4 **Mussau Island** *island* NE Papua New Guinea
98 P7 **Musselkanaal** Groningen, NE Netherlands 52°55′N 07°01′E
33 V9 **Musselshell River** ≈ Montana, NW USA
82 C12 **Mussende** Cuanza Sul, NW Angola 10°33′S 16°02′E
102 L12 **Mussidan** Dordogne, SW France 45°03′N 00°22′E
99 L25 **Musson** Luxembourg, SE Belgium 49°33′N 05°42′E
152 J9 **Mussoorie** Uttarakhand, N India 30°26′N 78°04′E
Musta *see* Mosta
152 M13 **Mustafābād** Uttar Pradesh, N India 25°54′N 81°17′E
136 D12 **Mustafakemalpaşa** Bursa, NW Turkey 40°03′N 28°25′E
Mustafa-Pasha *see* Svilengrad
81 M15 **Mustahīl** Sumalē, E Ethiopia 05°18′N 44°34′E
24 M7 **Mustang Draw** *valley* Texas, SW USA
25 T14 **Mustang Island** *island* Texas, SW USA
Mustasaari *see* Korsholm
Mustér *see* Disentis
63 I19 **Musters, Lago** ◎ S Argentina
45 Y14 **Mustique** *island* C Saint Vincent and the Grenadines
118 I6 **Mustla** Viljandimaa, S Estonia 58°12′N 25°50′E
118 J4 **Mustvee** *Ger.* Tschorna. Jõgevamaa, E Estonia 58°51′N 26°59′E
42 L9 **Musún, Cerro** ▲ NE Nicaragua 13°01′N 85°02′W
183 T7 **Muswellbrook** New South Wales, SE Australia 32°17′S 150°55′E
111 M18 **Muszyna** Małopolskie, SE Poland 49°21′N 20°54′E
75 V10 **Mūţ** *var.* Mut. C Egypt 25°28′N 28°58′E
136 I17 **Mut** İçel, S Turkey 36°38′N 33°27′E
109 V9 **Muta** N Slovenia 46°37′N 15°09′E
190 B15 **Mutalau** N Niue 18°56′S 169°50′E
Mu-tan-chiang *see* Mudanjiang
82 I13 **Mutanda** North Western, NW Zambia 12°24′S 26°13′E
59 O17 **Mutá, Ponta do** *headland* E Brazil 13°54′S 38°54′W
83 L17 **Mutare** *var.* Mutari; *prev.* Umtali. Manicaland, E Zimbabwe 18°55′S 32°36′E
Mutari *see* Mutare
54 D8 **Mutatá** Antioquia, NW Colombia 07°16′N 76°32′W
Mutina *see* Modena
83 L16 **Mutoko** *prev.* Mtoko. Mashonaland East, NE Zimbabwe 17°24′S 32°13′E
81 J20 **Mutomo** Eastern, S Kenya 01°50′S 38°13′E
Mutrah *see* Maţraḩ
Mutsamudu *see* Moutsamoudou
79 M24 **Mutshatsha** Katanga, S Dem. Rep. Congo 10°40′S 24°26′E
165 R6 **Mutsu** *var.* Mutu. Aomori, Honshū, N Japan 41°18′N 141°11′E
165 R6 **Mutsu-wan** *bay* N Japan
108 E6 **Muttenz** Basel-Land, NW Switzerland 47°31′N 07°39′E
185 A26 **Muttonbird Islands** *island group* SW New Zealand
Muttra *see* Mathura
Mutu *see* Mutsu
83 O15 **Mutuáli** Nampula, N Mozambique 14°51′S 37°01′E
82 D13 **Mutumbo** Bié, C Angola 13°10′S 17°22′E
189 Y14 **Mutunte, Mount** *var.* Mount Buache. ▲ Kosrae, E Micronesia 05°21′N 163°00′E
155 K24 **Mutur** Eastern Province, E Sri Lanka 08°27′N 81°15′E
92 L13 **Muurola** Lappi, NW Finland 66°22′N 25°20′E
162 M14 **Mu Us Shadi** *var.* Ordos Desert; *prev.* Mu Us Shamo. *desert* N China
Mu Us Shamo *see* Mu Us Shadi
82 B11 **Muxima** Bengo, NW Angola 09°33′S 13°58′E
124 I8 **Muyezerskiy** Respublika Kareliya, NW Russian Federation 63°54′N 32°00′E
81 E20 **Muyinga** NE Burundi 02°54′S 30°19′E
42 K9 **Muy Muy** Matagalpa, C Nicaragua 12°43′N 85°35′W
Muynak *see* Mo'ynoq
79 N22 **Muyumba** Katanga, SE Dem. Rep. Congo 07°13′S 27°02′E
149 V5 **Muzaffarābād** Jammu and Kashmir, NE Pakistan 34°23′N 73°34′E
149 S10 **Muzaffargarh** Punjab, E Pakistan 30°04′N 71°15′E
152 J9 **Muzaffarnagar** Uttar Pradesh, N India 29°28′N 77°42′E
153 P13 **Muzaffarpur** Bihār, N India 26°07′N 85°23′E
158 H6 **Muzat He** ≈ W China
83 L15 **Muze** Tete, NW Mozambique 15°05′S 31°16′E
122 H8 **Muzhi** Yamalo-Nenetskiy Avtonomnyy Okrug, N Russian Federation 65°25′N 64°28′E
102 H7 **Muzillac** Morbihan, NW France 47°34′N 02°30′W
Muzkol, Khrebet *see* Muzqŭl, Qatorkŭhi
112 L9 **Mužlja** *Hung.* Felsőmuzslya; *prev.* Gornja Mužlja. Vojvodina, N Serbia 45°21′N 20°25′E
54 F9 **Muzo** Boyacá, C Colombia 05°34′N 74°07′W
83 J15 **Muzoka** Southern, S Zambia 16°39′S 27°18′E
39 Y15 **Muzon, Cape** *headland* Dall Island, Alaska, USA 54°39′N 132°41′W
40 M6 **Múzquiz** Coahuila, NE Mexico 27°54′N 101°30′W
147 U13 **Muzqŭl, Qatorkŭhi** *Rus.* Khrebet Muzkol. ▲ SE Tajikistan
158 G10 **Muz Tag** ▲ NW China 36°02′N 80°13′E
158 K10 **Muztag** ▲ W China 36°26′N 87°15′E
158 D8 **Muztagata** ▲ NW China 38°16′N 75°03′E
83 K17 **Mvuma** *prev.* Umvuma. Midlands, C Zimbabwe 19°17′S 30°32′E
172 H13 **Mwali** *var.* Moili, *Fr.* Mohéli. *island* S Comoros
82 L13 **Mwanya** Eastern, E Zambia 12°40′S 32°15′E
79 N23 **Mwanza** Katanga, SE Dem. Rep. Congo 07°49′S 26°49′E
81 G20 **Mwanza** Mwanza, NW Tanzania 02°31′S 32°56′E
81 F20 **Mwanza** ◈ *region* N Tanzania
82 M13 **Mwase Lundazi** Eastern, E Zambia 12°26′S 33°20′E
97 B17 **Mweelrea** *Ir.* Caoc Maol Réidh. ▲ W Ireland 53°37′N 09°47′W
79 K21 **Mweka** Kasai-Occidental, C Dem. Rep. Congo 04°52′S 21°38′E
82 K12 **Mwenda** Luapula, N Zambia 10°30′S 30°21′E
79 L22 **Mwene-Ditu** Kasai-Oriental, S Dem. Rep. Congo 07°06′S 23°34′E
83 L18 **Mwenezi** ≈ S Zimbabwe
79 O20 **Mwenga** Sud-Kivu, E Dem. Rep. Congo 03°00′S 28°28′E
82 K11 **Mweru, Lake** *var.* Lac Moero. ◎ Dem. Rep. Congo/Zambia
82 H13 **Mwinilunga** North Western, NW Zambia 11°44′S 24°24′E
189 V16 **Mwokil Atoll** *prev.* Mokil Atoll. *atoll* Caroline Islands, E Micronesia
Myadel' *see* Myadzyel
118 J13 **Myadzyel** *Pol.* Miadzioł Nowy, *Rus.* Myadel'. Minskaya Voblasts', N Belarus 54°51′N 26°51′E
152 C12 **Myājlār** *var.* Miajlar. Rājasthān, NW India 26°16′N 70°21′E
123 T9 **Myakit** Magadanskaya Oblast', E Russian Federation 61°23′N 151°58′E
23 W13 **Myakka River** ≈ Florida, SE USA
124 L14 **Myaksa** Vologodskaya Oblast', NW Russian Federation 58°54′N 38°15′E
183 U8 **Myall Lake** ◎ New South Wales, SE Australia
166 L7 **Myanaung** Ayeyarwady, SW Burma (Myanmar) 18°17′N 95°19′E
Myanmar *see* Burma
166 K8 **Myaungmya** Ayeyarwady, SW Burma (Myanmar) 16°33′N 94°55′E
Myaydo *see* Aunglan
118 N11 **Myazha** *Rus.* Mezha. Vitsyebskaya Voblasts', NE Belarus 55°41′N 30°25′E
167 N12 **Myeik** *var.* Mergui. Tanintharyi, S Burma (Myanmar) 12°26′N 98°34′E
119 O18 **Myerkulavichy** *Rus.* Merkulovichi. Homyel'skaya Voblasts', SE Belarus 52°58′N 30°36′E
119 N14 **Myezhava** *Rus.* Mezhëvo. Vitsyebskaya Voblasts', NE Belarus 54°38′N 30°20′E
Myggenaes *see* Mykines
166 L5 **Myingyan** Mandalay, C Burma (Myanmar) 21°25′N 95°20′E
167 N12 **Myitkyina** Kachin State, N Burma (Myanmar) 25°24′N 97°25′E
166 M5 **Myittha** Mandalay, C Burma (Myanmar) 21°21′N 96°06′E
111 H19 **Myjava** *Hung.* Miava. Trenčiansky Kraj, W Slovakia 48°45′N 17°35′E
Myjeldino *see* Myyëldino
117 U9 **Mykhaylivka** *Rus.* Mikhaylovka. Zaporiz'ka Oblast', SE Ukraine 47°16′N 35°14′E
95 A18 **Mykines** *Dan.* Myggenaes. *island* W Faeroe Islands
116 I5 **Mykolayiv** L'vivs'ka Oblast', W Ukraine 49°34′N 23°58′E
117 Q10 **Mykolayiv** *Rus.* Nikolayev. Mykolayivs'ka Oblast', S Ukraine 46°58′N 31°59′E
117 Q10 **Mykolayiv** ✈ Mykolayivs'ka Oblast', S Ukraine 47°02′N 31°54′E
Mykolayiv *see* Mykolayivs'ka Oblast'
117 P9 **Mykolayivka** Odes'ka Oblast', SW Ukraine 47°34′N 30°48′E
117 S13 **Mykolayivka** Respublika Krym, S Ukraine 44°58′N 33°37′E
117 P9 **Mykolayivs'ka Oblast'** *var.* Mykolayiv, *Rus.* Nikolayevskaya Oblast'. ◈ *province* S Ukraine
115 J20 **Mýkonos** Mýkonos, Kykládes, Greece, Aegean Sea 37°27′N 25°20′E
115 K20 **Mýkonos** *var.* Míkonos. *island* Kykládes, Greece, Aegean Sea
125 R7 **Myla** Respublika Komi, NW Russian Federation 65°24′N 50°51′E
Mylae *see* Milazzo
93 M19 **Myllykoski** Etelä-Suomi, S Finland 60°45′N 26°52′E
153 U14 **Mymensing** *var.* Mymensingh. Dhaka, N Bangladesh 24°45′N 90°23′E
Mymensingh *see* Mymensing
93 K19 **Mynämäki** Länsi-Suomi, SW Finland 60°41′N 22°00′E
145 S14 **Mynaral** *Kaz.* Myngaral. Zhambyl, S Kazakhstan 45°25′N 73°37′E
Mynbulak *see* Mingbuloq
Mynbulak, Vpadina *see* Mingbuloq Botig'i
Myngaral *see* Mynaral
Myohaung *see* Mrauk-oo
163 W13 **Myohyang-sanmaek** ▲ C North Korea
164 M11 **Myōkō-san** ▲ Honshū, S Japan 36°54′N 138°05′E
83 J15 **Myooye** Central, C Zambia 15°11′S 27°10′E
118 K12 **Myory** *prev.* Miyory. Vitsyebskaya Voblasts', N Belarus 55°39′N 27°39′E
92 J4 **Mýrdalsjökull** *glacier* S Iceland
92 G10 **Myre** Nordland, C Norway 68°54′N 15°04′E
117 S5 **Myrhorod** *Rus.* Mirgorod. Poltavs'ka Oblast', NE Ukraine 49°58′N 33°37′E
115 J15 **Mýrina** *var.* Mírina. Límnos, SE Greece 39°52′N 25°04′E
117 P5 **Myronivka** *Rus.* Mironovka. Kyyivs'ka Oblast', N Ukraine 49°40′N 30°59′E
21 U13 **Myrtle Beach** South Carolina, SE USA 33°41′N 78°53′W
32 F14 **Myrtle Creek** Oregon, NW USA 43°01′N 123°19′W
183 P11 **Myrtleford** Victoria, SE Australia 36°34′S 146°45′E
32 E14 **Myrtle Point** Oregon, NW USA 43°04′N 124°08′W
115 K25 **Mýrtos** Kríti, Greece, E Mediterranean Sea 35°00′N 25°34′E
Myrtoum Mare *see* Mirtóo Pélagos
93 G17 **Myrviken** Jämtland, C Sweden 62°59′N 14°19′E
95 I15 **Mysen** Østfold, S Norway 59°33′N 11°20′E
124 L15 **Myshkin** Yaroslavskaya Oblast', NW Russian Federation 57°47′N 38°28′E
111 K17 **Myślenice** Małopolskie, S Poland 49°50′N 19°55′E
110 D10 **Myślibórz** Zachodnio-pomorskie, NW Poland 52°55′N 14°51′E
155 G20 **Mysore** *var.* Maisur. Karnātaka, W India 12°18′N 76°37′E
Mysore *see* Karnātaka
115 F21 **Mystrás** *var.* Mistras. Pelopónnisos, S Greece 37°03′N 22°22′E
111 K15 **Myszków** Śląskie, S Poland 50°36′N 19°20′E
167 T14 **My Tho** *var.* Mi Tho. Tiền Giang, S Vietnam 10°21′N 106°21′E
Mytilene *see* Mytilíni
115 L17 **Mytilíni** *var.* Mitilíni; *anc.* Mytilene. Lésvos, E Greece 39°06′N 26°33′E
126 K3 **Mytishchi** Moskovskaya Oblast', W Russian Federation 56°00′N 37°51′E
37 N3 **Myton** Utah, W USA 40°11′N 110°03′W
92 K2 **Mývatn** ◎ C Iceland
125 T11 **Myyëldino** *var.* Myjeldino. Respublika Komi, NW Russian Federation 61°46′N 54°48′E
82 M13 **Mzimba** Northern, NW Malawi 11°56′S 33°36′E
82 M12 **Mzuzu** Northern, N Malawi 11°23′S 34°03′E

N

101 M19 **Naab** ≈ SE Germany
98 G12 **Naaldwijk** Zuid-Holland, W Netherlands 52°00′N 04°13′E
38 G12 **Nā'ālehu** *var.* Naalehu. Hawaii, USA, C Pacific Ocean 19°04′N 155°36′W
93 K19 **Naantali** *Swe.* Nådendal. Länsi-Suomi, SW Finland 60°28′N 22°05′E
98 J10 **Naarden** Noord-Holland, C Netherlands 52°18′N 05°10′E
109 U4 **Naarn** ≈ N Austria
97 F18 **Naas** *Ir.* An Nás, Nás na Ríogh. Kildare, C Ireland 53°13′N 06°39′W
92 M9 **Näätämöjoki** *Lapp.* Njávdám. ≈ NE Finland
83 E23 **Nababeep** *var.* Nababiep. Northern Cape, W South Africa 29°36′S 17°46′E
Nababiep *see* Nababeep
Nabadwip *see* Navadwip
155 L14 **Nabarangapur** *var.* Nowrangapur. Orissa, E India 19°13′N 82°33′E
164 J14 **Nabari** Mie, Honshū, SW Japan 34°37′N 136°05′E
Nabatié *see* Nabatîyé
138 G8 **Nabatîyé** *var.* An Nabatīyah at Taḩtā, Nabatié, Nabatiyet et Tahta. SW Lebanon 33°18′N 35°36′E
Nabatiyet et Tahta *see* Nabatîyé
187 X14 **Nabavatu** Vanua Levu, N Fiji 16°35′S 178°55′E
190 I2 **Nabeina** *island* Tungaru, W Kiribati
127 T4 **Naberezhnyye Chelny** *prev.* Brezhnev. Respublika Tatarstan, W Russian Federation 55°43′N 52°21′E
39 T10 **Nabesna** Alaska, USA 62°22′N 143°00′W
39 T10 **Nabesna River** ≈ Alaska, USA
75 N5 **Nabeul** *var.* Nābul. NE Tunisia 36°32′N 10°45′E
152 I9 **Nābha** Punjab, NW India 30°22′N 76°12′E
171 W13 **Nabire** Papua, E Indonesia 03°23′S 135°31′E
141 O15 **Nabī Shu'ayb, Jabal an** ▲ W Yemen 15°24′N 44°04′E
138 F10 **Nablus** *var.* Nābulus, *Heb.* Shekhem; *anc.* Neapolis, *Bibl.* Shechem. N West Bank 32°13′N 35°16′E
187 X14 **Nabouwalu** Vanua Levu, N Fiji 17°00′S 178°43′E
Nābul *see* Nabeul
Nābulus *see* Nablus
187 Y13 **Nabuna** Vanua Levu, N Fiji 16°13′S 179°46′E
83 Q14 **Nacala** Nampula, NE Mozambique 14°30′S 40°37′E
42 H8 **Nacaome** Valle, S Honduras 13°30′N 87°31′W
Na Cealla Beaga *see* Killybegs
Na-Ch'i *see* Nagqu
164 J15 **Nachikatsuura** *var.* Nachi-Katsuura. Wakayama, Honshū, SE Japan 33°37′N 135°54′E
Nachi-Katsuura *see* Nachikatsuura
81 J24 **Nachingwea** Lindi, SE Tanzania 10°21′S 38°46′E
111 F16 **Náchod** Královéhradecký Kraj, N Czech Republic 50°26′N 16°10′E
Na Clocha Liatha *see* Greystones
40 G3 **Naco** Sonora, NW Mexico 31°16′N 109°56′W
25 X8 **Nacogdoches** Texas, SW USA 31°36′N 94°40′W
40 G4 **Nacozari de García** Sonora, NW Mexico 30°27′N 109°43′W
Nada *see* Danzhou
77 O14 **Nadawli** NW Ghana 10°30′N 02°40′W
104 I3 **Nadela** Galicia, NW Spain 42°58′N 07°33′W
Nådendal *see* Naantali
144 M7 **Nadezhdinka** *prev.* Nadezhdinskiy. Kostanay, N Kazakhstan 53°46′N 63°44′E
Nadezhdinskiy *see* Nadezhdinka
Nadgan *see* Nadqān, Qalamat
187 W14 **Nadi** *prev.* Nandi. Viti Levu, W Fiji 17°47′S 177°32′E
187 X14 **Nadi** *prev.* Nandi. ✈ Viti Levu, W Fiji 17°46′S 177°28′E
154 D10 **Nadiād** Gujarāt, W India 22°42′N 72°55′E
Nadikdik *see* Knox Atoll
116 E11 **Nădlac** *Ger.* Nadlak, *Hung.* Nagylak. Arad, W Romania 46°10′N 20°47′E
Nadlak *see* Nădlac
74 H6 **Nador** *prev.* Villa Nador. NE Morocco 35°10′N 05°22′W
141 S9 **Nadqān, Qalamat** *var.* Nadgan. *well* E Saudi Arabia
111 N22 **Nádudvar** Hajdú-Bihar, E Hungary 47°36′N 21°09′E
121 O15 **Nadur** Gozo, N Malta 36°03′N 14°18′E
187 X13 **Naduri** *prev.* Nanduri. Vanua Levu, N Fiji 16°26′S 179°08′E
116 I7 **Nadvirna** *Pol.* Nadwórna, *Rus.* Nadvornaya. Ivano-Frankivs'ka Oblast', W Ukraine 48°27′N 24°30′E
124 J8 **Nadvoitsy** Respublika Kareliya, NW Russian Federation 63°53′N 34°17′E
Nadvornaya/Nadwórna *see* Nadvirna
122 I9 **Nadym** Yamalo-Nenetskiy Avtonomnyy Okrug, N Russian Federation 65°25′N 72°40′E
122 I9 **Nadym** ≈ C Russian Federation
186 E7 **Nadzab** Morobe, C Papua New Guinea 06°36′S 146°46′E
95 C17 **Nærbø** Rogaland, S Norway 58°40′N 05°39′E
95 I24 **Næstved** Storstrøm, SE Denmark 55°12′N 11°47′E
77 X13 **Nafada** Gombe, E Nigeria 11°02′N 11°18′E
108 H8 **Näfels** Glarus, NE Switzerland 47°06′N 09°04′E
115 E18 **Náfpaktos** *var.* Návpaktos. Dytikí Elláda, C Greece 38°23′N 21°50′E
115 F20 **Náfplio** *prev.* Návplion. Pelopónnisos, S Greece 37°34′N 22°50′E
139 U6 **Naft Khāneh** Diyālá, E Iraq 34°01′N 45°26′E
149 N13 **Nāg** Baluchistān, SW Pakistan 27°43′N 65°31′E
171 P4 **Naga** *off.* Naga City; *prev.* Nueva Caceres. Luzon, N Philippines 13°36′N 123°10′E
Nagaarzê *see* Nagarzê
Naga City *see* Naga
12 F11 **Nagagami** ≈ Ontario, S Canada
164 F14 **Nagahama** Ehime, Shikoku, SW Japan 33°36′N 132°29′E
153 X12 **Nāga Hills** ▲ NE India
165 P10 **Nagai** Yamagata, Honshū, C Japan 38°08′N 140°00′E
Na Gaibhlte *see* Galty Mountains
39 N16 **Nagai Island** *island* Shumagin Islands, Alaska, USA
153 X12 **Nāgāland** ◈ *state* NE India
164 M11 **Nagano** Nagano, Honshū, S Japan 36°39′N 138°11′E
164 M12 **Nagano** *off.* Nagano-ken. ◈ *prefecture* Honshū, S Japan
Nagano-ken *see* Nagano
165 N11 **Nagaoka** Niigata, Honshū, C Japan 37°26′N 138°48′E
153 W12 **Nagaon** *prev.* Nowgong. Assam, NE India 26°21′N 92°41′E
155 J21 **Nāgappattinam** *var.* Negapatam, Negappattinam. Tamil Nādu, SE India 10°45′N 79°50′E
Nagara Nayok *see* Nakhon Nayok
Nagara Panom *see* Nakhon Phanom
Nagara Pathom *see* Nakhon Pathom
Nagara Sridharmaraj *see* Nakhon Si Thammarat
Nagara Svarga *see* Nakhon Sawan
155 H16 **Nāgārjuna Sāgar** ⊠ E India
42 I10 **Nagarote** León, SW Nicaragua 12°15′N 86°35′W
158 M16 **Nagarzê** *var.* Nagaarzê. Xizang Zizhiqu, W China 28°57′N 90°26′E
164 C14 **Nagasaki** Nagasaki, Kyūshū, SW Japan 32°45′N 129°52′E
164 C14 **Nagasaki** *off.* Nagasaki-ken. ◈ *prefecture* Kyūshū, SW Japan
Nagasaki-ken *see* Nagasaki
Nagashima *see* Kii-Nagashima
164 E12 **Nagato** Yamaguchi, Honshū, SW Japan 34°22′N 131°10′E
152 F11 **Nāgaur** Rājasthān, NW India 27°12′N 73°48′E
154 F10 **Nāgda** Madhya Pradesh, C India 23°30′N 75°29′E
98 L8 **Nagele** Flevoland, N Netherlands 52°39′N 05°43′E
155 H24 **Nāgercoil** Tamil Nādu, SE India 08°11′N 77°30′E
153 X12 **Nāginimāra** Nāgāland, NE India 26°44′N 94°51′E
Na Gleannta *see* Glenties
165 T16 **Nago** Okinawa, Okinawa, SW Japan 26°36′N 127°59′E
154 K9 **Nāgod** Madhya Pradesh, C India 24°34′N 80°34′E
155 J26 **Nagoda** Southern Province, S Sri Lanka 06°13′N 80°13′E
101 G22 **Nagold** Baden-Württemberg, SW Germany 48°33′N 08°43′E
137 V12 **Nagorno-Karabakh** *var.* Nagorno- Karabakhskaya Avtonomnaya Oblast, *Arm.* Lerrnayin Gharabakh, *Az.* Dağliq Quarabağ, *Rus.* Nagornyy Karabakh. *former autonomous region* SW Azerbaijan
Nagorno- Karabakhskaya Avtonomnaya Oblast *see* Nagorno-Karabakh
123 Q12 **Nagornyy** Respublika Sakha (Yakutiya), NE Russian Federation 55°53′N 124°58′E
Nagornyy Karabakh *see* Nagorno-Karabakh
125 R13 **Nagorsk** Kirovskaya Oblast', NW Russian Federation 59°18′N 50°49′E
164 K13 **Nagoya** Aichi, Honshū, SW Japan 35°10′N 136°53′E
154 I12 **Nāgpur** Mahārāshtra, C India 21°09′N 79°06′E
156 K10 **Nagqu** *Chin.* Na-Ch'ii; *prev.* Hei-ho. Xizang Zizhiqu, W China 31°30′N 91°57′E
152 J8 **Nāg Tibba Range** ▲ N India
45 O8 **Nagua** NE Dominican Republic 19°25′N 69°49′W
111 H25 **Nagyatád** Somogy, SW Hungary 46°15′N 17°25′E
Nagybánya *see* Baia Mare
Nagybecskerek *see* Zrenjanin
Nagydisznód *see* Cisnădie
Nagyenyed *see* Aiud
111 N21 **Nagykálló** Szabolcs-Szatmár-Bereg, E Hungary 47°50′N 21°47′E
111 G25 **Nagykanizsa** *Ger.* Grosskanizsa. Zala, SW Hungary 46°27′N 17°E
Nagykároly *see* Carei
111 K22 **Nagykáta** Pest, C Hungary 47°25′N 19°45′E
Nagykikinda *see* Kikinda
111 K23 **Nagykőrös** Pest, C Hungary 47°01′N 19°46′E
Nagy-Küküllő *see* Târnava Mare
Nagylak *see* Nădlac
Nagymihály *see* Michalovce
Nagyrőce *see* Revúca
Nagysomkút *see* Şomcuta Mare
Nagysurány *see* Šurany
Nagyszalonta *see* Salonta
Nagyszeben *see* Sibiu
Nagyszentmiklós *see* Sânnicolau Mare
Nagyszöllös *see* Vynohradiv
Nagyszombat *see* Trnava
Nagytapolcsány *see* Topoľčany
Nagyvárad *see* Oradea
165 S17 **Naha** Okinawa, Okinawa, SW Japan 26°10′N 127°40′E
152 J8 **Nāhan** Himāchal Pradesh, NW India 30°33′N 77°18′E
Nahang, Rūd-e *see* Nihing
138 F8 **Nahariya** *prev.* Nahariyya. Northern, N Israel 33°01′N 35°05′E
Nahariyya *see* Nahariya
142 L6 **Nahāvand** *var.* Nehavend. Hamadān, W Iran 34°13′N 48°21′E
101 F19 **Nahe** ≈ SW Germany
Na H-Iarmhidhe *see* Westmeath
189 O13 **Nahnalaud** ▲ Pohnpei, E Micronesia
Nahoi, Cape *see* Cumberland, Cape
Nahtavárr *see* Nattavaara
63 H16 **Nahuel Huapí, Lago** ◎ W Argentina
23 W7 **Nahunta** Georgia, SE USA 31°11′N 81°58′W
40 J6 **Naica** Chihuahua, N Mexico 27°53′N 105°30′W
11 U15 **Naicam** Saskatchewan, S Canada 52°26′N 104°30′W
Naiman Qi *see* Daqin Tal
158 M4 **Naimin Bulak** *spring* NW China
13 P6 **Nain** Newfoundland and Labrador, NE Canada 56°33′N 61°46′W
143 P8 **Nā'īn** Eşfahān, C Iran 32°52′N 53°05′E
152 K10 **Naini Tāl** Uttarakhand, N India 29°22′N 79°26′E
154 J11 **Nainpur** Madhya Pradesh, C India 22°26′N 80°10′E
96 J8 **Nairn** N Scotland, United Kingdom 57°36′N 03°51′W
96 I8 **Nairn** *cultural region* NE Scotland, United Kingdom
81 I19 **Nairobi** ● (Kenya) Nairobi Area, S Kenya 01°17′S 36°50′E
81 I19 **Nairobi** ✈ Nairobi Area, S Kenya 01°21′S 37°01′E
82 P13 **Nairoto** Cabo Delgado, NE Mozambique 12°22′S 39°05′E
118 G3 **Naissaar** *island* N Estonia
Naissus *see* Niš
187 Z14 **Naitaba** *var.* Naitauba; *prev.* Naitamba. *island* Lau Group, E Fiji
Naitamba/Naitauba *see* Naitaba
81 I19 **Naivasha** Rift Valley, SW Kenya 00°44′S 36°26′E
81 H19 **Naivasha, Lake** ◎ SW Kenya
Najaf *see* An Najaf
143 N8 **Najafābād** *var.* Nejafabad. Eşfahān, C Iran 32°38′N 51°23′E
141 N7 **Najd** *var.* Nejd. *cultural region* C Saudi Arabia
105 O4 **Nájera** La Rioja, N Spain 42°25′N 02°45′W
105 P4 **Najerilla** ≈ N Spain
163 U7 **Naji** *var.* Arun Qi. Nei Mongol Zizhiqu, N China 48°05′N 123°28′E
152 J9 **Najībābād** Uttar Pradesh, N India 29°37′N 78°19′E
Najima *see* Fukuoka
163 Y11 **Najin** NE North Korea 42°13′N 130°16′E
139 T9 **Najm al Ḩassūn** Bābil, C Iraq 32°24′N 44°13′E
141 O13 **Najrān** *var.* Abā as Su'ūd. Najrān, S Saudi Arabia 17°31′N 44°09′E
141 P12 **Najrān** *var.* Minţaqat al Najrān. ◈ *province* S Saudi Arabia
Najrān, Minţaqat al *see* Najrān
165 T2 **Nakagawa** Hokkaidō, NE Japan 44°49′N 142°04′E
38 F9 **Nākālele Point** *var.* Nakalele Point. *headland* Maui, Hawai'i, USA 21°01′N 156°35′W
164 D13 **Nakama** Fukuoka, Kyūshū, SW Japan 33°53′N 130°48′E
Nakambé *see* White Volta
Nakamti *see* Nek'emtē
164 F15 **Nakamura** *var.* Shimanto. Kōchi, Shikoku, SW Japan 33°00′N 132°55′E
186 H7 **Nakanai Mountains** ▲ New Britain, E Papua New Guinea
164 H11 **Nakano-shima** *island* Oki-shotō, SW Japan
165 Q6 **Nakasato** Aomori, Honshū, C Japan 40°58′N 140°26′E
165 T5 **Nakasatsunai** Hokkaidō, NE Japan 42°42′N 143°09′E
165 W4 **Nakashibetsu** Hokkaidō, NE Japan 43°31′N 144°58′E
81 F18 **Nakasongola** C Uganda 01°19′N 32°28′E
165 T1 **Nakatonbetsu** Hokkaidō, NE Japan 44°58′N 142°18′E
164 L13 **Nakatsugawa** *var.* Nakatugawa. Gifu, Honshū, SW Japan 35°30′N 137°29′E
Nakatugawa *see* Nakatsugawa
Nakdong *see* Naktong-gang
Nakel *see* Nakło nad Notecią
Nakfa *see* Nak'fa
80 J8 **Nak'fa** *var.* Nakfa. N Eritrea 16°38′N 38°26′E
Nakhichevan' *see* Naxçıvan
123 S15 **Nakhodka** Primorskiy Kray, SE Russian Federation 42°46′N 132°48′E
122 J8 **Nakhodka** Yamalo-Nenetskiy Avtonomnyy Okrug, N Russian Federation 67°48′N 77°48′E
Nakhon Navok *see* Nakhon Nayok
167 P11 **Nakhon Nayok** *var.* Nagara Nayok, Nakhon Navok. Nakhon Nayok, C Thailand 14°15′N 101°12′E
167 O11 **Nakhon Pathom** *var.* Nagara Pathom, Nakorn Pathom. Nakhon Pathom, W Thailand 13°49′N 100°06′E
167 R8 **Nakhon Phanom** *var.* Nagara Panom. Nakhon Phanom, E Thailand 17°22′N 104°46′E
167 Q10 **Nakhon Ratchasima** *var.* Khorat, Korat. Nakhon Ratchasima, E Thailand 15°N 102°06′E
167 O9 **Nakhon Sawan** *var.* Muang Nakhon Sawan, Nagara Svarga. Nakhon Sawan, W Thailand 15°42′N 100°06′E
167 N15 **Nakhon Si Thammarat** *var.* Nagara Sridharmaraj, Nakhon Sithamnaraj. Nakhon Si Thammarat, SW Thailand 08°24′N 99°58′E
Nakhon Sithamnaraj *see* Nakhon Si Thammarat
139 Y11 **Nakhrash** Al Başrah, SE Iraq 31°13′N 47°24′E
10 I9 **Nakina** British Columbia, W Canada 59°12′N 132°48′W
110 H9 **Nakło nad Notecią** *Ger.* Nakel. Kujawsko-pomorskie, C Poland 53°08′N 17°35′E
39 P13 **Naknek** Alaska, USA 58°45′N 157°01′W
152 H8 **Nakodar** Punjab, NW India 31°06′N 75°31′E
82 M11 **Nakonde** Northern, NE Zambia 09°22′S 42°47′E
Nakorn Pathom *see* Nakhon Pathom
95 H24 **Nakskov** Storstrøm, SE Denmark 54°50′N 11°10′E
163 Y15 **Naktong-gang** *var.* Nakdong, *Jap.* Rakutō-kō. ≈ C South Korea
81 H18 **Nakuru** Rift Valley, SW Kenya 0°16′S 36°04′E
81 H19 **Nakuru, Lake** ◎ Rift Valley, C Kenya
11 O17 **Nakusp** British Columbia, SW Canada 50°15′N 117°48′W
149 N15 **Nāl** ≈ W Pakistan
162 M7 **Nalayh** Töv, C Mongolia 47°48′N 107°17′E
153 V12 **Nalbāri** Assam, NE India 26°36′N 91°49′E
63 G19 **Nalcayec, Isla** *island* Archipiélago de los Chonos, S Chile
127 N15 **Nal'chik** Kabardino-Balkarskaya Respublika, SW Russian Federation 43°30′N 43°39′E
155 I16 **Nalgonda** Andhra Pradesh, C India 17°04′N 79°15′E
153 S14 **Nalhāti** West Bengal, NE India 24°19′N 87°53′E
153 U14 **Nalitabari** Dhaka, N Bangladesh 25°06′N 90°11′E
155 J17 **Nallamala Hills** ▲ E India
136 G12 **Nallıhan** Ankara, NW Turkey 40°12′N 31°22′E
104 K2 **Nalón** ≈ NW Spain
167 N3 **Nalong** Kachin State, N Burma (Myanmar) 24°42′N 97°27′E
75 N8 **Nālūt** NW Libya 31°52′N 10°59′E
171 T16 **Nama** Pulau Manawoka, E Indonesia 04°07′S 131°22′E
189 Q16 **Nama** *island* C Micronesia
83 O16 **Namacurra** Zambézia, NE Mozambique 17°31′S 37°03′E
188 F9 **Namai Bay** *bay* Babeldaob, N Palau
Namakal *see* Nāmakkal
29 W2 **Namakan Lake** ◎ Canada/USA
143 O6 **Namak, Daryācheh-ye** *marsh* N Iran
155 H22 **Nāmakkal** *var.* Namakal. Tamil Nādu, SE India 11°13′N 78°10′E
143 T6 **Namak, Kavīr-e** *salt pan* NE Iran
167 O6 **Namaklwe** Shan State, E Burma (Myanmar) 19°45′N 99°01′E
Namaksār, Kowl-e/Namakzār, Daryācheh-ye *see* Namakzar
148 I5 **Namakzar** *Pash.* Daryācheh-ye Namakzār, Kowl-e Namaksār. *marsh* Afghanistan/Iran
171 V15 **Namalau** Pulau Jursian, E Indonesia 05°50′S 134°43′E
81 I20 **Namanga** Rift Valley, S Kenya 02°33′S 36°48′E
147 S10 **Namangan** Namangan Viloyati, E Uzbekistan 40°59′N 71°34′E
Namanganskaya Oblast' *see* Namangan Viloyati
147 R10 **Namangan Viloyati** *Rus.* Namanganskaya Oblast'. ◈ *province* E Uzbekistan
83 Q14 **Namapa** Nampula, NE Mozambique 13°43′S 39°48′E
83 C21 **Namaqualand** *physical region* S Namibia
81 G18 **Namasagali** C Uganda 01°02′N 32°58′E
186 H6 **Namatanai** New Ireland, NE Papua New Guinea 03°40′S 152°26′E
83 I14 **Nambala** Central, C Zambia 15°04′S 26°56′E
81 J23 **Nambanje** Lindi, SE Tanzania 08°37′S 38°21′E
183 V2 **Nambour** Queensland, E Australia 26°40′S 152°52′E
183 V6 **Nambucca Heads** New South Wales, SE Australia 30°37′S 153°00′E
159 N15 **Nam Co** ◎ W China
167 R5 **Nâm Cum** Lai Châu, N Vietnam 22°37′N 103°12′E
Namdik *see* Namorik Atoll
167 T6 **Nam Định** Nam Ha, N Vietnam 20°25′N 106°12′E
99 I20 **Namêche** Namur, SE Belgium 50°29′N 05°02′E
30 J4 **Namekagon Lake** ◎ Wisconsin, N USA
188 F10 **Namekakl Passage** *passage* Babeldaob, N Palau
Namen *see* Namur
83 P15 **Nametil** Nampula, NE Mozambique 15°46′S 39°21′E
163 X14 **Nam-gang** ≈ C North Korea
163 Y16 **Nam-gang** ≈ C South Korea
163 Y17 **Namhae-do** *Jap.* Nankai-tō. *island* S South Korea

◆ Country ● Country Capital ◇ Dependent Territory ○ Dependent Territory Capital ◈ Administrative Regions ✈ International Airport ▲ Mountain ▲ Mountain Range △ Volcano ≈ River ◎ Lake ⊠ Reservoir
293

NAMHOI – NEÁPOLI

Namhoi see Foshan
83 C19 Namib Desert desert W Namibia
83 A15 Namibe Port. Moçâmedes, Mossâmedes. Namibe, SW Angola 15°10′S 12°09′E
83 A15 Namibe ◆ province SE Angola
83 C18 Namibia off. Republic of Namibia, var. South West Africa, Afr. Suidwes-Afrika, Ger. Deutsch-Südwestafrika; prev. German Southwest Africa, South-West Africa. ◆ republic S Africa
65 O17 Namibia Plain undersea feature S Atlantic Ocean
Namibia, Republic of see Namibia
165 Q11 Namie Fukushima, Honshū, C Japan 37°29′N 140°58′E
165 Q7 Namioka Aomori, Honshū, C Japan 40°43′N 140°34′E
40 I5 Namiquipa Chihuahua, N Mexico 29°15′N 107°25′W
159 P15 Namjagbarwa Feng ▲ W China 29°39′N 95°00′E
Namka see Doilungdêqên
171 R13 Namlea Pulau Buru, E Indonesia 03°12′S 127°06′E
158 L16 Namling Xizang Zizhiqu, W China 29°40′N 88°58′E
Namnetes see Nantes
167 R8 Nam Ngum ≈ C Laos
Namo see Namu Atoll
183 R5 Namoi River ≈ New South Wales, SE Australia
189 Q17 Namoluk Atoll atoll Mortlock Islands, C Micronesia
189 O15 Namonuito Atoll atoll Caroline Islands, C Micronesia
189 T9 Namorik Atoll var. Namdik. atoll Ralik Chain, S Marshall Islands
167 Q6 Nam Ou ≈ N Laos
32 M14 Nampa Idaho, NW USA 43°32′N 116°33′W
76 M11 Nampala Ségou, W Mali 15°21′N 05°32′W
163 W14 Namp'o SW North Korea 38°46′N 125°25′E
83 P15 Nampula Nampula, NE Mozambique 15°09′S 39°14′E
83 P15 Nampula off. Província de Nampula. ◆ province NE Mozambique
Nampula, Província de see Nampula
163 W13 Namsan-ni NW North Korea 40°25′N 125°01′E
Namslau see Namysłów
93 E15 Namsos Nord-Trøndelag, C Norway 64°28′N 11°31′E
93 F14 Namsskogan Nord-Trøndelag, C Norway 64°57′N 13°04′E
167 O6 Nam Teng ≈ E Burma (Myanmar)
167 P6 Nam Tha ≈ N Laos
123 Q10 Namtsy Respublika Sakha (Yakutiya), NE Russian Federation 62°42′N 129°30′E
167 N4 Namtu Shan State, E Burma (Myanmar) 23°04′N 97°26′E
10 J15 Namu British Columbia, SW Canada 51°46′N 127°49′W
189 T7 Namu Atoll var. Namo. atoll Ralik Chain, C Marshall Islands
187 Y15 Namuka-i-lau island Lau Group, E Fiji
83 O15 Namuli, Mont ▲ NE Mozambique 15°15′S 37°33′E
83 P14 Namuno Cabo Delgado, N Mozambique 13°39′S 38°50′E
99 I20 Namur Dut. Namen. Namur, SE Belgium 50°28′N 04°52′E
99 H21 Namur Dut. Namen. ◆ province S Belgium
83 D17 Namutoni Kunene, N Namibia 18°49′S 16°55′E
163 Y16 Namwŏn Jap. Nangen. S South Korea 35°24′N 127°20′E
111 H14 Namysłów Ger. Namslau. Opole, SW Poland 51°03′N 17°41′E
167 P7 Nan var. Muang Nan. Nan, NW Thailand 18°47′N 100°50′E
79 G15 Nana ≈ W Central African Republic
165 R5 Nanae Hokkaidō, NE Japan 41°55′N 140°40′E
79 I14 Nana-Grébizi ◆ prefecture N Central African Republic
10 L17 Nanaimo Vancouver Island, British Columbia, SW Canada 49°08′N 123°58′W
38 C9 Nānākuli var. Nanakuli. Oʻahu, Hawaii, USA, C Pacific Ocean 21°23′N 158°09′W
79 G15 Nana-Mambéré ◆ prefecture W Central African Republic
161 R13 Nan'an Fujian, SE China 24°57′N 118°22′E
183 U2 Nanango Queensland, E Australia 26°42′S 151°58′E
164 L11 Nanao Ishikawa, Honshū, SW Japan 37°03′N 136°58′E
161 Q14 Nan'ao Dao island S China
164 L10 Nanatsu-shima island SW Japan
56 F8 Nanay, Río ≈ NE Peru
160 J8 Nanbu Sichuan, C China 31°19′N 106°02′E
163 X7 Nancha Heilongjiang, NE China 47°09′N 129°17′E
161 P10 Nanchang var. Nan-ch'ang, Nanch'ang-hsien. province capital Jiangxi, S China 28°38′N 115°58′E
Nan-ch'ang see Nanchang
Nanch'ang-hsien see Nanchang
161 P11 Nancheng var. Jianchang. Jiangxi, S China 27°37′N 116°37′E
Nan-ching see Nanjing
160 J9 Nanchong Sichuan, C China 30°47′N 106°03′E
160 J10 Nanchuan Chongqing Shi, C China 29°06′N 107°13′E
103 T5 Nancy Meurthe-et-Moselle, NE France 48°40′N 06°11′E
185 A22 Nancy Sound sound South Island, New Zealand
152 L9 Nanda Devi ▲ NW India 30°27′N 80°00′E
42 J11 Nandaime Granada, SW Nicaragua 11°45′N 86°02′W
160 K13 Nandan var. Minami-Awaji. Guangxi Zhuangzu Zizhiqu, S China 25°03′N 107°31′E
155 H14 Nānded Mahārāshtra, C India 19°11′N 77°21′E
183 S5 Nandewar Range ▲▲ New South Wales, SE Australia
Nandi see Nadi
160 E13 Nanding He ≈ China/Vietnam
Nándorhgy see Oţelu Roşu
154 E11 Nandurbār Mahārāshtra, W India 21°22′N 74°18′E
Nanduri see Naduri
155 I17 Nandyāl Andhra Pradesh, E India 15°30′N 78°28′E
161 P11 Nanfeng var. Qincheng. Jiangxi, S China 27°15′N 116°16′E
Nang see Nangxian
79 E15 Nanga Eboko Centre, C Cameroon 04°38′N 12°21′E
Nangah Serawai see Nangaserawai
149 W4 Nanga Parbat ▲ India/Pakistan 35°15′N 74°36′E
169 R11 Nangapinoh Borneo, C Indonesia 0°21′S 111°44′E
149 R5 Nangarhār ◆ province E Afghanistan
169 S11 Nangaserawai var. Nangah Serawai. Borneo, C Indonesia 0°20′S 112°26′E
169 Q12 Nangatayap Borneo, C Indonesia 01°30′S 110°33′E
Nangen see Namwŏn
103 P5 Nangis Seine-et-Marne, N France 48°36′N 03°02′E
163 X13 Nangnim-sanmaek ▲▲ C North Korea
161 O4 Nangong Hebei, E China 37°22′N 115°20′E
159 Q14 Nangqên var. Xangda. Qinghai, C China 32°05′N 96°28′E
167 Q10 Nang Rong Buri Ram, E Thailand 14°37′N 102°48′E
159 O16 Nangxian var. Nang. Xizang Zizhiqu, W China 29°04′N 93°03′E
Nan Hai see South China Sea
160 L8 Nan He ≈ C China
160 F12 Nanhua var. Longchuan. Yunnan, SW China 25°15′N 101°15′E
Naniwa see Ōsaka
155 G20 Nanjangūd Karnātaka, W India 12°07′N 76°40′E
161 Q8 Nanjing var. Nan-ching, Nanking; prev. Chianning, Chian-ning, Kiang-ning, Jiangsu. province capital Jiangsu, E China 32°03′N 118°47′E
Nankai-tō see Namhae-do
161 O12 Nankang var. Rongjiang. Jiangxi, S China 25°42′N 114°45′E
Nanking see Nanjing
161 N13 Nan Ling ▲▲ S China
160 L15 Nanliu Jiang ≈ S China
189 P13 Nan Madol ruins Temwen Island, E Micronesia
160 K15 Nanning var. Nan-ning; prev. Yung-ning. Guangxi Zhuangzu Zizhiqu, S China 22°50′N 108°19′E
Nan-ning see Nanning
196 M15 Nanortalik Kitaa, S Greenland 60°12′N 44°53′W
Nanouki see Aranuka
160 H13 Nanpan Jiang ≈ S China
152 M11 Nānpāra Uttar Pradesh, N India 27°51′N 81°30′E
161 Q12 Nanping var. Nan-p'ing; prev. Yenping. Fujian, SE China 26°40′N 118°07′E
Nan-p'ing see Nanping
Nanping see Jiuzhaigou
Nanpu see Pucheng
161 R12 Nanri Dao island SE China
165 S16 Nansei-shotō Eng. Ryukyu Islands. island group SW Japan
Nansei Syotō Trench see Ryukyu Trench
197 T10 Nansen Basin undersea feature Arctic Ocean
197 T10 Nansen Cordillera var. Arctic Mid Oceanic Ridge, Nansen Ridge. undersea feature Arctic Ocean 87°00′N 90°00′E
Nansen Ridge see Nansen Cordillera
129 T9 Nan Shan ▲▲ C China
Nansha Qundao see Spratly Islands
12 K3 Nantais, Lac ◎ Québec, NE Canada
103 N5 Nanterre Hauts-de-Seine, N France 48°53′N 02°13′E
102 I8 Nantes Bret. Naoned; anc. Condivincum, Namnetes. Loire-Atlantique, NW France 47°12′N 01°32′W
14 G17 Nanticoke Ontario, S Canada 42°49′N 80°04′W
18 H13 Nanticoke Pennsylvania, NE USA 41°12′N 76°00′W
21 Y4 Nanticoke River ≈ Delaware/Maryland, NE USA
11 Q17 Nanton Alberta, SW Canada 50°21′N 113°47′W
161 S8 Nantong Jiangsu, E China 32°00′N 120°52′E
161 S13 Nant'ou W Taiwan 23°54′N 120°51′E
103 S10 Nantua Ain, E France 46°10′N 05°34′E
19 Q13 Nantucket Nantucket Island, Massachusetts, NE USA 41°15′N 70°05′W
19 Q13 Nantucket Island island Massachusetts, NE USA
19 Q13 Nantucket Sound sound Massachusetts, NE USA
82 P13 Nantulo Cabo Delgado, N Mozambique 12°30′S 39°03′E
189 O12 Nanuh Pohnpei, E Micronesia
190 D6 Nanumanga var. Nanumaga. atoll NW Tuvalu
Nanumanga see Nanumaga
190 D5 Nanumea Atoll atoll NW Tuvalu
59 O19 Nanuque Minas Gerais, SE Brazil 17°49′S 40°21′W
171 R10 Nanusa, Kepulauan island group N Indonesia
163 U4 Nanweng He ≈ NE China
160 I10 Nanxi Sichuan, C China 28°54′N 104°59′E
161 N10 Nanxian var. Nan Xian, Nanzhou. Hunan, S China 29°23′N 112°18′E
Nan Xian see Nanxian
161 N7 Nanyang var. Nan-yang. Henan, C China 32°59′N 112°29′E
Nan-yang see Nanyang
161 P6 Nanyang Hu ◎ E China
165 P10 Nan'yō Yamagata, Honshū, C Japan 38°04′N 140°06′E
81 I18 Nanyuki Central, C Kenya 0°01′N 37°05′E
160 M8 Nanzhang Hubei, C China 31°47′N 111°48′E
Nanzhou see Nanxian
105 T11 Nao, Cabo de La headland E Spain 38°43′N 00°13′E
12 M9 Naococane, Lac ◎ Québec, E Canada
153 S14 Naogaon Rajshahi, NW Bangladesh 24°49′N 88°59′E
Naokot see Naukot
187 R13 Naone Maewo, C Vanuatu 15°03′S 168°06′E
Naoned see Nantes
115 E14 Náousa Kentrikí Makedonía, N Greece 40°38′N 22°04′E
35 N8 Napa California, W USA 38°15′N 122°17′W
39 O11 Napaimiut Alaska, USA 61°32′N 158°46′W
39 N12 Napakiak Alaska, USA 60°42′N 161°57′W
122 J7 Napalkovo Yamalo-Nenetskiy Avtonomnyy Okrug, N Russian Federation 70°06′N 73°43′E
12 I16 Napanee Ontario, SE Canada 44°13′N 76°57′W
39 N12 Napaskiak Alaska, USA 60°42′N 161°46′W
167 S5 Na Phac Cao Băng, N Vietnam 22°24′N 105°54′E
184 O11 Napier Hawke's Bay, North Island, New Zealand 39°30′S 176°55′E
195 X3 Napier Mountains ▲▲ Antarctica
15 O13 Napierville Québec, SE Canada 45°12′N 73°25′W
23 W15 Naples Florida, SE USA 26°08′N 81°48′W
25 W5 Naples Texas, SW USA 33°12′N 94°40′W
Naples see Napoli
160 I14 Napo Guangxi Zhuangzu Zizhiqu, S China 23°21′N 105°47′E
56 C6 Napo ◆ province NE Ecuador
29 O6 Napoleon North Dakota, N USA 46°30′N 99°46′W
31 R11 Napoleon Ohio, N USA 41°23′N 84°07′W
Napoléon-Vendée see la Roche-sur-Yon
22 J9 Napoleonville Louisiana, S USA 29°55′N 91°01′W
107 K17 Napoli Eng. Naples, Ger. Neapel; anc. Neapolis. Campania, S Italy 40°52′N 14°15′E
107 J18 Napoli, Golfo di gulf S Italy
57 F7 Napo, Río ≈ Ecuador/Peru
191 W9 Napuka island Îles Tuamotu, C French Polynesia
142 J3 Naqadeh Āžarbāyjān-e Bākhtarī, NW Iran 36°57′N 45°24′E
139 U6 Naqnah Diyālá, E Iraq 34°13′N 45°33′E
Nar see Nera
164 J14 Nara Nara, Honshū, SW Japan 34°41′N 135°49′E
76 L11 Nara Koulikoro, W Mali 15°04′N 07°19′W
149 R14 Nāra Canal irrigation canal S Pakistan
182 K11 Naracoorte South Australia 37°02′S 140°45′E
183 P8 Naradhan New South Wales, SE Australia 33°37′S 146°19′E
Naradhivas see Narathiwat
56 B8 Naranjal Guayas, W Ecuador 02°43′S 79°38′W
57 Q19 Naranjos Santa Cruz, E Bolivia
41 Q12 Naranjos Veracruz-Llave, E Mexico 21°21′N 97°41′W
159 Q6 Naran Sebstein Bulag spring NW China
164 B14 Narao Nagasaki, Nakadōri-jima, SW Japan 32°40′N 129°03′E
155 J16 Narasaraopet Andhra Pradesh, E India 16°16′N 80°06′E
158 J5 Narat Xinjiang Uygur Zizhiqu, W China 43°20′N 84°02′E
167 P17 Narathiwat var. Naradhivas. Narathiwat, SW Thailand 06°25′N 101°48′E
37 V10 Nara Visa New Mexico, SW USA 35°35′N 103°06′W
Nārāyāni see Gandak
Narbada see Narmada
Narbo Martius see Narbonne
103 P16 Narbonne anc. Narbo Martius. Aude, S France 43°11′N 03°E
Narborough Island see Fernandina, Isla
104 J2 Narcea ≈ NW Spain
152 J9 Narendranagar Uttarakhand, N India 30°10′N 78°21′E
Nares Abyssal Plain see Nares Plain
64 G11 Nares Plain var. Nares Abyssal Plain. undersea feature NW Atlantic Ocean 23°30′N 63°00′W
Nares Stræde see Nares Strait
197 P10 Nares Strait Dan. Nares Stræde. strait Canada/Greenland
110 O9 Narew ≈ E Poland
155 F17 Nargund Karnātaka, W India 15°43′N 75°23′E
83 D20 Narib Hardap, S Namibia 24°11′S 17°46′E
Narikrik see Knox Atoll
Narin Gol see Dong He
54 B13 Nariño off. Departamento de Nariño. ◆ province SW Colombia
165 P13 Narita Chiba, Honshū, S Japan 35°46′N 140°20′E
165 P13 Narita ✈ (Tōkyō) Chiba, Honshū, S Japan 35°45′N 140°23′E
Nariya see An Nuʻayrīyah
162 F5 Nariyn Gol ≈ Mongolia/Russian Federation
162 J8 Nariynteel var. Tsagaan-Ovoo. Övörhangay, C Mongolia 45°57′N 101°25′E
152 J8 Nārkanda Himāchal Pradesh, NW India 31°14′N 77°27′E
92 L13 Narkaus Lappi, NW Finland 66°13′N 26°09′E
154 E11 Narmada var. Narbada. ≈ C India
152 H11 Narnaul var. Nārnaul. Haryāna, N India 28°04′N 76°10′E
107 I14 Narni Umbria, C Italy 42°31′N 12°31′E
107 J24 Naro Sicilia, Italy, C Mediterranean Sea 37°18′N 13°48′E
Narodichi see Narodychi
125 V7 Narodnaya, Gora ▲ NW Russian Federation 65°04′N 60°12′E
117 N3 Narodychi Rus. Narodichi. Zhytomyrs'ka Oblast', N Ukraine 51°11′N 29°01′E
126 J4 Naro-Fominsk Moskovskaya Oblast', W Russian Federation 55°25′N 36°41′E
81 H19 Narok Rift Valley, SW Kenya 01°04′S 35°54′E
104 H2 Narón Galicia, NW Spain 43°31′N 08°08′W
183 S11 Narooma New South Wales, SE Australia 36°16′S 150°08′E
Narova see Narva
Narovlya see Narowlya
149 W8 Nārowāl Punjab, E Pakistan 32°04′N 74°54′E
119 N20 Narowlya Rus. Narovlya. Homyel'skaya Voblasts', SE Belarus 51°48′N 29°30′E
93 J17 Närpes Fin. Närpiö. Länsi-Suomi, W Finland 62°28′N 21°19′E
Närpiö see Närpes
183 S5 Narrabri New South Wales, SE Australia 30°21′S 149°48′E
183 P9 Narrandera New South Wales, SE Australia 34°46′S 146°32′E
183 Q4 Narran Lake ◎ New South Wales, SE Australia
183 Q4 Narran River ≈ New South Wales/Queensland, SE Australia
180 J13 Narrogin Western Australia 32°53′S 117°17′E
183 Q7 Narromine New South Wales, SE Australia 32°16′S 148°15′E
21 R6 Narrows Virginia, NE USA 37°19′N 80°48′W
196 M15 Narsarsuaq ✈ Kitaa, S Greenland 61°07′N 45°03′W
154 I10 Narsimhapur Madhya Pradesh, C India 22°58′N 79°15′E
153 U15 Narsingdi var. Narsinghdi. Dhaka, C Bangladesh 23°56′N 90°40′E
Narsinghdi see Narsingdi
154 H9 Narsinghgarh Madhya Pradesh, C India 23°42′N 77°08′E
163 Q11 Nart Nei Mongol Zizhiqu, N China 42°54′N 115°55′E
Nartës, Gjol i/Nartës, Laguna e see Nartës, Liqeni i
113 J22 Nartës, Liqeni i var. Gjol i Nartës, Laguna e Nartës. ◎ SW Albania
115 F17 Narthákí ▲ C Greece 39°12′N 22°24′E
127 O15 Nartkala Kabardino-Balkarskaya Respublika, SW Russian Federation 43°34′N 43°55′E
118 K3 Narva Ida-Virumaa, NE Estonia 59°23′N 28°12′E
118 K4 Narva prev. Narova. ≈ Estonia/Russian Federation
118 J3 Narva Bay Est. Narva Laht, Ger. Narwa-Bucht, Rus. Narvskiy Zaliv. bay Estonia/Russian Federation
Narva Laht see Narva Bay
124 F13 Narva Reservoir Est. Narva Veehoidla, Rus. Narvskoye Vodokhranilishche. ⊠ Estonia/Russian Federation
Narva Veehoidla see Narva Reservoir
92 H10 Narvik Nordland, C Norway 68°26′N 17°24′E
Narvskiy Zaliv see Narva Bay
Narvskoye Vodokhranilishche see Narva Reservoir
Narwa-Bucht see Narva Bay
152 I9 Narwāna Haryāna, NW India 29°36′N 76°11′E
125 R4 Nar'yan-Mar prev. Beloshchel'ye, Dzerzhinskiy. Nenetskiy Avtonomnyy Okrug, NW Russian Federation 67°38′N 53°E
122 J12 Narym Tomskaya Oblast', C Russian Federation 58°59′N 81°20′E
145 Y10 Narymskiy Khrebet Kaz. Naryn Zhotasy. ▲▲ E Kazakhstan
147 W9 Naryn Narynskaya Oblast', C Kyrgyzstan 41°24′N 76°E
147 U8 Naryn ≈ Kyrgyzstan/Uzbekistan
145 W16 Narynkol Kaz. Narynqol. Almaty, SE Kazakhstan 42°45′N 80°12′E
Naryn Oblasty see Narynskaya Oblast'
Narynqol see Narynkol
147 V9 Narynskaya Oblast' Kir. Naryn Oblasty. ◆ province C Kyrgyzstan
Naryn Zhotasy see Narymskiy Khrebet
126 J6 Naryshkino Orlovskaya Oblast', W Russian Federation 53°00′N 35°41′E
95 L14 Nås Dalarna, C Sweden 60°28′N 14°30′E
10 J11 Nass ≈ British Columbia, SW Canada
92 G13 Nasafjellet Lapp. Násávárre. ▲ C Norway 66°29′N 15°23′E
93 H16 Näsåker Västernorrland, C Sweden 63°27′N 16°55′E
44 H2 Nassau ● (Bahamas) New Providence, N Bahamas 25°03′N 77°21′W
187 Y14 Nasau Koro, C Fiji 17°20′S 179°26′E
44 H2 Nassau ✈ New Providence, C Bahamas 25°00′N 77°26′W
190 J13 Nassau island N Cook Islands
116 I9 Năsăud Ger. Nussdorf, Hung. Naszód. Bistriţa-Năsăud, N Romania 47°16′N 24°24′E
Násávárre see Nasafjellet
103 P13 Nasbinals Lozère, S France 44°40′N 03°03′E
Na Sceirí see Skerries
Nase see Naze
185 E22 Naseby Otago, South Island, New Zealand 45°02′S 170°09′E
143 R10 Nāṣerīyeh Kermān, C Iran
25 X5 Nash Texas, SW USA 33°26′N 94°04′W
154 E13 Nāshik prev. Nāsik. Mahārāshtra, W India 20°05′N 73°48′E
56 E7 Nashiño, Río ≈ Ecuador/Peru
29 W12 Nashua Iowa, C USA 42°57′N 92°32′W
33 W7 Nashua Montana, NW USA 48°06′N 106°16′W
19 O10 Nashua New Hampshire, NE USA 42°45′N 71°26′W
27 S13 Nashville Arkansas, C USA 33°57′N 93°50′W
23 U7 Nashville Georgia, SE USA 31°12′N 83°15′W
30 L16 Nashville Illinois, N USA 38°20′N 89°22′W
31 O14 Nashville Indiana, N USA 39°13′N 86°15′W
21 V9 Nashville North Carolina, SE USA 35°58′N 78°00′W
20 J8 Nashville state capital Tennessee, S USA 36°11′N 86°48′W
20 J9 Nashville ✈ Tennessee, S USA 36°06′N 86°44′W
64 H10 Nashville Seamount undersea feature NW Atlantic Ocean 30°00′N 57°20′W
112 H9 Našice Osijek-Baranja, E Croatia 45°29′N 18°05′E
110 M11 Nasielsk Mazowieckie, C Poland 52°33′N 20°46′E
93 K18 Näsijärvi ◎ SW Finland
Nāsik see Nāshik
80 G13 Nasir Upper Nile, SE Sudan 08°37′N 33°06′E
148 K15 Nasīrābād Baluchistān, SW Pakistan 26°15′N 62°32′E
Nasir, Buhayrat/Nâşir, Buheiret see Nasser, Lake
Nāsiri see Ahvāz
Nasiriya see An Nāṣirīyah
Nás na Ríogh see Naas
107 L23 Naso Sicilia, Italy, C Mediterranean Sea 38°07′N 14°46′E
Nasratabad see Zābol
77 V15 Nassarawa Nassarawa, C Nigeria 08°33′N 07°42′E
23 W8 Nassau Sound sound Florida, SE USA
108 L7 Nassereith Tirol, W Austria 47°19′N 10°51′E
80 F5 Nasser, Lake var. Buhayrat Nasir, Buḥayrat Nāṣir, Buheiret Nâşir. ◎ Egypt/Sudan
95 L19 Nässjö Jönköping, S Sweden 57°39′N 14°40′E
99 K22 Nassogne Luxembourg, SE Belgium 50°08′N 05°19′E
12 J6 Nastapoka Islands island group Northwest Territories, C Canada
93 M19 Nastola Etelä-Suomi, S Finland 60°57′N 25°56′E
171 O4 Nasugbu Luzon, N Philippines 14°03′N 120°39′E
94 N11 Näsviken Gävleborg, C Sweden 61°46′N 16°55′E
Naszód see Năsăud
83 I17 Nata Central, NE Botswana 20°11′S 26°10′E
54 E11 Natagaima Tolima, C Colombia 03°38′N 75°07′W
59 Q14 Natal state capital Rio Grande do Norte, E Brazil 05°46′S 35°15′W
168 I11 Natal Sumatera, N Indonesia 0°32′N 99°07′E
Natal see KwaZulu/Natal
173 L10 Natal Basin var. Mozambique Basin. undersea feature W Indian Ocean 30°00′S 40°00′E
25 R12 Natalia Texas, SW USA 29°11′N 98°51′W
67 W15 Natal Valley undersea feature SW Indian Ocean 31°00′S 33°15′E
Natanya see Netanya
143 O7 Naṭanz Eşfahān, C Iran 33°31′N 51°55′E
13 Q11 Natashquan Québec, E Canada 50°10′N 61°50′W
13 Q10 Natashquan ≈ Newfoundland and Labrador/Québec, E Canada
22 J7 Natchez Mississippi, S USA 31°34′N 91°24′W
22 G6 Natchitoches Louisiana, S USA 31°45′N 93°05′W
108 E10 Naters Valais, S Switzerland 46°22′N 08°00′E
Nathanya see Netanya
92 O3 Nathorst Land physical region W Svalbard
186 E9 National Capital District ◆ province S Papua New Guinea
35 U17 National City California, W USA 32°40′N 117°06′W
184 M10 National Park Manawatu-Wanganui, North Island, New Zealand 39°11′S 175°22′E
77 R14 Natitingou NW Benin 10°21′N 01°26′E
40 B5 Natividad, Isla island NW Mexico
165 Q10 Natori Miyagi, Honshū, C Japan 38°12′N 140°51′E
18 C14 Natrona Heights Pennsylvania, NE USA 40°37′N 79°42′W
81 H20 Natron, Lake ◎ Kenya/Tanzania
Natsrat see Natzrat
166 L7 Nattalin Bago, C Burma (Myanmar) 18°25′N 95°34′E
92 J12 Nattavaara Lapp. Nahtavárr. Norrbotten, N Sweden 66°45′N 20°58′E
109 S3 Natternbach Oberösterreich, N Austria 48°26′N 13°44′E
95 M22 Nättraby Blekinge, S Sweden 56°12′N 15°30′E
169 P10 Natuna Besar, Pulau island Kepulauan Natuna, W Indonesia
Natuna Islands see Natuna, Kepulauan
169 O9 Natuna, Kepulauan var. Natuna Islands. island group W Indonesia
169 N9 Natuna, Laut Eng. Natuna Sea. sea W Indonesia
Natuna Sea see Natuna, Laut
21 N6 Natural Bridge tourist site Kentucky, C USA
173 V11 Naturaliste Fracture Zone tectonic feature E Indian Ocean
174 J10 Naturaliste Plateau undersea feature E Indian Ocean
138 G9 Natzrat var. Natsrat, Ar. En Nazira, Eng. Nazareth; prev. Nagerat. Northern, N Israel 32°42′N 35°18′E
Nau see Nov
103 O14 Naucelle Aveyron, S France 44°10′N 02°19′E
83 D20 Nauchas Hardap, C Namibia 23°40′S 16°19′E
108 K9 Nauders Tirol, W Austria 46°52′N 10°31′E
Naugard see Nowogard
153 N12 Naugarh Uttar Pradesh, N India 24°50′N 83°17′E
118 F12 Naujamiestis Panevėžys, C Lithuania 55°42′N 24°10′E
118 E10 Naujoji Akmenė Siauliai, NW Lithuania 56°20′N 22°57′E
149 R16 Naukot var. Naokot. Sind, SE Pakistan 24°52′N 69°27′E
101 L16 Naumburg var. Naumburg an der Saale. Sachsen-Anhalt, C Germany 51°09′N 11°48′E
Naumburg am Queis see Nowogrodziec
Naumburg an der Saale see Naumburg
191 W15 Naunau ancient monument Easter Island, Chile, E Pacific Ocean
Nauparha see Nūāparha
138 G10 Nāʻūr ʻAmmān, W Jordan 31°52′N 35°50′E
189 Q8 Nauru off. Republic of Nauru; prev. Pleasant Island. ◆ republic W Pacific Ocean
175 P5 Nauru island W Pacific Ocean
189 Q9 Nauru International ✈ S Nauru
Nauru, Republic of see Nauru
Nausari see Navsāri
19 Q12 Nauset Beach beach Massachusetts, NE USA
Naushahra see Nowshera
149 P14 Naushahro Fīroz Sind, SE Pakistan 26°51′N 68°11′E
Naushara see Nowshera
187 X14 Nausori Viti Levu, W Fiji 18°01′S 178°31′E
56 F9 Nauta Loreto, N Peru 04°31′S 73°36′W
153 O12 Nautanwa Uttar Pradesh, N India 27°26′N 83°25′E
41 R13 Nautla Veracruz-Llave, E Mexico 20°15′N 96°45′W
Nauzad see Now Zād
41 N6 Nava Coahuila, NE Mexico 28°28′N 100°45′W
Navabad see Navobod
104 L6 Nava del Rey Castilla-León, N Spain 41°19′N 05°04′W
153 S15 Navadwīp prev. Nabadwip. West Bengal, NE India 23°24′N 88°23′E
104 M9 Navahermosa Castilla-La Mancha, C Spain 39°39′N 04°25′W
119 I16 Navahrudak Pol. Nowogródek, Rus. Novogrudok. Hrodzyenskaya Voblasts', W Belarus 53°36′N 25°50′E
119 I16 Navahrudskaye Wzvyshsha ▲ W Belarus
36 M8 Navajo Mount ▲ Utah, W USA 37°00′N 110°52′W
37 Q9 Navajo Reservoir ⊠ New Mexico, SW USA
104 K9 Navalmoral de la Mata Extremadura, W Spain 39°54′N 05°33′W
104 K10 Navalvillar de Pelea Extremadura, W Spain 39°05′N 05°27′W
97 F17 Navan Ir. An Uaimh. E Ireland 53°39′N 06°41′W
Navanagar see Jāmnagar
118 L12 Navapolatsk Rus. Novopolotsk. Vitsyebskaya Voblasts', N Belarus 55°34′N 28°35′E
149 P6 Nāvar, Dasht-e Pash. Dasht-i-Nawar. desert C Afghanistan
123 W6 Navarin, Mys headland NE Russian Federation 62°18′N 179°06′E
63 I25 Navarino, Isla island S Chile
105 Q4 Navarra Eng./Fr. Navarre. ◆ autonomous community N Spain
Navarre see Navarra
105 P4 Navarrete La Rioja, N Spain 42°26′N 02°34′W
61 C20 Navarro Buenos Aires, E Argentina 35°00′S 59°15′W
105 O12 Navas de San Juan Andalucía, S Spain 38°11′N 03°19′W
127 N4 Navashino Nizhegorodskaya Oblast', W Russian Federation 55°33′N 42°11′E
25 V10 Navasota Texas, SW USA 30°23′N 96°05′W
25 U9 Navasota River ≈ Texas, SW USA
44 I9 Navassa Island ◇ US unincorporated territory C West Indies
119 L19 Navasyolki Rus. Novosëlki. Homyel'skaya Voblasts', SE Belarus 52°24′N 28°33′E
119 H17 Navayel'nya Pol. Nowojelnia, Rus. Novoyel'nya. Hrodzyenskaya Voblasts', W Belarus 53°28′N 25°35′E
171 Y13 Naver Papua, E Indonesia 03°27′S 139°45′E
118 H5 Navesti ≈ C Estonia
104 J2 Navia Asturias, N Spain 43°33′N 06°43′W
104 J2 Navia ≈ NW Spain
59 I21 Naviraí Mato Grosso do Sul, SW Brazil 23°01′S 54°09′W
126 I6 Navlya Bryanskaya Oblast', W Russian Federation 52°47′N 34°28′E
187 X13 Navoalevu Vanua Levu, N Fiji 16°22′S 179°28′E
147 R12 Navobod Rus. Navabad, Novabad. C Tajikistan 39°00′N 70°06′E
147 P13 Navobod Rus. Navabad. W Tajikistan 38°37′N 68°42′E
Navoi see Navoiy
146 M11 Navoiy Rus. Navoi. Navoiy Viloyati, C Uzbekistan 40°05′N 65°23′E
Navoiyskaya Oblast' see Navoiy Viloyati
146 K8 Navoiy Viloyati Rus. Navoiyskaya Oblast'. ◆ province N Uzbekistan
40 G7 Navojoa Sonora, NW Mexico 27°04′N 109°28′W
Navolat see Navolato
40 H9 Navolato var. Navolat. Sinaloa, C Mexico 24°46′N 107°42′W
187 Q13 Navonda Ambae, C Vanuatu 15°21′S 167°58′E
Návpaktos see Náfpaktos
Návplion see Náfplio
77 P14 Navrongo N Ghana 10°51′N 01°03′W
154 D12 Navsāri var. Nausari. Gujarāt, W India 20°55′N 72°55′E
187 X15 Navua Viti Levu, W Fiji 18°15′S 178°10′E
138 H8 Nawá Darʻā, S Syria 32°53′N 36°03′E
Nawabashah see Nawābshāh
153 S14 Nawabganj Rajshahi, NW Bangladesh 24°35′N 88°21′E
153 S14 Nawābganj Uttar Pradesh, N India 26°52′N 82°09′E
149 Q15 Nawābshāh var. Nawabashah. Sind, S Pakistan 26°15′N 68°26′E
153 P14 Nawāda Bihār, N India 24°54′N 85°33′E
152 H11 Nawalgarh Rājasthān, N India 27°48′N 75°21′E
Nawāl, Sabkhat an see Noual, Sebkhet en
Nawapara see Nuāparha
Nawar, Dasht-i- see Nāvar, Dasht-e
167 N4 Nawnghkio var. Nawngkio. Shan State, C Burma (Myanmar) 22°17′N 96°50′E
Nawngkio see Nawnghkio
137 U13 Naxçıvan Rus. Nakhichevan'. SW Azerbaijan 39°14′N 45°24′E
160 I10 Naxi Sichuan, C China 28°50′N 105°20′E
115 K21 Náxos var. Naxos. Náxos, Kykládes, Greece, Aegean Sea 36°07′N 25°24′E
115 K21 Náxos island Kykládes, Greece, Aegean Sea
40 J11 Nayarit ◆ state C Mexico
187 Y14 Nayau island Lau Group, E Fiji
143 S8 Nāy Band Yazd, E Iran 32°26′N 57°30′E
165 T2 Nayoro Hokkaidō, NE Japan 44°22′N 142°27′E
104 F9 Nazaré var. Nazare. Leiria, C Portugal 39°36′N 09°04′W
Nazare see Nazaré
24 M4 Nazareth Texas, SW USA 34°32′N 102°06′W
Nazareth see Natzrat
173 O8 Nazareth Bank undersea feature W Indian Ocean
40 K9 Nazas Durango, C Mexico 25°15′N 104°06′W
57 F16 Nazca Ica, S Peru 14°53′S 74°54′W
0 L17 Nazca Plate tectonic feature
193 U9 Nazca Ridge undersea feature E Pacific Ocean 22°00′S 82°00′W
165 V15 Naze var. Nase. Kagoshima, Amami-ōshima, SW Japan 28°21′N 129°30′E
Nazerat see Natzrat
137 R14 Nazık Gölü ◎ E Turkey
136 C15 Nazilli Aydın, SW Turkey 37°55′N 28°20′E
137 P14 Nazimiye Tunceli, E Turkey 39°12′N 39°51′E
Nazinon see Red Volta
10 L15 Nazko British Columbia, SW Canada 52°57′N 123°44′W
127 O16 Nazran' Respublika Ingushetiya, SW Russian Federation 43°14′N 44°47′E
80 J13 Nazrēt var. Adama, Hadama. Oromīya, C Ethiopia 08°31′N 39°20′E
Nazwāh see Nizwa
82 J13 Nchanga Copperbelt, C Zambia 12°30′S 27°53′E
82 J11 Nchelenge Luapula, N Zambia 09°20′S 28°50′E
Ncheu see Ntcheu
83 J25 Nciba Eng. Great Kei; prev. Groot-Kei. ≈ S South Africa
Ndaghamcha, Sebkra de see Te-n-Dghâmcha, Sebkhet
81 G21 Ndala Tabora, C Tanzania 04°45′S 33°15′E
82 B11 N'Dalatando Port. Salazar, Vila Salazar. Cuanza Norte, NW Angola 09°19′S 14°48′E
77 S14 Ndali C Benin 09°50′N 02°46′E
81 E18 Ndeke SW Uganda 0°11′S 30°04′E
78 J13 Ndélé Bamingui-Bangoran, N Central African Republic 08°24′N 20°41′E
79 E19 Ndendé Ngounié, S Gabon 02°21′S 11°20′E
79 E20 Ndindi Nyanga, S Gabon 03°47′S 11°06′E
78 G11 Ndjamena var. N'Djamena; prev. Fort-Lamy. ● (Chad) Chari-Baguirmi, W Chad 12°08′N 15°02′E
78 G11 Ndjamena ✈ Chari-Baguirmi, W Chad 12°09′N 15°00′E
N'Djamena see Ndjamena
79 D18 Ndjolé Moyen-Ogooué, W Gabon 0°07′S 10°45′E
82 J13 Ndola Copperbelt, C Zambia 12°59′S 28°35′E
Ndrhamcha, Sebkha de see Te-n-Dghâmcha, Sebkhet
79 L15 Ndu Orientale, N Dem. Rep. Congo 04°36′N 22°49′E
81 H21 Nduguti Singida, C Tanzania 04°19′S 34°40′E
186 M9 Nduindui Guadalcanal, C Solomon Islands 09°46′S 159°54′E
Nduke see Kolombangara
Ndzouani see Anjouan
115 F16 Néa Anchíalos var. Nea Anhialos, Néa Ankhíalos. Thessalía, C Greece 39°16′N 22°49′E
Nea Anhialos/Néa Ankhíalos see Néa Anchíalos
115 H18 Néa Artáki Évvoia, C Greece 38°31′N 23°39′E
97 F15 Neagh, Lough ◎ E Northern Ireland, United Kingdom
32 F7 Neah Bay Washington, NW USA 48°21′N 124°39′W
115 J22 Nea Kaméni island Kykládes, Greece, Aegean Sea
181 O8 Neale, Lake ◎ Northern Territory, C Australia
182 G2 Neales River seasonal river South Australia
115 G14 Néa Moudanía var. Néa Moudhaniá. Kentrikí Makedonía, N Greece 40°14′N 23°17′E
Néa Moudhaniá see Néa Moudanía
116 K10 Neamţ ◆ county NE Romania
Neapel see Napoli
115 D14 Neápoli prev. Neápolis. Dytikí Makedonía, N Greece 40°19′N 21°23′E
115 K25 Neápoli Kríti, Greece, E Mediterranean Sea 35°15′N 25°37′E

◆ Country ● Country Capital ◇ Dependent Territory ○ Dependent Territory Capital ◆ Administrative Regions ✈ International Airport ▲ Mountain ▲▲ Mountain Range Volcano ≈ River ◎ Lake ⊠ Reservoir

Neápoli – New Port Richey

115 G22 Neápoli Pelopónnisos, S Greece 36°29′N 23°05′E
Neápolis see Neápoli, Greece
Neapolis see Napoli, Italy
Neapolis see Nablus, West Bank
38 D16 Near Islands island group Aleutian Islands, Alaska, USA
97 J21 Neath S Wales, United Kingdom 51°40′N 03°48′W
114 H13 Néa Zíchni var. Néa Zikhni; prev. Néa Zíkhna. Kentrikí Makedonía, NE Greece 41°02′N 23°50′E
Néa Zíkhna/Néa Zíkhni see Néa Zíchni
42 C5 Nebaj Quiché, W Guatemala 15°25′N 91°05′W
77 P13 Nebbou S Burkina 11°22′N 01°49′W
Nebitdag see Balkanabat
54 M13 Neblina, Pico da ▲ NW Brazil 0°49′N 66°31′W
124 I13 Nebolchi Novgorodskaya Oblast', W Russian Federation 59°08′N 33°19′E
36 L4 Nebo, Mount ▲ Utah, W USA 39°47′N 111°46′W
28 L14 Nebraska off. State of Nebraska, also known as Blackwater State, Cornhusker State, Tree Planters State. ◆ state C USA
29 S16 Nebraska City Nebraska, C USA 40°38′N 95°52′W
107 K23 Nebrodi, Monti var. Monti Caronie. ▲▲ Sicilia, Italy, C Mediterranean Sea
10 L14 Nechako ≈ British Columbia, SW Canada
29 Q2 Neche North Dakota, N USA 48°57′N 97°33′W
25 V8 Neches Texas, SW USA 31°51′N 95°28′W
25 W8 Neches River ≈ Texas, SW USA
101 H20 Neckar ≈ SW Germany
101 H20 Neckarsulm Baden-Württemberg, SW Germany 49°12′N 09°13′E
192 L5 Necker Island island C British Virgin Islands
175 U3 Necker Ridge undersea feature N Pacific Ocean
61 D23 Necochea Buenos Aires, E Argentina 38°34′S 58°42′W
104 H2 Neda Galicia, NW Spain 43°29′N 08°09′W
115 E20 Néda var. Nédas. ≈ S Greece
Nédas see Néda
114 J12 Nedelino Smolyan, S Bulgaria 41°27′N 25°05′E
25 Y11 Nederland Texas, SW USA 29°58′N 93°59′W
Nederland see Netherlands
98 K12 Neder Rijn Eng. Lower Rhine. ≈ C Netherlands
99 L16 Nederweert Limburg, SE Netherlands 51°17′N 05°45′E
159 N17 Nêdong var. Zêtang. Xizang Zizhiqu, W China 29°11′N 91°48′E
95 G16 Nedre Tokke ◎ S Norway
Nedrigaylov see Nedryhayliv
117 S3 Nedryhayliv Rus. Nedrigaylov. Sums'ka Oblast', NE Ukraine 50°51′N 33°54′E
98 O11 Neede Gelderland, E Netherlands 52°08′N 06°36′E
33 T13 Needle Mountain ▲ Wyoming, C USA 44°03′N 109°33′W
35 Y14 Needles California, W USA 34°50′N 114°37′W
97 M24 Needles, The rocks S England, United Kingdom
62 O7 Ñeembucú off. Departamento de Ñeembucú. ◆ department SW Paraguay
Ñeembucú, Departamento de see Ñeembucú
30 M7 Neenah Wisconsin, N USA 44°09′N 88°26′W
11 W16 Neepawa Manitoba, S Canada 50°14′N 99°29′W
99 K16 Neerpelt Limburg, NE Belgium 51°13′N 05°26′E
74 M6 Nefta ✈ W Tunisia 34°03′N 08°05′E
126 L15 Neftegorsk Krasnodarskiy Kray, SW Russian Federation 44°21′N 39°40′E
127 S6 Neftegorsk Samarskaya Oblast', W Russian Federation 52°48′N 51°04′E
127 U3 Neftekamsk Respublika Bashkortostan, W Russian Federation 56°07′N 54°13′E
127 O14 Neftekumsk Stavropol'skiy Kray, SW Russian Federation 44°45′N 45°00′E
Neftezavodsk see Seýdi
82 C10 Negage var. N'Gage. Uíge, NW Angola 07°47′S 15°27′E
Negapatam/Negapattinam see Nāgappattinam
169 T17 Negara Bali, Indonesia 08°21′S 114°35′E
169 T13 Negara Borneo, C Indonesia 02°40′S 115°05′E
Negara Brunei Darussalam see Brunei
31 N4 Negaunee Michigan, N USA 46°30′N 87°36′W
81 J15 Negēlē var. Negelli, It. Neghelli. Oromīya, C Ethiopia 05°13′N 39°43′E
Negelli see Negēlē
Negeri Pahang Darul Makmur see Pahang
Negeri Selangor Darul Ehsan see Selangor
168 K9 Negeri Sembilan var. Negri Sembilan. ◆ state Peninsular Malaysia
92 P3 Negerpynten headland S Svalbard 77°15′N 22°40′E
Negev see HaNegev
Neghelli see Negēlē
116 I12 Negoiu var. Negoiul. ▲ S Romania 45°34′N 24°34′E
Negoiul see Negoiu
82 P13 Negomane var. Negomano. Cabo Delgado, N Mozambique 11°22′S 38°32′E
Negomano see Negomane
155 J25 Negombo Western Province, SW Sri Lanka 07°13′N 79°51′E
Negoreloye see Nyeharelaye
112 P12 Negotin Serbia, E Serbia 44°14′N 22°31′E
113 P19 Negotino C Macedonia 41°29′N 22°04′E
56 A10 Negra, Punta headland NW Peru 06°03′S 81°08′W
104 G3 Negreira Galicia, NW Spain 42°54′N 08°46′W
116 L10 Negrești Vaslui, E Romania 46°50′N 27°28′E
Negrești see Negrești-Oaș
116 H8 Negrești-Oaș Hung. Avasfelsőfalu; prev. Negrești. Satu Mare, NE Romania 47°56′N 23°22′E
44 H12 Negril W Jamaica 18°16′N 78°21′W
Negri Sembilan see Negeri Sembilan
63 K15 Negro, Río ≈ E Argentina
62 N7 Negro, Río ≈ NE Argentina
57 N17 Negro, Río ≈ E Bolivia
48 F6 Negro, Río ≈ N South America
61 E18 Negro, Río ≈ Brazil/Uruguay
62 O5 Negro, Río ≈ C Paraguay
Negro, Río see Chixoy, Río, Guatemala/Mexico
Negro, Río see Sico Tinto, Río, Honduras
171 P6 Negros island C Philippines
116 M15 Negru Vodă Constanța, SE Romania 43°49′N 28°12′E
13 P13 Neguac New Brunswick, SE Canada 47°16′N 65°04′W
14 B7 Negwazu, Lake ◎ Ontario, S Canada
Négyfalu see Săcele
32 F10 Nehalem Oregon, NW USA 45°42′N 123°55′W
32 F10 Nehalem River ≈ Oregon, NW USA
Nehavend see Nahāvand
143 V9 Nehbandān Khorāsān, E Iran 31°00′N 60°00′E
163 V6 Nehe Heilongjiang, NE China 48°28′N 124°52′E
193 Y14 Neiafu 'Uta Vava'u, N Tonga 18°36′S 173°58′W
45 N9 Neiba var. Neyba. SW Dominican Republic 18°31′N 71°25′W
Néid, Carn Uí see Mizen Head
92 M9 Neiden Finnmark, N Norway 69°41′N 29°23′E
Neidín see Kenmare
Néifinn see Nephin
103 S10 Neige, Crêt de la ▲ E France 46°18′N 05°58′E
173 O16 Neiges, Piton des ▲ C Réunion 21°05′S 55°28′E
15 R9 Neiges, Rivière des ≈ Québec, SE Canada
160 I10 Neijiang Sichuan, C China 29°32′N 105°03′E
30 K6 Neillsville Wisconsin, N USA 44°34′N 90°36′W
Nei Monggol Zizhiqu/Nei Mongol see Nei Mongol Zizhiqu
163 Q10 Nei Mongol Gaoyuan plateau NE China
163 O12 Nei Mongol Zizhiqu var. Nei Mongol, Eng. Inner Mongolia, Inner Mongolian Autonomous Region; prev. Nei Monggol Zizhiqu. ◆ autonomous region N China
161 O4 Neiqiu Hebei, E China 37°22′N 114°34′E
Neiriz see Neyrīz
101 Q16 Neisse Cz. Lužická Nisa Pol. Nisa, Ger. Lausitzer Neisse, Nysa Łużycka. ≈ C Europe
Neisse see Nysa
54 E11 Neiva Huila, S Colombia 02°58′N 75°15′W
160 M7 Neixiang Henan, C China 33°08′N 111°50′E
Nejafabad see Najafābād
11 V9 Nejanilini Lake ◎ Manitoba, C Canada
Nejd see Najd
80 I13 Nek'emtē var. Lakemti, Nakamti. Oromīya, C Ethiopia 09°06′N 36°31′E
126 M9 Nekhayevskaya Volgogradskaya Oblast', SW Russian Federation 50°25′N 41°44′E
30 K7 Nekoosa Wisconsin, N USA 44°19′N 89°54′W
Nekső Bornholm see Nexø
104 H7 Nelas Viseu, N Portugal 40°32′N 07°52′W
124 H16 Nelidovo Tverskaya Oblast', W Russian Federation 56°13′N 32°45′E
29 P13 Neligh Nebraska, C USA 42°07′N 98°01′W
123 R11 Nel'kan Khabarovskiy Kray, E Russian Federation 57°44′N 136°09′E
92 M10 Nellim var. Nellimö, Lapp. Njellim. Lappi, N Finland 68°49′N 28°18′E
Nellimö see Nellim
155 J18 Nellore Andhra Pradesh, E India 14°29′N 80°E
61 B17 Nelson Santa Fe, C Argentina 31°16′S 60°45′W
11 O17 Nelson British Columbia, SW Canada 49°29′N 117°17′W
185 I14 Nelson Nelson, South Island, New Zealand 41°17′S 173°17′E
97 L17 Nelson NW England, United Kingdom 53°51′N 02°13′W
29 P17 Nelson Nebraska, C USA 40°12′N 98°04′W
185 J14 Nelson ◆ unitary authority South Island, New Zealand
11 X12 Nelson ≈ Manitoba, C Canada
183 U8 Nelson Bay New South Wales, SE Australia 32°48′S 152°10′E
182 K13 Nelson, Cape headland Victoria, SE Australia 38°25′S 141°33′E
63 G23 Nelson, Estrecho strait SE Pacific Ocean
11 W12 Nelson House Manitoba, C Canada 55°49′N 98°51′W
30 J4 Nelson Lake ◎ Wisconsin, N USA
31 T14 Nelsonville Ohio, N USA 39°27′N 82°13′W
27 S2 Nelsoon River ≈ Iowa/Missouri, C USA
83 K21 Nelspruit Mpumalanga, NE South Africa 25°28′S 30°58′E
76 L10 Néma Hodh ech Chargui, SE Mauritania 16°32′N 07°12′W
118 D13 Neman Ger. Ragnit. Kaliningradskaya Oblast', W Russian Federation 55°01′N 22°00′E
84 I9 Neman Bel. Nyoman, Ger. Memel, Lith. Nemunas, Pol. Niemen. ≈ NE Europe
Nemausus see Nîmes
115 F19 Neméa Pelopónnisos, S Greece 37°49′N 22°40′E
Německý Brod see Havlíčkův Brod
14 D7 Nemegosenda ≈ Ontario, S Canada
14 D8 Nemegosenda Lake ◎ Ontario, S Canada
119 H14 Nemencinė Vilnius, SE Lithuania 54°50′N 25°29′E
Nemetocenna see Arras
Nemirov see Nemyriv
103 O6 Nemours Seine-et-Marne, N France 48°16′N 02°41′E
Nemunas see Neman
165 W4 Nemuro Hokkaidō, NE Japan 43°20′N 145°35′E
165 W4 Nemuro-hantō peninsula Hokkaidō, NE Japan
165 W3 Nemuro-kaikyō strait Japan/Russian Federation
165 W4 Nemuro-wan bay N Japan
116 H5 Nemyriv Rus. Nemirov. L'vivs'ka Oblast', NW Ukraine 50°08′N 23°28′E
117 N7 Nemyriv Rus. Nemirov. Vinnyts'ka Oblast', C Ukraine 48°58′N 28°50′E
97 D19 Nenagh Ir. An tAonach. Tipperary, C Ireland 52°52′N 08°12′W
39 R9 Nenana Alaska, USA 64°33′N 149°05′W
39 R9 Nenana River ≈ Alaska, USA
187 P10 Nendö var. Swallow Island. island Santa Cruz Islands, E Solomon Islands
97 O19 Nene ≈ E England, United Kingdom
125 R4 Nenetskiy Avtonomnyy Okrug ◆ autonomous district Arkhangel'skaya Oblast', NW Russian Federation
191 W11 Nengonengo atoll Îles Tuamotu, C French Polynesia
163 V6 Nenjiang Heilongjiang, NE China 49°11′N 125°18′E
163 U6 Nen Jiang var. Nonni. ≈ NE China
189 P16 Neoch atoll Caroline Islands, C Micronesia
115 D18 Neochóri Dytikí Ellás, C Greece 38°23′N 21°14′E
27 Q7 Neodesha Kansas, C USA 37°25′N 95°40′W
29 S14 Neola Iowa, C USA 41°27′N 95°40′W
115 E16 Néon Monastíri var. Néon Monastiri. Thessalía, C Greece 39°22′N 21°55′E
Néon Karlovasi/Néon Karlovásion see Karlovási
Néon Monastiri see Néon Monastíri
27 R8 Neosho Missouri, C USA 36°53′N 94°24′W
27 Q7 Neosho River ≈ Kansas/Oklahoma, C USA
123 N12 Nepa ≈ C Russian Federation
153 N10 Nepal off. Nepal. ◆ monarchy S Asia
Nepal see Nepal
152 M11 Nepālganj Mid Western, SW Nepal 28°04′N 81°37′E
14 L13 Nepean Ontario, SE Canada 45°19′N 75°54′W
36 L4 Nephi Utah, W USA 39°43′N 111°50′W
97 B16 Nephin Ir. Néifinn. ▲ W Ireland 54°00′N 09°21′W
67 T9 Nepoko ≈ NE Dem. Rep. Congo
18 K15 Neptune New Jersey, NE USA 40°10′N 74°03′W
182 G10 Neptune Islands island group South Australia
107 I14 Nera anc. Nar. ≈ C Italy
102 L14 Nérac Lot-et-Garonne, SW France 44°08′N 00°21′E
111 D16 Neratovice Ger. Neratowitz. Středočeský Kraj, C Czech Republic 50°16′N 14°31′E
Neratowitz see Neratovice
123 O13 Nercha ≈ S Russian Federation
123 O13 Nerchinsk Chitinskaya Oblast', S Russian Federation 52°01′N 116°25′E
123 P14 Nerchinskiy Zavod Chitinskaya Oblast', S Russian Federation 51°13′N 119°25′E
124 M15 Nerekhta Kostromskaya Oblast', NW Russian Federation 57°27′N 40°33′E
118 H10 Nereta Aizkraukle, S Latvia 56°12′N 25°18′E
106 K13 Nereto Abruzzo, C Italy 42°49′N 13°50′E
113 H15 Neretva ≈ Bosnia and Herzegovina/Croatia
115 C17 Nerikós ruins Lefkáda, Iónia Nisiá, Greece, C Mediterranean Sea
83 F15 Neriquinha Cuando Cubango, SE Angola 15°44′S 21°34′E
118 I13 Neris Bel. Viliya, Pol. Wilia; prev. Pol. Wilja. ≈ Belarus/Lithuania
Neris see Viliya
105 N15 Nerja Andalucía, S Spain 36°45′N 03°35′W
124 L16 Nerl' ≈ W Russian Federation
105 P12 Nerpio Castilla-La Mancha, C Spain 38°08′N 02°18′W
104 J13 Nerva Andalucía, S Spain 37°40′N 06°31′W
98 L4 Nes Friesland, N Netherlands 53°28′N 05°46′E
94 G13 Nesbyen Buskerud, S Norway 60°36′N 09°35′E
114 M9 Nesebŭr Burgas, E Bulgaria 42°40′N 27°43′E
92 L2 Neskaupstadhur Austurland, E Iceland 65°08′N 13°45′W
92 F13 Nesna Nordland, C Norway 66°11′N 12°54′E
26 K5 Ness City Kansas, C USA 38°27′N 99°54′W
Nesselsdorf see Kopřivnice
108 H7 Nesslau Sankt Gallen, NE Switzerland 47°13′N 09°12′E
96 I9 Ness, Loch ◎ N Scotland, United Kingdom
Nesterov see Zhovkva
114 I12 Néstos Bul. Mesta, Turk. Kara Su. ≈ Bulgaria/Greece see also Mesta
Néstos see Mesta
95 C14 Nesttun Hordaland, S Norway 60°19′N 05°16′E
Nesvizh see Nyasvizh
138 F9 Netanya var. Natanya, Nathanya. Central, C Israel 32°20′N 34°51′E
98 I9 Netherlands off. Kingdom of the Netherlands, var. Holland, Dut. Koninkrijk der Nederlanden, Nederland. ◆ monarchy NW Europe
45 S9 Netherlands Antilles prev. Dutch West Indies. ◇ Dutch autonomous region S Caribbean Sea
Netherlands East Indies see Indonesia
Netherlands Guiana see Surinam
Netherlands, Kingdom of the see Netherlands
Netherlands New Guinea see Papua
116 L4 Netishyn Khmel'nyts'ka Oblast', W Ukraine 50°20′N 26°38′E
138 E11 Netivot Southern, S Israel 31°26′N 34°36′E
107 O21 Neto ≈ S Italy
9 Q6 Nettilling Lake ◎ Baffin Island, Nunavut, N Canada
29 V3 Nett Lake ◎ Minnesota, N USA
107 I16 Nettuno Lazio, C Italy 41°27′N 12°40′E
Netum see Noto
41 U16 Netzahualcóyotl, Presa ⊠ SE Mexico
Netze see Noteć
Neu Amerika see Puławy
Neubetsche see Novi Bečej
Neubidschow see Nový Bydžov
Neubistritz see Nová Bystřice
100 N9 Neubrandenburg Mecklenburg-Vorpommern, NE Germany 53°33′N 13°16′E
101 K22 Neuburg an der Donau Bayern, S Germany 48°43′N 11°10′E
108 C8 Neuchâtel Ger. Neuenburg. Neuchâtel, W Switzerland 46°59′N 06°55′E
108 C8 Neuchâtel Ger. Neuenburg. ◆ canton W Switzerland
108 C8 Neuchâtel, Lac de Ger. Neuenburger See. ◎ W Switzerland
Neudorf see Spišská Nová Ves
100 L10 Neue Elde canal N Germany
Neuenburg see Neuchâtel
Neuenburg an der Elbe see Nymburk
Neuenburger See see Neuchâtel, Lac de
108 F7 Neuenhof Aargau, N Switzerland 47°27′N 08°17′E
100 H11 Neuenland ✈ (Bremen) Bremen, NW Germany 53°03′N 08°46′E
Neuenstadt see La Neuveville
101 C18 Neuerburg Rheinland-Pfalz, W Germany 50°01′N 06°13′E
99 K24 Neufchâteau Luxembourg, SE Belgium 49°50′N 05°26′E
103 S6 Neufchâteau Vosges, NE France 48°21′N 05°42′E
102 M3 Neufchâtel-en-Bray Seine-Maritime, N France 49°44′N 01°26′E
109 S3 Neufelden Oberösterreich, N Austria 48°27′N 14°01′E
Neugradisk see Nova Gradiška
Neuhaus see Jindřichův Hradec
Neuhäusel see Nové Zámky
108 G6 Neuhausen var. Neuhausen am Rheinfall. Schaffhausen, N Switzerland 47°24′N 08°37′E
Neuhausen am Rheinfall see Neuhausen
101 I17 Neuhof Hessen, C Germany 50°26′N 09°34′E
Neuhof see Zgierz
Neukuhren see Pionerskiy
Neu-Langenburg see Tukuyu
109 W4 Neulengbach Niederösterreich, NE Austria 48°10′N 15°53′E
113 G15 Neum Federacija Bosna I Hercegovina, S Bosnia and Herzegovina 42°57′N 17°33′E
Neumark see Nowy Targ, Małopolskie, Poland
Neumark see Nowe Miasto Lubawskie, Warmińsko-Mazurskie, Poland
Neumarkt see Neumarkt im Hausruckkreis, Oberösterreich, Austria
Neumarkt see Neumarkt am Wallersee, Salzburg, Austria
Neumarkt see Środa Śląska, Dolnośląskie, Poland
Neumarkt see Târgu Secuiesc, Covasna, Romania
Neumarkt see Târgu Mureș
109 Q5 Neumarkt am Wallersee var. Neumarkt. Salzburg, NW Austria 47°55′N 13°16′E
109 R4 Neumarkt im Hausruckkreis var. Neumarkt. Oberösterreich, N Austria 48°16′N 13°40′E
101 L20 Neumarkt in der Oberpfalz Bayern, SE Germany 49°16′N 11°28′E
Neumarktl see Tržič
Neumoldowa see Moldova Nouă
100 J8 Neumünster Schleswig-Holstein, N Germany 54°04′N 09°59′E
109 X5 Neunkirchen var. Neunkirchen am Steinfeld. Niederösterreich, E Austria 47°44′N 16°05′E
101 E20 Neunkirchen Saarland, SW Germany 49°21′N 07°11′E
Neunkirchen am Steinfeld see Neunkirchen
Neuoderberg see Bohumín
63 I15 Neuquén Neuquén, SE Argentina 39°03′S 68°36′W
63 H14 Neuquén off. Provincia de Neuquén. ◆ province W Argentina
Neuquén, Provincia de see Neuquén
63 H14 Neuquén, Río ≈ W Argentina
Neurode see Nowa Ruda
100 N11 Neuruppin Brandenburg, NE Germany 52°56′N 12°49′E
Neusalz an der Oder see Nowa Sól
Neu Sandec see Nowy Sącz
101 K22 Neusäss Bayern, S Germany 48°24′N 10°49′E
Neusatz see Novi Sad
Neuschliss see Gherla
21 N8 Neuse River ≈ North Carolina, SE USA
109 Z5 Neusiedl am See Burgenland, E Austria 47°58′N 16°51′E
111 G22 Neusiedler See Hung. Fertő. ◎ Austria/Hungary
Neusohl see Banská Bystrica
101 D15 Neuss anc. Novaesium, Novesium. Nordrhein-Westfalen, W Germany 51°12′N 06°42′E
Neuss see Nyon
Neustadt see Neustadt bei Coburg, Bayern, Germany
Neustadt see Neustadt an der Aisch, Bayern, Germany
Neustadt see Prudnik, Opole, Poland
Neustadt see Baia Mare, Maramureș, Romania
100 I12 Neustadt am Rübenberge Niedersachsen, N Germany 52°30′N 09°28′E
101 J19 Neustadt an der Aisch var. Neustadt. Bayern, C Germany 49°34′N 10°36′E
Neustadt an der Haardt see Neustadt an der Weinstrasse
101 F20 Neustadt an der Weinstrasse prev. Neustadt an der Haardt, hist. Niewenstat; anc. Nova Civitas. Rheinland-Pfalz, SW Germany 49°21′N 08°09′E
101 K18 Neustadt bei Coburg var. Neustadt. Bayern, C Germany 50°19′N 11°06′E
Neustadt bei Pinne see Lwówek
Neustadt in Oberschlesien see Prudnik
Neustadtl see Novo mesto
Neustadtl in Mähren see Nové Město na Moravě
Neustettin see Szczecinek
108 M8 Neustift im Stubaital var. Stubaital. Tirol, W Austria 47°07′N 11°26′E
100 N10 Neustrelitz Mecklenburg-Vorpommern, NE Germany 53°22′N 13°05′E
Neutitschein see Nový Jičín
Neutra see Nitra
101 J22 Neu-Ulm Bayern, S Germany 48°23′N 10°02′E
Neuveville see La Neuveville
103 N12 Neuvic Corrèze, C France 45°23′N 02°16′E
Neuwarp see Nowe Warpno
100 G9 Neuwerk island NW Germany
101 E17 Neuwied Rheinland-Pfalz, W Germany 50°26′N 07°28′E
Neuzen see Terneuzen
124 H12 Neva ≈ NW Russian Federation
29 V14 Nevada Iowa, C USA 42°01′N 93°27′W
27 R6 Nevada Missouri, C USA 37°51′N 94°22′W
35 R5 Nevada off. State of Nevada, also known as Battle Born State, Sagebrush State, Silver State. ◆ state W USA
35 P6 Nevada City California, W USA 39°15′N 121°02′W
105 O14 Nevada, Sierra ▲▲ S Spain
35 P6 Nevada, Sierra ▲▲ W USA
62 I13 Nevado, Sierra del ▲▲ W Argentina
124 G16 Nevel' Pskovskaya Oblast', W Russian Federation 56°01′N 29°54′E
123 T14 Nevel'sk Ostrov Sakhalin, Sakhalinskaya Oblast', SE Russian Federation 46°41′N 141°54′E
123 Q13 Never Amurskaya Oblast', SE Russian Federation 53°58′N 124°04′E
127 Q6 Neverkino Penzenskaya Oblast', W Russian Federation 52°53′N 46°46′E
103 P9 Nevers anc. Noviodunum. Nièvre, C France 47°N 03°09′E
18 J12 Neversink River ≈ New York, NE USA
183 Q6 Nevertire New South Wales, SE Australia 31°52′S 147°42′E
113 H15 Nevesinje ◆ Republika Srpska, S Bosnia and Herzegovina
118 G12 Nevėžis ≈ C Lithuania
138 F11 Neve Zohar prev. Newé Zohar. Southern, E Israel 31°07′N 35°23′E
126 M14 Nevinnomyssk Stavropol'skiy Kray, SW Russian Federation 44°39′N 41°57′E
45 W10 Nevis island Saint Kitts and Nevis
Nevoso, Monte see Veliki Snežnik
Nevrokop see Gotse Delchev
136 J14 Nevşehir var. Nevshehr. Nevşehir, C Turkey 38°38′N 34°43′E
136 J14 Nevşehir var. Nevshehr. ◆ province C Turkey
Nevshehr see Nevşehir
122 G10 Nev'yansk Sverdlovskaya Oblast', C Russian Federation 57°26′N 60°15′E
81 J25 Newala Mtwara, SE Tanzania 10°59′S 39°18′E
31 P16 New Albany Indiana, N USA 38°17′N 85°50′W
22 M2 New Albany Mississippi, S USA 34°29′N 89°00′W
29 Y11 New Albin Iowa, C USA 43°30′N 91°17′W
55 U8 New Amsterdam E Guyana 06°17′N 57°31′W
183 Q4 New Angledool New South Wales, SE Australia 29°06′S 147°54′E
21 Y2 Newark Delaware, NE USA 39°42′N 75°45′W
18 K14 Newark New Jersey, NE USA 40°42′N 74°12′W
18 G10 Newark New York, NE USA 43°01′N 77°04′W
31 T13 Newark Ohio, N USA 40°03′N 82°24′W
Newark see Newark-on-Trent
35 W5 Newark Lake ◎ Nevada, W USA
97 N18 Newark-on-Trent var. Newark. C England, United Kingdom 53°05′N 00°49′W
22 M7 New Augusta Mississippi, S USA 31°12′N 89°03′W
19 P12 New Bedford Massachusetts, NE USA 41°38′N 70°55′W
32 G11 Newberg Oregon, NW USA 45°18′N 122°58′W
21 X10 New Bern North Carolina, SE USA 35°05′N 77°04′W
20 F8 Newbern Tennessee, S USA 36°06′N 89°15′W
31 P4 Newberry Michigan, N USA 46°21′N 85°30′W
21 Q12 Newberry South Carolina, SE USA 34°17′N 81°39′W
18 F15 New Bloomfield Pennsylvania, NE USA 40°24′N 77°08′W
25 X5 New Boston Texas, SW USA 33°27′N 94°25′W
25 S11 New Braunfels Texas, SW USA 29°43′N 98°09′W
31 Q13 New Bremen Ohio, N USA 40°26′N 84°22′W
97 F18 Newbridge Ir. An Droichead Nua. Kildare, C Ireland 53°11′N 06°48′W
18 B14 New Brighton Pennsylvania, NE USA 40°44′N 80°18′W
18 M12 New Britain Connecticut, NE USA 41°37′N 72°45′W
186 G7 New Britain island E Papua New Guinea
192 I8 New Britain Trench undersea feature W Pacific Ocean
18 J15 New Brunswick New Jersey, NE USA 40°29′N 74°27′W
15 V8 New Brunswick Fr. Nouveau-Brunswick. ◆ province SE Canada
18 K13 Newburgh New York, NE USA 41°30′N 74°00′W
97 M22 Newbury S England, United Kingdom 51°25′N 01°20′W
19 P10 Newburyport Massachusetts, NE USA 42°49′N 70°53′W
77 T14 New Bussa Niger, W Nigeria 09°50′N 04°32′E
187 O17 New Caledonia var. Kanaky, Fr. Nouvelle-Calédonie. ◇ French overseas territory SW Pacific Ocean
187 O15 New Caledonia island SW Pacific Ocean
175 O10 New Caledonia Basin undersea feature W Pacific Ocean
183 T8 Newcastle New South Wales, SE Australia 32°55′S 151°46′E
13 O14 Newcastle New Brunswick, SE Canada 47°01′N 65°36′W
14 I15 Newcastle Ontario, SE Canada 43°55′N 78°35′W
83 K22 Newcastle KwaZulu/Natal, E South Africa 27°45′S 29°55′E
97 G16 Newcastle Ir. An Caisleán Nua. SE Northern Ireland, United Kingdom 54°12′N 05°54′W
31 P13 New Castle Indiana, N USA 39°56′N 85°21′W
20 L5 New Castle Kentucky, S USA 38°28′N 85°10′W
27 N11 Newcastle Oklahoma, C USA 35°15′N 97°36′W
18 B13 New Castle Pennsylvania, NE USA 41°00′N 80°22′W
25 R6 Newcastle Texas, SW USA 33°11′N 98°44′W
36 J7 Newcastle Utah, W USA 37°40′N 113°31′W
21 S6 New Castle Virginia, NE USA 37°31′N 80°09′W
33 Z13 Newcastle Wyoming, C USA 43°52′N 104°14′W
45 W10 Newcastle ✈ Nevis, Saint Kitts and Nevis 17°08′N 62°36′W
97 L14 Newcastle ✈ NE England, United Kingdom 55°03′N 01°42′W
Newcastle see Newcastle upon Tyne
97 L18 Newcastle-under-Lyme C England, United Kingdom 53°N 02°14′W
97 M14 Newcastle upon Tyne var. Newcastle, hist. Monkchester, Lat. Pons Aelii. NE England, United Kingdom 54°59′N 01°35′W
181 Q4 Newcastle Waters Northern Territory, N Australia 17°20′S 133°26′E
Newchwang see Yingkou
18 K13 New City New York, NE USA 41°08′N 73°57′W
31 U13 Newcomerstown Ohio, N USA 40°16′N 81°36′W
18 G15 New Cumberland Pennsylvania, NE USA 40°13′N 76°52′W
21 R1 New Cumberland West Virginia, NE USA 40°30′N 80°35′W
152 I10 New Delhi ● (India) Delhi, N India 28°35′N 77°15′E
11 O17 New Denver British Columbia, SW Canada 49°58′N 117°21′W
28 J9 Newell South Dakota, N USA 44°42′N 103°25′W
21 Q13 New Ellenton South Carolina, SE USA 33°25′N 81°41′W
22 J6 Newellton Louisiana, S USA 32°04′N 91°14′W
28 K6 New England North Dakota, N USA 46°32′N 102°52′W
19 P8 New England cultural region NE USA
New England of the West see Minnesota
183 U5 New England Range ▲▲ New South Wales, SE Australia
64 G9 New England Seamounts var. Bermuda-New England Seamount Arc. undersea feature W Atlantic Ocean 38°00′N 61°00′W
38 M14 Newenham, Cape headland Alaska, USA 58°39′N 162°10′W
Newé Zohar see Neve Zohar
18 D9 Newfane New York, NE USA 43°16′N 78°40′W
97 M23 New Forest physical region S England, United Kingdom
13 T12 Newfoundland Fr. Terre-Neuve. island Newfoundland and Labrador, SE Canada
13 R9 Newfoundland and Labrador Fr. Terre Neuve. ◆ province E Canada
65 J8 Newfoundland Basin undersea feature NW Atlantic Ocean 45°00′N 40°00′W
64 I8 Newfoundland Ridge undersea feature NW Atlantic Ocean
64 J8 Newfoundland Seamounts undersea feature N Sargasso Sea
18 G16 New Freedom Pennsylvania, NE USA 39°43′N 76°41′W
186 K9 New Georgia island New Georgia Islands, NW Solomon Islands
186 K8 New Georgia Islands island group NW Solomon Islands
186 L8 New Georgia Sound var. The Slot. sound E Solomon Sea
30 L9 New Glarus Wisconsin, N USA 42°50′N 89°38′W
13 Q15 New Glasgow Nova Scotia, SE Canada 45°36′N 62°38′W
New Goa see Panaji
186 A6 New Guinea Dut. Nieuw Guinea, Ind. Irian. island Indonesia/Papua New Guinea
192 H8 New Guinea Trench undersea feature SW Pacific Ocean
32 I6 Newhalem Washington, NW USA 48°40′N 121°18′W
39 P13 Newhalen Alaska, USA 59°43′N 154°54′W
29 X13 Newhall Iowa, C USA 42°00′N 91°58′W
14 F16 New Hamburg Ontario, S Canada 43°24′N 80°37′W
19 N9 New Hampshire off. State of New Hampshire, also known as Granite State. ◆ state NE USA
29 W12 New Hampton Iowa, C USA 43°03′N 92°19′W
186 G5 New Hanover island NE Papua New Guinea
97 P23 Newhaven SE England, United Kingdom 50°48′N 00°00′E
18 M13 New Haven Connecticut, NE USA 41°18′N 72°55′W
31 Q12 New Haven Indiana, N USA 41°02′N 84°59′W
27 W5 New Haven Missouri, C USA 38°34′N 91°15′W
10 K13 New Hazelton British Columbia, SW Canada 55°15′N 127°30′W
New Hebrides see Vanuatu
175 P9 New Hebrides Trench undersea feature N Coral Sea
18 H15 New Holland Pennsylvania, NE USA 40°06′N 76°05′W
22 I9 New Iberia Louisiana, S USA 30°00′N 91°51′W
186 G5 New Ireland ◆ province NE Papua New Guinea
186 G5 New Ireland island NE Papua New Guinea
65 A24 New Island island W Falkland Islands
18 J15 New Jersey off. State of New Jersey, also known as The Garden State. ◆ state NE USA
18 C14 New Kensington Pennsylvania, NE USA 40°33′N 79°45′W
21 W6 New Kent Virginia, NE USA 37°32′N 76°59′W
27 O8 Newkirk Oklahoma, C USA 36°54′N 97°03′W
21 Q9 Newland North Carolina, SE USA 36°04′N 81°50′W
28 L6 New Leipzig North Dakota, N USA 46°21′N 101°54′W
14 H9 New Liskeard Ontario, S Canada 47°31′N 79°41′W
22 G7 Newllano Louisiana, S USA 31°06′N 93°16′W
19 N13 New London Connecticut, NE USA 41°21′N 72°04′W
29 Y15 New London Iowa, C USA 40°55′N 91°24′W
29 T8 New London Minnesota, N USA 45°18′N 94°56′W
27 V3 New London Missouri, C USA 39°34′N 91°24′W
30 M7 New London Wisconsin, N USA 44°25′N 88°44′W
27 Y8 New Madrid Missouri, C USA 36°34′N 89°32′W
180 J8 Newman Western Australia 23°18′S 119°45′E
194 M13 Newman Island island Antarctica
14 H15 Newmarket Ontario, S Canada 44°03′N 79°27′W
97 P20 Newmarket E England, United Kingdom 52°18′N 00°28′E
19 P10 Newmarket New Hampshire, NE USA 43°04′N 70°53′W
21 U4 New Market Virginia, NE USA 38°39′N 78°40′W
21 R2 New Martinsville West Virginia, NE USA 39°39′N 80°52′W
31 U14 New Matamoras Ohio, N USA 39°32′N 81°04′W
32 M12 New Meadows Idaho, NW USA 44°57′N 116°16′W
26 R12 New Mexico off. State of New Mexico, also known as Land of Enchantment, Sunshine State. ◆ state SW USA
149 V6 New Mirpur var. Mirpur. Sind, SE Pakistan 33°11′N 73°46′E
151 N15 New Moore Island Island E India
23 S4 Newnan Georgia, SE USA 33°22′N 84°48′W
183 P17 New Norfolk Tasmania, SE Australia 42°46′S 147°02′E
22 K9 New Orleans Louisiana, S USA 30°00′N 90°01′W
22 K9 New Orleans ✈ Louisiana, S USA 29°59′N 90°17′W
18 K12 New Paltz New York, NE USA 41°44′N 74°04′W
31 U12 New Philadelphia Ohio, N USA 40°29′N 81°27′W
184 K10 New Plymouth Taranaki, North Island, New Zealand 39°04′S 174°06′E
97 M24 Newport S England, United Kingdom 50°42′N 01°18′W
97 K22 Newport SE Wales, United Kingdom 51°35′N 03°00′W
27 W10 Newport Arkansas, C USA 35°36′N 91°16′W
31 N13 Newport Indiana, N USA 39°52′N 87°24′W
20 M3 Newport Kentucky, S USA 39°05′N 84°27′W
29 W9 Newport Minnesota, N USA 44°52′N 93°00′W
32 F12 Newport Oregon, NW USA 44°39′N 124°04′W
19 O13 Newport Rhode Island, NE USA 41°29′N 71°17′W
21 O9 Newport Tennessee, S USA 35°58′N 83°13′W
19 N6 Newport Vermont, NE USA 44°56′N 72°13′W
32 M7 Newport Washington, NW USA 48°08′N 117°05′W
21 X7 Newport News Virginia, NE USA 36°59′N 76°26′W
97 N20 Newport Pagnell SE England, United Kingdom 52°05′N 00°44′W
23 U12 New Port Richey Florida, SE USA 28°14′N 82°42′W

◆ Country
● Country Capital
◇ Dependent Territory
○ Dependent Territory Capital
◆ Administrative Regions
✈ International Airport
▲ Mountain
▲▲ Mountain Range
☼ Volcano
≈ River
◎ Lake
⊠ Reservoir

New Prague – Nogent-le-Rotrou

29 V9 **New Prague** Minnesota, N USA 44°32′N 93°34′W
44 H3 **New Providence** *island* N Bahamas
97 I20 **New Quay** SW Wales, United Kingdom 52°13′N 04°22′W
97 H24 **Newquay** SW England, United Kingdom 50°27′N 05°03′W
29 V10 **New Richland** Minnesota, N USA 43°53′N 93°29′W
15 X7 **New-Richmond** Québec, SE Canada 48°12′N 65°52′W
31 R15 **New Richmond** Ohio, N USA 38°57′N 84°16′W
30 I5 **New Richmond** Wisconsin, N USA 45°09′N 92°31′W
42 G1 **New River** ⇝ N Belize
55 T12 **New River** ⇝ SE Guyana
21 R6 **New River** ⇝ West Virginia, NE USA
42 G1 **New River Lagoon** ◎ N Belize
22 J8 **New Roads** Louisiana, S USA 30°42′N 91°26′W
18 L14 **New Rochelle** New York, NE USA 40°55′N 73°44′W
29 O4 **New Rockford** North Dakota, N USA 47°40′N 99°08′W
97 P23 **New Romney** SE England, United Kingdom 50°58′N 00°56′E
97 F20 **New Ross** *Ir.* Ros Mhic Thriúin. Wexford, SE Ireland 52°24′N 06°56′W
97 F16 **Newry** *Ir.* An tIúr. SE Northern Ireland, United Kingdom 54°11′N 06°20′W
28 M5 **New Salem** North Dakota, N USA 46°51′N 101°24′W
New Sarum *see* Salisbury
29 W14 **New Sharon** Iowa, C USA 41°28′N 92°39′W
New Siberian Islands *see* Novosibirskiye Ostrova
23 X11 **New Smyrna Beach** Florida, SE USA 29°01′N 80°55′W
183 O7 **New South Wales** ◈ *state* SE Australia
39 O13 **New Stuyahok** Alaska, USA 59°27′N 157°18′W
21 N8 **New Tazewell** Tennessee, S USA 36°26′N 83°36′W
New Tehri *see* Tehri
38 M12 **Newtok** Alaska, USA 60°56′N 164°37′W
23 S7 **Newton** Georgia, SE USA 31°18′N 84°20′W
29 W14 **Newton** Iowa, C USA 41°42′N 93°03′W
27 N6 **Newton** Kansas, C USA 38°02′N 97°22′W
19 O11 **Newton** Massachusetts, NE USA 42°19′N 71°10′W
22 M5 **Newton** Mississippi, S USA 32°19′N 89°09′W
18 J14 **Newton** New Jersey, NE USA 41°03′N 74°45′W
21 R9 **Newton** North Carolina, SE USA 35°42′N 81°14′W
25 Y9 **Newton** Texas, SW USA 30°51′N 93°45′W
97 J24 **Newton Abbot** SW England, United Kingdom 50°33′N 03°34′W
96 K13 **Newton St Boswells** SE Scotland, United Kingdom 55°34′N 02°40′W
97 I14 **Newton Stewart** S Scotland, United Kingdom 54°58′N 04°30′W
92 O2 **Newtontoppen** ▲ C Svalbard 78°57′N 17°34′E
97 J20 **Newtown** E Wales, United Kingdom 52°32′N 03°19′W
28 K3 **New Town** North Dakota, N USA 47°58′N 102°30′W
97 G15 **Newtownabbey** *Ir.* Baile na Mainistreach. E Northern Ireland, United Kingdom 54°40′N 05°57′W
97 G15 **Newtownards** *Ir.* Baile Nua na hArda. SE Northern Ireland, United Kingdom 54°36′N 05°41′W
29 U10 **New Ulm** Minnesota, N USA 44°20′N 94°28′W
28 K10 **New Underwood** South Dakota, N USA 44°05′N 102°46′W
25 V10 **New Waverly** Texas, SW USA 30°32′N 95°28′W
18 K14 **New York** New York, NE USA 40°45′N 73°57′W
18 G10 **New York** ◈ *state* NE USA
35 X13 **New York Mountains** ▲▲ California, W USA
184 K12 **New Zealand** ◆ *commonwealth republic* SW Pacific Ocean
95 M24 **Nexø** *var.* Neksø Bornholm. E Denmark 55°04′N 15°09′E
125 O15 **Neya** Kostromskaya Oblast', NW Russian Federation 58°19′N 43°51′E
Neyba *see* Neiba
143 Q12 **Neyrīz** *var.* Neiriz, Niriz. Fārs, S Iran 29°14′N 54°18′E
143 T4 **Neyshābūr** *var.* Nishapur. Khorāsān-Razavī, NE Iran 36°15′N 58°47′E
155 J21 **Neyveli** Tamil Nādu, SE India 11°36′N 79°26′E
Nezhin *see* Nizhyn
33 N10 **Nezperce** Idaho, NW USA 46°14′N 116°15′W
22 H8 **Nezpique, Bayou** ⇝ Louisiana, S USA
77 Y13 **Ngadda** ⇝ NE Nigeria
N'Gage *see* Negage
185 G16 **Ngahere** West Coast, South Island, New Zealand 42°22′S 171°29′E
77 Z12 **Ngala** Borno, NE Nigeria 12°19′N 14°11′E
158 K16 **Ngamring** Xizang Zizhiqu, W China 29°16′N 87°10′E
81 K19 **Ngangerabeli Plain** *plain* SE Kenya
158 I14 **Ngangla Ringco** ◎ W China
158 H13 **Nganglong Kangri** ▲ W China 32°55′N 81°00′E
158 K15 **Ngangzê Co** ◎ W China
79 F14 **Ngaoundéré** *var.* N'Gaoundéré. Adamaoua, N Cameroon 07°20′N 13°35′E
N'Gaoundéré *see* Ngaoundéré
81 E20 **Ngara** Kagera, NW Tanzania 02°30′S 30°40′E
188 F8 **Ngardmau Bay** *bay* Babeldaob, N Palau
188 F7 **Ngaregur** *island* Palau Islands, N Palau
Ngarrab *see* Gyaca
184 L7 **Ngaruawahia** Waikato, North Island, New Zealand 37°41′S 175°10′E
184 N11 **Ngaruroro** ⇝ North Island, New Zealand
190 I16 **Ngatangiia** Rarotonga, S Cook Islands 21°14′S 159°44′W
184 M6 **Ngatea** Waikato, North Island, New Zealand 37°16′S 175°29′E
166 L8 **Ngathainggyaung** Ayeyarwady, SW Burma (Myanmar) 17°22′N 95°04′E
Ngatik *see* Ngetik Atoll
Ngau *see* Gau
Ngawa *see* Aba
172 G12 **Ngazidja** *Fr.* Grande-Comore. *island* NW Comoros
188 C7 **Ngcheangel** *var.* Kayangel Islands. *island* Palau Islands, N Palau
188 E10 **Ngchemiangel** Babeldaob, N Palau
188 C8 **Ngeaur** *var.* Angaur. *island* Palau Islands, S Palau
188 E10 **Ngerkeai** Babeldaob, N Palau
188 F9 **Ngermechau** Babeldaob, N Palau 07°35′N 134°39′E
188 C8 **Ngeruktabel** *prev.* Urukthapel. *island* Palau Islands, S Palau
188 F8 **Ngetbong** Babeldaob, N Palau 07°37′N 134°35′E
189 T17 **Ngetik Atoll** *var.* Ngatik; *prev.* Los Jardines. *atoll* Caroline Islands, E Micronesia
188 E10 **Ngetkip** Babeldaob, N Palau
Nghia Dan *see* Thai Hoa
83 C16 **N'Giva** *var.* Ondjiva, *Port.* Vila Pereira de Eça. Cunene, S Angola 17°02′S 15°42′E
79 G20 **Ngo** Plateaux, SE Congo 02°28′S 15°43′E
43 P16 **Ngöbe-Buglé** ◈ *special territory* W Panama
167 S7 **Ngoc Lac** Thanh Hoa, N Vietnam 20°06′N 105°21′E
79 G17 **Ngoko** ⇝ Cameroon/Congo
81 H19 **Ngorengore** Rift Valley, SW Kenya 01°01′S 35°26′E
159 Q11 **Ngoring Hu** ◎ C China
Ngorolaka *see* Banifing
81 H20 **Ngorongoro Crater** *crater* N Tanzania
79 D19 **Ngounié** *off.* Province de la Ngounié, *var.* La Ngounié. ◈ *province* S Gabon
79 D19 **Ngounié** ⇝ Congo/Gabon
Ngounié, Province de la *see* Ngounié
78 H10 **Ngoura** *var.* NGoura. Chari-Baguirmi, W Chad 12°52′N 16°27′E
NGoura *see* Ngoura
78 G10 **Ngouri** *var.* NGouri; *prev.* Fort-Millot. Lac, W Chad 13°42′N 15°19′E
NGouri *see* Ngouri
77 Y10 **Ngourti** Diffa, E Niger 15°22′N 13°13′E
77 Y11 **Nguigmi** *var.* N'Guigmi. Diffa, SE Niger 14°17′N 13°07′E
N'Guigmi *see* Nguigmi
Nguimbo *see* Lumbala N'Guimbo
188 F15 **Ngulu Atoll** *atoll* Caroline Islands, W Micronesia
187 R14 **Nguna** *island* C Vanuatu
N'Gunza *see* Sumbe
169 U17 **Ngurah Rai** ✕ (Bali) Bali, S Indonesia 8°40′S 115°14′E
77 W12 **Nguru** Yobe, NE Nigeria 12°55′N 10°31′E
Ngwaketze *see* Southern
83 I16 **Ngweze** ⇝ S Zambia
83 M17 **Nhamatanda** Sofala, C Mozambique 19°16′S 34°10′E
58 G12 **Nhamundá, Rio** *var.* Jamundá, Yamundá. ⇝ N Brazil
60 J7 **Nhandeara** São Paulo, S Brazil 20°40′S 50°03′W
82 D12 **Nharêa** *var.* N'Harea, Nhareia. Bié, W Angola 11°38′S 16°58′E
N'Harea *see* Nharêa
Nhareia *see* Nharêa
167 V12 **Nha Trang** Khanh Hoa, S Vietnam 12°15′N 109°10′E
182 L11 **Nhill** Victoria, SE Australia 36°21′S 141°38′E
83 L22 **Nhlangano** *prev.* Goedgegun. SW Swaziland 27°06′S 31°12′E
181 S1 **Nhulunbuy** Northern Territory, N Australia 12°16′S 136°46′E
77 N10 **Niafounké** Tombouctou, W Mali 15°54′N 03°58′W
31 N5 **Niagara** Wisconsin, N USA 45°45′N 87°57′W
14 H16 **Niagara** ⇝ Ontario, S Canada
14 G15 **Niagara Escarpment** *hill range* Ontario, S Canada
14 H16 **Niagara Falls** Ontario, S Canada 43°05′N 79°06′W
18 D9 **Niagara Falls** New York, NE USA 43°06′N 79°04′W
14 H16 **Niagara Falls** *waterfall* Canada/USA
76 K12 **Niagassola** *var.* Nyagassola. Haute-Guinée, NE Guinea 12°24′N 09°03′W
77 R12 **Niamey** ● (Niger) Niamey, SW Niger 13°28′N 02°03′E
77 R12 **Niamey** ✕ Niamey, SW Niger 13°28′N 02°14′E
77 R14 **Niamtougou** N Togo 09°50′N 01°08′E
79 O16 **Niangara** Orientale, NE Dem. Rep. Congo 03°45′N 27°54′E
77 O10 **Niangay, Lac** ◎ E Mali
77 N14 **Niangoloko** SW Burkina 10°15′N 04°53′W
27 U6 **Niangua River** ⇝ Missouri, C USA
79 O17 **Nia-Nia** Orientale, NE Dem. Rep. Congo 01°26′N 27°38′E
19 N13 **Niantic** Connecticut, NE USA 41°19′N 72°11′W
163 U7 **Nianzishan** Heilongjiang, NE China 47°31′N 122°53′E
79 E20 **Niari** ◈ *province* SW Congo
168 H10 **Nias, Pulau** *island* W Indonesia
82 O13 **Niassa** *off.* Província do Niassa. ◈ *province* N Mozambique
Niassa, Província do *see* Niassa
191 U10 **Niau** *island* Îles Tuamotu, C French Polynesia
95 G20 **Nibe** Nordjylland, N Denmark 56°59′N 09°39′E
189 Q8 **Nibok** N Nauru 0°31′S 166°55′E
118 C10 **Nīca** Liepāja, W Latvia 56°21′N 21°03′E
Nicaea *see* Nice
42 J9 **Nicaragua** *off.* Republic of Nicaragua. ◆ *republic* Central America
42 K11 **Nicaragua, Lago de** *var.* Cocibolca, Gran Lago, *Eng.* Lake Nicaragua. ◎ S Nicaragua
Nicaragua, Lake *see* Nicaragua, Lago de
64 D11 **Nicaraguan Rise** *undersea feature* NW Caribbean Sea 16°00′N 80°00′W
Nicaragua, Republic of *see* Nicaragua
Nicaria *see* Ikaría
107 N21 **Nicastro** Calabria, SW Italy 38°59′N 16°20′E
103 V15 **Nice** *It.* Nizza; *anc.* Nicaea. Alpes-Maritimes, SE France 43°43′N 07°13′E
Nice *see* Côte d'Azur
Nicephorium *see* Ar Raqqah
12 M9 **Nichicun, Lac** ◎ Québec, E Canada
164 D16 **Nichinan** *var.* Nitinan. Miyazaki, Kyūshū, SW Japan 31°36′N 131°23′E
44 E4 **Nicholas Channel** *channel* N Cuba
Nicholas II Land *see* Severnaya Zemlya
149 U2 **Nicholas Range** *Pash.* Selselehye Kuhe Vākhān, *Taj.* Qatorkŭhi Vakhon. ▲▲ Afghanistan/Tajikistan
20 M6 **Nicholasville** Kentucky, S USA 37°52′N 84°34′W
44 G2 **Nicholls Town** Andros Island, NW Bahamas 25°07′N 78°01′W
21 U12 **Nichols** South Carolina, SE USA 34°13′N 79°09′W
55 U9 **Nickerie** ◈ *district* NW Surinam
55 V9 **Nickerie Rivier** ⇝ NW Surinam
151 P22 **Nicobar Islands** *island group* India, E Indian Ocean
116 L9 **Nicolae Bălcescu** Botoșani, NE Romania 47°33′N 26°52′E
15 P11 **Nicolet** Québec, SE Canada 46°13′N 72°37′W
15 Q12 **Nicolet** ⇝ Québec, SE Canada
31 Q4 **Nicolet, Lake** ◎ Michigan, N USA
29 U10 **Nicollet** Minnesota, N USA 44°16′N 94°11′W
61 F19 **Nico Pérez** Florida, S Uruguay 33°30′S 55°10′W
Nicopolis *see* Nikopol, Bulgaria
Nicopolis *see* Nikópoli, Greece
121 P2 **Nicosia** *Gk.* Lefkosía, *Turk.* Lefkoşa. ● (Cyprus) C Cyprus 35°10′N 33°23′E
107 K24 **Nicosia** Sicilia, Italy, C Mediterranean Sea 37°45′N 14°24′E
107 N22 **Nicotera** Calabria, SW Italy 38°33′N 15°55′E
42 K13 **Nicoya** Guanacaste, W Costa Rica 10°09′N 85°26′W
42 L14 **Nicoya, Golfo de** *gulf* W Costa Rica
42 L14 **Nicoya, Península de** *peninsula* NW Costa Rica
Nictheroy *see* Niterói
118 B12 **Nida** *Ger.* Nidden. Klaipėda, SW Lithuania 55°20′N 21°00′E
111 L15 **Nida** ⇝ S Poland
Nidaros *see* Trondheim
108 D8 **Nidau** Bern, W Switzerland 47°07′N 07°15′E
101 H17 **Nidda** ⇝ W Germany
Nidden *see* Nida
95 F17 **Nidelva** ⇝ S Norway
110 L9 **Nidzica** *Ger.* Niedenburg. Warmińsko-Mazurskie, NE Poland 53°22′N 20°27′E
100 H6 **Niebüll** Schleswig-Holstein, N Germany 54°47′N 08°51′E
Niedenburg *see* Nidzica
99 N25 **Niederanven** Luxembourg, C Luxembourg 49°39′N 06°15′E
103 V4 **Niederbronn-les-Bains** Bas-Rhin, NE France 48°57′N 07°37′E
Niederdonau *see* Niederösterreich
109 S7 **Niedere Tauern** ▲▲ C Austria
101 P14 **Niederlausitz** *Eng.* Lower Lusatia, *Lus.* Donja Łužica. *physical region* E Germany
109 U5 **Niederösterreich** *off.* Land Niederösterreich, *Eng.* Lower Austria, *Ger.* Niederdonau; *prev.* Lower Danube. ◈ *state* NE Austria
Niederösterreich, Land *see* Niederösterreich
100 G12 **Niedersachsen** *Eng.* Lower Saxony, *Fr.* Basse-Saxe. ◈ *state* NW Germany
79 D17 **Niefang** *var.* Sevilla de Niefang. NW Equatorial Guinea 01°52′N 10°12′E
83 G23 **Niekerkshoop** Northern Cape, W South Africa 29°21′S 22°49′E
99 G17 **Niel** Antwerpen, N Belgium 51°07′N 04°20′E
Niélé *see* Niellé
76 M14 **Niellé** *var.* Niélé. N Ivory Coast 10°12′N 05°38′W
79 O22 **Niemba** Katanga, E Dem. Rep. Congo 05°58′S 28°24′E
111 G15 **Niemcza** *Ger.* Nimptsch. Dolnośląskie, SW Poland 50°45′N 16°52′E
Niemen *see* Neman
92 J13 **Niemisel** Norrbotten, N Sweden 66°00′N 22°00′E
111 H15 **Niemodlin** *Ger.* Falkenberg. Opolskie, SW Poland 50°37′N 17°45′E
76 M13 **Niéna** Sikasso, SW Mali 11°24′N 06°20′W
100 H12 **Nienburg** Niedersachsen, N Germany 52°37′N 09°12′E
100 N13 **Nieplitz** ⇝ NE Germany
111 L16 **Niepołomice** Malopolskie, S Poland 50°02′N 20°12′E
101 D14 **Niers** ⇝ Germany/Netherlands
101 Q15 **Niesky** *Lus.* Niska. Sachsen, E Germany 51°16′N 14°49′E
Nieśwież *see* Nyasvizh
Nieuport *see* Nieuwpoort
98 O8 **Nieuw-Amsterdam** Drenthe, NE Netherlands 52°43′N 06°52′E
55 W9 **Nieuw Amsterdam** Commewijne, NE Surinam 05°53′N 55°05′W
99 M14 **Nieuw-Bergen** Limburg, SE Netherlands 51°36′N 06°04′E
98 O7 **Nieuw-Buinen** Drenthe, NE Netherlands 52°57′N 06°55′E
98 J12 **Nieuwegein** Utrecht, C Netherlands 52°03′N 05°06′E
98 P6 **Nieuwe Pekela** Groningen, NE Netherlands 53°04′N 06°58′E
98 P5 **Nieuweschans** Groningen, NE Netherlands 53°10′N 07°10′E
Nieuw Guinea *see* New Guinea
98 I11 **Nieuwkoop** Zuid-Holland, C Netherlands 52°09′N 04°46′E
98 M9 **Nieuwleusen** Overijssel, S Netherlands 52°34′N 06°16′E
98 J11 **Nieuw-Loosdrecht** Noord-Holland, C Netherlands 52°12′N 05°08′E
55 U9 **Nieuw Nickerie** Nickerie, NW Surinam 05°56′N 57°W
98 P5 **Nieuwolda** Groningen, NE Netherlands 53°15′N 06°58′E
99 B17 **Nieuwpoort** *var.* Nieuport. West-Vlaanderen, W Belgium 51°08′N 02°45′E
99 G14 **Nieuw-Vossemeer** Noord-Brabant, S Netherlands 51°34′N 04°13′E
98 P7 **Nieuw-Weerdinge** Drenthe, NE Netherlands 52°51′N 07°00′E
40 L10 **Nieves** Zacatecas, C Mexico 24°00′N 102°57′W
64 O11 **Nieves, Pico de las** ▲ Gran Canaria, Islas Canarias, Spain, NE Atlantic Ocean 27°58′N 15°34′W
103 P8 **Nièvre** ◈ *department* C France
Niewenstat *see* Neustadt an der Weinstrasse
136 J15 **Niğde** Niğde, C Turkey 37°58′N 34°42′E
136 J15 **Niğde** ◈ *province* C Turkey
83 J21 **Nigel** Gauteng, NE South Africa 26°25′S 28°28′E
77 V10 **Niger** *off.* Republic of Niger. ◆ *republic* W Africa
77 T14 **Niger** ◈ *state* C Nigeria
67 P8 **Niger** ⇝ W Africa
Niger Cone *see* Niger Fan
67 P9 **Niger Delta** *delta* S Nigeria
67 P9 **Niger Fan** *var.* Niger Cone. *undersea feature* E Atlantic Ocean 04°15′N 05°00′E
77 T13 **Nigeria** *off.* Federal Republic of Nigeria. ◆ *federal republic* W Africa
Nigeria, Federal Republic of *see* Nigeria
77 T17 **Niger, Mouths of the** *delta* S Nigeria
Niger, Republic of *see* Niger
185 C24 **Nightcaps** Southland, South Island, New Zealand 45°58′S 168°03′E
14 F7 **Night Hawk Lake** ◎ Ontario, S Canada
65 M19 **Nightingale Island** *island* S Tristan da Cunha, S Atlantic Ocean
38 M12 **Nightmute** Alaska, USA 60°28′N 164°43′W
114 G13 **Nigrita** Kentrikí Makedonía, NE Greece 40°54′N 23°29′E
148 J15 **Nihing** *Per.* Rūd-e Nahang. ⇝ Iran/Pakistan
191 V10 **Nihiru** *atoll* Îles Tuamotu, C French Polynesia
Nihommatsu *see* Nihonmatsu
Nihon *see* Japan
165 P11 **Nihonmatsu** *var.* Nihommatsu, Nihonmatu. Fukushima, Honshū, C Japan 37°34′N 140°25′E
Nihonmatu *see* Nihonmatsu
62 I12 **Nihuil, Embalse del** ◎ W Argentina
165 O10 **Niigata** Niigata, Honshū, C Japan 37°55′N 139°01′E
165 O11 **Niigata** *off.* Niigata-ken. ◈ *prefecture* Honshū, C Japan
Niigata-ken *see* Niigata
165 G14 **Niihama** Ehime, Shikoku, SW Japan 33°57′N 133°15′E
38 A8 **Ni'ihau** *var.* Niihau. *island* Hawai'i, USA, C Pacific Ocean
165 X12 **Nii-jima** *island* E Japan
165 H12 **Niimi** Okayama, Honshū, SW Japan 35°00′N 133°27′E
165 O10 **Niitsu** *var.* Niitu. Niigata, Honshū, C Japan 37°48′N 139°09′E
Niitu *see* Niitsu
105 P15 **Níjar** Andalucía, S Spain 36°57′N 02°13′W
98 K11 **Nijkerk** Gelderland, C Netherlands 52°13′N 05°30′E
99 H16 **Nijlen** Antwerpen, N Belgium 51°10′N 04°40′E
98 L13 **Nijmegen** *Ger.* Nimwegen; *anc.* Noviomagus. Gelderland, SE Netherlands 51°50′N 05°52′E
98 N10 **Nijverdal** Overijssel, E Netherlands 52°22′N 06°28′E
190 G16 **Nikao** Rarotonga, S Cook Islands
Nikaria *see* Ikaría
124 I2 **Nikel'** *Finn.* Kolosjoki. Murmanskaya Oblast', NW Russian Federation 69°25′N 30°12′E
171 Q17 **Nikiniki** Timor, S Indonesia 10°S 124°30′E
129 Q15 **Nikitin Seamount** *undersea feature* E Indian Ocean 05°48′S 83°48′E
77 S14 **Nikki** E Benin 09°55′N 03°12′E
Niklasmarkt *see* Gheorgheni
39 P10 **Nikolai** Alaska, USA 63°00′N 154°22′W
Nikolaiken *see* Mikołajki
Nikolainkaupunki *see* Vaasa
Nikolayev *see* Mykolayiv
145 O6 **Nikolayevka** Severnyy Kazakhstan, N Kazakhstan
Nikolayevka *see* Zhetigen
127 P9 **Nikolayevsk** Volgogradskaya Oblast', SW Russian Federation 50°03′N 45°30′E
Nikolayevskaya Oblast' *see* Mykolayivs'ka Oblast'
123 S12 **Nikolayevsk-na-Amure** Khabarovskiy Kray, SE Russian Federation 53°04′N 140°39′E
127 P6 **Nikol'sk** Penzenskaya Oblast', W Russian Federation 53°46′N 46°03′E
125 O13 **Nikol'sk** Vologodskaya Oblast', NW Russian Federation 59°35′N 45°31′E
Nikol'sk *see* Ussuriysk
38 K17 **Nikolski** Umnak Island, Alaska, USA 52°56′N 168°52′W
Nikol'skiy *see* Satpayev
127 V7 **Nikol'skoye** Orenburgskaya Oblast', W Russian Federation 52°01′N 55°48′E
Nikol'sk-Ussuriyskiy *see* Ussuriysk
114 J7 **Nikopol** *anc.* Nicopolis. Pleven, N Bulgaria 43°43′N 24°55′E
117 S9 **Nikopol'** Dnipropetrovs'ka Oblast', SE Ukraine 47°34′N 34°23′E
115 C17 **Nikópoli** *anc.* Nicopolis. *site of ancient city* Ípeiros, W Greece
136 M12 **Niksar** Tokat, N Turkey 40°35′N 36°59′E
143 V14 **Nīkshahr** Sīstān va Balūchestān, SE Iran 26°15′N 60°10′E
113 J16 **Nikšić** C Montenegro 42°47′N 18°56′E
191 R4 **Nikumaroro** ; *prev.* Gardner Island. *atoll* Phoenix Islands, C Kiribati
191 P3 **Nikunau** *var.* Nukunau; *prev.* Byron Island. *atoll* Tungaru, W Kiribati
155 G21 **Nilambūr** Kerala, SW India 11°17′N 76°15′E
35 X16 **Niland** California, W USA 33°14′N 115°31′W
80 G8 **Nile** *former province* NW Uganda
67 T3 **Nile** *Ar.* Nahr an Nīl. ⇝ N Africa
75 W7 **Nile Delta** *delta* N Egypt
67 T3 **Nile Fan** *undersea feature* E Mediterranean Sea 33°00′N 31°00′E
31 O11 **Niles** Michigan, N USA 41°49′N 86°15′W
31 V11 **Niles** Ohio, N USA 41°10′N 80°46′W
155 F20 **Nīleswaram** Kerala, SW India 12°18′N 75°07′E
14 K10 **Nilgaut, Lac** ◎ Québec, SE Canada
149 O6 **Nīlī** Dāykondī, C Afghanistan 33°43′N 66°07′E
158 I5 **Nilka** Xinjiang Uygur Zizhiqu, NW China 43°46′N 82°33′E
Nīl, Nahr an *see* Nile
93 N16 **Nilsiä** Itä-Suomi, C Finland 63°13′N 28°00′E
154 F9 **Nīmach** Madhya Pradesh, C India 24°27′N 74°56′E
152 G14 **Nīmbāhera** Rājasthān, N India 24°38′N 74°45′E
76 L15 **Nimba, Monts** *var.* Nimba Mountains. ▲▲ W Africa
Nimba Mountains *see* Nimba, Monts
Nimburg *see* Nymburk
103 Q15 **Nîmes** *anc.* Nemausus, Nismes. Gard, S France 43°49′N 04°20′E
152 H11 **Nīm ka Thāna** Rājasthān, N India 27°42′N 75°50′E
183 R11 **Nimmitabel** New South Wales, SE Australia 36°34′S 149°18′E
Nimptsch *see* Niemcza
195 R11 **Nimrod Glacier** *glacier* Antarctica
Nimroze *see* Nīmrūz
148 K8 **Nīmrūz** *var.* Nimroze; *prev.* Chakhānsūr. ◈ *province* SW Afghanistan
81 F16 **Nimule** Eastern Equatoria, S Sudan 03°35′N 32°03′E
Nimwegen *see* Nijmegen
139 P3 **Ninawá** ◈ *governorate* NW Iraq
155 C23 **Nine Degree Channel** *channel* India/Maldives
18 G9 **Ninemile Point** *headland* New York, NE USA 43°31′N 76°22′W
173 S8 **Ninetyeast Ridge** *undersea feature* E Indian Ocean 04°00′S 90°00′E
183 P13 **Ninety Mile Beach** *beach* Victoria, SE Australia
184 I2 **Ninety Mile Beach** *beach* North Island, New Zealand
21 P12 **Ninety Six** South Carolina, SE USA 34°10′N 82°01′W
163 Y9 **Ning'an** Heilongjiang, NE China 44°20′N 129°28′E
161 S9 **Ningbo** *var.* Ning-po, Yin-hsien; *prev.* Ninghsien. Zhejiang, SE China 29°54′N 121°33′E
161 U12 **Ningde** Fujian, SE China 26°48′N 119°33′E
161 P12 **Ningdu** *var.* Meijiang. Jiangxi, S China 26°28′N 115°53′E
Ning'er *see* Pu'er
186 A7 **Ningerum** Western, SW Papua New Guinea 05°40′S 141°10′E
161 R9 **Ningguo** Anhui, E China 30°33′N 118°58′E
161 S9 **Ninghai** Zhejiang, SE China 29°18′N 121°26′E
Ning-hsia *see* Ningxia
Ninghsien *see* Ningbo
159 S15 **Ningjing Shan** ▲▲ W China
160 J15 **Ningming** *var.* Chengzhong. Guangxi Zhuangzu Zizhiqu, S China 22°07′N 106°43′E
160 H11 **Ningnan** *var.* Pisha. Sichuan, C China 26°59′N 102°49′E
Ning-po *see* Ningbo
Ningsia/Ningsia Hui/Ningsia Hui Autonomous Region *see* Ningxia
160 J5 **Ningxia** *off.* Ningxia Huizu Zizhiqu, *var.* Ning-hsia, Ningsia, *Eng.* Ningsia Hui, Ningsia Hui Autonomous Region. ◈ *autonomous region* N China
Ningxia Huizu Zizhiqu *see* Ningxia
159 X10 **Ningxian** *var.* Xinning. Gansu, N China 35°30′N 108°05′E
167 T7 **Ninh Binh** Ninh Binh, N Vietnam 20°14′N 106°00′E
167 V12 **Ninh Hoa** Khanh Hoa, S Vietnam 12°28′N 109°07′E
186 C4 **Ninigo Group** *island group* N Papua New Guinea
39 Q12 **Ninilchik** Alaska, USA 60°03′N 151°40′W
27 N7 **Ninnescah River** ⇝ Kansas, C USA
195 U16 **Ninnis Glacier** *glacier* Antarctica
165 R8 **Ninohe** Iwate, Honshū, C Japan 40°16′N 141°18′E
99 F18 **Ninove** Oost-Vlaanderen, C Belgium 50°50′N 04°02′E
171 O4 **Ninoy Aquino** ✕ (Manila) Luzon, N Philippines 14°26′N 121°00′E
Nio *see* Íos
29 P12 **Niobrara** Nebraska, C USA 42°43′N 97°59′W
28 M12 **Niobrara River** ⇝ Nebraska/Wyoming, C USA
79 I20 **Nioki** Bandundu, W Dem. Rep. Congo 02°44′S 17°42′E
76 M11 **Niono** Ségou, C Mali 14°18′N 05°59′W
76 K11 **Nioro** *var.* Nioro du Sahel. Kayes, W Mali 15°13′N 09°39′W
76 G11 **Nioro du Rip** SW Senegal 13°44′N 15°48′W
Nioro du Sahel *see* Nioro
102 K10 **Niort** Deux-Sèvres, W France 46°21′N 00°25′W
172 H14 **Nioumachoua** Mohéli, S Comoros 12°21′S 43°43′E
186 C7 **Nipa** Southern Highlands, W Papua New Guinea 06°11′S 143°27′E
11 U14 **Nipawin** Saskatchewan, S Canada 52°23′N 104°01′W
12 D12 **Nipigon** Ontario, S Canada 49°02′N 88°15′W
12 D11 **Nipigon, Lake** ◎ Ontario, S Canada
11 S13 **Nipin** ⇝ Saskatchewan, C Canada
14 G11 **Nipissing, Lake** ◎ Ontario, S Canada
35 P13 **Nipomo** California, W USA 35°02′N 120°28′W
Nippon *see* Japan
138 K6 **Niqniqīyah, Jabal an** ▲ C Syria
61 A16 **Niquivil** San Juan, W Argentina 30°25′S 68°42′W
171 Y13 **Nirabotong** Papua, E Indonesia 02°35′S 140°08′E
Niriz *see* Neyrīz
163 U7 **Nirji** *var.* Morin Dawa Daurzu Zizhiqi. Nei Mongol Zizhiqu, N China 48°21′N 124°32′E
155 I14 **Nirmal** Andhra Pradesh, C India 19°04′N 78°21′E
153 Q13 **Nirmāli** Bihār, NE India 26°18′N 86°35′E
113 O14 **Niš** *Eng.* Nish, *Ger.* Nisch; *anc.* Naissus. Serbia, SE Serbia 43°21′N 21°53′E
104 H9 **Nisa** Portalegre, C Portugal 39°31′N 07°39′W
Nisa *see* Neisse
141 P4 **Nişab** Al Ḥudūd ash Shamālīyah, N Saudi Arabia 29°11′N 44°43′E
141 Q15 **Niṣāb** *var.* Anṣāb. SW Yemen 14°24′N 46°47′E
113 P14 **Nišava** *Bul.* Nishava. ⇝ Bulgaria/Serbia *see also* Nishava
Nišava *see* Nishava
107 K25 **Niscemi** Sicilia, Italy, C Mediterranean Sea 37°09′N 14°23′E
Nisch/Nish *see* Niš
165 R4 **Niseko** Hokkaidō, NE Japan 42°50′N 140°43′E
Nishapur *see* Neyshābūr
114 G9 **Nishava** *var.* Nišava. ⇝ Bulgaria/Serbia *see also* Nišava
Nishava *see* Nišava
118 L11 **Nishcha** ⇝ N Belarus
165 C17 **Nishinoomote** Kagoshima, Tanega-shima, SW Japan 30°42′N 130°59′E
165 X15 **Nishino-shima** *Eng.* Rosario. *island* Ogasawara-shotō, SE Japan
165 I13 **Nishiwaki** *var.* Nisiwaki. Hyōgo, Honshū, SW Japan 34°59′N 134°58′E
141 U14 **Nishtūn** SE Yemen 15°47′N 52°08′E
Nisibin *see* Nusaybin
Nisiros *see* Nísyros
Nisiwaki *see* Nishiwaki
Niska *see* Niesky
113 O14 **Niška Banja** Serbia, SE Serbia 43°18′N 22°01′E
12 D6 **Niskibi** ⇝ Ontario, C Canada
111 O15 **Nisko** Podkrapackie, SE Poland 50°31′N 22°09′E
10 H7 **Nisling** ⇝ Yukon Territory, W Canada
99 H22 **Nismes** Namur, S Belgium 50°04′N 04°31′E
Nismes *see* Nîmes
116 M10 **Nisporeni** *Rus.* Nisporeny. W Moldova 47°04′N 28°10′E
Nisporeny *see* Nisporeni
95 K20 **Nissan** ⇝ S Sweden
Nissan Islands *see* Green Islands
95 F16 **Nisser** ◎ S Norway
95 E21 **Nissum Bredning** *inlet* NW Denmark
29 U6 **Nisswa** Minnesota, N USA 46°31′N 94°17′W
Nistru *see* Dniester
115 M22 **Nísyros** *var.* Nisiros. *island* Dodekánisa, Greece, Aegean Sea
118 H8 **Nītaure** Cēsis, C Latvia 57°05′N 25°12′E
60 P10 **Niterói** *prev.* Nictheroy. Rio de Janeiro, SE Brazil 22°54′S 43°06′W
14 F16 **Nith** ⇝ Ontario, S Canada
96 J13 **Nith** ⇝ S Scotland, United Kingdom
Nitinan *see* Nichinan
111 I21 **Nitra** *Ger.* Neutra, *Hung.* Nyitra. Nitriansky Kraj, SW Slovakia 48°20′N 18°05′E
111 I20 **Nitra** *Ger.* Neutra, *Hung.* Nyitra. ⇝ W Slovakia
111 I21 **Nitriansky Kraj** ◈ *region* SW Slovakia
21 Q5 **Nitro** West Virginia, NE USA 38°24′N 81°50′W
95 H14 **Nittedal** Akershus, S Norway 60°08′N 10°45′E
Niuatobutabu *see* Niuatoputapu
193 X13 **Niuatoputapu** *var.* Niuatobutabu; *prev.* Keppel Island. *island* N Tonga
193 U15 **Niu'Aunofo** *headland* Tongatapu, S Tonga 21°03′S 175°19′W
Niuchwang *see* Yingkou
190 B16 **Niue** ◇ *self-governing territory in free association with New Zealand* S Pacific Ocean
190 F10 **Niulakita** *var.* Nurakita. *atoll* S Tuvalu
190 E6 **Niutao** *atoll* NW Tuvalu
93 L15 **Nivala** Oulu, C Finland 63°56′N 25°00′E
102 I15 **Nive** ⇝ SW France
99 G19 **Nivelles** Walloon Brabant, C Belgium 50°36′N 04°04′E
103 P8 **Nivernais** *cultural region* C France
15 N8 **Niverville, Lac** ◎ Québec, SE Canada
27 T7 **Nixa** Missouri, C USA 37°02′N 93°17′W
35 R5 **Nixon** Nevada, W USA 39°48′N 119°24′W
25 S12 **Nixon** Texas, SW USA 29°16′N 97°45′W
Niya *see* Minfeng
Niyazov *see* Nyýazow
155 H14 **Nizāmābād** Andhra Pradesh, C India 18°40′N 78°05′E
155 H15 **Nizām Sāgar** ◎ C India
125 N16 **Nizhegorodskaya Oblast'** ◈ *province* W Russian Federation
Nizhnegorskiy *see* Nyzhn'ohirs'kyy
127 S4 **Nizhnekamsk** Respublika Tatarstan, W Russian Federation 55°36′N 51°45′E
127 U3 **Nizhnekamskoye Vodokhranilishche** ▨ W Russian Federation
123 S14 **Nizhneleninskoye** Yevreyskaya Avtonomnaya Oblast', SE Russian Federation 47°50′N 132°30′E
122 L13 **Nizhneudinsk** Irkutskaya Oblast', S Russian Federation 54°48′N 98°51′E
122 I10 **Nizhnevartovsk** Khanty-Mansiyskiy Avtonomnyy Okrug-Yugra, C Russian Federation 60°57′N 76°40′E
123 Q7 **Nizhneyansk** Respublika Sakha (Yakutiya), NE Russian Federation 71°25′N 135°59′E
127 Q11 **Nizhniy Baskunchak** Astrakhanskaya Oblast', SW Russian Federation 48°15′N 46°49′E
127 O6 **Nizhniy Lomov** Penzenskaya Oblast', W Russian Federation 53°32′N 43°39′E
127 P3 **Nizhniy Novgorod** *prev.* Gor'kiy. Nizhegorodskaya Oblast', W Russian Federation 56°17′N 44°E
125 T8 **Nizhniy Odes** Respublika Komi, NW Russian Federation 63°42′N 54°59′E
Nizhniy Pyandzh *see* Panji Poyon
122 G10 **Nizhniy Tagil** Sverdlovskaya Oblast', C Russian Federation 57°57′N 59°51′E
127 T4 **Nizhnyaya Maktama** Respublika Tatarstan, W Russian Federation 54°51′N 52°22′E
125 T9 **Nizhnyaya-Omra** Respublika Komi, NW Russian Federation
125 P5 **Nizhnyaya Pesha** Nenetskiy Avtonomnyy Okrug, NW Russian Federation 66°54′N 47°37′E
117 Q3 **Nizhyn** *Rus.* Nezhin. Chernihivs'ka Oblast', NE Ukraine 51°03′N 31°54′E
136 M17 **Nizip** Gaziantep, S Turkey 37°02′N 37°47′E
141 X8 **Nizwa** *var.* Nazwāh. NE Oman 23°00′N 57°50′E
Nizza *see* Nice
106 C9 **Nizza Monferrato** Piemonte, NE Italy 44°47′N 08°22′E
Njávdám *see* Näätämöjoki
Njellim *see* Nellim
81 H24 **Njombe** Iringa, S Tanzania 09°20′S 34°47′E
81 G23 **Njombe** ⇝ C Tanzania
Njuk, Ozero *see* Nyuk, Ozero
Njuksenica *see* Nyuksenitsa
92 I10 **Njunis** ▲ N Norway 68°47′N 19°24′E
93 H17 **Njurunda** Västernorrland, C Sweden 62°15′N 17°24′E
94 N11 **Njutånger** Gävleborg, C Sweden 61°37′N 17°04′E
79 D14 **Nkambe** Nord-Ouest, NW Cameroon 06°35′N 10°44′E
Nkata Bay *see* Nkhata Bay
79 F21 **Nkayi** *prev.* Jacob. Bouenza, S Congo 04°11′S 13°17′E
83 J17 **Nkayi** Matabeleland North, W Zimbabwe 19°00′S 28°54′E
82 N13 **Nkhata Bay** *var.* Nkata Bay. Northern, N Malawi 11°37′S 34°20′E
81 E22 **Nkonde** Kigoma, N Tanzania 06°16′S 30°17′E
79 D15 **Nkongsamba** *var.* N'Kongsamba. Littoral, W Cameroon 04°59′N 09°53′E
N'Kongsamba *see* Nkongsamba
83 E16 **Nkurenkuru** Okavango, N Namibia 17°38′S 18°39′E
77 Q15 **Nkwanta** E Ghana 08°18′N 00°27′E
167 O2 **Nmai Hka** *var.* Me Hka. ⇝ N Burma (Myanmar)
Noardwâlde *see* Noordwolde
39 N7 **Noatak** Alaska, USA 67°34′N 162°58′W
39 N7 **Noatak River** ⇝ Alaska, USA
164 E15 **Nobeoka** Miyazaki, Kyūshū, SW Japan 32°34′N 131°37′E
27 N11 **Noble** Oklahoma, C USA 35°08′N 97°23′W
31 P13 **Noblesville** Indiana, N USA 40°03′N 86°00′W
165 R5 **Noboribetsu** *var.* Noboribetu. Hokkaidō, NE Japan 42°27′N 141°08′E
Noboribetu *see* Noboribetsu
59 H18 **Nobres** Mato Grosso, W Brazil 14°44′S 56°15′W
107 N21 **Nocera Terinese** Calabria, S Italy 39°03′N 16°10′E
41 Q16 **Nochixtlán** *var.* Asunción Nochixtlán. Oaxaca, SE Mexico 17°29′N 97°17′W
25 S5 **Nocona** Texas, SW USA 33°47′N 97°43′W
63 K21 **Nodales, Bahía de los** *bay* S Argentina
27 Q2 **Nodaway River** ⇝ Iowa/Missouri, C USA
27 R8 **Noel** Missouri, C USA 36°33′N 94°29′W
40 H3 **Nogales** Chihuahua, NW Mexico 18°50′N 97°12′W
40 F3 **Nogales** Sonora, NW Mexico 31°17′N 110°53′W
36 M17 **Nogales** Arizona, SW USA 31°20′N 110°55′W
Nogal Valley *see* Dooxo Nugaaleed
102 K15 **Nogaro** Gers, S France 43°46′N 00°01′W
110 J7 **Nogat** ⇝ N Poland
164 D12 **Nōgata** Fukuoka, Kyūshū, SW Japan 33°46′N 130°42′E
127 P15 **Nogayskaya Step'** *steppe* SW Russian Federation
102 M6 **Nogent-le-Rotrou** Eure-et-Loir, C France 48°19′N 00°50′E

◆ Country
● Country Capital
◇ Dependent Territory
○ Dependent Territory Capital
◈ Administrative Regions
✕ International Airport
▲ Mountain
▲▲ Mountain Range
Volcano
⇝ River
◎ Lake
▨ Reservoir

NOGENT-SUR-OISE – NOTRE-DAME-DU-LAC

103 O4 **Nogent-sur-Oise** Oise, N France 49°16′N 02°28′E
103 P6 **Nogent-sur-Seine** Aube, N France 48°30′N 03°31′E
122 L10 **Noginsk** Evenkiyskiy Avtonomnyy Okrug, N Russian Federation 64°28′N 91°09′E
126 L3 **Noginsk** Moskovskaya Oblast', W Russian Federation 55°51′N 38°23′E
123 T12 **Nogliki** Ostrov Sakhalin, Sakhalinskaya Oblast', SE Russian Federation 51°44′N 143°14′E
164 K12 **Nōgōhaku-san** ▲ Honshū, SW Japan 35°46′N 136°30′E
162 D5 **Nogoonnuur** Bayan-Ölgiy, NW Mongolia 49°31′N 89°48′E
61 C18 **Nogoyá** Entre Ríos, E Argentina 32°25′S 59°50′W
111 K21 **Nógrád** *off.* Nógrád Megye. ◆ *county* N Hungary
Nógrád Megye *see* Nógrád
105 U5 **Noguera Pallaresa** ≈ NE Spain
105 U4 **Noguera Ribagorçana** ≈ NE Spain
101 E19 **Nohfelden** Saarland, SW Germany 49°35′N 07°08′E
38 A8 **Nohili Point** *headland* Kaua'i, Hawai'i, USA 22°03′N 159°48′W
104 G3 **Noia** Galicia, NW Spain 42°48′N 08°52′W
103 N16 **Noire, Montagne** ▲▲ S France
14 J10 **Noire, Rivière** ≈ Québec, SE Canada
15 P12 **Noire, Rivière** ≈ Québec, SE Canada
Noire, Rivi`ere *see* Black River
102 G6 **Noires, Montagnes** ▲▲ NW France
102 H8 **Noirmoutier-en-l'Île** Vendée, NW France 47°00′N 02°15′W
102 H8 **Noirmoutier, Île de** *island* NW France
187 Q10 **Noka** Nendö, E Solomon Islands 10°42′S 165°57′E
83 G17 **Nokaneng** North West, NW Botswana 19°40′S 22°12′E
93 L18 **Nokia** Länsi-Suomi, W Finland 61°29′N 23°30′E
148 K11 **Nok Kundi** Baluchistān, SW Pakistan 28°49′N 62°39′E
30 L14 **Nokomis** Illinois, N USA 39°18′N 89°17′W
30 K5 **Nokomis, Lake** ▣ Wisconsin, N USA
78 G9 **Nokou** Kanem, W Chad 14°36′N 14°45′E
187 Q12 **Nokuku** Espiritu Santo, W Vanuatu 14°56′S 166°34′E
95 J18 **Nol** Västra Götaland, S Sweden 57°55′N 12°03′E
79 H16 **Nola** Sangha-Mbaéré, SW Central African Republic 03°29′N 16°05′E
25 P7 **Nolan** Texas, SW USA 32°15′N 100°15′W
125 R15 **Nolinsk** Kirovskaya Oblast', NW Russian Federation 57°35′N 49°54′E
Nolsø *see* Nólsoy
95 B19 **Nólsoy** *Dan.* Nolsø. *island* E Faeroe Islands
186 B7 **Nomad** Western, SW Papau New Guinea 06°11′S 142°13′E
164 B16 **Noma-zaki** Kyūshū, SW Japan
40 K10 **Nombre de Dios** Durango, C Mexico 23°51′N 104°14′W
42 I5 **Nombre de Dios, Cordillera** ▲▲ N Honduras
38 M9 **Nome** Alaska, USA 64°30′N 165°24′W
29 Q6 **Nome** North Dakota, N USA 46°39′N 97°49′W
38 M9 **Nome, Cape** *headland* Alaska, USA 64°25′N 165°00′W
162 K11 **Nomgon** *var.* Sangiyn Dalay. Ömnögovĭ, S Mongolia 42°50′N 105°04′E
14 M11 **Nominingue, Lac** ◎ Québec, SE Canada
Nomoi Islands *see* Mortlock Islands
164 B16 **Nomo-zaki** *headland* Kyūshū, SW Japan 32°34′N 129°45′E
162 G6 **Nömrög** *var.* Hödrögö. Dzavhan, N Mongolia 48°51′N 96°48′E
193 X15 **Nomuka** *island* Nomuka Group, C Tonga
193 X15 **Nomuka Group** *island group* W Tonga
189 Q15 **Nomwin Atoll** *atoll* Hall Islands, C Micronesia
8 L10 **Nonacho Lake** ◎ Northwest Territories, NW Canada
Nondaburi *see* Nonthaburi
39 P12 **Nondalton** Alaska, USA 59°58′N 154°51′W
163 V10 **Nong'an** Jilin, NE China 44°25′N 125°10′E
169 P10 **Nong Bua Khok** Nakhon Ratchasima, C Thailand 15°23′N 101°51′E
167 Q9 **Nong Bua Lamphu** Udon Thani, E Thailand 17°11′N 102°27′E
167 R7 **Nông Hèt** Xiangkhoang, N Laos 19°27′N 104°02′E
Nongkaya *see* Nong Khai
167 Q8 **Nong Khai** *var.* Mi Chai, Nongkaya. Nong Khai, E Thailand 17°52′N 102°44′E
167 N14 **Nong Met** Surat Thani, SW Thailand 09°27′N 99°09′E
83 L22 **Nongoma** KwaZulu/Natal, E South Africa 27°54′S 31°40′E
167 P9 **Nong Phai** Phetchabun, C Thailand 15°58′N 101°02′E
153 U13 **Nongstoin** Meghālaya, NE India 25°24′N 91°19′E
83 C19 **Nonidas** Erongo, N Namibia 22°36′S 14°40′E
Nonni *see* Nen Jiang
40 I7 **Nonoava** Chihuahua, N Mexico 27°24′N 106°18′W
191 O3 **Nonouti** *prev.* Sydenham Island. *atoll* Tungaru, W Kiribati
167 O11 **Nonthaburi** *var.* Nondaburi, Nontha Buri. Nonthaburi, C Thailand 13°48′N 100°11′E
Nontha Buri *see* Nonthaburi
102 L11 **Nontron** Dordogne, SW France 45°34′N 00°41′E
181 P1 **Noonamah** Northern Territory, N Australia 12°46′S 131°08′E
28 K2 **Noonan** North Dakota, N USA 48°51′N 102°57′W
Noonu *see* South Miladhunmadulu Atoll
99 E14 **Noord-Beveland** *var.* North Beveland. *island* SW Netherlands
99 J14 **Noord-Brabant** *Eng.* North Brabant. ◈ *province* S Netherlands
98 H7 **Noorder Haaks** *spit* NW Netherlands
98 H9 **Noord-Holland** *Eng.* North Holland. ◈ *province* NW Netherlands
Noordhollandsch Kanaal *see* Noordhollands Kanaal
98 H8 **Noordhollands Kanaal** *var.* Noordhollandsch Kanaal. *canal* NW Netherlands
Noord-Kaap *see* Northern Cape
98 L8 **Noordoostpolder** *island* N Netherlands
45 P16 **Noordpunt** *headland* Curaçao, C Netherlands Antilles 12°21′N 69°08′W
98 I8 **Noord-Scharwoude** Noord-Holland, NW Netherlands 52°42′N 04°48′E
Noordwes *see* North-West
98 G11 **Noordwijk aan Zee** Zuid-Holland, W Netherlands 52°15′N 04°25′E
98 H11 **Noordwijkerhout** Zuid-Holland, W Netherlands 52°16′N 04°30′E
98 M7 **Noordwolde** *Fris.* Noordwâlde. Friesland, N Netherlands 52°54′N 06°10′E
Noordzee *see* North Sea
98 H10 **Noordzee-Kanaal** *canal* NW Netherlands
93 K18 **Noormarkku** *Swe.* Norrmark. Länsi-Suomi, SW Finland 61°35′N 21°54′E
39 N8 **Noorvik** Alaska, USA 66°50′N 161°01′W
10 J17 **Nootka Sound** *inlet* British Columbia, W Canada
82 A9 **Nóqui** Dem. Rep. Congo, NW Angola 05°54′S 13°30′E
95 L15 **Nora** Örebro, C Sweden 59°31′N 15°02′E
147 Q13 **Norak** *Rus.* Nurek. W Tajikistan 38°23′N 69°14′E
13 I13 **Noranda** Québec, SE Canada 48°16′N 79°03′W
29 W12 **Nora Springs** Iowa, C USA 43°08′N 93°00′W
95 M14 **Norberg** Västmanland, C Sweden 60°04′N 15°56′E
14 K13 **Norcan Lake** ◎ Ontario, SE Canada
197 R12 **Nord** Avannaarsua, N Greenland 81°38′N 12°51′W
78 F13 **Nord** *Eng.* North. ◈ *province* N Cameroon
103 P2 **Nord** ◈ *department* N France
92 P1 **Nordaustlandet** *island* NE Svalbard
95 G24 **Nordborg** *Ger.* Nordburg. Sønderjylland, SW Denmark 55°04′N 09°41′E
Nordburg *see* Nordborg
95 F23 **Nordby** Ribe, W Denmark 55°27′N 08°25′E
11 P15 **Nordegg** Alberta, SW Canada 52°27′N 116°06′W
79 E9 **Norden** Niedersachsen, NW Germany 53°36′N 07°12′E
100 G10 **Nordenham** Niedersachsen, NW Germany 53°30′N 08°29′E
122 M6 **Nordenshel'da, Arkhipelag** *island group* N Russian Federation
92 O3 **Nordenskiold Land** *physical region* W Svalbard
100 E9 **Norderney** *island* NW Germany
100 J9 **Norderstedt** Schleswig-Holstein, N Germany 53°42′N 09°59′E
94 D11 **Nordfjord** *fjord* S Norway
94 C11 **Nordfjord** *physical region* S Norway
94 D11 **Nordfjordeid** Sogn og Fjordane, S Norway 61°54′N 06°E
92 G11 **Nordfold** Nordland, C Norway 67°48′N 15°16′E
Nordfriesische Inseln *see* North Frisian Islands
100 H7 **Nordfriesland** *cultural region* N Germany
101 K15 **Nordhausen** Thüringen, C Germany 51°31′N 10°48′E
25 T13 **Nordheim** Texas, SW USA 28°55′N 97°36′W
94 C13 **Nordhordland** *physical region* S Norway
100 E12 **Nordhorn** Niedersachsen, NW Germany 52°26′N 07°04′E
92 I1 **Nordhurfjördhur** Vestfirdhir, NW Iceland 66°01′N 21°33′W
92 J1 **Nordhurland Eystra** ◈ *region* N Iceland
92 I2 **Nordhurland Vestra** ◈ *region* N Iceland
172 H16 **Nord, Île du** *island* Inner Islands, NE Seychelles
95 F20 **Nordjylland** *var.* Nordjyllands Amt. ◈ *county* N Denmark
Nordjyllands Amt *see* Nordjylland
92 K7 **Nordkapp** *Eng.* North Cape. *headland* N Norway 25°47′E 71°10′N
92 O1 **Nordkapp** *headland* N Svalbard 80°31′N 19°58′E
92 L7 **Nordkinn** *headland* N Norway 71°07′N 27°40′E
79 N19 **Nord-Kivu** *off.* Région du Nord Kivu. ◈ *region* E Dem. Rep. Congo
Nord Kivu, Région du *see* Nord-Kivu
92 G12 **Nordland** ◈ *county* C Norway
101 J21 **Nördlingen** Bayern, S Germany 48°49′N 10°28′E
93 I16 **Nordmaling** Västerbotten, N Sweden 63°35′N 19°30′E
95 K15 **Nordmark** Värmland, C Sweden 59°52′N 14°04′E
Nord, Mer du *see* North Sea
94 F8 **Nordmøre** *physical region* S Norway
100 I8 **Nord-Ostee-Kanal** *canal* N Germany
0 J3 **Nordostrundingen** *cape* NE Greenland
79 D14 **Nord-Ouest** *Eng.* North-West. ◈ *province* NW Cameroon
Nord-Ouest, Territoires du *see* Northwest Territories
103 N2 **Nord-Pas-de-Calais** ◈ *region* N France
101 F19 **Nordpfälzer Bergland** ▲▲ W Germany
Nord, Pointe *see* Fatua, Pointe
187 P16 **Nord, Province** ◈ *province* C New Caledonia
101 D14 **Nordrhein-Westfalen** *Eng.* North Rhine-Westphalia, *Fr.* Rhénanie du Nord-Westphalie. ◈ *state* W Germany
Nordsee/Nordsjøen/Nordsøen *see* North Sea
100 H7 **Nordstrand** *island* N Germany
93 E15 **Nord-Trøndelag** ◈ *county* C Norway
97 E19 **Nore** *Ir.* An Fheoir. ≈ S Ireland
29 Q14 **Norfolk** Nebraska, C USA 42°01′N 97°25′W
21 X7 **Norfolk** Virginia, NE USA 36°51′N 76°17′W
97 P19 **Norfolk** *cultural region* E England, United Kingdom
192 K10 **Norfolk Island** ◇ *Australian external territory* SW Pacific Ocean
175 P9 **Norfolk Ridge** *undersea feature* W Pacific Ocean
27 U8 **Norfork Lake** ▣ Arkansas/Missouri, C USA
98 N6 **Norg** Drenthe, NE Netherlands 53°04′N 06°28′E
Norge *see* Norway
95 D14 **Norheimsund** Hordaland, S Norway 60°22′N 06°09′E
25 S16 **Norias** Texas, SW USA 26°47′N 97°45′W
164 L12 **Norikura-dake** ▲ Honshū, S Japan 36°06′N 137°33′E
122 K8 **Noril'sk** Taymyrskiy (Dolgano-Nenetskiy) Avtonomnyy Okrug, N Russian Federation 69°21′N 88°02′E
14 I13 **Norland** Ontario, SE Canada 44°46′N 78°48′W
21 V8 **Norlina** North Carolina, SE USA 36°26′N 78°11′W
30 L13 **Normal** Illinois, N USA 40°30′N 88°59′W
27 N11 **Norman** Oklahoma, C USA 35°13′N 97°27′W
Norman *see* Tulita
186 G9 **Normanby Island** *island* SE Papua New Guinea
Normandes, Îles *see* Channel Islands
58 G9 **Normandia** Roraima, N Brazil 03°57′N 59°39′W
102 L5 **Normandie** *Eng.* Normandy. *cultural region* N France
102 J5 **Normandie, Collines de** *hill range* NW France
Normandy *see* Normandie
25 V9 **Normangee** Texas, SW USA 31°01′N 96°06′W
21 Q10 **Norman, Lake** ▣ North Carolina, SE USA
44 K13 **Norman Manley** ✈ (Kingston) E Jamaica 17°55′N 76°46′W
181 U5 **Norman River** ≈ Queensland, NE Australia
181 U4 **Normanton** Queensland, NE Australia 17°49′S 141°08′E
8 I8 **Norman Wells** Northwest Territories, NW Canada 65°18′N 126°42′W
12 H12 **Normétal** Québec, S Canada 48°59′N 79°23′W
163 O7 **Norovlin** *var.* Uldz. Hentiy, NE Mongolia 48°47′N 112°01′E
11 V15 **Norquay** Saskatchewan, S Canada 51°51′N 102°04′W
94 N11 **Norra Dellen** ◎ C Sweden
93 G15 **Norråker** Jämtland, C Sweden 64°25′N 15°40′E
94 N12 **Norrala** Gävleborg, C Sweden 61°22′N 17°04′E
Norra Ny *see* Stöllet
92 G13 **Norra Storfjället** ▲ N Sweden 65°57′N 15°15′E
92 I13 **Norrbotten** ◈ *county* N Sweden
95 G23 **Nørre Aaby** *var.* Nørre Åby. Fyn, C Denmark 55°28′N 09°53′E
Nørre Åby *see* Nørre Aaby
95 I24 **Nørre Alslev** Storstrøm, SE Denmark 54°54′N 11°53′E
95 E23 **Nørre Nebel** Ribe, W Denmark 55°45′N 08°16′E
95 G20 **Nørresundby** Nordjylland, N Denmark 57°05′N 09°55′E
21 N8 **Norris Lake** ▣ Tennessee, S USA
18 I15 **Norristown** Pennsylvania, NE USA 40°07′N 75°20′W
95 N17 **Norrköping** Östergötland, S Sweden 58°35′N 16°10′E
Norrmark *see* Noormarkku
94 N13 **Norrsundet** Gävleborg, C Sweden 60°55′N 17°09′E
95 P15 **Norrtälje** Stockholm, C Sweden 59°46′N 18°42′E
180 L12 **Norseman** Western Australia 32°16′S 121°46′E
93 I14 **Norsjö** Västerbotten, N Sweden 64°55′N 19°30′E
95 G16 **Norsjø** ◎ S Norway
123 R13 **Norsk** Amurskaya Oblast', SE Russian Federation 52°20′N 129°57′E
Norske Havet *see* Norwegian Sea
187 Q13 **Norsup** Malekula, C Vanuatu 16°05′S 167°24′E
191 V15 **Norte, Cabo** *headland* Easter Island, Chile, E Pacific Ocean 27°03′S 109°24′W
54 F7 **Norte de Santander** *off.* Departamento de Norte de Santander. ◈ *province* N Colombia
Norte de Santander, Departamento de *see* Norte de Santander
61 E21 **Norte, Punta** *headland* E Argentina 36°17′S 56°46′W
21 R13 **North** South Carolina, SE USA 33°37′N 81°06′W
North *see* Nord
18 L10 **North Adams** Massachusetts, NE USA 42°40′N 73°06′W
113 L17 **North Albanian Alps** *Alb.* Bjeshkët e Namuna, *SCr.* Prokletije. ▲▲ SE Europe
97 M15 **Northallerton** N England, United Kingdom 54°20′N 01°26′W
180 J12 **Northam** Western Australia 31°40′S 116°40′E
83 J20 **Northam** Northern, N South Africa 24°56′S 27°18′E
1 **North America** *continent*
1 N12 **North American Basin** *undersea feature* W Sargasso Sea 30°00′N 60°00′W
0 C5 **North American Plate** *tectonic feature*
18 M11 **North Amherst** Massachusetts, NE USA 42°24′N 72°31′W
97 N20 **Northampton** C England, United Kingdom 52°14′N 00°54′W
97 M20 **Northamptonshire** *cultural region* C England, United Kingdom
151 P18 **North Andaman** *island* Andaman Islands, India, NE Indian Ocean
65 D25 **North Arm** East Falkland, Falkland Islands 52°06′S 59°21′W
21 Q13 **North Augusta** South Carolina, SE USA 33°30′N 81°58′W
173 W8 **North Australian Basin** *Fr.* Bassin Nord de l' Australie. *undersea feature* E Indian Ocean
31 R11 **North Baltimore** Ohio, N USA 41°10′N 83°40′W
11 T15 **North Battleford** Saskatchewan, S Canada 52°47′N 108°19′W
14 H11 **North Bay** Ontario, S Canada 46°20′N 79°28′W
12 H6 **North Belcher Islands** *island group* Belcher Islands, Nunavut, C Canada
29 R15 **North Bend** Nebraska, C USA 41°27′N 96°46′W
32 E14 **North Bend** Oregon, NW USA 43°24′N 124°13′W
96 K12 **North Berwick** SE Scotland, United Kingdom 56°04′N 02°44′W
North Beveland *see* Noord-Beveland
North Borneo *see* Sabah
183 P5 **North Bourke** New South Wales, SE Australia 30°03′S 145°56′E
North Brabant *see* Noord-Brabant
182 F2 **North Branch Neales** *seasonal river* South Australia
44 M6 **North Caicos** *island* NW Turks and Caicos Islands
26 L10 **North Canadian River** ≈ Oklahoma, C USA
31 U12 **North Canton** Ohio, N USA 40°52′N 81°24′W
13 R13 **North, Cape** *headland* Cape Breton Island, Nova Scotia, SE Canada 47°06′N 60°24′W
184 I1 **North Cape** *headland* North Island, New Zealand 34°23′S 173°02′E
186 G5 **North Cape** *headland* New Ireland, NE Papua New Guinea 02°33′S 150°48′E
North Cape *see* Nordkapp
18 J17 **North Cape May** New Jersey, NE USA 38°59′N 74°55′W
12 C9 **North Caribou Lake** ◎ Ontario, C Canada
21 U10 **North Carolina** *off.* State of North Carolina, *also known as* Old North State, Tar Heel State, Turpentine State. ◈ *state* SE USA
North Celebes *see* Sulawesi Utara
155 J24 **North Central** ◈ *province* N Sri Lanka
31 S4 **North Channel** *lake channel* Canada/USA
97 G14 **North Channel** *strait* Northern Ireland/Scotland, United Kingdom
21 S14 **North Charleston** South Carolina, SE USA 32°53′N 79°59′W
31 N10 **North Chicago** Illinois, N USA 42°19′N 87°50′W
195 Y10 **Northcliffe Glacier** *glacier* Antarctica
31 Q14 **North College Hill** Ohio, N USA 39°13′N 84°33′W
25 O8 **North Concho River** ≈ Texas, SW USA
19 O8 **North Conway** New Hampshire, NE USA 44°03′N 71°06′W
27 V14 **North Crossett** Arkansas, C USA 33°10′N 91°56′W
28 L4 **North Dakota** *off.* State of North Dakota, *also known as* Flickertail State, Peace Garden State, Sioux State. ◈ *state* N USA
North Devon Island *see* Devon Island
97 O22 **North Downs** *hill range* SE England, United Kingdom
18 C11 **North East** Pennsylvania, NE USA 42°13′N 79°49′W
83 I18 **North East** ◈ *district* NE Botswana
65 G15 **North East Bay** *bay* Ascension Island, C Atlantic Ocean
38 L10 **Northeast Cape** *headland* Saint Lawrence Island, Alaska, USA 63°16′N 168°50′W
81 J17 **North Eastern** ◈ *province* Kenya
North East Frontier Agency/North East Frontier Agency of Assam *see* Arunāchal Pradesh
189 V11 **Northeast Island** *island* Chuuk, C Micronesia
44 L6 **Northeast Point** *headland* Great Inagua, S Bahamas 21°18′N 73°01′W
44 K5 **Northeast Point** *headland* Acklins Island, SE Bahamas 22°43′N 73°50′W
44 L12 **North East Point** *headland* E Jamaica 18°09′N 76°19′W
191 Z2 **Northeast Point** *headland* Kiritimati, E Kiribati 10°23′S 105°45′E
44 H2 **Northeast Providence Channel** *channel* N Bahamas
101 J14 **Northeim** Niedersachsen, C Germany 51°42′N 10°E
29 X14 **North English** Iowa, C USA 41°30′N 92°04′W
138 G8 **Northern** ◈ *district* N Israel
82 M12 **Northern** ◈ *region* N Malawi
186 F8 **Northern** ◈ *province* S Papua New Guinea
155 J23 **Northern** ◈ *province* N Sri Lanka
80 D7 **Northern** ◈ *state* N Sudan
83 K12 **Northern** ◈ *province* NE Zambia
Northern *see* Limpopo
80 B13 **Northern Bahr el Ghazal** ◈ *state* SW Sudan
Northern Border Region *see* Al Ḥudūd ash Shamālīyah
83 F24 **Northern Cape** *off.* Northern Cape Province, *Afr.* Noord-Kaap. ◈ *province* W South Africa
Northern Cape Province *see* Northern Cape
190 K14 **Northern Cook Islands** *island group* N Cook Islands
80 B8 **Northern Darfur** ◈ *state* NW Sudan
Northern Dvina *see* Severnaya Dvina
97 F14 **Northern Ireland** *var.* The Six Counties. *cultural region* Northern Ireland, United Kingdom
97 F14 **Northern Ireland** *var.* The Six Counties. ◈ *political division* Northern Ireland, United Kingdom
80 D9 **Northern Kordofan** ◈ *state* C Sudan
187 Z14 **Northern Lau Group** *island group* Lau Group, NE Fiji
188 K3 **Northern Mariana Islands** ◇ *US commonwealth territory* W Pacific Ocean
Northern Rhodesia *see* Zambia
Northern Sporades *see* Vóreies Sporádes
182 D1 **Northern Territory** ◈ *territory* N Australia
Northern Transvaal *see* Limpopo
Northern Ural Hills *see* Severnyye Uvaly
84 I9 **North European Plain** *plain* N Europe
27 V2 **North Fabius River** ≈ Missouri, C USA
65 D24 **North Falkland Sound** *sound* N Falkland Islands
29 V9 **Northfield** Minnesota, N USA 44°27′N 93°10′W
19 O9 **Northfield** New Hampshire, NE USA 43°26′N 71°34′W
175 Q8 **North Fiji Basin** *undersea feature* N Coral Sea
97 Q22 **North Foreland** *headland* SE England, United Kingdom 51°22′N 01°26′E
35 P6 **North Fork American River** ≈ California, W USA
39 R7 **North Fork Chandalar River** ≈ Alaska, USA
28 K7 **North Fork Grand River** ≈ North Dakota/South Dakota, N USA
21 O6 **North Fork Kentucky River** ≈ Kentucky, S USA
39 Q7 **North Fork Koyukuk River** ≈ Alaska, USA
39 Q10 **North Fork Kuskokwim River** ≈ Alaska, USA
26 K11 **North Fork Red River** ≈ Oklahoma/Texas, SW USA
26 K3 **North Fork Solomon River** ≈ Kansas, C USA
23 W14 **North Fort Myers** Florida, SE USA 26°40′N 81°52′W
31 P5 **North Fox Island** *island* Michigan, N USA
100 G6 **North Frisian Islands** *var.* Nordfriesische Inseln. *island group* N Germany
197 N9 **North Geomagnetic Pole** *pole* Arctic Ocean
18 M13 **North Haven** Connecticut, NE USA 41°25′N 72°51′W
184 J5 **North Head** *headland* North Island, New Zealand 36°23′S 174°01′E
18 L6 **North Hero** Vermont, NE USA 44°49′N 73°14′W
35 O7 **North Highlands** California, W USA 38°40′N 121°25′W
North Holland *see* Noord-Holland
81 I16 **North Horr** Eastern, N Kenya 03°17′N 37°08′E
151 K21 **North Huvadhu Atoll** *var.* Gaafu Alifu Atoll. *atoll* S Maldives
184 N9 **North Island** *island* N New Zealand
21 U14 **North Island** *island* South Carolina, SE USA
31 O11 **North Judson** Indiana, N USA 41°12′N 86°44′W
North Kazakhstan *see* Severnyy Kazakhstan
31 V10 **North Kingsville** Ohio, N USA 41°54′N 80°41′W
163 Y13 **North Korea** *off.* Democratic People's Republic of Korea, *Kor.* Chosŏn-minjujuŭi-inmin-kanghwaguk. ◆ *republic* E Asia
153 X11 **North Lakhimpur** Assam, NE India 27°10′N 94°00′E
184 J3 **Northland** *off.* Northland Region. ◈ *region* North Island, New Zealand
192 K11 **Northland Plateau** *undersea feature* S Pacific Ocean
Northland Region *see* Northland
35 X11 **North Las Vegas** Nevada, W USA 36°12′N 115°07′W
31 O11 **North Liberty** Indiana, N USA 41°36′N 86°22′W
29 X14 **North Liberty** Iowa, C USA 41°45′N 91°36′W
27 V12 **North Little Rock** Arkansas, C USA 34°46′N 92°15′W
28 M13 **North Loup River** ≈ Nebraska, C USA
151 K18 **North Maalhosmadulu Atoll** *var.* North Malosmadulu Atoll, Raa Atoll. *atoll* N Maldives
31 U10 **North Madison** Ohio, N USA 41°48′N 81°03′W
North Malosmadulu Atoll *see* North Maalhosmadulu Atoll
31 P12 **North Manchester** Indiana, N USA 41°00′N 85°45′W
31 P6 **North Manitou Island** *island* Michigan, N USA
29 U10 **North Mankato** Minnesota, N USA 44°11′N 94°03′W
23 Z15 **North Miami** Florida, SE USA 25°54′N 80°11′W
151 K18 **North Miladhunmadulu Atoll** *var.* Shaviyani Atoll. *atoll* N Maldives
North Minch *see* Minch, The
23 W15 **North Naples** Florida, SE USA 26°13′N 81°47′W
175 P8 **North New Hebrides Trench** *undersea feature* N Coral Sea
23 Y15 **North New River Canal** ≈ Florida, SE USA
151 K20 **North Nilandhe Atoll** *atoll* C Maldives
36 L2 **North Ogden** Utah, W USA 41°18′N 111°57′W
North Ossetia *see* Severnaya Osetiya-Alaniya, Respublika
35 S10 **North Palisade** ▲ California, W USA 37°06′N 118°31′W
189 U11 **North Pass** *passage* Chuuk Islands, C Micronesia
28 M15 **North Platte** Nebraska, C USA 41°07′N 100°46′W
33 X17 **North Platte River** ≈ C USA
65 G14 **North Point** *headland* Ascension Island, C Atlantic Ocean
172 I16 **North Point** *headland* Mahé, NE Seychelles 04°23′S 55°28′E
31 R5 **North Point** *headland* Michigan, N USA 45°21′N 83°30′W
31 S6 **North Point** *headland* Michigan, N USA 45°01′N 83°16′W
39 S9 **North Pole** Alaska, USA 64°42′N 147°09′W
197 R9 **North Pole** *pole* Arctic Ocean
23 O4 **Northport** Alabama, S USA 33°13′N 87°34′W
23 W14 **North Port** Florida, SE USA 27°03′N 82°15′W
32 L6 **Northport** Washington, NW USA 48°54′N 117°48′W
32 L12 **North Powder** Oregon, NW USA 45°00′N 117°56′W
29 U13 **North Raccoon River** ≈ Iowa, C USA
North Rhine-Westphalia *see* Nordrhein-Westfalen
97 M16 **North Riding** *cultural region* N England, United Kingdom
96 G5 **North Rona** *island* NW Scotland, United Kingdom
96 K4 **North Ronaldsay** *island* NE Scotland, United Kingdom
36 L2 **North Salt Lake** Utah, W USA 40°51′N 111°54′W
11 P15 **North Saskatchewan** ≈ Alberta/Saskatchewan, S Canada
35 X5 **North Schell Peak** ▲ Nevada, W USA 39°25′N 114°34′W
North Scotia Ridge *see* South Georgia Ridge
86 D10 **North Sea** *Dan.* Nordsøen, *Dut.* Noordzee, *Fr.* Mer du Nord, *Ger.* Nordsee, *Nor.* Nordsjøen; *prev.* German Ocean, *Lat.* Mare Germanicum. *sea* NW Europe
35 T6 **North Shoshone Peak** ▲ Nevada, W USA 39°08′N 117°28′W
North Siberian Lowland/North Siberian Plain *see* Severo-Sibirskaya Nizmennost'
29 R13 **North Sioux City** South Dakota, N USA 42°31′N 96°28′W
96 K4 **North Sound, The** *sound* N Scotland, United Kingdom
183 T4 **North Star** New South Wales, SE Australia 28°55′S 150°25′E
North Star State *see* Minnesota
183 V3 **North Stradbroke Island** *island* Queensland, E Australia
North Sulawesi *see* Sulawesi Utara
North Sumatra *see* Sumatera Utara
14 D17 **North Sydenham** ≈ Ontario, S Canada
18 H9 **North Syracuse** New York, NE USA 43°07′N 76°07′W
184 K9 **North Taranaki Bight** *gulf* North Island, New Zealand
12 H9 **North Twin Island** *island* Nunavut, C Canada
96 E8 **North Uist** *island* NW Scotland, United Kingdom
97 L14 **Northumberland** *cultural region* N England, United Kingdom
181 Y7 **Northumberland Isles** *island group* Queensland, NE Australia
13 Q14 **Northumberland Strait** *strait* SE Canada
32 G14 **North Umpqua River** ≈ Oregon, NW USA
45 Q13 **North Union** Saint Vincent, Saint Vincent and the Grenadines 13°15′N 61°07′W
10 L17 **North Vancouver** British Columbia, SW Canada 49°21′N 123°05′W
18 K9 **Northville** New York, NE USA 43°13′N 74°08′W
97 Q19 **North Walsham** E England, United Kingdom 52°49′N 01°22′E
39 T10 **Northway** Alaska, USA 62°57′N 141°56′W
149 R7 **North Wazīristān** ◈ *federally administered tribal area* NW Pakistan
83 G17 **North-West** ◈ *district* NW Botswana
83 G21 **North-West** *off.* North-West Province, *Afr.* Noordwes. ◈ *province* N South Africa
North-West *see* Nord-Ouest
64 I6 **Northwest Atlantic Mid-Ocean Canyon** *undersea feature* N Atlantic Ocean
180 G8 **North West Cape** *cape* Western Australia
38 J9 **Northwest Cape** *headland* Saint Lawrence Island, Alaska, USA 63°46′N 171°45′W
155 J24 **North Western** ◈ *province* W Sri Lanka
82 H13 **North Western** ◈ *province* W Zambia
149 U4 **North-West Frontier Province** ◈ *province* NW Pakistan
96 H8 **North West Highlands** ▲▲ N Scotland, United Kingdom
192 J4 **Northwest Pacific Basin** *undersea feature* NW Pacific Ocean 40°00′N 150°00′E
191 Y2 **Northwest Point** *headland* Kiritimati, E Kiribati 10°25′S 105°35′E
44 G1 **Northwest Providence Channel** *channel* N Bahamas
North-West Province *see* North-West
13 Q8 **North West River** Newfoundland and Labrador, E Canada 53°30′N 60°10′W
8 J9 **Northwest Territories** *Fr.* Territoires du Nord-Ouest. ◈ *territory* NW Canada
97 K18 **Northwich** C England, United Kingdom 53°16′N 02°32′W
25 Q5 **North Wichita River** ≈ Texas, SW USA
18 J17 **North Wildwood** New Jersey, NE USA 39°00′N 74°45′W
21 R9 **North Wilkesboro** North Carolina, SE USA 36°09′N 81°09′W
19 P8 **North Windham** Maine, NE USA 43°51′N 70°25′W
197 Q6 **Northwind Plain** *undersea feature* Arctic Ocean
29 V11 **Northwood** Iowa, C USA 43°26′N 93°13′W
29 Q4 **Northwood** North Dakota, N USA 47°43′N 97°34′W
97 M15 **North York Moors** *moorland* N England, United Kingdom
25 V9 **North Zulch** Texas, SW USA 30°54′N 96°06′W
26 K2 **Norton** Kansas, C USA 39°51′N 99°53′W
31 S13 **Norton** Ohio, N USA 40°25′N 83°04′W
21 P7 **Norton** Virginia, NE USA 36°56′N 82°37′W
39 N9 **Norton Bay** *bay* Alaska, USA
Norton de Matos *see* Balombo
31 O9 **Norton Shores** Michigan, N USA 43°10′N 86°15′W
38 M10 **Norton Sound** *inlet* Alaska, USA
27 Q3 **Nortonville** Kansas, C USA 39°25′N 95°19′W
102 I8 **Nort-sur-Erdre** Loire-Atlantique, NW France 47°27′N 01°30′W
195 N2 **Norvegia, Cape** *headland* Antarctica 71°16′S 12°25′W
18 L13 **Norwalk** Connecticut, NE USA 41°08′N 73°28′W
29 V14 **Norwalk** Iowa, C USA 41°28′N 93°40′W
31 S11 **Norwalk** Ohio, N USA 41°14′N 82°37′W
19 P7 **Norway** Maine, NE USA 44°13′N 70°30′W
31 N5 **Norway** Michigan, N USA 45°47′N 87°54′W
93 E17 **Norway** *off.* Kingdom of Norway, *Nor.* Norge. ◆ *monarchy* N Europe
11 X13 **Norway House** Manitoba, C Canada 53°59′N 97°50′W
Norway, Kingdom of *see* Norway
197 R16 **Norwegian Basin** *undersea feature* NW Norwegian Sea 68°00′N 02°00′W
84 D6 **Norwegian Sea** *var.* Norske Havet. *sea* NE Atlantic Ocean
197 S17 **Norwegian Trench** *undersea feature* NE North Sea 59°00′N 04°30′E
14 F16 **Norwich** Ontario, S Canada 42°57′N 80°37′W
97 Q19 **Norwich** E England, United Kingdom 52°38′N 01°18′E
19 N13 **Norwich** Connecticut, NE USA 41°30′N 72°02′W
18 I11 **Norwich** New York, NE USA 42°31′N 75°31′W
29 U9 **Norwood** Minnesota, N USA 44°46′N 93°55′W
31 Q15 **Norwood** Ohio, N USA 39°07′N 84°27′W
14 H11 **Nosbonsing, Lake** ◎ Ontario, S Canada
Nösen *see* Bistriţa
165 T1 **Noshappu-misaki** *headland* Hokkaidō, NE Japan 45°26′N 141°38′E
165 P7 **Noshiro** *var.* Nosiro; *prev.* Noshirominato. Akita, Honshū, C Japan 40°11′N 140°02′E
Noshirominato/Nosiro *see* Noshiro
117 Q3 **Nosivka** *Rus.* Nosovka. Chernihivs'ka Oblast', NE Ukraine 50°55′N 31°37′E
67 T14 **Nosop** *var.* Nossob, Nossop. ≈ Botswana/Namibia
83 E20 **Nossop** ≈ E Namibia
125 S4 **Nosovaya** Nenetskiy Avtonomnyy Okrug, NW Russian Federation 68°12′N 54°33′E
Nosovka *see* Nosivka
143 V11 **Noşratābād** Sīstān va Balūchestān, E Iran 29°53′N 59°57′E
95 J18 **Nossebro** Västra Götaland, S Sweden 58°12′N 12°42′E
96 K6 **Noss Head** *headland* N Scotland, United Kingdom 58°29′N 03°03′W
Nossi-Bé *see* Be, Nosy
81 E20 **Nossob** ≈ Namibia
Nossob/Nossop *see* Nosop
172 J2 **Nosy Be** ✈ Antsirănana, N Madagascar 23°36′S 47°36′E
172 J6 **Nosy Varika** Fianarantsoa, SE Madagascar 20°36′S 48°31′E
14 L10 **Notawassi** ≈ Québec, SE Canada
14 M9 **Notawassi, Lac** ◎ Québec, SE Canada
36 J5 **Notch Peak** ▲ Utah, W USA 39°08′N 113°24′W
110 G10 **Noteć** *Ger.* Netze. ≈ NW Poland
Nóties Sporádes *see* Dodekánisa
115 J22 **Nótion Aigaíon** *Eng.* Aegean South. ◈ *region* E Greece
115 H18 **Nótios Evvoïkós Kólpos** *gulf* E Greece
115 B16 **Nótio Stenó Kérkyras** *strait* W Greece
107 L25 **Noto** *anc.* Netum. Sicilia, Italy, C Mediterranean Sea 36°53′N 15°05′E
164 M10 **Noto** Ishikawa, Honshū, SW Japan 37°18′N 137°11′E
95 G15 **Notodden** Telemark, S Norway 59°35′N 09°18′E
107 L25 **Noto, Golfo di** *gulf* Sicilia, Italy, C Mediterranean Sea
164 L10 **Noto-hantō** *peninsula* Honshū, SW Japan
164 L11 **Noto-jima** *island* SW Japan
13 T11 **Notre Dame Bay** *bay* Newfoundland, Newfoundland and Labrador, E Canada
15 P6 **Notre-Dame-de-Lorette** Québec, SE Canada 49°05′N 72°24′W
14 L11 **Notre-Dame-de-Pontmain** Québec, SE Canada 46°18′N 75°37′W
15 T8 **Notre-Dame-du-Lac** Québec, SE Canada 47°36′N 68°48′W

◆ Country ● Country Capital ◇ Dependent Territory ○ Dependent Territory Capital ◈ Administrative Regions ✈ International Airport ▲ Mountain ▲▲ Mountain Range ⛰ Volcano ≈ River ◎ Lake ▣ Reservoir

Notre-Dame-du-Rosaire – Nymboida River

15 Q6 Notre-Dame-du-Rosaire Québec, SE Canada 48°48´N 71°27´W
15 U8 Notre-Dame, Monts ⛰ Québec, S Canada
77 R16 Notsé S Togo 06°59´N 01°12´E
14 G14 Nottawasaga ∽ Ontario, S Canada
14 G14 Nottawasaga Bay lake bay Ontario, S Canada
12 I11 Nottaway ∽ Québec, SE Canada
23 S1 Nottely Lake ⊠ Georgia, SE USA
95 H16 Nøtterøy island S Norway
97 M19 Nottingham C England, United Kingdom 52°58´N 01°10´W
9 E14 Nottingham Island island Nunavut, NE Canada
97 N18 Nottinghamshire cultural region C England, United Kingdom
21 V7 Nottoway Virginia, NE USA 37°07´N 78°03´W
21 V7 Nottoway River ∽ Virginia, NE USA
76 G7 Nouâdhibou prev. Port-Étienne. Dakhlet Nouâdhibou, W Mauritania 20°54´N 17°01´W
76 G7 Nouâdhibou ✈ Dakhlet Nouâdhibou, W Mauritania 20°59´N 17°02´W
76 F7 Nouâdhibou, Dakhlet prev. Baie du Lévrier. bay W Mauritania
76 F7 Nouâdhibou, Râs prev. Cap Blanc. headland NW Mauritania 20°48´N 17°03´W
76 G9 Nouakchott ● (Mauritania) Nouakchott District, SW Mauritania 18°09´N 15°58´W
76 G9 Nouakchott ✈ Trarza, SW Mauritania 18°18´N 15°54´W
120 J11 Noual, Sebkhet en var. Sabkhat an Nawāl. salt flat C Tunisia
76 G8 Nouâmghâr var. Nouamrhar. Dakhlet Nouâdhibou, W Mauritania 19°22´N 16°31´W
Nouamrhar see Nouâmghâr
Nouă Sulița see Novoselytsya
187 Q17 Nouméa ○ (New Caledonia) Province Sud, S New Caledonia 22°13´S 166°29´E
79 E15 Noun ∽ C Cameroon
77 N12 Nouna W Burkina 12°44´N 03°54´W
83 H24 Noupoort Northern Cape, C South Africa 31°11´S 24°57´E
Nouveau-Brunswick see New Brunswick
Nouveau-Comptoir see Wemindji
15 T4 Nouvel, Lacs ◎ Québec, SE Canada
15 W7 Nouvelle Québec, SE Canada 48°07´N 66°16´W
15 W7 Nouvelle ∽ Québec, SE Canada
Nouvelle-Calédonie see New Caledonia
Nouvelle Écosse see Nova Scotia
103 R3 Nouzonville Ardennes, N France 49°49´N 04°45´E
147 Q11 Nov Rus. Nau. NW Tajikistan 40°10´N 69°16´E
59 I21 Nova Alvorada Mato Grosso do Sul, SW Brazil 21°25´S 54°19´W
Novabad see Navobod
111 D19 Nová Bystřice Ger. Neubistritz. Jihočeský Kraj, S Czech Republic 49°N 15°05´E
116 H13 Novaci Gorj, SW Romania 45°07´N 23°37´E
Nova Civitas see Neustadt an der Weinstrasse
Novaesium see Neuss
60 H10 Nova Esperança Paraná, S Brazil 23°09´S 52°13´W
106 H11 Novafeltria Marche, C Italy 43°54´N 12°18´E
60 Q9 Nova Friburgo Rio de Janeiro, SE Brazil 22°16´S 42°34´W
82 D12 Nova Gaia var. Cambundi-Catembo. Malanje, NE Angola 10°09´S 17°31´E
109 S12 Nova Gorica W Slovenia 45°57´N 13°40´E
112 G10 Nova Gradiška Ger. Neugradisk, Hung. Újgradiska. Brod-Posavina, NE Croatia 45°15´N 17°23´E
60 K7 Nova Granada São Paulo, S Brazil 20°33´S 49°19´W
60 O10 Nova Iguaçu Rio de Janeiro, SE Brazil 22°31´S 44°05´W
117 S10 Nova Kakhovka Rus. Novaya Kakhovka. Khersons'ka Oblast', SE Ukraine 46°45´N 33°20´E
Nová Karvinná see Karviná
Nova Lamego see Gabú
Nova Lisboa see Huambo
112 C11 Novalja Lika-Senj, W Croatia 44°33´N 14°53´E
119 M14 Novalukoml' Rus. Novolukoml'. Vitsyebskaya Voblasts', N Belarus 54°40´N 29°09´E
Nova Mambone see Mambone
83 P16 Nova Nabúri Zambézia, NE Mozambique 16°47´S 38°55´E
117 Q9 Nova Odesa var. Novaya Odessa. Mykolayivs'ka Oblast', S Ukraine 47°19´N 31°45´E
60 H10 Nova Olímpia Paraná, S Brazil 23°28´S 53°12´W
61 I15 Nova Prata Rio Grande do Sul, S Brazil 28°45´S 51°37´W
14 H12 Novar Ontario, S Canada 45°26´N 79°14´W
106 C7 Novara anc. Novaria. Piemonte, NW Italy 45°27´N 08°36´E
Novaria see Novara
117 P7 Novarkanels'k Kirovohrads'ka Oblast', C Ukraine 48°39´N 30°48´E
13 P15 Nova Scotia Fr. Nouvelle Écosse. ⬖ province SE Canada
0 M9 Nova Scotia physical region SE Canada
34 M8 Novato California, W USA 38°06´N 122°35´W
192 M7 Nova Trough undersea feature W Pacific Ocean
116 L7 Nova Ushtsya Khmel'nyts'ka Oblast', W Ukraine 48°50´N 27°16´E
83 M17 Nova Vanduzi Manica, C Mozambique 18°54´S 33°18´E
117 U5 Nova Vodolaha Rus. Novaya Vodolaga. Kharkivs'ka Oblast', E Ukraine 49°43´N 35°49´E
123 O12 Novaya Chara Chitinskaya Oblast', S Russian Federation 56°45´N 117°58´E
122 M12 Novaya Igirma Irkutskaya Oblast', C Russian Federation 57°08´N 103°52´E
Novaya Kakhovka see Nova Kakhovka
144 E10 Novaya Kazanka Zapadnyy Kazakhstan, W Kazakhstan 48°57´N 49°34´E
124 I12 Novaya Ladoga Leningradskaya Oblast', NW Russian Federation 60°03´N 32°15´E
127 R5 Novaya Malykla Ul'yanovskaya Oblast', W Russian Federation 54°13´N 49°55´E
Novaya Odessa see Nova Odesa
123 Q5 Novaya Sibir', Ostrov island Novosibirskiye Ostrova, NE Russian Federation
Novaya Vodolaga see Nova Vodolaha
119 P17 Novaya Yel'nya Mahilyowskaya Voblasts', E Belarus 53°16´N 31°14´E
122 I6 Novaya Zemlya island group N Russian Federation
Novaya Zemlya Trough see East Novaya Zemlya Trough
114 K10 Nova Zagora Sliven, C Bulgaria 42°29´N 26°00´E
105 S12 Novelda País Valenciano, E Spain 38°24´N 00°45´W
111 H19 Nové Mesto nad Váhom Ger. Waagneustadtl, Hung. Vágújhely. Trenčiansky Kraj, W Slovakia 48°46´N 17°50´E
111 F17 Nové Město na Moravě Ger. Neustadtl in Mähren. Vysočina, C Czech Republic 49°34´N 16°05´E
Novesium see Neuss
111 I21 Nové Zámky Ger. Neuhäusel, Hung. Érsekújvár. Nitriansky Kraj, SW Slovakia 49°00´N 18°10´E
Novgorod see Velikiy Novgorod
Novgorod-Severskiy see Novhorod-Sivers'kyy
122 C7 Novgorodskaya Oblast' ⬖ province W Russian Federation
117 R8 Novhorodka Kirovohrads'ka Oblast', C Ukraine 48°21´N 32°38´E
117 R2 Novhorod-Sivers'kyy Rus. Novgorod-Severskiy. Chernihivs'ka Oblast', NE Ukraine 52°00´N 33°15´E
31 R10 Novi Michigan, N USA 42°28´N 83°28´W
Novi see Novi Vinodolski
112 L9 Novi Bečej prev. Új-Becse, Vološinovo, Ger. Neubetsche, Hung. Törökbecse. Vojvodina, N Serbia 45°36´N 20°09´E
116 M3 Novi Bilokorovychi Rus. Belokorovichi. Zhytomyrs'ka Oblast', N Ukraine 51°07´N 28°02´E
25 Q8 Novice Texas, SW USA 32°00´N 99°38´W
112 A9 Novigrad Istra, NW Croatia 45°19´N 13°33´E
Novi Grad see Bosanski Novi
114 G9 Novi Iskŭr Sofiya-Grad, W Bulgaria 42°46´N 23°19´E
106 C9 Novi Ligure Piemonte, NW Italy 44°46´N 08°47´E
99 L22 Noville Luxembourg, SE Belgium 50°04´N 05°46´E
194 I10 Noville Peninsula peninsula Thurston Island, Antarctica
Noviodunum see Soissons, Aisne, France
Noviodunum see Nevers, Nièvre, France
Noviodunum see Nyon, Vaud, Switzerland
Noviomagus see Lisieux, Calvados, France
Noviomagus see Nijmegen, Netherlands
114 M8 Novi Pazar Shumen, NE Bulgaria 43°20´N 27°12´E
113 M15 Novi Pazar Turk. Yenipazar. Serbia, S Serbia 43°09´N 20°31´E
112 K10 Novi Sad Ger. Neusatz, Hung. Újvidék. Vojvodina, N Serbia 45°16´N 19°49´E
117 T6 Novi Sanzhary Poltavs'ka Oblast', C Ukraine 49°21´N 34°18´E
112 H12 Novi Travnik prev. Pučarevo. Federacija Bosna I Hercegovina, C Bosnia and Herzegovina 44°12´N 17°39´E
112 B10 Novi Vinodolski var. Novi. Primorje-Gorski Kotar, NW Croatia 45°08´N 14°46´E
58 F12 Novo Airão Amazonas, N Brazil 02°06´S 61°20´W
Novoalekseyevka see Khobda
127 N9 Novoanninskiy Volgogradskaya Oblast', SW Russian Federation 50°31´N 42°43´E
58 F13 Novo Aripuanã Amazonas, N Brazil 05°05´S 60°20´W
117 Y6 Novoaydar Luhans'ka Oblast', E Ukraine 49°00´N 39°00´E
117 X9 Novoazovs'k Rus. Novoazovsk. Donets'ka Oblast', E Ukraine 47°07´N 38°06´E
123 R14 Novobureyskiy Amurskaya Oblast', SE Russian Federation 49°42´N 129°46´E
127 Q3 Novocheboksarsk Chuvashskaya Respublika, W Russian Federation 56°07´N 47°33´E
127 R5 Novocheremshansk Ul'yanovskaya Oblast', W Russian Federation 54°23´N 50°08´E
126 L12 Novocherkassk Rostovskaya Oblast', SW Russian Federation 47°23´N 40°00´E
127 R6 Novodevich'ye Samarskaya Oblast', W Russian Federation 53°33´N 48°51´E
124 M8 Novodvinsk Arkhangel'skaya Oblast', NW Russian Federation 64°22´N 40°49´E
Novograd-Volynskiy see Novohrad-Volyns'kyy
Novogrudok see Navahrudak
61 I15 Novo Hamburgo Rio Grande do Sul, S Brazil 29°42´S 51°07´W
59 H16 Novo Horizonte Mato Grosso, W Brazil 11°19´S 57°11´W
60 K8 Novo Horizonte São Paulo, S Brazil 21°27´S 49°14´W
116 M4 Novohrad-Volyns'kyy Rus. Novograd-Volynskiy. Zhytomyrs'ka Oblast', N Ukraine 50°34´N 27°32´E
145 O7 Novoishimskiy prev. Kuybyshevskiy. Severnyy Kazakhstan, N Kazakhstan 53°15´N 66°51´E
Novokazalinsk see Ayteke Bi
126 M8 Novokhopersk Voronezhskaya Oblast', W Russian Federation 51°09´N 41°34´E
127 R6 Novokuybyshevsk Samarskaya Oblast', W Russian Federation 53°06´N 49°56´E
122 J13 Novokuznetsk prev. Stalinsk. Kemerovskaya Oblast', S Russian Federation 53°45´N 87°12´E
195 R1 Novolazarevskaya Russian research station Antarctica 70°42´S 11°31´E
Novolukoml' see Novalukoml'
109 V12 Novo mesto Ger. Rudolfswert; prev. Ger. Neustadtl. SE Slovenia 45°49´N 15°09´E
126 K15 Novomikhaylovskiy Krasnodarskiy Kray, SW Russian Federation 44°18´N 38°49´E
112 L8 Novo Miloševo Vojvodina, N Serbia 45°43´N 20°20´E
Novomirgorod see Novomyrhorod
126 L5 Novomoskovsk Tul'skaya Oblast', W Russian Federation 54°05´N 38°23´E
117 U7 Novomoskovs'k Rus. Novomoskovsk. Dnipropetrovs'ka Oblast', E Ukraine 48°38´N 35°15´E
117 V8 Novomykolayivka Zaporiz'ka Oblast', SE Ukraine 47°58´N 35°54´E
117 Q7 Novomyrhorod Rus. Novomirgorod. Kirovohrads'ka Oblast', S Ukraine 48°46´N 31°39´E
127 N8 Novonikolayevskiy Volgogradskaya Oblast', SW Russian Federation 50°55´N 42°24´E
127 P10 Novonikol'skoye Volgogradskaya Oblast', SW Russian Federation 49°23´N 45°06´E
127 X7 Novoorsk Orenburgskaya Oblast', W Russian Federation 51°21´N 59°03´E
126 M13 Novopokrovskaya Krasnodarskiy Kray, SW Russian Federation 45°58´N 40°43´E
Novopolotsk see Navapolatsk
117 Y5 Novopskov Luhans'ka Oblast', E Ukraine 49°33´N 39°07´E
Novoradomsk see Radomsko
Novo Redondo see Sumbe
127 R8 Novorepnoye Saratovskaya Oblast', W Russian Federation 51°04´N 48°34´E
126 K14 Novorossiysk Krasnodarskiy Kray, SW Russian Federation 44°50´N 37°38´E
Novorossiyskiy/Novorossiyskoye see Akzhar
124 F15 Novorzhev Pskovskaya Oblast', W Russian Federation 57°01´N 29°19´E
Novoselitsa see Novoselytsya
117 S12 Novoselivs'ke Respublika Krym, S Ukraine 45°26´N 33°37´E
Novosëlki see Navasyolki
114 G6 Novo Selo Vidin, NW Bulgaria 44°08´N 22°48´E
113 M14 Novo Selo Serbia, C Serbia 43°39´N 20°54´E
116 K8 Novoselytsya Rom. Nouă Sulița, Rus. Novoselitsa. Chernivets'ka Oblast', W Ukraine 48°14´N 26°18´E
127 U7 Novosergiyevka Orenburgskaya Oblast', W Russian Federation 52°04´N 53°10´E
126 L11 Novoshakhtinsk Rostovskaya Oblast', SW Russian Federation 47°48´N 39°51´E
122 J12 Novosibirsk Novosibirskaya Oblast', C Russian Federation 55°04´N 83°05´E
122 J12 Novosibirskaya Oblast' ⬖ province C Russian Federation
122 M4 Novosibirskiye Ostrova Eng. New Siberian Islands. island group N Russian Federation
126 K6 Novosil' Orlovskaya Oblast', W Russian Federation 53°00´N 37°59´E
124 G16 Novosokol'niki Pskovskaya Oblast', W Russian Federation 56°21´N 30°07´E
127 Q6 Novospasskoye Ul'yanovskaya Oblast', W Russian Federation 53°08´N 47°48´E
Novotroickoje see Brlik
127 X8 Novotroitsk Orenburgskaya Oblast', W Russian Federation 51°10´N 58°18´E
Novotroitskoye see Brlik, Kazakhstan
Novotroitskoye see Novotroyits'ke, Ukraine
117 T11 Novotroyits'ke Rus. Novotroitskoye. Khersons'ka Oblast', S Ukraine 46°21´N 34°21´E
Novoukrainka see Novoukrayinka
117 Q8 Novoukrayinka Rus. Novoukrainka. Kirovohrads'ka Oblast', C Ukraine 48°19´N 31°33´E
127 Q5 Novoul'yanovsk Ul'yanovskaya Oblast', W Russian Federation 54°10´N 48°19´E
127 W8 Novoural'sk Orenburgskaya Oblast', W Russian Federation 51°19´N 56°57´E
Novo-Urgench see Urganch
127 Q9 Novouzensk Saratovskaya Oblast', W Russian Federation 50°28´N 48°07´E
116 I4 Novovolyns'k Rus. Novovolynsk. Volyns'ka Oblast', NW Ukraine 50°46´N 24°09´E
117 S9 Novovorontsovka Khersons'ka Oblast', S Ukraine 47°28´N 33°55´E
147 Y7 Novovoznesenovka Issyk-Kul'skaya Oblast', E Kyrgyzstan 42°36´N 78°44´E
125 R14 Novovyatsk Kirovskaya Oblast', NW Russian Federation 58°30´N 49°42´E
Novoyel'nya see Navayel'nya
117 O6 Novozhyvotiv Vinnyts'ka Oblast', C Ukraine 49°16´N 29°31´E
126 H6 Novozybkov Bryanskaya Oblast', W Russian Federation 52°36´N 31°58´E
112 F9 Novska Sisak-Moslavina, NE Croatia 45°20´N 16°58´E
Nový Bohumín see Bohumín
111 D15 Nový Bor Ger. Haida; prev. Bor u České Lípy, Hajda. Liberecký Kraj, N Czech Republic 50°46´N 14°32´E
111 E16 Nový Bydžov Ger. Neubidschow. Královéhradecký Kraj, N Czech Republic 50°15´N 15°27´E
119 G18 Novy Dvor Rus. Novyy Dvor. Hrodzyenskaya Voblasts', W Belarus 53°48´N 24°34´E
111 I17 Nový Jičín Ger. Neutitschein. Moravskoslezský Kraj, E Czech Republic 49°36´N 18°00´E
118 K12 Novy Pahost Rus. Novyy Pogost. Vitsyebskaya Voblasts', NW Belarus 55°30´N 27°29´E
Novyy Bug see Novyy Buh
117 R9 Novyy Buh Rus. Novyy Bug. Mykolayivs'ka Oblast', S Ukraine 47°40´N 32°30´E
117 Q4 Novyy Bykiv Chernihivs'ka Oblast', N Ukraine 50°36´N 31°39´E
Novyy Dvor see Novy Dvor
Novyye Aneny see Anenii Noi
127 P7 Novyye Burasy Saratovskaya Oblast', W Russian Federation 52°10´N 46°00´E
Novyy Margilan see Farg'ona
126 K8 Novyy Oskol Belgorodskaya Oblast', W Russian Federation 50°43´N 37°55´E
Novyy Pogost see Novy Pahost
127 R2 Novyy Tor''yal Respublika Mariy El, W Russian Federation 56°59´N 48°53´E
123 N12 Novyy Uoyan Respublika Buryatiya, S Russian Federation 56°06´N 111°27´E
122 J9 Novyy Urengoy Yamalo-Nenetskiy Avtonomnyy Okrug, N Russian Federation 66°06´N 76°25´E
Novyy Uzen' see Zhanaozen
111 N16 Nowa Dęba Podkarpackie, SE Poland 50°31´N 21°53´E
111 G15 Nowa Ruda Ger. Neurode. Dolnośląskie, SW Poland 50°34´N 16°30´E
110 F12 Nowa Sól var. Nowasól, Ger. Neusalz an der Oder. Lubuskie, W Poland 51°47´N 15°43´E
Nowasól see Nowa Sól
27 Q8 Nowata Oklahoma, C USA 36°42´N 95°36´W
142 M6 Nowbarān Markazī, W Iran 35°07´N 49°51´E
110 I8 Nowe Kujawski-pomorskie, N Poland 53°40´N 18°44´E
110 K9 Nowe Miasto Lubawskie Ger. Neumark. Warmińsko-Mazurskie, NE Poland 53°24´N 19°36´E
110 L13 Nowe Miasto nad Pilicą Mazowieckie, C Poland 51°37´N 20°34´E
110 D8 Nowe Warpno Ger. Neuwarp. Zachodnio-pomorskie, NW Poland 53°52´N 14°12´E
Nowgong see Nagaon
110 E8 Nowogard var. Nowógard, Ger. Naugard. Zachodnio-pomorskie, NW Poland 53°41´N 15°09´E
110 N9 Nowogród Podlaskie, NE Poland 53°14´N 21°52´E
Nowogródek see Navahrudak
111 E14 Nowogrodziec Ger. Naumburg am Queis. Dolnośląskie, SW Poland 51°12´N 15°24´E
Nowojelnia see Navayel'nya
Nowo-Minsk see Mińsk Mazowiecki
33 V13 Nowood River ∽ Wyoming, C USA
Nowo-Święciany see Švenčionėliai
183 S10 Nowra-Bomaderry New South Wales, SE Australia 34°51´S 150°41´E
Nowrangapur see Nabarangapur
149 T5 Nowshera var. Naushahra, Naushara. North-West Frontier Province, NE Pakistan 34°00´N 72°00´E
110 J7 Nowy Dwór Gdański Ger. Tiegenhof. Pomorskie, N Poland 54°12´N 19°03´E
110 L11 Nowy Dwór Mazowiecki Mazowieckie, C Poland 52°26´N 20°43´E
111 M17 Nowy Sącz Ger. Neu Sandec. Małopolskie, S Poland 49°36´N 20°42´E
111 L18 Nowy Targ Ger. Neumark. Małopolskie, S Poland 49°29´N 20°00´E
110 F11 Nowy Tomyśl var. Nowy Tomysl. Wielkopolskie, C Poland 52°18´N 16°07´E
Nowy Tomysl see Nowy Tomyśl
148 M7 Now Zād var. Nauzad. Helmand, S Afghanistan 32°22´N 64°32´E
23 N4 Noxubee River ∽ Alabama/Mississippi, S USA
122 I10 Noyabr'sk Yamalo-Nenetskiy Avtonomnyy Okrug, N Russian Federation 63°08´N 75°19´E
102 L8 Noyant Maine-et-Loire, NW France 47°28´N 00°08´W
39 X14 Noyes Island island Alexander Archipelago, Alaska, USA
103 O3 Noyon Oise, N France 49°35´N 03°E
102 I7 Nozay Loire-Atlantique, NW France 47°34´N 01°36´W
82 L12 Nsando Northern, NE Zambia 10°22´S 31°14´E
83 N16 Nsanje Southern, S Malawi 16°57´S 35°10´E
77 Q17 Nsawam SE Ghana 05°47´N 00°19´W
79 E16 Nsimalen ✈ Centre, C Cameroon 19°15´N 81°22´E
82 K12 Nsombo Northern, NE Zambia 10°35´S 29°58´E
82 H13 Ntambu North Western, NW Zambia 12°21´S 25°03´E
83 N14 Ntcheu var. Ncheu. Central, S Malawi 14°49´S 34°37´E
79 D17 Ntem prev. Campo, Kampo. ∽ Cameroon/Equatorial Guinea
83 I14 Ntemwa North Western, NW Zambia 14°03´S 26°13´E
Ntlenyana, Mount see Thabana Ntlenyana
79 I19 Ntomba, Lac var. Lac Tumba. ◎ NW Dem. Rep. Congo
115 I19 Ntóro, Kávo prev. Akrotírio Kafiréas. cape Évvoia, C Greece
81 E19 Ntungamo SW Uganda 0°54´S 30°16´E
81 E18 Ntusi SW Uganda 0°05´N 31°13´E
83 H18 Ntwetwe Pan salt lake NE Botswana
154 L13 Nūāparha var. Nauparha, Nawapara. Orissa, SW India 20°43´N 82°42´E
93 M15 Nuasjärvi ◎ C Finland
80 F11 Nuba Mountains ⛰ C Sudan
68 J9 Nubian Desert desert NE Sudan
116 G10 Nucet Hung. Diófás. Bihor, W Romania 46°28´N 22°35´E
Nu Chiang see Salween
145 U9 Nuclear Testing Ground nuclear site Pavlodar, E Kazakhstan
56 E9 Nucuray, Río ∽ N Peru
25 R14 Nueces River ∽ Texas, SW USA
9 V9 Nueltin Lake ◎ Manitoba/Northwest Territories, C Canada
99 K15 Nuenen Noord-Brabant, S Netherlands 51°29´N 05°36´E
62 G6 Nuestra Señora, Bahía bay N Chile
61 D14 Nuestra Señora Rosario de Caa Catí Corrientes, NE Argentina 27°48´S 57°42´W
54 J9 Nueva Antioquia Vichada, E Colombia 06°04´N 69°30´W
Nueva Caceres see Naga
41 O7 Nueva Ciudad Guerrera Tamaulipas, C Mexico 26°32´N 99°13´W
55 N4 Nueva Esparta off. Estado Nueva Esparta. ⬖ state NE Venezuela
Nueva Esparta, Estado see Nueva Esparta
44 C5 Nueva Gerona Isla de la Juventud, S Cuba 21°49´N 82°49´W
42 H8 Nueva Guadalupe San Miguel, E El Salvador 13°30´N 88°21´W
42 M11 Nueva Guinea Región Autónoma Atlántico Sur, SE Nicaragua 11°40´N 84°22´W
61 D19 Nueva Helvecia Colonia, SW Uruguay 34°16´S 57°53´W
63 J25 Nueva, Isla island S Chile
40 M14 Nueva Italia Michoacán, SW Mexico 19°01´N 102°06´W
56 D6 Nueva Loja var. Lago Agrio. Sucumbíos, NE Ecuador
42 F6 Nueva Ocotepeque prev. Ocotepeque. Ocotepeque, W Honduras 14°25´N 89°10´W
61 D19 Nueva Palmira Colonia, SW Uruguay 33°53´S 58°25´W
41 N6 Nueva Rosita Coahuila, NE Mexico 27°58´N 101°11´W
42 E7 Nueva San Salvador prev. Santa Tecla. La Libertad, SW El Salvador 13°40´N 89°18´W
42 J8 Nueva Segovia ⬖ department NW Nicaragua
Nueva Tabarca see Plana, Isla
Nueva Villa de Padilla see Nuevo Padilla
61 B21 Nueve de Julio Buenos Aires, E Argentina 35°29´S 60°52´W
44 H6 Nuevitas Camagüey, E Cuba 21°34´N 77°18´W
61 D18 Nuevo Berlín Río Negro, W Uruguay 32°59´S 58°03´W
40 I4 Nuevo Casas Grandes Chihuahua, N Mexico 30°23´N 107°54´W
43 T14 Nuevo Chagres Colón, C Panama 09°14´N 80°05´W
41 W15 Nuevo Coahuila Campeche, E Mexico 17°53´N 90°46´W
63 K17 Nuevo, Golfo gulf S Argentina
41 O7 Nuevo Laredo Tamaulipas, NE Mexico 27°28´N 99°32´W
41 N8 Nuevo León ⬖ state NE Mexico
41 P10 Nuevo Padilla var. Nueva Villa de Padilla. Tamaulipas, C Mexico 24°01´N 98°48´W
56 E6 Nuevo Rocafuerte Orellana, E Ecuador 0°59´S 75°27´W
Nuga see Dzavhanmandal
80 O13 Nugaal off. Gobolka Nugaal. ⬖ region N Somalia
Nugaal, Gobolka see Nugaal
185 E24 Nugget Point headland South Island, New Zealand 46°26´S 169°49´E
186 J5 Nuguria Islands island group E Papua New Guinea
184 P10 Nuhaka Hawke's Bay, North Island, New Zealand 39°03´S 177°43´E
138 M10 Nuhaydayn, Wādī an dry watercourse W Iraq
190 E7 Nui Atoll atoll W Tuvalu
Nu Jiang see Salween
Nûk see Nuuk
182 G7 Nukey Bluff hill South Australia
Nukha see Şäki
123 T9 Nukh Yablonevyy, Gora ▲ E Russian Federation 60°26´N 151°45´E
186 K7 Nukiki Choiseul Island, NW Solomon Islands 06°45´S 156°30´E
186 B6 Nuku Sandaun, NW Papua New Guinea 03°48´S 142°23´E
193 W15 Nuku island Tongatapu Group, NE Tonga
193 Y16 Nuku'alofa ● (Tonga) Tongatapu, S Tonga 21°08´S 175°13´W
193 U15 Nuku'alofa Tongatapu, S Tonga 21°09´S 175°14´W
190 G12 Nukuatea island N Wallis and Futuna
190 F7 Nukufetau Atoll atoll C Tuvalu
190 G12 Nukuhifala island E Wallis and Futuna
191 W7 Nuku Hiva island Îles Marquises, NE French Polynesia
191 W7 Nuku Hiva Island island Îles Marquises, N French Polynesia
190 F9 Nukulaelae Atoll var. Nukulailai. atoll E Tuvalu
Nukulailai see Nukulaelae Atoll
190 G11 Nukuloa island N Wallis and Futuna
186 L6 Nukumanu Islands prev. Tasman Group. island group NE Papua New Guinea
Nukunau see Nikunau
190 J9 Nukunonu Atoll island C Tokelau
190 J9 Nukunonu Village Nukunonu Atoll, C Tokelau
189 S18 Nukuoro Atoll atoll Caroline Islands, S Micronesia
146 H8 Nukus Qoraqalpog'iston Respublikasi, W Uzbekistan 42°29´N 59°32´E
190 G11 Nukutapu island N Wallis and Futuna
39 O9 Nulato Alaska, USA 64°43´N 158°06´W
39 O10 Nulato Hills ⛰ Alaska, USA
105 T9 Nules País Valenciano, E Spain 39°52´N 00°10´W
Nuling see Sultan Kudarat
182 C6 Nullarbor South Australia 31°28´S 130°57´E
180 M11 Nullarbor Plain plateau South Australia/Western Australia
163 S12 Nulu'erhu Shan ⛰ N China
77 X14 Numan Adamawa, E Nigeria 09°26´N 11°58´E
165 S3 Numata Hokkaidō, NE Japan 43°48´N 141°55´E
81 C15 Numatinna ∽ W Sudan
95 F14 Numedalen valley S Norway
95 G14 Numedalslågen var. Laagen. ∽ S Norway
93 L19 Nummela Etelä-Suomi, S Finland 60°21´N 24°20´E
183 O11 Numurkah Victoria, SE Australia 36°04´S 145°28´E
196 L16 Nunap Isua var. Uummannarsuaq, Dan. Kap Farvel, Eng. Cape Farewell. cape S Greenland
9 N8 Nunavut ⬖ territory N Canada
54 H9 Nunchia Casanare, C Colombia 05°37´N 72°13´W
97 M20 Nuneaton C England, United Kingdom 52°32´N 01°28´W
153 W14 Nungba Manipur, NE India 24°46´N 93°25´E
38 L12 Nunivak Island island Alaska, USA
152 I5 Nun Kun ▲ NW India 34°01´N 76°04´E
98 L10 Nunspeet Gelderland, E Netherlands 52°21´N 05°45´E
107 C18 Nuoro Sardegna, Italy, C Mediterranean Sea 40°20´N 09°20´E
75 R12 Nuqayy, Jabal hill range S Libya
54 C9 Nuquí Chocó, W Colombia 05°44´N 77°16´W
143 O4 Nūr Māzandarān, N Iran 36°32´N 52°00´E
145 Q9 Nura ∽ N Kazakhstan
143 N11 Nūrābād Fārs, C Iran 30°08´N 51°30´E
Nurakita see Niulakita
Nurata see Nurota
Nuratau, Khrebet see Nurota Tizmasi
136 L17 Nur Dağları ⛰ S Turkey
Nurek see Norak
Nuremberg see Nürnberg
149 S4 Nūrestān ⬖ province C Afghanistan
136 M15 Nurhak Kahramanmaraş, S Turkey 37°57´N 37°21´E
182 J9 Nuriootpa South Australia 34°28´S 139°00´E
127 S5 Nurlat Respublika Tatarstan, W Russian Federation 54°26´N 50°48´E
93 N15 Nurmes Itä-Suomi, E Finland 63°31´N 29°10´E
101 K20 Nürnberg Eng. Nuremberg. Bayern, S Germany 49°27´N 11°05´E
101 K20 Nürnberg ✈ Bayern, SE Germany 49°29´N 11°04´E
146 M10 Nurota Rus. Nurata. Navoiy Viloyati, C Uzbekistan 40°41´N 65°43´E
147 N10 Nurota Tizmasi Rus. Khrebet Nuratau. ⛰ C Uzbekistan
149 T8 Nūrpur Punjab, E Pakistan 31°54´N 71°55´E
183 P6 Nurri, Mount hill New South Wales, SE Australia
25 T13 Nursery Texas, SW USA 28°55´N 97°05´W
169 V17 Nusa Tenggara Barat off. Propinsi Nusa Tenggara Barat, Eng. West Nusa Tenggara. ⬖ province S Indonesia
Nusa Tenggara Barat, Propinsi see Nusa Tenggara Barat
171 O16 Nusa Tenggara Timur off. Propinsi Nusa Tenggara Timur, Eng. East Nusa Tenggara. ⬖ province S Indonesia
Nusa Tenggara Timur, Propinsi see Nusa Tenggara Timur
171 U14 Nusawulan Papua, E Indonesia 04°03´S 132°56´E
137 Q16 Nusaybin var. Nisibin. Manisa, SE Turkey 37°08´N 41°11´E
39 O14 Nushagak Bay bay Alaska, USA
39 O13 Nushagak Peninsula headland Alaska, USA 58°39´N 159°03´W
39 O13 Nushagak River ∽ Alaska, USA
160 E11 Nu Shan ⛰ SW China
149 N11 Nushki Baluchistān, SW Pakistan 29°33´N 66°01´E
Nussdorf see Năsăud
112 J9 Nuštar Vukovar-Srijem, E Croatia 45°20´N 18°48´E
99 L18 Nuth Limburg, SE Netherlands 50°55´N 05°52´E
100 N13 Nuthe ∽ NE Germany
Nutmeg State see Connecticut
39 T10 Nutzotin Mountains ⛰ Alaska, USA
64 I5 Nuuk var. Nûk, Dan. Godthaab, Godthåb. ○ (Greenland) Kitaa, SW Greenland 64°15´N 51°35´W
92 L13 Nuupas Lappi, NW Finland 66°01´N 26°19´E
191 O7 Nuupere, Pointe headland Moorea, W French Polynesia 17°35´S 149°47´W
191 O7 Nuuroa, Pointe headland Tahiti, W French Polynesia
Nüürst see Baganuur
Nuwara see Nuwara Eliya
155 K25 Nuwara Eliya var. Nuwara. Central Province, S Sri Lanka 06°58´N 80°46´E
182 E7 Nuyts Archipelago island group South Australia
83 F17 Nxaunxau North West, NW Botswana 18°57´S 21°18´E
39 N12 Nyac Alaska, USA 61°00´N 159°56´W
122 H9 Nyagan' Khanty-Mansiyskiy Avtonomnyy Okrug-Yugra, N Russian Federation 62°10´N 65°32´E
Nyagassola see Niagassola
Nyagquka see Yajiang
81 I18 Nyahururu Central, W Kenya 0°04´N 36°22´E
182 M10 Nyah West Victoria, SE Australia 35°14´S 143°18´E
158 M15 Nyainqêntanglha Feng ▲ W China 30°20´N 90°28´E
159 N15 Nyainqêntanglha Shan ⛰ W China
159 O13 Nyainrong Xizang Zizhiqu, W China 32°02´N 92°20´E
80 B11 Nyala Southern Darfur, W Sudan 12°01´N 24°50´E
158 J17 Nyalam Xizang Zizhiqu, SW China 28°10´N 85°57´E
83 M16 Nyamapanda Mashonaland East, NE Zimbabwe 16°59´S 32°52´E
81 H25 Nyamtumbo Ruvuma, S Tanzania 10°33´S 36°08´E
Nyanda see Masvingo
124 M11 Nyandoma Arkhangel'skaya Oblast', NW Russian Federation 61°39´N 40°10´E
83 M16 Nyanga prev. Inyanga. Manicaland, E Zimbabwe 18°13´S 32°46´E
79 D20 Nyanga off. Province de la Nyanga, var. La Nyanga. ⬖ province SW Gabon
79 E20 Nyanga ∽ Congo/Gabon
Nyanga, Province de la see Nyanga
81 F20 Nyantakara Kagera, NW Tanzania 03°05´S 31°23´E
81 G19 Nyanza ⬖ province W Kenya
81 E21 Nyanza-Lac S Burundi 04°16´S 29°38´E
68 J14 Nyasa, Lake var. Lake Malawi; prev. Lago Nyassa. ◎ E Africa
Nyasaland/Nyasaland Protectorate see Malawi
Nyassa, Lago see Nyasa, Lake
119 J17 Nyasvizh Pol. Nieśwież, Rus. Nesvizh. Minskaya Voblasts', C Belarus 53°13´N 26°40´E
166 M8 Nyaunglebin Bago, SW Burma (Myanmar) 17°59´N 94°44´E
166 M5 Nyaung-u Magway, C Burma (Myanmar) 21°03´N 95°44´E
95 H24 Nyborg Fyn, C Denmark 55°19´N 10°48´E
95 N21 Nybro Kalmar, S Sweden 56°45´N 15°54´E
119 J16 Nyeharelaye Rus. Negoreloye. Minskaya Voblasts', C Belarus 53°36´N 27°04´E
158 M16 Nyêmo var. Tarrong. Xizang Zizhiqu, W China 29°25´N 90°10´E
195 W3 Nye Mountains ⛰ Antarctica
81 I19 Nyeri Central, C Kenya 0°25´S 36°56´E
118 M11 Nyeshcharda, Vozyera ◎ N Belarus
92 O2 Ny-Friesland physical region N Svalbard
95 L14 Nyhammar Dalarna, C Sweden 60°19´N 14°55´E
160 F7 Nyikog Qu ∽ C China
158 K14 Nyima Xizang Zizhiqu, W China 31°56´N 87°16´E
83 L14 Nyimba Eastern, E Zambia 14°33´S 30°49´E
159 P15 Nyingchi var. Pula. Xizang Zizhiqu, W China 29°34´N 94°33´E
159 P15 Nyingchi Xizang Zizhiqu, W China 29°27´N 94°43´E
Nyinma see Maqu
111 O21 Nyírbátor Szabolcs-Szatmár-Bereg, E Hungary 47°50´N 22°09´E
111 N21 Nyíregyháza Szabolcs-Szatmár-Bereg, NE Hungary 47°57´N 21°43´E
Nyiro see Ewaso Ng'iro
Nyitra see Nitra
Nyitrabánya see Handlová
93 K16 Nykarleby Fin. Uusikaarlepyy. Länsi-Suomi, W Finland 63°22´N 22°30´E
95 I25 Nykøbing Storstrøm, SE Denmark 54°47´N 11°53´E
95 I22 Nykøbing Vestsjælland, C Denmark 55°56´N 11°41´E
95 F21 Nykøbing Viborg, NW Denmark 56°48´N 08°52´E
95 N17 Nyköping Södermanland, S Sweden 58°45´N 17°03´E
95 L15 Nykroppa Värmland, C Sweden 59°37´N 14°18´E
Nylstroom see Modimolle
183 P7 Nymagee New South Wales, SE Australia 32°06´S 146°19´E
183 V5 Nymboida New South Wales, SE Australia 29°57´S 152°45´E
183 U5 Nymboida River ∽ New South Wales, SE Australia

◆ Country
● Country Capital
◇ Dependent Territory
○ Dependent Territory Capital
⬖ Administrative Regions
✈ International Airport
▲ Mountain
⛰ Mountain Range
🌋 Volcano
∽ River
◎ Lake
⊠ Reservoir

◆ Country   ◇ Dependent Territory   ◆ Administrative Regions   ▲ Mountain   ▲ Volcano   ⊠ Lake
● Country Capital   ○ Dependent Territory Capital   ✈ International Airport   ▲ Mountain Range   ↝ River   ⊠ Reservoir

Orenburg – Ouidah

127 V7 Orenburg ✈ Orenburgskaya Oblast', W Russian Federation 51°54′N 55°15′E
127 T7 Orenburgskaya Oblast' ⬖ province W Russian Federation
Orense see Ourense
188 C8 Oreor var. Koror. island N Palau
185 B24 Orepuki Southland, South Island, New Zealand 46°17′S 167°45′E
114 L12 Orestiáda prev. Orestiás. Anatolikí Makedonía kai Thráki, NE Greece 41°30′N 26°31′E
Orestiás see Orestiáda
Öresund/Øresund see Sound, The
185 C23 Oreti ≈ South Island, New Zealand
184 L5 Orewa Auckland, North Island, New Zealand 36°34′S 174°43′E
65 A25 Orford, Cape headland West Falkland, Falkland Islands 52°00′S 61°04′W
44 B5 Órganos, Sierra de los ▲▲ W Cuba
37 R15 Organ Peak ▲ New Mexico, SW USA 32°17′N 106°35′W
105 N9 Orgaz Castilla-La Mancha, C Spain 39°39′N 03°52′W
Orgeyev see Orhei
Orgil see Jargalant
105 O15 Orgiva var. Orjiva. Andalucía, S Spain 36°54′N 03°25′W
163 O10 Örgön var. Senj. Dornogovĭ, SE Mongolia 44°34′N 110°58′E
Örgön see Bayangovĭ
Orgražden see Ograzhden
117 N9 Orhei var. Orheiu, Rus. Orgeyev. N Moldova 47°25′N 28°48′E
Orheiu see Orhei
105 R3 Orhi var. Orhy, Pico de Orhy, Pic d'Orhy. ▲ France/Spain 42°55′N 01°01′W see also Orhy
Orhi see Orhy
Orhomenos see Orchómenos
162 K6 Orhon ⬖ province N Mongolia
162 L6 Orhon Gol ≈ N Mongolia
102 J16 Orhy var. Orhi, Pico de Orhy, Pic d'Orhy. ▲ France/Spain 43°00′N 01°00′W see also Orhi
Orhy see Orhi
Orhy, Pic d'/Orhy, Pico de see Orhi/Orhy
34 L2 Orick California, W USA 41°16′N 124°03′W
32 L6 Orient Washington, NW USA 48°51′N 118°14′W
48 D6 Oriental, Cordillera ▲▲ Bolivia/Peru
48 D6 Oriental, Cordillera ▲▲ C Colombia
57 H16 Oriental, Cordillera ▲▲ C Peru
63 M15 Oriente Buenos Aires, E Argentina 38°45′S 60°37′W
105 R12 Orihuela País Valenciano, E Spain 38°05′N 00°56′W
117 V9 Orikhiv Rus. Orekhov. Zaporiz'ka Oblast', SE Ukraine 47°32′N 35°48′E
113 K22 Orikum var. Orikumi. Vlorë, SW Albania 40°20′N 19°28′E
Orikumi see Orikum
117 V6 Oril' Rus. Orel. ≈ E Ukraine
14 H14 Orillia Ontario, S Canada 44°36′N 79°26′W
93 M19 Orimattila Etelä-Suomi, S Finland 60°48′N 25°40′E
33 Y15 Orin Wyoming, C USA 42°39′N 105°10′W
47 R4 Orinoco, Río ≈ Colombia/Venezuela
186 C9 Oriomo Western, SW Papua New Guinea 08°53′S 143°13′E
30 K11 Orion Illinois, N USA 41°21′N 90°22′W
29 Q5 Oriska North Dakota, N USA 46°54′N 97°46′W
153 P17 Orissa ⬖ state NE India
Orissaar see Orissaare
118 E5 Orissaare Ger. Orissaar. Saaremaa, W Estonia 58°34′N 23°05′E
107 B19 Oristano Sardegna, Italy, C Mediterranean Sea 39°54′N 08°35′E
107 A19 Oristano, Golfo di gulf Sardegna, Italy, C Mediterranean Sea
54 D13 Orito Putumayo, SW Colombia 0°49′N 76°57′W
93 L18 Orivesi Häme, W Finland 61°39′N 24°21′E
93 N17 Orivesi ◎ Länsi-Suomi, SE Finland
58 H12 Oriximiná Pará, NE Brazil 01°45′S 55°50′W
41 Q14 Orizaba Veracruz-Llave, E Mexico 18°51′N 97°08′W
41 Q14 Orizaba, Volcán Pico de var. Citlaltépetl. ▲ S Mexico 19°00′N 97°15′W
95 I16 Ørje Østfold, S Norway 59°28′N 11°40′E
113 I16 Orjen ▲ Bosnia and Herzegovina/Montenegro
Orjiva see Orgiva
Orjonikidzeobod see Kofarnihon
94 G8 Orkanger Sør-Trøndelag, S Norway 63°17′N 09°52′E
94 G8 Orkdalen valley S Norway
95 K22 Örkelljunga Skåne, S Sweden 56°17′N 13°20′E
Orkhaniye see Botevgrad
Orkhómenos see Orchómenos
94 H9 Orkla ≈ S Norway
Orkney see Orkney Islands
65 J22 Orkney Deep undersea feature Scotia Sea/Weddell Sea
96 J4 Orkney Islands var. Orkney, Orkneys. island group N Scotland, United Kingdom
Orkneys see Orkney Islands
24 K8 Orla Texas, SW USA 31°48′N 103°55′W
35 N5 Orland California, W USA 39°43′N 122°12′W
23 X11 Orlando Florida, SE USA 28°32′N 81°23′W
23 X12 Orlando ✈ Florida, SE USA 28°24′N 81°16′W
107 K23 Orlando, Capo d' headland Sicilia, Italy, C Mediterranean Sea 38°10′N 14°44′E
Orlau see Orlová
103 N6 Orléanais cultural region C France
103 N7 Orléans anc. Aurelianum. Loiret, C France 47°54′N 01°53′E
34 L2 Orleans California, W USA 41°16′N 123°36′W
19 Q12 Orleans Massachusetts, NE USA 41°48′N 69°57′W
15 R10 Orléans, Île d' island Québec, SE Canada
Orléansville see Chlef
111 F16 Orlice Ger. Adler. ≈ NE Czech Republic
122 L13 Orlik Respublika Buryatiya, S Russian Federation 52°32′N 99°36′E
125 Q14 Orlov prev. Khalturin. Kirovskaya Oblast', NW Russian Federation 58°34′N 48°57′E
111 I17 Orlová Ger. Orlau, Pol. Orłowa. Moravskoslezský Kraj, E Czech Republic 49°50′N 18°21′E
Orlov, Mys see Orlovskiy, Mys
126 I6 Orlovskaya Oblast' ⬖ province W Russian Federation
124 M5 Orlovskiy, Mys var. Mys Orlov. headland NW Russian Federation 67°14′N 41°17′E
Orłowa see Orlová
103 O5 Orly ✈ (Paris) Essonne, N France 48°43′N 02°24′E
119 G16 Orlya Hrodzyenskaya Voblasts', W Belarus 53°30′N 24°59′E
114 M7 Orlyak prev. Makenzen, Trubchular, Rom. Trupcilar. Dobrich, NE Bulgaria 43°39′N 27°21′E
148 L16 Ormāra Baluchistān, SW Pakistan 25°14′N 64°36′E
171 P5 Ormoc off. Ormoc City, var. MacArthur. Leyte, C Philippines 11°02′N 124°35′E
Ormoc City see Ormoc
23 X10 Ormond Beach Florida, SE USA 29°16′N 81°04′W
109 X10 Ormož Ger. Friedau. NE Slovenia 46°24′N 16°09′E
14 J13 Ormsby Ontario, SE Canada 44°52′N 77°45′W
97 K17 Ormskirk NW England, United Kingdom 53°35′N 02°54′W
Ormsö see Vormsi
15 N13 Ormstown Québec, SE Canada 45°08′N 73°57′W
Ormuz, Strait of see Hormuz, Strait of
103 T8 Ornans Doubs, E France 47°06′N 06°06′E
102 K5 Orne ⬖ department N France
102 K5 Orne ≈ N France
92 G12 Ørnes Nordland, C Norway 66°51′N 13°43′E
110 L7 Orneta Warmińsko-Mazurskie, NE Poland 54°07′N 20°10′E
95 P16 Ornö Stockholm, C Sweden 59°03′N 18°28′E
37 Q3 Orno Peak ▲ Colorado, C USA 40°06′N 107°06′W
93 I16 Örnsköldsvik Västernorrland, C Sweden 63°16′N 18°45′E
163 X13 Oro E North Korea 39°59′N 127°27′E
45 T6 Orocovis C Puerto Rico 18°13′N 66°22′W
54 H10 Orocué Casanare, E Colombia 04°51′N 71°21′W
77 N13 Orodara SW Burkina 11°00′N 04°54′W
105 S4 Oroel, Peña de ▲ N Spain 42°30′N 00°31′W
33 N10 Orofino Idaho, NW USA 46°28′N 116°15′W
162 I9 Orog Nuur ◎ S Mongolia
35 U14 Oro Grande California, W USA 34°36′N 117°19′W
37 S15 Orogrande New Mexico, SW USA 32°24′N 106°04′W
191 Q7 Orohena, Mont Ѫ Tahiti, W French Polynesia 17°37′S 149°27′W
Orolaunum see Arlon
Orol Dengizi see Aral Sea
189 S15 Oroluk Atoll atoll Caroline Islands, C Micronesia
80 J13 Oromīya ⬖ federal region C Ethiopia
Oromo see Goba
13 O15 Oromocto New Brunswick, SE Canada 45°50′N 66°28′W
191 S4 Orona prev. Hull Island. atoll Phoenix Islands, C Kiribati
191 V17 Orongo ancient monument Easter Island, Chile, E Pacific Ocean
138 I3 Orontes var. Ononte, Nahr el Aassi, Ar. Nahr al 'Aṣī. ≈ SW Asia
104 L9 Oropesa Castilla-La Mancha, C Spain 39°55′N 05°10′W
Oropesa see Oropesa del Mar
105 T8 Oropesa del Mar var. Oropesa, Cat. Orpes. País Valenciano, E Spain 40°06′N 00°07′E
Oropeza see Cochabamba
Oroqen Zizhiqi see Alihe
171 P7 Oroquieta var. Oroquieta City. Mindanao, S Philippines 08°27′N 123°46′E
Oroquieta City see Oroquieta
40 J8 Oro, Río del ≈ C Mexico
59 O14 Orós, Açude ⊠ E Brazil
107 D18 Orosei, Golfo di gulf Tyrrhenian Sea, C Mediterranean Sea
111 M24 Orosháza Békés, SE Hungary 46°33′N 20°40′E
Orosirá Rodhópis see Rhodope Mountains
111 I22 Oroszlány Komárom-Esztergom, W Hungary 47°28′N 18°16′E
188 B16 Orote Peninsula peninsula W Guam
123 T9 Orotukan Magadanskaya Oblast', E Russian Federation 62°18′N 150°46′E
35 O5 Oroville California, W USA 39°29′N 121°35′W
32 K6 Oroville Washington, NW USA 48°56′N 119°25′W
35 O5 Oroville, Lake ⊠ California, W USA
0 G15 Orozco Fracture Zone tectonic feature E Pacific Ocean
Orpes see Oropesa del Mar
64 I7 Orphan Knoll undersea feature NW Atlantic Ocean 51°00′N 47°00′W
29 V3 Orr Minnesota, N USA 48°03′N 92°48′W
95 M21 Orrefors Kalmar, S Sweden 56°48′N 15°45′E
182 I7 Orroroo South Australia 32°46′S 138°38′E
31 T12 Orrville Ohio, N USA 40°50′N 81°45′W
94 L12 Orsa Dalarna, C Sweden 61°07′N 14°40′E
Orschowa see Orşova
Orschütz see Orzyc
119 O14 Orsha Vitsyebskaya Voblasts', NE Belarus 54°30′N 30°26′E
127 Q2 Orshanka Respublika Mariy El, W Russian Federation 56°54′N 47°54′E
108 C11 Orsières Valais, SW Switzerland 46°00′N 07°09′E
127 X8 Orsk Orenburgskaya Oblast', W Russian Federation 51°13′N 58°35′E
116 F13 Orşova Ger. Orschowa, Hung. Orsova. Mehedinţi, SW Romania 44°42′N 22°22′E
94 D10 Ørsta Møre og Romsdal, S Norway 62°12′N 06°09′E
95 O15 Örsundsbro Uppsala, C Sweden 59°45′N 17°19′E
136 D16 Ortaca Muğla, SW Turkey 36°49′N 28°43′E
83 I21 O.R. Tambo ✈ (Johannesburg) Gauteng, NE South Africa 26°08′S 28°01′E
107 M16 Orta Nova Puglia, SE Italy 41°20′N 15°43′E
136 I17 Orta Toroslar ▲▲ S Turkey
54 E11 Ortega Tolima, W Colombia 03°57′N 75°11′W
104 H1 Ortegal, Cabo headland NW Spain 43°46′N 07°54′W
Ortelsburg see Szczytno
102 J15 Orthez Pyrénées-Atlantiques, SW France 43°29′N 00°46′W
57 K14 Orthon, Río ≈ N Bolivia
60 J10 Ortigueira Paraná, S Brazil 24°10′S 50°55′W
104 H1 Ortigueira Galicia, NW Spain 43°40′N 07°50′W
106 H5 Ortisei Ger. Sankt-Ulrich. Trentino-Alto Adige, N Italy 46°35′N 11°42′E
40 F6 Ortiz Sonora, NW Mexico 28°18′N 110°40′W
54 L5 Ortiz Guárico, N Venezuela 09°37′N 67°20′W
Ortler see Ortles
106 F5 Ortles Ger. Ortler. ▲ N Italy 46°29′N 10°33′E
107 K14 Ortona Abruzzo, C Italy 42°21′N 14°24′E
29 R8 Ortonville Minnesota, N USA 45°18′N 96°26′W
147 W8 Orto-Tokoy Issyk-Kul'skaya Oblast', NE Kyrgyzstan 42°20′N 76°03′E
93 I15 Örträsk Västerbotten, N Sweden 64°10′N 19°00′E
100 J12 Örtze ≈ NW Germany
Oruba see Aruba
142 I3 Orūmīyeh var. Rizaiyeh, Urmia, Urmiyeh; prev. Reẕā'īyeh. Āẕarbāyjān-e Gharbī, NW Iran 37°33′N 45°06′E
142 J3 Orūmīyeh, Daryācheh-ye var. Matianus, Sha Hi, Urumi Yeh, Eng. Lake Urmia; prev. Daryācheh-ye Reẕā'īyeh. ◎ NW Iran
57 K19 Oruro Oruro, W Bolivia 17°58′S 67°06′W
57 J19 Oruro ⬖ department W Bolivia
95 J18 Orust island S Sweden
149 O7 Orūzgān var. Oruzgān, Pash. Ūrūzgān. Orūzgān, C Afghanistan 32°58′N 66°39′E
149 N6 Orūzgān Pash. Urūzgān. ⬖ province C Afghanistan
106 H13 Orvieto anc. Velsuna. Umbria, C Italy 42°43′N 12°06′E
194 K7 Orville Coast physical region Antarctica
114 H7 Oryakhovo Vratsa, NW Bulgaria 43°44′N 23°58′E
Oryokko see Yalu
117 R5 Orzhytsya Poltavs'ka Oblast', C Ukraine 49°48′N 32°40′E
110 M9 Orzyc Ger. Orschütz. ≈ NE Poland
110 N8 Orzysz Ger. Arys. Warmińsko-Mazurskie, NE Poland 53°49′N 21°54′E
98 K13 Oss Noord-Brabant, S Netherlands 51°46′N 05°32′E
94 I10 Os Hedmark, S Norway 62°29′N 11°14′E
125 U15 Osa Permskaya Oblast', NW Russian Federation 57°16′N 55°22′E
115 F15 Óssa ▲ C Greece
104 H11 Óssa ▲ S Portugal 38°43′N 07°33′W
29 W11 Osage Iowa, C USA 43°16′N 92°48′W
27 U5 Osage Beach Missouri, C USA 38°09′N 92°37′W
27 P5 Osage City Kansas, C USA 38°37′N 95°49′W
27 U7 Osage Fork River ≈ Missouri, C USA
27 U5 Osage River ≈ Missouri, C USA
164 J13 Ōsaka hist. Naniwa. Ōsaka, Honshū, SW Japan 34°38′N 135°28′E
164 I13 Ōsaka off. Ōsaka-fu, var. Ōsaka Hu. ⬖ urban prefecture Honshū, SW Japan
Ōsaka-fu/Ōsaka Hu see Ōsaka
145 R10 Osakarovka Karaganda, C Kazakhstan 50°32′N 72°39′E
Ōsaki see Furukawa
29 T7 Osakis Minnesota, N USA 45°51′N 95°08′W
43 N16 Osa, Península de peninsula S Costa Rica
60 M10 Osasco São Paulo, S Brazil 23°32′S 46°46′W
27 R5 Osawatomie Kansas, C USA 38°30′N 94°57′W
26 L3 Osborne Kansas, C USA 39°26′N 98°42′W
173 S8 Osborn Plateau undersea feature E Indian Ocean
95 L21 Osby Skåne, S Sweden 56°24′N 14°00′E
Osca see Huesca
92 N2 Oscar II Land physical region W Svalbard
29 Y10 Osceola Arkansas, C USA 35°43′N 89°58′W
29 V15 Osceola Iowa, C USA 41°01′N 93°45′W
27 S6 Osceola Missouri, C USA 38°01′N 93°41′W
29 Q15 Osceola Nebraska, C USA 41°09′N 97°28′W
101 N15 Oschatz Sachsen, E Germany 51°17′N 13°10′E
100 K13 Oschersleben Sachsen-Anhalt, C Germany 52°02′N 11°14′E
31 R7 Oscoda Michigan, N USA 44°25′N 83°19′W
Ösel see Saaremaa
94 H6 Osen Sør-Trøndelag, S Norway 64°17′N 10°29′E
94 I12 Osensjøen ◎ S Norway
164 A14 Ōse-zaki Fukue-jima, SW Japan
147 T10 Osh Oshskaya Oblast', SW Kyrgyzstan 40°34′N 72°46′E
83 C16 Oshakati Oshana, N Namibia 17°46′S 15°43′E
83 C16 Oshana ⬖ district N Namibia
14 H15 Oshawa Ontario, SE Canada 43°54′N 78°50′W
165 R10 Oshika-hantō peninsula Honshū, C Japan
83 C16 Oshikango Ohangwena, N Namibia 17°29′S 15°54′E
Oshikoto see Otjikoto
165 P5 Ō-shima island NE Japan
165 N14 Ō-shima island S Japan
165 Q5 Oshima-hantō ▲ Hokkaidō, NE Japan
83 D17 Oshivelo Otjikoto, N Namibia 18°37′S 17°10′E
28 K14 Oshkosh Nebraska, C USA 41°25′N 102°21′W
30 M7 Oshkosh Wisconsin, N USA 44°01′N 88°32′W
Oshmyany see Ashmyany
Osh Oblasty see Oshskaya Oblast'
77 T16 Oshogbo var. Osogbo. Osun, W Nigeria 07°42′N 04°31′E
147 S11 Oshskaya Oblast' Kir. Osh Oblasty. ⬖ province SW Kyrgyzstan
Ōshū see Mizusawa
Oshun see Osun
79 J20 Oshwe Bandundu, C Dem. Rep. Congo 03°24′S 19°32′E
Osiek see Osijek
112 I9 Osijek prev. Osiek, Osjek, Ger. Esseg, Hung. Eszék. Osijek-Baranja, E Croatia 45°33′N 18°41′E
112 I9 Osijek-Baranja off. Osječko-Baranjska Županija. ⬖ province E Croatia
106 J12 Osimo Marche, C Italy 43°28′N 13°29′E
122 M12 Osinovka Irkutskaya Oblast', C Russian Federation 56°19′N 101°55′E
Osintorf see Asintorf
112 N11 Osipaonica Serbia, NE Serbia 44°34′N 21°00′E
Osipenko see Berdyans'k
Osipovichi see Asipovichy
Osječko-Baranjska Županija see Osijek-Baranja
Osjek see Osijek
29 W15 Oskaloosa Iowa, C USA 41°17′N 92°38′W
27 Q4 Oskaloosa Kansas, C USA 39°14′N 95°21′W
95 N20 Oskarshamn Kalmar, S Sweden 57°16′N 16°25′E
95 J21 Oskarström Halland, S Sweden 56°48′N 13°00′E
14 M8 Oskélanéo Québec, SE Canada 48°06′N 75°12′W
Öskemen see Ust'-Kamenogorsk
117 W5 Oskil Rus. Oskil. ≈ Russian Federation/Ukraine
Oskil see Oskil
93 D20 Oslo prev. Christiania, Kristiania. ● (Norway) Oslo, S Norway 59°54′N 10°44′E
93 D20 Oslo ⬖ county S Norway
93 D21 Oslofjorden fjord S Norway
155 G15 Osmānābād Mahārāshtra, C India 18°09′N 76°06′E
136 J11 Osmancık Çorum, N Turkey 40°58′N 34°50′E
136 L16 Osmaniye Osmaniye, S Turkey 37°04′N 36°15′E
136 L16 Osmaniye ⬖ province S Turkey
95 O16 Ösmo Stockholm, C Sweden 58°58′N 17°55′E
118 E3 Osmussaar island W Estonia
100 G13 Osnabrück Niedersachsen, NW Germany 52°09′N 07°42′E
110 D11 Ośno Lubuskie Ger. Drossen. Lubuskie, W Poland 52°28′N 14°51′E
Osogbo see Oshogbo
113 P19 Osogov Mountains var. Osogovske Planine, Osogovski Planina, Mac. Osogovski Planini. ▲▲ Bulgaria/FYR Macedonia
Osogovske Planine/Osogovski Planina/Osogovski Planini see Osogov Mountains
165 R6 Osore-zan ▲ Honshū, C Japan 41°18′N 141°06′E
Oșorhei see Târgu Mureș
61 J16 Osório Rio Grande do Sul, S Brazil 29°53′S 50°17′W
63 G16 Osorno Los Lagos, C Chile 40°39′S 73°05′W
104 M4 Osorno Castilla-León, N Spain 42°24′N 04°22′W
11 N17 Osoyoos British Columbia, SW Canada 49°02′N 119°31′W
95 C14 Osøyro Hordaland, S Norway 60°11′N 05°30′E
54 J6 Ospino Portuguesa, N Venezuela 09°17′N 69°26′W
23 X6 Ossabaw Island island Georgia, SE USA
23 X6 Ossabaw Sound sound Georgia, SE USA
183 O16 Ossa, Mount ▲ Tasmania, SE Australia 41°55′S 146°03′E
104 H11 Ossa, Serra d' ▲ SE Portugal
77 U16 Osse ≈ S Nigeria
30 J6 Osseo Wisconsin, N USA 44°33′N 91°13′W
109 S9 Ossiacher See ◎ S Austria
18 K13 Ossining New York, NE USA 41°10′N 73°50′W
123 V9 Ossora Koryakskiy Avtonomnyy Okrug, E Russian Federation 59°16′N 163°02′E
124 I15 Ostashkov Tverskaya Oblast', W Russian Federation 57°08′N 33°10′E
100 H9 Oste ≈ NW Germany
Ostee see Baltic Sea
Ostend/Ostende see Oostende
117 P3 Oster Chernihivs'ka Oblast', N Ukraine 50°57′N 30°55′E
95 O14 Österbybruk Uppsala, C Sweden 60°13′N 17°55′E
95 M19 Österbymo Östergötland, S Sweden 57°49′N 15°15′E
94 K12 Österdalälven ≈ C Sweden
94 I12 Østerdalen valley S Norway
95 L18 Östergötland ⬖ county S Sweden
100 H10 Osterholz-Scharmbeck Niedersachsen, NW Germany 53°13′N 08°46′E
Östermark see Teuva
Östermyra see Seinäjoki
Østerø see Eysturoy
101 J14 Osterode am Harz Niedersachsen, C Germany 51°43′N 10°15′E
Osterode/Osterode in Ostpreussen see Ostróda
94 C13 Osterøy island S Norway
Österreich see Austria
93 G16 Östersund Jämtland, C Sweden 63°10′N 14°44′E
95 N14 Östervåla Västmanland, C Sweden 60°10′N 17°13′E
101 H22 Ostfildern Baden-Württemberg, SW Germany 48°43′N 09°16′E
95 H16 Østfold ⬖ county S Norway
100 E9 Ostfriesische Inseln Eng. East Frisian Islands. island group NW Germany
100 F10 Ostfriesland historical region NW Germany
95 P14 Östhammar Uppsala, C Sweden 60°15′N 18°25′E
Ostia Aterni see Pescara
106 G8 Ostiglia Lombardia, N Italy 45°04′N 11°09′E
95 J14 Östmark Värmland, C Sweden 60°15′N 12°45′E
95 K22 Östra Ringsjön ◎ S Sweden
111 I17 Ostrava Moravskoslezský Kraj, E Czech Republic 49°50′N 18°15′E
Ostravský Kraj see Moravskoslezský Kraj
94 J11 Østrehogna Swe. Härjahågnen, Härjehågna. ▲ Norway/Sweden 61°43′N 12°07′E
110 K8 Ostróda Ger. Osterode, Osterode in Ostpreussen. Warmińsko-Mazurskie, NE Poland 53°42′N 19°59′E
Ostrog/Ostróg see Ostroh
126 L8 Ostrogozhsk Voronezhskaya Oblast', W Russian Federation 50°52′N 39°00′E
116 L4 Ostroh Pol. Ostróg, Rus. Ostrog. Rivnens'ka Oblast', NW Ukraine 50°20′N 26°29′E
110 N9 Ostrołęka Ger. Wiesenhof, Rus. Ostrolenka. Mazowieckie, C Poland 53°06′N 21°34′E
Ostrolenka see Ostrołęka
111 A16 Ostrov Ger. Schlackenwerth. Karlovarský Kraj, W Czech Republic 50°18′N 12°56′E
124 F15 Ostrov Latv. Austrava. Pskovskaya Oblast', W Russian Federation 57°21′N 28°18′E
Ostrovets see Ostrowiec Świętokrzyski
113 M21 Ostrovicës, Mali i ▲ SE Albania 40°36′N 20°25′E
165 Z2 Ostrov Iturup island NE Russian Federation
124 M4 Ostrovnoy Murmanskaya Oblast', NW Russian Federation 68°00′N 39°40′E
114 L7 Ostrovo prev. Golema Ada. Razgrad, N Bulgaria 43°40′N 26°37′E
125 N15 Ostrovskoye Kostromskaya Oblast', NW Russian Federation 57°46′N 42°18′E
Ostrów see Ostrów Wielkopolski
Ostrowiec see Ostrowiec Świętokrzyski
111 M14 Ostrowiec Świętokrzyski var. Ostrowiec, Rus. Ostrovets. Świętokrzyskie, C Poland 50°55′N 21°23′E
110 P13 Ostrów Lubelski Lubelskie, E Poland 51°29′N 22°57′E
110 N10 Ostrów Mazowiecka var. Ostrów Mazowiecki. Mazowieckie, NE Poland 52°49′N 21°53′E
Ostrów Mazowiecki see Ostrów Mazowiecka
Ostrowo see Ostrów Wielkopolski
110 H13 Ostrów Wielkopolski var. Ostrów, Ger. Ostrowo. Wielkopolskie, C Poland 51°40′N 17°47′E
Ostryna see Astryna
110 I13 Ostrzeszów Wielkopolskie, C Poland 51°25′N 17°55′E
107 P18 Ostuni Puglia, SE Italy 40°44′N 17°35′E
Ostyako-Voguls'k see Khanty-Mansiysk
114 I9 Osŭm ≈ N Bulgaria
Osum see Osumit, Lumi i
164 C17 Ōsumi-hantō ▲ Kyūshū, SW Japan
164 C17 Ōsumi-kaikyō strait SW Japan
113 L22 Osumit, Lumi i var. Osum. ≈ SE Albania
77 T16 Osun var. Oshun. ⬖ state SW Nigeria
104 L14 Osuna Andalucía, S Spain 37°14′N 05°06′W
60 J8 Osvaldo Cruz São Paulo, S Brazil 21°49′S 50°52′W
Osveya see Asveya
18 J7 Oswegatchie River ≈ New York, NE USA
27 Q7 Oswego Kansas, C USA 37°11′N 95°10′W
18 H9 Oswego New York, NE USA 43°27′N 76°13′W
97 K19 Oswestry W England, United Kingdom 52°51′N 03°06′W
111 J16 Oświęcim Ger. Auschwitz. Małopolskie, S Poland 50°02′N 19°11′E
185 E22 Otago off. Otago Region. ⬖ region South Island, New Zealand
185 F23 Otago Peninsula peninsula South Island, New Zealand
Otago Region see Otago
165 F13 Ōtake Hiroshima, Honshū, SW Japan 34°13′N 132°12′E
184 L13 Otaki Wellington, North Island, New Zealand 40°46′S 175°08′E
93 M15 Otanmäki Oulu, C Finland 64°07′N 27°04′E
145 T15 Otar Zhambyl, SE Kazakhstan 43°30′N 75°13′E
165 R4 Otaru Hokkaidō, NE Japan 43°14′N 140°59′E
185 C24 Otatara Southland, South Island, New Zealand 46°26′S 168°18′E
185 C24 Otautau Southland, South Island, New Zealand 46°10′S 168°01′E
93 M18 Otava Itä-Suomi, E Finland 61°37′N 27°07′E
111 B18 Otava Ger. Wottawa. ≈ SW Czech Republic
56 C6 Otavalo Imbabura, N Ecuador 0°13′N 78°15′W
83 D17 Otavi Otjozondjupa, N Namibia 19°35′S 17°25′E
165 P12 Ōtawara Tochigi, Honshū, S Japan 36°52′N 140°01′E
83 B16 Otchinjau Cunene, SW Angola 16°31′S 13°54′E
116 F12 Oțelu Roșu Ger. Ferdinandsberg, Hung. Nándorhgy. Caraș-Severin, SW Romania 45°30′N 22°22′E
185 E21 Otematata Canterbury, South Island, New Zealand 44°37′S 170°12′E
118 I6 Otepää Ger. Odenpäh. Valgamaa, SE Estonia 58°01′N 26°30′E
162 H7 Otgon var. Buyant. Dzavhan, C Mongolia 47°14′N 97°14′E
32 K9 Othello Washington, NW USA 46°49′N 119°10′W
115 A15 Othonoí island Iónia Nisiá, Greece, C Mediterranean Sea
Othris see Óthrys
115 F17 Óthrys var. Othris. ▲▲ C Greece
77 Q14 Oti ≈ N Togo
40 K10 Otinapa Durango, C Mexico 24°01′N 104°58′W
185 G17 Otira West Coast, South Island, New Zealand 42°52′S 171°33′E
37 V3 Otis Colorado, C USA 40°09′N 102°57′W
12 L10 Otish, Monts ▲▲ Québec, E Canada
83 C17 Otjikondo Kunene, N Namibia 19°50′S 15°23′E
83 C17 Otjikoto var. Oshikoto. ⬖ district N Namibia
83 E18 Otjinene Omaheke, NE Namibia 21°10′S 18°43′E
83 D18 Otjiwarongo Otjozondjupa, N Namibia 20°29′S 16°36′E
83 D18 Otjosondu var. Otjosundu. Otjozondjupa, C Namibia 21°19′S 17°51′E
Otjosundu see Otjosondu
83 D18 Otjozondjupa ⬖ district C Namibia
112 C11 Otočac Lika-Senj, W Croatia 44°52′N 15°13′E
Otog Qi see Ulan
112 J10 Otok Vukovar-Srijem, E Croatia 45°10′N 18°52′E
116 K14 Otopeni ✈ (București) Ilfov, S Romania 44°34′N 26°09′E
184 L8 Otorohanga Waikato, North Island, New Zealand 38°10′S 175°14′E
12 D9 Otoskwin ≈ Ontario, C Canada
165 G14 Ōtoyo Kōchi, Shikoku, SW Japan 33°45′N 133°42′E
95 E16 Otra ≈ S Norway
107 R19 Otranto Puglia, SE Italy 40°08′N 18°28′E
Otranto, Canale d' see Otranto, Strait of
107 Q18 Otranto, Strait of It. Canale d'Otranto. strait Albania/Italy
111 H18 Otrokovice Ger. Otrokowitz. Zlínský Kraj, E Czech Republic 49°13′N 17°33′E
Otrokowitz see Otrokovice
31 P10 Otsego Michigan, N USA 42°27′N 85°42′W
31 Q6 Otsego Lake ◎ Michigan, N USA
18 I11 Otselic River ≈ New York, NE USA
164 J14 Ōtsu var. Ōtu. Shiga, Honshū, SW Japan 35°03′N 135°49′E
94 G11 Otta Oppland, S Norway 61°46′N 09°33′E
189 U13 Otta island Chuuk, C Micronesia
94 F11 Otta ≈ S Norway
189 U13 Otta Pass passage Chuuk Islands, C Micronesia
95 J22 Ottarp Skåne, S Sweden 55°55′N 12°55′E
14 L12 Ottawa ● (Canada) Ontario, SE Canada 45°24′N 75°41′W
30 L11 Ottawa Illinois, N USA 41°21′N 88°50′W
27 Q5 Ottawa Kansas, C USA 38°35′N 95°16′W
31 R12 Ottawa Ohio, N USA 41°01′N 84°03′W
14 L12 Ottawa var. Uplands. ✈ Ontario, SE Canada 45°19′N 75°39′W
14 M12 Ottawa Fr. Outaouais. ≈ Ontario/Québec, SE Canada
9 R10 Ottawa Islands island group Nunavut, C Canada
18 L8 Otter Creek ≈ Vermont, NE USA
36 L6 Otter Creek Reservoir ⊠ Utah, W USA
98 L11 Otterlo Gelderland, E Netherlands 52°06′N 05°46′E
94 D9 Otterøya island S Norway
29 S6 Otter Tail Lake ◎ Minnesota, N USA
29 R7 Otter Tail River ≈ Minnesota, C USA
95 H23 Otterup Fyn, C Denmark 55°31′N 10°25′E
99 H19 Ottignies Wallon Brabant, C Belgium 50°40′N 04°34′E
101 L23 Ottobrunn Bayern, SE Germany 48°02′N 11°40′E
29 X15 Ottumwa Iowa, C USA 41°00′N 92°24′W
Ōtu see Ōtsu
83 B16 Otuazuma Kunene, NW Namibia 17°52′S 13°16′E
77 V16 Oturkpo Benue, S Nigeria 07°12′N 08°06′E
193 Y15 Otu Tolu Group island group SE Tonga
182 M13 Otway, Cape headland Victoria, SE Australia 38°52′S 143°31′E
63 H24 Otway, Seno inlet S Chile
Otz see Ötz
108 L8 Ötztaler Ache ≈ W Austria
108 L9 Ötztaler Alpen It. Alpi Venoste. ▲▲ SW Austria
27 S12 Ouachita, Lake ⊠ Arkansas, C USA
27 R11 Ouachita Mountains ▲▲ Arkansas/Oklahoma, C USA
27 U13 Ouachita River ≈ Arkansas/Louisiana, C USA
Ouadaï see Ouaddaï
76 J7 Ouadâne var. Ouadane. Adrar, C Mauritania 20°57′N 11°35′W
78 K13 Ouadda Haute-Kotto, N Central African Republic 08°02′N 22°22′E
78 J10 Ouaddaï off. Préfecture du Ouaddaï, var. Ouadaï, Wadai. ⬖ prefecture SE Chad
Ouaddaï, Préfecture du see Ouaddaï
77 P13 Ouagadougou var. Wagadugu. ● (Burkina) C Burkina 12°20′N 01°32′W
77 P13 Ouagadougou ✈ C Burkina 12°21′N 01°27′W
77 O12 Ouahigouya NW Burkina 13°31′N 02°20′W
Ouahran see Oran
79 J14 Ouaka ⬖ prefecture C Central African Republic
79 J15 Ouaka ≈ S Central African Republic
Oualam see Ouallam
76 M9 Oualâta var. Oualata. Hodh ech Chargui, SE Mauritania 17°18′N 07°00′W
77 R11 Ouallam var. Oualam. Tillabéri, W Niger 14°23′N 02°09′E
172 H14 Ouanani Mohéli, S Comoros 12°19′S 93°98′E
55 Z10 Ouanary E French Guiana 04°11′N 51°40′W
78 L13 Ouanda Djallé Vakaga, NE Central African Republic 08°53′N 22°47′E
79 N14 Ouando Haut-Mbomou, SE Central African Republic 05°57′N 25°57′E
79 L15 Ouango Mbomou, S Central African Republic 04°19′N 22°30′E
77 N14 Ouangolodougou var. Wangolodougou. N Ivory Coast 09°58′N 05°09′W
172 I13 Ouani Anjouan, SE Comoros
79 M15 Ouara ≈ E Central African Republic
76 K7 Ouarâne desert C Mauritania
15 O11 Ouareau ≈ Québec, SE Canada
74 K7 Ouargla var. Wargla. NE Algeria 32°N 05°16′E
74 F8 Ouarzazate S Morocco 30°54′N 06°55′W
77 Q11 Ouatagouna Gao, E Mali 15°06′N 00°41′E
74 G6 Ouazzane var. Ouezzane, Ar. Wazan, Wazzan. N Morocco 34°52′N 05°35′W
Oubangui see Ubangi
Oubangui-Chari see Central African Republic
Oubangui-Chari, Territoire de l' see Central African Republic
Oubari, Edeyen d' see Awbāri, Idhān
98 G13 Oud-Beijerland Zuid-Holland, SW Netherlands 51°50′N 04°25′E
98 F13 Ouddorp Zuid-Holland, SW Netherlands 51°49′N 03°55′E
77 P9 Oudeïka oasis C Mali
98 G13 Oude Maas ≈ SW Netherlands
99 E18 Oudenaarde Fr. Audenarde. Oost-Vlaanderen, SW Belgium 50°50′N 03°37′E
99 H14 Oudenbosch Noord-Brabant, S Netherlands 51°35′N 04°32′E
98 P6 Oude Pekela Groningen, NE Netherlands 53°06′N 07°00′E
Ouderkerk see Ouderkerk aan den Amstel
98 I10 Ouderkerk aan den Amstel var. Ouderkerk. Noord-Holland, C Netherlands 52°18′N 04°54′E
98 I6 Oudeschild Noord-Holland, NW Netherlands 53°01′N 04°51′E
99 G14 Oude-Tonge Zuid-Holland, SW Netherlands 51°40′N 04°13′E
98 I12 Oudewater Utrecht, C Netherlands 52°02′N 04°54′E
Oudjda see Oujda
98 L5 Oudkerk Friesland, N Netherlands 53°16′N 05°52′E
102 J7 Oudon ≈ NW France
98 I9 Oudorp Noord-Holland, NW Netherlands 52°39′N 04°47′E
83 G25 Oudtshoorn Western Cape, SW South Africa 33°35′S 22°14′E
99 I16 Oud-Turnhout Antwerpen, N Belgium 51°19′N 05°01′E
74 F7 Oued-Zem C Morocco 32°53′N 06°30′W
187 P16 Ouégoa Province Nord, C New Caledonia 20°22′S 164°25′E
76 L13 Ouéléssébougou var. Ouolossébougou. Koulikoro, SW Mali 11°58′N 07°51′W
77 N16 Ouéllé E Ivory Coast 07°18′N 04°01′W
77 R16 Ouémé ≈ C Benin
77 O13 Ouessa S Burkina 11°02′N 02°44′W
102 D5 Ouessant, Île d' Eng. Ushant. island NW France
79 H17 Ouésso Sangha, NW Congo 01°38′N 16°03′E
79 D15 Ouest Eng. West. ⬖ province W Cameroon
190 G11 Ouest, Baie del' bay Îles Wallis, E Wallis and Futuna
15 Y7 Ouest, Pointe de l' headland Québec, SE Canada 48°08′N 64°57′W
Ouezzane see Ouazzane
99 K20 Ouffet Liège, E Belgium 50°30′N 05°31′E
79 H14 Ouham ⬖ prefecture NW Central African Republic
78 I13 Ouham ≈ Central African Republic/Chad
79 G14 Ouham-Pendé ⬖ prefecture W Central African Republic
77 R16 Ouidah Eng. Whydah, Wida. S Benin 06°23′N 02°08′E

◆ Country
● Country Capital
◇ Dependent Territory
○ Dependent Territory Capital
⬖ Administrative Regions
✈ International Airport
▲ Mountain
▲▲ Mountain Range
Ѫ Volcano
≈ River
◎ Lake
⊠ Reservoir

OUJDA – PAMA

74 H6 **Oujda** *Ar.* Oudjda, Ujda. NE Morocco 34°45′N 01°53′W
76 I7 **Oujeft** Adrar, C Mauritania 20°05′N 13°00′W
93 L15 **Oulainen** Oulu, C Finland 64°14′N 24°50′E
Ould Yanja *see* Ould Yenjé
76 J10 **Ould Yenjé** *var.* Ould Yanja. Guidimaka, S Mauritania 15°33′N 11°43′W
93 L14 **Oulu** *Swe.* Uleåborg. Oulu, C Finland 65°01′N 25°28′E
93 M14 **Oulu** *Swe.* Uleåborg. ◐ *province* N Finland
93 L15 **Oulujärvi** *Swe.* Uleträsk. ◎ C Finland
93 M14 **Oulujoki** *Swe.* Uleälv. ∽ C Finland
93 L14 **Oulunsalo** Oulu, C Finland 64°55′N 25°19′E
106 A8 **Oulx** Piemonte, NE Italy 45°05′N 06°41′E
78 J9 **Oum-Chalouba** Borkou-Ennedi-Tibesti, NE Chad 15°48′N 20°46′E
76 M16 **Oumé** C Ivory Coast 06°25′N 05°23′W
74 F7 **Oum er Rbia** ∽ C Morocco
78 J10 **Oum-Hadjer** Batha, E Chad 13°18′N 19°41′E
92 K10 **Ounasjoki** ∽ N Finland
78 J7 **Ounianga Kébir** Borkou-Ennedi-Tibesti, N Chad 19°06′N 20°29′E
Ouolossébougou *see* Ouéléssébougou
Oup *see* Auob
99 K19 **Oupeye** Liège, E Belgium 50°42′N 05°38′E
99 N21 **Our** ∽ NW Europe
37 Q7 **Ouray** Colorado, C USA 38°01′N 107°40′W
103 R7 **Ource** ∽ C France
104 G9 **Ourém** Santarém, C Portugal 39°40′N 08°32′W
104 H4 **Ourense** *Cast.* Orense, *Lat.* Aurium. Galicia, NW Spain 42°20′N 07°52′W
104 I4 **Ourense** *Cast.* Orense. ◐ *province* Galicia, NW Spain
59 O15 **Ouricuri** Pernambuco, E Brazil 07°51′S 40°05′W
60 J9 **Ourinhos** São Paulo, S Brazil 22°59′S 49°52′W
104 G13 **Ourique** Beja, S Portugal 37°38′N 08°13′W
59 M20 **Ouro Preto** Minas Gerais, NE Brazil 20°25′S 43°30′W
Ours, Grand Lac de l' *see* Great Bear Lake
99 K20 **Ourthe** ∽ E Belgium
165 Q9 **Ou-sanmyaku** ▲▲ Honshū, C Japan
97 M17 **Ouse** ∽ N England, United Kingdom
Ouse *see* Great Ouse
102 H7 **Oust** ∽ NW France
Outaouais *see* Ottawa
15 T4 **Outardes Quatre, Réservoir** ⊡ Québec, SE Canada
15 T5 **Outardes, Rivière aux** ∽ Québec, SE Canada
96 E8 **Outer Hebrides** *var.* Western Isles. *island group* NW Scotland, United Kingdom
30 K3 **Outer Island** *island* Apostle Islands, Wisconsin, N USA
35 S16 **Outer Santa Barbara Passage** *passage* California, SW USA
104 G3 **Outes** Galicia, NW Spain 42°50′N 08°54′W
83 C18 **Outjo** Kunene, N Namibia 20°08′S 16°08′E
11 T16 **Outlook** Saskatchewan, S Canada 51°30′N 107°03′W
93 N16 **Outokumpu** Itä-Suomi, E Finland 62°43′N 29°05′E
96 M2 **Out Skerries** *island group* NE Scotland, United Kingdom
187 Q16 **Ouvéa** *island* Îles Loyauté, NE New Caledonia
103 S14 **Ouvèze** ∽ SE France
182 L9 **Ouyen** Victoria, SE Australia 35°07′S 142°19′E
39 Q14 **Ouzinkie** Kodiak Island, Alaska, USA 57°54′N 152°27′W
137 O13 **Ovacık** Tunceli, E Turkey 39°23′N 39°13′E
106 C9 **Ovada** Piemonte, NE Italy 44°41′N 08°39′E
187 X14 **Ovalau** *island* C Fiji
62 G9 **Ovalle** Coquimbo, N Chile 30°33′S 71°16′W
83 C17 **Ovamboland** *physical region* N Namibia
54 L10 **Ovana, Cerro** ▲ S Venezuela 04°41′N 66°54′W
104 G7 **Ovar** Aveiro, N Portugal 40°52′N 08°38′W
114 L10 **Ovcharitsa, Yazovir** ⊡ SE Bulgaria
54 E6 **Ovejas** Sucre, NW Colombia 09°32′N 75°14′W
101 E16 **Overath** Nordrhein-Westfalen, W Germany 50°55′N 07°16′E
98 F13 **Overflakkee** *island* SW Netherlands
99 H19 **Overijse** Vlaams Brabant, C Belgium 50°46′N 04°32′E
98 N10 **Overijssel** ◐ *province* E Netherlands
98 M9 **Overijssels Kanaal** *canal* E Netherlands
92 K13 **Överkalix** Norrbotten, N Sweden 66°19′N 22°49′E
27 R4 **Overland Park** Kansas, C USA 38°57′N 94°41′W
99 L14 **Overloon** Noord-Brabant, SE Netherlands 51°35′N 05°54′E
99 K16 **Overpelt** Limburg, NE Belgium 51°13′N 05°24′E
35 Y10 **Overton** Nevada, W USA 36°32′N 114°25′W
25 W7 **Overton** Texas, SW USA 32°16′N 94°58′W
92 K13 **Övertorneå** Norrbotten, N Sweden 66°22′N 23°40′E
95 N18 **Överum** Kalmar, S Sweden 57°58′N 16°20′E
92 G13 **Överuman** ◎ N Sweden
117 P11 **Ovidiopol'** Odes'ka Oblast', SW Ukraine 46°15′N 30°27′E
116 M14 **Ovidiu** Constanța, SE Romania 44°16′N 28°34′E
45 N10 **Oviedo** SW Dominican Republic 17°47′N 71°22′W
104 K2 **Oviedo** *anc.* Asturias. Asturias, NW Spain 43°21′N 05°50′W
104 K2 **Oviedo** ✕ Asturias, N Spain 43°21′N 05°50′W
Ovilava *see* Wels
118 D7 **Ovišì** Ventspils, W Latvia 57°34′N 21°43′E
146 K10 **Ovminzatovo Tog'lari** *Rus.* Gory Auminzatau. ▲▲ N Uzbekistan
Övögdiy *see* Telmen
Ovoot *see* Darīganga
157 O4 **Övörhangay** ◐ *province* C Mongolia
94 E12 **Øvre Årdal** Sogn Og Fjordane, S Norway 61°18′N 07°48′E
95 J14 **Övre Fryken** ◎ C Sweden
92 J11 **Övre Soppero** *Lapp.* Badje-Sohppar. Norrbotten, N Sweden 68°07′N 21°40′E
117 N3 **Ovruch** Zhytomyrs'ka Oblast', N Ukraine 51°20′N 28°50′E
Övt *see* Bat-Öldziy
185 E24 **Owaka** Otago, South Island, New Zealand 46°27′S 169°42′E
79 H18 **Owando** *prev.* Fort Rousset. Cuvette, C Congo 0°29′S 15°55′E
164 J14 **Owase** Mie, Honshū, SW Japan 34°04′N 136°11′E
27 P9 **Owasso** Oklahoma, C USA 36°16′N 95°51′W
29 V10 **Owatonna** Minnesota, N USA 44°04′N 93°13′W
173 O4 **Owen Fracture Zone** *tectonic feature* W Arabian Sea
185 H15 **Owen, Mount** ▲ South Island, New Zealand 41°32′S 172°33′E
185 H15 **Owen River** Tasman, South Island, New Zealand 41°40′S 172°28′E
44 D8 **Owen Roberts** ✕ Grand Cayman, Cayman Islands 19°15′N 81°22′W
20 I6 **Owensboro** Kentucky, S USA 37°46′N 87°07′W
35 T11 **Owens Lake** *salt flat* California, W USA
14 F14 **Owen Sound** Ontario, S Canada 44°34′N 80°56′W
14 F13 **Owen Sound** ◎ Ontario, S Canada
35 T10 **Owens River** ∽ California, W USA
186 F9 **Owen Stanley Range** ▲▲ S Papua New Guinea
27 V5 **Owensville** Missouri, C USA 38°21′N 91°30′W
20 M4 **Owenton** Kentucky, S USA 38°33′N 84°50′W
77 U17 **Owerri** Imo, S Nigeria 05°19′N 07°07′E
184 M10 **Owhango** Manawatu-Wanganui, North Island, New Zealand 39°01′S 175°22′E
21 N5 **Owingsville** Kentucky, S USA 38°09′N 83°46′W
77 T16 **Owo** Ondo, SW Nigeria 07°10′N 05°31′E
31 R9 **Owosso** Michigan, N USA 43°00′N 84°10′W
35 V1 **Owyhee** Nevada, W USA 41°57′N 116°07′W
32 L14 **Owyhee, Lake** ◎ Oregon, NW USA
32 L15 **Owyhee River** ∽ Idaho/Oregon, NW USA
92 K1 **Öxarfjördhur** *var.* Axarfjördhur. *fjord* N Iceland
94 K12 **Oxberg** Dalarna, C Sweden 61°07′N 14°10′E
11 V17 **Oxbow** Saskatchewan, S Canada 49°16′N 102°12′W
95 O17 **Oxelösund** Södermanland, S Sweden 58°40′N 17°10′E
185 H18 **Oxford** Canterbury, South Island, New Zealand 43°18′S 172°10′E
97 M21 **Oxford** *Lat.* Oxonia. S England, United Kingdom 51°46′N 01°15′W
23 Q3 **Oxford** Alabama, S USA 33°36′N 85°50′W
22 L2 **Oxford** Mississippi, S USA 34°23′N 89°30′W
29 N16 **Oxford** Nebraska, C USA 40°15′N 99°37′W
18 I11 **Oxford** New York, NE USA 42°21′N 75°39′W
21 U8 **Oxford** North Carolina, SE USA 36°22′N 78°37′W
31 Q14 **Oxford** Ohio, N USA 39°30′N 84°45′W
18 H16 **Oxford** Pennsylvania, NE USA 39°46′N 75°57′W
11 X12 **Oxford House** Manitoba, C Canada 54°55′N 95°13′W
29 Y13 **Oxford Junction** Iowa, C USA 41°58′N 90°57′W
11 X12 **Oxford Lake** ◎ Manitoba, C Canada
97 M21 **Oxfordshire** *cultural region* S England, United Kingdom
Oxia *see* Oxyá
41 X12 **Oxkutzcab** Yucatán, SE Mexico 20°18′N 89°26′W
35 R15 **Oxnard** California, W USA 34°12′N 119°10′W
Oxonia *see* Oxford
14 I12 **Oxtongue** ∽ Ontario, SE Canada
Oxus *see* Amu Darya
115 E15 **Oxyá** *var.* Oxia. ▲ C Greece 39°46′N 21°56′E
164 L11 **Oyabe** Toyama, Honshū, SW Japan 36°42′N 136°52′E
Oyahue/Oyahue, Volcán *see* Ollagüe, Volcán
165 O12 **Oyama** Tochigi, Honshū, S Japan 36°19′N 139°46′E
47 U5 **Oyapock** ∽ E French Guiana
Oyapock *see* Oiapoque, Rio/Oyapok, Fleuve l'
55 Z10 **Oyapok, Baie de l'** *bay* Brazil/French Guiana South America W Atlantic Ocean
55 Z11 **Oyapok, Fleuve l'** *var.* Rio Oiapoque, Oyapock. ∽ Brazil/French Guiana *see also* Oiapoque, Rio
Oyapok, Fleuve l' *see* Oiapoque, Rio
79 E17 **Oyem** Woleu-Ntem, N Gabon 01°34′N 11°31′E
11 R16 **Oyen** Alberta, SW Canada 51°20′N 110°28′W
95 I15 **Øyeren** ◎ S Norway
Oygon *see* Tüdevtey
96 I7 **Oykel** ∽ N Scotland, United Kingdom
123 R9 **Oymyakon** Respublika Sakha (Yakutiya), NE Russian Federation 63°28′N 142°22′E
79 H19 **Oyo** Cuvette, C Congo 01°17′S 16°00′E
77 S15 **Oyo** Oyo, W Nigeria 07°51′N 03°57′E
77 S15 **Oyo** ◐ *state* SW Nigeria
56 D13 **Oyón** Lima, C Peru 10°39′S 76°44′W
103 S10 **Oyonnax** Ain, E France 46°16′N 05°39′E
146 L10 **Oyoqog'itma** *Rus.* Ayakagytma. Buxoro Viloyati, C Uzbekistan 40°37′N 64°26′E
146 M9 **Oyoqquduq** *Rus.* Ayakkuduk. Navoiy Viloyati, N Uzbekistan 41°16′N 65°12′E
32 F9 **Oysterville** Washington, NW USA 46°33′N 124°03′W
95 D14 **Øystese** Hordaland, S Norway 60°23′N 06°13′E
145 S16 **Oytal** Zhambyl, S Kazakhstan 42°54′N 73°21′E
147 U10 **Oy-Tal** Oshskaya Oblast', SW Kyrgyzstan 40°23′N 74°04′E
147 T10 **Oy-Tal** ∽ SW Kyrgyzstan
Oyyl *see* Uil
Ozarichi *see* Azarychy
23 R7 **Ozark** Alabama, S USA 31°27′N 85°38′W
27 S10 **Ozark** Arkansas, C USA 35°30′N 93°50′W
27 T8 **Ozark** Missouri, C USA 37°01′N 93°12′W
27 T8 **Ozark Plateau** *plain* Arkansas/Missouri, C USA
27 T6 **Ozarks, Lake of the** ⊡ Missouri, C USA
192 L10 **Ozbourn Seamount** *undersea feature* W Pacific Ocean 26°00′S 174°49′W
111 L20 **Ózd** Borsod-Abaúj-Zemplén, NE Hungary 48°15′N 20°18′E
112 D11 **Ozeblin** ▲ C Croatia 44°37′N 15°52′E
123 V11 **Ozernovskiy** Kamchatskaya Oblast', E Russian Federation 51°28′N 156°32′E
144 M7 **Ozërnoye** *var.* Ozërnyy. Kostanay, N Kazakhstan 53°29′N 63°14′E
124 J15 **Ozërnyy** Tverskaya Oblast', W Russian Federation 57°55′N 33°45′E
Ozërnyy *see* Ozërnoye
115 D18 **Ozerós, Límni** ◎ W Greece
122 G11 **Ozërsk** Chelyabinskaya Oblast', C Russian Federation 55°44′N 60°59′E
119 D14 **Ozërsk** *prev.* Darkehnen, *Ger.* Angerapp. Kaliningradskaya Oblast', W Russian Federation 54°23′N 21°59′E
126 L4 **Ozery** Moskovskaya Oblast', W Russian Federation 54°51′N 38°37′E
Özgön *see* Uzgen
107 C17 **Ozieri** Sardegna, Italy, C Mediterranean Sea 40°35′N 09°01′E
111 I15 **Ozimek** *Ger.* Malapane. Opolskie, SW Poland 50°41′N 18°16′E
127 R8 **Ozinki** Saratovskaya Oblast', W Russian Federation 51°16′N 49°45′E
25 O10 **Ozona** Texas, SW USA 30°43′N 101°13′W
Ozorkov *see* Ozorków
110 J12 **Ozorków** *Rus.* Ozorkov. Łódź, C Poland 52°00′N 19°17′E
164 F14 **Ōzu** Ehime, Shikoku, SW Japan 33°30′N 132°33′E
137 R10 **Ozurget'i** *prev.* Makharadze. W Georgia 41°57′N 42°01′E

P

99 J17 **Paal** Limburg, NE Belgium 51°03′N 05°08′E
196 M14 **Paamiut** *var.* Pâmiut, *Dan.* Frederikshåb. S Greenland 62°22′N 49°52′W
Pa-an *see* Hpa-an
101 L22 **Paar** ∽ SE Germany
83 E26 **Paarl** Western Cape, SW South Africa 33°45′S 18°58′E
93 L15 **Paavola** Oulu, C Finland 64°34′N 25°15′E
96 E8 **Pabbay** *island* NW Scotland, United Kingdom
153 T15 **Pabna** Rajshahi, W Bangladesh 24°02′N 89°15′E
109 U4 **Pabneukirchen** Oberösterreich, N Austria 48°19′N 14°49′E
118 H13 **Pabradė** *Pol.* Podbrodzie. Vilnius, SE Lithuania 54°58′N 25°03′E
56 L13 **Pacahuaras, Río** ∽ N Bolivia
Pacaraima, Sierra/Pacaraim, Serra *see* Pakaraima Mountains
56 B11 **Pacasmayo** La Libertad, W Peru 07°27′S 79°33′W
42 D6 **Pacaya, Volcán de** ⅄ S Guatemala 14°19′N 90°36′W
115 K23 **Pacheía** *var.* Pachía. *island* Kykládes, Greece, Aegean Sea
Pachía *see* Pacheía
107 L26 **Pachino** Sicilia, Italy, C Mediterranean Sea 36°43′N 15°06′E
56 F12 **Pachitea, Río** ∽ C Peru
154 I11 **Pachmarhi** Madhya Pradesh, C India 22°36′N 78°18′E
121 P3 **Páchna** *var.* Pakhna. SW Cyprus 34°47′N 32°48′E
115 H25 **Páchnes** ▲ Kríti, Greece, E Mediterranean Sea 35°19′N 24°00′E
54 F9 **Pacho** Cundinamarca, C Colombia 05°09′N 74°08′W
154 F12 **Pāchora** Mahārāshtra, C India 20°52′N 75°28′E
41 P13 **Pachuca** *var.* Pachuca de Soto. Hidalgo, C Mexico 20°05′N 98°46′W
Pachuca de Soto *see* Pachuca
27 W5 **Pacific** Missouri, C USA 38°28′N 90°44′W
192 L14 **Pacific-Antarctic Ridge** *undersea feature* S Pacific Ocean 62°00′S 157°00′W
32 F8 **Pacific Beach** Washington, NW USA 47°09′N 124°12′W
35 N10 **Pacific Grove** California, W USA 36°35′N 121°54′W
29 S15 **Pacific Junction** Iowa, C USA 41°01′N 95°48′W
192-193 **Pacific Ocean** *ocean*
129 Z10 **Pacific Plate** *tectonic feature*
113 J15 **Pačir** ▲ N Montenegro 43°19′N 19°07′E
182 L5 **Packsaddle** New South Wales, SE Australia 30°42′S 141°55′E
32 H9 **Packwood** Washington, NW USA 46°37′N 121°38′W
Padalung *see* Phatthalung
168 J12 **Padang** Sumatera, W Indonesia 01°S 100°21′E
168 L9 **Padang Endau** Pahang, Peninsular Malaysia 02°38′N 103°37′E
Padangpandjang *see* Padangpanjang
168 I11 **Padangpanjang** *prev.* Padangpandjang. Sumatera, W Indonesia 0°30′S 100°26′E
168 I10 **Padangsidempuan** *prev.* Padangsidimpoean. Sumatera, W Indonesia 01°23′N 99°15′E
Padangsidimpoean *see* Padangsidempuan
124 I9 **Padany** Respublika Kareliya, NW Russian Federation 63°18′N 33°20′E
93 M18 **Padasjoki** Etelä-Suomi, S Finland 61°20′N 25°21′E
57 M22 **Padcaya** Tarija, S Bolivia 21°52′S 64°46′W
101 H14 **Paderborn** Nordrhein-Westfalen, NW Germany 51°43′N 08°45′E
Padeșul/Padeș, Vîrful *see* Padeș, Vârful
116 F12 **Padeș, Vârful** *var.* Padeșul; *prev.* Vîrful Padeș. ▲ W Romania 45°39′N 22°19′E
112 L10 **Padinska Skela** Serbia, N Serbia 44°58′N 20°25′E
153 S14 **Padma** *var.* Ganges. ∽ Bangladesh/India *see also* Ganges
Padma *see* Brahmaputra
Padma *see* Ganges
106 H8 **Padova** *Eng.* Padua; *anc.* Patavium. Veneto, NE Italy 45°24′N 11°52′E
82 A10 **Padrão, Ponta do** *headland* NW Angola 06°06′S 12°18′E
25 T16 **Padre Island** *island* Texas, SW USA
104 G3 **Padrón** Galicia, NW Spain 42°44′N 08°40′W
118 K13 **Padsvillye** *Rus.* Podsvil'ye. Vitsyebskaya Voblasts', N Belarus 55°09′N 27°58′E
182 K11 **Padthaway** South Australia 36°39′S 140°30′E
Padua *see* Padova
20 G7 **Paducah** Kentucky, S USA 37°03′N 88°36′W
25 P4 **Paducah** Texas, SW USA 34°01′N 100°18′W
105 N15 **Padul** Andalucía, S Spain 37°02′N 03°37′W
191 P8 **Paea** Tahiti, W French Polynesia 17°41′S 149°35′W
185 L14 **Paekakariki** Wellington, North Island, New Zealand 41°00′S 174°58′E
163 X11 **Paektu-san** *var.* Baitou Shan. ▲ China/North Korea 42°00′N 128°03′E
163 V15 **Paengnyŏng-do** *island* NW South Korea
184 M7 **Paeroa** Waikato, North Island, New Zealand 37°23′S 175°39′E
54 D12 **Páez** Cauca, SW Colombia 02°37′N 76°00′W
121 O3 **Páfos** *var.* Paphos. W Cyprus 34°46′N 32°26′E
121 O3 **Páfos** ✕ SW Cyprus 34°46′N 32°25′E
83 L19 **Pafúri** Gaza, SW Mozambique 22°27′S 31°21′E
112 C12 **Pag** *It.* Pago. Lika-Senj, SW Croatia 44°26′N 15°01′E
112 B11 **Pag** *It.* Pago. *island* Zadar, C Croatia
171 P7 **Pagadian** Mindanao, S Philippines 07°47′N 123°22′E
168 J13 **Pagai Selatan, Pulau** *island* Kepulauan Mentawai, W Indonesia
168 J13 **Pagai Utara, Pulau** *island* Kepulauan Mentawai, W Indonesia
188 K4 **Pagan** *island* C Northern Mariana Islands
115 G16 **Pagasitikós Kólpos** *gulf* E Greece
36 L8 **Page** Arizona, SW USA 36°54′N 111°28′W
29 Q5 **Page** North Dakota, N USA 47°09′N 97°33′W
118 D13 **Pagėgiai** *Ger.* Pogegen. Tauragė, SW Lithuania 55°08′N 21°54′E
21 S11 **Pageland** South Carolina, SE USA 34°46′N 80°23′W
81 G16 **Pager** ∽ NE Uganda
149 Q5 **Paghmān** Kābol, E Afghanistan 34°33′N 68°55′E
Pago *see* Pag
188 C16 **Pago Bay** *bay* E Guam, W Pacific Ocean
115 M20 **Pagóndas** *var.* Pagóndhas. Sámos, Dodekánisa, Greece, Aegean Sea 37°41′N 26°50′E
Pagóndhas *see* Pagóndas
192 J16 **Pago Pago** ○ (American Samoa) Tutuila, W American Samoa 14°16′S 170°43′W
37 R8 **Pagosa Springs** Colorado, C USA 37°13′N 107°01′W
Pagqên *see* Gadê
38 H12 **Pāhala** *var.* Pahala. Hawaii, USA, C Pacific Ocean 19°12′N 155°28′W
168 K8 **Pahang** *var.* Negeri Pahang Darul Makmur. ◐ *state* Peninsular Malaysia
Pahang *see* Pahang, Sungai
168 L8 **Pahang, Sungai** *var.* Pahang, Sungei Pahang. ∽ Peninsular Malaysia
149 S8 **Pahārpur** North-West Frontier Province, NW Pakistan 32°06′N 71°00′E
185 B24 **Pahia Point** *headland* South Island, New Zealand 46°19′S 167°42′E
184 M13 **Pahiatua** Manawatu-Wanganui, North Island, New Zealand 40°30′S 175°49′E
38 H12 **Pāhoa** *var.* Pahoa. Hawaii, USA, C Pacific Ocean 19°29′N 154°56′W
23 Y14 **Pahokee** Florida, SE USA 26°49′N 80°40′W
35 X9 **Pahranagat Range** ▲▲ Nevada, W USA
35 W11 **Pahrump** Nevada, W USA 36°11′N 115°58′W
Pahsien *see* Chongqing
35 V9 **Pahute Mesa** ▲ Nevada, W USA
167 N7 **Pai** Mae Hong Son, NW Thailand 19°24′N 98°26′E
38 F10 **Pa'ia** *var.* Paia. Maui, Hawaii, USA, C Pacific Ocean 20°54′N 156°22′W
Paia *see* Pa'ia
Pai-ch'eng *see* Baicheng
118 H4 **Paide** *Ger.* Weissenstein. Järvamaa, N Estonia 58°55′N 25°36′E
97 J24 **Paignton** SW England, United Kingdom 50°26′N 03°34′W
184 K3 **Paihia** Northland, North Island, New Zealand 35°18′S 174°06′E
93 M18 **Päijänne** ◎ S Finland
114 F13 **Páïko** ▲▲ N Greece
57 M17 **Paila, Río** ∽ C Bolivia
167 Q12 **Pailin** Bătdâmbâng, W Cambodia 12°51′N 102°34′E
Pailing *see* Chun'an
54 F6 **Pailitas** Cesar, N Colombia 08°58′N 73°38′W
38 F9 **Pailolo Channel** *channel* Hawai'i, USA, C Pacific Ocean
93 K19 **Paimio** *Swe.* Pemar. Länsi-Suomi, SW Finland 60°27′N 22°42′E
165 O16 **Paimi-saki** *var.* Yaeme-saki. *headland* Iriomote-jima, SW Japan 24°18′N 123°40′E
102 G5 **Paimpol** Côtes d'Armor, NW France 48°47′N 03°03′W
168 J12 **Painan** Sumatera, W Indonesia 01°22′S 100°33′E
155 G23 **Painävu** Kerala, SW India 9°50′N 76°56′E
63 G23 **Paine, Cerro** ▲ S Chile 51°01′S 72°57′W
31 U11 **Painesville** Ohio, N USA 41°43′N 81°15′W
31 S14 **Paint Creek** ∽ Ohio, N USA
36 L10 **Painted Desert** *desert* Arizona, SW USA
Paint Hills *see* Wemindji
30 M4 **Paint River** ∽ Michigan, N USA
25 P8 **Paint Rock** Texas, SW USA 31°32′N 99°56′W
21 O6 **Paintsville** Kentucky, S USA 37°48′N 82°48′W
Paisance *see* Piacenza
96 I12 **Paisley** W Scotland, United Kingdom 55°50′N 04°26′W
32 I15 **Paisley** Oregon, NW USA 42°40′N 120°31′W
105 R10 **País Valenciano** *var.* Valencia, *Cat.* València; *anc.* Valentia. ◐ *autonomous community* NE Spain
105 O3 **País Vasco** *Basq.* Euskadi, *Eng.* The Basque Country, *Sp.* Provincias Vascongadas. ◐ *autonomous community* N Spain
56 A9 **Paita** Piura, NW Peru 05°11′S 81°09′W
169 V6 **Paitan, Teluk** *bay* Sabah, East Malaysia
104 H7 **Paiva, Rio** ∽ N Portugal
92 K12 **Pajala** Norrbotten, N Sweden 67°12′N 23°19′E
104 K3 **Pajares, Puerto de** *pass* NW Spain
54 G9 **Pajarito** Boyacá, C Colombia 05°18′N 72°43′W
54 G4 **Pajaro** La Guajira, S Colombia 11°41′N 72°37′W
Pakanbaru *see* Pekanbaru
55 Q10 **Pakaraima Mountains** *var.* Serra Pacaraim, Sierra Pacaraima. ▲▲ South America
153 S14 **Pakaur** *var.* Pakur. Jharkhand, N India 24°48′N 87°14′E
167 P10 **Pak Chong** Nakhon Ratchasima, C Thailand 14°38′N 101°22′E
123 V8 **Pakhachi** Koryakskiy Avtonomnyy Okrug, E Russian Federation 60°36′N 168°59′E
Pakhna *see* Páchna
189 U16 **Pakin Atoll** *atoll* Caroline Islands, E Micronesia
149 Q12 **Pakistan** *off.* Islamic Republic of Pakistan, *var.* Islami Jamhuriya e Pakistan. ◆ *republic* S Asia
Pakistan, Islamic Republic of *see* Pakistan
Pakistan, Islami Jamhuriya e *see* Pakistan
167 P8 **Pak Lay** *var.* Muang Pak Lay. Xaignabouli, C Laos 18°06′N 101°21′E
Pakmil *see* Samut Prakan
166 L5 **Pakokku** Magway, C Burma (Myanmar) 21°20′N 95°05′E
110 I10 **Pakość** *Ger.* Pakosch. Kujawski-pomorskie, C Poland 52°47′N 18°03′E
Pakosch *see* Pakość
149 V10 **Pākpattan** Punjab, E Pakistan 30°20′N 73°27′E
167 O15 **Pak Phanang** *var.* Ban Pak Phanang. Nakhon Si Thammarat, SW Thailand 08°20′N 100°10′E
112 G9 **Pakrac** *Hung.* Pakrácz. Požega-Slavonija, NE Croatia 45°26′N 17°09′E
Pakrácz *see* Pakrac
118 F11 **Pakruojis** Šiauliai, N Lithuania 56°N 23°51′E
111 J24 **Paks** Tolna, S Hungary 46°38′N 18°51′E
Pak Sane *see* Pakxan
Paksé *see* Pakxé
167 Q10 **Pak Thong Chai** Nakhon Ratchasima, C Thailand 14°43′N 102°01′E
149 R6 **Paktīkā** ◐ *province* SE Afghanistan
149 Q7 **Paktīā** ◐ *province* SE Afghanistan
171 N12 **Pakuli** Sulawesi, C Indonesia 01°14′S 119°55′E
Pakur *see* Pakaur
81 F17 **Pakwach** NW Uganda 02°28′N 31°28′E
167 R8 **Pakxan** *var.* Muang Pakxan, Pak Sane. Bolikhamxai, C Laos 18°27′N 103°38′E
167 S10 **Pakxé** *var.* Paksé. Champasak, S Laos 15°09′N 105°49′E
78 G12 **Pala** Mayo-Kébbi, SW Chad 09°22′N 14°54′E
61 A17 **Palacios** Santa Fe, C Argentina 30°43′S 61°37′W
25 V13 **Palacios** Texas, SW USA 28°42′N 96°13′W
105 X5 **Palafrugell** Cataluña, NE Spain 41°55′N 03°10′E
107 L24 **Palagonia** Sicilia, Italy, C Mediterranean Sea 37°20′N 14°45′E
113 E17 **Palagruža** *It.* Pelagosa. *island* SW Croatia
115 G20 **Palaiá Epídavros** Pelopónnisos, S Greece 37°38′N 23°09′E
121 P3 **Palaichóri** *var.* Palekhori. C Cyprus 34°55′N 33°06′E
115 H25 **Palaiochóra** Kríti, Greece, E Mediterranean Sea 35°14′N 23°37′E
115 A15 **Palaiolastritsa** *religious building* Kérkyra, Iónia Nisiá, Greece, C Mediterranean Sea
115 J19 **Palaiópoli** Ándros, Kykládes, Greece, Aegean Sea 37°49′N 24°49′E
103 N5 **Palaiseau** Essonne, N France 48°41′N 02°14′E
155 G21 **Palakkad** *var.* Pālghāt. Kerala, SW India 10°46′N 76°42′E *see also* Pālghāt
154 N11 **Pāla Laharha** Orissa, E India 21°25′N 85°18′E
83 G19 **Palamakoloi** Ghanzi, C Botswana 23°10′S 22°22′E
115 E16 **Palamás** Thessalía, C Greece 39°28′N 22°05′E
105 X5 **Palamós** Cataluña, NE Spain 41°51′N 03°06′E
118 J5 **Palamuse** *Ger.* Sankt-Bartholomäi. Jõgevamaa, E Estonia 58°41′N 26°35′E
183 Q14 **Palana** Tasmania, SE Australia 39°48′S 147°54′E
123 U9 **Palana** Koryakskiy Avtonomnyy Okrug, E Russian Federation 59°05′N 159°59′E
118 C11 **Palanga** *Ger.* Polangen. Klaipėda, NW Lithuania 05°54′N 21°05′E
143 V10 **Palangān, Kūh-e** ▲▲ E Iran
Palangkaraja *see* Palangkaraya
169 T12 **Palangkaraya** *prev.* Palangkaraja. Borneo, C Indonesia 02°16′S 113°55′E
155 H22 **Palani** Tamil Nādu, SE India 10°30′N 77°24′E
Palanka *see* Bačka Palanka
154 D9 **Pālanpur** Gujarāt, W India 24°12′N 72°29′E
Palantia *see* Palencia
83 I19 **Palapye** Central, SE Botswana 22°37′S 27°06′E
155 J19 **Pālār** ∽ SE India
104 H3 **Palas de Rei** Galicia, NW Spain 42°52′N 07°51′W
123 T9 **Palatka** Magadanskaya Oblast', E Russian Federation 60°09′N 150°33′E
23 W10 **Palatka** Florida, SE USA 29°39′N 81°38′W
188 B9 **Palau** *var.* Belau. ◆ *republic* W Pacific Ocean
Palau *see* Palau Islands
129 Y14 **Palau Islands** *var.* Palau. *island group* N Palau
192 G16 **Palauli Bay** *bay* Savai'i, C Samoa, C Pacific Ocean
167 N11 **Palaw** Tanintharyi, S Burma (Myanmar) 12°57′N 98°39′E
170 M6 **Palawan** *island* W Philippines
171 N6 **Palawan Passage** *passage* W Philippines
192 E7 **Palawan Trough** *undersea feature* S South China Sea 07°00′N 115°00′E
155 H23 **Pālayankottai** Tamil Nādu, SE India 08°42′N 77°46′E
107 L25 **Palazzola Acreide** *anc.* Acrae. Sicilia, Italy, C Mediterranean Sea 37°04′N 14°54′E
118 G3 **Paldiski** *prev.* Baltiski, *Eng.* Baltic Port, *Ger.* Baltischport. Harjumaa, NW Estonia 59°22′N 24°08′E
112 I13 **Pale** Republika Srpska, SE Bosnia and Herzegovina 43°49′N 18°35′E
Palekhori *see* Palaichóri
168 L13 **Palembang** Sumatera, W Indonesia 02°59′S 104°45′E
63 G18 **Palena** Los Lagos, S Chile 43°40′S 71°50′W
63 G18 **Palena, Río** ∽ S Chile
104 M5 **Palencia** *anc.* Palantia, Pallantia. Castilla-León, NW Spain 42°23′N 04°32′W
104 M3 **Palencia** ◐ *province* Castilla-León, N Spain
35 X15 **Palen Dry Lake** ◎ California, W USA
41 V15 **Palenque** Chiapas, SE Mexico 17°32′N 91°59′W
41 V15 **Palenque** *var.* Ruinas de Palenque. *ruins* Chiapas, SE Mexico
45 O9 **Palenque, Punta** *headland* S Dominican Republic 18°13′N 70°08′W
Palenque, Ruinas de *see* Palenque
Palerme *see* Palermo
107 I23 **Palermo** *Fr.* Palerme; *anc.* Panhormus, Panormus. Sicilia, Italy, C Mediterranean Sea 38°08′N 13°23′E
25 V8 **Palestine** Texas, SW USA 31°45′N 95°39′W
25 V7 **Palestine, Lake** ◎ Texas, SW USA
107 I15 **Palestrina** Lazio, C Italy 41°49′N 12°53′E
166 K5 **Paletwa** Chin State, W Burma (Myanmar) 21°25′N 92°49′E
155 G21 **Pālghāt** *var.* Palakkad. Kerala, SW India 10°46′N 76°42′E *see also* Palakkad
152 F13 **Pāli** Rājasthān, N India 25°48′N 73°21′E
167 N16 **Palian** Trang, SW Thailand 07°11′N 99°40′E
189 O12 **Palikir** ● (Micronesia) Pohnpei, E Micronesia 06°58′N 158°13′E
Palimé *see* Kpalimé
107 L19 **Palinuro, Capo** *headland* S Italy 40°02′N 15°16′E
115 H15 **Palioúri, Akrotírio** *var.* Akrotírio Kanestron. *headland* N Greece 39°55′N 23°45′E
33 R14 **Palisades Reservoir** ⊡ Idaho, NW USA
99 J23 **Paliseul** Luxembourg, SE Belgium 49°55′N 05°09′E
154 C11 **Pālitāna** Gujarāt, W India 21°30′N 71°50′E
118 F4 **Palivere** Läänemaa, W Estonia 58°59′N 23°58′E
41 V14 **Palizada** Campeche, SE Mexico 18°15′N 92°03′W
93 L18 **Pälkäne** Länsi-Suomi, W Finland 61°22′N 24°16′E
155 J22 **Palk Strait** *strait* India/Sri Lanka
155 J23 **Pallai** Northern Province, NW Sri Lanka 09°35′N 80°20′E
Pallantia *see* Palencia
106 C6 **Pallanza** Piemonte, NE Italy 45°57′N 08°32′E
127 Q9 **Pallasovka** Volgogradskaya Oblast', SW Russian Federation 50°06′N 46°52′E
Pallene/Pallíni *see* Kassándra
185 L15 **Palliser Bay** *bay* North Island, New Zealand
185 L15 **Palliser, Cape** *headland* North Island, New Zealand 41°37′S 175°16′E
191 U9 **Palliser, Îles** *island group* Îles Tuamotu, C French Polynesia
82 Q12 **Palma** Cabo Delgado, N Mozambique 10°46′S 40°30′E
105 X9 **Palma** *var.* Palma de Mallorca. Mallorca, Spain, W Mediterranean Sea 39°35′N 02°39′E
105 X9 **Palma** ✕ Mallorca, Spain, W Mediterranean Sea
105 X10 **Palma, Badia de** *bay* Mallorca, Spain, W Mediterranean Sea
104 L13 **Palma del Río** Andalucía, S Spain 37°42′N 05°16′W
Palma de Mallorca *see* Palma
107 J25 **Palma di Montechiaro** Sicilia, Italy, C Mediterranean Sea 37°12′N 13°46′E
106 J7 **Palmanova** Friuli-Venezia Giulia, NE Italy 45°54′N 13°20′E
54 J7 **Palmarito** Apure, C Venezuela 07°36′N 70°08′W
43 N15 **Palmar Sur** Puntarenas, SE Costa Rica 08°54′N 83°27′W
60 I12 **Palmas** Paraná, S Brazil 26°29′S 52°00′W
59 K16 **Palmas** *var.* Palmas do Tocantins. Tocantins, C Brazil 10°24′S 48°19′W
76 L18 **Palmas, Cape** *Fr.* Cap des Palmès. *headland* SW Ivory Coast 04°18′N 07°31′W
Palmas do Tocantins *see* Palmas
54 D11 **Palmaseca** ✕ (Cali) Valle del Cauca, SW Colombia 03°31′N 76°27′W
107 B21 **Palmas, Golfo di** *gulf* Sardegna, Italy, C Mediterranean Sea
44 I7 **Palma Soriano** Santiago de Cuba, E Cuba 20°10′N 76°00′W
23 Y12 **Palm Bay** Florida, SE USA 28°01′N 80°35′W
35 T14 **Palmdale** California, W USA 34°34′N 118°07′W
61 H14 **Palmeira das Missões** Rio Grande do Sul, S Brazil 27°54′S 53°20′W
82 A11 **Palmeirinhas, Ponta das** *headland* NW Angola 09°04′S 13°02′E
39 R11 **Palmer** Alaska, USA 61°36′N 149°06′W
19 N11 **Palmer** Massachusetts, NE USA 42°09′N 72°19′W
25 U7 **Palmer** Texas, SW USA 32°25′N 96°40′W
194 H4 **Palmer** *US research station* Antarctica 64°37′S 64°01′W
15 R11 **Palmer** ∽ Québec, SE Canada
37 T5 **Palmer Lake** Colorado, C USA 39°07′N 104°55′W
194 J6 **Palmer Land** *physical region* Antarctica
14 F15 **Palmerston** Ontario, SE Canada 43°51′N 80°49′W
185 F22 **Palmerston** Otago, South Island, New Zealand 45°27′S 170°42′E
190 K15 **Palmerston** *island* S Cook Islands
Palmerston *see* Darwin
184 M12 **Palmerston North** Manawatu-Wanganui, North Island, New Zealand 40°20′S 175°52′E
23 V13 **Palmetto** Florida, SE USA 27°31′N 82°34′W
The Palmetto State *see* South Carolina
107 M22 **Palmi** Calabria, SW Italy 38°21′N 15°51′E
54 D11 **Palmira** Valle del Cauca, W Colombia 03°33′N 76°17′W
56 F8 **Palmira, Río** ∽ N Peru
61 D19 **Palmitas** Soriano, SW Uruguay 33°27′S 57°48′W
Palmnicken *see* Yantarnyy
35 V15 **Palm Springs** California, W USA 33°48′N 116°33′W
27 V2 **Palmyra** Missouri, C USA 39°48′N 91°31′W
18 G10 **Palmyra** New York, NE USA 43°02′N 77°13′W
18 G15 **Palmyra** Pennsylvania, NE USA 40°18′N 76°35′W
21 V5 **Palmyra** Virginia, NE USA 37°53′N 78°17′W
Palmyra *see* Tudmur
192 L7 **Palmyra Atoll** ◇ *US privately owned unincorporated territory* C Pacific Ocean
154 P12 **Palmyras Point** *headland* E India 20°46′N 87°00′E
35 N9 **Palo Alto** California, W USA 37°26′N 122°08′W
25 O1 **Palo Duro Creek** ∽ Texas, SW USA
Paloe *see* Denpasar, Bali, C Indonesia
Paloe *see* Palu
168 L9 **Paloh** Johor, Peninsular Malaysia 02°10′N 103°11′E
80 F12 **Paloich** Upper Nile, SE Sudan 10°29′N 32°31′E
40 I3 **Palomas** Chihuahua, N Mexico 31°45′N 107°38′W
107 I15 **Palombara Sabina** Lazio, C Italy 42°04′N 12°45′E
105 S13 **Palos, Cabo de** *headland* SE Spain 37°38′N 00°42′W
104 I14 **Palos de la Frontera** Andalucía, S Spain 37°14′N 06°53′W
60 G11 **Palotina** Paraná, S Brazil 24°16′S 53°49′W
32 M9 **Palouse** Washington, NW USA 46°54′N 117°04′W
32 L9 **Palouse River** ∽ Washington, NW USA
35 Y16 **Palo Verde** California, W USA 33°25′N 114°43′W
57 E16 **Palpa** Ica, W Peru 14°35′S 75°09′W
95 M16 **Pålsboda** Örebro, C Sweden 59°04′N 15°21′E
93 M15 **Paltamo** Oulu, C Finland 64°25′N 27°50′E
171 N12 **Palu** *prev.* Paloe. Sulawesi, C Indonesia 0°54′S 119°52′E
137 P14 **Palu** Elazığ, E Turkey 38°43′N 39°56′E
152 I11 **Palwal** Haryāna, N India 28°15′N 77°18′E
123 U6 **Palyavaam** ∽ NE Russian Federation
77 Q13 **Pama** SE Burkina 11°13′N 00°46′E

◆ Country
● Country Capital
◇ Dependent Territory
○ Dependent Territory Capital
◐ Administrative Regions
✕ International Airport
▲ Mountain
▲▲ Mountain Range
⅄ Volcano
∽ River
◎ Lake
⊡ Reservoir

PAMANDZI – PATHĀNKOT

172 J14 **Pamandzi** ✈ (Mamoudzou) Petite-Terre, E Mayotte
Pamangkat see Pemangkat
143 R11 **Pā Mazār** Kermān, C Iran
83 N19 **Pambarra** Inhambane, SE Mozambique 21°57′S 35°06′E
171 X12 **Pamdai** Papua, E Indonesia 01°58′S 137°19′E
103 N16 **Pamiers** Ariège, S France 43°07′N 01°37′E
147 T14 **Pamir** var. Daryā-ye Pāmīr, Taj. Dar"yoi Pomir. ≈ Afghanistan/Tajikistan see also Pāmīr, Daryā-ye
Pamir see Pāmīr, Daryā-ye
149 U1 **Pāmīr, Daryā-ye** var. Pamir, Taj. Dar"yoi Pomir. ≈ Afghanistan/Tajikistan see also Pamir
Pāmīr, Daryā-ye see Pamir
Pāmīr-e Khord see Little Pamir
Pamir/Pāmīr, Daryā-ye see Pamirs
129 Q8 **Pamirs** Pash. Daryā-ye Pāmīr, Rus. Pamir. ▲▲ C Asia
Pâmiut see Paamiut
21 X10 **Pamlico River** ≈ North Carolina, SE USA
21 Y10 **Pamlico Sound** sound North Carolina, SE USA
25 O2 **Pampa** Texas, SW USA 35°32′N 100°58′W
Pampa Aullagas, Lago see Poopó, Lago
61 B21 **Pampa Húmeda** grassland E Argentina
56 A10 **Pampa las Salinas** salt lake NW Peru
57 F15 **Pampas** Huancavelica, C Peru 12°22′S 74°53′W
62 K13 **Pampas** plain C Argentina
55 O4 **Pampatar** Nueva Esparta, NE Venezuela 11°03′N 63°51′W
Pampeluna see Pamplona
104 H8 **Pampilhosa da Serra** var. Pampilhosa de Serra. Coimbra, N Portugal 40°03′N 07°58′W
173 Y15 **Pamplemousses** N Mauritius 20°06′S 57°34′E
54 G7 **Pamplona** Norte de Santander, N Colombia 07°24′N 72°38′W
105 Q3 **Pamplona** Basq. Iruña, prev. Pampeluna; anc. Pompaelo. Navarra, N Spain 42°49′N 01°39′W
114 I11 **Pamporovo** prev. Vasil Kolarov. Smolyan, S Bulgaria 41°39′N 24°45′E
136 D15 **Pamukkale** Denizli, W Turkey 37°51′N 29°13′E
21 W5 **Pamunkey River** ≈ Virginia, NE USA
152 K5 **Pamzal** Jammu and Kashmir, NW India 34°17′N 78°50′E
30 L14 **Pana** Illinois, N USA 39°23′N 89°04′W
41 Y11 **Panabá** Yucatán, SE Mexico 21°20′N 88°16′W
35 Y8 **Panaca** Nevada, W USA 37°47′N 114°24′W
115 E19 **Panachaikó** ▲▲ S Greece
14 F11 **Panache Lake** ◎ Ontario, S Canada
114 I10 **Panagyurishte** Pazardzhik, C Bulgaria 42°30′N 24°11′E
168 M16 **Panaitan, Pulau** island S Indonesia
115 D18 **Panaitolikó** ▲▲ C Greece
155 E17 **Panaji** var. Pangim, Panjim, New Goa. state capital Goa, W India 15°31′N 73°52′E
43 T15 **Panamá** var. Ciudad de Panama, Eng. Panama City. ● (Panama) Panamá, C Panama 08°57′N 79°33′W
43 T14 **Panama** off. Republic of Panama. ◆ republic Central America
43 U14 **Panamá** off. Provincia de Panamá. ◈ province E Panama
43 U15 **Panamá, Bahía de** bay N Gulf of Panama
193 T7 **Panama Basin** undersea feature E Pacific Ocean 05°00′N 83°30′W
43 T15 **Panama Canal** canal E Panama
23 R9 **Panama City** Florida, SE USA 30°09′N 85°39′W
43 T14 **Panama City** ✈ Panamá, C Panama 09°02′N 79°24′W
Panama City see Panamá
23 Q9 **Panama City Beach** Florida, SE USA 30°10′N 85°48′W
43 T17 **Panamá, Golfo de** var. Gulf of Panama. gulf S Panama
Panama, Gulf of see Panamá, Golfo de
Panama, Isthmus of see Panama, Istmo de
43 T15 **Panama, Istmo de** Eng. Isthmus of Panama; prev. Isthmus of Darien. isthmus E Panama
Panamá, Provincia de see Panamá
Panama, Republic of see Panama
35 U11 **Panamint Range** ▲▲ California, W USA
107 L22 **Panarea, Isola** island Isole Eolie, S Italy
106 G9 **Panaro** ≈ N Italy
171 P5 **Panay Island** island C Philippines
35 W7 **Pancake Range** ▲▲ Nevada, W USA
112 M11 **Pančevo** Ger. Pantschowa, Hung. Pancsova. Vojvodina, N Serbia 44°53′N 20°40′E
113 M15 **Pančićev Vrh** ▲ SW Serbia 43°16′N 20°49′E
116 L12 **Panciu** Vrancea, E Romania 45°54′N 27°08′E
116 F10 **Pâncota** Hung. Pankota; prev. Pîncota. Arad, W Romania 46°20′N 21°45′E
Pancsova see Pančevo
83 N20 **Panda** Inhambane, SE Mozambique 24°02′S 34°45′E
171 X12 **Pandaidori, Kepulauan** island group E Indonesia
25 N11 **Pandale** Texas, SW USA 30°09′N 101°34′W
169 P12 **Pandang Tikar, Pulau** island N Indonesia
61 F20 **Pan de Azúcar** Maldonado, S Uruguay 34°45′S 55°14′W
118 H11 **Pandėlys** Panevėžys, NE Lithuania 56°04′N 25°18′E
155 F15 **Pandharpur** Mahārāshtra, W India 17°42′N 75°24′E
182 J1 **Pandie Pandie** South Australia 26°06′S 139°26′E
171 O12 **Pandiri** Sulawesi, C Indonesia 01°32′S 120°47′E
61 F20 **Pando** Canelones, S Uruguay 34°44′S 55°58′W
57 J14 **Pando** ◈ department N Bolivia
192 K9 **Pandora Bank** undersea feature W Pacific Ocean
95 G20 **Pandrup** Nordjylland, N Denmark 57°14′N 09°42′E
79 J15 **Pandu** Equateur, NW Dem. Rep. Congo 05°03′N 19°14′E
153 V12 **Pandu** Assam, NE India 26°08′N 91°37′E
Paneas see Bāniyās
59 F15 **Panelas** Mato Grosso, W Brazil 09°06′S 60°41′W
118 G12 **Panevėžys** Panevėžys, C Lithuania 55°44′N 24°21′E
118 G11 **Panevėžys** ◈ province NW Lithuania
Panfilov see Zharkent
127 N9 **Panfilovo** Volgogradskaya Oblast', SW Russian Federation 50°25′N 42°55′E
79 N17 **Panga** Orientale, N Dem. Rep. Congo 01°52′N 26°18′E
193 Y15 **Pangai** Lifuka, C Tonga 19°50′S 174°23′W
114 H13 **Pangaío** ▲▲ N Greece
79 G20 **Pangala** Pool, S Congo 03°26′S 14°38′E
81 J22 **Pangani** Tanga, E Tanzania 05°27′S 39°00′E
81 I21 **Pangani** ≈ NE Tanzania
186 K8 **Panggoe** Choiseul Island, NW Solomon Islands 07°00′S 157°05′E
79 N20 **Pangi** Maniema, E Dem. Rep. Congo 03°12′S 26°39′E
Pangim see Panaji
168 H8 **Pangkalanbrandan** Sumatera, W Indonesia 04°00′N 98°15′E
Pangkalanbun see Pangkalanbuun
169 R13 **Pangkalanbuun** var. Pangkalanbun. Borneo, C Indonesia 02°43′S 111°38′E
169 N12 **Pangkalpinang** Pulau Bangka, W Indonesia 02°05′S 106°09′E
11 U17 **Pangman** Saskatchewan, S Canada 49°37′N 104°33′W
Pang-Nga see Phang-Nga
9 S6 **Pangnirtung** Baffin Island, Nunavut, NE Canada 66°05′N 65°45′W
152 K6 **Pangong Tso** var. Bangong Co. ◎ China/India see also Bangong Co
Pangong Tso see Banggong Co
36 K7 **Panguitch** Utah, W USA 37°49′N 112°26′W
186 J7 **Panguna** Bougainville Island, NE Papua New Guinea 06°22′S 155°20′E
171 N8 **Pangutaran Group** island group Sulu Archipelago, SW Philippines
25 N2 **Panhandle** Texas, SW USA 35°21′N 101°24′W
Panhormus see Palermo
171 W14 **Paniai, Danau** ◎ Papua, E Indonesia
79 L21 **Pania-Mutombo** Kasai-Oriental, C Dem. Rep. Congo 05°09′S 23°49′E
187 P16 **Panié, Mont** ▲ C New Caledonia 20°33′S 164°41′E
Panikoilli see Jājapur
152 I10 **Pānīpat** Haryāna, N India 29°18′N 77°00′E
147 Q14 **Panj** Rus. Pyandzh; prev. Kirovabad. SW Tajikistan 37°39′N 69°55′E
147 P15 **Panj** Rus. Pyandzh. ≈ Afghanistan/Tajikistan
149 O5 **Panjāb** Bāmīān, C Afghanistan 34°21′N 67°00′E
147 O12 **Panjakent** Rus. Pendzhikent. W Tajikistan 39°28′N 67°33′E
148 L14 **Panjgūr** Baluchistān, SW Pakistan 26°58′N 64°05′E
Panjim see Panaji
163 U12 **Panjin** Liaoning, NE China 41°11′N 122°05′E
147 P14 **Panji Poyon** Rus. Nizhniy Pyandzh. SW Tajikistan 37°14′N 68°32′E
149 S4 **Panjshīr** ◈ province NE Afghanistan
149 Q4 **Panjshīr** ≈ E Afghanistan
Pankota see Pâncota
77 W14 **Pankshin** Plateau, C Nigeria 09°21′N 09°27′E
163 Y10 **Pan Ling** ▲▲ N China
Panlong Jiang see Lô, Sông
154 J9 **Panna** Madhya Pradesh, C India 24°43′N 80°11′E
99 M16 **Panningen** Limburg, SE Netherlands 51°20′N 05°59′E
149 R13 **Pāno Āqil** Sind, SE Pakistan 27°55′N 69°18′E
121 P3 **Páno Léfkara** S Cyprus 34°52′N 33°18′E
121 O3 **Páno Panagiá** var. Pano Panayia. W Cyprus 34°55′N 32°38′E
Pano Panayia see Páno Panagiá
Panopolis see Akhmīm
29 U14 **Panora** Iowa, C USA 41°41′N 94°21′W
60 I8 **Panorama** São Paulo, S Brazil 21°22′S 51°51′W
115 I24 **Pánormos** Kríti, Greece, E Mediterranean Sea 35°24′N 24°42′E
Panormus see Palermo
163 W11 **Panshi** Jilin, NE China 42°56′N 126°02′E
59 H19 **Pantanal** var. Pantanalmato-Grossense. swamp SW Brazil
Pantanalmato-Grossense see Pantanal
61 H16 **Pântano Grande** Rio Grande do Sul, S Brazil 30°12′S 52°24′W
171 Q16 **Pantar, Pulau** island Kepulauan Alor, S Indonesia
21 X9 **Pantego** North Carolina, SE USA 35°34′N 76°39′E
107 G25 **Pantelleria** anc. Cossyra, Cosyra. Sicilia, Italy, C Mediterranean Sea 36°47′N 12°00′E
107 G25 **Pantelleria, Isola di** island SW Italy
Pante Makasar/Pante Macassar/Pante Makassar see Ponte Macassar
152 K10 **Pantnagar** Uttarakhand, N India 29°00′N 79°28′E
115 A15 **Pantokrátoras** ▲ Kérkyra, Iónia Nisiá, Greece, C Mediterranean Sea 39°45′N 19°51′E
Pantschowa see Pančevo
41 P11 **Pánuco** Veracruz-Llave, E Mexico 22°01′N 98°13′W
41 P11 **Pánuco, Río** ≈ C Mexico
160 I12 **Panxian** Guizhou, S China 25°45′N 104°39′E
168 I10 **Panyabungan** Sumatera, N Indonesia 0°55′N 99°30′E
77 W14 **Panyam** Plateau, C Nigeria 09°28′N 09°13′E
157 N13 **Panzhihua** prev. Dukou, Tu-k'ou. Sichuan, C China 26°35′N 101°41′E
79 I22 **Panzi** Bandundu, SW Dem. Rep. Congo 07°10′S 17°55′E
42 E5 **Panzós** Alta Verapaz, E Guatemala 15°21′N 89°40′W
Pao-chi/Paoki see Baoji
Pao-king see Shaoyang
107 N20 **Paola** Calabria, SW Italy 39°21′N 16°03′E
121 P16 **Paola** E Malta 35°52′N 14°30′E
27 R5 **Paola** Kansas, C USA 38°34′N 94°54′W
31 O15 **Paoli** Indiana, N USA 38°35′N 86°25′W
187 R14 **Paonangisu** Éfaté, C Vanuatu 17°33′S 168°23′E
171 S13 **Paoni** var. Pauni. Pulau Seram, E Indonesia 02°48′S 129°03′E
37 Q5 **Paonia** Colorado, C USA 38°52′N 107°35′W
191 O7 **Paopao** Moorea, W French Polynesia 17°28′S 149°48′W
Pao-shan see Baoshan
Pao-ting see Baoding
Pao-t'ou/Paotow see Baotou
79 H14 **Paoua** Ouham-Pendé, W Central African Republic 07°22′N 16°25′E
Pap see Pop
111 H23 **Pápa** Veszprém, W Hungary 47°20′N 17°29′E
42 J12 **Papagayo, Golfo de** gulf NW Costa Rica
38 H11 **Pāpa'ikou** var. Papaikou. Hawaii, USA, C Pacific Ocean 19°45′N 155°06′W
41 R15 **Papaloapan, Río** ≈ S Mexico
184 L6 **Papakura** Auckland, North Island, New Zealand 37°03′S 174°57′E
41 Q13 **Papantla** var. Papantla de Olarte. Veracruz-Llave, E Mexico 20°30′N 97°21′W
Papantla de Olarte see Papantla
191 P8 **Papara** Tahiti, W French Polynesia 17°45′S 149°33′W
184 K4 **Paparoa** Northland, North Island, New Zealand 36°06′S 174°12′E
185 G16 **Paparoa Range** ▲▲ South Island, New Zealand
115 K20 **Pápas, Akrotírio** headland Ikaría, Dodekánisa, Greece, Aegean Sea 37°31′N 25°58′E
96 L2 **Papa Stour** island NE Scotland, United Kingdom
184 L6 **Papatoetoe** Auckland, North Island, New Zealand 36°58′S 174°52′E
185 E25 **Papatowai** Otago, South Island, New Zealand 46°33′S 169°33′E
96 K4 **Papa Westray** island NE Scotland, United Kingdom
191 T10 **Papeete** ○ (French Polynesia) Tahiti, W French Polynesia 17°32′S 149°34′W
100 F11 **Papenburg** Niedersachsen, NW Germany 53°04′N 07°24′E
98 H13 **Papendrecht** Zuid-Holland, SW Netherlands 51°50′N 04°42′E
191 Q7 **Papenoo** Tahiti, W French Polynesia 17°29′S 149°25′W
191 Q7 **Papenoo Rivière** ≈ Tahiti, W French Polynesia
191 N7 **Papetoai** Moorea, W French Polynesia 17°29′S 149°52′W
92 L3 **Papey** island E Iceland
Paphos see Páfos
40 H5 **Papigochic, Río** ≈ NW Mexico
118 E10 **Papilė** Šiaulai, NW Lithuania 56°08′N 22°51′E
29 S15 **Papillion** Nebraska, C USA 41°09′N 96°02′W
15 T5 **Papinachois** ≈ Québec, SE Canada
171 X13 **Papua** var. Irian Barat, West Irian, West New Guinea, West Papua; prev. Dutch New Guinea, Irian Jaya, Netherlands New Guinea. ◈ province E Indonesia
Papua and New Guinea, Territory of see Papua New Guinea
186 C9 **Papua, Gulf of** gulf S Papua New Guinea
186 C8 **Papua New Guinea** off. Independent State of Papua New Guinea; prev. Territory of Papua and New Guinea. ◆ commonwealth republic NW Melanesia
Papua New Guinea, Independent State of see Papua New Guinea
192 H8 **Papua Plateau** undersea feature N Coral Sea
112 G9 **Papuk** ▲▲ NE Croatia
167 N8 **Papun** Kayin State, S Burma (Myanmar) 18°05′N 97°26′E
42 L14 **Paquera** Puntarenas, W Costa Rica 09°52′N 84°56′W
58 I13 **Pará** off. Estado do Pará. ◈ state NE Brazil
55 V9 **Para** ◈ district N Surinam
Pará see Belém
180 I8 **Paraburdoo** Western Australia 23°07′S 117°40′E
57 E16 **Paracas, Península de** peninsula W Peru
59 L19 **Paracatu** Minas Gerais, NE Brazil 17°14′S 46°52′W
192 E6 **Paracel Islands** ◇ disputed territory SE Asia
182 I6 **Parachilna** South Australia 31°09′S 138°23′E
149 R6 **Pārachinār** North-West Frontier Province, NW Pakistan 33°56′N 70°04′E
112 N13 **Paraćin** Serbia, C Serbia 43°51′N 21°25′E
14 K8 **Paradis** Québec, SE Canada 48°13′N 76°36′W
39 N11 **Paradise** var. Paradise Hill. Alaska, USA 62°28′N 160°09′W
35 O5 **Paradise** California, W USA 39°42′N 121°39′W
35 X11 **Paradise** Nevada, W USA 36°05′N 115°10′W
Paradise Hill see Paradise
37 R11 **Paradise Hills** New Mexico, SW USA 35°12′N 106°42′W
Paradise of the Pacific see Hawai'i
36 L13 **Paradise Valley** Arizona, SW USA 33°31′N 111°56′W
35 T2 **Paradise Valley** Nevada, W USA 41°30′N 117°30′W
115 O22 **Paradisi** ✈ (Ródos) Ródos, Dodekánisa, Greece, Aegean Sea 36°24′N 28°08′E
154 P12 **Pārādwīp** Orissa, E India 20°17′N 86°42′E
Pará, Estado do see Pará
Paraetonium see Mersá Maṭrûḥ
117 R4 **Parafiyivka** Chernihivs'ka Oblast', N Ukraine 50°53′N 32°40′E
36 K7 **Paragonah** Utah, W USA 37°53′N 112°46′W
27 X9 **Paragould** Arkansas, C USA 36°02′N 90°30′W
47 X8 **Paraguaçu** var. Paraguassú. ≈ E Brazil
60 J9 **Paraguaçu Paulista** São Paulo, S Brazil 22°22′S 50°35′W
54 H4 **Paraguaipoa** Zulia, NW Venezuela 11°21′N 71°58′W
62 O6 **Paraguarí** Paraguarí, S Paraguay 25°36′S 57°06′W
62 O7 **Paraguarí** off. Departamento de Paraguarí. ◈ department S Paraguay
Paraguarí, Departamento de see Paraguarí
57 O16 **Paraguá, Río** ≈ NE Bolivia
55 O8 **Paragua, Río** ≈ SE Venezuela
Paraguassú see Paraguaçu
62 N5 **Paraguay** ◆ republic C South America
47 U10 **Paraguay** var. Río Paraguay. ≈ C South America
Paraguay, Río see Paraguay
Parahiba/Parahyba see Paraíba
59 P15 **Paraíba** off. Estado da Paraíba; prev. Parahiba, Parahyba. ◈ state E Brazil
Paraíba see João Pessoa
60 P9 **Paraíba do Sul, Rio** ≈ SE Brazil
Paraíba, Estado da see Paraíba
Parainen see Pargas
43 N14 **Paraíso** Cartago, C Costa Rica 09°51′N 83°50′W
41 U14 **Paraíso** Tabasco, SE Mexico 18°26′N 93°10′W
57 O17 **Paraiso, Río** ≈ E Bolivia
Parajd see Praid
77 S14 **Parakou** C Benin 09°23′N 02°40′E
115 F20 **Paralía Tyrou** Pelopónnisos, S Greece 37°17′N 22°50′E
121 Q2 **Paralímni** E Cyprus 35°02′N 34°00′E
115 G18 **Paralímni, Límni** ◎ C Greece
55 W8 **Paramaribo** ● (Surinam) Paramaribo, N Surinam 05°52′N 55°14′W
55 W9 **Paramaribo** ◈ district N Surinam
55 W9 **Paramaribo** ✈ Paramaribo, N Surinam 05°52′N 55°14′W
Paramithiá see Paramythiá
56 C13 **Paramonga** Lima, W Peru 10°42′S 77°50′W
123 V12 **Paramushir, Ostrov** island SE Russian Federation
115 C16 **Paramythiá** var. Paramithiá. Ípeiros, W Greece 39°28′N 20°31′E
62 M10 **Paraná** Entre Ríos, E Argentina 31°48′S 60°29′W
60 H11 **Paraná** off. Estado do Paraná. ◈ state S Brazil
47 U11 **Paraná** var. Alto Paraná. ≈ C South America
Paraná, Estado do see Paraná
60 K12 **Paranaguá** Paraná, S Brazil 25°32′S 48°36′W
59 J20 **Paranaíba, Rio** ≈ E Brazil
61 C19 **Paraná Ibicuy, Río** ≈ E Argentina
59 H15 **Paranaíta** Mato Grosso, W Brazil 09°35′S 57°01′W
60 H9 **Paranapanema, Rio** ≈ S Brazil
60 K11 **Paranapiacaba, Serra do** ▲▲ S Brazil
60 H9 **Paranavaí** Paraná, S Brazil 23°02′S 52°36′W
143 N5 **Parandak** Markazī, W Iran 35°19′N 50°40′E
114 I12 **Paranésti** var. Paranestio. Anatolikí Makedonía kai Thráki, NE Greece 41°16′N 24°31′E
Paranestio see Paranésti
191 W11 **Paraoa** atoll Îles Tuamotu, C French Polynesia
184 L13 **Paraparaumu** Wellington, North Island, New Zealand 40°55′S 175°01′E
57 N20 **Parapetí, Río** ≈ SE Bolivia
54 L10 **Paraque, Cerro** ▲ W Venezuela 06°00′S 67°00′W
154 I11 **Parāsiya** Madhya Pradesh, C India 22°11′N 78°50′E
115 M23 **Paraspóri, Akrotírio** headland Kárpathos, SE Greece 35°54′N 27°15′E
60 O10 **Parati** Rio de Janeiro, SE Brazil 23°15′S 44°42′W
59 K14 **Parauapebas** Pará, N Brazil 06°03′S 49°48′W
103 Q10 **Paray-le-Monial** Saône-et-Loire, C France 46°27′N 04°07′E
Parbatsar see Parvatsar
154 G13 **Parbhani** Mahārāshtra, C India 19°16′N 76°51′E
100 L10 **Parchim** Mecklenburg-Vorpommern, N Germany 53°26′N 11°51′E
Parchwitz see Prochowice
110 P13 **Parczew** Lubelskie, E Poland 51°40′N 23°E
60 L8 **Pardo, Rio** ≈ S Brazil
111 E16 **Pardubice** Ger. Pardubitz. Pardubický Kraj, C Czech Republic 50°01′N 15°47′E
111 E17 **Pardubický Kraj** ◈ region N Czech Republic
Pardubitz see Pardubice
119 F16 **Parechcha** Pol. Porzecze, Rus. Porech'ye. Hrodzyenskaya Voblasts', W Belarus 53°53′N 24°08′E
59 F17 **Parecis, Chapada dos** var. Serra dos Parecis. ▲▲ W Brazil
Parecis, Serra dos see Parecis, Chapada dos
104 M4 **Paredes de Nava** Castilla-León, N Spain 42°09′N 04°42′W
189 U12 **Parem** island Chuuk, C Micronesia
189 O12 **Parem Island** island E Micronesia
184 I1 **Parengarenga Harbour** inlet North Island, New Zealand
15 N8 **Parent** Québec, SE Canada 47°55′N 74°36′W
102 J14 **Parentis-en-Born** Landes, SW France 44°22′N 01°04′W
Parenzo see Poreč
185 G20 **Pareora** Canterbury, South Island, New Zealand 44°28′S 171°12′E
171 N14 **Parepare** Sulawesi, C Indonesia 04°S 119°40′E
115 B16 **Párga** Ípeiros, W Greece 39°18′N 20°19′E
93 K20 **Pargas** Swe. Parainen. Länsi-Suomi, SW Finland 60°18′N 22°20′E
64 O5 **Pargo, Ponta do** headland Madeira, Portugal, NE Atlantic Ocean 32°48′N 17°17′W
Paria, Golfo de see Paria, Gulf of
55 N6 **Pariaguán** Anzoátegui, NE Venezuela 08°51′N 64°43′W
45 X17 **Paria, Gulf of** var. Golfo de Paria. gulf Trinidad and Tobago/Venezuela
57 I15 **Pariamanu, Río** ≈ E Peru
36 L8 **Paria River** ≈ Utah, W USA
Parichi see Parychy
40 M14 **Paricutín, Volcán** ⛰ C Mexico 19°25′N 102°20′W
43 P16 **Parida, Isla** island SW Panama
55 T8 **Parika** NE Guyana 06°51′N 58°25′W
93 O18 **Parikkala** Etelä-Suomi, SE Finland 61°33′N 29°34′E
58 E10 **Parima, Serra** var. Sierra Parima. ▲ Brazil/Venezuela see also Parima, Sierra
55 N11 **Parima, Sierra** var. Serra Parima. ▲ Brazil/Venezuela see also Parima, Serra
57 F17 **Parinacochas, Laguna** ◎ SW Peru
56 A9 **Pariñas, Punta** headland NW Peru 04°45′S 81°22′W
58 H12 **Parintins** Amazonas, N Brazil 02°38′S 56°45′W
103 O5 **Paris** anc. Lutetia, Lutetia Parisiorum, Parisii. ● (France) Paris, N France 48°52′N 02°19′E
191 Y2 **Paris** Kiritimati, E Kiribati 01°55′N 157°30′W
27 S11 **Paris** Arkansas, C USA 35°17′N 93°46′W
33 S16 **Paris** Idaho, NW USA 42°14′N 111°24′W
31 N14 **Paris** Illinois, N USA 39°36′N 87°42′W
20 M5 **Paris** Kentucky, S USA 38°13′N 84°15′W
27 V3 **Paris** Missouri, C USA 39°28′N 92°00′W
20 H8 **Paris** Tennessee, S USA 36°19′N 88°20′W
25 V5 **Paris** Texas, SW USA 33°41′N 95°33′W
Parisii see Paris
43 S16 **Parita** Herrera, S Panama 08°01′N 80°30′W
43 S16 **Parita, Bahía de** bay S Panama
93 K18 **Parkano** Länsi-Suomi, W Finland 62°03′N 23°E
Parkan/Párkány see Štúrovo
27 N6 **Park City** Kansas, C USA 37°48′N 97°19′W
36 L3 **Park City** Utah, W USA 40°39′N 111°30′W
36 I12 **Parker** Arizona, SW USA 34°07′N 114°16′W
23 R9 **Parker** Florida, SE USA 30°07′N 85°36′W
29 R11 **Parker** South Dakota, N USA 43°24′N 97°08′W
35 Z14 **Parker Dam** California, W USA 34°17′N 114°08′W
29 W13 **Parkersburg** Iowa, C USA 42°34′N 92°47′W
21 Q3 **Parkersburg** West Virginia, NE USA 39°17′N 81°33′W
29 T7 **Parkers Prairie** Minnesota, N USA 46°09′N 95°19′W
171 P8 **Parker Volcano** ⛰ Mindanao, S Philippines 06°09′N 124°52′E
181 W13 **Parkes** New South Wales, SE Australia 33°10′S 148°10′E
30 K4 **Park Falls** Wisconsin, N USA 45°57′N 90°25′W
Parkhar see Farkhor
14 E16 **Parkhill** Ontario, S Canada 43°11′N 81°39′W
29 T5 **Park Rapids** Minnesota, N USA 46°55′N 95°03′W
29 Q3 **Park River** North Dakota, N USA 48°24′N 97°44′W
29 Q11 **Parkston** South Dakota, N USA 43°24′N 97°58′W
10 L17 **Parksville** Vancouver Island, British Columbia, SW Canada 49°13′N 124°13′W
37 S3 **Parkview Mountain** ▲ Colorado, C USA 40°19′N 106°08′W
105 N8 **Parla** Madrid, C Spain 40°13′N 03°48′W
155 N14 **Parlākimidi** Andhra Pradesh, E India 18°46′N 84°05′E
29 S8 **Parle, Lac qui** ⊠ Minnesota, N USA
155 G14 **Parli Vaijnāth** Mahārāshtra, C India 18°53′N 76°36′E
106 F9 **Parma** Emilia-Romagna, N Italy 44°50′N 10°20′E
31 T11 **Parma** Ohio, N USA 41°24′N 81°43′W
Parnahyba see Parnaíba
58 N13 **Parnaíba** var. Parnahyba. Piauí, E Brazil 02°58′S 41°46′W
65 J14 **Parnaíba Ridge** undersea feature C Atlantic Ocean
58 N13 **Parnaíba, Rio** ≈ NE Brazil
115 F18 **Parnassós** ▲▲ C Greece
185 J17 **Parnassus** Canterbury, South Island, New Zealand 42°41′S 173°18′E
182 H10 **Parndana** South Australia 35°48′S 137°13′E
115 H19 **Párnitha** ▲▲ C Greece
Parnon see Párnonas
115 F21 **Párnonas** var. Parnon. ▲▲ S Greece
118 G5 **Pärnu** Ger. Pernau, Latv. Pērnava; prev. Rus. Pernov. Pärnumaa, SW Estonia 58°24′N 24°32′E
118 G6 **Pärnu** var. Parnu Jõgi, Ger. Pernau. ≈ SW Estonia
118 G5 **Pärnu-Jaagupi** Ger. Sankt-Jakobi. Pärnumaa, SW Estonia 58°36′N 24°30′E
Parnu Jõgi see Pärnu
118 G5 **Pärnu Laht** Ger. Pernauer Bucht. bay SW Estonia
118 F5 **Pärnumaa** var. Pärnu Maakond. ◈ province SW Estonia
Pärnu Maakond see Pärnumaa
153 T11 **Paro** W Bhutan 27°23′N 89°31′E
153 T11 **Paro** ✈ (Thimphu) W Bhutan 27°23′N 89°31′E
185 G17 **Paroa** West Coast, South Island, New Zealand 42°31′S 171°10′E
163 X14 **P'aro-ho** var. Hwach'ŏn-chŏsuji. ⊠ N South Korea
115 J21 **Pároikiá** prev. Páros. Páros, Kykládes, Greece, Aegean Sea 37°04′N 25°06′E
183 N6 **Paroo River** seasonal river New South Wales/Queensland, SE Australia
Paropamisus Range see Sefīd Kūh, Selseleh-ye
Paropamisus Range see Sefīd Kūh, Selseleh-ye
115 J21 **Páros** island Kykládes, Greece, Aegean Sea
Páros see Pároikiá
36 K7 **Parowan** Utah, W USA 37°50′N 112°49′W
103 U13 **Parpaillon** ▲▲ SE France
108 I9 **Parpan** Graubünden, S Switzerland 46°46′N 09°32′E
62 G13 **Parral** Maule, C Chile 36°08′S 71°52′W
Parral see Hidalgo del Parral
183 T9 **Parramatta** New South Wales, SE Australia 33°49′S 150°59′E
21 Y6 **Parramore Island** island Virginia, NE USA
40 M8 **Parras** var. Parras de la Fuente. Coahuila, NE Mexico 25°26′N 102°07′W
Parras de la Fuente see Parras
42 M14 **Parrita** Puntarenas, S Costa Rica 09°30′N 84°20′W
Parry group see Mukojima-rettō
14 G13 **Parry Island** island Ontario, S Canada
197 O9 **Parry Islands** island group Nunavut, NW Canada
14 G12 **Parry Sound** Ontario, S Canada 45°21′N 80°03′W
110 F7 **Parsęta** Ger. Persante. ≈ NW Poland
28 L3 **Parshall** North Dakota, N USA 47°57′N 102°07′W
27 Q7 **Parsons** Kansas, C USA 37°20′N 95°15′W
20 H9 **Parsons** Tennessee, S USA 35°39′N 88°07′W
21 T3 **Parsons** West Virginia, NE USA 39°06′N 79°43′W
Parsonstown see Birr
100 P11 **Parsteiner See** ◎ NE Germany
107 I24 **Partanna** Sicilia, Italy, C Mediterranean Sea 37°43′N 12°54′E
108 J8 **Partenen** Graubünden, E Switzerland 46°58′N 10°01′E
102 K9 **Parthenay** Deux-Sèvres, W France 46°39′N 00°13′W
95 J19 **Partille** Västra Götaland, S Sweden 57°43′N 12°12′E
107 I23 **Partinico** Sicilia, Italy, C Mediterranean Sea 38°03′N 13°07′E
111 I20 **Partizánske** prev. Šimonovany, Hung. Simony. Trenčiansky Kraj, W Slovakia 48°35′N 18°23′E
58 H11 **Paru de Oeste, Rio** ≈ N Brazil
182 K9 **Paruna** South Australia 34°45′S 140°43′E
58 I11 **Paru, Rio** ≈ N Brazil
149 Q5 **Parvān** Pash. Parwān. ◈ province E Afghanistan
155 M14 **Pārvatipuram** Andhra Pradesh, E India 17°01′N 81°47′E
152 G12 **Parvatsar** prev. Parbatsar. Rājasthān, N India 26°52′N 74°49′E
Parwān see Parvān
158 I15 **Paryang** Xizang Zizhiqu, W China 30°04′N 83°28′E
119 M18 **Parychy** Rus. Parichi. Homyel'skaya Voblasts', SE Belarus 52°48′N 29°25′E
83 J21 **Parys** Free State, C South Africa 26°55′S 27°28′E
35 T15 **Pasadena** California, W USA 34°09′N 118°09′W
25 W11 **Pasadena** Texas, SW USA 29°41′N 95°13′W
56 B8 **Pasaje** El Oro, SW Ecuador 03°23′S 79°50′W
137 T9 **P'asanauri** N Georgia 42°21′N 44°40′E
168 I13 **Pasapuat** Pulau Pagai Utara, W Indonesia 02°36′S 99°58′E
167 N7 **Pasawng** Kayah State, C Burma (Myanmar) 18°50′N 97°16′E
114 L13 **Paşayiğit** Edirne, NW Turkey 40°58′N 26°38′E
23 N9 **Pascagoula** Mississippi, S USA 30°21′N 88°32′W
22 M8 **Pascagoula River** ≈ Mississippi, S USA
116 F12 **Paşcani** Hung. Páskán. Iaşi, NE Romania 47°14′N 26°46′E
109 T4 **Pasching** Oberösterreich, N Austria 48°16′N 14°10′E
32 K10 **Pasco** Washington, NW USA 46°13′N 119°06′W
56 E13 **Pasco** off. Departamento de Pasco. ◈ department C Peru
Pasco, Departamento de see Pasco
191 N11 **Pascua, Isla de** var. Rapa Nui, Easter Island. island E Pacific Ocean
63 G21 **Pascua, Río** ≈ S Chile
103 N1 **Pas-de-Calais** ◈ department N France
100 P10 **Pasewalk** Mecklenburg-Vorpommern, NE Germany 53°31′N 13°59′E
11 T10 **Pasfield Lake** ◎ Saskatchewan, C Canada
Pa-shih Hai-hsia see Bashi Channel
Pashkeni see Bolyarovo
Pashmakli see Smolyan
153 X10 **Pāsighāt** Arunāchel Pradesh, NE India 28°08′N 95°13′E
137 Q12 **Pasinler** Erzurum, NE Turkey 39°59′N 41°41′E
Pasi Oloy, Qatorkŭhi see Zaalayskiy Khrebet
42 E3 **Pasión, Río de la** ≈ N Guatemala
168 J12 **Pasirganting** Sumatera, W Indonesia 02°04′S 100°51′E
Pasirpangarayan see Bagansiapiapi
168 K6 **Pasir Puteh** var. Pasir Putih. Kelantan, Peninsular Malaysia 05°50′N 102°24′E
Pasir Putih see Pasir Puteh
169 R9 **Pasir, Tanjung** headland East Malaysia 02°24′N 111°12′E
95 N20 **Påskallavik** Kalmar, S Sweden 57°10′N 16°25′E
Páskán see Paşcani
Paskevicha, Zaliv see Tushchybas, Zaliv
110 K7 **Pasłęk** Ger. Preußisch Holland. Warmińsko-Mazurskie, NE Poland 54°03′N 19°40′E
110 K7 **Pasłęka** Ger. Passarge. ≈ N Poland
148 K16 **Pasni** Baluchistān, SW Pakistan 25°13′N 63°30′E
63 I18 **Paso de Indios** Chubut, S Argentina 43°52′S 69°06′W
54 L7 **Paso del Caballo** Guárico, N Venezuela 08°19′N 67°08′W
61 E15 **Paso de los Libres** Corrientes, NE Argentina 29°43′S 57°09′W
61 E18 **Paso de los Toros** Tacuarembó, C Uruguay 32°45′S 56°30′W
Pasoeroean see Pasuruan
35 P12 **Paso Robles** California, W USA 35°37′N 120°42′W
15 Y7 **Paspébiac** Québec, SE Canada 48°03′N 65°10′W
11 U14 **Pasquia Hills** ▲▲ Saskatchewan, S Canada
149 W7 **Pasrūr** Punjab, E Pakistan 32°12′N 74°42′E
30 M1 **Passage Island** island Michigan, N USA
65 B24 **Passage Islands** island group W Falkland Islands
8 K5 **Passage Point** headland Banks Island, Northwest Territories, NW Canada 73°31′N 115°12′W
Passarge see Pasłęka
115 C15 **Passarón** ancient monument Ípeiros, W Greece
Passarowitz see Požarevac
101 O22 **Passau** Bayern, SE Germany 48°34′N 13°28′E
22 M9 **Pass Christian** Mississippi, S USA 30°19′N 89°15′W
107 L26 **Passero, Capo** headland Sicilia, Italy, C Mediterranean Sea 36°40′N 15°09′E
171 P5 **Passi** Panay Island, C Philippines 11°05′N 122°37′E
61 H14 **Passo Fundo** Rio Grande do Sul, S Brazil 28°16′S 52°20′W
60 H13 **Passo Fundo, Barragem de** ⊠ S Brazil
61 H15 **Passo Real, Barragem de** ⊠ S Brazil
59 L20 **Passos** Minas Gerais, NE Brazil 20°45′S 46°38′W
167 X10 **Passu Keah** island S Paracel Islands
118 J13 **Pastavy** Pol. Postawy, Rus. Postavy. Vitsyebskaya Voblasts', NW Belarus 55°07′N 26°50′E
56 D7 **Pastaza** ◈ province E Ecuador
56 D9 **Pastaza, Río** ≈ Ecuador/Peru
61 A21 **Pasteur** Buenos Aires, E Argentina 35°10′S 62°14′W
15 V3 **Pasteur** ≈ Québec, SE Canada
147 Q12 **Pastigav** Rus. Pastigov. W Tajikistan 39°27′N 69°16′E
Pastigov see Pastigav
54 C13 **Pasto** Nariño, SW Colombia 01°12′N 77°17′W
38 M10 **Pastol Bay** bay Alaska, USA
37 O8 **Pastora Peak** ▲ Arizona, SW USA 36°48′N 109°10′W
105 O8 **Pastrana** Castilla-La Mancha, C Spain 40°24′N 02°55′W
169 S16 **Pasuruan** prev. Pasoeroean. Jawa, C Indonesia 07°38′S 112°44′E
118 F11 **Pasvalys** Panevėžys, N Lithuania 56°03′N 24°24′E
111 K21 **Pásztó** Nógrád, N Hungary 47°57′N 19°41′E
189 U12 **Pata** var. Patta. atoll Chuuk Islands, C Micronesia
36 M16 **Patagonia** Arizona, SW USA 31°32′N 110°45′W
63 H20 **Patagonia** physical region Argentina/Chile
Patalung see Phatthalung
154 D9 **Pātan** Gujarāt, W India 23°51′N 72°11′E
154 J10 **Pātan** Madhya Pradesh, C India 23°19′N 79°41′E
171 S11 **Patani** Pulau Halmahera, E Indonesia 0°19′N 128°46′E
Patani see Pattani
15 V7 **Patapédia Est** ≈ Québec, SE Canada
116 K13 **Pătâriagele** prev. Pătîriagele. Buzău, SE Romania 45°19′N 26°21′E
Patavium see Padova
182 I5 **Patawarta Hill** ▲ South Australia 30°57′S 138°42′E
182 L10 **Patchewollock** Victoria, SE Australia 35°24′S 142°11′E
184 K11 **Patea** Taranaki, North Island, New Zealand 39°48′S 174°35′E
184 K11 **Patea** ≈ North Island, New Zealand
77 U15 **Pategi** Kwara, C Nigeria 08°39′N 05°46′E
81 K20 **Pate Island** var. Patta Island. island SE Kenya
105 S10 **Paterna** País Valenciano, E Spain 39°30′N 00°24′W
109 R9 **Paternion** Slvn. Špatrjan. Kärnten, S Austria 46°40′N 13°43′E
107 L24 **Paternò** anc. Hybla, Hybla Major. Sicilia, Italy, C Mediterranean Sea 37°34′N 14°55′E
32 J7 **Pateros** Washington, NW USA 48°01′N 119°55′W
18 J14 **Paterson** New Jersey, NE USA 40°55′N 74°12′W
32 J10 **Paterson** Washington, NW USA 45°56′N 119°37′W
185 C25 **Paterson Inlet** inlet Stewart Island, New Zealand
98 N6 **Paterswolde** Drenthe, NE Netherlands 53°07′N 06°32′E
155 G24 **Pathanāmthitta** Kerala, SW India 9°05′N 76°38′E
152 H7 **Pathānkot** Himāchal Pradesh, N India 32°16′N 75°43′E

◆ Country ● Country Capital ◇ Dependent Territory ○ Dependent Territory Capital ◈ Administrative Regions ✈ International Airport ▲ Mountain ▲▲ Mountain Range ⛰ Volcano ≈ River ◎ Lake ⊠ Reservoir

PATHEIN – PERNIÖ

166 K8 **Pathein** *var.* Bassein. Ayeyarwady, SW Burma (Myanmar) 16°46´N 94°45´E
33 W15 **Pathfinder Reservoir** ⊠ Wyoming, C USA
167 O11 **Pathum Thani** *var.* Patumdhani, Prathum Thani. Pathum Thani, C Thailand 14°03´N 100°29´E
54 C12 **Patía** *var.* El Bordo. Cauca, SW Colombia 02°07´N 76°57´W
152 I9 **Patiāla** *var.* Puttiala. Punjab, NW India 30°21´N 76°27´E
54 B12 **Patía, Río** ≈ SW Colombia
188 D15 **Pati Point** *headland* NE Guam 13°36´N 144°39´E
Pătîriagele *see* Pătâriagele
56 C13 **Pativilca** Lima, W Peru 10°44´S 77°45´W
166 M1 **Pātkai Bum** *var.* Patkai Range. ▲▲ Burma (Myanmar)/India
Patkai Range *see* Pātkai Bum
115 L20 **Pátmos** Pátmos, Dodekánisa, Greece, Aegean Sea 37°18´N 26°32´E
115 L20 **Pátmos** *island* Dodekánisa, Greece, Aegean Sea
153 P13 **Patna** *var.* Azimabad. *state capital* Bihār, N India 25°36´N 85°11´E
154 M12 **Patnāgarh** Orissa, E India 20°42´N 83°12´E
171 O5 **Patnongon** Panay Island, C Philippines 10°56´N 122°03´E
137 S13 **Patnos** Ağrı, E Turkey 39°14´N 42°52´E
60 H12 **Pato Branco** Paraná, S Brazil 26°20´S 52°40´W
31 O16 **Patoka Lake** ◎ Indiana, N USA
92 L9 **Patoniva** *Lapp.* Buoddobohki. Lappi, N Finland 69°44´N 27°01´E
113 K21 **Patos** *var.* Patosi. Fier, SW Albania 40°40´N 19°37´E
Patos *see* Patos de Minas
59 K19 **Patos de Minas** *var.* Patos. Minas Gerais, NE Brazil 18°35´S 46°32´W
Patosi *see* Patos
61 I17 **Patos, Lagoa dos** *lagoon* S Brazil
62 J9 **Patquía** La Rioja, C Argentina 30°02´S 66°54´W
115 E19 **Pátra** *Eng.* Patras; *prev.* Pátrai. Dytikí Ellás, S Greece 38°14´N 21°45´E
115 D18 **Patraïkós Kólpos** *gulf* S Greece
Pátrai/Patras *see* Pátra
92 G2 **Patreksfjördhur** Vestfirdhir, W Iceland 65°33´N 23°54´W
24 M7 **Patricia** Texas, SW USA 32°34´N 102°00´W
63 F21 **Patricio Lynch, Isla** *island* S Chile
Patta *see* Pata
Patta Island *see* Pate Island
167 O16 **Pattani** *var.* Patani. Pattani, SW Thailand 06°50´N 101°20´E
167 P12 **Pattaya** Chon Buri, S Thailand 12°57´N 100°53´E
19 S4 **Patten** Maine, NE USA 45°58´N 68°27´W
35 O9 **Patterson** California, W USA 37°27´N 121°07´W
22 J10 **Patterson** Louisiana, S USA 29°41´N 91°18´W
35 R7 **Patterson, Mount** ▲ California, W USA 38°27´N 119°16´W
31 P4 **Patterson, Point** *headland* Michigan, N USA 45°58´N 85°39´W
107 L23 **Patti** Sicilia, Italy, C Mediterranean Sea 38°08´N 14°58´E
107 L23 **Patti, Golfo di** *gulf* Sicilia, Italy
93 L14 **Pattijoki** Oulu, W Finland 64°41´N 24°40´E
193 Q4 **Patton Escarpment** *undersea feature* E Pacific Ocean
27 S2 **Pattonsburg** Missouri, C USA 40°03´N 94°08´W
0 D6 **Patton Seamount** *undersea feature* NE Pacific Ocean 54°40´N 150°30´W
10 J12 **Pattullo, Mount** ▲ British Columbia, W Canada 56°18´N 129°43´W
153 U16 **Patuakhali** *var.* Patukhali. Barisal, S Bangladesh 22°20´N 90°20´E
42 M5 **Patuca, Río** ≈ E Honduras
Patukhali *see* Patuakhali
Patumdhani *see* Pathum Thani
40 M14 **Pátzcuaro** Michoacán, SW Mexico 19°30´N 101°38´W
42 C6 **Patzicía** Chimaltenango, S Guatemala 14°38´N 90°52´W
102 K16 **Pau** Pyrénées-Atlantiques, SW France 43°18´N 00°22´W
102 J12 **Pauillac** Gironde, SW France 45°12´N 00°44´W
166 L5 **Pauk** Magway, W Burma (Myanmar) 21°25´N 94°30´E
8 I6 **Paulatuk** Northwest Territories, NW Canada 69°23´N 124°W
42 K5 **Paulayá, Río** ≈ NE Honduras
22 M6 **Paulding** Mississippi, S USA 32°01´N 89°01´W
31 Q12 **Paulding** Ohio, N USA 41°08´N 84°34´W
29 S12 **Paullina** Iowa, C USA 42°58´N 95°41´W
59 P15 **Paulo Afonso** Bahia, E Brazil 09°21´S 38°14´W
38 M16 **Pauloff Harbor** *var.* Pavlor Harbour. Sanak Island, Alaska, USA 54°26´N 162°43´W
27 N12 **Pauls Valley** Oklahoma, C USA 34°46´N 97°14´W
166 L7 **Paungde** Bago, C Burma (Myanmar) 18°30´N 95°30´E
Pauni *see* Paoni
152 K9 **Pauri** Uttaranchal, N India 30°08´N 78°48´E
Pautalia *see* Kyustendil
142 J5 **Pāveh** Kermānshāhān, NW Iran 35°02´N 46°15´E
114 I9 **Pavel Banya** Stara Zagora, C Bulgaria 42°35´N 25°19´E
126 L5 **Pavelets** Ryazanskaya Oblast', W Russian Federation 53°47´N 39°22´E
106 D8 **Pavia** *anc.* Ticinum. Lombardia, N Italy 45°10´N 09°10´E
118 C9 **Pāvilosta** Liepāja, W Latvia 56°52´N 21°12´E
125 P14 **Pavino** Kostromskaya Oblast', NW Russian Federation 59°10´N 46°09´E
114 J8 **Pavlikeni** Veliko Tŭrnovo, N Bulgaria 43°14´N 25°20´E
145 T8 **Pavlodar** Pavlodar, NE Kazakhstan 52°21´N 76°59´E
145 S9 **Pavlodar** *off.* Pavlodarskaya Oblast', *Kaz.* Pavlodar Oblysy. ◈ *province* NE Kazakhstan
Pavlodar Oblysy/ Pavlodarskaya Oblast' *see* Pavlodar
Pavlograd *see* Pavlohrad
117 U7 **Pavlohrad** *Rus.* Pavlograd. Dnipropetrovs'ka Oblast', E Ukraine 48°32´N 35°50´E
Pavlor Harbour *see* Pauloff Harbor
145 R9 **Pavlovka** Akmola, C Kazakhstan 51°22´N 72°35´E
127 V4 **Pavlovka** Respublika Bashkortostan, W Russian Federation 55°28´N 56°36´E
127 Q7 **Pavlovka** Ul'yanovskaya Oblast', W Russian Federation 52°40´N 47°08´E
127 N3 **Pavlovo** Nizhegorodskaya Oblast', W Russian Federation 55°59´N 43°03´E
126 L9 **Pavlovsk** Voronezhskaya Oblast', W Russian Federation 50°26´N 40°08´E
126 L13 **Pavlovskaya** Krasnodarskiy Kray, SW Russian Federation 46°06´N 39°52´E
117 S7 **Pavlysh** Kirovohrads'ka Oblast', C Ukraine 48°54´N 33°20´E
106 F10 **Pavullo nel Frignano** Emilia-Romagna, C Italy 44°19´N 10°52´E
27 P8 **Pawhuska** Oklahoma, C USA 36°42´N 96°21´W
21 U13 **Pawleys Island** South Carolina, SE USA 33°27´N 79°07´W
167 N6 **Pawn** ≈ C Burma (Myanmar)
30 K14 **Pawnee** Illinois, N USA 39°35´N 89°34´W
27 O9 **Pawnee** Oklahoma, C USA 36°21´N 96°50´W
37 U2 **Pawnee Buttes** ▲ Colorado, C USA 40°49´N 103°58´W
29 S17 **Pawnee City** Nebraska, C USA 40°06´N 96°09´W
26 K5 **Pawnee River** ≈ Kansas, C USA
31 O10 **Paw Paw** Michigan, N USA 42°12´N 86°09´W
31 O10 **Paw Paw Lake** Michigan, N USA 42°12´N 86°16´W
19 O12 **Pawtucket** Rhode Island, NE USA 41°52´N 71°22´W
Pax Augusta *see* Badajoz
115 I25 **Paximádia** *island* SE Greece
Pax Julia *see* Beja
115 B16 **Paxoí** *island* Iónia Nisiá, Greece, C Mediterranean Sea
39 S10 **Paxson** Alaska, USA 62°58´N 145°27´W
147 O11 **Paxtakor** Jizzax Viloyati, C Uzbekistan 40°21´N 67°54´E
30 M13 **Paxton** Illinois, N USA 40°27´N 88°06´W
124 J11 **Pay** Respublika Kareliya, NW Russian Federation 61°10´N 34°24´E
166 M8 **Payagyi** Bago, SW Burma (Myanmar) 17°28´N 96°32´E
108 C9 **Payerne** *Ger.* Peterlingen. Vaud, W Switzerland 46°49´N 06°57´E
32 M13 **Payette** Idaho, NW USA 44°04´N 116°55´W
32 M13 **Payette River** ≈ Idaho, NW USA
125 V2 **Pay-Khoy, Khrebet** ▲▲ NW Russian Federation
Payne *see* Kangirsuk
12 K4 **Payne, Lac** ◎ Québec, NE Canada
29 T8 **Paynesville** Minnesota, N USA 45°22´N 94°42´W
169 S8 **Payong, Tanjung** *cape* East Malaysia
Payo Obispo *see* Chetumal
61 D18 **Paysandú** Paysandú, W Uruguay 32°21´S 58°05´W
61 D17 **Paysandú** ◈ *department* W Uruguay
102 I7 **Pays de la Loire** ◈ *region* NW France
36 L12 **Payson** Arizona, SW USA 34°13´N 111°19´W
36 L4 **Payson** Utah, W USA 40°02´N 111°43´W
125 W4 **Payyer, Gora** ▲ NW Russian Federation 66°49´N 64°33´E
Payzawat *see* Jiashi
137 Q11 **Pazar** Rize, NE Turkey 41°10´N 40°53´E
136 F10 **Pazarbaşı Burnu** *headland* NW Turkey 41°12´N 30°18´E
136 M16 **Pazarcık** Kahramanmaraş, S Turkey 37°31´N 37°19´E
114 I10 **Pazardzhik** *prev.* Tatar Pazardzhik. Pazardzhik, SW Bulgaria 42°11´N 24°21´E
64 H11 **Pazardzhik** ◈ *province* C Bulgaria
54 H9 **Paz de Ariporo** Casanare, E Colombia 05°54´N 71°52´W
112 A10 **Pazin** *Ger.* Mitterburg, *It.* Pisino. Istra, NW Croatia 45°14´N 13°56´E
42 D7 **Paz, Río** ≈ El Salvador/Guatemala
113 O18 **Pčinja** ≈ N Macedonia
193 V15 **Pea** Tongatapu, S Tonga 21°10´S 175°14´W
27 O6 **Peabody** Kansas, C USA 38°10´N 97°06´W
11 O12 **Peace** ≈ Alberta/British Columbia, W Canada
Peace Garden State *see* North Dakota
11 Q10 **Peace Point** Alberta, C Canada 59°11´N 112°12´W
11 O12 **Peace River** Alberta, W Canada 56°15´N 117°18´W
23 W13 **Peace River** ≈ Florida, SE USA
11 N17 **Peachland** British Columbia, SW Canada 49°49´N 119°48´W
36 J10 **Peach Springs** Arizona, SW USA 35°33´N 113°27´W
Peach State *see* Georgia
23 S4 **Peachtree City** Georgia, SE USA 33°24´N 84°36´W
189 Y13 **Peacock Point** *point* SE Wake Island
97 M18 **Peak District** *physical region* C England, United Kingdom
183 Q7 **Peak Hill** New South Wales, SE Australia 32°39´S 148°12´E
65 G15 **Peak, The** ▲ C Ascension Island
105 O13 **Peal de Becerro** Andalucía, S Spain 37°55´N 03°08´W
189 X11 **Peale Island** *island* N Wake Island
37 O6 **Peale, Mount** ▲ Utah, W USA 38°26´N 109°13´W
39 O4 **Peard Bay** *bay* Alaska, USA
23 Q7 **Pea River** ≈ Alabama/Florida, S USA
25 W11 **Pearland** Texas, SW USA 29°33´N 95°17´W
38 D9 **Pearl City** O'ahu, Hawaii, USA, C Pacific Ocean 21°24´N 157°58´W
38 D9 **Pearl Harbor** *inlet* O'ahu, Hawai'i, USA, C Pacific Ocean
Pearl Islands *see* Perlas, Archipiélago de las
Pearl Lagoon *see* Perlas, Laguna de
22 M5 **Pearl River** ≈ Louisiana/Mississippi, S USA
25 Q13 **Pearsall** Texas, SW USA 28°54´N 99°07´W
23 U7 **Pearson** Georgia, SE USA 31°18´N 82°51´W
25 P4 **Pease River** ≈ Texas, SW USA
12 F7 **Peawanuk** Ontario, C Canada 54°55´N 85°31´W
12 E8 **Peawanuk** ≈ Ontario, S Canada
83 P16 **Pebane** Zambézia, NE Mozambique 17°14´S 38°10´E
65 C23 **Pebble Island** *island* N Falkland Islands
Peć *see* Pejë
25 R8 **Pecan Bayou** ≈ Texas, SW USA
22 H10 **Pecan Island** Louisiana, S USA 29°39´N 92°26´W
60 L12 **Peças, Ilha das** *island* S Brazil
30 L10 **Pecatonica River** ≈ Illinois/Wisconsin, N USA
108 G10 **Peccia** Ticino, S Switzerland 46°24´N 08°39´E
Pechenegi *see* Pechenihy
Pechenezhskoye Vodokhranilishche *see* Pecheniz'ke Vodoskhovyshche
124 I2 **Pechenga** *Fin.* Petsamo. Murmanskaya Oblast', NW Russian Federation 69°34´N 31°14´E
117 V5 **Pechenihy** *Rus.* Pechenegi. Kharkivs'ka Oblast', E Ukraine 49°49´N 36°57´E
117 V5 **Pecheniz'ke Vodoskhovyshche** *Rus.* Pechenezhskoye Vodokhranilishche. ⊠ E Ukraine
125 U7 **Pechora** Respublika Komi, NW Russian Federation 65°09´N 57°09´E
125 R6 **Pechora** ≈ NW Russian Federation
Pechora Bay *see* Pechorskaya Guba
Pechora Sea *see* Pechorskoye More
125 S3 **Pechorskaya Guba** *Eng.* Pechora Bay. *bay* NW Russian Federation
122 H7 **Pechorskoye More** *Eng.* Pechora Sea. *sea* NW Russian Federation
124 F14 **Pechory** *Est.* Petseri. Pskovskaya Oblast', W Russian Federation 57°49´N 27°37´E
116 E11 **Pecica** *Ger.* Petschka, *Hung.* Ópécska. Arad, W Romania 46°09´N 21°06´E
24 K8 **Pecos** Texas, SW USA 31°25´N 103°30´W
25 N11 **Pecos River** ≈ New Mexico/Texas, SW USA
111 I25 **Pécs** *Ger.* Fünfkirchen, *Lat.* Sopianae. Baranya, SW Hungary 46°05´N 18°11´E
43 T17 **Pedasí** Los Santos, S Panama 07°36´N 80°04´W
Pedde *see* Pedja
183 O17 **Pedder, Lake** ◎ Tasmania, SE Australia
44 M10 **Pedernales** SW Dominican Republic 18°02´N 71°41´W
55 Q5 **Pedernales** Delta Amacuro, NE Venezuela 09°58´N 62°15´W
25 R10 **Pedernales River** ≈ Texas, SW USA
62 H6 **Pedernales, Salar de** *salt lake* N Chile
Pedhoulas *see* Pedoulás
55 X11 **Pédima** *var.* Malavate. SW French Guiana 03°15´N 54°08´W
182 F1 **Pedirka** South Australia 26°41´S 135°11´E
171 S11 **Pediwang** Pulau Halmahera, E Indonesia 01°29´N 127°57´E
118 I5 **Pedja** *var.* Pedja Jõgi, *Ger.* Pedde. ≈ E Estonia
Pedja Jõgi *see* Pedja
121 O3 **Pedoulás** *var.* Pedhoulas. W Cyprus 34°58´N 32°51´E
59 N18 **Pedra Azul** Minas Gerais, NE Brazil 16°02´S 41°17´W
104 I3 **Pedrafita, Porto de** *var.* Puerto de Piedrafita. *pass* NW Spain
76 E9 **Pedra Lume** Sal, NE Cape Verde 16°47´N 22°54´W
43 P16 **Pedregal** Chiriquí, W Panama 09°04´N 79°25´W
54 J4 **Pedregal** Falcón, N Venezuela 11°04´N 70°08´W
40 L9 **Pedriceña** Durango, C Mexico 25°08´N 103°46´W
60 L11 **Pedro Barros** São Paulo, S Brazil 24°12´S 47°22´W
39 Q13 **Pedro Bay** Alaska, USA 59°47´N 154°06´W
62 H4 **Pedro de Valdivia** *var.* Oficina Pedro de Valdivia. Antofagasta, N Chile 22°33´S 69°38´W
62 P4 **Pedro Juan Caballero** Amambay, E Paraguay 22°34´S 55°41´W
63 L15 **Pedro Luro** Buenos Aires, E Argentina 39°30´S 62°38´W
105 O10 **Pedro Muñoz** Castilla-La Mancha, C Spain 39°25´N 02°56´W
155 J22 **Pedro, Point** *headland* NW Sri Lanka 09°54´N 80°08´E
182 K9 **Peebinga** South Australia 34°56´S 140°56´E
96 J13 **Peebles** SE Scotland, United Kingdom 55°40´N 03°15´W
31 S15 **Peebles** Ohio, N USA 38°57´N 83°23´W
96 J12 **Peebles** *cultural region* SE Scotland, United Kingdom
18 K13 **Peekskill** New York, NE USA 41°17´N 73°54´W
97 I16 **Peel** W Isle of Man 54°13´N 04°04´W
8 G7 **Peel** ≈ Northwest Territories/Yukon Territory, NW Canada
8 K5 **Peel Point** *headland* Victoria Island, Northwest Territories, NW Canada 73°22´N 114°33´W
8 M5 **Peel Sound** *passage* Nunavut, N Canada
100 N9 **Peene** ≈ NE Germany
99 K17 **Peer** Limburg, NE Belgium 51°08´N 05°29´E
14 H14 **Pefferlaw** Ontario, S Canada 44°18´N 79°11´W
185 I18 **Pegasus Bay** *bay* South Island, New Zealand
121 O3 **Pégeia** *var.* Peyia. SW Cyprus 34°52´N 32°24´E
109 V7 **Peggau** Steiermark, SE Austria 47°10´N 15°20´E
101 L19 **Pegnitz** Bayern, SE Germany 49°45´N 11°33´E
101 L19 **Pegnitz** ≈ SE Germany
105 T11 **Pego** País Valenciano, E Spain 38°51´N 00°08´W
Pegu *see* Bago
Pegu *see* Bago
189 N13 **Pehleng** Pohnpei, E Micronesia
114 M12 **Pehlivanköy** Kırklareli, NW Turkey 41°21´N 26°55´E
77 R14 **Péhonko** C Benin 10°14´N 01°57´E
61 B21 **Pehuajó** Buenos Aires, E Argentina 35°48´S 61°53´W
Pei-ching *see* Beijing/Beijing Shi
100 J13 **Peine** Niedersachsen, C Germany 52°19´N 10°14´E
Pei-p'ing *see* Beijing/Beijing Shi
Peipsi Järv/Peipus-See *see* Peipus, Lake
118 J5 **Peipus, Lake** *Est.* Peipsi Järv, *Ger.* Peipus-See, *Rus.* Chudskoye Ozero. ◎ Estonia/Russian Federation
115 H19 **Peiraías** *prev.* Piraiévs, *Eng.* Piraeus. Attikí, C Greece 37°57´N 23°42´E
Peisern *see* Pyzdry
60 I8 **Peixe, Rio do** ≈ S Brazil
59 I16 **Peixoto de Azevedo** Mato Grosso, W Brazil 10°18´S 55°03´W
168 O11 **Pejantan, Pulau** *island* W Indonesia
113 L16 **Pejë** *Serb.* Peć. W Kosovo 42°40´N 20°19´E
167 R7 **Pèk** *var.* Xieng Khouang; *prev.* Xiangkhoang. Xiangkhoang, N Laos 19°19´N 103°23´E
112 N11 **Pek** ≈ E Serbia
169 Q16 **Pekalongan** Jawa, C Indonesia 06°54´S 109°37´E
168 K11 **Pekanbaru** *var.* Pakanbaru. Sumatera, W Indonesia 0°31´N 101°27´E
30 L12 **Pekin** Illinois, N USA 40°34´N 89°38´W
Peking *see* Beijing/Beijing Shi
Pelabohan Kelang/ Pelabuhan Kelang *see* Pelabuhan Klang
168 J9 **Pelabuhan Klang** *var.* Kuala Pelabohan Kelang, Pelabohan Kelang, Pelabuhan Kelang, Port Klang, Port Swettenham. Selangor, Peninsular Malaysia 02°57´N 101°24´E
120 L11 **Pelagie, Isole** *island group* SW Italy
Pelagosa *see* Palagruža
22 L5 **Pelahatchie** Mississippi, S USA 32°19´N 89°48´W
169 T14 **Pelaihari** *var.* Pleihari. Borneo, C Indonesia 03°48´S 114°45´E
103 U14 **Pelat, Mont** ▲ SE France 44°16´N 06°46´E
116 F12 **Peleaga, Vârful** *prev.* Vîrful Peleaga. ▲ W Romania 45°23´N 22°52´E
Peleaga, Vîrful *see* Peleaga, Vârful
123 O11 **Peleduy** Respublika Sakha (Yakutiya), NE Russian Federation 59°39´N 112°36´E
14 C18 **Pelee Island** *island* Ontario, S Canada
45 Q11 **Pelée, Montagne** ▲ N Martinique 14°47´N 61°10´W
14 D18 **Pelee, Point** *headland* Ontario, S Canada 41°56´N 82°30´W
171 P12 **Pelei** Pulau Peleng, N Indonesia 01°26´S 123°27´E
Peleliu *see* Beliliou
171 P12 **Peleng, Pulau** *island* Kepulauan Banggai, N Indonesia
23 T7 **Pelham** Georgia, SE USA 31°07´N 84°09´W
111 E18 **Pelhřimov** *Ger.* Pilgram. Vysočina, C Czech Republic 49°26´N 15°14´E
39 W13 **Pelican** Chichagof Island, Alaska, USA 57°52´N 136°05´W
191 Z3 **Pelican Lagoon** ◎ Kiritimati, E Kiribati
29 U6 **Pelican Lake** ◎ Minnesota, N USA
29 V3 **Pelican Lake** ◎ Minnesota, N USA
30 L5 **Pelican Lake** ◎ Wisconsin, N USA
44 G1 **Pelican Point** Grand Bahama Island, N Bahamas 26°39´N 78°09´W
83 B19 **Pelican Point** *headland* W Namibia 22°55´S 14°25´E
29 S6 **Pelican Rapids** Minnesota, N USA 46°34´N 96°04´W
Pelican State *see* Louisiana
11 U13 **Pelikan Narrows** Saskatchewan, C Canada 55°11´N 102°51´W
115 L18 **Pelinaío** ▲ Chíos, E Greece 38°31´N 26°01´E
Pelinnaeum *see* Pelinnaío
115 E16 **Pelinnaío** *anc.* Pelinnaeum. *ruins* Thessalía, C Greece
113 N20 **Pelister** ▲ SW FYR Macedonia 41°00´N 21°12´E
113 G15 **Pelješac** *peninsula* S Croatia
92 M12 **Pelkosenniemi** Lappi, NE Finland 67°06´N 27°30´E
29 W15 **Pella** Iowa, C USA 41°24´N 92°55´W
114 F13 **Pélla** *site of ancient city* Kentrikí Makedonía, N Greece
23 Q3 **Pell City** Alabama, S USA 33°35´N 86°17´W
61 A22 **Pellegrini** Buenos Aires, E Argentina 36°16´S 63°07´W
92 K12 **Pello** Lappi, NW Finland 66°47´N 24°E
100 G7 **Pellworm** *island* N Germany
10 H6 **Pelly** ≈ Yukon Territory, NW Canada
Pelly Bay *see* Kugaaruk
10 I8 **Pelly Mountains** ▲▲ Yukon Territory, W Canada
Pélmonostor *see* Beli Manastir
37 P13 **Pelona Mountain** ▲ New Mexico, SW USA 33°40´N 108°06´W
Peloponnese/Peloponnesus *see* Pelopónnisos
115 E20 **Pelopónnisos** *Eng.* Peloponnese. ◈ *region* S Greece
115 E20 **Pelopónnisos** *var.* Morea, *Eng.* Peloponnese; *anc.* Peloponnesus. *peninsula* S Greece
107 L23 **Peloritani, Monti** *anc.* Pelorus and Neptunius. ▲▲ Sicilia, Italy, C Mediterranean Sea
107 M22 **Peloro, Capo** *var.* Punta del Faro. *headland* S Italy 38°15´N 15°39´E
Pelorus and Neptunius *see* Peloritani, Monti
61 H17 **Pelotas** Rio Grande do Sul, S Brazil 31°45´S 52°20´W
61 I14 **Pelotas, Rio** ≈ S Brazil
92 K10 **Peltovuoma** *Lapp.* Bealdovuopmi. Lappi, N Finland 68°23´N 24°12´E
19 R4 **Pemadumcook Lake** ◎ Maine, NE USA
169 Q16 **Pemalang** Jawa, C Indonesia 06°53´S 109°07´E
169 P10 **Pemangkat** *var.* Pamangkat. Borneo, C Indonesia 01°11´N 109°00´E
Pemar *see* Paimio
168 I9 **Pematangsiantar** Sumatera, W Indonesia 02°59´N 99°01´E
83 Q14 **Pemba** *prev.* Port Amelia, Porto Amélia. Cabo Delgado, NE Mozambique 13°S 40°35´E
81 J22 **Pemba** ◈ *region* E Tanzania
81 K21 **Pemba** *island* E Tanzania
83 Q14 **Pemba, Baia de** *inlet* NE Mozambique
81 J21 **Pemba Channel** *channel* E Tanzania
81 J22 **Pemba North** ◈ *region* E Tanzania
81 J22 **Pemba South** ◈ *region* E Tanzania
180 J14 **Pemberton** Western Australia 34°27´S 116°09´E
10 M16 **Pemberton** British Columbia, SW Canada 50°19´N 122°49´W
29 Q2 **Pembina** North Dakota, N USA 48°58´N 97°14´W
11 P15 **Pembina** ≈ Alberta, SW Canada
29 Q2 **Pembina** ≈ Canada/USA
171 X16 **Pembre** Papua, E Indonesia 07°49´S 138°01´E
14 K12 **Pembroke** Ontario, SE Canada 45°49´N 77°08´W
97 H21 **Pembroke** SW Wales, United Kingdom 51°41´N 04°55´W
23 W6 **Pembroke** Georgia, SE USA 32°09´N 81°35´W
21 U11 **Pembroke** North Carolina, SE USA 34°40´N 79°12´W
21 R7 **Pembroke** Virginia, NE USA 37°19´N 80°38´W
97 H21 **Pembroke** *cultural region* SW Wales, United Kingdom
Pembuang, Sungai *see* Seruyan, Sungai
43 S15 **Peña Blanca, Cerro** ▲ C Panama 08°39´N 80°39´W
104 K8 **Peña de Francia, Sierra de la** ▲▲ W Spain
104 G6 **Penafiel** *var.* Peñafiel. Porto, N Portugal 41°12´N 08°17´W
105 N6 **Peñafiel** Castilla-León, N Spain 41°36´N 04°07´W
Peñafiel *see* Penafiel
105 S8 **Peñagolosa** ▲ E Spain 40°10´N 00°15´W
105 N7 **Peñalara, Pico de** ▲ C Spain 40°52´N 03°55´W
171 X16 **Penambo, Banjaran** *var.* Banjaran Tama Abu, Penambo Range. ▲▲ Indonesia/Malaysia
Penambo Range *see* Penambo, Banjaran
41 O10 **Peña Nevada, Cerro** ▲ C Mexico 23°46´N 99°52´W
Penang *see* Pinang
Penang *see* George Town
Penang *see* Pinang, Pulau, Peninsular Malaysia
60 J8 **Penápolis** São Paulo, S Brazil 21°23´S 50°02´W
104 L7 **Peñaranda de Bracamonte** Castilla-León, N Spain 40°54´N 05°13´W
105 S8 **Peñarroya** ▲ E Spain 40°24´N 00°42´W
104 L12 **Peñarroya-Pueblonuevo** Andalucía, S Spain 38°21´N 05°18´W
97 K22 **Penarth** S Wales, United Kingdom 51°27´N 03°11´W
104 K1 **Peñas, Cabo de** *headland* N Spain 43°39´N 05°52´W
63 F20 **Penas, Golfo de** *gulf* S Chile
Pen-ch'i *see* Benxi
79 H14 **Pendé** *var.* Logone Oriental. ≈ Central African Republic/Chad
76 I14 **Pendembu** E Sierra Leone 09°06´N 12°12´W
29 R13 **Pender** Nebraska, C USA 42°06´N 96°42´W
Penderma *see* Bandırma
32 K11 **Pendleton** Oregon, NW USA 45°40´N 118°47´W
32 M7 **Pend Oreille, Lake** ◎ Idaho, NW USA
32 M7 **Pend Oreille River** ≈ Idaho/Washington, NW USA
Pendzhikent *see* Panjakent
Peneius *see* Pineiós
104 G8 **Penela** Coimbra, N Portugal 40°02´N 08°23´W
14 G13 **Penetanguishene** Ontario, S Canada 44°45´N 79°55´W
151 H15 **Penganga** ≈ C India
161 T12 **P'engchia Yu** *island* N Taiwan
79 M21 **Penge** Kasai-Oriental, C Dem. Rep. Congo 05°29´S 24°38´E
Penghu Archipelago/ P'enghu Ch'üntao/Penghu Islands *see* P'enghu Liehtao
161 R14 **P'enghu Liehtao** *var.* P'enghu Ch'üntao, Penghu Islands, *Eng.* Penghu Archipelago, Pescadores, *Jap.* Hoko-guntō, Hoko-shotō. *island group* W Taiwan
Penghu Shuidao/P'enghu Shuitao *see* Pescadores Channel
161 R4 **Penglai** *var.* Dengzhou. Shandong, E China 37°50´N 120°45´E
Peng-pu *see* Bengbu
Penhsihu *see* Benxi
Penibético, Sistema *see* Béticos, Sistemas
104 F10 **Peniche** Leiria, W Portugal 39°21´N 09°23´W
169 U17 **Penida, Nusa** *island* S Indonesia
Peninsular State *see* Florida
105 T8 **Peñíscola** País Valenciano, E Spain 40°22´N 00°24´E
40 M13 **Pénjamo** Guanajuato, C Mexico 20°26´N 101°44´W
Penki *see* Benxi
102 F7 **Penmarch, Pointe de** *headland* NW France 47°46´N 04°34´W
107 L15 **Penna, Punta della** *headland* C Italy 42°10´N 14°43´E
107 K14 **Penne** Abruzzo, C Italy 42°28´N 13°57´E
Penner *see* Penneru
155 J18 **Penneru** *var.* Penner. ≈ C India
182 I10 **Penneshaw** South Australia 35°45´S 137°57´E
18 C14 **Penn Hills** Pennsylvania, NE USA 40°28´N 79°53´W
Penninae, Alpes/Pennine, Alpi *see* Pennine Alps
108 D11 **Pennine Alps** *Fr.* Alpes Pennines, *It.* Alpi Pennine, *Lat.* Alpes Penninae. ▲▲ Italy/Switzerland
Pennine Chain *see* Pennines
97 L15 **Pennines** *var.* Pennine Chain. ▲▲ N England, United Kingdom
Pennines, Alpes *see* Pennine Alps
21 O8 **Pennington Gap** Virginia, NE USA 36°45´N 83°01´W
18 I16 **Penns Grove** New Jersey, NE USA 39°42´N 75°27´W
18 I16 **Pennsville** New Jersey, NE USA 39°37´N 75°29´W
18 E14 **Pennsylvania** *off.* Commonwealth of Pennsylvania, *also known as* Keystone State. ◈ *state* NE USA
18 G10 **Penn Yan** New York, NE USA 42°39´N 77°02´W
124 H16 **Peno** Tverskaya Oblast', W Russian Federation 56°55´N 32°44´E
19 R7 **Penobscot Bay** *bay* Maine, NE USA
19 S5 **Penobscot River** ≈ Maine, NE USA
182 K12 **Penola** South Australia 37°24´S 140°50´E
40 K9 **Peñón Blanco** Durango, C Mexico 25°12´N 100°50´W
182 E7 **Penong** South Australia 31°57´S 133°01´E
43 S16 **Penonomé** Coclé, C Panama 08°29´N 80°22´W
190 L13 **Penrhyn** *atoll* N Cook Islands
192 M9 **Penrhyn Basin** *undersea feature* C Pacific Ocean
183 S9 **Penrith** New South Wales, SE Australia 33°45´S 150°48´E
97 K15 **Penrith** NW England, United Kingdom 54°40´N 02°44´W
23 O9 **Pensacola** Florida, SE USA 30°25´N 87°13´W
23 O9 **Pensacola Bay** *bay* Florida, SE USA
195 N7 **Pensacola Mountains** ▲▲ Antarctica
182 L12 **Penshurst** Victoria, SE Australia 37°54´S 142°19´E
187 R13 **Pentecost** *Fr.* Pentecôte. *island* C Vanuatu
15 V4 **Pentecôte** ≈ Québec, SE Canada
Pentecôte *see* Pentecost
15 V4 **Pentecôte, Lac** ◎ Québec, SE Canada
8 H15 **Penticton** British Columbia, SW Canada 49°29´N 119°38´W
96 J6 **Pentland Firth** *strait* N Scotland, United Kingdom
96 J12 **Pentland Hills** *hill range* S Scotland, United Kingdom
171 Q12 **Penu** Pulau Taliabu, E Indonesia 01°43´S 125°09´E
155 H18 **Penukonda** Andhra Pradesh, E India 14°04´N 77°38´E
166 L7 **Penwegon** Bago, C Burma (Myanmar) 18°14´N 96°34´E
24 M8 **Penwell** Texas, SW USA 31°45´N 102°32´W
97 J21 **Pen y Fan** ▲ SE Wales, United Kingdom 51°52´N 03°25´W
97 L16 **Pen-y-ghent** ▲ N England, United Kingdom 54°11´N 02°15´W
127 O6 **Penza** Penzenskaya Oblast', W Russian Federation 53°11´N 45°E
97 G25 **Penzance** SW England, United Kingdom 50°08´N 05°33´W
127 N6 **Penzenskaya Oblast'** ◈ *province* W Russian Federation
123 U7 **Penzhina** ≈ E Russian Federation
123 U9 **Penzhinskaya Guba** *bay* E Russian Federation
Penzig *see* Pieńsk
36 K13 **Peoria** Arizona, SW USA 33°34´N 112°14´W
30 L12 **Peoria** Illinois, N USA 40°42´N 89°35´W
30 L12 **Peoria Heights** Illinois, N USA 40°45´N 89°34´W
31 N11 **Peotone** Illinois, N USA 41°19´N 87°47´W
18 J11 **Pepacton Reservoir** ⊠ New York, NE USA
76 I15 **Pepel** W Sierra Leone 08°39´N 13°04´W
30 I6 **Pepin, Lake** ⊠ Minnesota/Wisconsin, N USA
99 L20 **Pepinster** Liège, E Belgium 50°34´N 05°49´E
113 L20 **Peqin** *var.* Peqini. Elbasan, C Albania 41°03´N 19°46´E
Peqini *see* Peqin
40 D7 **Pequeña, Punta** *headland* NW Mexico 26°13´N 112°34´W
168 J8 **Perak** ◈ *state* Peninsular Malaysia
105 R7 **Perales del Alfambra** Aragón, NE Spain 40°38´N 01°00´W
115 C15 **Pérama** *var.* Perama. Ípeiros, W Greece 39°42´N 20°51´E
Perama *see* Pérama
155 I22 **Perambalūr** Tamil Nādu, SE India 11°14´N 78°51´E
92 M13 **Perä-Posio** Lappi, NE Finland 66°10´N 27°56´E
15 Z6 **Percé** Québec, SE Canada 48°32´N 64°14´W
15 Z6 **Percé, Rocher** *island* Québec, S Canada
102 L5 **Perche, Collines de** ▲▲ N France
109 X4 **Perchtoldsdorf** Niederösterreich, NE Austria 48°06´N 16°16´E
180 L6 **Percival Lakes** *lakes* Western Australia
105 T3 **Perdido, Monte** ▲ NE Spain 42°41´N 00°01´E
23 O8 **Perdido River** ≈ Alabama/Florida, S USA
Perece Vela Basin *see* West Mariana Basin
116 G7 **Perechyn** Zakarpats'ka Oblast', W Ukraine 48°45´N 22°28´E
54 E10 **Pereira** Risaralda, W Colombia 04°47´N 75°46´W
60 I7 **Pereira Barreto** São Paulo, S Brazil 20°37´S 51°07´W
59 G15 **Pereirinha** Pará, N Brazil 08°18´S 57°30´W
127 N10 **Perelazovskiy** Volgogradskaya Oblast', SW Russian Federation 49°10´N 42°30´E
127 S7 **Perelyub** Saratovskaya Oblast', W Russian Federation 51°52´N 50°19´E
31 P7 **Pere Marquette River** ≈ Michigan, N USA
Peremyshl *see* Przemyśl
116 I5 **Peremyshlyany** L'vivs'ka Oblast', W Ukraine 49°42´N 24°33´E
Pereshchepino *see* Pereshchepyne
116 L9 **Pereshchepyne** *Rus.* Pereshchepino. Dnipropetrovs'ka Oblast', E Ukraine 48°59´N 35°22´E
124 L16 **Pereslavl'-Zalesskiy** Yaroslavskaya Oblast', W Russian Federation 56°42´N 38°45´E
117 Y7 **Pereval's'k** Luhans'ka Oblast', E Ukraine 48°28´N 38°54´E
127 U7 **Perevolotskiy** Orenburgskaya Oblast', W Russian Federation 51°54´N 54°05´E
Pereyaslav-Khmel'nitskiy *see* Pereyaslav-Khmel'nyts'kyy
117 Q5 **Pereyaslav-Khmel'nyts'kyy** *Rus.* Pereyaslav-Khmel'nitskiy. Kyyivs'ka Oblast', N Ukraine 50°05´N 31°28´E
109 U4 **Perg** Oberösterreich, N Austria 48°15´N 14°38´E
61 B19 **Pergamino** Buenos Aires, E Argentina 33°56´S 60°38´W
106 G6 **Pergine Valsugana** *Ger.* Persen. Trentino-Alto Adige, N Italy 46°04´N 11°13´E
29 S6 **Perham** Minnesota, N USA 46°35´N 95°34´W
93 L16 **Perho** Länsi-Suomi, W Finland 63°15´N 24°25´E
116 E11 **Periam** *Ger.* Perjamosch, *Hung.* Perjámos. Timiș, W Romania 46°02´N 20°54´E
15 Q6 **Péribonca** ≈ Québec, SE Canada
12 L11 **Péribonca, Lac** ◎ Québec, SE Canada
15 Q6 **Péribonca, Petite Rivière** ≈ Québec, SE Canada
15 Q7 **Péribonka** Québec, SE Canada 48°45´N 72°01´W
40 I9 **Pericos** Sinaloa, C Mexico 25°03´N 107°42´W
169 Q10 **Perigi** Borneo, C Indonesia
102 L12 **Périgueux** *anc.* Vesuna. Dordogne, SW France 45°12´N 00°41´E
54 G5 **Perijá, Serranía de** ▲▲ Columbia/Venezuela
115 H17 **Peristéra** *island* Vóreies Sporádes, Greece, Aegean Sea
63 H20 **Perito Moreno** Santa Cruz, S Argentina 46°35´S 71°W
155 G22 **Periyāl** *var.* Periyār. ≈ SW India
Periyār *see* Periyāl
155 G23 **Periyār Lake** ◎ S India
Perjámos/Perjamosch *see* Periam
27 O9 **Perkins** Oklahoma, C USA 35°58´N 97°01´W
116 L7 **Perkivtsi** Chernivets'ka Oblast', W Ukraine 48°28´N 26°48´E
43 U15 **Perlas, Archipiélago de las** *Eng.* Pearl Islands. *island group* SE Panama
43 O10 **Perlas, Cayos de** *reef* SE Nicaragua
43 N9 **Perlas, Laguna de** *Eng.* Pearl Lagoon. *lagoon* E Nicaragua
43 N10 **Perlas, Punta de** *headland* E Nicaragua 12°22´N 83°30´W
100 L11 **Perleberg** Brandenburg, N Germany 53°04´N 11°52´E
Perlepe *see* Prilep
168 I6 **Perlis** ◈ *state* Peninsular Malaysia
125 U14 **Perm'** *prev.* Molotov. Permskaya Oblast', NW Russian Federation 58°01´N 56°10´E
113 M22 **Përmet** *var.* Përmeti, Prëmet. Gjirokastër, S Albania 40°12´N 20°24´E
Përmeti *see* Përmet
125 U15 **Permskaya Oblast'** ◈ *province* NW Russian Federation
59 P15 **Pernambuco** *off.* Estado de Pernambuco. ◈ *state* E Brazil
Pernambuco *see* Recife
Pernambuco Abyssal Plain *see* Pernambuco Plain
Pernambuco, Estado de *see* Pernambuco
47 Y6 **Pernambuco Plain** *var.* Pernambuco Abyssal Plain. *undersea feature* E Atlantic Ocean 07°30´S 27°00´W
65 K15 **Pernambuco Seamounts** *undersea feature* C Atlantic Ocean
182 H6 **Pernatty Lagoon** *salt lake* South Australia
Pernau *see* Pärnu
Pernauer Bucht *see* Pärnu Laht
Pērnava *see* Pärnu
114 G9 **Pernik** *prev.* Dimitrovo. Pernik, W Bulgaria 42°36´N 23°02´E
114 G10 **Pernik** ◈ *province* W Bulgaria
93 K20 **Perniö** *Swe.* Bjärnå. Länsi-Suomi, SW Finland 60°13´N 23°10´E

◆ Country
● Country Capital
◇ Dependent Territory
○ Dependent Territory Capital
◈ Administrative Regions
✕ International Airport
▲ Mountain
▲▲ Mountain Range
Volcano
≈ River
◎ Lake
⊠ Reservoir

PERNITZ – PINDUS MOUNTAINS

109 X5 Pernitz Niederösterreich, E Austria 47°54′N 15°58′E
Pernov see Pärnu
103 O3 Péronne Somme, N France 49°56′N 02°57′E
14 L8 Péronne, Lac ◎ Québec, SE Canada
106 A8 Perosa Argentina Piemonte, NE Italy 45°02′N 07°10′E
41 Q14 Perote Veracruz-Llave, E Mexico 19°32′N 97°16′W
Pérouse see Perugia
191 W15 Pérouse, Bahía de la bay Easter Island, Chile, E Pacific Ocean
Perovsk see Kzylorda
103 O17 Perpignan Pyrénées-Orientales, S France 42°41′N 02°53′E
113 M20 Përrenjas var. Përrenjasi, Prrenjas, Prenjasi. Elbasan, E Albania 41°04′N 20°34′E
Përrenjasi see Përrenjas
92 O2 Perriertoppen ▲ C Svalbard 79°10′N 17°01′E
25 S6 Perrin Texas, SW USA 32°59′N 98°03′W
23 Y16 Perrine Florida, SE USA 25°36′N 80°21′W
37 S12 Perro, Laguna del ◎ New Mexico, SW USA
102 G5 Perros-Guirec Côtes d'Armor, NW France 48°49′N 03°28′W
23 T9 Perry Florida, SE USA 30°07′N 83°34′W
23 T5 Perry Georgia, SE USA 32°27′N 83°43′W
29 U14 Perry Iowa, C USA 41°50′N 94°06′W
18 E10 Perry New York, NE USA 42°43′N 78°00′W
27 N9 Perry Oklahoma, C USA 36°17′N 97°18′W
27 Q3 Perry Lake ⊠ Kansas, C USA
31 R11 Perrysburg Ohio, N USA 41°33′N 83°37′W
25 O1 Perryton Texas, SW USA 36°23′N 100°48′W
39 O15 Perryville Alaska, USA 55°55′N 159°08′W
27 U11 Perryville Arkansas, C USA 35°00′N 92°48′W
27 Y6 Perryville Missouri, C USA 37°43′N 89°51′W
Persante see Parsęta
Persen see Pergine Valsugana
Pershay see Pyarshai
117 V7 Pershotravens'k Dnipropetrovs'ka Oblast', E Ukraine 48°19′N 36°22′E
Pershotravneve see Manhush
Persia see Iran
141 T5 Persian Gulf var. The Gulf, Ar. Khalīj al 'Arabī, Per. Khalīj-e Fars. Gulf SW Asia see also Gulf, The
Persis see Fārs
95 K22 Perstorp Skåne, S Sweden 56°08′N 13°23′E
137 O14 Pertek Tunceli, C Turkey 38°53′N 39°19′E
183 P16 Perth Tasmania, SE Australia 41°39′S 147°11′E
180 I13 Perth state capital Western Australia 31°58′S 115°49′E
14 L13 Perth Ontario, SE Canada 44°54′N 76°15′W
96 J11 Perth C Scotland, United Kingdom 56°24′N 03°28′W
96 J10 Perth cultural region C Scotland, United Kingdom
180 I12 Perth ✈ Western Australia 31°51′S 116°06′E
173 V10 Perth Basin undersea feature SE Indian Ocean 28°30′S 110°00′E
103 S15 Pertuis Vaucluse, SE France 43°42′N 05°30′E
103 Y16 Pertusato, Capo headland Corse, France, C Mediterranean Sea 41°22′N 09°10′E
30 L11 Peru Illinois, N USA 41°18′N 89°09′W
31 P12 Peru Indiana, N USA 40°45′N 86°04′W
57 E13 Peru off. Republic of Peru. ◆ republic W South America
Peru see Beru
193 T9 Peru Basin undersea feature E Pacific Ocean 15°00′S 85°00′W
193 U8 Peru-Chile Trench undersea feature E Pacific Ocean 20°00′S 73°00′W
112 F13 Perućko Jezero ◎ S Croatia
106 H13 Perugia Fr. Pérouse; anc. Perusia. Umbria, C Italy 43°06′N 12°24′E
Perugia, Lake of see Trasimeno, Lago
61 D15 Perugorría Corrientes, NE Argentina 29°21′S 58°35′W
60 M11 Peruíbe São Paulo, S Brazil 24°18′S 47°01′W
155 B21 Perumalpār reef India, N Indian Ocean
Peru, Republic of see Peru
Perusia see Perugia
99 D20 Péruwelz Hainaut, SW Belgium 50°30′N 03°35′E
137 R15 Pervari Siirt, SE Turkey 37°55′N 42°32′E
127 O4 Pervomaysk Nizhegorodskaya Oblast', W Russian Federation 54°52′N 43°49′E
117 X7 Pervomays'k Luhans'ka Oblast', E Ukraine 48°38′N 38°36′E
117 P8 Pervomays'k prev. Ol'viopol'. Mykolayivs'ka Oblast', S Ukraine 48°02′N 30°51′E
117 S12 Pervomays'ke Respublika Krym, S Ukraine 45°43′N 33°49′E
127 V7 Pervomayskiy Orenburgskaya Oblast', W Russian Federation 51°32′N 54°58′E
126 M6 Pervomayskiy Tambovskaya Oblast', W Russian Federation 53°15′N 40°20′E
117 V6 Pervomays'kyy Kharkivs'ka Oblast', E Ukraine 49°24′N 36°12′E
122 F10 Pervoural'sk Sverdlovskaya Oblast', C Russian Federation 56°58′N 59°50′E
123 V11 Pervyy Kuril'skiy Proliv strait E Russian Federation
99 I19 Perwez Walloon Brabant, C Belgium 50°39′N 04°49′E
106 I11 Pesaro anc. Pisaurum. Marche, C Italy 43°55′N 12°53′E
35 N9 Pescadero California, W USA 37°15′N 122°23′W
Pescadores see P'enghu Liehtao
161 S14 Pescadores Channel var. Penghu Shuidao, P'enghu Shuitao. channel W Taiwan
107 K14 Pescara anc. Aternum, Ostia Aterni. Abruzzo, C Italy 42°28′N 14°13′E
107 K15 Pescara ∽ C Italy
106 F11 Pescia Toscana, C Italy 43°54′N 10°41′E
108 C8 Peseux Neuchâtel, W Switzerland 46°59′N 06°53′E
125 P6 Pësha ∽ NW Russian Federation
149 T5 Peshāwar North-West Frontier Province, N Pakistan 34°01′N 71°33′E
149 T6 Peshāwar ✈ North-West Frontier Province, N Pakistan 34°01′N 71°40′E
113 M19 Peshkopi var. Peshkopia, Peshkopija. Dibër, NE Albania 41°40′N 20°25′E
Peshkopia/Peshkopija see Peshkopi
114 I11 Peshtera Pazardzhik, C Bulgaria 42°02′N 24°18′E
31 N6 Peshtigo Wisconsin, N USA 45°04′N 87°43′W
31 N6 Peshtigo River ∽ Wisconsin, N USA
Peski see Pyeski
125 S13 Peskovka Kirovskaya Oblast', NW Russian Federation 59°04′N 52°17′E
103 S8 Pesmes Haute-Saône, E France 47°17′N 05°33′E
104 H6 Peso da Régua var. Pêso da Regua. Vila Real, N Portugal 41°10′N 07°47′W
40 F5 Pesqueira Sonora, NW Mexico 29°22′N 110°58′W
102 J13 Pessac Gironde, SW France 44°46′N 00°42′W
111 J23 Pest off. Pest Megye. ◈ county C Hungary
Pest Megye see Pest
124 J14 Pestovo Novgorodskaya Oblast', W Russian Federation 58°37′N 35°48′E
40 M15 Petacalco, Bahía bay W Mexico
Petach-Tikva see Petah Tikva
138 F10 Petah Tikva var. Petach-Tikva, Petah Tiqva, Petakh Tikva; prev. Petaḥ Tiqwa. Tel Aviv, C Israel 32°05′N 34°53′E
Petaḥ Tiqwa see Petah Tikva
93 L17 Petäjävesi Länsi-Suomi, C Finland 62°17′N 25°10′E
Petakh Tikva/Petah Tiqva see Petah Tikva
22 M7 Petal Mississippi, S USA 31°21′N 89°15′W
115 I19 Petalioí island C Greece
115 H19 Petalión, Kólpos gulf E Greece
115 J19 Pétalo ▲ Ándros, Kykládes, Greece, Aegean Sea 37°51′N 24°50′E
34 M8 Petaluma California, W USA 38°15′N 122°37′W
99 L25 Pétange Luxembourg, SW Luxembourg 49°33′N 05°53′E
54 M5 Petare Miranda, N Venezuela 10°31′N 66°50′W
41 N16 Petatlán Guerrero, S Mexico 17°31′N 101°16′W
83 L14 Petauke Eastern, E Zambia 14°12′S 31°16′E
14 J12 Petawawa Ontario, SE Canada 45°54′N 77°18′W
14 J11 Petawawa ∽ Ontario, SE Canada
Petchaburi see Phetchaburi
42 D2 Petén off. Departamento del Petén. ◈ department N Guatemala
Petén, Departamento del see Petén
42 D2 Petén Itzá, Lago var. Lago de Flores. ◎ N Guatemala
30 K7 Petenwell Lake ⊠ Wisconsin, N USA
14 D6 Peterbell Ontario, S Canada 48°34′N 83°19′W
182 I7 Peterborough South Australia 32°59′S 138°51′E
14 I14 Peterborough Ontario, SE Canada 44°19′N 78°20′W
97 N20 Peterborough prev. Medeshamstede. E England, United Kingdom 52°35′N 00°15′W
19 N10 Peterborough New Hampshire, NE USA 42°51′N 71°54′W
96 L8 Peterhead NE Scotland, United Kingdom 57°30′N 01°46′W
Peterhof see Luboń
Peter I øy see Peter I Øy
193 Q14 Peter I Øy ◇ Norwegian dependency Antarctica
194 H9 Peter I Øy var. Peter I øy. island Antarctica
97 M14 Peterlee N England, United Kingdom 54°45′N 01°18′W
Peterlingen see Payerne
197 P14 Petermann Bjerg ▲ C Greenland 73°16′N 27°59′W
11 S12 Peter Pond Lake ◎ Saskatchewan, C Canada
39 X13 Petersburg Mytkof Island, Alaska, USA 56°43′N 132°51′W
30 K13 Petersburg Illinois, N USA 40°01′N 89°52′W
31 N16 Petersburg Indiana, N USA 38°30′N 87°16′W
29 Q3 Petersburg North Dakota, N USA 47°59′N 97°59′W
25 N5 Petersburg Texas, SW USA 33°52′N 101°36′W
21 V7 Petersburg Virginia, NE USA 37°14′N 77°24′W
21 T4 Petersburg West Virginia, NE USA 39°01′N 79°09′W
100 H12 Petershagen Nordrhein-Westfalen, NW Germany 52°22′N 08°58′E
55 S9 Peters Mine var. Peter's Mine. N Guyana 06°13′N 59°18′W
107 O21 Petilia Policastro Calabria, SW Italy 39°07′N 16°48′E
44 M9 Pétionville S Haiti 18°29′N 72°16′W
45 X6 Petit-Bourg Basse Terre, C Guadeloupe 16°12′N 61°36′W
15 Y5 Petit-Cap Québec, SE Canada 49°00′N 64°26′W
45 Y6 Petit Cul-de-Sac Marin bay C Guadeloupe
44 M9 Petite-Rivière-de-l'Artibonite C Haiti 19°10′N 72°30′W
173 X16 Petite Rivière Noire, Piton de la ▲ C Mauritius
15 R9 Petite-Rivière-St-François Québec, SE Canada 47°18′N 70°34′W
44 L9 Petit-Goâve S Haiti 18°27′N 72°51′W
Petitjean see Sidi-Kacem
13 N10 Petit Lac Manicouagan ◎ Québec, E Canada
19 T7 Petit Manan Point headland Maine, NE USA 44°23′N 67°54′W
Petit Mécatina, Rivière du see Little Mecatina
11 N10 Petitot ∽ Alberta/British Columbia, W Canada
45 S12 Petit Piton ▲ SW Saint Lucia 13°49′N 61°03′W
Petit-Popo see Aného
Petit St-Bernard, Col du see Little Saint Bernard Pass
13 O8 Petitsikapau Lake ◎ Newfoundland and Labrador, E Canada
92 L11 Petkula Lappi, N Finland 67°41′N 26°44′E
41 X12 Peto Yucatán, SE Mexico 20°09′N 88°55′W
62 G10 Petorca Valparaíso, C Chile 32°18′S 70°49′W
31 Q5 Petoskey Michigan, N USA 45°51′N 88°03′W
138 G14 Petra archaeological site Ma'ān, W Jordan
Petra see Wādī Mūsā
115 F14 Pétras, Sténa pass N Greece
123 S16 Petra Velikogo, Zaliv bay SE Russian Federation
Petrel see Petrer
14 K15 Petre, Point headland Ontario, SE Canada 43°49′N 77°07′W
105 S12 Petrer var. Petrel. País Valenciano, E Spain 38°28′N 00°46′W
125 U11 Petretsovo Permskaya Oblast', NW Russian Federation 61°22′N 57°21′E
114 G12 Petrich Blagoevgrad, SW Bulgaria 41°25′N 23°12′E
187 P15 Petrie, Récif reef N New Caledonia
37 N11 Petrified Forest prehistoric site Arizona, SW USA
Petrikau see Piotrków Trybunalski
Petrikov see Pyetrykaw
116 H12 Petrila Hung. Petrilla. Hunedoara, W Romania 45°27′N 23°25′E
Petrilla see Petrila
112 E9 Petrinja Sisak-Moslavina, C Croatia 45°27′N 16°14′E
Petroaleksandrovsk see To'rtkok'l
Petrőcz see Bački Petrovac
124 G12 Petrodvorets Fin. Pietarhovi. Leningradskaya Oblast', NW Russian Federation 59°53′N 29°52′E
Petrograd see Sankt-Peterburg
Petrokov see Piotrków Trybunalski
54 G6 Petrólea Norte de Santander, NE Colombia 08°30′N 72°35′W
14 D16 Petrolia Ontario, S Canada 42°54′N 82°07′W
25 S4 Petrolia Texas, SW USA 34°00′N 98°13′W
59 O15 Petrolina Pernambuco, E Brazil 09°22′S 40°30′W
45 T6 Petrona, Punta headland C Puerto Rico 17°57′N 66°23′W
Petropavl see Petropavlovsk
117 V7 Petropavlivka Dnipropetrovs'ka Oblast', E Ukraine 48°28′N 36°28′E
145 P6 Petropavlovsk Kaz. Petropavl. Severnyy Kazakhstan, N Kazakhstan 54°47′N 69°06′E
123 V11 Petropavlovsk-Kamchatskiy Kamchatskaya Oblast', E Russian Federation 53°03′N 158°43′E
60 P9 Petrópolis Rio de Janeiro, SE Brazil 22°30′S 43°28′W
116 H12 Petroşani var. Petroşeni, Ger. Petroschen, Hung. Petrozsény. Hunedoara, W Romania 45°25′N 23°22′E
Petroschen/Petroşeni see Petroşani
Petroskoi see Petrozavodsk
112 N12 Petrovac Serbia, E Serbia 42°22′N 21°25′E
Petrovac see Bosanski Petrovac
113 J17 Petrovac na Moru S Montenegro 42°11′N 19°00′E
Petrovac/Petrovácz see Bački Petrovac
117 S8 Petrove Kirovohrads'ka Oblast', C Ukraine 48°22′N 33°12′E
113 O18 Petrovec C FYR Macedonia 41°57′N 21°37′E
Petrovgrad see Zrenjanin
127 P7 Petrovsk Saratovskaya Oblast', W Russian Federation 52°20′N 45°23′E
Petrovsk-Port see Makhachkala
127 P9 Petrov Val Volgogradskaya Oblast', SW Russian Federation 50°10′N 45°16′E
124 J11 Petrozavodsk Fin. Petroskoi. Respublika Kareliya, NW Russian Federation 61°46′N 34°19′E
Petrozsény see Petroşani
83 D20 Petrusdal Hardap, C Namibia 23°42′S 17°23′E
117 T7 Petrykivka Dnipropetrovs'ka Oblast', E Ukraine 48°44′N 34°42′E
Petsamo see Pechenga
Petschka see Pecica
Petseri see Pechory
Pettau see Ptuj
109 S5 Pettenbach Oberösterreich, C Austria 47°58′N 14°03′E
25 S13 Pettus Texas, SW USA 28°34′N 97°49′W
122 G12 Petukhovo Kurganskaya Oblast', C Russian Federation 55°04′N 67°49′E
Petuna see Songyuan
109 R4 Peuerbach Oberösterreich, N Austria 48°19′N 13°45′E
62 G12 Peumo Libertador, C Chile 34°20′S 71°12′W
123 T6 Pevek Chukotskiy Avtonomnyy Okrug, NE Russian Federation 69°41′N 170°19′E
27 X5 Pevely Missouri, C USA 38°16′N 90°24′W
Peyia see Pégeia
102 J15 Peyrehorade Landes, SW France 43°33′N 01°05′W
124 J14 Peza ∽ NW Russian Federation
103 P16 Pézenas Hérault, S France 43°28′N 03°25′E
111 H20 Pezinok Ger. Bösing, Hung. Bazin. Bratislavský Kraj, W Slovakia 48°17′N 17°15′E
101 L22 Pfaffenhofen an der Ilm Bayern, SE Germany 48°31′N 11°30′E
108 G7 Pfäffikon Schwyz, C Switzerland 47°11′N 08°46′E
101 F20 Pfälzer Wald hill range W Germany
101 N22 Pfarrkirchen Bayern, SE Germany 48°25′N 12°56′E
101 G21 Pforzheim Baden-Württemberg, SW Germany 48°53′N 08°42′E
101 H24 Pfullendorf Baden-Württemberg, S Germany 47°55′N 09°16′E
108 K8 Pfunds Tirol, W Austria 46°56′N 10°30′E
101 G19 Pfungstadt Hessen, W Germany 49°48′N 08°36′E
83 L20 Phalaborwa Limpopo, NE South Africa 23°59′S 31°04′E
152 E11 Phalodi Rājasthān, NW India 27°06′N 72°22′E
152 E12 Phalsund Rājasthān, NW India 26°22′N 71°56′E
155 E15 Phaltan Mahārāshtra, W India 18°01′N 74°31′E
167 O7 Phan var. Muang Phan. Chiang Rai, NW Thailand 19°34′N 99°44′E
167 O14 Phangan, Ko island SW Thailand
166 M15 Phang-Nga var. Pang-Nga, Phangnga. Phangnga, SW Thailand 08°29′N 98°31′E
Phangnga see Phang-Nga
Phan Rang/Phanrang see Phan Rang-Thap Cham
167 V13 Phan Rang-Thap Cham var. Phanrang, Phan Rang, Phan Rang Thap Cham. Ninh Thuân, S Vietnam 11°34′N 109°00′E
167 U13 Phan Ri Binh Thuận, S Vietnam 11°11′N 108°31′E
167 U13 Phan Thiêt Bình Thuân, S Vietnam 10°56′N 108°06′E
25 S17 Pharr Texas, SW USA 26°11′N 98°10′W
Pharus see Hvar
167 N16 Phatthalung var. Padalung, Patalung. Phatthalung, SW Thailand 07°38′N 100°04′E
167 O7 Phayao var. Muang Phayao. Phayao, NW Thailand 19°10′N 99°55′E
11 U10 Phelps Lake ◎ Saskatchewan, C Canada
21 X9 Phelps Lake ◎ North Carolina, SE USA
23 R5 Phenix City Alabama, S USA 32°28′N 85°00′W
167 T8 Pheo Quang Bình, C Vietnam 17°42′N 105°58′E
Phet Buri see Phetchaburi
167 O11 Phetchaburi var. Bejraburi, Petchaburi, Phet Buri. Phetchaburi, SW Thailand 13°05′N 99°58′E
167 O9 Phichit var. Bichitra, Muang Phichit, Pichit. Phichit, C Thailand 16°29′N 100°21′E
22 M5 Philadelphia Mississippi, S USA 32°45′N 89°06′W
18 I7 Philadelphia New York, NE USA 44°10′N 75°40′W
18 I16 Philadelphia Pennsylvania, NE USA 40°N 75°10′W
18 I16 Philadelphia ✈ Pennsylvania, NE USA 39°51′N 75°13′W
Philadelphia see 'Ammān
28 L10 Philip South Dakota, N USA 44°02′N 101°39′W
99 H22 Philippeville Namur, S Belgium 50°12′N 04°33′E
Philippeville see Skikda
21 S3 Philippi West Virginia, NE USA 39°08′N 80°03′W
Philippi see Fílippoi
195 Y9 Philippi Glacier glacier Antarctica
192 G6 Philippine Basin undersea feature W Pacific Ocean 17°00′N 132°00′E
129 X12 Philippine Plate tectonic feature
171 O5 Philippines off. Republic of the Philippines. ◆ republic SE Asia
129 X13 Philippines island group W Pacific Ocean
171 P3 Philippine Sea sea W Pacific Ocean
Philippines, Republic of the see Philippines
192 F6 Philippine Trench undersea feature W Philippine Sea
83 H23 Philippolis Free State, C South Africa 30°16′S 25°16′E
Philippopolis see Plovdiv
Philippopolis see Shahbā', Syria
45 V9 Philipsburg Sint Maarten, N Netherlands Antilles 17°58′N 63°02′W
33 P10 Philipsburg Montana, NW USA 46°19′N 113°17′W
39 R6 Philip Smith Mountains ▲▲ Alaska, USA
152 H8 Phillaur Punjab, N India 31°02′N 75°50′E
183 N13 Phillip Island island Victoria, SE Australia
25 N2 Phillips Texas, SW USA 35°39′N 101°21′W
30 K5 Phillips Wisconsin, N USA 45°42′N 90°23′W
26 K3 Phillipsburg Kansas, C USA 39°45′N 99°19′W
18 I14 Phillipsburg New Jersey, NE USA 40°39′N 75°09′W
21 S7 Philpott Lake ⊠ Virginia, NE USA
Phintias see Licata
167 P9 Phitsanulok var. Bisnulok, Muang Phitsanulok, Pitsanulok. Phitsanulok, C Thailand 16°49′N 100°15′E
Phlórina see Flórina
Phnom Penh see Phnum Penh
167 S13 Phnum Penh var. Phnom Penh. ● (Cambodia) Phnum Penh, S Cambodia 11°35′N 104°55′E
167 S11 Phnum Tbêng Meanchey Preăh Vihéar, N Cambodia 13°45′N 104°58′E
36 K13 Phoenix state capital Arizona, SW USA 33°27′N 112°04′W
Phoenix Island see Rawaki
191 R3 Phoenix Islands island group C Kiribati
18 I15 Phoenixville Pennsylvania, NE USA 40°07′N 75°31′W
83 K22 Phofung var. Mont-aux-Sources. ▲ N Lesotho 28°47′S 28°52′E
167 Q10 Phon Khon Kaen, E Thailand 15°47′N 102°35′E
167 Q5 Phôngsali var. Phong Saly. Phôngsali, N Laos 21°40′N 102°04′E
Phong Saly see Phôngsali
167 Q8 Phônhông C Laos 18°29′N 102°26′E
167 R5 Phô Rang var. Bao Yèn. Lao Cai, N Vietnam 22°12′N 104°27′E
Phort Láirge, Cuan see Waterford Harbour
167 N10 Phra Chedi Sam Ong Kanchanaburi, W Thailand 15°18′N 98°26′E
167 O8 Phrae var. Muang Phrae, Prae. Phrae, NW Thailand 18°07′N 100°09′E
Phra Nakhon Si Ayutthaya see Ayutthaya
167 M14 Phra Thong, Ko island SW Thailand
Phu Cường see Thu Dâu Môt
166 M15 Phuket var. Bhuket, Puket, Mal. Ujung Salang; prev. Junkseylon, Salang. Phuket, SW Thailand 07°52′N 98°22′E
166 M15 Phuket ✈ Phuket, SW Thailand 08°03′N 98°16′E
166 M15 Phuket, Ko island SW Thailand
154 N12 Phulabāni prev. Phulbani. Orissa, E India 20°30′N 84°18′E
Phulbani see Phulabāni
167 U9 Phu Lôc Th,a Thiên-Huê, C Vietnam 16°13′N 107°53′E
167 S13 Phumĭ Banam Prey Vêng, S Cambodia 11°14′N 105°18′E
167 R13 Phumĭ Chŏâm Kâmpóng Spœ, SW Cambodia 11°42′N 103°58′E
167 T11 Phumĭ Kalêng Stœng Trêng, NE Cambodia 13°57′N 106°17′E
167 S12 Phumĭ Kâmpóng Trâbêk prev. Phum Kompong Trabek. Kâmpóng Thum, C Cambodia 13°06′N 105°16′E
167 Q11 Phumĭ Koŭk Kduŏch Bătdâmbâng, NW Cambodia 13°16′N 103°08′E
167 T11 Phumĭ Labăng Rôtânôkiri, NE Cambodia 13°51′N 107°01′E
167 S11 Phumĭ Mlu Prey Preăh Vihéar, N Cambodia 13°48′N 105°16′E
167 R11 Phumĭ Moŭng Siĕmréab, NW Cambodia 13°45′N 103°35′E
167 Q12 Phumĭ Prâmaôy Poŭthĭsăt, W Cambodia 12°13′N 103°05′E
167 Q13 Phumĭ Samĭt Kaôh Kŏng, SW Cambodia 10°54′N 103°09′E
167 R11 Phumĭ Sâmraông prev. Phum Samrong. Siĕmréab, NW Cambodia 14°11′N 103°31′E
167 S12 Phumĭ Siĕmbok Stœng Trêng, N Cambodia 13°28′N 105°59′E
167 S11 Phumĭ Thalabârĭvăt Stœng Trêng, N Cambodia 13°34′N 105°57′E
167 R13 Phumĭ Veal Renh Kâmpôt, SW Cambodia 10°43′N 103°49′E
167 P13 Phumĭ Yeay Sên Kaôh Kŏng, SW Cambodia 11°09′N 103°09′E
Phum Kompong Trabek see Phumĭ Kâmpóng Trâbêk
Phum Samrong see Phumĭ Sâmraông
167 V11 Phu My Bình Định, C Vietnam 14°07′N 109°05′E
167 S14 Phung Hiêp Cân Thơ, S Vietnam 09°50′N 105°48′E
153 T12 Phuntsholing SW Bhutan 26°52′N 89°26′E
167 R15 Phước Long Minh Hai, S Vietnam 09°27′N 105°25′E
Phươc Sơn see Khâm Đưc
167 R14 Phu Quôc, Đao var. Phu Quoc Island. island S Vietnam
Phu Quoc Island see Phu Quôc, Đao
167 S6 Phu Tho Vinh Phu, N Vietnam 21°23′N 105°13′E
Phu Vinh see Tra Vinh
166 M7 Phyu var. Hpyu, Pyu. Bago, C Burma (Myanmar) 18°29′N 96°28′E
189 T13 Piaanu Pass passage Chuuk Islands, C Micronesia
106 E8 Piacenza Fr. Paisance; anc. Placentia. Emilia-Romagna, N Italy 45°02′N 09°42′E
107 K14 Pianella Abruzzo, C Italy 42°23′N 14°04′E
107 M15 Pianosa, Isola island Archipelago Toscano, C Italy
171 U13 Piar Papua, E Indonesia 02°49′S 132°46′E
45 U14 Piarco var. Port of Spain. ✈ (Port-of-Spain) Trinidad, Trinidad and Tobago 10°36′N 61°21′W
110 M12 Piaseczno Mazowieckie, C Poland 52°03′N 21°00′E
116 I15 Piatra Teleorman, S Romania 43°49′N 25°10′E
116 L10 Piatra-Neamţ Hung. Karácsonkő. Neamţ, NE Romania 46°54′N 26°23′E
Piauhy see Piauí
59 N15 Piauí off. Estado do Piauí; prev. Piauhy. ◈ state E Brazil
Piauí, Estado do see Piauí
106 I7 Piave ∽ NE Italy
107 K24 Piazza Armerina var. Chiazza. Sicilia, Italy, C Mediterranean Sea 37°23′N 14°22′E
81 G14 Pibor Amh. Pībor Wenz. ∽ Ethiopia/Sudan
81 G14 Pibor Post Jonglei, SE Sudan 06°50′N 33°06′E
Pībor Wenz see Pibor
Pibrans see Příbram
36 K11 Picacho Butte ▲ Arizona, SW USA 35°12′N 112°44′W
40 D4 Picachos, Cerro ▲ NW Mexico 29°15′N 114°04′W
103 O4 Picardie Eng. Picardy. ◈ region N France
Picardy see Picardie
22 L8 Picayune Mississippi, S USA 30°31′N 89°40′W
Piccolo San Bernardo, Colle di see Little Saint Bernard Pass
PicdeBälaïtous see Balaïtous
62 K5 Pichanal Salta, N Argentina 23°18′S 64°10′W
147 P12 Pichandar W Tajikistan 38°44′N 68°51′E
27 R8 Picher Oklahoma, C USA 36°59′N 94°49′W
62 G12 Pichilemu Libertador, C Chile 34°25′S 72°00′W
40 F9 Pichilingue Baja California Sur, NW Mexico 24°20′N 110°17′W
56 B6 Pichincha ◈ province N Ecuador
56 C6 Pichincha ▲ N Ecuador 0°12′S 78°39′W
Pichit see Phichit
41 U15 Pichucalco Chiapas, SE Mexico 17°32′N 93°07′W
22 L5 Pickens Mississippi, S USA 32°52′N 89°58′W
21 O11 Pickens South Carolina, SE USA 34°53′N 82°42′W
14 G11 Pickerel ∽ Ontario, S Canada
14 H15 Pickering Ontario, S Canada 43°50′N 79°03′W
97 N16 Pickering N England, United Kingdom 54°14′N 00°47′W
31 S13 Pickerington Ohio, N USA 39°52′N 82°45′W
12 C10 Pickle Lake Ontario, C Canada 51°30′N 90°10′W
29 P12 Pickstown South Dakota, N USA 43°02′N 98°31′W
25 V6 Pickton Texas, SW USA 33°01′N 95°19′W
23 N1 Pickwick Lake ⊠ S USA
64 N2 Pico var. Ilha do Pico. island Azores, Portugal, NE Atlantic Ocean
63 I19 Pico de Salamanca Chubut, SE Argentina 45°26′S 67°26′W
1 P9 Pico Fracture Zone tectonic feature NW Atlantic Ocean
Pico, Ilha do see Pico
59 O14 Picos Piauí, E Brazil 07°05′S 41°24′W
63 I20 Pico Truncado Santa Cruz, SE Argentina 46°45′S 68°00′W
183 S9 Picton New South Wales, SE Australia 34°12′S 150°36′E
14 K15 Picton Ontario, SE Canada 43°59′N 77°09′W
185 K14 Picton Marlborough, South Island, New Zealand 41°18′S 174°00′E
63 H15 Pićun Leufú, Arroyo ∽ SW Argentina
Pidálion see Gkréko, Akrotíri
155 K25 Pidurutalagala ▲ S Sri Lanka 07°03′N 80°47′E
116 K6 Pidvolochys'k Ternopil's'ka Oblast', W Ukraine 49°31′N 26°09′E
107 K16 Piedimonte Matese Campania, S Italy 41°20′N 14°30′E
27 X7 Piedmont Missouri, C USA 37°09′N 90°42′W
21 P11 Piedmont South Carolina, SE USA 34°42′N 82°27′W
17 S12 Piedmont escarpment E USA
Piedmont see Piemonte
31 U13 Piedmont Lake ⊠ Ohio, N USA
104 M11 Piedrabuena Castilla-La Mancha, C Spain 39°02′N 04°10′W
Piedrafita, Puerto de see Pedrafita, Porto de
104 L8 Piedrahita Castilla-León, N Spain 40°27′N 05°20′W
41 N6 Piedras Negras var. Ciudad Porfirio Díaz. Coahuila, NE Mexico 28°40′N 100°32′W
61 E21 Piedras, Punta headland E Argentina 35°27′S 57°04′W
57 I14 Piedras, Río de las ∽ E Peru
111 J16 Piekary Śląskie Śląskie, S Poland 50°24′N 18°58′E
93 M17 Pieksämäki Itä-Suomi, E Finland 62°18′N 27°10′E
109 V5 Pielach ∽ NE Austria
93 M16 Pielavesi Itä-Suomi, C Finland 63°14′N 26°45′E
93 M16 Pielavesi ◎ C Finland
93 N16 Pielinen var. Pielisjärvi. ◎ E Finland
Pielisjärvi see Pielinen
106 A8 Piemonte Eng. Piedmont. ◈ region NW Italy
111 L18 Pieniny ▲ S Poland
111 E14 Pieńsk Ger. Penzig. Dolnośląskie, SW Poland 51°14′N 15°03′E
29 Q13 Pierce Nebraska, C USA 42°12′N 97°31′W
11 R14 Pierceland Saskatchewan, C Canada
115 E14 Piéria ▲ N Greece
29 N10 Pierre state capital South Dakota, N USA 44°22′N 100°21′W
102 K16 Pierrefitte-Nestalas Hautes-Pyrénées, S France 42°57′N 00°04′W
103 R14 Pierrelatte Drôme, E France 44°22′N 04°40′E
15 P11 Pierreville Québec, SE Canada 46°05′N 72°48′W
15 O7 Pierriche ∽ Québec, SE Canada
111 H20 Piešťany Ger. Pistyan, Hung. Pöstyén. Tranavský Kraj, W Slovakia 48°37′N 17°48′E
109 X5 Piesting ∽ E Austria
Pietarhovi see Petrodvorets
Pietari see Sankt-Peterburg
Pietarsaari see Jakobstad
83 K23 Pietermaritzburg var. Maritzburg. KwaZulu/Natal, E South Africa 29°35′S 30°23′E
Pietersburg see Polokwane
107 K24 Pietraperzia Sicilia, Italy, C Mediterranean Sea 37°25′N 14°08′E
107 N22 Pietra Spada, Passo della pass SW Italy
83 K22 Piet Retief Mpumalanga, E South Africa 27°00′S 30°49′E
116 J10 Pietrosul, Vârful prev. Vîrful Pietrosu. ▲ N Romania 47°06′N 25°09′E
106 I6 Pieve di Cadore Veneto, NE Italy 46°27′N 12°22′E
14 C18 Pigeon Bay lake bay Ontario, S Canada
27 X8 Piggott Arkansas, C USA 36°22′N 90°11′W
83 L21 Piggs Peak NW Swaziland 25°58′S 31°17′E
Pigs, Bay of see Cochinos, Bahía de
61 A23 Pigüé Buenos Aires, E Argentina 37°38′S 62°27′W
41 O12 Piguícas ▲ C Mexico 21°08′N 99°37′W
193 W15 Piha Passage passage S Tonga
Pihkva Järv see Pskov, Lake
93 N18 Pihlajavesi ◎ SE Finland
93 J18 Pihlava Länsi-Suomi, SW Finland 61°33′N 21°36′E
93 L16 Pihtipudas Länsi-Suomi, C Finland 63°20′N 25°37′E
40 L14 Pihuamo Jalisco, SW Mexico 19°20′N 103°21′W
189 U11 Piis Moen var. Pis. atoll Chuuk Islands, C Micronesia
41 U17 Pijijiapán Chiapas, SE Mexico 15°42′N 93°12′W
98 G12 Pijnacker Zuid-Holland, W Netherlands 52°01′N 04°26′E
42 H5 Pijol, Pico ▲ NW Honduras 15°07′N 87°39′W
Pikaar see Bikar Atoll
124 I13 Pikalevo Leningradskaya Oblast', NW Russian Federation 59°33′N 34°04′E
188 M15 Pikelot island Caroline Islands, C Micronesia
30 M5 Pike River ∽ Wisconsin, N USA
37 T5 Pikes Peak ▲ Colorado, C USA 38°51′N 105°06′W
21 P6 Pikeville Kentucky, S USA 37°29′N 82°33′W
20 L9 Pikeville Tennessee, S USA 35°35′N 85°11′W
Pikinni see Bikini Atoll
79 H18 Pikounda Sangha, C Congo 0°30′N 16°44′E
110 G9 Piła Ger. Schneidemühl. Wielkopolskie, C Poland 53°09′N 16°44′E
62 N6 Pilagá, Riacho ∽ NE Argentina
61 D20 Pilar Buenos Aires, E Argentina 34°28′S 58°55′W
62 N7 Pilar var. Villa del Pilar. Ñeembucú, S Paraguay 26°55′S 58°20′W
62 N6 Pilcomayo, Rio ∽ C South America
147 R12 Pildon Rus. Pil'don. C Tajikistan 39°10′N 71°00′E
Piles see Pylés
Pilgram see Pelhřimov
152 L10 Pīlībhīt Uttar Pradesh, N India 28°37′N 79°48′E
110 M13 Pilica ∽ C Poland
115 G16 Pílio ▲▲ C Greece
111 J22 Pilisvörösvár Pest, N Hungary 47°38′N 18°55′E
65 G15 Pillar Bay bay Ascension Island, C Atlantic Ocean
183 P17 Pillar, Cape headland Tasmania, SE Australia 43°13′S 147°58′E
Pillau see Baltiysk
183 R5 Pilliga New South Wales, SE Australia 30°22′S 148°53′E
44 H8 Pilón Granma, E Cuba 19°54′N 77°20′W
Pilos see Pýlos
11 W17 Pilot Mound Manitoba, S Canada 49°12′N 98°49′W
21 S8 Pilot Mountain North Carolina, SE USA 36°23′N 80°28′W
39 O14 Pilot Point Alaska, USA 57°33′N 157°34′W
25 T5 Pilot Point Texas, SW USA 33°24′N 96°57′W
32 K11 Pilot Rock Oregon, NW USA 45°28′N 118°49′W
38 M11 Pilot Station Alaska, USA 61°56′N 162°52′W
Pilsen see Plzeň
111 K18 Pilsko ▲ N Slovakia 49°31′N 19°21′E
Pilten see Piltene
118 D8 Piltene Ger. Pilten. Ventspils, W Latvia 57°14′N 21°41′E
111 M16 Pilzno Podkarpackie, SE Poland 49°58′N 21°18′E
Pilzno see Plzeň
37 N14 Pima Arizona, SW USA 32°49′N 109°50′W
58 H13 Pimenta Pará, N Brazil 04°32′S 56°17′W
59 F16 Pimenta Bueno Rondônia, W Brazil 11°40′S 61°14′W
56 B11 Pimentel Lambayeque, W Peru 06°51′S 79°53′W
105 S6 Pina Aragón, NE Spain 41°28′N 00°31′W
119 I20 Pina ∽ SW Belarus
40 E2 Pinacate, Sierra del ▲ NW Mexico 31°49′N 113°30′W
63 H22 Pináculo, Cerro ▲ S Argentina 50°46′S 72°07′W
191 X11 Pinaki atoll Îles Tuamotu, E French Polynesia
37 N15 Pinaleno Mountains ▲▲ Arizona, SW USA
171 P4 Pinamalayan Mindoro, N Philippines 13°00′N 121°30′E
169 Q10 Pinang Borneo, C Indonesia 0°36′N 109°11′W
168 J7 Pinang var. Penang. ◈ state Peninsular Malaysia
Pinang see Pinang, Pulau, Peninsular Malaysia
Pinang see George Town
168 J7 Pinang, Pulau var. Penang, Pinang; prev. Prince of Wales Island. island Peninsular Malaysia
44 B5 Pinar del Río Pinar del Río, W Cuba 22°24′N 83°42′W
114 N11 Pınarhisar Kırklareli, NW Turkey 41°37′N 27°32′E
171 O3 Pinatubo, Mount Ѫ Luzon, N Philippines 15°08′N 120°21′E
11 Y16 Pinawa Manitoba, S Canada 50°09′N 95°52′W
11 Q17 Pincher Creek Alberta, SW Canada 49°31′N 113°53′W
30 L16 Pinckneyville Illinois, N USA 38°04′N 89°22′W
Pińczota see Pâncota
111 L15 Pińczów Świętokrzyskie, C Poland 50°30′N 20°30′E
149 U7 Pind Dādan Khān Punjab, E Pakistan 32°36′N 73°07′E
Píndhos/Píndhos Óros see Píndos
149 V8 Pindi Bhattiān Punjab, E Pakistan 31°54′N 73°20′E
149 U6 Pindi Gheb Punjab, E Pakistan 33°16′N 72°21′E
115 D15 Píndos var. Píndhos Óros, Eng. Pindus Mountains; prev. Píndhos. ▲▲ C Greece
Pindus Mountains see Píndos

◆ Country
● Country Capital
◇ Dependent Territory
○ Dependent Territory Capital
◈ Administrative Regions
✈ International Airport
▲ Mountain
▲▲ Mountain Range
Ѫ Volcano
∽ River
◎ Lake
⊠ Reservoir

PINE BARRENS – POKHARĀ

18 J16 **Pine Barrens** physical region New Jersey, NE USA
27 V12 **Pine Bluff** Arkansas, C USA 34°15'N 92°00'W
23 X11 **Pine Castle** Florida, SE USA 28°28'N 81°22'W
29 V7 **Pine City** Minnesota, N USA 45°49'N 92°55'W
181 P2 **Pine Creek** Northern Territory, N Australia 13°51'S 131°51'E
35 V4 **Pine Creek** ≈ Nevada, W USA
18 F13 **Pine Creek** ≈ Pennsylvania, NE USA
27 Q13 **Pine Creek Lake** ▣ Oklahoma, C USA
33 T15 **Pinedale** Wyoming, C USA 42°52'N 109°51'W
11 X15 **Pine Dock** Manitoba, S Canada 51°34'N 96°47'W
11 Y16 **Pine Falls** Manitoba, S Canada 50°29'N 96°12'W
35 R10 **Pine Flat Lake** ▣ California, W USA
125 N8 **Pinega** Arkhangel'skaya Oblast', NW Russian Federation 64°40'N 43°24'E
125 N8 **Pinega** ≈ NW Russian Federation
15 N12 **Pine Hill** Québec, SE Canada 45°44'N 74°30'W
11 T12 **Pinehouse Lake** ◎ Saskatchewan, C Canada
21 T10 **Pinehurst** North Carolina, SE USA 35°12'N 79°28'W
115 D19 **Pineiós** ≈ S Greece
115 E16 **Pineiós** var. Piniós; anc. Peneius. ≈ C Greece
29 W10 **Pine Island** Minnesota, N USA 44°12'N 92°39'W
23 V15 **Pine Island** island Florida, SE USA
194 K10 **Pine Island Glacier** glacier Antarctica
25 X9 **Pineland** Texas, SW USA 31°15'N 93°58'W
23 V13 **Pinellas Park** Florida, SE USA 27°50'N 82°42'W
10 M13 **Pine Pass** pass British Columbia, W Canada
8 J10 **Pine Point** Northwest Territories, W Canada 60°52'N 114°30'W
28 K12 **Pine Ridge** South Dakota, N USA 43°01'N 102°33'W
29 U6 **Pine River** Minnesota, N USA 46°43'N 94°24'W
31 Q8 **Pine River** ≈ Michigan, N USA
30 M4 **Pine River** ≈ Wisconsin, N USA
106 A8 **Pinerolo** Piemonte, NE Italy 44°56'N 07°21'E
115 I15 **Pines, Akrotírio** var. Akrotírio Pínnes. headland N Greece 40°06'N 24°19'E
25 W6 **Pines, Lake O' the** ▣ Texas, SW USA
Pines, The Isle of the see Juventud, Isla de la
Pine Tree State see Maine
21 N7 **Pineville** Kentucky, S USA 36°47'N 83°43'W
22 H7 **Pineville** Louisiana, S USA 31°19'N 92°25'W
27 R8 **Pineville** Missouri, C USA 36°36'N 94°23'W
21 R10 **Pineville** North Carolina, SE USA 35°04'N 80°53'W
21 Q6 **Pineville** West Virginia, NE USA 37°35'N 81°34'W
33 W8 **Piney Buttes** physical region Montana, NW USA
163 W9 **Ping'an** Jilin, NE China 44°36'N 127°13'E
160 H14 **Pingbian** var. Pingbian Miaozu Zizhixian, Yuping. Yunnan, SW China 22°51'N 103°28'E
Pingbian Miaozu Zizhixian see Pingbian
157 S9 **Pingdingshan** Henan, C China 33°52'N 113°20'E
161 R4 **Pingdu** Shandong, E China 36°50'N 119°55'E
189 W16 **Pingelap Atoll** atoll Caroline Islands, E Micronesia
160 K14 **Pingguo** var. Matou. Guangxi Zhuangzu Zizhiqu, S China 23°24'N 107°30'E
161 Q13 **Pinghe** var. Xiaoxi. Fujian, SE China 24°30'N 117°19'E
P'ing-hsiang see Pingxiang
161 N10 **Pingjiang** Hunan, S China 28°44'N 113°33'E
Pingkiang see Harbin
160 L8 **Pingli** Shaanxi, C China 32°27'N 109°21'E
159 W10 **Pingliang** var. Kongtong, P'ing-liang. Gansu, C China 35°27'N 106°38'E
P'ing-liang see Pingliang
159 W8 **Pingluo** Ningxia, N China 38°55'N 106°31'E
Pingma see Tiandong
167 O7 **Ping, Mae Nam** ≈ W Thailand
161 Q1 **Pingquan** Hebei, E China 41°02'N 118°35'E
29 P5 **Pingree** North Dakota, N USA 47°07'N 98°54'W
Pingsiang see Pingxiang
161 S14 **P'ingtung** Jap. Heitō. S Taiwan 22°40'N 120°30'E
160 I8 **Pingwu** var. Long'an. Sichuan, C China 32°33'N 104°32'E
160 J15 **Pingxiang** Guangxi Zhuangzu Zizhiqu, S China 22°03'N 106°44'E
161 O11 **Pingxiang** var. P'ing-hsiang; prev. Pingsiang. Jiangxi, S China 27°42'N 113°50'E
Pingxiang see Tongwei
161 S11 **Pingyang** var. Kunyang. Zhejiang, SE China 27°46'N 120°37'E
161 P5 **Pingyi** Shandong, E China 35°30'N 117°38'E
161 P5 **Pingyin** Shandong, E China 36°18'N 116°24'E
60 H13 **Pinhalzinho** Santa Catarina, S Brazil 26°53'S 52°57'W
60 I12 **Pinhão** Paraná, S Brazil 25°46'S 51°32'W
61 H17 **Pinheiro Machado** Rio Grande do Sul, S Brazil 31°34'S 53°22'W
104 I7 **Pinhel** Guarda, N Portugal 40°47'N 07°03'W
Piniós see Pineiós
168 I11 **Pini, Pulau** island Kepulauan Batu, W Indonesia
109 Y7 **Pinka** ≈ SE Austria
109 X7 **Pinkafeld** Burgenland, SE Austria 47°23'N 16°08'E
Pinkiang see Harbin
10 M12 **Pink Mountain** British Columbia, W Canada 57°10'N 122°36'W
166 M3 **Pinlebu** Sagaing, N Burma (Myanmar) 24°02'N 95°21'E
38 J12 **Pinnacle Island** island Alaska, USA
180 I12 **Pinnacles, The** tourist site Western Australia
182 K10 **Pinnaroo** South Australia 35°17'S 140°54'E
Pinne see Pniewy
100 I9 **Pinneberg** Schleswig-Holstein, N Germany 53°40'N 09°49'E
Pínnes, Akrotírio see Pínes, Akrotírio
Pinos, Isla de see Juventud, Isla de la
35 R14 **Pinos, Mount** ▲ California, W USA 34°48'N 119°09'W
105 R12 **Pinoso** País Valenciano, E Spain 38°25'N 01°02'W
105 N14 **Pinos-Puente** Andalucía, S Spain 37°16'N 03°46'W
41 Q17 **Pinotepa Nacional** var. Santiago Pinotepa Nacional. Oaxaca, SE Mexico 16°20'N 98°02'W
114 F13 **Pinovo** ▲ N Greece 41°06'N 22°19'E
187 R17 **Pins, Île des** var. Kunyé. island E New Caledonia
119 I20 **Pinsk** Pol. Pińsk. Brestskaya Voblasts', SW Belarus 52°07'N 26°07'E
14 D18 **Pins, Pointe aux** headland Ontario, S Canada 42°14'N 81°53'W
57 B16 **Pinta, Isla** var. Abingdon. island Galapagos Islands, Ecuador, E Pacific Ocean
125 Q12 **Pinyug** Kirovskaya Oblast', NW Russian Federation 60°12'N 47°45'E
57 B17 **Pinzón, Isla** var. Duncan Island. island Galapagos Islands, Ecuador, E Pacific Ocean
35 Y8 **Pioche** Nevada, W USA 37°57'N 114°30'W
106 F13 **Piombino** Toscana, C Italy 42°54'N 10°30'E
0 C9 **Pioneer Fracture Zone** tectonic feature NE Pacific Ocean
122 L5 **Pioner, Ostrov** island Severnaya Zemlya, N Russian Federation
118 A13 **Pionerskiy** Ger. Neukuhren. Kaliningradskaya Oblast', W Russian Federation 54°57'N 20°16'E
110 N13 **Pionki** Mazowieckie, C Poland 51°30'N 21°27'E
184 L9 **Piopio** Waikato, North Island, New Zealand 38°27'S 175°00'E
110 K13 **Piotrków Trybunalski** Ger. Petrikau, Rus. Petrokov. Łodzkie, C Poland 51°25'N 19°42'E
152 F12 **Pīpār Road** Rājasthān, N India 26°25'N 73°29'E
115 I16 **Pipéri** island Vóreies Sporádes, Greece, Aegean Sea
29 S10 **Pipestone** Minnesota, N USA 44°00'N 96°19'W
12 C9 **Pipestone** ≈ Ontario, C Canada
61 E21 **Pipinas** Buenos Aires, E Argentina 35°32'S 57°20'W
149 T7 **Piplān** prev. Liaqatabad. Punjab, E Pakistan 32°17'N 71°24'E
15 R5 **Pipmuacan, Réservoir** ▣ Québec, SE Canada
Piqan see Shanshan
31 R13 **Piqua** Ohio, N USA 40°08'N 84°14'W
105 P5 **Piqueras, Puerto de** pass N Spain
60 H11 **Piquiri, Rio** ≈ S Brazil
60 L9 **Piracicaba** São Paulo, S Brazil 22°45'S 47°40'W
Piraeus/Piraiévs see Peiraías
60 K10 **Piraju** São Paulo, S Brazil 23°12'S 49°24'W
60 K9 **Pirajuí** São Paulo, S Brazil 21°58'S 49°27'W
63 G21 **Pirámide, Cerro** ▲ S Chile 49°06'S 73°32'W
Piramiva see Pyramíva
109 R13 **Piran** It. Pirano. SW Slovenia 45°35'N 13°35'E
62 N6 **Pirané** Formosa, N Argentina 25°42'S 59°06'W
59 J18 **Piranhas** Goiás, S Brazil 16°24'S 51°51'W
Pirano see Piran
142 I4 **Pīrānshahr** Āzarbāyjān-e Gharbī, NW Iran 36°41'N 45°08'E
59 M19 **Pirapora** Minas Gerais, NE Brazil 17°20'S 44°54'W
60 I9 **Pirapòzinho** São Paulo, S Brazil 22°17'S 51°31'W
61 G19 **Piraraja** Lavalleja, S Uruguay 33°44'S 54°45'W
60 L9 **Pirassununga** São Paulo, S Brazil 21°58'S 47°23'W
45 V6 **Pirata, Monte** ▲ E Puerto Rico 18°06'N 65°33'W
60 I13 **Piratuba** Santa Catarina, S Brazil 27°26'S 51°47'W
114 I9 **Pirdop** prev. Strednogorie. Sofiya, W Bulgaria 42°44'N 24°09'E
191 P7 **Pirea** Tahiti, W French Polynesia
59 K18 **Pirenópolis** Goiás, S Brazil 15°48'S 49°00'W
153 S13 **Pirganj** Rajshahi, NW Bangladesh 25°51'N 88°25'E
Pirgi see Pyrgí
Pírgos see Pýrgos
61 F20 **Piriápolis** Maldonado, S Uruguay 34°51'S 55°15'W
114 G11 **Pirin** ▲▲ SW Bulgaria
Pirineos see Pyrenees
58 N13 **Piripiri** Piauí, E Brazil 04°15'S 41°46'W
118 H4 **Pirita** var. Pirita Jõgi. ≈ NW Estonia
Pirita Jõgi see Pirita
54 J6 **Píritu** Portuguesa, N Venezuela 09°21'N 69°16'W
93 L18 **Pirkkala** Länsi-Suomi, W Finland 61°27'N 23°47'E
101 F20 **Pirmasens** Rheinland-Pfalz, SW Germany 49°12'N 07°37'E
101 P16 **Pirna** Sachsen, E Germany 50°57'N 13°56'E
Piroe see Piru
113 Q15 **Pirot** Serbia, SE Serbia 43°12'N 22°34'E
152 H6 **Pīr Panjāl Range** ▲▲ NE India
43 W16 **Pirre, Cerro** ▲ SE Panama 07°54'N 77°42'W
137 Y11 **Pirsaat** Rus. Pirsagat. ≈ E Azerbaijan
Pirsagat see Pirsaat
143 V11 **Pīr Shūrān, Selseleh-ye** ▲ SE Iran
92 M12 **Pirttikoski** Lappi, N Finland 66°20'N 27°08'E
Pirttikylä see Pörtom
171 R13 **Piru** prev. Piroe. Pulau Seram, E Indonesia 03°01'S 128°10'E
Piryatin see Pyryatyn
Pis see Piis Moen
106 F11 **Pisa** var. Pisae. Toscana, C Italy 43°43'N 10°23'E
Pisae see Pisa
189 V12 **Pisar** atoll Chuuk Islands, C Micronesia
Pisaurum see Pesaro
14 M10 **Piscatosine, Lac** ◎ Québec, SE Canada
109 W7 **Pischeldorf** Steiermark, SE Austria 47°11'N 15°48'E
Pischk see Simeria
107 L19 **Pisciotta** Campania, S Italy 40°07'N 15°13'E
57 E16 **Pisco** Ica, SW Peru 13°46'S 76°12'W
116 G9 **Pişcolt** Hung. Piskolt. Satu Mare, NW Romania 47°35'N 22°18'E
57 E16 **Pisco, Río** ≈ E Peru
111 C18 **Písek** Budějovický Kraj, S Czech Republic 49°19'N 14°07'E
31 R14 **Pisgah** Ohio, N USA 39°19'N 84°22'W
Pisha see Ningnan
158 F9 **Pishan** var. Guma. Xinjiang Uygur Zizhiqu, NW China 37°36'N 78°45'E
117 N8 **Pishchanka** Vinnyts'ka Oblast', C Ukraine 48°12'N 28°52'E
113 K21 **Pishë** Fier, SW Albania 40°40'N 19°22'E
143 X14 **Pīshīn** Sīstān va Balūchestān, SE Iran 26°05'N 61°46'E
149 O9 **Pishin** North-West Frontier Province, NW Pakistan 30°33'N 67°01'E
149 N11 **Pishin Lora** var. Psein Lora, Pash. Pseyn Bowr. ≈ SW Pakistan
Pishma see Pizhma
Pishpek see Bishkek
171 O14 **Pising** Pulau Kabaena, C Indonesia 05°07'S 121°50'E
Pisino see Pazin
Piski see Simeria
Piskolt see Pişcolt
147 Q9 **Piskom** Rus. Pskem. ≈ E Uzbekistan
Piskom Tizmasi see Pskemskiy Khrebet
35 P13 **Pismo Beach** California, W USA 35°08'N 120°38'W
77 P12 **Pissila** C Burkina 13°07'N 00°51'W
62 H8 **Pissis, Monte** ▲ N Argentina 27°45'S 68°43'W
41 X12 **Piste** Yucatán, E Mexico 20°40'N 88°34'W
107 O18 **Pisticci** Basilicata, S Italy 40°23'N 16°33'E
106 F11 **Pistoia** anc. Pistoria, Pistoriæ. Toscana, C Italy 43°57'N 10°53'E
32 E15 **Pistol River** Oregon, NW USA 42°13'N 124°23'W
Pistoria/Pistoriæ see Pistoia
15 U5 **Pistuacanis** ≈ Québec, SE Canada
Pistyan see Piešt'any
104 M5 **Pisuerga** ≈ N Spain
110 N8 **Pisz** Ger. Johannisburg. Warmińsko-Mazurskie, NE Poland 53°37'N 21°49'E
76 I13 **Pita** NW Guinea 11°05'N 12°15'W
54 D12 **Pitalito** Huila, S Colombia 01°51'N 76°01'W
60 I11 **Pitanga** Paraná, S Brazil 24°45'S 51°43'W
182 M9 **Pitarpunga Lake** salt lake New South Wales, SE Australia
193 P10 **Pitcairn Island** island S Pitcairn Islands
193 P10 **Pitcairn Islands** ◇ UK dependent territory C Pacific Ocean
93 J15 **Piteå** Norrbotten, N Sweden 65°19'N 21°30'E
92 I13 **Piteälven** ≈ N Sweden
116 I13 **Piteşti** Argeş, S Romania 44°53'N 24°49'E
Pithagorio see Pythagóreio
180 I12 **Pithara** Western Australia 30°31'S 116°38'E
103 N6 **Pithiviers** Loiret, C France 48°10'N 02°15'E
152 L9 **Pithorāgarh** Uttarakhand, N India 29°35'N 80°12'E
188 B16 **Piti** W Guam 13°28'N 144°42'E
106 G13 **Pitigliano** Toscana, C Italy 42°38'N 11°40'E
40 F3 **Pitiquito** Sonora, NW Mexico 30°39'N 112°00'W
Pitkäranta see Pitkyaranta
38 M11 **Pitkas Point** Alaska, USA 62°01'N 163°17'W
124 H11 **Pitkyaranta** Fin. Pitkäranta. Respublika Kareliya, NW Russian Federation 61°34'N 31°27'E
96 J10 **Pitlochry** C Scotland, United Kingdom 56°47'N 03°48'W
18 I16 **Pitman** New Jersey, NE USA 39°43'N 75°06'W
146 I9 **Pitnak** var. Drujba, Rus. Druzhba. Xorazm Viloyati, W Uzbekistan 41°14'N 61°13'E
112 G8 **Pitomača** Virovitica-Podravina, NE Croatia 45°57'N 17°14'E
35 O2 **Pit River** ≈ California, W USA
63 G15 **Pitrufquén** Araucanía, S Chile 38°59'S 72°40'W
Pitsanulok see Phitsanulok
Pitschen see Byczyna
Pitsunda see Bichvint'a
109 X6 **Pitten** ≈ E Austria
10 J14 **Pitt Island** island British Columbia, W Canada
Pitt Island see Makin
22 M3 **Pittsboro** Mississippi, S USA 33°55'N 89°20'W
21 T9 **Pittsboro** North Carolina, SE USA 35°46'N 79°12'W
27 R7 **Pittsburg** Kansas, C USA 37°24'N 94°42'W
25 W6 **Pittsburg** Texas, SW USA 33°00'N 94°58'W
18 B14 **Pittsburgh** Pennsylvania, NE USA 40°26'N 80°W
30 J14 **Pittsfield** Illinois, N USA 39°36'N 90°48'W
19 R6 **Pittsfield** Maine, NE USA 44°46'N 69°22'W
18 L11 **Pittsfield** Massachusetts, NE USA 42°27'N 73°15'W
183 U3 **Pittsworth** Queensland, E Australia 27°43'S 151°36'E
62 I8 **Pituil** La Rioja, NW Argentina 28°33'S 67°24'W
56 A10 **Piura** Piura, NW Peru 05°11'S 80°41'W
56 A9 **Piura** off. Departamento de Piura. ◈ department NW Peru
Piura, Departamento de see Piura
35 S13 **Piute Peak** ▲ California, W USA 35°27'N 118°24'W
113 J15 **Piva** ≈ NW Montenegro
117 V5 **Pivdenne** Kharkivs'ka Oblast', E Ukraine 49°52'N 36°04'E
117 P8 **Pivdennyy Buh** Rus. Yuzhnyy Bug. ≈ S Ukraine
54 F5 **Pivijay** Magdalena, N Colombia 10°31'N 74°36'W
109 T13 **Pivka** prev. Šent Peter, Ger. Sankt Peter, It. San Pietro del Carso. SW Slovenia 45°41'N 14°12'E
117 U13 **Pivnichno-Kryms'kyy Kanal** canal S Ukraine
113 J15 **Pivsko Jezero** ◎ NW Montenegro
111 M18 **Piwniczna** Małopolskie, S Poland 49°26'N 20°43'E
35 R12 **Pixley** California, W USA 35°58'N 119°18'W
125 Q15 **Pizhma** var. Pishma. ≈ NW Russian Federation
13 U13 **Placentia** Newfoundland, Newfoundland and Labrador, SE Canada 47°12'N 53°58'W
Placentia see Piacenza
13 U13 **Placentia Bay** inlet Newfoundland, Newfoundland and Labrador, SE Canada
171 P5 **Placer** Masbate, N Philippines 11°54'N 123°54'E
35 P7 **Placerville** California, W USA 38°42'N 120°48'W
44 F5 **Placetas** Villa Clara, C Cuba 22°18'N 79°40'W
113 Q18 **Plačkovica** ▲ E Macedonia
36 L2 **Plain City** Utah, W USA 41°18'N 112°05'W
22 G4 **Plain Dealing** Louisiana, S USA 32°54'N 93°42'W
31 O14 **Plainfield** Indiana, N USA 39°42'N 86°18'W
18 K14 **Plainfield** New Jersey, NE USA 40°37'N 74°25'W
33 O8 **Plains** Montana, NW USA 47°27'N 114°52'W
24 L6 **Plains** Texas, SW USA 33°12'N 102°50'W
29 X10 **Plainview** Minnesota, N USA 44°10'N 92°10'W
29 Q13 **Plainview** Nebraska, C USA 42°21'N 97°47'W
25 N4 **Plainview** Texas, SW USA 34°12'N 101°43'W
26 K4 **Plainville** Kansas, C USA 39°13'N 99°18'W
115 I22 **Pláka** var. Mílos. Mílos, Kykládes, Greece, Aegean Sea 36°44'N 24°25'E
115 J15 **Pláka, Akrotírio** headland Límnos, E Greece 40°02'N 25°25'E
113 N19 **Plakenska Planina** ▲▲ SW Macedonia
44 K5 **Plana Cays** islets SE Bahamas
105 S12 **Plana, Isla** var. Nueva Tabarca. island E Spain
59 L18 **Planaltina** Goiás, S Brazil 15°35'S 47°28'W
83 O14 **Planalto Moçambicano** plateau N Mozambique
112 N10 **Plandište** Vojvodina, NE Serbia 45°13'N 21°07'E
100 N13 **Plane** ≈ NE Germany
54 E6 **Planeta Rica** Córdoba, NW Colombia 08°24'N 75°39'W
29 P11 **Plankinton** South Dakota, N USA 43°43'N 98°28'W
30 M11 **Plano** Illinois, N USA 41°39'N 88°32'W
25 U6 **Plano** Texas, SW USA 33°01'N 96°42'W
23 W12 **Plant City** Florida, SE USA 28°01'N 82°06'W
22 J9 **Plaquemine** Louisiana, S USA 30°17'N 91°13'W
104 K9 **Plasencia** Extremadura, W Spain 40°02'N 06°05'W
110 P7 **Płaska** Podlaskie, NE Poland 53°55'N 23°18'E
112 C10 **Plaški** Karlovac, C Croatia 45°04'N 15°21'E
113 N19 **Plasnica** SW FYR Macedonia 41°28'N 21°07'E
13 N14 **Plaster Rock** New Brunswick, SE Canada 46°55'N 67°24'W
107 J24 **Platani** anc. Halycus. ≈ Sicilia, Italy, C Mediterranean Sea
115 G17 **Plataniá** Thessalía, C Greece 39°09'N 23°15'E
115 G24 **Plátanos** Kríti, Greece, E Mediterranean Sea 35°27'N 23°34'E
65 H18 **Plata, Río de la** var. River Plate. estuary Argentina/Uruguay
77 V15 **Plateau** ◈ state C Nigeria
79 G19 **Plateaux** var. Région des Plateaux. ◈ province C Congo
Plateaux, Région des see Plateaux
Plate, Île see Flat Island
92 P1 **Platen, Kapp** headland NE Svalbard 80°30'N 22°46'E
Plate, River see Plata, Río de la
99 G22 **Plate Taille, Lac de la** var. L'Eau d'Heure. ◎ SE Belgium
Plathe see Płoty
39 N13 **Platinum** Alaska, USA 59°01'N 161°49'W
54 F5 **Plato** Magdalena, N Colombia 09°47'N 74°47'W
29 O11 **Platte** South Dakota, N USA 43°20'N 98°51'W
27 R3 **Platte City** Missouri, C USA 39°22'N 94°47'W
Plattensee see Balaton
27 R3 **Platte River** ≈ Iowa/Missouri, USA
29 Q15 **Platte River** ≈ Nebraska, C USA
37 T3 **Platteville** Colorado, C USA 40°13'N 104°49'W
30 K9 **Platteville** Wisconsin, N USA 42°44'N 90°27'W
101 N21 **Plattling** Bayern, SE Germany 48°45'N 12°52'E
27 R3 **Plattsburg** Missouri, C USA 39°33'N 94°27'W
18 L6 **Plattsburgh** New York, NE USA 44°42'N 73°29'W
29 S15 **Plattsmouth** Nebraska, C USA 41°00'N 95°52'W
101 M17 **Plauen** var. Plauen im Vogtland. Sachsen, E Germany 50°31'N 12°08'E
Plauen im Vogtland see Plauen
100 M10 **Plauer See** ◎ NE Germany
113 L16 **Plav** E Montenegro 42°36'N 19°57'E
118 I10 **Pļaviņas** Ger. Stockmannshof. Aizkraukle, S Latvia 56°37'N 25°40'E
126 K5 **Plavsk** Tul'skaya Oblast', W Russian Federation 53°42'N 37°21'E
41 Z12 **Playa del Carmen** Quintana Roo, E Mexico 20°37'N 87°04'W
40 J12 **Playa Los Corchos** Nayarit, SW Mexico 21°91'N 105°28'W
37 P16 **Playas Lake** ◎ New Mexico, SW USA
41 S15 **Playa Vicenté** Veracruz-Llave, SE Mexico 17°42'N 95°01'W
167 U11 **Plây Cu** var. Pleiku. Gia Lai, C Vietnam 13°57'N 108°01'E
28 L3 **Plaza** North Dakota, N USA 48°00'N 102°00'W
63 I15 **Plaza Huincul** Neuquén, C Argentina 38°55'S 69°14'W
36 L3 **Pleasant Grove** Utah, W USA 40°21'N 111°44'W
29 V14 **Pleasant Hill** Iowa, C USA 41°34'N 93°31'W
27 R4 **Pleasant Hill** Missouri, C USA 38°47'N 94°16'W
Pleasant Island see Nauru
36 K13 **Pleasant, Lake** ▣ Arizona, SW USA
19 P8 **Pleasant Mountain** ▲ Maine, NE USA 44°01'N 70°47'W
27 R5 **Pleasanton** Kansas, C USA 38°09'N 94°43'W
25 R12 **Pleasanton** Texas, SW USA 28°58'N 98°28'W
185 G20 **Pleasant Point** Canterbury, South Island, New Zealand 44°16'S 171°09'E
19 R5 **Pleasant River** ≈ Maine, NE USA
18 J17 **Pleasantville** New Jersey, NE USA 39°22'N 74°31'W
103 N12 **Pléaux** Cantal, C France 45°08'N 02°10'E
111 B19 **Plechý** var. Plöckenstein. ▲ Austria/Czech Republic 48°45'N 13°50'E
Pleebo see Plibo
Pleihari see Pelaihari
Pleiku see Plây Cu
101 M16 **Pleisse** ≈ E Germany
Plencia see Plentzia
184 O7 **Plenty, Bay of** bay North Island, New Zealand
33 Y6 **Plentywood** Montana, NW USA 48°46'N 104°33'W
105 O2 **Plentzia** var. Plencia. País Vasco, N Spain 43°25'N 02°56'W
102 H5 **Plérin** Côtes d'Armor, NW France 48°33'N 02°46'W
124 M10 **Plesetsk** Arkhangel'skaya Oblast', NW Russian Federation 62°41'N 40°14'E
Pleshchenitsy see Plyeshchanitsy
Pleskau see Pskov
Pleskauer See see Pskov, Lake
Pleskava see Pskov
112 E8 **Pleso International** ✈ (Zagreb) Zagreb, NW Croatia 45°45'N 16°00'E
Pless see Pszczyna
15 Q11 **Plessisville** Québec, SE Canada 46°14'N 71°46'W
110 H12 **Pleszew** Wielkopolskie, C Poland 51°54'N 17°47'E
12 L10 **Plétipi, Lac** ◎ Québec, SE Canada
101 F15 **Plettenberg** Nordrhein-Westfalen, W Germany 51°13'N 07°52'E
114 I8 **Pleven** prev. Plevna. Pleven, N Bulgaria 43°25'N 24°36'E
114 I8 **Pleven** ◈ province N Bulgaria
Plevlja/Plevlje see Pljevlja
Plevna see Pleven
Plezzo see Bovec
Pliberk see Bleiburg
76 L17 **Plibo** var. Pleebo. SE Liberia 04°38'N 07°41'W
121 R11 **Pliny Trench** undersea feature C Mediterranean Sea
118 K13 **Plisa** Rus. Plissa. Vitsyebskaya Voblasts', N Belarus 55°13'N 27°57'E
Plissa see Plisa
112 D11 **Plitvica Selo** Lika-Senj, W Croatia 44°53'N 15°36'E
112 D11 **Plješevica** ▲ C Croatia
113 K14 **Pljevlja** prev. Plevlja, Plevlje. N Montenegro 43°21'N 19°21'E
Ploça see Ploçë
Plocce see Ploče
113 K22 **Ploçë** var. Ploça. Vlorë, SW Albania 40°24'N 19°41'E
113 G15 **Ploče** It. Plocce; prev. Kardeljevo. Dubrovnik-Neretva, SE Croatia 43°02'N 17°25'E
110 K11 **Płock** Ger. Plozk. Mazowieckie, C Poland 52°32'N 19°40'E
109 Q10 **Plöcken Pass** Ger. Plöckenpass, It. Passo di Monte Croce Carnico. pass SW Austria
Plöckenpass see Plöcken Pass
Plöckenstein see Plechý
99 B19 **Ploegsteert** Hainaut, W Belgium 50°45'N 02°52'E
102 H6 **Ploërmel** Morbihan, NW France 47°57'N 02°24'W
Ploeşti see Ploieşti
116 K13 **Ploieşti** prev. Ploeşti. Prahova, SE Romania 44°56'N 26°03'E
115 L17 **Plomári** prev. Plomárion. Lésvos, E Greece 38°58'N 26°24'E
Plomárion see Plomári
103 O12 **Plomb du Cantal** ▲ C France 45°03'N 02°48'E
183 V6 **Plomer, Point** headland New South Wales, SE Australia 31°19'S 153°00'E
100 J8 **Plön** Schleswig-Holstein, N Germany 54°10'N 10°25'E
110 L11 **Płońsk** Mazowieckie, C Poland 52°38'N 20°23'E
119 J20 **Plotnitsa** Brestskaya Voblasts', SW Belarus 52°03'N 26°39'E
110 E8 **Płoty** Ger. Plathe. Zachodnio-pomorskie, NW Poland 53°48'N 15°16'E
102 G7 **Plouay** Morbihan, NW France 47°54'N 03°14'W
111 D15 **Ploučnice** Ger. Polzen. ≈ NE Czech Republic
114 I10 **Plovdiv** prev. Eumolpias; anc. Evmolpia, Philippopolis, Lat. Trimontium. Plovdiv, C Bulgaria 42°09'N 24°47'E
114 I11 **Plovdiv** ◈ province C Bulgaria
30 L6 **Plover** Wisconsin, N USA 44°30'N 89°33'W
Plozk see Płock
27 U11 **Plumerville** Arkansas, C USA 35°09'N 92°38'W
19 P10 **Plum Island** island Massachusetts, NE USA
32 M9 **Plummer** Idaho, NW USA 47°19'N 116°54'W
83 J18 **Plumtree** Matabeleland South, SW Zimbabwe 20°30'S 27°50'E
118 D11 **Plungė** Telšiai, W Lithuania 55°55'N 21°53'E
113 J15 **Plužine** NW Montenegro 43°08'N 18°49'E
119 K14 **Plyeshchanitsy** Rus. Pleshchenitsy. Minskaya Voblasts', N Belarus 54°25'N 27°50'E
45 V10 **Plymouth** ○ (Montserrat) SW Montserrat 16°44'N 62°14'W
97 I24 **Plymouth** SW England, United Kingdom 50°23'N 04°10'W
31 O11 **Plymouth** Indiana, N USA 41°20'N 86°19'W
19 P12 **Plymouth** Massachusetts, NE USA 41°57'N 70°40'W
19 N8 **Plymouth** New Hampshire, NE USA 43°43'N 71°39'W
21 X9 **Plymouth** North Carolina, SE USA 35°53'N 76°46'W
30 M8 **Plymouth** Wisconsin, N USA 43°48'N 87°58'W
97 J20 **Plynlimon** ▲ C Wales, United Kingdom 52°27'N 03°48'W
124 G14 **Plyussa** Pskovskaya Oblast', W Russian Federation 58°27'N 29°21'E
111 B17 **Plzeň** Ger. Pilsen, Pol. Pilzno. Plzeňský Kraj, W Czech Republic 49°45'N 13°23'E
111 B17 **Plzeňský Kraj** ◈ region W Czech Republic
110 F11 **Pniewy** Ger. Pinne. Wielkolpolskie, W Poland 52°31'N 16°14'E
77 P13 **Pô** S Burkina 11°11'N 01°10'W
106 D8 **Po** ≈ N Italy
42 M13 **Poás, Volcán** ⛰ NW Costa Rica 10°12'N 84°12'W
77 S16 **Pobè** S Benin 07°00'N 02°41'E
123 S8 **Pobeda, Gora** ▲ NE Russian Federation 65°28'N 145°44'E
Pobeda Peak see Pobedy, Pik/Tomur Feng
147 Z7 **Pobedy, Pik** Chin. Tomür Feng. ▲ China/Kyrgyzstan 42°02'N 80°02'E see also Tomür Feng
Pobedy, Pik see Tomür Feng
110 H11 **Pobiedziska** Ger. Pudewitz. Wielkolpolskie, C Poland 52°30'N 17°19'E
Po, Bocche del see Po, Foci del
27 W9 **Pocahontas** Arkansas, C USA 36°15'N 91°00'W
29 U12 **Pocahontas** Iowa, C USA 42°44'N 94°40'W
33 Q15 **Pocatello** Idaho, NW USA 42°52'N 112°27'W
167 S13 **Pochentong** ✈ (Phnum Penh) Phnum Penh, S Cambodia 11°24'N 104°52'E
126 I6 **Pochep** Bryanskaya Oblast', W Russian Federation 52°56'N 33°20'E
126 H4 **Pochinok** Smolenskaya Oblast', W Russian Federation 54°21'N 32°29'E
41 R17 **Pochutla** var. San Pedro Pochutla. Oaxaca, SE Mexico 15°45'N 96°30'W
62 I6 **Pocitos, Salar** var. Salar Quiróm. salt lake NW Argentina
101 O22 **Pocking** Bayern, SE Germany 48°22'N 13°17'E
186 I10 **Pocklington Reef** reef SE Papua New Guinea
59 P15 **Poço da Cruz, Açude** ▣ E Brazil
27 R11 **Pocola** Oklahoma, C USA 35°13'N 94°28'W
21 Y5 **Pocomoke City** Maryland, NE USA 38°04'N 75°34'W
59 L21 **Poços de Caldas** Minas Gerais, NE Brazil 21°48'S 46°33'W
124 H14 **Podberez'ye** Novgorodskaya Oblast', NW Russian Federation 58°42'N 31°22'E
Podbrodzie see Pabradė
125 U8 **Podcher'ye** Respublika Komi, NW Russian Federation 63°55'N 57°34'E
111 E16 **Poděbrady** Ger. Podiebrad. Středočeský Kraj, C Czech Republic 50°10'N 15°06'E
126 L9 **Podgorenskiy** Voronezhskaya Oblast', W Russian Federation 50°22'N 39°43'E
113 J17 **Podgorica** prev. Titograd. ● S Montenegro 42°25'N 19°16'E
113 K17 **Podgorica** ✈ S Montenegro 42°22'N 19°16'E
109 T13 **Podgrad** SW Slovenia 45°31'N 14°09'E
Podiebrad see Poděbrady
116 M5 **Podil's'ka Vysochina** plateau W Ukraine
Podium Anicensis see le Puy
122 L11 **Podkamennaya Tunguska** Eng. Stony Tunguska. ≈ C Russian Federation
111 N17 **Podkarpackie** ◈ province SE Poland
Pod Klošter see Arnoldstein
110 P9 **Podlaskie** ◈ province Mazowieckie, C Poland
127 Q8 **Podlesnoye** Saratovskaya Oblast', W Russian Federation 51°51'N 47°03'E
126 K4 **Podol'sk** Moskovskaya Oblast', W Russian Federation 55°24'N 37°30'E
76 H10 **Podor** N Senegal 16°40'N 14°57'W
125 P12 **Podosinovets** Kirovskaya Oblast', NW Russian Federation 60°15'N 47°06'E
124 I12 **Podporozh'ye** Leningradskaya Oblast', NW Russian Federation 60°52'N 34°00'E
Podravska Slatina see Slatina
112 J13 **Podromanlja** Republika Srpska, SE Bosnia and Herzegovina 43°55'N 18°46'E
Podsvil'ye see Padsvilly
116 L9 **Podu Iloaiei** prev. Podul Iloaei. Iaşi, NE Romania 47°13'N 27°16'E
113 N15 **Podujevë** Serb. Podujevo. N Kosovo 42°56'N 21°13'E
Podujevo see Podujevë
Podul Iloaei see Podu Iloaiei
Podunajská Rovina see Little Alföld
124 M12 **Podyuga** Arkhangel'skaya Oblast', NW Russian Federation 61°04'N 40°46'E
56 A9 **Poechos, Embalse** ◎ NW Peru
55 W10 **Poeketi** Sipaliwini, E Surinam
100 L8 **Poel** island N Germany
83 M20 **Poelela, Lagoa** ◎ S Mozambique
Poerwodadi see Purwodadi
Poerwokerto see Purwokerto
Poerworedjo see Purworejo
Poetovio see Ptuj
83 E23 **Pofadder** Northern Cape, W South Africa 29°09'S 19°25'E
106 I9 **Po, Foci del** var. Bocche del Po. ≈ NE Italy
116 E12 **Pogăniş** ≈ W Romania
Pogegen see Pagėgiai
106 G12 **Poggibonsi** Toscana, C Italy 43°28'N 11°09'E
107 I14 **Poggio Mirteto** Lazio, C Italy 42°17'N 12°42'E
109 V4 **Pöggstall** Niederösterreich, N Austria 48°19'N 15°10'E
116 L13 **Pogoanele** Buzău, SE Romania 44°55'N 27°00'E
Pogónion see Delvináki
113 M21 **Pogradec** var. Pogradeci. Korçë, SE Albania 40°54'N 20°40'E
Pogradeci see Pogradec
123 S15 **Pogranichnyy** Primorskiy Kray, SE Russian Federation 44°18'N 131°33'E
38 M16 **Pogromni Volcano** ⛰ Unimak Island, Alaska, USA 54°34'N 164°41'W
163 Z15 **P'ohang** Jap. Hokō. E South Korea 36°02'N 129°20'E
15 T9 **Pohénégamook, Lac** ◎ Québec, SE Canada
93 L20 **Pohja** Swe. Pojo. Etelä-Suomi, SW Finland 60°07'N 23°30'E
Pohjanlahti see Bothnia, Gulf of
189 U16 **Pohnpei** ◈ state E Micronesia
189 O12 **Pohnpei** ✈ Pohnpei, E Micronesia
189 O12 **Pohnpei** prev. Ponape Ascension Island. island E Micronesia
111 F19 **Pohořelice** Ger. Pohrlitz. Jihomoravský Kraj, SE Czech Republic 48°58'N 16°30'E
109 V10 **Pohorje** Ger. Bacher. ▲▲ N Slovenia
117 N6 **Pohrebyshche** Vinnyts'ka Oblast', C Ukraine 49°31'N 29°16'E
Pohrlitz see Pohořelice
161 P9 **Po Hu** ◎ E China
116 G15 **Poiana Mare** Dolj, S Romania 43°55'N 23°02'E
Poictiers see Poitiers
127 N6 **Poim** Penzenskaya Oblast', W Russian Federation 53°03'N 43°11'E
159 N15 **Poindo** Xizang Zizhiqu, W China 29°58'N 91°20'E
195 Y13 **Poinsett, Cape** headland Antarctica 65°35'S 113°00'E
29 R9 **Poinsett, Lake** ◎ South Dakota, N USA
22 I10 **Point Au Fer Island** island Louisiana, S USA
39 X14 **Point Baker** Prince of Wales Island, Alaska, USA 56°19'N 133°31'W
25 U13 **Point Comfort** Texas, SW USA 28°40'N 96°33'W
Pointe de Galle see Galle
44 K10 **Pointe à Gravois** headland SW Haiti 18°00'N 73°53'W
22 L10 **Pointe a la Hache** Louisiana, S USA 29°34'N 89°48'W
45 Y6 **Pointe-à-Pitre** Grande Terre, C Guadeloupe 16°14'N 61°32'W
15 U7 **Pointe-au-Père** Québec, SE Canada 48°31'N 68°27'W
15 V5 **Pointe-aux-Anglais** Québec, SE Canada 49°40'N 67°09'W
45 T10 **Pointe Du Cap** headland N Saint Lucia 14°06'N 60°56'W
79 E21 **Pointe-Noire** Kouilou, S Congo 04°46'S 11°53'E
45 X6 **Pointe Noire** Basse Terre, W Guadeloupe 16°14'N 61°47'W
79 E21 **Pointe-Noire** ✈ Kouilou, S Congo 04°45'S 11°55'E
45 U15 **Point Fortin** Trinidad, Trinidad and Tobago 10°12'N 61°41'W
38 M6 **Point Hope** Alaska, USA 68°21'N 166°48'W
39 N5 **Point Lay** Alaska, USA 69°42'N 162°57'W
18 B16 **Point Marion** Pennsylvania, NE USA 39°44'N 79°53'W
18 K16 **Point Pleasant** New Jersey, NE USA 40°04'N 74°00'W
21 P4 **Point Pleasant** West Virginia, NE USA 38°53'N 82°07'W
45 R14 **Point Salines** ✈ (St. George's) SW Grenada 12°00'N 61°47'W
102 L9 **Poitiers** prev. Poictiers; anc. Limonum. Vienne, W France 46°35'N 00°19'E
102 K9 **Poitou** cultural region W France
102 K10 **Poitou-Charentes** ◈ region W France
103 N3 **Poix-de-Picardie** Somme, N France 49°47'N 01°58'E
Pojo see Pohja
37 S10 **Pojoaque** New Mexico, SW USA 35°52'N 106°01'W
152 E11 **Pokaran** Rājasthān, NW India 26°55'N 71°55'E
183 R4 **Pokataroo** New South Wales, SE Australia 29°37'S 148°43'E
119 P18 **Pokats'** Rus. Pokot'. ≈ SE Belarus
29 V5 **Pokegama Lake** ◎ Minnesota, N USA
184 L6 **Pokeno** Waikato, North Island, New Zealand 37°15'S 175°01'E
153 O11 **Pokharā** Western, C Nepal 28°14'N 84°E

◆ Country
● Country Capital
◇ Dependent Territory
○ Dependent Territory Capital
◈ Administrative Regions
✈ International Airport
▲ Mountain
▲▲ Mountain Range
⛰ Volcano
≈ River
◎ Lake
▣ Reservoir

Pokhvistnevo – Port Rois

127 T6 **Pokhvistnevo** Samarskaya Oblast', W Russian Federation 53°38'N 52°07'E
55 W10 **Pokigron** Sipaliwini, C Surinam 04°31'N 55°23'W
92 L10 **Pokka** *Lapp.* Bohkká. Lappi, N Finland 68°11'N 25°45'E
79 N16 **Poko** Orientale, NE Dem. Rep. Congo 03°08'N 26°52'E
Pokot' *see* Pokats'
Po-ko-to Shan *see* Bogda Shan
147 S7 **Pokrovka** Talasskaya Oblast', NW Kyrgyzstan 42°45'N 71°33'E
Pokrovka *see* Kyzyl-Suu
117 V8 **Pokrovs'ke** *Rus.* Pokrovskoye. Dnipropetrovs'ka Oblast', E Ukraine 47°58'N 36°15'E
Pokrovskoye *see* Pokrovs'ke
Pola *see* Pula
37 N10 **Polacca** Arizona, SW USA 35°49'N 110°21'W
104 L2 **Pola de Laviana** Asturias, N Spain 43°15'N 05°33'W
104 K2 **Pola de Lena** Asturias, N Spain 43°10'N 05°49'W
104 L2 **Pola de Siero** Asturias, N Spain 43°24'N 05°39'W
191 Y3 **Poland** Kiritimati, E Kiribati 01°52'N 157°33'W
110 H12 **Poland** *off.* Republic of Poland, *var.* Polish Republic, *Pol.* Polska, Rzeczpospolita Polska; *prev. Pol.* Polska Rzeczpospolita Ludowa, The Polish People's Republic. ◆ *republic* C Europe
Poland, Republic of *see* Poland
Polangen *see* Palanga
110 G7 **Polanów** *Ger.* Pollnow. Zachodnio-pomorskie, NW Poland 54°07'N 16°38'E
136 H13 **Polatlı** Ankara, C Turkey 39°34'N 32°08'E
118 L12 **Polatsk** *Rus.* Polotsk. Vitsyebskaya Voblasts', N Belarus 55°29'N 28°47'E
125 U14 **Polazna** Permskaya Oblast', NW Russian Federation 58°18'N 56°22'E
110 F8 **Połczyn-Zdrój** *Ger.* Bad Polzin. Zachodnio-pomorskie, NW Poland 53°44'N 16°02'E
149 R5 **Pol-e-'Alam** Lowgar, E Afghanistan 33°59'N 69°02'E
Polekhatum *see* Pulhatyn
149 Q3 **Pol-e Khomrī** *var.* Pul-i-Khumri. Baghlān, NE Afghanistan 35°55'N 68°45'E
197 S10 **Pole Plain** *undersea feature* Arctic Ocean
Pol-e-Safid *see* Pol-e Sefīd
143 P5 **Pol-e Sefīd** *var.* Pol-e-Safid, Pul-i-Sefid. Māzandarān, N Iran 36°05'N 53°01'E
118 B13 **Polessk** *Ger.* Labiau. Kaliningradskaya Oblast', W Russian Federation 54°52'N 21°06'E
Polesskoye *see* Polis'ke
171 N13 **Polewali** Sulawesi, C Indonesia 03°26'S 119°23'E
114 G11 **Polezhan** ▲ SW Bulgaria 41°42'N 23°28'E
78 F13 **Poli** Nord, N Cameroon 09°31'N 13°10'E
Poli *see* Pólis
107 M19 **Policastro, Golfo di** *gulf* S Italy
110 D8 **Police** *Ger.* Politz. Zachodnio-pomorskie, NW Poland 53°34'N 14°34'E
172 I17 **Police, Pointe** *headland* Mahé, NE Seychelles 04°48'S 55°31'E
115 L17 **Polichnítos** *var.* Polihnitos, Políkhnitos. Lésvos, E Greece 39°04'N 26°10'E
Poligiros *see* Polýgyros
107 P17 **Polignano a Mare** Puglia, SE Italy 40°59'N 17°13'E
103 S9 **Poligny** Jura, E France 46°51'N 05°42'E
Polihnitos *see* Polichnítos
Polikastro/Políkastron *see* Polýkastro
Políkhnitos *see* Polichnítos
171 O3 **Polillo Islands** *island group* N Philippines
109 Q9 **Polinik** ▲ SW Austria 46°54'N 13°10'E
115 J15 **Políochni** *var.* Polýochni. *site of ancient city* Límnos, E Greece
121 O2 **Pólis** *var.* Poli. W Cyprus 35°02'N 32°27'E
Polish People's Republic, The *see* Poland
Polish Republic *see* Poland
117 O3 **Polis'ke** *Rus.* Polesskoye. Kyyivs'ka Oblast', N Ukraine 51°16'N 29°27'E
107 N22 **Polistena** Calabria, SW Italy 38°25'N 16°05'E
Politz *see* Police
Políyiros *see* Polýgyros
29 V14 **Polk City** Iowa, C USA 41°46'N 93°42'W
110 F13 **Polkowice** *Ger.* Heerwegen. Dolnośląskie, W Poland 51°32'N 16°06'E
155 G22 **Pollāchi** Tamil Nādu, SE India 10°38'N 77°00'E
109 W7 **Pöllau** Steiermark, SE Austria 47°18'N 15°46'E
189 T13 **Polle** *atoll* Chuuk Islands, C Micronesia
105 X9 **Pollença** Mallorca, Spain, W Mediterranean Sea 39°52'N 03°01'E
Pollnow *see* Polanów
29 N7 **Pollock** South Dakota, N USA 45°53'N 100°15'W
92 L8 **Polmak** Finnmark, N Norway 70°01'N 28°04'E
30 L10 **Polo** Illinois, N USA 41°59'N 89°34'W
193 V15 **Poloa** *island* Tongatapu Group, N Tonga
42 E5 **Polochic, Río** ≈ C Guatemala
Pologi *see* Polohy
117 V9 **Polohy** *Rus.* Pologi. Zaporiz'ka Oblast', SE Ukraine 47°30'N 36°18'E
83 K20 **Polokwane** *prev.* Pietersburg. Limpopo, NE South Africa 23°54'S 29°23'E
14 M10 **Polonais, Lac des** ◎ Québec, SE Canada
61 G20 **Polonio, Cabo** *headland* E Uruguay 34°22'S 53°46'W
155 K24 **Polonnaruwa** North Central Province, C Sri Lanka 07°56'N 81°02'E
116 L5 **Polonne** *Rus.* Polonnoye. Khmel'nyts'ka Oblast', NW Ukraine 50°10'N 27°30'E
Polonnoye *see* Polonne
Polotsk *see* Polatsk
Polovinka *see* Ugleural'skiy
109 T7 **Pöls** *var.* Pölsbach. ≈ E Austria
Pölsbach *see* Pöls
Polska/Polska, Rzeczpospolita/Polska Rzeczpospolita Ludowa *see* Poland
114 L10 **Polski Gradets** Stara Zagora, C Bulgaria 42°12'N 26°06'E
114 K8 **Polski Trŭmbesh** Ruse, N Bulgaria 43°22'N 25°38'E
33 P8 **Polson** Montana, NW USA 47°41'N 114°09'W
117 T6 **Poltava** Poltavs'ka Oblast', NE Ukraine 49°33'N 34°32'E
Poltava *see* Poltavs'ka Oblast'
117 R5 **Poltavs'ka Oblast'** *var.* Poltava, *Rus.* Poltavskaya Oblast'. ◈ *province* NE Ukraine
Poltavskaya Oblast' *see* Poltavs'ka Oblast'
Poltoratsk *see* Aşgabat
118 I5 **Põltsamaa** *Ger.* Oberpahlen. Jõgevamaa, E Estonia 58°40'N 26°00'E
118 I4 **Põltsamaa** *var.* Põltsamaa Jõgi. ≈ C Estonia
Põltsamaa Jõgi *see* Põltsamaa
122 I8 **Poluy** ≈ N Russian Federation
118 J6 **Põlva** *Ger.* Põlwe. Põlvamaa, SE Estonia 58°04'N 27°06'E
93 N16 **Polvijärvi** Itä-Suomi, SE Finland 62°53'N 29°20'E
Pölwe *see* Põlva
115 I22 **Polýaigos** *island* Kykládes, Greece, Aegean Sea
115 I22 **Polyaígou Folégandrou, Stenó** *strait* Kykládes, Greece, Aegean Sea
124 J3 **Polyarnyy** Murmanskaya Oblast', NW Russian Federation 69°10'N 33°21'E
124 I5 **Polyarnyye Zori** Murmanskaya Oblast', NW Russian Federation 67°22'N 32°31'E
125 W5 **Polyarnyy Ural** ▲▲ NW Russian Federation
115 G14 **Polýgyros** *var.* Poligiros, Políyiros. Kentrikí Makedonía, N Greece 40°21'N 23°27'E
114 F13 **Polýkastro** *var.* Polikastro; *prev.* Políkastron. Kentrikí Makedonía, N Greece 41°01'N 22°33'E
193 O9 **Polynesia** *island group* C Pacific Ocean
Polýochni *see* Políochni
41 Y13 **Polyuc** Quintana Roo, E Mexico
109 V10 **Polzela** C Slovenia 46°18'N 15°04'E
Polzen *see* Ploučnice
56 D12 **Pomabamba** Ancash, C Peru 08°48'S 77°30'W
185 D23 **Pomahaka** ≈ South Island, New Zealand
106 F12 **Pomarance** Toscana, C Italy 43°19'N 10°53'E
104 G9 **Pombal** Leiria, C Portugal 39°55'N 08°38'W
76 D9 **Pombas** Santo Antão, NW Cape Verde 17°09'N 25°02'W
83 N19 **Pomene** Inhambane, SE Mozambique 22°57'S 35°34'E
110 G8 **Pomerania** *cultural region* Germany/Poland
110 D7 **Pomeranian Bay** *Ger.* Pommersche Bucht, *Pol.* Zatoka Pomorska. *bay* Germany/Poland
31 T15 **Pomeroy** Ohio, N USA 39°01'N 82°01'W
32 L10 **Pomeroy** Washington, NW USA 46°28'N 117°36'W
117 Q8 **Pomichna** Kirovohrads'ka Oblast', C Ukraine 48°07'N 31°25'E
186 H7 **Pomio** New Britain, E Papua New Guinea 05°31'S 151°30'E
Pomir, Dar"yoi *see* Pamir/Pāmīr, Daryā-ye
27 T6 **Pomme de Terre Lake** ⊠ Missouri, C USA
29 S8 **Pomme de Terre River** ≈ Minnesota, N USA
Pommersche Bucht *see* Pomeranian Bay
35 T15 **Pomona** California, W USA 34°03'N 117°45'W
114 N9 **Pomorie** Burgas, E Bulgaria 42°32'N 27°39'E
Pomorska, Zatoka *see* Pomeranian Bay
110 H8 **Pomorskie** ◈ *province* N Poland
125 Q4 **Pomorskiy Proliv** *strait* NW Russian Federation
125 T10 **Pomozdino** Respublika Komi, NW Russian Federation 62°11'N 54°13'E
Pompaelo *see* Pamplona
23 Z15 **Pompano Beach** Florida, SE USA 26°14'N 80°06'W
107 K18 **Pompei** Campania, S Italy 40°45'N 14°27'E
33 V10 **Pompeys Pillar** Montana, NW USA 45°58'N 107°55'W
Ponape Ascension Island *see* Pohnpei
29 R13 **Ponca** Nebraska, C USA 42°35'N 96°42'W
27 O8 **Ponca City** Oklahoma, C USA 36°41'N 97°04'W
45 T6 **Ponce** C Puerto Rico 18°01'N 66°36'W
23 X10 **Ponce de Leon Inlet** *inlet* Florida, SE USA
22 K8 **Ponchatoula** Louisiana, S USA 30°26'N 90°26'W
26 M8 **Pond Creek** Oklahoma, C USA 36°40'N 97°48'W
155 J20 **Pondicherry** *var.* Puduchcheri, *Fr.* Pondichéry. Pondicherry, SE India 11°59'N 79°50'E
151 I20 **Pondicherry** *var.* Puduchcheri, *Fr.* Pondichéry. ◈ *union territory* India
Pondichéry *see* Pondicherry
197 N11 **Pond Inlet** Baffin Island, Nunavut, NE Canada 72°37'N 77°56'W
187 P16 **Ponérihouen** Province Nord, C New Caledonia 21°04'S 165°24'E
104 J4 **Ponferrada** Castilla-León, NW Spain 42°33'N 06°35'W
184 N13 **Pongaroa** Manawatu-Wanganui, North Island, New Zealand 40°36'S 176°08'E
167 Q12 **Pong Nam Ron** Chantaburi, S Thailand 12°55'N 102°15'E
81 C14 **Pongo** ≈ S Sudan
152 I7 **Pong Reservoir** ⊠ N India
111 N14 **Poniatowa** Lubelskie, E Poland 51°11'N 22°05'E
167 R12 **Pônley** Kâmpóng Chhnăng, C Cambodia 12°26'N 104°25'E
155 I20 **Ponnaiyār** ≈ SE India
11 Q15 **Ponoka** Alberta, SW Canada 52°42'N 113°33'W
127 U6 **Ponomarevka** Orenburgskaya Oblast', W Russian Federation 53°16'N 54°10'E
169 Q17 **Ponorogo** Jawa, C Indonesia 07°51'S 111°30'E
124 M5 **Ponoy** Murmanskaya Oblast', NW Russian Federation 67°00'N 41°06'E
122 F6 **Ponoy** ≈ NW Russian Federation
102 K11 **Pons** Charente-Maritime, W France 45°31'N 00°31'W
Pons *see* Ponts
Pons Aelii *see* Newcastle upon Tyne
Pons Vetus *see* Pontevedra
99 G20 **Pont-à-Celles** Hainaut, S Belgium 50°31'N 04°21'E
102 K16 **Pontacq** Pyrénées-Atlantiques, SW France 43°11'N 00°06'W
64 P3 **Ponta Delgada** São Miguel, Azores, Portugal, NE Atlantic Ocean 37°29'N 25°40'W
64 P3 **Ponta Delgado** ✈ São Miguel, Azores, Portugal, NE Atlantic Ocean 37°28'N 25°40'W
64 N2 **Ponta do Pico** ▲ Pico, Azores, Portugal, NE Atlantic Ocean 38°28'N 28°25'W
60 J11 **Ponta Grossa** Paraná, S Brazil 25°07'S 50°09'W
103 S5 **Pont-à-Mousson** Meurthe-et-Moselle, NE France 48°55'N 06°03'E
103 T9 **Pontarlier** Doubs, E France 46°54'N 06°20'E
106 G11 **Pontassieve** Toscana, C Italy 43°46'N 11°28'E
102 L4 **Pont-Audemer** Eure, N France 49°22'N 00°31'E
22 K9 **Pontchartrain, Lake** ◎ Louisiana, S USA
102 I8 **Pontchâteau** Loire-Atlantique, NW France 47°26'N 02°04'W
103 R10 **Pont-de-Vaux** Ain, E France 46°25'N 04°57'E
104 G4 **Ponteareas** Galicia, NW Spain 42°11'N 08°29'W
106 J6 **Pontebba** Friuli-Venezia Giulia, NE Italy 46°32'N 13°18'E
104 G4 **Ponte Caldelas** Galicia, NW Spain 42°23'N 08°30'W
107 J16 **Pontecorvo** Lazio, C Italy 41°27'N 13°40'E
104 G5 **Ponte da Barca** Viana do Castelo, N Portugal 41°48'N 08°25'W
104 G5 **Ponte de Lima** Viana do Castelo, N Portugal 41°46'N 08°35'W
106 F11 **Pontedera** Toscana, C Italy 43°40'N 10°38'E
104 H10 **Ponte de Sor** Portalegre, C Portugal 39°15'N 08°01'W
104 H2 **Pontedeume** Galicia, NW Spain 43°22'N 08°09'W
106 F6 **Ponte di Legno** Lombardia, N Italy 46°16'N 10°31'E
11 T17 **Ponteix** Saskatchewan, S Canada 49°43'N 107°22'W
171 Q16 **Ponte Macassar** *var.* Pante Macassar, Pante Makasar, Pante Makassar. W East Timor 09°11'S 124°27'E
59 N20 **Ponte Nova** Minas Gerais, NE Brazil 20°25'S 42°54'W
59 G18 **Pontes e Lacerda** Mato Grosso, W Brazil 15°14'S 59°21'W
104 G4 **Pontevedra** *anc.* Pons Vetus. Galicia, NW Spain 42°25'N 08°39'W
104 G3 **Pontevedra** ◈ *province* Galicia, NW Spain
104 G4 **Pontevedra, Ría de** *estuary* NW Spain
30 M12 **Pontiac** Illinois, N USA 40°54'N 88°36'W
31 R9 **Pontiac** Michigan, N USA 42°38'N 83°17'W
169 P11 **Pontianak** Borneo, C Indonesia 0°05'S 109°16'E
107 I16 **Pontino, Agro** *plain* C Italy
Pontisarae *see* Pontoise
102 H6 **Pontivy** Morbihan, NW France 48°04'N 02°58'W
102 F6 **Pont-l'Abbé** Finistère, NW France 47°52'N 04°14'W
103 N4 **Pontoise** *anc.* Briva Isarae, Cergy-Pontoise, Pontisarae. Val-d'Oise, N France 49°03'N 02°05'E
11 W13 **Ponton** Manitoba, C Canada 54°36'N 99°02'W
102 J5 **Pontorson** Manche, N France 48°33'N 01°31'W
22 M2 **Pontotoc** Mississippi, S USA 34°15'N 89°00'W
25 R9 **Pontotoc** Texas, SW USA 30°52'N 98°57'W
106 E10 **Pontremoli** Toscana, C Italy 44°24'N 09°55'E
108 J10 **Pontresina** Graubünden, S Switzerland 46°29'N 09°52'E
105 U5 **Ponts** *var.* Pons. Cataluña, NE Spain 41°55'N 01°12'E
103 R14 **Pont-St-Esprit** Gard, S France 44°15'N 04°37'E
97 K21 **Pontypool** *Wel.* Pontypŵl. SE Wales, United Kingdom 51°43'N 03°02'W
97 J22 **Pontypridd** S Wales, United Kingdom 51°37'N 03°22'W
Pontypŵl *see* Pontypool
43 R17 **Ponuga** Veraguas, SE Panama 07°50'N 80°58'W
184 L6 **Ponui Island** *island* N New Zealand
119 K14 **Ponya** ≈ N Belarus
107 I17 **Ponza, Isola di** *island* Isole Ponziane, S Italy
107 I17 **Ponziane, Isole** *island* C Italy
182 F7 **Poochera** South Australia 32°45'S 134°51'E
97 L24 **Poole** S England, United Kingdom 50°43'N 01°59'W
25 S6 **Poolville** Texas, SW USA 33°00'N 97°55'W
Poona *see* Pune
182 M8 **Pooncarie** New South Wales, SE Australia 33°26'S 142°37'E
183 N6 **Poopelloe Lake** *seasonal lake* New South Wales, SE Australia
57 K19 **Poopó** Oruro, C Bolivia 18°23'S 66°58'W
57 K19 **Poopó, Lago** *var.* Lago Pampa Aullagas. ◎ W Bolivia
184 L3 **Poor Knights Islands** *island* N New Zealand
39 P10 **Poorman** Alaska, USA 64°05'N 155°34'W
182 E3 **Pootnoura** South Australia 28°31'S 134°09'E
147 R10 **Pop** *Rus.* Pap. Namangan Viloyati, E Uzbekistan 40°49'N 71°06'E
117 X5 **Popasna** *Rus.* Popasnaya. Luhans'ka Oblast', E Ukraine 48°38'N 38°24'E
Popasnaya *see* Popasna
54 D12 **Popayán** Cauca, SW Colombia 02°27'N 76°32'W
99 B18 **Poperinge** West-Vlaanderen, W Belgium 50°52'N 02°44'E
123 N7 **Popigay** Taymyrskiy (Dolgano-Nenetskiy) Avtonomnyy Okrug, N Russian Federation 71°54'N 110°45'E
123 N7 **Popigay** ≈ N Russian Federation
117 O5 **Popil'nya** Zhytomyrs'ka Oblast', N Ukraine 49°57'N 29°24'E
182 K8 **Popiltah Lake** *seasonal lake* New South Wales, SE Australia
33 X7 **Poplar** Montana, NW USA 48°06'N 105°12'W
11 Y14 **Poplar** ≈ Manitoba, C Canada
27 X8 **Poplar Bluff** Missouri, C USA 36°45'N 90°23'W
33 X6 **Poplar River** ≈ Montana, NW USA
41 P14 **Popocatépetl** ⛰ S Mexico 18°59'N 98°37'W
79 H21 **Popokabaka** Bandundu, SW Dem. Rep. Congo 05°42'S 16°35'E
107 J15 **Popoli** Abruzzo, C Italy 42°09'N 13°51'E
186 F9 **Popondetta** Northern, S Papua New Guinea 08°45'S 148°15'E
112 F9 **Popovača** Sisak-Moslavina, NE Croatia 45°35'N 16°37'E
114 L8 **Popovo** Tŭrgovishte, N Bulgaria 43°20'N 26°14'E
Popovo *see* Iskra
Poppberg *see* Poprad
30 M5 **Popple River** ≈ Wisconsin, N USA
111 L19 **Poprad** *Ger.* Deutschendorf, *Hung.* Poprád. Prešovský Kraj, E Slovakia 49°04'N 20°16'E
111 L18 **Poprad** *Ger.* Popper, *Hung.* Poprád. ≈ Poland/Slovakia
111 L19 **Poprad-Tatry** ✈ (Poprad) Prešovský Kraj, E Slovakia 49°04'N 20°21'E
21 X7 **Poquoson** Virginia, NE USA 37°08'N 76°21'W
149 O15 **Porāli** ≈ SW Pakistan
184 N12 **Porangahau** Hawke's Bay, North Island, New Zealand 40°19'S 176°36'E
59 K17 **Porangatu** Goiás, C Brazil 13°28'S 49°14'W
119 G18 **Porazava** *Pol.* Porozow, *Rus.* Porozovo. Hrodzyenskaya Voblasts', W Belarus 52°56'N 24°22'E
154 A11 **Porbandar** Gujarāt, W India 21°40'N 69°40'E
10 I13 **Porcher Island** *island* British Columbia, SW Canada
104 M13 **Porcuna** Andalucía, S Spain 37°52'N 04°12'W
14 F7 **Porcupine** Ontario, S Canada 48°31'N 81°07'W
64 M6 **Porcupine Bank** *undersea feature* N Atlantic Ocean
11 V15 **Porcupine Hills** ▲▲ Manitoba/Saskatchewan, S Canada
30 L3 **Porcupine Mountains** *hill range* Michigan, N USA
64 M7 **Porcupine Plain** *undersea feature* E Atlantic Ocean 16°00'W 49°00'N
8 G7 **Porcupine River** ≈ Canada/USA
106 I7 **Pordenone** *anc.* Portenau. Friuli-Venezia Giulia, NE Italy 45°58'N 12°39'E
54 H9 **Pore** Casanare, E Colombia 05°42'N 71°59'W
112 A9 **Poreč** *It.* Parenzo. Istra, NW Croatia 45°16'N 13°36'E
60 I9 **Porecatu** Paraná, S Brazil 22°46'S 51°22'W
Porech'ye *see* Parechcha
127 P4 **Poretskoye** Chuvashskaya Respublika, W Russian Federation 55°12'N 46°20'E
77 Q13 **Porga** N Benin 11°04'N 00°58'E
186 B7 **Porgera** Enga, W Papua New Guinea 05°32'S 143°08'E
93 K18 **Pori** *Swe.* Björneborg. Länsi-Suomi, SW Finland 61°28'N 21°50'E
185 L14 **Porirua** Wellington, North Island, New Zealand 41°08'S 174°51'E
92 I12 **Porjus** *Lapp.* Bårjås. Norrbotten, N Sweden 66°55'N 19°55'E
124 G14 **Porkhov** Pskovskaya Oblast', W Russian Federation 57°46'N 29°27'E
55 O4 **Porlamar** Nueva Esparta, NE Venezuela 10°57'N 63°51'W
102 I8 **Pornic** Loire-Atlantique, NW France 47°07'N 02°07'W
186 B7 **Poroma** Southern Highlands, W Papua New Guinea 06°15'S 143°34'E
123 T13 **Poronaysk** Ostrov Sakhalin, Sakhalinskaya Oblast', SE Russian Federation 49°15'N 143°00'E
115 G20 **Póros** Póros, S Greece 37°30'N 23°27'E
115 C19 **Póros** Kefallinía, Iónia Nisiá, Greece, C Mediterranean Sea 38°09'N 20°46'E
115 G20 **Póros** *island* S Greece
81 G24 **Poroto Mountains** ▲▲ SW Tanzania
112 B10 **Porozina** Primorje-Gorski Kotar, NW Croatia 45°07'N 14°17'E
Porozovo/Porozow *see* Porazava
195 X15 **Porpoise Bay** *bay* Antarctica
65 G15 **Porpoise Point** *headland* NE Ascension Island 07°54'S 14°22'W
108 C6 **Porrentruy** Jura, NW Switzerland 47°25'N 07°06'E
106 F10 **Porretta Terme** Emilia-Romagna, C Italy 44°10'N 11°01'E
Porriño *see* O Porriño
Pors *see* Porsangenfjorden
92 L7 **Porsangenfjorden** *Lapp.* Pors. *fjord* N Norway
92 K8 **Porsangerhalvøya** *peninsula* N Norway
95 G16 **Porsgrunn** Telemark, S Norway 59°08'N 09°38'E
136 E13 **Porsuk Çayı** ≈ C Turkey
Porsy *see* Boldumsaz
57 N18 **Portachuelo** Santa Cruz, C Bolivia 17°21'S 63°24'W
182 I9 **Port Adelaide** South Australia 34°49'S 138°31'E
97 F15 **Portadown** *Ir.* Port An Dúnáin. S Northern Ireland, United Kingdom 54°26'N 06°27'W
31 P10 **Portage** Michigan, N USA 42°12'N 85°34'W
18 D15 **Portage** Pennsylvania, NE USA 40°23'N 78°40'W
30 K8 **Portage** Wisconsin, N USA 43°33'N 89°29'W
30 M3 **Portage Lake** ◎ Michigan, N USA
11 X16 **Portage la Prairie** Manitoba, S Canada 49°58'N 98°20'W
31 R11 **Portage River** ≈ Ohio, N USA
27 Y8 **Portageville** Missouri, C USA 36°25'N 89°42'W
28 L2 **Portal** North Dakota, N USA 48°57'N 102°33'W
10 L17 **Port Alberni** Vancouver Island, British Columbia, SW Canada 49°11'N 124°49'W
14 E15 **Port Albert** Ontario, S Canada 43°51'N 81°42'W
104 I10 **Portalegre** *anc.* Ammaia, Amoea. Portalegre, E Portugal 39°17'N 07°25'W
104 H10 **Portalegre** ◈ *district* C Portugal
37 V12 **Portales** New Mexico, SW USA 34°11'N 103°19'W
39 X14 **Port Alexander** Baranof Island, Alaska, USA 56°15'N 134°39'W
83 I25 **Port Alfred** Eastern Cape, S South Africa 33°31'S 26°55'E
10 J16 **Port Alice** Vancouver Island, British Columbia, SW Canada 50°23'N 127°24'W
22 J8 **Port Allen** Louisiana, S USA 30°27'N 91°12'W
Port Amelia *see* Pemba
Port An Dúnáin *see* Portadown
32 G7 **Port Angeles** Washington, NW USA 48°06'N 123°26'W
44 L12 **Port Antonio** NE Jamaica 18°10'N 76°27'W
115 D16 **Pórta Panagiá** *religious building* Thessalía, C Greece
25 T14 **Port Aransas** Texas, SW USA 27°49'N 97°03'W
97 E18 **Portarlington** *Ir.* Cúil an tSúdaire. Laois/Offaly, C Ireland 53°10'N 07°11'W
183 P17 **Port Arthur** Tasmania, SE Australia 43°09'S 147°51'E
25 Y11 **Port Arthur** Texas, SW USA 29°55'N 93°56'W
96 G12 **Port Askaig** W Scotland, United Kingdom 55°51'N 06°06'W
182 I7 **Port Augusta** South Australia 32°29'S 137°44'E
44 M9 **Port-au-Prince** ● (Haiti) C Haiti 18°33'N 72°20'W
44 M9 **Port-au-Prince** ✈ E Haiti 18°38'N 72°13'W
22 I8 **Port Barre** Louisiana, S USA 30°33'N 91°57'W
Port Bergé *see* Boriziny
151 Q19 **Port Blair** Andaman and Nicobar Islands, SE India 11°40'N 92°44'E
25 X12 **Port Bolivar** Texas, SW USA 29°21'N 94°45'W
105 X4 **Portbou** Cataluña, NE Spain 42°26'N 03°10'E
77 N17 **Port Bouet** ✈ (Abidjan) SE Ivory Coast 05°17'N 03°55'W
182 I8 **Port Broughton** South Australia 33°39'S 137°55'E
14 F17 **Port Burwell** Ontario, S Canada 42°39'N 80°47'W
12 G17 **Port Burwell** Québec, NE Canada 60°25'N 64°49'W
182 M13 **Port Campbell** Victoria, SE Australia 38°37'S 143°00'E
15 V4 **Port-Cartier** Québec, SE Canada 50°00'N 66°55'W
185 F23 **Port Chalmers** Otago, South Island, New Zealand 45°46'S 170°37'E
23 W14 **Port Charlotte** Florida, SE USA 27°00'N 82°07'W
38 L9 **Port Clarence** Alaska, USA 65°15'N 166°51'W
10 I13 **Port Clements** Graham Island, British Columbia, SW Canada 53°37'N 132°12'W
31 S11 **Port Clinton** Ohio, N USA 41°30'N 82°56'W
14 H17 **Port Colborne** Ontario, S Canada 42°51'N 79°16'W
15 Y7 **Port-Daniel** Québec, SE Canada 48°10'N 64°58'W
Port Darwin *see* Darwin
183 O17 **Port Davey** *headland* Tasmania, SE Australia 43°19'S 145°54'E
44 K8 **Port-de-Paix** NW Haiti 19°56'N 72°52'W
181 W4 **Port Douglas** Queensland, NE Australia 16°33'S 145°27'E
10 J13 **Port Edward** British Columbia, SW Canada 54°11'N 130°16'W
83 K24 **Port Edward** KwaZulu/Natal, SE South Africa 31°03'S 30°14'E
58 J12 **Portel** Pará, NE Brazil 01°58'S 50°45'W
104 H12 **Portel** Évora, S Portugal 38°18'N 07°42'W
14 E14 **Port Elgin** Ontario, S Canada 44°26'N 81°22'W
45 Y14 **Port Elizabeth** Bequia, Saint Vincent and the Grenadines 13°01'N 61°15'W
83 I26 **Port Elizabeth** Eastern Cape, S South Africa 33°58'S 25°36'E
96 G13 **Port Ellen** W Scotland, United Kingdom 55°37'N 06°12'W
Portenau *see* Pordenone
97 H16 **Port Erin** SW Isle of Man 54°05'N 04°47'W
45 Q13 **Porter Point** *headland* Saint Vincent, Saint Vincent and the Grenadines 13°22'N 61°10'W
185 G18 **Porters Pass** *pass* South Island, New Zealand
83 E25 **Porterville** Western Cape, SW South Africa 33°03'S 19°00'E
35 R12 **Porterville** California, W USA 36°03'N 119°03'W
Port-Étienne *see* Nouâdhibou
182 L13 **Port Fairy** Victoria, SE Australia 38°24'S 142°13'E
184 M4 **Port Fitzroy** Great Barrier Island, Auckland, NE New Zealand 36°10'S 175°21'E
Port Florence *see* Kisumu
Port-Francqui *see* Ilebo
79 C18 **Port-Gentil** Ogooué-Maritime, W Gabon 0°40'S 08°50'E
182 I7 **Port Germein** South Australia 33°02'S 138°01'E
22 J6 **Port Gibson** Mississippi, S USA 31°57'N 90°58'W
39 Q13 **Port Graham** Alaska, USA 59°21'N 151°49'W
77 U17 **Port Harcourt** Rivers, S Nigeria 04°43'N 07°02'E
10 J16 **Port Hardy** Vancouver Island, British Columbia, SW Canada 50°41'N 127°30'W
Port Harrison *see* Inukjuak
13 R14 **Port Hawkesbury** Cape Breton Island, Nova Scotia, SE Canada 45°36'N 61°22'W
180 I6 **Port Hedland** Western Australia 20°23'S 118°40'E
39 O15 **Port Heiden** Alaska, USA 56°54'N 158°40'W
97 I19 **Porthmadog** *var.* Portmadoc. NW Wales, United Kingdom 52°55'N 04°08'W
14 I15 **Port Hope** Ontario, SE Canada 43°58'N 78°18'W
13 S9 **Port Hope Simpson** Newfoundland and Labrador, E Canada 52°30'N 56°18'W
65 C24 **Port Howard Settlement** West Falkland, Falkland Islands
31 T9 **Port Huron** Michigan, N USA 42°58'N 82°25'W
107 K17 **Portici** Campania, S Italy 40°48'N 14°20'E
137 Y13 **Port-İliç** *Rus.* Port Il'ich. SE Azerbaijan 38°54'N 48°49'E
Port Il'ich *see* Port-İliç
104 G14 **Portimão** *var.* Vila Nova de Portimão. Faro, S Portugal 37°08'N 08°32'W
25 T17 **Port Isabel** Texas, SW USA 26°04'N 97°13'W
18 J13 **Port Jervis** New York, NE USA 41°22'N 74°39'W
55 S7 **Port Kaituma** NW Guyana 07°42'N 59°52'W
126 K12 **Port Katon** Rostovskaya Oblast', SW Russian Federation 46°52'N 38°46'E
183 S9 **Port Kembla** New South Wales, SE Australia 34°30'S 150°54'E
182 F8 **Port Kenny** South Australia 33°09'S 134°38'E
Port Klang *see* Pelabuhan Klang
Port Láirge *see* Waterford
183 S8 **Portland** New South Wales, SE Australia 33°24'S 150°00'E
182 L13 **Portland** Victoria, SE Australia 38°21'S 141°38'E
184 K4 **Portland** Northland, North Island, New Zealand 35°48'S 174°19'E
31 Q13 **Portland** Indiana, N USA 40°25'N 84°58'W
19 P8 **Portland** Maine, NE USA 43°41'N 70°16'W
31 Q9 **Portland** Michigan, N USA 42°51'N 84°52'W
29 Q4 **Portland** North Dakota, N USA 47°28'N 97°22'W
32 G11 **Portland** Oregon, NW USA 45°31'N 122°41'W
20 J8 **Portland** Tennessee, S USA 36°34'N 86°31'W
25 T14 **Portland** Texas, SW USA 27°52'N 97°19'W
32 G11 **Portland** ✈ Oregon, NW USA 45°36'N 122°34'W
182 L13 **Portland Bay** *bay* Victoria, SE Australia
44 K13 **Portland Bight** *bay* S Jamaica
97 L24 **Portland Bill** *var.* Bill of Portland. *headland* S England, United Kingdom 50°31'N 02°28'W
Portland, Bill of *see* Portland Bill
183 P15 **Portland, Cape** *headland* Tasmania, SE Australia 40°46'S 147°58'E
10 J12 **Portland Inlet** *inlet* British Columbia, W Canada
184 P11 **Portland Island** *island* E New Zealand
65 F15 **Portland Point** *headland* SW Ascension Island
44 J13 **Portland Point** *headland* C Jamaica 17°42'N 77°10'W
103 P16 **Port-la-Nouvelle** Aude, S France 43°01'N 03°04'E
Portlaoighise *see* Port Laoise
97 E18 **Port Laoise** *var.* Portlaoise, *Ir.* Portlaoighise; *prev.* Maryborough. C Ireland 53°02'N 07°17'W
Portlaoise *see* Port Laoise
25 U13 **Port Lavaca** Texas, SW USA 28°36'N 96°39'W
182 G9 **Port Lincoln** South Australia 34°43'S 135°49'E
39 Q14 **Port Lions** Kodiak Island, Alaska, USA 57°55'N 152°48'W
76 I15 **Port Loko** W Sierra Leone 08°50'N 12°50'W
65 E24 **Port Louis** East Falkland, Falkland Islands 51°31'S 58°07'W
45 Y5 **Port-Louis** Grande Terre, N Guadeloupe 16°25'N 61°32'W
173 X16 **Port Louis** ● (Mauritius) NW Mauritius 20°10'S 57°30'E
Port Louis *see* Scarborough
Port-Lyautey *see* Kénitra
182 K12 **Port MacDonnell** South Australia 38°04'S 140°40'E
183 U7 **Port Macquarie** New South Wales, SE Australia 31°26'S 152°55'E
Portmadoc *see* Porthmadog
Port Mahon *see* Mahón
44 K12 **Port Maria** C Jamaica 18°22'N 76°54'W
10 K16 **Port McNeill** Vancouver Island, British Columbia, SW Canada 50°34'N 127°06'W
13 P11 **Port-Menier** Île d'Anticosti, Québec, E Canada 49°49'N 64°19'W
39 N15 **Port Moller** Alaska, USA 56°00'N 160°31'W
44 L13 **Port Morant** E Jamaica 17°53'N 76°20'W
44 K13 **Portmore** C Jamaica 17°58'N 76°52'W
186 D9 **Port Moresby** ● (Papua New Guinea) Central/National Capital District, SW Papua New Guinea 09°28'S 147°12'E
Port Natal *see* Durban
25 Y11 **Port Neches** Texas, SW USA 29°59'N 93°57'W
182 G9 **Port Neill** South Australia 34°06'S 136°19'E
15 S6 **Portneuf** ≈ Québec, SE Canada
15 R6 **Portneuf, Lac** ◎ Québec, SE Canada
83 D23 **Port Nolloth** Northern Cape, W South Africa 29°17'S 16°51'E
18 J17 **Port Norris** New Jersey, NE USA 39°13'N 75°00'W
Port-Nouveau-Québec *see* Kangiqsualujjuaq
104 G6 **Porto** *Eng.* Oporto; *anc.* Portus Cale. Porto, NW Portugal 41°09'N 08°37'W
104 G6 **Porto** *var.* Pôrto. ◈ *district* N Portugal
104 G6 **Porto** ✈ Porto, W Portugal 41°09'N 08°37'W
Pôrto *see* Porto
61 I16 **Porto Alegre** *var.* Pôrto Alegre. *state capital* Rio Grande do Sul, S Brazil 30°03'S 51°10'W
Porto Alexandre *see* Tombua
82 B12 **Porto Amboim** Cuanza Sul, NW Angola 10°47'S 13°43'E
Porto Amélia *see* Pemba
Porto Bello *see* Portobelo
43 T14 **Portobelo** *var.* Porto Bello, Puerto Bello. Colón, N Panama 09°33'N 79°37'W
60 G10 **Pôrto Camargo** Paraná, S Brazil 23°23'S 53°47'W
25 U13 **Port O'Connor** Texas, SW USA 28°26'N 96°26'W
Pôrto de Mós *see* Porto de Moz
58 J12 **Porto de Moz** *var.* Pôrto de Mós. Pará, NE Brazil 01°45'S 52°15'W
64 O5 **Porto do Moniz** Madeira, Portugal, NE Atlantic Ocean
59 H16 **Porto dos Gaúchos** Mato Grosso, W Brazil 11°32'S 57°16'W
Porto Edda *see* Sarandë
107 J24 **Porto Empedocle** Sicilia, Italy, C Mediterranean Sea 37°18'N 13°32'E
59 H20 **Porto Esperança** Mato Grosso do Sul, SW Brazil 19°36'S 57°24'W
106 E13 **Portoferraio** Toscana, C Italy 42°49'N 10°18'E
96 G6 **Port of Ness** NW Scotland, United Kingdom 58°29'N 06°15'W
45 U14 **Port-of-Spain** ● (Trinidad and Tobago) Trinidad, Trinidad and Tobago 10°39'N 61°30'W
Port of Spain *see* Piarco
103 X15 **Porto, Golfe de** *gulf* Corse, France, C Mediterranean Sea
Porto Grande *see* Mindelo
106 I7 **Portogruaro** Veneto, NE Italy 45°46'N 12°50'E
35 P5 **Portola** California, W USA 39°48'N 120°28'W
187 Q13 **Port-Olry** Espiritu Santo, C Vanuatu 15°03'S 167°04'E
93 J17 **Pörtom** *Fin.* Pirttikylä. Länsi-Suomi, W Finland 62°42'N 21°40'E
Port Omna *see* Portumna
59 G21 **Porto Murtinho** Mato Grosso do Sul, SW Brazil 21°42'S 57°52'W
59 K16 **Porto Nacional** Tocantins, C Brazil 10°41'S 48°19'W
77 S16 **Porto-Novo** ● (Benin) S Benin 06°29'N 02°37'E
23 X10 **Port Orange** Florida, SE USA 29°06'N 80°59'W
32 G8 **Port Orchard** Washington, NW USA 47°32'N 122°38'W
Porto Re *see* Kraljevica
32 E15 **Port Orford** Oregon, NW USA 42°45'N 124°30'W
Porto Rico *see* Puerto Rico
106 J13 **Porto San Giorgio** Marche, C Italy 43°10'N 13°47'E
107 F14 **Porto San Stefano** Toscana, C Italy 42°26'N 11°09'E
64 P5 **Porto Santo** *var.* Vila Baleira. Porto Santo, Madeira, Portugal, NE Atlantic Ocean 33°04'N 16°20'W
64 Q5 **Porto Santo** ✈ Porto Santo, Madeira, Portugal, NE Atlantic Ocean 33°04'N 16°20'W
64 P5 **Porto Santo** *var.* Ilha do Porto Santo. *island* Madeira, Portugal, NE Atlantic Ocean
Porto Santo, Ilha do *see* Porto Santo
60 H9 **Porto São José** Paraná, S Brazil 22°43'S 53°10'W
59 O19 **Porto Seguro** Bahia, E Brazil 16°25'S 39°07'W
107 B17 **Porto Torres** Sardegna, Italy, C Mediterranean Sea 40°50'N 08°23'E
59 J23 **Porto União** Santa Catarina, S Brazil 26°15'S 51°04'W
103 Y16 **Porto-Vecchio** Corse, France, C Mediterranean Sea 41°35'N 09°17'E
59 E15 **Porto Velho** *var.* Velho. *state capital* Rondônia, W Brazil 08°45'S 63°54'W
56 A6 **Portoviejo** *var.* Puertoviejo. Manabí, W Ecuador 01°03'S 80°31'W
185 B26 **Port Pegasus** *bay* Stewart Island, New Zealand
14 H15 **Port Perry** Ontario, SE Canada 44°08'N 78°57'W
183 N12 **Port Phillip Bay** *harbour* Victoria, SE Australia
182 I8 **Port Pirie** South Australia 33°11'S 138°01'E
96 G9 **Portree** N Scotland, United Kingdom 57°26'N 06°12'W
Port Rex *see* East London
Port Rois *see* Portrush

◆ Country
● Country Capital
◇ Dependent Territory
○ Dependent Territory Capital
◈ Administrative Regions
✈ International Airport
▲ Mountain
▲▲ Mountain Range
⛰ Volcano
≈ River
◎ Lake
⊠ Reservoir

PORT ROYAL – PRYDZ BAY

44 K13 **Port Royal** E Jamaica 17°55′N 76°52′W
21 R15 **Port Royal** South Carolina, SE USA 32°22′N 80°41′W
21 R15 **Port Royal Sound** *inlet* South Carolina, SE USA
97 F14 **Portrush** *Ir.* Port Rois. N Northern Ireland, United Kingdom 55°12′N 06°40′W
Port Said *see* Būr Sa'īd
23 R9 **Port Saint Joe** Florida, SE USA 29°49′N 85°18′W
23 Y11 **Port Saint John** Florida, SE USA 28°28′N 80°46′W
103 R16 **Port-St-Louis-du-Rhône** Bouches-du-Rhône, SE France 43°22′N 04°48′E
44 K10 **Port Salut** SW Haiti 18°04′N 73°55′W
65 E24 **Port Salvador** *inlet* East Falkland, Falkland Islands
65 D24 **Port San Carlos** East Falkland, Falkland Islands 51°30′S 58°59′W
13 S10 **Port Saunders** Newfoundland, Newfoundland and Labrador, SE Canada 50°40′N 57°17′W
83 K24 **Port Shepstone** KwaZulu/Natal, E South Africa 30°44′S 30°28′E
45 O11 **Portsmouth** *var.* Grand-Anse. NW Dominica 15°34′N 61°27′W
97 N24 **Portsmouth** S England, United Kingdom 50°48′N 01°05′W
19 P10 **Portsmouth** New Hampshire, NE USA 43°04′N 70°47′W
31 S15 **Portsmouth** Ohio, N USA 38°43′N 83°00′W
21 X7 **Portsmouth** Virginia, NE USA 36°50′N 76°18′W
14 E17 **Port Stanley** Ontario, S Canada 42°39′N 81°12′W
Port Stanley *see* Stanley
65 B25 **Port Stephens** *inlet* West Falkland, Falkland Islands
65 B25 **Port Stephens Settlement** West Falkland, Falkland Islands
97 F14 **Portstewart** *Ir.* Port Stíobhaird. N Northern Ireland, United Kingdom 55°11′N 06°43′W
Port Stíobhaird *see* Portstewart
83 K24 **Port St. Johns** Eastern Cape, SE South Africa 31°37′S 29°32′E
80 I7 **Port Sudan** Red Sea, NE Sudan 19°37′N 37°14′E
22 L10 **Port Sulphur** Louisiana, S USA 29°28′N 89°41′W
Port Swettenham *see* Klang/Pelabuhan Klang
97 J22 **Port Talbot** S Wales, United Kingdom 51°36′N 03°47′W
92 L11 **Porttipahdan Tekojärvi** ◎ N Finland
32 G7 **Port Townsend** Washington, NW USA 48°07′N 122°45′W
104 H9 **Portugal** *off.* Portuguese Republic. ◆ *republic* SW Europe
105 O2 **Portugalete** País Vasco, N Spain 43°19′N 03°01′W
54 J6 **Portuguesa** *off.* Estado Portuguesa. ⬖ *state* N Venezuela
Portuguesa, Estado *see* Portuguesa
Portuguese East Africa *see* Mozambique
Portuguese Guinea *see* Guinea-Bissau
Portuguese Republic *see* Portugal
Portuguese Timor *see* East Timor
Portuguese West Africa *see* Angola
97 D18 **Portumna** *Ir.* Port Omna. Galway, W Ireland 53°06′N 08°13′W
Portus Cale *see* Porto
Portus Magnus *see* Almería
Portus Magonis *see* Mahón
103 P17 **Port-Vendres** *var.* Port Vendres. Pyrénées-Orientales, S France 42°31′N 03°06′E
182 H9 **Port Victoria** South Australia 34°34′S 137°31′E
187 Q14 **Port-Vila** *var.* Vila. ● (Vanuatu) Éfaté, C Vanuatu 17°45′S 168°21′E
Port Vila *see* Bauer Field
182 I9 **Port Wakefield** South Australia 34°13′S 138°10′E
31 N8 **Port Washington** Wisconsin, N USA 43°23′N 87°54′W
57 J14 **Porvenir** Pando, NW Bolivia 11°15′S 68°43′W
63 I24 **Porvenir** Magallanes, S Chile 53°18′S 70°22′W
61 D18 **Porvenir** Paysandú, W Uruguay 32°23′S 57°59′W
93 M19 **Porvoo** *Swe.* Borgå. Etelä-Suomi, S Finland 60°25′N 25°40′E
Porzecze *see* Parechcha
104 M10 **Porzuna** Castilla-La Mancha, C Spain 39°10′N 04°10′W
61 E14 **Posadas** Misiones, NE Argentina 27°27′S 55°52′W
104 L13 **Posadas** Andalucía, S Spain 37°48′N 05°06′W
Poschega *see* Požega
108 J11 **Poschiavino** ≈ Italy/Switzerland
108 J10 **Poschiavo** *Ger.* Puschlav. Graubünden, S Switzerland 46°19′N 10°02′E
112 D12 **Posedarje** Zadar, SW Croatia 44°12′N 15°27′E
Posen *see* Poznań
124 L14 **Poshekhon'ye** Yaroslavskaya Oblast', W Russian Federation 58°31′N 39°07′E
92 M13 **Posio** Lappi, NE Finland 66°06′N 28°16′E
Poskam *see* Zepu
Posnania *see* Poznań
1713 O12 **Poso** Sulawesi, C Indonesia 01°23′S 120°45′E
171 O12 **Poso, Danau** ◎ Sulawesi, C Indonesia
137 R10 **Posof** Ardahan, NE Turkey 41°30′N 42°33′E
25 R6 **Possum Kingdom Lake** ▣ Texas, SW USA
25 N6 **Post** Texas, SW USA 33°14′N 101°24′W
Postavy/Postawy *see* Pastavy
12 I7 **Poste-de-la-Baleine** Québec, NE Canada 55°13′N 77°54′W
99 M17 **Posterholt** Limburg, SE Netherlands 51°07′N 06°02′E
83 G22 **Postmasburg** Northern Cape, N South Africa 28°20′S 23°05′E
Pôsto Diuarum *see* Campo de Diauarum
59 I16 **Pôsto Jacaré** Mato Grosso, W Brazil 12°S 53°27′W
109 T12 **Postojna** *Ger.* Adelsberg, *It.* Postumia. SW Slovenia 45°48′N 14°12′E
Postumia *see* Postojna
29 X12 **Postville** Iowa, C USA 43°04′N 91°34′W
Pöstyén *see* Piešťany
113 G14 **Posušje** Federacija Bosna I Hercegovina, SW Bosnia and Herzegovina 43°28′N 17°20′E
171 O16 **Pota** Flores, C Indonesia 08°21′S 120°50′E
115 G23 **Potamós** Antikýthira, S Greece 35°53′N 23°17′E
55 S9 **Potaru River** ≈ C Guyana
83 I21 **Potchefstroom** North-West, N South Africa 26°42′S 27°06′E
27 R11 **Poteau** Oklahoma, C USA 35°03′N 94°36′W
25 R12 **Poteet** Texas, SW USA 29°02′N 98°34′W
115 G14 **Poteídaia** *site of ancient city* Kentrikí Makedonía, N Greece
Potentia *see* Potenza
107 M18 **Potenza** *anc.* Potentia. Basilicata, S Italy 40°40′N 15°50′E
185 A24 **Poteriteri, Lake** ◎ South Island, New Zealand
104 M2 **Potes** Cantabria, N Spain 43°10′N 04°41′W
Potgietersrus *see* Mokopane
25 S12 **Poth** Texas, SW USA 29°04′N 98°04′W
32 J9 **Potholes Reservoir** ▣ Washington, NW USA
137 Q9 **P'ot'i** W Georgia 42°10′N 41°42′E
77 X13 **Potiskum** Yobe, NE Nigeria 11°38′N 11°07′E
Potkozarje *see* Ivanjska
32 M9 **Potlatch** Idaho, NW USA 46°55′N 116°51′W
33 N9 **Pot Mountain** ▲ Idaho, NW USA 46°44′N 115°24′W
113 H14 **Potoci** Federacija Bosna I Hercegovina, S Bosnia and Herzegovina 43°24′N 17°52′E
21 V3 **Potomac River** ≈ NE USA
57 L20 **Potosí** Potosí, S Bolivia 19°35′S 65°51′W
42 H9 **Potosí** Chinandega, NW Nicaragua 12°58′N 87°30′W
27 W6 **Potosi** Missouri, C USA 37°57′N 90°49′W
57 K21 **Potosí** ⬖ *department* SW Bolivia
62 H7 **Potrerillos** Atacama, N Chile 26°30′S 69°25′W
42 H5 **Potrerillos** Cortés, NW Honduras 15°10′N 87°58′W
62 H8 **Potro, Cerro del** ▲ N Chile 28°22′S 69°34′W
100 N12 **Potsdam** Brandenburg, NE Germany 52°24′N 13°04′E
18 J7 **Potsdam** New York, NE USA 44°40′N 74°58′W
109 X5 **Pottendorf** Niederösterreich, E Austria 47°55′N 16°23′E
109 X5 **Pottenstein** Niederösterreich, E Austria 47°58′N 16°07′E
18 I15 **Pottstown** Pennsylvania, NE USA 40°15′N 75°39′W
18 H14 **Pottsville** Pennsylvania, NE USA 40°40′N 76°10′W
155 L25 **Pottuvil** Eastern Province, SE Sri Lanka 06°53′N 81°49′E
149 U6 **Potwar Plateau** *plateau* NE Pakistan
102 J7 **Pouancé** Maine-et-Loire, W France 47°46′N 01°11′W
15 R6 **Poulin de Courval, Lac** ◎ Québec, SE Canada
18 L9 **Poultney** Vermont, NE USA 43°31′N 73°12′W
187 O16 **Poum** Province Nord, W New Caledonia 20°15′S 164°03′E
59 L21 **Pouso Alegre** Minas Gerais, NE Brazil 22°13′S 45°56′W
192 I16 **Poutasi** Upolu, SE Samoa 14°00′S 171°43′W
167 R12 **Poŭthĭsăt** *prev.* Pursat. Poŭthĭsăt, W Cambodia 12°32′N 103°55′E
167 R12 **Poŭthĭsăt, Stœng** *prev.* Pursat. ≈ W Cambodia
102 J9 **Pouzauges** Vendée, NW France 46°47′N 00°54′W
Po, Valle del *see* Po Valley
106 F8 **Po Valley** *It.* Valle del Po. *valley* N Italy
111 I19 **Považská Bystrica** *Ger.* Waagbistritz, *Hung.* Vágbeszterce. Trenčiansky Kraj, W Slovakia 49°07′N 18°26′E
124 J10 **Povenets** Respublika Kareliya, NW Russian Federation 62°50′N 34°47′E
184 Q9 **Poverty Bay** *inlet* North Island, New Zealand
112 K12 **Povlen** ▲▲ W Serbia
104 G6 **Póvoa de Varzim** Porto, NW Portugal 41°22′N 08°46′W
127 N8 **Povorino** Voronezhskaya Oblast', W Russian Federation 51°10′N 42°16′E
Povungnituk *see* Puvirnituq
12 J3 **Povungnituk, Rivière de** ≈ Québec, NE Canada
14 H11 **Powassan** Ontario, S Canada 46°05′N 79°21′W
35 U17 **Poway** California, W USA 32°57′N 117°02′W
33 W14 **Powder River** Wyoming, C USA 43°01′N 106°57′W
33 Y10 **Powder River** ≈ Montana/Wyoming, NW USA
32 L12 **Powder River** ≈ Oregon, NW USA
33 W13 **Powder River Pass** *pass* Wyoming, C USA
33 U12 **Powell** Wyoming, C USA 44°45′N 108°45′W
65 I22 **Powell Basin** *undersea feature* NW Weddell Sea
36 M8 **Powell, Lake** ◎ Utah, W USA
37 R4 **Powell, Mount** ▲ Colorado, C USA 39°25′N 106°20′W
10 L17 **Powell River** British Columbia, SW Canada 49°54′N 124°34′W
31 N5 **Powers** Michigan, N USA 45°40′N 87°29′W
28 K2 **Powers Lake** North Dakota, N USA 48°33′N 102°37′W
21 V6 **Powhatan** Virginia, NE USA 37°33′N 77°56′W
31 V13 **Powhatan Point** Ohio, N USA 39°49′N 80°49′W
97 J20 **Powys** *cultural region* E Wales, United Kingdom
187 P17 **Poya** Province Nord, C New Caledonia 21°19′S 165°07′E
161 P10 **Poyang Hu** ◎ S China
30 L7 **Poygan, Lake** ◎ Wisconsin, N USA
109 Y2 **Poysdorf** Niederösterreich, NE Austria 48°40′N 16°38′E
112 N11 **Požarevac** *Ger.* Passarowitz. Serbia, NE Serbia 44°37′N 21°11′E
41 Q13 **Poza Rica** *var.* Poza Rica de Hidalgo. Veracruz-Llave, E Mexico 20°34′N 97°26′W
Poza Rica de Hidalgo *see* Poza Rica
112 L13 **Požega** *prev.* Slavonska Požega, *Ger.* Poschega, *Hung.* Pozsega. Požega-Slavonija, NE Croatia 45°19′N 17°42′E
112 H9 **Požega-Slavonija** *off.* Požeško-Slavonska Županija. ⬖ *province* NE Croatia
Požeško-Slavonska Županija *see* Požega-Slavonija
125 U13 **Pozhva** Komi-Permyatskiy Avtonomnyy Okrug, NW Russian Federation 59°07′N 56°04′E
110 G11 **Poznań** *Ger.* Posen, Posnania. Wielkolpolskie, C Poland 52°24′N 16°56′E
105 O13 **Pozo Alcón** Andalucía, S Spain 37°43′N 02°55′W
62 H3 **Pozo Almonte** Tarapacá, N Chile 20°16′S 69°50′W
104 L12 **Pozoblanco** Andalucía, S Spain 38°23′N 04°48′W
105 Q11 **Pozo Cañada** Castilla-La Mancha, C Spain 38°49′N 01°45′W
62 N5 **Pozo Colorado** Presidente Hayes, C Paraguay 23°26′S 58°51′W
63 J20 **Pozos, Punta** *headland* S Argentina 47°55′S 65°46′W
Pozsega *see* Požega
Pozsony *see* Bratislava
55 N5 **Pozuelos** Anzoátegui, NE Venezuela 10°11′N 64°39′W
107 L26 **Pozzallo** Sicilia, Italy, C Mediterranean Sea 36°44′N 14°51′E
107 K17 **Pozzuoli** *anc.* Puteoli. Campania, S Italy 40°49′N 14°07′E
77 P17 **Pra** ≈ S Ghana
111 C19 **Prachatice** *Ger.* Prachatitz. Jihočeský Kraj, S Czech Republic 49°01′N 14°02′E
Prachatitz *see* Prachatice
167 P11 **Prachin Buri** *var.* Prachinburi. Prachin Buri, C Thailand 14°05′N 101°23′E
Prachinburi *see* Prachin Buri
Prachuab Girikhand *see* Prachuap Khiri Khan
167 O12 **Prachuap Khiri Khan** *var.* Prachuab Girikhand. Prachuap Khiri Khan, SW Thailand 11°50′N 99°49′E
111 H16 **Praděd** *Ger.* Altvater. ▲ NE Czech Republic 50°06′N 17°14′E
54 D11 **Pradera** Valle del Cauca, SW Colombia 03°23′N 76°11′W
103 O17 **Prades** Pyrénées-Orientales, S France 42°36′N 02°22′E
59 O19 **Prado** Bahia, SE Brazil 17°13′S 39°15′W
54 E11 **Prado** Tolima, C Colombia 03°45′N 74°55′W
Prado del Ganso *see* Goose Green
Prae *see* Phrae
95 I24 **Præstø** Storstrøm, SE Denmark 55°08′N 12°03′E
Prag/Praga/Prague *see* Praha
27 O10 **Prague** Oklahoma, C USA 35°29′N 96°40′W
111 D16 **Praha** *Eng.* Prague, *Ger.* Prag, *Pol.* Praga. ● (Czech Republic) Středočeský Kraj, NW Czech Republic 50°06′N 14°26′E
116 J13 **Prahova** ⬖ *county* SE Romania
116 J13 **Prahova** ≈ S Romania
76 E10 **Praia** ● (Cape Verde) Santiago, S Cape Verde 14°55′N 23°31′W
83 M21 **Praia do Bilene** Gaza, S Mozambique 25°18′S 33°10′E
83 M20 **Praia do Xai-Xai** Gaza, S Mozambique 25°04′S 33°43′E
116 J10 **Praid** *Hung.* Parajd. Harghita, C Romania 46°33′N 25°06′E
26 J3 **Prairie Dog Creek** ≈ Kansas/Nebraska, C USA
30 J9 **Prairie du Chien** Wisconsin, N USA 43°02′N 91°08′W
27 S9 **Prairie Grove** Arkansas, C USA 35°58′N 94°19′W
31 P10 **Prairie River** ≈ Michigan, N USA
Prairie State *see* Illinois
25 V11 **Prairie View** Texas, SW USA 30°05′N 95°59′W
167 Q10 **Prakhon Chai** Buri Ram, E Thailand 14°36′N 103°04′E
109 R4 **Pram** ≈ N Austria
109 S4 **Prambachkirchen** Oberösterreich, N Austria 48°18′N 13°50′E
118 H2 **Prangli** *island* N Estonia
154 J13 **Prānhita** ≈ C India
127 O14 **Praskoveya** Stavropol'skiy Kray, SW Russian Federation 44°45′N 44°11′E
172 I15 **Praslin** *island* Inner Islands, NE Seychelles
115 O23 **Prasonísi, Akrotírio** *cape* Ródos, Dodekánisa, Greece, Aegean Sea
111 I14 **Praszka** Opolskie, S Poland 51°05′N 18°29′E
152 M13 **Pratāpgarh** Uttar Pradesh, N India 25°53′N 81°56′E
Pratas Island *see* Tungsha Tao
119 M18 **Pratasy** *Rus.* Protasy. Homyel'skaya Voblasts', SE Belarus 52°47′N 29°05′E
167 Q10 **Prathai** Nakhon Ratchasima, E Thailand 15°31′N 102°42′E
Prathet Thai *see* Thailand
Prathum Thani *see* Pathum Thani
63 F21 **Prat, Isla** *island* S Chile
106 G11 **Prato** Toscana, C Italy 43°53′N 11°05′E
103 O17 **Prats-de-Mollo-la-Preste** Pyrénées-Orientales, S France 42°25′N 02°28′E
26 L6 **Pratt** Kansas, C USA 37°40′N 98°45′W
108 E6 **Pratteln** Basel-Land, NW Switzerland 47°32′N 07°42′E
193 O2 **Pratt Seamount** *undersea feature* N Pacific Ocean 56°09′N 142°30′W
23 P5 **Prattville** Alabama, S USA 32°27′N 86°27′W
Praust *see* Pruszcz Gdański
119 B14 **Pravdinsk** *Ger.* Friedland. Kaliningradskaya Oblast', W Russian Federation 54°26′N 21°01′E
104 K2 **Pravia** Asturias, N Spain 43°30′N 06°06′W
118 L12 **Prazaroki** *Rus.* Prozoroki. Vitsyebskaya Voblasts', N Belarus 55°18′N 28°13′E
Prázsmár *see* Prejmer
167 S11 **Preăh Vihéar** Preăh Vihéar, N Cambodia 13°57′N 104°48′E
116 J12 **Predeal** *Hung.* Predeál. Brașov, C Romania 45°30′N 25°31′E
109 S8 **Predlitz** Steiermark, SE Austria 47°04′N 13°54′E
11 V15 **Preeceville** Saskatchewan, S Canada 51°58′N 102°40′W
Preenkuln *see* Priekule
102 K6 **Pré-en-Pail** Mayenne, NW France 48°27′N 00°15′W
109 T4 **Pregarten** Oberösterreich, N Austria 48°21′N 14°31′E
54 H7 **Pregonero** Táchira, NW Venezuela 08°02′N 71°35′W
118 J10 **Preiļi** *Ger.* Preli. Preiļi, SE Latvia 56°17′N 26°52′E
116 J12 **Prejmer** *Ger.* Tartlau, *Hung.* Prázsmár. Brașov, S Romania 45°42′N 25°49′E
113 J16 **Prekornica** ▲▲ C Montenegro
Preli *see* Preiļi
Prëmet *see* Përmet
100 M12 **Premnitz** Brandenburg, NE Germany 52°33′N 12°22′E
25 S15 **Premont** Texas, SW USA 27°21′N 98°07′W
113 H14 **Prenj** ▲▲ S Bosnia and Herzegovina
Prenjas/Prenjasi *see* Përrenjas
22 L7 **Prentiss** Mississippi, S USA 31°36′N 89°52′W
Preny *see* Prienai
100 O10 **Prenzlau** Brandenburg, NE Germany 53°19′N 13°52′E
123 N11 **Preobrazhenka** Irkutskaya Oblast', C Russian Federation 60°01′N 108°00′E
166 J9 **Preparis Island** *island* SW Burma (Myanmar)
Prerau *see* Přerov
111 H18 **Přerov** *Ger.* Prerau. Olomoucký Kraj, E Czech Republic 49°27′N 17°27′E
Preschau *see* Prešov
14 M14 **Prescott** Ontario, SE Canada 44°43′N 75°33′W
36 K12 **Prescott** Arizona, SW USA 34°33′N 112°26′W
27 T13 **Prescott** Arkansas, C USA 33°49′N 93°25′W
32 L10 **Prescott** Washington, NW USA 46°17′N 118°21′W
30 H6 **Prescott** Wisconsin, N USA 44°46′N 92°45′W
185 A24 **Preservation Inlet** *inlet* South Island, New Zealand
112 O7 **Preševo** Serbia, SE Serbia 42°20′N 21°38′E
29 N10 **Presho** South Dakota, N USA 43°54′N 100°03′W
58 M13 **Presidente Dutra** Maranhão, E Brazil 05°17′S 44°30′W
60 I8 **Presidente Epitácio** São Paulo, S Brazil 21°45′S 52°07′W
62 N5 **Presidente Hayes** *off.* Departamento de Presidente Hayes. ⬖ *department* C Paraguay
Presidente Hayes, Departamento de *see* Presidente Hayes
60 I9 **Presidente Prudente** São Paulo, S Brazil 22°09′S 51°24′W
Presidente Stroessner *see* Ciudad del Este
Presidente Vargas *see* Itabira
60 I8 **Presidente Venceslau** São Paulo, S Brazil 21°52′S 51°51′W
193 O10 **President Thiers Seamount** *undersea feature* C Pacific Ocean 24°39′S 145°50′W
24 J11 **Presidio** Texas, SW USA 29°33′N 104°22′W
Preslav *see* Veliki Preslav
111 M19 **Prešov** *var.* Preschau, *Ger.* Eperies, *Hung.* Eperjes. Prešovský Kraj, E Slovakia 49°N 21°14′E
111 M19 **Prešovský Kraj** ⬖ *region* E Slovakia
113 N20 **Prespa, Lake** *Alb.* Liqen i Prespës, *Gk.* Límni Megáli Préspa, Limni Prespa, *Mac.* Prespansko Ezero, *Serb.* Prespansko Jezero. ◎ SE Europe
Prespa, Limni/Prespansko Ezero/Prespansko Jezero/Prespës, Liqen i *see* Prespa, Lake
19 S2 **Presque Isle** Maine, NE USA 46°40′N 68°01′W
18 B11 **Presque Isle** *headland* Pennsylvania, NE USA 42°09′N 80°06′W
Pressburg *see* Bratislava
77 P17 **Prestea** SW Ghana 05°22′N 02°07′W
111 B17 **Přeštice** *Ger.* Pschestitz. Plzeňský Kraj, W Czech Republic 49°36′N 13°19′E
97 K17 **Preston** NW England, United Kingdom 53°46′N 02°42′W
23 S6 **Preston** Georgia, SE USA 32°03′N 84°32′W
33 R16 **Preston** Idaho, NW USA 42°06′N 111°52′W
29 Z13 **Preston** Iowa, C USA 42°03′N 90°24′W
29 X11 **Preston** Minnesota, N USA 43°41′N 92°06′W
21 O6 **Prestonsburg** Kentucky, S USA 37°40′N 82°46′W
96 I13 **Prestwick** W Scotland, United Kingdom 55°31′N 04°39′W
83 I45 **Pretoria** *var.* Epitoli, Tshwane. ● Gauteng, NE South Africa 25°41′S 28°12′E *see also* Tshwane
Pretoria-Witwatersrand-Vereeniging *see* Gauteng
Pretusha *see* Pretushë
113 M21 **Pretushë** *var.* Pretusha. Korçë, SE Albania 40°50′N 20°45′E
Preussisch Eylau *see* Bagrationovsk
Preußisch Holland *see* Pasłęk
Preussisch-Stargard *see* Starogard Gdański
115 C17 **Préveza** Ípeiros, W Greece 38°59′N 20°44′E
37 V3 **Prewitt Reservoir** ▣ Colorado, C USA
167 S13 **Prey Vêng** Prey Vêng, S Cambodia 11°30′N 105°20′E
144 M12 **Priaral'skiye Karakumy, Peski** *desert* SW Kazakhstan
123 P14 **Priargunsk** Chitinskaya Oblast', S Russian Federation 50°25′N 119°12′E
38 K14 **Pribilof Islands** *island group* Alaska, USA
113 K14 **Priboj** Serbia, W Serbia 43°34′N 19°33′E
111 C17 **Příbram** *Ger.* Pibrans. Středočeský Kraj, W Czech Republic 49°41′N 14°02′E
36 M4 **Price** Utah, W USA 39°35′N 110°49′W
37 N5 **Price River** ≈ Utah, W USA
23 N8 **Prichard** Alabama, S USA 30°44′N 88°04′W
25 R8 **Priddy** Texas, SW USA 31°39′N 98°30′W
105 P8 **Priego** Castilla-La Mancha, C Spain 40°26′N 02°19′W
104 M14 **Priego de Córdoba** Andalucía, S Spain 37°27′N 04°12′W
118 C10 **Priekule** *Ger.* Preenkuln. Liepāja, SW Latvia 56°26′N 21°36′E
118 C12 **Priekulė** *Ger.* Prökuls. Klaipėda, W Lithuania 55°36′N 21°16′E
119 F14 **Prienai** *Pol.* Preny. Kaunas, S Lithuania 54°37′N 23°56′E
83 G23 **Prieska** Northern Cape, C South Africa 29°40′S 22°45′E
32 M7 **Priest Lake** ▣ Idaho, NW USA
32 M7 **Priest River** Idaho, NW USA 48°10′N 117°02′W
104 M3 **Prieta, Peña** ▲ N Spain 43°01′N 04°42′W
40 J10 **Prieto, Cerro** ▲ C Mexico 24°10′N 105°21′W
111 J19 **Prievidza** *var.* Priewitz, *Ger.* Priwitz, *Hung.* Privigye. Trenčiansky Kraj, W Slovakia 48°47′N 18°35′E
Priewitz *see* Prievidza
112 F10 **Prijedor** ⬖ Republika Srpska, NW Bosnia and Herzegovina
113 K14 **Prijepolje** Serbia, W Serbia 43°24′N 19°39′E
Prikaspiyskaya Nizmennost' *see* Caspian Depression
113 O19 **Prilep** *Turk.* Perlepe. S FYR Macedonia 41°21′N 21°34′E
108 B9 **Prilly** Vaud, SW Switzerland 46°32′N 06°38′E
Priluki *see* Pryluky
62 L10 **Primero, Río** ≈ C Argentina
29 S12 **Primghar** Iowa, C USA 43°05′N 95°37′W
112 B9 **Primorje-Gorski Kotar** *off.* Primorsko-Goranska Županija. ⬖ *province* NW Croatia
118 A13 **Primorsk** *Ger.* Fischhausen. Kaliningradskaya Oblast', W Russian Federation 54°45′N 20°00′E
124 G12 **Primorsk** *Fin.* Koivisto. Leningradskaya Oblast', NW Russian Federation 60°20′N 28°39′E
123 S14 **Primorskiy Kray** *prev.* *Eng.* Maritime Territory. ⬖ *territory* SE Russian Federation
114 N10 **Primorsko** *prev.* Keupriya. Burgas, E Bulgaria 42°15′N 27°45′E
126 K13 **Primorsko-Akhtarsk** Krasnodarskiy Kray, SW Russian Federation 46°03′N 38°44′E
Primorsko-Goranska Županija *see* Primorje-Gorski Kotar
Primorsk/Primorskoye *see* Prymors'k
117 U13 **Primors'kyy** Respublika Krym, S Ukraine 45°09′N 35°33′E
113 D14 **Primošten** Šibenik-Knin, S Croatia 43°34′N 15°57′E
11 R13 **Primrose Lake** ◎ Saskatchewan, C Canada
11 T14 **Prince Albert** Saskatchewan, S Canada 53°09′N 105°43′W
83 G25 **Prince Albert** Western Cape, SW South Africa 33°13′S 22°03′E
8 J5 **Prince Albert Peninsula** *peninsula* Victoria Island, Northwest Territories, NW Canada
8 J6 **Prince Albert Sound** *inlet* Northwest Territories, N Canada
J5 8 **Prince Alfred, Cape** *headland* Northwest Territories, NW Canada
9 P6 **Prince Charles Island** *island* Nunavut, NE Canada
195 W6 **Prince Charles Mountains** ▲▲ Antarctica
Prince-Édouard, Île-du *see* Prince Edward Island
172 M13 **Prince Edward Fracture Zone** *tectonic feature* SW Indian Ocean
13 P14 **Prince Edward Island** *Fr.* Île-du Prince-Édouard. ⬖ *province* SE Canada
13 Q14 **Prince Edward Island** *Fr.* Île-du Prince-Édouard. *island* SE Canada
173 M12 **Prince Edward Islands** *island group* S South Africa
21 X4 **Prince Frederick** Maryland, NE USA 38°32′N 76°35′W
10 M14 **Prince George** British Columbia, SW Canada 53°55′N 122°49′W
21 W6 **Prince George** Virginia, NE USA 37°13′N 77°13′W
197 O8 **Prince Gustaf Adolf Sea** *sea* Nunavut, N Canada
197 Q3 **Prince of Wales, Cape** *headland* Alaska, USA 65°39′N 168°12′W
181 V1 **Prince of Wales Island** *island* Queensland, E Australia
8 L5 **Prince of Wales Island** *island* Queen Elizabeth Islands, Nunavut, NW Canada
39 Y14 **Prince of Wales Island** *island* Alexander Archipelago, Alaska, USA
Prince of Wales Island *see* Pinang, Pulau
8 J5 **Prince of Wales Strait** *strait* Northwest Territories, N Canada
197 O8 **Prince Patrick Island** *island* Parry Islands, Northwest Territories, NW Canada
9 N5 **Prince Regent Inlet** *channel* Nunavut, N Canada
10 J13 **Prince Rupert** British Columbia, SW Canada 54°18′N 130°17′W
Prince's Island *see* Príncipe
21 Y5 **Princess Anne** Maryland, NE USA 38°12′N 75°42′W
181 W2 **Princess Charlotte Bay** *bay* Queensland, NE Australia
195 W7 **Princess Elizabeth Land** *physical region* Antarctica
10 J14 **Princess Royal Island** *island* British Columbia, SW Canada
45 U15 **Princes Town** Trinidad, Trinidad and Tobago 10°16′N 61°23′W
11 N17 **Princeton** British Columbia, SW Canada 49°25′N 120°35′W
30 L11 **Princeton** Illinois, N USA 41°22′N 89°27′W
31 N16 **Princeton** Indiana, N USA 38°21′N 87°33′W
29 Z14 **Princeton** Iowa, C USA 41°40′N 90°21′W
20 H7 **Princeton** Kentucky, S USA 37°06′N 87°52′W
29 V8 **Princeton** Minnesota, N USA 45°34′N 93°34′W
27 S1 **Princeton** Missouri, C USA 40°22′N 93°37′W
18 J15 **Princeton** New Jersey, NE USA 40°21′N 74°39′W
21 R6 **Princeton** West Virginia, NE USA 37°23′N 81°06′W
39 S12 **Prince William Sound** *inlet* Alaska, USA
67 P9 **Príncipe** *var.* Príncipe Island, *Eng.* Prince's Island. *island* N Sao Tome and Principe
Príncipe Island *see* Príncipe
32 I13 **Prineville** Oregon, NW USA 44°19′N 120°50′W
28 J11 **Pringle** South Dakota, N USA 43°34′N 103°34′W
25 N1 **Pringle** Texas, SW USA 35°55′N 101°28′W
99 H14 **Prinsenbeek** Noord-Brabant, S Netherlands 51°36′N 04°42′E
98 L6 **Prinses Margriet Kanaal** *canal* N Netherlands
195 R1 **Prinsesse Astrid Kyst** *physical region* Antarctica
195 T2 **Prinsesse Ragnhild Kyst** *physical region* Antarctica
195 U2 **Prins Harald Kyst** *physical region* Antarctica
92 N2 **Prins Karls Forland** *island* W Svalbard
43 N8 **Prinzapolka** Región Autónoma Atlántico Norte, NE Nicaragua 13°19′N 83°35′W
42 L8 **Prinzapolka, Río** ≈ NE Nicaragua
122 H9 **Priob'ye** Khanty-Mansiyskiy Avtonomnyy Okrug-Yugra, N Russian Federation 62°25′N 65°36′E
104 H1 **Prior, Cabo** *headland* NW Spain 43°33′N 08°21′W
29 V9 **Prior Lake** Minnesota, N USA 44°42′N 93°25′W
124 H11 **Priozersk** *Fin.* Käkisalmi. Leningradskaya Oblast', NW Russian Federation 61°02′N 30°07′E
119 J20 **Pripet** *Bel.* Prypyats', *Ukr.* Pryp"yat'. ≈ Belarus/Ukraine
119 J20 **Pripet Marshes** *wetland* Belarus/Ukraine
113 N16 **Prishtinë** *Eng.* Pristina, *Serb.* Priština. C Kosovo 42°40′N 21°10′E
126 J8 **Pristen'** Kurskaya Oblast', W Russian Federation 51°15′N 36°47′E
Priština *see* Prishtinë
Pristina *see* Prishtinë
100 M10 **Pritzwalk** Brandenburg, NE Germany 53°10′N 12°11′E
103 R13 **Privas** Ardèche, E France 44°45′N 04°35′E
107 I16 **Priverno** Lazio, C Italy 41°28′N 13°11′E
Privigye *see* Prievidza
112 C12 **Privlaka** Zadar, SW Croatia 44°15′N 15°07′E
124 M15 **Privolzhsk** Ivanovskaya Oblast', NW Russian Federation 57°24′N 41°16′E
127 P7 **Privolzhskaya Vozvyshennost'** *var.* Volga Uplands. ▲▲ W Russian Federation
127 P8 **Privolzhskiy** Saratovskaya Oblast', W Russian Federation 51°24′N 46°02′E
127 P8 **Privolzhskoye** Saratovskaya Oblast', W Russian Federation 51°08′N 45°57′E
Priwitz *see* Prievidza
127 N13 **Priyutnoye** Respublika Kalmykiya, SW Russian Federation 46°08′N 43°33′E
127 U5 **Priyutovo** Respublika Bashkortostan, W Russian Federation 53°54′N 53°56′E
113 M17 **Prizren** S Kosovo 42°14′N 20°46′E
107 I24 **Prizzi** Sicilia, Italy, C Mediterranean Sea 37°44′N 13°26′E
113 P18 **Probištip** NE FYR Macedonia 42°00′N 22°06′E
169 S16 **Probolinggo** Jawa, C Indonesia 07°45′S 113°12′E
Probstberg *see* Wyszków
111 F14 **Prochowice** *Ger.* Parchwitz. Dolnośląskie, SW Poland 51°15′N 16°22′E
29 W5 **Proctor** Minnesota, N USA 46°46′N 92°13′W
25 R8 **Proctor** Texas, SW USA 31°57′N 98°25′W
25 R8 **Proctor Lake** ▣ Texas, SW USA
155 I18 **Proddatūr** Andhra Pradesh, E India 14°45′N 78°34′E
104 H9 **Proença-a-Nova** *var.* Proença a Nova. Castelo Branco, C Portugal 39°45′N 07°56′W
Proença a Nova *see* Proença-a-Nova
99 I21 **Profondeville** Namur, SE Belgium 50°22′N 04°52′E
41 W11 **Progreso** Yucatán, SE Mexico 21°14′N 89°41′W
123 R14 **Progress** Amurskaya Oblast', SE Russian Federation 49°40′N 129°30′E
127 O15 **Prokhladnyy** Kabardino-Balkarskaya Respublika, SW Russian Federation 43°48′N 44°02′E
Prokletije *see* North Albanian Alps
Prökuls *see* Priekulė
113 O15 **Prokuplje** Serbia, SE Serbia 43°15′N 21°35′E
124 H14 **Proletariy** Novgorodskaya Oblast', W Russian Federation 58°24′N 31°40′E
126 M12 **Proletarsk** Rostovskaya Oblast', SW Russian Federation 46°42′N 41°48′E
127 N13 **Proletarskoye Vodokhranilishche** *salt lake* SW Russian Federation
Prome *see* Pyay
60 J8 **Promissão** São Paulo, S Brazil 21°33′S 49°51′W
60 J8 **Promissão, Represa de** ▣ S Brazil
125 V4 **Promyshlennyy** Respublika Komi, NW Russian Federation 67°36′N 64°E
119 O16 **Pronya** ≈ E Belarus
10 M11 **Prophet River** British Columbia, W Canada 58°07′N 122°39′W
30 K11 **Prophetstown** Illinois, N USA 41°40′N 89°56′W
Propinsi Kepulauan Riau *see* Kepulauan Riau
59 P16 **Propriá** Sergipe, E Brazil 10°15′S 36°51′W
103 X16 **Propriano** Corse, France, C Mediterranean Sea 41°41′N 08°54′E
Prościejów *see* Prostějov
Proskurov *see* Khmel'nyts'kyy
114 H12 **Prosotsáni** Anatolikí Makedonía kai Thráki, NE Greece 41°11′N 23°59′E
171 Q7 **Prosperidad** Mindanao, S Philippines 08°36′N 125°54′E
32 J10 **Prosser** Washington, NW USA 46°12′N 119°46′W
Prossnitz *see* Prostějov
111 G18 **Prostějov** *Ger.* Prossnitz, *Pol.* Prościejów. Olomoucký Kraj, E Czech Republic 49°29′N 17°08′E
117 V8 **Prosyana** Dnipropetrovs'ka Oblast', E Ukraine 48°07′N 36°22′E
111 L16 **Proszowice** Małopolskie, S Poland 50°12′N 20°15′E
Protasy *see* Pratasy
172 J11 **Protea Seamount** *undersea feature* SW Indian Ocean 36°50′S 18°05′E
115 D21 **Próti** *island* S Greece
114 N8 **Provadiya** Varna, E Bulgaria 43°10′N 27°29′E
103 T14 **Provence** *cultural region* SE France
103 S15 **Provence** *prev.* Marseille-Marignane. ✈ (Marseille) Bouches-du-Rhône, SE France 43°25′N 05°15′E
103 T14 **Provence-Alpes-Côte d'Azur** ⬖ *region* SE France
20 H6 **Providence** Kentucky, S USA 37°23′N 87°47′W
19 N12 **Providence** *state capital* Rhode Island, NE USA 41°50′N 71°26′W
36 L1 **Providence** Utah, W USA 41°42′N 111°49′W
Providence *see* Fort Providence
Providence *see* Providence Atoll
67 X10 **Providence Atoll** *var.* Providence. *atoll* S Seychelles
14 D12 **Providence Bay** Manitoulin Island, Ontario, S Canada 45°39′N 82°16′W
23 R6 **Providence Canyon** *valley* Alabama/Georgia, S USA
22 I5 **Providence, Lake** ◎ Louisiana, S USA
35 X13 **Providence Mountains** ▲▲ California, W USA
43 Q7 **Providencia, Isla de** *island* NW Colombia, Caribbean Sea
44 L6 **Providenciales** *island* W Turks and Caicos Islands
19 Q12 **Provincetown** Massachusetts, NE USA 42°01′N 70°10′W
103 P5 **Provins** Seine-et-Marne, N France 48°34′N 03°18′E
36 L3 **Provo** Utah, W USA 40°14′N 111°39′W
11 R15 **Provost** Alberta, SW Canada 52°24′N 110°16′W
112 G13 **Prozor** Federacija Bosna I Hercegovina, SW Bosnia and Herzegovina 43°46′N 17°38′E
Prozoroki *see* Prazaroki
60 I11 **Prudentópolis** Paraná, S Brazil 25°12′S 50°58′W
39 R5 **Prudhoe Bay** Alaska, USA 70°16′N 148°18′W
39 R4 **Prudhoe Bay** *bay* Alaska, USA
111 H16 **Prudnik** *Ger.* Neustadt, Neustadt in Oberschlesien. Opole, SW Poland 50°20′N 17°34′E
119 J16 **Prudy** Minskaya Voblasts', C Belarus 53°47′N 26°32′E
101 D18 **Prüm** Rheinland-Pfalz, W Germany 50°15′N 06°27′E
101 D18 **Prüm** ≈ W Germany
Prusa *see* Bursa
110 J7 **Pruszcz Gdański** *Ger.* Praust. Pomorskie, N Poland 54°16′N 18°36′E
110 M12 **Pruszków** *Ger.* Kaltdorf. Mazowieckie, C Poland 52°09′N 20°49′E
116 K8 **Prut** *Ger.* Pruth. ≈ E Europe
Pruth *see* Prut
108 L8 **Prutz** Tirol, W Austria 47°07′N 10°42′E
Pružana *see* Pruzhany
119 G19 **Pruzhany** *Pol.* Prużana. Brestskaya Voblasts', SW Belarus 52°33′N 24°28′E
124 I11 **Pryazha** Respublika Kareliya, NW Russian Federation 61°42′N 33°39′E
117 U10 **Pryazovs'ke** Zaporiz'ka Oblast', SE Ukraine 46°43′N 35°39′E
Prychornomor'ska Nyzovyna *see* Black Sea Lowland
Prydniprovs'ka Nyzovyna/Prydnyaprowskaya Nizina *see* Dnieper Lowland
195 Y7 **Prydz Bay** *bay* Antarctica

◆ Country
● Country Capital
◇ Dependent Territory
○ Dependent Territory Capital
⬖ Administrative Regions
✈ International Airport
▲ Mountain
▲▲ Mountain Range
Volcano
≈ River
◎ Lake
▣ Reservoir

Pryluky – Qapqal Xibe Zizhixian

117 R4 Pryluky Rus. Priluki. Chernihivs'ka Oblast', NE Ukraine 50°35'N 32°23'E
117 V10 Prymors'k Rus. Primorsk; prev. Primorskoye. Zaporiz'ka Oblast', SE Ukraine 46°44'N 36°19'E
27 Q9 Pryor Oklahoma, C USA 36°19'N 95°19'W
33 U11 Pryor Creek ≈ Montana, NW USA
Pryp"yat'/Prypyats' see Pripet
110 M10 Przasnysz Mazowieckie, C Poland 53°01'N 20°51'E
111 K14 Przedbórz Łodzkie, S Poland 51°04'N 19°51'E
111 P17 Przemyśl Rus. Peremyshl. Podkarpackie, C Poland 49°47'N 22°47'E
111 O16 Przeworsk Podkarpackie, SE Poland 50°04'N 22°30'E
Przheval'sk see Karakol
110 L13 Przysucha Mazowieckie, SE Poland 51°22'N 20°36'E
115 H18 Psachná var. Psahna, Psakhná. Évvoia, C Greece 38°35'N 23°39'E
Psahna/Psakhná see Psachná
115 K18 Psará island E Greece
115 I16 Psathoúra island Vóreies Sporádes, Greece, Aegean Sea
Pschestitz see Přeštice
Psein Lora see Pishin Lora
117 S5 Psel Rus. Psël. ≈ Russian Federation/Ukraine
Psël see Psel
115 M21 Psérimos island Dodekánisa, Greece, Aegean Sea
Pseyn Bowr see Pishin Lora
Pskem see Piskom
147 R8 Pskemskiy Khrebet Uzb. Piskom Tizmasi. ▲▲ Kyrgyzstan/Uzbekistan
124 F14 Pskov Ger. Pleskau, Latv. Pleskava. Pskovskaya Oblast', W Russian Federation 58°32'N 31°15'E
118 K6 Pskov, Lake Est. Pihkva Järv, Ger. Pleskauer See, Rus. Pskovskoye Ozero. ◎ Estonia/Russian Federation
124 F15 Pskovskaya Oblast' ◈ province W Russian Federation
Pskovskoye Ozero see Pskov, Lake
112 G9 Psunj ▲▲ NE Croatia
111 J17 Pszczyna Ger. Pless. Śląskie, S Poland 49°59'N 18°54'E
Ptačnik/Ptacsnik see Vtáčnik
115 D17 Ptéri ▲ C Greece 39°08'N 21°32'E
Ptich' see Ptsich
115 E14 Ptolemaïda prev. Ptolemaïs. Dytikí Makedonía, N Greece 40°34'N 21°42'E
Ptolemaïs see Ptolemaïda, Greece
Ptolemaïs see 'Akko, Israel
119 M19 Ptsich Rus. Ptich'. Homyel'skaya Voblasts', SE Belarus 52°11'N 28°49'E
119 M18 Ptsich Rus. Ptich'. ≈ SE Belarus
109 X10 Ptuj Ger. Pettau; anc. Poetovio. NE Slovenia 46°26'N 15°54'E
61 A23 Puán Buenos Aires, E Argentina 37°35'S 62°45'W
192 H15 Pu'apu'a Savai'i, C Samoa 13°32'S 172°09'W
192 G15 Puava, Cape headland Savai'i, NW Samoa
Pubao see Baingoin
56 F12 Pucallpa Ucayali, C Peru 08°21'S 74°33'W
57 J17 Pucarani La Paz, NW Bolivia 16°25'S 68°29'W
Pučarevo see Novi Travnik
157 U12 Pucheng Shaanxi, SE China 35°00'N 109°34'E
160 L6 Pucheng var. Nanpu. Fujian, C China 27°59'N 118°31'E
125 N16 Puchezh Ivanovskaya Oblast', W Russian Federation 56°58'N 41°08'E
111 I19 Púchov Hung. Puhó. Trenčiansky Kraj, W Slovakia 49°08'N 18°15'E
116 J13 Pucioasa Dâmboviţa, S Romania 45°04'N 25°23'E
110 I6 Puck Pomorskie, N Poland 54°43'N 18°24'E
30 L8 Puckaway Lake ◎ Wisconsin, N USA
63 G15 Pucón Araucanía, S Chile 39°18'S 71°52'W
93 M14 Pudasjärvi Oulu, C Finland 65°20'N 27°02'E
148 L8 Pūdeh Tal, Shelleh-ye ≈ SW Afghanistan
127 S1 Pudem Udmurtskaya Respublika, NW Russian Federation 58°18'N 52°08'E
Pudewitz see Pobiedziska
124 K11 Pudozh Respublika Kareliya, NW Russian Federation 61°48'N 36°30'E
97 M17 Pudsey N England, United Kingdom 53°48'N 01°40'W
Puduchcheri see Pondicherry
151 H21 Pudukkottai Tamil Nādu, SE India 10°23'N 78°47'E
171 Z13 Pue Papua, E Indonesia 02°42'S 140°36'E
41 P14 Puebla var. Puebla de Zaragoza. Puebla, S Mexico 19°02'N 98°13'W
41 P15 Puebla ◈ state S Mexico
104 L11 Puebla de Alcocer Extremadura, W Spain 38°59'N 05°14'W
Puebla de Don Fabrique see Puebla de Don Fadrique
105 P13 Puebla de Don Fadrique var. Puebla de Don Fabrique. Andalucía, S Spain 37°58'N 02°25'W
104 J11 Puebla de la Calzada Extremadura, W Spain 38°54'N 06°38'W
104 J5 Puebla de Sanabria Castilla-León, N Spain 42°04'N 06°38'W
Puebla de Trives see A Pobla de Trives
Puebla de Zaragoza see Puebla
37 T6 Pueblo Colorado, C USA 38°15'N 104°37'W
37 N10 Pueblo Colorado Wash valley Arizona, SW USA
61 C16 Pueblo Libertador Corrientes, NE Argentina 30°13'S 59°23'W
40 J10 Pueblo Nuevo Durango, C Mexico 23°24'N 105°21'W
42 J8 Pueblo Nuevo Estelí, NW Nicaragua 13°21'N 86°30'W
54 J3 Pueblo Nuevo Falcón, N Venezuela 11°59'N 69°57'W
42 B6 Pueblo Nuevo Tiquisate var. Tiquisate. Escuintla, SW Guatemala 14°16'N 91°21'W
41 Q11 Pueblo Viejo, Laguna de lagoon E Mexico
63 J14 Puelches La Pampa, C Argentina 38°08'S 65°56'W
104 L14 Puente-Genil Andalucía, S Spain 37°23'N 04°45'W
105 Q3 Puente la Reina Bas. Gares. Navarra, N Spain 42°40'N 01°49'W
104 L12 Puente Nuevo, Embalse de ⊠ S Spain
57 D14 Puente Piedra Lima, W Peru 11°49'S 77°01'W
160 F14 Pu'er var. Ning'er. Yunnan, SW China 23°09'N 100°58'E
45 V6 Puerca, Punta headland E Puerto Rico 18°13'N 65°36'W
37 R12 Puerco, Rio ≈ New Mexico, SW USA
57 J17 Puerto Acosta La Paz, W Bolivia 15°33'S 69°15'W
63 G19 Puerto Aisén Aisén, S Chile 45°24'S 72°42'W
41 R17 Puerto Ángel Oaxaca, SE Mexico 15°39'N 96°29'W
Puerto Argentino see Stanley
41 T17 Puerto Arista Chiapas, SE Mexico 15°55'N 93°47'W
43 O16 Puerto Armuelles Chiriquí, SW Panama 08°19'N 82°51'W
Puerto Arrecife see Arrecife
54 D14 Puerto Asís Putumayo, SW Colombia 0°31'N 76°31'W
54 L9 Puerto Ayacucho Amazonas, SW Venezuela 05°45'N 67°37'W
57 C18 Puerto Ayora Galapagos Islands, Ecuador, E Pacific Ocean 0°45'S 90°19'W
57 C18 Puerto Baquerizo Moreno var. Baquerizo Moreno. Galapagos Islands, Ecuador, E Pacific Ocean 0°54'S 89°37'W
42 G4 Puerto Barrios Izabal, E Guatemala 15°42'N 88°34'W
Puerto Bello see Portobelo
54 F8 Puerto Berrío Antioquia, C Colombia 06°28'N 74°28'W
54 F9 Puerto Boyacá Boyacá, C Colombia 05°58'N 74°36'W
54 K4 Puerto Cabello Carabobo, N Venezuela 10°29'N 68°02'W
43 N7 Puerto Cabezas var. Bilwi. Región Autónoma Atlántico Norte, NE Nicaragua 14°05'N 83°22'W
54 L9 Puerto Carreño Vichada, E Colombia 06°08'N 67°30'W
54 E4 Puerto Colombia Atlántico, N Colombia 10°59'N 74°57'W
42 H4 Puerto Cortés Cortés, NW Honduras 15°50'N 87°55'W
54 J4 Puerto Cumarebo Falcón, N Venezuela 11°29'N 69°21'W
Puerto de Cabras see Puerto del Rosario
55 Q5 Puerto de Hierro Sucre, NE Venezuela 10°40'N 62°03'W
64 O11 Puerto de la Cruz Tenerife, Islas Canarias, Spain, NE Atlantic Ocean 28°24'N 16°33'W
64 Q11 Puerto del Rosario var. Puerto de Cabras. Fuerteventura, Islas Canarias, Spain, NE Atlantic Ocean 28°29'N 13°52'W
63 J20 Puerto Deseado Santa Cruz, SE Argentina 47°46'S 65°53'W
40 F8 Puerto Escondido Baja California Sur, NW Mexico 25°48'N 111°20'W
41 R17 Puerto Escondido Oaxaca, SE Mexico 15°48'N 96°57'W
60 G12 Puerto Esperanza Misiones, NE Argentina 26°01'S 54°39'W
54 H10 Puerto Gaitán Meta, C Colombia 04°20'N 72°10'W
Puerto Gallegos see Río Gallegos
60 G12 Puerto Iguazú Misiones, NE Argentina 25°39'S 54°35'W
56 F12 Puerto Inca Huánuco, N Peru 09°22'S 74°54'W
54 L11 Puerto Inírida var. Obando. Guainía, E Colombia 03°48'N 67°54'W
42 K13 Puerto Jesús Guanacaste, NW Costa Rica 10°08'N 85°26'W
41 Z11 Puerto Juárez Quintana Roo, SE Mexico 21°06'N 86°46'W
55 N5 Puerto La Cruz Anzoátegui, NE Venezuela 10°14'N 64°40'W
54 E14 Puerto Leguízamo Putumayo, S Colombia 0°14'S 74°45'W
43 N5 Puerto Lempira Gracias a Dios, E Honduras 15°14'N 83°48'W
Puerto Libertad see La Libertad
54 I11 Puerto Limón Meta, E Colombia 04°00'N 71°09'W
54 D13 Puerto Limón Putumayo, SW Colombia 01°02'N 76°30'W
Puerto Limón see Limón
105 N11 Puertollano Castilla-La Mancha, C Spain 38°41'N 04°07'W
63 K17 Puerto Lobos Chubut, SE Argentina 42°00'S 64°58'W
54 I3 Puerto López La Guajira, N Colombia 11°54'N 71°21'W
105 Q14 Puerto Lumbreras Murcia, SE Spain 37°35'N 01°49'W
41 V17 Puerto Madero Chiapas, SE Mexico 14°44'N 92°25'W
63 K17 Puerto Madryn Chubut, S Argentina 42°45'S 65°02'W
Puerto Magdalena see Bahía Magdalena
57 J15 Puerto Maldonado Madre de Dios, E Peru 12°37'S 69°11'W
Puerto Masachapa see Masachapa
Puerto México see Coatzacoalcos
63 G17 Puerto Montt Los Lagos, C Chile 41°28'S 72°57'W
41 Z12 Puerto Morelos Quintana Roo, SE Mexico 20°47'N 86°54'W
54 L10 Puerto Nariño Vichada, E Colombia 04°57'N 67°51'W
63 H23 Puerto Natales Magallanes, S Chile 51°42'S 72°28'W
43 X15 Puerto Obaldía Kuna Yala, NE Panama 08°38'N 77°26'W
44 H6 Puerto Padre Las Tunas, E Cuba 21°13'N 76°35'W
54 L9 Puerto Páez Apure, C Venezuela 06°10'N 67°30'W
40 E3 Puerto Peñasco Sonora, NW Mexico 31°20'N 113°35'W
55 N5 Puerto Píritu Anzoátegui, NE Venezuela 10°04'N 65°00'W
45 N8 Puerto Plata var. San Felipe de Puerto Plata. N Dominican Republic 19°46'N 70°42'W
45 N8 Puerto Plata ✈ N Dominican Republic 19°43'N 70°43'W
Puerto Presidente Stroessner see Ciudad del Este
171 N6 Puerto Princesa off. Puerto Princesa City. Palawan, W Philippines 09°48'N 118°43'E
Puerto Princesa City see Puerto Princesa
Puerto Príncipe see Camagüey
Puerto Quellón see Quellón
60 F13 Puerto Rico Misiones, NE Argentina 26°48'S 54°59'W
57 K14 Puerto Rico Pando, N Bolivia 11°07'S 67°32'W
54 E12 Puerto Rico Caquetá, S Colombia 01°54'N 75°13'W
45 U5 Puerto Rico off. Commonwealth of Puerto Rico; prev. Porto Rico. ◇ US commonwealth territory C West Indies
64 F11 Puerto Rico island C West Indies
Puerto Rico, Commonwealth of see Puerto Rico
64 G11 Puerto Rico Trench undersea feature NE Caribbean Sea
54 I8 Puerto Rondón Arauca, E Colombia 06°16'N 71°05'W
Puerto San José see San José
63 J21 Puerto San Julián var. San Julián. Santa Cruz, SE Argentina 49°14'S 67°41'W
63 I22 Puerto Santa Cruz var. Santa Cruz. Santa Cruz, SE Argentina 50°05'S 68°31'W
Puerto Sauce see Juan L. Lacaze
57 Q20 Puerto Suárez Santa Cruz, E Bolivia 18°59'S 57°47'W
54 D13 Puerto Umbría Putumayo, SW Colombia 0°52'N 76°36'W
40 J13 Puerto Vallarta Jalisco, SW Mexico 20°36'N 105°15'W
63 G16 Puerto Varas Los Lagos, C Chile 41°20'S 73°00'W
42 M13 Puerto Viejo Heredia, NE Costa Rica 10°27'N 84°00'W
Puertoviejo see Portoviejo
57 B18 Puerto Villamil var. Villamil. Galapagos Islands, Ecuador, E Pacific Ocean 0°57'S 91°00'W
54 F8 Puerto Wilches Santander, N Colombia 07°22'N 73°53'W
63 H20 Pueyrredón, Lago var. Lago Cochrane. ◎ S Argentina
127 R7 Pugachëv Saratovskaya Oblast', W Russian Federation 52°06'N 48°50'E
127 T3 Pugachëvo Udmurtskaya Respublika, NW Russian Federation 56°38'N 53°03'E
32 H8 Puget Sound sound Washington, NW USA
107 O17 Puglia var. Le Puglie, Eng. Apulia. ◈ region SE Italy
107 N17 Puglia, Canosa di anc. Canusium. Puglia, SE Italy 41°13'N 16°04'E
118 I6 Puhja Ger. Kawelecht. Tartumaa, SE Estonia 58°20'N 26°19'E
Puhó see Púchov
105 V4 Puigcerdà Cataluña, NE Spain 42°25'N 01°53'E
Puigmal see Puigmal d'Err
103 N17 Puigmal d'Err var. Puigmal. ▲ S France 42°24'N 02°07'E
76 I16 Pujehun S Sierra Leone 07°23'N 11°44'W
Puka see Pukë
185 E20 Pukaki, Lake ◎ South Island, New Zealand
38 F10 Pukalani Maui, Hawaii, USA, C Pacific Ocean 20°50'N 156°20'W
190 J13 Pukapuka atoll N Cook Islands
191 X9 Pukapuka atoll Îles Tuamotu, E French Polynesia
Pukari Neem see Purekkari Neem
191 X11 Pukarua var. Pukaruha. atoll Îles Tuamotu, E French Polynesia
Pukaruha see Pukarua
14 A7 Pukaskwa ≈ Ontario, S Canada
11 V12 Pukatawagan Manitoba, C Canada 55°46'N 101°14'W
191 X16 Pukatikei, Maunga ⋀ Easter Island, Chile, E Pacific Ocean
182 C1 Pukatja var. Ernabella. South Australia 26°18'S 132°13'E
163 Y12 Pukch'ŏng E North Korea 40°13'N 128°20'E
113 L18 Pukë var. Puka. Shkodër, N Albania 42°03'N 19°53'E
184 L6 Pukekohe Auckland, North Island, New Zealand 37°12'S 174°54'E
184 L7 Pukemiro Waikato, North Island, New Zealand 37°37'S 175°02'E
190 D12 Puke, Mont ▲ Île Futuna, W Wallis and Futuna
Puket see Phuket
185 C20 Puketeraki Range ▲▲ South Island, New Zealand
184 N13 Puketoi Range ▲▲ North Island, New Zealand
185 F21 Pukeuri Junction Otago, South Island, New Zealand 45°01'S 171°01'E
119 L16 Pukhavichy Rus. Pukhovichi. Minskaya Voblasts', C Belarus 53°32'N 28°15'E
Pukhovichi see Pukhavichy
124 M10 Puksoozero Arkhangel'skaya Oblast', NW Russian Federation 62°37'N 40°29'E
112 A10 Pula It. Pola; prev. Pulj. Istra, NW Croatia 44°53'N 13°51'E
Pula see Nyingchi
163 U14 Pulandian var. Xinjin. Liaoning, NE China 39°25'N 121°58'E
163 T14 Pulandian Wan bay NE China
189 O15 Pulap Atoll atoll Caroline Islands, C Micronesia
18 H9 Pulaski New York, NE USA 43°34'N 76°06'W
20 I10 Pulaski Tennessee, S USA 35°11'N 87°00'W
21 R7 Pulaski Virginia, NE USA 37°03'N 80°47'W
171 Y14 Pulau, Sungai ≈ Papua, E Indonesia
110 N13 Puławy Ger. Neu Amerika. Lubelskie, E Poland 51°25'N 21°57'E
146 I16 Pulhatyn Rus. Polekhatum; prev. Pul'-I-Khatum. Ahal Welaýaty, S Turkmenistan 36°01'N 61°08'E
101 E16 Pulheim Nordrhein-Westfalen, W Germany 51°00'N 06°48'E
155 J19 Pulicat Lake lagoon SE India
Pul'-I-Khatum see Pulhatyn
Pul-i-Khumri see Pol-e Khomrī
Pul-i-Sefid see Pol-e Sefīd
Pulj see Pula
109 W2 Pulkau ≈ NE Austria
93 L15 Pulkkila Oulu, C Finland 64°15'N 25°53'E
122 C7 Pulkovo ✈ (Sankt-Peterburg) Leningradskaya Oblast', NW Russian Federation 60°06'N 30°23'E
32 M9 Pullman Washington, NW USA 46°43'N 117°10'W
108 B10 Pully Vaud, SW Switzerland 46°31'N 06°40'E
40 F7 Púlpita, Punta headland NW Mexico 26°30'N 111°28'W
110 M10 Pułtusk Mazowieckie, C Poland 52°41'N 21°04'E
158 H10 Pulu Xinjiang Uygur Zizhiqu, W China 36°10'N 81°29'E
137 P13 Pülümür Tunceli, E Turkey 39°30'N 39°54'E
189 N16 Pulusuk island Caroline Islands, C Micronesia
189 N16 Puluwat Atoll atoll Caroline Islands, C Micronesia
25 N11 Pumpville Texas, SW USA 29°55'N 101°43'W
191 P7 Punaauia var. Hakapehi. Tahiti, W French Polynesia 17°38'S 149°37'W
56 B8 Puná, Isla island SW Ecuador
185 G16 Punakaiki West Coast, South Island, New Zealand 42°07'S 171°21'E
153 T11 Punakha C Bhutan 27°38'N 89°50'E
57 L18 Punata Cochabamba, C Bolivia 17°32'S 65°50'W
155 E14 Pune prev. Poona. Mahārāshtra, W India 18°32'N 73°52'E
83 M17 Pungoè, Rio var. Púnguè, Pungwe. ≈ C Mozambique
21 X10 Pungo River ≈ North Carolina, SE USA
Púnguè/Pungwe see Pungoè, Rio
79 N19 Punia Maniema, E Dem. Rep. Congo 01°28'S 26°25'E
62 H8 Punilla, Sierra de la ▲▲ W Argentina
161 P14 Puning Guangdong, S China 23°24'N 116°14'E
62 G10 Punitaqui Coquimbo, C Chile 30°50'S 71°29'W
149 T9 Punjab prev. West Punjab, Western Punjab. ◈ province E Pakistan
152 H8 Punjab state NW India
129 Q9 Punjab Plains plain N India
93 O17 Punkaharju var. Punkasalmi. Itä-Suomi, E Finland 61°45'N 29°21'E
Punkasalmi see Punkaharju
57 I17 Puno Puno, SE Peru 15°53'S 70°03'W
57 H17 Puno off. Departamento de Puno. ◈ department S Peru
Puno, Departamento de see Puno
61 B24 Punta Alta Buenos Aires, E Argentina 38°54'S 62°01'W
63 H24 Punta Arenas prev. Magallanes. Magallanes, S Chile 53°10'S 70°56'W
45 T6 Punta, Cerro de ▲ C Puerto Rico 18°10'N 66°36'W
43 T15 Punta Chame Panamá, C Panama 08°39'N 79°42'W
57 G17 Punta Colorada Arequipa, SW Peru 16°17'S 72°31'W
40 F9 Punta Coyote Baja California Sur, NW Mexico
62 G8 Punta de Díaz Atacama, N Chile 28°03'S 70°36'W
61 G20 Punta del Este Maldonado, S Uruguay 34°59'S 54°58'W
63 K17 Punta Delgada Chubut, SE Argentina 42°46'S 63°40'W
55 O5 Punta de Mata Monagas, NE Venezuela 09°48'N 63°38'W
55 O4 Punta de Piedras Nueva Esparta, NE Venezuela 10°57'N 64°06'W
42 F4 Punta Gorda Toledo, SE Belize 16°07'N 88°47'W
43 N11 Punta Gorda Región Autónoma Atlántico Sur, SE Nicaragua 11°31'N 83°46'W
23 W14 Punta Gorda Florida, SE USA 26°55'N 82°03'W
42 M11 Punta Gorda, Río ≈ SE Nicaragua
62 H6 Punta Negra, Salar de salt lake N Chile
40 D5 Punta Prieta Baja California Norte, NW Mexico 28°56'N 114°11'W
42 L13 Puntarenas Puntarenas, W Costa Rica 09°58'N 84°50'W
42 L13 Puntarenas off. Provincia de Puntarenas. ◈ province W Costa Rica
Puntarenas, Provincia de see Puntarenas
80 P13 Puntland cultural region NE Somalia
54 J4 Punto Fijo Falcón, N Venezuela 11°42'N 70°13'W
105 S4 Puntón de Guara ▲ N Spain 42°18'N 00°13'W
18 D14 Punxsutawney Pennsylvania, NE USA 40°55'N 78°57'W
93 M14 Puolanka Oulu, C Finland 64°51'N 27°42'E
57 J17 Pupuya, Nevado ▲ W Bolivia 15°04'S 69°01'W
Puqi see Chibi
57 F16 Puquio Ayacucho, S Peru 14°44'S 74°07'W
122 J9 Pur ≈ N Russian Federation
186 D7 Purari ≈ S Papua New Guinea
27 N11 Purcell Oklahoma, C USA 35°00'N 97°21'W
11 O16 Purcell Mountains ▲▲ British Columbia, SW Canada
105 P14 Purchena Andalucía, S Spain 37°21'N 02°21'W
27 S8 Purdy Missouri, C USA 36°49'N 93°55'W
118 I2 Purekkari Neem prev. Pukari Neem. headland N Estonia 59°33'N 24°49'E
37 U7 Purgatoire River ≈ Colorado, C USA
Purgstall see Purgstall an der Erlauf
109 V5 Purgstall an der Erlauf var. Purgstall. Niederösterreich, NE Austria 48°01'N 15°08'E
154 O13 Puri var. Jagannath. Orissa, E India 19°52'N 85°49'E
Puriramya see Buriram
109 X4 Purkersdorf Niederösterreich, NE Austria 48°13'N 16°12'E
98 I9 Purmerend Noord-Holland, C Netherlands 52°30'N 04°56'E
151 G16 Pūrna ≈ C India
Purnea see Pūrnia
153 R13 Pūrnia prev. Purnea. Bihār, NE India 25°47'N 87°28'E
Pursat see Poŭthĭsăt, Stœ̆ng, W, Cambodia
Pursat see Poŭthĭsăt, W Cambodia
Purulia see Puruliya
150 L13 Puruliya prev. Purulia. West Bengal, NE India 23°20'N 86°24'E
47 G7 Purus, Rio var. Río Purús. ≈ Brazil/Peru
186 C9 Purutu Island island SW Papua New Guinea
93 N17 Puruvesi ◎ SE Finland
22 L7 Purvis Mississippi, S USA 31°08'N 89°24'W
114 J11 Pŭrvomay prev. Borisovgrad. Plovdiv, C Bulgaria 42°06'N 25°13'E
169 R16 Purwodadi prev. Poerwodadi. Jawa, C Indonesia 07°05'S 110°53'E
169 P16 Purwokerto prev. Poerwokerto. Jawa, C Indonesia 07°25'S 109°14'E
169 P16 Purworejo prev. Poerworedjo. Jawa, C Indonesia 07°45'S 110°04'E
20 H8 Puryear Tennessee, S USA 36°25'N 88°21'W
154 H13 Pusad Mahārāshtra, C India 19°56'N 77°40'E
163 Z16 Pusan off. Pusan-gwangyŏksi, var. Busan, Jap. Fusan. SE South Korea 35°11'N 129°04'E
Pusan see Kim Hae
Pusan-gwangyŏksi see Pusan
168 H7 Pusatgajo, Pegunungan ▲▲ Sumatera, NW Indonesia
Puschlav see Poschiavo
124 G13 Pushkin prev. Tsarskoye Selo. Leningradskaya Oblast', NW Russian Federation 59°42'N 30°24'E
126 L3 Pushkino Moskovskaya Oblast', W Russian Federation 55°57'N 37°45'E
127 Q8 Pushkino Saratovskaya Oblast', W Russian Federation 51°09'N 47°00'E
Pushkino see Biläsuvar
111 M22 Püspökladány Hajdú-Bihar, E Hungary 47°20'N 21°05'E
118 J3 Püssi Ger. Isenhof. Ida-Virumaa, NE Estonia 59°22'N 27°04'E
116 I5 Pustomyty L'vivs'ka Oblast', W Ukraine 49°43'N 23°55'E
124 F16 Pustoshka Pskovskaya Oblast', W Russian Federation 56°21'N 29°16'E
Puszcza Mazowiecka see Mazowiecka, Puszcza
Pusztakalán see Călan
167 N1 Putao prev. Fort Hertz. Kachin State, N Burma (Myanmar) 27°22'N 97°24'E
184 M8 Putaruru Waikato, North Island, New Zealand 38°03'S 175°48'E
Puteoli see Pozzuoli
161 R12 Putian Fujian, SE China 25°32'N 119°02'E
107 O17 Putignano Puglia, SE Italy 40°51'N 17°08'E
Puting see De'an
Putivl' see Putyvl'
41 Q16 Putla var. Putla de Guerrero. Oaxaca, SE Mexico 17°01'N 97°56'W
Putla de Guerrero see Putla
19 N12 Putnam Connecticut, NE USA 41°56'N 71°52'W
25 Q7 Putnam Texas, SW USA 32°22'N 99°11'W
18 M10 Putney Vermont, NE USA 42°59'N 72°30'W
111 L20 Putnok Borsod-Abaúj-Zemplén, NE Hungary 48°18'N 20°25'E
Putorana, Gory/Putorana Mountains see Putorana, Plato
122 L8 Putorana, Plato var. Gory Putorana, Eng. Putorana Mountains. ▲▲ N Russian Federation
168 K9 Putrajaya ● (Malaysia) Kuala Lumpur, Peninsular Malaysia 02°57'N 101°42'E
62 H2 Putre Tarapacá, N Chile 18°11'S 69°30'W
155 J24 Puttalam North Western Province, W Sri Lanka 08°02'N 79°55'E
155 J24 Puttalam Lagoon lagoon W Sri Lanka
99 H17 Putte Antwerpen, C Belgium 51°04'N 04°39'E
94 E10 Puttegga ▲ S Norway 62°13'N 07°40'E
98 K11 Putten Gelderland, C Netherlands 52°15'N 05°36'E
100 K7 Puttgarden Schleswig-Holstein, N Germany 54°30'N 11°13'E
Puttiala see Patiāla
101 D20 Püttlingen Saarland, SW Germany 49°16'N 06°52'E
54 D14 Putumayo off. Intendencia del Putumayo. ◈ province S Colombia
Putumayo, Intendencia del see Putumayo
48 E7 Putumayo, Río var. Içá, Rio. ≈ NW South America see also Içá, Rio
Putumayo, Rio see Içá, Rio
169 P11 Putus, Tanjung headland Borneo, N Indonesia 0°27'S 109°04'E
116 J8 Putyla Chernivets'ka Oblast', W Ukraine 47°59'N 25°04'E
117 S3 Putyvl' Rus. Putivl'. Sums'ka Oblast', NE Ukraine 51°21'N 33°53'E
93 M18 Puula ◎ SE Finland
93 N18 Puumala Itä-Suomi, E Finland 61°31'N 28°12'E
118 I5 Puurmani Ger. Talkhof. Jõgevamaa, E Estonia 58°36'N 26°17'E
99 G17 Puurs Antwerpen, N Belgium 51°05'N 04°17'E
38 F10 Pu'u 'Ula'ula var. Red Hill. ▲ Maui, Hawai'i, USA 20°42'N 156°16'W
38 A8 Pu'uwai var. Puuwai. Ni'ihau, Hawaii, USA, C Pacific Ocean 21°54'N 160°11'W
12 J4 Puvirnituq prev. Povungnituk. Québec, NE Canada 60°10'N 77°20'W
32 H8 Puyallup Washington, NW USA 47°11'N 122°17'W
161 O5 Puyang Henan, C China 35°40'N 115°00'E
161 R9 Puyang Jiang var. Tsien Tang. ≈ SE China
103 O11 Puy-de-Dôme ◈ department C France
103 N15 Puylaurens Tarn, S France 43°33'N 02°01'E
102 M13 Puy-l'Evêque Lot, S France 44°31'N 01°10'E
103 N17 Puymorens, Col de pass S France
56 C7 Puyo Pastaza, C Ecuador 01°30'S 77°58'W
185 A24 Puysegur Point headland South Island, New Zealand 46°09'S 166°38'E
148 J8 Pūzak, Hāmūn-e Pash. Hāmūn-i-Puzak. ◎ SW Afghanistan
Puzak, Hāmūn-i- see Pūzak, Hāmūn-e
81 J23 Pwani Eng. Coast. ◈ region E Tanzania
79 O23 Pweto Katanga, SE Dem. Rep. Congo 08°28'S 28°52'E
97 I19 Pwllheli NW Wales, United Kingdom 52°54'N 04°23'W
189 O14 Pwok Pohnpei, E Micronesia
122 I9 Pyakupur ≈ N Russian Federation
124 M6 Pyalitsa Murmanskaya Oblast', NW Russian Federation 66°17'N 39°56'E
124 K10 Pyal'ma Respublika Kareliya, NW Russian Federation 62°24'N 35°56'E
Pyandzh see Panj
124 I6 Pyaozero, Ozero ◎ NW Russian Federation
166 L9 Pyapon Ayeyarwady, SW Burma (Myanmar) 16°15'N 95°40'E
119 J15 Pyarshai Rus. Pershay. Minskaya Voblasts', C Belarus 54°02'N 26°41'E
122 K8 Pyasina ≈ N Russian Federation
114 I10 Pyasŭchnik, Yazovir ⊠ C Bulgaria
Pyatikhatki see P"yatykhatky
117 S7 P"yatykhatky Rus. Pyatikhatki. Dnipropetrovs'ka Oblast', E Ukraine 48°23'N 33°43'E
166 M6 Pyawbwe Mandalay, C Burma (Myanmar) 20°39'N 96°04'E
166 L7 Pyay var. Prome, Pye. Bago, C Burma (Myanmar) 18°50'N 95°14'E
127 T3 Pychas Udmurtskaya Respublika, NW Russian Federation 56°30'N 52°33'E
Pye see Pyay
166 K6 Pyechin Chin State, W Burma (Myanmar) 20°01'N 93°36'E
119 G17 Pyeski Rus. Peski. Hrodzyenskaya Voblasts', W Belarus 53°21'N 24°38'E
119 L19 Pyetrykaw Rus. Petrikov. Homyel'skaya Voblasts', SE Belarus 52°08'N 28°30'E
93 O17 Pyhäjärvi ◎ SE Finland
93 M16 Pyhäjärvi ◎ C Finland
93 L15 Pyhäjoki Oulu, W Finland 64°28'N 24°15'E
93 L15 Pyhäjoki ≈ W Finland
93 M15 Pyhäntä Oulu, C Finland 64°07'N 26°19'E
93 M16 Pyhäsalmi Oulu, C Finland 63°38'N 26°E
93 O17 Pyhäselkä ◎ SE Finland
93 M19 Pyhtää Swe. Pyttis. Etelä-Suomi, S Finland 60°29'N 26°40'E
166 M5 Pyin-Oo-Lwin var. Maymyo. Mandalay, C Burma (Myanmar) 22°03'N 96°30'E
115 N24 Pylés var. Piles. Kárpathos, SE Greece 35°31'N 27°08'E
115 D21 Pýlos var. Pilos. Pelopónnisos, S Greece 36°55'N 21°42'E
18 B12 Pymatuning Reservoir ⊠ Ohio/Pennsylvania, NE USA
163 X15 P'yŏngt'aek NW South Korea 37°00'N 127°04'E
163 V14 P'yŏngyang var. P'yŏngyang-si, Eng. Pyongyang. ● (North Korea) SW North Korea 39°04'N 125°46'E
P'yŏngyang-si see P'yŏngyang
35 Q4 Pyramid Lake ◎ Nevada, W USA
37 P15 Pyramid Mountains ▲▲ New Mexico, SW USA
37 R5 Pyramid Peak ▲ Colorado, C USA 39°04'N 106°57'W
115 D17 Pyramíva var. Piramiva. ▲ C Greece 39°08'N 21°18'E
Pyrenaei Montes see Pyrenees
86 B12 Pyrenees Fr. Pyrénées, Sp. Pirineos; anc. Pyrenaei Montes. ▲▲ SW Europe
102 J16 Pyrénées-Atlantiques ◈ department SW France
103 N17 Pyrénées-Orientales ◈ department S France
115 L19 Pyrgí var. Pirgi. Chíos, E Greece 38°13'N 26°01'E
115 D20 Pýrgos var. Pírgos. Dytikí Ellás, S Greece 37°40'N 21°27'E
Pyritz see Pyrzyce
115 E19 Pýrros ≈ S Greece
117 R4 Pyryatyn Rus. Piryatin. Poltavs'ka Oblast', NE Ukraine 50°14'N 32°31'E
110 D9 Pyrzyce Ger. Pyritz. Zachodnio-pomorskie, NW Poland 53°09'N 14°53'E
124 F15 Pytalovo Latv. Abrene; prev. Jaunlatgale. Pskovskaya Oblast', W Russian Federation 57°06'N 27°55'E
115 M20 Pythagóreio var. Pithagorio. Sámos, Dodekánisa, Greece, Aegean Sea 37°42'N 26°57'E
14 L11 Pythonga, Lac ◎ Québec, SE Canada
Pyttis see Pyhtää
Pyu see Phyu
166 M8 Pyuntaza Bago, SW Burma (Myanmar) 17°51'N 96°44'E
153 N11 Pyuthān Mid Western, W Nepal 28°09'N 82°50'E
110 H12 Pyzdry Ger. Peisern. Wielkopolskie, C Poland 52°10'N 17°42'E

Q

138 H13 Qā' al Jafr ◎ S Jordan
197 O11 Qaanaaq var. Qânâq, Dan. Thule. ◈ Avannaarsua, N Greenland
Qabanbay see Kabanbay
138 G7 Qabb Eliâs E Lebanon 33°46'N 35°49'E
Qabil see Al Qābil
Qabırrı see Iori
Qābis see Gabès
Qābis, Khalīj see Gabès, Golfe de
Qabqa see Gonghe
141 S14 Qabr Hūd C Yemen 16°02'N 49°36'E
Qacentina see Constantine
148 L4 Qādes Bādghīs, NW Afghanistan 34°48'N 63°26'E
139 T11 Qādisīyah Al Qādisīyah, S Iraq 31°43'N 44°28'E
139 Q6 Qādisīyah, Buḩayrat al ⊠ NW Iraq
143 O4 Qā'emshahr prev. 'Aliābad, Shāhī. Māzandarān, N Iran 36°31'N 52°49'E
143 U7 Qā'en var. Qain, Qāyen. Khorāsān-Razavī, E Iran 33°43'N 59°07'E
141 U13 Qafa spring/well SW Oman 17°46'N 52°55'E
Qafṣah see Gafsa
163 Q12 Qagan Nur var. Xulun Hobot Qagan, Zhengxiangbai Qi. Nei Mongol Zizhiqu, N China 42°10'N 114°57'E
163 V9 Qagan Nur ◎ NE China
163 Q11 Qagan Nur ◎ N China
Qagan Us see Dulan
158 H13 Qagcaka Xizang Zizhiqu, W China 32°32'N 81°52'E
Qagchêng see Xiangcheng
Qahremānshahr see Kermānshāh
159 Q10 Qaidam He ≈ C China
156 L8 Qaidam Pendi basin C China
Qain see Qā'en
Qala Āhangarān see Chaghcharān
139 U3 Qalā Diza var. Qal 'at Dīzah. As Sulaymānīyah, NE Iraq 36°11'N 45°07'E
Qal'ah Sālih see Qal'at Şāliḩ
147 R13 Qal'aikhum Rus. Kalaikhum. S Tajikistan 38°28'N 70°49'E
Qala Nau see Qal'eh-ye Now
141 V17 Qalansīyah Suquṭrā, W Yemen 12°40'N 53°30'E
Qala Panja see Qal'eh-ye Panjeh
Qala Shāhar see Qal'eh Shahr
149 O8 Qalāt Per. Kalāt. Zābol, S Afghanistan 32°10'N 66°54'E
139 W9 Qal'at Aḩmad Maysān, E Iraq 32°24'N 46°46'E
141 N11 Qal'at Bīshah 'Asīr, SW Saudi Arabia 19°59'N 42°38'E
138 H4 Qal'at Burzay Ḩamāh, W Syria 35°37'N 36°16'E
Qal 'at Dīzah see Qalā Diza
139 W9 Qal'at Ḩusayn Maysān, E Iraq 32°19'N 46°46'E
139 V10 Qal'at Majnūnah Al Qādisīyah, S Iraq 31°39'N 45°44'E
139 X11 Qal'at Şāliḩ var. Qal'ah Sālih. Maysān, E Iraq 31°30'N 47°24'E
139 V10 Qal'at Sukkar Dhī Qār, SE Iraq 31°52'N 46°05'E
Qalba Zhotasy see Kalbinskiy Khrebet
143 Q12 Qal'eh Bīābān Fārs, S Iran
149 N4 Qal'eh Shahr Pash. Qala Shāhar. Sar-e Pol, N Afghanistan 35°34'N 65°38'E
148 L4 Qal'eh-ye Now var. Qala Nau. Bādghīs, NW Afghanistan 35°N 63°08'E
149 T2 Qal'eh-ye Panjeh var. Qala Panja. Badakhshān, NE Afghanistan 36°56'N 72°15'E
Qalqaman see Kalkaman
Qalzhat see Kol'zhat
Qamar Bay see Qamar, Ghubbat al
141 U14 Qamar, Ghubbat al Eng. Qamar Bay. bay Oman/Yemen
141 V13 Qamar, Jabal al ▲▲ SW Oman
147 N12 Qamashi Qashqadaryo Viloyati, S Uzbekistan 38°52'N 66°30'E
Qambar see Kambar
159 R14 Qamdo Xizang Zizhiqu, W China 31°09'N 97°09'E
75 R7 Qaminis NE Libya 31°48'N 20°04'E
Qamishly see Al Qāmishlī
Qânâq see Qaanaaq
Qandahār see Kandahār
80 Q11 Qandala Bari, NE Somalia 11°30'N 50°00'E
Qandyaghash see Kandyagash
138 L2 Qanţarī Ar Raqqah, N Syria 36°24'N 39°16'E
Qapiciğ Dağı see Qazangödağ
158 H5 Qapqal var. Qapqal Xibe Zizhixian. Xinjiang Uygur Zizhiqu, NW China 43°46'N 81°09'E
Qapqal Xibe Zizhixian see Qapqal

◆ Country ● Country Capital ◇ Dependent Territory ○ Dependent Territory Capital ◈ Administrative Regions ✈ International Airport ▲ Mountain ▲▲ Mountain Range ⋀ Volcano ≈ River ◎ Lake ⊠ Reservoir
309

QAPSHAGAY BÖYENI – RADUN'

Qapshagay Böyeni see Kapchagayskoye Vodokhranilishche
Qapshaghay see Kapchagay
Qapugtang see Zadoi
196 M15 Qaqortoq Dan. Julianehåb. ◈ Kitaa, S Greenland
139 T4 Qara Anjīr At Ta'mīm, N Iraq 35°30′N 44°37′E
Qarabāgh see Qarah Bāgh
Qarabaū see Karabau
Qaraböget see Karaboget
Qarabulaq see Karabulak
Qarabutaq see Karabutak
Qaraghandy/Qaraghandy Oblysy see Karaganda
Qaraghayly see Karagayly
139 U4 Qara Gol As Sulaymānīyah, NE Iraq 35°21′N 45°38′E
75 U8 Qārah var. Qâra. NW Egypt 29°34′N 26°28′E
Qârah see Qārah
148 J4 Qarah Bāgh var. Qarabāgh. Herāt, NW Afghanistan 35°06′N 61°33′E
138 G7 Qaraoun, Lac de var. Buḩayrat al Qir'awn. ⊚ S Lebanon
Qaraoy see Karaoy
Qaraqoyyn see Karakoyyn, Ozero
Qara Qum see Garagum
Qarasū see Karasu
Qaratal see Karatal
Qarataū see Karatau, Khrebet, Kazakhstan
Qarataū see Karatau, Zhambyl, Kazakhstan
Qaraton see Karaton
Qarazhal see Karazhal
80 P13 Qardho var. Kardh, It. Gardo. Bari, N Somalia 09°34′N 49°30′E
142 M6 Qareh Chāy ≈ N Iran
142 K2 Qareh Sū ≈ NW Iran
Qariateïne see Al Qaryatayn
Qarkilik see Ruoqiang
147 O13 Qarluq Rus. Karluk. Surkhondaryo Viloyati, S Uzbekistan 38°17′N 67°39′E
147 U12 Qarokŭl Rus. Karakul'. E Tajikistan 39°07′N 73°33′E
147 T12 Qarokŭl Rus. Ozero Karakul'. ⊚ E Tajikistan
Qarqan see Qiemo
158 K9 Qarqan He ≈ NW China
Qarqannah, Juzur see Kerkenah, Îles de
Qarqaraly see Karkaralinsk
149 O1 Qarqīn Jowzjān, N Afghanistan 37°25′N 66°03′E
Qars see Kars
Qarsaqbay see Karsakpay
146 M12 Qarshi Rus. Karshi; prev. Bek-Budi. Qashqadaryo Viloyati, S Uzbekistan 38°54′N 65°48′E
146 L12 Qarshi Cho'li Rus. Karshinskaya Step. grassland S Uzbekistan
146 M13 Qarshi Kanali Rus. Karshinskiy Kanal. canal Turkmenistan/Uzbekistan
Qaryatayn see Al Qaryatayn
Qāsh, Nahr al see Gash
146 M12 Qashqadaryo Viloyati Rus. Kashkadar'inskaya Oblast'. ◈ province S Uzbekistan
Qasigianguit see Qasigiannguit
197 N13 Qasigiannguit var. Qasigianguit, Dan. Christianshåb. ◈ Kitaa, C Greenland
Qaşim, Mintaqat see Al Qaşim
75 V10 Qaşr al Farāfirah var. Qasr Farâfra. W Egypt 27°00′N 27°59′E
139 P8 Qaşr 'Amīj Al Anbār, C Iraq 33°30′N 41°52′E
139 R9 Qaşr Darwīshāh Karbalā', C Iraq 32°36′N 43°27′E
142 J6 Qaşr-e Shīrīn Kermānshāhān, W Iran 34°32′N 45°36′E
Qasr Farâfra see Qaşr al Farāfirah
Qassim see Al Qaşim
141 O16 Qa'ṭabah SW Yemen 13°51′N 44°42′E
138 H7 Qaṭanā var. Katana. Dimashq, S Syria 33°27′N 36°04′E
143 N15 Qatar off. State of Qatar, Ar. Dawlat Qaṭar. ◆ monarchy SW Asia
Qatar, State of see Qatar
Qatrana see Al Qaṭrānah
143 Q12 Qaṭrūyeh Fārs, S Iran 29°08′N 54°42′E
Qattara Depression/Qaṭṭārah, Munkhafaḍ al see Qaṭṭārah, Munkhafaḍ al
75 U8 Qaṭṭārah, Munkhafaḍ al var. Munkhafaḍ al Qaṭṭārah var. Monkhafad el Qaṭṭâra, Eng. Qattara Depression. desert NW Egypt
Qaṭṭâra, Monkhafad el see Qaṭṭārah, Munkhafaḍ al
Qattinah, Buhayrat see Ḩimş, Buḩayrat
Qausuittuq see Resolute
Qaydār see Qeydār
Qāyen see Qā'en
Qaynar see Kaynar
147 Q11 Qayroqqum Rus. Kayrakkum. NW Tajikistan 40°16′N 69°46′E
147 Q10 Qayroqqum, Obanbori Rus. Kayrakkumskoye Vodokhranilishche. ⊠ NW Tajikistan
159 O17 Qayū Xizang Zizhiqu, W China 28°17′N 92°46′E
137 V13 Qazangödağ Rus. Gora Kapydzhik, Turk. Qapiciğ Dağı. ▲ SW Azerbaijan 39°18′N 46°00′E
139 U7 Qazānīyah var. Dhū Shaykh. Diyālá, E Iraq 33°39′N 45°33′E
Qazaqstan/Qazaqstan Respublikasy see Kazakhstan
137 T9 Qazbegi Rus. Kazbegi. NE Georgia 42°39′N 44°36′E
149 P15 Qāzi Ahmad var. Kazi Ahmad. Sind, SE Pakistan 26°19′N 68°08′E
137 Y12 Qazimämmäd Rus. Kazi Magomed. SE Azerbaijan 40°03′N 48°56′E
Qazris see Cáceres
142 M4 Qazvīn var. Kazvin. Qazvīn, N Iran 36°16′N 50°E
142 M5 Qazvīn ◈ province N Iran
187 Z13 Qelelevu Lagoon lagoon NE Fiji
Qena see Qinā
113 L23 Qeparo Vlorë, S Albania 40°04′N 19°49′E
Qeqertarssuaq see Qeqertarsuaq
197 N13 Qeqertarssuaq var. Qeqertarsuaq, Dan. Godhavn. ◈ Kitaa, S Greenland
196 M13 Qeqertarsuaq island W Greenland
197 N13 Qeqertarsuup Tunua Dan. Disko Bugt. inlet W Greenland
Qerveh see Qorveh
143 S14 Qeshm Hormozgān, S Iran 26°58′N 56°17′E
143 R14 Qeshm var. Jazīreh-ye Qeshm, Qeshm Island. island S Iran
Qeshm Island/Qeshm, Jazīreh-ye see Qeshm
Qey see Kīsh, Jazīreh-ye
142 L4 Qeydār var. Qaydār. Zanjān, NW Iran 36°50′N 47°40′E
142 K5 Qezel Owzan, Rūd-e var. Ki Zil Uzen, Qi Zil Uzun. ≈ NW Iran
Qian see Guizhou
161 Q2 Qian'an Hebei, E China 40°01′N 118°43′E
Qiandao Hu see Xin'anjiang Shuiku
Qiandaohu see Chun'an
Qian Gorlo/Qian Gorlos/Qian Gorlos Mongolzu Zizhixian/Quianguozhen see Qianguo
163 V9 Qianguo var. Qian Gorlo, Qian Gorlos, Qian Gorlos Mongolzu Zizhixian, Quianguozhen. Jilin, NE China 45°05′N 124°52′E
161 N9 Qianjiang Hubei, C China 30°23′N 112°58′E
160 K10 Qianjiang Sichuan, C China 29°30′N 108°45′E
160 L14 Qian Jiang ≈ S China
160 G9 Qianning var. Gartar. Sichuan, C China 30°27′N 101°24′E
163 U13 Qian Shan ▲▲ NE China
160 H10 Qianwei var. Yujin. Sichuan, C China 29°15′N 103°52′E
160 J11 Qianxi Guizhou, S China 27°00′N 106°01′E
Qiaotou see Datong
Qiaowa see Muli
159 Q7 Qiaowan Gansu, N China 40°37′N 96°40′E
Qibili see Kebili
158 K9 Qiemo var. Qarqan. Xinjiang Uygur Zizhiqu, NW China 38°09′N 85°30′E
160 J10 Qijiang var. Gunan. Chongqing Shi, C China 29°01′N 106°40′E
159 N5 Qijiaojing Xinjiang Uygur Zizhiqu, NW China 43°29′N 91°35′E
Qike see Xunke
9 R5 Qikiqtarjuaq prev. Broughton Island. Nunavut, NE Canada 67°35′N 63°55′W
149 P9 Qila Saifullāh Baluchistān, SW Pakistan 30°45′N 68°08′E
159 S9 Qilian var. Babao. Qinghai, C China 38°09′N 100°08′E
159 N8 Qilian Shan var. Kilien Mountains. ▲▲ N China
197 O11 Qimusseriarsuaq Dan. Melville Bugt, Eng. Melville Bay. bay NW Greenland
75 X10 Qinā var. Qena; anc. Caene, Caenepolis. E Egypt 26°12′N 32°49′E
159 W11 Qin'an Gansu, C China 34°49′N 105°50′E
159 X10 Qingcheng Gansu, N China 36°01′N 107°53′E
Qincheng see Nanfeng
Qing see Qinghai
163 W7 Qing'an Heilongjiang, NE China 46°53′N 127°29′E
161 R5 Qingdao var. Ching-Tao, Ch'ing-tao, Tsingtao, Tsintao, Ger. Tsingtau. Shandong, E China 36°31′N 120°55′E
163 V8 Qinggang Heilongjiang, NE China 46°41′N 126°05′E
Qinggil see Qinghe
159 P11 Qinghai var. Chinghai, Koko Nor, Qing, Qinghai Sheng, Tsinghai. ◈ province C China
159 S10 Qinghai Hu var. Ch'ing Hai, Tsing Hai, Mong. Koko Nor. ⊚ C China
Qinghai Sheng see Qinghai
158 M3 Qinghe var. Qinggil. Xinjiang Uygur Zizhiqu, NW China 46°42′N 90°19′E
160 L4 Qingjian var. Kuanzhou; prev. Xiuyan. Shaanxi, C China 37°10′N 110°09′E
160 L9 Qing Jiang ≈ C China
Qingjiang see Huai'an
Qingkou see Ganyu
160 I12 Qinglong var. Liancheng. Guizhou, S China 25°49′N 105°10′E
161 Q2 Qinglong Hebei, E China 40°24′N 118°57′E
Qingshan see Wudalianchi
159 R12 Qingshuihe Qinghai, C China 33°47′N 97°10′E
159 X10 Qingyang var. Xifeng. Gansu, C China 35°46′N 107°35′E
Qingyang see Jinjiang
161 N14 Qingyuan Guangdong, S China 23°42′N 113°02′E
163 V11 Qingyuan var. Qingyuan Manzu Zizhixian. Liaoning, NE China 42°08′N 124°55′E
Qingyuan see Shandan
Qingyuan see Weiyuan
Qingyuan Manzu Zizhixian see Qingyuan
158 L13 Qingzang Gaoyuan var. Xizang Gaoyuan, Eng. Plateau of Tibet. plateau W China
161 Q4 Qingzhou prev. Yidu. Shandong, E China 36°41′N 118°29′E
157 R9 Qin He ≈ C China
161 Q2 Qinhuangdao Hebei, E China 39°57′N 119°31′E
160 K7 Qin Ling ▲▲ C China
161 N5 Qinxian var. Dingchang, Qin Xian. Shanxi, C China 36°46′N 112°42′E
Qin Xian see Qinxian
161 N6 Qinyang Henan, C China 35°05′N 112°56′E
160 K15 Qinzhou Guangxi Zhuangzu Zizhiqu, S China 22°09′N 108°36′E
Qiong see Hainan
160 L17 Qionghai prev. Jiaji. Hainan, S China 19°12′N 110°26′E
160 H9 Qionglai Sichuan, C China 30°24′N 103°28′E
160 H8 Qionglai Shan ▲▲ C China
160 L17 Qiongzhou Haixia var. Hainan Strait. strait S China
163 U7 Qiqihar var. Ch'i-ch'i-ha-erh, Tsitsihar; prev. Lungkiang. Heilongjiang, NE China 47°23′N 124°E
Qir see Qīr-va-Kārzīn
158 H10 Qira Xinjiang Uygur Zizhiqu, NW China 37°05′N 80°45′E
Qir'awn, Buḩayrat al see Qaraoun, Lac de
143 P12 Qīr-va-Kārzīn var. Qir. Fārs, S Iran 28°27′N 53°04′E
Qiryat Gat see Kiryat Gat
Qiryat Shemona see Kiryat Shmona
Qishlaq see Garmsār
141 U14 Qishn SE Yemen 15°29′N 51°44′E
Qishon, Nahal see Kishon, Nahal
Qita Ghazzah see Gaza Strip
156 K5 Qitai Xinjiang Uygur Zizhiqu, NW China 44°N 89°34′E
163 Y8 Qitaihe Heilongjiang, NE China 45°45′N 130°53′E
141 W12 Qiṭbīt, Wādī dry watercourse S Oman
161 O5 Qixian var. Qi Xian, Zhaoge. Henan, C China 35°35′N 114°10′E
Qi Xian see Qixian
Qīzān see Jīzān
Qizil Orda see Kzylorda
Qizil Qum/Qizilqum see Kyzyl Kum
147 V14 Qizilrabot Rus. Kyzylrabot. SE Tajikistan 37°29′N 74°44′E
146 J10 Qizilravote Rus. Kyzylrabat. Buxoro Viloyati, C Uzbekistan 40°35′N 62°09′E
Qi Zil Uzun see Qezel Owzan, Rūd-e
139 S4 Qizil Yār At Ta'mīm, N Iraq 35°26′N 44°12′E
Qoghaly see Kugaly
Qogir Feng see K2
143 N6 Qom var. Kum, Qum. Qom, N Iran 34°43′N 50°54′E
143 N6 Qom ◈ province N Iran
Qomisheh see Shahreẓā
Qomolangma Feng see Everest, Mount
142 M7 Qom, Rūd-e ≈ C Iran
Qomul see Hami
Qondūz see Kondoz
159 N16 Qonggyai Xizang Zizhiqu, W China 29°03′N 91°39′E
146 G7 Qo'ng'irot Rus. Kungrad. Qoraqalpog'iston Respublikasi, NW Uzbekistan 43°01′N 58°49′E
Qongyrat see Konyrat
Qoqek see Tacheng
147 R10 Qo'qon var. Khokand, Rus. Kokand. Farg'ona Viloyati, E Uzbekistan 40°34′N 70°55′E
Qorabowur Kirlari see Karabaur', Uval
Qoradaryo see Karadar'ya
146 G6 Qorajar Rus. Karadzhar. Qoraqalpog'iston Respublikasi, NW Uzbekistan 43°34′N 58°35′E
146 K12 Qorako'l Rus. Karakul'. Buxoro Viloyati, C Uzbekistan 39°27′N 63°45′E
146 H7 Qoraqo'zak Rus. Karauzyak. Qoraqalpog'iston Respublikasi, NW Uzbekistan 43°07′N 60°03′E
146 E5 Qoraqalpog'iston Rus. Karakalpakya. Qoraqalpog'iston Respublikasi, NW Uzbekistan 44°45′N 56°06′E
146 G7 Qoraqalpog'iston Respublikasi Rus. Respublika Karakalpakstan. ◈ autonomous republic NW Uzbekistan
Qorghalzhyn see Korgalzhyn
138 H6 Qornet es Saouda ▲ NE Lebanon 36°06′N 34°06′E
146 L12 Qorowulbozor Rus. Karaulbazar. Buxoro Viloyati, C Uzbekistan 39°28′N 64°49′E
142 K5 Qorveh var. Qerveh. Kordestān, W Iran 35°09′N 47°48′E
147 N11 Qo'shrabot Rus. Kushrabat. Samarqand Viloyati, C Uzbekistan 40°15′N 66°40′E
Qosköl see Koskol'
Qosshaghyl see Koschagyl
Qostanay/Qostanay Oblysy see Kostanay
143 P12 Qoṭbābād Fārs, S Iran 28°52′N 53°40′E
143 R13 Qoṭbābād Hormozgān, S Iran 27°49′N 56°00′E
138 H6 Qoubaïyât var. Al Qubayyāt. N Lebanon 37°00′N 34°30′E
Qoussantîna see Constantine
Qowowuyag see Cho Oyu
147 O11 Qo'ytosh Rus. Koytash. Jizzax Viloyati, C Uzbekistan 40°13′N 67°19′E
146 G7 Qozonketkan Rus. Kazanketken. Qoraqalpog'iston Respublikasi, W Uzbekistan 42°59′N 59°21′E
146 H6 Qozoqdaryo Rus. Kazakdar'ya. Qoraqalpog'iston Respublikasi, NW Uzbekistan 43°26′N 59°47′E
19 N11 Quabbin Reservoir ⊠ Massachusetts, NE USA
100 F12 Quakenbrück Niedersachsen, NW Germany 52°41′N 07°57′E
18 I15 Quakertown Pennsylvania, NE USA 40°26′N 75°17′W
182 M10 Quambatook Victoria, SE Australia 35°52′S 143°28′E
25 Q4 Quanah Texas, SW USA 34°17′N 99°46′W
167 V10 Quang Ngai var. Quangngai, Quang Nghia. Quang Ngai, C Vietnam 15°09′N 108°50′E
Quangngai see Quang Ngai
Quang Nghia see Quang Ngai
167 T9 Quang Tri var. Trieu Hai. Quang Tri, C Vietnam 16°46′N 107°11′E
Quanjiang see Suichuan
Quan Long see Ca Mau
152 L4 Quanshuigou China/India 35°40′N 79°28′E
161 R13 Quanzhou var. Ch'uan-chou, Tsinkiang; prev. Chin-chiang. Fujian, SE China 24°56′N 118°31′E
160 M12 Quanzhou Guangxi Zhuangzu Zizhiqu, S China 25°59′N 111°02′E
11 V16 Qu'Appelle ≈ Saskatchewan, S Canada
12 M3 Quaqtaq prev. Koartac. Québec, NE Canada 60°50′N 69°30′W
61 E16 Quaraí Rio Grande do Sul, S Brazil 30°38′S 56°25′W
59 H24 Quaraí, Rio Sp. Río Cuareim. ≈ Brazil/Uruguay see also Cuareim, Río
Quaraí, Rio see Cuareim, Río
171 N13 Quarles, Pegunungan ▲▲ Sulawesi, C Indonesia
Quarnero see Kvarner
107 C20 Quartu Sant' Elena Sardegna, Italy, C Mediterranean Sea 39°15′N 09°12′E
29 X13 Quasqueton Iowa, C USA 42°23′N 91°45′W
173 X16 Quatre Bornes W Mauritius 20°15′S 57°28′E
172 I17 Quatre Bornes Mahé, NE Seychelles
137 X10 Quba Rus. Kuba. N Azerbaijan 41°22′N 48°30′E
Qubba see Ba'qūbah
143 T3 Qūchān var. Kuchan. Khorāsān-Razavī, NE Iran 37°12′N 58°28′E
183 R10 Queanbeyan New South Wales, SE Australia 35°24′S 149°17′E
15 Q10 Québec var. Quebec. province capital Québec, SE Canada 46°50′N 71°15′W
14 K10 Québec var. Quebec. ◈ province SE Canada
61 D17 Quebracho Paysandú, W Uruguay 31°58′S 57°53′W
43 P16 Quebrada Guabo Ngöbe-Buglé, W Panama 08°19′N 81°50′W
101 K14 Quedlinburg Sachsen-Anhalt, C Germany 51°48′N 11°09′E
138 H10 Queen Alia ✈ ('Ammān) 'Ammān, C Jordan
10 L16 Queen Bess, Mount ▲ British Columbia, SW Canada 51°15′N 124°29′W
10 I14 Queen Charlotte British Columbia, SW Canada 53°18′N 132°04′W
65 B24 Queen Charlotte Bay bay West Falkland, W Falkland Islands
10 H14 Queen Charlotte Islands Fr. Îles de la Reine-Charlotte. island group British Columbia, SW Canada
10 I15 Queen Charlotte Sound sea area British Columbia, W Canada
10 J16 Queen Charlotte Strait strait British Columbia, W Canada
27 U1 Queen City Missouri, C USA 40°24′N 92°34′W
25 X5 Queen City Texas, SW USA 33°09′N 94°09′W
197 O9 Queen Elizabeth Islands Fr. Îles de la Reine-Élisabeth. island group Nunavut, N Canada
195 Y10 Queen Mary Coast physical region Antarctica
65 N24 Queen Mary's Peak ▲ C Tristan da Cunha
196 M8 Queen Maud Gulf gulf Arctic Ocean
195 P11 Queen Maud Mountains ▲▲ Antarctica
Queen's County see Laois
181 U7 Queensland ◈ state N Australia
192 I9 Queensland Plateau undersea feature N Coral Sea
183 O16 Queenstown Tasmania, SE Australia 42°06′S 145°33′E
185 C22 Queenstown Otago, South Island, New Zealand 45°01′S 168°44′E
83 I24 Queenstown Eastern Cape, S South Africa 31°52′S 26°50′E
Queenstown see Cobh
32 F8 Queets Washington, NW USA 47°31′N 124°19′W
61 D18 Queguay Grande, Río ≈ W Uruguay
59 O16 Queimadas Bahia, E Brazil 10°59′S 39°38′W
82 D11 Quela Malanje, NW Angola 09°18′S 17°07′E
83 O16 Quelimane var. Kilimane, Kilmain, Quilimane. Zambézia, NE Mozambique 17°53′S 36°51′E
63 G18 Quellón var. Puerto Quellón. Los Lagos, S Chile 43°05′S 73°38′W
Quelpart see Cheju-do
37 P12 Quemado New Mexico, SW USA 34°18′N 108°29′W
25 O12 Quemado Texas, SW USA 28°58′N 100°36′W
44 K7 Quemado, Punta de headland E Cuba 20°13′N 74°07′W
Quemoy see Chinmen Tao
62 K13 Quemú Quemú La Pampa, E Argentina 36°03′S 63°36′W
155 E17 Quepem Goa, W India 15°13′N 74°03′E
42 M14 Quepos Puntarenas, S Costa Rica 09°28′N 84°10′W
Que Que see Kwekwe
61 D23 Quequén Buenos Aires, E Argentina 38°30′S 58°44′W
61 D23 Quequén Grande, Río ≈ E Argentina
61 C23 Quequén Salado, Río ≈ E Argentina
Quera see Chur
41 N13 Querétaro Querétaro de Arteaga, C Mexico 20°36′N 100°24′W
40 F4 Querobabi Sonora, NW Mexico 30°02′N 111°02′W
42 M13 Quesada var. Ciudad Quesada, San Carlos. Alajuela, N Costa Rica 10°19′N 84°26′W
105 O13 Quesada Andalucía, S Spain 37°52′N 03°05′W
161 O7 Queshan Henan, C China 32°48′N 114°03′E
10 M15 Quesnel British Columbia, SW Canada 53°05′N 122°30′W
37 S9 Questa New Mexico, SW USA 36°41′N 105°37′W
102 H7 Questembert Morbihan, NW France 47°39′N 02°24′W
57 K22 Quetena, Río ≈ SW Bolivia
149 O10 Quetta Baluchistān, SW Pakistan 30°15′N 67°E
Quetzalcoalco see Coatzacoalcos
Quetzaltenango see Quezaltenango
56 B6 Quevedo Los Ríos, C Ecuador 01°02′S 79°27′W
42 B6 Quezaltenango var. Quetzaltenango. Quezaltenango, W Guatemala 14°50′N 91°30′W
42 A2 Quezaltenango off. Departamento de Quezaltenango, var. Quetzaltenango. ◈ department SW Guatemala
Quezaltenango, Departamento de see Quezaltenango
42 E6 Quezaltepeque Chiquimula, SE Guatemala 14°38′N 89°25′W
170 M6 Quezon Palawan, W Philippines 09°13′N 118°01′E
161 P5 Qufu Shandong, E China 35°37′N 117°05′E
82 B12 Quibala Cuanza Sul, NW Angola 10°44′S 14°58′E
82 B11 Quibaxe var. Quibaxi. Cuanza Norte, NW Angola 08°30′S 14°36′E
Quibaxi see Quibaxe
54 D9 Quibdó Chocó, W Colombia 05°40′N 76°38′W
102 G7 Quiberon Morbihan, NW France 47°30′N 03°07′W
102 G7 Quiberon, Baie de bay NW France
54 J5 Quíbor Lara, N Venezuela 09°55′N 69°35′W
42 C4 Quiché off. Departamento del Quiché. ◈ department W Guatemala
Quiché, Departamento del see Quiché
99 E21 Quiévrain Hainaut, S Belgium 50°25′N 03°41′E
40 I9 Quila Sinaloa, C Mexico 24°24′N 107°11′W
83 B14 Quilengues Huíla, SW Angola 14°09′S 14°04′E
Quilimane see Quelimane
57 G15 Quillabamba Cusco, C Peru 12°49′S 72°41′W
57 L18 Quillacollo Cochabamba, C Bolivia 17°26′S 66°16′W
62 H4 Quillagua Antofagasta, N Chile 21°33′S 69°32′W
103 N17 Quillan Aude, S France 42°52′N 02°11′E
11 U15 Quill Lakes ⊚ Saskatchewan, S Canada
62 G11 Quillota Valparaíso, C Chile 32°54′S 71°16′W
155 G23 Quilon var. Kollam. Kerala, SW India 08°57′N 76°37′E see also Kollam
181 V9 Quilpie Queensland, C Australia 26°39′S 144°15′E
149 O4 Quil-Qala Bāmīān, N Afghanistan 35°13′N 67°02′E
62 L7 Quimilí Santiago del Estero, C Argentina 27°35′S 62°25′W
57 O19 Quimome Santa Cruz, E Bolivia 17°45′S 61°15′W
102 F6 Quimper anc. Quimper Corentin. Finistère, NW France 48°00′N 04°05′W
Quimper Corentin see Quimper
102 G7 Quimperlé Finistère, NW France 47°52′N 03°33′W
32 F8 Quinault Washington, NW USA 47°27′N 123°53′W
32 F8 Quinault River ≈ Washington, NW USA
35 P5 Quincy California, W USA 39°56′N 120°56′W
23 S8 Quincy Florida, SE USA 30°35′N 84°34′W
30 I13 Quincy Illinois, N USA 39°56′N 91°24′W
19 O11 Quincy Massachusetts, NE USA 42°15′N 71°00′W
32 J9 Quincy Washington, NW USA 47°13′N 119°51′W
54 E10 Quindío off. Departamento del Quindío. ◈ province C Colombia
54 E10 Quindío, Nevado del ▲ C Colombia 04°42′N 75°25′W
62 J10 Quines San Luis, C Argentina 32°15′S 65°46′W
39 N13 Quinhagak Alaska, USA 59°45′N 161°55′W
76 G13 Quinhámel W Guinea-Bissau 11°52′N 15°52′W
Qui Nhon/Quinhon see Quy Nhon
Quinindé see Rosa Zárate
25 U6 Quinlan Texas, SW USA 32°54′N 96°08′W
61 H17 Quinta Rio Grande do Sul, S Brazil 32°05′S 52°18′W
105 O10 Quintanar de la Orden Castilla-La Mancha, C Spain 39°36′N 03°03′W
41 X13 Quintana Roo ◈ state SE Mexico
105 S6 Quinto Aragón, NE Spain 41°25′N 00°31′W
108 G10 Quinto Ticino, S Switzerland 46°32′N 08°44′E
27 Q11 Quinton Oklahoma, C USA 35°07′N 95°22′W
62 K12 Quinto, Río ≈ C Argentina
82 A10 Quinzau Dem. Rep. Congo, NW Angola 06°50′S 12°48′E
14 H8 Quinze, Lac des ⊚ Québec, SE Canada
83 B15 Quipungo Huíla, C Angola 14°49′S 14°29′E
62 G13 Quirihue Bío Bío, C Chile 36°15′S 72°35′W
82 D12 Quirima Malanje, NW Angola 10°51′S 18°06′E
183 T6 Quirindi New South Wales, SE Australia 31°29′S 150°40′E
55 P5 Quiriquire Monagas, NE Venezuela 09°59′N 63°14′W
14 D10 Quirke Lake ⊚ Ontario, S Canada
61 B21 Quiroga Buenos Aires, E Argentina 35°18′S 61°22′W
104 I4 Quiroga Galicia, NW Spain 42°28′N 07°15′W
Quiróm, Salar see Pocitos, Salar
56 B9 Quiroz, Río ≈ NW Peru
82 Q13 Quissanga Cabo Delgado, NE Mozambique 12°24′S 40°33′E
83 M20 Quissico Inhambane, S Mozambique 24°42′S 34°44′E
25 O4 Quitaque Texas, SW USA 34°22′N 101°03′W
82 Q13 Quiterajo Cabo Delgado, NE Mozambique 11°37′S 40°22′E
23 T6 Quitman Georgia, SE USA 30°46′N 83°33′W
22 M6 Quitman Mississippi, S USA 32°02′N 88°43′W
25 V6 Quitman Texas, SW USA 32°37′N 95°26′W
56 C6 Quito ● (Ecuador) Pichincha, N Ecuador 0°14′S 78°30′W
Quito see Mariscal Sucre
58 P13 Quixadá Ceará, E Brazil 04°57′S 39°04′W
83 Q15 Quixaxe Nampula, NE Mozambique 15°15′S 40°07′E
161 N13 Qujiang var. Maba. Guangdong, S China 24°47′N 113°34′E
160 J9 Qu Jiang ≈ C China
161 R10 Qu Jiang ≈ SE China
160 H12 Qujing Yunnan, SW China 25°39′N 103°52′E
Qulan see Kulan
163 T8 Qulin Gol prev. Chaor He. ≈ NE China
146 L10 Quljuqtov-Tog'lari Rus. Gory Kul'dzhuktau. ▲ C Uzbekistan
Qulsary see Kul'sary
Qulyndy Zhazyghy see Kulunda Steppe
Qum see Qom
Qumälisch see Lubartów
159 P11 Qumar He ≈ C China
159 Q12 Qumarlêb var. Yuegai; prev. Yuegaitan. Qinghai, C China 34°06′N 95°54′E
159 Q15 Qumdo Xizang Zizhiqu, W China 30°03′N 95°33′E
Qumisheh see Shahreẓā
147 O14 Qumqo'rg'on Rus. Kumkurgan. Surkhondaryo Viloyati, S Uzbekistan 37°54′N 67°31′E
Qunaytirah/Quneitra, Muḩāfaẓat al see Al Qunayṭirah
189 V12 Quoi island Chuuk, C Micronesia
9 N8 Quoich ≈ Nunavut, NE Canada
83 E26 Quoin Point headland SW South Africa 34°48′S 19°39′E
182 I7 Quorn South Australia 32°22′S 138°03′E
Qurein see Al Kuwayt
147 P14 Qŭrghonteppa Rus. Kurgan-Tyube. SW Tajikistan 37°51′N 68°42′E
Qurlurtuuq see Kugluktuk
Qurveh see Qorveh
Quryq see Kuryk
Quşair see Al Quşayr
137 X10 Qusar Rus. Kusary. NE Azerbaijan 41°26′N 48°27′E
Quşayr see Al Quşayr
Quseir see Al Quşayr
142 I2 Qūshchī Āẕarbāyjān-e Gharbī, N Iran 37°59′N 45°05′E
Qusmuryn see Kushmurun, Kostanay, Kazakhstan
Qusmuryn see Kushmurun, Ozero
159 O16 Qusum Xizang Zizhiqu, W China 29°02′N 92°09′E
Quṭayfah/Qutayfe/Quteife see Al Quṭayfah
Quthing see Moyeni
147 S10 Quvasoy Rus. Kuvasay. Farg'ona Viloyati, E Uzbekistan 40°17′N 71°53′E
Quwair see Guwēr
Quxar see Lhazê
Qu Xian see Quzhou
159 N16 Qüxü var. Xoi. Xizang Zizhiqu, W China 29°25′N 90°48′E
Quyang see Jingzhou
167 V13 Quy Chanh Ninh Thuận, S Vietnam 11°28′N 108°53′E
167 V11 Quy Nhơn var. Quinhon, Qui Nhon. Binh Đinh, C Vietnam 13°47′N 109°11′E
161 R10 Quzhou var. Qu Xian. Zhejiang, SE China 28°55′N 118°54′E
Qyteti Stalin see Kuçovë
Qyzylagash see Kyzylagash
Qyzylorda see Kzylorda
Qyzyltū see Kishkenekol'
Qyzylzhar see Kyzylzhar

R

Raa Atoll see North Maalhosmadulu Atoll
109 R4 Raab Oberösterreich, N Austria 48°19′N 13°40′E
109 X8 Raab Hung. Rába. ≈ Austria/Hungary see also Rába
Raab see Rába
Raab see Győr
109 V2 Raabs an der Thaya Niederösterreich, E Austria 48°51′N 15°28′E
93 L14 Raahe Swe. Brahestad. Oulu, W Finland 64°42′N 24°31′E
98 M10 Raalte Overijssel, E Netherlands 52°23′N 06°16′E
99 I14 Raamsdonksveer Noord-Brabant, S Netherlands 51°42′N 04°54′E
92 L12 Raanujärvi Lappi, NW Finland 66°39′N 24°40′E
96 G9 Raasay island NW Scotland, United Kingdom
118 H3 Raasiku Ger. Rasik. Harjumaa, NW Estonia 59°22′N 25°11′E
112 B11 Rab It. Arbe. Primorje-Gorski Kotar, NW Croatia 44°46′N 14°46′E
112 B11 Rab It. Arbe. island NW Croatia
171 N16 Raba Sumbawa, S Indonesia 08°27′S 118°45′E
111 G22 Rába Ger. Raab. ≈ Austria/Hungary see also Raab
Rába see Raab
112 A10 Rabac Istra, NW Croatia 45°03′N 14°09′E
104 I2 Rábade Galicia, NW Spain 43°07′N 07°37′W
80 F10 Rabak White Nile, C Sudan 13°12′N 32°44′E
186 G9 Rabaraba Milne Bay, SE Papua New Guinea 10°00′S 149°50′E
102 K16 Rabastens-de-Bigorre Hautes-Pyrénées, S France 43°23′N 00°10′E
121 O16 Rabat W Malta 35°51′N 14°25′E
74 F6 Rabat var. al Dar al Baida. ● (Morocco) NW Morocco 34°02′N 06°51′W
Rabat see Victoria
186 H6 Rabaul New Britain, E Papua New Guinea 04°13′S 152°11′E
Rabbah Ammon/Rabbath Ammon see 'Ammān
28 K8 Rabbit Creek ≈ South Dakota, N USA
14 H10 Rabbit Lake ⊚ Ontario, S Canada
187 Y14 Rabi prev. Rambi. island N Fiji
140 K9 Rābigh Makkah, W Saudi Arabia 22°51′N 39°E
42 D5 Rabinal Baja Verapaz, C Guatemala 15°05′N 90°26′W
168 G9 Rabi, Pulau island NW Indonesia, East Indies
111 L17 Rabka Małopolskie, S Poland 49°38′N 20°E
155 F16 Rabkavi Karnātaka, W India 16°40′N 75°03′E
Râbnița see Rîbnița
109 Y6 Rabnitz ≈ E Austria
124 J7 Rabocheostrovsk Respublika Kareliya, NW Russian Federation 64°58′N 34°46′E
23 U1 Rabun Bald ▲ Georgia, SE USA 34°58′N 83°18′W
75 S11 Rabyānah SE Libya 24°07′N 21°58′E
75 S11 Rabyānah, Ramlat var. Rebiana Sand Sea, Şaḩrā' Rabyānah. desert SE Libya
Rabyānah, Şaḩrā' see Rabyānah, Ramlat
116 L11 Răcăciuni Bacău, E Romania 46°20′N 27°00′E
Racaka see Riwoqê
107 J24 Racalmuto Sicilia, Italy, C Mediterranean Sea 37°25′N 13°44′E
116 J14 Răcari Dâmbovița, SE Romania 44°37′N 25°43′E
Răcari see Durankulak
116 F13 Răcășdia Hung. Rakasd. Caraș-Severin, SW Romania 44°58′N 21°36′E
106 B9 Racconigi Piemonte, NE Italy 44°45′N 07°41′E
31 T15 Raccoon Creek ≈ Ohio, N USA
13 V13 Race, Cape headland Newfoundland, Newfoundland and Labrador, E Canada 46°40′N 53°05′W
22 K10 Raceland Louisiana, S USA 29°43′N 90°36′W
19 Q12 Race Point headland Massachusetts, NE USA 42°03′N 70°14′W
167 S14 Rach Gia Kiên Giang, S Vietnam 10°01′N 105°05′E
167 S14 Rach Gia, Vinh bay S Vietnam
76 J8 Rachid Tagant, C Mauritania 18°48′N 11°41′W
110 L10 Raciąż Mazowieckie, C Poland 52°46′N 20°04′E
111 I16 Racibórz Ger. Ratibor. Śląskie, S Poland 50°05′N 18°10′E
31 N9 Racine Wisconsin, N USA 42°42′N 87°50′W
14 D7 Racine Lake ⊚ Ontario, S Canada
111 J23 Ráckeve Pest, C Hungary 47°10′N 18°58′E
Rácz-Becse see Bečej
141 O15 Radā' var. Ridā'. W Yemen 14°24′N 44°49′E
113 O15 Radan ▲ SE Serbia 42°59′N 21°31′E
63 J19 Rada Tilly Chubut, SE Argentina 45°54′S 67°33′W
116 K8 Rădăuți Ger. Radautz, Hung. Rádóc. Suceava, N Romania 47°49′N 25°58′E
116 L8 Rădăuți-Prut Botoșani, NE Romania 48°14′N 26°47′E
Radautz see Rădăuți
Radbusa see Radbuza
111 A17 Radbuza Ger. Radbusa. ≈ SE Czech Republic
20 K6 Radcliff Kentucky, S USA 37°50′N 85°57′W
139 O2 Radd, Wādī ar dry watercourse N Syria
95 H16 Råde Østfold, S Norway 59°21′N 10°53′E
101 N17 Radebeul Sachsen, E Germany 51°06′N 13°41′E
109 V11 Radeče Ger. Ratschach. C Slovenia 46°01′N 15°10′E
Radein see Radenci
116 J4 Radekhiv Pol. Radziechów, Rus. Radekhov. L'vivs'ka Oblast', W Ukraine 50°17′N 24°39′E
Radekhov see Radekhiv
109 X9 Radenci Ger. Radein; prev. Radinci. NE Slovenia 46°36′N 16°02′E
109 S9 Radenthein Kärnten, S Austria 46°48′N 13°42′E
Rádeyilikóé see Fort Good Hope
21 R7 Radford Virginia, NE USA 37°07′N 80°34′W
154 C9 Rādhanpur Gujarāt, W India 23°52′N 71°49′E
Radinci see Radenci
127 Q6 Radishchevo Ul'yanovskaya Oblast', W Russian Federation 52°49′N 47°54′E
12 I9 Radisson Québec, E Canada 53°47′N 77°35′W
11 P16 Radium Hot Springs British Columbia, SW Canada 50°39′N 116°09′W
116 F11 Radna Hung. Máriaradna. Arad, W Romania 46°05′N 21°41′E
114 K10 Radnevo Stara Zagora, C Bulgaria 42°17′N 25°58′E
97 J20 Radnor cultural region E Wales, United Kingdom
Radnót see Iernut
Rádóc see Rădăuți
101 H24 Radolfzell am Bodensee Baden-Württemberg, S Germany 47°43′N 08°58′E
110 M13 Radom Mazowieckie, C Poland 51°23′N 21°08′E
116 I14 Radomirești Olt, S Romania 44°06′N 24°41′E
111 K14 Radomsko Rus. Novoradomsk. Łódzkie, C Poland 51°04′N 19°25′E
117 N4 Radomyshl' Zhytomyrs'ka Oblast', N Ukraine 50°30′N 29°16′E
113 P19 Radoviš prev. Radovište. E Macedonia 41°39′N 22°26′E
Radovište see Radoviš
94 B13 Radøy island S Norway
109 R7 Radstadt Salzburg, NW Austria 47°24′N 13°31′E
182 E8 Radstock, Cape headland South Australia 33°11′S 134°18′E
109 U10 Raduha ▲ N Slovenia 46°24′N 14°46′E
119 G15 Radun' Hrodzyenskaya Voblasts', W Belarus 54°03′N 25°00′E

◆ Country
● Country Capital
◇ Dependent Territory
○ Dependent Territory Capital
◈ Administrative Regions
✈ International Airport
▲ Mountain
▲▲ Mountain Range
Volcano
≈ River
⊚ Lake
⊠ Reservoir

RADUZHNYY – RED RIVER

126 M3 **Raduzhnyy** Vladimirskaya Oblast', W Russian Federation 55°59′N 40°15′E
118 F11 **Radviliškis** Šiaulai, N Lithuania 55°48′N 23°32′E
11 U17 **Radville** Saskatchewan, S Canada 49°28′N 104°19′W
140 K7 **Raḍwá, Jabal** ▲ W Saudi Arabia 24°31′N 38°21′E
111 P16 **Radymno** Podkarpackie, SE Poland 49°57′N 22°49′E
116 J5 **Radyvyliv** Rivnens'ka Oblast', NW Ukraine 50°07′N 25°12′E
Radziechów *see* Radekhiv
110 I11 **Radziejów** Kujawsko-pomorskie, C Poland 52°36′N 18°33′E
110 O12 **Radzyń Podlaski** Lubelskie, E Poland 51°48′N 22°37′E
8 J7 **Rae** ≈ Nunavut, NW Canada
152 M13 **Rāe Bareli** Uttar Pradesh, N India 26°14′N 81°14′E
Rae-Edzo *see* Edzo
21 T11 **Raeford** North Carolina, SE USA 34°59′N 79°15′W
99 M19 **Raeren** Liège, E Belgium 50°42′N 06°06′E
9 N7 **Rae Strait** *strait* Nunavut, N Canada
184 L11 **Raetihi** Manawatu-Wanganui, North Island, New Zealand 39°29′S 175°16′E
Raevavae *see* Raivavae
Rafa *see* Rafah
62 M10 **Rafaela** Santa Fe, E Argentina 31°16′S 61°25′W
138 E11 **Rafah** *var.* Rafa, Rafaḥ, *Heb.* Rafiaḥ, Raphiah. SW Gaza Strip 31°18′N 34°15′E
79 L15 **Rafaï** Mbomou, SE Central African Republic 05°01′N 23°51′E
141 O4 **Rafḥah** Al Ḥudūd ash Shamālīyah, N Saudi Arabia 29°41′N 43°29′E
Rafiaḥ *see* Rafah
143 R10 **Rafsanjān** Kermān, C Iran 30°25′N 56°E
80 B13 **Raga** Western Bahr el Ghazal, SW Sudan 08°28′N 25°41′E
19 S8 **Ragged Island** *island* Maine, NE USA
44 I5 **Ragged Island Range** *island group* S Bahamas
184 L7 **Raglan** Waikato, North Island, New Zealand 37°48′S 174°54′E
22 G8 **Ragley** Louisiana, S USA 30°31′N 93°13′W
Ragnit *see* Neman
107 K25 **Ragusa** Sicilia, Italy, C Mediterranean Sea 36°56′N 14°42′E
Ragusa *see* Dubrovnik
Ragusavecchia *see* Cavtat
171 P14 **Raha** Pulau Muna, C Indonesia 04°50′S 122°43′E
119 N17 **Rahachow** *Rus.* Rogachëv. Homyel'skaya Voblasts', SE Belarus 53°03′N 30°03′E
67 U6 **Rahad** *var.* Nahr ar Rahad. ≈ W Sudan
Rahad, Nahr ar *see* Rahad
Rahaeng *see* Tak
138 F11 **Rahat** Southern, C Israel 31°20′N 34°43′E
140 L8 **Rahaṭ, Ḥarrat** *lava flow* W Saudi Arabia
149 S12 **Rahīmyār Khān** Punjab, SE Pakistan 28°27′N 70°21′E
95 I14 **Råholt** Akershus, S Norway 60°16′N 11°10′E
113 M17 **Rahovec** *Serb.* Orahovac. W Kosovo 42°24′N 20°40′E
191 S10 **Raiatea** *island* Îles Sous le Vent, W French Polynesia
155 H16 **Rāichūr** Karnātaka, C India 16°15′N 77°20′E
Raidestos *see* Tekirdağ
153 S13 **Rāiganj** West Bengal, NE India 25°38′N 88°11′E
154 M11 **Raigarh** Chhattīsgarh, C India 21°53′N 83°28′E
183 O16 **Railton** Tasmania, SE Australia 41°24′S 146°28′E
36 L8 **Rainbow Bridge** *natural arch* Utah, W USA
23 Q3 **Rainbow City** Alabama, S USA 33°57′N 86°02′W
11 N11 **Rainbow Lake** Alberta, W Canada 58°30′N 119°24′W
21 R5 **Rainelle** West Virginia, NE USA 37°57′N 80°46′W
32 G10 **Rainier** Oregon, NW USA 46°05′N 122°55′W
32 H9 **Rainier, Mount** ⛰ Washington, NW USA 46°51′N 121°45′W
23 Q2 **Rainsville** Alabama, S USA 34°29′N 85°51′W
12 B11 **Rainy Lake** ⊚ Canada/USA
12 A11 **Rainy River** Ontario, C Canada 48°44′N 94°33′W
Raippaluoto *see* Replot
154 K12 **Raipur** Chhattīsgarh, C India 21°16′N 81°42′E
154 H10 **Raisen** Madhya Pradesh, C India 23°21′N 77°49′E
15 N13 **Raisin** ≈ Ontario, SE Canada
31 R11 **Raisin, River** ≈ Michigan, N USA
191 U13 **Raivavae** *var.* Raevavae. Îles Australes, SW French Polynesia
149 W9 **Rāiwind** Punjab, E Pakistan 31°14′N 74°10′E
171 T12 **Raja Ampat, Kepulauan** *island group* E Indonesia
155 L16 **Rājahmundry** Andhra Pradesh, E India 17°05′N 81°42′E
155 I18 **Rājampet** Andhra Pradesh, E India 14°09′N 79°10′E
Rajang *see* Rajang, Batang
169 S9 **Rajang, Batang** *var.* Rajang. ≈ East Malaysia
149 S11 **Rājanpur** Punjab, E Pakistan 29°05′N 70°25′E
155 H23 **Rājapālaiyam** Tamil Nādu, SE India 09°26′N 77°36′E
152 E12 **Rājasthān** ◈ *state* NW India
153 T15 **Rajbari** Dhaka, C Bangladesh 23°47′N 89°39′E
153 R12 **Rajbiraj** Eastern, E Nepal 26°34′N 86°52′E
154 G9 **Rājgarh** Madhya Pradesh, C India 24°01′N 76°42′E
152 H10 **Rājgarh** Rājasthān, NW India 28°38′N 75°21′E
153 P14 **Rājgīr** Bihār, N India 25°01′N 85°26′E
110 O8 **Rajgród** Podlaskie, NE Poland 53°43′N 22°40′E
154 L12 **Rājim** Chhattīsgarh, C India 20°57′N 81°58′E
112 C11 **Rajinac, Mali** ▲ W Croatia 44°47′N 15°04′E
154 B10 **Rājkot** Gujarāt, W India 22°18′N 70°47′E
153 R14 **Rājmahal** Jhārkhand, NE India 25°03′N 87°49′E
153 Q14 **Rājmahal Hills** *hill range* N India
154 K12 **Rāj Nāndgaon** Chhattīsgarh, C India 21°06′N 81°02′E
154 E12 **Rājpīpla** Gujarāt, W India 21°49′N 73°36′E
152 I8 **Rājpura** Punjab, NW India 30°29′N 76°40′E
152 E14 **Rājsamand** Rājasthān, N India 23°04′N 73.53°00′E
153 S14 **Rajshahi** *prev.* Rampur Boalia. Rajshahi, W Bangladesh 24°24′N 88°40′E
153 S13 **Rajshahi** ◈ *division* NW Bangladesh
158 J16 **Raka** Xizang Zizhiqu, W China 29°27′N 85°48′E
190 K13 **Rakahanga** *atoll* N Cook Islands
185 H19 **Rakaia** Canterbury, South Island, New Zealand 43°45′S 172°02′E
185 G19 **Rakaia** ≈ South Island, New Zealand
152 H3 **Rakaposhi** ▲ N India 36°06′N 74°31′E
Rakasd *see* Răcăşdia
169 N15 **Rakata, Pulau** *var.* Pulau Krakatau. *island* S Indonesia
141 U10 **Rakbah, Qalamat ar** *well* SE Saudi Arabia
Rakhine State *see* Arakan State
116 I8 **Rakhiv** Zakarpats'ka Oblast', W Ukraine 48°05′N 24°15′E
141 V13 **Rakhyūt** SW Oman 16°41′N 53°09′E
190 K9 **Rakiraki** Viti Levu, W Fiji 17°22′S 178°10′E
126 J8 **Rakitnoye** Belgorodskaya Oblast', W Russian Federation 50°50′N 35°51′E
Rakka *see* Ar Raqqah
118 I4 **Rakke** Lääne-Virumaa, NE Estonia 58°58′N 26°14′E
95 I16 **Rakkestad** Østfold, S Norway 59°25′N 11°17′E
110 F12 **Rakoniewice** *Ger.* Rakwitz. Wielkopolskie, C Poland 52°09′N 16°10′E
Rakonitz *see* Rakovník
83 H18 **Rakops** Central, C Botswana 21°01′S 24°20′E
111 C16 **Rakovník** *Ger.* Rakonitz. Středočeský Kraj, W Czech Republic 50°07′N 13°44′E
114 J10 **Rakovski** Plovdiv, C Bulgaria 42°16′N 24°58′E
Rakutō-kō *see* Naktong-gang
118 I3 **Rakvere** *Ger.* Wesenberg. Lääne-Virumaa, N Estonia 59°21′N 26°20′E
Rakwitz *see* Rakoniewice
22 L6 **Raleigh** Mississippi, S USA 32°01′N 89°30′W
21 U9 **Raleigh** *state capital* North Carolina, SE USA 35°46′N 78°38′W
21 Y11 **Raleigh Bay** *bay* North Carolina, SE USA
21 U9 **Raleigh-Durham** ✈ North Carolina, SE USA 35°54′N 78°45′W
189 S6 **Ralik Chain** *island group* Ralik Chain, W Marshall Islands
25 N5 **Ralls** Texas, SW USA 33°40′N 101°23′W
18 G13 **Ralston** Pennsylvania, NE USA 41°29′N 76°57′W
141 O16 **Ramādah** W Yemen 13°35′N 43°50′E
Ramadi *see* Ar Ramādī
105 N2 **Ramales de la Victoria** Cantabria, N Spain 43°15′N 03°28′W
138 F10 **Ramallah** C West Bank 31°55′N 35°12′E
61 C19 **Ramallo** Buenos Aires, E Argentina 33°30′S 60°01′W
155 H20 **Rāmanagaram** Karnātaka, E India 12°45′N 77°16′E
155 I23 **Rāmanāthapuram** Tamil Nādu, SE India 09°23′N 78°53′E
154 N12 **Rāmapur** Orissa, E India 21°48′N 84°00′E
155 I14 **Rāmāreddi** *var.* Kāmāreddi, Kamareddy. Andhra Pradesh, C India 18°19′N 78°23′E
138 F10 **Ramat Gan** Tel Aviv, W Israel 32°04′N 34°48′E
103 T6 **Rambervillers** Vosges, NE France 48°15′N 06°50′E
Rambi *see* Rabi
103 N5 **Rambouillet** Yvelines, N France 48°39′N 01°50′E
186 E5 **Rambutyo Island** *island* N Papua New Guinea
153 Q12 **Ramechhāp** Central, C Nepal 27°20′N 86°05′E
183 R12 **Rame Head** *headland* Victoria, SE Australia 37°48′S 149°30′E
126 L4 **Ramenskoye** Moskovskaya Oblast', W Russian Federation 55°31′N 38°24′E
124 J15 **Rameshki** Tverskaya Oblast', W Russian Federation 57°21′N 36°05′E
153 P14 **Rāmgarh** Jhārkhand, N India 23°37′N 85°32′E
152 D11 **Rāmgarh** Rājasthān, NW India 27°29′N 70°38′E
142 M9 **Rāmhormoz** *var.* Ram Hormuz, Ramuz. Khūzestān, SW Iran 31°15′N 49°38′E
Ram Hormuz *see* Rāmhormoz
Ram, Jebel *see* Ramm, Jabal
138 F10 **Ramla** *var.* Ramle, Ramleh, *Ar.* Er Ramle. Central, C Israel 31°56′N 34°52′E
Ramle/Ramleh *see* Ramla
138 F14 **Ramm, Jabal** *var.* Jebel Ram. ▲ SW Jordan 29°34′N 35°24′E
152 K10 **Rāmnagar** Uttarakhand, N India 29°23′N 79°07′E
95 N15 **Ramnäs** Västmanland, C Sweden 59°46′N 16°16′E
Râmnicul-Sărat *see* Râmnicu Sărat
116 L12 **Râmnicu Sărat** *prev.* Râmnicul-Sărat, Rîmnicu-Sărat. Buzău, E Romania 45°24′N 27°06′E
116 I13 **Râmnicu Vâlcea** *prev.* Rîmnicu Vîlcea. Vâlcea, C Romania 45°04′N 24°32′E
Ramokgwebana *see* Ramokgwebane
83 J18 **Ramokgwebane** *var.* Ramokgwebana. Central, NE Botswana 20°38′S 27°40′E
126 L7 **Ramon'** Voronezhskaya Oblast', W Russian Federation 51°51′N 39°18′E
35 V17 **Ramona** California, W USA 33°02′N 116°52′W
56 A10 **Ramón, Laguna** ⊚ NW Peru
14 G7 **Ramore** Ontario, S Canada 48°26′N 80°19′W
40 M11 **Ramos** San Luis Potosí, C Mexico 22°48′N 101°55′W
41 N8 **Ramos Arizpe** Coahuila, NE Mexico 25°35′N 100°59′W
40 J9 **Ramos, Río de** ≈ C Mexico
83 J21 **Ramotswa** South East, S Botswana 24°56′S 25°50′E
39 R8 **Rampart** Alaska, USA 65°30′N 150°10′W
8 H8 **Ramparts** ≈ Northwest Territories, NW Canada
152 K10 **Rāmpur** Uttar Pradesh, N India 28°48′N 79°03′E
154 F9 **Rāmpura** Madhya Pradesh, C India 24°30′N 75°32′E
Rampura *see* Rudrapur
Rampur Boalia *see* Rajshahi
166 K6 **Ramree Island** *island* W Burma (Myanmar)
141 W6 **Rams** *var.* Ar Rams. Ra's al Khaymah, NE United Arab Emirates 25°52′N 56°01′E
143 N4 **Rāmsar** *prev.* Sakhtsar. Māzandarān, N Iran 36°55′N 50°39′E
93 H16 **Ramsele** Västernorrland, N Sweden 63°33′N 16°35′E
21 T9 **Ramseur** North Carolina, SE USA 35°43′N 79°39′W
97 I16 **Ramsey** NE Isle of Man 54°19′N 04°24′W
97 I16 **Ramsey Bay** *bay* NE Isle of Man
14 E9 **Ramsey Lake** ⊚ Ontario, S Canada
97 Q22 **Ramsgate** SE England, United Kingdom 51°20′N 01°25′E
94 M10 **Ramsjö** Gävleborg, C Sweden 62°10′N 15°40′E
154 I12 **Rāmtek** Mahārāshtra, C India 21°28′N 79°28′E
Ramtha *see* Ar Ramthā
Ramuz *see* Rāmhormoz
118 G12 **Ramygala** Panevėžys, C Lithuania 55°30′N 24°18′E
152 H14 **Rāna Pratāp Sāgar** ⊚ N India
169 V7 **Ranau** Sabah, East Malaysia 05°56′N 116°43′E
168 L14 **Ranau, Danau** ⊚ Sumatera, W Indonesia
62 H12 **Rancagua** Libertador, C Chile 34°10′S 70°45′W
99 G22 **Rance** Hainaut, S Belgium 50°09′N 04°16′E
102 H6 **Rance** ≈ NW France
60 J9 **Rancharia** São Paulo, S Brazil 22°13′S 50°53′W
153 P15 **Rānchi** Jhārkhand, N India 23°22′N 85°20′E
61 D21 **Ranchos** Buenos Aires, E Argentina 35°32′S 58°22′W
37 S9 **Ranchos De Taos** New Mexico, SW USA 36°21′N 105°36′W
63 G16 **Ranco, Lago** ⊚ C Chile
95 C16 **Randaberg** Rogaland, S Norway 59°00′N 05°38′E
29 U7 **Randall** Minnesota, N USA 46°05′N 94°30′W
107 L23 **Randazzo** Sicilia, Italy, C Mediterranean Sea 37°52′N 14°57′E
95 G21 **Randers** Århus, C Denmark 56°28′N 10°03′E
92 I12 **Randijaure** ⊚ N Sweden
21 T9 **Randleman** North Carolina, SE USA 35°49′N 79°48′W
19 O11 **Randolph** Massachusetts, NE USA 42°09′N 71°02′W
29 Q13 **Randolph** Nebraska, C USA 42°25′N 97°05′W
36 M1 **Randolph** Utah, W USA 41°40′N 111°10′W
100 P9 **Randow** ≈ NE Germany
95 H14 **Randsfjorden** ⊚ S Norway
93 K13 **Råneå** Norrbotten, N Sweden 65°52′N 22°17′E
92 G12 **Ranelva** ≈ C Norway
93 F15 **Ranemsletta** Nord-Trøndelag, C Norway 64°36′N 11°55′E
76 H10 **Ranérou** C Senegal 15°17′N 14°00′W
Råneš *see* Ringvassøya
185 E22 **Ranfurly** Otago, South Island, New Zealand 45°07′S 170°06′E
167 P17 **Rangae** Narathiwat, SW Thailand 06°15′N 101°45′E
153 V16 **Rangamati** Chittagong, SE Bangladesh 22°40′N 92°10′E
184 I2 **Rangaunu Bay** *bay* North Island, New Zealand
19 P6 **Rangeley** Maine, NE USA 44°58′N 70°37′W
37 O4 **Rangely** Colorado, C USA 40°05′N 108°48′W
25 R7 **Ranger** Texas, SW USA 32°28′N 98°40′W
14 C9 **Ranger Lake** Ontario, S Canada 46°51′N 83°34′W
14 C9 **Ranger Lake** ⊚ Ontario, S Canada
153 V12 **Rangia** Assam, NE India 26°26′N 91°38′E
185 I18 **Rangiora** Canterbury, South Island, New Zealand 43°19′S 172°34′E
191 T9 **Rangiroa** *atoll* Îles Tuamotu, W French Polynesia
184 N9 **Rangitaiki** ≈ North Island, New Zealand
185 F19 **Rangitata** ≈ South Island, New Zealand
184 M12 **Rangitikei** ≈ North Island, New Zealand
184 L6 **Rangitoto Island** *island* N New Zealand
Rangkasbitoeng *see* Rangkasbitung
169 N16 **Rangkasbitung** *prev.* Rangkasbitoeng. Jawa, SW Indonesia 06°21′S 106°12′E
167 P9 **Rang, Khao** ▲ C Thailand 16°13′N 99°03′E
147 V13 **Rangkŭl** *Rus.* Rangkul'. SE Tajikistan 38°30′N 74°24′E
Rangkul' *see* Rangkŭl
Rangoon *see* Yangon
153 T13 **Rangpur** Rajshahi, N Bangladesh 25°46′N 89°20′E
155 F18 **Rānibennur** Karnātaka, W India 14°36′N 75°39′E
153 R15 **Rāniganj** West Bengal, NE India 23°34′N 87°13′E
149 Q13 **Rānīpur** Sind, SE Pakistan 27°17′N 68°34′E
Rāniyah *see* Rānya
25 N9 **Rankin** Texas, SW USA 31°14′N 101°56′W
9 O9 **Rankin Inlet** Nunavut, C Canada 62°52′N 92°14′W
183 P8 **Rankins Springs** New South Wales, SE Australia 33°51′S 146°16′E
Rankovićevo *see* Kraljevo
108 I7 **Rankweil** Vorarlberg, W Austria 47°17′N 09°40′E
Rann *see* Brežice
127 T8 **Ranneye** Orenburgskaya Oblast', W Russian Federation 51°28′N 52°29′E
96 I10 **Rannoch, Loch** ⊚ C Scotland, United Kingdom
191 U17 **Rano Kau** *var.* Rano Kao. *crater* Easter Island, Chile, E Pacific Ocean
167 N14 **Ranong** Ranong, SW Thailand 09°59′N 98°40′E
186 J8 **Ranongga** *var.* Ghanongga. *island* NW Solomon Islands
191 W16 **Rano Raraku** *ancient monument* Easter Island, Chile, E Pacific Ocean
171 V12 **Ransiki** Papua, E Indonesia 01°27′S 134°12′E
92 K12 **Rantajärvi** Norrbotten, N Sweden 66°45′N 23°39′E
93 N17 **Rantasalmi** Itä-Suomi, SE Finland 62°02′N 28°22′E
169 U13 **Rantau** Borneo, C Indonesia 02°56′S 115°09′E
168 L10 **Rantau, Pulau** *var.* Pulau Tebingtinggi. *island* W Indonesia
171 N13 **Rantepao** Sulawesi, C Indonesia 02°58′S 119°58′E
30 M13 **Rantoul** Illinois, N USA 40°19′N 88°08′W
93 L15 **Rantsila** Oulu, C Finland 64°31′N 25°40′E
92 L13 **Ranua** Lappi, NW Finland 65°55′N 26°34′E
139 T3 **Rānya** *var.* Rāniyah. As Sulaymānīyah, NE Iraq 36°15′N 44°53′E
157 X3 **Raohe** Heilongjiang, NE China 46°49′N 134°00′E
74 H9 **Raoui, Erg er** *desert* W Algeria
193 O10 **Rapa** *island* Îles Australes, S French Polynesia
191 V14 **Rapa Iti** *island* Îles Australes, SW French Polynesia
106 D10 **Rapallo** Liguria, NW Italy 44°21′N 09°13′E
Rapa Nui *see* Pascua, Isla de
Raphiah *see* Rafah
21 V5 **Rapidan River** ≈ Virginia, NE USA
28 J10 **Rapid City** South Dakota, N USA 44°05′N 103°14′W
15 P8 **Rapide-Blanc** Québec, SE Canada 47°48′N 72°57′W
14 I8 **Rapide-Deux** Québec, SE Canada 47°56′N 78°33′W
118 K6 **Räpina** *Ger.* Rappin. Põlvamaa, SE Estonia 58°06′N 27°27′E
118 G4 **Rapla** *Ger.* Rappel. Raplamaa, NW Estonia 59°00′N 24°46′E
118 G4 **Raplamaa** *var.* Rapla Maakond. ◈ *province* NW Estonia
Rapla Maakond *see* Raplamaa
21 X6 **Rappahannock River** ≈ Virginia, NE USA
Rappel *see* Rapla
108 G7 **Rapperswil** Sankt Gallen, NE Switzerland 47°14′N 08°50′E
Rappin *see* Räpina
153 N12 **Rāpti** ≈ N India
57 K16 **Rapulo, Río** ≈ E Bolivia
Raqqah/Raqqah, Muḥāfaẓat al *see* Ar Raqqah
18 J8 **Raquette Lake** ⊚ New York, NE USA
18 J6 **Raquette River** ≈ New York, NE USA
191 V10 **Raraka** *atoll* Îles Tuamotu, C French Polynesia
191 V10 **Raroia** *atoll* Îles Tuamotu, C French Polynesia
190 H15 **Rarotonga** ✈ Rarotonga, S Cook Islands, C Pacific Ocean 21°15′S 159°45′W
190 H16 **Rarotonga** *island* S Cook Islands, C Pacific Ocean
147 P12 **Rarz** W Tajikistan 39°23′N 68°43′E
Ras al'Ain *see* Ra's al 'Ayn
139 N2 **Ra's al 'Ayn** *var.* Ras al'Ain. Al Ḥasakah, N Syria 36°52′N 40°05′E
138 H3 **Ra's al Basīṭ** Al Lādhiqīyah, W Syria 35°57′N 35°55′E
Ra's al-Hafğī *see* Ra's al Khafjī
141 R5 **Ra's al Khafjī** *var.* Ra's al-Hafğī. Ash Sharqīyah, NE Saudi Arabia 28°22′N 48°30′E
Ras al-Khaimah/Ras al Khaimah *see* Ra's al Khaymah
143 R15 **Ra's al Khaymah** *var.* Ras al Khaimah. Ra's al Khaymah, NE United Arab Emirates 25°44′N 55°55′E
143 R15 **Ra's al Khaymah** *var.* Ras al-Khaimah. ✈ Ra's al Khaymah, NE United Arab Emirates 25°37′N 55°51′E
138 G13 **Ra's an Naqb** Ma'ān, S Jordan 30°00′N 35°29′E
61 B26 **Rasa, Punta** *headland* E Argentina 40°50′S 62°15′W
171 V12 **Rasawi** Papua, E Indonesia 02°04′S 134°02′E
Râşcani *see* Rîşcani
80 J10 **Ras Dashen Terara** ▲ N Ethiopia 13°12′N 38°09′E
Rasdhoo Atoll *see* Rasdu Atoll
151 K19 **Rasdu Atoll** *var.* Rasdhoo Atoll. *atoll* C Maldives
118 E12 **Raseiniai** Kaunas, C Lithuania 55°23′N 23°06′E
75 X8 **Ra's Ghārib** *var.* Râs Ghârib. E Egypt 28°16′N 33°01′E
Râs Ghârib *see* Ra's Ghārib
162 J6 **Rashaant** Hövsgöl, N Mongolia 49°08′N 101°27′E
Rashaant *see* Delüün, Bayan-Ölgiy, Mongolia
Rashaant *see* Öldziyt, Dundgovĭ, Mongolia
80 F12 **Rashad** Southern Kordofan, C Sudan 11°55′N 31°05′E
75 V7 **Rashīd** *Eng.* Rosetta. N Egypt 31°25′N 30°25′E
139 Y11 **Rashīd** Al Başrah, E Iraq 31°15′N 47°31′E
142 M3 **Rasht** *var.* Resht. Gīlān, NW Iran 37°18′N 49°38′E
139 S2 **Rashwan** Arbil, N Iraq 36°28′N 43°54′E
Rasik *see* Raasiku
143 W14 **Rāsk** Sīstān va Balūchestān, SE Iran 26°13′N 61°25′E
113 M15 **Raška** Serbia, C Serbia 43°18′N 20°37′E
119 P15 **Rasna** *Rus.* Ryasna. Mahilyowskaya Voblasts', E Belarus 54°01′N 31°12′E
116 J12 **Râşnov** *prev.* Rişno, Rozsnyó, *Hung.* Barcarozsnyó. Braşov, C Romania 45°35′N 25°27′E
118 L11 **Rasony** *Rus.* Rossony. Vitsyebskaya Voblasts', N Belarus 55°53′N 28°50′E
Ra's Shamrah *see* Ugarit
127 N7 **Rasskazovo** Tambovskaya Oblast', W Russian Federation 52°42′N 41°45′E
119 O16 **Rasta** ≈ E Belarus
Rastadt *see* Rastatt
Rastâne *see* Ar Rastān
141 S6 **Ra's Tannūrah** *Eng.* Ras Tanura. Ash Sharqīyah, NE Saudi Arabia 26°44′N 50°04′E
Ras Tanura *see* Ra's Tannūrah
101 G21 **Rastatt** *var.* Rastadt. Baden-Württemberg, SW Germany 48°51′N 08°13′E
Rastenburg *see* Kętrzyn
149 V7 **Rasūlnagar** Punjab, E Pakistan 32°20′N 73°51′E
189 U6 **Ratak Chain** *island group* Ratak Chain, E Marshall Islands
119 K15 **Ratamka** *Rus.* Ratomka. Minskaya Voblasts', C Belarus 53°56′N 27°21′E
93 G17 **Ratän** Jämtland, C Sweden 62°28′N 14°35′E
152 G11 **Ratangarh** Rājasthān, NW India 28°02′N 74°39′E
Rat Buri *see* Ratchaburi
167 O11 **Ratchaburi** *var.* Rat Buri. Ratchaburi, W Thailand 13°30′N 99°50′E
29 W15 **Rathbun Lake** ⊠ Iowa, C USA
Ráth Caola *see* Rathkeale
166 K5 **Rathedaung** Rakhine State, W Burma (Myanmar) 20°30′N 92°48′E
100 M12 **Rathenow** Brandenburg, NE Germany 52°37′N 12°21′E
97 C19 **Rathkeale** *Ir.* Ráth Caola. Limerick, SW Ireland 52°32′N 08°56′W
96 F13 **Rathlin Island** *Ir.* Reachlainn. *island* N Northern Ireland, United Kingdom
97 C20 **Ráth Luirc** *Ir.* An Ráth. Cork, SW Ireland 52°22′N 08°44′W
Ratibor *see* Racibórz
Ratisbon/Ratisbona/Ratisbonne *see* Regensburg
Rätische Alpen *see* Rhaetian Alps
38 E17 **Rat Island** *island* Aleutian Islands, Alaska, USA
38 E17 **Rat Islands** *island group* Aleutian Islands, Alaska, USA
154 F10 **Ratlām** *prev.* Rutlam. Madhya Pradesh, C India 23°23′N 75°04′E
155 D15 **Ratnāgiri** Mahārāshtra, W India 17°00′N 73°20′E
155 K26 **Ratnapura** Sabaragamuwa Province, S Sri Lanka 06°41′N 80°25′E
116 J2 **Ratne** *var.* Ratno. Volyns'ka Oblast', NW Ukraine 51°40′N 24°33′E
Ratno *see* Ratne
Ratomka *see* Ratamka
37 U8 **Raton** New Mexico, SW USA 36°54′N 104°27′W
139 O7 **Ratqah, Wādī ar** *dry watercourse* W Iraq
Ratschach *see* Radeče
167 O16 **Rattaphum** Songkhla, SW Thailand 07°07′N 100°16′E
26 L6 **Rattlesnake Creek** ≈ Kansas, C USA
94 L13 **Rättvik** Dalarna, C Sweden 60°53′N 15°12′E
100 K9 **Ratzeburg** Mecklenburg-Vorpommern, N Germany 53°41′N 10°48′E
100 K9 **Ratzeburger See** ⊚ N Germany
10 J10 **Ratz, Mount** ▲ British Columbia, SW Canada 57°22′N 132°17′W
61 D22 **Rauch** Buenos Aires, E Argentina 36°45′S 59°05′W
41 U16 **Raudales** Chiapas, SE Mexico
Raudhatain *see* Ar Rawdatayn
Raudnitz an der Elbe *see* Roudnice nad Labem
92 K1 **Raufarhöfn** Nordhurland Eystra, NE Iceland 66°27′N 15°58′W
94 H13 **Raufoss** Oppland, S Norway 60°44′N 10°39′E
Raukawa *see* Cook Strait
184 Q8 **Raukumara** ▲ North Island, New Zealand 37°46′S 178°07′E
192 K11 **Raukumara Plain** *undersea feature* N Coral Sea
184 P8 **Raukumara Range** ▲▲ North Island, New Zealand
154 N11 **Rāulakela** *var.* Raurkela; *prev.* Rourkela. Orissa, E India 22°13′N 84°53′E
95 F15 **Rauland** Telemark, S Norway 59°41′N 07°57′E
93 J19 **Rauma** *Swe.* Raumo. Länsi-Suomi, SW Finland 61°09′N 21°30′E
94 F10 **Rauma** ≈ S Norway
Raumo *see* Rauma
118 H8 **Rauna** Cēsis, C Latvia 57°19′N 25°34′E
169 T17 **Raung, Gunung** ▲ Jawa, S Indonesia 08°00′S 114°07′E
Raurkela *see* Rāulakela
95 J22 **Raus** Skåne, S Sweden 56°01′N 12°48′E
165 W3 **Rausu** Hokkaidō, NE Japan 44°00′N 145°06′E
165 W3 **Rausu-dake** ▲ Hokkaidō, NE Japan 44°06′N 145°04′E
116 M9 **Răut** *var.* Răuţel. ≈ C Moldova
93 M17 **Rautalampi** Itä-Suomi, C Finland 62°37′N 26°48′E
93 N16 **Rautavaara** Itä-Suomi, C Finland 63°30′N 28°19′E
Răuţel *see* Răut
93 O18 **Rautjärvi** Etelä-Suomi, SE Finland 61°21′N 29°20′E
Rautu *see* Sosnovo
191 V11 **Ravahere** *atoll* Îles Tuamotu, C French Polynesia
107 J25 **Ravanusa** Sicilia, Italy, C Mediterranean Sea 37°16′N 13°59′E
143 S9 **Rāvar** Kermān, C Iran 31°15′N 56°51′E
147 Q11 **Ravat** Batkenskaya Oblast', SW Kyrgyzstan 39°54′N 70°06′E
18 K11 **Ravena** New York, NE USA 42°28′N 73°49′W
106 H10 **Ravenna** Emilia-Romagna, N Italy 44°28′N 12°15′E
29 O15 **Ravenna** Nebraska, C USA 41°01′N 98°54′W
31 U11 **Ravenna** Ohio, N USA 41°09′N 81°14′W
101 I24 **Ravensburg** Baden-Württemberg, S Germany 47°47′N 09°37′E
181 W4 **Ravenshoe** Queensland, NE Australia 17°29′S 145°28′E
180 K13 **Ravensthorpe** Western Australia 33°37′S 120°03′E
21 Q4 **Ravenswood** West Virginia, NE USA 38°57′N 81°45′W
149 U9 **Rāvi** ≈ India/Pakistan
112 C9 **Ravna Gora** Primorje-Gorski Kotar, NW Croatia 45°20′N 14°54′E
109 U10 **Ravne na Koroškem** *Ger.* Gutenstein. N Slovenia 46°33′N 14°57′E
139 P6 **Rāwah** Al Anbār, W Iraq 34°32′N 41°54′E
191 T4 **Rawaki** *prev.* Phoenix Island. *atoll* Phoenix Islands, C Kiribati
149 U6 **Rāwalpindi** Punjab, NE Pakistan 33°38′N 73°06′E
110 L13 **Rawa Mazowiecka** Łódzkie, C Poland 51°47′N 20°16′E
139 T2 **Rawāndiz** *var.* Rawandoz, Rawāndūz. Arbīl, N Iraq 36°38′N 44°32′E
Rawandoz/Rawāndūz *see* Rawāndiz
171 U12 **Rawas** Papua, E Indonesia 01°07′S 132°12′E
139 O4 **Rawdah** ⊚ E Syria
110 G13 **Rawicz** *Ger.* Rawitsch. Wielkopolskie, C Poland 51°37′N 16°51′E
Rawitsch *see* Rawicz
180 M11 **Rawlinna** Western Australia 31°01′S 125°36′E
33 W16 **Rawlins** Wyoming, C USA 41°47′N 107°14′W
63 K17 **Rawson** Chubut, SE Argentina 43°22′S 65°01′W
159 R16 **Rawu** Xizang Zizhiqu, W China 29°30′N 96°42′E
153 P12 **Raxaul** Bihār, N India 26°58′N 84°51′E
28 K3 **Ray** North Dakota, N USA 48°19′N 103°11′W
169 S11 **Raya, Bukit** ▲ Borneo, C Indonesia 0°40′S 112°40′E
155 I18 **Rāyachoti** Andhra Pradesh, E India 14°03′N 78°43′E
Rāyadrug *see* Rāyagada
155 M14 **Rāyagada** *prev.* Rāyadrug. Orissa, E India 19°10′N 83°28′E
138 H7 **Rayak** *var.* Rayaq, Riyāq. E Lebanon 33°51′N 36°03′E
Rayaq *see* Rayak
139 T2 **Rāyat** Arbīl, E Iraq 36°39′N 44°56′E
169 N12 **Raya, Tanjung** *cape* Pulau Bangka, W Indonesia
13 R13 **Ray, Cape** *headland* Newfoundland, Newfoundland and Labrador, E Canada 47°38′N 59°15′W
123 Q13 **Raychikhinsk** Amurskaya Oblast', SE Russian Federation 49°47′N 129°19′E
127 U5 **Rayevskiy** Respublika Bashkortostan, W Russian Federation 54°04′N 54°58′E
11 Q17 **Raymond** Alberta, SW Canada 49°30′N 112°41′W
22 K6 **Raymond** Mississippi, S USA 32°15′N 90°25′W
32 F9 **Raymond** Washington, NW USA 46°41′N 123°43′W
183 T8 **Raymond Terrace** New South Wales, SE Australia 32°47′S 151°45′E
25 T17 **Raymondville** Texas, SW USA 26°30′N 97°48′W
11 U16 **Raymore** Saskatchewan, S Canada 51°24′N 104°34′W
39 Q8 **Ray Mountains** ▲▲ Alaska, USA
22 H9 **Rayne** Louisiana, S USA 30°13′N 92°15′W
41 O12 **Rayón** San Luis Potosí, C Mexico 21°54′N 99°33′W
40 G4 **Rayón** Sonora, NW Mexico 29°45′N 110°33′W
167 P12 **Rayong** Rayong, S Thailand 12°42′N 101°17′E
25 T5 **Ray Roberts, Lake** ⊚ Texas, SW USA
18 E15 **Raystown Lake** ⊠ Pennsylvania, NE USA
141 V13 **Raysūt** SW Oman 16°58′N 54°02′E
27 R4 **Raytown** Missouri, C USA 39°00′N 94°27′W
22 I5 **Rayville** Louisiana, S USA 32°29′N 91°45′W
142 L5 **Razan** Hamadān, W Iran 35°22′N 48°58′E
139 S9 **Razāzah, Buḥayrat ar** *var.* Baḥr al Milḥ. ⊚ C Iraq
114 L9 **Razboyna** ▲ E Bulgaria 42°54′N 26°31′E
Razdan *see* Hrazdan
Razdolnoye *see* Rozdol'ne
Razelm, Lacul *see* Razim, Lacul
139 U2 **Razga** As Sulaymānīyah, E Iraq 36°25′N 45°06′E
114 L8 **Razgrad** Razgrad, N Bulgaria 43°33′N 26°31′E
114 L8 **Razgrad** ◈ *province* NE Bulgaria
117 N13 **Razim, Lacul** *prev.* Lacul Razelm. *lagoon* NW Black Sea
114 G11 **Razlog** Blagoevgrad, SW Bulgaria 41°53′N 23°28′E
118 K10 **Rāznas Ezers** ⊚ SE Latvia
102 E6 **Raz, Pointe du** *headland* NW France 48°06′N 04°52′W
Reachlainn *see* Rathlin Island
Reachrainn *see* Lambay Island
97 N22 **Reading** S England, United Kingdom 51°28′N 00°59′W
18 H15 **Reading** Pennsylvania, NE USA 40°20′N 75°55′W
48 C7 **Real, Cordillera** ▲▲ C Ecuador
62 K12 **Realicó** La Pampa, C Argentina 35°02′S 64°14′W
25 R15 **Realitos** Texas, SW USA 27°26′N 98°31′W
108 G9 **Realp** Uri, C Switzerland 46°36′N 08°32′E
167 Q12 **Reăng Kesei** Bătdâmbâng, W Cambodia 12°57′N 103°15′E
191 Y11 **Reao** *atoll* Îles Tuamotu, E French Polynesia
Reate *see* Rieti
Greater Antarctica *see* East Antarctica
180 L11 **Rebecca, Lake** ⊚ Western Australia
Rebiana Sand Sea *see* Rabyānah, Ramlat
124 H8 **Reboly** *Finn.* Repola. Respublika Kareliya, NW Russian Federation 63°51′N 30°49′E
165 S1 **Rebun** Rebun-tō, NE Japan 45°19′N 141°02′E
165 S1 **Rebun-tō** *island* NE Japan
106 J12 **Recanati** Marche, C Italy 43°23′N 13°34′E
Rechitsa *see* Rechytsa
109 Y7 **Rechnitz** Burgenland, SE Austria 47°19′N 16°26′E
119 J20 **Rechytsa** *Rus.* Rechitsa. Brestskaya Voblasts', SW Belarus 51°51′N 26°48′E
119 O19 **Rechytsa** *Rus.* Rechitsa. Homyel'skaya Voblasts', SE Belarus 52°22′N 30°23′E
59 Q15 **Recife** *prev.* Pernambuco. *state capital* Pernambuco, E Brazil 08°06′S 34°53′W
83 I26 **Recife, Cape** *Afr.* Kaap Recife. *headland* S South Africa 34°03′S 25°37′E
Recife, Kaap *see* Recife, Cape
172 I16 **Récifs, Îles aux** *island* Inner Islands, NE Seychelles
101 E14 **Recklinghausen** Nordrhein-Westfalen, W Germany 51°37′N 07°12′E
100 M8 **Recknitz** ≈ NE Germany
99 K23 **Recogne** Luxembourg, SE Belgium 49°56′N 05°20′E
61 C15 **Reconquista** Santa Fe, C Argentina 29°08′S 59°38′W
195 O6 **Recovery Glacier** *glacier* Antarctica
59 G15 **Recreio** Mato Grosso, W Brazil 08°13′S 58°15′W
27 X9 **Rector** Arkansas, C USA 36°15′N 90°17′W
110 E9 **Recz** *Ger.* Reetz Neumark. Zachodnio-pomorskie, NW Poland 53°16′N 15°32′E
99 L24 **Redange** *var.* Redange-sur-Attert. Diekirch, W Luxembourg 49°46′N 05°53′E
Redange-sur-Attert *see* Redange
18 C13 **Redbank Creek** ≈ Pennsylvania, NE USA
13 S9 **Red Bay** Québec, E Canada 51°40′N 56°37′W
23 N2 **Red Bay** Alabama, S USA 34°26′N 88°08′W
35 N4 **Red Bluff** California, W USA 40°09′N 122°14′W
24 J8 **Red Bluff Reservoir** ⊠ New Mexico/Texas, SW USA
30 K16 **Red Bud** Illinois, N USA 38°12′N 89°59′W
30 J5 **Red Cedar River** ≈ Wisconsin, N USA
11 R17 **Redcliff** Alberta, SW Canada 50°06′N 110°48′W
83 K17 **Redcliff** Midlands, C Zimbabwe 19°00′S 29°49′E
182 L9 **Red Cliffs** Victoria, SE Australia 34°21′S 142°12′E
29 P17 **Red Cloud** Nebraska, C USA 40°05′N 98°31′W
22 L8 **Red Creek** ≈ Mississippi, S USA
11 P15 **Red Deer** Alberta, SW Canada 52°15′N 113°48′W
11 Q16 **Red Deer** ≈ Alberta, SW Canada
39 O11 **Red Devil** Alaska, USA 61°45′N 157°18′W
35 N3 **Redding** California, W USA 40°33′N 122°26′W
97 L20 **Redditch** W England, United Kingdom 52°19′N 01°56′W
29 P9 **Redfield** South Dakota, N USA 44°51′N 98°31′W
24 J12 **Redford** Texas, SW USA 29°31′N 104°19′W
45 V13 **Redhead** Trinidad, Trinidad and Tobago 10°44′N 60°58′W
182 I8 **Red Hill** South Australia 33°34′S 138°13′E
Red Hill *see* Pu'u 'Ula'ula
26 K7 **Red Hills** *hill range* Kansas, C USA
13 T12 **Red Indian Lake** ⊚ Newfoundland, Newfoundland and Labrador, E Canada
124 J16 **Redkino** Tverskaya Oblast', W Russian Federation 56°41′N 36°07′E
12 A10 **Red Lake** Ontario, C Canada 51°00′N 93°55′W
36 I10 **Red Lake** *salt flat* Arizona, SW USA
29 S4 **Red Lake Falls** Minnesota, N USA 47°52′N 96°16′W
29 R4 **Red Lake River** ≈ Minnesota, N USA
35 U15 **Redlands** California, W USA 34°03′N 117°10′W
18 G16 **Red Lion** Pennsylvania, NE USA 39°53′N 76°36′W
33 U11 **Red Lodge** Montana, NW USA 45°11′N 109°15′W
32 H13 **Redmond** Oregon, NW USA 44°16′N 121°10′W
36 L5 **Redmond** Utah, W USA 39°00′N 111°51′W
32 H8 **Redmond** Washington, NW USA 47°40′N 122°07′W
Rednitz *see* Regnitz
29 T15 **Red Oak** Iowa, C USA 41°00′N 95°10′W
18 K12 **Red Oaks Mill** New York, NE USA 41°39′N 73°52′W
102 I7 **Redon** Ille-et-Vilaine, NW France 47°39′N 02°05′W
45 W10 **Redonda** *island* SW Antigua and Barbuda
104 G4 **Redondela** Galicia, NW Spain 42°17′N 08°36′W
104 H11 **Redondo** Évora, S Portugal 38°38′N 07°32′W
39 Q12 **Redoubt Volcano** ⛰ Alaska, USA 60°29′N 152°44′W
11 Y16 **Red River** ≈ Canada/USA
129 U12 **Red River** *var.* Yuan, *Chin.* Yuan Jiang, *Vtn.* Sông Hông Hà. ≈ China/Vietnam
25 W4 **Red River** ≈ S USA
22 H7 **Red River** ≈ Louisiana, S USA
30 M6 **Red River** ≈ Wisconsin, N USA

◆ Country
● Country Capital
◇ Dependent Territory
○ Dependent Territory Capital
◈ Administrative Regions
✈ International Airport
▲ Mountain
▲▲ Mountain Range
⛰ Volcano
≈ River
⊚ Lake
⊠ Reservoir

RED ROCK, LAKE – RIO DELL

Red Rock, Lake see Red Rock Reservoir
29 W14 **Red Rock Reservoir** var. Lake Red Rock. ⊠ Iowa, C USA
80 H7 **Red Sea** ❖ state NE Sudan
75 Y9 **Red Sea** var. Sinus Arabicus. sea Africa/Asia
21 T11 **Red Springs** North Carolina, SE USA 34°49′N 79°10′W
8 I9 **Redstone** ≈ Northwest Territories, NW Canada
11 V17 **Redvers** Saskatchewan, S Canada 49°31′N 101°33′W
77 P13 **Red Volta** var. Nazinon, Fr. Volta Rouge. ≈ Burkina/Ghana
11 Q14 **Redwater** Alberta, SW Canada 53°57′N 113°06′W
28 M16 **Red Willow Creek** ≈ Nebraska, C USA
29 W9 **Red Wing** Minnesota, N USA 44°33′N 92°31′W
35 N9 **Redwood City** California, W USA 37°29′N 122°13′W
29 T9 **Redwood Falls** Minnesota, N USA 44°33′N 95°07′W
31 P7 **Reed City** Michigan, N USA 43°52′N 85°30′W
28 K6 **Reeder** North Dakota, N USA 46°03′N 102°55′W
35 R11 **Reedley** California, W USA 36°35′N 119°27′W
33 T11 **Reedpoint** Montana, NW USA 45°41′N 109°33′W
30 K8 **Reedsburg** Wisconsin, N USA 43°33′N 90°03′W
32 E13 **Reedsport** Oregon, NW USA 43°42′N 124°06′W
187 Q9 **Reef Islands** island group Santa Cruz Islands, E Solomon Islands
185 H16 **Reefton** West Coast, South Island, New Zealand 42°07′S 171°53′E
20 F8 **Reelfoot Lake** ◎ Tennessee, S USA
97 D17 **Ree, Lough** Ir. Loch Rí. ◎ C Ireland
Reengus see Rīngas
35 U4 **Reese River** ≈ Nevada, W USA
98 M8 **Reest** ≈ E Netherlands
Reetz Neumark see Recz
Reevhtse see Røsvatnet
137 N13 **Refahiye** Erzincan, C Turkey 39°54′N 38°45′E
23 N4 **Reform** Alabama, S USA 33°22′N 88°01′W
95 K20 **Reftele** Jönköping, S Sweden 57°10′N 13°34′E
25 T14 **Refugio** Texas, SW USA 28°19′N 97°18′W
110 E8 **Rega** ≈ NW Poland
Regar see Tursunzoda
101 O21 **Regen** Bayern, SE Germany 48°57′N 13°10′E
101 M20 **Regen** ≈ SE Germany
101 M21 **Regensburg** Eng. Ratisbon, Fr. Ratisbonne, hist. Ratisbona; anc. Castra Regina, Reginum. Bayern, SE Germany 49°01′N 12°06′E
101 M21 **Regenstauf** Bayern, SE Germany 49°06′N 12°07′E
74 I10 **Reggane** C Algeria 26°46′N 00°09′E
98 N9 **Regge** ≈ E Netherlands
Reggio see Reggio nell'Emilia
Reggio Calabria see Reggio di Calabria
107 M23 **Reggio di Calabria** var. Reggio Calabria, Gk. Rhegion; anc. Regium, Rhegium. Calabria, SW Italy 38°06′N 15°39′E
Reggio Emilia see Reggio nell'Emilia
106 F9 **Reggio nell'Emilia** var. Reggio Emilia, abbrev. Reggio; anc. Regium Lepidum. Emilia-Romagna, N Italy 44°42′N 10°37′E
116 I10 **Reghin** Ger. Sächsisch-Reen, Hung. Szászrégen; prev. Reghinul Săsesc, Ger. Sächsisch-Regen. Mureş, C Romania 46°46′N 24°41′E
Reghinul Săsesc see Reghin
11 U16 **Regina** province capital Saskatchewan, S Canada 50°25′N 104°39′W
55 Z10 **Régina** E French Guiana 04°20′N 52°07′W
11 U16 **Regina** ✈ Saskatchewan, S Canada 50°21′N 104°43′W
11 U16 **Regina Beach** Saskatchewan, S Canada 50°44′N 105°03′W
Reginum see Regensburg
Région du Haut-Congo see Haut-Congo
Registan see Rīgestān
60 L11 **Registro** São Paulo, S Brazil 24°30′S 47°50′W
Regium see Reggio di Calabria
Regium Lepidum see Reggio nell'Emilia
101 K19 **Regnitz** var. Rednitz. ≈ SE Germany
40 K10 **Regocijo** Durango, W Mexico 23°35′N 105°11′W
104 H12 **Reguengos de Monsaraz** Évora, S Portugal 38°25′N 07°32′W
101 M18 **Rehau** Bayern, E Germany 50°15′N 12°03′E
83 D19 **Rehoboth** Hardap, C Namibia 23°18′S 17°03′E
21 Z4 **Rehoboth Beach** Delaware, NE USA 38°42′N 75°03′W
138 F10 **Rehovot**; prev. Reḥovot. Central, C Israel 31°54′N 34°49′E
Reḥovot see Rehovot
81 J20 **Rei** spring/well S Kenya 03°24′S 39°18′E
Reichenau see Rychnov nad Kněžnou
Reichenau see Bogatynia, Poland
101 M17 **Reichenbach** var. Reichenbach im Vogtland. Sachsen, E Germany 50°36′N 12°18′E
Reichenbach see Dzierżoniów
Reichenbach im Vogtland see Reichenbach
Reichenberg see Liberec
181 O11 **Reid** Western Australia 30°49′S 128°24′E
23 V6 **Reidsville** Georgia, SE USA 32°05′N 82°07′W
21 T8 **Reidsville** North Carolina, SE USA 36°21′N 79°39′W
Reifnitz see Ribnica
97 O22 **Reigate** SE England, United Kingdom 51°14′N 00°13′W
Reikjavik see Reykjavík
102 I10 **Ré, Île de** island W France
37 N15 **Reiley Peak** ▲ Arizona, SW USA 32°24′N 110°09′W
103 Q4 **Reims** Eng. Rheims; anc. Durocortorum, Remi. Marne, N France 49°16′N 04°01′E
63 G23 **Reina Adelaida, Archipiélago** island group S Chile
45 O16 **Reina Beatrix** ✈ (Oranjestad) C Aruba 12°30′N 69°57′W
108 F7 **Reinach** Aargau, W Switzerland 47°16′N 08°12′E
108 E6 **Reinach** Basel-Land, NW Switzerland 47°30′N 07°36′E
64 O11 **Reina Sofía** ✈ (Tenerife) Tenerife, Islas Canarias, Spain, NE Atlantic Ocean
29 W13 **Reinbeck** Iowa, C USA 42°19′N 92°36′W
100 J10 **Reinbek** Schleswig-Holstein, N Germany 53°31′N 10°15′E
11 U12 **Reindeer** ≈ Saskatchewan, C Canada
11 U11 **Reindeer Lake** ◎ Manitoba/Saskatchewan, C Canada
Reine-Charlotte, Îles de la see Queen Charlotte Islands
Reine-Élisabeth, Îles de la see Queen Elizabeth Islands
94 F13 **Reineskarvet** ▲ S Norway 60°38′N 07°48′E
184 H1 **Reinga, Cape** headland North Island, New Zealand 34°24′S 172°40′E
105 N3 **Reinosa** Cantabria, N Spain 43°01′N 04°09′W
109 R8 **Reisseck** ▲ S Austria 46°57′N 13°21′E
21 W3 **Reisterstown** Maryland, NE USA 39°27′N 76°46′W
Reisui see Yŏsu
98 N5 **Reitdiep** ≈ NE Netherlands
191 V10 **Reitoru** atoll Îles Tuamotu, C French Polynesia
95 M17 **Rejmyre** Östergötland, S Sweden 58°49′N 15°55′E
Reka see Rijeka
Reka Ili see Ile/Ili He
95 N16 **Rekarne** Västmanland, C Sweden 59°25′N 16°04′E
Rekhovot see Rehovot
8 K9 **Reliance** Northwest Territories, C Canada 62°45′N 109°08′W
33 U16 **Reliance** Wyoming, C USA 41°42′N 109°13′W
74 I5 **Relizane** var. Ghelîzâne, Ghilizane. NW Algeria 35°45′N 00°33′E
182 I7 **Remarkable, Mount** ▲ South Australia 32°46′S 138°08′E
54 E8 **Remedios** Antioquia, N Colombia 07°02′N 74°42′W
43 Q16 **Remedios** Veraguas, W Panama 08°13′N 81°48′W
42 D8 **Remedios, Punta** headland SW El Salvador 13°31′N 89°48′W
Remi see Reims
99 N25 **Remich** Grevenmacher, SE Luxembourg 49°33′N 06°23′E
99 J19 **Remicourt** Liège, E Belgium 50°40′N 05°19′E
14 H8 **Rémigny, Lac** ◎ Québec, SE Canada
55 Z10 **Rémire** NE French Guiana 04°52′N 52°16′W
127 N13 **Remontnoye** Rostovskaya Oblast', SW Russian Federation 46°35′N 43°38′E
171 U14 **Remoon** Pulau Kur, E Indonesia 05°18′S 131°59′E
99 L20 **Remouchamps** Liège, E Belgium 50°29′N 05°43′E
103 R15 **Remoulins** Gard, S France 43°56′N 04°34′E
173 X16 **Rempart, Mont du** hill W Mauritius
101 E15 **Remscheid** Nordrhein-Westfalen, W Germany 51°10′N 07°11′E
29 S12 **Remsen** Iowa, C USA 42°48′N 95°58′W
94 I12 **Rena** Hedmark, S Norway 61°08′N 11°21′E
94 I11 **Renåa** ≈ S Norway
Renaix see Ronse
118 H7 **Renčēni** Valmiera, N Latvia 57°43′N 25°25′E
118 D9 **Renda** Kuldīga, W Latvia 57°04′N 22°18′E
107 N20 **Rende** Calabria, SW Italy 39°19′N 16°10′E
99 K21 **Rendeux** Luxembourg, SE Belgium 50°15′N 05°28′E
Rendina see Rentína
30 L16 **Rend Lake** ⊠ Illinois, N USA
186 K9 **Rendova** island New Georgia Islands, NW Solomon Islands
100 I8 **Rendsburg** Schleswig-Holstein, N Germany 54°18′N 09°40′E
108 B9 **Renens** Vaud, SW Switzerland 46°32′N 06°36′E
14 K12 **Renfrew** Ontario, SE Canada 45°28′N 76°44′W
96 I12 **Renfrew** cultural region SW Scotland, United Kingdom
168 L11 **Rengat** Sumatera, W Indonesia 0°26′S 102°38′E
153 W12 **Rengma Hills** ▲▲ NE India
62 H12 **Rengo** Libertador, C Chile 34°24′S 70°50′W
116 M12 **Reni** Odes'ka Oblast', SW Ukraine 45°30′N 28°18′E
80 F11 **Renk** Upper Nile, E Sudan 11°48′N 32°49′E
93 L19 **Renko** Etelä-Suomi, S Finland 60°52′N 24°16′E
98 L12 **Renkum** Gelderland, SE Netherlands 51°58′N 05°43′E
182 K9 **Renmark** South Australia 34°12′S 140°43′E
186 L10 **Rennell** var. Mu Nggava. island S Solomon Islands
181 Q4 **Renner Springs Roadhouse** Northern Territory, N Australia 18°12′S 133°48′E
102 I6 **Rennes** Bret. Roazon; anc. Condate. Ille-et-Vilaine, NW France 48°08′N 01°40′W
195 S16 **Rennick Glacier** glacier Antarctica
11 Y16 **Rennie** Manitoba, S Canada 49°51′N 95°28′W
35 Q5 **Reno** Nevada, W USA 39°32′N 119°49′W
106 H10 **Reno** ≈ N Italy
35 Q5 **Reno-Cannon** ✈ Nevada, W USA 39°26′N 119°42′W
83 F24 **Renoster** ≈ SW South Africa
15 T5 **Renouard, Lac** ◎ Québec, SE Canada
18 F13 **Renovo** Pennsylvania, NE USA 41°19′N 77°42′W
161 O3 **Renqiu** Hebei, E China 38°49′N 116°02′E
160 I9 **Renshou** Sichuan, C China 30°02′N 104°09′E
31 N12 **Rensselaer** Indiana, N USA 40°57′N 87°09′W
18 L11 **Rensselaer** New York, NE USA 42°38′N 73°44′W
Rentería see Errenteria
115 E17 **Rentína** var. Rendina. Thessalía, C Greece 39°04′N 21°58′E
29 T9 **Renville** Minnesota, N USA 44°48′N 95°13′W
77 O13 **Réo** W Burkina 12°20′N 02°28′W
15 O12 **Repentigny** Québec, SE Canada 45°42′N 73°28′W
146 K13 **Repetek** Lebap Welaýaty, E Turkmenistan 38°40′N 63°12′E
93 J16 **Replot** Fin. Raippaluoto. island W Finland
Repola see Reboly
Reppen see Rzepin
Reps see Rupea
27 T7 **Republic** Missouri, C USA 37°07′N 93°28′W
32 K7 **Republic** Washington, NW USA 48°39′N 118°44′W
27 N3 **Republican River** ≈ Kansas/Nebraska, C USA
9 O7 **Repulse Bay** Northwest Terretories, N Canada 66°35′N 86°20′W
56 F9 **Requena** Loreto, NE Peru 05°05′S 73°52′W
105 R10 **Requena** País Valenciano, E Spain 39°29′N 01°08′W
103 O14 **Réquista** Aveyron, S France 44°00′N 02°31′E
136 M12 **Reşadiye** Tokat, N Turkey 40°24′N 37°19′E
Reschenpass see Resia, Passo di
Reschitza see Reşiţa
113 N20 **Resen** Turk. Resne. SW FYR Macedonia 41°07′N 21°00′E
60 J11 **Reserva** Paraná, S Brazil 24°40′S 50°52′W
11 V15 **Reserve** Saskatchewan, S Canada 52°24′N 102°37′W
37 P13 **Reserve** New Mexico, SW USA 33°42′N 108°45′W
Reshetilovka see Reshetylivka
117 S6 **Reshetylivka** Rus. Reshetilovka. Poltavs'ka Oblast', NE Ukraine 49°34′N 34°05′E
Resht see Rasht
106 F5 **Resia, Passo di** Ger. Reschenpass. pass Austria/Italy
Resicabánya see Reşiţa
62 N7 **Resistencia** Chaco, NE Argentina 27°27′S 58°56′W
116 F12 **Reşiţa** Ger. Reschitza, Hung. Resicabánya. Caraş-Severin, W Romania 45°14′N 21°58′E
Resne see Resen
197 N9 **Resolute** Inuit Qausuittuq. Cornwallis Island, Nunavut, N Canada 74°41′N 94°54′W
Resolution see Fort Resolution
9 T7 **Resolution Island** island Nunavut, NE Canada
185 A23 **Resolution Island** island SW New Zealand
15 W7 **Restigouche** Québec, SE Canada 48°02′N 66°42′W
11 W17 **Reston** Manitoba, S Canada 49°33′N 101°03′W
14 H11 **Restoule Lake** ◎ Ontario, S Canada
54 F10 **Restrepo** Meta, C Colombia 04°20′N 73°29′W
42 B6 **Retalhuleu** Retalhuleu, SW Guatemala 14°31′N 91°40′W
42 A1 **Retalhuleu** off. Departamento de Retalhuleu. ❖ department SW Guatemala
Retalhuleu, Departamento de see Retalhuleu
97 N18 **Retford** C England, United Kingdom 53°18′N 00°52′W
103 Q3 **Rethel** Ardennes, N France 49°31′N 04°22′E
Rethimno/Réthimnon see Réthymno
115 I25 **Réthymno** prev. Rethimno, Réthimnon. Kriti, Greece, E Mediterranean Sea 35°21′N 24°29′E
Retiche, Alpi see Rhaetian Alps
99 J16 **Retie** Antwerpen, N Belgium 51°18′N 05°05′E
111 J21 **Rétság** Nógrád, N Hungary 47°57′N 19°08′E
109 W2 **Retz** Niederösterreich, NE Austria 48°46′N 15°58′E
173 N15 **Réunion** off. La Réunion. ◇ French overseas department W Indian Ocean
128 L17 **Réunion** island W Indian Ocean
105 U6 **Reus** Cataluña, E Spain 41°10′N 01°06′E
108 F7 **Reuss** ≈ NW Switzerland
99 J15 **Reusel** Noord-Brabant, S Netherlands 51°21′N 05°10′E
Reuţel see Ciuhuru
101 H22 **Reutlingen** Baden-Württemberg, S Germany 48°30′N 09°13′E
108 L7 **Reutte** Tirol, W Austria 47°30′N 10°44′E
99 M16 **Reuver** Limburg, SE Netherlands 51°17′N 06°05′E
28 K7 **Reva** South Dakota, N USA 45°30′N 103°03′W
Reval/Revel see Tallinn
124 J4 **Revda** Murmanskaya Oblast', NW Russian Federation 67°57′N 34°29′E
122 F6 **Revda** Sverdlovskaya Oblast', C Russian Federation 56°48′N 59°42′E
103 N16 **Revel** Haute-Garonne, S France 43°27′N 01°59′E
11 O16 **Revelstoke** British Columbia, SW Canada 51°02′N 118°12′W
43 N13 **Reventazón, Río** ≈ E Costa Rica
106 G9 **Revere** Lombardia, N Italy 45°03′N 11°07′E
39 Y14 **Revillagigedo Island** island Alexander Archipelago, Alaska, USA
193 R7 **Revillagigedo Islands** Mexico
103 R3 **Revin** Ardennes, N France 49°57′N 04°39′E
92 O3 **Revnosa** headland C Svalbard 78°03′N 18°52′E
Revolyutsii, Pik see Revolyutsiya, Qullai
147 T13 **Revolyutsiya, Qullai** Rus. Pik Revolyutsii. ▲ SE Tajikistan 38°40′N 72°26′E
111 L19 **Revúca** Ger. Grossrauschenbach, Hung. Nagyrőce. Banskobystrický Kraj, C Slovakia 48°40′N 20°10′E
154 K9 **Rewa** Madhya Pradesh, C India 24°32′N 81°18′E
152 I11 **Rewāri** Haryāna, N India 28°14′N 76°38′E
33 R14 **Rexburg** Idaho, NW USA 43°49′N 111°47′W
78 G13 **Rey Bouba** Nord, NE Cameroon 08°40′N 14°11′E
92 L3 **Reydharfjördhur** Austurland, E Iceland 65°02′N 14°12′W
57 K16 **Reyes** Beni, NW Bolivia 14°17′S 67°18′W
34 L8 **Reyes, Point** headland California, W USA 37°59′N 123°01′W
54 B12 **Reyes, Punta** headland SW Colombia 02°44′N 78°08′W
136 L17 **Reyhanlı** Hatay, S Turkey 36°16′N 36°35′E
43 U16 **Rey, Isla del** island Archipiélago de las Perlas, SE Panama
92 H2 **Reykhólar** Vestfirdhir, W Iceland 65°28′N 22°12′W
92 K2 **Reykjahlídh** Nordhurland Eystra, NE Iceland 65°37′N 16°54′W
92 I4 **Reykjanes** ❖ region SW Iceland
197 O16 **Reykjanes Basin** var. Irminger Basin. undersea feature N Atlantic Ocean 62°30′N 33°30′W
197 N17 **Reykjanes Ridge** undersea feature N Atlantic Ocean 62°00′N 27°00′W
92 H4 **Reykjavík** var. Reikjavik. ● (Iceland) Höfudhborgarsvaedhi, W Iceland 64°08′N 21°54′W
18 D13 **Reynoldsville** Pennsylvania, NE USA 41°04′N 78°51′W
41 P8 **Reynosa** Tamaulipas, C Mexico 26°03′N 98°19′W
Reẕā'īyeh see Orūmīyeh
Reẕā'īyeh, Daryācheh-ye see Orūmīyeh, Daryācheh-ye
102 I8 **Rezé** Loire-Atlantique, NW France 47°10′N 01°36′W
118 K10 **Rēzekne** Ger. Rositten; prev. Rus. Rezhitsa. Rēzekne, SE Latvia 56°31′N 27°22′E
Rezhitsa see Rēzekne
117 N9 **Rezina** NE Moldova 47°44′N 28°58′E
114 N11 **Rezovo** Turk. Rezve. Burgas, E Bulgaria 42°00′N 28°00′E
114 N11 **Rezovska Reka** Turk. Rezve Deresi. ≈ Bulgaria/Turkey see also Rezve Deresi
Rezovska Reka see Rezve Deresi
Rezve see Rezovo
114 N11 **Rezve Deresi** Bul. Rezovska Reka. ≈ Bulgaria/Turkey see also Rezovska Reka
Rezve Deresi see Rezovska Reka
Rhadames see Ghadāmis
Rhaedestus see Tekirdağ
108 J10 **Rhaetian Alps** Fr. Alpes Rhétiques, Ger. Rätische Alpen, It. Alpi Retiche. ▲▲ C Europe
108 I8 **Rhätikon** ▲▲ C Europe
101 G14 **Rheda-Wiedenbrück** Nordrhein-Westfalen, W Germany 51°51′N 08°17′E
98 M12 **Rheden** Gelderland, E Netherlands 52°01′N 06°03′E
Rhegion/Rhegium see Reggio di Calabria
Rheims see Reims
Rhein see Rhine
101 E17 **Rheinbach** Nordrhein-Westfalen, W Germany 50°37′N 06°57′E
100 F13 **Rheine** var. Rheine in Westfalen. Nordrhein-Westfalen, NW Germany 52°17′N 07°27′E
Rheine in Westfalen see Rheine
Rheinfeld see Rheinfelden
101 F24 **Rheinfelden** Baden-Württemberg, S Germany 47°34′N 07°46′E
108 E6 **Rheinfelden** var. Rheinfeld. Aargau, N Switzerland 47°33′N 07°47′E
101 E17 **Rheinisches Schiefergebirge** var. Rhine State Uplands, Eng. Rhenish Slate Mountains. ▲▲ W Germany
101 D18 **Rheinland-Pfalz** Eng. Rhineland-Palatinate, Fr. Rhénanie-Palatinat. ❖ state W Germany
101 G18 **Rhein Main** ✈ (Frankfurt am Main) Hessen, W Germany 50°03′N 08°33′E
Rhénanie du Nord-Westphalie see Nordrhein-Westfalen
Rhénanie-Palatinat see Rheinland-Pfalz
98 K12 **Rhenen** Utrecht, C Netherlands 52°01′N 06°02′E
Rhenish Slate Mountains see Rheinisches Schiefergebirge
Rhétiques, Alpes see Rhaetian Alps
100 N10 **Rhin** ≈ NE Germany
Rhin see Rhine
84 F10 **Rhine** Dut. Rijn, Fr. Rhin, Ger. Rhein. ≈ W Europe
30 L5 **Rhinelander** Wisconsin, N USA 45°39′N 89°23′W
Rhineland-Palatinate see Rheinland-Pfalz
Rhine State Uplands see Rheinisches Schiefergebirge
100 N11 **Rhinkanal** canal NE Germany
81 F17 **Rhino Camp** NW Uganda 02°58′N 31°24′E
74 D7 **Rhir, Cap** headland W Morocco 30°40′N 09°54′W
106 D7 **Rho** Lombardia, N Italy 45°32′N 09°02′E
19 N12 **Rhode Island** off. State of Rhode Island and Providence Plantations, also known as Little Rhody, Ocean State. ❖ state NE USA
19 O13 **Rhode Island** island Rhode Island, NE USA
19 O13 **Rhode Island Sound** sound Maine/Rhode Island, NE USA
Rhodes see Ródos
Rhode-Saint-Genèse see Sint-Genesius-Rode
84 L14 **Rhodes Basin** undersea feature E Mediterranean Sea 35°55′N 28°30′E
Rhodesia see Zimbabwe
114 I12 **Rhodope Mountains** var. Rodhópi Óri, Bul. Rhodope Planina, Rodopi, Gk. Orosirá Rodhópis, Turk. Dospad Dagh. ▲▲ Bulgaria/Greece
Rhodope Planina see Rhodope Mountains
101 I18 **Rhön** ▲▲ C Germany
103 Q10 **Rhône** ❖ department E France
86 C12 **Rhône** ≈ France/Switzerland
103 R12 **Rhône-Alpes** ❖ region E France
98 G13 **Rhoon** Zuid-Holland, SW Netherlands 51°52′N 04°25′E
96 G9 **Rhum** var. Rum. island W Scotland, United Kingdom
Rhuthun see Ruthin
97 J18 **Rhyl** NE Wales, United Kingdom 53°19′N 03°28′W
59 K18 **Rialma** Goiás, S Brazil 15°22′S 49°35′W
104 L3 **Riaño** Castilla-León, N Spain 42°59′N 05°00′W
105 O9 **Riansáres** ≈ C Spain
152 H6 **Riāsi** Jammu and Kashmir, NW India 33°03′N 74°51′E
168 K10 **Riau** off. Propinsi Riau. ❖ province W Indonesia
Riau Archipelago see Riau, Kepulauan
168 M11 **Riau, Kepulauan** var. Riau Archipelago, Dut. Riouw-Archipel. island group W Indonesia
Riau, Propinsi see Riau
105 O6 **Riaza** Castilla-León, N Spain 41°17′N 03°29′W
105 N6 **Riaza** ≈ N Spain
81 K17 **Riba** spring/well NE Kenya 01°56′N 40°38′E
104 H4 **Ribadavia** Galicia, NW Spain 42°17′N 08°08′W
104 J2 **Ribadeo** Galicia, NW Spain 43°32′N 07°04′W
104 L2 **Ribadesella** Asturias, N Spain 43°27′N 05°04′W
104 G10 **Ribatejo** former province C Portugal
83 P15 **Ribáuè** Nampula, N Mozambique 14°56′S 38°19′E
97 K17 **Ribble** ≈ NW England, United Kingdom
95 F23 **Ribe** Ribe, W Denmark 55°20′N 08°47′E
95 F23 **Ribe** off. Ribe Amt, var. Ripen. ❖ county W Denmark
Ribe Amt see Ribe
104 G3 **Ribeira** Galicia, NW Spain 42°33′N 09°01′W
64 O5 **Ribeira Brava** Madeira, Portugal, NE Atlantic Ocean 32°39′N 17°04′W
64 P3 **Ribeira Grande** São Miguel, Azores, Portugal, NE Atlantic Ocean 37°34′N 25°32′W
60 L8 **Ribeirão Preto** São Paulo, S Brazil 21°09′S 47°48′W
60 L11 **Ribeira, Rio** ≈ S Brazil
107 I24 **Ribera** Sicilia, Italy, C Mediterranean Sea 37°31′N 13°16′E
57 L14 **Riberalta** Beni, N Bolivia 11°01′S 66°04′W
105 W4 **Ribes de Freser** Cataluña, NE Spain 42°18′N 02°11′E
30 L6 **Rib Mountain** ▲ Wisconsin, N USA 44°55′N 89°41′W
109 U12 **Ribnica** Ger. Reifnitz. S Slovenia 45°46′N 14°40′E
117 N9 **Rîbniţa** var. Râbniţa, Rus. Rybnitsa. NE Moldova 47°46′N 29°01′E
100 M8 **Ribnitz-Damgarten** Mecklenburg-Vorpommern, NE Germany 54°14′N 12°25′E
111 D16 **Říčany** Ger. Ritschan. Středočeský Kraj, W Czech Republic 49°59′N 14°40′E
29 U7 **Rice** Minnesota, N USA 45°42′N 94°10′W
30 J5 **Rice Lake** Wisconsin, N USA 45°33′N 91°43′W
14 I15 **Rice Lake** ◎ Ontario, SE Canada
14 E8 **Rice Lake** ◎ Ontario, S Canada
23 V3 **Richard B. Russell Lake** ⊠ Georgia, SE USA
25 U6 **Richardson** Texas, SW USA 32°55′N 96°44′W
11 R11 **Richardson** ≈ Alberta, C Canada
10 I3 **Richardson Mountains** ▲▲ Yukon Territory, NW Canada
185 C21 **Richardson Mountains** ▲▲ South Island, New Zealand
42 F3 **Richardson Peak** ▲ SE Belize 16°34′N 88°46′W
76 G10 **Richard Toll** N Senegal 16°28′N 15°44′W
28 L5 **Richardton** North Dakota, N USA 46°52′N 102°19′W
14 F13 **Rich, Cape** headland Ontario, S Canada 44°42′N 80°37′W
102 L8 **Richelieu** Indre-et-Loire, C France 47°01′N 00°18′E
33 P15 **Richfield** Idaho, NW USA 43°03′N 114°11′W
36 K5 **Richfield** Utah, W USA 38°45′N 112°05′W
18 J10 **Richfield Springs** New York, NE USA 42°52′N 74°57′W
18 M6 **Richford** Vermont, NE USA 44°59′N 72°37′W
27 R6 **Rich Hill** Missouri, C USA 38°06′N 94°22′W
13 P14 **Richibucto** New Brunswick, SE Canada 46°42′N 64°54′W
108 G8 **Richisau** Glarus, NE Switzerland 47°00′N 08°54′E
23 S6 **Richland** Georgia, SE USA 32°05′N 84°40′W
27 U6 **Richland** Missouri, C USA 37°51′N 92°24′W
25 U8 **Richland** Texas, SW USA 31°55′N 96°25′W
32 K10 **Richland** Washington, NW USA 46°17′N 119°16′W
30 K8 **Richland Center** Wisconsin, N USA 43°22′N 90°24′W
21 W11 **Richlands** North Carolina, SE USA 34°52′N 77°33′W
21 Q7 **Richlands** Virginia, NE USA 37°05′N 81°47′W
25 R9 **Richland Springs** Texas, SW USA 31°16′N 98°56′W
183 S8 **Richmond** New South Wales, SE Australia 33°36′S 150°44′E
10 L17 **Richmond** British Columbia, SW Canada 49°07′N 123°09′W
14 L13 **Richmond** Ontario, SE Canada 45°12′N 75°49′W
15 Q12 **Richmond** Québec, SE Canada 45°39′N 72°07′W
185 I14 **Richmond** Tasman, South Island, New Zealand 41°25′S 173°04′E
35 N8 **Richmond** California, W USA 37°57′N 122°22′W
31 Q14 **Richmond** Indiana, N USA 39°50′N 84°51′W
20 M6 **Richmond** Kentucky, S USA 37°45′N 84°19′W
27 S4 **Richmond** Missouri, C USA 39°15′N 93°59′W
25 V11 **Richmond** Texas, SW USA 29°36′N 95°48′W
36 L1 **Richmond** Utah, W USA 41°55′N 111°51′W
21 W6 **Richmond** state capital Virginia, NE USA 37°33′N 77°28′W
14 H15 **Richmond Hill** Ontario, S Canada 43°51′N 79°24′W
185 J15 **Richmond Range** ▲▲ South Island, New Zealand
27 S12 **Rich Mountain** ▲ Arkansas, C USA 34°37′N 94°17′W
31 S13 **Richwood** Ohio, N USA 40°25′N 83°18′W
21 R5 **Richwood** West Virginia, NE USA 38°13′N 80°31′W
104 K5 **Ricobayo, Embalse de** ⊠ NW Spain
Ricomagus see Riom
Ridā' see Radā'
145 X9 **Ridder** Kaz. Leningor. Vostochnyy Kazakhstan, E Kazakhstan 50°20′N 83°34′E
98 H13 **Ridderkerk** Zuid-Holland, SW Netherlands 51°52′N 04°35′E
33 N16 **Riddle** Idaho, NW USA 42°07′N 116°09′W
32 F14 **Riddle** Oregon, NW USA 42°57′N 123°21′W
14 L13 **Rideau** ≈ Ontario, SE Canada
35 T12 **Ridgecrest** California, W USA 35°37′N 117°40′W
18 L13 **Ridgefield** Connecticut, NE USA 41°16′N 73°30′W
22 K5 **Ridgeland** Mississippi, S USA 32°25′N 90°07′W
21 R15 **Ridgeland** South Carolina, SE USA 32°30′N 80°59′W
20 F8 **Ridgely** Tennessee, S USA 36°15′N 89°29′W
14 D17 **Ridgetown** Ontario, S Canada 42°27′N 81°52′W
21 R12 **Ridgeway** South Carolina, SE USA 34°17′N 80°56′W
Ridgeway see Ridgway
18 D13 **Ridgway** var. Ridgeway. Pennsylvania, NE USA 41°24′N 78°40′W
11 W16 **Riding Mountain** ▲▲ Manitoba, S Canada
Ried see Ried im Innkreis
109 R4 **Ried im Innkreis** var. Ried. Oberösterreich, NW Austria 48°13′N 13°29′E
109 X8 **Riegersburg** Steiermark, SE Austria 47°03′N 15°52′E
108 E6 **Riehen** Basel-Stadt, NW Switzerland 47°35′N 07°39′E
92 J9 **Riehppegáisá** var. Rieppe. ▲ N Norway 69°38′N 21°31′E
99 K18 **Riemst** Limburg, NE Belgium 50°49′N 05°36′E
Rieppe see Riehppegáisá
101 O15 **Riesa** Sachsen, E Germany 51°18′N 13°18′E
63 H24 **Riesco, Isla** island S Chile
107 K25 **Riesi** Sicilia, Italy, C Mediterranean Sea 37°17′N 14°05′E
83 F25 **Riet** ≈ SW South Africa
83 I23 **Riet** ≈ SW South Africa
118 D11 **Rietavas** Telšiai, W Lithuania 55°43′N 21°56′E
83 F19 **Rietfontein** Omaheke, E Namibia 21°58′S 20°58′E
107 I14 **Rieti** anc. Reate. Lazio, C Italy 42°24′N 12°51′E
84 D14 **Rif** var. Riff, Er Rif, Er Riff. ▲▲ N Morocco
Riff see Rif
37 Q4 **Rifle** Colorado, C USA 39°30′N 107°46′W
31 R7 **Rifle River** ≈ Michigan, N USA
81 H18 **Rift Valley** ❖ province Kenya
Rift Valley see Great Rift Valley
118 F9 **Rīga** Eng. Riga. ● (Latvia) Rīga, C Latvia 56°57′N 24°08′E
Rigaer Bucht see Riga, Gulf of
118 F6 **Riga, Gulf of** Est. Liivi Laht, Ger. Rigaer Bucht, Latv. Rīgas Jūras Līcis, Rus. Rizhskiy Zaliv; prev. Est. Riia Laht. gulf Estonia/Latvia
Rīgas Jūras Līcis see Riga, Gulf of
15 N12 **Rigaud** ≈ Ontario/Québec, SE Canada
33 R14 **Rigby** Idaho, NW USA 43°40′N 111°54′W
148 M10 **Rīgestān** var. Registan. desert region S Afghanistan
32 M11 **Riggins** Idaho, NW USA 45°24′N 116°18′W
13 R8 **Rigolet** Newfoundland and Labrador, NE Canada 54°10′N 58°25′W
78 G9 **Rig-Rig** Kanem, W Chad 14°16′N 14°21′E
118 F4 **Riguldi** Läänemaa, W Estonia 59°07′N 23°34′E
Riia Laht see Riga, Gulf of
93 L19 **Riihimäki** Etelä-Suomi, S Finland 60°45′N 24°45′E
195 O2 **Riiser-Larsenisen** ice shelf Antarctica
195 U2 **Riiser-Larsen Peninsula** peninsula Antarctica
65 P22 **Riiser-Larsen Sea** sea Antarctica
40 D2 **Riito** Sonora, NW Mexico 32°06′N 114°57′W
112 B9 **Rijeka** Ger. Sankt Veit am Flaum, It. Fiume, Slvn. Reka; anc. Tarsatica. Primorje-Gorski Kotar, NW Croatia 45°20′N 14°26′E
99 I14 **Rijen** Noord-Brabant, S Netherlands 51°35′N 04°55′E
99 H15 **Rijkevorsel** Antwerpen, N Belgium 51°23′N 04°43′E
Rijn see Rhine
98 G11 **Rijnsburg** Zuid-Holland, W Netherlands 52°12′N 04°27′E
Rijssel see Lille
98 N10 **Rijssen** Overijssel, E Netherlands 52°19′N 06°30′E
98 G12 **Rijswijk** Eng. Ryswick. Zuid-Holland, W Netherlands 52°03′N 04°20′E
92 I10 **Riksgränsen** Norrbotten, N Sweden 68°24′N 18°15′E
165 U4 **Rikubetsu** Hokkaidō, NE Japan 43°30′N 143°43′E
165 R9 **Rikuzen-Takata** Iwate, Honshū, C Japan 39°03′N 141°38′E
27 O4 **Riley** Kansas, C USA 39°18′N 96°49′W
99 I17 **Rillaar** Vlaams Brabant, C Belgium 50°58′N 04°58′E
Rí, Loch see Ree, Lough
114 G11 **Rilska Reka** ≈ W Bulgaria
77 T12 **Rima** ≈ N Nigeria
141 N7 **Rimah, Wādī ar** var. Wādī ar Rummah. dry watercourse C Saudi Arabia
Rimaszombat see Rimavská Sobota
191 R12 **Rimatara** island Îles Australes, SW French Polynesia
111 L20 **Rimavská Sobota** Ger. Gross-Steffelsdorf, Hung. Rimaszombat. Bankobystrický Kraj, C Slovakia 48°24′N 20°01′E
11 Q15 **Rimbey** Alberta, SW Canada 52°39′N 114°10′W
95 P15 **Rimbo** Stockholm, C Sweden 59°44′N 18°21′E
95 M18 **Rimforsa** Östergötland, S Sweden 58°06′N 15°40′E
106 I11 **Rimini** anc. Ariminum. Emilia-Romagna, N Italy 44°03′N 12°33′E
Rîmnicu-Sărat see Râmnicu Sărat
Rîmnicu Vîlcea see Râmnicu Vâlcea
149 Y3 **Rimo Muztāgh** ▲▲ India/Pakistan
15 U7 **Rimouski** Québec, SE Canada 48°26′N 68°32′W
158 M16 **Rinbung** Xizang Zizhiqu, W China 29°15′N 89°40′E
Rinchinlhumbe see Dzöölön
62 I5 **Rincón, Cerro** ▲ N Chile 24°01′S 67°19′W
104 M15 **Rincón de la Victoria** Andalucía, S Spain 36°43′N 04°18′W
Rincón del Bonete, Lago Artificial de see Río Negro, Embalse del
105 Q4 **Rincón de Soto** La Rioja, N Spain 42°15′N 01°50′W
94 G8 **Rindal** Møre og Romsdal, S Norway 63°02′N 09°09′E
115 J20 **Ríneia** island Kykládes, Greece, Aegean Sea
152 H11 **Rīngas** prev. Reengus, Rīngus. Rājasthān, N India 27°18′N 75°27′E
95 H24 **Ringe** Fyn, C Denmark 55°14′N 10°30′E
94 H11 **Ringebu** Oppland, S Norway 61°31′N 10°09′E
Ringen see Rõngu
186 K8 **Ringgi** Kolombangara, NW Solomon Islands 08°03′S 157°08′E
23 R1 **Ringgold** Georgia, SE USA 34°55′N 85°06′W
22 G5 **Ringgold** Louisiana, S USA 32°19′N 93°16′W
25 S5 **Ringgold** Texas, SW USA 33°47′N 97°56′W
95 E22 **Ringkøbing** Ringkøbing, W Denmark 56°04′N 08°22′E
95 E21 **Ringkøbing** var. Ringkøbing Amt. ❖ county W Denmark
Ringkøbing Amt see Ringkøbing
95 E22 **Ringkøbing Fjord** fjord W Denmark
33 S10 **Ringling** Montana, NW USA 46°15′N 110°48′W
27 N13 **Ringling** Oklahoma, C USA 34°12′N 97°35′W
94 H13 **Ringsaker** Hedmark, S Norway 60°54′N 10°45′E
95 I23 **Ringsted** Vestsjælland, E Denmark 55°28′N 11°48′E
Ringus see Rīngas
92 I9 **Ringvassøya** Lapp. Ráneš. island N Norway
18 K13 **Ringwood** New Jersey, NE USA 41°06′N 74°15′W
Rinn Duáin see Hook Head
100 H13 **Rinteln** Niedersachsen, NW Germany 52°10′N 09°04′E
115 E18 **Río** Dytikí Ellás, S Greece 38°18′N 21°48′E
Rio see Rio de Janeiro
56 C7 **Riobamba** Chimborazo, C Ecuador 01°44′S 78°40′W
60 P9 **Rio Bonito** Rio de Janeiro, SE Brazil 22°42′S 42°38′W
59 C16 **Rio Branco** state capital Acre, W Brazil 09°59′S 67°49′W
61 H18 **Río Branco** Cerro Largo, NE Uruguay 32°32′S 53°28′W
Rio Branco, Território de see Roraima
41 P8 **Río Bravo** Tamaulipas, C Mexico 25°57′N 98°03′W
63 G16 **Río Bueno** Los Lagos, C Chile 40°20′S 72°55′W
55 P5 **Río Caribe** Sucre, NE Venezuela 10°43′N 63°06′W
54 M5 **Río Chico** Miranda, N Venezuela 10°18′N 66°00′W
63 H18 **Río Cisnes** Aisén, S Chile 44°29′S 71°15′W
60 L9 **Rio Claro** São Paulo, S Brazil 22°19′S 47°35′W
45 V14 **Rio Claro** Trinidad, Trinidad and Tobago 10°18′N 61°11′W
54 J5 **Río Claro** Lara, N Venezuela 09°54′N 69°23′W
63 K15 **Río Colorado** Río Negro, E Argentina 39°01′S 64°05′W
62 K11 **Río Cuarto** Córdoba, C Argentina 33°06′S 64°20′W
60 P10 **Rio de Janeiro** var. Rio. state capital Rio de Janeiro, SE Brazil 22°53′S 43°17′W
60 P9 **Rio de Janeiro** off. Estado do Rio de Janeiro. ❖ state SE Brazil
Rio de Janeiro, Estado do see Rio de Janeiro
43 R17 **Río de Jesús** Veraguas, S Panama 07°58′N 81°01′W
34 K3 **Rio Dell** California, W USA 40°30′N 124°07′W

◆ Country ● Country Capital ◇ Dependent Territory ○ Dependent Territory Capital ❖ Administrative Regions ✈ International Airport ▲ Mountain ▲▲ Mountain Range Volcano ≈ River ◎ Lake ⊠ Reservoir

RIO DO SUL – ROSALIE

60 K13 **Rio do Sul** Santa Catarina, S Brazil 27°15′S 49°37′W
63 I23 **Río Gallegos** *var.* Gallegos, Puerto Gallegos. Santa Cruz, S Argentina 51°40′S 69°21′W
63 J24 **Río Grande** Tierra del Fuego, S Argentina 53°45′S 67°46′W
61 I18 **Rio Grande** *var.* São Pedro do Rio Grande do Sul. Rio Grande do Sul, S Brazil 32°03′S 52°08′W
40 L10 **Río Grande** Zacatecas, C Mexico 23°50′N 103°20′W
42 J9 **Río Grande** León, NW Nicaragua 12°59′N 86°34′W
45 V5 **Río Grande** E Puerto Rico 18°23′N 65°51′W
24 I9 **Rio Grande** ≈ Texas, SW USA
25 R17 **Rio Grande City** Texas, SW USA 26°24′N 98°50′W
59 P14 **Rio Grande do Norte** *off.* Estado do Rio Grande do Norte. ⬖ *state* E Brazil
Rio Grande do Norte, Estado do *see* Rio Grande do Norte
61 G15 **Rio Grande do Sul** *off.* Estado do Rio Grande do Sul. ⬖ *state* S Brazil
Rio Grande do Sul, Estado do *see* Rio Grande do Sul
65 M17 **Rio Grande Fracture Zone** *tectonic feature* C Atlantic Ocean
65 J18 **Rio Grande Gap** *undersea feature* S Atlantic Ocean
Rio Grande Plateau *see* Rio Grande Rise
65 J18 **Rio Grande Rise** *var.* Rio Grande Plateau. *undersea feature* SW Atlantic Ocean 31°00′S 35°00′W
54 G4 **Ríohacha** La Guajira, N Colombia 11°23′N 72°47′W
43 S16 **Río Hato** Coclé, C Panama 08°21′N 80°10′W
25 T17 **Rio Hondo** Texas, SW USA 26°14′N 97°34′W
56 D10 **Rioja** San Martín, N Peru 06°02′S 77°10′W
41 Y11 **Río Lagartos** Yucatán, SE Mexico 21°35′N 88°08′W
103 P11 **Riom** *anc.* Ricomagus. Puy-de-Dôme, C France 45°54′N 03°06′E
104 F10 **Rio Maior** Santarém, C Portugal 39°20′N 08°55′W
103 O12 **Riom-ès-Montagnes** Cantal, C France 45°15′N 02°39′E
60 J12 **Rio Negro** Paraná, S Brazil 26°06′S 49°46′W
63 I15 **Río Negro** *off.* Provincia de Río Negro. ⬖ *province* C Argentina
61 D18 **Río Negro** ⬖ *department* W Uruguay
47 V12 **Río Negro, Embalse del** *var.* Lago Artificial de Rincón del Bonete. ⊠ C Uruguay
Río Negro, Provincia de *see* Río Negro
107 M17 **Rionero in Vulture** Basilicata, S Italy 40°55′N 15°40′E
137 S9 **Rioni** ≈ W Georgia
105 P12 **Riópar** Castilla-La Mancha, C Spain 38°31′N 02°27′W
61 H16 **Rio Pardo** Rio Grande do Sul, S Brazil 29°41′S 52°25′W
37 R11 **Rio Rancho Estates** New Mexico, SW USA 35°14′N 106°40′W
42 L11 **Río San Juan** ⬖ *department* S Nicaragua
54 E9 **Ríosucio** Caldas, W Colombia 05°26′N 75°44′W
54 C7 **Ríosucio** Chocó, NW Colombia 07°25′N 77°05′W
62 K10 **Río Tercero** Córdoba, C Argentina 32°15′S 64°08′W
42 K5 **Río Tinto, Sierra** ▲▲ NE Honduras
54 J5 **Río Tocuyo** Lara, N Venezuela 10°18′N 70°00′W
Riouw-Archipel *see* Riau, Kepulauan
59 J19 **Rio Verde** Goiás, C Brazil 17°50′S 50°55′W
41 O12 **Río Verde** *var.* Rioverde. San Luis Potosí, C Mexico 21°58′N 100°W
Rioverde *see* Río Verde
35 O8 **Rio Vista** California, W USA 38°09′N 121°42′W
112 M11 **Ripanj** Serbia, N Serbia 44°37′N 20°30′E
106 J13 **Ripatransone** Marche, C Italy 43°00′N 13°45′E
Ripen *see* Ribe
22 M2 **Ripley** Mississippi, S USA 34°43′N 88°57′W
31 R15 **Ripley** Ohio, N USA 38°45′N 83°51′W
20 F9 **Ripley** Tennessee, S USA 35°43′N 89°30′W
21 Q4 **Ripley** West Virginia, NE USA 38°49′N 81°44′W
105 W4 **Ripoll** Cataluña, NE Spain 42°12′N 02°12′E
97 M16 **Ripon** N England, United Kingdom 54°07′N 01°31′W
30 M7 **Ripon** Wisconsin, N USA 43°52′N 88°48′W
107 L24 **Riposto** Sicilia, Italy, C Mediterranean Sea 37°44′N 15°13′E
99 L14 **Rips** Noord-Brabant, SE Netherlands 51°31′N 05°49′E
54 D9 **Risaralda** *off.* Departamento de Risaralda. ⬖ *province* C Colombia
Risaralda, Departamento de *see* Risaralda
116 L8 **Rîşcani** *var.* Râşcani, *Rus.* Ryshkany. NW Moldova 47°55′N 27°31′E
152 J9 **Rishikesh** Uttarakhand, N India 30°06′N 78°16′E
165 S1 **Rishiri-tō** *var.* Risiri Tô. *island* NE Japan
165 S1 **Rishiri-yama** ※ Rishiri-tō, NE Japan 45°11′N 141°11′E
25 R7 **Rising Star** Texas, SW USA 32°06′N 98°57′W
31 Q15 **Rising Sun** Indiana, N USA 38°58′N 84°53′W
Risiri Tô *see* Rishiri-tō
102 L4 **Risle** ≈ N France
Rîşno *see* Râşnov
27 V13 **Rison** Arkansas, C USA 33°58′N 92°11′W
95 G17 **Risør** Aust-Agder, S Norway 58°44′N 09°15′E
92 H10 **Risøyhamn** Nordland, C Norway 69°00′N 15°37′E
101 I23 **Riss** ≈ S Germany
118 G4 **Risti** *Ger.* Kreuz. Läänemaa, W Estonia 59°01′N 24°01′E
15 V8 **Ristigouche** ≈ Québec, SE Canada
93 N18 **Ristiina** Itä-Suomi, E Finland 61°32′N 27°15′E
93 N14 **Ristijärvi** Oulu, C Finland 64°30′N 28°15′E
188 C14 **Ritidian Point** *headland* N Guam 13°39′N 144°51′E
Ritschan *see* Říčany
35 R9 **Ritter, Mount** ▲ California, W USA 37°40′N 119°10′W
31 T12 **Rittman** Ohio, N USA 40°58′N 81°46′W
32 L9 **Ritzville** Washington, NW USA 47°07′N 118°22′W
Riva *see* Riva del Garda
61 A21 **Rivadavia** Buenos Aires, E Argentina 35°29′S 62°59′W
106 F7 **Riva del Garda** *var.* Riva. Trentino-Alto Adige, N Italy 45°54′N 10°50′E
106 B8 **Rivarolo Canavese** Piemonte, W Italy 45°21′N 07°42′E
42 K11 **Rivas** Rivas, SW Nicaragua 11°26′N 85°50′W
42 J11 **Rivas** ⬖ *department* SW Nicaragua
103 R11 **Rive-de-Gier** Loire, E France 45°31′N 04°36′E
61 A22 **Rivera** Buenos Aires, E Argentina 37°13′S 63°14′W
61 F16 **Rivera** Rivera, NE Uruguay 30°54′S 55°31′W
61 F17 **Rivera** ⬖ *department* NE Uruguay
35 P9 **Riverbank** California, W USA 37°43′N 120°59′W
76 K17 **River Cess** SW Liberia 05°28′N 09°32′W
28 M4 **Riverdale** North Dakota, N USA 47°29′N 101°22′W
30 I6 **River Falls** Wisconsin, N USA 44°52′N 92°38′W
11 T16 **Riverhurst** Saskatchewan, S Canada 50°52′N 106°49′W
183 O10 **Riverina** *physical region* New South Wales, SE Australia
80 G8 **River Nile** ⬖ *state* NE Sudan
63 F19 **Rivero, Isla** *island* Archipiélago de los Chonos, S Chile
11 W16 **Rivers** Manitoba, S Canada 50°02′N 100°14′W
77 U17 **Rivers** ⬖ *state* S Nigeria
185 D23 **Riversdale** Southland, South Island, New Zealand 45°54′S 168°44′E
83 F26 **Riversdale** Western Cape, SW South Africa 34°05′S 21°15′E
35 U15 **Riverside** California, W USA 33°58′N 117°25′W
25 W9 **Riverside** Texas, SW USA 30°51′N 95°24′W
37 U3 **Riverside Reservoir** ⊠ Colorado, C USA
10 K15 **Rivers Inlet** British Columbia, SW Canada 51°43′N 127°19′W
10 K15 **Rivers Inlet** *inlet* British Columbia, SW Canada
11 X15 **Riverton** Manitoba, S Canada 51°00′N 97°00′W
185 C24 **Riverton** Southland, South Island, New Zealand 46°20′S 168°02′E
30 L13 **Riverton** Illinois, N USA 39°50′N 89°31′W
36 L3 **Riverton** Utah, W USA 40°32′N 111°57′W
33 V15 **Riverton** Wyoming, C USA 43°01′N 108°22′W
14 G10 **River Valley** Ontario, S Canada 46°36′N 80°09′W
13 P14 **Riverview** New Brunswick, SE Canada 46°03′N 64°47′W
103 O17 **Rivesaltes** Pyrénées-Orientales, S France 42°46′N 02°48′E
36 H11 **Riviera** Arizona, SW USA 35°06′N 114°36′W
25 S15 **Riviera** Texas, SW USA 27°15′N 97°48′W
23 Z14 **Riviera Beach** Florida, SE USA 26°46′N 80°03′W
15 Q10 **Rivière-à-Pierre** Québec, SE Canada 46°59′N 72°12′W
15 T9 **Rivière-Bleue** Québec, SE Canada 47°26′N 69°02′W
15 T8 **Rivière-du-Loup** Québec, SE Canada 47°49′N 69°32′W
173 Y15 **Rivière du Rempart** NE Mauritius 20°06′S 57°41′E
45 R12 **Rivière-Pilote** S Martinique 14°29′N 60°54′W
173 O17 **Rivière St-Etienne, Point de la** *headland* SW Réunion
13 S10 **Rivière-St-Paul** Québec, E Canada 51°26′N 57°52′W
Rivière Sèche *see* Bel Air
116 K4 **Rivne** *Pol.* Równe, *Rus.* Rovno. Rivnens'ka Oblast', NW Ukraine 50°37′N 26°16′E
Rivne *see* Rivnens'ka Oblast'
116 K3 **Rivnens'ka Oblast'** *var.* Rivne, *Rus.* Rovenskaya Oblast'. ⬖ *province* NW Ukraine
106 B8 **Rivoli** Piemonte, NW Italy 45°04′N 07°31′E
159 Q14 **Riwoqê** *var.* Racaka. Xizang Zizhiqu, W China 31°10′N 96°25′E
99 H19 **Rixensart** Walloon Brabant, C Belgium 50°43′N 04°32′E
Riyadh/Riyāḍ, Minṭaqat ar *see* Ar Riyāḍ
Riyāq *see* Rayak
Rizaiyeh *see* Orūmīyeh
137 P11 **Rize** Rize, NE Turkey 41°03′N 40°33′E
137 P11 **Rize** *prev.* Çoruh. ⬖ *province* NE Turkey
161 R5 **Rizhao** Shandong, E China 35°23′N 119°31′E
Rizhskiy Zaliv *see* Riga, Gulf of
Rizokarpaso/Rizokárpason *see* Dipkarpaz
107 O21 **Rizzuto, Capo** *headland* S Italy 38°54′N 17°05′E
95 F15 **Rjukan** Telemark, S Norway 59°54′N 08°33′E
95 D16 **Rjuven** ▲▲ S Norway
76 H9 **Rkîz** Trarza, W Mauritania 16°50′N 15°20′W
115 Q23 **Ro** *prev.* Ágios Geórgios. *island* SE Greece
95 H14 **Roa** Oppland, S Norway 60°16′N 10°38′E
105 N5 **Roa** Castilla-León, N Spain 41°42′N 03°55′W
45 T9 **Road Town** ○ (British Virgin Islands) Tortola, C British Virgin Islands 18°28′N 64°39′W
96 F6 **Roag, Loch** *inlet* NW Scotland, United Kingdom
37 O5 **Roan Cliffs** *cliff* Colorado/Utah, W USA
21 P9 **Roan High Knob** *var.* Roan Mountain. ▲ North Carolina/Tennessee, SE USA 36°09′N 82°07′W
Roan Mountain *see* Roan High Knob
103 Q10 **Roanne** *anc.* Rodunma. Loire, E France 46°03′N 04°04′E
23 R4 **Roanoke** Alabama, S USA 33°09′N 85°22′W
21 S7 **Roanoke** Virginia, NE USA 37°16′N 79°57′W
21 Z9 **Roanoke Island** *island* North Carolina, SE USA
21 W8 **Roanoke Rapids** North Carolina, SE USA 36°27′N 77°39′W
21 X9 **Roanoke River** ≈ North Carolina/Virginia, SE USA
37 O4 **Roan Plateau** *plain* Utah, W USA
37 R5 **Roaring Fork River** ≈ Colorado, C USA
25 O5 **Roaring Springs** Texas, SW USA 33°54′N 100°51′W
42 J4 **Roatán** *var.* Coxen Hole, Coxin Hole. Islas de la Bahía, N Honduras 16°19′N 86°33′W
42 I4 **Roatán, Isla de** *island* Islas de la Bahía, N Honduras
Roat Kampuchea *see* Cambodia
Roazon *see* Rennes
143 T7 **Robāṭ-e Chāh Gonbad** Yazd, E Iran 33°24′N 57°43′E
143 R7 **Robāṭ-e Khān** Yazd, C Iran 33°24′N 56°04′E
143 T7 **Robāṭ-e Khvosh Āb** Yazd, E Iran
143 R8 **Robāṭ-e Posht-e Bādām** Yazd, NE Iran 33°01′N 55°34′E
143 Q8 **Robaṭ-e Rīzāb** Yazd, C Iran
175 S8 **Robbie Ridge** *undersea feature* W Pacific Ocean
21 T10 **Robbins** North Carolina, SE USA 35°25′N 79°35′W
183 N15 **Robbins Island** *island* Tasmania, SE Australia
21 N10 **Robbinsville** North Carolina, SE USA 35°18′N 83°49′W
182 J12 **Robe** South Australia 37°11′S 139°48′E
21 W9 **Robersonville** North Carolina, SE USA 35°49′N 77°15′W
25 P8 **Robert Lee** Texas, SW USA 31°50′N 100°30′W
35 V5 **Roberts Creek Mountain** ▲ Nevada, W USA 39°52′N 116°16′W
93 J15 **Robertsfors** Västerbotten, N Sweden 64°12′N 20°50′E
153 N14 **Robertsganj** Uttar Pradesh, N India 24°41′N 83°04′E
27 R11 **Robert S. Kerr Reservoir** ⊠ Oklahoma, C USA
38 L12 **Roberts Mountain** ▲ Nunivak Island, Alaska, USA 60°01′N 166°15′W
83 F26 **Robertson** Western Cape, SW South Africa 33°48′S 19°53′E
194 H4 **Robertson Island** *island* Antarctica
76 J16 **Robertsport** W Liberia 06°45′N 11°15′W
182 J8 **Robertstown** South Australia 34°00′S 139°04′E
Robert Williams *see* Caála
15 P7 **Roberval** Québec, SE Canada 48°31′N 72°16′W
31 N15 **Robinson** Illinois, N USA 39°00′N 87°44′W
193 U11 **Róbinson Crusoe, Isla** *island* Islas Juan Fernández, Chile, E Pacific Ocean
180 J9 **Robinson Range** ▲▲ Western Australia
182 M9 **Robinvale** Victoria, SE Australia 34°37′S 142°45′E
105 P11 **Robledo** Castilla-La Mancha, C Spain 38°45′N 02°27′W
54 G5 **Robles** *var.* La Paz, Robles La Paz. Cesar, N Colombia 10°24′N 73°11′W
Robles La Paz *see* Robles
11 V15 **Roblin** Manitoba, S Canada 51°15′N 101°20′W
11 S17 **Robsart** Saskatchewan, S Canada 49°22′N 109°15′W
11 N15 **Robson, Mount** ▲ British Columbia, SW Canada 53°09′N 119°16′W
25 T14 **Robstown** Texas, SW USA 27°47′N 97°40′W
25 P6 **Roby** Texas, SW USA 32°42′N 100°23′W
104 E11 **Roca, Cabo da** *cape* C Portugal
Rocadas *see* Xangongo
41 S14 **Roca Partida, Punta** *headland* C Mexico 18°43′N 95°11′W
47 X6 **Rocas, Atol das** *island* E Brazil
107 L18 **Roccadaspide** *var.* Rocca d'Aspide. Campania, S Italy 40°25′N 15°12′E
Rocca d'Aspide *see* Roccadaspide
107 K15 **Roccaraso** Abruzzo, C Italy 41°49′N 14°01′E
106 H10 **Rocca San Casciano** Emilia-Romagna, C Italy 44°06′N 11°51′E
106 G13 **Roccastrada** Toscana, C Italy 43°00′N 11°09′E
61 G20 **Rocha** Rocha, E Uruguay 34°30′S 54°22′W
61 G19 **Rocha** ⬖ *department* E Uruguay
97 L17 **Rochdale** NW England, United Kingdom 53°38′N 02°09′W
102 L11 **Rochechouart** Haute-Vienne, C France 45°49′N 00°49′E
99 J22 **Rochefort** Namur, SE Belgium 50°10′N 05°13′E
102 J11 **Rochefort** *var.* Rochefort sur Mer. Charente-Maritime, W France 45°57′N 00°58′W
Rochefort sur Mer *see* Rochefort
125 N10 **Rochegda** Arkhangel'skaya Oblast', NW Russian Federation 62°37′N 43°21′E
30 L10 **Rochelle** Illinois, N USA 41°54′N 89°03′W
25 Q9 **Rochelle** Texas, SW USA 31°13′N 99°10′W
15 V3 **Rochers Ouest, Rivière aux** ≈ Québec, SE Canada
97 O22 **Rochester** *anc.* Durobrivae. SE England, United Kingdom 51°24′N 00°30′E
31 O12 **Rochester** Indiana, N USA 41°03′N 86°13′W
29 W10 **Rochester** Minnesota, N USA 44°01′N 92°28′W
19 O9 **Rochester** New Hampshire, NE USA 43°18′N 70°58′W
18 F9 **Rochester** New York, NE USA 43°09′N 77°37′W
25 P5 **Rochester** Texas, SW USA 33°19′N 99°51′W
31 S9 **Rochester Hills** Michigan, N USA 42°39′N 83°04′W
Rocheuses, Montagnes/Rockies *see* Rocky Mountains
64 M6 **Rockall** *island* N Atlantic Ocean, United Kingdom
64 L6 **Rockall Bank** *undersea feature* N Atlantic Ocean
84 B8 **Rockall Rise** *undersea feature* N Atlantic Ocean 59°00′N 14°00′W
84 C9 **Rockall Trough** *undersea feature* N Atlantic Ocean 57°00′N 12°00′W
35 U2 **Rock Creek** ≈ Nevada, W USA
25 T10 **Rockdale** Texas, SW USA 30°39′N 96°58′W
195 N12 **Rockefeller Plateau** *plateau* Antarctica
30 K11 **Rock Falls** Illinois, N USA 41°46′N 89°41′W
23 Q5 **Rockford** Alabama, S USA 32°53′N 86°11′W
30 L10 **Rockford** Illinois, N USA 42°16′N 89°06′W
15 Q12 **Rock Forest** Québec, SE Canada 45°21′N 71°58′W
11 T17 **Rockglen** Saskatchewan, S Canada 49°11′N 105°57′W
181 Y8 **Rockhampton** Queensland, E Australia 23°31′S 150°31′E
21 R11 **Rock Hill** South Carolina, SE USA 34°55′N 81°01′W
180 I13 **Rockingham** Western Australia 32°16′S 115°21′E
21 T11 **Rockingham** North Carolina, SE USA 34°56′N 79°47′W
30 J11 **Rock Island** Illinois, N USA 41°30′N 90°34′W
25 U12 **Rock Island** Texas, SW USA 29°31′N 96°33′W
14 C10 **Rock Lake** Ontario, S Canada 46°25′N 83°49′W
29 O2 **Rock Lake** North Dakota, N USA 48°45′N 99°12′W
14 I12 **Rock Lake** ◎ Ontario, SE Canada
14 M12 **Rockland** Ontario, SE Canada 45°33′N 75°16′W
19 R7 **Rockland** Maine, NE USA 44°08′N 69°06′W
182 L11 **Rocklands Reservoir** ⊠ Victoria, SE Australia
35 O7 **Rocklin** California, W USA 38°48′N 121°13′W
23 R3 **Rockmart** Georgia, SE USA 34°00′N 85°02′W
31 N16 **Rockport** Indiana, N USA 37°53′N 87°04′W
27 Q1 **Rock Port** Missouri, C USA 40°26′N 95°30′W
25 T14 **Rockport** Texas, SW USA 28°02′N 99°04′W
32 I7 **Rockport** Washington, NW USA 48°28′N 121°36′W
29 S11 **Rock Rapids** Iowa, C USA 43°25′N 96°10′W
30 K11 **Rock River** ≈ Illinois/Wisconsin, N USA
44 I3 **Rock Sound** Eleuthera Island, C Bahamas 24°52′N 76°10′W
25 P11 **Rocksprings** Texas, SW USA 30°02′N 100°14′W
33 U17 **Rock Springs** Wyoming, C USA 41°35′N 109°12′W
55 T9 **Rockstone** C Guyana 05°58′N 58°33′W
29 S12 **Rock Valley** Iowa, C USA 43°12′N 96°17′W
31 N14 **Rockville** Indiana, N USA 39°45′N 87°15′W
21 W3 **Rockville** Maryland, NE USA 39°05′N 77°10′W
25 U6 **Rockwall** Texas, SW USA 32°56′N 96°27′W
29 U13 **Rockwell City** Iowa, C USA 42°24′N 94°37′W
31 S10 **Rockwood** Michigan, N USA 42°04′N 83°15′W
20 M9 **Rockwood** Tennessee, S USA 35°52′N 84°41′W
25 Q8 **Rockwood** Texas, SW USA 31°29′N 99°23′W
37 U6 **Rocky Ford** Colorado, C USA 38°03′N 103°45′W
14 D9 **Rocky Island Lake** ◎ Ontario, S Canada
21 V9 **Rocky Mount** North Carolina, SE USA 35°56′N 77°48′W
21 S7 **Rocky Mount** Virginia, NE USA 37°00′N 79°53′W
33 Q8 **Rocky Mountain** ▲ Montana, NW USA 47°45′N 112°46′W
11 P15 **Rocky Mountain House** Alberta, SW Canada 52°24′N 114°52′W
37 T3 **Rocky Mountain National Park** *national park* Colorado, C USA
2 E12 **Rocky Mountains** *var.* Rockies, *Fr.* Montagnes Rocheuses. ▲▲ Canada/USA
42 H1 **Rocky Point** *headland* NE Belize 18°21′N 88°04′W
83 A17 **Rocky Point** *headland* NW Namibia 19°01′S 12°27′E
95 F14 **Rødberg** Buskerud, S Norway 60°16′N 09°00′E
95 I25 **Rødby** Storstrøm, SE Denmark 54°42′N 11°24′E
95 I25 **Rødbyhavn** Storstrøm, SE Denmark 54°39′N 11°24′E
13 T10 **Roddickton** Newfoundland, Newfoundland and Labrador, SE Canada 50°51′N 56°03′W
95 F23 **Rødding** Sønderjylland, SW Denmark 55°22′N 09°04′E
95 M22 **Rödeby** Blekinge, S Sweden 56°16′N 15°35′E
98 N6 **Roden** Drenthe, NE Netherlands 53°08′N 06°26′E
62 H9 **Rodeo** San Juan, W Argentina 30°12′S 69°06′W
103 O14 **Rodez** *anc.* Segodunum. Aveyron, S France 44°21′N 02°34′E
Rodholívos *see* Rodolívos
Rodhópi Óri *see* Rhodope Mountains
Ródhos/Rodi *see* Ródos
107 N15 **Rodi Gargancio** Puglia, SE Italy 41°54′N 15°51′E
101 N20 **Roding** Bayern, SE Germany 49°12′N 12°30′E
113 J19 **Rodinit, Kepi i** *headland* W Albania 41°35′N 19°27′E
116 I9 **Rodnei, Munţii** ▲▲ N Romania
184 L4 **Rodney, Cape** *headland* North Island, New Zealand 36°16′S 174°48′E
38 L9 **Rodney, Cape** *headland* Alaska, USA 64°39′N 166°24′W
124 M16 **Rodniki** Ivanovskaya Oblast', W Russian Federation 57°04′N 41°45′E
119 Q16 **Rodnya** Mahilyowskaya Voblasts', E Belarus 53°31′N 32°07′E
Rodó *see* José Enrique Rodó
114 H13 **Rodolívos** *var.* Rodholívos. Kentrikí Makedonía, NE Greece 40°55′N 24°00′E
Rodopi *see* Rhodope Mountains
115 O22 **Ródos** *var.* Ródhos, *Eng.* Rhodes, *It.* Rodi. Ródos, Dodekánisa, Greece, Aegean Sea 36°26′N 28°14′E
115 O22 **Ródos** *var.* Ródhos, *Eng.* Rhodes, *It.* Rodi; *anc.* Rhodos. *island* Dodekánisa, Greece, Aegean Sea
Rodosto *see* Tekirdağ
59 A14 **Rodrigues** Amazonas, W Brazil 06°50′S 73°45′W
173 P8 **Rodrigues** *var.* Rodriquez. *island* E Mauritius
Rodriquez *see* Rodrigues
Rodunma *see* Roanne
180 I7 **Roebourne** Western Australia 20°49′S 117°04′E
83 J20 **Roedtan** Limpopo, NE South Africa 24°37′S 29°05′E
98 H11 **Roelofarendsveen** Zuid-Holland, W Netherlands 52°12′N 04°37′E
Roepat *see* Rupat, Pulau
Roer *see* Rur
99 M16 **Roermond** Limburg, SE Netherlands 51°12′N 06°E
99 C18 **Roeselare** *Fr.* Roulers; *prev.* Rousselaere. West-Vlaanderen, W Belgium 50°57′N 03°08′E
9 P8 **Roes Welcome Sound** *strait* Nunavut, N Canada
Roeteng *see* Ruteng
Rofreit *see* Rovereto
Rogachëv *see* Rahachow
57 L15 **Rogagua, Laguna** ◎ NW Bolivia
95 C16 **Rogaland** ⬖ *county* S Norway
25 Y9 **Roganville** Texas, SW USA 30°49′N 93°54′W
109 W11 **Rogaška Slatina** *Ger.* Rohitsch-Sauerbrunn; *prev.* Rogatec-Slatina. E Slovenia 46°13′N 15°38′E
Rogatec-Slatina *see* Rogaška Slatina
112 J13 **Rogatica** Republika Srpska, SE Bosnia and Herzegovina 43°50′N 18°55′E
Rogatin *see* Rohatyn
93 F17 **Rogen** ◎ C Sweden
27 S9 **Rogers** Arkansas, C USA 36°19′N 94°07′W
29 P5 **Rogers** North Dakota, N USA 47°03′N 98°12′W
25 T9 **Rogers** Texas, SW USA 30°53′N 97°10′W
31 R5 **Rogers City** Michigan, N USA 45°25′N 83°49′W
Roger Simpson Island *see* Abemama
35 T14 **Rogers Lake** *salt flat* California, W USA
21 Q8 **Rogers, Mount** ▲ Virginia, NE USA 36°39′N 81°32′W
33 O16 **Rogerson** Idaho, NW USA 42°11′N 114°36′W
11 O16 **Rogers Pass** *pass* British Columbia, SW Canada
21 O8 **Rogersville** Tennessee, S USA 36°26′N 83°01′W
99 L16 **Roggel** Limburg, SE Netherlands 51°16′N 05°55′E
Roggeveen *see* Roggewein, Cabo
193 R10 **Roggeveen Basin** *undersea feature* E Pacific Ocean 31°30′S 95°30′W
191 X16 **Roggewein, Cabo** *var.* Roggeveen. *headland* Easter Island, Chile, E Pacific Ocean 27°07′S 109°15′W
103 Y13 **Rogliano** Corse, France, C Mediterranean Sea 42°58′N 09°25′E
107 N21 **Rogliano** Calabria, SW Italy 39°09′N 16°18′E
92 G12 **Rognan** Nordland, C Norway 67°04′N 15°21′E
100 K10 **Rögnitz** ≈ N Germany
Rogozhina/Rogozhinë *see* Rrogozhinë
110 G10 **Rogoźno** Wielkopolskie, C Poland 52°46′N 16°58′E
32 E15 **Rogue River** ≈ Oregon, NW USA
116 I6 **Rohatyn** *Rus.* Rogatin. Ivano-Frankivs'ka Oblast', W Ukraine 49°25′N 24°35′E
189 O14 **Rohi** Pohnpei, E Micronesia
Rohitsch-Sauerbrunn *see* Rogaška Slatina
149 Q13 **Rohri** Sind, SE Pakistan 27°39′N 68°57′E
152 I10 **Rohtak** Haryāna, N India 28°57′N 76°38′E
Roi Ed *see* Roi Et
167 R9 **Roi Et** *var.* Muang Roi Et, Roi Ed. Roi Et, E Thailand 16°05′N 103°38′E
191 U9 **Roi Georges, Îles du** *island group* Îles Tuamotu, C French Polynesia
153 Y10 **Roing** Arunāchal Pradesh, NE India 28°06′N 95°46′E
118 E7 **Roja** Talsi, NW Latvia 57°31′N 22°44′E
61 B20 **Rojas** Buenos Aires, E Argentina 34°10′S 60°45′W
149 R12 **Rojhān** Punjab, E Pakistan 28°39′N 70°00′E
41 Q12 **Rojo, Cabo** *headland* C Mexico 21°33′N 97°19′W
45 Q10 **Rojo, Cabo** *headland* W Puerto Rico 17°57′N 67°10′W
168 K10 **Rokan Kiri, Sungai** ≈ Sumatera, W Indonesia
118 I11 **Rokiškis** Panevėžys, NE Lithuania 55°58′N 25°35′E
165 R7 **Rokkasho** Aomori, Honshū, C Japan 40°59′N 141°22′E
111 B17 **Rokycany** *Ger.* Rokytzan. Plzeňský Kraj, W Czech Republic 49°45′N 13°36′E
117 P6 **Rokytne** Kyyivs'ka Oblast', N Ukraine 49°40′N 30°29′E
116 L3 **Rokytne** Rivnens'ka Oblast', NW Ukraine 51°19′N 27°09′E
Rokytzan *see* Rokycany
158 L11 **Rola Co** ◎ W China
29 V13 **Roland** Iowa, C USA 42°10′N 93°30′W
95 D15 **Røldal** Hordaland, S Norway 59°52′N 06°49′E
98 O7 **Rolde** Drenthe, NE Netherlands 52°58′N 06°39′E
29 O2 **Rolette** North Dakota, N USA 48°39′N 99°50′W
27 V6 **Rolla** Missouri, C USA 37°56′N 91°47′W
29 O2 **Rolla** North Dakota, N USA 48°51′N 99°37′W
108 A10 **Rolle** Vaud, W Switzerland 46°27′N 06°19′E
181 X8 **Rolleston** Queensland, E Australia 24°30′S 148°36′E
185 H19 **Rolleston** Canterbury, South Island, New Zealand 43°34′S 172°24′E
185 G18 **Rolleston Range** ▲▲ South Island, New Zealand
14 H8 **Rollet** Québec, SE Canada 47°56′N 79°14′W
22 J4 **Rolling Fork** Mississippi, S USA 32°54′N 90°52′W
20 L6 **Rolling Fork** ≈ Kentucky, S USA
14 J11 **Rolphton** Ontario, SE Canada 46°09′N 77°43′W
Röm *see* Rømø
181 X10 **Roma** Queensland, E Australia 26°37′S 148°54′E
107 I15 **Roma** *Eng.* Rome. ● (Italy) Lazio, C Italy 41°53′N 12°30′E
95 P19 **Roma** Gotland, SE Sweden 57°31′N 18°28′E
21 T14 **Romain, Cape** *headland* South Carolina, SE USA 33°00′N 79°21′W
13 P11 **Romaine** ≈ Newfoundland and Labrador/Québec, E Canada
25 R17 **Roma Los Saenz** Texas, SW USA 26°24′N 99°01′W
114 H8 **Roman** Vratsa, NW Bulgaria 43°09′N 23°56′E
116 L10 **Roman** *Hung.* Románvásár. Neamţ, NE Romania 46°46′N 26°56′E
64 M13 **Romanche Fracture Zone** *tectonic feature* E Atlantic Ocean
61 C15 **Romang** Santa Fe, C Argentina 29°30′S 59°46′W
171 R15 **Romang, Pulau** *var.* Pulau Roma. *island* Kepulauan Damar, E Indonesia
171 R15 **Romang, Selat** *strait* Nusa Tenggara, S Indonesia
116 J11 **Romania** *Bul.* Rumŭniya, *Ger.* Rumänien, *Hung.* Románia, *Rom.* România, *SCr.* Rumunjska, *Ukr.* Rumuniya, *prev.* Republica Socialistă România, Roumania, Rumania, Socialist Republic of Romania, *prev.Rom.* Romînia. ◆ *republic* SE Europe
România, Republica Socialistă *see* Romania
Romania, Socialist Republic of *see* Romania
117 T7 **Romaniv** *Rus.* Dneprodzerzhinsk, *prev.* Dniprodzerzhyns'k, *prev.* Kamenskoye. Dnipropetrovs'ka Oblast', E Ukraine 48°30′N 34°35′E
23 W16 **Romano, Cape** *headland* Florida, SE USA 25°51′N 81°40′W
44 G5 **Romano, Cayo** *island* C Cuba
123 O13 **Romanovka** Respublika Buryatiya, S Russian Federation 53°10′N 112°34′E
127 N8 **Romanovka** Saratovskaya Oblast', W Russian Federation 51°45′N 42°45′E
108 I6 **Romanshorn** Thurgau, NE Switzerland 47°34′N 09°23′E
103 R12 **Romans-sur-Isère** Drôme, E France 45°03′N 05°03′E
189 U12 **Romanum** *island* Chuuk, C Micronesia
Románvásár *see* Roman
39 S5 **Romanzof Mountains** ▲▲ Alaska, USA
Roma, Pulau *see* Romang, Pulau
103 S4 **Rombas** Moselle, NE France 49°15′N 06°04′E
23 R2 **Rome** Georgia, SE USA 34°01′N 85°02′W
18 I9 **Rome** New York, NE USA 43°13′N 75°28′W
Rome *see* Roma
31 S9 **Romeo** Michigan, N USA 42°48′N 83°00′W
Römerstadt *see* Rýmařov
Rometan *see* Romiton
103 P5 **Romilly-sur-Seine** Aube, N France 48°31′N 03°44′E
Romînia *see* Romania
146 L11 **Romiton** *Rus.* Rometan. Buxoro Viloyati, C Uzbekistan 39°56′N 64°21′E
21 U3 **Romney** West Virginia, NE USA 39°21′N 78°44′W
117 S4 **Romny** Sums'ka Oblast', NE Ukraine 50°45′N 33°30′E
95 E24 **Rømø** *Ger.* Röm. *island* SW Denmark
117 S5 **Romodan** Poltavs'ka Oblast', NE Ukraine 50°00′N 33°20′E
127 P5 **Romodanovo** Respublika Mordoviya, W Russian Federation 54°25′N 45°24′E
Romorantin *see* Romorantin-Lanthenay
103 N8 **Romorantin-Lanthenay** *var.* Romorantin. Loir-et-Cher, C France 47°22′N 01°44′E
94 F9 **Romsdal** *physical region* S Norway
94 F10 **Romsdalen** *valley* S Norway
94 E9 **Romsdalsfjorden** *fjord* S Norway
33 P8 **Ronan** Montana, NW USA 47°31′N 114°06′W
59 M14 **Roncador** Maranhão, E Brazil 05°48′S 45°08′W
186 M7 **Roncador Reef** *reef* N Solomon Islands
59 J17 **Roncador, Serra do** ▲▲ C Brazil
21 S6 **Ronceverte** West Virginia, NE USA 37°45′N 80°27′W
107 H14 **Ronciglione** Lazio, C Italy 42°16′N 12°15′E
104 L15 **Ronda** Andalucía, S Spain 36°45′N 05°10′W
94 G11 **Rondane** ▲▲ S Norway
104 L15 **Ronda, Serranía de** ▲▲ S Spain
95 H22 **Rønde** Århus, C Denmark 56°18′N 10°28′E
Ronde, Île *see* Round Island
Rōṇdik *see* Rongrik Atoll
59 E16 **Rondônia** *off.* Estado de Rondônia; *prev.* Território de Rondônia. ⬖ *state* W Brazil
Rondônia, Estado de *see* Rondônia
Rondônia, Território de *see* Rondônia
59 I18 **Rondonópolis** Mato Grosso, W Brazil 16°29′S 54°37′W
94 G11 **Rondslottet** ▲ S Norway 61°54′N 09°48′E
95 P20 **Ronehamn** Gotland, SE Sweden 57°10′N 18°30′E
160 L13 **Rong'an** *var.* Chang'an, Rongan. Guangxi Zhuangzu Zizhiqu, S China 25°14′N 109°20′E
Rongan *see* Rong'an
Rongcheng *see* Rongxian, Guangxi, China
Rongcheng *see* Jianli, Hubei, China
189 R4 **Rongelap Atoll** *var.* Rōnlap. *atoll* Ralik Chain, NW Marshall Islands
Rongerik *see* Rongrik Atoll
160 K12 **Rongjiang** *var.* Guzhou. Guizhou, S China 25°59′N 108°27′E
160 L13 **Rong Jiang** ≈ S China
Rongjiang *see* Nankang
Rong, Kas *see* Rŭng, Kaôh
167 P8 **Rong Kwang** Phrae, NW Thailand 18°19′N 100°18′E
189 T4 **Rongrik Atoll** *var.* Rōṇdik, Rongerik. *atoll* Ralik Chain, N Marshall Islands
189 X2 **Rongrong** *island* SE Marshall Islands
160 L13 **Rongshui** *var.* Rongshui Miaozu Zizhixian. Guangxi Zhuangzu Zizhiqu, S China 25°05′N 109°09′E
Rongshui Miaozu Zizhixian *see* Rongshui
118 I6 **Rõngu** *Ger.* Ringen. Tartumaa, SE Estonia 58°10′N 26°17′E
Rongwo *see* Tongren
160 L15 **Rongxian** *var.* Rongzhou; *prev.* Rongcheng. Guangxi Zhuangzu Zizhiqu, S China 22°52′N 110°33′E
Rongzhag *see* Danba
Rongzhou *see* Rongxian
Roniu *see* Ronui, Mont
189 N13 **Ronkiti** Pohnpei, E Micronesia 06°48′N 158°10′E
Rōnlap *see* Rongelap Atoll
95 L24 **Rønne** Bornholm, E Denmark 55°07′N 14°43′E
95 M22 **Ronneby** Blekinge, S Sweden 56°12′N 15°18′E
194 J7 **Ronne Entrance** *inlet* Antarctica
194 L6 **Ronne Ice Shelf** *ice shelf* Antarctica
99 E19 **Ronse** *Fr.* Renaix. Oost-Vlaanderen, SW Belgium 50°45′N 03°36′E
191 R8 **Ronui, Mont** *var.* Roniu. ※ Tahiti, W French Polynesia 17°49′S 149°12′W
30 K14 **Roodhouse** Illinois, N USA 39°28′N 90°22′W
83 C19 **Rooibank** Erongo, W Namibia 23°04′S 14°34′E
Rooke Island *see* Umboi Island
65 N24 **Rookery Point** *headland* NE Tristan da Cunha 37°03′S 12°15′W
171 V13 **Roon, Pulau** *island* E Indonesia
173 V7 **Roo Rise** *undersea feature* E Indian Ocean
152 J9 **Roorkee** Uttarakhand, N India 29°51′N 77°54′E
99 H15 **Roosendaal** Noord-Brabant, S Netherlands 51°32′N 04°29′E
25 P10 **Roosevelt** Texas, SW USA 30°28′N 100°06′W
37 N3 **Roosevelt** Utah, W USA 40°18′N 109°59′W
47 T8 **Roosevelt** ≈ W Brazil
195 O13 **Roosevelt Island** *island* Antarctica
10 L10 **Roosevelt, Mount** ▲ British Columbia, W Canada 58°28′N 125°22′W
11 P17 **Roosville** British Columbia, SW Canada 48°59′N 115°03′W
29 X10 **Root River** ≈ Minnesota, N USA
Ropar *see* Rūpnagar
111 N16 **Ropczyce** Podkarpackie, SE Poland 50°04′N 21°31′E
181 Q3 **Roper Bar** Northern Territory, N Australia 14°45′S 134°30′E
24 M5 **Ropesville** Texas, SW USA 33°24′N 102°09′W
102 K14 **Roquefort** Landes, SW France 44°01′N 00°18′W
61 C21 **Roque Pérez** Buenos Aires, E Argentina 35°25′S 59°24′W
58 E10 **Roraima** *off.* Estado de Roraima; *prev.* Território de Rio Branco, Território de Roraima. ⬖ *state* N Brazil
Roraima, Estado de *see* Roraima
58 F9 **Roraima, Mount** ▲ N South America 05°10′N 60°36′W
Roraima, Território de *see* Roraima
94 I9 **Røros** Sør-Trøndelag, S Norway 62°37′N 11°25′E
108 I7 **Rorschach** Sankt Gallen, NE Switzerland 47°28′N 09°30′E
93 E14 **Rørvik** Nord-Trøndelag, C Norway 64°54′N 11°15′E
119 G17 **Ros'** *Rus.* Ross'. Hrodzyenskaya Voblasts', W Belarus 53°25′N 24°24′E
185 F17 **Ross** West Coast, South Island, New Zealand 42°54′S 170°52′E
119 G17 **Ros'** *Rus.* Ross'. ≈ W Belarus
10 J7 **Ross** ≈ Yukon Territory, W Canada
117 O6 **Ros'** ≈ N Ukraine
44 K7 **Rosa, Lake** ◎ Great Inagua, S Bahamas
32 M9 **Rosalia** Washington, NW USA 47°14′N 117°22′W
191 W15 **Rosalia, Punta** *headland* Easter Island, Chile, E Pacific Ocean 27°04′S 109°19′W
45 P12 **Rosalie** E Dominica 15°22′N 61°15′W

◆ Country
● Country Capital
◇ Dependent Territory
○ Dependent Territory Capital
⬖ Administrative Regions
✕ International Airport
▲ Mountain
▲▲ Mountain Range
※ Volcano
≈ River
◎ Lake
⊠ Reservoir

ROSAMOND – RYBNITSA

35 T14 Rosamond California, W USA 34°51′N 118°09′W
35 S14 Rosamond Lake salt flat California, W USA
96 H8 Ross and Cromarty cultural region N Scotland, United Kingdom
61 B18 Rosario Santa Fe, C Argentina 32°56′S 60°39′W
40 J11 Rosario Sinaloa, C Mexico 23°00′N 105°51′W
40 G6 Rosario Sonora, NW Mexico 27°53′N 109°18′W
62 O6 Rosario San Pedro, C Paraguay 24°26′S 57°06′W
61 E20 Rosario Colonia, SW Uruguay 34°20′S 57°26′W
54 H5 Rosario Zulia, NW Venezuela 10°18′N 72°19′W
Rosario see Nishino-shima
Rosario see Rosarito
40 B4 Rosario, Bahía del bay NW Mexico
62 K6 Rosario de la Frontera Salta, N Argentina 25°50′S 65°00′W
61 C18 Rosario del Tala Entre Ríos, E Argentina 32°20′S 59°10′W
61 F16 Rosário do Sul Rio Grande do Sul, S Brazil 30°15′S 54°55′W
59 H18 Rosário Oeste Mato Grosso, W Brazil 14°50′S 56°25′W
40 B1 Rosarito var. Rosario. Baja California Norte, NW Mexico 32°25′N 117°04′W
40 D5 Rosarito Baja California Norte, NW Mexico 28°27′N 113°58′W
40 F7 Rosarito Baja California Sur, NW Mexico 26°28′N 111°41′W
104 L9 Rosarito, Embalse del ⊠ W Spain
107 N22 Rosarno Calabria, SW Italy 38°29′N 15°59′E
56 B5 Rosa Zárate var. Quinindé. Esmeraldas, SW Ecuador 0°14′N 79°28′W
Roscianum see Rossano
29 O8 Roscoe South Dakota, N USA 45°24′N 99°19′W
25 P7 Roscoe Texas, SW USA 32°27′N 100°32′W
102 F5 Roscoff Finistère, NW France 48°43′N 04°00′W
Ros Comáin see Roscommon
97 C17 Roscommon Ir. Ros Comáin. C Ireland 53°38′N 08°11′W
31 Q7 Roscommon Michigan, N USA 44°30′N 84°35′W
97 C17 Roscommon Ir. Ros Comáin. cultural region C Ireland
Ros. Cré see Roscrea
97 D19 Roscrea Ir. Ros. Cré. C Ireland 52°57′N 07°47′W
14 H13 Rosseau Ontario, S Canada 45°15′N 79°38′W
45 X12 Roseau prev. Charlotte Town. ● (Dominica) SW Dominica 15°17′N 61°23′W
29 S2 Roseau Minnesota, N USA 48°51′N 95°45′W
173 Y16 Rose Belle SE Mauritius 20°24′S 57°36′E
183 O16 Rosebery Tasmania, SE Australia 41°51′S 145°33′E
21 U11 Roseboro North Carolina, SE USA 34°58′N 78°31′W
25 T9 Rosebud Texas, SW USA 31°04′N 96°58′W
33 W10 Rosebud Creek ≈ Montana, NW USA
32 F14 Roseburg Oregon, NW USA 43°13′N 123°21′W
22 J3 Rosedale Mississippi, S USA 33°51′N 91°01′W
99 H21 Rosée Namur, S Belgium 50°15′N 04°43′E
55 U8 Rose Hall E Guyana 06°14′N 57°30′W
173 X16 Rose Hill W Mauritius 20°14′S 57°29′E
80 H12 Roseires, Reservoir var. Lake Rusayris. ⊠ E Sudan
Rosenau see Rožnov pod Radhoštěm
Rosenau see Rožňava
25 V11 Rosenberg Texas, SW USA 29°33′N 95°48′W
Rosenberg see Olesno, Poland
Rosenberg see Ružomberok, Slovakia
100 I10 Rosengarten Niedersachsen, N Germany 53°24′N 09°54′E
101 M24 Rosenheim Bayern, S Germany 47°51′N 12°08′E
Rosenhof see Zilupe
105 X4 Roses Cataluña, NE Spain 42°15′N 03°11′E
105 X4 Roses, Golf de gulf NE Spain
107 K14 Roseto degli Abruzzi Abruzzo, C Italy 42°39′N 14°01′E
11 S16 Rosetown Saskatchewan, S Canada 51°34′N 107°59′W
Rosetta see Rashîd
35 O7 Roseville California, W USA 38°44′N 121°16′W
30 J12 Roseville Illinois, N USA 40°42′N 90°40′W
29 V8 Roseville Minnesota, N USA 45°00′N 93°09′W
29 R7 Rosholt South Dakota, N USA 45°51′N 96°42′W
106 F12 Rosignano Marittimo Toscana, C Italy 43°24′N 10°28′E
116 I14 Roșiori de Vede Teleorman, S Romania 44°06′N 25°00′E
114 K8 Rositsa ≈ N Bulgaria
Rositten see Rēzekne
95 J23 Roskilde Roskilde, E Denmark 55°39′N 12°07′E
95 I23 Roskilde off. Roskilde Amt. ◐ county E Denmark
Roskilde Amt see Roskilde
Ros Láir see Rosslare
126 H5 Roslavl' Smolenskaya Oblast', W Russian Federation 54°N 32°57′E
124 J3 Roslyakovo Murmanskaya Oblast', NW Russian Federation 69°03′N 33°12′E
32 I8 Roslyn Washington, NW USA 47°13′N 120°52′W
99 K14 Rosmalen Noord-Brabant, S Netherlands 51°43′N 05°21′E
Ros Mhic Thriúin see New Ross
113 P19 Rosoman C FYR Macedonia 41°31′N 21°55′E
102 F6 Rosporden Finistère, NW France 47°58′N 03°54′W
Ross' see Ros'
107 O20 Rossano anc. Roscianum. Calabria, SW Italy 39°35′N 16°38′E
22 L5 Ross Barnett Reservoir ⊠ Mississippi, S USA
11 W16 Rossburn Manitoba, S Canada 50°42′N 100°49′W
14 H13 Rosseau, Lake ◎ Ontario, S Canada
186 I10 Rossel Island prev. Yela Island. island SE Papua New Guinea
195 P12 Ross Ice Shelf ice shelf Antarctica
15 P16 Rossignol, Lake ◎ Nova Scotia, SE Canada
83 C19 Rössing Erongo, W Namibia 22°31′S 14°52′E
195 Q14 Ross Island island Antarctica
Rossitten see Rybachiy
Rossiyskaya Federatsiya see Russian Federation
11 N17 Rossland British Columbia, SW Canada 49°03′N 117°49′W
97 F20 Rosslare Ir. Ros Láir. Wexford, SE Ireland 52°16′N 06°23′W
97 F20 Rosslare Harbour Wexford, SE Ireland 52°15′N 06°20′W
101 M14 Rosslau Sachsen-Anhalt, E Germany 51°52′N 12°15′E
76 G10 Rosso Trarza, SW Mauritania 16°36′N 15°50′W
103 X14 Rosso, Cap headland Corse, France, C Mediterranean Sea 42°25′N 08°22′E
93 H16 Rossön Jämtland, C Sweden 63°54′N 16°21′E
97 K21 Ross-on-Wye W England, United Kingdom 51°55′N 02°34′W
Rossony see Rasony
126 L9 Rossosh' Voronezhskaya Oblast', W Russian Federation 50°10′N 39°34′E
181 Q7 Ross River Northern Territory, N Australia 23°36′S 134°30′E
10 J7 Ross River Yukon Territory, W Canada 61°57′N 132°26′W
195 O15 Ross Sea sea Antarctica
92 G13 Røsvatnet Lapp. Reevhtse. ◎ C Norway
23 R1 Rossville Georgia, SE USA 34°59′N 85°22′W
Rostak see Ar Rustāq
143 P14 Rostāq Hormozgān, S Iran 26°48′N 53°50′E
117 N5 Rostavytsya ≈ N Ukraine
11 T15 Rosthern Saskatchewan, S Canada 52°40′N 106°20′W
100 M8 Rostock Mecklenburg-Vorpommern, NE Germany 54°05′N 12°08′E
124 L16 Rostov Yaroslavskaya Oblast', W Russian Federation 57°11′N 39°19′E
Rostov see Rostov-na-Donu
126 L12 Rostov-na-Donu var. Rostov, Eng. Rostov-on-Don. Rostovskaya Oblast', SW Russian Federation 47°16′N 39°45′E
Rostov-on-Don see Rostov-na-Donu
126 L10 Rostovskaya Oblast' ◐ province SW Russian Federation
93 J14 Rosvik Norrbotten, N Sweden 65°26′N 21°48′E
23 S3 Roswell Georgia, SE USA 34°01′N 84°21′W
37 U14 Roswell New Mexico, SW USA 33°23′N 104°31′W
94 K12 Rot Dalarna, C Sweden 61°16′N 14°04′E
101 I23 Rot ≈ S Germany
104 J15 Rota Andalucía, S Spain 36°39′N 06°20′W
188 K9 Rota island S Northern Mariana Islands
25 P6 Rotan Texas, SW USA 32°51′N 100°28′W
Rotcher Island see Tamana
100 I11 Rotenburg Niedersachsen, NW Germany 53°06′N 09°25′E
Rotenburg see Rotenburg an der Fulda
101 I16 Rotenburg an der Fulda var. Rotenburg. Thüringen, C Germany 51°00′N 09°43′E
101 L18 Roter Main ≈ E Germany
101 K20 Roth Bayern, SE Germany 49°15′N 11°06′E
101 G16 Rothaargebirge ▲▲ W Germany
Rothenburg see Rothenburg ob der Tauber
101 J20 Rothenburg ob der Tauber var. Rothenburg. Bayern, S Germany 49°23′N 10°10′E
194 H6 Rothera UK research station Antarctica 67°28′S 68°31′W
185 I17 Rotherham Canterbury, South Island, New Zealand 42°42′S 172°56′E
97 M17 Rotherham N England, United Kingdom 53°26′N 01°20′W
96 H12 Rothesay W Scotland, United Kingdom 55°49′N 05°03′W
108 E7 Rothrist Aargau, N Switzerland 47°18′N 07°54′E
194 H6 Rothschild Island island Antarctica
171 P17 Roti, Pulau island S Indonesia
183 O8 Roto New South Wales, SE Australia 33°04′S 145°27′E
184 N8 Rotoiti, Lake ◎ North Island, New Zealand
Rotomagus see Rouen
107 N19 Rotondella Basilicata, S Italy 40°12′N 16°30′E
103 X15 Rotondo, Monte ▲ Corse, France, C Mediterranean Sea 42°15′N 09°03′E
185 I15 Rotoroa, Lake ◎ South Island, New Zealand
184 N8 Rotorua Bay of Plenty, North Island, New Zealand 38°10′S 176°14′E
184 N8 Rotorua, Lake ◎ North Island, New Zealand
101 N22 Rott ≈ SE Germany
108 F10 Rotten ≈ S Switzerland
109 T6 Rottenmann Steiermark, E Austria 47°31′N 14°18′E
98 H12 Rotterdam Zuid-Holland, SW Netherlands 51°55′N 04°30′E
18 K10 Rotterdam New York, NE USA 42°46′N 73°57′W
95 M21 Rottnen ◎ S Sweden
98 N4 Rottumeroog island Waddeneilanden, NE Netherlands
98 N4 Rottumerplaat island Waddeneilanden, NE Netherlands
101 G23 Rottweil Baden-Württemberg, S Germany 48°10′N 08°38′E
191 O7 Rotui, Mont Ѫ Moorea, W French Polynesia 17°30′S 149°50′W
103 P1 Roubaix Nord, N France 50°42′N 03°10′E
111 C15 Roudnice nad Labem Ger. Raudnitz an der Elbe. Ústecký Kraj, NW Czech Republic 50°25′N 14°14′E
102 M4 Rouen anc. Rotomagus. Seine-Maritime, N France 49°26′N 01°05′E
171 X13 Rouffaer Reserves reserve Papua, E Indonesia
15 N10 Rouge, Rivière ≈ Québec, SE Canada
20 J6 Rough River ≈ Kentucky, S USA
20 J6 Rough River Lake ⊠ Kentucky, S USA
Rouhaïbé see Ar Ruḩaybah
102 K11 Rouillac Charente, W France 45°46′N 00°04′W
Roulers see Roeselare
Roumania see Romania
173 Y15 Round Island var. Île Ronde. island NE Mauritius
14 J12 Round Lake ◎ Ontario, SE Canada
35 U7 Round Mountain Nevada, W USA 38°42′N 117°04′W
25 R10 Round Mountain Texas, SW USA 30°25′N 98°20′W
183 U5 Round Mountain ▲ New South Wales, SE Australia 30°22′S 152°13′E
25 S10 Round Rock Texas, SW USA 30°30′N 97°40′W
33 U10 Roundup Montana, NW USA 46°27′N 108°32′W
55 Y10 Roura NE French Guiana 04°44′N 52°16′W
Rourkela see Rāulakela
96 J4 Rousay island N Scotland, United Kingdom
Rousselaere see Roeselare
103 O17 Roussillon cultural region S France
15 V7 Routhierville Québec, SE Canada 48°09′N 67°07′W
99 K25 Rouvroy Luxembourg, SE Belgium 49°33′N 05°28′E
14 I7 Rouyn-Noranda Québec, SE Canada 48°16′N 79°03′W
Rouyuan see Huachi
Rouyuanchengzi see Huachi
92 L12 Rovaniemi Lappi, N Finland 66°29′N 25°40′E
106 E7 Rovato Lombardia, N Italy 45°34′N 10°03′E
125 N11 Rovdino Arkhangel'skaya Oblast', NW Russian Federation 61°36′N 42°28′E
Roven'ki see Roven'ky
117 Y8 Roven'ky var. Roven'ki. Luhans'ka Oblast', E Ukraine 48°05′N 39°20′E
Rovenskaya Oblast' see Rivnens'ka Oblast'
Rovenskaya Sloboda see Rovyenskaya Slabada
106 G7 Rovereto Ger. Rofreit. Trentino-Alto Adige, N Italy 45°53′N 11°03′E
167 S12 Rôviĕng Tbong Preăh Vihéar, N Cambodia 13°18′N 105°06′E
Rovigno see Rovinj
106 H8 Rovigo Veneto, NE Italy 45°04′N 11°48′E
112 A10 Rovinj It. Rovigno. Istra, NW Croatia 45°06′N 13°39′E
54 E10 Rovira Tolima, C Colombia 04°15′N 75°15′W
Rovno see Rivne
127 P9 Rovnoye Saratovskaya Oblast', W Russian Federation 50°43′N 46°03′E
82 Q12 Rovuma, Rio var. Ruvuma. ≈ Mozambique/Tanzania see also Ruvuma
Rovuma, Rio see Ruvuma
119 O19 Rovyenskaya Slabada Rus. Rovenskaya Sloboda. Homyel'skaya Voblasts', SE Belarus 52°13′N 30°19′E
183 R5 Rowena New South Wales, SE Australia 29°51′S 148°55′E
21 T11 Rowland North Carolina, SE USA 34°32′N 79°17′W
9 P5 Rowley ≈ Baffin Island, Nunavut, NE Canada
9 P6 Rowley Island island Nunavut, NE Canada
173 W8 Rowley Shoals reef NW Australia
Równe see Rivne
171 O4 Roxas Mindoro, N Philippines 12°36′N 121°29′E
171 P5 Roxas City Panay Island, C Philippines 11°33′N 122°43′E
21 U8 Roxboro North Carolina, SE USA 36°24′N 79°00′W
185 D23 Roxburgh Otago, South Island, New Zealand 45°32′S 169°18′E
96 K13 Roxburgh cultural region SE Scotland, United Kingdom
182 H5 Roxby Downs South Australia 30°29′S 136°56′E
95 M17 Roxen ◎ S Sweden
25 V5 Roxton Texas, SW USA 33°33′N 95°43′W
15 P12 Roxton-Sud Québec, SE Canada 45°30′N 72°35′W
33 U8 Roy Montana, NW USA 47°19′N 108°55′W
37 U10 Roy New Mexico, SW USA 35°56′N 104°12′W
97 E17 Royal Canal Ir. An Chanáil Ríoga. canal C Ireland
30 L1 Royale, Isle island Michigan, N USA
37 S6 Royal Gorge valley Colorado, C USA
97 M20 Royal Leamington Spa var. Leamington, Leamington Spa. C England, United Kingdom 52°18′N 01°31′W
97 O23 Royal Tunbridge Wells var. Tunbridge Wells. SE England, United Kingdom 51°08′N 00°16′E
24 L9 Royalty Texas, SW USA 31°21′N 102°51′W
102 J11 Royan Charente-Maritime, W France 45°37′N 01°01′W
65 B24 Roy Cove Settlement West Falkland, Falkland Islands 51°32′S 60°23′W
103 O3 Roye Somme, N France 49°42′N 02°46′E
95 H15 Røyken Buskerud, S Norway 59°47′N 10°21′E
93 F14 Røyrvik Nord-Trøndelag, C Norway 64°53′N 13°30′E
25 U6 Royse City Texas, SW USA 32°58′N 96°19′W
97 O21 Royston E England, United Kingdom 52°05′N 00°01′W
23 U2 Royston Georgia, SE USA 34°17′N 83°06′W
114 L10 Roza prev. Gyulovo. Yambol, E Bulgaria 42°29′N 26°30′E
113 L16 Rožaje E Montenegro 42°51′N 20°11′E
110 M10 Różan Mazowieckie, C Poland 52°36′N 21°27′E
117 O10 Rozdil'na Odes'ka Oblast', SW Ukraine 46°51′N 30°03′E
117 S12 Rozdol'ne Rus. Razdolnoye. Respublika Krym, S Ukraine 45°45′N 33°27′E
145 Q9 Rozhdestvenka Akmola, C Kazakhstan 50°51′N 71°25′E
116 I6 Rozhnyativ Ivano-Frankivs'ka Oblast', W Ukraine 48°58′N 24°07′E
116 J3 Rozhyshche Volyns'ka Oblast', NW Ukraine 50°54′N 25°16′E
Roznau am Radhost see Rožnov pod Radhoštěm
111 L19 Rožňava Ger. Rosenau, Hung. Rozsnyó. Košický Kraj, E Slovakia 48°41′N 20°32′E
116 K10 Roznov Neamţ, NE Romania 46°47′N 26°33′E
111 I18 Rožnov pod Radhoštěm Ger. Rosenau, Roznau am Radhost. Zlínský Kraj, E Czech Republic 49°28′N 18°09′E
Rózsahegy see Ružomberok
Rozsnyó see Râşnov, Romania
Rozsnyó see Rožňava, Slovakia
113 K18 Rranxë Shkodër, NW Albania 41°58′N 19°27′E
113 L18 Rrëshen var. Rresheni, Rrshen. Lezhë, C Albania 41°46′N 19°54′E
Rresheni see Rrëshen
Rrogozhina see Rrogozhinë
113 K20 Rrogozhinë var. Rrogozhina, Rogozhinë, Rrogozhina. Tiranë, W Albania 41°04′N 19°40′E
Rrshen see Rrëshen
112 O13 Rtanj ▲ E Serbia 43°45′N 21°54′E
127 O7 Rtishchevo Saratovskaya Oblast', W Russian Federation 52°16′N 43°46′E
184 N12 Ruahine Range var. Ruarine. ▲▲ North Island, New Zealand
185 L14 Ruamahanga ≈ North Island, New Zealand
Ruanda see Rwanda
184 M10 Ruapehu, Mount Ѫ North Island, New Zealand 39°15′S 175°33′E
185 C25 Ruapuke Island island SW New Zealand
Ruarine see Ruahine Range
184 O9 Ruatahuna Bay of Plenty, North Island, New Zealand 38°38′S 176°56′E
184 Q8 Ruatoria Gisborne, North Island, New Zealand 37°54′S 178°18′E
184 K4 Ruawai Northland, North Island, New Zealand 36°08′S 174°04′E
15 N8 Ruban ≈ Québec, SE Canada
81 I22 Rubeho Mountains ▲▲ C Tanzania
165 U3 Rubeshibe Hokkaidō, NE Japan 43°49′N 143°37′E
Rubezhnoye see Rubizhne
113 L18 Rubik Lezhë, C Albania 41°46′N 19°48′E
54 H7 Rubio Táchira, W Venezuela 07°42′N 72°23′W
117 X6 Rubizhne Rus. Rubezhnoye. Luhans'ka Oblast', E Ukraine 49°01′N 38°22′E
81 F20 Rubondo Island island N Tanzania
122 I13 Rubtsovsk Altayskiy Kray, S Russian Federation 51°34′N 81°11′E
39 P9 Ruby Alaska, USA 64°44′N 155°29′W
35 W3 Ruby Dome ▲ Nevada, W USA 40°35′N 115°25′W
35 W4 Ruby Lake ◎ Nevada, W USA
35 W4 Ruby Mountains ▲▲ Nevada, W USA
33 Q12 Ruby Range ▲▲ Montana, NW USA
118 C10 Rucava Liepāja, SW Latvia 56°09′N 21°10′E
143 S13 Rūdān var. Dehbārez. Hormozgān, S Iran 27°30′N 57°10′E
Rudelstadt see Ciechanowiec
Rudensk see Rudzyensk
119 G14 Rūdiškės Vilnius, S Lithuania 54°31′N 24°49′E
95 H24 Rudkøbing Fyn, C Denmark 54°57′N 10°43′E
125 S13 Rudnichnyy Kirovskaya Oblast', NW Russian Federation 59°37′N 52°28′E
Rūdnîchnyy see Koksu
Rudny see Rudnyy
126 H4 Rudnya Smolenskaya Oblast', W Russian Federation 54°55′N 31°10′E
127 O8 Rudnya Volgogradskaya Oblast', SW Russian Federation 50°54′N 44°27′E
144 M7 Rudnyy var. Rudny. Kostanay, N Kazakhstan 53°N 63°05′E
122 K3 Rudol'fa, Ostrov island Zemlya Frantsa-Iosifa, NW Russian Federation
Rudolf, Lake see Turkana, Lake
Rudolfswert see Novo mesto
101 L17 Rudolstadt Thüringen, C Germany 50°44′N 11°20′E
152 K9 Rudraprayāg Uttarakhand, N India 28°51′N 79°01′E
152 K10 Rudrapur var. Rampura. Uttarakhand, N India 28°58′N 79°23′E
31 Q4 Rudyard Michigan, N USA 46°15′N 84°36′W
33 S7 Rudyard Montana, NW USA 48°33′N 110°37′W
119 K16 Rudzyensk Rus. Rudensk. Minskaya Voblasts', C Belarus 53°36′N 27°52′E
104 L6 Rueda Castilla-León, N Spain 41°24′N 04°58′W
114 F10 Ruen ▲ Bulgaria/FYR Macedonia 42°10′N 22°31′E
80 G10 Rufa'a Gezira, C Sudan 14°49′N 33°21′E
102 L10 Ruffec Charente, W France 46°01′N 00°10′E
21 R14 Ruffin South Carolina, SE USA 33°00′N 80°48′W
81 J23 Rufiji ≈ E Tanzania
61 A20 Rufino Santa Fe, C Argentina 34°16′S 62°45′W
76 F11 Rufisque W Senegal 14°44′N 17°18′W
83 K14 Rufunsa Lusaka, C Zambia 15°02′S 29°35′E
118 J9 Rugāji Balvi, E Latvia 57°01′N 27°07′E
161 R7 Rugao Jiangsu, E China 32°27′N 120°35′E
97 M20 Rugby C England, United Kingdom 52°22′N 01°18′W
29 N3 Rugby North Dakota, N USA 48°24′N 100°00′W
100 N7 Rügen headland NE Germany 54°25′N 13°21′E
Ruhaybeh see Ar Ruḩaybah
81 E19 Ruhengeri NW Rwanda 01°39′S 29°16′E
Ruhja see Rūjiena
100 M10 Ruhner Berg hill N Germany
118 F7 Ruhnu var. Ruhnu Saar, Swe. Runö. island SW Estonia
Ruhnu Saar see Ruhnu
101 G15 Ruhr ≈ W Germany
91 W6 Ruhr Valley industrial region W Germany
161 S11 Rui'an var. Rui an. Zhejiang, SE China 27°51′N 120°39′E
Rui an see Rui'an
161 P10 Ruichang Jiangxi, S China 29°46′N 115°37′E
24 J11 Ruidosa Texas, SW USA 30°00′N 104°40′W
37 S14 Ruidoso New Mexico, SW USA 33°19′N 105°40′W
161 P12 Ruijin Jiangxi, S China 25°52′N 116°01′E
160 D13 Ruili Yunnan, SW China 24°04′N 97°49′E
98 N8 Ruinen Drenthe, NE Netherlands 52°46′N 06°19′E
99 D17 Ruiselede West-Vlaanderen, W Belgium 51°03′N 03°21′E
64 P5 Ruivo de Santana, Pico ▲ Madeira, Portugal, NE Atlantic Ocean 32°46′N 16°57′W
40 J12 Ruiz Nayarit, SW Mexico 22°00′N 105°09′W
54 E10 Ruiz, Nevado del Ѫ W Colombia 04°53′N 75°22′W
138 J9 Rujaylah, Ḩarrat ar salt lake N Jordan
Rujen see Rūjiena
118 H7 Rūjiena Est. Ruhja, Ger. Rujen. Valmiera, N Latvia 57°54′N 25°22′E
79 I18 Ruki ≈ W Dem. Rep. Congo
81 E22 Rukwa ◐ region SW Tanzania
81 F23 Rukwa, Lake ◎ SE Tanzania
25 P6 Rule Texas, SW USA 33°10′N 99°53′W
22 K3 Ruleville Mississippi, S USA 33°43′N 90°33′W
Rum see Rhum
112 K10 Ruma Vojvodina, N Serbia 45°02′N 19°51′E
Rumadiya see Ar Ramādī
141 Q7 Rumāḩ Ar Riyāḑ, C Saudi Arabia 25°35′N 47°09′E
Rumaitha see Ar Rumaythah
Rumania/Rumänien see Romania
Rumänisch-Sankt-Georgen see Sângeorz-Băi
139 Y13 Rumaylah Al Başrah, SE Iraq 30°16′N 47°22′E
139 P2 Rumaylah, Wādī dry watercourse NE Syria
171 U13 Rumbati Papua, E Indonesia 02°44′S 132°04′E
81 E14 Rumbek El Buhayrat, S Sudan 06°50′N 29°42′E
Rumburg see Rumburk
111 D14 Rumburk Ger. Rumburg. Ústecký Kraj, NW Czech Republic 50°58′N 14°35′E
44 J4 Rum Cay island C Bahamas
99 M26 Rumelange Luxembourg, S Luxembourg 49°28′N 06°02′E
99 D20 Rumes Hainaut, SW Belgium 50°33′N 03°19′E
19 P7 Rumford Maine, NE USA 44°31′N 70°31′W
110 I6 Rumia Pomorskie, N Poland 54°36′N 18°21′E
113 J17 Rumija ▲▲ S Montenegro
103 T11 Rumilly Haute-Savoie, E France 45°52′N 05°57′E
139 O5 Rūmiyah Al Anbār, W Iraq 34°28′N 41°17′E
Rummah, Wādī ar see Rimah, Wādī ar
Rummelsburg in Pommern see Miastko
165 S3 Rumoi Hokkaidō, NE Japan 43°57′N 141°40′E
82 M12 Rumphi var. Rumpi. Northern, N Malawi 11°00′S 33°51′E
Rumpi see Rumphi
29 V7 Rum River ≈ Minnesota, N USA
188 F16 Rumung island Caroline Islands, W Micronesia
Rumuniya/Rumŭniya/Rumunjska see Romania
185 G16 Runanga West Coast, South Island, New Zealand 42°25′S 171°15′E
184 P7 Runaway, Cape headland North Island, New Zealand 37°33′S 177°59′E
97 K18 Runcorn C England, United Kingdom 53°20′N 02°44′W
118 K10 Rundāni var. Rundāni. Ludza, E Latvia 56°19′N 27°51′E
Rundāni see Rundāni
83 L18 Runde var. Lundi. ≈ SE Zimbabwe
83 E16 Rundu var. Runtu. Okavango, NE Namibia 17°55′S 19°45′E
93 I16 Rundvik Västerbotten, N Sweden 63°31′N 19°22′E
81 G20 Runere Mwanza, N Tanzania 03°06′S 33°18′E
25 S13 Runge Texas, SW USA 28°52′N 97°42′W
167 Q13 Rŭng, Kaôh prev. Kas Rong. island SW Cambodia
79 O16 Rungu Orientale, NE Dem. Rep. Congo 03°11′N 27°52′E
81 F23 Rungwa Rukwa, W Tanzania 07°18′S 31°40′E
81 G22 Rungwa Singida, C Tanzania 06°54′S 33°33′E
94 M14 Runn ◎ C Sweden
24 M4 Running Water Draw valley New Mexico/Texas, SW USA
Runö see Ruhnu
Runtu see Rundu
189 V12 Ruo island Caroline Islands, C Micronesia
158 L9 Ruoqiang var. Jo-ch'iang, Uigh. Charkhlik, Charkhliq, Qarkilik. Xinjiang Uygur Zizhiqu, NW China 38°59′N 88°08′E
159 S7 Ruo Shui ≈ N China
92 L8 Ruostekfielbmá var. Rustefjelbma Finnmark. Finnmark, N Norway 70°25′N 28°10′E
93 L18 Ruovesi Länsi-Suomi, W Finland 61°59′N 24°05′E
112 B9 Rupa Primorje-Gorski Kotar, NW Croatia 45°29′N 14°15′E
182 M11 Rupanyup Victoria, SE Australia 36°38′S 142°37′E
168 K9 Rupat, Pulau prev. Roepat. island W Indonesia
168 K10 Rupat, Selat strait Sumatera, W Indonesia
116 J11 Rupea Ger. Reps, Hung. Kőhalom; prev. Cohalm. Braşov, C Romania 46°02′N 25°13′E
99 G17 Rupel ≈ N Belgium
Rupella see la Rochelle
33 P15 Rupert Idaho, NW USA 42°37′N 113°40′W
21 R5 Rupert West Virginia, NE USA 37°57′N 80°40′W
Rupert House see Waskaganish
12 J10 Rupert, Rivière de ≈ Québec, C Canada
152 I8 Rūpnagar var. Ropar. Punjab, India
194 M13 Ruppert Coast physical region Antarctica
100 N11 Ruppiner Kanal canal NE Germany
55 S11 Rupununi River ≈ S Guyana
101 D16 Rur Dut. Roer. ≈ Germany/Netherlands
58 H13 Rurópolis Presidente Medici Pará, N Brazil 04°05′S 55°26′W
191 S12 Rurutu island Îles Australes, SW French Polynesia
Rusaddir see Melilla
83 L17 Rusape Manicaland, E Zimbabwe 18°32′S 32°07′E
Rusayris, Lake see Roseires, Reservoir
Ruschuk/Rusçuk see Ruse
114 K7 Ruse var. Ruschuk, Rustchuk, Turk. Ruşçuk. Ruse, N Bulgaria 43°50′N 25°59′E
109 W10 Ruše NE Slovenia 46°31′N 15°30′E
114 L7 Ruse ◐ province N Bulgaria
114 K7 Rusenski Lom ≈ N Bulgaria
97 G17 Rush Ir. An Ros. Dublin, E Ireland 53°32′N 06°06′W
161 S4 Rushan var. Xiacun. Shandong, E China 36°55′N 121°26′E
Rushan see Rŭshon
Rushanskiy Khrebet see Rushon, Qatorkŭhi
29 V7 Rush City Minnesota, N USA 45°41′N 92°56′W
37 V5 Rush Creek ≈ Colorado, C USA
29 X10 Rushford Minnesota, N USA 43°48′N 91°45′W
154 N13 Rushikulya ≈ E India
14 D8 Rush Lake ◎ Ontario, S Canada
30 M7 Rush Lake ◎ Wisconsin, N USA
28 J10 Rushmore, Mount ▲ South Dakota, N USA 43°52′N 103°27′W
147 S13 Rŭshon Rus. Rushan. S Tajikistan 37°58′N 71°31′E
147 S14 Rushon, Qatorkŭhi Rus. Rushanskiy Khrebet. ▲▲ SE Tajikistan
26 M12 Rush Springs Oklahoma, C USA 34°46′N 97°57′W
45 V15 Rushville Trinidad, Trinidad and Tobago 10°07′N 61°03′W
30 J13 Rushville Illinois, N USA 40°07′N 90°33′W
28 K12 Rushville Nebraska, C USA 42°41′N 102°28′W
183 O11 Rushworth Victoria, SE Australia 36°36′S 145°03′E
25 W8 Rusk Texas, SW USA 31°49′N 95°11′W
93 I14 Ruskele Västerbotten, N Sweden 64°49′N 18°55′E
118 C12 Rusnė Klaipėda, W Lithuania 55°18′N 21°19′E
114 M10 Rusokastrenska Reka ≈ E Bulgaria
Russadir see Melilla
109 X3 Russbach ≈ NE Austria
11 V16 Russell Manitoba, S Canada 50°47′N 101°17′W
184 K2 Russell Northland, North Island, New Zealand 35°17′S 174°07′E
26 L4 Russell Kansas, C USA 38°54′N 98°51′W
21 O4 Russell Kentucky, S USA 38°30′N 82°43′W
20 L7 Russell Springs Kentucky, S USA 37°02′N 85°03′W
23 O2 Russellville Alabama, S USA 34°30′N 87°43′W
27 T11 Russellville Arkansas, C USA 35°17′N 93°06′W
20 J7 Russellville Kentucky, S USA 36°50′N 86°54′W
101 G18 Rüsselsheim Hessen, W Germany 50°00′N 08°25′E
Russia see Russian Federation
Russian America see Alaska
122 J11 Russian Federation off. Russian Federation, var. Russia, Latv. Krievija, Rus. Rossiyskaya Federatsiya. ◆ republic Asia/Europe
Russian Federation see Russian Federation
39 N11 Russian Mission Alaska, USA 61°48′N 161°23′W
34 M7 Russian River ≈ California, W USA
122 J5 Russkaya Gavan' Novaya Zemlya, Arkhangel'skaya Oblast', N Russian Federation 76°13′N 62°48′E
122 J5 Russkiy, Ostrov island N Russian Federation
109 Y5 Rust Burgenland, E Austria 47°48′N 16°42′E
Rustaq see Ar Rustāq
137 U10 Rust'avi SE Georgia 41°36′N 45°00′E
21 T7 Rustburg Virginia, NE USA 37°17′N 79°07′W
Rustchuk see Ruse
Rustefjelbma Finnmark see Ruostekfielbmá
83 I21 Rustenburg North-West, N South Africa 25°40′S 27°15′E
22 H5 Ruston Louisiana, S USA 32°31′N 92°38′W
81 E21 Rutana SE Burundi 04°01′S 30°01′E
62 I4 Rutana, Volcán Ѫ N Chile 22°43′S 67°52′W
Rutanzige, Lake see Edward, Lake
Rutba see Ar Ruṭbah
104 M14 Rute Andalucía, S Spain 37°20′N 04°23′W
171 N16 Ruteng prev. Roeteng. Flores, C Indonesia 08°35′S 120°28′E
194 L8 Rutford Ice Stream ice feature Antarctica
35 X6 Ruth Nevada, W USA 39°15′N 115°00′W
101 G15 Rüthen Nordrhein-Westfalen, W Germany 51°30′N 08°28′E
14 D17 Rutherford Ontario, S Canada 42°39′N 82°06′W
21 Q10 Rutherfordton North Carolina, SE USA 35°23′N 81°57′W
97 J18 Ruthin Wel. Rhuthun. NE Wales, United Kingdom 53°05′N 03°18′W
108 G7 Rüti Zürich, N Switzerland 47°16′N 08°51′E
Rutlam see Ratlām
18 M9 Rutland Vermont, NE USA 43°37′N 72°59′W
97 N19 Rutland cultural region C England, United Kingdom
21 N8 Rutledge Tennessee, S USA 36°16′N 83°31′W
158 G12 Rutog var. Rutög, Rutok. Xizang Zizhiqu, W China 33°27′N 79°43′E
Rutok see Rutog
79 P19 Rutshuru Nord-Kivu, E Dem. Rep. Congo 01°11′S 29°28′E
98 L8 Rutten Flevoland, N Netherlands 52°49′N 05°44′E
127 Q17 Rutul Respublika Dagestan, SW Russian Federation 41°35′N 47°30′E
93 L14 Ruukki Oulu, C Finland 64°40′N 25°35′E
98 N11 Ruurlo Gelderland, E Netherlands 52°04′N 06°27′E
143 S15 Ru'ūs al Jibāl cape Oman/United Arab Emirates
138 I7 Ru'ūs aṭ Ṭiwāl, Jabal ▲▲ W Syria
81 H23 Ruvuma ◐ region SE Tanzania
81 I25 Ruvuma var. Rio Rovuma. ≈ Mozambique/Tanzania see also Rovuma, Rio
Ruvuma see Rovuma, Rio
Ruwais see Ar Ruways
138 L9 Ruwayshid, Wadi ar dry watercourse NE Jordan
141 Z10 Ruways, Ra's ar headland E Oman 20°58′N 59°00′E
79 P18 Ruwenzori ▲▲ Dem. Rep. Congo/Uganda
141 Y8 Ruwī NE Oman 23°33′N 58°31′E
114 F9 Ruy ▲ Bulgaria/Serbia 42°52′N 22°35′E
Ruya see Luia, Rio
81 E20 Ruyigi E Burundi 03°28′S 30°19′E
127 P5 Ruzayevka Respublika Mordoviya, W Russian Federation 54°04′N 44°56′E
119 G18 Ruzhany Brestskaya Voblasts', SW Belarus 52°52′N 24°53′E
114 I10 Rŭzhevo Konare Plovdiv, C Bulgaria 42°16′N 24°58′E
Ruzhin see Ruzhyn
114 G7 Ruzhintsi Vidin, NW Bulgaria 43°38′N 22°50′E
161 N6 Ruzhou Henan, C China 34°10′N 112°51′E
117 N5 Ruzhyn Rus. Ruzhin. Zhytomyrs'ka Oblast', N Ukraine 49°42′N 29°01′E
111 K19 Ružomberok Ger. Rosenberg, Hung. Rózsahegy. Žilinský Kraj, N Slovakia 49°04′N 19°19′E
111 C16 Ruzyně ✈ (Praha) Praha, C Czech Republic
81 D19 Rwanda off. Rwandese Republic; prev. Ruanda. ◆ republic C Africa
Rwandese Republic see Rwanda
95 G22 Ry Århus, C Denmark 56°06′N 09°46′E
Ryasna see Rasna
126 L5 Ryazan' Ryazanskaya Oblast', W Russian Federation 54°37′N 39°37′E
126 L5 Ryazanskaya Oblast' ◐ province W Russian Federation
126 M6 Ryazhsk Ryazanskaya Oblast', W Russian Federation 53°42′N 40°09′E
118 B13 Rybachiy Ger. Rossitten. Kaliningradskaya Oblast', W Russian Federation 55°09′N 20°49′E
124 J2 Rybachiy, Poluostrov peninsula NW Russian Federation
Rybach'ye see Balykchy
124 L15 Rybinsk prev. Andropov. Yaroslavskaya Oblast', W Russian Federation 58°03′N 38°53′E
124 K14 Rybinskoye Vodokhranilishche Eng. Rybinsk Reservoir, Rybinsk Sea. ⊠ W Russian Federation
Rybinsk Reservoir/Rybinsk Sea see Rybinskoye Vodokhranilishche
111 I16 Rybnik Śląskie, S Poland 50°05′N 18°31′E
Rybnitsa see Rîbniţa

314
◆ Country ● Country Capital ◇ Dependent Territory ○ Dependent Territory Capital ◐ Administrative Regions ✈ International Airport ▲ Mountain ▲▲ Mountain Range Ѫ Volcano ≈ River ◎ Lake ⊠ Reservoir

RYCHNOV NAD KNĚŽNOU – ST. JOSEPH, LAKE

111 F16 **Rychnov nad Kněžnou** *Ger.* Reichenau. Královéhradecký Kraj, N Czech Republic 50°10′N 16°17′E
110 I12 **Rychwał** Wielkopolskie, C Poland 52°04′N 18°10′E
11 O13 **Rycroft** Alberta, W Canada 55°45′N 118°42′W
95 L21 **Ryd** Kronoberg, S Sweden 56°27′N 14°44′E
95 L20 **Rydaholm** Jönköping, S Sweden 56°57′N 14°19′E
194 I8 **Rydberg Peninsula** *peninsula* Antarctica
97 P23 **Rye** SE England, United Kingdom 50°57′N 00°42′E
33 T10 **Ryegate** Montana, NW USA 46°21′N 109°12′W
35 S3 **Rye Patch Reservoir** ⊠ Nevada, W USA
95 D15 **Ryfylke** *physical region* S Norway
95 H16 **Rygge** Østfold, S Norway 59°22′N 10°45′E
110 N13 **Ryki** Lubelskie, E Poland 51°38′N 21°57′E
Rykovo *see* Yenakiyeve
126 I7 **Ryl'sk** Kurskaya Oblast', W Russian Federation 51°34′N 34°41′E
183 S8 **Rylstone** New South Wales, SE Australia 32°48′S 149°58′E
111 H17 **Rýmařov** *Ger.* Römerstadt. Moravskoslezský Kraj, E Czech Republic 49°56′N 17°15′E
144 E11 **Ryn-Peski** *desert* W Kazakhstan
165 N10 **Ryōtsu** *var.* Ryôtu. Niigata, Sado, C Japan 38°06′N 138°28′E
Ryôtu *see* Ryōtsu
110 K10 **Rypin** Kujawsko-pomorskie, C Poland 53°03′N 19°25′E
Ryshkany *see* Rîşcani
Ryssel *see* Lille
Ryswick *see* Rijswijk
95 M24 **Rytterknægten** *hill* E Denmark
Ryukyu Islands *see* Nansei-shotō
192 G5 **Ryukyu Trench** *var.* Nansei Syotō Trench. *undersea feature* S East China Sea 24°45′N 128°00′E
110 D11 **Rzepin** *Ger.* Reppen. Lubuskie, W Poland 52°20′N 14°48′E
111 N16 **Rzeszów** Podkarpackie, SE Poland 50°03′N 22°01′E
124 I16 **Rzhev** Tverskaya Oblast', W Russian Federation 56°17′N 34°22′E
Rzhishchev *see* Rzhyshchiv
117 P5 **Rzhyshchiv** *Rus.* Rzhishchev. Kyyivs'ka Oblast', N Ukraine 49°58′N 31°02′E

S

138 E11 **Sa'ad** Southern, W Israel 31°27′N 34°31′E
109 P7 **Saalach** ≈ W Austria
101 L14 **Saale** ≈ C Germany
101 L17 **Saalfeld** *var.* Saalfeld an der Saale. Thüringen, C Germany 50°39′N 11°22′E
Saalfeld *see* Zalewo
Saalfeld an der Saale *see* Saalfeld
108 C8 **Saane** ≈ W Switzerland
101 D19 **Saar** *Fr.* Sarre. ≈ France/Germany
101 E20 **Saarbrücken** *Fr.* Sarrebruck. Saarland, SW Germany 49°13′N 07°01′E
Saarburg *see* Sarrebourg
118 D6 **Sääre** *var.* Sjar. Saaremaa, W Estonia 57°57′N 21°53′E
Saare *see* Saaremaa
118 D5 **Saaremaa** *off.* Saare Maakond. ◆ *province* W Estonia
118 E6 **Saaremaa** *Ger.* Oesel, Ösel; *prev.* Saare. *island* W Estonia
Saare Maakond *see* Saaremaa
92 L12 **Saarenkylä** Lappi, N Finland 66°31′N 25°51′E
Saargemund *see* Sarreguemines
93 L17 **Saarijärvi** Länsi-Suomi, C Finland 62°42′N 25°16′E
Saar in Mähren *see* Žďár nad Sázavou
92 M10 **Saariselkä** *Lapp.* Suoločielgi. Lappi, N Finland 68°27′N 27°29′E
92 L10 **Saariselkä** *hill range* NE Finland
101 D20 **Saarland** *Fr.* Sarre. ◆ *state* SW Germany
Saarlautern *see* Saarlouis
101 D20 **Saarlouis** *prev.* Saarlautern. Saarland, SW Germany 49°19′N 06°45′E
108 E11 **Saaser Vispa** ≈ S Switzerland
137 X12 **Saatlı** *Rus.* Saatly. C Azerbaijan 39°57′N 48°24′E
Saatly *see* Saatlı
Saaz *see* Žatec
45 V9 **Saba** *island* N Netherlands Antilles
138 J7 **Sab' Ābār** *var.* Sab'a Biyar, Sa'b Bi'ār. Ḥimṣ, C Syria 33°46′N 37°41′E
Sab'a Biyar *see* Sab' Ābār
112 K11 **Šabac** Serbia, W Serbia 44°45′N 19°42′E
105 W5 **Sabadell** Cataluña, E Spain 41°33′N 02°07′E
164 K12 **Sabae** Fukui, Honshū, SW Japan 36°00′N 136°12′E
169 V7 **Sabah** *prev.* British North Borneo, North Borneo. ◆ *state* East Malaysia
168 J8 **Sabak** *var.* Sabak Bernam. Selangor, Peninsular Malaysia 03°45′N 100°59′E
Sabak Bernam *see* Sabak
38 D16 **Sabak, Cape** *headland* Agattu Island, Alaska, USA 52°21′N 173°43′E
81 J20 **Sabaki** ≈ S Kenya
142 L2 **Sabalān, Kuhhā-ye** ▲ NW Iran 38°21′N 47°47′E
154 H7 **Sabalgarh** Madhya Pradesh, C India 26°18′N 77°28′E
44 E4 **Sabana, Archipiélago de** *island group* C Cuba
42 H7 **Sabanagrande** *var.* Sabana Grande. Francisco Morazán, S Honduras 13°48′N 87°15′W
Sabana Grande *see* Sabanagrande
54 E5 **Sabanalarga** Atlántico, N Colombia 10°38′N 74°55′W
41 W14 **Sabancuy** Campeche, SE Mexico 18°58′N 91°11′W
45 N8 **Sabaneta** NW Dominican Republic 19°30′N 71°21′W
54 J4 **Sabaneta** Falcón, N Venezuela 11°17′N 70°00′W
188 H4 **Sabaneta, Puntan** *prev.* Ushi Point. *headland* Saipan, S Northern Mariana Islands 15°17′N 145°49′E
171 X14 **Sabang** Papua, E Indonesia 04°33′S 138°42′E
116 L10 **Săbăoani** Neamţ, NE Romania 47°01′N 26°51′E
155 J26 **Sabaragamuwa** ◆ *province* C Sri Lanka
Sabaria *see* Szombathely
154 D10 **Sābarmati** ≈ NW India
171 S10 **Sabatai** Pulau Morotai, E Indonesia 02°04′N 128°23′E
141 Q15 **Sab'atayn, Ramlat as** *desert* C Yemen
107 I16 **Sabaudia** Lazio, C Italy 41°17′N 13°02′E
57 J19 **Sabaya** Oruro, S Bolivia 19°09′S 68°21′W
Sa'b Bi'ār *see* Sab' Ābār
Sabbioncello *see* Orebić
148 I8 **Şāberi, Hāmūn-e** *var.* Daryācheh-ye Hāmun, Daryācheh-ye Sīstān. ⊚ Afghanistan/Iran *see also* Sīstān, Daryācheh-ye
Şāberi, Hāmūn-e *see* Sīstān, Daryācheh-ye
27 P2 **Sabetha** Kansas, C USA 39°54′N 95°48′W
75 P10 **Sabhā** C Libya 27°02′N 14°26′E
67 V13 **Sabi** *var.* Save. ≈ Mozambique/Zimbabwe *see also* Save
Sabi *see* Save
118 E8 **Sabile** *Ger.* Zabeln. Talsi, NW Latvia 57°03′N 22°33′E
31 R14 **Sabina** Ohio, N USA 39°29′N 83°38′W
40 I3 **Sabinal** Chihuahua, N Mexico 30°59′N 107°29′W
25 Q12 **Sabinal** Texas, SW USA 29°19′N 99°28′W
25 Q11 **Sabinal River** ≈ Texas, SW USA
105 S4 **Sabiñánigo** Aragón, NE Spain 42°31′N 00°22′W
41 N6 **Sabinas** Coahuila, NE Mexico 27°52′N 101°04′W
41 O8 **Sabinas Hidalgo** Nuevo León, NE Mexico 26°29′N 100°09′W
41 N6 **Sabinas, Río** ≈ NE Mexico
22 F9 **Sabine Lake** ⊚ Louisiana/Texas, S USA
92 O3 **Sabine Land** *physical region* C Svalbard
25 W7 **Sabine River** ≈ Louisiana/Texas, SW USA
137 X12 **Sabirabad** C Azerbaijan 40°00′N 48°27′E
Sabkha *see* As Sabkhah
171 O4 **Sablayan** Mindoro, N Philippines 12°48′N 120°48′E
13 P16 **Sable, Cape** *headland* Newfoundland and Labrador, SE Canada 43°21′N 65°40′W
23 X17 **Sable, Cape** *headland* Florida, SE USA 25°12′N 81°06′W
13 R16 **Sable Island** *island* Nova Scotia, SE Canada
14 L11 **Sables, Lac des** ⊚ Québec, SE Canada
14 E10 **Sables, Rivière aux** ≈ Ontario, S Canada
102 K7 **Sablé-sur-Sarthe** Sarthe, NW France 47°49′N 00°19′W
125 U7 **Sablya, Gora** ▲ NW Russian Federation 64°46′N 58°52′E
77 U14 **Sabon Birnin Gwari** Kaduna, C Nigeria 10°43′N 06°39′E
77 V11 **Sabon Kafi** Zinder, C Niger 14°37′N 08°46′E
104 I6 **Sabor, Rio** ≈ N Portugal
14 J8 **Sabourin, Lac** ⊚ Québec, SE Canada
102 J14 **Sabres** Landes, SW France 44°07′N 00°46′W
195 X13 **Sabrina Coast** *physical region* Antarctica
140 M11 **Sabt al Ulayā** 'Asīr, SW Saudi Arabia 19°33′N 41°58′E
104 I8 **Sabugal** Guarda, N Portugal 40°20′N 07°05′W
29 Z13 **Sabula** Iowa, C USA 42°04′N 90°10′W
141 N13 **Şabyā** Jīzān, SW Saudi Arabia 17°50′N 42°50′E
Sabzawar *see* Sabzevār
Sabzawaran *see* Jīroft
143 S4 **Sabzevār** *var.* Sabzawar. Khorāsān-Razavī, NE Iran 36°13′N 57°38′E
Sabzvārān *see* Jīroft
Sacajawea Peak *see* Matterhorn
82 C9 **Sacandica** Uíge, NW Angola 06°01′S 15°57′E
42 A2 **Sacatepéquez** *off.* Departamento de Sacatepéquez. ◆ *department* S Guatemala
Sacatepéquez, Departamento de *see* Sacatepéquez
104 F11 **Sacavém** Lisboa, W Portugal 38°47′N 09°06′W
29 T13 **Sac City** Iowa, C USA 42°25′N 94°59′W
105 P8 **Sacedón** Castilla-La Mancha, C Spain 40°29′N 02°44′W
116 J12 **Săcele** *Ger.* Vierdörfer, *Hung.* Négyfalu; *prev. Ger.* Sieben Dörfer, *Hung.* Hétfalu. Braşov, C Romania 45°36′N 25°40′E
12 C8 **Sachigo** Ontario, C Canada 53°52′N 92°16′W
12 C7 **Sachigo** ≈ Ontario, C Canada
12 C8 **Sachigo Lake** ⊚ Ontario, C Canada
163 Y16 **Sach'ŏn** *Jap.* Sansenhō; *prev.* Samch'ŏnpŏ. S South Korea 34°55′N 128°07′E
101 O15 **Sachsen** *Eng.* Saxony, *Fr.* Saxe. ◆ *state* E Germany
101 K14 **Sachsen-Anhalt** *Eng.* Saxony-Anhalt. ◆ *state* C Germany
109 R9 **Sachsenburg** Salzburg, S Austria 46°49′N 13°23′E
Sachsenfeld *see* Žalec
8 I5 **Sachs Harbour** *var.* Ikaahuk. Banks Island, Northwest Territories, N Canada 72°N 125°14′W
Sächsisch-Reen/Sächsisch-Regen *see* Reghin
18 H8 **Sackets Harbor** New York, NE USA 43°57′N 76°06′W
13 P14 **Sackville** New Brunswick, SE Canada 45°54′N 64°23′W
19 P9 **Saco** Maine, NE USA 43°32′N 70°25′W
19 P8 **Saco River** ≈ Maine/New Hampshire, NE USA
35 O7 **Sacramento** *state capital* California, W USA 38°35′N 121°30′W
37 T14 **Sacramento Mountains** ▲▲ New Mexico, SW USA
35 N6 **Sacramento River** ≈ California, W USA
35 N5 **Sacramento Valley** *valley* California, W USA
36 I10 **Sacramento Wash** *valley* Arizona, SW USA
105 N15 **Sacratif, Cabo** *headland* S Spain 36°41′N 03°30′W
116 F9 **Săcueni** *prev.* Săcuieni, *Hung.* Székelyhid. Bihor, W Romania 47°20′N 22°05′E
Săcuieni *see* Săcueni
105 R4 **Sádaba** Aragón, NE Spain 42°15′N 01°16′W
Sá da Bandeira *see* Lubango
138 I6 **Şadad** Ḥimş, W Syria 34°19′N 36°52′E
141 O13 **Şa'dah** NW Yemen 16°59′N 43°45′E
167 O16 **Sadao** Songkhla, SW Thailand 06°39′N 100°30′E
142 L8 **Sadd-e Dez, Daryācheh-ye** ⊚ W Iran
19 S3 **Saddleback Mountain** *hill* Maine, NE USA
19 P6 **Saddleback Mountain** ▲ Maine, NE USA 44°57′N 70°27′W
141 W13 **Sadh** S Oman 17°11′N 55°08′E
76 J11 **Sadiola** Kayes, W Mali 13°48′N 11°47′W
149 R12 **Sādiqābād** Punjab, E Pakistan 28°16′N 70°10′E
153 Y10 **Sadiya** Assam, NE India 27°49′N 95°38′E
139 W9 **Sa'dīyah, Hawr as** ⊚ E Iraq
165 N9 **Sado** *var.* Sadoga-shima. *island* C Japan
Sadoga-shima *see* Sado
104 F12 **Sado, Rio** ≈ S Portugal
114 I8 **Sadovets** Pleven, N Bulgaria 43°19′N 24°21′E
114 J11 **Sadovo** Plovdiv, C Bulgaria 42°07′N 24°56′E
127 O11 **Sadovoye** Respublika Kalmykiya, SW Russian Federation 47°51′N 44°34′E
105 W9 **Sa Dragonera** *var.* Isla Dragonera. *island* Islas Baleares, Spain, W Mediterranean Sea
105 P9 **Saelices** Castilla-La Mancha, C Spain 39°55′N 02°49′W
Saena Julia *see* Siena
Saetabicula *see* Alzira
114 O12 **Safaalan** Tekirdağ, NW Turkey 41°26′N 28°07′E
Safad *see* Tsefat
Şafāqis *see* Sfax
143 P10 **Şafāshahr** *var.* Deh Bīd. Fārs, C Iran 30°50′N 53°50′E
192 I16 **Safata Bay** *bay* Upolu, Samoa, C Pacific Ocean
Safed *see* Tsefat
139 X11 **Şaffāf, Ḩawr aş** *marshy lake* S Iraq
95 J16 **Säffle** Värmland, C Sweden 59°08′N 12°55′E
37 N15 **Safford** Arizona, SW USA 32°46′N 109°41′W
74 E7 **Safi** W Morocco 32°19′N 09°14′W
126 I4 **Safonovo** Smolenskaya Oblast', W Russian Federation 55°05′N 33°12′E
136 H11 **Safranbolu** Karabük, NW Turkey 41°16′N 32°41′E
139 Y13 **Safwān** Al Başrah, SE Iraq 30°06′N 47°44′E
158 J16 **Saga** *var.* Gya'gya. Xizang Zizhiqu, W China 29°22′N 85°19′E
164 C14 **Saga** Saga, Kyūshū, SW Japan 33°14′N 130°16′E
164 C13 **Saga** *off.* Saga-ken. ◆ *prefecture* Kyūshū, SW Japan
165 P10 **Sagae** Yamagata, Honshū, C Japan 38°22′N 140°12′E
166 L3 **Sagaing** Sagaing, C Burma (Myanmar) 21°55′N 95°56′E
166 L5 **Sagaing** ◆ *division* N Burma (Myanmar)
Saga-ken *see* Saga
165 N13 **Sagamihara** Kanagawa, Honshū, S Japan 35°34′N 139°22′E
165 N14 **Sagami-nada** *inlet* SW Japan
Sagan *see* Żagań
29 Y3 **Saganaga Lake** ⊚ Minnesota, N USA
155 F18 **Sāgar** Karnātaka, W India 14°09′N 75°02′E
154 I9 **Sāgar** *prev.* Saugor. Madhya Pradesh, C India 23°53′N 78°46′E
15 S8 **Sagard** Québec, SE Canada 48°01′N 70°03′W
Sagarmāthā *see* Everest, Mount
Sagebrush State *see* Nevada
143 V11 **Sāghand** Yazd, C Iran 32°33′N 55°12′E
19 N14 **Sag Harbor** Long Island, New York, NE USA 40°59′N 72°15′W
Saghez *see* Saqqez
Saghyz *see* Sagiz
31 R8 **Saginaw** Michigan, N USA 43°25′N 83°57′W
31 R8 **Saginaw Bay** *lake bay* Michigan, N USA
144 H11 **Sagiz** *Kaz.* Saghyz. Atyrau, W Kazakhstan 48°12′N 54°56′E
64 H6 **Saglek Bank** *undersea feature* W Labrador Sea
13 P5 **Saglek Bay** *bay* SW Labrador Sea
Saglouc/Sagluk *see* Salluit
103 X15 **Sagone, Golfe de** *gulf* Corse, France, C Mediterranean Sea
105 P13 **Sagra** ▲ S Spain 37°59′N 02°33′W
104 F14 **Sagres** Faro, S Portugal 37°01′N 08°56′W
37 S7 **Saguache** Colorado, C USA 38°05′N 106°05′W
44 J7 **Sagua de Tánamo** Holguín, E Cuba 20°38′N 75°14′W
44 E5 **Sagua la Grande** Villa Clara, C Cuba 22°48′N 80°06′W
15 R7 **Saguenay** ≈ Québec, SE Canada
74 C9 **Saguia al Hamra** *var.* As Saqia al Hamra. ≈ N Western Sahara
105 S9 **Sagunt** *Cas.* Sagunto, *Ar.* Murviedro; *anc.* Saguntum. País Valenciano, E Spain 39°40′N 00°17′W
Sagunt/Saguntum *see* Sagunto
158 L16 **Sa'gya** Xizang Zizhiqu, W China 28°51′N 88°00′E
138 H10 **Saḩāb** 'Ammān, NW Jordan 31°52′N 36°00′E
54 E6 **Sahagún** Córdoba, NW Colombia 08°58′N 75°30′W
104 L4 **Sahagún** Castilla-León, N Spain 42°23′N 05°02′W
141 X8 **Saḩam** N Oman 24°06′N 56°52′E
68 F9 **Sahara** *desert* Libya/Algeria
Sahara el Gharbîya *see* Şaḩrā' al Gharbīyah
75 X9 **Sahara el Sharqîya** *var.* Aş Şaḩrā' ash Sharqīyah, *Eng.* Arabian Desert, Eastern Desert. *desert* E Egypt
Saharan Atlas *see* Atlas Saharien
152 J9 **Sahāranpur** Uttar Pradesh, N India 29°58′N 77°33′E
64 L10 **Saharan Seamounts** *var.* Saharian Seamounts. *undersea feature* E Atlantic Ocean 25°00′N 20°00′W
Saharian Seamounts *see* Saharan Seamounts
153 Q13 **Saharsa** Bihār, NE India 25°54′N 86°36′E
67 O7 **Sahel** *physical region* C Africa
153 R14 **Sāhibganj** Jhārkhand, NE India 25°15′N 87°40′E
80 N12 **Sahil** *off.* Gobolka Sahil. ◆ *region* N Somalia
139 Q7 **Saḩīlīyah** Al Anbār, C Iraq 33°43′N 42°42′E
138 H4 **Saḩilīyah, Jibāl as** ▲▲ NW Syria
114 M13 **Şahin** Tekirdağ, NW Turkey 41°01′N 26°51′E
149 U8 **Sāhīwāl** Punjab, E Pakistan 31°57′N 72°22′E
149 U9 **Sāhīwāl** *prev.* Montgomery. Punjab, E Pakistan 30°40′N 73°05′E
141 W11 **Şaḩmah, Ramlat as** *desert* C Oman
75 U9 **Şaḩrā' al Gharbīyah** *var.* Sahara el Gharbîya, *Eng.* Western Desert. *desert* C Egypt
139 T13 **Şaḩrā' al Ḩijārah** *desert* S Iraq
40 H5 **Sahuaripa** Sonora, NW Mexico 29°02′N 109°14′W
36 M16 **Sahuarita** Arizona, SW USA 31°24′N 110°55′W
40 L13 **Sahuayo** *var.* Sahuayo de José Mariá Morelos; *prev.* Sahuayo de Díaz, Sahuayo de Porfirio Díaz. Michoacán, SW Mexico 20°05′N 102°42′W
Sahuayo de Díaz/Sahuayo de José Mariá Morelos/ Sahuayo de Porfirio Díaz *see* Sahuayo
173 W8 **Sahul Shelf** *undersea feature* N Timor Sea
167 P17 **Sai Buri** Pattani, SW Thailand 06°42′N 101°37′E
74 I6 **Saïda** NW Algeria 32°50′N 00°10′E
138 G7 **Saïda** *var.* Şaydā, Sayida; *anc.* Sidon. W Lebanon 33°20′N 35°24′E
Sa'īdābād *see* Sīrjān
80 B13 **Sa'id Bundas** Western Bahr el Ghazal, SW Sudan 08°24′N 24°53′E
186 E7 **Saidor** Madang, N Papua New Guinea 05°38′S 146°28′E
153 S13 **Saidpur** *var.* Syedpur. Rajshahi, NW Bangladesh 25°48′N 89°E
149 U5 **Saidu Sharif** *var.* Mingora, Mongora. North-West Frontier Province, N Pakistan 34°45′N 72°21′E
108 C7 **Saignelégier** Jura, NW Switzerland 47°18′N 07°03′E
164 H11 **Saigō** Shimane, Dōgo, SW Japan 36°12′N 133°18′E
Saigon *see* Hô Chi Minh
163 P11 **Saihan Tal** *var.* Sonid Youqi. Nei Mongol Zizhiqu, N China 42°45′N 112°36′E
162 I12 **Saihan Toroi** Nei Mongol Zizhiqu, N China 41°44′N 100°29′E
Sai Hun *see* Syr Darya
92 M11 **Saija** Lappi, NE Finland 67°07′N 28°46′E
164 G14 **Saijō** Ehime, Shikoku, SW Japan 33°55′N 133°10′E
164 E15 **Saiki** Ōita, Kyūshū, SW Japan 32°57′N 131°52′E
93 N18 **Saimaa** ⊚ SE Finland
93 N18 **Saimaa Canal** *Fin.* Saimaan Kanava, *Rus.* Saymenskiy Kanal. *canal* Finland/Russian Federation
Saimaan Kanava *see* Saimaa Canal
40 L10 **Saín Alto** Zacatecas, C Mexico 23°36′N 103°14′W
96 L12 **St Abb's Head** *headland* SE Scotland, United Kingdom 55°54′N 02°07′W
11 Y16 **St. Adolphe** Manitoba, S Canada 49°39′N 96°55′W
103 O15 **St-Affrique** Aveyron, S France 43°57′N 02°52′E
15 Q10 **St-Agapit** Québec, SE Canada 46°22′N 71°37′W
97 O21 **St Albans** *anc.* Verulamium. E England, United Kingdom 51°46′N 00°21′W
18 L6 **Saint Albans** Vermont, NE USA 44°49′N 73°07′W
21 Q5 **Saint Albans** West Virginia, NE USA 38°21′N 81°47′W
St. Alban's Head *see* St Aldhelm's Head
11 Q14 **St. Albert** Alberta, SW Canada 53°38′N 113°38′W
97 M24 **St Aldhelm's Head** *var.* St. Alban's Head. *headland* S England, United Kingdom 50°34′N 02°04′W
15 O11 **St-Alexis-des-Monts** Québec, SE Canada 46°30′N 73°08′W
103 P2 **St-Amand-les-Eaux** Nord, N France 50°27′N 03°25′E
103 O9 **St-Amand-Montrond** *var.* St-Amand-Mont-Rond. Cher, C France 46°43′N 02°29′E
173 P16 **St-André** NE Réunion
14 M12 **St-André-Avellin** Québec, SE Canada 45°45′N 75°04′W
Saint-André, Cap *see* Vilanandro, Tanjona
102 K12 **St-André-de-Cubzac** Gironde, SW France 45°01′N 00°26′W
96 K11 **St Andrews** E Scotland, United Kingdom 56°20′N 02°49′W
23 Q9 **Saint Andrews Bay** *bay* Florida, SE USA
23 W7 **Saint Andrew Sound** *sound* Georgia, SE USA
Saint Anna Trough *see* Svyataya Anna Trough
44 J11 **St. Ann's Bay** C Jamaica 18°26′N 77°12′W
13 T10 **St. Anthony** Newfoundland and Labrador, SE Canada 51°22′N 55°34′W
33 R13 **Saint Anthony** Idaho, NW USA 43°56′N 111°38′W
182 M11 **Saint Arnaud** Victoria, SE Australia 36°39′S 143°15′E
185 I15 **St.Arnaud Range** ▲▲ South Island, New Zealand
13 R10 **St-Augustin** Québec, E Canada 51°13′N 58°39′W
23 X9 **Saint Augustine** Florida, SE USA 29°54′N 81°19′W
97 H24 **St Austell** SW England, United Kingdom 50°21′N 04°47′W
103 T4 **St-Avold** Moselle, NE France 49°06′N 06°43′E
45 R3 **St-Barthélemy** ▲ S France
102 M17 **St-Béat** Haute-Garonne, S France 42°55′N 00°39′E
97 I15 **St Bees Head** *headland* NW England, United Kingdom 54°30′N 03°39′W
173 P16 **St-Benoit** E Réunion
103 T13 **St-Bonnet** Hautes-Alpes, SE France 44°41′N 06°04′E
St.Botolph's Town *see* Boston
97 G21 **St Brides Bay** *inlet* SW Wales, United Kingdom
102 H5 **St-Brieuc** Côtes d'Armor, NW France 48°31′N 02°45′W
102 H5 **St-Brieuc, Baie de** *bay* NW France
102 L7 **St-Calais** Sarthe, NW France 47°55′N 00°48′E
15 Q10 **St-Casimir** Québec, SE Canada 46°40′N 72°05′W
14 H16 **St. Catharines** Ontario, S Canada 43°10′N 79°15′W
45 S14 **St. Catherine, Mount** ▲ N Grenada 12°10′N 61°41′W
64 C11 **St Catherine Point** *headland* E Bermuda
23 X6 **Saint Catherines Island** *island* Georgia, SE USA
97 M24 **St Catherine's Point** *headland* S England, United Kingdom 50°34′N 01°17′W
103 N13 **St-Céré** Lot, S France 44°52′N 01°53′E
108 A10 **St. Cergue** Vaud, W Switzerland 46°25′N 06°10′E
103 R11 **St-Chamond** Loire, E France 45°29′N 04°32′E
33 S16 **Saint Charles** Idaho, NW USA 42°05′N 111°23′W
27 X4 **Saint Charles** Missouri, C USA 38°48′N 90°29′W
103 P13 **St-Chély-d'Apcher** Lozère, S France 44°51′N 03°16′E
Saint Christopher and Nevis, Federation of *see* Saint Kitts and Nevis
Saint Christopher-Nevis *see* Saint Kitts and Nevis
31 S9 **Saint Clair** Michigan, N USA 42°49′N 82°29′W
183 O17 **St. Clair, Lake** ⊚ Tasmania, SE Australia
14 C17 **St. Clair, Lake** *var.* Lac à L'Eau Claire. ⊚ Canada/USA
31 S10 **Saint Clair Shores** Michigan, N USA 42°30′N 82°53′W
103 S10 **St-Claude** *anc.* Condate. Jura, E France 46°23′N 05°52′E
45 X6 **St-Claude** Basse Terre, SW Guadeloupe 16°02′N 61°42′W
23 X12 **Saint Cloud** Florida, SE USA 28°15′N 81°15′W
29 U8 **Saint Cloud** Minnesota, N USA 45°34′N 94°10′W
45 T9 **Saint Croix** *island* S Virgin Islands (US)
30 J4 **Saint Croix Flowage** ⊠ Wisconsin, N USA
19 T5 **Saint Croix River** ≈ Canada/USA
29 W7 **Saint Croix River** ≈ Minnesota/Wisconsin, N USA
45 S14 **St. David's** SE Grenada 12°01′N 61°40′W
97 H21 **St David's** SW Wales, United Kingdom 51°53′N 05°16′W
97 G21 **St David's Head** *headland* SW Wales, United Kingdom 51°54′N 05°19′W
64 C12 **St David's Island** *island* E Bermuda
173 O16 **St-Denis** ○ (Réunion) NW Réunion 20°55′S 14°34′E
103 U6 **St-Dié** Vosges, NE France 48°17′N 06°57′E
103 R5 **St-Dizier** *anc.* Desiderii Fanum. Haute-Marne, N France 48°39′N 05°00′E
15 N11 **St-Donat** Québec, SE Canada 46°19′N 74°15′W
15 N11 **Ste-Adèle** Québec, SE Canada 45°58′N 74°10′W
15 N11 **Ste-Agathe-des-Monts** Québec, SE Canada 46°03′N 74°19′W
11 Y16 **Ste. Anne** Manitoba, S Canada 49°40′N 96°40′W
45 R12 **Ste-Anne** Grande Terre, E Guadeloupe 16°13′N 61°23′W
45 Y6 **Ste-Anne** SE Martinique 14°26′N 60°53′W
15 Q10 **Ste-Anne** ≈ Québec, SE Canada
172 I16 **Sainte Anne** *island* Inner Islands, NE Seychelles
15 W6 **Ste-Anne-des-Monts** Québec, SE Canada 49°07′N 66°29′W
14 M10 **Ste-Anne-du-Lac** Québec, SE Canada 46°51′N 75°20′W
15 S10 **Ste-Apolline** Québec, SE Canada 46°47′N 70°15′W
15 R10 **Ste-Claire** Québec, SE Canada 46°30′N 70°40′W
15 Q10 **Ste-Croix** Québec, SE Canada 46°36′N 71°42′W
108 B8 **Ste. Croix** Vaud, SW Switzerland 46°50′N 06°31′E
103 P14 **Ste-Énimie** Lozère, S France 44°21′N 03°26′E
27 Y6 **Sainte Genevieve** Missouri, C USA 37°57′N 90°01′W
103 S12 **St-Egrève** Isère, E France 45°15′N 05°41′E
39 T12 **Saint Elias, Cape** *headland* Kayak Island, Alaska, USA 59°48′N 144°36′W
39 U11 **St Elias, Mount** ▲ Alaska, USA 60°18′N 140°57′W
10 G8 **Saint Elias Mountains** ▲▲ Canada/USA
55 Y10 **St-Élie** N French Guiana 04°50′N 53°21′W
103 O10 **St-Eloy-les-Mines** Puy-de-Dôme, C France 46°07′N 02°50′E
15 R10 **Ste-Marie** Québec, SE Canada 46°28′N 71°00′W
45 Q11 **Ste-Marie** NE Martinique 14°47′N 61°00′W
173 P16 **Ste-Marie** NE Réunion
103 U6 **Ste-Marie-aux-Mines** Haut-Rhin, NE France 48°16′N 07°12′E
Sainte Marie, Cap *see* Vohimena, Tanjona
102 L8 **Ste-Maure-de-Touraine** Indre-et-Loire, C France 47°06′N 00°38′E
103 R4 **Ste-Menehould** Marne, NE France 49°06′N 04°54′E
Ste-Perpétue *see* Ste-Perpétue-de-l'Islet
15 S9 **Ste-Perpétue-de-l'Islet** *var.* Ste-Perpétue. Québec, SE Canada 47°02′N 69°58′W
45 X11 **Ste-Rose** Basse Terre, N Guadeloupe 16°20′N 61°42′W
173 P16 **Ste-Rose** E Réunion
11 W15 **Ste. Rose du Lac** Manitoba, S Canada 51°04′N 99°31′W
102 J11 **Saintes** *anc.* Mediolanum. Charente-Maritime, W France 45°45′N 00°37′W
45 X7 **Saintes, Canal des** *channel* SW Guadeloupe
Saintes, Îles des *see* les Saintes
173 P16 **Ste-Suzanne** N Réunion
15 P10 **Ste-Thècle** Québec, SE Canada 46°48′N 72°31′W
103 Q12 **St-Étienne** Loire, E France 45°26′N 04°23′E
102 M4 **St-Étienne-du-Rouvray** Seine-Maritime, N France 49°22′N 01°07′E
Saint Eustatius *see* Sint Eustatius
15 R7 **Ste-Marguerite** ≈ Québec, SE Canada
14 M11 **Ste-Véronique** Québec, SE Canada 46°30′N 74°58′W
15 P7 **St-Félicien** Québec, SE Canada 48°38′N 72°29′W
15 O11 **St-Félix-de-Valois** Québec, SE Canada 46°10′N 73°26′W
103 Y14 **St-Florent** Corse, France, C Mediterranean Sea 42°41′N 09°19′E
103 Y14 **St-Florent, Golfe de** *gulf* Corse, France, C Mediterranean Sea
103 P6 **St-Florentin** Yonne, C France 48°00′N 03°46′E
103 N9 **St-Florent-sur-Cher** Cher, C France 47°00′N 02°13′E
103 P12 **St-Flour** Cantal, C France 45°02′N 03°05′E
26 H2 **Saint Francis** Kansas, C USA 39°45′N 101°31′W
83 H26 **St. Francis, Cape** *headland* S South Africa 34°11′S 24°45′E
27 X10 **Saint Francis River** ≈ Arkansas/Missouri, C USA
22 J8 **Saint Francisville** Louisiana, S USA 30°46′N 91°22′W
45 Y6 **St-François** Grande Terre, E Guadeloupe 16°15′N 61°17′W
15 Q12 **St-François** ≈ Québec, SE Canada
27 X7 **Saint Francois Mountains** ▲▲ Missouri, C USA
St-Gall *see* St-Gall/Saint Gall/ St.Gallen
St-Gall/Saint Gall/St. Gallen *see* Sankt Gallen
102 L16 **St-Gaudens** Haute-Garonne, S France 43°07′N 00°43′E
15 R12 **St-Gédéon** Québec, SE Canada 45°51′N 70°36′W
181 X10 **Saint George** Queensland, E Australia 28°05′S 148°40′E
64 B12 **St George** N Bermuda 32°24′N 64°42′W
38 K15 **Saint George** Saint George Island, Alaska, USA 56°34′N 169°30′W
21 S14 **Saint George** South Carolina, SE USA 33°12′N 80°34′W
36 J8 **Saint George** Utah, W USA 37°06′N 113°35′W
13 R12 **St. George, Cape** *headland* Newfoundland and Labrador, E Canada 48°26′N 59°17′W
186 I6 **St. George, Cape** *headland* New Ireland, NE Papua New Guinea 04°49′S 152°52′E
38 J15 **Saint George Island** *island* Pribilof Islands, Alaska, USA
23 S10 **Saint George Island** *island* Florida, SE USA
99 J19 **Saint-Georges** Liège, E Belgium 50°36′N 05°20′E
15 R12 **St-Georges** Québec, SE Canada 46°08′N 70°40′W
55 Z11 **St-Georges** E French Guiana 03°55′N 51°49′W
45 R14 **St. George's** ● (Grenada) SW Grenada 12°04′N 61°45′W
13 R12 **St. George's Bay** *inlet* Newfoundland and Labrador, E Canada
97 G21 **Saint George's Channel** *channel* Ireland/Wales, United Kingdom
186 H6 **St. George's Channel** *channel* NE Papua New Guinea
64 B11 **St George's Island** *island* E Bermuda
99 I21 **Saint-Gérard** Namur, S Belgium 50°20′N 04°47′E
St-Germain *see* St-Germain-en-Laye
15 P12 **St-Germain-de-Grantham** Québec, SE Canada 45°49′N 72°32′W
103 N5 **St-Germain-en-Laye** *var.* St-Germain. Yvelines, N France 48°53′N 02°04′E
102 H8 **St-Gildas, Pointe du** *headland* NW France 47°09′N 02°25′W
103 R15 **St-Gilles** Gard, S France 43°41′N 04°24′E
102 I9 **St-Gilles-Croix-de-Vie** Vendée, NW France 46°41′N 01°55′W
173 O16 **St-Gilles-les-Bains** W Réunion 21°02′S 55°14′E
102 M16 **St-Girons** Ariège, S France 42°58′N 01°07′E
Saint Gotthard *see* Szentgotthárd
108 G9 **St. Gotthard Tunnel** *tunnel* Ticino, S Switzerland
97 H22 **St Govan's Head** *headland* SW Wales, United Kingdom 51°35′N 04°55′W
34 M7 **Saint Helena** California, W USA 38°29′N 122°30′W
65 F24 **Saint Helena** ◇ *UK dependent territory* C Atlantic Ocean
67 O12 **Saint Helena** *island* C Atlantic Ocean
65 M16 **Saint Helena Fracture Zone** *tectonic feature* C Atlantic Ocean
34 M7 **Saint Helena, Mount** ▲ California, W USA 38°40′N 122°39′W
21 S15 **Saint Helena Sound** *inlet* South Carolina, SE USA
31 Q7 **Saint Helen, Lake** ⊚ Michigan, N USA
183 Q16 **Saint Helens** Tasmania, SE Australia 41°21′S 148°15′E
97 K18 **St Helens** NW England, United Kingdom 53°28′N 02°44′W
32 G10 **Saint Helens** Oregon, NW USA 45°54′N 122°50′W
32 H10 **Saint Helens, Mount** ⛰ Washington, NW USA 46°24′N 121°49′W
97 L26 **St Helier** ○ (Jersey) S Jersey, Channel Islands 49°12′N 02°07′W
15 S9 **St-Hilarion** Québec, SE Canada 47°34′N 70°24′W
99 K22 **Saint-Hubert** Luxembourg, SE Belgium 50°02′N 05°23′E
15 P12 **St-Hyacinthe** Québec, SE Canada 45°38′N 72°57′W
St.Iago de la Vega *see* Spanish Town
31 Q4 **Saint Ignace** Michigan, N USA 45°53′N 84°44′W
15 O10 **St-Ignace-du-Lac** Québec, SE Canada 46°43′N 73°49′W
12 D12 **St. Ignace Island** *island* Ontario, S Canada
108 C7 **St. Imier** Bern, W Switzerland 47°09′N 06°55′E
97 G25 **St Ives** SW England, United Kingdom 50°12′N 05°29′W
29 U10 **Saint James** Minnesota, N USA 44°00′N 94°36′W
10 I15 **St. James, Cape** *headland* Graham Island, British Columbia, SW Canada 51°57′N 131°04′W
15 O13 **St-Jean** *var.* St-Jean-sur-Richelieu. Québec, SE Canada 45°15′N 73°16′W
55 X9 **St-Jean** NW French Guiana 05°25′N 54°05′W
Saint-Jean-d'Acre *see* Akko
102 K11 **St-Jean-d'Angély** Charente-Maritime, W France 45°57′N 00°31′W
103 N7 **St-Jean-de-Braye** Loiret, C France 47°54′N 01°58′E
102 I16 **St-Jean-de-Luz** Pyrénées-Atlantiques, SW France 43°24′N 01°40′W
103 T12 **St-Jean-de-Maurienne** Savoie, E France 45°17′N 06°21′E
102 I9 **St-Jean-de-Monts** Vendée, NW France 46°45′N 02°00′W
103 Q14 **St-Jean-du-Gard** Gard, S France 44°06′N 03°49′E
15 Q7 **St-Jean, Lac** ⊚ Québec, SE Canada
102 I16 **St-Jean-Pied-de-Port** Pyrénées-Atlantiques, SW France 43°10′N 01°14′W
15 S9 **St-Jean-Port-Joli** Québec, SE Canada 47°13′N 70°16′W
St-Jean-sur-Richelieu *see* St-Jean
15 N12 **St-Jérôme** Québec, SE Canada 45°47′N 74°01′W
25 T5 **Saint Jo** Texas, SW USA 33°42′N 97°33′W
13 O15 **St. John** New Brunswick, SE Canada 45°16′N 66°03′W
26 L6 **Saint John** Kansas, C USA 37°59′N 98°44′W
19 Q2 **Saint John** *Fr.* Saint-John. ≈ Canada/USA
76 K16 **Saint John** ≈ C Liberia
45 T9 **Saint John** *island* C Virgin Islands (US)
Saint-John *see* Saint John
22 I6 **Saint John, Lake** ⊚ Louisiana, S USA
45 W10 **St John's** ● (Antigua and Barbuda) Antigua, Antigua and Barbuda 17°06′N 61°50′W
13 V12 **St. John's** *province capital* Newfoundland and Labrador, E Canada 47°34′N 52°41′W
37 O12 **Saint Johns** Arizona, SW USA 34°28′N 109°22′W
31 Q9 **Saint Johns** Michigan, N USA 43°01′N 84°31′W
13 V12 **St. John's** ✕ Newfoundland and Labrador, E Canada 47°22′N 52°45′W
23 X11 **Saint Johns River** ≈ Florida, SE USA
103 Q11 **St-Jost-St-Rambert** Loire, E France 45°30′N 04°13′E
45 N12 **St. Joseph** W Dominica 15°24′N 61°26′W
173 P17 **St-Joseph** S Réunion
22 J6 **Saint Joseph** Louisiana, S USA 31°56′N 91°14′W
31 O10 **Saint Joseph** Michigan, N USA 42°05′N 86°30′W
27 R3 **Saint Joseph** Missouri, C USA 39°46′N 94°49′W
20 I10 **Saint Joseph** Tennessee, S USA 35°02′N 87°29′W
22 R9 **Saint Joseph Bay** *bay* Florida, SE USA
15 R11 **St-Joseph-de-Beauce** Québec, SE Canada 46°20′N 70°52′W
12 C10 **St. Joseph, Lake** ⊚ Ontario, C Canada

◆ Country ● Country Capital ◇ Dependent Territory ○ Dependent Territory Capital ◆ Administrative Regions ✕ International Airport ▲ Mountain ▲▲ Mountain Range ⛰ Volcano ≈ River ⊚ Lake ⊠ Reservoir

SAINT JOSEPH RIVER – SAMARKANDSKOYE

31 Q11 Saint Joseph River ≈ N USA
14 C11 Saint Joseph's Island island Ontario, S Canada
15 N11 St-Jovite Québec, SE Canada 46°07′N 74°35′W
121 P16 St Julian's N Malta 35°55′N 14°29′E
St-Julien see St-Julien-en-Genevois
103 T10 St-Julien-en-Genevois var. St-Julien. Haute-Savoie, E France 46°07′N 06°06′E
102 M11 St-Junien Haute-Vienne, C France 45°52′N 00°54′E
96 D8 St Kilda island NW Scotland, United Kingdom
45 V10 Saint Kitts island Saint Kitts and Nevis
45 U10 Saint Kitts and Nevis off. Federation of Saint Christopher and Nevis, var. Saint Christopher-Nevis. ◆ commonwealth republic E West Indies
11 X16 St. Laurent Manitoba, S Canada 50°20′N 97°55′W
St-Laurent see St-Laurent-du-Maroni
55 X9 St-Laurent-du-Maroni var. St-Laurent. NW French Guiana 05°29′N 54°03′W
St-Laurent, Fleuve see St. Lawrence
102 J12 St-Laurent-Médoc Gironde, SW France 45°11′N 00°50′W
13 N12 St. Lawrence Fr. Fleuve St-Laurent. ≈ Canada/USA
13 Q12 St. Lawrence, Gulf of gulf NW Atlantic Ocean
38 K10 Saint Lawrence Island island Alaska, USA
14 M14 Saint Lawrence River ≈ Canada/USA
99 L25 Saint-Léger Luxembourg, SE Belgium 49°36′N 05°39′E
13 N14 St. Léonard New Brunswick, SE Canada 47°10′N 67°55′W
15 P11 St-Léonard Québec, SE Canada 46°06′N 72°18′W
173 O17 St-Leu W Réunion 21°09′S 55°17′E
102 J4 St-Lô anc. Briovera, Laudus. Manche, N France 49°07′N 01°08′W
11 T15 St. Louis Saskatchewan, S Canada 52°50′N 105°43′W
103 V7 St-Louis Haut-Rhin, NE France 47°35′N 07°34′E
173 O17 St-Louis S Réunion
76 G10 Saint Louis NW Senegal 15°59′N 16°30′W
27 X4 Saint Louis Missouri, C USA 38°38′N 90°15′W
29 W5 Saint Louis River ≈ Minnesota, N USA
103 T7 St-Loup-sur-Semouse Haute-Saône, E France 47°53′N 06°15′E
15 O12 St-Luc Québec, SE Canada 45°19′N 73°18′W
45 X13 Saint Lucia ◆ commonwealth republic SE West Indies
47 S3 Saint Lucia island SE West Indies
83 L22 St. Lucia, Cape headland E South Africa 28°29′S 32°26′E
45 Y13 Saint Lucia Channel channel Martinique/Saint Lucia
23 Y14 Saint Lucie Canal canal Florida, SE USA
23 Z13 Saint Lucie Inlet inlet Florida, SE USA
96 L2 St Magnus Bay bay N Scotland, United Kingdom
102 K10 St-Maixent-l'École Deux-Sèvres, W France 46°24′N 00°13′W
11 Y16 St. Malo Manitoba, S Canada 49°16′N 96°58′W
102 I5 St-Malo Ille-et-Vilaine, NW France 48°39′N 02°W
102 H4 St-Malo, Golfe de gulf NW France
44 L9 St-Marc C Haiti 19°08′N 72°41′W
44 L9 St-Marc, Canal de channel W Haiti
103 S12 St-Marcellin-le-Mollard Isère, E France 45°12′N 05°18′E
55 Y12 Saint-Marcel, Mont ▲ S French Guiana 2°32′N 53°00′E
96 K5 St Margaret's Hope NE Scotland, United Kingdom 58°50′N 02°57′W
32 M9 Saint Maries Idaho, NW USA 47°19′N 116°37′W
23 T9 Saint Marks Florida, SE USA 30°09′N 84°12′W
108 D11 St. Martin Valais, SW Switzerland 46°09′N 07°27′E
Saint Martin see Sint Maarten
31 O5 Saint Martin Island island Michigan, N USA
22 I9 Saint Martinville Louisiana, S USA 30°09′N 91°51′W
185 E20 St. Mary, Mount ▲ South Island, New Zealand 44°16′S 169°42′E
186 E8 St. Mary, Mount ▲ S Papua New Guinea 08°06′S 147°00′E
182 I6 Saint Mary Peak ▲ South Australia 31°25′S 138°39′E
183 Q16 Saint Marys Tasmania, SE Australia 41°34′S 148°13′E
14 E16 St. Marys Ontario, S Canada 43°15′N 81°08′W
38 M11 Saint Marys Alaska, USA 62°03′N 163°10′W
23 W8 Saint Marys Georgia, SE USA 30°44′N 81°30′W
27 P4 Saint Marys Kansas, C USA 39°09′N 96°00′W
31 Q4 Saint Marys Ohio, N USA 40°31′N 84°22′W
21 R3 Saint Marys West Virginia, NE USA 39°24′N 81°13′W
23 W8 Saint Marys River ≈ Florida/Georgia, SE USA
31 Q4 Saint Marys River ≈ Michigan, N USA
102 D6 St-Mathieu, Pointe headland NW France 48°17′N 04°56′W
38 J12 Saint Matthew Island island Alaska, USA
21 R13 Saint Matthews South Carolina, SE USA 33°40′N 80°44′W
St.Matthew's Island see Zadetkyi Kyun
186 G4 St.Matthias Group island group NE Papua New Guinea
108 C11 St. Maurice Valais, SW Switzerland 46°09′N 07°28′E
15 P9 St-Maurice ≈ Québec, SE Canada
102 J13 St-Médard-en-Jalles Gironde, SW France 44°54′N 00°43′W
39 N10 Saint Michael Alaska, USA 63°28′N 162°02′W
15 N10 St-Michel-des-Saints Québec, SE Canada 46°39′N 73°54′W
103 S5 St-Mihiel Meuse, NE France 48°57′N 05°33′E
108 J10 St. Moritz Ger. Sankt Moritz, Rmsch. San Murezzan. Graubünden, SE Switzerland 46°30′N 09°51′E
102 H8 St-Nazaire Loire-Atlantique, NW France 47°17′N 02°12′W
Saint Nicholas see São Nicolau
Saint-Nicolas see Sint-Niklaas
103 N1 St-Omer Pas-de-Calais, N France 50°45′N 02°15′E
102 J11 Saintonge cultural region W France
15 S9 St-Pacôme Québec, SE Canada 47°22′N 69°56′W
15 S10 St-Pamphile Québec, SE Canada 46°57′N 69°46′W
15 S9 St-Pascal Québec, SE Canada 47°32′N 69°48′W
14 J11 St-Patrice, Lac ◎ Québec, SE Canada
11 R14 St. Paul Alberta, SW Canada 54°00′N 111°18′W
173 O16 St-Paul NW Réunion
38 K14 Saint Paul Saint Paul Island, Alaska, USA 57°08′N 170°13′W
29 V8 Saint Paul state capital Minnesota, N USA 45°N 93°10′W
29 P15 Saint Paul Nebraska, C USA 41°13′N 98°26′W
21 P7 Saint Paul Virginia, NE USA 36°53′N 82°18′W
77 Q17 Saint Paul, Cape headland S Ghana 05°44′N 00°55′E
103 O17 St-Paul-de-Fenouillet Pyrénées-Orientales, S France 42°49′N 02°29′E
65 K14 Saint Paul Fracture Zone tectonic feature E Atlantic Ocean
38 J14 Saint Paul Island island Pribilof Islands, Alaska, USA
102 J15 St-Paul-les-Dax Landes, SW France 43°45′N 01°01′W
21 U11 Saint Pauls North Carolina, SE USA 34°45′N 78°56′W
Saint Paul's Bay see San Pawl il-Bahar
191 R16 St Paul's Point headland Pitcairn Island, Pitcairn Islands
29 U10 Saint Peter Minnesota, N USA 44°21′N 93°58′W
97 L26 St Peter Port ○ (Guernsey) C Guernsey, Channel Islands 49°28′N 02°33′W
23 V13 Saint Petersburg Florida, SE USA 27°47′N 82°37′W
Saint Petersburg see Sankt-Peterburg
23 V13 Saint Petersburg Beach Florida, SE USA 27°43′N 82°43′W
173 P17 St-Philippe SE Réunion 21°21′S 55°46′E
45 Q11 St-Pierre NW Martinique 14°44′N 61°11′W
173 O17 St-Pierre SW Réunion
13 S13 St-Pierre and Miquelon Fr. Îles St-Pierre et Miquelon. ◇ French territorial collectivity NE North America
15 P11 St-Pierre, Lac ◎ Québec, SE Canada
102 F5 St-Pol-de-Léon Finistère, NW France 48°42′N 04°00′W
103 O2 St-Pol-sur-Ternoise Pas-de-Calais, N France 50°22′N 02°21′E
St. Pons see St-Pons-de-Thomières
103 O16 St-Pons-de-Thomières var. St. Pons. Hérault, S France 43°28′N 02°48′E
103 P10 St-Pourçain-sur-Sioule Allier, C France 46°19′N 03°16′E
15 S11 St-Prosper Québec, SE Canada 46°14′N 70°28′W
103 P3 St-Quentin Aisne, N France 49°51′N 03°17′E
15 R10 St-Raphaël Québec, SE Canada 46°47′N 70°46′W
103 U15 St-Raphaël Var, SE France 43°26′N 06°46′E
15 Q10 St-Raymond Québec, SE Canada 46°53′N 71°49′W
33 O9 Saint Regis Montana, NW USA 47°18′N 115°06′W
18 J7 Saint Regis River ≈ New York, NE USA
103 R15 St-Rémy-de-Provence Bouches-du-Rhône, SE France 43°48′N 04°49′E
102 M9 St-Savin Vienne, W France 46°34′N 00°53′E
Saint-Sébastien,Cap see Anorontany, Tanjona
23 X7 Saint Simons Island island Georgia, SE USA
191 Y2 Saint Stanislas Bay bay Kiritimati, E Kiribati
13 O15 St. Stephen New Brunswick, SE Canada 45°12′N 67°18′W
39 X12 Saint Terese Alaska, USA 58°28′N 134°46′W
14 E17 St. Thomas Ontario, S Canada 42°46′N 81°12′W
29 Q2 Saint Thomas North Dakota, N USA 48°37′N 97°28′W
45 T9 Saint Thomas island W Virgin Islands (US)
Saint Thomas see São Tomé, Sao Tome and Principe
Saint Thomas see Charlotte Amalie, Virgin Islands (US)
15 P10 St-Tite Québec, SE Canada 46°42′N 72°32′W
Saint-Trond see Sint-Truiden
103 U16 St-Tropez Var, SE France 43°16′N 06°39′E
Saint Ubes see Setúbal
102 L3 St-Valéry-en-Caux Seine-Maritime, N France 49°53′N 00°42′E
103 Q9 St-Vallier Saône-et-Loire, C France 46°39′N 04°19′E
106 B7 St-Vincent Valle d'Aosta, NW Italy 45°47′N 07°42′E
45 Q14 Saint Vincent island N Saint Vincent and the Grenadines
Saint Vincent see São Vicente
45 W14 Saint Vincent and the Grenadines ◆ commonwealth republic SE West Indies
Saint-Vincent, Cap see Ankaboa, Tanjona
Saint Vincent, Cape see São Vicente, Cabo de
102 I15 St-Vincent-de-Tyrosse Landes, SW France 43°39′N 01°16′W
182 I9 Saint Vincent, Gulf gulf South Australia
23 R10 Saint Vincent Island island Florida, SE USA
45 T12 Saint Vincent Passage passage Saint Lucia/Saint Vincent and the Grenadines
183 N18 Saint Vincent, Point headland Tasmania, SE Australia 43°19′S 145°50′E
Saint-Vith see Sankt-Vith
11 S14 St. Walburg Saskatchewan, S Canada 53°38′N 109°12′W
St Wolfgangsee see Wolfgangsee
102 M11 St-Yrieix-la-Perche Haute-Vienne, C France 45°31′N 01°12′E
Saint Yves see Setúbal
188 H5 Saipan island ● (Northern Mariana Islands) S Northern Mariana Islands
188 H6 Saipan Channel channel S Northern Mariana Islands
188 H6 Saipan International ✕ Saipan, S Northern Mariana Islands
74 G6 Saïs ✕ (Fès) C Morocco 33°58′N 04°48′W
Saishū see Cheju-do
Saishū see Cheju
102 J16 Saison ≈ SW France
169 R10 Sai, Sungai ≈ Borneo, N Indonesia
165 N13 Saitama off. Saitama-ken. ◆ prefecture Honshū, S Japan
Saitama see Urawa
Saitama-ken see Saitama
Saiyid Abid see Sayyid 'Abid
57 J19 Sajama, Nevado ▲ W Bolivia 17°57′S 68°51′W
141 V13 Sājir, Ras headland S Oman 16°42′N 53°40′E
111 M20 Sajószentpéter Borsod-Abaúj-Zemplén, NE Hungary 48°13′N 20°43′E
83 F24 Sak ≈ SW South Africa
81 J18 Saka Coast, E Kenya 0°11′S 39°27′E
167 P11 Sa Kaeo Prachin Buri, C Thailand 13°47′N 102°03′E
164 J14 Sakai Ōsaka, Honshū, SW Japan 34°35′N 135°28′E
164 H14 Sakaide Kagawa, Shikoku, SW Japan 34°19′N 133°50′E
164 H12 Sakaiminato Tottori, Honshū, SW Japan 35°34′N 133°12′E
140 M3 Sakākah Al Jawf, NW Saudi Arabia 29°56′N 40°10′E
28 L4 Sakakawea, Lake ⊠ North Dakota, N USA
12 J9 Sakami, Lac ◎ Québec, C Canada
79 O26 Sakania Katanga, SE Dem. Rep. Congo 12°44′S 28°34′E
146 K12 Sakar Lebap Welaýaty, E Turkmenistan 38°57′N 63°46′E
172 H7 Sakaraha Toliara, SW Madagascar 22°54′S 44°31′E
146 I14 Sakarçäge var. Sakarchäge, Rus. Sakar-Chaga. Mary Welaýaty, C Turkmenistan 37°40′N 61°33′E
Sakar-Chaga/Sakarchäge see Sakarçäge
Sak'art'velo see Georgia
136 F11 Sakarya ◆ province NW Turkey
136 F12 Sakarya Nehri ≈ NW Turkey
165 P9 Sakata Yamagata, Honshū, C Japan 38°54′N 139°51′E
145 S11 Saken Seyfullin Kaz. Säken Seyfullïn; prev. Zharyk. Karaganda, C Kazakhstan 48°52′N 72°51′E
Säken Seyfullïn see Saken Seyfullin
123 P9 Sakha (Yakutiya), Respublika var. Respublika Yakutiya, Eng. Yakutia. ◆ autonomous republic NE Russian Federation
Sakhalin see Sakhalin, Ostrov
192 I3 Sakhalin, Ostrov var. Sakhalin. island SE Russian Federation
123 U12 Sakhalinskaya Oblast' ◆ province SE Russian Federation
123 T12 Sakhalinskiy Zaliv gulf E Russian Federation
Sakhnovshchina see Sakhnovshchyna
117 U6 Sakhnovshchyna Rus. Sakhnovshchina. Kharkivs'ka Oblast', E Ukraine 49°08′N 35°52′E
Sakhon Nakhon see Sakon Nakhon
Sakhtsar see Rāmsar
137 W10 Şäki Rus. Sheki; prev. Nukha. NW Azerbaijan 41°09′N 47°10′E
Saki see Saky
118 E13 Šakiai Ger. Schaken. Marijampolė, S Lithuania 54°57′N 23°04′E
165 O16 Sakishima-shotō var. Sakisima Syotō. island group SW Japan
Sakisima Syotô see Sakishima-shotō
Sakiz see Saqqez
Sakiz-Adasi see Chíos
155 F19 Sakleshpur Karnātaka, E India 12°58′N 75°45′E
167 S9 Sakon Nakhon var. Muang Sakon Nakhon, Sakhon Nakhon. Sakon Nakhon, E Thailand 17°10′N 104°08′E
149 P15 Sakrand Sind, SE Pakistan 26°06′N 68°20′E
83 F24 Sak River Afr. Sakrivier. Northern Cape, W South Africa 30°49′S 20°24′E
Sakrivier see Sak River
Saksaul'skiy see Saksaul'skoye
144 K13 Saksaul'skoye var. Saksaul'skiy, Kaz. Sekseüil. Kzylorda, S Kazakhstan 47°07′N 61°06′E
95 I25 Sakskøbing Storstrøm, SE Denmark 54°48′N 11°39′E
165 N12 Saku Nagano, Honshū, S Japan 36°17′N 138°29′E
117 S13 Saky Rus. Saki. Respublika Krym, S Ukraine 45°09′N 33°36′E
76 E9 Sal island Ilhas de Barlavento, NE Cape Verde
127 N12 Sal ≈ SW Russian Federation
111 I21 Sal'a Hung. Sellye, Vágsellye. Nitriansky Kraj, SW Slovakia 48°09′N 17°51′E
95 N15 Sala Västmanland, C Sweden 59°55′N 16°38′E
15 N13 Salaberry-de-Valleyfield var. Valleyfield. Québec, SE Canada 45°15′N 74°07′W
118 G7 Salacgrīva Est. Salatsi. Limbaži, N Latvia 57°45′N 24°21′E
107 M18 Sala Consilina Campania, S Italy 40°23′N 15°35′E
40 C2 Salada, Laguna ◎ NW Mexico
61 D14 Saladas Corrientes, NE Argentina 28°15′S 58°40′W
61 C21 Saladillo Buenos Aires, E Argentina 35°40′S 59°50′W
61 B16 Saladillo, Río ≈ C Argentina
25 T9 Salado Texas, SW USA 30°57′N 97°32′W
63 J16 Salado, Arroyo ≈ SE Argentina
61 D21 Salado, Río ≈ E Argentina
62 J12 Salado, Río ≈ C Argentina
41 N7 Salado, Río ≈ NE Mexico
37 Q12 Salado, Río ≈ New Mexico, SW USA
143 N6 Salafchegān var. Sarafjagān. Quom, N Iran 34°28′N 50°28′E
77 Q15 Salaga C Ghana 08°31′N 00°37′W
139 S6 Şalāḩ ad Dīn ◆ governorate C Iraq
192 G5 Sala'ilua Savai'i, W Samoa 13°39′S 172°33′W
116 G9 Sălaj ◆ county NW Romania
83 H20 Salajwe Kweneng, SE Botswana 23°40′S 24°46′E
78 H9 Salal Kanem, W Chad 14°48′N 17°12′E
80 I6 Salala Red Sea, NE Sudan 21°17′N 36°16′E
141 V13 Şalālah SW Oman 17°01′N 54°04′E
42 D5 Salamá Baja Verapaz, C Guatemala 15°06′N 90°18′W
42 J6 Salamá Olancho, C Honduras 14°48′N 86°34′W
62 G10 Salamanca Coquimbo, C Chile 31°47′S 70°58′W
41 N13 Salamanca Guanajuato, C Mexico 20°34′N 101°12′W
104 K7 Salamanca anc. Helmantica, Salmantica. Castilla-León, NW Spain 40°58′N 05°40′W
18 D11 Salamanca New York, NE USA 42°09′N 78°43′W
104 J7 Salamanca ◆ province Castilla-León, W Spain
63 J19 Salamanca, Pampa de plain S Argentina
78 J12 Salamat off. Préfecture du Salamat. ◆ prefecture SE Chad
78 I12 Salamat, Bahr ≈ S Chad
Salamat, Préfecture du see Salamat
54 F5 Salamina Magdalena, N Colombia 10°30′N 74°48′W
115 G19 Salamína var. Salamís. Salamína, C Greece 37°58′N 23°29′E
115 G19 Salamína island C Greece
Salamís see Salamína
138 I5 Salamīyah var. As Salamīyah. Ḩamāh, W Syria 35°01′N 37°02′E
31 P12 Salamonie Lake ⊠ Indiana, N USA
31 P12 Salamonie River ≈ Indiana, N USA
Salang see Phuket
192 I16 Salani Upolu, SE Samoa 14°00′S 171°35′W
118 C11 Salantai Klaipėda, NW Lithuania 56°05′N 21°36′E
104 K2 Salas Asturias, N Spain 43°25′N 06°15′W
105 O5 Salas de los Infantes Castilla-León, N Spain 42°02′N 03°17′W
102 M16 Salat ≈ S France
189 V13 Salat island Chuuk, C Micronesia
169 Q16 Salatiga Jawa, C Indonesia 07°15′S 110°34′E
189 V13 Salat Pass passage W Pacific Ocean
Salatsi see Salacgrīva
167 T10 Salavan var. Saravan, Saravane. Salavan, S Laos 15°43′N 106°26′E
127 V6 Salavat Respublika Bashkortostan, W Russian Federation 53°20′N 55°54′E
56 C12 Salaverry La Libertad, N Peru 08°14′S 78°55′W
171 T12 Salawati, Pulau island E Indonesia
193 R10 Sala y Gomez island Chile, E Pacific Ocean
Sala y Gomez Fracture Zone see Sala y Gomez Ridge
193 S10 Sala y Gomez Ridge var. Sala y Gomez Fracture Zone. tectonic feature SE Pacific Ocean
61 A22 Salazar Buenos Aires, E Argentina 36°20′S 62°11′W
54 G7 Salazar Norte de Santander, N Colombia 07°46′N 72°46′W
Salazar see N'Dalatando
173 P16 Salazie C Réunion 21°02′S 55°33′E
103 N8 Salbris Loir-et-Cher, C France 47°25′N 02°02′E
57 G15 Salcantay, Nevado ▲ C Peru 13°21′S 72°31′W
45 O8 Salcedo N Dominican Republic 19°26′N 70°25′W
39 S9 Salcha River ≈ Alaska, USA
119 H15 Šalčininkai Vilnius, SE Lithuania 54°20′N 25°26′E
Saldae see Béjaïa
54 E11 Saldaña Tolima, C Colombia 03°57′N 75°01′W
104 M4 Saldaña Castilla-León, N Spain 42°31′N 04°44′W
83 E25 Saldanha Western Cape, SW South Africa 33°00′S 17°56′E
Salduba see Zaragoza
61 B23 Saldungaray Buenos Aires, E Argentina 38°15′S 61°45′W
118 D9 Saldus Ger. Frauenburg. Saldus, W Latvia 56°40′N 22°29′E
183 P13 Sale Victoria, SE Australia 38°06′S 147°06′E
74 F6 Salé NW Morocco 34°07′N 06°40′W
74 F6 Salé ✕ (Rabat) W Morocco 34°09′N 06°30′W
Salehābād see Andīmeshk
170 M16 Saleh, Teluk bay Nusa Tenggara, S Indonesia
122 H8 Salekhard prev. Obdorsk. Yamalo-Nenetskiy Avtonomnyy Okrug, N Russian Federation 66°33′N 66°35′E
192 H16 Sālelologa Savai'i, C Samoa 13°42′S 172°10′W
155 H21 Salem Tamil Nādu, SE India 11°38′N 78°08′E
27 V9 Salem Arkansas, C USA 36°21′N 91°49′W
30 L15 Salem Illinois, N USA 38°37′N 88°57′W
31 P15 Salem Indiana, N USA 38°38′N 86°06′W
19 P11 Salem Massachusetts, NE USA 42°30′N 70°51′W
27 V6 Salem Missouri, C USA 37°39′N 91°32′W
18 I16 Salem New Jersey, NE USA 39°33′N 75°26′W
31 U12 Salem Ohio, N USA 40°52′N 80°51′W
32 G12 Salem state capital Oregon, NW USA 44°57′N 123°01′W
29 Q11 Salem South Dakota, N USA 43°43′N 97°23′W
36 L4 Salem Utah, W USA 40°03′N 111°40′W
21 S7 Salem Virginia, NE USA 37°16′N 80°00′W
21 R3 Salem West Virginia, NE USA 39°15′N 80°32′W
107 H23 Salemi Sicilia, Italy, C Mediterranean Sea 37°48′N 12°48′E
Salemy see As Sālimī
94 K12 Sälen Dalarna, C Sweden 61°11′N 13°14′E
107 Q18 Salentina, Campi Puglia, SE Italy 40°23′N 18°01′E
107 Q18 Salentina, Penisola peninsula SE Italy
107 L18 Salerno anc. Salernum. Campania, S Italy 40°40′N 14°44′E
107 L18 Salerno, Golfo di Eng. Gulf of Salerno. gulf S Italy
Salerno, Gulf of see Salerno, Golfo di
Salernum see Salerno
97 K17 Salford NW England, United Kingdom 53°30′N 02°16′W
Salgir see Salhyr
111 K21 Salgótarján Nógrád, N Hungary 48°07′N 19°47′E
59 O15 Salgueiro Pernambuco, E Brazil 08°04′S 39°05′W
94 C13 Salhus Hordaland, S Norway 60°30′N 05°15′E
117 T12 Salhyr Rus. Salgir. ≈ S Ukraine
171 Q9 Salibabu, Pulau island N Indonesia
37 S6 Salida Colorado, C USA 38°29′N 105°57′W
102 J15 Salies-de-Béarn Pyrénées-Atlantiques, SW France 43°28′N 00°55′W
136 C14 Salihli Manisa, W Turkey 38°29′N 28°08′E
119 K18 Salihorsk Rus. Soligorsk. Minskaya Voblasts', S Belarus 52°48′N 27°32′E
119 K18 Salihorskaye Vodaskhovishcha ⊠ C Belarus
83 N14 Salima Central, C Malawi 13°44′S 34°21′E
166 L5 Salin Magway, W Burma (Myanmar) 20°30′N 94°40′E
27 N4 Salina Kansas, C USA 38°53′N 97°36′W
36 L5 Salina Utah, W USA 38°57′N 111°54′W
41 S17 Salina Cruz Oaxaca, SE Mexico 16°11′N 95°12′W
107 L22 Salina, Isola island Isole Eolie, S Italy
44 J5 Salina Point headland Acklins Island, SE Bahamas 22°10′N 74°16′W
56 A7 Salinas Guayas, W Ecuador 02°15′S 80°58′W
40 M11 Salinas var. Salinas de Hidalgo. San Luis Potosí, C Mexico 22°36′N 101°41′W
45 T6 Salinas C Puerto Rico 17°57′N 66°18′W
35 O10 Salinas California, W USA 36°41′N 121°40′W
Salinas, Cabo de see Salines, Cap de ses
Salinas de Hidalgo see Salinas
82 A13 Salinas, Ponta das headland W Angola 12°50′S 12°57′E
45 O10 Salinas, Punta headland S Dominican Republic 18°11′N 70°32′W
Salinas, Río see Chixoy, Río
35 O11 Salinas River ≈ California, W USA
22 H6 Saline Lake ◎ Louisiana, S USA
25 R17 Salineno Texas, SW USA 26°29′N 99°06′W
27 V14 Saline River ≈ Arkansas, C USA
30 M17 Saline River ≈ Illinois, N USA
105 X10 Salines, Cap de ses var. Cabo de Salinas. headland Mallorca, Spain, W Mediterranean Sea 39°15′N 03°03′E
Salisburg see Mazsalaca
45 O12 Salisbury var. Baroui. W Dominica 15°26′N 61°27′W
97 M23 Salisbury var. New Sarum. S England, United Kingdom 51°05′N 01°48′W
21 Y4 Salisbury Maryland, NE USA 38°22′N 75°37′W
27 T3 Salisbury Missouri, C USA 39°25′N 92°48′W
21 S9 Salisbury North Carolina, SE USA 35°40′N 80°28′W
Salisbury see Harare
9 Q7 Salisbury Island island Nunavut, NE Canada
Salisbury, Lake see Bisina, Lake
97 L23 Salisbury Plain plain S England, United Kingdom
21 R14 Salkehatchie River ≈ South Carolina, SE USA
138 I9 Şalkhad As Suwaydā', SW Syria 32°29′N 36°42′E
92 M12 Salla Lappi, NE Finland 66°50′N 28°40′E
Sállan see Sørøya
103 U11 Sallanches Haute-Savoie, E France 45°55′N 06°37′E
105 V5 Sallent Cataluña, NE Spain 41°48′N 01°52′E
61 A22 Salliqueló Buenos Aires, E Argentina 36°45′S 62°55′W
27 R10 Sallisaw Oklahoma, C USA 35°27′N 94°49′W
80 I7 Sallom Red Sea, NE Sudan 19°17′N 37°02′E
12 J2 Salluit prev. Saglouc, Sagluk. Québec, NE Canada 62°10′N 75°40′W
Sallyana see Salyān
13 S11 Sally's Cove Newfoundland and Labrador, E Canada 49°43′N 58°00′W
139 W9 Salmān Bin 'Arāzah Maysān, E Iraq 32°33′N 46°36′E
Salmantica see Salamanca
142 I2 Salmās prev. Dilman, Shāpūr. Āžarbāyjān-e Gharbī, NW Iran 38°13′N 44°50′E
124 I11 Salmi Respublika Kareliya, NW Russian Federation 61°21′N 31°55′E
33 P12 Salmon Idaho, NW USA 45°10′N 113°54′W
11 N16 Salmon Arm British Columbia, SW Canada 50°41′N 119°18′W
192 L5 Salmon Bank undersea feature N Pacific Ocean 26°55′N 176°28′W
Salmon Leap see Leixlip
34 L2 Salmon Mountains ▲▲ California, W USA
14 J15 Salmon Point headland Ontario, SE Canada 43°51′N 77°15′W
33 N11 Salmon River ≈ Idaho, NW USA
18 K6 Salmon River ≈ New York, NE USA
33 N12 Salmon River Mountains ▲▲ Idaho, NW USA
18 I9 Salmon River Reservoir ⊠ New York, NE USA
93 K19 Salo Länsi-Suomi, SW Finland 60°23′N 23°10′E
106 F7 Salò Lombardia, N Italy 45°37′N 10°30′E
Salona/Salonae see Solin
103 S15 Salon-de-Provence Bouches-du-Rhône, SE France 43°39′N 05°05′E
Salonica/Salonika see Thessaloníki
115 I14 Salonikiós, Akrotírio var. Akrotírio Salonikós. headland Thásos, E Greece 40°34′N 24°39′E
Salonikós, Akrotírio see Salonikiós, Akrotírio
116 F10 Salonta Hung. Nagyszalonta. Bihor, W Romania 46°49′N 21°40′E
104 I9 Salor ≈ W Spain
105 U6 Salou Cataluña, NE Spain 41°05′N 01°08′E
76 H11 Saloum ≈ C Senegal
42 H4 Sal, Punta headland NW Honduras 15°55′N 87°36′W
92 N3 Salpynten headland W Svalbard 78°12′N 12°11′E
138 I3 Salqīn Idlib, W Syria 36°09′N 36°27′E
93 F14 Salsbruket Nord-Trøndelag, C Norway 64°49′N 11°48′E
126 M13 Sal'sk Rostovskaya Oblast', SW Russian Federation 46°30′N 41°31′E
107 K25 Salso ≈ Sicilia, Italy, C Mediterranean Sea
107 J25 Salso ≈ Sicilia, Italy, C Mediterranean Sea
106 E9 Salsomaggiore Terme Emilia-Romagna, N Italy 44°49′N 09°58′E
Salt see As Salț
62 J6 Salta Salta, NW Argentina 24°47′S 65°23′W
62 K6 Salta off. Provincia de Salta. ◆ province N Argentina
Salta, Provincia de see Salta
97 I24 Saltash SW England, United Kingdom 50°26′N 04°14′W
24 I8 Salt Basin basin Texas, SW USA
11 V16 Saltcoats Saskatchewan, S Canada 51°06′N 102°12′W
30 L13 Salt Creek ≈ Illinois, N USA
24 J9 Salt Draw ≈ Texas, SW USA
97 F21 Saltee Islands island group SE Ireland
92 G12 Saltfjorden inlet C Norway
24 I8 Salt Flat Texas, SW USA 31°43′N 105°05′W
27 N8 Salt Fork Arkansas River ≈ Oklahoma, C USA
31 T13 Salt Fork Lake ⊠ Ohio, N USA
26 J11 Salt Fork Red River ≈ Oklahoma/Texas, C USA
95 J23 Saltholm island E Denmark
41 N8 Saltillo Coahuila, NE Mexico 25°30′N 101°W
182 L5 Salt Lake salt lake New South Wales, SE Australia
37 V15 Salt Lake ◎ New Mexico, SW USA
36 K2 Salt Lake City state capital Utah, W USA 40°45′N 111°54′W
61 C20 Salto Buenos Aires, E Argentina 34°18′S 60°17′W
61 D17 Salto Salto, N Uruguay 31°23′S 57°58′W
61 E17 Salto ◆ department N Uruguay
107 I14 Salto ≈ C Italy
62 Q6 Salto del Guairá Canindeyú, E Paraguay 24°06′S 54°22′W
61 D17 Salto Grande, Embalse de var. Lago de Salto Grande. ⊠ Argentina/Uruguay
Salto Grande, Lago de see Salto Grande, Embalse de
35 W16 Salton Sea ◎ California, W USA
60 I12 Salto Santiago, Represa de ⊠ S Brazil
149 U7 Salt Range ▲▲ E Pakistan
36 M13 Salt River ≈ Arizona, SW USA
20 L5 Salt River ≈ Kentucky, S USA
27 V3 Salt River ≈ Missouri, C USA
95 F17 Saltrød Aust-Agder, S Norway 58°28′N 08°49′E
95 P16 Saltsjöbaden Stockholm, C Sweden 59°15′N 18°20′E
92 G12 Saltstraumen Nordland, C Norway 67°16′N 14°42′E
21 Q7 Saltville Virginia, NE USA 36°52′N 81°48′W
Saluces/Saluciae see Saluzzo
21 Q12 Saluda South Carolina, SE USA 34°00′N 81°47′W
21 X6 Saluda Virginia, NE USA 37°36′N 76°36′W
21 Q12 Saluda River ≈ South Carolina, SE USA
Salûm see As Sallūm
152 F14 Sālūmbar Rājasthān, N India 24°16′N 74°04′E
Salûm, Gulf of see Khalīj as Sallūm
171 O11 Salumpaga Sulawesi, N Indonesia 01°18′N 120°58′E
155 M14 Sālūr Andhra Pradesh, E India 18°31′N 83°16′E
55 Y9 Salut, Îles du island group N French Guiana
106 A9 Saluzzo Fr. Saluces; anc. Saluciae. Piemonte, NW Italy 44°39′N 07°29′E
63 F23 Salvación, Bahía bay S Chile
59 P17 Salvador prev. São Salvador. state capital Bahia, E Brazil 12°58′S 38°29′W
65 E24 Salvador East Falkland, Falkland Islands 51°28′S 58°22′W
22 K10 Salvador, Lake ◎ Louisiana, S USA
Salvaleón de Higüey see Higüey
104 F10 Salvaterra de Magos Santarém, C Portugal 39°01′N 08°47′W
41 N13 Salvatierra Guanajuato, C Mexico 20°14′N 100°52′W
105 P3 Salvatierra Basq. Agurain. País Vasco, N Spain 42°52′N 02°23′W
Salwa/Salwah see As Salwā
166 M7 Salween Bur. Thanlwin, Chin. Nu Chiang, Nu Jiang. ≈ SE Asia
137 Y12 Salyan Rus. Sal'yany. SE Azerbaijan 39°36′N 48°57′E
153 N11 Salyān var. Sallyana. Mid Western, W Nepal 28°22′N 82°10′E
Sal'yany see Salyan
21 O6 Salyersville Kentucky, S USA 37°43′N 83°06′W
109 V6 Salza ≈ E Austria
109 Q7 Salzach ≈ Austria/Germany
109 Q6 Salzburg anc. Juvavum. Salzburg, N Austria 47°48′N 13°03′E
109 O8 Salzburg off. Land Salzburg. ◆ state C Austria
Salzburg see Ocna Sibiului
Salzburg Alps see Salzburger Kalkalpen
109 Q7 Salzburger Kalkalpen Eng. Salzburg Alps. ▲▲ C Austria
Salzburg, Land see Salzburg
100 J13 Salzgitter prev. Watenstedt-Salzgitter. Niedersachsen, C Germany 52°07′N 10°24′E
101 G14 Salzkotten Nordrhein-Westfalen, W Germany 51°40′N 08°36′E
100 K11 Salzwedel Sachsen-Anhalt, N Germany 52°51′N 11°10′E
152 D11 Sām Rājasthān, NW India 26°50′N 70°30′E
Šamac see Bosanski Šamac
54 G9 Samacá Boyacá, C Colombia 05°28′N 73°33′W
40 I7 Samachique Chihuahua, N Mexico 27°17′N 107°28′W
141 Y8 Şamad NE Oman 22°47′N 58°12′E
Sama de Langreo see Sama, Spain
Samaden see Samedan
57 M19 Samaipata Santa Cruz, C Bolivia 18°08′S 63°53′W
167 T10 Samakhixai var. Attapu, Attopeu. Attapu, S Laos 14°48′N 106°51′E
Samakov see Samokov
42 B6 Samalá, Río ≈ SW Guatemala
40 J3 Samalayuca Chihuahua, N Mexico 31°25′N 106°30′W
155 L16 Sāmalkot Andhra Pradesh, E India 17°03′N 82°15′E
45 P8 Samaná var. Santa Bárbara de Samaná. E Dominican Republic 19°14′N 69°20′W
45 P8 Samaná, Bahía de bay E Dominican Republic
44 K4 Samana Cay island SE Bahamas
136 K17 Samandağı Hatay, S Turkey 36°07′N 35°55′E
149 P3 Samangān ◆ province N Afghanistan
Samangān see Āybak
165 T5 Samani Hokkaidō, NE Japan 42°07′N 142°57′E
54 C13 Samaniego Nariño, SW Colombia 01°22′N 77°35′W
171 Q5 Samar island C Philippines
127 S6 Samara prev. Kuybyshev. Samarskaya Oblast', W Russian Federation 53°15′N 50°15′E
127 T7 Samara ≈ W Russian Federation
127 S6 Samara ✕ Samarskaya Oblast', W Russian Federation 53°11′N 50°27′E
117 V7 Samara ≈ E Ukraine
186 G10 Samarai Milne Bay, SE Papua New Guinea 10°36′S 150°39′E
Samarang see Semarang
123 T14 Samarga Khabarovskiy Kray, SE Russian Federation 47°43′N 139°08′E
138 G9 Samarian Hills hill range N Israel
54 L9 Samariapo Amazonas, C Venezuela 05°16′N 67°43′W
169 V11 Samarinda Borneo, C Indonesia 0°30′S 117°09′E
Samarkand see Samarqand
Samarkandskaya Oblast' see Samarqand Viloyati
Samarkandski/Samarkandskoye see Temirtau

◆ Country ● Country Capital ◇ Dependent Territory ○ Dependent Territory Capital ◆ Administrative Regions ✕ International Airport ▲ Mountain ▲▲ Mountain Range Volcano ≈ River ◎ Lake ⊠ Reservoir

Samarobriva – San Juan Bautista Tuxtepec

Samarobriva see Amiens
147 N11 **Samarqand** Rus. Samarkand. Samarqand Viloyati, C Uzbekistan 39°40′N 66°56′E
146 M11 **Samarqand Viloyati** Rus. Samarkandskaya Oblast'. ⬖ province C Uzbekistan
139 S6 **Sāmarrā'** Ṣalāḥ ad Dīn, C Iraq 34°13′N 43°52′E
127 R7 **Samarskaya Oblast'** prev. Kuybyshevskaya Oblast'. ⬖ province W Russian Federation
153 Q13 **Samastipur** Bihār, N India 25°52′N 85°47′E
76 L14 **Samatiguila** NW Ivory Coast 09°51′N 07°36′W
Samawa see As Samāwah
137 Y11 **Şamaxı** Rus. Shemakha. E Azerbaijan 40°38′N 48°34′E
79 K18 **Samba** Equateur, NW Dem. Rep. Congo 0°13′N 21°17′E
79 N21 **Samba** Maniema, E Dem. Rep. Congo 04°41′S 26°23′E
152 H6 **Samba** Jammu and Kashmir, NW India 32°32′N 75°08′E
169 W10 **Sambaliung, Pegunungan** ⛰ Borneo, N Indonesia
154 M11 **Sambalpur** Orissa, E India 21°28′N 84°04′E
67 X12 **Sambao** ≈ W Madagascar
169 Q10 **Sambas, Sungai** ≈ Borneo, N Indonesia
172 K2 **Sambava** Antsiranana, NE Madagascar 14°16′S 50°10′E
152 J10 **Sambhal** Uttar Pradesh, N India 28°35′N 78°34′E
152 H12 **Sāmbhar Salt Lake** ◎ N India
107 N21 **Sambiase** Calabria, SW Italy 38°58′N 16°16′E
116 H5 **Sambir** Rus. Sambor. L'vivs'ka Oblast', NW Ukraine 49°31′N 23°10′E
82 C13 **Sambo** Huambo, C Angola 13°07′S 16°06′E
Sambor see Sambir
61 E21 **Samborombón, Bahía** bay NE Argentina
99 H20 **Sambre** ≈ Belgium/France
43 V16 **Sambú, Río** ≈ SE Panama
163 Z14 **Samch'ŏk** Jap. Sanchoku. NE South Korea 37°21′N 129°12′E
Samch'ŏnpŏ see Sach'ŏn
81 I21 **Same** Kilimanjaro, NE Tanzania 04°04′S 37°41′E
108 J10 **Samedan** Ger. Samaden. Graubünden, S Switzerland 46°31′N 09°51′E
82 K12 **Samfya** Luapula, N Zambia 11°22′S 29°34′E
141 W13 **Samḥān, Jabal** ⛰ SW Oman
115 C18 **Sámi** Kefallonía, Iónia Nisiá, Greece, C Mediterranean Sea 38°15′N 20°39′E
56 F10 **Samiria, Río** ≈ N Peru
Samirum see Semīrom
137 V11 **Şämkir** Rus. Shamkhor. NW Azerbaijan 40°51′N 46°03′E
167 S7 **Sam, Nam** Vtn. Sông Chu. ≈ Laos/Vietnam
Samnān see Semnān
Sam Neua see Xam Nua
75 P10 **Samnū** C Libya 27°19′N 15°01′E
192 H15 **Samoa** off. Independent State of Western Samoa, var. Sāmoa; prev. Western Samoa. ◆ monarchy W Polynesia
192 L9 **Sāmoa** island group American Samoa
Sāmoa see Samoa
175 T9 **Samoa Basin** undersea feature W Pacific Ocean
112 D8 **Samobor** Zagreb, N Croatia 45°48′N 15°38′E
114 H10 **Samokov** var. Samakov. Sofiya, W Bulgaria 42°19′N 23°34′E
111 H21 **Šamorín** Ger. Sommerein, Hung. Somorja. Trnavský Kraj, W Slovakia 48°01′N 17°18′E
115 M19 **Sámos** prev. Limín Vathéos. Sámos, Dodekánisa, Greece, Aegean Sea 37°45′N 26°58′E
115 M20 **Sámos** island Dodekánisa, Greece, Aegean Sea
Samosch see Szamos
168 I9 **Samosir, Pulau** island W Indonesia
Samothrace see Samothráki
115 K14 **Samothráki** Samothráki, NE Greece 40°28′N 25°31′E
115 J14 **Samothráki** anc. Samothrace. island NE Greece
115 A15 **Samothráki** island Iónia Nisiá, Greece, C Mediterranean Sea
Samotschin see Szamocin
Sampê see Xiangcheng
169 S13 **Sampit** Borneo, C Indonesia 02°30′S 112°30′E
169 S12 **Sampit, Sungai** ≈ Borneo, N Indonesia
Sampoku see Sanpoku
186 H7 **Sampun** New Britain, E Papua New Guinea 05°19′S 152°06′E
79 N24 **Sampwe** Katanga, SE Dem. Rep. Congo 09°17′S 27°22′E
25 X8 **Sam Rayburn Reservoir** ⊠ Texas, SW USA
158 H15 **Samsang** Xizang Zizhiqu, W China 30°23′N 82°49′E
167 Q6 **Sam Sao, Phou** ⛰ Laos/Thailand
95 H22 **Samsø** island E Denmark
95 H23 **Samsø Bælt** channel E Denmark
167 T7 **Sâm Sơn** Thanh Hoa, N Vietnam 19°44′N 105°53′E
136 L11 **Samsun** anc. Amisus. Samsun, N Turkey 41°17′N 36°22′E
136 K11 **Samsun** ⬖ province N Turkey
137 R9 **Samtredia** W Georgia 42°09′N 42°20′E
59 E15 **Samuel, Represa de** ⊠ W Brazil
167 O14 **Samui, Ko** island SW Thailand
Samundari see Samundri
149 U9 **Samundri** var. Samundari. Punjab, E Pakistan 31°04′N 72°58′E
137 X10 **Samur** ≈ Azerbaijan/Russian Federation
137 Y11 **Samur-Abşeron Kanalı** Rus. Sam ur-Apsheronskiy Kanal. canal E Azerbaijan
Sam ur-Apsheronskiy Kanal see Samur-Abşeron Kanalı
167 O11 **Samut Prakan** var. Muang Samut Prakan, Paknam. Samut Prakan, C Thailand 13°36′N 100°36′E
167 O11 **Samut Sakhon** var. Maha Chai, Samut Sakorn, Tha Chin. Samut Sakhon, C Thailand 13°31′N 100°15′E
Samut Sakorn see Samut Sakhon
167 O11 **Samut Songhram** prev. Meklong. Samut Songkhram, SW Thailand 13°25′N 100°01′E
77 N12 **San** Ségou, C Mali 13°21′N 04°57′W
111 O15 **San** ≈ SE Poland
141 O15 **Şan'ā'** Eng. Sana. ● (Yemen) W Yemen 15°24′N 44°14′E
112 F11 **Sana** ≈ NW Bosnia and Herzegovina
80 O12 **Sanaag** off. Gobolka Sanaag. ⬖ region N Somalia
Sanaag, Gobolka see Sanaag
114 J8 **Sanadinovo** Pleven, N Bulgaria 43°33′N 25°00′E
195 P1 **Sanae** South African research station Antarctica 70°19′S 01°31′W
139 Y10 **Sanāf, Hawr as** ◎ S Iraq
79 E15 **Sanaga** ≈ C Cameroon
54 D12 **San Agustín** Huila, SW Colombia 01°53′N 76°14′W
171 R8 **San Agustin, Cape** headland Mindanao, S Philippines 06°17′N 126°12′E
37 Q13 **San Agustin, Plains of** plain New Mexico, SW USA
38 M16 **Sanak Islands** island Aleutian Islands, Alaska, USA
San Alessandro see Kita-Iō-jima
193 U10 **San Ambrosio, Isla** Eng. San Ambrosio Island. island W Chile
San Ambrosio Island see San Ambrosio, Isla
171 Q12 **Sanana** Pulau Sanana, E Indonesia 02°04′S 125°58′E
171 Q12 **Sanana, Pulau** island Maluku, E Indonesia
142 K5 **Sanandaj** prev. Sinneh. Kordestān, W Iran 35°18′N 47°01′E
35 P8 **San Andreas** California, W USA 38°10′N 120°40′W
2 C13 **San Andreas Fault** fault W USA
54 G8 **San Andrés** Santander, C Colombia 06°52′N 72°53′W
61 C20 **San Andrés de Giles** Buenos Aires, E Argentina 34°27′S 59°27′W
43 Q7 **San Andrés, Isla de** island NW Colombia, Caribbean Sea
43 Q7 **San Andrés y Providencia** ⬖ province Colombia, Caribbean Sea
37 R14 **San Andres Mountains** ⛰ New Mexico, SW USA
41 S15 **San Andrés Tuxtla** var. Tuxtla. Veracruz-Llave, E Mexico 18°28′N 95°15′W
25 P8 **San Angelo** Texas, SW USA 31°28′N 100°26′W
107 A20 **San Antioco, Isola di** island W Italy
42 F4 **San Antonio** Toledo, S Belize 16°13′N 89°02′W
62 G11 **San Antonio** Valparaíso, C Chile 33°35′S 71°38′W
188 H6 **San Antonio** Saipan, S Northern Mariana Islands
37 R13 **San Antonio** New Mexico, SW USA 33°53′N 106°52′W
25 R12 **San Antonio** Texas, SW USA 29°25′N 98°30′W
54 M11 **San Antonio** Amazonas, S Venezuela 03°31′N 66°47′W
54 I7 **San Antonio** Barinas, C Venezuela 07°24′N 71°28′W
55 O5 **San Antonio** Monagas, NE Venezuela 10°03′N 63°45′W
25 S12 **San Antonio** ✈ Texas, SW USA 29°31′N 98°11′W
San Antonio see San Antonio del Táchira
San Antonio Abad see Sant Antoni de Portmany
25 U13 **San Antonio Bay** inlet Texas, SW USA
61 E22 **San Antonio, Cabo** headland E Argentina 36°45′S 56°40′W
44 A5 **San Antonio, Cabo de** headland W Cuba 21°51′N 84°58′W
105 T11 **San Antonio, Cabo de** headland E Spain 38°50′N 00°09′E
54 H7 **San Antonio de Caparo** Táchira, W Venezuela 07°34′N 71°28′W
62 J5 **San Antonio de los Cobres** Salta, NE Argentina 24°10′S 66°17′W
54 H7 **San Antonio del Táchira** var. San Antonio. Táchira, W Venezuela 07°48′N 72°28′W
35 T15 **San Antonio, Mount** ▲ California, W USA 34°18′N 117°37′W
63 K16 **San Antonio Oeste** Río Negro, E Argentina 40°45′S 64°58′W
25 T13 **San Antonio River** ≈ Texas, SW USA
54 J5 **Sanare** Lara, N Venezuela 09°45′N 69°39′W
103 T16 **Sanary-sur-Mer** Var, SE France 43°07′N 05°48′E
25 X8 **San Augustine** Texas, SW USA 31°32′N 94°09′W
San Augustine see Minami-Iō-jima
141 T13 **Sanāw** var. Sanaw. NE Yemen 18°N 51°E
41 O11 **San Bartolo** San Luis Potosí, C Mexico 22°20′N 100°05′W
107 L16 **San Bartolomeo in Galdo** Campania, S Italy 41°24′N 15°01′E
106 K13 **San Benedetto del Tronto** Marche, C Italy 42°57′N 13°53′E
42 E3 **San Benito** Petén, N Guatemala 16°56′N 89°53′W
25 T17 **San Benito** Texas, SW USA 26°07′N 97°37′W
54 E6 **San Benito Abad** Sucre, N Colombia 08°56′N 75°02′W
35 P11 **San Benito Mountain** ▲ California, W USA 36°21′N 120°37′W
35 O10 **San Benito River** ≈ California, W USA
108 H10 **San Bernardino** Graubünden, S Switzerland 46°21′N 09°13′E
35 U15 **San Bernardino** California, W USA 34°06′N 117°15′W
35 U15 **San Bernardino Mountains** ⛰ California, W USA
62 H11 **San Bernardo** Santiago, C Chile 33°37′S 70°45′W
40 J8 **San Bernardo** Durango, C Mexico 25°58′N 105°27′W
164 G12 **Sanbe-san** ▲ Kyūshū, SW Japan 35°09′N 132°36′E
San Bizenti-Barakaldo see San Vicente de Barakaldo
40 J12 **San Blas** Nayarit, C Mexico 21°35′N 105°20′W
40 H8 **San Blas** Sinaloa, C Mexico 26°05′N 108°44′W
San Blas see Kuna Yala
43 U14 **San Blas, Archipiélago de** island group NE Panama
23 Q10 **San Blas, Cape** headland Florida, SE USA 29°39′N 85°21′W
43 V14 **San Blas, Cordillera de** ⛰ NE Panama
62 J8 **San Blas de los Sauces** Catamarca, NW Argentina 28°18′S 67°12′W
106 G8 **San Bonifacio** Veneto, NE Italy 45°22′N 11°14′E
29 S12 **Sanborn** Iowa, C USA 43°10′N 95°39′W
40 M7 **San Buenaventura** Coahuila, NE Mexico 27°04′N 101°32′W
105 S5 **San Caprasio** ▲ N Spain 41°45′N 00°26′W
62 G13 **San Carlos** Bío Bío, C Chile 36°25′S 71°58′W
40 E9 **San Carlos** Baja California Sur, NW Mexico 24°52′N 112°15′W
41 N5 **San Carlos** Coahuila, NE Mexico 29°00′N 100°51′W
41 P9 **San Carlos** Tamaulipas, C Mexico 24°36′N 98°42′W
42 L12 **San Carlos** Río San Juan, S Nicaragua 11°06′N 84°46′W
43 T16 **San Carlos** Panamá, C Panama 08°29′N 79°58′W
171 N3 **San Carlos** off. San Carlos City. Luzon, N Philippines 15°57′N 120°18′E
61 G20 **San Carlos** Maldonado, S Uruguay 34°46′S 54°58′W
36 M14 **San Carlos** Arizona, SW USA 33°21′N 110°27′W
54 K5 **San Carlos** Cojedes, N Venezuela 09°39′N 68°35′W
San Carlos see Quesada, Costa Rica
San Carlos see Luba, Equatorial Guinea
61 B17 **San Carlos Centro** Santa Fe, C Argentina 31°45′S 61°05′W
171 P6 **San Carlos City** Negros, C Philippines 10°34′N 123°24′E
San Carlos City see San Carlos
San Carlos de Ancud see Ancud
63 H16 **San Carlos de Bariloche** Río Negro, SW Argentina 41°08′S 71°15′W
61 B21 **San Carlos de Bolívar** Buenos Aires, E Argentina 36°15′S 61°06′W
54 H6 **San Carlos del Zulia** Zulia, W Venezuela 09°01′N 71°58′W
54 L12 **San Carlos de Río Negro** Amazonas, S Venezuela 01°54′N 67°54′W
San Carlos, Estrecho de see Falkland Sound
36 M14 **San Carlos Reservoir** ⊠ Arizona, SW USA
42 M12 **San Carlos, Río** ≈ N Costa Rica
65 D24 **San Carlos Settlement** East Falkland, Falkland Islands
61 C23 **San Cayetano** Buenos Aires, E Argentina 38°20′S 59°37′W
103 O8 **Sancerre** Cher, C France 47°19′N 02°53′E
158 G7 **Sanchakou** Xinjiang Uygur Zizhiqu, NW China 39°56′N 78°28′E
Sanchoku see Samch'ŏk
41 O12 **San Ciro** San Luis Potosí, C Mexico 21°40′N 99°50′W
105 P10 **San Clemente** Castilla-La Mancha, C Spain 39°24′N 02°25′W
35 T16 **San Clemente** California, W USA 33°25′N 117°36′W
61 E21 **San Clemente del Tuyú** Buenos Aires, E Argentina 36°22′S 56°43′W
35 S17 **San Clemente Island** island Channel Islands, California, W USA
103 O9 **Sancoins** Cher, C France 46°49′N 03°00′E
61 B16 **San Cristóbal** Santa Fe, C Argentina 30°20′S 61°14′W
44 B4 **San Cristóbal** Pinar del Río, W Cuba 22°43′N 83°03′W
45 O9 **San Cristóbal** var. Benemérita de San Cristóbal. S Dominican Republic 18°27′N 70°07′W
54 H7 **San Cristóbal** Táchira, W Venezuela 07°46′N 72°15′W
187 N10 **San Cristobal** var. Makira. island SE Solomon Islands
San Cristóbal see San Cristóbal de Las Casas
41 U16 **San Cristóbal de Las Casas** var. San Cristóbal. Chiapas, SE Mexico 16°44′N 92°40′W
187 N10 **San Cristóbal, Isla** var. Chatham Island. island Galapagos Islands, Ecuador, E Pacific Ocean
42 D5 **San Cristóbal Verapaz** Alta Verapaz, C Guatemala 15°21′N 90°22′W
44 F6 **Sancti Spíritus** Sancti Spíritus, C Cuba 21°54′N 79°27′W
103 O11 **Sancy, Puy de** ▲ C France 45°33′N 02°48′E
95 D15 **Sand** Rogaland, S Norway 59°28′N 06°16′E
169 W7 **Sandakan** Sabah, East Malaysia 05°52′N 118°04′E
182 K9 **Sandalwood** South Australia 34°51′S 140°13′E
Sandalwood Island see Sumba, Pulau
94 D11 **Sandane** Sogn Og Fjordane, S Norway 61°47′N 06°14′E
114 G12 **Sandanski** prev. Sveti Vrach. Blagoevgrad, SW Bulgaria 41°36′N 23°19′E
Sandaohezi see Shawan
76 J11 **Sandaré** Kayes, W Mali 14°36′N 10°22′W
95 J19 **Sandared** Västra Götaland, S Sweden 57°43′N 12°47′E
94 N12 **Sandarne** Gävleborg, C Sweden 61°15′N 17°10′E
186 B5 **Sandaun** prev. West Sepik. ⬖ province NW Papua New Guinea
96 K4 **Sanday** island NE Scotland, United Kingdom
31 P15 **Sand Creek** ≈ Indiana, N USA
95 H15 **Sande** Vestfold, S Norway 59°34′N 10°13′E
95 H16 **Sandefjord** Vestfold, S Norway 59°10′N 10°15′E
77 O15 **Sandégué** E Ivory Coast 07°59′N 03°33′W
77 P14 **Sandema** N Ghana 10°42′N 01°17′W
37 O11 **Sanders** Arizona, SW USA 35°13′N 109°21′W
24 M11 **Sanderson** Texas, SW USA 30°08′N 102°25′W
23 U4 **Sandersville** Georgia, SE USA 32°58′N 82°48′W
92 H4 **Sandgerdhi** Sudhurland, SW Iceland 64°01′N 22°42′W
28 K14 **Sand Hills** ⛰ Nebraska, C USA
25 S14 **Sandia** Texas, SW USA 27°59′N 97°52′W
35 T17 **San Diego** California, W USA 32°43′N 117°09′W
25 S14 **San Diego** Texas, SW USA 27°47′N 98°15′W
136 F14 **Sandıklı** Afyon, W Turkey 38°28′N 30°17′E
152 L12 **Sandila** Uttar Pradesh, N India 27°05′N 80°37′E
San Dimitri Point see San Dimitri, Ras
121 N15 **San Dimitri, Ras** var. San Dimitri Point. headland Gozo, NW Malta 36°04′N 14°12′E
168 J13 **Sanding, Selat** strait W Indonesia
30 J3 **Sand Island** island Apostle Islands, Wisconsin, N USA
95 C16 **Sandnes** Rogaland, S Norway 58°51′N 05°45′E
92 F13 **Sandnessjøen** Nordland, C Norway 66°00′N 12°37′E
Sandø see Sandoy
79 L24 **Sandoa** Katanga, S Dem. Rep. Congo 09°41′S 22°56′E
111 N15 **Sandomierz** Rus. Sandomir. Świętokrzyskie, C Poland 50°42′N 21°45′E
Sandomir see Sandomierz
54 C13 **Sandoná** Nariño, SW Colombia 01°18′N 77°28′W
106 I7 **San Donà di Piave** Veneto, NE Italy 45°38′N 12°34′E
124 K14 **Sandovo** Tverskaya Oblast', W Russian Federation 58°26′N 36°30′E
Sandoway see Thandwe
97 M24 **Sandown** S England, United Kingdom 50°40′N 01°11′W
95 B19 **Sandoy** Dan. Sandø. island C Faeroe Islands
39 N16 **Sand Point** Popof Island, Alaska, USA 55°20′N 160°30′W
32 M7 **Sandpoint** Idaho, NW USA 48°16′N 116°33′W
65 N24 **Sand Point** headland E Tristan da Cunha
31 R7 **Sand Point** headland Michigan, N USA 43°54′N 83°24′W
93 H14 **Sandsele** Västerbotten, N Sweden 65°16′N 17°40′E
10 I14 **Sandspit** Moresby Island, British Columbia, SW Canada 53°14′N 131°50′W
27 P9 **Sand Springs** Oklahoma, C USA 36°08′N 96°06′W
29 W7 **Sandstone** Minnesota, N USA 46°07′N 92°51′W
36 K15 **Sand Tank Mountains** ⛰ Arizona, SW USA
31 S8 **Sandusky** Michigan, N USA 43°26′N 82°50′W
31 S11 **Sandusky** Ohio, N USA 41°27′N 82°42′W
31 S12 **Sandusky River** ≈ Ohio, N USA
83 D22 **Sandverhaar** Karas, S Namibia 26°50′S 17°25′E
95 L24 **Sandvig** Bornholm, E Denmark 55°15′N 14°45′E
95 H15 **Sandvika** Akershus, S Norway 59°54′N 10°29′E
94 N13 **Sandviken** Gävleborg, C Sweden 60°38′N 16°50′E
30 M11 **Sandwich** Illinois, N USA 41°39′N 88°37′W
Sandwich Island see Efate
Sandwich Islands see Hawaiian Islands
153 V16 **Sandwip** island SE Bangladesh
11 U12 **Sandy Bay** Saskatchewan, C Canada 55°31′N 102°14′W
183 N16 **Sandy Cape** headland Tasmania, SE Australia 41°27′S 144°43′E
36 L3 **Sandy City** Utah, W USA 40°36′N 111°53′W
31 U12 **Sandy Creek** ≈ Ohio, N USA
21 O5 **Sandy Hook** Kentucky, S USA 38°05′N 83°09′W
18 K15 **Sandy Hook** headland New Jersey, NE USA 40°27′N 73°59′W
Sandykachi/Sandykgachy see Sandykgaçy
146 J15 **Sandykaçy** var. Sandykgachy. Maryyskiy Velayat, S Turkmenistan 36°34′N 62°28′E
Sandykgachy see Sandykaçy
146 J15 **Sandykgaçy** var. Sandykgachy, Rus. Sandykachi. Mary Welaýaty, S Turkmenistan 36°34′N 62°28′E
146 L13 **Sandykly Gumy** Rus. Peski Sandykly. desert E Turkmenistan
Sandykly, Peski see Sandykly Gumy
11 Q13 **Sandy Lake** Alberta, W Canada 55°50′N 113°30′W
12 B8 **Sandy Lake** Ontario, C Canada 53°00′N 93°25′W
12 B8 **Sandy Lake** ◎ Ontario, C Canada
65 N25 **Sandy Point** headland E Tristan da Cunha
23 S3 **Sandy Springs** Georgia, SE USA 33°57′N 84°23′W
24 H8 **San Elizario** Texas, SW USA 31°35′N 106°16′W
99 L25 **Sanem** Luxembourg, SW Luxembourg 49°33′N 05°56′E
42 K5 **San Esteban** Olancho, C Honduras 15°19′N 85°52′W
105 O6 **San Esteban de Gormaz** Castilla-León, N Spain 41°34′N 03°13′W
40 E5 **San Esteban, Isla** island NW Mexico
San Eugenio/San Eugenio del Cuareim see Artigas
62 H11 **San Felipe** var. San Felipe de Aconcagua. Valparaíso, C Chile 32°45′S 70°42′W
40 D3 **San Felipe** Baja California Norte, NW Mexico 31°03′N 114°52′W
40 N12 **San Felipe** Guanajuato, C Mexico 21°30′N 101°15′W
54 K5 **San Felipe** Yaracuy, NW Venezuela 10°25′N 68°40′W
44 B5 **San Felipe, Cayos de** island group W Cuba
San Felipe de Aconcagua see San Felipe
San Felipe de Puerto Plata see Puerto Plata
37 R11 **San Felipe Pueblo** New Mexico, SW USA 35°25′N 106°27′W
San Feliú de Guixols see Sant Feliu de Guíxols
193 T10 **San Félix, Isla** Eng. San Felix Island. island W Chile
San Felix Island see San Félix, Isla
54 L11 **San Fernando de Atabapo** Amazonas, S Venezuela 04°00′N 67°42′W
40 C4 **San Fernando** var. Misión San Fernando. Baja California Norte, NW Mexico 29°58′N 115°14′W
41 P9 **San Fernando** Tamaulipas, C Mexico 24°50′N 98°10′W
171 N2 **San Fernando** Luzon, N Philippines 16°45′N 120°21′E
171 O3 **San Fernando** Luzon, N Philippines 15°01′N 120°41′E
104 J16 **San Fernando** prev. Isla de León. Andalucía, S Spain 36°28′N 06°12′W
45 U14 **San Fernando** Trinidad, Trinidad and Tobago 10°17′N 61°27′W
35 S15 **San Fernando** California, W USA 34°16′N 118°26′W
54 L7 **San Fernando** var. San Fernando de Apure. Apure, C Venezuela 07°54′N 67°28′W
San Fernando de Apure see San Fernando
62 L8 **San Fernando del Valle de Catamarca** var. Catamarca. Catamarca, NW Argentina 28°28′S 65°46′W
San Fernando de Monte Cristi see Monte Cristi
41 P9 **San Fernando, Río** ≈ C Mexico
23 X11 **Sanford** Florida, SE USA 28°48′N 81°16′W
19 P9 **Sanford** Maine, NE USA 43°26′N 70°46′W
21 T10 **Sanford** North Carolina, SE USA 35°29′N 79°10′W
25 N2 **Sanford** Texas, SW USA 35°42′N 101°31′W
39 T10 **Sanford, Mount** ▲ Alaska, USA 62°21′N 144°12′W
42 G8 **San Francisco** var. Gotera, San Francisco Gotera. Morazán, E El Salvador 13°41′N 88°06′W
43 R16 **San Francisco** Veraguas, C Panama 08°19′N 80°59′W
171 N2 **San Francisco** var. Aurora. Luzon, N Philippines 13°22′N 122°31′E
35 L8 **San Francisco** California, W USA 37°47′N 122°25′W
54 H5 **San Francisco** Zulia, NW Venezuela 10°36′N 71°39′W
34 M8 **San Francisco** ✈ California, W USA 37°37′N 122°23′W
35 N9 **San Francisco Bay** bay California, W USA
61 C24 **San Francisco de Bellocq** Buenos Aires, E Argentina 38°42′S 60°01′W
40 I6 **San Francisco de Borja** Chihuahua, N Mexico 27°57′N 106°42′W
42 J6 **San Francisco de la Paz** Olancho, C Honduras 14°55′N 86°14′W
40 J7 **San Francisco del Oro** Chihuahua, N Mexico 26°52′N 105°50′W
40 M12 **San Francisco del Rincón** Jalisco, SW Mexico 21°00′N 101°51′W
45 O8 **San Francisco de Macorís** C Dominican Republic 19°19′N 70°15′W
San Francisco de Satipo see Satipo
San Francisco Gotera see San Francisco
San Francisco Telixtlahuaca see Telixtlahuaca
107 K23 **San Fratello** Sicilia, Italy, C Mediterranean Sea 38°00′N 14°35′E
San Fructuoso see Tacuarembó
82 C12 **Sanga** Cuanza Sul, NW Angola 11°10′S 15°27′E
56 C5 **San Gabriel** Carchi, N Ecuador 0°35′N 77°48′W
159 S15 **Sa'ngain** Xizang Zizhiqu, W China 30°47′N 98°45′E
154 E13 **Sangamner** Mahārāshtra, W India 19°37′N 74°18′E
152 H12 **Sāngāner** Rājasthān, N India 26°48′N 75°48′E
Sangan, Koh-i- see Sangān, Kūh-e
149 N6 **Sangān, Kūh-e** Pash. Koh-i-Sangan. ⛰ C Afghanistan
123 P10 **Sangar** Respublika Sakha (Yakutiya), NE Russian Federation 63°48′N 127°37′E
155 H18 **Sāngāreddi** Andhra Pradesh, India 17°37′N 78°04′E
169 V11 **Sangasanga** Borneo, C Indonesia 0°36′S 117°12′E
103 N1 **Sangatte** Pas-de-Calais, N France 50°56′N 01°41′E
107 B19 **San Gavino Monreale** Sardegna, Italy, C Mediterranean Sea 39°33′N 08°47′E
57 D16 **Sangayan, Isla** island W Peru
30 L14 **Sangchris Lake** ⊠ Illinois, N USA
171 N16 **Sangeang, Pulau** island S Indonesia
116 I10 **Sângeorgiu de Pădure** prev. Erdăt-Sângeorz, Sîngeorgiu de Pădure, Hung. Erdőszentgyörgy. Mureş, C Romania 46°27′N 24°50′E
116 I9 **Sângeorz-Băi** var. Singeroz Băi, Ger. Rumänisch-Sankt-Georgen, Hung. Oláhszentgyőrgy; prev. Sîngeorz-Băi. Bistriţa-Năsăud, N Romania 47°24′N 24°40′E
35 R10 **Sanger** California, W USA 36°42′N 119°33′W
25 T5 **Sanger** Texas, SW USA 33°21′N 97°10′W
Sângerei see Singerei
101 L15 **Sangerhausen** Sachsen-Anhalt, C Germany 51°29′N 11°18′E
45 S6 **San Germán** W Puerto Rico 18°05′N 67°02′W
San Germano see Cassino
161 N2 **Sanggan He** ≈ E China
169 Q11 **Sanggau** Borneo, C Indonesia 0°08′N 110°35′E
79 G17 **Sangha** ⬖ province N Congo
79 H16 **Sangha** ≈ Central African Republic/Congo
79 G16 **Sangha-Mbaéré** ⬖ prefecture SW Central African Republic
149 Q15 **Sānghar** Sind, SE Pakistan 26°10′N 68°59′E
115 F22 **Sangiás** ▲ S Greece 36°39′N 22°24′E
Sangihe, Kepulauan see Sangir, Kepulauan
171 Q9 **Sangihe, Pulau** var. Sangir. island N Indonesia
54 G8 **San Gil** Santander, C Colombia 06°35′N 73°08′W
106 F12 **San Gimignano** Toscana, C Italy 43°30′N 11°00′E
148 M8 **Sangin** var. Sangin. Helmand, S Afghanistan 32°03′N 64°50′E
Sangin see Sangin
107 O21 **San Giovanni in Fiore** Calabria, SW Italy 39°15′N 16°42′E
107 M16 **San Giovanni Rotondo** Puglia, SE Italy 41°43′N 15°44′E
106 G12 **San Giovanni Valdarno** Toscana, C Italy 43°34′N 11°31′E
Sangir see Sangihe, Pulau
171 Q10 **Sangir, Kepulauan** var. Kepulauan Sangihe. island group N Indonesia
Sangiyn Dalay see Erdenedalay, Dundgovĭ, Mongolia
Sangiyn Dalay see Erdene, Govĭ-Altay, Mongolia
Sangiyn Dalay see Nomgon, Ömnögovĭ, Mongolia
Sangiyn Dalay see Öldziyt, Övörhangay, Mongolia
163 Y15 **Sangju** Jap. Shōshū. C South Korea 36°26′N 128°09′E
167 R11 **Sangkha** Surin, E Thailand 14°36′N 103°43′E
169 W10 **Sangkulirang** Borneo, N Indonesia 01°00′N 117°56′E
169 W10 **Sangkulirang, Teluk** bay Borneo, N Indonesia
155 E16 **Sāngli** Mahārāshtra, W India 16°55′N 74°37′E
79 E16 **Sangmélima** Sud, S Cameroon 02°57′N 11°56′E
35 V15 **San Gorgonio Mountain** ▲ California, W USA 34°06′N 116°50′W
37 T8 **Sangre de Cristo Mountains** ⛰ Colorado/New Mexico, USA
61 A20 **San Gregorio** Santa Fe, C Argentina 34°18′S 62°02′W
61 F18 **San Gregorio de Polanco** Tacuarembó, C Uruguay 32°37′S 55°50′W
45 V14 **Sangre Grande** Trinidad, Trinidad and Tobago 10°35′N 61°08′W
159 N16 **Sangri** Xizang Zizhiqu, W China 29°17′N 92°01′E
152 H9 **Sangrūr** Punjab, NW India 30°16′N 75°52′E
158 K16 **Sangsang** Xizang Zizhiqu, W China 29°45′N 86°42′E
44 I11 **Sangster** off. Sir Donald Sangster International Airport, var. Montego Bay. ✈ (Montego Bay) W Jamaica 18°30′N 77°54′W
59 G17 **Sangue, Rio do** ≈ W Brazil
105 R4 **Sangüesa** Navarra, N Spain 42°34′N 01°17′W
61 C16 **San Gustavo** Entre Ríos, E Argentina 30°41′S 59°23′W
Sangyuan see Wuqiao
40 C6 **San Hipólito, Punta** headland NW Mexico 26°57′N 114°00′W
23 W15 **Sanibel** Sanibel Island, Florida, SE USA 26°27′N 82°01′W
23 V15 **Sanibel Island** island Florida, SE USA
60 F13 **San Ignacio** Misiones, NE Argentina 27°15′S 55°32′W
42 F2 **San Ignacio** prev. Cayo, El Cayo. Cayo, W Belize 17°09′N 89°02′W
57 L16 **San Ignacio** Beni, N Bolivia 14°54′S 65°35′W
57 O18 **San Ignacio** Santa Cruz, E Bolivia 16°23′S 60°59′W
42 M14 **San Ignacio** var. San Ignacio de Acosta. San José, W Costa Rica 09°46′N 84°10′W
40 E6 **San Ignacio** Baja California Sur, NW Mexico 27°18′N 112°51′W
40 J10 **San Ignacio** Sinaloa, W Mexico 23°55′N 106°25′W
56 B9 **San Ignacio** Cajamarca, N Peru 05°09′S 79°00′W
San Ignacio de Acosta see San Ignacio
40 D7 **San Ignacio, Laguna** lagoon W Mexico
12 I6 **Sanikiluaq** Belcher Islands, Nunavut, C Canada 55°20′N 77°50′W
171 O3 **San Ildefonso Peninsula** peninsula Luzon, N Philippines
Saniquillie see Sanniquellie
61 D20 **San Isidro** Buenos Aires, E Argentina 34°28′S 58°31′W
43 N14 **San Isidro** var. San Isidro de El General. San José, SE Costa Rica 09°28′N 83°42′W
San Isidro de El General see San Isidro
54 E5 **San Jacinto** Bolívar, N Colombia 09°53′N 75°06′W
35 U16 **San Jacinto** California, W USA 33°47′N 116°58′W
35 V15 **San Jacinto Peak** ▲ California, W USA 33°48′N 116°40′W
61 F14 **San Javier** Misiones, NE Argentina 27°50′S 55°06′W
61 C16 **San Javier** Santa Fe, C Argentina 30°35′S 59°59′W
105 S13 **San Javier** Murcia, SE Spain 37°49′N 00°50′W
61 D18 **San Javier** Río Negro, W Uruguay 32°41′S 58°08′W
61 C16 **San Javier, Río** ≈ C Argentina
160 L12 **Sanjiang** var. Guyi, Sanjiang Dongzu Zizhixian. Guangxi Zhuangzu Zizhiqu, S China 25°46′N 109°26′E
Sanjiang see Jinping, Guizhou
Sanjiang Dongzu Zizhixian see Sanjiang
Sanjiaocheng see Haiyan
165 N11 **Sanjō** var. Sanzyô. Niigata, Honshū, C Japan 37°39′N 139°00′E
57 M15 **San Joaquín** Beni, N Bolivia 13°06′S 64°46′W
55 O6 **San Joaquín** Anzoátegui, NE Venezuela 09°21′N 64°30′W
35 O9 **San Joaquin River** ≈ California, W USA
35 P10 **San Joaquin Valley** valley California, W USA
61 A18 **San Jorge** Santa Fe, C Argentina 31°50′S 61°50′W
40 D3 **San Jorge, Bahía de** bay NW Mexico
63 J19 **San Jorge, Golfo** var. Gulf of San Jorge. gulf S Argentina
San Jorge, Gulf of see San Jorge, Golfo
San Jorge, Isla de see Weddell Island
61 F14 **San José** Misiones, NE Argentina 27°46′S 55°47′W
57 P19 **San José** var. San José de Chiquitos. Santa Cruz, E Bolivia 14°13′S 68°05′W
42 M14 **San José** ● (Costa Rica) San José, C Costa Rica 09°55′N 84°05′W
42 C7 **San José** var. Puerto San José. Escuintla, S Guatemala 14°00′N 90°50′W
40 G6 **San José** Sonora, NW Mexico 27°32′N 110°09′W
188 K8 **San Jose** Tinian, S Northern Mariana Islands 15°00′S 145°38′E
105 U11 **San José** Eivissa, Spain, W Mediterranean Sea 38°55′N 01°18′E
35 N9 **San Jose** California, W USA 37°18′N 121°53′W
54 H5 **San José** Zulia, NW Venezuela 10°02′N 72°24′W
42 M14 **San José** off. Provincia de San José. ⬖ province W Costa Rica
61 E19 **San José** ⬖ department S Uruguay
42 M13 **San José** ✈ Alajuela, C Costa Rica 10°03′N 84°12′W
San José see San José del Guaviare, Colombia
San Jose see Oleai
San Jose see Sant Josep de sa Talaia, Ibiza, Spain
San José see San José de Mayo, Uruguay
171 O3 **San Jose City** Luzon, N Philippines 15°49′N 120°57′E
San José de Chiquitos see San José
San José de Cúcuta see Cúcuta
61 D16 **San José de Feliciano** Entre Ríos, E Argentina 30°26′S 58°46′W
55 O6 **San José de Guanipa** var. El Tigrito. Anzoátegui, NE Venezuela 08°54′N 64°10′W
62 I9 **San José de Jáchal** San Juan, W Argentina 30°15′S 68°46′W
40 G10 **San José del Cabo** Baja California Sur, NW Mexico 23°01′N 109°40′W
54 G12 **San José del Guaviare** var. San José. Guaviare, S Colombia 02°34′N 72°38′W
61 E20 **San José de Mayo** var. San José. San José, S Uruguay 34°20′S 56°42′W
54 I10 **San José de Ocuné** Vichada, E Colombia 04°10′N 70°21′W
41 O9 **San José de Raíces** Nuevo León, NE Mexico 24°32′N 100°15′W
63 K17 **San José, Golfo** gulf E Argentina
40 F9 **San José, Isla** island NW Mexico
43 U16 **San José, Isla** island SE Panama
25 U14 **San Jose Island** island Texas, SW USA
San José, Provincia de see San José
62 I10 **San Juan** San Juan, W Argentina 31°37′S 68°27′W
45 N9 **San Juan** var. San Juan de la Maguana. C Dominican Republic 18°49′N 71°12′W
57 E17 **San Juan** Ica, S Peru 15°22′S 75°07′W
45 U5 **San Juan** O (Puerto Rico) NE Puerto Rico 18°28′N 66°06′W
62 H10 **San Juan** off. Provincia de San Juan. ⬖ province W Argentina
45 U5 **San Juan** var. Luis Muñoz Marin. ✈ NE Puerto Rico 18°27′N 66°05′W
San Juan see San Juan de los Morros
62 O7 **San Juan Bautista** Misiones, S Paraguay 26°40′S 57°08′W
35 O10 **San Juan Bautista** California, W USA 36°50′N 121°34′W
San Juan Bautista see Villahermosa
San Juan Bautista Cuicatlán see Cuicatlán
San Juan Bautista Tuxtepec see Tuxtepec

◆ Country
● Country Capital
◇ Dependent Territory
○ Dependent Territory Capital
⬖ Administrative Regions
✈ International Airport
▲ Mountain
⛰ Mountain Range
Volcano
≈ River
◎ Lake
⊠ Reservoir

San Juan, Cabo – Santa Rosa

79 C17 **San Juan, Cabo** *headland* S Equatorial Guinea 01°09′N 09°25′E
105 S12 **San Juan de Alicante** País Valenciano, E Spain 38°26′N 00°27′W
54 H7 **San Juan de Colón** Táchira, NW Venezuela 08°02′N 72°17′W
40 L9 **San Juan de Guadalupe** Durango, C Mexico 25°12′N 100°50′W
San Juan de la Maguana *see* San Juan
54 G4 **San Juan del Cesar** La Guajira, N Colombia 10°45′N 73°00′W
40 L15 **San Juan de Lima, Punta** *headland* SW Mexico 18°34′N 103°40′W
42 I8 **San Juan de Limay** Estelí, NW Nicaragua 13°10′N 86°36′W
43 N12 **San Juan del Norte** *var.* Greytown. Río San Juan, SE Nicaragua 10°58′N 83°40′W
54 K4 **San Juan de los Cayos** Falcón, N Venezuela 11°11′N 68°27′W
40 M12 **San Juan de los Lagos** Jalisco, C Mexico 21°15′N 102°15′W
54 L5 **San Juan de los Morros** *var.* San Juan. Guárico, N Venezuela 09°53′N 67°23′W
40 K9 **San Juan del Río** Durango, C Mexico 25°12′N 100°50′W
41 O13 **San Juan del Río** Querétaro de Arteaga, C Mexico 20°24′N 100°00′W
42 J11 **San Juan del Sur** Rivas, SW Nicaragua 11°16′N 85°51′W
54 M9 **San Juan de Manapiare** Amazonas, S Venezuela 05°15′N 66°05′W
40 E7 **San Juanico** Baja California Sur, NW Mexico
40 D7 **San Juanico, Punta** *headland* NW Mexico 26°01′N 112°17′W
32 G6 **San Juan Islands** *island group* Washington, NW USA
40 I6 **San Juanito** Chihuahua, N Mexico
40 I12 **San Juanito, Isla** *island* C Mexico
37 R8 **San Juan Mountains** ▲▲ Colorado, C USA
54 E5 **San Juan Nepomuceno** Bolívar, NW Colombia 09°57′N 75°06′W
44 E5 **San Juan, Pico** ▲ C Cuba 21°58′N 80°10′W
San Juan, Provincia de *see* San Juan
191 W15 **San Juan, Punta** *headland* Easter Island, Chile, E Pacific Ocean 27°03′S 109°22′W
42 M12 **San Juan, Río** Costa Rica/Nicaragua
41 S15 **San Juan, Río** SE Mexico
37 O8 **San Juan River** Colorado/Utah, W USA
San Julián *see* Puerto San Julián
61 B17 **San Justo** Santa Fe, C Argentina 30°47′S 60°32′W
109 W5 **Sankt Aegyd am Neuwalde** Niederösterreich, E Austria 47°51′N 15°34′E
109 U9 **Sankt Andrä** *Slvn.* Šent Andraž. Kärnten, S Austria 46°46′N 14°49′E
Sankt Andrä *see* Szentendre
Sankt Anna *see* Sântana
108 K8 **Sankt Anton-am-Arlberg** Vorarlberg, W Austria 47°08′N 10°11′E
101 E16 **Sankt Augustin** Nordrhein-Westfalen, W Germany 50°46′N 07°10′E
Sankt-Bartholomäi *see* Palamuse
101 F24 **Sankt Blasien** Baden-Württemberg, SW Germany 47°43′N 08°09′E
109 R3 **Sankt Florian am Inn** Oberösterreich, N Austria 48°24′N 13°27′E
108 I7 **Sankt Gallen** *var.* St. Gallen, *Eng.* Saint Gall, *Fr.* St-Gall. Sankt Gallen, NE Switzerland 47°25′N 09°23′E
108 H8 **Sankt Gallen** *var.* St.Gallen, *Eng.* Saint Gall, *Fr.* St-Gall. ◈ *canton* NE Switzerland
108 J8 **Sankt Gallenkirch** Vorarlberg, W Austria 47°00′N 10°59′E
109 Q5 **Sankt Georgen** Salzburg, N Austria 47°59′N 12°57′E
Sankt Georgen *see* Đurđevac
Sankt-Georgen *see* Sfântu Gheorghe
109 R6 **Sankt Gilgen** Salzburg, NW Austria 47°46′N 13°21′E
Sankt Gotthard *see* Szentgotthárd
101 E20 **Sankt Ingbert** Saarland, SW Germany 49°17′N 07°07′E
Sankt-Jakobi *see* Viru-Jaagupi, Lääne-Virumaa, Estonia
Sankt-Jakobi *see* Pärnu-Jaagupi, Pärnumaa, Estonia
Sankt Johann *see* Sankt Johann in Tirol
109 T7 **Sankt Johann am Tauern** Steiermark, E Austria 47°20′N 14°27′E
109 Q7 **Sankt Johann im Pongau** Salzburg, NW Austria 47°22′N 13°13′E
109 P6 **Sankt Johann in Tirol** *var.* Sankt Johann. Tirol, W Austria 47°32′N 12°26′E
Sankt-Johannis *see* Järva-Jaani
108 L8 **Sankt Leonhard** Tirol, W Austria 47°05′N 10°53′E
Sankt Margarethen *see* Sankt Margarethen im Burgenland
109 Y5 **Sankt Margarethen im Burgenland** *var.* Sankt Margarethen. Burgenland, E Austria 47°49′N 16°38′E
Sankt Martin *see* Martin
109 X8 **Sankt Martin an der Raab** Burgenland, SE Austria 46°59′N 16°12′E
109 U7 **Sankt Michael in Obersteiermark** Steiermark, SE Austria 47°21′N 14°59′E
Sankt Michel *see* Mikkeli
Sankt Moritz *see* St. Moritz
108 E11 **Sankt Niklaus** Valais, S Switzerland 46°09′N 07°48′E
109 S7 **Sankt Nikolai** *var.* Sankt Nikolai im Sölktal. Steiermark, SE Austria 47°18′N 14°04′E
Sankt Nikolai im Sölktal *see* Sankt Nikolai
109 U9 **Sankt Paul** *var.* Sankt Paul im Lavanttal. Kärnten, S Austria 46°42′N 14°53′E
Sankt Paul im Lavanttal *see* Sankt Paul
Sankt Peter *see* Pivka
109 W9 **Sankt Peter am Ottersbach** Steiermark, SE Austria 46°49′N 15°48′E
124 J13 **Sankt-Peterburg** *prev.* Leningrad, Petrograd, *Eng.* Saint Petersburg, *Fin.* Pietari. Leningradskaya Oblast', NW Russian Federation 59°55′N 30°25′E
100 H8 **Sankt Peter-Ording** Schleswig-Holstein, N Germany 54°18′N 08°37′E
109 V4 **Sankt Pölten** Niederösterreich, N Austria 48°14′N 15°38′E
109 W7 **Sankt Ruprecht** *var.* Sankt Ruprecht an der Raab. Steiermark, SE Austria 47°10′N 15°41′E
Sankt Ruprecht an der Raab *see* Sankt Ruprecht
Sankt-Ulrich *see* Ortisei
109 T4 **Sankt Valentin** Niederösterreich, C Austria 48°11′N 14°33′E
Sankt Veit am Flaum *see* Rijeka
109 T9 **Sankt Veit an der Glan** *Slvn.* Št. Vid. Kärnten, S Austria 46°47′N 14°22′E
99 M21 **Sankt-Vith** *var.* Saint-Vith. Liège, E Belgium 50°17′N 06°07′E
101 E20 **Sankt Wendel** Saarland, SW Germany 49°28′N 07°10′E
109 R6 **Sankt Wolfgang** Salzburg, NW Austria 47°43′N 13°30′E
79 K21 **Sankuru** C Dem. Rep. Congo
40 D8 **San Lázaro, Cabo** *headland* NW Mexico 24°46′N 112°15′W
137 O16 **Şanlıurfa** *prev.* Sanli Urfa, Urfa; *anc.* Edessa. şanlıurfa, S Turkey 37°08′N 38°45′E
137 O16 **Şanlıurfa** *prev.* Urfa. ◈ *province* SE Turkey
Sanli Urfa *see* Şanlıurfa
137 O16 **Şanlıurfa Yaylası** *plateau* SE Turkey
61 B18 **San Lorenzo** Santa Fe, C Argentina 32°45′S 60°45′W
57 M21 **San Lorenzo** Tarija, S Bolivia 21°25′S 64°45′W
56 C5 **San Lorenzo** Esmeraldas, N Ecuador 01°15′N 78°51′W
42 H8 **San Lorenzo** Valle, S Honduras 13°24′N 87°27′W
56 A6 **San Lorenzo, Cabo** *headland* W Ecuador 0°57′S 80°49′W
105 N8 **San Lorenzo de El Escorial** *var.* El Escorial. Madrid, C Spain 40°36′N 04°07′W
40 E5 **San Lorenzo, Isla** *island* NW Mexico
57 C14 **San Lorenzo, Isla** *island* W Peru
63 G20 **San Lorenzo, Monte** ▲ S Argentina 47°40′S 72°12′W
40 I9 **San Lorenzo, Río** C Mexico
104 J15 **Sanlúcar de Barrameda** Andalucía, S Spain 36°46′N 06°21′W
104 J14 **Sanlúcar la Mayor** Andalucía, S Spain 37°24′N 06°13′W
40 F11 **San Lucas** Baja California Sur, NW Mexico 22°50′N 109°52′W
40 E6 **San Lucas** *var.* Cabo San Lucas. Baja California Sur, NW Mexico 27°14′N 112°15′W
40 G11 **San Lucas, Cabo** *var.* San Lucas Cape. *headland* NW Mexico 22°52′N 109°53′W
San Lucas Cape *see* San Lucas, Cabo
62 J11 **San Luis** San Luis, C Argentina 33°18′S 66°18′W
42 E4 **San Luis** Petén, NE Guatemala 16°16′N 89°27′W
40 D2 **San Luis** *var.* San Luis Río Colorado. Sonora, NW Mexico 32°26′N 114°48′W
42 M7 **San Luis** Región Autónoma Atlántico Norte, NE Nicaragua 13°59′N 84°10′W
36 H15 **San Luis** Arizona, SW USA 32°27′N 114°45′W
37 T8 **San Luis** Colorado, C USA 37°09′N 105°24′W
54 J4 **San Luis** Falcón, N Venezuela 11°09′N 69°39′W
62 J11 **San Luis** *off.* Provincia de San Luis. ◈ *province* C Argentina
41 N12 **San Luis de la Paz** Guanajuato, C Mexico 21°15′N 100°33′W
40 K8 **San Luis del Cordero** Durango, C Mexico 25°25′N 104°09′W
40 D4 **San Luis, Isla** *island* NW Mexico
42 E6 **San Luis Jilotepeque** Jalapa, SE Guatemala 14°40′N 89°42′W
57 M16 **San Luis, Laguna de** NW Bolivia
35 P13 **San Luis Obispo** California, W USA 35°17′N 120°40′W
37 R7 **San Luis Peak** ▲ Colorado, C USA 37°59′N 106°55′W
41 N11 **San Luis Potosí** San Luis Potosí, C Mexico 22°10′N 100°57′W
41 N11 **San Luis Potosí** ◈ *state* C Mexico
San Luis, Provincia de *see* San Luis
35 O10 **San Luis Reservoir** California, W USA
San Luis Río Colorado *see* San Luis
37 S8 **San Luis Valley** *basin* Colorado, C USA
107 C19 **Sanluri** Sardegna, Italy, C Mediterranean Sea 39°34′N 08°54′E
61 D23 **San Manuel** Buenos Aires, E Argentina 37°47′S 58°50′W
36 M15 **San Manuel** Arizona, SW USA 32°36′N 110°37′W
106 F11 **San Marcello Pistoiese** Toscana, C Italy 44°03′N 10°46′E
107 N20 **San Marco Argentano** Calabria, SW Italy 39°31′N 16°07′E
54 E6 **San Marcos** Sucre, N Colombia 08°38′N 75°10′W
42 M14 **San Marcos** San José, C Costa Rica 09°39′N 84°00′W
42 B5 **San Marcos** San Marcos, W Guatemala 14°58′N 91°48′W
42 F6 **San Marcos** Ocotepeque, SW Honduras 14°23′N 88°57′W
41 O16 **San Marcos** Guerrero, S Mexico 16°45′N 99°22′W
25 S11 **San Marcos** Texas, SW USA 29°54′N 97°57′W
42 A5 **San Marcos** *off.* Departamento de San Marcos. ◈ *department* W Guatemala
San Marcos de Arica *see* Arica
San Marcos, Departamento de *see* San Marcos
40 E6 **San Marcos, Isla** *island* NW Mexico
106 H11 **San Marino** ● (San Marino) C San Marino 43°54′N 12°27′E
106 I11 **San Marino** *off.* Republic of San Marino. ◆ *republic* S Europe
San Marino, Republic of *see* San Marino
62 I11 **San Martín** Mendoza, C Argentina 33°05′S 68°28′W
54 F11 **San Martín** Meta, C Colombia 03°43′N 73°42′W
56 D11 **San Martín** *off.* Departamento de San Martín. ◈ *department* C Peru
194 I5 **San Martín** *Argentinian research station* Antarctica 68°18′S 67°03′W
63 H16 **San Martín de los Andes** Neuquén, W Argentina 40°11′S 71°22′W
San Martín, Departamento de *see* San Martín
104 M8 **San Martín de Valdeiglesias** Madrid, C Spain 40°21′N 04°24′W
63 G21 **San Martín, Lago** *var.* Lago O'Higgins. S Argentina
106 H6 **San Martino di Castrozza** Trentino-Alto Adige, N Italy 46°16′N 11°50′E
57 N16 **San Martín, Río** N Bolivia
San Martín Texmelucan *see* Texmelucan
35 N9 **San Mateo** California, W USA 37°33′N 122°19′W
55 O6 **San Mateo** Anzoátegui, NE Venezuela 09°48′N 64°36′W
42 B4 **San Mateo Ixtatán** Huehuetenango, W Guatemala 15°50′N 91°30′W
57 Q18 **San Matías** Santa Cruz, E Bolivia 16°20′S 58°24′W
63 K16 **San Matías, Golfo** *var.* Gulf of San Matías. *gulf* E Argentina
San Matías, Gulf of *see* San Matías, Golfo
15 O8 **Sanmaur** Québec, SE Canada 47°52′N 73°47′W
161 T10 **Sanmen Wan** *bay* E China
160 M6 **Sanmenxia** *var.* Shan Xian. Henan, C China 34°46′N 111°17′E
Sânmiclăuş Mare *see* Sânnicolau Mare
61 D14 **San Miguel** Corrientes, NE Argentina 28°02′S 57°41′W
57 L16 **San Miguel** Beni, N Bolivia 16°43′S 61°06′W
42 G8 **San Miguel** San Miguel, SE El Salvador 13°27′N 88°11′W
40 L6 **San Miguel** Coahuila, N Mexico 29°10′N 101°28′W
40 J9 **San Miguel** *var.* San Miguel de Cruces. Durango, C Mexico 24°25′N 105°55′W
43 U16 **San Miguel** Panamá, SE Panama 08°27′N 78°51′W
35 P12 **San Miguel** California, W USA 35°45′N 120°42′W
42 B9 **San Miguel** ◈ *department* E El Salvador
41 N13 **San Miguel de Allende** Guanajuato, C Mexico 20°56′N 100°48′W
San Miguel de Cruces *see* San Miguel
San Miguel de Ibarra *see* Ibarra
61 D21 **San Miguel del Monte** Buenos Aires, E Argentina 35°26′S 58°50′W
62 J7 **San Miguel de Tucumán** *var.* Tucumán. Tucumán, N Argentina 26°47′S 65°15′W
43 V16 **San Miguel, Golfo de** *gulf* S Panama
35 P15 **San Miguel Island** *island* California, W USA
42 L11 **San Miguelito** Río San Juan, S Nicaragua 11°22′N 84°54′W
43 T15 **San Miguelito** Panamá, C Panama 08°58′N 79°31′W
57 N18 **San Miguel, Río** E Bolivia
56 D6 **San Miguel, Río** Colombia/Ecuador
40 I7 **San Miguel, Río** N Mexico
42 G8 **San Miguel, Volcán de** SE El Salvador 13°27′N 88°18′W
161 Q12 **Sanming** Fujian, SE China 26°11′N 117°37′E
106 F11 **San Miniato** Toscana, C Italy 43°40′N 10°53′E
San Murezzan *see* St. Moritz
Sannār *see* Sennar
107 M15 **Sannicandro Garganico** Puglia, SE Italy 41°50′N 15°32′E
40 H6 **San Nicolás** Sonora, NW Mexico 28°31′N 109°24′W
61 C19 **San Nicolás de los Arroyos** Buenos Aires, E Argentina 33°20′S 60°13′W
35 R16 **San Nicolas Island** *island* Channel Islands, California, W USA
Sânnicolaul-Mare *see* Sânnicolau Mare
116 E11 **Sânnicolau Mare** *var.* Sânnicolaul-Mare, *Hung.* Nagyszentmiklós; *prev.* Sânmiclăuş Mare, Sînnicolau Mare. Timiş, W Romania 46°05′N 20°38′E
123 Q6 **Sannikova, Proliv** *strait* NE Russian Federation
76 K16 **Sanniquellie** *var.* Saniquillie. NE Liberia 07°24′N 08°45′W
165 R7 **Sannohe** Aomori, Honshū, C Japan 40°23′N 141°16′E
Sanntaler Alpen *see* Kamniško-Savinjske Alpe
111 O17 **Sanok** Podkarpackie, SE Poland 49°31′N 22°14′E
54 E5 **San Onofre** Sucre, NW Colombia 09°45′N 75°33′W
57 K21 **San Pablo** Potosí, S Bolivia 21°43′S 66°38′W
171 O4 **San Pablo** *off.* San Pablo City. Luzon, N Philippines 14°04′N 121°16′E
San Pablo Balleza *see* Balleza
35 N8 **San Pablo Bay** *bay* California, W USA
San Pablo City *see* San Pablo
40 C6 **San Pablo, Punta** *headland* NW Mexico 27°12′N 114°30′W
43 R16 **San Pablo, Río** C Panama
171 P4 **San Pascual** Burias Island, C Philippines 13°06′N 122°59′E
121 Q16 **San Pawl il-Baħar** *Eng.* Saint Paul's Bay. E Malta 35°57′N 14°24′E
61 C19 **San Pedro** Buenos Aires, E Argentina 33°43′S 59°45′W
62 K5 **San Pedro** Jujuy, N Argentina 24°12′S 64°55′W
60 G13 **San Pedro** Misiones, NE Argentina 26°38′S 54°12′W
42 H1 **San Pedro** Corozal, NE Belize 17°58′N 87°55′W
76 M17 **San-Pédro** S Ivory Coast 04°45′N 06°37′W
40 L8 **San Pedro** *var.* San Pedro de las Colonias. Coahuila, NE Mexico 25°47′N 102°57′W
62 O5 **San Pedro** San Pedro, SE Paraguay 24°08′S 57°08′W
62 O6 **San Pedro** *off.* Departamento de San Pedro. ◈ *department* C Paraguay
44 G6 **San Pedro** C Cuba
77 N16 **San Pedro** ✈ (Yamoussoukro) C Ivory Coast 06°49′N 05°14′W
San Pedro *see* San Pedro del Pinatar
42 D5 **San Pedro Carchá** Alta Verapaz, C Guatemala 15°30′N 90°12′W
35 S16 **San Pedro Channel** *channel* California, W USA
62 I5 **San Pedro de Atacama** Antofagasta, N Chile 22°52′S 68°10′W
San Pedro de Durazno *see* Durazno
40 G5 **San Pedro de la Cueva** Sonora, NW Mexico 29°17′N 109°47′W
San Pedro de las Colonias *see* San Pedro
56 B11 **San Pedro de Lloc** La Libertad, NW Peru 07°26′S 79°31′W
105 S13 **San Pedro del Pinatar** *var.* San Pedro. Murcia, SE Spain 37°50′N 00°47′W
45 P9 **San Pedro de Macorís** SE Dominican Republic 18°30′N 69°18′W
San Pedro, Departamento de *see* San Pedro
40 C3 **San Pedro Mártir, Sierra** ▲▲ NW Mexico
San Pedro Pochutla *see* Pochutla
42 D2 **San Pedro, Río** Guatemala/Mexico
40 K10 **San Pedro, Río** C Mexico
104 J10 **San Pedro, Sierra de** ▲▲ W Spain
42 G5 **San Pedro Sula** Cortés, NW Honduras 15°26′N 88°01′W
San Pedro Tapanatepec *see* Tapanatepec
62 I4 **San Pedro, Volcán** N Chile 21°46′S 68°13′W
106 E7 **San Pellegrino Terme** Lombardia, N Italy 45°53′N 09°42′E
25 T16 **San Perlita** Texas, SW USA 26°30′N 97°38′W
San Pietro *see* Supetar
San Pietro del Carso *see* Pivka
107 A20 **San Pietro, Isola di** *island* W Italy
32 K7 **Sanpoil River** Washington, NW USA
165 O9 **Sanpoku** *var.* Sampoku. Niigata, Honshū, C Japan 38°32′N 139°33′E
40 C3 **San Quintín** Baja California Norte, NW Mexico 30°28′N 115°58′W
40 B3 **San Quintín, Bahía de** *bay* NW Mexico
40 B3 **San Quintín, Cabo** *headland* NW Mexico 30°22′N 116°01′W
62 I12 **San Rafael** Mendoza, W Argentina 34°44′S 68°15′W
41 N9 **San Rafael** Nuevo León, NE Mexico 25°01′N 100°33′W
34 M8 **San Rafael** California, W USA 37°58′N 122°31′W
37 Q11 **San Rafael** New Mexico, SW USA 35°03′N 107°52′W
54 H4 **San Rafael** *var.* El Moján. Zulia, NW Venezuela 10°58′N 71°45′W
42 J8 **San Rafael del Norte** Jinotega, NW Nicaragua 13°12′N 86°06′W
42 J10 **San Rafael del Sur** Managua, SW Nicaragua 11°51′N 86°24′W
36 M5 **San Rafael Knob** ▲ Utah, W USA 38°46′N 110°45′W
35 Q14 **San Rafael Mountains** ▲▲ California, W USA
42 M13 **San Ramón** Alajuela, C Costa Rica 10°04′N 84°31′W
57 E14 **San Ramón** Junín, C Peru 11°08′S 75°18′W
61 F19 **San Ramón** Canelones, S Uruguay 34°18′S 55°55′W
62 K5 **San Ramón de la Nueva Orán** Salta, N Argentina 23°08′S 64°20′W
57 O16 **San Ramón, Río** E Bolivia
106 B11 **San Remo** Liguria, NW Italy 43°48′N 07°47′E
54 J3 **San Román, Cabo** *headland* NW Venezuela 12°10′N 70°01′W
61 C15 **San Roque** Corrientes, NE Argentina 28°35′S 58°45′W
188 I4 **San Roque** Saipan, S Northern Mariana Islands 15°15′S 145°47′E
104 K16 **San Roque** Andalucía, S Spain 36°13′N 05°23′W
25 R9 **San Saba** Texas, SW USA 31°13′N 98°44′W
25 Q9 **San Saba River** Texas, SW USA
61 D17 **San Salvador** Entre Ríos, E Argentina 31°38′S 58°30′W
42 F7 **San Salvador** ● (El Salvador) San Salvador, SW El Salvador 13°42′N 89°12′W
42 A10 **San Salvador** ◈ *department* C El Salvador
44 K4 **San Salvador** *prev.* Watlings Island. *island* E Bahamas
42 F8 **San Salvador** ✈ La Paz, S El Salvador 13°27′N 89°04′W
62 J5 **San Salvador de Jujuy** *var.* Jujuy. Jujuy, N Argentina 24°10′S 65°20′W
57 B18 **San Salvador, Isla** *island* Ecuador
42 F7 **San Salvador, Volcán de** C El Salvador 13°58′N 89°14′W
77 Q14 **Sansanné-Mango** *var.* Mango. N Togo 10°21′N 00°28′E
45 S5 **San Sebastián** W Puerto Rico 18°21′N 67°00′W
63 J24 **San Sebastián, Bahía** *bay* S Argentina
Sansenhō *see* Sach'ŏn
106 H12 **Sansepolcro** Toscana, C Italy 43°35′N 12°12′E
107 M16 **San Severo** Puglia, SE Italy 41°41′N 15°23′E
112 F11 **Sanski Most** ◈ Federacija Bosna I Hercegovina, NW Bosnia and Herzegovina
171 W12 **Sansundi** Papua, E Indonesia 0°42′S 135°48′E
162 K9 **Sant** *var.* Mayhan. Övörhangay, C Mongolia 46°02′N 104°00′E
104 K11 **Santa Amalia** Extremadura, W Spain 39°00′N 06°01′W
60 F13 **Santa Ana** Misiones, NE Argentina 27°22′S 55°34′W
57 L16 **Santa Ana** Beni, N Bolivia 13°43′S 65°37′W
42 E7 **Santa Ana** Santa Ana, NW El Salvador 13°59′N 89°34′W
40 F4 **Santa Ana** Sonora, NW Mexico 30°31′N 111°08′W
35 T16 **Santa Ana** California, W USA 33°45′N 117°52′W
55 N6 **Santa Ana** Nueva Esparta, NE Venezuela 09°15′N 64°39′W
42 A9 **Santa Ana** ◈ *department* NW El Salvador
Santa Ana de Coro *see* Coro
35 U16 **Santa Ana Mountains** ▲▲ California, W USA
42 E7 **Santa Ana, Volcán de** *var.* La Matepec. W El Salvador 13°49′N 89°36′W
42 G6 **Santa Bárbara** Santa Bárbara, W Honduras 14°56′N 88°11′W
40 J7 **Santa Barbara** Chihuahua, N Mexico 26°46′N 105°46′W
35 Q14 **Santa Barbara** California, W USA 34°24′N 119°40′W
54 L11 **Santa Bárbara** Amazonas, S Venezuela 03°55′N 67°06′W
54 I7 **Santa Bárbara** Barinas, W Venezuela 07°48′N 71°10′W
42 F5 **Santa Bárbara** ◈ *department* NW Honduras
Santa Bárbara *see* Iscuandé
35 Q15 **Santa Barbara Channel** *channel* California, W USA
Santa Bárbara de Samaná *see* Samaná
35 R16 **Santa Barbara Island** *island* Channel Islands, California, W USA
54 E5 **Santa Catalina** Bolívar, N Colombia 10°36′N 75°17′W
43 R15 **Santa Catalina** Ngöbe Bugle, W Panama 08°46′N 81°18′W
35 T17 **Santa Catalina, Gulf of** *gulf* California, W USA
43 Q7 **Santa Catalina, Isla** *island* NW Colombia, Caribbean Sea
40 F8 **Santa Catalina, Isla** *island* NW Mexico
35 S16 **Santa Catalina Island** *island* Channel Islands, California, W USA
41 N8 **Santa Catarina** Nuevo León, NE Mexico 25°39′N 100°30′W
60 H13 **Santa Catarina** *off.* Estado de Santa Catarina. ◈ *state* S Brazil
Santa Catarina de Tepehuanes *see* Tepehuanes
Santa Catarina, Estado de *see* Santa Catarina
60 L13 **Santa Catarina, Ilha de** *island* S Brazil
45 Q16 **Santa Catherina** Curaçao, C Netherlands Antilles 12°07′N 68°46′W
44 E5 **Santa Clara** Villa Clara, C Cuba 22°25′N 78°01′W
35 N9 **Santa Clara** California, W USA 37°20′N 121°57′W
36 J8 **Santa Clara** Utah, W USA 37°07′N 113°39′W
Santa Clara *see* Santa Clara de Olimar
61 F18 **Santa Clara de Olimar** *var.* Santa Clara. Cerro Largo, NE Uruguay 32°50′S 54°54′W
61 A17 **Santa Clara de Saguier** Santa Fe, C Argentina 31°21′S 61°50′W
Santa Coloma *see* Santa Coloma de Gramanet
105 X5 **Santa Coloma de Farners** *var.* Santa Coloma de Farnés. Cataluña, NE Spain 41°52′N 02°39′E
Santa Coloma de Farnés *see* Santa Coloma de Farners
105 W6 **Santa Coloma de Gramanet** *var.* Santa Coloma. Cataluña, NE Spain 41°28′N 02°14′E
104 G2 **Santa Comba** Galicia, NW Spain 43°02′N 08°49′W
Santa Comba *see* Uaco Cungo
104 H8 **Santa Comba Dão** Viseu, N Portugal 40°23′N 08°07′W
82 C10 **Santa Cruz** Uíge, NW Angola 06°56′S 16°25′E
57 N19 **Santa Cruz** *var.* Santa Cruz de la Sierra. Santa Cruz, C Bolivia 17°49′S 63°11′W
62 G12 **Santa Cruz** Libertador, C Chile 34°38′S 71°27′W
42 K13 **Santa Cruz** Guanacaste, W Costa Rica 10°15′N 85°35′W
44 I12 **Santa Cruz** W Jamaica 18°03′N 77°43′W
64 P6 **Santa Cruz** Madeira, Portugal, NE Atlantic Ocean 32°43′N 16°47′W
35 N10 **Santa Cruz** California, W USA 36°58′N 122°01′W
63 H20 **Santa Cruz** *off.* Provincia de Santa Cruz. ◈ *province* S Argentina
57 O18 **Santa Cruz** ◈ *department* E Bolivia
Santa Cruz *see* Puerto Santa Cruz
Santa Cruz *see* Viru-Viru
Santa Cruz Barillas *see* Barillas
59 O18 **Santa Cruz Cabrália** Bahia, E Brazil 16°17′S 39°03′W
Santa Cruz de El Seibo *see* El Seibo
64 N11 **Santa Cruz de la Palma** La Palma, Islas Canarias, Spain, NE Atlantic Ocean 28°41′N 17°46′W
Santa Cruz de la Sierra *see* Santa Cruz
105 O9 **Santa Cruz de la Zarza** Castilla-La Mancha, C Spain 39°59′N 03°10′W
42 C5 **Santa Cruz del Quiché** Quiché, W Guatemala 15°02′N 91°06′W
105 N8 **Santa Cruz del Retamar** Castilla-La Mancha, C Spain 40°08′N 04°14′W
Santa Cruz del Seibo *see* El Seibo
44 G7 **Santa Cruz del Sur** Camagüey, C Cuba 20°44′N 78°00′W
105 O11 **Santa Cruz de Mudela** Castilla-La Mancha, C Spain 38°37′N 03°27′W
64 Q11 **Santa Cruz de Tenerife** Tenerife, Islas Canarias, Spain, NE Atlantic Ocean 28°28′N 16°15′W
64 P11 **Santa Cruz de Tenerife** ◈ *province* Islas Canarias, Spain, NE Atlantic Ocean
60 K9 **Santa Cruz do Rio Pardo** São Paulo, S Brazil 22°52′S 49°37′W
61 H15 **Santa Cruz do Sul** Rio Grande do Sul, S Brazil 29°42′S 52°25′W
57 C17 **Santa Cruz, Isla** *var.* Indefatigable Island, Isla Chávez. *island* Galapagos Islands, Ecuador, E Pacific Ocean
40 F8 **Santa Cruz, Isla** *island* NW Mexico
35 Q15 **Santa Cruz Island** *island* California, W USA
187 Q10 **Santa Cruz Islands** *island group* E Solomon Islands
Santa Cruz, Provincia de *see* Santa Cruz
63 I22 **Santa Cruz, Río** S Argentina
36 L15 **Santa Cruz River** Arizona, SW USA
61 C17 **Santa Elena** Entre Ríos, E Argentina 30°58′S 59°47′W
42 F2 **Santa Elena** Cayo, W Belize 17°08′N 89°04′W
25 R16 **Santa Elena** Texas, SW USA 26°43′N 98°30′W
56 A7 **Santa Elena, Bahía de** *bay* W Ecuador
55 R10 **Santa Elena de Uairén** Bolívar, E Venezuela 04°40′N 61°03′W
42 K12 **Santa Elena, Península** *peninsula* NW Costa Rica
56 A7 **Santa Elena, Punta** *headland* W Ecuador 02°11′S 81°00′W
104 L11 **Santa Eufemia** Andalucía, S Spain 38°36′N 04°54′W
107 N21 **Santa Eufemia, Golfo di** *gulf* S Italy
105 S4 **Santa Eulalia de Gállego** Aragón, NE Spain 42°16′N 00°46′W
105 V11 **Santa Eulalia del Río** Ibiza, Spain, W Mediterranean Sea 39°00′N 01°33′E
61 B17 **Santa Fe** Santa Fe, C Argentina 31°36′S 60°47′W
44 C6 **Santa Fé** *var.* La Fe. Isla de la Juventud, W Cuba 21°45′N 82°45′W
43 R16 **Santa Fé** Veraguas, C Panama 08°29′N 80°50′W
105 N14 **Santa Fe** Andalucía, S Spain 37°11′N 03°43′W
37 S10 **Santa Fe** *state capital* New Mexico, SW USA 35°41′N 105°56′W
61 B15 **Santa Fe** *off.* Provincia de Santa Fe. ◈ *province* C Argentina
Santa Fe *see* Bogotá
Santa Fe de Bogotá *see* Bogotá
60 J7 **Santa Fé do Sul** São Paulo, S Brazil 20°13′S 50°56′W
57 B18 **Santa Fe, Isla** *var.* Barrington Island. *island* Galapagos Islands, Ecuador, E Pacific Ocean
Santa Fe, Provincia de *see* Santa Fe
23 V9 **Santa Fe River** Florida, SE USA
59 M15 **Santa Filomena** Piauí, E Brazil 09°06′S 45°52′W
40 G10 **Santa Genoveva** ▲ NW Mexico 23°07′N 109°56′W
153 S14 **Santahar** Rajshahi, NW Bangladesh 24°45′N 89°03′E
60 G11 **Santa Helena** Paraná, S Brazil 24°53′S 54°19′W
54 J5 **Santa Inés** Lara, N Venezuela 10°37′N 69°18′W
63 G24 **Santa Inés, Isla** *island* S Chile
62 J13 **Santa Isabel** La Pampa, C Argentina 36°11′S 66°59′W
43 U14 **Santa Isabel** Colón, N Panama 09°31′N 79°12′W
186 L8 **Santa Isabel** *var.* Bughotu. *island* N Solomon Islands
Santa Isabel *see* Malabo
58 D11 **Santa Isabel do Rio Negro** Amazonas, NW Brazil 0°40′S 64°56′W
61 C15 **Santa Lucia** Corrientes, NE Argentina 28°58′S 59°05′W
57 I17 **Santa Lucía** Puno, S Peru 15°45′S 70°34′W
61 F20 **Santa Lucía** *var.* Santa Lucia. Canelones, S Uruguay 34°26′S 56°25′W
42 B6 **Santa Lucía Cotzumalguapa** Escuintla, SW Guatemala 14°20′N 91°00′W
107 L23 **Santa Lucia del Mela** Sicilia, Italy, C Mediterranean Sea 38°08′N 15°17′E
35 O11 **Santa Lucia Range** ▲▲ California, W USA
40 D9 **Santa Margarita, Isla** *island* NW Mexico
62 J7 **Santa María** Catamarca, N Argentina 26°51′S 66°02′W
61 G15 **Santa Maria** Rio Grande do Sul, S Brazil 29°41′S 53°48′W
35 P13 **Santa Maria** California, W USA 34°56′N 120°25′W
64 Q4 **Santa Maria** ✈ Santa Maria, Azores, Portugal, NE Atlantic Ocean
64 P3 **Santa Maria** *island* Azores, Portugal, NE Atlantic Ocean
Santa Maria *see* Gaua
Santa María Asunción Tlaxiaco *see* Tlaxiaco
40 G9 **Santa María, Bahía** *bay* W Mexico
83 L21 **Santa Maria, Cabo de** *headland* S Mozambique 26°05′S 32°58′E
104 G15 **Santa Maria, Cabo de** *headland* S Portugal 36°57′N 07°55′W
44 J4 **Santa Maria, Cape** *headland* Long Island, C Bahamas 23°40′N 75°20′W
107 J17 **Santa Maria Capua Vetere** Campania, S Italy 41°05′N 14°15′E
104 G7 **Santa Maria da Feira** Aveiro, N Portugal 40°55′N 08°32′W
59 M17 **Santa Maria da Vitória** Bahia, E Brazil 13°26′S 44°09′W
55 N9 **Santa Maria de Erebato** Bolívar, SE Venezuela 05°09′N 64°50′W
55 N6 **Santa María de Ipire** Guárico, C Venezuela 08°51′N 65°21′W
Santa Maria del Buen Aire *see* Buenos Aires
40 J8 **Santa María del Oro** Durango, C Mexico 25°57′N 105°22′W
41 N12 **Santa María del Río** San Luis Potosí, C Mexico 21°48′N 100°42′W
Santa Maria di Castellabate *see* Castellabate
107 Q20 **Santa Maria di Leuca, Capo** *headland* SE Italy 39°48′N 18°21′E
108 K10 **Santa Maria-im-Munstertal** Graubünden, SE Switzerland 46°36′N 10°25′E
57 B18 **Santa María, Isla** *var.* Isla Floreana, Charles Island. *island* Galapagos Islands, Ecuador, E Pacific Ocean
40 J3 **Santa María, Laguna de** N Mexico
61 G16 **Santa Maria, Rio** S Brazil
43 R16 **Santa María, Río** C Panama
36 J12 **Santa Maria River** Arizona, SW USA
107 G15 **Santa Marinella** Lazio, C Italy 42°01′N 11°51′E
54 F4 **Santa Marta** Magdalena, N Colombia 11°14′N 74°13′W
104 J11 **Santa Marta** Extremadura, W Spain 38°37′N 06°39′W
54 F4 **Santa Marta, Sierra Nevada de** ▲▲ NE Colombia
Santa Maura *see* Lefkáda
35 S15 **Santa Monica** California, W USA 34°01′N 118°29′W
116 F10 **Sântana** *Ger.* Sankt Anna, *Hung.* Újszentanna; *prev.* Sîntana. Arad, W Romania 46°20′N 21°30′E
61 F16 **Santana, Coxilha de** *hill range* S Brazil
61 H16 **Santana da Boa Vista** Rio Grande do Sul, S Brazil 30°52′S 53°03′W
61 F16 **Santana do Livramento** *prev.* Livramento. Rio Grande do Sul, S Brazil 30°52′S 55°30′W
105 N2 **Santander** Cantabria, N Spain 43°28′N 03°48′W
54 F8 **Santander** *off.* Departamento de Santander. ◈ *province* C Colombia
Santander, Departamento de *see* Santander
Santander Jiménez *see* Jiménez
Sant'Andrea *see* Svetac
107 B20 **Sant'Antioco** Sardegna, Italy, C Mediterranean Sea 39°03′N 08°28′E
105 V11 **Sant Antoni de Portmany** *Cas.* San Antonio Abad. Ibiza, Spain, W Mediterranean Sea 38°58′N 01°18′E
105 Y10 **Santanyí** Mallorca, Spain, W Mediterranean Sea 39°22′N 03°07′E
104 J13 **Santa Olalla del Cala** Andalucía, S Spain 37°54′N 06°13′W
35 R15 **Santa Paula** California, W USA 34°21′N 119°03′W
36 L4 **Santaquin** Utah, W USA 39°58′N 111°46′W
58 I12 **Santarém** Pará, N Brazil 02°26′S 54°41′W
104 G10 **Santarém** *anc.* Scalabis. Santarém, W Portugal 39°14′N 08°40′W
104 G10 **Santarém** ◈ *district* C Portugal
44 F4 **Santaren Channel** *channel* W Bahamas
54 K10 **Santa Rita** Vichada, E Colombia 04°51′N 68°27′W
188 B16 **Santa Rita** SW Guam
42 H5 **Santa Rita** Cortés, NW Honduras 15°10′N 87°54′W
40 E9 **Santa Rita** Baja California Sur, NW Mexico 27°29′N 100°33′W
54 H5 **Santa Rita** Zulia, NW Venezuela 10°35′N 71°30′W
59 I19 **Santa Rita de Araguaia** Goiás, S Brazil 17°17′S 53°13′W
Santa Rita de Cassia *see* Cássia
61 D14 **Santa Rosa** Corrientes, NE Argentina 28°18′S 58°04′W

◆ Country
● Country Capital
◇ Dependent Territory
○ Dependent Territory Capital
◈ Administrative Regions
✈ International Airport
▲ Mountain
▲▲ Mountain Range
Volcano
River
Lake
Reservoir

SANTA ROSA – SATKHIRA

62 K13 **Santa Rosa** La Pampa, C Argentina 36°38′S 64°15′W
61 G14 **Santa Rosa** Rio Grande do Sul, S Brazil 27°50′S 54°29′W
58 E10 **Santa Rosa** Roraima, N Brazil 03°41′N 62°29′W
56 B8 **Santa Rosa** El Oro, SW Ecuador 03°29′S 79°57′W
57 I16 **Santa Rosa** Puno, S Peru 14°38′S 70°45′W
34 M7 **Santa Rosa** California, W USA 38°27′N 122°42′W
37 U11 **Santa Rosa** New Mexico, SW USA 34°54′N 104°43′W
55 O6 **Santa Rosa** Anzoátegui, NE Venezuela 09°37′N 64°20′W
42 A3 **Santa Rosa** *off.* Departamento de Santa Rosa. ⬖ *department* SE Guatemala
Santa Rosa *see* Santa Rosa de Copán
63 J15 **Santa Rosa, Bajo de** *basin* E Argentina
42 F6 **Santa Rosa de Copán** *var.* Santa Rosa. Copán, W Honduras 14°48′N 88°43′W
54 E8 **Santa Rosa de Osos** Antioquia, C Colombia 06°40′N 75°27′W
Santa Rosa, Departamento de *see* Santa Rosa
35 Q15 **Santa Rosa Island** *island* California, W USA
23 O9 **Santa Rosa Island** *island* Florida, SE USA
40 E6 **Santa Rosalía** Baja California Sur, NW Mexico 27°20′N 112°20′W
54 K6 **Santa Rosalía** Portuguesa, NW Venezuela 09°02′N 69°01′W
188 C15 **Santa Rosa, Mount** ▲ NE Guam
35 V16 **Santa Rosa Mountains** ▲▲ California, W USA
35 T2 **Santa Rosa Range** ▲▲ Nevada, W USA
62 M8 **Santa Sylvina** Chaco, N Argentina 27°49′S 61°09′W
Santa Tecla *see* Nueva San Salvador
61 B19 **Santa Teresa** Santa Fe, C Argentina 33°30′S 60°45′W
59 O20 **Santa Teresa** Espírito Santo, SE Brazil 19°51′S 40°49′W
61 E21 **Santa Teresita** Buenos Aires, E Argentina 36°32′S 56°41′W
61 H19 **Santa Vitória do Palmar** Rio Grande do Sul, S Brazil 33°32′S 53°25′W
35 Q14 **Santa Ynez River** ≈ California, W USA
Sant Carles de la Rápida *see* Sant Carles de la Ràpita
105 U7 **Sant Carles de la Ràpita** *var.* Sant Carles de la Rápida. Cataluña, NE Spain 40°37′N 00°36′E
105 W5 **Sant Celoni** Cataluña, NE Spain 41°39′N 02°25′E
35 U17 **Santee** California, W USA 32°50′N 116°58′W
21 T13 **Santee River** ≈ South Carolina, SE USA
40 K15 **San Telmo, Punta** *headland* SW Mexico 18°19′N 103°30′W
107 O17 **Santeramo in Colle** Puglia, SE Italy 40°47′N 16°45′E
107 M23 **San Teresa di Riva** Sicilia, Italy, C Mediterranean Sea 38°00′N 15°25′E
105 X5 **Sant Feliu de Guíxols** *var.* San Feliú de Guixols. Cataluña, NE Spain 41°47′N 03°02′E
105 W6 **Sant Feliu de Llobregat** Cataluña, NE Spain 41°22′N 02°00′E
106 C7 **Santhià** Piemonte, NE Italy 45°21′N 08°11′E
61 F15 **Santiago** Rio Grande do Sul, S Brazil 29°11′S 54°52′W
62 H11 **Santiago** *var.* Gran Santiago. ● (Chile) Santiago, C Chile 33°30′S 70°40′W
45 N8 **Santiago** *var.* Santiago de los Caballeros. N Dominican Republic 19°27′N 70°42′W
40 G10 **Santiago** Baja California Sur, NW Mexico 23°32′N 109°47′W
41 O8 **Santiago** Nuevo León, NE Mexico 25°22′N 100°09′W
43 R16 **Santiago** Veraguas, S Panama 08°06′N 80°59′W
57 E16 **Santiago** Ica, SW Peru 14°14′S 75°44′W
104 G3 **Santiago** *var.* Santiago de Compostela, *Eng.* Compostella; *anc.* Campus Stellae. Galicia, NW Spain 42°52′N 08°33′W
62 H11 **Santiago** *off.* Región Metropolitana de Santiago, *var.* Metropolitan. ⬖ *region* C Chile
76 D10 **Santiago** *var.* São Tiago. *island* Ilhas de Sotavento, S Cape Verde
62 H11 **Santiago** ✕ Santiago, C Chile 33°27′S 70°40′W
104 G3 **Santiago** ✕ Galicia, NW Spain
Santiago *see* Santiago de Cuba, Cuba
Santiago *see* Grande de Santiago, Río, Mexico
42 B6 **Santiago Atitlán** Sololá, SW Guatemala 14°39′N 91°12′W
43 Q16 **Santiago, Cerro** ▲ W Panama 08°27′N 81°42′W
Santiago de Compostela *see* Santiago
44 I8 **Santiago de Cuba** *var.* Santiago. Santiago de Cuba, E Cuba 20°01′N 75°51′W
Santiago de Guayaquil *see* Guayaquil
62 K8 **Santiago del Estero** Santiago del Estero, C Argentina 27°51′S 64°16′W
61 A15 **Santiago del Estero** *off.* Provincia de Santiago del Estero. ⬖ *province* N Argentina
Santiago del Estero, Provincia de *see* Santiago del Estero
40 I8 **Santiago de los Caballeros** Sinaloa, W Mexico 25°33′N 107°22′W
Santiago de los Caballeros *see* Santiago, Dominican Republic
Santiago de los Caballeros *see* Ciudad de Guatemala, Guatemala
42 F8 **Santiago de María** Usulután, SE El Salvador 13°28′N 88°28′W
104 F12 **Santiago do Cacém** Setúbal, S Portugal 38°01′N 08°42′W
40 J12 **Santiago Ixcuintla** Nayarit, C Mexico 21°50′N 105°11′W
Santiago Jamiltepec *see* Jamiltepec
24 L11 **Santiago Mountains** ▲▲ Texas, SW USA
40 J9 **Santiago Papasquiaro** Durango, C Mexico 25°00′N 105°27′W
Santiago Pinotepa Nacional *see* Pinotepa Nacional
Santiago, Región Metropolitana de *see* Santiago
56 C8 **Santiago, Río** ≈ N Peru
40 M10 **San Tiburcio** Zacatecas, C Mexico 24°08′N 101°29′W
105 N2 **Santillana** Cantabria, N Spain 43°24′N 04°06′W
54 I5 **San Timoteo** Zulia, NW Venezuela 09°50′N 71°05′W
Santi Quaranta *see* Sarandë
Santissima Trinidad *see* Chilung
105 O12 **Santisteban del Puerto** Andalucía, S Spain 38°15′N 03°11′W
105 U7 **Sant Jordi, Golf de** *gulf* NE Spain
105 U11 **Sant Josep de sa Talaia** *var.* San José. Ibiza, Spain, W Mediterranean Sea 38°55′N 1°18′E
162 G6 **Santmargats** *var.* Holboo. Dzavhan, W Mongolia 48°35′N 95°25′E
105 T8 **Sant Mateu** País Valenciano, E Spain 40°28′N 00°10′E
25 S7 **Santo** Texas, SW USA 32°35′N 98°06′W
Santo *see* Espiritu Santo
60 M10 **Santo Amaro, Ilha de** *island* SE Brazil
61 G14 **Santo Ângelo** Rio Grande do Sul, S Brazil 28°17′S 54°15′W
76 C9 **Santo Antão** *island* Ilhas de Barlavento, N Cape Verde
60 J10 **Santo Antônio da Platina** Paraná, S Brazil 23°20′S 50°05′W
58 C13 **Santo Antônio do Içá** Amazonas, N Brazil 03°05′S 67°56′W
57 Q18 **Santo Corazón, Río** ≈ E Bolivia
44 E5 **Santo Domingo** Villa Clara, C Cuba 22°35′N 80°15′W
45 O9 **Santo Domingo** *prev.* Ciudad Trujillo. ● (Dominican Republic) SE Dominican Republic 18°30′N 69°57′W
40 E8 **Santo Domingo** Baja California Sur, NW Mexico 25°34′N 112°00′W
40 M10 **Santo Domingo** San Luis Potosí, C Mexico 23°18′N 101°42′W
42 L10 **Santo Domingo** Chontales, S Nicaragua 12°15′N 84°59′W
105 P4 **Santo Domingo de la Calzada** La Rioja, N Spain 42°26′N 02°57′W
56 B6 **Santo Domingo de los Colorados** Pichincha, NW Ecuador 00°13′S 79°09′W
Santo Domingo Tehuantepec *see* Tehuantepec
55 O6 **San Tomé** Anzoátegui, NE Venezuela 08°58′N 64°08′W
San Tomé de Guayana *see* Ciudad Guayana
105 R13 **Santomera** Murcia, SE Spain 38°03′N 01°05′W
105 O2 **Santoña** Cantabria, N Spain 43°27′N 03°28′W
Santorin *see* Santoríni
115 K22 **Santoríni** *var.* Santorin, *prev.* Thíra; *anc.* Thera. *island* Kykládes, Greece, Aegean Sea
60 M10 **Santos** São Paulo, S Brazil 23°56′S 46°22′W
65 J17 **Santos Plateau** *undersea feature* SW Atlantic Ocean 25°00′S 43°00′W
104 G6 **Santo Tirso** Porto, N Portugal 41°20′N 08°25′W
40 B2 **Santo Tomás** Baja California Norte, NW Mexico 31°32′N 116°26′W
42 L10 **Santo Tomás** Chontales, S Nicaragua 12°04′N 85°02′W
42 G5 **Santo Tomás de Castilla** Izabal, E Guatemala 15°40′N 88°36′W
40 B2 **Santo Tomás, Punta** *headland* NW Mexico 31°30′N 116°40′W
57 H16 **Santo Tomás, Río** ≈ C Peru
57 B18 **Santo Tomás, Volcán** Ѫ Galapagos Islands, Ecuador, E Pacific Ocean 0°46′S 91°01′W
61 F14 **Santo Tomé** Corrientes, NE Argentina 28°31′S 56°03′W
Santo Tomé de Guayana *see* Ciudad Guayana
98 H10 **Santpoort** Noord-Holland, W Netherlands 52°26′N 04°38′E
Santurce *see* Santurtzi
105 O2 **Santurtzi** *var.* Santurce, Santurzi. País Vasco, N Spain 43°20′N 03°03′W
Santurzi *see* Santurtzi
63 G20 **San Valentín, Cerro** ▲ S Chile 46°36′S 73°17′W
42 F8 **San Vicente** San Vicente, C El Salvador 13°38′N 88°42′W
40 C2 **San Vicente** Baja California Norte, NW Mexico 31°20′N 116°15′W
188 H6 **San Vicente** Saipan, S Northern Mariana Islands
42 B9 **San Vicente** ⬖ *department* E El Salvador
104 I10 **San Vicente de Alcántara** Extremadura, W Spain 39°21′N 07°07′W
105 N2 **San Vicente de Barakaldo** *var.* Baracaldo, *Basq.* San Bizenti-Barakaldo. País Vasco, N Spain 43°17′N 02°59′W
57 E15 **San Vicente de Cañete** *var.* Cañete. Lima, W Peru 13°06′S 76°23′W
104 M2 **San Vicente de la Barquera** Cantabria, N Spain 43°23′N 04°24′W
54 E12 **San Vicente del Caguán** Caquetá, S Colombia 02°07′N 74°47′W
42 F8 **San Vicente, Volcán de** Ѫ C El Salvador 13°34′N 88°50′W
43 O15 **San Vito** Puntarenas, SE Costa Rica 08°49′N 82°58′W
106 I7 **San Vito al Tagliamento** Friuli-Venezia Giulia, NE Italy 45°54′N 12°55′E
107 H23 **San Vito, Capo** *headland* Sicilia, Italy, C Mediterranean Sea 38°11′N 12°41′E
107 P18 **San Vito dei Normanni** Puglia, SE Italy 40°40′N 17°42′E
160 L17 **Sanya** *var.* Ya Xian. Hainan, S China 18°25′N 109°27′E
83 J16 **Sanyati** ≈ N Zimbabwe
25 Q16 **San Ygnacio** Texas, SW USA 27°04′N 99°26′W
160 L6 **Sanyuan** Shaanxi, C China 34°40′N 108°56′E
123 P11 **Sanyyakhtakh** Respublika Sakha (Yakutiya), NE Russian Federation 60°34′N 124°09′E
146 J15 **S. A.Nyýazow Adyndaky** *Rus.* Imeni S. A. Niyazova. Maryyskiy Velayat, S Turkmenistan 36°44′N 62°23′E
82 C10 **Sanza Pombo** Uíge, NW Angola 07°20′S 16°00′E
Sanzyô *see* Sanjō
104 G14 **São Bartolomeu de Messines** Faro, S Portugal 37°12′N 08°16′W
60 M10 **São Bernardo do Campo** São Paulo, S Brazil 23°45′S 46°34′W
61 F15 **São Borja** Rio Grande do Sul, S Brazil 28°35′S 56°01′W
104 H14 **São Brás de Alportel** Faro, S Portugal 37°09′N 07°55′W
60 M10 **São Caetano do Sul** São Paulo, S Brazil 23°37′S 46°34′W
60 L9 **São Carlos** São Paulo, S Brazil 22°02′S 47°53′W
59 P16 **São Cristóvão** Sergipe, E Brazil 10°59′S 37°10′W
61 F15 **São Francisco de Assis** Rio Grande do Sul, S Brazil 29°32′S 55°07′W
58 K13 **São Félix** Pará, NE Brazil 06°43′S 51°56′W
São Félix *see* São Félix do Araguaia
59 J16 **São Félix do Araguaia** *var.* São Félix. Mato Grosso, W Brazil 11°36′S 50°40′W
59 J14 **São Félix do Xingu** Pará, NE Brazil 06°38′S 51°59′W
60 Q9 **São Fidélis** Rio de Janeiro, SE Brazil 21°37′S 41°40′W
76 D10 **São Filipe** Fogo, S Cape Verde 14°52′N 24°29′W
60 K12 **São Francisco do Sul** Santa Catarina, S Brazil 26°17′S 48°39′W
60 K12 **São Francisco, Ilha de** *island* S Brazil
59 P16 **São Francisco, Rio** ≈ E Brazil
61 G16 **São Gabriel** Rio Grande do Sul, S Brazil 30°17′S 54°17′W
60 P10 **São Gonçalo** Rio de Janeiro, SE Brazil 22°48′S 43°03′W
81 H23 **Sao Hill** Iringa, S Tanzania 08°19′S 35°11′E
60 R9 **São João da Barra** Rio de Janeiro, SE Brazil 21°39′S 41°04′W
104 G7 **São João da Madeira** Aveiro, N Portugal 40°52′N 08°28′W
58 M12 **São João de Cortes** Maranhão, E Brazil 02°30′S 44°27′W
59 M21 **São João del Rei** Minas Gerais, NE Brazil 21°08′S 44°15′W
59 N15 **São João do Piauí** Piauí, E Brazil 08°21′S 42°14′W
59 N14 **São João dos Patos** Maranhão, E Brazil 06°29′S 43°44′W
58 C11 **São Joaquim** Amazonas, NW Brazil 0°08′S 67°10′W
61 J14 **São Joaquim** Santa Catarina, S Brazil 28°20′S 49°55′W
60 L7 **São Joaquim da Barra** São Paulo, S Brazil 20°36′S 47°50′W
64 N2 **São Jorge** *island* Azores, Portugal, NE Atlantic Ocean
61 K14 **São José** Santa Catarina, S Brazil 27°34′S 48°39′W
60 M8 **São José do Rio Pardo** São Paulo, S Brazil 21°37′S 46°52′W
60 K8 **São José do Rio Preto** São Paulo, S Brazil 20°50′S 49°20′W
60 N10 **São Jose dos Campos** São Paulo, S Brazil 23°07′S 45°52′W
61 I17 **São Lourenço do Sul** Rio Grande do Sul, S Brazil 31°25′S 52°00′W
58 M12 **São Luís** *state capital* Maranhão, NE Brazil 02°34′S 44°16′W
58 F11 **São Luis** Roraima, N Brazil 01°11′N 60°15′W
58 M12 **São Luís, Ilha de** *island* NE Brazil
61 F14 **São Luiz Gonzaga** Rio Grande do Sul, S Brazil 28°24′S 54°58′W
São Mandol *see* São Manuel, Rio
47 U8 **São Manuel** ≈ C Brazil
59 H15 **São Manuel, Rio** *var.* São Mandol, Teles Pirés. ≈ C Brazil
58 C11 **São Marcelino** Amazonas, NW Brazil 0°53′N 67°16′W
58 N12 **São Marcos, Baía de** *bay* N Brazil
59 O20 **São Mateus** Espírito Santo, SE Brazil 18°44′S 39°53′W
60 J12 **São Mateus do Sul** Paraná, S Brazil 25°58′S 50°29′W
64 P3 **São Miguel** *island* Azores, Portugal, NE Atlantic Ocean
60 G13 **São Miguel d'Oeste** Santa Catarina, S Brazil 26°45′S 53°34′W
45 P9 **Saona, Isla** *island* SE Dominican Republic
172 H12 **Saondzou** ▲ Grande Comore, NW Comoros
103 R10 **Saône** ≈ E France
103 Q9 **Saône-et-Loire** ⬖ *department* C France
76 D9 **São Nicolau** *Eng.* Saint Nicholas. *island* Ilhas de Barlavento, N Cape Verde
60 M10 **São Paulo** *state capital* São Paulo, S Brazil 23°33′S 46°39′W
60 K9 **São Paulo** *off.* Estado de São Paulo. ⬖ *state* S Brazil
São Paulo de Loanda *see* Luanda
São Paulo, Estado de *see* São Paulo
São Pedro do Rio Grande do Sul *see* Rio Grande
104 H7 **São Pedro do Sul** Viseu, N Portugal 40°46′N 07°58′W
64 K13 **São Pedro e São Paulo** *undersea feature* C Atlantic Ocean 01°25′N 28°54′W
59 M14 **São Raimundo das Mangabeiras** Maranhão, E Brazil 07°00′S 45°30′W
59 Q14 **São Roque, Cabo de** *headland* E Brazil 05°29′S 35°16′W
São Salvador *see* Salvador, Brazil
São Salvador/São Salvador do Congo *see* M'Banza Congo, Angola
60 N10 **São Sebastião, Ilha de** *island* S Brazil
83 N19 **São Sebastião, Ponta** *headland* C Mozambique 22°09′S 35°33′E
104 F13 **São Teotónio** Beja, S Portugal 37°30′N 08°41′W
São Tiago *see* Santiago
79 B18 **São Tomé** ● (Sao Tome and Principe) São Tomé, S Sao Tome and Principe 0°22′N 06°41′E
79 B18 **São Tomé** ✕ São Tomé, S Sao Tome and Principe 0°24′N 06°39′E
79 B18 **São Tomé** *Eng.* Saint Thomas. *island* S Sao Tome and Principe
79 B17 **Sao Tome and Principe** *off.* Democratic Republic of Sao Tome and Principe. ◆ *republic* E Atlantic Ocean
Sao Tome and Principe, Democratic Republic of *see* Sao Tome and Principe
74 H9 **Saoura, Oued** ≈ NW Algeria
60 M10 **São Vicente** *Eng.* Saint Vincent. São Paulo, S Brazil 23°55′S 46°25′W
64 O5 **São Vicente** Madeira, Portugal, NE Atlantic Ocean 32°48′N 17°03′W
76 C9 **São Vicente** *Eng.* Saint Vincent. *island* Ilhas de Barlavento, N Cape Verde
104 F14 **São Vicente, Cabo de** *Eng.* Cape Saint Vincent, *Port.* Cabode São Vicente. *cape* S Portugal
São Vicente, Cabo de *see* São Vicente, Cabo de
Sápai *see* Sápes
Sapaleri, Cerro *see* Zapaleri, Cerro
Saparoea *see* Saparua
171 S13 **Saparua** *prev.* Saparoea. Pulau Saparau, C Indonesia 03°35′S 128°37′E
168 L11 **Sapat** Sumatera, W Indonesia 0°18′S 103°18′E
77 U17 **Sapele** Delta, S Nigeria 05°54′N 05°43′E
23 X7 **Sapelo Island** *island* Georgia, SE USA
23 X7 **Sapelo Sound** *sound* Georgia, SE USA
114 K13 **Sápes** *var.* Sápai. Anatolikí Makedonía kai Thráki, NE Greece 41°02′N 25°44′E
Sapiénza *see* Sapiénza
115 D22 **Sapiénza** *var.* Sapiénza. *island* S Greece
138 F12 **Sapir** *prev.* Sappir. Southern, S Israel 30°43′N 35°11′E
61 I15 **Sapiranga** Rio Grande do Sul, S Brazil 29°39′S 50°58′W
114 K13 **Sápka** ▲▲ NE Greece
105 X9 **Sa Pobla** Mallorca, Spain, W Mediterranean Sea 39°46′N 03°03′E
56 D11 **Saposoa** San Martín, N Peru 06°53′S 76°45′W
119 F16 **Sapotskin** *Pol.* Sopockinie, *Rus.* Sapotskino, Sopotskin. Hrodzyenskaya Voblasts', W Belarus 53°50′N 23°39′E
77 P13 **Sapoui** *var.* Sapouy. S Burkina 11°34′N 01°44′W
Sapouy *see* Sapoui
Sappir *see* Sapir
165 S4 **Sapporo** Hokkaidō, NE Japan 43°05′N 141°21′E
107 M19 **Sapri** Campania, S Italy 40°05′N 15°36′E
169 T16 **Sapudi, Pulau** *island* S Indonesia
27 P9 **Sapulpa** Oklahoma, C USA 36°00′N 96°06′W
142 J4 **Saqqez** *var.* Saghez, Sakiz, Saqqiz. Kordestān, NW Iran 36°31′N 46°16′E
Saqqiz *see* Saqqez
139 U8 **Sarābādī** Wāsiţ, E Iraq 33°00′N 44°52′E
167 P10 **Sara Buri** *var.* Saraburi. Saraburi, C Thailand 14°32′N 100°53′E
Saraburi *see* Sara Buri
Sarafjagān *see* Salafchegān
24 K9 **Saragosa** Texas, SW USA 31°03′N 103°39′W
Saragossa *see* Zaragoza
Saragt *see* Sarahs
56 B8 **Saraguro** Loja, S Ecuador 03°42′S 79°18′W
146 I15 **Sarahs** *var.* Saragt, *Rus.* Serakhs. Ahal Welaýaty, S Turkmenistan 36°33′N 61°10′E
126 M6 **Sarai** Ryazanskaya Oblast', W Russian Federation 53°43′N 39°59′E
Sarāi *see* Sarāy
154 M12 **Saraipāli** Chhattīsgarh, C India 21°21′N 83°01′E
149 T9 **Sarāi Sidhu** Punjab, E Pakistan 30°35′N 72°02′E
93 M15 **Säräisniemi** Oulu, C Finland 64°25′N 26°50′E
113 I14 **Sarajevo** ● (Bosnia and Herzegovina) Federacija Bosna I Hercegovina, SE Bosnia and Herzegovina 43°53′N 18°24′E
112 I13 **Sarajevo** ✕ Federacija Bosna I Hercegovina, C Bosnia and Herzegovina 43°49′N 18°21′E
143 V4 **Sarakhs** Khorāsān-Razavī, NE Iran 36°50′N 61°00′E
115 H17 **Sarakíniko, Akrotírio** *headland* Évvia, C Greece 38°46′N 23°43′E
115 I18 **Sarakinó** *island* Vóreies Sporádes, Greece, Aegean Sea
127 V7 **Saraktash** Orenburgskaya Oblast', W Russian Federation 51°46′N 56°23′E
30 L15 **Sara, Lake** ⊠ Illinois, N USA
23 N8 **Saraland** Alabama, S USA 30°49′N 88°04′W
55 V9 **Saramacca** ⬖ *district* N Surinam
55 V10 **Saramacca Rivier** ≈ C Surinam
166 M2 **Saramati** ▲ N Burma (Myanmar) 25°46′N 95°01′E
145 R10 **Saran'** *Kaz.* Saran. Karaganda, C Kazakhstan 49°47′N 73°02′E
18 K7 **Saranac Lake** New York, NE USA 44°18′N 74°06′W
18 K7 **Saranac River** ≈ New York, NE USA
Saranda *see* Sarandë
113 L23 **Sarandë** *var.* Saranda, *It.* Porto Edda; *prev.* Santi Quaranta. Vlorë, S Albania 39°53′N 20°E
61 H14 **Sarandi** Rio Grande do Sul, S Brazil 27°57′S 52°58′W
61 F19 **Sarandí del Yí** Durazno, C Uruguay 33°18′S 55°38′W
61 F19 **Sarandí Grande** Florida, S Uruguay 33°43′S 56°19′W
171 Q8 **Sarangani Islands** *island group* S Philippines
127 P5 **Saransk** Respublika Mordoviya, W Russian Federation 54°11′N 45°10′E
115 C14 **Sarantáporos** ≈ N Greece
114 H9 **Sarantsi** Sofiya, W Bulgaria 42°43′N 23°46′E
127 T3 **Sarapul** Udmurtskaya Respublika, NW Russian Federation 56°26′N 53°52′E
Sarāqeb *see* Sarāqib
138 I3 **Sarāqib** *Fr.* Saraqeb. Idlib, N Syria 35°52′N 36°48′E
54 J5 **Sarare** Lara, N Venezuela 09°47′N 69°10′W
55 O10 **Sarariña** Amazonas, S Venezuela 04°10′N 64°31′W
143 S10 **Sar Ashk** Kermān, C Iran
23 V13 **Sarasota** Florida, SE USA 27°20′N 82°31′W
117 O11 **Sarata** Odes'ka Oblast', SW Ukraine 46°01′N 29°40′E
116 I10 **Sărăţel** *Hung.* Szeretfalva. Bistriţa-Năsăud, N Romania 47°02′N 24°24′E
25 X10 **Saratoga** Texas, SW USA 30°15′N 94°31′W
18 K10 **Saratoga Springs** New York, NE USA 43°04′N 73°47′W
127 P8 **Saratov** Saratovskaya Oblast', W Russian Federation 51°33′N 45°58′E
127 P8 **Saratovskaya Oblast'** ⬖ *province* W Russian Federation
127 Q7 **Saratovskoye Vodokhranilishche** ⊠ W Russian Federation
143 X13 **Sarāvān** Sīstān va Balūchestān, SE Iran 27°11′N 62°35′E
Saravan/Saravane *see* Salavan
169 S9 **Sarawak** ⬖ *state* East Malaysia
Sarawak *see* Kuching
139 U6 **Sarāy** *var.* Sarāi. Diyālá, E Iraq 34°06′N 45°06′E
136 D10 **Saray** Tekirdağ, NW Turkey 41°27′N 27°56′E
76 J12 **Saraya** SE Senegal 12°50′N 11°45′W
143 W14 **Sarbāz** Sīstān va Balūchestān, SE Iran 26°38′N 61°13′E
143 U8 **Sarbīsheh** Khorāsān-e Janūbī, E Iran 32°35′N 59°50′E
111 J24 **Sárbogárd** Fejér, C Hungary 46°54′N 18°36′E
Şarcad *see* Sarkad
27 S7 **Sarcoxie** Missouri, C USA 37°04′N 94°07′W
152 L11 **Sārda** *Nep.* Kali. ≈ India/Nepal
152 G10 **Sardārshahr** Rājasthān, NW India 28°30′N 74°30′E
107 C18 **Sardegna** *Eng.* Sardinia. ⬖ *region* Italy, C Mediterranean Sea
107 A18 **Sardegna** *Eng.* Sardinia. *island* Italy, C Mediterranean Sea
42 K13 **Sardinal** Guanacaste, NW Costa Rica 10°30′N 85°38′W
54 G7 **Sardinata** Norte de Santander, N Colombia 08°07′N 72°47′W
Sardinia *see* Sardegna
120 K8 **Sardinia-Corsica Trough** *undersea feature* Tyrrhenian Sea, C Mediterranean Sea
22 L2 **Sardis** Mississippi, S USA 34°25′N 89°55′W
22 L2 **Sardis Lake** ⊠ Mississippi, S USA
27 P12 **Sardis Lake** ⊠ Oklahoma, C USA
92 H12 **Sarek** ▲▲ N Sweden
92 H11 **Sarektjåhkkå** ▲ N Sweden 67°28′N 17°56′E
149 N3 **Sar-e Pol** *var.* Sar-i-Pul. Sar-e Pol, N Afghanistan 36°16′N 65°55′E
149 O3 **Sar-e Pol** ⬖ *province* N Afghanistan
Sar-e Pol *see* Sar-e Pol-e Žahāb
142 J6 **Sar-e Pol-e Žahāb** *var.* Sar-e Pol, Sar-i Pul. Kermānshāhān, W Iran 34°28′N 45°52′E
Sarera, Teluk *see* Cenderawasih, Teluk
147 T13 **Sarez, Kŭli** *Rus.* Sarezskoye Ozero. ◎ SE Tajikistan
Sarezskoye Ozero *see* Sarez, Kŭli
64 G10 **Sargasso Sea** *sea* W Atlantic Ocean
149 U8 **Sargodha** Punjab, NE Pakistan 32°06′N 72°48′E
78 I13 **Sarh** *prev.* Fort-Archambault. Moyen-Chari, S Chad 09°08′N 18°22′E
143 P4 **Sārī** *var.* Sari, Sāri. Māzandarān, N Iran 36°37′N 53°05′E
115 N23 **Saría** *island* SE Greece
Sariasiya *see* Sariosiyo
40 F3 **Saric** Sonora, NW Mexico 31°08′N 111°22′W
188 K6 **Sarigan** *island* C Northern Mariana Islands
136 D14 **Sarıgöl** Manisa, SW Turkey 38°16′N 28°41′E
139 T6 **Sārihah** At Ta'mīn, E Iraq 34°34′N 44°38′E
137 R12 **Sarıkamış** Kars, NE Turkey 40°18′N 42°36′E
169 R9 **Sarikei** Sarawak, East Malaysia 02°07′N 111°30′E
147 U12 **Sarikol Range** *Rus.* Sarykol'skiy Khrebet. ▲▲ China/Tajikistan
181 Y7 **Sarina** Queensland, NE Australia 21°34′S 149°12′E
Sarine *see* La Sarine
105 S5 **Sariñena** Aragón, NE Spain 41°47′N 00°10′W
147 O13 **Sariosiyo** *Rus.* Sariasiya. Surkhondaryo Viloyati, S Uzbekistan 38°25′N 67°51′E
Sar-i-Pul *see* Sar-e Pol, Afghanistan
Sar-i Pul *see* Sar-e Pol-e Žahāb, Iran
Sariqamish Kŭli *see* Sarygamyş Köli
149 V1 **Sari Qŭl** *Rus.* Ozero Zurkul', *Taj.* Zŭrkŭl. ◎ Afghanistan/Tajikistan *see also* Zŭrkŭl
Sari Qŭl *see* Zŭrkŭl
75 Q12 **Sarīr Tibistī** *var.* Serir Tibesti. *desert* S Libya
25 S15 **Sarita** Texas, SW USA 27°14′N 97°48′W
163 W14 **Sariwŏn** SW North Korea 38°30′N 125°52′E
114 P12 **Sarıyer** İstanbul, NW Turkey 41°11′N 29°03′E
97 L26 **Sark** *Fr.* Sercq. *island* Channel Islands
111 N24 **Sarkad** *Rom.* Şărcad. Békés, SE Hungary 46°44′N 21°25′E
145 W14 **Sarkand** *Kaz.* Sarqan. Almaty, SW Kazakhstan 45°24′N 79°55′E
Sarkaņi *see* Krasnogorskoye
152 D11 **Sarkāri Tala** Rājasthān, NW India 27°39′N 70°52′E
136 G15 **Şarkikaraağaç** *var.* Şarki Karaağaç. Isparta, SW Turkey 38°04′N 31°22′E
Şarki Karaağaç *see* Şarkikaraağaç
136 L13 **Şarkışla** Sivas, C Turkey 39°21′N 36°27′E
136 C11 **Şarköy** Tekirdağ, NW Turkey 40°37′N 27°07′E
Sarkŏrz *see* Livada
Sarlat *see* Sarlat-la-Canéda
102 M13 **Sarlat-la-Canéda** *var.* Sarlat. Dordogne, SW France 44°54′N 01°12′E
109 S3 **Sarleinsbach** Oberösterreich, N Austria 48°33′N 13°55′E
Şarma *see* Ash Sharmah
171 Y12 **Sarmi** Papua, E Indonesia 01°51′S 138°45′E
63 I19 **Sarmiento** Chubut, S Argentina 45°38′S 69°07′W
63 H25 **Sarmiento, Monte** ▲ S Chile 54°28′S 70°49′W
94 J11 **Särna** Dalarna, C Sweden 61°40′N 13°10′E
108 F8 **Sarnen** Obwalden, C Switzerland 46°54′N 08°15′E
108 F9 **Sarner See** ◎ C Switzerland
14 D16 **Sarnia** Ontario, S Canada 42°58′N 82°23′W
116 L3 **Sarny** Rivnens'ka Oblast', NW Ukraine 51°20′N 26°35′E
171 O13 **Saroako** Sulawesi, C Indonesia 02°31′S 121°18′E
118 L13 **Sarochyna** *Rus.* Sorochino. Vitsyebskaya Voblasts', N Belarus 55°12′N 28°45′E
168 L12 **Sarolangun** Sumatera, W Indonesia 02°17′S 102°39′E
165 U3 **Saroma** Hokkaidō, NE Japan 44°01′N 143°43′E
165 V3 **Saroma-ko** ◎ Hokkaidō, NE Japan
Saronic Gulf *see* Saronikós Kólpos
115 H20 **Saronikós Kólpos** *Eng.* Saronic Gulf. *gulf* S Greece
106 D7 **Saronno** Lombardia, N Italy 45°38′N 09°02′E
136 B11 **Saros Körfezi** *gulf* NW Turkey
111 N20 **Sárospatak** Borsod-Abaúj-Zemplén, NE Hungary 48°18′N 21°30′E
127 O4 **Sarov** *prev.* Sarova. Respublika Mordoviya, SW Russian Federation 54°39′N 43°09′E
Sarova *see* Sarov
127 P12 **Sarpa** Respublika Kalmykiya, SW Russian Federation 47°00′N 45°42′E
127 P12 **Sarpa, Ozero** ◎ SW Russian Federation
113 M18 **Šar Planina** ▲▲ FYR Macedonia/Serbia
95 I16 **Sarpsborg** Østfold, S Norway 59°16′N 11°07′E
139 U5 **Sarqalā** At Ta'mīn, N Iraq
Sarqan *see* Sarkand
103 U4 **Sarralbe** Moselle, NE France 49°02′N 07°01′E
Sarre *see* Saar, France/Germany
Sarre *see* Saarland, Germany
103 U5 **Sarrebourg** *Ger.* Saarburg. Moselle, NE France 48°43′N 07°03′E
Sarrebruck *see* Saarbrücken
103 U4 **Sarreguemines** *prev.* Saargemund. Moselle, NE France 49°06′N 07°04′E
104 I3 **Sarria** Galicia, NW Spain 42°47′N 07°25′W
105 S8 **Sarrión** Aragón, NE Spain 40°09′N 00°49′W
42 F4 **Sarstoon** *Sp.* Río Sarstún. ≈ Belize/Guatemala
Sarstún, Río *see* Sarstoon
123 Q9 **Sartang** ≈ NE Russian Federation
103 X16 **Sartène** Corse, France, C Mediterranean Sea 41°38′N 08°58′E
102 K7 **Sarthe** ⬖ *department* NW France
102 K7 **Sarthe** ≈ N France
115 H15 **Sártí** Kentrikí Makedonía, N Greece 40°05′N 24°E
Sartu *see* Daqing
165 T1 **Sarufutsu** Hokkaidō, NE Japan 45°20′N 142°03′E
Saruhan *see* Manisa
152 G9 **Sarūpsar** Rājasthān, NW India 29°25′N 73°50′E
137 U13 **Şärur** *prev.* Il'ichevsk. SW Azerbaijan 39°30′N 44°59′E
Sarvani *see* Marneuli
111 G23 **Sárvár** Vas, W Hungary 47°15′N 16°59′E
143 P11 **Sarvestān** Fārs, S Iran 29°16′N 53°13′E
171 W12 **Sarwon** Papua, E Indonesia 0°58′S 136°08′E
145 P17 **Saryagash** *Kaz.* Saryaghash. Yuzhnyy Kazakhstan, S Kazakhstan 41°29′N 69°10′E
Saryaghash *see* Saryagash
Saryarqa *see* Kazakhskiy Melkosopochnik
147 W8 **Sary-Bulak** Narynskaya Oblast', C Kyrgyzstan 41°56′N 75°44′E
147 U10 **Sary-Bulak** Oshskaya Oblast', SW Kyrgyzstan 40°49′N 73°44′E
117 S14 **Sarych, Mys** *headland* S Ukraine 44°23′N 33°44′E
147 Z7 **Sary-Dzhaz** *var.* Aksu He. ≈ China/Kyrgyzstan *see also* Aksu He
Sary-Dzhaz *see* Aksu He
146 F8 **Sarygamyş Köli** *Rus.* Sarykamyshkoye Ozero, *Uzb.* Sariqamish Kŭli. *salt lake* Kazakhstan/Uzbekistan
144 G13 **Sarykamys** *Kaz.* Saryqamys. Mangistau, SW Kazakhstan 45°58′N 53°30′E
Sarykamyshkoye Ozero *see* Sarygamyş Köli
145 N7 **Sarykol'** *prev.* Uritskiy. Kustanay, N Kazakhstan 53°19′N 65°34′E
Sarykol'skiy Khrebet *see* Sarikol Range
144 M10 **Sarykopa, Ozero** ◎ C Kazakhstan
145 V15 **Saryozek** *Kaz.* Saryözek. Almaty, SE Kazakhstan 44°22′N 77°57′E
Saryqamys *see* Sarykamys
145 S13 **Saryshagan** *Kaz.* Saryshaghan. Karaganda, SE Kazakhstan 46°05′N 73°38′E
Saryshaghan *see* Saryshagan
145 O13 **Sarysu** ≈ S Kazakhstan
147 T11 **Sary-Tash** Oshskaya Oblast', SW Kyrgyzstan 39°44′N 73°14′E
145 T12 **Saryterek** Karaganda, C Kazakhstan 47°46′N 74°06′E
Saryyazynskoye Vodokhranilishche *see* Saryýazy Suw Howdany
146 J15 **Saryýazy Suw Howdany** *Rus.* Saryyazynskoye Vodokhranilishche. ⊠ S Turkmenistan
145 T14 **Saryyesik-Atyrau, Peski** *desert* E Kazakhstan
106 E10 **Sarzana** Liguria, NW Italy 44°07′N 09°59′E
188 B17 **Sasalaguan, Mount** ▲ S Guam
153 O14 **Sasarām** Bihār, N India 24°58′N 84°01′E
186 M8 **Sasari, Mount** ▲ Santa Isabel, N Solomon Islands 08°09′S 159°32′E
164 C13 **Sasebo** Nagasaki, Kyūshū, SW Japan 33°10′N 129°42′E
14 I9 **Saseginaga, Lac** ◎ Québec, SE Canada
Saseno *see* Sazan
11 R13 **Saskatchewan** ⬖ *province* SW Canada
11 U14 **Saskatchewan** ≈ Manitoba/Saskatchewan, C Canada
11 T15 **Saskatoon** Saskatchewan, S Canada 52°10′N 106°40′W
11 T15 **Saskatoon** ✕ Saskatchewan, S Canada 52°15′N 107°05′W
123 N7 **Saskylakh** Respublika Sakha (Yakutiya), NE Russian Federation 71°56′N 114°07′E
42 L7 **Saslaya, Cerro** ▲ N Nicaragua 13°52′N 85°06′W
38 G17 **Sasmik, Cape** *headland* Tanaga Island, Alaska, USA 51°36′N 177°55′W
119 N19 **Sasnovy Bor** *Rus.* Sosnovyy Bor. Homyel'skaya Voblasts', SE Belarus 52°32′N 29°35′E
127 N5 **Sasovo** Ryazanskaya Oblast', W Russian Federation 54°19′N 41°54′E
25 S12 **Saspamco** Texas, SW USA 29°13′N 98°18′W
109 W9 **Sass** *var.* Sassbach. SE Austria
76 M17 **Sassandra** S Ivory Coast 04°58′N 06°08′W
76 M17 **Sassandra** *var.* Ibo, Sassandra Fleuve. ≈ S Ivory Coast
Sassandra Fleuve *see* Sassandra
107 B17 **Sassari** Sardegna, Italy, C Mediterranean Sea 40°44′N 08°33′E
Sassbach *see* Sass
98 H11 **Sassenheim** Zuid-Holland, W Netherlands 52°14′N 04°31′E
Sassmacken *see* Valdemārpils
100 O7 **Sassnitz** Mecklenburg-Vorpommern, NE Germany 54°32′N 13°39′E
99 E16 **Sas van Gent** Zeeland, SW Netherlands 51°13′N 03°48′E
145 W12 **Sasykkol', Ozero** ◎ E Kazakhstan
117 O12 **Sasyk, Ozero** *Rus.* Ozero Kunduk. ◎ SW Ukraine
76 J12 **Satadougou** Kayes, SW Mali 12°40′N 11°25′W
164 C17 **Sata-misaki** Kyūshū, SW Japan
26 I7 **Satanta** Kansas, C USA 37°23′N 102°00′W
155 E15 **Sātāra** Mahārāshtra, W India 17°41′N 73°59′E
192 G15 **Sātaua** Savai'i, NW Samoa 13°26′S 172°40′W
188 M16 **Satawal** *island* Caroline Islands, C Micronesia
189 R17 **Satawan Atoll** *atoll* Mortlock Islands, C Micronesia
Sätbaev *see* Satpayev
23 Y12 **Satellite Beach** Florida, SE USA 28°10′N 80°35′W
95 M14 **Säter** Dalarna, C Sweden 60°21′N 15°45′E
Sathmar *see* Satu Mare
23 V7 **Satilla River** ≈ Georgia, SE USA
57 F14 **Satipo** *var.* San Francisco de Satipo. Junín, C Peru 11°19′S 74°37′W
122 F11 **Satka** Chelyabinskaya Oblast', C Russian Federation 55°08′N 58°54′E
153 T16 **Satkhira** Khulna, SW Bangladesh 22°43′N 89°06′E

◆ Country
● Country Capital
◇ Dependent Territory
○ Dependent Territory Capital
⬖ Administrative Regions
✕ International Airport
▲ Mountain
▲▲ Mountain Range
Ѫ Volcano
≈ River
◎ Lake
⊠ Reservoir

ŞATLYK – SEHWĀN

146 J13 **Şatlyk** *Rus.* Shatlyk. Mary Welaýaty, C Turkmenistan 37°55′N 61°00′E
154 K9 **Satna** *prev.* Sutna. Madhya Pradesh, C India 24°33′N 80°50′E
103 R11 **Satolas** ✈ (Lyon) Rhône, E France 45°44′N 05°01′E
111 N20 **Sátoraljaújhely** Borsod-Abaúj-Zemplén, NE Hungary 48°24′N 21°39′E
145 O12 **Satpayev** *Kaz.* Sätbaev; *prev.* Nikol'skiy. Karaganda, C Kazakhstan 47°59′N 67°27′E
154 G11 **Sātpura Range** ▲▲ C India
Satsuma-Sendai *see* Sendai
167 P12 **Sattahip** *var.* Ban Sattahip, Ban Sattahipp. Chon Buri, S Thailand 12°36′N 100°56′E
92 L11 **Sattanen** Lappi, NE Finland 67°31′N 26°35′E
Satul *see* Satun
116 H9 **Satulung** *Hung.* Kővárhosszúfalu. Maramureş, N Romania 47°34′N 23°26′E
Satul-Vechi *see* Staro Selo
116 G8 **Satu Mare** *Ger.* Sathmar, *Hung.* Szatmárnémeti. Satu Mare, NW Romania 47°46′N 22°55′E
116 G8 **Satu Mare** ◐ *county* NW Romania
167 N16 **Satun** *var.* Satul, Setul. Satun, SW Thailand 06°40′N 100°01′E
192 G16 **Satupa'itea** Savai'i, W Samoa 13°46′S 172°26′W
Sau *see* Sava
14 F14 **Sauble** ≈ Ontario, S Canada
14 F13 **Sauble Beach** Ontario, S Canada 44°36′N 81°15′W
61 C16 **Sauce** Corrientes, NE Argentina 30°05′S 58°46′W
Sauce *see* Juan L. Lacaze
36 K15 **Sauceda Mountains** ▲▲ Arizona, SW USA
61 C17 **Sauce de Luna** Entre Ríos, E Argentina 31°15′S 59°09′W
63 L15 **Sauce Grande, Río** ≈ E Argentina
40 K6 **Saucillo** Chihuahua, N Mexico 28°01′N 105°17′W
95 D15 **Sauda** Rogaland, S Norway 59°38′N 06°23′E
145 Q16 **Saudakent** *Kaz.* Saūdakent; *prev.* Baykadam, *Kaz.* Bayqadam. Zhambyl, S Kazakhstan 43°49′N 69°56′E
92 J2 **Saudhárkrókur** Nordhurland Vestra, N Iceland 65°45′N 19°39′W
141 P9 **Saudi Arabia** *off.* Kingdom of Saudi Arabia, Al 'Arabīyah as Su'ūdīyah, *Ar.* Al Mamlakah al 'Arabīyah as Su'ūdīyah. ◆ *monarchy* SW Asia
Saudi Arabia, Kingdom of *see* Saudi Arabia
101 D19 **Sauer** *var.* Sûre. ≈ NW Europe *see also* Sûre
Sauer *see* Sûre
101 F15 **Sauerland** *forest* W Germany
14 F14 **Saugeen** ≈ Ontario, S Canada
18 K12 **Saugerties** New York, NE USA 42°04′N 73°55′W
Saugor *see* Sāgar
10 K15 **Saugstad, Mount** ▲ British Columbia, SW Canada 52°12′N 126°35′W
Sāūjbulāgh *see* Mahābād
102 J11 **Saujon** Charente-Maritime, W France 45°40′N 00°54′W
29 T7 **Sauk Centre** Minnesota, N USA 45°44′N 94°57′W
30 L8 **Sauk City** Wisconsin, N USA 43°16′N 89°43′W
29 U7 **Sauk Rapids** Minnesota, N USA 45°35′N 94°09′W
55 Y11 **Saül** C French Guiana 03°37′N 53°12′W
103 O7 **Sauldre** ≈ C France
101 I23 **Saulgau** Baden-Württemberg, SW Germany 48°03′N 09°28′E
103 Q8 **Saulieu** Côte d'Or, C France 47°15′N 04°15′E
118 G8 **Saulkrasti** Riga, C Latvia 57°14′N 24°25′E
15 S6 **Sault-aux-Cochons, Rivière du** ≈ Québec, SE Canada
31 Q4 **Sault Sainte Marie** Michigan, N USA 46°29′N 84°22′W
12 F14 **Sault Ste. Marie** Ontario, S Canada 46°30′N 84°17′W
145 P7 **Saumalkol'** *prev.* Volodarskoye. Severnyy Kazakhstan, N Kazakhstan 53°19′N 68°05′E
190 E13 **Sauma, Pointe** *headland* Île Alofi, W Wallis and Futuna 14°21′S 177°58′W
171 T16 **Saumlaki** *var.* Saumlakki. Pulau Yamdena, E Indonesia 07°53′S 131°18′E
Saumlakki *see* Saumlaki
15 R12 **Saumon, Rivière au** ≈ Québec, SE Canada
102 K8 **Saumur** Maine-et-Loire, NW France 47°16′N 00°04′W
185 F23 **Saunders, Cape** *headland* South Island, New Zealand 45°53′S 170°40′E
195 N13 **Saunders Coast** *physical region* Antarctica
65 C24 **Saunders Island Settlement** Saunders Island, NW Falkland Islands 51°22′S 60°05′W
82 F11 **Saurimo** *Port.* Henrique de Carvalho, Vila Henrique de Carvalho. Lunda Sul, NE Angola 09°39′S 20°24′E
55 S11 **Sauriwaunawa** S Guyana 03°10′N 59°51′W
82 D12 **Sautar** Malanje, NW Angola 11°10′S 18°26′E
45 S13 **Sauteurs** N Grenada 12°14′N 61°38′W
102 K13 **Sauveterre-de-Guyenne** Gironde, SW France 44°43′N 00°02′W
119 O14 **Sava** Mahilyowskaya Voblasts', E Belarus 54°22′N 30°49′E
42 J5 **Savá** Colón, N Honduras 15°30′N 86°16′W
84 H11 **Sava** *Eng.* Save, *Ger.* Sau, *Hung.* Száva. ≈ SE Europe
33 Y8 **Savage** Montana, NW USA 47°28′N 104°17′W
183 N16 **Savage River** Tasmania, SE Australia 41°34′S 145°15′E
77 R15 **Savalou** S Benin 07°59′N 01°58′E
30 K10 **Savanna** Illinois, N USA 42°05′N 90°09′W
23 X6 **Savannah** Georgia, SE USA 32°02′N 81°01′W
27 R2 **Savannah** Missouri, C USA 39°57′N 94°49′W
20 H10 **Savannah** Tennessee, S USA 35°12′N 88°15′W
21 O12 **Savannah River** ≈ Georgia/South Carolina, SE USA
Savannakhét *see* Khanthabouli
44 H12 **Savanna-La-Mar** W Jamaica 18°13′N 78°08′W
12 B10 **Savant Lake** ◎ Ontario, S Canada
155 F17 **Savanūr** Karnātaka, W India 14°58′N 75°19′E
93 J16 **Sävar** Västerbotten, N Sweden 63°52′N 20°33′E
Savaria *see* Szombathely
154 C11 **Sāvarkundla** *var.* Kundla. Gujarāt, W India 21°21′N 71°20′E
116 F11 **Săvârşin** *Hung.* Soborsin; *prev.* Săvirşin. Arad, W Romania 46°00′N 22°15′E
136 C13 **Savaştepe** Balıkesir, W Turkey 39°20′N 27°38′E
147 P11 **Savat** *Rus.* Savat. Sirdaryo Viloyati, E Uzbekistan 40°03′N 68°35′E
Savat *see* Savat
Sāvdijāri *see* Skaulo
77 R15 **Savè** SE Benin 08°04′N 02°29′E
83 N18 **Save** Inhambane, E Mozambique 21°07′S 34°35′E
102 L16 **Save** ≈ S France
83 L17 **Save** *var.* Sabi. ≈ Mozambique/Zimbabwe *see also* Sabi
Save *see* Sava
Save *see* Sabi
142 M6 **Sāveh** Markazī, W Iran 35°00′N 50°22′E
116 L8 **Săveni** Botoşani, NE Romania 47°57′N 26°52′E
103 N16 **Saverdun** Ariège, S France 43°15′N 01°34′E
103 U5 **Saverne** *var.* Zabern; *anc.* Tres Tabernae. Bas-Rhin, NE France 48°45′N 07°22′E
106 B9 **Savigliano** Piemonte, NW Italy 44°39′N 07°39′E
Savigsivik *see* Savissivik
Savinichi *see* Savinichy
119 Q16 **Savinichy** *Rus.* Savinichi. Mahilyowskaya Voblasts', E Belarus 53°28′N 31°46′E
109 U10 **Savinja** ≈ N Slovenia
106 H11 **Savio** ≈ C Italy
Săvirşin *see* Săvârşin
197 O11 **Savissivik** *var.* Savigsivik. ◐ Avannaarsua, N Greenland
93 N18 **Savitaipale** Etelä-Suomi, SE Finland 61°12′N 27°43′E
113 J15 **Šavnik** C Montenegro 42°57′N 19°04′E
108 I9 **Savognin** Graubünden, S Switzerland 46°34′N 09°35′E
103 T12 **Savoie** ◐ *department* E France
106 C10 **Savona** Liguria, NW Italy 44°18′N 08°29′E
93 N17 **Savonlinna** *Swe.* Nyslott. Itä-Suomi, E Finland 61°51′N 28°56′E
93 N17 **Savonranta** Itä-Suomi, E Finland 62°10′N 29°10′E
38 K10 **Savoonga** Saint Lawrence Island, Alaska, USA 63°40′N 170°29′W
30 M13 **Savoy** Illinois, N USA 40°03′N 88°15′W
117 O8 **Savran'** Odes'ka Oblast', SW Ukraine 48°07′N 30°00′E
137 R11 **Şavşat** Artvin, NE Turkey 41°15′N 42°30′E
95 L19 **Sävsjö** Jönköping, S Sweden 57°25′N 14°40′E
Savu, Kepulauan *see* Sawu, Kepulauan
92 M11 **Savukoski** Lappi, NE Finland 67°17′N 28°14′E
Savu, Pulau *see* Sawu, Pulau
187 Y14 **Savusavu** Vanua Levu, N Fiji 16°48′S 179°20′E
171 O17 **Savu Sea** *Ind.* Laut Sawu. *sea* S Indonesia
83 H17 **Savute** North-West, N Botswana 18°33′S 24°06′E
139 N7 **Şawāb Uqlat'** *well* W Iraq
138 M7 **Şawāb, Wādī aş** *dry watercourse* W Iraq
152 H13 **Sawai Mādhopur** Rājasthān, N India 26°00′N 76°22′E
Sawakin *see* Suakin
167 R8 **Sawang Daen Din** Sakon Nakhon, E Thailand 17°28′N 103°27′E
167 O8 **Sawankhalok** *var.* Swankalok. Sukhothai, NW Thailand 17°19′N 99°50′E
165 P13 **Sawara** Chiba, Honshū, S Japan 35°52′N 140°31′E
37 R5 **Sawatch Range** ▲▲ Colorado, C USA
141 N12 **Sawdā', Jabal** ▲ SW Saudi Arabia 18°15′N 42°26′E
75 P9 **Sawdā', Jabal as** ▲▲ C Libya
Sawdirī *see* Sodiri
97 F14 **Sawel Mountain** ▲ C Northern Ireland, United Kingdom 54°49′N 07°04′W
75 X10 **Sawhāj** *var.* Sawhāj *var.* Sohâg, Suliag. C Egypt 26°28′N 31°44′E
Sawhāj *see* Sawhāj
77 O15 **Sawla** N Ghana 09°14′N 02°26′W
141 X12 **Şawqirah** *var.* Suqrah. S Oman 18°16′N 56°34′E
141 X12 **Şawqirah, Dawhat** *var.* Ghubbat Sawqirah, Sukra Bay, Suqrah Bay. *bay* S Oman
Şawqirah, Ghubbat *see* Şawqirah, Dawhat
183 V5 **Sawtell** New South Wales, SE Australia 30°22′S 153°04′E
138 K7 **Şawt, Wādī aş** *dry watercourse* S Syria
171 O17 **Sawu, Kepulauan** *var.* Kepulauan Savu. *island group* S Indonesia
Sawu, Laut *see* Savu Sea
171 O17 **Sawu, Pulau** *var.* Pulau Savu. *island* Kepulauan Sawu, S Indonesia
105 S12 **Sax** País Valenciano, E Spain 38°33′N 00°49′W
Saxe *see* Sachsen
108 C11 **Saxon** Valais, SW Switzerland 46°07′N 07°09′E
Saxony *see* Sachsen
Saxony-Anhalt *see* Sachsen-Anhalt
77 R12 **Say** Niamey, SW Niger 13°08′N 02°20′E
15 V7 **Sayabec** Québec, SE Canada 48°33′N 67°42′W
Sayaboury *see* Xaignabouli
145 U12 **Sayak** *Kaz.* Sayaq. Karaganda, E Kazakhstan 46°54′N 77°17′E
57 D14 **Sayán** Lima, W Peru 11°10′S 77°08′W
129 T6 **Sayanskiy Khrebet** ▲▲ S Russian Federation
Sayaq *see* Sayak
146 K13 **Saýat** *Rus.* Sayat. Lebap Welaýaty, E Turkmenistan 38°44′N 63°51′E
42 D3 **Sayaxché** Petén, N Guatemala 16°34′N 90°14′W
Şaydā/Sayida *see* Saïda
162 J7 **Sayhan** *var.* Hüremt. Bulgan, C Mongolia 48°40′N 102°33′E
163 N10 **Sayhandulaan** *var.* Öldziyt. Dornogovĭ, SE Mongolia 44°42′N 109°10′E
162 K9 **Sayhan-Ovoo** *var.* Ongi. Dundgovĭ, C Mongolia 45°27′N 103°58′E
141 T15 **Sayḩūt** E Yemen 15°18′N 51°16′E
29 U14 **Saylorville Lake** ⊡ Iowa, C USA
Saymenskiy Kanal *see* Saimaa Canal
163 N10 **Saynshand** Dornogovĭ, SE Mongolia 44°51′N 110°07′E
Saynshand *see* Sevrey
Sayn-Ust *see* Hohmorit
Say-Ötesh *see* Say-Utës
138 J7 **Şayqal, Bahr** ◎ S Syria
Sayrab *see* Sayrob
158 H4 **Sayram Hu** ◎ NW China
26 K11 **Sayre** Oklahoma, C USA 35°18′N 99°38′W
18 H12 **Sayre** Pennsylvania, NE USA 41°57′N 76°30′W
18 K15 **Sayreville** New Jersey, NE USA 40°27′N 74°19′W
147 N13 **Sayrob** *Rus.* Sayrab. Surkhondaryo Viloyati, S Uzbekistan 38°03′N 66°54′E
40 L13 **Sayula** Jalisco, SW Mexico 19°52′N 103°36′W
141 R14 **Say'ūn** *var.* Saywūn. C Yemen 15°53′N 48°32′E
144 G14 **Say-Utës** *Kaz.* Say-Ötesh. Mangistau, SW Kazakhstan 44°20′N 53°32′E
10 K16 **Sayward** Vancouver Island, British Columbia, SW Canada 50°20′N 126°01′W
Saywūn *see* Say'ūn
Sayyāl *see* Sayyāl
139 U8 **Sayyid 'Abīd** *var.* Saiyid Abīd. Wāsiţ, E Iraq 32°51′N 45°07′E
113 J22 **Sazan** *var.* Ishulli i Sazanit, *It.* Saseno. *island* SW Albania
Sazanit, Ishulli i *see* Sazan
Sazau/Sazawa *see* Sázava
111 E17 **Sázava** *var.* Sazau, *Ger.* Sazawa. ≈ C Czech Republic
124 J14 **Sazonovo** Vologodskaya Oblast', NW Russian Federation 59°04′N 35°10′E
102 G6 **Scaër** Finistère, NW France 48°00′N 03°40′W
97 J15 **Scafell Pike** ▲ NW England, United Kingdom 54°26′N 03°10′W
Scalabis *see* Santarém
96 M2 **Scalloway** N Scotland, United Kingdom 60°10′N 01°17′W
38 M11 **Scammon Bay** Alaska, USA 61°50′N 165°34′W
Scammon Lagoon/ Scammon, Laguna *see* Ojo de Liebre, Laguna
84 F7 **Scandinavia** *geophysical region* NW Europe
Scania *see* Skåne
96 K5 **Scapa Flow** *sea basin* N Scotland, United Kingdom
107 K26 **Scaramia, Capo** *headland* Sicilia, Italy, C Mediterranean Sea 36°46′N 14°29′E
14 H15 **Scarborough** Ontario, SE Canada 43°46′N 79°14′W
45 Z16 **Scarborough** *prev.* Port Louis. Tobago, Trinidad and Tobago 11°11′N 60°45′W
97 N16 **Scarborough** N England, United Kingdom 54°17′N 00°24′W
185 I17 **Scargill** Canterbury, South Island, New Zealand 42°57′S 172°57′E
96 E7 **Scarp** *island* NW Scotland, United Kingdom
Scarpanto *see* Kárpathos
Scarpanto Strait *see* Karpathou, Stenó
107 G25 **Scauri** Sicilia, Italy, C Mediterranean Sea 36°45′N 12°06′E
Scealg, Bá na *see* Ballinskelligs Bay
Scebeli *see* Shebeli
100 K10 **Schaale** ≈ N Germany
100 K9 **Schaalsee** ◎ N Germany
99 G18 **Schaerbeek** Brussels, C Belgium 50°52′N 04°21′E
108 G6 **Schaffhausen** *Fr.* Schaffhouse. Schaffhausen, N Switzerland 47°42′N 08°38′E
108 G6 **Schaffhausen** *Fr.* Schaffhouse. ◐ *canton* N Switzerland
Schaffhouse *see* Schaffhausen
98 I8 **Schagen** Noord-Holland, NW Netherlands 52°47′N 04°47′E
Schaken *see* Šakiai
98 M10 **Schalkhaar** Overijssel, E Netherlands 52°16′N 06°10′E
109 R3 **Schärding** Oberösterreich, N Austria 48°27′N 13°26′E
100 G9 **Scharhörn** *island* NW Germany
Schässburg *see* Sighişoara
Schaulen *see* Šiauliai
30 M10 **Schaumburg** Illinois, N USA 42°01′N 88°04′W
Schebschi Mountains *see* Shebshi Mountains
98 P6 **Scheemda** Groningen, NE Netherlands 53°10′N 06°58′E
100 I10 **Scheessel** Niedersachsen, NW Germany 53°11′N 09°33′E
13 N8 **Schefferville** Québec, E Canada 54°50′N 67°W
Schelde *see* Scheldt
99 D18 **Scheldt** *Dut.* Schelde, *Fr.* Escaut. ≈ W Europe
35 X5 **Schell Creek Range** ▲▲ Nevada, W USA
18 K10 **Schenectady** New York, NE USA 42°48′N 73°57′W
99 I17 **Scherpenheuvel** *Fr.* Montaigu. Vlaams Brabant, C Belgium 51°00′N 04°57′E
98 K11 **Scherpenzeel** Gelderland, C Netherlands 52°07′N 05°30′E
25 S12 **Schertz** Texas, SW USA 29°33′N 98°16′W
98 G11 **Scheveningen** Zuid-Holland, W Netherlands 52°07′N 04°18′E
98 G12 **Schiedam** Zuid-Holland, SW Netherlands 51°55′N 04°25′E
99 M24 **Schieren** Diekirch, NE Luxembourg 49°50′N 06°06′E
98 M4 **Schiermonnikoog** *Fris.* Skiermûntseach. Friesland, N Netherlands 53°28′N 06°09′E
98 M4 **Schiermonnikoog** *Fris.* Skiermûntseach. *island* Waddeneilanden, N Netherlands
99 K14 **Schijndel** Noord-Brabant, S Netherlands 51°37′N 05°27′E
Schil *see* Jiu
99 H16 **Schilde** Antwerpen, N Belgium 51°14′N 04°35′E
Schillen *see* Zhilino
103 V5 **Schiltigheim** Bas-Rhin, NE France 48°38′N 07°47′E
106 G7 **Schio** Veneto, NE Italy 45°42′N 11°21′E
98 H10 **Schiphol** ✈ (Amsterdam) Noord-Holland, C Netherlands 52°18′N 04°48′E
Schippenbeil *see* Sępopol
Schiria *see* Şiria
Schivelbein *see* Świdwin
115 D22 **Schíza** *island* S Greece
175 U3 **Schjetman Reef** *reef* Antarctica
Schlackenwerth *see* Ostrov
109 R7 **Schladming** Steiermark, SE Austria 47°24′N 13°42′E
Schlan *see* Slaný
Schlanders *see* Silandro
100 I7 **Schlei** *inlet* N Germany
101 D17 **Schleiden** Nordrhein-Westfalen, W Germany 50°31′N 06°30′E
Schlelau *see* Szydłowiec
100 I7 **Schleswig** Schleswig-Holstein, N Germany 54°31′N 09°34′E
29 T13 **Schleswig** Iowa, C USA 42°10′N 95°27′W
100 H8 **Schleswig-Holstein** ◐ *state* N Germany
Schlettstadt *see* Sélestat
108 F7 **Schlieren** Zürich, N Switzerland 47°23′N 08°27′E
Schlochau *see* Człuchów
Schloppe *see* Człopa
101 I18 **Schlüchtern** Hessen, C Germany 50°19′N 09°27′E
101 J17 **Schmalkalden** Thüringen, C Germany 50°42′N 10°26′E
109 W2 **Schmida** ≈ NE Austria
65 P19 **Schmidt-Ott Seamount** *var.* Schmitt-Ott Seamount, Schmitt-Ott Tablemount. *undersea feature* SW Indian Ocean 39°37′S 13°00′E
Schmiegel *see* Śmigiel
Schmitt-Ott Seamount/ Schmitt-Ott Tablemount *see* Schmidt-Ott Seamount
15 V3 **Schmon** ≈ Québec, SE Canada
101 M18 **Schneeberg** ▲ W Germany 50°03′N 11°51′E
Schneeberg *see* Veliki Snežnik
Schnee-Eifel *see* Schneifel
Schneekoppe *see* Sněžka
Schneidemühl *see* Piła
101 D18 **Schneifel** *var.* Schnee-Eifel. *plateau* W Germany
Schnelle Körös/Schnelle Kreisch *see* Crişul Repede
100 I11 **Schneverdingen** *var.* Schneverdingen (Wümme). Niedersachsen, NW Germany 53°07′N 09°48′E
Schneverdingen (Wümme) *see* Schneverdingen
Schoden *see* Skuodas
45 Q12 **Schœlcher** W Martinique 14°37′N 61°08′W
18 K10 **Schoharie** New York, NE USA 42°40′N 74°20′W
18 K11 **Schoharie Creek** ≈ New York, NE USA
115 J21 **Schoinoússa** *island* Kykládes, Greece, Aegean Sea
100 L13 **Schönebeck** Sachsen-Anhalt, C Germany 52°01′N 11°45′E
Schöneck *see* Skarszewy
100 O12 **Schönefeld** ✈ (Berlin) Berlin, NE Germany 52°23′N 13°29′E
101 K24 **Schongau** Bayern, S Germany 47°49′N 10°54′E
100 K13 **Schöningen** Niedersachsen, C Germany 52°07′N 10°58′E
Schönlanke *see* Trzcianka
Schönsee *see* Kowalewo Pomorskie
31 P10 **Schoolcraft** Michigan, N USA 42°05′N 85°39′W
98 O8 **Schoonebeek** Drenthe, NE Netherlands 52°39′N 06°57′E
98 I12 **Schoonhoven** Zuid-Holland, C Netherlands 51°57′N 04°51′E
98 H8 **Schoorl** Noord-Holland, NW Netherlands 52°42′N 04°40′E
Schooten *see* Schoten
101 F24 **Schopfheim** Baden-Württemberg, SW Germany 47°39′N 07°49′E
101 I21 **Schorndorf** Baden-Württemberg, S Germany 48°48′N 09°31′E
100 F10 **Schortens** Niedersachsen, NW Germany 53°31′N 07°57′E
99 H16 **Schoten** *var.* Schooten. Antwerpen, N Belgium 51°15′N 04°30′E
183 Q17 **Schouten Island** *island* Tasmania, SE Australia
186 C5 **Schouten Islands** *island group* NW Papua New Guinea
98 E13 **Schouwen** *island* SW Netherlands
Schreiberhau *see* Szklarska Poręba
109 U2 **Schrems** Niederösterreich, E Austria 48°48′N 15°05′E
101 L22 **Schrobenhausen** Bayern, SE Germany 48°33′N 11°14′E
18 L8 **Schroon Lake** ◎ New York, NE USA
108 J8 **Schruns** Vorarlberg, W Austria 47°04′N 09°54′E
Schubin *see* Szubin
25 U11 **Schulenburg** Texas, SW USA 29°40′N 96°54′W
Schuls *see* Scuol
108 E8 **Schüpfheim** Luzern, C Switzerland 47°02′N 07°23′E
35 S6 **Schurz** Nevada, W USA 38°55′N 118°48′W
101 I24 **Schussen** ≈ S Germany
Schüttenhofen *see* Sušice
29 R15 **Schuyler** Nebraska, C USA 41°25′N 97°04′W
18 L10 **Schuylerville** New York, NE USA 43°05′N 73°34′W
101 K20 **Schwabach** Bayern, SE Germany 49°20′N 11°02′E
Schwabenalb *see* Schwäbische Alb
101 I23 **Schwäbische Alb** *var.* Schwabenalb, *Eng.* Swabian Jura. ▲▲ S Germany
101 I22 **Schwäbisch Gmünd** *var.* Gmünd. Baden-Württemberg, SW Germany 48°49′N 09°48′E
101 I21 **Schwäbisch Hall** *var.* Hall. Baden-Württemberg, SW Germany 49°07′N 09°45′E
101 H16 **Schwalm** ≈ C Germany
109 V9 **Schwanberg** Steiermark, SE Austria 46°46′N 15°12′E
108 H8 **Schwanden** Glarus, E Switzerland 47°02′N 09°04′E
101 M20 **Schwandorf** Bayern, SE Germany 49°20′N 12°07′E
109 S5 **Schwanenstadt** Oberösterreich, NW Austria 48°03′N 13°47′E
169 S11 **Schwaner, Pegunungan** ▲▲ Borneo, N Indonesia
109 W5 **Schwarza** ≈ E Austria
109 P9 **Schwarzach** ≈ S Austria
101 M20 **Schwarzach** *Cz.* Černice. ≈ Czech Republic/Germany
Schwarzach *see* Schwarzach im Pongau
109 Q7 **Schwarzach im Pongau** *var.* Schwarzach. Salzburg, NW Austria 47°19′N 13°09′E
Schwarzawa *see* Svratka
101 N14 **Schwarze Elster** ≈ E Germany
Schwarze Körös *see* Crişul Negru
108 D9 **Schwarzenburg** Bern, W Switzerland 46°51′N 07°28′E
83 D21 **Schwarzrand** ▲▲ S Namibia
101 G23 **Schwarzwald** *Eng.* Black Forest. ▲▲ SW Germany
Schwarzwasser *see* Wda
39 P7 **Schwatka Mountains** ▲▲ Alaska, USA
109 N7 **Schwaz** Tirol, W Austria 47°21′N 11°44′E
109 Y4 **Schwechat** Niederösterreich, NE Austria 48°09′N 16°29′E
109 Y4 **Schwechat** ✈ (Wien) Wien, E Austria 48°04′N 16°31′E
100 P11 **Schwedt** Brandenburg, NE Germany 53°04′N 14°16′E
101 D19 **Schweich** Rheinland-Pfalz, SW Germany 49°49′N 06°44′E
Schweidnitz *see* Świdnica
101 J18 **Schweinfurt** Bayern, SE Germany 50°03′N 10°13′E
Schweiz *see* Switzerland
100 L9 **Schwerin** Mecklenburg-Vorpommern, N Germany 53°38′N 11°25′E
Schwerin *see* Skwierzyna
100 L9 **Schweriner See** ◎ N Germany
Schwertberg *see* Świecie
101 F15 **Schwerte** Nordrhein-Westfalen, W Germany 51°27′N 07°34′E
Schwiebus *see* Świebodzin
100 P13 **Schwielochsee** ◎ NE Germany
Schwihau *see* Švihov
Schwiz *see* Schwyz
108 G8 **Schwyz** *var.* Schwiz. Schwyz, C Switzerland 47°02′N 08°39′E
108 G8 **Schwyz** *var.* Schwiz. ◐ *canton* C Switzerland
14 J11 **Schyan** ≈ Québec, SE Canada
Schyl *see* Jiu
107 I24 **Sciacca** Sicilia, Italy, C Mediterranean Sea 37°31′N 13°05′E
Sciasciamana *see* Shashemenē
107 L26 **Scicli** Sicilia, Italy, C Mediterranean Sea 36°48′N 14°43′E
97 F25 **Scilly, Isles of** *island group* SW England, United Kingdom
111 H17 **Ścinawa** *Ger.* Steinau an der Elbe. Dolnośląskie, SW Poland 51°22′N 16°27′E
Scio *see* Chíos
31 S14 **Scioto River** ≈ Ohio, N USA
36 L5 **Scipio** Utah, W USA 39°15′N 112°06′W
33 X6 **Scobey** Montana, NW USA 48°47′N 105°25′W
183 T7 **Scone** New South Wales, SE Australia 32°02′S 150°51′E
Scoresby Sound/ Scoresbysund *see* Ittoqqortoormiit
Scoresby Sund *see* Kangertittivaq
Scorno, Punta dello *see* Caprara, Punta
34 K3 **Scotia** California, W USA 40°34′N 124°07′W
47 Y14 **Scotia Plate** *tectonic feature*
47 V15 **Scotia Ridge** *undersea feature* S Atlantic Ocean
194 H2 **Scotia Sea** *sea* SW Atlantic Ocean
29 Q12 **Scotland** South Dakota, N USA 43°09′N 97°43′W
25 R5 **Scotland** Texas, SW USA 33°37′N 98°27′W
96 H11 **Scotland** ◐ *national region* Scotland, U K
21 W8 **Scotland Neck** North Carolina, SE USA 36°07′N 77°25′W
195 R13 **Scott Base** *NZ research station* Antarctica 77°52′S 167°18′E
10 J16 **Scott, Cape** *headland* Vancouver Island, British Columbia, SW Canada 50°43′N 128°24′W
26 I5 **Scott City** Kansas, C USA 38°28′N 100°55′W
27 Y7 **Scott City** Missouri, C USA 37°13′N 89°31′W
195 R14 **Scott Coast** *physical region* Antarctica
18 C15 **Scottdale** Pennsylvania, NE USA 40°05′N 79°35′W
195 Y11 **Scott Glacier** *glacier* Antarctica
195 Q17 **Scott Island** *island* Antarctica
26 L11 **Scott, Mount** ▲ Oklahoma, USA 34°52′N 98°34′W
32 G15 **Scott, Mount** ▲ Oregon, NW USA 42°53′N 122°06′W
34 M1 **Scott River** ≈ California, W USA
28 I13 **Scottsbluff** Nebraska, C USA 41°52′N 103°40′W
23 Q2 **Scottsboro** Alabama, S USA 34°40′N 86°01′W
31 P15 **Scottsburg** Indiana, N USA 38°42′N 85°47′W
183 P16 **Scottsdale** Tasmania, SE Australia 41°13′S 147°30′E
36 L13 **Scottsdale** Arizona, SW USA 33°31′N 111°54′W
45 O12 **Scotts Head Village** *var.* Cachacrou. S Dominica 15°12′N 61°22′W
192 L14 **Scott Shoal** *undersea feature* S Pacific Ocean
20 K7 **Scottsville** Kentucky, S USA 36°45′N 86°11′W
29 U14 **Scranton** Iowa, C USA 42°01′N 94°33′W
18 I13 **Scranton** Pennsylvania, NE USA 41°25′N 75°40′W
186 B6 **Screw** ≈ NW Papua New Guinea
29 R14 **Scribner** Nebraska, C USA 41°40′N 96°40′W
Scrobesbyrig' *see* Shrewsbury
14 I14 **Scugog** ≈ Ontario, SE Canada
14 I14 **Scugog, Lake** ◎ Ontario, SE Canada
97 N17 **Scunthorpe** E England, United Kingdom 53°35′N 00°39′W
108 K9 **Scuol** *Ger.* Schuls. Graubünden, E Switzerland 46°51′N 10°21′E
Scupi *see* Skopje
Scutari *see* Shkodër
113 K17 **Scutari, Lake** *Alb.* Liqeni i Shkodrës, *SCr.* Skadarsko Jezero. ◎ Albania/ Montenegro
Scyros *see* Skýros
Scythopolis *see* Beit She'an
138 E11 **Sderot** *prev.* Sederot. Southern, S Israel 31°31′N 34°35′E
25 U13 **Seadrift** Texas, SW USA 28°25′N 96°42′W
21 Y4 **Seaford** *var.* Seaford City. Delaware, NE USA 38°39′N 75°35′W
Seaford City *see* Seaford
14 E15 **Seaforth** Ontario, S Canada 43°33′N 81°25′W
24 M6 **Seagraves** Texas, SW USA 32°56′N 102°33′W
11 X9 **Seal** ≈ Manitoba, C Canada
182 M10 **Sea Lake** Victoria, SE Australia 35°34′S 142°51′E
83 G26 **Seal, Cape** *headland* S South Africa 34°06′S 23°18′E
65 D26 **Sea Lion Islands** *island group* SE Falkland Islands
19 S8 **Seal Island** *island* Maine, NE USA
25 V11 **Sealy** Texas, SW USA 29°46′N 96°09′W
35 X12 **Searchlight** Nevada, W USA 35°27′N 114°54′W
27 V11 **Searcy** Arkansas, C USA 35°14′N 91°43′W
19 R7 **Searsport** Maine, NE USA 44°28′N 68°54′W
35 N10 **Seaside** California, W USA 36°36′N 121°51′W
32 F10 **Seaside** Oregon, NW USA 45°57′N 123°55′W
18 K16 **Seaside Heights** New Jersey, NE USA 39°56′N 74°03′W
32 H8 **Seattle** Washington, NW USA 47°35′N 122°20′W
32 H9 **Seattle-Tacoma** ✈ Washington, NW USA 47°04′N 122°27′W
185 J16 **Seaward Kaikoura Range** ▲▲ South Island, New Zealand
42 J9 **Sébaco** Matagalpa, W Nicaragua 12°51′N 86°08′W
19 P8 **Sebago Lake** ◎ Maine, NE USA
169 S13 **Sebangan, Teluk** *bay* Borneo, C Indonesia
169 S13 **Sebanganu, Teluk** *bay* Borneo, C Indonesia
Sebaste/Sebastia *see* Sivas
23 Y12 **Sebastian** Florida, SE USA 27°55′N 80°31′W
40 C5 **Sebastían Vizcaíno, Bahía** *bay* NW Mexico
19 R6 **Sebasticook Lake** ◎ Maine, NE USA
34 M7 **Sebastopol** California, W USA 38°22′N 122°50′W
Sebastopol *see* Sevastopol'
169 W8 **Sebatik, Pulau** *island* N Indonesia
19 R5 **Sebec Lake** ◎ Maine, NE USA
76 K12 **Sébékoro** Kayes, W Mali 13°00′N 09°03′W
Sebenico *see* Šibenik
40 G6 **Seberi, Cerro** ▲ NW Mexico 27°49′N 110°18′W
116 H11 **Sebeş** *Ger.* Mühlbach, *Hung.* Szászsebes; *prev.* Sebeşu Săsesc. Alba, W Romania 45°58′N 23°34′E
Sebes-Körös *see* Crişul Repede
Sebeşu Săsesc *see* Sebeş
31 R8 **Sebewaing** Michigan, N USA 43°43′N 83°27′W
124 F16 **Sebezh** Pskovskaya Oblast', W Russian Federation 56°19′N 28°31′E
137 N12 **Şebinkarahisar** Giresun, N Turkey 40°19′N 38°25′E
116 F11 **Sebiş** *Hung.* Borossebes. Arad, W Romania 46°21′N 22°09′E
Sebkra Azz el Matti *see* Azzel Matti, Sebkha
19 Q4 **Seboomook Lake** ◎ Maine, NE USA
74 G6 **Sebou** *var.* Sebu. ≈ N Morocco
20 I6 **Sebree** Kentucky, S USA 37°34′N 87°30′W
23 X13 **Sebring** Florida, SE USA 27°30′N 81°26′W
Sebta *see* Ceuta
Sebu *see* Sebou
169 U13 **Sebuku, Pulau** *island* N Indonesia
169 W8 **Sebuku, Teluk** *bay* Borneo, N Indonesia
106 F10 **Secchia** ≈ N Italy
10 L17 **Sechelt** British Columbia, SW Canada 49°25′N 123°37′W
56 C12 **Sechin, Río** ≈ W Peru
56 A10 **Sechura, Bahía de** *bay* NW Peru
185 A22 **Secretary Island** *island* SW New Zealand
155 I15 **Secunderābād** *var.* Sikandarabad. Andhra Pradesh, C India 17°30′N 78°33′E
57 L17 **Sécure, Río** ≈ C Bolivia
118 D10 **Seda** Telšiai, NW Lithuania 56°10′N 22°04′E
27 T5 **Sedalia** Missouri, C USA 38°42′N 93°15′W
103 R3 **Sedan** Ardennes, N France 49°42′N 04°56′E
27 P7 **Sedan** Kansas, C USA 37°07′N 96°11′W
105 N3 **Sedano** Castilla-León, N Spain 42°43′N 03°43′W
104 H10 **Seda, Ribeira de** *stream* C Portugal
185 K15 **Seddon** Marlborough, South Island, New Zealand 41°42′S 174°05′E
185 H15 **Seddonville** West Coast, South Island, New Zealand 41°35′S 171°59′E
143 U7 **Sedeh** Khorāsān-e Janūbī, E Iran 33°18′N 59°12′E
Sederot *see* Sderot
65 B23 **Sedge Island** *island* NW Falkland Islands
76 G12 **Sédhiou** SW Senegal 12°39′N 15°33′W
11 U16 **Sedley** Saskatchewan, S Canada 50°06′N 103°51′W
Sedlez *see* Siedlce
117 Q2 **Sedniv** Chernihivs'ka Oblast', N Ukraine 51°39′N 31°34′E
36 L11 **Sedona** Arizona, SW USA 34°52′N 111°45′W
Sedunum *see* Sion
118 F12 **Šeduva** Šiaulai, N Lithuania 55°45′N 23°46′E
141 Y8 **Seeb** *var.* Muscat Sīb Airport. ✈ (Masqaţ) NE Oman 23°36′N 58°27′E
Seeb *see* As Sīb
108 M7 **Seefeld-in-Tirol** Tirol, W Austria 47°19′N 11°16′E
83 E22 **Seeheim Noord** Karas, S Namibia 26°50′S 17°45′E
Seeland *see* Sjælland
195 N9 **Seelig, Mount** ▲ Antarctica 81°45′S 102°15′W
Seenu Atoll *see* Addu Atoll
Seeonee *see* Seoni
Seer *see* Dörgön
102 L5 **Sées** Orne, N France 48°36′N 00°11′E
101 J14 **Seesen** Niedersachsen, C Germany 51°54′N 10°11′E
Seesker Höhe *see* Szeska Góra
100 J10 **Seevetal** Niedersachsen, N Germany 53°24′N 10°01′E
109 V6 **Seewiesen** Steiermark, E Austria 47°37′N 15°16′E
136 J13 **Şefaatli** *var.* Kızılkoca. Yozgat, C Turkey 39°32′N 34°45′E
143 V9 **Sefīdābeh** Khorāsān-e Janūbī, E Iran 31°05′N 60°30′E
149 N3 **Sefīd, Darya-ye** *Pash.* Āb-i-safed. ≈ N Afghanistan
148 K5 **Sefīd Kūh, Selseleh-ye** *Eng.* Paropamisus Range. ▲ W Afghanistan 34°00′N 61°40′E
148 K5 **Sefīd Kūh, Selseleh-ye** *Eng.* Paropamisus Range. ▲▲ W Afghanistan
142 M4 **Sefīd, Rūd-e** ≈ NW Iran
74 G6 **Sefrou** N Morocco 33°51′N 04°49′W
185 E19 **Sefton, Mount** ▲ South Island, New Zealand 43°43′S 169°58′E
171 S13 **Segaf, Kepulauan** *island group* E Indonesia
169 W7 **Segama, Sungai** ≈ East Malaysia
168 L9 **Segamat** Johor, Peninsular Malaysia 02°30′N 102°48′E
77 S13 **Ségbana** NE Benin 10°56′N 03°42′E
Segestica *see* Sisak
Segesvár *see* Sighişoara
171 T12 **Seget** Papua, E Indonesia 01°21′S 131°04′E
Segewold *see* Sigulda
124 J9 **Segezha** Respublika Kareliya, NW Russian Federation 63°39′N 34°24′E
Seghedin *see* Szeged
Segna *see* Senj
107 I16 **Segni** Lazio, C Italy 41°41′N 13°02′E
Segodunum *see* Rodez
105 S9 **Segorbe** País Valenciano, E Spain 39°51′N 00°30′W
76 M12 **Ségou** *var.* Segu. Ségou, C Mali 13°26′N 06°12′W
76 M12 **Ségou** ◐ *region* SW Mali
54 E8 **Segovia** Antioquia, N Colombia 07°08′N 74°39′W
105 N7 **Segovia** Castilla-León, C Spain 40°57′N 04°07′W
104 M6 **Segovia** ◐ *province* Castilla-León, N Spain
Segoviao Wangkí *see* Coco, Río
124 J9 **Segozerskoye Vodokhranilishche** ⊡ NW Russian Federation
102 J7 **Segré** Maine-et-Loire, NW France 47°41′N 00°51′W
105 U5 **Segre** ≈ NE Spain
Segu *see* Ségou
38 I17 **Seguam Island** *island* Aleutian Islands, Alaska, USA
38 I17 **Seguam Pass** *strait* Aleutian Islands, Alaska, USA
77 Y7 **Séguédine** Agadez, NE Niger 20°12′N 13°03′E
76 M15 **Séguéla** W Ivory Coast 07°58′N 06°44′W
25 S11 **Seguin** Texas, SW USA 29°34′N 97°58′W
38 E17 **Segula Island** *island* Aleutian Islands, Alaska, USA
62 K10 **Segundo, Río** ≈ C Argentina
105 Q12 **Segura** ≈ S Spain
105 P13 **Segura, Sierra de** ▲▲ S Spain
83 G18 **Sehithwa** North-West, N Botswana 20°28′S 22°43′E
154 H10 **Sehore** Madhya Pradesh, C India 23°12′N 77°08′E
186 G9 **Sehulea** Normanby Island, S Papua New Guinea 09°55′S 151°10′E
149 P15 **Sehwān** Sind, SE Pakistan 26°26′N 67°52′N

◆ Country
● Country Capital
◇ Dependent Territory
○ Dependent Territory Capital
◐ Administrative Regions
✈ International Airport
▲ Mountain
▲▲ Mountain Range
Volcano
≈ River
◎ Lake
⊡ Reservoir

SEIERSBERG – SHAHREZ̲Ā

109 V8 **Seiersberg** Steiermark, SE Austria 47°01′N 15°22′E
26 L9 **Seiling** Oklahoma, C USA 36°09′N 98°55′W
103 S9 **Seille** ≈ E France
99 J20 **Seilles** Namur, SE Belgium 50°31′N 05°12′E
93 K17 **Seinäjoki** *Swe.* Östermyra. Länsi-Suomi, W Finland 62°45′N 22°55′E
12 B12 **Seine** ≈ Ontario, S Canada
102 M4 **Seine** ≈ N France
102 K4 **Seine, Baie de la** *bay* N France
Seine, Banc de la *see* Seine Seamount
103 O5 **Seine-et-Marne** ◈ *department* N France
102 L3 **Seine-Maritime** ◈ *department* N France
84 B14 **Seine Plain** *undersea feature* E Atlantic Ocean 34°00′N 12°15′W
84 B15 **Seine Seamount** *var.* Banc de la Seine. *undersea feature* E Atlantic Ocean 33°45′N 14°25′W
102 E6 **Sein, Île de** *island* NW France
171 Y14 **Seinma** Papua, E Indonesia 04°10′S 138°54′E
Seisbierrum *see* Sexbierum
109 U5 **Seitenstetten Markt** Niederösterreich, C Austria 48°03′N 14°41′E
Seiyo *see* Uwa
Seiyu *see* Chŏnju
95 H22 **Sejerø** *island* E Denmark
110 P7 **Sejny** Podlaskie, NE Poland 54°09′N 23°21′E
81 G20 **Seke** Shinyanga, N Tanzania 03°16′S 33°31′E
164 L13 **Seki** Gifu, Honshū, SW Japan 35°30′N 136°54′E
161 U12 **Sekibi-sho** *island* China/Japan/Taiwan
165 U3 **Sekihoku-tōge** *pass* Hokkaidō, NE Japan
Sekondi *see* Sekondi-Takoradi
77 P17 **Sekondi-Takoradi** *var.* Sekondi. S Ghana 04°55′N 01°45′W
80 J11 **Sek'ot'a** Āmara, N Ethiopia 12°41′N 39°05′E
Sekseüil *see* Saksaul'skoye
32 I9 **Selah** Washington, NW USA 46°39′N 120°31′W
168 J8 **Selangor** *var.* Negeri Selangor Darul Ehsan. ◈ *state* Peninsular Malaysia
Selânik *see* Thessaloníki
168 K10 **Selapanjang** Pulau Rantau, W Indonesia 01°00′N 102°44′E
167 R10 **Selaphum** Roi Et, E Thailand 16°00′N 103°54′E
171 T16 **Selaru, Pulau** *island* Kepulauan Tanimbar, E Indonesia
171 U13 **Selassi** Papua, E Indonesia 03°16′S 132°50′E
168 J7 **Selatan, Selat** *strait* Peninsular Malaysia
39 N8 **Selawik** Alaska, USA 66°36′N 160°00′W
39 N8 **Selawik Lake** ◎ Alaska, USA
171 N14 **Selayar, Selat** *strait* Sulawesi, C Indonesia
95 C14 **Selbjørnsfjorden** *fjord* S Norway
94 H8 **Selbusjøen** ◎ S Norway
97 M17 **Selby** N England, United Kingdom 53°49′N 01°06′W
29 N8 **Selby** South Dakota, N USA 45°30′N 100°01′W
21 Z4 **Selbyville** Delaware, NE USA 38°28′N 75°12′W
136 B15 **Selçuk** *var.* Akıncılar. İzmir, SW Turkey 37°56′N 27°25′E
39 Q13 **Seldovia** Alaska, USA 59°26′N 151°42′W
107 M18 **Sele** *anc.* Silarius. ≈ S Italy
83 J19 **Selebi-Phikwe** Central, E Botswana 21°58′S 27°48′E
42 B5 **Selegua, Río** ≈ W Guatemala
129 X7 **Selemdzha** ≈ SE Russian Federation
129 U7 **Selenga** *Mong.* Selenge Mörön. ≈ Mongolia/Russian Federation
79 I19 **Selenge** Bandundu, W Dem. Rep. Congo 01°58′S 18°11′E
162 K6 **Selenge** *var.* Ingettolgoy. Bulgan, N Mongolia 49°27′N 103°59′E
162 L6 **Selenge** ◈ *province* N Mongolia
Selenge *see* Hyalganat, Bulgan, Mongolia
Selenge *see* Ih-Uul, Hövsgöl, Mongolia
Selenge Mörön *see* Selenga
123 N14 **Selenginsk** Respublika Buryatiya, S Russian Federation 52°00′N 106°40′E
Selenica *see* Selenicë
113 K22 **Selenicë** *var.* Selenica. Vlorë, SW Albania 40°32′N 19°38′E
123 Q8 **Selennyakh** ≈ NE Russian Federation
100 J8 **Selenter See** ◎ N Germany
Sele Sound *see* Soela Väin
103 U6 **Sélestat** *Ger.* Schlettstadt. Bas-Rhin, NE France 48°16′N 07°28′E
Selety *see* Sileti
Seleucia *see* Silifke
92 I4 **Selfoss** Sudhurland, SW Iceland 63°56′N 20°59′W
28 M7 **Selfridge** North Dakota, N USA 46°01′N 100°52′W
76 I15 **Seli** ≈ N Sierra Leone
76 I11 **Sélibabi** *var.* Sélibaby. Guidimaka, S Mauritania 15°14′N 12°11′W
Sélibaby *see* Sélibabi
Selidovka/Selidovo *see* Selydove
124 I15 **Seliger, Ozero** ◎ W Russian Federation
36 J11 **Seligman** Arizona, SW USA 35°20′N 112°56′W
27 S8 **Seligman** Missouri, C USA 36°31′N 93°56′W
80 E6 **Selima Oasis** *oasis* N Sudan
76 L13 **Sélingué, Lac de** ⊠ S Mali
Selinoús *see* Kréstena
18 G14 **Selinsgrove** Pennsylvania, NE USA 40°47′N 76°51′W
Selishche *see* Syelishcha
124 I16 **Selizharovo** Tverskaya Oblast', W Russian Federation 56°50′N 33°24′E
94 C10 **Selje** Sogn Og Fjordane, S Norway 62°02′N 05°22′E
11 X16 **Selkirk** Manitoba, S Canada 50°10′N 96°52′W
96 K13 **Selkirk** SE Scotland, United Kingdom 55°36′N 02°48′W
96 K13 **Selkirk** *cultural region* SE Scotland, United Kingdom
11 O16 **Selkirk Mountains** ▲▲ British Columbia, SW Canada
193 T11 **Selkirk Rise** *undersea feature* SE Pacific Ocean
115 F21 **Sellasía** Pelopónnisos, S Greece 37°14′N 22°24′E
44 M9 **Selle, Pic de la** *var.* La Selle. ▲ SE Haiti 18°18′N 71°55′W
102 M8 **Selles-sur-Cher** Loir-et-Cher, C France 47°16′N 01°31′E
36 K16 **Sells** Arizona, SW USA 31°54′N 111°52′W
Sellye *see* Sal'a
23 P5 **Selma** Alabama, S USA 32°24′N 87°01′W
35 Q11 **Selma** California, W USA 36°33′N 119°37′W
20 G10 **Selmer** Tennessee, S USA 35°10′N 88°34′W
173 N17 **Sel, Pointe au** *headland* W Réunion
Selselehye Kuhe Vākhān *see* Nicholas Range
127 S2 **Selty** Udmurtskaya Respublika, NW Russian Federation 57°19′N 52°09′E
Selukwe *see* Shurugwi
62 L9 **Selva** Santiago del Estero, N Argentina 29°46′S 62°02′W
11 T9 **Selwyn Lake** ◎ Northwest Territories/Saskatchewan, C Canada
10 K6 **Selwyn Mountains** ▲▲ Yukon Territory, NW Canada
181 T6 **Selwyn Range** ▲▲ Queensland, C Australia
117 W8 **Selydove** *var.* Selidovka, *Rus.* Selidovo. Donets'ka Oblast', SE Ukraine 48°06′N 37°16′E
Selzaete *see* Zelzate
Seman *see* Semanit, Lumi i
168 M15 **Semangka, Teluk** *bay* Sumatera, SW Indonesia
113 D22 **Semanit, Lumi i** *var.* Seman. ≈ W Albania
169 Q16 **Semarang** *var.* Samarang. Jawa, C Indonesia 06°58′S 110°29′E
169 Q10 **Sematan** Sarawak, East Malaysia 01°50′N 109°44′E
171 P17 **Semau, Pulau** *island* S Indonesia
169 V8 **Sembakung, Sungai** ≈ Borneo, N Indonesia
79 G17 **Sembé** Sangha, NW Congo 01°38′N 14°35′E
169 S13 **Sembulu, Danau** ◎ Borneo, N Indonesia
Semendria *see* Smederevo
117 R1 **Semenivka** Chernihivs'ka Oblast', N Ukraine 52°10′N 32°37′E
117 S6 **Semenivka** *Rus.* Semenovka. Poltavs'ka Oblast', NE Ukraine 49°36′N 33°10′E
127 O3 **Semenov** Nizhegorodskaya Oblast', W Russian Federation 56°47′N 44°27′E
Semenovka *see* Semenivka
169 S17 **Semeru, Gunung** *var.* Mahameru. ▲ Jawa, S Indonesia 08°01′S 112°53′E
Semey *see* Semipalatinsk
Semezhevo *see* Syemyezhava
126 L7 **Semiluki** Voronezhskaya Oblast', W Russian Federation 51°46′N 39°00′E
33 W16 **Seminoe Reservoir** ⊠ Wyoming, C USA
27 O11 **Seminole** Oklahoma, C USA 35°13′N 96°40′W
24 M6 **Seminole** Texas, SW USA 32°43′N 102°39′W
23 S8 **Seminole, Lake** ⊠ Florida/Georgia, SE USA
Semiozernoye *see* Auliyekol'
145 V9 **Semipalatinsk** *Kaz.* Semey. Vostochnyy Kazakhstan, E Kazakhstan 50°26′N 80°16′E
143 O9 **Semīrom** *var.* Samirum. Eşfahān, C Iran 31°20′N 51°50′E
38 F17 **Semisopochnoi Island** *island* Aleutian Islands, Alaska, USA
169 R11 **Semitau** Borneo, C Indonesia 0°30′N 111°59′E
81 E18 **Semliki** ≈ Uganda/Dem. Rep. Congo
143 P5 **Semnān** *var.* Samnān. Semnān, N Iran 35°37′N 53°21′E
143 Q5 **Semnān** *off.* Ostān-e Semnān. ◈ *province* N Iran
Semnān, Ostān-e *see* Semnān
99 K24 **Semois** ≈ SE Belgium
108 E8 **Sempacher See** ◎ C Switzerland
Sena *see* Vila de Sena
30 L12 **Senachwine Lake** ◎ Illinois, N USA
59 O14 **Senador Pompeu** Ceará, E Brazil 05°30′S 39°25′W
Sena Gallica *see* Senigallia
59 C15 **Sena Madureira** Acre, W Brazil 09°05′S 68°41′W
155 L25 **Senanayake Samudra** ◎ E Sri Lanka
83 G15 **Senanga** Western, SW Zambia 16°09′S 23°16′E
27 Y9 **Senath** Missouri, C USA 36°07′N 90°09′W
22 L2 **Senatobia** Mississippi, S USA 34°37′N 89°58′W
164 C16 **Sendai** *var.* Satsuma-Sendai. Kagoshima, Kyūshū, SW Japan 31°49′N 130°17′E
165 Q10 **Sendai** Miyagi, Honshū, C Japan 38°16′N 140°52′E
165 Q11 **Sendai-wan** *bay* E Japan
101 J23 **Senden** Bayern, S Germany 48°18′N 10°04′E
154 F11 **Sendhwa** Madhya Pradesh, C India 21°38′N 75°04′E
111 H21 **Senec** *Ger.* Wartberg, *Hung.* Szenc; *prev.* Szempcz. Bratislavský Kraj, W Slovakia 48°14′N 17°24′E
27 P3 **Seneca** Kansas, C USA 39°50′N 96°04′W
27 R8 **Seneca** Missouri, C USA 36°50′N 94°36′W
32 K13 **Seneca** Oregon, NW USA 44°06′N 118°57′W
21 O11 **Seneca** South Carolina, SE USA 34°41′N 82°57′W
18 G11 **Seneca Lake** ◎ New York, NE USA
31 U13 **Senecaville Lake** ⊠ Ohio, N USA
76 G11 **Senegal** *off.* Republic of Senegal, *Fr.* Sénégal. ◆ *republic* W Africa
76 H9 **Senegal** *Fr.* Sénégal. ≈ W Africa
Senegal, Republic of *see* Senegal
31 O4 **Seney Marsh** *wetland* Michigan, N USA
101 P14 **Senftenberg** Brandenburg, E Germany 51°31′N 14°01′E
82 L11 **Senga Hill** Northern, NE Zambia 09°26′S 31°12′E
158 G13 **Sênggê Zangbo** ≈ W China
171 Z13 **Senggi** Papua, E Indonesia 03°26′S 140°46′E
127 R5 **Sengiley** Ul'yanovskaya Oblast', W Russian Federation 53°54′N 48°51′E
63 I19 **Senguerr, Río** ≈ S Argentina
83 J16 **Sengwa** ≈ C Zimbabwe
Senia *see* Senj
111 H19 **Senica** *Ger.* Senitz, *Hung.* Szenice. Trnavský Kraj, W Slovakia 48°40′N 17°22′E
Seniça *see* Sjenica
106 J11 **Senigallia** *anc.* Sena Gallica. Marche, C Italy 43°43′N 13°13′E
136 F15 **Senirkent** Isparta, SW Turkey 38°07′N 30°34′E
Senitz *see* Senica
112 C10 **Senj** *Ger.* Zengg, *It.* Segna; *anc.* Senia. Lika-Senj, NW Croatia 44°58′N 14°55′E
Senj *see* Örgön
92 H9 **Senja** *prev.* Senjen. *island* N Norway
Senjen *see* Senja
161 U12 **Senkaku-shotō** *island group* SW Japan
137 R12 **Şenkaya** Erzurum, NE Turkey 40°33′N 42°17′E
83 I16 **Senkobo** Southern, S Zambia 17°38′S 25°58′E
103 O4 **Senlis** Oise, N France 49°13′N 02°33′E
167 T12 **Senmonorom** Môndól Kiri, E Cambodia 12°27′N 107°12′E
80 G10 **Sennar** *var.* Sannār. Sinnar, C Sudan 13°31′N 33°38′E
Senno *see* Syanno
Senones *see* Sens
109 W11 **Senovo** E Slovenia 46°01′N 15°24′E
103 P6 **Sens** *anc.* Agendicum, Senones. Yonne, C France 48°12′N 03°17′E
Sensburg *see* Mrągowo
167 S11 **Sên, Stœng** ≈ C Cambodia
42 F7 **Sensuntepeque** Cabañas, NE El Salvador 13°52′N 88°38′W
112 L8 **Senta** *Hung.* Zenta. Vojvodina, N Serbia 45°57′N 20°04′E
Šent Andraž *see* Sankt Andrä
171 Y13 **Sentani, Danau** ◎ Papua, E Indonesia
28 J5 **Sentinel Butte** ▲ North Dakota, N USA 46°52′N 103°50′W
10 M13 **Sentinel Peak** ▲ British Columbia, W Canada 54°51′N 122°02′W
59 N16 **Sento Sé** Bahia, E Brazil 09°51′S 41°56′W
Šent Peter *see* Pivka
Št. Vid *see* Sankt Veit an der Glan
Seo de Urgel *see* La See d'Urgel
154 I7 **Seondha** Madhya Pradesh, C India 26°09′N 78°47′E
154 J11 **Seoni** *prev.* Seeonee. Madhya Pradesh, C India 22°06′N 79°36′E
Seoul *see* Sŏul
83 I17 **Sepako** Central, NE Botswana 19°50′S 26°29′E
184 I13 **Separation Point** *headland* South Island, New Zealand 40°46′S 172°58′E
169 V10 **Sepasu** Borneo, N Indonesia 0°44′N 117°38′E
186 B6 **Sepik** ≈ Indonesia/Papua New Guinea
Sepone *see* Muang Xépôn
110 M7 **Sępopol** *Ger.* Schippenbeil. Warmińsko-Mazurskie, N Poland 54°16′N 21°09′E
116 F10 **Şepreuş** *Hung.* Seprős. Arad, W Romania 46°34′N 21°44′E
Seprős *see* Şepreuş
Şepşi-Sângeorz/Sepsiszentgyörgy *see* Sfântu Gheorghe
15 W4 **Sept-Îles** Québec, SE Canada 50°11′N 66°19′W
105 N6 **Sepúlveda** Castilla-León, N Spain 41°18′N 03°45′W
104 K8 **Sequeros** Castilla-León, N Spain 40°31′N 06°04′W
104 L5 **Sequillo** ≈ NW Spain
32 G7 **Sequim** Washington, NW USA 48°04′N 123°06′W
35 S11 **Sequoia National Park** *national park* California, W USA
137 Q14 **Şerafettin Dağları** ▲▲ E Turkey
127 N10 **Serafimovich** Volgogradskaya Oblast', SW Russian Federation 49°34′N 42°43′E
127 U5 **Serafimovskiy** Respublika Bashkortostan, W Russian Federation 54°26′N 53°49′E
171 Q10 **Serai** Sulawesi, N Indonesia 01°45′N 124°58′E
99 K19 **Seraing** Liège, E Belgium 50°37′N 05°31′E
Sêraitang *see* Baima
Serakhs *see* Sarahs
171 W13 **Serami** Papua, E Indonesia 02°11′S 136°46′E
Seram, Laut *see* Ceram Sea
Serampore/Serampur *see* Shrīrāmpur
171 S13 **Seram, Pulau** *var.* Serang, *Eng.* Ceram. *island* Maluku, E Indonesia
169 N15 **Serang** Jawa, C Indonesia 06°07′S 106°09′E
Serang *see* Seram, Pulau
169 P9 **Serasan, Pulau** *island* Kepulauan Natuna, W Indonesia
169 P9 **Serasan, Selat** *strait* Indonesia/Malaysia
112 M13 **Serbia** *off.* Federal Republic of Serbia; *prev.* Yugoslavia, *SCr.* Jugoslavija. ◆ *federal republic* SE Europe
112 M12 **Serbia** *Ger.* Serbien, *Serb.* Srbija. ◈ *republic* Serbia
Serbia, Federal Republic of *see* Serbia
Serbien *see* Serbia
Sercq *see* Sark
146 D12 **Serdar** *prev. Rus.* Gyzyrlabat, Kizyl-Arvat. Balkan Welaýaty, W Turkmenistan 39°02′N 56°15′E
Serdica *see* Sofiya
Serdobol' *see* Sortavala
127 O7 **Serdobsk** Penzenskaya Oblast', W Russian Federation 52°30′N 44°16′E
145 X9 **Serebryansk** Vostochnyy Kazakhstan, E Kazakhstan 49°44′N 83°16′E
123 Q12 **Serebryanyy Bor** Respublika Sakha (Yakutiya), NE Russian Federation 56°40′N 124°46′E
111 H20 **Sered'** *Hung.* Szered. Trnavský Kraj, W Slovakia 48°19′N 17°45′E
117 S1 **Seredyna-Buda** Sums'ka Oblast', NE Ukraine 52°09′N 34°00′E
118 E13 **Seredžius** Tauragė, C Lithuania 55°04′N 23°24′E
136 I14 **Şereflikoçhisar** Ankara, C Turkey 38°56′N 33°31′E
106 D7 **Seregno** Lombardia, N Italy 45°39′N 09°12′E
103 P7 **Serein** ≈ C France
168 K9 **Seremban** Negeri Sembilan, Peninsular Malaysia 02°42′N 101°54′E
81 H20 **Serengeti Plain** *plain* N Tanzania
82 K13 **Serenje** Central, E Zambia 13°12′S 30°15′E
Seres *see* Sérres
116 J5 **Seret** ≈ W Ukraine
Seret/Sereth *see* Siret
115 I21 **Serfopoúla** *island* Kykládes, Greece, Aegean Sea
127 P4 **Sergach** Nizhegorodskaya Oblast', W Russian Federation 55°31′N 45°29′E
29 S13 **Sergeant Bluff** Iowa, C USA 42°24′N 96°19′W
163 P7 **Sergelen** Dornod, NE Mongolia 48°31′N 114°01′E
Sergelen *see* Tuvshinshiree
168 H8 **Sergeulangit, Pegunungan** ▲▲ Sumatera, NW Indonesia
122 L5 **Sergeya Kirova, Ostrova** *island* N Russian Federation
Sergeyevichi *see* Syarhyeyevichy
145 O7 **Sergeyevka** Severnyy Kazakhstan, N Kazakhstan 53°53′N 67°25′E
Sergiopol *see* Ayagoz
59 P16 **Sergipe** *off.* Estado de Sergipe. ◈ *state* E Brazil
Sergipe, Estado de *see* Sergipe
126 L3 **Sergiyev Posad** Moskovskaya Oblast', W Russian Federation 56°21′N 38°10′E
124 K5 **Sergozero, Ozero** ◎ NW Russian Federation
146 J17 **Serhetabat** *prev. Rus.* Gushgy, Kushka. Mary Welaýaty, S Turkmenistan 35°19′N 62°17′E
169 Q10 **Serian** Sarawak, East Malaysia 01°10′N 110°35′E
115 I21 **Sérifos** *anc.* Seriphos. *island* Kykládes, Greece, Aegean Sea
115 I21 **Sérifou, Stenó** *strait* SE Greece
136 F16 **Serik** Antalya, SW Turkey 36°55′N 31°06′E
106 E7 **Serio** ≈ N Italy
Seriphos *see* Sérifos
Serir Tibesti *see* Sarīr Tībistī
Sêrkog *see* Sêrtar
127 S5 **Sernovodsk** Samarskaya Oblast', W Russian Federation 53°56′N 51°16′E
127 R2 **Sernur** Respublika Mariy El, W Russian Federation 56°55′N 49°09′E
110 M11 **Serock** Mazowieckie, C Poland 52°30′N 21°03′E
61 B18 **Serodino** Santa Fe, C Argentina 32°33′S 60°52′W
Seroei *see* Serui
105 P14 **Serón** Andalucía, S Spain 37°20′N 02°28′W
99 E14 **Serooskerke** Zeeland, SW Netherlands 51°42′N 03°52′E
105 T6 **Seròs** Cataluña, NE Spain 41°27′N 00°24′E
122 G10 **Serov** Sverdlovskaya Oblast', C Russian Federation 59°42′N 60°32′E
83 I19 **Serowe** Central, SE Botswana 22°26′S 26°44′E
104 H13 **Serpa** Beja, S Portugal 37°56′N 07°36′W
Serpa Pinto *see* Menongue
182 A4 **Serpentine Lakes** *salt lake* South Australia
45 T15 **Serpent's Mouth, The** *Sp.* Boca de la Serpiente. *strait* Trinidad and Tobago/Venezuela
Serpiente, Boca de la *see* Serpent's Mouth, The
126 K4 **Serpukhov** Moskovskaya Oblast', W Russian Federation 54°54′N 37°26′E
104 I10 **Serra de São Mamede** ▲ C Portugal 39°18′N 07°19′W
60 K13 **Serra do Mar** ▲▲
Sérrai *see* Sérres
107 N22 **Serra San Bruno** Calabria, SW Italy 38°32′N 16°18′E
103 S14 **Serres** Hautes-Alpes, SE France 44°26′N 05°42′E
114 H13 **Sérres** *var.* Seres; *prev.* Sérrai. Kentrikí Makedonía, NE Greece 41°03′N 23°33′E
62 J9 **Serrezuela** Córdoba, C Argentina 30°38′S 65°26′W
59 O16 **Serrinha** Bahia, E Brazil 11°38′S 38°56′W
59 M19 **Serro** *var.* Sêrro. Minas Gerais, NE Brazil 18°38′S 43°22′W
Sêrro *see* Serro
Sert *see* Siirt
104 H9 **Sertã** *var.* Sertá. Castelo Branco, C Portugal 39°48′N 08°05′W
Sertá *see* Sertã
60 L8 **Sertãozinho** São Paulo, S Brazil 21°04′S 47°55′W
160 F7 **Sêrtar** *var.* Sêrkog. Sichuan, C China 32°18′N 100°18′E
124 G12 **Sertolovo** Leningradskaya Oblast', NW Russian Federation 60°08′N 30°06′E
171 W13 **Serui** *prev.* Seroei. Papua, E Indonesia 01°53′S 136°15′E
83 J19 **Serule** Central, E Botswana 21°58′S 27°20′E
169 S12 **Seruyan, Sungai** *var.* Sungai Pembuang. ≈ Borneo, N Indonesia
115 E14 **Sérvia** Dytikí Makedonía, N Greece 40°12′N 22°01′E
160 E7 **Sêrxü** *var.* Jugar. Sichuan, C China 32°54′N 98°06′E
123 R13 **Seryshevo** Amurskaya Oblast', SE Russian Federation 51°03′N 128°16′E
Sesana *see* Sežana
169 V8 **Sesayap, Sungai** ≈ Borneo, N Indonesia
Sesdlets *see* Siedlce
79 N17 **Sese** Orientale, N Dem. Rep. Congo 02°13′N 25°52′E
81 F18 **Sese Islands** *island group* S Uganda
83 H16 **Sesheke** *var.* Sesheko. Western, SE Zambia 17°28′S 24°20′E
Sesheko *see* Sesheke
106 C8 **Sesia** *anc.* Sessites. ≈ NW Italy
104 F11 **Sesimbra** Setúbal, S Portugal 38°26′N 09°06′W
115 N22 **Seskló** *island* Dodekánisa, Greece, Aegean Sea
30 L16 **Sesser** Illinois, N USA 38°05′N 89°03′W
Sessites *see* Sesia
106 G11 **Sesto Fiorentino** Toscana, C Italy 43°50′N 11°12′E
106 E7 **Sesto San Giovanni** Lombardia, N Italy 45°32′N 09°14′E
106 A8 **Sestriere** Piemonte, NE Italy 45°00′N 06°54′E
106 D10 **Sestri Levante** Liguria, NW Italy 44°16′N 09°22′E
124 G12 **Sestroretsk** Leningradskaya Oblast', NW Russian Federation 60°05′N 29°57′E
107 C20 **Sestu** Sardegna, Italy, C Mediterranean Sea 39°15′N 09°06′E
112 E8 **Sesvete** Zagreb, N Croatia 45°50′N 16°03′E
118 G12 **Šeta** Kaunas, C Lithuania 55°17′N 24°16′E
Setabis *see* Xàtiva
165 Q4 **Setana** Hokkaidō, NE Japan 42°27′N 139°52′E
103 Q16 **Sète** *prev.* Cette. Hérault, S France 43°24′N 03°42′E
58 J11 **Sete Ilhas** Amapá, NE Brazil 01°06′N 52°06′W
59 L20 **Sete Lagoas** Minas Gerais, NE Brazil 19°29′S 44°15′W
60 G10 **Sete Quedas, Ilha das** *island* S Brazil
92 I10 **Setermoen** Troms, N Norway 68°51′N 18°20′E
95 E17 **Setesdal** *valley* S Norway
43 W16 **Setetule, Cerro** ▲ SE Panama 07°51′N 77°37′W
21 Q5 **Seth** West Virginia, NE USA 38°06′N 81°40′W
Setia *see* Sezze
74 K5 **Sétif** *var.* Stif. N Algeria 36°11′N 05°24′E
164 L5 **Seto** Aichi, Honshū, SW Japan 35°14′N 137°06′E
164 G13 **Seto-naikai** *Eng.* Inland Sea. *sea* S Japan
165 V16 **Setouchi** *var.* Setoushi. Kagoshima, Amami-Ō-shima, SW Japan 44°19′N 142°58′E
Setoushi *see* Setouchi
74 F6 **Settat** W Morocco 33°03′N 07°37′W
79 D20 **Setté Cama** Ogooué-Maritime, SW Gabon 02°32′S 09°46′E
11 W13 **Setting Lake** ◎ Manitoba, C Canada
97 L16 **Settle** N England, United Kingdom 54°04′N 02°17′W
189 Y12 **Settlement** E Wake Island 19°17′N 166°38′E
104 F11 **Setúbal** *Eng.* Saint Ubes, Saint Yves. Setúbal, W Portugal 38°31′N 08°54′W
104 F11 **Setúbal** ◈ *district* S Portugal
104 F12 **Setúbal, Baía de** *bay* W Portugal
Setul *see* Satun
12 B10 **Seul, Lac** ◎ Ontario, S Canada
103 R8 **Seurre** Côte d'Or, C France 47°00′N 05°09′E
137 U11 **Sevan** C Armenia 40°32′N 44°56′E
137 V12 **Sevana Lich** *Eng.* Lake Sevan, *Rus.* Ozero Sevan. ◎ E Armenia
Sevan, Lake/Sevan, Ozero *see* Sevana Lich
77 N11 **Sévaré** Mopti, C Mali 14°32′N 04°06′W
117 S14 **Sevastopol'** *Eng.* Sebastopol. Respublika Krym, S Ukraine 44°36′N 33°33′E
25 R14 **Seven Sisters** Texas, SW USA 27°57′N 98°34′W
10 K13 **Seven Sisters Peaks** ▲ British Columbia, SW Canada 54°57′N 128°10′W
99 M15 **Sevenum** Limburg, SE Netherlands 51°25′N 06°01′E
103 P14 **Séverac-le-Château** Aveyron, S France 44°18′N 03°03′E
14 H13 **Severn** ≈ Ontario, S Canada
97 L21 **Severn** *Wel.* Hafren. ≈ England/Wales, United Kingdom
125 O11 **Severnaya Dvina** *var.* Northern Dvina. ≈ NW Russian Federation
127 N16 **Severnaya Osetiya-Alaniya, Respublika** *Eng.* North Ossetia; *prev.* Respublika Severnaya Osetiya, Severo-Osetinskaya SSR. ◈ *autonomous republic* SW Russian Federation
Severnaya Osetiya, Respublika *see* Severnaya Osetiya-Alaniya, Respublika
122 M5 **Severnaya Zemlya** *var.* Nicholas II Land. *island group* N Russian Federation
127 T5 **Severnoye** Orenburgskaya Oblast', W Russian Federation 54°03′N 52°31′E
35 S3 **Severn Troughs Range** ▲▲ Nevada, W USA
125 W3 **Severnyy** Respublika Komi, NW Russian Federation 67°38′N 64°13′E
144 I13 **Severnyy Chink Ustyurta** ▲▲ W Kazakhstan
125 Q13 **Severnyye Uvaly** *var.* Northern Ural Hills. *hill range* NW Russian Federation
145 O6 **Severnyy Kazakhstan** *off.* Severo-Kazakhstanskaya Oblast', *var.* North Kazakhstan, *Kaz.* Soltüstik Qazaqstan Oblysy. ◈ *province* N Kazakhstan
125 V9 **Severnyy Ural** ▲▲ NW Russian Federation
Severo-Alichurskiy Khrebet *see* Alichuri Shimolí, Qatorkŭhi
123 N12 **Severobaykal'sk** Respublika Buryatiya, S Russian Federation 55°39′N 109°17′E
Severodonetsk *see* Syeverodonets'k
124 M8 **Severodvinsk** *prev.* Molotov, Sudostroy. Arkhangel'skaya Oblast', NW Russian Federation 64°32′N 39°50′E
Severo-Kazakhstanskaya Oblast' *see* Severnyy Kazakhstan
123 U11 **Severo-Kuril'sk** Sakhalinskaya Oblast', SE Russian Federation 50°38′N 155°57′E
124 J3 **Severomorsk** Murmanskaya Oblast', NW Russian Federation 69°00′N 33°16′E
Severo-Osetinskaya SSR *see* Severnaya Osetiya-Alaniya, Respublika
122 M7 **Severo-Sibirskaya Nizmennost'** *var.* North Siberian Plain, *Eng.* North Siberian Lowland. *lowlands* N Russian Federation
122 G10 **Severoural'sk** Sverdlovskaya Oblast', C Russian Federation 60°09′N 59°58′E
122 L11 **Severo-Yeniseyskiy** Krasnoyarskiy Kray, C Russian Federation 60°29′N 93°13′E
122 J12 **Seversk** Tomskaya Oblast', C Russian Federation 53°37′N 84°47′E
126 M11 **Severskiy Donets** *Ukr.* Sivers'kyy Donets'. ≈ Russian Federation/Ukraine *see also* Sivers'kyy Donets'
Severskiy Donets *see* Sivers'kyy Donets'
92 M9 **Sevettijärvi** Lappi, N Finland 69°31′N 28°40′E
36 M5 **Sevier Bridge Reservoir** ⊠ Utah, W USA
36 J4 **Sevier Desert** *plain* Utah, W USA
36 J5 **Sevier Lake** ◎ Utah, W USA
21 N9 **Sevierville** Tennessee, S USA 35°53′N 83°34′W
104 J14 **Sevilla** *Eng.* Seville; *anc.* Hispalis. Andalucía, SW Spain 37°24′N 05°59′W
104 J13 **Sevilla** ◈ *province* Andalucía, SW Spain
Sevilla de Niefang *see* Niefang
43 O16 **Sevilla, Isla** *island* SW Panama
Seville *see* Sevilla
114 J9 **Sevlievo** Gabrovo, N Bulgaria 43°01′N 25°06′E
Sevluš/Sevlyush *see* Vynohradiv
109 V11 **Sevnica** *Ger.* Lichtenwald. E Slovenia 46°00′N 15°20′E
162 J11 **Sevrey** *var.* Saynshand. Ömnögovĭ, S Mongolia 43°30′N 102°08′E
126 I7 **Sevsk** Bryanskaya Oblast', W Russian Federation 52°03′N 34°31′E
76 J15 **Sewa** ≈ E Sierra Leone
39 R12 **Seward** Alaska, USA 60°06′N 149°26′W
29 R15 **Seward** Nebraska, C USA 40°52′N 97°06′W
10 G8 **Seward Glacier** *glacier* Yukon Territory, W Canada
197 Q3 **Seward Peninsula** *peninsula* Alaska, USA
Seward's Folly *see* Alaska
62 H12 **Sewell** Libertador, C Chile 34°05′S 70°25′W
98 K5 **Sexbierum** *Fris.* Seisbierrum. Friesland, N Netherlands 53°13′N 05°28′E
11 O13 **Sexsmith** Alberta, W Canada 55°18′N 118°45′W
41 W13 **Seybaplaya** Campeche, SE Mexico 19°39′N 90°36′W
173 N6 **Seychelles** *off.* Republic of Seychelles. ◆ *republic* W Indian Ocean
67 Z9 **Seychelles** *island group* NE Seychelles
173 N6 **Seychelles Bank** *var.* Le Banc des Seychelles. *undersea feature* W Indian Ocean 04°45′S 55°30′E
Seychelles, Le Banc des *see* Seychelles Bank
Seychelles, Republic of *see* Seychelles
172 H17 **Seychellois, Morne** ▲ Mahé, NE Seychelles
92 L2 **Seydhisfjördhur** Austurland, E Iceland 65°15′N 14°00′W
146 J12 **Seýdi** *Rus.* Seydi; *prev.* Neftezavodsk. Lebap Welaýaty, E Turkmenistan 39°31′N 62°53′E
136 G16 **Seydişehir** Konya, SW Turkey 37°25′N 31°51′E
136 J13 **Seyfe Gölü** ◎ C Turkey
Seyhan *see* Adana
136 K16 **Seyhan Barajı** ⊠ S Turkey
136 K17 **Seyhan Nehri** ≈ S Turkey
136 F13 **Seyitgazi** Eskişehir, W Turkey 39°27′N 30°42′E
126 J7 **Seym** ≈ W Russian Federation
117 S3 **Seym** ≈ N Ukraine
123 T9 **Seymchan** Magadanskaya Oblast', E Russian Federation 62°54′N 152°27′E
114 N12 **Seymen** Tekirdağ, NW Turkey 41°06′N 27°56′E
183 O11 **Seymour** Victoria, SE Australia 37°01′S 145°10′E
83 I25 **Seymour** Eastern Cape, S South Africa 32°33′S 26°46′E
29 W16 **Seymour** Iowa, C USA 40°40′N 93°07′W
27 U7 **Seymour** Missouri, C USA 37°09′N 92°46′W
25 Q5 **Seymour** Texas, SW USA 33°36′N 99°16′W
114 M12 **Şeytan Deresi** ≈ NW Turkey
109 S12 **Sežana** *It.* Sesana. SW Slovenia 45°42′N 13°52′E
103 P5 **Sézanne** Marne, N France 48°43′N 03°41′E
107 I16 **Sezze** *anc.* Setia. Lazio, C Italy 41°29′N 13°04′E
Sfákia *see* Chóra Sfakíon
115 D21 **Sfaktiría** *island* S Greece
116 J11 **Sfântu Gheorghe** *Ger.* Sankt-Georgen, *Hung.* Sepsiszentgyőrgy; *prev.* Şepşi-Sângeorz, Sfîntu Gheorghe. Covasna, C Romania 45°52′N 25°49′E
117 N13 **Sfântu Gheorghe, Braţul** *var.* Gheorghe Braţul. ≈ E Romania
75 N6 **Sfax** *Ar.* Şafāqis. E Tunisia 34°45′N 10°45′E
75 N6 **Sfax** ✈ E Tunisia 34°43′N 10°37′E
Sfîntu Gheorghe *see* Sfântu Gheorghe
98 H13 **'s-Gravendeel** Zuid-Holland, SW Netherlands 51°48′N 04°36′E
98 F11 **'s-Gravenhage** *var.* Den Haag, *Eng.* The Hague, *Fr.* La Haye. ● (Netherlands-seat of government) Zuid-Holland, W Netherlands 52°07′N 04°17′E
98 G12 **'s-Gravenzande** Zuid-Holland, W Netherlands 52°00′N 04°10′E
Shaan/Shaanxi Sheng *see* Shaanxi
159 X11 **Shaanxi** *var.* Shaan, Shaanxi Sheng, Shan-hsi, Shenshi, Shensi. ◈ *province* C China
Shaartuz *see* Shahrtuz
Shaba *see* Katanga
Shabani *see* Zvishavane
81 N17 **Shabeellaha Dhexe** *off.* Gobolka Shabeellaha Dhexe. ◈ *region* E Somalia
Shabeellaha Dhexe, Gobolka *see* Shabeellaha Dhexe
81 L17 **Shabeellaha Hoose** *off.* Gobolka Shabeellaha Hoose. ◈ *region* S Somalia
Shabeellaha Hoose, Gobolka *see* Shabeellaha Hoose
Shabeelle, Webi *see* Shebeli
114 O7 **Shabla** Dobrich, NE Bulgaria 43°33′N 28°31′E
114 O7 **Shabla, Nos** *headland* NE Bulgaria 43°30′N 28°36′E
13 N9 **Shabogama Lake** ◎ Newfoundland and Labrador, E Canada
79 N20 **Shabunda** Sud-Kivu, E Dem. Rep. Congo 02°42′S 27°20′E
141 Q15 **Shabwah** C Yemen 15°09′N 46°46′E
158 F8 **Shache** *var.* Yarkant. Xinjiang Uygur Zizhiqu, NW China 38°27′N 77°16′E
Shacheng *see* Huailai
195 R12 **Shackleton Coast** *physical region* Antarctica
195 Z10 **Shackleton Ice Shelf** *ice shelf* Antarctica
Shaddādī *see* Ash Shadādah
28 K7 **Shadehill Reservoir** ⊠ South Dakota, N USA
122 G11 **Shadrinsk** Kurganskaya Oblast', C Russian Federation 56°08′N 63°18′E
31 O12 **Shafer, Lake** ⊠ Indiana, N USA
35 R13 **Shafter** California, W USA 35°27′N 119°15′W
24 J11 **Shafter** Texas, SW USA 29°49′N 104°18′W
97 L23 **Shaftesbury** S England, United Kingdom 51°01′N 02°12′W
185 F22 **Shag** ≈ South Island, New Zealand
145 V9 **Shagan** ≈ E Kazakhstan
39 O11 **Shageluk** Alaska, USA 62°40′N 159°33′W
122 K14 **Shagonar** Respublika Tyva, S Russian Federation 51°31′N 93°06′E
185 F22 **Shag Point** *headland* South Island, New Zealand 45°28′S 170°50′E
144 J12 **Shagyray, Plato** *plain* SW Kazakhstan
Shāhābād *see* Eslāmābād
168 K9 **Shah Alam** Selangor, Peninsular Malaysia 03°02′N 101°31′E
117 O12 **Shahany, Ozero** ◎ SW Ukraine
138 H9 **Shahbā'** *anc.* Philippopolis. As Suwaydā', S Syria 32°50′N 36°38′E
Shahbān *see* Ad Dayr
149 P17 **Shāh Bandar** Sind, SE Pakistan 23°59′N 67°54′E
149 P13 **Shahdād Kot** Sind, SW Pakistan 27°49′N 67°49′E
143 T10 **Shahdād, Namakzār-e** *salt pan* E Iran
149 Q15 **Shāhdādpur** Sind, SE Pakistan 25°56′N 68°40′E
154 K10 **Shahdol** Madhya Pradesh, C India 23°19′N 81°26′E
161 N7 **Sha He** ≈ C China
Shahe *see* Linze
Shahepu *see* Linze
153 N13 **Shāhganj** Uttar Pradesh, N India 26°03′N 82°41′E
152 C11 **Shāhgarh** Rājasthān, NW India 27°08′N 69°56′E
Sha Hi *see* Orūmīyeh, Daryācheh-ye
Shāhī *see* Qā'emshahr
Shahjahanabad *see* Delhi
152 L11 **Shāhjahānpur** Uttar Pradesh, N India 27°53′N 79°55′E
149 U7 **Shāhpur** Punjab, E Pakistan 32°15′N 72°32′E
Shāhpur *see* Shāhpur Chākar
152 G13 **Shāhpura** Rājasthān, N India 25°38′N 75°01′E
149 Q15 **Shāhpur Chākar** *var.* Shāhpur. Sind, SE Pakistan 26°11′N 68°44′E
148 M5 **Shahrak** Ghowr, C Afghanistan 34°09′N 64°16′E
143 Q11 **Shahr-e Bābak** Kermān, C Iran 30°08′N 55°04′E
143 N8 **Shahr-e Kord** *var.* Shahr Kord. Chahār Maḩall va Bakhtīārī, C Iran 32°20′N 50°52′E
143 O9 **Shahreẕā** *var.* Qomisheh, Qumisheh, Shahriza; *prev.* Qomsheh. Eşfahān, C Iran 32°01′N 51°51′E

◆ Country
● Country Capital
◇ Dependent Territory
○ Dependent Territory Capital
◈ Administrative Regions
✈ International Airport
▲ Mountain
▲▲ Mountain Range
Ѧ Volcano
≈ River
◎ Lake
⊠ Reservoir

SHAHRIKHON – SHŌDO-SHIMA

147 S10 Shahrikhon Rus. Shakhrikhan. Andijon Viloyati, E Uzbekistan 40°42′N 72°03′E
147 P11 Shahriston Rus. Shakhristan. NW Tajikistan 39°45′N 68°47′E
Shahriza see Shahreẓā
Shahr-i-Zabul see Zābol
Shahr Kord see Shahr-e Kord
147 P14 Shahrtuz Rus. Shaartuz. SW Tajikistan 37°13′N 68°05′E
143 Q4 Shāhrūd prev. Emāmrūd, Emāmshahr. Semnān, N Iran 36°30′N 55°E
Shahsavār/Shahsawar see Tonekābon
Shaidara see Step' Nardara
Shaikh Ābid see Shaykh 'Ābid
Shaikh Fāris see Shaykh Fāris
Shaikh Najm see Shaykh Najm
138 K5 Shā'īr, Jabal ▲ C Syria 34°51′N 37°49′E
154 G10 Shājāpur Madhya Pradesh, C India 23°27′N 76°21′E
80 J8 Shakal, Ras headland NE Sudan 18°04′N 38°34′E
83 G17 Shakawe North West, NW Botswana 18°25′S 21°53′E
Shakhdarinskiy Khrebet see Shokhdara, Qatorkŭhi
Shakhrikhan see Shahrikhon
Shakhrisabz see Sharixon
Shakhristan see Shahriston
Shakhtërsk see Shakmars'k
145 R10 Shakhtinsk Karaganda, C Kazakhstan 49°40′N 72°37′E
126 L11 Shakhty Rostovskaya Oblast', SW Russian Federation 47°45′N 40°14′E
127 P2 Shakhun'ya Nizhegorodskaya Oblast', W Russian Federation 57°42′N 46°36′E
77 S15 Shaki Oyo, W Nigeria 08°37′N 03°25′E
81 J15 Shakiso Oromīya, C Ethiopia 05°33′N 38°48′E
117 X8 Shakmars'k Rus. Shakhtërsk. Donets'ka Oblast', SE Ukraine 48°02′N 38°18′E
29 V9 Shakopee Minnesota, N USA 44°48′N 93°31′W
165 R3 Shakotan-misaki headland Hokkaidō, NE Japan 43°22′N 140°28′E
39 N9 Shaktoolik Alaska, USA 64°19′N 161°05′W
81 J14 Shala Hāyk' ◎ C Ethiopia
124 M10 Shalakusha Arkhangel'skaya Oblast', NW Russian Federation 62°16′N 40°16′E
145 U8 Shalday Pavlodar, NE Kazakhstan 51°57′N 78°51′E
127 P16 Shali Chechenskaya Respublika, SW Russian Federation 43°03′N 45°55′E
141 W12 Shalīm var. Shelim. S Oman 18°07′N 55°39′E
Shaliuhe see Gangca
144 K12 Shalkar var. Chelkar. Aktyubinsk, W Kazakhstan 47°50′N 59°29′E
144 F9 Shalkar, Ozero prev. Chelkar Ozero. ◎ W Kazakhstan
21 V12 Shallotte North Carolina, SE USA 33°58′N 78°21′W
25 N5 Shallowater Texas, SW USA 33°41′N 102°00′W
124 K11 Shal'skiy Respublika Kareliya, NW Russian Federation 61°45′N 36°02′E
160 F9 Shaluli Shan ▲▲ C China
81 F22 Shama ≈ C Tanzania
11 Z11 Shamattawa Manitoba, C Canada 55°52′N 92°05′W
12 F8 Shamattawa ≈ Ontario, C Canada
Shām, Bādiyat ash see Syrian Desert
Shamiya see Ash Shāmīyah
141 X8 Shām, Jabal ash var. Jebel Sham. ▲ NW Oman 23°21′N 57°08′E
Sham, Jebel see Shām, Jabal ash
Shamkhor see Şämkir
18 G14 Shamokin Pennsylvania, NE USA 40°47′N 76°33′W
25 P2 Shamrock Texas, SW USA 35°12′N 100°15′W
Shana see Kuril'sk
Sha'nabī, Jabal ash see Chambi, Jebel
139 Y12 Shanāwah Al Başrah, E Iraq 30°57′N 47°25′E
Shancheng see Taining
159 T8 Shandan var. Qingyuan. Gansu, N China 38°50′N 101°08′E
Shandī see Shendi
161 Q5 Shandong var. Lu, Shandong Sheng, Shantung. ◈ province E China
161 R4 Shandong Bandao var. Shantung Peninsula. peninsula E China
Shandong Sheng see Shandong
139 U8 Shandrūkh Diyālá, E Iraq 33°20′N 45°19′E
83 J17 Shangani ≈ W Zimbabwe
161 O15 Shangchuan Dao island S China
Shangchuankou see Minhe
163 P12 Shangdu Nei Mongol Zizhiqu, N China 41°32′N 113°33′E
161 O11 Shanggao var. Aoyang. Jiangxi, S China 28°16′N 114°55′E
Shangguan see Daixian
161 S8 Shanghai var. Shang-hai. Shanghai Shi, E China 31°14′N 121°28′E
161 S8 Shanghai Shi var. Hu, Shanghai. ◈ municipality E China
161 P13 Shanghang var. Linjiang. Fujian, SE China 25°03′N 116°25′E
160 K14 Shanglin var. Dafeng. Guangxi Zhuangzu Zizhiqu, S China 23°26′N 108°32′E
160 L7 Shangluo prev. Shangxian, Shangzhou. Shaanxi, C China 33°51′N 109°55′E
83 G15 Shangombo Western, W Zambia 16°28′S 22°10′E
Shangpai/Shangpaihe see Feixi
161 O6 Shangqiu var. Zhuji. Henan, C China 34°24′N 115°37′E
161 Q10 Shangrao Jiangxi, S China 28°27′N 117°57′E
Shangxian see Shangluo
161 S9 Shangyu var. Baiguan. Zhejiang, SE China 30°03′N 120°52′E
163 X9 Shangzhi Heilongjiang, NE China 45°13′N 127°59′E
Shangzhou see Shangluo
Shanhe see Zhengning
163 W9 Shanhetun Heilongjiang, NE China 44°42′N 127°12′E
Shan-hsi see Shaanxi, China
Shan-hsi see Shanxi, China
159 O6 Shankou Xinjiang Uygur Zizhiqu, W China 42°02′N 94°08′E
184 M13 Shannon Manawatu-Wanganui, North Island, New Zealand 40°32′S 175°24′E
97 C17 Shannon Ir. An tSionainn. ≈ W Ireland
97 B19 Shannon ✕ W Ireland 52°42′N 08°57′W
167 N6 Shan Plateau plateau E Burma (Myanmar)
158 M6 Shanshan var. Piqan. Xinjiang Uygur Zizhiqu, NW China 42°53′N 90°18′E
Shansi see Shanxi
167 N5 Shan State ◈ state E Burma (Myanmar)
Shantar Islands see Shantarskiye Ostrova
123 S12 Shantarskiye Ostrova Eng. Shantar Islands. island group E Russian Federation
161 Q14 Shantou var. Shan-t'ou, Swatow. Guangdong, S China 23°23′N 116°39′E
Shan-t'ou see Shantou
Shantung see Shandong
Shantung Peninsula see Shandong Bandao
161 O15 Shanwei Guangdong, China 22°28′N 115°13′E
163 O14 Shanxi var. Jin, Shan-hsi, Shansi, Shanxi Sheng. ◈ province C China
161 P6 Shanxian var. Shan Xian. Shandong, E China 34°51′N 116°09′E
Shan Xian see Sanmenxia
Shan Xian see Shanxian
Shanxi Sheng see Shanxi
160 L7 Shanyang Shaanxi, C China 33°35′N 109°48′E
161 N13 Shanyin var. Daiyue. Shanxi, C China E Asia 39°30′N 112°56′E
161 O13 Shaoguan var. Shao-kuan, Cant. Kukong; prev. Ch'ü-chiang. Guangdong, S China 24°57′N 113°38′E
Shao-kuan see Shaoguan
161 Q11 Shaowu Fujian, SE China 27°24′N 117°26′E
161 S9 Shaoxing Zhejiang, SE China 30°02′N 120°35′E
160 M11 Shaoyang var. Baoqing, Shao-yang; prev. Pao-king. Hunan, S China 27°13′N 111°31′E
160 M12 Shaoyang var. Tangdukou. Hunan, S China 26°54′N 111°14′E
Shao-yang see Shaoyang
96 K5 Shapinsay island NE Scotland, United Kingdom
125 S4 Shapkina ≈ NW Russian Federation
Shāpūr see Salmās
158 M4 Shaqiuhe Xinjiang Uygur Zizhiqu, W China 45°00′N 88°52′E
139 T2 Shaqlāwa var. Shaqlāwah. Arbīl, E Iraq 36°24′N 44°21′E
Shaqlāwah see Shaqlāwa
138 I8 Shaqqā As Suwaydā', S Syria 32°53′N 36°42′E
141 P7 Shaqrā' Ar Riyāḑ, C Saudi Arabia 25°11′N 45°08′E
Shaqrā see Shuqrah
145 W10 Shar var. Charsk. Vostochnyy Kazakhstan, E Kazakhstan 49°33′N 81°03′E
149 O6 Sharan Dāykondī, SE Afghanistan 33°28′N 66°19′E
149 Q7 Sharan var. Zareh Sharan. Paktīkā, E Afghanistan 33°08′N 68°47′E
Sharaqpur see Sharqpur
Sharbaqty see Shcherbakty
141 X12 Sharbatāt S Oman 17°57′N 56°14′E
Sharbatāt, Ra's see Sharbithāt, Ras
141 X12 Sharbithāt, Ras var. Ra's Sharbatāt. headland S Oman 17°55′N 56°30′E
14 K14 Sharbot Lake Ontario, SE Canada 44°45′N 76°46′W
145 P17 Shardara var. Chardara. Yuzhnyy Kazakhstan, S Kazakhstan 41°15′N 68°01′E
Shardara Dalasy see Step' Nardara
162 F8 Sharga Govĭ-Altay, W Mongolia 46°16′N 95°32′E
Sharga see Tsagaan-Uul
116 M7 Sharhorod Vinnyts'ka Oblast', C Ukraine 48°46′N 28°05′E
Sharhulsan see Mandal-Ovoo
165 V3 Shari Hokkaidō, NE Japan 43°54′N 144°42′E
Shari see Chari
139 T6 Shārī, Buḩayrat ◎ C Iraq
147 N12 Sharixon Rus. Shakhrisabz. Qashqadaryo Viloyati, S Uzbekistan 39°01′N 66°45′E
Sharjah see Ash Shāriqah
118 K12 Sharkawshchyna var. Sharkowshchyna, Pol. Szarkowszczyzna, Rus. Sharkovshchina. Vitsyebskaya Voblasts', NW Belarus 55°27′N 27°28′E
180 G9 Shark Bay bay Western Australia
141 Y9 Sharkh E Oman 21°20′N 59°04′E
Sharkovshchina/Sharkowshchyna see Sharkawshchyna
127 U6 Sharlyk Orenburgskaya Oblast', W Russian Federation 52°52′N 54°45′E
75 Y9 Sharm ash Shaykh var. Ofiral, Sharm el Sheikh. E Egypt 27°51′N 34°16′E
Sharm el Sheikh see Sharm ash Shaykh
18 B13 Sharon Pennsylvania, NE USA 41°12′N 80°28′W
26 H4 Sharon Springs Kansas, C USA 38°54′N 101°46′W
31 Q14 Sharonville Ohio, N USA 39°16′N 84°24′W
Sharourah see Sharūrah
29 O10 Sharpe, Lake ⊞ South Dakota, N USA
Sharqī, Al Jabal ash/Sharqi, Jebel esh see Anti-Lebanon
Sharqīyah, Al Minṭaqah ash see Ash Sharqīyah
138 I6 Sharqīyat an Nabk, Jabal ▲ W Syria
149 W8 Sharqpur var. Sharaqpur. Punjab, E Pakistan 31°29′N 74°08′E
141 Q13 Sharūrah var. Sharourah. Najrān, S Saudi Arabia 17°29′N 47°05′E
125 O14 Shar'ya Kostromskaya Oblast', NW Russian Federation 58°22′N 45°30′E
145 V15 Sharyn var. Charyn. ≈ SE Kazakhstan
Sharyn see Charyn
122 K13 Sharypovo Krasnoyarskiy Kray, C Russian Federation 55°33′N 89°12′E
83 J18 Shashe Central, NE Botswana 21°25′S 27°28′E
83 J18 Shashe var. Shashi. ≈ Botswana/Zimbabwe
81 J14 Shashemenē var. Shashemenne, Shashhamana, It. Sciasciamana. Oromīya, C Ethiopia 07°16′N 38°38′E
Shashemenne/Shashhamana see Shashemenē
Shashi see Shashe
Shashi/Sha-shih/Shasi see Jingzhou, Hubei
35 N3 Shasta Lake ⊞ California, W USA
35 N2 Shasta, Mount ▲ California, W USA 41°24′N 122°11′W
127 O4 Shatki Nizhegorodskaya Oblast', W Russian Federation 55°09′N 44°04′E
Shatlyk see Şatlyk
Shatra see Ash Shaṭrah
119 K17 Shatsk Minskaya Voblasts', C Belarus 53°25′N 27°41′E
127 N5 Shatsk Ryazanskaya Oblast', W Russian Federation 54°02′N 41°38′E
26 J9 Shattuck Oklahoma, C USA 36°16′N 99°52′W
145 P16 Shaul'der Yuzhnyy Kazakhstan, S Kazakhstan 42°45′N 68°21′E
11 S17 Shaunavon Saskatchewan, S Canada 49°49′N 108°25′W
Shavat see Shovot
Shaviyani Atoll see North Miladhunmadulu Atoll
158 K4 Shawan var. Sandaohezi. Xinjiang Uygur Zizhiqu, NW China 44°21′N 85°37′E
14 G12 Shawanaga Ontario, S Canada 45°29′N 80°16′W
30 M6 Shawano Wisconsin, N USA 44°46′N 88°38′W
30 M6 Shawano Lake ◎ Wisconsin, N USA
15 P10 Shawinigan prev. Shawinigan Falls. Québec, SE Canada 46°33′N 72°45′W
Shawinigan Falls see Shawinigan
15 P10 Shawinigan-Sud Québec, SE Canada 46°30′N 72°43′W
138 J5 Shawmarīyah, Jabal ash ▲ C Syria
27 O11 Shawnee Oklahoma, C USA 35°20′N 96°55′W
14 K12 Shawville Québec, SE Canada 45°37′N 76°31′W
145 Q16 Shayan var. Chayan. Yuzhnyy Kazakhstan, S Kazakhstan 42°59′N 69°22′E
Shaykh see Ash Shakk
139 W9 Shaykh 'Ābid var. Shaikh Ābid. Wāsiţ, E Iraq 32°40′N 46°09′E
139 Y10 Shaykh Fāris var. Shaikh Fāris. Maysān, E Iraq 32°06′N 47°39′E
139 T7 Shaykh Ḩātim Baghdād, E Iraq 33°29′N 44°15′E
Shaykh, Jabal ash see Hermon, Mount
139 X10 Shaykh Najm var. Shaikh Najm. Maysān, E Iraq 32°04′N 46°54′E
139 W9 Shaykh Sa'd Maysān, E Iraq 32°35′N 46°16′E
147 T14 Shazud SE Tajikistan 37°45′N 72°22′E
119 N18 Shchadryn Rus. Shchedrin. Homyel'skaya Voblasts', SE Belarus 52°53′N 29°33′E
119 H18 Shchara ≈ SW Belarus
Shchedrin see Shchadryn
Shcheglovsk see Kemerovo
126 K5 Shchëkino Tul'skaya Oblast', W Russian Federation 53°57′N 37°33′E
125 S7 Shchel'yayur Respublika Komi, NW Russian Federation 65°19′N 53°27′E
145 U8 Shcherbakty Kaz. Sharbaqty. Pavlodar, E Kazakhstan 52°28′N 78°00′E
126 K7 Shchigry Kurskaya Oblast', W Russian Federation 51°53′N 36°49′E
Shchitkovichi see Shchytkavichy
117 Q2 Shchors Chernihivs'ka Oblast', N Ukraine 51°49′N 31°58′E
117 T8 Shchors'k Dnipropetrovs'ka Oblast', E Ukraine 48°20′N 34°07′E
Shchuchin see Shchuchyn
145 Q7 Shchuchinsk prev. Shchuchye. Akmola, N Kazakhstan 52°57′N 70°10′E
Shchuchye see Shchuchinsk
119 G16 Shchuchyn Pol. Szczuczyn Nowogródzki, Rus. Shchuchin. Hrodzyenskaya Voblasts', W Belarus 53°36′N 24°45′E
119 K17 Shchytkavichy Rus. Shchitkovichi. Minskaya Voblasts', C Belarus 53°13′N 27°59′E
122 J13 Shebalino Respublika Altay, S Russian Federation 51°16′N 85°41′E
126 J9 Shebekino Belgorodskaya Oblast', W Russian Federation 50°25′N 36°55′E
Shebelē Wenz, Wabē see Shebeli
81 L14 Shebeli Amh. Wabē Shebelē Wenz, It. Scebeli, Som. Webi Shabeelle. ≈ Ethiopia/Somalia
113 M20 Shebenikut, Maja e ▲ E Albania 41°13′N 20°27′E
149 N2 Sheberghān var. Shibarghān, Shiberghan, Shiberghān. Jowzjān, N Afghanistan 36°41′N 65°45′E
144 F14 Shebir Mangistau, SW Kazakhstan 44°52′N 52°01′E
31 N8 Sheboygan Wisconsin, N USA 43°46′N 87°44′W
77 X15 Shebshi Mountains var. Schebschi Mountains. ▲▲ E Nigeria
Shechem see Nablus
Shedadi see Ash Shadādah
13 P14 Shediac New Brunswick, SE Canada 46°13′N 64°35′W
126 L15 Shedok Krasnodarskiy Kray, SW Russian Federation 44°12′N 40°49′E
80 N12 Sheekh Togdheer, N Somalia 10°01′N 45°21′E
38 M11 Sheenjek River ≈ Alaska, USA
96 D13 Sheep Haven Ir. Cuan na gCaorach. inlet N Ireland
35 X10 Sheep Range ▲▲ Nevada, W USA
98 M13 's-Heerenberg Gelderland, E Netherlands 51°52′N 06°15′E
97 P22 Sheerness SE England, United Kingdom 51°27′N 00°45′E
13 Q15 Sheet Harbour Nova Scotia, SE Canada 44°56′N 62°31′W
185 H18 Sheffield Canterbury, South Island, New Zealand 43°22′S 172°01′E
97 M18 Sheffield N England, United Kingdom 53°23′N 01°30′W
23 O2 Sheffield Alabama, S USA 34°46′N 87°42′W
29 V12 Sheffield Iowa, C USA 42°53′N 93°13′W
25 N10 Sheffield Texas, SW USA 30°42′N 101°49′W
63 H22 Shehuen, Río ≈ S Argentina
Shekhem see Nablus
149 V8 Shekhūpura Punjab, NE Pakistan 31°42′N 74°08′E
Sheki see Şäki
124 L14 Sheksna Vologodskaya Oblast', NW Russian Federation 59°11′N 38°32′E
123 T5 Shelagskiy, Mys headland NE Russian Federation 70°04′N 170°39′E
27 V3 Shelbina Missouri, C USA 39°41′N 92°02′W
13 P16 Shelburne Nova Scotia, SE Canada 43°47′N 65°20′W
14 G14 Shelburne Ontario, S Canada 44°04′N 80°12′W
33 R7 Shelby Montana, NW USA 48°30′N 111°52′W
21 Q10 Shelby North Carolina, SE USA 35°15′N 81°34′W
31 S12 Shelby Ohio, N USA 40°52′N 82°39′W
30 L14 Shelbyville Illinois, N USA 39°24′N 88°47′W
31 P14 Shelbyville Indiana, N USA 39°31′N 85°46′W
20 L5 Shelbyville Kentucky, S USA 38°13′N 85°12′W
27 V2 Shelbyville Missouri, C USA 39°48′N 92°01′W
20 J10 Shelbyville Tennessee, S USA 35°29′N 86°30′W
25 X8 Shelbyville Texas, SW USA 31°42′N 94°03′W
30 L14 Shelbyville, Lake ⊞ Illinois, N USA
29 S12 Sheldon Iowa, C USA 43°10′N 95°51′W
38 M11 Sheldons Point Alaska, USA 62°31′N 165°03′W
Shelek see Chilik
Shelekhov Gulf see Shelikhova, Zaliv
123 U9 Shelikhova, Zaliv Eng. Shelekhov Gulf. gulf E Russian Federation
39 P14 Shelikof Strait strait Alaska, USA
Shelim see Shalīm
11 T14 Shellbrook Saskatchewan, S Canada 53°14′N 106°24′W
28 L3 Shell Creek ≈ North Dakota, N USA
Shellif see Chelif, Oued
22 I10 Shell Keys island group Louisiana, S USA
30 I4 Shell Lake Wisconsin, N USA 45°44′N 91°56′W
29 W12 Shell Rock Iowa, C USA 42°42′N 92°34′W
185 C26 Shelter Point headland Stewart Island, New Zealand 47°04′S 168°13′E
18 L13 Shelton Connecticut, NE USA 41°19′N 73°06′W
32 G8 Shelton Washington, NW USA 47°13′N 123°06′W
Shemakha see Şamaxı
145 W9 Shemonaikha Vostochnyy Kazakhstan, E Kazakhstan 50°38′N 81°55′E
127 Q4 Shemursha Chuvashskaya Respublika, W Russian Federation 54°57′N 47°27′E
38 D16 Shemya Island island Aleutian Islands, Alaska, USA
29 T16 Shenandoah Iowa, C USA 40°46′N 95°23′W
21 U4 Shenandoah Virginia, NE USA 38°26′N 78°34′W
21 U4 Shenandoah Mountains ridge West Virginia, NE USA
21 V3 Shenandoah River ≈ West Virginia, NE USA
77 W15 Shendam Plateau, C Nigeria 08°52′N 09°30′E
80 G8 Shendi var. Shandī. River Nile, NE Sudan 16°41′N 33°22′E
76 I15 Shenge SW Sierra Leone 07°54′N 12°54′W
146 L10 Shengeldi Rus. Chingildi. Navoiy Viloyati, N Uzbekistan 40°59′N 64°13′E
145 U15 Shengel'dy Almaty, SE Kazakhstan 44°04′N 77°31′E
113 K18 Shëngjin var. Shëngjini. Lezhë, NW Albania 41°49′N 19°34′E
Shëngjini see Shëngjin
Shengking see Liaoning
Sheng Xian/Shengxian see Shengzhou
161 S9 Shengzhou var. Shengxian, Sheng Xian. Zhejiang, SE China 29°36′N 120°42′E
Shenking see Liaoning
125 N11 Shenkursk Arkhangel'skaya Oblast', NW Russian Federation 62°10′N 42°58′E
160 L3 Shenmu Shaanxi, C China 38°49′N 110°27′E
113 L19 Shën Noj i Madh ▲ C Albania 41°23′N 20°07′E
160 L8 Shennong Ding ▲ C China 31°24′N 110°16′E
Shenshi/Shensi see Shaanxi
163 V12 Shenyang Chin. Shen-yang, Eng. Moukden, Mukden; prev. Fengtien. province capital Liaoning, NE China 41°50′N 123°26′E
Shen-yang see Shenyang
161 O15 Shenzhen Guangdong, S China 22°39′N 114°02′E
154 G8 Sheopur Madhya Pradesh, C India 25°41′N 76°42′E
116 L5 Shepetivka Rus. Shepetovka. Khmel'nyts'ka Oblast', NW Ukraine 50°12′N 27°01′E
Shepetovka see Shepetivka
25 W10 Shepherd Texas, SW USA 30°30′N 95°00′W
187 R14 Shepherd Islands island group C Vanuatu
20 K5 Shepherdsville Kentucky, S USA 38°00′N 85°42′W
183 O11 Shepparton Victoria, SE Australia 36°25′S 145°26′E
97 P22 Sheppey, Isle of island SE England, United Kingdom
Sherabad see Sherobod
9 O4 Sherard, Cape headland Nunavut, N Canada 74°36′N 80°10′W
97 L23 Sherborne S England, United Kingdom 50°58′N 02°30′W
76 H16 Sherbro Island island SW Sierra Leone
15 Q12 Sherbrooke Québec, SE Canada 45°23′N 71°55′W
29 T11 Sherburn Minnesota, N USA 43°39′N 94°43′W
78 H6 Sherda Borkou-Ennedi-Tibesti, N Chad 20°04′N 16°48′E
80 G7 Shereik River Nile, N Sudan 18°44′N 33°37′E
126 K3 Sheremet'yevo ✕ (Moskva) Moskovskaya Oblast', W Russian Federation 56°05′N 37°10′E
153 P14 Sherghāti Bihār, N India 24°35′N 84°51′E
27 U12 Sheridan Arkansas, C USA 34°18′N 92°22′W
33 W12 Sheridan Wyoming, C USA 44°47′N 106°59′W
182 G8 Sheringa South Australia 33°51′S 135°13′E
25 U5 Sherman Texas, SW USA 33°39′N 96°35′W
194 J10 Sherman Island island Antarctica
19 S4 Sherman Mills Maine, NE USA 45°51′N 68°23′W
29 O15 Sherman Reservoir ⊞ Nebraska, C USA
147 N14 Sherobod Rus. Sherabad. Surkhondaryo Viloyati, S Uzbekistan 37°43′N 66°59′E
147 O13 Sherobod Rus. Sherabad. ≈ S Uzbekistan
153 T14 Sherpur Dhaka, N Bangladesh 25°00′N 90°01′E
37 T4 Sherrelwood Colorado, C USA 39°49′N 105°00′W
99 J14 's-Hertogenbosch Fr. Bois-le-Duc, Ger. Herzogenbusch. Noord-Brabant, S Netherlands 51°41′N 05°19′E
28 M2 Sherwood North Dakota, N USA 48°55′N 101°36′W
11 Q14 Sherwood Park Alberta, SW Canada 53°34′N 113°04′W
56 F13 Sheshea, Río ≈ E Peru
143 T5 Sheshtamad Khorāsān-Razavī, NE Iran 36°03′N 57°45′E
29 S10 Shetek, Lake ◎ Minnesota, N USA
96 M2 Shetland Islands island group NE Scotland, United Kingdom
144 F14 Shetpe Mangistau, SW Kazakhstan 44°06′N 52°03′E
154 C11 Shetrunji ≈ W India
Shevchenko see Aktau
117 W5 Shevchenkove Kharkivs'ka Oblast', E Ukraine 49°40′N 37°13′E
81 H14 Shewa Gīmīra Southern Nationalities, S Ethiopia 07°12′N 35°49′E
161 Q9 Shexian var. Huicheng, She Xian. Anhui, E China 29°53′N 118°27′E
She Xian see Shexian
161 R6 Sheyang prev. Hede. Jiangsu, E China 33°49′N 120°13′E
29 O4 Sheyenne North Dakota, N USA 47°49′N 99°08′W
29 P4 Sheyenne ≈ North Dakota, N USA
96 G7 Shiant Islands island group NW Scotland, United Kingdom
123 U12 Shiashkotan, Ostrov island Kuril'skiye Ostrova, SE Russian Federation
31 R9 Shiawassee River ≈ Michigan, N USA
141 R14 Shibām C Yemen 15°49′N 48°24′E
Shibarghān see Sheberghān
165 O10 Shibata var. Sibata. Niigata, Honshū, C Japan 37°57′N 139°20′E
Shiberghan/Shiberghān see Sheberghān
Shibh Jazīrat Sīnā' see Sinai
75 W8 Shibīn al Kawm var. Shibîn el Kôm. N Egypt 30°33′N 31°00′E
Shibîn el Kôm see Shibīn al Kawm
143 O13 Shīb, Kūh-e ▲ S Iran
12 D8 Shibogama Lake ◎ Ontario, C Canada
Shibotsu-jima see Zelënyy, Ostrov
164 B16 Shibushi Kagoshima, Kyūshū, SW Japan 31°27′N 131°05′E
189 U13 Shichiyo Islands island group Chuuk, C Micronesia
Shickshock Mountains see Chic-Chocs, Monts
145 S8 Shiderti var. Shiderty. Pavlodar, NE Kazakhstan 51°40′N 74°50′E
145 S9 Shiderti ≈ N Kazakhstan
Shiderty see Shiderti
Shieli see Chiili
96 G10 Shiel, Loch ◎ N Scotland, United Kingdom
164 J13 Shiga off. Shiga-ken, var. Siga. ◈ prefecture Honshū, SW Japan
Shiga-ken see Shiga
Shigatse see Xigazê
141 U13 Shiḩan oasis NE Yemen
Shih-chia-chuang/Shihmen see Shijiazhuang
158 K4 Shihezi Xinjiang Uygur Zizhiqu, NW China 44°21′N 85°59′E
Shiichi see Shyichy
113 K19 Shijak var. Shijaku. Durrës, W Albania 41°21′N 19°34′E
Shijaku see Shijak
161 O4 Shijiazhuang var. Shih-chia-chuang; prev. Shihmen. province capital Hebei, E China 38°04′N 114°28′E
165 R5 Shikabe Hokkaidō, NE Japan 42°03′N 140°45′E
149 Q13 Shikārpur Sind, S Pakistan 27°59′N 68°39′E
127 Q7 Shikhany Saratovskaya Oblast', W Russian Federation 52°07′N 47°13′E
189 V12 Shiki Islands island group Chuuk, C Micronesia
164 G14 Shikoku var. Sikoku. island SW Japan
192 H5 Shikoku Basin var. Sikoku Basin. undersea feature N Philippine Sea 28°00′N 137°00′E
164 G14 Shikoku-sanchi ▲▲ Shikoku, SW Japan
165 X4 Shikotan, Ostrov Jap. Shikotan-tō. island NE Russian Federation
Shikotan-tō see Shikotan, Ostrov
165 R4 Shikotsu-ko var. Sikotu Ko. ◎ Hokkaidō, NE Japan
81 N15 Shilabo Sumalē, E Ethiopia 06°05′N 44°48′E
127 X7 Shil'da Orenburgskaya Oblast', W Russian Federation 51°46′N 59°48′E
139 V3 Shilēr, Āw-e ≈ E Iraq
153 S12 Shiliguri prev. Siliguri. West Bengal, NE India 26°46′N 88°24′E
Shiliu see Changjiang
129 V7 Shilka ≈ S Russian Federation
18 H15 Shillington Pennsylvania, NE USA 40°18′N 75°57′W
153 V13 Shillong state capital Meghālaya, NE India 25°37′N 91°54′E
126 M5 Shilovo Ryazanskaya Oblast', W Russian Federation 54°18′N 40°53′E
164 C14 Shimabara var. Simabara. Nagasaki, Kyūshū, SW Japan 32°48′N 130°20′E
164 C14 Shimabara-wan bay SW Japan
164 F12 Shimane off. Shimane-ken, var. Simane. ◈ prefecture Honshū, SW Japan
164 G11 Shimane-hantō peninsula Honshū, SW Japan
Shimane-ken see Shimane
123 Q13 Shimanovsk Amurskaya Oblast', SE Russian Federation 52°00′N 127°36′E
Shimanto see Nakamura
Shimbir Berris see Shimbiris
80 O12 Shimbiris var. Shimbir Berris. ▲ N Somalia 10°43′N 47°10′E
165 T4 Shimizu Hokkaidō, NE Japan 42°58′N 142°54′E
164 M14 Shimizu var. Simizu. Shizuoka, Honshū, S Japan 35°01′N 138°29′E
152 I8 Shimla prev. Simla. state capital Himāchal Pradesh, N India 31°07′N 77°09′E
165 N14 Shimoda var. Simoda. Shizuoka, Honshū, S Japan 34°40′N 138°55′E
165 O13 Shimodate var. Simodate. Ibaraki, Honshū, S Japan 36°20′N 140°00′E
155 F18 Shimoga Karnātaka, W India 13°56′N 75°31′E
164 C15 Shimo-jima island SW Japan
164 B15 Shimo-Koshiki-jima island SW Japan
81 J21 Shimoni Coast, S Kenya 04°40′S 39°22′E
164 D13 Shimonoseki var. Simonoseki, hist. Akamagaseki, Bakan. Yamaguchi, Honshū, SW Japan 33°57′N 130°54′E
124 G14 Shimsk Novgorodskaya Oblast', NW Russian Federation 58°12′N 30°43′E
141 W7 Shināş N Oman 24°45′N 56°24′E
148 J6 Shīndand Herāt, W Afghanistan 33°19′N 62°09′E
Shinei see Hsinying
162 H10 Shinejinst var. Dzalaa. Bayanhongor, C Mongolia 44°29′N 99°19′E
25 T12 Shiner Texas, SW USA 29°25′N 97°10′W
167 N1 Shingbwiyang Kachin State, N Burma (Myanmar) 26°40′N 96°14′E
145 W11 Shingozha Vostochnyy Kazakhstan, E Kazakhstan 47°46′N 80°38′E
164 J15 Shingū var. Singû. Wakayama, Honshū, SW Japan 33°41′N 135°57′E
14 F8 Shining Tree Ontario, S Canada 47°36′N 81°12′W
165 P9 Shinjō var. Sinzyô. Yamagata, Honshū, C Japan 38°47′N 140°17′E
96 I7 Shin, Loch ◎ N Scotland, United Kingdom
21 S3 Shinnston West Virginia, NE USA 39°22′N 80°19′W
138 I6 Shinshār Fr. Chinnchâr. Ḩimş, W Syria 34°36′N 36°45′E
Shinshū see Chinju
165 T4 Shintoku Hokkaidō, NE Japan 43°03′N 142°50′E
81 G20 Shinyanga Shinyanga, NW Tanzania 03°40′S 33°25′E
81 G20 Shinyanga ◈ region N Tanzania
165 Q10 Shiogama var. Siogama. Miyagi, Honshū, C Japan 38°19′N 141°00′E
164 M12 Shiojiri var. Sioziri. Nagano, Honshū, S Japan 36°08′N 137°58′E
164 I15 Shiono-misaki headland Honshū, SW Japan 33°25′N 135°45′E
165 Q12 Shioya-zaki headland Honshū, C Japan 37°00′N 140°57′E
114 J9 Shipchenski Prokhod pass C Bulgaria
160 G14 Shiping Yunnan, SW China 23°45′N 102°23′E
13 P13 Shippagan var. Shippegan. New Brunswick, SE Canada 47°45′N 64°44′W
Shippegan see Shippagan
18 F15 Shippensburg Pennsylvania, NE USA 40°03′N 77°31′W
37 P9 Shiprock New Mexico, SW USA 36°47′N 108°41′W
37 O9 Ship Rock ▲ New Mexico, SW USA 36°41′N 108°50′W
15 R6 Shipshaw ≈ Québec, SE Canada
123 V10 Shipunskiy, Mys headland E Russian Federation 53°04′N 159°57′E
160 K7 Shiquan Shaanxi, C China 33°05′N 108°15′E
122 K13 Shira Respublika Khakasiya, S Russian Federation 54°35′N 89°58′E
Shirajganj Ghat see Sirajganj
165 P12 Shirakawa var. Sirakawa. Fukushima, Honshū, C Japan 37°07′N 140°11′E
164 M13 Shirane-san ▲ Honshū, S Japan 35°39′N 138°13′E
165 U14 Shiranuka Hokkaidō, NE Japan 42°57′N 144°01′E
195 N12 Shirase Coast physical region Antarctica
165 U3 Shirataki Hokkaidō, NE Japan 43°55′N 143°14′E
143 O11 Shīrāz var. Shirāz. Fārs, S Iran 29°38′N 52°34′E
83 N15 Shire var. Chire. ≈ Malawi/Mozambique
Shiree see Tsagaanhayrhan
Shireet see Bayandelger
165 W3 Shiretoko-hantō headland Hokkaidō, NE Japan 44°06′N 145°07′E
165 W3 Shiretoko-misaki headland Hokkaidō, NE Japan 44°20′N 145°19′E
127 N5 Shiringushi Respublika Mordoviya, W Russian Federation 53°50′N 42°49′E
148 M3 Shīrīn Tagāb Fāryāb, N Afghanistan 36°49′N 65°01′E
149 N2 Shīrīn Tagāb ≈ N Afghanistan
165 R6 Shiriya-zaki headland Honshū, C Japan 41°24′N 141°27′E
144 I12 Shirkala, Gryada plain W Kazakhstan
165 P10 Shiroishi var. Siroisi. Miyagi, Honshū, C Japan 38°00′N 140°38′E
Shirokoye see Shyroke
165 O10 Shirone var. Sirone. Niigata, Honshū, C Japan 37°46′N 139°00′E
164 L12 Shirotori Gifu, Honshū, SW Japan 35°53′N 136°52′E
197 T1 Shirshov Ridge undersea feature W Bering Sea
Shirshütür/Shirshyutyur, Peski see Şirşütür Gumy
143 T3 Shīrvān var. Shirwān. Khorāsān, NE Iran 37°25′N 57°55′E
Shirwa, Lake see Chilwa, Lake
Shirwān see Shīrvān
159 N5 Shisanjianfang Xinjiang Uygur Zizhiqu, W China 43°10′N 91°15′E
38 M16 Shishaldin Volcano Ѫ Unimak Island, Alaska, USA 54°45′N 163°58′W
Shishchitsy see Shyshchytsy
83 G16 Shishikola North West, N Botswana 18°09′S 23°08′E
38 M8 Shishmaref Alaska, USA 66°15′N 166°04′W
Shisur see Ash Shişar
164 L13 Shitara Aichi, Honshū, SW Japan 35°06′N 137°33′E
152 D12 Shiv Rājasthān, NW India 26°11′N 71°14′E
Shivāji Sāgar see Konya Reservoir
154 H8 Shivpuri Madhya Pradesh, C India 25°28′N 77°41′E
36 J9 Shivwits Plateau plain Arizona, SW USA
Shiwalik Range see Siwalik Range
160 M8 Shiyan Hubei, C China 32°31′N 110°45′E
Shizilu see Junan
160 H13 Shizong var. Danfeng. Yunnan, SW China 24°53′N 104°E
165 R10 Shizugawa Miyagi, Honshū, NE Japan 38°40′N 141°26′E
159 W8 Shizuishan var. Dawukou. Ningxia, N China 39°04′N 106°22′E
165 T5 Shizunai Hokkaidō, NE Japan 42°20′N 142°24′E
165 M14 Shizuoka var. Sizuoka. Shizuoka, Honshū, S Japan 34°59′N 138°20′E
164 M13 Shizuoka off. Shizuoka-ken, var. Sizuoka. ◈ prefecture Honshū, S Japan
Shizuoka-ken see Shizuoka
Shklov see Shklow
119 N15 Shklow Rus. Shklov. Mahilyowskaya Voblasts', E Belarus 54°13′N 30°18′E
113 K18 Shkodër var. Shkodra, It. Scutari, SCr. Skadar. Shkodër, NW Albania 42°03′N 19°31′E
113 K17 Shkodër ◈ district NW Albania
Shkodra see Shkodër
Shkodrës, Liqeni i see Scutari, Lake
113 L20 Shkumbinit, Lumi i var. Shkumbî, Shkumbin. ≈ C Albania
Shkumbi/Shkumbin see Shkumbinit, Lumi i
Shligigh, Cuan see Sligo Bay
122 L4 Shmidta, Ostrov island Severnaya Zemlya, N Russian Federation
183 S10 Shoalhaven River ≈ New South Wales, SE Australia
11 W16 Shoal Lake Manitoba, S Canada 50°28′N 100°36′W
31 O15 Shoals Indiana, N USA 38°40′N 86°47′W
164 I13 Shōdo-shima island SW Japan

◆ Country
● Country Capital
◇ Dependent Territory
○ Dependent Territory Capital
◈ Administrative Regions
✕ International Airport
▲ Mountain
▲▲ Mountain Range
Ѫ Volcano
≈ River
◎ Lake
⊞ Reservoir

Shōka – Sint Eustatius

Shōka see Changhua
122 M5 Shokal'skogo, Proliv strait N Russian Federation
147 T14 Shokhdara, Qatorkŭhi Rus. Shakhdarinskiy Khrebet. ▲▲ SE Tajikistan
145 P15 Sholakkorgan var. Chulakkurgan. Yuzhnyy Kazakhstan, S Kazakhstan 43°45′N 69°10′E
145 N9 Sholaksay Kostanay, N Kazakhstan 51°45′N 64°45′E
Sholāpur see Solāpur
Sholdaneshty see Şoldăneşti
Shonzhy see Chundzha
Shoqpar see Chokpar
155 G21 Shoranūr Kerala, SW India 10°53′N 76°06′E
155 G16 Shorāpur Karnātaka, C India 16°34′N 76°48′E
147 O14 Sho'rchi Rus. Shurchi. Surkhondaryo Viloyati, S Uzbekistan 37°58′N 67°40′E
30 M11 Shorewood Illinois, N USA 41°31′N 88°12′W
Shorkazakhly, Solonchak see Kazakhlyshor, Solonchak
145 Q9 Shortandy Akmola, C Kazakhstan 51°45′N 71°01′E
Shortepa/Shor Tepe see Shūr Tappeh
186 J7 Shortland Island var. Alu. island Shortland Islands, NW Solomon Islands
Shosambetsu see Shosanbetsu
165 S2 Shosanbetsu var. Shosambetsu. Hokkaidō, NE Japan 44°31′N 141°47′E
33 O15 Shoshone Idaho, NW USA 42°56′N 114°24′W
35 T6 Shoshone Mountains ▲▲ Nevada, W USA
33 U12 Shoshone River ≈ Wyoming, C USA
83 I19 Shoshong Central, SE Botswana 23°02′S 26°31′E
33 V14 Shoshoni Wyoming, C USA 43°13′N 108°06′W
Shōshū see Sangju
117 S2 Shostka Sums'ka Oblast', NE Ukraine 51°52′N 33°30′E
185 C21 Shotover ≈ South Island, New Zealand
146 H9 Shovot Rus. Shavat. Xorazm Viloyati, W Uzbekistan 41°41′N 60°13′E
37 N12 Show Low Arizona, SW USA 34°15′N 110°01′W
Show Me State see Missouri
125 O4 Shoyna Nenetskiy Avtonomnyy Okrug, NW Russian Federation 67°50′N 44°09′E
124 M11 Shozhma Arkhangel'skaya Oblast', NW Russian Federation 61°57′N 40°10′E
117 Q7 Shpola Cherkas'ka Oblast', N Ukraine 49°00′N 31°27′E
Shqipëria/Shqipërisë, Republika e see Albania
22 G5 Shreveport Louisiana, S USA 32°32′N 93°45′W
97 K19 Shrewsbury hist. Scrobesbyrig'. W England, United Kingdom 52°43′N 02°45′W
152 D11 Shri Mohangarh prev. Sri Mohangorh. Rājasthān, NW India 27°17′N 71°18′E
153 S16 Shrīrāmpur prev. Serampore, Serampur. West Bengal, NE India 22°44′N 88°20′E
97 K19 Shropshire cultural region W England, United Kingdom
113 N17 Shtime Serb. Štimlje. C Kosovo 42°27′N 21°03′E
145 S16 Shu Kaz. Shū. Zhambyl, SE Kazakhstan 43°34′N 73°41′E
160 G13 Shuangbai var. Tuodian. Yunnan, SW China 24°45′N 101°38′E
163 W9 Shuangcheng Heilongjiang, NE China 45°20′N 126°21′E
Shuangcheng see Zherong
160 E14 Shuangjiang var. Weiyuan. Yunnan, SW China 23°28′N 99°43′E
Shuangjiang see Jiangkou
Shuangjiang see Tongdao
163 U10 Shuangliao var. Zhengjiatun. Jilin, NE China 43°31′N 123°32′E
Shuang-liao see Liaoyuan
Shuangshipu see Fengxian
163 Y7 Shuangyashan var. Shuang-ya-shan. Heilongjiang, NE China 46°37′N 131°10′E
Shuang-ya-shan see Shuangyashan
Shu'aymiah see Shu'aymīyah
141 W12 Shu'aymīyah var. Shu'aymiah. S Oman 17°55′N 55°39′E
144 I10 Shubarkuduk Kaz. Shubarqudyq. Aktyubinsk, W Kazakhstan 49°09′N 56°31′E
Shubarqudyq see Shubarkuduk
145 N12 Shubar-Tengiz, Ozero ◎ C Kazakhstan
39 S5 Shublik Mountains ▲▲ Alaska, USA
Shubrā al Khaymah see Shubrâ el Kheima
121 U13 Shubrâ el Kheima var. Shubrā al Khaymah. N Egypt 30°06′N 31°15′E
158 E8 Shufu var. Tuokezhake. Xinjiang Uygur Zizhiqu, NW China 39°18′N 75°43′E
147 S14 Shughnon, Qatorkŭhi Rus. Shugnanskiy Khrebet. ▲▲ SE Tajikistan
Shugnanskiy Khrebet see Shughnon, Qatorkŭhi
161 Q6 Shu He ≈ E China
Shuicheng see Lupanshui
Shuiding see Huocheng
Shuidong see Dianbai
Shuiji see Laixi
Shū-Ile Taūlary see Chu-Iliyskiye Gory
Shuilocheng see Zhuanglang
Shuiluo see Zhuanglang
149 T10 Shujāābād Punjab, E Pakistan 29°53′N 71°23′E
Shū, Kazakhstan see Shu
Shū, Kazakhstan/Kyrgyzstan see Chu
163 W9 Shulan Jilin, NE China 44°28′N 126°57′E
158 E8 Shule Xinjiang Uygur Zizhiqu, NW China 39°19′N 76°06′E
Shuleh see Shule He
159 Q8 Shule He var. Shuleh, Sulo. ≈ C China
30 K9 Shullsburg Wisconsin, N USA 42°37′N 90°12′W
Shulu see Xinji
39 N16 Shumagin Islands island group Alaska, USA
146 G7 Shumanay Qoraqalpog'iston Respublikasi, W Uzbekistan 42°42′N 58°56′E
114 M8 Shumen Shumen, NE Bulgaria 43°17′N 26°57′E
114 M8 Shumen ◈ province NE Bulgaria
127 P4 Shumerlya Chuvashskaya Respublika, W Russian Federation 55°31′N 46°24′E
122 G11 Shumikha Kurganskaya Oblast', C Russian Federation 55°12′N 63°09′E
118 M12 Shumilina Rus. Shumilino. Vitsyebskaya Voblasts', NE Belarus 55°18′N 29°37′E
Shumilino see Shumilina
123 V11 Shumshu, Ostrov island SE Russian Federation
116 K5 Shums'k Ternopil's'ka Oblast', W Ukraine 50°06′N 26°04′E
Shūnan see Tokuyama
39 O7 Shungnak Alaska, USA 66°53′N 157°08′W
Shunsen see Ch'unch'ŏn
Shuoxian see Shuozhou
161 N3 Shuozhou var. Shuoxian. Shanxi, C China 39°20′N 112°25′E
141 P16 Shuqrah var. Shaqrā. SW Yemen 13°26′N 45°44′E
Shurab see Shŭrob
Shurchi see Sho'rchi
147 R11 Shŭrob Rus. Shurab. NW Tajikistan 40°02′N 70°31′E
143 T10 Shūr, Rūd-e ≈ E Iran
149 O2 Shūr Tappeh var. Shortepa, Shor Tepe. Balkh, N Afghanistan 37°22′N 66°49′E
83 K17 Shurugwi prev. Selukwe. Midlands, C Zimbabwe 19°40′S 30°00′E
142 L8 Shūsh anc. Susa, Bibl. Shushan. Khūzestān, SW Iran 32°12′N 48°20′E
Shushan see Shūsh
142 L9 Shūshtar var. Shustar, Shushter. Khūzestān, SW Iran 32°03′N 48°51′E
Shushter/Shustar see Shūshtar
141 T9 Shuṭfah, Qalamat well E Saudi Arabia
139 V9 Shuwayjah, Hawr ash var. Hawr as Suwayqiyah. ◎ E Iraq
124 M16 Shuya Ivanovskaya Oblast', W Russian Federation 56°51′N 41°24′E
39 Q14 Shuyak Island island Alaska, USA
166 M4 Shwebo Sagaing, C Burma (Myanmar) 22°35′N 95°42′E
166 L7 Shwedaung Bago, W Burma (Myanmar) 18°44′N 95°12′E
166 M7 Shwegyin Bago, SW Burma (Myanmar) 17°56′N 96°59′E
167 N4 Shweli Chin. Longchuan Jiang. ≈ Burma (Myanmar)/China
166 M6 Shwemyo Mandalay, C Burma (Myanmar) 20°04′N 96°13′E
Shyghanaq see Chiganak
Shyghys Qazagastan Oblysy see Vostochnyy Kazakhstan
Shyghys Qongyrat see Vostochno-Kounradskiy
Shyghys Qongyrat see Shygys Konyrat
145 T12 Shygys Konyrat , Kaz. Shyghys Qongyrat. Karaganda, C Kazakhstan 47°01′N 75°05′E
119 M19 Shyichy Rus. Shiichi. Homyel'skaya Voblasts', SE Belarus 52°15′N 29°14′E
145 Q17 Shymkent prev. Chimkent. Yuzhnyy Kazakhstan, S Kazakhstan 42°19′N 69°36′E
Shyngghyrlaū see Chingirlau
152 J5 Shyok Jammu and Kashmir, NW India 34°13′N 78°12′E
117 S9 Shyroke Rus. Shirokoye. Dnipropetrovs'ka Oblast', E Ukraine 47°41′N 33°16′E
117 O9 Shyryayeve Odes'ka Oblast', SW Ukraine 47°21′N 30°11′E
117 S5 Shyshaky Poltavs'ka Oblast', C Ukraine 49°54′N 34°00′E
119 K17 Shyshchytsy Rus. Shishchitsy. Minskaya Voblasts', C Belarus 53°13′N 27°33′E
149 Y3 Siachen Muztāgh ▲▲ NE Pakistan
Siadehan see Tākestān
148 M13 Siāhān Range ▲▲ W Pakistan
142 I1 Sīāh Chashmeh var. Chālderān. Āzarbāyjān-e Gharbī, N Iran 39°02′N 44°22′E
149 W7 Siālkot Punjab, NE Pakistan 32°29′N 74°35′E
186 E7 Sialum Morobe, C Papua New Guinea 06°02′S 147°37′E
Siam see Thailand
Siam, Gulf of see Thailand, Gulf of
Sian see Xi'an
Siang see Brahmaputra
Siangtan see Xiangtan
169 N8 Siantan, Pulau island Kepulauan Anambas, W Indonesia
54 H11 Siare, Río ≈ C Colombia
171 R6 Siargao Island island S Philippines
186 F72 Siassi Umboi Island, C Papua New Guinea 05°34′S 147°50′E
115 D14 Siátista Dytikí Makedonía, N Greece 40°16′N 21°34′E
166 K4 Siatlai Chin State, W Burma (Myanmar) 22°05′N 93°36′E
171 P6 Siaton Negros, C Philippines 09°03′N 123°03′E
171 P6 Siaton Point headland Negros, C Philippines 09°03′N 123°00′E
118 F11 Šiauliai Ger. Schaulen. Šiauliai, N Lithuania 55°55′N 23°21′E
118 E11 Šiauliai ◈ province N Lithuania
171 Q10 Siau, Pulau island N Indonesia
83 J15 Siavonga Southern, SE Zambia 16°33′S 28°42′E
Siazan' see Siyäzän
Sibah see As Sībah
107 N20 Sibari Calabria, S Italy 39°45′N 16°26′E
Sibata see Shibata
127 X6 Sibay Respublika Bashkortostan, W Russian Federation 52°40′N 58°39′E
93 M19 Sibbo Fin. Sipoo. Etelä-Suomi, S Finland 60°22′N 25°20′E
112 D13 Šibenik It. Sebenico. Šibenik-Knin, S Croatia 43°43′N 15°54′E
Sibenik see Šibenik-Knin
112 E13 Šibenik-Knin off. Šibenska Županija, var. Sibenik. ◈ province S Croatia
Šibenik-Knin see Drniš
Šibenska Županija see Šibenik-Knin
Siberia see Sibir'
Siberoet see Siberut, Pulau
168 H12 Siberut, Pulau prev. Siberoet. island Kepulauan Mentawai, W Indonesia
168 I12 Siberut, Selat strait W Indonesia
149 P11 Sibi Baluchistān, SW Pakistan 29°31′N 67°54′E
186 B9 Sibidiri Western, SW Papua New Guinea 08°58′S 142°14′E
123 N10 Sibir' var. Siberia. physical region NE Russian Federation
79 F20 Sibiti Lékoumou, S Congo 03°41′S 13°20′E
81 G21 Sibiti ≈ C Tanzania
116 I12 Sibiu Ger. Hermannstadt, Hung. Nagyszeben. Sibiu, C Romania 45°48′N 24°09′E
116 I11 Sibiu ◈ county C Romania
29 S11 Sibley Iowa, C USA 43°24′N 95°45′W
153 X11 Sibsāgar Assam, NE India 26°59′N 94°38′E
169 R9 Sibu Sarawak, East Malaysia 02°18′N 111°49′E
42 G2 Sibun ≈ E Belize
79 I15 Sibut prev. Fort-Sibut. Kémo, S Central African Republic 05°44′N 19°07′E
171 P4 Sibuyan Island island C Philippines
189 U1 Sibylla Island island N Marshall Islands
11 N16 Sicamous British Columbia, SW Canada 50°49′N 118°52′W
Sichelburger Gerbirge see Gorjanci
167 N14 Sichon var. Ban Sichon, Si Chon. Nakhon Si Thammarat, SW Thailand 09°03′N 99°51′E
Si Chon see Sichon
160 H9 Sichuan var. Chuan, Sichuan Sheng, Ssu-ch'uan, Szechuan, Szechwan. ◈ province C China
160 I9 Sichuan Pendi basin C China
Sichuan Sheng see Sichuan
103 S16 Sicie, Cap headland SE France 43°03′N 05°50′E
107 J24 Sicilia Eng. Sicily; anc. Trinacria. ◈ region Italy, C Mediterranean Sea
107 M24 Sicilia Eng. Sicily; anc. Trinacria. island Italy, C Mediterranean Sea
Sicilian Channel see Sicily, Strait of
107 H24 Sicily, Strait of var. Sicilian Channel. strait C Mediterranean Sea
42 K5 Sico Tinto, Río var. Río Negro. ≈ NE Honduras
57 H16 Sicuani Cusco, S Peru 14°21′S 71°13′W
112 J10 Šid Vojvodina, NW Serbia 45°07′N 19°13′E
115 A15 Sidári Kérkyra, Iónia Nisiá, Greece, C Mediterranean Sea 39°47′N 19°43′E
169 Q11 Sidas Borneo, C Indonesia 0°24′N 109°46′E
98 O5 Siddeburen Groningen, NE Netherlands 53°15′N 06°52′E
154 D9 Siddhapur prev. Siddhpur, Sidhpur. Gujarāt, W India 23°57′N 72°28′E
Siddhpur see Siddhapur
155 I15 Siddipet Andhra Pradesh, C India 18°10′N 78°54′E
77 N14 Sidéradougou SW Burkina 10°39′N 04°16′W
107 N23 Siderno Calabria, SW Italy 38°18′N 16°19′E
Siders see Sierre
154 L9 Sidhi Madhya Pradesh, C India 24°24′N 81°54′E
Sidhirókastron see Sidirókastro
Sidhpur see Siddhapur
75 U7 Sîdi Barrâni NW Egypt 31°38′N 25°58′E
74 I6 Sidi Bel Abbès var. Sidi bel Abbès, Sidi-Bel-Abbès. NW Algeria 35°12′N 00°43′W
74 E7 Sidi-Bennour W Morocco 32°39′N 08°28′W
74 M6 Sidi Bouzid var. Gammouda, Sīdī Bu Zayd. C Tunisia 35°05′N 09°20′E
Sīdī Bu Zayd see Sidi Bouzid
74 D8 Sidi-Ifni SW Morocco 29°33′N 10°04′W
74 G6 Sidi-Kacem prev. Petitjean. N Morocco 34°21′N 05°46′W
114 G12 Sidirókastro prev. Sidhirókastron. Kentrikí Makedonía, NE Greece 41°14′N 23°23′E
194 L12 Sidley, Mount ▲ Antarctica 76°39′S 124°48′W
29 S16 Sidney Iowa, C USA 40°45′N 95°39′W
33 Y7 Sidney Montana, NW USA 47°42′N 104°10′W
28 J15 Sidney Nebraska, C USA 41°09′N 102°57′W
18 I11 Sidney New York, NE USA 42°18′N 75°21′W
31 R13 Sidney Ohio, N USA 40°16′N 84°09′W
23 T2 Sidney Lanier, Lake ▣ Georgia, SE USA
Sidon see Saïda
122 J9 Sidorovsk Yamalo-Nenetskiy Avtonomnyy Okrug, N Russian Federation 66°34′N 82°12′E
Sidra see Surt
Sidra/Sidra, Gulf of see Surt, Khalīj, N Libya
Siebenbürgen see Transylvania
Sieben Dörfer see Săcele
110 O12 Siedlce Ger. Sedlez, Rus. Sesdlets. Mazowieckie, C Poland 52°10′N 22°18′E
101 E16 Sieg ≈ W Germany
101 F16 Siegen Nordrhein-Westfalen, W Germany 50°53′N 08°02′E
109 X4 Sieghartskirchen Niederösterreich, E Austria 48°13′N 16°01′E
110 O11 Siemiatycze Podlaskie, NE Poland 52°27′N 22°52′E
167 T11 Siĕmpang Stœ̆ng Trêng, NE Cambodia 14°07′N 106°24′E
167 R11 Siĕmréab prev. Siemreap. Siĕmréab, NW Cambodia 13°21′N 103°50′E
Siemreap see Siĕmréab
106 G12 Siena Fr. Sienne; anc. Saena Julia. Toscana, C Italy 43°20′N 11°20′E
Sienne see Siena
92 K12 Sieppijärvi Lappi, NW Finland 67°09′N 23°58′E
110 J13 Sieradz Sieradz, C Poland 51°36′N 18°42′E
110 K10 Sierpc Mazowieckie, C Poland 52°51′N 19°44′E
24 I9 Sierra Blanca Texas, SW USA 31°10′N 105°22′W
37 S14 Sierra Blanca Peak ▲ New Mexico, SW USA 33°22′N 105°48′W
35 P5 Sierra City California, W USA 39°34′N 120°35′W
63 I16 Sierra Colorada Río Negro, S Argentina 40°37′S 67°48′W
63 J16 Sierra Grande Río Negro, E Argentina 41°34′S 65°21′W
76 G15 Sierra Leone off. Republic of Sierra Leone. ◆ republic W Africa
64 M13 Sierra Leone Basin undersea feature E Atlantic Ocean 05°00′N 17°00′W
66 K8 Sierra Leone Fracture Zone tectonic feature E Atlantic Ocean
Sierra Leone, Republic of see Sierra Leone
Sierra Leone Ridge see Sierra Leone Rise
64 L13 Sierra Leone Rise var. Sierra Leone Ridge, Sierra Leone Schwelle. undersea feature E Atlantic Ocean 05°30′N 21°00′W
Sierra Leone Schwelle see Sierra Leone Rise
40 L7 Sierra Mojada Coahuila, NE Mexico 27°13′N 103°42′W
37 N16 Sierra Vista Arizona, SW USA 31°33′N 110°18′W
108 D10 Sierre Ger. Siders. Valais, SW Switzerland 46°18′N 07°33′E
36 L16 Sierrita Mountains ▲▲ Arizona, SW USA
Siete Moai see Ahu Akivi
76 M15 Sifié W Ivory Coast 07°59′N 06°55′W
115 I21 Sífnos anc. Siphnos. island Kykládes, Greece, Aegean Sea
115 I21 Sífnou, Stenó strait SE Greece
Siga see Shiga
103 P16 Sigean Aude, S France 43°02′N 02°58′E
Sighet see Sighetu Marmaţiei
Sighetul Marmaţiei see Sighetu Marmaţiei
116 I8 Sighetu Marmaţiei var. Sighet, Sighetul Marmaţiei, Hung. Máramarossziget. Maramureş, N Romania 47°56′N 23°53′E
116 I11 Sighişoara Ger. Schässburg, Hung. Segesvár. Mureş, C Romania 46°12′N 24°48′E
168 G7 Sigli Sumatera, W Indonesia 05°21′N 95°56′E
92 J1 Siglufjördhur Nordhurland Vestra, N Iceland 66°09′N 18°56′W
101 H23 Sigmaringen Baden-Württemberg, S Germany 48°04′N 09°12′E
101 N20 Signalberg ▲ SE Germany 49°30′N 12°34′E
36 I13 Signal Peak ▲ Arizona, SW USA 33°20′N 114°03′W
Signan see Xi'an
194 H1 Signy UK research station South Orkney Islands, Antarctica 60°27′S 45°35′W
29 X15 Sigourney Iowa, C USA 41°19′N 92°12′W
115 K17 Sígri, Akrotírio headland Lésvos, E Greece 39°12′N 25°49′E
Sigsbee Deep see Mexico Basin
47 N2 Sigsbee Escarpment undersea feature N Gulf of Mexico 26°00′N 92°30′W
56 C8 Sigsig Azuay, S Ecuador 03°04′S 78°50′W
95 O15 Sigtuna Stockholm, C Sweden 59°36′N 17°44′E
42 H6 Siguatepeque Comayagua, W Honduras 14°39′N 87°48′W
105 P7 Sigüenza Castilla-La Mancha, C Spain 41°04′N 02°38′W
105 R4 Sigües Aragón, NE Spain 42°39′N 01°00′W
76 K13 Siguiri NE Guinea 11°26′N 09°08′W
118 G8 Sigulda Ger. Segewold. Rīga, C Latvia 57°08′N 24°51′E
Sihanoukville see Kâmpóng Saôm
108 G8 Sihlsee ◎ NW Switzerland
93 K18 Siikainen Länsi-Suomi, SW Finland 61°52′N 21°49′E
93 M16 Siilinjärvi Itä-Suomi, C Finland 63°05′N 27°40′E
137 R15 Siirt var. Sert; anc. Tigranocerta. Siirt, SE Turkey 37°56′N 41°56′E
137 R15 Siirt var. Sert. ◈ province SE Turkey
187 N8 Sikaiana var. Stewart Islands. island group W Solomon Islands
Sikandarabad see Secunderābād
152 J11 Sikandra Rao Uttar Pradesh, N India 27°42′N 78°21′E
10 M11 Sikanni Chief British Columbia, W Canada 57°16′N 122°44′W
10 M11 Sikanni Chief ≈ British Columbia, W Canada
152 H11 Sīkar Rājasthān, N India 27°33′N 75°12′E
76 M13 Sikasso Sikasso, S Mali 11°21′N 05°43′W
76 L13 Sikasso ◈ region SW Mali
167 N3 Sikaw Kachin State, C Burma (Myanmar) 23°50′N 97°04′E
83 H14 Sikelenge Western, W Zambia 14°51′S 24°13′E
27 Y7 Sikeston Missouri, C USA 36°52′N 89°35′W
93 J14 Sikfors Norrbotten, N Sweden 65°29′N 21°17′E
123 T14 Sikhote-Alin', Khrebet ▲▲ SE Russian Federation
Siking see Xi'an
115 J22 Síkinos island Kykládes, Greece, Aegean Sea
153 S11 Sikkim Tib. Denjong. ◈ state N India
111 I26 Siklós Baranya, SW Hungary 45°51′N 18°18′E
Sikoku see Shikoku
Sikoku Basin see Shikoku Basin
83 G14 Sikongo Western, W Zambia 15°03′S 22°07′E
Sikotu Ko see Shikotsu-ko
Sikouri/Sikoúrion see Sykoúrio
123 P8 Siktyakh Respublika Sakha (Yakutiya), NE Russian Federation 69°45′N 124°42′E
118 D12 Šilalė Tauragė, W Lithuania 55°29′N 22°10′E
106 G5 Silandro Ger. Schlanders. Trentino-Alto Adige, N Italy 46°39′N 10°55′E
41 N12 Silao Guanajuato, C Mexico 20°56′N 101°28′W
Silarius see Sele
153 W14 Silchar Assam, NE India 24°49′N 92°48′E
108 G9 Silenen Uri, C Switzerland 46°49′N 08°39′E
21 T9 Siler City North Carolina, SE USA 35°43′N 79°27′W
33 U11 Silesia Montana, NW USA 45°32′N 108°52′W
110 F13 Silesia physical region SW Poland
74 K12 Silet S Algeria 22°45′N 04°51′E
145 R8 Sileti var. Selety. ≈ N Kazakhstan
Siletitengiz see Siletiteniz, Ozero
145 R7 Siletiteniz, Ozero Kaz. Siletitengiz. ◎ N Kazakhstan
172 H16 Silhouette island Inner Islands, SE Seychelles
136 I17 Silifke anc. Seleucia. İçel, S Turkey 36°22′N 33°57′E
Siliguri see Shiliguri
156 J10 Siling Co ◎ W China
Silinhot see Xilinhot
192 G14 Silisili, Mauga ▲ Savai'i, C Samoa 13°37′S 172°26′W
114 M6 Silistra var. Silistria; anc. Durostorum. Silistra, NE Bulgaria 44°06′N 27°17′E
114 M7 Silistra ◈ province NE Bulgaria
Silistria see Silistra
136 D10 Silivri İstanbul, NW Turkey 41°05′N 28°15′E
94 L13 Siljan ◎ C Sweden
95 G22 Silkeborg Århus, C Denmark 56°10′N 09°34′E
108 M8 Sill ≈ W Austria
105 S10 Silla País Valenciano, E Spain 39°22′N 00°25′W
62 H3 Sillajguay, Cordillera ▲ N Chile 19°45′S 68°39′W
118 K3 Sillamäe Ger. Sillamäggi. Ida-Virumaa, NE Estonia 59°23′N 27°45′E
Sillamäggi see Sillamäe
Sillein see Žilina
109 P9 Sillian Tirol, W Austria 46°45′N 12°25′E
112 B10 Šilo Primorje-Gorski Kotar, NW Croatia 45°09′N 14°39′E
27 R9 Siloam Springs Arkansas, C USA 36°11′N 94°32′W
25 X10 Silsbee Texas, SW USA 30°21′N 94°10′W
143 W15 Sīlūp, Rūd-e ≈ SE Iran
118 C12 Šilutė Ger. Heydekrug. Klaipėda, W Lithuania 55°20′N 21°30′E
137 Q15 Silvan Dıyarbakır, SE Turkey 38°08′N 41°E
108 J10 Silvaplana Graubünden, S Switzerland 46°27′N 09°45′E
Silva Porto see Kuito
58 M12 Silva, Recife do reef E Brazil
154 D12 Silvassa Dādra and Nagar Haveli, W India 20°13′N 73°03′E
29 X4 Silver Bay Minnesota, N USA 47°17′N 91°15′W
37 P15 Silver City New Mexico, SW USA 32°47′N 108°16′W
18 D10 Silver Creek New York, NE USA 42°32′N 79°10′W
37 N12 Silver Creek ≈ Arizona, SW USA
27 P4 Silver Lake Kansas, C USA 39°06′N 95°51′W
32 I14 Silver Lake Oregon, NW USA 43°07′N 121°04′W
35 T9 Silver Peak Range ▲▲ Nevada, W USA
21 W3 Silver Spring Maryland, NE USA 39°00′N 77°01′W
Silver State see Colorado
Silver State see Nevada
37 Q7 Silverton Colorado, C USA 37°48′N 107°39′W
18 K16 Silverton New Jersey, NE USA 40°00′N 74°09′W
32 G11 Silverton Oregon, NW USA 45°00′N 122°46′W
25 N4 Silverton Texas, SW USA 34°28′N 101°18′W
104 G14 Silves Faro, S Portugal 37°11′N 08°26′W
54 D12 Silvia Cauca, SW Colombia 02°37′N 76°24′W
108 J9 Silvrettagruppe ▲▲ Austria/Switzerland
Sily-Vajdej see Vulcan
108 L7 Silz Tirol, W Austria 47°17′N 11°00′E
172 I13 Sima Anjouan, SE Comoros 12°11′S 44°18′E
Simabara see Shimabara
83 H15 Simakando Western, W Zambia 16°43′S 24°46′E
Simane see Shimane
119 L20 Simanichy Rus. Simonichi. Homyel'skaya Voblasts', SE Belarus 51°53′N 28°05′E
160 F14 Simao Yunnan, SW China 22°30′N 101°06′E
153 P12 Simarā Central, C Nepal 27°14′N 85°00′E
14 I8 Simard, Lac ◎ Québec, SE Canada
136 D13 Simav Kütahya, W Turkey 39°05′N 28°59′E
136 D13 Simav Çayı ≈ NW Turkey
79 L18 Simba Orientale, N Dem. Rep. Congo 0°46′N 22°54′E
186 C7 Simbai Madang, N Papua New Guinea 05°12′S 144°33′E
Simbirsk see Ul'yanovsk
14 F17 Simcoe Ontario, S Canada 42°50′N 80°19′W
14 H14 Simcoe, Lake ◎ Ontario, S Canada
80 J11 Sīmēn ▲▲ N Ethiopia
114 K11 Simeonovgrad prev. Maritsa. Khaskovo, S Bulgaria 42°03′N 25°36′E
116 G11 Simeria Ger. Pischk, Hung. Piski. Hunedoara, W Romania 45°51′N 23°00′E
107 L24 Simeto ≈ Sicilia, Italy, C Mediterranean Sea
168 G9 Simeulue, Pulau island NW Indonesia
117 T13 Simferopol' Respublika Krym, S Ukraine 44°55′N 33°06′E
117 T13 Simferopol' ✈ Respublika Krym, S Ukraine 44°55′N 34°04′E
Simi see Sými
152 M9 Simikot Far Western, NW Nepal 30°02′N 81°49′E
54 F7 Simití Bolívar, N Colombia 07°57′N 73°57′W
114 G11 Simitla Blagoevgrad, SW Bulgaria 41°57′N 23°06′E
35 S15 Simi Valley California, W USA 34°16′N 118°47′W
Simizu see Shimizu
Simla see Shimla
Şimlăul Silvaniei/Şimleul Silvaniei see Şimleu Silvaniei
116 G9 Şimleu Silvaniei Hung. Szilágysomlyó; prev. Şimlăul Silvaniei, Şimleul Silvaniei. Sălaj, NW Romania 47°12′N 22°49′E
Simmer see Simmerbach
101 E19 Simmerbach var. Simmer. ≈ W Germany
101 F18 Simmern Rheinland-Pfalz, W Germany 50°00′N 07°30′E
22 I7 Simmesport Louisiana, S USA 30°58′N 91°48′W
119 F14 Simnas Alytus, S Lithuania 54°23′N 23°40′E
92 L13 Simo Lappi, NW Finland 65°40′N 25°04′E
Simoda see Shimoda
Simodate see Shimodate
92 M13 Simojärvi ◎ N Finland
92 L13 Simojoki ≈ NW Finland
41 U15 Simojovel var. Simojovel de Allende. Chiapas, SE Mexico 17°14′N 92°40′W
Simojovel de Allende see Simojovel
56 B7 Simon Bolivar var. Guayaquil. ✈ (Quayaquil) Guayas, W Ecuador 02°16′S 79°54′W
54 L5 Simon Bolívar ✈ (Caracas) Vargas, N Venezuela 10°33′N 66°54′W
Simonichi see Simanichy
14 M12 Simon, Lac ◎ Québec, SE Canada
Simonoseki see Shimonoseki
Šimonovany see Partizánske
Simonstad see Simon's Town
83 E26 Simon's Town var. Simonstad. Western Cape, SW South Africa 34°12′S 18°26′E
Simony see Partizánske
Simpeln see Simplon
99 M18 Simpelveld Limburg, SE Netherlands 50°50′N 05°59′E
108 E11 Simplon var. Simpeln. Valais, SW Switzerland 46°13′N 08°01′E
108 E11 Simplon Pass pass S Switzerland
106 C6 Simplon Tunnel tunnel Italy/Switzerland
Simpson see Fort Simpson
182 G1 Simpson Desert desert Northern Territory/South Australia
10 J9 Simpson Peak ▲ British Columbia, W Canada 59°43′N 131°29′W
9 N7 Simpson Peninsula peninsula Nunavut, NE Canada
21 P11 Simpsonville South Carolina, SE USA 34°44′N 82°15′W
95 L23 Simrishamn Skåne, S Sweden 55°34′N 14°20′E
123 U13 Simushir, Ostrov island Kuril'skiye Ostrova, SE Russian Federation
168 G9 Sinabang Sumatera, W Indonesia 02°27′N 96°24′E
81 N15 Sina Dhaqa Galguduud, C Somalia 05°21′N 46°21′E
75 X8 Sinai var. Sinai Peninsula, Ar. Shibh Jazirat Sīnā', Sīnā. physical region NE Egypt
116 J12 Sinaia Prahova, SE Romania 45°20′N 25°33′E
188 B16 Sinajana C Guam 13°28′N 144°45′E
40 H8 Sinaloa ◈ state C Mexico
54 H4 Sinamaica Zulia, NW Venezuela 11°06′N 71°52′W
163 X14 Sinan-ni SE North Korea 38°37′N 127°43′E
Sīnā/Sinai Peninsula see Sinai
Sīnāwan see Sīnāwin
75 N8 Sīnāwin var. Sīnāwan. NW Libya 31°00′N 10°37′E
83 J16 Sinazongwe Southern, S Zambia 17°14′S 27°27′E
166 L6 Sinbaungwe Magway, W Burma (Myanmar) 19°44′N 95°10′E
166 L5 Sinbyugyun Magway, W Burma (Myanmar) 20°38′N 94°40′E
54 E6 Since Sucre, NW Colombia 09°14′N 75°08′W
54 E6 Sincelejo Sucre, NW Colombia 09°17′N 75°23′W
166 J5 Sinchaingbyin var. Zullapara. Rakhine State, W Burma (Myanmar) 20°51′N 92°23′E
23 U4 Sinclair, Lake ▣ Georgia, SE USA
10 M14 Sinclair Mills British Columbia, SW Canada 54°03′N 121°37′W
149 Q14 Sind var. Sindh. ◈ province SE Pakistan
154 I8 Sind ≈ N India
95 H19 Sindal Nordjylland, N Denmark 57°29′N 10°13′E
171 P7 Sindañgan Mindanao, S Philippines 08°09′N 122°59′E
79 D19 Sindara Ngounié, W Gabon 01°07′S 10°41′E
152 E13 Sindari prev. Sindri. Rājasthān, N India 25°32′N 71°58′E
114 N8 Sindel Varna, E Bulgaria 43°07′N 27°35′E
101 H22 Sindelfingen Baden-Württemberg, SW Germany 48°43′N 09°E
155 G16 Sindgi Karnātaka, C India 17°01′N 76°22′E
Sindh see Sind
118 G5 Sindi Ger. Zintenhof. Pärnumaa, SW Estonia 58°28′N 24°41′E
136 C13 Sındırgı Balıkesir, W Turkey 39°13′N 28°10′E
77 N14 Sindou SW Burkina 10°35′N 05°04′W
Sindri see Sindari
149 T9 Sind Sāgar Doāb desert E Pakistan
126 M11 Sinegorskiy Rostovskaya Oblast', SW Russian Federation 48°01′N 40°52′E
123 S9 Sinegor'ye Magadanskaya Oblast', E Russian Federation 62°04′N 150°33′E
114 O12 Sinekli İstanbul, NW Turkey 41°13′N 28°13′E
104 F12 Sines Setúbal, S Portugal 37°58′N 08°52′W
104 F12 Sines, Cabo de headland S Portugal 37°57′N 08°55′W
92 L12 Sinettä Lappi, NW Finland 66°39′N 25°25′E
186 H6 Sinewit, Mount ▲ New Britain, C Papua New Guinea 04°42′S 151°58′E
80 G11 Singa var. Sinja, Sinjah. Sinnar, E Sudan 13°11′N 33°55′E
78 J12 Singako Moyen-Chari, S Chad 09°52′N 19°31′E
Singan see Xi'an
168 K10 Singapore ● (Singapore) S Singapore 01°17′N 103°48′E
168 L10 Singapore off. Republic of Singapore. ◆ republic SE Asia
Singapore, Republic of see Singapore
169 U17 Singaraja Bali, C Indonesia 08°06′S 115°04′E
167 O10 Sing Buri var. Singhaburi. Sing Buri, C Thailand 14°56′N 100°21′E
101 H24 Singen Baden-Württemberg, S Germany 47°46′N 08°50′E
Sîngeorgiu de Pădure see Sângeorgiu de Pădure
Sîngeorz-Băi/Singeroz Băi see Sângeorz-Băi
116 M9 Sîngerei var. Sângerei; prev. Lazovsk. N Moldova 47°38′N 28°08′E
Singhaburi see Sing Buri
81 H21 Singida Singida, C Tanzania 04°45′S 34°48′E
81 G22 Singida ◈ region C Tanzania
Singidunum see Beograd
166 M2 Singkaling Hkamti Sagaing, N Burma (Myanmar) 26°00′N 95°43′E
171 N14 Singkang Sulawesi, C Indonesia 04°09′S 119°58′E
168 J11 Singkarak, Danau ◎ Sumatera, W Indonesia
169 N10 Singkawang Borneo, C Indonesia 0°57′N 108°57′E
168 M11 Singkep, Pulau island Kepulauan Lingga, W Indonesia
168 H9 Singkilbaru Sumatera, W Indonesia 02°18′N 97°47′E
183 T7 Singleton New South Wales, SE Australia 32°38′S 151°00′E
Singora see Songkhla
Singû see Shingū
Sining see Xining
107 D17 Siniscola Sardegna, Italy, C Mediterranean Sea 40°34′N 09°42′E
113 F14 Sinj Split-Dalmacija, SE Croatia 43°41′N 16°37′E
Sinjajevina see Sinjavina
139 P3 Sinjār Nīnawýa, NW Iraq 36°20′N 41°51′E
139 P2 Sinjār, Jabal ▲▲ N Iraq
Sinja/Sinjah see Singa
113 K15 Sinjavina var. Sinjajevina. ▲▲ C Montenegro
80 I7 Sinkat Red Sea, NE Sudan 18°52′N 36°51′E
Sinkiang/Sinkiang Uighur Autonomous Region see Xinjiang Uygur Zizhiqu
Sînmartin see Târnăveni
163 V13 Sinmi-do island NW North Korea
101 I18 Sinn ≈ C Germany
Sinnamarie see Sinnamary
55 Y9 Sinnamary var. Sinnamarie. N French Guiana 05°23′N 53°00′W
80 G11 Sinnar ◈ state E Sudan
Sinneh see Sanandaj
18 E13 Sinnemahoning Creek ≈ Pennsylvania, NE USA
Sînnicolau Mare see Sânnicolau Mare
Sinoe, Lacul see Sinoie, Lacul
Sinoia see Chinhoyi
117 N14 Sinoie, Lacul prev. Lacul Sinoe. lagoon SE Romania
59 H16 Sinop Mato Grosso, W Brazil 11°38′S 55°27′W
136 K10 Sinop anc. Sinope. Sinop, N Turkey 42°02′N 35°09′E
136 J10 Sinop ◈ province N Turkey
136 K10 Sinop Burnu headland N Turkey 42°02′N 35°12′E
Sinope see Sinop
Sino/Sinoe see Greenville
163 Y12 Sinp'o E North Korea 40°01′N 128°10′E
101 H20 Sinsheim Baden-Württemberg, SW Germany 49°15′N 08°53′E
Sîntana see Sântana
169 R11 Sintang Borneo, C Indonesia 0°03′N 111°31′E
99 F14 Sint Annaland Zeeland, SW Netherlands 51°36′N 04°07′E
98 L5 Sint Annaparochie Friesland, N Netherlands 53°20′N 05°46′E
45 V9 Sint Eustatius Eng. Saint Eustatius. island N Netherlands Antilles

◆ Country
● Country Capital
◇ Dependent Territory
○ Dependent Territory Capital
◈ Administrative Regions
✈ International Airport
▲ Mountain
▲▲ Mountain Range
Volcano
≈ River
◎ Lake
▣ Reservoir

Sint-Genesius-Rode – Snækollur

99 G19 **Sint-Genesius-Rode** *Fr.* Rhode-Saint-Genèse. Vlaams Brabant, C Belgium 50°45′N 04°21′E
99 F16 **Sint-Gillis-Waas** Oost-Vlaanderen, N Belgium 51°14′N 04°08′E
99 H17 **Sint-Katelijne-Waver** Antwerpen, C Belgium 51°05′N 04°31′E
99 E18 **Sint-Lievens-Houtem** Oost-Vlaanderen, NW Belgium 50°55′N 03°52′E
45 V9 **Sint Maarten** *Eng.* Saint Martin. *island* N Netherlands Antilles
99 F14 **Sint Maartensdijk** Zeeland, SW Netherlands 51°33′N 04°05′E
99 L19 **Sint-Martens-Voeren** *Fr.* Fouron-Saint-Martin. Limburg, NE Belgium 50°46′N 05°49′E
99 J14 **Sint-Michielsgestel** Noord-Brabant, S Netherlands 51°38′N 05°21′E
Sîn-Miclăuş *see* Gheorgheni
45 O16 **Sint Nicolaas** S Aruba 12°25′N 69°52′W
99 F16 **Sint-Niklaas** *Fr.* Saint-Nicolas. Oost-Vlaanderen, N Belgium 51°10′N 04°09′E
99 K14 **Sint-Oedenrode** Noord-Brabant, S Netherlands 51°34′N 05°28′E
25 T14 **Sinton** Texas, SW USA 28°02′N 97°33′W
99 G14 **Sint Philipsland** Zeeland, SW Netherlands 51°37′N 04°11′E
99 G19 **Sint-Pieters-Leeuw** Vlaams Brabant, C Belgium 50°47′N 04°16′E
104 E11 **Sintra** *prev.* Cintra. Lisboa, W Portugal 38°48′N 09°22′W
99 J18 **Sint-Truiden** *Fr.* Saint-Trond. Limburg, NE Belgium 50°48′N 05°13′E
99 H14 **Sint Willebrord** Noord-Brabant, S Netherlands 51°33′N 04°35′E
163 V13 **Sinŭiju** W North Korea 40°08′N 124°33′E
80 P13 **Sinujiif** Nugaal, NE Somalia 08°33′N 49°05′E
Sinus Aelaniticus *see* Aqaba, Gulf of
Sinus Gallicus *see* Lion, Golfe du
Sinyang *see* Xinyang
Sinyavka *see* Sinyawka
119 I18 **Sinyawka** *Rus.* Sinyavka. Minskaya Voblasts', SW Belarus 52°57′N 26°29′E
Sinying *see* Hsinying
Sinyukha *see* Synyukha
Sinzyô *see* Shinjō
111 I24 **Sió** ≈ W Hungary
171 O7 **Siocon** Mindanao, S Philippines 07°37′N 122°09′E
111 I24 **Siófok** Somogy, Hungary 46°54′N 18°03′E
Siogama *see* Shiogama
83 G15 **Sioma** Western, SW Zambia 16°39′S 23°36′E
108 D11 **Sion** *Ger.* Sitten; *anc.* Sedunum. Valais, SW Switzerland 46°15′N 07°23′E
103 O11 **Sioule** ≈ C France
29 S12 **Sioux Center** Iowa, C USA 43°04′N 96°10′W
29 R13 **Sioux City** Iowa, C USA 42°30′N 96°24′W
29 R11 **Sioux Falls** South Dakota, N USA 43°33′N 96°45′W
12 B11 **Sioux Lookout** Ontario, S Canada 49°27′N 94°06′W
29 T12 **Sioux Rapids** Iowa, C USA 42°53′N 95°09′W
Sioux State *see* North Dakota
Siozir *see* Shiojiri
171 P6 **Sipalay** Negros, C Philippines 09°46′N 122°25′E
55 V11 **Sipaliwini** ⬖ *district* S Surinam
45 U15 **Siparia** Trinidad, Trinidad and Tobago 10°08′N 61°31′W
Siphnos *see* Sífnos
163 V11 **Siping** *var.* Ssu-p'ing, Szeping; *prev.* Ssu-p'ing-chieh. Jilin, NE China 43°09′N 124°22′E
11 X12 **Sipiwesk** Manitoba, C Canada 55°28′N 97°16′W
11 W13 **Sipiwesk Lake** ◎ Manitoba, C Canada
195 O11 **Siple Coast** *physical region* Antarctica
194 K12 **Siple Island** *island* Antarctica
194 K13 **Siple, Mount** ▲ Siple Island, Antarctica 73°25′S 126°24′W
Sipoo *see* Sibbo
112 G12 **Šipovo** Republika Srpska, W Bosnia and Herzegovina 44°16′N 17°05′E
23 O4 **Sipsey River** ≈ Alabama, S USA
168 I13 **Sipura, Pulau** *island* W Indonesia
0 G16 **Siqueiros Fracture Zone** *tectonic feature* E Pacific Ocean
42 L10 **Siquia, Río** ≈ SE Nicaragua
43 N13 **Siquirres** Limón, E Costa Rica 10°05′N 83°30′W
54 J5 **Siquisique** Lara, N Venezuela 10°36′N 69°45′W
155 G19 **Sīra** Karnātaka, W India 13°46′N 76°54′E
95 D16 **Sira** ≈ S Norway
167 P12 **Siracha** *var.* Ban Si Racha, Si Racha. Chon Buri, S Thailand 13°10′N 100°57′E
Si Racha *see* Siracha
107 L25 **Siracusa** *Eng.* Syracuse. Sicilia, Italy, C Mediterranean Sea 37°04′N 15°17′E
153 T14 **Sirajganj** *var.* Shirajganj Ghat. Rajshahi, C Bangladesh 24°27′N 89°42′E
Sirakawa *see* Shirakawa
11 N14 **Sir Alexander, Mount** ▲ British Columbia, W Canada 54°00′N 120°33′W
137 O12 **Şiran** Gümüşhane, NE Turkey 40°12′N 39°07′E
77 Q12 **Sirba** ≈ E Burkina
143 O17 **Şīr Banī Yās** *island* W United Arab Emirates
95 D17 **Sirdalsvatnet** ◎ S Norway
Sir Darya/Sirdaryo *see* Syr Darya
147 P10 **Sirdaryo** Sirdaryo Viloyati, E Uzbekistan 40°46′N 68°34′E
147 O11 **Sirdaryo Viloyati** *Rus.* Syrdar'inskaya Oblast'. ⬖ *province* E Uzbekistan
Sir Donald Sangster International Airport *see* Sangster
181 S3 **Sir Edward Pellew Group** *island group* Northern Territory, NE Australia
116 K8 **Siret** *Ger.* Sereth, *Hung.* Szeret. Suceava, N Romania 47°55′N 26°05′E
116 K8 **Siret** *var.* Siretul, *Ger.* Sereth, *Rus.* Seret. ≈ Romania/Ukraine
Siretul *see* Siret
140 K3 **Sirḥān, Wādī as** *dry watercourse* Jordan/Saudi Arabia
152 I8 **Sirhind** Punjab, N India 30°39′N 76°28′E
116 F11 **Şiria** *Ger.* Schiria. Arad, W Romania 46°16′N 21°38′E
Siria *see* Syria
143 S14 **Sīrīk** Hormozgān, SE Iran 26°32′N 57°07′E
167 P8 **Sirikit Reservoir** ⊠ N Thailand
58 K12 **Sirituba, Ilha** *island* NE Brazil
143 R11 **Sīrjān** *prev.* Sa'īdābād. Kermān, S Iran 29°29′N 55°39′E
182 H9 **Sir Joseph Banks Group** *island group* South Australia
92 K11 **Sirkka** Lappi, N Finland 67°49′N 24°48′E
Sirna *see* Sýrna
137 R16 **Şırnak** Şırnak, SE Turkey 37°33′N 42°27′E
137 S16 **Şırnak** ⬖ *province* SE Turkey
152 E14 **Sirohi** Rājasthān, N India 25°53′N 72°58′E
Siroisi *see* Shiroishi
155 J14 **Sironcha** Mahārāshtra, C India 18°51′N 80°03′E
Sirone *see* Shirone
Síros *see* Sýros
Sirotino *see* Sirotsina
118 M12 **Sirotsina** *Rus.* Sirotino. Vitsyebskaya Voblasts', N Belarus 55°23′N 29°37′E
152 H9 **Sirsa** Haryāna, NW India 29°32′N 75°04′E
173 Y17 **Sir Seewoosagur Ramgoolam** ✈ (port Louis) SE Mauritius
155 E18 **Sirsi** Karnātaka, W India 14°46′N 74°49′E
146 K12 **Şirşütür Gumy** *var.* Shirshütür, *Rus.* Peski Shirshyutyur. *desert* E Turkmenistan
Sirte *see* Surt
182 A2 **Sir Thomas, Mount** ▲ South Australia 27°09′S 129°49′E
Sirti, Gulf of *see* Surt, Khalīj
142 J5 **Sīrvān, Rūdkhāneh-ye** *var.* Nahr Diyālá, Sirwan. ≈ Iran/Iraq *see also* Diyālá, Nahr
Sīrvān, Rudkhaneh-ye *see* Diyālá, Sirwan Nahr
118 H13 **Širvintos** Vilnius, SE Lithuania 55°01′N 24°58′E
Sīrwān *see* Diyālá, Nahr/Sīrvān, Rudkhaneh-ye
11 N15 **Sir Wilfrid Laurier, Mount** ▲ British Columbia, SW Canada 52°45′N 119°51′W
14 M10 **Sir-Wilfrid, Mont** ▲ Québec, SE Canada 46°57′N 75°33′W
Sisačko-Moslavačka Županija *see* Sisak-Moslavina
112 E9 **Sisak** *var.* Siscia, *Ger.* Sissek, *Hung.* Sziszek; *anc.* Segestica. Sisak-Moslavina, C Croatia 45°28′N 16°21′E
167 R10 **Si Sa Ket** *var.* Sisaket, Sri Saket. Si Sa Ket, E Thailand 15°08′N 104°18′E
Sisaket *see* Si Sa Ket
112 E9 **Sisak-Moslavina** *off.* Sisačko-Moslavačka Županija. ⬖ *province* C Croatia
167 O8 **Si Satchanala** Sukhothai, NW Thailand
Siscia *see* Sisak
83 G22 **Sishen** Northern Cape, NW South Africa 27°47′S 22°59′E
137 V13 **Sisian** SE Armenia 39°31′N 46°03′E
197 N13 **Sisimiut** *var.* Holsteinborg, Holsteinsborg, Holstenborg, Holstensborg. Kitaa, S Greenland 67°07′N 53°42′W
30 M1 **Siskiwit Bay** *lake bay* Michigan, N USA
34 L1 **Siskiyou Mountains** ▲▲ California/Oregon, W USA
167 Q11 **Sisŏphŏn** Bătdâmbâng, NW Cambodia 13°37′N 102°58′E
108 E7 **Sissach** Basel-Land, NW Switzerland 47°28′N 07°48′E
186 B5 **Sissano** Sandaun, NW Papua New Guinea 03°02′S 142°01′E
Sissek *see* Sisak
29 R7 **Sisseton** South Dakota, N USA 45°39′N 97°03′W
143 W9 **Sīstān, Daryācheh-ye** *var.* Daryācheh-ye Hāmūn, Hāmūn-e Şāberī. ◎ Afghanistan/Iran *see also* Şāberī, Hāmūn-e
Sīstān, Daryācheh-ye *see* Şāberī, Hāmūn-e
143 V12 **Sīstān va Balūchestān** *off.* Ostān-e Sīstān va Balūchestān, *var.* Balūchestān va Sīstān. ⬖ *province* SE Iran
Sīstān va Balūchestān, Ostān-e *see* Sīstān va Balūchestān
103 T14 **Sisteron** Alpes-de-Haute-Provence, SE France 44°12′N 05°55′E
32 H13 **Sisters** Oregon, NW USA 44°17′N 121°33′W
65 G15 **Sisters Peak** ▲ N Ascension Island 07°56′S 14°23′W
21 R3 **Sistersville** West Virginia, NE USA 39°33′N 81°00′W
Sistova *see* Svishtov
Sitakund *see* Sitakunda
153 V16 **Sitakunda** *var.* Sitakund. Chittagong, SE Bangladesh 22°35′N 91°40′E
153 P12 **Sītāmarhi** Bihār, N India 26°36′N 85°30′E
152 L11 **Sītāpur** Uttar Pradesh, N India 27°33′N 80°40′E
Sitaş Cristuru *see* Cristuru Secuiesc
115 L25 **Siteía** *var.* Sitía. Kríti, Greece, E Mediterranean Sea 35°13′N 26°06′E
105 V6 **Sitges** Cataluña, NE Spain 41°14′N 01°49′E
115 H15 **Sithonía** *peninsula* NE Greece
Sitía *see* Siteía
54 F4 **Sitionuevo** Magdalena, N Colombia 10°46′N 74°43′W
39 X13 **Sitka** Baranof Island, Alaska, USA 57°03′N 135°19′W
39 Q15 **Sitkinak Island** *island* Trinity Islands, Alaska, USA
Sittang *see* Sittoung
99 L17 **Sittard** Limburg, SE Netherlands 51°00′N 05°52′E
Sitten *see* Sion
108 H7 **Sitter** ≈ NW Switzerland
109 U10 **Sittersdorf** Kärnten, S Austria 46°31′N 14°34′E
166 M7 **Sittoung** *var.* Sittang. ≈ S Burma (Myanmar)
166 K6 **Sittwe** *var.* Akyab. Rakhine State, W Burma (Myanmar) 22°09′N 92°51′E
42 L8 **Siuna** Región Autónoma Atlántico Norte, NE Nicaragua 13°44′N 84°46′W
153 R15 **Siuri** West Bengal, NE India 23°54′N 87°32′E
Siut *see* Asyūţ
155 I23 **Sivaganga** Tamil Nādu, SE India 09°59′N 78°30′E
123 Q13 **Sivaki** Amurskaya Oblast', SE Russian Federation 52°39′N 126°43′E
136 M13 **Sivas** *anc.* Sebastia, Sebaste. Sivas, C Turkey 39°44′N 37°01′E
136 M13 **Sivas** ⬖ *province* C Turkey
137 O15 **Siverek** Şanlıurfa, S Turkey 37°46′N 39°19′E
117 X6 **Sivers'k** Donets'ka Oblast', E Ukraine 48°52′N 38°07′E
124 G13 **Siverskiy** Leningradskaya Oblast', NW Russian Federation 59°21′N 30°01′E
117 X6 **Sivers'kyy Donets'** *Rus.* Severskiy Donets. ≈ Russian Federation/Ukraine *see also* Severskiy Donets
Sivers'kyy Donets' *see* Severskiy Donets
125 W5 **Sivomaskinskiy** Respublika Komi, NW Russian Federation 66°42′N 62°33′E
136 G13 **Sivrihisar** Eskişehir, W Turkey 39°29′N 31°32′E
99 F22 **Sivry** Hainaut, S Belgium 50°10′N 04°11′E
123 V9 **Sivuchiy, Mys** *headland* E Russian Federation 56°45′N 163°13′E
Siwa *see* Sīwah
75 U9 **Sīwah** *var.* Siwa. NW Egypt 29°11′N 25°32′E
152 J9 **Siwalik Range** *var.* Shiwalik Range. ▲▲ India/Nepal
153 O13 **Siwān** Bihār, N India 26°14′N 84°21′E
43 O14 **Sixaola, Río** ≈ Costa Rica/Panama
Six Counties, The *see* Northern Ireland
103 T16 **Six-Fours-les-Plages** Var, SE France 43°05′N 05°50′E
161 Q7 **Sixian** *var.* Si Xian. Anhui, E China 33°29′N 117°53′E
Si Xian *see* Sixian
22 J9 **Six Mile Lake** ◎ Louisiana, S USA
139 V3 **Sīyāh Gūz** As Sulaymānīyah, E Iraq 35°49′N 45°45′E
155 L25 **Siyambalanduwa** Uva Province, SE Sri Lanka 06°54′N 81°32′E
137 Y10 **Siyäzän** *Rus.* Siazan'. NE Azerbaijan 41°05′N 49°05′E
Sizebolu *see* Sozopol
Siziwang Qi *see* Shizuoka
95 I24 **Sjælland** *Eng.* Zealand, *Ger.* Seeland. *island* E Denmark
Sjar *see* Sääre
113 L15 **Sjenica** *Turk.* Seniça. Serbia, SW Serbia 43°16′N 20°01′E
94 G11 **Sjoa** ≈ S Norway
95 K23 **Sjöbo** Skåne, S Sweden 55°37′N 13°45′E
94 E9 **Sjøholt** Møre og Romsdal, S Norway 62°29′N 06°50′E
92 O1 **Sjuøyane** *island group* N Svalbard
Skadar *see* Shkodër
Skadarsko Jezero *see* Scutari, Lake
117 R11 **Skadovs'k** Khersons'ka Oblast', S Ukraine 46°07′N 32°53′E
95 I24 **Skælskør** Vestsjælland, E Denmark 55°16′N 11°18′E
92 J2 **Skagaströnd** *prev.* Höfdhakaupstadhur. Nordhurland Vestra, N Iceland 65°49′N 20°18′W
95 H19 **Skagen** Nordjylland, N Denmark 57°44′N 10°37′E
Skagerak *see* Skagerrak
95 L16 **Skagern** ◎ C Sweden
197 T17 **Skagerrak** *var.* Skagerak. *channel* N Europe
94 G12 **Skagget** ▲ S Norway 61°19′N 09°07′E
32 H7 **Skagit River** ≈ Washington, NW USA
39 W12 **Skagway** Alaska, USA 59°27′N 135°18′W
92 K8 **Skaidi** Finnmark, N Norway 70°26′N 24°31′E
115 F21 **Skála** Pelopónnisos, S Greece 36°51′N 22°39′E
116 K6 **Skalat** *Pol.* Skałat. Ternopil's'ka Oblast', W Ukraine 49°27′N 25°59′E
95 J22 **Skälderviken** *inlet* Denmark/Sweden
92 I12 **Skalka** ◎ N Sweden
114 I12 **Skalotí** Anatolikí Makedonía kai Thráki, NE Greece 41°24′N 24°16′E
95 G22 **Skanderborg** Århus, C Denmark 56°02′N 09°57′E
95 K22 **Skåne** *prev. Eng.* Scania. ⬖ *county* S Sweden
75 N6 **Skanès** ✈ (Sousse) E Tunisia 35°36′N 10°56′E
95 C15 **Skånevik** Hordaland, S Norway 59°43′N 06°35′E
95 M18 **Skänninge** Östergötland, S Sweden 58°24′N 15°05′E
95 J23 **Skanör med Falsterbo** Skåne, S Sweden 55°24′N 12°48′E
115 H17 **Skantzoúra** *island* Vóreies Sporádes, Greece, Aegean Sea
95 K18 **Skara** Västra Götaland, S Sweden 58°23′N 13°25′E
95 M17 **Skärblacka** Östergötland, S Sweden 58°34′N 15°54′E
152 I5 **Skārdu** Jammu and Kashmīr, India 35°18′N 75°44′E
95 I18 **Skärhamn** Västra Götaland, S Sweden 57°59′N 11°33′E
95 I14 **Skarnes** Hedmark, S Norway 60°14′N 11°41′E
119 M21 **Skarodnaye** *Rus.* Skorodnoye. Homyel'skaya Voblasts', SE Belarus 51°38′N 28°50′E
110 I8 **Skarszewy** *Ger.* Schöneck. Pomorskie, NW Poland 54°04′N 18°25′E
111 M14 **Skarżysko-Kamienna** Świętokrzyskie, C Poland 51°07′N 20°52′E
95 K16 **Skattkärr** Värmland, C Sweden 59°25′N 13°42′E
118 D12 **Skaudvilė** Tauragė, SW Lithuania 55°25′N 22°33′E
92 J12 **Skaulo** *Lapp.* Sávdijári. Norrbotten, N Sweden 67°21′N 21°03′E
111 K17 **Skawina** Małopolskie, S Poland 49°59′N 19°49′E
10 K12 **Skeena** ≈ British Columbia, SW Canada
10 J11 **Skeena Mountains** ▲▲ British Columbia, W Canada
97 O18 **Skegness** E England, United Kingdom 53°10′N 00°21′E
92 J4 **Skeidharársandur** *coast* S Iceland
93 J15 **Skellefteå** Västerbotten, N Sweden 64°45′N 20°58′E
93 I14 **Skellefteälven** ≈ N Sweden
93 J15 **Skelleftehamn** Västerbotten, N Sweden 64°41′N 21°13′E
25 O2 **Skellytown** Texas, SW USA 35°34′N 101°10′W
95 J19 **Skene** Västra Götaland, S Sweden 57°30′N 12°34′E
97 G17 **Skerries** *Ir.* Na Sceirí. Dublin, E Ireland 53°35′N 06°07′W
95 H15 **Ski** Akershus, S Norway 59°43′N 10°50′E
115 G17 **Skíathos** Skíathos, Vóreies Sporádes, Greece, Aegean Sea 39°10′N 23°30′E
115 G17 **Skíathos** *island* Vóreies Sporádes, Greece, Aegean Sea
27 P9 **Skiatook** Oklahoma, C USA 36°22′N 96°00′W
27 P9 **Skiatook Lake** ⊠ Oklahoma, C USA
97 B22 **Skibbereen** *Ir.* An Sciobairín. Cork, SW Ireland 51°33′N 09°15′W
92 I10 **Skibotn** Troms, N Norway 69°22′N 20°18′E
119 F16 **Skidal'** *Rus.* Skidel'. Hrodzyenskaya Voblasts', W Belarus 53°35′N 24°15′E
97 K15 **Skiddaw** ▲ NW England, United Kingdom 54°37′N 03°07′W
Skidel' *see* Skidal'
25 T14 **Skidmore** Texas, SW USA 28°13′N 97°40′W
95 G16 **Skien** Telemark, S Norway 59°14′N 09°37′E
Skiermûntseach *see* Schiermonnikoog
110 L12 **Skierniewice** Łódzkie, C Poland 51°58′N 20°10′E
74 L5 **Skikda** *prev.* Philippeville. NE Algeria 36°51′N 07°E
30 M16 **Skillet Fork** ≈ Illinois, N USA
95 L19 **Skillingaryd** Jönköping, S Sweden 57°27′N 14°05′E
115 B19 **Skinári, Akrotírio** *headland* Iónia Nisiá, Greece 37°55′N 20°57′E
95 M15 **Skinnskatteberg** Västmanland, C Sweden 59°50′N 15°41′E
182 M12 **Skipton** Victoria, SE Australia 37°44′S 143°21′E
97 L16 **Skipton** N England, United Kingdom 53°57′N 02°W
Skiropoula *see* Skyropoúla
Skiros *see* Skýros
95 F21 **Skive** Viborg, NW Denmark 56°34′N 09°02′E
94 F11 **Skjåk** Oppland, S Norway 61°52′N 08°21′E
92 K2 **Skjálfandafljót** ≈ C Iceland
95 F22 **Skjern** Ringkøbing, W Denmark 55°57′N 08°30′E
95 F22 **Skjern Å** *var.* Skjern Aa. ≈ W Denmark
Skjern Aa *see* Skjern Å
92 G12 **Skjerstad** Nordland, C Norway 67°14′N 15°00′E
92 J8 **Skjervøy** Troms, N Norway 70°03′N 20°56′E
92 I10 **Skjold** Troms, N Norway 69°03′N 19°18′E
111 I17 **Skoczów** Śląskie, S Poland 49°49′N 18°45′E
109 T11 **Škofja Loka** *Ger.* Bischoflack. NW Slovenia 46°12′N 14°16′E
94 N12 **Skog** Gävleborg, C Sweden 61°10′N 16°49′E
95 K16 **Skoghall** Värmland, C Sweden 59°20′N 13°30′E
31 N10 **Skokie** Illinois, N USA 42°01′N 87°43′W
116 H6 **Skole** L'vivs'ka Oblast', W Ukraine 49°04′N 23°29′E
115 D19 **Skóllis** ▲ S Greece 37°58′N 21°33′E
167 S13 **Skon** Kâmpóng Cham, C Cambodia 12°56′N 104°36′E
115 H17 **Skópelos** Skópelos, Vóreies Sporádes, Greece, Aegean Sea 39°07′N 23°43′E
115 H17 **Skópelos** *island* Vóreies Sporádes, Greece, Aegean Sea
126 L5 **Skopin** Ryazanskaya Oblast', W Russian Federation 53°46′N 39°37′E
113 N18 **Skopje** *var.* Üsküb, *Turk.* Üsküp, *prev.* Skoplje; *anc.* Scupi. ● (FYR Macedonia) N FYR Macedonia 42°N 21°28′E
113 O18 **Skopje** ✈ N FYR Macedonia 41°58′N 21°35′E
Skoplje *see* Skopje
110 I8 **Skórcz** *Ger.* Skurz. Pomorskie, N Poland 53°46′N 18°43′E
Skorodnoye *see* Skarodnaye
93 H16 **Skorped** Västernorrland, C Sweden 63°23′N 17°55′E
95 G21 **Skørping** Nordjylland, N Denmark 56°50′N 09°55′E
95 K18 **Skövde** Västra Götaland, S Sweden 58°24′N 13°52′E
123 Q13 **Skovorodino** Amurskaya Oblast', SE Russian Federation 54°03′N 123°47′E
19 Q6 **Skowhegan** Maine, NE USA 44°46′N 69°41′W
11 W15 **Skownan** Manitoba, S Canada 51°55′N 99°34′W
94 H13 **Skreia** Oppland, S Norway 60°37′N 11°00′E
Skripón *see* Orchómenos
118 H9 **Skrīveri** Aizkraukle, S Latvia 56°39′N 25°08′E
118 J11 **Skrudaliena** Daugvapils, SE Latvia 55°50′N 26°42′E
118 D9 **Skrunda** Kuldīga, W Latvia 56°39′N 22°01′E
95 C16 **Skudeneshavn** Rogaland, S Norway 59°10′N 05°16′E
83 L20 **Skukuza** Mpumalanga, NE South Africa 25°01′S 31°35′E
97 B22 **Skull** *Ir.* An Scoil. SW Ireland 51°32′N 09°34′W
22 L3 **Skuna River** ≈ Mississippi, S USA
29 X15 **Skunk River** ≈ Iowa, C USA
Skuø *see* Skúvoy
118 C10 **Skuodas** *Ger.* Schoden, *Pol.* Szkudy. Klaipėda, NW Lithuania 56°16′N 21°30′E
95 K23 **Skurup** Skåne, S Sweden 55°28′N 13°30′E
Skurz *see* Skórcz
114 H8 **Skut** ≈ NW Bulgaria
94 O13 **Skutskär** Uppsala, C Sweden 60°39′N 17°25′E
95 B19 **Skúvoy** *Dan.* Skuø. *island* C Faeroe Islands
Skvira *see* Skvyra
117 O5 **Skvyra** *Rus.* Skvira. Kyyivs'ka Oblast', N Ukraine 49°44′N 29°42′E
39 Q11 **Skwentna** Alaska, USA 61°56′N 151°03′W
110 E11 **Skwierzyna** *Ger.* Schwerin. Lubuskie, W Poland 52°37′N 15°27′E
194 J7 **SkyBlu** *UK research station* Antarctica74°51′N 71°77′W
96 G9 **Skye, Isle of** *island* NW Scotland, United Kingdom
36 K13 **Sky Harbor** ✈ (Phoenix) Arizona, SW USA 32°26′N 112°00′W
32 I8 **Skykomish** Washington, NW USA 47°40′N 121°20′W
Skylge *see* Terschelling
63 F19 **Skyring, Peninsula** *peninsula* S Chile
63 H24 **Skyring, Seno** *inlet* S Chile
115 H17 **Skyropoúla** *var.* Skiropoula. *island* Vóreies Sporádes, Greece, Aegean Sea
115 I17 **Skýros** *var.* Skíros. Skýros, Vóreies Sporádes, Greece, Aegean Sea 38°55′N 24°34′E
115 I17 **Skýros** *var.* Skíros; *anc.* Scyros. *island* Vóreies Sporádes, Greece, Aegean Sea
118 J12 **Slabodka** *Rus.* Slobodka. Vitsyebskaya Voblasts', NW Belarus 55°41′N 27°11′E
95 I23 **Slagelse** Vestsjælland, E Denmark 55°25′N 11°22′E
93 I14 **Slagnäs** Norrbotten, N Sweden 65°36′N 18°10′E
39 T10 **Slana** Alaska, USA 62°46′N 144°00′W
97 F20 **Slaney** *Ir.* An tSláine. ≈ SE Ireland
116 J13 **Slănic** Prahova, SE Romania 45°14′N 25°58′E
116 K11 **Slănic Moldova** Bacău, E Romania 46°12′N 26°23′E
113 H16 **Slano** Dubrovnik-Neretva, SE Croatia 42°47′N 17°54′E
124 F13 **Slantsy** Leningradskaya Oblast', NW Russian Federation 59°06′N 28°00′E
111 C16 **Slaný** *Ger.* Schlan. Střední Čechy, NW Czech Republic 50°14′N 14°05′E
111 K16 **Śląskie** ⬖ *province* S Poland
12 C10 **Slate Falls** Ontario, S Canada 51°11′N 91°32′W
27 T4 **Slater** Missouri, C USA 39°13′N 93°04′W
112 H9 **Slatina** *Hung.* Szlatina; *prev.* Podravska Slatina. Virovitica-Podravina, NE Croatia 45°40′N 17°46′E
116 I14 **Slatina** Olt, S Romania 45°27′N 24°21′E
25 N5 **Slaton** Texas, SW USA 33°26′N 101°38′W
95 H14 **Slattum** Akershus, S Norway 60°00′N 10°55′E
11 R10 **Slave** ≈ Alberta/Northwest Territories, C Canada
68 E12 **Slave Coast** *coastal region* W Africa
11 P13 **Slave Lake** Alberta, SW Canada 55°17′N 114°46′W
122 I13 **Slavgorod** Altayskiy Kray, S Russian Federation 52°55′N 78°46′E
Slavgorod *see* Slawharad
Slavonia *see* Slavonija
112 G9 **Slavonija** *Eng.* Slavonia, *Ger.* Slawonien, *Hung.* Szlavonia, Szlavonország. *cultural region* NE Croatia
112 H10 **Slavonski Brod** *Ger.* Brod, *Hung.* Bród; *prev.* Brod, Brod na Savi. Brod-Posavina, NE Croatia 45°09′N 18°00′E
Slavonski Brod-Posavina *see* Brod-Posavina
116 L4 **Slavuta** Khmel'nyts'ka Oblast', NW Ukraine 50°18′N 26°52′E
117 P2 **Slavutych** Chernihivs'ka Oblast', N Ukraine 51°31′N 30°47′E
123 R15 **Slavyanka** Primorskiy Kray, SE Russian Federation 42°46′N 131°19′E
114 J8 **Slavyanovo** Pleven, N Bulgaria 43°28′N 24°52′E
Slavyansk *see* Slov"yans'k
126 K14 **Slavyansk-na-Kubani** Krasnodarskiy Kray, SW Russian Federation 45°16′N 38°09′E
119 N20 **Slavyechna** *Rus.* Slovechna. ≈ Belarus/Ukraine
119 O16 **Slawharad** *Rus.* Slavgorod. Mahilyowskaya Voblasts', E Belarus 53°27′N 31°00′E
110 G7 **Sławno** Zachodnio-pomorskie, NW Poland 54°23′N 16°43′E
Slawonien *see* Slavonija
29 S10 **Slayton** Minnesota, N USA 43°59′N 95°45′W
97 N18 **Sleaford** E England, United Kingdom 53°00′N 00°28′W
97 A20 **Slea Head** *Ir.* Ceann Sléibhe. *headland* SW Ireland 52°05′N 10°25′W
96 G9 **Sleat, Sound of** *strait* NW Scotland, United Kingdom
Sledyuki *see* Slyedzyuki
12 I5 **Sleeper Islands** *island group* Nunavut, C Canada
31 O6 **Sleeping Bear Point** *headland* Michigan, N USA 44°54′N 86°02′W
29 T10 **Sleepy Eye** Minnesota, N USA 44°18′N 94°43′W
39 O11 **Sleetmute** Alaska, USA 61°42′N 157°10′W
Sléibhe, Ceann *see* Slea Head
Slēmānī *see* As Sulaymānīyah
195 O5 **Slessor Glacier** *glacier* Antarctica
22 L9 **Slidell** Louisiana, S USA 30°16′N 89°46′W
18 K12 **Slide Mountain** ▲ New York, NE USA 42°00′N 74°23′W
98 I13 **Sliedrecht** Zuid-Holland, C Netherlands 51°50′N 04°46′E
121 P16 **Sliema** N Malta 35°54′N 14°31′E
97 G16 **Slieve Donard** ▲ SE Northern Ireland, United Kingdom 54°10′N 05°57′W
Sligeach *see* Sligo
97 D16 **Sligo** *Ir.* Sligeach. Sligo, NW Ireland 54°17′N 08°28′W
97 C16 **Sligo** *Ir.* Sligeach. *cultural region* NW Ireland
97 C15 **Sligo Bay** *Ir.* Cuan Shligigh. *inlet* NW Ireland
18 B13 **Slippery Rock** Pennsylvania, NE USA 41°02′N 80°02′W
95 P19 **Slite** Gotland, SE Sweden 57°37′N 18°46′E
114 L9 **Sliven** *var.* Slivno. Sliven, C Bulgaria 42°42′N 26°21′E
114 L10 **Sliven** ⬖ *province* C Bulgaria
114 G9 **Slivnitsa** Sofiya, W Bulgaria 42°51′N 23°01′E
Slivno *see* Sliven
114 L7 **Slivo Pole** Ruse, N Bulgaria 43°57′N 26°15′E
29 S13 **Sloan** Iowa, C USA 42°13′N 96°13′W
35 X12 **Sloan** Nevada, W USA 35°56′N 115°13′W
Slobodka *see* Slabodka
125 R14 **Slobodskoy** Kirovskaya Oblast', NW Russian Federation 58°43′N 50°12′E
Slobodzeya *see* Slobozia
117 O10 **Slobozia** *Rus.* Slobodzeya. E Moldova 46°45′N 29°42′E
116 L14 **Slobozia** Ialomiţa, SE Romania 44°34′N 27°23′E
98 O5 **Slochteren** Groningen, NE Netherlands 53°13′N 06°48′E
119 H17 **Slonim** *Pol.* Słonim. Hrodzyenskaya Voblasts', W Belarus 53°06′N 25°19′E
Słonim *see* Slonim
98 K7 **Sloter Meer** ◎ N Netherlands
Slot, The *see* New Georgia Sound
97 N22 **Slough** S England, United Kingdom 51°31′N 00°36′W
111 J20 **Slovakia** *off.* Slovenská Republika, *Ger.* Slowakei, *Hung.* Szlovákia, *Slvk.* Slovensko. ◆ *republic* C Europe
Slovak Ore Mountains *see* Slovenské rudohorie
Slovechna *see* Slavyechna
109 S12 **Slovenia** *off.* Republic of Slovenia, *Ger.* Slowenien, *Slvn.* Slovenija. ◆ *republic* SE Europe
Slovenia, Republic of *see* Slovenia
Slovenija *see* Slovenia
109 V10 **Slovenj Gradec** *Ger.* Windischgraz. N Slovenia 46°29′N 15°05′E
109 W10 **Slovenska Bistrica** *Ger.* Windischfeistritz. NE Slovenia 46°21′N 15°27′E
Slovenská Republika *see* Slovakia
109 W10 **Slovenske Konjice** E Slovenia 46°21′N 15°28′E
111 K20 **Slovenské rudohorie** *Eng.* Slovak Ore Mountains, *Ger.* Slowakisches Erzgebirge, Ungarisches Erzgebirge. ▲▲ C Slovakia
Slovensko *see* Slovakia
117 Y7 **Slov"yanoserbs'k** Luhans'ka Oblast', E Ukraine 48°41′N 39°00′E
117 W6 **Slov"yans'k** *Rus.* Slavyansk. Donets'ka Oblast', E Ukraine 48°51′N 37°38′E
Slowakei *see* Slovakia
Slowakisches Erzgebirge *see* Slovenské rudohorie
Slowenien *see* Slovenia
110 D11 **Słubice** *Ger.* Frankfurt. Lubuskie, W Poland 52°20′N 14°35′E
119 K19 **Sluch** *Rus.* Sluch'. ≈ C Belarus
116 L4 **Sluch** ≈ NW Ukraine
99 D16 **Sluis** Zeeland, SW Netherlands 51°18′N 03°22′E
112 D10 **Slunj** *Hung.* Szluin. Karlovac, C Croatia 45°06′N 15°35′E
110 I11 **Słupca** Wielkopolskie, C Poland 52°17′N 17°52′E
110 G6 **Słupia** *Ger.* Stolpe. ≈ NW Poland
110 G6 **Słupsk** *Ger.* Stolp. Pomorskie, N Poland 54°28′N 17°01′E
119 K18 **Slutsk** Minskaya Voblasts', S Belarus 53°02′N 27°32′E
119 O16 **Slyedzyuki** *Rus.* Sledyuki. Mahilyowskaya Voblasts', E Belarus 53°35′N 30°22′E
97 A17 **Slyne Head** *Ir.* Ceann Léime. *headland* W Ireland 53°25′N 10°11′W
27 U14 **Smackover** Arkansas, C USA 33°21′N 92°43′W
95 L20 **Småland** *cultural region* S Sweden
95 K20 **Smålandsstenar** Jönköping, S Sweden 57°10′N 13°24′E
Small Malaita *see* Maramasike
13 O8 **Smallwood Reservoir** ⊠ Newfoundland and Labrador, S Canada
119 N14 **Smalyany** *Rus.* Smolyany. Vitsyebskaya Voblasts', NE Belarus 54°36′N 30°04′E
119 L15 **Smalyavichy** *Rus.* Smolevichi. Minskaya Voblasts', C Belarus 54°02′N 28°05′E
74 C9 **Smara** *var.* Es Semara. N Western Sahara 26°45′N 11°44′W
119 I14 **Smarhon'** *Pol.* Smorgonie, *Rus.* Smorgon'. Hrodzyenskaya Voblasts', W Belarus 54°29′N 26°24′E
112 M11 **Smederevo** *Ger.* Semendria. Serbia, N Serbia 44°41′N 20°56′E
112 M12 **Smederevska Palanka** Serbia, C Serbia 44°24′N 20°56′E
95 M14 **Smedjebacken** Dalarna, C Sweden 60°08′N 15°25′E
116 L13 **Smeeni** Buzău, SE Romania 45°00′N 26°52′E
Smela *see* Smila
107 D16 **Smeralda, Costa** *cultural region* Sardegna, Italy, C Mediterranean Sea
111 J22 **Śmigiel** *Ger.* Schmiegel. Wielkopolskie, C Poland 52°02′N 16°33′E
117 Q6 **Smila** *Rus.* Smela. Cherkas'ka Oblast', C Ukraine 49°15′N 31°54′E
98 N7 **Smilde** Drenthe, NE Netherlands 52°57′N 06°28′E
11 S16 **Smiley** Saskatchewan, S Canada 51°40′N 109°24′W
25 T12 **Smiley** Texas, SW USA 29°16′N 97°38′W
Smilten *see* Smiltene
118 I8 **Smiltene** *Ger.* Smilten. Valka, N Latvia 57°25′N 25°53′E
123 T13 **Smirnykh** Ostrov Sakhalin, Sakhalinskaya Oblast', SE Russian Federation 49°43′N 142°48′E
11 Q13 **Smith** Alberta, W Canada 55°06′N 113°57′W
39 P4 **Smith Bay** *bay* Alaska, NW USA
12 I3 **Smith, Cape** *headland* Québec, NE Canada 60°50′N 78°06′W
26 L3 **Smith Center** Kansas, C USA 39°46′N 98°46′W
10 K13 **Smithers** British Columbia, SW Canada 54°45′N 127°10′W
21 V10 **Smithfield** North Carolina, SE USA 35°30′N 78°21′W
36 L1 **Smithfield** Utah, W USA 41°50′N 111°49′W
21 X7 **Smithfield** Virginia, NE USA 36°41′N 76°38′W
12 I3 **Smith Island** *island* Nunavut, C Canada
Smith Island *see* Sumisu-jima
20 H7 **Smithland** Kentucky, S USA 37°06′N 88°24′W
21 T7 **Smith Mountain Lake** *var.* Leesville Lake. ⊠ Virginia, NE USA
34 L1 **Smith River** California, W USA 41°54′N 124°09′W
33 R9 **Smith River** ≈ Montana, NW USA
14 L13 **Smiths Falls** Ontario, SE Canada 44°54′N 76°01′W
33 N13 **Smiths Ferry** Idaho, NW USA 44°19′N 116°04′W
20 K7 **Smiths Grove** Kentucky, S USA 37°01′N 86°14′W
183 N15 **Smithton** Tasmania, SE Australia 40°54′S 145°06′E
18 L14 **Smithtown** Long Island, New York, NE USA 40°52′N 73°13′W
20 K9 **Smithville** Tennessee, S USA 35°59′N 85°49′W
25 T11 **Smithville** Texas, SW USA 30°04′N 97°32′W
Šmohor *see* Hermagor
35 Q4 **Smoke Creek Desert** *desert* Nevada, W USA
11 O14 **Smoky** ≈ Alberta, W Canada
182 E7 **Smoky Bay** South Australia 32°22′S 133°57′E
183 V6 **Smoky Cape** *headland* New South Wales, SE Australia 30°54′S 153°06′E
26 L4 **Smoky Hill River** ≈ Kansas, C USA
26 L4 **Smoky Hills** *hill range* Kansas, C USA
11 Q14 **Smoky Lake** Alberta, SW Canada 54°08′N 112°26′W
94 E8 **Smøla** *island* W Norway
126 H4 **Smolensk** Smolenskaya Oblast', W Russian Federation 54°48′N 32°08′E
126 H4 **Smolenskaya Oblast'** ⬖ *province* W Russian Federation
Smolensk-Moscow Upland *see* Smolensko-Moskovskaya Vozvyshennost'
126 J3 **Smolensko-Moskovskaya Vozvyshennost'** *var.* Smolensk-Moscow Upland. ▲▲ W Russian Federation
Smolevichi *see* Smalyavichy
115 C15 **Smólikas** *var.* Smolikás. ▲ W Greece 40°06′N 20°54′E
114 I12 **Smolyan** *prev.* Pashmakli. Smolyan, S Bulgaria 41°34′N 24°42′E
114 I12 **Smolyan** ⬖ *province* S Bulgaria
Smolyany *see* Smalyany
33 S15 **Smoot** Wyoming, C USA 42°37′N 110°55′W
12 G12 **Smooth Rock Falls** Ontario, S Canada 49°17′N 81°37′W
Smorgon'/Smorgonie *see* Smarhon'
114 M9 **Smyadovo** Shumen, NE Bulgaria 43°04′N 27°01′E
95 K23 **Smygehamn** Skåne, S Sweden 55°19′N 13°25′E
194 I7 **Smyley Island** *island* Antarctica
21 Y3 **Smyrna** Delaware, NE USA 39°18′N 75°36′W
23 S3 **Smyrna** Georgia, SE USA 33°52′N 84°30′W
20 J9 **Smyrna** Tennessee, S USA 36°00′N 86°30′W
Smyrna *see* İzmir
97 I16 **Snaefell** ▲ C Isle of Man 54°15′N 04°29′W
92 H3 **Snaefellsjökull** ▲ W Iceland 64°51′N 23°51′W
92 J3 **Snækollur** ▲ C Iceland 64°38′N 19°18′W

◆ Country ● Country Capital ◇ Dependent Territory ○ Dependent Territory Capital ⬖ Administrative Regions ✈ International Airport ▲ Mountain ▲▲ Mountain Range ⛛ Volcano ≈ River ◎ Lake ⊠ Reservoir

Snake – Souris

10 J4 **Snake** ≈ Yukon Territory, NW Canada
29 O8 **Snake Creek** ≈ South Dakota, N USA
183 P13 **Snake Island** island Victoria, SE Australia
35 Y6 **Snake Range** ▲▲ Nevada, W USA
32 K10 **Snake River** ≈ NW USA
29 V6 **Snake River** ≈ Minnesota, N USA
28 L12 **Snake River** ≈ Nebraska, C USA
33 Q14 **Snake River Plain** plain Idaho, NW USA
93 F15 **Snåsa** Nord-Trøndelag, C Norway 64°16′N 12°25′E
21 O8 **Sneedville** Tennessee, S USA 36°31′N 83°13′W
98 K6 **Sneek** Friesland, N Netherlands 53°02′N 05°40′E
Sneeuw-gebergte see Maoke, Pegunungan
95 F22 **Snejbjerg** Ringkøbing, C Denmark 56°08′N 08°55′E
124 J3 **Snezhnogorsk** Murmanskaya Oblast', NW Russian Federation 69°12′N 33°20′E
122 K9 **Snezhnogorsk** Taymyrskiy (Dolgano-Nenetskiy) Avtonomnyy Okrug, N Russian Federation 68°06′N 87°37′E
Snezhnoye see Snizhne
111 G15 **Sněžka** Ger. Schneekoppe, Pol. Śnieżka. ▲ N Czech Republic/Poland 50°42′N 15°55′E
110 N8 **Śniardwy, Jezioro** Ger. Spirdingsee. ◎ NE Poland
Sniečkus see Visaginas
Śnieżka see Sněžka
117 R10 **Snihurivka** Mykolayivs'ka Oblast', S Ukraine 47°05′N 32°48′E
116 I5 **Snilov** ✈ (L'viv) L'vivs'ka Oblast', W Ukraine 49°45′N 23°59′E
111 O19 **Snina** Hung. Szinna. Prešovský Kraj, E Slovakia 49°N 22°10′E
117 Y8 **Snizhne** Rus. Snezhnoye. Donets'ka Oblast', SE Ukraine 48°01′N 38°46′E
94 G10 **Snøhetta** var. Snohetta. ▲ S Norway 62°22′N 09°08′E
92 G12 **Snøtinden** ▲ C Norway 66°39′N 13°50′E
97 I18 **Snowdon** ▲ NW Wales, United Kingdom 53°04′N 04°04′W
97 I18 **Snowdonia** ▲▲ NW Wales, United Kingdom
8 K10 **Snowdrift** ≈ Northwest Territories, NW Canada
Snowdrift see Łutselk'e
37 N12 **Snowflake** Arizona, SW USA 34°30′N 110°04′W
21 Y5 **Snow Hill** Maryland, NE USA 38°11′N 75°23′W
21 W10 **Snow Hill** North Carolina, SE USA 35°26′N 77°39′W
194 H3 **Snowhill Island** island Antarctica
11 V13 **Snow Lake** Manitoba, C Canada 54°56′N 100°02′W
37 R5 **Snowmass Mountain** ▲ Colorado, C USA 39°07′N 107°04′W
18 M10 **Snow, Mount** ▲ Vermont, NE USA 42°56′N 72°52′W
34 M5 **Snow Mountain** ▲ California, W USA 39°44′N 123°01′W
Snow Mountains see Maoke, Pegunungan
33 N7 **Snowshoe Peak** ▲ Montana, NW USA 48°15′N 115°44′W
182 I8 **Snowtown** South Australia 33°49′S 138°13′E
36 K1 **Snowville** Utah, W USA 41°59′N 112°42′W
35 X3 **Snow Water Lake** ◎ Nevada, W USA
183 Q11 **Snowy Mountains** ▲▲ New South Wales/Victoria, SE Australia
183 Q12 **Snowy River** ≈ New South Wales/Victoria, SE Australia
44 K5 **Snug Corner** Acklins Island, SE Bahamas 22°31′N 73°51′W
167 T13 **Snuŏl** Krâchéh, E Cambodia 12°04′N 106°26′E
116 J7 **Snyatyn** Ivano-Frankivs'ka Oblast', W Ukraine 48°30′N 25°50′E
26 L12 **Snyder** Oklahoma, C USA 34°37′N 98°56′W
25 O6 **Snyder** Texas, SW USA 32°43′N 100°54′W
172 H3 **Soalala** Mahajanga, W Madagascar 16°05′S 45°21′E
172 J4 **Soanierana-Ivongo** Toamasina, E Madagascar 16°53′S 49°35′E
171 R11 **Soasiu** var. Tidore. Pulau Tidore, E Indonesia 0°40′N 127°25′E
54 G8 **Soatá** Boyacá, C Colombia 06°23′N 72°40′W
172 I5 **Soavinandriana** Antananarivo, C Madagascar 19°09′S 46°43′E
77 V13 **Soba** Kaduna, C Nigeria 10°58′N 08°06′E
163 Y16 **Sobaek-sanmaek** ▲▲ S South Korea
80 F13 **Sobat** ≈ E Sudan
171 Z14 **Sobger, Sungai** ≈ Papua, E Indonesia
171 V13 **Sobiei** Papua, E Indonesia 02°31′S 134°30′E
126 M3 **Sobinka** Vladimirskaya Oblast', W Russian Federation 56°00′N 39°55′E
127 S7 **Sobolevo** Orenburgskaya Oblast', W Russian Federation 51°57′N 51°42′E
Soborsin see Săvârşin
164 D15 **Sobo-san** ▲ Kyūshū, SW Japan 32°50′N 131°16′E
111 G14 **Sobótka** Dolnośląskie, SW Poland 50°53′N 16°48′E
59 O15 **Sobradinho** Bahia, E Brazil 09°33′S 40°56′W
Sobradinho, Barragem de see Sobradinho, Represa de
59 O16 **Sobradinho, Represa de** var. Barragem de Sobradinho. ⊠ E Brazil
58 O13 **Sobral** Ceará, E Brazil 03°45′S 40°20′W
105 T4 **Sobrarbe** physical region NE Spain
109 R10 **Soča** It. Isonzo. ≈ Italy/Slovenia
110 L11 **Sochaczew** Mazowieckie, C Poland 52°15′N 20°15′E
126 L15 **Sochi** Krasnodarskiy Kray, SW Russian Federation 43°35′N 39°46′E
114 G13 **Sochós** var. Sohos, Sokhós. Kentrikí Makedonía, N Greece 40°49′N 23°23′E
191 R11 **Société, Archipel de la** var. Archipel de Tahiti, Îles de la Société, Eng. Society Islands. island group W French Polynesia
Société, Îles de la/Society Islands see Société, Archipel de la
21 T11 **Society Hill** South Carolina, SE USA 34°28′N 79°54′W
175 W9 **Society Ridge** undersea feature C Pacific Ocean
62 I5 **Socompa, Volcán** ☗ N Chile 24°18′S 68°03′W
Soconusco, Sierra de see Madre, Sierra
54 G8 **Socorro** Santander, C Colombia 06°30′N 73°16′W
37 R13 **Socorro** New Mexico, SW USA 33°58′N 106°55′W
Socotra see Suquṭrā
167 S14 **Soc Trăng** var. Khanh Hung. Soc Trăng, S Vietnam 09°36′N 105°58′E
105 P10 **Socuéllamos** Castilla-La Mancha, C Spain 39°18′N 02°48′W
35 W13 **Soda Lake** salt flat California, W USA
92 L11 **Sodankylä** Lappi, N Finland 67°26′N 26°35′E
Sodari see Sodiri
33 R15 **Soda Springs** Idaho, NW USA 42°39′N 111°36′W
Soddo/Soddu see Sodo
20 L10 **Soddy Daisy** Tennessee, S USA 35°14′N 85°11′W
95 N14 **Söderfors** Uppsala, C Sweden 60°23′N 17°14′E
94 N12 **Söderhamn** Gävleborg, C Sweden 61°19′N 17°10′E
95 N17 **Söderköping** Östergötland, S Sweden 58°28′N 16°20′E
95 N17 **Södermanland** ◈ county C Sweden
95 O16 **Södertälje** Stockholm, C Sweden 59°11′N 17°39′E
80 D10 **Sodiri** var. Sawdirī, Sodari. Northern Kordofan, C Sudan 14°23′N 29°06′E
81 I14 **Sodo** var. Soddo, Soddu. Southern Nationalities, S Ethiopia 06°49′N 37°43′E
94 N11 **Södra Dellen** ◎ C Sweden
95 M19 **Södra Vi** Kalmar, S Sweden 57°45′N 15°45′E
18 G9 **Sodus Point** headland New York, NE USA 43°16′N 76°59′W
171 Q17 **Soe** prev. Soë. Timor, C Indonesia 09°51′S 124°29′E
Soebang see Subang
Soekaboemi see Sukabumi
169 N15 **Soekarno-Hatta** ✈ (Jakarta) Jawa, S Indonesia
Soëla-Sund see Soela Väin
118 E5 **Soela Väin** prev. Eng. Sele Sound, Ger. Dagden-Sund, Soëla-Sund. strait W Estonia
Soemba see Sumba, Pulau
Soembawa see Sumbawa
Soemenep see Sumenep
Soengaipenoeh see Sungaipenuh
Soerabaja see Surabaya
Soerakarta see Surakarta
101 G14 **Soest** Nordrhein-Westfalen, W Germany 51°34′N 08°06′E
98 J11 **Soest** Utrecht, C Netherlands 52°10′N 05°20′E
100 F11 **Soeste** ≈ NW Germany
98 J11 **Soesterberg** Utrecht, C Netherlands 52°07′N 05°17′E
115 E16 **Sofádes** var. Sofádhes. Thessalía, C Greece 39°20′N 22°06′E
Sofádhes see Sofádes
83 N18 **Sofala** Sofala, C Mozambique 20°04′S 34°43′E
83 N17 **Sofala** ◈ province C Mozambique
83 N18 **Sofala, Baia de** bay C Mozambique
172 J3 **Sofia** seasonal river NW Madagascar
Sofia see Sofiya
115 G19 **Sofikó** Pelopónnisos, S Greece 37°46′N 23°04′E
Sofi-Kurgan see Sopu-Korgon
114 G10 **Sofiya** var. Sophia, Eng. Sofia, Lat. Serdica. ● (Bulgaria) Sofiya-Grad, W Bulgaria 42°42′N 23°20′E
114 H9 **Sofiya** ◈ province W Bulgaria
114 G9 **Sofiya** ✈ Sofiya-Grad, W Bulgaria 42°42′N 23°26′E
114 G9 **Sofiya, Grad** ◈ municipality W Bulgaria
Sofiyevka see Sofiyivka
117 S8 **Sofiyivka** Rus. Sofiyevka. Dnipropetrovs'ka Oblast', E Ukraine 48°04′N 33°55′E
123 R12 **Sofiysk** Khabarovskiy Kray, SE Russian Federation 51°32′N 139°46′E
123 R13 **Sofiysk** Khabarovskiy Kray, SE Russian Federation 52°20′N 133°37′E
124 I6 **Sofporog** Respublika Kareliya, NW Russian Federation 65°48′N 31°30′E
115 L23 **Sofraná** prev. Záfora. island Kykládes, Greece, Aegean Sea
165 Y14 **Sōfu-gan** island Izu-shotō, SE Japan
156 K10 **Sog** Xizang Zizhiqu, W China 31°52′N 93°40′E
54 G9 **Sogamoso** Boyacá, C Colombia 05°43′N 72°56′W
136 I11 **Soğanlı Çayı** ≈ N Turkey
94 E12 **Sogn** physical region S Norway
Sogndal see Sogndalsfjøra
94 E12 **Sogndalsfjøra** var. Sogndal. Sogn Og Fjordane, S Norway 61°13′N 07°05′E
95 E18 **Søgne** Vest-Agder, S Norway 58°05′N 07°49′E
94 D12 **Sognefjorden** fjord NE North Sea
94 C12 **Sogn Og Fjordane** ◈ county S Norway
162 I11 **Sogo Nur** ◎ N China
159 T12 **Sogruma** Qinghai, W China 32°32′N 100°52′E
163 X17 **Sŏgwip'o** S South Korea 33°14′N 126°33′E
Sohâg see Sawhāj
Sohar see Şuḩār
64 H9 **Sohm Plain** undersea feature NW Atlantic Ocean
100 H7 **Soholmer Au** ≈ N Germany
Sohos see Sochós
Sohrau see Żory
99 F20 **Soignies** Hainaut, SW Belgium 50°35′N 04°04′E
159 R15 **Sola** Xizang Zizhiqu, W China 30°40′N 97°07′E
103 P4 **Soissons** anc. Augusta Suessionum, Noviodunum. Aisne, N France 49°23′N 03°20′E
164 H13 **Sōja** Okayama, Honshū, SW Japan 34°40′N 133°42′E
152 F13 **Sojat** Rājasthān, N India 25°53′N 73°45′E
163 W13 **Sojosŏn-man** inlet W North Korea
116 I4 **Sokal'** Rus. Sokal. L'vivs'ka Oblast', NW Ukraine 50°29′N 24°17′E
163 Y14 **Sokch'o** N South Korea 38°07′N 128°34′E
136 B15 **Söke** Aydın, SW Turkey 37°46′N 27°24′E
189 N12 **Sokehs Island** island E Micronesia
79 M24 **Sokele** Katanga, SE Dem. Rep. Congo 09°54′S 24°38′E
147 R11 **Sokh** Uzb. Sŭkh. ≈ Kyrgyzstan/Uzbekistan
Sokh see So'x
Sokhós see Sochós
137 Q8 **Sokhumi** Rus. Sukhumi. NW Georgia 43°02′N 41°01′E
113 O14 **Sokobanja** Serbia, E Serbia 43°39′N 21°51′E
77 R15 **Sokodé** C Togo 08°58′N 01°10′E
123 T10 **Sokol** Magadanskaya Oblast', E Russian Federation 59°51′N 150°56′E
124 M13 **Sokol** Vologodskaya Oblast', NW Russian Federation 59°26′N 40°09′E
110 P9 **Sokółka** Podlaskie, NE Poland 53°24′N 23°31′E
76 M11 **Sokolo** Ségou, W Mali 14°43′N 06°02′W
111 A16 **Sokolov** Ger. Falkenau an der Eger; prev. Falknov nad Ohří. Karlovarský Kraj, W Czech Republic 50°10′N 12°38′E
111 O16 **Sokołów Małopolski** Podkarpackie, SE Poland 50°12′N 22°07′E
110 O11 **Sokołów Podlaski** Mazowieckie, C Poland 52°26′N 22°14′E
76 G11 **Sokone** W Senegal 13°53′N 16°22′W
77 T12 **Sokoto** Sokoto, NW Nigeria 13°05′N 05°16′E
77 T12 **Sokoto** ◈ state NW Nigeria
77 S12 **Sokoto** ≈ NW Nigeria
Sokotra see Suquṭrā
147 U7 **Sokuluk** Chuyskaya Oblast', N Kyrgyzstan 42°53′N 74°19′E
116 L7 **Sokyryany** Chernivets'ka Oblast', W Ukraine 48°28′N 27°25′E
95 C16 **Sola** Rogaland, S Norway 58°53′N 05°36′E
187 R12 **Sola** Vanua Lava, N Vanuatu 13°51′S 167°34′E
95 C17 **Sola** ✈ (Stavanger) Rogaland, S Norway 58°54′N 05°36′E
81 H18 **Solai** Rift Valley, W Kenya 0°02′N 36°03′E
152 I8 **Solan** Himāchal Pradesh, N India 30°54′N 77°06′E
185 A25 **Solander Island** island SW New Zealand
Solano see Bahía Solano
155 F15 **Solāpur** var. Sholāpur. Mahārāshtra, W India 17°43′N 75°54′E
93 H16 **Solberg** Västernorrland, C Sweden 63°48′N 17°40′E
116 K9 **Solca** Ger. Solka. Suceava, N Romania 47°40′N 25°50′E
105 O16 **Sol, Costa del** coastal region S Spain
106 F5 **Solda** Ger. Sulden. Trentino-Alto Adige, N Italy 46°33′N 10°35′E
117 N9 **Şoldăneşti** Rus. Sholdaneshty. N Moldova 47°49′N 28°45′E
Soldau see Wkra
108 L8 **Sölden** Tirol, W Austria 46°58′N 11°01′E
27 P3 **Soldier Creek** ≈ Kansas, C USA
39 R12 **Soldotna** Alaska, USA 60°29′N 151°03′W
110 I10 **Solec Kujawski** Kujawsko-pomorskie, C Poland 53°04′N 18°09′E
61 B16 **Soledad** Santa Fe, C Argentina 30°38′S 60°52′W
55 E4 **Soledad** Atlántico, N Colombia 10°54′N 74°48′W
35 O11 **Soledad** California, W USA 36°25′N 121°19′W
55 O7 **Soledad** Anzoátegui, NE Venezuela 08°10′N 63°36′W
61 H15 **Soledade** Rio Grande do Sul, S Brazil 28°50′S 52°30′W
Isla Soledad see East Falkland
103 Y15 **Solenzara** Corse, France, C Mediterranean Sea 41°55′N 09°24′E
Soleure see Solothurn
94 C12 **Solheim** Hordaland, S Norway 60°54′N 05°30′E
125 N14 **Soligalich** Kostromskaya Oblast', NW Russian Federation 59°05′N 42°15′E
Soligorsk see Salihorsk
97 L20 **Solihull** C England, United Kingdom 52°25′N 01°45′W
125 U13 **Solikamsk** Permskaya Oblast', NW Russian Federation 59°37′N 56°46′E
127 V8 **Sol'-Iletsk** Orenburgskaya Oblast', W Russian Federation 51°09′N 55°05′E
57 G17 **Solimana, Nevado** ▲ S Peru 15°24′S 72°49′W
58 E13 **Solimões, Rio** ≈ C Brazil
113 E14 **Solin** It. Salona; anc. Salonae. Split-Dalmacija, S Croatia 43°33′N 16°29′E
101 E15 **Solingen** Nordrhein-Westfalen, W Germany 51°10′N 07°05′E
Solka see Solca
93 H16 **Sollefteå** Västernorrland, C Sweden 63°09′N 17°15′E
95 O15 **Sollentuna** Stockholm, C Sweden 59°26′N 17°56′E
105 X9 **Sóller** Mallorca, Spain, W Mediterranean Sea 39°46′N 02°42′E
94 L13 **Sollerön** Dalarna, C Sweden 60°55′N 14°34′E
101 I14 **Solling** hill range C Germany
95 O16 **Solna** Stockholm, C Sweden 59°22′N 17°58′E
126 K3 **Solnechnogorsk** Moskovskaya Oblast', W Russian Federation 56°07′N 37°04′E
123 R10 **Solnechnyy** Khabarovskiy Kray, SE Russian Federation 50°41′N 136°42′E
123 S13 **Solnechnyy** Respublika Sakha (Yakutiya), NE Russian Federation 60°13′N 137°42′E
Solo see Surakarta
107 L17 **Solofra** Campania, S Italy 40°49′N 14°48′E
168 J11 **Solok** Sumatera, W Indonesia 0°45′S 100°42′E
42 C6 **Sololá** Sololá, W Guatemala 14°46′N 91°09′W
42 A2 **Sololá** off. Departamento de Sololá. ◈ department SW Guatemala
Sololá, Departamento de see Sololá
81 J16 **Sololo** Eastern, N Kenya 03°31′N 38°39′E
42 C4 **Soloma** Huehuetenango, W Guatemala 15°38′N 91°25′W
38 M9 **Solomon** Alaska, USA 64°33′N 164°26′W
27 N4 **Solomon** Kansas, C USA 38°55′N 97°22′W
187 N9 **Solomon Islands** prev. British Solomon Islands Protectorate. ◆ commonwealth republic W Solomon Islands N Melanesia W Pacific Ocean
186 L7 **Solomon Islands** island group Papua New Guinea/Solomon Islands
26 M3 **Solomon River** ≈ Kansas, C USA
186 H8 **Solomon Sea** sea W Pacific Ocean
31 U11 **Solon** Ohio, N USA 41°23′N 81°26′W
117 T8 **Solone** Dnipropetrovs'ka Oblast', E Ukraine 48°12′N 34°49′E
171 P16 **Solor, Kepulauan** island group S Indonesia
126 M4 **Solotcha** Ryazanskaya Oblast', W Russian Federation 54°43′N 39°50′E
108 D7 **Solothurn** Fr. Soleure. Solothurn, NW Switzerland 47°13′N 07°32′E
108 D7 **Solothurn** Fr. Soleure. ◈ canton NW Switzerland
124 J7 **Solovetskiye Ostrova** island group NW Russian Federation
105 V5 **Solsona** Cataluña, NE Spain 42°00′N 01°31′E
113 E14 **Šolta** It. Solta. island S Croatia
Solṭānābād see Kāshmar
142 L4 **Solṭānīyeh** Zanjān, NW Iran 36°24′N 48°50′E
100 I11 **Soltau** Niedersachsen, NW Germany 52°59′N 09°50′E
124 G14 **Sol'tsy** Novgorodskaya Oblast', W Russian Federation 58°09′N 30°23′E
Soltüstik Qazaqstan Oblysy see Severnyy Kazakhstan
Solun see Thessaloníki
113 O19 **Solunska Glava** ▲ C FYR Macedonia 41°43′N 21°24′E
95 L22 **Sölvesborg** Blekinge, S Sweden 56°04′N 14°35′E
97 J15 **Solway Firth** inlet England/Scotland, United Kingdom
82 I13 **Solwezi** North Western, NW Zambia 12°11′S 26°23′E
165 Q11 **Sōma** Fukushima, Honshū, C Japan 37°49′N 140°52′E
136 C13 **Soma** Manisa, W Turkey 39°10′N 27°36′E
81 O15 **Somalia** off. Somali Democratic Republic, Som. Jamuuriyada Demuqraadiga Soomaaliyeed, Soomaaliya; prev. Italian Somaliland, Somaliland Protectorate. ◆ republic E Africa
173 N6 **Somali Basin** undersea feature W Indian Ocean 0°00′N 52°00′E
Somali Democratic Republic see Somalia
80 N12 **Somaliland** ◈ disputed territory N Somalia
Somaliland Protectorate see Somalia
67 Y8 **Somali Plain** undersea feature W Indian Ocean 01°00′N 51°30′E
112 J8 **Sombor** Hung. Zombor. Vojvodina, NW Serbia 45°46′N 19°07′E
99 H20 **Sombreffe** Namur, S Belgium 50°32′N 04°39′E
40 L10 **Sombrerete** Zacatecas, C Mexico 23°38′N 103°40′W
45 V8 **Sombrero** island N Anguilla
151 Q21 **Sombrero Channel** channel Nicobar Islands, India
116 H9 **Şomcuta Mare** Hung. Nagysomkút; prev. Somcuţa Mare. Maramureş, N Romania 47°29′N 23°30′E
Somcuţa Mare see Şomcuta Mare
167 R9 **Somdet** Kalasin, E Thailand 16°41′N 103°44′E
99 L15 **Someren** Noord-Brabant, SE Netherlands 51°23′N 05°42′E
93 L19 **Somero** Länsi-Suomi, SW Finland 60°37′N 23°30′E
33 P7 **Somers** Montana, NW USA 48°04′N 114°16′W
64 A12 **Somerset** var. Somerset Village. W Bermuda 32°18′N 64°53′W
37 Q5 **Somerset** Colorado, C USA 38°55′N 107°27′W
20 M7 **Somerset** Kentucky, S USA 37°05′N 84°36′W
19 O12 **Somerset** Massachusetts, NE USA 41°46′N 71°07′W
97 K23 **Somerset** cultural region SW England, United Kingdom
Somerset East see Somerset-Oos
64 A12 **Somerset Island** island W Bermuda
197 N9 **Somerset Island** island Queen Elizabeth Islands, Nunavut, NW Canada
Somerset Nile see Victoria Nile
83 I25 **Somerset-Oos** var. Somerset East. Eastern Cape, S South Africa 32°44′S 25°35′E
Somerset Village see Somerset
83 E26 **Somerset-Wes** var. Somerset West. Western Cape, SW South Africa 34°05′S 18°51′E
Somerset West see Somerset-Wes
Somers Islands see Bermuda
18 J17 **Somers Point** New Jersey, NE USA 39°18′N 74°34′W
19 P9 **Somersworth** New Hampshire, NE USA 43°15′N 70°52′W
36 H15 **Somerton** Arizona, SW USA 32°36′N 114°42′W
18 J14 **Somerville** New Jersey, NE USA 40°34′N 74°36′W
20 F10 **Somerville** Tennessee, S USA 35°14′N 89°24′W
25 U10 **Somerville** Texas, SW USA 30°21′N 96°31′W
25 T10 **Somerville Lake** ⊠ Texas, SW USA
Someş/Somesch/Someşul see Szamos
103 N2 **Somme** ◈ department N France
103 N2 **Somme** ≈ N France
95 L18 **Sommen** Jönköping, S Sweden 58°07′N 14°58′E
95 M18 **Sommen** ◎ S Sweden
101 K16 **Sömmerda** Thüringen, C Germany 51°10′N 11°07′E
Sommerein see Šamorín
Sommerfeld see Lubsko
55 Y11 **Sommet Tabulaire** var. Mont Itoupé. ▲ S French Guiana
111 H25 **Somogy** off. Somogy Megye. ◈ county SW Hungary
Somogy Megye see Somogy
Somorja see Šamorín
105 N7 **Somosierra, Puerto de** pass N Spain
187 Y14 **Somosomo** Taveuni, N Fiji 16°46′S 179°57′W
42 I9 **Somotillo** Chinandega, NW Nicaragua 13°01′N 86°53′W
42 J8 **Somoto** Madriz, NW Nicaragua 13°29′N 86°36′W
110 I11 **Sompolno** Wielkopolskie, C Poland 52°24′N 18°30′E
102 J17 **Somport, Col du** var. Puerto de Somport, Sp. Somport; anc. Summus Portus. pass France/Spain see also Somport
99 K15 **Son** Noord-Brabant, S Netherlands 51°32′N 05°34′E
95 H15 **Son** Akershus, S Norway 59°32′N 10°42′E
154 L9 **Son** var. Sone. ≈ C India
43 R16 **Soná** Veraguas, W Panama 08°00′N 81°20′W
Sonag see Zêkog
154 M12 **Sonapur** prev. Sonepur. Orissa, E India 20°50′N 83°58′E
95 G24 **Sønderborg** Ger. Sonderburg. Sønderjylland, SW Denmark 54°55′N 09°48′E
Sonderburg see Sønderborg
95 F24 **Sønderjylland** var. Sønderjyllands Amt. ◈ county SW Denmark
Sønderjyllands Amt see Sønderjylland
101 K15 **Sondershausen** Thüringen, C Germany 51°22′N 10°52′E
Søndre Strømfjord see Kangerlussuaq
106 E6 **Sondrio** Lombardia, N Italy 46°11′N 09°52′E
Sone see Son
Sonepur see Sonapur
57 K22 **Sonequera** ▲ S Bolivia 22°06′S 67°10′W
167 V12 **Sông Câu** Phu Yên, C Vietnam 13°26′N 109°12′E
167 R15 **Sông Đôc** Minh Hai, S Vietnam 09°03′N 104°51′E
81 H25 **Songea** Ruvuma, S Tanzania 10°42′S 35°39′E
163 X10 **Songhua Hu** ◎ NE China
163 Y7 **Songhua Jiang** var. Sungari. ≈ NE China
161 S8 **Songjiang** Shanghai Shi, E China 31°01′N 121°14′E
Sŏngjin see Kimch'aek
167 O16 **Songkhla** var. Songkla, Mal. Singora. Songkhla, SW Thailand 07°12′N 100°35′E
Songkla see Songkhla
163 T13 **Song Ling** ▲▲ NE China
129 U12 **Sông Ma** Laos Ma, Nam. ≈ Laos/Vietnam
163 W14 **Songnim** SW North Korea 38°43′N 125°40′E
82 B10 **Songo** Uíge, NW Angola 07°30′S 14°56′E
83 M15 **Songo** Tete, NW Mozambique 15°36′S 32°45′E
79 F21 **Songololo** Bas-Congo, SW Dem. Rep. Congo 05°40′S 14°05′E
160 H7 **Songpan** var. Jin'an, Tib. Sungpu. Sichuan, C China 32°49′N 103°39′E
163 Y17 **Sŏngsan** S South Korea 33°25′N 126°54′E
161 R11 **Songxi** Fujian, SE China 27°33′N 118°46′E
160 M6 **Songxian** var. Song Xian. Henan, C China 34°11′N 112°04′E
Song Xian see Songxian
161 R10 **Songyang** var. Xiping; prev. Songyin. Zhejiang, SE China 28°29′N 119°27′E
Songyin see Songyang
163 V9 **Songyuan** var. Fu-yü, Petuna; prev. Fuyu. Jilin, NE China 45°10′N 124°52′E
Sonid Youqi see SaihanTal
Sonid Zuoqi see Mandalt
152 I10 **Sonīpat** Haryāna, N India 29°00′N 77°01′E
93 M15 **Sonkajärvi** Itä-Suomi, C Finland 63°40′N 27°30′E
167 R6 **Son La** Sơn La, N Vietnam 21°20′N 103°55′E
149 O16 **Sonmiāni** Baluchistān, S Pakistan 25°24′N 66°37′E
149 O16 **Sonmiāni Bay** bay S Pakistan
101 K18 **Sonneberg** Thüringen, C Germany 50°22′N 11°10′E
101 N24 **Sonntagshorn** ▲ Austria/Germany 47°40′N 12°42′E
Sonoita see Sonoyta
40 E3 **Sonoita, Río** var. Río Sonoyta. ≈ Mexico/USA
35 N7 **Sonoma** California, W USA 38°16′N 122°28′W
35 T3 **Sonoma Peak** ▲ Nevada, W USA 40°50′N 117°34′W
35 P8 **Sonora** California, W USA 37°58′N 120°22′W
25 O10 **Sonora** Texas, SW USA 30°34′N 100°39′W
40 F5 **Sonora** ◈ state NW Mexico
35 X17 **Sonoran Desert** var. Desierto de Altar. desert Mexico/USA see also Altar, Desierto de
40 G5 **Sonora, Río** ≈ NW Mexico
40 E2 **Sonoyta** var. Sonoita. Sonora, NW Mexico 31°49′N 112°50′W
Sonoyta, Río see Sonoita, Río
142 K6 **Sonqor** var. Sunqur. Kermānshāhān, W Iran 34°45′N 47°39′E
105 N9 **Sonseca** var. Sonseca con Casalgordo. Castilla-La Mancha, C Spain 39°40′N 03°59′W
Sonseca con Casalgordo see Sonseca
54 E9 **Sonsón** Antioquia, W Colombia 05°45′N 75°18′W
42 E7 **Sonsonate** Sonsonate, W El Salvador 13°44′N 89°43′W
42 A9 **Sonsonate** ◈ department SW El Salvador
188 A10 **Sonsorol Islands** island group S Palau
112 J9 **Sonta** Hung. Szond; prev. Szonta. Vojvodina, NW Serbia 45°34′N 19°06′E
167 S6 **Sơn Tây** var. Sontay. Ha Tây, N Vietnam 21°06′N 105°32′E
Sontay see Sơn Tây
101 J25 **Sonthofen** Bayern, S Germany 47°31′N 10°16′E
Soochow see Suzhou
80 O13 **Sool** off. Gobolka Sool. ◈ region N Somalia
Soomaaliya/Soomaaliyeed, Jamuuriyada Demuqraadiga see Somalia
Soome Laht see Finland, Gulf of
23 V5 **Soperton** Georgia, SE USA 32°22′N 82°35′W
167 S6 **Sop Hao** Houaphan, N Laos 20°33′N 104°25′E
Sophia see Sofiya
171 S10 **Sopi** Pulau Morotai, E Indonesia 02°36′N 128°32′E
Sopianae see Pécs
171 U13 **Sopinusa** Papua, E Indonesia 03°31′S 132°55′E
81 B14 **Sopo** ≈ W Sudan
Sopockinie/Sopotskin/Sopotskino see Sapotskin
114 J9 **Sopot** Plovdiv, C Bulgaria 42°39′N 24°43′E
110 I7 **Sopot** Ger. Zoppot. Pomorskie, N Poland 54°26′N 18°33′E
167 O8 **Sop Prap** var. Ban Sop Prap. Lampang, NW Thailand 17°55′N 99°20′E
111 G22 **Sopron** Ger. Ödenburg. Győr-Moson-Sopron, NW Hungary 47°40′N 16°35′E
147 U11 **Sopu-Korgon** var. Sofi-Kurgan. Oshskaya Oblast', SW Kyrgyzstan 40°03′N 73°30′E
152 H5 **Sopur** Jammu and Kashmir, NW India 34°19′N 74°30′E
107 J15 **Sora** Lazio, C Italy 41°43′N 13°37′E
154 N13 **Sorada** Orissa, E India 19°46′N 84°29′E
93 H17 **Söråker** Västernorrland, C Sweden 62°32′N 17°32′E
57 J17 **Sorata** La Paz, W Bolivia 15°47′S 68°38′W
Sorau/Sorau in der Niederlausitz see Żary
105 Q14 **Sorbas** Andalucía, S Spain 37°06′N 02°06′W
Sord/Sórd Choluim Chille see Swords
15 O11 **Sorel** Québec, SE Canada 46°03′N 73°06′W
183 P17 **Sorell** Tasmania, SE Australia 42°49′S 147°34′E
183 O17 **Sorell, Lake** ◎ Tasmania, SE Australia
106 E8 **Soresina** Lombardia, N Italy 45°17′N 09°51′E
95 D14 **Sørfjorden** fjord S Norway
94 N11 **Sörforsa** Gävleborg, C Sweden 61°45′N 17°00′E
103 R14 **Sorgues** Vaucluse, SE France 44°N 04°52′E
136 K13 **Sorgun** Yozgat, C Turkey 39°49′N 35°10′E
105 P5 **Soria** Castilla-León, N Spain 41°47′N 02°26′W
105 P6 **Soria** ◈ province Castilla-León, N Spain
61 D19 **Soriano** Soriano, SW Uruguay 33°25′S 58°21′W
61 D19 **Soriano** ◈ department SW Uruguay
92 O4 **Sørkapp** headland SW Svalbard 76°34′N 16°33′E
143 T5 **Sorkh, Kūh-e** ▲▲ NE Iran
95 I23 **Sorø** Vestsjælland, E Denmark 55°26′N 11°34′E
Soro see Ghazal, Bahr el
116 M8 **Soroca** Rus. Soroki. N Moldova 48°10′N 28°18′E
60 L10 **Sorocaba** São Paulo, S Brazil 23°29′S 47°27′W
Sorochino see Sarochyna
127 T7 **Sorochinsk** Orenburgskaya Oblast', W Russian Federation 52°26′N 53°10′E
Soroki see Soroca
188 H15 **Sorol** atoll Caroline Islands, W Micronesia
171 T12 **Sorong** Papua, E Indonesia 0°49′S 131°16′E
81 G17 **Soroti** C Uganda 01°42′N 33°37′E
Sørøy see Sørøya
92 J8 **Sørøya** var. Sørøy, Lapp. Sállan. island N Norway
104 G11 **Sorraia, Rio** ≈ C Portugal
92 I10 **Sørreisa** Troms, N Norway 69°08′N 18°09′E
107 K18 **Sorrento** anc. Surrentum. Campania, S Italy 40°37′N 14°23′E
104 H10 **Sor, Ribeira de** stream C Portugal
195 T3 **Sør Rondane** ▲▲ Antarctica
93 H14 **Sorsele** Västerbotten, N Sweden 65°31′N 17°34′E
107 B17 **Sorso** Sardegna, Italy, C Mediterranean Sea 40°46′N 08°33′E
171 P4 **Sorsogon** Luzon, N Philippines 12°57′N 124°04′E
105 U4 **Sort** Cataluña, NE Spain 42°25′N 01°07′E
124 H11 **Sortavala** prev. Serdobol'. Respublika Kareliya, NW Russian Federation 61°45′N 30°37′E
107 L25 **Sortino** Sicilia, Italy, C Mediterranean Sea 37°10′N 15°02′E
92 G10 **Sortland** Nordland, C Norway 68°44′N 15°25′E
94 G9 **Sør-Trøndelag** ◈ county S Norway
95 I15 **Sørumsand** Akershus, S Norway 59°58′N 11°13′E
118 D6 **Sõrve Säär** headland SW Estonia 57°54′N 22°02′E
95 K22 **Sösdala** Skåne, S Sweden 56°00′N 13°36′E
105 R4 **Sos del Rey Católico** Aragón, NE Spain 42°30′N 01°13′W
93 F15 **Sösjöfjällen** ▲ C Sweden 63°51′N 13°15′E
126 K7 **Sosna** ≈ W Russian Federation
62 H12 **Sosneado, Cerro** ▲ W Argentina 34°44′S 69°52′W
125 S9 **Sosnogorsk** Respublika Komi, NW Russian Federation 63°33′N 53°55′E
124 J8 **Sosnovets** Respublika Kareliya, NW Russian Federation 64°25′N 34°23′E
Sosnovets see Sosnowiec
127 Q3 **Sosnovka** Chuvashskaya Respublika, W Russian Federation 56°18′N 47°14′E
125 S16 **Sosnovka** Kirovskaya Oblast', NW Russian Federation 56°15′N 51°20′E
124 M6 **Sosnovka** Murmanskaya Oblast', NW Russian Federation 66°28′N 40°31′E
126 M6 **Sosnovka** Tambovskaya Oblast', W Russian Federation 53°14′N 41°19′E
124 H12 **Sosnovo** Fin. Rautu. Leningradskaya Oblast', NW Russian Federation 60°30′N 30°13′E
124 G13 **Sosnovyy Bor** Leningradskaya Oblast', NW Russian Federation 59°53′N 29°07′E
127 V3 **Sosnovyy Bor** Respublika Bashkortostan, W Russian Federation 55°51′N 57°09′E
Sosnovyy Bor see Sasnovy Bor
111 J16 **Sosnowiec** Ger. Sosnowitz, Rus. Sosnovets. Śląskie, S Poland 50°16′N 19°07′E
Sosnowitz see Sosnowiec
117 R2 **Sosnytsya** Chernihivs'ka Oblast', N Ukraine 51°31′N 32°30′E
109 V10 **Šoštanj** N Slovenia 46°23′N 15°03′E
122 G10 **Sos'va** Sverdlovskaya Oblast', C Russian Federation 59°13′N 61°58′E
54 D12 **Sotará, Volcán** ☗ S Colombia 02°04′N 76°40′W
76 D10 **Sotavento, Ilhas de** var. Leeward Islands. island group S Cape Verde
93 N15 **Sotkamo** Oulu, C Finland 64°06′N 28°30′E
109 W11 **Sotla** ≈ E Slovenia
41 P10 **Soto la Marina** Tamaulipas, C Mexico 23°44′N 98°10′W
41 P10 **Soto la Marina, Río** ≈ C Mexico
95 B14 **Sotra** island S Norway
41 X12 **Sotuta** Yucatán, SE Mexico 20°34′N 89°00′W
79 F17 **Souanké** Sangha, NW Congo 02°03′N 14°02′E
76 M17 **Soubré** S Ivory Coast 05°50′N 06°35′W
115 H24 **Soúda** var. Soúdha, Eng. Suda. Kríti, Greece, E Mediterranean Sea 35°29′N 24°04′E
Soúdha see Soúda
Soueida see As Suwaydā'
114 L12 **Souflí** prev. Souflíon. Anatolikí Makedonía kai Thráki, NE Greece 41°12′N 26°18′E
Souflíon see Souflí
45 S11 **Soufrière** W Saint Lucia 13°51′N 61°03′W
45 X6 **Soufrière** ☗ Basse Terre, S Guadeloupe 16°03′N 61°39′W
102 M13 **Souillac** Lot, S France 44°53′N 01°29′E
173 Y17 **Souillac** S Mauritius 20°31′S 57°31′E
74 M5 **Souk Ahras** NE Algeria 36°14′N 08°00′E
Souk el Arba du Rharb/Souk-el-Arba-du-Rharb/Souk-el-Arba-el-Rhab see Souk-el-Arba-Rharb
74 E6 **Souk-el-Arba-Rharb** var. Souk el Arba du Rharb, Souk-el-Arba-du-Rharb, Souk-el-Arba-el-Rhab. NW Morocco 34°38′N 06°00′W
Soukhné see As Sukhnah
163 X14 **Sŏul** off. Sŏul-t'ŭkpyŏlsi, Eng. Seoul, Jap. Keijō; prev. Kyŏngsŏng. ● (South Korea) NW South Korea 37°30′N 126°58′E
102 J11 **Soulac-sur-Mer** Gironde, SW France 45°31′N 01°06′W
Sŏul-t'ŭkpyŏlsi see Sŏul
99 L19 **Soumagne** Liège, E Belgium 50°36′N 05°48′E
18 M14 **Sound Beach** Long Island, New York, NE USA 40°56′N 72°58′W
95 J22 **Sound, The** Dan. Øresund, Swe. Öresund. strait Denmark/Sweden
115 H20 **Soúnio, Akrotírio** headland C Greece 37°39′N 24°01′E
138 F8 **Soûr** var. Şūr; anc. Tyre. SW Lebanon 33°18′N 35°30′E
Sources, Mont-aux- see Phofung
104 G8 **Soure** Coimbra, N Portugal 40°04′N 08°38′W
11 W17 **Souris** Manitoba, S Canada 49°38′N 100°17′W
13 Q14 **Souris** Prince Edward Island, SE Canada 46°22′N 62°16′W

◆ Country ● Country Capital ◇ Dependent Territory ○ Dependent Territory Capital ◈ Administrative Regions ✈ International Airport ▲ Mountain ▲▲ Mountain Range ☗ Volcano ≈ River ◎ Lake ⊠ Reservoir

Souris River – Stamford

28 L2 **Souris River** var. Mouse River. ≈ Canada/USA
25 X10 **Sour Lake** Texas, SW USA 30°08′N 94°24′W
115 F17 **Soúrpi** Thessalía, C Greece 39°07′N 22°55′E
104 H11 **Sousel** Portalegre, C Portugal 38°57′N 07°40′W
75 N6 **Sousse** var. Sūsah. NE Tunisia 35°46′N 10°38′E
14 H11 **South** ≈ Ontario, S Canada
South see Sud
83 G23 **South Africa** off. Republic of South Africa, Afr. Suid-Afrika. ◆ republic S Africa
South Africa, Republic of see South Africa
46-47 **South America** continent
2 J17 **South American Plate** tectonic feature
97 M23 **Southampton** hist. Hamwih, Lat. Clausentum. S England, United Kingdom 50°54′N 01°23′W
19 N14 **Southampton** Long Island, New York, NE USA 40°52′N 72°22′W
9 P8 **Southampton Island** island Nunavut, NE Canada
151 P20 **South Andaman** island Andaman Islands, India, NE Indian Ocean
13 Q6 **South Aulatsivik Island** island Newfoundland and Labrador, E Canada
182 E4 **South Australia** ◐ state S Australia
South Australian Abyssal Plain see South Australian Plain
192 G11 **South Australian Basin** undersea feature SW Indian Ocean 38°00′S 126°00′E
173 X12 **South Australian Plain** var. South Australian Abyssal Plain. undersea feature SE Indian Ocean
37 R13 **South Baldy** ▲ New Mexico, SW USA 33°59′N 107°11′W
23 Y14 **South Bay** Florida, SE USA 26°39′N 80°43′W
14 E12 **South Baymouth** Manitoulin Island, Ontario, S Canada 45°33′N 82°01′W
30 L10 **South Beloit** Illinois, N USA 42°29′N 89°02′W
31 O11 **South Bend** Indiana, N USA 41°40′N 86°15′W
25 R6 **South Bend** Texas, SW USA 32°58′N 98°39′W
32 F9 **South Bend** Washington, NW USA 46°38′N 123°48′W
South Beveland see Zuid-Beveland
South Borneo see Kalimantan Selatan
21 U7 **South Boston** Virginia, NE USA 36°42′N 78°58′W
182 F2 **South Branch Neales** seasonal river South Australia
21 U3 **South Branch Potomac River** ≈ West Virginia, NE USA
185 H19 **Southbridge** Canterbury, South Island, New Zealand 43°49′S 172°17′E
19 N12 **Southbridge** Massachusetts, NE USA 42°03′N 72°00′W
183 P17 **South Bruny Island** island Tasmania, SE Australia
18 L7 **South Burlington** Vermont, NE USA 44°27′N 73°08′W
44 M6 **South Caicos** island S Turks and Caicos Islands
South Cape see Ka Lae
23 V3 **South Carolina** off. State of South Carolina, also known as The Palmetto State. ◐ state SE USA
South Carpathians see Carpații Meridionali
South Celebes see Sulawesi Selatan
21 Q5 **South Charleston** West Virginia, NE USA 38°22′N 81°42′W
192 D7 **South China Basin** undersea feature SE South China Sea 15°00′N 115°00′E
169 R8 **South China Sea** Chin. Nan Hai, Ind. Laut Cina Selatan, Vtn. Biên Đông. sea SE Asia
33 Z10 **South Dakota** off. State of South Dakota, also known as The Coyote State, Sunshine State. ◐ state N USA
23 X10 **South Daytona** Florida, SE USA 29°09′N 81°01′W
37 R10 **South Domingo Pueblo** New Mexico, SW USA 35°28′N 106°24′W
97 N23 **South Downs** hill range SE England, United Kingdom
83 I21 **South East** ◐ district SE Botswana
65 H15 **South East Bay** bay Ascension Island, C Atlantic Ocean
183 O17 **South East Cape** headland Tasmania, SE Australia 43°36′S 146°52′E
38 K10 **Southeast Cape** headland Saint Lawrence Island, Alaska, USA 62°56′N 169°39′W
South-East Celebes see Sulawesi Tenggara
192 G12 **Southeast Indian Ridge** undersea feature Indian Ocean/Pacific Ocean 50°00′S 110°00′E
Southeast Island see Tagula Island
193 P13 **Southeast Pacific Basin** var. Belling Hausen Mulde. undersea feature SE Pacific Ocean 60°00′S 115°00′W
65 H15 **South East Point** headland SE Ascension Island
183 O14 **South East Point** headland Victoria, S Australia 39°10′S 146°21′E
44 L5 **Southeast Point** headland Mayaguana, SE Bahamas 22°15′N 72°44′W
191 Z3 **South East Point** headland Kiritimati, NE Kiribati 01°42′N 157°10′W
South-East Sulawesi see Sulawesi Tenggara
11 U12 **Southend** Saskatchewan, C Canada 56°20′N 103°14′W
97 P22 **Southend-on-Sea** E England, United Kingdom 51°33′N 00°43′E
83 H20 **Southern** var. Bangwaketse, Ngwaketze. ◐ district SE Botswana
138 E13 **Southern** ◐ district S Israel
83 N15 **Southern** ◐ region S Malawi
155 J26 **Southern** ◐ province S Sri Lanka
83 I15 **Southern** ◐ province S Zambia
185 E19 **Southern Alps** ▲▲ South Island, New Zealand
190 K15 **Southern Cook Islands** island group S Cook Islands
180 K12 **Southern Cross** Western Australia 31°17′S 119°15′E
80 A12 **Southern Darfur** ◐ state W Sudan
186 B7 **Southern Highlands** ◐ province W Papua New Guinea
11 V11 **Southern Indian Lake** ◎ Manitoba, C Canada
80 E11 **Southern Kordofan** ◐ state C Sudan
187 Z15 **Southern Lau Group** island group Lau Group, SE Fiji
81 I15 **Southern Nationalities** ◐ region S Ethiopia
173 S13 **Southern Ocean** ocean
21 T10 **Southern Pines** North Carolina, SE USA 35°10′N 79°23′W
96 I13 **Southern Uplands** ▲▲ S Scotland, United Kingdom
Southern Urals see Yuzhnyy Ural
183 P16 **South Esk River** ≈ Tasmania, SE Australia
11 U16 **Southey** Saskatchewan, S Canada 50°53′N 104°27′W
27 V2 **South Fabius River** ≈ Missouri, C USA
31 S10 **Southfield** Michigan, N USA 42°28′N 83°12′W
192 K10 **South Fiji Basin** undersea feature S Pacific Ocean 26°00′S 175°00′E
97 Q22 **South Foreland** headland SE England, United Kingdom 51°08′N 01°22′E
35 P7 **South Fork American River** ≈ California, W USA
28 K7 **South Fork Grand River** ≈ South Dakota, N USA
35 T12 **South Fork Kern River** ≈ California, W USA
39 Q7 **South Fork Koyukuk River** ≈ Alaska, USA
39 Q11 **South Fork Kuskokwim River** ≈ Alaska, USA
26 H2 **South Fork Republican River** ≈ C USA
26 L3 **South Fork Solomon River** ≈ Kansas, C USA
31 P5 **South Fox Island** island Michigan, N USA
20 G8 **South Fulton** Tennessee, S USA 36°28′N 88°53′W
195 U10 **South Geomagnetic Pole** pole Antarctica
65 J20 **South Georgia** island South Georgia and the South Sandwich Islands, SW Atlantic Ocean
65 K21 **South Georgia and the South Sandwich Islands** ◇ UK Dependent Territory SW Atlantic Ocean
47 Y14 **South Georgia Ridge** var. North Scotia Ridge. undersea feature SW Atlantic Ocean 54°00′S 40°00′W
181 Q1 **South Goulburn Island** island Northern Territory, N Australia
153 U16 **South Hatia Island** island SE Bangladesh
31 O10 **South Haven** Michigan, N USA 42°24′N 86°16′W
21 V7 **South Hill** Virginia, NE USA 36°43′N 78°07′W
South Holland see Zuid-Holland
21 P8 **South Holston Lake** ⊠ Tennessee/Virginia, S USA
175 N1 **South Honshu Ridge** undersea feature W Pacific Ocean
26 M6 **South Hutchinson** Kansas, C USA 38°01′N 97°56′W
151 K21 **South Huvadhu Atoll** atoll S Maldives
173 U14 **South Indian Basin** undersea feature Indian Ocean/Pacific Ocean 60°00′S 120°00′E
11 W11 **South Indian Lake** Manitoba, C Canada 56°48′N 98°56′W
81 I17 **South Island** island NW Kenya
185 C20 **South Island** island S New Zealand
South Kalimantan see Kalimantan Selatan
South Kazakhstan see Yuzhnyy Kazakhstan
163 X15 **South Korea** off. Republic of Korea, Kor. Taehan Min'guk. ◆ republic E Asia
35 Q6 **South Lake Tahoe** California, W USA 38°56′N 119°57′W
25 N6 **Southland** Texas, SW USA 33°16′N 101°31′W
185 B23 **Southland** off. Southland Region. ◐ region South Island, New Zealand
Southland Region see Southland
29 N15 **South Loup River** ≈ Nebraska, C USA
151 K19 **South Maalhosmadulu Atoll** atoll N Maldives
14 E15 **South Maitland** ≈ Ontario, S Canada
192 E8 **South Makassar Basin** undersea feature E Java Sea
31 O6 **South Manitou Island** island Michigan, N USA
151 K18 **South Miladhunmadulu Atoll** var. Noonu. atoll N Maldives
21 X8 **South Mills** North Carolina, SE USA 36°28′N 76°18′W
8 H9 **South Nahanni** ≈ Northwest Territories, NW Canada
39 P13 **South Naknek** Alaska, USA 58°39′N 157°01′W
14 M13 **South Nation** ≈ Ontario, SE Canada
44 F9 **South Negril Point** headland W Jamaica 18°14′N 78°21′W
151 K20 **South Nilandhe Atoll** var. Dhaalu Atoll. atoll C Maldives
36 L2 **South Ogden** Utah, W USA 41°09′N 111°58′W
18 M14 **Southold** Long Island, New York, NE USA 41°03′N 72°24′W
194 H1 **South Orkney Islands** island group Antarctica
137 S9 **South Ossetia** former autonomous region SW Georgia
South Pacific Basin see Southwest Pacific Basin
19 P7 **South Paris** Maine, NE USA 44°14′N 70°33′W
189 U13 **South Pass** passage Chuuk Islands, C Micronesia
33 U15 **South Pass** pass Wyoming, C USA
20 K10 **South Pittsburg** Tennessee, S USA 35°00′N 85°42′W
28 K15 **South Platte River** ≈ Colorado/Nebraska, C USA
31 T16 **South Point** Ohio, N USA 38°25′N 82°35′W
65 G15 **South Point** headland S Ascension Island
31 R6 **South Point** headland Michigan, N USA 44°51′N 83°17′W
South Point see Ka Lae
195 Q9 **South Pole** pole Antarctica
183 P17 **Southport** Tasmania, SE Australia 43°26′S 146°57′E
97 K17 **Southport** NW England, United Kingdom 53°39′N 03°01′W
21 V12 **Southport** North Carolina, SE USA 33°55′N 78°00′W
19 P8 **South Portland** Maine, NE USA 43°38′N 70°14′W
14 H12 **South River** Ontario, S Canada 45°50′N 79°23′W
21 U11 **South River** ≈ North Carolina, SE USA
96 K5 **South Ronaldsay** island NE Scotland, United Kingdom
36 L2 **South Salt Lake** Utah, W USA 40°40′N 111°52′W
65 L21 **South Sandwich Islands** island group SW Atlantic Ocean
65 K21 **South Sandwich Trench** undersea feature SW Atlantic Ocean 56°30′S 25°00′W
11 S16 **South Saskatchewan** ≈ Alberta/Saskatchewan, S Canada
65 I21 **South Scotia Ridge** undersea feature S Scotia Sea
11 V10 **South Seal** ≈ Manitoba, C Canada
194 G4 **South Shetland Islands** island group Antarctica
65 H22 **South Shetland Trough** undersea feature Atlantic Ocean/Pacific Ocean 61°00′S 59°30′W
97 M14 **South Shields** NE England, United Kingdom 55°01′N 01°25′W
29 R13 **South Sioux City** Nebraska, C USA 42°28′N 96°24′W
192 J9 **South Solomon Trench** undersea feature W Pacific Ocean
183 V3 **South Stradbroke Island** island Queensland, E Australia
South Sulawesi see Sulawesi Selatan
South Sumatra see Sumatera Selatan
184 K11 **South Taranaki Bight** bight SE Tasman Sea
South Tasmania Plateau see Tasman Plateau
36 M15 **South Tucson** Arizona, SW USA 32°11′N 110°56′W
12 H9 **South Twin Island** island Nunavut, C Canada
96 E9 **South Uist** island NW Scotland, United Kingdom
149 R8 **South Wazīristān** ◐ federally administered tribal area NW Pakistan
South-West see Sud-Ouest
South-West Africa/South West Africa see Namibia
65 F15 **South West Bay** bay Ascension Island, C Atlantic Ocean
183 N18 **South West Cape** headland Tasmania, SE Australia 43°34′S 146°01′E
185 B26 **South West Cape** headland Stewart Island, New Zealand 47°15′S 167°28′E
38 J10 **Southwest Cape** headland Saint Lawrence Island, Alaska, USA 63°19′N 171°27′W
Southwest Indian Ocean Ridge see Southwest Indian Ridge
173 N11 **Southwest Indian Ridge** var. Southwest Indian Ocean Ridge. undersea feature SW Indian Ocean 43°00′S 40°00′E
192 L10 **Southwest Pacific Basin** var. South Pacific Basin. undersea feature SE Pacific Ocean 40°00′S 150°00′W
44 H2 **Southwest Point** headland Great Abaco, N Bahamas 25°50′N 77°12′W
191 X3 **South West Point** headland Kiritimati, NE Kiribati 01°53′N 157°34′E
65 G25 **South West Point** headland SW Saint Helena 16°00′S 05°48′W
25 P5 **South Wichita River** ≈ Texas, SW USA
97 Q20 **Southwold** E England, United Kingdom 52°15′N 01°36′E
19 Q12 **South Yarmouth** Massachusetts, NE USA 41°38′N 70°09′W
116 J10 **Sovata** Hung. Szováta. Mureș, C Romania 46°36′N 25°04′E
107 N22 **Soverato** Calabria, SW Italy 38°40′N 16°31′E
121 O4 **Sovereign Base Area** uk military installation S Cyprus
Sovetabad see Ghafurov
126 C2 **Sovetsk** Ger. Tilsit. Kaliningradskaya Oblast', W Russian Federation 55°04′N 21°52′E
125 Q15 **Sovetsk** Kirovskaya Oblast', NW Russian Federation 57°37′N 49°02′E
127 N10 **Sovetskaya** Rostovskaya Oblast', SW Russian Federation 49°00′N 42°09′E
127 P3 **Sovetskiy** Respublika Mariy El, W Russian Federation 56°45′N 48°30′E
Sovetskoye see Ketchenery
146 I15 **Sovet"yab** prev. Sovet"yap. Ahal Welaýaty, S Turkmenistan 36°29′N 61°13′E
Sovet"yap see Sovet"yab
117 U12 **Sovyets'kyy** Respublika Krym, S Ukraine 45°20′N 34°54′E
83 I18 **Sowa** var. Sua. Central, NE Botswana 20°33′S 26°18′E
83 I18 **Sowa Pan** var. Sua Pan. salt lake NE Botswana
83 J21 **Soweto** Gauteng, NE South Africa 26°08′S 27°54′E
147 R11 **So'x** Rus. Sokh. Farg'ona Viloyati, E Uzbekistan 39°56′N 71°10′E
Sōya-kaikyō see La Perouse Strait
165 T1 **Sōya-misaki** headland Hokkaidō, NE Japan 45°31′N 141°55′E
125 N7 **Soyana** ≈ NW Russian Federation
146 A8 **Soye, Mys** var. Mys Suz. headland NW Turkmenistan 41°47′N 52°27′E
82 A10 **Soyo** Dem. Rep. Congo, NW Angola 06°07′S 12°18′E
80 J10 **Soyra** ▲ C Eritrea 14°46′N 39°29′E
Sozaq see Suzak
119 P16 **Sozh** ≈ NE Europe
114 N10 **Sozopol** prev. Sizebolu; anc. Apollonia. Burgas, E Bulgaria 42°25′N 27°42′E
99 L20 **Spa** Liège, E Belgium 50°29′N 05°52′E
194 I7 **Spaatz Island** island Antarctica
144 M14 **Space Launching Centre** space station Kzylorda, S Kazakhstan
105 O7 **Spain** off. Kingdom of Spain, Sp. España; anc. Hispania, Iberia, Lat. Hispana. ◆ monarchy SW Europe
Spain, Kingdom of see Spain
Spalato see Split
97 O19 **Spalding** E England, United Kingdom 52°49′N 00°06′W
14 D11 **Spanish** Ontario, S Canada 46°12′N 82°21′W
36 L3 **Spanish Fork** Utah, W USA 40°09′N 111°40′W
64 B12 **Spanish Point** headland C Bermuda 32°18′N 64°49′W
14 E9 **Spanish River** ≈ Ontario, S Canada
44 K13 **Spanish Town** hist. St.Iago de la Vega. C Jamaica 18°N 76°57′W
Spánta, Akrotírio see Spátha, Akrotírio
35 Q5 **Sparks** Nevada, W USA 39°32′N 119°45′W
Sparnacum see Épernay
95 N16 **Sparreholm** Södermanland, C Sweden 59°04′N 16°51′E
23 U4 **Sparta** Georgia, SE USA 33°16′N 82°58′W
30 K16 **Sparta** Illinois, N USA 38°07′N 89°42′W
31 P9 **Sparta** Michigan, N USA 43°09′N 85°42′W
21 R8 **Sparta** North Carolina, SE USA 36°30′N 81°07′W
20 L9 **Sparta** Tennessee, S USA 35°55′N 85°30′W
30 I7 **Sparta** Wisconsin, N USA 43°57′N 90°50′W
Sparta see Spárti
21 Q11 **Spartanburg** South Carolina, SE USA 34°56′N 81°57′W
115 F21 **Spárti** Eng. Sparta. Pelopónnisos, S Greece 37°05′N 22°25′E
107 B21 **Spartivento, Capo** headland Sardegna, Italy, C Mediterranean Sea 38°52′N 08°50′E
11 P17 **Sparwood** British Columbia, SW Canada 49°45′N 114°45′W
126 I4 **Spas-Demensk** Kaluzhskaya Oblast', W Russian Federation 54°22′N 34°16′E
126 M4 **Spas-Klepiki** Ryazanskaya Oblast', W Russian Federation 55°08′N 40°15′E
Spasovo see Kulen Vakuf
123 R15 **Spassk-Dal'niy** Primorskiy Kray, SE Russian Federation 44°34′N 132°52′E
126 M5 **Spassk-Ryazanskiy** Ryazanskaya Oblast', W Russian Federation 54°25′N 40°21′E
115 H19 **Spáta** Attikí, C Greece 37°58′N 23°55′E
121 Q11 **Spátha, Akrotírio** var. Akrotírio Spánta. headland Kríti, Greece, E Mediterranean Sea 35°42′N 23°44′E
Špatrjan see Paternion
28 I9 **Spearfish** South Dakota, N USA 44°29′N 103°51′W
25 O1 **Spearman** Texas, SW USA 36°12′N 101°13′W
65 C25 **Speedwell Island** island S Falkland Islands
65 G25 **Speery Island** island S Saint Helena
45 N14 **Speightstown** NW Barbados 13°15′N 59°39′W
106 I13 **Spello** Umbria, C Italy 43°00′N 12°41′E
39 R12 **Spenard** Alaska, USA 61°09′N 150°03′W
Spence Bay see Taloyoak
31 O14 **Spencer** Indiana, N USA 39°18′N 86°46′W
29 T12 **Spencer** Iowa, C USA 43°09′N 95°07′W
29 P12 **Spencer** Nebraska, C USA 42°52′N 98°42′W
21 S9 **Spencer** North Carolina, SE USA 35°41′N 80°26′W
20 L9 **Spencer** Tennessee, S USA 35°46′N 85°27′W
21 Q4 **Spencer** West Virginia, NE USA 38°48′N 81°22′W
30 K6 **Spencer** Wisconsin, N USA 44°46′N 90°17′W
182 G10 **Spencer, Cape** headland South Australia 35°17′S 136°52′E
39 V13 **Spencer, Cape** headland Alaska, USA 58°12′N 136°39′W
182 H9 **Spencer Gulf** gulf South Australia
18 F9 **Spencerport** New York, NE USA 43°11′N 77°48′W
31 Q12 **Spencerville** Ohio, N USA 40°42′N 84°21′W
115 E17 **Spercheiáda** var. Sperhiada, Sperkhiás. Stereá Ellás, C Greece 38°54′N 22°07′E
115 E17 **Spercheiós** ≈ C Greece
Sperhiada see Spercheiáda
95 G14 **Sperillen** ◎ S Norway
Sperkhiás see Spercheiáda
101 I18 **Spessart** hill range C Germany
Spétsai see Spétses
115 G21 **Spétses** prev. Spétsai. Spétses, S Greece 37°16′N 23°09′E
115 G21 **Spétses** island S Greece
96 J8 **Spey** ≈ NE Scotland, United Kingdom
101 G20 **Speyer** Eng. Spires; anc. Civitas Nemetum, Spira. Rheinland-Pfalz, SW Germany 49°18′N 08°26′E
101 G20 **Speyerbach** ≈ W Germany
107 N20 **Spezzano Albanese** Calabria, SW Italy 39°40′N 16°17′E
Spice Islands see Maluku
100 F9 **Spiekeroog** island NW Germany
109 W9 **Spielfeld** Steiermark, SE Austria 46°43′N 15°36′E
65 N21 **Spiess Seamount** undersea feature S Atlantic Ocean 53°00′S 02°00′W
108 E9 **Spiez** Bern, W Switzerland 46°42′N 07°41′E
98 G13 **Spijkenisse** Zuid-Holland, SW Netherlands 51°52′N 04°19′E
39 T6 **Spike Mountain** ▲ Alaska, USA 67°42′N 141°39′W
115 I25 **Spíli** Kríti, Greece, E Mediterranean Sea 35°12′N 24°33′E
108 D10 **Spillgerten** ▲ W Switzerland 46°34′N 07°25′E
118 F9 **Spilva** ✈ (Rīga) Rīga, C Latvia 56°55′N 24°03′E
107 N17 **Spinazzola** Puglia, SE Italy 40°58′N 16°06′E
149 O9 **Spīn Būldak** Kandahār, S Afghanistan 31°01′N 66°23′E
Spira see Speyer
Spirdingsee see Śniardwy, Jezioro
Spires see Speyer
29 T11 **Spirit Lake** Iowa, C USA 43°25′N 95°06′W
29 T11 **Spirit Lake** ◎ Iowa, C USA
11 N13 **Spirit River** Alberta, W Canada 55°46′N 118°51′W
11 S14 **Spiritwood** Saskatchewan, S Canada 53°18′N 107°33′W
27 R11 **Spiro** Oklahoma, C USA 35°14′N 94°37′W
111 L19 **Spišská Nová Ves** Ger. Neudorf, Zipser Neudorf, Hung. Igló. Košický Kraj, E Slovakia 48°58′N 20°35′E
137 T11 **Spitak** NW Armenia 40°51′N 44°17′E
92 O2 **Spitsbergen** island NW Svalbard
Spittal see Spittal an der Drau
109 R9 **Spittal an der Drau** var. Spittal. Kärnten, S Austria 46°48′N 13°30′E
109 V3 **Spitz** Niederösterreich, NE Austria 48°24′N 15°22′E
94 D9 **Spjelkavik** Møre og Romsdal, S Norway 62°28′N 06°22′E
25 W10 **Splendora** Texas, SW USA 30°13′N 95°09′W
113 E14 **Split** It. Spalato. Split-Dalmacija, S Croatia 43°31′N 16°27′E
113 E14 **Split** ✈ Split-Dalmacija, S Croatia 43°33′N 16°19′E
113 E14 **Split-Dalmacija** off. Splitsko-Dalmatinska Županija. ◐ province S Croatia
11 X12 **Split Lake** ◎ Manitoba, C Canada
Splitsko-Dalmatinska Županija see Split-Dalmacija
108 H10 **Splügen** Graubünden, S Switzerland 46°33′N 09°18′E
Spodnji Dravograd see Dravograd
25 P12 **Spofford** Texas, SW USA 29°10′N 100°24′W
118 J11 **Špoģi** Daugvapils, SE Latvia 56°03′N 26°47′E
32 L8 **Spokane** Washington, NW USA 47°40′N 117°26′W
32 L8 **Spokane River** ≈ Washington, NW USA
106 I13 **Spoleto** Umbria, C Italy 42°44′N 12°44′E
30 I4 **Spooner** Wisconsin, N USA 45°51′N 91°49′W
30 K12 **Spoon River** ≈ Illinois, N USA
21 W5 **Spotsylvania** Virginia, NE USA 38°12′N 77°35′W
32 L8 **Sprague** Washington, NW USA 47°19′N 117°55′W
170 J5 **Spratly Island** island SW Spratly Islands
192 E6 **Spratly Islands** Chin. Nansha Qundao. ◇ disputed territory SE Asia
32 J12 **Spray** Oregon, NW USA 44°30′N 119°38′W
112 I11 **Spreča** ≈ N Bosnia and Herzegovina
100 P13 **Spree** ≈ E Germany
100 P13 **Spreewald** wetland NE Germany
101 P14 **Spremberg** Brandenburg, E Germany 51°34′N 14°22′E
25 W11 **Spring** Texas, SW USA 30°03′N 95°24′W
31 Q10 **Spring Arbor** Michigan, N USA 42°12′N 84°33′W
83 E23 **Springbok** Northern Cape, W South Africa 29°44′S 17°56′E
18 I15 **Spring City** Pennsylvania, NE USA 40°10′N 75°33′W
20 L9 **Spring City** Tennessee, S USA 35°41′N 84°51′W
36 L4 **Spring City** Utah, W USA 39°28′N 111°30′W
35 W3 **Spring Creek** Nevada, W USA 40°45′N 115°40′W
27 S9 **Springdale** Arkansas, C USA 36°11′N 94°07′W
31 Q14 **Springdale** Ohio, N USA 39°17′N 84°29′W
100 I13 **Springe** Niedersachsen, N Germany 52°13′N 09°33′E
37 U9 **Springer** New Mexico, SW USA 36°21′N 104°35′W
37 W7 **Springfield** Colorado, C USA 37°24′N 102°36′W
23 W5 **Springfield** Georgia, SE USA 32°21′N 81°20′W
30 K14 **Springfield** state capital Illinois, N USA 39°48′N 89°39′W
20 L6 **Springfield** Kentucky, S USA 37°42′N 85°18′W
18 M12 **Springfield** Massachusetts, NE USA 42°06′N 72°32′W
29 T10 **Springfield** Minnesota, N USA 44°15′N 94°58′W
27 T7 **Springfield** Missouri, C USA 37°13′N 93°18′W
31 R13 **Springfield** Ohio, N USA 39°55′N 83°49′W
32 G13 **Springfield** Oregon, NW USA 44°03′N 123°01′W
29 Q12 **Springfield** South Dakota, N USA 42°51′N 97°54′W
20 J8 **Springfield** Tennessee, S USA 36°30′N 86°54′W
18 M9 **Springfield** Vermont, NE USA 43°18′N 72°27′W
30 K14 **Springfield, Lake** ⊠ Illinois, N USA
55 T8 **Spring Garden** NE Guyana 06°58′N 58°34′W
30 K8 **Spring Green** Wisconsin, N USA 43°10′N 90°02′W
29 X11 **Spring Grove** Minnesota, N USA 43°33′N 91°38′W
13 P15 **Springhill** Nova Scotia, SE Canada 45°40′N 64°04′W
23 V12 **Spring Hill** Florida, SE USA 28°28′N 82°36′W
27 R4 **Spring Hill** Kansas, C USA 38°44′N 94°49′W
22 G4 **Springhill** Louisiana, S USA 33°01′N 93°27′W
20 I9 **Spring Hill** Tennessee, S USA 35°46′N 86°55′W
21 U10 **Spring Lake** North Carolina, SE USA 35°10′N 78°58′W
24 M4 **Springlake** Texas, SW USA 34°13′N 102°18′W
35 W11 **Spring Mountains** ▲▲ Nevada, W USA
27 W9 **Spring River** ≈ Arkansas/Missouri, C USA
27 S7 **Spring River** ≈ Missouri/Oklahoma, C USA
83 J21 **Springs** Gauteng, NE South Africa 26°16′S 28°26′E
185 H16 **Springs Junction** West Coast, South Island, New Zealand 42°21′S 172°11′E
181 X8 **Springsure** Queensland, E Australia 24°09′S 148°06′E
29 W11 **Spring Valley** Minnesota, N USA 43°41′N 92°23′W
18 K13 **Spring Valley** New York, NE USA 41°10′N 73°58′W
29 N12 **Springview** Nebraska, C USA 42°49′N 99°45′W
18 D11 **Springville** New York, NE USA 42°27′N 78°52′W
36 L3 **Springville** Utah, W USA 40°10′N 111°36′W
Sprottau see Szprotawa
15 V4 **Sproule, Pointe** headland Québec, SE Canada 49°47′N 67°02′W
11 Q14 **Spruce Grove** Alberta, SW Canada 53°36′N 113°55′W
21 T4 **Spruce Knob** ▲ West Virginia, NE USA 38°40′N 79°37′W
35 X3 **Spruce Mountain** ▲ Nevada, W USA 40°33′N 114°46′W
21 P9 **Spruce Pine** North Carolina, SE USA 35°55′N 82°03′W
98 G13 **Spui** ≈ SW Netherlands
107 O19 **Spulico, Capo** headland S Italy 39°57′N 16°38′E
25 O5 **Spur** Texas, SW USA 33°28′N 100°51′W
97 O17 **Spurn Head** headland E England, United Kingdom 53°34′N 00°06′E
99 H20 **Spy** Namur, S Belgium 50°29′N 04°43′E
95 I15 **Spydeberg** Østfold, S Norway 59°36′N 11°04′E
185 J17 **Spy Glass Point** headland South Island, New Zealand 42°33′S 173°31′E
10 L17 **Squamish** British Columbia, SW Canada 49°41′N 123°11′W
19 O8 **Squam Lake** ◎ New Hampshire, NE USA
19 S2 **Squa Pan Mountain** ▲ Maine, NE USA 46°36′N 68°09′W
39 N16 **Squaw Harbor** Unga Island, Alaska, USA 55°12′N 160°41′W
14 E11 **Squaw Island** island Ontario, S Canada
107 O22 **Squillace, Golfo di** gulf S Italy
107 Q18 **Squinzano** Puglia, SE Italy 40°26′N 18°03′E
Sráid na Cathrach see Milltown Malbay
167 S11 **Srâlau** Stœng Trêng, N Cambodia 14°03′N 105°46′E
Srath an Urláir see Stranorlar
112 G10 **Srbac** ◐ Republika Srpska, N Bosnia and Herzegovina
Srbija see Serbia
Srbinje see Foča
112 K9 **Srbobran** var. Bácsszenttamás, Hung. Szenttamás. Vojvodina, N Serbia 45°33′N 19°46′E
Srbobran see Donji Vakuf
167 R13 **Srê Âmbĕl** Kaôh Kông, SW Cambodia 11°07′N 103°46′E
112 K13 **Srebrenica** Republika Srpska, E Bosnia and Herzegovina 44°04′N 19°18′E
112 I11 **Srebrenik** Federacija Bosna I Hercegovina, NE Bosnia and Herzegovina 44°42′N 18°30′E
114 K10 **Sredets** prev. Syulemeshlii. Stara Zagora, C Bulgaria 42°16′N 25°40′E
114 M10 **Sredets** prev. Grudovo. ◐ Burgas, E Bulgaria
114 M10 **Sredetska Reka** ≈ SE Bulgaria
123 U9 **Sredinnyy Khrebet** ▲▲ E Russian Federation
114 N7 **Sredishte** Rom. Beibunar; prev. Knyazhevo. Dobrich, NE Bulgaria 43°51′N 27°30′E
114 I10 **Sredna Gora** ▲▲ C Bulgaria
123 R7 **Srednekolymsk** Respublika Sakha (Yakutiya), NE Russian Federation 67°28′N 153°52′E
126 K7 **Srednerusskaya Vozvyshennost'** Eng. Central Russian Upland. ▲▲ W Russian Federation
122 L9 **Srednesibirskoye Ploskogor'ye** var. Central Siberian Uplands, Eng. Central Siberian Plateau. ▲▲ N Russian Federation
125 V13 **Sredniy Ural** ▲▲ NW Russian Federation
167 T12 **Srê Khtŭm** Môndól Kiri, E Cambodia 12°10′N 106°52′E
110 G12 **Śrem** Wielkopolskie, C Poland 52°07′N 17°00′E
112 K10 **Sremska Mitrovica** prev. Mitrovica, Ger. Mitrowitz. Vojvodina, NW Serbia 44°58′N 19°37′E
167 R11 **Srêng, Stœng** ≈ NW Cambodia
167 R11 **Srê Noy** Siĕmréab, NW Cambodia 13°47′N 104°03′E
Srepok, Sông see Srêpôk, Tônle
167 T12 **Srêpôk, Tônle** var. Sông Srepok. ≈ Cambodia/Vietnam
123 P13 **Sretensk** Chitinskaya Oblast', S Russian Federation 52°14′N 117°33′E
169 R10 **Sri Aman** Sarawak, East Malaysia 01°13′N 111°25′E
117 R4 **Sribne** Chernihivs'ka Oblast', N Ukraine 50°40′N 32°55′E
Sri Jayawardanapura see Sri Jayawardanapura Kotte
155 I25 **Sri Jayewardanapura Kotte** var. Sri Jayawardanapura. Western Province, W Sri Lanka 06°54′N 79°58′E
155 M14 **Srīkākulam** Andhra Pradesh, E India 18°18′N 83°54′E
155 I25 **Sri Lanka** off. Democratic Socialist Republic of Sri Lanka; prev. Ceylon. ◆ republic S Asia
130 F14 **Sri Lanka** island S Asia
Sri Lanka, Democratic Socialist Republic of see Sri Lanka
153 V14 **Srimangal** Sylhet, E Bangladesh 24°19′N 91°40′E
Sri Mohangorh see Shri Mohangarh
152 H5 **Srinagar** state capital Jammu and Kashmir, N India 34°07′N 74°50′E
167 N10 **Srinagarind Reservoir** ⊠ W Thailand
155 F19 **Sringeri** Karnātaka, W India 13°26′N 75°13′E
155 K25 **Sri Pada** Eng. Adam's Peak. ▲ S Sri Lanka 06°49′N 80°25′E
Sri Saket see Si Sa Ket
111 G14 **Środa Śląska** Ger. Neumarkt. Dolnośląskie, SW Poland 51°10′N 16°30′E
110 H12 **Środa Wielkopolska** Wielkopolskie, C Poland 52°13′N 17°17′E
Srpska Kostajnica see Bosanska Kostajnica
113 G14 **Srpska, Republika** ◐ republic Bosnia and Herzegovina
Srpski Brod see Bosanski Brod
Ssu-ch'uan see Sichuan
Ssu-p'ing/Ssu-p'ing-chieh see Siping
Stablo see Stavelot
99 G15 **Stabroek** Antwerpen, N Belgium 51°21′N 04°22′E
Stackeln see Strenči
96 I5 **Stack Skerry** island N Scotland, United Kingdom
100 I9 **Stade** Niedersachsen, N Germany 53°36′N 09°29′E
94 C10 **Stadlandet** peninsula S Norway
109 R5 **Stadl-Paura** Oberösterreich, NW Austria 48°05′N 13°52′E
119 L20 **Stadolichy** Rus. Stodolichi. Homyel'skaya Voblasts', SE Belarus 51°44′N 28°30′E
98 P7 **Stadskanaal** Groningen, NE Netherlands 53°N 06°55′E
101 H16 **Stadtallendorf** Hessen, C Germany 50°49′N 09°01′E
101 K23 **Stadtbergen** Bayern, S Germany 48°21′N 10°50′E
108 G7 **Stäfa** Zürich, NE Switzerland 47°14′N 08°45′E
95 K23 **Staffanstorp** Skåne, S Sweden 55°38′N 13°13′E
101 K18 **Staffelstein** Bayern, C Germany 50°05′N 11°00′E
97 L19 **Stafford** C England, United Kingdom 52°48′N 02°07′W
26 L6 **Stafford** Kansas, C USA 37°57′N 98°36′W
21 W4 **Stafford** Virginia, NE USA 38°26′N 77°27′W
97 L19 **Staffordshire** cultural region C England, United Kingdom
19 N12 **Stafford Springs** Connecticut, NE USA 41°57′N 72°18′W
115 H14 **Stágira** Kentrikí Makedonía, N Greece 40°31′N 23°46′E
118 G7 **Staicele** Limbaži, N Latvia 57°52′N 24°48′E
Ştaierdorf-Anina see Anina
109 V8 **Stainz** Steiermark, SE Austria 46°55′N 15°18′E
Stájerlakanina see Anina
117 Y7 **Stakhanov** Luhans'ka Oblast', E Ukraine 48°30′N 38°42′E
108 E11 **Stalden** Valais, SW Switzerland 46°12′N 07°55′E
15 S8 **St-Alexandre** Québec, SE Canada 47°39′N 69°36′W
Stalin see Varna
Stalinabad see Dushanbe
Stalingrad see Volgograd
Staliniri see Ts'khinvali
Stalino see Donets'k
Stalinobod see Dushanbe
Stalinov Štít see Gerlachovský štít
Stalinsk see Novokuznetsk
Stalins'kaya Oblast' see Donets'ka Oblast'
Stalinski Zaliv see Varnenski Zaliv
Stalin, Yazovir see Iskŭr, Yazovir
111 N15 **Stalowa Wola** Podkarpackie, SE Poland 50°35′N 22°02′E
114 I11 **Stamboliyski** Plovdiv, C Bulgaria 42°09′N 24°32′E
114 J8 **Stamboliyski, Yazovir** ⊠ N Bulgaria
15 Q7 **St-Ambroise** Québec, SE Canada 48°35′N 71°19′W
97 N19 **Stamford** E England, United Kingdom 52°39′N 00°32′W

326
◆ Country ● Country Capital ◇ Dependent Territory ○ Dependent Territory Capital ◐ Administrative Regions ✈ International Airport ▲ Mountain ▲▲ Mountain Range Volcano ≈ River ◎ Lake ⊠ Reservoir

Stamford – Stroudsburg

18 L14 **Stamford** Connecticut, NE USA 41°03′N 73°32′W
25 P6 **Stamford** Texas, SW USA 32°55′N 99°49′W
25 Q6 **Stamford, Lake** ⊠ Texas, SW USA
108 I10 **Stampa** Graubünden, SE Switzerland 46°21′N 09°35′E
Stampalia *see* Astypálaia
27 T14 **Stamps** Arkansas, C USA 33°22′N 93°30′W
92 G11 **Stamsund** Nordland, C Norway 68°07′N 13°50′E
27 R2 **Stanberry** Missouri, C USA 40°12′N 94°33′W
195 O3 **Stancomb-Wills Glacier** *glacier* Antarctica
83 K21 **Standerton** Mpumalanga, E South Africa 26°57′S 29°14′E
31 R7 **Standish** Michigan, N USA 43°59′N 83°58′W
20 M6 **Stanford** Kentucky, S USA 37°30′N 84°40′W
33 S9 **Stanford** Montana, NW USA 47°08′N 110°15′W
95 P19 **Stånga** Gotland, SE Sweden 57°16′N 18°30′E
94 I13 **Stange** Hedmark, S Norway 60°40′N 11°05′E
83 L23 **Stanger** KwaZulu/Natal, E South Africa 29°20′S 31°18′E
Stanimaka *see* Asenovgrad
Stanislau *see* Ivano-Frankivs'k
35 P8 **Stanislaus River** ≈ California, W USA
Stanislav *see* Ivano-Frankivs'k
Stanislavskaya Oblast' *see* Ivano-Frankivs'ka Oblast'
Stanisławów *see* Ivano-Frankivs'k
Stanke Dimitrov *see* Dupnitsa
183 O15 **Stanley** Tasmania, SE Australia 40°48′S 145°18′E
65 E24 **Stanley** *var.* Port Stanley, Puerto Argentino. ○ (Falkland Islands) East Falkland, Falkland Islands 51°45′S 57°56′W
33 O13 **Stanley** Idaho, NW USA 44°12′N 114°58′W
28 L3 **Stanley** North Dakota, N USA 48°19′N 102°23′W
21 U4 **Stanley** Virginia, NE USA 38°34′N 78°30′W
30 J6 **Stanley** Wisconsin, N USA 44°58′N 90°54′W
79 G21 **Stanley Pool** *var.* Pool Malebo. ◎ Congo/Dem. Rep. Congo
155 H20 **Stanley Reservoir** ⊠ S India
Stanleyville *see* Kisangani
42 G3 **Stann Creek** ◈ *district* SE Belize
Stann Creek *see* Dangriga
123 Q12 **Stanovoy Khrebet** ▲▲ SE Russian Federation
108 F8 **Stans** Unterwalden, C Switzerland 46°57′N 08°23′E
97 O21 **Stansted** ✈ (London) Essex, E England, United Kingdom 51°53′N 00°16′E
183 U4 **Stanthorpe** Queensland, E Australia 28°35′S 151°52′E
21 N6 **Stanton** Kentucky, S USA 37°51′N 83°51′W
31 Q8 **Stanton** Michigan, N USA 43°19′N 85°04′W
29 Q14 **Stanton** Nebraska, C USA 41°57′N 97°13′W
28 L5 **Stanton** North Dakota, N USA 47°19′N 101°22′W
25 N7 **Stanton** Texas, SW USA 32°07′N 101°47′W
32 H7 **Stanwood** Washington, NW USA 48°14′N 122°22′W
117 Y7 **Stanychno-Luhans'ke** Luhans'ka Oblast', E Ukraine 48°39′N 39°30′E
108 K7 **Stanzach** Tirol, W Austria 47°24′N 10°36′E
98 M9 **Staphorst** Overijssel, E Netherlands 52°38′N 06°12′E
14 D18 **Staples** Ontario, S Canada 42°09′N 82°34′W
29 T6 **Staples** Minnesota, N USA 46°21′N 94°47′W
28 M14 **Stapleton** Nebraska, C USA 41°29′N 100°40′W
25 S8 **Star** Texas, SW USA 31°27′N 98°16′W
111 M14 **Starachowice** Świętokrzyskie, C Poland 51°04′N 21°02′E
Stara Kanjiža *see* Kanjiža
111 M18 **Stará L'ubovňa** *Ger.* Altlublau, *Hung.* Ólubló. Prešovský Kraj, E Slovakia 49°19′N 20°40′E
112 L10 **Stara Pazova** *Ger.* Altpasua, *Hung.* Ópazova. Vojvodina, N Serbia 44°59′N 20°10′E
Stara Planina *see* Balkan Mountains
114 L9 **Stara Reka** ≈ C Bulgaria
116 M5 **Stara Synyava** Khmel'nyts'ka Oblast', W Ukraine 49°39′N 27°39′E
116 I2 **Stara Vyzhivka** Volyns'ka Oblast', NW Ukraine 51°27′N 24°25′E
Staraya Belitsa *see* Staraya Byelitsa
119 M14 **Staraya Byelitsa** *Rus.* Staraya Belitsa. Vitsyebskaya Voblasts', NE Belarus 54°42′N 29°38′E
127 R5 **Staraya Mayna** Ul'yanovskaya Oblast', W Russian Federation 54°36′N 48°57′E
119 O18 **Staraya Rudnya** Homyel'skaya Voblasts', SE Belarus 52°50′N 30°17′E
124 H14 **Staraya Russa** Novgorodskaya Oblast', W Russian Federation 57°59′N 31°18′E
114 K10 **Stara Zagora** *Lat.* Augusta Trajana. Stara Zagora, C Bulgaria 42°26′N 25°39′E
114 K10 **Stara Zagora** ◈ *province* C Bulgaria
29 S8 **Starbuck** Minnesota, N USA 45°36′N 95°31′W
191 W4 **Starbuck Island** *prev.* Volunteer Island. *island* E Kiribati
27 V13 **Star City** Arkansas, C USA 33°56′N 91°52′W
112 F13 **Staretina** ▲▲ W Bosnia and Herzegovina
Stargard in Pommern *see* Stargard Szczeciński
110 E9 **Stargard Szczeciński** *Ger.* Stargard in Pommern. Zachodnio-pomorskie, NW Poland 53°20′N 15°02′E
187 N10 **Star Harbour** *harbour* San Cristobal, SE Solomon Islands
Stari Bečej *see* Bečej
113 F15 **Stari Grad** *It.* Cittavecchia. Split-Dalmacija, S Croatia 43°11′N 16°36′E
124 J16 **Staritsa** Tverskaya Oblast', W Russian Federation 56°28′N 34°51′E
23 V9 **Starke** Florida, SE USA 29°56′N 82°07′W
22 M4 **Starkville** Mississippi, S USA 33°27′N 88°49′W
186 B7 **Star Mountains** *Ind.* Pegunungan Sterren. ▲▲ Indonesia/Papua New Guinea
101 L23 **Starnberg** Bayern, SE Germany 48°00′N 11°19′E
101 L24 **Starnberger See** ◎ SE Germany
Starobel'sk *see* Starobil's'k
117 X8 **Starobesheve** Donets'ka Oblast', E Ukraine 47°45′N 38°01′E
117 Y6 **Starobil's'k** *Rus.* Starobel'sk. Luhans'ka Oblast', E Ukraine 49°16′N 38°56′E
119 K18 **Starobin** *var.* Starobyn. Minskaya Voblasts', S Belarus 52°44′N 27°28′E
Starobyn *see* Starobin
126 H6 **Starodub** Bryanskaya Oblast', W Russian Federation 52°30′N 32°56′E
110 I8 **Starogard Gdański** *Ger.* Preussisch-Stargard. Pomorskie, N Poland 53°57′N 18°29′E
145 P16 **Staroikan** Yuzhnyy Kazakhstan, S Kazakhstan 43°09′N 68°34′E
Starokonstantinov *see* Starokostyantyniv
116 L5 **Starokostyantyniv** *Rus.* Starokonstantinov. Khmel'nyts'ka Oblast', NW Ukraine 49°43′N 27°13′E
126 K12 **Starominskaya** Krasnodarskiy Kray, SW Russian Federation 46°31′N 39°03′E
114 L7 **Staro Selo** *Rom.* Satul-Vechi; *prev.* Star-Smil. Silistra, NE Bulgaria 43°58′N 26°32′E
126 K12 **Staroshcherbinovskaya** Krasnodarskiy Kray, SW Russian Federation 46°36′N 38°42′E
127 V6 **Starosubkhangulovo** Respublika Bashkortostan, W Russian Federation 53°05′N 57°22′E
35 S4 **Star Peak** ▲ Nevada, W USA 40°31′N 118°09′W
15 T8 **St-Arsène** Québec, SE Canada 47°55′N 69°21′W
Star-Smil *see* Staro Selo
97 J25 **Start Point** *headland* SW England, United Kingdom 50°13′N 03°38′W
Startsy *see* Kirawsk
Starum *see* Stavoren
119 L18 **Staryya Darohi** *Rus.* Staryye Dorogi. Minskaya Voblasts', S Belarus 53°02′N 28°16′E
Staryye Dorogi *see* Staryya Darohi
127 T2 **Staryye Zyattsy** Udmurtskaya Respublika, NW Russian Federation 57°22′N 52°42′E
117 U13 **Staryy Krym** Respublika Krym, S Ukraine 45°03′N 35°06′E
126 K8 **Staryy Oskol** Belgorodskaya Oblast', W Russian Federation 51°21′N 37°52′E
116 H6 **Staryy Sambir** L'vivs'ka Oblast', W Ukraine 49°27′N 23°00′E
101 L14 **Stassfurt** *var.* Staßfurt. Sachsen-Anhalt, C Germany 51°51′N 11°35′E
Staßfurt *see* Stassfurt
111 M15 **Staszów** Świętokrzyskie, C Poland 50°33′N 21°07′E
29 W13 **State Center** Iowa, C USA 42°01′N 93°09′W
18 E14 **State College** Pennsylvania, NE USA 40°48′N 77°52′W
18 K15 **Staten Island** *island* New York, NE USA
Staten Island *see* Estados, Isla de los
23 U8 **Statenville** Georgia, SE USA 30°42′N 83°00′W
23 W5 **Statesboro** Georgia, SE USA 32°28′N 81°47′W
States, The *see* United States of America
21 R9 **Statesville** North Carolina, SE USA 35°46′N 80°54′W
95 G16 **Stathelle** Telemark, S Norway 59°01′N 09°40′E
30 K15 **Staunton** Illinois, N USA 39°00′N 89°47′W
21 T5 **Staunton** Virginia, NE USA 38°10′N 79°05′W
95 C16 **Stavanger** Rogaland, S Norway 58°58′N 05°43′E
99 L21 **Stavelot** *Dut.* Stablo. Liège, E Belgium 50°24′N 05°56′E
95 G16 **Stavern** Vestfold, S Norway 59°00′N 10°01′E
Stavers Island *see* Vostok Island
98 J7 **Stavoren** *Fris.* Starum. Friesland, N Netherlands 52°52′N 05°22′E
115 K21 **Stavrí, Akrotírio** *var.* Akrotírio Stavrós. *headland* Náxos, Kykládes, Greece, Aegean Sea 37°12′N 25°32′E
126 M14 **Stavropol'** *prev.* Voroshilovsk. Stavropol'skiy Kray, SW Russian Federation 45°02′N 41°58′E
Stavropol' *see* Tol'yatti
126 M14 **Stavropol'skaya Vozvyshennost'** ▲▲ SW Russian Federation
126 M14 **Stavropol'skiy Kray** ◈ *territory* SW Russian Federation
115 H14 **Stavrós** Kentrikí Makedonía, N Greece 40°39′N 23°43′E
115 J24 **Stavrós, Akrotírio** *headland* Kríti, Greece, E Mediterranean Sea 35°25′N 24°57′E
Stavrós, Akrotírio *see* Stavrí, Akrotírio
114 I12 **Stavroúpoli** *prev.* Stavroúpolis. Anatolikí Makedonía kai Thráki, NE Greece 41°12′N 24°45′E
Stavroúpolis *see* Stavroúpoli
117 O6 **Stavyshche** Kyyivs'ka Oblast', N Ukraine 49°23′N 30°10′E
182 M11 **Stawell** Victoria, SE Australia 37°06′S 142°52′E
110 N9 **Stawiski** Podlaskie, NE Poland 53°22′N 22°08′E
14 G14 **Stayner** Ontario, S Canada 44°25′N 80°05′W
14 D17 **St. Clair** ≈ Canada/USA
37 R3 **Steamboat Springs** Colorado, C USA 40°28′N 106°51′W
15 U4 **Ste-Anne, Lac** ◎ Québec, SE Canada
20 M8 **Stearns** Kentucky, S USA 36°39′N 84°27′W
39 N10 **Stebbins** Alaska, USA 63°30′N 162°15′W
15 U7 **Ste-Blandine** Québec, SE Canada 48°22′N 68°27′W
108 K7 **Steeg** Tirol, W Austria 47°15′N 10°18′E
27 Y9 **Steele** Missouri, C USA 36°04′N 89°49′W
29 N5 **Steele** North Dakota, N USA 46°51′N 99°55′W
194 J5 **Steele Island** *island* Antarctica
30 K16 **Steeleville** Illinois, N USA 38°00′N 89°39′W
27 W6 **Steelville** Missouri, C USA 37°57′N 91°21′W
99 G14 **Steenbergen** Noord-Brabant, S Netherlands 51°35′N 04°19′E
Steenkool *see* Bintuni
11 O10 **Steen River** Alberta, W Canada 59°37′N 117°17′W
98 M8 **Steenwijk** Overijssel, N Netherlands 52°47′N 06°07′E
174 J8 **Steep Point** *headland* Western Australia 26°09′S 113°11′E
116 L9 **Ştefăneşti** Botoşani, NE Romania 47°44′N 27°15′E
Stefanie, Lake *see* Ch'ew Bahir
8 L5 **Stefansson Island** *island* Nunavut, N Canada
117 O10 **Ştefan Vodă** *Rus.* Suvorovo. SE Moldova 46°33′N 29°39′E
63 H18 **Steffen, Cerro** ▲ S Chile 44°27′S 71°42′W
108 D9 **Steffisburg** Bern, C Switzerland 46°47′N 07°38′E
95 J24 **Stege** Storstrøm, SE Denmark 54°59′N 12°18′E
116 G10 **Ştei** *Hung.* Vaskohsziklás. Bihor, W Romania 46°34′N 22°28′E
Steier *see* Steyr
Steierdorf/Steierdorf-Anina *see* Anina
109 T7 **Steiermark** *off.* Land Steiermark, *Eng.* Styria. ◈ *state* C Austria
Steiermark, Land *see* Steiermark
101 J19 **Steigerwald** *hill range* C Germany
99 L17 **Stein** Limburg, SE Netherlands 50°58′N 05°45′E
Stein *see* Stein an der Donau
Stein *see* Kamnik, Slovenia
108 M8 **Steinach** Tirol, W Austria 47°07′N 11°30′E
Steinamanger *see* Szombathely
109 W3 **Stein an der Donau** *var.* Stein. Niederösterreich, NE Austria 48°25′N 15°35′E
Steinau an der Elbe *see* Ścinawa
11 Y16 **Steinbach** Manitoba, S Canada 49°32′N 96°40′W
Steiner Alpen *see* Kamniško-Savinjske Alpe
99 L24 **Steinfort** Luxembourg, W Luxembourg 49°39′N 05°55′E
100 H12 **Steinhuder Meer** ◎ NW Germany
93 E15 **Steinkjer** Nord-Trøndelag, C Norway 64°01′N 11°29′E
Stejarul *see* Karapelit
99 F16 **Stekene** Oost-Vlaanderen, NW Belgium 51°13′N 04°04′E
83 E26 **Stellenbosch** Western Cape, SW South Africa 33°56′S 18°51′E
98 F13 **Stellendam** Zuid-Holland, SW Netherlands 51°48′N 04°01′E
39 T12 **Steller, Mount** ▲ Alaska, USA 60°36′N 142°49′W
103 Y14 **Stello, Monte** ▲ Corse, France, C Mediterranean Sea 42°49′N 09°24′E
106 F5 **Stelvio, Passo dello** *pass* Italy/Switzerland
15 S7 **Ste-Marguerite Nord-Est** ≈ Québec, SE Canada
15 V4 **Ste-Marguerite, Pointe** *headland* Québec, SE Canada 50°01′N 66°43′W
12 J14 **Ste-Marie, Lac** ⊠ Québec, S Canada
103 R3 **Stenay** Meuse, NE France 49°29′N 05°12′E
100 L12 **Stendal** Sachsen-Anhalt, C Germany 52°36′N 11°52′E
118 E8 **Stende** Talsi, NW Latvia 57°09′N 22°33′E
182 H10 **Stenhouse Bay** South Australia 35°15′S 136°58′E
95 J23 **Stenløse** Frederiksborg, E Denmark 55°47′N 12°13′E
95 L19 **Stensjön** Jönköping, S Sweden 57°36′N 14°42′E
95 K18 **Stenstorp** Västra Götaland, S Sweden 58°15′N 13°45′E
95 I18 **Stenungsund** Västra Götaland, S Sweden 58°05′N 11°49′E
Stepanakert *see* Xankändi
137 T11 **Step'anavan** N Armenia 41°00′N 44°27′E
100 K9 **Stepenitz** ≈ N Germany
29 O10 **Stephan** South Dakota, N USA 44°12′N 99°25′W
29 R3 **Stephen** Minnesota, N USA 48°27′N 96°54′W
27 T14 **Stephens** Arkansas, C USA 33°25′N 93°04′W
184 J13 **Stephens, Cape** *headland* D'Urville Island, Marlborough, SW New Zealand 40°42′S 173°56′E
21 V3 **Stephens City** Virginia, NE USA 39°03′N 78°10′W
182 L6 **Stephens Creek** New South Wales, SE Australia 31°51′S 141°30′E
184 K13 **Stephens Island** *island* C New Zealand
31 N5 **Stephenson** Michigan, N USA 45°27′N 87°36′W
13 S12 **Stephenville** Newfoundland, Newfoundland and Labrador, SE Canada 48°33′N 58°34′W
25 S7 **Stephenville** Texas, SW USA 32°12′N 98°13′W
145 P17 **Step' Nardara** *Kaz.* Shardara Dalasy; *prev.* Shaidara. *grassland* S Kazakhstan
145 R8 **Stepnogorsk** Akmola, C Kazakhstan 52°04′N 72°18′E
127 O15 **Stepnoye** Stavropol'skiy Kray, SW Russian Federation 44°18′N 44°34′E
145 Q8 **Stepnyak** Akmola, N Kazakhstan 52°52′N 70°49′E
192 J17 **Steps Point** *headland* Tutuila, W American Samoa 14°23′S 170°46′W
115 F17 **Stereá Elláς** *Eng.* Greece Central. ◈ *region* C Greece
83 J24 **Sterkspruit** Eastern Cape, SE South Africa 30°31′S 27°22′E
127 U6 **Sterlibashevo** Respublika Bashkortostan, W Russian Federation 53°19′N 55°12′E
39 R12 **Sterling** Alaska, USA 60°32′N 150°51′W
37 V3 **Sterling** Colorado, C USA 40°37′N 103°12′W
30 K11 **Sterling** Illinois, N USA 41°47′N 89°42′W
26 M5 **Sterling** Kansas, C USA 38°12′N 98°12′W
25 O8 **Sterling City** Texas, SW USA 31°50′N 101°00′W
31 S9 **Sterling Heights** Michigan, N USA 42°34′N 83°01′W
21 W3 **Sterling Park** Virginia, NE USA 39°00′N 77°24′W
37 V2 **Sterling Reservoir** ⊠ Colorado, C USA
22 I5 **Sterlington** Louisiana, S USA 32°42′N 92°05′W
127 U6 **Sterlitamak** Respublika Bashkortostan, W Russian Federation 53°39′N 56°00′E
Sternberg *see* Šternberk
111 H17 **Šternberk** *Ger.* Sternberg. Olomoucký Kraj, E Czech Republic 49°45′N 17°20′E
141 V17 **Stēroh** Suquṭrā, S Yemen 12°21′N 53°50′E
Sterren, Pegunungan *see* Star Mountains
110 G11 **Stęszew** Wielkopolskie, C Poland 52°16′N 16°41′E
Stettin *see* Szczecin
Stettiner Haff *see* Szczeciński, Zalew
11 Q15 **Stettler** Alberta, SW Canada 52°21′N 112°40′W
31 V13 **Steubenville** Ohio, N USA 40°21′N 80°37′W
97 O21 **Stevenage** E England, United Kingdom 51°55′N 00°14′W
23 Q1 **Stevenson** Alabama, S USA 34°52′N 85°50′W
32 H11 **Stevenson** Washington, NW USA 45°43′N 121°54′W
182 E1 **Stevenson Creek** *seasonal river* South Australia
39 Q13 **Stevenson Entrance** *strait* Alaska, USA
30 L6 **Stevens Point** Wisconsin, N USA 44°32′N 89°33′W
39 R8 **Stevens Village** Alaska, USA 66°01′N 149°02′W
33 P10 **Stevensville** Montana, NW USA 46°30′N 114°05′W
93 E25 **Stevns Klint** *headland* E Denmark 55°15′N 12°25′E
10 J12 **Stewart** British Columbia, W Canada 55°58′N 129°52′W
10 I6 **Stewart** ≈ Yukon Territory, NW Canada
10 I6 **Stewart Crossing** Yukon Territory, NW Canada 63°22′N 136°37′W
63 H25 **Stewart, Isla** *island* S Chile
185 B25 **Stewart Island** *island* S New Zealand
Stewart Islands *see* Sikaiana
181 W6 **Stewart, Mount** ▲ Queensland, E Australia 20°11′S 145°29′E
10 H6 **Stewart River** Yukon Territory, NW Canada 63°17′N 139°24′W
27 R3 **Stewartsville** Missouri, C USA 39°45′N 94°30′W
11 S16 **Stewart Valley** Saskatchewan, S Canada 50°34′N 107°47′W
29 W10 **Stewartville** Minnesota, N USA 43°51′N 92°29′W
Steyerlak-Anina *see* Anina
109 T5 **Steyr** *var.* Steier. Oberösterreich, N Austria 48°02′N 14°26′E
109 T5 **Steyr** ≈ NW Austria
15 T7 **St-Fabien** Québec, SE Canada 48°19′N 68°51′W
15 R11 **St-François, Lac** ◎ Québec, SE Canada
83 E25 **St. Helena Bay** *bay* SW South Africa
15 T8 **St-Hubert** Québec, SE Canada 47°46′N 69°15′W
29 P11 **Stickney** South Dakota, N USA 43°24′N 98°23′W
98 L5 **Stiens** Friesland, N Netherlands 53°15′N 05°45′E
Stif *see* Sétif
27 Q11 **Stigler** Oklahoma, C USA 35°16′N 95°08′W
107 N18 **Stigliano** Basilicata, S Italy 40°24′N 16°13′E
95 N17 **Stigtomta** Södermanland, C Sweden 58°48′N 16°47′E
10 I11 **Stikine** ≈ British Columbia, W Canada
Stilida/Stilís *see* Stylída
95 G22 **Stilling** Århus, C Denmark 56°04′N 10°00′E
29 W8 **Stillwater** Minnesota, N USA 45°03′N 92°48′W
27 O9 **Stillwater** Oklahoma, C USA 36°07′N 97°03′W
35 S5 **Stillwater Range** ▲▲ Nevada, W USA
18 I8 **Stillwater Reservoir** ⊠ New York, NE USA
107 O22 **Stilo, Punta** *headland* S Italy 38°27′N 16°36′E
27 R10 **Stilwell** Oklahoma, C USA 35°48′N 94°37′W
Štimlje *see* Shtime
25 N1 **Stinnett** Texas, SW USA 35°49′N 101°27′W
113 P18 **Štip** E FYR Macedonia 41°45′N 22°10′E
Stira *see* Stýra
96 J12 **Stirling** C Scotland, United Kingdom 56°07′N 03°57′W
96 I12 **Stirling** *cultural region* C Scotland, United Kingdom
180 J14 **Stirling Range** ▲▲ Western Australia
15 R8 **St-Jean** ≈ Québec, SE Canada
93 E16 **Stjørdalshalsen** Nord-Trøndelag, C Norway 63°27′N 10°57′E
83 L22 **St. Lucia** KwaZulu/Natal, E South Africa 28°22′S 32°25′E
Stochód *see* Stokhid
101 H24 **Stockach** Baden-Württemberg, S Germany 47°51′N 09°01′E
25 S12 **Stockdale** Texas, SW USA 29°14′N 97°57′W
109 X3 **Stockerau** Niederösterreich, NE Austria 48°24′N 16°13′E
93 H20 **Stockholm** ● (Sweden) Stockholm, C Sweden 59°17′N 18°03′E
95 O15 **Stockholm** ◈ *county* C Sweden
Stockmannshof *see* Pļaviņas
97 L18 **Stockport** NW England, United Kingdom 53°25′N 02°10′W
65 K15 **Stocks Seamount** *undersea feature* C Atlantic Ocean 11°42′S 33°48′W
35 O8 **Stockton** California, W USA 37°56′N 121°19′W
26 L3 **Stockton** Kansas, C USA 39°27′N 99°17′W
27 S6 **Stockton** Missouri, C USA 37°43′N 93°49′W
30 K3 **Stockton Island** *island* Apostle Islands, Wisconsin, N USA
27 S7 **Stockton Lake** ⊠ Missouri, C USA
97 M15 **Stockton-on-Tees** *var.* Stockton on Tees. N England, United Kingdom 54°34′N 01°19′W
Stockton on Tees *see* Stockton-on-Tees
24 M10 **Stockton Plateau** *plain* Texas, SW USA
28 M16 **Stockville** Nebraska, C USA 40°33′N 100°20′W
93 H17 **Stöde** Västernorrland, C Sweden 62°27′N 16°34′E
Stodolichi *see* Stadolichy
113 M19 **Stogovo Karaorman** ▲ W FYR Macedonia
Stoke *see* Stoke-on-Trent
97 L19 **Stoke-on-Trent** *var.* Stoke. C England, United Kingdom 53°N 02°10′W
182 M15 **Stokes Point** *headland* Tasmania, SE Australia 40°09′S 143°55′E
116 J2 **Stokhid** *Pol.* Stochód, *Rus.* Stokhod. ≈ NW Ukraine
Stokhod *see* Stokhid
92 I4 **Stokkseyri** Sudhurland, SW Iceland 63°49′N 21°00′W
92 G10 **Stokmarknes** Nordland, C Norway 68°34′N 14°55′E
Stol *see* Veliki Krš
113 H15 **Stolac** Federacija Bosna I Hercegovina, S Bosnia and Herzegovina 43°04′N 17°58′E
Stolbce *see* Stowbtsy
101 D16 **Stolberg** *var.* Stolberg im Rheinland. Nordrhein-Westfalen, W Germany 50°45′N 06°15′E
Stolberg im Rheinland *see* Stolberg
123 P6 **Stolbovoy, Ostrov** *island* NE Russian Federation
Stolbtsy *see* Stowbtsy
119 J20 **Stolin** Brestskaya Voblasts', SW Belarus 51°53′N 26°51′E
95 K14 **Stöllet** *var.* Norra Ny. Värmland, C Sweden 60°24′N 13°15′E
Stolp *see* Słupsk
Stolpe *see* Słupia
Stolpmünde *see* Ustka
115 F15 **Stómio** Thessalía, C Greece 39°51′N 22°45′E
14 J11 **Stonecliffe** Ontario, SE Canada 46°12′N 77°58′W
96 L10 **Stonehaven** NE Scotland, United Kingdom 56°59′N 02°14′W
97 M23 **Stonehenge** *ancient monument* Wiltshire, S England, United Kingdom
23 T3 **Stone Mountain** ▲ Georgia, SE USA 33°48′N 84°10′W
11 X16 **Stonewall** Manitoba, S Canada 50°08′N 97°20′W
21 S3 **Stonewood** West Virginia, NE USA 39°15′N 80°18′W
14 D17 **Stoney Point** Ontario, S Canada 42°18′N 82°32′W
92 H10 **Stonglandseidet** Troms, N Norway 69°03′N 17°06′E
65 N25 **Stonybeach Bay** *bay* Tristan da Cunha, SE Atlantic Ocean
35 N5 **Stony Creek** ≈ California, W USA
65 N25 **Stonyhill Point** *headland* S Tristan da Cunha
14 I14 **Stony Lake** ◎ Ontario, SE Canada
11 Q14 **Stony Plain** Alberta, SW Canada 53°31′N 114°04′W
21 R9 **Stony Point** North Carolina, SE USA 35°51′N 81°04′W
18 G8 **Stony Point** *headland* New York, NE USA 43°50′N 76°18′W
11 T10 **Stony Rapids** Saskatchewan, C Canada 59°14′N 105°48′W
39 P11 **Stony River** Alaska, USA 61°48′N 156°37′W
Stony Tunguska *see* Podkamennaya Tunguska
12 G10 **Stooping** ≈ Ontario, C Canada
100 I9 **Stör** ≈ N Germany
95 M16 **Storå** Örebro, S Sweden 59°44′N 15°10′E
95 J16 **Stora Gla** ◎ C Sweden
95 I16 **Stora Le** *Nor.* Store Le. ◎ Norway/Sweden
92 I12 **Stora Lulevatten** ◎ N Sweden
92 H13 **Storavan** ◎ N Sweden
93 I20 **Storby** Åland, SW Finland 60°12′N 19°33′E
94 E10 **Stordalen** Møre og Romsdal, S Norway 62°22′N 07°00′E
95 H23 **Storebælt** *var.* Store Bælt, *Eng.* Great Belt, Storebelt. *channel* Baltic Sea/Kattegat
Store Bælt *see* Storebælt
Storebelt *see* Storebælt
95 M19 **Storebro** Kalmar, S Sweden 57°36′N 15°30′E
95 J24 **Store Heddinge** Storstrøm, SE Denmark 55°19′N 12°24′E
Store Le *see* Stora Le
93 E16 **Støren** Sør-Trøndelag, S Norway 63°02′N 10°16′E
92 O4 **Storfjorden** *fjord* S Norway
95 L15 **Storfors** Värmland, C Sweden 59°33′N 14°16′E
92 G13 **Storforshei** Nordland, C Norway 66°25′N 14°25′E
Storhammer *see* Hamar
100 L10 **Störkanal** *canal* N Germany
93 F16 **Storlien** Jämtland, C Sweden 63°18′N 12°10′E
183 P17 **Storm Bay** *inlet* Tasmania, SE Australia
29 T12 **Storm Lake** Iowa, C USA 42°38′N 95°12′W
29 S13 **Storm Lake** ◎ Iowa, C USA
96 G7 **Stornoway** NW Scotland, United Kingdom 58°13′N 06°23′W
Storojineț *see* Storozhynets'
92 P1 **Storøya** *island* NE Svalbard
125 S10 **Storozhevsk** Respublika Komi, NW Russian Federation 61°56′N 52°18′E
Storozhinets *see* Storozhynets'
116 K8 **Storozhynets'** *Ger.* Storozynetz, *Rom.* Storojineț, *Rus.* Storozhinets. Chernivets'ka Oblast', W Ukraine 48°11′N 25°42′E
Storozynetz *see* Storozhynets'
92 H11 **Storriten** ▲ C Norway 68°09′N 17°12′E
19 N12 **Storrs** Connecticut, NE USA 41°48′N 72°15′W
94 I11 **Storsjøen** ◎ S Norway
94 N13 **Storsjön** ◎ C Sweden
93 F16 **Storsjön** ◎ C Sweden
92 J9 **Storslett** Troms, N Norway 69°45′N 21°03′E
94 H11 **Storsølnkletten** ▲ S Norway 61°52′N 11°32′E
92 I9 **Storsteinnes** Troms, N Norway 69°13′N 19°14′E
95 I24 **Storstrøm** *var.* Storstrøms Amt. ◈ *county* SE Denmark
Storstrøms Amt *see* Storstrøm
93 J14 **Storsund** Norrbotten, N Sweden 65°36′N 20°40′E
94 J9 **Storsylen** *Swe.* Sylarna. ▲ Norway/Sweden 63°00′N 12°14′E
92 H11 **Stortoppen** ▲ N Sweden 67°33′N 17°27′E
93 H14 **Storuman** Västerbotten, N Sweden 65°05′N 17°10′E
93 H14 **Storuman** ◎ N Sweden
94 N13 **Storvik** Gävleborg, C Sweden 60°37′N 16°30′E
95 O14 **Storvreta** Uppsala, C Sweden 59°58′N 17°42′E
29 V13 **Story City** Iowa, C USA 42°10′N 93°36′W
11 V17 **Stoughton** Saskatchewan, S Canada 49°40′N 103°01′W
19 O11 **Stoughton** Massachusetts, NE USA 42°07′N 71°06′W
30 L9 **Stoughton** Wisconsin, N USA 42°56′N 89°12′W
97 L23 **Stour** ≈ E England, United Kingdom
97 P21 **Stour** ≈ S England, United Kingdom
27 T5 **Stover** Missouri, C USA 38°26′N 92°59′W
95 G21 **Støvring** Nordjylland, N Denmark 56°53′N 09°52′E
119 J17 **Stowbtsy** *Pol.* Stolbce, *Rus.* Stolbtsy. Minskaya Voblasts', C Belarus 53°29′N 26°44′E
25 X11 **Stowell** Texas, SW USA 29°47′N 94°22′W
97 P20 **Stowmarket** E England, United Kingdom 52°05′N 00°54′E
114 N8 **Stozher** Dobrich, NE Bulgaria 43°27′N 27°49′E
97 E14 **Strabane** *Ir.* An Srath Bán. W Northern Ireland, United Kingdom 54°49′N 07°27′W
121 S11 **Strabo Trench** *undersea feature* C Mediterranean Sea
27 T7 **Strafford** Missouri, C USA 37°16′N 93°07′W
183 N17 **Strahan** Tasmania, SE Australia 42°10′S 145°18′E
111 C18 **Strakonice** *Ger.* Strakonitz. Jihočeský Kraj, S Czech Republic 49°14′N 13°55′E
Strakonitz *see* Strakonice
100 N8 **Stralsund** Mecklenburg-Vorpommern, NE Germany 54°18′N 13°06′E
99 L16 **Stramproy** Limburg, SE Netherlands 51°12′N 05°43′E
83 E26 **Strand** Western Cape, SW South Africa 34°06′S 18°50′E
94 E10 **Stranda** Møre og Romsdal, S Norway 62°18′N 06°56′E
97 G15 **Strangford Lough** *Ir.* Loch Cuan. *inlet* E Northern Ireland, United Kingdom
95 N16 **Strängnäs** Södermanland, C Sweden 59°22′N 17°02′E
97 E14 **Stranorlar** *Ir.* Srath an Urláir. NW Ireland 54°48′N 07°46′W
97 H14 **Stranraer** S Scotland, United Kingdom 54°54′N 05°02′W
11 U16 **Strasbourg** Saskatchewan, S Canada 51°05′N 104°58′W
103 V5 **Strasbourg** *Ger.* Strassburg; *anc.* Argentoratum. Bas-Rhin, NE France 48°35′N 07°45′E
109 T8 **Strassburg** Kärnten, S Austria 46°54′N 14°21′E
37 U4 **Strasburg** Colorado, C USA 39°42′N 104°13′W
29 N7 **Strasburg** North Dakota, N USA 46°07′N 100°10′W
31 U12 **Strasburg** Ohio, N USA 40°35′N 81°31′W
21 U3 **Strasburg** Virginia, NE USA 38°59′N 78°21′W
117 N10 **Strășeni** *var.* Strasheny. C Moldova 47°07′N 28°37′E
Strasheny *see* Strășeni
Strassburg *see* Strasbourg, France
Strassburg *see* Aiud, Romania
99 M25 **Strassen** Luxembourg, S Luxembourg 49°37′N 06°05′E
109 R5 **Strasswalchen** Salzburg, C Austria 47°59′N 13°19′E
14 F16 **Stratford** Ontario, S Canada 43°22′N 81°00′W
184 K10 **Stratford** Taranaki, North Island, New Zealand 39°20′S 174°16′E
35 Q11 **Stratford** California, W USA 36°10′N 119°47′W
29 V13 **Stratford** Iowa, C USA 42°16′N 93°55′W
27 O12 **Stratford** Oklahoma, C USA 34°48′N 96°57′W
25 N1 **Stratford** Texas, SW USA 36°21′N 102°05′W
30 K6 **Stratford** Wisconsin, N USA 44°53′N 90°13′W
Stratford *see* Stratford-upon-Avon
97 M20 **Stratford-upon-Avon** *var.* Stratford. C England, United Kingdom 52°12′N 01°41′W
183 O17 **Strathgordon** Tasmania, SE Australia 42°49′S 146°04′E
11 Q16 **Strathmore** Alberta, SW Canada 51°05′N 113°20′W
35 R11 **Strathmore** California, W USA 36°07′N 119°04′W
14 E16 **Strathroy** Ontario, S Canada 42°57′N 81°40′W
96 I6 **Strathy Point** *headland* N Scotland, United Kingdom 58°36′N 04°04′W
37 W4 **Stratton** Colorado, C USA 39°16′N 102°34′W
19 P6 **Stratton** Maine, NE USA 45°08′N 70°25′W
18 M10 **Stratton Mountain** ▲ Vermont, NE USA 43°05′N 72°55′W
101 N21 **Straubing** Bayern, SE Germany 48°53′N 12°35′E
100 O12 **Strausberg** Brandenburg, E Germany 52°34′N 13°52′E
32 K13 **Strawberry Mountain** ▲ Oregon, NW USA 44°18′N 118°43′W
29 X12 **Strawberry Point** Iowa, C USA 42°40′N 91°31′W
36 M3 **Strawberry Reservoir** ⊠ Utah, W USA
36 M4 **Strawberry River** ≈ Utah, W USA
25 R7 **Strawn** Texas, SW USA 32°33′N 98°30′W
113 P17 **Straža** ▲ Bulgaria/FYR Macedonia 42°16′N 22°13′E
111 I19 **Strážov** *Hung.* Sztrazsó. ▲ NW Slovakia 48°59′N 18°29′E
182 F7 **Streaky Bay** South Australia 32°49′S 134°13′E
182 E7 **Streaky Bay** *bay* South Australia
30 L12 **Streator** Illinois, N USA 41°07′N 88°50′W
Streckenbach *see* Świdnik
Strednogorie *see* Pirdop
111 C17 **Středočeský Kraj** ◈ *region* C Czech Republic
29 O6 **Streeter** North Dakota, N USA 46°37′N 99°23′W
25 U8 **Streetman** Texas, SW USA 31°52′N 96°19′W
116 G13 **Strehaia** Mehedinți, SW Romania 44°37′N 23°10′E
Strehlen *see* Strzelin
114 I10 **Strelcha** Pazardzhik, C Bulgaria 42°28′N 24°21′E
122 L12 **Strelka** Krasnoyarskiy Kray, C Russian Federation 58°05′N 92°54′E
124 L6 **Strel'na** ≈ NW Russian Federation
118 H7 **Strenči** *Ger.* Stackeln. Valka, N Latvia 57°38′N 25°42′E
15 V6 **St-René-de-Matane** Québec, SE Canada 48°42′N 67°22′W
108 K8 **Strengen** Tirol, W Austria 47°07′N 10°25′E
106 C6 **Stresa** Piemonte, NE Italy 45°52′N 08°32′E
Streshin *see* Streshyn
119 N18 **Streshyn** *Rus.* Streshin. Homyel'skaya Voblasts', SE Belarus 52°43′N 30°07′E
95 B18 **Streymoy** *Dan.* Strømø. *island* N Faeroe Islands
95 G23 **Strib** Fyn, C Denmark 55°33′N 09°47′E
111 A17 **Stříbro** *Ger.* Mies. Plzeňský Kraj, W Czech Republic 49°44′N 12°55′E
186 B7 **Strickland** ≈ SW Papua New Guinea
Striegau *see* Strzegom
Strigonium *see* Esztergom
98 H13 **Strijen** Zuid-Holland, SW Netherlands 51°45′N 04°34′E
63 H21 **Strobel, Lago** ◎ S Argentina
61 B25 **Stroeder** Buenos Aires, E Argentina 40°11′S 62°35′W
115 C20 **Strofádes** *island* Iónia Nisiá, Greece, C Mediterranean Sea
Strofilia *see* Strofyliá
115 G17 **Strofyliá** *var.* Strofilia. Évvoia, C Greece 38°49′N 23°25′E
100 O10 **Strom** ≈ NE Germany
107 L22 **Stromboli** ⛰ Isola Stromboli, SW Italy 38°48′N 15°13′E
107 L22 **Stromboli, Isola** *island* Isole Eolie, S Italy
96 H9 **Stromeferry** N Scotland, United Kingdom 57°20′N 05°35′W
96 J5 **Stromness** N Scotland, United Kingdom 58°57′N 03°18′W
Strømø *see* Streymoy
94 N11 **Strömsbruk** Gävleborg, C Sweden 61°52′N 17°19′E
29 Q15 **Stromsburg** Nebraska, C USA 41°06′N 97°36′W
95 K21 **Strömsnäsbruk** Kronoberg, S Sweden 56°35′N 13°45′E
95 I17 **Strömstad** Västra Götaland, S Sweden 58°56′N 11°11′E
93 G16 **Strömsund** Jämtland, C Sweden 63°51′N 15°35′E
93 G15 **Ströms Vattudal** *valley* N Sweden
27 V14 **Strong** Arkansas, C USA 33°06′N 92°19′W
Strongilí *see* Strongylí
107 O21 **Strongoli** Calabria, SW Italy 39°17′N 17°03′E
31 T11 **Strongsville** Ohio, N USA 41°18′N 81°50′W
115 Q23 **Strongylí** *var.* Strongilí. *island* SE Greece
96 K5 **Stronsay** *island* NE Scotland, United Kingdom
97 L21 **Stroud** C England, United Kingdom 51°46′N 02°15′W
27 O10 **Stroud** Oklahoma, C USA 35°45′N 96°39′W
18 I14 **Stroudsburg** Pennsylvania, NE USA 40°59′N 75°12′W

◆ Country
● Country Capital
◇ Dependent Territory
○ Dependent Territory Capital
◈ Administrative Regions
✈ International Airport
▲ Mountain
▲▲ Mountain Range
⛰ Volcano
≈ River
◎ Lake
⊠ Reservoir
327

STRUER – SUROVIKINO

95 F21 **Struer** Ringkøbing, W Denmark 56°29′N 08°37′E
113 M20 **Struga** SW FYR Macedonia 41°11′N 20°40′E
Strugi-Kranyse *see* Strugi-Krasnyye
124 G14 **Strugi-Krasnyye** *var.* Strugi-Kranyse. Pskovskaya Oblast', W Russian Federation 58°19′N 29°09′E
114 G11 **Struma** *Gk.* Strymónas. ∽ Bulgaria/Greece *see also* Strymónas
Struma *see* Strymónas
97 G21 **Strumble Head** *headland* SW Wales, United Kingdom 52°01′N 05°05′W
Strumeshnitsa *see* Strumica
113 Q19 **Strumica** E FYR Macedonia 41°27′N 22°39′E
113 Q19 **Strumica** *Bulg.* Strumeshnitsa. ∽ Bulgaria/FYR Macedonia
114 G11 **Strumyani** Blagoevgrad, SW Bulgaria 41°41′N 23°13′E
31 V12 **Struthers** Ohio, N USA 41°03′N 80°36′W
114 I10 **Stryama** ∽ C Bulgaria
114 G13 **Strymónas** *Bul.* Struma. ∽ Bulgaria/Greece *see also* Struma
Strymónas *see* Struma
115 H14 **Strymonikós Kólpos** *gulf* N Greece
116 I6 **Stryy** L'vivs'ka Oblast', NW Ukraine 49°16′N 23°51′E
116 H6 **Stryy** ∽ W Ukraine
111 F14 **Strzegom** *Ger.* Striegau. Wałbrzych, SW Poland 50°59′N 16°20′E
110 E10 **Strzelce Krajeńskie** *Ger.* Friedeberg Neumark. Lubuskie, W Poland 52°52′N 15°30′E
111 I15 **Strzelce Opolskie** *Ger.* Gross Strehlitz. Opolskie, SW Poland 50°31′N 18°19′E
182 K3 **Strzelecki Creek** *seasonal river* South Australia
182 J3 **Strzelecki Desert** *desert* South Australia
111 G15 **Strzelin** *Ger.* Strehlen. Dolnośląskie, SW Poland 50°48′N 17°03′E
110 I11 **Strzelno** Kujawsko-pomorski, C Poland 52°38′N 18°11′E
111 N17 **Strzyżów** Podkarpackie, SE Poland 49°52′N 21°46′E
15 S8 **St-Siméon** Québec, SE Canada 47°50′N 69°55′W
Stua Laighean *see* Leinster, Mount
23 Y13 **Stuart** Florida, SE USA 27°12′N 80°15′W
29 U14 **Stuart** Iowa, C USA 41°30′N 94°19′W
29 O13 **Stuart** Nebraska, C USA 42°36′N 99°08′W
21 S8 **Stuart** Virginia, NE USA 36°38′N 80°19′W
10 L13 **Stuart** ∽ British Columbia, SW Canada
39 N10 **Stuart Island** *island* Alaska, USA
10 L13 **Stuart Lake** ◎ British Columbia, SW Canada
185 B22 **Stuart Mountains** ▲ South Island, New Zealand
182 F3 **Stuart Range** *hill range* South Australia
Stubaital *see* Neustift im Stubaital
95 I24 **Stubbekøbing** Storstrøm, SE Denmark 54°53′N 12°04′E
45 P14 **Stubbs** Saint Vincent, Saint Vincent and the Grenadines 13°08′N 61°09′W
109 V6 **Stübming** ∽ E Austria
114 J11 **Studen Kladenets, Yazovir** ⊠ S Bulgaria
185 G21 **Studholme** Canterbury, South Island, New Zealand 44°44′S 171°08′E
Stuhlweissenberg *see* Székesfehérvár
Stuhm *see* Sztum
12 C7 **Stull Lake** ◎ Ontario, C Canada
126 L4 **Stupino** Moskovskaya Oblast', W Russian Federation 54°54′N 38°06′E
27 U4 **Sturgeon** Missouri, C USA 39°13′N 92°16′W
14 G10 **Sturgeon** ∽ Ontario, S Canada
31 N6 **Sturgeon Bay** Wisconsin, N USA 44°51′N 87°21′W
14 G11 **Sturgeon Falls** Ontario, S Canada 46°22′N 79°57′W
12 C11 **Sturgeon Lake** ◎ Ontario, S Canada
30 M3 **Sturgeon River** ∽ Michigan, N USA
20 H6 **Sturgis** Kentucky, S USA 37°33′N 87°58′W
31 P11 **Sturgis** Michigan, N USA 41°48′N 85°25′W
28 J9 **Sturgis** South Dakota, N USA 44°24′N 103°30′W
112 D10 **Šturlić** ◈ Federacija Bosna I Hercegovina, NW Bosnia and Herzegovina
111 J22 **Štúrovo** *Hung.* Párkány; *prev.* Parkan. Nitriansky Kraj, SW Slovakia 47°49′N 18°40′E
182 L4 **Sturt, Mount** *hill* New South Wales, SE Australia
181 P4 **Sturt Plain** *plain* Northern Territory, N Australia
181 T9 **Sturt Stony Desert** *desert* South Australia
83 J25 **Stutterheim** Eastern Cape, S South Africa 32°35′S 27°26′E
101 H21 **Stuttgart** Baden-Württemberg, SW Germany 48°47′N 09°12′E
27 W12 **Stuttgart** Arkansas, C USA 34°30′N 91°32′W
92 H2 **Stykkishólmur** Vesturland, W Iceland 65°04′N 22°43′W
115 F17 **Stylída** *var.* Stilida, Stilís. Stereá Ellás, C Greece 38°55′N 22°37′E
116 K2 **Styr** *Rus.* Styr'. ∽ Belarus/Ukraine
115 I19 **Stýra** *var.* Stira. Évvoia, C Greece 38°10′N 24°13′E
Styria *see* Steiermark
15 Y5 **St-Yvon** Québec, SE Canada 49°09′N 64°51′W
Su *see* Jiangsu
Sua *see* Sowa
171 Q17 **Suai** W East Timor 09°19′S 125°16′E
54 G9 **Suaita** Santander, C Colombia 06°07′N 73°30′W
80 I7 **Suakin** *var.* Sawakin. Red Sea, NE Sudan 19°06′N 37°17′E
161 T13 **Suao** *Jap.* Suō. N Taiwan 24°33′N 121°48′E
Suao *see* Suau
Sua Pan *see* Sowa Pan
40 G6 **Suaqui Grande** Sonora, NW Mexico 28°22′N 109°52′W
61 A16 **Suardi** Santa Fe, C Argentina 30°32′S 61°58′W
54 D11 **Suárez** Cauca, SW Colombia 02°55′N 76°41′W
186 G10 **Suau** *var.* Suao. Suaul Island, SE Papua New Guinea 10°39′S 150°03′E
118 G12 **Subačius** Panevėžys, NE Lithuania 55°46′N 24°45′E
168 K9 **Subang** *prev.* Soebang. Jawa, C Indonesia 06°32′S 107°45′E
169 O16 **Subang** ✕ (Kuala Lumpur) Pahang, Peninsular Malaysia
129 S10 **Subansiri** ∽ NE India
118 I11 **Subate** Daugvapils, SE Latvia 56°00′N 25°54′E
139 N5 **Subaykhān** Dayr az Zawr, E Syria 34°52′N 40°35′E
Subei/Subei Mongolzu Zizhixian *see* Dangchengwan
169 P9 **Subi Besar, Pulau** *island* Kepulauan Natuna, W Indonesia
Subiyah *see* Aş Şubayhiyah
26 I7 **Sublette** Kansas, C USA 37°28′N 100°52′W
112 K8 **Subotica** *Ger.* Maria-Theresiopel, *Hung.* Szabadka. Vojvodina, N Serbia 46°06′N 19°41′E
116 K9 **Suceava** *Ger.* Suczawa, *Hung.* Szucsava. Suceava, NE Romania 47°41′N 26°16′E
116 J9 **Suceava** ◈ *county* NE Romania
116 K9 **Suceava** *Ger.* Suczawa. ∽ N Romania
112 E12 **Sučević** Zadar, SW Croatia 44°13′N 16°04′E
111 K17 **Sucha Beskidzka** Małopolskie, S Poland 49°44′N 19°36′E
111 M14 **Suchedniów** Świętokrzyskie, C Poland 51°01′N 20°49′E
42 A2 **Suchitepéquez** *off.* Departamento de Suchitepéquez. ◈ *department* SW Guatemala
Suchitepéquez, Departamento de *see* Suchitepéquez
Su-chou *see* Suzhou
Suchow *see* Xuzhou, Jiangsu, China
Suchow *see* Suzhou, Jiangsu, China
97 D17 **Suck** ∽ C Ireland
Sucker State *see* Illinois
186 F9 **Suckling, Mount** ▲ S Papua New Guinea 09°36′S 149°00′E
57 L19 **Sucre** *hist.* Chuquisaca, La Plata. ● (Bolivia-legal capital) Chuquisaca, S Bolivia 18°53′S 65°25′W
54 E6 **Sucre** Santander, N Colombia 08°50′N 74°22′W
56 A7 **Sucre** Manabí, W Ecuador 01°21′S 80°27′W
54 E6 **Sucre** *off.* Departamento de Sucre. ◈ *province* N Colombia
55 O5 **Sucre** *off.* Estado Sucre. ◈ *state* NE Venezuela
Sucre, Departamento de *see* Sucre
Sucre, Estado *see* Sucre
56 D6 **Sucumbíos** ◈ *province* NE Ecuador
113 G15 **Sućuraj** Split-Dalmacija, S Croatia 43°07′N 17°10′E
58 K10 **Sucuriju** Amapá, NE Brazil 01°31′N 50°W
Suczawa *see* Suceava
79 E16 **Sud** *Eng.* South. ◈ *province* S Cameroon
124 K13 **Suda** ∽ NW Russian Federation
Suda *see* Soúda
117 U13 **Sudak** Respublika Krym, S Ukraine 44°52′N 34°57′E
24 M4 **Sudan** Texas, SW USA 34°04′N 102°32′W
80 C10 **Sudan** *off.* Republic of Sudan, *Ar.* Jumhuriyat as-Sudan; *prev.* Anglo-Egyptian Sudan. ◆ *republic* N Africa
Sudanese Republic *see* Mali
Sudan, Jumhuriyat as- *see* Sudan
Sudan, Republic of *see* Sudan
14 F10 **Sudbury** Ontario, S Canada 46°29′N 81°W
97 P20 **Sudbury** E England, United Kingdom 52°04′N 00°43′E
Sud, Canal de *see* Gonâve, Canal de la
80 E13 **Sudd** *swamp region* S Sudan
100 K10 **Sude** ∽ N Germany
Suderø *see* Suðuroy
Sudest Island *see* Tagula Island
111 E15 **Sudeten** *var.* Sudetes, Sudetic Mountains, *Cz./Pol.* Sudety. ▲ Czech Republic/Poland
Sudetes/Sudetic Mountains/Sudety *see* Sudeten
92 G1 **Suðhureyri** Vestfirdhir, NW Iceland 66°08′N 23°31′W
92 J4 **Suðhurland** ◈ *region* S Iceland
95 B19 **Suðhuroy** *Dan.* Suderø. *island* S Faeroe Islands
124 M15 **Sudislavl'** Kostromskaya Oblast', NW Russian Federation 57°55′N 41°45′E
Südkarpaten *see* Carpaţii Meridionalii
79 N20 **Sud-Kivu** *off.* Région Sud Kivu. ◈ *region* E Dem. Rep. Congo
Sud Kivu, Région *see* Sud-Kivu
Südliche Morava *see* Južna Morava
100 E12 **Süd-Nord-Kanal** *canal* NW Germany
126 M3 **Sudogda** Vladimirskaya Oblast', W Russian Federation 55°58′N 40°57′E
Sudostroy *see* Severodvinsk
79 C15 **Sud-Ouest** *Eng.* South-West. ◈ *province* W Cameroon
173 X17 **Sud Ouest, Pointe** *headland* SW Mauritius 20°27′S 57°18′E
187 P17 **Sud, Province** ◈ *province* S New Caledonia
126 J8 **Sudzha** Kurskaya Oblast', W Russian Federation 51°12′N 35°19′E
81 D15 **Sue** ∽ S Sudan
105 S10 **Sueca** País Valenciano, E Spain 39°13′N 00°19′W
114 I10 **Sŭedinenie** Plovdiv, C Bulgaria 42°14′N 24°36′E
Suero *see* Alzira
75 X8 **Suez** *Ar.* As Suways. NE Egypt 29°59′N 32°33′E
75 W7 **Suez Canal** *Ar.* Qanāt as Suways. *canal* NE Egypt
Suez, Gulf of *see* Khalīj as Suways
11 R17 **Suffield** Alberta, SW Canada 50°15′N 111°05′W
21 X7 **Suffolk** Virginia, NE USA 36°44′N 76°37′W
97 P20 **Suffolk** *cultural region* E England, United Kingdom
142 J2 **Şūfiān** Āzarbāyjān-e Sharqī, N Iran 38°15′N 45°59′E
31 N12 **Sugar Creek** ∽ Illinois, N USA
30 L13 **Sugar Creek** ∽ Illinois, N USA
31 R3 **Sugar Island** *island* Michigan, N USA
25 V11 **Sugar Land** Texas, SW USA 29°37′N 95°37′W
19 P6 **Sugarloaf Mountain** ▲ Maine, NE USA 45°01′N 70°18′W
65 G24 **Sugar Loaf Point** *headland* N Saint Helena 15°54′S 05°43′W
136 G16 **Suğla Gölü** ◎ SW Turkey
123 T8 **Sugoy** ∽ E Russian Federation
158 F7 **Sugun** Xinjiang Uygur Zizhiqu, W China 39°46′N 76°45′E
147 U11 **Sugut, Gora** ▲ SW Kyrgyzstan 39°52′N 73°36′E
169 V6 **Sugut, Sungai** ∽ East Malaysia
159 O9 **Suhai Hu** ◎ C China
162 K14 **Suhait** Nei Mongol Zizhiqu, N China 39°29′N 105°11′E
141 X7 **Şuḩār** *var.* Sohar. N Oman 24°20′N 56°43′E
113 M17 **Suharekë** *Serb.* Suva Reka. S Kosovo 42°23′N 20°50′E
162 L6 **Sühbaatar** Selenge, N Mongolia 50°12′N 106°14′E
163 P8 **Sühbaatar** *var.* Haylaastay. Sühbaatar, E Mongolia 46°44′N 113°51′E
163 P9 **Sühbaatar** ◈ *province* E Mongolia
101 K17 **Suhl** Thüringen, C Germany 50°37′N 10°43′E
108 F7 **Suhr** Aargau, N Switzerland 47°23′N 08°05′E
Sui'an *see* Zhangpu
Suicheng *see* Suixi
160 I12 **Suichuan** *var.* Quanjiang. Jiangxi, S China 26°26′N 114°34′E
Suid-Afrika *see* South Africa
160 L4 **Suide** *var.* Mingzhou. Shaanxi, C China 37°30′N 110°10′E
Suidwes-Afrika *see* Namibia
163 Y9 **Suifenhe** Heilongjiang, NE China 44°22′N 131°12′E
Suigen *see* Suwŏn
163 W8 **Suihua** Heilongjiang, NE China 46°40′N 127°00′E
Súilí, Loch *see* Swilly, Lough
161 Q6 **Suining** Jiangsu, E China 33°54′N 117°58′E
160 I9 **Suining** Sichuan, C China 30°31′N 105°33′E
103 Q4 **Suippes** Marne, N France 49°08′N 04°31′E
97 E20 **Suir** *Ir.* An tSiúir. ∽ S Ireland
165 J13 **Suita** Ōsaka, Honshū, SW Japan 34°39′N 135°27′E
160 L16 **Suixi** *var.* Suicheng. Guangdong, S China 21°23′N 110°14′E
Sui Xian *see* Suizhou
163 T13 **Suizhong** Liaoning, NE China 40°19′N 120°22′E
161 N8 **Suizhou** *prev.* Sui Xian. Hubei, C China 31°46′N 113°20′E
149 P17 **Sujāwal** Sind, SE Pakistan 24°36′N 68°06′E
169 O16 **Sukabumi** *prev.* Soekaboemi. Jawa, C Indonesia 06°55′S 106°56′E
169 Q12 **Sukadana, Teluk** *bay* Borneo, W Indonesia
165 P11 **Sukagawa** Fukushima, Honshū, C Japan 37°16′N 140°20′E
Sukarnapura *see* Jayapura
Sukarno, Puntjak *see* Jaya, Puncak
Sŭkh *see* Sokh
114 N8 **Sukha Reka** ∽ NE Bulgaria
114 J8 **Sukhindol** Veliko Turnovo, N Bulgaria 43°11′N 24°10′E
126 J5 **Sukhinichi** Kaluzhskaya Oblast', W Russian Federation 54°06′N 35°22′E
Sukhne *see* As Sukhnah
127 S5 **Sukhodol** Samarskaya Oblast', W Russian Federation 53°53′N 51°13′E
129 Q4 **Sukhona** *var.* Tot'ma. ∽ NW Russian Federation
167 O8 **Sukhothai** *var.* Sukotai. Sukhothai, W Thailand 17°00′N 99°51′E
Sukhumi *see* Sokhumi
Sukkertoppen *see* Maniitsoq
149 Q13 **Sukkur** Sind, SE Pakistan 27°45′N 68°46′E
Sukotai *see* Sukhothai
Sukra Bay *see* Şawqirah, Dawhat
125 V15 **Suksun** Permskaya Oblast', NW Russian Federation 57°10′N 57°27′E
165 F15 **Sukumo** Kōchi, Shikoku, SW Japan 32°55′N 132°42′E
94 B12 **Sula** *island* S Norway
125 Q5 **Sula** ∽ NW Russian Federation
117 R5 **Sula** ∽ N Ukraine
42 H6 **Sulaco, Río** ∽ NW Honduras
Sulaimaniya *see* As Sulaymānīyah
149 S10 **Sulaimān Range** ▲ C Pakistan
127 Q16 **Sulak** Respublika Dagestan, SW Russian Federation 43°19′N 47°28′E
127 Q16 **Sulak** ∽ SW Russian Federation
171 Q13 **Sula, Kepulauan** *island group* C Indonesia
136 I12 **Sulakyurt** *var.* Konur. Kırıkkale, N Turkey 40°10′N 33°42′E
171 P17 **Sulamu** Timor, S Indonesia 09°57′S 123°33′E
96 F5 **Sula Sgeir** *island* NW Scotland, United Kingdom
171 N13 **Sulawesi** *Eng.* Celebes. *island* C Indonesia
Sulawesi, Laut *see* Celebes Sea
171 N14 **Sulawesi Selatan** *off.* Propinsi Sulawesi Selatan, *Eng.* South Celebes, South Sulawesi. ◈ *province* C Indonesia
Sulawesi Selatan, Propinsi *see* Sulawesi Selatan
171 P12 **Sulawesi Tengah** *off.* Propinsi Sulawesi Tengah, *Eng.* Central Celebes, Central Sulawesi. ◈ *province* N Indonesia
Sulawesi Tengah, Propinsi *see* Sulawesi Tengah
171 O14 **Sulawesi Tenggara** *off.* Propinsi Sulawesi Tenggara, *Eng.* South-East Celebes, South-East Sulawesi. ◈ *province* C Indonesia
Sulawesi Tenggara, Propinsi *see* Sulawesi Tenggara
171 P11 **Sulawesi Utara** *off.* Propinsi Sulawesi Utara, *Eng.* North Celebes, North Sulawesi. ◈ *province* N Indonesia
Sulawesi Utara, Propinsi *see* Sulawesi Utara
139 T5 **Sulaymān Beg** At Ta'mīn, N Iraq
Sulaymānīyah, Muḩāfaz̧at as *see* As Sulaymānīyah
95 D15 **Suldalsvatnet** ◎ S Norway
Sulden *see* Solda
110 E12 **Sulechów** *Ger.* Züllichau. Lubuskie, W Poland 52°05′N 15°37′E
110 E11 **Sulęcin** Lubuskie, W Poland 52°29′N 15°06′E
77 U14 **Suleja** Niger, C Nigeria 09°15′N 07°10′E
111 K14 **Sulejów** Łodzkie, S Poland 51°21′N 19°57′E
96 I5 **Sule Skerry** *island* N Scotland, United Kingdom
Sulia *see* Sawhāj
76 J16 **Sulima** S Sierra Leone 06°59′N 11°34′W
117 O13 **Sulina** Tulcea, SE Romania 45°07′N 29°40′E
117 N13 **Sulina, Braţul** ∽ SE Romania
100 H12 **Sulingen** Niedersachsen, NW Germany 52°40′N 08°48′E
Sulisjielmmá *see* Sulitjelma
92 H12 **Suliskongen** ▲ C Norway 67°10′N 16°16′E
92 H12 **Sulitjelma** *Lapp.* Sulisjielmmá. Nordland, C Norway 67°10′N 16°05′E
56 A9 **Sullana** Piura, NW Peru 04°54′S 80°42′W
23 N3 **Sulligent** Alabama, S USA 33°54′N 88°07′W
30 M14 **Sullivan** Illinois, N USA 39°36′N 88°36′W
31 N15 **Sullivan** Indiana, N USA 39°05′N 87°24′W
27 W5 **Sullivan** Missouri, C USA 38°12′N 91°09′W
Sullivan Island *see* Lanbi Kyun
96 M1 **Sullom Voe** NE Scotland, United Kingdom 60°24′N 01°09′W
103 O7 **Sully-sur-Loire** Loiret, C France 47°46′N 02°21′E
Sulmo *see* Sulmona
107 K15 **Sulmona** *anc.* Sulmo. Abruzzo, C Italy 42°03′N 13°56′E
Sulo *see* Shule He
114 M11 **Süloğlu** Edirne, NW Turkey 41°46′N 26°55′E
22 G9 **Sulphur** Louisiana, S USA 30°14′N 93°22′W
27 O12 **Sulphur** Oklahoma, C USA 34°31′N 96°58′W
28 K9 **Sulphur Creek** ∽ South Dakota, N USA
24 M5 **Sulphur Draw** ∽ Texas, SW USA
25 W5 **Sulphur River** ∽ Arkansas/Texas, SW USA
25 V6 **Sulphur Springs** Texas, SW USA 33°09′N 95°36′W
24 M6 **Sulphur Springs Draw** ∽ Texas, SW USA
14 D8 **Sultan** Ontario, S Canada 47°34′N 82°45′W
Sultānābād *see* Arāk
Sultan Alonto, Lake *see* Lanao, Lake
136 G15 **Sultan Dağları** ▲ C Turkey
114 N13 **Sultanköy** Tekirdağ, NW Turkey 41°01′N 27°58′E
171 Q7 **Sultan Kudarat** *var.* Nuling. Mindanao, S Philippines 07°20′N 124°16′E
152 M13 **Sultānpur** Uttar Pradesh, N India 26°15′N 82°04′E
171 O9 **Sulu Archipelago** *island group* SW Philippines
192 F7 **Sulu Basin** *undersea feature* SE South China Sea 08°00′N 121°30′E
Sülükta *see* Sulyukta
Sulu, Laut *see* Sulu Sea
169 X6 **Sulu Sea** *var.* Laut Sulu. *sea* SW Philippines
145 O15 **Sulutobe** *Kaz.* Sulūtöbe. Kzylorda, S Kazakhstan 44°31′N 66°17′E
Sulūtöbe *see* Sulutobe
147 Q11 **Sulyukta** *Kir.* Sülüktü. Batkenskaya Oblast', SW Kyrgyzstan 39°57′N 69°31′E
Sulz *see* Sulz am Neckar
101 G22 **Sulz am Neckar** *var.* Sulz. Baden-Württemberg, SW Germany 48°22′N 08°37′E
101 L20 **Sulzbach-Rosenberg** Bayern, SE Germany 49°30′N 11°43′E
195 N14 **Sulzberger Bay** *bay* Antarctica
Sumail *see* Summēl
81 M14 **Sumalē** ◈ *federal region* E Ethiopia
113 F15 **Sumartin** Split-Dalmacija, S Croatia 43°17′N 16°52′E
32 H6 **Sumas** Washington, NW USA 49°00′N 122°15′W
168 J10 **Sumatera** *Eng.* Sumatra. *island* W Indonesia
168 J12 **Sumatera Barat** *off.* Propinsi Sumatera Barat, *Eng.* West Sumatra. ◈ *province* W Indonesia
Sumatera Barat, Propinsi *see* Sumatera Barat
168 L13 **Sumatera Selatan** *off.* Propinsi Sumatera Selatan, *Eng.* South Sumatra. ◈ *province* W Indonesia
Sumatera Selatan, Propinsi *see* Sumatera Selatan
168 H10 **Sumatera Utara** *off.* Propinsi Sumatera Utara, *Eng.* North Sumatra. ◈ *province* W Indonesia
Sumatera Utara, Propinsi *see* Sumatera Utara
Sumatra *see* Sumatera
Šumava *see* Bohemian Forest
Sumayl *see* Summēl
139 U7 **Sumayr al Muḩammad** Diyālá, E Iraq 33°34′N 45°06′E
171 N17 **Sumba, Pulau** *Eng.* Sandalwood Island; *prev.* Soemba. *island* Nusa Tenggara, C Indonesia
146 D12 **Sumbar** ∽ W Turkmenistan
192 E9 **Sumbawa** *prev.* Soembawa. *island* Nusa Tenggara, C Indonesia
170 L16 **Sumbawabesar** Sumbawa, S Indonesia 08°30′S 117°25′E
81 F23 **Sumbawanga** Rukwa, W Tanzania 07°57′S 31°37′E
82 B12 **Sumbe** *var.* N'Gunza, *Port.* Novo Redondo. Cuanza Sul, W Angola 11°13′S 13°53′E
96 M3 **Sumburgh Head** *headland* NE Scotland, United Kingdom 59°51′N 01°16′W
111 H23 **Sümeg** Veszprém, W Hungary 47°01′N 17°13′E
80 C12 **Sumeih** Southern Darfur, S Sudan 09°50′N 27°39′E
169 T16 **Sumenep** *prev.* Soemenep. Pulau Madura, C Indonesia 07°01′S 113°51′E
Sumgait *see* Sumqayıtçay, Azerbaijan
Sumgait *see* Sumqayıt, Azerbaijan
165 Y14 **Sumisu-jima** *Eng.* Smith Island. *island* SE Japan
139 Q2 **Summēl** *var.* Sumail, Sumayl. Dahūk, N Iraq 36°52′N 42°51′E
31 O5 **Summer Island** *island* Michigan, N USA
32 H15 **Summer Lake** ◎ Oregon, NW USA
11 N17 **Summerland** British Columbia, SW Canada 49°35′N 119°45′W
13 P14 **Summerside** Prince Edward Island, SE Canada 46°24′N 63°46′W
21 R5 **Summersville** West Virginia, NE USA 38°17′N 80°52′W
21 R5 **Summersville Lake** ⊠ West Virginia, NE USA
21 S13 **Summerton** South Carolina, SE USA 33°36′N 80°21′W
23 R2 **Summerville** Georgia, SE USA 34°28′N 85°21′W
21 S14 **Summerville** South Carolina, SE USA 33°01′N 80°10′W
39 R10 **Summit** Alaska, USA 63°21′N 148°50′W
35 V6 **Summit Mountain** ▲ Nevada, W USA 39°23′N 116°25′W
37 R8 **Summit Peak** ▲ Colorado, C USA 37°21′N 106°42′W
Summus Portus *see* Somport, Col du
29 X12 **Sumner** Iowa, C USA 42°51′N 92°05′W
22 K3 **Sumner** Mississippi, S USA 33°58′N 90°22′W
185 H17 **Sumner, Lake** ◎ South Island, New Zealand
37 U12 **Sumner, Lake** ⊠ New Mexico, SW USA
111 G17 **Šumperk** *Ger.* Mährisch-Schönberg. Olomoucký Kraj, E Czech Republic 49°58′N 17°00′E
42 F7 **Sumpul, Río** ∽ El Salvador/Honduras
137 Z11 **Sumqayıt** *Rus.* Sumgait. E Azerbaijan 40°33′N 49°41′E
137 Y11 **Sumqayıtçay** *Rus.* Sumgait. ∽ E Azerbaijan
147 R9 **Sumsar** Dzhalal-Abadskaya Oblast', W Kyrgyzstan 41°12′N 71°16′E
117 S3 **Sums'ka Oblast'** *var.* Sumy, *Rus.* Sumskaya Oblast'. ◈ *province* NE Ukraine
Sumskaya Oblast' *see* Sums'ka Oblast'
124 J8 **Sumskiy Posad** Respublika Kareliya, NW Russian Federation 64°12′N 35°22′E
21 S12 **Sumter** South Carolina, SE USA 33°54′N 80°22′W
117 T3 **Sumy** Sums'ka Oblast', NE Ukraine 50°54′N 34°49′E
Sumy *see* Sums'ka Oblast'
159 Q15 **Sumzom** Xizang Zizhiqu, W China 29°45′N 96°14′E
125 R15 **Suna** Kirovskaya Oblast', NW Russian Federation 57°53′N 50°04′E
124 I10 **Suna** ∽ NW Russian Federation
165 S3 **Sunagawa** Hokkaidō, NE Japan 43°30′N 141°55′E
153 V13 **Sunamganj** Sylhet, NE Bangladesh 25°04′N 91°24′E
163 W14 **Sunan** ✕ (P'yŏngyang) SW North Korea 39°12′N 125°40′E
Sunan/Sunan Yugurzu Zizhixian *see* Hongwansi
19 N9 **Sunapee Lake** ◎ New Hampshire, NE USA
139 P4 **Sunaysilah** *salt marsh* N Iraq
20 M8 **Sunbright** Tennessee, S USA 36°12′N 84°39′W
33 R6 **Sunburst** Montana, NW USA 48°51′N 111°54′W
183 N12 **Sunbury** Victoria, SE Australia 37°36′S 144°45′E
21 X8 **Sunbury** North Carolina, SE USA 36°27′N 76°34′W
18 G14 **Sunbury** Pennsylvania, NE USA 40°51′N 76°47′W
61 A17 **Sunchales** Santa Fe, C Argentina 30°58′S 61°35′W
163 W13 **Sunch'ŏn** SW North Korea 39°28′N 125°48′E
163 Y16 **Sunch'ŏn** *Jap.* Junten. S South Korea 34°56′N 127°29′E
36 K13 **Sun City** Arizona, SW USA 33°36′N 112°16′W
19 O9 **Suncook** New Hampshire, NE USA 43°07′N 71°25′W
161 P5 **Suncun** *prev.* Xinwen. Shandong, E China 35°49′N 117°36′E
Sunda Islands *see* Greater Sunda Islands
33 Z12 **Sundance** Wyoming, C USA 44°24′N 104°22′W
153 T17 **Sundarbans** *wetland* Bangladesh/India
154 M11 **Sundargarh** Orissa, E India 22°07′N 84°02′E
129 U15 **Sunda Shelf** *undersea feature* S South China Sea 05°00′N 107°00′E
Sunda Trench *see* Java Trench
129 U17 **Sunda Trough** *undersea feature* E Indian Ocean 08°50′S 109°30′E
95 O16 **Sundbyberg** Stockholm, C Sweden 59°22′N 17°58′E
97 M14 **Sunderland** *var.* Wearmouth. NE England, United Kingdom 54°55′N 01°23′W
101 F15 **Sundern** Nordrhein-Westfalen, W Germany 51°19′N 08°00′E
136 F12 **Sündiken Dağları** ▲ C Turkey
24 M5 **Sundown** Texas, SW USA 33°27′N 102°29′W
11 P16 **Sundre** Alberta, SW Canada 51°49′N 114°46′W
14 H12 **Sundridge** Ontario, S Canada 45°45′N 79°25′W
93 H17 **Sundsvall** Västernorrland, C Sweden 62°22′N 17°20′E
26 H4 **Sunflower, Mount** ▲ Kansas, C USA 39°01′N 102°02′W
Sunflower State *see* Kansas
169 N14 **Sungaibuntu** Sumatera, SW Indonesia 04°04′S 105°37′E
168 K12 **Sungaidareh** Sumatera, W Indonesia 0°58′S 101°30′E
167 P17 **Sungai Kolok** *var.* Sungai Ko-Lok. Narathiwat, SW Thailand 06°02′N 101°58′E
Sungai Ko-Lok *see* Sungai Kolok
168 K12 **Sungaipenuh** *prev.* Soengaipenoeh. Sumatera, W Indonesia 02°S 101°28′E
169 P11 **Sungaipinyuh** Borneo, C Indonesia 0°16′N 109°06′E
Sungari *see* Songhua Jiang
Sungaria *see* Dzungaria
Sungei Pahang *see* Pahang, Sungai
167 O8 **Sung Men** Phrae, NW Thailand 17°59′N 100°07′E
83 M15 **Sungo** Tete, NW Mozambique 16°31′S 33°58′E
Sungpu *see* Songpan
168 M13 **Sungsang** Sumatera, W Indonesia 02°22′S 104°50′E
114 M9 **Sungurlare** Burgas, E Bulgaria 42°47′N 26°46′E
136 J12 **Sungurlu** Çorum, N Turkey 40°10′N 34°23′E
112 F9 **Sunja** Sisak-Moslavina, C Croatia 45°21′N 16°33′E
153 Q12 **Sun Koshi** ∽ E Nepal
94 F9 **Sunndalen** *valley* S Norway
94 F9 **Sunndalsøra** Møre og Romsdal, S Norway 62°39′N 08°37′E
95 K15 **Sunne** Värmland, C Sweden 59°52′N 13°05′E
95 O15 **Sunnersta** Uppsala, C Sweden 59°46′N 17°40′E
94 C11 **Sunnfjord** *physical region* S Norway
95 C15 **Sunnhordland** *physical region* S Norway
94 D10 **Sunnmøre** *physical region* S Norway
37 N4 **Sunnyside** Utah, W USA 39°33′N 110°23′W
32 J10 **Sunnyside** Washington, NW USA 46°01′N 119°58′W
35 N9 **Sunnyvale** California, W USA 37°22′N 122°02′W
30 L8 **Sun Prairie** Wisconsin, N USA 43°12′N 89°12′W
Sunqur *see* Sonqor
25 N1 **Sunray** Texas, SW USA 36°01′N 101°49′W
22 I8 **Sunset** Louisiana, S USA 30°24′N 92°04′W
25 S5 **Sunset** Texas, SW USA 33°24′N 97°45′W
Sunset State *see* Oregon
181 Z10 **Sunshine Coast** *cultural region* Queensland, E Australia
Sunshine State *see* Florida
Sunshine State *see* New Mexico
Sunshine State *see* South Dakota
123 O10 **Suntar** Respublika Sakha (Yakutiya), NE Russian Federation 62°10′N 117°34′E
39 R10 **Suntrana** Alaska, USA 63°51′N 148°51′W
148 J15 **Suntsar** Baluchistān, SW Pakistan 25°30′N 62°03′E
163 W15 **Sunwi-do** *island* SW North Korea
163 W6 **Sunwu** Heilongjiang, NE China 49°29′N 127°15′E
77 O16 **Sunyani** W Ghana 07°22′N 02°18′W
Suō *see* Suao
93 M17 **Suolahti** Länsi-Suomi, C Finland 62°32′N 25°51′E
Suoločielgi *see* Saariselkä
Suomenlahti *see* Finland, Gulf of
Suomen Tasavalta/Suomi *see* Finland
93 N14 **Suomussalmi** Oulu, E Finland 64°54′N 29°05′E
165 E13 **Suō-nada** *sea* SW Japan
93 M17 **Suonenjoki** Itä-Suomi, C Finland 62°36′N 27°07′E
167 S13 **Suŏng** Kâmpóng Cham, C Cambodia 11°53′N 105°41′E
124 I10 **Suoyarvi** Respublika Kareliya, NW Russian Federation 62°02′N 32°24′E
Supanburi *see* Suphan Buri
57 D14 **Supe** Lima, W Peru 10°49′S 77°40′W
15 V7 **Supérieur, Lac** ◎ Québec, SE Canada
Supérieur, Lac *see* Superior, Lake
36 M14 **Superior** Arizona, SW USA 33°17′N 111°06′W
33 O9 **Superior** Montana, NW USA 47°11′N 114°53′W
29 P17 **Superior** Nebraska, C USA 40°01′N 98°04′W
30 I3 **Superior** Wisconsin, N USA 46°42′N 92°04′W
41 S17 **Superior, Laguna** *lagoon* S Mexico
31 N2 **Superior, Lake** *Fr.* Lac Supérieur. ◎ Canada/USA
36 L13 **Superstition Mountains** ▲ Arizona, SW USA
113 F14 **Supetar** *It.* San Pietro. Split-Dalmacija, S Croatia 43°22′N 16°34′E
167 O10 **Suphan Buri** *var.* Supanburi. Suphan Buri, W Thailand 14°29′N 100°10′E
171 V12 **Supiori, Pulau** *island* E Indonesia
188 K2 **Supply Reef** *reef* N Northern Mariana Islands
195 O7 **Support Force Glacier** *glacier* Antarctica
137 R10 **Sup'sa** *var.* Supsa. ∽ W Georgia
Supsa *see* Sup'sa
Sūq 'Abs *see* 'Abs
139 W12 **Sūq ash Shuyūkh** Dhī Qār, SE Iraq 30°53′N 46°28′E
138 H4 **Şuqaylibīyah** Ḩamāh, W Syria 35°21′N 36°24′E
161 Q6 **Suqian** Jiangsu, E China 33°57′N 118°18′E
Suqrah *see* Şawqirah
Suqrah Bay *see* Şawqirah, Dawḩat
141 V16 **Suquţrā** *var.* Sokotra, *Eng.* Socotra. *island* SE Yemen
141 Z8 **Şūr** NE Oman 22°32′N 59°33′E
Şūr *see* Soûr
127 P5 **Sura** Penzenskaya Oblast', W Russian Federation 53°23′N 45°03′E
127 P4 **Sura** ∽ W Russian Federation
149 N12 **Sūrāb** Baluchistān, SW Pakistan 28°28′N 66°15′E
Surabaja *see* Surabaya
192 E8 **Surabaya** *prev.* Surabaja, Soerabaja. Jawa, C Indonesia 07°14′S 112°45′E
95 N15 **Surahammar** Västmanland, C Sweden 59°43′N 16°13′E
169 Q16 **Surakarta** *Eng.* Solo; *prev.* Soerakarta. Jawa, S Indonesia 07°32′S 110°50′E
Surakhany *see* Suraxanı
137 S10 **Surami** C Georgia 41°59′N 43°36′E
143 X13 **Sūrān** Sīstān va Balūchestān, SE Iran 27°18′N 61°58′E
111 I21 **Šurany** *Hung.* Nagysurány. Nitriansky Kraj, SW Slovakia 48°05′N 18°10′E
154 D12 **Sūrat** Gujarāt, W India 21°10′N 72°54′E
Suratdhani *see* Surat Thani
152 G9 **Sūratgarh** Rājasthān, NW India 29°20′N 73°59′E
167 N14 **Surat Thani** *var.* Suratdhani. Surat Thani, SW Thailand 09°09′N 99°20′E
119 Q16 **Suraw** *Rus.* Surov. ∽ E Belarus
137 Z11 **Suraxanı** *Rus.* Surakhany. E Azerbaijan 40°25′N 49°59′E
141 Y11 **Surayr** E Oman 19°56′N 57°47′E
138 K2 **Suraysāt** Ḩalab, N Syria 36°42′N 38°01′E
118 O12 **Surazh** Vitsyebskaya Voblasts', NE Belarus 55°25′N 30°44′E
126 H6 **Surazh** Bryanskaya Oblast', W Russian Federation 53°04′N 32°29′E
191 V17 **Sur, Cabo** *headland* Easter Island, Chile, E Pacific Ocean 27°11′S 109°26′W
112 L11 **Surčin** Serbia, N Serbia 44°48′N 20°19′E
116 H9 **Surduc** *Hung.* Szurduk. Sălaj, NW Romania 47°13′N 23°20′E
113 P16 **Surdulica** Serbia, SE Serbia 42°43′N 22°10′E
99 L24 **Sûre** *var.* Sauer. ∽ W Europe *see also* Sauer
Sûre *see* Sauer
154 C10 **Surendranagar** Gujarāt, W India 22°44′N 71°43′E
18 K16 **Surf City** New Jersey, NE USA 39°21′N 74°24′W
183 V3 **Surfers Paradise** Queensland, E Australia 27°54′S 153°18′E
21 U13 **Surfside Beach** South Carolina, SE USA 33°36′N 78°58′W
102 J10 **Surgères** Charente-Maritime, W France 46°07′N 00°44′W
122 H10 **Surgut** Khanty-Mansiyskiy Avtonomnyy Okrug-Yugra, C Russian Federation 61°13′N 73°28′E
122 K10 **Surgutikha** Krasnoyarskiy Kray, N Russian Federation 64°44′N 87°13′E
98 M6 **Surhuisterveen** Friesland, N Netherlands 53°11′N 06°10′E
105 V5 **Súria** Cataluña, NE Spain 41°50′N 01°45′E
143 P10 **Sūrīān** Fārs, S Iran
155 J15 **Suriāpet** Andhra Pradesh, C India 17°10′N 79°42′E
171 Q6 **Surigao** Mindanao, S Philippines 09°43′N 125°31′E
167 R10 **Surin** Surin, E Thailand 14°53′N 103°29′E
55 U11 **Surinam** *off.* Republic of Suriname, *var.* Suriname; *prev.* Dutch Guiana, Netherlands Guiana. ◆ *republic* N South America
Suriname *see* Surinam
Suriname, Republic of *see* Surinam
Sūrīya/Sūrīyah, Al-Jumhūrīyah al-'Arabīyah as- *see* Syria
Surkhab, Darya-i- *see* Kahmard, Daryā-ye
Surkhandar'inskaya Oblast' *see* Surxondaryo Viloyati
Surkhandar'ya *see* Surxondaryo
Surkhet *see* Birendranagar
147 R12 **Surkhob** ∽ C Tajikistan
137 P11 **Sürmene** Trabzon, NE Turkey 40°56′N 40°03′E
Surov *see* Suraw
127 N11 **Surovikino** Volgogradskaya Oblast', SW Russian Federation 48°39′N 42°46′E

◆ Country ● Country Capital ◇ Dependent Territory ○ Dependent Territory Capital ◈ Administrative Regions ✕ International Airport ▲ Mountain ▲ Mountain Range Volcano ∽ River ◎ Lake ⊠ Reservoir

SUR, POINT – TAGANT

35 N11 **Sur, Point** *headland* California, W USA 36°18′N 121°54′W
187 N15 **Surprise, Île** *island* N New Caledonia
61 E22 **Sur, Punta** *headland* E Argentina 50°59′S 69°10′W
Surrentum *see* Sorrento
28 M3 **Surrey** North Dakota, N USA 48°13′N 101°05′W
97 O22 **Surrey** *cultural region* SE England, United Kingdom
21 X7 **Surry** Virginia, NE USA 37°08′N 81°34′W
108 F8 **Sursee** Luzern, W Switzerland 47°11′N 08°07′E
127 P6 **Sursk** Penzenskaya Oblast', W Russian Federation 53°06′N 45°46′E
127 P5 **Surskoye** Ul'yanovskaya Oblast', W Russian Federation 54°28′N 46°47′E
75 P8 **Surt** *var.* Sidra, Sirte. N Libya 31°13′N 16°35′E
95 I19 **Surte** Västra Götaland, S Sweden 57°49′N 12°01′E
75 Q8 **Surt, Khalīj** *Eng.* Gulf of Sidra, Gulf of Sirti, Sidra. *gulf* N Libya
92 I5 **Surtsey** *island* S Iceland
137 N17 **Suruç** Şanlıurfa, S Turkey 36°58′N 38°24′E
168 L13 **Surulangun** Sumatera, W Indonesia 02°35′S 102°47′E
147 P13 **Surxondaryo** *Rus.* Surkhandar'ya. ⌇ Tajikistan/Uzbekistan
147 N13 **Surxondaryo Viloyati** *Rus.* Surkhandar'inskaya Oblast'. ◆ *province* S Uzbekistan
Süs *see* Susch
106 A8 **Susa** Piemonte, NE Italy 45°10′N 07°01′E
165 E12 **Susa** Yamaguchi, Honshū, SW Japan 34°35′N 131°34′E
Susa *see* Shūsh
113 E16 **Sušac** *It.* Cazza. *island* SW Croatia
Süsah *see* Sousse
164 G14 **Susaki** Kōchi, Shikoku, SW Japan 33°22′N 133°13′E
165 I15 **Susami** Wakayama, Honshū, SW Japan 33°32′N 135°32′E
142 K9 **Süsangerd** *var.* Susangird. Khūzestān, SW Iran 31°40′N 48°06′E
Susangird *see* Süsangerd
35 P4 **Susanville** California, W USA 40°25′N 120°39′W
108 J9 **Susch** *var.* Süs. Graubünden, SE Switzerland 46°45′N 10°04′E
137 N12 **Suşehri** Sivas, N Turkey 40°11′N 38°06′E
Susiana *see* Khūzestān
111 B18 **Sušice** *Ger.* Schüttenhofen. Plzeňský Kraj, W Czech Republic 49°14′N 13°32′E
39 R11 **Susitna** Alaska, USA 61°32′N 150°30′W
39 R11 **Susitna River** ⌇ Alaska, USA
127 Q3 **Suslonger** Respublika Mariy El, W Russian Federation 56°18′N 48°16′E
105 N14 **Suspiro del Moro, Puerto del** *pass* S Spain
18 H16 **Susquehanna River** ⌇ New York/Pennsylvania, NE USA
13 O15 **Sussex** New Brunswick, SE Canada 45°43′N 65°32′W
18 J13 **Sussex** New Jersey, NE USA 41°12′N 74°34′W
21 W7 **Sussex** Virginia, NE USA 36°54′N 77°16′W
97 O23 **Sussex** *cultural region* S England, United Kingdom
183 S10 **Sussex Inlet** New South Wales, SE Australia 35°10′S 150°35′E
99 L17 **Susteren** Limburg, SE Netherlands 51°04′N 05°50′E
10 K12 **Sustut Peak** ▲ British Columbia, W Canada 56°25′N 126°34′W
123 S9 **Susuman** Magadanskaya Oblast', E Russian Federation 62°46′N 148°08′E
188 H6 **Susupe** ● (Northern Mariana Islands-judicial capital) Saipan, S Northern Mariana Islands
136 D12 **Susurluk** Balıkesir, NW Turkey 39°55′N 28°10′E
114 M13 **Susuzmüsellim** Tekirdağ, NW Turkey 41°04′N 27°03′E
136 F15 **Sütçüler** Isparta, SW Turkey 37°31′N 31°00′E
116 L13 **Şuţeşti** Brăila, SE Romania 45°13′N 27°27′E
83 F25 **Sutherland** Western Cape, SW South Africa 32°24′S 20°40′E
28 L15 **Sutherland** Nebraska, C USA 41°09′N 101°07′W
96 I7 **Sutherland** *cultural region* N Scotland, United Kingdom
185 B21 **Sutherland Falls** *waterfall* South Island, New Zealand
32 F14 **Sutherlin** Oregon, NW USA 43°23′N 123°18′W
149 V10 **Sutlej** ⌇ India/Pakistan
Sutna *see* Satna
35 P7 **Sutter Creek** California, W USA 38°22′N 120°49′W
39 R11 **Sutton** Alaska, USA 61°42′N 148°53′W
29 Q16 **Sutton** Nebraska, C USA 40°36′N 97°52′W
21 R4 **Sutton** West Virginia, NE USA 38°41′N 80°43′W
12 F8 **Sutton** ⌇ Ontario, C Canada
97 M19 **Sutton Coldfield** C England, United Kingdom 52°34′N 01°48′W
21 R4 **Sutton Lake** ⊠ West Virginia, NE USA
15 P13 **Sutton, Monts** *hill range* Québec, SE Canada
12 F8 **Sutton Ridges** ▲▲ Ontario, C Canada
165 Q4 **Suttsu** Hokkaidō, NE Japan 42°46′N 140°12′E
39 P15 **Sutwik Island** *island* Alaska, USA
Süüj *see* Dashinchilen
118 H5 **Suure-Jaani** *Ger.* Gross-Sankt-Johannis. Viljandimaa, S Estonia 58°34′N 25°28′E
118 J7 **Suur Munamägi** *var.* Munamägi, *Ger.* Eier-Berg. ▲ SE Estonia 57°42′N 27°03′E
118 F5 **Suur Väin** *Ger.* Grosser Sund. *strait* W Estonia
147 U8 **Suusamyr** Chuyskaya Oblast', C Kyrgyzstan 42°07′N 73°55′E
187 X14 **Suva** ● (Fiji) Viti Levu, W Fiji 18°08′S 178°27′E
187 X15 **Suva** ✈ Viti Levu, C Fiji 18°01′S 178°30′E
113 N18 **Suva Gora** ▲▲ W FYR Macedonia
118 H11 **Suvainiškis** Panevėžys, NE Lithuania 56°09′N 25°15′E
Suvalkai/Suvalki *see* Suwałki
113 P15 **Suva Planina** ▲▲ SE Serbia
Suva Reka *see* Suharekë
126 K5 **Suvorov** Tul'skaya Oblast', W Russian Federation 54°08′N 36°33′E
117 N12 **Suvorove** Odes'ka Oblast', SW Ukraine 45°35′N 28°58′E
114 M8 **Suvorovo** Varna, E Bulgaria 43°19′N 27°26′E
Suvorovo *see* Ştefan Vodă
Suwaik *see* As Suwayq
Suwaira *see* Aş Şuwayrah
110 O7 **Suwałki** *Lith.* Suvalkai, *Rus.* Suvalki. Podlaskie, NE Poland 54°06′N 22°56′E
167 R10 **Suwannaphum** Roi Et, E Thailand 15°36′N 103°46′E
23 V8 **Suwannee River** ⌇ Florida/Georgia, SE USA
Şuwār *see* Aş Şuwār
190 K14 **Suwarrow** *atoll* N Cook Islands
143 R16 **Suwaydān** *var.* Sweiham. Abū Ẓaby, E United Arab Emirates 24°30′N 55°19′E
Suwaydá/Suwaydā', **Muḥāfaẓat as** *see* As Suwaydā'
Suwayqiyah, Hawr as *see* Shuwayjah, Hawr ash
Suways, Qanāt as *see* Suez Canal
Suweida *see* As Suwaydā'
Suweon *see* Suwŏn
163 X15 **Suwŏn** *var.* Suweon, *Jap.* Suigen. NW South Korea 37°17′N 127°03′E
Su Xian *see* Suzhou
143 R14 **Sūzā** Hormozgān, S Iran 26°50′N 56°05′E
145 P15 **Suzak** *Kaz.* Sozaq. Yuzhnyy Kazakhstan, S Kazakhstan 44°09′N 68°28′E
165 N12 **Suzaka** *var.* Suzaka. Nagano, Honshū, S Japan 36°38′N 138°20′E
Suzaka *see* Suzaka
126 M3 **Suzdal'** Vladimirskaya Oblast', W Russian Federation 56°27′N 40°29′E
161 P7 **Suzhou** *var.* Su Xian. Anhui, E China 33°38′N 117°02′E
161 R8 **Suzhou** *var.* Soochow, Su-chou, Suchow; *prev.* Wuhsien. Jiangsu, E China 31°23′N 120°34′E
Suzhou *see* Jiuquan
163 V12 **Suzi He** ⌇ NE China
Suz, Mys *see* Soye, Mys
165 M10 **Suzu** Ishikawa, Honshū, SW Japan 37°24′N 137°12′E
165 K14 **Suzuka** Mie, Honshū, SW Japan 34°52′N 136°37′E
165 M10 **Suzu-misaki** *headland* Honshū, SW Japan 37°31′N 137°19′E
Svågälv *see* Svågan
94 M10 **Svågan** *var.* Svågälv. ⌇ C Sweden
Svalava/Svaljava *see* Svalyava
92 O2 **Svalbard** ◇ *Norwegian dependency* Arctic Ocean
92 J2 **Svalbardhseyri** Nordhurland Eystra, N Iceland 65°43′N 18°03′W
95 K22 **Svalöv** Skåne, S Sweden 55°55′N 13°06′E
116 H7 **Svalyava** *Cz.* Svalava, Svaljava, *Hung.* Szolyva. Zakarpats'ka Oblast', W Ukraine 48°33′N 23°00′E
92 O2 **Svanbergfjellet** ▲ C Svalbard 78°40′N 18°10′E
95 M24 **Svaneke** Bornholm, E Denmark 55°07′N 15°08′E
95 L22 **Svängsta** Blekinge, S Sweden 56°16′N 14°46′E
95 J16 **Svanskog** Värmland, C Sweden 59°10′N 12°34′E
95 L16 **Svartå** Örebro, C Sweden 59°13′N 14°07′E
95 L15 **Svartälven** ⌇ C Sweden
92 G12 **Svartisen** *glacier* C Norway
117 X6 **Svatove** *Rus.* Svatovo. Luhans'ka Oblast', E Ukraine 49°24′N 38°11′E
Svatovo *see* Svatove
Sväty Kríž nad Hronom *see* Žiar nad Hronom
167 Q11 **Svay Chék, Stœng** ⌇ Cambodia/Thailand
167 S13 **Svay Riĕng** Svay Riĕng, S Cambodia 11°05′N 105°48′E
92 O3 **Sveagruva** Spitsbergen, W Svalbard 77°53′N 16°42′E
95 K23 **Svedala** Skåne, S Sweden 55°30′N 13°15′E
118 H12 **Svėdesai** Utena, NE Lithuania 55°42′N 25°22′E
93 G18 **Sveg** Jämtland, C Sweden 62°02′N 14°20′E
118 C12 **Švėkšna** Klaipėda, W Lithuania 55°31′N 21°37′E
94 C11 **Svelgen** Sogn Og Fjordane, S Norway 61°47′N 05°18′E
95 H15 **Svelvik** Vestfold, S Norway 59°37′N 10°24′E
118 I13 **Švenčionėliai** *Pol.* Nowo-Święciany. Vilnius, SE Lithuania 55°10′N 26°00′E
118 I13 **Švenčionys** *Pol.* Swięciany. Vilnius, SE Lithuania 55°08′N 26°08′E
95 H24 **Svendborg** Fyn, C Denmark 55°04′N 10°38′E
95 K19 **Svenljunga** Västra Götaland, S Sweden 57°30′N 13°05′E
92 P2 **Svenskøya** *island* E Svalbard
93 G17 **Svenstavik** Jämtland, C Sweden 62°40′N 14°24′E
95 G20 **Svenstrup** Nordjylland, N Denmark 56°58′N 09°52′E
118 H12 **Šventoji** ⌇ C Lithuania
117 Z8 **Sverdlovs'k** *Rus.* Sverdlovsk; *prev.* Imeni Sverdlova Rudnik. Luhans'ka Oblast', E Ukraine 48°05′N 39°37′E
Sverdlovsk *see* Yekaterinburg
127 W2 **Sverdlovskaya Oblast'** ◆ *province* C Russian Federation
122 K6 **Sverdrupa, Ostrov** *island* N Russian Federation
Sverige *see* Sweden
113 D15 **Svetac** *prev.* Sveti Andrea, *It.* Sant'Andrea. *island* SW Croatia
Sveti Andrea *see* Svetac
Sveti Nikola *see* Sveti Nikole
113 O18 **Sveti Nikole** *prev.* Sveti Nikola. C FYR Macedonia 41°54′N 21°55′E
Sveti Vrach *see* Sandanski
123 T14 **Svetlaya** Primorskiy Kray, SE Russian Federation 46°33′N 138°20′E
126 B2 **Svetlogorsk** Kaliningradskaya Oblast', W Russian Federation 54°56′N 20°09′E
122 K9 **Svetlogorsk** Krasnoyarskiy Kray, N Russian Federation 66°51′N 88°29′E
Svetlogorsk *see* Svyetlahorsk
127 N14 **Svetlograd** Stavropol'skiy Kray, SW Russian Federation 45°20′N 42°53′E
Svetlovodsk *see* Svitlovods'k
119 A14 **Svetlyy** *Ger.* Zimmerbude. Kaliningradskaya Oblast', W Russian Federation 54°42′N 20°07′E
127 Y8 **Svetlyy** Orenburgskaya Oblast', W Russian Federation 50°34′N 60°42′E
127 P7 **Svetlyy** Saratovskaya Oblast', W Russian Federation 51°42′N 45°40′E
124 G11 **Svetogorsk** *Fin.* Enso. Leningradskaya Oblast', NW Russian Federation 61°06′N 28°52′E
Svetozarevo *see* Jagodina
111 B18 **Švihov** *Ger.* Schwihau. Plzeňský Kraj, W Czech Republic 49°31′N 13°18′E
112 E13 **Svilaja** ▲▲ SE Croatia
112 N12 **Svilajnac** Serbia, C Serbia 44°15′N 21°12′E
114 L11 **Svilengrad** *prev.* Mustafa-Pasha. Khaskovo, S Bulgaria 41°45′N 26°14′E
Svinecea Mare, Munte *see* Svinecea Mare, Vârful
116 F13 **Svinecea Mare, Vârful** *var.* Munte Svinecea Mare. ▲ SW Romania 44°47′N 22°10′E
Svinø *see* Svínoy
95 B18 **Svínoy** *Dan.* Svinø. *island* NE Faeroe Islands
147 N14 **Svintsovyy Rudnik** *Turkm.* Swintsowyy Rudnik. Lebap Welaýaty, E Turkmenistan 37°54′N 66°25′E
118 I13 **Svir** *Rus.* Svir'. Minskaya Voblasts', NW Belarus 54°51′N 26°24′E
124 I12 **Svir'** *canal* NW Russian Federation
Svir', Ozero *see* Svir, Vozyera
119 I14 **Svir, Vozyera** *Rus.* Ozero Svir'. ◎ C Belarus
114 J7 **Svishtov** *prev.* Sistova. Veliko Tŭrnovo, N Bulgaria 43°37′N 25°20′E
119 F18 **Svislach** *Pol.* Świsłocz, *Rus.* Svisloch'. Hrodzyenskaya Voblasts', W Belarus 53°02′N 24°06′E
119 M17 **Svislach** *Rus.* Svisloch'. Mahilyowskaya Voblasts', E Belarus 53°26′N 28°59′E
119 L17 **Svislach** *Rus.* Svisloch'. ⌇ E Belarus
Svisloch' *see* Svislach
111 F17 **Svitavy** *Ger.* Zwittau. Pardubický Kraj, C Czech Republic 49°45′N 16°27′E
117 S6 **Svitlovods'k** *Rus.* Svetlovodsk. Kirovohrads'ka Oblast', C Ukraine 49°05′N 33°15′E
Svizzera *see* Switzerland
123 Q13 **Svobodnyy** Amurskaya Oblast', SE Russian Federation 51°24′N 128°05′E
114 G9 **Svoge** Sofiya, W Bulgaria 42°58′N 23°20′E
92 G11 **Svolvær** Nordland, C Norway 68°15′N 14°40′E
111 F18 **Svratka** *Ger.* Schwarzawa. ⌇ SE Czech Republic
113 P14 **Svrljig** Serbia, E Serbia 43°26′N 22°07′E
197 U10 **Svyataya Anna Trough** *var.* Saint Anna Trough. *undersea feature* N Kara Sea
124 M4 **Svyatoy Nos, Mys** *headland* NW Russian Federation 68°07′N 39°49′E
119 N18 **Svyetlahorsk** *Rus.* Svetlogorsk. Homyel'skaya Voblasts', SE Belarus 52°38′N 29°46′E
Swabian Jura *see* Schwäbische Alb
149 U5 **Swābi** North-West Frontier Province, N Pakistan 34°07′N 72°28′E
97 P19 **Swaffham** E England, United Kingdom 52°39′N 00°40′E
23 V5 **Swainsboro** Georgia, SE USA 32°36′N 82°19′W
83 C19 **Swakop** ⌇ W Namibia
83 C19 **Swakopmund** Erongo, W Namibia 22°40′S 14°34′E
97 M15 **Swale** ⌇ N England, United Kingdom
Swallow Island *see* Nendö
99 M16 **Swalmen** Limburg, SE Netherlands 51°13′N 06°02′E
12 G8 **Swan** ⌇ Ontario, C Canada
97 L24 **Swanage** S England, United Kingdom 50°37′N 01°59′W
182 M10 **Swan Hill** Victoria, SE Australia 35°23′S 143°37′E
11 P13 **Swan Hills** Alberta, W Canada 54°41′N 116°20′W
65 D24 **Swan Island** *island* C Falkland Islands
Swankalok *see* Sawankhalok
29 U10 **Swan Lake** ◎ Minnesota, N USA
21 Y10 **Swanquarter** North Carolina, SE USA 35°24′N 76°20′W
182 J9 **Swan Reach** South Australia 34°39′S 139°35′E
11 V15 **Swan River** Manitoba, S Canada 52°06′N 101°17′W
183 P17 **Swansea** Tasmania, SE Australia 42°09′S 148°03′E
97 J22 **Swansea** *Wel.* Abertawe. S Wales, United Kingdom 51°38′N 03°57′W
21 R13 **Swansea** South Carolina, SE USA 33°47′N 81°06′W
19 S7 **Swans Island** *island* Maine, NE USA
28 L17 **Swanson Lake** ⊠ Nebraska, C USA
31 R11 **Swanton** Ohio, N USA 41°35′N 83°53′W
110 G11 **Swarzędz** Poznań, W Poland 52°24′N 17°05′E
Swatow *see* Shantou
83 L22 **Swaziland** *off.* Kingdom of Swaziland. ◆ *monarchy* S Africa
Swaziland, Kingdom of *see* Swaziland
93 G18 **Sweden** *off.* Kingdom of Sweden, *Swe.* Sverige. ◆ *monarchy* N Europe
Sweden, Kingdom of *see* Sweden
Swedru *see* Agona Swedru
25 V12 **Sweeny** Texas, SW USA 29°02′N 95°42′W
33 R6 **Sweetgrass** Montana, NW USA 48°58′N 111°58′W
32 G12 **Sweet Home** Oregon, NW USA 44°24′N 122°44′W
25 T12 **Sweet Home** Texas, SW USA 29°21′N 97°04′W
27 T4 **Sweet Springs** Missouri, C USA 38°57′N 93°24′W
20 M10 **Sweetwater** Tennessee, S USA 35°36′N 84°27′W
25 P7 **Sweetwater** Texas, SW USA 32°27′N 100°25′W
33 V15 **Sweetwater River** ⌇ Wyoming, C USA
Sweiham *see* Suwaydān
83 F26 **Swellendam** Western Cape, SW South Africa 34°01′S 20°26′E
111 G15 **Świdnica** *Ger.* Schweidnitz. Wałbrzych, SW Poland 50°51′N 16°29′E
111 O14 **Świdnik** *Ger.* Streckenbach. Lubelskie, E Poland 51°14′N 22°41′E
110 F8 **Świdwin** *Ger.* Schivelbein. Zachodnio-pomorskie, NW Poland 53°47′N 15°44′E
111 F15 **Świebodzice** *Ger.* Freiburg in Schlesien, Swiebodzice. Wałbrzych, SW Poland 50°54′N 16°23′E
110 E11 **Świebodzin** *Ger.* Schwiebus. Lubuskie, W Poland 52°15′N 15°31′E
Święciany *see* Švenčionys
110 I9 **Świecie** *Ger.* Schwertberg. Kujawsko-pomorskie, C Poland 53°24′N 18°24′E
111 L15 **Świętokrzyskie** ◆ *province* S Poland
11 T16 **Swift Current** Saskatchewan, S Canada 50°17′N 107°49′W
98 K9 **Swifterbant** Flevoland, C Netherlands 52°36′N 05°33′E
183 Q12 **Swifts Creek** Victoria, SE Australia 37°17′S 147°41′E
96 E13 **Swilly, Lough** *Ir.* Loch Súilí. *inlet* N Ireland
97 M22 **Swindon** S England, United Kingdom 51°34′N 01°47′W
Swinemünde *see* Świnoujście
110 D8 **Świnoujście** *Ger.* Swinemünde. Zachodnio-pomorskie, NW Poland 53°54′N 14°13′E
Swintsowyy Rudnik *see* Svintsovyy Rudnik
Świsłocz *see* Svislach
Swiss Confederation *see* Switzerland
108 E9 **Switzerland** *off.* Swiss Confederation, *Fr.* La Suisse, *Ger.* Schweiz, *It.* Svizzera; *anc.* Helvetia. ◆ *federal republic* C Europe
97 F17 **Swords** *Ir.* Sord, Sórd Choluim Chille. Dublin, E Ireland 53°28′N 06°13′W
18 H13 **Swoyerville** Pennsylvania, NE USA 41°18′N 75°48′W
124 I10 **Syamozera, Ozero** ◎ NW Russian Federation
124 M13 **Syamzha** Vologodskaya Oblast', NW Russian Federation 60°02′N 41°09′E
118 N13 **Syanno** *Rus.* Senno. Vitsyebskaya Voblasts', NE Belarus 54°49′N 29°43′E
119 K16 **Syarhyeyevichy** *Rus.* Sergeyevichi. Minskaya Voblasts', C Belarus 53°30′N 27°45′E
124 I12 **Syas'stroy** Leningradskaya Oblast', NW Russian Federation 60°05′N 32°37′E
Sycaminum *see* Hefa
30 M10 **Sycamore** Illinois, N USA 41°59′N 88°41′W
126 J3 **Sychëvka** Smolenskaya Oblast', W Russian Federation 55°52′N 34°19′E
111 H14 **Syców** *Ger.* Gross Wartenberg. Dolnośląskie, SW Poland 51°18′N 17°42′E
14 E17 **Sydenham** ⌇ Ontario, S Canada
Sydenham Island *see* Nonouti
183 T9 **Sydney** *state capital* New South Wales, SE Australia 33°55′S 151°10′E
13 R14 **Sydney** Cape Breton Island, Nova Scotia, SE Canada 46°10′N 60°10′W
Sydney Island *see* Manra
13 R14 **Sydney Mines** Cape Breton Island, Nova Scotia, SE Canada 46°14′N 60°19′W
Syedpur *see* Saidpur
119 K18 **Syelishcha** *Rus.* Selishche. Minskaya Voblasts', C Belarus 53°01′N 27°25′E
119 J18 **Syemyezhava** *Rus.* Semezhevo. Minskaya Voblasts', C Belarus 52°58′N 27°00′E
Syene *see* Aswân
117 X6 **Syeverodonets'k** *Rus.* Severodonetsk. Luhans'ka Oblast', E Ukraine 48°59′N 38°28′E
161 T6 **Sÿiao Shan** *island* SE China
100 H11 **Syke** Niedersachsen, NW Germany 52°55′N 08°49′E
94 D10 **Sykkylven** Møre og Romsdal, S Norway 62°23′N 06°35′E
Sykoúri *see* Sykoúrio
115 F15 **Sykoúrio** *var.* Sikouri, Sykoúri; *prev.* Sikoúrion. Thessalía, C Greece 39°46′N 22°35′E
125 R11 **Syktyvkar** *prev.* Ust'-Sysol'sk. Respublika Komi, NW Russian Federation 61°42′N 50°45′E
23 Q4 **Sylacauga** Alabama, S USA 33°10′N 86°15′W
Sylarna *see* Storsylen
153 V14 **Sylhet** Sylhet, NE Bangladesh 24°53′N 91°51′E
153 V13 **Sylhet** ◆ *division* NE Bangladesh
100 G6 **Sylt** *island* NW Germany
21 O10 **Sylva** North Carolina, SE USA 35°23′N 83°13′W
125 V15 **Sylva** ⌇ NW Russian Federation
23 W5 **Sylvania** Georgia, SE USA 32°45′N 81°38′W
31 R11 **Sylvania** Ohio, N USA 41°43′N 83°42′W
11 Q15 **Sylvan Lake** Alberta, SW Canada 52°18′N 114°02′W
33 T13 **Sylvan Pass** *pass* Wyoming, C USA
23 T7 **Sylvester** Georgia, SE USA 31°31′N 83°50′W
25 P6 **Sylvester** Texas, SW USA 32°42′N 100°15′W
10 L11 **Sylvia, Mount** ▲ British Columbia, W Canada 58°03′N 124°26′W
122 K11 **Sym** ⌇ C Russian Federation
115 N22 **Sými** *var.* Simi. *island* Dodekánisa, Greece, Aegean Sea
117 U8 **Synel'nykove** Dnipropetrovs'ka Oblast', E Ukraine 48°19′N 35°32′E
125 U6 **Synya** Respublika Komi, NW Russian Federation 65°21′N 58°01′E
117 P7 **Synyukha** *Rus.* Sinyukha. ⌇ S Ukraine
195 V2 **Syowa** *Japanese research station* Antarctica 68°58′S 40°07′E
26 H6 **Syracuse** Kansas, C USA 38°00′N 101°43′W
29 S16 **Syracuse** Nebraska, C USA 40°39′N 96°11′W
18 H10 **Syracuse** New York, NE USA 43°03′N 76°09′W
Syracuse *see* Siracusa
Syrdar'inskaya Oblast' *see* Sirdaryo Viloyati
Syrdariya *see* Syr Darya
144 L14 **Syr Darya** *var.* Sai Hun, Sir Darya, Syrdarya, *Kaz.* Syrdariya, *Rus.* Syrdar'ya, *Uzb.* Sirdaryo; *anc.* Jaxartes. ⌇ C Asia
Syrdarya *see* Syr Darya
138 J6 **Syria** *off.* Syrian Arab Republic, *var.* Siria, Syrie, *Ar.* Al-Jumhūrīyah al-'Arabīyah as-Sūrīyah, Sūrīya. ◆ *republic* SW Asia
Syrian Arab Republic *see* Syria
138 L9 **Syrian Desert** *Ar.* Al Hamad, Bādiyat ash Shām. *desert* SW Asia
Syrie *see* Syria
115 L22 **Sýrna** *var.* Sirna. *island* Kykládes, Greece, Aegean Sea
115 I20 **Sýros** *var.* Síros. *island* Kykládes, Greece, Aegean Sea
93 M18 **Sysmä** Etelä-Suomi, S Finland 61°28′N 25°37′E
125 R12 **Sysola** ⌇ NW Russian Federation
Syulemeshlii *see* Sredets
127 S2 **Syumsi** Udmurtskaya Respublika, NW Russian Federation 57°07′N 51°35′E
114 K10 **Syuyutliyka** ⌇ C Bulgaria
Syvash, Zaliv *see* Syvash, Zatoka
117 U12 **Syvash, Zatoka** *Rus.* Zaliv Syvash. *inlet* S Ukraine
127 Q6 **Syzran'** Samarskaya Oblast', W Russian Federation 53°10′N 48°23′E
Szabadka *see* Subotica
111 N21 **Szabolcs-Szatmár-Bereg** *off.* Szabolcs-Szatmár-Bereg Megye. ◆ *county* E Hungary
Szabolcs-Szatmár-Bereg Megye *see* Szabolcs-Szatmár-Bereg
110 G10 **Szamocin** *Ger.* Samotschin. Wielkopolskie, C Poland 53°02′N 17°04′E
116 H8 **Szamos** *var.* Someş, Someşul, *Ger.* Samosch, Somesch. ⌇ Hungary/Romania
Szamosújvár *see* Gherla
110 G11 **Szamotuły** Poznań, W Poland 52°35′N 16°36′E
Szarkowszczyzna *see* Sharkawshchyna
111 M24 **Szarvas** Békés, SE Hungary 46°51′N 20°35′E
Szászmagyarós *see* Măieruş
Szászrégen *see* Reghin
Szászsebes *see* Sebeş
Szászváros *see* Orăştie
Szatmárrnémeti *see* Satu Mare
Száva *see* Sava
111 P15 **Szczebrzeszyn** Lubelskie, E Poland 50°43′N 23°00′E
110 D9 **Szczecin** *Eng./Ger.* Stettin. Zachodnio-pomorskie, NW Poland 53°25′N 14°32′E
110 G8 **Szczecinek** *Ger.* Neustettin. Zachodnio-pomorskie, NW Poland 53°43′N 16°40′E
110 D8 **Szczeciński, Zalew** *var.* Stettiner Haff, *Ger.* Oderhaff. *bay* Germany/Poland
111 K15 **Szczekociny** Śląskie, S Poland 50°38′N 19°46′E
110 N8 **Szczuczyn** Podlaskie, NE Poland 53°34′N 22°17′E
Szczuczyn Nowogródzki *see* Shchuchyn
110 M8 **Szczytno** *Ger.* Ortelsburg. Warmińsko-Mazurskie, NE Poland 53°34′N 21°E
Szechuan/Szechwan *see* Sichuan
111 K21 **Szécsény** Nógrád, N Hungary 48°07′N 19°30′E
111 L25 **Szeged** *Ger.* Szegedin, *Rom.* Seghedin. Csongrád, SE Hungary 46°17′N 20°06′E
Szegedin *see* Szeged
111 N23 **Szeghalom** Békés, SE Hungary 47°01′N 21°09′E
Székelyhid *see* Săcueni
Székelykeresztúr *see* Cristuru Secuiesc
111 I23 **Székesfehérvár** *Ger.* Stuhlweissenberg; *anc.* Alba Regia. Fejér, W Hungary 47°13′N 18°24′E
Szeklerburg *see* Miercurea-Ciuc
Szekler Neumarkt *see* Târgu Secuiesc
111 J25 **Szekszárd** Tolna, S Hungary 46°21′N 18°41′E
Szempcz/Szenc *see* Senec
Szenice *see* Senica
Szentágota *see* Agnita
111 J22 **Szentendre** *Ger.* Sankt Andrä. Pest, N Hungary 47°40′N 19°02′E
111 L24 **Szentes** Csongrád, SE Hungary 46°40′N 20°17′E
111 F23 **Szentgotthárd** *Eng.* Saint Gotthard, *Ger.* Sankt Gotthard. Vas, W Hungary 46°57′N 16°18′E
Szentgyörgy *see* Đurđevac
Szenttamás *see* Srbobran
Széphely *see* Jebel
Szeping *see* Siping
Szered *see* Sereď
111 N21 **Szerencs** Borsod-Abaúj-Zemplén, NE Hungary 48°10′N 21°11′E
Szeret *see* Siret
Szeretfalva *see* Sărăţel
110 N7 **Szeska Góra** *var.* Szeskie Wygórza, *Ger.* Seesker Höhe. *hill* NE Poland
Szeskie Wygórza *see* Szeska Góra
111 H25 **Szigetvár** Baranya, SW Hungary 46°01′N 17°50′E
Szilágysomlyó *see* Şimleu Silvaniei
Szinna *see* Snina
Sziszek *see* Sisak
Szitás-Keresztúr *see* Cristuru Secuiesc
111 E15 **Szklarska Poręba** *Ger.* Schreiberhau. Dolnośląskie, SW Poland 50°50′N 15°30′E
Szkudy *see* Skuodas
Szlatina *see* Slatina
Szlavonia/Szlavonország *see* Slavonija
Szlovákia *see* Slovakia
Szluin *see* Slunj
111 L23 **Szolnok** Jász-Nagykun-Szolnok, C Hungary 47°11′N 20°12′E
Szolyva *see* Svalyava
111 G23 **Szombathely** *Ger.* Steinamanger; *anc.* Sabaria, Savaria. Vas, W Hungary 47°14′N 16°38′E
Szond/Szonta *see* Sonta
Szováta *see* Sovata
110 F13 **Szprotawa** *Ger.* Sprottau. Lubuskie, W Poland 51°33′N 15°32′E
Sztálinváros *see* Dunaújváros
Sztrazsó *see* Strážov
110 J8 **Sztum** *Ger.* Stuhm. Pomorskie, N Poland 53°54′N 19°01′E
110 H10 **Szubin** *Ger.* Schubin. Kujawsko-pomorskie, C Poland 53°04′N 17°49′E
Szucsava *see* Suceava
Szurduk *see* Surduc
111 M14 **Szydłowiec** *Ger.* Schlelau. Mazowieckie, C Poland 51°14′N 20°50′E

T

190 I17 **Taakoka** *island* S Cook Islands
Taalintehdas *see* Dalsbruk
171 O4 **Taal, Lake** ◎ Luzon, NW Philippines
95 J23 **Taastrup** *var.* Tåstrup. København, E Denmark 55°39′N 12°19′E
111 I24 **Tab** Somogy, W Hungary 46°45′N 18°01′E
171 P4 **Tabaco** Luzon, N Philippines 13°22′N 123°42′E
186 G4 **Tabar Island** *island* NE Papua New Guinea 01°22′S 149°37′E
104 K5 **Tábara** Castilla-León, N Spain 41°49′N 05°57′W
186 H5 **Tabar Islands** *island group* NE Papua New Guinea
Tabariya, Bahrat *see* Tiberias, Lake
143 S7 **Ţabas** *var.* Golshan. Yazd, C Iran 33°37′N 56°54′E
43 P15 **Tabasará, Serranía de** ▲▲ W Panama
41 U15 **Tabasco** ◆ *state* SE Mexico
Tabasco *see* Grijalva, Río
127 Q2 **Tabashino** Respublika Mariy El, W Russian Federation 57°00′N 47°47′E
58 B13 **Tabatinga** Amazonas, N Brazil 04°14′S 69°44′W
74 G9 **Tabelbala** W Algeria 29°22′N 03°01′W
11 Q17 **Taber** Alberta, SW Canada 49°48′N 112°09′W
171 V15 **Taberfane** Pulau Trangan, E Indonesia 06°14′S 134°08′E
95 L19 **Taberg** Jönköping, S Sweden 57°42′N 14°05′E
191 O3 **Tabiteuea** *prev.* Drummond Island. *atoll* Tungaru, W Kiribati
171 O5 **Tablas Island** *island* C Philippines
184 Q10 **Table Cape** *headland* North Island, New Zealand 39°07′S 178°00′E
13 S13 **Table Mountain** ▲ Newfoundland, Newfoundland and Labrador, E Canada 47°39′N 59°15′W
173 P17 **Table, Pointe de la** *headland* SE Réunion 21°19′S 55°49′E
27 S8 **Table Rock Lake** ⊠ Arkansas/Missouri, C USA
36 K14 **Table Top** ▲ Arizona, SW USA 32°45′N 112°07′W
186 D8 **Tabletop, Mount** ▲ C Papua New Guinea 06°51′S 146°00′E
111 D18 **Tábor** Jihočeský Kraj, S Czech Republic 49°25′N 14°41′E
123 R7 **Tabor** Respublika Sakha (Yakutiya), NE Russian Federation 71°14′N 150°23′E
29 S15 **Tabor** Iowa, C USA 40°54′N 95°40′W
81 F21 **Tabora** Tabora, W Tanzania 05°04′S 32°49′E
81 F21 **Tabora** ◆ *region* C Tanzania
21 U12 **Tabor City** North Carolina, SE USA 34°09′N 78°52′W
147 Q10 **Taboshar** NW Tajikistan 40°37′N 69°33′E
76 L18 **Tabou** *var.* Tabu. S Ivory Coast 04°28′N 07°20′W
142 J2 **Tabrīz** *var.* Tebriz; *anc.* Tauris. Āzarbāyjān-e Sharqī, NW Iran 38°05′N 46°18′E
Tabu *see* Tabou
191 W1 **Tabuaeran** *prev.* Fanning Island. *atoll* Line Islands, E Kiribati
171 O2 **Tabuk** Luzon, N Philippines 17°26′N 121°25′E
140 J4 **Tabūk** Tabūk, NW Saudi Arabia 28°25′N 36°34′E
140 J5 **Tabūk** *off.* Minţaqat Tabūk. ◆ *province* NW Saudi Arabia
Tabūk, Minţaqat *see* Tabūk
187 Q13 **Tabwemasana, Mount** ▲ Espiritu Santo, W Vanuatu 15°22′S 166°44′E
95 O15 **Täby** Stockholm, C Sweden 59°29′N 18°04′E
41 N14 **Tacámbaro** Michoacán, SW Mexico 19°12′N 101°27′W
42 A5 **Tacaná, Volcán** ⛰ Guatemala/Mexico 15°07′N 92°06′W
43 X16 **Tacarcuna, Cerro** ▲ SE Panama 08°08′N 77°15′W
Tachau *see* Tachov
158 J3 **Tacheng** *var.* Qoqek. Xinjiang Uygur Zizhiqu, NW China 46°45′N 82°55′E
54 H7 **Táchira** *off.* Estado Táchira. ◆ *state* W Venezuela
Táchira, Estado *see* Táchira
161 T13 **Tachoshui** N Taiwan 24°26′N 121°43′E
111 A17 **Tachov** *Ger.* Tachau. Plveňský Kraj, W Czech Republic 49°48′N 12°38′E
171 Q5 **Tacloban** *off.* Tacloban City. Leyte, C Philippines 11°15′N 125°E
Tacloban City *see* Tacloban
57 I19 **Tacna** Tacna, SE Peru 18°S 70°15′W
57 H18 **Tacna** *off.* Departamento de Tacna. ◆ *department* S Peru
Tacna, Departamento de *see* Tacna
32 H8 **Tacoma** Washington, NW USA 47°15′N 122°27′W
18 L11 **Taconic Range** ▲▲ NE USA
62 L6 **Taco Pozo** Formosa, N Argentina 25°35′S 63°15′W
57 M20 **Tacsara, Cordillera de** ▲▲ S Bolivia
61 F17 **Tacuarembó** *prev.* San Fructuoso. Tacuarembó, C Uruguay 31°42′S 56°W
61 E18 **Tacuarembó** ◆ *department* C Uruguay
61 F17 **Tacuarembó, Río** ⌇ C Uruguay
83 I14 **Taculi** North Western, NW Zambia 14°17′S 26°51′E
171 Q8 **Tacurong** Mindanao, S Philippines 06°42′N 124°40′E
77 V8 **Tadek** ⌇ NW Niger
74 J9 **Tademaït, Plateau du** *plateau* C Algeria
187 R17 **Tadine** Province des Îles Loyauté, E New Caledonia 21°33′S 167°54′E
80 M11 **Tadjoura, Golfe de** *Eng.* Gulf of Tajura. *inlet* E Djibouti
80 L11 **Tadjourah** E Djibouti 11°47′N 42°51′E
Tadmor/Tadmur *see* Tudmur
11 W10 **Tadoule Lake** ◎ Manitoba, C Canada
15 S8 **Tadoussac** Québec, SE Canada 48°09′N 69°43′W
155 H18 **Tādpatri** Andhra Pradesh, E India 14°55′N 77°59′E
Tadzhikabad *see* Tojikobod
Tadzhikistan *see* Tajikistan
163 Y14 **T'aebaek-sanmaek** ▲▲ E South Korea
163 V15 **Taechŏng-do** *island* NW South Korea
163 X13 **Taedong-gang** ⌇ C North Korea
163 Y16 **Taegu** *off.* Taegu-gwangyŏksi, *var.* Daegu, *Jap.* Taikyū. SE South Korea 35°55′N 128°33′E
Taegu-gwangyŏksi *see* Taegu
Taehan-haehyŏp *see* Korea Strait
Taehan Min'guk *see* South Korea
163 Y15 **Taejŏn** *off.* Taejŏn-gwangyŏksi, *Jap.* Taiden. C South Korea 36°20′N 127°28′E
Taejŏn-gwangyŏksi *see* Taejŏn
193 Z13 **Tafahi** *island* N Tonga
105 Q4 **Tafalla** Navarra, N Spain 42°32′N 01°41′W
77 W7 **Tafassâsset, Ténéré du** *desert* N Niger
75 M12 **Tafassâsset, Oued** ⌇ SE Algeria
55 U11 **Tafelberg** ▲ S Surinam 03°55′N 56°09′W
97 J21 **Taff** ⌇ SE Wales, United Kingdom
Tafila/Ţafīlah, Muḥāfaẓat at *see* Aţ Ţafīlah
77 N15 **Tafiré** N Ivory Coast 09°04′N 05°10′W
142 M6 **Tafresh** Markazī, W Iran 34°40′N 50°00′E
143 Q9 **Taft** Yazd, C Iran 31°45′N 54°14′E
35 R13 **Taft** California, W USA 35°08′N 119°27′W
25 T14 **Taft** Texas, SW USA 27°58′N 97°24′W
143 W12 **Taftān, Kūh-e** ▲ SE Iran 28°38′N 61°06′E
35 R13 **Taft Heights** California, W USA 35°06′N 119°29′W
189 Y14 **Tafunsak** Kosrae, E Micronesia 05°21′N 162°58′E
192 G16 **Tāga** Savai'i, SW Samoa 13°46′S 172°31′W
149 O6 **Tagāb** Dāikondī, E Afghanistan 33°53′N 66°23′E
39 O8 **Tagagawik River** ⌇ Alaska, USA
165 Q10 **Tagajō** *var.* Tagazyô. Miyagi, Honshū, C Japan 38°18′N 140°58′E
126 K12 **Taganrog** Rostovskaya Oblast', SW Russian Federation 47°10′N 38°55′E
126 K12 **Taganrog, Gulf of** *Rus.* Taganrogskiy Zaliv, *Ukr.* Tahanroz'ka Zatoka. *gulf* Russian Federation/Ukraine
Taganrogskiy Zaliv *see* Taganrog, Gulf of
76 J8 **Tagant** ◆ *region* C Mauritania

◆ Country
● Country Capital
◇ Dependent Territory
○ Dependent Territory Capital
◆ Administrative Regions
✈ International Airport
▲ Mountain
▲▲ Mountain Range
⛰ Volcano
⌇ River
◎ Lake
⊠ Reservoir

TAGAS – TAPIRAPECÓ, SERRA

148 M14 **Tagas** Baluchistān, SW Pakistan 27°09′N 64°36′E
171 O4 **Tagaytay** Luzon, N Philippines 14°04′N 120°55′E
Tagazyô *see* Tagajō
171 P6 **Tagbilaran** *var.* Tagbilaran City. Bohol, C Philippines 09°41′N 123°54′E
Tagbilaran City *see* Tagbilaran
106 B10 **Taggia** Liguria, NW Italy 43°51′N 07°48′E
77 V9 **Taghouaji, Massif de** ▲ C Niger 17°13′N 08°37′E
107 J15 **Tagliacozzo** Lazio, C Italy 42°03′N 13°15′E
106 J7 **Tagliamento** ≈ NE Italy
149 N3 **Tagow Bāy** *var.* Bai. Sar-e Pol, N Afghanistan 35°41′N 66°01′E
146 H9 **Tagta** *var.* Tahta, *Rus.* Takhta. Daşoguz Welaýaty, N Turkmenistan 41°40′N 59°51′E
146 J16 **Tagtabazar** *var.* Takhtabazar. Mary Welaýaty, S Turkmenistan 35°57′N 62°49′E
59 L17 **Taguatinga** Tocantins, C Brazil 12°16′S 46°25′W
186 I10 **Tagula** Tagula Island, SE Papua New Guinea 11°21′S 153°11′E
186 I11 **Tagula Island** *prev.* Southeast Island, Sudest Island. *island* SE Papua New Guinea
171 Q7 **Tagum** Mindanao, S Philippines 07°22′N 125°51′E
54 C7 **Tagún, Cerro** *elevation* Colombia/Panama
105 P7 **Tagus** *Port.* Rio Tejo, *Sp.* Río Tajo. ≈ Portugal/Spain
64 M9 **Tagus Plain** *undersea feature* E Atlantic Ocean 37°30′N 12°00′W
191 S10 **Tahaa** *island* Îles Sous le Vent, W French Polynesia
191 U10 **Tahanea** *atoll* Îles Tuamotu, C French Polynesia
Tahanroz'ka Zatoka *see* Taganrog, Gulf of
74 K12 **Tahat** ▲ SE Algeria 23°15′N 05°34′E
163 U4 **Tahe** Heilongjiang, NE China 52°21′N 124°42′E
Tahilt *see* Tsogt
191 T10 **Tahiti** *island* Îles du Vent, W French Polynesia
Tahiti, Archipel de *see* Société, Archipel de la
118 E4 **Tahkuna Nina** *headland* W Estonia 59°06′N 22°35′E
148 K12 **Tāhlāb** ≈ W Pakistan
148 K12 **Tāhlāb, Dasht-i** *desert* SW Pakistan
27 R10 **Tahlequah** Oklahoma, C USA 35°57′N 94°58′W
35 Q6 **Tahoe City** California, W USA 39°09′N 120°09′W
35 P6 **Tahoe, Lake** ◎ California/Nevada, W USA
25 N6 **Tahoka** Texas, SW USA 33°10′N 101°47′W
32 F8 **Taholah** Washington, NW USA 47°19′N 124°17′W
77 T11 **Tahoua** Tahoua, W Niger 14°53′N 05°18′E
77 T11 **Tahoua** ◐ *department* W Niger
31 P3 **Tahquamenon Falls** *waterfall* Michigan, N USA
31 P4 **Tahquamenon River** ≈ Michigan, N USA
139 V10 **Taḩrīr** Al Qādisīyah, S Iraq 31°58′N 45°34′E
10 K17 **Tahsis** Vancouver Island, British Columbia, SW Canada 49°42′N 126°31′W
75 W9 **Ṭahṭa** *var.* Ṭahṭa. C Egypt 26°47′N 31°31′E
Tahta *see* Tagta
136 L15 **Tahtalı Dağları** ▲▲ C Turkey
57 I14 **Tahuamanu, Río** ≈ Bolivia/Peru
56 F13 **Tahuanía, Río** ≈ E Peru
191 X7 **Tahuata** *island* Îles Marquises, NE French Polynesia
76 L17 **Taï** SW Ivory Coast 05°52′N 07°28′W
161 P5 **Tai'an** Shandong, E China 36°13′N 117°12′E
191 R8 **Taiarapu, Presqu'île de** *peninsula* Tahiti, W French Polynesia
Taibad *see* Tāybād
160 K7 **Taibai Shan** ▲ C China 33°57′N 107°31′E
105 Q12 **Taibilla, Sierra de** ▲▲ S Spain
Taibus Qi *see* Baochang
Taichū *see* T'aichung
161 S13 **T'aichung** *Jap.* Taichū; *prev.* Taiwan. C Taiwan 24°09′N 120°40′E
Taiden *see* Taejŏn
185 E23 **Taieri** ≈ South Island, New Zealand
115 E21 **Taïgetos** ▲▲ S Greece
161 N4 **Taihang Shan** ▲▲ C China
184 M11 **Taihape** Manawatu-Wanganui, North Island, New Zealand 39°41′S 175°47′E
161 O7 **Taihe** Anhui, E China 33°14′N 115°35′E
161 O12 **Taihe** *var.* Chengjiang. Jiangxi, S China 26°47′N 114°52′E
Taihoku *see* T'aipei
161 P9 **Taihu** Anhui, E China 30°22′N 116°20′E
161 R8 **Tai Hu** ◎ E China
159 O9 **Taikang** *var.* Dorbod, Dorbod Mongolzu Zizhixian. Heilongjiang, NE China 46°50′N 124°25′E
161 O6 **Taikang** Henan, C China 34°01′N 114°59′E
165 T5 **Taiki** Hokkaidō, NE Japan 42°29′N 143°15′E
166 L8 **Taikkyi** Yangon, SW Burma (Myanmar) 17°16′N 95°55′E
Taikyū *see* Taegu
163 U8 **Tailai** Heilongjiang, NE China 46°25′N 123°25′E
168 I12 **Taileleo** Pulau Siberut, W Indonesia 01°45′S 99°06′E
182 J10 **Tailem Bend** South Australia 35°20′S 139°34′E
96 I8 **Tain** N Scotland, United Kingdom 57°49′N 04°04′W
161 S14 **T'ainan** *Jap.* Tainan; *prev.* Dainan. S Taiwan 23°01′N 120°05′E
115 E22 **Taínaro, Akrotírio** *cape* S Greece
161 Q11 **Taining** *var.* Shancheng. Fujian, SE China 26°55′N 117°13′E
191 W7 **Taiohae** *prev.* Madisonville. Nuku Hiva, NE French Polynesia 08°55′S 140°04′W
161 T13 **T'aipei** *Jap.* Taihoku; *prev.* Daihoku. ● (Taiwan) N Taiwan 25°02′N 121°28′E
168 J7 **Taiping** Perak, Peninsular Malaysia 04°54′N 100°42′E
Taiping *see* Chongzuo
163 S8 **Taiping Ling** ▲ NE China 47°27′N 120°27′E
165 Q4 **Taisei** Hokkaidō, NE Japan 42°13′N 139°52′E
165 G12 **Taisha** Shimane, Honshū, SW Japan 35°23′N 132°40′E
109 R4 **Taiskirchen** Oberösterreich, NW Austria 48°15′N 13°33′E
63 F20 **Taitao, Peninsula de** *peninsula* S Chile
Taitō *see* T'aitung
161 T14 **T'aitung** *Jap.* Taitō. S Taiwan 22°43′N 121°10′E
92 M13 **Taivalkoski** Oulu, E Finland 65°35′N 28°20′E
93 K19 **Taivassalo** Länsi-Suomi, SW Finland 60°35′N 21°36′E
161 T14 **Taiwan** *off.* Republic of China, *var.* Formosa, Formo'sa. ◆ *republic* E Asia
192 F5 **Taiwan** *var.* Formosa. *island* E Asia
Taiwan *see* T'aichung
T'aiwan Haihsia/Taiwan Haixia *see* Taiwan Strait
Taiwan Shan *see* Chungyang Shanmo
161 R13 **Taiwan Strait** *var.* Formosa Strait, *Chin.* T'aiwan Haihsia, Taiwan Haixia. *strait* China/Taiwan
161 N4 **Taiyuan** *var.* T'ai-yuan, T'ai-yüan; *prev.* Yangku. *province capital* Shanxi, C China 37°48′N 112°33′E
T'ai-yuan/T'ai-yüan *see* Taiyuan
161 R7 **Taizhou** Jiangsu, E China 32°36′N 119°52′E
161 S10 **Taizhou** *var.* Jiaojiang; *prev.* Haimen. Zhejiang, SE China 28°36′N 121°19′E
Taizhou *see* Linhai
141 O16 **Ta'izz** SW Yemen 13°36′N 44°04′E
141 O16 **Ta'izz** ✈ SW Yemen 13°40′N 44°10′E
75 P12 **Tajarhī** SW Libya 24°21′N 14°28′E
147 P13 **Tajikistan** *off.* Republic of Tajikistan, *Rus.* Tadzhikistan, *Taj.* Jumhurii Tojikiston; *prev.* Tajik S.S.R. ◆ *republic* C Asia
Tajikistan, Republic of *see* Tajikistan
Tajik S.S.R *see* Tajikistan
165 O11 **Tajima** Fukushima, Honshū, C Japan 37°10′N 139°46′E
Tajoe *see* Tayu
Tajo, Río *see* Tagus
42 B5 **Tajumulco, Volcán** ▲ W Guatemala 15°04′N 91°50′W
105 P7 **Tajuña** ≈ C Spain
Tajura, Gulf of *see* Tadjoura, Golfe de
167 O9 **Tak** *var.* Rahaeng. Tak, W Thailand 16°51′N 99°08′E
189 U4 **Taka Atoll** *var.* Tōke. *atoll* Ratak Chain, N Marshall Islands
165 P12 **Takahagi** Ibaraki, Honshū, S Japan 36°42′N 140°42′E
165 H13 **Takahashi** *var.* Takahasi. Okayama, Honshū, SW Japan 34°48′N 133°38′E
Takahasi *see* Takahashi
189 P12 **Takaieu Island** *island* E Micronesia
184 I13 **Takaka** Tasman, South Island, New Zealand 40°52′S 172°49′E
170 M14 **Takalar** Sulawesi, C Indonesia 05°28′S 119°24′E
165 H13 **Takamatsu** *var.* Takamatu. Kagawa, Shikoku, SW Japan 34°19′N 133°59′E
Takamatu *see* Takamatsu
165 D14 **Takamori** Kumamoto, Kyūshū, SW Japan 32°50′N 131°08′E
165 D16 **Takanabe** Miyazaki, Kyūshū, SW Japan 32°13′N 131°31′E
170 M16 **Takan, Gunung** ▲ Pulau Sumba, S Indonesia 08°52′S 117°32′E
165 Q7 **Takanosu** *var.* Kita-Akita. Akita, Honshū, C Japan 40°13′N 140°23′E
Takao *see* Kaohsiung
165 L11 **Takaoka** Toyama, Honshū, SW Japan 36°44′N 137°02′E
184 N12 **Takapau** Hawke's Bay, North Island, New Zealand 40°01′S 176°21′E
191 U9 **Takapoto** *atoll* Îles Tuamotu, C French Polynesia
184 L5 **Takapuna** Auckland, North Island, New Zealand 36°48′S 174°46′E
165 J3 **Takarazuka** Hyōgo, Honshū, SW Japan 34°49′N 135°21′E
191 U9 **Takaroa** *atoll* Îles Tuamotu, C French Polynesia
165 N12 **Takasaki** Gunma, Honshū, S Japan 36°20′N 139°00′E
164 L12 **Takayama** Gifu, Honshū, SW Japan 36°09′N 137°16′E
164 K12 **Takefu** *var.* Echizen, Takehu. Fukui, Honshū, SW Japan 35°55′N 136°11′E
Takehu *see* Takefu
164 C14 **Takeo** Saga, Kyūshū, SW Japan 33°13′N 130°00′E
Takeo *see* Takêv
164 C17 **Take-shima** *island* Nansei-shotō, SW Japan
142 M5 **Tākestān** *var.* Takistan; *prev.* Siadehan. Qazvin, N Iran 36°02′N 49°40′E
164 D14 **Taketa** Ōita, Kyūshū, SW Japan 33°00′N 131°23′E
167 R13 **Takêv** *prev.* Takeo. Takêv, S Cambodia 10°59′N 104°47′E
167 O10 **Tak Fah** Nakhon Sawan, C Thailand
139 T13 **Takhādīd** *well* S Iraq
149 R3 **Takhār** ◐ *province* NE Afghanistan
Takhiatash *see* Taxiatosh
167 S13 **Ta Khmau** Kândal, S Cambodia 11°30′N 104°59′E
Takhta *see* Tagta
Takhtabazar *see* Tagtabazar
145 O8 **Takhtabrod** Severnyy Kazakhstan, N Kazakhstan 52°35′N 67°37′E
Takhtakupyr *see* Taxtako'pir
142 M8 **Takht-e Shāh, Kūh-e** ▲▲ C Iran
77 V12 **Takiéta** Zinder, S Niger 13°43′N 08°33′E
8 J8 **Takijuq Lake** ◎ Nunavut, NW Canada
165 S3 **Takikawa** Hokkaidō, NE Japan 43°35′N 141°54′E
165 U3 **Takinoue** Hokkaidō, NE Japan 44°10′N 143°09′E
Takistan *see* Tākestān
185 B23 **Takitimu Mountains** ▲▲ South Island, New Zealand
Takkaze *see* Tekezē
165 R7 **Takko** Aomori, Honshū, C Japan 40°19′N 141°11′E
10 L13 **Takla Lake** ◎ British Columbia, SW Canada
Takla Makan Desert *see* Taklimakan Shamo
158 H9 **Taklimakan Shamo** *Eng.* Takla Makan Desert. *desert* NW China
167 T12 **Takôk** Môndól Kiri, E Cambodia 12°37′N 106°30′E
39 P10 **Takotna** Alaska, USA 62°59′N 156°03′W
Takow *see* Kaohsiung
123 O12 **Taksimo** Respublika Buryatiya, S Russian Federation 56°18′N 114°53′E
164 C13 **Taku** Saga, Kyūshū, SW Japan 33°19′N 130°06′E
10 I10 **Taku** ≈ British Columbia, W Canada
166 M15 **Takua Pa** *var.* Ban Takua Pa. Phangnga, SW Thailand 08°55′N 98°20′E
77 W16 **Takum** Taraba, E Nigeria 07°16′N 10°00′E
191 V10 **Takume** *atoll* Îles Tuamotu, C French Polynesia
190 L16 **Takutea** *island* S Cook Islands
186 K6 **Takuu Islands** *prev.* Mortlock Group. *island group* NE Papua New Guinea
119 L18 **Tal'** Minskaya Voblasts', S Belarus 52°52′N 27°58′E
40 L13 **Tala** Jalisco, C Mexico 20°39′N 103°45′W
61 F19 **Tala** Canelones, S Uruguay 34°24′S 55°45′W
Talabriga *see* Aveiro, Portugal
Talabriga *see* Talavera de la Reina, Spain
119 N14 **Talachyn** *Rus.* Tolochin. Vitsyebskaya Voblasts', NE Belarus 54°25′N 29°42′E
149 U7 **Talagang** Punjab, E Pakistan 32°55′N 72°29′E
105 V11 **Talaiassa** ▲ Ibiza, Spain, W Mediterranean Sea 38°55′N 1°17′E
155 J23 **Talaimannar** Northern Province, NW Sri Lanka 09°05′N 79°43′E
117 R3 **Talalayivka** Chernihivs'ka Oblast', N Ukraine 50°51′N 33°09′E
43 O15 **Talamanca, Cordillera de** ▲▲ S Costa Rica
56 A9 **Talara** Piura, NW Peru 04°31′S 81°17′W
104 L11 **Talarrubias** Extremadura, W Spain 39°03′N 05°14′W
147 S8 **Talas** Talasskaya Oblast', NW Kyrgyzstan 42°29′N 72°21′E
147 S8 **Talas** ≈ NW Kyrgyzstan
186 G7 **Talasea** New Britain, E Papua New Guinea 05°20′S 150°01′E
Talas Oblasty *see* Talasskaya Oblast'
147 S8 **Talasskaya Oblast'** *Kir.* Talas Oblasty. ◐ *province* NW Kyrgyzstan
147 S8 **Talasskiy Alatau, Khrebet** ▲▲ Kazakhstan/Kyrgyzstan
77 U12 **Talata Mafara** Zamfara, NW Nigeria 12°33′N 06°01′E
171 R9 **Talaud, Kepulauan** *island group* E Indonesia
104 M9 **Talavera de la Reina** *anc.* Caesarobriga, Talabriga. Castilla-La Mancha, C Spain 39°58′N 04°50′W
104 J11 **Talavera la Real** Extremadura, W Spain 38°53′N 06°46′W
186 F7 **Talawe, Mount** ▲ New Britain, C Papua New Guinea 05°30′S 148°24′E
23 S5 **Talbotton** Georgia, SE USA 32°40′N 84°32′W
183 R7 **Talbragar River** ≈ New South Wales, SE Australia
62 G13 **Talca** Maule, C Chile 35°28′S 71°42′W
62 F13 **Talcahuano** Bío Bío, C Chile 36°43′S 73°07′W
154 N12 **Tālcher** Orissa, E India 20°57′N 85°13′E
25 W5 **Talco** Texas, SW USA 33°21′N 95°06′W
145 V14 **Taldykorgan** *Kaz.* Taldyqorghan; *prev.* Taldy-Kurgan. Taldykorgan, SE Kazakhstan 45°N 78°23′E
Taldy-Kurgan/Taldyqorghan *see* Taldykorgan
147 Y7 **Taldy-Suu** Issyk-Kul'skaya Oblast', E Kyrgyzstan 42°49′N 78°33′E
147 U10 **Taldy-Suu** Oshskaya Oblast', SW Kyrgyzstan 40°33′N 73°52′E
Tal-e Khosravī *see* Yāsūj
193 Y15 **Taleki Tonga** *island* Otu Tolu Group, C Tonga
193 Y15 **Taleki Vavu'u** *island* Otu Tolu Group, C Tonga
102 J13 **Talence** Gironde, SW France 44°49′N 00°35′W
145 U16 **Talgar** *Kaz.* Talghar. Almaty, SE Kazakhstan 43°17′N 77°15′E
Talghar *see* Talgar
171 Q12 **Taliabu, Pulau** *island* Kepulauan Sula, C Indonesia
115 L22 **Taliarós, Akrotírio** *headland* Astypálaia, Kykládes, Greece, Aegean Sea 36°31′N 26°18′E
Ta-lien *see* Dalian
27 Q12 **Talihina** Oklahoma, C USA 34°45′N 95°03′W
Talimardzhan *see* Tollimarjon
137 T12 **T'alin** *Rus.* Talin; *prev.* Verin T'alin. W Armenia 40°23′N 43°51′E
Talin *see* T'alin
81 E15 **Tali Post** Bahr el Gabel, S Sudan 05°55′N 30°44′E
Taliq-an *see* Tāloqān
Talış Dağları *see* Talish Mountains
142 L2 **Talish Mountains** *Az.* Talış Dağları, *Per.* Kūhhā-ye Ṭavālesh, *Rus.* Talyshskiye Gory. ▲▲ Azerbaijan/Iran
170 M16 **Taliwang** Sumbawa, C Indonesia 08°45′S 116°55′E
119 L17 **Tal'ka** Minskaya Voblasts', C Belarus 53°22′N 28°21′E
39 R11 **Talkeetna** Alaska, USA 62°19′N 150°06′W
39 R11 **Talkeetna Mountains** ▲▲ Alaska, USA
Talkhof *see* Puurmani
92 H2 **Tálknafjördhur** Vestfirdhir, W Iceland 65°38′N 23°51′W
139 Q3 **Tall 'Abṭah** Nīnawá, N Iraq 35°52′N 42°40′E
138 M2 **Tall Abyaḍ** *var.* Tell Abiad. Ar Raqqah, N Syria 36°42′N 38°56′E
23 Q4 **Talladega** Alabama, S USA 33°26′N 86°06′W
139 Q2 **Tall 'Afar** Nīnawýa, N Iraq 36°22′N 42°27′E
23 S8 **Tallahassee** *prev.* Muskogean. *state capital* Florida, SE USA 30°26′N 84°17′W
22 L2 **Tallahatchie River** ≈ Mississippi, S USA
Tall al Abyaḍ *see* At Tall al Abyaḍ
139 W12 **Tall al Laḥm** Dhī Qār, S Iraq 30°46′N 46°22′E
183 P11 **Tallangatta** Victoria, SE Australia 36°15′S 147°13′E
23 R4 **Tallapoosa River** ≈ Alabama/Georgia, S USA
103 T13 **Tallard** Hautes-Alpes, SE France 44°30′N 06°04′E
139 Q3 **Tall ash Sha'īr** Nīnawá, N Iraq 36°11′N 42°26′E
23 Q5 **Tallassee** Alabama, S USA 32°32′N 85°53′W
139 R4 **Tall 'Azbah** Nīnawýa, NW Iraq 35°47′N 43°13′E
138 I5 **Tall Bīsah** Ḥimṣ, W Syria 34°50′N 36°44′E
139 R3 **Tall Ḥassūnah** Al Anbār, N Iraq 36°05′N 43°10′E
139 Q2 **Tall Ḥuqnah** *var.* Tell Huqnah. Nīnawá, N Iraq 36°33′N 42°34′E
Tallin *see* Tallinn
118 G3 **Tallinn** *Ger.* Reval, *Rus.* Tallin; *prev.* Revel. ● (Estonia) Harjumaa, NW Estonia 59°26′N 24°42′E
118 H3 **Tallinn** ✈ Harjumaa, NW Estonia 59°23′N 24°52′E
138 H5 **Tall Kalakh** *var.* Tell Kalakh. Ḥimṣ, C Syria 34°40′N 36°18′E
139 R2 **Tall Kayf** Nīnawýa, NW Iraq 36°30′N 43°08′E
Tall Kūchak *see* Tall Kūshik
139 P2 **Tall Kūshik** *var.* Tall Kūchak. Al Ḥasakah, E Syria 36°48′N 42°01′E
31 U12 **Tallmadge** Ohio, N USA 41°06′N 81°26′W
22 J5 **Tallulah** Louisiana, S USA 32°22′N 91°12′W
139 Q2 **Tall 'Uwaynāt** Nīnawýa, NW Iraq 36°43′N 42°18′E
139 Q2 **Tall Ẕāhir** Nīnawá, N Iraq 36°51′N 42°29′E
122 J13 **Tal'menka** Altayskiy Kray, S Russian Federation 53°55′N 83°26′E
122 K8 **Talnakh** Taymyrskiy (Dolgano-Nenetskiy) Avtonomnyy Okrug, N Russian Federation 69°26′N 88°27′E
117 P7 **Tal'ne** *Rus.* Tal'noye. Cherkas'ka Oblast', C Ukraine 48°55′N 30°40′E
Tal'noye *see* Tal'ne
80 E12 **Talodi** Southern Kordofan, C Sudan 10°40′N 30°25′E
188 B16 **Talofofo** SE Guam 13°21′N 144°45′E
188 B16 **Talofofo Bay** *bay* SE Guam
26 L9 **Taloga** Oklahoma, C USA 36°02′N 98°58′W
123 T10 **Talon** Magadanskaya Oblast', E Russian Federation 59°47′N 148°46′E
14 H11 **Talon, Lake** ◎ Ontario, S Canada
149 R2 **Tāloqān** *var.* Taliq-an. Takhār, NE Afghanistan 36°44′N 69°33′E
126 M8 **Talovaya** Voronezhskaya Oblast', W Russian Federation 51°07′N 40°46′E
9 N6 **Taloyoak** *prev.* Spence Bay. Nunavut, N Canada 69°30′N 93°25′W
25 Q8 **Talpa** Texas, SW USA 31°46′N 99°42′W
40 K13 **Talpa de Allende** Jalisco, C Mexico 20°22′N 104°51′W
23 S9 **Talquin, Lake** ▣ Florida, SE USA
Talsen *see* Talsi
Talshand *see* Chandmanī
118 E8 **Talsi** *Ger.* Talsen. Talsi, NW Latvia 57°14′N 22°35′E
143 V11 **Tal Sīāh** Sīstān va Balūchestān, SE Iran 28°19′N 57°43′E
62 G6 **Taltal** Antofagasta, N Chile 25°22′S 70°27′W
8 K10 **Taltson** ≈ Northwest Territories, NW Canada
168 K11 **Taluk** Sumatera, W Indonesia 0°32′S 101°35′E
92 J8 **Talvik** Finnmark, N Norway 70°02′N 22°59′E
182 M7 **Talyawalka Creek** ≈ New South Wales, SE Australia
Talyshskiye Gory *see* Talish Mountains
29 W14 **Tama** Iowa, C USA 41°58′N 92°34′W
Tama Abu, Banjaran *see* Penambo, Banjaran
169 U9 **Tamabo, Banjaran** ▲▲ East Malaysia
190 B16 **Tamakautoga** SW Niue 19°05′S 169°55′W
127 N7 **Tamala** Penzenskaya Oblast', W Russian Federation 52°32′N 43°18′E
77 P15 **Tamale** C Ghana 09°21′N 00°54′W
191 P3 **Tamana** *prev.* Rotcher Island. *atoll* Tungaru, W Kiribati
74 K12 **Tamanrasset** *var.* Tamenghest. S Algeria 22°49′N 05°32′E
74 J13 **Tamanrasset** *wadi* Algeria/Mali
166 M2 **Tamanthi** Sagaing, N Burma (Myanmar) 25°17′N 95°18′E
97 I24 **Tamar** ≈ SW England, United Kingdom
Tamar *see* Tudmur
54 H9 **Támara** Casanare, C Colombia 05°51′N 72°09′W
54 F7 **Tamar, Alto de** ▲ C Colombia 07°25′N 74°28′W
173 X16 **Tamarin** E Mauritius 20°20′S 57°22′E
105 T5 **Tamarite de Litera** *var.* Tararite de Llitera. Aragón, NE Spain 41°52′N 00°25′E
111 I24 **Tamási** Tolna, S Hungary 46°39′N 18°17′E
Tamatave *see* Toamasina
41 O9 **Tamaulipas** ◐ *state* C Mexico
41 P10 **Tamaulipas, Sierra de** ▲▲ C Mexico
56 F12 **Tamaya, Río** ≈ E Peru
40 I9 **Tamazula** Durango, C Mexico 24°43′N 106°33′W
40 L14 **Tamazula** Jalisco, C Mexico 19°41′N 103°18′W
Tamazulápam *see* Tamazulapán
41 Q15 **Tamazulapán** *var.* Tamazulápam. Oaxaca, SE Mexico 17°41′N 97°33′W
41 P12 **Tamazunchale** San Luis Potosí, C Mexico 21°17′N 98°46′W
76 H11 **Tambacounda** SE Senegal 13°44′N 13°43′W
83 M16 **Tambara** Manica, C Mozambique 16°42′S 34°14′E
77 T13 **Tambawel** Sokoto, NW Nigeria 12°24′N 04°42′E
186 M9 **Tambea** Guadalcanal, C Solomon Islands 09°19′S 159°42′E
169 N10 **Tambelan, Kepulauan** *island group* W Indonesia
57 E15 **Tambo de Mora** Ica, W Peru 13°30′S 76°08′W
170 L16 **Tambora, Gunung** Ѫ Sumbawa, S Indonesia 08°16′S 117°59′E
61 E17 **Tambores** Paysandú, W Uruguay 31°50′S 56°17′W
57 F14 **Tambo, Río** ≈ C Peru
56 F7 **Tamboryacu, Río** ≈ N Peru
126 M7 **Tambov** Tambovskaya Oblast', W Russian Federation 52°43′N 41°28′E
126 L6 **Tambovskaya Oblast'** ◐ *province* W Russian Federation
104 H3 **Tambre** ≈ NW Spain
169 V7 **Tambunan** Sabah, East Malaysia 05°40′N 116°22′E
81 C15 **Tambura** Western Equatoria, SW Sudan 05°38′N 27°30′E
Tamchaket *see* Tâmchekkeṭ
76 J9 **Tâmchekkeṭ** *var.* Tamchaket. Hodh el Gharbi, S Mauritania 17°23′N 10°37′W
167 T7 **Tam Điệp** Ninh Binh, N Vietnam 20°09′N 105°54′E
Tamdybulak *see* Tomdibuloq
54 H8 **Tame** Arauca, C Colombia 06°27′N 71°42′W
104 H6 **Tâmega, Rio** *Sp.* Río Támega. ≈ Portugal/Spain
Támega, Río *see* Tâmega, Rio
115 H20 **Tamélos, Akrotírio** *headland* Tziá, Kykládes, Greece, Aegean Sea 37°31′N 24°16′E
Tamenghest *see* Tamanrasset
77 V8 **Tamgak, Adrar** ▲ C Niger 19°10′N 08°39′E
76 I13 **Tamgue** ▲ NW Guinea 12°14′N 12°18′W
41 Q12 **Tamiahua** Veracruz-Llave, E Mexico 21°15′N 97°27′W
41 Q12 **Tamiahua, Laguna de** *lagoon* E Mexico
23 Y16 **Tamiami Canal** *canal* Florida, SE USA
188 F17 **Tamil Harbor** *harbour* Yap, W Micronesia
155 H21 **Tamil Nādu** *prev.* Madras. ◐ *state* SE India
Ta'mīm, Muḩāfaẓat at *see* At Ta'mīn
99 H20 **Tamines** Namur, S Belgium 50°27′N 04°37′E
116 E12 **Tamiš** *Ger.* Temesch, *Hung.* Temes. ≈ Romania/Serbia
167 U10 **Tam Ky** Quang Nam-Đa Năng, C Vietnam 15°32′N 108°30′E
Tammerfors *see* Tampere
Tammisaari *see* Ekenäs
95 N14 **Tämnaren** ◎ C Sweden
191 Q7 **Tamotoe, Passe** *passage* Tahiti, W French Polynesia
23 V12 **Tampa** Florida, SE USA 27°57′N 82°27′W
23 V12 **Tampa** ✈ Florida, SE USA 27°57′N 82°29′W
23 V13 **Tampa Bay** *bay* Florida, SE USA
93 L18 **Tampere** *Swe.* Tammerfors. Länsi-Suomi, W Finland 61°30′N 23°45′E
41 Q11 **Tampico** Tamaulipas, C Mexico 22°18′N 97°52′W
171 P14 **Tampo** Pulau Muna, C Indonesia 04°38′S 122°40′E
167 V11 **Tam Quan** Binh Đinh, C Vietnam 14°34′N 109°00′E
162 J13 **Tamsag Muchang** Nei Mongol Zizhiqu, N China 40°28′N 102°34′E
Tamsal *see* Tamsalu
118 I4 **Tamsalu** *Ger.* Tamsal. Lääne-Virumaa, NE Estonia 59°10′N 26°07′E
109 S8 **Tamsweg** Salzburg, SW Austria 47°08′N 13°49′E
41 P12 **Tamuín** San Luis Potosí, C Mexico 22°00′N 98°44′W
188 C15 **Tamuning** NW Guam 13°29′N 144°47′E
183 T6 **Tamworth** New South Wales, SE Australia 31°07′S 150°54′E
97 M19 **Tamworth** C England, United Kingdom 52°39′N 01°40′W
81 K19 **Tana** ≈ SE Kenya
Tana *see* Deatnu/Tana
164 I15 **Tanabe** Wakayama, Honshū, SW Japan 33°43′N 135°22′E
92 L8 **Tana Bru** Finnmark, N Norway 70°11′N 28°06′E
39 T10 **Tanacross** Alaska, USA 63°30′N 143°21′W
92 L7 **Tanafjorden** *Lapp.* Deanuvuotna. *fjord* N Norway
38 G17 **Tanaga Island** *island* Aleutian Islands, Alaska, USA
38 G17 **Tanaga Volcano** ▲ Tanaga Island, Alaska, USA 51°53′N 178°08′W
107 M18 **Tanagro** ≈ S Italy
80 H11 **T'ana Hāyk'** *var.* Lake Tana. ◎ NW Ethiopia
168 H11 **Tanahbela, Pulau** *island* Kepulauan Batu, W Indonesia
171 H15 **Tanahjampea, Pulau** *island* W Indonesia
168 H11 **Tanahmasa, Pulau** *island* Kepulauan Batu, W Indonesia
Tanais *see* Don
152 L10 **Tanakpur** Uttarakhand, N India 29°04′N 80°06′E
Tana, Lake *see* T'ana Hāyk'
181 P5 **Tanami Desert** *desert* Northern Territory, N Australia
167 T14 **Tân An** Long An, S Vietnam 10°32′N 106°24′E
39 Q9 **Tanana** Alaska, USA 65°12′N 152°00′W
Tananarive *see* Antananarivo
39 Q9 **Tanana River** ≈ Alaska, USA
95 C16 **Tananger** Rogaland, S Norway 58°55′N 05°34′E
188 H5 **Tanapag** Saipan, S Northern Mariana Islands 15°14′S 145°45′E
188 H5 **Tanapag, Puetton** *bay* Saipan, S Northern Mariana Islands
106 C9 **Tanaro** ≈ N Italy
163 Y12 **Tanch'ŏn** E North Korea 40°22′N 128°49′E
40 M14 **Tancitaro, Cerro** Ѫ C Mexico 19°16′N 102°25′W
153 N12 **Tānda** Uttar Pradesh, N India 26°33′N 82°39′E
77 O15 **Tanda** E Ivory Coast 07°48′N 03°10′W
116 L14 **Ţăndărei** Ialomiţa, SE Romania 44°39′N 27°40′E
63 N14 **Tandil** Buenos Aires, E Argentina 37°18′S 59°10′W
78 H12 **Tandjilé** *off.* Préfecture du Tandjilé. ◐ *prefecture* SW Chad
Tandjilé, Préfecture du *see* Tandjilé
Tandjoeng *see* Tanjung
Tandjoengkarang *see* Bandar Lampung
Tandjoengpandan *see* Tanjungpandan
Tandjoengpinang *see* Tanjungpinang
Tandjoengredeb *see* Tanjungredeb
149 Q16 **Tando Allāhyār** Sind, SE Pakistan 25°28′N 68°44′E
149 Q17 **Tando Bāgo** Sind, SE Pakistan 24°48′N 68°59′E
149 Q16 **Tando Muhammad Khān** Sind, SE Pakistan 25°07′N 68°35′E
182 L7 **Tandou Lake** *seasonal lake* New South Wales, SE Australia
94 L11 **Tandsjöborg** Gävleborg, C Sweden 61°40′N 14°40′E
155 H15 **Tāndūr** Andhra Pradesh, C India 17°16′N 77°37′E
164 C17 **Tanega-shima** *island* Nansei-shotō, SW Japan
165 R7 **Taneichi** Iwate, Honshū, C Japan 40°23′N 141°42′E
Tanen Taunggyi *see* Tane Range
167 N8 **Tane Range** *Bur.* Tanen Taunggyi. ▲▲ W Thailand
111 P15 **Tanew** ≈ SE Poland
21 W2 **Taneytown** Maryland, NE USA 39°39′N 77°10′W
74 H12 **Tanezrouft** *desert* Algeria/Mali
138 L7 **Ţanf, Jabal aţ** ▲ SE Syria 33°32′N 38°43′E
81 J21 **Tanga** Tanga, E Tanzania 05°07′S 39°05′E
81 I22 **Tanga** ◐ *region* E Tanzania
153 T14 **Tangail** Dhaka, C Bangladesh 24°15′N 89°55′E
186 I5 **Tanga Islands** *island group* NE Papua New Guinea
155 K26 **Tangalla** Southern Province, S Sri Lanka 06°02′N 80°47′E
Tanganyika and Zanzibar *see* Tanzania
68 J13 **Tanganyika, Lake** ◎ E Africa
56 E7 **Tangarana, Río** ≈ N Peru
191 V16 **Tangaroa, Maunga** Ѫ Easter Island, Chile, E Pacific Ocean
Tangdukou *see* Shaoyang
74 G5 **Tanger** *var.* Tangiers, Tangier, *Fr./Ger.* Tangerk, *Sp.* Tánger; *anc.* Tingis. NW Morocco 35°49′N 05°49′W
169 N15 **Tangerang** Jawa, C Indonesia 06°14′S 106°36′E
Tangerk *see* Tanger
100 M12 **Tangermünde** Sachsen-Anhalt, C Germany 52°35′N 11°57′E
159 O12 **Tanggulashan** *var.* Togton Heyan, Tuotuoheyan. Qinghai, C China 34°13′N 92°25′E
156 K10 **Tanggula Shan** *var.* Dangla, Tangla Range. ▲▲ W China
159 N13 **Tanggula Shan** ▲ W China 33°18′N 91°10′E
156 K10 **Tanggula Shankou** *Tib.* Dang La. *pass* W China
161 N7 **Tanghe** Henan, C China 32°40′N 112°53′E
149 T5 **Tāngi** North-West Frontier Province, NW Pakistan 34°18′N 71°42′E
Tangier *see* Tanger
21 Y5 **Tangier Island** *island* Virginia, NE USA
Tangiers *see* Tanger
22 K8 **Tangipahoa River** ≈ Louisiana, S USA
Tangla Range *see* Tanggula Shan
164 J12 **Tango-hantō** *peninsula* Honshū, SW Japan
156 I10 **Tangra Yumco** *var.* Tangro Tso. ◎ W China
Tangro Tso *see* Tangra Yumco
157 T7 **Tangshan** *var.* T'ang-shan. Hebei, E China 39°39′N 118°15′E
T'ang-shan *see* Tangshan
77 R14 **Tanguiéta** NW Benin 10°35′N 01°19′E
163 X7 **Tangwang He** ≈ NE China
163 X7 **Tangyuan** Heilongjiang, NE China 46°45′N 129°52′E
92 M11 **Tanhua** Lappi, N Finland 67°31′N 27°30′E
159 R15 **Taniantaweng Shan** ▲▲ W China
171 U16 **Tanimbar, Kepulauan** *island group* Maluku, E Indonesia
Tanintharyi *see* Tenasserim
139 U4 **Tānjarō** ≈ E Iraq
129 T15 **Tanjong Piai** *headland* Peninsular Malaysia
Tanjore *see* Thanjāvūr
169 U12 **Tanjung** *prev.* Tandjoeng. Borneo, C Indonesia 02°08′S 115°23′E
169 W9 **Tanjungbatu** Borneo, N Indonesia 02°19′N 118°03′E
Tanjungkarang/Tanjungkarang-Telukbetung *see* Bandar Lampung
169 N13 **Tanjungpandan** *prev.* Tandjoengpandan. Pulau Belitung, W Indonesia 02°44′S 107°36′E
168 M10 **Tanjungpinang** *prev.* Tandjoengpinang. Pulau Bintan, W Indonesia 0°55′N 104°28′E
169 V9 **Tanjungredeb** *var.* Tanjungredep; *prev.* Tandjoengredeb. Borneo, C Indonesia 02°09′N 117°29′E
Tanjungredep *see* Tanjungredeb
149 S8 **Tānk** North-West Frontier Province, NW Pakistan 32°14′N 70°29′E
187 S15 **Tanna** *island* S Vanuatu
93 F17 **Tännäs** Jämtland, C Sweden 62°27′N 12°40′E
Tannenhof *see* Krynica
108 K7 **Tannheim** Tirol, W Austria 47°30′N 10°32′E
Tannu-Tuva *see* Tyva, Respublika
171 Q12 **Tano** Pulau Taliabu, E Indonesia 01°51′S 124°55′E
77 O17 **Tano** ≈ S Ghana
152 D10 **Tanot** Rājasthān, NW India 27°44′N 70°17′E
77 V11 **Tanout** Zinder, C Niger 14°58′N 08°54′E
Tân Phu *see* Đinh Quan
41 P12 **Tanquián** San Luis Potosí, C Mexico 21°38′N 98°39′W
77 R13 **Tansarga** E Burkina 11°51′N 01°51′E
167 T13 **Tan Son Nhat** ✈ (Hô Chi Minh) Tây Ninh, S Vietnam 10°52′N 106°38′E
75 V8 **Ṭanṭā** *var.* Tanta, Tantâ, Tantā. N Egypt 30°42′N 31°00′E
74 D9 **Tan-Tan** SW Morocco 28°30′N 11°11′W
41 P12 **Tantoyuca** Veracruz-Llave, E Mexico 21°21′N 98°12′W
152 J12 **Tāntpur** Uttar Pradesh, N India 26°51′N 77°29′E
Tan-tung *see* Dandong
38 M12 **Tanunak** Alaska, USA 60°35′N 165°15′W
166 L5 **Ta-nyaung** Magway, W Burma (Myanmar) 20°49′N 94°40′E
167 S5 **Tân Yên** Tuyên Quang, N Vietnam 22°08′N 104°58′E
81 F22 **Tanzania** *off.* United Republic of Tanzania, *Swa.* Jamhuri ya Muungano wa Tanzania; *prev.* German East Africa, Tanganyika and Zanzibar. ◆ *republic* E Africa
Tanzania, Jamhuri ya Muungano wa *see* Tanzania
Tanzania, United Republic of *see* Tanzania
Tao'an *see* Taonan
163 T8 **Tao'er He** ≈ NE China
159 U11 **Tao He** ≈ C China
163 U9 **Taonan** *var.* Tao'an. Jilin, NE China 45°20′N 122°46′E
T'aon-an *see* Baicheng
Taongi *see* Bokaak Atoll
107 M23 **Taormina** *anc.* Tauromenium. Sicilia, Italy, C Mediterranean Sea 37°54′N 15°18′E
37 S9 **Taos** New Mexico, SW USA 36°24′N 105°35′W
Taoudenit *see* Taoudenni
77 O6 **Taoudenni** *var.* Taoudenit. Tombouctou, N Mali 22°46′N 03°54′W
74 G6 **Taounate** N Morocco 34°33′N 04°39′N
Taoyang *see* Lintao
161 S13 **T'aoyüan** *Jap.* Tōen. N Taiwan 25°00′N 121°15′E
118 I3 **Tapa** *Ger.* Taps. Lääne-Virumaa, NE Estonia 59°15′N 26°E
41 V17 **Tapachula** Chiapas, SE Mexico 14°53′N 92°18′W
Tapaiu *see* Gvardeysk
59 H14 **Tapajós, Rio** *var.* Tapajóz. ≈ NW Brazil
Tapajóz *see* Tapajós, Rio
61 C21 **Tapalqué** *var.* Tapalquén. Buenos Aires, E Argentina 36°21′S 60°01′W
Tapalquén *see* Tapalqué
Tapanahoni *see* Tapanahony Rivier
55 W11 **Tapanahony Rivier** *var.* Tapanahoni. ≈ E Surinam
41 T16 **Tapanatepec** *var.* San Pedro Tapanatepec. Oaxaca, SE Mexico 16°23′N 94°09′W
185 D23 **Tapanui** Otago, South Island, New Zealand 45°55′S 169°16′E
59 E14 **Tapauá** Amazonas, N Brazil 05°42′S 64°15′W
47 R7 **Tapauá, Rio** ≈ W Brazil
185 I14 **Tapawera** Tasman, South Island, New Zealand 41°24′S 172°50′E
61 I16 **Tapes** Rio Grande do Sul, S Brazil 30°40′S 51°25′W
76 K16 **Tapeta** C Liberia 06°36′N 08°52′W
154 H11 **Tāpi** *prev.* Tāpti. ≈ W India
104 J2 **Tapia de Casariego** Asturias, N Spain 43°34′N 06°56′W
56 F10 **Tapiche, Río** ≈ N Peru
167 N15 **Tapi, Mae Nam** *var.* Luang. ≈ SW Thailand
186 E8 **Tapini** Central, S Papua New Guinea 08°16′S 146°09′E
Tapirapecó, Serra *see* Tapirapecó, Sierra

◆ Country
● Country Capital
◇ Dependent Territory
○ Dependent Territory Capital
◐ Administrative Regions
✈ International Airport
▲ Mountain
▲▲ Mountain Range
Ѫ Volcano
≈ River
◎ Lake
▣ Reservoir

TAPIRAPECÓ, SIERRA – TEHRI

55 N13 **Tapirapecó, Sierra** Port. Serra Tapirapecó. ▲▲ Brazil/Venezuela

77 R13 **Tapoa** ≈ Benin/Niger

188 H5 **Tapochau, Mount** ▲ Saipan, S Northern Mariana Islands

111 H24 **Tapolca** Veszprém, W Hungary 46°54′N 17°29′E

21 X5 **Tappahannock** Virginia, NE USA 37°55′N 76°54′W

31 U13 **Tappan Lake** ⊠ Ohio, N USA

165 Q6 **Tappi-zaki** headland Honshū, C Japan 41°15′N 140°19′E

Tāps see Tapa

Tāpti see Tāpi

Tapuaemanu see Maiao

185 J16 **Tapuaenuku** ▲ South Island, New Zealand 42°00′S 173°39′E

171 N8 **Tapul Group** island group Sulu Archipelago, SW Philippines

58 E11 **Tapurmcuará** var. Tapuruquara. Amazonas, NW Brazil 0°17′S 65°00′W

Tapuruquara see Tapurmcuará

192 J17 **Taputapu, Cape** headland Tutuila, W American Samoa 14°20′S 170°51′W

141 W13 **Ṭāqah** S Oman 17°02′N 54°23′E

139 T3 **Taqtaq** Arbīl, N Iraq 35°54′N 44°36′E

61 J15 **Taquara** Rio Grande do Sul, S Brazil 29°36′S 50°46′W

59 H19 **Taquari, Rio** ≈ C Brazil

60 L8 **Taquaritinga** São Paulo, S Brazil 21°22′S 48°29′W

122 I11 **Tara** Omskaya Oblast', C Russian Federation 56°54′N 74°17′E

83 I16 **Tara** Southern, S Zambia 16°56′S 26°50′E

113 J15 **Tara** ≈ Montenegro

112 K13 **Tara** ▲▲ W Serbia

77 W15 **Taraba** ◐ state E Nigeria

77 X15 **Taraba** ≈ E Nigeria

75 O7 **Tarābulus** var. Ṭarābulus al Gharb, Eng. Tripoli. ● (Libya) NW Libya 32°54′N 13°11′E

75 O7 **Tarābulus** ✈ NW Libya 32°37′N 13°07′E

Ṭarābulus al Gharb see Ṭarābulus

Tarābulus/Ṭarābulus ash Shām see Tripoli

105 O7 **Taracena** Castilla-La Mancha, C Spain 40°39′N 03°08′W

117 N12 **Taraclia** Rus. Tarakilya. S Moldova 45°55′N 28°40′E

139 V10 **Tarād al Kahf** Dhī Qār, SE Iraq 31°58′N 45°58′E

183 R10 **Tarago** New South Wales, SE Australia 35°04′S 149°40′E

162 J8 **Taragt** var. Hüremt. Övörhangay, C Mongolia 46°18′N 102°27′E

169 V8 **Tarakan** Borneo, C Indonesia 03°20′N 117°38′E

169 V9 **Tarakan, Pulau** island N Indonesia

Tarakilya see Taraclia

165 P16 **Tarama-jima** island Sakishima-shotō, SW Japan

184 K10 **Taranaki** off. Taranaki Region. ◐ region North Island, New Zealand

184 K10 **Taranaki, Mount** var. Egmont. ✱ North Island, New Zealand 39°16′S 174°04′E

Taranaki Region see Taranaki

105 O9 **Tarancón** Castilla-La Mancha, C Spain 40°01′N 03°01′W

188 M15 **Tarang Reef** reef C Micronesia

96 E7 **Taransay** island NW Scotland, United Kingdom

107 P18 **Taranto** var. Tarentum. Puglia, SE Italy 40°30′N 17°11′E

107 O19 **Taranto, Golfo di** Eng. Gulf of Taranto. gulf S Italy

Taranto, Gulf of see Taranto, Golfo di

62 G3 **Tarapacá** off. Región de Tarapacá. ◐ region N Chile

Tarapacá, Región de see Tarapacá

187 N9 **Tarapaina** Maramasike Island, N Solomon Islands 09°28′S 161°24′E

56 D10 **Tarapoto** San Martín, N Peru 06°31′S 76°23′W

138 M6 **Ṭaraq an Naʻjah** hill range E Syria

138 M6 **Ṭaraq Sidāwī** hill range E Syria

103 Q11 **Tarare** Rhône, E France 45°54′N 04°26′E

Tararite de Llitera see Tamarite de Litera

184 M13 **Tararua Range** ▲▲ North Island, New Zealand

151 Q22 **Tarāsa Dwīp** island Nicobar Islands, India, NE Indian Ocean

103 Q15 **Tarascon** Bouches-du-Rhône, SE France 43°48′N 04°39′E

102 M17 **Tarascon-sur-Ariège** Ariège, S France 42°51′N 01°35′E

117 P6 **Tarashcha** Kyyivs'ka Oblast', N Ukraine 49°34′N 30°31′E

57 L18 **Tarata** Cochabamba, C Bolivia 17°35′S 66°04′W

57 I18 **Tarata** Tacna, SW Peru 17°30′S 70°00′W

190 H2 **Taratai** atoll Tungaru, W Kiribati

59 B15 **Tarauacá** Acre, W Brazil 08°06′S 70°45′W

59 B15 **Tarauacá, Rio** ≈ NW Brazil

191 Q8 **Taravao** Tahiti, W French Polynesia 17°44′S 149°19′W

191 R8 **Taravao, Baie de** bay Tahiti, W French Polynesia

191 Q8 **Taravao, Isthme de** isthmus Tahiti, W French Polynesia

103 X16 **Taravo** ≈ Corse, France, C Mediterranean Sea

190 J3 **Tarawa** ✈ Tarawa, W Kiribati 0°53′S 169°32′E

190 H2 **Tarawa** atoll Tungaru, W Kiribati

184 N10 **Tarawera** Hawke's Bay, North Island, New Zealand 39°03′S 176°34′E

184 N8 **Tarawera, Lake** ◎ North Island, New Zealand

184 N8 **Tarawera, Mount** ▲ North Island, New Zealand 38°13′S 176°29′E

105 S8 **Tarayuela** ▲ N Spain 40°28′N 00°22′W

145 R16 **Taraz** prev. Aulie Ata, Auliye-Ata, Dzhambul, Zhambyl. Zhambyl, S Kazakhstan 42°55′N 71°27′E

105 Q5 **Tarazona** Aragón, NE Spain 41°54′N 01°44′W

105 Q10 **Tarazona de la Mancha** Castilla-La Mancha, C Spain 39°16′N 01°55′W

145 X12 **Tarbagatay, Khrebet** ▲▲ China/Kazakhstan

96 J8 **Tarbat Ness** headland N Scotland, United Kingdom 57°51′N 03°48′W

149 U5 **Tarbela Reservoir** ⊠ N Pakistan

96 H12 **Tarbert** W Scotland, United Kingdom 55°52′N 05°26′W

96 F7 **Tarbert** NW Scotland, United Kingdom 57°54′N 06°48′W

102 K16 **Tarbes** anc. Bigorra. Hautes-Pyrénées, S France 43°14′N 00°04′E

21 W9 **Tarboro** North Carolina, SE USA 35°54′N 77°34′W

Tarca see Torysa

106 J6 **Tarcento** Friuli-Venezia Giulia, NE Italy 46°13′N 13°13′E

182 F5 **Tarcoola** South Australia 30°44′S 134°34′E

105 S5 **Tardienta** Aragón, NE Spain 41°58′N 00°31′W

102 L11 **Tardoire** ≈ W France

183 U7 **Taree** New South Wales, SE Australia 31°56′S 152°29′E

92 K12 **Tärendö** Lapp. Deargget. Norrbotten, N Sweden 67°10′N 22°40′E

Tarentum see Taranto

74 C9 **Tarfaya** SW Morocco 27°56′N 12°55′W

116 J13 **Târgoviște** prev. Tîrgoviște. Dâmbovița, S Romania 44°54′N 25°29′E

Târgoviște see Türgovishte

116 M12 **Târgu Bujor** prev. Tîrgu Bujor. Galați, E Romania 45°52′N 27°55′E

116 H13 **Târgu Cărbunești** prev. Tîrgu. Gorj, SW Romania 44°57′N 23°32′E

116 L9 **Târgu Frumos** prev. Tîrgu Frumos. Iași, NE Romania 47°12′N 27°00′E

116 H13 **Târgu Jiu** prev. Tîrgu Jiu. Gorj, W Romania 45°03′N 23°20′E

116 H9 **Târgu Lăpuș** prev. Tîrgu Lăpuș. Maramureș, N Romania 47°28′N 23°54′E

Târgul-Neamț see Târgu-Neamț

Târgul-Săcuiesc see Târgu Secuiesc

116 I10 **Târgu Mureș** prev. Oșorhei, Tîrgu Mures, Ger. Neumarkt, Hung. Marosvásárhely. Mureș, C Romania 46°33′N 24°36′E

116 K9 **Târgu-Neamț** var. Târgul-Neamț; prev. Tîrgu-Neamț. Neamț, NE Romania 47°12′N 26°25′E

116 K11 **Târgu Ocna** Hung. Aknavásár; prev. Tîrgu Ocna. Bacău, E Romania 46°17′N 26°37′E

116 K11 **Târgu Secuiesc** Ger. Neumarkt, Szekler Neumarkt, Hung. Kezdivásárhely; prev. Chezdi-Oșorheiu, Târgul-Săcuiesc, Tîrgu Secuiesc. Covasna, E Romania 46°00′N 26°08′E

145 X10 **Targyn** Vostochnyy Kazakhstan, E Kazakhstan 49°32′N 82°47′E

Tar Heel State see North Carolina

186 C7 **Tari** Southern Highlands, W Papua New Guinea 05°52′S 142°58′E

162 J6 **Tarialan** var. Badrah. Hövsgöl, N Mongolia 49°33′N 101°58′E

162 I7 **Tariat** var. Horgo. Arhangay, C Mongolia 48°06′N 99°52′E

143 P17 **Ṭarīf** Abū Ẓaby, C United Arab Emirates 24°02′N 53°47′E

104 K16 **Tarifa** Andalucía, S Spain 36°01′N 05°36′W

84 C14 **Tarifa, Punta de** headland SW Spain 36°01′N 05°39′W

57 M21 **Tarija** Tarija, S Bolivia 21°33′S 64°42′W

57 M21 **Tarija** ◐ department S Bolivia

141 R14 **Tarīm** C Yemen 16°N 48°50′E

Tarim Basin see Tarim Pendi

81 G19 **Tarime** Mara, N Tanzania 01°20′S 34°24′E

129 S8 **Tarim He** ≈ NW China

159 H8 **Tarim Pendi** Eng. Tarim Basin. basin NW China

149 N7 **Tarīn Kowt** var. Terinkot. Orūzgān, C Afghanistan 32°38′N 65°52′E

171 O12 **Taripa** Sulawesi, C Indonesia 01°51′S 120°46′E

117 Q12 **Tarkhankut, Mys** headland S Ukraine 45°20′N 32°32′E

27 Q1 **Tarkio** Missouri, C USA 40°25′N 95°24′W

122 J9 **Tarko-Sale** Yamalo-Nenetskiy Avtonomnyy Okrug, N Russian Federation 64°55′N 77°34′E

77 P17 **Tarkwa** S Ghana 05°16′N 01°59′W

171 O3 **Tarlac** Luzon, N Philippines 15°29′N 120°34′E

95 F22 **Tarm** Ringkøbing, W Denmark 55°55′N 08°32′E

57 E14 **Tarma** Junín, C Peru 11°28′S 75°41′W

103 N15 **Tarn** ◐ department S France

102 M15 **Tarn** ≈ S France

111 L22 **Tarna** ≈ C Hungary

92 G13 **Tärnaby** Västerbotten, N Sweden 65°44′N 15°20′E

149 P8 **Tarnak Rūd** ≈ SE Afghanistan

116 J11 **Târnava Mare** Ger. Grosse Kokel, Hung. Nagy-Küküllő; prev. Tîrnava Mare. ≈ S Romania

116 I11 **Târnava Mică** Ger. Kleine Kokel, Hung. Kis-Küküllő; prev. Tîrnava Mică. ≈ C Romania

116 I11 **Târnăveni** Ger. Marteskirch, Martinskirch, Hung. Dicsőszentmárton; prev. Sînmartin, Tîrnăveni. Mureș, C Romania 46°20′N 24°17′E

102 L14 **Tarn-et-Garonne** ◐ department S France

111 P18 **Tarnica** ▲ SE Poland 49°05′N 22°43′E

111 N15 **Tarnobrzeg** Podkarpackie, SE Poland 50°35′N 21°40′E

125 N12 **Tarnogskiy Gorodok** Vologodskaya Oblast', NW Russian Federation 60°28′N 43°45′E

Tarnopol see Ternopil'

111 M16 **Tarnów** Małopolskie, S Poland 50°01′N 20°59′E

Tarnowice/Tarnowitz see Tarnowskie Góry

111 J16 **Tarnowskie Góry** var. Tarnowice, Tarnowskie Gory, Ger. Tarnowitz. Śląskie, S Poland 50°27′N 18°52′E

95 N14 **Tärnsjö** Västmanland, C Sweden 60°10′N 16°57′E

106 E9 **Taro** ≈ NW Italy

186 I6 **Taron** New Ireland, NE Papua New Guinea 04°22′S 153°04′E

74 E8 **Taroudannt** var. Taroudant. SW Morocco 30°31′N 08°50′W

Taroudant see Taroudannt

23 V12 **Tarpon, Lake** ◎ Florida, SE USA

23 V12 **Tarpon Springs** Florida, SE USA 28°09′N 82°45′W

107 G14 **Tarquinia** anc. Tarquinii, hist. Corneto. Lazio, C Italy 42°23′N 11°45′E

Tarquinii see Tarquinia

Tarraco see Tarragona

76 D10 **Tarrafal** Santiago, S Cape Verde 15°16′N 23°45′W

105 V6 **Tarragona** anc. Tarraco. Cataluña, E Spain 41°07′N 01°15′E

105 T7 **Tarragona** ◐ province Cataluña, NE Spain

183 O17 **Tarraleah** Tasmania, SE Australia 42°11′S 146°29′E

23 P3 **Tarrant City** Alabama, S USA 33°34′N 86°45′W

185 D21 **Tarras** Otago, South Island, New Zealand 44°48′S 169°25′E

Tarrasa see Terrassa

105 U5 **Tàrrega** var. Tarrega. Cataluña, NE Spain 41°39′N 01°09′E

21 W9 **Tar River** ≈ North Carolina, SE USA

Tarrong see Nyêmo

Tarsatica see Rijeka

136 J17 **Tarsus** İçel, S Turkey 36°52′N 34°52′E

62 K4 **Tartagal** Salta, N Argentina 22°32′S 63°50′W

137 V12 **Tärtär** Rus. Terter. ≈ SW Azerbaijan

102 J15 **Tartas** Landes, SW France 43°52′N 00°45′W

Tartlau see Prejmer

Tartous/Tartouss see Ṭarṭūs

118 J5 **Tartu** Ger. Dorpat; prev. Rus. Yurev, Yury'ev. Tartumaa, SE Estonia 58°20′N 26°44′E

118 I5 **Tartumaa** off. Tartu Maakond. ◐ province E Estonia

Tartu Maakond see Tartumaa

138 H5 **Ṭarṭūs** Fr. Tartouss; anc. Tortosa. Ṭarṭūs, W Syria 34°55′N 35°52′E

138 H5 **Ṭarṭūs** off. Muḥāfaẓat Ṭarṭūs, var. Tartous, Tartus. ◐ governorate W Syria

Ṭarṭūs, Muḥāfaẓat see Ṭarṭūs

164 C16 **Tarumizu** Kagoshima, Kyūshū, SW Japan 31°30′N 130°40′E

126 K4 **Tarusa** Kaluzhskaya Oblast', W Russian Federation 54°45′N 37°10′E

117 N11 **Tarutyne** Odes'ka Oblast', SW Ukraine 46°11′N 29°09′E

162 I7 **Tarvagatyn Nuruu** ▲▲ N Mongolia

106 J6 **Tarvisio** Friuli-Venezia Giulia, NE Italy 46°31′N 13°33′E

Tarvisium see Treviso

57 O16 **Tarvo, Río** ≈ E Bolivia

14 G8 **Tarzwell** Ontario, S Canada 48°00′N 79°58′W

40 K5 **Tasajera, Sierra de la** ▲▲ N Mexico

145 S13 **Tasaral** Karaganda, C Kazakhstan 46°17′N 73°54′E

Tasböget see Tasbuget

145 N15 **Tasbuget** Kaz. Tasböget. Kzylorda, S Kazakhstan 44°46′N 65°38′E

108 E11 **Tasch** Valais, SW Switzerland 46°04′N 07°43′E

Tasek Kenyir see Kenyir, Tasik

122 J14 **Tashanta** Respublika Altay, S Russian Federation 49°42′N 89°15′E

Tashauz see Daşoguz

Tashi Chho Dzong see Thimphu

153 U11 **Tashigang** E Bhutan 27°19′N 91°33′E

137 T11 **Tashir** prev. Kalinino. N Armenia 41°07′N 44°16′E

143 Q11 **Ṭashk, Daryācheh-ye** ◎ C Iran

Tashkent see Toshkent

Tashkentskaya Oblast' see Toshkent Viloyati

Tashkepri see Daşköpri

Tash-Kömür see Tash-Kumyr

147 S9 **Tash-Kumyr** Kir. Tash-Kömür. Dzhalal-Abadskaya Oblast', W Kyrgyzstan 41°22′N 72°09′E

127 T7 **Tashla** Orenburgskaya Oblast', W Russian Federation 51°42′N 52°33′E

Tashqurghan see Kholm

122 J13 **Tashtagol** Kemerovskaya Oblast', S Russian Federation 52°49′N 88°00′E

95 H24 **Tåsinge** island C Denmark

12 M5 **Tasiujaq** Québec, E Canada 58°43′N 69°58′W

77 W11 **Tasker** Zinder, C Niger 15°06′N 10°42′E

145 W12 **Taskesken** Vostochnyy Kazakhstan, E Kazakhstan 47°15′N 80°45′E

136 J10 **Taşköprü** Kastamonu, N Turkey 41°30′N 34°12′E

Taskuduk, Peski see Tosquduq Qumlari

186 G5 **Taskul** New Ireland, NE Papua New Guinea 02°34′S 150°25′E

137 S13 **Taşlıçay** Ağrı, E Turkey 39°37′N 43°23′E

185 H14 **Tasman** off. Tasman District. ◐ unitary authority South Island, New Zealand

192 J12 **Tasman Basin** var. East Australian Basin. undersea feature S Tasman Sea

185 I14 **Tasman Bay** inlet South Island, New Zealand

Tasman District see Tasman

192 I13 **Tasman Fracture Zone** tectonic feature S Indian Ocean

185 E19 **Tasman Glacier** glacier South Island, New Zealand

Tasman Group see Nukumanu Islands

183 N15 **Tasmania** prev. Van Diemen's Land. ◐ state SE Australia

183 Q16 **Tasmania** island SE Australia

185 H14 **Tasman Mountains** ▲▲ South Island, New Zealand

183 P17 **Tasman Peninsula** peninsula Tasmania, SE Australia

192 I11 **Tasman Plain** undersea feature W Tasman Sea

192 I12 **Tasman Plateau** var. South Tasmania Plateau. undersea feature SW Tasman Sea

192 I11 **Tasman Sea** sea SW Pacific Ocean

116 G9 **Tășnad** Ger. Trestenberg, Trestendorf, Hung. Tasnád. Satu Mare, NW Romania 47°30′N 22°33′E

136 L11 **Taşova** Amasya, N Turkey 40°45′N 36°20′E

77 T10 **Tassara** Tahoua, W Niger 16°40′N 05°34′E

12 K4 **Tassialouc, Lac** ◎ Québec, C Canada

Tassili du Hoggar see Tassili ta-n-Ahaggar

74 L11 **Tassili-n-Ajjer** plateau E Algeria

74 K14 **Tassili ta-n-Ahaggar** var. Tassili du Hoggar. plateau S Algeria

59 M15 **Tasso Fragoso** Maranhão, E Brazil 08°22′S 45°53′W

Tåstrup see Taastrup

145 O9 **Tasty-Taldy** Akmola, C Kazakhstan 50°47′N 66°31′E

143 W10 **Tāsūkī** Sīstān va Balūchestān, SE Iran

111 I22 **Tata** Ger. Totis. Komárom-Esztergom, NW Hungary 47°39′N 18°19′E

74 E8 **Tata** SW Morocco 29°38′N 08°04′W

Tataaihoa, Pointe see Vénus, Pointe

111 I22 **Tatabánya** Komárom-Esztergom, NW Hungary 47°33′N 18°23′E

191 X10 **Tatakoto** atoll Îles Tuamotu, E French Polynesia

75 N7 **Tataouine** var. Taṭāwīn. SE Tunisia 32°48′N 10°27′E

55 O5 **Tataracual, Cerro** ▲ NE Venezuela 10°13′N 64°20′W

117 O12 **Tatarbunary** Odes'ka Oblast', SW Ukraine 45°50′N 29°37′E

119 M17 **Tatarka** Mahilyowskaya Voblasts', E Belarus 53°15′N 28°50′E

Tatar Pazardzhik see Pazardzhik

122 I12 **Tatarsk** Novosibirskaya Oblast', C Russian Federation 55°08′N 75°58′E

Tatarskaya ASSR see Tatarstan, Respublika

123 T13 **Tatarskiy Proliv** Eng. Tatar Strait. strait SE Russian Federation

127 R4 **Tatarstan, Respublika** prev. Tatarskaya ASSR. ◐ autonomous republic W Russian Federation

Tatar Strait see Tatarskiy Proliv

Taṭāwīn see Tataouine

171 N12 **Tate** Sulawesi, N Indonesia 0°12′S 119°44′E

141 N11 **Tathlīth** 'Asīr, S Saudi Arabia 19°38′N 43°32′E

141 O11 **Tathlīth, Wādī** dry watercourse S Saudi Arabia

183 R11 **Tathra** New South Wales, SE Australia 36°46′S 149°58′E

127 P8 **Tatishchevo** Saratovskaya Oblast', W Russian Federation 51°43′N 45°35′E

39 S12 **Tatitlek** Alaska, USA 60°49′N 146°29′W

10 L15 **Tatla Lake** British Columbia, SW Canada 51°54′N 124°39′W

121 Q2 **Tatlısu** Gk. Akanthoú. N Cyprus 35°21′N 33°45′E

11 Z10 **Tatnam, Cape** headland Manitoba, C Canada 57°16′N 91°03′W

111 K18 **Tatra Mountains** Ger. Tatra, Hung. Tátra, Pol./Slvk. Tatry. ▲▲ Poland/Slovakia

Tatra/Tátra see Tatra Mountains

Tatry see Tatra Mountains

164 I13 **Tatsuno** var. Tatuno. Hyōgo, Honshū, SW Japan 34°54′N 134°30′E

145 S16 **Tatti** var. Tatty. Zhambyl, S Kazakhstan 43°11′N 73°22′E

Tatty see Tatti

60 L10 **Tatuí** São Paulo, S Brazil 23°21′S 47°49′W

37 V14 **Tatum** New Mexico, SW USA 33°15′N 103°19′W

25 X7 **Tatum** Texas, SW USA 32°19′N 94°31′W

Ta-t'ung/Tatung see Datong

Tatuno see Tatsuno

137 R14 **Tatvan** Bitlis, SE Turkey 38°31′N 42°15′E

95 C16 **Tau** Rogaland, S Norway 59°04′N 05°55′E

192 L17 **Ta'ū** var. Tau. island Manua Islands, E American Samoa

193 W15 **Tau** island Tongatapu Group, N Tonga

59 O14 **Tauá** Ceará, E Brazil 06°04′S 40°26′W

60 N10 **Taubaté** São Paulo, S Brazil 23°S 45°36′W

101 I19 **Tauber** ≈ SW Germany

101 I19 **Tauberbischofsheim** Baden-Württemberg, C Germany 49°37′N 09°39′E

144 E14 **Tauchik** Kaz. Taūshyq. Mangistau, SW Kazakhstan 44°17′N 51°22′E

191 W10 **Tauere** atoll Îles Tuamotu, C French Polynesia

101 H17 **Taufstein** ▲ C Germany 50°31′N 09°18′E

190 I17 **Taukoka** island SE Cook Islands

145 T15 **Taukum, Peski** desert SE Kazakhstan

184 L10 **Taumarunui** Manawatu-Wanganui, North Island, New Zealand 38°52′S 175°14′E

59 A15 **Taumaturgo** Acre, W Brazil 08°54′S 72°48′W

27 X6 **Taum Sauk Mountain** ▲ Missouri, C USA 37°34′N 90°43′W

83 H22 **Taung** North-West, N South Africa 27°32′S 24°48′E

166 L6 **Taungdwingyi** Magway, C Burma (Myanmar) 20°01′N 95°20′E

166 M6 **Taunggyi** Shan State, C Burma (Myanmar) 20°47′N 97°00′E

166 M7 **Taungoo** Bago, C Burma (Myanmar) 18°57′N 96°26′E

166 L5 **Taungtha** Mandalay, C Burma (Myanmar) 21°16′N 95°25′E

166 K7 **Taungup** Rakhine State, W Burma (Myanmar) 18°50′N 94°14′E

149 S9 **Taunsa** Punjab, E Pakistan 30°43′N 70°41′E

97 K23 **Taunton** SW England, United Kingdom 51°01′N 03°06′W

19 O12 **Taunton** Massachusetts, NE USA 41°54′N 71°03′W

101 F18 **Taunus** ▲▲ W Germany

101 G18 **Taunusstein** Hessen, W Germany 50°09′N 08°09′E

184 N9 **Taupo** Waikato, North Island, New Zealand 38°42′S 176°05′E

184 M9 **Taupo, Lake** ◎ North Island, New Zealand

109 R8 **Taurach** var. Taurachbach. ≈ E Austria

Taurachbach see Taurach

118 D12 **Tauragė** Ger. Tauroggen. Tauragė, SW Lithuania 55°16′N 22°17′E

118 D13 **Tauragė** ◐ province Lithuania

54 G10 **Tauramena** Casanare, C Colombia 05°02′N 72°43′W

184 N7 **Tauranga** Bay of Plenty, North Island, New Zealand 37°42′S 176°09′E

15 O10 **Taureau, Réservoir** ⊠ Québec, SE Canada

107 N22 **Taurianova** Calabria, SW Italy 38°22′N 16°01′E

Tauris see Tabrīz

184 I2 **Tauroa Point** headland North Island, New Zealand 35°09′S 173°02′E

Tauroggen see Tauragė

Tauromenium see Taormina

Taurus Mountains see Toros Dağları

Taus see Domažlice

Taūshyq see Tauchik

105 R5 **Tauste** Aragón, NE Spain 41°55′N 01°15′W

191 V16 **Tautara, Motu** island Easter Island, Chile, E Pacific Ocean

191 R8 **Tautira** Tahiti, W French Polynesia 17°45′S 149°10′W

Tauz see Tovuz

Ṭavālesh, Kūhhā-ye see Talish Mountains

136 D15 **Tavas** Denizli, SW Turkey 37°33′N 29°04′E

Tavastehus see Hämeenlinna

Tavau see Davos

122 G10 **Tavda** Sverdlovskaya Oblast', C Russian Federation 58°01′N 65°07′E

122 G10 **Tavda** ≈ C Russian Federation

105 T11 **Tavernes de la Valldigna** País Valenciano, E Spain 39°03′N 00°13′W

81 I20 **Taveta** Coast, S Kenya 03°23′S 37°40′E

187 Y14 **Taveuni** island N Fiji

147 R13 **Tavildara** Rus. Tavil'dara, Tovil'-Dora. C Tajikistan 38°42′N 70°27′E

Tavin see Adaatsag

104 H14 **Tavira** Faro, S Portugal 37°07′N 07°39′W

97 I24 **Tavistock** SW England, United Kingdom 50°33′N 04°08′W

Tavoy see Dawei

Tavoy Island see Mali Kyun

115 E16 **Tavropoú, Technítí Límni** ⊠ C Greece

136 E13 **Tavşanlı** Kütahya, NW Turkey 39°34′N 29°28′E

187 X14 **Tavua** Viti Levu, W Fiji 17°27′S 177°51′E

97 J23 **Taw** ≈ SW England, United Kingdom

185 L14 **Tawa** Wellington, North Island, New Zealand 41°10′S 174°50′E

25 V6 **Tawakoni, Lake** ⊠ Texas, SW USA

153 V11 **Tawang** Arunāchal Pradesh, NE India 27°34′N 91°54′E

169 R17 **Tawang, Teluk** bay Jawa, S Indonesia

31 R7 **Tawas Bay** ◎ Michigan, N USA

31 R7 **Tawas City** Michigan, N USA 44°16′N 83°33′W

169 V8 **Tawau** Sabah, East Malaysia 04°16′N 117°54′E

141 U10 **Ṭawīl, Qalamat aṭ** well SE Saudi Arabia

171 N9 **Tawitawi** island Tawitawi Group, SW Philippines

Ṭawkar see Tokar

Tawūq see Dāqūq

Tawzar see Tozeur

41 O15 **Taxco** var. Taxco de Alarcón. Guerrero, S Mexico 18°32′N 99°37′W

Taxco de Alarcón see Taxco

146 H8 **Taxiatosh** Rus. Takhiatash. Qoraqalpog'iston Respublikasi, W Uzbekistan 42°27′N 59°27′E

158 D9 **Taxkorgan** var. Taxkorgan Tajik Zizhixian. Xinjiang Uygur Zizhiqu, NW China 37°43′N 75°13′E

Taxkorgan Tajik Zizhixian see Taxkorgan

146 H7 **Taxtako'pir** Rus. Takhtakupyr. Qoraqalpog'iston Respublikasi, NW Uzbekistan 43°04′N 60°23′E

96 J10 **Tay** ≈ C Scotland, United Kingdom

143 V6 **Tāybād** var. Taibad, Tāyybād, Tayyebāt. Khorāsān-Razavī, NE Iran 34°48′N 60°46′E

Taybert at Turkz see Ṭayyibat at Turkī

124 J3 **Taybola** Murmanskaya Oblast', NW Russian Federation 68°30′N 33°18′E

81 M16 **Tayeeglow** Bakool, C Somalia 04°01′N 44°25′E

96 K11 **Tay, Firth of** inlet E Scotland, United Kingdom

122 J12 **Tayga** Kemerovskaya Oblast', S Russian Federation 56°02′N 85°26′E

Taygan see Delger

123 T9 **Taygonos, Mys** headland E Russian Federation 60°36′N 160°09′E

96 I11 **Tay, Loch** ◎ C Scotland, United Kingdom

11 N12 **Taylor** British Columbia, W Canada 56°09′N 120°43′W

29 O14 **Taylor** Nebraska, C USA 41°47′N 99°23′W

18 I13 **Taylor** Pennsylvania, NE USA 41°22′N 75°41′W

25 T10 **Taylor** Texas, SW USA 30°34′N 97°24′W

37 Q11 **Taylor, Mount** ▲ New Mexico, SW USA 35°14′N 107°36′W

37 R5 **Taylor Park Reservoir** ⊠ Colorado, C USA

37 R6 **Taylor River** ≈ Colorado, C USA

21 P11 **Taylors** South Carolina, SE USA 34°55′N 82°18′W

20 L5 **Taylorsville** Kentucky, S USA 38°01′N 85°21′W

21 R6 **Taylorsville** North Carolina, SE USA 35°56′N 81°10′W

30 L14 **Taylorville** Illinois, N USA 39°33′N 89°17′W

140 K5 **Taymā'** Tabūk, NW Saudi Arabia 27°39′N 38°32′E

122 M10 **Taymura** ≈ C Russian Federation

123 O7 **Taymylyr** Respublika Sakha (Yakutiya), NE Russian Federation 72°32′N 121°54′E

122 L7 **Taymyr, Ozero** ◎ N Russian Federation

122 M6 **Taymyr, Poluostrov** peninsula N Russian Federation

122 L8 **Taymyrskiy (Dolgano-Nenetskiy) Avtonomnyy Okrug** ◐ autonomous district Krasnoyarskiy Kray, N Russian Federation

167 S13 **Tây Ninh** Tây Ninh, S Vietnam 11°21′N 106°07′E

122 L12 **Tayshet** Irkutskaya Oblast', S Russian Federation 55°51′N 98°04′E

162 G8 **Tayshir** var. Tsagaan-Olom. Govĭ-Altay, C Mongolia 46°42′N 96°30′E

171 N5 **Taytay** Palawan, W Philippines 10°49′N 119°30′E

169 Q16 **Tayu** prev. Tajoe. Jawa, C Indonesia 06°32′S 111°02′E

Tāyybād/Tayyebāt see Tāybād

138 L5 **Ṭayyibah** var. At Taybé. Ḥimṣ, C Syria 35°13′N 38°51′E

138 I4 **Ṭayyibat at Turkī** var. Taybert at Turkz. Ḥamāh, W Syria 35°16′N 36°55′E

145 P7 **Tayynsha** prev. Krasnoarmeysk. Severnyy Kazakhstan, N Kazakhstan 53°52′N 69°51′E

122 I10 **Taz** ≈ N Russian Federation

74 G6 **Taza** NE Morocco 34°13′N 04°06′W

139 T4 **Tāza Khurmātū** At Ta'mīn, E Iraq 35°18′N 44°22′E

165 Q8 **Tazawa-ko** ◎ Honshū, C Japan

21 N8 **Tazewell** Tennessee, S USA 36°27′N 83°34′W

21 Q7 **Tazewell** Virginia, NE USA 37°08′N 81°34′W

75 S11 **Tāzirbū** SE Libya 25°43′N 21°16′E

39 S11 **Tazlina Lake** ◎ Alaska, USA

122 J8 **Tazovskiy** Yamalo-Nenetskiy Avtonomnyy Okrug, N Russian Federation 67°33′N 78°21′E

137 U10 **T'bilisi** Eng. Tiflis. ● (Georgia) SE Georgia 41°41′N 44°55′E

137 T10 **T'bilisi** ✈ S Georgia 41°43′N 44°49′E

79 E14 **Tchabal Mbabo** ▲ NW Cameroon 07°12′N 12°16′E

Tchad see Chad

Tchad, Lac see Chad, Lake

77 S15 **Tchaourou** E Benin 08°58′N 02°40′E

79 E20 **Tchibanga** Nyanga, S Gabon 02°49′S 11°00′E

Tchien see Zwedru

77 Z6 **Tchigaï, Plateau du** ▲ NE Niger

77 V9 **Tchighozérine** Agadez, C Niger 17°15′N 07°48′E

77 T10 **Tchin-Tabaradene** Tahoua, W Niger 15°57′N 05°49′E

78 G13 **Tcholliré** Nord, NE Cameroon 08°48′N 14°00′E

Tchongking see Chongqing

22 K4 **Tchula** Mississippi, S USA 33°10′N 90°13′W

110 I7 **Tczew** Ger. Dirschau. Pomorskie, N Poland 54°05′N 18°46′E

116 I10 **Teaca** Ger. Tekendorf, Hung. Teke; prev. Ger. Teckendorf. Bistrița-Năsăud, N Romania 46°55′N 24°30′E

40 J11 **Teacapán** Sinaloa, C Mexico 22°33′N 105°44′W

190 A10 **Teafuafou** island Funafuti Atoll, C Tuvalu

25 U8 **Teague** Texas, SW USA 31°37′N 96°16′W

191 R9 **Teahupoo** Tahiti, W French Polynesia 17°51′S 149°15′W

190 H15 **Te Aiti Point** headland Rarotonga, S Cook Islands 21°11′S 59°47′W

185 B22 **Te Anau** Southland, South Island, New Zealand 45°25′S 167°45′E

185 B22 **Te Anau, Lake** ◎ South Island, New Zealand

41 U15 **Teapa** Tabasco, SE Mexico 17°36′N 92°57′W

184 Q7 **Te Araroa** Gisborne, North Island, New Zealand 37°37′S 178°21′E

184 M7 **Te Aroha** Waikato, North Island, New Zealand 37°32′S 175°58′E

Teate see Chieti

190 A9 **Te Ava Fuagea** channel Funafuti Atoll, SE Tuvalu

190 B8 **Te Ava I Te Lape** channel Funafuti Atoll, SE Tuvalu

190 B9 **Te Ava Pua Pua** channel Funafuti Atoll, SE Tuvalu

184 M8 **Te Awamutu** Waikato, North Island, New Zealand 38°00′S 177°18′E

171 X12 **Teba** Papua, E Indonesia 01°27′S 137°54′E

104 L15 **Teba** Andalucía, S Spain 36°59′N 04°54′W

126 M15 **Teberda** Karachayevo-Cherkesskaya Respublika, SW Russian Federation 43°28′N 41°45′E

74 M6 **Tébessa** NE Algeria 35°21′N 08°06′E

62 O7 **Tebicuary, Río** ≈ S Paraguay

168 I8 **Tebingtinggi** Sumatera, N Indonesia 03°20′N 99°08′E

168 L13 **Tebingtinggi** Sumatera, W Indonesia 03°33′S 103°00′E

Tebingtinggi, Pulau see Rantau, Pulau

Tebriz see Tabrīz

137 U9 **Tebulosmta** Rus. Gora Tebulosmta. ▲ Georgia/Russian Federation 42°33′N 45°21′E

Tebulosmta, Gora see Tebulosmta

41 Q14 **Tecamachalco** Puebla, S Mexico 18°52′N 97°44′W

40 B1 **Tecate** Baja California Norte, NW Mexico 32°33′N 116°38′W

136 M13 **Tecer Dağları** ▲▲ C Turkey

103 O17 **Tech** ≈ S France

77 P16 **Techiman** W Ghana 07°35′N 01°56′W

117 N15 **Techirghiol** Constanța, SE Romania 44°03′N 28°37′E

74 A12 **Techla** var. Techlé. SW Western Sahara 21°39′N 14°57′W

Techlé see Techla

63 H18 **Tecka, Sierra de** ▲▲ SW Argentina

Teckendorf see Teaca

40 K13 **Tecolotlán** Jalisco, SW Mexico 20°10′N 104°07′W

40 K14 **Tecomán** Colima, SW Mexico 18°53′N 103°54′W

35 V12 **Tecopa** California, W USA 35°51′N 116°14′W

40 G5 **Tecoripa** Sonora, NW Mexico 28°38′N 109°58′W

41 N16 **Tecpan** var. Tecpan de Galeana. Guerrero, S Mexico 17°12′N 100°39′W

Tecpan de Galeana see Tecpan

40 J11 **Tecuala** Nayarit, C Mexico 22°24′N 105°30′W

116 L12 **Tecuci** Galați, E Romania 45°50′N 27°27′E

31 R10 **Tecumseh** Michigan, N USA 42°00′N 83°57′W

29 S16 **Tecumseh** Nebraska, C USA 40°22′N 96°12′W

27 O11 **Tecumseh** Oklahoma, C USA 35°15′N 96°56′W

Tedzhen see Harīrūd/Tejen

Tedzhen see Tejen

146 H15 **Tedzhenstroy** Turkm. Tejenstroy. Ahal Welaýaty, S Turkmenistan 36°57′N 60°49′E

Teel see Öndör-Ulaan

97 L15 **Tees** ≈ N England, United Kingdom

14 E15 **Teeswater** Ontario, S Canada 44°00′N 81°17′W

190 A10 **Tefala** island Funafuti Atoll, C Tuvalu

58 D13 **Tefé** Amazonas, N Brazil 03°24′S 64°45′W

74 K11 **Tefedest** ▲▲ S Algeria

136 E16 **Tefenni** Burdur, SW Turkey 37°19′N 29°45′E

58 D13 **Tefé, Rio** ≈ NW Brazil

169 P16 **Tegal** Jawa, C Indonesia 06°52′S 109°07′E

100 O12 **Tegel** ✈ (Berlin) Berlin, NE Germany 52°33′N 13°16′E

99 M15 **Tegelen** Limburg, SE Netherlands 51°20′N 06°09′E

101 L24 **Tegernsee** ◎ SE Germany

107 M18 **Teggiano** Campania, S Italy 40°25′N 15°28′E

77 U14 **Tegina** Niger, C Nigeria 10°06′N 06°10′E

42 I7 **Tegucigalpa** ● (Honduras) Francisco Morazán, SW Honduras 14°04′N 87°11′W

42 H7 **Tegucigalpa** ✈ Central District, C Honduras 14°03′N 87°20′W

Tegucigalpa see Central District

Tegucigalpa see Francisco Morazán

77 U9 **Teguidda-n-Tessoumt** Agadez, C Niger 17°27′N 06°40′E

64 Q11 **Teguise** Lanzarote, Islas Canarias, Spain, NE Atlantic Ocean 29°04′N 13°38′W

122 K12 **Tegul'det** Tomskaya Oblast', C Russian Federation 57°16′N 87°58′E

35 S13 **Tehachapi** California, W USA 35°07′N 118°27′W

35 S13 **Tehachapi Mountains** ▲▲ California, W USA

Tehama see Tihāmah

Teheran see Tehrān

77 O14 **Téhini** NE Ivory Coast 09°36′N 03°40′W

143 N5 **Tehrān** var. Teheran. ● (Iran) Tehrān, N Iran 35°44′N 51°27′E

143 N6 **Tehrān** off. Ostān-e Tehrān, var. Tehran. ◐ province N Iran

Tehrān, Ostān-e see Tehrān

152 K9 **Tehri** var. New Tehri. Uttarakhand, N India 30°12′N 78°29′E

◆ Country ● Country Capital ◇ Dependent Territory ○ Dependent Territory Capital ◐ Administrative Regions ✈ International Airport ▲ Mountain ▲▲ Mountain Range ✱ Volcano ≈ River ◎ Lake ⊠ Reservoir

TEHRI – THAU, BASSIN DE

Tehri see Tikamgarh
41 Q15 **Tehuacán** Puebla, S Mexico 18°29′N 97°24′W
41 S17 **Tehuantepec** var. Santo Domingo Tehuantepec. Oaxaca, SE Mexico 16°18′N 95°14′W
41 S17 **Tehuantepec, Golfo de** var. Gulf of Tehuantepec. gulf S Mexico
Tehuantepec, Gulf of see Tehuantepec, Golfo de
Tehuantepec, Isthmus of see Tehuantepec, Istmo de
41 T16 **Tehuantepec, Istmo de** var. Isthmus of Tehuantepec. isthmus SE Mexico
0 I16 **Tehuantepec Ridge** undersea feature E Pacific Ocean 13°30′N 98°00′W
41 S16 **Tehuantepec, Río** ≈ SE Mexico
191 W10 **Tehuata** atoll Îles Tuamotu, C French Polynesia
64 O11 **Teide, Pico del** ▲ Gran Canaria, Islas Canarias, Spain, NE Atlantic Ocean 28°16′N 16°39′W
97 I21 **Teifi** ≈ SW Wales, United Kingdom
80 B9 **Teiga Plateau** plateau W Sudan
97 J24 **Teignmouth** SW England, United Kingdom 50°34′N 03°29′W
Teisen see Chech'ŏn
116 H11 **Teiuş** Ger. Dreikirchen, Hung. Tövis. Alba, C Romania 46°12′N 23°40′E
169 U17 **Tejakula** Bali, C Indonesia 08°09′S 115°19′E
146 H14 **Tejen** Rus. Tedzhen. Ahal Welaýaty, S Turkmenistan 37°24′N 60°29′E
146 I15 **Tejen** Per. Harīrūd, Rus. Tedzhen. ≈ Afghanistan/Iran see also Harīrūd
Tejen see Harīrūd
Tejenstroy see Tedzhenstroy
35 S14 **Tejon Pass** pass California, W USA
Tejo, Rio see Tagus
41 O14 **Tejupilco** var. Tejupilco de Hidalgo. México, S Mexico 18°55′N 100°10′W
Tejupilco de Hidalgo see Tejupilco
184 P7 **Te Kaha** Bay of Plenty, North Island, New Zealand 37°45′S 177°42′E
29 S14 **Tekamah** Nebraska, C USA 41°46′N 96°13′W
184 I1 **Te Kao** Northland, North Island, New Zealand 34°40′S 172°57′E
185 F20 **Tekapo** ≈ South Island, New Zealand
185 F19 **Tekapo, Lake** ◎ South Island, New Zealand
184 P9 **Te Karaka** Gisborne, North Island, New Zealand 38°30′S 177°52′E
184 L7 **Te Kauwhata** Waikato, North Island, New Zealand 37°22′S 175°07′E
41 X12 **Tekax** var. Tekax de Álvaro Obregón. Yucatán, SE Mexico 20°07′N 89°10′W
Tekax de Álvaro Obregón see Tekax
136 A14 **Teke Burnu** headland W Turkey 38°06′N 26°35′E
114 M12 **Teke Deresi** ≈ NW Turkey
146 D10 **Tekedzhik, Gory** hill range NW Turkmenistan
145 V14 **Tekeli** Almaty, SE Kazakhstan 44°50′N 78°47′E
145 R7 **Teke, Ozero** ◎ N Kazakhstan
158 I5 **Tekes** Xinjiang Uygur Zizhiqu, NW China 43°15′N 81°43′E
145 W16 **Tekes** Almaty, SE Kazakhstan 42°40′N 80°01′E
Tekes see Tekes He
158 H5 **Tekes He** Rus. Tekes. ≈ China/Kazakhstan
Teke/Tekendorf see Teaca
80 I10 **Tekezē** var. Takkaze. ≈ Eritrea/Ethiopia
Tekhtin see Tsyakhtsin
136 C10 **Tekirdağ** It. Rodosto; anc. Bisanthe, Raidestos, Rhaedestus. Tekirdağ, NW Turkey 40°59′N 27°31′E
136 C10 **Tekirdağ** ◈ province NW Turkey
155 N14 **Tekkali** Andhra Pradesh, E India 18°37′N 84°15′E
115 K15 **Tekke Burnu** Turk. İlyasbaba Burnu. headland NW Turkey 40°03′N 26°12′E
137 Q13 **Tekman** Erzurum, NE Turkey 39°39′N 41°31′E
32 M9 **Tekoa** Washington, NW USA 47°13′N 117°05′W
190 H16 **Te Kou** ▲ Rarotonga, S Cook Islands 21°14′S 159°46′W
Tekrit see Tikrīt
171 P12 **Teku** Sulawesi, N Indonesia 0°46′S 123°25′E
184 L9 **Te Kuiti** Waikato, North Island, New Zealand 38°21′S 175°10′E
42 H4 **Tela** Atlántida, NW Honduras 15°46′N 87°25′W
138 F12 **Telalim** Southern, S Israel 30°58′N 34°47′E
Telanaipura see Jambi
137 U10 **T'elavi** E Georgia 41°55′N 45°29′E
138 F10 **Tel Aviv** ◈ district W Israel
Tel Aviv-Jaffa see Tel Aviv-Yafo
138 F10 **Tel Aviv-Yafo** var. Tel Aviv-Jaffa. Tel Aviv, C Israel 32°05′N 34°46′E
111 E18 **Telč** Ger. Teltsch. Vysočina, C Czech Republic 49°10′N 15°28′E
186 B6 **Telefomin** Sandaun, NW Papua New Guinea 05°08′S 141°31′E
10 J10 **Telegraph Creek** British Columbia, W Canada 57°56′N 131°10′W
190 B10 **Telele** island Funafuti Atoll, C Tuvalu
60 J11 **Telêmaco Borba** Paraná, S Brazil 24°20′S 50°44′W
95 E15 **Telemark** ◈ county S Norway
62 J13 **Telén** La Pampa, C Argentina 36°20′S 65°31′W
Teleneshty see Teleneşti
116 M9 **Teleneşti** Rus. Teleneshty. C Moldova 47°35′N 28°20′E
104 J4 **Teleno, El** ▲ NW Spain 42°19′N 06°21′W
116 I15 **Teleorman** ◈ county S Romania
116 I14 **Teleorman** ≈ S Romania
25 V5 **Telephone** Texas, SW USA 33°48′N 96°00′W
35 U11 **Telescope Peak** ▲ California, W USA 36°09′N 117°03′W
Teles Pirés see São Manuel, Rio
97 L19 **Telford** W England, United Kingdom 52°42′N 02°28′W
108 L7 **Telfs** Tirol, W Austria 47°19′N 11°05′E
42 I9 **Telica** León, NW Nicaragua 12°30′N 86°52′W
42 J6 **Telica, Río** ≈ C Honduras
76 I13 **Télimélé** W Guinea 10°45′N 13°02′W
43 O14 **Telire, Río** ≈ Costa Rica/Panama
114 I8 **Telish** prev. Azizie. Pleven, N Bulgaria 43°20′N 24°15′E
41 R16 **Telixtlahuaca** var. San Francisco Telixtlahuaca. Oaxaca, SE Mexico 17°18′N 96°54′W
10 K13 **Telkwa** British Columbia, SW Canada 54°39′N 126°51′W
25 P4 **Tell** Texas, SW USA 34°18′N 100°20′W
Tell Abiad see Tall Abyaḍ
Tell Abiad/Tell Abyad see At Tall al Abyaḍ
31 O16 **Tell City** Indiana, N USA 37°56′N 86°47′W
38 M9 **Teller** Alaska, USA 65°15′N 166°21′W
Tell Huqnah see Tall Ḥuqnah
155 F20 **Tellicherry** var. Thalashsheri, Thalassery. Kerala, SW India 11°44′N 75°29′E see also Thalassery
20 M10 **Tellico Plains** Tennessee, S USA 35°19′N 84°18′W
Tell Kalakh see Tall Kalakh
Tell Mardīkh see Ebla
54 E11 **Tello** Huila, C Colombia 03°06′N 75°08′W
Tell Shedadi see Ash Shadādah
37 Q7 **Telluride** Colorado, C USA 37°56′N 107°48′W
117 X9 **Tel'manove** Donets'ka Oblast', E Ukraine 47°24′N 38°03′E
Tel'man/Tel'mansk see Gubadag
162 H6 **Telmen** var. Övögdiy. Dzavhan, C Mongolia 48°38′N 97°39′E
162 H6 **Telmen Nuur** ◎ NW Mongolia
Teloekbetoeng see Bandar Lampung
41 O15 **Teloloapán** Guerrero, S Mexico 18°21′N 99°52′W
Telo Martius see Toulon
125 V8 **Telposiz, Gora** ▲ NW Russian Federation 63°52′N 59°15′E
Telschen see Telšiai
63 J17 **Telsen** Chubut, S Argentina 42°27′S 66°59′W
118 D11 **Telšiai** Ger. Telschen. Telšiai, NW Lithuania 55°59′N 22°21′E
118 D11 **Telšiai** ◈ province NW Lithuania
Teltsch see Telč
Telukbetung see Bandar Lampung
168 H10 **Telukdalam** Pulau Nias, W Indonesia 0°34′N 97°47′E
14 H9 **Temagami** Ontario, S Canada 47°03′N 79°47′W
14 G9 **Temagami, Lake** ◎ Ontario, S Canada
190 H16 **Te Manga** ▲ Rarotonga, S Cook Islands 21°13′S 159°45′W
191 W12 **Tematangi** atoll Îles Tuamotu, S French Polynesia
41 X11 **Temax** Yucatán, SE Mexico 21°10′N 88°53′W
171 E14 **Tembagapura** Papua, E Indonesia 04°10′S 137°19′E
129 U5 **Tembenchi** ≈ N Russian Federation
55 P6 **Temblador** Monagas, NE Venezuela 08°59′N 62°44′W
105 N9 **Tembleque** Castilla-La Mancha, C Spain 39°41′N 03°30′W
Temboni see Mitemele, Río
35 U16 **Temecula** California, W USA 33°29′N 117°09′W
168 K7 **Temengor, Tasik** ◎ Peninsular Malaysia
112 L9 **Temerin** Vojvodina, N Serbia 45°25′N 19°54′E
Temeschburg/Temeschwar see Timişoara
Temes-Kubin see Kovin
Temes/Temesch see Tamiš
Temesvár/Temeswar see Timişoara
Teminaboean see Teminabuan
171 U12 **Teminabuan** prev. Teminaboean. Papua, E Indonesia 01°30′S 131°59′E
145 P17 **Temirlanovka** Yuzhnyy Kazakhstan, S Kazakhstan 42°36′N 69°17′E
145 R10 **Temirtau** prev. Samarkandski, Samarkandskoye. Karaganda, C Kazakhstan 50°05′N 72°55′E
14 H10 **Témiscaming** Québec, SE Canada 46°40′N 79°04′W
Témiscamingue, Lac see Timiskaming, Lake
15 T8 **Témiscouata, Lac** ◎ Québec, SE Canada
127 N5 **Temnikov** Respublika Mordoviya, W Russian Federation 54°39′N 43°09′E
191 Y13 **Temoe** island Îles Gambier, E French Polynesia
183 Q9 **Temora** New South Wales, SE Australia 34°28′S 147°33′E
40 H7 **Témoris** Chihuahua, W Mexico 27°16′N 108°15′W
40 I5 **Temósachic** Chihuahua, N Mexico 28°55′N 107°42′W
187 Q10 **Temotu** var. Temotu Province. ◈ province E Solomon Islands
Temotu Province see Temotu
36 L14 **Tempe** Arizona, SW USA 33°24′N 111°54′W
Tempelburg see Czaplinek
107 C17 **Tempio Pausania** Sardegna, Italy, C Mediterranean Sea 40°55′N 09°07′E
42 K12 **Tempisque, Río** ≈ NW Costa Rica
25 T9 **Temple** Texas, SW USA 31°06′N 97°22′W
100 O12 **Templehof** ✖ (Berlin) Berlin, NE Germany 52°28′N 13°24′E
97 D19 **Templemore** Ir. An Teampall Mór. Tipperary, C Ireland 52°48′N 07°50′W
100 O11 **Templin** Brandenburg, NE Germany 53°07′N 13°31′E
41 P12 **Tempoal** var. Tempoal de Sánchez. Veracruz-Llave, E Mexico 21°32′N 98°23′W
Tempoal de Sánchez see Tempoal
41 P13 **Tempoal, Río** ≈ C Mexico
83 E14 **Tempué** Moxico, C Angola 13°36′S 18°56′E
126 J14 **Temryuk** Krasnodarskiy Kray, SW Russian Federation 45°15′N 37°26′E
99 G17 **Temse** Oost-Vlaanderen, N Belgium 51°08′N 04°13′E
63 F15 **Temuco** Araucanía, C Chile 38°45′S 72°37′W
185 G20 **Temuka** Canterbury, South Island, New Zealand 44°14′S 171°17′E
189 P13 **Temwen Island** island E Micronesia
56 C6 **Tena** Napo, C Ecuador 01°00′S 77°48′W
41 W13 **Tenabo** Campeche, E Mexico 20°02′N 90°12′W
Tenaghau see Aola
25 X7 **Tenaha** Texas, SW USA 31°56′N 94°14′W
39 X13 **Tenake** Chichagof Island, Alaska, USA 57°46′N 135°13′W
155 K16 **Tenāli** Andhra Pradesh, E India 16°13′N 80°36′E
Tenan see Ch'ŏnan
41 O14 **Tenancingo** var. Tenencingo de Degollado. México, S Mexico 18°57′N 99°39′W
191 X12 **Tenararo** island Groupe Actéon, SE French Polynesia
167 N12 **Tenasserim** Tanintharyi, S Burma (Myanmar) 12°05′N 99°00′E
167 N11 **Tenasserim** var. Tanintharyi. ◈ division S Burma (Myanmar)
98 O5 **Ten Boer** Groningen, NE Netherlands 53°16′N 06°42′E
97 I21 **Tenby** SW Wales, United Kingdom 51°41′N 04°43′W
80 K11 **Tendaho** Āfar, NE Ethiopia 11°39′N 40°59′E
103 V14 **Tende** Alpes Maritimes, SE France 44°04′N 07°34′E
151 Q20 **Ten Degree Channel** strait Andaman and Nicobar Islands, India, E Indian Ocean
80 F11 **Tendelti** White Nile, E Sudan 13°01′N 31°55′E
76 G8 **Te-n-Dghâmcha, Sebkhet** var. Sebkha de Ndrhamcha, Sebkra de Ndaghamcha. salt lake W Mauritania
165 P10 **Tendō** Yamagata, Honshū, C Japan 38°22′N 140°22′E
74 H7 **Tendrara** NE Morocco 33°06′N 01°58′W
117 Q11 **Tendrivs'ka Kosa** spit S Ukraine
117 Q11 **Tendrivs'ka Zatoka** gulf S Ukraine
Tenencingo de Degollado see Tenancingo
77 N11 **Ténenkou** Mopti, C Mali 14°28′N 04°55′W
77 W9 **Ténéré** physical region C Niger
77 W9 **Ténére, Erg du** desert C Niger
64 O11 **Tenerife** island Islas Canarias, Spain, NE Atlantic Ocean
74 J5 **Ténès** NW Algeria 36°35′N 01°18′E
170 M15 **Tengah, Kepulauan** island group C Indonesia
Tengcheng see Tengxian
169 V11 **Tenggarong** Borneo, C Indonesia 0°23′S 117°00′E
162 J15 **Tengger Shamo** desert N China
168 L8 **Tenggul, Pulau** island Peninsular Malaysia
Tengiz Köl see Tengiz, Ozero
145 P9 **Tengiz, Ozero** Kaz. Tengiz Köl. salt lake C Kazakhstan
76 M14 **Tengréla** var. Tingréla. N Ivory Coast 10°26′N 06°20′W
160 M14 **Tengxian** var. Tengcheng, Tengxian, Teng Xian. Guangxi Zhuangzu Zizhiqu, S China 23°24′N 110°49′E
Teng Xian see Tengxian
Tengxian see Tengxian
155 H23 **Teni** var. Theni. Tamil Nādu, SE India 10°00′N 77°29′E
194 H2 **Teniente Rodolfo Marsh** Chilean research station South Shetland Islands, Antarctica 61°57′S 58°23′W
32 G9 **Tenino** Washington, NW USA 46°51′N 122°51′W
112 I9 **Tenja** Osijek-Baranja, E Croatia 45°30′N 18°45′E
188 B16 **Tenjo, Mount** ▲ W Guam
155 H23 **Tenkāsi** Tamil Nādu, SE India 08°58′N 77°22′E
79 N24 **Tenke** Katanga, SE Dem. Rep. Congo 10°34′S 26°12′E
Tenke see Tinca
123 Q7 **Tenkeli** Respublika Sakha (Yakutiya), NE Russian Federation 70°09′N 140°39′E
27 R10 **Tenkiller Ferry Lake** ▣ Oklahoma, C USA
77 Q13 **Tenkodogo** S Burkina 11°54′N 00°19′W
181 Q5 **Tennant Creek** Northern Territory, C Australia 19°40′S 134°16′E
20 G9 **Tennessee** off. State of Tennessee, also known as The Volunteer State. ◈ state SE USA
37 R5 **Tennessee Pass** pass Colorado, C USA
20 H10 **Tennessee River** ≈ S USA
23 N2 **Tennessee Tombigbee Waterway** canal Alabama/Mississippi, S USA
99 K22 **Tenneville** Luxembourg, SE Belgium 50°05′N 05°31′E
92 M11 **Tenniöjoki** ≈ NE Finland
92 L9 **Tenojoki** Lapp. Deatnu, Nor. Tana. ≈ Finland/Norway see also Deatnu
169 U7 **Tenom** Sabah, East Malaysia 05°07′N 115°57′E
Tenos see Tínos
41 V15 **Tenosique** var. Tenosique de Pino Suárez. Tabasco, SE Mexico 17°30′N 91°24′W
Tenosique de Pino Suárez see Tenosique
22 I6 **Tensas River** ≈ Louisiana, S USA
23 O8 **Tensaw River** ≈ Alabama, S USA
74 E7 **Tensift** seasonal river W Morocco
171 O12 **Tentena** var. Tenteno. Sulawesi, C Indonesia 01°46′S 120°40′E
Tenteno see Tentena
183 U4 **Tenterfield** New South Wales, SE Australia 29°04′S 152°02′E
23 X16 **Ten Thousand Islands** island group Florida, SE USA
60 H9 **Teodoro Sampaio** São Paulo, S Brazil 22°30′S 52°13′W
59 N19 **Teófilo Otoni** var. Theophilo Ottoni. Minas Gerais, NE Brazil 17°52′S 41°31′W
116 K5 **Teofipol'** Khmel'nyts'ka Oblast', W Ukraine 50°00′N 26°22′E
191 Q8 **Teohatu** Tahiti, W French Polynesia
41 P14 **Teotihuacán** ruins México, S Mexico
Teotilán see Teotitlán del Camino
41 Q15 **Teotitlán del Camino** var. Teotilán. Oaxaca, S Mexico 18°10′N 97°08′W
190 G12 **Tepa** Île Uvea, E Wallis and Futuna 13°19′S 176°09′W
191 P8 **Tepaee, Récif** reef Tahiti, W French Polynesia
40 L14 **Tepalcatepec** Michoacán, SW Mexico 19°11′N 102°50′W
190 A16 **Tepa Point** headland SW Niue 19°07′S 169°56′E
40 L13 **Tepatitlán** var. Tepatitlán de Morelos. Jalisco, SW Mexico 20°50′N 102°46′W
Tepatitlán de Morelos see Tepatitlán
40 J9 **Tepehuanes** var. Santa Catarina de Tepehuanes. Durango, C Mexico 25°22′N 105°42′W
Tepelena see Tepelenë
113 L22 **Tepelenë** var. Tepelena, It. Tepeleni. Gjirokastër, S Albania 40°18′N 20°00′E
Tepeleni see Tepelenë
40 K12 **Tepic** Nayarit, C Mexico 21°30′N 104°55′W
111 C15 **Teplice** Ger. Teplitz; prev. Teplice-Šanov, Teplitz-Schönau. Ústecký Kraj, NW Czech Republic 50°38′N 13°49′E
Teplice-Šanov/Teplitz/Teplitz-Schönau see Teplice
117 O7 **Teplyk** Vinnyts'ka Oblast', C Ukraine 48°40′N 29°46′E
123 R10 **Teplyy Klyuch** Respublika Sakha (Yakutiya), NE Russian Federation 62°46′N 137°01′E
40 E5 **Tepoca, Cabo** headland NW Mexico 29°19′N 112°24′W
191 W9 **Tepoto** island Îles du Désappointement, C French Polynesia
92 L11 **Tepsa** Lappi, N Finland 67°34′N 25°36′E
190 B8 **Tepuka** atoll Funafuti Atoll, C Tuvalu
184 N7 **Te Puke** Bay of Plenty, North Island, New Zealand 37°48′S 176°19′E
40 L13 **Tequila** Jalisco, SW Mexico 20°52′N 103°48′W
41 O13 **Tequisquiapan** Querétaro de Arteaga, C Mexico 20°34′N 99°52′W
77 Q12 **Téra** Tillabéri, W Niger 14°01′N 00°45′E
104 J5 **Tera** ≈ NW Spain
191 V1 **Teraina** prev. Washington Island. atoll Line Islands, E Kiribati
81 F15 **Terakeka** Bahr el Gabel, S Sudan 05°26′N 31°45′E
107 J14 **Teramo** anc. Interamna. Abruzzi, C Italy 42°40′N 13°43′E
98 P7 **Ter Apel** Groningen, NE Netherlands 52°52′N 07°05′E
104 H11 **Tera, Ribeira de** ≈ S Portugal
185 K14 **Terawhiti, Cape** headland North Island, New Zealand 41°17′S 174°36′E
98 N12 **Terborg** Gelderland, E Netherlands 51°55′N 06°22′E
137 P13 **Tercan** Erzincan, NE Turkey 39°47′N 40°23′E
64 O2 **Terceira** ✖ Terceira, Azores, Portugal, NE Atlantic Ocean 38°43′N 27°13′W
64 O2 **Terceira** var. Ilha Terceira. island Azores, Portugal, NE Atlantic Ocean
Terceira, Ilha see Terceira
116 K6 **Terebovlya** Ternopil's'ka Oblast', W Ukraine 49°18′N 25°44′E
127 O15 **Terek** ≈ SW Russian Federation
Terekhovka see Tsyerakhowka
147 R9 **Terek-Say** Dzhalal-Abadskaya Oblast', W Kyrgyzstan 41°28′N 71°06′E
145 Z10 **Terekty** prev. Alekseevka, Alekseyevka. Vostochnyy Kazakhstan, E Kazakhstan 48°25′N 85°38′E
168 L7 **Terengganu** var. Trengganu. ◈ state Peninsular Malaysia
127 X7 **Terensay** Orenburgskaya Oblast', W Russian Federation 51°35′N 59°28′E
58 N13 **Teresina** var. Therezina. state capital Piauí, NE Brazil 05°09′S 42°46′W
60 P9 **Teresópolis** Rio de Janeiro, SE Brazil 22°25′S 42°59′W
110 P12 **Terespol** Lubelskie, E Poland 52°05′N 23°37′E
191 V16 **Terevaka, Maunga** ⋏ Easter Island, Chile, E Pacific Ocean 27°05′S 109°23′W
103 P3 **Tergnier** Aisne, N France 49°39′N 03°18′E
43 O14 **Teribe, Río** ≈ NW Panama
124 K3 **Teriberka** Murmanskaya Oblast', NW Russian Federation 69°10′N 35°18′E
Terinkot see Tarīn Kowt
Terisaqqan see Tersakkan
24 K12 **Terlingua** Texas, SW USA 29°18′N 103°36′W
24 K11 **Terlingua Creek** ≈ Texas, SW USA
62 K7 **Termas de Río Hondo** Santiago del Estero, N Argentina 27°29′S 64°52′W
136 M11 **Terme** Samsun, N Turkey 41°12′N 37°00′E
Termez see Termiz
Termia see Kýthnos
107 J23 **Termini Imerese** anc. Thermae Himerenses. Sicilia, Italy, C Mediterranean Sea 37°59′N 13°42′E
41 V14 **Términos, Laguna de** lagoon SE Mexico
77 X10 **Termit-Kaoboul** Zinder, C Niger 15°34′N 11°31′E
147 O14 **Termiz** Rus. Termez. Surkhondaryo Viloyati, S Uzbekistan 37°17′N 67°12′E
107 L15 **Termoli** Molise, C Italy 42°00′N 14°58′E
Termonde see Dendermonde
98 P5 **Termunten** Groningen, NE Netherlands 53°18′N 07°02′E
171 R11 **Ternate** Pulau Ternate, E Indonesia 0°48′N 127°23′E
109 T5 **Ternberg** Oberösterreich, N Austria 47°57′N 14°22′E
99 E15 **Terneuzen** var. Neuzen. Zeeland, SW Netherlands 51°20′N 03°50′E
123 T14 **Terney** Primorskiy Kray, SE Russian Federation 45°03′N 136°43′E
107 I14 **Terni** anc. Interamna Nahars. Umbria, C Italy 42°34′N 12°38′E
109 X6 **Ternitz** Niederösterreich, E Austria 47°43′N 16°02′E
117 V7 **Ternivka** Dnipropetrovs'ka Oblast', E Ukraine 48°30′N 36°05′E
116 K6 **Ternopil'** Pol. Tarnopol, Rus. Ternopol'. Ternopil's'ka Oblast', W Ukraine 49°32′N 25°38′E
Ternopil' see Ternopil's'ka Oblast'
116 I6 **Ternopil's'ka Oblast'** var. Ternopil', Rus. Ternopol'skaya Oblast'. ◈ province NW Ukraine
Ternopol' see Ternopil'
Ternopol'skaya Oblast' see Ternopil's'ka Oblast'
123 U13 **Terpeniya, Mys** headland Ostrov Sakhalin, SE Russian Federation 48°37′N 144°40′E
Térraba, Río see Grande de Térraba, Río
10 J13 **Terrace** British Columbia, W Canada 54°31′N 128°32′W
12 D12 **Terrace Bay** Ontario, S Canada 48°47′N 87°06′W
107 I16 **Terracina** Lazio, C Italy 41°18′N 13°13′E
93 F14 **Terråk** Troms, N Norway 65°03′N 12°22′E
26 M13 **Terral** Oklahoma, C USA 33°55′N 97°54′W
107 B19 **Terralba** Sardegna, Italy, C Mediterranean Sea 39°47′N 08°35′E
Terranova di Sicilia see Gela
Terranova Pausania see Olbia
105 W5 **Terrassa** Cast. Tarrasa. Cataluña, E Spain 41°34′N 02°01′E
15 O12 **Terrebonne** Québec, SE Canada 45°42′N 73°37′W
22 J11 **Terrebonne Bay** bay Louisiana, SE USA
31 N14 **Terre Haute** Indiana, N USA 39°27′N 87°24′W
25 U6 **Terrell** Texas, SW USA 32°44′N 96°16′W
Terre Neuve see Newfoundland and Labrador
33 Q14 **Terreton** Idaho, NW USA 43°49′N 112°25′W
103 T7 **Territoire-de-Belfort** ◈ department E France
33 X9 **Terry** Montana, NW USA 46°46′N 105°16′W
28 I9 **Terry Peak** ▲ South Dakota, N USA 44°19′N 103°49′W
136 H14 **Tersakan Gölü** ◎ C Turkey
145 O10 **Tersakkan** Kaz. Terisaqqan. ≈ C Kazakhstan
98 J4 **Terschelling** Fris. Skylge. island Waddeneilanden, N Netherlands
78 H10 **Tersef** Chari-Baguirmi, C Chad 12°55′N 16°49′E
147 X8 **Terskey Ala-Too, Khrebet** ⛰ Kazakhstan/Kyrgyzstan
Terter see Tärtär
105 R8 **Teruel** anc. Turba. Aragón, E Spain 40°21′N 01°06′W
105 R7 **Teruel** ◈ province Aragón, E Spain
114 M7 **Tervel** prev. Kurtbunar, Rom. Curtbunar. Dobrich, NE Bulgaria 43°45′N 27°25′E
93 M16 **Tervo** Itä-Suomi, C Finland 62°57′N 26°48′E
92 L13 **Tervola** Lappi, NW Finland 66°04′N 24°49′E
Tervueren see Tervuren
99 H18 **Tervuren** var. Tervueren. Vlaams Brabant, C Belgium 50°48′N 04°28′E
162 G5 **Tes** var. Dzür. Dzavhan, W Mongolia 49°37′N 95°46′E
112 H11 **Tešanj** Federacija Bosna I Hercegovina, N Bosnia and Herzegovina 44°37′N 18°00′E
Teschen see Cieszyn
83 M19 **Tesenane** Inhambane, S Mozambique 22°48′S 34°02′E
80 I9 **Teseney** var. Tessenei. W Eritrea 15°05′N 36°42′E
39 P5 **Teshekpuk Lake** ◎ Alaska, USA
162 K6 **Teshig** Bulgan, N Mongolia 49°51′N 102°45′E
165 T2 **Teshio** Hokkaidō, NE Japan 44°49′N 141°46′E
165 T2 **Teshio-sanchi** ⛰ Hokkaidō, NE Japan
14 L7 **Tessier, Lac** ◎ Québec, SE Canada
Těšín see Cieszyn
Tesiyn Gol see Tes-Khem
129 T7 **Tes-Khem** var. Tesiyn Gol. ≈ Mongolia/Russian Federation
112 H11 **Teslić** Republika Srpska, N Bosnia and Herzegovina 44°35′N 17°50′E
10 I9 **Teslin** Yukon Territory, W Canada 60°12′N 132°44′W
10 I8 **Teslin** ≈ British Columbia/Yukon Territory, W Canada
77 Q8 **Tessalit** Kidal, NE Mali 20°12′N 00°58′E
77 V12 **Tessaoua** Maradi, S Niger 13°46′N 07°55′E
99 J17 **Tessenderlo** Limburg, NE Belgium 51°05′N 05°04′E
Tessenei see Teseney
Tessin see Ticino
97 M23 **Test** ≈ S England, United Kingdom
Testama see Tõstamaa
55 P4 **Testigos, Islas los** island group N Venezuela
37 S10 **Tesuque** New Mexico, SW USA 35°45′N 105°55′W
103 O17 **Têt** var. Tet. ≈ S France
Tet see Têt
54 G5 **Tetas, Cerro de las** ▲ NW Venezuela 09°58′N 73°00′W
83 M15 **Tete** Tete, NW Mozambique 16°14′S 33°34′E
83 M15 **Tete** off. Província de Tete. ◈ province NW Mozambique
11 N15 **Tête Jaune Cache** British Columbia, SW Canada 52°52′N 119°22′W
184 O8 **Te Teko** Bay of Plenty, North Island, New Zealand 38°03′S 176°48′E
186 K9 **Tetepare** island New Georgia Islands, NW Solomon Islands
Tete, Província de see Tete
Teterev see Teteriv
116 M5 **Teteriv** Rus. Teterev. ≈ N Ukraine
100 M9 **Teterow** Mecklenburg-Vorpommern, NE Germany 53°47′N 12°34′E
114 I9 **Teteven** Lovech, N Bulgaria 42°54′N 24°18′E
191 T10 **Tetiaroa** atoll Îles du Vent, W French Polynesia
105 P14 **Tetica de Bacares** ▲ S Spain 37°15′N 02°24′W
Tetiyev see Tetiyiv
117 O6 **Tetiyiv** Rus. Tetiyev. Kyyivs'ka Oblast', N Ukraine 49°21′N 29°40′E
39 T10 **Tetlin** Alaska, USA 63°08′N 142°31′W
33 R8 **Teton River** ≈ Montana, NW USA
74 G5 **Tétouan** var. Tetouan, Tetuán. N Morocco 35°33′N 05°22′W
Tetova/Tetovë see Tetovo
114 L7 **Tetovo** Razgrad, N Bulgaria 43°49′N 26°21′E
113 N18 **Tetovo** Alb. Tetova, Tetovë, Turk. Kalkandelen. NW FYR Macedonia 42°01′N 20°58′E
115 E20 **Tetrázio** ▲ S Greece
Tetschen see Děčín
Tetuán see Tétouan
191 Q8 **Tetufera, Mont** ▲ Tahiti, W French Polynesia 17°40′S 149°26′W
127 R4 **Tetyushi** Respublika Tatarstan, W Russian Federation 54°55′N 48°46′E
108 I7 **Teufen** Sankt Gallen, NE Switzerland 47°24′N 09°24′E
40 L12 **Teul** var. Teul de Gonzáles Ortega. Zacatecas, C Mexico 21°30′N 103°28′W
107 B21 **Teulada** Sardegna, Italy, C Mediterranean Sea 38°58′N 08°46′E
Teul de Gonzáles Ortega see Teul
11 X16 **Teulon** Manitoba, S Canada 50°20′N 97°14′W
42 I7 **Teupasenti** El Paraíso, S Honduras 14°13′N 86°42′W
165 S2 **Teuri-tō** island NE Japan
100 G13 **Teutoburger Wald** Eng. Teutoburg Forest. hill range NW Germany
Teutoburg Forest see Teutoburger Wald
93 K17 **Teuva** Swe. Östermark. Länsi-Suomi, W Finland 62°29′N 21°45′E
107 H15 **Tevere** Eng. Tiber. ≈ C Italy
Teverya see Tverya
96 K13 **Teviot** ≈ SE Scotland, United Kingdom
Tevli see Tewli
122 H11 **Tevriz** Omskaya Oblast', C Russian Federation 57°30′N 72°13′E
185 B24 **Te Waewae Bay** bay South Island, New Zealand
97 L21 **Tewkesbury** C England, United Kingdom 51°59′N 02°09′W
119 F19 **Tewli** Rus. Tevli. Brestskaya Voblasts', SW Belarus 52°20′N 24°15′E
159 U12 **Têwo** var. Dêngka; prev. Dêngkagoin. Gansu, C China 34°05′N 103°15′E
Tewulike see Hoxud
25 U12 **Texana, Lake** ◎ Texas, SW USA
27 S14 **Texarkana** Arkansas, C USA 33°26′N 94°02′W
25 X5 **Texarkana** Texas, SW USA 33°26′N 94°03′W
25 N9 **Texas** off. State of Texas, also known as Lone Star State. ◈ state S USA
25 W12 **Texas City** Texas, SW USA 29°23′N 94°55′W
41 P14 **Texcoco** México, C Mexico 19°32′N 98°52′W
98 I6 **Texel** island Waddeneilanden, NW Netherlands
26 H8 **Texhoma** Oklahoma, C USA 36°30′N 101°46′W
25 N1 **Texhoma** Texas, SW USA 36°30′N 101°46′W
37 W12 **Texico** New Mexico, SW USA 34°23′N 103°03′W
24 L1 **Texline** Texas, SW USA 36°22′N 103°01′W
41 P14 **Texmelucan** var. San Martín Texmelucan. Puebla, S Mexico 19°46′N 98°53′W
27 O13 **Texoma, Lake** ▣ Oklahoma/Texas, C USA
25 N9 **Texon** Texas, SW USA 31°13′N 101°42′W
83 J23 **Teyateyaneng** NW Lesotho 29°04′S 27°51′E
124 M16 **Teykovo** Ivanovskaya Oblast', W Russian Federation 56°49′N 40°31′E
124 M16 **Teza** ≈ W Russian Federation
41 Q13 **Teziutlán** Puebla, S Mexico 19°49′N 97°22′W
153 W12 **Tezpur** Assam, NE India 26°39′N 92°47′E
153 Y11 **Tezu** Arunāchal Pradesh, NE India 27°55′N 96°09′E
Thaa Atoll see Kolhumadulu
9 N10 **Tha-Anne** ≈ Nunavut, NE Canada
83 K23 **Thabana Ntlenyana** var. Thabantshonyana, Mount Ntlenyana. ▲ E Lesotho 29°26′S 29°16′E
Thabantshonyana see Thabana Ntlenyana
83 J23 **Thaba Putsoa** ▲ C Lesotho 29°48′S 27°46′E
167 Q8 **Tha Bo** Nong Khai, E Thailand 17°52′N 102°34′E
103 T12 **Thabor, Pic du** ▲ E France 45°07′N 06°34′E
Tha Chin see Samut Sakhon
166 M7 **Thagaya** Bago, C Burma (Myanmar) 19°19′N 96°16′E
Thai, Ao see Thailand, Gulf of
167 T6 **Thai Binh** Thai Binh, N Vietnam 20°27′N 106°20′E
167 S7 **Thai Hoa** var. Nghia Dan. Nghê An, N Vietnam 19°21′N 105°26′E
167 P9 **Thailand** off. Kingdom of Thailand, Th. Prathet Thai; prev. Siam. ◆ monarchy SE Asia
167 P13 **Thailand, Gulf of** var. Gulf of Siam, Th. Ao Thai, Vtn. Vinh Thai Lan. gulf SE Asia
Thailand, Kingdom of see Thailand
Thai Lan, Vinh see Thailand, Gulf of
167 T6 **Thai Nguyên** Bắc Thai, N Vietnam 21°36′N 105°50′E
167 S8 **Thakhèk** var. Muang Khammouan. Khammouan, C Laos 17°25′N 104°51′E
153 S13 **Thakurgaon** Rajshahi, NW Bangladesh 26°05′N 88°34′E
149 S6 **Thal** North-West Frontier Province, NW Pakistan 33°24′N 70°32′E
166 M15 **Thalang** Phuket, SW Thailand 08°00′N 98°21′E
Thalashsheri see Tellicherry/Thalassery
155 F20 **Thalassery** var. Tellicherry, Thalashsheri. Kerala, SW India 11°44′N 75°29′E see also Tellicherry
167 Q10 **Thalat Khae** Nakhon Ratchasima, C Thailand 15°15′N 102°24′E
109 Q5 **Thalgau** Salzburg, NW Austria 47°49′N 13°19′E
108 G7 **Thalwil** Zürich, NW Switzerland 47°17′N 08°35′E
83 I20 **Thamaga** Kweneng, SE Botswana 24°41′S 25°31′E
Thamarīd see Thamarīt
141 V13 **Thamarīt** var. Thamarīd, Thumrayt. SW Oman 17°39′N 54°02′E
141 P16 **Thamar, Jabal** ▲ SW Yemen 13°46′N 45°32′E
184 M6 **Thames** Waikato, North Island, New Zealand 37°10′S 175°33′E
14 D17 **Thames** ≈ Ontario, S Canada
97 O22 **Thames** ≈ S England, United Kingdom
184 M6 **Thames, Firth of** gulf North Island, New Zealand
14 D17 **Thamesville** Ontario, S Canada 42°33′N 81°58′W
141 S13 **Thamūd** N Yemen 17°18′N 49°57′E
167 N9 **Thanbyuzayat** Mon State, S Burma (Myanmar) 15°58′N 97°44′E
166 K7 **Thandwe** var. Sandoway. Rakhine State, W Burma (Myanmar) 18°28′N 94°20′E
152 I9 **Thānesar** Haryāna, NW India 29°58′N 76°48′E
167 T7 **Thanh Hoa** Thanh Hoa, N Vietnam 19°49′N 105°48′E
Thanintari Taungdan see Bilauktaung Range
155 I21 **Thanjāvūr** prev. Tanjore. Tamil Nādu, SE India 10°46′N 79°09′E
Thanlwin see Salween
103 U7 **Thann** Haut-Rhin, NE France 47°51′N 07°04′E
167 O16 **Tha Nong Phrom** Phatthalung, SW Thailand 07°24′N 100°04′E
167 N13 **Thap Sakae** var. Thap Sakau. Prachuap Khiri Khan, SW Thailand 11°30′N 99°35′E
Thap Sakau see Thap Sakae
98 L10 **'t Harde** Gelderland, E Netherlands 52°25′N 05°53′E
152 D11 **Thar Desert** var. Great Indian Desert, Indian Desert. desert India/Pakistan
181 V10 **Thargomindah** Queensland, C Australia 28°00′S 143°47′E
150 D11 **Thar Pārkar** desert SE Pakistan
139 S7 **Tharthār al Furāt, Qanāt ath** canal C Iraq
139 R7 **Tharthār, Buḥayrat ath** ◎ C Iraq
139 R5 **Tharthār, Wādī ath** dry watercourse N Iraq
167 N13 **Tha Sae** Chumphon, SW Thailand
167 N15 **Tha Sala** Nakhon Si Thammarat, SW Thailand 08°43′N 99°54′E
114 I13 **Thásos** Thásos, E Greece 40°47′N 24°43′E
115 I14 **Thásos** island E Greece
37 N14 **Thatcher** Arizona, SW USA 32°47′N 109°46′W
167 T5 **Thât Khê** var. Trâng Dinh. Lang Son, N Vietnam 22°15′N 106°26′E
166 M8 **Thaton** Mon State, S Burma (Myanmar) 16°56′N 97°20′E
167 S9 **That Phanom** Nakhon Phanom, E Thailand 16°52′N 104°41′E
167 R10 **Tha Tum** Surin, E Thailand 15°18′N 103°39′E
103 P16 **Thau, Bassin de** var. Étang de Thau. ◎ S France

◆ Country
● Country Capital
◇ Dependent Territory
○ Dependent Territory Capital
◈ Administrative Regions
✖ International Airport
▲ Mountain
⛰ Mountain Range
⋏ Volcano
≈ River
◎ Lake
▣ Reservoir

THAU, ÉTANG DE – TISA

Thau, Étang de *see* Thau, Bassin de
166 L3 **Thaungdut** Sagaing, N Burma (Myanmar) 24°26′N 94°45′E
167 O8 **Thaungyin** *Th.* Mae Nam Moei. ≈ Burma (Myanmar)/Thailand
167 R8 **Tha Uthen** Nakhon Phanom, E Thailand 17°32′N 104°34′E
109 W2 **Thaya** *var.* Dyje. ≈ Austria/Czech Republic *see also* Dyje
Thaya *see* Dyje
27 V8 **Thayer** Missouri, C USA 36°31′N 91°34′W
166 L6 **Thayetmyo** Magway, C Burma (Myanmar) 19°20′N 95°10′E
33 S15 **Thayne** Wyoming, C USA 42°54′N 111°01′W
166 M5 **Thazi** Mandalay, C Burma (Myanmar) 20°50′N 96°04′E
Thebes *see* Thíva
44 L5 **The Carlton** *var.* Abraham Bay. Mayaguana, SE Bahamas 22°21′N 72°56′W
45 O14 **The Crane** *var.* Crane. S Barbados 13°06′N 59°27′W
32 I11 **The Dalles** Oregon, NW USA 45°36′N 121°10′W
28 M14 **Thedford** Nebraska, C USA 41°59′N 100°32′W
The Flatts Village *see* Flatts Village
The Hague *see* 's-Gravenhage
Theiss *see* Tisa/Tisza
8 M9 **Thelon** ≈ Northwest Territories, N Canada
Theni *see* Teni
11 V15 **Theodore** Saskatchewan, S Canada 51°25′N 103°01′W
23 N8 **Theodore** Alabama, S USA 30°33′N 88°10′W
36 L13 **Theodore Roosevelt Lake** ⊞ Arizona, SW USA
Theodosia *see* Feodosiya
Theophilo Ottoni *see* Teófilo Otoni
11 V13 **The Pas** Manitoba, C Canada 53°49′N 101°09′W
31 T14 **The Plains** Ohio, N USA 39°22′N 82°07′W
Thera *see* Santoríni
172 H17 **Thérèse, Île** *island* Inner Islands, NE Seychelles
Therezina *see* Teresina
115 L20 **Thérma** Ikaría, Dodekánisa, Greece, Aegean Sea 37°37′N 26°18′E
Thermae Himerenses *see* Termini Imerese
Thermae Pannonicae *see* Baden
Thermaic Gulf/Thermaicus Sinus *see* Thermaïkós Kólpos
121 Q8 **Thermaïkós Kólpos** *Eng.* Thermaic Gulf; *anc.* Thermaicus Sinus. *gulf* N Greece
Thermiá *see* Kýthnos
115 L17 **Thermís** Lésvos, E Greece 39°08′N 26°32′E
115 E18 **Thérmo** Dytikí Ellás, C Greece 38°32′N 21°42′E
33 V14 **Thermopolis** Wyoming, C USA 43°39′N 108°12′W
183 P10 **The Rock** New South Wales, SE Australia 35°18′S 147°07′E
195 O5 **Theron Mountains** ▲▲ Antarctica
The Sooner State *see* Oklahoma
115 G18 **Thespiés** Stereá Ellás, C Greece 38°18′N 23°08′E
115 E16 **Thessalía** *Eng.* Thessaly. ◈ *region* C Greece
14 C10 **Thessalon** Ontario, S Canada 46°15′N 83°34′W
115 G14 **Thessaloníki** *Eng.* Salonica, Salonika, *SCr.* Solun, *Turk.* Selânik. Kentrikí Makedonía, N Greece 40°38′N 22°58′E
115 G14 **Thessaloníki** ✈ Kentrikí Makedonía, N Greece 40°30′N 22°58′E
Thessaly *see* Thessalía
84 B12 **Theta Gap** *undersea feature* E Atlantic Ocean 12°40′W 43°30′N
97 P20 **Thetford** E England, United Kingdom 52°25′N 00°45′E
15 R11 **Thetford-Mines** Québec, SE Canada 46°07′N 71°16′W
113 K17 **Theth** *var.* Thethi. Shkodër, N Albania 42°25′N 19°45′E
Thethi *see* Theth
99 L20 **Theux** Liège, E Belgium 50°33′N 05°48′E
45 V9 **The Valley** ○ (Anguilla) E Anguilla 18°13′N 63°00′W
27 N10 **The Village** Oklahoma, C USA 35°33′N 97°33′W
The Volunteer State *see* Tennessee
25 W10 **The Woodlands** Texas, SW USA 30°09′N 95°27′E
Thiamis *see* Kalamás
Thian Shan *see* Tien Shan
Thibet *see* Xizang Zizhiqu
22 J9 **Thibodaux** Louisiana, S USA 29°48′N 90°49′W
29 S3 **Thief Lake** ◎ Minnesota, N USA
29 S3 **Thief River** ≈ Minnesota, C USA
29 S3 **Thief River Falls** Minnesota, N USA 48°07′N 96°10′W
Thièle *see* La Thielle
32 G14 **Thielsen, Mount** ▲ Oregon, NW USA 43°09′N 122°04′W
Thielt *see* Tielt
106 G7 **Thiene** Veneto, NE Italy 45°43′N 11°29′E
Thienen *see* Tienen
103 P11 **Thiers** Puy-de-Dôme, C France 45°51′N 03°33′E
76 F11 **Thiès** W Senegal 14°49′N 16°52′W
81 I19 **Thika** Central, S Kenya 01°03′S 37°05′E
Thikombia *see* Cikobia
151 K18 **Thiladhunmathi Atoll** *var.* Tiladummati Atoll. *atoll* N Maldives
Thimbu *see* Thimphu
153 T11 **Thimphu** *var.* Thimbu; *prev.* Tashi Chho Dzong. ● (Bhutan) W Bhutan 27°28′N 89°37′E
92 H2 **Thingeyri** Vestfirdhir, NW Iceland 65°52′N 23°28′W
92 I3 **Thingvellir** Sudhurland, SW Iceland 64°15′N 21°06′W
187 Q17 **Thio** Province Sud, C New Caledonia 21°37′S 166°13′E
103 T4 **Thionville** *Ger.* Diedenhofen. Moselle, NE France 49°22′N 06°11′E
77 O12 **Thiou** NW Burkina 13°42′N 02°34′W
115 K22 **Thíra** Santorini, Kykládes, Greece, Aegean Sea 36°25′N 25°26′E
Thíra *see* Santoríni
115 J22 **Thirasía** *island* Kykládes, Greece, Aegean Sea
97 M16 **Thirsk** N England, United Kingdom 54°07′N 01°17′W
14 F12 **Thirty Thousand Islands** *island group* Ontario, S Canada
155 G24 **Thiruvanathapuram** *var.* Tiruvantapuram, Trivandrum. *state capital* Kerala, SW India 08°30′N 76°57′E
155 H22 **Thiruvārūr** *var.* Tiruvarur. Tamil Nādu, SE India 10°46′N 79°39′E
95 F20 **Thisted** Viborg, NW Denmark 56°58′N 08°42′E
Thistil Fjord *see* Thistilfjördhur
92 L1 **Thistilfjördhur** *var.* Thistil Fjord. *fjord* NE Iceland
182 G9 **Thistle Island** *island* South Australia
Thithia *see* Cicia
Thiukhaoluang Phrahang *see* Luang Prabang Range
115 G18 **Thíva** *Eng.* Thebes; *prev.* Thívai. Stereá Ellás, C Greece 38°19′N 23°19′E
Thívai *see* Thíva
102 M12 **Thiviers** Dordogne, SW France 45°24′N 00°54′E
92 J4 **Thjórsá** ≈ C Iceland
9 N10 **Thlewiaza** ≈ Nunavut, NE Canada
8 L10 **Thoa** ≈ Northwest Territories, NW Canada
99 G14 **Tholen** Zeeland, SW Netherlands 51°31′N 04°13′E
99 F14 **Tholen** *island* SW Netherlands
26 L10 **Thomas** Oklahoma, C USA 35°44′N 98°45′W
21 T3 **Thomas** West Virginia, NE USA 39°09′N 79°28′W
27 U3 **Thomas Hill Reservoir** ⊞ Missouri, C USA
23 S5 **Thomaston** Georgia, SE USA 32°53′N 84°19′W
19 R7 **Thomaston** Maine, NE USA 44°06′N 69°10′W
25 T12 **Thomaston** Texas, SW USA 28°56′N 97°07′W
23 O6 **Thomasville** Alabama, S USA 31°54′N 87°42′W
23 T8 **Thomasville** Georgia, SE USA 30°49′N 83°57′W
21 S9 **Thomasville** North Carolina, SE USA 35°52′N 80°04′W
35 N5 **Thomes Creek** ≈ California, W USA
11 W12 **Thompson** Manitoba, C Canada 55°45′N 97°54′W
29 R4 **Thompson** North Dakota, N USA 47°45′N 97°07′W
0 F8 **Thompson** ≈ Alberta/British Columbia, SW Canada
33 O8 **Thompson Falls** Montana, NW USA 47°36′N 115°20′W
29 Q10 **Thompson, Lake** ◎ South Dakota, N USA
34 M3 **Thompson Peak** ▲ California, W USA 41°00′N 123°01′W
27 S2 **Thompson River** ≈ Missouri, C USA
185 A22 **Thompson Sound** *sound* South Island, New Zealand
8 J5 **Thomsen** ≈ Banks Island, Northwest Territories, NW Canada
23 V4 **Thomson** Georgia, SE USA 33°28′N 82°30′W
103 T10 **Thonon-les-Bains** Haute-Savoie, E France 46°22′N 06°30′E
103 O15 **Thoré** *var.* Thore. ≈ S France
Thore *see* Thoré
37 P11 **Thoreau** New Mexico, SW USA 35°24′N 108°13′W
Thorenburg *see* Turda
92 J3 **Thórisvatn** ◎ C Iceland
92 P4 **Thor, Kapp** *headland* S Svalbard 76°25′N 25°01′E
92 I4 **Thorlákshöfn** Sudhurland, SW Iceland 63°52′N 21°24′W
Thorn *see* Toruń
25 T10 **Thorndale** Texas, SW USA 30°36′N 97°12′W
14 H10 **Thorne** Ontario, S Canada 46°38′N 79°04′W
97 J14 **Thornhill** S Scotland, United Kingdom 55°13′N 03°46′W
25 U8 **Thornton** Texas, SW USA 31°24′N 96°34′W
Thornton Island *see* Millennium Island
14 H16 **Thorold** Ontario, S Canada 43°07′N 79°15′W
32 I9 **Thorp** Washington, NW USA 47°03′N 120°40′W
Thorshavn *see* Tórshavn
195 S3 **Thorshavnheiane** *physical region* Antarctica
92 L1 **Thórshöfn** Nordhurland Eystra, NE Iceland 66°09′N 15°18′W
Thospitis *see* Van Gölü
167 S14 **Thôt Nôt** Cân Thơ, S Vietnam 10°17′N 105°31′E
102 K8 **Thouars** Deux-Sèvres, W France 46°59′N 00°13′W
153 X14 **Thoubal** Manipur, NE India 24°40′N 94°00′E
102 K9 **Thouet** ≈ W France
Thoune *see* Thun
18 H7 **Thousand Islands** *island* Canada/USA
35 S15 **Thousand Oaks** California, W USA 34°10′N 118°50′W
114 L12 **Thrace** *cultural region* SE Europe
114 J13 **Thracian Sea** *Gk.* Thrakikó Pélagos; *anc.* Thracium Mare. *sea* Greece/Turkey
Thracium Mare/Thrakikó Pélagos *see* Thracian Sea
Thrá Lí, Bá *see* Tralee Bay
33 R11 **Three Forks** Montana, NW USA 45°53′N 111°34′W
162 M8 **Three Gorges Dam** *dam* Hubei, C China
160 L9 **Three Gorges Reservoir** ⊞ C China
11 Q16 **Three Hills** Alberta, SW Canada 51°43′N 113°15′W
183 N15 **Three Hummock Island** *island* Tasmania, SE Australia
184 H1 **Three Kings Islands** *island group* N New Zealand
175 P10 **Three Kings Rise** *undersea feature* W Pacific Ocean
77 O18 **Three Points, Cape** *headland* S Ghana 04°43′N 02°03′W
31 P10 **Three Rivers** Michigan, N USA 41°56′N 85°37′W
25 S13 **Three Rivers** Texas, SW USA 28°27′N 98°10′W
83 G24 **Three Sisters** Northern Cape, SW South Africa 31°51′S 23°04′E
32 H13 **Three Sisters** ▲ Oregon, NW USA 44°08′N 121°46′W
187 N10 **Three Sisters Islands** *island group* SE Solomon Islands
155 G22 **Thrissur** *var.* Trichūr. Kerala, SW India 10°32′N 76°14′E *see also* Trichūr
25 Q6 **Throckmorton** Texas, SW USA 33°11′N 99°12′W
180 M10 **Throssell, Lake** *salt lake* Western Australia
115 K25 **Thryptís** *var.* Thrýptis. ▲ Kríti, Greece, E Mediterranean Sea 35°06′N 25°51′E
167 T13 **Thu Dâu Một** *var.* Phu Cŭơng. Sông Be, S Vietnam 10°58′N 106°40′E
167 S6 **Thu Do** ✈ (Ha Nôi) Ha Nôi, N Vietnam 21°13′N 105°46′E
99 G21 **Thuin** Hainaut, S Belgium 50°21′N 04°18′E
149 Q12 **Thul** Sind, SE Pakistan 28°14′N 68°50′E
Thule *see* Qaanaaq
83 J18 **Thuli** *var.* Tuli. ≈ S Zimbabwe
Thumrayt *see* Thamarīt
108 D9 **Thun** *Fr.* Thoune. Bern, W Switzerland 46°46′N 07°38′E
12 C12 **Thunder Bay** Ontario, S Canada 48°27′N 89°12′W
30 M1 **Thunder Bay** *lake bay* S Canada
31 R6 **Thunder Bay** *lake bay* Michigan, N USA
31 R6 **Thunder Bay River** ≈ Michigan, N USA
27 N11 **Thunderbird, Lake** ⊞ Oklahoma, C USA
28 L8 **Thunder Butte Creek** ≈ South Dakota, N USA
108 E9 **Thuner See** ◎ C Switzerland
167 N15 **Thung Song** *var.* Cha Mai. Nakhon Si Thammarat, SW Thailand 08°10′N 99°41′E
108 H7 **Thur** ≈ N Switzerland
108 G6 **Thurgau** *Fr.* Thurgovie. ◈ *canton* NE Switzerland
Thurgovie *see* Thurgau
Thuringe *see* Thüringen
108 J7 **Thüringen** Vorarlberg, W Austria 47°12′N 09°48′E
101 J17 **Thüringen** *Eng.* Thuringia, *Fr.* Thuringe. ◈ *state* C Germany
101 J17 **Thüringer Wald** *Eng.* Thuringian Forest. ▲▲ C Germany
Thuringia *see* Thüringen
Thuringian Forest *see* Thüringer Wald
97 D19 **Thurles** *Ir.* Durlas. S Ireland 52°41′N 07°49′W
21 W2 **Thurmont** Maryland, NE USA 39°36′N 77°22′W
Thurø *see* Thurø By
95 H24 **Thurø By** *var.* Thurø. Fyn, C Denmark 55°03′N 10°43′E
14 M12 **Thurso** Québec, SE Canada 45°36′N 75°13′W
96 J6 **Thurso** N Scotland, United Kingdom 58°35′N 03°32′W
194 I10 **Thurston Island** *island* Antarctica
108 I9 **Thusis** Graubünden, S Switzerland 46°40′N 09°27′E
Thýamis *see* Kalamás
95 E21 **Thyborøn** *var.* Tyborøn. Ringkøbing, W Denmark 56°40′N 08°12′E
195 U3 **Thyer Glacier** *glacier* Antarctica
115 L20 **Thýmaina** *island* Dodekánisa, Greece, Aegean Sea
83 N15 **Thyolo** *var.* Cholo. Southern, S Malawi 16°03′S 35°11′E
183 U6 **Tia** New South Wales, SE Australia 31°14′S 151°51′E
54 H5 **Tía Juana** Zulia, NW Venezuela 10°18′N 71°24′W
Tiancheng *see* Chongyang
160 J14 **Tiandong** *var.* Pingma. Guangxi Zhuangzu Zizhiqu, S China 23°37′N 107°06′E
161 O3 **Tianjin** *var.* Tientsin. Tianjin Shi, E China 39°13′N 117°06′E
Tianjin *see* Tianjin Shi
161 P3 **Tianjin Shi** *var.* Jin, Tianjin, T'ien-ching, Tientsin. ◈ *municipality* E China
159 S10 **Tianjun** *var.* Xinyuan. Qinghai, C China 37°16′N 99°03′E
160 J13 **Tianlin** *var.* Leli. Guangxi Zhuangzu Zizhiqu, S China 24°27′N 106°03′E
Tian Shan *see* Tien Shan
159 W11 **Tianshui** Gansu, C China 34°33′N 105°51′E
150 I7 **Tianshuihai** Xinjiang Uygur Zizhiqu, W China 35°17′N 79°30′E
161 S10 **Tiantai** Zhejiang, SE China 29°11′N 121°01′E
160 J14 **Tianyang** *var.* Tianzhou. Guangxi Zhuangzu Zizhiqu, S China 23°50′N 106°52′E
Tianzhou *see* Tianyang
159 U9 **Tianzhu** *var.* Huazangsi, Tianzhu Zangzu Zizhixian. Gansu, C China 37°01′N 103°04′E
Tianzhu Zangzu Zizhixian *see* Tianzhu
191 Q7 **Tiarei** Tahiti, W French Polynesia 17°32′S 149°20′W
74 J6 **Tiaret** *var.* Tihert. NW Algeria 35°20′N 01°20′E
77 N17 **Tiassalé** S Ivory Coast 05°54′N 04°50′W
192 I16 **Ti'avea** Upolu, SE Samoa 13°58′S 171°30′W
Tiba *see* Chiba
60 J11 **Tibagi** *var.* Tibaji. Paraná, S Brazil 24°29′S 50°29′W
60 J10 **Tibagi, Rio** *var.* Rio Tibají. ≈ S Brazil
Tibaji *see* Tibagi
Tibají, Rio *see* Tibagi, Rio
139 Q9 **Tibal, Wādī** *dry watercourse* S Iraq
54 G9 **Tibaná** Boyacá, C Colombia 05°19′N 73°25′W
79 F14 **Tibati** Adamaoua, N Cameroon 06°25′N 12°33′E
76 K15 **Tibé, Pic de** ▲ SE Guinea 08°39′N 08°58′W
Tiber *see* Tevere, Italy
Tiber *see* Tivoli, Italy
Tiberias *see* Tverya
138 G8 **Tiberias, Lake** *var.* Chinnereth, Sea of Bahr Tabariya, Sea of Galilee, *Ar.* Bahrat Tabariya, *Heb.* Yam Kinneret. ◎ N Israel
67 Q5 **Tibesti** *var.* Tibesti Massif, *Ar.* Tībistī. ▲▲ N Africa
Tibesti Massif *see* Tibesti
Tibet *see* Xizang Zizhiqu
Tibetan Autonomous Region *see* Xizang Zizhiqu
Tibet, Plateau of *see* Qingzang Gaoyuan
Tībistī *see* Tibesti
14 K7 **Tiblemont, Lac** ◎ Québec, SE Canada
139 X9 **Ţīb, Nahr aţ** ≈ S Iraq
Tibnī *see* At Tibnī
182 L4 **Tibooburra** New South Wales, SE Australia 29°24′S 142°01′E
95 L18 **Tibro** Västra Götaland, S Sweden 58°25′N 14°11′E
40 E5 **Tiburón, Isla** *var.* Isla del Tiburón. *island* NW Mexico
Tiburón, Isla del *see* Tiburón, Isla
23 W14 **Tice** Florida, SE USA 26°40′N 81°49′W
Tichau *see* Tychy
114 L8 **Ticha, Yazovir** ◎ NE Bulgaria
76 K9 **Tîchît** *var.* Tichitt. Tagant, C Mauritania 18°26′N 09°31′W
Tichitt *see* Tîchît
108 G11 **Ticino** *Fr./Ger.* Tessin. ◈ *canton* S Switzerland
106 D8 **Ticino** ≈ Italy/Switzerland
108 H11 **Ticino** *Ger.* Tessin. ≈ SW Switzerland
Ticinum *see* Pavia
41 X12 **Ticul** Yucatán, SE Mexico 20°22′N 89°30′W
95 K18 **Tidaholm** Västra Götaland, S Sweden 58°12′N 13°55′E
Tidjikdja *see* Tidjikja
76 J8 **Tidjikja** *var.* Tidjikdja; *prev.* Fort-Cappolani. Tagant, C Mauritania 18°31′N 11°24′W
Tidore *see* Soasiu
171 R11 **Tidore, Pulau** *island* E Indonesia
Tîdra, Ile *see* Et Tîdra
77 N16 **Tiébissou** *var.* Tiebissou. C Ivory Coast 07°10′N 05°10′W
Tiebissou *see* Tiébissou
Tiefa *see* Diaobingshan
108 I9 **Tiefencastel** Graubünden, S Switzerland 46°40′N 09°33′E
Tiegenhof *see* Nowy Dwór Gdański
T'ieh-ling *see* Tieling
98 K13 **Tiel** Gelderland, C Netherlands 51°53′N 05°26′E
163 W7 **Tieli** Heilongjiang, NE China 46°57′N 128°01′E
163 V11 **Tieling** *var.* T'ieh-ling. Liaoning, NE China 42°19′N 123°52′E
152 L4 **Tielongtan** China/India 35°10′N 79°32′E
99 D17 **Tielt** *var.* Thielt. West-Vlaanderen, W Belgium 51°00′N 03°20′E
T'ien-ching *see* Tianjin Shi
99 I18 **Tienen** *var.* Thienen, *Fr.* Tirlemont. Vlaams Brabant, C Belgium 50°48′N 04°56′E
Tiên Giang, Sông *see* Mekong
147 X9 **Tien Shan** *Chin.* Thian Shan, Tian Shan, T'ien Shan, *Rus.* Tyan'-Shan'. ▲▲ C Asia
Tientsin *see* Tianjin
167 U6 **Tiên Yên** Quang Ninh, N Vietnam 21°19′N 107°24′E
95 O14 **Tierp** Uppsala, C Sweden 60°20′N 17°30′E
62 H7 **Tierra Amarilla** Atacama, N Chile 27°28′S 70°17′W
37 R9 **Tierra Amarilla** New Mexico, SW USA 36°42′N 106°31′W
41 R15 **Tierra Blanca** Veracruz-Llave, E Mexico 18°28′N 96°21′W
41 O16 **Tierra Colorada** Guerrero, S Mexico 17°10′N 99°30′W
63 J17 **Tierra Colorada, Bajo de la** *basin* SE Argentina
63 I25 **Tierra del Fuego** *off.* Provincia de la Tierra del Fuego. ◈ *province* S Argentina
63 J24 **Tierra del Fuego** *island* Argentina/Chile
Tierra del Fuego, Provincia de la *see* Tierra del Fuego
54 D7 **Tierralta** Córdoba, NW Colombia 08°10′N 76°04′W
104 K9 **Tiétar** ≈ W Spain
60 L10 **Tietê** São Paulo, S Brazil 23°04′S 47°41′W
60 J8 **Tietê, Rio** ≈ S Brazil
32 I9 **Tieton** Washington, NW USA 46°41′N 120°43′W
32 J6 **Tiffany Mountain** ▲ Washington, NW USA 48°40′N 119°55′W
31 S12 **Tiffin** Ohio, N USA 41°06′N 83°10′W
31 Q11 **Tiffin River** ≈ Ohio, N USA
Tiflis *see* T'bilisi
23 U7 **Tifton** Georgia, SE USA 31°27′N 83°31′W
171 R13 **Tifu** Pulau Buru, E Indonesia 03°46′S 126°36′E
38 L17 **Tigalda Island** *island* Aleutian Islands, Alaska, USA
115 I15 **Tigáni, Akrotírio** *headland* Límnos, E Greece 39°50′N 25°03′E
169 V6 **Tiga Tarok** Sabah, East Malaysia 06°57′N 117°07′E
117 O10 **Tighina** *Rus.* Bendery; *prev.* Bender. E Moldova 46°51′N 29°28′E
145 X9 **Tigiretskiy Khrebet** ▲▲ E Kazakhstan
79 F14 **Tignère** Adamaoua, N Cameroon 07°24′N 12°35′E
13 P14 **Tignish** Prince Edward Island, SE Canada 46°58′N 64°03′W
Tigranocerta *see* Siirt
80 I11 **Tigray** ◈ *federal region* N Ethiopia
41 O11 **Tigre, Cerro del** ▲ C Mexico 23°06′N 99°13′W
56 F8 **Tigre, Río** ≈ N Peru
139 X10 **Tigris** *Ar.* Dijlah, *Turk.* Dicle. ≈ Iraq/Turkey
76 G9 **Tiguent** Trarza, SW Mauritania 17°15′N 16°00′W
74 M10 **Tiguentourine** E Algeria 27°59′N 09°16′E
77 V10 **Tiguidit, Falaise de** *ridge* C Niger
141 N13 **Tihāmah** *var.* Tehama. *plain* Saudi Arabia/Yemen
Tihert *see* Tiaret
Ti-hua/Tihwa *see* Ürümqi
41 Q13 **Tihuatlán** Veracruz-Llave, E Mexico 20°44′N 97°30′W
40 B1 **Tijuana** Baja California Norte, NW Mexico 32°32′N 117°01′W
42 E2 **Tikal** Petén, N Guatemala 17°11′N 89°36′W
154 I9 **Tīkamgarh** *prev.* Tehri. Madhya Pradesh, C India 24°44′N 78°50′E
158 L7 **Tikanlik** Xinjiang Uygur Zizhiqu, NW China 40°34′N 87°37′E
77 P12 **Tikaré** N Burkina 13°16′N 01°39′W
39 O12 **Tikchik Lakes** *lakes* Alaska, USA
191 T9 **Tikehau** *atoll* Îles Tuamotu, C French Polynesia
191 V9 **Tikei** *island* Îles Tuamotu, C French Polynesia
126 L13 **Tikhoretsk** Krasnodarskiy Kray, SW Russian Federation 45°51′N 40°07′E
124 I13 **Tikhvin** Leningradskaya Oblast', NW Russian Federation 59°37′N 33°30′E
193 P9 **Tiki Basin** *undersea feature* S Pacific Ocean
76 K13 **Tikinsso** ≈ NE Guinea
184 Q8 **Tikitiki** Gisborne, North Island, New Zealand 37°49′S 178°23′E
79 D16 **Tiko** Sud-Ouest, SW Cameroon 04°02′N 09°19′E
139 S6 **Tikrīt** *var.* Tekrit. Şalāḩ ad Dīn, N Iraq 34°36′N 43°42′E
124 I8 **Tiksha** Respublika Kareliya, NW Russian Federation 64°07′N 32°31′E
124 I6 **Tikshozero, Ozero** ◎ NW Russian Federation
123 P7 **Tiksi** Respublika Sakha (Yakutiya), NE Russian Federation 71°40′N 128°47′E
Tiladummati Atoll *see* Thiladhunmathi Atoll
42 A6 **Tilapa** San Marcos, SW Guatemala 14°31′N 92°11′W
42 L13 **Tilarán** Guanacaste, NW Costa Rica 10°28′N 84°57′W
99 J14 **Tilburg** Noord-Brabant, S Netherlands 51°34′N 05°05′E
14 D17 **Tilbury** Ontario, S Canada 42°15′N 82°26′W
182 K4 **Tilcha** South Australia 29°37′S 140°52′E
Tilcha Creek *see* Callabonna Creek
29 Q14 **Tilden** Nebraska, C USA 42°03′N 97°49′W
25 R13 **Tilden** Texas, SW USA 28°27′N 98°43′W
14 H10 **Tilden Lake** Ontario, S Canada 46°35′N 79°36′W
116 G9 **Tileagd** *Hung.* Mezőtelegd. Bihor, W Romania 47°03′N 22°11′E
77 Q8 **Tîlemsi, Vallée de** ≈ C Mali
123 V8 **Tilichiki** Koryakskiy Avtonomnyy Okrug, E Russian Federation 60°25′N 165°55′E
Tiligul *see* Tilihul
Tiligul'skiy Liman *see* Tilihul's'kyy Lyman
117 P9 **Tilihul** *Rus.* Tiligul. ≈ SW Ukraine
117 P10 **Tilihul's'kyy Lyman** *Rus.* Tiligul'skiy Liman. ◎ S Ukraine
Tilimsen *see* Tlemcen
Tilio Martius *see* Toulon
77 R11 **Tillabéri** *var.* Tillabéry. Tillabéri, W Niger 14°13′N 01°27′E
77 R11 **Tillabéri** ◈ *department* SW Niger
Tillabéry *see* Tillabéri
32 F11 **Tillamook** Oregon, NW USA 45°28′N 123°50′W
32 E11 **Tillamook Bay** *inlet* Oregon, NW USA
151 Q22 **Tillanchāng Dwīp** *island* Nicobar Islands, India, NE Indian Ocean
95 N15 **Tillberga** Västmanland, C Sweden 59°41′N 16°37′E
Tillenberg *see* Dyleń
21 S10 **Tillery, Lake** ⊞ North Carolina, SE USA
77 T10 **Tillia** Tahoua, W Niger 16°13′N 04°51′E
23 N8 **Tillmans Corner** Alabama, S USA 30°35′N 88°10′W
14 F17 **Tillsonburg** Ontario, S Canada 42°53′N 80°44′W
115 N22 **Tílos** *island* Dodekánisa, Greece, Aegean Sea
183 N5 **Tilpa** New South Wales, SE Australia 30°56′S 144°24′E
Tilsit *see* Sovetsk
31 N13 **Tilton** Illinois, N USA 40°06′N 87°39′W
126 K7 **Tim** Kurskaya Oblast', W Russian Federation 51°39′N 37°11′E
54 D12 **Timaná** Huila, S Colombia 01°58′N 75°55′W
Timan Ridge *see* Timanskiy Kryazh
125 Q6 **Timanskiy Kryazh** *Eng.* Timan Ridge. *ridge* NW Russian Federation
185 G20 **Timaru** Canterbury, South Island, New Zealand 44°23′S 171°15′E
127 S6 **Timashevo** Samarskaya Oblast', W Russian Federation 53°22′N 51°13′E
126 K13 **Timashevsk** Krasnodarskiy Kray, SW Russian Federation 45°37′N 38°57′E
Timbaki/Timbákion *see* Tympáki
22 K10 **Timbalier Bay** *bay* Louisiana, S USA
22 K11 **Timbalier Island** *island* Louisiana, S USA
76 L10 **Timbedgha** *var.* Timbédra. Hodh ech Chargui, SE Mauritania 16°17′N 08°14′W
Timbédra *see* Timbedgha
32 G10 **Timber** Oregon, NW USA 45°42′N 123°19′W
181 O3 **Timber Creek** Northern Territory, N Australia 15°35′S 130°21′E
28 M8 **Timber Lake** South Dakota, N USA 45°25′N 101°01′W
54 D12 **Timbío** Cauca, SW Colombia 02°20′N 76°40′W
54 C12 **Timbiquí** Cauca, SW Colombia 02°43′N 77°45′W
83 O17 **Timbue, Ponta** *headland* C Mozambique 18°49′S 36°22′E
Timbuktu *see* Tombouctou
169 W8 **Timbun Mata, Pulau** *island* E Malaysia
77 P8 **Timétrine** *var.* Ti-n-Kâr. *oasis* C Mali
Timfi *see* Týmfi
Timfristos *see* Tymfristós
77 V9 **Tîmia** Agadez, C Niger 18°07′N 08°49′E
171 X14 **Timika** Papua, E Indonesia 04°39′S 137°15′E
74 I9 **Timimoun** C Algeria 29°18′N 00°21′E
Timiris, Cap *see* Timirist, Râs
76 F8 **Timirist, Râs** *var.* Cap Timiris. *headland* NW Mauritania 19°18′N 16°28′W
145 O7 **Timiryazevo** Severnyy Kazakhstan, N Kazakhstan 53°45′N 66°33′E
116 E11 **Timiş** ◈ *county* SW Romania
14 H9 **Timiskaming, Lake** *Fr.* Lac Témiscamingue. ◎ Ontario/Québec, SE Canada
116 E11 **Timişoara** *Ger.* Temeschwar, Temeswar, *Hung.* Temesvár; *prev.* Temeschburg. Timiş, W Romania 45°46′N 21°17′E
116 E11 **Timisoara** ✈ Timiş, SW Romania 45°50′N 21°21′E
Timkovichi *see* Tsimkavichy
77 U8 **Ti-m-Meghsoï** ≈ NW Niger
100 K8 **Timmerdorfer Strand** Schleswig-Holstein, N Germany 53°59′N 10°50′E
14 F7 **Timmins** Ontario, S Canada 48°09′N 80°01′W
21 S12 **Timmonsville** South Carolina, SE USA 34°07′N 79°56′W
30 K5 **Timms Hill** ▲ Wisconsin, N USA 45°27′N 90°12′W
112 P12 **Timok** ≈ E Serbia
58 N13 **Timon** Maranhão, E Brazil 05°08′S 42°52′W
171 Q17 **Timor Sea** *sea* E Indian Ocean
Timor Timur *see* East Timor
Timor Trench *see* Timor Trough
192 G8 **Timor Trough** *var.* Timor Trench. *undersea feature* NE Timor Sea
61 A21 **Timote** Buenos Aires, E Argentina 35°22′S 62°13′W
54 I6 **Timotes** Mérida, NW Venezuela 08°57′N 70°46′W
25 X8 **Timpson** Texas, SW USA 31°54′N 94°24′W
123 Q11 **Timpton** ≈ NE Russian Federation
93 H17 **Timrå** Västernorrland, C Sweden 62°29′N 17°20′E
20 J10 **Tims Ford Lake** ⊞ Tennessee, S USA
168 L7 **Timur, Banjaran** ▲▲ Peninsular Malaysia
149 T4 **Timurgara** North-West Frontier Province, N Pakistan 34°50′N 71°55′E
171 Q8 **Tinaca Point** *headland* Mindanao, S Philippines 05°35′N 125°18′E
54 K5 **Tinaco** Cojedes, N Venezuela 09°44′N 68°28′W
64 Q11 **Tinajo** Lanzarote, Islas Canarias, Spain, NE Atlantic Ocean 29°03′N 13°41′W
187 P10 **Tinakula** *island* Santa Cruz Islands, E Solomon Islands
54 K5 **Tinaquillo** Cojedes, N Venezuela 09°57′N 68°20′W
116 F10 **Tinca** *Hung.* Tenke. Bihor, W Romania 46°46′N 21°58′E
155 J20 **Tīndivanam** Tamil Nādu, SE India 12°15′N 79°41′E
74 E9 **Tindouf** W Algeria 27°43′N 08°09′W
74 E9 **Tindouf, Sebkha de** *salt lake* W Algeria
104 J2 **Tineo** Asturias, N Spain 43°20′N 06°25′W
77 R9 **Ti-n-Essako** Kidal, E Mali 18°30′N 02°27′E
183 T5 **Tingha** New South Wales, SE Australia 29°56′S 151°13′E
Tingis *see* Tanger
Tinglett *see* Tinglev
95 F24 **Tinglev** *Ger.* Tinglett. Sønderjylland, SW Denmark 54°57′N 09°15′E
56 E12 **Tingo María** Huánuco, C Peru 09°10′S 76°00′W
Tingréla *see* Tengréla
158 K16 **Tingri** *var.* Xêgar. Xizang Zizhiqu, W China 28°40′N 87°04′E
95 M21 **Tingsryd** Kronoberg, S Sweden 56°30′N 15°E
95 P19 **Tingstäde** Gotland, SE Sweden 57°45′N 18°36′E
62 H12 **Tinguiririca, Volcán** ⛰ C Chile 34°52′S 70°24′W
94 F9 **Tingvoll** Møre og Romsdal, S Norway 62°55′N 08°13′E
188 K8 **Tinian** *island* S Northern Mariana Islands
Ti-n-Kâr *see* Timétrine
Tinnevelly *see* Tirunelveli
95 G15 **Tinnoset** Telemark, S Norway 59°43′N 09°03′E
95 F15 **Tinnsjø** ◎ S Norway
Tino *see* Chino
115 J20 **Tínos** Tínos, Kykládes, Greece, Aegean Sea 37°33′N 25°08′E
115 J20 **Tínos** *anc.* Tenos. *island* Kykládes, Greece, Aegean Sea
153 R14 **Tinpahar** Jhārkhand, NE India 25°00′N 87°43′E
153 X11 **Tinsukia** Assam, NE India 27°28′N 95°20′E
76 K10 **Tîntâne** Hodh el Gharbi, S Mauritania 16°25′N 10°08′W
62 L7 **Tintina** Santiago del Estero, N Argentina 27°00′S 62°45′W
182 K10 **Tintinara** South Australia 35°54′S 140°04′E
104 I14 **Tinto** ≈ SW Spain
77 S8 **Ti-n-Zaouâtene** Kidal, NE Mali 19°56′N 02°45′E
Tiobraid Árann *see* Tipperary
28 K3 **Tioga** North Dakota, N USA 48°24′N 102°56′W
18 G12 **Tioga** Pennsylvania, NE USA 41°54′N 77°07′W
25 T5 **Tioga** Texas, SW USA 33°28′N 96°55′W
35 Q8 **Tioga Pass** *pass* California, W USA
18 G12 **Tioga River** ≈ New York/Pennsylvania, NE USA
Tioman Island *see* Tioman, Pulau
168 M9 **Tioman, Pulau** *var.* Tioman Island. *island* Peninsular Malaysia
18 C12 **Tionesta** Pennsylvania, NE USA 41°31′N 79°30′W
18 D12 **Tionesta Creek** ≈ Pennsylvania, NE USA
168 J13 **Tiop** Pulau Pagai Selatan, W Indonesia 03°12′S 100°21′E
18 H11 **Tioughnioga River** ≈ New York, NE USA
74 J5 **Tipasa** *var.* Tipaza. N Algeria 36°35′N 02°27′E
Tipaza *see* Tipasa
42 J10 **Tipitapa** Managua, W Nicaragua 12°08′N 86°04′W
31 R13 **Tipp City** Ohio, N USA 39°57′N 84°10′W
31 O12 **Tippecanoe River** ≈ Indiana, N USA
97 D20 **Tipperary** *Ir.* Tiobraid Árann. S Ireland 52°29′N 08°10′W
97 D19 **Tipperary** *Ir.* Tiobraid Árann. *cultural region* S Ireland
35 R12 **Tipton** California, W USA 36°02′N 119°19′W
31 P13 **Tipton** Indiana, N USA 40°19′N 86°00′W
29 Y14 **Tipton** Iowa, C USA 41°46′N 91°07′W
27 U5 **Tipton** Missouri, C USA 38°39′N 92°46′W
36 I10 **Tipton, Mount** ▲ Arizona, SW USA 35°32′N 114°11′W
20 F8 **Tiptonville** Tennessee, S USA 36°21′N 89°30′W
12 E12 **Tip Top Mountain** ▲ Ontario, S Canada 48°18′N 86°06′W
155 G19 **Tiptūr** Karnātaka, W India 13°17′N 76°31′E
Tiquisate *see* Pueblo Nuevo Tiquisate
58 L13 **Tiracambu, Serra do** ▲▲ E Brazil
Tirana *see* Tiranë
113 K19 **Tirana Rinas** ✈ Durrës, W Albania 41°25′N 19°41′E
113 L20 **Tiranë** *var.* Tirana. ● (Albania) Tiranë, C Albania 41°20′N 19°50′E
113 K20 **Tiranë** ◈ *district* W Albania
140 I5 **Tirān, Jazīrat** *island* Egypt/Saudi Arabia
106 F6 **Tirano** Lombardia, N Italy 46°13′N 10°10′E
182 I2 **Tirari Desert** *desert* South Australia
117 O10 **Tiraspol** *Rus.* Tiraspol'. E Moldova 46°50′N 29°35′E
Tiraspol' *see* Tiraspol
184 M8 **Tirau** Waikato, North Island, New Zealand 37°59′S 175°44′E
136 C14 **Tire** İzmir, SW Turkey 38°04′N 27°45′E
137 O11 **Tirebolu** Giresun, N Turkey 41°01′N 38°49′E
96 F11 **Tiree** *island* W Scotland, United Kingdom
Tîrgovişte *see* Târgovişte
Tîrgu *see* Târgu Cărbuneşti
Tîrgu Bujor *see* Târgu Bujor
Tîrgu Frumos *see* Târgu Frumos
Tîrgu Jiu *see* Targu Jiu
Tîrgu Lăpuş *see* Târgu Lăpuş
Tîrgu Mures *see* Târgu Mureş
Tîrgu-Neamţ *see* Târgu-Neamţ
Tîrgu Ocna *see* Târgu Ocna
Tîrgu Secuiesc *see* Târgu Secuiesc
149 T3 **Tirich Mīr** ▲ NW Pakistan 36°12′N 71°51′E
76 J5 **Tiris Zemmour** ◈ *region* N Mauritania
Tirlemont *see* Tienen
127 W5 **Tirlyanskiy** Respublika Bashkortostan, W Russian Federation 54°09′N 58°32′E
Tîrnava Mare *see* Târnava Mare
Tîrnava Mică *see* Târnava Mică
Tîrnăveni *see* Târnăveni
Tírnavos *see* Týrnavos
Tirnovo *see* Veliko Tŭrnovo
154 J11 **Tirodi** Madhya Pradesh, C India 21°40′N 79°44′E
108 K8 **Tirol** *off.* Land Tirol, *var.* Tyrol, *It.* Tirolo. ◈ *state* W Austria
Tirol, Land *see* Tirol
Tirolo *see* Tirol
Tirreno, Mare *see* Tyrrhenian Sea
107 B19 **Tirso** ≈ Sardegna, Italy, C Mediterranean Sea
95 H22 **Tirstrup** ✈ (Århus) Århus, C Denmark 56°17′N 10°36′E
155 I21 **Tiruchchirāppalli** *prev.* Trichinopoly. Tamil Nādu, SE India 10°50′N 78°43′E
155 H23 **Tirunelveli** *var.* Tinnevelly. Tamil Nādu, SE India 08°45′N 77°43′E
155 J19 **Tirupati** Andhra Pradesh, E India 13°39′N 79°25′E
155 I20 **Tiruppattūr** Tamil Nādu, SE India 12°28′N 78°31′E
155 H21 **Tiruppur** Tamil Nādu, SW India 11°05′N 77°20′E
155 J20 **Tiruvallūr** *var.* Tirvellore. Tamil Nādu, SE India 13°08′N 79°54′E
Tiruvantapuram *see* Thiruvanathapuram/Trivandrum
Tiruvarur *see* Thiruvārūr
155 I20 **Tiruyannāmalai** Tamil Nādu, SE India 12°13′N 79°07′E
Tirvellore *see* Tiruvallūr
112 L10 **Tisa** *Ger.* Theiss, *Hung.* Tisza, *Rus.* Tissa, *Ukr.* Tysa. ≈ SE Europe *see also* Tisza

◆ Country
● Country Capital
◇ Dependent Territory
○ Dependent Territory Capital
◈ Administrative Regions
✈ International Airport
▲ Mountain
▲▲ Mountain Range
⛰ Volcano
≈ River
◎ Lake
⊞ Reservoir

Tisa *see* Tisza
Tischnowitz *see* Tišnov
11 U14 **Tisdale** Saskatchewan, S Canada 52°51′N 104°01′W
27 O13 **Tishomingo** Oklahoma, C USA 34°15′N 96°41′W
95 M17 **Tisnaren** ◎ S Sweden
111 F18 **Tišnov** *Ger.* Tischnowitz. Jihomoravský Kraj, SE Czech Republic 49°22′N 16°24′E
Tissa *see* Tisa/Tisza
74 J6 **Tissemsilt** N Algeria 35°37′N 01°48′E
153 S12 **Tista** ≈ NE India
112 L8 **Tisza** *Ger.* Theiss, *Rom./Slvn./SCr.* Tisa, *Rus.* Tissa, *Ukr.* Tysa. ≈ SE Europe *see also* Tisa
Tisza *see* Tisa
111 L23 **Tiszaföldvár** Jász-Nagykun-Szolnok, E Hungary 47°00′N 20°16′E
111 M22 **Tiszafüred** Jász-Nagykun-Szolnok, E Hungary 47°38′N 20°45′E
111 L23 **Tiszakécske** Bács-Kiskun, C Hungary 46°56′N 20°04′E
111 M21 **Tiszaújváros** *prev.* Leninváros. Borsod-Abaúj-Zemplén, NE Hungary 47°56′N 21°03′E
111 N21 **Tiszavasvári** Szabolcs-Szatmár-Bereg, NE Hungary 47°56′N 21°21′E
57 I17 **Titicaca, Lake** ◎ Bolivia/Peru
190 H17 **Titikaveka** Rarotonga, S Cook Islands 21°16′S 159°45′W
154 M13 **Titilāgarh** *var.* Titlagarh. Orissa, E India 20°18′N 83°09′E
168 K8 **Titiwangsa, Banjaran** ▲▲ Peninsular Malaysia
Titlagarh *see* Titilāgarh
Titograd *see* Podgorica
Titose *see* Chitose
Titova Mitrovica *see* Mitrovicë
Titovo Užice *see* Užice
113 M18 **Titov Vrv** ▲ NW FYR Macedonia 41°58′N 20°49′E
94 F7 **Titran** Sør-Trøndelag, S Norway 63°40′N 08°20′E
31 Q8 **Tittabawassee River** ≈ Michigan, N USA
116 J13 **Titu** Dâmbovița, S Romania 44°40′N 25°32′E
79 M16 **Titule** Orientale, N Dem. Rep. Congo 03°20′N 25°23′E
23 X11 **Titusville** Florida, SE USA 28°37′N 80°50′W
18 C12 **Titusville** Pennsylvania, NE USA 41°36′N 79°39′W
76 G11 **Tivaouane** W Senegal 14°59′N 16°50′W
113 I17 **Tivat** SW Montenegro 42°25′N 18°43′E
14 E14 **Tiverton** Ontario, S Canada 44°15′N 81°31′W
97 J23 **Tiverton** SW England, United Kingdom 50°54′N 03°30′W
19 O12 **Tiverton** Rhode Island, NE USA 41°38′N 71°10′W
107 I15 **Tivoli** *anc.* Tiber. Lazio, C Italy 41°58′N 12°45′E
25 U13 **Tivoli** Texas, SW USA 28°26′N 96°54′W
141 Z8 **Ţīwī** NE Oman 22°43′N 59°20′E
41 Y11 **Tizimín** Yucatán, SE Mexico 21°10′N 88°09′W
74 K5 **Tizi Ouzou** *var.* Tizi-Ouzou. N Algeria 36°44′N 04°06′E
Tizi-Ouzou *see* Tizi Ouzou
74 D8 **Tiznit** SW Morocco 29°43′N 09°39′W
95 F23 **Tjæreborg** Ribe, W Denmark 55°28′N 08°35′E
113 I14 **Tjentište** Republika Srpska, SE Bosnia and Herzegovina 43°23′N 18°42′E
98 L7 **Tjeukemeer** ◎ N Netherlands
Tjiamis *see* Ciamis
Tjiandjoer *see* Cianjur
Tjilatjap *see* Cilacap
Tjirebon *see* Cirebon
95 I18 **Tjörn** *island* S Sweden
92 O3 **Tjuvfjorden** *fjord* S Svalbard
Tkvarcheli *see* Tqvarch'eli
40 L8 **Tlahualillo** Durango, N Mexico 26°06′N 103°25′W
41 P14 **Tlalnepantla** México, C Mexico 19°34′N 99°12′W
41 Q13 **Tlapacoyán** Veracruz-Llave, E Mexico 19°58′N 97°13′W
41 P16 **Tlapa de Comonfort** Guerrero, S Mexico 17°33′N 98°33′W
40 L13 **Tlaquepaque** Jalisco, C Mexico 20°36′N 103°19′W
Tlascala *see* Tlaxcala
41 P14 **Tlaxcala** *var.* Tlascala, Tlaxcala de Xicohténcatl. Tlaxcala, C Mexico 19°17′N 98°16′W
41 P14 **Tlaxcala** ⬖ *state* S Mexico
Tlaxcala de Xicohténcatl *see* Tlaxcala
41 P14 **Tlaxco** *var.* Tlaxco de Morelos. Tlaxcala, S Mexico 19°38′N 98°06′W
Tlaxco de Morelos *see* Tlaxco
41 Q16 **Tlaxiaco** *var.* Santa María Asunción Tlaxiaco. Oaxaca, S Mexico 17°18′N 97°42′W
74 I6 **Tlemcen** *var.* Tilimsen, Tlemsen. NW Algeria 34°53′N 01°21′W
Tlemsen *see* Tlemcen
138 L4 **Tlété Ouâte Rharbi, Jebel** ▲ N Syria
116 J7 **Tlumach** Ivano-Frankivs'ka Oblast', W Ukraine 48°53′N 25°00′E
127 P17 **Tlyarata** Respublika Dagestan, SW Russian Federation 42°10′N 46°30′E
116 K10 **Toaca, Vârful** *prev.* Vîrful Toaca. ▲ NE Romania 46°58′N 25°55′E
Toaca, Vîrful *see* Toaca, Vârful
187 R13 **Toak** Ambrym, C Vanuatu 16°21′S 168°16′E
172 J4 **Toamasina** *var.* Tamatave. Toamasina, E Madagascar 18°10′S 49°23′E
172 J4 **Toamasina** ⬖ *province* E Madagascar
172 J4 **Toamasina** ✈ Toamasina, E Madagascar 18°10′S 49°23′E
21 X6 **Toano** Virginia, NE USA 37°22′N 76°46′W
191 U10 **Toau** *atoll* Îles Tuamotu, C French Polynesia
45 T6 **Toa Vaca, Embalse** ⊠ C Puerto Rico
62 K13 **Toay** La Pampa, C Argentina 36°43′S 64°22′W
159 R14 **Toba** Xizang Zizhiqu, W China 31°17′N 97°37′E
164 K14 **Toba** Mie, Honshū, SW Japan 34°29′N 136°51′E
168 I9 **Toba, Danau** ◎ Sumatera, W Indonesia
45 Y16 **Tobago** *island* NE Trinidad and Tobago
149 Q9 **Toba Kākar Range** ▲▲ NW Pakistan
105 Q12 **Tobarra** Castilla-La Mancha, C Spain 38°36′N 01°41′W
149 U9 **Toba Tek Singh** Punjab, E Pakistan 30°54′N 72°30′E
171 R11 **Tobelo** Pulau Halmahera, E Indonesia 01°45′N 127°59′E
14 E12 **Tobermory** Ontario, S Canada 45°15′N 81°39′W
96 G10 **Tobermory** W Scotland, United Kingdom 56°37′N 06°12′W
165 S4 **Tōbetsu** Hokkaidō, NE Japan 43°12′N 141°28′E
180 M6 **Tobin Lake** ◎ Western Australia
11 U14 **Tobin Lake** ◎ Saskatchewan, C Canada
35 T4 **Tobin, Mount** ▲ Nevada, W USA 40°25′N 117°28′W
165 O9 **Tobi-shima** *island* C Japan
169 N13 **Toboali** Pulau Bangka, W Indonesia 03°00′S 106°30′E
144 M8 **Tobol** *Kaz.* Tobyl. Kustanay, N Kazakhstan 52°42′N 62°36′E
144 L8 **Tobol** *Kaz.* Tobyl. ≈ Kazakhstan/Russian Federation
122 H11 **Tobol'sk** Tyumenskaya Oblast', C Russian Federation 58°15′N 68°12′E
Tobruch/Tobruk *see* Ţubruq
125 R3 **Tobseda** Nenetskiy Avtonomnyy Okrug, NW Russian Federation 68°37′N 52°24′E
Tobyl *see* Tobol
125 Q6 **Tobysh** ≈ NW Russian Federation
54 F10 **Tocaima** Cundinamarca, C Colombia 04°30′N 74°38′W
59 K16 **Tocantins** *off.* Estado do Tocantins. ⬖ *state* C Brazil
Tocantins, Estado do *see* Tocantins
59 K15 **Tocantins, Rio** ≈ N Brazil
23 T2 **Toccoa** Georgia, SE USA 34°34′N 83°19′W
165 O12 **Tochigi** *off.* Tochigi-ken, *var.* Totigi. ⬖ *prefecture* Honshū, S Japan
Tochigi-ken *see* Tochigi
165 O11 **Tochio** *var.* Totio. Niigata, Honshū, C Japan 37°27′N 139°00′E
95 I15 **Töcksfors** Värmland, C Sweden 59°30′N 11°49′E
42 J5 **Tocoa** Colón, N Honduras 15°40′N 86°01′W
62 H4 **Tocopilla** Antofagasta, N Chile 22°06′S 70°08′W
62 I4 **Tocorpuri, Cerro de** ▲ Bolivia/Chile 22°26′S 67°53′W
183 O10 **Tocumwal** New South Wales, SE Australia 35°53′S 145°35′E
54 K4 **Tocuyo de La Costa** Falcón, NW Venezuela 11°04′N 68°23′W
152 H13 **Toda Rāisingh** Rājasthān, N India 26°02′N 75°35′E
106 H13 **Todi** Umbria, C Italy 42°47′N 12°25′E
108 G9 **Tödi** ▲ NE Switzerland 46°52′N 08°53′E
171 T12 **Todlo** Papua, E Indonesia 0°46′S 130°50′E
165 S9 **Todoga-saki** *headland* Honshū, C Japan 39°33′N 142°02′E
59 P17 **Todos os Santos, Baía de** *bay* E Brazil
40 F10 **Todos Santos** Baja California Sur, NW Mexico 23°28′N 110°14′W
40 B2 **Todos Santos, Bahía de** *bay* NW Mexico
Toeban *see* Tuban
Toekang Besi Eilanden *see* Tukangbesi, Kepulauan
Toeloengagoeng *see* Tulungagung
Tōen *see* T'aoyüan
185 D25 **Toetoes Bay** *bay* South Island, New Zealand
11 Q14 **Tofield** Alberta, SW Canada 53°22′N 112°39′W
10 K17 **Tofino** Vancouver Island, British Columbia, SW Canada 49°05′N 125°51′W
189 X17 **Tofol** Kosrae, E Micronesia
95 J20 **Tofta** Halland, S Sweden 57°10′N 12°19′E
95 H15 **Tofte** Buskerud, S Norway 59°31′N 10°33′E
95 F24 **Toftlund** Sønderjylland, SW Denmark 55°12′N 09°04′E
193 X15 **Tofua** *island* Ha'apai Group, C Tonga
187 Q12 **Toga** *island* Torres Islands, N Vanuatu
80 N13 **Togdheer** *off.* Gobolka Togdheer. ⬖ *region* NW Somalia
Togdheer, Gobolka *see* Togdheer
Toghyzaq *see* Toguzak
164 L11 **Togi** Ishikawa, Honshū, SW Japan 37°06′N 136°44′E
39 N13 **Togiak** Alaska, USA 59°03′N 160°31′W
171 O11 **Togian, Kepulauan** *island group* C Indonesia
77 Q15 **Togo** *off.* Togolese Republic; *prev.* French Togoland. ◆ *republic* W Africa
Togolese Republic *see* Togo
162 F8 **Tögrög** Govĭ-Altay, SW Mongolia 45°51′N 95°04′E
162 F8 **Tögrög** *var.* Hoolt. Övörhangay, C Mongolia 45°31′N 103°06′E
Tögrög *see* Manhan
159 N12 **Togton He** *var.* Tuotuo He. ≈ C China
Togton Heyan *see* Tanggulashan
144 L7 **Toguzak** *Kaz.* Toghyzaq. ≈ Kazakhstan/Russian Federation
37 P10 **Tohatchi** New Mexico, SW USA 35°51′N 108°45′W
191 O7 **Tohiea, Mont** 🌋 Moorea, W French Polynesia 17°33′S 149°48′W
137 N14 **Tohma Çayı** ≈ C Turkey
93 O17 **Tohmajärvi** Itä-Suomi, SE Finland 62°12′N 30°19′E
93 L16 **Toholampi** Länsi-Suomi, W Finland 63°46′N 24°15′E
Töhöm *see* Mandah
23 X12 **Tohopekaliga, Lake** ◎ Florida, SE USA
164 M14 **Toi** Shizuoka, Honshū, S Japan 34°55′N 138°45′E
190 B15 **Toi** N Niue 18°57′S 169°51′W
93 L19 **Toijala** Länsi-Suomi, SW Finland 61°09′N 23°51′E
171 P12 **Toima** Sulawesi, N Indonesia 0°48′S 122°21′E
164 D17 **Toi-misaki** Kyūshū, SW Japan
171 Q17 **Toineke** Timor, S Indonesia 10°06′S 124°22′E
Toirc, Inis *see* Inishturk
35 U6 **Toiyabe Range** ▲▲ Nevada, W USA
Tojikiston, Jumhurii *see* Tajikistan
147 R12 **Tojikobod** *Rus.* Tadzhikabad. C Tajikistan 39°08′N 70°54′E
164 G12 **Tōjō** Hiroshima, Honshū, SW Japan 34°54′N 133°15′E
39 T10 **Tok** Alaska, USA 63°20′N 142°59′W
164 K13 **Tōkai** Aichi, Honshū, SW Japan 35°01′N 136°51′E
111 N21 **Tokaj** Borsod-Abaúj-Zemplén, NE Hungary 48°08′N 21°25′E
165 N11 **Tōkamachi** Niigata, Honshū, C Japan 37°08′N 138°44′E
185 D25 **Tokanui** Southland, South Island, New Zealand 46°33′S 169°02′E
80 I7 **Tokar** *var.* Ţawkar. Red Sea, NE Sudan 18°27′N 37°41′E
136 L12 **Tokat** Tokat, N Turkey 40°20′N 36°35′E
136 L12 **Tokat** ⬖ *province* N Turkey
163 X15 **Tŏkchŏk-kundo** *island group* NW South Korea
Tōke *see* Taka Atoll
190 J9 **Tokelau** ◇ *NZ overseas territory* W Polynesia
Tőketerebes *see* Trebišov
Tokhtamyshbek *see* Tŭkhtamish
24 M6 **Tokio** Texas, SW USA 33°09′N 102°31′W
Tokio *see* Tōkyō
189 W11 **Toki Point** *point* NW Wake Island
Tokkuztara *see* Gongliu
147 V7 **Tokmak** *Kir.* Tokmok. Chuyskaya Oblast', N Kyrgyzstan 42°50′N 75°18′E
117 V9 **Tokmak** *var.* Velykyy Tokmak. Zaporiz'ka Oblast', SE Ukraine 47°13′N 35°43′E
Tokmok *see* Tokmak
184 Q8 **Tokomaru Bay** Gisborne, North Island, New Zealand 38°10′S 178°18′E
184 M8 **Tokoroa** Waikato, North Island, New Zealand 38°14′S 175°52′E
76 K14 **Tokounou** C Guinea 09°43′N 09°46′W
38 M12 **Toksook Bay** Alaska, USA 60°33′N 165°01′W
Toksu *see* Xinhe
Toksum *see* Toksun
158 L6 **Toksun** *var.* Toksum. Xinjiang Uygur Zizhiqu, NW China 42°47′N 88°38′E
147 T8 **Toktogul** Talasskaya Oblast', NW Kyrgyzstan 41°51′N 72°56′E
147 T9 **Toktogul'skoye Vodokhranilishche** ⊠ W Kyrgyzstan
Toktomush *see* Tŭkhtamish
193 Y14 **Toku** *island* Vava'u Group, N Tonga
165 U16 **Tokunoshima** Kagoshima, Tokuno-shima, SW Japan
165 U16 **Tokuno-shima** *island* Nansei-shotō, SW Japan
164 I14 **Tokushima** *var.* Tokusima. Tokushima, Shikoku, SW Japan 34°04′N 134°28′E
164 H14 **Tokushima** *off.* Tokushima-ken, *var.* Tokusima. ⬖ *prefecture* Shikoku, SW Japan
Tokushima-ken *see* Tokushima
Tokusima *see* Tokushima
164 E13 **Tokuyama** *var.* Shūnan. Yamaguchi, Honshū, SW Japan 34°04′N 131°48′E
165 N13 **Tōkyō** *var.* Tokio. ● (Japan) Tōkyō, Honshū, S Japan 35°40′N 139°45′E
165 O13 **Tōkyō** *off.* Tōkyō-to. ⬖ *capital district* Honshū, S Japan
Tōkyō-to *see* Tōkyō
145 T12 **Tokyrau** ≈ C Kazakhstan
149 O3 **Tokzār** *Pash.* Tukzār. Sar-e Pol, N Afghanistan 35°47′N 66°28′E
145 W13 **Tokzhaylau** *prev.* Dzerzhinskoye. Almaty, SE Kazakhstan 45°49′N 81°04′E
145 W13 **Tokzhaylau** *var.* Dzerzhinskoye. Taldykorgan, SE Kazakhstan 45°49′N 81°04′E
189 U12 **Tol** *atoll* Chuuk Islands, C Micronesia
184 Q9 **Tolaga Bay** Gisborne, North Island, New Zealand 38°22′S 178°17′E
172 I7 **Tôlañaro** *prev.* Faradofay, Fort-Dauphin. Toliara, SE Madagascar
162 D6 **Tolbo** Bayan-Ölgiy, W Mongolia 48°22′N 90°22′E
Tolbukhin *see* Dobrich
60 G11 **Toledo** Paraná, S Brazil 24°45′S 53°41′W
54 G8 **Toledo** Norte de Santander, N Colombia 07°16′N 72°28′W
105 N9 **Toledo** *anc.* Toletum. Castilla-La Mancha, C Spain 39°52′N 04°02′W
30 M14 **Toledo** Illinois, N USA 39°16′N 88°15′W
29 W13 **Toledo** Iowa, C USA 42°00′N 92°34′W
31 R11 **Toledo** Ohio, N USA 41°40′N 83°33′W
32 F12 **Toledo** Oregon, NW USA 44°37′N 123°56′W
32 G9 **Toledo** Washington, NW USA 46°27′N 122°49′W
42 F3 **Toledo** ⬖ *district* S Belize
104 M9 **Toledo** ⬖ *province* Castilla-La Mancha, C Spain
25 Y7 **Toledo Bend Reservoir** ⊠ Louisiana/Texas, SW USA
104 M10 **Toledo, Montes de** ▲▲ C Spain
106 J12 **Tolentino** Marche, C Italy 43°08′N 13°17′E
Toletum *see* Toledo
94 H10 **Tolga** Hedmark, S Norway 62°25′N 11°00′E
158 J3 **Toli** Xinjiang Uygur Zizhiqu, NW China 45°55′N 83°33′E
172 H7 **Toliara** *var.* Toliary; *prev.* Tuléar. Toliara, SW Madagascar 23°20′S 43°41′E
172 H7 **Toliara** ⬖ *province* SW Madagascar
Toliary *see* Toliara
54 D11 **Tolima** *off.* Departamento del Tolima. ⬖ *province* C Colombia
Tolima, Departamento del *see* Tolima
171 N11 **Tolitoli** Sulawesi, C Indonesia 01°05′N 120°50′E
95 K22 **Tollarp** Skåne, S Sweden 55°55′N 14°00′E
100 N9 **Tollense** ≈ NE Germany
100 N10 **Tollensesee** ◎ NE Germany
36 K13 **Tolleson** Arizona, SW USA 33°25′N 112°15′W
146 M13 **Tollimarjon** *Rus.* Talimardzhan. Qashqadaryo Viloyati, S Uzbekistan 38°22′N 65°31′E
Tolmein *see* Tolmin
106 J6 **Tolmezzo** Friuli-Venezia Giulia, NE Italy 46°27′N 13°01′E
109 S11 **Tolmin** *Ger.* Tolmein, *It.* Tolmino. W Slovenia 46°12′N 13°39′E
Tolmino *see* Tolmin
111 J25 **Tolna** *Ger.* Tolnau. Tolna, S Hungary 46°26′N 18°47′E
111 I24 **Tolna** *off.* Tolna Megye. ⬖ *county* SW Hungary
Tolna Megye *see* Tolna
Tolnau *see* Tolna
79 I20 **Tolo** Bandundu, W Dem. Rep. Congo 02°57′S 18°35′E
Tolochin *see* Talachyn
190 D12 **Toloke** Île Futuna, W Wallis and Futuna
30 M13 **Tolono** Illinois, N USA 39°59′N 88°16′W
105 Q3 **Tolosa** País Vasco, N Spain 43°09′N 02°04′W
Tolosa *see* Toulouse
171 O13 **Tolo, Teluk** *bay* Sulawesi, C Indonesia
39 R9 **Tolovana River** ≈ Alaska, USA
123 U10 **Tolstoy, Mys** *headland* E Russian Federation 59°12′N 155°04′E
63 G15 **Toltén** Araucanía, C Chile 39°13′S 73°15′W
63 G15 **Toltén, Río** ≈ S Chile
54 E6 **Tolú** Sucre, NW Colombia 09°32′N 75°34′W
41 O14 **Toluca** *var.* Toluca de Lerdo. México, S Mexico 19°20′N 99°40′W
Toluca de Lerdo *see* Toluca
41 O14 **Toluca, Nevado de** 🌋 C Mexico 19°05′N 99°45′W
127 R6 **Tol'yatti** *prev.* Stavropol'. Samarskaya Oblast', W Russian Federation 53°32′N 49°27′E
77 O12 **Toma** NW Burkina 12°46′N 02°51′W
30 K7 **Tomah** Wisconsin, N USA 43°59′N 90°31′W
30 L5 **Tomahawk** Wisconsin, N USA 45°27′N 89°40′W
117 T8 **Tomakivka** Dnipropetrovs'ka Oblast', E Ukraine 47°47′N 34°45′E
165 S4 **Tomakomai** Hokkaidō, NE Japan 42°38′N 141°32′E
165 S2 **Tomamae** Hokkaidō, NE Japan 44°18′N 141°38′E
104 G9 **Tomar** Santarém, W Portugal 39°36′N 08°25′W
123 T13 **Tomari** Ostrov Sakhalin, Sakhalinskaya Oblast', SE Russian Federation 47°47′N 142°09′E
115 C16 **Tómaros** ▲ W Greece 39°31′N 20°45′E
Tomaschow *see* Tomaszów Mazowiecki
Tomaschow *see* Tomaszów Lubelski
61 E16 **Tomás Gomensoro** Artigas, N Uruguay 30°28′S 57°28′W
117 N7 **Tomashpil'** Vinnyts'ka Oblast', C Ukraine 48°32′N 28°31′E
Tomaszów *see* Tomaszów Mazowiecki
111 P15 **Tomaszów Lubelski** *Ger.* Tomaschow. Lubelskie, E Poland 50°29′N 23°23′E
Tomaszów Mazowiecka *see* Tomaszów Mazowiecki
110 L13 **Tomaszów Mazowiecki** *var.* Tomaszów Mazowiecka; *prev.* Tomaszów, *Ger.* Tomaschow. Łódzkie, C Poland 51°33′N 20°E
40 J13 **Tomatlán** Jalisco, C Mexico 19°53′N 105°18′W
81 F15 **Tombe** Jonglei, S Sudan 05°52′N 31°40′E
23 N4 **Tombigbee River** ≈ Alabama/Mississippi, S USA
82 A10 **Tomboco** Dem. Rep. Congo, NW Angola 06°50′S 13°20′E
77 O10 **Tombouctou** *Eng.* Timbuktu. Tombouctou, N Mali 16°47′N 03°03′W
77 N9 **Tombouctou** ⬖ *region* W Mali
37 N16 **Tombstone** Arizona, SW USA 31°42′N 110°04′W
83 A15 **Tombua** *Port.* Porto Alexandre. Namibe, SW Angola 15°49′S 11°53′E
83 J19 **Tom Burke** Limpopo, NE South Africa 23°07′S 28°01′E
146 L9 **Tomdibuloq** *Rus.* Tamdybulak. Navoiy Viloyati, N Uzbekistan 41°48′N 64°33′E
146 L9 **Tomditov-Tog'lari** ▲▲ N Uzbekistan
62 G13 **Tomé** Bío Bío, C Chile 36°38′S 72°57′W
58 L12 **Tomé-Açu** Pará, NE Brazil 02°25′S 48°09′W
95 L23 **Tomelilla** Skåne, S Sweden 55°33′N 14°00′E
105 O10 **Tomelloso** Castilla-La Mancha, C Spain 39°09′N 03°01′W
14 H10 **Tomiko Lake** ◎ Ontario, S Canada
77 N12 **Tominian** Ségou, C Mali 13°18′N 04°39′W
171 N12 **Tomini, Gulf of** *var.* Teluk Tomini; *prev.* Teluk Gorontalo. *bay* Sulawesi, C Indonesia
Tomini, Teluk *see* Tomini, Gulf of
165 Q11 **Tomioka** Fukushima, Honshū, C Japan 37°19′N 140°57′E
113 G14 **Tomislavgrad** Federacija Bosna I Hercegovina, SW Bosnia and Herzegovina 43°43′N 17°15′E
181 O9 **Tomkinson Ranges** ▲▲ South Australia/Western Australia
123 Q11 **Tommot** Respublika Sakha (Yakutiya), NE Russian Federation 58°57′N 126°24′E
171 Q11 **Tomohon** Sulawesi, N Indonesia 01°19′N 124°49′E
54 K9 **Tomo, Río** ≈ E Colombia
113 L21 **Tomorrit, Mali i** ▲ S Albania 40°43′N 20°12′E
11 S17 **Tompkins** Saskatchewan, S Canada 50°03′N 108°49′W
20 K8 **Tompkinsville** Kentucky, S USA 36°43′N 85°41′W
171 N11 **Tompo** Sulawesi, N Indonesia 0°56′N 120°16′E
180 I8 **Tom Price** Western Australia 22°48′S 117°49′E
122 J12 **Tomsk** Tomskaya Oblast', C Russian Federation 56°30′N 85°05′E
122 I11 **Tomskaya Oblast'** ⬖ *province* C Russian Federation
18 K16 **Toms River** New Jersey, NE USA 39°56′N 74°09′W
Tom Steed Lake *see* Tom Steed Reservoir
26 L12 **Tom Steed Reservoir** *var.* Tom Steed Lake. ⊠ Oklahoma, C USA
171 U13 **Tomu** Papua, E Indonesia 02°07′S 133°01′E
158 H6 **Tomür Feng** *var.* Pobeda Peak, *Rus.* Pik Pobedy. ▲ China/Kyrgyzstan 42°02′N 80°07′E *see also* Pobedy, Pik
Tomür Feng *see* Pobedy, Pik
189 N13 **Tomworoahlang** Pohnpei, E Micronesia
41 U17 **Tonalá** Chiapas, SE Mexico 16°08′N 93°41′W
106 F6 **Tonale, Passo del** *pass* N Italy
164 I11 **Tonami** Toyama, Honshū, SW Japan 36°40′N 136°55′E
58 C12 **Tonantins** Amazonas, W Brazil 02°58′S 67°30′W
32 K6 **Tonasket** Washington, NW USA 48°41′N 119°27′W
55 Y9 **Tonate** *var.* Macouria. N French Guiana 05°00′N 52°28′W
18 D10 **Tonawanda** New York, NE USA 43°00′N 78°51′W
171 Q11 **Tondano** Sulawesi, C Indonesia 01°19′N 124°56′E
104 H7 **Tondela** Viseu, N Portugal 40°31′N 08°05′W
95 F24 **Tønder** *Ger.* Tondern. Sønderjylland, SW Denmark 54°57′N 08°53′E
Tondern *see* Tønder
143 N4 **Tonekābon** *var.* Shahsawar, Tonkābon; *prev.* Shahsavār. Māzandarān, N Iran 36°40′N 51°25′E
Tonezh *see* Tonyezh
193 Y14 **Tonga** *off.* Kingdom of Tonga, *var.* Friendly Islands. ◆ *monarchy* SW Pacific Ocean
175 R9 **Tonga** *island group* SW Pacific Ocean
83 K23 **Tongaat** KwaZulu/Natal, E South Africa 29°35′S 31°07′E
Tonga, Kingdom of *see* Tonga
161 Q13 **Tong'an** *var.* Datong, Tong an. Fujian, SE China 24°43′N 118°07′E
Tong an *see* Tong'an
27 Q4 **Tonganoxie** Kansas, C USA 39°06′N 95°05′W
39 Y13 **Tongass National Forest** *reserve* Alaska, USA
193 Y16 **Tongatapu** ✈ Tongatapu, S Tonga 21°10′S 175°10′W
193 Y16 **Tongatapu** *island* Tongatapu Group, S Tonga
193 Y16 **Tongatapu Group** *island group* S Tonga
175 S9 **Tonga Trench** *undersea feature* S Pacific Ocean
161 N8 **Tongbai Shan** ▲▲ C China
161 P8 **Tongcheng** Anhui, E China 31°16′N 117°00′E
160 L6 **Tongchuan** Shaanxi, C China 35°10′N 109°03′E
160 L12 **Tongdao** *var.* Tongdao Dongzu Zizhixian; *prev.* Shuangjiang. Hunan, S China 26°06′N 109°46′E
Tongdao Dongzu Zizhixian *see* Tongdao
159 T11 **Tongde** *var.* Gabasumdo. Qinghai, C China 35°13′N 100°39′E
99 K19 **Tongeren** *Fr.* Tongres. Limburg, NE Belgium 50°47′N 05°28′E
163 Y14 **Tonghae** NE South Korea 37°26′N 129°09′E
160 G13 **Tonghai** *var.* Xiushan. Yunnan, SW China 24°06′N 102°45′E
163 X8 **Tonghe** Heilongjiang, NE China 46°00′N 128°45′E
163 W11 **Tonghua** Jilin, NE China 41°45′N 125°50′E
163 Z6 **Tongjiang** Heilongjiang, NE China 47°39′N 132°29′E
163 Y13 **Tongjosŏn-man** *prev.* Broughton Bay. *bay* E North Korea
163 V7 **Tongken He** ≈ NE China
167 T7 **Tongking, Gulf of** *Chin.* Beibu Wan, *Vtn.* Vinh Băc Bô. *gulf* China/Vietnam
163 U10 **Tongliao** Nei Mongol Zizhiqu, N China 43°37′N 122°15′E
161 Q9 **Tongling** Anhui, E China 30°55′N 117°50′E
161 R9 **Tonglu** Zhejiang, SE China 29°50′N 119°38′E
187 R14 **Tongoa** *island* Shepherd Islands, S Vanuatu
62 G9 **Tongoy** Coquimbo, C Chile 30°16′S 71°31′W
160 L11 **Tongren** *var.* Rongwo. Guizhou, S China 27°44′N 109°10′E
159 T11 **Tongren** *var.* Rongwo. Qinghai, C China 35°31′N 101°58′E
Tongres *see* Tongeren
153 U11 **Tongsa** *var.* Tongsa Dzong. C Bhutan 27°33′N 90°30′E
Tongsa Dzong *see* Tongsa
Tongshan *see* Fuding, Fujian, China
Tongshan *see* Xuzhou, Jiangsu, China
Tongshi *see* Wuzhishan
159 P12 **Tongtian He** ≈ C China
96 I6 **Tongue** N Scotland, United Kingdom 58°30′N 04°25′W
44 H3 **Tongue of the Ocean** *strait* C Bahamas
33 X10 **Tongue River** ≈ Montana, NW USA
33 W11 **Tongue River Resevoir** ⊠ Montana, NW USA
159 V11 **Tongwei** *var.* Pingxiang. Gansu, C China 35°09′N 105°15′E
159 W9 **Tongxin** Ningxia, N China 37°00′N 105°41′E
163 U9 **Tongyu** *var.* Kaitong. Jilin, NE China 44°49′N 123°08′E
160 J11 **Tongzi** *var.* Loushanguan. Guizhou, S China 28°08′N 106°49′E
162 F8 **Tonhil** *var.* Dzüyl. Govĭ-Altay, SW Mongolia 46°09′N 93°55′E
40 G5 **Tónichi** Sonora, NW Mexico 28°37′N 109°34′W
81 D14 **Tonj** Warab, SW Sudan 07°18′N 28°41′E
152 H13 **Tonk** Rājasthān, N India 26°10′N 75°50′E
Tonkābon *see* Tonekābon
27 N8 **Tonkawa** Oklahoma, C USA 36°40′N 97°18′W
167 Q12 **Tônlé Sap** *Eng.* Great Lake. ◎ W Cambodia
102 L14 **Tonneins** Lot-et-Garonne, SW France 44°21′N 00°21′E
103 Q7 **Tonnerre** Yonne, C France 47°50′N 04°00′E
Tonoas *see* Dublon
35 U8 **Tonopah** Nevada, W USA 38°04′N 117°13′W
164 H13 **Tonoshō** Okayama, Shōdo-shima, SW Japan 34°29′N 134°10′E
43 S17 **Tonosí** Los Santos, S Panama 07°23′N 80°26′W
95 H16 **Tønsberg** Vestfold, S Norway 59°16′N 10°25′E
39 T11 **Tonsina** Alaska, USA 61°39′N 145°10′W
95 D17 **Tonstad** Vest-Agder, S Norway 58°40′N 06°42′E
193 X15 **Tonumea** *island* Nomuka Group, W Tonga
137 O11 **Tonya** Trabzon, NE Turkey 40°52′N 39°17′E
119 K20 **Tonyezh** *Rus.* Tonezh. Homyel'skaya Voblasts', SE Belarus 51°50′N 27°48′E
36 L3 **Tooele** Utah, W USA 40°32′N 112°18′W
122 L13 **Toora-Khem** Respublika Tyva, S Russian Federation 52°25′N 96°01′E
183 O5 **Toorale East** New South Wales, SE Australia 30°29′S 145°25′E
83 H25 **Toorberg** ▲ S South Africa 32°02′S 24°02′E
118 G5 **Tootsi** Pärnumaa, SW Estonia 58°34′N 24°43′E
183 U3 **Toowoomba** Queensland, E Australia 27°35′S 151°54′E
27 Q4 **Topeka** *state capital* Kansas, C USA 39°03′N 95°41′W
122 J12 **Topki** Kemerovskaya Oblast', S Russian Federation 55°12′N 85°40′E
111 M18 **Topľa** *Hung.* Toplya. ≈ NE Slovakia
Toplicza *see* Toplița
116 J10 **Toplița** *Ger.* Töplitz, *Hung.* Maroshevíz; *prev.* Toplița Română, *Hung.* Oláh-Toplicza, Toplicza. Harghita, C Romania 45°56′N 25°20′E
Toplița Română/Töplitz *see* Toplița
Toplya *see* Topľa
111 I20 **Topoľčany** *Hung.* Nagytapolcsány. Nitriansky Kraj, W Slovakia 48°33′N 18°10′E
40 G8 **Topolobampo** Sinaloa, C Mexico 25°36′N 109°04′W
116 I13 **Topoloveni** Argeș, S Romania 44°49′N 25°02′E
114 L11 **Topolovgrad** *prev.* Kavakli. Khaskovo, S Bulgaria 42°06′N 26°20′E
Topolya *see* Bačka Topola
124 I6 **Topozero, Ozero** ◎ NW Russian Federation
32 J10 **Toppenish** Washington, NW USA 46°22′N 120°18′W
181 P4 **Top Springs Roadhouse** Northern Territory, N Australia 16°37′S 131°49′E
189 U11 **Tora** *island* Chuuk, C Micronesia
Toraigh *see* Tory Island
189 U11 **Tora Island Pass** *passage* Chuuk Islands, C Micronesia
143 U5 **Torbat-e Ḩeydarīyeh** *var.* Turbat-i-Haidari. Khorāsān-Razavī, NE Iran 35°18′N 59°12′E
143 V5 **Torbat-e Jām** *var.* Turbat-i-Jam. Khorāsān-Razavī, NE Iran 35°16′N 60°36′E
39 Q11 **Torbert, Mount** ▲ Alaska, USA 61°30′N 152°15′W
31 P6 **Torch Lake** ◎ Michigan, N USA
Törcsvár *see* Bran
Torda *see* Turda
104 L6 **Tordesillas** Castilla-León, N Spain 41°30′N 05°00′W
92 K13 **Töre** Norrbotten, N Sweden 65°55′N 22°40′E
95 L17 **Töreboda** Västra Götaland, S Sweden 58°41′N 14°07′E
95 J21 **Torekov** Skåne, S Sweden 56°25′N 12°39′E
92 O3 **Torell Land** *physical region* SW Svalbard
117 Y8 **Torez** Donets'ka Oblast', SE Ukraine 48°00′N 38°38′E
101 N14 **Torgau** Sachsen, E Germany 51°34′N 13°01′E
Torgay *see* Turgay
Torgay Üstirti *see* Turgayskaya Stolovaya Strana
Torghay *see* Turgay
95 N22 **Torhamn** Blekinge, S Sweden 56°04′N 15°49′E
99 C17 **Torhout** West-Vlaanderen, W Belgium 51°04′N 03°06′E
106 B8 **Torino** *Eng.* Turin. Piemonte, NW Italy 45°03′N 07°39′E
165 U15 **Tori-shima** *island* Izu-shotō, SE Japan
81 F16 **Torit** Eastern Equatoria, S Sudan 04°27′N 32°31′E
186 H6 **Toriu** New Britain, E Papua New Guinea 04°39′S 151°42′E
148 M4 **Torkestān, Selseleh-ye Band-e** *var.* Bandi-i Turkistan. ▲▲ NW Afghanistan
104 L7 **Tormes** ≈ W Spain
Tornacum *see* Tournai
Torneå *see* Tornio
92 K12 **Torneälven** *var.* Torniojoki, *Fin.* Tornionjoki. ≈ Finland/Sweden
92 I11 **Torneträsk** ◎ N Sweden
13 O4 **Torngat Mountains** ▲▲ Newfoundland and Labrador, NE Canada
24 H8 **Tornillo** Texas, SW USA 31°26′N 106°06′W
92 K13 **Tornio** *Swe.* Torneå. Lappi, NW Finland 65°50′N 24°18′E
Torniojoki/Tornionjoki *see* Torneälven
61 B23 **Tornquist** Buenos Aires, E Argentina 38°08′S 62°15′W
104 L6 **Toro** Castilla-León, N Spain 41°31′N 05°24′W
62 H9 **Toro, Cerro del** ▲ N Chile 29°10′S 69°43′W
77 R12 **Torodi** Tillabéri, SW Niger 13°05′N 01°46′E
Törökbecse *see* Novi Bečej
186 J7 **Torokina** Bougainville Island, NE Papua New Guinea 06°12′S 155°04′E
111 L23 **Törökszentmiklós** Jász-Nagykun-Szolnok, E Hungary 47°11′N 20°26′E
42 G7 **Torola, Río** ≈ El Salvador/Honduras
Toronaíos, Kólpos *see* Kassándras, Kólpos
14 H15 **Toronto** *province capital* Ontario, S Canada 43°42′N 79°25′W
31 V12 **Toronto** Ohio, N USA 40°27′N 80°36′W
Toronto *see* Lester B. Pearson
27 P6 **Toronto Lake** ⊠ Kansas, C USA
35 V16 **Toro Peak** ▲ California, W USA 33°31′N 116°25′W
124 H16 **Toropets** Tverskaya Oblast', W Russian Federation 56°29′N 31°37′E
81 G18 **Tororo** E Uganda 0°42′N 34°12′E
136 H16 **Toros Dağları** *Eng.* Taurus Mountains. ▲▲ S Turkey
183 N13 **Torquay** Victoria, SE Australia 38°21′S 144°18′E
97 J24 **Torquay** SW England, United Kingdom 50°28′N 03°30′W
104 M5 **Torquemada** Castilla-León, N Spain 42°02′N 04°17′W
35 S16 **Torrance** California, W USA 33°50′N 118°20′W
104 G12 **Torrão** Setúbal, S Portugal 38°18′N 08°13′W
104 H8 **Torre, Alto da** ▲ C Portugal 40°21′N 07°31′W
107 K18 **Torre Annunziata** Campania, S Italy 40°45′N 14°27′E
105 T8 **Torreblanca** País Valenciano, E Spain 40°14′N 00°12′E
104 L15 **Torrecilla** ▲ S Spain 36°38′N 04°54′W
105 P4 **Torrecilla en Cameros** La Rioja, N Spain 42°18′N 02°33′W
105 N13 **Torredelcampo** Andalucía, S Spain 37°45′N 03°52′W
107 K17 **Torre del Greco** Campania, S Italy 40°46′N 14°22′E
104 I6 **Torre de Moncorvo** *var.* Moncorvo, Tôrre de Moncorvo. Bragança, N Portugal 41°10′N 07°03′W
104 J9 **Torrejoncillo** Extremadura, W Spain 39°54′N 06°28′W
105 O8 **Torrejón de Ardoz** Madrid, C Spain 40°27′N 03°29′W
105 N7 **Torrelaguna** Madrid, C Spain 40°50′N 03°33′W
105 N2 **Torrelavega** Cantabria, N Spain 43°21′N 04°03′W
107 M16 **Torremaggiore** Puglia, SE Italy 41°42′N 15°17′E
104 M15 **Torremolinos** Andalucía, S Spain 36°38′N 04°30′W
182 I6 **Torrens, Lake** *salt lake* South Australia
105 S10 **Torrent** *Cas.* Torrente, *var.* Torrent de l'Horta. País Valenciano, E Spain 39°27′N 00°28′W
Torrent de l'Horta/Torrente *see* Torrent
40 L8 **Torreón** Coahuila, NE Mexico 25°47′N 103°21′W
105 R13 **Torre Pacheco** Murcia, SE Spain 37°43′N 00°57′W
106 A8 **Torre Pellice** Piemonte, NE Italy 44°49′N 07°12′E
105 O13 **Torreperogil** Andalucía, S Spain 38°02′N 03°17′W
61 J15 **Torres** Rio Grande do Sul, S Brazil 29°20′S 49°43′W
Torrès, Îles *see* Torres Islands
187 Q11 **Torres Islands** *Fr.* Îles Torrès. *island group* N Vanuatu
104 G9 **Torres Novas** Santarém, C Portugal 39°28′N 08°32′W
181 V1 **Torres Strait** *strait* Australia/Papua New Guinea
104 F10 **Torres Vedras** Lisboa, C Portugal 39°05′N 09°15′W
105 S13 **Torrevieja** País Valenciano, E Spain 37°59′N 00°40′W
186 B6 **Torricelli Mountains** ▲▲ NW Papua New Guinea
96 G8 **Torridon, Loch** *inlet* NW Scotland, United Kingdom
106 D9 **Torriglia** Liguria, NW Italy 44°31′N 09°08′E
104 M9 **Torrijos** Castilla-La Mancha, C Spain 39°59′N 04°18′W
18 L12 **Torrington** Connecticut, NE USA 41°48′N 73°07′W

◆ Country ● Country Capital ◇ Dependent Territory ○ Dependent Territory Capital ⬖ Administrative Regions ✈ International Airport ▲ Mountain ▲▲ Mountain Range 🌋 Volcano ≈ River ◎ Lake ⊠ Reservoir

Torrington – Truchas Peak

33 Z15 **Torrington** Wyoming, C USA 42°04′N 104°10′W
Torröjen see Torrön
94 F16 **Torrön** prev. Torröjen. ◎ C Sweden
105 N15 **Torrox** Andalucía, S Spain 36°45′N 03°58′W
94 N13 **Torsåker** Gävleborg, C Sweden 60°31′N 16°30′E
95 N21 **Torsås** Kalmar, S Sweden 56°24′N 16°00′E
95 J14 **Torsby** Värmland, C Sweden 60°07′N 13°E
95 N16 **Torshälla** Södermanland, C Sweden 59°25′N 16°28′E
95 B19 **Tórshavn** Dan. Thorshavn. ○ Faeroe Islands 62°02′N 06°47′W
Torshiz see Kāshmar
146 I9 **To'rtkok'l** var. Türtkül, Rus. Turtkul'; prev. Petroaleksandrovsk. Qoraqalpog'iston Respublikasi, W Uzbekistan 41°35′N 61°E
Tortoise Islands see Colón, Archipiélago de
45 T9 **Tortola** island C British Virgin Islands
106 D9 **Tortona** anc. Dertona. Piemonte, NW Italy 44°54′N 08°52′E
107 L23 **Tortorici** Sicilia, Italy, C Mediterranean Sea 38°02′N 14°49′E
105 U7 **Tortosa** anc. Dertosa. Cataluña, E Spain 40°49′N 00°31′E
Tortosa see Ţarţūs
105 U7 **Tortosa, Cap** cape E Spain
44 L8 **Tortue, Île de la** var. Tortuga Island. island N Haiti
55 Y10 **Tortue, Montagne** ▲▲ C French Guiana
Tortuga, Isla see La Tortuga, Isla
Tortuga Island see Tortue, Île de la
54 C11 **Tortugas, Golfo** gulf W Colombia
45 T5 **Tortuguero, Laguna** lagoon N Puerto Rico
137 Q12 **Tortum** Erzurum, NE Turkey 40°20′N 41°36′E
Torugart, Pereval see Turugart Shankou
137 O12 **Torul** Gümüşhane, NE Turkey 40°35′N 39°18′E
110 J10 **Toruń** Ger. Thorn. Toruń, Kujawsko-pomorskie, C Poland 53°02′N 18°36′E
95 K20 **Torup** Halland, S Sweden 56°57′N 13°04′E
118 I6 **Tõrva** Ger. Törwa. Valgamaa, S Estonia 58°00′N 25°54′E
Törwa see Tõrva
96 D13 **Tory Island** Ir. Toraigh. island NW Ireland
111 N19 **Torysa** Hung. Tarca. ≈ NE Slovakia
Törzburg see Bran
124 J16 **Torzhok** Tverskaya Oblast', W Russian Federation 57°04′N 34°55′E
164 F15 **Tosa-Shimizu** var. Tosasimizu. Kōchi, Shikoku, SW Japan 32°47′N 132°58′E
Tosasimizu see Tosa-Shimizu
164 G15 **Tosa-wan** bay SW Japan
83 H21 **Tosca** North-West, N South Africa 25°51′S 23°56′E
106 F12 **Toscana** Eng. Tuscany. ◈ region C Italy
107 E14 **Toscano, Archipelago** Eng. Tuscan Archipelago. island group C Italy
106 G10 **Tosco-Emiliano, Appennino** Eng. Tuscan-Emilian Mountains. ▲▲ C Italy
Tōsei see Tungshih
165 N15 **To-shima** island Izu-shotō, SE Japan
147 Q9 **Toshkent** Eng./Rus. Tashkent. ● Toshkent Viloyati, E Uzbekistan 41°19′N 69°17′E
147 Q9 **Toshkent** ✈ Toshkent Viloyati, E Uzbekistan 41°13′N 69°15′E
147 P9 **Toshkent Viloyati** Rus. Tashkentskaya Oblast'. ◈ province E Uzbekistan
124 H13 **Tosno** Leningradskaya Oblast', NW Russian Federation 59°34′N 30°48′E
159 Q10 **Toson Hu** ◎ C China
162 H6 **Tosontsengel** Dzavhan, NW Mongolia 48°42′N 98°14′E
162 J6 **Tosontsengel** var. Tsengel. Hövsgöl, N Mongolia 49°29′N 101°09′E
146 I8 **Tosquduq Qumlari** var. Goshquduq Qum, Taskuduk, Peski. desert W Uzbekistan
105 U4 **Tossal de l'Orri** var. Llorri. ▲ NE Spain 42°24′N 01°15′E
61 A15 **Tostado** Santa Fe, C Argentina 29°15′S 61°45′W
118 F6 **Tõstamaa** Ger. Testama. Pärnumaa, SW Estonia 58°20′N 23°59′E
100 I10 **Tostedt** Niedersachsen, N Germany 53°16′N 09°42′E
136 J11 **Tosya** Kastamonu, N Turkey 41°02′N 34°02′E
95 F15 **Totak** ◎ S Norway
105 R13 **Totana** Murcia, SE Spain 37°45′N 01°30′W
94 H13 **Toten** physical region S Norway
83 G18 **Toteng** North-West, C Botswana 20°25′S 23°00′E
102 M3 **Tôtes** Seine-Maritime, N France 49°40′N 01°02′E
Totigi see Tochigi
Totio see Tochio
Totis see Tata
189 U13 **Totiw** island Chuuk, C Micronesia
125 N13 **Tot'ma** var. Totma. Vologodskaya Oblast', NW Russian Federation 59°58′N 42°42′E
Tot'ma see Sukhona
55 V9 **Totness** Coronie, N Surinam 05°53′N 56°19′W
42 C5 **Totonicapán** Totonicapán, W Guatemala 14°58′N 91°12′W
42 A2 **Totonicapán** off. Departamento de Totonicapán. ◈ department W Guatemala
Totonicapán, Departamento de see Totonicapán
61 B18 **Totoras** Santa Fe, C Argentina 32°35′S 61°11′W
187 Y15 **Totoya** island S Fiji
183 Q7 **Tottenham** New South Wales, SE Australia 32°16′S 147°23′E
164 I12 **Tottori** Tottori, Honshū, SW Japan 35°29′N 134°14′E
164 H12 **Tottori** off. Tottori-ken. ◈ prefecture Honshū, SW Japan
Tottori-ken see Tottori
76 I6 **Touâjîl** Tiris Zemmour, N Mauritania 22°03′N 12°40′W
76 L15 **Touba** W Ivory Coast 08°17′N 07°41′W
76 G11 **Touba** W Senegal 14°55′N 15°53′W
74 E7 **Toubkal, Jbel** ▲ W Morocco 31°00′N 07°50′W
32 K10 **Touchet** Washington, NW USA 46°03′N 118°40′W
103 P7 **Toucy** Yonne, C France 47°45′N 03°18′E
77 O12 **Tougan** W Burkina 13°06′N 03°03′W
74 L7 **Touggourt** NE Algeria 33°08′N 06°04′E
77 Q12 **Tougouri** N Burkina 13°22′N 00°25′W
76 J13 **Tougué** NW Guinea 11°29′N 11°48′W
76 K12 **Toukoto** Kayes, W Mali 13°27′N 09°52′W
103 S5 **Toul** Meurthe-et-Moselle, NE France 48°41′N 05°54′E
76 L16 **Toulépleu** var. Toulobli. W Ivory Coast 06°37′N 08°27′W
161 S14 **Touliu** C Taiwan 23°44′N 120°27′E
15 U3 **Toulnustouc** ≈ Québec, SE Canada
Toulobli see Toulépleu
103 T16 **Toulon** anc. Telo Martius, Tilio Martius. Var, SE France 43°07′N 05°56′E
30 K12 **Toulon** Illinois, N USA 41°05′N 89°54′W
102 M15 **Toulouse** anc. Tolosa. Haute-Garonne, S France 43°37′N 01°25′E
102 M15 **Toulouse** ✈ Haute-Garonne, S France 43°38′N 01°19′E
77 N16 **Toumodi** C Ivory Coast 06°34′N 05°01′W
74 G9 **Tounassine, Hamada** hill range W Algeria
Toungoo see Taungoo
102 L8 **Touraine** cultural region C France
Tourane see Đà Nẵng
103 P1 **Tourcoing** Nord, N France 50°44′N 03°10′E
104 F2 **Touriñán, Cabo** headland NW Spain 43°02′N 09°20′W
76 J6 **Tourine** Tiris Zemmour, N Mauritania 22°23′N 11°50′W
102 J3 **Tourlaville** Manche, N France 49°38′N 01°34′W
99 D19 **Tournai** var. Tournay, Dut. Doornik; anc. Tornacum. Hainaut, SW Belgium 50°36′N 03°24′E
102 L16 **Tournay** Hautes-Pyrénées, S France 43°10′N 00°16′E
Tournay see Tournai
103 R12 **Tournon** Ardèche, E France 45°05′N 04°49′E
103 R9 **Tournus** Saône-et-Loire, C France 46°33′N 04°53′E
59 Q14 **Touros** Rio Grande do Norte, E Brazil 05°10′S 35°29′W
102 L8 **Tours** anc. Caesarodunum, Turoni. Indre-et-Loire, C France 47°22′N 00°40′E
183 Q17 **Tourville, Cape** headland Tasmania, SE Australia 42°09′S 148°20′E
162 I8 **Töv** ◈ province C Mongolia
54 H7 **Tovar** Mérida, NW Venezuela 08°22′N 71°50′W
126 L5 **Tovarkovskiy** Tul'skaya Oblast', W Russian Federation 53°41′N 38°18′E
Tovil'-Dora see Tavildara
Tövis see Teiuş
137 V11 **Tovuz** Rus. Tauz. W Azerbaijan 40°58′N 45°41′E
165 R7 **Towada** Aomori, Honshū, C Japan 40°35′N 141°13′E
184 K3 **Towai** Northland, North Island, New Zealand 35°29′S 174°06′E
18 H12 **Towanda** Pennsylvania, NE USA 41°45′N 76°25′W
29 W4 **Tower** Minnesota, N USA 47°48′N 92°16′W
171 N12 **Towera** Sulawesi, N Indonesia 0°29′S 120°01′E
Tower Island see Genovesa, Isla
180 M13 **Tower Peak** ▲ Western Australia 33°23′S 123°27′E
35 U11 **Towne Pass** pass California, W USA
29 N3 **Towner** North Dakota, N USA 48°20′N 100°27′W
33 R10 **Townsend** Montana, NW USA 46°19′N 111°31′W
181 X6 **Townsville** Queensland, NE Australia 19°24′S 146°53′E
Towoeti Meer see Towuti, Danau
148 K4 **Towraghoudī** Herāt, NW Afghanistan 35°13′N 62°19′E
21 X3 **Towson** Maryland, NE USA 39°25′N 76°36′W
171 O13 **Towuti, Danau** Dut. Towoeti Meer. ◎ Sulawesi, C Indonesia
Toxkan He see Ak-say
24 K9 **Toyah** Texas, SW USA 31°18′N 103°47′W
165 R4 **Tōya-ko** ◎ Hokkaidō, NE Japan
164 L11 **Toyama** Toyama, Honshū, SW Japan 36°41′N 137°13′E
164 L11 **Toyama** off. Toyama-ken. ◈ prefecture Honshū, SW Japan
Toyama-ken see Toyama
164 L11 **Toyama-wan** bay W Japan
164 H15 **Tōyo** Kōchi, Shikoku, SW Japan 33°22′N 134°18′E
Toyohara see Yuzhno-Sakhalinsk
164 L14 **Toyohashi** var. Toyohasi. Aichi, Honshū, SW Japan 34°46′N 137°22′E
Toyohasi see Toyohashi
164 L14 **Toyokawa** Aichi, Honshū, SW Japan 34°47′N 137°24′E
164 I14 **Toyooka** Hyōgo, Honshū, SW Japan 35°35′N 134°48′E
164 L13 **Toyota** Aichi, Honshū, SW Japan 35°04′N 137°09′E
165 T1 **Toyotomi** Hokkaidō, NE Japan 45°07′N 141°45′E
147 Q10 **To'ytepa** Rus. Toytepa. Toshkent Viloyati, E Uzbekistan 41°04′N 69°22′E
Toytepa see To'ytepa
74 M6 **Tozeur** var. Tawzar. W Tunisia 34°00′N 08°09′E
39 Q8 **Tozi, Mount** ▲ Alaska, USA 65°45′N 151°01′W
137 Q9 **Tqvarch'eli** Rus. Tkvarcheli. NW Georgia 42°51′N 41°42′E
Trâblous see Tripoli
137 O11 **Trabzon** Eng. Trebizond; anc. Trapezus. Trabzon, NE Turkey 41°N 39°43′E
137 O11 **Trabzon** Eng. Trebizond. ◈ province NE Turkey
13 P13 **Tracadie** New Brunswick, SE Canada 47°32′N 64°57′W
Trachenberg see Żmigród
15 O11 **Tracy** Québec, SE Canada 45°59′N 73°07′W
35 O8 **Tracy** California, W USA 37°43′N 121°27′W
29 S10 **Tracy** Minnesota, N USA 44°14′N 95°37′W
20 K10 **Tracy City** Tennessee, S USA 35°15′N 85°44′W
106 D7 **Tradate** Lombardia, N Italy 45°43′N 08°57′E
84 F6 **Traena Bank** undersea feature E Norwegian Sea 66°15′N 09°45′E
29 W13 **Traer** Iowa, C USA 42°11′N 92°28′W
104 J16 **Trafalgar, Cabo de** headland SW Spain 36°10′N 06°03′W
Traiectum ad Mosam/Traiectum Tungorum see Maastricht
Tráigh Mhór see Tramore
11 O17 **Trail** British Columbia, SW Canada 49°94′N 117°39′W
58 B11 **Traíra, Serra do** ▲▲ NW Brazil
109 V5 **Traisen** Niederösterreich, NE Austria 48°03′N 15°37′E
109 W4 **Traisen** ≈ NE Austria
109 X4 **Traiskirchen** Niederösterreich, NE Austria 48°01′N 16°18′E
Trajani Portus see Civitavecchia
Trajectum ad Rhenum see Utrecht
119 H14 **Trakai** Ger. Traken, Pol. Troki. Vilnius, SE Lithuania 54°39′N 24°58′E
Traken see Trakai
97 B20 **Tralee** Ir. Trá Lí. SW Ireland 52°16′N 09°42′W
97 A20 **Tralee Bay** Ir. Bá Thrá Lí. bay SW Ireland
Trá Lí see Tralee
Trälleborg see Trelleborg
Tralles Aydin see Aydın
61 J16 **Tramandaí** Rio Grande do Sul, S Brazil 30°01′S 50°11′W
108 C7 **Tramelan** Bern, W Switzerland 47°13′N 07°07′E
Trá Mhór see Tramore
97 E20 **Tramore** Ir. Tráigh Mhór, Trá Mhór. Waterford, S Ireland 52°10′N 07°10′W
95 L18 **Tranås** Jönköping, S Sweden 58°03′N 15°00′E
62 J7 **Trancas** Tucumán, N Argentina 26°11′S 65°20′W
104 I7 **Trancoso** Guarda, N Portugal 40°46′N 07°21′W
95 H22 **Tranebjerg** Århus, C Denmark 55°51′N 10°36′E
95 K19 **Tranemo** Västra Götaland, S Sweden 57°30′N 13°20′E
167 N16 **Trang** Trang, S Thailand 07°33′N 99°36′E
171 V15 **Trangan, Pulau** island Kepulauan Aru, E Indonesia
Trang Dinh see Thất Khê
183 Q7 **Trangie** New South Wales, SE Australia 32°01′S 147°58′E
94 K12 **Trängslet** Dalarna, C Sweden 61°22′N 13°43′E
107 N16 **Trani** Puglia, SE Italy 41°17′N 16°25′E
61 F17 **Tranqueras** Rivera, NE Uruguay 31°13′S 55°45′W
63 G17 **Tranqui, Isla** island S Chile
39 V6 **Trans-Alaska pipeline** oil pipeline Alaska, USA
195 Q10 **Transantarctic Mountains** ▲▲ Antarctica
Transcarpathian Oblast see Zakarpats'ka Oblast'
122 E9 **Trans-Siberian Railway** railway Russian Federation
Transilvania see Transylvania
Transilvaniei, Alpi see Carpaţii Meridionalii
Transjordan see Jordan
172 L11 **Transkei Basin** undersea feature SW Indian Ocean 35°30′S 29°00′E
117 O10 **Transnistria** cultural region E Moldavia
Transsylvanische Alpen/Transylvanian Alps see Carpaţii Meridionalii
94 K12 **Transtrand** Dalarna, C Sweden 61°06′N 13°19′E
116 G10 **Transylvania** Eng. Ardeal, Transilvania, Ger. Siebenbürgen, Hung. Erdély. cultural region NW Romania
167 S14 **Tra Ôn** Vinh Long, S Vietnam 09°58′N 105°58′E
107 H23 **Trapani** anc. Drepanum. Sicilia, Italy, C Mediterranean Sea 38°02′N 12°32′E
167 S12 **Trâpeăng Vêng** Kâmpóng Thum, C Cambodia 12°37′N 104°58′E
Trapezus see Trabzon
114 L9 **Trapoklovo** Sliven, C Bulgaria 42°40′N 26°36′E
183 P13 **Traralgon** Victoria, SE Australia 38°15′S 146°36′E
76 H9 **Trarza** ◈ region SW Mauritania
Trasimenischersee see Trasimeno, Lago
106 H12 **Trasimeno, Lago** Eng. Lake of Perugia, Ger. Trasimenischersee. ◎ C Italy
95 J20 **Träslövsläge** Halland, S Sweden 57°02′N 12°18′E
Trás-os-Montes see Cucumbi
104 I6 **Trás-os-Montes e Alto Douro** former province N Portugal
167 Q12 **Trat** var. Bang Phra. Trat, S Thailand 12°16′N 102°30′E
Trá Tholl, Inis see Inishtrahull
Traù see Trogir
109 T4 **Traun** Oberösterreich, N Austria 48°14′N 14°15′E
109 S5 **Traun** ≈ N Austria
Traun, Lake see Traunsee
101 N23 **Traunreut** Bayern, SE Germany 47°58′N 12°36′E
109 S5 **Traunsee** var. Gmundner See, Eng. Lake Traun. ◎ N Austria
Trautenau see Trutnov
21 P11 **Travelers Rest** South Carolina, SE USA 34°58′N 82°26′W
182 L8 **Travellers Lake** seasonal lake New South Wales, SE Australia
31 P6 **Traverse City** Michigan, N USA 44°45′N 85°37′W
29 R7 **Traverse, Lake** ◎ Minnesota/South Dakota, N USA
185 I16 **Travers, Mount** ▲ South Island, New Zealand 42°01′S 172°46′E
11 P17 **Travers Reservoir** ⊠ Alberta, SW Canada
167 T14 **Tra Vinh** var. Phu Vinh. Tra Vinh, S Vietnam 09°57′N 106°20′E
25 S10 **Travis, Lake** ⊠ Texas, SW USA
112 H12 **Travnik** Federacija Bosna I Hercegovina, C Bosnia and Herzegovina 44°14′N 17°40′E
109 V11 **Trbovlje** Ger. Trifail. C Slovenia 46°10′N 15°03′E
23 V13 **Treasure Island** Florida, SE USA 27°46′N 82°46′W
Treasure State see Montana
186 I8 **Treasury Islands** island group NW Solomon Islands
106 D9 **Trebbia** anc. Trebia. ≈ NW Italy
100 N8 **Trebel** ≈ NE Germany
103 O16 **Trèbes** Aude, S France 43°12′N 02°26′E
Trebia see Trebbia
111 F18 **Třebíč** Ger. Trebitsch. Vysočina, C Czech Republic 49°13′N 15°52′E
113 I16 **Trebinje** Republika Srpska, S Bosnia and Herzegovina 42°42′N 18°19′E
Trebišnica see Trebišnjica
113 H16 **Trebišnjica** var. Trebišnica. ≈ S Bosnia and Herzegovina
111 N20 **Trebišov** Hung. Tőketerebes. Košický Kraj, E Slovakia 48°37′N 21°44′E
Trebitsch see Třebíč
Trebizond see Trabzon
Trebnitz see Trzebnica
109 V12 **Trebnje** SE Slovenia 45°54′N 15°01′E
111 D19 **Třeboň** Ger. Wittingau. Jihočeský Kraj, S Czech Republic 49°00′N 14°46′E
104 J15 **Trebujena** Andalucía, S Spain 36°52′N 06°11′W
100 I7 **Treene** ≈ N Germany
Tree Planters State see Nebraska
109 S9 **Treffen** Kärnten, S Austria 46°40′N 13°51′E
Trefynwy see Monmouth
102 G5 **Tréguier** Côtes d'Armor, NW France 48°50′N 03°12′W
61 G18 **Treinta y Tres** Treinta y Tres, E Uruguay 33°16′S 54°17′W
61 F18 **Treinta y Tres** ◈ department E Uruguay
122 F11 **Trëkhgornyy** Chelyabinskaya Oblast', C Russian Federation 54°42′N 58°25′E
114 F9 **Treklyanska Reka** ≈ W Bulgaria
102 K8 **Trélazé** Maine-et-Loire, NW France 47°27′N 00°28′W
63 K17 **Trelew** Chubut, SE Argentina 43°13′S 65°15′W
95 K23 **Trelleborg** var. Trälleborg. Skåne, S Sweden 55°22′N 13°10′E
113 P15 **Trem** ▲ SE Serbia 43°10′N 22°12′E
15 N11 **Tremblant, Mont** ▲ Québec, SE Canada 46°13′N 74°34′W
99 H17 **Tremelo** Vlaams Brabant, C Belgium 51°N 04°34′E
107 M15 **Tremiti, Isole** island group SE Italy
30 K12 **Tremont** Illinois, N USA 40°30′N 89°31′W
36 L1 **Tremonton** Utah, W USA 41°42′N 112°09′W
105 U4 **Tremp** Cataluña, NE Spain 42°09′N 00°53′E
30 J7 **Trempealeau** Wisconsin, N USA 44°00′N 91°25′W
15 P8 **Trenche** ≈ Québec, SE Canada
15 O7 **Trenche, Lac** ◎ Québec, SE Canada
111 I20 **Trenčiansky Kraj** ◈ region W Slovakia
111 I19 **Trenčín** Ger. Trentschin, Hung. Trencsén. Trenčiansky Kraj, W Slovakia 48°54′N 18°03′E
Trencsén see Trenčín
Trengganu see Terengganu
Trengganu, Kuala see Kuala Terengganu
61 A21 **Trenque Lauquen** Buenos Aires, E Argentina 35°56′S 62°43′W
14 J14 **Trent** ≈ Ontario, SE Canada
97 N18 **Trent** ≈ C England, United Kingdom
Trent see Trento
106 F5 **Trentino-Alto Adige** prev. Venezia Tridentina. ◈ region N Italy
106 G6 **Trento** Eng. Trent, Ger. Trient; anc. Tridentum. Trentino-Alto Adige, N Italy 46°05′N 11°08′E
14 J15 **Trenton** Ontario, SE Canada 44°07′N 77°34′W
23 V10 **Trenton** Florida, SE USA 29°36′N 82°49′W
23 R1 **Trenton** Georgia, SE USA 34°52′N 85°27′W
31 S10 **Trenton** Michigan, N USA 42°08′N 83°10′W
27 S2 **Trenton** Missouri, C USA 40°04′N 93°37′W
28 M17 **Trenton** Nebraska, C USA 40°10′N 101°00′W
18 J15 **Trenton** state capital New Jersey, NE USA 40°13′N 74°45′W
21 W10 **Trenton** North Carolina, SE USA 35°03′N 77°20′W
20 G9 **Trenton** Tennessee, S USA 35°59′N 88°59′W
36 L1 **Trenton** Utah, W USA 41°53′N 111°57′W
Trentschin see Trenčín
Treptow an der Rega see Trzebiatów
61 C23 **Tres Arroyos** Buenos Aires, E Argentina 38°22′S 60°17′W
61 J15 **Três Cachoeiras** Rio Grande do Sul, S Brazil 29°21′S 49°48′W
106 E7 **Trescore Balneario** Lombardia, N Italy 45°43′N 09°52′E
41 V17 **Tres Cruces, Cerro** ▲ SE Mexico 15°28′N 92°27′W
57 K18 **Tres Cruces, Cordillera** ▲▲ W Bolivia
113 N18 **Treska** ≈ NW FYR Macedonia
113 I14 **Treskavica** ▲▲ SE Bosnia and Herzegovina
59 J20 **Três Lagoas** Mato Grosso do Sul, SW Brazil 20°46′S 51°43′W
40 H12 **Tres Marías, Islas** island group C Mexico
59 M19 **Três Marias, Represa** ⊠ SE Brazil
63 F20 **Tres Montes, Península** headland S Chile 46°49′S 75°29′W
105 O3 **Trespaderne** Castilla-León, N Spain 42°47′N 03°24′W
60 G13 **Três Passos** Rio Grande do Sul, S Brazil 27°33′S 53°55′W
61 A23 **Tres Picos, Cerro** ▲ E Argentina 38°10′S 61°54′W
63 G17 **Tres Picos, Cerro** ▲ SW Argentina 42°22′S 71°51′W
60 I12 **Três Pinheiros** Paraná, S Brazil 25°25′S 51°57′W
59 M21 **Três Pontas** Minas Gerais, SE Brazil 21°33′S 45°18′W
Tres Puntas, Cabo see Manabique, Punta
60 P9 **Três Rios** Rio de Janeiro, SE Brazil 22°06′S 43°15′W
Tres Tabernae see Saverne
Trestenberg/Trestendorf see Tăşnad
41 R15 **Tres Valles** Veracruz-Llave, SE Mexico 18°14′N 96°03′W
94 H12 **Tretten** Oppland, S Norway 61°19′N 10°19′E
Treuburg see Olecko
101 K21 **Treuchtlingen** Bayern, S Germany 48°57′N 10°55′E
100 N13 **Treuenbrietzen** Brandenburg, E Germany 52°06′N 12°52′E
95 F16 **Treungen** Telemark, S Norway 59°00′N 08°34′E
63 H17 **Trevelín** Chubut, SW Argentina 43°02′S 71°27′W
Treves/Trèves see Trier
106 I13 **Trevi** Umbria, C Italy 42°52′N 12°46′E
106 E7 **Treviglio** Lombardia, N Italy 45°32′N 09°35′E
104 J4 **Trevinca, Peña** ▲ NW Spain 42°10′N 06°49′W
105 P3 **Treviño** Castilla-León, N Spain 42°45′N 02°41′W
106 I7 **Treviso** anc. Tarvisium. Veneto, NE Italy 45°40′N 12°15′E
97 G24 **Trevose Head** headland SW England, United Kingdom 50°33′N 05°03′W
Trg see Feldkirchen in Kärnten
183 P17 **Triabunna** Tasmania, SE Australia 42°33′S 147°55′E
21 W4 **Triangle** Virginia, NE USA 38°30′N 77°17′W
83 L18 **Triangle** Masvingo, SE Zimbabwe 20°58′S 31°28′E
115 L23 **Tría Nisía** island Kykládes, Greece, Aegean Sea
Triberg see Triberg im Schwarzwald
101 G23 **Triberg im Schwarzwald** var. Triberg. Baden-Württemberg, SW Germany 48°07′N 08°13′E
153 P11 **Tribhuvan** ✈ (Kathmandu) Central, C Nepal
54 C9 **Tribugá, Golfo de** gulf W Colombia
181 W4 **Tribulation, Cape** headland Queensland, NE Australia 16°14′S 145°48′E
108 M8 **Tribulaun** ▲ SW Austria 46°59′N 11°18′E
11 U17 **Tribune** Saskatchewan, S Canada 49°16′N 103°50′W
26 H5 **Tribune** Kansas, C USA 38°27′N 101°46′W
107 N18 **Tricarico** Basilicata, S Italy 40°37′N 16°09′E
107 Q19 **Tricase** Puglia, SE Italy 39°56′N 18°21′E
Trichinopoly see Tiruchchirāppalli
115 D18 **Trichonída, Límni** ◎ C Greece
155 G22 **Trichūr** var. Thrissur. Kerala, SW India 10°32′N 76°14′E see also Thrissur
Tricorno see Triglav
183 O8 **Trida** New South Wales, SE Australia 33°02′S 145°03′E
35 S1 **Trident Peak** ▲ Nevada, W USA 41°52′N 118°22′W
Tridentum/Trient see Trento
109 T6 **Trieben** Steiermark, SE Austria 47°29′N 14°30′E
101 D19 **Trier** Eng. Treves, Fr. Trèves; anc. Augusta Treverorum. Rheinland-Pfalz, SW Germany 49°45′N 06°39′E
106 K7 **Trieste** Slvn. Trst. Friuli-Venezia Giulia, NE Italy 45°39′N 13°45′E
Trieste, Golfo di/Triest, Golf von see Trieste, Gulf of
106 J8 **Trieste, Gulf of** Cro. Tršćanski Zaljev, Ger. Golf von Triest, It. Golfo di Trieste, Slvn. Tržaški Zaliv. gulf S Europe
109 W4 **Triesting** ≈ W Austria
Triêu Hai see Quang Tri
Trifail see Trbovlje
116 L9 **Trifeşti** Iaşi, NE Romania 47°30′N 27°31′E
109 S10 **Triglav** It. Tricorno. ▲ NW Slovenia 46°22′N 13°40′E
104 I14 **Trigueros** Andalucía, S Spain 37°24′N 06°50′W
115 E16 **Tríkala** prev. Trikkala. Thessalía, C Greece 39°33′N 21°46′E
115 E17 **Trikeriótis** ≈ C Greece
Trikkala see Tríkala
Trikomo/Trikomon see İskele
97 F17 **Trim** Ir. Baile Átha Troim. Meath, E Ireland 53°34′N 06°47′W
108 E7 **Trimbach** Solothurn, NW Switzerland 47°22′N 07°53′E
109 Q5 **Trimmelkam** Oberösterreich, N Austria 48°02′N 12°55′E
29 U11 **Trimont** Minnesota, N USA 43°45′N 94°42′W
Trimontium see Plovdiv
Trinacria see Sicilia
155 K24 **Trincomalee** var. Trinkomali. Eastern Province, NE Sri Lanka 08°34′N 81°13′E
65 K16 **Trindade, Ilha da** island Brazil, W Atlantic Ocean
47 Y9 **Trindade Spur** undersea feature SW Atlantic Ocean 21°00′S 35°00′W
111 J17 **Třinec** Ger. Trzynietz. Moravskoslezský Kraj, E Czech Republic 49°41′N 18°39′E
57 M16 **Trinidad** Beni, N Bolivia 14°52′S 64°54′W
54 H9 **Trinidad** Casanare, E Colombia 05°25′N 71°39′W
44 E6 **Trinidad** Sancti Spíritus, C Cuba 21°48′N 80°00′W
61 E19 **Trinidad** Flores, S Uruguay 33°35′S 56°54′W
37 U8 **Trinidad** Colorado, C USA 37°11′N 104°31′W
45 Y17 **Trinidad** island C Trinidad and Tobago
Trinidad see Jose Abad Santos
45 Y16 **Trinidad and Tobago** off. Republic of Trinidad and Tobago. ◆ republic SE West Indies
Trinidad and Tobago, Republic of see Trinidad and Tobago
63 F22 **Trinidad, Golfo** gulf S Chile
61 B24 **Trinidad, Isla** island E Argentina
107 N16 **Trinitapoli** Puglia, SE Italy 41°22′N 16°06′E
55 X10 **Trinité, Montagnes de la** ▲▲ C French Guiana
25 W9 **Trinity** Texas, SW USA 30°57′N 95°22′W
13 U12 **Trinity Bay** inlet Newfoundland, Newfoundland and Labrador, E Canada
39 P15 **Trinity Islands** island group Alaska, USA
35 N2 **Trinity Mountains** ▲▲ California, W USA
35 S4 **Trinity Peak** ▲ Nevada, W USA 40°13′N 118°43′W
35 S5 **Trinity Range** ▲▲ Nevada, W USA
35 N2 **Trinity River** ≈ California, W USA
25 V8 **Trinity River** ≈ Texas, SW USA
Trinkomali see Trincomalee
173 Y15 **Triolet** NW Mauritius 20°05′S 57°32′E
107 O20 **Trionto, Capo** headland S Italy 39°37′N 16°46′E
Tripiti, Ákra see Trypití, Akrotírio
115 F20 **Trípoli** prev. Trípolis. Pelopónnisos, S Greece 37°31′N 22°22′E
138 G6 **Tripoli** var. Tarābulus, Ţarābulus ash Shām, Trâblous; anc. Tripolis. N Lebanon 34°30′N 35°42′E
29 X12 **Tripoli** Iowa, C USA 42°48′N 92°15′W
Tripoli see Ţarābulus
Trípolis see Trípoli, Greece
Tripolis see Tripoli, Lebanon
75 O8 **Tripolitania** ◈ cultural region NW Libya
29 Q12 **Tripp** South Dakota, N USA 43°12′N 97°57′W
153 V15 **Tripura** var. Hill Tippera. ◈ state NE India
108 K8 **Trisanna** ≈ W Austria
100 H8 **Trischen** island NW Germany
65 M24 **Tristan da Cunha** ◇ dependency of Saint Helena SE Atlantic Ocean
67 P15 **Tristan da Cunha** island SE Atlantic Ocean
65 L18 **Tristan da Cunha Fracture Zone** tectonic feature S Atlantic Ocean
167 S14 **Tri Tôn** An Giang, S Vietnam 10°26′N 105°01′E
167 W10 **Triton Island** island S Paracel Islands
155 G24 **Trivandrum** var. Thiruvanathapuram, Tiruvantapuram. state capital Kerala, SW India 08°30′N 76°57′E
111 H20 **Trnava** Ger. Tyrnau, Hung. Nagyszombat. Trnavský Kraj, W Slovakia 48°22′N 17°36′E
111 H20 **Trnavský Kraj** ◈ region W Slovakia
Trnovo see Veliko Tŭrnovo
Trobriand Island see Kiriwina Island
Trobriand Islands see Kiriwina Islands
11 Q16 **Trochu** Alberta, SW Canada 51°48′N 113°12′W
109 U7 **Trofaiach** Steiermark, SE Austria 47°25′N 15°01′E
93 F14 **Trofors** Troms, N Norway 65°31′N 13°19′E
113 E14 **Trogir** It. Traù. Split-Dalmacija, S Croatia 43°32′N 16°13′E
112 F13 **Troglav** ▲ Bosnia and Herzegovina/Croatia 44°00′N 16°36′E
107 M16 **Troia** Puglia, SE Italy 41°21′N 15°19′E
107 K24 **Troina** Sicilia, Italy, C Mediterranean Sea 37°47′N 14°37′E
173 O16 **Trois-Bassins** W Réunion 21°05′S 55°18′E
101 E17 **Troisdorf** Nordrhein-Westfalen, W Germany 50°49′N 07°09′E
74 H5 **Trois Fourches, Cap des** headland NE Morocco 35°27′N 02°58′W
15 T8 **Trois-Pistoles** Québec, SE Canada 48°08′N 69°10′W
99 L21 **Trois-Ponts** Liège, E Belgium 50°22′N 05°52′E
15 P11 **Trois-Rivières** Québec, SE Canada 46°21′N 72°34′W
55 Y12 **Trois Sauts** S French Guiana 02°15′N 52°52′W
99 M22 **Troisvierges** Diekirch, N Luxembourg 50°07′N 06°00′E
122 F11 **Troitsk** Chelyabinskaya Oblast', S Russian Federation 54°04′N 61°31′E
125 T9 **Troitsko-Pechorsk** Respublika Komi, NW Russian Federation 62°39′N 56°06′E
127 V7 **Troitskoye** Orenburgskaya Oblast', W Russian Federation 52°23′N 56°24′E
Troki see Trakai
94 F9 **Trolla** ▲ S Norway 62°41′N 09°47′E
95 J18 **Trollhättan** Västra Götaland, S Sweden 58°17′N 12°20′E
94 G9 **Trollheimen** ▲▲ S Norway
94 E9 **Trolltindane** ▲ S Norway 62°30′N 07°43′E
58 H11 **Trombetas, Rio** ≈ NE Brazil
128 L16 **Tromelin, Île** island N Réunion
92 I9 **Troms** ◈ county N Norway
92 I9 **Tromsø** Fin. Tromssa. Troms, N Norway 69°39′N 19°01′E
84 F5 **Tromsøflaket** undersea feature W Barents Sea 18°30′E 71°30′N
Tromssa see Tromsø
94 H10 **Tron** ▲ S Norway 62°12′N 10°46′E
35 U12 **Trona** California, W USA 35°46′N 117°21′W
63 G16 **Tronador, Cerro** ▲ S Chile 41°12′S 71°51′W
94 H8 **Trondheim** Ger. Drontheim; prev. Nidaros, Trondhjem. Sør-Trøndelag, S Norway 63°25′N 10°24′E
94 H7 **Trondheimsfjorden** fjord S Norway
Trondhjem see Trondheim
107 J14 **Tronto** ≈ C Italy
121 P3 **Troódos** var. Troodos Mountains. ▲▲ C Cyprus
Troodos see Ólympos
Troodos Mountains see Troódos
96 I13 **Troon** W Scotland, United Kingdom 55°32′N 04°41′W
107 M22 **Tropea** Calabria, SW Italy 38°40′N 15°52′E
36 L7 **Tropic** Utah, W USA 37°37′N 112°04′W
64 L10 **Tropic Seamount** var. Banc du Tropique. undersea feature E Atlantic Ocean 23°50′N 20°40′W
Tropique, Banc du see Tropic Seamount
Tropoja see Tropojë
113 L17 **Tropojë** var. Tropoja. Kukës, N Albania 42°25′N 20°09′E
Troppau see Opava
95 O16 **Trosa** Södermanland, C Sweden 58°54′N 17°35′E
118 H12 **Troškūnai** Utena, E Lithuania 55°36′N 24°55′E
101 G23 **Trossingen** Baden-Württemberg, SW Germany 48°04′N 08°37′E
117 T4 **Trostyanets'** Rus. Trostyanets. Sums'ka Oblast', NE Ukraine 50°30′N 34°59′E
117 N7 **Trostyanets'** Rus. Trostyanets. Vinnyts'ka Oblast', C Ukraine 48°35′N 29°10′E
Trostyanets see Trostyanets'
116 L11 **Trotuş** ≈ E Romania
44 M8 **Trou-du-Nord** N Haiti 19°34′N 71°57′W
25 W7 **Troup** Texas, SW USA 32°08′N 95°07′W
8 I10 **Trout** ≈ Northwest Territories, NW Canada
33 N8 **Trout Creek** Montana, NW USA 47°51′N 115°40′W
32 H10 **Trout Lake** Washington, NW USA 45°59′N 121°33′W
12 B9 **Trout Lake** ◎ Ontario, S Canada
33 T12 **Trout Peak** ▲ Wyoming, C USA 44°36′N 109°33′W
102 L4 **Trouville** Calvados, N France 49°21′N 00°07′E
97 L22 **Trowbridge** S England, United Kingdom 51°20′N 02°13′W
23 Q6 **Troy** Alabama, S USA 31°48′N 85°58′W
27 Q3 **Troy** Kansas, C USA 39°45′N 95°06′W
27 W4 **Troy** Missouri, C USA 38°59′N 90°59′W
18 L10 **Troy** New York, NE USA 42°43′N 73°37′W
21 S10 **Troy** North Carolina, SE USA 35°23′N 79°54′W
31 R13 **Troy** Ohio, N USA 40°02′N 84°12′W
25 T9 **Troy** Texas, SW USA 31°12′N 97°18′W
114 I9 **Troyan** Lovech, N Bulgaria 42°52′N 24°42′E
114 I9 **Troyanski Prokhod** pass N Bulgaria
145 N6 **Troyebratskiy** Severnyy Kazakhstan, N Kazakhstan 54°25′N 66°03′E
103 Q6 **Troyes** anc. Augustobona Tricassium. Aube, N France 48°18′N 04°04′E
117 X5 **Troyits'ke** Luhans'ka Oblast', E Ukraine 49°55′N 38°18′E
35 W7 **Troy Peak** ▲ Nevada, W USA 38°18′N 115°27′W
113 G15 **Trpanj** Dubrovnik-Neretva, S Croatia 43°00′N 17°18′E
Tršćanski Zaljev see Trieste, Gulf of
Trst see Trieste
113 N14 **Trstenik** Serbia, C Serbia 43°38′N 21°01′E
126 I6 **Trubchevsk** Bryanskaya Oblast', W Russian Federation 52°33′N 33°45′E
Trubchular see Orlyak
37 S10 **Truchas Peak** ▲ New Mexico, SW USA 35°57′N 105°38′W

◆ Country ● Country Capital ◇ Dependent Territory ○ Dependent Territory Capital ◈ Administrative Regions ✈ International Airport ▲ Mountain ▲▲ Mountain Range Volcano ≈ River ◎ Lake ⊠ Reservoir

143 P16 **Trucial Coast** *physical region* C United Arab Emirates
Trucial States *see* United Arab Emirates
35 Q6 **Truckee** California, W USA 39°18´N 120°10´W
35 R5 **Truckee River** ♦ Nevada, W USA
127 Q13 **Trudfront** Astrakhanskaya Oblast´, SW Russian Federation 45°56´N 47°42´E
14 I9 **Truite, Lac à la** ⊚ Québec, SE Canada
42 K4 **Trujillo** Colón, NE Honduras 15°59´N 85°54´W
56 C12 **Trujillo** La Libertad, NW Peru 08°04´S 79°02´W
104 K10 **Trujillo** Extremadura, W Spain 39°28´N 05°53´W
54 I6 **Trujillo** NW Venezuela 09°20´N 70°38´W
54 I6 **Trujillo** *off.* Estado Trujillo. ♦ *state* W Venezuela
Trujillo, Estado *see* Trujillo
Truk *see* Chuuk
Truk Islands *see* Chuuk Islands
29 U10 **Truman** Minnesota, N USA 43°49´N 94°26´W
27 X10 **Trumann** Arkansas, C USA 35°40´N 90°30´W
36 J9 **Trumbull, Mount** ▲ Arizona, SW USA 36°22´N 113°09´W
114 F9 **Trŭn** Pernik, W Bulgaria 42°51´N 22°37´E
183 Q8 **Trundle** New South Wales, SE Australia 32°55´S 147°43´E
129 U13 **Trung Phân** *physical region* S Vietnam
Trupcilar *see* Orlyak
13 Q15 **Truro** Nova Scotia, SE Canada 45°24´N 63°18´W
97 H25 **Truro** SW England, United Kingdom 50°16´N 05°03´W
25 P5 **Truscott** Texas, SW USA 33°45´N 99°48´W
116 K9 **Truşeşti** Botoşani, NE Romania 47°45´N 27°01´E
116 H6 **Truskavets'** L'vivs'ka Oblast´, W Ukraine 49°15´N 23°30´E
95 H22 **Trustrup** Århus, C Denmark 56°20´N 10°46´E
10 M11 **Trutch** British Columbia, W Canada 57°42´N 123°00´W
37 Q14 **Truth Or Consequences** New Mexico, SW USA 33°07´N 107°15´W
111 F15 **Trutnov** *Ger.* Trautenau. Královéhradecký Kraj, N Czech Republic 50°34´N 15°55´E
103 P13 **Truyère** ♦ C France
114 K9 **Tryavna** Lovech, N Bulgaria 42°52´N 25°30´E
28 M14 **Tryon** Nebraska, C USA 41°33´N 100°57´W
115 J16 **Trypíti, Akrotírio** *var.* Ákra Tripíti. *headland* Ágios Efstrátios, E Greece 38°N 24°58´E
94 J12 **Trysil** Hedmark, S Norway 61°18´N 12°16´E
94 I11 **Trysilelva** ♦ S Norway
112 D10 **Tržac** Federacija Bosna I Hercegovina, NW Bosnia and Herzegovina 44°58´N 15°48´E
Tržaški Zaliv *see* Trieste, Gulf of
110 G10 **Trzcianka** *Ger.* Schönlanke. Piła, Wielkopolskie, C Poland 53°02´N 16°24´E
110 E7 **Trzebiatów** *Ger.* Treptow an der Rega. Zachodnio-pomorskie, NW Poland 54°04´N 15°14´E
111 G14 **Trzebnica** *Ger.* Trebnitz. Dolnośląskie, SW Poland 51°19´N 17°03´E
109 T10 **Tržič** *Ger.* Neumarktl. NW Slovenia 46°22´N 14°17´E
Trzynietz *see* Třinec
83 G21 **Tsabong** *var.* Tshabong. Kgalagadi, SW Botswana 26°03´S 22°27´E
162 G7 **Tsagaanchuluut** Dzavhan, C Mongolia 47°06´N 96°48´E
162 M8 **Tsagaandelger** *var.* Haraat. Dundgovĭ, C Mongolia 46°30´N 107°39´E
Tsagaanders *see* Bayantümen
162 G7 **Tsagaanhayrhan** *var.* Shiree. Dzavhan, W Mongolia 47°30´N 96°48´E
Tsagaannuur *see* Halhgol
Tsagaan-Olom *see* Tayshir
Tsagaan-Ovoo *see* Altantsögts
Tsagaantüngi *see* Altantsögts
162 H6 **Tsagaan-Uul** *var.* Sharga. Hövsgöl, N Mongolia 49°33´N 98°36´E
162 J5 **Tsagaan-Üür** *var.* Bulgan. Hövsgöl, N Mongolia 50°30´N 101°28´E
127 P12 **Tsagan Aman** Respublika Kalmykiya, SW Russian Federation 47°37´N 46°43´E
23 V11 **Tsala Apopka Lake** ⊚ Florida, SE USA
Tsamkong *see* Zhanjiang
Tsangpo *see* Brahmaputra
Tsant *see* Deren
Tsao *see* Tsau
172 I4 **Tsaratanana** Mahajanga, C Madagascar 16°46´S 47°40´E
114 N10 **Tsarevo** *prev.* Michurin. Burgas, E Bulgaria 42°10´N 27°51´E
Tsarigrad *see* Istanbul
114 K7 **Tsar Kaloyan** Ruse, N Bulgaria 43°36´N 26°14´E
Tsaritsyn *see* Volgograd
Tsarskoye Selo *see* Pushkin
117 T7 **Tsarychanka** Dnipropetrovs'ka Oblast´, E Ukraine 48°56´N 34°29´E
83 H21 **Tsatsu** Southern, S Botswana 25°21´S 24°45´E
83 G17 **Tsau** *var.* Tsao. North-West, NW Botswana 20°08´S 22°29´E
81 J20 **Tsavo** Coast, S Kenya 02°59´S 38°28´E
83 E21 **Tsawisis** Karas, S Namibia 25°58´S 18°08´E
Tschakathurn *see* Čakovec
Tschaslau *see* Čáslav
Tschenstochau *see* Częstochowa
28 K6 **Tschida, Lake** ⊚ North Dakota, N USA
Tschorna *see* Mustvee
162 G8 **Tseel** Govĭ-Altay, SW Mongolia 45°45´N 95°54´E

138 G8 **Tsefat** *var.* Safed, *Ar.* Safad; *prev.* Zefat. Northern, N Israel 32°57´N 35°27´E
126 M13 **Tselina** Rostovskaya Oblast´, SW Russian Federation 46°31´N 41°01´E
Tselinograd *see* Astana
Tselinogradskaya Oblast *see* Akmola
Tsengel *see* Tosontsengel
162 J8 **Tsenher** *var.* Altan-Ovoo. Arhangay, C Mongolia 47°24´N 101°51´E
163 N8 **Tsenhermandal** *var.* Modot. Hentiy, C Mongolia 47°45´N 109°03´E
Tsentral'nyy Nizmennyye Garagumy *see* Merkezi Garagumy
83 E21 **Tses** Karas, S Namibia 25°58´S 18°08´E
Tseshevlya *see* Tsyeshawlya
162 E7 **Tsetseg** *var.* Tsetsegnuur. Hovd, W Mongolia 46°30´N 93°16´E
Tsetsegnuur *see* Tsetseg
Tsetsen Khan *see* Öndörhaan
162 J8 **Tsetserleg** Arhangay, C Mongolia 47°29´N 101°19´E
162 H6 **Tsetserleg** *var.* Halban. Hövsgöl, N Mongolia 49°30´N 97°33´E
162 J8 **Tsetserleg** *var.* Hujirt. Övörhangay, C Mongolia 46°50´N 102°38´E
77 R16 **Tsévié** S Togo 06°25´N 01°13´E
83 G20 **Tshabong** *see* Tsabong
83 G20 **Tshane** Kgalagadi, SW Botswana 24°05´S 21°54´E
Tshangalele, Lac *see* Lufira, Lac de Retenue de la
83 H7 **Tshauxaba** Central, C Botswana 19°56´S 25°09´E
79 F21 **Tshela** Bas-Congo, W Dem. Rep. Congo 04°57´S 13°02´E
79 K22 **Tshibala** Kasai-Occidental, S Dem. Rep. Congo 06°53´S 22°01´E
79 J22 **Tshikapa** Kasai-Occidental, SW Dem. Rep. Congo 06°23´S 20°47´E
79 L22 **Tshilenge** Kasai Oriental, S Dem. Rep. Congo 06°17´S 23°48´E
79 L24 **Tshimbalanga** Katanga, S Dem. Rep. Congo 09°42´S 23°04´E
79 L22 **Tshimbulu** Kasai-Occidental, S Dem. Rep. Congo 06°27´S 22°54´E
Tshiumbe *see* Chiumbe
79 M21 **Tshofa** Kasai-Oriental, C Dem. Rep. Congo 05°13´S 25°13´E
79 K18 **Tshuapa** ♦ C Dem. Rep. Congo
83 J21 **Tshwane** *var.* Epitoli; *prev.* Pretoria. ● Gauteng, NE South Africa 25°41´S 28°12´E *see also* Pretoria
114 G7 **Tsibritsa** ♦ NW Bulgaria
Tsien Tang *see* Puyang Jiang
114 I12 **Tsigansko Gradishte** ▲ Bulgaria/Greece 41°24´N 24°41´E
8 H7 **Tsihombe** *see* Tsiombe
8 H7 **Tsiigehtchic** *prev.* Arctic Red River. Northwest Territories, NW Canada 67°24´N 133°40´W
125 Q7 **Tsil'ma** ♦ NW Russian Federation
119 J17 **Tsimkavichy** *Rus.* Timkovichi. Minskaya Voblasts´, S Belarus 53°04´N 26°59´E
126 M11 **Tsimlyansk** Rostovskaya Oblast´, SW Russian Federation 47°39´N 42°05´E
127 N11 **Tsimlyanskoye Vodokhranilishche** *var.* Tsimlyansk Vodoskhovshche, *Eng.* Tsimlyansk Reservoir. ◙ SW Russian Federation
Tsimlyansk Reservoir *see* Tsimlyanskoye Vodokhranilishche
Tsimlyansk Vodoskhovshche *see* Tsimlyanskoye Vodokhranilishche
Tsinan *see* Jinan
Tsing Hai *see* Qinghai Hu, China
Tsingtao/Tsingtau *see* Qingdao
99 G19 **Tsinkenakow** *see* Qingdao
83 D17 **Tsintsabis** Otjikoto, N Namibia 18°45´S 17°51´E
172 H8 **Tsiombe** *var.* Tsihombe. Toliara, S Madagascar 25°16´S 45°29´E
123 O13 **Tsipa** ♦ S Russian Federation
172 H5 **Tsiribihina** ♦ W Madagascar
172 I5 **Tsiroanomandidy** Antananarivo, C Madagascar 18°44´S 46°02´E
189 U13 **Tsis** *island* Chuuk, C Micronesia
127 Q3 **Tsivil'sk** Chuvashskaya Respublika, W Russian Federation 55°51´N 47°33´E
137 T9 **Ts'khinvali** *prev.* Staliniri. C Georgia 42°12´N 43°58´E
119 J19 **Tsna** ♦ S Belarus
127 N5 **Tsna** *var.* Tzna. ♦ W Russian Federation
162 J8 **Tsogt** *var.* Tahilt. Govĭ-Altay, W Mongolia 46°N 96°42´E
162 K10 **Tsogt-Ovoo** *var.* Doloon. Ömnögovĭ, S Mongolia 44°28´N 105°22´E
162 L10 **Tsogttsetsiy** *var.* Baruunsuu. Ömnögovĭ, S Mongolia 43°46´N 105°28´E
164 K14 **Tsu** *var.* Tu. Mie, Honshū, SW Japan 34°41´N 136°30´E
165 O10 **Tsubame** *var.* Tubame. Niigata, Honshū, C Japan 37°40´N 138°56´E
165 V3 **Tsubetsu** Hokkaidō, NE Japan 43°43´N 144°01´E
165 O15 **Tsuchiura** *var.* Tutiura. Ibaraki, Honshū, S Japan 36°05´N 140°12´E
165 Q6 **Tsugaru-kaikyō** *strait* N Japan

164 E14 **Tsukumi** *var.* Tukumi. Ōita, Kyūshū, SW Japan 33°04´N 131°51´E
Tsul-Ulaan *see* Bayannuur
Tsul-Ulaan *see* Bayannuur
83 D17 **Tsumeb** Otjikoto, N Namibia 19°13´S 17°42´E
83 F17 **Tsumkwe** Otjozondjupa, NE Namibia 19°37´S 20°30´E
164 D15 **Tsuno** Miyazaki, Kyūshū, SW Japan 32°15´N 131°32´E
164 D12 **Tsuno-shima** *island* SW Japan
164 K12 **Tsuruga** *var.* Turuga. Fukui, Honshū, SW Japan 35°38´N 136°01´E
164 H12 **Tsurugi-san** ▲ Shikoku, SW Japan 33°51´N 134°04´E
165 P9 **Tsuruoka** *var.* Turuoka. Yamagata, Honshū, C Japan 38°44´N 139°48´E
164 C12 **Tsushima** *var.* Tsushima-tō, Tusima. *island group* SW Japan
164 H12 **Tsuyama** *var.* Tuyama. Okayama, Honshū, SW Japan 35°04´N 134°01´E
83 G19 **Tswaane** Ghanzi, W Botswana 22°21´S 21°52´E
119 N16 **Tsyakhtsin** *Rus.* Tekhtin. Mahilyowskaya Voblasts´, E Belarus 53°51´N 29°44´E
119 P19 **Tsyerakhowka** *Rus.* Terekhovka. Homyel'skaya Voblasts´, SE Belarus 52°13´N 31°24´E
119 I17 **Tsyeshawlya** *Rus.* Cheshevlya, Tseshevlya. Brestskaya Voblasts´, SW Belarus 53°14´N 25°49´E
Tsyurupinsk *see* Tsyurupyns'k
117 R10 **Tsyurupyns'k** *Rus.* Tsyurupinsk. Khersons'ka Oblast´, S Ukraine 46°35´N 32°43´E
186 C7 **Tua** ♦ C Papua New Guinea
184 L6 **Tuakau** Waikato, North Island, New Zealand 37°16´S 174°56´E
97 C17 **Tuam** *Ir.* Tuaim. Galway, W Ireland 53°31´N 08°50´W
185 K14 **Tuamarina** Marlborough, South Island, New Zealand 41°27´S 174°00´E
Tuamotu, Archipel des *see* Tuamotu, Îles
193 Q9 **Tuamotu Fracture Zone** *tectonic feature* E Pacific Ocean
191 W9 **Tuamotu, Îles** *var.* Archipel des Tuamotu, Dangerous Archipelago, Tuamotu Islands. *island group* N French Polynesia
Tuamotu Islands *see* Tuamotu, Îles
175 X10 **Tuamotu Ridge** *undersea feature* C Pacific Ocean
167 R5 **Tuân Giao** Lai Châu, N Vietnam 21°34´N 103°24´E
171 O2 **Tuao** Luzon, N Philippines 17°42´N 121°25´E
190 B15 **Tuapa** NW Niue 18°57´S 169°59´W
43 N7 **Tuapí** Región Autónoma Atlántico Norte, NE Nicaragua 14°10´N 83°20´W
126 K15 **Tuapse** Krasnodarskiy Kray, SW Russian Federation 44°08´N 39°07´E
169 U6 **Tuaran** Sabah, East Malaysia 06°12´N 116°12´E
104 I6 **Tua, Rio de** ♦ N Portugal
192 H15 **Tuasivi** Savai'i, C Samoa 13°38´S 172°08´W
185 B24 **Tuatapere** Southland, South Island, New Zealand 46°09´S 167°43´E
36 M9 **Tuba City** Arizona, SW USA 36°08´N 111°14´W
138 H11 **Tūbah, Qaşr aţ** *castle* 'Ammān, C Jordan
Tubame *see* Tsubame
169 R16 **Tuban** *prev.* Toeban. Jawa, C Indonesia 06°55´S 112°01´E
141 O16 **Tuban, Wādī** *dry watercourse* SW Yemen
61 K14 **Tubarão** Santa Catarina, S Brazil 28°29´S 49°00´W
98 O10 **Tubbergen** Overijssel, E Netherlands 52°25´N 06°46´E
Tubeke *see* Tubize
101 H22 **Tübingen** *var.* Tuebingen. Baden-Württemberg, SW Germany 48°32´N 09°04´E
99 F19 **Tubize** *Dut.* Tubeke. Walloon Brabant, C Belgium 50°43´N 04°14´E
76 J16 **Tubmanburg** NW Liberia 06°50´N 10°53´W
75 T7 **Ţubruq** *Eng.* Tobruk, *It.* Tobruch. NE Libya 32°05´N 23°59´E
191 T13 **Tubuai** *island* Îles Australes, SW French Polynesia
Tubuai, Îles/Tubuai Islands *see* Australes, Îles
Tubuai-Manu *see* Maiao
54 F3 **Tubutama** Sonora, NW Mexico 30°51´N 111°31´W
54 K4 **Tucacas** Falcón, N Venezuela 10°50´N 68°22´W
59 P16 **Tucano** Bahia, E Brazil 10°51´N 38°48´W
57 P19 **Tucavaca, Río** ♦ E Bolivia
110 H8 **Tuchola** Kujawsko-pomorskie, C Poland 53°35´N 17°50´E
111 M17 **Tuchów** Małopolskie, S Poland 49°53´N 21°04´E
23 S3 **Tucker** Georgia, SE USA 33°43´N 91°12´W
27 W10 **Tuckerman** Arkansas, C USA 35°43´N 91°12´W
64 B12 **Tucker's Town** E Bermuda 32°20´N 64°42´W
36 M15 **Tucson** Arizona, SW USA 32°13´N 110°58´W
62 J7 **Tucumán** *off.* Provincia de Tucumán. ♦ *province* N Argentina
Tucumán *see* San Miguel de Tucumán
Tucumán, Provincia de *see* Tucumán
37 V11 **Tucumcari** New Mexico, SW USA 35°11´N 103°44´W
58 H13 **Tucunaré** Pará, N Brazil

55 Q6 **Tucupita** Delta Amacuro, NE Venezuela 09°02´N 62°04´W
58 K13 **Tucuruí, Represa de** ◙ NE Brazil
110 F9 **Tuczno** Zachodnio-pomorskie, NW Poland 53°12´N 16°08´E
105 Q5 **Tudela** *Basq.* Tutera; *anc.* Tutela. Navarra, N Spain 42°04´N 01°37´W
104 M6 **Tudela de Duero** Castilla-León, N Spain 41°35´N 04°34´W
162 G6 **Tüdevtey** *var.* Oygon. Dzavhan, N Mongolia 48°57´N 96°31´E
138 K6 **Tudmur** *var.* Tadmur, Tamar, *Gk.* Palmyra, *Bibl.* Tadmor. Ḥimş, C Syria 34°36´N 38°15´E
118 J4 **Tudu** *Ger.* Tuddo. Lääne-Virumaa, NE Estonia 59°12´N 26°52´E
Tuebingen *see* Tübingen
122 J14 **Tuekta** Respublika Altay, S Russian Federation 50°51´N 85°52´E
153 X12 **Tuensang** Nāgāland, NE India 26°16´N 94°45´E
136 L15 **Tufanbeyli** Adana, C Turkey 38°15´N 36°13´E
Tüffer *see* Laško
186 F9 **Tufi** Northern, S Papua New Guinea 09°08´S 149°15´E
193 O3 **Tufts Plain** *undersea feature* N Pacific Ocean
Tugalan *see* Kolkhozobod
67 V14 **Tugela** ♦ SE South Africa
21 P6 **Tug Fork** ♦ S USA
39 P15 **Tugidak Island** *island* Trinity Islands, Alaska, USA
171 O2 **Tuguegarao** Luzon, N Philippines 17°37´N 121°48´E
123 S12 **Tugur** Khabarovskiy Kray, SE Russian Federation 53°43´N 137°00´E
161 I7 **Tuhai He** ♦ E China
104 G4 **Tui** Galicia, NW Spain 42°02´N 08°37´W
77 O13 **Tui** *var.* Grand Balé. ♦ W Burkina
57 J16 **Tuichi, Río** ♦ W Bolivia
64 Q11 **Tuineje** Fuerteventura, Islas Canarias, Spain, NE Atlantic Ocean 28°18´N 14°03´W
43 X16 **Tuira, Río** ♦ SE Panama
127 W5 **Tuisarkan** *see* Tūysarkān
Tujiabu *see* Yongxiu
171 P14 **Tukangbesi, Kepulauan** *Dut.* Toekang Besi Eilanden. *island group* C Indonesia
147 V13 **Tükhtamish** *Rus.* Toktomush; *prev.* Tokhtamyshbek. SE Tajikistan 37°51´N 74°41´E
184 O12 **Tukituki** ♦ North Island, New Zealand
167 Q12 **Tumbot, Phnum** ▲ W Cambodia
121 P12 **Ţukrah** NE Libya 32°32´N 20°35´E
182 G9 **Tumby Bay** South Australia 34°22´S 136°05´E
163 Y10 **Tumen** Jilin, NE China 42°56´N 129°47´E
163 Y11 **Tumen** *Chin.* Tumen Jiang, *Kor.* Tuman-gang, *Rus.* Tumyn'tszyan. ♦ E Asia
Tumen Jiang *see* Tumen
55 Q8 **Tumeremo** Bolívar, E Venezuela 07°17´N 61°30´W
96 I10 **Tummel** ♦ C Scotland, United Kingdom
188 B15 **Tumon Bay** *bay* W Guam
77 P14 **Tumu** NW Ghana 10°55´N 01°59´W
58 I10 **Tumuc-Humac Mountains** *var.* Serra Tumucumaque. ▲ N South America
Tumucumaque, Serra *see* Tumuc-Humac Mountains
183 Q10 **Tumut** New South Wales, SE Australia 35°20´S 148°14´E
158 F7 **Tumxuk** *var.* Urad Qianqi. Xinjiang Uygur Zizhiqu, NW China 78°40´N 39°54´E
Tumyn'tszyan *see* Tumen
45 U14 **Tunapuna** Trinidad, Trinidad and Tobago 10°38´N 61°23´W
60 K11 **Tunas** Paraná, S Brazil 24°57´S 49°05´W
Tunbridge Wells *see* Royal Tunbridge Wells
114 L11 **Tundzha** *Bul.* Tundzha; *Turk.* Tunca Nehri. ♦ Bulgaria/Turkey *see also* Tunca Nehri
Tundzha *see* Tunca Nehri
162 I6 **Tünel** *var.* Bulag. Hövsgöl, N Mongolia 49°51´N 100°41´E
155 H17 **Tungabhadra** ♦ S India
155 F17 **Tungabhadra Reservoir** ◙ S India
Tungaru *prev.* Gilbert Islands. *island group* W Kiribati
171 P7 **Tungawan** Mindanao, S Philippines 07°33´N 122°22´E
Tungdor *see* Mainling
Tung-shan *see* Xuzhou
161 Q16 **Tungshih** *Jap.* Tōsei. N Taiwan 24°13´N 120°54´E
161 S13 **Tungshih** *Jap.* Tōsei. N Taiwan 24°13´N 120°54´E
8 H9 **Tungsten** Northwest Territories, W Canada 62°N 128°09´W
Tung-t'ing Hu *see* Dongting Hu
110 I12 **Turek** Wielkopolskie, C Poland 52°01´N 18°30´E
191 X12 **Tureia** *atoll* Îles Tuamotu, SE French Polynesia
93 J17 **Turenki** Etelä-Suomi, SW Finland 60°55´N 24°38´E
Turfan *see* Turpan
Turgay *Kaz.* Torghay. ♦ C Kazakhstan
145 R8 **Turgay** *Kaz.* Torgay. Akmola, N Kazakhstan 51°46´N 72°45´E
144 M8 **Turgayskaya Stolovaya Strana** *Kaz.* Torghay Ustirti. *plateau* Kazakhstan/Russian Federation

22 H6 **Tullos** Louisiana, S USA 31°48´N 92°19´W
97 F19 **Tullow** *Ir.* An Tullach. Carlow, SE Ireland 52°48´N 06°44´W
181 W5 **Tully** Queensland, NE Australia 18°03´S 145°56´E
124 J3 **Tuloma** ♦ NW Russian Federation
27 P9 **Tulsa** Oklahoma, C USA 36°09´N 96°W
153 N11 **Tulsipur** Mid Western, W Nepal 28°01´N 82°22´E
126 K6 **Tul'skaya Oblast'** ♦ *province* W Russian Federation
126 L14 **Tul'skiy** Respublika Adygeya, SW Russian Federation 44°26´N 40°12´E
186 E5 **Tulu** Manus Island, N Papua New Guinea 01°58´S 146°50´E
54 D10 **Tuluá** Valle del Cauca, W Colombia 04°01´N 76°16´W
116 M12 **Tulucești** Galaţi, E Romania 45°35´N 28°01´E
39 N12 **Tuluksak** Alaska, USA 61°06´N 160°57´W
41 Z12 **Tulum, Ruinas de** *ruins* Quintana Roo, SE Mexico
169 R17 **Tulungagung** Jawa, C Indonesia 08°03´S 111°54´E
186 J6 **Tulun Islands** *var.* Kilinailau Islands; *prev.* Carteret Islands. *island group* NE Papua New Guinea
126 M4 **Tuma** Ryazanskaya Oblast´, W Russian Federation 55°09´N 40°27´E
54 B12 **Tumaco** Nariño, SW Colombia 01°51´N 78°46´W
54 B12 **Tumaco, Bahía de** *bay* SW Colombia
42 L8 **Tuma, Río** ♦ N Nicaragua
95 O16 **Tumba** Stockholm, C Sweden 59°12´N 17°49´E
79 H20 **Tumba, Lac** *var.* Lake Ntomba, Lac Ntomba. ⊚ NW Dem. Rep. Congo
169 S12 **Tumbangsenamang** Borneo, C Indonesia 01°17´S 112°21´E
183 Q10 **Tumbarumba** New South Wales, SE Australia 35°47´S 148°03´E
56 A8 **Tumbes** Tumbes, NW Peru 03°33´S 80°27´W
56 A9 **Tumbes** *off.* Departamento de Tumbes. ♦ *department* NW Peru
Tumbes, Departamento de *see* Tumbes
19 P5 **Tumbledown Mountain** ▲ Maine, NE USA 45°27´N 70°28´W
11 N13 **Tumbler Ridge** British Columbia, W Canada 55°06´N 120°51´W
62 H11 **Tunuyán, Río** ♦ W Argentina
62 I11 **Tunuyán** ♦ W Argentina
54 D7 **Turbo** Antioquia, NW Colombia 08°06´N 76°44´W
116 H10 **Turda** *Ger.* Thorenburg, *Hung.* Torda. Cluj, NW Romania 46°35´N 23°50´E
111 N14 **Türeh** Markazī, W Iran
110 I12 **Turek** Wielkopolskie, C Poland 52°01´N 18°30´E
93 K19 **Turku** *Swe.* Åbo. Länsi-Suomi, SW Finland 60°27´N 22°17´E
81 H17 **Turkwel** *seasonal river* NW Kenya
27 P9 **Turley** Oklahoma, C USA 36°14´N 95°58´W
35 Q9 **Turlock** California, W USA 37°29´N 120°52´W
118 I12 **Turmantas** Utena, NE Lithuania 55°41´N 26°27´E
119 K20 **Turaw** *Rus.* Turov. Homyel'skaya Voblasts´, SE Belarus 51°59´N 27°44´E
54 L5 **Turmero** Aragua, N Venezuela South America 10°14´N 67°22´W
184 N13 **Turnagain, Cape** *headland* North Island, New Zealand 40°30´S 176°36´E
42 F2 **Turneffe Islands** *island group* E Belize
18 M11 **Turners Falls** Massachusetts, NE USA
11 P16 **Turner Valley** Alberta, SW Canada 50°43´N 114°19´W
99 G16 **Turnhout** Antwerpen, N Belgium 51°19´N 04°57´E
109 V5 **Türnitz** Niederösterreich, E Austria 47°56´N 15°30´E
11 S12 **Turnor Lake** ⊚ Saskatchewan, C Canada
111 E15 **Turnov** *Ger.* Turnau. Liberecký Kraj, N Czech Republic 50°36´N 15°10´E
116 I15 **Turnu Măgurele** *var.* Turnu-Măgurele. Teleorman, S Romania 43°44´N 24°53´E
116 F12 **Turnu Severin** *see* Drobeta-Turnu Severin
Turócszentmárton *see* Martin
175 R9 **Turoni** *see* Tours
175 R9 **Turov** *see* Turaw
Turpakka *see* Tuproqqal'a
144 M8 **Turgayskaya Stolovaya Strana**
158 M6 **Turpan** *var.* T'u-lu-p'an, Turfan. Xinjiang Uygur Zizhiqu, NW China 42°55´N 89°06´E
158 M6 **Turpan Depression** *see* Turpan Pendi

75 N6 **Tunisia** *off.* Tunisian Republic, *Ar.* Al Jumhūrīyah at Tūnisīyah, *Fr.* République Tunisienne. ♦ *republic* N Africa
Tunisian Republic *see* Tunisia
75 N6 **Tunis, Golfe de** *Ar.* Khalīj Tūnis. *gulf* NE Tunisia
54 G9 **Tunja** Boyacá, C Colombia 05°33´N 73°23´W
93 F14 **Tunnsjøen** *Lapp.* Dätnejavrie. ⊚ C Norway
39 N12 **Tununak** Alaska, USA 60°37´N 165°20´W
62 H11 **Tunuyán, Río** ♦ W Argentina
62 I11 **Tunuyán** ♦ W Argentina
197 P14 **Tunu** ♦ *province* E Greenland
147 U8 **Tunuk** Chuyskaya Oblast´, C Kyrgyzstan 42°31´N 73°55´E
13 O9 **Tunungayualok Island** *island* Newfoundland and Labrador, E Canada
62 H11 **Tunuyán** ♦ W Argentina 33°35´S 69°00´W
62 I11 **Tunuyán, Río** ♦ W Argentina
147 Q12 **Turkestan Range** *Rus.* Turkestanskiy Khrebet. ▲ C Asia
Turkestanskiy Khrebet *see* Turkestan Range
111 M23 **Túrkeve** Jász-Nagykun-Szolnok, E Hungary 47°06´N 20°42´E
25 O4 **Turkey** Texas, SW USA 34°23´N 100°54´W
136 H14 **Turkey** *off.* Republic of Turkey, *Turk.* Türkiye Cumhuriyeti. ♦ *republic* SW Asia
181 N4 **Turkey Creek** Western Australia 16°54´S 128°12´E
26 M9 **Turkey Creek** Oklahoma, C USA
37 T9 **Turkey Mountains** ▲ New Mexico, SW USA
Turkey, Republic of *see* Turkey
29 X11 **Turkey River** ♦ Iowa, C USA
127 N7 **Turki** Saratovskaya Oblast´, W Russian Federation 52°00´N 43°16´E
121 O7 **Turkish Republic of Northern Cyprus** ◇ *disputed territory* Cyprus
Türkistan *see* Turkestan
Turkistan, Bandi-i *see* Torkestān, Selseleh-ye Band-e
Türkiye Cumhuriyeti *see* Turkey
146 K12 **Türkmenabat** *prev. Rus.* Chardzhev, Chardzhou, Chardzhui, Lenin-Turkmenski, *Turkm.* Chärjew. Lebap Welaýaty, E Turkmenistan 39°07´N 63°30´E
146 A11 **Türkmen Aýlagy** *Rus.* Turkmenskiy Zaliv. *lake gulf* W Turkmenistan
Turkmenbashi *see* Türkmenbaşy
146 A10 **Türkmenbaşy** *prev. Rus.* Krasnovodsk. Balkan Welaýaty, W Turkmenistan 40°N 53°04´E
146 A10 **Türkmenbaşy Aýlagy** *prev. Rus.* Krasnovodskiy Zaliv, *Turkm.* Krasnowodsk Aýlagy. *lake gulf* W Turkmenistan
146 J14 **Türkmengala** *Rus.* Turkmen-kala; *prev. Rus.* Turkmen-Kala. Mary Welaýaty, S Turkmenistan 37°25´N 62°19´E
Turkmenistan ; *prev.* Turkmenskaya Soviet Socialist Republic. ♦ *republic* C Asia
Turkmen-kala/Turkmen-Kala *see* Türkmengala
Turkmenskaya Soviet Socialist Republic *see* Turkmenistan
Turkmenskiy Zaliv *see* Türkmen Aýlagy
136 L16 **Türkoğlu** Kahramanmaraş, S Turkey 37°24´N 36°50´E
44 L7 **Turks and Caicos Islands** ◇ *UK dependent territory* W Indies
64 G10 **Turks and Caicos Islands** *UK dependant territory* W Indies
45 N6 **Turks Islands** *island group* SE Turks and Caicos Islands
93 K19 **Turku** *Swe.* Åbo. Länsi-Suomi, SW Finland 60°27´N 22°17´E
81 H17 **Turkwel** *seasonal river* NW Kenya
27 P9 **Turley** Oklahoma, C USA 36°14´N 95°58´W
35 Q9 **Turlock** California, W USA 37°29´N 120°52´W
118 I12 **Turmantas** Utena, NE Lithuania 55°41´N 26°27´E
119 K20 **Turaw** *Rus.* Turov. Homyel'skaya Voblasts´, SE Belarus 51°59´N 27°44´E

Turpan Pendi – Ummas Samīn

158 M6 Turpan Pendi Eng. Turpan Depression. depression NW China
158 M5 Turpan Zhan Xinjiang Uygur Zizhiqu, W China 43°10′N 89°06′E
Turpentine State see North Carolina
44 H8 Turquino, Pico ▲ E Cuba 19°54′N 76°55′W
27 Y10 Turrell Arkansas, C USA 35°22′N 90°13′W
43 N14 Turrialba Cartago, E Costa Rica 09°56′N 83°40′W
96 K8 Turriff NE Scotland, United Kingdom 57°32′N 02°28′W
139 V7 Tursāq Diyālá, E Iraq 33°27′N 45°47′E
Turshiz see Kāshmar
Tursunzade see Tursunzoda
147 P13 Tursunzoda Rus. Tursunzade; prev. Regar. W Tajikistan 38°30′N 68°10′E
Turt see Hanh
Türtkül/Turtkul' see To'rtko'l
29 O9 Turtle Creek ≈ South Dakota, N USA
30 K4 Turtle Flambeau Flowage ▣ Wisconsin, N USA
11 S14 Turtleford Saskatchewan, S Canada 53°21′N 108°48′W
28 M4 Turtle Lake North Dakota, N USA 47°31′N 100°53′W
92 K12 Turtola Lappi, NW Finland 66°39′N 23°55′E
122 M10 Turu ≈ N Russian Federation
Turuga see Tsuruga
147 V10 Turugart Pass pass China/ Kyrgyzstan
158 E7 Turugart Shankou var. Pereval Torugart. pass China/Kyrgyzstan
122 K9 Turukhan ≈ N Russian Federation
122 K9 Turukhansk Krasnoyarskiy Kray, N Russian Federation 65°50′N 87°48′E
139 N3 Ṭurumbah well NE Syria
Turuoka see Tsuruoka
144 H14 Turush Mangistau, SW Kazakhstan 45°24′N 56°02′E
60 K7 Turvo, Rio ≈ S Brazil
116 J2 Tur"ya Pol. Turja, Rus. Tur'ya. ≈ NW Ukraine
23 O4 Tuscaloosa Alabama, S USA 33°13′N 87°34′W
23 O4 Tuscaloosa, Lake ◎ Alabama, S USA
Tuscan Archipelago see Toscano, Archipelago
Tuscan-Emilian Mountains see Tosco-Emiliano, Appennino
Tuscany see Toscana
35 V2 Tuscarora Nevada, W USA 41°16′N 116°13′W
18 F15 Tuscarora Mountain ridge Pennsylvania, NE USA
30 M14 Tuscola Illinois, N USA 39°46′N 88°19′W
25 P7 Tuscola Texas, SW USA 32°12′N 99°48′W
23 O2 Tuscumbia Alabama, S USA 34°43′N 87°42′W
92 O4 Tusenøyane island group S Svalbard
144 K13 Tushchybas, Zaliv prev. Zaliv Paskevicha. lake gulf SW Kazakhstan
Tusima see Tsushima
171 Y15 Tusirah Papua, E Indonesia 06°46′S 140°19′E
23 Q5 Tuskegee Alabama, S USA 32°25′N 85°41′W
94 E8 Tustna island S Norway
39 R12 Tustumena Lake ◎ Alaska, USA
110 K13 Tuszyn Łódzkie, C Poland 51°36′N 19°31′E
137 S13 Tutak Ağrı, E Turkey 39°34′N 42°48′E
185 C20 Tutamoe Range ▲▲ North Island, New Zealand
Tutasev see Tutayev
124 L15 Tutayev var. Tutasev. Yaroslavskaya Oblast', W Russian Federation 57°51′N 39°29′E
Tutela see Tulle, France
Tutela see Tudela, Spain
Tutera see Tudela
155 H23 Tuticorin Tamil Nādu, SE India 08°48′N 78°10′E
113 L15 Tutin Serbia, S Serbia 43°00′N 20°20′E
184 O10 Tutira Hawke's Bay, North Island, New Zealand 39°14′S 176°53′E
Tutiura see Tsuchiura
122 K10 Tutonchny Evenkiyskiy Avtonomnyy Okrug, N Russian Federation 64°12′N 93°52′E
114 L6 Tutrakan Silistra, NE Bulgaria 44°03′N 26°38′E
29 N5 Tuttle North Dakota, N USA 47°07′N 99°58′W
26 M11 Tuttle Oklahoma, C USA 35°17′N 97°48′W
27 O3 Tuttle Creek Lake ▣ Kansas, C USA
101 H23 Tuttlingen Baden-Württemberg, S Germany 47°59′N 08°49′E
171 R16 Tutuala East Timor 08°23′S 127°12′E
192 K17 Tutuila island W American Samoa
83 I18 Tutume Central, E Botswana 20°26′S 27°02′E
39 N7 Tututalak Mountain ▲ Alaska, USA 67°51′N 161°27′W
22 K3 Tutwiler Mississippi, S USA 34°00′N 90°25′W
162 J8 Tuul Gol ≈ N Mongolia
93 O16 Tuupovaara Itä-Suomi, E Finland 62°30′N 30°40′E
Tuva see Tyva, Respublika
190 E7 Tuvalu prev. Ellice Islands. ◆ commonwealth republic SW Pacific Ocean
Tuvinskaya ASSR see Tyva, Respublika
163 O9 Tuvshinshiree var. Sergelen. Sühbaatar, E Mongolia 46°12′N 111°48′E
141 P9 Ṭuwayq, Jabal ▲▲ C Saudi Arabia
138 H13 Ṭuwayyil ash Shihāq desert S Jordan
11 U16 Tuxford Saskatchewan, S Canada 50°33′N 105°32′W
167 U12 Tu Xoay Đăc Lăc, S Vietnam 12°18′N 107°33′E
40 L14 Tuxpan Jalisco, C Mexico 19°33′N 103°21′W
40 J12 Tuxpan Nayarit, C Mexico 21°57′N 105°12′W
41 Q12 Tuxpán var. Tuxpán de Rodríguez Cano. Veracruz-Llave, E Mexico 20°58′N 97°23′W
Tuxpán de Rodríguez Cano see Tuxpán
41 R15 Tuxtepec var. San Juan Bautista Tuxtepec. Oaxaca, S Mexico 18°02′N 96°05′W
41 U16 Tuxtla var. Tuxtla Gutiérrez. Chiapas, SE Mexico 16°44′N 93°03′W
Tuxtla see San Andrés Tuxtla
Tuxtla Gutiérrez see Tuxtla
Tuyama see Tsuyama
167 T5 Tuyên Quang Tuyên Quang, N Vietnam 21°48′N 105°18′E
167 U13 Tuy Hoa Bình Thuận, S Vietnam 11°03′N 108°12′E
167 V12 Tuy Hoa Phu Yên, S Vietnam 13°02′N 109°15′E
127 U5 Tuymazy Respublika Bashkortostan, W Russian Federation 54°36′N 53°40′E
Tuy Phong see Liên Hương
142 L6 Tūysarkān var. Tuisarkan, Tuyserkān. Hamadān, W Iran 34°31′N 48°30′E
Tuyserkān see Tūysarkān
145 W16 Tuyuk Kaz. Tuyyq. Taldykorgan, SE Kazakhstan 43°07′N 79°24′E
Tuyyq see Tuyuk
136 I14 Tuz Gölü ◎ C Turkey
125 Q15 Tuzha Kirovskaya Oblast', NW Russian Federation 57°37′N 48°02′E
113 K17 Tuzi S Montenegro 42°22′N 19°21′E
139 T5 Ṭūz Khurmātū At Ta'mīn, N Iraq 34°56′N 44°38′E
112 I11 Tuzla Federacija Bosna I Hercegovina, NE Bosnia and Herzegovina 44°33′N 18°40′E
117 N15 Tuzla Constanța, SE Romania 43°58′N 28°38′E
137 T12 Tuzluca Iğdır, E Turkey 40°02′N 43°39′E
95 J20 Tvååker Halland, S Sweden 57°04′N 12°25′E
95 F17 Tvedestrand Aust-Agder, S Norway 58°36′N 08°55′E
124 J16 Tver' prev. Kalinin. Tverskaya Oblast', W Russian Federation 56°53′N 35°52′E
126 I15 Tverskaya Oblast' ◐ province W Russian Federation
124 I15 Tvertsa ≈ W Russian Federation
138 G9 Tverya var. Tiberias; prev. Teverya. Northern, N Israel 32°48′N 35°32′E
110 H13 Twardogóra Ger. Festenberg. Dolnośląskie, SW Poland 51°21′N 17°27′E
14 J14 Tweed Ontario, SE Canada 44°29′N 77°19′W
96 K13 Tweed ≈ England/ Scotland, United Kingdom
98 O7 Tweede-Exloërmond Drenthe, NE Netherlands 52°55′N 06°55′E
183 V3 Tweed Heads New South Wales, SE Australia 28°10′S 153°32′E
98 M11 Twello Gelderland, E Netherlands 52°14′N 06°07′E
35 W15 Twentynine Palms California, W USA 34°08′N 116°03′W
25 P9 Twin Buttes Reservoir ▣ Texas, SW USA
33 O15 Twin Falls Idaho, NW USA 42°34′N 114°28′W
39 N13 Twin Hills Alaska, USA 59°06′N 160°21′W
11 O11 Twin Lakes Alberta, W Canada 57°47′N 117°30′W
33 O12 Twin Peaks ▲ Idaho, NW USA 44°37′N 114°24′W
185 I14 Twins, The ▲ South Island, New Zealand 41°14′S 172°38′E
29 S5 Twin Valley Minnesota, N USA 47°15′N 96°15′W
100 G11 Twistringen Niedersachsen, NW Germany 52°48′N 08°39′E
185 E20 Twizel Canterbury, South Island, New Zealand 44°04′S 171°12′E
29 X5 Two Harbors Minnesota, N USA 47°01′N 91°40′W
11 R14 Two Hills Alberta, SW Canada 53°40′N 111°43′W
31 N7 Two Rivers Wisconsin, N USA 44°10′N 87°33′W
116 H8 Tyachiv Zakarpats'ka Oblast', W Ukraine 48°02′N 23°35′E
Tyan'-Shan' see Tien Shan
166 L3 Tyao ≈ Burma (Myanmar)/ India
117 R6 Tyasmyn ≈ N Ukraine
23 X6 Tybee Island Georgia, SE USA 32°00′N 80°51′W
Tyborøn see Thyborøn
111 J16 Tychy Ger. Tichau. Śląskie, S Poland 50°12′N 19°01′E
111 O16 Tyczyn Podkarpackie, SE Poland 49°58′N 22°03′E
94 I8 Tydal Sør-Trøndelag, S Norway 63°01′N 11°36′E
115 H24 Tyflós ≈ Kríti, Greece, E Mediterranean Sea
21 S3 Tygart Lake ▣ West Virginia, NE USA
123 Q13 Tygda Amurskaya Oblast', SE Russian Federation 53°07′N 126°12′E
21 Q11 Tyger River ≈ South Carolina, SE USA
32 I11 Tygh Valley Oregon, NW USA 45°15′N 121°12′W
94 F12 Tyin ◎ S Norway
29 S10 Tyler Minnesota, N USA 44°16′N 96°07′W
25 W7 Tyler Texas, SW USA 32°21′N 95°18′W
25 W7 Tyler, Lake ▣ Texas, SW USA
22 K7 Tylertown Mississippi, S USA 31°07′N 90°08′W
117 P10 Tylihuls'kyy Lyman ◎ SW Ukraine
Tylos see Bahrain
115 C15 Týmfi var. Timfi. ▲ W Greece 39°58′N 20°51′E
115 E17 Tymfristós var. Timfristos. ▲ C Greece 38°57′N 21°49′E
115 J25 Tympáki var. Timbaki; prev. Timbákion. Kríti, Greece, E Mediterranean Sea 35°04′N 24°47′E
123 Q12 Tynda Amurskaya Oblast', SE Russian Federation 55°09′N 124°44′E
29 Q12 Tyndall South Dakota, N USA 42°57′N 97°52′W
97 L14 Tyne ≈ N England, United Kingdom
97 M14 Tynemouth NE England, United Kingdom 55°01′N 01°24′W
97 L14 Tyneside cultural region NE England, United Kingdom
94 H10 Tynset Hedmark, S Norway 61°45′N 10°49′E
39 Q12 Tyonek Alaska, USA 61°04′N 151°08′W
Tyôsi see Chōshi
Tyras see Dniester
Tyras see Bilhorod-Dnistrovs'kyy
Tyre see Soûr
95 G14 Tyrifjorden ◎ S Norway
95 K22 Tyringe Skåne, S Sweden 56°09′N 13°35′E
123 R13 Tyrma Khabarovskiy Kray, SE Russian Federation 50°00′N 132°04′E
Tyrnau see Trnava
115 F15 Týrnavos var. Tírnavos. Thessalía, C Greece 39°45′N 22°18′E
127 N16 Tyrnyauz Kabardino-Balkarskaya Respublika, SW Russian Federation 43°19′N 42°55′E
Tyrol see Tirol
18 E14 Tyrone Pennsylvania, NE USA 40°41′N 78°12′W
97 E15 Tyrone cultural region W Northern Ireland, United Kingdom
Tyros see Bahrain
182 M10 Tyrrell, Lake salt lake Victoria, SE Australia
84 H14 Tyrrhenian Basin undersea feature Tyrrhenian Sea, C Mediterranean Sea 39°30′N 13°00′E
120 L8 Tyrrhenian Sea It. Mare Tirreno. sea N Mediterranean Sea
94 J12 Tyrsil ≈ Hedmark, S Norway
Tysa see Tisa/Tisza
116 J7 Tysmenytsya Ivano-Frankivs'ka Oblast', W Ukraine 48°54′N 24°50′E
95 C14 Tysnesøya island S Norway
95 C14 Tysse Hordaland, S Norway 60°23′N 05°46′E
95 D14 Tyssedal Hordaland, S Norway 60°07′N 06°36′E
95 O17 Tystberga Södermanland, C Sweden 58°51′N 17°15′E
118 E12 Tytuvėnai Šiauliai, C Lithuania 55°36′N 23°14′E
144 D14 Tyub-Karagan, Mys headland SW Kazakhstan 44°40′N 50°19′E
147 V8 Tyugel'-Say Narynskaya Oblast', C Kyrgyzstan 41°57′N 74°40′E
122 H11 Tyukalinsk Omskaya Oblast', C Russian Federation 55°56′N 72°02′E
127 V7 Tyul'gan Orenburgskaya Oblast', W Russian Federation 52°27′N 56°08′E
122 G11 Tyumen' Tyumenskaya Oblast', C Russian Federation 57°11′N 65°29′E
122 H11 Tyumenskaya Oblast' ◐ province C Russian Federation
147 Y7 Tyup Kir. Tüp. Issyk-Kul'skaya Oblast', NE Kyrgyzstan 42°44′N 78°18′E
122 L14 Tyva, Respublika prev. Tannu-Tuva, Tuva, Tuvinskaya ASSR. ◐ autonomous republic C Russian Federation
117 N7 Tyvriv Vinnyts'ka Oblast', C Ukraine 49°01′N 28°28′E
97 J21 Tywi ≈ S Wales, United Kingdom
97 I19 Tywyn W Wales, United Kingdom 52°35′N 04°06′W
83 K20 Tzaneen Limpopo, NE South Africa 23°50′S 30°09′E
Tzekung see Zigong
115 I20 Tziá prev. Kéa, Kéos; anc. Ceos. island Kykládes, Greece, Aegean Sea
41 X12 Tzucacab Yucatán, SE Mexico 20°04′N 89°03′W

U

82 B12 Uaco Cungo var. Waku Kungo, Port. Santa Comba. Cuanza Sul, C Angola 11°21′S 15°04′E
UAE see United Arab Emirates
191 X7 Ua Huka island Îles Marquises, NE French Polynesia
58 E10 Uaiacás Roraima, N Brazil 03°28′N 63°13′W
Uamba see Wamba
Uanle Uen see Wanlaweyn
191 W7 Ua Pu island Îles Marquises, NE French Polynesia
81 L17 Uar Garas spring/well SW Somalia 01°19′N 41°22′E
58 G12 Uatumã, Rio ≈ C Brazil
Ua Uíbh Fhailí see Offaly
58 C11 Uaupés, Rio var. Río Vaupés. ≈ Brazil/Colombia see also Vaupés, Río
Uaupés, Rio see Vaupés, Río
145 X9 Uba ≈ E Kazakhstan
145 N6 Ubagan Kaz. Obagan. ≈ Kazakhstan/Russian Federation
186 G7 Ubai New Britain, E Papua New Guinea 05°38′S 150°45′E
79 J15 Ubangi Fr. Oubangui. ≈ C Africa
Ubangi-Shari see Central African Republic
116 M3 Ubarts' Ukr. Ubort'. ≈ Belarus/Ukraine see also Ubort'
Ubarts' see Ubort'
54 F9 Ubaté Cundinamarca, C Colombia 05°20′N 73°50′W
60 N10 Ubatuba São Paulo, S Brazil 23°26′S 45°04′W
149 R12 Ubauro Sind, SE Pakistan 28°08′N 69°43′E
171 Q6 Ubay Bohol, C Philippines 10°02′N 124°29′E
103 U14 Ubaye ≈ SE France
Ubayid, Wadi al see Ubayyiḍ, Wādī al
139 N8 Ubaylah Al Anbār, W Iraq 33°06′N 40°13′E
139 O10 Ubayyiḍ, Wādī al var. Wadi al Ubayid. dry watercourse SW Iraq
98 L13 Ubbergen Gelderland, E Netherlands 51°49′N 05°54′E
164 E13 Ube Yamaguchi, Honshū, SW Japan 33°57′N 131°15′E
105 O13 Úbeda Andalucía, S Spain 38°01′N 03°22′W
109 V7 Übelbach var. Markt-Übelbach. Steiermark, SE Austria 47°13′N 15°15′E
59 L20 Uberaba Minas Gerais, SE Brazil 19°47′S 47°57′W
57 Q19 Uberaba, Laguna ◎ E Bolivia
59 K19 Uberlândia Minas Gerais, SE Brazil 18°17′S 48°17′W
101 H24 Überlingen Baden-Württemberg, S Germany 47°46′N 09°10′E
77 U16 Ubiaja Edo, S Nigeria 06°39′N 06°23′E
104 K3 Ubiña, Peña ▲ NW Spain 43°01′N 05°58′W
57 H17 Ubinas, Volcán ⛰ S Peru 16°16′S 70°49′W
Ubol Rajadhani/Ubol Ratchathani see Ubon Ratchathani
167 P9 Ubolratna Reservoir ▣ C Thailand
167 S10 Ubon Ratchathani var. Muang Ubon, Ubol Rajadhani, Ubol Ratchathani, Udon Ratchathani. Ubon Ratchathani, E Thailand 15°15′N 104°50′E
119 L20 Ubort' Bel. Ubarts'. ≈ Belarus/Ukraine see also Ubarts'
Ubort' see Ubarts'
104 K15 Ubrique Andalucía, S Spain 36°42′N 05°27′W
Ubsu-Nur, Ozero see Uvs Nuur
79 M18 Ubundu Orientale, C Dem. Rep. Congo 0°24′S 25°30′E
146 J13 Üçajy var. Üchajy, Rus. Uch-Adzhi. Mary Welaýaty, C Turkmenistan 38°06′N 62°44′E
137 X11 Ucar Rus. Udzhary. C Azerbaijan 40°31′N 47°40′E
56 G13 Ucayali off. Departamento de Ucayali. ◐ department E Peru
Ucayali, Departamento de see Ucayali
56 F10 Ucayali, Río ≈ C Peru
Uccle see Ukkel
Uch-Adzhi/Üchajy see Üçajy
127 X4 Uchaly Respublika Bashkortostan, W Russian Federation 54°19′N 59°33′E
145 W13 Ucharal Kaz. Üsharal. Almaty, E Kazakhstan 46°08′N 80°55′E
164 C17 Uchinoura Kagoshima, Kyūshū, SW Japan 31°16′N 131°04′E
165 R5 Uchiura-wan bay NW Pacific Ocean
Uchkuduk see Uchquduq
147 S9 Uchqo'rg'on Rus. Uchkurghan. Namangan Viloyati, E Uzbekistan 41°06′N 72°04′E
146 K8 Uchquduq Rus. Uchkuduk. Navoiy Viloyati, N Uzbekistan 42°12′N 63°27′E
Uchsay see Uchsoy
146 G6 Uchsoy Rus. Uchsay. Qoraqalpog'iston Respublikasi, NW Uzbekistan 43°51′N 58°51′E
Uchtagan Gumy/Uchtagan, Peski see Uçtagan Gumy
123 R11 Uchur ≈ E Russian Federation
100 O10 Uckermark cultural region E Germany
10 K17 Ucluelet Vancouver Island, British Columbia, SW Canada 48°55′N 125°34′W
146 D10 Uçtagan Gumy var. Uchtagan Gumy, Rus. Peski Uchtagan. desert NW Turkmenistan
122 M13 Uda ≈ S Russian Federation
123 R12 Uda ≈ E Russian Federation
123 N6 Udachnyy Respublika Sakha (Yakutiya), NE Russian Federation 66°27′N 112°18′E
155 G21 Udagamandalam var. Ooty, Udhagamandalam; prev. Ootacamund. Tamil Nādu, SW India 11°28′N 76°42′E
152 F14 Udaipur prev. Oodeypore. Rājasthān, N India 24°35′N 73°41′E
Udayadhani see Uthai Thani
143 N16 'Udayd, Khawr al var. Khor al Udeid. inlet Qatar/Saudi Arabia
112 D11 Udbina Lika-Senj, W Croatia 44°33′N 15°46′E
95 I18 Uddevalla Västra Götaland, S Sweden 58°20′N 11°56′E
Uddjaur see Uddjaure
92 H13 Uddjaure var. Uddjaur. ◎ N Sweden
Udeid, Khor al see 'Udayd, Khawr al
99 K14 Uden Noord-Brabant, SE Netherlands 51°40′N 05°37′E
Uden see Udenhout
99 J14 Udenhout var. Uden. Noord-Brabant, S Netherlands 51°37′N 05°09′E
155 H14 Udgīr Mahārāshtra, C India 18°23′N 77°06′E
Udhagamandalam see Udagamandalam
152 H6 Udhampur Jammu and Kashmir, NW India 32°55′N 75°07′E
139 X14 'Udhaybah, 'Uqlat al well S Iraq
106 J7 Udine anc. Utina. Friuli-Venezia Giulia, NE Italy 46°05′N 13°10′E
175 T14 Udintsev Fracture Zone tectonic feature S Pacific Ocean
Udipi see Udupi
Udmurtia see Udmurtskaya Respublika
127 S2 Udmurtskaya Respublika Eng. Udmurtia. ◐ autonomous republic NW Russian Federation
124 J15 Udomlya Tverskaya Oblast', W Russian Federation 57°53′N 34°59′E
Udon Ratchathani see Ubon Ratchathani
167 Q8 Udon Thani var. Ban Mak Khaeng, Udorndhani. Udon Thani, N Thailand 17°25′N 102°45′E
Udorndhani see Udon Thani
189 U12 Udot atoll Chuuk Islands, C Micronesia
123 S12 Udskaya Guba bay E Russian Federation
123 R12 Udskoye Khabarovskiy Kray, SE Russian Federation 54°32′N 134°26′E
155 E19 Udupi var. Udipi. Karnātaka, SW India 13°18′N 74°46′E
Udzhary see Ucar
100 O9 Uecker ≈ NE Germany
100 P9 Ueckermünde Mecklenburg-Vorpommern, NE Germany 53°43′N 14°03′E
164 M12 Ueda var. Uyeda. Nagano, Honshū, S Japan 36°27′N 138°13′E
79 L16 Uele var. Welle. ≈ NE Dem. Rep. Congo
123 W5 Uelen Chukotskiy Avtonomnyy Okrug, NE Russian Federation 66°01′N 169°52′W
Uele (upper course) see Kibali, Dem. Rep. Congo
Uele (upper course) see Uolo, Río, Equatorial Guinea/ Gabon
100 J11 Uelzen Niedersachsen, N Germany 52°58′N 10°34′E
164 J14 Ueno Mie, Honshū, SW Japan 34°45′N 136°08′E
127 V4 Ufa Respublika Bashkortostan, W Russian Federation 54°46′N 56°02′E
127 V4 Ufa ≈ W Russian Federation
Ufra see Kenar
83 C18 Ugab ≈ C Namibia
118 D8 Ugāle Ventspils, NW Latvia 57°16′N 21°58′E
81 F17 Uganda off. Republic of Uganda. ◆ republic E Africa
Uganda, Republic of see Uganda
138 G4 Ugarit Ar. Ra's Shamrah. site of ancient city Al Lādhiqīyah, NW Syria
39 O14 Ugashik Alaska, USA 57°30′N 157°24′W
107 Q19 Ugento Puglia, SE Italy 39°53′N 18°09′E
105 O15 Ugíjar Andalucía, S Spain 36°58′N 03°03′W
103 T11 Ugine Savoie, E France 45°45′N 06°25′E
123 R13 Uglegorsk Amurskaya Oblast', S Russian Federation 51°40′N 128°05′E
Ugleural'sk see Ugleural'skiy
125 V13 Ugleural'skiy var. Ugleural'sk, earlier Polovinka. Permskaya Oblast', NW Russian Federation 58°57′N 57°37′E
124 L15 Uglich Yaroslavskaya Oblast', W Russian Federation 57°33′N 38°23′E
126 J4 Ugra ≈ W Russian Federation
147 V9 Ugyut Narynskaya Oblast', C Kyrgyzstan 41°22′N 74°49′E
111 H19 Uherské Hradiště Ger. Ungarisch-Hradisch. Zlínský Kraj, E Czech Republic 49°05′N 17°26′E
111 H19 Uherský Brod Ger. Ungarisch-Brod. Zlínský Kraj, E Czech Republic 49°01′N 17°40′E
111 B17 Uhlava Ger. Angel. ≈ W Czech Republic
Uhorshchyna see Hungary
31 T13 Uhrichsville Ohio, N USA 40°23′N 81°21′W
Uhuru Peak see Kilimanjaro
96 G8 Uig N Scotland, United Kingdom 57°35′N 06°22′W
82 B10 Uíge Port. Carmona, Vila Marechal Carmona. Uíge, NW Angola 07°37′S 15°02′E
82 B10 Uíge ◐ province N Angola
193 Y15 Uiha island Ha'apai Group, C Tonga
189 U13 Uijec island Chuuk, C Micronesia
163 X14 Ŭijŏngbu Jap. Giseifu. NW South Korea 37°42′N 127°02′E
144 H10 Uil Kaz. Oyyl. Aktyubinsk, W Kazakhstan 49°06′N 54°41′E
144 H10 Uil Kaz. Oyyl. ≈ W Kazakhstan
36 M3 Uinta Mountains ▲▲ Utah, W USA
83 C18 Uis Erongo, NW Namibia 21°08′S 14°49′E
83 I25 Uitenhage Eastern Cape, S South Africa 33°44′S 25°27′E
98 H9 Uitgeest Noord-Holland, W Netherlands 52°32′N 04°43′E
98 I11 Uithoorn Noord-Holland, C Netherlands 52°14′N 04°50′E
98 O4 Uithuizen Groningen, NE Netherlands 53°24′N 06°40′E
98 O4 Uithuizermeeden Groningen, NE Netherlands 53°25′N 06°43′E
189 R6 Ujae Atoll var. Wūjae. atoll Ralik Chain, W Marshall Islands
Ujain see Ujjain
111 I16 Ujazd Opolskie, S Poland 50°22′N 18°20′E
Új-Becse see Novi Bečej
Ujda see Oujda
189 N5 Ujelang Atoll var. Wujlān. atoll Ralik Chain, W Marshall Islands
111 N21 Újfehértó Szabolcs-Szatmár-Bereg, E Hungary 47°48′N 21°40′E
Újgradiska see Nova Gradiška
164 J13 Uji var. Uzi. Kyōto, Honshū, SW Japan 34°54′N 135°48′E
81 E21 Ujiji Kigoma, W Tanzania 04°55′S 29°39′E
154 G10 Ujjain prev. Ujain. Madhya Pradesh, C India 23°11′N 75°50′E
Újlak see Ilok
'Ujmān see 'Ajmān
Újmoldova see Moldova Nouă
Újszentanna see Sântana
Ujungpandang see Makassar
Ujung Salang see Phuket
Újvidék see Novi Sad
UK see United Kingdom
154 E11 Ukāi Reservoir ▣ W India
81 G19 Ukara Island island N Tanzania
'Ukash, Wādī see 'Akāsh, Wādī
81 F19 Ukerewe Island island N Tanzania
139 S9 Ukhayḍir Al Anbār, C Iraq 32°28′N 43°36′E
153 X13 Ukhrul Manipur, NE India 25°08′N 94°24′E
125 S9 Ukhta Respublika Komi, NW Russian Federation 63°31′N 53°48′E
34 L6 Ukiah California, W USA 39°07′N 123°14′W
32 K12 Ukiah Oregon, NW USA 45°06′N 118°57′W
99 G18 Ukkel Fr. Uccle. Brussels, C Belgium 50°47′N 04°19′E
118 G13 Ukmergė Pol. Wiłkomierz. Vilnius, C Lithuania 55°16′N 24°46′E
Ukraina see Ukraine
116 L6 Ukraine off. Ukraine, Rus. Ukraina, Ukr. Ukrayina; prev. Ukrainian Soviet Socialist Republic, Ukrainskay S.S.R. ◆ republic SE Europe
Ukraine see Ukraine
Ukrainian Soviet Socialist Republic see Ukraine
Ukrainskay S.S.R/ Ukrayina see Ukraine
82 B13 Uku Cuanza Sul, NW Angola 11°25′S 14°18′E
164 B13 Uku-jima island Gotō-rettō, SW Japan
83 F20 Ukwi Kgalagadi, SW Botswana 23°41′S 20°26′E
118 M13 Ula Rus. Ulla. Vitsyebskaya Voblasts', N Belarus 55°14′N 29°15′E
136 C16 Ula Muğla, SW Turkey 37°08′N 28°25′E
118 M13 Ula Rus. Ulla. ≈ N Belarus
162 L7 Ulaanbaatar Eng. Ulan Bator; prev. Urga. ● (Mongolia) Töv, C Mongolia 47°55′N 106°57′E
Ulaan-Ereg see Bayanmönh
162 E5 Ulaangom Uvs, NW Mongolia 49°56′N 92°06′E
162 D5 Ulaanhus var. Bilüü. Bayan-Ölgiy, W Mongolia 48°54′N 89°40′E
Ulaantolgoy see Möst
Ulaan-Uul see Öldziyt, Bayanhongor, Mongolia
Ulaan-Uul see Erdene, Dornogovi, Mongolia
162 M14 Ulan var. Otog Qi. Nei Mongol Zizhiqu, N China 39°05′N 107°58′E
159 R10 Ulan var. Xireg; prev. Xiligou. Qinghai, C China 36°59′N 98°21′E
Ulan Bator see Ulaanbaatar
162 L13 Ulan Buh Shamo desert N China
Ulanhad see Chifeng
163 T8 Ulanhot Nei Mongol Zizhiqu, N China 46°02′N 122°E
127 Q14 Ulan Khol Respublika Kalmykiya, SW Russian Federation 45°27′N 46°48′E
163 P13 Ulan Qab var. Jining. Nei Mongol Zizhiqu, N China 40°59′N 113°08′E
162 M13 Ulansuhai Nur ◎ N China
123 N14 Ulan-Ude prev. Verkhneudinsk. Respublika Buryatiya, S Russian Federation 51°55′N 107°40′E
159 N12 Ulan Ul Hu ◎ C China
187 N9 Ulawa Island island SE Solomon Islands
138 J7 'Ulayyānīyah, Bi'r al var. Al Hilbeh. well S Syria
123 S12 Ul'banskiy Zaliv strait E Russian Federation
Ulbo see Olib
113 J18 Ulcinj S Montenegro 41°56′N 19°14′E
Uldz see Norovlin
Uleåborg see Oulu
Uleälv see Oulujoki
95 G16 Ulefoss Telemark, S Norway 59°17′N 09°15′E
Uleträsk see Oulujärvi
113 L19 Ulëz var. Ulëza. Dibër, C Albania 41°42′N 19°52′E
Ulëza see Ulëz
95 F22 Ulfborg Ringkøbing, W Denmark 56°16′N 08°21′E
98 N13 Ulft Gelderland, E Netherlands 51°53′N 06°23′E
162 G7 Uliastay prev. Jibhalanta. Dzavhan, W Mongolia 47°47′N 96°53′E
188 F8 Ulimang Babeldaob, N Palau
67 T10 Ulindi ≈ W Dem. Rep. Congo
188 H14 Ulithi Atoll atoll Caroline Islands, W Micronesia
112 N10 Uljma Vojvodina, NE Serbia 45°04′N 21°08′E
144 L11 Ul'kayak Kaz. Ölkeyek. ≈ C Kazakhstan
145 Q7 Ul'ken-Karoy, Ozero ◎ N Kazakhstan
Ülkenözen see Bol'shoy Uzen'
Ülkenqobda see Bol'shaya Khobda
104 G3 Ulla ≈ NW Spain
Ulla see Ula
183 S10 Ulladulla New South Wales, SE Australia 35°21′S 150°25′E
153 T14 Ullapara Rajshahi, W Bangladesh 24°20′N 89°34′E
96 H7 Ullapool N Scotland, United Kingdom 57°54′N 05°10′W
95 J20 Ullared Halland, S Sweden 57°07′N 12°45′E
105 T7 Ulldecona Cataluña, NE Spain 40°36′N 00°27′E
92 I9 Ullsfjorden fjord N Norway
97 K15 Ullswater ◎ NW England, United Kingdom
101 I22 Ulm Baden-Württemberg, S Germany 48°24′N 09°59′E
33 R8 Ulm Montana, NW USA 47°27′N 111°32′W
183 V5 Ulmarra New South Wales, SE Australia 29°37′S 153°06′E
116 K13 Ulmeni Buzău, C Romania 45°08′N 26°43′E
116 K14 Ulmeni Călărași, S Romania 44°08′N 26°43′E
42 L7 Ulmukhuás Región Autónoma Atlántico Norte, NE Nicaragua 14°20′N 84°30′W
188 C8 Ulong var. Aulong. island Palau Islands, N Palau
83 N14 Ulonguè var. Ulongwé. Tete, NW Mozambique 14°34′S 34°21′E
Ulongwé see Ulonguè
95 K19 Ulricehamn Västra Götaland, S Sweden 57°47′N 13°25′E
98 N5 Ulrum Groningen, NE Netherlands 53°24′N 06°20′E
163 Z16 Ulsan Jap. Urusan. SE South Korea 35°33′N 129°19′E
94 D10 Ulsteinvik Møre og Romsdal, S Norway 62°21′N 05°53′E
97 D15 Ulster ◐ province Northern Ireland, United Kingdom/ Ireland
171 Q10 Ulu Pulau Siau, N Indonesia 02°46′N 125°22′E
123 Q11 Ulu Respublika Sakha (Yakutiya), NE Russian Federation 60°18′N 127°27′E
42 H5 Ulúa, Río ≈ NW Honduras
136 D12 Ulubat Gölü ◎ NW Turkey
136 E12 Uludağ ▲ NW Turkey 40°08′N 29°13′E
158 D7 Ulugqat Xinjiang Uygur Zizhiqu, W China 39°45′N 74°10′E
136 J16 Ulukışla Niğde, S Turkey 37°33′N 34°29′E
189 O15 Ulul island Caroline Islands, C Micronesia
83 L22 Ulundi KwaZulu/Natal, E South Africa 28°18′S 31°26′E
158 M3 Ulungur He ≈ NW China
158 K2 Ulungur Hu ◎ NW China
181 P8 Uluru var. Ayers Rock. monolith Northern Territory, C Australia
97 K16 Ulverston NW England, United Kingdom 54°13′N 03°08′W
183 O16 Ulverstone Tasmania, SE Australia 41°09′S 146°10′E
94 D13 Ulvik Hordaland, S Norway 60°34′N 06°53′E
93 J18 Ulvila Länsi-Suomi, W Finland 61°26′N 21°55′E
117 O8 Ulyanivka Rus. Ul'yanovka. Kirovohrads'ka Oblast', C Ukraine 48°18′N 30°15′E
Ul'yanovka see Ulyanivka
127 Q5 Ul'yanovsk prev. Simbirsk. Ul'yanovskaya Oblast', W Russian Federation 54°17′N 48°21′E
127 Q5 Ul'yanovskaya Oblast' ◐ province W Russian Federation
145 S10 Ul'yanovskiy Karaganda, C Kazakhstan 50°05′N 73°45′E
Ul'yanovskiy Kanal see Ul'yanow Kanali
146 M13 Ul'yanow Kanali Rus. Ul'yanovskiy Kanal. canal Turkmenistan/Uzbekistan
Ulyshylanshyq see Uly-Zhylanshyk
26 H6 Ulysses Kansas, C USA 37°36′N 101°23′W
145 O12 Ulytau, Gory ▲▲ C Kazakhstan
145 N11 Uly-Zhylanshyk Kaz. Ulyshylanshyq. ≈ C Kazakhstan
112 A9 Umag It. Umago. Istra, NW Croatia 45°25′N 13°32′E
Umago see Umag
41 W12 Umán Yucatán, SE Mexico 20°51′N 89°43′W
117 O7 Uman' Rus. Uman. Cherkas'ka Oblast', C Ukraine 48°45′N 30°10′E
189 V13 Uman atoll Chuuk Islands, C Micronesia
Uman see Uman'
Umanak/Umanaq see Uummannaq
'Umān, Khalīj see Oman, Gulf of
'Umān, Salṭanat see Oman
154 K10 Umaria Madhya Pradesh, C India 23°34′N 80°49′E
149 R16 Umarkot Sind, SE Pakistan 25°22′N 69°48′E
188 B17 Umatac SW Guam 13°17′N 144°40′E
188 A17 Umatac Bay bay SW Guam
139 S6 Umayqah Ṣalāḥ ad Dīn, C Iraq 34°32′N 43°45′E
124 J5 Umba Murmanskaya Oblast', NW Russian Federation 66°39′N 34°24′E
138 I8 Umbāshī, Khirbat al ruins As Suwaydā', S Syria
80 A12 Umbelasha ≈ W Sudan
106 H12 Umbertide Umbria, C Italy 43°16′N 12°21′E
61 B17 Umberto var. Humberto. Santa Fe, C Argentina 30°52′S 61°19′W
186 E7 Umboi Island var. Rooke Island. island C Papua New Guinea
124 J4 Umbozero, Ozero ◎ NW Russian Federation
106 H13 Umbria ◐ region C Italy
Umbrian-Machigian Mountains see Umbro-Marchigiano, Appennino
106 I12 Umbro-Marchigiano, Appennino Eng. Umbrian-Machigian Mountains. ▲▲ C Italy
93 J16 Umeå Västerbotten, N Sweden 63°50′N 20°15′E
93 H14 Umeälven ≈ N Sweden
39 Q5 Umiat Alaska, USA 69°22′N 152°09′W
83 K23 Umlazi KwaZulu/Natal, E South Africa 29°58′S 30°50′E
139 X10 Umm al Baqar, Hawr var. Birkat ad Dawaymah. spring S Iraq
139 Q5 Umm al Faṭūr var. Umm al Tūz. Ṣalāḥ ad Dīn, C Iraq 34°53′N 42°42′E
141 U12 Umm al Ḥayt, Wādī var. Wādī Amilḥayt. seasonal river SW Oman
Umm al Qaiwain see Umm al Qaywayn
143 R15 Umm al Qaywayn var. Umm al Qaiwain. Umm al Qaywayn, NE United Arab Emirates 25°43′N 55°55′E
Umm al Tūz see Umm al Faṭūr
138 J3 Umm 'Āmūd Ḥalab, N Syria 35°57′N 37°39′E
141 Y10 Umm ar Ruṣāṣ var. Umm Ruṣayṣ. W Oman 20°26′N 58°48′E
141 X9 Ummas Samīn salt flat C Oman

◆ Country ◇ Dependent Territory ◐ Administrative Regions ▲ Mountain ⛰ Volcano ◎ Lake
● Country Capital ○ Dependent Territory Capital ✈ International Airport ▲▲ Mountain Range ≈ River ▣ Reservoir

UMM AZ ZUMŪL – VÅGØ

141 V9 **Umm az Zumūl** *oasis* E Saudi Arabia
80 A9 **Umm Buru** Western Darfur, W Sudan *15°01′N 23°36′E*
80 A12 **Umm Dafag** Southern Darfur, W Sudan *10°28′N 23°20′E*
Umm Durmān *see* Omdurman
138 F9 **Umm el Fahm** Haifa, N Israel *32°30′N 35°06′E*
80 F9 **Umm Inderab** Northern Kordofan, C Sudan *15°12′N 31°54′E*
80 C10 **Umm Keddada** Northern Darfur, W Sudan *13°36′N 26°42′E*
140 J7 **Umm Lajj** Tabūk, W Saudi Arabia *25°02′N 37°19′E*
138 L10 **Umm Maḥfur** ≈ N Jordan
139 Y13 **Umm Qaṣr** Al Baṣrah, SE Iraq *30°02′N 47°55′E*
Umm Ruṣayṣ *see* Umm ar Ruṣāṣ
80 F11 **Umm Ruwaba** *var.* Umm Ruwābah, Um Ruwāba. Northern Kordofan, C Sudan *12°54′N 31°13′E*
Umm Ruwābah *see* Umm Ruwaba
143 N16 **Umm Sa'īd** *var.* Musay'īd. S Qatar *24°57′N 51°32′E*
139 Y10 **Umm Sawān, Hawr** ◎ S Iraq
138 K10 **Umm Ṭuways, Wādī** *dry watercourse* N Jordan
38 J17 **Umnak Island** *island* Aleutian Islands, Alaska, USA
32 F13 **Umpqua River** ≈ Oregon, NW USA
82 D13 **Umpulo** Bié, C Angola *12°43′S 17°42′E*
154 I12 **Umred** Mahārāshtra, C India *20°54′N 79°19′E*
Um Ruwāba *see* Umm Ruwaba
Umtali *see* Mutare
83 J24 **Umtata** Eastern Cape, SE South Africa *31°33′S 28°47′E*
77 V17 **Umuahia** Abia, SW Nigeria *05°30′N 07°33′E*
60 H10 **Umuarama** Paraná, S Brazil *23°45′S 53°20′W*
Umvuma *see* Mvuma
83 K18 **Umzingwani** ≈ S Zimbabwe
112 D11 **Una** ≈ Bosnia and Herzegovina/Croatia
Una *see* Unna
112 E12 **Unac** ≈ W Bosnia and Herzegovina
23 T6 **Unadilla** Georgia, SE USA *32°15′N 83°44′W*
18 I10 **Unadilla River** ≈ New York, NE USA
59 L18 **Unaí** Minas Gerais, SE Brazil *16°24′S 46°49′W*
39 N10 **Unalakleet** Alaska, USA *63°52′N 160°47′W*
38 K17 **Unalaska Island** *island* Aleutian Islands, Alaska, USA
185 I16 **Una, Mount** ▲ South Island, New Zealand *42°12′S 172°34′E*
82 N13 **Unango** Niassa, N Mozambique *12°45′S 35°28′E*
Unao *see* Unnāo
92 L12 **Unari** Lappi, N Finland *67°07′N 25°37′E*
141 O6 **'Unayzah** *var.* Anaiza. Al Qaşīm, C Saudi Arabia *26°03′N 44°00′E*
138 L10 **'Unayzah, Jabal** ▲ Jordan/Saudi Arabia *32°09′N 39°11′E*
Unci *see* Almería
57 K19 **Uncía** Potosí, C Bolivia *18°30′S 66°29′W*
37 Q7 **Uncompahgre Peak** ▲ Colorado, C USA *38°04′N 107°27′W*
37 P6 **Uncompahgre Plateau** *plain* Colorado, C USA
95 J17 **Unden** ◎ S Sweden
28 M4 **Underwood** North Dakota, N USA *47°25′N 101°09′W*
171 T13 **Undur** Pulau Seram, E Indonesia *03°41′S 130°38′E*
Undur Khan *see* Öndörhaan
126 H6 **Unecha** Bryanskaya Oblast', W Russian Federation *52°51′N 32°38′E*
39 N16 **Unga** Unga Island, Alaska, USA *55°14′N 160°34′W*
Ungaria *see* Hungary
183 P8 **Ungarie** New South Wales, SE Australia *33°39′S 146°54′E*
Ungarisch-Brod *see* Uherský Brod
Ungarisches Erzgebirge *see* Slovenské rudohorie
Ungarisch-Hradisch *see* Uherské Hradiště
Ungarn *see* Hungary
12 M4 **Ungava Bay** *bay* Québec, E Canada
12 J2 **Ungava, Péninsule d'** *peninsula* Québec, SE Canada
Ungeny *see* Ungheni
116 M9 **Ungheni** *Rus.* Ungeny. W Moldova *47°13′N 27°48′E*
Unguja *see* Zanzibar
146 G10 **Üngüz Angyrsyndaky Garagum** *Rus.* Zaunguzskiye Garagumy. *desert* N Turkmenistan
146 H11 **Unguz, Solonchakovyye Vpadiny** *salt marsh* C Turkmenistan
Ungvár *see* Uzhhorod
60 I12 **União da Vitória** Paraná, S Brazil *26°13′S 51°05′W*
111 G17 **Uničov** *Ger.* Mährisch-Neustadt. Olomoucký Kraj, E Czech Republic *49°48′N 17°05′E*
110 J12 **Uniejów** Łódzkie, C Poland *51°58′N 18°46′E*
112 A11 **Unije** *island* W Croatia
38 L16 **Unimak Island** *island* Aleutian Islands, Alaska, USA
38 L16 **Unimak Pass** *strait* Aleutian Islands, Alaska, USA
62 J12 **Unión** San Luis, C Argentina *35°09′S 65°55′W*
27 W5 **Union** Missouri, C USA *38°27′N 91°01′W*
32 L12 **Union** Oregon, NW USA *45°12′N 117°51′W*
21 Q11 **Union** South Carolina, SE USA *34°42′N 81°37′W*
21 R6 **Union** West Virginia, NE USA *37°36′N 80°34′W*
61 B25 **Unión, Bahía** *bay* E Argentina
31 Q13 **Union City** Indiana, N USA *40°12′N 84°50′W*
31 Q10 **Union City** Michigan, N USA *42°03′N 85°06′W*
18 C12 **Union City** Pennsylvania, NE USA *41°54′N 79°51′W*
20 G8 **Union City** Tennessee, S USA *36°26′N 89°03′W*
32 G14 **Union Creek** Oregon, NW USA *42°54′N 122°26′W*
83 G25 **Uniondale** Western Cape, SW South Africa *33°40′S 23°07′E*
40 K13 **Unión de Tula** Jalisco, SW Mexico *19°58′N 104°16′W*
30 M9 **Union Grove** Wisconsin, N USA *42°39′N 88°03′W*
45 Y15 **Union Island** *island* S Saint Vincent and the Grenadines
Union of Myanmar *see* Burma
46 K5 **Union Reefs** *reef* SW Mexico
0 D7 **Union Seamount** *undersea feature* NE Pacific Ocean *49°35′N 132°45′W*
23 Q6 **Union Springs** Alabama, S USA *32°08′N 85°43′W*
20 H6 **Uniontown** Kentucky, S USA *37°46′N 87°55′W*
18 C16 **Uniontown** Pennsylvania, NE USA *39°54′N 79°44′W*
27 T1 **Unionville** Missouri, C USA *40°28′N 93°00′W*
141 V8 **United Arab Emirates** *Ar.* Al Imārāt al 'Arabīyah al Muttaḥidah, *abbrev.* UAE; *prev.* Trucial States. ◆ *federation* SW Asia
United Arab Republic *see* Egypt
97 H14 **United Kingdom** *off.* United Kingdom of Great Britain and Northern Ireland, *abbrev.* UK. ◆ *monarchy* NW Europe
United Kingdom of Great Britain and Northern Ireland *see* United Kingdom
United Mexican States *see* Mexico
United Provinces *see* Uttar Pradesh
16 L10 **United States of America** *off.* United States of America, *var.* America, The States, *abbrev.* U.S., USA. ◆ *federal republic* North America
United States of America *see* United States of America
124 J10 **Unitsa** Respublika Kareliya, NW Russian Federation *62°31′N 34°31′E*
11 S15 **Unity** Saskatchewan, S Canada *52°27′N 109°10′W*
Unity State *see* Wahda
105 Q8 **Universales, Montes** ▲▲ C Spain
27 X4 **University City** Missouri, C USA *38°40′N 90°19′W*
187 Q13 **Unmet** Malekula, C Vanuatu *16°09′S 167°16′E*
101 F15 **Unna** Nordrhein-Westfalen, W Germany *51°32′N 07°41′E*
152 H8 **Unnāo** *var.* Una. Uttarakhand, N India *31°27′N 76°16′E*
Unnan *see* Kisuki
152 L12 **Unnāo** *prev.* Unao. Uttar Pradesh, N India *26°32′N 80°30′E*
187 R15 **Unpongkor** Erromango, S Vanuatu *18°48′S 169°01′E*
Unruhstadt *see* Kargowa
96 M1 **Unst** *island* NE Scotland, United Kingdom
101 K16 **Unstrut** ≈ C Germany
Unterdrauburg *see* Dravograd
Unterlimbach *see* Lendava
101 L23 **Unterschleissheim** Bayern, SE Germany *48°16′N 11°34′E*
101 H24 **Untersee** ◎ Germany/Switzerland
100 O10 **Unterueckersee** ◎ NE Germany
108 F9 **Unterwalden** ◆ *canton* C Switzerland
55 N12 **Unturán, Sierra de** ▲▲ Brazil/Venezuela
159 N11 **Unuli Horog** Qinghai, W China *35°10′N 91°50′E*
136 M11 **Ünye** Ordu, W Turkey *41°08′N 37°14′E*
Unza *see* Unzha
125 O14 **Unzha** *var.* Unza. ≈ NW Russian Federation
79 E17 **Uolo, Río** *var.* Eyo (lower course), Mbini, Uele (upper course), Woleu; *prev.* Benito. ≈ Equatorial Guinea/Gabon
55 Q10 **Uonán** Bolívar, SE Venezuela *04°33′N 62°10′W*
161 T12 **Uotsuri-shima** *island* China/Japan/Taiwan
165 M11 **Uozu** Toyama, Honshū, SW Japan *36°50′N 137°25′E*
42 L12 **Upala** Alajuela, NW Costa Rica *10°52′N 85°W*
55 P7 **Upata** Bolívar, E Venezuela *08°02′N 62°25′W*
79 M23 **Upemba, Lac** ◎ SE Dem. Rep. Congo
197 O12 **Upernavik** *var.* Upernivik. Kitaa, C Greenland *73°06′N 55°42′W*
Upernivik *see* Upernavik
83 F22 **Upington** Northern Cape, W South Africa *28°28′S 21°14′E*
Uplands *see* Ottawa
192 I16 **'Upolu** *island* SE Samoa
38 G11 **'Upolu Point** *var.* Upolu Point. *headland* Hawai'i, USA, C Pacific Ocean *20°15′N 155°51′W*
Upper Austria *see* Oberösterreich
Upper Bann *see* Bann
14 M13 **Upper Canada Village** *tourist site* Ontario, SE Canada
18 I16 **Upper Darby** Pennsylvania, NE USA *39°57′N 75°15′W*
28 L2 **Upper Des Lacs Lake** ⊡ North Dakota, N USA
185 L14 **Upper Hutt** Wellington, North Island, New Zealand *41°06′S 175°06′E*
29 X11 **Upper Iowa River** ≈ Iowa, C USA
32 H15 **Upper Klamath Lake** ◎ Oregon, NW USA
34 M6 **Upper Lake** California, W USA *39°07′N 122°53′W*
35 Q1 **Upper Lake** ◎ California, W USA
10 K9 **Upper Liard** Yukon Territory, W Canada *60°01′N 128°59′W*
97 E16 **Upper Lough Erne** ◎ SW Northern Ireland, United Kingdom
80 F12 **Upper Nile** ◆ *state* E Sudan
29 T3 **Upper Red Lake** ◎ Minnesota, N USA
31 S12 **Upper Sandusky** Ohio, N USA *40°49′N 83°16′W*
Upper Volta *see* Burkina
95 O15 **Upplands Väsby** *var.* Upplands Väsby. Stockholm, C Sweden *59°29′N 18°04′E*
Upplands Väsby *see* Upplandsväsby
95 O15 **Uppsala** Uppsala, C Sweden *59°52′N 17°38′E*
95 O14 **Uppsala** ◆ *county* C Sweden
38 J12 **Upright Cape** *headland* Saint Matthew Island, Alaska, USA *60°19′N 172°15′W*
20 K6 **Upton** Kentucky, S USA *37°25′N 85°53′W*
33 Y13 **Upton** Wyoming, C USA *44°06′N 104°37′W*
141 N7 **'Uqlat aş Şuqūr** Al Qaşīm, W Saudi Arabia *25°51′N 42°13′E*
Uqsuqtuuq *see* Gjoa Haven
Uqturpan *see* Wushi
54 C7 **Urabá, Golfo de** *gulf* NW Colombia
Uracas *see* Farallon de Pajaros
uradqianqi *see* Wulashan, N China
Uradar'ya *see* O'radaryo
Urad Qianqi *see* Xishanzui, N China
165 U5 **Urahoro** Hokkaidō, NE Japan *42°47′N 143°41′E*
165 T5 **Urakawa** Hokkaidō, NE Japan *42°11′N 142°42′E*
127 X6 **Ural** *Kaz.* Zayyq. ≈ Kazakhstan/Russian Federation
183 T6 **Uralla** New South Wales, SE Australia *30°39′S 151°30′E*
Ural Mountains *see* Ural'skiye Gory
144 F8 **Ural'sk** *Kaz.* Oral. Zapadnyy Kazakhstan, NW Kazakhstan *51°12′N 51°17′E*
Ural'skaya Oblast' *see* Zapadnyy Kazakhstan
127 W5 **Ural'skiye Gory** *var.* Ural'skiy Khrebet, *Eng.* Ural Mountains. ▲▲ Kazakhstan/Russian Federation
Ural'skiy Khrebet *see* Ural'skiye Gory
138 I3 **Urām aş Şughrá** Ḥalab, N Syria *36°10′N 36°55′E*
183 P10 **Urana** New South Wales, SE Australia *35°22′S 146°16′E*
11 S10 **Uranium City** Saskatchewan, C Canada *59°30′N 108°46′W*
58 F10 **Uraricoera** Roraima, N Brazil *03°26′N 60°54′W*
47 S5 **Uraricoera, Rio** ≈ N Brazil
Ura-Tyube *see* Üroteppa
165 O13 **Urawa** *var.* Saitama. Saitama, Honshū, S Japan *35°52′N 139°40′E*
122 H10 **Uray** Khanty-Mansiyskiy Avtonomnyy Okrug-Yugra, C Russian Federation *60°07′N 64°38′E*
141 R7 **'Uray'irah** Ash Sharqīyah, E Saudi Arabia *25°59′N 48°52′E*
30 M13 **Urbana** Illinois, N USA *40°06′N 88°12′W*
31 R13 **Urbana** Ohio, N USA *40°04′N 83°46′W*
29 V14 **Urbandale** Iowa, C USA *41°37′N 93°42′W*
106 I11 **Urbania** Marche, C Italy *43°40′N 12°33′E*
106 I11 **Urbino** Marche, C Italy *43°45′N 12°38′E*
57 H16 **Urcos** Cusco, S Peru *13°40′S 71°38′W*
144 D10 **Urda** Zapadnyy Kazakhstan, W Kazakhstan *48°52′N 47°31′E*
105 N10 **Urda** Castilla-La Mancha, C Spain *39°25′N 03°43′W*
Urdgol *see* Chandmanï
105 O3 **Urduña** *var.* Orduña. País Vasco, N Spain *43°00′N 03°00′W*
Urdunn *see* Jordan
145 X12 **Urdzhar** *Kaz.* Ürzhar. Vostochnyy Kazakhstan, E Kazakhstan *47°06′N 81°33′E*
97 L16 **Ure** ≈ N England, United Kingdom
119 K18 **Urechcha** *Rus.* Urech'ye. Minskaya Voblasts', S Belarus *52°57′N 27°54′E*
Urech'ye *see* Urechcha
127 P2 **Uren'** Nizhegorodskaya Oblast', W Russian Federation *57°30′N 45°48′E*
122 J9 **Urengoy** Yamalo-Nenetskiy Avtonomnyy Okrug, N Russian Federation *65°52′N 78°42′E*
184 K10 **Urenui** Taranaki, North Island, New Zealand *38°59′S 174°25′E*
187 Q12 **Ureparapara** *island* Banks Islands, N Vanuatu
40 G5 **Ures** Sonora, NW Mexico *29°26′N 110°24′W*
Urfa *see* Şanlıurfa
Urga *see* Ulaanbaatar
162 F6 **Urgamal** *var.* Hungiy. Dzavhan, W Mongolia *48°31′N 94°15′E*
146 H9 **Urganch** *Rus.* Urgench; *prev.* Novo-Urgench. Xorazm Viloyati, W Uzbekistan *41°40′N 60°32′E*
Urgench *see* Urganch
136 J14 **Ürgüp** Nevşehir, C Turkey *38°39′N 34°55′E*
147 O12 **Urgut** Samarqand Viloyati, C Uzbekistan *39°26′N 67°15′E*
158 K3 **Urho** Xinjiang Uygur Zizhiqu, W China *46°05′N 84°51′E*
152 G5 **Uri** Jammu and Kashmir, NW India *34°05′N 74°03′E*
108 G9 **Uri** ◆ *canton* C Switzerland
54 F11 **Uribe** Meta, C Colombia *03°01′N 74°33′W*
54 H4 **Uribia** La Guajira, N Colombia *11°45′N 72°19′W*
116 G12 **Uricani** *Hung.* Hobicaurikány. Hunedoara, SW Romania *45°18′N 23°03′E*
57 M21 **Uriondo** Tarija, S Bolivia *21°43′S 64°40′W*
40 I7 **Urique** Chihuahua, N Mexico *27°16′N 107°51′W*
40 I7 **Urique, Río** ≈ N Mexico
56 E9 **Urituyacu, Río** ≈ N Peru
Uritskiy *see* Sarykol'
98 K8 **Urk** Flevoland, N Netherlands *52°40′N 05°35′E*
136 B14 **Urla** İzmir, W Turkey *38°19′N 26°47′E*
116 K13 **Urlaţi** Prahova, SE Romania *44°59′N 26°15′E*
127 V4 **Urman** Respublika Bashkortostan, W Russian Federation *54°53′N 56°52′E*
147 P12 **Urmetan** W Tajikistan *39°27′N 68°13′E*
Urmia *see* Orūmīyeh
Urmia, Lake *see* Orūmīyeh, Daryācheh-ye
Urmīyeh *see* Orūmīyeh
Uroševac *see* Ferizaj
147 P11 **Üroteppa** *Rus.* Ura-Tyube. NW Tajikistan *39°55′N 68°57′E*
54 D8 **Urrao** Antioquia, W Colombia *06°16′N 76°10′W*
Ursat'yevskaya *see* Xovos
Urt *see* Gurvantes
127 X7 **Urtazym** Orenburgskaya Oblast', W Russian Federation *52°12′N 58°48′E*
59 K18 **Uruaçu** Goiás, C Brazil *14°38′S 49°06′W*
40 M14 **Uruapan** *var.* Uruapan del Progreso. Michoacán, SW Mexico *19°26′N 102°04′W*
Uruapan del Progreso *see* Uruapan
57 G15 **Urubamba, Cordillera** ▲▲ C Peru
57 G14 **Urubamba, Río** ≈ C Peru
58 G12 **Urucará** Amazonas, N Brazil *02°30′S 57°45′W*
61 E16 **Uruguaiana** Rio Grande do Sul, S Brazil *29°45′S 57°05′W*
Uruguai, Rio *see* Uruguay
61 E18 **Uruguay** *off.* Oriental Republic of Uruguay; *prev.* La Banda Oriental. ◆ *republic* E South America
61 E15 **Uruguay** *var.* Rio Uruguai, Río Uruguay. ≈ E South America
Uruguay, Oriental Republic of *see* Uruguay
Uruguay, Río *see* Uruguay
Urukthapel *see* Ngeruktabel
Urumchi *see* Ürümqi
Urumi Yeh *see* Orūmīyeh, Daryācheh-ye
158 L5 **Ürümqi** *var.* Tihwa, Urumchi, Urumqi, Urumtsi, Wu-lu-k'o-mu-shi, Wu-lu-mu-ch'i; *prev.* Ti-hua. Xinjiang Uygur Zizhiqu, NW China *43°52′N 87°31′E*
Urumtsi *see* Ürümqi
Urundi *see* Burundi
183 V6 **Urunga** New South Wales, SE Australia *30°33′S 152°58′E*
188 C15 **Uruno Point** *headland* NW Guam *13°37′N 144°50′E*
123 U13 **Urup, Ostrov** *island* Kuril'skiye Ostrova, SE Russian Federation
141 P11 **'Uruq al Mawārid** *desert* S Saudi Arabia
Urusan *see* Ulsan
127 O16 **Urus-Martan** Chechenskaya Respublika, SW Russian Federation *43°08′N 45°33′E*
127 T5 **Urussu** Respublika Tatarstan, W Russian Federation *54°34′N 53°23′E*
184 K10 **Uruti** Taranaki, North Island, New Zealand *38°57′S 174°32′E*
57 K19 **Uru Uru, Lago** ◎ W Bolivia
55 P9 **Uruyén** Bolívar, SE Venezuela *05°40′N 62°26′W*
Ürüzgān *see* Orūzgān
165 T3 **Uryū-gawa** ≈ Hokkaidō, NE Japan
165 T2 **Uryū-ko** ◎ Hokkaidō, NE Japan
127 N8 **Uryupinsk** Volgogradskaya Oblast', SW Russian Federation *50°51′N 41°59′E*
Ürzhar *see* Urdzhar
125 R16 **Urzhum** Kirovskaya Oblast', NW Russian Federation *57°09′N 49°56′E*
116 K13 **Urziceni** Ialomiţa, SE Romania *44°43′N 26°39′E*
164 E14 **Usa** Ōita, Kyūshū, SW Japan *33°31′N 131°22′E*
119 K16 **Usa** ≈ C Belarus
125 T6 **Usa** ≈ NW Russian Federation
136 E14 **Uşak** *prev.* Ushak. Uşak, W Turkey *38°42′N 29°25′E*
136 D14 **Uşak** *var.* Ushak. ◆ *province* W Turkey
83 C19 **Usakos** Erongo, W Namibia *22°01′S 15°32′E*
81 J21 **Usambara Mountains** ▲▲ NE Tanzania
81 G23 **Usangu Flats** *wetland* SW Tanzania
65 D24 **Usborne, Mount** ▲ East Falkland, Falkland Islands *51°35′S 58°57′W*
100 O8 **Usedom** *island* NE Germany
99 M24 **Useldange** Diekirch, C Luxembourg *49°47′N 05°59′E*
118 L13 **Ushachy** *Rus.* Ushachi. Vitsyebskaya Voblasts', N Belarus *55°11′N 28°37′E*
Ushak *see* Uşak
122 L4 **Ushakova, Ostrov** *island* Severnaya Zemlya, N Russian Federation
Ushant *see* Ouessant, Île d'
Usharal *see* Ucharal
164 B15 **Ushibuka** *var.* Usibuka. Kumamoto, Shimo-jima, SW Japan *32°12′N 130°00′E*
Ushi Point *see* Sabaneta, Puntan
145 V14 **Ushtobe** *Kaz.* Üshtöbe. Almaty, SE Kazakhstan *45°15′N 77°59′E*
Üshtöbe *see* Ushtobe
63 I25 **Ushuaia** Tierra del Fuego, S Argentina *54°48′S 68°19′W*
39 R10 **Usibelli** Alaska, USA *63°54′N 148°41′W*
Usibuka *see* Ushibuka
Usichi *see* Ushachy
186 D7 **Usino** Madang, N Papua New Guinea *05°40′S 145°31′E*
125 U6 **Usinsk** Respublika Komi, NW Russian Federation *66°01′N 57°37′E*
97 K22 **Usk** *Wel.* Wysg. ≈ SE Wales, United Kingdom
Uskočke Planine/ Uskokengebirge *see* Gorjanci
Uskoplje *see* Gornji Vakuf
Üsküb/Üsküp *see* Skopje
114 M11 **Üsküpdere** Kırklareli, NW Turkey *41°41′N 27°21′E*
126 L7 **Usman'** Lipetskaya Oblast', W Russian Federation *52°04′N 39°41′E*
118 D8 **Usmas Ezers** ◎ NW Latvia
125 U13 **Usol'ye** Permskaya Oblast', NW Russian Federation *59°27′N 56°33′E*
41 T16 **Uspanapa, Río** ≈ SE Mexico
145 R11 **Uspenskiy** Karaganda, C Kazakhstan *48°45′N 72°46′E*
103 O11 **Ussel** Corrèze, C France *45°33′N 02°18′E*
153 Z6 **Ussuri** *var.* Usuri, Wusuri, *Chin.* Wusuli Jiang. ≈ China/Russian Federation
123 S15 **Ussuriysk** *prev.* Nikol'sk, Nikol'sk-Ussuriyskiy, Voroshilov. Primorskiy Kray, SE Russian Federation *43°48′N 131°59′E*
136 J10 **Usta Burnu** *headland* N Turkey *41°58′N 34°30′E*
149 P13 **Usta Muhammad** Baluchistān, SW Pakistan *28°07′N 68°00′E*
123 V11 **Ust'-Bol'sheretsk** Kamchatskaya Oblast', E Russian Federation *52°48′N 156°12′E*
127 N9 **Ust'-Buzulukskaya** Volgogradskaya Oblast', SW Russian Federation *50°12′N 42°06′E*
111 C16 **Ústecký Kraj** ◆ *region* NW Czech Republic
108 G7 **Uster** Zürich, NE Switzerland *47°21′N 08°49′E*
107 I22 **Ustica, Isola d'** *island* S Italy
122 M11 **Ust'-Ilimsk** Irkutskaya Oblast', C Russian Federation *57°57′N 102°30′E*
111 C15 **Ústí nad Labem** *Ger.* Aussig. Ústecký Kraj, NW Czech Republic *50°41′N 14°04′E*
111 F17 **Ústí nad Orlicí** *Ger.* Wildenschwert. Pardubický Kraj, C Czech Republic *49°58′N 16°24′E*
Ustinov *see* Izhevsk
113 J14 **Ustiprača** ◆ Republika Srpska, SE Bosnia and Herzegovina
122 H11 **Ust'-Ishim** Omskaya Oblast', C Russian Federation *57°42′N 70°58′E*
110 G6 **Ustka** *Ger.* Stolpmünde. Pomorskie, N Poland *54°35′N 16°50′E*
123 V9 **Ust'-Kamchatsk** Kamchatskaya Oblast', E Russian Federation *56°14′N 162°28′E*
145 X9 **Ust'-Kamenogorsk** *Kaz.* Öskemen. Vostochnyy Kazakhstan, E Kazakhstan *49°58′N 82°36′E*
123 T10 **Ust'-Khayryuzovo** Koryakskiy Avtonomnyy Okrug, E Russian Federation *57°07′N 156°37′E*
122 I14 **Ust'-Koksa** Respublika Altay, S Russian Federation *50°15′N 85°45′E*
125 S11 **Ust'-Kulom** Respublika Komi, NW Russian Federation *61°42′N 53°42′E*
123 Q8 **Ust'-Kuyga** Respublika Sakha (Yakutiya), NE Russian Federation *69°59′N 135°27′E*
126 L14 **Ust'-Labinsk** Krasnodarskiy Kray, SW Russian Federation *44°40′N 40°46′E*
123 R10 **Ust'-Maya** Respublika Sakha (Yakutiya), NE Russian Federation *60°27′N 134°28′E*
123 R9 **Ust'-Nera** Respublika Sakha (Yakutiya), NE Russian Federation *64°28′N 143°01′E*
123 P12 **Ust'-Nyukzha** Amurskaya Oblast', S Russian Federation *56°30′N 121°32′E*
123 O7 **Ust'-Olenëk** Respublika Sakha (Yakutiya), NE Russian Federation *73°03′N 119°34′E*
123 T9 **Ust'-Omchug** Magadanskaya Oblast', E Russian Federation *61°07′N 149°17′E*
122 M13 **Ust'-Ordynskiy** Ust'-Ordynskiy Buryatskiy Avtonomnyy Okrug, S Russian Federation *52°50′N 104°42′E*
122 M13 **Ust'-Ordynskiy Buryatskiy Avtonomnyy Okrug** ◆ *autonomous district* S Russian Federation
125 N8 **Ust'-Pinega** Arkhangel'skaya Oblast', NW Russian Federation *64°09′N 41°55′E*
122 K8 **Ust'-Port** Taymyrskiy (Dolgano-Nenetskiy) Avtonomnyy Okrug, N Russian Federation *69°42′N 84°25′E*
114 L11 **Ustrem** *prev.* Vakav. Yambol, E Bulgaria *42°01′N 26°28′E*
111 O18 **Ustrzyki Dolne** Podkarpackie, SE Poland *49°26′N 22°36′E*
Ust'-Sysol'sk *see* Syktyvkar
125 R7 **Ust'-Tsil'ma** Respublika Komi, NW Russian Federation *65°25′N 52°09′E*
Ust Urt *see* Ustyurt Plateau
125 O11 **Ust'ya** ≈ NW Russian Federation
124 K6 **Ust'ye Varzugi** Murmanskaya Oblast', NW Russian Federation *66°16′N 36°47′E*
123 V10 **Ust'yevoye** *prev.* Kirovskiy. Kamchatskaya Oblast', E Russian Federation *54°06′N 155°48′E*
117 R8 **Ustynivka** Kirovohrads'ka Oblast', C Ukraine *47°58′N 32°32′E*
144 H15 **Ustyurt Plateau** *var.* Ust Urt, *Uzb.* Ustyurt Platosi. *plateau* Kazakhstan/Uzbekistan
Ustyurt Platosi *see* Ustyurt Plateau
124 K14 **Ustyuzhna** Vologodskaya Oblast', NW Russian Federation *58°50′N 36°25′E*
158 J4 **Usu** Xinjiang Uygur Zizhiqu, NW China *44°27′N 84°37′E*
171 O13 **Usu** Sulawesi, C Indonesia *02°34′S 120°58′E*
164 E14 **Usuki** Ōita, Kyūshū, SW Japan *33°07′N 131°48′E*
42 G8 **Usulután** Usulután, SE El Salvador *13°20′N 88°26′W*
42 B9 **Usulután** ◆ *department* SE El Salvador
41 W16 **Usumacinta, Río** ≈ Guatemala/Mexico
Usumbura *see* Bujumbura
Usuri *see* Ussuri
U.S./USA *see* United States of America
171 W14 **Uta** Papua, E Indonesia *04°28′S 136°03′E*
36 K5 **Utah** *off.* State of Utah, *also known as* Beehive State, Mormon State. ◆ *state* W USA
36 L3 **Utah Lake** ◎ Utah, W USA
Utaidhani *see* Uthai Thani
93 M14 **Utajärvi** Oulu, C Finland *64°45′N 26°25′E*
Utamboni *see* Mitemele, Río
Utaradit *see* Uttaradit
165 T3 **Utashinai** *var.* Utasinai. Hokkaidō, NE Japan *43°32′N 142°03′E*
Utasinai *see* Utashinai
193 Y14 **'Uta Vava'u** *island* Vava'u Group, N Tonga
37 V9 **Ute Creek** ≈ New Mexico, SW USA
118 H12 **Utena** Utena, E Lithuania *55°30′N 25°34′E*
118 H12 **Utena** ◆ *province* Lithuania
37 V10 **Ute Reservoir** ⊡ New Mexico, SW USA
167 O10 **Uthai Thani** *var.* Muang Uthai Thani, Udayadhani, Utaidhani. Uthai Thani, W Thailand *15°22′N 100°03′E*
149 O15 **Uthal** Baluchistān, SW Pakistan *25°53′N 66°37′E*
18 I10 **Utica** New York, NE USA *43°06′N 75°15′W*
105 R10 **Utiel** País Valenciano, E Spain *39°33′N 01°13′W*
11 O13 **Utikuma Lake** ◎ Alberta, W Canada
42 I4 **Utila, Isla de** *island* Islas de la Bahía, N Honduras
Utina *see* Udine
59 O17 **Utinga** Bahia, E Brazil *12°05′S 41°07′W*
Utirik *see* Utrik Atoll
95 M22 **Utlängan** *island* S Sweden
117 U11 **Utlyuts'kyy Lyman** *bay* S Ukraine
95 P16 **Utö** Stockholm, C Sweden *58°55′N 18°19′E*
25 Q12 **Utopia** Texas, SW USA *29°30′N 99°31′W*
98 J11 **Utrecht** *Lat.* Trajectum ad Rhenum. Utrecht, C Netherlands *52°06′N 05°07′E*
83 K22 **Utrecht** KwaZulu/Natal, E South Africa *27°40′S 30°20′E*
98 I11 **Utrecht** ◆ *province* C Netherlands
104 K14 **Utrera** Andalucía, S Spain *37°10′N 05°47′W*
189 V4 **Utrik Atoll** *var.* Utirik, Utrōk, Utrōnk. *atoll* Ratak Chain, N Marshall Islands
Utrōk/Utrōnk *see* Utrik Atoll
95 B16 **Utsira** *island* SW Norway
92 L8 **Utsjoki** *var.* Ohcejohka. Lappi, N Finland *69°54′N 27°01′E*
165 O12 **Utsunomiya** *var.* Utunomiya. Tochigi, Honshū, S Japan *36°36′N 139°53′E*
127 P13 **Utta** Respublika Kalmykiya, SW Russian Federation *46°22′N 46°03′E*
167 O8 **Uttaradit** *var.* Utaradit. Uttaradit, N Thailand *17°38′N 100°05′E*
152 J9 **Uttarakhand** ◆ *state* N India
152 J8 **Uttarkāshi** Uttarakhand, N India *30°45′N 78°19′E*
152 K11 **Uttar Pradesh** *prev.* United Provinces, United Provinces of Agra and Oudh. ◆ *state* N India
45 T5 **Utuado** C Puerto Rico *18°17′N 66°41′W*
158 K3 **Utubulak** Xinjiang Uygur Zizhiqu, W China *46°50′N 86°15′E*
39 N5 **Utukok River** ≈ Alaska, USA
Utunomiya *see* Utsunomiya
187 P10 **Utupua** *island* Santa Cruz Islands, E Solomon Islands
144 G9 **Utva** ≈ NW Kazakhstan
189 Y15 **Utwe** Kosrae, E Micronesia
189 X15 **Utwe Harbor** *harbour* Kosrae, E Micronesia
Uubulan *see* Hayrhan
163 O8 **Uulbayan** *var.* Dzüünbulag. Sühbaatar, E Mongolia *46°30′N 112°22′E*
118 G6 **Uulu** Pärnumaa, SW Estonia *58°15′N 24°32′E*
197 N13 **Uummannaq** *var.* Umanak, Umanaq. ◆ Kitaa, C Greenland
Uummannarsuaq *see* Nunap Isua
162 E4 **Üüreg Nuur** ◎ NW Mongolia
Uusikaarlepyy *see* Nykarleby
93 J19 **Uusikaupunki** *Swe.* Nystad. Länsi-Suomi, SW Finland *60°48′N 21°25′E*
127 S2 **Uva** Udmurtskaya Respublika, NW Russian Federation *56°41′N 52°15′E*
155 K25 **Uva** ◆ *province* SE Sri Lanka
113 L14 **Uvac** ≈ W Serbia
25 Q12 **Uvalde** Texas, SW USA *29°14′N 99°49′W*
119 O18 **Uvaravichy** *Rus.* Uvarovichi. Homyel'skaya Voblasts', SE Belarus *52°36′N 30°44′E*
54 J11 **Uvá, Río** ≈ E Colombia
Uvarovichi *see* Uvaravichy
127 N7 **Uvarovo** Tambovskaya Oblast', W Russian Federation *51°58′N 42°13′E*
122 H10 **Uvat** Tyumenskaya Oblast', C Russian Federation *59°11′N 68°37′E*
190 G12 **Uvea, Île** *island* N Wallis and Futuna
81 E21 **Uvinza** Kigoma, W Tanzania *05°08′S 30°23′E*
79 O20 **Uvira** Sud-Kivu, E Dem. Rep. Congo *03°24′S 29°05′E*
162 E5 **Uvs** ◆ *province* NW Mongolia
162 F5 **Uvs Nuur** *var.* Ozero Ubsu-Nur. ◎ Mongolia/Russian Federation
Uxin Qi *see* Dabqig
164 F14 **Uwa** *var.* Seiyo. Ehime, Shikoku, SW Japan *33°22′N 132°29′E*
164 F14 **Uwajima** *var.* Uwazima. Ehime, Shikoku, SW Japan *33°13′N 132°32′E*
80 B5 **'Uwaynāt, Jabal al** *var.* Jebel Uweinat. ▲ Libya/Sudan *21°51′N 25°01′E*
Uwazima *see* Uwajima
Uweinat, Jebel *see* 'Uwaynāt, Jabal al
14 H14 **Uxbridge** Ontario, S Canada *44°07′N 79°07′W*
Uxellodunum *see* Issoudun
Uxin Qi *see* Dabqig, N China
41 X12 **Uxmal, Ruinas** *ruins* Yucatán, SE Mexico
129 Q5 **Uy** ≈ Kazakhstan/Russian Federation
144 K15 **Uyaly** Kzylorda, S Kazakhstan *44°22′N 61°16′E*
123 R8 **Uyandina** ≈ NE Russian Federation
162 J8 **Uyanga** *var.* Ongi. Övörhangay, C Mongolia *46°30′N 102°18′E*
Üydzen *see* Manlay
Uyeda *see* Ueda
122 K5 **Uyedineniya, Ostrov** *island* N Russian Federation
77 V17 **Uyo** Akwa Ibom, S Nigeria *05°00′N 07°57′E*
162 D8 **Üyönch** Hovd, W Mongolia *46°04′N 92°05′E*
145 Q15 **Uyuk** Zhambyl, S Kazakhstan *43°46′N 70°55′E*
141 V13 **'Uyūn** SW Oman *17°19′N 53°50′E*
57 K20 **Uyuni** Potosí, W Bolivia *20°27′S 66°48′W*
57 J20 **Uyuni, Salar de** *wetland* SW Bolivia
146 I9 **Uzbekistan** *off.* Republic of Uzbekistan. ◆ *republic* C Asia
Uzbekistan, Republic of *see* Uzbekistan
158 D8 **Uzbel Shankou** *Rus.* Pereval Kyzyl-Dzhiik. *pass* China/Tajikistan
146 B11 **Uzboý** *prev. Rus.* Imeni 26 Bakinskikh Komissarov, *Turkm.* 26 Baku Komissarlary Adyndaky. Balkan Welaýaty, W Turkmenistan *39°24′N 54°04′E*
119 J17 **Uzda** Minskaya Voblasts', C Belarus *53°29′N 27°10′E*
103 N12 **Uzerche** Corrèze, C France *45°24′N 01°35′E*
103 R14 **Uzès** Gard, S France *44°00′N 04°25′E*
147 T10 **Uzgen** *Kir.* Özgön. Oshskaya Oblast', SW Kyrgyzstan *40°42′N 73°17′E*
117 O3 **Uzh** ≈ N Ukraine
Uzhgorod *see* Uzhhorod
116 G7 **Uzhhorod** *Rus.* Uzhgorod; *prev.* Ungvár. Zakarpats'ka Oblast', W Ukraine *48°36′N 22°19′E*
Uzi *see* Uji
112 K13 **Užice** *prev.* Titovo Užice. Serbia, W Serbia *43°52′N 19°51′E*
Uzin *see* Uzyn
126 L5 **Uzlovaya** Tul'skaya Oblast', W Russian Federation *54°01′N 38°15′E*
108 H7 **Uznach** Sankt Gallen, NE Switzerland *47°12′N 09°00′E*
145 U16 **Uzunagach** Almaty, SE Kazakhstan *43°08′N 76°20′E*
136 B10 **Uzunköprü** Edirne, NW Turkey *41°18′N 26°40′E*
118 D11 **Užventis** Šiauliai, C Lithuania *55°49′N 22°38′E*
117 P5 **Uzyn** *Rus.* Uzin. Kyyivs'ka Oblast', N Ukraine *49°52′N 30°27′E*
145 N7 **Uzynkol'** Kostanay, N Kazakhstan
145 N7 **Uzynkol'** *prev.* Lenin, Leninskoye. Kustanay, N Kazakhstan *54°05′N 65°23′E*

V

Vääksy *see* Asikkala
83 H23 **Vaal** ≈ C South Africa
93 M14 **Vaala** Oulu, C Finland *64°34′N 26°49′E*
93 N19 **Vaalimaa** Etelä-Suomi, SE Finland *60°34′N 27°49′E*
99 M19 **Vaals** Limburg, SE Netherlands *50°46′N 06°01′E*
93 J16 **Vaasa** *Swe.* Vasa; *prev.* Nikolainkaupunki. Länsi-Suomi, W Finland *63°07′N 21°39′E*
98 L10 **Vaassen** Gelderland, E Netherlands *52°18′N 05°59′E*
118 G11 **Vabalninkas** Panevėžys, NE Lithuania *55°59′N 24°45′E*
Vabkent *see* Vobkent
111 J22 **Vác** *Ger.* Waitzen. Pest, N Hungary *47°46′N 19°08′E*
61 I14 **Vacaria** Rio Grande do Sul, S Brazil *28°31′S 50°52′W*
35 N7 **Vacaville** California, W USA *38°21′N 121°59′W*
103 R15 **Vaccarès, Étang de** ◎ SE France
44 L10 **Vache, Île à** *island* SW Haiti
173 Y16 **Vacoas** W Mauritius *20°18′S 57°29′E*
155 F21 **Vadakara** *var.* Badagara. Kerala, SW India *11°36′N 75°34′E* *see also* Badagara
32 G10 **Vader** Washington, NW USA *46°23′N 122°58′W*
94 D12 **Vadheim** Sogn Og Fjordane, S Norway *61°12′N 05°48′E*
154 D11 **Vadodara** *prev.* Baroda. Gujarāt, W India *22°19′N 73°14′E*
92 M8 **Vadsø** *Fin.* Vesisaari. Finnmark, N Norway *70°07′N 29°47′E*
95 L17 **Vadstena** Östergötland, S Sweden *58°26′N 14°55′E*
108 I8 **Vaduz** ● (Liechtenstein) W Liechtenstein *47°08′N 09°32′E*
Våg *see* Váh
125 N12 **Vaga** ≈ NW Russian Federation
94 G11 **Vågåmo** Oppland, S Norway *61°52′N 09°06′E*
112 D12 **Vaganski Vrh** ▲ W Croatia *44°24′N 15°32′E*
95 A19 **Vágar** *Dan.* Vågø. *island* W Faeroe Islands
Vágbeszterce *see* Považská Bystrica
95 L19 **Vaggeryd** Jönköping, S Sweden *57°30′N 14°10′E*
137 T12 **Vagharshapat** *var.* Ejmiadzin, Ejmiatsin, Etchmiadzin, *Rus.* Echmiadzin. W Armenia *40°10′N 44°17′E*
95 O16 **Vaggarön** Södermanland, C Sweden *58°57′N 17°32′E*
Vågø *see* Vágar

◆ Country ● Country Capital ◇ Dependent Territory ○ Dependent Territory Capital ◆ Administrative Regions ✈ International Airport ▲ Mountain ▲▲ Mountain Range ⛰ Volcano ≈ River ◎ Lake ⊡ Reservoir

- 104 G7 **Vagos** Aveiro, N Portugal 40°33´N 08°42´W
- **Vágsellye** see Šal´a
- 92 H10 **Vågsfjorden** fjord N Norway
- 94 C10 **Vågsøy** island S Norway
- **Vágújhely** see Nové Mesto nad Váhom
- 111 I21 **Váh** Ger. Waag, Hung. Vág. ≈ W Slovakia
- 93 K16 **Vähäkyrö** Länsi-Suomi, W Finland 63°04´N 22°05´E
- 191 X11 **Vahitahi** atoll Îles Tuamotu, E French Polynesia
- **Váhtjer** see Gällivare
- **Vaidei** see Vulcan
- 22 L4 **Vaiden** Mississippi, S USA 33°19´N 89°42´W
- 155 I23 **Vaigai** ≈ SE India
- 191 V16 **Vaihu** Easter Island, Chile, E Pacific Ocean 27°10´S 109°22´W
- 118 I6 **Väike Emajõgi** ≈ S Estonia
- 118 I4 **Väike-Maarja** Klein-Marien. Lääne-Virumaa, NE Estonia 59°07´N 26°16´E
- **Väike-Salatsi** see Mazsalaca
- 37 R4 **Vail** Colorado, C USA 39°36´N 106°20´W
- 193 V15 **Vaina** Tongatapu, S Tonga 21°12´S 175°10´W
- 118 E5 **Väinameri** prev. Muhu Väin, Ger. Moon-Sund. sea E Baltic Sea
- 93 N18 **Vainikkala** Etelä-Suomi, SE Finland 60°54´N 28°18´E
- 118 D10 **Vaiņode** Liepāja, SW Latvia 56°25´N 21°52´E
- 155 H23 **Vaippār** ≈ SE India
- 191 W11 **Vairaatea** atoll Îles Tuamotu, C French Polynesia
- 191 R8 **Vairao** Tahiti, W French Polynesia 17°48´S 149°17´W
- 103 R14 **Vaison-la-Romaine** Vaucluse, SE France 44°15´N 05°04´E
- 190 G11 **Vaitupu** Île Uvea, E Wallis and Futuna 13°14´S 176°09´W
- 190 F7 **Vaitupu** atoll C Tuvalu
- **Vajdahunyad** see Hunedoara
- **Vajdej** see Vulcan
- 78 K12 **Vakaga** ◊ prefecture NE Central African Republic
- 114 H10 **Vakarel** Sofiya, W Bulgaria 42°35´N 23°42´E
- **Vakav** see Ustrem
- 137 O11 **Vakfıkebir** Trabzon, NE Turkey 41°03´N 39°19´E
- 122 J10 **Vakh** ≈ C Russian Federation
- **Vakhon, Qatorkühi** see Nicholas Range
- 147 P14 **Vakhsh** SW Tajikistan 37°46´N 68°48´E
- 147 Q12 **Vakhsh** ≈ SW Tajikistan
- 127 P1 **Vakhtan** Nizhegorodskaya Oblast´, W Russian Federation 58°00´N 46°43´E
- 94 C13 **Vaksdal** Hordaland, S Norway 60°29´N 05°45´E
- 125 O8 **Vaksha** ≈ NW Russian Federation
- **Valachia** see Wallachia
- 108 D11 **Valais** Ger. Wallis. ◊ canton SW Switzerland
- 113 M21 **Valamarës, Mali i** ▲ SE Albania 40°48´N 20°31´E
- 127 S2 **Valamaz** Udmurtskaya Respublika, NW Russian Federation 57°36´N 52°07´E
- 113 Q19 **Valandovo** ◊ FYR Macedonia 41°20´N 22°33´E
- 111 I18 **Valašské Meziříčí** Ger. Wallachisch-Meseritsch, Pol. Wałachische-Międzyrzecze. Zlínský Kraj, E Czech Republic 49°29´N 17°57´E
- 115 I17 **Valáxa** island Vóreies Sporádes, Greece, Aegean Sea
- 95 K16 **Vålberg** Värmland, C Sweden 59°24´N 13°12´E
- 116 H12 **Vâlcea** prev. Vîlcea. ◊ county SW Romania
- 63 J16 **Valcheta** Río Negro, E Argentina 40°42´S 66°08´W
- 15 P12 **Valcourt** Québec, SE Canada 45°28´N 72°18´W
- **Valdai Hills** see Valdayskaya Vozvyshennost´
- 124 M3 **Valdaia** ≈ N Spain
- 124 I15 **Valday** Novgorodskaya Oblast´, W Russian Federation 57°57´N 33°20´E
- 124 I15 **Valdayskaya Vozvyshennost´** var. Valdai Hills. hill range NW Russian Federation
- 105 L9 **Valdecañas, Embalse de** ▨ W Spain
- 118 E8 **Valdemārpils** Ger. Sassmacken. Talsi, NW Latvia 57°23´N 22°36´E
- 95 N18 **Valdemarsvik** Östergötland, S Sweden 58°13´N 16°35´E
- 105 N8 **Valdemoro** Madrid, C Spain 40°12´N 03°40´W
- 105 O11 **Valdepeñas** Castilla-La Mancha, C Spain 38°46´N 03°24´W
- 104 L5 **Valderaduey** ≈ NE Spain
- 104 L5 **Valderas** Castilla-León, N Spain 42°05´N 05°27´W
- 105 T7 **Valderrobres** var. Vall-de-roures. Aragón, NE Spain
- 63 K17 **Valdés, Península** peninsula SE Argentina
- 56 C5 **Valdez** var. Limones. Esmeraldas, NW Ecuador 01°13´N 79°00´W
- 39 S11 **Valdez** Alaska, USA 61°08´N 146°21´W
- 103 U11 **Val d'Isère** Savoie, E France 45°30´N 06°58´E
- 63 G15 **Valdivia** Los Lagos, C Chile 39°50´S 73°13´W
- **Valdivia Bank** see Valdivia Seamount
- 65 P10 **Valdivia Seamount** var. Valdivia Bank. undersea feature E Atlantic Ocean 26°15´S 06°25´E
- 103 N4 **Val-d'Oise** ◊ department N France
- 14 J8 **Val-d'Or** Québec, SE Canada 48°06´N 77°42´W
- 23 U8 **Valdosta** Georgia, SE USA 30°49´N 83°16´W
- 94 G13 **Valdres** physical region S Norway
- 32 L13 **Vale** Oregon, NW USA 43°59´N 117°15´W
- 116 F9 **Vale lui Mihai** Hung. Érmihályfalva. Bihor, NW Romania 47°31´N 22°08´E

- 11 N15 **Valemount** British Columbia, SW Canada 52°46´N 119°17´W
- 59 O17 **Valença** Bahia, E Brazil 13°22´S 39°06´W
- 104 F4 **Valença do Minho** Viana do Castelo, N Portugal 42°02´N 08°38´W
- 59 N14 **Valença do Piauí** Piauí, E Brazil 06°26´S 41°46´W
- 103 N8 **Valençay** Indre, C France 47°10´N 01°31´E
- 103 R13 **Valence** anc. Valentia, Valentia Julia, Ventia. Drôme, E France 44°56´N 04°54´E
- 105 S10 **País Valenciano** ◊ Spain
- 54 K5 **Valencia** Carabobo, N Venezuela 10°12´N 68°02´W
- 105 R10 **Valencia** Cat. València. ◊ province País Valenciano, E Spain
- 105 S10 **Valencia ✈** Valencia, E Spain
- 104 I10 **Valencia de Alcántara** Extremadura, W Spain 39°25´N 07°14´W
- 104 L4 **Valencia de Don Juan** Castilla-León, N Spain 42°17´N 05°31´W
- 105 U9 **Valencia, Golfo de** var. Gulf of Valencia. gulf E Spain
- **Valencia, Gulf of** see Valencia, Golfo de
- 97 A21 **Valencia Island** Ir. Dairbhre. island SW Ireland
- **Valencia/Valenciana** see País Valenciano
- 103 P2 **Valenciennes** Nord, N France 50°21´N 03°32´E
- 116 K13 **Valea lui Munte** Prahova, SE Romania 45°11´N 26°02´E
- **Valentia** see Valence
- **Valentia** see País Valenciano
- 103 T8 **Valentigney** Doubs, E France 47°27´N 06°49´E
- 28 M12 **Valentine** Nebraska, C USA 42°53´N 100°31´W
- 24 J10 **Valentine** Texas, SW USA 30°35´N 104°30´W
- **Valentine State** see Oregon
- 106 D8 **Valenza** Piemonte, NW Italy 45°01´N 08°37´E
- 94 I13 **Våler** Hedmark, S Norway 60°39´N 11°52´E
- 54 I12 **Valera** Trujillo, NW Venezuela 09°21´N 70°38´W
- 192 M11 **Valerie Guyot** undersea feature S Pacific Ocean 33°00´S 164°00´W
- 118 I7 **Valga** Ger. Walk, Latv. Valka. Valgamaa, S Estonia 57°48´N 26°04´E
- 118 I7 **Valgamaa** var. Valga Maakond. ◊ province S Estonia
- **Valga Maakond** see Valgamaa
- 43 Q15 **Valiente, Península** peninsula NW Panama
- 103 X16 **Valinco, Golfe de** gulf Corse, France, C Mediterranean Sea
- 112 L12 **Valjevo** Serbia, W Serbia 44°17´N 19°54´E
- **Valjok** see Válljohka
- 118 I7 **Valka** Ger. Walk. Valka, N Latvia 57°48´N 26°01´E
- 93 L18 **Valkeakoski** Länsi-Suomi, W Finland 61°17´N 24°05´E
- 93 M19 **Valkeala** Etelä-Suomi, S Finland 60°55´N 26°49´E
- 99 L15 **Valkenburg** Limburg, SE Netherlands 50°52´N 05°50´E
- 99 K15 **Valkenswaard** Noord-Brabant, S Netherlands 51°21´N 05°29´E
- 119 G15 **Valkininkai** Alytus, S Lithuania 54°22´N 24°51´E
- 117 U5 **Valky** Kharkivs'ka Oblast', E Ukraine 49°51´N 35°40´E
- 41 Y12 **Valladolid** Yucatán, SE Mexico 20°39´N 88°13´W
- 104 M5 **Valladolid** Castilla-León, NW Spain 41°39´N 04°45´W
- 104 L5 **Valladolid** ◊ province Castilla-León, N Spain
- 103 U15 **Vallauris** Alpes-Maritimes, SE France 43°34´N 07°07´E
- **Vall-de-roures** see Valderrobres
- **Vall D'Uxó** see La Vall d'Uixó
- 95 E16 **Valle** Aust-Agder, S Norway 59°13´N 07°33´E
- 105 N2 **Valle** Cantabria, N Spain 43°14´N 04°16´W
- 42 H8 **Valle** ◊ department S Honduras
- 104 L12 **Vallecas** Madrid, C Spain 61°07´N 14°30´E
- 37 Q8 **Vallecito Reservoir** ▨ Colorado, C USA
- 106 A7 **Valle d'Aosta** ◊ region NW Italy
- 41 O14 **Valle de Bravo** México, S Mexico 19°09´N 100°08´W
- 54 I7 **Valle de Guanape** Anzoátegui, N Venezuela 09°54´N 65°41´W
- 54 M6 **Valle de La Pascua** Guárico, N Venezuela 09°15´N 66°00´W
- 54 E10 **Valle del Cauca** off. Departamento del Valle del Cauca. ◊ province W Colombia
- **Valle del Cauca, Departamento del** see Valle del Cauca
- 41 N13 **Valle de Santiago** Guanajuato, C Mexico
- 40 J7 **Valle de Zaragoza** Chihuahua, N Mexico 27°25´N 105°50´W
- 54 G5 **Valledupar** Cesar, N Colombia 10°31´N 73°16´W
- 76 G10 **Vallée de Ferlo** ≈ NW Senegal
- 57 M19 **Vallegrande** Santa Cruz, C Bolivia 18°30´S 64°06´W
- 41 N9 **Valle Hermoso** Tamaulipas, C Mexico 25°39´N 97°49´W
- 35 N8 **Vallejo** California, W USA 38°08´N 122°16´W
- 62 G11 **Vallenar** Atacama, N Chile 28°35´S 70°44´W
- 95 O15 **Vallentuna** Stockholm, C Sweden 59°32´N 18°04´E
- 121 P16 **Valletta** prev. Valetta. ● (Malta) E Malta 35°54´N 14°31´E

- 27 N6 **Valley Center** Kansas, C USA 37°49´N 97°22´W
- 29 Q5 **Valley City** North Dakota, N USA 46°57´N 97°58´W
- 32 I15 **Valley Falls** Oregon, NW USA 42°28´N 120°16´W
- **Valleyfield** see Salaberry-de-Valleyfield
- 21 S4 **Valley Head** West Virginia, NE USA 38°33´N 80°01´W
- 25 T8 **Valley Mills** Texas, SW USA 31°36´N 97°27´W
- 75 W10 **Valley of the Kings** ancient monument E Egypt
- 29 R11 **Valley Springs** South Dakota, N USA
- 20 K5 **Valley Station** Kentucky, S USA 38°06´N 85°52´W
- 11 O13 **Valleyview** Alberta, W Canada 55°02´N 117°17´W
- 25 T5 **Valley View** Texas, SW USA 33°29´N 97°09´W
- 61 C21 **Vallimanca, Arroyo** ≈ E Argentina
- 92 L9 **Válljohka** var. Valjok. Finnmark, N Norway 69°42´N 25°52´E
- 107 M19 **Vallo della Lucania** Campania, S Italy 40°13´N 15°15´E
- 108 B9 **Vallorbe** Vaud, W Switzerland 46°43´N 06°21´E
- 105 V6 **Valls** Cataluña, NE Spain 41°18´N 01°15´E
- 94 N11 **Vallsta** Gävleborg, C Sweden 61°30´N 16°25´E
- 94 N12 **Vallvik** Gävleborg, C Sweden 61°10´N 17°15´E
- 11 T17 **Val Marie** Saskatchewan, S Canada 49°15´N 107°44´W
- 118 H7 **Valmiera** Est. Volmari, Ger. Wolmar. Valmiera, N Latvia 57°34´N 25°26´E
- 105 N3 **Valnera** ▲ N Spain 43°08´N 03°39´W
- 102 J3 **Valognes** Manche, N France 49°31´N 01°28´W
- 104 G6 **Valonga** var. Valongo de Gaia. Porto, N Portugal 41°11´N 08°30´W
- **Valongo de Gaia** see Valonga
- 104 M5 **Valoria la Buena** Castilla-León, N Spain 41°48´N 04°33´W
- 119 J15 **Valozhyn** Pol. Wołożyn, Rus. Volozhin. Minskaya Voblasts', C Belarus 54°05´N 26°32´E
- 104 I5 **Valpaços** Vila Real, N Portugal 41°36´N 07°17´W
- 62 G11 **Valparaíso** Valparaíso, C Chile 33°05´S 71°18´W
- 40 J11 **Valparaíso** Zacatecas, C Mexico 22°49´N 103°28´W
- 31 N11 **Valparaiso** Florida, SE USA 30°30´N 86°28´W
- 31 N11 **Valparaiso** Indiana, N USA 41°28´N 87°04´W
- 62 G11 **Valparaíso** off. Región de Valparaíso. ◊ region C Chile
- **Valparaíso, Región de** see Valparaíso
- **Valpo** see Valpovo
- 112 I9 **Valpovo** Valpo. Osijek-Baranja, E Croatia 45°40´N 18°25´E
- 112 I9 **Valpovo** Valpo
- 154 D12 **Valsad** prev. Bulsar. Gujarāt, W India 20°40´N 72°55´E
- **Valsbaai** see False Bay
- 171 T12 **Valse Pisang, Kepulauan** island group E Indonesia
- 108 H9 **Vals-Platz** var. Vals. Graubünden, S Switzerland
- 171 X16 **Vals, Tanjung** headland Papua, SE Indonesia 08°26´S 137°35´E
- 115 N15 **Valtimo** Itä-Suomi, E Finland 63°39´N 28°49´E
- 113 O17 **Valtou** ▲ C Greece
- 127 O12 **Valuyevka** Rostovskaya Oblast', SW Russian Federation 46°48´N 43°49´E
- 126 K9 **Valuyki** Belgorodskaya Oblast', W Russian Federation 50°11´N 38°07´E
- 103 U15 **Vallauris** Alpes-Maritimes, SE France 43°34´N 07°07´E
- 36 L2 **Val Verda** Utah, W USA 40°51´N 111°53´W
- 64 **Valverde** Hierro, Islas Canarias, Spain, NE Atlantic Ocean 27°48´N 17°55´W
- 32 J9 **Vantage** Washington, NW USA 46°56´N 119°55´W
- 187 Z14 **Vanua Balavu** prev. Vanua Mbalavu. island Lau Group, E Fiji
- 187 Q13 **Vanua Lava** island Banks Islands, N Vanuatu
- 187 Y13 **Vanua Levu** island N Fiji
- 187 R12 **Vanuatu** off. Republic of Vanuatu; prev. New Hebrides. ◆ republic SW Pacific Ocean
- 175 P8 **Vanuatu** island group SW Pacific Ocean
- **Vanuatu, Republic of** see Vanuatu
- 31 Q12 **Van Wert** Ohio, N USA 40°52´N 84°34´W
- 137 T14 **Van** prev. E Turkey
- 187 Q17 **Vao** Province Sud, S New Caledonia 22°40´S 167°29´E
- 117 N7 **Vapnyarka** Vinnyts'ka Oblast', C Ukraine 48°31´N 28°43´E
- 104 H13 **Vascão, Ribeira de** ≈ S Portugal
- 116 F10 **Vaşcău** Hung. Vaskoh. Bihor, NE Romania 46°28´N 22°32´E
- **Vască** see Vittangi
- 143 V13 **Vazhgort** var. Chasovo. Respublika Komi, NW Russian Federation 64°06´N 46°44´E
- 118 B9 **V. C. Bird ✈** (St. John's) Antigua, Antigua and Barbuda 17°07´N 61°49´W
- 124 C16 **Vecht** Ger. Vechte. ≈ Germany/Netherlands see also Vechte
- 100 J10 **Vecht** see Vechte
- 100 I11 **Vechta** Niedersachsen, NW Germany 52°43´N 08°16´E
- 100 E12 **Vechte** Dut. Vecht. ≈ Germany/Netherlands see also Vecht
- **Vechte** see Vecht
- 118 I8 **Vecpiebalga** Cēsis, C Latvia 57°03´N 25°47´E
- 118 F9 **Vecumnieki** Bauska, C Latvia 56°36´N 24°31´E

- 32 G11 **Vancouver** Washington, NW USA 45°38´N 122°39´W
- 10 L17 **Vancouver ✈** British Columbia, SW Canada 49°03´N 123°00´W
- 10 **Vancouver Island** island British Columbia, SW Canada
- **Vanda** see Vantaa
- 171 X13 **Van Daalen** ≈ Papua, E Indonesia
- 30 L15 **Vandalia** Illinois, N USA 38°57´N 89°05´W
- 27 V3 **Vandalia** Missouri, C USA 39°18´N 91°29´W
- 31 R13 **Vandalia** Ohio, N USA 39°53´N 84°12´W
- 25 U13 **Vanderbilt** Texas, SW USA 28°45´N 96°37´W
- 31 Q10 **Vandercook Lake** Michigan, N USA 42°11´N 84°23´W
- 10 L14 **Vanderhoof** British Columbia, SW Canada 53°54´N 124°00´W
- 181 P1 **Vanderlin Island** island Sir Edward Pellew Group, Northern Territory, N Australia
- **Van Diemen Gulf** gulf Northern Territory, N Australia
- **Van Diemen's Land** see Tasmania
- 18 H5 **Vanderwhacker Mountain** ▲ New York, NE USA 43°54´N 74°07´W
- 98 I12 **Vandsburg** see Więcbork
- 95 F23 **Varde** Ribe, W Denmark 55°38´N 08°29´E
- 137 V12 **Vardenis** E Armenia 40°11´N 45°43´E
- 92 N8 **Vardø** Fin. Vuoreija. Finnmark, N Norway 70°22´N 31°06´E
- 115 D18 **Vardoúsia** ▲ C Greece 42°07´N 14°43´E
- **Vareia** see Logroño
- 100 J10 **Varel** Niedersachsen, NW Germany 53°24´N 08°07´E
- 119 G15 **Varėna** Pol. Orany. Alytus, S Lithuania 54°13´N 24°35´E
- 103 P10 **Varennes-sur-Allier** Allier, C France 46°17´N 03°24´E
- 112 I12 **Vareš** Federacija Bosna I Hercegovina, E Bosnia and Herzegovina 44°12´N 18°19´E
- 106 D7 **Varese** Lombardia, N Italy 45°49´N 08°50´E
- 95 J18 **Vårförö Moldoveanu** var. Moldoveanul; prev. Vîrful Moldoveanu. ▲ C Romania 45°35´N 24°48´E
- 95 J18 **Vårgårda** Västra Götaland, S Sweden 58°00´N 12°49´E
- 54 L4 **Vargas** ◊ state N Venezuela
- 95 C17 **Varhaug** Rogaland, S Norway 58°37´N 05°39´E
- 95 N17 **Varkaus** Itä-Suomi, C Finland 62°20´N 27°50´E
- 114 N8 **Varna** prev. Stalin; anc. Odessus. Varna, E Bulgaria 43°14´N 27°56´E
- 114 N8 **Varna** ◊ province E Bulgaria
- 114 N8 **Varna ✕** Varna, E Bulgaria 43°16´N 27°52´E
- 95 L20 **Varnamo** Jönköping, S Sweden 57°11´N 14°03´E
- 114 N8 **Varnenski Zaliv** prev. Stalinski Zaliv. bay E Bulgaria
- 114 N8 **Varnensko Ezero** estuary E Bulgaria
- 118 D11 **Varniai** Telšiai, W Lithuania 55°45´N 22°22´E
- 98 J11 **Varnsdorf** Ger. Warnsdorf. Ústecký Kraj, NW Czech Republic 50°57´N 14°35´E
- 54 I14 **Vaupés** off. Comisaría del Vaupés. ◊ province SE Colombia
- **Vaupés, Comisaría del** see Vaupés
- 54 J13 **Vaupés, Río** var. Rio Uaupés. ≈ Brazil/Colombia see also Uaupés, Rio
- **Vaupés, Rio** see Uaupés, Rio
- 103 T13 **Vauvert** Gard, S France 43°42´N 04°16´E
- 99 K23 **Vaux-sur-Sûre** Luxembourg, SE Belgium 49°55´N 05°34´E
- 172 J4 **Vavatenina** Toamasina, E Madagascar 17°28´S 49°11´E
- 193 Y14 **Vava'u Group** island group N Tonga
- 76 M16 **Vavoua** W Ivory Coast 07°23´N 06°29´W
- 155 K23 **Vavuniya** Northern Province, N Sri Lanka 08°45´N 80°30´E
- 119 G17 **Vawkavysk Pol.** Wołkowysk, Rus. Volkovysk. Hrodzyenskaya Voblasts', W Belarus 53°10´N 24°28´E
- 119 F19 **Vawkavyskaya Wzvyshsha** Rus. Volkovyskiye Vysoty. hill range W Belarus
- 95 P15 **Vaxholm** Stockholm, C Sweden 59°25´N 18°21´E
- 95 L21 **Växjö** var. Vexiö. Kronoberg, S Sweden 56°52´N 14°50´E
- 125 T1 **Vaygach, Ostrov** island NW Russian Federation
- 137 V13 **Vayk'** prev. Azizbekov. S Armenia 39°41´N 45°28´E
- 128 L3 **Vaygach** island NW Russian Federation

- 118 M15 **Varano, Lago di** ⊚ SE Italy
- 118 J13 **Varapayeva Rus.** Voropayevo. Vitsyebskaya Voblasts', NW Belarus 55°09´N 27°13´E
- 112 E7 **Varaždin** Ger. Warasdin, Hung. Varasd. Varaždin, N Croatia 46°18´N 16°21´E
- 112 E7 **Varaždin** off. Varaždinska Županija. ◊ province N Croatia
- 106 C7 **Varazze** Liguria, NW Italy 44°21´N 08°35´E
- 95 J20 **Varberg** Halland, S Sweden 57°06´N 12°15´E
- 149 P7 **Vardak Pash.** var. Wardak, Pash. Wardag. ◊ province E Afghanistan
- 113 P20 **Vardar Gk.** Axiós. ≈ FYR Macedonia/Greece see also Axiós
- **Vardar** see Axiós
- 112 J12 **Varzzin** ...
- 122 I11 **Vasyugan** ≈ C Russian Federation
- 103 N8 **Vatan** Indre, C France 47°06´N 01°49´E
- **Vaté** see Efate
- 105 C18 **Vathy** prev. Itháki. Itháki, Iónia Nisiá, Greece, C Mediterranean Sea 38°22´N 20°43´E
- 92 G15 **Vatican City** off. ● papal state S Europe. Vatican City see Vatican City
- 107 M22 **Vaticano, Capo** headland S Italy 38°37´N 15°49´E
- 92 K3 **Vatnajökull** glacier SE Iceland
- 95 P15 **Vätö** Stockholm, C Sweden 59°48´N 18°55´E
- 187 Z16 **Vatoa** island Lau Group, SE Fiji
- 172 J5 **Vatomandry** Toamasina, E Madagascar 19°22´S 48°59´E
- 116 J9 **Vatra Dornei** Ger. Dorna Watra. Suceava, NE Romania 47°20´N 25°22´E
- 116 J9 **Vatra Moldoviței** Suceava, NE Romania 47°37´N 25°36´E
- 95 L18 **Vättern** Eng. Lake Vetter. ⊚ S Sweden
- 187 X5 **Vatulele** island SW Fiji
- 187 P7 **Vatutine** Cherkas'ka Oblast', C Ukraine 49°01´N 31°04´E
- 187 W15 **Vatu Vara** island Lau Group, E Fiji
- 103 R14 **Vaucluse** ◊ department SE France
- 103 S5 **Vaucouleurs** Meuse, NE France 48°37´N 05°38´E
- 108 B9 **Vaud** Ger. Waadt. ◊ canton SW Switzerland
- 15 N12 **Vaudreuil** Québec, SE Canada 45°24´N 74°01´W
- 37 T12 **Vaughn** New Mexico, SW USA 34°36´N 105°12´W
- **Vaupés, Río** var. Rio Uaupés. ≈ Brazil/Colombia
- 103 R14 **Vaucluse** ≈ SE France
- 113 M20 **Veleshta** ▲ SW FYR Macedonia 41°16´N 20°37´E
- 115 F16 **Velestíno** prev. Velestínon. Thessalía, C Greece 39°23´N 22°45´E
- **Velestínon** see Velestíno
- **Velevshchina** see Vyelyevshchyna
- 54 F9 **Vélez** Santander, C Colombia 06°02´N 73°43´W
- 104 M17 **Vélez de la Gomera, Peñon de** island group S Spain
- 105 N15 **Vélez-Málaga** Andalucía, S Spain 36°47´N 04°06´W
- 105 Q13 **Vélez Rubio** Andalucía, S Spain 37°39´N 02°05´W
- **Velha Goa** see Goa
- **Velho** see Porto Velho
- 112 E8 **Velika Gorica** Zagreb, N Croatia 45°43´N 16°03´E
- 112 C9 **Velika Kapela** ▲ NW Croatia
- **Velika Kikinda** see Kikinda
- 112 D10 **Velika Kladuša** Federacija Bosna I Hercegovina, NW Bosnia and Herzegovina 45°11´N 15°48´E
- 112 N11 **Velika Morava** var. Glavn'a Morava, Morava, Ger. Grosse Morava. ≈ C Serbia
- 112 L12 **Velika Plana** Serbia, C Serbia 44°20´N 21°01´E
- 109 U10 **Velika Raduha** ▲ N Slovenia 46°23´N 14°46´E
- 123 V7 **Velikaya** ≈ NE Russian Federation
- 124 F15 **Velikaya** ≈ W Russian Federation
- **Velikaya Berestovitsa** see Vyalikaya Byerastavitsa
- **Velikaya Lepetikha** see Velyka Lepetykha
- **Veliki Bečkerek** see Zrenjanin
- 112 P12 **Veliki Krš** var. Stol. ▲ E Serbia 44°10´N 22°09´E
- 114 L8 **Veliki Preslav** prev. Preslav. Shumen, NE Bulgaria 43°09´N 26°50´E
- 112 B9 **Veliki Risnjak** ▲
- 109 T13 **Veliki Snežnik** Ger. Schneeberg, It. Monte Nevoso. ▲ SW Slovenia 45°34´N 14°26´E
- 112 J13 **Veliki Stolac** ▲ E Bosnia and Herzegovina 43°53´N 19°15´E
- 116 G16 **Velikiye Luki** Pskovskaya Oblast', W Russian Federation
- 124 H14 **Velikiy Novgorod** prev. Novgorod. Novgorodskaya Oblast', W Russian Federation 58°32´N 31°15´E
- 125 P12 **Velikiy Ustyug** Vologodskaya Oblast', NW Russian Federation 60°46´N 46°18´E
- 112 N11 **Veliko Gradište** Serbia, NE Serbia 44°46´N 21°28´E
- 155 I18 **Velikonda Range** ▲ SE India

- 116 M10 **Vaskoh** see Vaşcău
- **Vaskohsziklás** see Ştei
- 116 M10 **Vaslui** Vaslui, C Romania 46°38´N 27°44´E
- 116 L11 **Vaslui** ◊ county NE Romania
- **Vas Megye** see Vas
- 31 R9 **Vassar** Michigan, N USA 43°22´N 83°34´W
- 95 E15 **Vassdalsegga** ▲ S Norway 59°47´N 07°07´E
- 60 P9 **Vassouras** Rio de Janeiro, SE Brazil 22°24´S 43°30´W
- 95 K12 **Västerås** Västmanland, C Sweden 59°37´N 16°33´E
- 93 G15 **Västerbotten** ◊ county N Sweden
- 94 K12 **Västerdalälven** ≈ C Sweden
- 95 O16 **Västerhaninge** Stockholm, C Sweden 59°07´N 18°06´E
- 95 M10 **Västernorrland** ◊ county N Sweden
- 95 N19 **Västervik** Kalmar, S Sweden 57°44´N 16°40´E
- 95 M15 **Västmanland** ◊ county C Sweden
- 107 L15 **Vasto** anc. Histonium. Abruzzo, C Italy 42°07´N 14°43´E
- 95 J19 **Västra Götaland** ◊ county S Sweden
- 95 J16 **Västra Silen** ⊚ S Sweden
- 111 G23 **Vasvár** Ger. Eisenburg. Vas, W Hungary 47°03´N 16°49´E
- 117 V9 **Vasylivka** Zaporiz'ka Oblast', SE Ukraine 47°26´N 35°18´E
- 117 O5 **Vasyl'kiv** var. Vasil'kov. Kyyivs'ka Oblast', N Ukraine 50°12´N 30°18´E
- 122 I11 **Vasyugan** ≈ C Russian Federation
- 103 N8 **Vatan** Indre, C France 47°06´N 01°49´E
- 95 F23 **Vejen** Ribe, W Denmark 55°29´N 09°13´E
- 104 K16 **Vejer de la Frontera** Andalucía, S Spain 36°15´N 05°58´W
- 95 G23 **Vejle** Vejle, C Denmark 55°43´N 09°33´E
- 95 F23 **Vejle** var. Vejle Amt. ◊ county C Denmark
- **Vejle Amt** see Vejle
- 114 M7 **Vekilski** Shumen, NE Bulgaria 43°33´N 27°19´E
- 54 G3 **Vela, Cabo de la** headland N Colombia 12°14´N 72°13´W
- **Vela Goa** see Goa
- 113 F15 **Vela Luka** Dubrovnik-Neretva, S Croatia 42°57´N 16°43´E
- 61 G19 **Velázquez** Rocha, E Uruguay 34°05´S 54°16´W
- 101 E15 **Velbert** Nordrhein-Westfalen, W Germany 51°22´N 07°03´E
- 109 S9 **Velden** Kärnten, S Austria 46°37´N 13°59´E
- **Velden** see Bled
- 99 K15 **Veldhoven** Noord-Brabant, S Netherlands 51°24´N 05°24´E
- 112 C11 **Velebit** ▲ C Croatia
- 114 N11 **Velele** ▲ SE Bulgaria
- 109 V10 **Velenje Ger.** Wöllan. N Slovenia 46°22´N 15°07´E
- 190 E12 **Vele, Pointe** headland Île Futuna, S Wallis and Futuna
- 113 O18 **Veles Turk.** Köprülü. C FYR Macedonia 41°43´N 21°49´E
- 113 M20 **Veleshta** ▲ SW FYR Macedonia 41°16´N 20°37´E

- 95 J20 **Veddige** Halland, S Sweden 57°16´N 12°19´E
- 116 J15 **Vedea** ≈ S Romania
- 127 P16 **Vedeno** Chechenskaya Respublika, SW Russian Federation 42°57´N 46°02´E
- 95 C16 **Vedvågen** Rogaland, S Norway 59°18´N 05°13´E
- 98 O6 **Veendam** Groningen, NE Netherlands 53°05´N 06°53´E
- 98 K12 **Veenendaal** Utrecht, C Netherlands 52°03´N 05°33´E
- 99 E14 **Veere** Zeeland, SW Netherlands 51°33´N 03°40´E
- 24 M2 **Vega** Texas, SW USA 35°14´N 102°26´W
- 92 F13 **Vega** island C Norway
- 45 T5 **Vega Baja** C Puerto Rico
- 38 D17 **Vega Point** headland Kiska Island, Alaska, USA 51°49´N 177°19´E
- 95 F17 **Vegår** ⊚ S Norway
- 99 K14 **Veghel** Noord-Brabant, S Netherlands 51°37´N 05°33´E
- 109 S9 **Veglia** see Krk
- 114 E13 **Vegoritída, Límni** var. Límni Vegorítis. N Greece
- **Vegorítis, Límni** see Vegoritída, Límni
- 11 Q14 **Vegreville** Alberta, SW Canada 53°30´N 112°02´W
- 95 K21 **Veinge** Halland, S Sweden 56°33´N 13°04´E
- 61 B21 **Veinticinco de Mayo** var. 25 de Mayo. Buenos Aires, E Argentina 35°27´S 60°11´W
- 63 I14 **Veinticinco de Mayo** La Pampa, C Argentina 37°45´S 67°40´W
- 119 F15 **Veisiejai** Alytus, S Lithuania 54°06´N 23°42´E
- 95 F23 **Vejen** Ribe, W Denmark 55°29´N 09°13´E
- 104 K16 **Vejer de la Frontera** Andalucía, S Spain
- 95 G23 **Vejle** Vejle, C Denmark 55°43´N 09°33´E

VELIKO TŬRNOVO – VILA MARECHAL CARMONA

114 K9 **Veliko Tŭrnovo** *prev.* Tirnovo, Trnovo, Tŭrnovo. Veliko Tŭrnovo, N Bulgaria 43°05´N 25°40´E
114 K8 **Veliko Tŭrnovo** ⬖ *province* N Bulgaria
Velikovec *see* Völkermarkt
125 R5 **Velikovisochnoye** Nenetskiy Avtonomnyy Okrug, NW Russian Federation 67°13´N 52°00´E
76 H12 **Vélingara** C Senegal 15°00´N 14°39´W
76 H11 **Vélingara** S Senegal 13°12´N 14°05´W
114 H11 **Velingrad** Pazardzhik, C Bulgaria 42°01´N 24°00´E
126 H3 **Velizh** Smolenskaya Oblast', W Russian Federation 55°30´N 31°06´E
111 F16 **Velká Deštná** *var.* Deštná, Grosskoppe, *Ger.* Deschnaer Koppe. ▲ NE Czech Republic 50°18´N 16°25´E
111 F18 **Velké Meziříčí** *Ger.* Grossmeseritsch. Vysočina, C Czech Republic 49°22´N 16°02´E
92 N1 **Velkomstpynten** *headland* NW Svalbard 79°51´N 11°37´E
111 K21 **Veľký Krtíš** Banskobystrický Kraj, C Slovakia 48°13´N 19°21´E
186 J8 **Vella Lavella** *var.* Mbilua. *island* New Georgia Islands, NW Solomon Islands
107 I15 **Velletri** Lazio, C Italy 41°41´N 12°47´E
95 K23 **Vellinge** Skåne, S Sweden 55°29´N 13°00´E
155 I19 **Vellore** Tamil Nādu, SE India 12°56´N 79°09´E
Velobriga *see* Viana do Castelo
115 G21 **Velopoúla** *island* S Greece
98 M12 **Velp** Gelderland, SE Netherlands 52°00´N 05°59´E
Velsen *see* Velsen-Noord
98 H9 **Velsen-Noord** *var.* Velsen. Noord-Holland, W Netherlands 52°27´N 04°40´E
125 N12 **Vel'sk** *var.* Velsk. Arkhangel'skaya Oblast', NW Russian Federation 61°03´N 42°01´E
Velsuna *see* Orvieto
98 K10 **Veluwemeer** *lake channel* C Netherlands
28 M3 **Velva** North Dakota, N USA 48°03´N 100°55´W
Velvendos/Velvendós *see* Velventós
115 E14 **Velventós** *var.* Velvendos, Velvendós. Dytikí Makedonía, N Greece 40°15´N 22°04´E
117 S5 **Velyka Bahachka** Poltavs'ka Oblast', C Ukraine 49°46´N 33°44´E
117 S9 **Velyka Lepetykha** *Rus.* Velikaya Lepetikha. Khersons'ka Oblast', S Ukraine 47°09´N 33°59´E
117 O10 **Velyka Mykhaylivka** Odes'ka Oblast', SW Ukraine 47°07´N 29°49´E
117 W8 **Velyka Novosilka** Donets'ka Oblast', E Ukraine 47°49´N 36°49´E
117 S9 **Velyka Oleksandrivka** Khersons'ka Oblast', S Ukraine 47°17´N 33°16´E
117 T4 **Velyka Pysarivka** Sums'ka Oblast', NE Ukraine 50°25´N 35°28´E
116 G6 **Velykyy Bereznyy** Zakarpats'ka Oblast', W Ukraine 48°54´N 22°27´E
117 W4 **Velykyy Burluk** Kharkivs'ka Oblast', E Ukraine 50°04´N 37°25´E
Velykyy Tokmak *see* Tokmak
173 P7 **Vema Fracture Zone** *tectonic feature* W Indian Ocean
65 P18 **Vema Seamount** *undersea feature* SW Indian Ocean 31°38´S 08°19´E
93 F17 **Vemdalen** Jämtland, C Sweden 62°26´N 13°50´E
95 N19 **Vena** Kalmar, S Sweden 57°31´N 16°00´E
41 N11 **Venado** San Luis Potosí, C Mexico 22°56´N 101°05´W
62 L11 **Venado Tuerto** Entre Ríos, E Argentina 33°45´S 61°56´W
61 A19 **Venado Tuerto** Santa Fe, C Argentina 33°46´S 61°57´W
107 K16 **Venafro** Molise, C Italy 41°28´N 14°03´E
55 Q9 **Venamo, Cerro** ▲ E Venezuela 05°56´N 61°25´W
106 B8 **Venaria** Piemonte, NW Italy 45°09´N 07°40´E
103 U15 **Vence** Alpes-Maritimes, SE France 43°45´N 07°07´E
104 H5 **Venda Nova** Vila Real, N Portugal 41°40´N 07°58´W
104 G11 **Vendas Novas** Évora, S Portugal 38°41´N 08°27´W
102 J9 **Vendée** ⬖ *department* NW France
103 Q6 **Vendeuvre-sur-Barse** Aube, NE France 48°08´N 04°17´E
102 M7 **Vendôme** Loir-et-Cher, C France 47°48´N 01°04´E
Venedig *see* Venezia
Vener, Lake *see* Vänern
106 I8 **Veneta, Laguna** *lagoon* NE Italy
Venetia *see* Venezia
39 S7 **Venetie** Alaska, USA 67°00´N 146°25´W
106 H8 **Veneto** *var.* Venezia Euganea. ⬖ *region* NE Italy
114 M7 **Venets** Shumen, NE Bulgaria 43°33´N 26°56´E
126 L5 **Venev** Tul'skaya Oblast', W Russian Federation 54°18´N 38°16´E
106 I8 **Venezia** *Eng.* Venice, *Fr.* Venise, *Ger.* Venedig; *anc.* Venetia. Veneto, NE Italy 45°26´N 12°20´E
Venezia Euganea *see* Veneto
Venezia, Golfo di *see* Venice, Gulf of
Venezia Tridentina *see* Trentino-Alto Adige
54 K8 **Venezuela** *off.* Republic of Venezuela; *prev.* Estados Unidos de Venezuela, United States of Venezuela. ◆ *republic* N South America
Venezuela, Cordillera de *see* Costa, Cordillera de la
Venezuela, Estados Unidos de *see* Venezuela
54 I4 **Venezuela, Golfo de** *Eng.* Gulf of Maracaibo, Gulf of Venezuela. *gulf* NW Venezuela
Venezuela, Gulf of *see* Venezuela, Golfo de
64 F11 **Venezuelan Basin** *undersea feature* E Caribbean Sea
Venezuela, Republic of *see* Venezuela
Venezuela, United States of *see* Venezuela
155 D16 **Vengurla** Mahārāshtra, W India 15°55´N 73°39´E
39 O15 **Veniaminof, Mount** ▲ Alaska, USA 56°12´N 159°24´W
23 V14 **Venice** Florida, SE USA 27°06´N 82°27´W
22 L10 **Venice** Louisiana, S USA 29°15´N 89°20´W
Venice *see* Venezia
106 J8 **Venice, Gulf of** *It.* Golfo di Venezia, *Slvn.* Beneški Zaliv. *gulf* N Adriatic Sea
Venise *see* Venezia
94 K13 **Venjan** Dalarna, C Sweden 60°58´N 13°55´E
94 K13 **Venjansjön** ◎ C Sweden
155 J18 **Venkatagiri** Andhra Pradesh, E India 14°00´N 79°39´E
99 M15 **Venlo** *prev.* Venloo. Limburg, SE Netherlands 51°22´N 06°11´E
Venloo *see* Venlo
95 E18 **Vennesla** Vest-Agder, S Norway 58°15´N 08°00´E
107 M17 **Venosa** *anc.* Venusia. Basilicata, S Italy 40°57´N 15°49´E
Venoste, Alpi *see* Ötztaler Alpen
Venraij *see* Venray
99 M14 **Venray** *var.* Venraij. Limburg, SE Netherlands 51°32´N 05°59´E
118 C8 **Venta** *Ger.* Windau. ⤳ Latvia/Lithuania
Venta Belgarum *see* Winchester
40 G9 **Ventana, Punta Arena de la** *var.* Punta de la Ventana. *headland* NW Mexico 24°03´N 109°49´W
Ventana, Punta de la *see* Ventana, Punta Arena de la
61 B23 **Ventana, Sierra de la** *hill range* E Argentina
Ventia *see* Valence
191 S11 **Vent, Îles du** *var.* Windward Islands. *island group* Archipel de la Société, W French Polynesia
191 R10 **Vent, Îles Sous le** *var.* Leeward Islands. *island group* Archipel de la Société, W French Polynesia
106 B11 **Ventimiglia** Liguria, NW Italy 43°47´N 07°37´E
97 M24 **Ventnor** S England, United Kingdom 50°36´N 01°11´W
18 J17 **Ventnor City** New Jersey, NE USA 39°19´N 74°27´W
103 S14 **Ventoux, Mont** ▲ SE France 44°12´N 05°21´E
118 C8 **Ventspils** *Ger.* Windau. Ventspils, NW Latvia 57°22´N 21°34´E
54 M10 **Ventuari, Río** ⤳ S Venezuela
35 R15 **Ventura** California, W USA 34°15´N 119°18´W
182 F8 **Venus Bay** South Australia 33°15´S 134°42´E
Venusia *see* Venosa
191 P7 **Vénus, Pointe** *var.* Pointe Tataaihoa. *headland* Tahiti, W French Polynesia 17°28´S 149°29´W
41 V16 **Venustiano Carranza** Chiapas, SE Mexico 16°21´N 92°33´W
41 N7 **Venustiano Carranza, Presa** ⊠ NE Mexico
61 B15 **Vera** Santa Fe, C Argentina 29°28´S 60°10´W
105 Q14 **Vera** Andalucía, S Spain 37°15´N 01°51´W
63 K18 **Vera, Bahía** *bay* E Argentina
41 R14 **Veracruz** *var.* Veracruz Llave. Veracruz-Llave, E Mexico 19°10´N 96°09´W
Veracruz *see* Veracruz-Llave
41 Q13 **Veracruz-Llave** *var.* Veracruz. ⬖ *state* E Mexico
Veracruz Llave *see* Veracruz
43 Q16 **Veraguas** *off.* Provincia de Veraguas. ⬖ *province* W Panama
Veraguas, Provincia de *see* Veraguas
Veramin *see* Varāmīn
154 B12 **Verāval** Gujarāt, W India 20°54´N 70°22´E
106 C6 **Verbania** Piemonte, NW Italy 45°56´N 08°34´E
107 N20 **Verbicaro** Calabria, SW Italy 39°44´N 15°51´E
108 D11 **Verbier** Valais, SW Switzerland 46°06´N 07°14´E
Vercellae *see* Vercelli
106 C8 **Vercelli** *anc.* Vercellae. Piemonte, NW Italy 45°19´N 08°25´E
103 S13 **Vercors** *physical region* E France
Verdal *see* Verdalsøra
93 E16 **Verdalsøra** *var.* Verdal. Nord-Trøndelag, C Norway 63°47´N 11°27´E
Verde, Cabo *see* Cape Verde
44 J5 **Verde, Cape** *headland* Long Island, C Bahamas 22°51´N 75°50´W
104 M2 **Verde, Costa** *coastal region* N Spain
Verde Grande, Río/Verde Grande y de Belem, Río *see* Verde, Río
100 H11 **Verden** Niedersachsen, NW Germany 52°55´N 09°14´E
57 P16 **Verde, Río** ⤳ Bolivia/Brazil
59 J19 **Verde, Río** ⤳ SE Brazil
40 M12 **Verde, Río** *var.* Río Verde Grande, Río Verde Grande y de Belem. ⤳ C Mexico
41 Q16 **Verde, Río** ⤳ SE Mexico
36 L13 **Verde River** ⤳ Arizona, SW USA
Verdhikoúsa/Verdhikoússa *see* Verdikoússa
27 Q8 **Verdigris River** ⤳ Kansas/Oklahoma, C USA
115 E15 **Verdikoússa** *var.* Verdhikoúsa, Verdhikoússa. Thessalía, C Greece 39°47´N 21°59´E
103 S15 **Verdon** ⤳ SE France
15 O12 **Verdun** Québec, SE Canada 45°27´N 73°36´W
103 S4 **Verdun** *var.* Verdun-sur-Meuse; *anc.* Verodunum. Meuse, NE France 49°09´N 05°25´E
Verdun-sur-Meuse *see* Verdun
83 J21 **Vereeniging** Gauteng, NE South Africa 26°41´S 27°56´E
Veremeyki *see* Vyeramyeyki
125 T14 **Vereshchagino** Permskaya Oblast', NW Russian Federation 58°06´N 54°38´E
76 G14 **Verga, Cap** *headland* W Guinea 10°12´N 14°27´W
61 G18 **Vergara** Treinta y Tres, E Uruguay 32°58´S 53°54´W
108 G11 **Vergeletto** Ticino, S Switzerland 46°13´N 08°34´E
18 L8 **Vergennes** Vermont, NE USA 44°09´N 73°13´W
Veria *see* Véroia
104 I5 **Verín** Galicia, NW Spain 41°55´N 07°26´W
Verin T'alin *see* T'alin
118 K6 **Veriora** Põlvamaa, SE Estonia 57°57´N 27°23´E
117 T7 **Verkhivtseve** Dnipropetrovs'ka Oblast', E Ukraine 48°27´N 34°15´E
Verkhnedvinsk *see* Vyerkhnyadzvinsk
122 K10 **Verkhneimbatsk** Krasnoyarskiy Kray, N Russian Federation 63°06´N 88°03´E
124 I3 **Verkhnetulomskiy** Murmanskaya Oblast', NW Russian Federation 68°37´N 31°46´E
124 I3 **Verkhnetulomskoye Vodokhranilishche** ⊠ NW Russian Federation
Verkhneudinsk *see* Ulan-Ude
123 P10 **Verkhnevilyuysk** Respublika Sakha (Yakutiya), NE Russian Federation 63°44´N 119°59´E
127 W5 **Verkhniy Avzyan** Respublika Bashkortostan, W Russian Federation 53°31´N 57°26´E
127 Q11 **Verkhniy Baskunchak** Astrakhanskaya Oblast', SW Russian Federation 48°14´N 46°43´E
127 W3 **Verkhniye Kigi** Respublika Bashkortostan, W Russian Federation 55°25´N 58°40´E
117 T9 **Verkhniy Rohachyk** Khersons'ka Oblast', S Ukraine 47°16´N 34°16´E
123 Q11 **Verkhnyaya Amga** Respublika Sakha (Yakutiya), NE Russian Federation 59°34´N 127°07´E
125 V6 **Verkhnyaya Inta** Respublika Komi, NW Russian Federation 65°55´N 60°07´E
125 O10 **Verkhnyaya Toyma** Arkhangel'skaya Oblast', NW Russian Federation 62°12´N 44°57´E
126 K6 **Verkhov'ye** Orlovskaya Oblast', W Russian Federation 52°49´N 37°20´E
116 I8 **Verkhovyna** Ivano-Frankivs'ka Oblast', W Ukraine 48°09´N 24°48´E
123 P8 **Verkhoyanskiy Khrebet** ▲▲ NE Russian Federation
117 T7 **Verkh'odniprovs'k** Dnipropetrovs'ka Oblast', E Ukraine 48°40´N 34°17´E
101 G14 **Verl** Nordrhein-Westfalen, NW Germany 51°52´N 08°30´E
92 N1 **Verlegenhuken** *headland* N Svalbard 80°03´N 16°15´E
82 A9 **Vermelha, Ponta** *headland* NW Angola 05°40´S 12°09´E
103 P7 **Vermenton** Yonne, C France 47°40´N 03°43´E
11 R14 **Vermilion** Alberta, SW Canada 53°21´N 110°52´W
31 T11 **Vermilion** Ohio, N USA 41°25´N 82°21´W
22 I10 **Vermilion Bay** *bay* Louisiana, S USA
29 V4 **Vermilion Lake** ◎ Minnesota, N USA
14 F9 **Vermilion River** ⤳ Ontario, S Canada
30 L12 **Vermilion River** ⤳ Illinois, N USA
29 R12 **Vermillion** South Dakota, N USA 42°46´N 96°55´W
29 R12 **Vermillion River** ⤳ South Dakota, N USA
15 O9 **Vermillon, Rivière** ⤳ Québec, SE Canada
115 E14 **Vérmio** ▲ N Greece
18 L8 **Vermont** *off.* State of Vermont, *also known as* Green Mountain State. ⬖ *state* NE USA
113 K16 **Vermosh** *var.* Vermoshi. Shkodër, N Albania 42°37´N 19°42´E
Vermoshi *see* Vermosh
37 O3 **Vernal** Utah, W USA 40°27´N 109°31´W
14 G11 **Verner** Ontario, S Canada 46°24´N 80°04´W
102 M5 **Verneuil-sur-Avre** Eure, N France 48°44´N 00°55´E
114 D13 **Vérno** ▲ N Greece
11 N17 **Vernon** British Columbia, SW Canada 50°17´N 119°19´W
102 M4 **Vernon** Eure, N France 49°04´N 01°28´E
23 N3 **Vernon** Alabama, S USA 33°45´N 88°06´W
31 P15 **Vernon** Indiana, N USA 38°59´N 85°39´W
25 Q4 **Vernon** Texas, SW USA 34°11´N 99°17´W
32 G10 **Vernonia** Oregon, NW USA 45°51´N 123°11´W
14 G12 **Vernon, Lake** ◎ Ontario, S Canada
22 G7 **Vernon Lake** ⊠ Louisiana, S USA
23 Y13 **Vero Beach** Florida, SE USA 27°38´N 80°24´W
Verőcze *see* Virovitica
Verodunum *see* Verdun
115 E14 **Véroia** *var.* Veria, Vérroia, *Turk.* Karaferiye. Kentrikí Makedonía, N Greece 40°32´N 22°11´E
106 E8 **Verolanuova** Lombardia, N Italy 45°20´N 10°06´E
14 K14 **Verona** Ontario, SE Canada 44°30´N 76°42´W
106 G8 **Verona** Veneto, NE Italy 45°27´N 11°E
29 P6 **Verona** North Dakota, N USA 46°19´N 98°03´W
30 L9 **Verona** Wisconsin, N USA 42°59´N 89°33´W
61 E20 **Verónica** Buenos Aires, E Argentina 35°25´S 57°16´W
22 J9 **Verret, Lake** ◎ Louisiana, S USA
Vérroia *see* Véroia
103 N5 **Versailles** Yvelines, N France 48°48´N 02°08´E
31 P15 **Versailles** Indiana, N USA 39°04´N 85°16´W
20 M5 **Versailles** Kentucky, S USA 38°02´N 84°45´W
27 U5 **Versailles** Missouri, C USA 38°25´N 92°51´W
31 Q13 **Versailles** Ohio, N USA 40°13´N 84°28´W
Versecz *see* Vršac
108 A10 **Versoix** Genève, SW Switzerland 46°17´N 06°10´E
15 Z6 **Verte, Pointe** *headland* Québec, SE Canada 48°36´N 64°10´W
111 I22 **Vértes** ▲▲ NW Hungary
44 G6 **Vertientes** Camagüey, C Cuba 21°18´N 78°11´W
114 G13 **Vertiskos** ▲▲ N Greece
102 I8 **Vertou** Loire-Atlantique, NW France 47°10´N 01°28´W
Verulamium *see* St Albans
99 L19 **Verviers** Liège, E Belgium 50°36´N 05°52´E
103 Y14 **Vescovato** Corse, France, C Mediterranean Sea 42°30´N 09°27´E
99 L20 **Vesdre** ⤳ E Belgium
117 U10 **Vesele** *Rus.* Veseloye. Zaporiz'ka Oblast', S Ukraine 47°00´N 34°52´E
111 D18 **Veselí nad Lužnicí** *var.* Weseli an der Lainsitz, *Ger.* Frohenbruck. Jihočeský Kraj, S Czech Republic 49°11´N 14°40´E
114 M9 **Veselinovo** Shumen, NE Bulgaria 43°01´N 27°02´E
126 L12 **Veselovskoye Vodokhranilishche** ⊠ SW Russian Federation
Veseloye *see* Vesele
117 Q9 **Veselynove** Mykolayivs'ka Oblast', S Ukraine 47°21´N 31°15´E
Veseya *see* Vyasyeya
126 M10 **Veshenskaya** Rostovskaya Oblast', SW Russian Federation 49°37´N 41°43´E
127 Q5 **Veshkayma** Ul'yanovskaya Oblast', W Russian Federation 54°04´N 47°06´E
Vesisaari *see* Vadsø
Vesontio *see* Besançon
103 T7 **Vesoul** *anc.* Vesulium, Vesulum. Haute-Saône, E France 47°37´N 06°09´E
95 J20 **Vessigebro** Halland, S Sweden 56°58´N 12°40´E
95 D17 **Vest-Agder** ⬖ *county* S Norway
23 P4 **Vestavia Hills** Alabama, S USA 33°27´N 86°47´W
84 F6 **Vesterålen** *island* NW Norway
92 G10 **Vesterålen** *island group* N Norway
87 V3 **Vestervig** Viborg, NW Denmark 56°46´N 08°20´E
92 H2 **Vestfirdhir** ⬖ *region* NW Iceland
92 G11 **Vestfjorden** *fjord* C Norway
95 G16 **Vestfold** ⬖ *county* S Norway
Vestmanhavn *see* Vestmanna
95 B18 **Vestmanna** *Dan.* Vestmanhavn. Streymoy, N Faeroe Islands 62°09´N 07°11´W
92 I4 **Vestmannaeyjar** Sudhurland, S Iceland 63°26´N 20°14´W
94 E9 **Vestnes** Møre og Romsdal, S Norway 62°39´N 07°00´E
95 I23 **Vestsjælland** *off.* Vestsjællands Amt. ⬖ *county* E Denmark
Vestsjællands Amt *see* Vestsjælland
92 H3 **Vesturland** ⬖ *region* W Iceland
92 G11 **Vestvågøya** *island* C Norway
Vesulium/Vesulum *see* Vesoul
Vesuna *see* Périgueux
107 K17 **Vesuvio** *Eng.* Vesuvius. ⛰ S Italy 40°48´N 14°29´E
Vesuvius *see* Vesuvio
124 K14 **Ves'yegonsk** Tverskaya Oblast', W Russian Federation 58°40´N 37°13´E
111 I23 **Veszprém** *Ger.* Veszprim. Veszprém, W Hungary 47°06´N 17°54´E
111 H23 **Veszprém** *off.* Veszprém Megye. ⬖ *county* W Hungary
Veszprém Megye *see* Veszprém
Veszprim *see* Veszprém
Vetka *see* Vyetka
95 M19 **Vetlanda** Jönköping, S Sweden 57°26´N 15°05´E
127 P1 **Vetluga** Nizhegorodskaya Oblast', W Russian Federation 57°51´N 45°45´E
125 P14 **Vetluga** ⤳ NW Russian Federation
125 O14 **Vetluzhskiy** Kostromskaya Oblast', NW Russian Federation 58°21´N 45°25´E
127 P2 **Vetluzhskiy** Nizhegorodskaya Oblast', W Russian Federation 57°10´N 45°07´E
114 K7 **Vetovo** Ruse, N Bulgaria 43°42´N 26°16´E
107 H14 **Vetralla** Lazio, C Italy 42°18´N 12°03´E
Vetrino *see* Vyetryna
122 L7 **Vetrovaya, Gora** ▲ N Russian Federation 73°54´N 95°00´E
Vetter, Lake *see* Vättern
106 J13 **Vettore, Monte** ▲ C Italy 42°49´N 13°15´E
99 A17 **Veurne** *var.* Furnes. West-Vlaanderen, W Belgium 51°04´N 02°40´E
31 Q15 **Vevay** Indiana, N USA 38°45´N 85°08´W
108 C10 **Vevey** *Ger.* Vivis; *anc.* Vibiscum. Vaud, SW Switzerland 46°28´N 06°51´E
Vexiö *see* Växjö
103 S13 **Veynes** Hautes-Alpes, SE France 44°33´N 05°51´E
103 N11 **Vézère** ⤳ W France
114 I9 **Vezhen** ▲ C Bulgaria 42°45´N 24°22´E
136 K11 **Vezirköprü** Samsun, N Turkey 41°09´N 35°27´E
57 J18 **Viacha** La Paz, W Bolivia 16°40´S 68°17´W
27 R10 **Vian** Oklahoma, C USA 35°30´N 94°56´W
Viana de Castelo *see* Viana do Castelo
104 H12 **Viana do Alentejo** Évora, S Portugal 38°20´N 08°00´W
104 I4 **Viana do Bolo** Galicia, NW Spain 42°10´N 07°06´W
104 G5 **Viana do Castelo** *var.* Viana de Castelo; *anc.* Velobriga. Viana do Castelo, NW Portugal 41°41´N 08°50´W
104 G5 **Viana do Castelo** *var.* Viana de Castelo. ⬖ *district* N Portugal
98 J12 **Vianen** Utrecht, C Netherlands 52°N 05°06´E
167 Q8 **Viangchan** *Eng./Fr.* Vientiane. ● (Laos) C Laos 17°58´N 102°38´E
167 P6 **Viangphoukha** *var.* Vieng Pou Kha. Louang Namtha, N Laos 20°41´N 101°03´E
104 K13 **Viar** ⤳ SW Spain
106 E11 **Viareggio** Toscana, C Italy 43°52´N 10°15´E
103 O14 **Viaur** ⤳ S France
Vibiscum *see* Vevey
95 G21 **Viborg** Viborg, NW Denmark 56°28´N 09°25´E
29 R12 **Viborg** South Dakota, N USA 43°10´N 97°04´W
95 F21 **Viborg** *off.* Viborg Amt. ⬖ *county* NW Denmark
Viborg Amt *see* Viborg
107 N22 **Vibo Valentia** *prev.* Monteleone di Calabria; *anc.* Hipponium. Calabria, SW Italy 38°40´N 16°06´E
105 W5 **Vic** *var.* Vich; *anc.* Ausa, Vicus Ausonensis. Cataluña, NE Spain 41°56´N 02°16´E
102 K16 **Vic-en-Bigorre** Hautes-Pyrénées, S France 43°23´N 00°04´E
40 K10 **Vicente Guerrero** Durango, C Mexico 23°30´N 104°24´W
41 P10 **Vicente Guerrero, Presa** *var.* Presa de las Adjuntas. ⊠ NE Mexico
Vicentia *see* Vicenza
106 G8 **Vicenza** *anc.* Vicentia. Veneto, NE Italy 45°32´N 11°31´E
Vich *see* Vic
54 J10 **Vichada** *off.* Comisaría del Vichada. ⬖ *province* E Colombia
Vichada, Comisaría del *see* Vichada
54 K10 **Vichada, Río** ⤳ E Colombia
61 G17 **Vichadero** Rivera, NE Uruguay 31°45´S 54°41´W
Vichegda *see* Vychegda
124 M16 **Vichuga** Ivanovskaya Oblast', W Russian Federation 57°13´N 41°51´E
103 P10 **Vichy** Allier, C France 46°08´N 03°26´E
26 K9 **Vici** Oklahoma, C USA 36°09´N 99°18´W
31 P10 **Vicksburg** Michigan, N USA 42°07´N 85°31´W
22 J5 **Vicksburg** Mississippi, S USA 32°21´N 90°52´W
103 O12 **Vic-sur-Cère** Cantal, C France 45°00´N 02°36´E
59 I21 **Víctor** Mato Grosso do Sul, SW Brazil 21°39´S 53°21´W
29 X14 **Victor** Iowa, C USA 41°45´N 92°18´W
182 I10 **Victor Harbor** South Australia 35°33´S 138°37´E
61 C18 **Victoria** Entre Ríos, E Argentina 32°40´S 60°10´W
10 L17 **Victoria** *province capital* Vancouver Island, British Columbia, SW Canada 48°25´N 123°22´W
45 R14 **Victoria** NW Grenada 12°12´N 61°42´W
42 H6 **Victoria** Yoro, NW Honduras 15°01´N 87°28´W
121 O15 **Victoria** *var.* Rabat. Gozo, NW Malta 36°02´N 14°14´E
116 I12 **Victoria** *Ger.* Viktoriastadt. Braşov, C Romania 45°44´N 24°41´E
172 H17 **Victoria** ● (Seychelles) Mahé, SW Seychelles 04°38´S 28°28´E
25 U13 **Victoria** Texas, SW USA 28°47´N 96°59´W
183 N12 **Victoria** ⬖ *state* SE Australia
174 K7 **Victoria** ⤳ Western Australia
Victoria *see* Labuan, East Malaysia
Victoria *see* Masvingo, Zimbabwe
Victoria Bank *see* Vitória Seamount
11 Y15 **Victoria Beach** Manitoba, S Canada 50°40´N 96°30´W
Victoria de Durango *see* Durango
Victoria de las Tunas *see* Las Tunas
83 I16 **Victoria Falls** Matabeleland North, W Zimbabwe 17°55´S 25°51´E
83 I15 **Victoria Falls** *waterfall* Zambia/Zimbabwe
83 I16 **Victoria Falls** ✈ Matabeleland North, W Zimbabwe 18°03´S 25°48´E
Victoria Falls *see* Iguaçu, Salto do
63 F19 **Victoria, Isla** *island* Archipiélago de los Chonos, S Chile
8 K6 **Victoria Island** *island* Northwest Territories/Nunavut, NW Canada
182 L8 **Victoria, Lake** ◎ New South Wales, SE Australia
68 I12 **Victoria, Lake** *var.* Victoria Nyanza. ◎ E Africa
195 S13 **Victoria Land** *physical region* Antarctica
187 X14 **Victoria, Mount** ▲ Viti Levu, W Fiji 17°37´S 178°00´E
166 L5 **Victoria, Mount** ▲ W Burma (Myanmar) 21°13´N 93°53´E
186 E9 **Victoria, Mount** ▲ S Papua New Guinea 08°51´S 147°36´E
81 F17 **Victoria Nile** *var.* Somerset Nile. ⤳ C Uganda
Victoria Nyanza *see* Victoria, Lake
42 G3 **Victoria Peak** ▲ SE Belize 16°50´N 88°38´W
185 H16 **Victoria Range** ▲▲ South Island, New Zealand
181 O3 **Victoria River** ⤳ Northern Territory, N Australia
181 P3 **Victoria River Roadhouse** Northern Territory, N Australia 15°37´S 131°07´E
15 Q11 **Victoriaville** Québec, SE Canada 46°04´N 71°57´W
Victoria-Wes *see* Victoria West
83 G24 **Victoria West** *Afr.* Victoria-Wes. Northern Cape, W South Africa 31°25´S 23°08´E
62 J13 **Victorica** La Pampa, C Argentina 36°15´S 65°25´W
Victor, Mount *see* Belgicafjella
35 U14 **Victorville** California, W USA 34°32´N 117°17´W
62 G9 **Vicuña** Coquimbo, N Chile 30°00´S 70°44´W
62 K11 **Vicuña Mackenna** Córdoba, C Argentina 33°53´S 64°25´W
Vicus Ausonensis *see* Vic
Vicus Elbii *see* Viterbo
33 X7 **Vida** Montana, NW USA 47°52´N 105°30´W
23 V6 **Vidalia** Georgia, SE USA 32°13´N 82°24´W
22 J7 **Vidalia** Louisiana, S USA 31°34´N 91°25´W
95 F22 **Videbæk** Ringkøbing, C Denmark 56°08´N 08°38´E
60 I13 **Videira** Santa Catarina, S Brazil 27°00´S 51°08´W
116 J14 **Videle** Teleorman, S Romania 44°15´N 25°27´E
Videm-Krško *see* Krško
Vídeň *see* Wien
104 H12 **Vidigueira** Beja, S Portugal 38°12´N 07°48´W
114 F7 **Vidima** ⤳ N Bulgaria
114 G7 **Vidin** *anc.* Bononia. Vidin, NW Bulgaria 44°00´N 22°52´E
114 F8 **Vidin** ⬖ *province* NW Bulgaria
154 H10 **Vidisha** Madhya Pradesh, C India 23°30´N 77°50´E
25 Y10 **Vidor** Texas, SW USA 30°07´N 94°01´W
95 L20 **Vidöstern** ◎ S Sweden
92 J13 **Vidsel** Norrbotten, N Sweden 65°49´N 20°31´E
118 H9 **Vidzemes Augstiene** ▲ C Latvia
118 J12 **Vidzy** Vitsyebskaya Voblasts', NW Belarus 55°24´N 26°38´E
63 L16 **Viedma** Río Negro, E Argentina 40°50´S 62°58´W
63 H22 **Viedma, Lago** ◎ S Argentina
45 O11 **Vieille Case** *var.* Itassi. N Dominica 15°36´N 61°24´W
104 M2 **Vieja, Peña** ▲ N Spain 43°09´N 04°47´W
24 J10 **Vieja, Sierra** ▲▲ Texas, SW USA
40 E4 **Viejo, Cerro** ▲ NW Mexico 30°16´N 112°18´W
56 B9 **Viejo, Cerro** ▲ N Peru 04°54´S 79°24´W
118 E10 **Viekšniai** Telšiai, NW Lithuania 56°14´N 22°33´E
105 U3 **Vielha** *var.* Viella. Cataluña, NE Spain 42°41´N 00°47´E
Viella *see* Vielha
99 L21 **Vielsalm** Luxembourg, E Belgium 50°17´N 05°55´E
Vieng Pou Kha *see* Viangphoukha
23 T6 **Vienna** Georgia, SE USA 32°05´N 83°48´W
30 L17 **Vienna** Illinois, N USA 37°24´N 88°55´W
27 V5 **Vienna** Missouri, C USA 38°12´N 91°59´W
21 Q3 **Vienna** West Virginia, NE USA 39°19´N 81°33´W
Vienna *see* Wien, Austria
Vienna *see* Vienne, France
103 R11 **Vienne** *anc.* Vienna. Isère, E France 45°32´N 04°53´E
102 L10 **Vienne** ⬖ *department* W France
102 L9 **Vienne** ⤳ W France
Vientiane *see* Viangchan
Vientos, Paso de los *see* Windward Passage
45 V6 **Vieques** *var.* Isabel Segunda. E Puerto Rico 18°08´N 65°25´W
45 V6 **Vieques, Isla de** *island* E Puerto Rico
45 V6 **Vieques, Pasaje de** *passage* E Puerto Rico
45 V5 **Vieques, Sonda de** *sound* E Puerto Rico
Vierdörfer *see* Săcele
93 M15 **Vieremä** Itä-Suomi, C Finland 63°42´N 27°02´E
99 M14 **Vierlingsbeek** Noord-Brabant, SE Netherlands 51°36´N 06°01´E
101 G20 **Viernheim** Hessen, W Germany 49°32´N 08°35´E
101 D15 **Viersen** Nordrhein-Westfalen, W Germany 51°16´N 06°24´E
108 G8 **Vierwaldstätter See** *Eng.* Lake of Lucerne. ◎ C Switzerland
103 N8 **Vierzon** Cher, C France 47°13´N 02°04´E
40 L8 **Viesca** Coahuila, NE Mexico 25°25´N 102°45´W
118 H10 **Viesīte** *Ger.* Eckengraf. Jēkabpils, S Latvia 56°21´N 25°30´E
107 N15 **Vieste** Puglia, SE Italy 41°52´N 16°11´E
167 T8 **Vietnam** *off.* Socialist Republic of Vietnam, *Vtn.* Công Hoa Xa Hôi Chu Nghia Việt Nam. ◆ *republic* SE Asia
Vietnam, Socialist Republic of *see* Vietnam
167 S5 **Viêt Quang** Ha Giang, N Vietnam 22°24´N 104°48´E
Vietri *see* Viêt Tri
167 S6 **Viêt Tri** *var.* Vietri. Vinh Phu, N Vietnam 21°20´N 105°26´E
30 L4 **Vieux Desert, Lac** ◎ Michigan/Wisconsin, N USA
45 Y13 **Vieux Fort** S Saint Lucia 13°43´N 60°57´W
45 X6 **Vieux-Habitants** Basse Terre, SW Guadeloupe 16°04´N 61°45´W
119 G14 **Vievis** Vilnius, S Lithuania 54°46´N 24°51´E
171 N2 **Vigan** Luzon, N Philippines 17°34´N 102°21´E
106 D8 **Vigevano** Lombardia, N Italy 45°19´N 08°51´E
107 N18 **Viggiano** Basilicata, S Italy 40°21´N 15°54´E
58 L12 **Vigia** Pará, NE Brazil 0°50´S 48°07´W
41 Y12 **Vigía Chico** Quintana Roo, SE Mexico 19°49´N 87°31´W
45 T11 **Vigie** *prev.* George F L Charles. ✈ (Castries) NE Saint Lucia 14°01´N 60°59´W
102 K17 **Vignemale** *var.* Pic de Vignemale. ▲ France/Spain 42°48´N 00°06´W
Vignemale, Pic de *see* Vignemale
106 G10 **Vignola** Emilia-Romagna, C Italy 44°28´N 11°00´E
104 G4 **Vigo** Galicia, NW Spain 42°15´N 08°44´W
104 G4 **Vigo, Ría de** *estuary* NW Spain
94 D9 **Vigra** *island* S Norway
95 C17 **Vigrestad** Rogaland, S Norway 58°34´N 05°42´E
93 L15 **Vihanti** Oulu, C Finland 64°29´N 25°E
149 U10 **Vihāri** Punjab, E Pakistan 30°03´N 72°32´E
102 K8 **Vihiers** Maine-et-Loire, NW France 47°09´N 00°37´W
111 O19 **Vihorlat** ▲ E Slovakia 48°54´N 22°09´E
93 L19 **Vihti** Etelä-Suomi, S Finland 60°25´N 24°16´E
Viipuri *see* Vyborg
93 M16 **Viitasaari** Länsi-Suomi, C Finland 63°05´N 25°52´E
118 K3 **Viivikonna** Ida-Virumaa, NE Estonia 59°19´N 27°41´E
155 K16 **Vijayawāda** *prev.* Bezwada. Andhra Pradesh, SE India 16°34´N 80°40´E
Vijosa/Vijosë *see* Aóos, Albania/Greece
Vijosa/Vijosë *see* Vjosës, Lumi i, Albania/Greece
92 J4 **Vík** Sudhurland, S Iceland 63°25´N 18°58´W
Vík *see* Vikøyri
94 L13 **Vika** Dalarna, C Sweden 60°55´N 14°30´E
92 L12 **Vikajärvi** Lappi, N Finland 66°37´N 26°10´E
94 L13 **Vikarbyn** Dalarna, C Sweden 60°57´N 15°00´E
95 J22 **Viken** Skåne, S Sweden 56°09´N 12°36´E
95 L17 **Viken** ◎ C Sweden
95 G15 **Vikersund** Buskerud, S Norway 59°58´N 09°59´E
114 G11 **Vikhren** ▲ SW Bulgaria 41°45´N 23°24´E
11 R15 **Viking** Alberta, SW Canada 53°07´N 111°50´W
84 E7 **Viking Bank** *undersea feature* N North Sea 60°35´N 02°35´E
95 M14 **Vikmanshyttan** Dalarna, C Sweden 60°19´N 15°55´E
94 D12 **Vikøyri** *var.* Vik. Sogn Og Fjordane, S Norway 61°04´N 06°34´E
93 H17 **Viksjö** Västernorrland, C Sweden 62°45´N 17°30´E
Viktoriastadt *see* Victoria
Vila *see* Port-Vila
Vila Arriaga *see* Bibala
Vila Artur de Paiva *see* Cubango
Vila Baleira *see* Porto Santo
Vila Bela da Santíssima Trindade *see* Mato Grosso
58 B12 **Vila Bittencourt** Amazonas, NW Brazil 01°25´S 69°24´W
Vila da Ponte *see* Cubango
64 O2 **Vila da Praia da Vitória** Terceira, Azores, Portugal, NE Atlantic Ocean 38°44´N 27°04´W
Vila de Aljustrel *see* Cangamba
Vila de Almoster *see* Chiange
Vila de João Belo *see* Xai-Xai
Vila de Macia *see* Macia
Vila de Manhiça *see* Manhiça
Vila de Manica *see* Manica
Vila de Mocímboa da Praia *see* Mocímboa da Praia
83 N16 **Vila de Sena** *var.* Sena. Sofala, C Mozambique 17°25´S 34°59´E
104 F14 **Vila do Bispo** Faro, S Portugal 37°05´N 08°53´W
104 G6 **Vila do Conde** Porto, NW Portugal 41°21´N 08°45´W
Vila do Maio *see* Maio
64 P3 **Vila do Porto** Santa Maria, Azores, Portugal, NE Atlantic Ocean 36°57´N 25°10´W
83 K15 **Vila do Zumbo** *prev.* Vila do Zumbu, Zumbo. Tete, NW Mozambique 15°36´S 30°30´E
Vila do Zumbu *see* Vila do Zumbo
104 I6 **Vila Flor** *var.* Vila Flôr. Bragança, N Portugal 41°18´N 07°09´W
105 V6 **Vilafranca del Penedès** *var.* Villafranca del Panadés. Cataluña, NE Spain 41°21´N 01°42´E
104 F10 **Vila Franca de Xira** *var.* Vilafranca de Xira. Lisboa, C Portugal 38°57´N 08°59´W
Vila Gago Coutinho *see* Lumbala N'Guimbo
104 G3 **Vilagarcía de Arousa** *var.* Villagarcía de Arosa. Galicia, NW Spain 42°35´N 08°45´W
Vila General Machado *see* Camacupa
Vila Henrique de Carvalho *see* Saurimo
102 I7 **Vilaine** ⤳ NW France
Vila João de Almeida *see* Chibia
118 K8 **Viļaka** *Ger.* Marienhausen. Balvi, NE Latvia 57°12´N 27°43´E
104 I2 **Vilalba** Galicia, NW Spain 43°17´N 07°41´W
Vila Marechal Carmona *see* Uíge

◆ Country
● Country Capital
◇ Dependent Territory
○ Dependent Territory Capital
⬖ Administrative Regions
✈ International Airport
▲ Mountain
▲▲ Mountain Range
⛰ Volcano
⤳ River
◎ Lake
⊠ Reservoir

Vila Mariano Machado – Volta Rouge

Vila Mariano Machado *see* Ganda
172 *G3* **Vilanandro, Tanjona** *Fr.* Cap Saint-André. *headland* W Madagascar *16°10′S 44°27′E*
Vilanculos *see* Vilankulo
118 *J10* **Viļāni** Rēzekne, E Latvia *56°33′N 26°55′E*
83 *N19* **Vilankulo** *var.* Vilanculos. Inhambane, E Mozambique *22°01′S 35°19′E*
Vila Norton de Matos *see* Balombo
104 *G6* **Vila Nova de Famalicão** *var.* Vila Nova de Famalicao. Braga, N Portugal *41°24′N 08°31′W*
104 *I6* **Vila Nova de Foz Côa** *var.* Vila Nova de Fozcôa. Guarda, N Portugal *41°05′N 07°09′W*
Vila Nova de Fozcôa *see* Vila Nova de Foz Côa
104 *F6* **Vila Nova de Gaia** Porto, NW Portugal *41°08′N 08°37′W*
Vila Nova de Portimão *see* Portimão
105 *V6* **Vilanova i La Geltrú** Cataluña, NE Spain *41°15′N 01°42′E*
Vila Pereira de Eça *see* N'Giva
104 *H6* **Vila Pouca de Aguiar** Vila Real, N Portugal *41°30′N 07°38′W*
104 *H6* **Vila Real** *var.* Vila Rial. Vila Real, N Portugal *41°17′N 07°45′W*
104 *H6* **Vila Real** ◆ *district* N Portugal
Vila-real de los Infantes *see* Villarreal
104 *H14* **Vila Real de Santo António** Faro, S Portugal *37°12′N 07°25′W*
104 *J7* **Vilar Formoso** Guarda, N Portugal *40°37′N 06°50′W*
Vila Rial *see* Vila Real
59 *J15* **Vila Rica** Mato Grosso, W Brazil *09°52′S 50°44′W*
Vila Robert Williams *see* Caála
Vila Salazar *see* N'Dalatando
Vila Serpa Pinto *see* Menongue
Vila Teixeira da Silva *see* Bailundo
Vila Teixeira de Sousa *see* Luau
104 *H9* **Vila Velha de Ródão** Castelo Branco, C Portugal *39°39′N 07°40′W*
104 *G5* **Vila Verde** Braga, N Portugal *41°39′N 08°27′W*
104 *H11* **Vila Viçosa** Évora, S Portugal *38°46′N 07°25′W*
57 *G15* **Vilcabamba, Cordillera de** ▲ C Peru
Vîlcea *see* Vâlcea
122 *J4* **Vil'cheka, Zemlya** *Eng.* Wilczek Land. *island* Zemlya Frantsa-Iosifa, NW Russian Federation
95 *F22* **Vildbjerg** Ringkøbing, C Denmark *56°12′N 08°47′E*
Vileyka *see* Vilyeyka
93 *H15* **Vilhelmina** Västerbotten, N Sweden *64°38′N 16°40′E*
59 *F17* **Vilhena** Rondônia, W Brazil *12°40′S 60°08′W*
115 *G19* **Vília** Attikí, C Greece *38°09′N 23°21′E*
119 *I14* **Viliya** *Lith.* Neris. ↝ W Belarus
Viliya *see* Neris
118 *H5* **Viljandi** *Ger.* Fellin. Viljandimaa, S Estonia *58°22′N 25°30′E*
118 *H5* **Viljandimaa** *var.* Viljandi Maakond. ◆ *province* SW Estonia
Viljandi Maakond *see* Viljandimaa
119 *E14* **Vilkaviškis** *Pol.* Wyłkowyszki. Marijampolė, SW Lithuania *54°39′N 23°03′E*
118 *F13* **Vilkija** Kaunas, C Lithuania *55°02′N 23°36′E*
197 *V9* **Vil'kitskogo, Proliv** *strait* N Russian Federation
Vilkovo *see* Vylkove
57 *L21* **Villa Abecia** Chuquisaca, S Bolivia *21°00′S 65°18′W*
41 *N5* **Villa Acuña** *var.* Ciudad Acuña. Coahuila, NE Mexico *29°18′N 100°58′W*
40 *J4* **Villa Ahumada** Chihuahua, N Mexico *30°38′N 106°30′W*
45 *O9* **Villa Altagracia** C Dominican Republic *18°43′N 70°13′W*
56 *L13* **Villa Bella** Beni, N Bolivia *10°21′S 65°25′W*
104 *J3* **Villablino** Castilla-León, N Spain *42°55′N 06°21′W*
54 *K6* **Villa Bruzual** Portuguesa, N Venezuela *09°20′N 69°06′W*
105 *O9* **Villacañas** Castilla-La Mancha, C Spain *39°38′N 03°20′W*
105 *O12* **Villacarrillo** Andalucía, S Spain *38°07′N 03°05′W*
104 *M7* **Villacastín** Castilla-León, N Spain *40°46′N 04°25′W*
Villa Cecilia *see* Ciudad Madero
109 *S9* **Villach** *Slvn.* Beljak. Kärnten, S Austria *46°36′N 13°49′E*
107 *B20* **Villacidro** Sardegna, Italy, C Mediterranean Sea *39°28′N 08°43′E*
Villa Concepción *see* Concepción
104 *L4* **Villada** Castilla-León, N Spain *42°15′N 04°59′W*
40 *M10* **Villa de Cos** Zacatecas, C Mexico *23°20′N 102°20′W*
54 *L5* **Villa de Cura** *var.* Cura. Aragua, N Venezuela *10°00′N 67°30′W*
Villa del Nevoso *see* Ilirska Bistrica
Villa del Pilar *see* Pilar
104 *M13* **Villa del Río** Andalucía, S Spain *37°59′N 04°17′W*
Villa de Méndez *see* Méndez
42 *H6* **Villa de San Antonio** Comayagua, W Honduras *14°24′N 87°37′W*
105 *N4* **Villadiego** Castilla-León, N Spain *42°31′N 04°01′W*
105 *T8* **Villafames** País Valenciano, E Spain *40°07′N 00°03′W*
41 *U16* **Villa Flores** Chiapas, SE Mexico *16°12′N 93°16′W*
104 *J3* **Villafranca del Bierzo** Castilla-León, N Spain *42°36′N 06°49′W*
105 *S8* **Villafranca del Cid** País Valenciano, E Spain *40°25′N 00°15′W*
104 *J11* **Villafranca de los Barros** Extremadura, W Spain *38°34′N 06°20′W*
105 *N10* **Villafranca de los Caballeros** Castilla-La Mancha, C Spain *39°26′N 03°21′W*
Villafranca del Panadés *see* Vilafranca del Penedès
106 *F8* **Villafranca di Verona** Veneto, NE Italy *45°22′N 10°51′E*
107 *J23* **Villafrati** Sicilia, Italy, C Mediterranean Sea *37°53′N 13°30′E*
Villagarcía de Arosa *see* Vilagarcía de Arousa
41 *O9* **Villagrán** Tamaulipas, C Mexico *24°29′N 99°30′W*
61 *C17* **Villaguay** Entre Ríos, E Argentina *31°55′S 59°01′W*
62 *O6* **Villa Hayes** Presidente Hayes, S Paraguay *25°05′S 57°25′W*
41 *U15* **Villahermosa** *prev.* San Juan Bautista. Tabasco, SE Mexico *17°56′N 92°50′W*
105 *O11* **Villahermosa** Castilla-La Mancha, C Spain *38°46′N 02°52′W*
64 *O11* **Villahermoso** Gomera, Islas Canarias, Spain, NE Atlantic Ocean *38°46′N 02°52′W*
Villa Hidalgo *see* Hidalgo
105 *T12* **Villajoyosa** *Cat.* La Vila Joíosa. País Valenciano, E Spain *38°31′N 00°14′W*
Villa Juárez *see* Juárez
Villalba *see* Collado Villalba
41 *N8* **Villaldama** Nuevo León, NE Mexico *26°29′N 100°27′W*
104 *L5* **Villalón de Campos** Castilla-León, N Spain *42°05′N 05°03′W*
61 *A25* **Villalonga** Buenos Aires, E Argentina *39°55′S 62°35′W*
104 *L5* **Villalpando** Castilla-León, N Spain *41°51′N 05°25′W*
40 *K9* **Villa Madero** *var.* Francisco I. Madero. Durango, C Mexico *24°28′N 104°20′W*
41 *O9* **Villa Mainero** Tamaulipas, C Mexico *24°32′N 99°39′W*
Villamaña *see* Villamañán
104 *L4* **Villamañán** *var.* Villamaña. Castilla-León, N Spain *42°19′N 05°35′W*
62 *L10* **Villa María** Córdoba, C Argentina *32°23′S 63°15′W*
61 *C17* **Villa María Grande** Entre Ríos, E Argentina *31°39′S 59°54′W*
57 *K21* **Villa Martín** Potosí, SW Bolivia *20°46′S 67°45′W*
104 *K15* **Villamartín** Andalucía, S Spain *36°52′N 05°38′W*
62 *J8* **Villa Mazán** La Rioja, NW Argentina *28°43′S 66°25′W*
62 *J11* **Villa Mercedes** *var.* Mercedes. San Luis, C Argentina *33°40′S 65°25′W*
Villamil *see* Puerto Villamil
Villa Nador *see* Nador
54 *G5* **Villanueva** La Guajira, N Colombia *10°37′N 72°58′W*
42 *H5* **Villanueva** Cortés, NW Honduras *15°14′N 88°00′W*
40 *L11* **Villanueva** Zacatecas, C Mexico *22°24′N 102°53′W*
42 *I9* **Villa Nueva** Chinandega, NW Nicaragua *12°58′N 86°46′W*
37 *T11* **Villanueva** New Mexico, SW USA *35°18′N 105°20′W*
104 *M12* **Villanueva de Córdoba** Andalucía, S Spain *38°20′N 04°38′W*
105 *O12* **Villanueva del Arzobispo** Andalucía, S Spain *38°10′N 03°00′W*
104 *K11* **Villanueva de la Serena** Extremadura, W Spain *38°58′N 05°48′W*
104 *L5* **Villanueva del Campo** Castilla-León, N Spain *41°59′N 05°25′W*
105 *O11* **Villanueva de los Infantes** Castilla-La Mancha, C Spain *38°45′N 03°01′W*
61 *C14* **Villa Ocampo** Santa Fe, C Argentina *28°28′S 59°22′W*
40 *J8* **Villa Ocampo** Durango, C Mexico *26°29′N 105°30′W*
40 *J7* **Villa Orestes Pereyra** Durango, C Mexico *26°30′N 105°38′W*
105 *N3* **Villarcayo** Castilla-León, N Spain *42°56′N 03°34′W*
104 *L5* **Villardefrades** Castilla-León, N Spain *41°43′N 05°15′W*
105 *S9* **Villar del Arzobispo** País Valenciano, E Spain *39°44′N 00°50′W*
105 *Q6* **Villaroya de la Sierra** Aragón, NE Spain *41°28′N 01°46′W*
105 *T9* **Villarreal** *var.* Vila-real de los Infantes. País Valenciano, E Spain *39°56′N 00°08′W*
62 *P6* **Villarrica** Guairá, SE Paraguay *25°45′S 56°28′W*
63 *G15* **Villarrica, Volcán** ⋏ S Chile *39°28′S 71°57′W*
105 *P10* **Villarrobledo** Castilla-La Mancha, C Spain *39°16′N 02°36′W*
105 *N10* **Villarrubia de los Ojos** Castilla-La Mancha, C Spain *39°14′N 03°36′W*
18 *J17* **Villas** New Jersey, NE USA *39°01′N 74°54′W*
105 *O3* **Villasana de Mena** Castilla-León, N Spain *43°05′N 03°16′W*
107 *M23* **Villa San Giovanni** Calabria, S Italy *38°12′N 15°39′E*
61 *D18* **Villa San José** Entre Ríos, E Argentina *32°01′S 58°20′W*
Villa Sanjurjo *see* Al-Hoceïma
105 *P6* **Villasayas** Castilla-León, N Spain *41°19′N 02°36′W*
107 *C20* **Villasimius** Sardegna, Italy, C Mediterranean Sea *39°10′N 09°30′E*
41 *N6* **Villa Unión** Coahuila, NE Mexico *28°18′N 100°43′W*
40 *K10* **Villa Unión** Durango, C Mexico *23°59′N 104°01′W*
40 *J10* **Villa Unión** Sinaloa, C Mexico *23°10′N 106°12′W*
62 *K12* **Villa Valeria** Córdoba, C Argentina *34°21′S 64°56′W*
105 *N8* **Villaverde** Madrid, C Spain *40°21′N 03°43′W*
54 *F10* **Villavicencio** Meta, C Colombia *04°09′N 73°38′W*
104 *L2* **Villaviciosa** Asturias, N Spain *43°29′N 05°26′W*
104 *L12* **Villaviciosa de Córdoba** Andalucía, S Spain *38°04′N 05°00′W*
57 *L22* **Villazón** Potosí, S Bolivia *22°05′S 65°35′W*
14 *J8* **Villebon, Lac** ⊗ Québec, SE Canada
Ville de Kinshasa *see* Kinshasa
102 *J5* **Villedieu-les-Poêles** Manche, N France *48°51′N 01°12′W*
Villefranche *see* Villefranche-sur-Saône
103 *N16* **Villefranche-de-Lauragais** Haute-Garonne, S France *43°24′N 01°42′E*
103 *N14* **Villefranche-de-Rouergue** Aveyron, S France *44°21′N 02°02′E*
103 *R10* **Villefranche-sur-Saône** *var.* Villefranche. Rhône, E France *46°00′N 04°40′E*
14 *H9* **Ville-Marie** Québec, SE Canada *47°21′N 79°26′W*
102 *M15* **Villemur-sur-Tarn** Haute-Garonne, S France *43°50′N 01°32′E*
105 *S11* **Villena** País Valenciano, E Spain *38°39′N 00°52′W*
Villeneuve-d'Agen *see* Villeneuve-sur-Lot
102 *L13* **Villeneuve-sur-Lot** *var.* Villeneuve-d'Agen, *hist.* Gajac. Lot-et-Garonne, SW France *44°24′N 00°43′E*
103 *P6* **Villeneuve-sur-Yonne** Yonne, C France *48°04′N 03°21′E*
22 *H8* **Ville Platte** Louisiana, S USA *30°41′N 92°16′W*
103 *R11* **Villeurbanne** Rhône, E France *45°46′N 04°54′E*
101 *G23* **Villingen-Schwenningen** Baden-Württemberg, S Germany *48°04′N 08°27′E*
29 *T15* **Villisca** Iowa, C USA *40°55′N 94°58′W*
Villmanstrand *see* Lappeenranta
Vilna *see* Vilnius
119 *H15* **Vilnius** ◆ *province* Lithuania
119 *H14* **Vilnius** *Pol.* Wilno, *Ger.* Wilna; *prev. Rus.* Vilna. ● (Lithuania) Vilnius, SE Lithuania *54°41′N 25°20′E*
119 *H14* **Vilnius** ✈ Vilnius, SE Lithuania *54°33′N 25°17′E*
117 *S7* **Vil'nohirs'k** Dnipropetrovs'ka Oblast', E Ukraine *48°31′N 34°01′E*
117 *U8* **Vil'nyans'k** Zaporiz'ka Oblast', SE Ukraine *47°56′N 35°22′E*
93 *L17* **Vilppula** Länsi-Suomi, W Finland *62°02′N 24°30′E*
101 *M20* **Vils** ↝ SE Germany
118 *C5* **Vilsandi** *island* W Estonia
117 *P8* **Vil'shanka** *Rus.* Olshanka. Kirovohrads'ka Oblast', C Ukraine *48°12′N 30°54′E*
101 *O22* **Vilshofen** Bayern, SE Germany *48°36′N 13°10′E*
155 *J20* **Viluppuram** Tamil Nādu, SE India *12°54′N 79°40′E*
113 *I16* **Vilusi** W Montenegro *42°44′N 18°34′E*
99 *G18* **Vilvoorde** *Fr.* Vilvorde. Vlaams Brabant, C Belgium *50°56′N 04°25′E*
Vilvorde *see* Vilvoorde
119 *J14* **Vilyeyka** *Pol.* Wilejka, *Rus.* Vileyka. Minskaya Voblasts', NW Belarus *54°30′N 26°55′E*
122 *V11* **Vilyuchinsk** Kamchatskaya Oblast', E Russian Federation *52°55′N 158°28′E*
123 *P10* **Vilyuy** ↝ NE Russian Federation
123 *P10* **Vilyuysk** Respublika Sakha (Yakutiya), NE Russian Federation *63°42′N 121°20′E*
123 *N10* **Vilyuyskoye Vodokhranilishche** ⊠ NE Russian Federation
104 *G2* **Vimianzo** Galicia, NW Spain *43°06′N 09°03′W*
95 *M19* **Vimmerby** Kalmar, S Sweden *57°40′N 15°50′E*
102 *L5* **Vimoutiers** Orne, N France *48°56′N 00°10′E*
93 *L16* **Vimpeli** Länsi-Suomi, W Finland *63°10′N 23°50′E*
79 *G14* **Vina** ↝ Cameroon/Chad
62 *G11* **Viña del Mar** Valparaíso, C Chile *33°02′S 71°35′W*
19 *R8* **Vinalhaven Island** *island* Maine, NE USA
105 *T8* **Vinaròs** País Valenciano, E Spain *40°29′N 00°28′E*
Vinàtori *see* Vânători
31 *N15* **Vincennes** Indiana, N USA *38°42′N 87°30′W*
195 *Y12* **Vincennes Bay** *bay* Antarctica
25 *O7* **Vincent** Texas, SW USA *32°30′N 101°10′W*
95 *H24* **Vindeby** Fyn, C Denmark *54°55′N 11°09′E*
93 *I15* **Vindeln** Västerbotten, N Sweden *64°11′N 19°42′E*
95 *F21* **Vinderup** Ringkøbing, C Denmark *56°29′N 08°48′E*
Vindhya Mountains *see* Vindhya Range
153 *N14* **Vindhya Range** *var.* Vindhya Mountains. ▲ N India
Vindobona *see* Wien
20 *K6* **Vine Grove** Kentucky, S USA *37°48′N 85°58′W*
18 *J17* **Vineland** New Jersey, NE USA *39°29′N 75°02′W*
116 *E11* **Vinga** Arad, W Romania *46°00′N 21°14′E*
95 *M16* **Vingåker** Södermanland, C Sweden *59°02′N 15°52′E*
167 *S8* **Vinh** Nghệ An, N Vietnam *18°42′N 105°41′E*
104 *I5* **Vinhais** Bragança, N Portugal *41°50′N 07°00′W*
167 *T9* **Vinh Linh** Quang Tri, C Vietnam *17°02′N 107°03′E*
Vinh Loi *see* Bac Liêu
167 *S14* **Vinh Long** *var.* Vinhlong. Vinh Long, S Vietnam *10°15′N 105°59′E*
Vinhlong *see* Vinh Long
113 *Q18* **Vinica** NE FYR Macedonia *41°53′N 22°30′E*
109 *V13* **Vinica** SE Slovenia *45°28′N 15°12′E*
114 *G8* **Vinishte** Montana, NW Bulgaria *43°30′N 23°04′E*
27 *Q8* **Vinita** Oklahoma, C USA *36°38′N 95°09′W*
Vinju Mare *see* Vânju Mare
98 *I11* **Vinkeveen** Utrecht, C Netherlands *52°13′N 04°55′E*
116 *L6* **Vin'kivtsi** Khmel'nyts'ka Oblast', W Ukraine *49°02′N 27°13′E*
112 *I10* **Vinkovci** *Ger.* Winkowitz, *Hung.* Vinkovcze. Vukovar-Srijem, E Croatia *45°18′N 18°45′E*
Vinkovcze *see* Vinkovci
Vinnitsa *see* Vinnytsya
Vinnitskaya Oblast'/Vinnytsya *see* Vinnyts'ka Oblast'
116 *M7* **Vinnyts'ka Oblast'** *var.* Vinnytsya, *Rus.* Vinnitskaya Oblast'. ◆ *province* C Ukraine
117 *N6* **Vinnytsya** *Rus.* Vinnitsa. Vinnyts'ka Oblast', C Ukraine *49°14′N 28°30′E*
117 *N6* **Vinnytsya** ✈ Vinnyts'ka Oblast', N Ukraine *49°13′N 28°40′E*
Vinogradov *see* Vynohradiv
194 *L8* **Vinson Massif** ▲ Antarctica *78°45′S 85°19′W*
94 *G11* **Vinstra** Oppland, S Norway *61°36′N 09°45′E*
116 *K12* **Vintilă Vodă** Buzău, SE Romania *45°28′N 26°43′E*
29 *X13* **Vinton** Iowa, C USA *42°10′N 92°01′W*
22 *F9* **Vinton** Louisiana, S USA *30°10′N 93°37′W*
155 *J17* **Vinukonda** Andhra Pradesh, E India *16°03′N 79°41′E*
Vioara *see* Ocnele Mari
83 *E23* **Vioolsdrif** Northern Cape, SW South Africa *28°50′S 17°38′E*
109 *S12* **Vipava** ↝ Italy/Slovenia
82 *M13* **Viphya Mountains** ▲ C Malawi
171 *Q4* **Virac** Catanduanes Island, N Philippines *13°39′N 124°17′E*
124 *K8* **Virandozero** Respublika Kareliya, NW Russian Federation *63°59′N 36°00′E*
137 *P16* **Viranşehir** Şanlıurfa, SE Turkey *37°13′N 39°32′E*
154 *D13* **Virār** Mahārāshtra, W India *19°30′N 72°48′E*
11 *W16* **Virden** Manitoba, S Canada *49°50′N 100°57′W*
30 *K14* **Virden** Illinois, N USA *39°30′N 89°46′W*
Virdois *see* Virrat
102 *J5* **Vire** Calvados, N France *48°50′N 00°53′W*
102 *J4* **Vire** ↝ N France
83 *A15* **Virei** Namibe, SW Angola *15°43′S 12°54′E*
Virful Moldoveanu *see* Vârful Moldoveanu
35 *R5* **Virginia Peak** ▲ Nevada, W USA *39°46′N 119°26′W*
45 *U9* **Virgin Gorda** *island* C British Virgin Islands
83 *I22* **Virginia** Free State, C South Africa *28°06′S 26°53′E*
30 *K13* **Virginia** Illinois, N USA *39°57′N 90°12′W*
29 *W4* **Virginia** Minnesota, N USA *47°31′N 92°32′W*
21 *T6* **Virginia** *off.* Commonwealth of Virginia, *also known as* Mother of Presidents, Mother of States, Old Dominion. ◆ *state* NE USA
21 *Y7* **Virginia Beach** Virginia, NE USA *36°51′N 75°59′W*
33 *R11* **Virginia City** Montana, NW USA *45°17′N 111°54′W*
35 *Q6* **Virginia City** Nevada, W USA *39°19′N 119°39′W*
14 *H8* **Virginiatown** Ontario, S Canada *48°09′N 79°35′W*
Virgin Islands *see* British Virgin Islands
45 *T9* **Virgin Islands (US)** *var.* Virgin Islands of the United States; *prev.* Danish West Indies. ◇ *US unincorporated territory* E West Indies
Virgin Islands of the United States *see* Virgin Islands (US)
45 *T9* **Virgin Passage** *passage* Puerto Rico/Virgin Islands (US)
35 *Y10* **Virgin River** ↝ Nevada/Utah, W USA
Virihaur *see* Virihaure
92 *H12* **Virihaure** *var.* Virihaur. ⊗ N Sweden
167 *T11* **Virôchey** Rôtânôkiri, NE Cambodia *13°59′N 106°49′E*
93 *N19* **Virolahti** Etelä-Suomi, S Finland *60°33′N 27°37′E*
30 *J8* **Viroqua** Wisconsin, N USA *43°33′N 90°54′W*
112 *G8* **Virovitica** *Ger.* Virovititz, *Hung.* Verőcze; *prev. Ger.* Werowitz. Virovitica-Podravina, NE Croatia *45°49′N 17°25′E*
112 *G8* **Virovitica-Podravina** *off.* Virovitičko-Podravska Županija. ◆ *province* NE Croatia
Virovitičko-Podravska Županija *see* Virovitica-Podravina
Virovititz *see* Virovitica
113 *J17* **Virpazar** S Montenegro *42°15′N 19°06′E*
93 *L17* **Virrat** *Swe.* Virdois. Länsi-Suomi, W Finland *62°14′N 23°50′E*
95 *M20* **Virserum** Kalmar, S Sweden *57°17′N 15°18′E*
99 *K25* **Virton** Luxembourg, SE Belgium *49°34′N 05°32′E*
118 *F5* **Virtsu** *Ger.* Werder. Läänemaa, W Estonia *58°35′N 23°33′E*
56 *C12* **Virú** La Libertad, C Peru *08°24′S 78°40′W*
Virudhunagar *see* Virudunagar
155 *H23* **Virudunagar** *var.* Virudhunagar; *prev.* Virudupatti. Tamil Nādu, SE India *09°35′N 77°57′E*
Virudupatti *see* Virudunagar
118 *I3* **Viru-Jaagupi** *Ger.* Sankt-Jakobi. Lääne-Virumaa, NE Estonia *59°14′N 26°29′E*
57 *N19* **Viru-Viru** *var.* Santa Cruz. ✈ (Santa Cruz) Santa Cruz, C Bolivia *17°49′S 63°12′W*
113 *E15* **Vis** *It.* Lissa; *anc.* Issa. *island* S Croatia
Vis *see* Fish
118 *I12* **Visaginas** *prev.* Sniečkus. Utena, E Lithuania *55°36′N 26°22′E*
155 *M15* **Visākhapatnam** *var.* Vishakhapatnam. Andhra Pradesh, SE India *17°45′N 83°19′E*
35 *R11* **Visalia** California, W USA *36°19′N 119°19′W*
Višau *see* Vişeu
95 *P19* **Visby** *Ger.* Wisby. Gotland, SE Sweden *57°37′N 18°20′E*
197 *N9* **Viscount Melville Sound** *prev.* Melville Sound. *sound* Northwest Territories, N Canada
99 *L19* **Visé** Liège, E Belgium *50°44′N 05°42′E*
112 *K13* **Višegrad** Republika Srpska, SE Bosnia and Herzegovina *43°46′N 19°18′E*
58 *L12* **Viseu** Pará, NE Brazil *01°10′S 46°09′W*
104 *H7* **Viseu** *prev.* Vizeu. Viseu, N Portugal *40°40′N 07°55′W*
104 *H7* **Viseu** *var.* Vizeu. ◆ *district* N Portugal
116 *I8* **Vişeu** *Hung.* Visó; *prev.* Vişău. ↝ NW Romania
116 *I8* **Vişeu de Sus** *var.* Vişeul de Sus, *Ger.* Oberwischau, *Hung.* Felsővisó. Maramureş, N Romania *47°43′N 23°24′E*
Vişeul de Sus *see* Vişeu de Sus
Vishakhapatnam *see* Visākhapatnam
125 *R10* **Vishera** ↝ NW Russian Federation
95 *J19* **Viskafors** Västra Götaland, S Sweden *57°37′N 12°50′E*
95 *J20* **Viskan** ↝ S Sweden
95 *L21* **Vislanda** Kronoberg, S Sweden *56°46′N 14°30′E*
Vislinskiy Zaliv *see* Vistula Lagoon
Visó *see* Vişeu
112 *H13* **Visoko** ◆ Federacija Bosna I Hercegovina, C Bosnia and Herzegovina
106 *A9* **Viso, Monte** ▲ NW Italy *44°42′N 07°04′E*
108 *E10* **Visp** Valais, SW Switzerland *46°18′N 07°53′E*
108 *E10* **Vispa** ↝ S Switzerland
95 *M21* **Vissefjärda** Kalmar, S Sweden *56°31′N 15°34′E*
100 *I11* **Visselhövede** Niedersachsen, NW Germany *52°58′N 09°36′E*
95 *G23* **Vissenbjerg** Fyn, C Denmark *55°23′N 10°08′E*
35 *U17* **Vista** California, W USA *33°12′N 117°14′W*
58 *C11* **Vista Alegre** Amazonas, NW Brazil *01°23′N 68°13′W*
114 *J13* **Vistonída, Límni** ⊗ NE Greece
92 *K12* **Visttasjohka** ↝ N Sweden
Vistula *see* Wisła
119 *A14* **Vistula Lagoon** *Ger.* Frisches Haff, *Pol.* Zalew Wiślany, *Rus.* Vislinskiy Zaliv. *lagoon* Poland/Russian Federation
114 *I8* **Vit** ↝ NW Bulgaria
Vitebsk *see* Vitsyebsk
Vitebskaya Oblast' *see* Vitsyebskaya Voblasts'
107 *H14* **Viterbo** *anc.* Vicus Elbii. Lazio, C Italy *42°25′N 12°08′E*
112 *H12* **Vitez** Federacija Bosna I Hercegovina, C Bosnia and Herzegovina *44°08′N 17°47′E*
167 *S14* **Vi Thanh** Cần Thơ, S Vietnam *09°45′N 105°28′E*
Viti *see* Fiji
186 *E7* **Vitiaz Strait** *strait* NE Papua New Guinea
104 *J7* **Vitigudino** Castilla-León, N Spain *41°00′N 06°26′W*
187 *W15* **Viti Levu** *island* W Fiji
123 *O11* **Vitim** ↝ C Russian Federation
123 *O12* **Vitimskiy** Irkutskaya Oblast', C Russian Federation *58°12′N 113°10′E*
109 *V2* **Vitis** Niederösterreich, N Austria *48°45′N 15°09′E*
59 *O20* **Vitória** *state capital* Espírito Santo, SE Brazil *20°19′S 40°21′W*
Vitoria *see* Vitoria-Gasteiz
Vitoria Bank *see* Vitória Seamount
59 *N18* **Vitória da Conquista** Bahia, E Brazil *14°53′S 40°52′W*
105 *P3* **Vitoria-Gasteiz** *var.* Vitoria, *Eng.* Vittoria. País Vasco, N Spain *42°51′N 02°40′W*
65 *J16* **Vitória Seamount** *var.* Victoria Bank, Vitoria Bank. *undersea feature* C Atlantic Ocean *18°48′S 37°24′W*
112 *F13* **Vitorog** ▲ SW Bosnia and Herzegovina *44°06′N 17°03′E*
102 *J6* **Vitré** Ille-et-Vilaine, NW France *48°07′N 01°12′W*
103 *R5* **Vitry-le-François** Marne, N France *48°43′N 04°36′E*
114 *D13* **Vítsi** *var.* Vítsoi. ▲ N Greece *40°39′N 21°23′E*
Vítsoi *see* Vítsi
118 *N13* **Vitsyebsk** *Rus.* Vitebsk. Vitsyebskaya Voblasts', NE Belarus *55°11′N 30°10′E*
118 *K13* **Vitsyebskaya Voblasts'** *prev. Rus.* Vitebskaya Oblast'. ◆ *province* N Belarus
92 *J11* **Vittangi** *Lapp.* Vazáš. Norrbotten, N Sweden *67°40′N 21°39′E*
103 *R8* **Vitteaux** Côte d'Or, C France *47°24′N 04°31′E*
103 *S6* **Vittel** Vosges, NE France *48°13′N 05°57′E*
95 *N15* **Vittinge** Västmanland, C Sweden *59°52′N 17°04′E*
107 *K25* **Vittoria** Sicilia, Italy, C Mediterranean Sea *36°56′N 14°30′E*
Vittoria *see* Vitoria-Gasteiz
106 *I7* **Vittorio Veneto** Veneto, NE Italy *45°59′N 12°18′E*
175 *Q9* **Vitu Levu** *island* W Fiji
175 *Q7* **Vityaz Trench** *undersea feature* W Pacific Ocean
108 *G8* **Vitznau** Luzern, W Switzerland *47°01′N 08°28′E*
104 *I1* **Viveiro** Galicia, NW Spain *43°39′N 07°35′W*
105 *S9* **Viver** País Valenciano, E Spain *39°55′N 00°36′W*
103 *Q13* **Viverais, Monts du** ▲ C France
122 *L9* **Vivi** ↝ N Russian Federation
22 *F4* **Vivian** Louisiana, S USA *32°52′N 93°59′W*
29 *N10* **Vivian** South Dakota, N USA *43°53′N 100°16′W*
103 *R13* **Viviers** Ardèche, E France *44°31′N 04°40′E*
Vivis *see* Vevey
83 *K19* **Vivo** Limpopo, NE South Africa *22°58′S 29°13′E*
102 *L10* **Vivonne** Vienne, W France *46°25′N 00°15′E*
Vizakna *see* Ocna Sibiului
105 *O2* **Vizcaya** *Basq.* Bizkaia. ◆ *province* País Vasco, N Spain
Vizcaya, Golfo de *see* Biscay, Bay of
136 *C10* **Vize** Kırklareli, NW Turkey *41°34′N 27°45′E*
122 *K4* **Vize, Ostrov** *island* Severnaya Zemlya, N Russian Federation
Vizeu *see* Viseu
155 *M15* **Vizianagaram** *var.* Vizianagram. Andhra Pradesh, E India *18°07′N 83°25′E*
Vizianagram *see* Vizianagaram
103 *S12* **Vizille** Isère, E France *45°05′N 05°46′E*
125 *R11* **Vizinga** Respublika Komi, NW Russian Federation *61°06′N 50°09′E*
116 *M13* **Viziru** Brăila, SE Romania *45°00′N 27°43′E*
113 *K21* **Vjosës, Lumi i** *var.* Vijosa, Vijosë, *Gk.* Aóos. ↝ Albania/Greece *see also* Aóos
Vjosës, Lumi i *see* Aóos
99 *H18* **Vlaams Brabant** ◆ *province* C Belgium
Vlaanderen *see* Flanders
98 *G12* **Vlaardingen** Zuid-Holland, SW Netherlands *51°55′N 04°21′E*
116 *F10* **Vlădeasa, Vârful** *prev.* Vîrful Vlădeasa. ▲ NW Romania *46°45′N 22°46′E*
Vlădeasa, Vîrful *see* Vlădeasa, Vârful
113 *P16* **Vladičin Han** Serbia, SE Serbia *42°44′N 22°04′E*
127 *O16* **Vladikavkaz** *prev.* Dzaudzhikau, Ordzhonikidze. Respublika Severnaya Osetiya, SW Russian Federation *42°58′N 44°41′E*
126 *M3* **Vladimir** Vladimirskaya Oblast', W Russian Federation *56°09′N 40°21′E*
144 *M7* **Vladimirovka** Kostanay, N Kazakhstan *53°30′N 64°02′E*
Vladimirovka *see* Yuzhno-Sakhalinsk
126 *L3* **Vladimirskaya Oblast'** ◆ *province* W Russian Federation
126 *I3* **Vladimirskiy Tupik** Smolenskaya Oblast', W Russian Federation *55°45′N 33°25′E*
Vladimir-Volynskiy *see* Volodymyr-Volyns'kyy
123 *Q7* **Vladivostok** Primorskiy Kray, SE Russian Federation *43°09′N 131°53′E*
117 *U13* **Vladyslavivka** Respublika Krym, S Ukraine *45°09′N 35°25′E*
98 *P6* **Vlagtwedde** Groningen, NE Netherlands *53°02′N 07°07′E*
Vlajna *see* Kukavica
112 *J12* **Vlasenica** ◆ Republika Srpska, E Bosnia and Herzegovina
112 *G12* **Vlašić** ▲ C Bosnia and Herzegovina *44°18′N 17°40′E*
111 *D17* **Vlašim** *Ger.* Wlaschim. Středočeský Kraj, C Czech Republic *49°42′N 14°54′E*
113 *P15* **Vlasotince** Serbia, SE Serbia *42°58′N 22°07′E*
123 *Q7* **Vlasovo** Respublika Sakha (Yakutiya), NE Russian Federation *70°41′N 134°49′E*
98 *I11* **Vleuten** Utrecht, C Netherlands *52°07′N 05°01′E*
98 *I5* **Vlieland** *Fris.* Flylân. *island* Waddeneilanden, N Netherlands
98 *I5* **Vliestroom** *strait* NW Netherlands
99 *J14* **Vlijmen** Noord-Brabant, S Netherlands *51°42′N 05°14′E*
99 *E15* **Vlissingen** *Eng.* Flushing, *Fr.* Flessingue. Zeeland, SW Netherlands *51°26′N 03°34′E*
Vlodava *see* Włodawa
Vlonë/Vlora *see* Vlorë
113 *K22* **Vlorë** *prev.* Vlonë, *It.* Valona, Vlora. Vlorë, SW Albania *40°28′N 19°31′E*
113 *K22* **Vlorë** ◆ *district* SW Albania
113 *K22* **Vlorës, Gjiri i** *var.* Valona Bay. *bay* SW Albania
Vlotslavsk *see* Włocławek
111 *C16* **Vltava** *Ger.* Moldau. ↝ W Czech Republic
126 *K3* **Vnukovo** ✈ (Moskva) Gorod Moskva, W Russian Federation *55°30′N 36°52′E*
146 *L11* **Vobkent** *Rus.* Vabkent. Buxoro Viloyati, C Uzbekistan *40°01′N 64°25′E*
25 *Q9* **Voca** Texas, SW USA *30°58′N 99°09′W*
109 *R5* **Vöcklabruck** Oberösterreich, NW Austria *48°01′N 13°38′E*
112 *D13* **Vodice** Šibenik-Knin, S Croatia *43°46′N 15°46′E*
124 *K10* **Vodlozero, Ozero** ⊗ NW Russian Federation
112 *A10* **Vodnjan** *It.* Dignano d'Istria. Istra, NW Croatia *44°57′N 13°51′E*
125 *S9* **Vodnyy** Respublika Komi, NW Russian Federation *63°31′N 53°21′E*
95 *G20* **Vodskov** Nordjylland, N Denmark *57°07′N 10°02′E*
92 *H4* **Vogar** Sudhurland, SW Iceland *63°58′N 22°20′W*
Vogelkop *see* Doberai, Jazirah
77 *X15* **Vogel Peak** *prev.* Dimlang. ▲ E Nigeria *08°16′N 11°44′E*
101 *H17* **Vogelsberg** ▲ C Germany
106 *D8* **Voghera** Lombardia, N Italy *44°59′N 09°01′E*
112 *I13* **Vogošća** Federacija Bosna I Hercegovina, SE Bosnia and Herzegovina *43°55′N 18°20′E*
101 *M17* **Vogtland** *historical region* E Germany
125 *V12* **Vogul'skiy Kamen', Gora** ▲ NW Russian Federation *60°10′N 58°41′E*
187 *P16* **Voh** Province Nord, C New Caledonia *20°57′S 164°41′E*
Vohémar *see* Iharaña
172 *H8* **Vohimena, Tanjona** *Fr.* Cap Sainte Marie. *headland* S Madagascar *25°20′S 45°06′E*
172 *J6* **Vohipeno** Fianarantsoa, SE Madagascar *22°21′S 47°51′E*
118 *H5* **Võhma** *Ger.* Wöchma. Viljandimaa, S Estonia *58°37′N 25°34′E*
81 *J20* **Voi** Coast, S Kenya *03°23′S 38°35′E*
76 *K15* **Voinjama** N Liberia *08°25′N 09°42′W*
103 *S12* **Voiron** Isère, E France *45°22′N 05°35′E*
109 *V8* **Voitsberg** Steiermark, SE Austria *47°04′N 15°09′E*
95 *F24* **Vojens** *Ger.* Woyens. Sønderjylland, SW Denmark *55°15′N 09°19′E*
112 *K9* **Vojvodina** *Ger.* Wojwodina. Vojvodina, N Serbia
15 *S6* **Volant** ↝ Québec, SE Canada
Volaterrae *see* Volterra
43 *P15* **Volcán** *var.* Hato del Volcán. Chiriquí, W Panama *08°45′N 82°38′W*
Volcano Islands *see* Kazan-rettō
Volchansk *see* Vovchans'k
Volchya *see* Vovcha
94 *D10* **Volda** Møre og Romsdal, S Norway *62°07′N 06°04′E*
98 *J9* **Volendam** Noord-Holland, C Netherlands *52°30′N 05°04′E*
124 *L15* **Volga** Yaroslavskaya Oblast', W Russian Federation *57°56′N 38°23′E*
29 *R10* **Volga** South Dakota, N USA *44°19′N 96°55′W*
122 *C11* **Volga** ↝ NW Russian Federation
Volga-Baltic Waterway *see* Volgo-Baltiyskiy Kanal
Volga Uplands *see* Privolzhskaya Vozvyshennost'
124 *L13* **Volgo-Baltiyskiy Kanal** *var.* Volga-Baltic Waterway. *canal* NW Russian Federation
126 *M12* **Volgodonsk** Rostovskaya Oblast', SW Russian Federation *47°35′N 42°03′E*
127 *O10* **Volgograd** *prev.* Stalingrad, Tsaritsyn. Volgogradskaya Oblast', SW Russian Federation *48°42′N 44°29′E*
127 *N9* **Volgogradskaya Oblast'** ◆ *province* SW Russian Federation
127 *P10* **Volgogradskoye Vodokhranilishche** ⊠ SW Russian Federation
101 *J19* **Volkach** Bayern, C Germany *49°51′N 10°15′E*
109 *U9* **Völkermarkt** *Slvn.* Velikovec. Kärnten, S Austria *46°40′N 14°38′E*
124 *I12* **Volkhov** Leningradskaya Oblast', NW Russian Federation *59°56′N 32°19′E*
101 *D20* **Völklingen** Saarland, SW Germany *49°15′N 06°51′E*
Volkovysk *see* Vawkavysk
Volkovyskiye Vysoty *see* Vawkavyskaye Wzvyshsha
83 *K22* **Volksrust** Mpumalanga, E South Africa *27°22′S 29°54′E*
98 *L8* **Vollenhove** Overijssel, N Netherlands *52°40′N 05°58′E*
119 *L16* **Volma** ↝ C Belarus
Volmari *see* Valmiera
117 *W9* **Volnovakha** Donets'ka Oblast', SE Ukraine *47°36′N 37°32′E*
116 *K6* **Volochys'k** Khmel'nyts'ka Oblast', W Ukraine *49°32′N 26°14′E*
117 *O6* **Volodarka** Kyyivs'ka Oblast', N Ukraine *49°31′N 29°55′E*
117 *W9* **Volodars'ke** Donets'ka Oblast', E Ukraine *47°11′N 37°19′E*
127 *R13* **Volodarskiy** Astrakhanskaya Oblast', SW Russian Federation *46°23′N 48°39′E*
Volodarskoye *see* Saumalkol'
117 *N8* **Volodars'k-Volyns'kyy** Zhytomyrs'ka Oblast', N Ukraine *50°37′N 28°28′E*
116 *K3* **Volodymerets'** Rivnens'ka Oblast', NW Ukraine *51°24′N 25°52′E*
116 *I3* **Volodymyr-Volyns'kyy** *Pol.* Włodzimierz, *Rus.* Vladimir-Volynskiy. Volyns'ka Oblast', NW Ukraine *50°51′N 24°19′E*
124 *L14* **Vologda** Vologodskaya Oblast', W Russian Federation *59°10′N 39°55′E*
124 *L12* **Vologodskaya Oblast'** ◆ *province* NW Russian Federation
126 *K3* **Volokolamsk** Moskovskaya Oblast', W Russian Federation *56°03′N 35°57′E*
126 *K9* **Volokonovka** Belgorodskaya Oblast', W Russian Federation *50°30′N 37°54′E*
115 *G16* **Vólos** Thessalía, C Greece *39°21′N 22°58′E*
124 *M11* **Voloshka** Arkhangel'skaya Oblast', NW Russian Federation *61°19′N 40°06′E*
Vološinovo *see* Novi Bečej
116 *H7* **Volovets'** Zakarpats'ka Oblast', W Ukraine *48°42′N 23°12′E*
Volozhin *see* Valozhyn
127 *Q7* **Vol'sk** Saratovskaya Oblast', W Russian Federation *52°04′N 47°20′E*
77 *Q17* **Volta** ↝ SE Ghana
Volta Blanche *see* White Volta
77 *P16* **Volta, Lake** ⊠ SE Ghana
Volta Noire *see* Black Volta
60 *O9* **Volta Redonda** Rio de Janeiro, SE Brazil *22°31′S 44°05′W*
Volta Rouge *see* Red Volta

◆ Country ● Country Capital ◇ Dependent Territory ○ Dependent Territory Capital ◆ Administrative Regions ✈ International Airport ▲ Mountain ▲ Mountain Range ⋏ Volcano ↝ River ⊗ Lake ⊠ Reservoir

VOLTERRA – WALK

106 *F12* **Volterra** *anc.* Volaterrae. Toscana, C Italy 43°23′N 10°52′E
107 *K17* **Volturno** ≈ S Italy
113 *I15* **Volujak** ▲▲ NW Montenegro
Volunteer Island *see* Starbuck Island
114 *H13* **Vólvi, Límni** ◎ N Greece
Volyn *see* Volyns'ka Oblast'
116 *I3* **Volyns'ka Oblast'** *var.* Volyn, *Rus.* Volynskaya Oblast'. ◆ *province* NW Ukraine
Volynskaya Oblast' *see* Volyns'ka Oblast'
127 *Q3* **Volzhsk** Respublika Mariy El, W Russian Federation 55°53′N 48°21′E
127 *O10* **Volzhskiy** Volgogradskaya Oblast', SW Russian Federation 48°49′N 44°40′E
172 *I7* **Vondrozo** Fianarantsoa, SE Madagascar 22°50′S 47°20′E
39 *P10* **Von Frank Mountain** ▲ Alaska, USA 63°36′N 154°29′W
115 *C17* **Vónitsa** Dytikí Ellás, W Greece 38°55′N 20°53′E
118 *J6* **Võnnu** *Ger.* Wendau. Tartumaa, SE Estonia 58°17′N 27°06′E
98 *G12* **Voorburg** Zuid-Holland, W Netherlands 52°04′N 04°22′E
98 *H11* **Voorschoten** Zuid-Holland, W Netherlands 52°08′N 04°26′E
98 *M11* **Voorst** Gelderland, E Netherlands 52°10′N 06°10′E
98 *K11* **Voorthuizen** Gelderland, C Netherlands 52°12′N 05°36′E
92 *L2* **Vopnafjörður** Austurland, E Iceland 65°45′N 14°51′W
92 *L2* **Vopnafjördhur** *bay* E Iceland
Vora *see* Vorë
119 *H15* **Voranava** *Pol.* Werenów, *Rus.* Voronovo. Hrodzyenskaya Voblasts', W Belarus 54°09′N 25°19′E
108 *I8* **Vorarlberg** *off.* Land Vorarlberg. ◆ *state* W Austria
Vorarlberg, Land *see* Vorarlberg
109 *X7* **Vorau** Steiermark, E Austria 47°22′N 15°55′E
98 *N11* **Vorden** Gelderland, E Netherlands 52°07′N 06°18′E
108 *H9* **Vorderrhein** ≈ SE Switzerland
92 *J2* **Vordhufell** ▲ N Iceland 65°42′N 18°45′W
95 *I24* **Vordingborg** Storstrøm, SE Denmark 55°01′N 11°55′E
113 *K19* **Vorë** *var.* Vora. Tiranë, W Albania 41°23′N 19°37′E
115 *H17* **Vóreies Sporádes** *var.* Vóreioi Sporádes, Vórioi Sporádhes, *Eng.* Northern Sporades. *island group* E Greece
Vóreioi Sporádes *see* Vóreies Sporádes
115 *J17* **Vóreion Aigaíon** *Eng.* Aegean North. ◆ *region* SE Greece
115 *G18* **Vóreios Evvoïkós Kólpos** *var.* Voreiós Evvoïkós Kólpos. *gulf* E Greece
197 *S16* **Voring Plateau** *undersea feature* N Norwegian Sea 67°00′N 04°00′E
Vórioi Sporádhes *see* Vóreies Sporádes
125 *W4* **Vorkuta** Respublika Komi, NW Russian Federation 67°27′N 64°E
95 *I14* **Vorma** ≈ S Norway
118 *E4* **Vormsi** *var.* Vormsi Saar, *Ger.* Worms, *Swed.* Ormsö. *island* W Estonia
Vormsi Saar *see* Vormsi
127 *N7* **Vorona** ≈ W Russian Federation
126 *L7* **Voronezh** Voronezhskaya Oblast', W Russian Federation 51°40′N 39°13′E
126 *L7* **Voronezh** ≈ W Russian Federation
126 *K8* **Voronezhskaya Oblast'** ◆ *province* W Russian Federation
Voronovitsya *see* Voronovytsya
Voronovo *see* Voranava
117 *N6* **Voronovytsya** *Rus.* Voronovitsya. Vinnyts'ka Oblast', C Ukraine 49°06′N 28°49′E
122 *K7* **Vorontsovo** Taymyrskiy (Dolgano-Nenetskiy) Avtonomnyy Okrug, N Russian Federation 71°45′N 83°31′E
124 *K3* **Voron'ya** ≈ NW Russian Federation
Voropayevo *see* Varapayeva
Voroshilov *see* Ussuriysk
Voroshilovgrad *see* Luhans'ka Oblast', Ukraine
Voroshilovgrad *see* Luhans'k, Ukraine
Voroshilovgradskaya Oblast' *see* Luhans'ka Oblast'
Voroshilovsk *see* Stavropol', Russian Federation
Voroshilovsk *see* Alchevs'k
137 *V13* **Vorotan** *Az.* Bärgušad. ≈ Armenia/Azerbaijan
127 *P3* **Vorotynets** Nizhegorodskaya Oblast', W Russian Federation 56°06′N 46°06′E
117 *S3* **Vorozhba** Sums'ka Oblast', NE Ukraine 51°10′N 34°15′E
117 *T5* **Vorskla** ≈ Russian Federation/Ukraine
99 *I17* **Vorst** Antwerpen, N Belgium 51°06′N 05°01′E
83 *G21* **Vorstershoop** North-West, N South Africa 25°46′S 22°57′E
118 *H6* **Võrtsjärv** *Ger.* Wirz-See. ◎ SE Estonia
118 *J7* **Võru** *Ger.* Werro. Võrumaa, SE Estonia 57°51′N 27°01′E
147 *R11* **Vorukh** N Tajikistan 39°51′N 70°34′E
118 *I7* **Võrumaa** *off.* Võru Maakond. ◆ *province* SE Estonia
Võru Maakond *see* Võrumaa
83 *G24* **Vosburg** Northern Cape, W South Africa 30°35′S 22°52′E
147 *Q14* **Vose'** *Rus.* Vose; *prev.* Aral. SW Tajikistan 37°51′N 69°31′E
103 *S6* **Vosges** ◆ *department* NE France
103 *U6* **Vosges** ▲▲ NE France
124 *K13* **Voskresenkoye** Vologodskaya Oblast', NW Russian Federation 59°25′N 37°56′E
126 *L4* **Voskresensk** Moskovskaya Oblast', W Russian Federation 55°19′N 38°42′E
127 *P2* **Voskresenskoye** Nizhegorodskaya Oblast', W Russian Federation 57°00′N 45°33′E
127 *V6* **Voskresenskoye** Respublika Bashkortostan, W Russian Federation 53°07′N 56°07′E
94 *D13* **Voss** Hordaland, S Norway 60°38′N 06°25′E
94 *D13* **Voss** *physical region* S Norway
99 *I16* **Vosselaar** Antwerpen, N Belgium 51°19′N 04°55′E
94 *D13* **Vosso** ≈ S Norway
Vostochno-Kazakhstanskaya Oblast' *see* Vostochnyy Kazakhstan
145 *T12* **Vostochno-Kounradskiy** *Kaz.* Shyghys Qongyrat. Zhezkazgan, C Kazakhstan
123 *S5* **Vostochno-Sibirskoye More** *Eng.* East Siberian Sea. *sea* Arctic Ocean
145 *X10* **Vostochnyy Kazakhstan** *off.* Vostochno-Kazakhstanskaya Oblast', *var.* East Kazakhstan, *Kaz.* Shyghys Qazagastan Oblysy. ◆ *province* E Kazakhstan
Vostochnyy Sayan *see* Eastern Sayans
Vostock Island *see* Vostok Island
195 *U10* **Vostok** *Russian research station* Antarctica 77°18′S 105°32′E
191 *X5* **Vostok Island** *var.* Vostock Island; *prev.* Stavers Island. *island* Line Islands, SE Kiribati
127 *T2* **Votkinsk** Udmurtskaya Respublika, NW Russian Federation 57°04′N 54°00′E
125 *U15* **Votkinskoye Vodokhranilishche** *var.* Votkinsk Reservoir. ▣ NW Russian Federation
Votkinsk Reservoir *see* Votkinskoye Vodokhranilishche
60 *J7* **Votuporanga** São Paulo, S Brazil 20°26′S 49°53′W
104 *H7* **Vouga, Rio** ≈ N Portugal
115 *E14* **Voúrinos** ▲ N Greece
115 *G24* **Voúxa, Akrotírio** *headland* Kríti, Greece, E Mediterranean Sea 35°37′N 23°34′E
103 *R4* **Vouziers** Ardennes, N France 49°24′N 04°42′E
117 *V7* **Vovcha** *Rus.* Volchya. ≈ E Ukraine
117 *V4* **Vovchans'k** *Rus.* Volchansk. Kharkivs'ka Oblast', E Ukraine 50°19′N 36°55′E
103 *N6* **Voves** Eure-et-Loir, C France 48°18′N 01°39′E
79 *M14* **Vovodo** ≈ S Central African Republic
94 *M12* **Voxna** Gävleborg, C Sweden 61°21′N 15°35′E
94 *L11* **Voxnan** ≈ C Sweden
114 *F7* **Voynishka Reka** ≈ NW Bulgaria
125 *T9* **Voyvozh** Respublika Komi, NW Russian Federation 62°54′N 54°52′E
124 *M12* **Vozhega** Vologodskaya Oblast', NW Russian Federation 60°27′N 40°11′E
124 *L12* **Vozhe, Ozero** ◎ NW Russian Federation
117 *Q9* **Voznesens'k** *Rus.* Voznesensk. Mykolayivs'ka Oblast', S Ukraine 47°34′N 31°21′E
124 *J12* **Voznesen'ye** Leningradskaya Oblast', NW Russian Federation 61°00′N 35°24′E
144 *J14* **Vozrozhdeniya, Ostrov** *Uzb.* Wozrojdeniye Oroli. *island* Kazakhstan/Uzbekistan
95 *G20* **Vrå** *var.* Vraa. Nordjylland, N Denmark 57°21′N 09°57′E
Vraa *see* Vrå
114 *H9* **Vrachesh** Sofiya, W Bulgaria 42°52′N 23°45′E
115 *C19* **Vrachíonas** ▲ Zákynthos, Iónia Nisiá, Greece, C Mediterranean Sea 37°49′N 20°43′E
117 *P8* **Vradiyivka** Mykolayivs'ka Oblast', S Ukraine 47°51′N 30°37′E
113 *G14* **Vran** ▲ SW Bosnia and Herzegovina 43°35′N 17°30′E
116 *K12* **Vrancea** ◆ *county* E Romania
147 *T14* **Vrang** SE Tajikistan 37°03′N 72°26′E
123 *T4* **Vrangelya, Ostrov** *Eng.* Wrangel Island. *island* NE Russian Federation
112 *H13* **Vranica** ▲ C Bosnia and Herzegovina 43°57′N 17°43′E
113 *O16* **Vranje** Serbia, SE Serbia 42°33′N 21°55′E
Vranov *see* Vranov nad Topl'ou
111 *N19* **Vranov nad Topl'ou** *var.* Vranov, *Hung.* Varannó. Prešovský Kraj, E Slovakia 48°54′N 21°41′E
114 *H8* **Vratsa** Vratsa, NW Bulgaria 43°13′N 23°34′E
114 *H8* **Vratsa** ◆ *province* NW Bulgaria
114 *F10* **Vrattsa** *prev.* Mirovo. Kyustendil, W Bulgaria 42°15′N 22°33′E
112 *G11* **Vrbanja** ≈ NW Bosnia and Herzegovina
112 *K9* **Vrbas** Vojvodina, NW Serbia 45°34′N 19°39′E
112 *G13* **Vrbas** ≈ N Bosnia and Herzegovina
112 *E8* **Vrbovec** Zagreb, N Croatia 45°53′N 16°24′E
112 *C9* **Vrbovsko** Primorje-Gorski Kotar, NW Croatia 45°22′N 15°06′E
111 *E15* **Vrchlabí** *Ger.* Hohenelbe. Královéhradecký Kraj, N Czech Republic 50°38′N 15°35′E
83 *J22* **Vrede** Free State, E South Africa 27°25′S 29°10′E
100 *E13* **Vreden** Nordrhein-Westfalen, NW Germany 52°01′N 06°50′E
83 *E25* **Vredenburg** Western Cape, SW South Africa 32°55′S 18°00′E
99 *I23* **Vresse-sur-Semois** Namur, SE Belgium 49°52′N 04°56′E
95 *L16* **Vretstorp** Örebro, C Sweden 59°03′N 14°51′E
113 *G15* **Vrgorac** *prev.* Vrhgorac. Split-Dalmacija, SE Croatia 43°10′N 17°24′E
Vrhgorac *see* Vrgorac
109 *T12* **Vrhnika** *Ger.* Oberlaibach. W Slovenia 45°57′N 14°18′E
155 *I21* **Vriddhāchalam** Tamil Nādu, SE India 11°33′N 79°18′E
98 *N6* **Vries** Drenthe, NE Netherlands 53°04′N 06°34′E
98 *O10* **Vriezenveen** Overijssel, E Netherlands 52°25′N 06°37′E
95 *L20* **Vrigstad** Jönköping, S Sweden 57°19′N 14°30′E
108 *H9* **Vrin** Graubünden, S Switzerland 46°40′N 09°06′E
112 *E13* **Vrlika** Split-Dalmacija, S Croatia 43°54′N 16°24′E
113 *M14* **Vrnjačka Banja** Serbia, C Serbia 43°36′N 20°55′E
Vrondádhes/Vrondados *see* Vrontádos
115 *L18* **Vrontádos** *var.* Vrondados; *prev.* Vrondádhes. Chíos, E Greece 38°25′N 26°08′E
98 *N9* **Vroomshoop** Overijssel, E Netherlands 52°28′N 06°35′E
112 *N10* **Vršac** *Ger.* Werschetz, *Hung.* Versecz. Vojvodina, NE Serbia 45°08′N 21°18′E
112 *M10* **Vršački Kanal** *canal* N Serbia
83 *H21* **Vryburg** North-West, N South Africa 26°57′S 24°44′E
83 *K22* **Vryheid** KwaZulu/Natal, E South Africa 27°45′S 30°48′E
111 *I18* **Vsetín** *Ger.* Wsetin. Zlínský Kraj, E Czech Republic 49°21′N 17°57′E
111 *J20* **Vtáčnik** *Hung.* Madaras, Ptacsnik; *prev.* Ptačnik. ▲ W Slovakia 48°38′N 18°38′E
Vuadil' *see* Wodil
114 *I11* **Vŭcha** ≈ SW Bulgaria
Vučitrn *see* Vushtrri
99 *J14* **Vught** Noord-Brabant, S Netherlands 51°37′N 05°19′E
117 *W8* **Vuhledar** Donets'ka Oblast', E Ukraine 47°48′N 37°11′E
112 *I9* **Vuka** ≈ E Croatia
113 *K17* **Vukël** *var.* Vukli. Shkodër, N Albania 42°29′N 19°39′E
Vukli *see* Vukël
112 *J9* **Vukovar** *Hung.* Vukovár. Vukovar-Srijem, E Croatia 45°18′N 18°45′E
Vukovarsko-Srijemska Županija *see* Vukovar-Srijem
112 *I10* **Vukovar-Srijem** *off.* Vukovarsko-Srijemska Županija. ◆ *province* E Croatia
125 *U8* **Vuktyl'** Respublika Komi, NW Russian Federation 63°49′N 57°07′E
11 *Q17* **Vulcan** Alberta, SW Canada 50°27′N 113°12′W
116 *G12* **Vulcan** *Ger.* Wulkan, *Hung.* Zsilyvajdevulkán; *prev.* Crivadia Vulcanului, Vaidei, *Hung.* Sily-Vajdej, Vajdej. Hunedoara, W Romania 45°22′N 23°16′E
116 *M12* **Vulcănești** *Rus.* Vulkaneshty. S Moldova 45°41′N 28°25′E
107 *L22* **Vulcano, Isola** *island* Isole Eolie, S Italy
114 *G7* **Vŭlchedrŭm** Montana, NW Bulgaria 43°42′N 23°25′E
114 *N8* **Vŭlchidol** *prev.* Kurt-Dere. Varna, E Bulgaria 43°25′N 27°33′E
Vulkaneshty *see* Vulcănești
123 *V11* **Vulkannyy** Kamchatskaya Oblast', E Russian Federation 53°01′N 158°26′E
36 *J13* **Vulture Mountains** ▲▲ Arizona, SW USA
167 *T14* **Vung Tau** *prev. Fr.* Cape Saint Jacques, Cap Saint-Jacques. Ba Ria-Vung Tau, S Vietnam 10°21′N 107°04′E
187 *X15* **Vunisea** Kadavu, SE Fiji 19°04′S 178°10′E
Vuohčču *see* Vuotso
93 *N15* **Vuokatti** Oulu, C Finland 64°08′N 28°16′E
93 *M15* **Vuolijoki** Oulu, C Finland 64°09′N 27°00′E
Vuolleriebme *see* Vuollerim
92 *J13* **Vuollerim** *Lapp.* Vuolleriebme. Norrbotten, N Sweden 66°24′N 20°36′E
Vuoreija *see* Vardø
92 *L10* **Vuotso** *Lapp.* Vuohčču. Lappi, N Finland 68°04′N 27°05′E
114 *J11* **Vŭrbitsa** *prev.* Filevo. Khaskovo, S Bulgaria 42°02′N 25°25′E
114 *J12* **Vŭrbitsa** ≈ S Bulgaria
127 *Q4* **Vurnary** Chuvashskaya Respublika, W Russian Federation 55°30′N 46°59′E
114 *G8* **Vŭrshets** Montana, NW Bulgaria 43°14′N 23°20′E
113 *N16* **Vushtrri** *Serb.* Vučitrn. N Kosovo 42°49′N 21°00′E
119 *F17* **Vyalikaya Byerastavitsa** *Pol.* Brzostowica Wielka, *Rus.* Bol'shaya Berëstovitsa; *prev.* Velikaya Berestovitsa. Hrodzyenskaya Voblasts', SW Belarus 53°12′N 24°03′E
119 *N20* **Vyaliki Bor** *Rus.* Velikiy Bor. Homyel'skaya Voblasts', SE Belarus 52°02′N 29°56′E
119 *J18* **Vyaliki Rozhan** *Rus.* Bol'shoy Rozhan. Minskaya Voblasts', S Belarus 52°46′N 27°07′E
124 *H10* **Vyartsilya** *Fin.* Värtsilä. Respublika Kareliya, NW Russian Federation 62°07′N 30°43′E
119 *K17* **Vyasyeya** *Rus.* Veseya. Minskaya Voblasts', C Belarus 53°04′N 27°41′E
125 *R15* **Vyatka** ≈ NW Russian Federation
Vyatka *see* Kirov
125 *S16* **Vyatskiye Polyany** Kirovskaya Oblast', NW Russian Federation 56°15′N 51°06′E
123 *S14* **Vyazemskiy** Khabarovskiy Kray, SE Russian Federation 47°28′N 134°39′E
126 *I4* **Vyaz'ma** Smolenskaya Oblast', W Russian Federation 55°09′N 34°20′E
127 *N3* **Vyazniki** Vladimirskaya Oblast', W Russian Federation 56°15′N 42°06′E
127 *O8* **Vyazovka** Volgogradskaya Oblast', SW Russian Federation 50°57′N 43°57′E
119 *J14* **Vyazyn'** Minskaya Voblasts', NW Belarus 54°25′N 27°10′E
124 *G11* **Vyborg** *Fin.* Viipuri. Leningradskaya Oblast', NW Russian Federation 60°44′N 28°47′E
125 *P11* **Vychegda** *var.* Vichegda. ≈ NW Russian Federation
125 *P11* **Vychegodskiy** Arkhangel'skaya Oblast', NW Russian Federation 61°14′N 46°53′E
119 *L14* **Vyelyewshchyna** *Rus.* Velevshchina. Vitsyebskaya Voblasts', N Belarus 54°44′N 28°35′E
119 *P16* **Vyeramyeyki** *Rus.* Veremeyki. Mahilyowskaya Voblasts', E Belarus 53°46′N 31°17′E
118 *K11* **Vyerkhnyadzvinsk** *Rus.* Verkhnedvinsk. Vitsyebskaya Voblasts', N Belarus 55°47′N 27°56′E
119 *P18* **Vyetka** *Rus.* Vetka. Homyel'skaya Voblasts', SE Belarus 52°33′N 31°10′E
118 *L12* **Vyetryna** *Rus.* Vetrino. Vitsyebskaya Voblasts', N Belarus 55°25′N 28°28′E
Vygonovskoye, Ozero *see* Vyhanawskaye, Vozyera
124 *J9* **Vygozero, Ozero** ◎ NW Russian Federation
Vyhanashchanskaye Vozyera *see* Vyhanawskaye, Vozyera
119 *I18* **Vyhanawskaye, Vozyera** *var.* Vyhanashchanskaye Vozyera, *Rus.* Ozero Vygonovskoye. ◎ SW Belarus
127 *N4* **Vyksa** Nizhegorodskaya Oblast', W Russian Federation 55°21′N 42°10′E
117 *O12* **Vylkove** *Rus.* Vilkovo. Odes'ka Oblast', SW Ukraine 45°24′N 29°37′E
125 *R9* **Vym'** ≈ NW Russian Federation
116 *H8* **Vynohradiv** *Cz.* Sevluš, *Hung.* Nagyszöllös, *Rus.* Vinogradov; *prev.* Sevlyush. Zakarpats'ka Oblast', W Ukraine 48°09′N 23°01′E
124 *G13* **Vyritsa** Leningradskaya Oblast', NW Russian Federation 59°25′N 30°20′E
97 *J19* **Vyrnwy** *Wel.* Afon Efyrnwy. ≈ E Wales, United Kingdom
145 *X9* **Vyshe Ivanovskiy Belak, Gora** ▲ E Kazakhstan 50°16′N 83°46′E
117 *P4* **Vyshhorod** Kyyivs'ka Oblast', N Ukraine 50°36′N 30°28′E
124 *I15* **Vyshniy Volochek** Tverskaya Oblast', W Russian Federation 57°37′N 34°33′E
111 *G18* **Vyškov** *Ger.* Wischau. Jihomoravský Kraj, SE Czech Republic 49°17′N 17°01′E
111 *E18* **Vysočina** *prev.* Jihlavský Kraj. ◆ *region* N Czech Republic
119 *E19* **Vysokaye** *Rus.* Vysokoye. Brestskaya Voblasts', SW Belarus 52°20′N 23°18′E
111 *F17* **Vysoké Mýto** *Ger.* Hohenmauth. Pardubický Kraj, C Czech Republic 49°57′N 16°10′E
117 *S9* **Vysokopillya** Khersons'ka Oblast', S Ukraine 47°28′N 33°30′E
126 *K3* **Vysokovsk** Moskovskaya Oblast', W Russian Federation 56°12′N 36°42′E
Vysokoye *see* Vysokaye
124 *K12* **Vytegra** Vologodskaya Oblast', NW Russian Federation 60°59′N 36°27′E
116 *J8* **Vyzhnytsya** Chernivets'ka Oblast', W Ukraine 48°14′N 25°10′E

W

77 *O14* **Wa** NW Ghana 10°07′N 02°28′W
Waadt *see* Vaud
Waag *see* Váh
Waagbistritz *see* Považská Bystrica
Waagneustadtl *see* Nové Mesto nad Váhom
81 *M16* **Waajid** Gedo, SW Somalia 03°37′N 43°19′E
98 *L13* **Waal** ≈ S Netherlands
187 *O16* **Waala** Province Nord, W New Caledonia 19°46′S 163°41′E
99 *I14* **Waalwijk** Noord-Brabant, S Netherlands 51°42′N 05°04′E
99 *E16* **Waarschoot** Oost-Vlaanderen, NW Belgium 51°09′N 03°35′E
186 *C7* **Wabag** Enga, W Papua New Guinea 05°28′S 143°40′E
15 *N7* **Wabano** ≈ Québec, SE Canada
11 *P11* **Wabasca** ≈ Alberta, SW Canada
31 *P12* **Wabash** Indiana, N USA 40°47′N 85°48′W
29 *X9* **Wabasha** Minnesota, N USA 44°22′N 92°01′W
31 *N13* **Wabash River** ≈ N USA
14 *C7* **Wabatongushi Lake** ◎ Ontario, S Canada
81 *L15* **Wabē Gestro Wenz** ≈ SE Ethiopia
14 *B9* **Wabos** Ontario, S Canada 46°48′N 84°06′W
11 *W13* **Wabowden** Manitoba, C Canada 54°57′N 98°38′W
110 *J9* **Wąbrzeźno** Kujawsko-pomorskie, C Poland 53°18′N 18°55′E
21 *U12* **Waccamaw River** ≈ South Carolina, SE USA
23 *U11* **Waccasassa Bay** *bay* Florida, SE USA
99 *F16* **Wachtebeke** Oost-Vlaanderen, NW Belgium 51°10′N 03°52′E
25 *T8* **Waco** Texas, SW USA 31°33′N 97°10′W
26 *M3* **Waconda Lake** *var.* Great Elder Reservoir. ▣ Kansas, C USA
Wadai *see* Ouaddaï
Wad Al-Hajarah *see* Guadalajara
164 *I12* **Wadayama** Hyōgo, Honshū, SW Japan 35°19′N 134°51′E
80 *D10* **Wad Banda** Western Kordofan, C Sudan 13°08′N 27°56′E
75 *P9* **Waddān** NW Libya 29°10′N 16°08′E
98 *J4* **Waddeneilanden** *Eng.* West Frisian Islands. *island group* N Netherlands
98 *J6* **Waddenzee** *var.* Wadden Zee. *sea* SE North Sea
Wadden Zee *see* Waddenzee
10 *L16* **Waddington, Mount** ▲ British Columbia, SW Canada 51°17′N 125°16′W
98 *H12* **Waddinxveen** Zuid-Holland, C Netherlands 52°03′N 04°38′E
11 *U15* **Wadena** Saskatchewan, S Canada 51°57′N 103°48′W
29 *T6* **Wadena** Minnesota, N USA 46°27′N 95°07′W
108 *G7* **Wädenswil** Zürich, N Switzerland 47°14′N 08°41′E
21 *S11* **Wadesboro** North Carolina, SE USA 34°59′N 80°03′W
155 *G16* **Wādi** Karnātaka, C India 17°00′N 76°58′E
138 *G10* **Wādī as Sīr** *var.* Wadi es Sir. 'Ammān, NW Jordan 31°57′N 35°49′E
Wadi es Sir *see* Wādī as Sīr
80 *F5* **Wadi Halfa** *var.* Wādī Ḥalfā'. Northern, N Sudan 21°46′N 31°17′E
138 *G13* **Wādī Mūsā** *var.* Petra. Ma'ān, S Jordan 30°19′N 35°29′E
23 *V4* **Wadley** Georgia, SE USA 32°52′N 82°24′W
Wad Madanī *see* Wad Medani
80 *G10* **Wad Medani** *var.* Wad Madanī. Gezira, C Sudan 14°24′N 33°30′E
80 *F10* **Wad Nimr** White Nile, C Sudan 14°32′N 32°10′E
165 *U16* **Wadomari** Kagoshima, Okinoerabu-jima, SW Japan 27°25′N 128°40′E
111 *K17* **Wadowice** Małopolskie, S Poland 49°54′N 19°29′E
35 *R5* **Wadsworth** Nevada, W USA 39°39′N 119°16′W
31 *T12* **Wadsworth** Ohio, N USA 41°01′N 81°43′W
25 *T11* **Waelder** Texas, SW USA 29°42′N 97°16′W
Waereghem *see* Waregem
163 *U13* **Wafangdian** *var.* Fuxian. Liaoning, NE China 39°36′N 122°00′E
171 *R13* **Waflia** Pulau Buru, E Indonesia 03°10′S 126°05′E
Wagadugu *see* Ouagadougou
98 *K12* **Wageningen** Gelderland, SE Netherlands 51°58′N 05°40′E
55 *V9* **Wageningen** Nickerie, NW Surinam 05°44′N 56°45′W
9 *O8* **Wager Bay** *inlet* Nunavut, N Canada
183 *P10* **Wagga Wagga** New South Wales, SE Australia 35°11′S 147°22′E
180 *J13* **Wagin** Western Australia 33°16′S 117°26′E
108 *H8* **Wägitaler See** ◎ SW Switzerland
29 *P12* **Wagner** South Dakota, N USA 43°04′N 98°17′W
27 *Q9* **Wagoner** Oklahoma, C USA 35°58′N 92°23′W
37 *U10* **Wagon Mound** New Mexico, SW USA 36°00′N 104°42′W
32 *J14* **Wagontire** Oregon, NW USA 43°15′N 119°51′W
110 *H10* **Wągrowiec** Wielkopolskie, C Poland 52°49′N 17°11′E
149 *U6* **Wāh** Punjab, NE Pakistan 33°50′N 72°44′E
171 *S13* **Wahai** Pulau Seram, E Indonesia 02°48′S 129°29′E
169 *V10* **Wahau, Sungai** ≈ Borneo, C Indonesia
Wahaybah, Ramlat Al *see* Wahībah, Ramlat Āl
80 *D13* **Wahda** *var.* Unity State. ◆ *state* S Sudan
38 *D9* **Wahiawā** *var.* Wahiawa. O'ahu, Hawaii, USA, C Pacific Ocean 21°30′N 158°01′W
Wahībah, Ramlat Ahl *see* Wahībah, Ramlat Āl
141 *Y9* **Wahībah, Ramlat Āl** *var.* Ramlat Ahl Wahībah, Ramlat Al Wahaybah, *Eng.* Wahibah Sands. *desert* N Oman
Wahībah Sands *see* Wahībah, Ramlat Āl
101 *E16* **Wahn** ✈ (Köln) Nordrhein-Westfalen, W Germany 50°51′N 07°09′E
29 *R15* **Wahoo** Nebraska, C USA 41°12′N 96°37′W
29 *R6* **Wahpeton** North Dakota, N USA 46°16′N 96°36′W
Wahran *see* Oran
36 *J6* **Wah Wah Mountains** ▲▲ Utah, W USA
38 *D9* **Waialua** O'ahu, Hawaii, USA, C Pacific Ocean 21°34′N 158°07′W
38 *D9* **Wai'anae** *var.* Waianae. O'ahu, Hawaii, USA, C Pacific Ocean 21°26′N 158°11′W
184 *Q8* **Waiapu** ≈ North Island, New Zealand
185 *I17* **Waiau** Canterbury, South Island, New Zealand 42°39′S 173°03′E
185 *I17* **Waiau** ≈ South Island, New Zealand
185 *B23* **Waiau** ≈ South Island, New Zealand
101 *H21* **Waiblingen** Baden-Württemberg, S Germany 48°49′N 09°19′E
Waidhofen *see* Waidhofen an der Thaya, Niederösterreich, Austria
Waidhofen *see* Waidhofen an der Ybbs, Niederösterreich, Austria
109 *V2* **Waidhofen an der Thaya** *var.* Waidhofen. Niederösterreich, NE Austria 48°49′N 15°17′E
109 *U5* **Waidhofen an der Ybbs** *var.* Waidhofen. Niederösterreich, E Austria 47°58′N 14°47′E
171 *T11* **Waigeo, Pulau** *island* Maluku, E Indonesia
184 *L5* **Waiheke Island** *island* N New Zealand
184 *M7* **Waihi** Waikato, North Island, New Zealand 37°22′S 175°51′E
185 *C20* **Waihou** ≈ North Island, New Zealand
Waikaboebak *see* Waikabubak
171 *N17* **Waikabubak** *prev.* Waikaboebak. Pulau Sumba, C Indonesia 09°40′S 119°25′E
185 *D23* **Waikaia** ≈ South Island, New Zealand
185 *D23* **Waikaka** Southland, South Island, New Zealand 45°55′S 168°59′E
184 *L13* **Waikanae** Wellington, North Island, New Zealand 40°52′S 175°03′E
184 *M7* **Waikare, Lake** ◎ North Island, New Zealand
184 *O9* **Waikaremoana, Lake** ◎ North Island, New Zealand
185 *I17* **Waikari** Canterbury, South Island, New Zealand 42°50′S 172°41′E
184 *L8* **Waikato** *off.* Waikato Region. ◆ *region* North Island, New Zealand
184 *M8* **Waikato** ≈ North Island, New Zealand
Waikato Region *see* Waikato
182 *J9* **Waikerie** South Australia 34°12′S 139°57′E
185 *F23* **Waikouaiti** Otago, South Island, New Zealand 45°36′S 170°39′E
38 *H11* **Wailea** Hawaii, USA, C Pacific Ocean 19°53′N 155°07′W
38 *F10* **Wailuku** Maui, Hawaii, USA, C Pacific Ocean 20°53′N 156°30′W
185 *H18* **Waimakariri** ≈ South Island, New Zealand
38 *D9* **Waimānalo Beach** *var.* Waimanalo Beach. O'ahu, Hawaii, USA, C Pacific Ocean 21°20′N 157°42′W
185 *G15* **Waimangaroa** West Coast, South Island, New Zealand 41°41′S 171°49′E
185 *G21* **Waimate** Canterbury, South Island, New Zealand 44°44′S 171°03′E
38 *G11* **Waimea** *var.* Kamuela. Hawaii, USA, C Pacific Ocean 20°02′N 155°20′W
38 *D9* **Waimea** *var.* Maunawai. O'ahu, Hawaii, USA, C Pacific Ocean 21°39′N 158°04′W
38 *B8* **Waimea** Kaua'i, Hawaii, USA, C Pacific Ocean 21°57′N 159°40′W
99 *M20* **Waimes** Liège, E Belgium 50°25′N 06°10′E
154 *J11* **Wainganga** *var.* Wain River. ≈ C India
Waingapoe *see* Waingapu
171 *N17* **Waingapu** *prev.* Waingapoe. Pulau Sumba, C Indonesia 09°40′S 120°16′E
55 *S7* **Waini** ≈ N Guyana
55 *S7* **Waini Point** *headland* NW Guyana 08°24′N 59°48′W
Wain River *see* Wainganga
11 *R15* **Wainwright** Alberta, SW Canada 52°50′N 110°51′W
39 *O5* **Wainwright** Alaska, USA 70°38′N 160°02′W
184 *K4* **Waiotira** Northland, North Island, New Zealand 35°56′S 174°11′E
184 *M11* **Waiouru** Manawatu-Wanganui, North Island, New Zealand 39°28′S 175°41′E
171 *W14* **Waipa** Papua, E Indonesia 03°47′S 136°16′E
184 *L8* **Waipa** ≈ North Island, New Zealand
184 *P9* **Waipaoa** ≈ North Island, New Zealand
185 *D25* **Waipapa Point** *headland* South Island, New Zealand 46°39′S 168°51′E
185 *I18* **Waipara** Canterbury, South Island, New Zealand 43°04′S 172°45′E
184 *N12* **Waipawa** Hawke's Bay, North Island, New Zealand 39°57′S 176°36′E
184 *K4* **Waipu** Northland, North Island, New Zealand 35°58′S 174°25′E
184 *N12* **Waipukurau** Hawke's Bay, North Island, New Zealand 40°01′S 176°34′E
171 *U14* **Wair** Pulau Kai Besar, E Indonesia 05°16′S 133°09′E
Wairakai *see* Wairakei
184 *N9* **Wairakei** *var.* Wairakai. Waikato, North Island, New Zealand 38°37′S 176°05′E
185 *M14* **Wairarapa, Lake** ◎ North Island, New Zealand
185 *J15* **Wairau** ≈ South Island, New Zealand
184 *P10* **Wairoa** Hawke's Bay, North Island, New Zealand 39°03′S 177°26′E
184 *P10* **Wairoa** ≈ North Island, New Zealand
184 *J4* **Wairoa** ≈ North Island, New Zealand
184 *N9* **Waitahanui** Waikato, North Island, New Zealand 38°48′S 176°04′E
184 *M6* **Waitakaruru** Waikato, North Island, New Zealand 37°14′S 175°22′E
185 *F21* **Waitaki** ≈ South Island, New Zealand
184 *K10* **Waitara** Taranaki, North Island, New Zealand 39°01′S 174°14′E
184 *M7* **Waitoa** Waikato, North Island, New Zealand 37°36′S 175°37′E
184 *L8* **Waitomo Caves** Waikato, North Island, New Zealand 38°17′S 175°06′E
184 *L11* **Waitotara** Taranaki, North Island, New Zealand 39°49′S 174°43′E
184 *L11* **Waitotara** ≈ North Island, New Zealand
32 *L10* **Waitsburg** Washington, NW USA 46°16′N 118°09′W
Waitzen *see* Vác
184 *L6* **Waiuku** Auckland, North Island, New Zealand 37°15′S 174°45′E
164 *L10* **Wajima** *var.* Wazima. Ishikawa, Honshū, SW Japan 37°23′N 136°53′E
81 *K17* **Wajir** North Eastern, NE Kenya 01°46′N 40°05′E
79 *J17* **Waka** Equateur, NW Dem. Rep. Congo 01°04′N 20°11′E
81 *I14* **Waka** Southern Nationalities, S Ethiopia 07°12′N 37°19′E
14 *D9* **Wakami Lake** ◎ Ontario, S Canada
164 *I12* **Wakasa** Tottori, Honshū, SW Japan 35°18′N 134°25′E
164 *J12* **Wakasa-wan** *bay* C Japan
185 *C22* **Wakatipu, Lake** ◎ South Island, New Zealand
11 *T15* **Wakaw** Saskatchewan, S Canada 52°40′N 105°45′W
164 *I14* **Wakayama** Wakayama, Honshū, SW Japan 34°12′N 135°09′E
164 *I15* **Wakayama** *off.* Wakayama-ken. ◆ *prefecture* Honshū, SW Japan
Wakayama-ken *see* Wakayama
26 *K4* **Wa Keeney** Kansas, C USA 39°02′N 99°53′W
185 *I14* **Wakefield** Tasman, South Island, New Zealand 41°24′S 173°03′E
97 *M17* **Wakefield** N England, United Kingdom 53°42′N 01°29′W
27 *O4* **Wakefield** Kansas, C USA 39°12′N 97°00′W
30 *L4* **Wakefield** Michigan, N USA 46°27′N 89°55′W
21 *U9* **Wake Forest** North Carolina, SE USA 35°58′N 78°30′W
Wakeham Bay *see* Kangiqsujuaq
189 *Y11* **Wake Island** ◇ US *unincorporated territory* NW Pacific Ocean
189 *Y12* **Wake Island** ✈ NW Pacific Ocean
189 *Y12* **Wake Island** *atoll* NW Pacific Ocean
189 *X12* **Wake Lagoon** *lagoon* Wake Island, NW Pacific Ocean
166 *L8* **Wakema** Ayeyarwady, SW Burma (Myanmar) 16°36′N 95°11′E
Wakhan *see* Khandūd
164 *H14* **Waki** Tokushima, Shikoku, SW Japan 34°04′N 134°10′E
165 *T1* **Wakkanai** Hokkaidō, NE Japan 45°25′N 141°39′E
83 *K22* **Wakkerstroom** Mpumalanga, E South Africa 27°21′S 30°10′E
14 *C10* **Wakomata Lake** ◎ Ontario, S Canada
183 *N10* **Wakool** New South Wales, SE Australia 35°30′S 144°22′E
Wakra *see* Al Wakrah
Waku Kungo *see* Uaco Cungo
186 *J7* **Wakunai** Bougainville Island, NE Papua New Guinea 05°52′S 155°10′E
Walachei/Walachia *see* Wallachia
155 *K26* **Walawe Ganga** ≈ S Sri Lanka
111 *F15* **Wałbrzych** *Ger.* Waldenburg, Waldenburg in Schlesien. Dolnośląskie, SW Poland 50°45′N 16°20′E
183 *T6* **Walcha** New South Wales, SE Australia 31°01′S 151°38′E
101 *K24* **Walchensee** ◎ SE Germany
99 *D14* **Walcheren** *island* SW Netherlands
29 *Z14* **Walcott** Iowa, C USA 41°34′N 90°46′W
33 *W16* **Walcott** Wyoming, C USA 41°46′N 106°46′W
99 *G21* **Walcourt** Namur, S Belgium 50°16′N 04°26′E
110 *G9* **Wałcz** *Ger.* Deutsch Krone. Zachodnio-pomorskie, NW Poland 53°17′N 16°29′E
108 *H7* **Wald** Zürich, N Switzerland 47°17′N 08°56′E
109 *U3* **Waldaist** ≈ N Austria
180 *I9* **Walburg Range** ▲▲ Western Australia
37 *R3* **Walden** Colorado, C USA 40°43′N 106°16′W
18 *K13* **Walden** New York, NE USA 41°35′N 74°09′W
Waldenburg/Waldenburg in Schlesien *see* Wałbrzych
11 *T15* **Waldheim** Saskatchewan, S Canada 52°38′N 106°35′W
Waldia *see* Weldiya
101 *M23* **Waldkraiburg** Bayern, SE Germany 48°10′N 12°23′E
27 *T14* **Waldo** Arkansas, C USA 33°21′N 93°18′W
23 *V9* **Waldo** Florida, SE USA 29°47′N 82°07′W
19 *R7* **Waldoboro** Maine, NE USA 44°06′N 69°22′W
21 *W4* **Waldorf** Maryland, NE USA 38°36′N 76°54′W
32 *F12* **Waldport** Oregon, NW USA 44°25′N 124°04′W
27 *S11* **Waldron** Arkansas, C USA 34°54′N 94°09′W
195 *Y13* **Waldron, Cape** *headland* Antarctica 66°08′S 116°00′E
101 *F24* **Waldshut-Tiengen** Baden-Württemberg, S Germany 47°37′N 08°13′E
171 *P12* **Walea, Selat** *strait* Sulawesi, C Indonesia
Walecké Meziříčí *see* Valašské Meziříčí
108 *H8* **Walensee** ◎ NW Switzerland
38 *L8* **Wales** Alaska, USA 65°36′N 168°03′W
97 *J20* **Wales** *Wel.* Cymru. ◆ *national region* Wales, United Kingdom
9 *O7* **Wales Island** *island* Nunavut, NE Canada
77 *P14* **Walewale** N Ghana 10°21′N 00°48′W
99 *M24* **Walferdange** Luxembourg, C Luxembourg 49°39′N 06°08′E
183 *Q5* **Walgett** New South Wales, SE Australia 30°02′S 148°14′E
194 *K10* **Walgreen Coast** *physical region* Antarctica
29 *Q2* **Walhalla** North Dakota, N USA 48°55′N 97°55′W
21 *O11* **Walhalla** South Carolina, SE USA 34°46′N 83°05′W
79 *O19* **Walikale** Nord-Kivu, E Dem. Rep. Congo 01°29′S 28°05′E
Walk *see* Valga, Estonia

◆ Country ● Country Capital ◇ Dependent Territory ○ Dependent Territory Capital ◆ Administrative Regions ✈ International Airport ▲ Mountain ▲▲ Mountain Range ✕ Volcano ≈ River ◎ Lake ▣ Reservoir

WALK – WELLINGBOROUGH

Walk see Valka, Latvia
29 U5 **Walker** Minnesota, N USA 47°06′N 94°35′W
15 V4 **Walker, Lac** ◎ Québec, SE Canada
35 S7 **Walker Lake** ◎ Nevada, W USA
35 R6 **Walker River** ⇝ Nevada, W USA
28 K10 **Wall** South Dakota, N USA 43°58′N 102°12′W
173 U9 **Wallaby Plateau** undersea feature E Indian Ocean
33 N8 **Wallace** Idaho, NW USA 47°28′N 115°55′W
21 V11 **Wallace** North Carolina, SE USA 34°42′N 77°59′W
14 D17 **Wallaceburg** Ontario, S Canada 42°34′N 82°22′W
22 F5 **Wallace Lake** ⊠ Louisiana, S USA
11 P13 **Wallace Mountain** ▲ Alberta, W Canada 54°50′N 115°57′W
116 J14 **Wallachia** var. Walachia, Ger. Walachei, Rom. Valachia. cultural region S Romania
Wallachisch-Meseritsch see Valašské Meziříčí
183 U4 **Wallangarra** New South Wales, SE Australia 28°56′S 151°57′E
182 I8 **Wallaroo** South Australia 33°56′S 137°38′E
32 L10 **Walla Walla** Washington, NW USA 46°03′N 118°20′W
45 V9 **Wall Blake** ✈ (The Valley) C Anguilla 18°12′N 63°02′W
101 H19 **Walldürn** Baden-Württemberg, SW Germany 49°34′N 09°22′E
100 F12 **Wallenhorst** Niedersachsen, NW Germany 52°21′N 08°01′E
Wallenthal see Haţeg
109 S4 **Wallern** Oberösterreich, N Austria 48°13′N 13°58′E
Wallern see Wallern im Burgenland
109 Z5 **Wallern im Burgenland** var. Wallern. Burgenland, E Austria 47°44′N 16°57′E
18 M9 **Wallingford** Vermont, NE USA 43°27′N 72°56′W
25 V11 **Wallis** Texas, SW USA 29°38′N 96°05′W
Wallis see Valais
192 K9 **Wallis and Futuna** Fr. Territoire de Wallis et Futuna. ◇ French overseas territory C Pacific Ocean
108 G7 **Wallisellen** Zürich, N Switzerland 47°25′N 08°36′E
Wallis et Futuna, Territoire de see Wallis and Futuna
190 H11 **Wallis, Îles** island group N Wallis and Futuna
31 Q5 **Walloon Lake** ◎ Michigan, N USA
32 K10 **Wallula** Washington, NW USA 46°03′N 118°54′W
32 K10 **Wallula, Lake** ◎ Washington, NW USA
21 S8 **Walnut Cove** North Carolina, SE USA 36°18′N 80°08′W
35 N8 **Walnut Creek** California, W USA 37°52′N 122°04′W
26 K5 **Walnut Creek** ⇝ Kansas, C USA
27 W9 **Walnut Ridge** Arkansas, C USA 36°06′N 90°56′W
25 S7 **Walnut Springs** Texas, SW USA 32°05′N 97°42′W
182 L10 **Walpeup** Victoria, SE Australia 35°09′S 142°01′E
187 R17 **Walpole, Île** island SE New Caledonia
39 N13 **Walrus Islands** island group Alaska, USA
97 L19 **Walsall** C England, United Kingdom 52°35′N 01°58′W
37 T7 **Walsenburg** Colorado, C USA 37°37′N 104°46′W
11 S17 **Walsh** Alberta, SW Canada 49°58′N 110°03′W
37 W7 **Walsh** Colorado, C USA 37°20′N 102°17′W
100 I11 **Walsrode** Niedersachsen, NW Germany 52°52′N 09°36′E
Waltenberg see Zalău
21 R14 **Walterboro** South Carolina, SE USA 32°54′N 80°21′W
Walter F.George Lake see Walter F. George Reservoir
23 R6 **Walter F. George Reservoir** var. Walter F.George Lake. ⊠ Alabama/Georgia, SE USA
26 M12 **Walters** Oklahoma, C USA 34°22′N 98°18′W
101 J16 **Waltershausen** Thüringen, C Germany 50°53′N 10°33′E
173 N10 **Walters Shoal** var. Walters Shoals. reef S Madagascar
Walters Shoals see Walters Shoal
22 M3 **Walthall** Mississippi, S USA 33°36′N 89°16′W
20 M4 **Walton** Kentucky, S USA 38°52′N 84°36′W
18 J11 **Walton** New York, NE USA 42°10′N 75°07′W
159 R16 **Walung** Xizang Zizhiqu, W China 28°07′N 97°00′E
79 O20 **Walungu** Sud-Kivu, E Dem. Rep. Congo 02°40′S 28°37′E
Walvisbaai see Walvis Bay
83 C19 **Walvis Bay** Afr. Walvisbaai. Erongo, NW Namibia 22°59′S 14°31′E
83 B19 **Walvis Bay** bay NW Namibia
Walvish Ridge see Walvis Ridge
65 O17 **Walvis Ridge** var. Walvish Ridge. undersea feature E Atlantic Ocean 28°00′S 03°00′E
171 X16 **Wamal** Papua, E Indonesia 08°00′S 139°06′E
171 U15 **Wamar, Pulau** island Kepulauan Aru, E Indonesia
79 O17 **Wamba** Orientale, NE Dem. Rep. Congo 02°10′N 27°59′E
77 V15 **Wamba** Nassarawa, C Nigeria 08°57′N 08°35′E
79 H22 **Wamba** var. Uamba. ⇝ Angola/Dem. Rep. Congo
27 P4 **Wamego** Kansas, C USA 39°12′N 96°18′W
18 I10 **Wampsville** New York, NE USA 43°03′N 75°40′W
42 K6 **Wampú, Río** ⇝ E Honduras
171 X16 **Wan** Papua, E Indonesia 08°15′S 138°00′E
Wan see Anhui
183 N4 **Wanaaring** New South Wales, SE Australia 29°42′S 144°07′E
185 D21 **Wanaka** Otago, South Island, New Zealand 44°42′S 169°09′E
185 D20 **Wanaka, Lake** ◎ South Island, New Zealand
171 W14 **Wanapiri** Papua, E Indonesia 04°21′S 135°52′E
14 F9 **Wanapitei** ⇝ Ontario, S Canada
14 F10 **Wanapitei Lake** ◎ Ontario, S Canada
18 K14 **Wanaque** New Jersey, NE USA 41°02′N 74°17′W
171 U12 **Wanau** Papua, E Indonesia 01°20′S 132°40′E
185 F22 **Wanbrow, Cape** headland South Island, New Zealand 45°07′S 170°59′E
Wancheng see Wanning
Wanchuan see Zhangjiakou
171 W13 **Wandai** var. Komeyo. Papua, E Indonesia 03°35′S 136°15′E
163 Z8 **Wanda Shan** ▲▲ NE China
197 R11 **Wandel Sea** sea Arctic Ocean
160 D13 **Wanding** var. Wandingzhen. Yunnan, SW China 24°01′N 98°00′E
Wandingzhen see Wanding
99 H20 **Wanfercée-Baulet** Hainaut, S Belgium 50°27′N 04°37′E
184 L12 **Wanganui** Manawatu-Wanganui, North Island, New Zealand 39°56′S 175°02′E
184 L11 **Wanganui** ⇝ North Island, New Zealand
183 P11 **Wangaratta** Victoria, SE Australia 36°22′S 146°17′E
160 J8 **Wangcang** var. Donghe; prev. Fengjiaba, Hongjiang. Sichuan, C China 32°15′N 106°16′E
Wangda see Zogang
101 I24 **Wangen im Allgäu** Baden-Württemberg, S Germany 47°40′N 09°49′E
Wangerin see Węgorzyno
100 F9 **Wangerooge** island NW Germany
171 W13 **Wanggar** Papua, E Indonesia 03°22′S 135°15′E
160 J13 **Wangmo** var. Fuxing. Guizhou, S China 25°08′N 106°08′E
Wangolodougou see Ouangolodougou
161 S9 **Wangpan Yang** sea E China
163 Y10 **Wangqing** Jilin, NE China 43°19′N 129°42′E
167 P8 **Wang Saphung** Loei, C Thailand 17°18′N 101°45′E
167 O6 **Wan Hsa-la** Shan State, E Burma (Myanmar) 20°27′N 98°39′E
55 W9 **Wanica** ◈ district N Surinam
79 M18 **Wanie-Rukula** Orientale, C Dem. Rep. Congo 0°13′N 25°34′E
Wankie see Hwange
Wanki, Río see Coco, Río
81 N17 **Wanlaweyn** var. Wanle Weyn, It. Uanle Uen. Shabeellaha Hoose, SW Somalia 02°36′N 44°47′E
Wanle Weyn see Wanlaweyn
180 I12 **Wanneroo** Western Australia 31°40′S 115°35′E
160 L17 **Wanning** var. Wancheng. Hainan, S China 18°55′N 110°27′E
167 Q8 **Wanon Niwat** Sakon Nakhon, E Thailand 17°39′N 103°45′E
155 H16 **Wanparti** Andhra Pradesh, C India 16°19′N 78°06′E
Wansen see Wiązów
160 L11 **Wanshan** Guizhou, S China 27°45′N 109°12′E
99 M14 **Wanssum** Limburg, SE Netherlands 51°31′N 06°04′E
184 N12 **Wanstead** Hawke's Bay, North Island, New Zealand 40°09′S 176°31′E
Wanxian see Wanzhou
188 F16 **Wanyaan** Yap, Micronesia
160 K8 **Wanyuan** Sichuan, C China 32°05′N 108°08′E
161 O11 **Wanzai** var. Kangle. Jiangxi, S China 28°06′N 114°27′E
99 J20 **Wanze** Liège, E Belgium 50°32′N 05°16′E
160 K9 **Wanzhou** var. Wanxian. Chongqing Shi, C China 30°48′N 108°21′E
31 R12 **Wapakoneta** Ohio, N USA 40°34′N 84°11′W
12 D7 **Wapaseese** ⇝ Ontario, C Canada
32 I10 **Wapato** Washington, NW USA 46°27′N 120°25′W
29 Y15 **Wapello** Iowa, C USA 41°10′N 91°13′W
11 N13 **Wapiti** ⇝ Alberta/British Columbia, SW Canada
27 X7 **Wappapello Lake** ⊠ Missouri, C USA
18 K13 **Wappingers Falls** New York, NE USA 41°36′N 73°54′W
29 X13 **Wapsipinicon River** ⇝ Iowa, C USA
14 L9 **Wapus** ⇝ Québec, SE Canada
160 H7 **Waqên** Sichuan, C China 33°05′N 102°34′E
21 Q7 **War** West Virginia, NE USA 37°18′N 81°39′W
80 D13 **Warab** Warab, SW Sudan 08°08′N 28°37′E
81 D14 **Warab** ◈ state SW Sudan
155 J15 **Warangal** Andhra Pradesh, C India 18°N 79°35′E
Warasdin see Varaždin
183 O16 **Waratah** Tasmania, SE Australia 41°28′S 145°34′E
183 O14 **Waratah Bay** bay Victoria, SE Australia
101 H15 **Warburg** Nordrhein-Westfalen, W Germany 51°30′N 09°11′E
182 I1 **Warburton Creek** seasonal river South Australia
180 M9 **Warburton** Western Australia 26°17′S 126°18′E
99 M20 **Warche** ⇝ E Belgium
Wardag/Wardak see Vardak
32 K9 **Warden** Washington, NW USA 46°58′N 119°02′W
154 I12 **Wardha** Mahārāshtra, W India 20°41′N 78°40′E
Wardija Point see Wardija, Ras il-
121 N15 **Wardija, Ras il-** var. Wardija Point. headland Gozo, NW Malta 36°03′N 14°11′E
139 P3 **Wardiyah** Nīnawá, N Iraq 36°18′N 41°45′E
185 E19 **Ward, Mount** ▲ South Island, New Zealand 43°49′S 169°54′E
10 L11 **Ware** British Columbia, W Canada 57°26′N 125°41′W
99 D18 **Waregem** var. Waereghem. West-Vlaanderen, W Belgium 50°53′N 03°26′E
99 J19 **Waremme** Liège, E Belgium 50°41′N 05°15′E
100 N10 **Waren** Mecklenburg-Vorpommern, NE Germany 53°32′N 12°42′E
171 W13 **Waren** Papua, E Indonesia 02°13′S 136°21′E
101 F14 **Warendorf** Nordrhein-Westfalen, W Germany 51°57′N 08°00′E
21 P12 **Ware Shoals** South Carolina, SE USA 34°24′N 82°15′W
98 N4 **Warffum** Groningen, NE Netherlands 53°22′N 06°34′E
81 O15 **Wargalo** Mudug, E Somalia 06°06′N 47°40′E
146 M12 **Warganza** Rus. Varganzi. Qashqadaryo Viloyati, S Uzbekistan 39°18′N 66°00′E
Wargla see Ouargla
183 T4 **Warialda** New South Wales, SE Australia 29°34′S 150°35′E
154 F13 **Wāri Godri** Mahārāshtra, C India 19°28′N 75°43′E
167 R10 **Warin Chamrap** Ubon Ratchathani, E Thailand 15°11′N 104°51′E
25 R11 **Waring** Texas, SW USA 29°56′N 98°48′W
39 O8 **Waring Mountains** ▲▲ Alaska, USA
110 M12 **Warka** Mazowieckie, E Poland 51°45′N 21°12′E
184 L5 **Warkworth** Auckland, North Island, New Zealand 36°23′S 174°42′E
171 U12 **Warmandi** Papua, E Indonesia 0°21′S 132°38′E
83 E22 **Warmbad** Karas, S Namibia 28°29′S 18°41′E
98 H8 **Warmenhuizen** Noord-Holland, NW Netherlands 52°43′N 04°45′E
110 M8 **Warmińsko-Mazurskie** ◈ province C Poland
97 L22 **Warminster** S England, United Kingdom 51°13′N 02°12′W
18 I15 **Warminster** Pennsylvania, NE USA 40°11′N 75°04′W
35 V8 **Warm Springs** Nevada, W USA 38°10′N 116°21′W
32 H12 **Warm Springs** Oregon, NW USA 44°51′N 121°24′W
21 S5 **Warm Springs** Virginia, NE USA 38°03′N 79°48′W
100 M8 **Warnemünde** Mecklenburg-Vorpommern, NE Germany 54°10′N 12°03′E
27 Q10 **Warner** Oklahoma, C USA 35°29′N 95°18′W
35 Q2 **Warner Mountains** ▲▲ California, W USA
23 T5 **Warner Robins** Georgia, SE USA 32°38′N 83°38′W
57 N18 **Warnes** Santa Cruz, C Bolivia 17°30′S 63°11′W
100 M9 **Warnow** ⇝ NE Germany
Warnsdorf see Varnsdorf
98 M11 **Warnsveld** Gelderland, E Netherlands 52°08′N 06°14′E
154 I13 **Warora** Mahārāshtra, C India 20°12′N 79°01′E
182 L11 **Warracknabeal** Victoria, SE Australia 36°17′S 142°26′E
183 O13 **Warragul** Victoria, SE Australia 38°11′S 145°55′E
183 O4 **Warrego River** seasonal river New South Wales/Queensland, E Australia
183 Q6 **Warren** New South Wales, SE Australia 31°41′S 147°51′E
11 X16 **Warren** Manitoba, S Canada 50°05′N 97°33′W
27 V14 **Warren** Arkansas, C USA 33°38′N 92°05′W
31 S10 **Warren** Michigan, N USA 42°29′N 83°02′W
29 R3 **Warren** Minnesota, N USA 48°12′N 96°46′W
31 U11 **Warren** Ohio, N USA 41°14′N 80°49′W
18 D12 **Warren** Pennsylvania, NE USA 41°52′N 79°09′W
25 X10 **Warren** Texas, SW USA 30°33′N 94°24′W
97 G16 **Warrenpoint** Ir. An Pointe. SE Northern Ireland, United Kingdom 54°07′N 06°16′W
27 S4 **Warrensburg** Missouri, C USA 38°46′N 93°44′W
83 H22 **Warrenton** Northern Cape, N South Africa 28°07′S 24°51′E
23 U4 **Warrenton** Georgia, SE USA 33°24′N 82°39′W
27 W4 **Warrenton** Missouri, C USA 38°48′N 91°08′W
21 V8 **Warrenton** North Carolina, SE USA 36°24′N 78°11′W
21 V4 **Warrenton** Virginia, NE USA 38°43′N 77°48′W
77 U17 **Warri** Delta, S Nigeria 05°26′N 05°34′E
97 L18 **Warrington** C England, United Kingdom 53°24′N 02°37′W
23 O9 **Warrington** Florida, SE USA 30°22′N 87°16′W
23 P3 **Warrior** Alabama, S USA 33°49′N 86°49′W
182 L13 **Warrnambool** Victoria, SE Australia 38°23′S 142°30′E
29 T2 **Warroad** Minnesota, N USA 48°55′N 95°18′W
183 S6 **Warrumbungle Range** ▲▲ New South Wales, SE Australia
154 J12 **Wārsa** Mahārāshtra, C India 20°42′N 79°58′E
31 P11 **Warsaw** Indiana, N USA 41°13′N 85°52′W
20 L4 **Warsaw** Kentucky, S USA 38°47′N 84°55′W
27 T5 **Warsaw** Missouri, C USA 38°14′N 93°23′W
18 E10 **Warsaw** New York, NE USA 42°44′N 78°06′W
21 V10 **Warsaw** North Carolina, SE USA 35°00′N 78°05′W
21 X5 **Warsaw** Virginia, NE USA 37°57′N 76°46′W
Warsaw/Warschau see Warszawa
81 N17 **Warshiikh** Shabeellaha Dhexe, C Somalia 02°22′N 45°52′E
101 G15 **Warstein** Nordrhein-Westfalen, W Germany 51°27′N 08°21′E
110 M11 **Warszawa** Eng. Warsaw, Ger. Warschau, Rus. Varshava. ● (Poland) Mazowieckie, C Poland 52°15′N 21°E
110 J13 **Warta** Sieradz, C Poland 51°43′N 18°37′E
110 D11 **Warta** Ger. Warthe. ⇝ W Poland
Wartberg see Senec
20 M9 **Wartburg** Tennessee, S USA 36°08′N 84°37′W
108 J7 **Warth** Vorarlberg, NW Austria 47°16′N 10°11′E
Warthe see Warta
169 U12 **Waru** Borneo, C Indonesia 01°24′S 116°37′E
171 T13 **Waru** Pulau Seram, E Indonesia 03°24′S 130°38′E
139 N6 **Wa'r, Wādī al** dry watercourse E Syria
183 U3 **Warwick** Queensland, E Australia 28°12′S 152°E
15 Q11 **Warwick** Québec, SE Canada 45°55′N 72°00′W
97 M20 **Warwick** C England, United Kingdom 52°17′N 01°34′W
18 K13 **Warwick** New York, NE USA 41°15′N 74°21′W
29 P4 **Warwick** North Dakota, N USA 47°49′N 98°42′W
19 O12 **Warwick** Rhode Island, NE USA 41°40′N 71°21′W
97 L20 **Warwickshire** cultural region C England, United Kingdom
14 G14 **Wasaga Beach** Ontario, S Canada 44°30′N 80°00′W
77 U13 **Wasagu** Kebbi, NW Nigeria 11°25′N 05°48′E
36 M2 **Wasatch Range** ▲▲ W USA
35 R12 **Wasco** California, W USA 35°34′N 119°20′W
29 V10 **Waseca** Minnesota, N USA 44°04′N 93°30′W
14 H13 **Washago** Ontario, S Canada 44°46′N 79°48′W
19 S2 **Washburn** Maine, NE USA 46°46′N 68°08′W
28 M5 **Washburn** North Dakota, N USA 47°15′N 101°02′W
30 K3 **Washburn** Wisconsin, N USA 46°41′N 90°53′W
31 S14 **Washburn Hill** hill Ohio, N USA
154 H13 **Wāshīm** Mahārāshtra, C India 20°06′N 77°08′E
97 M14 **Washington** NE England, United Kingdom 54°54′N 01°31′W
23 U3 **Washington** Georgia, SE USA 33°44′N 82°44′W
30 L12 **Washington** Illinois, N USA 40°42′N 89°24′W
31 N15 **Washington** Indiana, N USA 38°40′N 87°10′W
29 X15 **Washington** Iowa, C USA 41°18′N 91°41′W
27 O3 **Washington** Kansas, C USA 39°49′N 97°03′W
27 W5 **Washington** Missouri, C USA 38°31′N 91°01′W
21 X9 **Washington** North Carolina, SE USA 35°33′N 77°04′W
18 B15 **Washington** Pennsylvania, NE USA 40°11′N 80°16′W
25 V10 **Washington** Texas, SW USA 30°18′N 96°08′W
36 J8 **Washington** Utah, W USA 37°07′N 113°30′W
21 V4 **Washington** Virginia, NE USA 38°43′N 78°11′W
32 I9 **Washington** off. State of Washington, also known as Chinook State, Evergreen State. ◈ state NW USA
Washington see Washington Court House
31 S14 **Washington Court House** var. Washington. Ohio, NE USA 39°32′N 83°29′W
21 W4 **Washington DC** ● (USA) District of Columbia, NE USA 38°54′N 77°02′W
31 O5 **Washington Island** island Wisconsin, N USA
Washington Island see Teraina
19 O7 **Washington, Mount** ▲ New Hampshire, NE USA 44°16′N 71°18′W
26 M11 **Washita River** ⇝ Oklahoma/Texas, C USA
97 O18 **Wash, The** inlet E England, United Kingdom
32 L9 **Washtucna** Washington, NW USA 46°44′N 118°19′W
Wasiliszki see Vasilishki
110 P9 **Wasilków** Podlaskie, NE Poland 53°12′N 23°15′E
39 R11 **Wasilla** Alaska, USA 61°34′N 149°26′W
139 V9 **Wāsiţ** ◈ governorate E Iraq
55 U9 **Wasjabo** Sipaliwini, NW Surinam 05°09′N 57°09′W
12 I10 **Waskaganish** prev. Fort Rupert, Rupert House. Québec, SE Canada 51°30′N 79°45′W
11 X11 **Waskaiowaka Lake** ◎ Manitoba, C Canada
11 T14 **Waskesiu Lake** Saskatchewan, C Canada 53°56′N 106°05′W
25 X7 **Waskom** Texas, SW USA 32°28′N 94°03′W
110 G13 **Wąsosz** Dolnośląskie, SW Poland 51°36′N 16°30′E
42 M6 **Waspam** var. Waspán. Región Autónoma Atlántico Norte, NE Nicaragua 14°41′N 84°04′W
Waspán see Waspam
165 T3 **Wassamu** Hokkaidō, NE Japan 44°01′N 142°25′E
108 G9 **Wassen** Uri, C Switzerland 46°42′N 08°34′E
98 G11 **Wassenaar** Zuid-Holland, W Netherlands 52°09′N 04°23′E
99 N24 **Wasserbillig** Grevenmacher, E Luxembourg 49°43′N 06°30′E
Wasserburg see Wasserburg am Inn
101 M23 **Wasserburg am Inn** var. Wasserburg. Bayern, SE Germany 48°02′N 12°12′E
101 I17 **Wasserkuppe** ▲ C Germany 50°30′N 09°55′E
103 R5 **Wassy** Haute-Marne, N France 48°32′N 04°54′E
171 N14 **Watampone** var. Bone. Sulawesi, C Indonesia 04°33′S 120°20′E
171 R13 **Watawa** Pulau Buru, E Indonesia 03°36′S 127°13′E
Watenstedt-Salzgitter see Salzgitter
18 M13 **Waterbury** Connecticut, NE USA 41°33′N 73°01′W
21 R11 **Wateree Lake** ⊠ South Carolina, SE USA
21 R12 **Wateree River** ⇝ South Carolina, SE USA
97 E20 **Waterford** Ir. Port Láirge. Waterford, S Ireland 52°15′N 07°08′W
31 S9 **Waterford** Michigan, N USA 42°42′N 83°24′W
97 E20 **Waterford** Ir. Port Láirge. cultural region S Ireland
97 E21 **Waterford Harbour** Ir. Cuan Phort Láirge. inlet S Ireland
98 G12 **Wateringen** Zuid-Holland, W Netherlands 52°02′N 04°16′E
99 G19 **Waterloo** Walloon Brabant, C Belgium 50°43′N 04°24′E
14 F16 **Waterloo** Ontario, S Canada 43°28′N 80°32′W
15 P12 **Waterloo** Québec, SE Canada 45°20′N 72°28′W
30 K16 **Waterloo** Illinois, N USA 38°20′N 90°09′W
29 X13 **Waterloo** Iowa, C USA 42°31′N 92°16′W
18 G10 **Waterloo** New York, NE USA 42°54′N 76°51′W
30 L4 **Watersmeet** Michigan, N USA 46°16′N 89°10′W
23 V9 **Watertown** Florida, SE USA 30°11′N 82°36′W
18 I8 **Watertown** New York, NE USA 43°37′N 75°56′W
29 R9 **Watertown** South Dakota, N USA 44°54′N 97°07′W
30 M8 **Watertown** Wisconsin, N USA 43°12′N 88°44′W
22 L3 **Water Valley** Mississippi, S USA 34°09′N 89°37′W
27 O3 **Waterville** Kansas, C USA 39°41′N 96°45′W
17 V6 **Waterville** Maine, NE USA 44°34′N 69°41′W
29 V10 **Waterville** Minnesota, N USA 44°13′N 93°34′W
18 I10 **Waterville** New York, NE USA 42°55′N 75°18′W
14 E16 **Watford** Ontario, S Canada 42°57′N 81°51′W
97 N21 **Watford** E England, United Kingdom 51°39′N 00°24′W
28 K4 **Watford City** North Dakota, N USA 47°48′N 103°16′W
141 X12 **Wāţif** S Oman 18°34′N 56°31′E
18 G11 **Watkins Glen** New York, NE USA 42°23′N 76°53′W
Watlings Island see San Salvador
171 U15 **Watnil** Pulau Kai Kecil, E Indonesia 05°45′S 132°39′E
26 M10 **Watonga** Oklahoma, C USA 35°52′N 98°26′W
11 T16 **Watrous** Saskatchewan, S Canada 51°40′N 105°29′W
37 T10 **Watrous** New Mexico, SW USA 35°48′N 104°58′W
79 P16 **Watsa** Orientale, NE Dem. Rep. Congo 03°00′N 29°31′E
31 N12 **Watseka** Illinois, N USA 40°46′N 87°44′W
79 J19 **Watsikengo** Equateur, C Dem. Rep. Congo 0°49′S 20°34′E
182 C5 **Watson** South Australia 30°32′S 131°29′E
11 U15 **Watson** Saskatchewan, S Canada 52°13′N 104°30′W
195 O10 **Watson Escarpment** ▲▲ Antarctica
10 K9 **Watson Lake** Yukon Territory, W Canada 60°05′N 128°47′W
35 N10 **Watsonville** California, W USA 36°53′N 121°43′W
167 Q8 **Wattay** ✈ (Viangchan) Viangchan, C Laos 18°03′N 102°36′E
109 N7 **Wattens** Tirol, W Austria 47°18′N 11°37′E
20 M9 **Watts Bar Lake** ⊠ Tennessee, S USA
108 H7 **Wattwil** Sankt Gallen, NE Switzerland 47°18′N 09°06′E
171 T14 **Watubela, Kepulauan** island group E Indonesia
101 N24 **Watzmann** ▲ SE Germany 47°32′N 12°56′E
186 E8 **Wau** Morobe, C Papua New Guinea 07°22′S 146°40′E
81 D14 **Wau** var. Wāw. Western Bahr el Ghazal, S Sudan 07°43′N 28°01′E
29 Q8 **Waubay** South Dakota, N USA 45°19′N 97°18′W
29 Q8 **Waubay Lake** ◎ South Dakota, N USA
183 U7 **Wauchope** New South Wales, SE Australia 31°30′S 152°46′E
23 W13 **Wauchula** Florida, SE USA 27°33′N 81°48′W
30 M10 **Wauconda** Illinois, N USA 42°15′N 88°08′W
182 J7 **Waukaringa** South Australia 32°19′S 139°27′E
31 N10 **Waukegan** Illinois, N USA 42°21′N 87°50′W
30 M9 **Waukesha** Wisconsin, N USA 43°01′N 88°14′W
29 X11 **Waukon** Iowa, C USA 43°16′N 91°28′W
30 L8 **Waunakee** Wisconsin, N USA 43°13′N 89°28′W
30 L7 **Waupaca** Wisconsin, N USA 44°23′N 89°04′W
30 M8 **Waupun** Wisconsin, N USA 43°40′N 88°43′W
26 M13 **Waurika** Oklahoma, C USA 34°10′N 98°00′W
26 M12 **Waurika Lake** ⊠ Oklahoma, C USA
30 L6 **Wausau** Wisconsin, N USA 44°58′N 89°40′W
31 R11 **Wauseon** Ohio, N USA 41°33′N 84°08′W
30 L7 **Wautoma** Wisconsin, N USA 44°05′N 89°17′W
30 M9 **Wauwatosa** Wisconsin, N USA 43°03′N 88°03′W
22 L9 **Waveland** Mississippi, S USA 30°17′N 89°22′W
97 Q20 **Waveney** ⇝ E England, United Kingdom
184 L11 **Waverley** Taranaki, North Island, New Zealand 39°45′S 174°35′E
29 W12 **Waverly** Iowa, C USA 42°43′N 92°28′W
27 T4 **Waverly** Missouri, C USA 39°12′N 93°31′W
29 R15 **Waverly** Nebraska, C USA 40°56′N 96°27′W
18 G12 **Waverly** New York, NE USA 42°00′N 76°33′W
20 H8 **Waverly** Tennessee, S USA 36°04′N 87°49′W
21 W7 **Waverly** Virginia, NE USA 37°02′N 77°06′W
99 H19 **Wavre** Walloon Brabant, C Belgium 50°43′N 04°37′E
166 M8 **Waw** Bago, SW Burma (Myanmar) 17°26′N 96°40′E
Wāw see Wau
14 B7 **Wawa** Ontario, S Canada 47°59′N 84°43′W
77 T14 **Wawa** Niger, W Nigeria 09°52′N 04°33′E
75 Q11 **Wāw al Kabīr** S Libya 25°21′N 16°41′E
43 N7 **Wawa, Río** var. Río Huahua. ⇝ NE Nicaragua
186 B8 **Wawoi** ⇝ SW Papua New Guinea
25 T7 **Waxahachie** Texas, SW USA 32°23′N 96°52′W
158 L9 **Waxxari** Xinjiang Uygur Zizhiqu, NW China 38°43′N 87°11′E
Wayaobu see Zichang
23 V7 **Waycross** Georgia, SE USA 31°13′N 82°21′W
180 K10 **Way, Lake** ◎ Western Australia
31 P9 **Wayland** Michigan, N USA 42°40′N 85°38′W
29 R13 **Wayne** Nebraska, C USA 42°13′N 97°01′W
18 K14 **Wayne** New Jersey, NE USA 40°57′N 74°16′W
21 P5 **Wayne** West Virginia, NE USA 38°14′N 82°27′W
23 V4 **Waynesboro** Georgia, SE USA 33°04′N 82°01′W
22 M7 **Waynesboro** Mississippi, S USA 31°40′N 88°39′W
20 H10 **Waynesboro** Tennessee, S USA 35°20′N 87°49′W
21 U5 **Waynesboro** Virginia, NE USA 38°04′N 78°54′W
18 B16 **Waynesburg** Pennsylvania, NE USA 39°51′N 80°10′W
27 U6 **Waynesville** Missouri, C USA 37°48′N 92°11′W
21 O10 **Waynesville** North Carolina, SE USA 35°29′N 82°59′W
26 L8 **Waynoka** Oklahoma, C USA 36°36′N 98°53′W
Wazan see Ouazzane
Wazima see Wajima
149 V7 **Wazīrābād** Punjab, NE Pakistan 32°28′N 74°04′E
Wazzan see Ouazzane
110 I8 **Wda** var. Czarna Woda, Ger. Schwarzwasser. ⇝ N Poland
187 Q16 **Wé** Province des Îles Loyauté, E New Caledonia 20°55′S 167°15′E
97 O23 **Weald, The** lowlands SE England, United Kingdom
186 A9 **Weam** Western, SW Papua New Guinea 08°33′S 141°10′E
97 L15 **Wear** ⇝ N England, United Kingdom
Wearmouth see Sunderland
26 L10 **Weatherford** Oklahoma, C USA 35°31′N 98°42′W
25 S6 **Weatherford** Texas, SW USA 32°47′N 97°48′W
34 M3 **Weaverville** California, W USA 40°42′N 122°57′W
27 R7 **Webb City** Missouri, C USA 37°07′N 94°28′W
192 G8 **Weber Basin** undersea feature S Ceram Sea
Webfoot State see Oregon
18 F9 **Webster** New York, NE USA 43°12′N 77°25′W
29 Q8 **Webster** South Dakota, N USA 45°19′N 97°31′W
29 V13 **Webster City** Iowa, C USA 42°28′N 93°49′W
27 X5 **Webster Groves** Missouri, C USA 38°32′N 90°20′W
21 S4 **Webster Springs** var. Addison. West Virginia, NE USA 38°29′N 80°52′W
171 S11 **Weda, Teluk** bay Pulau Halmahera, E Indonesia
65 B25 **Weddell Island** var. Isla de San Jorge. island W Falkland Islands
65 K22 **Weddell Plain** undersea feature SW Atlantic Ocean 65°00′S 40°00′W
65 K23 **Weddell Sea** sea SW Atlantic Ocean
182 M11 **Wedderburn** Victoria, SE Australia 36°26′S 143°37′E
100 I9 **Wedel** Schleswig-Holstein, N Germany 53°35′N 09°42′E
92 N3 **Wedel Jarlsberg Land** physical region SW Svalbard
100 I12 **Wedemark** Niedersachsen, NW Germany 52°33′N 09°43′E
10 M17 **Wedge Mountain** ▲ British Columbia, SW Canada 50°10′N 122°43′W
23 R4 **Wedowee** Alabama, S USA 33°16′N 85°28′W
171 U15 **Weduar** Pulau Kai Besar, E Indonesia 05°55′S 132°51′E
35 N2 **Weed** California, W USA 41°26′N 122°24′W
15 Q12 **Weedon Centre** Québec, SE Canada 45°40′N 71°28′W
18 E13 **Weedville** Pennsylvania, NE USA 41°15′N 78°28′W
100 F10 **Weener** Niedersachsen, NW Germany 53°09′N 07°19′E
29 S16 **Weeping Water** Nebraska, C USA 40°52′N 96°08′W
99 L16 **Weert** Limburg, SE Netherlands 51°15′N 05°43′E
98 I10 **Weesp** Noord-Holland, C Netherlands 52°18′N 05°03′E
183 S5 **Wee Waa** New South Wales, SE Australia 30°16′S 149°27′E
110 N7 **Węgorzewo** Ger. Angerburg. Warmińsko-Mazurskie, NE Poland 54°12′N 21°49′E
110 E9 **Węgorzyno** Ger. Wangerin. Zachodnio-pomorskie, NW Poland 53°34′N 15°35′E
110 N11 **Węgrów** Ger. Bingerau. Mazowieckie, C Poland 52°22′N 22°00′E
98 N5 **Wehe-Den Hoorn** Groningen, NE Netherlands 53°20′N 06°29′E
98 M12 **Wehl** Gelderland, E Netherlands 51°58′N 06°13′E
Wehlau see Znamensk
168 F7 **Weh, Pulau** island NW Indonesia
Wei see Weifang
161 P1 **Weichang** prev. Zhuizishan. Hebei, E China 41°55′N 117°45′E
Weichang see Weishan
Weichsel see Wisła
101 M16 **Weida** Thüringen, C Germany 50°46′N 12°05′E
Weiden see Weiden in der Oberpfalz
101 M19 **Weiden in der Oberpfalz** var. Weiden. Bayern, SE Germany 49°40′N 12°10′E
161 Q4 **Weifang** var. Wei, Wei-fang; prev. Weihsien. Shandong, E China 36°44′N 119°10′E
161 S4 **Weihai** Shandong, E China 37°30′N 122°04′E
160 K6 **Wei He** ⇝ C China
Weihsien see Weifang
101 G17 **Weilburg** Hessen, W Germany 50°31′N 08°18′E
101 K24 **Weilheim in Oberbayern** Bayern, SE Germany 47°50′N 11°09′E
183 P4 **Weilmoringle** New South Wales, SE Australia 29°13′S 146°51′E
101 L16 **Weimar** Thüringen, C Germany 50°59′N 11°20′E
25 U11 **Weimar** Texas, SW USA 29°42′N 96°46′W
160 L6 **Weinan** Shaanxi, C China 34°30′N 109°30′E
108 H6 **Weinfelden** Thurgau, NE Switzerland 47°33′N 09°09′E
101 I24 **Weingarten** Baden-Württemberg, S Germany 47°49′N 09°37′E
101 G20 **Weinheim** Baden-Württemberg, SW Germany 49°33′N 08°40′E
160 H11 **Weining** var. Caohai, Weining Yizu Huizu Miaozu Zizhixian. Guizhou, S China 26°51′N 104°16′E
Weining Yizu Huizu Miaozu Zizhixian see Weining
181 V2 **Weipa** Queensland, NE Australia 12°43′S 142°01′E
11 Y11 **Weir River** Manitoba, C Canada 56°44′N 94°06′W
21 R1 **Weirton** West Virginia, NE USA 40°24′N 80°37′W
32 M13 **Weiser** Idaho, NW USA 44°15′N 116°58′W
160 F12 **Weishan** var. Weichang. Yunnan, SW China 25°22′N 100°19′E
161 P6 **Weishan Hu** ◎ E China
101 M15 **Weisse Elster** Eng. White Elster. ⇝ Czech Republic/Germany
Weisse Körös/Weisse Kreisch see Crişul Alb
108 L7 **Weissenbach am Lech** Tirol, W Austria 47°27′N 10°39′E
Weissenburg see Wissembourg, France
Weissenburg see Alba Iulia, Romania
101 K21 **Weissenburg in Bayern** Bayern, SE Germany 49°02′N 10°59′E
101 M15 **Weissenfels** var. Weißenfels. Sachsen-Anhalt, C Germany 51°12′N 11°58′E
109 R9 **Weissensee** ◎ S Austria
Weissenstein see Paide
108 E11 **Weisshorn** var. Flüela Wisshorn. ▲ SW Switzerland 46°06′N 07°43′E
Weisskirchen see Bela Crkva
23 R3 **Weiss Lake** ⊠ Alabama, S USA
101 Q14 **Weisswasser** Lus. Běla Woda. Sachsen, E Germany 51°30′N 14°37′E
99 M22 **Weiswampach** Diekirch, N Luxembourg 50°08′N 06°05′E
109 U2 **Weitra** Niederösterreich, N Austria 48°41′N 14°54′E
161 O4 **Weixian** var. Wei Xian. Hebei, E China 36°59′N 115°15′E
Wei Xian see Weixian
159 V11 **Weiyuan** var. Qingyuan. Gansu, C China 35°07′N 104°12′E
Weiyuan see Shuangjiang
160 F14 **Weiyuan Jiang** ⇝ SW China
109 W7 **Weiz** Steiermark, SE Austria 47°13′N 15°38′E
Weizhou see Wenchuan
160 K16 **Weizhou Dao** island S China
110 I6 **Wejherowo** Pomorskie, NW Poland 54°36′N 18°12′E
27 Q8 **Welch** Oklahoma, C USA 36°52′N 95°06′W
24 M6 **Welch** Texas, SW USA 32°52′N 102°06′W
21 Q6 **Welch** West Virginia, NE USA 37°26′N 81°36′W
45 O14 **Welchman Hall** C Barbados 13°10′N 59°34′W
80 J11 **Weldiya** var. Waldia, It. Valdia. Āmara, N Ethiopia 11°45′N 39°39′E
21 W8 **Weldon** North Carolina, SE USA 36°25′N 77°36′W
25 V9 **Weldon** Texas, SW USA 31°00′N 95°33′W
99 M19 **Welkenraedt** Liège, E Belgium 50°40′N 05°58′E
193 O2 **Welker Seamount** undersea feature N Pacific Ocean 55°07′N 140°18′W
83 I22 **Welkom** Free State, C South Africa 27°59′S 26°44′E
14 H16 **Welland** Ontario, S Canada 42°59′N 79°14′W
14 G16 **Welland** ⇝ Ontario, S Canada
97 O19 **Welland** ⇝ C England, United Kingdom
14 H17 **Welland Canal** canal Ontario, S Canada
155 K25 **Wellawaya** Uva Province, SE Sri Lanka 06°44′N 81°07′E
Welle see Uele
181 T4 **Wellesley Islands** island group Queensland, N Australia
99 J22 **Wellin** Luxembourg, SE Belgium 50°06′N 05°05′E
97 N20 **Wellingborough** C England, United Kingdom 52°19′N 00°42′W

◆ Country ● Country Capital ◇ Dependent Territory ○ Dependent Territory Capital ◈ Administrative Regions ✈ International Airport ▲ Mountain ▲▲ Mountain Range Volcano ⇝ River ◎ Lake ⊠ Reservoir

Wellington – Wilczek Land

183 R7 **Wellington** New South Wales, SE Australia 32°33′S 148°59′E
14 J15 **Wellington** Ontario, SE Canada 43°59′N 77°21′W
185 L14 **Wellington** ● Wellington, North Island, New Zealand 41°17′S 174°47′E
83 E26 **Wellington** Western Cape, SW South Africa 33°39′S 19°00′E
37 T2 **Wellington** Colorado, C USA 40°42′N 105°00′W
27 N7 **Wellington** Kansas, C USA 37°17′N 97°25′W
35 R7 **Wellington** Nevada, W USA 38°45′N 119°22′W
31 T11 **Wellington** Ohio, N USA 41°10′N 82°13′W
25 P3 **Wellington** Texas, SW USA 34°52′N 100°13′W
36 M4 **Wellington** Utah, W USA 39°31′N 110°45′W
185 M14 **Wellington** *off.* Wellington Region. ⬖ *region* (New Zealand) North Island, New Zealand
185 L14 **Wellington** ✈ Wellington, North Island, New Zealand 41°19′S 174°48′E
Wellington *see* Wellington, Isla
63 F22 **Wellington, Isla** *var.* Wellington. *island* S Chile
183 P12 **Wellington, Lake** ◎ Victoria, SE Australia
Wellington Region *see* Wellington
29 X14 **Wellman** Iowa, C USA 41°27′N 91°50′W
24 M6 **Wellman** Texas, SW USA 33°03′N 102°25′W
97 K22 **Wells** SW England, United Kingdom 51°13′N 02°39′W
29 V11 **Wells** Minnesota, N USA 43°45′N 93°43′W
35 X2 **Wells** Nevada, W USA 41°07′N 114°58′W
25 W8 **Wells** Texas, SW USA 31°28′N 94°54′W
18 F12 **Wellsboro** Pennsylvania, NE USA 41°43′N 77°39′W
21 R1 **Wellsburg** West Virginia, NE USA 40°15′N 80°37′W
184 K4 **Wellsford** Auckland, North Island, New Zealand 36°17′S 174°30′E
180 L9 **Wells, Lake** ◎ Western Australia
181 N4 **Wells, Mount** ▲ Western Australia 17°39′S 127°08′E
97 P18 **Wells-next-the-Sea** E England, United Kingdom 52°58′N 00°48′E
31 T15 **Wellston** Ohio, N USA 39°07′N 82°31′W
27 O10 **Wellston** Oklahoma, C USA 35°41′N 97°03′W
18 E11 **Wellsville** New York, NE USA 42°06′N 77°55′W
31 V12 **Wellsville** Ohio, N USA 40°36′N 80°39′W
36 L1 **Wellsville** Utah, W USA 41°38′N 111°55′W
36 I14 **Wellton** Arizona, SW USA 32°40′N 114°09′W
109 S4 **Wels** *anc.* Ovilava. Oberösterreich, N Austria 48°10′N 14°02′E
99 K15 **Welschap** ✈ (Eindhoven) Noord-Brabant, S Netherlands 51°27′N 05°22′E
100 P10 **Welse** ≈ NE Germany
22 H9 **Welsh** Louisiana, S USA 30°12′N 92°49′W
97 K19 **Welshpool** *Wel.* Y Trallwng. E Wales, United Kingdom 52°38′N 03°06′W
97 O21 **Welwyn Garden City** E England, United Kingdom 51°48′N 00°13′W
79 K18 **Wema** Equateur, NW Dem. Rep. Congo 0°25′S 21°33′E
81 G21 **Wembere** ≈ C Tanzania
11 N13 **Wembley** Alberta, W Canada 55°07′N 119°12′W
12 I9 **Wemindji** *prev.* Nouveau-Comptoir, Paint Hills. Québec, C Canada 53°00′N 78°42′W
99 G18 **Wemmel** Vlaams Brabant, C Belgium 50°54′N 04°18′E
32 J8 **Wenatchee** Washington, NW USA 47°50′N 120°48′W
160 M17 **Wenchang** Hainan, S China 19°34′N 110°46′E
161 R11 **Wencheng** *var.* Daxue. Zhejiang, SE China 27°48′N 120°01′E
77 P16 **Wenchi** W Ghana 07°45′N 02°02′W
Wen-chou/Wenchow *see* Wenzhou
160 H8 **Wenchuan** *var.* Weizhou. Sichuan, C China 31°29′N 103°39′E
Wendau *see* Võnnu
Wenden *see* Cēsis
161 S4 **Wendeng** Shandong, E China 37°10′N 122°00′E
81 J14 **Wendo** Southern Nationalities, S Ethiopia 06°34′N 38°28′E
36 J2 **Wendover** Utah, W USA 40°41′N 114°00′W
14 D9 **Wenebegon** ≈ Ontario, S Canada
14 D8 **Wenebegon Lake** ◎ Ontario, S Canada
108 E9 **Wengen** Bern, W Switzerland 46°38′N 07°57′E
161 O13 **Wengyuan** *var.* Longxian. Guangdong, S China 24°22′N 114°06′E
189 P15 **Weno** *prev.* Moen. Chuuk, C Micronesia
189 V12 **Weno** *prev.* Moen. *atoll* Chuuk Islands, C Micronesia
158 N13 **Wenquan** Qinghai, C China 33°16′N 91°44′E
159 H4 **Wenquan** *var.* Arixang, Bogeda'er. Xinjiang Uygur Zizhiqu, NW China 45°00′N 81°02′E
Wenquan *see* Yingshan
160 H14 **Wenshan** *var.* Kaihua. Yunnan, SW China 23°22′N 104°21′E
158 H6 **Wensu** Xinjiang Uygur Zizhiqu, W China 41°15′N 80°11′E
182 L8 **Wentworth** New South Wales, SE Australia 34°04′S 141°53′E
27 W4 **Wentzville** Missouri, C USA 38°48′N 90°51′W
159 V12 **Wenxian** *var.* Wen Xian. Gansu, C China 32°57′N 104°42′E
Wen Xian *see* Wenxian
161 S10 **Wenzhou** *var.* Wen-chou, Wenchow. Zhejiang, SE China 28°02′N 120°36′E
34 L4 **Weott** California, W USA 40°19′N 123°57′W
99 I20 **Wépion** Namur, SE Belgium 50°24′N 04°53′E
100 O11 **Werbellinsee** ◎ NE Germany
99 L21 **Werbomont** Liège, E Belgium 50°22′N 05°43′E
83 G20 **Werda** Kgalagadi, S Botswana 25°13′S 23°16′E
81 N14 **Werder** Sumalē, E Ethiopia 06°59′N 45°20′E
Werder *see* Virtsu
Werenów *see* Voranava
171 U13 **Weri** Papua, E Indonesia 03°10′S 132°39′E
98 I13 **Werkendam** Noord-Brabant, S Netherlands 51°48′N 04°54′E
101 M20 **Wernberg-Köblitz** Bayern, SE Germany 49°31′N 12°10′E
101 J18 **Werneck** Bayern, C Germany 50°00′N 10°06′E
101 K14 **Wernigerode** Sachsen-Anhalt, C Germany 51°51′N 10°48′E
Werowitz *see* Virovitica
101 J16 **Werra** ≈ C Germany
183 N12 **Werribee** Victoria, SE Australia 37°55′S 144°39′E
183 T6 **Werris Creek** New South Wales, SE Australia 31°22′S 150°40′E
Werro *see* Võru
Werschetz *see* Vršac
101 K23 **Wertach** ≈ S Germany
101 I19 **Wertheim** Baden-Württemberg, SW Germany 49°45′N 09°31′E
98 J8 **Wervershoof** Noord-Holland, NW Netherlands 52°43′N 05°09′E
Wervicq *see* Wervik
99 C18 **Wervik** *var.* Wervicq, Werwick. West-Vlaanderen, W Belgium 50°47′N 03°03′E
Werwick *see* Wervik
101 D14 **Wesel** Nordrhein-Westfalen, W Germany 51°39′N 06°37′E
Weseli an der Lainsitz *see* Veselí nad Lužnicí
Wesenberg *see* Rakvere
100 H12 **Weser** ≈ NW Germany
Wes-Kaap *see* Western Cape
25 S17 **Weslaco** Texas, SW USA 26°09′N 97°59′W
14 J13 **Weslemkoon Lake** ◎ Ontario, SE Canada
181 R1 **Wessel Islands** *island group* Northern Territory, N Australia
29 P9 **Wessington** South Dakota, N USA 44°27′N 98°40′W
29 P10 **Wessington Springs** South Dakota, N USA 44°02′N 98°33′W
25 T8 **West** Texas, SW USA 31°48′N 97°05′W
West *see* Ouest
30 M9 **West Allis** Wisconsin, N USA 43°01′N 88°00′W
182 E8 **Westall, Point** *headland* South Australia 32°54′S 134°04′E
194 M10 **West Antarctica** *var.* Lesser Antarctica. *physical region* Antarctica
14 G11 **West Arm** Ontario, S Canada 46°16′N 80°25′W
West Australian Basin *see* Wharton Basin
West Azerbaijan *see* Āžarbāyjān-e Gharbī
11 N17 **Westbank** British Columbia, SW Canada 49°50′N 119°37′W
138 F10 **West Bank** *disputed region* SW Asia
14 E11 **West Bay** Manitoulin Island, Ontario, S Canada 45°48′N 82°09′W
22 L11 **West Bay** *bay* Louisiana, S USA
30 M8 **West Bend** Wisconsin, N USA 43°26′N 88°13′W
153 R16 **West Bengal** ⬖ *state* NE India
West Borneo *see* Kalimantan Barat
29 Y14 **West Branch** Iowa, C USA 41°40′N 91°21′W
31 R7 **West Branch** Michigan, N USA 44°16′N 84°14′W
18 F13 **West Branch Susquehanna River** ≈ Pennsylvania, NE USA
97 L20 **West Bromwich** C England, United Kingdom 52°29′N 01°59′W
19 P8 **Westbrook** Maine, NE USA 43°42′N 70°21′W
29 T10 **Westbrook** Minnesota, N USA 44°02′N 95°26′W
29 Y15 **West Burlington** Iowa, C USA 40°49′N 91°09′W
96 L2 **West Burra** *island* NE Scotland, United Kingdom
30 J8 **Westby** Wisconsin, N USA 43°39′N 90°52′W
44 L6 **West Caicos** *island* W Turks and Caicos Islands
185 A24 **West Cape** *headland* South Island, New Zealand 45°51′S 166°26′E
174 L4 **West Caroline Basin** *undersea feature* SW Pacific Ocean 04°00′N 138°00′E
18 I16 **West Chester** Pennsylvania, NE USA 39°56′N 75°35′W
185 E18 **West Coast** *off.* West Coast Region. ⬖ *region* South Island, New Zealand
West Coast Region *see* West Coast
25 V12 **West Columbia** Texas, SW USA 29°08′N 95°39′W
29 W10 **West Concord** Minnesota, N USA 44°09′N 92°54′W
29 V14 **West Des Moines** Iowa, C USA 41°33′N 93°42′W
37 Q6 **West Elk Peak** ▲ Colorado, C USA 38°43′N 107°12′W
44 F1 **West End** Grand Bahama Island, N Bahamas 26°36′N 78°55′W
44 F1 **West End Point** *headland* Grand Bahama Island, N Bahamas 26°40′N 78°58′W
98 O7 **Westerbork** Drenthe, NE Netherlands 52°49′N 06°36′E
98 N3 **Westereems** *strait* Germany/Netherlands
98 O9 **Westerhaar-Vriezenveensewijk** Overijssel, E Netherlands 52°28′N 06°38′E
100 G6 **Westerland** Schleswig-Holstein, N Germany 54°54′N 08°19′E
99 I17 **Westerlo** Antwerpen, N Belgium 51°05′N 04°55′E
19 N13 **Westerly** Rhode Island, NE USA 41°22′N 71°45′W
81 G18 **Western** ⬖ *province* W Kenya
153 N11 **Western** ⬖ *zone* C Nepal
186 A8 **Western** ⬖ *province* SW Papua New Guinea
186 J8 **Western** *off.* Western Province. ⬖ *province* NW Solomon Islands
155 J26 **Western** ⬖ *province* SW Sri Lanka
83 G15 **Western** ⬖ *province* SW Zambia
180 K8 **Western Australia** ⬖ *state* W Australia
80 A13 **Western Bahr el Ghazal** ⬖ *state* SW Sudan
Western Bug *see* Bug
83 F25 **Western Cape** *off.* Western Cape Province, *Afr.* Wes-Kaap. ⬖ *province* SW South Africa
Western Cape Province *see* Western Cape
80 A11 **Western Darfur** ⬖ *state* W Sudan
Western Desert *see* Şaḩrā' al Gharbīyah
118 G9 **Western Dvina** *Bel.* Dzvina, *Ger.* Düna, *Latv.* Daugava, *Rus.* Zapadnaya Dvina. ≈ W Europe
81 D15 **Western Equatoria** ⬖ *state* SW Sudan
155 E16 **Western Ghats** ▲▲ SW India
186 C7 **Western Highlands** ⬖ *province* C Papua New Guinea
Western Isles *see* Outer Hebrides
80 C12 **Western Kordofan** ⬖ *state* C Sudan
21 T3 **Westernport** Maryland, NE USA 39°29′N 79°03′W
Western Province *see* Western
Western Punjab *see* Punjab
74 B10 **Western Sahara** ◇ *disputed territory* N Africa
Western Samoa *see* Samoa
Western Samoa, Independent State of *see* Samoa
Western Sayans *see* Zapadnyy Sayan
Western Scheldt *see* Westerschelde
Western Sierra Madre *see* Madre Occidental, Sierra
99 E15 **Westerschelde** *Eng.* Western Scheldt; *prev.* Honte. *inlet* S North Sea
31 S13 **Westerville** Ohio, N USA 40°07′N 82°55′W
101 F17 **Westerwald** ▲▲ W Germany
65 C25 **West Falkland** *var.* Gran Malvina, Isla Gran Malvina. *island* W Falkland Islands
29 R5 **West Fargo** North Dakota, N USA 46°49′N 96°51′W
188 M15 **West Fayu Atoll** *atoll* Caroline Islands, C Micronesia
18 C11 **Westfield** New York, NE USA 42°18′N 79°34′W
30 L7 **Westfield** Wisconsin, N USA 43°56′N 89°31′W
West Flanders *see* West-Vlaanderen
27 S10 **West Fork** Arkansas, C USA 35°55′N 94°11′W
29 P16 **West Fork Big Blue River** ≈ Nebraska, C USA
29 U12 **West Fork Des Moines River** ≈ Iowa/Minnesota, C USA
25 S5 **West Fork Trinity River** ≈ Texas, SW USA
30 L16 **West Frankfort** Illinois, N USA 37°54′N 88°55′W
98 I8 **West-Friesland** *physical region* NW Netherlands
West Frisian Islands *see* Waddeneilanden
19 T5 **West Grand Lake** ◎ Maine, NE USA
18 M12 **West Hartford** Connecticut, NE USA 41°44′N 72°45′W
18 M13 **West Haven** Connecticut, NE USA 41°16′N 72°57′W
27 X12 **West Helena** Arkansas, C USA 34°33′N 90°38′W
28 M2 **Westhope** North Dakota, N USA 48°54′N 101°01′W
195 Y8 **West Ice Shelf** *ice shelf* Antarctica
47 R2 **West Indies** *island group* SE North America
West Irian *see* Papua
West Java *see* Jawa Barat
36 L3 **West Jordan** Utah, W USA 40°37′N 111°55′W
West Kalimantan *see* Kalimantan Barat
99 D14 **Westkapelle** Zeeland, SW Netherlands 51°32′N 03°26′E
West Kazakhstan *see* Zapadnyy Kazakhstan
31 O13 **West Lafayette** Indiana, N USA 40°24′N 86°54′W
31 T13 **West Lafayette** Ohio, N USA 40°16′N 81°45′W
West Lake *see* Kagera
29 Y14 **West Liberty** Iowa, C USA 41°34′N 91°15′W
21 O5 **West Liberty** Kentucky, S USA 37°56′N 83°16′W
Westliche Morava *see* Zapadna Morava
10 J13 **Westlock** Alberta, SW Canada 54°12′N 113°50′W
14 E17 **West Lorne** Ontario, S Canada 42°36′N 81°35′W
96 J12 **West Lothian** *cultural region* S Scotland, United Kingdom
99 H16 **Westmalle** Antwerpen, N Belgium 51°18′N 04°40′E
192 G6 **West Mariana Basin** *var.* Perece Vela Basin. *undersea feature* W Pacific Ocean 15°00′N 137°00′E
97 E17 **Westmeath** *Ir.* An Iarmhí, Na H-Iarmhidhe. *cultural region* C Ireland
27 Y11 **West Memphis** Arkansas, C USA 35°09′N 90°11′W
21 W2 **Westminster** Maryland, NE USA 39°34′N 77°00′W
21 O11 **Westminster** South Carolina, SE USA 34°39′N 83°06′W
22 I5 **West Monroe** Louisiana, S USA 32°31′N 92°09′W
18 D15 **Westmont** Pennsylvania, NE USA 40°16′N 78°55′W
27 O3 **Westmoreland** Kansas, C USA 39°23′N 96°30′W
35 W17 **Westmorland** California, W USA 33°02′N 115°37′W
186 E6 **West New Britain** ⬖ *province* E Papua New Guinea
West New Guinea *see* Papua
83 K18 **West Nicholson** Matabeleland South, S Zimbabwe 21°06′S 29°25′E
29 T14 **West Nishnabotna River** ≈ Iowa, C USA
175 P11 **West Norfolk Ridge** *undersea feature* W Pacific Ocean
25 P12 **West Nueces River** ≈ Texas, SW USA
West Nusa Tenggara *see* Nusa Tenggara Barat
29 T11 **West Okoboji Lake** ◎ Iowa, C USA
33 R16 **Weston** Idaho, NW USA 42°01′N 119°29′W
21 R4 **Weston** West Virginia, NE USA 39°03′N 80°28′W
97 J22 **Weston-super-Mare** SW England, United Kingdom 51°21′N 02°59′W
23 Z14 **West Palm Beach** Florida, SE USA 26°43′N 80°03′W
West Papua *see* Papua
188 E9 **West Passage** *passage* Babeldaob, N Palau
23 O9 **West Pensacola** Florida, SE USA 30°25′N 87°16′W
27 V8 **West Plains** Missouri, C USA 36°44′N 91°51′W
35 P7 **West Point** California, W USA 38°21′N 120°33′W
23 R5 **West Point** Georgia, SE USA 32°52′N 85°10′W
22 M3 **West Point** Mississippi, S USA 33°36′N 88°39′W
29 R14 **West Point** Nebraska, C USA 41°50′N 96°42′W
21 X6 **West Point** Virginia, NE USA 37°31′N 76°48′W
182 G10 **West Point** *headland* South Australia 35°01′S 135°58′E
23 R4 **West Point Lake** ⊠ Alabama/Georgia, SE USA
97 B16 **Westport** *Ir.* Cathair na Mart. Mayo, W Ireland 53°48′N 09°32′W
185 G15 **Westport** West Coast, South Island, New Zealand 41°46′S 171°37′E
32 F10 **Westport** Oregon, NW USA 46°07′N 123°22′W
32 F9 **Westport** Washington, NW USA 46°53′N 124°06′W
31 S15 **West Portsmouth** Ohio, N USA 38°45′N 83°01′W
West Punjab *see* Punjab
11 V14 **Westray** Manitoba, C Canada 53°30′N 101°19′W
96 J4 **Westray** *island* NE Scotland, United Kingdom
14 F9 **Westree** Ontario, S Canada 47°25′N 81°32′W
97 L16 **West Riding** *cultural region* N England, United Kingdom
West River *see* Xi Jiang
30 J7 **West Salem** Wisconsin, N USA 43°54′N 91°04′W
65 H21 **West Scotia Ridge** *undersea feature* W Scotia Sea
West Sepik *see* Sandaun
173 N4 **West Sheba Ridge** *undersea feature* W Indian Ocean 12°45′N 48°15′E
West Siberian Plain *see* Zapadno-Sibirskaya Ravnina
31 S11 **West Sister Island** *island* Ohio, N USA
West-Skylge *see* West-Terschelling
West Sumatra *see* Sumatera Barat
98 J5 **West-Terschelling** *Fris.* West-Skylge. Friesland, N Netherlands 53°23′N 05°15′E
64 J7 **West Thulean Rise** *undersea feature* N Atlantic Ocean
29 X12 **West Union** Iowa, C USA 42°57′N 91°48′W
31 R15 **West Union** Ohio, N USA 38°47′N 83°33′W
21 R3 **West Union** West Virginia, NE USA 39°18′N 80°47′W
31 N13 **Westville** Illinois, N USA 40°02′N 87°38′W
21 R3 **West Virginia** *off.* State of West Virginia, *also known as* Mountain State. ⬖ *state* NE USA
99 A17 **West-Vlaanderen** *Eng.* West Flanders. ⬖ *province* W Belgium
35 R7 **West Walker River** ≈ California/Nevada, W USA
35 P4 **Westwood** California, W USA 40°18′N 121°02′W
183 P9 **West Wyalong** New South Wales, SE Australia 33°56′S 147°10′E
171 Q16 **Wetar, Pulau** *island* Kepulauan Damar, E Indonesia
Wetar, Selat *see* Wetar Strait
171 R16 **Wetar Strait** *var.* SelatWetar. *strait* Nusa Tenggara, S Indonesia
11 Q15 **Wetaskiwin** Alberta, SW Canada 52°57′N 113°20′W
81 K21 **Wete** Pemba, E Tanzania 05°03′S 39°41′E
166 M4 **Wetlet** Sagaing, C Burma (Myanmar) 22°43′N 95°22′E
37 T6 **Wet Mountains** ▲▲ Colorado, C USA
101 E15 **Wetter** Nordrhein-Westfalen, W Germany 51°22′N 07°24′E
101 H17 **Wetter** ≈ W Germany
99 F17 **Wetteren** Oost-Vlaanderen, NW Belgium 51°06′N 03°59′E
108 F7 **Wettingen** Aargau, N Switzerland 47°28′N 08°20′E
27 P11 **Wetumka** Oklahoma, C USA 35°14′N 96°14′W
23 Q5 **Wetumpka** Alabama, S USA 32°32′N 86°12′W
108 G7 **Wetzikon** Zürich, N Switzerland 47°19′N 08°48′E
101 G17 **Wetzlar** Hessen, W Germany 50°33′N 08°30′E
99 C18 **Wevelgem** West-Vlaanderen, W Belgium 50°48′N 03°12′E
38 M6 **Wevok** *var.* Wewuk. Alaska, USA 68°52′N 166°05′W
23 R9 **Wewahitchka** Florida, SE USA 30°06′N 85°12′W
186 C6 **Wewak** East Sepik, NW Papua New Guinea 03°35′S 143°35′E
27 O11 **Wewoka** Oklahoma, C USA 35°09′N 96°30′W
Wewuk *see* Wevok
97 F20 **Wexford** *Ir.* Loch Garman. SE Ireland 52°21′N 06°31′W
97 F20 **Wexford** *Ir.* Loch Garman. *cultural region* SE Ireland
30 L7 **Weyauwega** Wisconsin, N USA 44°16′N 88°54′W
11 U17 **Weyburn** Saskatchewan, S Canada 49°39′N 103°51′W
Weyer *see* Weyer Markt
109 U5 **Weyer Markt** *var.* Weyer. Oberösterreich, N Austria 47°52′N 14°39′E
100 H11 **Weyhe** Niedersachsen, NW Germany 53°00′N 08°52′E
97 L24 **Weymouth** S England, United Kingdom 50°36′N 02°28′W
19 P11 **Weymouth** Massachusetts, NE USA 42°13′N 70°56′W
99 H18 **Wezembeek-Oppem** Vlaams Brabant, C Belgium 50°51′N 04°28′E
98 M9 **Wezep** Gelderland, E Netherlands 52°28′N 06°E
184 M9 **Whakamaru** Waikato, North Island, New Zealand 38°27′S 175°48′E
184 O8 **Whakatane** Bay of Plenty, North Island, New Zealand 37°58′S 177°E
184 O8 **Whakatane** ≈ North Island, New Zealand
9 O9 **Whale Cove** Nunavut, C Canada 62°14′N 92°10′W
96 M2 **Whalsay** *island* NE Scotland, United Kingdom
184 L11 **Whangaehu** ≈ North Island, New Zealand
184 M6 **Whangamata** Waikato, North Island, New Zealand 37°13′S 175°54′E
184 Q9 **Whangara** Gisborne, North Island, New Zealand 38°34′S 178°12′E
184 K3 **Whangarei** Northland, North Island, New Zealand 35°44′S 174°18′E
184 K3 **Whangaruru Harbour** *inlet* North Island, New Zealand
25 V12 **Wharton** Texas, SW USA 29°19′N 96°08′W
173 U8 **Wharton Basin** *var.* West Australian Basin. *undersea feature* E Indian Ocean
185 E18 **Whataroa** West Coast, South Island, New Zealand 43°17′S 170°20′E
8 J9 **Wha Ti** Northwest Territories, W Canada 63°10′N 117°12′W
8 K10 **Wha Ti** *prev.* Lac la Martre. Northwest Territories, W Canada 63°10′N 117°12′W
184 K6 **Whatipu** Auckland, North Island, New Zealand 37°17′S 174°44′E
33 Y16 **Wheatland** Wyoming, C USA 42°03′N 104°57′W
14 D18 **Wheatley** Ontario, S Canada 42°06′N 82°27′W
30 M10 **Wheaton** Illinois, N USA 41°52′N 88°06′W
29 R7 **Wheaton** Minnesota, N USA 45°48′N 96°30′W
37 T4 **Wheat Ridge** Colorado, C USA 39°44′N 105°06′W
25 F2 **Wheeler** Texas, SW USA 35°26′N 100°17′W
23 O2 **Wheeler Lake** ⊠ Alabama, S USA
35 Y6 **Wheeler Peak** ▲ Nevada, W USA 39°00′N 114°17′W
37 T9 **Wheeler Peak** ▲ New Mexico, SW USA 36°34′N 105°25′W
31 S15 **Wheelersburg** Ohio, N USA 38°43′N 82°51′W
21 R2 **Wheeling** West Virginia, NE USA 40°05′N 80°43′W
97 L16 **Whernside** ▲ N England, United Kingdom 54°13′N 02°27′W
182 F9 **Whidbey, Point** *headland* South Australia 34°36′S 135°08′E
180 I7 **Whim Creek** Western Australia 20°51′S 117°54′E
10 L17 **Whistler** British Columbia, SW Canada 50°07′N 122°57′W
21 W8 **Whitakers** North Carolina, SE USA 36°06′N 77°43′W
14 H15 **Whitby** Ontario, S Canada 43°52′N 78°56′W
97 N15 **Whitby** N England, United Kingdom 54°29′N 00°37′W
10 G6 **White** ≈ Yukon Territory, W Canada
13 T11 **White Bay** *bay* Newfoundland, Newfoundland and Labrador, E Canada
20 I8 **White Bluff** Tennessee, S USA 36°06′N 87°13′W
28 J6 **White Butte** ▲ North Dakota, N USA 46°23′N 103°18′W
19 R5 **White Cap Mountain** ▲ Maine, NE USA 45°33′N 69°15′W
22 J9 **White Castle** Louisiana, S USA 30°10′N 91°09′W
182 M5 **White Cliffs** New South Wales, SE Australia 30°52′S 143°04′E
31 P8 **White Cloud** Michigan, N USA 43°34′N 85°47′W
11 P14 **Whitecourt** Alberta, SW Canada 54°10′N 115°38′W
25 O2 **White Deer** Texas, SW USA 35°26′N 101°10′W
White Elster *see* Weisse Elster
24 M5 **Whiteface** Texas, SW USA 33°36′N 102°36′W
18 K7 **Whiteface Mountain** ▲ New York, NE USA 44°22′N 73°54′W
29 W5 **Whiteface Reservoir** ⊠ Minnesota, N USA
33 O7 **Whitefish** Montana, NW USA 48°24′N 114°20′W
31 N9 **Whitefish Bay** Wisconsin, N USA 43°09′N 87°54′W
31 Q3 **Whitefish Bay** *lake bay* Canada/USA
14 E11 **Whitefish Falls** Ontario, S Canada 46°06′N 81°42′W
14 B7 **Whitefish Lake** ◎ Ontario, S Canada
29 U6 **Whitefish Lake** ◎ Minnesota, C USA
31 Q3 **Whitefish Point** *headland* Michigan, N USA 46°46′N 84°57′W
31 O4 **Whitefish River** ≈ Michigan, N USA
25 O4 **Whiteflat** Texas, SW USA 34°06′N 100°55′W
27 V12 **White Hall** Arkansas, C USA 34°18′N 92°05′W
30 K14 **White Hall** Illinois, N USA 39°26′N 90°24′W
31 O8 **Whitehall** Michigan, N USA 43°24′N 86°21′W
18 L9 **Whitehall** New York, NE USA 43°33′N 73°24′W
31 S13 **Whitehall** Ohio, N USA 39°58′N 82°53′W
30 J7 **Whitehall** Wisconsin, N USA 44°22′N 91°20′W
97 J15 **Whitehaven** NW England, United Kingdom 54°33′N 03°35′W
10 I8 **Whitehorse** *territory capital* Yukon Territory, W Canada 60°41′N 135°08′W
184 O7 **White Island** *island* NE New Zealand
14 K13 **White Lake** ◎ Ontario, SE Canada
22 H10 **White Lake** ◎ Louisiana, S USA
186 G7 **Whiteman Range** ▲▲ New Britain, E Papua New Guinea
183 Q15 **Whitemark** Tasmania, SE Australia 40°10′S 148°01′E
35 S9 **White Mountains** ▲▲ California/Nevada, W USA
19 N7 **White Mountains** ▲▲ Maine/New Hampshire, NE USA
80 F11 **White Nile** ⬖ *state* C Sudan
67 U7 **White Nile** *var.* Bahr el Jebel. ≈ S Sudan
81 E14 **White Nile** *Ar.* Al Baḩr al Abyaḑ, An Nīl al Abyaḑ, Bahr el Jebel. ≈ SE Sudan
25 W5 **White Oak Creek** ≈ Texas, SW USA
10 H9 **White Pass** *pass* Canada/USA
32 I9 **White Pass** *pass* Washington, NW USA
21 O9 **White Pine** Tennessee, S USA 36°06′N 83°17′W
18 K14 **White Plains** New York, NE USA 41°01′N 73°45′W
37 N13 **Whiteriver** Arizona, SW USA 33°50′N 109°57′W
28 M11 **White River** South Dakota, N USA 43°34′N 100°45′W
27 W12 **White River** ≈ Arkansas, SE USA
37 P3 **White River** ≈ Colorado/Utah, C USA
31 N15 **White River** ≈ Indiana, N USA
31 O8 **White River** ≈ Michigan, N USA
28 K11 **White River** ≈ South Dakota, N USA
25 O5 **White River** ≈ Texas, SW USA
18 M8 **White River** ≈ Vermont, NE USA
25 O5 **White River Lake** ⊠ Texas, SW USA
32 H11 **White Salmon** Washington, NW USA 45°43′N 121°29′W
18 I10 **Whitesboro** New York, NE USA 43°07′N 75°17′W
25 T5 **Whitesboro** Texas, SW USA 33°39′N 96°54′W
21 O7 **Whitesburg** Kentucky, S USA 37°07′N 82°52′W
White Sea *see* Beloye More
White Sea-Baltic Canal/White Sea Canal *see* Belomorsko-Baltiyskiy Kanal
63 I25 **Whiteside, Canal** *channel* S Chile
33 S10 **White Sulphur Springs** Montana, NW USA 46°33′N 110°54′W
21 R6 **White Sulphur Springs** West Virginia, NE USA 37°48′N 80°18′W
20 J6 **Whitesville** Kentucky, S USA 37°40′N 86°48′W
32 I10 **White Swan** Washington, NW USA 46°22′N 120°46′W
21 U12 **Whiteville** North Carolina, SE USA 34°20′N 78°42′W
20 F10 **Whiteville** Tennessee, S USA 35°19′N 89°09′W
77 Q13 **White Volta** *var.* Nakambé, *Fr.* Volta Blanche. ≈ Burkina/Ghana
30 M9 **Whitewater** Wisconsin, N USA 42°51′N 88°43′W
37 P14 **Whitewater Baldy** ▲ New Mexico, SW USA 33°19′N 108°38′W
23 X17 **Whitewater Bay** *bay* Florida, SE USA
31 Q14 **Whitewater River** ≈ Indiana/Ohio, N USA
11 V16 **Whitewood** Saskatchewan, S Canada 50°19′N 102°16′W
28 J9 **Whitewood** South Dakota, N USA 44°27′N 103°38′W
25 U5 **Whitewright** Texas, SW USA 33°30′N 96°23′W
97 I15 **Whithorn** S Scotland, United Kingdom 54°44′N 04°26′W
184 M6 **Whitianga** Waikato, North Island, New Zealand 36°50′S 175°42′E
19 N11 **Whitinsville** Massachusetts, NE USA 42°06′N 71°40′W
20 M8 **Whitley City** Kentucky, S USA 36°45′N 84°29′W
21 Q11 **Whitmire** South Carolina, SE USA 34°30′N 81°36′W
31 R10 **Whitmore Lake** Michigan, N USA 42°26′N 83°44′W
195 N9 **Whitmore Mountains** ▲▲ Antarctica
14 I12 **Whitney** Ontario, SE Canada 45°29′N 78°11′W
25 T8 **Whitney** Texas, SW USA 31°56′N 97°20′W
25 S8 **Whitney, Lake** ⊠ Texas, SW USA
35 S11 **Whitney, Mount** ▲ California, W USA 37°45′N 119°55′W
181 Y6 **Whitsunday Group** *island group* Queensland, E Australia
25 S6 **Whitt** Texas, SW USA 32°55′N 98°01′W
29 U12 **Whittemore** Iowa, C USA 43°03′N 94°25′W
39 R12 **Whittier** Alaska, USA 60°46′N 148°40′W
35 T15 **Whittier** California, W USA 33°58′N 118°01′W
83 I25 **Whittlesea** Eastern Cape, S South Africa 32°08′S 26°51′E
20 K10 **Whitwell** Tennessee, S USA 35°12′N 85°31′W
8 L10 **Wholdaia Lake** ◎ Northwest Territories, NW Canada
182 H7 **Whyalla** South Australia 33°04′S 137°34′E
Whydah *see* Ouidah
14 F13 **Wiarton** Ontario, S Canada 44°44′N 81°10′W
171 O13 **Wiau** Sulawesi, C Indonesia 03°08′S 121°22′E
111 H15 **Wiązów** *Ger.* Wansen. Dolnośląskie, SW Poland 50°49′N 17°13′E
33 Y8 **Wibaux** Montana, NW USA 46°57′N 104°11′W
27 N6 **Wichita** Kansas, C USA 37°42′N 97°20′W
25 R5 **Wichita Falls** Texas, SW USA 33°55′N 98°30′W
26 L11 **Wichita Mountains** ▲▲ Oklahoma, C USA
25 R5 **Wichita River** ≈ Texas, SW USA
96 K6 **Wick** N Scotland, United Kingdom 58°26′N 03°06′W
36 K13 **Wickenburg** Arizona, SW USA 33°57′N 112°44′W
24 L8 **Wickett** Texas, SW USA 31°34′N 103°00′W
180 I7 **Wickham** Western Australia 20°40′S 117°11′E
182 M14 **Wickham, Cape** *headland* Tasmania, SE Australia 39°36′S 143°55′E
20 G7 **Wickliffe** Kentucky, S USA 36°58′N 89°04′W
97 G19 **Wicklow** *Ir.* Cill Mhantáin. E Ireland 52°59′N 06°03′W
97 F19 **Wicklow** *Ir.* Cill Mhantáin. *cultural region* E Ireland
97 G19 **Wicklow Head** *Ir.* Ceann Chill Mhantáin. *headland* E Ireland 52°57′N 06°00′W
97 F18 **Wicklow Mountains** *Ir.* Sléibhte Chill Mhantáin. ▲▲ E Ireland
14 H10 **Wicksteed Lake** ◎ Ontario, S Canada
Wida *see* Ouidah
65 G15 **Wideawake Airfield** ✈ (Georgetown) SW Ascension Island
97 K18 **Widnes** NW England, United Kingdom 53°22′N 02°44′W
110 H9 **Więcbork** *Ger.* Vandsburg. Kujawsko-pomorskie, C Poland 53°21′N 17°31′E
101 E17 **Wied** ≈ W Germany
101 F16 **Wiehl** Nordrhein-Westfalen, W Germany 50°57′N 07°33′E
111 L17 **Wieliczka** Małopolskie, S Poland 50°N 20°02′E
110 H12 **Wielkopolskie** ⬖ *province* SW Poland
111 J14 **Wieluń** Sieradz, C Poland 51°14′N 18°33′E
109 X4 **Wien** *Eng.* Vienna, *Hung.* Bécs, *Slvk.* Vídeň, *Slvn.* Dunaj; *anc.* Vindobona. ● (Austria) Wien, NE Austria 48°13′N 16°22′E
109 X4 **Wien** *off.* Land Wien, *Eng.* Vienna. ⬖ *state* NE Austria
109 X5 **Wiener Neustadt** Niederösterreich, E Austria 47°49′N 16°08′E
Wien, Land *see* Wien
110 G7 **Wieprza** *Ger.* Wipper. ≈ NW Poland
98 O10 **Wierden** Overijssel, E Netherlands 52°22′N 06°35′E
98 I7 **Wieringerwerf** Noord-Holland, NW Netherlands 52°51′N 05°01′E
Wieruschow *see* Wieruszów
111 I14 **Wieruszów** *Ger.* Wieruschow. Łódzkie, C Poland 51°18′N 18°09′E
109 V9 **Wies** Steiermark, SE Austria 46°40′N 15°16′E
Wiesbachhorn *see* Grosses Wiesbachhorn
101 G18 **Wiesbaden** Hessen, W Germany 50°06′N 08°14′E
Wieselburg and Ungarisch-Altenburg/Wieselburg-Ungarisch-Altenburg *see* Mosonmagyaróvár
Wiesenhof *see* Ostrołęka
101 G20 **Wiesloch** Baden-Württemberg, SW Germany 49°18′N 08°42′E
100 F10 **Wiesmoor** Niedersachsen, NW Germany 53°22′N 07°46′E
110 I7 **Wieżyca** *Ger.* Turmberg. *hill* Pomorskie, N Poland
97 L17 **Wigan** NW England, United Kingdom 53°33′N 02°38′W
37 U3 **Wiggins** Colorado, C USA 40°11′N 104°03′W
22 M8 **Wiggins** Mississippi, S USA 30°50′N 89°09′W
Wigorna Ceaster *see* Worcester
97 I14 **Wigtown** S Scotland, United Kingdom 54°53′N 04°27′W
97 H14 **Wigtown** *cultural region* SW Scotland, United Kingdom
97 I15 **Wigtown Bay** *bay* SW Scotland, United Kingdom
98 L13 **Wijchen** Gelderland, SE Netherlands 51°48′N 05°44′E
92 N1 **Wijdefjorden** *fjord* NW Svalbard
98 M10 **Wijhe** Overijssel, E Netherlands 52°22′N 06°07′E
98 J12 **Wijk bij Duurstede** Utrecht, C Netherlands 51°58′N 05°21′E
98 J13 **Wijk en Aalburg** Noord-Brabant, S Netherlands 51°46′N 05°06′E
99 H16 **Wijnegem** Antwerpen, N Belgium 51°13′N 04°32′E
14 E11 **Wikwemikong** Manitoulin Island, Ontario, S Canada 45°46′N 81°43′W
108 H7 **Wil** Sankt Gallen, NE Switzerland 47°28′N 09°03′E
29 R16 **Wilber** Nebraska, C USA 40°28′N 96°57′W
32 K8 **Wilbur** Washington, NW USA 47°45′N 118°42′W
27 Q11 **Wilburton** Oklahoma, C USA 34°57′N 95°20′W
182 M6 **Wilcannia** New South Wales, SE Australia 31°34′S 143°23′E
18 D12 **Wilcox** Pennsylvania, NE USA 41°34′N 78°40′W
Wilczek Land *see* Vil'cheka, Zemlya

◆ Country
● Country Capital
◇ Dependent Territory
○ Dependent Territory Capital
⬖ Administrative Regions
✈ International Airport
▲ Mountain
▲▲ Mountain Range
Volcano
≈ River
◎ Lake
⊠ Reservoir

WILDALPEN – WULKA

109 U6 **Wildalpen** Steiermark, E Austria 47°40′N 14°54′E
31 O13 **Wildcat Creek** ≈ Indiana, N USA
108 L9 **Wilde Kreuzspitze** *It.* Picco di Croce. ▲ Austria/Italy 46°53′N 10°51′E
Wildenschwert *see* Ústí nad Orlicí
98 O6 **Wildervank** Groningen, NE Netherlands 53°04′N 06°52′E
100 G11 **Wildeshausen** Niedersachsen, NW Germany 52°54′N 08°26′E
108 D10 **Wildhorn** ▲ SW Switzerland 46°21′N 07°22′E
11 R17 **Wild Horse** Alberta, SW Canada 49°00′N 110°19′W
27 N12 **Wildhorse Creek** ≈ Oklahoma, C USA
28 L14 **Wild Horse Hill** ▲ Nebraska, C USA 41°52′N 101°56′W
109 W8 **Wildon** Steiermark, SE Austria 46°53′N 15°29′E
24 M2 **Wildorado** Texas, SW USA 35°12′N 102°10′W
29 R6 **Wild Rice River** ≈ Minnesota/North Dakota, N USA
Wilejka *see* Vilyeyka
195 Y9 **Wilhelm II Coast** *physical region* Antarctica
195 X9 **Wilhelm II Land** *physical region* Antarctica
55 U11 **Wilhelmina Gebergte** ▲▲ C Surinam
18 B13 **Wilhelm, Lake** ⊠ Pennsylvania, NE USA
92 O2 **Wilhelmøya** *island* C Svalbard
Wilhelm-Pieck-Stadt *see* Guben
109 W4 **Wilhelmsburg** Niederösterreich, E Austria 48°07′N 15°37′E
100 G10 **Wilhelmshaven** Niedersachsen, NW Germany 53°31′N 08°07′E
Wilia/Wilja *see* Neris
18 H13 **Wilkes Barre** Pennsylvania, NE USA 41°15′N 75°50′W
21 R9 **Wilkesboro** North Carolina, SE USA 36°08′N 81°09′W
195 W15 **Wilkes Coast** *physical region* Antarctica
189 W12 **Wilkes Island** *island* N Wake Island
195 X12 **Wilkes Land** *physical region* Antarctica
11 S15 **Wilkie** Saskatchewan, S Canada 52°27′N 108°42′W
194 I6 **Wilkins Ice Shelf** *ice shelf* Antarctica
182 D4 **Wilkinsons Lakes** *salt lake* South Australia
Wiłkomierz *see* Ukmergė
182 K11 **Willalooka** South Australia 36°24′S 140°20′E
32 G11 **Willamette River** ≈ Oregon, NW USA
183 O8 **Willandra Billabong Creek** *seasonal river* New South Wales, SE Australia
32 F9 **Willapa Bay** *inlet* Washington, NW USA
27 T7 **Willard** Missouri, C USA 37°18′N 93°25′W
37 S12 **Willard** New Mexico, SW USA 34°36′N 106°01′W
31 S12 **Willard** Ohio, N USA 41°03′N 82°43′W
36 L1 **Willard** Utah, W USA 41°23′N 112°01′W
186 G6 **Willaumez Peninsula** *headland* New Britain, E Papua New Guinea 05°03′S 150°04′E
37 N15 **Willcox** Arizona, SW USA 32°13′N 109°49′W
37 N16 **Willcox Playa** *salt flat* Arizona, SW USA
99 G17 **Willebroek** Antwerpen, C Belgium 51°04′N 04°22′E
99 G14 **Willemstad** Noord-Brabant, S Netherlands 51°40′N 04°27′E
45 P16 **Willemstad** ○ (Netherlands Antilles) Curaçao, Netherlands Antilles 12°07′N 68°54′W
11 S11 **William** ≈ Saskatchewan, C Canada
23 O6 **William "Bill" Dannelly Reservoir** ⊠ Alabama, S USA
182 G3 **William Creek** South Australia 28°55′S 136°23′E
181 T15 **William, Mount** ▲ South Australia
36 K11 **Williams** Arizona, SW USA 35°15′N 112°11′W
29 X14 **Williamsburg** Iowa, C USA 41°39′N 92°00′W
20 M8 **Williamsburg** Kentucky, S USA 36°44′N 84°10′W
31 R15 **Williamsburg** Ohio, N USA 39°00′N 84°02′W
21 X6 **Williamsburg** Virginia, NE USA 37°17′N 76°43′W
10 M15 **Williams Lake** British Columbia, SW Canada 52°08′N 122°09′W
21 P6 **Williamson** West Virginia, NE USA 37°42′N 82°16′W
31 N13 **Williamsport** Indiana, N USA 40°18′N 87°18′W
18 G13 **Williamsport** Pennsylvania, NE USA 41°16′N 77°03′W
21 W9 **Williamston** North Carolina, SE USA 35°53′N 77°05′W
21 P11 **Williamston** South Carolina, SE USA 34°37′N 82°28′W
20 M4 **Williamstown** Kentucky, S USA 38°39′N 84°32′W
18 L10 **Williamstown** Massachusetts, NE USA 42°41′N 73°11′W
18 J16 **Willingboro** New Jersey, NE USA 40°01′N 74°52′W
11 Q14 **Willingdon** Alberta, SW Canada 53°49′N 112°08′W
25 W10 **Willis** Texas, SW USA 30°25′N 95°28′W
108 F8 **Willisau** Luzern, W Switzerland 47°07′N 08°00′E
83 F24 **Williston** Northern Cape, W South Africa 31°20′S 20°52′E
23 V10 **Williston** Florida, SE USA 29°23′N 82°27′W
28 J3 **Williston** North Dakota, N USA 48°07′N 103°37′W
21 Q13 **Williston** South Carolina, SE USA 33°24′N 81°25′W
10 L12 **Williston Lake** ⊠ British Columbia, W Canada
34 L5 **Willits** California, W USA 39°24′N 123°22′W
29 T8 **Willmar** Minnesota, N USA 45°07′N 95°02′W
10 K11 **Will, Mount** ▲ British Columbia, W Canada 57°31′N 128°48′W
31 T11 **Willoughby** Ohio, N USA 41°38′N 81°24′W
11 U17 **Willow Bunch** Saskatchewan, S Canada 49°30′N 105°41′W
32 J11 **Willow Creek** ≈ Oregon, NW USA
39 R11 **Willow Lake** Alaska, USA 61°44′N 150°02′W
8 I9 **Willowlake** ≈ Northwest Territories, NW Canada
83 H25 **Willowmore** Eastern Cape, S South Africa 33°18′S 23°30′E
30 L5 **Willow Reservoir** ⊠ Wisconsin, N USA
35 N5 **Willows** California, W USA 39°28′N 122°12′W
27 V7 **Willow Springs** Missouri, C USA 36°59′N 91°58′W
182 I7 **Wilmington** South Australia 32°42′S 138°08′E
21 Y2 **Wilmington** Delaware, NE USA 39°45′N 75°33′W
21 V12 **Wilmington** North Carolina, SE USA 34°14′N 77°55′W
31 R14 **Wilmington** Ohio, N USA 39°27′N 83°49′W
20 M6 **Wilmore** Kentucky, S USA 37°51′N 84°39′W
29 R8 **Wilmot** South Dakota, N USA 45°24′N 96°51′W
Wilna/Wilno *see* Vilnius
101 G16 **Wilnsdorf** Nordrhein-Westfalen, W Germany 50°49′N 08°06′E
99 G16 **Wilrijk** Antwerpen, N Belgium 51°11′N 04°25′E
100 I10 **Wilseder Berg** *hill* NW Germany
67 Z12 **Wilshaw Ridge** *undersea feature* W Indian Ocean 17°30′S 56°30′E
21 V9 **Wilson** North Carolina, SE USA 35°43′N 77°56′W
25 N5 **Wilson** Texas, SW USA 33°21′N 101°44′W
182 A7 **Wilson Bluff** *headland* South Australia/Western Australia 31°41′S 129°01′E
35 Y7 **Wilson Creek Range** ▲▲ Nevada, W USA
23 O1 **Wilson Lake** ⊠ Alabama, S USA
26 M4 **Wilson Lake** ⊠ Kansas, SE USA
37 P7 **Wilson, Mount** ▲ Colorado, C USA 37°50′N 107°59′W
183 P13 **Wilsons Promontory** *peninsula* Victoria, SE Australia
29 Y14 **Wilton** Iowa, C USA 41°35′N 91°01′W
19 P7 **Wilton** Maine, NE USA 44°35′N 70°15′W
28 M5 **Wilton** North Dakota, N USA 47°09′N 100°46′W
97 L22 **Wiltshire** *cultural region* S England, United Kingdom
99 M23 **Wiltz** Diekirch, NW Luxembourg 49°58′N 05°56′E
180 K9 **Wiluna** Western Australia 26°34′S 120°14′E
99 M23 **Wilwerwiltz** Diekirch, NE Luxembourg 49°59′N 06°00′E
29 P5 **Wimbledon** North Dakota, N USA 47°08′N 98°25′W
42 K7 **Wina** *var.* Güina. Jinotega, N Nicaragua 14°00′N 85°14′W
31 O12 **Winamac** Indiana, N USA 41°03′N 86°37′W
81 G19 **Winam Gulf** *var.* Kavirondo Gulf. *gulf* SW Kenya
83 I22 **Winburg** Free State, C South Africa 28°31′S 27°01′E
19 N10 **Winchendon** Massachusetts, NE USA 42°41′N 72°01′W
14 M13 **Winchester** Ontario, SE Canada 45°07′N 75°19′W
97 M23 **Winchester** *hist.* Wintanceaster, *Lat.* Venta Belgarum. S England, United Kingdom 51°04′N 01°19′W
32 M10 **Winchester** Idaho, NW USA 46°13′N 116°35′W
30 J14 **Winchester** Illinois, N USA 39°38′N 90°28′W
31 Q13 **Winchester** Indiana, N USA 40°11′N 84°57′W
20 M5 **Winchester** Kentucky, S USA 38°00′N 84°10′W
18 M10 **Winchester** New Hampshire, NE USA 42°46′N 72°21′W
20 K10 **Winchester** Tennessee, S USA 35°11′N 86°06′W
21 V3 **Winchester** Virginia, NE USA 39°11′N 78°12′W
99 L22 **Wincrange** Diekirch, NW Luxembourg 50°03′N 05°55′E
10 I5 **Wind** ≈ Yukon Territory, NW Canada
183 S8 **Windamere, Lake** ◎ New South Wales, SE Australia
Windau *see* Ventspils, Latvia
Windau *see* Venta, Latvia/Lithuania
18 D15 **Windber** Pennsylvania, NE USA 40°12′N 78°47′W
23 T3 **Winder** Georgia, SE USA 33°59′N 83°43′W
97 K15 **Windermere** NW England, United Kingdom 54°24′N 02°54′W
14 C7 **Windermere Lake** ◎ Ontario, S Canada
31 U11 **Windham** Ohio, N USA 41°14′N 81°03′W
83 D19 **Windhoek** *Ger.* Windhuk. ● (Namibia) Khomas, C Namibia 22°34′S 17°06′E
83 D20 **Windhoek** ✈ Khomas, C Namibia 22°31′S 17°04′E
Windhuk *see* Windhoek
15 O8 **Windigo** Québec, SE Canada 47°45′N 73°19′W
15 O8 **Windigo** ≈ Québec, SE Canada
Windischfeistritz *see* Slovenska Bistrica
109 T6 **Windischgarsten** Oberösterreich, W Austria 47°42′N 14°21′E
Windischgraz *see* Slovenj Gradec
37 T16 **Wind Mountain** ▲ New Mexico, SW USA 32°01′N 105°35′W
29 T10 **Windom** Minnesota, N USA 43°52′N 95°07′W
37 Q7 **Windom Peak** ▲ Colorado, C USA 37°37′N 107°35′W
181 U9 **Windorah** Queensland, C Australia 25°25′S 142°41′E
37 O10 **Window Rock** Arizona, SW USA 35°40′N 109°03′W
31 N9 **Wind Point** *headland* Wisconsin, N USA 42°46′N 87°46′W
33 U14 **Wind River** ≈ Wyoming, C USA
13 P15 **Windsor** Nova Scotia, SE Canada 45°00′N 64°09′W
14 C17 **Windsor** Ontario, S Canada 42°18′N 83°W
15 Q12 **Windsor** Québec, SE Canada 45°34′N 72°00′W
97 N22 **Windsor** S England, United Kingdom 51°29′N 00°39′W
37 T3 **Windsor** Colorado, C USA 40°28′N 104°54′W
18 M12 **Windsor** Connecticut, NE USA 41°51′N 72°38′W
27 T5 **Windsor** Missouri, C USA 38°31′N 93°31′W
21 X9 **Windsor** North Carolina, SE USA 36°00′N 76°57′W
18 M12 **Windsor Locks** Connecticut, NE USA 41°55′N 72°37′W
25 R5 **Windthorst** Texas, SW USA 33°34′N 98°26′W
45 Z14 **Windward Islands** *island group* E West Indies
Windward Islands *see* Barlavento, Ilhas de, Cape Verde
Windward Islands *see* Vent, Îles du, Archipel de la Société, French Polynesia
44 K8 **Windward Passage** *Sp.* Paso de los Vientos. *channel* Cuba/Haiti
55 T9 **Wineperu** C Guyana 06°10′N 58°34′W
23 O3 **Winfield** Alabama, S USA 33°55′N 87°49′W
29 Y15 **Winfield** Iowa, C USA 41°07′N 91°26′W
27 O7 **Winfield** Kansas, C USA 37°14′N 97°00′W
25 W6 **Winfield** Texas, SW USA 33°10′N 95°06′W
21 Q4 **Winfield** West Virginia, NE USA 38°30′N 81°54′W
29 N5 **Wing** North Dakota, N USA 47°06′N 100°16′W
183 U7 **Wingham** New South Wales, SE Australia 31°52′S 152°24′E
12 G16 **Wingham** Ontario, S Canada 43°54′N 81°19′W
33 T8 **Winifred** Montana, NW USA 47°33′N 109°26′W
12 E9 **Winisk Lake** ◎ Ontario, C Canada
24 L8 **Wink** Texas, SW USA 31°45′N 103°09′W
36 M14 **Winkelman** Arizona, SW USA 32°59′N 110°46′W
11 X17 **Winkler** Manitoba, S Canada 49°12′N 97°55′W
109 Q9 **Winklern** Tirol, W Austria 46°54′N 12°54′E
Winkowitz *see* Vinkovci
32 G9 **Winlock** Washington, NW USA 46°29′N 122°56′W
77 P17 **Winneba** SE Ghana 05°22′N 00°38′W
29 U11 **Winnebago** Minnesota, N USA 43°46′N 94°10′W
29 R13 **Winnebago** Nebraska, C USA 42°14′N 96°28′W
30 M7 **Winnebago, Lake** ◎ Wisconsin, N USA
30 M7 **Winneconne** Wisconsin, N USA 44°07′N 88°44′W
35 T3 **Winnemucca** Nevada, W USA 40°59′N 117°44′W
35 R4 **Winnemucca Lake** ◎ Nevada, W USA
101 H21 **Winnenden** Baden-Württemberg, SW Germany 48°52′N 09°22′E
29 N11 **Winner** South Dakota, N USA 43°22′N 99°51′W
33 U9 **Winnett** Montana, NW USA 47°00′N 108°18′W
14 I9 **Winneway** Québec, SE Canada 47°35′N 78°33′W
22 H6 **Winnfield** Louisiana, S USA 31°55′N 92°38′W
29 U4 **Winnibigoshish, Lake** ◎ Minnesota, N USA
25 X11 **Winnie** Texas, SW USA 29°49′N 94°22′W
11 Y16 **Winnipeg** *province capital* Manitoba, S Canada 49°53′N 97°10′W
11 X16 **Winnipeg** ✈ Manitoba, S Canada 49°56′N 97°16′W
0 J8 **Winnipeg** ≈ Manitoba, S Canada
11 X16 **Winnipeg Beach** Manitoba, S Canada 50°25′N 96°59′W
11 W14 **Winnipeg, Lake** ◎ Manitoba, C Canada
11 W15 **Winnipegosis** Manitoba, S Canada 51°36′N 99°59′W
11 W15 **Winnipegosis, Lake** ◎ Manitoba, C Canada
19 O8 **Winnipesaukee, Lake** ◎ New Hampshire, NE USA
22 I6 **Winnsboro** Louisiana, S USA 32°09′N 91°43′W
21 R12 **Winnsboro** South Carolina, SE USA 34°22′N 81°05′W
25 W6 **Winnsboro** Texas, SW USA 33°01′N 95°16′W
29 X10 **Winona** Minnesota, N USA 44°03′N 91°37′W
22 L4 **Winona** Mississippi, S USA 33°30′N 89°42′W
27 W7 **Winona** Missouri, C USA 37°00′N 91°19′W
25 W7 **Winona** Texas, SW USA 32°29′N 95°10′W
18 M7 **Winooski River** ≈ Vermont, NE USA
98 P6 **Winschoten** Groningen, NE Netherlands 53°09′N 07°03′E
100 J10 **Winsen** Niedersachsen, N Germany 53°22′N 10°13′E
36 M11 **Winslow** Arizona, SW USA 35°01′N 110°42′W
19 Q7 **Winslow** Maine, NE USA 44°33′N 69°35′W
18 M12 **Winsted** Connecticut, NE USA 41°55′N 73°03′W
32 F14 **Winston** Oregon, NW USA 43°07′N 123°24′W
21 S9 **Winston Salem** North Carolina, SE USA 36°06′N 80°15′W
98 N5 **Winsum** Groningen, NE Netherlands 53°20′N 06°31′E
Wintanceaster *see* Winchester
23 W11 **Winter Garden** Florida, SE USA 28°34′N 81°35′W
10 J16 **Winter Harbour** Vancouver Island, British Columbia, SW Canada 50°28′N 128°03′W
23 W12 **Winter Haven** Florida, SE USA 28°01′N 81°43′W
23 X11 **Winter Park** Florida, SE USA 28°36′N 81°20′W
25 P8 **Winters** Texas, SW USA 31°57′N 99°57′W
29 U15 **Winterset** Iowa, C USA 41°19′N 94°00′W
98 O12 **Winterswijk** Gelderland, E Netherlands 51°58′N 06°44′E
108 G6 **Winterthur** Zürich, NE Switzerland 47°30′N 08°43′E
29 U9 **Winthrop** Minnesota, N USA 44°32′N 94°22′W
32 J7 **Winthrop** Washington, NW USA 48°28′N 120°13′W
181 V7 **Winton** Queensland, E Australia 22°22′S 143°04′E
185 C24 **Winton** Southland, South Island, New Zealand 46°08′S 168°20′E
21 X8 **Winton** North Carolina, SE USA 36°24′N 76°57′W
101 K15 **Wipper** ≈ C Germany
101 K14 **Wipper** ≈ C Germany
Wipper *see* Wieprza
182 G6 **Wirraminna** South Australia 31°10′S 136°13′E
182 F4 **Wirrida** South Australia 29°34′S 134°33′E
182 F7 **Wirrulla** South Australia 32°27′S 134°33′E
Wirsitz *see* Wyrzysk
Wirz-See *see* Võrtsjärv
97 O19 **Wisbech** E England, United Kingdom 52°39′N 00°08′E
Wisby *see* Visby
19 Q8 **Wiscasset** Maine, NE USA 44°01′N 69°41′W
Wischau *see* Vyškov
30 J5 **Wisconsin** *off.* State of Wisconsin, *also known as* Badger State. ◈ *state* N USA
30 L8 **Wisconsin Dells** Wisconsin, N USA 43°37′N 89°43′W
30 L8 **Wisconsin, Lake** ⊠ Wisconsin, N USA
30 L7 **Wisconsin Rapids** Wisconsin, N USA 44°24′N 89°50′W
30 L7 **Wisconsin River** ≈ Wisconsin, N USA
33 P11 **Wisdom** Montana, NW USA 45°36′N 113°27′W
21 P7 **Wise** Virginia, NE USA 37°00′N 82°36′W
39 Q7 **Wiseman** Alaska, USA 67°24′N 150°06′W
96 J12 **Wishaw** W Scotland, United Kingdom 55°47′N 03°56′W
29 O6 **Wishek** North Dakota, N USA 46°12′N 99°33′W
32 I11 **Wishram** Washington, NW USA 45°40′N 120°53′W
111 J17 **Wisła** Śląskie, S Poland 49°39′N 18°50′E
110 K11 **Wisła** *Eng.* Vistula, *Ger.* Weichsel. ≈ C Poland
Wiślany, Zalew *see* Vistula Lagoon
111 M16 **Wisłoka** ≈ SE Poland
100 L9 **Wismar** Mecklenburg-Vorpommern, N Germany 53°54′N 11°28′E
29 R14 **Wisner** Nebraska, C USA 41°59′N 96°54′W
103 V4 **Wissembourg** *var.* Weissenburg. Bas-Rhin, NE France 49°03′N 07°57′E
30 J6 **Wissota, Lake** ⊠ Wisconsin, N USA
97 O18 **Witham** ≈ E England, United Kingdom
97 O17 **Withernsea** E England, United Kingdom 53°46′N 00°01′W
37 Q13 **Withington, Mount** ▲ New Mexico, SW USA 33°52′N 107°29′W
23 U8 **Withlacoochee River** ≈ Florida/Georgia, SE USA
110 H11 **Witkowo** Wielkopolskie, C Poland 52°27′N 17°49′E
97 M21 **Witney** S England, United Kingdom 51°47′N 01°30′W
101 E15 **Witten** Nordrhein-Westfalen, W Germany 51°25′N 07°19′E
101 N14 **Wittenberg** Sachsen-Anhalt, E Germany 51°53′N 12°39′E
30 L6 **Wittenberg** Wisconsin, N USA 44°53′N 89°20′W
100 L11 **Wittenberge** Brandenburg, N Germany 52°59′N 11°45′E
103 U7 **Wittenheim** Haut-Rhin, NE France 47°49′N 07°19′E
180 I7 **Wittenoom** Western Australia 22°17′S 118°22′E
Wittingau *see* Třeboň
100 K12 **Wittingen** Niedersachsen, C Germany 52°42′N 10°43′E
101 E18 **Wittlich** Rheinland-Pfalz, SW Germany 49°59′N 06°54′E
100 F9 **Wittmund** Niedersachsen, NW Germany 53°34′N 07°46′E
100 M10 **Wittstock** Brandenburg, NE Germany 53°10′N 12°29′E
186 F6 **Witu Islands** *island group* E Papua New Guinea
110 O7 **Wiżajny** Podlaskie, NE Poland 54°22′N 22°51′E
55 W10 **W. J. van Blommesteinmeer** ⊠ E Surinam
110 L11 **Wkra** *Ger.* Soldau. ≈ C Poland
110 I6 **Władysławowo** Pomorskie, N Poland 54°48′N 18°25′E
Wlaschim *see* Vlašim
111 E14 **Wleń** *Ger.* Lähn. Dolnośląskie, SW Poland 51°00′N 15°39′E
110 J11 **Włocławek** *Ger./Rus.* Vlotslavsk. Kujawsko-pomorskie, C Poland 52°39′N 19°03′E
110 P13 **Włodawa** *Rus.* Vlodava. Lubelskie, SE Poland 51°33′N 23°31′E
Włodzimierz *see* Volodymyr-Volyns'kyy
111 K15 **Włoszczowa** Świętokrzyskie, C Poland 50°51′N 19°58′E
83 C19 **Wlotzkasbaken** Erongo, W Namibia 22°26′S 14°30′E
15 R12 **Woburn** Québec, SE Canada 45°22′N 70°52′W
19 O11 **Woburn** Massachusetts, NE USA 42°28′N 71°09′W
Wocheiner Feistritz *see* Bohinjska Bistrica
Wöchma *see* Võhma
147 S11 **Wodil** *var.* Vuadil'. Farg'ona Viloyati, E Uzbekistan 40°10′N 71°43′E
181 V14 **Wodonga** Victoria, SE Australia 36°11′S 146°55′E
111 I17 **Wodzisław Śląski** *Ger.* Loslau. Śląskie, S Poland 49°59′N 18°27′E
98 I11 **Woerden** Zuid-Holland, C Netherlands 52°06′N 04°54′E
98 I8 **Wognum** Noord-Holland, NW Netherlands 52°40′N 05°01′E
Wohlau *see* Wołów
108 F7 **Wohlen** Aargau, NW Switzerland 47°21′N 08°17′E
195 R2 **Wohlthat Massivet** ▲▲ Antarctica
Wojerecy *see* Hoyerswerda
Wōjjā *see* Wotje Atoll
Wojwodina *see* Vojvodina
171 V15 **Wokam, Pulau** *island* Kepulauan Aru, E Indonesia
97 N22 **Woking** SE England, United Kingdom 51°20′N 00°34′W
Woldenberg Neumark *see* Dobiegniew
188 K15 **Woleai Atoll** *atoll* Caroline Islands, W Micronesia
Woleu *see* Uolo, Río
79 E17 **Woleu-Ntem** *off.* Province du Woleu-Ntem, *var.* Le Woleu-Ntem. ◈ *province* W Gabon
Woleu-Ntem, Province du *see* Woleu-Ntem
32 F15 **Wolf Creek** Oregon, NW USA 42°40′N 123°22′W
26 K9 **Wolf Creek** ≈ Oklahoma/Texas, SW USA
37 R7 **Wolf Creek Pass** *pass* Colorado, C USA
19 O9 **Wolfeboro** New Hampshire, NE USA 43°34′N 71°10′W
25 U5 **Wolfe City** Texas, SW USA 33°22′N 96°04′W
14 L15 **Wolfe Island** *island* Ontario, SE Canada
101 M14 **Wolfen** Sachsen-Anhalt, E Germany 51°40′N 12°16′E
100 J13 **Wolfenbüttel** Niedersachsen, C Germany 52°10′N 10°33′E
109 T4 **Wolfern** Oberösterreich, N Austria 48°06′N 14°16′E
109 Q6 **Wolfgangsee** *var.* Abersee, St Wolfgangsee. ◎ N Austria
39 P9 **Wolf Mountain** ▲ Alaska, USA 65°20′N 154°08′W
33 X7 **Wolf Point** Montana, NW USA 48°05′N 105°40′W
22 L8 **Wolf River** ≈ Mississippi, S USA
30 M7 **Wolf River** ≈ Wisconsin, N USA
109 U9 **Wolfsberg** Kärnten, SE Austria 46°50′N 14°50′E
100 K12 **Wolfsburg** Niedersachsen, N Germany 52°25′N 10°47′E
57 B17 **Wolf, Volcán** △ Galapagos Islands, Ecuador, E Pacific Ocean 0°01′N 91°22′W
100 O8 **Wolgast** Mecklenburg-Vorpommern, NE Germany 54°04′N 13°47′E
108 F8 **Wolhusen** Luzern, W Switzerland 47°04′N 08°06′E
110 D8 **Wolin** *Ger.* Wollin. Zachodnio-pomorskie, NW Poland 53°52′N 14°35′E
109 Y3 **Wolkersdorf** Niederösterreich, NE Austria 48°24′N 16°31′E
Wołkowysk *see* Vawkavysk
Wöllan *see* Velenje
8 J6 **Wollaston, Cape** *headland* Victoria Island, Northwest Territories, NW Canada 71°00′N 118°21′W
63 J25 **Wollaston, Isla** *island* S Chile
11 U11 **Wollaston Lake** Saskatchewan, C Canada 58°05′N 103°38′W
11 T10 **Wollaston Lake** ◎ Saskatchewan, C Canada
8 J6 **Wollaston Peninsula** *peninsula* Victoria Island, Northwest Territories/Nunavut NW Canada
Wollin *see* Wolin
183 S9 **Wollongong** New South Wales, SE Australia 34°25′S 150°52′E
Wolmar *see* Valmiera
100 L13 **Wolmirstedt** Sachsen-Anhalt, C Germany 52°15′N 11°37′E
110 M11 **Wołomin** Mazowieckie, C Poland 52°20′N 21°11′E
110 G!3 **Wołów** *Ger.* Wohlau. Dolnośląskie, SW Poland 51°21′N 16°40′E
Wołożyn *see* Valozhyn
14 G11 **Wolseley Bay** Ontario, S Canada 46°05′N 80°16′W
29 P10 **Wolsey** South Dakota, N USA 44°22′N 98°28′W
110 F12 **Wolsztyn** Wielkopolskie, C Poland 52°07′N 16°07′E
98 M7 **Wolvega** *Fris.* Wolvegea. Friesland, N Netherlands 52°53′N 06°E
Wolvegea *see* Wolvega
97 K19 **Wolverhampton** C England, United Kingdom 52°36′N 02°08′W
Wolverine State *see* Michigan
99 G18 **Wolvertem** Vlaams Brabant, C Belgium 50°55′N 04°19′E
99 H16 **Wommelgem** Antwerpen, N Belgium 51°12′N 04°32′E
186 D7 **Wonenara** *var.* Wonerara. Eastern Highlands, C Papua New Guinea 06°46′S 145°54′E
Wonerara *see* Wonenara
Wongalara Lake *see* Wongalarroo Lake
183 N6 **Wongalarroo Lake** *var.* Wongalara Lake. *seasonal lake* New South Wales, SE Australia
163 Y15 **Wŏnju** *Jap.* Genshū. N South Korea 37°21′N 127°57′E
10 M12 **Wonowon** British Columbia, W Canada 56°46′N 121°54′W
163 X13 **Wŏnsan** SE North Korea 39°11′N 127°21′E
183 O13 **Wonthaggi** Victoria, SE Australia 38°38′S 145°37′E
23 N2 **Woodall Mountain** ▲ Mississippi, S USA 34°47′N 88°14′W
23 W7 **Woodbine** Georgia, SE USA 30°58′N 81°43′W
29 S14 **Woodbine** Iowa, C USA 41°44′N 95°42′W
18 J17 **Woodbine** New Jersey, NE USA 39°12′N 74°47′W
21 W4 **Woodbridge** Virginia, NE USA 38°40′N 77°17′W
183 V4 **Woodburn** New South Wales, SE Australia 29°07′S 153°23′E
32 G11 **Woodburn** Oregon, NW USA 45°08′N 122°51′W
20 K9 **Woodbury** Tennessee, S USA 35°49′N 86°06′W
183 V5 **Wooded Bluff** *headland* New South Wales, SE Australia 29°24′S 153°22′E
183 V3 **Woodenbong** New South Wales, SE Australia 28°24′S 152°39′E
35 R11 **Woodlake** California, W USA 36°24′N 119°06′W
35 N7 **Woodland** California, W USA 38°41′N 121°46′W
19 T5 **Woodland** Maine, NE USA 45°10′N 67°25′W
32 G10 **Woodland** Washington, NW USA 45°54′N 122°44′W
37 T5 **Woodland Park** Colorado, C USA 38°59′N 105°03′W
186 I9 **Woodlark Island** *var.* Murua Island. *island* SE Papua New Guinea
Woodle Island *see* Kuria
11 T17 **Wood Mountain** ▲▲ Saskatchewan, S Canada
30 K15 **Wood River** Illinois, N USA 38°51′N 90°06′W
29 P16 **Wood River** Nebraska, C USA 40°48′N 98°33′W
39 R9 **Wood River** ≈ Alaska, USA
39 O13 **Wood River Lakes** *lakes* Alaska, USA
182 C1 **Woodroffe, Mount** ▲ South Australia 26°19′S 131°42′E
21 P11 **Woodruff** South Carolina, SE USA 34°44′N 82°02′W
30 K4 **Woodruff** Wisconsin, N USA 45°55′N 89°41′W
25 T14 **Woodsboro** Texas, SW USA 28°14′N 97°19′W
31 U13 **Woodsfield** Ohio, N USA 39°45′N 81°07′W
181 P4 **Woods, Lake** ◎ Northern Territory, N Australia
11 Z16 **Woods, Lake of the** *Fr.* Lac des Bois. ◎ Canada/USA
25 Q6 **Woodson** Texas, SW USA 33°00′N 99°01′W
13 N14 **Woodstock** New Brunswick, SE Canada 46°10′N 67°38′W
14 F16 **Woodstock** Ontario, S Canada 43°07′N 80°46′W
30 M10 **Woodstock** Illinois, N USA 42°18′N 88°27′W
18 M9 **Woodstock** Vermont, NE USA 43°37′N 72°33′W
21 U4 **Woodstock** Virginia, NE USA 38°55′N 78°31′W
19 N8 **Woodsville** New Hampshire, NE USA 44°08′N 72°02′W
184 M12 **Woodville** Manawatu-Wanganui, North Island, New Zealand 40°22′S 175°59′E
22 J7 **Woodville** Mississippi, S USA 31°06′N 91°18′W
25 X9 **Woodville** Texas, SW USA 30°47′N 94°26′W
26 K9 **Woodward** Oklahoma, C USA 36°26′N 99°25′W
29 O5 **Woodworth** North Dakota, N USA 47°06′N 99°19′W
171 W12 **Wool** Papua, E Indonesia 01°38′S 135°34′E
183 V5 **Woolgoolga** New South Wales, E Australia 30°04′S 153°09′E
182 H6 **Woomera** South Australia 31°12′S 136°52′E
19 O12 **Woonsocket** Rhode Island, NE USA 41°58′N 71°27′W
29 P10 **Woonsocket** South Dakota, N USA 44°03′N 98°16′W
31 T12 **Wooster** Ohio, N USA 40°48′N 81°56′W
80 L12 **Woqooyi Galbeed** *off.* Gobolka Woqooyi Galbeed. ◈ *region* NW Somalia
Woqooyi Galbeed, Gobolka *see* Woqooyi Galbeed
108 E8 **Worb** Bern, C Switzerland 46°54′N 07°36′E
83 F26 **Worcester** Western Cape, SW South Africa 33°41′S 19°22′E
97 L20 **Worcester** *hist.* Wigorna Ceaster. W England, United Kingdom 52°11′N 02°13′W
19 N11 **Worcester** Massachusetts, NE USA 42°17′N 71°48′W
97 L20 **Worcestershire** *cultural region* C England, United Kingdom
32 H16 **Worden** Oregon, NW USA 42°04′N 121°50′W
109 O6 **Wörgl** Tirol, W Austria 47°29′N 12°04′E
171 V15 **Workai, Pulau** *island* Kepulauan Aru, E Indonesia
97 J15 **Workington** NW England, United Kingdom 54°39′N 03°33′W
98 K7 **Workum** Friesland, N Netherlands 52°58′N 05°25′E
33 V13 **Worland** Wyoming, C USA 44°01′N 107°57′W
see São João de Cortes
Wormatia *see* Worms
99 N25 **Wormeldange** Grevenmacher, E Luxembourg 49°37′N 06°25′E
98 I9 **Wormer** Noord-Holland, C Netherlands 52°30′N 04°50′E
101 G19 **Worms** *anc.* Augusta Vangionum, Borbetomagus, Wormatia. Rheinland-Pfalz, SW Germany 49°38′N 08°22′E
Worms *see* Vormsi
101 K21 **Wörnitz** ≈ S Germany
25 U8 **Wortham** Texas, SW USA 31°47′N 96°27′W
101 G21 **Wörth am Rhein** Rheinland-Pfalz, SW Germany 49°04′N 08°16′E
109 S9 **Wörther See** ◎ S Austria
97 O23 **Worthing** SE England, United Kingdom 50°48′N 00°23′W
29 S11 **Worthington** Minnesota, N USA 43°37′N 95°37′W
31 S13 **Worthington** Ohio, N USA 40°05′N 83°01′W
35 W8 **Worthington Peak** ▲ Nevada, W USA 37°57′N 115°32′W
171 Y13 **Wosi** Papua, E Indonesia 03°55′S 138°54′E
171 V13 **Wosimi** Papua, E Indonesia 02°44′S 134°34′E
189 R5 **Wotho Atoll** *var.* Wōtto. *atoll* Ralik Chain, W Marshall Islands
189 V5 **Wotje Atoll** *var.* Wōjjā. *atoll* Ratak Chain, E Marshall Islands
Wotoe *see* Wotu
Wottawa *see* Otava
Wōtto *see* Wotho Atoll
171 O13 **Wotu** *prev.* Wotoe. Sulawesi, C Indonesia 02°34′S 120°46′E
98 K11 **Woudenberg** Utrecht, C Netherlands 52°05′N 05°25′E
98 I13 **Woudrichem** Noord-Brabant, S Netherlands 51°49′N 05°E
43 N8 **Wounta** *var.* Huaunta. Región Autónoma Atlántico Norte, NE Nicaragua 13°30′N 83°32′W
171 P14 **Wowoni, Pulau** *island* C Indonesia
81 J17 **Woyamdero Plain** *plain* E Kenya
Woyens *see* Vojens
Wozrojdeniye Oroli *see* Vozrozhdeniya, Ostrov
Wrangel Island *see* Vrangelya, Ostrov
39 Y13 **Wrangell** Wrangell Island, Alaska, USA 56°28′N 132°22′W
38 C15 **Wrangell, Cape** *headland* Attu Island, Alaska, USA 52°55′N 172°28′E
39 S11 **Wrangell, Mount** ▲ Alaska, USA 62°00′N 144°01′W
39 T11 **Wrangell Mountains** ▲▲ Alaska, USA
197 S7 **Wrangel Plain** *undersea feature* Arctic Ocean
96 H6 **Wrath, Cape** *headland* N Scotland, United Kingdom 58°37′N 05°01′W
37 W3 **Wray** Colorado, C USA 40°01′N 102°12′W
44 K13 **Wreck Point** *headland* C Jamaica 17°50′N 76°55′W
83 C23 **Wreck Point** *headland* W South Africa 28°52′S 16°17′E
23 V4 **Wrens** Georgia, SE USA 33°12′N 82°23′W
97 K18 **Wrexham** NE Wales, United Kingdom 53°03′N 03°W
27 R13 **Wright City** Oklahoma, C USA 34°03′N 95°00′W
194 J12 **Wright Island** *island* Antarctica
13 N9 **Wright, Mont** ▲ Québec, E Canada 52°36′N 67°40′W
25 X5 **Wright Patman Lake** ⊠ Texas, SW USA
36 M16 **Wrightson, Mount** ▲ Arizona, SW USA 31°42′N 110°51′W
23 U5 **Wrightsville** Georgia, SE USA 32°43′N 82°43′W
21 W12 **Wrightsville Beach** North Carolina, SE USA 34°12′N 77°48′W
35 T15 **Wrightwood** California, W USA 34°21′N 117°37′W
8 H9 **Wrigley** Northwest Territories, W Canada 63°16′N 123°39′W
111 G14 **Wrocław** *Eng./Ger.* Breslau. Dolnośląskie, SW Poland 51°07′N 17°01′E
110 F10 **Wronki** *Ger.* Fronicken. Wielkopolskie, C Poland 52°42′N 16°22′E
110 H11 **Września** Wielkopolskie, C Poland 52°19′N 17°34′E
110 F12 **Wschowa** Lubuskie, W Poland 51°49′N 16°15′E
Wsetin *see* Vsetín
161 O5 **Wu'an** Hebei, E China 36°45′N 114°12′E
180 I12 **Wubin** Western Australia 30°05′S 116°43′E
163 W9 **Wuchang** Heilongjiang, NE China 44°55′N 127°13′E
Wuchang *see* Wuhan
Wu-chou/Wuchow *see* Wuzhou
160 M16 **Wuchuan** *var.* Meilu. Guangdong, S China 21°28′N 110°49′E
160 K10 **Wuchuan** *var.* Duru, Gelaozu Miaozu Zhizhixian. Guizhou, S China 28°40′N 108°04′E
163 O13 **Wuchuan** Nei Mongol Zizhiqu, N China 41°04′N 111°28′E
163 V6 **Wudalianchi** *var.* Qingshan; *prev.* Dedu. Heilongjiang, NE China 48°40′N 126°06′E
159 O11 **Wudaoliang** Qinghai, C China 35°16′N 93°03′E
141 Q13 **Wuday'ah** *spring/well* S Saudi Arabia 17°03′N 47°06′E
77 V13 **Wudil** Kano, N Nigeria 11°46′N 08°49′E
160 G12 **Wuding** *var.* Jincheng. Yunnan, SW China 25°30′N 102°21′E
182 G8 **Wudinna** South Australia 33°06′S 135°30′E
Wudu *see* Longnan
160 L9 **Wufeng** Hubei, C China 30°09′N 110°31′E
161 O11 **Wugong Shan** ▲▲ S China
157 P7 **Wuhai** *var.* Haibowan. Nei Mongol Zizhiqu, N China 39°40′N 106°48′E
161 O9 **Wuhan** *var.* Han-kou, Han-k'ou, Hanyang, Wuchang, Wu-han; *prev.* Hankow. *province capital* Hubei, C China 30°35′N 114°19′E
Wu-han *see* Wuhan
161 Q7 **Wuhe** Anhui, E China 33°05′N 117°55′E
Wuhsien *see* Suzhou
Wuhsi/Wu-his *see* Wuxi
161 Q8 **Wuhu** *var.* Wu-na-mu. Anhui, E China 31°23′N 118°25′E
Wūjae *see* Ujae Atoll
160 K11 **Wu Jiang** ≈ C China
158 L5 **Wujiaqu** Xinjiang Uygur Zizhiqu, NW China 44°11′N 87°30′E
Wujlān *see* Ujelang Atoll
77 W15 **Wukari** Taraba, E Nigeria 07°51′N 09°49′E
Wulan *see* Jingyuan
152 H4 **Wular Lake** ◎ NE India
162 M13 **Wulashan** Nei Mongol Zizhiqu, N China 40°43′N 108°45′E
160 H11 **Wulian Feng** ▲▲ SW China
160 F13 **Wuliang Shan** ▲▲ SW China
160 K11 **Wuling Shan** ▲▲ S China
109 Y5 **Wulka** ≈ E Austria

◆ Country
● Country Capital
◇ Dependent Territory
○ Dependent Territory Capital
◈ Administrative Regions
✈ International Airport
▲ Mountain
▲▲ Mountain Range
△ Volcano
≈ River
◎ Lake
⊠ Reservoir

Column 1

Wulkan *see* Vulcan
109 T3 Wullowitz Oberösterreich, N Austria 48°37′N 14°27′E
Wu-lu-k'o-mu-shi/Wu-lu-mu-ch'i *see* Ürümqi
79 D14 Wum Nord-Ouest, NE Cameroon 06°24′N 10°04′E
160 K14 Wumeng Shan ▲ SW China
160 K14 Wuming Guangxi Zhuangzu Zizhiqu, S China 23°12′N 108°11′E
100 I10 Wümme ♒ NW Germany
Wu-na-mu *see* Wuhu
171 X13 Wunen Papua, E Indonesia 03°40′S 138°31′E
12 D9 Wunnummin Lake ◉ Ontario, C Canada
80 D13 Wun Rog Warab, S Sudan 09°00′N 28°20′E
101 M18 Wunsiedel Bayern, E Germany 50°02′N 12°00′E
100 I12 Wunstorf Niedersachsen, NW Germany 52°25′N 09°25′E
166 M3 Wuntho Sagaing, N Burma (Myanmar) 23°52′N 95°43′E
101 F15 Wupper ♒ W Germany
101 E15 Wuppertal *prev.* Barmen-Elberfeld. Nordrhein-Westfalen, W Germany 51°16′N 07°12′E
160 K5 Wuqi Shaanxi, C China 36°57′N 108°15′E
158 E7 Wuqia Xinjiang Uygur Zizhiqu, NW China 39°50′N 75°19′E
161 P4 Wuqiao *var.* Sangyuan. Hebei, E China 37°40′N 116°21′E
101 L23 Würm ♒ SE Germany
77 T12 Wurno Sokoto, NW Nigeria 13°15′N 05°24′E
101 I19 Würzburg Bayern, SW Germany 49°48′N 09°56′E
101 N15 Wurzen Sachsen, E Germany 51°21′N 12°48′E
159 V11 Wushan Gansu, C China 34°42′N 104°53′E
160 L9 Wu Shan ▲ C China
158 G7 Wushi *var.* Uqturpan. Xinjiang Uygur Zizhiqu, NW China 41°07′N 79°09′E
Wasih *see* Wuxi
65 N18 Wüst Seamount *undersea feature* S Atlantic Ocean 32°00′S 00°06′E
Wusuli Jiang/Wusuri *see* Ussuri
161 N3 Wutai Shan *var.* Beitai Ding. ▲ C China 39°00′N 114°00′E
160 H10 Wutongqiao Sichuan, C China 29°21′N 103°48′E
159 P6 Wutongwozi Quan *spring* NW China
99 H15 Wuustwezel Antwerpen, N Belgium 51°24′N 04°34′E
186 B4 Wuvulu Island *island* NW Papua New Guinea
159 U9 Wuwei *var.* Liangzhou. Gansu, C China 37°58′N 102°40′E
161 R8 Wuxi *var.* Wuhsi, Wu-hsi, Wusih. Jiangsu, E China 31°35′N 120°19′E
Wuxing *see* Huzhou
160 L14 Wuxuan Guangxi Zhuangzu Zizhiqu, S China 23°40′N 109°41′E
160 K11 Wuyang He ♒ S China
163 X6 Wuying Heilongjiang, NE China 48°36′N 129°24′E
161 Q11 Wuyishan *prev.* Chong'an. Fujian, SE China 27°48′N 118°03′E
157 T12 Wuyi Shan ▲ SE China
162 M13 Wuyuan Nei Mongol Zizhiqu, N China 41°05′N 108°15′E
160 L17 Wuzhishan *prev.* Tongshi. Hainan, S China 18°37′N 109°24′E
160 L17 Wuzhi Shan ▲ S China 18°52′N 109°36′E
159 W8 Wuzhong Ningxia, N China 37°58′N 106°09′E
160 M14 Wuzhou *var.* Wu-chou, Wuchow. Guangxi Zhuangzu Zizhiqu, S China 23°30′N 111°21′E
18 H12 Wyalusing Pennsylvania, NE USA 41°40′N 76°13′W
182 M10 Wycheproof Victoria, SE Australia 36°06′S 143°13′E
97 K21 Wye Wel. Gwy. ♒ England/Wales, United Kingdom
Wyłkowyszki *see* Vilkaviškis
97 P19 Wymondham E England, United Kingdom 52°29′N 01°10′E
29 R17 Wymore Nebraska, C USA 40°07′N 96°39′W
182 E5 Wynbring South Australia 30°34′S 133°27′E
181 N3 Wyndham Western Australia 15°28′S 128°08′E
29 R6 Wyndmere North Dakota, N USA 46°16′N 97°07′W
27 X11 Wynne Arkansas, C USA 35°14′N 90°48′W
27 N12 Wynnewood Oklahoma, C USA 34°39′N 97°09′W
183 O15 Wynyard Tasmania, SE Australia 40°57′S 145°33′E
11 U15 Wynyard Saskatchewan, S Canada 51°46′N 104°10′W
159 V11 Wyola Montana, NW USA 45°07′N 107°23′W
182 A4 Wyola Lake *salt lake* South Australia
31 P9 Wyoming Michigan, N USA 42°54′N 85°42′W
33 V14 Wyoming ◆ *State of Wyoming, also known as* Equality State. ◆ C USA
33 S15 Wyoming Range ▲ Wyoming, C USA
183 T8 Wyong New South Wales, SE Australia 33°18′S 151°27′E
110 O9 Wyrzysk Ger. Wirsitz. Wielkopolskie, C Poland 53°09′N 17°15′E
110 O10 Wysokie Mazowieckie Łomża, E Poland
110 M11 Wyszków Ger. Probstberg. Mazowieckie, NE Poland 52°36′N 21°28′E
110 L11 Wyszogród Mazowieckie, C Poland 52°24′N 20°14′E
21 R7 Wytheville Virginia, NE USA 36°57′N 81°07′W
111 L15 Wyżyna Małopolska *plateau*

Column 2 (X)

X

80 Q12 Xaafuun *It.* Hafun. Bari, NE Somalia 10°25′N 51°17′E
80 Q12 Xaafuun, Raas *var.* Ras Hafun. *cape* NE Somalia
Xàbia *see* Jávea
42 C4 Xaclbal, Río *var.* Xalbal. Guatemala/Mexico
137 Y10 Xaçmaz Rus. Khachmas. N Azerbaijan 41°26′N 48°47′E
80 O12 Xadeed *var.* Haded. *physical region* N Somalia
159 O14 Xagquka Xizang Zizhiqu, W China 31°47′N 92°46′E
167 Q6 Xai *var.* Muang Xay, Muong Sai. Oudômxai, N Laos 20°41′N 102°00′E
158 F10 Xaidulla Xinjiang Uygur Zizhiqu, W China 36°27′N 77°46′E
167 Q7 Xaignabouli *prev.* Muang Xaignabouri, *Fr.* Sayaboury. N Laos 19°13′N 101°43′E
167 R7 Xai Lai Leng, Phou ▲ Laos/Vietnam 19°13′N 104°09′E
158 L15 Xainza Xizang Zizhiqu, W China 30°54′N 88°36′E
158 L16 Xaitongmoin Xizang Zizhiqu, W China 29°27′N 88°13′E
83 F17 Xaixai *var.* Caecae. North-West, NW Botswana 19°52′S 21°04′E
83 M20 Xai-Xai *prev.* João Belo, Vila de João Belo. Gaza, S Mozambique 25°01′S 33°37′E
Xalbal *see* Xaclbal, Río
80 P13 Xalin Sool, N Somalia
146 H7 Xalqobod Rus. Khalkabad. Qoraqalpog'iston Respublikasi, W Uzbekistan
167 R6 Xam Nua *var.* Sam Neua. Houaphan, N Laos 20°24′N 104°03′E
83 D11 Xá-Muteba Port. Cinco de Outubro. Lunda Norte, NE Angola 09°07′N 17°50′E
83 C16 Xangongo Port. Rocadas. Cunene, SW Angola 16°43′S 15°01′E
137 W12 Xankändi Rus. Khankendi; *prev.* Stepanakert. SW Azerbaijan 39°50′N 46°44′E
137 V11 Xanlar Rus. Khanlar. NW Azerbaijan 40°39′N 46°18′E
114 J13 Xánthi Anatolikí Makedonía kai Thráki, NE Greece 41°09′N 24°54′E
60 H13 Xanxerê Santa Catarina, S Brazil 26°52′S 52°25′W
81 O15 Xarardheere Mudug, E Somalia 04°45′N 47°54′E
137 Z11 Xärä Zirä Adasi Rus. Ostrov Bulla. *island* E Azerbaijan
162 K13 Xar Burd *prev.* Bayan Nuru. Nei Mongol Zizhiqu, N China 40°09′N 104°48′E
163 T11 Xar Moron ♒ NE China
163 T11 Xar Moron ♒ N China
Xarsingma *see* Chomo/Yadong
113 L23 Xarrë *var.* Xarra. Vlorë, S Albania 39°45′N 20°01′E
82 D12 Xassengue Lunda Sul, NW Angola 10°28′S 18°32′E
105 S11 Xàtiva Cas. Xátiva; *anc.* Setabis, *var.* Jativa. País Valenciano, E Spain 39°N 00°32′W
60 K10 Xauen *see* Chefchaouen
Xavantes, Represa de *var.* Represa de Chavantes. ⊟ S Brazil
158 I7 Xayar Xinjiang Uygur Zizhiqu, W China 41°16′N 82°52′E
Xäzär Dänizi *see* Caspian Sea
159 U11 Xiahe *var.* Labrang. Gansu, C China 35°12′N 102°28′E
161 O3 Xiamen *var.* Hsia-men; *prev.* Amoy. Fujian, SE China 24°28′N 118°05′E
160 L6 Xi'an *var.* Changan, Sian, Signan, Siking, Singan, Xian. *province capital* Shaanxi, C China 34°16′N 108°54′E
160 L10 Xianfeng *var.* Gaoleshan. Hubei, C China 29°45′N 109°10′E
Xiang *see* Hunan
161 N7 Xiangcheng Henan, C China 33°51′N 113°27′E
162 D8 Xiangcheng Yunnan, SW China 28°52′N 99°45′E
160 M8 Xiangfan *var.* Xiangyang. Hubei, C China 32°07′N 112°00′E
Xianggang *see* Hong Kong
161 N10 Xiang Jiang ♒ S China
167 Q7 Xiangkhoang, Plateau de *var.* Plain of Jars. *plateau* N Laos
161 N11 Xiangxiang Hunan, S China 27°50′N 112°31′E
158 S10 Xianju Zhejiang, SE China 28°51′N 120°41′E
161 O9 Xianning Hubei, C China 29°58′N 114°17′E
161 F8 Xianshui He ♒ C China
161 N9 Xiantao *var.* Mianyang. Hubei, C China 30°20′N 113°31′E
160 L6 Xianyang Shaanxi, C China 34°17′N 108°44′E
158 L5 Xiaocaohu Xinjiang Uygur Zizhiqu, W China 45°44′N 90°07′E

Column 3

161 O9 Xiaogan Hubei, C China 30°55′N 113°54′E
Xiaogang *see* Dongxiang
163 W6 Xiao Hinggan Ling Eng. Lesser Khingan Range. ▲ NE China
160 M6 Xiao Shan ▲ C China
160 M12 Xiao Shui ♒ S China
161 P6 Xiaoxi *var.* Pinghe
160 Q3 Xiao Xian *see* Xiaoxian
34°11′N 116°56′E
160 G11 Xichang Sichuan, C China 27°53′N 102°18′E
41 P11 Xicoténcatl Tamaulipas, C Mexico 22°59′N 98°54′W
Xieng Khouang *see* Pèk
Xieng Ngeun *see* Muong Xiang Ngeun
160 J11 Xifeng *var.* Yongjing. Guizhou, S China 27°11′N 106°09′E
Xifeng *see* Qingyang
162 M13 Xigazê *var.* Jih-k'a-tse, Shigatse, Xigaze. Xizang Zizhiqu, W China 29°18′N 88°50′E
159 W11 Xihe *var.* Hanyuan. Gansu, C China 34°00′N 105°24′E
160 I8 Xi He ♒ C China
159 W10 Xiji Ningxia, N China 36°02′N 105°33′E
160 M14 Xi Jiang *var.* Hsi Chiang, Eng. West River. ♒ S China
159 Q7 Xijian Quan *spring* NW China
160 K15 Xijin Shuiku ⊟ S China
158 L16 Xilaganí *see* Xylaganí
Xiligou *see* Ulan
163 Q10 Xilin *var.* Bada. Guangxi Zhuangzu Zizhiqu, S China 24°30′N 105°00′E
Xilinhot *var.* Silinhot. Nei Mongol Zizhiqu, N China 43°58′N 116°07′E
Xilinji *see* Mohe
Xilokástro *see* Xylókastro
160 G11 Xin'an *see* Anlong
161 R10 Xin'anjiang Shuiku *var.* Qiandao Hu. ⊟ SE China
146 H8 Xin'anzhen *see* Xinyi
Xin Barag Youqi *see* Altan Emel
Xin Barag Zuoqi *see* Amgalang
163 W12 Xinbin *var.* Xinbin Manzu Zizhixian. Liaoning, NE China 41°44′N 125°02′E
Xinbin Manzu Zizhixian *see* Xinbin
161 O7 Xincai Henan, C China 32°47′N 114°58′E
Xincheng *see* Zhaojue
Xindu *see* Luhuo
161 O13 Xinfeng *var.* Jiading. Jiangxi, S China 25°23′N 114°48′E
161 O14 Xinfengjiang Shuiku ⊟ S China
Xing'an *see* Ankang
Xingba *see* Lhünzê
163 T13 Xingcheng Liaoning, NE China 40°38′N 120°47′E
Xingcheng *see* Xinbin
167 T9 Xuân Đức Quang Binh, C Vietnam 17°19′N 106°38′E
160 L9 Xuan'an *var.* Zhushan. Hubei, C China 30°03′N 109°26′E
160 K8 Xuanhan Sichuan, C China 31°25′N 107°41′E
160 O3 Xuanhua Hebei, E China 40°36′N 115°01′E
161 P4 Xuanwei *var.* Xuanwen. Yunnan, China
H12 Xuanwei Yunnan, China 26°08′N 104°04′E
Xuanzhou *see* Xuancheng
161 N7 Xuchang Henan, C China 34°03′N 113°48′E
Xuchengzhen *see* Xuwen
137 X10 Xudat Rus. Khudat. NE Azerbaijan 41°37′N 48°39′E
81 M16 Xuddur *var.* Hudur, It. Oddur. Bakool, SW Somalia 04°07′N 43°50′E
80 O13 Xudun Sool, N Somalia
160 L11 Xuefeng Shan ▲ S China
147 O13 Xufar Surkhondaryo Viloyati, S Uzbekistan 38°31′N 67°45′E
Xulun Hobot Qagan *see* Qagan Nur
42 F2 Xunantunich *ruins* Cayo, W Belize
163 W6 Xun He ♒ NE China
160 L7 Xun He ♒ C China
160 L14 Xun Jiang ♒ S China
163 W5 Xunke *var.* Bianjing; *prev.* Qike. Heilongjiang, NE China 49°36′N 128°25′E
159 T10 Xining *var.* Hsining, Hsi-ning, Sining. *province capital* Qinghai, C China 36°37′N 101°46′E
161 O4 Xinji *prev.* Shulu. Hebei, C China 37°55′N 115°14′E
161 P10 Xinjian Jiangxi, S China 28°37′N 115°46′E
Xinjiang *see* Xinjiang Uygur Zizhiqu
160 I11 Xuyong *var.* Yongning. Sichuan, C China 28°17′N 105°21′E
161 P6 Xuzhou *var.* Hsu-chou, Suchow, Tongshan; *prev.* T'ung-shan. Jiangsu, E China 34°17′N 117°09′E
K13 Xylaganí *var.* Xilaganí. Anatolikí Makedonía kai Thráki, NE Greece 40°58′N 25°27′E
115 F19 Xylókastro *var.* Xilokastro. Pelopónnisos, S Greece 38°04′N 22°36′E

Column 4

158 I5 Xinyuan *var.* Künes. Xinjiang Uygur Zizhiqu, NW China 43°25′N 83°12′E
162 M13 Xinzhao Shan ▲ N China 39°31′N 105°31′E
161 N3 Xinzhou *var.* Xin. Shanxi, C China 38°24′N 112°43′E
104 H4 Xinzo de Limia Galicia, NW Spain 42°05′N 07°45′W
Xions *see* Książ Wielkopolski
161 O7 Xiping Henan, C China 33°22′N 114°00′E
Xiping *see* Songyang
159 T11 Xiqing Shan ▲ C China
59 N16 Xique-Xique Bahia, E Brazil 10°47′S 42°44′W
Xireg *see* Ulan
115 E14 Xirovoúni ▲ N Greece 39°17′N 20°43′E
162 M13 Xishanzui *prev.* Urad Qianqi. Nei Mongol Zizhiqu, N China 40°43′N 108°41′E
Xishuangbanna *see* Jinghong
160 J11 Xishui *var.* Donghuang. Guizhou, S China 28°24′N 106°09′E
161 O3 Xi Ujimqin Qi *see* Bayan Ul
160 K11 Xiushan *var.* Zhonghe. Chongqing Shi, C China 28°23′N 108°52′E
161 O10 Xiu Shui ♒ S China
161 N7 Xiuyan *var.* Qingjian
146 H9 Xiuzhou *see* Qingjian
146 H9 Xixabangma Feng ▲ W China 28°25′N 85°47′E
160 M7 Xixia Henan, C China 33°30′N 111°25′E
Xixón *see* Gijón
Xixona *see* Jijona
Xizang *see* Xizang Zizhiqu
Xizang Gaoyuan *see* Qingzang Gaoyuan
160 E9 Xizang Zizhiqu *var.* Thibet, Tibetan Autonomous Region, Xizang, Eng. Tibet. ◆ *autonomous region* W China
163 U14 Xizhong Dao *island* N China
Xoi *see* Qüxü
146 H8 Xo'jayli Rus. Khodzheyli. Qoraqalpog'iston Respublikasi, W Uzbekistan 42°23′N 59°27′E
119 O14 Xorazm Viloyati Rus. Khorezmskaya Oblast'. ◆ *province* W Uzbekistan
159 N9 Xorkol Xinjiang Uygur Zizhiqu, NW China 38°45′N 91°07′E
163 S6 Xqeshi Nei Mongol Zizhiqu, N China 49°16′N 120°42′E
34 I9 Yakima Washington, NW USA 46°36′N 120°30′W
32 J10 Yakima River ♒ Washington, NW USA
41 X14 Xpujil Quintana Roo, E Mexico 18°30′N 89°24′W
161 Q8 Xuancheng *var.* Xuanzhou. Anhui, E China 30°57′N 118°53′E
147 N12 Xakkabog' Rus. Yakkabag. Qashqadaryo Viloyati, S Uzbekistan 38°57′N 66°35′E
148 L12 Xakmach Baluchistān, SW Pakistan 28°48′N 63°48′E
77 W10 Yako W Burkina 12°54′N 02°24′W
39 W13 Yakobi Island *island* Alexander Archipelago, Alaska, USA
79 K16 Yakoruda Blagoevgrad, SW Bulgaria 42°01′N 23°40′E
114 H11 Yakovlevichi *see* Yakovlevichi
159 N7 Yakshur-Bod'ya Udmurtskaya Respublika, NW Russian Federation 57°10′N 53°10′E
165 Q5 Yaku Hokkaidō, NE Japan 42°13′N 140°15′E
164 B17 Yaku-shima *island* Nansei-shotō, SW Japan
39 U12 Yakutat Alaska, USA 59°33′N 139°44′W
39 U12 Yakutat Bay *inlet* Alaska, USA
Yakutia/Yakutiya *see* Sakha (Yakutia), Respublika
122 Q10 Yakutsk Respublika Sakha (Yakutiya), NE Russian Federation 62°10′N 129°50′E
167 O17 Yala Yala, SW Thailand 06°32′N 101°19′E
182 I9 Yalata South Australia 31°30′S 131°53′E
31 T4 Yale Michigan, N USA 43°07′N 82°45′W
180 I11 Yalgoo Western Australia 28°23′S 116°43′E
114 O12 Yalıköy İstanbul, NW Turkey 41°19′N 29°51′E
79 L14 Yalinga Haute-Kotto, C Central African Republic 06°47′N 23°09′E
119 O11 Yalizava Rus. Yelizovo. Mahilyowskaya Voblasts', E Belarus 53°24′N 29°01′E
44 L13 Yallahs Hill ▲ E Jamaica 17°53′N 76°31′W
22 L3 Yalobusha River ♒ Mississippi, S USA
79 H15 Yaloké Ombella-Mpoko, W Central African Republic 05°15′N 17°12′E
160 D7 Yalong Jiang ♒ C China
114 M11 Yalova Yalova, NW Turkey 40°40′N 29°17′E
114 M11 Yalova ◆ *province* NW Turkey
158 M15 Yangbajain Xizang Zizhiqu, W China 30°05′N 90°35′E
117 N12 Yalpuh, Ozero Rus. Ozero Yalpug. ◉ SW Ukraine
117 N12 Yalpuh, Ozero *see* Yalpuh, Ozero
114 M11 Yalta Respublika Krym, S Ukraine 44°30′N 34°09′E
163 W13 Yalu Chin. Yalu Jiang, Jap. Oryokko, Kor. Amnok-kang. ♒ China/North Korea
158 H5 Yalu Jiang *see* Yalu
146 G13 Yalvaç Isparta, SW Turkey 38°16′N 31°09′E
43 N7 Yablis Región Autónoma Atlántico Norte, NE Nicaragua 14°08′N 83°44′W
165 Q6 Yamada Iwate, Honshū, C Japan 39°27′N 141°56′E
123 Q8 Yablonovyy Khrebet ▲ S Russian Federation
162 J14 Yabrai Shan ▲ NE China
U6 Yabucoa E Puerto Rico 18°02′N 65°53′W
165 Q9 Yamagata Yamagata, Honshū, C Japan 38°15′N 140°19′E

Column 5

160 J11 Yachi He ♒ S China
32 H10 Yacolt Washington, NW USA 45°49′N 122°22′W
54 M10 Yacuanquer Nariño, S Venezuela 04°12′N 06°40′W
57 M22 Yacuiba Tarija, S Bolivia 22°00′S 63°43′W
57 K16 Yacuma, Río ♒ C Bolivia
21 R8 Yadkin River ♒ North Carolina, SE USA
21 R9 Yadkinville North Carolina, SE USA 36°07′N 80°40′W
158 L17 Yadong *var.* Xarsingma. Xizang Zizhiqu, W China 27°31′N 88°58′E *see also* Chomo
127 P3 Yadrin Chuvashskaya Respublika, W Russian Federation 55°55′N 46°10′E
115 E14 Yaegama-shotō *see* Yaeyama-shotō
162 M13 Yaeme-saki *see* Paimi-saki
165 O16 Yafran NW Libya 32°04′N 12°31′E
165 S2 Yagashiri-tō *island* NE Japan
65 H21 Yaghan Basin *undersea feature* SE Pacific Ocean
123 S9 Yagodnoye Magadanskaya Oblast', E Russian Federation 62°37′N 149°18′E
78 G12 Yagoua Extrême-Nord, NE Cameroon 10°23′N 15°13′E
159 Q11 Yagradagzê Shan ▲ C China 35°06′N 95°41′E
Yaguachi *see* Yaguachi Nuevo
56 B7 Yaguachi Nuevo *var.* Yaguachi. Guayas, W Ecuador 02°06′S 79°43′W
Yaguarón, Río *see* Jaguarão, Rio
117 Q11 Yahorlyts'kyy Lyman *bay* S Ukraine
117 Q5 Yahotyn Rus. Yagotin. Kyyivs'ka Oblast', N Ukraine 50°15′N 31°48′E
40 L12 Yahualica Jalisco, SW Mexico 21°11′N 102°29′W
79 L17 Yahuma Orientale, N Dem. Rep. Congo 01°12′N 23°10′E
136 K15 Yahyalı Kayseri, C Turkey 38°08′N 35°23′E
167 N15 Yai, Khao ▲ SW Thailand
164 M14 Yaizu Shizuoka, Honshū, C Japan 34°52′N 138°20′E
160 G9 Yajiang *var.* Hekou, Tib. Nyagquka. Sichuan, C China 30°05′N 100°57′E
119 O14 Yakawlyevichi Rus. Yakovlevichi. Vitsyebskaya Voblasts', NE Belarus 54°20′N 30°31′E
Yaks *see* Yakovlevichi
165 P9 Yamagata *off.* Yamagata-ken. ◆ *prefecture* Honshū, C Japan
147 Q9 Yangiobod Rus. Yangiabad. Toshkent Viloyati, E Uzbekistan 41°10′N 70°01′E
147 Q9 Yangiqishloq Rus. Yangishlyak. Jizzax Viloyati, C Uzbekistan 40°27′N 67°06′E
147 P11 Yangiyer Sirdaryo Viloyati, E Uzbekistan 40°19′N 68°48′E
147 P9 Yangiyo'l Rus. Yangiyul'. Toshkent Viloyati, E Uzbekistan 41°12′N 69°05′E
Yangiyul *see* Yangiyo'l
160 M15 Yangjiang Guangdong, S China 21°50′N 112°02′E
Yangku *see* Taiyuan
Yang-Nishan *see* Yangi-Nishon
166 L13 Yangon Eng. Rangoon. Yangon, S Burma (Myanmar) 16°50′N 96°11′E
166 M8 Yangon ◆ *division* SW Burma (Myanmar)
161 N4 Yangquan Shanxi, C China
161 N13 Yangshan *var.* Yangcheng. Guangdong, S China 24°32′N 112°36′E
167 U12 Yang Sin, Chư ▲ S Vietnam 12°23′N 108°25′E
Yangtze *see* Chang Jiang/Jinsha Jiang
Yangtze Kiang *see* Chang Jiang
161 R7 Yangzhou *var.* Yangchow. Jiangsu, E China 32°22′N 119°22′E
160 L5 Yan He ♒ C China
163 Y10 Yanji Jilin, NE China 42°54′N 129°31′E
Yanji *see* Longjing
183 V5 Yanjing *see* Yanyuan
29 Q12 Yankton South Dakota, N USA 42°52′N 97°24′W
161 O12 Yanling *prev.* Lingxian, Ling Xian. Hunan, S China 26°32′N 113°48′E
Yannina *see* Ioánnina
123 Q7 Yano-Indigirskaya Nizmennost' *plain* N Russian Federation
155 K24 Yan Oya ♒ N Sri Lanka
158 K6 Yanqi *var.* Yanqi Huizu Zizhixian. Xinjiang Uygur Zizhiqu, NW China 42°04′N 86°32′E
Yanqi Huizu Zizhixian *see* Yanqi
161 Q10 Yanshan *var.* Hekou. Jiangxi, S China 28°18′N 117°43′E
160 H14 Yanshan *var.* Jiangna. Yunnan, China 23°36′N 104°20′E
161 P2 Yan Shan ▲ E China
163 X8 Yanshou Heilongjiang, NE China 45°27′N 128°18′E
123 Q7 Yanskiy Zaliv *bay* N Russian Federation
183 V4 Yantabulla New South Wales, SE Australia 29°22′S 145°00′E
161 R4 Yantai *var.* Yan-t'ai; *prev.* Chefoo, Chih-fu. Shandong, E China 37°30′N 121°22′E
118 A13 Yantarnyy Ger. Palmnicken. Kaliningradskaya Oblast', W Russian Federation 54°53′N 19°59′E
114 J9 Yantra Gabrovo, N Bulgaria 42°58′N 25°19′E
114 K9 Yantra ♒ N Bulgaria
160 G11 Yanyuan *var.* Yanjing. Sichuan, C China 27°30′N 101°22′E
161 P5 Yanzhou Shandong, C China 35°37′N 116°53′E
79 E16 Yaoundé *var.* Yaunde. ● (Cameroon) Centre, C Cameroon 03°51′N 11°31′E
188 I14 Yap ◆ *state* W Micronesia
188 F16 Yap *island* Caroline Islands, W Micronesia
57 M18 Yapacani, Río ♒ C Bolivia
171 W14 Yapa Kopra Papua, E Indonesia
Yapan *see* Yapen, Selat
Yapanskoye More *see* East Sea/Japan, Sea of
79 I9 Yapei N Ghana 09°10′N 01°08′W
8 M10 Yapeitso, Mont ▲ Québec, C Canada 52°18′N 70°24′W
171 W12 Yapen, Pulau *prev.* Japen. *island* E Indonesia
171 W12 Yapen, Selat *var.* Yapan. *strait* Papua, E Indonesia
61 E15 Yapeyú Corrientes, NE Argentina 29°28′S 56°50′W
136 I11 Yapraklı Çankırı, N Turkey 40°45′N 33°46′E
174 M3 Yap Trench *var.* Yap Trough. *undersea feature* SE Philippine Sea 08°30′N 138°00′E
Yap Trough *see* Yap Trench
183 O10 Yapurá *var.* Caquetá, Río, Brazil/Colombia
183 O6 Yanda Creek *seasonal river* New South Wales, SE Australia
Yapurá *see* Japurá, Rio
197 I12 Yaqaga *island* N Fiji
197 H12 Yaqeta *prev.* Yanggeta. *island* Yasawa Group, NW Fiji
40 G6 Yaqui Sonora, NW Mexico 27°21′N 109°59′W
32 E12 Yaquina Bay *bay* Oregon, NW USA
40 G6 Yaqui, Río ♒ NW Mexico
54 K5 Yaracuy *off.* Estado Yaracuy. ◆ *state* NW Venezuela
Yaracuy, Estado *see* Yaracuy
146 E13 Yaraji Rus. Yaradzhi. Ahal Welayaty, C Turkmenistan 38°12′N 57°46′E
Yaradzhi *see* Yaraji
123 Q15 Yaransk Kirovskaya Oblast', NW Russian Federation 57°18′N 47°52′E
136 N2 Yardımcı Burnu *headland* SW Turkey 36°10′N 30°25′E
97 Q19 Yare ♒ E England, United Kingdom
125 S9 Yarega Respublika Komi, NW Russian Federation 63°27′N 53°28′E
116 I7 Yaremcha Ivano-Frankivs'ka Oblast', W Ukraine 48°27′N 24°34′E
189 Q6 Yaren SW Nauru 0°33′S 166°54′E
125 Q10 Yarensk Arkhangel'skaya Oblast', NW Russian Federation 62°09′N 49°03′E

155 F16 **Yargatti** Karnātaka, W India 16°07′N 75°11′E
164 M12 **Yariga-take** ▲ Honshū, S Japan 36°20′N 137°38′E
141 O15 **Yarīm** W Yemen 14°15′N 44°23′E
54 F14 **Yarí, Río** ≈ SW Colombia
54 K5 **Yaritagua** Yaracuy, N Venezuela 10°05′N 69°07′W
Yarkand *see* Yarkant He
Yarkant *see* Shache
158 E9 **Yarkant He** *var.* Yarkand. ≈ NW China
149 U3 **Yarkhūn** ≈ NW Pakistan
Yarlung Zangbo Jiang *see* Brahmaputra
116 L6 **Yarmolyntsi** Khmel'nyts'ka Oblast', W Ukraine 49°13′N 26°53′E
13 O16 **Yarmouth** Nova Scotia, SE Canada 43°53′N 66°09′W
Yarmouth *see* Great Yarmouth
Yaroslav *see* Jarosław
124 L15 **Yaroslavl'** Yaroslavskaya Oblast', W Russian Federation 57°38′N 39°53′E
124 K14 **Yaroslavskaya Oblast'** ◐ *province* W Russian Federation
123 N11 **Yaroslavskiy** Respublika Sakha (Yakutiya), NE Russian Federation 60°10′N 114°12′E
183 P13 **Yarram** Victoria, SE Australia 38°36′S 146°40′E
183 O11 **Yarrawonga** Victoria, SE Australia 36°04′S 145°58′E
182 L4 **Yarriarraburra Swamp** *wetland* New South Wales, SE Australia
122 I8 **Yar-Sale** Yamalo-Nenetskiy Avtonomnyy Okrug, N Russian Federation 66°52′N 70°42′E
122 K11 **Yartsevo** Krasnoyarskiy Kray, C Russian Federation 60°15′N 90°09′E
126 I4 **Yartsevo** Smolenskaya Oblast', W Russian Federation 55°03′N 32°46′E
54 E8 **Yarumal** Antioquia, NW Colombia 06°59′N 75°25′W
187 W14 **Yasawa Group** *island group* NW Fiji
77 V12 **Yashi** Katsina, N Nigeria 12°21′N 07°56′E
77 S14 **Yashikera** Kwara, W Nigeria 09°40′N 03°19′E
147 T14 **Yashilkŭl** *Rus.* Ozero Yashil'kul'. ◎ SE Tajikistan
Yashil'kul', Ozero *see* Yashilkŭl
165 P9 **Yashima** Akita, Honshū, C Japan 39°10′N 140°10′E
127 P13 **Yashkul'** Respublika Kalmykiya, SW Russian Federation 46°09′N 45°22′E
146 F13 **Yashlyk** Ahal Welaýaty, C Turkmenistan 37°46′N 58°51′E
Yasinovataya *see* Yasynuvata
114 N10 **Yasna Polyana** Burgas, E Bulgaria 42°18′N 27°35′E
167 R10 **Yasothon** Yasothon, E Thailand 15°46′N 104°12′E
183 R10 **Yass** New South Wales, SE Australia 34°52′S 148°55′E
Yassy *see* Iaşi
164 H12 **Yasugi** Shimane, Honshū, SW Japan 35°25′N 133°12′E
143 N10 **Yāsūj** *var.* Yesuj; *prev.* Tal-e Khosravī. Kohkīlūyeh va Būyer AHmad, C Iran 30°40′N 51°34′E
136 M11 **Yasun Burnu** *headland* N Turkey 41°07′N 37°40′E
117 X8 **Yasynuvata** *Rus.* Yasinovataya. Donets'ka Oblast', SE Ukraine 48°05′N 37°57′E
136 C15 **Yatağan** Muğla, SW Turkey 37°22′N 28°08′E
165 Q7 **Yatate-tōge** *pass* Honshū, C Japan
187 Q17 **Yaté** Province Sud, S New Caledonia 22°10′S 166°56′E
27 P6 **Yates Center** Kansas, C USA 37°54′N 95°44′W
185 B21 **Yates Point** *headland* South Island, New Zealand 44°30′S 167°49′E
9 N9 **Yathkyed Lake** ◎ Nunavut, NE Canada
171 T16 **Yatoke** Pulau Babar, E Indonesia 07°51′S 129°49′E
79 M18 **Yatolema** Orientale, N Dem. Rep. Congo 0°25′N 24°35′E
164 C15 **Yatsushiro** *var.* Yatusiro. Kumamoto, Kyūshū, SW Japan 32°30′N 130°34′E
164 C15 **Yatsushiro-kai** *bay* SW Japan
138 F11 **Yatta** *var.* Yuta. S West Bank 31°29′N 35°10′E
81 J20 **Yatta Plateau** *plateau* SE Kenya
Yatusiro *see* Yatsushiro
57 F17 **Yauca, Río** ≈ SW Peru
45 S6 **Yauco** W Puerto Rico 18°02′N 66°51′W
Yaunde *see* Yaoundé
Yavan *see* Yovon
Yavarí *see* Javari, Rio
56 G9 **Yavari Mirim, Río** ≈ NE Peru
40 G7 **Yavaros** Sonora, NW Mexico 26°40′N 109°32′W
154 I13 **Yavatmāl** Mahārāshtra, C India 20°22′N 78°11′E
54 M9 **Yaví, Cerro** ▲ C Venezuela 05°43′N 65°51′W
43 W16 **Yaviza** Darién, SE Panama 08°09′N 77°41′W
138 F10 **Yavne** Central, W Israel 31°52′N 34°45′E
116 H5 **Yavoriv** *Pol.* Jaworów, *Rus.* Yavorov. L'vivs'ka Oblast', NW Ukraine 49°57′N 23°22′E
Yavorov *see* Yavoriv
164 F14 **Yawatahama** Ehime, Shikoku, SW Japan 33°27′N 132°24′E
Ya Xian *see* Sanya
136 L17 **Yayladaği** Hatay, S Turkey 35°55′N 36°00′E
125 V13 **Yayva** Permskaya Oblast', NW Russian Federation 59°19′N 57°15′E
125 V12 **Yayva** ≈ NW Russian Federation
143 Q9 **Yazd** *var.* Yezd. Yazd, C Iran 31°55′N 54°22′E
143 Q8 **Yazd** *off.* Ostān-e Yazd, *var.* Yezd. ◐ *province* C Iran
Yazd, Ostān-e *see* Yazd
Yazgulemskiy Khrebet *see* Yazgulom, Qatorkŭhi
147 S13 **Yazgulom, Qatorkŭhi** *Rus.* Yazgulemskiy Khrebet. ▲▲ S Tajikistan
22 K5 **Yazoo City** Mississippi, S USA 32°51′N 90°24′W
22 K5 **Yazoo River** ≈ Mississippi, S USA
127 Q5 **Yazykovka** Ul'yanovskaya Oblast', W Russian Federation 54°19′N 47°22′E
109 U4 **Ybbs** Niederösterreich, NE Austria 48°10′N 15°03′E
109 U4 **Ybbs** ≈ C Austria
95 G22 **Yding Skovhøj** *hill* C Denmark
115 G20 **Ýdra** *var.* Ídhra, Idra. Ýdra, S Greece 37°20′N 23°28′E
115 G21 **Ýdra** *var.* Ídhra. *island* Ýdra, S Greece
115 G20 **Ýdras, Kólpos** *strait* S Greece
167 N10 **Ye** Mon State, S Burma (Myanmar) 15°15′N 97°50′E
183 O12 **Yea** Victoria, SE Australia 37°15′S 145°27′E
Yebaishou *see* Jianping
78 I5 **Yebbi-Bou** Borkou-Ennedi-Tibesti, N Chad 21°12′N 17°55′E
158 F9 **Yecheng** *var.* Kargilik. Xinjiang Uygur Zizhiqu, NW China 37°54′N 77°26′E
105 R11 **Yecla** Murcia, SE Spain 38°36′N 01°07′W
40 H6 **Yécora** Sonora, NW Mexico 28°23′N 108°56′W
Yedintsy *see* Edineţ
124 J13 **Yefimovskiy** Leningradskaya Oblast', NW Russian Federation 59°32′N 34°34′E
126 K6 **Yefremov** Tul'skaya Oblast', W Russian Federation 53°10′N 38°02′E
159 T11 **Yêgainnyin** *var.* Henan Mongolzu Zizhixian. Qinghai, C China 34°42′N 101°36′E
137 U12 **Yegbhegis** *Rus.* Yekhegis. ≈ C Armenia
137 U12 **Yeghegnadzor** C Armenia 39°45′N 45°20′E
145 T10 **Yegindybulak** *Kaz.* Egindibulaq. Karaganda, C Kazakhstan 49°45′N 75°45′E
126 L4 **Yegor'yevsk** Moskovskaya Oblast', W Russian Federation 55°29′N 39°03′E
Yehuda, Haré *see* Judaean Hills
81 E15 **Yei** ≈ S Sudan
161 P8 **Yeji** *var.* Yejiaji. Anhui, E China 31°52′N 115°58′E
Yejiaji *see* Yeji
122 G10 **Yekaterinburg** *prev.* Sverdlovsk. Sverdlovskaya Oblast', C Russian Federation 56°52′N 60°35′E
Yekaterinodar *see* Krasnodar
Yekaterinoslav *see* Dnipropetrovs'k
123 R13 **Yekaterinoslavka** Amurskaya Oblast', SE Russian Federation 50°23′N 129°03′E
127 O7 **Yekaterinovka** Saratovskaya Oblast', W Russian Federation 52°01′N 44°11′E
76 K16 **Yekepa** NE Liberia 07°35′N 08°32′W
Yekhegis *see* Yegbhegis
127 T3 **Yelabuga** Respublika Tatarstan, W Russian Federation 55°46′N 52°07′E
Yela Island *see* Rossel Island
127 O8 **Yelan'** Volgogradskaya Oblast', SW Russian Federation 51°00′N 43°40′E
117 Q9 **Yelanets'** *Rus.* Yelanets. Mykolayivs'ka Oblast', S Ukraine 47°40′N 31°51′E
126 L7 **Yelets** Lipetskaya Oblast', W Russian Federation 52°37′N 38°29′E
125 W4 **Yeletskiy** Respublika Komi, NW Russian Federation 67°03′N 64°05′E
76 J11 **Yélimané** Kayes, W Mali 15°06′N 10°43′W
Yelisavetpol *see* Gäncä
Yelizavetgrad *see* Kirovohrad
123 T12 **Yelizavety, Mys** *headland* SE Russian Federation 54°20′N 142°39′E
Yelizovo *see* Yalizava
127 S5 **Yelkhovka** Samarskaya Oblast', W Russian Federation 53°51′N 50°16′E
96 M1 **Yell** *island* NE Scotland, United Kingdom
155 E17 **Yellāpur** Karnātaka, W India 15°06′N 74°50′E
11 U17 **Yellow Grass** Saskatchewan, S Canada 49°51′N 104°09′W
Yellowhammer State *see* Alabama
11 O15 **Yellowhead Pass** *pass* Alberta/British Columbia, SW Canada
8 K10 **Yellowknife** *territory capital* Northwest Territories, W Canada 62°30′N 114°29′W
8 K9 **Yellowknife** ≈ Northwest Territories, NW Canada
23 P8 **Yellow River** ≈ Alabama/Florida, S USA
30 J6 **Yellow River** ≈ Wisconsin, N USA
30 K7 **Yellow River** ≈ Wisconsin, N USA
30 I4 **Yellow River** ≈ Wisconsin, N USA
Yellow River *see* Huang He
157 V8 **Yellow Sea** *Chin.* Huang Hai, *Kor.* Hwang-Hae. *sea* E Asia
33 S13 **Yellowstone Lake** ◎ Wyoming, C USA
33 T13 **Yellowstone National Park** *national park* Wyoming, NW USA
33 Y8 **Yellowstone River** ≈ Montana/Wyoming, NW USA
96 L1 **Yell Sound** *strait* N Scotland, United Kingdom
27 U9 **Yellville** Arkansas, C USA 36°12′N 92°41′W
126 I4 **Yel'nya** Smolenskaya Oblast', W Russian Federation 54°34′N 33°11′E
122 K10 **Yelogui** ≈ C Russian Federation
Yëloten *see* Ýolöten
119 M20 **Yel'sk** Homyel'skaya Voblasts', SE Belarus 51°48′N 29°09′E
77 T13 **Yelwa** Kebbi, W Nigeria 10°52′N 04°46′E
21 R15 **Yemassee** South Carolina, SE USA 32°41′N 80°51′W
141 O15 **Yemen** *off.* Republic of Yemen, *Ar.* Al Jumhuriyah al Yamaniyah, Al Yaman. ◆ *republic* SW Asia
Yemen, Republic of *see* Yemen
116 M4 **Yemil'chyne** Zhytomyrs'ka Oblast', N Ukraine 50°51′N 27°49′E
124 M10 **Yemtsa** Arkhangel'skaya Oblast', NW Russian Federation 63°04′N 40°18′E
124 M10 **Yemtsa** ≈ NW Russian Federation
125 R10 **Yemva** *prev.* Zheleznodorozhnyy. Respublika Komi, NW Russian Federation 62°38′N 50°59′E
77 U17 **Yenagoa** Bayelsa, S Nigeria 4°58′N 6°16′E
117 X7 **Yenakiyeve** *Rus.* Yenakiyevo; *prev.* Ordzhonikidze, Rykovo. Donets'ka Oblast', E Ukraine 48°13′N 38°13′E
Yenakiyevo *see* Yenakiyeve
166 L6 **Yenangyaung** Magway, W Burma (Myanmar) 20°28′N 94°54′E
167 S5 **Yên Bai** Yên Bai, N Vietnam 21°43′N 104°54′E
183 P9 **Yenda** New South Wales, SE Australia 34°16′S 146°15′E
77 Q14 **Yendi** NE Ghana 09°30′N 00°01′W
Yêndum *see* Zhag'yab
158 E8 **Yengisar** Xinjiang Uygur Zizhiqu, NW China 38°50′N 76°11′E
136 H11 **Yenice Çayı** *var.* Filyos Çayı. ≈ N Turkey
121 R1 **Yenierenköy** *var.* Yialousa, *Gk.* Agialoúsa. NE Cyprus 35°33′N 34°13′E
Yenipazar *see* Novi Pazar
136 E12 **Yenişehir** Bursa, NW Turkey 40°17′N 29°38′E
Yenisei Bay *see* Yeniseyskiy Zaliv
122 K12 **Yeniseysk** Krasnoyarskiy Kray, C Russian Federation 58°23′N 92°06′E
197 W10 **Yeniseyskiy Zaliv** *var.* Yenisei Bay. *bay* N Russian Federation
127 Q12 **Yenotayevka** Astrakhanskaya Oblast', SW Russian Federation 47°16′N 47°01′E
124 L4 **Yenozero, Ozero** ◎ NW Russian Federation
Yenping *see* Nanping
39 Q11 **Yentna River** ≈ Alaska, USA
180 M10 **Yeo, Lake** *salt lake* Western Australia
183 R7 **Yeoval** New South Wales, SE Australia 32°45′S 148°39′E
97 K23 **Yeovil** SW England, United Kingdom 50°57′N 02°39′W
40 H6 **Yepachic** Chihuahua, N Mexico 28°27′N 108°25′W
181 Y8 **Yeppoon** Queensland, E Australia 23°05′S 150°42′E
126 M5 **Yeraktur** Ryazanskaya Oblast', W Russian Federation 54°45′N 41°09′E
Yeraliyev *see* Kuryk
146 F12 **Yerbent** Ahal Welaýaty, C Turkmenistan 39°19′N 58°34′E
123 N11 **Yerbogachën** Irkutskaya Oblast', C Russian Federation 61°07′N 108°03′E
137 T12 **Yerevan** *Eng.* Erivan. ● (Armenia) C Armenia 40°12′N 44°31′E
137 U12 **Yerevan** ✈ C Armenia 40°07′N 44°34′E
145 R9 **Yereymentau** *var.* Jermentau, *Kaz.* Ereymentaū. Akmola, C Kazakhstan 51°38′N 73°10′E
127 O12 **Yergeni** *hill range* SW Russian Federation
Yeriho *see* Jericho
35 R6 **Yerington** Nevada, W USA 38°58′N 119°10′W
136 J13 **Yerköy** Yozgat, C Turkey 39°39′N 34°28′E
114 L13 **Yerlisu** Edirne, NW Turkey 40°45′N 26°38′E
Yermak *see* Aksu
145 R9 **Yermentau, Gory** ▲▲ C Kazakhstan
125 R5 **Yërmitsa** Respublika Komi, NW Russian Federation 66°57′N 52°15′E
35 V14 **Yermo** California, W USA 34°54′N 116°49′W
123 P13 **Yerofey Pavlovich** Amurskaya Oblast', SE Russian Federation 53°58′N 121°49′E
99 F15 **Yerseke** Zeeland, SW Netherlands 51°30′N 04°03′E
127 Q8 **Yershov** Saratovskaya Oblast', W Russian Federation 51°18′N 48°16′E
125 P9 **Yërtom** Respublika Komi, NW Russian Federation 63°27′N 47°52′E
56 D13 **Yerupaja, Nevado** ▲ C Peru 10°23′S 76°58′W
Yerushalayim *see* Jerusalem
105 R4 **Yesa, Embalse de** ⊠ NE Spain
144 F9 **Yesensay** Zapadnyy Kazakhstan, NW Kazakhstan 49°59′N 51°19′E
144 F9 **Yesensay** Zapadnyy Kazakhstan, NW Kazakhstan 49°58′N 51°19′E
145 V15 **Yesik** *Kaz.* Esik; *prev.* Issyk. Almaty, SE Kazakhstan 42°23′N 77°25′E
145 O8 **Yesil'** *Kaz.* Esil. Akmola, C Kazakhstan 51°58′N 66°24′E
136 K15 **Yeşilhisar** Kayseri, C Turkey 38°22′N 35°08′E
136 L11 **Yeşilırmak** *var.* Iris. ≈ N Turkey
37 U12 **Yeso** New Mexico, SW USA 34°25′N 104°36′W
Yeso *see* Hokkaidō
127 N15 **Yessentuki** Stavropol'skiy Kray, SW Russian Federation 44°06′N 42°51′E
122 M9 **Yessey** Evenkiyskiy Avtonomnyy Okrug, N Russian Federation 68°18′N 101°49′E
105 P12 **Yeste** Castilla-La Mancha, C Spain 38°21′N 02°18′W
Yesuj *see* Yāsūj
183 T4 **Yetman** New South Wales, SE Australia 28°56′S 150°47′E
76 L4 **Yetti** *physical region* N Mauritania
166 M4 **Ye-u** Sagaing, C Burma (Myanmar) 22°49′N 95°26′E
102 H9 **Yeu, Île d'** *island* NW France
Yevlakh *see* Yevlax
137 W11 **Yevlax** *Rus.* Yevlakh. C Azerbaijan 40°36′N 47°10′E
117 S13 **Yevpatoriya** Respublika Krym, S Ukraine 45°12′N 33°23′E
Ye Xian *see* Laizhou
126 K12 **Yeya** ≈ SW Russian Federation
158 I10 **Yeyik** Xinjiang Uygur Zizhiqu, W China 36°44′N 83°14′E
126 K12 **Yeysk** Krasnodarskiy Kray, SW Russian Federation 46°41′N 38°15′E
Yezd *see* Yazd
Yezerishche *see* Yezyaryshcha
Yezhou *see* Jianshi
Yezo *see* Hokkaidō
118 N11 **Yezyaryshcha** *Rus.* Yezerishche. Vitsyebskaya Voblasts', NE Belarus 55°50′N 29°59′E
Yiali *see* Gyalí
Yialousa *see* Yenierenköy
163 V7 **Yi'an** Heilongjiang, NE China 47°52′N 125°13′E
Yiannitsá *see* Giannitsá
160 I10 **Yibin** Sichuan, C China 28°50′N 104°35′E
158 K13 **Yibug Caka** ◎ W China
160 M9 **Yichang** Hubei, C China 30°37′N 111°02′E
160 L5 **Yichuan** *var.* Danzhou. Shaanxi, C China 36°05′N 110°02′E
157 W3 **Yichun** Heilongjiang, NE China 47°41′N 129°10′E
161 O11 **Yichun** Jiangxi, S China 27°45′N 114°22′E
160 M9 **Yidu** *prev.* Zhicheng. Hubei, C China 30°21′N 111°27′E
Yidu *see* Qingzhou
188 C15 **Yigo** NE Guam 13°33′N 144°53′E
161 Q5 **Yi He** ≈ E China
163 X8 **Yilan** Heilongjiang, NE China 46°18′N 129°36′E
136 C9 **Yıldız Dağları** ▲▲ NW Turkey
136 L13 **Yıldızeli** Sivas, N Turkey 39°52′N 36°37′E
163 U4 **Yilehuli Shan** ▲▲ NE China
163 S7 **Yimin He** ≈ NE China
159 W8 **Yinchuan** *var.* Yinch'uan, Yin-ch'uan, Yinchwan. *province capital* Ningxia, N China 38°30′N 106°19′E
Yinchwan *see* Yinchuan
Yindu He *see* Indus
Yingcheng *see* Yingde
161 N14 **Yingde** *var.* Yingcheng. Guangdong, S China 24°08′N 113°21′E
161 O7 **Ying He** ≈ C China
163 U13 **Yingkou** *var.* Ying-k'ou, Yingkow; *prev.* Newchwang, Niuchwang. Liaoning, NE China 40°40′N 122°17′E
Yingkow *see* Yingkou
161 P9 **Yingshan** *var.* Wenquan. Hubei, C China 30°45′N 115°41′E
Yingshan *see* Guangshui
161 Q10 **Yingtan** Jiangxi, S China 28°17′N 117°03′E
Yin-hsien *see* Ningbo
158 H5 **Yining** *var.* I-ning, *Uigh.* Gulja, Kuldja. Xinjiang Uygur Zizhiqu, NW China 43°53′N 81°18′E
160 K11 **Yinjiang** *var.* Yinjiang Tujiazu Miaozu Zizhixian. Guizhou, S China 28°22′N 108°07′E
Yinjiang Tujiazu Miaozu Zizhixian *see* Yinjiang
166 L4 **Yinmabin** Sagaing, C Burma (Myanmar) 22°05′N 94°57′E
163 N13 **Yin Shan** ▲▲ N China
Yin-tu Ho *see* Indus
159 P15 **Yi'ong Zangbo** ≈ W China
Yioúra *see* Gyáros
81 J14 **Yirga 'Alem** *It.* Irgalem. Southern Nationalities, S Ethiopia 06°43′N 38°24′E
61 E19 **Yí, Río** ≈ C Uruguay
81 E14 **Yirol** El Buhayrat, S Sudan 06°34′N 30°33′E
163 S8 **Yirshi** *var.* Yirxie. Nei Mongol Zizhiqu, N China 47°16′N 119°51′E
Yirxie *see* Yirshi
Yishan *see* Guanyun
Yishi *see* Linyi
161 Q5 **Yishui** Shandong, E China 35°50′N 118°39′E
Yisrael/Yisra'el *see* Israel
Yíthion *see* Gýtheio
Yitiaoshan *see* Jingtai
163 W10 **Yitong** *var.* Yitong Manzu Zizhixian. Jilin, NE China 43°23′N 125°19′E
Yitong Manzu Zizhixian *see* Yitong
159 P5 **Yiwu** *var.* Aratürük. Xinjiang Uygur Zizhiqu, NW China 43°16′N 94°38′E
163 U12 **Yiwulü Shan** ▲▲ N China
163 T12 **Yixian** *var.* Yizhou. Liaoning, NE China 41°29′N 121°21′E
161 N10 **Yiyang** Hunan, S China 28°39′N 112°10′E
161 Q10 **Yiyang** Jiangxi, S China 28°21′N 117°23′E
161 N13 **Yizhang** Hunan, S China 25°24′N 112°51′E
Yizhou *see* Yixian
93 K19 **Ylāne** Länsi-Suomi, SW Finland 60°51′N 22°26′E
93 L14 **Yli-Ii** Oulu, C Finland 65°21′N 25°55′E
93 L14 **Ylikiiminki** Oulu, C Finland 65°00′N 26°10′E
92 N13 **Yli-Kitka** ◎ NE Finland
93 K17 **Ylistaro** Länsi-Suomi, W Finland 62°58′N 22°30′E
92 K13 **Ylitornio** Lappi, NW Finland 66°19′N 23°40′E
93 L15 **Ylivieska** Oulu, W Finland 64°05′N 24°30′E
93 L18 **Ylöjärvi** Länsi-Suomi, W Finland 61°31′N 23°37′E
95 N17 **Yngaren** ◎ C Sweden
25 T12 **Yoakum** Texas, SW USA 29°17′N 97°09′W
77 X13 **Yobe** ◐ *state* NE Nigeria
165 R3 **Yobetsu-dake** volcano Hokkaidō, NE Japan 43°15′N 140°27′E
80 L11 **Yoboki** C Djibouti 11°30′N 42°04′E
22 M4 **Yockanookany River** ≈ Mississippi, S USA
22 L2 **Yocona River** ≈ Mississippi, S USA
171 Y15 **Yodom** Papua, E Indonesia 07°12′S 139°24′E
169 Q16 **Yogyakarta** *prev.* Djokjakarta, Jogjakarta, Jokyakarta. Jawa, C Indonesia 07°48′S 110°24′E
169 P17 **Yogyakarta** *off.* Daerah Istimewa Yogyakarta, *var.* Djokjakarta, Jogjakarta, Jokyakarta. ◐ *autonomous district* S Indonesia
Yogyakarta, Daerah Istimewa *see* Yogyakarta
165 Q3 **Yoichi** Hokkaidō, NE Japan 43°11′N 140°45′E
42 G6 **Yojoa, Lago de** ◎ NW Honduras
79 G16 **Yokadouma** Est, SE Cameroon 03°26′N 15°06′E
164 K13 **Yokkaichi** *var.* Yokkaiti. Mie, Honshū, SW Japan 34°58′N 136°38′E
Yokkaiti *see* Yokkaichi
79 E15 **Yoko** Centre, C Cameroon 05°29′N 12°19′E
165 V15 **Yokoate-jima** *island* Nansei-shotō, SW Japan
165 R6 **Yokohama** Aomori, Honshū, C Japan 41°04′N 141°14′E
165 O14 **Yokosuka** Kanagawa, Honshū, S Japan 35°18′N 139°39′E
164 G12 **Yokota** Shimane, Honshū, SW Japan 35°10′N 133°03′E
165 Q9 **Yokote** Akita, Honshū, C Japan 39°20′N 140°33′E
77 Y14 **Yola** Adamawa, E Nigeria 09°08′N 12°24′E
79 L19 **Yolombo** Equateur, C Dem. Rep. Congo 01°36′S 23°13′E
146 J14 **Ýolöten** *Rus.* Yëloten; *prev.* Iolotan'. Mary Welaýaty, S Turkmenistan 37°15′N 62°18′E
165 Y15 **Yome-jima** *island* Ogasawara-shotō, SE Japan
76 K16 **Yomou** SE Guinea 07°30′N 09°13′W
171 Y15 **Yomuka** Papua, E Indonesia 07°25′S 138°36′E
188 C16 **Yona** E Guam 13°24′N 144°46′E
164 H12 **Yonago** Tottori, Honshū, SW Japan 35°30′N 134°15′E
165 N16 **Yonaguni** Okinawa, SW Japan 24°29′N 123°00′E
165 N16 **Yonaguni-jima** *island* Nansei-shotō, SW Japan
165 T16 **Yonaha-dake** ▲ Okinawa, SW Japan 26°43′N 128°13′E
163 X14 **Yŏnan** SW North Korea 37°50′N 126°15′E
165 P10 **Yonezawa** Yamagata, Honshū, C Japan 37°56′N 140°06′E
161 Q12 **Yong'an** *var.* Yongan. Fujian, SE China 25°58′N 117°26′E
Yong'an *see* Fengjie
159 T9 **Yongchang** Gansu, N China 38°15′N 101°56′E
161 P7 **Yongcheng** Henan, C China 33°56′N 116°21′E
163 Z15 **Yŏngch'ŏn** *Jap.* Eisen. SE South Korea 35°56′N 128°55′E
160 J10 **Yongchuan** Chongqing Shi, C China 29°27′N 105°56′E
159 U10 **Yongdeng** Gansu, C China 35°58′N 103°27′E
Yongding *see* Yongren
129 W9 **Yongding He** ≈ E China
161 P11 **Yongfeng** *var.* Enjiang. Jiangxi, S China 27°19′N 115°23′E
158 L5 **Yongfengqu** Xinjiang Uygur Zizhiqu, W China 43°28′N 87°09′E
160 L13 **Yongfu** Guangxi Zhuangzu Zizhiqu, S China 24°57′N 109°59′E
163 X13 **Yŏnghŭng** E North Korea 39°31′N 127°14′E
159 U10 **Yongjing** *var.* Liujiaxia. Gansu, C China 36°00′N 103°30′E
Yongjing *see* Xifeng
163 Y15 **Yŏngju** *Jap.* Eishū. C South Korea 36°48′N 128°37′E
Yongning *see* Xuyong
160 E12 **Yongping** Yunnan, SW China 25°30′N 99°28′E
160 G12 **Yongren** *var.* Yongding. Yunnan, SW China 26°09′N 101°40′E
160 L10 **Yongshun** *var.* Lingxi. Hunan, S China 29°02′N 109°46′E
161 P10 **Yongxiu** *var.* Tujiabu. Jiangxi, S China 29°09′N 115°47′E
160 M12 **Yongzhou** *var.* Lengshuitan. Hunan, S China 26°13′N 111°36′E
Yongzhou *see* Zhishan
18 K14 **Yonkers** New York, NE USA 40°56′N 73°51′W
103 Q7 **Yonne** ◐ *department* C France
103 P6 **Yonne** ≈ C France
54 H9 **Yopal** *var.* El Yopal. Casanare, C Colombia 05°20′N 72°19′W
158 E8 **Yopurga** *var.* Yukuriawat. Xinjiang Uygur Zizhiqu, NW China 39°13′N 76°44′E
147 S11 **Yordon** *var.* Iordan, *Rus.* Jardan. Farg'ona Viloyati, E Uzbekistan 39°59′N 71°44′E
180 J12 **York** Western Australia 31°55′S 116°52′E
97 M16 **York** *anc.* Eboracum, Eburacum. N England, United Kingdom 53°58′N 01°05′W
23 N5 **York** Alabama, S USA 32°29′N 88°18′W
29 Q15 **York** Nebraska, C USA 40°52′N 97°35′W
18 G16 **York** Pennsylvania, NE USA 39°57′N 76°44′W
21 R11 **York** South Carolina, SE USA 34°59′N 81°14′W
14 J13 **York** ≈ Ontario, SE Canada
15 X6 **York** ≈ Québec, SE Canada
181 V1 **York, Cape** *headland* Queensland, NE Australia 10°40′S 142°36′E
182 I9 **Yorke Peninsula** *peninsula* South Australia
182 I9 **Yorketown** South Australia 35°01′S 137°38′E
19 P9 **York Harbor** Maine, NE USA 43°10′N 70°37′W
York, Kap *see* Innaanganeq
21 X6 **York River** ≈ Virginia, NE USA
97 M16 **Yorkshire** *cultural region* N England, United Kingdom
97 L16 **Yorkshire Dales** *physical region* N England, United Kingdom
11 V16 **Yorkton** Saskatchewan, S Canada 51°12′N 102°29′W
25 T12 **Yorktown** Texas, SW USA 28°58′N 97°30′W
21 X6 **Yorktown** Virginia, NE USA 37°14′N 76°32′W
30 M11 **Yorkville** Illinois, N USA 41°38′N 88°27′W
42 I5 **Yoro** Yoro, C Honduras 15°08′N 87°10′W
42 H5 **Yoro** ◐ *department* N Honduras
165 T16 **Yoron-jima** *island* Nansei-shotō, SW Japan
77 N13 **Yorosso** Sikasso, S Mali 12°21′N 04°47′W
35 R8 **Yosemite National Park** *national park* California, W USA
127 Q3 **Yoshkar-Ola** Respublika Mariy El, W Russian Federation 56°38′N 47°54′E
Yösöndzüyl *see* Altay
162 K8 **Yösöndzüyl** *var.* Mönhbulag. Övörhangay, C Mongolia 46°48′N 103°25′E
171 Y16 **Yos Sudarso, Pulau** *var.* Pulau Dolak, Pulau Kolepom; *prev.* Jos Sudarso. *island* E Indonesia
163 Y17 **Yŏsu** *Jap.* Reisui. S South Korea 34°45′N 127°41′E
165 R4 **Yotei-zan** ▲ Hokkaidō, NE Japan 42°50′N 140°46′E
97 D21 **Youghal** *Ir.* Eochaill. Cork, S Ireland 51°57′N 07°50′W
97 D21 **Youghal Bay** *Ir.* Cuan Eochaille. *inlet* S Ireland
18 C15 **Youghiogheny River** ≈ Pennsylvania, NE USA
160 K14 **You Jiang** ≈ S China
183 Q9 **Young** New South Wales, SE Australia 34°19′S 148°20′E
11 T15 **Young** Saskatchewan, S Canada 51°44′N 105°44′W
61 E18 **Young** Río Negro, W Uruguay 32°44′S 57°36′W
182 G5 **Younghusband, Lake** *salt lake* South Australia
182 J10 **Younghusband Peninsula** *peninsula* South Australia
184 Q10 **Young Nicks Head** *headland* North Island, New Zealand 39°38′S 177°03′E
185 D20 **Young Range** ▲▲ South Island, New Zealand
191 Q15 **Young's Rock** *island* Pitcairn Island, Pitcairn Islands
11 R16 **Youngstown** Alberta, SW Canada 51°32′N 111°12′W
31 V12 **Youngstown** Ohio, N USA 41°06′N 80°39′W
159 N9 **Youshashan** Qinghai, C China 38°12′N 90°58′E
Youth, Isle of *see* Juventud, Isla de la
77 N11 **Youvarou** Mopti, C Mali 15°19′N 04°15′W
160 K10 **Youyang** *var.* Zhongduo. Chongqing Shi, C China 28°48′N 108°48′E
163 Y7 **Youyi** Heilongjiang, NE China 46°51′N 131°54′E
147 P13 **Yovon** *Rus.* Yavan. SW Tajikistan 38°19′N 69°02′E
136 J13 **Yozgat** Yozgat, C Turkey 39°49′N 34°48′E
136 K13 **Yozgat** ◐ *province* C Turkey
62 O6 **Ypacaraí** *var.* Ypacaray. Central, S Paraguay 25°23′S 57°16′W
Ypacaray *see* Ypacaraí
62 P5 **Ypané, Río** ≈ C Paraguay
Ypres *see* Ieper
114 I13 **Ypsário** *var.* Ipsario. ▲ Thásos, E Greece 40°43′N 24°39′E
31 R10 **Ypsilanti** Michigan, N USA 42°12′N 83°36′W
34 M1 **Yreka** California, W USA 41°43′N 122°39′W
Yrendagüé *see* General Eugenio A. Garay
Yrghyz *see* Irgiz
186 G5 **Ysabel Channel** *channel* N Papua New Guinea
14 K8 **Yser, Lac** ◎ Québec, SE Canada
147 Y8 **Ysthyk** Issyk-Kul'skaya Oblast', E Kyrgyzstan 41°34′N 78°21′E
109 U4 **Ysper** ≈ N Austria
Yssel *see* IJssel
103 Q12 **Yssingeaux** Haute-Loire, C France 45°09′N 04°07′E
95 K23 **Ystad** Skåne, S Sweden 55°25′N 13°51′E
Ysyk-Köl *see* Issyk-Kul', Ozero
Ysyk-Köl *see* Balykchy
Ysyk-Köl Oblasty *see* Issyk-Kul'skaya Oblast'
96 L8 **Ythan** ≈ NE Scotland, United Kingdom
Y Trallwng *see* Welshpool
94 C13 **Ytre Arna** Hordaland, S Norway 60°28′N 05°25′E
94 B12 **Ytre Sula** *island* S Norway
93 G17 **Ytterhogdal** Jämtland, C Sweden 62°10′N 14°55′E
Yu *see* Henan
Yuan *see* Red River
Yuancheng *see* Heyuan, Guangdong, S China
Yuan Jiang *see* Red River
161 S13 **Yüanlin** *Jap.* Inrin. C Taiwan 23°57′N 120°33′E
161 N3 **Yuanping** Shanxi, C China 38°26′N 112°42′E
Yuanquan *see* Anxi
Yuanshan *see* Lianping
161 O11 **Yuan Shui** ≈ S China
35 O6 **Yuba City** California, W USA 39°07′N 121°40′W
35 O6 **Yuba River** ≈ California, W USA
80 H13 **Yubdo** Oromīya, C Ethiopia 09°05′N 35°28′E
41 X12 **Yucatán** ◐ *state* SE Mexico
47 O3 **Yucatan Basin** *var.* Yucatan Deep. *undersea feature* N Caribbean Sea 20°00′N 84°00′W
Yucatán, Canal de *see* Yucatan Channel
41 Y10 **Yucatan Channel** *Sp.* Canal de Yucatán. *channel* Cuba/Mexico
Yucatan Deep *see* Yucatan Basin
Yucatan Peninsula *see* Yucatán, Península de
41 X13 **Yucatán, Península de** *Eng.* Yucatan Peninsula. *peninsula* Guatemala/Mexico
36 I11 **Yucca** Arizona, SW USA 34°49′N 114°06′W
35 V15 **Yucca Valley** California, W USA 34°06′N 116°30′W
161 P4 **Yucheng** Shandong, E China 37°01′N 116°37′E
Yuci *see* Jinzhong
129 X5 **Yudoma** ≈ E Russian Federation
161 P12 **Yudu** *var.* Gongjiang. Jiangxi, C China 26°02′N 115°24′E
Yue *see* Guangdong
Yuecheng *see* Yuexi
160 M12 **Yuecheng Ling** ▲▲ S China
Yuegai *see* Qumarlêb
Yuegaitan *see* Qumarlêb
181 P7 **Yuendumu** Northern Territory, N Australia 22°19′S 131°51′E
Yue Shan, Tai *see* Lantau Island
160 H10 **Yuexi** *var.* Yuecheng. Sichuan, C China 28°50′N 102°36′E
161 N10 **Yueyang** Hunan, S China 29°24′N 113°08′E
125 U14 **Yug** Permskaya Oblast', NW Russian Federation 57°49′N 56°08′E
125 P13 **Yug** ≈ NW Russian Federation
123 R10 **Yugorënok** Respublika Sakha (Yakutiya), NE Russian Federation 59°46′N 137°36′E
122 H9 **Yugorsk** Khanty-Mansiyskiy Avtonomnyy Okrug-Yugra, C Russian Federation 61°17′N 63°25′E
122 H7 **Yugorskiy Poluostrov** *peninsula* NW Russian Federation
Yugoslavia *see* Serbia
146 K14 **Yugo-Vostochnyye Garagumy** *prev.* Yugo-Vostochnyye Karakumy. *desert* E Turkmenistan
Yugo-Vostochnyye Karakumy *see* Yugo-Vostochnyye Garagumy
Yuhu *see* Eryuan
161 S10 **Yuhuan Dao** *island* SE China
160 L14 **Yu Jiang** ≈ S China
Yujin *see* Qianwei
123 S7 **Yukagirskoye Ploskogor'ye** *plateau* NE Russian Federation
118 L11 **Yukhavichy** *Rus.* Yukhovichi. Vitsyebskaya Voblasts', N Belarus 56°02′N 28°39′E
126 J4 **Yukhnov** Kaluzhskaya Oblast', W Russian Federation 54°43′N 35°15′E
Yukhovichi *see* Yukhavichy
79 J20 **Yuki** *var.* Yuki Kengunda. Bandundu, W Dem. Rep. Congo 03°57′S 19°30′E
Yuki Kengunda *see* Yuki
26 M10 **Yukon** Oklahoma, C USA 35°30′N 97°45′W
0 F4 **Yukon** ≈ Canada/USA
Yukon *see* Yukon Territory
39 S7 **Yukon Flats** *salt flat* Alaska, USA
Yukon, Territoire du *see* Yukon Territory
10 I5 **Yukon Territory** *var.* Yukon, *Fr.* Territoire du Yukon. ◐ *territory* NW Canada
137 T16 **Yüksekova** Hakkâri, SE Turkey 37°35′N 44°17′E
123 N10 **Yukta** Evenkiyskiy Avtonomnyy Okrug, C Russian Federation 63°16′N 106°04′E
165 O13 **Yukuhashi** *var.* Yukuhasi. Fukuoka, Kyūshū, SW Japan 33°41′N 131°00′E
Yukuhasi *see* Yukuhashi
Yukuriawat *see* Yopurga
125 O9 **Yula** ≈ NW Russian Federation
181 P8 **Yulara** Northern Territory, N Australia 25°15′S 130°57′E
127 W6 **Yuldybayevo** Respublika Bashkortostan, W Russian Federation 52°22′N 57°55′E
23 W8 **Yulee** Florida, SE USA 30°37′N 81°36′W
158 K7 **Yuli** *var.* Lopnur. Xinjiang Uygur Zizhiqu, NW China 41°24′N 86°12′E
161 T14 **Yüli** C Taiwan 23°23′N 121°18′E
160 L15 **Yulin** Guangxi Zhuangzu Zizhiqu, S China 22°37′N 110°08′E
160 L4 **Yulin** Shaanxi, C China 38°14′N 109°48′E
161 T14 **Yüli Shan** ▲ E Taiwan 23°23′N 121°14′E
160 F11 **Yulong Xueshan** ▲ SW China 27°09′N 100°10′E
36 H14 **Yuma** Arizona, SW USA 32°40′N 114°38′W
37 W3 **Yuma** Colorado, C USA 40°07′N 102°43′W
54 K5 **Yumare** Yaracuy, N Venezuela 10°37′N 68°41′W
63 G14 **Yumbel** Bío Bío, C Chile 37°05′S 72°40′W
79 N19 **Yumbi** Maniema, E Dem. Rep. Congo 01°14′S 26°14′E
159 Q7 **Yumen** *prev.* Yumenzhen. Gansu, N China 40°19′N 97°12′E
Yumenzhen *see* Yumen
158 J3 **Yumin** *var.* Karabura. Xinjiang Uygur Zizhiqu, NW China 46°14′N 82°52′E
Yun *see* Yunnan
136 G14 **Yunak** Konya, W Turkey 38°50′N 31°42′E
45 O8 **Yuna, Río** ≈ E Dominican Republic
38 I17 **Yunaska Island** *island* Aleutian Islands, Alaska, USA
160 M6 **Yuncheng** Shanxi, C China 35°07′N 110°45′E
Yuncheng *see* Yunfu
161 N14 **Yunfu** *var.* Yuncheng. Guangdong, S China 22°56′N 112°02′E

Yungas – Zhanadar'ya

57 L18 **Yungas** *physical region* E Bolivia
Yungki *see* Jilin
Yung-ning *see* Nanning
160 I12 **Yungui Gaoyuan** *plateau* SW China
Yunjinghong *see* Jinghong
160 M15 **Yunkai Dashan** ▲▲ S China
Yunki *see* Jilin
160 E11 **Yun Ling** ▲▲ SW China
Yunling *see* Yunxiao
161 N9 **Yunmeng** Hubei, C China 31°04′N 113°45′E
157 N14 **Yunnan** *var.* Yun, Yunnan Sheng, Yünnan, Yun-nan. ◈ *province* SW China
Yunnan *see* Kunming
Yunnan Sheng *see* Yunnan
Yünnan/Yun-nan *see* Yunnan
165 P15 **Yunomae** Kumamoto, Kyūshū, SW Japan 32°16′N 131°00′E
161 N8 **Yun Shui** ~ C China
182 J7 **Yunta** South Australia 32°37′S 139°33′E
161 Q14 **Yunxiao** *var.* Yunling. Fujian, SE China 23°56′N 117°16′E
160 K9 **Yunyang** Sichuan, C China 31°03′N 109°43′E
Yunzhong *see* Huairen
193 S9 **Yupanqui Basin** *undersea feature* E Pacific Ocean
Yuping *see* Libo, Guizhou, China
Yuping *see* Pingbian, Yunnan, China
Yuratishki *see* Yuratsishki
119 I15 **Yuratsishki** *Pol.* Juraciszki, *Rus.* Yuratishki. Hrodzyenskaya Voblasts', W Belarus 54°02′N 25°56′E
Yurev *see* Tartu
122 J12 **Yurga** Kemerovskaya Oblast', S Russian Federation 55°42′N 84°59′E
Yurihonjō *see* Honjō
56 E10 **Yurimaguas** Loreto, N Peru 05°54′S 76°07′W
127 P3 **Yurino** Respublika Mariy El, W Russian Federation 56°19′N 46°15′E
41 N13 **Yuriria** Guanajuato, C Mexico 20°12′N 101°09′W
125 T13 **Yurla** Komi-Permyatskiy Avtonomnyy Okrug, NW Russian Federation 59°18′N 54°19′E
Yuruá, Río *see* Juruá, Rio
114 M13 **Yürük** Tekirdağ, NW Turkey 40°58′N 27°09′E
158 G10 **Yurungkax He** ~ W China
125 Q14 **Yur'ya** *var.* Jarja. Kirovskaya Oblast', NW Russian Federation 59°01′N 49°22′E
Yury'ev *see* Tartu
125 N16 **Yur'yevets** Ivanovskaya Oblast', W Russian Federation 57°19′N 43°01′E
126 M3 **Yur'yev-Pol'skiy** Vladimirskaya Oblast', W Russian Federation 56°28′N 39°39′E
117 V7 **Yur"yivka** Dnipropetrovs'ka Oblast', E Ukraine 48°45′N 36°01′E
42 I7 **Yuscarán** El Paraíso, S Honduras 13°55′N 86°51′W
161 P12 **Yu Shan** ▲ S China
124 I7 **Yushkozero** Respublika Kareliya, NW Russian Federation 64°46′N 32°13′E
124 I7 **Yushkozerskoye Vodokhranilishche** *var.* Ozero Kujto. ▣ NW Russian Federation
169 W9 **Yushu** Jilin, China E Asia 44°48′N 126°31′E
159 R13 **Yushu** *var.* Gyêgu. Qinghai, C China 33°04′N 97°E
127 P12 **Yusta** Respublika Kalmykiya, SW Russian Federation 47°06′N 46°16′E
124 I10 **Yustozero** Respublika Kareliya, NW Russian Federation 62°44′N 33°31′E
137 Q11 **Yusufeli** Artvin, NE Turkey 40°50′N 41°31′E
164 F14 **Yusuhara** Kōchi, Shikoku, SW Japan 33°22′N 132°52′E
125 T14 **Yus'va** Permskaya Oblast', NW Russian Federation 58°48′N 54°59′E
Yuta *see* Yatta
161 P2 **Yutian** Hebei, E China 39°52′N 117°44′E
158 H10 **Yutian** *var.* Keriya, Mugalla. Xinjiang Uygur Zizhiqu, NW China 36°49′N 81°31′E
62 K5 **Yuto** Jujuy, NW Argentina 23°35′S 64°28′W
62 P7 **Yuty** Caazapá, S Paraguay 26°31′S 56°20′W
160 G13 **Yuxi** Yunnan, SW China 24°22′N 102°28′E
161 O2 **Yuxian** *prev.* Yu Xian. Hebei, E China 39°50′N 114°33′E
Yu Xian *see* Yuxian
165 Q9 **Yuzawa** Akita, Honshū, C Japan 39°11′N 140°29′E
125 N16 **Yuzha** Ivanovskaya Oblast', W Russian Federation 56°34′N 42°00′E
Yuzhno-Alichurskiy Khrebet *see* Alichuri Janubí, Qatorkŭhi
Yuzhno-Kazakhstanskaya Oblast' *see* Yuzhnyy Kazakhstan
123 T13 **Yuzhno-Sakhalinsk** *Jap.* Toyohara; *prev.* Vladimirovka. Ostrov Sakhalin, Sakhalinskaya Oblast', SE Russian Federation 46°58′N 142°45′E
127 P14 **Yuzhno-Sukhokumsk** Respublika Dagestan, SW Russian Federation 44°43′N 45°32′E
145 Z10 **Yuzhnyy Altay, Khrebet** ▲▲ E Kazakhstan
Yuzhnyy Bug *see* Pivdennyy Buh
145 O15 **Yuzhnyy Kazakhstan** *off.* Yuzhno-Kazakhstanskaya Oblast', *Eng.* South Kazakhstan, *Kaz.* Ongtüstik Qazaqstan Oblysy; *prev.* Chimkentskaya Oblast'. ◈ *province* S Kazakhstan
123 U10 **Yuzhnyy, Mys** *headland* E Russian Federation 57°44′N 156°49′E
127 W6 **Yuzhnyy Ural** *var.* Southern Urals. ▲▲ W Russian Federation
159 V10 **Yuzhong** Gansu, C China 35°52′N 104°09′E
Yuzhou *see* Chongqing
103 N5 **Yvelines** ◈ *department* N France
108 B9 **Yverdon** *var.* Yverdon-les-Bains, *Ger.* Iferten; *anc.* Eborodunum. Vaud, W Switzerland 46°47′N 06°38′E
Yverdon-les-Bains *see* Yverdon
102 M3 **Yvetot** Seine-Maritime, N France 49°37′N 00°48′E
Ÿylanly *see* Gurbansoltan Eje

Z

147 T12 **Zaalayskiy Khrebet** *Taj.* Qatorkŭhi Pasi Oloy. ▲▲ Kyrgyzstan/Tajikistan
Zaamin *see* Zomin
Zaandam *see* Zaanstad
98 I10 **Zaanstad** *prev.* Zaandam. Noord-Holland, C Netherlands 52°27′N 04°49′E
Zabadani *see* Az Zabdānī
119 L18 **Zabalatstsye** *Rus.* Zabolot'ye. Homyel'skaya Voblasts', SE Belarus 52°40′N 28°34′E
112 L9 **Žabalj** *Ger.* Josefsdorf, *Hung.* Zsablya; *prev.* Józseffalva. Vojvodina, N Serbia 45°22′N 20°01′E
Zāb aş Şaghīr, Nahraz *see* Little Zab
123 P14 **Zabaykal'sk** Chitinskaya Oblast', S Russian Federation 49°37′N 117°20′E
Zāb-e Kūchek, Rūdkhāneh-ye *see* Little Zab
Zabeln *see* Sabile
Zabéré *see* Zabré
Zabern *see* Saverne
141 N16 **Zabīd** W Yemen 14°N 43°E
141 O16 **Zabīd, Wādī** *dry watercourse* SW Yemen
Żabinka *see* Zhabinka
Ząbkowice *see* Ząbkowice Śląskie
111 G15 **Ząbkowice Śląskie** *var.* Ząbkowice, *Ger.* Frankenstein, Frankenstein in Schlesien. Dolnośląskie, SW Poland 50°35′N 16°48′E
110 P10 **Zabłudów** Podlaskie, NE Poland 53°00′N 23°21′E
112 D8 **Zabok** Krapina-Zagorje, N Croatia 46°00′N 15°48′E
143 W9 **Zābol** *var.* Shahr-i-Zabul, Zabul; *prev.* Nasratabad. Sīstān va Balūchestān, E Iran 31°N 61°32′E
149 O7 **Zābol** *Pash.* Zābul. ◈ *province* SE Afghanistan
143 W13 **Zābolī** Sīstān va Balūchestān, SE Iran 27°09′N 61°32′E
Zabolot'ye *see* Zabalatstsye
77 Q13 **Zabré** *var.* Zabéré. S Burkina 11°13′N 00°34′W
111 G17 **Zábřeh** *Ger.* Hohenstadt. Olomoucký Kraj, E Czech Republic 49°52′N 16°53′E
111 J16 **Zabrze** *Ger.* Hindenburg, Hindenburg in Oberschlesien. Śląskie, S Poland 50°18′N 18°47′E
Zabul/Zābul *see* Zābol
42 E6 **Zacapa** Zacapa, E Guatemala 14°59′N 89°33′W
42 A3 **Zacapa** *off.* Departamento de Zacapa. ◈ *department* E Guatemala
Zacapa, Departamento de *see* Zacapa
40 M14 **Zacapú** Michoacán, SW Mexico 19°49′N 101°48′W
41 V14 **Zacatal** Campeche, SE Mexico 18°40′N 91°52′W
40 M11 **Zacatecas** Zacatecas, C Mexico 22°46′N 102°33′W
40 L10 **Zacatecas** ◈ *state* C Mexico
42 F8 **Zacatecoluca** La Paz, S El Salvador 13°29′N 88°51′W
41 P15 **Zacatepec** Morelos, S Mexico 18°40′N 99°11′W
41 Q13 **Zacatlán** Puebla, S Mexico 19°56′N 97°58′W
144 F8 **Zachagansk** *Kaz.* Zashaghan. Zapadnyy Kazakhstan, NW Kazakhstan 51°04′N 51°13′E
115 D20 **Zacháro** *var.* Zaharo, Zakháro. Dytikí Elláda, S Greece 37°29′N 21°40′E
22 J8 **Zachary** Louisiana, S USA 30°39′N 91°09′W
117 U6 **Zachepylivka** Kharkivs'ka Oblast', E Ukraine 49°13′N 35°15′E
Zachist'ye *see* Zachystsye
110 E9 **Zachodnio-pomorskie** ◈ *province* NW Poland
119 L14 **Zachystsye** *Rus.* Zachist'ye. Minskaya Voblasts', NW Belarus 54°24′N 28°45′E
40 L13 **Zacoalco** *var.* Zacoalco de Torres. Jalisco, SW Mexico 20°14′N 103°33′W
Zacoalco de Torres *see* Zacoalco
41 P13 **Zacualtipán** Hidalgo, C Mexico 20°39′N 98°42′W
112 C12 **Zadar** *It.* Zara; *anc.* Iader. Zadar, SW Croatia 44°07′N 15°15′E
112 C12 **Zadar** *off.* Zadarsko-Kninska Županija, Zadar-Knin. ◈ *province* SW Croatia
Zadar-Knin *see* Zadar
Zadarsko-Kninska Županija *see* Zadar
166 M14 **Zadetkyi Kyun** *var.* St.Matthew's Island. *island* Mergui Archipelago, S Burma (Myanmar)
67 Q9 **Zadié** *var.* Djadié. ~ NE Gabon
159 Q13 **Zadoi** *var.* Qapugtang. Qinghai, C China 32°56′N 95°21′E
126 L7 **Zadonsk** Lipetskaya Oblast', W Russian Federation 52°25′N 38°55′E
Za'farāna *see* Za'farānah
75 X8 **Za'farānah** *var.* Za'farāna. E Egypt 29°06′N 32°34′E
149 W7 **Zafarwāl** Punjab, E Pakistan 32°20′N 74°53′E
121 Q1 **Zafer Burnu** *var.* Cape Andreas, Cape Apostolas Andreas, *Gk.* Akrotíri Apostólou Andréa. *cape* NE Cyprus
107 J23 **Zafferano, Capo** *headland* Sicilia, Italy, C Mediterranean Sea 38°06′N 13°31′E
114 M7 **Zafirovo** Silistra, NE Bulgaria 44°00′N 26°51′E
Záfora *see* Sofraná
104 J12 **Zafra** Extremadura, W Spain 38°25′N 06°27′W
110 E13 **Żagań** *var.* Zagań, Żegań, *Ger.* Sagan. Lubuskie, W Poland 51°37′N 15°20′E
118 F10 **Žagarė** *Pol.* Żagory. Siaulai, N Lithuania 56°22′N 23°16′E
Zagazig *see* Az Zaqāzīq
74 M5 **Zaghouan** *var.* Zaghwān. NE Tunisia 36°26′N 10°05′E
Zaghwān *see* Zaghouan
115 G16 **Zagorá** Thessalía, C Greece 39°27′N 23°06′E
Zagorod'ye *see* Zaharoddzye
Zagory *see* Žagarė
Zágráb *see* Zagreb
112 E8 **Zagreb** *Ger.* Agram, *Hung.* Zágráb. ● (Croatia) Zagreb, N Croatia 45°48′N 15°58′E
112 E8 **Zagreb** *prev.* Grad Zagreb. ◈ *province* N Croatia
142 L7 **Zāgros, Kūhhā-ye** *Eng.* Zagros Mountains. ▲▲ W Iran
Zagros Mountains *see* Zāgros, Kūhhā-ye
112 O12 **Žagubica** Serbia, E Serbia 44°13′N 21°47′E
Zagunao *see* Lixian
111 L22 **Zagyva** ~ N Hungary
Zaharo *see* Zacháro
119 G19 **Zaharoddzye** *Rus.* Zagorod'ye. *physical region* SW Belarus
143 W11 **Zāhedān** *var.* Zahidan; *prev.* Duzdab. Sīstān va Balūchestān, SE Iran 29°31′N 60°51′E
Zahidan *see* Zāhedān
Zahlah *see* Zahlé
138 H7 **Zahlé** *var.* Zaḩlah. C Lebanon 33°51′N 35°54′E
146 J14 **Zähmet** *Rus.* Zakhmet. Mary Welaýaty, C Turkmenistan 37°48′N 62°33′E
111 O20 **Záhony** Szabolcs-Szatmár-Bereg, NE Hungary 48°26′N 22°11′E
141 N13 **Ẓahrān** 'Asīr, S Saudi Arabia 17°48′N 43°28′E
139 R12 **Ẓahrat al Baṭn** *hill range* S Iraq
120 H11 **Zahrez Chergui** *var.* Zahrez Chergúi. *marsh* N Algeria
Zainlha *see* Xinjin
127 S4 **Zainsk** Respublika Tatarstan, W Russian Federation 55°12′N 52°01′E
82 A10 **Zaire** *prev.* Congo. ◈ *province* NW Angola
Zaire *see* Congo (river)
Zaire *see* Congo (Democratic Republic of)
112 P13 **Zaječar** Serbia, E Serbia 43°54′N 22°16′E
83 L18 **Zaka** Masvingo, E Zimbabwe 20°20′S 31°29′E
122 M14 **Zakamensk** Respublika Buryatiya, S Russian Federation 50°18′N 102°57′E
116 G7 **Zakarpats'ka Oblast'** *Eng.* Transcarpathian Oblast, *Rus.* Zakarpatskaya Oblast'. ◈ *province* W Ukraine
Zakarpatskaya Oblast' *see* Zakarpats'ka Oblast'
Zakataly *see* Zaqatala
Zakháro *see* Zacháro
Zakhidnyy Buh/Zakhodni Buh *see* Bug
Zakhmet *see* Zähmet
139 Q1 **Zākhō** *var.* Zākhū. Dahūk, N Iraq 37°09′N 42°40′E
Zākhū *see* Zākhō
Zákinthos *see* Zákynthos
111 L18 **Zakopane** Małopolskie, S Poland 49°17′N 19°57′E
78 J12 **Zakouma** Salamat, S Chad 10°47′N 19°51′E
115 L25 **Zákros** Kríti, Greece, E Mediterranean Sea 35°06′N 26°12′E
115 C19 **Zákynthos** *var.* Zákinthos. Zákynthos, W Greece 37°47′N 20°54′E
115 C20 **Zákynthos** *var.* Zákinthos, *It.* Zante. *island* Iónia Nísoi, Greece, C Mediterranean Sea
115 C19 **Zakýnthou, Porthmós** *strait* SW Greece
111 G24 **Zala** *off.* Zala Megye. ◈ *county* W Hungary
111 G24 **Zala** ~ W Hungary
138 M4 **Zalābīyah** Dayr az Zawr, C Syria 35°39′N 39°51′E
111 G24 **Zalaegerszeg** Zala, W Hungary 46°51′N 16°49′E
104 K11 **Zalamea de la Serena** Extremadura, W Spain 38°38′N 05°37′W
104 J13 **Zalamea la Real** Andalucía, S Spain 37°41′N 06°40′W
Zala Megye *see* Zala
163 U7 **Zalantun** *var.* Butha Qi. Nei Mongol Zizhiqu, N China 47°58′N 122°44′E
111 G23 **Zalaszentgrót** Zala, SW Hungary 46°57′N 17°05′E
Zalatna *see* Zlatna
116 G9 **Zalău** *Ger.* Waltenberg, *Hung.* Zilah; *prev. Ger.* Zillenmarkt. Sălaj, NW Romania 47°11′N 23°03′E
109 V10 **Žalec** *Ger.* Sachsenfeld. C Slovenia 46°15′N 15°08′E
110 K8 **Zalewo** *Ger.* Saalfeld. Warmińsko-Mazurskie, NE Poland 53°54′N 19°39′E
141 N9 **Ẓalim** Makkah, W Saudi Arabia 22°46′N 42°12′E
80 A11 **Zalingei** *var.* Zalinje. Western Darfur, W Sudan 12°51′N 23°29′E
Zalinje *see* Zalingei
116 K7 **Zalishchyky** Ternopil's'ka Oblast', W Ukraine 48°40′N 25°43′E
Zallah *see* Zillah
98 J13 **Zaltbommel** Gelderland, C Netherlands 51°49′N 05°15′E
124 H15 **Zaluch'ye** Novgorodskaya Oblast', NW Russian Federation 57°40′N 31°45′E
Zamak *see* Zamakh
141 Q14 **Zamakh** *var.* Zamak. N Yemen 16°26′N 47°35′E
136 K15 **Zamantı Irmağı** ~ C Turkey
Zambesi/Zambeze *see* Zambezi
83 G14 **Zambezi** North Western, W Zambia 13°34′S 23°08′E
83 K15 **Zambezi** *var.* Zambesi, *Port.* Zambeze. ~ S Africa
83 O15 **Zambézia** *off.* Província da Zambézia. ◈ *province* C Mozambique
Zambézia, Província da *see* Zambézia
83 I14 **Zambia** *off.* Republic of Zambia; *prev.* Northern Rhodesia. ◆ *republic* S Africa
Zambia, Republic of *see* Zambia
171 O8 **Zamboanga** *off.* Zamboanga City. Mindanao, S Philippines 06°56′N 122°03′E
Zamboanga City *see* Zamboanga
54 E5 **Zambrano** Bolívar, N Colombia 09°45′N 74°50′W
110 N10 **Zambrów** Łomża, E Poland 52°59′N 22°14′E
83 L14 **Zambuè** Tete, NW Mozambique 15°03′S 30°49′E
77 T13 **Zamfara** ~ NW Nigeria
Zamkog *see* Zamtang
56 C9 **Zamora** Zamora Chinchipe, S Ecuador 04°04′S 78°52′W
104 K6 **Zamora** Castilla-León, NW Spain 41°30′N 05°45′W
104 K5 **Zamora** ◈ *province* Castilla-León, NW Spain
Zamora *see* Barinas
56 A13 **Zamora Chinchipe** ◈ *province* S Ecuador
40 M13 **Zamora de Hidalgo** Michoacán, SW Mexico 20°N 102°18′W
111 P15 **Zamość** *Rus.* Zamoste. Lubelskie, E Poland 50°44′N 23°16′E
Zamoste *see* Zamość
160 G7 **Zamtang** *var.* Zamkog; *prev.* Gamba. Sichuan, C China 32°19′N 100°55′E
75 O8 **Zamzam, Wādī** *dry watercourse* NW Libya
79 F20 **Zanaga** Lékoumou, S Congo 02°50′S 13°53′E
41 T16 **Zanatepec** Oaxaca, SE Mexico 16°28′N 94°24′W
105 P9 **Záncara** ~ C Spain
Zancle *see* Messina
158 G14 **Zanda** Xizang Zizhiqu, W China 31°29′N 79°50′E
98 H10 **Zandvoort** Noord-Holland, W Netherlands 52°22′N 04°31′E
39 P8 **Zane Hills** *hill range* Alaska, USA
31 T13 **Zanesville** Ohio, N USA 39°55′N 82°02′W
Zanga *see* Hrazdan
Zangkaxa *see* Domar
142 L4 **Zanjān** *var.* Zenjan, Zinjan. Zanjān, NW Iran 36°40′N 48°30′E
142 L4 **Zanjān** *off.* Ostān-e Zanjān, *var.* Zenjan, Zinjan. ◈ *province* NW Iran
Zanjān, Ostān-e *see* Zanjān
Zante *see* Zákynthos
81 J22 **Zanzibar** Zanzibar, E Tanzania 06°10′S 39°12′E
81 J22 **Zanzibar** ◈ *region* E Tanzania
81 J22 **Zanzibar** *Swa.* Unguja. *island* E Tanzania
81 J22 **Zanzibar Channel** *channel* E Tanzania
81 J23 **Zanzibar North** ◈ *region* E Tanzania
81 J23 **Zanzibar South** ◈ *region* E Tanzania
81 J23 **Zanzibar West** ◈ *region* E Tanzania
161 N8 **Zaoyang** Hubei, C China 32°10′N 112°45′E
165 P10 **Zaō-zan** ▲ Honshū, C Japan 38°06′N 140°27′E
124 J2 **Zaozërsk** Murmanskaya Oblast', NW Russian Federation 69°25′N 32°25′E
161 Q6 **Zaozhuang** Shandong, E China 34°53′N 117°38′E
28 L4 **Zap** North Dakota, N USA 47°18′N 101°55′W
112 L13 **Zapadna Morava** *Ger.* Westliche Morava. ~ C Serbia
124 H16 **Zapadnaya Dvina** Tverskaya Oblast', W Russian Federation 56°17′N 32°03′E
Zapadnaya Dvina *see* Western Dvina
Zapadno-Kazakhstanskaya Oblast' *see* Zapadnyy Kazakhstan
122 I9 **Zapadno-Sibirskaya Ravnina** *Eng.* West Siberian Plain. *plain* C Russian Federation
Zapadnyy Bug *see* Bug
144 E9 **Zapadnyy Kazakhstan** *off.* Zapadno-Kazakhstanskaya Oblast', *Eng.* West Kazakhstan, *Kaz.* Batys Qazaqstan Oblysy; *prev.* Ural'skaya Oblast'. ◈ *province* NW Kazakhstan
122 K13 **Zapadnyy Sayan** *Eng.* Western Sayans. ▲▲ S Russian Federation
63 H15 **Zapala** Neuquén, W Argentina 38°54′S 70°06′W
62 I4 **Zapaleri, Cerro** *var.* Cerro Sapaleri. ▲ N Chile 22°51′S 67°10′W
25 Q16 **Zapata** Texas, SW USA 26°57′N 99°17′W
44 D5 **Zapata, Península de** *peninsula* W Cuba
61 G19 **Zapicán** Lavalleja, S Uruguay 33°31′S 54°55′W
65 J19 **Zapiola Ridge** *undersea feature* SW Atlantic Ocean
65 L19 **Zapiola Seamount** *undersea feature* S Atlantic Ocean 38°15′S 26°15′W
124 I2 **Zapolyarnyy** Murmanskaya Oblast', NW Russian Federation 69°24′N 30°53′E
117 U8 **Zaporizhzhya** *Rus.* Zaporozh'ye; *prev.* Aleksandrovsk. Zaporiz'ka Oblast', SE Ukraine 47°47′N 35°12′E
Zaporizhzhya *see* Zaporiz'ka Oblast'
117 U9 **Zaporiz'ka Oblast'** *var.* Zaporizhzhya, *Rus.* Zaporozhskaya Oblast'. ◈ *province* SE Ukraine
Zaporozhskaya Oblast' *see* Zaporiz'ka Oblast'
Zaporozh'ye *see* Zaporizhzhya
40 L14 **Zapotiltic** Jalisco, SW Mexico 19°40′N 103°29′W
158 G13 **Zapug** Xizang Zizhiqu, W China
137 V10 **Zaqatala** *Rus.* Zakataly. NW Azerbaijan 41°38′N 46°38′E
159 P13 **Zaqên** Qinghai, W China 33°23′N 94°31′E
159 Q13 **Za Qu** ~ C China
136 M13 **Zara** Sivas, C Turkey 39°55′N 37°44′E
Zara *see* Zadar
Zarafshan *see* Zarafshon
147 P12 **Zarafshon** *Rus.* Zeravshan. W Tajikistan 39°12′N 68°36′E
146 L9 **Zarafshon** *Rus.* Zarafshan. Navoiy Viloyati, N Uzbekistan 41°33′N 64°09′E
Zarafshon *see* Zeravshan
147 O12 **Zarafshon, Qatorkŭhi** *Rus.* Zeravshanskiy Khrebet, *Uzb.* Zarafshon Tizmasi. ▲▲ Tajikistan/Uzbekistan
Zarafshon Tizmasi *see* Zarafshon, Qatorkŭhi
54 E7 **Zaragoza** Antioquia, N Colombia 07°30′N 74°52′W
40 I5 **Zaragoza** Chihuahua, N Mexico 29°36′N 107°41′W
41 N6 **Zaragoza** Coahuila, NE Mexico 28°31′N 100°54′W
41 O10 **Zaragoza** Nuevo León, NE Mexico 23°59′N 99°49′W
105 R5 **Zaragoza** *Eng.* Saragossa; *anc.* Caesaraugusta, Salduba. Aragón, NE Spain 41°39′N 00°54′W
105 R6 **Zaragoza** ◈ *province* Aragón, NE Spain
105 R5 **Zaragoza** ✕ Aragón, NE Spain 41°38′N 00°53′W
143 S10 **Zarand** Kermān, C Iran 30°50′N 56°35′E
148 J9 **Zaranj** Nīmrūz, SW Afghanistan 30°59′N 61°54′E
118 I11 **Zarasai** Utena, E Lithuania 55°44′N 26°17′E
62 N12 **Zárate** *prev.* General José F.Uriburu. Buenos Aires, E Argentina 34°06′S 59°03′W
105 Q2 **Zarautz** *var.* Zarauz. País Vasco, N Spain 43°17′N 02°10′W
Zarauz *see* Zarautz
Zaravecchia *see* Biograd na Moru
Zarāyīn *see* Zarēn
126 L4 **Zaraysk** Moskovskaya Oblast', W Russian Federation 54°48′N 38°54′E
55 N6 **Zaraza** Guárico, N Venezuela 09°23′N 65°20′W
Zarbdar *see* Zarbdor
147 P11 **Zarbdor** *Rus.* Zarbdar. Jizzax Viloyati, C Uzbekistan 40°04′N 68°10′E
142 M8 **Zard Kūh** ▲ SW Iran 32°19′N 50°03′E
124 I5 **Zarechensk** Murmanskaya Oblast', NW Russian Federation 66°39′N 31°27′E
127 P6 **Zarechnyy** Penzenskaya Oblast', W Russian Federation 53°12′N 45°12′E
Zareh Sharan *see* Sharan
39 Y14 **Zarembo Island** *island* Alexander Archipelago, Alaska, USA
139 V4 **Zarēn** *var.* Zarāyīn. As Sulaymānīyah, E Iraq 35°16′N 45°43′E
149 Q7 **Zarghūn Shahr** *var.* Katawaz. Paktīkā, SE Afghanistan 32°40′N 68°20′E
77 V13 **Zaria** Kaduna, C Nigeria 11°06′N 07°42′E
116 K2 **Zarichne** Rivnens'ka Oblast', NW Ukraine 51°49′N 26°09′E
122 J13 **Zarinsk** Altayskiy Kray, S Russian Federation 53°34′N 85°22′E
116 J12 **Zărnești** *Hung.* Zernest. Brașov, C Romania 45°34′N 25°18′E
115 J25 **Zarós** Kríti, Greece, E Mediterranean Sea 35°08′N 24°54′E
100 O9 **Zarow** ~ NE Germany
Zarqa *see* Az Zarqā'
Zarqa/Muḩāfaẓat az Zarqā' *see* Az Zarqā'
111 G20 **Záruby** ▲ W Slovakia 48°30′N 17°24′E
56 B8 **Zaruma** El Oro, SW Ecuador 03°46′S 79°38′W
110 E13 **Żary** *Ger.* Sorau, Sorau in der Niederlausitz. Lubuskie, W Poland 51°44′N 15°09′E
54 D10 **Zarzal** Valle del Cauca, W Colombia 04°24′N 76°01′W
42 I7 **Zarzalar, Cerro** ▲ S Honduras 14°15′N 86°49′W
Zashaghan *see* Zachagansk
152 I5 **Zāskār** ~ NE India
152 I5 **Zāskār Range** ▲▲ NE India
119 K15 **Zaslawye** Minskaya Voblasts', C Belarus 54°01′N 27°16′E
116 K7 **Zastavna** Chernivets'ka Oblast', W Ukraine 48°30′N 25°51′E
111 B16 **Žatec** *Ger.* Saaz. Ústecký Kraj, NW Czech Republic 50°20′N 13°35′E
Zaumgarten *see* Chrzanów
Zaunguzskiye Garagumy *see* Üngüz Angyrsyndaky Garagum
25 X9 **Zavalla** Texas, SW USA 31°09′N 94°25′W
99 H18 **Zaventem** Vlaams Brabant, C Belgium 50°53′N 04°28′E
99 H18 **Zaventem** ✕ (Brussel/Bruxelles) Vlaams Brabant, C Belgium 50°55′N 04°28′E
Zavertse *see* Zawiercie
114 L7 **Zavet** Razgrad, NE Bulgaria 43°46′N 26°40′E
127 O12 **Zavetnoye** Rostovskaya Oblast', SW Russian Federation 47°10′N 43°54′E
156 M3 **Zavhan Gol** ~ W Mongolia
112 H12 **Zavidovići** Federacija Bosna I Hercegovina, N Bosnia and Herzegovina 44°26′N 18°07′E
123 R13 **Zavitinsk** Amurskaya Oblast', SE Russian Federation 50°23′N 128°57′E
Zawia *see* Az Zāwiyah
111 K15 **Zawiercie** *Rus.* Zavertse. Śląskie, S Poland 50°29′N 19°24′E
75 P11 **Zawīlah** *var.* Zuwaylah, *It.* Zueila. C Libya 26°10′N 15°07′E
138 I4 **Zāwiyah, Jabal az** ▲ NW Syria
109 Y3 **Zaya** ~ NE Austria
166 M8 **Zayatkyi** Bago, C Burma (Myanmar) 17°48′N 96°27′E
145 Y11 **Zaysan** Vostochnyy Kazakhstan, E Kazakhstan 47°30′N 84°55′E
Zaysan Köl *see* Zaysan, Ozero
145 Y11 **Zaysan, Ozero** *Kaz.* Zaysan Köl. ◎ E Kazakhstan
159 R16 **Zayü** *var.* Gyigang. Xizang Zizhiqu, W China 28°36′N 97°25′E
Zayyq *see* Ural
44 F6 **Zaza** ~ C Cuba
116 K5 **Zbarazh** Ternopil's'ka Oblast', W Ukraine 49°40′N 25°47′E
116 J5 **Zboriv** Ternopil's'ka Oblast', W Ukraine 49°40′N 25°07′E
111 F18 **Zbraslav** Jihomoravský Kraj, SE Czech Republic 49°13′N 16°19′E
116 K6 **Zbruch** ~ W Ukraine
Žďár *see* Žďár nad Sázavou
111 F17 **Žďár nad Sázavou** *Ger.* Saar in Mähren; *prev.* Žďár. Vysočina, C Czech Republic 49°34′N 16°00′E
116 K4 **Zdolbuniv** *Pol.* Zdołbunów, *Rus.* Zdolbunov. Rivnens'ka Oblast', NW Ukraine 50°33′N 26°15′E
Zdolbunov/Zdołbunów *see* Zdolbuniv
110 J13 **Zduńska Wola** Sieradz, C Poland 51°37′N 18°57′E
117 O4 **Zdvizh** ~ N Ukraine
Zdzięciół *see* Dzyatlava
111 I16 **Zdzieszowice** *Ger.* Odertal. Opolskie, SW Poland 50°24′N 18°06′E
Zealand *see* Sjælland
188 K6 **Zealandia Bank** *undersea feature* C Pacific Ocean
63 H20 **Zeballos, Monte** ▲ S Argentina 47°04′S 71°32′W
83 K20 **Zebediela** Limpopo, NE South Africa 24°16′S 29°21′E
113 L18 **Zebë, Mal** *var.* Mali i Zebës. ▲ NE Albania 41°57′N 20°16′E
Zebës, Mali i *see* Zebë, Mal
21 V9 **Zebulon** North Carolina, SE USA 35°49′N 78°19′W
112 K8 **Žednik** *Hung.* Bácsjózseffalva. Vojvodina, N Serbia 45°58′N 19°40′E
99 C15 **Zeebrugge** West-Vlaanderen, NW Belgium 51°20′N 03°13′E
183 N16 **Zeehan** Tasmania, SE Australia 41°54′S 145°19′E
99 L14 **Zeeland** Noord-Brabant, SE Netherlands 51°42′N 05°40′E
29 N7 **Zeeland** North Dakota, N USA 45°57′N 99°49′W
99 E14 **Zeeland** ◈ *province* SW Netherlands
83 I21 **Zeerust** North-West, N South Africa 25°33′S 26°06′E
98 K10 **Zeewolde** Flevoland, C Netherlands 52°20′N 05°32′E
Zefat *see* Tsefat
Żegań *see* Żagań
Zehden *see* Cedynia
100 O11 **Zehdenick** Brandenburg, NE Germany 52°58′N 13°19′E
Zē-i Bādīnān *see* Great Zab
Zeiden *see* Codlea
146 M14 **Zeidskoye Vodokhranilishche** ▣ E Turkmenistan
Zē-i Kōya *see* Little Zab
181 P7 **Zeil, Mount** ▲ Northern Territory, C Australia 23°31′S 132°41′E
98 J12 **Zeist** Utrecht, C Netherlands 52°05′N 05°15′E
101 M16 **Zeitz** Sachsen-Anhalt, E Germany 51°03′N 12°08′E
159 T11 **Zêkog** *var.* Zequ; *prev.* Sonag. Qinghai, C China 35°03′N 101°30′E
Zelaya Norte *see* Atlántico Norte, Región Autónoma
Zelaya Sur *see* Atlántico Sur, Región Autónoma
99 F17 **Zele** Oost-Vlaanderen, NW Belgium 51°04′N 04°02′E
110 N12 **Żelechów** Lubelskie, E Poland 51°49′N 21°57′E
113 H14 **Zelena Glava** ▲ SE Bosnia and Herzegovina 43°32′N 17°55′E
113 P20 **Zelen Breg** ▲ S Macedonia 41°10′N 22°14′E
113 I14 **Zelengora** ▲▲ S Bosnia and Herzegovina
124 I5 **Zelenoborskiy** Murmanskaya Oblast', NW Russian Federation 66°52′N 32°25′E
127 R3 **Zelenodol'sk** Respublika Tatarstan, W Russian Federation 55°52′N 48°49′E
117 S9 **Zelenodol's'k** Dnipropetrovs'ka Oblast', E Ukraine 47°38′N 33°41′E
122 J12 **Zelenogorsk** Krasnoyarskiy Kray, C Russian Federation 56°08′N 94°29′E
126 K3 **Zelenograd** Moskovskaya Oblast', W Russian Federation 56°02′N 37°08′E
118 B13 **Zelenogradsk** *Ger.* Cranz, Kranz. Kaliningradskaya Oblast', W Russian Federation 54°58′N 20°30′E
127 O15 **Zelenokumsk** Stavropol'skiy Kray, SW Russian Federation 44°22′N 43°48′E
165 X4 **Zelënyy, Ostrov** *var.* Shibotsu-jima. *island* NE Russian Federation
Železna Kapela *see* Eisenkappel
Železna Vrata *see* Demir Kapija
112 L11 **Železniki** Serbia, N Serbia 44°45′N 20°23′E
98 N12 **Zelhem** Gelderland, E Netherlands 52°00′N 06°21′E
113 N18 **Želino** NW FYR Macedonia 42°00′N 21°06′E
113 M14 **Željin** ▲ C Serbia
101 K17 **Zella-Mehlis** Thüringen, C Germany 50°40′N 10°40′E
109 P7 **Zell am See** *var.* Zell-am-See. Salzburg, S Austria 47°19′N 12°47′E
Zell-am-See *see* Zell am See
109 N7 **Zell am Ziller** Tirol, W Austria 47°13′N 11°52′E
Zelle *see* Celle
109 W2 **Zellerndorf** Niederösterreich, NE Austria 48°40′N 15°57′E
109 U7 **Zeltweg** Steiermark, S Austria 47°12′N 14°46′E
119 G17 **Zel'va** *Pol.* Zelwa. Hrodzyenskaya Voblasts', W Belarus 53°09′N 24°49′E
118 H13 **Želva** Vilnius, C Lithuania 55°13′N 25°07′E
Zelwa *see* Zel'va
99 E16 **Zelzate** *var.* Selzaete. Oost-Vlaanderen, NW Belgium 51°12′N 03°49′E
118 E11 **Žemaičių Aukštumas** *physical region* W Lithuania
118 C12 **Žemaičių Naumiestis** Klaipėda, SW Lithuania 55°22′N 21°39′E
119 L14 **Zembin** *var.* Zyembin. Minskaya Voblasts', C Belarus 54°22′N 28°13′E
127 N6 **Zemetchino** Penzenskaya Oblast', W Russian Federation 53°31′N 42°35′E
79 M15 **Zémio** Haut-Mbomou, E Central African Republic 05°04′N 25°07′E
41 R16 **Zempoaltepec, Cerro** ▲ SE Mexico 17°04′N 95°54′W
99 G17 **Zemst** Vlaams Brabant, C Belgium 50°59′N 04°28′E
112 L11 **Zemun** Serbia, N Serbia 44°52′N 20°25′E
Zendajan *see* Zendeh Jan
148 J5 **Zendeh Jan** *var.* Zendajan, Zindajān. Herāt, NW Afghanistan 34°55′N 61°53′E
Zengg *see* Senj
112 H12 **Zenica** Federacija Bosna I Hercegovina, C Bosnia and Herzegovina 44°12′N 17°53′E
Zenjan *see* Zanjān
Zen'kov *see* Zin'kiv
Zenshū *see* Chŏnju
Zenta *see* Senta
82 B11 **Zenza do Itombe** Cuanza Norte, NW Angola 09°22′S 14°10′E
112 H12 **Žepče** Federacija Bosna I Hercegovina, N Bosnia and Herzegovina 44°26′N 18°00′E
23 W12 **Zephyrhills** Florida, SE USA 28°13′N 82°10′W
158 F9 **Zepu** *var.* Poskam. Xinjiang Uygur Zizhiqu, NW China 38°10′N 77°18′E
Zequ *see* Zêkog
147 Q12 **Zeravshan** *Taj./Uzb.* Zarafshon. ~ Tajikistan/Uzbekistan
Zeravshan *see* Zarafshon
Zeravshanskiy Khrebet *see* Zarafshon, Qatorkŭhi
101 M14 **Zerbst** Sachsen-Anhalt, E Germany 51°57′N 12°05′E
145 P8 **Zerenda** Akmola, N Kazakhstan 52°56′N 69°09′E
110 H12 **Żerków** Wielkopolskie, C Poland 52°03′N 17°33′E
108 E11 **Zermatt** Valais, SW Switzerland 46°00′N 07°45′E
Zernest *see* Zărnești
108 J9 **Zernez** Graubünden, SE Switzerland 46°42′N 10°06′E
126 L12 **Zernograd** Rostovskaya Oblast', SW Russian Federation 46°52′N 40°13′E
Zestafoni *see* Zestap'oni
137 S9 **Zestap'oni** *Rus.* Zestafoni. C Georgia 42°09′N 43°00′E
98 H12 **Zestienhoven** ✕ (Rotterdam) Zuid-Holland, SW Netherlands 51°57′N 04°30′E
113 J16 **Zeta** ~ C Montenegro
8 L6 **Zeta Lake** ◎ Victoria Island, Northwest Territories, N Canada
Zētang *see* Nêdong
98 L12 **Zetten** Gelderland, SE Netherlands 51°55′N 05°43′E
101 M17 **Zeulenroda** Thüringen, C Germany 50°40′N 11°58′E
100 H10 **Zeven** Niedersachsen, NW Germany 53°17′N 09°16′E
98 M12 **Zevenaar** Gelderland, SE Netherlands 51°55′N 06°05′E
99 H14 **Zevenbergen** Noord-Brabant, S Netherlands 51°39′N 04°36′E
129 X6 **Zeya** ~ SE Russian Federation
Zeya Reservoir *see* Zeyskoye Vodokhranilishche
143 T11 **Zeynalābād** Kermān, C Iran 29°56′N 57°29′E
123 R12 **Zeyskoye Vodokhranilishche** *Eng.* Zeya Reservoir. ▣ SE Russian Federation
104 H8 **Zêzere, Rio** ~ C Portugal
Zgerzh *see* Zgierz
138 H6 **Zgharta** N Lebanon 34°24′N 35°54′E
110 K12 **Zgierz** *Ger.* Neuhof, *Rus.* Zgerzh. Łódź, C Poland 51°55′N 19°20′E
111 E14 **Zgorzelec** *Ger.* Görlitz. Dolnośląskie, SW Poland 51°10′N 15°E
119 F19 **Zhabinka** *Pol.* Żabinka. Brestskaya Voblasts', SW Belarus 52°12′N 24°01′E
Zhaggo *see* Luhuo
159 R15 **Zhag'yab** *var.* Yêndum. Xizang Zizhiqu, W China 30°42′N 97°33′E
144 L9 **Zhailma** *Kaz.* Zhayylma. Kostanay, N Kazakhstan 51°34′N 61°39′E
Zhalagash *see* Dzhalagash
145 V16 **Zhalanash** Almaty, SE Kazakhstan 43°04′N 78°08′E
145 S7 **Zhalauly, Ozero** ◎ NE Kazakhstan
144 E9 **Zhalpaktal** *Kaz.* Zhalpaqtal; *prev.* Furmanovo. Zapadnyy Kazakhstan, W Kazakhstan 49°43′N 49°28′E
Zhalpaqtal *see* Zhalpaktal
119 G16 **Zhaludok** *Rus.* Zheludok. Hrodzyenskaya Voblasts', W Belarus 53°36′N 24°59′E
Zhaman-Akkol', Ozero *see* Akkol', Ozero
145 Q14 **Zhambyl** *off.* Zhambylskaya Oblast', *Kaz.* Zhambyl Oblysy; *prev.* Dzhambulskaya Oblast'. ◈ *province* S Kazakhstan
Zhambyl *see* Taraz
Zhambyl Oblysy/Zhambylskaya Oblast' *see* Zhambyl
Zhamo *see* Bomi
145 S12 **Zhamshy** ~ C Kazakhstan
144 M15 **Zhanadar'ya** Kzylorda, S Kazakhstan 44°41′N 64°39′E

◆ Country ● Country Capital ◇ Dependent Territory ○ Dependent Territory Capital ◈ Administrative Regions ✕ International Airport ▲ Mountain ▲▲ Mountain Range Volcano ~ River ◎ Lake ▣ Reservoir

ZHANAKORGAN – ZYRYANOVSK

145 O15 **Zhanakorgan** *Kaz.* Zhangaqorghan. Kzylorda, S Kazakhstan *43°57′N 67°14′E*
159 N16 **Zhanang** *var.* Chatang. Xizang Zizhiqu, W China *29°15′N 91°20′E*
145 T12 **Zhanaortalyk** Karaganda, C Kazakhstan *47°31′N 75°42′E*
144 F15 **Zhanaozen** *Kaz.* Zhangaözen; *prev.* Novyy Uzen'. Mangistau, W Kazakhstan *43°22′N 52°50′E*
145 Q16 **Zhanatas** Zhambyl, S Kazakhstan *43°36′N 69°43′E*
Zhangaözen *see* Zhanaozen
Zhangaqazaly *see* Ayteke Bi
Zhangaqorghan *see* Zhanakorgan
161 O2 **Zhangbei** Hebei, E China *41°13′N 114°43′E*
Zhang-chia-k'ou *see* Zhangjiakou
Zhangdian *see* Zibo
Zhanggu *see* Danba
163 X9 **Zhangguangcai Ling** ▲▲ NE China
145 W10 **Zhangiztobe** Vostochnyy Kazakhstan, E Kazakhstan *49°15′N 81°16′E*
159 W11 **Zhangjiachuan** Gansu, N China *34°55′N 106°26′E*
160 L10 **Zhangjiajie** *var.* Dayong. Hunan, S China *29°10′N 110°22′E*
161 O2 **Zhangjiakou** *var.* Changkiakow, Zhang-chia-k'ou, *Eng.* Kalgan; *prev.* Wanchuan. Hebei, E China *40°48′N 114°51′E*
161 Q13 **Zhangping** Fujian, SE China *25°21′N 117°29′E*
161 Q13 **Zhangpu** *var.* Sui'an. Fujian, SE China *24°08′N 117°36′E*
163 U11 **Zhangwu** Liaoning, NE China *42°21′N 122°32′E*
159 S8 **Zhangye** *var.* Ganzhou. Gansu, N China *38°58′N 100°30′E*
161 Q13 **Zhangzhou** Fujian, SE China *24°31′N 117°40′E*
163 W6 **Zhan He** ≈ NE China
Zhänibek *see* Dzhanibek
160 L16 **Zhanjiang** *var.* Chanchiang, Chan-chiang, *Cant.* Tsamkong, *Fr.* Fort-Bayard. Guangdong, S China *21°10′N 110°20′E*
Zhansügirov *see* Dzhansugurov
163 V8 **Zhaodong** Heilongjiang, NE China *46°03′N 125°58′E*
Zhaoge *see* Qixian
160 H11 **Zhaojue** *var.* Xincheng. Sichuan, C China *28°03′N 102°50′E*
161 N14 **Zhaoqing** Guangdong, S China *23°08′N 112°26′E*
Zhaoren *see* Changwu
158 H5 **Zhaosu** *var.* Mongolküre. Xinjiang Uygur Zizhiqu, NW China *43°09′N 81°07′E*
160 H11 **Zhaotong** Yunnan, SW China *27°20′N 103°29′E*
163 V9 **Zhaoyuan** Heilongjiang, NE China *45°30′N 125°05′E*
163 V9 **Zhaozhou** Heilongjiang, NE China *45°42′N 125°11′E*
145 X13 **Zharbulak** Vostochnyy Kazakhstan, E Kazakhstan *46°04′N 82°05′E*
158 J15 **Zhari Namco** ◎ W China
144 I12 **Zharkamys** *Kaz.* Zharqamys. Aktyubinsk, W Kazakhstan *47°58′N 56°33′E*
145 W15 **Zharkent** *prev.* Panfilov. Taldykorgan, SE Kazakhstan *44°10′N 80°01′E*
124 H17 **Zharkovskiy** Tverskaya Oblast', W Russian Federation *55°51′N 32°19′E*
145 W11 **Zharma** Vostochnyy Kazakhstan, E Kazakhstan *48°48′N 80°55′E*
144 F14 **Zharmysh** Mangistau, SW Kazakhstan *44°12′N 52°27′E*
Zharqamys *see* Zharkamys
118 L13 **Zhary** Vitsyebskaya Voblasts', N Belarus *55°05′N 28°40′E*
Zharyk *see* Saken Seyfullin
Zhaslyk *see* Jasliq
158 J14 **Zhaxi Co** ◎ W China
Zhayylma *see* Zhailma
Zhdanov *see* Beyläqan
Zhdanov *see* Mariupol'
Zhe *see* Zhejiang
161 R10 **Zhejiang** *var.* Che-chiang, Chekiang, Zhe, Zhejiang Sheng. ◐ *province* SE China
Zhejiang Sheng *see* Zhejiang
145 S7 **Zhelezinka** Pavlodar, N Kazakhstan *53°35′N 75°16′E*
119 C14 **Zheleznodorozhnyy** *Ger.* Gerdauen. Kaliningradskaya Oblast', W Russian Federation *54°21′N 21°17′E*
Zheleznodorozhnyy *see* Yemva
122 K12 **Zheleznogorsk** Krasnoyarskiy, C Russian Federation *56°20′N 93°36′E*
126 J7 **Zheleznogorsk** Kurskaya Oblast', W Russian Federation *52°22′N 35°21′E*
127 N15 **Zheleznovodsk** Stavropol'skiy Kray, SW Russian Federation *44°12′N 43°01′E*
Zhëltyye Vody *see* Zhovti Vody
Zheludok *see* Zhaludok
Zhem *see* Emba
160 K7 **Zhenba** Shaanxi, C China *32°42′N 107°55′E*
160 I13 **Zhenfeng** *var.* Mingu. Guizhou, S China *25°27′N 105°38′E*
Zhengjiatun *see* Shuangliao
159 X10 **Zhengning** *var.* Shanhe. Gansu, N China *35°29′N 108°21′E*
Zhengxiangbai Qi *see* Qagan Nur
161 N6 **Zhengzhou** *var.* Ch'eng-chou, Chengchow; *prev.* Chenghsien. *province capital* Henan, C China *34°45′N 113°38′E*
161 R8 **Zhenjiang** *var.* Chenkiang. Jiangsu, E China *32°08′N 119°30′E*
163 U9 **Zhenlai** Jilin, NE China *45°52′N 123°11′E*
160 I11 **Zhenxiong** Yunnan, SW China *27°31′N 104°52′E*
160 K11 **Zhenyuan** *var.* Wuyang. Guizhou, S China *27°07′N 108°33′E*
161 R11 **Zherong** *var.* Shuangcheng. Fujian, SE China *27°16′N 119°54′E*
145 U15 **Zhetigen** *prev.* Nikolayevka. Almaty, SE Kazakhstan *43°39′N 77°10′E*
Zhetiqara *see* Zhitikara
144 F15 **Zhetybay** Mangistau, SW Kazakhstan *43°35′N 52°05′E*
145 P17 **Zhetysay** *var.* Dzhetysay. Yuzhnyy Kazakhstan *40°45′N 68°18′E*
160 M11 **Zhexi Shuiku** ⊠ C China
145 O12 **Zhezdy** Karaganda, C Kazakhstan *48°06′N 67°01′E*
145 O12 **Zhezkazgan** *Kaz.* Zhezqazghan; *prev.* Dzhezkazgan. Karaganda, C Kazakhstan *47°49′N 67°44′E*
Zhezqazghan *see* Zhezkazgan
Zhicheng *see* Yidu
Zhidachov *see* Zhydachiv
159 Q12 **Zhidoi** *var.* Gyaijêpozhanggê. Qinghai, C China *33°55′N 95°39′E*
122 M13 **Zhigalovo** Irkutskaya Oblast', S Russian Federation *54°47′N 105°00′E*
127 R6 **Zhigulevsk** Samarskaya Oblast', W Russian Federation *53°24′N 49°30′E*
118 D13 **Zhilino** *Ger.* Schillen. Kaliningradskaya Oblast', W Russian Federation *54°55′N 21°54′E*
Zhiloy, Ostrov *see* Çiloy Adası
127 O8 **Zhirnovsk** Volgogradskaya Oblast', SW Russian Federation *51°01′N 44°49′E*
160 M12 **Zhishan** *prev.* Yongzhou. Hunan, S China *26°12′N 111°36′E*
144 L8 **Zhitikara** *Kaz.* Zhetiqara; *prev.* Džetygara. Kostanay, NW Kazakhstan *52°14′N 61°12′E*
Zhitkovichi *see* Zhytkavichy
Zhitomir *see* Zhytomyr
Zhitomirskaya Oblast' *see* Zhytomyrs'ka Oblast'
126 J5 **Zhizdra** Kaluzhskaya Oblast', W Russian Federation *53°38′N 34°39′E*
119 N18 **Zhlobin** Homyel'skaya Voblasts', SE Belarus *52°53′N 30°01′E*
Zhmerinka *see* Zhmerynka
116 M7 **Zhmerynka** *Rus.* Zhmerinka. Vinnyts'ka Oblast', C Ukraine *49°00′N 28°02′E*
149 R9 **Zhob** *var.* Fort Sandeman. Baluchistān, SW Pakistan *31°21′N 69°31′E*
149 R8 **Zhob** ≈ C Pakistan
Zhodino *see* Zhodzina
119 L15 **Zhodzina** *Rus.* Zhodino. Minskaya Voblasts', C Belarus *54°06′N 28°21′E*
123 Q5 **Zhokhova, Ostrov** *island* Novosibirskiye Ostrova, NE Russian Federation
Zholkev/Zholkva *see* Zhovkva
Zhondor *see* Jondor
158 I15 **Zhongba** *var.* Tuoji. Xizang Zizhiqu, W China *29°37′N 84°11′E*
Zhongba *see* Jiangyou
160 F11 **Zhongdian** *var.* Larang. Yunnan, SW China *27°48′N 99°41′E*
Zhongduo *see* Youyang
Zhonghe *see* Xiushan
Zhonghua Renmin Gongheguo *see* China
159 V9 **Zhongning** Ningxia, N China *37°26′N 105°40′E*
Zhongping *see* Huize
161 N15 **Zhongshan** Guangdong, S China *22°30′N 113°20′E*
195 X7 **Zhongshan** *Chinese research station* Antarctica *69°23′S 76°34′E*
160 M6 **Zhongtiao Shan** ▲▲ C China
159 V9 **Zhongwei** Ningxia, N China *37°31′N 105°10′E*
160 K9 **Zhongxian** *var.* Zhongzhou. Chongqing Shi, C China *30°16′N 108°03′E*
161 N9 **Zhongxiang** Hubei, C China *31°12′N 112°35′E*
Zhongzhou *see* Zhongxian
Zhosaly *see* Dzhusaly
161 O7 **Zhoukou** *var.* Zhoukouzhen. Henan, C China *33°32′N 114°40′E*
Zhoukouzhen *see* Zhoukou
161 S9 **Zhoushan** Zhejiang, S China
Zhoushan Islands *see* Zhoushan Qundao
161 S9 **Zhoushan Qundao** *Eng.* Zhoushan Islands. *island group* SE China
116 I5 **Zhovkva** *Pol.* Żółkiew, *Rus.* Zholkev, Zholkva; *prev.* Nesterov. L'vivs'ka Oblast', NW Ukraine *50°04′N 24°E*
117 S7 **Zhovti Vody** *Rus.* Zhëltyye Vody. Dnipropetrovs'ka Oblast', E Ukraine *48°24′N 33°30′E*
117 Q10 **Zhovtneve** *Rus.* Zhovtnevoye. Mykolayivs'ka Oblast', S Ukraine *46°50′N 32°00′E*
Zhovtnevoye *see* Zhovtneve
114 K9 **Zhrebchevo, Yazovir** ⊠ C Bulgaria
163 V13 **Zhuanghe** Liaoning, NE China *39°42′N 123°00′E*
159 W11 **Zhuanglang** *var.* Shuiluo; *prev.* Shuilocheng. Gansu, C China *35°06′N 106°21′E*
145 P15 **Zhuantobe** *Kaz.* Zhūantöbe. Yuzhnyy Kazakhstan, S Kazakhstan *44°45′N 68°50′E*
161 Q5 **Zhucheng** Shandong, E China *35°58′N 119°24′E*
159 V12 **Zhugqu** Gansu, C China *33°51′N 104°14′E*
161 N15 **Zhuhai** Guangdong, S China *22°16′N 113°30′E*
Zhuizishan *see* Weichang
Zhuji *see* Shangqiu
126 I5 **Zhukovka** Bryanskaya Oblast', W Russian Federation *53°33′N 33°48′E*
161 N7 **Zhumadian** Henan, C China *32°58′N 114°03′E*
Zhuo Xian *see* Zhuozhou
161 O3 **Zhuozhou** *prev.* Zhuo Xian. Hebei, E China *39°22′N 115°40′E*
162 L14 **Zhuozi Shan** ▲ N China *39°28′N 106°58′E*
113 M17 **Zhur** *Serb.* Žur. S Kosovo *42°10′N 20°37′E*
Zhuravichi *see* Zhuravichy
119 O17 **Zhuravichy** *Rus.* Zhuravichi. Homyel'skaya Voblasts', SE Belarus *53°15′N 30°33′E*
145 Q8 **Zhuravlevka** Akmola, N Kazakhstan *52°00′N 69°59′E*
117 Q4 **Zhurivka** Kyyivs'ka Oblast', N Ukraine *50°28′N 31°48′E*
144 J11 **Zhuryn** Aktyubinsk, W Kazakhstan *49°13′N 57°36′E*
145 T15 **Zhusandala, Step'** *grassland* SE Kazakhstan
160 L8 **Zhushan** Hubei, C China *32°11′N 110°05′E*
Zhushan *see* Xuan'en
Zhuyang *see* Dazhu
161 N11 **Zhuzhou** Hunan, S China *27°52′N 112°52′E*
116 I6 **Zhydachiv** *Pol.* Żydaczów, *Rus.* Zhidachov. L'vivs'ka Oblast', NW Ukraine *49°20′N 24°08′E*
144 G9 **Zhympity** *Kaz.* Zhympīty; *prev.* Dzhambeyty. Zapadnyy, W Kazakhstan *50°16′N 52°34′E*
119 K19 **Zhytkavichy** *Rus.* Zhitkovichi. Homyel'skaya Voblasts', SE Belarus *52°14′N 27°52′E*
117 N4 **Zhytomyr** *Rus.* Zhitomir. Zhytomyrs'ka Oblast', NW Ukraine *50°17′N 28°40′E*
Zhytomyr *see* Zhytomyrs'ka Oblast'
116 M4 **Zhytomyrs'ka Oblast'** *var.* Zhytomyr, *Rus.* Zhitomirskaya Oblast'. ◐ *province* N Ukraine
153 U15 **Zia** ✈ (Dhaka) Dhaka, C Bangladesh
149 P10 **Ziārat** Baluchistān, SW Pakistan *30°23′N 67°43′E*
111 J20 **Žiar nad Hronom** *var.* Svätý Kríž nad Hronom, *Ger.* Heiligenkreuz, *Hung.* Garamszentkereszt. Banskobystrický Kraj, C Slovakia *48°36′N 18°52′E*
161 Q4 **Zibo** *var.* Zhangdian. Shandong, E China *36°51′N 118°01′E*
160 L4 **Zichang** *prev.* Wayaobu. Shaanxi, C China *37°08′N 109°40′E*
Zichenau *see* Ciechanów
111 G15 **Ziębice** *Ger.* Münsterberg in Schlesien. Dolnośląskie, SW Poland *50°37′N 17°01′E*
Ziebingen *see* Cybinka
Ziegenhais *see* Głuchołazy
110 E12 **Zielona Góra** *Ger.* Grünberg, Grünberg in Schlesien, Grüneberg. Lubuskie, W Poland *51°56′N 15°31′E*
99 F14 **Zierikzee** Zeeland, SW Netherlands *51°39′N 03°55′E*
160 I10 **Zigong** *var.* Tzekung. Sichuan, C China *29°20′N 104°48′E*
76 G12 **Ziguinchor** SW Senegal *12°34′N 16°20′W*
41 N16 **Zihuatanejo** Guerrero, S Mexico *17°39′N 101°33′W*
Ziketan *see* Xinghai
Zilah *see* Zalău
127 W7 **Zilair** Respublika Bashkortostan, W Russian Federation *52°12′N 57°15′E*
136 L12 **Zile** Tokat, N Turkey *40°18′N 35°52′E*
111 J18 **Žilina** *Ger.* Sillein, *Hung.* Zsolna. Zlínský Kraj, N Slovakia *49°13′N 18°44′E*
111 J19 **Žilinský Kraj** ◐ *region* N Slovakia
75 Q9 **Zillah** *var.* Zallah. C Libya *28°30′N 17°33′E*
Zillenmarkt *see* Zalău
109 N7 **Ziller** ≈ W Austria
Zillertal Alps *see* Zillertaler Alpen
109 N8 **Zillertaler Alpen** *Eng.* Zillertal Alps, *It.* Alpi Aurine. ▲▲ Austria/Italy
118 K10 **Zilupe** *Ger.* Rosenhof. Ludza, E Latvia *56°10′N 28°06′E*
41 O13 **Zimapán** Hidalgo, C Mexico *20°45′N 99°21′W*
83 I16 **Zimba** Southern, S Zambia *17°20′S 26°11′E*
83 J17 **Zimbabwe** *off.* Republic of Zimbabwe; *prev.* Rhodesia. ◆ *republic* S Africa
Zimbabwe, Republic of *see* Zimbabwe
116 H10 **Zimbor** *Hung.* Magyarzsombor. Sălaj, NW Romania *47°00′N 23°16′E*
Zimmerbude *see* Svetlyy
116 J15 **Zimnicea** Teleorman, S Romania *43°39′N 25°21′E*
114 L9 **Zimnitsa** Yambol, E Bulgaria *42°34′N 26°37′E*
127 N12 **Zimovniki** Rostovskaya Oblast', SW Russian Federation *47°07′N 42°29′E*
Zindajān *see* Zendeh Jan
77 V12 **Zinder** Zinder, S Niger *13°47′N 09°02′E*
77 W11 **Zinder** ◐ *department* S Niger
77 P12 **Ziniaré** C Burkina *12°35′N 01°18′W*
Zinjan *see* Zanjān
141 P16 **Zinjibār** SW Yemen *13°08′N 45°23′E*
117 T4 **Zin'kiv** *var.* Zen'kov. Poltavs'ka Oblast', NE Ukraine *50°11′N 34°22′E*
Zinov'yevsk *see* Kirovohrad
Zintenhof *see* Sindi
31 N10 **Zion** Illinois, N USA *42°27′N 87°49′W*
54 F10 **Zipaquirá** Cundinamarca, C Colombia *05°03′N 74°01′W*
Zipser Neudorf *see* Spišská Nová Ves
111 H23 **Zirc** Veszprém, W Hungary *47°16′N 17°52′E*
113 D14 **Žirje** *It.* Zuri. *island* S Croatia
Zirknitz *see* Cerknica
108 M7 **Zirl** Tirol, W Austria *47°17′N 11°16′E*
101 K20 **Zirndorf** Bayern, SE Germany *49°27′N 10°57′E*
153 Y11 **Ziro** Arunāchal Pradesh, NE India *27°35′N 93°50′E*
160 M11 **Zi Shui** ≈ C China
109 Y3 **Zistersdorf** Niederösterreich, NE Austria *48°32′N 16°45′E*
41 O14 **Zitácuaro** Michoacán, SW Mexico *19°28′N 100°21′W*
Zito *see* Lhorong
101 Q16 **Zittau** Sachsen, E Germany *50°53′N 14°48′E*
112 I12 **Živinice** Federacija Bosna I Hercegovina, E Bosnia and Herzegovina *44°26′N 18°39′E*
Ziwa Magharibi *see* Kagera
81 J14 **Ziway Hāyk'** ◎ C Ethiopia
161 N12 **Zixing** Hunan, S China *26°01′N 113°25′E*
127 W7 **Ziyanchurino** Orenburgskaya Oblast', W Russian Federation *51°36′N 56°58′E*
160 K8 **Ziyang** Shaanxi, C China *32°33′N 108°27′E*
111 I20 **Zlaté Moravce** *Hung.* Aranyosmarót. Nitriansky Kraj, SW Slovakia *48°24′N 18°20′E*
112 K13 **Zlatibor** ▲▲ W Serbia
114 L9 **Zlati Voyvoda** Sliven, C Bulgaria *42°36′N 26°13′E*
116 G11 **Zlatna** *Ger.* Kleinschlatten, *Hung.* Zalatna; *prev. Ger.* Goldmarkt. Alba, C Romania *46°08′N 23°11′E*
114 I8 **Zlatna Panega** Lovech, N Bulgaria *43°07′N 24°09′E*
114 N8 **Zlatni Pyasŭtsi** Dobrich, NE Bulgaria *43°19′N 28°03′E*
122 F11 **Zlatoust** Chelyabinskaya Oblast', C Russian Federation *55°12′N 59°33′E*
111 M19 **Zlatý Stôl** *Ger.* Goldener Tisch, *Hung.* Aranyosasztal. ▲ C Slovakia *48°45′N 20°39′E*
113 P18 **Zletovo** NE FYR Macedonia *42°00′N 22°14′E*
111 H18 **Zlín** *prev.* Gottwaldov. Zlínský Kraj, E Czech Republic *49°14′N 17°40′E*
111 H19 **Zlínský Kraj** ◐ *region* E Czech Republic
75 O7 **Zlīṭan** W Libya *32°28′N 14°34′E*
110 F9 **Złocieniec** *Ger.* Falkenburg in Pommern. Zachodnio-pomorskie, NW Poland *53°31′N 16°01′E*
110 J13 **Złoczew** Sieradz, S Poland *51°24′N 18°36′E*
Złoczów *see* Zolochev
111 F14 **Złotoryja** *Ger.* Goldberg. Dolnośląskie, W Poland *51°08′N 15°57′E*
110 G9 **Złotów** Wielkopolskie, C Poland *53°22′N 17°02′E*
110 G13 **Żmigród** *Ger.* Trachenberg. Dolnośląskie, SW Poland *51°31′N 16°55′E*
126 J6 **Zmiyevka** Orlovskaya Oblast', W Russian Federation *52°39′N 36°20′E*
117 V5 **Zmiyiv** Kharkivs'ka Oblast', E Ukraine *49°40′N 36°22′E*
Zna *see* Tsna
Znaim *see* Znojmo
126 M7 **Znamenka** Tambovskaya Oblast', W Russian Federation *52°24′N 42°28′E*
Znamenka *see* Znam"yanka
119 C14 **Znamens** Astrakhanskaya Oblast', W Russian Federation *54°37′N 21°13′E*
127 P10 **Znamensk** *Ger.* Wehlau. Kaliningradskaya Oblast', W Russian Federation *48°33′N 46°18′E*
117 R7 **Znam"yanka** *Rus.* Znamenka. Kirovohrads'ka Oblast', C Ukraine *48°41′N 32°40′E*
110 H10 **Żnin** Kujawsko-pomorskie, C Poland *52°50′N 17°41′E*
111 F19 **Znojmo** *Ger.* Znaim. Jihomoravský Kraj, SE Czech Republic *48°52′N 16°04′E*
79 N16 **Zobia** Orientale, N Dem. Rep. Congo *02°57′N 25°55′E*
83 N15 **Zóbuè** Tete, NW Mozambique *15°36′S 34°26′E*
98 G12 **Zoetermeer** Zuid-Holland, W Netherlands *52°04′N 04°30′E*
108 E7 **Zofingen** Aargau, N Switzerland *47°18′N 07°57′E*
159 R15 **Zogang** *var.* Wangda. Xizang Zizhiqu, W China *29°41′N 97°54′E*
106 E7 **Zogno** Lombardia, N Italy *45°49′N 09°42′E*
142 M10 **Zohreh, Rūd-e** ≈ SW Iran
160 H7 **Zoigê** *var.* Dagcagoin. Sichuan, C China *33°44′N 102°57′E*
Zółkiew *see* Zhovkva
108 D8 **Zollikofen** Bern, W Switzerland *47°00′N 07°24′E*
116 J5 **Zolochev** *Pol.* Złoczów, *Rus.* Zolochiv. L'vivs'ka Oblast', W Ukraine *49°48′N 24°51′E*
117 U4 **Zolochiv** *Rus.* Zolochev. Kharkivs'ka Oblast', E Ukraine *50°16′N 35°58′E*
Zolochiv *see* Zolochev
117 X7 **Zolote** *Rus.* Zolotoye. Luhans'ka Oblast', E Ukraine *48°42′N 38°33′E*
117 Q6 **Zolotonosha** Cherkas'ka Oblast', C Ukraine *49°39′N 32°05′E*
Zolotoye *see* Zolote
Zólyom *see* Zvolen
83 N15 **Zomba** Southern, S Malawi *15°22′S 35°23′E*
Zombor *see* Sombor
99 D17 **Zomergem** Oost-Vlaanderen, NW Belgium *51°07′N 03°31′E*
147 P11 **Zomin** *Rus.* Zaamin. Jizzax Viloyati, C Uzbekistan *39°56′N 68°16′E*
79 I15 **Zongo** Equateur, N Dem. Rep. Congo *04°18′N 18°42′E*
136 G10 **Zonguldak** Zonguldak, NW Turkey *41°26′N 31°47′E*
136 H10 **Zonguldak** ◐ *province* NW Turkey
99 K17 **Zonhoven** Limburg, NE Belgium *50°59′N 05°22′E*
142 J2 **Zonūz** Āżarbāyjān-e Khāvarī, NW Iran *38°32′N 45°54′E*
103 Y16 **Zonza** Corse, France, C Mediterranean Sea *41°49′N 09°13′E*
Zoppot *see* Sopot
Zorgho *see* Zorgo
77 Q13 **Zorgo** *var.* Zorgho. C Burkina *12°15′N 00°37′W*
104 K10 **Zorita** Extremadura, W Spain *39°18′N 05°42′W*
147 U14 **Zorkŭl** *Rus.* Ozero Zorkul'. ◎ SE Tajikistan
Zorkul', Ozero *see* Zorkŭl
56 A8 **Zorritos** Tumbes, N Peru *03°43′S 80°42′W*
111 J16 **Żory** *var.* Zory, *Ger.* Sohrau. Śląskie, S Poland *50°04′N 18°42′E*
76 K15 **Zorzor** N Liberia *07°46′N 09°28′W*
99 E18 **Zottegem** Oost-Vlaanderen, NW Belgium *50°52′N 03°49′E*
77 R15 **Zou** ≈ S Benin
78 H6 **Zouar** Borkou-Ennedi-Tibesti, N Chad *20°25′N 16°28′E*
76 J6 **Zouérat** *var.* Zouérate, Zouîrât. Tiris Zemmour, N Mauritania *22°44′N 12°29′W*
Zouérate *see* Zouérat
Zoug *see* Zug
Zouîrât *see* Zouérat
76 M16 **Zoukougbeu** C Ivory Coast *09°47′N 06°50′W*
98 M5 **Zoutkamp** Groningen, NE Netherlands *53°22′N 06°17′E*
99 J18 **Zoutleeuw** *Fr.* Leau. Vlaams Brabant, C Belgium *50°49′N 05°06′E*
112 L9 **Zrenjanin** *prev.* Petrovgrad, Veliki Bečkerek, *Ger.* Grossbetschkerek, *Hung.* Nagybecskerek. Vojvodina, N Serbia *45°23′N 20°24′E*
112 E10 **Zrinska Gora** ▲▲ C Croatia
Zsablya *see* Žabalj
101 N16 **Zschopau** ≈ E Germany
Zsebely *see* Jebel
Zsibó *see* Jibou
Zsilyvajdevulkán *see* Vulcan
Zsil/Zsily *see* Jiu
Zsolna *see* Žilina
Zsombolya *see* Jimbolia
Zsupanya *see* Županja
55 N7 **Zuata** Anzoátegui, NE Venezuela *08°24′N 65°13′W*
105 N14 **Zubia** Andalucía, S Spain *37°10′N 03°36′W*
127 N5 **Zubova Polyana** Respublika Mordoviya, W Russian Federation *54°05′N 42°50′E*
65 P16 **Zubov Seamount** *undersea feature* E Atlantic Ocean *20°45′S 08°45′E*
124 I16 **Zubtsov** Tverskaya Oblast', W Russian Federation *56°10′N 34°34′E*
108 M8 **Zuckerhütl** ▲ SW Austria *46°57′N 11°07′E*
Zueila *see* Zawīlah
76 M16 **Zuénoula** C Ivory Coast *07°26′N 06°03′W*
105 S5 **Zuera** Aragón, NE Spain *41°52′N 00°47′W*
141 V13 **Ẓufār** *Eng.* Dhofar. *physical region* SW Oman
108 G8 **Zug** *Fr.* Zoug. Zug, C Switzerland *47°11′N 08°31′E*
108 G8 **Zug** *Fr.* Zoug. ◐ *canton* C Switzerland
137 R9 **Zugdidi** W Georgia *42°30′N 41°52′E*
108 G8 **Zuger See** ◎ NW Switzerland
101 K25 **Zugspitze** ▲ S Germany *47°25′N 10°58′E*
99 E15 **Zuid-Beveland** *var.* South Beveland. *island* SW Netherlands
98 K10 **Zuidelijk-Flevoland** *polder* C Netherlands
Zuider Zee *see* IJsselmeer
98 G12 **Zuid-Holland** *Eng.* South Holland. ◐ *province* W Netherlands
98 N5 **Zuidhorn** Groningen, NE Netherlands *53°15′N 06°25′E*
98 O6 **Zuidlaardermeer** ◎ NE Netherlands
98 O6 **Zuidlaren** Drenthe, . NE Netherlands *53°06′N 06°41′E*
99 K14 **Zuid-Willemsvaart Kanaal** *canal* S Netherlands
98 N8 **Zuidwolde** Drenthe, NE Netherlands *52°40′N 06°25′E*
Zuitai/Zuitaizi *see* Kangxian
105 O14 **Zújar** Andalucía, S Spain *37°33′N 02°52′W*
104 L11 **Zújar** ≈ W Spain
104 L11 **Zújar, Embalse del** ⊠ W Spain
80 J9 **Zula** E Eritrea *15°19′N 39°40′E*
54 G6 **Zulia** *off.* Estado Zulia. ◐ *state* NW Venezuela
Zulia, Estado *see* Zulia
Zullapara *see* Sinchaingbyin
Züllichau *see* Sulechów
105 P3 **Zumárraga** País Vasco, N Spain *43°05′N 02°19′W*
112 D8 **Žumberačko Gorje** *var.* Gorjanči, Uskocke Planine, Žumberak, *Ger.* Uskokengebirge; *prev.* Sichelburger Gerbirge. ▲ Croatia/Slovenia *see also* Gorjanci
Žumberak *see* Gorjanci/Žumberačko Gorje
194 K7 **Zumberge Coast** *coastal feature* Antarctica
Zumbo *see* Vila do Zumbo
29 W10 **Zumbro Falls** Minnesota, N USA *44°15′N 92°25′W*
29 W10 **Zumbro River** ≈ Minnesota, N USA
29 W10 **Zumbrota** Minnesota, N USA *44°18′N 92°37′W*
99 H15 **Zundert** Noord-Brabant, S Netherlands *51°28′N 04°40′E*
Zungaria *see* Dzungaria
77 U14 **Zungeru** Niger, C Nigeria *09°49′N 06°10′E*
161 P2 **Zunhua** Hebei, E China *40°10′N 117°58′E*
37 O11 **Zuni** New Mexico, SW USA *35°03′N 108°52′W*
37 P11 **Zuni Mountains** ▲▲ New Mexico, SW USA
160 J11 **Zunyi** Guizhou, S China *27°40′N 106°56′E*
160 J15 **Zuo Jiang** ≈ China/Vietnam
108 J9 **Zuoz** Graubünden, SE Switzerland *46°37′N 09°58′E*
112 I10 **Županja** *Hung.* Zsupanya. Vukovar-Srijem, E Croatia *45°03′N 18°42′E*
Žur *see* Zhur
127 T2 **Zura** Udmurtskaya Respublika, NW Russian Federation *57°36′N 53°19′E*
139 V8 **Zurbāṭīyah** Wāsiṭ, E Iraq *33°13′N 46°07′E*
Zuri *see* Žirje
108 F7 **Zürich** *Eng./Fr.* Zurich, *It.* Zurigo. Zürich, N Switzerland *47°23′N 08°33′E*
108 G6 **Zürich** *Eng./Fr.* Zurich. ◐ *canton* N Switzerland
Zurich, Lake *see* Zürichsee
108 G7 **Zürichsee** *Eng.* Lake Zurich. ◎ NE Switzerland
Zurigo *see* Zürich
149 V1 **Zŭrkŭl** *Pash.* Sarī Qūl, *Rus.* Ozero Zurkul'. ◎ Afghanistan/Tajikistan *see also* Sarī Qūl
Zŭrkŭl *see* Sarī Qūl
Zurkul', Ozero *see* Sarī Qūl/Zŭrkŭl
110 K10 **Żuromin** Mazowieckie, C Poland *53°00′N 19°54′E*
108 J8 **Zürs** Vorarlberg, W Austria *47°11′N 10°11′E*
77 T13 **Zuru** Kebbi, W Nigeria *11°28′N 05°13′E*
108 F6 **Zurzach** Aargau, N Switzerland *47°33′N 08°21′E*
101 J22 **Zusam** ≈ S Germany
98 M11 **Zutphen** Gelderland, E Netherlands *52°09′N 06°12′E*
75 N7 **Zuwārah** NW Libya *32°56′N 12°06′E*
Zuwaylah *see* Zawīlah
125 R14 **Zuyevka** Kirovskaya Oblast', NW Russian Federation *58°24′N 51°08′E*
161 N10 **Zuzhou** Hunan, S China *27°52′N 113°00′E*
Zvenigorodka *see* Zvenyhorodka
117 P6 **Zvenyhorodka** *Rus.* Zvenigorodka. Cherkas'ka Oblast', C Ukraine *49°05′N 30°58′E*
123 N12 **Zvezdnyy** Irkutskaya Oblast', C Russian Federation *56°43′N 106°22′E*
125 U14 **Zvëzdnyy** Permskaya Oblast', NW Russian Federation *57°45′N 56°20′E*
83 K18 **Zvishavane** *prev.* Shabani. Matabeleland South, S Zimbabwe *20°20′S 30°02′E*
111 J20 **Zvolen** *Ger.* Altsohl, *Hung.* Zólyom. Banskobystrický Kraj, C Slovakia *48°35′N 19°06′E*
112 J12 **Zvornik** E Bosnia and Herzegovina *44°24′N 19°07′E*
98 M5 **Zwaagwesteinde** *Fris.* De Westerein. Friesland, N Netherlands *53°16′N 06°08′E*
98 H10 **Zwanenburg** Noord-Holland, C Netherlands *52°22′N 04°44′E*
98 L8 **Zwarte Meer** ◎ N Netherlands
98 M9 **Zwarte Water** ≈ N Netherlands
98 M8 **Zwartsluis** Overijssel, E Netherlands *52°39′N 06°04′E*
76 L17 **Zwedru** *var.* Tchien. E Liberia *06°04′N 08°07′W*
98 O8 **Zweeloo** Drenthe, NE Netherlands *52°48′N 06°45′E*
101 E20 **Zweibrücken** *Fr.* Deux-Ponts, *Lat.* Bipontium. Rheinland-Pfalz, SW Germany *49°15′N 07°22′E*
108 D9 **Zweisimmen** Fribourg, W Switzerland *46°33′N 07°22′E*
101 M15 **Zwenkau** Sachsen, E Germany *51°11′N 12°19′E*
109 V3 **Zwettl** Wien, NE Austria *48°28′N 14°17′E*
109 T3 **Zwettl an der Rodl** Oberösterreich, N Austria *48°28′N 14°17′E*
99 D18 **Zwevegem** West-Vlaanderen, W Belgium *50°48′N 03°20′E*
101 M17 **Zwickau** Sachsen, E Germany *50°43′N 12°31′E*
101 N16 **Zwickauer Mulde** ≈ E Germany
101 O21 **Zwiesel** Bayern, SE Germany *49°02′N 13°14′E*
98 H13 **Zwijndrecht** Zuid-Holland, SW Netherlands *51°49′N 04°39′E*
Zwischenwässern *see* Medvode
Zwittau *see* Svitavy
110 N13 **Zwoleń** Mazowieckie, SE Poland *51°21′N 21°37′E*
98 M9 **Zwolle** Overijssel, E Netherlands *52°31′N 06°06′E*
22 G6 **Zwolle** Louisiana, S USA *31°37′N 93°38′W*
110 K12 **Żychlin** Łódzkie, C Poland *52°15′N 19°38′E*
Żydaczów *see* Zhydachiv
Zyembin *see* Zembin
Zyôetu *see* Jōetsu
110 L12 **Żyrardów** Mazowieckie, C Poland *52°02′N 20°28′E*
123 S8 **Zyryanka** Respublika Sakha (Yakutiya), NE Russian Federation *65°45′N 150°43′E*
145 Y9 **Zyryanovsk** Vostochnyy Kazakhstan, E Kazakhstan *49°45′N 84°16′E*

◆ Country
● Country Capital
◇ Dependent Territory
○ Dependent Territory Capital
◐ Administrative Regions
✈ International Airport
▲ Mountain
▲▲ Mountain Range
Volcano
≈ River
◎ Lake
⊠ Reservoir

349

Picture Credits

DORLING KINDERSLEY *would like to express their thanks to the following individuals, companies, and institutions for their help in preparing this atlas.*

Earth Resource Mapping Ltd., Egham, Surrey
Brian Groombridge, World Conservation Monitoring Centre, Cambridge
The British Library, London
British Library of Political and Economic Science, London
The British Museum, London
The City Business Library, London
King's College, London
National Meteorological Library and Archive, Bracknell
The Printed Word, London
The Royal Geographical Society, London
University of London Library
Paul Beardmore
Philip Boyes
Hayley Crockford
Alistair Dougal
Reg Grant
Louise Keane
Zoe Livesley
Laura Porter
Jeff Eidenshink
Chris Hornby
Rachelle Smith
Ray Pinchard
Robert Meisner
Fiona Strawbridge

Every effort has been made to trace the copyright holders and we apologize in advance for any unintentional omissions. We would be pleased to insert the appropriate acknowledgment in any subsequent edition of this publication.

Adams Picture Library: 86CLA; **G Andrews:** 186CR; **Ardea London Ltd:** K Ghana 150C; M Iljima 132TC; R Waller 148TR; Art Directors **Aspect Picture Library:** P Carmichael 160TR; 131CR(below); G Tompkinson 190TRB; **Axiom:** C Bradley 148CA, 158CA; J Holmes xivCRA, xxivBCR, xxviiCRB, 150TCR, 165C(below), 166TL, J Morris 75TL, 77CRB, J Spaull 134BL; **Bridgeman Art Library, London / New York:** Collection of the Earl of Pembroke, Wilton House xxBC; **The J. Allan Cash Photolibrary:** xlBR, xliiCLA, xlivCL, 10BC, 60CL, 69CLB, 70CL, 72CLB, 75BR, 76BC, 87BL, 109BR, 138BCL, 141TL, 154CR, 178BR, 181TR; **Bruce Coleman Ltd:** 86BC, 98CL, 100TC; S Alden 192BC(below); Atlantide xxviTCR, 138BR; E Bjurstrom 141BR; S Bond 96CRB; T Buchholz xvCL, 92TR, 123TCL; J Burton xxiiiC; J Cancalosi 181TRB; B J Coates xxvBL, 192CL; B Coleman 63TL; B & C Colhoun 2TR, 36CB; A Compost xxiiiCBR; Dr S Coyne 45TL; G Cubitt xviTCL, 169BR, 178TR, 184TR; P Davey xxviiCLB, 121TL(below); N Devore 189CBL; S J Doylee xxiiCRR; H Flygare xviiCRA; M P L Fogden 17C(above) ; Jeff Foott Productions xxiiiCRB, 11CRA; M Freeman 91BRA; P van Gaalen 86TR; G Gualco 140C; B Henderson 194CR; Dr C Henneghien 69C; HPH Photography, H Van den Berg 69CR; C Hughes 69BCL; C James xxxixTC; J Johnson 39CR, 197TR; J Jurka 91CA; S C Kaufman 28C; S J Krasemann 33TR; H Lange 10TRB, 68CA; C Lockwood 32BC; L C Marigo xxiiBC, xxviiCLA, 49CRA, 59BR; M McCoy 187TR; D Meredith 3CR; J Murray xvCR, 179BR; Orion Press 165CR(above); Orion Services & Trading Co. Inc. 164CR; C Ott 17BL; Dr E Pott 9TR, 40CL, 87C, 93TL, 194CLB; F Prenzel 186BC, 193BC; M Read 42BR, 43CRB; H Reinhard xxiiCR, xxviiTR, 194BR; L Lee Rue III 151BCL; J Shaw xixTL; K N Swenson 194BC; P Terry 115CR; N Tomalin 54BCL; P Ward 78TC; S Widstrand 57TR; K Wothe 91C, 173TCL; J T Wright 127BR; **Colorific:** Black Star / L Mulvehil 156CL; Black Star / R Rogers 57BR; Black Star / J Rupp 161BCR; Camera Tres / C. Meyer 59BRA; R Caputo / Matrix 78CL; J. Hill 117CLB; M Koene 55TR; G Satterley xliiCLAR; M Yamashita 156BL, 167CR(above); **Comstock:** 108CRB; Corbis UK Ltd: 170TR, 170BL; **D Cousens:** 147 CRA; **Corbis:** Bob Daemmrich 6BL; **Sue Cunningham Photographic:** 51CR; S Alden 192BC(below) **James Davis Travel Photography:** xxxviTCB, xxxviTR, xxxviCL, 13CA, 19BC, 49TLB, 56BCR, 57CLA, 61BCL, 93BC, 94TC, 102TR, 120CB, 158BC, 179CRA, 191BR; **Dorling Kindersley:** Paul Harris xxiiTR; Nigel Hicks xxiiBM; Jamie Marshall 181TR; Bharath Ramamrutham 155BR; Colin Sinclair 133BMR; George Dunnet: 124CA; **Environmental Picture Library:** Chris Westwood 126C; **Eye Ubiquitous:** xlCA; L. Fordyce 12CLA; L Johnstone 6CRA, 28BLA, 30CB; S. Miller xxiCA; M Southern 73BLA; **Chris Fairclough Colour Library:** xliBR; **Ffotograff:** N. Tapsell 158CL; **FLPA -Images of nature:** 123TR; **Geoscience Features:** xviBCR, xviBR, 102CL, 108BC, 122BR; Solar Film 64TC; **Getty Images:** Kim Steele 161BCL; **gettyone stone**: 131BC, 133BR, 164CR(above); G Johnson 130BL; R Passmore 120TR; D Austen 187CL; G Allison 186CL; L Ulrich 17TL; M Vines 17BL; R Wells 193BL; **Robert Harding Picture Library:** xviiTC, xxivCR, xxxC, xxxvTC, 2TLB, 3CA, 15CRB, 15CR, 37BC, 38CRA, 50BL, 95BR, 99CR, 114CR, 122BL, 131CLA, 142CB, 143TL, 147TR, 168TR, 168CA, 166BR; P G. Adam 13TCB; D Atchison-Jones 70BLA; J Bayne 72BCL; B Schuster 80CR; C Bowman 50BR, 53CA, 62CL, 70CRL; C Campbell xxiBC; G Corrigan 159CRB, 161CRB; P Craven xxxvBL; R Cundy 69BR; Delu 79BC; A Durand 111BR; Financial Times 142BR; R Frerck 51BL; T Gervis 3BCL, 7CR; I Griffiths xxxCL, 77TL; T Hall 166CRA; D Harney 142CA; S Harris xliiiBCL; G Hellier xvCRB, 135BL; F Jackson 137BCR; Jacobs xxxviiTL; P Koch 139TR; F Joseph Land 122TR; Y Marcoux 9BR; S Massif xvBC; A Mills 88CLB; L Murray 114TR; R Rainford xlivBL; G Renner 74CB, 194C; C Rennie 48CL, 116BR; R Richardson 118CL; P Van Riel 48BR; E Rooney 124TR; Sassoon xxivCL, 148CLB; Jochen Schlenker 193CL; P Scholey 176TR; M Short 137TL; E Simanor xxviiCR; V Southwell 139CR; J Strachan 42TR, 111BL, 132BCR; C Tokeley 131CLA; A C Waltham 161C; T Waltham xviiBL, xxiiCLLL, 138CRB; Westlight 37CR; N Wheeler 139BL; A Williams xxxviiiBR, xlTR; A Woolfitt 95BRA; Paul Harris: 168TC; **Hutchison Library:** 131CR (above) 6BL; P. Collomb 137CR; C. Dodwell 130TR; S Errington 70BCL; P. Hellyer 142BC; J. Horner xxxiTC; R. Ian Lloyd 134CRA; N. Durrell McKenna xxviBCR; J. Nowell 135CLB, 143TC; A Zvoznikov xxiiCL; **Image Bank:** 87BR; J Banagan 190BCA; A Becker xxivBCL; M Khansa 121CR, M Isy-Schwart 193CR(above), 191CL; Khansa K Forest 163TR; Lomeo xxivTCR; T Madison 170TL(below); C Molyneux xxiiCRRR; C Navajas xviiiTR; Ocean Images Inc. 192CLB; J van Os xviiTCR; S Proehl 6CL; T Rakke xixTC, 64CL; M Reitz 196CA; M Romanelli 166CL(below); G A Rossi 151BCR, 176BLA; B Roussel 109TL; S Satushek xviiBCR; Stock Photos / J M Spielman xxivTRL; **Images Colour Library:** xxiiCLL, xxxixTR, xliCR, xliiiBL, 3BR, 19BR, 37TL, 44TL, 62TC, 91BR, 102CLB, 103CR, 150CL, 180CA; 164BC, 165TL; **Impact Photos:** J & G Andrews 186BL; C. Bluntzer 156BR; Cosmos / G. Buthaud 65BC; S Franklin 126BL; A. le Garsmeur 131C; A Indge xxviiTC; C Jones xxxiCB, 70BL; V. Nemirousky 137BR; J Nicholl 76TCR; C. Penn 187C(below); G Sweeney xviiBR, 196CB, 196TR, J & G Andrews 186TR; **JVZ Picture Library:** T Nilson 135TC; **Frank Lane Picture Agency:** xxiTCR, xxiiiBL, 93TR; A Christiansen 58CRA; J Holmes xivBL; S. McCutcheon 3C; Silvestris 173TCR; D Smith xxiiBCL; W Wisniewsli 195BR; **Leeds Castle Foundation:** xxxviiBC; **Magnum:** Abbas 83CR, 136CA; S Franklin 134CRB; D Hurn 4BCL; P. Jones-Griffiths 191BL; H Kubota xviBCL, 156CLB; F Maver xviBL; S McCurry 73CL, 133BCR; G. Rodger 74TR; C Steele Perkins 72BL; **Mountain Camera / John Cleare:** 153TR; C Monteath 153CR; **Nature Photographers:** E.A. Janes 112CL; **Natural Science Photos:** M Andera 110C; **Network Photographers Ltd.:** C Sappa / Rapho 119BL; **N.H.P.A.:** N. J. Dennis xxiiiCL; D Heuchlin xxiiiCLA; S Krasemann 15BL, 25BR, 38TC; K Schafer 49CB; R Tidman 160CLB; D Tomlinson 145CR; M Wendler 48TR; **Nottingham Trent University:** T Waltham xivCL, xvBR; **Novosti:** 144BLA; **Oxford Scientific Films:** D Allan xxiiTR; H R Bardarson xviiiBC; D Bown xxiiiCBLL; M Brown 140BL; M Colbeck 147CAR; W Faidley 3TL; L Gould xxiiiTRB; D Guravich xxiiiTR; P Hammerschmidy / Okapia 87CLA; M Hill 57TL, 195TR; C Menteath ; J Netherton 2CRB; S Osolinski 82CA; R Packwood 72CA; M Pitts 179TC; N Rosing xxiiiCBL, 9TR, 197BR; D Simonson 57C; Survival Anglia / C Catton 137TR; R Toms xxiiiBR; K Wothe xxiBL, xviiCLA; **Panos Pictures:** B Aris 133C; P Barker xxivBR; T Bolstao 153BR; N Cooper 82CB, 153TC; J-L Dugast 166C(below), 167BR; J Hartley 73CA, 90CL; J Holmes 149BC; J Morris 76CLB; M Rose 146TR; D Sansoni 155CL; C Stowers 163TL; **Edward Parker:** 49TL, 49CLB; **Pictor International:** xivBR, xvBRA, xixTCL, xxCL, 3CLA, 17BR, 20TR, 20CRB, 23BCA, 23CL, 26CB, 27BC, 30CA, 33TRB, 34BC, 34BR, 34CR, 38CB, 38CL, 43CL, 63BR, 65TC, 82CL, 83CLB, 99BR, 107CLA, 166TR, 171CL(above), 180CLB, 185TL; **Pictures Colour Library:** xxiBCL, xxiiBR, xxviBCL, 6BR, 15TR, 8TR, 16CL(above), 19TL, 20BL, 24C, 24CLA, 27TR, 32TRB, 36BC, 41CA, 43CRA, 68BL, 90TCB, 94BL, 99BL, 106CA, 107CLB, 107CR, 107BR, 117BL, 164BC, 192BL, K Forest 165TL(below); **Planet Earth Pictures:** 193CR(below); D Barrett 148CB, 184CA; R Coomber 16BL; G Douwma 172BR; E Edmonds 173BR; J Lythgoe 196BL; A Mounter 172CR; M Potts 6CA; P Scoones xxTR; J Walencik 110TR; J Waters 53BCL; **Popperfoto:** Reuters / J Drake xxxiiCLA; **Rex Features:** 165CR; Antelope xxxiiCLB; M Friedel xxiCR; I McIlgorm xxxCBR; J Shelley xxxCR; Sipa Press xxxCR; Sipa Press / Alix xxxCBL; Sipa Press / Chamussy 176BL; **Robert Harding Picture Library:** C. Tokeley 131TL; J Strachan 132BL; Franz Joseph Land 122TR; Franz Joseph Land 364/7088 123BL, 169C(above), 170C(above), 168CL, Tony Waltham 186CR(below), Y Marcoux 9BR; **Russia & Republics Photolibrary:** M Wadlow 118CR, 119CL, 124BC, 124CL, 125TL, 125BR, 126TCR; **Science Photo Library:** Earth Satellite Corporation xixTRB, xxxiCR, 49BCL; F Gohier xiCR; J Heseltine xviTCB; K Kent xvBLA; P Menzell xvBL; N.A.S.A. xBC; D Parker xivBC; University of Cambridge Collection Air Pictures 87CLB; RJ Wainscoat / P Arnold, Inc. xiBC; D Weintraub xiBL; **South American Pictures:** 57BL, 62TR; R Francis 52BL; Guyana Space Centre 50TR; T Morrison 49CRB, 49BL, 50CR, 52TR, 54TR, 60BL, 61C; **Southampton Oceanography:** xviiiBL; **Sovofoto / Eastfoto:** xxxiiCBR; **Spectrum Colour Library:** 50BC, 160BC; J King 145BR; **Frank Spooner Pictures:** Gamma-Liason/Vogel 131CL(above); 26CRB; E. Baitel xxxiiBC; Bernstein xxxiCL; Contrast 112CR; Diard / Photo News 113CL; Liaison / C. Hires xxxiiTCB; Liaison / Nickelsberg xxxiiTR; Marleen 113TL; Novosti 116CA; P. Piel xxxCA; N Quidu 135CL; H Stucke 188CLB, 190CA; Torrengo / Figaro 78BR; A Zamur 113BL; **Still Pictures:** C Caldicott 77TC; A Crump 189CL; M & C Denis-Huot xxiiBL, 78CR, 81BL; M Edwards xxiCRL, 53BL, 64CR, 69BLA, 155BR; J Frebet 53CLB; H Giradet 53TC; E Parker 52CL; M Gunther 121BC; **Tony Stone Images:** xxviTR, 4CA, 7BL, 7CL, 13CRB, 39BR, 58C, 97BC, 101BR, 106TR, 109CL, 109CRB, 164CLB, 165C,180CB, 181BR, 188BC, 192TR; G Allison 18TR, 31CRB, 187CRB; D Armand 14TCB; D Austen 180TR, 186CL, 187CL; J Beatty 74CL; O Benn xxviBR; K Biggs xxiTL; R Bradbury 44BR; R A Butcher xxviTL; J Callahan xxviiCRA; P Chesley 185BCL, 188C; W Clay 30BL, 31CRA; J Cornish 96BL, 107TL; C Condina 41CB; T Craddock xxivTR; P Degginger 36CLB; Demetrio 5BR; N DeVore xxivBC; A Diesendruck 60BR; S Egan 87CRA, 96BR; R Elliot xxiiBCR; S Elmore 19C; J Garrett 73CR; S Grandadam 14BR; R Grosskopf 28BL; D Hanson 104BC; C Harvey 69TL; G Hellier 110BL, 165CR; S Huber 103CRB; D Hughs xxxiBR; A Husmo 91TR; G Irvine 31BC; J Jangoux 58CL; D Johnston xviiTR; A Kehr 113C; R Koskas xviTR; J Lamb 96CRA; J Lawrence 75CRA; L Lefkowitz 7CA; M Lewis 45CLA; S Mayman 55BR; Murray & Associates 45CR; G Norways 104CA; N Parfitt xxviiCL, 68TCR, 81TL; R Passmore 121TR; N Press xviBCA; E Pritchard 88CA, 90CLR; T Raymond 21BL, 29TR; L Resnick 74BR; M Rogers 80BR; A Sacks 28TCB; C Saule 90CR; S Schulhof xxivTC; P Seaward 34CL; M Segal 32BL; V Shenai 152CL; R Sherman 26CL; H Sitton 136CR; R Smith xxvBLA, 56C; S Studd 108CLA; H Strand 49BR, 63TR; P Tweedie 177CR; L Ulrich 17BL; M Vines 17TC; A B Wadham 60CR; J Warden 63CLB; R Wells 23CRA, 193BL; G Yeowell 34BL; **Telegraph Colour Library:** 61CRB, 61TCR, 157TL; R Antrobus xxxixBR; J Sims 26BR; **Topham Picturepoint:** xxxiCBL, 162BR, 168TR, 168BC; **Travel Ink:** A Cowin 88TR; **Trip:** 140BR, 144CA, 155CRA; B Ashe 159TR; D Cole 190BCL, 190CR; D Davis 89BL; I Deineko xxxiTR; J Dennis 22BL; Dinodia 154CL; Eye Ubiquitous / L Fordyce 2CLB; A Gasson 149CR; W Jacobs 43TL, 54BL, 177BC, 178CLA, 185BCR, 186BL; P Kingsbury 112C; K Knight 177BR; V Kolpakov 147BL; T Noorits 87TL, 119BR, 146CL; R Power 41TR; N Ray 166BL, 168TC; C Rennie 116CLB; V Sidoropolev 145TR; E Smith 183BC, 183TL; **Woodfin Camp & Associates:** 92BLR; **World Pictures:** xvCRA, xviiCRA, 9CRB, 22CL, 23BC, 24BL, 35BL, 40TR, 51TR, 71BR, 80TCR, 82TR, 83BL, 86BCR, 96TC, 98BL, 100CR, 101CR, 103BC, 105TC, 157BL, 161BCL, 162CLB, 172CLB, 172BC, 179BL, 182CB, 183C, 184CL, 185CR; 121BR, 121TT; **Zefa Picture Library:** xviBLR, xviiBCL, xviiiCL, 3CL, 8BC, 8CT, 9CR, 13BC, 14TC, 16TR, 21TL, 22CRB, 25BL, 32TCR, 36BCR, 59BCL, 65TCL, 69CLA, 79TL, 81BR, 87CRB, 92C, 98C, 99TL, 100BL, 107TR, 118CRB, 120BL; 122C(below), 124CLA, 164BR, 183TR; Anatol 113BR; Barone 114BL; Brandenburg 5C; A J Brown 44TR; H J Clauss 55CLB; Damm 71BC; Evert 92BL; W Felger 3BL; J Fields 189CRA; R Frerck 4BL; G Heil 56BR; K Heibig 115BR; Heilman 28BC; Hunter 8C; Kitchen 10TR, 8CL, 8BL, 9TR; Dr H Kramarz 7BLA, 123CR(below); Mehlio 155BL; J F Raga 24TR; Rossenbach 105BR; Streichan 89TL; T Stewart 13TR, 19CR; Sunak 54BR, 162TR; D H Teuffen 95TL; B Zaunders 40BC. **Additional Photography:** Geoff Dann; Rob Reichenfeld; H Taylor; Jerry Young.

Map Credits

World Population Density map, page xxiv:

Source:LandScanTM Global Population Database. Oak Ridge, TN; Oak Ridge National Laboratory. Available at http://www.ornl.gov/landscan/.

NORTH AMERICA

CANADA
Pages 8–15

UNITED STATES OF AMERICA
Pages 16–39

MEXICO
Pages 40–41

BELIZE
Pages 42–43

COSTA RICA
Pages 42–43

EL SALVADOR
Pages 42–43

GUATEMALA
Pages 42–43

HONDURAS
Pages 42–43

SOUTH AMERIC

GRENADA
Pages 44–45

HAITI
Pages 44–45

JAMAICA
Pages 44–45

ST KITTS & NEVIS
Pages 44–45

ST LUCIA
Pages 44–45

ST VINCENT & THE GRENADINES
Pages 44–45

TRINIDAD & TOBAGO
Pages 44–45

COLOMBIA
Pages 54–55

AFRICA

URUGUAY
Pages 60–61

CHILE
Pages 62–63

PARAGUAY
Pages 62–63

ALGERIA
Pages 74–75

EGYPT
Pages 74–75

LIBYA
Pages 74–75

MOROCCO
Pages 74–75

TUNISIA
Pages 74–75

LIBERIA
Pages 76–77

MALI
Pages 76–77

MAURITANIA
Pages 76–77

NIGER
Pages 76–77

NIGERIA
Pages 76–77

SENEGAL
Pages 76–77

SIERRA LEONE
Pages 76–77

TOGO
Pages 76–77

BURUNDI
Pages 80–81

DJIBOUTI
Pages 80–81

ERITREA
Pages 80–81

ETHIOPIA
Pages 80–81

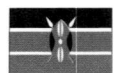
KENYA
Pages 80–81

RWANDA
Pages 80–81

SOMALIA
Pages 80–81

SUDAN
Pages 80–81

EUROPE

SOUTH AFRICA
Pages 82–83

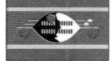
SWAZILAND
Pages 82–83

ZAMBIA
Pages 82–83

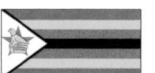
ZIMBABWE
Pages 82–83

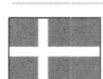
DENMARK
Pages 92–93

FINLAND
Pages 92–93

ICELAND
Pages 92–93

NORWAY
Pages 92–95

MONACO
Pages 102–103

ANDORRA
Pages 104–105

PORTUGAL
Pages 104–105

SPAIN
Pages 104–105

ITALY
Pages 106–107

SAN MARINO
Pages 106–107

VATICAN CITY
Pages 106–107

AUSTRIA
Pages 108–109

LIECHTENSTEIN
Pages 108–109

CROATIA
Pages 112–113

KOSOVO (disputed)
Pages 112–113

MACEDONIA
Pages 112–113

MONTENEGRO
Pages 112–113

SERBIA
Pages 112–113

BULGARIA
Pages 114–115

GREECE
Pages 114–115

MOLDOVA
Pages 116–117

ASIA

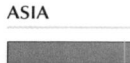
ARMENIA
Pages 136–137

AZERBAIJAN
Pages 136–137

GEORGIA
Pages 136–137

TURKEY
Pages 136–137/114–115

IRAQ
Pages 138–139

ISRAEL
Pages 138–139

JORDAN
Pages 138–139

LEBANON
Pages 138–139

IRAN
Pages 142–143

KAZAKHSTAN
Pages 144–145

KYRGYZSTAN
Pages 146–147

TAJIKISTAN
Pages 146–147

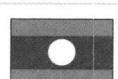
TURKMENISTAN
Pages 146–147

UZBEKISTAN
Pages 146–147

AFGHANISTAN
Pages 148–149

PAKISTAN
Pages 148–151

TAIWAN
Pages 160–161

JAPAN
Pages 164–165

BURMA
Pages 166–167

CAMBODIA
Pages 166–167

LAOS
Pages 166–167

PHILIPPINES
Pages 166–167

THAILAND
Pages 166–167

VIETNAM
Pages 166–167

AUSTRALASIA & OCEANIA

MAURITIUS
Pages 172–173

SEYCHELLES
Pages 172–173

AUSTRALIA
Pages 180–183

NEW ZEALAND
Pages 184–185

PAPUA NEW GUINEA
Pages 186–187

FIJI
Pages 186–187

SOLOMON ISLANDS
Pages 186–187

VANUATU
Pages 186–187